Canadian Environmental Resource Guide

Guide des ressources environnementales canadiennes

Additional Publications

For more detailed information or to place an order, see the back of the book.

ASSOCIATIONS CANADA 2011
Le répertoire des associations du Canada
1983 pages, 8 1/2 x 11, Hardcover
32nd edition, February 2011
ISBN 978-1-59237-764-0
ISSN 1186-9798

Nearly 20,000 entries profile Canadian and international organizations active in Canada. Over 2,000 subject classifications index activities, professions and interests served by associations. Includes listings of NGOs, institutes, coalitions, social agencies, federations, foundations, trade unions, fraternal orders, political parties. Fully indexed by subject, geographic location, budget, executive name, acronym, mailing list availability, conferences and registered charitable organizations.

FINANCIAL SERVICES CANADA 2011-2012
Services financiers au Canada
1550 pages, 8 1/2 x 11, Softcover
14th edition, May 2011
ISBN 978-1-59237-766-4
ISSN 1484-2408

This directory of Canadian financial institutions and organizations includes banks and depository institutions, non-depository institutions, investment management firms, financial planners, insurance companies, accountants, major law firms, government and regulatory agencies and associations. Fully indexed.

LIBRARIES CANADA 2010-2011
Bibliothèques Canada
928 pages, 8 1/2 x 11, Hardcover
25th edition, July 2010
ISBN 978-1-59237-572-1
ISSN 1920-2849

Offers comprehensive information on Canadian libraries, resource centres, business information centres, professional associations, regional library systems, archives, library schools, government libraries and library technical programs.

CANADIAN PARLIAMENTARY GUIDE 2011
Guide parlementaire canadien
1180 pages, 6 x 9, Hardcover
ISBN 978-1-59237-765-7
ISSN 0315-6168

Published annually since before Confederation, this indispensable guide to government in Canada provides information on federal and provincial governments with biographical sketches of government members, descriptions of government institutions, and historical text and charts. With significant bilingual sections, the Guide covers elections from Confederation to the present, with coverage through March 2011.

CANADIAN ALMANAC & DIRECTORY 2011
Répertoire et almanach canadien
1946 pages, 8 1/2 x 11, Hardcover
164th edition, November 2010
ISBN 978-1-59237-589-9
ISSN 0068-8193

A combination of textual material, charts, colour photographs and directory listings, the Canadian Almanac & Directory provides the most comprehensive picture of Canada, from physical attributes to economic and business summaries to leisure and recreation.

2011-2012
16th Edition

Canadian Environmental Resource Guide

Guide des ressources environnementales canadiennes

GREY HOUSE PUBLISHING CANADA

Grey House Publishing Canada
PUBLISHER: Leslie Mackenzie
GENERAL MANAGER: Bryon Moore
MANAGING EDITOR: Tannys Williams
ASSOCIATE EDITORS: Janet Hawtin; Terence Martin; Rachel Smeijers
OPERATIONS AND
  MARKETING COORDINATOR: Caitlin Beatty

Grey House Publishing New York
EDITORIAL DIRECTOR: Laura Mars
MARKETING DIRECTOR: Jessica Moody
COMPOSITION: David Garoogian

Grey House Publishing Canada
555 Richmond Street West, Suite 301
Toronto, ON M5V 3B1
866-433-4739
FAX 416-644-1904
www.greyhouse.ca
e-mail: info@greyhouse.ca

Grey House Publishing Canada is a wholly owned subsidiary of Grey House Publishing, Inc. USA.

While every effort has been made to ensure the reliability of the information presented in this publication, Grey House Publishing neither guarantees the accuracy of the data contained herein nor assumes any responsibility for errors, omissions or discrepancies. Grey House Publishing accepts no payment for listing; inclusion in the publication of any organization, agency, institution, publication, service or individual does not imply endorsement of the editors or publisher.

Errors brought to the attention of the publisher and verified to the satisfaction of the publisher will be corrected in future editions.

Except by express prior written permission of the Copyright Proprietor no part of this work may be copied by any means of publication or communication now known or developed hereafter including, but not limited to, use in any directory or compilation or other print publication, in any information storage and retrieval system, in any other electronic device, or in any visual or audio-visual device or product.

This publication is an original and creative work, copyrighted by Grey House Publishing, Inc. and is fully protected by all applicable copyright laws, as well as by laws covering misappropriation, trade secrets and unfair competition.

Grey House Publishing has added value to the underlying factual material through one or more of the following efforts: unique and original selection; expression; arrangement; coordination; and classification.

Grey House Publishing, Inc. will defend its rights in this publication.

Copyright © 2011 Grey House Publishing, Inc.
All rights reserved

Droits d'auteur © 2011 Grey House Publishing, Inc.
Tous droits réservés
16th edition published 2011
ISBN: 978-1-59237-768-8
ISSN: 1920-2725

CANADIAN CATALOGUING IN PUBLICATION DATA
The National Library of Canada has catalogued this publication as follows:
Main entry under title:
Canadian Environmental Resource Guide
Annual.
1991-
Continues: Canadian Environmental Directory, ISSN 1187-1202.

1. Environmental protection-Canada-Directories. 2. Environmental protection-Canada-Directories
3. Environmental sciences-Canada-Directories.
TD169.6.C36   363.7'0025'71   C91-032400-X

Table of Contents

SECTION 1: Environmental Up-Date 2011

Canadian Environmentalists E-3
Canadian Maps on Environmental Concerns E-7
Chronology of Environmental Events E-31
Environmental Abbreviations E-35
Environmental Rankings (Environmental Performance Index) E-39
Environmental Statistics E-71
Trade Shows, Conferences & Seminars E-133

SECTION 2: Environmental Products & Services Buyer's Guide

Company Listings 63
Individual indexes by Subject, Location, and ISO precede company listings

SECTION 3: Environmental Government Listings

Government Quick Reference Guide 441
Government Acts & Regulations 489
Federal/Provincial Government 507
Municipal Governments 669
Waste & Water Commissions 757
Intergovernmental Offices & Councils 763
Environmental Trade Representatives Abroad 767

SECTION 4: Environmental Resources

Associations/Organizations 813
Educational Programs 1029
Foundations & Grants 1039
Law Firms 1049
Libraries & Resource Centres 1099
Publications
    Non-government 1193
    Government Distribution Centres 1195
Research Centres 1199
Websites 1213
Individual indexes precede each category

SECTION 5: Master Indexes

Entry Name Index 1221
Executive Name Index 1261

Introduction

This is the 16th edition of the *Canadian Environmental Resource Guide,* previously *Canadian Environmental Directory*. It is the fifth edition to be published by Grey House Publishing Canada.

As its name indicates, this reference book is so much more than a directory. It includes colour maps, charts, rankings, a chronology, descriptions of environmental issues and prominent researchers, plus valuable profiles of government and private agencies, educational and research facilities, foundations, law firms, manufacturers and service providers—over 9500 ways to access information and knowledge about the environment in Canada. The wealth of information in this annual resource guide—essential for any business or agency with an interest in a wide spectrum of environmental issues—is arranged into four main sections and 22 subsections. All profiles include current contact information and key executives, plus valuable details, such as number of employees, financial and membership data, additional services and more. In addition, there are 13 indexes; two all-inclusive at the end of the book—Entry and Executive Name—and 11 others, conveniently arranged throughout these pages for quick and easy navigation.

Section 1: Environmental Update 2011

This section offers a current look at the Canadian environmental picture. With revised and expanded **Chronology, Statistics** and more, Update 2011 includes 25 Ranking Charts from Environmental Performance Indicators that show how Canada compares with the rest of the world in significant environmental issues. Also in this section are 24 **Biographies** of prominent Canadian environmentalists, 24 full-colour environmental **Maps, Abbreviations** of environmental terms, and updated and expanded **Trade Show, Conference & Seminar** profiles.

Section 2: Environmental Products & Services Buyer's Guide

The manufacturers and service providers listed here offer products that deal with environmental issues from Absorbents to Wood Recycling, from Agriculture Management to Wind Energy Conversion. Company profiles are current and comprehensive, with descriptions, corporate details and key executives. This valuable information is further accessed by three indexes: **Subject, Geographic** and **ISO**.

Section 3: Environmental Government Listings

Arranged in six subsections, this section starts with a **Quick Reference Guide** to environmental government agencies, followed by **Government Acts & Regulations** as they relate to environmental issues. Next is current, comprehensive information on all **Federal, Provincial** and **Municipal** agencies that deal with environmental concerns. Municipal listings include detailed descriptions on water and waste treatment information, landfill statistics and more. Section 3 also includes updated information on **Intergovernmental Offices & Councils** and **Environmental Trade Representatives Abroad**.

Section 4: Environmental Resources

Section 4 includes 2295 **Associations**, 944 **Special Libraries & Resource Centres**, and private and government environment **Publications**. You'll also find environmental **Educational Programs, Foundations & Grants** and **Research Centres**, all arranged by province. Rounding out this section are **Law Firms** across Canada with an interest in environmental law, and a comprehensive list of environmental **Websites** that will help you access a myriad of information, not only locally, but internationally as well. To facilitate access to this valuable information, this section has eight indexes—Associations by Acronym, Associations by Subject, Association Publications, Educational Programs, Foundations & Grants, Law Firms, Libraries & Resource Centres, and Research Centres.

Section 5: Master Indexes

Canadian Environmental Resource Guide ends with two master indexes: **Entry Name Index**, an alphabetical list of 9542 entries, providing a quick and easy way to access any listing in this edition; and **Executive Name Index**, which alphabetically lists 20,799 key executives in the environment industry.

This reference work is also available as part of Grey House Publishing Canada's **Canada Information Resource Centre (CIRC)** on the web (information available at www.greyhouse.ca). Subscribers have full access to this rich database right at their computer. Trial subscriptions to the CIRC database are available when you call 866-433-4739.

Grey House Publishing Canada also publishes annual editions of the *Canadian Parliamentary Guide, Canadian Almanac & Directory, Associations Canada, Financial Services Canada* and *Libraries Canada*. Look for our new directories on government and health services in 2011 and 2012.

Every effort has been made to assure the accuracy of the information included in this edition of the *Canadian Environmental Resource Guide*. We acknowledge the valuable contributions of those individuals and organizations that have responded to our information gathering process. Your help and responses to our phone calls, faxes and questionnaires are greatly appreciated. Do not hesitate to contact us with comments, or with revisions if necessary.

SECTION 1

Environmental Up-Date 2011

Included in this section:
- Canadian Environmentalists E-3
- Canadian Maps on Environmental Concerns E-7
- Chronology of Environmental Events E-31
- Environmental Abbreviations.................................... E-35
- Environmental Rankings (Environmental Performance Index) E-39
- Environmental Statistics E-69
- Trade Shows, Conferences & Seminars E-131

Canadian Environmentalists

Michael Bailey

Currently: Operational Advisor, The Climate Summit (theclimatesummit.org), and Producer/Director at Planetviews Productions, based in Honolulu, Hawaii. Bailey is a graduate of Al Gore's The Climate Project training program and is currently an authorized presenter for the program. In addition to his documentary film work, Bailey was an official observer at the International Whaling Commission and has been involved in anti-whaling and dolphin protection initiatives, and other environmental and wildlife conservation programs. He supervised the original *Rainbow Warrior*, flagship of Greenpeace.

Contact: Planetviews, 758 Kapahulu Ave., Suite 422, Honolulu, Hawaii, USA 96816; Phone: (808) 306-4386; Fax: (808) 733-7808; URL: planetviews.com

Maude Barlow

Born May 24, 1947.

Currently: National Chairperson, The Council of Canadians, a citizens' advocacy group with chapters across the country. Barlow is also the Chair of Food and Water Watch, based in Washington, DC, a member of the executive of the International Forum on Globalization, located in San Francisco, and a councillor of the World Future Council, based in Hamburg, Germany.

Career: Barlow served as Senior Advisor on Water to the 63rd President of the United Nations General Assembly, 2008-2009. She is the co-founder of the Blue Planet Project, a global initiative with a focus on securing the right to water, and sustainable solutions to the water crisis.

Books: Barlow has authored or co-authored numerous books and reports, including the bestseller, *Blue Covenant: The Global Water Crisis and the Fight for the Right to Water* (2007). She also contributes regularly to the *Water on the Table* blog (www.wateronthetable.com/blog/).

Awards: Recipient of several honourary degrees from Canadian universities, most recently from Trent University in Peterborough in 2009. Barlow was also bestowed with the 2005 Right Livelihood Award, the Citation of Lifetime Achievement at the 2008 Canadian Environment Awards, and the 2009 Earth Day Canada Outstanding Environmental Achievement Award. She is featured in Sam Bozzo's documentary film *Blue Gold: World Water Wars*, and is the subject of the National Film Board's documentary *Democracy à la Maude* (1998).

Contact: Council of Canadians, 170 Laurier Ave. West, Suite 700, Ottawa, ON K1P 5V5; Phone: (613) 233-2773; Fax: (613) 233-6776; URL: www.canadians.org

John Bennett

Currently: Executive Director, Sierra Club Canada, since 2007.

Career: Bennett has served Sierra Club Canada in various capacities since 1998. While a student at the University of Toronto, he was instrumental in establishing the Toronto office of Greenpeace. After working as a newspaper reporter for ten years, Bennett returned to Greenpeace in 1989, and also worked with Pollution Probe. In 1994, he was in charge of Belleville Green Check, which conducted energy audits on area homes. He played a role in opposing a coal-fired power plant at Point Aconi, Cape Breton. Bennett also headed the national Climate Action Network. He served as Communications Director for the Green Party of Canada and has worked closely with party leader Elizabeth May.

Contact: Sierra Club Canada, 1 Nicholas St., Suite 412, Ottawa, ON K1N 7B7; Phone: (613) 241-4611; URL: www.sierraclub.ca

David B. Brooks

Born in the U.S.; immigrated to Canada in 1970.

Currently: Senior Advisor-Fresh Water, for Friends of the Earth Canada and an Associate for the International Institute of Sustainable Development's Natural and Social Capital program

Career: Educated at MIT with a degree in Geology, studied at the California Institute of Technology, and at the University of Colorado with a Ph.D. in Economics. Dr. Brooks is the Founding President of Friends of the Earth Canada, a past President (1996-97), and a Director of Research for the organization. He is a past Acting Director for Environment and Natural Resources Management at the International Development Research Centre (IDRC), headquartered in Ottawa, the Founding Director of the Office of Energy Conservation at Energy, Mines and Resources Canada, and a member of the International Water Academy. His research, interdisciplinary in approach, has focused on ways to reduce the dependence on minerals, water and energy in economic production and other areas, while slowing or avoiding environmental degradation. Dr. Brooks has a particular interest in water soft paths, a method or system which targets current water use practices to foster conservation and efficiency (rather than a supply side or demand perspective) as the foundation for a long-term, sustainable strategy for managing water as a critical resource. He is a noted author and conference speaker.

Books: Author of: *Zero Energy Growth for Canada*; *Water-Local Level Management* (IDRC's in-focus series). Co-author of: *Watershed-The Role of Fresh Water in the Israeli-Palestinian Conflict*; and *Making the Most of the Water we Have: The Soft Path Approach to Water Management* (2009).

Contact: c/o Friends of the Earth Canada, 260 St. Patrick St., Suite 300, Ottawa, ON K1N 5K5; Phone: (613) 241-0085; Fax: (613) 241-7998; e-mail: foe@foecanada.org; URL: www.foecanada.org

Bruce Cox

Currently: Executive Director of Greenpeace Canada. Greenpeace Canada, founded in 1971, has its headquarters in Toronto and branch offices in Vancouver, Edmonton, and Montreal. It has more than 89,000 supporters in Canada.

Political Career: Held positions with the Ontario ministries of Energy and Environment and at Toronto City Hall.

Contact: 33 Cecil St., Toronto, ON M5T 1N1; Phone: (416) 597-8408; Fax: (416) 597-8422; URL: www.greenpeace.org/canada

Severn Cullis-Suzuki

Born November 30, 1979, in Vancouver, BC. Cullis-Suzuki is the daughter of geneticist and environmental advocate Dr. David Suzuki and Dr. Tara Cullis.

Currently: An environmental activist, author, speaker and presenter.

Career: Completed her B.Sc. in Ecology and Evolutionary Biology at Yale University, 2002, and a Masters degree in Ethnobotany at the University of Victoria. Cullis-Suzuki began her career as co-host of *Suzuki's Nature Quest*, which aired on the Discovery Channel in 2002. The same year, she helped found The Skyfish Project, an Internet-based think tank which presented their Recognition of Responsibility pledge to the World Summit on Sustainable Development, in Johannesburg, South Africa, in 2002. The group disbanded in 2004. While still in elementary school, Cullis-Suzuki established the Environmental children's Organization (ECO), a children's group which focused on learning and teaching young people about environmental issues. The group made a presentation to the 1992 Earth Summit in Rio de Janeiro, and Cullis-Suzuki's speech to the delegation earned her high praise. In 1993, she was named to the United Nations Environment Program's Global 500 Roll of Honor for her efforts. The same year, her book *Tell the World*, an environmental guide for families, was published by Doubleday.

Contact: c/o Speaker's Spotlight, 355 King Street West, 2nd Floor, Toronto, Ontario, M5V 1J6; Phone: 1-800-333-4453; Fax: 416.345.9589; URL: www.speakers.ca

Linda Duncan

Born June 25, 1949, in Edmonton, AB.

Currently: MLA for the constituency of Edmonton-Strathcona at the Alberta Legislative Assembly; lawyer and environmental consultant.

Political Career: NDP member for Edmonton-Strathcona at the Alberta provincial legislature since 2008. At the time of her election, she became the only non-Conservative MP in Alberta. Duncan has served as NDP Critic for the Environment, and as a member of the Standing Committee on Environment and Sustainable Development.

Career: Educated at the University of Alberta, and at Dalhousie University. Before entering politics, Duncan was best known for establishing Alberta's Environmental Law Centre in 1982. The Centre has a mandate to provide public programs, research services and other services for a fee, with the aim of promoting effective environmental laws and policies, and public participation in the law-making and decision-making process. In 1987, Duncan spent a year with Environment Canada, and later worked as the assistant Deputy Minister for Renewable Resources in the Yukon territorial government. Her main focus has been the development and implementation of enforcement guidelines and mechanisms. Duncan has served on the Edmonton Social Planning Council, Alberta's Clean Air Strategic Alliance, and was a member of the board of the Sierra Legal Defence Fund (now Ecojustice) for several years.

Contact: Linda Duncan, MP Edmonton-Strathcona, House of Commons, Ottawa, ON, K1A 0A6

Stewart Elgie

Currently: Associate Director, Institute of the Environment, University of Ottawa; Associate Professor, Faculty of Law, University of Ottawa.

Career: Educated at Duke University, the University of Western Ontario, Harvard University (Master's degree in Law), and Yale University (doctoral studies in Progress), Prof. Elgie's current research focus is on the economics of environmental protection. Elgie was a part time instructor at Osgoode Hall Law School, and at the law faculties of the University of Alberta and the University of British Columbia. He is a member of the Bars of Ontario, British Columbia and Alaska. Prof. Elgie is the founder of Ecojustice, formerly the Sierra Legal Defence Fund, a non-profit environmental law firm with a mandate to set legal precedents, and to represent environmental organizations and concerned individuals in the battle to preserve the Earth. The firm works at the grassroots level and will take on cases at any level of the courts. Ecojustice frequently partners with other advocacy groups and has worked with The David Suzuki Foundation, Greenpeace Canada, The World Wildlife Fund of Canada and The Pembina Institute, among others. Elgie is also the founding Executive Director of the Canadian Boreal Trust and a past Chair of Canada's National Advisory Committee under the NAFTA environmental side agreement. He is the founder and Chair of Sustainable Prosperity, a research and policy network at the University of Ottawa, dedicated to practical solutions and strategies for building a productive yet environmentally sustainable Canadian economy.

Awards: Medal for exceptional lifetime contributions, awarded by the Law Society of Upper Canada in 2001.

Contact: c/o Faculty of Law, University of Ottawa, 57 Louis Pasteur St., Rm. 343, Ottawa, ON K1N 6N5; Phone: (613) 562-5800, Ext. 2525; Fax (613) 562-5124, e-mail: steward.elgie@uottawa.ca; URL: www.commonlaw.uottawa.ca

Thomas Esakin

Currently: Executive Director, Canadian Institute for Environmental Law and Policy (CIELAP), author, and teacher. CIELAP is a not-for-profit environmental think tank, with a mandate to provide solutions-based research and education, and guidance to policy makers in government, business, and academia.

Career: Educated at Simon Fraser University, with a Bachelor's degree in Political Science and Philosophy; the University of Saskatchewan; and at Staffordshire University, with a Master's degree in Sustainable Development. Esakin is a former professor at Mexico's Universidad del Caribe, located in Cancun, where he taught in the Sustainable Tourism department and the English department. He is a past Executive Director of JUMP Math, and the inaugural Director of the Clayoquot Biosphere Trust. Esakin has served as policy advisor on sustainable development to the Canadian government and most recently designed and taught Toronto's George Brown College's first Sustainability course. Esakin has written with particular focus on the areas of sustainable development leadership and strategies, local agenda development and benchmarking, and educating for sustainability.

Contact: c/o CIELAP, 130 Spadina Ave., Suite 305, Toronto, ON M5V 2L4; Phone: (416) 923-3529; e-mail: cielap@cielap.org; URL: www.cielap.org; thomasesakin.com

Steven Guilbeault
Born 1970 in La Tuque, QC.

Currently: Environmental activist, journalist and speaker. Guilbeault is a deputy Executive Coordinator of Équiterre, which he co-founded, and a regular contributor to columns published by Transcontinental Media and Métro. He is also a Co-President of the Climate Action Network and chairs the Québec Ministry of Natural Resources' Energy Committee.

Career: Guilbeault is a past Coordinator for Greenpeace Canada's climate and energy campaign, and has served in the same capacity for Greenpeace International. He has been actively involved in United Nations initiatives and meetings on climate change.

Books: Alerte! Le Québec à l'heure des changements climatiques.

Awards: Québec Cercle des Phénix de l'environnement, 2009. France's Le Monde magazine named Guilbeault one of the top 50 newsmakers in global sustainable development.

Contact: c/o Équiterre, 2177, rue Masson, bureau 206, Montréal, QC H2H 1B1; Phone: (514) 522-2000; Fax: (514) 522-1227; e-mail: info@equiterre.org; URL: www.equiterre.org

Toby Heaps

Currently: Co-founder, President and Editor of Corporate Knights. Launched in 2002, and dubbed "the magazine for clean capitalism," Corporate Knights is now the world's largest circulation magazine with a focus on responsible corporate practices and social and environmental sustainability. Heaps makes regular appearances on the CBC and continues to provide commentary to national publications such as The Globe and Mail, Financial Times and the Toronto Star. He is a member of the Board of Directors of Friends of the Earth Canada.

Career: Educated at McGill University, with a Bachelor's degree in Economics, and at the London School of Economics and Political Science.

Contact: c/o Corporate Knights, 147 Spadina Ave., Suite 207, Toronto, ON M5V 2L7; Phone: (416) 203-4674; Fax: (416) 946-1770; e-mail: info@corporateknights.ca; URL: www.corporateknights.ca

Kathryn Holloway
Born October 18, 1968, in Montréal, QC.

Currently: A journalist, businesswoman and political activist, Ms. Holloway is the Executive Director of Element Village, a not-for-profit organization with a focus on supporting energy demand-reduction initiatives at a grassroots level. Element Village works with neighbourhoods, cooperatives and larger communities to promote renewable energy, alternatives to the use of fossil fuels, food security programs and similar projects. At present, the group is working on a Geothermal Energy Co-operative Feasibility Study, funded in part by the federal Department of Agriculture.

Political Career: Was a candidate for the Liberal Party in the Trinity-Spadina constituency in the 2007 Ontario general election, finishing second to the NDP incumbent Rosario Marchese. Holloway was also a staff organizer for the Green Party of Canada, 2004 to 2005, and later supported Elizabeth May in the race for the leadership of the Party. She joined the Liberal Party in late 2006.

Career: Educated at the University of Toronto. Holloway has been involved in a number of environmental organizations and initiatives, including the Steering Committee of Green Enterprise Toronto (a member of the BALLE network), the Civic Efficiency Group, the United Nations Environment Programme Sustainable Energy Finance Roundtable, and the United Nations Climate Change Conference. She is a founding member of the Toronto Women's Environmental Alliance, and BALLE Canada (Business Alliance for Local Living Economies). Holloway is a co-founder of Village Technologies, a Toronto-based renewable energy firm, and a past President and CEO of Carbonzero.

Contact: c/o Element Village Community Services Inc., 214 Campbell Ave., Toronto, ON M6P 3V4; Phone: (416) 930-4085; e-mail: info@elementvillage.net; URL: elementvillage.com

Thomas Homer-Dixon
Born 1956 in Victoria, BC.

Currently: Professor, Centre for Environment and Business, Faculty of Environment, University of Waterloo. Homer-Dixon is also the Centre for International Governance Innovation Chair of Global Systems at the Balsillie School of International Affairs, Waterloo. His research is interdisciplinary and focuses on the themes of global security; technological, economic and ecological change; and how human society will adapt to a complex and changing global picture as environmental and security issues continue to coalesce.

Career: Educated at Carleton University, with a bachelor's degree in Political Science, and at MIT, where he earned his Ph.D. in Political Science. At the University of Toronto, Homer-Dixon led research projects studying the connections between environmental problems and the internal security of developing countries. He remains at the forefront of an evolving global discourse on the links between threats to the environment and threats to human security. Before joining the Basillie School of International Affairs, he held the George Ignatieff Chair of Peace and Conflict Studies at the Trudeau Centre for Peace and Conflict Studies, University of Toronto, and was Professor in the Political Science department of the University.

Books: The Upside of Down: Catastrophe, Creativity, and the Renewal of Civilization (winner of the National Business Book Award for 2006); The Ingenuity Gap (winner of the Governor General's Award for Non-fiction, 2001); and Environment, Scarcity, and Violence (winner of the 2000 Lynton Caldwell Prize from the American Political Science Association). His other published works include Population and Conflict (1994), and Environmental Scarcity and Global Security (1993).

Contact: c/o Balsillie School of International Affairs, Centre for International Governance Innovation, 57 Erb St. West, Waterloo, ON N2L 6C2; Phone: (519) 885-2444, e-mail: tad@homerdixon.com; URL: www.homerdixon.com

Mark Jaccard

Currently: Professor at the School of Resource and Environmental Management at Simon Fraser University, and President, M.K. Jaccard and Associates, Energy Policy Consultants.

Career: Dr. Jaccard develops and applies energy-economy models to assess sustainable energy and materials policies. A professor in REM since 1986, Mark served as Chair and CEO of the B.C. Utilities Commission (1992-97), on the Intergovernmental Panel on Climate Change (1993-96), and on the China Council for International Cooperation on Environment and Development (1996-2001). Currently, he is a lead author on the Global Energy Assessment (due in 2010), a member of Canada's National Roundtable on the Environment and the Economy and a special advisor to Canada's Council of Chief Executive Officers. In 2007, he won the SFU President's Award for Media and his book, Sustainable Fossil Fuels, won the Donner Prize for best policy book in Canada. Dr. Jaccard is responsible for the Canadian Industrial Energy End-use Data and Analysis Centre, directed by Dr. John Nyboer, University Research Associate.

Books: Hot Air-Meeting Canada's Climate Change Challenge; Sustainable Fossil Fuels-The Unusual Suspect in the Quest for Clean and Enduring Energy; The Cost of Climate Policy.

Contact: School of Resource and Environmental Management, Simon Fraser University, 8888 University Drive, Burnaby, BC. Phone: (778)782-4219; Fax: (778) 782-4968; e-mail: jaccard@sfu.ca; URL: www.emrg.sfu.ca; www.mkja.ca

Harvey Locke
Born May 22, 1959, in Calgary, AB.

Currently: Locke, a lawyer by profession, is a well-known conservationist, lecturer, writer and photographer. He is recognized around the world as leader in the field of wilderness protection and the conservation of parklands. Locke's photographic work has been published widely in a variety of media, including The New York Times, Agence France Press, The Globe and Mail and Canadian Geographic. Currently, he is an advisor on conservation for the Canadian Parks and Wilderness Society (CPAWS), Vice President for Conservation Strategy at the WILD Foundation, based in Boulder, Colorado, and serves the boards of the Henry P. Kendall Foundation in Boston, Massachusetts, the Freedom to Roam Initiative, and the Eighth and Ninth World Wilderness Congress. Locke is an active member of the World Commission on Protected Areas.

Career: Educated at the University of Calgary, with a Bachelor's degree in French and a Bachelor of Laws degree. Locke is the founder of the Yellowstone to Yukon Conservation Initiative, which promotes the creation of a wildlife corridor from Yellowstone National Park to the Yukon. He practised law in Calgary for 14 years before changing careers to become a full time conservationist. Locke is a past President, and Vice President, of the Canadian Parks and Wilderness Society (CPAWS), a former board member of the Nature Conservancy of Montana, and has served various other environmental and conservation organizations such as the Wildlands Project (Wildlands Network), Tides Canada Foundation, and the Canadian Boreal Initiative. As a writer and photographer, his work has been published in national and international peer-reviewed journals. In 1999, Locke was named one of Canada's leaders for the 21st century by *Time Magazine*, and in 2009, he addressed the WILD9 Congress in Mérida, Mexico. Locke continues to contribute to the dialogue on current environment and climate change issues.

Contact: c/o The WILD Foundation, 717 Poplar Ave., Boulder, CO 80304 USA; Phone: (303) 442-8811; Fax: (303) 442-8877; e-mail: info@wild.org; URL: www.wild.org

Jim MacNeill
Born April 22, 1928, in Mazenod, SK.

Currently: Member of the Caspian Development Advisory Panel, Chair Emeritus of the IISD and board member of the Woods Hole Research Centre, Woods Hole, Massachusetts. He is still very involved in environmental diplomacy, and sustainable development.

Career: Officer of the Order of Canada. He was Director of Environment at OECD in Paris (1978-84), Secretary General of the World Commission on Environment and Development (Brundtland Commission) and principal author of its acclaimed landmark report *Our Common Future* (1984-87). MacNeill has held a number of senior positions with the Government of Canada, including Director of Policy and Planning for the Department of Energy, Mines and Resources (1965-68), and Acting Assistant Deputy Minister for Water and Renewable Resources (1968). He was instrumental in developing the Canadian government's position on environmental issues, and took a lead role in Canada's preparations for the 1972 Stockholm Conference on the Human Environment. In 1975, he was appointed Canadian Commissioner General to the first United Nations Conference on Human Settlements, held in Vancouver in 1976. MacNeill also served in various capacities the Institute for Research on Public Policy, the International Development Research Centre, and the United Nations Development Programme. He was a founding member, in 1990, of the International Institute for Sustainable Development, and a founding member of the Japanese Institute for Global Environmental Strategies. MacNeill is also a board member of the Wuppertal Institute on Climate and Energy Policy, in Wuppertal, Germany.

Books: *Environmental Management*; and *Beyond Interdependence: The Meshing of the World's Economy and the Earth's Ecology*.

Awards: In 1994, he received the Lifetime Achievement Award of Environment Canada. In 2002, UN Secretary General Kofi Annan presented him with the Candlelight Award for his distinguished service to the United Nations and his key role in promoting and advancing sustainable development. In 2006 he received the Elizabeth Haub Award for environmental diplomacy.

Contact: c/o National Environmental Treasure 99 Fifth Ave, Ste 265, Ottawa, ON, K1S 5P5; e-mail: info@oursafetynet.org.

Elizabeth May
Born June 9, 1954, in Hartford, Connecticut; moved to Nova Scotia in 1972.

Currently: Leader of the Green Party of Canada, MP for the riding of Saanich-Gulf Islands.

Political Career: Appointed Senior Policy Advisor to then federal Environment Minister, Tom McMillan in 1986. On August 26, 2006, May won the Green Party of Canada leadership election on the first ballot. May entered the 2008 federal election race in the Nova Scotia constituency Central Nova, losing to incumbent Peter MacKay. In the 2011 election, she won the riding of Saanich-Gulf Islands in Sidney, B.C.; she is now the first Green Party candidate to be elected to the House of Commons.

Career: May is a lawyer by profession, graduating from the Dalhousie University Law School in 1983. Officer of the Order of Canada since 2005. Executive Director of the Sierra Club of Canada, 1989-2006. Recipient of many awards including the Outstanding Achievement Award from the Sierra Club in 1989, the International Conservation Award from the Friends of Nature, and the United Nations Global 500 Award in 1990. In 1996, she was presented with the award for Outstanding Leadership in Environmental Education by the Ontario Society for Environmental Education. May, a co-founder of the Canadian Environmental Defence Fund, has been active with organizations such as the Public Interest Advocacy Centre, Pollution Probe, and Friends of the Earth. She is also a former Vice Chair of the National Round Table on the Environment and the Economy.

Books: *Budworm Battles; Paradise Won: The Struggle to Save South Moresby; At the Cutting Edge: The Crisis in Canada's Forests; Frederick Street; Life and Death on Canada's Love Canal; How to Save the World in Your Spare Time; Global Warming for Dummies;* and *Losing Confidence: Power, Politics and the Crisis in Canadian Democracy*.

Contact: SGI Green Party Community Centre, 101-2417 Beacon Ave., Sidney, BC V8L 1X5; Phone: (778) 426-4494; Fax: (778) 426-4495; e-mail: leader@greenparty.ca

Briony Penn
Born October 16, 1960, in Saanich, BC.

Currently: Adjunct Professor of Environmental Studies, University of Victoria. Her study program on the sandhill crane, a species at risk, continues under the aegis of University's Geography Department. Penn is an environmental activist, cartographer, artist, and businesswoman.

Career: Penn earned her B.A. in Geography and Anthropology from the University of British Columbia, and later a Ph.D. in Geography from Edinburgh University in Scotland. She established an environmental education consulting business in 1986 and was the host of the television program Enviro/Mental. Penn is the author of a number of books and articles on natural history and environmental issues. She is the co-founder of The Land Conservancy of British Columbia and has volunteered her time to many local and provincial organizations with a focus on conservation and related issues, including the Raincoast Conservation Foundation, Stewardship Pledge, and the Environment Advisory Committee, Islands Trust Saltspring Island Local Trust Committee. In 2007, she announced her intention to run as a Liberal candidate in the constituency of Saanich-Gulf Islands in the 2008 federal election. Penn was narrowly defeated by incumbent Gary Lunn. She maintains her membership in the Green Party of BC.

Books: *Islands in the Salish Sea: A Community Atlas* and *A Year on the Wild Side*.

Contact: 119 Clarinda Rd., Salt Spring Island, BC V8K 1W7; Phone: (250) 653-9996; e-mail: penn@saltspring.com; URL: www.thewildside.ca

Dianne Saxe
Currently: Certified Specialist in Environmental Law; head of Saxe Law Office (Envirolaw), since 1991; member of the City of Toronto's External Panel on Climate Change Risk Management.

Career: Educated at Osgoode Hall Law School, York University, Toronto, with a Ph.D. in Law, and called to the Ontario Bar in 1976, Dr. Saxe is among the top 25 environmental lawyers in the world. Before establishing her own law firm, she was senior legal counsel to the Ontario Ministry of the Environment. Her firm's core practice areas include due diligence, compliance, enforcement, renewable energy approvals, environmental assessments, ISO 14000, brownfields, and climate change. Dr. Saxe is a certified mediator and a consultant to business, government, environmental groups and individuals. She has been active on the boards of Evergreen, Pollution Probe, Windshare, and Algonquin Ecowatch, and is a life member of the Bruce Trail Conservancy. Dr. Saxe is a founding member of the Law Society of Upper Canada's Environmental Specialist Certification Committee, and a long-time member of the Ontario Bar Association Environmental Law section.

Books: *Ontario Environmental Protection Act Annotated*; Dr. Saxe is also the author of numerous articles and book chapters.

Awards: Ontario Bar Association Distinguished Service Award, 2010.

Contact: Saxe Law Office, 248 Russell Hill Rd., Toronto, ON M4V 2T2; Phone: (416) 962-5009; Fax: (416) 962-8817; e-mail: admin@envirolaw; URL: www.envirolaw.com

Rick Smith
Currently: Executive Director of Environmental Defence Canada, a charitable organization dedicated to protecting the environment and human health. Smith, along with others in the organization, worked towards passage of Ontario's new Clean Water Act, and the Endangered Species Act.

Political Career: Served as Chief of Staff to Jack Layton and the New Democratic Party in 2003.

Career: Former Executive Director of the UK and Canadian offices of the International Fund for Animal Welfare.

Books: Co-author, *Slow Death by Rubber Duck: How the Toxic Chemistry of Everyday Life Affects Our Health*.

Contact: 116 Spadina Ave, Suite 300, Toronto, ON M5V 2K6; Phone: (416) 323-9521; Fax: (416) 323-9301; email: info@environmental defence.ca; URL: www.environmentaldefence.ca

David Suzuki
Born March 24, 1936, in Vancouver, BC.

Currently: Co-founder, along with his wife Dr. Tara Cullis, of the David Suzuki Foundation, a non-profit organization dedicated to finding innovative solutions to help conserve the natural world. Host of CBC's long-running science programme *The Nature of Things*, now in syndication in 40+ countries. Active proponent of environmental sustainability and combating global warming. Professor Emeritus University of British Columbia, Vancouver, B.C., 2001 to present.

Career: Ph.D. in zoology from the University of Chicago. Professor in the Genetics Department of the University of British Columbia, 1963 to 2001. Established, and hosted from 1975 to 1979 the CBC radio program *Quirks and Quarks*. Director of the Canadian Civil Liberties Association, 1982-1987. Hosted the critically acclaimed PBS television series *The Secret of Life*, 1993.

Awards: Honours include the Governor General's Award for Conservation in 1985 and the Order of Canada in 1997. Lifetime Achievement Award, University of British Columbia Alumni Association, 2000; Commemorative Medal, 125th Anniversary of Canadian Confederation, 1992. Received ACTRA Award in 1985 and GEMINI Awards in 1986 and 1992 for his television programs. Dr. Suzuki is the recipient of a number of honourary degrees from Canadian and international universities, including most recently from Memorial University, the University of Western Ontario, and the University of Montreal at Québec.

Books: Canadian author of more than 32 books, including an autobiography, *The Balance, You are the Earth Sacred,* as well as a number of children's books. Also author of published columns discussing science, the environment, and nature.

Contact: Head Office: Suite 219, 2211 West 4th Avenue, Vancouver, BC, V6K 4S2; Phone: (604) 732-4228; Fax (604) 730-9672. URL: www.davidsuzuki.org

Peter Tabuns
Born October 3, 1951, in London, ON.

Currently: NDP Ontario MPP for the Toronto-Danforth constituency. Tabuns is the Deputy Third Party House Leader, and Critic for Environment, Energy and several other areas.

Political Career: He was City Councillor for the Riverdale portion of the Toronto-Danforth constituency from 1990 to 1997. On being sworn in to the Ontario Legislature, he was given responsibility for Environment, Infrastructure Renewal, Transportation, and the Greater Toronto Area, among several other portfolios.

Career: Was President of Citizens for a Safe Environment and helped end garbage incineration in the Toronto Portlands. He championed housing alternatives as Vice Chair of the Co-op Housing Federation of Toronto. Tabuns was also Chair of the Toronto Board of Health. He has long campaigned for protection of the environment. As Executive Director of Greenpeace Canada from 1999 to 2004, he advocated for environmental protection, including the adoption of the Kyoto Protocol. Tabuns served as special advisor on climate change to Jack Layton, 2004 to 2005.

Contact: 923 Danforth Avenue, Toronto, ON M4J 1L8; Phone: (416) 461-0223; Fax: (416) 461-9542; e-mail: tabunsp-co@ndp.on.ca; URL: peter tabunsndp.ca

Chris Tollefson
Born in Saskatchewan.

Currently: Professor, Faculty of Law, University of Victoria. Founding Executive Director of the Environmental Law Centre at the University of Victoria, home of the first clinical program in public interest environmental law in Canada. Fellow of LEAD International (Leadership through Environment and Development). Member of the Board of Directors of Ecojustice (formerly the Sierra Legal Defence Fund) since 1993.

Career: Educated at the University of Victoria Faculty of Law. Called to the Bar of British Columbia in 1987. Served as law clerk to Mr. Justice Lambert of the British Columbia Court of Appeal before practising law in the area of criminal defence and Charter litigation. Prof. Tollefson's research interests include aboriginal rights and environmental protection, water pollution and coastal zone ecology and management, forest protection and management, and citizen participation in environmental and trade issues. He is a member of Canada's National Advisory Committee under the NAFTA environmental side agreement, and a past member of the Academic Advisory Committee to the Deputy Minister of International Trade (2002-2004). Tollefson is also a Past Chair and President, 1997-2001, of Ecojustice.

Books: *Environmental Law: Cases and Materials* (2009); *Setting the Standard: Certification, Governance and the Forest Stewardship Council* (2008); *cleanair.ca: a citizen's action guide* (2000); and *The Wealth of Forests: Markets, Regulation and Sustainable Forestry* (1998).

Contact: Environmental Law Centre, University of Victoria, PO Box 2400, Stn CSC, Victoria, BC V8W 3H7; Phone: (250) 721-8170; e-mail: ctollef@uvic.ca; URL: www.law.uvic.ca

Sheila Watt-Cloutier
Born December 2, 1953 in Kuujjuaq, Nunavik, QC.

Currently: Activist, writer, lecturer and presenter. Watt-Cloutier is a Commissioner on The Aspen Institute's Commission on Arctic Climate Change.

Career: Educated at McGill University, with a focus on human development, education and counseling. Watt-Cloutier worked as an Inuktitut translator at Ungava Hospital, and played a key role in the review of the educational system in Northern Québec. She was Corporate Secretary for the Makivik Corporation, an Inuit land claims organization, from 1995-1998, and Past President of the Inuit Circumpolar Council (ICC), headquartered in Canada and representing Inuit interests in several countries. In this capacity, Watt-Cloutier advocated for the banning of the manufacture and use of persistent organic pollutants (POPs), which include polychlorinated biphenyls and DDT, and which have had a profound effect on the Arctic ecology and the families who rely on Arctic species for food. From 2002 to 2006, Watt-Cloutier was the International Chair of the ICC. She continues to advocate for the interests of Arctic peoples with particular reference to the effects of greenhouse gases and climate change on their wellbeing, as well as themes of human rights and the protection of indigenous cultures in an era of rapid change.

Awards: Among her many honours, Ms. Watt-Cloutier was named Officer of the Order of Canada in 2006, and is the holder of numerous honourary degrees from Canadian universities. In 2007, she was nominated along with former U.S. Vice President Al Gore for the Nobel Peace Prize, and was awarded the Rachel Carson Prize for exceptional achievement in work for environmental causes. In 2010, the Globe and Mail called her the Nation Builder of the Decade for the environment.

Canadian Maps on Environmental Concerns

Sensitivity of River Regions to Climate Change

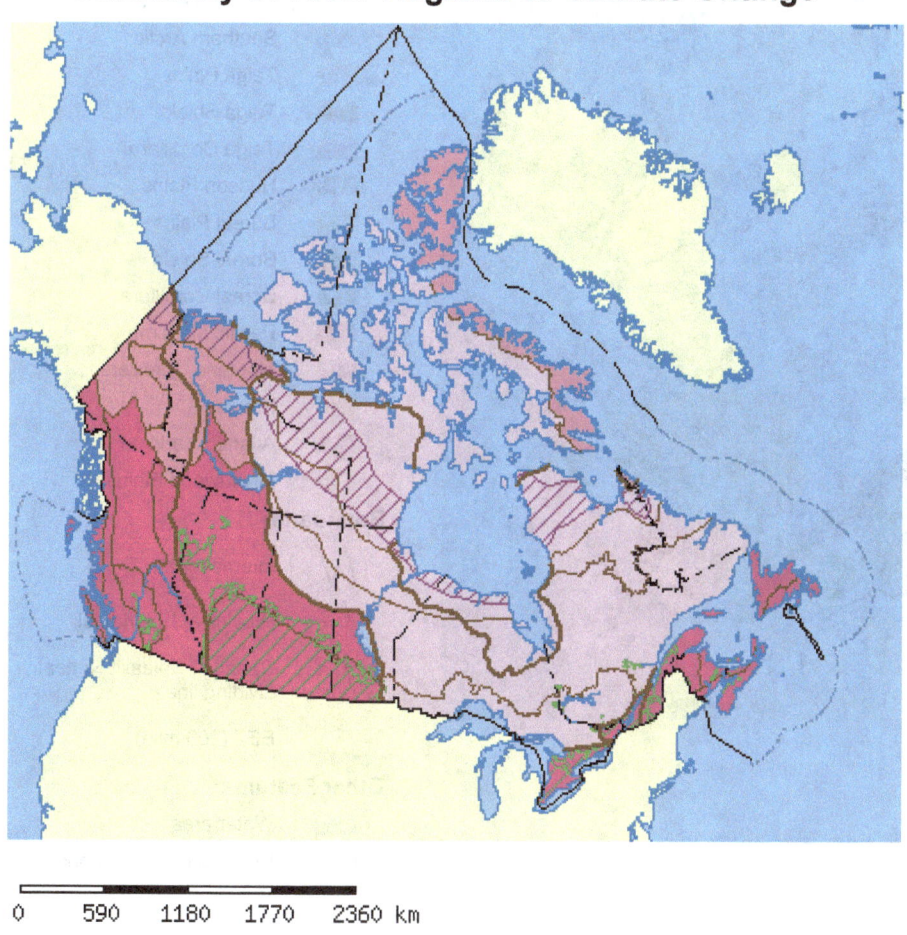

Boundaries of River Regions

 Boundaries of major river regions

Boundaries of river sub-regions

Agricultural and Urbanized Areas

Agricultural and urbanized areas

Area at Risk of Permafrost Reduction

Area at risk of permafrost reduction

Sensitivity of River Regions to Climate Change

Less sensitive and less vulnerable

Sensitive and less vulnerable

More sensitive and vulnerable

International Boundaries

 EEZ (200 mile)

 Canada / Kalaallit Nunaat dividing line

 International

Provincial and Territorial Boundaries

Provincial / Territorial

Drainage

Coast / Lake shoreline

Water areas

Water Area

Regions outside Canada

Land Area

Abstract:

The most sensitive river regions include the Atlantic coast, the Great Lakes-St. Lawrence Valley regions, the Rocky Mountains and the Prairies. The sensitivity projection for Canada's river regions in response to climate warming was derived based on an examination of the effects of projected precipitation changes on landscapes. Climate warming has the potential to cause substantial changes to flow in rivers. The most direct effects of projected climate change would be an increase in floods and river erosion.

© Her Majesty the Queen in Right of Canada, 2009.

Ecological Framework

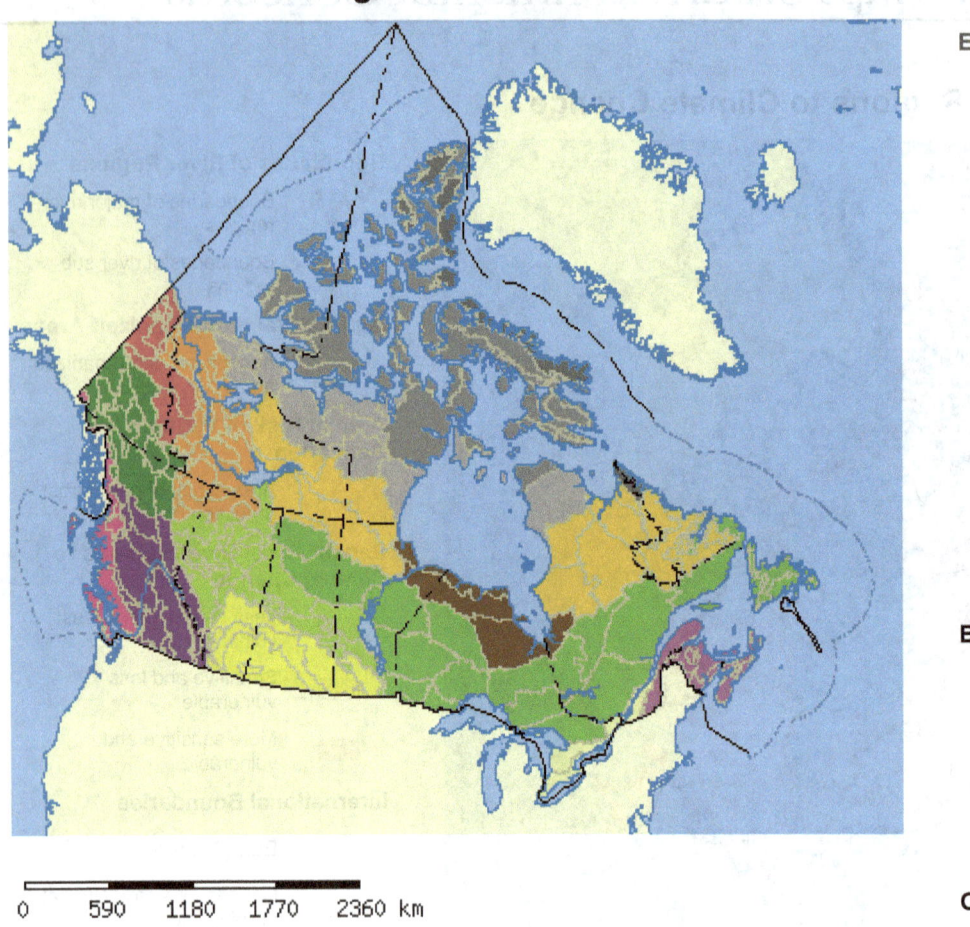

Abstract:

Fifteen ecozones make up terrestrial Canada, and five make up the marine waters bordering Canada. Canada's 15 terrestrial ecozones can be subdivided into 53 ecoprovinces, which can be further broken into 194 ecoregions. Ecozones are useful for general national reporting and for placing Canada's ecosystem diversity in a North American or global context. Ecoprovinces are useful units at an intermediate scale for national and regional planning and reporting purposes. Ecoregions are a useful ecosystem scale for national, provincial, and regional planning and reporting purposes. Regardless of the level in the hierarchy, each unit is distinguished from others by its unique mosaic of plants, wildlife, climate, landforms, and human activities.

© Her Majesty the Queen in Right of Canada, 2009.

Protecting Forests

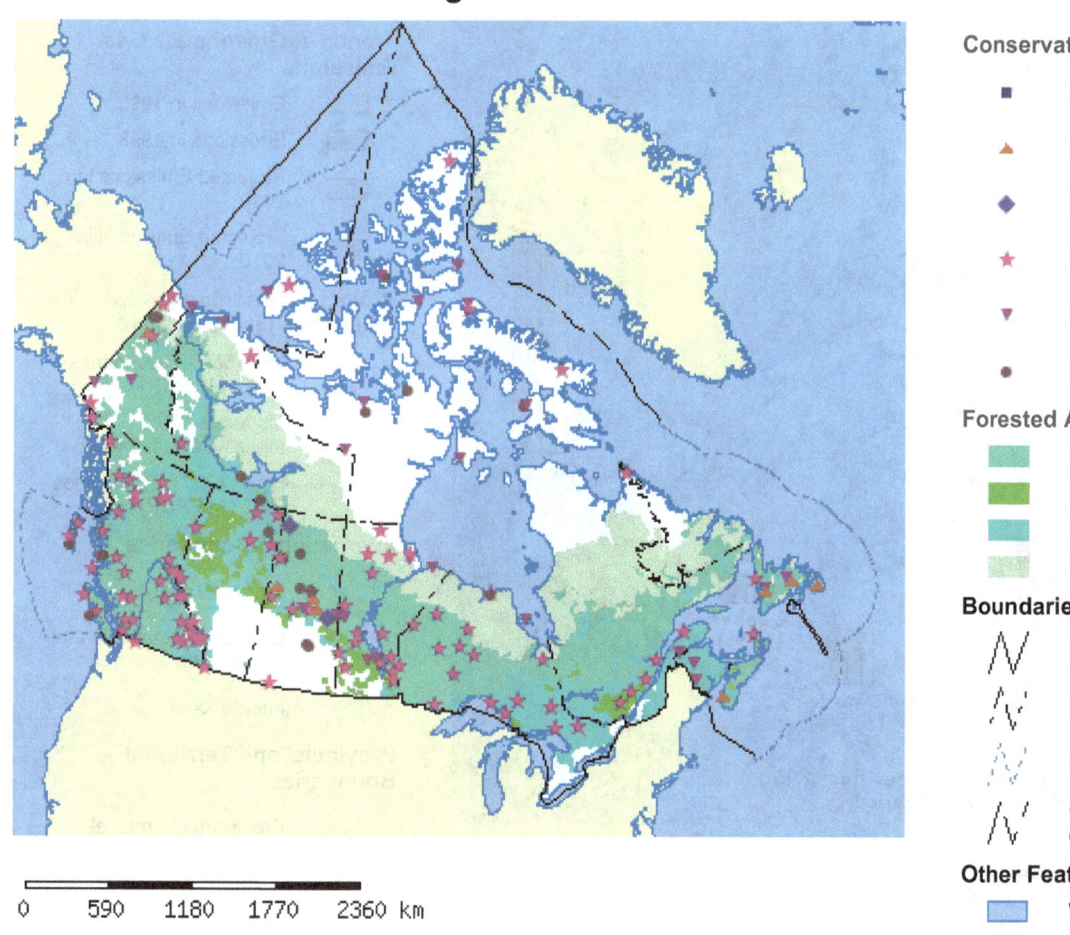

Abstract:

Approximately 7.6% of Canada's forest land is located in protected areas. Over 95% of protected forests are totally protected and the rest reflect degrees of human intervention such as logging, mining and agriculture. This map shows all the protected areas in Canada.

© Her Majesty the Queen in Right of Canada, 2009.

Canadian Maps on Environmental Concerns

Trends in Greenhouse Gas Emissions, 1998 to 2010

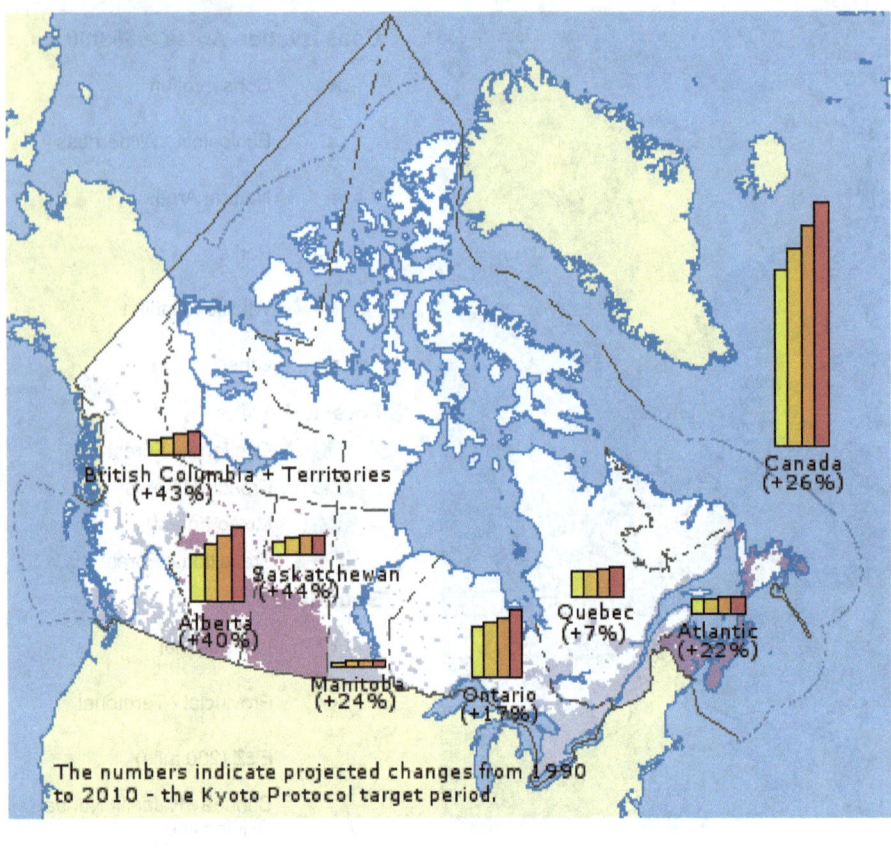

Abstract:

The regional trends of greenhouse gas emissions for the period 1990 to 2020 are shown here. Also shown is a projection of regional carbon intensity in terms of tonnes of carbon dioxide per million dollars of Real Domestic Product. This map shows long-term greenhouse gas emissions growth on a provincial and territorial basis. The pattern of emissions growth varies across provinces, largely reflecting the distribution of energy sources available, the existence of energy production, and the nature of manufacturing activities and projected population growth. In relative terms, the provinces of British Columbia, Alberta and Saskatchewan are expected to experience the largest increases between 1990 and 2010. In absolute terms, Alberta and Ontario are expected to experience the largest increases in emissions.

© Her Majesty the Queen in Right of Canada, 2009.

Rare Plant Diversity

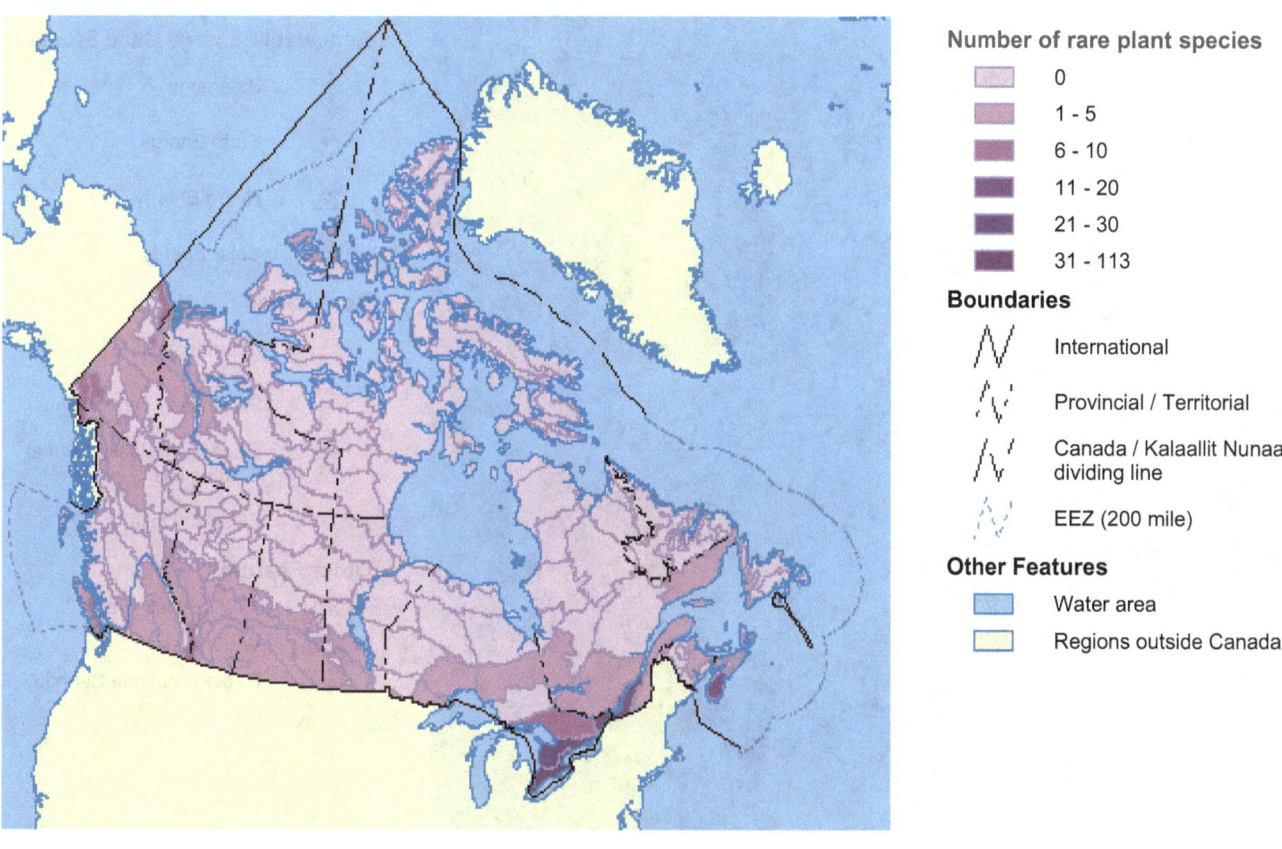

Abstract:

Some plants are rare because they naturally occur in very specialized habitats or in very low numbers; others may be rare because they have suffered setbacks because of natural processes or pressures from human activities. The highest number of rare plant species is in southern Ontario, where human activity is intensive and extensive. Farming, deforestation, draining of wetlands, and the use of insecticides and herbicides has reduced the populations and areas of distribution of numerous species.

© Her Majesty the Queen in Right of Canada, 2009.

Renewable Energy Case Studies

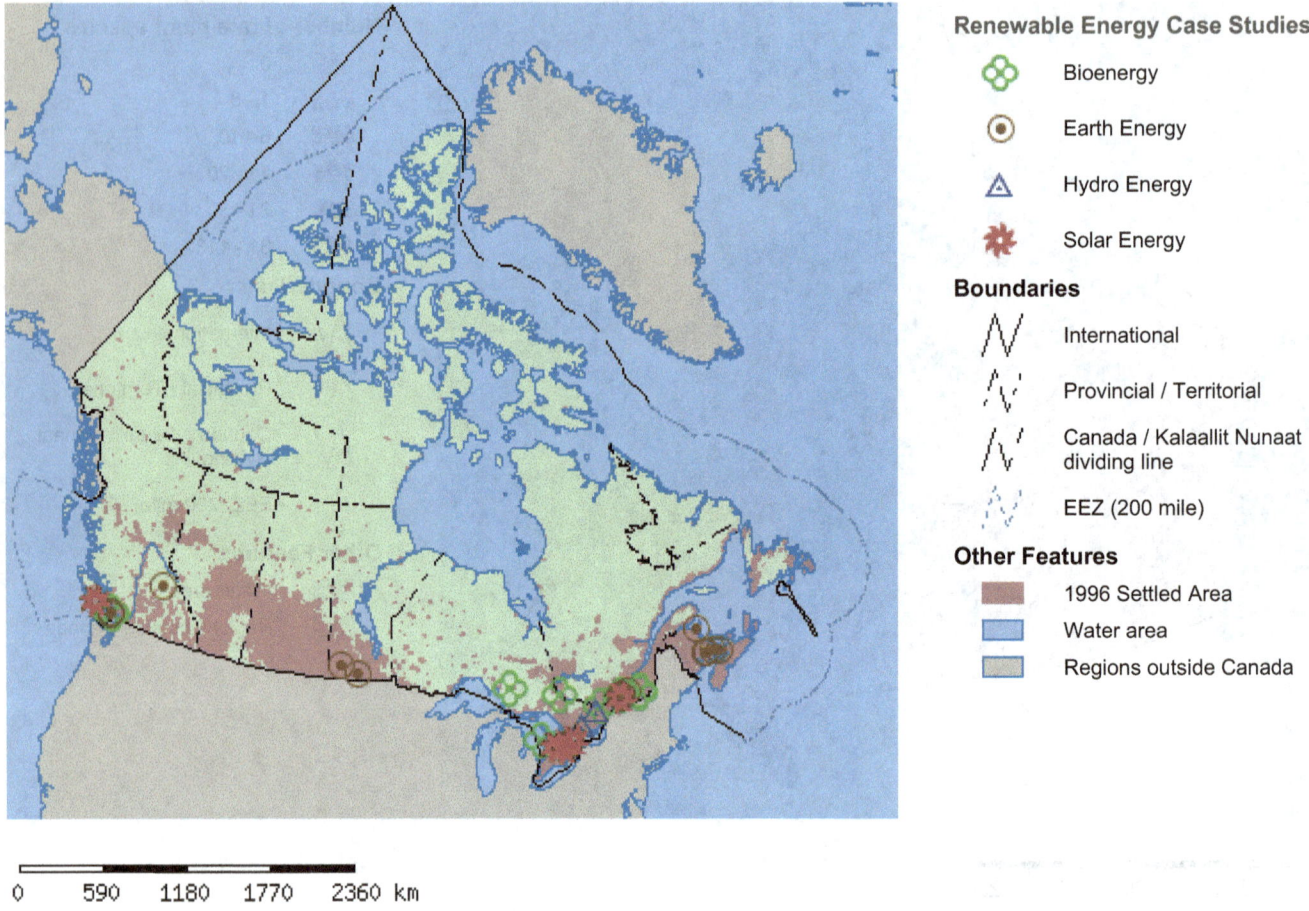

Abstract:

The 34 high-potential projects whose goal is to help accelerate the implementation of renewable energy technologies are shown here. Renewable energy refers to several energy sources that produce electrical, thermal or mechanical energy without unnecessarily depleting resources. The renewable energy sources are generally classified as water, biomass, wind, solar, earth and energy from wastes. The development and use of renewable energies is one of the two major strategies to reduce greenhouse gas emissions from energy consumptions. The 34 projects serve as prime examples of how renewable energy can be implemented into the Canadian energy market.

© Her Majesty the Queen in Right of Canada, 2009.

Light-Duty Vehicle Fuel Efficiency Scenario: Model Year 1990 to 2010

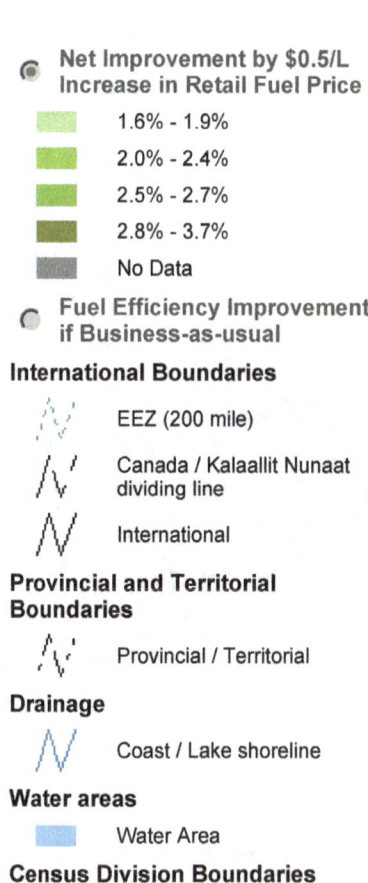

Abstract:

The likely effect of an unexpectedly large increase in the period 1990 to 2010 in retail fuel price on the average fuel efficiency of light-duty vehicles is shown here. Light-duty vehicles include all cars and light trucks. Because vehicles consume a substantial part of energy, average vehicle fuel efficiency is an important indicator for greenhouse gas emission and climate change policy making. The lower the fuel efficiency, the higher the emission per vehicle, and, consequently, the greater its contribution to greenhouse gas production. Gasoline cost is the major vehicle operating cost. An increase in gasoline price would, to some extent, cause users to choose more fuel-efficient vehicles in order to reduce vehicle-operating cost. The Prairie Provinces would have the most sensitive response in fuel efficiency improvement to retail fuel price.

© Her Majesty the Queen in Right of Canada, 2009.

Road Density

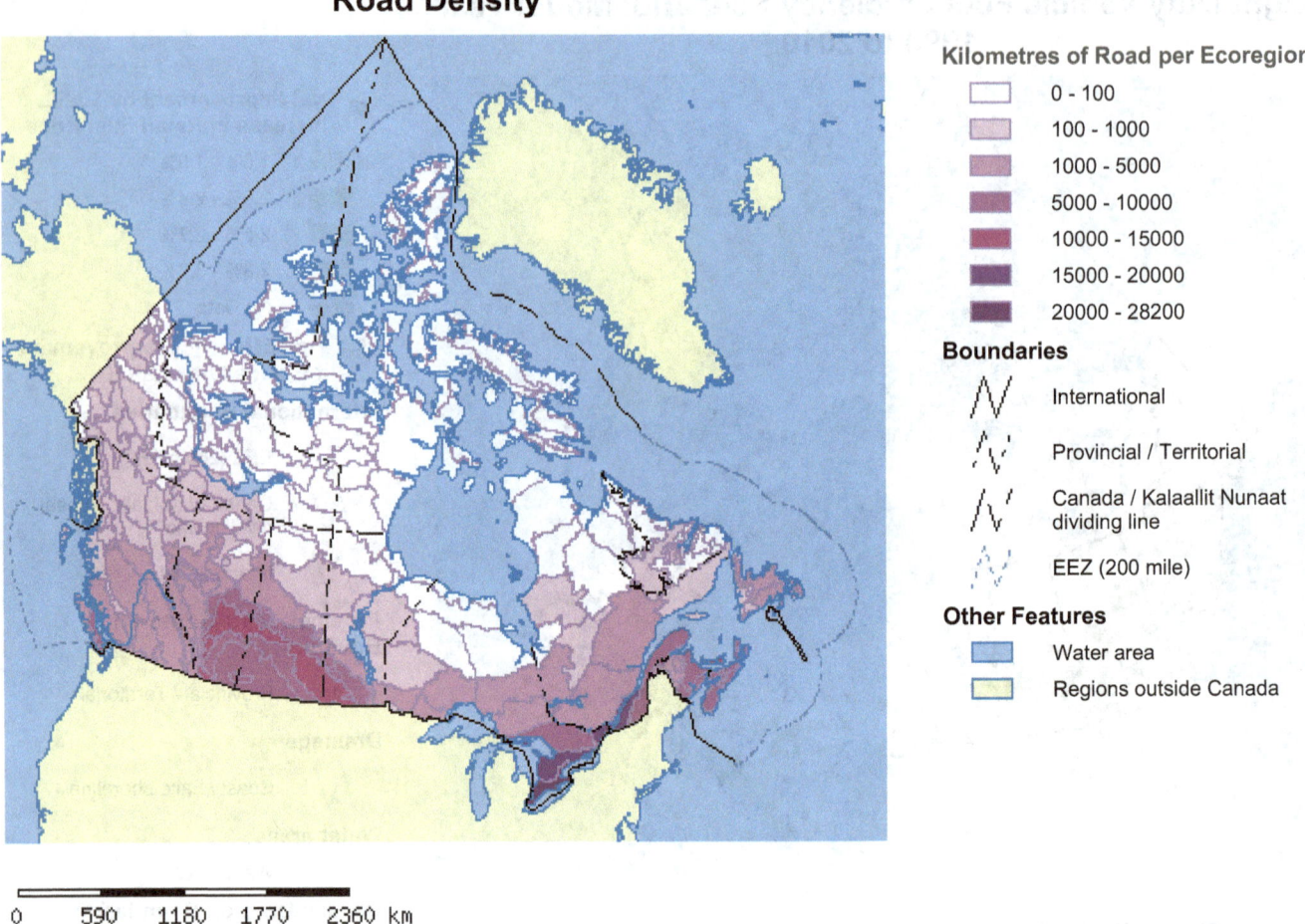

Abstract:

Transportation activities have a great impact on the environment because they fracture natural habitats and create pollution. Roads intrude into natural habitats, separating ecosystems and permanently altering the landscape. Road building has undesirable effects on species that require large tracts of undisturbed land.

The main impact of transportation is due to vehicles' large consumption of fossil fuels. This consumes the fossil fuel reserves, as well as releasing greenhouse gasses into the atmosphere. There is a radical difference between high road density in the settled parts of southern Canada, and virtually no roads in the Arctic ecosystems.

© *Her Majesty the Queen in Right of Canada, 2009.*

National Annual Temperature Scenario: 2050

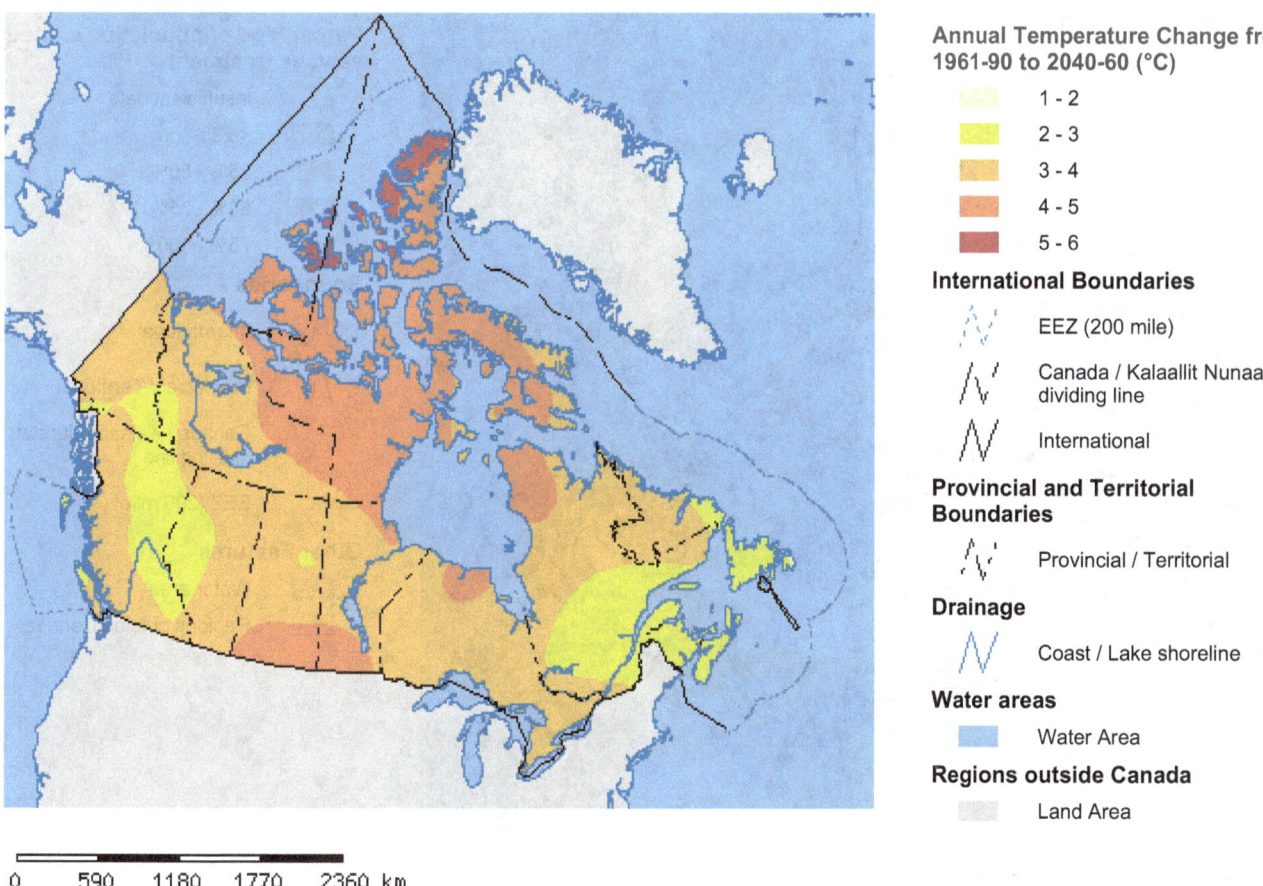

Abstract:

A simulation of projected changes in annual mean temperatures from the period 1961 to 1990 to the period 2040 to 2060 for Canadian lands is shown here. The temperature changes would not be evenly distributed geographically. The largest warming projected is for the interior and northern parts of the country. Temperatures are projected to continue increasing as the century progresses. Temperatures would generally increase as a consequence of the projected increase in greenhouse gas concentrations in the atmosphere. The results are based on climate change simulations made with the Coupled Global Climate Model developed by Environment Canada.

© *Her Majesty the Queen in Right of Canada, 2009.*

Sewage Treatment

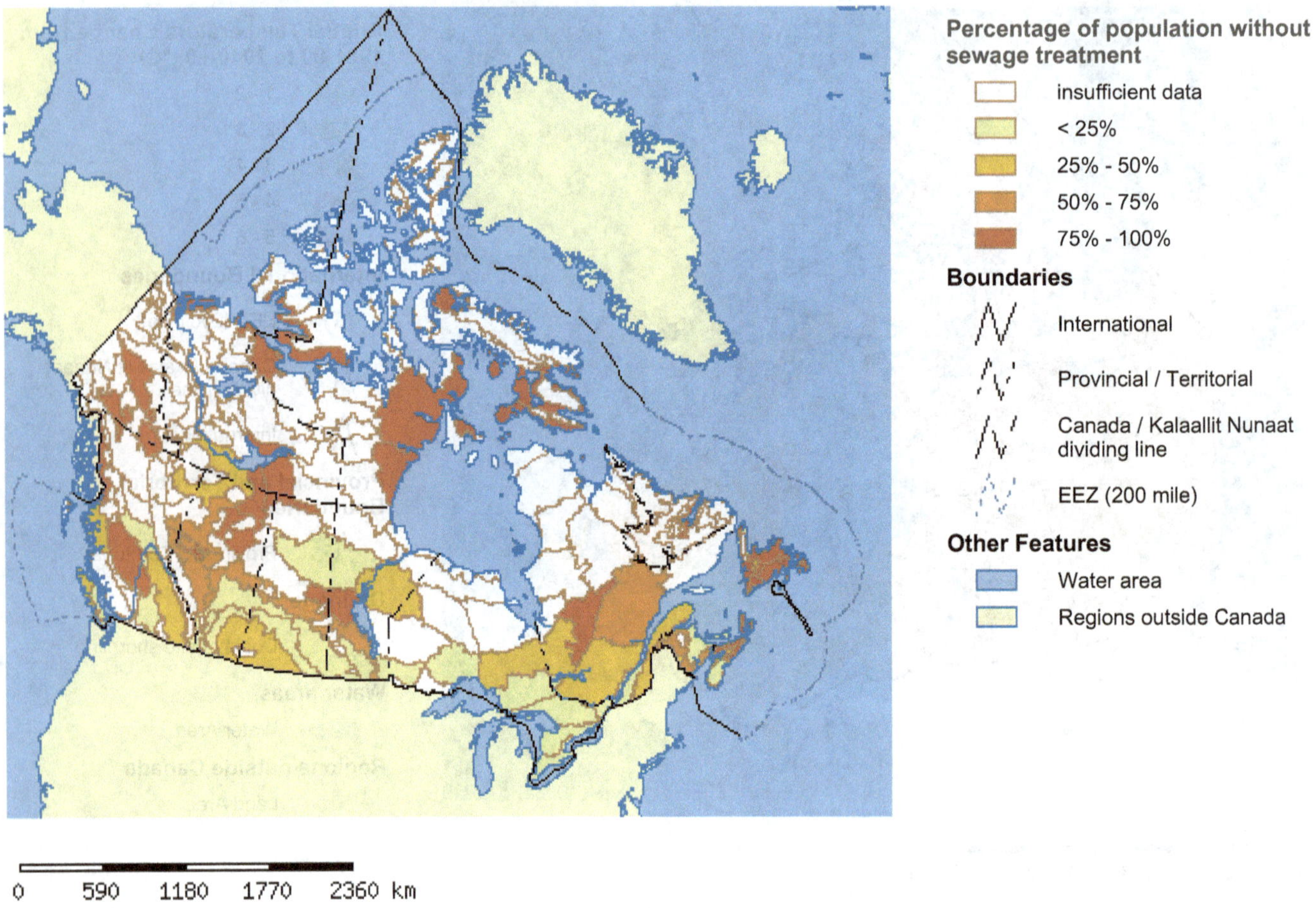

Percentage of population without sewage treatment
- insufficient data
- < 25%
- 25% - 50%
- 50% - 75%
- 75% - 100%

Boundaries
- International
- Provincial / Territorial
- Canada / Kalaallit Nunaat dividing line
- EEZ (200 mile)

Other Features
- Water area
- Regions outside Canada

0 590 1180 1770 2360 km

Abstract:

Urban living generates waste that is usually treated to some degree and then discharged into water bodies. Too much waste can pose a risk to aquatic ecosystems and species. Pollutants can remain environmentally damaging even after passing through conventional sewage treatment. Municipal wastewater, including residential, commercial and industrial wastewater, is the major source of contaminants in the marine environment. In southern Canada, where most Canadians live, much of the municipal wastewater is treated by reducing some of the oxygen, suspended solids, phosphorus and sometimes ammonia and nitrogen to reduce the environmental impact on the receiving aquatic ecosystems.

© Her Majesty the Queen in Right of Canada, 2009.

Tree Species by Ecoregion

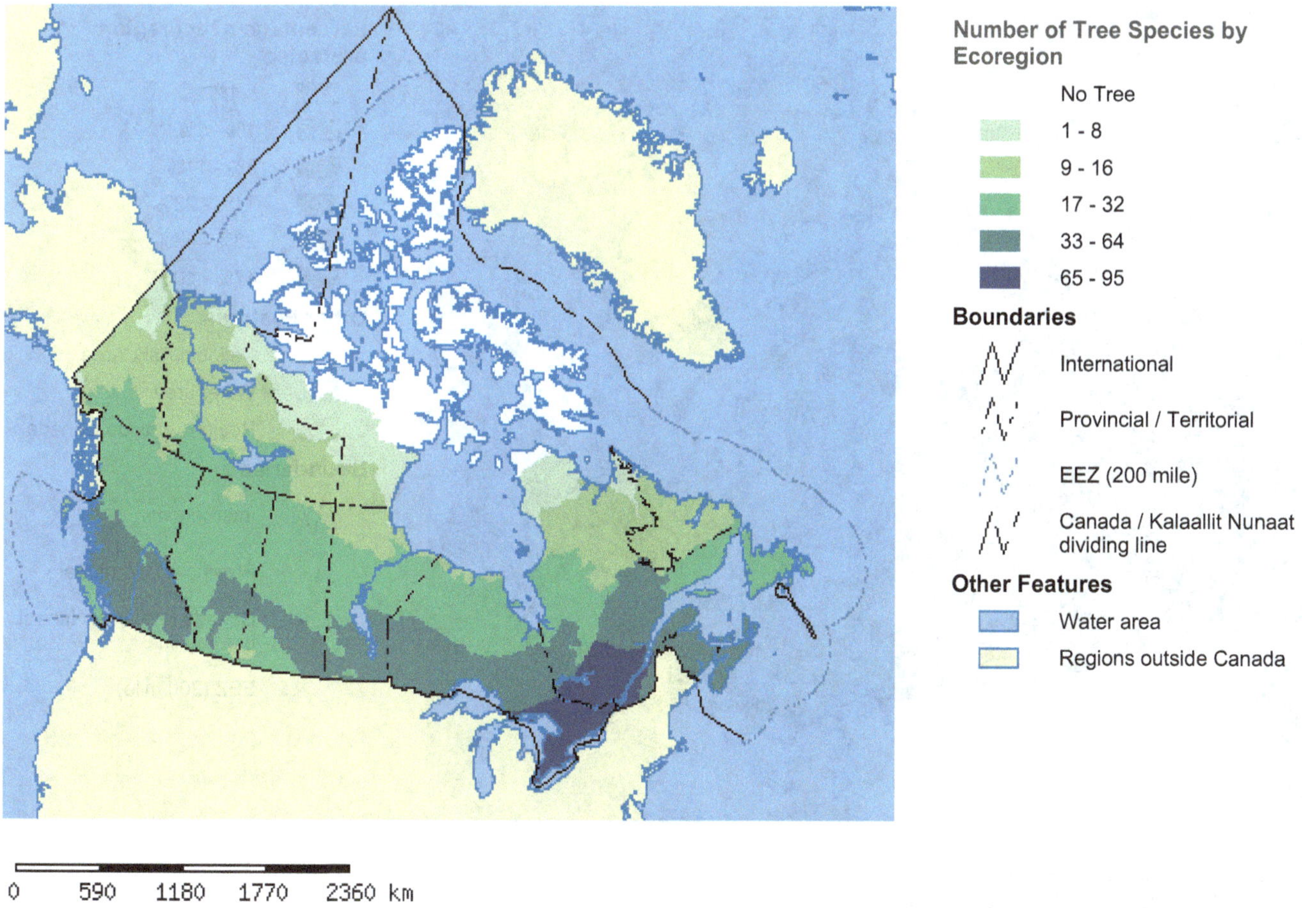

Abstract:

There are about 180 species of trees in Canada. More tree species are found in Southern Ontario and along the St. Lawrence River. The highest number of tree species is found in the Lake Erie Lowlands ecoregion.

© Her Majesty the Queen in Right of Canada, 2009.

Percentage of Ecoregion Protected

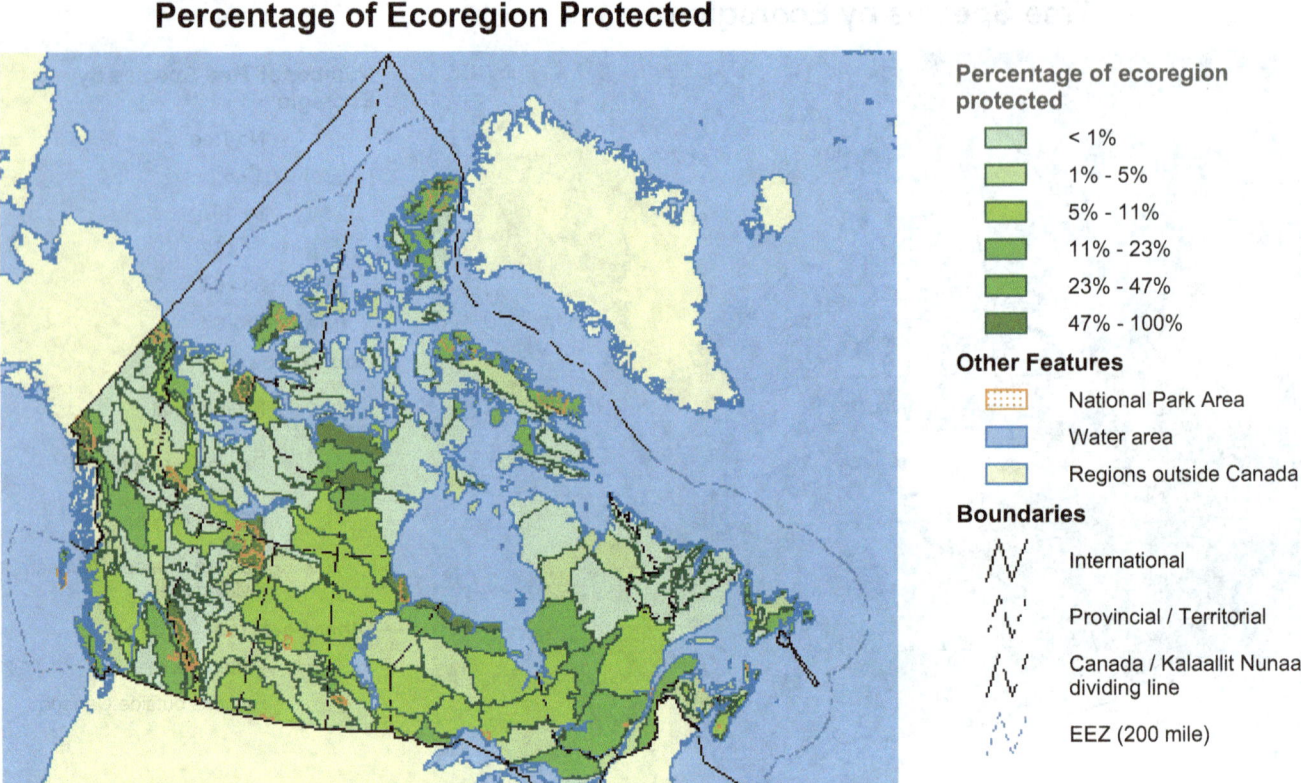

Abstract:

Protected areas are defined as legally established areas, both land and water, that are regulated and managed for conservation objectives. They include parks, wildlife and forest reserves, wilderness and other areas designated through federal, provincial, and territorial legislations.

© Her Majesty the Queen in Right of Canada, 2009.

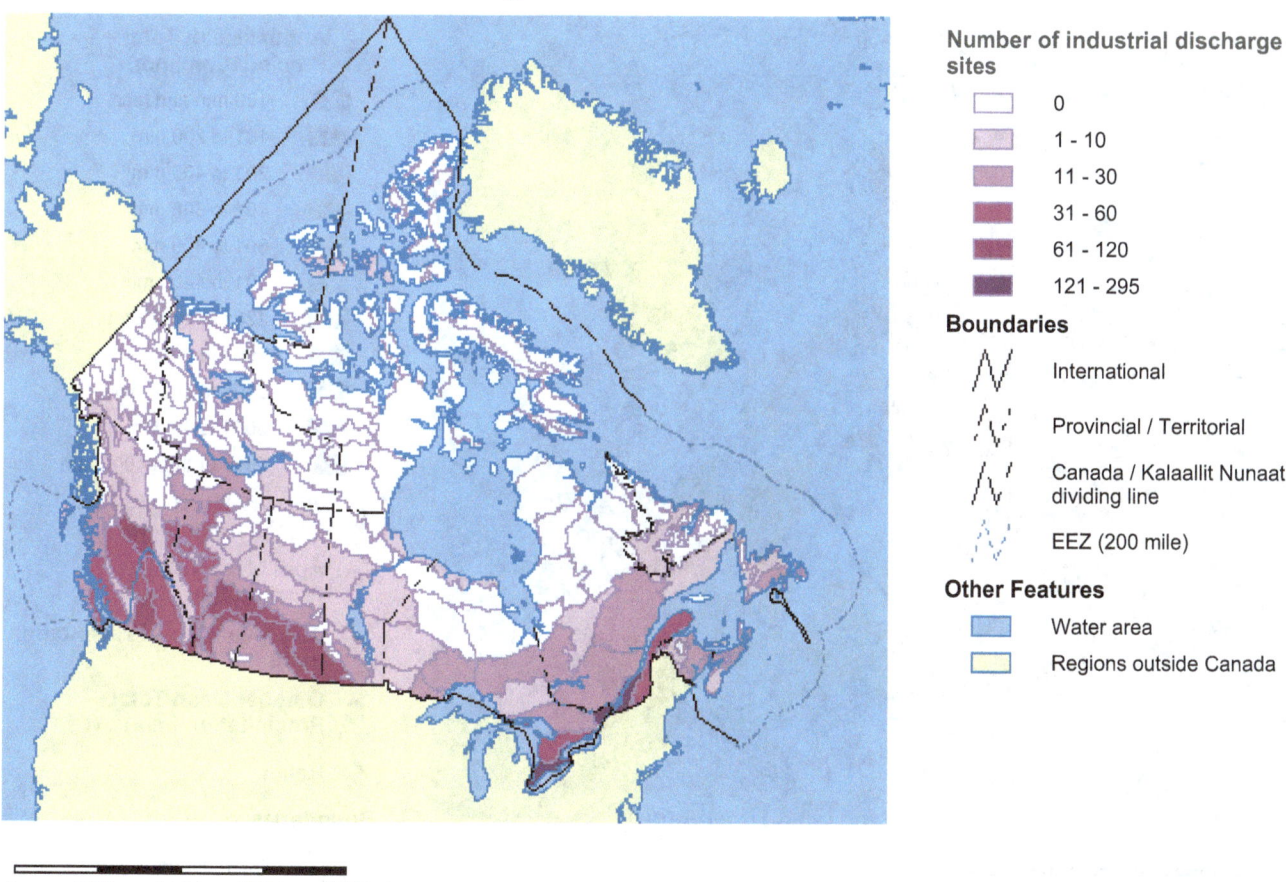

Abstract:

Industrial activities generate waste that is discharged into water bodies, the air or ends up in landfill sites. Air is the most common release medium. Ammonia, methanol, sulfur dioxide, and nitrogen dioxide are by far the most common industrial pollutants released in Canada. Industrial discharge sites are concentrated in southern Ontario and Quebec, and around major cities in British Columbia and the Prairies.

© Her Majesty the Queen in Right of Canada, 2009.

Mean Total Precipitation

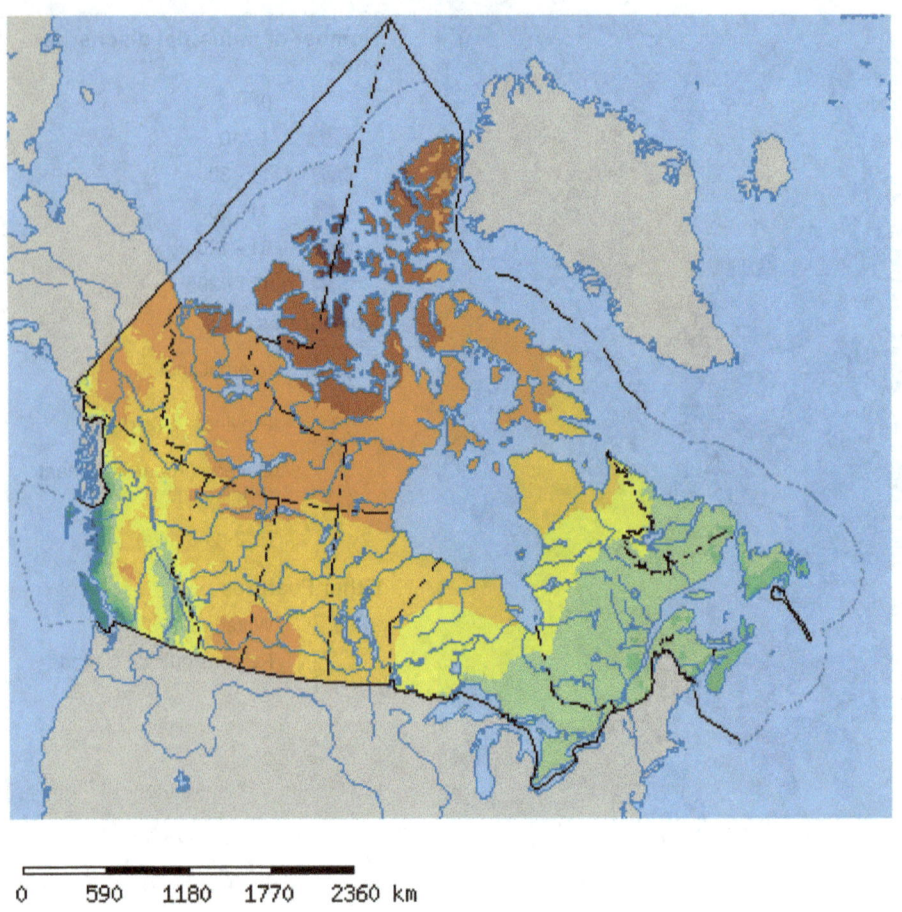

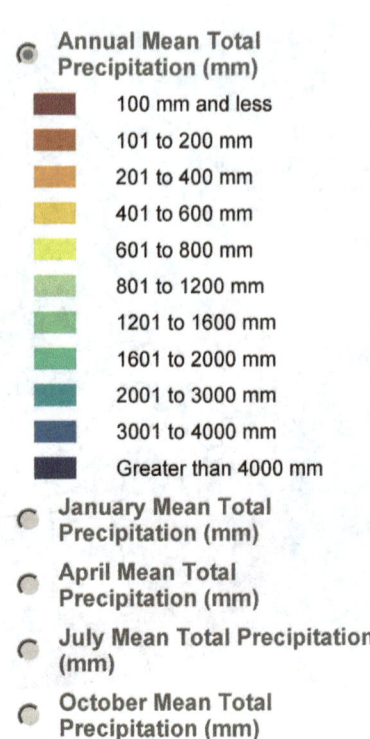

Abstract:

Over much of the continental interior of Canada, precipitation reaches its annual maximum in the summer months and falls as rain. October marks the transition from mainly rain to snowfall across northern Canada. The map shows the seasonal mean precipitation in the months of January, April, July and October.

© Her Majesty the Queen in Right of Canada, 2009.

Forest Fires

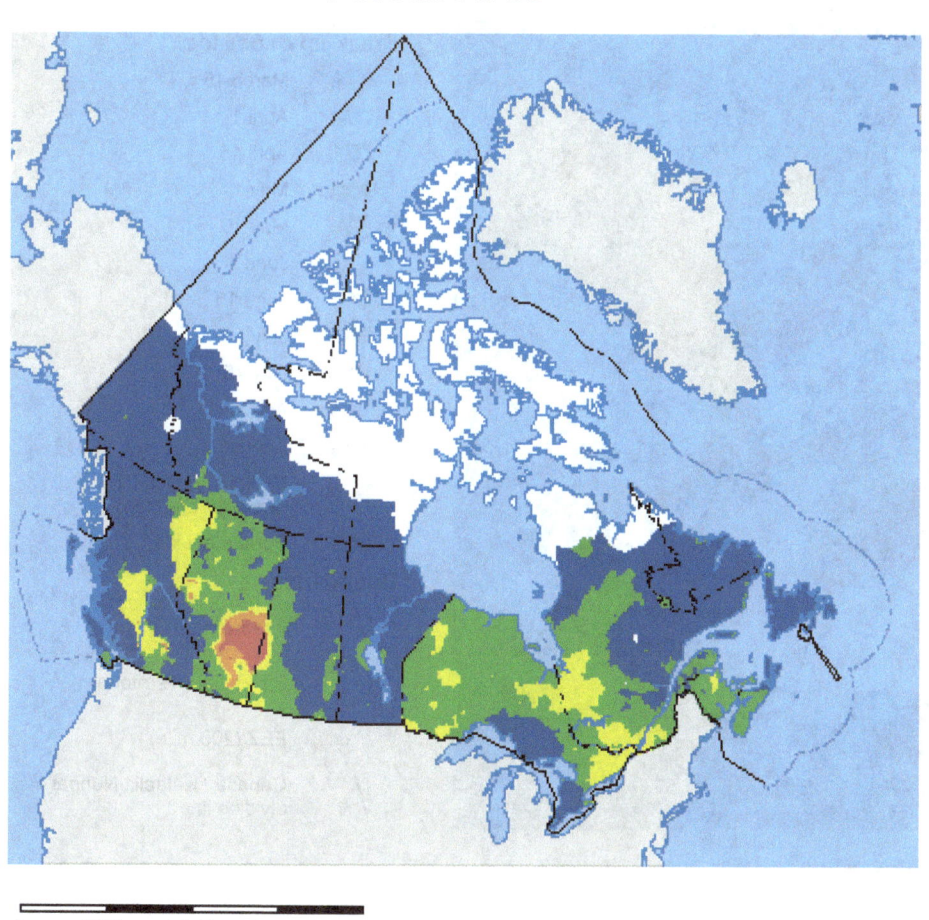
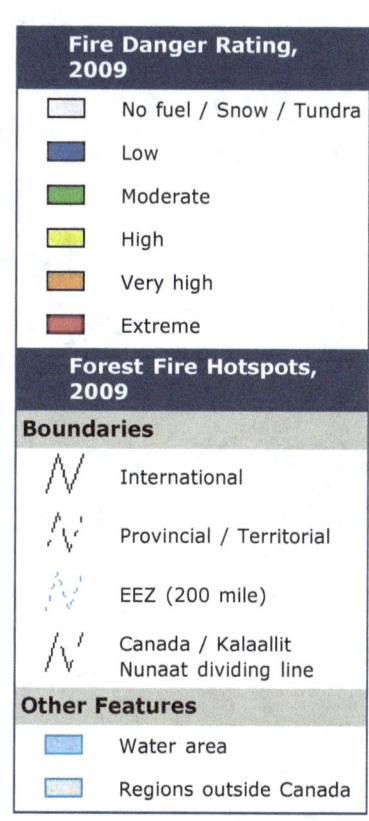

Abstract:

About 10 000 fires burn 2.5 million hectares of forest in Canada each year. This map focuses on two themes in fire science: monitoring the location and extent of fires (shown in the Hotspots map layer), and determining the fire danger based on weather conditions and vegetation types (shown in the Forest Fire Danger Rating map layer).

© Her Majesty the Queen in Right of Canada, 2011.

Canadian Maps on Environmental Concerns

Break-up of Sea Ice

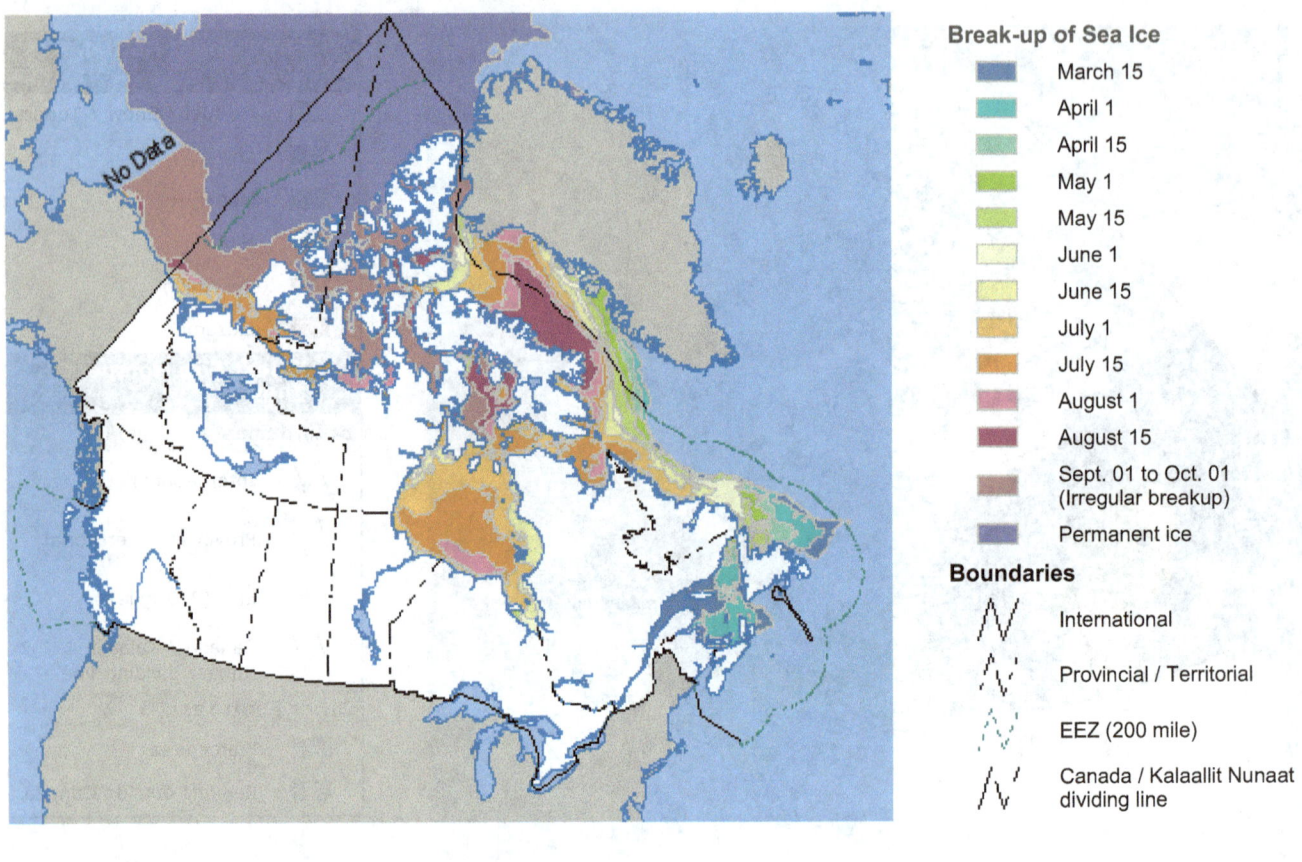

Abstract:

The typical retreat of the sea ice cover from the late winter to late summer is shown on this map. Sea ice is any form of ice that is found at sea and has originated from the freezing of seawater. Melting of sea ice begins in spring in the Gulf of St. Lawrence and East Newfoundland, retreating northward towards the Labrador coast. In June openings appear in Baffin Bay and the Beaufort Sea, while clearing is already underway in Hudson Bay. Break-up continues throughout the summer months, reaching a minimum extent around mid-September.

© Her Majesty the Queen in Right of Canada, 2009.

Species at Risk

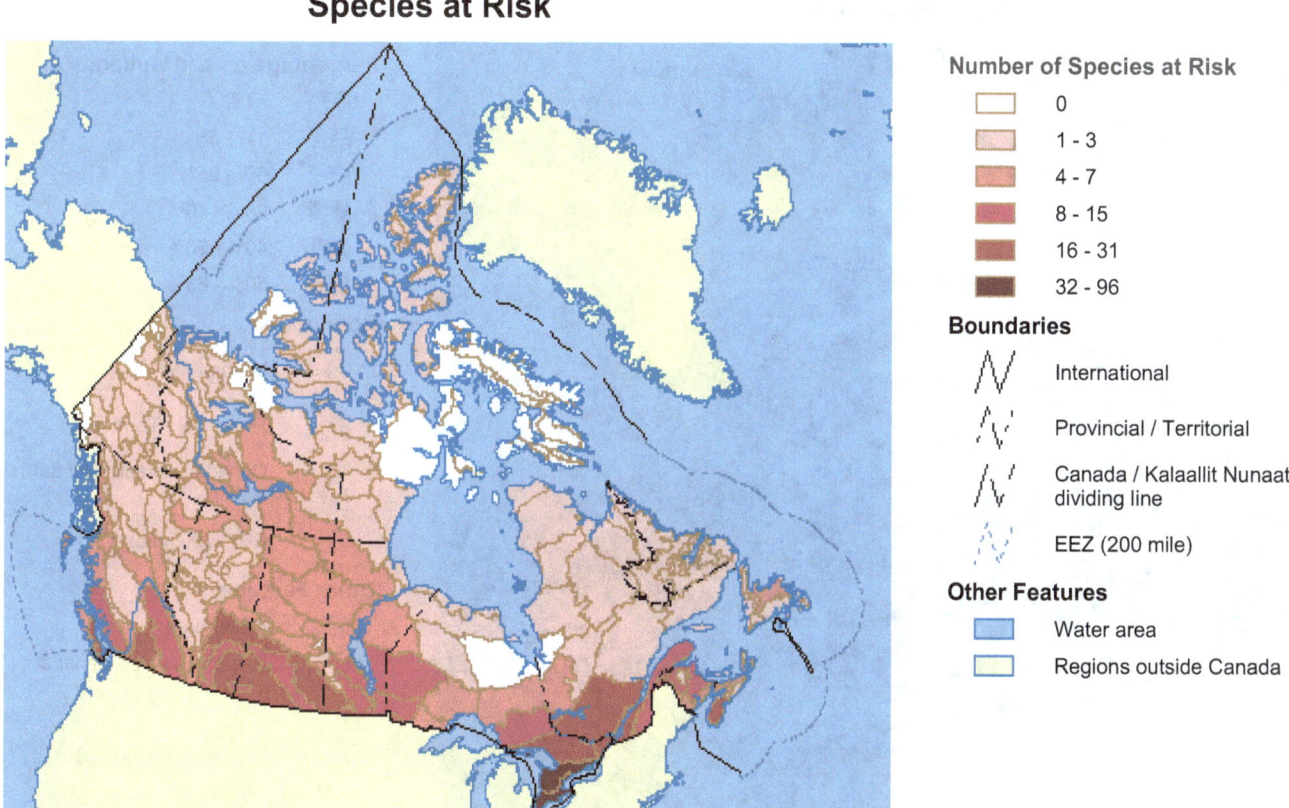

Abstract:

The highest number of species at risk is in the southern areas of Canada where human activity is most extensive and intensive. As of May 2002, 30 animal and plant species had disappeared in Canada. Eleven of these species are no longer found anywhere on the Earth. For most species the greatest threat is the alteration of habitat or essential growing conditions. The major national recovery program of endangered species in Canada is called RENEW. Canada is committed to implementing sustainable development, and establishment of protected areas representing all of Canada's landscapes and species.

© Her Majesty the Queen in Right of Canada, 2009.

Wetland Diversity

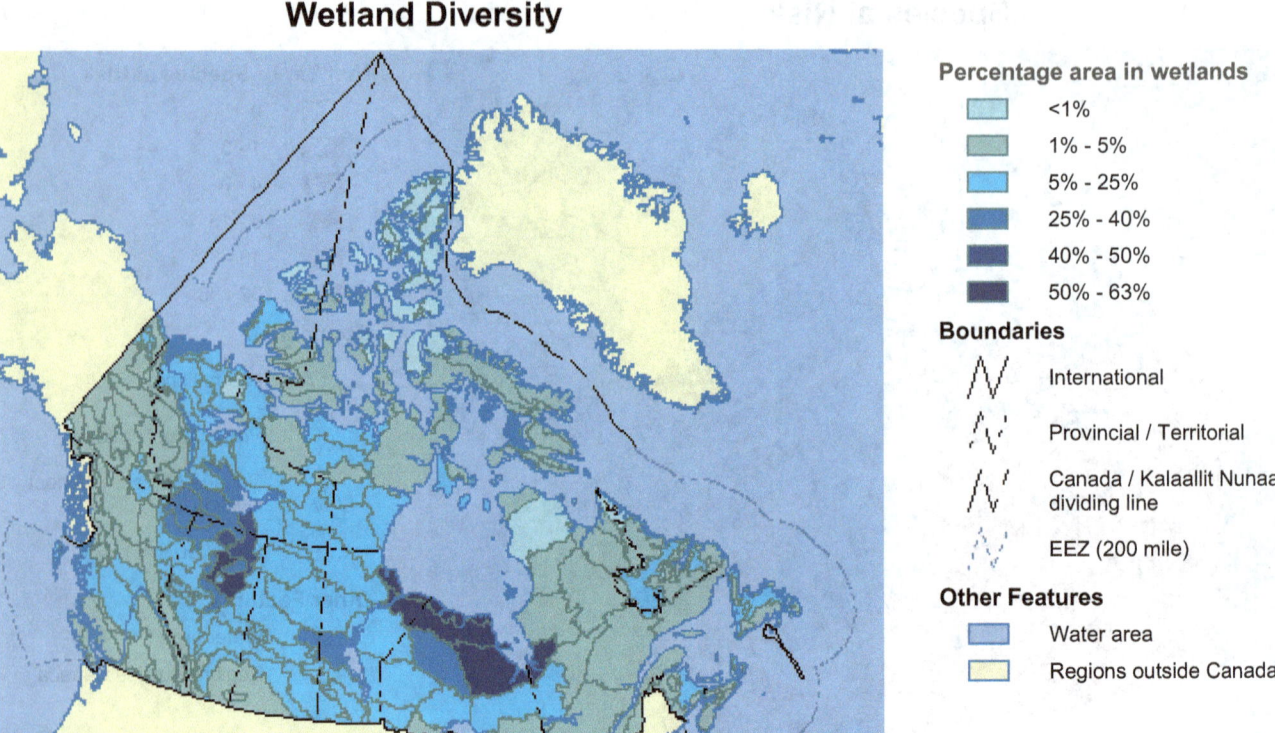

Abstract:

Wetlands are lands where water saturation is the dominant factor. Wetlands occupy about 18% of Canada, and Canada has about 25% of the world's wetlands. Wetlands foster the growth of hydrophytic vegetation and other biological activities such as the sustenance of large numbers of waterfowl, storage and release of large quantities of water, and the production of large amounts of energy in the form of peat. They offer food and shelter, slow down soil erosion, and contribute to the natural water purification process. Wetland conservation is important particularly in the human-dominated ecozones of southern Canada.

© Her Majesty the Queen in Right of Canada, 2009.

Coastal Sensitivity to Sea-Level Rise

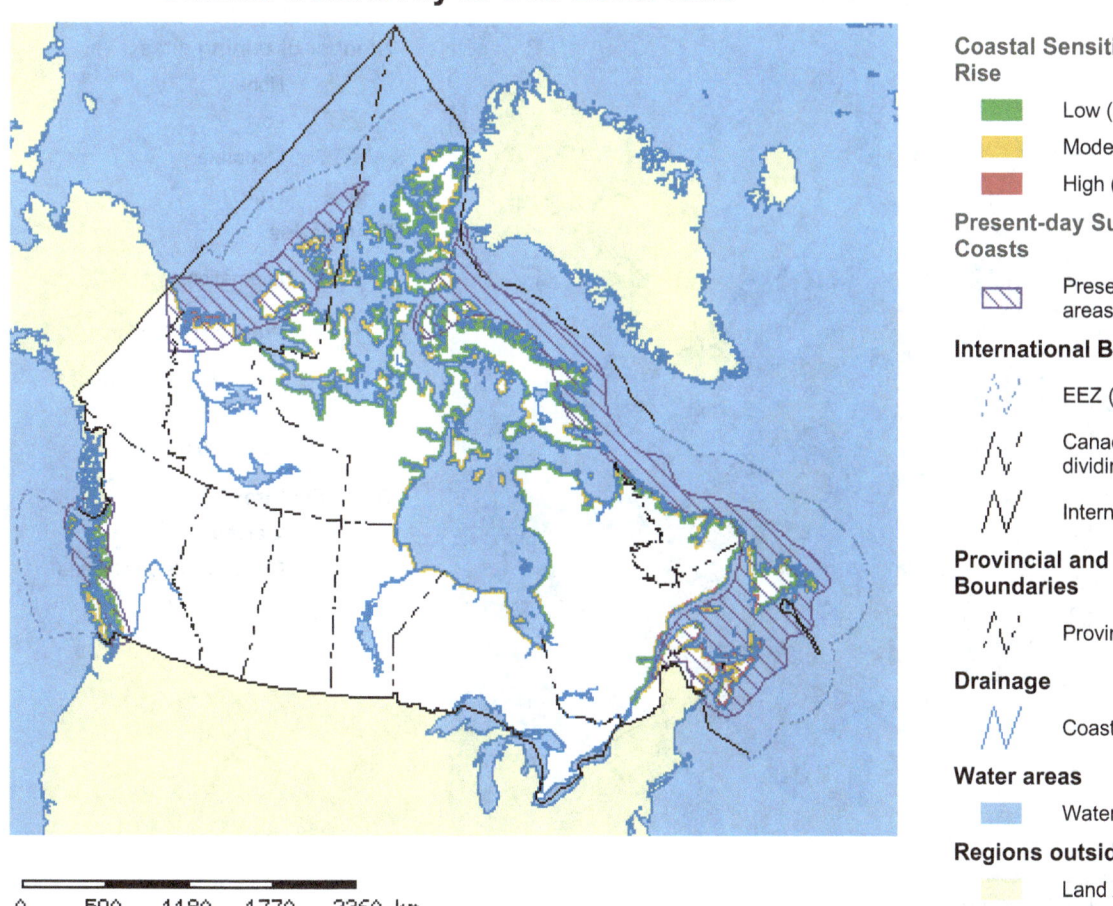

Abstract:

Sensitivity of the coastlines of Canada to the expected rise in sea level is shown here. Sensitivity here means the degree to which a coastline may experience physical changes such as flooding, erosion, beach migration, and coastal dune destabilization. Climate warming is expected to cause warming of the oceans and the partial melting of glaciers and ice-caps, resulting in a global rise in sea level. Two major regions of high sensitivity are identified: Atlantic Canada and parts of the Beaufort Sea coast.

© Her Majesty the Queen in Right of Canada, 2009.

Mining Sites

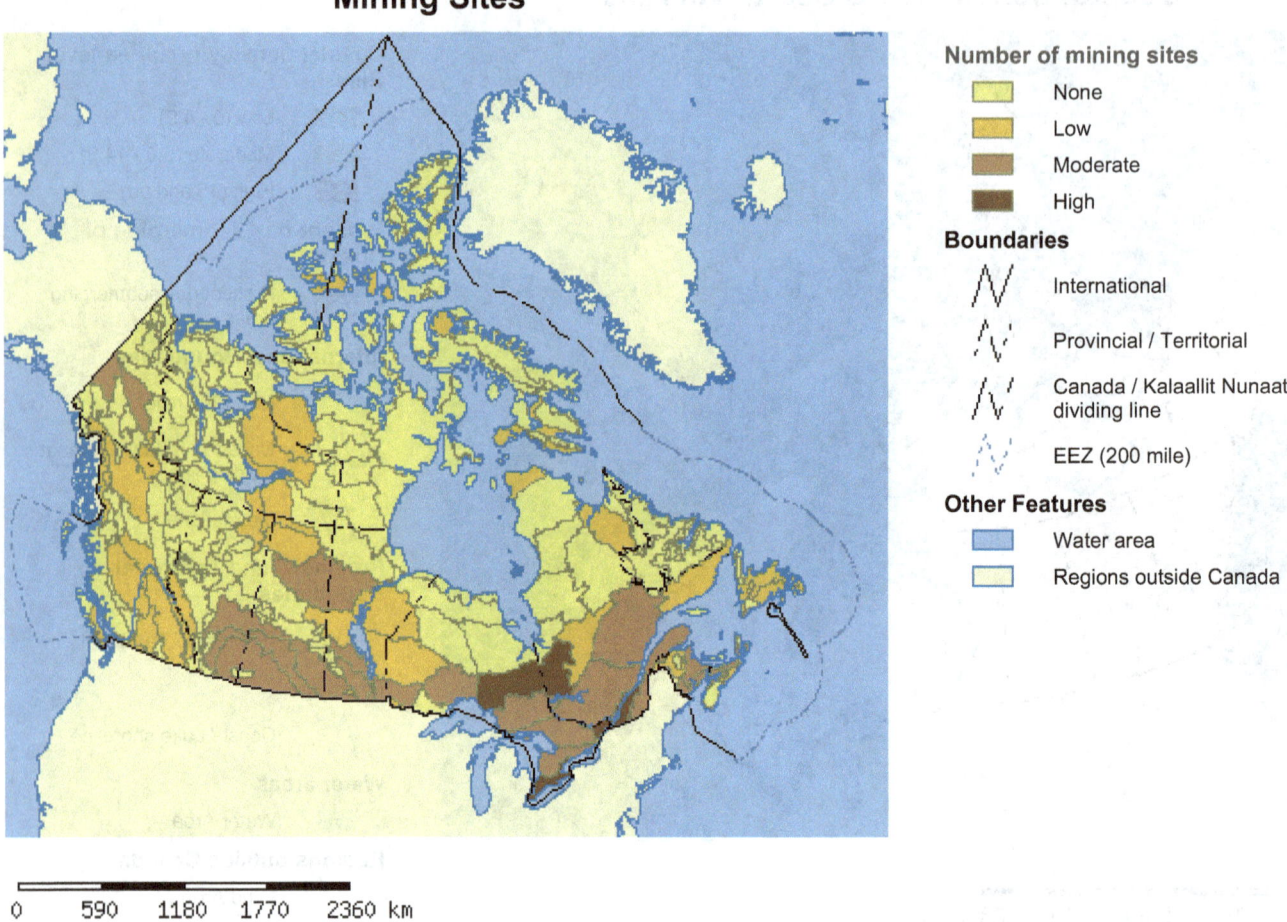

Abstract:

In Canada, mines are most heavily concentrated in the Mixedwood Plains, Boreal Shield, Prairie, and Montane Cordillera ecozones. Mines require accessibility, and are therefore strongly correlated with transportation routes. While most mines are designed as closed systems, occasionally water pollution results from problems in the mining, or milling processes, and aquatic ecosystems can be affected.

© Her Majesty the Queen in Right of Canada, 2009.

Sensitivity of Peatlands to Climate Change

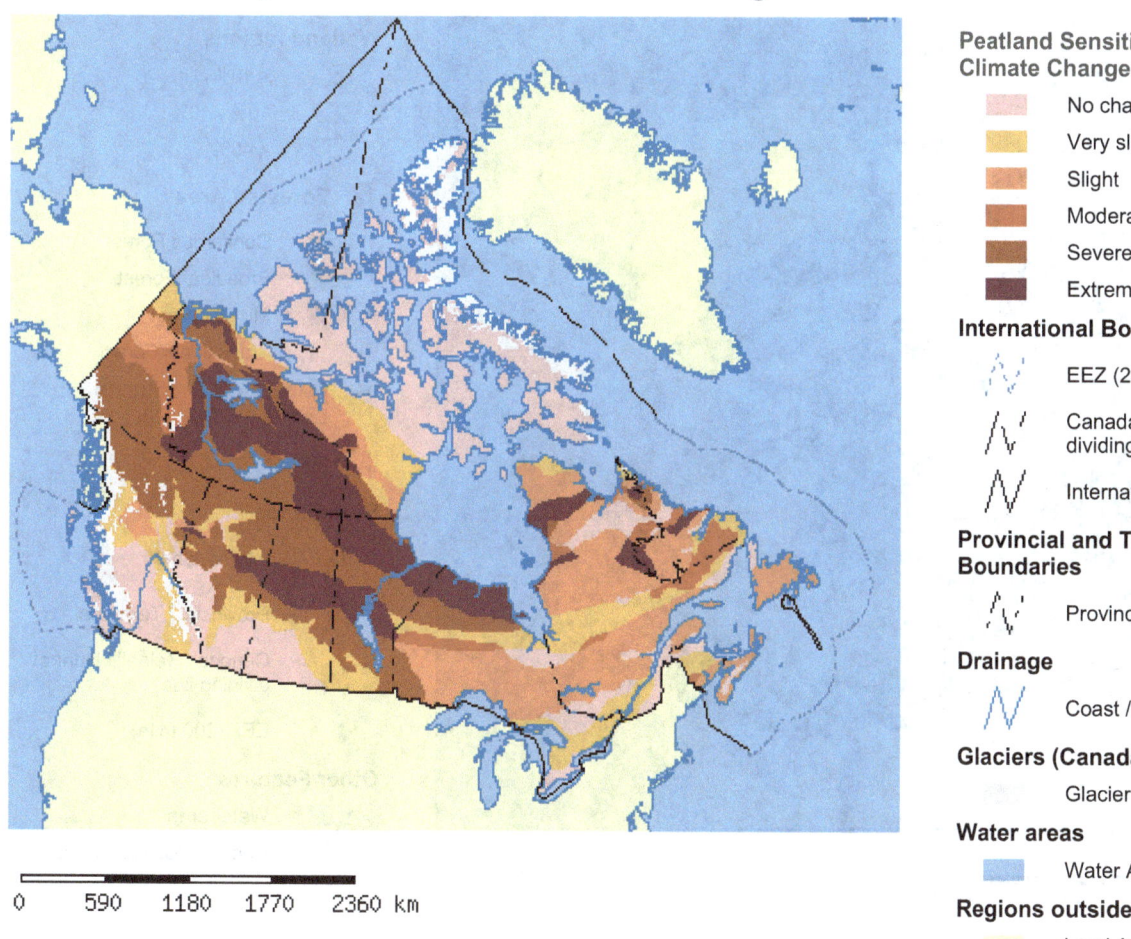

Abstract:

Sensitivity of peatlands to climate warming is shown here. Peatlands are massive deposits of peat, a material consisting largely of organic residue that acts as a natural sink for carbon. With global warming, however, they have the potential to become immense sources of greenhouse gases, and contribute significantly to further warming. The geographic areas where peatland will be most affected are the Hudson Bay lowlands, the Mackenzie River valley region and the northern parts of Alberta and Manitoba.

© Her Majesty the Queen in Right of Canada, 2009.

Wetlands and Forests

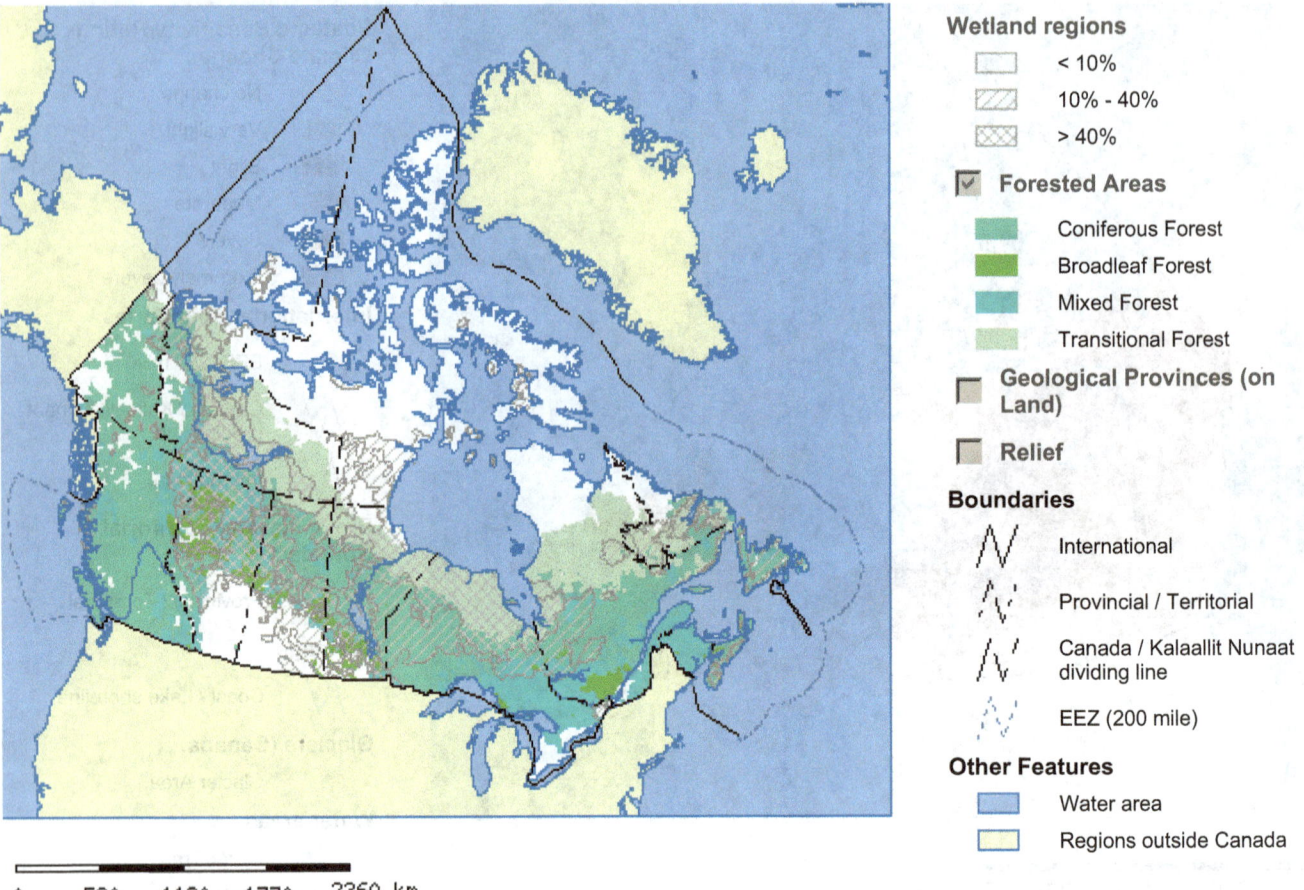

Abstract:

Wetlands are areas characterized by relatively shallow water. These areas play an extremely important role in Canada's ecology. Canada has one of the largest areas in the world with wetlands covering more than 1.2 million square kilometres. They occur across most of the country, and their location usually depends on local factors, which include drainage, topography and surface materials.

© Her Majesty the Queen in Right of Canada, 2009.

Productive Forest Land Use

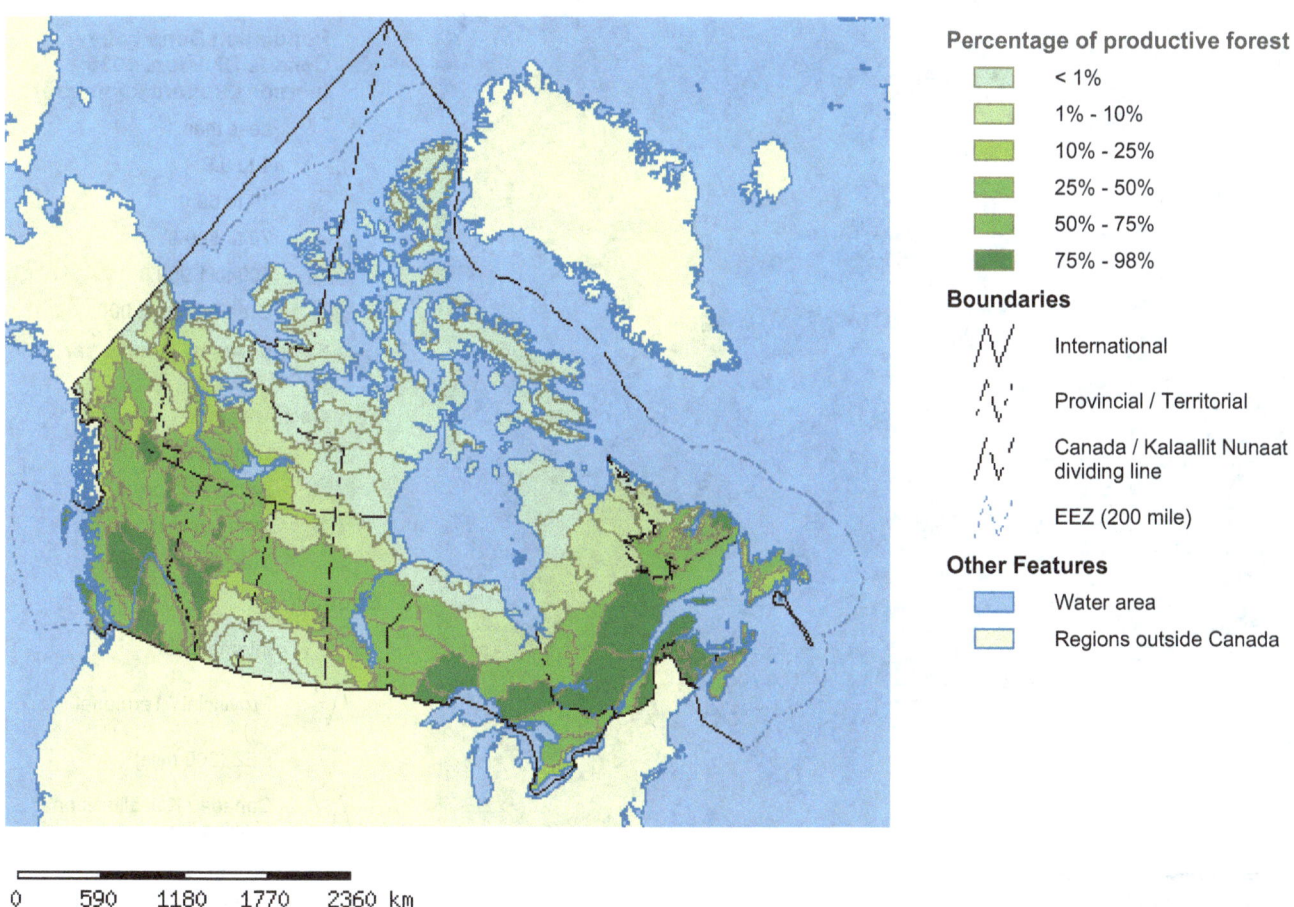

Abstract:

Forests sustain hundreds of economies across Canada. The forest industry is an active player in the conservation and sustainability of forested ecosystems. Forests are managed from a legal perspective by provincial and territorial legislation. The primary objective of forest management is timber production, which is achieved through harvesting and regenerating areas that have been harvested or damaged by fire or insects. Clearcutting has been the main method of harvesting in Canada. However, selective cutting methods are being promoted and investigated as alternatives where clearcutting may have negative impacts on wildlife habitat or water resources. Forested areas are managed for timber production, mostly in the Boreal Shield, Atlantic Maritime, Montane Cordillera, and Pacific Maritime ecozones.

© *Her Majesty the Queen in Right of Canada, 2009.*

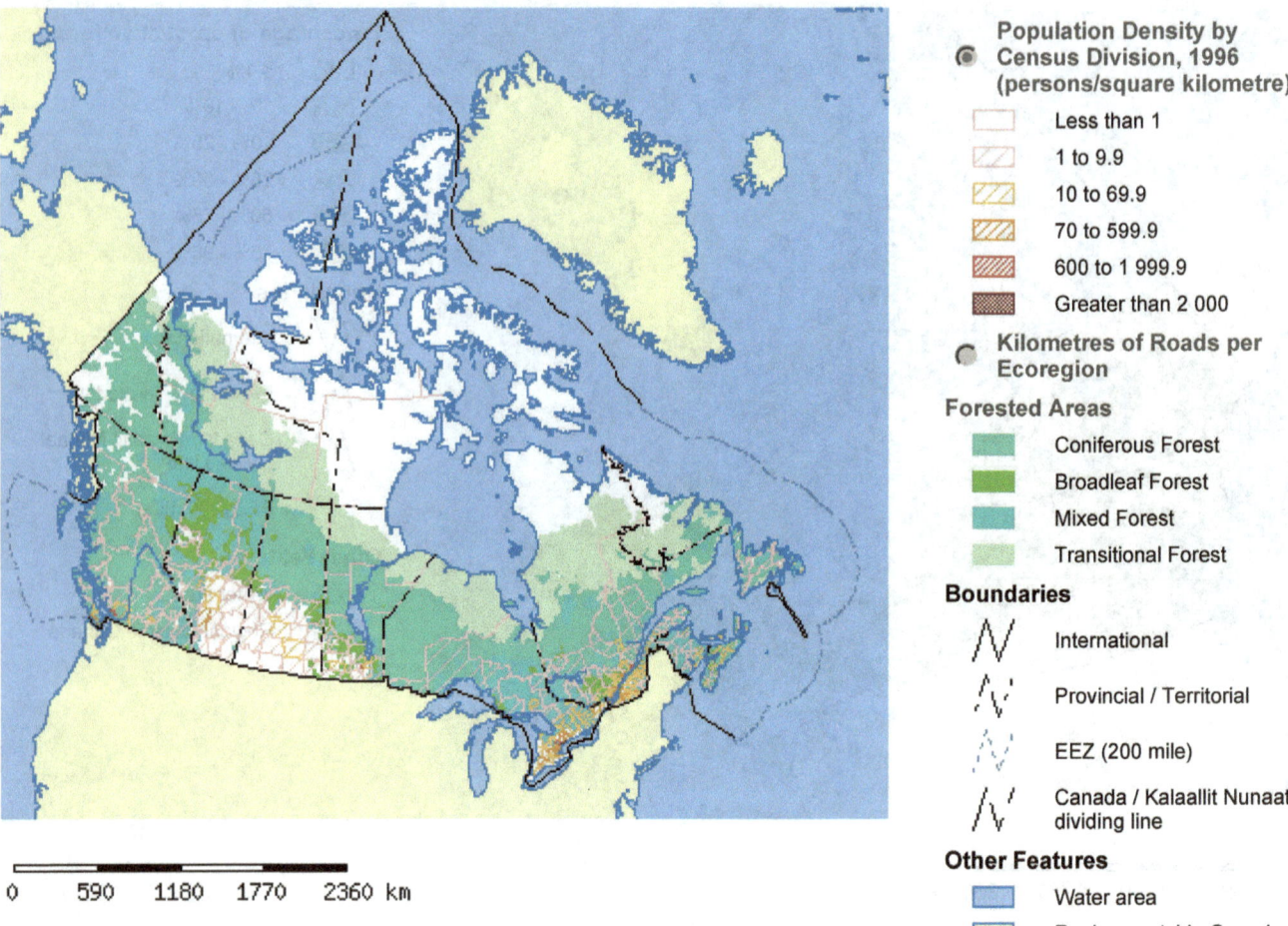

Abstract:

Increases in population, urbanisation and the development of the road network have replaced large forested lands and have created pressures on the remaining forests (or woodlands). Three principal Canadian forested regions have been most affected by these events: the Windsor-Québec corridor, the Prairies and the south-west of British Columbia.

© Her Majesty the Queen in Right of Canada, 2009.

Chronology of Environmental Events, June 2010 - March 2011

June 2010

Summit Greening
The Government of Canada made every effort to organize a sustainably managed G-8 summit when it planned this summer's meeting in Huntsville, Ontario. Consistent with the approach taken during previous high-level international events hosted by Canada, every effort was made to ensure the environmental equilibrium was maintained. Summit planners consulted with community partners and experts to understand and minimize any possible adverse impacts that hosting such an event might have on the natural environment.

The Plan
Our greening plan placed environmental concerns at the forefront of managing each facet of the G-8 Summit, including:

- **Muskoka 2010 G-8 Summit:** A Carbon-Neutral Summit: Through its carbon neutral strategy, the Government of Canada will offset greenhouse gas emissions resulting from the G-8 Summit.
- **Signature Project:** In consultation with the Town of Huntsville, a solar lighting system was chosen as the environmental signature project for the Muskoka 2010 G-8 Summit.
- **Ecosystem Impact Analysis:** The Muskoka 2010 G-8 Summit was held in an area that is prized for its pristine natural beauty. One of the first components of the sustainability plan for the Muskoka 2010 G-8 Summit was an ecosystem impact analysis that identified potential environmental impacts summit activities might have on the local environment.
- **Green Transportation:** Working to reduce the environmental impact of transportation associated with the Muskoka 2010 G-8 Summit was a key element of the summit sustainability strategy.
- **Green Venues:** The Government of Canada was pleased to host the Muskoka 2010 G-8 Summit in the Deerhurst Resort in Huntsville, Ontario, a venue that has taken a number of measures to reduce its overall environmental footprint.
- **Tree Planting:** The Government of Canada's commitment to hosting a sustainable Muskoka 2010 G-8 Summit included leaving a positive environmental legacy in Muskoka by planting several thousand trees that will contribute to the environmental health of the region.
- **Green Power:** In order to reduce greenhouse gas and other air emissions associated with the generation of electricity, the Government of Canada purchased "green" power for the Deerhurst Resort for the duration of the Summit.
- **Zero Waste:** The Government of Canada reduced and managed the solid waste generated as a result of the Muskoka 2010 G-8 Summit. The Summit diverted as much waste as possible from landfill.

Muskoka
Muskoka, the region where Huntsville is located, is the place where the farmland of southern Ontario gives way to the forests and ancient bedrock of the Canadian Shield, where the cities and towns begin dotting the landscape with decreased frequency.

To the west are the enigmatic expanses of Georgian Bay; to the east, the iconic highlands of Algonquin Park. Muskoka is justly known for its natural beauty—a place where year-round and seasonal residents alike enjoy the restorative and recreational benefits of plentiful lakes and forests. It is a place where balance between capitalizing on natural resources and protecting the land is increasingly a reality.

Muskoka boasts some of the cleanest, well-monitored freshwater in the world, and its residents are working to understand and balance the effects of day-to-day living in this unique, sensitive landscape. Muskoka is home to a world-class research station for acid rain and the University of Waterloo environmental research facility.

The G-8 Summit will unfold in full appreciation of the incalculable value of Muskoka's natural heritage.

Government of Canada. "Summit Greening." Summit Documents. 2010 Muskoka Summit. Last modified May 18, 2011. http://canadainternational.gc.ca/g8/summit-sommet/2010/muskoka-greening-muskoka.aspx?lang=eng.

July 2010

Government of Canada Announces Funding for Lake Simcoe Clean-up Projects
BARRIE, ON, July 13, 2010 – On behalf of Canada's Environment Minister, the Honourable Jim Prentice, Patrick Brown, Member of Parliament for Barrie, and Bruce Stanton, Member of Parliament for Simcoe North, today announced that eight projects will receive funding under round five of the Lake Simcoe Clean-Up Fund.

Initiatives funded by the Lake Simcoe Clean-Up Fund are designed to preserve and protect the environment of Lake Simcoe.

"Our Government is proud to be working in partnership with members of the Lake Simcoe community to restore the health of this important lake," said M.P. Brown. "These eight new projects, totaling of $1.6 million, will build on approximately one hundred other targeted projects which our Government has funded through the Lake Simcoe Clean-Up Fund since 2008."

"Projects funded under previous rounds of the Lake Simcoe Clean-Up Fund have produced positive results and are a great example of what we can achieve when we work in partnership," said M.P. Stanton. "Locally, this Fund is supporting important initiatives such as the Septic System Funding Program for Lake Simcoe Municipalities."

"Lake Simcoe is an important natural resource, as well as a regional economic driver, and this Government's Clean-Up Fund to restore the health of the lake is an investment in the future of the region," said Minister Prentice.

As part of this investment, the Septic System Funding Program will receive $760,000, for the third phase of a multi-year initiative. Building on the success of Phases 1 and 2, this program will continue to administer grant funds in order to encourage landowners within 300 metres of Lake Simcoe to upgrade and/or repair their current septic systems. This program will help to reduce high levels of phosphorus and other contaminants flowing directly into Lake Simcoe and nearby watercourses.

According to Lake Simcoe Region Conservation Authority Chair Virginia Hackson, the Lake Simcoe Clean-Up Fund "has been extraordinarily successful. We've undertaken more than 60 projects that would not have been possible otherwise. The positive impacts on the watershed will be felt for years to come."

This investment to clean up Lake Simcoe is part of the Government of Canada's Action Plan for Clean Water, which includes projects like the Health of the Oceans initiative to protect Canada's three oceans, the clean-up of contaminated sediment in Great Lakes Areas of Concern, and action on pollution in Lake Winnipeg.

Environment Canada, "Government of Canada Announces Funding for Lake Simcoe Clean-up Projects," news release, July 13, 2010, http://www.ec.gc.ca/default.asp?lang=En&n=714D9 AAE-1&news=41E3A324-0F7F-4969-82B2-FCCC8D780A26.

August 2010

Government of Canada and Nature Conservancy of Canada Conserve Valuable Habitat in Kawartha Lakes, Ontario
KAWARTHA LAKES, ON, August 18, 2010 – Barry Devolin, Member of Parliament for Haliburton-Kawartha Lakes-Brock, on behalf of Canada's Environment Minister, the Honourable Jim Prentice, today announced the Nature Conservancy of Canada's successful acquisition of the Little Bluestem Alvar-264.66 hectares (654 acres) of land in Kawartha Lakes, Ontario, secured in part with funding from Environment Canada's Natural Areas Conservation Program. The Government of Canada is a major contributor in this project, which has an overall budget of $543,885.

"As part of the International Year of Biodiversity, we are continuing to demonstrate real action in conserving our ecosystems and protecting sensitive species," said MP Barry Devolin. "Today, on behalf of the Government of Canada, I am proud to be here with our partners to announce the acquisition of this ecologically-significant land."

"This acquisition marks another achievement under our government's Natural Areas Conservation Program. With this investment, we are taking real action to protect and conserve our ecosystems and sensitive species for present and future generations," said Minister Jim Prentice. "Your actions, large or small, will help to protect the abundance and variety of life that is part of our natural heritage."

The Little Bluestem is a large piece of the Carden Alvar property in the City of Kawartha Lakes. It is adjacent to Nature Conservancy of Canada's 678-acre Prairie Smoke Nature Reserve. It is a relatively undisturbed area and similar in composition to the Prairie Smoke property. The acquisition of Little Bluestem will create a 538-hectare (1330-acre) natural reserve, which increases the protection of one of Ontario's rarest landscapes. The property also provides habitat for a number of species at risk including the Blanding's Turtle, the Milksnake, and the Common Nighthawk.

"These Gifts to Canadians are tangible examples of what we are able to achieve by working together. By designing and managing networks of protected areas, we fulfill our national and global responsibility to protect Canada's natural treasures for the future," said John Lounds, president and CEO of the Nature Conservancy of Canada. "What better way to celebrate our nation than by protecting the spectacular lands and wildlife that our country is known for around the world."

The Government of Canada's $225-million Natural Areas Conservation Program is an important on-the-ground initiative that takes real action to preserve Canada's environment and conserve its precious natural heritage for present and future generations. It is through the ongoing contribution from all donors that we can ensure the protection of natural areas in Canada. As of March 2010, under the Natural Areas Conservation Program over 138,600 hectares (342,500 acres) have been secured, protecting habitat for over 79 species at risk.

Environment Canada, "Government of Canada and Nature Conservancy of Canada Conserve Valuable Habitat in Kawartha Lakes, Ontario," news release, August 18, 2010, http://www.ec.gc.ca/default.asp?lang=En&n=714D9AAE-1&news=A56FD72E-991D-4C1B-9BB4-90230C3E3B1C.

September 2010

Environment Canada Receives International Award for Advancing Clean Technology with Zero Energy Housing Projects

WASHINGTON, DC, September 14, 2010 – Canada's Environment Minister, the Honourable Jim Prentice, accepted the International Star (I-Star) of Energy Efficiency Award from the Washington D.C.-based Alliance to Save Energy this evening. Environment Canada and Efficiency New Brunswick were jointly awarded the I-Star award for pioneering creative energy efficiency programs and solutions throughout Canada.

"We are working closely with our industry and international partners to demonstrate the role that zero energy housing can play in contributing to global greenhouse gas emission reductions," said Minister Prentice. "The Canadian-led demonstration projects currently underway in China and Mexico will help these major emerging economies to optimize performance of efficient buildings that integrate energy efficiency and renewable energy in a way that is both technically-feasible and cost-effective."

Environment Canada received the award for demonstrating leadership in advancing zero energy housing through the optimization of energy efficiency and integration of renewable energy into residential building design.

Through active participation in key international technology partnerships-including the Asia Pacific Partnership on Climate and Clean Development (APP) and the Renewable Energy & Energy Efficiency Partnership (REEEP)-and the Canada-Mexico Partnership, Environment Canada is partnering with the private sector to facilitate the exchange of energy-efficiency information and the development of demonstration homes in Mexico, China, India, Korea and Japan.

As an example, Canada was involved in the development of an international Zero Energy Housing roadmap. This project facilitated the construction of zero energy housing demonstration projects, and allowed APP partner countries to share knowledge and information, and identify different technologies for efficient building design.

As buildings worldwide-including residential housing-account for about 40 percent of global energy use and carbon dioxide emissions, Environment Canada's exemplary work on zero energy housing contributes to the Government of Canada's priority of promoting clean technology and energy efficiency as an important part of addressing climate change and reducing air emissions.

Environment Canada, "Environment Canada Receives International Award for Advancing Clean Technology with Zero Energy Housing Projects," news release, September 14, 2010, http://www.ec.gc.ca/default.asp?lang=En&n=714D9AAE-1&news=A1966AC2-3E88-44D3-AE52-79482FB5B583.

October 2010

Government of Canada Announces Details of Major Investment to International Climate Change

WATERLOO, ON, October 1, 2010 – Today, the Honourable Jim Prentice, Minister of the Environment, released the details of Canada's $400 million commitment for international climate change while speaking to the Centre for International Governance Innovation's annual conference.

"This represents Canada's largest ever contribution to support international efforts to address climate change and it will support three key areas in which Canada has considerable expertise: adaptation, clean energy, forests and agriculture," said Minister Prentice.

Funding for adaption will support critical on the ground projects that will build knowledge and adaptive capacity, while reducing vulnerability to natural disasters. Other funding will focus on mobilizing private sector investment in renewable energy and energy efficiency projects, and will provide technical assistance to developing countries as they work to implement these types of clean energy. Canada's contribution will also support projects in developing countries which are essential to laying the groundwork for ambitious global action on Reducing Emissions from Deforestation and Forest Degradation (REDD+).

Under the Copenhagen Accord, developed countries committed to provide fast-start financing approaching US$30 billion for 2010-2012 to support climate change mitigation, including financing for adaptation, capacity building, technology transfer and reducing greenhouse gas emissions from deforestation in developing countries.

As promised as part of the Accord, this investment represents the 2010 portion of Canada's fair share of the fast-start financing promised by developed countries under the Copenhagen Accord. While Canada contributes to 2 per cent of worldwide GHG emissions, it is contributing 4 per cent of the funding.

Environment Canada, "Government of Canada Announces Details of Major Investment to International Climate Change," news release, October 1, 2010, http://www.ec.gc.ca/default.asp?lang=En&n=714D9AAE-1&news=454E8F15-55C2-4A70-9FC0-249B35E5DD80.

November 2010

Senate Kills Climate Change Accountability Act

OTTAWA, ON, November 17, 2010 – The Climate Change Accountability Act—Bill C-311 twice won the support of elected members of Parliament, reflecting the views of the majority of Canadians who have been demanding stronger action on climate change.

Despite this, the Harper Conservatives used their new unelected majority in the Senate this week to vote down C-311 even before members of the upper house had time to debate or consider it.

In a trick procedural move, the Conservatives called for a sudden vote on Bill C-311 while many Liberal Senators were missing. Although there is precedent for ambushing absent members in Parliament, the fact that the bill was called for a vote before any debate had taken place was unprecedented.

Some MPs reported that Conservative senators were ordered not to speak on the bill at any time during the 193 days it was before the Senate. Even the Conservative speaker of the Senate was told to vote against the bill.

"This reckless approach to climate change must stop. Global warming is an urgent problem that requires urgent solutions," says Graham Saul, executive director of Climate Action Network Canada (CAN-C).

"Stephen Harper has done what he always promised never to do—use unelected officials to counter the will of Parliament and the Canadian public," Saul notes.

"As we head into the United Nations climate talks in Cancun later this month, it is unacceptable that Canada's only climate change legislation has been defeated after years of majority support from our elected members of parliament and their constituents."

Canada is the only country in the industrialize[d] world to:

- sign and ratify the Kyoto protocol and then announce that it has no intention of honouring its commitments;
- return from Copenhagen and announce that it is weakening its targets;
- allow its only major federal program supporting renewable energy to run out of money;
- allow its only major federal program supporting home efficiency to run out of money; and
- actively work to weaken climate change policy in the United States and Europe.

"The Harper government has been repeatedly promising to regulate industry and doing nothing in practice, all the while handing out billions of dollars in tax breaks to some of the biggest oil companies in the world," says Saul.

National Union of Public and General Employees. "Senate Kills Climate Change Accountability Act." Issues and Campaigns. Environment. Last modified November 17, 2010. http://www.nupge.ca/content/3761/senate-kills-climate-change-accountability-act-bill-c-311.

December 2010

Government of Canada Highlights Commitment to Renewable Fuels

OTTAWA, ON, December 15, 2010 – On behalf of Canada's Environment Minister, the Honourable John Baird, the Honourable Gerry Ritz, Minister of Agriculture and Agri-Food and Minister for the Canadian Wheat Board, highlighted today the Government of Canada's commitment to renewable fuels. Federal regulations requiring 5 per cent renewable fuel content in gasoline came into effect today, December 15, 2010.

"This initiative is one of Canada's contributions to the fight against climate change," said Minister Ritz. "We are proud to be moving forward with the Renewable Fuels Regulations as they will benefit Canada's economy, our farmers and our environment."

These Regulations are one pillar of the Government's broader Renewable Fuels Strategy. The Strategy will establish a demand for renewable fuels that will help stimulate Canadian biofuels production, create jobs and new market opportunities for farmers, and help create jobs in rural communities, while accelerating the commercialization of new biofuel technologies.

"This federal 5 per cent requirement is estimated to result in a reduction in greenhouse gas emissions of one megatonne per year over and above the reductions attributable to existing provincial requirements-the equivalent of taking a quarter million vehicles off the road," said Minister Baird.

"Biofuels can help reduce greenhouse gas emissions and air pollutants while sustaining economic growth and development," said the Honourable Christian Paradis, Minister of Natural Resources. "In the midst of a global economic slowdown, our Government is working to accelerate key investments in Canada in order to create jobs and help stimulate our economy."

These Regulations are a key initiative in support of the Government of Canada's commitment to reduce Canada's total greenhouse gas emissions by 17 per cent from 2005 levels by 2020. In addition, the Government of Canada has finalized vehicle tailpipe emissions regulations under the Canadian Environmental Protection Act, 1999, that are aligned with those of the United States, and is working to do the same for heavy-duty vehicles.

Environment Canada, "Government of Canada Highlights Commitment to Renewable Fuels," news release, December 15, 2010, http://www.ec.gc.ca/default.asp?lang=En&n=714D9AAE-1&news=41704C39-126F-40E0-862F-AEB77721B161.

January 2011

Joint Review Panel for the Enbridge Northern Gateway Project releases Panel Session Results and Decision

CALGARY, AB, January 19, 2011 – The Joint Review Panel (the Panel) conducting the review of the proposed Enbridge Northern Gateway Project has released its Panel Session Results and Decision based on comments received on the additional information which Northern Gateway should be required to file, the draft List of Issues, and comments related to potential hearing locations.

The Panel decided that:

1. Additional information on the design and risk assessment of the proposed project is required. Once the additional information is received a Hearing Order will be issued.

2. It would make changes to the draft List of Issues.

3. Hearing locations will be in proximity to the pipeline and marine components of the project. Specific hearing locations will be decided at a later date.

To view the complete response from the Panel or for detailed information about the public Panel sessions conducted in Whitecourt Alberta and Kitimat and Prince George British Columbia, or to learn about ways in which interested people may wish to become involved, please visit www.gatewaypanel.review.gc.ca.

The proposed Northern Gateway project involves the construction of two 1,170 kilometre long pipelines running from Bruderheim, Alberta to Kitimat, British Columbia and the construction and operation of the Kitimat Marine Terminal.

About the Joint Review Panel

The Joint Review Panel for the Enbridge Northern Gateway Project is an independent body, mandated by the Minister of the Environment and the National Energy Board. The Panel will assess the environmental effects of the proposed project and review the application under both the Canadian Environmental Assessment Act and the National Energy Board Act.

Canadian Environmental Assessment Agency, "Joint Review Panel for Enbridge Nothern Gateway Project Releases Panel Session Results and Decision," news release, January 19, 2011, http://gatewaypanel.review-examen.gc.ca/clf-nsi/nwsrls/2011/nwsrls01-eng.html.

February 2011

Government of Canada Moving Forward on Road to Historic Waste Cleanup in Port Hope

PORT HOPE, ON – The Port Hope Area Initiative will take a major step forward this spring with the construction of an access road to facilitate the construction and operation of a new long-term waste management facility.

The Honourable Christian Paradis, Minister of Natural Resources, and Rick Norlock, Member of Parliament for Northumberland-Quinte West, announced today that the Government of Canada will tender proposals to construct the access road in the coming weeks.

"The Government of Canada has a long-standing commitment to clean up historic low-level radioactive waste sites in this community, and I am pleased to see this progress," said Minister Paradis. "At the same time, the construction of this access road and other construction activities that will be part of the Port Hope Area Initiative will create both short- and long-term opportunities for economic development in this beautiful community."

"I am pleased to see that the hard work done by the Port Hope Area Initiative and the municipality over the last several years is beginning to show tangible results," said Mr. Norlock. "We look forward to continued collaboration with the people of Port Hope as we develop and implement a solution that will benefit the community and protect the environment for the long term."

Public Works and Government Services Canada, on behalf of Natural Resources Canada, will be competitively tendering the construction project on MERX, the Government of Canada's public electronic tendering service. The contract is expected to be awarded in spring 2011.

The Port Hope Area Initiative (PHAI) is dedicated to the safe cleanup and long-term management of historic low-level radioactive waste in the municipalities of Port Hope and Clarington. The PHAI Management Office is a partnership of Natural Resources Canada with Atomic Energy of Canada Limited and Public Works and Government Services Canada.

Natural Resources Canada, "Government of Canada Moving Forward on Road to Historic Waste Cleanup in Port Hope," news release, February 14, 2011, http://www.nrcan.gc.ca/media/newcom/2011/201123-eng.php.

March 2011

Shale Gas: Operations of This Industry will be Subject to the Development of Scientific Knowledge

MONTRÉAL, QC, March 8, 2011 – Minister of Sustainable Development, Environment and Parks Pierre Arcand announced that he has released the report issued by the Bureau d'audiences publiques sur l'environnement (BAPE) on the sustainable development of the shale gas industry in Québec. In so doing, the minister announced that he looks favourably on the BAPE report and will immediately take action on its main recommendation and move forward with the strategic environmental assessment.

"The commissioners have produced a rigorous report that sheds valuable light on this issue. I welcome its main recommendations, and I can state that it will guide our future actions," declared Minister Arcand.

The main recommendation: a strategic environmental assessment.

In its report, the BAPE puts forth 43 observations and issues 101 opinions that are chiefly addressed to the Government of Québec. These recommendations target three main directions for intervention:

- Address the knowledge deficit within the industry, government and the general population.
- Encourage the social acceptability of this development through innovation in the area of public hearings and dialogue with the various government and regional actors that are involved.
- Strengthen current regulatory provisions.

In order to immediately follow up on the report's main recommendation (move forward with a strategic environmental assessment on shale gas), the minister announced that a committee of experts and representatives from government, municipalities and industry would be soon created.

The BAPE recommends that development be controlled during the strategic environmental assessment process. Transitional regulations will be required, and will be adopted in the short term. New drilling will only be authorized when required to advance scientific knowledge for the strategic environmental assessment.

"The government is committed to ensuring that this industry develops properly, or else close down. The people of Québec need to know that we will abide no compromise on matters of health, safety or respect for the environment, and that we will take all the time needed to ensure that these conditions are fulfilled," the minister concluded.

Ministère du Développement durable, de l'Environnement et des Parcs (Quebec), "Shale Gas," news release, March 8, 2011, http://www.mddep.gouv.qc.ca/communiques_en/2011/c20110308-shale-gas.htm.

Environmental Abbreviations

Indicating academic degrees, memberships and honours particular to the sciences, engineering and other professional standings in environmental pursuits. This list is intended to add definition to abbreviations that may not be commonly encountered. For a complete list of abbreviations see the *Canadian Almanac and Directory*.

A.C.	"Advanced Certification" Canadian Association of Medical Radiation Technologists
A.C.I.C.	Associate of Canadian Institute of Chemistry
A.C.S.M.	— of Cambourne School of Mines
A.F.R.A.S.	Fellow of the Royal Aeronautical Society
A.L.S.	Commissioned Alberta Land Surveyor
A.M.E.I.C.	Associate Member of the Engineering Institute of Canada
A.M.I.C.E.	— Member of the Institution of Civil Engineers (British)
A.M.I.E.E.	— of the Institute of Electrical Engineers
A.M.I.Mech.E.	— of the Institution of Mechanical Engineers (British)
A.R.I.C.	— of the Royal Institute of Chemistry
A.R.S.H.	— of the Royal Society of Health
A.R.S.M.	— of the Royal School of Mines
A.Sc.T.	Applied Science Technologist
Assoc. Inst. M.M.	Associate of the Institute of Mining and Metallurgy (British)
B.A.S. (B.A.Sc.)	Bachelor of Applied Science
B.C.E.	— of Civil Engineering
B.E. (B.Eng.)	— of Engineering
B.E.D.S.	— of Environmental Design Studies
B.E.S.	— of Environmental Sciences/Studies
B.ès.Sc.	Bachelier ès Science
B.ès.Sc.App.	— ès Science Appliquée
B.L.A.	Bachelor of Landscape Architecture
B.S.A.	— of Science in Agriculture
B.Sc.	— of Science
B.Sc.E.	— of Science in Civil Engineering
B.Sc.F (B.S.F.)	— of Science in Forestry
B.Sc.F.E.	— of Science in Forestry Engineering
C.C.	Chartered Cartographer
C.C.E.P.	Canadian Certified Environmental Practitioner
C.E.A.	Certified Environmental Auditor
C.H.E.	Certified Health Executive
Chem. Ing.	Ingénieur Chimiste Diplomé (Swiss Fed. Inst. Technology)
C.I.F.	Canadian Institute of Forestry
C.I.M.	Certified Industrial Manager
C.I.S.&P.	Canadian Inst. of Surveying & Photogrammetry
C.L.S.	Canada Land Surveyor
C.M.M.	Certified Municipal Manager (Ontario)
C.M.O.S.	Canadian Meterological & Oceanographic Society Consultant
C.P.P.O.	Certified Public Purchasing Officer
C.P.P.	— Professional Purchaser
C.R.S.P.	Canadian Registered Safety Professional
D.A.	Doctor of Archaeology (Laval)
D.Arch.	— of Architecture
D.A.Sc.	— in Applied Sciences
D.Ch.E.	— of Chemical Engineering (American)
D.Eng.	— of Engineering
D. ès Sc. App.	Docteur ès science appliquée
D.F.	Doctor of Forestry (American)
Dip. Bact.	— in Bacteriology
D.L.S.	Dominion Land Surveyor
D.S.A. (D.Sc.A.)	Docteur ès science appliqués
D.Sc.	Doctor of Science
D.Sc.Nat.	— in Natural Science
E.E.	Electrical Engineer
E.M.	Mining Engineer
F.A.G.S.	Fellow of the American Geographical Society
F.A.O.U.	— of the American Ornithologists Union
F.A.P.H.A.	— of the American Public Health Association
F.C.I.C.	— of the Chemical Institute of Canada
F.C.M.R.T.	— of the Canadian Association of Medical Radiation Technologists
F.E.	Forest Engineer
F.E.I.C.	Fellow of the Engineering Institute of Canada
F.F.R.	— of the Faculty of Radiologists (British)
F.G.S.	— of the Geological Society (British)
F.G.S.A.	— of the Geological Society of America
F.I.C.	— of the Institute of Chemistry
F.I.C.E.	— of the Institution of Civil Engineers
F.I.E.E.	— of the Institution of Electrical Engineers
F.M.S.A.	— of the Mineralogical Society of America
F.R.A.I.	— of the Royal Anthropological Institute
F.R.A.I.C.	— of the Royal Architectural Institute of Canada
F.R.G.S.	— of the Royal Geographical Society
F.R.Hort.S.	— of the Royal Horticultural Society
F.R.I.B.A.	— of the Royal Institute of British Architects
F.R.I.C.	— of the Royal Institute of Chemistry
F.R.I.C.S.	— of the Royal Institution of Chartered Surveyors
F.R.M.S. (F.R.Met.S.)	— of the Royal Meteorological Society
F.R.S.H.	— of the Royal Society of Health
F.Z.S.	— of the Zoological Society (British)
L.S.	Land Surveyor
L.S.A.	Licentiate in Agricultural Science
M.A.I.E.E.	Member of American Institute of Electrical Engineers
M.A.I.M.E.	— of American Institute of Mining Engineers
M.A.P.	Maîtrise en administration publique
M.Arch.	Master of Architecture
M.A.Sc. (M.A.S.)	— of Applied Science
M.A.S.C.E.	Member of the American Society of Civil Engineers
M.A.S.M.E.	— of the American Society of Mechanical Engineers
M.C.E.	— of Civil Engineering
M.Ch.E.	— of Chemical Engineering (American)
M.C.I.C.	— of the Chemical Institute of Canada
M.C.I.F.	— of the Canadian Institute of Forestry
M.C.I.M.	— of the Canadian Institute of Mining
M.C.I.M.M.	— of the Canadian Institute of Mining and Metallurgy
M.E.D.S.	— Master of Environmental Design Studies
M.E.E.	— of Electrical Engineering (American)
M.E.I.C.	Member of the Engineering Institute of Canada
M.Eng.	Master of Engineering
M.E.S.	— of Environmental Sciences/Studies
M.F.	— of Forestry
M.I.C.E.	Member of the Institution of Civil Engineers (British)
M.I.E.E.	— of the Institution of Electrical Engineers (British)
M.I.M.M.	— of the Institute of Mining and Metallurgy (British)
M.Pl.	Master of Planning
M.P.M.	— of Pest Management
M.R.A.I.C.	Member of the Royal Architectural Institute of Canada
M.R.M.	Master of Resource Management
M.R.S.H.	Member of the Royal Society of Health
M.S.A.	Master of Science in Agriculture
M.Sc.	— of Science
M.Sc.A.	— of Applied Science
M.S.C.E.	— of Science in Civil Engineering
M.Sc.F.	— of Science in Forestry
M.U.P.	— of Urban Planning
M.U.R.P.	— of Urban and Rural Planning
M.V.	Médécin Vétérinaire
M.V.Sc.	Master of Veterinary Science
N.D.A.	National Diploma in Agriculture (Royal Ag. Soc. of Engineering)
O.L.S.	Ontario Land Surveyor
P.E.	Professional Engineer
P.Eng.	Registered Professional Engineer
P.P.	Professional Purchaser
P.P.B.	Public Buyer
P.T.I.C.	Patent & Trade Mark Institute of Canada
Q.L.S.	Québec Land Surveyor
R.P.Bio.	Registered Professional Biologist
R.P.F.	— Professional Forester

Environmental Abbreviations

Sc.D. . . . . Doctorat ès Sciences
Sc.L. . . . . Licence ès Sciences

Geographical Terms

Provinces

Alberta	AB	Alberta
British Columbia	BC	Colombie-Britannique
Manitoba	MB	Manitoba
New Brunswick	NB	Nouveau-Brunswick
Newfoundland (& Labrador)	NL	Terre-Neuve (et Labrador)
Nova Scotia	NS	Nouvelle-Écosse
Nunavut	NU	Nunavut
Ontario	ON	Ontario
Prince Edward Island	PE	Île-du-Prince-Édouard
Québec	PQ	Québec
Saskatchewan	SK	Saskatchewan
Northwest Territories	NT	Territoires du Nord-Ouest
Yukon	YT	Yukon

The United States

Alabama	AL
Alaska	AK
Arizona	AZ
Arkansas	AR
California	CA
Colorado	CO
Connecticut	CT
Delaware	DE
District of Columbia	DC
Florida	FL
Georgia	GA
Hawaii	HI
Idaho	ID
Illinois	IL
Indiana	IN
Iowa	IA
Kansas	KA
Kentucky	KY
Louisiana	LA
Maine	ME
Maryland	MD
Massachusetts	MA
Michigan	MI
Minnesota	MN
Mississippi	MS
Missouri	MO
Montana	MT
Nebraska	NE
Nevada	NV
New Hampshire	NH
New Jersey	NJ
New Mexico	NM
New York	NY
North Carolina	NC
North Dakota	ND
Ohio	OH
Oklahoma	OK
Oregon	OR
Pennsylvania	PA
Rhode Island	RI
South Carolina	SC
South Dakota	SD
Tennessee	TN
Texas	TX
Utah	UT
Vermont	VT
Virginia	VA
Washington	WA
West Virginia	WV
Wisconsin	WI
Wyoming	WY

Street Addresses

Avenue	Ave./av
Boulevard	Blvd./boul.
Building	Bldg./Édifice
Care of/au soins de	c/o a/s
Court	Ct.
Crescent	Cres.
Drive/Promenade	Dr./promenade
Floor/Étage	Fl./étage
Highway/Route	Hwy./Rte.
Parkway	Pkwy.
Place/Place	Pl.
Post Office Bag	PO Bag
Post Office Box/Case postal	PO Box/CP
Postal Sub-Station	Postal Sub-Stn./sous-station
Road/Chemin	Rd./ch
Retail Postal Outlet	RPO
Rural Route/Route rurale	RR
Square/Carré	Sq./carré
Station/Succursale	Stn/Succ
Suburban Service/Service	SS/suburbain
Street/Rue	St./rue

Days of the Week

Sunday	D	dimanche
Monday	M	lundi
Tuesday	T	mardi
Wednesday	W	mercredi
Thursday	R	jeudi
Friday	F	vendredi
Saturday	S	samedi

Months of the Year

January/janvier	Jan./jan.
February/février	Feb./fév.
March/mars	March/mars
April/avril	April/avril
May/mai	May/mai
June/juin	June/juin
July/juillet	July/juillet
August/août	Aug./août
September/septembre	Sept./sept.
October/octobre	Oct./oct.
November/novembre	Nov./nov.
December/décembre	Dec./déc.

Publications/Frequency

weekly/w	hebdomadaire
every two weeks/bi-weekly	quinzomadaire
twice a month/s-m.	bimensuel
monthly/m.	mensuel
every two months	bimestriel
quarterly/q.	trimestriel
twice a year/s-a.	semestriel
annual/a.	annuel
# per annum/# pa	# fois par an
every two years/biennial	tous les deux ans
every four years/quadrennial	tous les quatre ans
irregular/irreg.	irrég.

Translations

Selected titles, tags, phrases

Acronym	Acronyme
Activities, Task Forces, Programs, Services	Activités, groupes de travail, programmes, services
Administrator	Administrateur(trice)

Affiliation(s) . . . . .Affiliation(s)
Also known as. . . . . .Également appelé
Amount . . . . .Montant
Annual Operating Budget . . . . . . .Budget de fonctionnement annuel
Attendees . . . . .Participants
Author. . . . . .Auteur(e)
Awards . . . . .Attribution de prix
Awareness Events . . . . .Événements de sensibilisation
Business Agent. . . . . .Agent d'affaires
Chief Officers . . . . .Membres du bureau directeur
Commissioner. . . . . .Commissaire
Committees. . . . . .Comités
Communications Officer . . . . .Agent de communications
Conferences . . . . .Conférences
Contact/Library . . . . .Responsable/Bibliothèque
Contact Person . . . . .Personne ressource
Contact/Speakers . . . . .Responsable/Conférenciers
Contents (Publications). . . . . .Contenu(Publications)
Conventions . . . . .Congrès
Coordinator . . . . .Coordonnateur(trice)
Corresponding Secretary . . . . . . .Secrétaire correspondancier
Crisis-Line . . . . .Ligne secours
Deputy Secretary . . . . .Secrétaire adjoint(e)
Editor. . . . . .Rédacteur(trice)
Eligibility .Éligibilité
E-Mail . . . . .Courriel
EPT. . . . . .Employé(e) plein temps
Executive Assistant. . . . . .Adjoint(e) de direction
Executive Director. . . . . .Directeur(trice) général(e)
Executive Manager. . . . . .Directeur(trice)
Executive Secretary-Treasurer. . .Secrétaire-trésorier(ière) exécutif(ive)
FAX (Facsmile Transmission) . . . .Télécopieur
Financial Secretary . . . . .Secrétaire financier(ière)
Founding Date . . . . .Date de fondation
General Director . . . . .Directeur(trice) général(e)
General Organizer . . . . .Organisateur(trice) général(e)
Grants . . . . .Subventions
Info-Line .Infoligne
Interns . . . . .Stagiaires
ISBN . . . . .Numéro ISBN
ISSN . . . . .Numéro ISSN

Librarian .Bibliothécaire
Library Hours . . . . .Heures d'ouverture de la bibliothèque
Library (Permission Required) . . .Avec permission seulement
Licensing Body . . . . .Organisme de réglementation professionnelle
Mailing Lists . . . . .Listes de diffusion
Manager .Administrateur(trice) ou Gérant(e)
Meetings .Réunions
Member of. . . . . .Membre de
Membership . . . . .Nombre de membres
Membership criteria . . . . .Critères d'admissibilité
Membership fee . . . . .Montant de la cotisation
Merged from . . . . .Fusion de
National President. . . . . .Président(e) national(e)
National Secretary . . . . .Secrétaire national(e)
National Treasurer . . . . .Trésorier(ière) national(e)
Number of Pages . . . . .Nombre de pages
Organizational Profile . . . . .Description
Past President. . . . . .Président(e) sortant(e)
Predecessor name . . . . .Nom du prédécesseur
President .Président(e)
President-elect . . . . .Président(e) désigné(e)
Publications. . . . . .Publications
Recording Secretary . . . . .Secrétaire archiviste
Registrar .Secrétaire
Representative . . . . .Représentant(e), Délégué(e)
Schedule. . . . . .Tableau des cotisations
Scholarships . . . . .Bourses
Scope of Activity . . . . .Envergure des opérations
Secretary. . . . . .Secrétaire
Secretary General. . . . . .Secrétaire général(e)
Secretary-Treasurer . . . . .Secrétaire-trésorier(ière)
See . . . . .Voir
Source of Funding. . . . . .Fonds
Speakers Service . . . . .Service de conférenciers
Sponsors .Commanditaires
Staff. . . . . .Personnel
Toll-free(telephone number) . . . . .Ligne sans frais
Translated Name. . . . . .Nom traduit
Treasurer. . . . . .Trésorier(ière)
TTY (Text Telephone) . . . . .ATS
Volunteers . . . . .Bénévoles

Environmental Rankings

Result of the *2010 Environmental Performance Index* reprinted here is the work of both Yale University's **Yale Center for Environmental Law & Policy** and Columbia University's **Center for International Earth Science Information Network**, in collaboration with the **World Economic Forum** headquartered in Switzerland and the **Joint Research Centre of the European Commission** in Italy.

It uses 25 performance indicators, tracked in six policy categories, that score a country's performance as related to the EPI's two main objectives: 1.Reducing environmental stresses to human health; and 2. Promoting ecosystem vitality and sound natural resource management. These goals reflect the policy priorities of environmental authorities around the world. The EPI tracked national environmental results on a quantitative basis, measuring proximity to an established set of policy targets.

These tables show how 163 countries ranked in each of 25 indicators—listed below—from Access to Sanitation to Water Stress Index. In all cases, Canada is starred so you can easily see how it compares to the rest of the world.

2010 Environmental Performance Index
Canada Overview E-42
Indicators E-43
Overall Scores by Rank E-44

Indicators
Environmental Burden of Disease E-45
Access to Sanitation E-46
Access to Water E-47
Indoor Air Pollution E-48
Outdoor Air Pollution E-49
Sulfur Dioxide Emissions Per Populated Land Area E-50
Nitrogen Oxides Emissions Per Populated Land Area E-51
Non-Methane Volatile Organic Compound Emissions Per Populated Land Area E-52
Ecosystem Ozone E-53
Water Quality Index E-54
Water Stress Index E-55
Water Scarcity Index E-56
Biome Protection E-57
Marine Protection E-58
Critical Habitat Protection E-59
Annual Change in Forest Cover E-60
Growing Stock Rate E-61
MTI Slope E-62
Trawling and Dredging Intensity E-63
Agricultural Water Intensity E-64
Pesticide Regulation E-65
Agriculture Subsidies E-66
Greenhouse Gas Emissions Per Capita (Including Land Use Emissions) E-67
Industrial Greenhouse Gas Emissions Intensity E-68
CO_2 Emissions Per Electricity Generation E-69

Source: Emerson, J., D.C. Esty, M.A. Levy, C.H. Kim, V. Mara, A. de Sherbinin, and T. Srebotnjak. 2010. 2010 Environmental Performance Index. New Haven: Yale Center for Environmental Law and Policy.

Environmental Rankings

Canada

NORTH AMERICA

GDP/capita 2007 est. (PPP) $36,260
Income Decile 1 (1=high, 10=low)

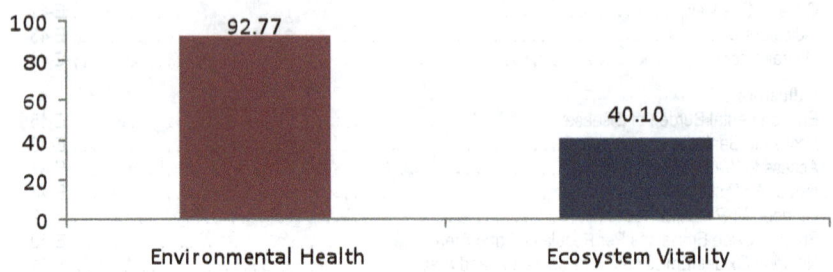

2010 ENVIRONMENTAL PERFORMANCE INDEX

Rank:	46
Score:	66.4
Income Group Average:	67.1
Geographic Group Average:	65.0

Environmental objectives:

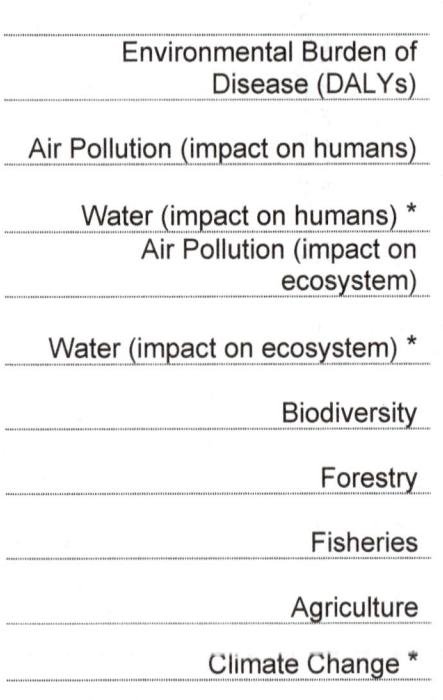

Policy Categories

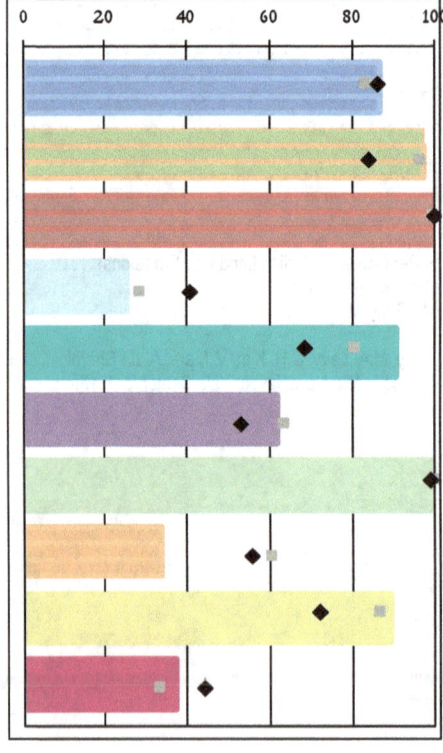

	Country	Income Group	Geographic Group
Environmental Burden of Disease (DALYs)	86.86	86.3	83.0
Air Pollution (impact on humans)	97.4	84.0	96.5
Water (impact on humans) *	100.0	99.9	99.6
Air Pollution (impact on ecosystem)	25.3	40.7	28.4
Water (impact on ecosystem) *	90.7	68.4	80.5
Biodiversity	61.9	53.1	63.9
Forestry	100.0	99.0	100.0
Fisheries	33.8	55.8	60.7
Agriculture	89.5	72.2	86.67
Climate Change *	37.3	44.3	33.4

* This indicator / policy category makes use of imputed data for certain countries. Please download the 2010 EPI data file in Excel format to determine whether this country's score relied upon imputed data.

Environmental Rankings

Indicators

Indicator	Value	Target	Proximity to Target (100=target met)
DALY: Environmental Burden of Disease (DALY)	15.0	0	86.9
INDOOR: Indoor air pollution (%)	5.0	100	94.7
OUTDOOR: Outdoor air pollution (μg/m³)	17.4	100	100.0
ACSAT: Access to sanitation (%)*	100.0	100	100.0
WATSUP: Access to water (%)	100.0	100	100.0
SO2: Sulfur dioxide emissions (Gg/1000 sq km)	8.3	<= 0.01	30.2
NOX: Nitrogen oxides emissions (Gg/1000 sq km)	6.8	<= 0.01	31.2
NMVOC: Non-methane volatile organic compound emissions (Gg/1000 sq km)	13.4	<= 0.01	20.6
OZONE: Ecosystem ozone (ppb)	65561497.6	0	9.3
WQI: Water quality index *	93.1	100	93.1
WSI: Water scarcity index	0.0	0	100.0
WATSTR: Water stress index	1.7	0	76.7
PACOV: Biome protection (%)	7.8	>= 10	77.7
MPAEEZ: Marine protection (%)	0.5	>= 10	17.3
AZE: Critical habitat protection (%)	75.0	100	75.0
FORGRO: Growing stock change (ratio)	1.0	>=1	100.0
FORCOV: Forest cover change (%)	0.0	>=0	100.0
MTI: Marine trophic index (slope)	-0.03	>=0	0.0
EEZTD: Trawling and dredging intensity (%)	32.5	0	67.5
AGWAT: Agricultural water intensity (%)	0.2	<=10	100.0
AGSUB: Agricultural subsidies (NRA)	0.1	0	65.1
AGPEST: Pesticide regulation	22.0	22	100.0
GHGCAP: Greenhouse gas emissions per capita including land use emissions (Mt CO2 eq) *	24.9	2.5	21.8
GHGIND: Industrial greenhouse gas emissions intensity(t CO2 per mill US$)	64.8	36.3	72.4
CO2KWH: CO2 emissions per electricity generation (CO2 per kWh) *	204.9	0	33.3

* This indicator / policy category makes use of imputed data for certain countries. Please download the 2010 EPI data file in Excel format to determine whether this country's score relied upon imputed data.

CANADIAN ENVIRONMENTAL RESOURCE GUIDE 2011-2012   E-41

Environmental Rankings

EPI Scores (by rank)*

Rank	Country	Score	Rank	Country	Score	Rank	Country	Score
1	Iceland	93.5	56	Syria	64.6	111	Tajikistan	51.3
2	Switzerland	89.1	57	Estonia	63.8	112	Mozambique	51.2
3	Costa Rica	86.4	58	Sri Lanka	63.7	113	Kuwait	51.1
4	Sweden	86.0	59	Georgia	63.6	114	Solomon Islands	51.1
5	Norway	81.1	60	Paraguay	63.5	115	South Africa	50.8
6	Mauritius	80.6	61	United States	63.5	116	Gambia	50.3
7	France	78.2	62	Brazil	63.4	117	Libya	50.1
8	Austria	78.1	63	Poland	63.1	118	Honduras	49.9
9	Cuba	78.1	64	Venezuela	62.9	119	Uganda	49.8
10	Colombia	76.8	65	Bulgaria	62.5	120	Madagascar	49.2
11	Malta	76.3	66	Israel	62.4	121	China	49.0
12	Finland	74.7	67	Thailand	62.2	122	Qatar	48.9
13	Slovakia	74.5	68	Egypt	62.0	123	India	48.3
14	United Kingdom	74.2	69	Russia	61.2	124	Yemen	48.3
15	New Zealand	73.4	70	Argentina	61.0	125	Pakistan	48.0
16	Chile	73.3	71	Greece	60.9	126	Tanzania	47.9
17	Germany	73.2	72	Brunei	60.8	127	Zimbabwe	47.8
18	Italy	73.1	73	Macedonia	60.6	128	Burkina Faso	47.3
19	Portugal	73.0	74	Tunisia	60.6	129	Sudan	47.1
20	Japan	72.5	75	Djibouti	60.5	130	Zambia	47.0
21	Latvia	72.5	76	Armenia	60.4	131	Oman	45.9
22	Czech Republic	71.6	77	Turkey	60.4	132	Guinea-Bissau	44.7
23	Albania	71.4	78	Iran	60.0	133	Cameroon	44.6
24	Panama	71.4	79	Kyrgyzstan	59.7	134	Indonesia	44.6
25	Spain	70.6	80	Laos	59.6	135	Rwanda	44.6
26	Belize	69.9	81	Namibia	59.3	136	Guinea	44.4
27	Antigua & Barbuda	69.8	82	Guyana	59.2	137	Bolivia	44.3
28	Singapore	69.6	83	Uruguay	59.1	138	Papua New Guinea	44.3
29	Serbia & Montenegro	69.4	84	Azerbaijan	59.1	139	Bangladesh	44.0
30	Ecuador	69.3	85	Viet Nam	59.0	140	Burundi	43.9
31	Peru	69.3	86	Moldova	58.8	141	Ethiopia	43.1
32	Denmark	69.2	87	Ukraine	58.2	142	Mongolia	42.8
33	Hungary	69.1	88	Belgium	58.1	143	Senegal	42.3
34	El Salvador	69.1	89	Jamaica	58.0	144	Uzbekistan	42.3
35	Croatia	68.7	90	Lebanon	57.9	145	Bahrain	42.0
36	Dominican Republic	68.4	91	Sao Tome & Principe	57.3	146	Equatorial Guinea	41.9
37	Lithuania	68.3	92	Kazakhstan	57.3	147	North Korea	41.8
38	Nepal	68.2	93	Nicaragua	57.1	148	Cambodia	41.7
39	Suriname	68.2	94	South Korea	57.0	149	Botswana	41.3
40	Bhutan	68.0	95	Gabon	56.4	150	Iraq	41.0
41	Luxembourg	67.8	96	Cyprus	56.3	151	Chad	40.8
42	Algeria	67.4	97	Jordan	56.1	152	United Arab Emirates	40.7
43	Mexico	67.3	98	Bosnia & Herzegovina	55.9	153	Nigeria	40.2
44	Ireland	67.1	99	Saudi Arabia	55.3	154	Benin	39.6
45	Romania	67.0	100	Eritrea	54.6	155	Haiti	39.5
★ 46	Canada	66.4	101	Swaziland	54.4	156	Mali	39.4
47	Netherlands	66.4	102	Côte d'Ivoire	54.3	157	Turkmenistan	38.4
48	Maldives	65.9	103	Trinidad and Tobago	54.2	158	Niger	37.6
49	Fiji	65.9	104	Guatemala	54.0	159	Togo	36.4
50	Philippines	65.7	105	Congo	54.0	160	Angola	36.3
51	Australia	65.7	106	Dem. Rep. Congo	51.6	161	Mauritania	33.7
52	Morocco	65.6	107	Malawi	51.4	162	Central African Rep.	33.3
53	Belarus	65.4	108	Kenya	51.4	163	Sierra Leone	32.1
54	Malaysia	65.0	109	Ghana	51.3			
55	Slovenia	65.0	110	Myanmar	51.3			

* Owing to changes in methodologies and underlying data, 2010 EPI scores and ranks cannot be directly compared to 2006 and 2008 scores and ranks.

Indicator: Environmental Burden of Disease

Rank	Country	Score	Rank	Country	Score	Rank	Country	Score
1	Iceland	91.5	56	Bosnia & Herzegovina	69.0	111	Sri Lanka	41.4
2	Israel	91.5	57	Malaysia	67.8	112	Bangladesh	39.9
3	Switzerland	89.1	58	Venezuela	67.8	113	Turkmenistan	39.9
4	Singapore	89.1	59	Tunisia	67.8	114	India	39.4
5	Kuwait	89.1	60	Trinidad & Tobago	67.8	115	Gabon	38.9
6	Qatar	89.1	61	Hungary	66.6	116	Tajikistan	38.4
7	United Arab Emirates	89.1	62	Albania	65.5	117	Myanmar	37.9
8	Sweden	86.9	63	Paraguay	65.5	118	South Africa	37.4
9	Austria	86.9	64	Bulgaria	65.5	119	Nepal	36.5
10	Malta	86.9	65	Turkey	65.5	120	Papua New Guinea	35.1
11	Italy	86.9	66	Romania	64.4	121	Laos	33.9
12	Japan	86.9	67	Morocco	64.4	122	Eritrea	33.4
★ 13	Canada	86.9	68	Lebanon	64.4	123	Sao Tome & Principe	31.4
14	Netherlands	86.9	69	Saudi Arabia	64.4	124	Congo	31.0
15	Brunei Darussalam	86.9	70	Colombia	63.3	125	Botswana	30.3
16	Cyprus	86.9	71	Fiji	63.3	126	Djibouti	29.9
17	Spain	84.8	72	Ecuador	62.3	127	Swaziland	29.9
18	Ireland	84.8	73	Armenia	62.3	128	Haiti	29.5
19	Australia	84.8	74	Viet Nam	62.3	129	Ghana	29.2
20	Bahrain	84.8	75	China	62.3	130	Yemen	27.7
21	Norway	82.8	76	Peru	61.3	131	Cambodia	27.7
22	France	82.8	77	El Salvador	61.3	132	Sudan	27.1
23	Finland	82.8	78	Algeria	61.3	133	Gambia	25.7
24	New Zealand	82.8	79	Egypt	61.3	134	Mauritania	25.7
25	Germany	82.8	80	Iran	61.3	135	Kenya	25.1
26	Luxembourg	82.8	81	Lithuania	60.3	136	Madagascar	22.6
27	Greece	82.8	82	Nicaragua	60.3	137	Zimbabwe	22.0
28	United Kingdom	81.0	83	Latvia	59.4	138	Togo	21.1
29	Denmark	81.0	84	Estonia	59.4	139	Iraq	20.3
30	Belgium	81.0	85	Moldova	59.4	140	Mozambique	20.0
31	Chile	79.2	86	Suriname	58.5	141	Senegal	19.8
32	Portugal	79.2	87	Brazil	58.5	142	Tanzania	18.2
33	United States	79.2	88	Belize	57.6	143	Cameroon	17.6
34	Costa Rica	77.5	89	Azerbaijan	57.6	144	Guinea	16.4
35	Slovenia	77.5	90	Honduras	56.7	145	Benin	16.4
36	Oman	77.5	91	Maldives	55.9	146	Uganda	15.2
37	Czech Republic	76.0	92	Thailand	55.9	147	Central African Rep.	14.0
38	South Korea	76.0	93	Solomon Islands	55.9	148	Ethiopia	13.1
39	Cuba	74.5	94	Dominican Republic	55.1	149	Zambia	11.6
40	Croatia	74.5	95	Philippines	55.1	150	Côte d'Ivoire	10.2
41	Antigua & Barbuda	73.0	96	Mongolia	54.3	151	Malawi	9.2
42	Mexico	73.0	97	Belarus	52.7	152	Nigeria	9.2
43	Syria	73.0	98	Ukraine	52.7	153	Equatorial Guinea	8.4
44	Argentina	71.6	99	Namibia	52.0	154	Chad	6.7
45	Mauritius	70.3	100	Uzbekistan	52.0	155	Rwanda	5.8
46	Slovakia	70.3	101	North Korea	52.0	156	Burkina Faso	4.9
47	Panama	70.3	102	Guatemala	51.3	157	Guinea-Bissau	4.4
48	Poland	70.3	103	Guyana	49.2	158	Burundi	4.1
49	Uruguay	70.3	104	Kyrgyzstan	48.5	159	Dem. Rep. Congo	2.0
50	Jamaica	70.3	105	Indonesia	45.4	160	Mali	1.4
51	Jordan	70.3	106	Russia	44.2	161	Niger	0.0
52	Libya	70.3	107	Kazakhstan	44.2	162	Angola	0.0
53	Serbia & Montenegro	69.0	108	Pakistan	43.0	163	Sierra Leone	0.0
54	Georgia	69.0	109	Bhutan	42.5			
55	Macedonia	69.0	110	Bolivia	41.9			

Environmental Rankings

Indicator: Access to sanitation

Rank	Country	Score	Rank	Country	Score	Rank	Country	Score
1	Australia	100.0	56	Georgia	92.1	111	Bhutan	46.1
2	Austria	100.0	57	Kyrgyzstan	92.1	112	Gambia	46.1
3	Bahrain	100.0	58	Ukraine	92.1	113	Zambia	46.1
4	Belgium	100.0	59	Serbia & Montenegro	91.0	114	Indonesia	46.1
5	Brunei Darussalam	100.0	60	Syria	91.0	115	Cameroon	45.0
★ 6	Canada	100.0	61	Trinidad & Tobago	91.0	116	Equatorial Guinea	45.0
7	Cyprus	100.0	62	Tajikistan	91.0	117	Swaziland	43.9
8	Denmark	100.0	63	Argentina	89.9	118	Mongolia	43.9
9	Finland	100.0	64	Armenia	89.9	119	Angola	43.9
10	France	100.0	65	Saudi Arabia	89.6	120	Laos	41.6
11	Germany	100.0	66	Macedonia	87.7	121	Nicaragua	41.6
12	Hungary	100.0	67	Turkey	86.5	122	Belize	40.5
13	Iceland	100.0	68	South Korea	85.5	123	Botswana	40.5
14	Ireland	100.0	69	Russia	85.4	124	Yemen	39.4
15	Israel	100.0	70	Oman	85.4	125	Zimbabwe	39.4
16	Italy	100.0	71	El Salvador	84.3	126	Papua New Guinea	38.3
17	Japan	100.0	72	Sri Lanka	84.3	127	Mali	38.3
18	Kuwait	100.0	73	Venezuela	84.3	128	Bolivia	36.0
19	Luxembourg	100.0	74	Tunisia	83.2	129	Kenya	34.9
20	Malta	100.0	75	Jordan	83.2	130	Burundi	33.8
21	Netherlands	100.0	76	Ecuador	82.0	131	Gabon	28.2
22	New Zealand	100.0	77	Guatemala	82.0	132	Bangladesh	28.2
23	Norway	100.0	78	Poland	80.9	133	Namibia	27.0
24	Qatar	100.0	79	Iran	80.9	134	Sudan	27.0
25	Singapore	100.0	80	Jamaica	80.9	135	Uganda	24.8
26	Slovakia	100.0	81	Suriname	79.8	136	Tanzania	24.8
27	Slovenia	100.0	82	Myanmar	79.8	137	Guinea-Bissau	24.8
28	Spain	100.0	83	Lithuania	78.7	138	Solomon Islands	23.7
29	Sweden	100.0	84	Mexico	78.7	139	Dem. Rep. Congo	22.6
30	Switzerland	100.0	85	Guyana	78.7	140	Mozambique	22.6
31	United Kingdom	100.0	86	Azerbaijan	77.6	141	Central African Rep.	22.6
32	United States	100.0	87	Dominican Republic	76.4	142	Nigeria	21.4
33	Uruguay	100.0	88	Moldova	76.4	143	Benin	21.4
34	Portugal	98.9	89	Colombia	75.3	144	India	19.2
35	Czech Republic	98.9	90	Latvia	75.3	145	Senegal	19.2
36	Croatia	98.9	91	Philippines	75.3	146	Cambodia	19.2
37	Bulgaria	98.9	92	Brazil	74.2	147	Nepal	18.1
38	Cuba	97.8	93	Iraq	73.1	148	Sao Tome & Principe	14.7
39	Greece	97.8	94	Panama	70.8	149	Côte d'Ivoire	14.7
40	Lebanon	97.8	95	Peru	68.6	150	Mauritania	14.7
41	Albania	96.6	96	Romania	68.6	151	Rwanda	13.6
42	Kazakhstan	96.6	97	Morocco	68.6	152	Congo	10.2
43	Libya	96.6	98	Fiji	67.5	153	Guinea	9.1
44	United Arab Emirates	96.6	99	Paraguay	66.3	154	Haiti	9.1
45	Costa Rica	95.5	100	Djibouti	63.0	155	Burkina Faso	2.4
46	Thailand	95.5	101	Egypt	61.8	156	Madagascar	1.2
47	Uzbekistan	95.5	102	Honduras	61.8	157	Togo	1.2
48	Antigua & Barbuda	94.4	103	Viet Nam	60.7	158	Ethiopia	0.1
49	Estonia	94.4	104	China	60.7	159	Sierra Leone	0.1
50	Bosnia & Herzegovina	94.4	105	Turkmenistan	57.4	160	Chad	0.0
51	Mauritius	93.3	106	Malawi	55.1	161	Eritrea	0.0
52	Chile	93.3	107	Maldives	54.0	162	Ghana	0.0
53	Algeria	93.3	108	South Africa	54.0	163	Niger	0.0
54	Malaysia	93.3	109	North Korea	54.0			
55	Belarus	92.1	110	Pakistan	52.9			

Indicator: Access to water

Rank	Country	Score	Rank	Country	Score	Rank	Country	Score
1	Australia	100.0	56	Albania	94.8	111	Bhutan	67.2
2	Austria	100.0	57	Russia	94.8	112	Côte d'Ivoire	67.2
3	Bahrain	100.0	58	Turkey	94.8	113	Zimbabwe	67.2
4	Belarus	100.0	59	Ukraine	94.8	114	Ghana	65.5
5	Belgium	100.0	60	Argentina	93.1	115	Myanmar	65.5
6	Brunei Darussalam	100.0	61	Kazakhstan	93.1	116	Indonesia	65.5
★ 7	Canada	100.0	62	Guatemala	93.1	117	Bangladesh	65.5
8	Cyprus	100.0	63	Botswana	93.1	118	Nicaragua	63.8
9	Czech Republic	100.0	64	Chile	91.4	119	Azerbaijan	62.1
10	Denmark	100.0	65	Ecuador	91.4	120	Paraguay	60.3
11	Estonia	100.0	66	Dominican Republic	91.4	121	Senegal	60.3
12	Finland	100.0	67	Mexico	91.4	122	Iraq	60.3
13	France	100.0	68	Tunisia	89.7	123	Malawi	58.6
14	Germany	100.0	69	Iran	89.7	124	Burkina Faso	51.7
15	Greece	100.0	70	Trinidad & Tobago	89.7	125	Mongolia	51.7
16	Hungary	100.0	71	Colombia	87.9	126	Turkmenistan	51.7
17	Iceland	100.0	72	Philippines	87.9	127	Congo	50.0
18	Ireland	100.0	73	Namibia	87.9	128	Libya	50.0
19	Israel	100.0	74	Guyana	87.9	129	Burundi	50.0
20	Italy	100.0	75	Jamaica	87.9	130	Solomon Islands	48.3
21	Japan	100.0	76	South Africa	87.9	131	Sudan	48.3
22	Kuwait	100.0	77	Panama	86.2	132	Cameroon	48.3
23	Lebanon	100.0	78	Suriname	86.2	133	Guinea	48.3
24	Luxembourg	100.0	79	Djibouti	86.2	134	Tajikistan	43.1
25	Macedonia	100.0	80	Viet Nam	86.2	135	Yemen	41.4
26	Malta	100.0	81	South Korea	86.2	136	Central African Rep.	41.4
27	Mauritius	100.0	82	Cuba	84.5	137	Rwanda	39.7
28	Netherlands	100.0	83	Belize	84.5	138	Cambodia	39.7
29	New Zealand	100.0	84	Antigua & Barbuda	84.5	139	Benin	39.7
30	North Korea	100.0	85	Brazil	84.5	140	Uganda	37.9
31	Norway	100.0	86	Venezuela	82.8	141	Laos	31.0
32	Qatar	100.0	87	Moldova	82.8	142	Eritrea	31.0
33	Singapore	100.0	88	Saudi Arabia	82.8	143	Swaziland	31.0
34	Slovakia	100.0	89	Pakistan	82.8	144	Mali	31.0
35	Slovenia	100.0	90	Nepal	81.0	145	Mauritania	31.0
36	Spain	100.0	91	Syria	81.0	146	Togo	29.3
37	Sweden	100.0	92	Kyrgyzstan	81.0	147	Zambia	27.6
38	Switzerland	100.0	93	India	81.0	148	Haiti	27.6
39	United Arab Emirates	100.0	94	Lithuania	79.9	149	Kenya	25.9
40	United Kingdom	100.0	95	Romania	79.3	150	Guinea-Bissau	25.9
41	Uruguay	100.0	96	China	79.3	151	Tanzania	22.4
42	Portugal	98.3	97	Uzbekistan	79.3	152	Sierra Leone	19.0
43	Latvia	98.3	98	Poland	77.6	153	Angola	15.5
44	Serbia & Montenegro	98.3	99	Gabon	77.6	154	Chad	10.3
45	Croatia	98.3	100	Sao Tome & Principe	75.9	155	Fiji	8.6
46	Malaysia	98.3	101	Gambia	75.9	156	Madagascar	8.6
47	Georgia	98.3	102	Bolivia	75.9	157	Nigeria	8.6
48	United States	98.3	103	Algeria	74.1	158	Dem. Rep. Congo	6.9
49	Bulgaria	98.3	104	Peru	72.4	159	Equatorial Guinea	1.7
50	Bosnia & Herzegovina	98.3	105	El Salvador	72.4	160	Ethiopia	0.0
51	Costa Rica	96.6	106	Honduras	72.4	161	Mozambique	0.0
52	Thailand	96.6	107	Maldives	70.7	162	Niger	0.0
53	Egypt	96.6	108	Morocco	70.7	163	Papua New Guinea	0.0
54	Armenia	96.6	109	Sri Lanka	69.0			
55	Jordan	96.6	110	Oman	69.0			

Indicator: Indoor air pollution

Rank	Country	Score	Rank	Country	Score	Rank	Country	Score
1	Algeria	94.7	56	Turkmenistan	94.7	111	Namibia	38.4
2	Antigua & Barbuda	94.7	57	United Arab Emirates	94.7	112	India	37.2
3	Argentina	94.7	58	United Kingdom	94.7	113	Viet Nam	36.6
4	Armenia	94.7	59	United States	94.7	114	Mauritania	36.3
5	Australia	94.7	60	Uruguay	94.7	115	Swaziland	36.0
6	Austria	94.7	61	Venezuela	94.7	116	Eritrea	34.0
7	Bahrain	94.7	62	Ukraine	94.3	117	Guatemala	30.5
8	Belarus	94.7	63	Iraq	94.3	118	Pakistan	29.3
9	Belgium	94.7	64	Morocco	92.8	119	Kenya	27.7
10	Brunei Darussalam	94.7	65	Dominican Republic	91.9	120	Zimbabwe	25.1
★ 11	Canada	94.7	66	Russia	91.8	121	Sri Lanka	22.3
12	Chile	94.7	67	Slovenia	91.1	122	Mongolia	19.2
13	Cuba	94.7	68	Guyana	90.1	123	Côte d'Ivoire	18.7
14	Cyprus	94.7	69	Maldives	89.9	124	Nigeria	17.1
15	Czech Republic	94.7	70	Azerbaijan	89.7	125	Cameroon	15.2
16	Denmark	94.7	71	Latvia	89.2	126	Nepal	14.7
17	Ecuador	94.7	72	Brazil	88.5	127	Congo	11.7
18	Egypt	94.7	73	Turkey	88.4	128	Zambia	9.8
19	Finland	94.7	74	Kazakhstan	88.1	129	Ghana	9.6
20	France	94.7	75	Croatia	87.0	130	Papua New Guinea	5.6
21	Germany	94.7	76	Costa Rica	86.6	131	Bangladesh	5.6
22	Greece	94.7	77	Colombia	86.2	132	Sudan	5.4
23	Hungary	94.7	78	Djibouti	86.0	133	Cambodia	4.2
24	Iceland	94.7	79	Belize	85.2	134	Haiti	2.1
25	Iran	94.7	80	Moldova	84.5	135	Chad	1.5
26	Ireland	94.7	81	Uzbekistan	83.0	136	Benin	0.8
27	Israel	94.7	82	Estonia	82.7	137	Gambia	0.4
28	Italy	94.7	83	Mexico	82.6	138	Burkina Faso	0.0
29	Japan	94.7	84	Bulgaria	82.1	139	Burundi	0.0
30	Jordan	94.7	85	South Africa	81.8	140	Central African Rep.	0.0
31	Kuwait	94.7	86	Tajikistan	77.0	141	Dem. Rep. Congo	0.0
32	Lebanon	94.7	87	El Salvador	75.9	142	Ethiopia	0.0
33	Libya	94.7	88	Romania	75.9	143	Guinea	0.0
34	Lithuania	94.7	89	Thailand	75.7	144	Guinea-Bissau	0.0
35	Luxembourg	94.7	90	Gabon	71.1	145	Laos	0.0
36	Malaysia	94.7	91	Panama	65.3	146	Madagascar	0.0
37	Malta	94.7	92	Bolivia	65.2	147	Malawi	0.0
38	Mauritius	94.7	93	Yemen	62.2	148	Mali	0.0
39	Netherlands	94.7	94	Macedonia	61.5	149	Mozambique	0.0
40	New Zealand	94.7	95	Kyrgyzstan	60.6	150	Myanmar	0.0
41	Norway	94.7	96	Fiji	57.9	151	Niger	0.0
42	Oman	94.7	97	Peru	57.3	152	Rwanda	0.0
43	Poland	94.7	98	Botswana	55.3	153	Sierra Leone	0.0
44	Portugal	94.7	99	Georgia	55.0	154	Tanzania	0.0
45	Qatar	94.7	100	Jamaica	52.6	155	Togo	0.0
46	Saudi Arabia	94.7	101	Philippines	50.4	156	Uganda	0.0
47	Singapore	94.7	102	Angola	49.7	157	Serbia & Montenegro	..
48	Slovakia	94.7	103	China	48.4	158	Suriname	..
49	South Korea	94.7	104	Bosnia & Herzegovina	48.2	159	Bhutan	..
50	Spain	94.7	105	Albania	47.4	160	Sao Tome & Principe	..
51	Sweden	94.7	106	Paraguay	47.1	161	Solomon Islands	..
52	Switzerland	94.7	107	Honduras	43.5	162	Equatorial Guinea	..
53	Syria	94.7	108	Senegal	41.4	163	North Korea	..
54	Trinidad & Tobago	94.7	109	Nicaragua	39.9			
55	Tunisia	94.7	110	Indonesia	38.6			

Indicator: Outdoor air pollution

Rank	Country	Score	Rank	Country	Score	Rank	Country	Score
1	Antigua & Barbuda	100.0	56	Nicaragua	83.1	111	Qatar	50.4
2	Australia	100.0	57	Suriname	82.9	112	Brunei Darussalam	47.6
3	Belarus	100.0	58	Mozambique	82.3	113	Peru	47.2
4	Belize	100.0	59	Burundi	80.3	114	Uzbekistan	47.1
5	Bosnia & Herzegovina	100.0	60	Japan	79.3	115	Turkmenistan	46.7
★ 6	Canada	100.0	61	Slovenia	78.5	116	Viet Nam	46.4
7	Cuba	100.0	62	Tunisia	78.5	117	Eritrea	45.5
8	Denmark	100.0	63	Guyana	77.8	118	Bulgaria	44.4
9	Dominican Republic	100.0	64	Croatia	77.8	119	Myanmar	44.1
10	Equatorial Guinea	100.0	65	Israel	76.1	120	Armenia	42.6
11	Estonia	100.0	66	Spain	75.9	121	Azerbaijan	42.0
12	Finland	100.0	67	Maldives	75.9	122	Cameroon	40.4
13	France	100.0	68	Swaziland	73.9	123	Guatemala	40.3
14	Gabon	100.0	69	Austria	73.6	124	Congo	38.8
15	Germany	100.0	70	Malawi	73.5	125	India	37.9
16	Hungary	100.0	71	El Salvador	73.2	126	Angola	37.2
17	Iceland	100.0	72	Netherlands	72.5	127	Botswana	36.2
18	Ireland	100.0	73	Madagascar	72.3	128	Bahrain	35.7
19	Kazakhstan	100.0	74	Ghana	71.3	129	Ethiopia	35.7
20	Latvia	100.0	75	Nepal	71.3	130	North Korea	35.4
21	Lithuania	100.0	76	South Korea	70.9	131	Guinea	33.8
22	Luxembourg	100.0	77	Panama	70.4	132	Thailand	33.3
23	Mauritius	100.0	78	Togo	70.1	133	Algeria	33.2
24	New Zealand	100.0	79	Greece	69.1	134	Guinea-Bissau	32.6
25	Norway	100.0	80	Moldova	68.9	135	China	31.7
26	Romania	100.0	81	Costa Rica	68.6	136	Argentina	31.7
27	Russia	100.0	82	Lebanon	68.5	137	Syria	30.5
28	Serbia & Montenegro	100.0	83	Kenya	68.4	138	Paraguay	28.8
29	Slovakia	100.0	84	Côte d'Ivoire	68.4	139	Yemen	25.6
30	Sweden	100.0	85	Mexico	68.4	140	Sri Lanka	25.5
31	Uganda	100.0	86	Solomon Islands	68.3	141	Indonesia	25.1
32	United Kingdom	100.0	87	Haiti	67.6	142	Burkina Faso	24.1
33	Venezuela	100.0	88	Poland	67.1	143	Gambia	23.2
34	Ukraine	98.6	89	Sao Tome & Principe	64.4	144	Mauritania	22.9
35	South Africa	98.6	90	Turkey	63.8	145	Libya	22.1
36	Czech Republic	97.5	91	Zambia	63.7	146	Bolivia	18.4
37	Macedonia	97.4	92	Singapore	62.3	147	Senegal	17.9
38	Morocco	97.4	93	Honduras	59.6	148	Kuwait	16.6
39	United States	96.6	94	Jamaica	59.3	149	Trinidad & Tobago	14.7
40	Papua New Guinea	96.3	95	Cyprus	59.0	150	Oman	10.9
41	Fiji	95.9	96	Albania	58.6	151	Chad	10.4
42	Kyrgyzstan	94.5	97	Central African Rep.	58.4	152	Mongolia	9.9
43	Colombia	94.0	98	Jordan	57.6	153	Saudi Arabia	8.8
44	Belgium	93.9	99	Nigeria	57.3	154	Iraq	7.7
45	Philippines	93.0	100	Djibouti	56.8	155	Egypt	5.9
46	Malaysia	92.9	101	Cambodia	56.4	156	Pakistan	5.4
47	Portugal	91.9	102	Benin	56.1	157	United Arab Emirates	2.5
48	Brazil	91.9	103	Georgia	55.5	158	Niger	0.4
49	Ecuador	88.8	104	Dem. Rep. Congo	55.2	159	Bangladesh	0.0
50	Tanzania	87.4	105	Namibia	54.8	160	Mali	0.0
51	Switzerland	87.2	106	Chile	54.1	161	Sudan	0.0
52	Rwanda	86.1	107	Laos	52.9	162	Uruguay	0.0
53	Bhutan	85.8	108	Sierra Leone	52.0	163	Malta	..
54	Italy	84.8	109	Tajikistan	51.7			
55	Zimbabwe	84.6	110	Iran	51.1			

Environmental Rankings

Indicator: Sulfur dioxide emissions per populated land area

Rank	Country	Score	Rank	Country	Score	Rank	Country	Score
1	Kazakhstan	100.0	56	Togo	60.6	111	Azerbaijan	45.3
2	Solomon Islands	90.6	57	Zimbabwe	60.4	112	North Korea	44.9
3	Equatorial Guinea	86.5	58	Nicaragua	59.9	113	Syria	44.9
4	Eritrea	85.4	59	Armenia	59.5	114	Mexico	44.9
5	Bolivia	85.4	60	Colombia	59.4	115	Thailand	44.5
6	Laos	85.1	61	Paraguay	59.2	116	Portugal	44.4
7	Latvia	82.2	62	Brunei Darussalam	59.2	117	Japan	44.2
8	Niger	78.8	63	Argentina	59.1	118	Dominican Republic	44.0
9	Luxembourg	78.4	64	Sao Tome & Principe	59.0	119	Peru	44.0
10	Tajikistan	76.3	65	Lithuania	59.0	120	Tunisia	43.8
11	Mali	76.2	66	Finland	58.5	121	India	43.6
12	Burkina Faso	76.0	67	Denmark	58.4	122	Romania	43.4
13	Papua New Guinea	75.2	68	Namibia	58.3	123	Philippines	43.2
14	Macedonia	74.4	69	Botswana	58.3	124	Austria	43.2
15	Chad	73.9	70	Costa Rica	57.8	125	Congo	43.0
16	Bhutan	73.2	71	Belarus	57.0	126	Libya	42.2
17	Djibouti	72.8	72	Morocco	56.8	127	Ukraine	42.0
18	Myanmar	71.9	73	Albania	56.6	128	Spain	41.5
19	Fiji	71.5	74	Angola	56.5	129	United Kingdom	41.5
20	Georgia	71.4	75	Central African Rep.	55.4	130	Estonia	41.5
21	Madagascar	71.3	76	Slovenia	55.3	131	Czech Republic	41.4
22	Sweden	71.3	77	Uzbekistan	54.6	132	Cuba	41.2
23	Tanzania	71.3	78	Rwanda	54.4	133	United States	39.6
24	Haiti	71.2	79	Ireland	54.2	134	Poland	38.7
25	Norway	70.4	80	Saudi Arabia	54.2	135	Jordan	38.5
26	Sudan	70.4	81	Guatemala	54.1	136	Greece	37.0
27	Kyrgyzstan	70.4	82	Viet Nam	53.7	137	Mauritius	36.0
28	Mauritania	70.2	83	Bangladesh	53.5	138	Serbia & Montenegro	33.9
29	Nepal	69.3	84	Nigeria	53.2	139	China	33.5
30	Ethiopia	69.0	85	France	53.1	140	South Africa	32.9
31	Russia	68.6	86	Brazil	52.9	141	Bosnia & Herzegovina	32.0
32	Dem. Rep. Congo	68.3	87	Ecuador	52.9	142	Cyprus	31.8
33	Turkmenistan	67.7	88	Algeria	52.7	143	Qatar	31.4
34	Cambodia	67.1	89	Iraq	52.5	144	Trinidad & Tobago	30.6
35	Mozambique	66.5	90	Iran	52.2	145	South Korea	30.3
36	Benin	66.5	91	Suriname	52.0	★146	Canada	30.2
37	Kenya	66.5	92	Indonesia	51.9	147	Egypt	30.1
38	Guinea	66.2	93	Malaysia	51.8	148	Mongolia	28.0
39	Senegal	66.0	94	Hungary	51.4	149	Lebanon	27.8
40	Guinea-Bissau	65.8	95	Italy	50.7	150	Chile	27.7
41	Uruguay	65.5	96	New Zealand	49.9	151	Bulgaria	27.6
42	Uganda	65.2	97	Croatia	49.4	152	Israel	27.5
43	Burundi	65.0	98	Turkey	49.3	153	Jamaica	27.1
44	Malawi	64.4	99	Germany	48.9	154	United Arab Emirates	25.8
45	Honduras	63.5	100	Zambia	48.8	155	Australia	25.7
46	Ghana	63.4	101	Yemen	48.4	156	Maldives	25.6
47	Guyana	63.3	102	Slovakia	48.2	157	Kuwait	22.3
48	Swaziland	63.2	103	Pakistan	48.1	158	Iceland	20.6
49	Belize	62.6	104	Sri Lanka	47.8	159	Antigua & Barbuda	18.2
50	Switzerland	62.5	105	Oman	47.0	160	Malta	13.7
51	Sierra Leone	62.0	106	Panama	47.0	161	Belgium	13.3
52	Côte d'Ivoire	62.0	107	Venezuela	46.9	162	Bahrain	1.4
53	Gambia	61.8	108	Gabon	46.7	163	Singapore	0.0
54	Moldova	61.6	109	Netherlands	46.6			
55	Cameroon	61.6	110	El Salvador	46.3			

Indicator: Nitrogen oxides emissions per populated land area

Rank	Country	Score	Rank	Country	Score	Rank	Country	Score
1	Serbia & Montenegro	93.8	56	Ecuador	51.1	111	Switzerland	43.3
2	Solomon Islands	83.2	57	Lithuania	51.1	112	Jordan	43.0
3	Mauritania	77.9	58	Estonia	50.8	113	Costa Rica	42.8
4	Equatorial Guinea	77.8	59	Malawi	50.7	114	Brazil	42.8
5	Eritrea	77.1	60	Burundi	50.6	115	Slovenia	42.6
6	Laos	77.0	61	Algeria	50.5	116	China	42.4
7	Niger	74.2	62	Mexico	50.4	117	Venezuela	41.9
8	Tajikistan	72.9	63	Guinea-Bissau	50.3	118	Cuba	41.8
9	Luxembourg	70.3	64	Mozambique	50.1	119	Paraguay	41.8
10	Djibouti	70.0	65	Moldova	50.1	120	Panama	41.7
11	Myanmar	70.0	66	Guinea	50.1	121	France	41.3
12	Bhutan	68.0	67	Ghana	50.0	122	Austria	41.3
13	Fiji	66.7	68	Colombia	49.8	123	New Zealand	40.9
14	Uruguay	65.7	69	Nigeria	49.6	124	Namibia	40.9
15	Bolivia	65.6	70	Uzbekistan	49.6	125	Angola	40.8
16	Turkmenistan	65.6	71	Nicaragua	49.5	126	Poland	40.5
17	Burkina Faso	63.5	72	Armenia	49.5	127	Portugal	40.3
18	Nepal	63.4	73	Finland	49.4	128	Greece	40.1
19	Mali	62.5	74	Suriname	49.2	129	Dominican Republic	39.8
20	Cambodia	61.8	75	Chile	49.0	130	El Salvador	39.6
21	Kyrgyzstan	60.7	76	Gambia	48.7	131	Spain	38.0
22	Morocco	60.5	77	Guyana	48.6	132	Germany	37.9
23	Yemen	60.2	78	Viet Nam	48.3	133	Czech Republic	37.7
24	Papua New Guinea	59.8	79	Thailand	48.3	134	Central African Rep.	37.7
25	Georgia	58.5	80	Côte d'Ivoire	48.2	135	Italy	37.2
26	Chad	57.7	81	Bulgaria	48.1	136	Denmark	37.1
27	Ethiopia	57.7	82	Honduras	48.0	137	United States	36.5
28	Kenya	57.0	83	Croatia	47.8	138	Brunei Darussalam	36.5
29	Saudi Arabia	56.4	84	Macedonia	47.8	139	Mongolia	35.2
30	Senegal	55.7	85	Syria	47.7	140	Cyprus	34.7
31	Madagascar	55.6	86	Bangladesh	47.4	141	Antigua & Barbuda	34.0
32	Latvia	55.1	87	Romania	47.2	142	Jamaica	33.8
33	Swaziland	54.5	88	Zambia	47.0	143	Japan	33.8
34	Argentina	54.5	89	Turkey	46.8	144	South Africa	33.6
35	Peru	54.2	90	Indonesia	46.7	145	Lebanon	33.2
36	Gabon	54.2	91	Togo	46.7	146	Mauritius	31.3
37	Sudan	54.2	92	India	46.4	★147	Canada	31.2
38	Zimbabwe	54.1	93	Russia	46.4	148	United Kingdom	31.1
39	Sweden	54.0	94	Ukraine	46.3	149	Egypt	29.8
40	Haiti	54.0	95	Belize	46.3	150	Kuwait	29.5
41	Cameroon	53.7	96	Norway	46.0	151	Netherlands	29.2
42	Belarus	53.3	97	Sierra Leone	45.9	152	Belgium	28.9
43	Tanzania	53.0	98	Botswana	45.9	153	Iceland	28.4
44	Kazakhstan	52.4	99	Slovakia	45.7	154	Israel	27.6
45	Iran	52.4	100	Philippines	45.7	155	Trinidad & Tobago	26.3
46	Dem. Rep. Congo	52.3	101	Congo	45.5	156	Australia	24.7
47	Azerbaijan	52.0	102	North Korea	45.4	157	United Arab Emirates	24.5
48	Iraq	51.9	103	Ireland	45.4	158	South Korea	21.3
49	Pakistan	51.6	104	Malaysia	45.0	159	Maldives	18.6
50	Benin	51.5	105	Sri Lanka	44.7	160	Malta	16.7
51	Sao Tome & Principe	51.4	106	Libya	44.4	161	Qatar	15.7
52	Oman	51.3	107	Rwanda	44.2	162	Bahrain	2.2
53	Albania	51.1	108	Hungary	44.1	163	Singapore	0.0
54	Tunisia	51.1	109	Guatemala	43.5			
55	Uganda	51.1	110	Bosnia & Herzegovina	43.4			

Indicator: Non-methane volatile organic compound emissions per populated land area

Rank	Country	Score	Rank	Country	Score	Rank	Country	Score
1	Kazakhstan	100.0	56	Greece	44.0	111	Saudi Arabia	36.6
2	Tajikistan	79.3	57	Kenya	43.9	112	Viet Nam	35.7
3	Solomon Islands	67.1	58	Georgia	43.9	113	Portugal	35.6
4	Equatorial Guinea	66.7	59	Turkey	43.7	114	Jamaica	35.5
5	Bolivia	66.6	60	Armenia	43.7	115	Iraq	35.5
6	Eritrea	64.6	61	Cameroon	43.6	116	Germany	35.2
7	Djibouti	63.1	62	Costa Rica	43.3	117	Philippines	35.1
8	Laos	62.4	63	Norway	43.2	118	Sri Lanka	35.1
9	Morocco	62.1	64	North Korea	42.9	119	Bangladesh	34.6
10	Uruguay	62.0	65	Nepal	42.9	120	Guatemala	34.5
11	Niger	60.2	66	Dem. Rep. Congo	42.6	121	Brazil	34.4
12	Mauritania	59.3	67	Hungary	42.6	122	United States	34.2
13	Kyrgyzstan	58.4	68	Pakistan	42.4	123	El Salvador	33.9
14	Bhutan	55.7	69	Sudan	42.4	124	South Africa	33.9
15	Fiji	55.1	70	Guinea-Bissau	42.1	125	Italy	33.8
16	Bulgaria	53.2	71	Poland	42.1	126	Namibia	33.3
17	Ireland	52.9	72	Tanzania	42.0	127	United Kingdom	33.0
18	Mali	52.9	73	Honduras	41.7	128	Netherlands	32.8
19	Burkina Faso	52.0	74	Albania	41.6	129	France	32.8
20	Turkmenistan	51.9	75	Mozambique	41.6	130	Japan	32.7
21	Estonia	51.6	76	Benin	41.6	131	Malaysia	32.6
22	Peru	51.4	77	Iran	41.5	132	Nigeria	32.5
23	Belarus	51.3	78	Slovenia	41.4	133	Thailand	32.4
24	Sweden	51.2	79	Luxembourg	41.3	134	Indonesia	31.7
25	Finland	51.0	80	Ghana	41.2	135	Congo	31.5
26	Cambodia	50.4	81	Guinea	41.0	136	Switzerland	31.0
27	Argentina	50.4	82	Austria	40.8	137	Gabon	31.0
28	Papua New Guinea	50.1	83	Croatia	40.6	138	Paraguay	30.7
29	Chad	49.9	84	Czech Republic	40.3	139	Angola	30.6
30	Senegal	49.7	85	Syria	40.2	140	Serbia & Montenegro	29.9
31	Latvia	49.6	86	Spain	40.1	141	Central African Rep.	29.6
32	Uzbekistan	49.0	87	Uganda	40.1	142	Belgium	29.0
33	Zimbabwe	48.3	88	Cuba	39.9	143	Rwanda	28.5
34	Suriname	48.0	89	Iceland	39.9	144	Antigua & Barbuda	27.6
35	Macedonia	47.9	90	Malawi	39.7	145	Libya	27.1
36	Ethiopia	47.9	91	Guyana	39.7	146	Venezuela	26.5
37	Swaziland	47.8	92	Ecuador	39.6	147	Lebanon	26.3
38	Tunisia	47.3	93	Colombia	39.5	148	Brunei Darussalam	25.9
39	Romania	47.2	94	Denmark	39.3	149	Egypt	25.7
40	Myanmar	47.2	95	Gambia	39.0	150	Malta	25.1
41	Jordan	47.2	96	Zambia	39.0	151	Oman	24.6
42	Ukraine	47.2	97	Botswana	38.4	152	Mauritius	22.9
43	Mexico	47.1	98	Dominican Republic	38.4	153	Israel	22.9
44	Lithuania	46.6	99	Mongolia	38.3	154	Maldives	22.2
45	Chile	46.6	100	Azerbaijan	38.1	155	Australia	22.1
46	Madagascar	46.0	101	Cyprus	38.1	156	South Korea	21.8
47	Sao Tome & Principe	45.7	102	China	37.9	★157	Canada	20.6
48	Panama	45.0	103	Burundi	37.7	158	United Arab Emirates	18.9
49	Bosnia & Herzegovina	44.9	104	Côte d'Ivoire	37.7	159	Trinidad & Tobago	14.7
50	Yemen	44.9	105	Belize	37.5	160	Kuwait	4.0
51	Slovakia	44.6	106	New Zealand	37.2	161	Singapore	0.0
52	Haiti	44.6	107	Togo	37.2	162	Qatar	0.0
53	Russia	44.4	108	Algeria	36.7	163	Bahrain	0.0
54	Nicaragua	44.2	109	India	36.7			
55	Moldova	44.1	110	Sierra Leone	36.6			

Indicator: Ecosystem ozone

Rank	Country	Score	Rank	Country	Score	Rank	Country	Score
1	Antigua & Barbuda	100.0	56	Hungary	69.9	111	Peru	22.8
2	Armenia	100.0	57	Singapore	64.3	112	Guatemala	22.7
3	Azerbaijan	100.0	58	Bulgaria	63.8	113	Tanzania	22.7
4	Bahrain	100.0	59	Finland	55.9	114	Uganda	22.1
5	Belarus	100.0	60	Honduras	55.1	115	Cambodia	20.3
6	Brunei Darussalam	100.0	61	Australia	52.8	116	Germany	20.2
7	Costa Rica	100.0	62	Romania	52.1	117	Gabon	20.1
8	Cyprus	100.0	63	Norway	48.3	118	Pakistan	19.6
9	Djibouti	100.0	64	Ireland	48.1	119	Colombia	19.3
10	Dominican Republic	100.0	65	Malta	47.9	120	Senegal	19.1
11	Ecuador	100.0	66	Kazakhstan	47.2	121	France	18.6
12	Egypt	100.0	67	Luxembourg	44.2	122	Mozambique	18.0
13	El Salvador	100.0	68	Tunisia	44.2	123	North Korea	17.8
14	Eritrea	100.0	69	Kenya	43.6	124	South Africa	16.0
15	Estonia	100.0	70	Ukraine	43.5	125	Bangladesh	15.4
16	Fiji	100.0	71	Iraq	40.9	126	Indonesia	15.1
17	Georgia	100.0	72	Panama	40.1	127	Mali	13.2
18	Guyana	100.0	73	Czech Republic	39.7	128	Togo	12.6
19	Haiti	100.0	74	Malawi	38.8	129	Viet Nam	12.5
20	Iceland	100.0	75	Turkey	38.7	130	Ethiopia	12.4
21	Israel	100.0	76	Cuba	38.6	131	Sierra Leone	12.1
22	Jamaica	100.0	77	Denmark	38.3	132	South Korea	11.6
23	Jordan	100.0	78	Poland	38.0	133	Zimbabwe	11.5
24	Kuwait	100.0	79	Bosnia & Herzegovina	37.4	134	Italy	10.6
25	Latvia	100.0	80	Uzbekistan	37.1	135	Japan	9.3
26	Lebanon	100.0	81	Swaziland	36.3	★136	Canada	9.3
27	Libya	100.0	82	Sweden	36.1	137	Benin	9.2
28	Lithuania	100.0	83	Gambia	35.2	138	Mexico	8.9
29	Macedonia	100.0	84	Malaysia	35.2	139	Botswana	8.8
30	Madagascar	100.0	85	United Kingdom	33.9	140	India	8.6
31	Maldives	100.0	86	Uruguay	33.7	141	Burkina Faso	8.6
32	Mauritania	100.0	87	Iran	33.4	142	Laos	8.3
33	Mauritius	100.0	88	Slovenia	33.0	143	Congo	8.2
34	Moldova	100.0	89	Greece	33.0	144	Argentina	7.1
35	Mongolia	100.0	90	Nepal	32.5	145	Ghana	6.9
36	Morocco	100.0	91	Saudi Arabia	32.5	146	Chad	6.8
37	New Zealand	100.0	92	Rwanda	32.4	147	Namibia	6.6
38	Nicaragua	100.0	93	Albania	32.3	148	Cameroon	5.8
39	Oman	100.0	94	Belize	32.2	149	Côte d'Ivoire	5.7
40	Papua New Guinea	100.0	95	Kyrgyzstan	31.7	150	Guinea	5.6
41	Philippines	100.0	96	Bhutan	31.6	151	Thailand	5.3
42	Qatar	100.0	97	Russia	31.3	152	Myanmar	5.0
43	Sao Tome & Principe	100.0	98	Belgium	30.9	153	Paraguay	4.8
44	Serbia & Montenegro	100.0	99	Tajikistan	30.4	154	Sudan	4.0
45	Slovakia	100.0	100	Netherlands	29.8	155	Zambia	2.1
46	Solomon Islands	100.0	101	Croatia	29.7	156	Nigeria	2.0
47	Sri Lanka	100.0	102	Burundi	28.4	157	Central African Rep.	0.7
48	Suriname	100.0	103	Niger	27.8	158	China	0.2
49	Syria	100.0	104	Austria	27.3	159	Angola	0.0
50	Trinidad & Tobago	100.0	105	Algeria	27.1	160	Bolivia	0.0
51	Turkmenistan	100.0	106	Switzerland	25.2	161	Brazil	0.0
52	Yemen	100.0	107	Spain	25.1	162	Dem. Rep. Congo	0.0
53	United Arab Emirates	83.3	108	Portugal	23.7	163	United States	0.0
54	Equatorial Guinea	75.9	109	Venezuela	23.0			
55	Chile	74.6	110	Guinea-Bissau	22.9			

Indicator: Water quality index

Rank	Country	Score	Rank	Country	Score	Rank	Country	Score
1	Iceland	100.0	56	Czech Republic	74.5	111	Myanmar	45.7
2	New Zealand	99.2	57	Hungary	74.0	112	Namibia	45.7
3	Singapore	98.0	58	Netherlands	73.2	113	Guinea	45.5
4	Sweden	96.2	59	Viet Nam	72.7	114	Guinea-Bissau	45.5
5	Austria	95.1	60	Zimbabwe	71.9	115	Central African Rep.	45.2
6	Norway	95.1	61	Luxembourg	70.3	116	Tajikistan	45.1
7	Estonia	94.3	62	China	68.0	117	Turkmenistan	45.0
8	Bosnia & Herzegovina	93.5	63	Belgium	66.3	118	Mongolia	45.0
★ 9	Canada	93.1	64	Sudan	65.2	119	Syria	45.0
10	Slovenia	93.0	65	Uruguay	63.4	120	Nigeria	44.8
11	Croatia	92.5	66	Tunisia	63.0	121	Chad	44.7
12	Panama	92.2	67	Morocco	62.9	122	Azerbaijan	44.3
13	Ireland	91.9	68	Pakistan	62.6	123	Belarus	44.3
14	Sri Lanka	91.7	69	Egypt	62.4	124	Togo	44.2
15	Latvia	90.5	70	Indonesia	62.2	125	Oman	44.2
16	Cambodia	90.0	71	Australia	61.7	126	North Korea	44.1
17	Philippines	89.3	72	Mexico	61.4	127	Sao Tome & Principe	43.7
18	Slovakia	89.2	73	Guatemala	59.9	128	Kazakhstan	43.4
19	Cuba	88.6	74	Macedonia	59.7	129	Botswana	42.9
20	Japan	87.8	75	Algeria	58.3	130	Bhutan	42.8
21	Fiji	87.7	76	Turkey	57.9	131	Guyana	42.8
22	Finland	87.6	77	Kenya	57.9	132	Ethiopia	42.8
23	Bangladesh	87.2	78	Israel	57.7	133	Iraq	42.7
24	Switzerland	86.9	79	Malaysia	54.6	134	Eritrea	42.5
25	France	86.5	80	Colombia	54.6	135	Saudi Arabia	42.4
26	Lithuania	85.9	81	Cameroon	52.9	136	Nicaragua	42.3
27	Brazil	85.4	82	Chile	52.6	137	Niger	42.2
28	Laos	85.1	83	Angola	51.8	138	Gabon	42.1
29	Tanzania	85.0	84	Paraguay	51.8	139	Antigua & Barbuda	41.7
30	South Korea	84.9	85	Armenia	51.0	140	Zambia	41.7
31	Argentina	84.3	86	Côte d'Ivoire	50.9	141	Kyrgyzstan	41.3
32	South Africa	84.2	87	Burkina Faso	50.5	142	Lebanon	40.6
33	Senegal	83.6	88	El Salvador	49.8	143	Venezuela	40.5
34	Serbia & Montenegro	83.6	89	Iran	49.8	144	Georgia	40.2
35	Ecuador	83.4	90	Honduras	49.7	145	Maldives	39.9
36	Peru	83.4	91	Libya	49.4	146	Burundi	39.8
37	Bolivia	83.4	92	Congo	49.0	147	Haiti	39.7
38	Spain	83.1	93	Sierra Leone	49.0	148	Papua New Guinea	39.6
39	Thailand	82.7	94	Belize	48.9	149	Uganda	39.5
40	Albania	82.5	95	Moldova	48.8	150	Suriname	38.7
41	Russia	82.4	96	Mauritius	48.8	151	Uzbekistan	38.0
42	Italy	82.2	97	Solomon Islands	48.7	152	Benin	37.2
43	Poland	81.6	98	Gambia	48.6	153	Djibouti	34.4
44	United Kingdom	81.6	99	Brunei Darussalam	48.6	154	Malawi	30.3
45	Romania	81.5	100	Dem. Rep. Congo	47.9	155	Jordan	30.0
46	Bulgaria	81.1	101	Costa Rica	47.7	156	Ukraine	29.8
47	India	78.9	102	Madagascar	47.6	157	Malta	23.9
48	Mali	78.6	103	Mozambique	46.6	158	Bahrain	..
49	Germany	78.6	104	Dominican Republic	46.5	159	Kuwait	..
50	Portugal	77.9	105	Trinidad & Tobago	46.3	160	Qatar	..
51	Ghana	77.8	106	Jamaica	46.2	161	Swaziland	..
52	United States	77.5	107	Equatorial Guinea	46.2	162	United Arab Emirates	..
53	Greece	77.1	108	Rwanda	46.1	163	Yemen	..
54	Cyprus	75.3	109	Nepal	46.0			
55	Denmark	74.9	110	Mauritania	45.8			

Indicator: Water stress index

Rank	Country	Score	Rank	Country	Score	Rank	Country	Score
1	Albania	100.0	56	Haiti	77.6	111	Ethiopia	29.6
2	Austria	100.0	57	Serbia & Montenegro	77.5	112	Ecuador	28.3
3	Belize	100.0	★ 58	Canada	76.7	113	Qatar	28.1
4	Benin	100.0	59	Papua New Guinea	75.8	114	China	27.9
5	Bhutan	100.0	60	Belarus	75.5	115	Kazakhstan	27.2
6	Bosnia & Herzegovina	100.0	61	Côte d'Ivoire	75.1	116	Dominican Republic	26.9
7	Burundi	100.0	62	Myanmar	74.5	117	Zimbabwe	26.9
8	Cambodia	100.0	63	Russia	73.3	118	Kyrgyzstan	26.8
9	Cameroon	100.0	64	Bolivia	72.9	119	United States	26.0
10	Congo	100.0	65	Denmark	71.7	120	Paraguay	23.7
11	Costa Rica	100.0	66	Brazil	71.7	121	Djibouti	23.7
12	Croatia	100.0	67	Honduras	71.4	122	Argentina	23.1
13	Cyprus	100.0	68	Estonia	70.0	123	Netherlands	23.1
14	Dem. Rep. Congo	100.0	69	Panama	69.8	124	Ukraine	23.0
15	El Salvador	100.0	70	Czech Republic	69.7	125	Algeria	22.8
16	Equatorial Guinea	100.0	71	Colombia	68.0	126	Hungary	22.7
17	Eritrea	100.0	72	Philippines	67.0	127	Libya	22.6
18	Fiji	100.0	73	Viet Nam	66.8	128	Iran	22.0
19	Gabon	100.0	74	North Korea	63.2	129	Egypt	21.9
20	Gambia	100.0	75	Swaziland	61.5	130	Iraq	21.4
21	Ghana	100.0	76	Greece	59.6	131	Turkmenistan	19.7
22	Guatemala	100.0	77	Nigeria	58.7	132	Cuba	19.1
23	Guinea	100.0	78	Lithuania	55.9	133	Niger	19.1
24	Guinea-Bissau	100.0	79	Angola	55.4	134	Botswana	17.7
25	Guyana	100.0	80	Poland	55.1	135	Azerbaijan	17.0
26	Ireland	100.0	81	Japan	54.9	136	Mexico	17.0
27	Jamaica	100.0	82	Georgia	50.3	137	Pakistan	15.6
28	Laos	100.0	83	France	46.6	138	India	15.5
29	Latvia	100.0	84	United Kingdom	46.6	139	Bulgaria	13.5
30	Luxembourg	100.0	85	Thailand	45.6	140	Spain	13.2
31	Macedonia	100.0	86	Bangladesh	45.5	141	Oman	12.9
32	Malta	100.0	87	Venezuela	43.4	142	United Arab Emirates	10.5
33	Mauritius	100.0	88	South Korea	43.4	143	Uzbekistan	10.2
34	Nicaragua	100.0	89	Portugal	42.9	144	Australia	8.3
35	Norway	100.0	90	Lebanon	42.8	145	Morocco	7.4
36	Rwanda	100.0	91	Sudan	41.4	146	Belgium	6.3
37	Sierra Leone	100.0	92	Tanzania	41.0	147	Saudi Arabia	5.5
38	Slovakia	100.0	93	Mongolia	40.2	148	Tunisia	5.3
39	Slovenia	100.0	94	Madagascar	39.0	149	Namibia	5.3
40	Solomon Islands	100.0	95	Burkina Faso	38.5	150	Moldova	4.1
41	Suriname	100.0	96	Senegal	36.5	151	South Africa	4.0
42	Switzerland	100.0	97	Mozambique	36.3	152	Syria	3.7
43	Togo	100.0	98	Mali	36.2	153	Yemen	3.6
44	Trinidad & Tobago	100.0	99	Kenya	35.6	154	Armenia	0.0
45	Uruguay	100.0	100	Turkey	35.6	155	Israel	0.0
46	Zambia	97.7	101	Malawi	35.6	156	Jordan	0.0
47	Indonesia	95.3	102	Tajikistan	35.4	157	Kuwait	0.0
48	Sweden	92.8	103	Mauritania	32.6	158	Antigua & Barbuda	..
49	Finland	91.6	104	Germany	32.5	159	Bahrain	..
50	Central African Rep.	90.5	105	Chad	31.8	160	Brunei Darussalam	..
51	Malaysia	86.8	106	Chile	31.7	161	Maldives	..
52	Iceland	84.4	107	Sri Lanka	31.7	162	Sao Tome & Principe	..
53	Nepal	84.4	108	Peru	31.5	163	Singapore	..
54	New Zealand	81.5	109	Romania	30.7			
55	Uganda	79.6	110	Italy	30.2			

Environmental Rankings

Indicator: Water scarcity index

Rank	Country	Score	Rank	Country	Score	Rank	Country	Score
1	Albania	100.0	56	Haiti	100.0	111	South Korea	100.0
2	Angola	100.0	57	Honduras	100.0	112	Spain	100.0
3	Antigua & Barbuda	100.0	58	Hungary	100.0	113	Sri Lanka	100.0
4	Argentina	100.0	59	Iceland	100.0	114	Suriname	100.0
5	Armenia	100.0	60	India	100.0	115	Swaziland	100.0
6	Australia	100.0	61	Indonesia	100.0	116	Sweden	100.0
7	Austria	100.0	62	Ireland	100.0	117	Switzerland	100.0
8	Azerbaijan	100.0	63	Italy	100.0	118	Tanzania	100.0
9	Bangladesh	100.0	64	Jamaica	100.0	119	Thailand	100.0
10	Belarus	100.0	65	Japan	100.0	120	Togo	100.0
11	Belize	100.0	66	Kazakhstan	100.0	121	Trinidad & Tobago	100.0
12	Benin	100.0	67	Kenya	100.0	122	Turkey	100.0
13	Bhutan	100.0	68	Laos	100.0	123	Uganda	100.0
14	Bolivia	100.0	69	Latvia	100.0	124	Ukraine	100.0
15	Botswana	100.0	70	Lebanon	100.0	125	United Kingdom	100.0
16	Brazil	100.0	71	Lithuania	100.0	126	United States	100.0
17	Brunei Darussalam	100.0	72	Luxembourg	100.0	127	Uruguay	100.0
18	Burkina Faso	100.0	73	Macedonia	100.0	128	Venezuela	100.0
19	Burundi	100.0	74	Madagascar	100.0	129	Viet Nam	100.0
20	Cambodia	100.0	75	Malawi	100.0	130	Zambia	100.0
21	Cameroon	100.0	76	Malaysia	100.0	131	Zimbabwe	100.0
★ 22	Canada	100.0	77	Maldives	100.0	132	Bulgaria	99.0
23	Central African Rep.	100.0	78	Mali	100.0	133	Kyrgyzstan	96.8
24	Chad	100.0	79	Malta	100.0	134	Morocco	95.3
25	Chile	100.0	80	Mauritania	100.0	135	Belgium	87.2
26	China	100.0	81	Mauritius	100.0	136	Algeria	83.8
27	Colombia	100.0	82	Mexico	100.0	137	Sudan	75.6
28	Congo	100.0	83	Moldova	100.0	138	Tunisia	71.2
29	Costa Rica	100.0	84	Mongolia	100.0	139	Iran	62.2
30	Cuba	100.0	85	Mozambique	100.0	140	Tajikistan	52.3
31	Cyprus	100.0	86	Myanmar	100.0	141	Pakistan	51.8
32	Czech Republic	100.0	87	Namibia	100.0	142	Israel	48.7
33	Dem. Rep. Congo	100.0	88	Nepal	100.0	143	Oman	46.5
34	Denmark	100.0	89	Netherlands	100.0	144	Syria	43.8
35	Djibouti	100.0	90	New Zealand	100.0	145	Iraq	38.0
36	Dominican Republic	100.0	91	Nicaragua	100.0	146	Jordan	37.8
37	Ecuador	100.0	92	Niger	100.0	147	Egypt	29.1
38	El Salvador	100.0	93	Nigeria	100.0	148	Turkmenistan	18.5
39	Equatorial Guinea	100.0	94	North Korea	100.0	149	Bahrain	0.0
40	Eritrea	100.0	95	Norway	100.0	150	Kuwait	0.0
41	Estonia	100.0	96	Panama	100.0	151	Libya	0.0
42	Ethiopia	100.0	97	Papua New Guinea	100.0	152	Qatar	0.0
43	Fiji	100.0	98	Paraguay	100.0	153	Saudi Arabia	0.0
44	Finland	100.0	99	Peru	100.0	154	United Arab Emirates	0.0
45	France	100.0	100	Philippines	100.0	155	Uzbekistan	0.0
46	Gabon	100.0	101	Poland	100.0	156	Yemen	0.0
47	Gambia	100.0	102	Portugal	100.0	157	Bosnia & Herzegovina	..
48	Georgia	100.0	103	Romania	100.0	158	Côte d'Ivoire	..
49	Germany	100.0	104	Russia	100.0	159	Croatia	..
50	Ghana	100.0	105	Rwanda	100.0	160	Serbia & Montenegro	..
51	Greece	100.0	106	Sao Tome & Principe	100.0	161	Slovakia	..
52	Guatemala	100.0	107	Senegal	100.0	162	Slovenia	..
53	Guinea	100.0	108	Sierra Leone	100.0	163	Solomon Islands	..
54	Guinea-Bissau	100.0	109	Singapore	100.0			
55	Guyana	100.0	110	South Africa	100.0			

Indicator: Biome protection

Rank	Country	Score	Rank	Country	Score	Rank	Country	Score
1	Austria	100.0	56	Thailand	94.4	111	South Africa	49.8
2	Belize	100.0	57	Brazil	94.0	112	Sierra Leone	49.4
3	Bhutan	100.0	58	Sri Lanka	94.0	113	Singapore	48.4
4	Bolivia	100.0	59	Ecuador	93.8	114	Mauritius	48.1
5	Botswana	100.0	60	Gabon	93.4	115	Eritrea	48.1
6	Brunei Darussalam	100.0	61	Pakistan	92.8	116	India	45.2
7	Burkina Faso	100.0	62	Oman	91.9	117	Lithuania	44.1
8	Cambodia	100.0	63	Guatemala	90.9	118	Macedonia	40.2
9	Central African Rep.	100.0	64	Bulgaria	89.1	119	South Korea	39.0
10	Costa Rica	100.0	65	Jordan	88.5	120	Argentina	39.0
11	Côte d'Ivoire	100.0	66	Congo	88.2	121	Sudan	38.6
12	Cyprus	100.0	67	Iceland	87.3	122	Tajikistan	38.1
13	Czech Republic	100.0	68	Kenya	86.7	123	Greece	37.9
14	Equatorial Guinea	100.0	69	New Zealand	86.5	124	Georgia	35.2
15	Estonia	100.0	70	Peru	86.3	125	Kyrgyzstan	34.4
16	France	100.0	71	China	85.7	126	Ukraine	34.3
17	Germany	100.0	72	Rwanda	85.0	127	Morocco	31.8
18	Guinea-Bissau	100.0	73	Russia	83.7	128	Guyana	30.9
19	Indonesia	100.0	74	Finland	82.9	129	Madagascar	30.5
20	Jamaica	100.0	75	Cameroon	81.7	130	Turkmenistan	30.4
21	Japan	100.0	76	Italy	81.4	131	Swaziland	30.1
22	Laos	100.0	77	Mongolia	80.7	132	Belgium	26.6
23	Latvia	100.0	78	Dominican Republic	80.5	133	Mali	24.3
24	Luxembourg	100.0	79	Nepal	79.6	134	El Salvador	23.9
25	Malaysia	100.0	80	Spain	79.1	135	Kazakhstan	22.7
26	Malta	100.0	81	Israel	78.2	136	Uzbekistan	21.8
27	Netherlands	100.0	82	Nicaragua	77.9	137	North Korea	21.6
28	Philippines	100.0	★ 83	Canada	77.7	138	Papua New Guinea	21.3
29	Poland	100.0	84	Croatia	77.3	139	Serbia & Montenegro	20.2
30	Saudi Arabia	100.0	85	Australia	75.6	140	Turkey	18.7
31	Slovakia	100.0	86	Armenia	73.8	141	Fiji	18.5
32	Switzerland	100.0	87	Chad	73.5	142	Bangladesh	18.0
33	Tanzania	100.0	88	Belarus	70.1	143	Kuwait	15.9
34	Togo	100.0	89	Mexico	69.1	144	Gambia	14.6
35	Uganda	100.0	90	Niger	68.9	145	Moldova	12.8
36	United Kingdom	100.0	91	Iran	68.5	146	Bahrain	12.7
37	Venezuela	100.0	92	Guinea	67.6	147	Tunisia	12.6
38	Zambia	100.0	93	Azerbaijan	67.6	148	Ireland	9.3
39	Zimbabwe	100.0	94	Chile	67.0	149	Syria	6.4
40	Ethiopia	99.9	95	Cuba	65.9	150	Mauritania	5.4
41	Dem. Rep. Congo	99.9	96	Portugal	64.8	151	Lebanon	4.4
42	Senegal	99.6	97	Sweden	63.7	152	Qatar	4.0
43	Ghana	99.4	98	Algeria	63.1	153	Bosnia & Herzegovina	3.8
44	Nigeria	99.3	99	Slovenia	62.5	154	Haiti	2.7
45	Benin	98.9	100	Norway	61.0	155	Uruguay	2.4
46	Angola	98.4	101	United States	60.8	156	Libya	1.1
47	Namibia	98.1	102	Egypt	59.0	157	Solomon Islands	0.9
48	Honduras	97.5	103	Viet Nam	56.0	158	Djibouti	0.0
49	Mozambique	97.5	104	Myanmar	56.0	159	Iraq	0.0
50	Malawi	97.3	105	Romania	55.7	160	Maldives	0.0
51	Trinidad & Tobago	97.2	106	Antigua & Barbuda	53.5	161	Sao Tome & Principe	0.0
52	Panama	96.7	107	Paraguay	53.0	162	United Arab Emirates	0.0
53	Albania	96.3	108	Burundi	51.5	163	Yemen	0.0
54	Suriname	95.4	109	Denmark	50.5			
55	Colombia	95.1	110	Hungary	50.0			

Environmental Rankings

Indicator: Marine protection

Rank	Country	Score	Rank	Country	Score	Rank	Country	Score
1	Cameroon	100.0	56	Algeria	18.3	111	Solomon Islands	0.2
2	Dominican Republic	100.0	57	India	17.5	112	Ireland	0.2
3	Ecuador	100.0	★ 58	Canada	17.3	113	Guinea-Bissau	0.1
4	Germany	100.0	59	Jamaica	17.1	114	Benin	0.0
5	Jordan	100.0	60	Slovenia	17.0	115	Bosnia & Herzegovina	0.0
6	South Africa	100.0	61	Greece	16.9	116	Dem. Rep. Congo	0.0
7	Colombia	93.2	62	Bahrain	16.3	117	Eritrea	0.0
8	Australia	90.7	63	United Kingdom	15.2	118	Ghana	0.0
9	Belize	87.2	64	Syria	14.8	119	Guinea	0.0
10	Romania	87.0	65	Iceland	13.6	120	Guyana	0.0
11	United States	84.2	66	Senegal	13.5	121	Haiti	0.0
12	Mauritania	67.3	67	Qatar	12.8	122	Iraq	0.0
13	Venezuela	60.0	68	Guatemala	11.6	123	Namibia	0.0
14	Egypt	59.6	69	New Zealand	11.3	124	Nigeria	0.0
15	Denmark	59.3	70	Suriname	11.0	125	North Korea	0.0
16	Estonia	54.1	71	China	9.8	126	Sao Tome & Principe	0.0
17	Lithuania	53.9	72	Peru	9.3	127	Sierra Leone	0.0
18	Russia	53.6	73	Equatorial Guinea	8.3	128	Armenia	..
19	Sweden	53.2	74	Sri Lanka	8.0	129	Austria	..
20	Mozambique	45.5	75	Libya	7.9	130	Azerbaijan	..
21	Saudi Arabia	45.4	76	Japan	7.6	131	Belarus	..
22	Panama	41.7	77	Argentina	7.0	132	Bhutan	..
23	Ukraine	40.0	78	Djibouti	6.9	133	Bolivia	..
24	Serbia & Montenegro	38.8	79	Brunei Darussalam	6.6	134	Botswana	..
25	Croatia	38.6	80	Morocco	6.6	135	Burkina Faso	..
26	Angola	37.0	81	Yemen	6.4	136	Burundi	..
27	Tanzania	36.6	82	Myanmar	6.3	137	Central African Rep.	..
28	Thailand	36.0	83	Madagascar	5.9	138	Chad	..
29	Israel	34.6	84	Nicaragua	5.7	139	Czech Republic	..
30	Iran	32.2	85	Bangladesh	5.7	140	Ethiopia	..
31	Kenya	32.1	86	Papua New Guinea	5.5	141	Hungary	..
32	Singapore	31.8	87	Latvia	5.2	142	Kazakhstan	..
33	Turkey	31.1	88	United Arab Emirates	4.7	143	Kyrgyzstan	..
34	Mexico	30.9	89	Oman	4.6	144	Laos	..
35	Malaysia	29.6	90	Norway	3.6	145	Luxembourg	..
36	Indonesia	29.4	91	Antigua & Barbuda	3.5	146	Macedonia	..
37	Gabon	28.0	92	Togo	3.4	147	Malawi	..
38	Cambodia	26.9	93	Viet Nam	3.0	148	Mali	..
39	Italy	26.7	94	Portugal	2.3	149	Moldova	..
40	Brazil	26.2	95	Tunisia	2.2	150	Mongolia	..
41	Finland	25.9	96	Trinidad & Tobago	1.9	151	Nepal	..
42	Pakistan	25.8	97	Georgia	1.8	152	Niger	..
43	Congo	25.3	98	Côte d'Ivoire	1.7	153	Paraguay	..
44	Gambia	22.2	99	Chile	1.2	154	Rwanda	..
45	Honduras	21.9	100	Belgium	1.1	155	Slovakia	..
46	Poland	21.8	101	Lebanon	0.9	156	Swaziland	..
47	Spain	20.8	102	Fiji	0.8	157	Switzerland	..
48	Kuwait	20.8	103	Cyprus	0.7	158	Tajikistan	..
49	Philippines	20.3	104	Sudan	0.5	159	Turkmenistan	..
50	Netherlands	20.2	105	Maldives	0.5	160	Uganda	..
51	Cuba	19.8	106	Bulgaria	0.4	161	Uzbekistan	..
52	France	19.7	107	Uruguay	0.3	162	Zambia	..
53	South Korea	19.6	108	Malta	0.2	163	Zimbabwe	..
54	Albania	19.2	109	Mauritius	0.2			
55	Costa Rica	18.6	110	El Salvador	0.2			

Indicator: Critical habitat protection

Rank	Country	Score	Rank	Country	Score	Rank	Country	Score
1	Equatorial Guinea	100.0	56	Haiti	7.1	111	Kazakhstan	..
2	Ghana	100.0	57	Angola	0.0	112	Kuwait	..
3	Israel	100.0	58	Antigua & Barbuda	0.0	113	Laos	..
4	Italy	100.0	59	Armenia	0.0	114	Latvia	..
5	Kenya	100.0	60	Djibouti	0.0	115	Lebanon	..
6	Malawi	100.0	61	Guatemala	0.0	116	Libya	..
7	Nigeria	100.0	62	Iran	0.0	117	Lithuania	..
8	Portugal	100.0	63	Kyrgyzstan	0.0	118	Luxembourg	..
9	Russia	100.0	64	Mozambique	0.0	119	Macedonia	..
10	Sri Lanka	100.0	65	Oman	0.0	120	Maldives	..
11	Tanzania	85.7	66	Pakistan	0.0	121	Mali	..
12	Mauritius	83.3	67	Sao Tome & Principe	0.0	122	Malta	..
13	Dominican Republic	83.3	68	Solomon Islands	0.0	123	Mauritania	..
14	New Zealand	78.6	69	Turkey	0.0	124	Moldova	..
15	Costa Rica	75.0	70	Albania	..	125	Mongolia	..
★ 16	Canada	75.0	71	Algeria	..	126	Morocco	..
17	Zimbabwe	75.0	72	Austria	..	127	Namibia	..
18	Ethiopia	75.0	73	Azerbaijan	..	128	Nepal	..
19	Australia	69.4	74	Bahrain	..	129	Netherlands	..
20	United Kingdom	66.7	75	Bangladesh	..	130	Nicaragua	..
21	Malaysia	66.7	76	Belarus	..	131	Niger	..
22	Madagascar	59.4	77	Belgium	..	132	North Korea	..
23	United States	57.9	78	Belize	..	133	Norway	..
24	Venezuela	52.8	79	Benin	..	134	Paraguay	..
25	France	50.0	80	Bhutan	..	135	Poland	..
26	Panama	50.0	81	Bosnia & Herzegovina	..	136	Qatar	..
27	Spain	50.0	82	Botswana	..	137	Romania	..
28	Greece	50.0	83	Brunei Darussalam	..	138	Rwanda	..
29	Viet Nam	50.0	84	Bulgaria	..	139	Saudi Arabia	..
30	Côte d'Ivoire	50.0	85	Burkina Faso	..	140	Senegal	..
31	Trinidad & Tobago	50.0	86	Burundi	..	141	Serbia & Montenegro	..
32	South Africa	50.0	87	Cambodia	..	142	Sierra Leone	..
33	Uganda	50.0	88	Central African Rep.	..	143	Singapore	..
34	Guinea	50.0	89	Chad	..	144	Slovakia	..
35	China	47.7	90	Congo	..	145	Slovenia	..
36	Colombia	47.1	91	Croatia	..	146	South Korea	..
37	Cuba	47.1	92	Cyprus	..	147	Sudan	..
38	India	46.7	93	Czech Republic	..	148	Suriname	..
39	Japan	45.0	94	Denmark	..	149	Swaziland	..
40	Ecuador	44.1	95	Egypt	..	150	Sweden	..
41	Bolivia	42.9	96	El Salvador	..	151	Switzerland	..
42	Argentina	40.0	97	Eritrea	..	152	Syria	..
43	Jamaica	40.0	98	Estonia	..	153	Tajikistan	..
44	Philippines	36.4	99	Finland	..	154	Thailand	..
45	Mexico	35.3	100	Gabon	..	155	Togo	..
46	Dem. Rep. Congo	33.3	101	Gambia	..	156	Tunisia	..
47	Honduras	32.1	102	Georgia	..	157	Turkmenistan	..
48	Brazil	31.0	103	Germany	..	158	Ukraine	..
49	Fiji	30.0	104	Guinea-Bissau	..	159	United Arab Emirates	..
50	Peru	29.3	105	Guyana	..	160	Uruguay	..
51	Chile	28.6	106	Hungary	..	161	Uzbekistan	..
52	Indonesia	23.3	107	Iceland	..	162	Yemen	..
53	Myanmar	16.7	108	Iraq	..	163	Zambia	..
54	Cameroon	16.7	109	Ireland	..			
55	Papua New Guinea	14.3	110	Jordan	..			

Indicator: Annual change in forest cover

Rank	Country	Score	Rank	Country	Score	Rank	Country	Score
1	Albania	100.0	56	Oman	100.0	111	Papua New Guinea	84.4
2	Algeria	100.0	57	Poland	100.0	112	Senegal	84.4
3	Antigua & Barbuda	100.0	58	Portugal	100.0	113	Brazil	81.3
4	Austria	100.0	59	Qatar	100.0	114	Venezuela	81.3
5	Azerbaijan	100.0	60	Rwanda	100.0	115	Malaysia	78.2
6	Bahrain	100.0	61	Sao Tome & Principe	100.0	116	Brunei Darussalam	78.2
7	Belarus	100.0	62	Saudi Arabia	100.0	117	Chad	78.2
8	Belgium	100.0	63	Serbia & Montenegro	100.0	118	Haiti	78.2
9	Belize	100.0	64	Singapore	100.0	119	Sierra Leone	78.2
10	Bhutan	100.0	65	Slovakia	100.0	120	Sudan	75.1
11	Bosnia & Herzegovina	100.0	66	Slovenia	100.0	121	Mongolia	75.1
12	Bulgaria	100.0	67	South Africa	100.0	122	Mali	75.1
★ 13	Canada	100.0	68	Spain	100.0	123	Paraguay	72.0
14	Chile	100.0	69	Suriname	100.0	124	Namibia	72.0
15	China	100.0	70	Swaziland	100.0	125	Malawi	72.0
16	Costa Rica	100.0	71	Switzerland	100.0	126	Equatorial Guinea	72.0
17	Côte d'Ivoire	100.0	72	Syria	100.0	127	Zambia	68.9
18	Croatia	100.0	73	Tajikistan	100.0	128	Cameroon	68.9
19	Cuba	100.0	74	Tunisia	100.0	129	Botswana	68.9
20	Cyprus	100.0	75	Turkey	100.0	130	Niger	68.9
21	Czech Republic	100.0	76	Turkmenistan	100.0	131	Tanzania	65.8
22	Denmark	100.0	77	Ukraine	100.0	132	Ethiopia	65.8
23	Djibouti	100.0	78	United Arab Emirates	100.0	133	Nicaragua	59.6
24	Dominican Republic	100.0	79	United Kingdom	100.0	134	Guatemala	59.6
25	Egypt	100.0	80	United States	100.0	135	Nepal	56.5
26	Estonia	100.0	81	Uruguay	100.0	136	Myanmar	56.5
27	Fiji	100.0	82	Uzbekistan	100.0	137	Sri Lanka	53.3
28	France	100.0	83	Viet Nam	100.0	138	Armenia	53.3
29	Gambia	100.0	84	Yemen	100.0	139	Ecuador	47.1
30	Germany	100.0	85	Colombia	96.9	140	El Salvador	47.1
31	Greece	100.0	86	Panama	96.9	141	Solomon Islands	47.1
32	Guyana	100.0	87	Peru	96.9	142	Zimbabwe	47.1
33	Hungary	100.0	88	Australia	96.9	143	North Korea	40.9
34	Iceland	100.0	89	Jamaica	96.9	144	Ghana	37.8
35	Iran	100.0	90	South Korea	96.9	145	Indonesia	37.8
36	Iraq	100.0	91	Congo	96.9	146	Cambodia	37.8
37	Ireland	100.0	92	Central African Rep.	96.9	147	Philippines	34.7
38	Israel	100.0	93	Kazakhstan	93.8	148	Pakistan	34.7
39	Italy	100.0	94	Trinidad & Tobago	93.8	149	Uganda	31.6
40	Jordan	100.0	95	Dem. Rep. Congo	93.8	150	Benin	22.2
41	Kuwait	100.0	96	Angola	93.8	151	Honduras	3.6
42	Kyrgyzstan	100.0	97	Eritrea	90.7	152	Burundi	0.0
43	Latvia	100.0	98	Kenya	90.7	153	Mauritania	0.0
44	Lebanon	100.0	99	Mozambique	90.7	154	Nigeria	0.0
45	Libya	100.0	100	Madagascar	90.7	155	Togo	0.0
46	Lithuania	100.0	101	Burkina Faso	90.7	156	Finland	..
47	Luxembourg	100.0	102	Bangladesh	90.7	157	Gabon	..
48	Macedonia	100.0	103	Mexico	87.6	158	Georgia	..
49	Maldives	100.0	104	Thailand	87.6	159	India	..
50	Malta	100.0	105	Argentina	87.6	160	Japan	..
51	Moldova	100.0	106	Mauritius	84.4	161	Romania	..
52	Morocco	100.0	107	Laos	84.4	162	Russia	..
53	Netherlands	100.0	108	Guinea-Bissau	84.4	163	Sweden	..
54	New Zealand	100.0	109	Guinea	84.4			
55	Norway	100.0	110	Bolivia	84.4			

Indicator: Growing stock rate

Rank	Country	Score	Rank	Country	Score	Rank	Country	Score
1	Albania	100.0	56	Russia	100.0	111	Namibia	81.3
2	Algeria	100.0	57	Rwanda	100.0	112	Botswana	81.0
3	Austria	100.0	58	Sao Tome & Principe	100.0	113	Cameroon	80.3
4	Azerbaijan	100.0	59	Saudi Arabia	100.0	114	Zambia	79.8
5	Belarus	100.0	60	Serbia & Montenegro	100.0	115	Argentina	78.1
6	Belgium	100.0	61	Slovakia	100.0	116	Panama	77.4
7	Belize	100.0	62	Slovenia	100.0	117	Tanzania	75.6
8	Bhutan	100.0	63	South Africa	100.0	118	Nicaragua	74.6
9	Bosnia & Herzegovina	100.0	64	South Korea	100.0	119	Guatemala	74.3
10	Bulgaria	100.0	65	Spain	100.0	120	Nepal	72.9
★ 11	Canada	100.0	66	Suriname	100.0	121	Armenia	72.7
12	Chile	100.0	67	Sweden	100.0	122	Ethiopia	72.4
13	China	100.0	68	Switzerland	100.0	123	North Korea	68.0
14	Costa Rica	100.0	69	Trinidad & Tobago	100.0	124	Burkina Faso	67.6
15	Côte d'Ivoire	100.0	70	Tunisia	100.0	125	Zimbabwe	67.5
16	Croatia	100.0	71	Turkey	100.0	126	Ghana	64.8
17	Cuba	100.0	72	Turkmenistan	100.0	127	Philippines	61.2
18	Cyprus	100.0	73	Ukraine	100.0	128	Cambodia	60.0
19	Czech Republic	100.0	74	United Arab Emirates	100.0	129	Honduras	57.6
20	Denmark	100.0	75	United Kingdom	100.0	130	Uganda	56.6
21	Djibouti	100.0	76	United States	100.0	131	Sri Lanka	55.8
22	Dominican Republic	100.0	77	Uzbekistan	100.0	132	Pakistan	50.7
23	Egypt	100.0	78	Viet Nam	100.0	133	Nigeria	44.1
24	Finland	100.0	79	Yemen	100.0	134	Mauritania	36.9
25	France	100.0	80	Gabon	99.1	135	Indonesia	0.0
26	Gambia	100.0	81	Congo	98.5	136	Antigua & Barbuda	..
27	Georgia	100.0	82	Central African Rep.	97.5	137	Australia	..
28	Germany	100.0	83	Swaziland	95.9	138	Bahrain	..
29	Greece	100.0	84	Angola	95.8	139	Benin	..
30	Hungary	100.0	85	Dem. Rep. Congo	95.3	140	Burundi	..
31	Iceland	100.0	86	Mozambique	94.9	141	Colombia	..
32	India	100.0	87	Madagascar	94.3	142	Ecuador	..
33	Iran	100.0	88	Guinea-Bissau	92.2	143	El Salvador	..
34	Ireland	100.0	89	Thailand	92.1	144	Eritrea	..
35	Israel	100.0	90	Kenya	91.3	145	Fiji	..
36	Italy	100.0	91	Bolivia	91.0	146	Guyana	..
37	Jamaica	100.0	92	Estonia	90.7	147	Iraq	..
38	Japan	100.0	93	Laos	90.6	148	Kuwait	..
39	Jordan	100.0	94	Papua New Guinea	90.5	149	Lebanon	..
40	Kazakhstan	100.0	95	Senegal	90.4	150	Maldives	..
41	Kyrgyzstan	100.0	96	Myanmar	89.9	151	Mexico	..
42	Latvia	100.0	97	Guinea	89.5	152	New Zealand	..
43	Libya	100.0	98	Mauritius	88.5	153	Oman	..
44	Lithuania	100.0	99	Chad	87.6	154	Paraguay	..
45	Luxembourg	100.0	100	Haiti	87.6	155	Peru	..
46	Macedonia	100.0	101	Brunei Darussalam	86.1	156	Qatar	..
47	Malaysia	100.0	102	Tajikistan	84.9	157	Sierra Leone	..
48	Malta	100.0	103	Bangladesh	84.6	158	Singapore	..
49	Moldova	100.0	104	Mongolia	84.5	159	Solomon Islands	..
50	Morocco	100.0	105	Mali	84.4	160	Syria	..
51	Netherlands	100.0	106	Niger	83.9	161	Togo	..
52	Norway	100.0	107	Brazil	83.5	162	Uruguay	..
53	Poland	100.0	108	Sudan	83.3	163	Venezuela	..
54	Portugal	100.0	109	Equatorial Guinea	82.1			
55	Romania	100.0	110	Malawi	81.6			

Environmental Rankings

Indicator: MTI slope

Rank	Country	Score	Rank	Country	Score	Rank	Country	Score
1	Albania	100.0	56	Solomon Islands	100.0	111	Mauritania	68.0
2	Australia	100.0	57	South Korea	100.0	112	Denmark	67.1
3	Benin	100.0	58	Spain	100.0	113	Uruguay	66.1
4	Bosnia & Herzegovina	100.0	59	Sudan	100.0	114	Italy	63.0
5	Brazil	100.0	60	Syria	100.0	115	Mozambique	60.0
6	Cambodia	100.0	61	Thailand	100.0	116	Sweden	56.2
7	Chile	100.0	62	Trinidad & Tobago	100.0	117	Antigua & Barbuda	52.5
8	China	100.0	63	United Arab Emirates	100.0	118	Bangladesh	52.0
9	Congo	100.0	64	United Kingdom	100.0	119	Finland	48.7
10	Costa Rica	100.0	65	United States	100.0	120	Estonia	39.0
11	Côte d'Ivoire	100.0	66	Togo	99.0	121	Poland	36.9
12	Croatia	100.0	67	Angola	99.0	122	Latvia	36.4
13	Cuba	100.0	68	Bulgaria	98.7	123	Lithuania	34.1
14	Cyprus	100.0	69	Viet Nam	97.5	124	Jamaica	31.3
15	Djibouti	100.0	70	Belgium	97.5	125	Oman	22.0
16	Ecuador	100.0	71	Morocco	96.5	★126	Canada	0.0
17	Egypt	100.0	72	Ukraine	96.0	127	Gambia	0.0
18	El Salvador	100.0	73	Georgia	95.8	128	Armenia	..
19	Equatorial Guinea	100.0	74	Brunei Darussalam	95.8	129	Austria	..
20	Eritrea	100.0	75	Greece	95.2	130	Azerbaijan	..
21	Fiji	100.0	76	Dominican Republic	94.0	131	Belarus	..
22	France	100.0	77	Maldives	93.4	132	Bhutan	..
23	Gabon	100.0	78	Ghana	93.0	133	Bolivia	..
24	India	100.0	79	Cameroon	92.6	134	Botswana	..
25	Indonesia	100.0	80	Jordan	90.9	135	Burkina Faso	..
26	Iran	100.0	81	Tunisia	90.7	136	Burundi	..
27	Ireland	100.0	82	Netherlands	90.5	137	Central African Rep.	..
28	Israel	100.0	83	Romania	90.1	138	Chad	..
29	Japan	100.0	84	South Africa	89.6	139	Czech Republic	..
30	Kenya	100.0	85	Guinea-Bissau	89.5	140	Ethiopia	..
31	Lebanon	100.0	86	Sri Lanka	88.2	141	Hungary	..
32	Libya	100.0	87	Belize	87.9	142	Kazakhstan	..
33	Madagascar	100.0	88	Algeria	87.9	143	Kyrgyzstan	..
34	Malaysia	100.0	89	Dem. Rep. Congo	87.9	144	Laos	..
35	Malta	100.0	90	Guinea	87.3	145	Luxembourg	..
36	Mauritius	100.0	91	Haiti	86.6	146	Macedonia	..
37	Mexico	100.0	92	Iceland	86.4	147	Malawi	..
38	Myanmar	100.0	93	Guatemala	85.9	148	Mali	..
39	Namibia	100.0	94	Senegal	85.0	149	Moldova	..
40	New Zealand	100.0	95	Yemen	83.7	150	Mongolia	..
41	Nicaragua	100.0	96	Kuwait	83.6	151	Nepal	..
42	North Korea	100.0	97	Tanzania	83.5	152	Niger	..
43	Norway	100.0	98	Papua New Guinea	83.0	153	Paraguay	..
44	Pakistan	100.0	99	Venezuela	82.2	154	Rwanda	..
45	Panama	100.0	100	Nigeria	79.0	155	Slovakia	..
46	Peru	100.0	101	Argentina	78.6	156	Swaziland	..
47	Philippines	100.0	102	Colombia	78.2	157	Switzerland	..
48	Portugal	100.0	103	Turkey	76.9	158	Tajikistan	..
49	Qatar	100.0	104	Iraq	76.7	159	Turkmenistan	..
50	Russia	100.0	105	Suriname	75.8	160	Uganda	..
51	Sao Tome & Principe	100.0	106	Sierra Leone	73.0	161	Uzbekistan	..
52	Saudi Arabia	100.0	107	Honduras	72.7	162	Zambia	..
53	Serbia & Montenegro	100.0	108	Guyana	71.1	163	Zimbabwe	..
54	Singapore	100.0	109	Bahrain	70.7			
55	Slovenia	100.0	110	Germany	70.6			

Indicator: Trawling and dredging intensity

Rank	Country	Score	Rank	Country	Score	Rank	Country	Score
1	Sao Tome and Principe	100.0	56	France	75.2	111	Denmark	5.9
2	Maldives	99.4	57	United States of America	75.1	112	Malaysia	5.7
3	Mauritius	99.1	58	Italy	75.1	113	Germany	2.1
4	Colombia	99.0	59	Angola	74.5	114	Jordan	1.3
5	Antigua and Barbuda	98.6	60	Senegal	73.9	115	Bahrain	0.0
6	Costa Rica	98.2	61	Sierra Leone	73.7	116	Bangladesh	0.0
7	Romania	98.1	62	Haiti	72.9	117	Belgium	0.0
8	Estonia	96.8	63	New Zealand	72.7	118	Bosnia and Herzegovina	0.0
9	Fiji	95.9	64	Mozambique	72.3	119	Cambodia	0.0
10	Papua New Guinea	95.7	65	Madagascar	72.1	120	Guyana	0.0
11	Equatorial Guinea	95.5	66	India	71.9	121	Iraq	0.0
12	Cyprus	95.3	67	Syria	71.4	122	Kuwait	0.0
13	Solomon Islands	95.2	68	South Africa	70.5	123	Myanmar	0.0
14	Ecuador	94.8	69	Oman	69.0	124	Netherlands	0.0
15	Portugal	94.6	70	Venezuela	68.4	125	Singapore	0.0
16	Australia	93.1	71	Mauritania	68.1	126	Slovenia	0.0
17	Jamaica	92.3	72	Pakistan	67.8	127	United Arab Emirates	0.0
18	Nicaragua	91.9	★ 73	Canada	67.5	128	Armenia	..
19	Kenya	91.3	74	Yemen	66.7	129	Austria	..
20	Honduras	91.3	75	Togo	65.8	130	Azerbaijan	..
21	Lebanon	91.0	76	Congo	64.6	131	Belarus	..
22	Finland	90.3	77	Guinea-Bissau	64.0	132	Bhutan	..
23	Cuba	88.6	78	Gambia	61.8	133	Bolivia	..
24	Bulgaria	87.7	79	Croatia	61.0	134	Botswana	..
25	Chile	87.2	80	Greece	59.9	135	Burkina Faso	..
26	Dem. Rep. Congo	86.9	81	Poland	58.9	136	Burundi	..
27	Georgia	85.2	82	Guinea	56.1	137	Central African Republic	..
28	Latvia	85.0	83	Saudi Arabia	55.5	138	Chad	..
29	Trinidad and Tobago	84.4	84	Morocco	55.1	139	Czech Republic	..
30	Russia	83.9	85	Namibia	54.8	140	Ethiopia	..
31	Belize	83.7	86	Egypt	53.6	141	Hungary	..
32	Israel	83.3	87	Philippines	52.5	142	Kazakhstan	..
33	Algeria	83.3	88	United Kingdom	52.5	143	Kyrgyzstan	..
34	Tanzania	83.3	89	Nigeria	52.2	144	Laos	..
35	Dominican Republic	83.0	90	Lithuania	50.3	145	Luxembourg	..
36	Benin	83.0	91	North Korea	49.0	146	Macedonia	..
37	Panama	82.9	92	Iceland	46.5	147	Malawi	..
38	Côte d'Ivoire	82.4	93	Norway	44.8	148	Mali	..
39	Libyan Arab Jamahiriya	82.0	94	Suriname	44.6	149	Moldova	..
40	Serbia and Montenegro	81.9	95	Indonesia	40.8	150	Mongolia	..
41	Ghana	81.1	96	Ireland	39.0	151	Nepal	..
42	Sri Lanka	79.9	97	Uruguay	35.2	152	Niger	..
43	Spain	79.6	98	Turkey	34.4	153	Paraguay	..
44	Brazil	79.4	99	Qatar	32.1	154	Rwanda	..
45	Mexico	79.2	100	Albania	25.1	155	Slovakia	..
46	Sudan	78.6	101	Brunei Darussalam	25.0	156	Swaziland	..
47	Malta	78.5	102	Djibouti	23.9	157	Switzerland	..
48	Eritrea	78.2	103	Thailand	20.3	158	Tajikistan	..
49	Guatemala	77.8	104	South Korea	19.9	159	Turkmenistan	..
50	Peru	77.1	105	Argentina	17.5	160	Uganda	..
51	Ukraine	77.0	106	Iran	14.7	161	Uzbekistan	..
52	Gabon	76.9	107	China	13.1	162	Zambia	..
53	Sweden	76.8	108	Cameroon	9.4	163	Zimbabwe	..
54	El Salvador	76.6	109	Viet Nam	6.5			
55	Japan	75.3	110	Tunisia	6.3			

Indicator: Agricultural water intensity

Rank	Country	Score	Rank	Country	Score	Rank	Country	Score
1	Albania	100.0	56	Indonesia	100.0	111	Mauritania	89.0
2	Angola	100.0	57	Ireland	100.0	112	Mexico	88.8
3	Antigua and Barbuda	100.0	58	Jamaica	100.0	113	Turkey	86.9
4	Argentina	100.0	59	Kenya	100.0	114	Ukraine	86.1
5	Australia	100.0	60	Laos	100.0	115	Cuba	84.2
6	Austria	100.0	61	Latvia	100.0	116	China	83.4
7	Bangladesh	100.0	62	Lithuania	100.0	117	South Africa	81.8
8	Belarus	100.0	63	Madagascar	100.0	118	Zimbabwe	79.5
9	Belgium	100.0	64	Malawi	100.0	119	Lebanon	77.7
10	Belize	100.0	65	Malaysia	100.0	120	Mauritius	76.4
11	Benin	100.0	66	Maldives	100.0	121	Thailand	72.8
12	Bhutan	100.0	67	Mali	100.0	122	Malta	72.1
13	Bolivia	100.0	68	Moldova	100.0	123	Spain	68.2
14	Botswana	100.0	69	Mongolia	100.0	124	Swaziland	67.1
15	Brazil	100.0	70	Mozambique	100.0	125	Cyprus	66.9
16	Bulgaria	100.0	71	Myanmar	100.0	126	Armenia	64.2
17	Burkina Faso	100.0	72	Namibia	100.0	127	Sri Lanka	64.1
18	Burundi	100.0	73	Nepal	100.0	128	Kazakhstan	60.5
19	Cambodia	100.0	74	Netherlands	100.0	129	Azerbaijan	59.3
20	Cameroon	100.0	75	New Zealand	100.0	130	India	55.1
★ 21	Canada	100.0	76	Nicaragua	100.0	131	Algeria	49.7
22	Central African Republic	100.0	77	Niger	100.0	132	Morocco	44.7
23	Chad	100.0	78	Nigeria	100.0	133	Kyrgyzstan	41.4
24	Chile	100.0	79	North Korea	100.0	134	Tunisia	35.4
25	Colombia	100.0	80	Norway	100.0	135	Sudan	28.1
26	Congo	100.0	81	Panama	100.0	136	Iran	23.3
27	Costa Rica	100.0	82	Papua New Guinea	100.0	137	Israel	22.7
28	Côte d'Ivoire	100.0	83	Paraguay	100.0	138	Jordan	21.5
29	Czech Republic	100.0	84	Peru	100.0	139	Tajikistan	19.3
30	Dem. Rep. Congo	100.0	85	Philippines	100.0	140	Iraq	19.2
31	Denmark	100.0	86	Poland	100.0	141	Pakistan	17.1
32	Djibouti	100.0	87	Romania	100.0	142	Oman	10.8
33	Ecuador	100.0	88	Russia	100.0	143	Syria	8.9
34	El Salvador	100.0	89	Rwanda	100.0	144	Turkmenistan	4.2
35	Equatorial Guinea	100.0	90	Senegal	100.0	145	Egypt	1.7
36	Eritrea	100.0	91	Sierra Leone	100.0	146	Bahrain	0.0
37	Estonia	100.0	92	Singapore	100.0	147	Kuwait	0.0
38	Ethiopia	100.0	93	Suriname	100.0	148	Libyan Arab Jamahiriya	0.0
39	Fiji	100.0	94	Sweden	100.0	149	Qatar	0.0
40	Finland	100.0	95	Switzerland	100.0	150	Saudi Arabia	0.0
41	France	100.0	96	Tanzania	100.0	151	United Arab Emirates	0.0
42	Gabon	100.0	97	Togo	100.0	152	Uzbekistan	0.0
43	Gambia	100.0	98	Trinidad and Tobago	100.0	153	Yemen	0.0
44	Georgia	100.0	99	Uganda	100.0	154	Bosnia and Herzegovina	..
45	Germany	100.0	100	United Kingdom	100.0	155	Brunei Darussalam	..
46	Ghana	100.0	101	United States of America	100.0	156	Croatia	..
47	Greece	100.0	102	Uruguay	100.0	157	Luxembourg	..
48	Guatemala	100.0	103	Venezuela	100.0	158	Macedonia	..
49	Guinea	100.0	104	Viet Nam	100.0	159	Sao Tome and Principe	..
50	Guinea-Bissau	100.0	105	Zambia	100.0	160	Serbia and Montenegro	..
51	Guyana	100.0	106	Italy	98.2	161	Slovakia	..
52	Haiti	100.0	107	Dominican Republic	97.4	162	Slovenia	..
53	Honduras	100.0	108	South Korea	90.1	163	Solomon Islands	..
54	Hungary	100.0	109	Portugal	90.0			
55	Iceland	100.0	110	Japan	90.0			

Indicator: Pesticide regulation

Rank	Country	Score	Rank	Country	Score	Rank	Country	Score
1	Armenia	100.0	56	Indonesia	90.9	111	Tanzania	18.2
2	Australia	100.0	57	Ireland	90.9	112	Gabon	18.2
3	Austria	100.0	58	Argentina	90.9	113	Senegal	18.2
4	Belgium	100.0	59	Viet Nam	90.9	114	Nigeria	18.2
5	Benin	100.0	60	Malaysia	90.9	115	Oman	18.2
6	Bulgaria	100.0	61	Netherlands	90.9	116	United Arab Emirates	18.2
7	Burundi	100.0	62	Turkey	90.9	117	Serbia and Montenegro	13.6
★ 8	Canada	100.0	63	Lebanon	90.9	118	Malawi	13.6
9	Chile	100.0	64	Thailand	90.9	119	Botswana	13.6
10	Congo	100.0	65	Yemen	90.9	120	Maldives	13.6
11	Czech Republic	100.0	66	Saudi Arabia	90.9	121	Georgia	13.6
12	Denmark	100.0	67	Slovenia	86.4	122	Eritrea	13.6
13	Dominican Republic	100.0	68	Laos	86.4	123	Venezuela	13.6
14	Finland	100.0	69	Ecuador	86.4	124	Guinea-Bissau	13.6
15	Gambia	100.0	70	Trinidad and Tobago	86.4	125	Namibia	13.6
16	Germany	100.0	71	United States of America	86.4	126	Cameroon	13.6
17	Japan	100.0	72	Mexico	86.4	127	Guyana	13.6
18	Jordan	100.0	73	Morocco	86.4	128	Mauritania	13.6
19	Lithuania	100.0	74	Kyrgyzstan	86.4	129	India	13.6
20	New Zealand	100.0	75	Egypt	86.4	130	Tunisia	13.6
21	Norway	100.0	76	Brunei Darussalam	81.8	131	Tajikistan	13.6
22	Panama	100.0	77	Mongolia	81.8	132	Pakistan	13.6
23	Peru	100.0	78	Costa Rica	81.8	133	Libyan Arab Jamahiriya	13.6
24	Romania	100.0	79	Ghana	81.8	134	Qatar	13.6
25	Slovakia	100.0	80	Philippines	81.8	135	Sao Tome and Principe	9.1
26	South Korea	100.0	81	Myanmar	81.8	136	Bosnia and Herzegovina	9.1
27	Sweden	100.0	82	Sri Lanka	81.8	137	Belarus	9.1
28	Switzerland	100.0	83	Côte d'Ivoire	77.3	138	Antigua and Barbuda	9.1
29	Syria	100.0	84	El Salvador	77.3	139	Equatorial Guinea	9.1
30	Colombia	95.5	85	Madagascar	77.3	140	Belize	9.1
31	Croatia	95.5	86	Ukraine	77.3	141	Angola	9.1
32	Cyprus	95.5	87	Togo	72.7	142	Sierra Leone	9.1
33	Estonia	95.5	88	Djibouti	72.7	143	Mozambique	9.1
34	France	95.5	89	Cuba	72.7	144	North Korea	9.1
35	Greece	95.5	90	Central African Republic	68.2	145	Suriname	9.1
36	Hungary	95.5	91	Algeria	68.2	146	Albania	9.1
37	Iran	95.5	92	Burkina Faso	63.6	147	Bangladesh	9.1
38	Italy	95.5	93	South Africa	63.6	148	Cambodia	9.1
39	Jamaica	95.5	94	Nepal	59.1	149	Bahrain	9.1
40	Kuwait	95.5	95	Niger	59.1	150	Solomon Islands	4.5
41	Latvia	95.5	96	China	59.1	151	Papua New Guinea	4.5
42	Luxembourg	95.5	97	Chad	54.5	152	Honduras	4.5
43	Malta	95.5	98	Guinea	54.5	153	Guatemala	4.5
44	Mauritius	95.5	99	Uruguay	54.5	154	Swaziland	4.5
45	Moldova	95.5	100	Kazakhstan	50.0	155	Azerbaijan	4.5
46	Paraguay	95.5	101	Macedonia	45.5	156	Israel	4.5
47	Poland	95.5	102	Zambia	45.5	157	Bhutan	0.0
48	Portugal	95.5	103	Nicaragua	31.8	158	Haiti	0.0
49	Singapore	95.5	104	Ethiopia	22.7	159	Iraq	0.0
50	Spain	95.5	105	Uganda	18.2	160	Russia	0.0
51	Sudan	95.5	106	Rwanda	18.2	161	Turkmenistan	0.0
52	United Kingdom	95.5	107	Bolivia	18.2	162	Uzbekistan	0.0
53	Fiji	90.9	108	Mali	18.2	163	Zimbabwe	0.0
54	Brazil	90.9	109	Kenya	18.2			
55	Iceland	90.9	110	Dem. Rep. Congo	18.2			

Indicator: Agriculture subsidies

Rank	Country	Score	Rank	Country	Score	Rank	Country	Score
1	Albania	100.0	56	Maldives	100.0	111	Australia	90.6
2	Algeria	100.0	57	Mauritania	100.0	112	Chile	89.3
3	Angola	100.0	58	Mauritius	100.0	113	Bulgaria	84.8
4	Antigua and Barbuda	100.0	59	Moldova	100.0	114	Brazil	84.3
5	Argentina	100.0	60	Mongolia	100.0	115	Ecuador	83.7
6	Armenia	100.0	61	Morocco	100.0	116	Kazakhstan	80.7
7	Azerbaijan	100.0	62	Myanmar	100.0	117	Philippines	78.9
8	Bahrain	100.0	63	Namibia	100.0	118	China	76.1
9	Bangladesh	100.0	64	Nepal	100.0	119	Indonesia	70.8
10	Belarus	100.0	65	Nicaragua	100.0	120	Ukraine	69.9
11	Belize	100.0	66	Niger	100.0	121	United States of America	68.8
12	Bhutan	100.0	67	Nigeria	100.0	122	Latvia	66.0
13	Bolivia	100.0	68	North Korea	100.0	★123	Canada	65.1
14	Bosnia and Herzegovina	100.0	69	Oman	100.0	124	Mexico	64.7
15	Botswana	100.0	70	Pakistan	100.0	125	Kenya	64.3
16	Brunei Darussalam	100.0	71	Panama	100.0	126	Finland	63.3
17	Burundi	100.0	72	Papua New Guinea	100.0	127	Italy	63.1
18	Cambodia	100.0	73	Paraguay	100.0	128	Viet Nam	61.9
19	Central African Republic	100.0	74	Peru	100.0	129	Sweden	60.4
20	Congo	100.0	75	Qatar	100.0	130	Estonia	60.1
21	Costa Rica	100.0	76	Rwanda	100.0	131	India	59.5
22	Côte d'Ivoire	100.0	77	Sao Tome and Principe	100.0	132	Romania	58.6
23	Croatia	100.0	78	Saudi Arabia	100.0	133	Denmark	58.2
24	Cuba	100.0	79	Senegal	100.0	134	Spain	55.9
25	Dem. Rep. Congo	100.0	80	Serbia and Montenegro	100.0	135	Slovakia	55.8
26	Djibouti	100.0	81	Sierra Leone	100.0	136	France	54.6
27	Egypt	100.0	82	Singapore	100.0	137	South Africa	53.6
28	El Salvador	100.0	83	Solomon Islands	100.0	138	Portugal	53.5
29	Equatorial Guinea	100.0	84	Sri Lanka	100.0	139	Netherlands	52.3
30	Eritrea	100.0	85	Sudan	100.0	140	Russia	51.9
31	Ethiopia	100.0	86	Suriname	100.0	141	Lithuania	50.8
32	Fiji	100.0	87	Swaziland	100.0	142	Germany	49.2
33	Gabon	100.0	88	Syria	100.0	143	Hungary	49.2
34	Gambia	100.0	89	Tajikistan	100.0	144	Austria	48.5
35	Georgia	100.0	90	Tanzania	100.0	145	Czech Republic	45.4
36	Ghana	100.0	91	Thailand	100.0	146	United Kingdom	38.3
37	Guatemala	100.0	92	Togo	100.0	147	Slovenia	33.1
38	Guinea	100.0	93	Trinidad and Tobago	100.0	148	Ireland	32.8
39	Guinea-Bissau	100.0	94	Tunisia	100.0	149	Poland	29.5
40	Guyana	100.0	95	Turkmenistan	100.0	150	Colombia	28.1
41	Haiti	100.0	96	United Arab Emirates	100.0	151	Turkey	4.3
42	Honduras	100.0	97	Uruguay	100.0	152	Mozambique	0.8
43	Iran	100.0	98	Uzbekistan	100.0	153	Belgium	0.0
44	Iraq	100.0	99	Venezuela	100.0	154	Cyprus	0.0
45	Israel	100.0	100	Yemen	100.0	155	Dominican Republic	0.0
46	Jamaica	100.0	101	Zambia	100.0	156	Greece	0.0
47	Jordan	100.0	102	Zimbabwe	100.0	157	Iceland	0.0
48	Kuwait	100.0	103	Benin	99.3	158	Japan	0.0
49	Kyrgyzstan	100.0	104	Chad	99.2	159	Luxembourg	0.0
50	Laos	100.0	105	Mali	98.7	160	Malta	0.0
51	Lebanon	100.0	106	Uganda	98.6	161	Norway	0.0
52	Libyan Arab Jamahiriya	100.0	107	Malaysia	97.7	162	South Korea	0.0
53	Macedonia	100.0	108	Cameroon	97.5	163	Switzerland	0.0
54	Madagascar	100.0	109	Burkina Faso	97.3			
55	Malawi	100.0	110	New Zealand	97.3			

Indicator: Greenhouse gas emissions per capita (including land use emissions)

Rank	Country	Score	Rank	Country	Score	Rank	Country	Score
1	Bangladesh	100.0	56	Panama	80.1	111	Japan	52.5
2	Burkina Faso	100.0	57	Peru	79.3	112	Ukraine	52.4
3	Burundi	100.0	58	Iraq	76.9	113	United Kingdom	52.0
4	Chad	100.0	59	Cameroon	76.1	114	Singapore	50.7
5	Costa Rica	100.0	60	Thailand	75.8	115	Greece	48.6
6	Cuba	100.0	61	China	75.7	116	Germany	48.5
7	Djibouti	100.0	62	Dominican Republic	75.7	117	Slovakia	47.8
8	El Salvador	100.0	63	Turkey	74.6	118	South Korea	47.8
9	Eritrea	100.0	64	Myanmar	74.4	119	Gabon	47.6
10	Ethiopia	100.0	65	Zimbabwe	74.2	120	Uruguay	46.7
11	Gambia	100.0	66	Belize	73.9	121	Denmark	44.9
12	Ghana	100.0	67	Antigua and Barbuda	72.8	122	Israel	44.4
13	Guinea-Bissau	100.0	68	Benin	72.7	123	Jamaica	44.1
14	Iceland	100.0	69	Laos	71.7	124	Austria	44.1
15	India	100.0	70	Albania	70.5	125	Russia	43.7
16	Kenya	100.0	71	Guatemala	70.0	126	Libyan Arab Jamahiriya	42.8
17	Malawi	100.0	72	Mexico	69.8	127	Malaysia	41.9
18	Maldives	100.0	73	Namibia	68.3	128	Netherlands	41.8
19	Mali	100.0	74	Guyana	68.0	129	Macedonia	41.3
20	Mozambique	100.0	75	Malta	68.0	130	Zambia	41.0
21	Niger	100.0	76	Lebanon	68.0	131	Norway	41.0
22	Pakistan	100.0	77	Georgia	67.7	132	Kazakhstan	40.1
23	Rwanda	100.0	78	Serbia and Montenegro	67.4	133	Argentina	39.7
24	Sao Tome and Principe	100.0	79	Romania	67.2	134	Czech Republic	39.5
25	Senegal	100.0	80	Congo	67.2	135	Armenia	39.4
26	Sierra Leone	100.0	81	Suriname	66.7	136	Ireland	39.0
27	Sri Lanka	100.0	82	North Korea	66.6	137	Belgium	38.3
28	Swaziland	100.0	83	Lithuania	65.7	138	Venezuela	37.9
29	Togo	100.0	84	Uzbekistan	65.7	139	Slovenia	37.9
30	Tunisia	100.0	85	Nicaragua	64.6	140	Angola	37.8
31	Uganda	100.0	86	Portugal	63.5	141	Finland	35.5
32	Viet Nam	100.0	87	Azerbaijan	63.4	142	Saudi Arabia	35.5
33	Yemen	100.0	88	Cambodia	62.6	143	Brazil	30.4
34	Philippines	99.8	89	Bulgaria	62.5	144	Botswana	25.8
35	Morocco	98.7	90	Honduras	62.4	145	Estonia	24.7
36	Egypt	98.2	91	Chile	61.7	146	United States of America	24.7
37	Nepal	97.0	92	Iran	61.6	147	Turkmenistan	24.3
38	Madagascar	96.6	93	Jordan	60.7	148	Equatorial Guinea	23.9
39	Côte d'Ivoire	94.6	94	Solomon Islands	59.4	149	New Zealand	23.2
40	Mauritania	94.4	95	Switzerland	59.4	150	Mongolia	22.8
41	Guinea	94.4	96	Hungary	59.2	★151	Canada	21.8
42	Mauritius	94.2	97	Ecuador	59.1	152	Bolivia	19.4
43	Tanzania	93.9	98	South Africa	58.6	153	Luxembourg	19.2
44	Nigeria	92.8	99	Paraguay	58.1	154	Oman	19.2
45	Fiji	92.2	100	France	58.1	155	Kuwait	18.2
46	Moldova	91.7	101	Papua New Guinea	56.8	156	Australia	16.6
47	Sudan	89.4	102	Italy	56.6	157	Cyprus	12.9
48	Syria	87.8	103	Indonesia	55.7	158	Central African Republic	6.5
49	Haiti	84.5	104	Spain	55.7	159	United Arab Emirates	0.9
50	Dem. Rep. Congo	84.3	105	Sweden	55.5	160	Bahrain	0.0
51	Algeria	83.9	106	Bosnia and Herzegovina	55.4	161	Brunei Darussalam	0.0
52	Bhutan	82.6	107	Poland	54.8	162	Qatar	0.0
53	Kyrgyzstan	82.4	108	Belarus	54.7	163	Trinidad and Tobago	0.0
54	Tajikistan	81.1	109	Latvia	54.6			
55	Colombia	80.1	110	Croatia	53.4			

Environmental Rankings

Indicator: Industrial greenhouse gas emissions intensity

Rank	Country	Score	Rank	Country	Score	Rank	Country	Score
1	Angola	100.0	56	Cameroon	87.5	111	Syria	58.9
2	Antigua and Barbuda	100.0	57	Algeria	87.3	112	Macedonia	58.6
3	Bahrain	100.0	58	Peru	86.8	113	France	57.8
4	Belize	100.0	59	Libyan Arab Jamahiriya	86.2	114	Costa Rica	57.8
5	Botswana	100.0	60	Zimbabwe	86.0	115	United States of America	56.6
6	Brunei Darussalam	100.0	61	Saudi Arabia	84.8	116	Uruguay	55.6
7	Burkina Faso	100.0	62	Zambia	84.3	117	Netherlands	54.9
8	Burundi	100.0	63	Germany	84.3	118	Slovakia	54.4
9	Cambodia	100.0	64	Finland	83.4	119	Spain	54.0
10	Central African Republic	100.0	65	Armenia	82.3	120	Portugal	53.0
11	Chad	100.0	66	New Zealand	81.4	121	Romania	52.3
12	Chile	100.0	67	Colombia	81.2	122	Pakistan	51.8
13	Dem. Rep. Congo	100.0	68	Norway	80.8	123	Rwanda	51.4
14	Djibouti	100.0	69	Singapore	80.7	124	Haiti	51.3
15	Equatorial Guinea	100.0	70	Ecuador	80.4	125	Luxembourg	51.3
16	Eritrea	100.0	71	Venezuela	80.2	126	Panama	50.9
17	Gabon	100.0	72	Indonesia	79.1	127	Turkey	50.8
18	Gambia	100.0	73	Malawi	78.6	128	Tanzania	50.3
19	Guinea-Bissau	100.0	74	Austria	78.5	129	Thailand	48.1
20	Guyana	100.0	75	Serbia and Montenegro	78.3	130	Honduras	47.9
21	Iraq	100.0	76	United Arab Emirates	78.2	131	Georgia	43.6
22	Laos	100.0	77	Guinea	77.5	132	Ukraine	43.4
23	Maldives	100.0	78	Czech Republic	77.5	133	Kenya	42.9
24	Mali	100.0	79	El Salvador	77.2	134	Philippines	42.3
25	Malta	100.0	80	Australia	76.8	135	Bhutan	41.9
26	Mauritius	100.0	81	Malaysia	76.6	136	Belgium	41.4
27	Namibia	100.0	82	Bangladesh	75.7	137	Sierra Leone	41.3
28	Niger	100.0	83	Iran	74.9	138	India	41.0
29	Nigeria	100.0	84	Latvia	74.7	139	Fiji	39.5
30	Papua New Guinea	100.0	85	Mexico	74.5	140	Ethiopia	38.8
31	Qatar	100.0	86	Paraguay	73.7	141	South Africa	38.6
32	Sao Tome and Principe	100.0	87	Bolivia	72.8	142	Mauritania	36.6
33	Solomon Islands	100.0	★ 88	Canada	72.4	143	Ghana	36.5
34	Sri Lanka	100.0	89	Japan	72.2	144	Israel	36.3
35	Sudan	100.0	90	Oman	72.2	145	Egypt	36.2
36	Suriname	100.0	91	Belarus	71.6	146	South Korea	35.5
37	Swaziland	100.0	92	Denmark	71.2	147	Croatia	33.3
38	Sweden	100.0	93	Russia	70.3	148	Greece	27.4
39	Trinidad and Tobago	100.0	94	Ireland	70.0	149	Tunisia	24.2
40	Congo	99.6	95	Slovenia	69.6	150	Morocco	23.3
41	Yemen	99.5	96	Brazil	68.8	151	Bulgaria	21.8
42	Argentina	97.6	97	Benin	67.2	152	North Korea	18.9
43	Côte d'Ivoire	97.1	98	Albania	66.9	153	Viet Nam	15.1
44	Kuwait	95.8	99	Poland	66.9	154	Lebanon	7.8
45	Switzerland	95.1	100	Dominican Republic	66.2	155	Kyrgyzstan	7.3
46	Madagascar	94.5	101	Hungary	65.1	156	Cyprus	6.8
47	Nepal	91.5	102	Cuba	64.5	157	China	4.8
48	Kazakhstan	91.4	103	Nicaragua	62.7	158	Uzbekistan	1.9
49	Mongolia	91.3	104	Lithuania	61.4	159	Moldova	0.6
50	United Kingdom	89.6	105	Iceland	61.2	160	Jordan	0.0
51	Myanmar	89.1	106	Bosnia and Herzegovina	59.7	161	Senegal	0.0
52	Azerbaijan	88.9	107	Jamaica	59.6	162	Tajikistan	0.0
53	Uganda	88.5	108	Italy	59.4	163	Togo	0.0
54	Turkmenistan	88.2	109	Mozambique	59.4			
55	Estonia	88.0	110	Guatemala	59.1			

Indicator: CO2 emissions per electricity generation

Rank	Country	Score	Rank	Country	Score	Rank	Country	Score
1	Dem. Rep. Congo	100.0	56	Slovenia	20.1	111	Swaziland	8.3
2	Iceland	100.0	57	Chile	19.5	112	Lebanon	8.2
3	Mozambique	100.0	58	Portugal	19.5	113	Serbia and Montenegro	8.0
4	Nepal	100.0	59	Croatia	19.4	114	Kuwait	8.0
5	Norway	100.0	60	Italy	19.2	115	Eritrea	7.3
6	Paraguay	100.0	61	Spain	19.1	116	Bangladesh	7.2
7	Zambia	100.0	62	Sri Lanka	18.8	117	Poland	7.2
8	Switzerland	81.5	63	Togo	18.3	118	Yemen	6.8
9	Bhutan	79.6	64	Netherlands	18.2	119	Belize	6.7
10	Tajikistan	74.4	65	Nigeria	17.8	120	Estonia	6.5
11	Ethiopia	71.5	66	Viet Nam	17.8	121	Indonesia	6.4
12	Sweden	69.4	67	Honduras	17.5	122	Rwanda	6.4
13	Albania	68.0	68	Germany	17.1	123	Benin	6.4
14	Costa Rica	56.4	69	Fiji	16.8	124	Sao Tome and Principe	6.2
15	Brazil	56.1	70	Pakistan	16.8	125	Morocco	5.8
16	Kyrgyzstan	52.8	71	Azerbaijan	16.6	126	Senegal	5.7
17	France	51.4	72	Romania	16.5	127	Burkina Faso	5.3
18	Namibia	49.2	73	Gabon	16.1	128	Saudi Arabia	5.0
19	Congo	48.8	74	Philippines	16.0	129	Trinidad and Tobago	4.9
20	Uruguay	48.2	75	Japan	15.9	130	Macedonia	4.9
21	Lithuania	45.7	76	Egypt	15.9	131	Greece	4.7
22	Colombia	43.8	77	Uzbekistan	15.8	132	China	4.4
23	Angola	39.7	78	South Korea	15.7	133	Cyprus	4.3
24	Georgia	38.5	79	North Korea	15.0	134	Israel	4.2
25	Armenia	38.3	80	Turkey	14.6	135	Jamaica	3.6
26	Latvia	38.2	81	Kazakhstan	14.5	136	Turkmenistan	3.3
27	Peru	35.4	82	Bolivia	13.7	137	Mauritius	3.2
28	Austria	33.6	83	United Kingdom	13.6	138	Iraq	2.9
★ 29	Canada	33.3	84	Mali	13.6	139	United Arab Emirates	2.4
30	Venezuela	32.9	85	Ireland	13.4	140	Brunei Darussalam	2.1
31	Laos	31.8	86	Moldova	13.3	141	Mauritania	2.1
32	Slovakia	30.8	87	Haiti	13.1	142	South Africa	2.0
33	Finland	30.7	88	Bulgaria	12.9	143	Libyan Arab Jamahiriya	2.0
34	Tanzania	29.1	89	Sudan	12.9	144	Bahrain	2.0
35	Belgium	28.7	90	Guinea	12.7	145	Equatorial Guinea	2.0
36	Malawi	28.4	91	Nicaragua	12.5	146	Antigua and Barbuda	1.9
37	New Zealand	27.0	92	Singapore	12.1	147	Cuba	1.9
38	Uganda	26.0	93	Burundi	12.1	148	Guyana	1.8
39	El Salvador	25.8	94	Thailand	12.1	149	Maldives	1.8
40	Belarus	25.4	95	Iran	12.1	150	Solomon Islands	1.8
41	Cameroon	24.8	96	Mexico	11.6	151	Djibouti	1.7
42	Kenya	24.5	97	United States of America	11.5	152	Chad	1.7
43	Panama	23.7	98	Tunisia	11.2	153	Gambia	1.7
44	Denmark	23.7	99	Czech Republic	11.2	154	Sierra Leone	1.6
45	Russia	23.3	100	Mongolia	11.0	155	Niger	1.6
46	Ecuador	23.2	101	Madagascar	11.0	156	Oman	1.6
47	Luxembourg	22.9	102	Central African Republic	10.8	157	Guinea-Bissau	1.6
48	Hungary	21.8	103	Zimbabwe	10.6	158	Australia	0.4
49	Myanmar	21.7	104	Papua New Guinea	10.0	159	Malta	0.0
50	Argentina	21.4	105	Jordan	10.0	160	Bosnia and Herzegovina	0.0
51	Ukraine	20.9	106	Algeria	9.7	161	Botswana	0.0
52	Ghana	20.9	107	Syria	9.4	162	Cambodia	0.0
53	Suriname	20.9	108	Malaysia	8.9	163	India	0.0
54	Guatemala	20.8	109	Dominican Republic	8.8			
55	Côte d'Ivoire	20.4	110	Qatar	8.7			

Environmental Statistics

2009 Air Pollutant Emissions for Canada

SECTORS	TPM (tonnes)	PM 10 (tonnes)	PM 2.5 (tonnes)	SOX (tonnes)	NOX (tonnes)	VOC (tonnes)	CO (tonnes)	NH3 (tonnes)	Pb (kg)	Cd (kg)	Hg (kg)	D/F (gTEQ)	B(a)p (kg)	B(b)f (kg)	B(k)f (kg)	I(1,2,3-cd)p (kg)	HCB (g)
Industrial Sources																	
Abrasives Manufacture	11	9	4			23											
Aluminum Industry	9,818	6,279	5,019	64,153	1,535	1,455	389,028				23.9	1.038	5,642.7	13,125.4	4,862	3,218.2	
Alumina (Bauxite Refining)	139	58	43	1,028	576	20	305				3.3						
Primary Aluminum Smelting & Refining	9,639	6,183	4,939	63,125	959	1,435	388,723				20.6		5,642.7	13,125.4	4,862	3,218.2	
Secondary Aluminum (Includes Recycling)	40	38	37									1.038					
Asbestos Industry	104	23	9	162	54		4										
Asphalt Paving Industry	38,273	7,608	1,491	761	1,127	4,489	4,199		1,140.86	22.77	21.47	0.005	2.03	7.11	2.52	2.03	
Bakeries	2	2	2			9,040											
Cement and Concrete Industry	50,516	16,651	7,860	24,577	31,310	263	11,874	237	568.33	19.04	269.7	0.758	0.04	0.1	0.07	0.07	469.543
Cement Manufacture	2,701	1,684	797	20,224	26,465	222	9,406	224	438.2	17.6	263.1	0.758		0.1	0.1	0.1	469.543
Lime Manufacture	1,576	811	427	4,273	4,653	41	2,208	13	0.8	0.2	6.6						
Concrete Batching & Products	46,239	14,157	6,635	80	192		260		129.3	1.2							
Chemicals Industry	4,123	2,886	1,354	13,816	22,116	11,059	13,492	10,117	1,614.5	3.3	15.3	0.239	2.7	14.3	6.3	4.3	0.173
Chemical Manufacture	1,146	866	672	9,245	6,674	3,899	6,758	163	1.7	0.2	14.9	0.239	2.6	14.3	6.3	4.2	
Paint & Varnish Manufacturing	22	19	14		2	892	1	1	1,604.8								
Petrochemical Industry	1,145	1,122	269	2,498	6,256	2,641	2,420		7.9	3.1	0.4		0.1	0.1		0.2	
Plastics & Synthetic Resins Fabrication	109	96	79	31	278	2,649	254	24									0.173
Fertilizer Production	1,452	691	247	2,042	5,758	366	3,399	7,768									
Other (Chemical Industries)	249	91	72		3,148	612	661	2,161									
Mineral Products Industry	1,292	1,001	799	1,506	457	194	3,395	203									
Clay Products	66	45	23	458		23	70										
Brick Products																	
Other Mineral Products	1,226	956	777	1,048	457	171	3,325	203									
Foundries	6,391	5,964	5,421	50	151	378	51,245		430.4	0.1							
Ferrous Foundries	6,362	5,943	5,403	50	151	376	51,245		384.9								
Non-ferrous Foundries	11	8	7			2			45.4	0.1							
Die Casting	18	13	10					10									
Grain Industries	48,513	12,382	2,256	582	1,006	2,818	487		4,902.9	249.5	677.3	1.691	189.5	200.2	122	70.2	862.138
Iron and Steel Industries	4,698	2,388	1,600	21,789	8,680	644	19,607	85									

Environmental Statistics / Air Quality

2009 Air Pollutant Emissions for Canada – continued

SECTORS	TPM (tonnes)	PM 10 (tonnes)	PM 2.5 (tonnes)	SOX (tonnes)	NOX (tonnes)	VOC (tonnes)	CO (tonnes)	NH3 (tonnes)	Pb (kg)	Cd (kg)	Hg (kg)	D/F (gTEQ)	B(a)p (kg)	B(b)f (kg)	B(k)f (kg)	I(1,2,3-cd)p (kg)	HCB (g)
Primary (Blast furnace and DRI)	4,296	2,165	1,445	21,382	7,750	521	17,593	85	2,754	197.1	70.9	1.019	189.5	200.2	122	70.2	107.274
Secondary (Electric Arc Furnaces)	402	224	155	407	930	123	2,015		2,148.9	52.4	508.5	0.672					754.864
Steel Recycling											97.9						
Other (Iron and Steel Industries)																	
Iron Ore Mining Industry	8,956	3,739	1,285	10,992	9,982	40	17,822		1,217	18.8	70.1			7.9			
Iron Ore Mining Industry	1,117	769	228	659	341		283		18	1.9	0.2						
Pelletizing	7,839	2,971	1,057	10,333	9,641	40	17,539		1,199	16.9	69.9			7.9			11.441
Mining and Rock Quarrying	171,930	35,641	10,444	4,720	18,149	1,982	9,259	1,209	7,810.3	279.3	100.7	0.001					
Rock, Sand and Gravel	103,310	13,501	2,645		859		131										
Metal Mining	33,807	9,325	4,169	581	5,436	101	4,217	1,163	7,795.1	275.7	6.7	0.001					3.467
Coal Mining Industry	25,750	9,083	2,056	3,122	3,588	986	1,936		0.5								
Potash	2,944	1,611	766		1,099	270	487										
Other Minerals	6,118	2,121	809	1,017	7,167	625	2,488	47	14.6	3.5	94						7.974
Non-Ferrous Smelting and Refining Industry	4,803	3,019	1,835	401,307	2,052	54	9,136	356	181,103.8	17,366.1	839.8	0.463		0.2	0.1		724.347
Primary Ni, Cu, Zn, Pb	4,779	3,000	1,820	400,854	2,002	25	9,136	318	180,751.6	17,366.1	839.8	0.451					724.34
Secondary Pb, Cu	17	14	10	453	49	29		38	352.2			0.011		0.2	0.1		0.007
Other metals	7	6	5														
Pulp and Paper Industry	17,723	12,720	9,073	29,346	30,443	15,789	52,945	1,464	1,641.8	232.7	49.5	1.918	54	29.2	28.2	19.5	408.184
Wood Industry	20,411	11,077	6,149	1,938	10,312	55,251	322,227	1,291	101.5	5.2	0.3	0.38	1.2	0.1	0.1	1.1	6.648
Upstream Petroleum Industry	13,748	10,932	8,288	295,086	411,293	454,047	477,590	3,038	781.7	291.7	107.6		1.3	1.8	1.1	1.1	
Crude Oil and Natural Gas Production and Processing	7,169	6,986	6,182	135,798	363,905	339,957	445,950	2,410									
Petroleum Liquids Storage	546	142	18			2,810											
Oil Sands In-Situ Extraction and Processing	350	342	341	14,062	12,494	966	8,574			47.8	6.8						
Oil Sands Mining Extraction and Processing	192	192	186	10,572	2,984	34,369	2,205		66	149	35						
Bitumen and Heavy Oil Upgrading	5,400	3,182	1,473	107,640	27,044	37,041	12,931	599	715.7	94.9	65.8		1.3	1.8	1.1	1.1	
Other Upstream Petroleum Industry	91	89	88	27,015	4,866	38,904	7,931	28									
Downstream Petroleum Industry	4,665	3,415	2,225	71,050	24,123	42,347	20,497	75	499	128.4	56.4		23.6	5.4	2.7	3.2	
Petroleum Refining	4,600	3,364	2,187	69,112	23,243	12,929	20,288	75	499	128.4	56.4		23.6	5.4	2.7	3.2	
Refined Petroleum Products Bulk Storage and Distribution	11	8	7			28,073											
Other Downstream Petroleum Industry	54	43	32	1,938	880	1,345	209				0.1						
Other Industries	6,048	4,005	2,809	5,214	5,299	42,526	7,564	278	7,887.3	339.9	115.3	0.622	0.4	0.9	0.9	0.1	
Metal Fabrication	1,253	772	625	1,176	883	5,631	3,682	10	7,349.5	329.6	10.6	0.618	0.4	0.9	0.9	0.1	

2009 Air Pollutant Emissions for Canada - continued

SECTORS	TPM (tonnes)	PM 10 (tonnes)	PM 2.5 (tonnes)	SOX (tonnes)	NOX (tonnes)	VOC (tonnes)	CO (tonnes)	NH3 (tonnes)	Pb (kg)	Cd (kg)	Hg (kg)	D/F (gTEQ)	B(a)p (kg)	B(b)f (kg)	B(k)f (kg)	I(1,2,3-cd)p (kg)	HCB (g)
Glass Manufacture	660	270	247	603	988	311	248		0.7								
Vehicle Manufacture (Engines, Parts, Assembly, Painting)	508	349	242	430	689	6,147	1,665	24	132.9		0.2	0.004					
Electronics				7	1	49	2	8	33.6		104						
Plastics Manufacture	171	113	78	566	235	10,935	166		10.7	5.5							
Food Preparation	3,000	2,169	1,396	2,251	1,840	16,783	1,008	224									
Paint and Varnish Formulation						376											
Textiles	9	7	5	61	46	2,295	793	12		4.8							
Other (Other Industries)	448	326	214	119	617				359.9		0.5						
Petroleum Product Transportation and Distribution	138	135	134	1,295	27,219	175	14,719										
Natural Gas Transmission	109	106	106		14,935	112	6,116										
Natural Gas Distribution	26	25	25	1,295	12,183	35	8,603										
Petroleum Product Pipelines	3	3	3		102	29											
TOTAL INDUSTRIAL SOURCES	**412,162**	**139,879**	**68,057**	**948,343**	**605,309**	**642,576**	**1,425,090**	**18,362**	**209,699.3**	**18,956.9**	**2,347.5**	**7.114**	**5,917.3**	**13,392.6**	**5,026**	**3,318.7**	**2,482.474**
Non-Industrial Sources																	
Commercial Fuel Combustion	5,299	3,947	2,991	39,383	35,182	1,498	19,685	416	623.3	351.6	49.1	0.395	0.5	0.8	0.8	1	
Electric Power Generation (Utilities)	22,987	11,501	7,013	384,897	205,348	2,719	40,816	464	2,572.3	405.7	1,647.6	2.893	1	1.6	1.6	0.9	2,731.809
Coal	18,923	7,774	3,709	365,162	149,135	491	12,510	34	1,938.1	265.4	1,588.8	1.886					2,603.063
Natural Gas	2,117	2,364	2,222	415	23,337	1,676	17,897	306	34.6	83.9	29	0.001	0.1	0.1	0.1	0.1	49.9
Other (EPG)	1,947	1,363	1,082	19,319	32,876	551	10,409	123	599.7	56.4	29.8	1.005	0.9	1.5	1.5	0.8	78.846
Residential Fuel Combustion	3,758	2,864	2,616	7,307	33,261	1,770	13,226	358	309.7	385.8	82.4	1.547	0.6	0.8	0.8	0.9	
Residential Fuel Wood Combustion	111,321	105,399	105,271	1,466	10,261	151,821	690,843	923	1,429.5	80.6	21.8	3.665	14,658.3	21,987.4	7,329.1	11,392.7	
TOTAL NON-INDUSTRIAL SOURCES	**143,366**	**123,712**	**117,890**	**433,052**	**284,052**	**157,808**	**764,570**	**2,162**	**4,934.9**	**1,223.7**	**1,801**	**8.5**	**14,660.3**	**21,990.7**	**7,332.4**	**11,395.5**	**2,731.809**
Mobile Sources																	
Air Transportation	1,102	1,102	1,075	5,287	74,377	11,950	65,801	39	43,562.7				32.1	41.3	41.3	30.5	
Heavy-duty diesel vehicles	4,697	4,697	4,325	569	207,885	8,573	44,246	635			2	6.47	56.2	47.5	47.5	4.3	
Heavy-duty gasoline trucks	305	296	250	85	20,357	6,855	83,663	258					29.4	34.9	34.9	22.1	
Light-duty diesel trucks	336	336	309	40	3,960	1,830	3,297	26				1.05	15	26.3	26.3	7.2	
Light-duty diesel vehicles	101	101	93	9	1,017	359	1,583	12				0.47	4.5	7.9	7.9	2.2	
Light-duty gasoline trucks	612	595	503	712	96,715	100,126	1,853,697	8,962			0.1	0.23	59.2	70.3	70.3	44.4	
Light-duty gasoline vehicles	520	505	468	663	82,945	99,615	1,767,964	11,762			0.1	0.31	50.3	59.8	59.8	37.8	
Marine Transportation	11,089	10,658	9,773	82,766	119,368	3,941	9,982	127	317.4	65.9			27.3	40.2	34.7	11.3	
Motorcycles	26	25	17	3	1,435	3,364	20,482	14					2.5	2.9	2.9	1.9	
Off-road use of diesel	32,026	32,026	30,906	2,875	388,803	36,274	208,168	574					13.1	18.4	13.1	25.3	
Off-road use of gasoline/LPG/CNG	8,670	8,670	7,992	106	36,386	233,867	2,530,752	91					167.9	161.4	157.2	18.6	
Rail Transportation	3,895	3,895	3,583	2,241	98,831	2,822	16,063	99	160.5	53.5			4.9	11.6	9.4	4.8	

2009 Air Pollutant Emissions for Canada – *continued*

SECTORS	TPM (tonnes)	PM 10 (tonnes)	PM 2.5 (tonnes)	SOX (tonnes)	NOX (tonnes)	VOC (tonnes)	CO (tonnes)	NH3 (tonnes)	Pb (kg)	Cd (kg)	Hg (kg)	D/F (gTEQ)	B(a)p (kg)	B(b)f (kg)	B(k)f (kg)	I(1,2,3-cd)p (kg)	HCB (g)
Tire wear & Brake Lining	5,381	5,321	1,855														
TOTAL MOBILE SOURCES	**68,760**	**68,227**	**61,151**	**95,355**	**1,132,079**	**509,575**	**6,605,699**	**22,600**	**44,040.6**	**119.4**	**2.1**	**8.53**	**462.3**	**522.3**	**505.1**	**210.2**	
Incineration Sources																	
Crematorium	6	6	6	12	20	2	17		5	0.8	250.6	2.863					
Industrial & Commercial Incineration	115	75	32	525	639	637	1,899	72	371.5	1.9	155.9	0.35					0.817
Municipal Incineration	677	480	443	350	1,364	602	1,330	19	95.1	25.1	303.4	18.107					1,199.302
Other Incineration & Utilities	218	22	16	1,648	394	144	1,933	47	40.9	7.4	254.5	0.02					43.007
TOTAL INCINERATION	**1,016**	**583**	**497**	**2,535**	**2,417**	**1,386**	**5,179**	**138**	**512.5**	**35.3**	**964.5**	**21.34**					**1,243.126**
Miscellaneous Sources																	
Cigarette Smoking	479	479	479			8	2,264	86	1.3	3.5	0.1	0.011	0.3	0.3	0.1		
Dry Cleaning	2	2	2			300											
General Solvent Use						253,539											
Marine Cargo Handling Industry	201	82	30			16				1.3							
Meat Cooking	8,473	8,473	8,473						29				2.7				
Refined Petroleum Products Retail						51,128											
Printing	16	15	14		33	43,189	6	0.055									
Structural Fires	261	261	242			266	1,451	15	0.8								
Surface Coatings						77,397											
Human								567			16.9						
Other Miscellaneous Sources								1,045			600.2						
TOTAL MISCELLANEOUS	**9,431**	**9,311**	**9,238**		**33**	**425,843**	**3,720**	**1,713**	**31.2**	**4.8**	**617.2**	**0.011**	**3**	**0.3**	**0.1**		
Open Sources																	
Agriculture	1,717,015	879,405	48,140			257,381		413,765									
Agriculture (Animals)	270,239	172,953	27,024			257,381		301,579									
Agriculture Tilling and Wind Erosion	1,435,802	701,075	19,579														
Fertilizer Application	10,974	5,377	1,536					112,186									
Construction Operations	3,685,768	1,100,422	218,012	661	2,080	24	342	38	2.3	9.6	7.5	0.015		0.1			
Dust from Paved Roads	3,444,827	660,259	157,964														
Dust from Unpaved Roads	8,979,137	2,837,591	421,565														
Waste	5,658	2,521	2,338	532	3,085	17,190	13,936	4,046	106.7	13.7	613.8	20.291	199.8	240.3	97.7	258.2	4,684.467
Landfills	3,424	306	132	161	648	12,779	1,865	107	80	0.2	307.9	0.996	18.2		10.4	93.3	112.801
Water and Sewage Treatment	38	29	27	185	1,026	403	307	3,854	9.4	10.4	185.3						
Energy from Waste	67	56	49	53	613	15	583		17.3	3.1	9.2						0.129
Open Burning	2,130	2,130	2,130	133	799	3,993	11,181	85			111.5	19.295	181.5	240.3	87.3	164.8	4,571.537
Mine Tailings	32,966	2,637	659														
Prescribed Burning	1,574	1,343	940	4	205	574	9,823	17			0.227		84.1	5.7	10.2	193.3	
TOTAL OPEN SOURCES	**17,866,946**	**5,484,178**	**849,618**	**1,197**	**5,369**	**275,169**	**24,100**	**417,866**	**109.1**	**23.3**	**621.3**	**20.533**	**283.9**	**246**	**108**	**451.5**	**4,684.467**
Natural Sources	105,431	89,620	73,802	65	146,090	23,151,774	868,257	1,861				24.807	9,178.7	620.2	1,116.3	21,086.2	
Biogenics (Vegetation, soils)					118,430	23,032,699											
Forest Fires	105,431	89,620	73,802	65	27,660	119,075	868,257	1,861				24.807	9,178.7	620.2	1,116.3	21,086.2	

2009 Air Pollutant Emissions for Canada - *continued*

SECTORS	TPM (tonnes)	PM 10 (tonnes)	PM 2.5 (tonnes)	SOX (tonnes)	NOX (tonnes)	VOC (tonnes)	CO (tonnes)	NH3 (tonnes)	Pb (kg)	Cd (kg)	Hg (kg)	D/F (gTEQ)	B(a)p (kg)	B(b)f (kg)	B(k)f (kg)	I(1,2,3-cd)p (kg)	HCB (g)
TOTAL NATURAL SOURCES	105,431	89,620	73,802	65	146,090	23,151,774	868,257	1,861				24.807	9,178.7	620.2	1,116.3	21,086.2	
GRAND TOTAL	18,607,112	5,915,509	1,180,253	1,480,547	2,175,349	25,164,130	9,696,616	464,702	259,327.5	20,363.5	6,353.6	90.835	30,505.6	36,772.2	14,087.9	36,462.1	11,141.876
WITHOUT OPEN AND NATURAL SOURCES	634,736	341,711	256,834	1,479,285	2,023,889	1,737,187	8,804,258	44,975	259,218.4	20,340.2	5,732.3	45.494	21,042.9	35,905.9	12,863.6	14,924.4	6,457.409

Notes:

1. A blank space indicates that no emissions data is available or applicable.
2. "0" indicates that the value was approximated to zero, as the value was very small in the context of the sector and pollutant.
3. The emission totals and sub-totals may not add up exactly, due to rounding.
4. The air pollutant emissions data was compiled in collaboration with provincial, territorial and regional environmental agencies using the latest emission estimation methodologies. It represents the most comprehensive information on emissions of key air pollutants available in Canada.
5. Emission summaries and trends for a given year may be different from those previously published by Environment Canada, other governmental agencies and international organizations.
6. A portion of emissions from the Marine Transportation sector is attributed to movement ("innocent passage") of domestic and international commercial vehicles through provincial waters. These emissions have been proportionally allocated to the provinces nearest to the release of the emissions in the different waterways.
7. Mercury emissions from products are included in the 2007, 2008 and 2009 estimates, however, emissions from products are not yet included in the estimates for previous years. Updates to historical trends are currently being compiled and will be published in the near future.
8. Particulate matter emission estimates for the woods products sector have been updated based on new methodologies developed in collaboration with Environment Canada's Forestry, Agriculture and Aquaculture Division.
9. Information on other considerations for the use and interpretation of NPRI data for industrial and non-industrial sources is available at: http://www.ec.gc.ca/inrp-npri/default.asp?lang=En&n=B5C1EAB8-1.

Environmental Statistics / Air Quality

Ground-level ozone exposure indicator, Canada, 1990 to 2006

Parts per billion (population-weighted)

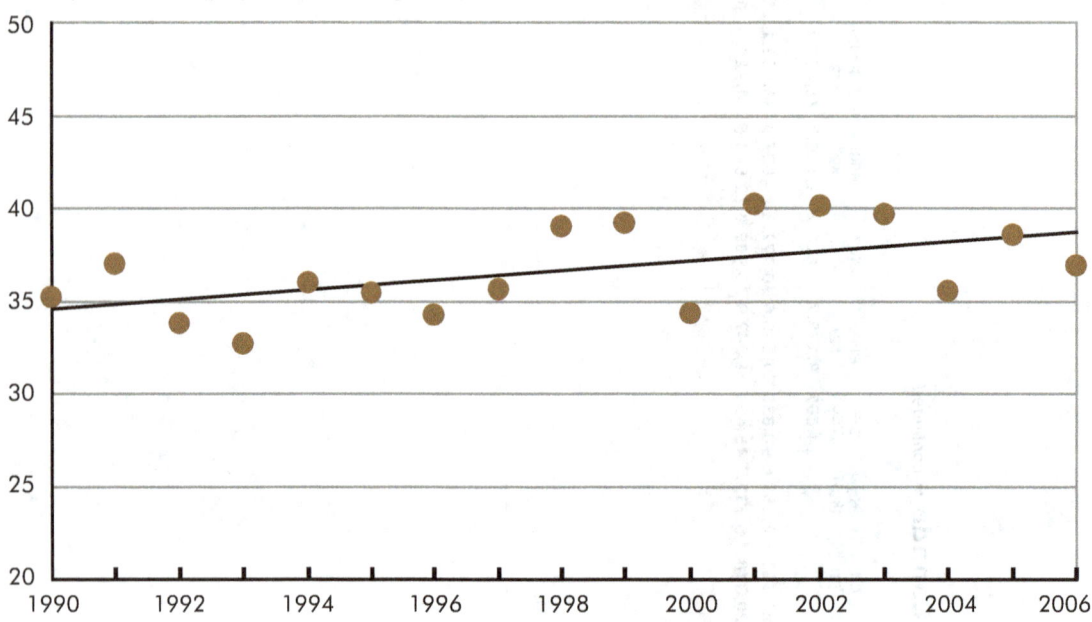

Note: The ozone exposure indicator is based on the average of the 8-hour daily maximum concentrations recorded at monitoring stations across Canada during the warm season (April 1 – September 30). Ambient data were collected from 74 monitoring stations. A trend line indicates a statistically significant trend at the 90% confidence level. The national average increase between 1990 and 2006 is 11.3%. Because of statistical uncertainty the increase could range from 1.7% to 19.0% 90% of the time. Additional technical information on the indicator is available in the Data Sources and Methods section.

Source: National Air Pollution Surveillance (NAPS) Network and the Canadian Air and Precipitation Monitoring Network (CAPMoN); Statistics Canada Census of Population.

Fine particulate matter ($PM_{2.5}$) exposure indicator, Canada, 2000 to 2006

Micrograms per cubic metre (population-weighted)

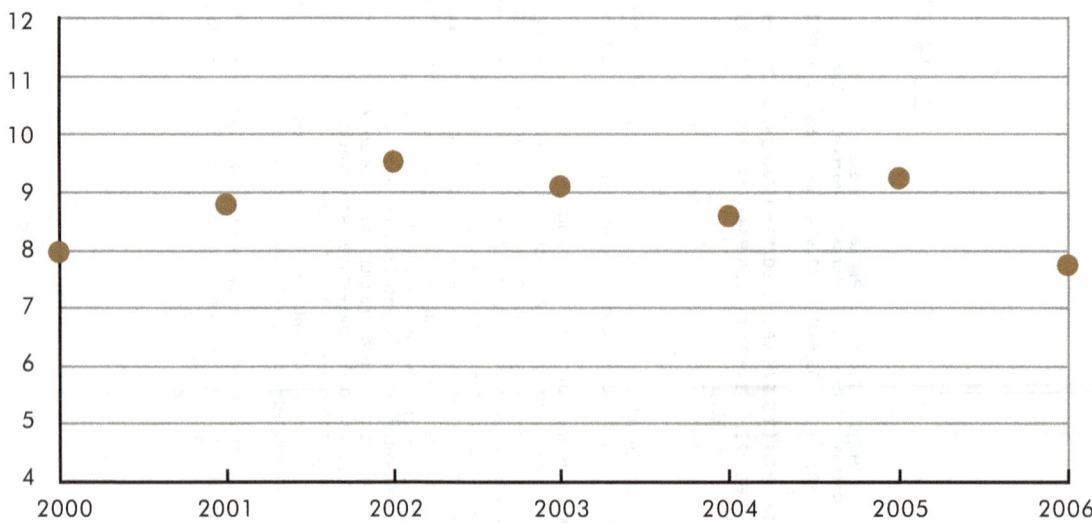

Note: The $PM_{2.5}$ exposure indicator is based on the 24-hour daily average concentrations recorded at monitoring stations across Canada during the warm season (April 1 – September 30). Ambient data were collected from 64 monitoring stations. Additional technical information on the indicator is available in the Data Sources and Methods section.

Source: The National Air Pollution Surveillance (NAPS) Network and Statistics Canada Census of Population.

Environmental Statistics / Children's Environmental Issues

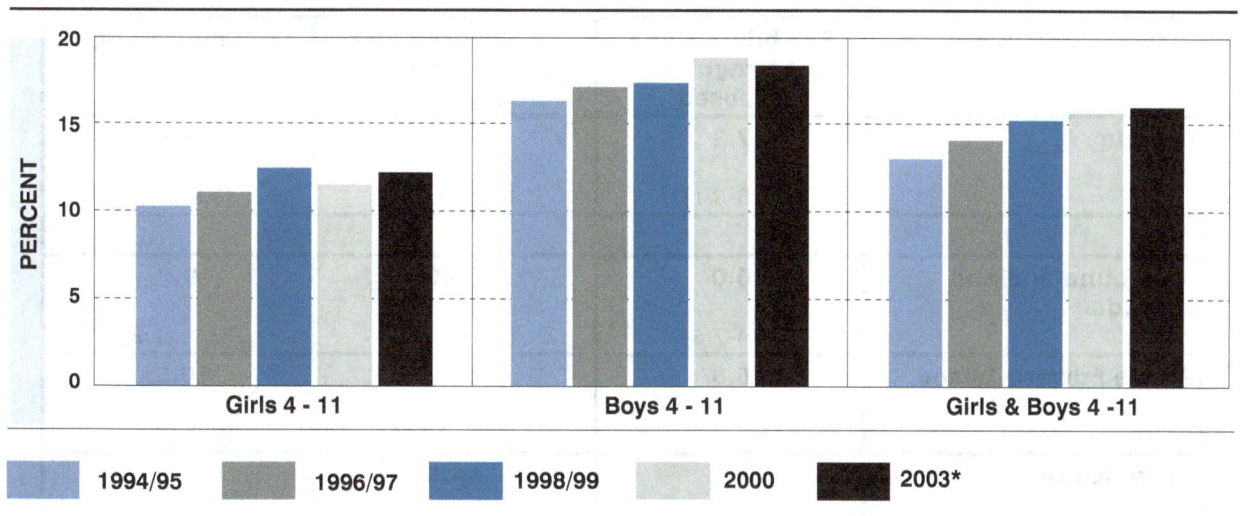

Prevalence of physician diagnosed asthma (ever), children aged 4-11 years, Canada, 1994/95 to 2003.

Source: Centre for Chronic Disease Prevention and Control, Public Health Agency of Canada, using data from National Longitudinal Survey of Children and Youth (cross-sectional component), Statistics Canada.

★ For 2003, the cross sectional component included only ages 5 and under. Ages 7 and over are from the longitudinal component, and individuals age 6 were not included in either samples.

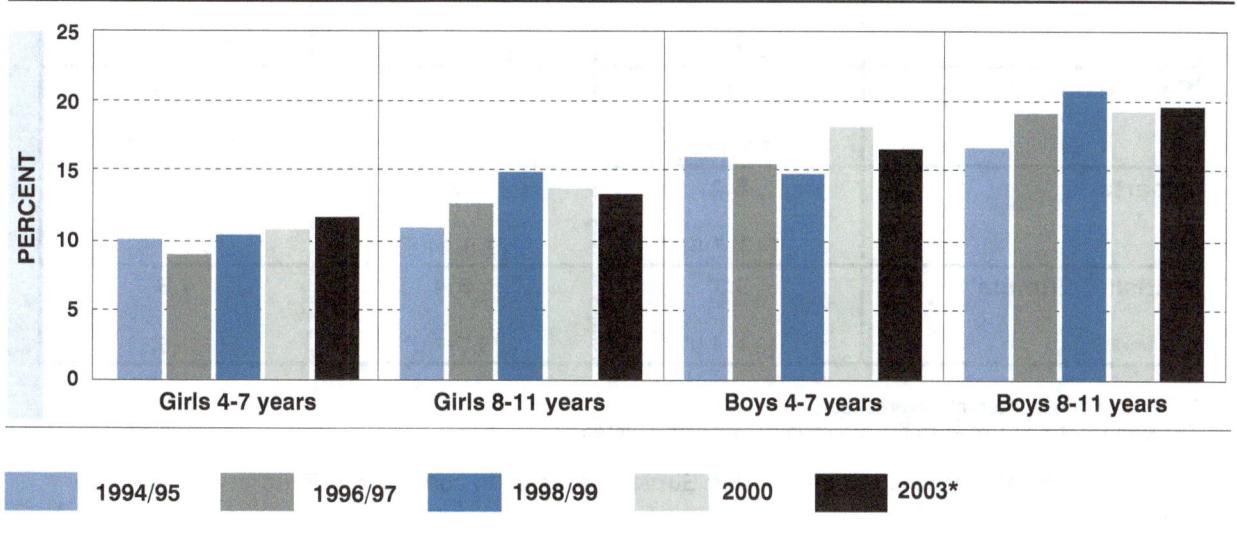

Prevalence of physician diagnosed asthma (ever), children aged 4-11 years by age group, Canada, 1994/95 to 2003.

Source: Centre for Chronic Disease Prevention and Control, Public Health Agency of Canada, using data from National Longitudinal Survey of Children and Youth (cross-sectional component), Statistics Canada.

★ For 2003, the cross sectional component included only ages 5 and under. Ages 8 and over are from the longitudinal component, and age 4-7 includes only 4-5.

Exposure of children at home to Environmental Tobacco Smoke (ETS), by province and age group, Canada 2007

Province	% Children Age 0-11 regularly exposed	% Children Age 12-17 regularly exposed	% Children Age 0-17 regularly exposed
Canada	7.3 [6.5-8.1]	13.0 [11.7-14.2]	9.5↑ [8.8-10.3]
Newfoundland and Labrador	6.0 [4.4-7.6]	15.0 [12.6-17.3]	9.7 [8.3-11.2]
Prince Edward Island	6.6 [5.0-8.3]	15.7 [13.1-18.3]	10.5↑ [8.9-12.1]
Nova Scotia	6.6 [5.0-8.2]	14.8 [12.1-17.4]	9.9 [8.3-11.5]
New Brunswick	10.5↓ [8.3-12.7]	16.7 [13.7-19.6]	12.6 [10.7-14.5]
Quebec	13.6 [11.3-15.9]	22.1 [19.0-25.2]	17.3 [15.3-19.2]
Ontario	4.9 [3.5-6.4]	9.4 [7.2-11.7]	6.7 [5.3-8.0]
Manitoba	7.9 [6.2-9.6]	12.6 [10.1-15.1]	9.6 [8.0-11.2]
Saskatchewan	10.3 [8.5-12.2]	16.4 [13.8-19.1]	12.4 [10.7-14.0]
Alberta	6.2 [4.7-7.8]	12.3 [9.8-14.8]	8.3 [6.9-9.8]
British Columbia	3.7 [2.4-4.9]	5.4 [3.7-7.0]	4.3 [3.2-5.5]

[95% confidence intervals in brackets]
The symbols ↑ and ↓ refer to the direction of rounding to integers.

Source: Canadian Tobacco Use Monitoring Survey, Household component, February - December 2007

Primary type of drinking water consumed, Canada and provinces

	Municipal and non-municipal water supply [1]			Municipal water supply [2]			Non-municipal water supply [3]		
	Tap water	Bottled	Both tap water and bottled water	Tap water	Bottled	Both tap water and bottled water	Tap water	Bottled	Both tap water and bottled water
	percent								
Canada	59	30	10	59	30	10	61	30	7
Newfoundland and Labrador	57	28	7 E	55	30	6 E	69	F	F
Prince Edward Island	72	20	F	64	28	F	79	F	F
Nova Scotia	63	28	7 E	60	31	F	67	24	F
New Brunswick	65	29	4 E	59	35	F	72	23	F
Quebec	59	28	11	59	28	12	64	26	8 E
Ontario	53	34	12	53	34	12	55	36	8
Manitoba	55	37	8 E	54	37	8 E	59	33	F
Saskatchewan	65	28	7	66	26	7	54	39	F
Alberta	62	29	8	62	29	9	60	36	F
British Columbia	68	24	8	68	24	7	64	24	F

1. As a percentage of all households.
2. As a percentage of all households that had a municipal water supply.
3. As a percentage of all households that had a non-municipal water supply.

Source(s): Statistics Canada, Environment Accounts and Statistics Division, Households and the Environment Survey, 2007, CANSIM Table 153-0063.

Households with a non-municipal water supply that had their water tested by a laboratory, Canada and provinces

	Non-municipal water supply	Water tested by a laboratory in last twelve months [1]	No problem found [2]
	percent		
Canada	13	35	87
Newfoundland and Labrador	11 E	F	F
Prince Edward Island	51	35	90
Nova Scotia	44	28	80
New Brunswick	50	26	81
Quebec	11	26	79
Ontario	11	48	93
Manitoba	18	34	84
Saskatchewan	9 E	25 E	93
Alberta	10 E	32	87
British Columbia	8	30	84

1. As a percentage of all households that had a non-municipal water supply.
2. As a percentage of households that had their water tested by a laboratory.

Source(s): Statistics Canada, Environment Accounts and Statistics Division, Households and the Environment Survey, 2007, CANSIM Table 153-0062.

Treatment of drinking water by households that had a municipal water supply, Canada and provinces

	Municipal water supply[1]	Households that had a municipal water supply						
		Primary type of drinking water, tap water[2]	Treated water prior to consumption[3]	Used an on-tap filter or purifier[3]	Used a filter or purifier on the main supply pipe[3]	Used a filter[3]	Used a jug filter[3]	Boiled water in order to make it safe to drink in the last twelve months[3]
	percent							
Canada	86	59	54	12	6	47	34	11
Newfoundland and Labrador	88	55	66	16	7 E	57	44	21
Prince Edward Island	49	64	43	F	F	41	29	F
Nova Scotia	56	60	52	F	F	47	38	F
New Brunswick	50	59	52	F	F	47	41	F
Quebec	88	59	37	9 E	3	31	21	9
Ontario	87	53	64	14	9	58	41	11
Manitoba	80	54	53	11	8 E	48	36	9 E
Saskatchewan	90	66	48	11	9	44	29	8 E
Alberta	89	62	56	13	6 E	52	38	9 E
British Columbia	91	68	60	13	5	47	32	21

1. As a percentage of all households.
2. As a percentage of all households that had a municipal water supply.
3. Information relates only to households that reported primarily consuming tap water, or tap water and bottled water.

Source(s): Statistics Canada, Environment Accounts and Statistics Division, Households and the Environment Survey, 2007, CANSIM Tables 153-0062, 153-0063 and 153-0066.

Treatment of drinking water by households that had a non-municipal water supply, Canada and provinces

	Non-municipal water supply[1]	Households that had a non-municipal water supply						
		Primary type of drinking water, tap water[2]	Treated water prior to consumption[3]	Used an on-tap filter or purifier[3]	Used a filter or purifier on the main supply pipe[3]	Used a filter[3]	Used a jug filter[3]	Boiled water in order to make it safe to drink in the last twelve months[3]
	percent							
Canada	13	61	49	10	31	48	17	3
Newfoundland and Labrador	11 E	69	F	F	F	F	F	F
Prince Edward Island	51	79	34	F	19 E	33	F	F
Nova Scotia	44	67	54	F	34	52	20 E	F
New Brunswick	50	72	43	F	21	42	23	F
Quebec	11	64	34	F	25	33	7 E	F
Ontario	11	55	60	12	39	58	20	F
Manitoba	18	59	50	13 E	31	49	19	F
Saskatchewan	9 E	54	50 E	F	F	49 E	F	F
Alberta	10 E	60	54	F	23 E	52	F	F
British Columbia	8	64	49	12 E	33	47	12 E	F

1. As a percentage of all households.
2. As a percentage of all households that had a non-municipal water supply.
3. Information relates only to households that reported primarily consuming tap water, or tap water and bottled water.

Source(s): Statistics Canada, Environment Accounts and Statistics Division, Households and the Environment Survey, 2007, CANSIM Tables 153-0062, 153-0063 and 153-0066.

Reasons why households with a municipal water supply treated their tap water before using it, Canada and provinces

	Treated water prior to consumption [1]	Reasons for treating [2]				
		To improve appearance, taste or odour	To remove water treatment chemicals such as chlorine	To remove metals or minerals	To remove possible bacterial contamination	Other reasons
		percent				
Canada	**54**	**58**	**51**	**40**	**43**	**12**
Newfoundland and Labrador	66	44	45	33	36	22 E
Prince Edward Island	43	64	70	F	F	F
Nova Scotia	52	59	57	26 E	28	F
New Brunswick	52	68	51	28	35	F
Quebec	37	50	50	42	42	13
Ontario	64	62	49	41	42	11
Manitoba	53	73	52	33	41	11 E
Saskatchewan	48	62	50	37	40	17
Alberta	56	60	57	44	46	13
British Columbia	60	52	51	38	50	11

1. As a percentage of households with a municipal water supply reporting that tap water was used.
2. Relates only to households reporting that tap water was used.
Source(s): Statistics Canada, Environment Accounts and Statistics Division, Households and the Environment Survey, 2007, CANSIM Table 153-0066.

Reasons why households with a non-municipal water supply treated their tap water before using it, Canada and provinces

	Treated water prior to consumption [1]	Reasons for treating [2]				
		To improve appearance, taste or odour	To remove water treatment chemicals such as chlorine	To remove metals or minerals	To remove possible bacterial contamination	Other reasons
		percent				
Canada	**49**	**42**	**11**	**51**	**31**	**17**
Newfoundland and Labrador	F	F	F	F	F	F
Prince Edward Island	34	F	F	F	F	F
Nova Scotia	54	33	F	38	F	35
New Brunswick	43	39	F	48	28	F
Quebec	34	41	F	57	21 E	14 E
Ontario	60	42	13 E	50	39	14
Manitoba	50	55	F	56	35	F
Saskatchewan	50 E	F	F	F	F	F
Alberta	54	59 E	F	71	F	F
British Columbia	49	37	F	50	38	F

1. As a percentage of households with a non-municipal water supply reporting that tap water was used.
2. Relates only to households reporting that tap water was used.
Source(s): Statistics Canada, Environment Accounts and Statistics Division, Households and the Environment Survey, 2007, CANSIM Table 153-0066.

Environmental Statistics / Emissions & Toxic Releases

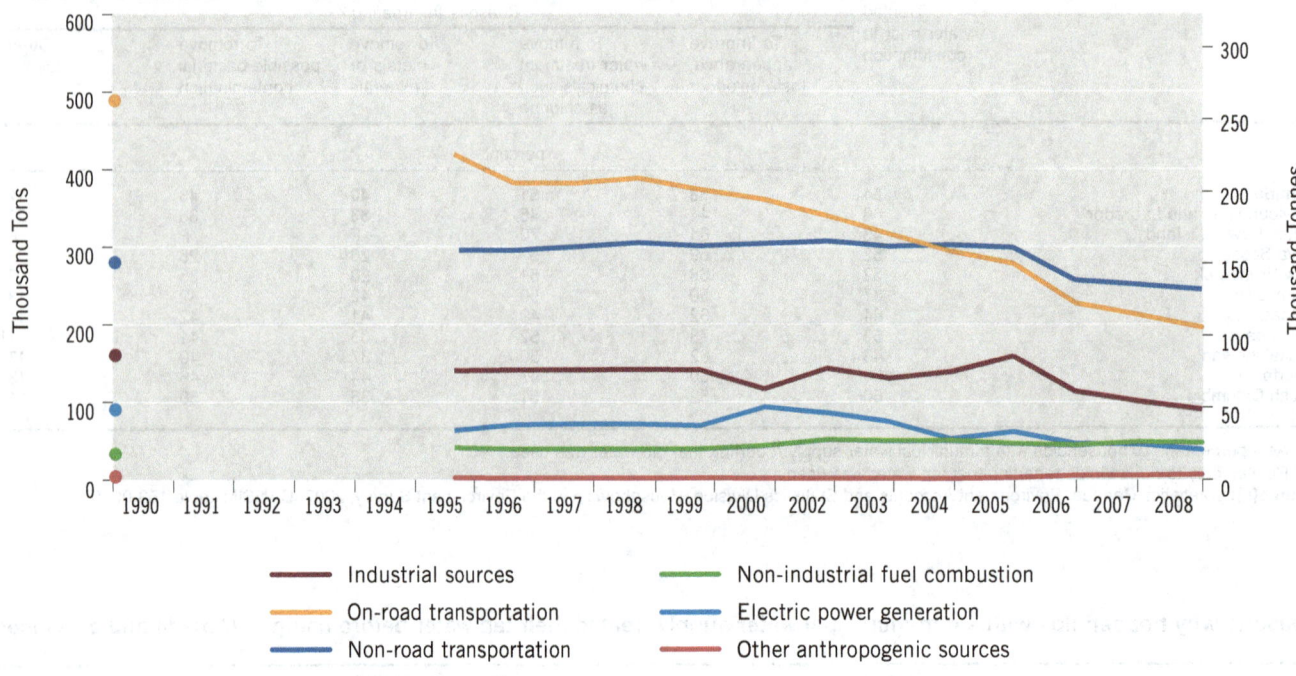

Note: The scales in Figures 18–19 and 20–21 are significantly different.

Source: Environment Canada 2010

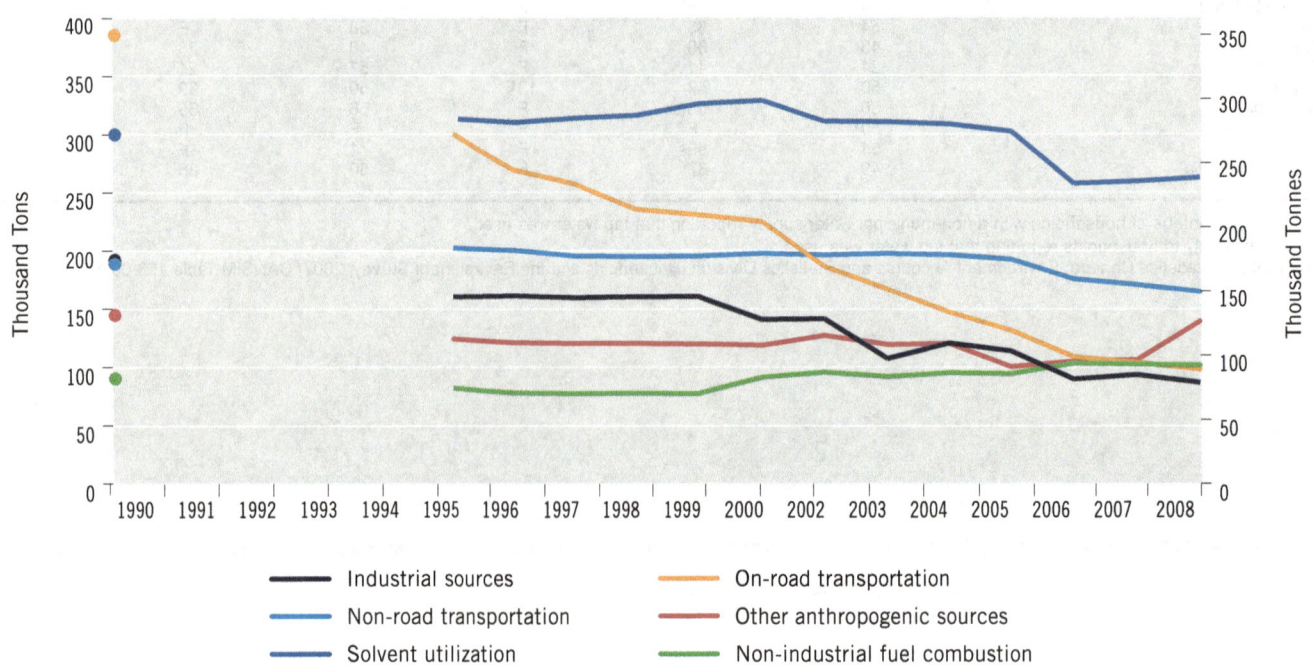

Note: The scales in Figures 18–19 and 20–21 are significantly different.

Source: Environment Canada 2010

Ozone Concentrations along the Canada–U.S. Border
(Three-Year Average of the Fourth-highest Daily Maximum 8-hour Average), 2006–2008

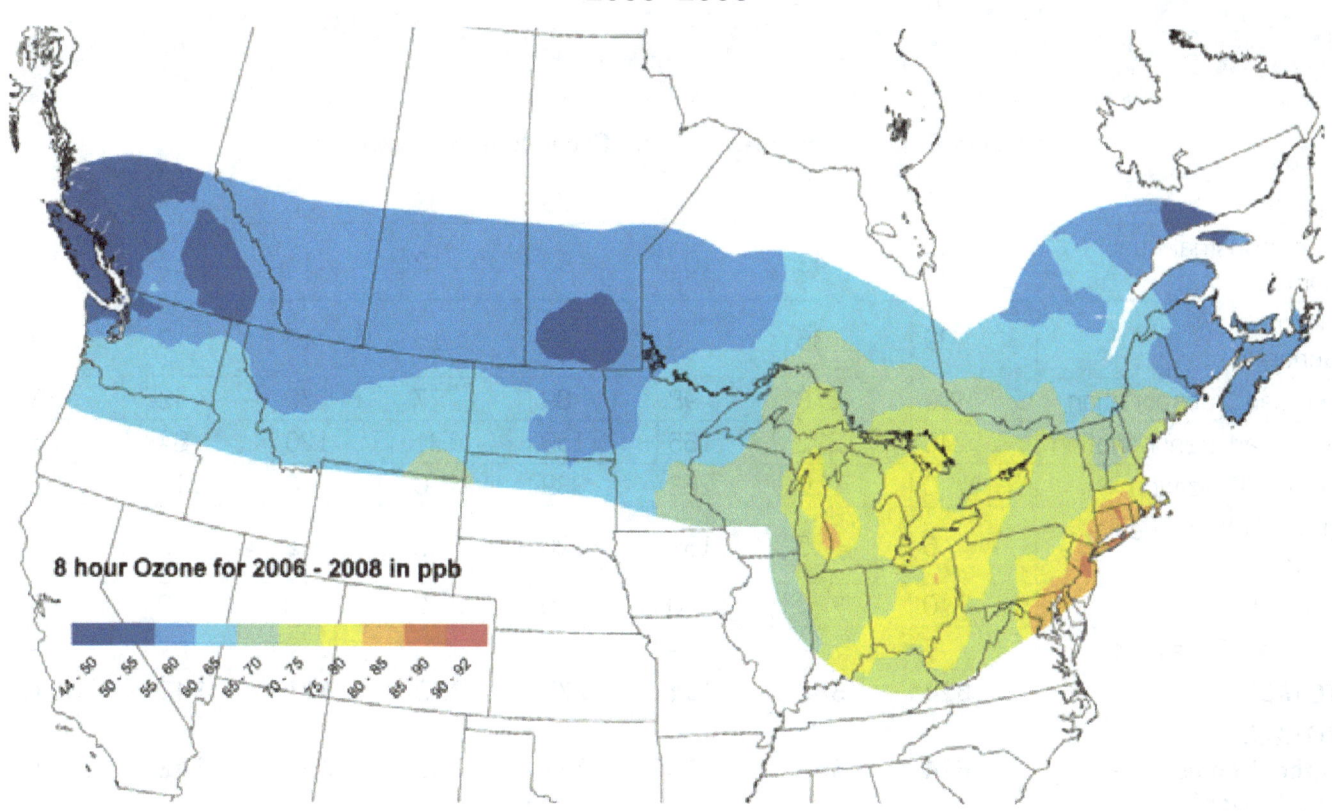

Note: Data contoured are the 2006–2008 averages of annual fourth-highest daily values, where the daily value is the highest running 8-hour average for the day. Sites used had at least 75% of possible daily values for the period.

Sources: Environment Canada National Air Pollution Surveillance (NAPS) Network Canada-wide Database, 2008 (http://www.ec.gc.ca/rnspa-naps/Default.asp?lang=En&n=5C0D33CF-1)); EPA Aerometric Information Retrieval System (AIRS) Database (www.epa.gov/air/data/index.html)

PEMA Emissions, 2008

Emissions Category	2008 Annual				2008 Ozone Season			
	NOx		VOCs		NOx		VOCs	
	1000 Tons	1000 Tonnes	1000 Tons	1000 Tonnes	1000 Tons	1000 Tonnes	1000 Tons	1000 Tonnes
Canadian PEMA Region: Annual and Ozone Season Emissions								
Industrial Sources	91	83	87	79	39	36	37	34
Non-industrial Fuel Combustion	48	43	102	93	12	11	17	15
Electric Power Generation	39	36	0	0	16	15	0	0
On-road Transportation	196	178	98	89	77	70	42	38
Non-road Transportation	245	222	165	150	131	120	84	76
Solvent Utilization	0	0	263	239	0	0	112	102
Other Anthropogenic Sources	6	5	139	126	3	2	83	75
Forest Fires	0	0	0	0	0	0	0	0
Biogenic Emissions	–	–	–	–	–	–	–	–
TOTALS	**624**	**568**	**854**	**777**	**353**	**321**	**342**	**311**
TOTALS without Forest Fires and Biogenics	**624**	**568**	**854**	**777**	**353**	**321**	**342**	**311**
U.S. PEMA States: Annual and Ozone Season Emissions								
Industrial Sources	608	552	261	236	253	230	109	99
Non-industrial Fuel Combustion	382	346	655	594	159	144	273	248
Electric Power Generation	1,236	1,122	17	16	515	467	7	6
On-road Transportation	1,747	1,585	1,179	1,070	728	660	491	446
Non-road Transportation	1,254	1,138	995	903	523	474	415	376
Solvent Utilization	1	0	1,728	1,568	0	0	720	653
Other Anthropogenic Sources	64	58	552	501	27	24	230	209
Forest Fires*	1	1	14	12	–	–	–	–
Biogenic Emissions*	149	139	4,445	4,038	–	–	–	–
TOTALS	**5,443**	**4,938**	**9,846**	**8,932**	**2,205**	**2,000**	**2,245**	**2,036**
TOTALS without Forest Fires and Biogenics	**5,292**	**4,801**	**5,387**	**4,887**	**2,205**	**2,000**	**2,245**	**2,036**

*Data are for 2005.
Note: Tons and tonnes are rounded to the nearest thousand. Totals in final rows may not equal the sum of the individual columns.

Source: Environment Canada and US EPA 2010

U.S. and Canadian National Emissions by Sector for Selected Pollutants, 2008

U.S. SO₂ Emissions – 2008
Total: 11.5 million tons/year
(10.4 million tonnes/year)

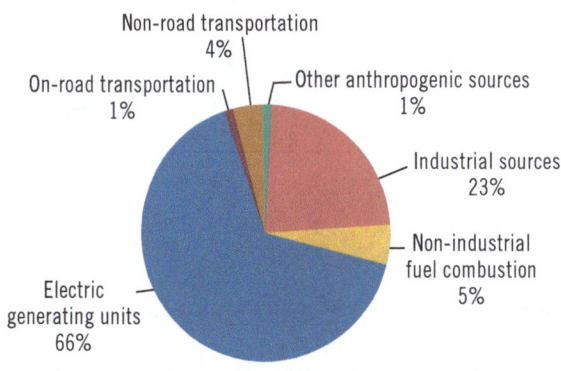

Canadian Emissions – 2008
Sulphur Dioxide
Total: 1.7 million tonnes/year
(1.9 million tons/year)

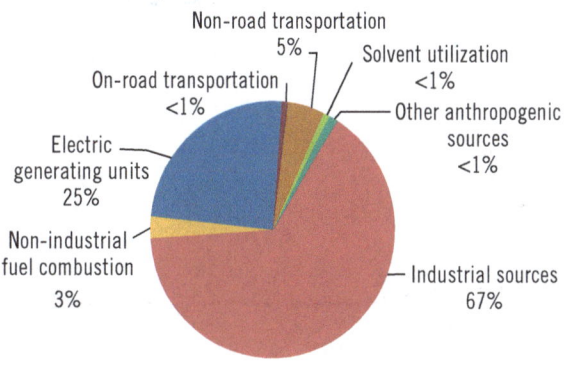

U.S. NOₓ Emissions – 2008
Total: 16.2 million tons/year
(14.7 million tonnes/year)

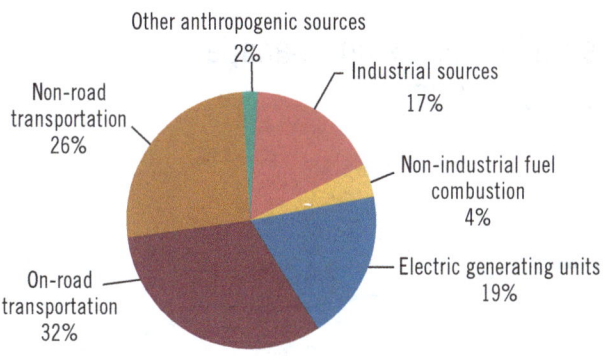

Canadian Emissions – 2008
Nitrogen Oxides
Total: 2.2 million tonnes/year
(2.4 million tons/year)

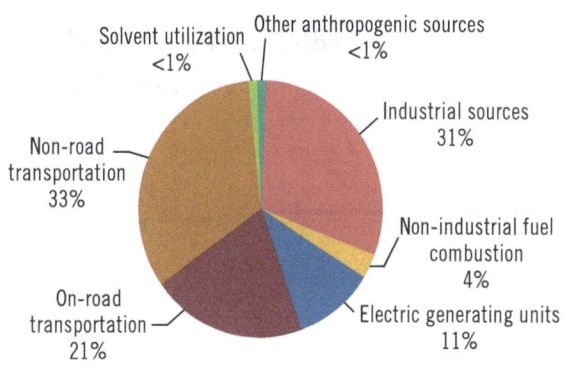

U.S. VOC Emissions – 2008
Total: 15.4 million tons/year
(14 million tonnes/year)

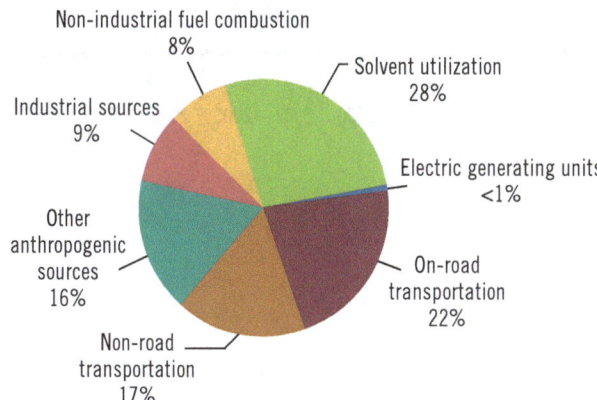

Canadian Emissions – 2008
Volatile Organic Compounds
Total: 2.4 million tonnes/year
(2.6 million tons/year)

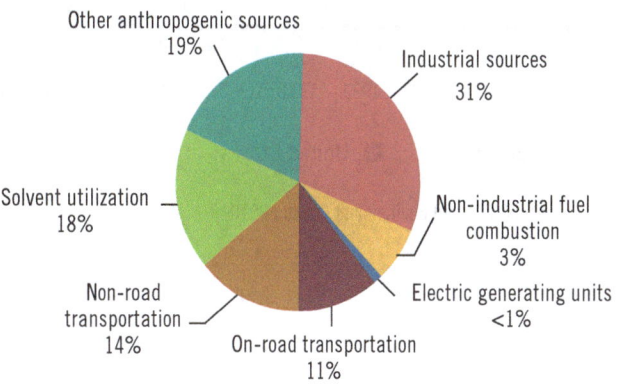

Source: US EPA and Environment Canada 2010

Environmental Statistics / Emissions & Toxic Releases

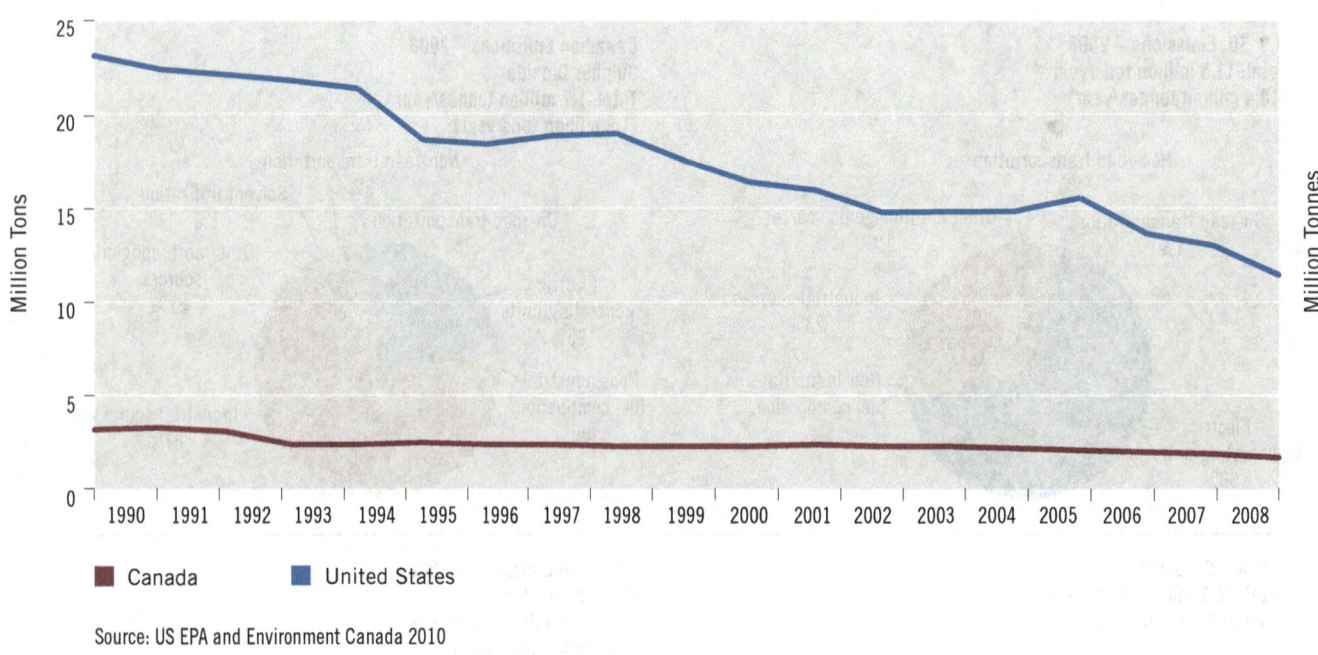

National SO$_2$ Emissions in the United States and Canada from All Sources, 1990–2008

Source: US EPA and Environment Canada 2010

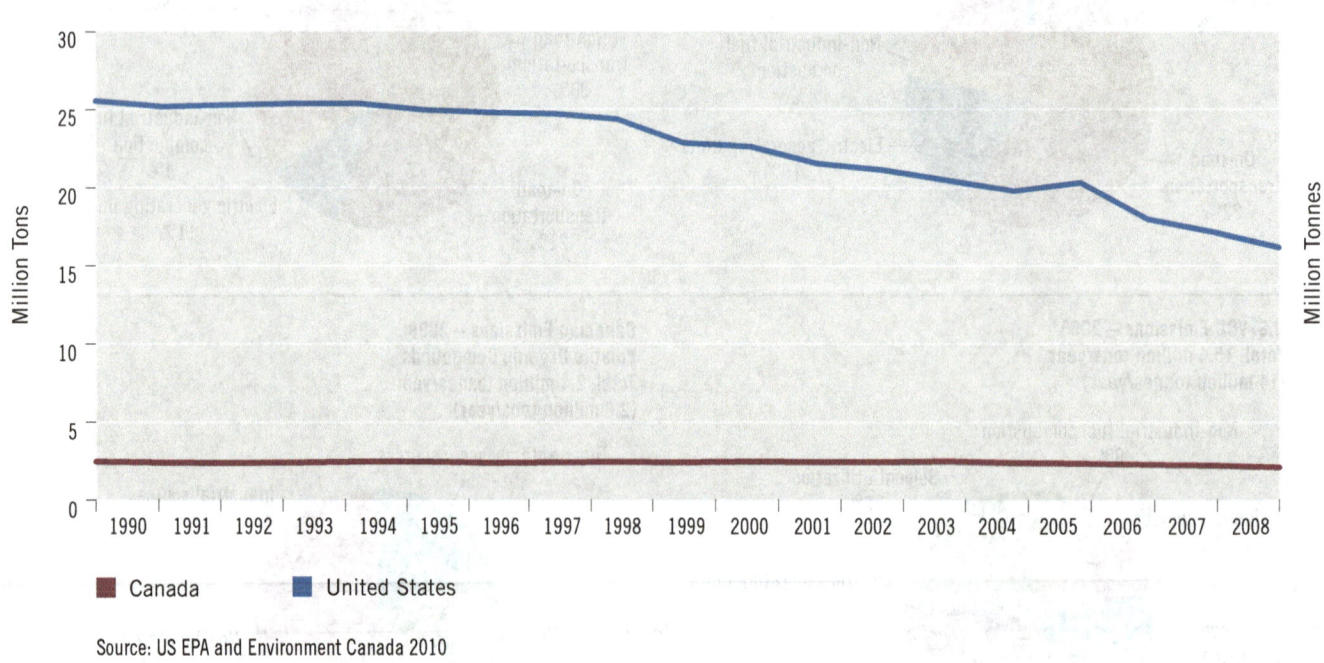

National NO$_x$ Emissions in the United States and Canada from All Sources, 1990–2008

Source: US EPA and Environment Canada 2010

Wildlife species extinct and extirpated from Canada, 2008

Species	Group	Date of extinction[1] or extirpation[2]	Probable cause(s) of extinction[1] or extirpation[2]
Extinct [1]			
Benthic Hadley Lake stickleback	fishes (freshwater)	1999	introduced predators
Limnetic Hadley Lake stickleback	fishes (freshwater)	1999	introduced predators
Banff longnose dace	fishes (freshwater)	1986	introduced predators; habitat alteration
Blue walleye	fishes (freshwater)	1965	commercial fishing; introduced predators
Lake Ontario kiyi	fishes (freshwater)	1964	commercial fishing; introduced predators
Deepwater cisco	fishes (freshwater)	1952	commercial fishing; introduced predators
Eelgrass limpet	molluscs	1929	loss of food source
Caribou (dawsoni subspecies)	mammals (terrestrial)	1920s	unknown
Passenger pigeon	birds	1914	hunting and predation
Sea mink	mammals (marine)	1894	trapping
Labrador duck	birds	1875	hunting; habitat alteration
Macoun's shining moss	mosses	after 1864	habitat alteration
Great auk	birds	1844	hunting
Extirpated [2]			
Karner blue	arthropods	1991	loss of food source; habitat alteration
Frosted elfin	arthropods	1988	successional change
Greater prairie-chicken	birds	after 1987	habitat alteration
Black-footed ferret	mammals (terrestrial)	1974	loss of food source
Striped bass (St. Lawrence Estuary population)	fishes (freshwater)	after 1968	illegal fishing
Dwarf wedgemussel	molluscs	1968	habitat alteration
Greater sage grouse (phaios subspecies)	birds	1960s	hunting; habitat alteration
Pacific pond turtle	reptiles	after 1959	commercial harvesting; habitat alteration
Gravel chub	fishes (freshwater)	after 1958	habitat alteration
Pacific gophersnake	reptiles	after 1957	habitat alteration
Spring blue-eyed Mary	plants	after 1954	habitat alteration
Timber rattlesnake	reptiles	1941	hunting; habitat alteration
Oregon lupine	plants	after 1929	habitat alteration
Paddlefish	fishes (freshwater)	1917	habitat alteration; over-fishing
Tiger salamander (Great Lakes population)	amphibians	1915	habitat alteration
Island marble	arthropods	before 1910	loss of food source; habitat alteration
Puget Oregonian snail	molluscs	after 1905	unknown
Pygmy short-horned lizard	reptiles	after 1898	habitat alteration
Atlantic salmon (Lake Ontario population)	fishes (freshwater)	after 1898	habitat destruction and over-exploitation by a food and commercial fishery
Illinois tick-trefoil	plants	after 1888	habitat alteration
Grizzly bear (Prairie population)	mammals (terrestrial)	1880s	hunting
Incurved grizzled moss	mosses	1828	unknown
Grey whale (Atlantic population)	mammals (marine)	1800s	hunting

1. A wildlife species that no longer exists.
2. A wildlife species that no longer exists in the wild in Canada, but exists elsewhere.

Source(s): Committee on the Status of Endangered Wildlife in Canada, 2008, *Canadian Wildlife Species at Risk*, www.cosewic.gc.ca/eng/sct0/rpt/dsp_booklet_e.htm (accessed January 29, 2009).

Wildlife species extinct and at risk in Canada, 2008

	Assessment of the Committee on the Status of Endangered Wildlife in Canada					Total
	Extinct [1]	Extirpated [2]	Endangered [3]	Threatened [4]	Special concern [5]	
	number					
Total	**13**	**23**	**238**	**146**	**157**	**577**
Mammals	2	3	21	18	26	70
Birds	3	2	27	18	23	73
Fishes	6	4	37	25	41	113
Amphibians	0	1	7	6	7	21
Reptiles	0	4	14	13	9	40
Molluscs	1	2	17	3	4	27
Arthropods [6]	0	3	17	6	5	31
Vascular plants	0	3	89	52	33	177
Lichens	0	0	2	2	5	9
Mosses	1	1	7	3	4	16

1. A wildlife species that no longer exists.
2. A wildlife species that no longer exists in the wild in Canada, but exists elsewhere.
3. A wildlife species facing imminent extirpation or extinction.
4. A wildlife species that is likely to become endangered if nothing is done to reverse the factors leading to its extirpation or extinction.
5. A wildlife species that may become threatened or endangered because of a combination of biological characteristics and identified threats.
6. Formerly described as lepidopterans.

Source(s): Committee on the Status of Endangered Wildlife in Canada, 2008, *Canadian Wildlife Species at Risk*, www.cosewic.gc.ca/eng/sct0/rpt/dsp_booklet_e.htm (accessed January 29, 2009).

Thermostat use by households during the winter, by province

	Households reporting at least one thermostat	Winter temperature lowered when asleep [1]	Main thermostat, programmable [1]	Programmable thermostat		Not programmed or non-programmable
				Programmed thermostat [2]	Winter temperature lowered when asleep [3]	Winter temperature lowered when asleep [4]
	percent					
Canada	91	61	49	84	74	53
Newfoundland and Labrador	92	60	20	74	75	59
Prince Edward Island	97	66	25	86	76	63
Nova Scotia	96	63	25	77	57	64
New Brunswick	95	58	28	72	60	57
Quebec	92	62	46	81	76	54
Ontario	88	59	61	87	70	46
Manitoba	92	58	45	75	81	47
Saskatchewan	96	65	49	83	82	53
Alberta	97	63	47	85	79	52
British Columbia	92	64	38	86	78	58

1. As a percentage of all households that had a thermostat.
2. As a percentage of all households that had a programmable thermostat.
3. As a percentage of all households that had a programmable thermostat that was programmed.
4. As a percentage of all households that had an unprogrammed or non-programmable thermostat.

Source(s): Statistics Canada, Environment Accounts and Statistics Division, Households and the Environment, 2009 CANSIM Table 153-0060.

Energy-saving light bulbs, Canada and provinces

	At least one type of energy-saving light	Compact fluorescent lights	Fluorescent tubes	Halogen lights
	percent			
Canada	84	69	46	35
Newfoundland and Labrador	72	65	31	20
Prince Edward Island	82	73	43	16
Nova Scotia	85	77	43	21
New Brunswick	81	70	39	23
Quebec	81	63	36	42
Ontario	87	76	50	33
Manitoba	78	62	53	29
Saskatchewan	84	64	55	26
Alberta	80	64	46	34
British Columbia	87	71	53	36

Note(s): As a percentage of all households.
Source(s): Statistics Canada, Environment Accounts and Statistics Division, Households and the Environment Survey, 2007, CANSIM Table 153-0059.

Adoption and impact of new or significantly improved systems or equipment to improve energy efficiency by industry and province or territory, 2006[1]

	Introduced new or significantly improved systems or equipment	Impact on energy use [2]		
	Yes	Low	Moderate	High
	percent			
Industry				
Logging	12	34	66	0
Oil and gas extraction	43	36	52	13
Mining	28	33	53	14
Electric power generation, transmission and distribution	41	57	24	20
Natural gas distribution	19	x	76	x
Food	24	45	42	13
Beverage and tobacco products	25	13	34	54
Wood products	18	54	32	13
Paper manufacturing	22	24	54	22
Petroleum and coal products	33	19	74	x
Chemicals	30	28	68	4
Non-metallic mineral products	23	46	45	9
Primary metals	39	51	28	21
Fabricated metal products	20	21	65	14
Transportation equipment	38	40	58	2
Other manufacturing	18	39	36	25
Pipeline transportation	42	17	78	x
Total	**22**	**37**	**46**	**16**
Province or territory				
Newfoundland and Labrador	19	20	80	0
Prince Edward Island	9	51	x	x
Nova Scotia	19	10	82	8
New Brunswick	16	23	68	9
Quebec	18	41	38	21
Ontario	28	36	46	19
Manitoba	19	50	45	5
Saskatchewan	15	28	58	15
Alberta	15	38	56	7
British Columbia	18	46	45	9
Yukon, Northwest Territories and Nunavut	45	74	x	0
Total	**22**	**37**	**46**	**16**

1. Adoption of new or significantly improved systems or equipment within a three-year period, 2004 to 2006.
2. Respondents who answered 'yes' to the adoption of new or significantly improved systems or equipment were asked to rank the impact on energy efficiency as being low, moderate or high.

Source(s): Statistics Canada, Environment Accounts and Statistics Division.

Adoption and impact of new or significantly improved systems or equipment to improve energy efficiency by establishment size, 2006[1]

	Introduced new or significantly improved systems or equipment	Impact on energy use [2]		
	Yes	Low	Moderate	High
	percent			
Number of employees per establishment				
Fewer than 50	16	42	46	11
50 to 99	19	31	55	14
100 to 499	34	39	40	21
500 to 999	33	24	44	32
More than 999	56	25	54	21
Total	**22**	**38**	**46**	**16**

1. Adoption of new or significantly improved systems or equipment within a three-year period, 2004 to 2006.
2. Respondents who answered 'yes' to the adoption of new or significantly improved systems or equipment were asked to rank the impact on energy efficiency as being low, moderate or high.

Note(s): This table excludes the 'pipeline transportation' industry category.
Source(s): Statistics Canada, Environment Accounts and Statistics Division.

Average proportion of total capital expenditures spent on machinery and equipment to improve energy efficiency by industry and province or territory, 2006

	Average proportion of total capital expenditures
	percent
Industry	
Logging	3
Oil and gas extraction	6
Mining	3
Electric power generation, transmission and distribution	12
Natural gas distribution	7
Food	F
Beverage and tobacco products	7
Wood products	2
Paper manufacturing	4
Petroleum and coal products	11
Chemicals	4
Non-metallic mineral products	1
Primary metals	6
Fabricated metal products	5
Transportation equipment	F
Other manufacturing	3
Pipeline transportation	12
Total	**3**
Province or territory	
Newfoundland and Labrador	6
Prince Edward Island	2
Nova Scotia	1
New Brunswick	1
Quebec	3
Ontario	5
Manitoba	4
Saskatchewan	3
Alberta	3
British Columbia	1
Yukon, Northwest Territories and Nunavut	9
Total	**3**

Source(s): Statistics Canada, Environment Accounts and Statistics Division.

Obstacles to the adoption of technologies to improve energy efficiency by industry and province or territory, 2006[1]

	Lack of information or knowledge	Lack of available new and improved technology	Lack of skilled personnel	High cost of equipment	Lack of financing	Regulatory and policy barriers	Other	Share of establishments in industry, province or territory that reported encountering one or more obstacles	Industry, province or territory share of reported obstacles
	percent								
Industry									
Logging	26	43	34	77	54	10	7	59	3
Oil and gas extraction	34	40	26	69	30	25	17	82	2
Mining	42	50	20	58	42	9	12	74	1
Electric power generation, transmission and distribution	25	36	5	86	35	38	8	70	1
Natural gas distribution	8	9	x	57	45	77	x	72	0 s
Food	50	22	21	50	37	10	11	74	12
Beverage and tobacco products	34	16	4	72	29	0	21	74	1
Wood products	46	22	11	74	35	12	3	59	7
Paper manufacturing	29	30	10	60	42	3	4	76	3
Petroleum and coal products	31	29	32	74	32	14	12	87	1
Chemicals	31	39	22	80	49	19	11	74	5
Non-metallic mineral products	29	35	17	78	43	19	7	67	4
Primary metals	32	26	22	84	49	2	6	79	2
Fabricated metal products	46	30	8	52	37	4	8	68	15
Transportation equipment	46	46	15	59	45	6	24	72	6
Other manufacturing	52	33	24	62	41	6	4	56	36
Pipeline transportation	21	61	12	58	x	24	9	77	0 s
Total	**45**	**32**	**19**	**63**	**40**	**8**	**8**	**64**	**100**
Province or territory									
Newfoundland and Labrador	31	27	17	81	47	8	4	41	1
Prince Edward Island	53	28	15	68	45	10	3	64	0 s
Nova Scotia	36	10	26	76	52	2	4	54	2
New Brunswick	31	25	17	73	52	4	5	70	2
Quebec	57	28	19	57	31	7	9	59	21
Ontario	45	33	16	63	47	7	6	68	46
Manitoba	39	34	20	61	43	8	17	63	3
Saskatchewan	49	36	34	71	28	12	11	68	2
Alberta	41	35	31	65	22	6	14	56	9
British Columbia	34	32	16	65	41	18	6	65	13
Yukon, Northwest Territories and Nunavut	17	64	0	75	30	23	8	66	0 s
Total	**45**	**32**	**19**	**63**	**40**	**8**	**8**	**64**	**100**

1. Adoption of new or significantly improved systems or equipment within a three-year period, 2004 to 2006.
Source(s): Statistics Canada, Environment Accounts and Statistics Division.

Drivers to the adoption of technologies to improve energy efficiency by industry and province or territory, 2006[1]

	Sufficient return on investment	Regulations	Voluntary agreement	Public relations	Corporate policy, culture and awareness	Other	Share of establishments in industry, province or territory that reported encountering one or more drivers	Industry, province or territory share of reported drivers
					percent			
Industry								
Logging	67	45	16	17	49	7	46	3
Oil and gas extraction	73	74	38	52	63	4	79	2
Mining	72	57	34	35	68	9	67	1
Electric power generation, transmission and distribution	68	61	34	46	76	10	83	1
Natural gas distribution	83	78	33	67	82	0	62	0 s
Food	83	39	7	15	45	2	59	10
Beverage and tobacco products	99	63	19	40	69	0	80	1
Wood products	74	42	12	17	31	7	59	8
Paper manufacturing	89	30	7	13	38	4	63	3
Petroleum and coal products	76	44	25	29	63	x	80	1
Chemicals	80	38	24	16	38	18	65	5
Non-metallic mineral products	84	41	23	25	43	2	61	4
Primary metals	91	50	26	29	53	4	76	2
Fabricated metal products	80	39	16	8	37	1	61	15
Transportation equipment	81	39	35	13	37	27	59	5
Other manufacturing	72	26	7	11	45	3	50	36
Pipeline transportation	88	79	39	36	48	x	77	0 s
Total	**77**	**36**	**14**	**15**	**43**	**5**	**57**	**100**
Province or territory								
Newfoundland and Labrador	74	45	20	37	49	0	39	1
Prince Edward Island	74	37	9	18	44	0	51	0 s
Nova Scotia	92	34	22	31	44	3	56	2
New Brunswick	76	24	15	22	41	6	59	2
Quebec	77	29	13	14	50	5	57	23
Ontario	79	36	13	11	33	6	59	45
Manitoba	77	43	19	16	48	4	43	3
Saskatchewan	86	60	31	37	54	4	53	2
Alberta	73	40	16	17	55	2	54	10
British Columbia	71	45	13	24	55	5	56	13
Yukon, Northwest Territories and Nunavut	82	46	29	34	51	x	89	0 s
Total	**77**	**36**	**14**	**15**	**43**	**5**	**57**	**100**

1. Adoption of new or significantly improved systems or equipment within a three-year period, 2004 to 2006.
Source(s): Statistics Canada, Environment Accounts and Statistics Division.

Household participation rates for environmental behaviours, by province, 2006

	Low-flow showerhead	Reduced volume toilet	Compact fluorescent light bulbs	Composting	Recycling	Lowering temperatures
			percent[1]			
Newfoundland and Labrador	58	27	53	23	94	62
Prince Edward Island	55	27	59	92	99	59
Nova Scotia	54	30	60	71	99	58
New Brunswick	55	31	61	37	96	48
Quebec	59	29	48	14	95	55
Ontario	60	43	65	38	98	51
Manitoba	46	35	50	23	88	50
Saskatchewan	37	34	53	29	96	63
Alberta	49	41	59	24	96	59
British Columbia	53	35	65	31	99	56
Canada	**56**	**37**	**59**	**30**	**97**	**54**

1. As a percentage of all households that have a thermostat and that have access to at least one recycling program.

Source(s):
Statistics Canada, Households and the Environment Survey, 2006, Special tabulation.

Environmental activity level, by dwelling type, 2006

	Less active	Moderately active	Very active
		percent	
Apartments	24	59	17
Multi-unit	9	50	41
Single-detached	6	39	55

Note(s):
Other types of dwellings such as mobile homes and camps were excluded from this analysis because they make up a small portion of total dwellings.

Source(s):
Statistics Canada, Households and the Environment Survey, 2006, Special tabulation.

Environmental Statistics / Environmental Enforcement

Enforcement Activities and Measures Carried Out under Fisheries Act during Fiscal Year 2008-2009

National	Spill/Release Occurrences	Non spill/Release Occurrences[1]	Inspections[2]				Enforcement measures						Investigations[3]	Enforcement measures								
			Total	Off-site	On-site	Tickets	Written Directives	Written Warnings	Injunctions	Ministerial Orders	EPCOs			Tickets	Written Directives	Written Warnings	Injunctions	Ministerial Orders	Prosecutions	Charges	Counts	Convictions
FA – Fisheries Act	1,481	435	3,280	2,507	773	-	29	98	-	-	1	47		2	2	177	-	-	16	24	28	5
Alice Arm Tailings Deposit	-	-	-	-	-	-	-	-	-	-	-			-	-	-	-	-	-	-	-	-
Chlor-Alkali Mercury Liquid Effluent and Guideline	-	-	4	4	-	-	-	-	-	-	-			-	-	-	-	-	-	-	-	-
General Prohibition	1,424	347	1,082	457	625	-	29	42	-	-	1	41		2	2	75	-	-	16	24	28	5
Guidelines for Effluent Quality and Wastewater Treatment at Federal Establishments	-	-	1	-	1	-	-	-	-	-	-			-	-	-	-	-	-	-	-	-
Meat and Poultry Products Plant Liquid Effluent and Guidelines	-	-	5	3	2	-	-	-	-	-	-			-	-	-	-	-	-	-	-	-
Metal Mining Effluent	22	27	577	504	73	-	-	22	-	-	-	6		1	-	72	-	-	-	-	-	-
Petroleum Refinery Liquid Effluent and Guidelines	-	-	144	141	3	-	-	-	-	-	-			-	-	-	-	-	-	-	-	-
Port Alberni Pulp and Paper Effluent	-	-	-	-	-	-	-	-	-	-	-			-	-	-	-	-	-	-	-	-
Potato Processing Plant Liquid Effluent and Guidelines	-	-	34	32	2	-	-	-	-	-	-			-	-	-	-	-	-	-	-	-
Pulp and Paper Effluent	57	65	1,433	1,366	67	-	-	34	-	-	-	8		-	-	30	-	-	-	-	-	-

Additional statistics:
There were 128 Referrals to an other federal/provincial or municipal government or department.

Investigation Breakdown:

	# of Investigations
Investigation Started and Ended in FY 2007-2008	10
Investigation Started in FY 2007-2008 and still on-going at end of FY 2007-2008	37
Investigation Started before FY 2007-2008 and ended in FY 2007-2008	24
Investigation Started before FY 2007-2008 and still ongoing at end of FY 2007-2008	45

Explanatory notes: The statistics are tabulated as follows

The measures such as Inspection Tickets, Written Warnings, Written Directions, Injunctions, Ministerial Orders and EPCOs are tabulated at the section level of a regulation. An occurrence file may include one or more regulations, therefore is it possible that the data at the regulation level, may not add to the total at the legislation level.

Prosecutions: The number of prosecutions is represented by the number of Occurrence files, based on Reported Date, for all categories except Spill/Release. An occurrence file may include one or more regulations, therefore is it possible that the data at the regulation level, may not add to the total at the legislation level.
EPAMs: The number of EPAMs is represented by the number of regulatees whom signed EPAMs by the charged date regardless of the number of regulations involved. (including Tickets)
Charges: The number of charges (excluding tickets) is tabulated at the section level of the regulation by charge date, by regulatee.
Counts: The number of counts (excluding tickets) is tabulated at the section level of the regulation, by offence date relating to the regulatee's charge.
Convictions: The number of convictions (excluding tickets) is represented by the number of counts where the regulatee was found guilty or pleaded guilt.
Investigation Tickets: It is tabulated at the section level of the regulation by charge date, by regulatee.

- Means no activity or measure for the report period

[1] **Number of Occurrences:** Is tabulated by the number of Occurrence files, based on Reported Date, for all categories except Spill/Release. An occurrence file may include one or more regulations, therefore it may not add to the total at the legislation level.
[2] **Number of Inspections - new way of counting:** Only closed files using the end date are tabulated. The number of inspections relates to the number of regulatees inspected for compliance under each of the applicable regulations. is the issuance of a written warning which relates to 3 sections of a given regulation the number of written warnings is 3.
[3] **Number of Investigations:** Investigations are tabulated by number of investigations files, based on Start Date of the investigation. An investigation file may include activities relating also to another legislation and may include one or more regulations. Therefore, the total number of investigations shown by regulation may not add to the total at the legislation level.

Summary of inspections, investigations and enforcement measures from April 2009 to March 2010

CEPA Tool	Inspections			Investigations	Enforcement Measures										
	Total	On-site	Off-site		Tickets	Written Directions	Written Warnings	Injunctions	Ministerial Orders	EPOCs	EPAMs	Prosecutions	Charges	Counts	Convictions
Regulations															
Asbestos Mines and Mills Release															
Benzene in Gasoline	294	252	42												
Chlor-Alkali Mercury Release	1	1													
Chlorobiphenyls (inactive)	3	1	2												
Chromium Electroplating, Chromium Anodizing and Reverse Etching	42	19	23				17								
Disposal at Sea	79	51	28	2			27					2	2	2	3
Environmental Emergency	66	24	42				39		2						
Export and Import of Hazardous Waste and Hazardous Recyclable Material	753	127	626	5			400					9	9	9	4
Export and Import of Hazardous Waste (inactive)	7	5	2												
Export of Substances Under the Rotterdam Convention	1		1												
Federal Halocarbon, 2003	667	341	326	4			519			1					
Federal Halocarbon (inactive)	183	157	26	1			22								
Federal Mobile PCB Treatment and Destruction															
Federal Registration of Storage Tank Systems for Petroleum Products and Allied Petroleum Products on Federal Lands or Aboriginal Lands (inactive)	1		1												

Summary of inspections, investigations and enforcement measures from April 2009 to March 2010 - continued

CEPA Tool	Inspections			Investigations	Enforcement Measures									
	Total	On-site	Off-site		Tickets	Written Directions	Written Warnings	Injunctions	Ministerial Orders	EPOCs	EPAMs	Prosecutions	Charges	Counts	Convictions
Fuels Information, No. 1	221	214	7				5								
Gasoline and Gasoline Blend Dispensing Flow Rate	146	1	145				16								
Gasoline	38	31	7				3								
Interprovincial Movement of Hazardous Waste	37	17	20	2			2								
New Substances Notification – Biotechnology Products (inactive)	3		3												
New Substances Notification (inactive)	2		2	1											
New Substances Notification (Chemicals and Polymers)	35	11	24	1			13								
New Substances Notification Regulations (Organisms)	17	7	10	1											
Off-Road Compression-Ignition Engine Emission	8	1	7	1			10								
Off-Road Small Spark-Ignition Engine Emission	46	5	41	2	10		14			1		2	2	2	
On-Road Vehicle and Engine Emission	11	2	9	1											
Ozone-Depleting Substances, 1998	53	24	29	2											
PCB	167	98	69	2			8								
PCB Waste Export, 1996	1		1												
Perfluorooctane Sulfonate and its Salts and Certain Other Compounds	1		1												
Phosphorus Concentration	1		1												
Pulp and Paper Mill Defoamer and Wood Chip	54	49	5												
Pulp and Paper Mill Effluent Chlorinated Dioxins and Furans	85	82	3												
Regulations Respecting Applications for Permits for Disposal at Sea															
Secondary Lead Smelter Release	5	2	3		1										
Solvent Degreasing	44	11	33	1			14					1	1	1	1
Storage of PCB Material (inactive)	21	17	4												
Storage Tank Systems for Petroleum Products and Allied Petroleum Products	35	10	25				8								

Summary of inspections, investigations and enforcement measures from April 2009 to March 2010 - *continued*

CEPA Tool	Inspections			Investigations	Enforcement Measures										
	Total	On-site	Off-site		Tickets	Written Directions	Written Warnings	Injunctions	Ministerial Orders	EPOCs	EPAMs	Prosecutions	Charges	Counts	Convictions
Sulphur in Diesel Fuel	336	290	46				12			4					
Sulphur in Gasoline	107	63	44												
Tetrachloro-ethylene (Use in Dry Cleaning and Reporting Requirements)	1216	813	403	15			474			47		7	8	8	3
Vinyl Chloride Release, 1992	5	4	1												
Other tools*															
CEPA 1999	339			12			31		1			4	4	4	
CEPA section 46 notices – greenhouse gases															
CEPA section 56 notices – P2 plans	14						6								
CEPA section 71 notices – toxics	7						1								
Glycol Guidelines (inactive)	1		1												
National Pollutant Release Inventory	127	73	54				166								
Total	5280	2914	2366	44	1	10	1810			56		25	26	26	11

Explanatory Notes:

* Includes activities related to enforceable provisions of CEPA 1999.

Tickets, written warnings, written directions, injunctions, ministerial orders and Environmental Protection Compliance Orders (EPCOs) are tabulated at the section level of a regulation. For example, if the outcome of an inspection is the issuance of a written warning that relates to three sections of a given regulation, the number of written warnings is three.

Inspections – The number of regulatees who were inspected for compliance where inspections were completed during the fiscal year.

Investigations – The total number of investigations is the number of investigation files started in the fiscal year. An investigation file may include activities relating to another law or to more than one regulation. Therefore, the total number of investigations shown does not add up to the total number of investigations by regulation.

EPAMs – The number of regulatees who signed Environmental Protection Alternative Measures, regardless of the number of regulations involved.

Prosecutions – The number of regulatees who were prosecuted, regardless of the number of regulations involved.

Charges – The number of charges (excluding tickets) is tabulated at the section level of the regulation by charge date, by regulatee.

Counts – The number of counts is tabulated at the section level of the regulation, by offence date relating to the regulatee's charge.

Convictions – The number of convictions is represented by the number of counts for which the regulatee was found guilty or pleaded guilty.

Additional Statistics:

There were 22 referrals to other federal, provincial or municipal governments or departments.

Of the 44 investigations started in 2009–2010, 13 ended in 2009–2010 and 31 are ongoing. In addition, of 68 investigations started before 2008–2009, 42 were completed in 2008–2009 and 26 are ongoing.

Canadian Environmental Protection Act, 1999 Annual Report for April 2009 to March 2010

Federal government research and development expenditures by socio-economic objective

	Intramural [1]									
	1997/1998	1998/1999	1999/2000	2000/2001	2001/2002	2002/2003	2003/2004	2004/2005	2005/2006	2006/2007
	millions of dollars									
Total	**1,588**	**1,627**	**1,734**	**1,957**	**2,000**	**2,075**	**1,976**	**1,983**	**2,298**	**2,391**
Exploration and exploitation of the earth	178	179	186	207	125	141	85	98	110	98
Infrastructure and general planning of land use										
Transport	34	38	42	37	71	65	56	53	58	50
Telecommunications	33	32	24	28	44	37	35	43	52	51
Other	54	50	42	48	30	39	38	38	46	40
Control and care of the environment	97	98	122	143	142	174	178	181	216	188
Protection and improvement of human health	80	87	103	116	152	186	196	203	210	217
Production, distribution and rational utilization of energy	209	170	171	187	248	214	245	199	229	339
Agricultural production and technology										
Agriculture	317	308	334	333	345	287	275	269	336	340
Fishing	30	42	43	51	47	55	42	44	47	47
Forestry	73	74	77	83	75	74	72	71	75	76
Industrial production and technology	119	123	137	165	164	189	189	174	198	196
Social structures and relationships	110	125	50	53	47	61	60	62	59	81
Exploration and exploitation of space	59	92	68	187	175	179	121	125	162	163
Non-oriented research	51	54	150	150	181	202	206	208	219	219
Other civil research	15	13	14	16	15	14	14	15	23	24
Defence	127	136	167	150	134	152	157	191	245	261
Other	3	4	4	3	5	6	6	10	13	0

	Extramural [2]									
	1997/1998	1998/1999	1999/2000	2000/2001	2001/2002	2002/2003	2003/2004	2004/2005	2005/2006	2006/2007
	millions of dollars									
Total	**1,659**	**1,835**	**2,030**	**2,070**	**2,887**	**2,737**	**3,379**	**3,371**	**3,628**	**3,577**
Exploration and exploitation of the earth	25	29	99	46	69	59	75	55	78	58
Infrastructure and general planning of land use										
Transport	32	28	23	20	24	25	19	27	28	26
Telecommunications	21	35	34	15	23	24	27	30	31	21
Other	13	15	16	20	25	28	31	28	29	29
Control and care of the environment	73	83	88	112	148	141	171	155	185	175
Protection and improvement of human health	282	318	390	519	709	866	960	988	1,106	1,160
Production, distribution and rational utilization of energy	57	65	68	64	117	75	210	181	103	89
Agricultural production and technology										
Agriculture	37	44	67	70	75	90	86	79	102	130
Fishing	8	10	13	14	15	16	23	26	25	19
Forestry	24	24	43	27	27	41	56	49	44	46
Industrial production and technology	429	406	398	518	741	657	778	732	884	831
Social structures and relationships	31	90	87	106	130	149	170	189	203	196
Exploration and exploitation of space	190	270	269	154	193	179	197	190	164	179
Non-oriented research	237	229	256	188	365	213	376	428	496	535
Other civil research	1	2	1	17	17	2	1	2	4	10
Defence	124	120	121	119	142	100	116	94	93	72
Other	74	68	57	62	67	72	82	119	54	0

1. The research and development intramural expenditures are managed and carried out primarily by federal government employees. Non-program (indirect costs) are excluded.
2. The management and conduct of the research and development extramural expenditures are entrusted to a non-federal organization.

Source(s): Statistics Canada, Science, Innovation and Electronic Information Division, *Science Statistics*, Catalogue no. 88-001-X, various issues.

Expenditures on environmental protection by type of activity and province or territory, 2008

	Total capital expenditures	Share of total capital expenditures	Total operating expenditures	Share of total operating expenditures
	millions of dollars	percent	millions of dollars	percent
Newfoundland and Labrador	18.5	0.5	163.9	3.1
Prince Edward Island	1.8	0.0 s	5.4	0.1
Nova Scotia	58.0	1.5	70.2	1.3
New Brunswick	76.8	2.0	213.4	4.1
Quebec	439.0	11.5	1,002.9	19.1
Ontario	579.5	15.1	1,580.5	30.2
Manitoba	364.3	9.5	83.3	1.6
Saskatchewan	347.5	9.1	231.8	4.4
Alberta	1,677.4	43.8	1,430.1	27.3
British Columbia	x	x	428.5	8.2
Yukon, Northwest Territories and Nunavut	x	x	31.4	0.6
Total	**3,828.6**	**100.0**	**5,241.4**	**100.0**

Note(s): Figures may not add up to totals due to rounding.
Source(s): Statistics Canada, Environment Accounts and Statistics Division.

Capital expenditures on environmental protection by establishment size, 2008

	Number of employees per establishment			
	Fewer than 100	100 to 499	500 to 999	1,000 or more
	millions of dollars			
Environmental monitoring	13.7	x	x	9.0
Environmental assessments and audits	16.5	34.2	20.6	36.7
Reclamation and decommissioning	161.2	239.7	46.0	49.7
Wildlife and habitat protection	16.2	x	x	28.9
Waste management and sewerage services	166.5	133.0	42.6	55.7
Pollution abatement and control processes (end-of-pipe)	122.2	636.2	255.1	668.6
Pollution prevention processes	136.9	369.6	128.4	324.2
Other	7.4	22.7	12.3	9.3
Total	**640.6**	**1,481.5**	**524.3**	**1,182.1**

Note(s): Figures may not add up to totals due to rounding.
Source(s): Statistics Canada, Environment Accounts and Statistics Division, CANSIM table 153-0056.

Capital expenditures on environmental protection per employee by establishment size, 2008

	Number of employees per establishment				Total
	Fewer than 100	100 to 499	500 to 999	1,000 or more	
	dollars per employee				
Environmental monitoring	26.4	x	x	23.0	23.8
Environmental assessments and audits	31.8	46.4	93.3	93.9	57.9
Reclamation and decommissioning	311.2	325.5	208.2	127.0	266.0
Wildlife and habitat protection	31.4	x	x	73.8	47.6
Waste management and sewerage services	321.4	180.5	192.9	142.3	213.1
Pollution abatement and control processes (end-of-pipe)	236.0	863.8	1,155.7	1,708.8	901.2
Pollution prevention processes	264.4	501.8	581.7	828.6	513.9
Other	14.2	30.8	55.8	23.9	27.7
Total	**1,236.8**	**2,011.4**	**2,375.3**	**3,021.4**	**2,051.2**

Note(s): Figures may not add up to totals due to rounding.
Source(s): Statistics Canada, Environment Accounts and Statistics Division.

Capital expenditures on environmental protection by type of activity and industry

	Environmental monitoring	Environmental assessments and audits	Reclamation and decommissioning	Wildlife and habitat protection	Waste management and sewerage services	Pollution abatement and control processes (end-of-pipe)	Pollution prevention processes	Total
	millions of dollars							
2006								
Total, all industries	**171.9**	**87.9**	**433.8**	**153.7**	**519.3**	**908.7**	**1,561.1**	**3,836.4**
Logging	F	F	F	F	0.5	0.8	F	F
Oil and gas extraction	132.2	43.1	356.2	126.6	286.1	409.8	377.1	1,730.9
Mining and quarrying	5.3	x	9.3	x	26.0	174.5	49.2	269.9
Electric power generation, transmission and distribution	4.1	30.7	13.9	13.5	18.2	65.8	105.9	252.1
Natural gas distribution	x	2.9	x	x	x	3.0	54.1	65.7
Food manufacturing	1.4	0.4	F	x	F	12.8	41.0	123.8
Beverage and tobacco product manufacturing	x	0.0	F	0.0	x	x	3.1	5.4
Wood product manufacturing	F	F	F	F	1.8	30.7	18.3	55.5
Paper manufacturing	1.8	0.1	3.2	0.2	9.5	21.3	52.0	88.0
Petroleum and coal product manufacturing	x	F	x	0.0	10.4	45.7	533.1	596.4
Chemical manufacturing	0.6	x	3.0	x	8.8	25.8	44.0	82.4
Non-metallic mineral product manufacturing	F	F	F	3.3	0.5	16.1	22.7	61.1
Primary metal manufacturing	0.8	x	12.8	x	8.1	68.9	31.1	122.6
Fabricated metal product manufacturing	F	x	x	0.0	10.1	3.0	F	F
Transportation equipment manufacturing	0.1	x	x	x	x	15.7	18.7	42.2
Other manufacturing industries	0.8	F	0.4	x	F	12.8	73.0	150.2
Pipeline transportation	1.6	5.6	21.9	4.8	x	x	39.2	75.3

Note(s): Figures may not add up to totals due to rounding.
Source(s): Statistics Canada, CANSIM table 153-0052.

Capital expenditures on pollution prevention by medium and industry

	2008					
	Total	Air	Surface water	On-site contained solid and liquid waste	Noise, radiation and vibration	Other
	$ millions					
Total, all industries	**959.1**	422.2	178.8	232.8	F	100.6
Logging	F	F	F	F	F	F
Oil and gas extraction	**118.1**	F	F	19.4	F	0.9
Mining	**134.2**	18.9	83.6	30.7	x	x
Electric power generation, transmission and distribution	**276.3**	81.3	21.3	142.3	F	F
Natural gas distribution	x	x	0.1	1.1	0.0	0.0
Food	**42.3**	10.8	8.3	F	F	16.2
Beverage and tobacco products	x	1.4	1.4	0.0	F	1.5
Wood products	**6.8**	3.1	0.6	1.6	0.0	1.6
Paper manufacturing	**30.5**	20.9	x	2.9	x	3.9
Petroleum and coal products	**42.5**	26.8	x	4.6	x	x
Chemicals	**47.4**	23.9	4.0	8.3	F	F
Non-metallic mineral products	**38.2**	30.9	2.7	x	F	4.2
Primary metals	**72.6**	60.5	5.7	5.4	x	x
Fabricated metal products	**14.3**	7.5	1.7	2.0	0.2	2.9
Transportation equipment	**14.6**	x	F	x	0.0	4.6
Other manufacturing industries	F	F	F	F	0.2	12.0

x : suppressed to meet the confidentiality requirements of the *Statistics Act*
F : too unreliable to be published.
Notes:
Figures may not add up to totals due to rounding.
North American Industry Classification System (NAICS), 2007.
Source: Statistics Canada, CANSIM table (for fee) 153-0054, Catalogue no. 16F0006X.
Last modified: 2011-01-06.

Operating expenditures on environmental protection by establishment size, 2008

	Number of employees per establishment			
	Fewer than 100	100 to 499	500 to 999	1,000 or more
	millions of dollars			
Environmental monitoring	79.7	97.6	45.8	61.4
Environmental assessments and audits	24.3	36.4	19.9	31.7
Reclamation and decommissioning	130.8	216.8	95.5	195.6
Wildlife and habitat protection	8.3	29.3	5.4	9.0
Waste management and sewerage services	517.6	552.3	242.6	312.1
Pollution abatement and control processes (end-of-pipe)	111.9	559.0	187.9	402.3
Pollution prevention processes	224.1	312.0	69.9	344.5
Fees, fines and licences	10.8	51.4	26.8	8.2
Other	36.1	78.2	36.5	69.8
Total	**1,143.5**	**1,933.0**	**730.4**	**1,434.5**

Note(s): Figures may not add up to totals due to rounding.
Source(s): Statistics Canada, Environment Accounts and Statistics Division, CANSIM table 153-0056.

Operating expenditures on environmental protection per employee by establishment size, 2008

	Number of employees per establishment				Total
	Fewer than 100	100 to 499	500 to 999	1,000 or more	
	dollars per employee				
Environmental monitoring	153.9	132.6	207.7	157.0	152.5
Environmental assessments and audits	46.9	49.5	89.9	81.0	60.1
Reclamation and decommissioning	252.5	294.4	432.7	499.9	342.2
Wildlife and habitat protection	16.0	39.8	24.4	23.0	27.9
Waste management and sewerage services	999.3	749.9	1,099.1	797.7	870.4
Pollution abatement and control processes (end-of-pipe)	216.0	758.9	851.4	1,028.2	675.6
Pollution prevention processes	432.6	423.6	316.5	880.4	509.2
Fees, fines and licences	20.9	69.7	121.5	20.9	52.1
Other	69.7	106.2	165.5	178.3	118.2
Total	**2,207.8**	**2,624.5**	**3,308.6**	**3,666.4**	**2,808.2**

Note(s): Figures may not add up to totals due to rounding.
Source(s): Statistics Canada, Environment Accounts and Statistics Division.

Operating expenditures on environmental protection by type of activity and industry

	Environmental monitoring	Environmental assessments and audits	Reclamation and decommis- sioning	Wildlife and habitat protection	Waste management and sewerage services	Pollution abatement and control processes (end-of-pipe)	Pollution prevention processes	Fees, fines and licences	Other	Total
	millions of dollars									
2006										
Total, all industries	244.3	116.1	533.6	106.7	1,728.2	1,039.8	661.7	117.5	221.1	4,769.0
Logging	2.6	2.5	6.5	32.2	9.3	0.8	5.4	0.8	2.4	62.6
Oil and gas extraction	50.5	43.3	344.1	16.4	198.4	183.6	117.6	25.3	103.4	1,082.6
Mining and quarrying	20.8	8.3	49.8	2.1	54.5	71.3	48.9	11.1	10.2	277.0
Electric power generation, transmission and distribution	37.9	13.5	58.8	14.5	80.1	43.6	78.7	24.9	29.2	381.2
Natural gas distribution	0.8	3.4	1.2	0.1	4.1	x	6.7	x	2.2	22.4
Food manufacturing	10.8	4.7	F	x	239.5	24.4	19.6	9.2	8.2	317.9
Beverage and tobacco product manufacturing	0.2	x	F	x	10.5	F	0.8	3.0	0.2	15.5
Wood product manufacturing	4.1	2.4	12.4	F	F	18.8	9.4	2.8	3.4	181.8
Paper manufacturing	31.1	x	7.8	x	219.0	165.5	56.2	12.3	9.0	508.5
Petroleum and coal product manufacturing	7.6	2.0	6.1	x	48.1	123.7	103.1	x	4.7	297.1
Chemical manufacturing	18.8	5.5	10.1	x	123.7	59.8	32.2	F	13.0	280.5
Non-metallic mineral product manufacturing	6.2	1.5	2.8	0.1	33.9	16.6	6.4	2.7	2.7	73.0
Primary metal manufacturing	34.5	8.6	16.8	1.4	168.6	290.0	76.3	4.5	10.3	610.9
Fabricated metal product manufacturing	2.4	2.9	2.1	F	45.7	5.0	8.0	0.7	1.6	68.5
Transportation equipment manufacturing	3.6	4.0	x	x	94.9	18.8	6.8	x	10.2	142.1
Other manufacturing industries	9.6	5.5	F	F	294.1	13.1	F	2.5	3.8	379.0
Pipeline transportation	2.6	2.7	6.6	2.0	6.6	1.3	39.4	0.4	6.7	68.3

Note(s): Figures may not add up to totals due to rounding.
Source(s): Statistics Canada, CANSIM table 153-0052.

Canadian environment and sustainable development indicators

Population indicators

	2004	2005	2006	2007	2008	2009
Population						
Persons [1]	31,940,676	32,245,209	32,576,074	32,929,733	33,315,976	33,720,184
Percent change from previous year	1.0	1.0	1.0	1.1	1.2	1.2
Aged 65 and over (percent of total)	13.0	13.1	13.3	13.5	13.7	13.9
Census metropolitan areas and census agglomerations (percent of total) [2]	..	..	81.1	..	..	..
Density (per square kilometre)	3.5	3.6	3.6	3.7	3.7	3.7

1. Population data is based on the Estimates of Population program, except for data on population in census metropolitan areas and census agglomerations, which is based on the Census of Population.
2. Area consisting of one or more neighbouring municipalities situated around a major urban core. A census metropolitan area must have a total population of at least 100,000 of which 50,000 or more live in the urban core. A census agglomeration must have an urban core population of at least 10,000.

Source(s): Statistics Canada, CANSIM table 051-0001 (accessed February 28, 2011). Statistics Canada, 2007, *Population and Dwelling Count Highlight Tables, 2006 Census*, Catalogue no. 97-550-X2006002.

Economy indicators

	2004	2005	2006	2007	2008	2009
Gross Domestic Product (GDP)						
GDP (millions of chained 2002 dollars)	1,211,239	1,247,807	1,283,033	1,311,260	1,318,055	1,285,604
Percent change from previous year	3.1	3.0	2.8	2.2	0.5	-2.5
Per capita (chained 2002 dollars)	37,922	38,697	39,386	39,820	39,562	38,126
Consumer Price Index (2002 = 100)	104.7	107.0	109.1	111.5	114.1	114.4
Unemployment rate (percent)	7.2	6.8	6.3	6.0	6.1	8.3

Source(s): Statistics Canada, CANSIM tables 380-0017, 051-0001, 326-0021 and 282-0002 (accessed March 4, 2011).

Social indicators

	2004	2005	2006	2007	2008	2009
Average household spending [1]						
Total (current dollars)	62,464	65,575	67,736	69,946	71,364	71,117
Water and sewage (current dollars)	204	211	221	253	251	259
Electricity (current dollars)	1,040	1,070	1,111	1,147	1,162	1,183
Food (current dollars)	6,772	6,978	7,046	7,305	7,435	7,262
Gasoline and other motor fuels (current dollars)	1,854	2,024	2,079	2,223	2,233	2,218
Personal expenditure on consumer goods and services						
(millions of chained 2002 dollars)	697,566	723,146	753,263	787,765	810,723	814,344
Residential waste						
Production per capita (kilograms)	386	..	387	..	387	..
Disposal (tonnes)	8,961,583	..	8,893,494	..	8,536,891	..
Disposal per capita (kilograms)	281	..	273	..	256	..
Diversion (tonnes)	3,363,803	..	3,722,843	..	4,360,505	..
Diversion per capita (kilograms)	105	..	114	..	131	..
Diversion rate (percent of waste production)	27	..	30	..	34	..
Distance driven by light vehicles [2] (millions of kilometres)	285,164	289,717	296,871	300,203	294,361	303,576
Asthma (percent of population age 12 and over)	..	8.3	..	8.1	8.4	8.1

1. Data on average household spending is based on the Survey of Household Spending (SHS). For information on the difference between the SHS and personal expenditure data please see: Statistics Canada, 2008, *Guide to the Income and Expenditure Accounts*, Catalogue no. 13-017-X.
2. Distance driven for vehicles weighing less than 4.5 tonnes, excluding the territories.

Source(s): Statistics Canada, CANSIM tables 203-0001, 203-0003, 203-0002, 203-0007, 380-0017, 153-0041, 153-0042, 051-0001, 405-0063 and 105-0501 (accessed March 4, 2011).

Energy indicators

	2004	2005	2006	2007	2008	2009
Primary energy availability (terajoules)	11,527,500	11,307,113	11,176,879	11,969,050	11,179,124	10,962,914
Primary and secondary energy						
Exports (terajoules)	9,810,695	9,641,137	9,833,549	10,308,635	10,265,704	8,816,828
Residential consumption (terajoules)	1,313,015	1,296,644	1,243,425	1,336,452	1,356,259	1,316,207
Established reserve						
Crude bitumen (closing stock, [1] millions of cubic metres)	1,660	1,620	3,340	3,500	4,300	4,220
Crude oil (closing stock, [1] millions of cubic metres)	603.8	752.3	712.6	721.8	688.8	..
Natural gas (closing stock, [1] billions of cubic metres)	1,497.5	1,553.7	1,577.7	1,534.3	1,671.2	..
Recoverable reserves						
Coal (closing stock, [1] millions of tonnes)	4,666.3	4,560.4	4,468.8	4,395.1	4,331.5	..
Uranium (closing stock, [1] tonnes)	444,000	431,000	423,400	482,000	447,000	..
Electricity generation						
Total (megawatt hours)	571,291,905	597,810,875	585,097,531	603,572,420	601,719,256	575,414,339
Hydro-electric (percent of total)	58.7	60.1	60.0	60.6	62.0	63.1
Nuclear (percent of total)	14.9	14.5	15.8	14.6	14.7	14.8
Fossil fuel and other fuel combustion (percent of total)	26.4	25.4	24.2	24.8	23.3	22.1

1. The size of the reserve at year-end.

Source(s): Statistics Canada, CANSIM tables 128-0009, 153-0012, 153-0013, 153-0014, 153-0017, 153-0018, 153-0019, 127-0001 and 127-0002 (accessed March 4, 2011).

Environment and natural resources indicators

	2004	2005	2006	2007	2008	2009
Greenhouse gas (GHG) emissions (megatonnes of carbon dioxide equivalent (CO_2eq))	741	731	718	750	734	..
GHG emissions per capita (tonnes of CO_2eq)	23.2	22.7	22.0	22.8	22.0	..
GHG emissions by final demand						
Total household [1] (megatonnes of CO_2eq)	423	415	411 p	..	..	..
Total household per capita (tonnes of CO_2eq)	13.2	12.9	12.6 p	..	..	..
Direct household [2] (megatonnes of CO_2eq)	110	111	109 p	..	..	..
Indirect household [3] (megatonnes of CO_2eq)	313	304	302 p	..	..	..
Exports (megatonnes of CO_2eq)	277	274	264 p	..	..	..
Value of selected natural resources						
Land (millions of current dollars)	1,227,819	1,367,002	1,532,193	1,708,196	1,824,120	1,891,438
Timber (millions of current dollars)	311,771	283,572	265,747	246,713	236,556	192,660
Subsoil resource stocks (millions of current dollars)	566,179	805,761	931,530	941,765	1,543,864	914,173
Average farm pesticide expenditures (current dollars)	7,602	7,792	8,268	9,147	11,361	11,572
Air quality [4]						
Ozone (population weighted, parts per billion)	36	40	38	39	37	..
$PM_{2.5}$ (population weighted, micrograms per cubic metre)	9	10	8	8	8	..

1. Total household greenhouse gas emissions are the sum of direct plus indirect household greenhouse gas emissions.
2. Direct household greenhouse gas emissions include all greenhouse gas emissions due to energy use in the home and for private motor vehicles.
3. Indirect household greenhouse gas emissions are those business-sector emissions due to the production of the goods and services purchased by households. An estimate of the greenhouse gas emissions from foreign companies due to the production of the imported goods purchased by Canadian households is included.
4. Ground level ozone and fine particulate matter ($PM_{2.5}$) are two key components of smog that have been linked to health impacts ranging from minor respiratory problems to hospitalizations and premature death. Exposure studies indicate that adverse health effects can occur even with low concentrations of these pollutants in the air. Annual data are revised, based on the latest release of the Canadian Environmental Sustainability Indicators report.

Source(s): Statistics Canada, CANSIM tables 051-0001, 153-0046, 378-0005 and 002-0044 (accessed February 28, 2011). Environment Canada, 2010, *National Inventory Report 1990-2008: Greenhouse Gas Sources and Sinks in Canada*, Catalogue no. En81-4/2008E-PDF. Environment Canada, 2010, *Environmental Indicators - Air Quality Data*, www.ec.gc.ca/indicateurs-indicators/default.asp?lang=en&n=B1385495-1#air1_en (accessed February 28, 2011). Statistics Canada, Environment Accounts and Statistics Division, Material and Energy Flow Accounts.

Status of freshwater quality for protection of aquatic life at monitoring stations in Canada, 2006 to 2008

Note: Water quality in Canada's 16 drainage regions where human activity is most intensive was assessed using the Canadian Council of Ministers of the Environment's Water Quality Index. Some data for Newfoundland and Labrador cover the period from December 2005 to January 2009 due to sampling constraints. Five stations in Manitoba have 11 rather than 12 samples for the 2006-2008 period.

Source: Data assembled by Environment Canada from federal, provincial, territorial and joint water quality monitoring programs.

Environmental Statistics / Freshwater Quality

Status of freshwater quality for protection of aquatic life at monitoring stations in selected drainage regions in Canada, 2006 to 2008

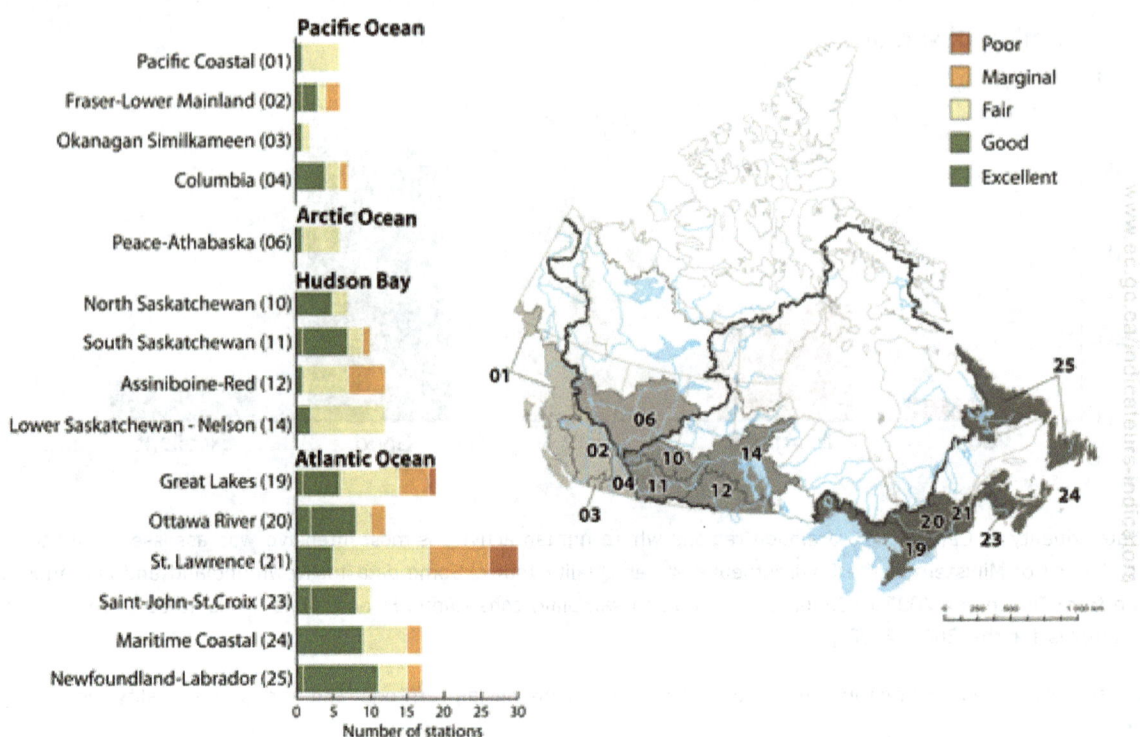

Note: Water quality was assessed using the Canadian Council of Ministers of the Environment's Water Quality Index. Care must be taken in comparing rankings among basins as methodological differences exist among jurisdictions.
Source: Data assembled by Environment Canada from federal, provincial, territorial and joint water quality monitoring programs.

Environmental Statistics / Freshwater Quality

Water quality ratings for protection of aquatic life at individual stations, Canada, 2006 to 2008

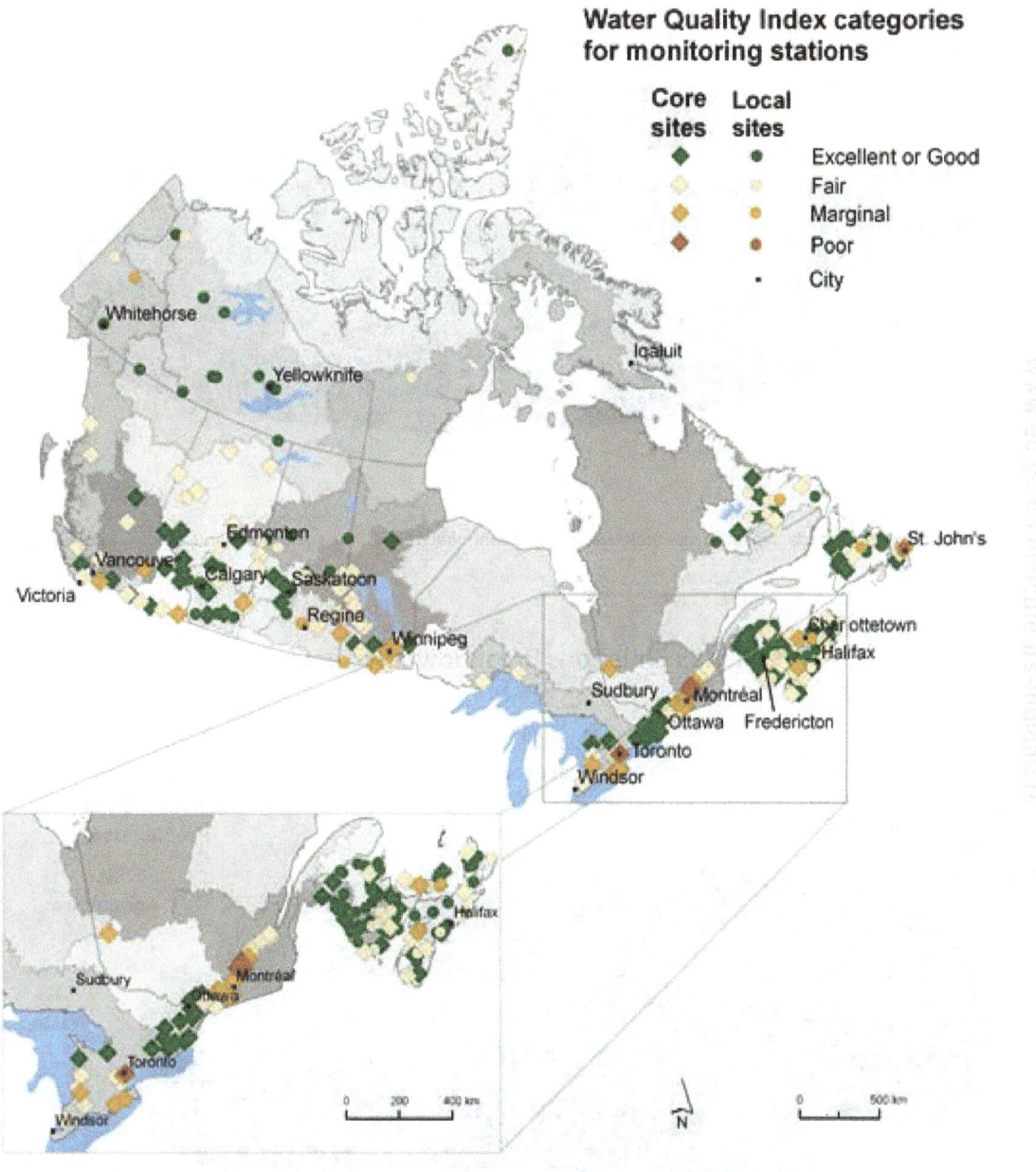

Note: Water quality was assessed using the Canadian Council of Ministers of the Environment's Water Quality Index. Care must be taken in comparing rankings among basins as methodological differences exist among jurisdictions.
Source: Data were assembled by Environment Canada from existing federal, provincial, territorial and joint water quality monitoring programs.

Environmental Statistics / Green House Gas Emissions

Canada's Total Emissions Breakdown by Gas

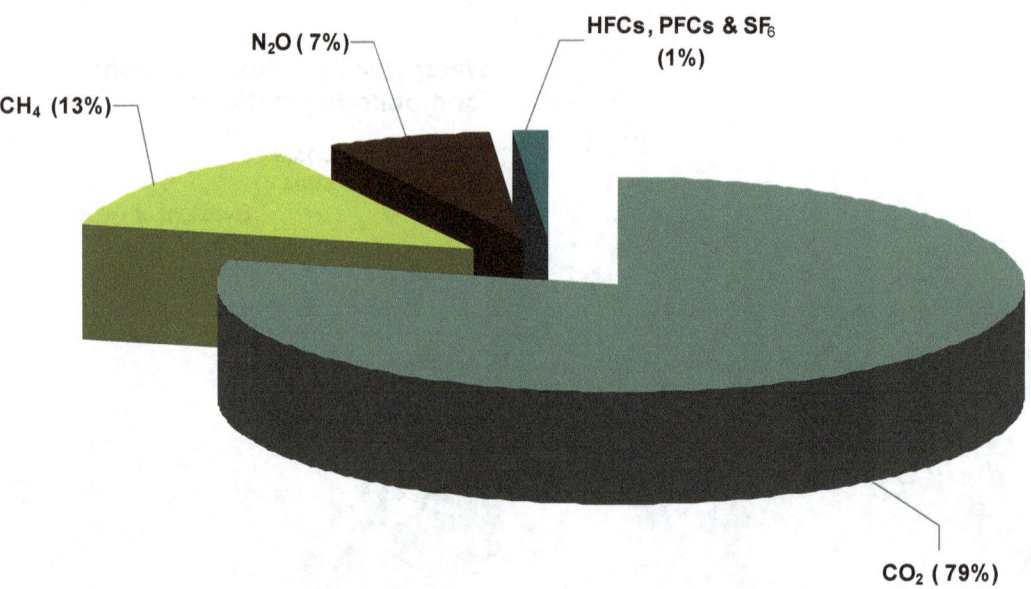

Source: Environment Canada, National Inventory Report, Greenhouse Gas Sources and Sinks in Canada, 1990-2009

Canada's Emissions Breakdown by Sector

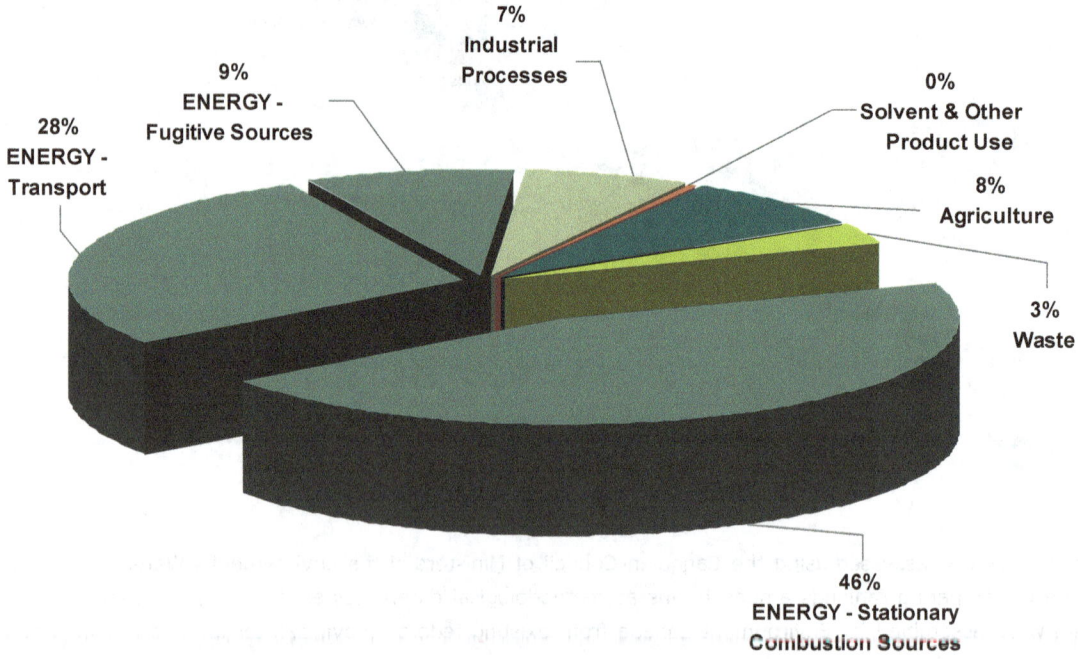

Source: Environment Canada, National Inventory Report, Greenhouse Gas Sources and Sinks in Canada, 1990-2009

Canada's GHG Emissions 1990–2009

Greenhouse Gas Categories		1990	1995	2000	2005	2008	2009
				kt CO_2 equivalent			
TOTAL[1]		590 000	640 000	716 000	731 000	732 000	690 000
ENERGY		468 000	508 000	586 000	595 000	597 000	566 000
a.	Stationary Combustion Sources	279 000	292 000	343 000	339 000	339 000	315 000
	Electricity and Heat Generation	91 600	96 100	127 000	123 000	116 000	97 900
	Fossil Fuel Production and Refining	51 000	54 000	67 000	66 000	69 000	64 000
	Petroleum Refining and Upgrading	18 000	17 000	16 000	19 000	20 000	20 000
	Fossil Fuel Production	34 000	37 000	50 000	48 000	49 000	44 000
	Mining & Oil and Gas Extraction	6 650	8 520	12 400	18 600	27 600	31 300
	Manufacturing Industries	56 000	55 800	56 000	48 800	43 700	42 600
	Iron and Steel	5 270	6 050	6 330	5 770	4 750	4 030
	Non-ferrous Metals	3 260	3 150	3 220	3 290	3 680	3 120
	Chemical	8 220	10 200	10 000	7 040	7 270	7 570
	Pulp and Paper	14 400	12 800	12 000	7 920	5 160	4 510
	Cement	3 820	4 030	4 240	5 020	4 630	3 610
	Other Manufacturing	21 000	19 500	20 200	19 800	18 200	19 700
	Construction	1 870	1 170	1 070	1 360	1 260	1 080
	Commercial & Institutional	25 700	28 900	33 100	36 700	35 200	36 000
	Residential	43 000	45 000	45 000	42 000	43 000	41 000
	Agriculture & Forestry	2 390	2 750	2 540	1 970	2 260	2 050
b.	Transport[2]	146 000	160 000	180 000	193 000	196 000	190 000
	Civil Aviation (Domestic Aviation)	7 200	6 600	7 500	7 700	7 800	7 200
	Road Transportation	96 700	107 000	118 000	130 000	132 000	131 000
	Light-duty Gasoline Vehicles	45 500	43 800	41 900	40 000	39 700	41 400
	Light-duty Gasoline Trucks	20 300	27 300	36 300	42 500	42 600	41 300
	Heavy-duty Gasoline Vehicles	7 440	6 230	5 460	6 540	6 840	6 990
	Motorcycles	152	125	161	254	264	245
	Light-duty Diesel Vehicles	469	429	466	574	652	663
	Light-duty Diesel Trucks	702	1 310	1 660	1 930	2 020	1 940
	Heavy-duty Diesel Vehicles	20 000	26 100	30 900	37 600	39 200	38 200
	Propane & Natural Gas Vehicles	2 200	2 100	1 100	720	880	780
	Railways	7 000	6 000	7 000	6 000	7 000	7 000
	Navigation (Domestic Marine)	5 000	4 400	5 100	6 400	5 900	5 100
	Other Transportation	30 000	36 000	43 000	43 000	43 000	40 000
	Off-road Gasoline	7 800	7 700	8 800	8 300	7 400	7 600
	Off-road Diesel	16 000	16 000	23 000	24 000	28 000	26 000
	Pipelines	6 850	11 900	11 200	10 100	7 460	6 320
c.	Fugitive Sources	42 100	55 600	63 000	63 100	62 300	60 700
	Coal Mining	2 000	2 000	900	700	800	700
	Oil and Natural Gas	40 200	53 900	62 100	62 400	61 500	60 000
	Oil	4 190	5 150	5 440	5 650	5 550	5 530
	Natural Gas	11 400	14 900	17 700	19 200	19 700	19 400
	Venting	20 200	28 800	33 500	32 100	30 700	28 700
	Flaring	4 400	5 100	5 400	5 500	5 500	6 400
INDUSTRIAL PROCESSES		56 800	58 900	53 500	57 200	54 500	46 300
a.	Mineral Products	8 300	8 800	9 600	9 500	8 600	6 800
	Cement Production	5 400	6 100	6 700	7 200	6 600	5 100
	Lime Production	1 800	1 900	1 900	1 700	1 500	1 200
	Mineral Product Use[3]	1 090	877	1 020	589	489	449
b.	Chemical Industry	17 000	18 000	9 000	10 000	10 000	8 100
	Ammonia Production	5 000	6 500	6 800	6 300	6 700	6 200
	Nitric Acid Production	1 010	1 000	1 230	1 250	1 230	1 150
	Adipic Acid Production	11 000	11 000	900	2 600	2 400	660
	Petrochemical Production[4]	110	90	97	79	73	63
c.	Metal Production	22 600	22 600	22 500	19 600	18 500	15 000
	Iron and Steel Production	10 200	11 300	11 500	10 100	10 600	7 650
	Aluminum Production	9 300	9 200	8 200	8 200	7 400	7 200
	SF_6 Used in Magnesium Smelters and Casters	3 110	2 110	2 780	1 290	462	193
d.	Production and Consumption of Halocarbons and SF_6[5]	990	730	3 200	5 400	5 700	7 000
e.	Other & Undifferentiated Production	8 000	8 400	9 200	12 000	11 000	9 400
SOLVENT & OTHER PRODUCT USE		180	210	250	180	340	260
AGRICULTURE		47 000	53 000	55 000	58 000	58 000	56 000
a.	Enteric Fermentation	16 000	19 000	20 000	22 000	20 000	19 000
b.	Manure Management	5 700	6 500	6 900	7 500	6 800	6 600
c.	Agriculture Soils	25 000	27 000	29 000	28 000	31 000	30 000
	Direct Sources	14 000	14 000	15 000	15 000	17 000	16 000
	Pasture, Range and Paddock Manure	2 200	2 800	3 100	3 400	3 200	3 000
	Indirect Sources	9 000	10 000	10 000	10 000	10 000	10 000
d.	Field Burning of Agricultural Residues	210	170	120	41	45	45
WASTE		19 000	20 000	20 000	21 000	21 000	22 000
a.	Solid Waste Disposal on Land	18 000	19 000	19 000	20 000	20 000	20 000
b.	Wastewater Handling	780	860	930	980	1 000	1 000
c.	Waste Incineration	400	350	250	240	250	260
Land Use, Land-use Change and Forestry		-67 000	190 000	-62 000	54 000	-17 000	-12 000
a.	Forest Land	-93 000	170 000	-74 000	46 000	-22 000	-17 000
b.	Cropland	11 000	4 700	-140	-4 300	-6 300	-6 900
c.	Grassland	-	-	-	-	-	-
d.	Wetlands	5 000	3 000	3 000	3 000	3 000	2 000
e.	Settlements	9 000	8 000	9 000	9 000	9 000	9 000
LAND USE, LAND-USE CHANGE AND FORESTRY							
Activities under the Kyoto Protocol							
a.	Article 3.3						
	Afforestation / reforestation	NA	NA	NA	NA	-738	-797
	Deforestation	NA	NA	NA	NA	14 533	14 699
b.	Article 3.4						
	Cropland Management	3 732	NA	NA	NA	-11 711	-12 406

Notes:
1. National totals exclude all GHGs from the Land Use, Land-use Change and Forestry Sector. The estimates for LULUCF activities under the Kyoto Protocol will be accounted for over the five years (2008–2012) of the first commitment period under the Protocol.
2. Emissions from Fuel Ethanol are reported within the gasoline transportation subcategories.
3. The category Mineral Product Use includes CO_2 emissions coming from the use of limestone & dolomite, soda ash and magnesite.
4. The category Petrochemical Production includes emissions coming from production of silicon/calcium carbides, carbon black, ethylene, methanol, ethylene dichloride and styrene. CO_2 emissions are included in Other & Undifferentiated Production.
5. Production of HFCs (HCFC-22 exclusively) only occurred in Canada from 1990 to 1992. HFC consumption began in 1995.

Source: Environment Canada, National Inventory Report, Greenhouse Gas Sources and Sinks in Canada, 1990-2009

Environmental Statistics / Green House Gas Emissions

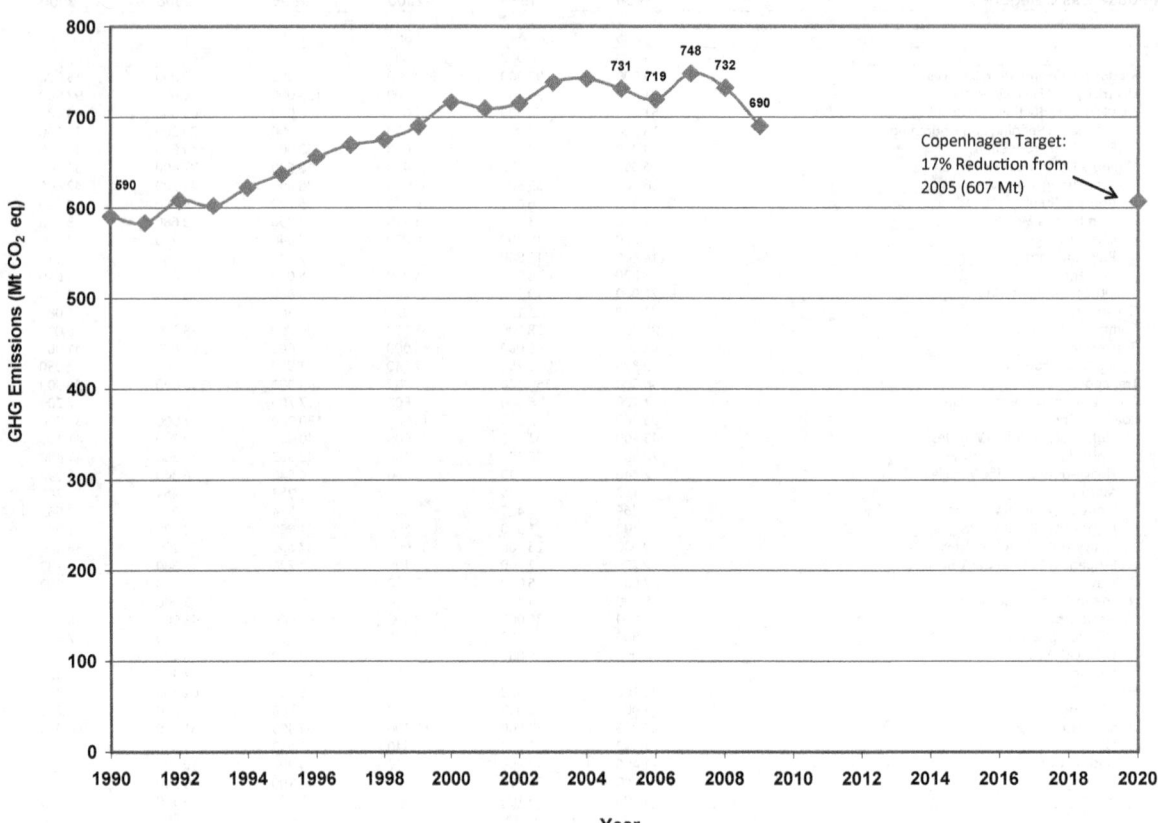

* Under the Copenhagen Accord, Canada committed to reducing emissions to 17% below 2005 levels by 2020.

Source: Environment Canada, National Inventory Report, Greenhouse Gas Sources and Sinks in Canada, 1990-2009

Environmental Statistics / Green House Gas Emissions

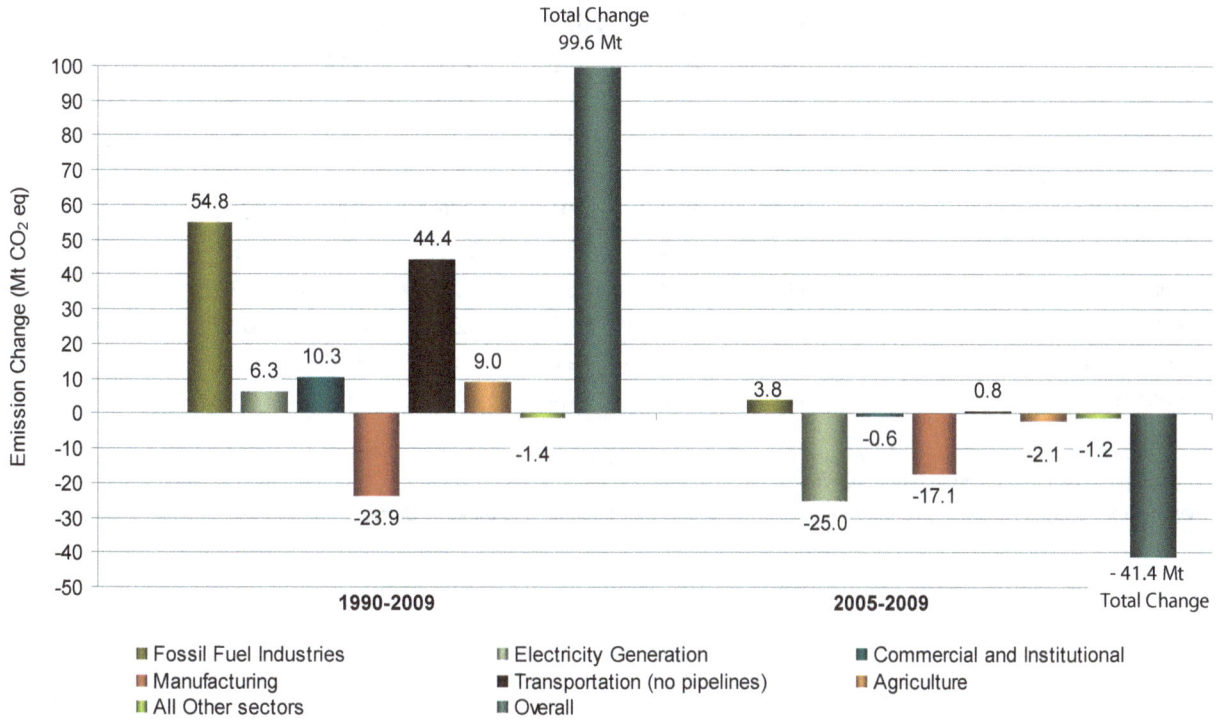

Source: Environment Canada, National Inventory Report, Greenhouse Gas Sources and Sinks in Canada, 1990-2009

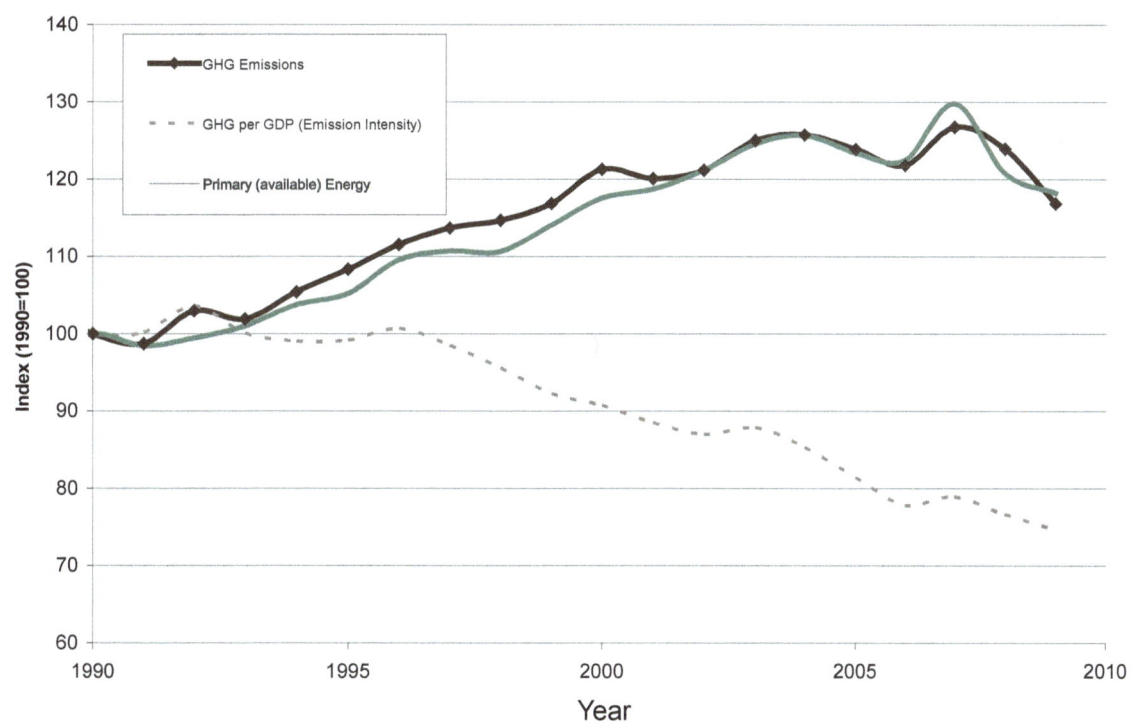

Source: Environment Canada, National Inventory Report, Greenhouse Gas Sources and Sinks in Canada, 1990-2009

Environmental Statistics / Green House Gas Emissions

Trends in Emissions and Economic Indicators for Selected Years (1990–2009)

	1990	1995	2000	2005	2006	2007	2008	2009
Total GHG (Mt)	590	637	716	731	719	748	732	690
Change Since 1990 (%)	NA	7.9	21.3	23.9	21.8	26.7	23.9	16.9
Annual Change (%)	NA	2.4	3.8	-1.5	-1.7	4.0	-2.2	-5.7
Average Annual Change (%)*	NA	1.6	2.1	1.6	1.4	1.6	1.3	0.9
GDP (Billions 2002$)	825	899	1101	1248	1283	1311	1318	1286
Change Since 1990 (%)	NA	8.9	33.3	51.2	55.5	58.9	59.7	55.8
Annual Change (%)	NA	2.8	5.2	3.0	2.8	2.2	0.5	-2.5
GHG Intensity (Mt/$B GDP)	0.72	0.71	0.65	0.59	0.56	0.57	0.56	0.54
Change Since 1990 (%)	NA	-0.9	-9.0	-18.1	-21.6	-20.2	-22.4	-25.0
Annual Change (%)	NA	-0.4	-1.4	-4.4	-4.4	1.8	-2.7	-3.3

*Average annual change since 1990.
GDP: Statistics Canada - Table 384-0002 - Expenditure-based, annual, chained (billions)
Annual Change: Implies change over previous calendar year.

Source: Environment Canada, National Inventory Report, Greenhouse Gas Sources and Sinks in Canada, 1990-2009

Environmental Statistics / Green House Gas Emissions

Contribution of Constituent Source Categories to Overall Industrial Processes Sector Emissions

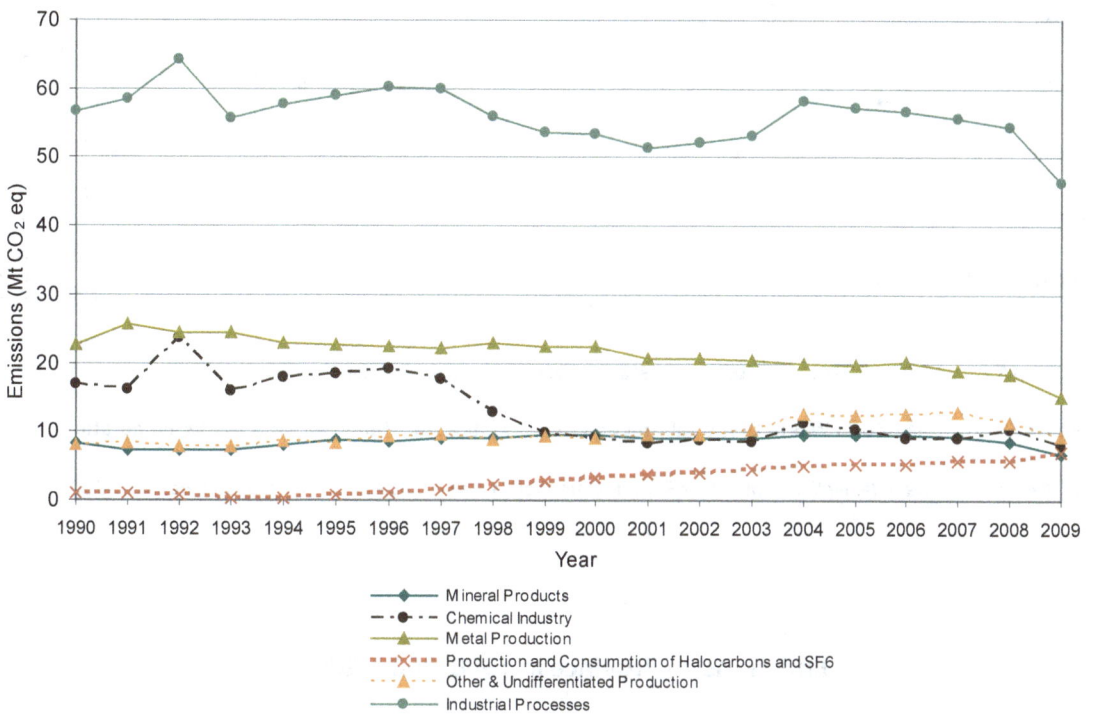

Source: Environment Canada, National Inventory Report, Greenhouse Gas Sources and Sinks in Canada, 1990-2009

Relative GHG Contribution from Livestock and Crop Production and Total Agricultural Emissions, 1990–2009

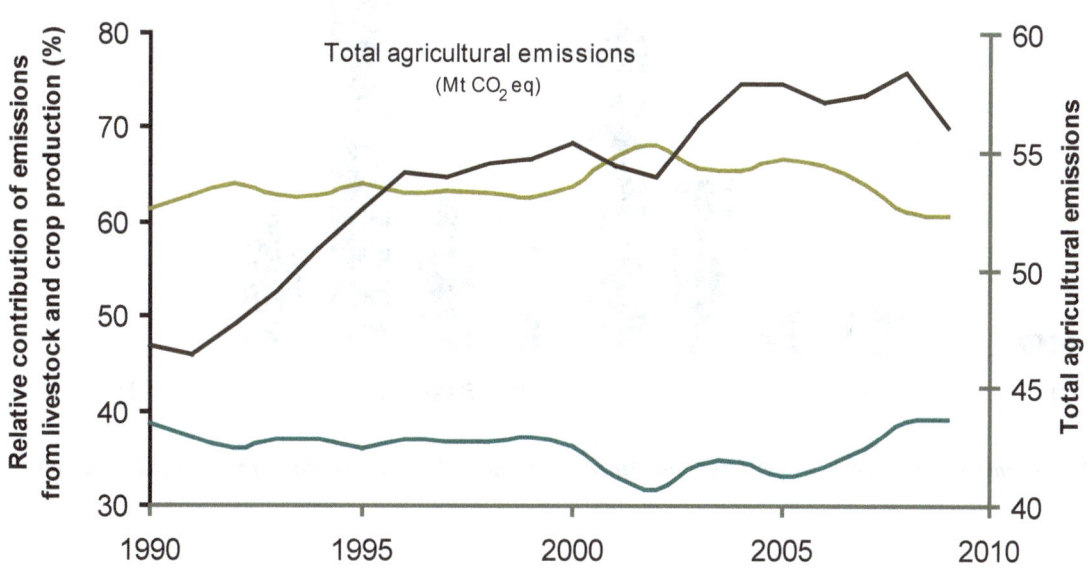

Source: Environment Canada, National Inventory Report, Greenhouse Gas Sources and Sinks in Canada, 1990-2009

Environmental Statistics / Green House Gas Emissions

GHG Emissions from Waste, 1990–2009

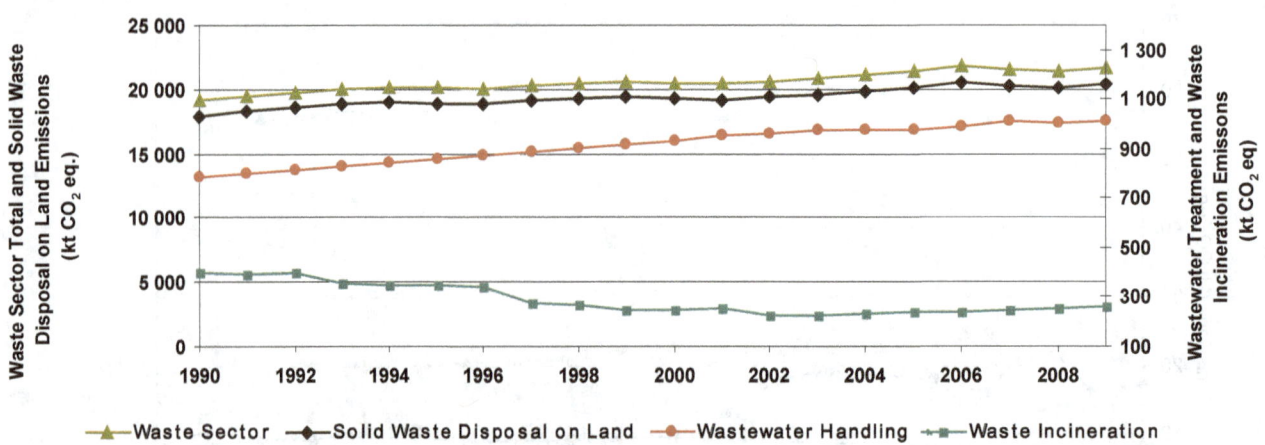

Source: Environment Canada, National Inventory Report, Greenhouse Gas Sources and Sinks in Canada, 1990-2009

Emissions by Province in 1990, 2008, 2009

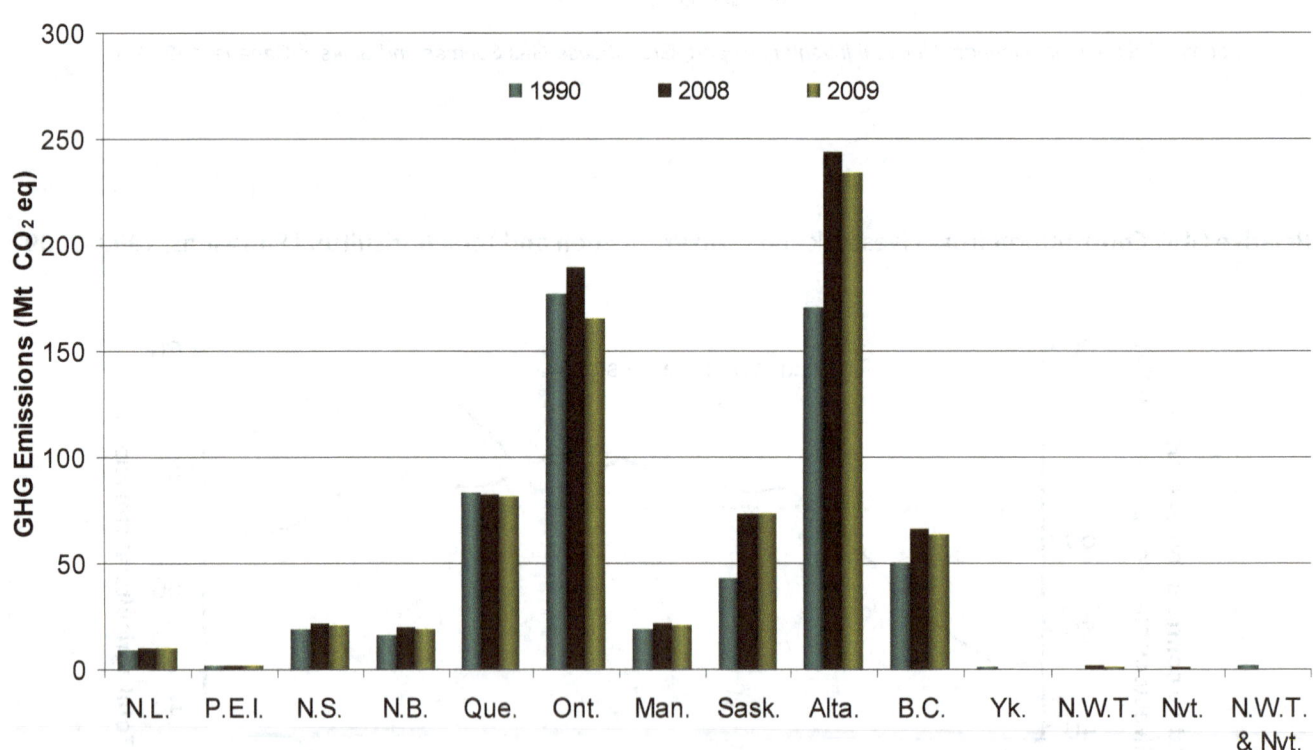

Source: Environment Canada, National Inventory Report, Greenhouse Gas Sources and Sinks in Canada, 1990-2009

Land cover by ecozone, 2005

	Evergreen needleleaf forest	Deciduous broadleaf forest	Mixed forest	Disturbance[1]	Shrubland	Grassland	Low vegetation and barren	Cropland	Cropland with Woodland	Other[2]	Total
					thousands of square kilometres						
Total	2,552	35	1,122	267	1,006	49	2,857	419	237	1,432	9,976
Arctic Cordillera	0s	0	0	0s	0	0	101	0	0	143	245
Northern Arctic	2	0	0	0s	9	0	1,322	0	0	191	1,523
Southern Arctic	52	0	0s	1	38	0	612	0	0	150	852
Taiga Plains	305	1	68	28	122	0	43	0s	1	89	658
Taiga Shield	497	0	1	73	123	0	429	0	0s	271	1,393
Boreal Shield	862	13	456	86	183	0s	33	2	8	278	1,921
Atlantic Maritime	20	11	137	1	3	0s	0s	8	12	10	203
Mixed Wood Plains	0	1	25	0s	4	0s	0s	17	56	65	168
Boreal Plains	181	5	220	24	84	1	2	92	62	72	744
Prairies	0	0s	4	0s	4	46	0s	297	90	25	466
Taiga Cordillera	21	0	3	9	82	0	140	0	0	13	267
Boreal Cordillera	172	0s	19	18	136	0	93	0	0	30	467
Pacific Maritime	18	3	70	3	48	0	15	1	1	47	205
Montane Cordillera	185	1	118	11	75	2	55	2	5	34	487
Hudson Plains	236	0	2	12	95	0	14	0	0s	16	376

1. The disturbance area category refers to forest disturbance, which can be caused by changes in forest structure or composition resulting from natural events such as fire, flood or wind, from mortality caused by insect or disease outbreaks, or from human-caused events such as forest harvesting.
2. 'Other' consists of water, snow/ice, urban and built-up land and statistical error.

Note(s): Figures may not add up to totals due to rounding.

Source(s): Latifovic, Rasim and Darren Pouliot, 2005, "Multi-temporal land cover mapping for Canada: Methodology and Products," Canadian Journal of Remote Sensing, Vol. 31, no. 5, p. 347-363. Natural Resources Canada, Canada Centre for Remote Sensing. Agriculture and Agri-Food Canada and Environment Canada, 2003, Framework Data - National Resolution - Ecological Units, http://sis.agr.gc.ca/cansis/nsdb/ecostrat/gis_data.html (accessed December 5, 2007). Statistics Canada, Environment Accounts and Statistics Division.

Total terrestrial protected areas by province and territory, 2005

	Protected areas[1]	Area protected[2]	Amount of land[3]	Percentage of land protected[4]
	number	km²	km²	percent
Canada	8,475	855,973	9,093,507	9.4
Newfoundland and Labrador	63	18,383	373,872	4.9
Prince Edward Island	184	161	5,660	2.8
Nova Scotia	75	4,557	53,338	8.5
New Brunswick	106	2,321	71,450	3.2
Quebec[5]	1,096	75,652	1,365,128	5.5
Ontario[6]	666	94,614	917,741	10.3
Manitoba[7]	122	42,755	553,556	7.7
Saskatchewan	4,608	53,375	591,670	9.0
Alberta	537	82,501	642,317	12.8
British Columbia	948	120,882	925,186	13.1
Yukon Territory	24	52,348	474,391	11.0
Northwest Territories	19	94,894	1,183,085	8.0
Nunavut Territory	27	213,530	1,936,113	11.0

1. Includes protected areas administered federally, provincially and territorially, as well as Aboriginal or privately held conservation lands that are recognized by protected area agencies as being part of their network.
2. These figures include a number of terrestrial protected areas that have a marine component totalling 28,995 km².
3. Includes only land area. For example, when freshwater is included, the total area of the country is 9,984,670 km².
4. Percent of land protected differs from the Canadian Protected Areas Status because only land area (not land and water) was used as referenced below.
5. Includes the terrestrial portion of Environment Canada's 28 Migratory Bird Sanctuaries that are found in Quebec, and the marine portion of these Sanctuaries (431 km²).
6. Included are 19 sites or 322 km² of National Wildlife Areas (NWAs) and Migratory Bird Sanctuaries (MBSs) that are located in Ontario and administered by Environment Canada.
7. Manitoba does not currently recognize Environment Canada administered National Wildlife Areas as part of their protected areas network. Excluded are 1,682 km² of Agriculture Canada administered PFRA pastures. These lands will be reviewed in the near future.

Source(s): Government of Canada. 2007, Canadian Protected Areas Status Report 2000-2005, http://www.cws-scf.ec.gc.ca/publications/habitat/cpa-apc/index_e.cfm, (accessed July 18, 2007). Statistics Canada, Land and freshwater area, by province and territory, http://www40.statcan.ca/l01/cst01/phys01.htm?sdi=land%20 area (accessed November 16, 2007). Statistics Canada, Environmental Accounts and Statistics Division.

Biophysical characteristics of terrestrial ecozones

Ecozone code	Terrestrial ecozone	Land area (km^2)	Landforms	Vegetation and productivity	Surface materials and soils	Climate and oceanographic characteristics
1	Arctic Cordillera	234,708	Mountains	Mainly unvegetated; some shrub-herb tundra	Ice; snow; colluvium; rock; cryosols[1]	Extremely cold; dry; continuous permafrost
2	Northern Arctic	1,371,340	Plains; hills	Herb-lichen tundra	Moraine; rock; marine; cryosols[1]	Very cold; dry; continuous permafrost
3	Southern Arctic	702,542	Plains; hills	Shrub-herb tundra	Moraine; rock; marine; cryosols[1]	Cold; dry; continuous permafrost
4	Taiga Plains	569,363	Plains; some foothills	Open to closed mixed evergreen-deciduous forest	Organic; moraine; lacustrine; cryosols;[1] brunisols[2]	Cold; semiarid to moist; discontinuous permafrost
5	Taiga Shield	1,122,504	Plains; some hills	Open evergreen-deciduous trees; some lichen-shrub tundra	Canadian Shield rock; moraine; cryosols;[1] brunisols[2]	Cold; moist to semi-arid; discontinuous permafrost
6	Boreal Shield	1,640,949	Plains; some hills	Evergreen forest; mixed evergreen-deciduous forest	Canadian Shield rock; moraine; lacustrine; podzols;[3] brunisols[2]	Cold; moist
7	Atlantic Maritime	192,017	Hills and coastal plains	Mixed deciduous-evergreen forest stands	Moraine; colluvium; marine; brunisols;[2] podzols;[3] luvisols[4]	Cool; wet
8	Mixed Wood Plains	107,017	Plains; some hills	Mixed deciduous-evergreen forest	Moraine; marine; rock; luvisols;[4] brunisols[2]	Cool to mild; moist
9	Boreal Plains	668,664	Plains; some foothills	Mixed evergreen-deciduous forest	Moraine; lacustrine; organic; luvisols;[4] brunisols[2]	Cold; moist
10	Prairies	443,159	Plains; some hills	Grass; scattered deciduous forest (aspen parkland)	Moraine; chernozems[5]	Cold; semiarid
11	Taiga Cordillera	264,213	Mountains	Shrub-herb-moss-lichen tundra	Colluvium; moraine; rock; cryosols;[1] gleysols[6]	Very cold winters; cool summers; minimal precipitation
12	Boreal Cordillera	459,864	Mountains; some hills	Largely evergreen forest; some tundra; open woodland	Colluvium; moraine; rock; podzols;[3] cryosols[1]	Moderately cold; moist
13	Pacific Maritime	196,200	Mountains; minor coastal plains	Coastal evergreen forest	Colluvium; moraine; rock; podzols;[3] brunisols[2]	Mild; temperate; very wet to cold alpine
14	Montane Cordillera	474,753	Mountains; interior plains	Evergreen forest; alpine tundra; interior grassland	Moraine; colluvium; rock; luvisols;[4] brunisols[2]	Moderately cold; moist to arid
15	Hudson Plains	359,546	Plains	Wetlands; some herb-moss-lichen tundra; evergreen forest	Organic; marine; cryosols[1]	Cold to mild; semiarid; discontinuous permafrost

Notes:
1. Cryosols are frozen soils.
2. Brunisols are soils with minimal weathering.
3. Podzols are acid and well-weathered soils.
4. Luvisols are temperate-region soils with clay-rich sublayers.
5. Chernozems are organically rich, relatively fertile grassland soils.
6. Gleysols are soils developed under wet conditions and characterized by reduced iron and other elements.

Sources:
Environment Canada, 1996, *The State of Canada's Environment Part II: Canadian Ecozones,* www.ec.gc.ca/soer-ree/English/SOER/1996report/Doc/1-1.cfm (accessed June 3, 2008).
Wiken, E.B. et al., 1996, *A Perspective on Canada's Ecosystems: An Overview of the Terrestrial and Marine Ecozones,* Canadian Council on Ecological Areas, Occasional paper, No.14.

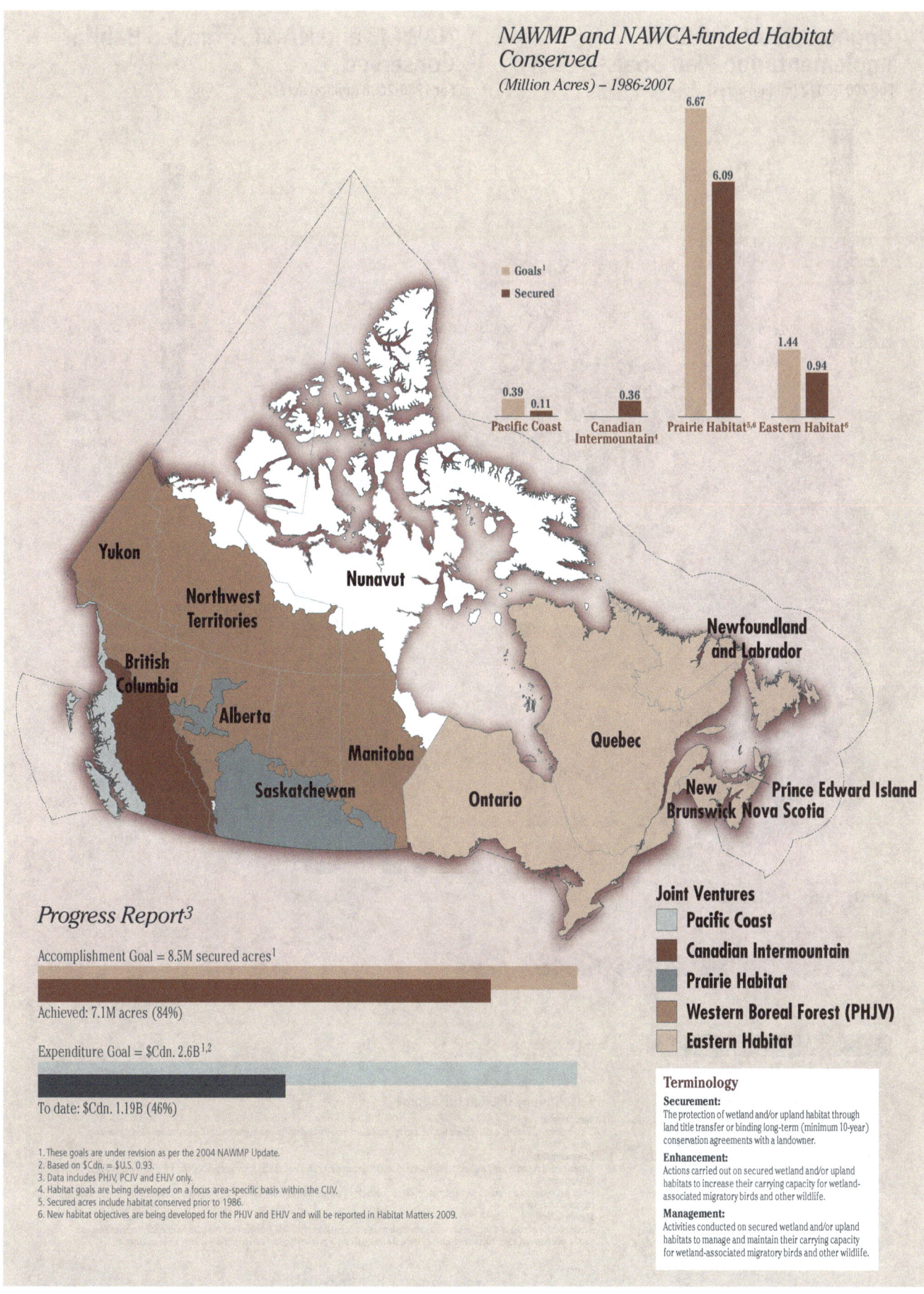

Environmental Statistics / Habitat

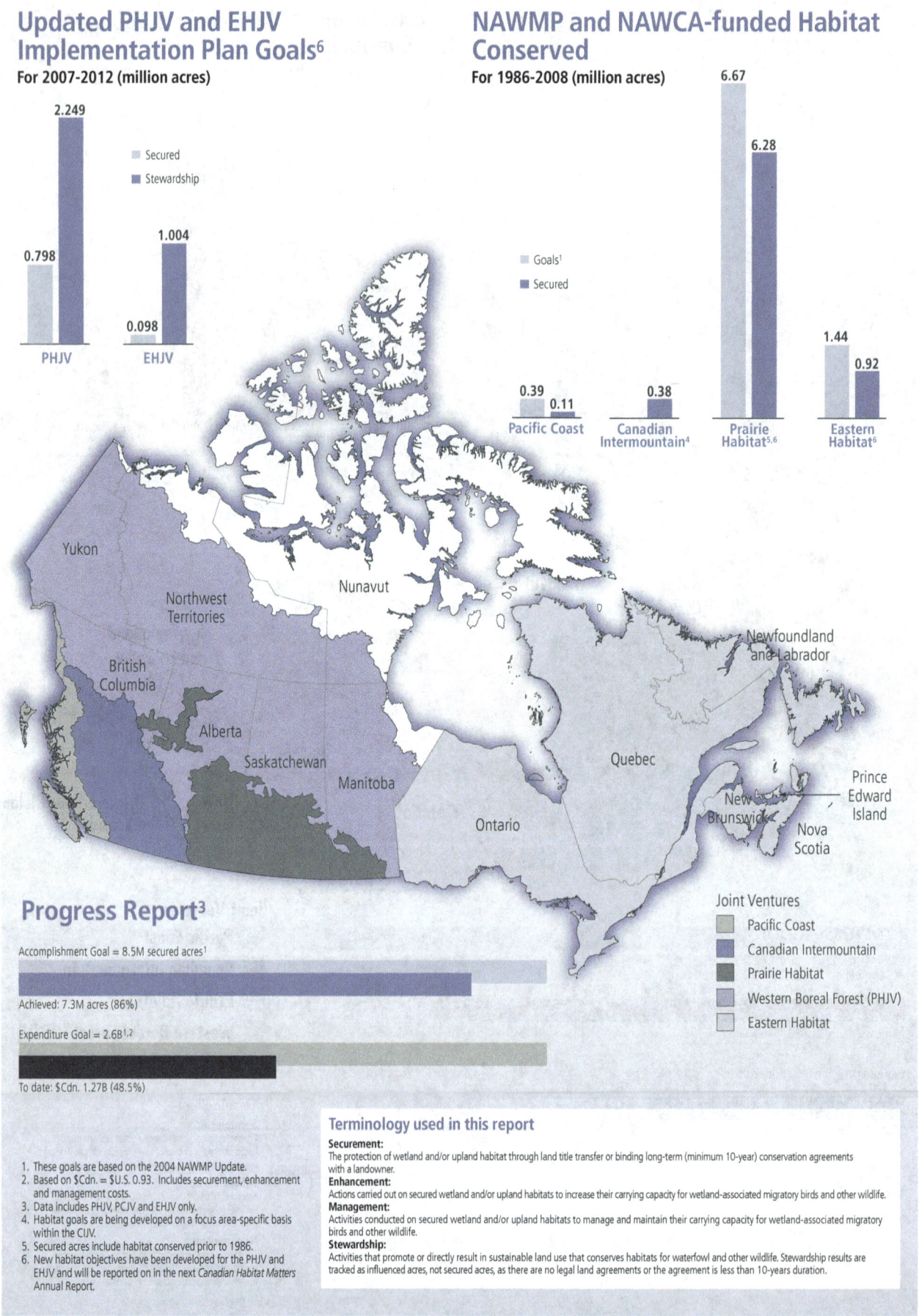

Updated PHJV and EHJV Implementation Plan Goals[6]
For 2007-2012 (million acres)

- Secured
- Stewardship

PHJV: 0.798 / 2.249
EHJV: 0.098 / 1.004

NAWMP and NAWCA-funded Habitat Conserved
For 1986-2008 (million acres)

- Goals[1]
- Secured

Pacific Coast: 0.39 / 0.11
Canadian Intermountain[4]: — / 0.38
Prairie Habitat[5,6]: 6.67 / 6.28
Eastern Habitat[6]: 1.44 / 0.92

Joint Ventures
- Pacific Coast
- Canadian Intermountain
- Prairie Habitat
- Western Boreal Forest (PHJV)
- Eastern Habitat

Progress Report[3]

Accomplishment Goal = 8.5M secured acres[1]
Achieved: 7.3M acres (86%)

Expenditure Goal = 2.6B[1,2]
To date: $Cdn. 1.27B (48.5%)

1. These goals are based on the 2004 NAWMP Update.
2. Based on $Cdn. = $U.S. 0.93. Includes securement, enhancement and management costs.
3. Data includes PHJV, PCJV and EHJV only.
4. Habitat goals are being developed on a focus area-specific basis within the CIJV.
5. Secured acres include habitat conserved prior to 1986.
6. New habitat objectives have been developed for the PHJV and EHJV and will be reported on in the next *Canadian Habitat Matters* Annual Report.

Terminology used in this report

Securement:
The protection of wetland and/or upland habitat through land title transfer or binding long-term (minimum 10-year) conservation agreements with a landowner.

Enhancement:
Actions carried out on secured wetland and/or upland habitats to increase their carrying capacity for wetland-associated migratory birds and other wildlife.

Management:
Activities conducted on secured wetland and/or upland habitats to manage and maintain their carrying capacity for wetland-associated migratory birds and other wildlife.

Stewardship:
Activities that promote or directly result in sustainable land use that conserves habitats for waterfowl and other wildlife. Stewardship results are tracked as influenced acres, not secured acres, as there are no legal land agreements or the agreement is less than 10-years duration.

Environmental Statistics / Pesticides

Pesticide use, Canada and provinces

	Households reporting having a lawn or a garden [1]	Applied chemical or organic pesticide [2]	Applied chemical pesticide [2]	Applied only chemical pesticide [2]	Type of chemical pesticides applied [3]			Applied organic pesticide [2]	Applied only organic pesticide [2]	Applied both chemical and organic pesticides [2]
					Herbicide	Insecticide	Fungicide			
	percent									
Canada	95	33	25	21	80	29	6	12	8	3
Newfoundland and Labrador	95	25	20	17	61	43	F	8 E	F	F
Prince Edward Island	98	21	16	12	46	60	F	8 E	F	F
Nova Scotia	98	21	15	13	58	48	F	8 E	6 E	F
New Brunswick	97	23	17	13	61	43	F	9	5 E	F
Quebec	90	19	4	3	46	49	F	16	15	1 E
Ontario	98	37	30	26	79	32	7	11	7	4
Manitoba	96	47	43	38	89	17	F	8	4 E	5 E
Saskatchewan	96	48	46	41	91	14	F	8	F	5 E
Alberta	96	47	42	38	88	23	F	9	5 E	4
British Columbia	91	33	25	20	79	27	7 E	13	7	5

1. As a percentage of all households that did not live in an apartment.
2. As a percentage of all households that had a lawn or garden.
3. As a percentage of those households who applied chemical pesticides.
Source(s): Statistics Canada, Environment Accounts and Statistics Division, Households and the Environment Survey, 2007, CANSIM Table 153-0064.

Fertilizer use, Canada and provinces

	Households reporting having a lawn or a garden [1]	Applied chemical fertilizer [2]	Applied only chemical fertilizer [2]	Applied organic fertilizer [2]	Applied only organic fertilizer [2]	Applied chemical or organic fertilizer [2]	Fertilizer applied by: [3]		
							Household member	Lawn maintenance company	Someone else
	percent								
Canada	95	27	18	34	24	51	76	23	3
Newfoundland and Labrador	95	25	18	27	20 E	45	87	F	F
Prince Edward Island	98	15	8 E	30	23	38	90	F	F
Nova Scotia	98	18	9	35	27	45	88	9 E	F
New Brunswick	97	21	13	28	20	41	82	15	F
Quebec	90	8	4	44	41	49	70	28	4 E
Ontario	98	32	21	32	22	53	72	28	3
Manitoba	96	35	24	24	12	48	73	27	F
Saskatchewan	96	47	35	25	13	60	86	11	F
Alberta	96	45	32	27	14	59	82	17	3 E
British Columbia	91	26	15	33	22	48	82	17	F

1. As a percentage of all households that did not live in an apartment.
2. As a percentage of all households that had a lawn or garden.
3. As a percentage of those households who applied either chemical or organic fertilizer.
Source(s): Statistics Canada, Environment Accounts and Statistics Division, Households and the Environment Survey, 2007, CANSIM Table 153-0064.

Pesticide application strategies, Canada and provinces

	Pesticide application strategy							Pesticide applied by:		
	All pesticides			Applied organic pesticide		Applied chemical pesticide		Household member[1]	Lawn maintenance company[1]	Someone else[1]
	Regular schedule[1]	To address a specific problem[1]	Both regular maintenance and to address a specific problem[1]	Regular schedule[2]	To address a specific problem[2]	Regular schedule[3]	To address a specific problem[3]			
	percent									
Canada	39	61	2	45	54	38	63	70	27	3
Newfoundland and Labrador	36	65	F	F	F	39 E	59	76	F	F
Prince Edward Island	F	79	F	F	F	F	76	82	F	F
Nova Scotia	32	66	F	F	F	F	70	82	F	F
New Brunswick	40	56	F	F	F	40	54	68	26	F
Quebec	46	52	F	52	46	F	82	52	45	F
Ontario	47	54	3	47	55	46	54	63	35	3 E
Manitoba	28	73	F	F	65	27	73	81	17	F
Saskatchewan	33	68	F	F	F	34	67	86	11 E	F
Alberta	29	72	F	F	76	31	70	85	13	F
British Columbia	31	68	F	32	63	32	68	81	17	F

1. As a percentage of those households who applied either chemical or organic fertilizer.
2. As a percentage of those households that applied only organic pesticides.
3. As a percentage of those households who applied only chemical pesticides.

Source(s): Statistics Canada, Environment Accounts and Statistics Division, Households and the Environment Survey, 2007, CANSIM Table 153-0064.

Awareness of air quality advisories, Canada and provinces

	Aware of air quality advisories[1]	Changed behaviour due to advisory[2]	Did not change behaviour[2]
	percent		
Canada	34	44	55
Newfoundland and Labrador	F	F	F
Prince Edward Island	F	F	F
Nova Scotia	9	F	72
New Brunswick	14	49	49
Quebec	30	32	68
Ontario	58	51	49
Manitoba	16	46	54
Saskatchewan	3 E	F	56 E
Alberta	10	34	66
British Columbia	18	33	67

1. As a percentage of all households.
2. As a percentage of those households aware of air quality advisories.

Source(s): Statistics Canada, Environment Accounts and Statistics Division, Households and the Environment Survey, 2007, CANSIM Table 153-0065.

Pollution prevention methods by industry

	Product design or reformulation	Equipment or process modifications	Recirculation, recovery, reuse or recycling	Materials, feedstock or solvent substitution	Improved management or purchasing techniques	Prevention of leaks and spills	Good operating practices or training	Energy conservation	Other
					percent [1]				
1995	**10**	**32**	**64**	**33**	..	**50**	..	**37**	**5**
Logging	0	25	31	6	..	38	..	19	6
Crude petroleum and natural gas	7	39	48	42	..	71	..	77	10
Mining	5	25	50	36	..	59	..	39	7
Electric power systems	18	27	73	82	..	46	..	73	18
Food	4	26	69	13	..	51	..	33	1
Beverage	13	33	75	17	..	33	..	46	4
Pulp and paper	11	46	44	16	..	54	..	25	3
Refined petroleum and coal products	8	0	39	15	..	54	..	46	0
Chemicals	20	37	69	41	..	59	..	30	8
Non-metallic mineral products	19	23	68	34	..	49	..	38	9
Primary metals	9	51	65	42	..	42	..	37	7
Pipeline transport and gas distribution systems	8	23	62	39	..	69	..	77	0
Other manufacturing [2]	7	28	69	43	..	42	..	36	3
1996	**11**	**31**	**66**	**37**	..	**49**	..	**42**	**8**
Logging	4	4	46	17	..	63	..	25	0
Crude petroleum and natural gas	3	41	66	41	..	79	..	76	0
Mining	5	23	58	27	..	49	..	42	21
Electric power systems	12	24	77	59	..	47	..	82	6
Food and tobacco products	12	25	60	29	..	52	..	43	7
Beverage	13	43	83	15	..	38	..	43	5
Pulp and paper	5	41	47	27	..	51	..	37	13
Refined petroleum and coal products	13	13	50	19	..	75	..	44	13
Chemicals	20	36	71	43	..	62	..	30	17
Non-metallic mineral products	9	30	73	39	..	42	..	39	9
Primary metals	5	37	70	39	..	49	..	38	6
Transportation equipment	18	43	80	57	..	51	..	57	6
Pipeline transport and gas distribution systems	4	7	68	43	..	75	..	71	4
Other manufacturing [2]	13	29	72	40	..	39	..	38	4
1997	**15**	**24**	**64**	**37**	..	**51**	..	**42**	**10**
Logging	9	3	34	14	..	80	..	6	6
Crude petroleum and natural gas	34	40	74	49	..	94	..	66	6
Mining	4	23	59	24	..	50	..	54	3
Electric power systems	7	20	53	53	..	93	..	73	13
Food and tobacco products	14	30	67	30	..	63	..	59	6
Beverage	25	18	57	21	..	50	..	32	14
Wood products [3]	16	21	58	35	..	61	..	35	9
Pulp and paper	8	27	72	31	..	58	..	41	12
Refined petroleum and coal products	39	44	72	50	..	78	..	61	0
Chemicals	27	23	61	36	..	69	..	39	5
Non-metallic mineral products	12	25	75	31	..	39	..	33	8
Primary metals	11	43	70	37	..	51	..	54	2
Transportation equipment	19	32	64	56	..	57	..	56	5
Pipeline transport and gas distribution systems	17	11	50	44	..	78	..	72	11
Other manufacturing [2]	12	18	63	41	..	30	..	33	18
1998 [4]	**17**	**23**	**66**	**31**	..	**59**	..	**45**	**10**
Logging	0	15	33	3	..	82	..	12	3
Oil and gas extraction	27	35	71	40	..	88	..	75	6
Mining	6	18	67	21	..	53	..	42	8
Electric power generation, transmission and distribution	13	22	65	52	..	87	..	74	4
Natural gas distribution	0	25	38	25	..	75	..	63	0
Food	13	26	72	34	..	55	..	61	3
Beverage and tobacco products	8	16	50	24	..	63	..	50	11
Wood products [3]	23	25	62	22	..	58	..	40	12
Pulp, paper and paperboard mills	10	24	76	38	..	73	..	54	7
Petroleum and coal products	26	32	74	26	..	79	..	63	0
Chemicals	30	24	72	27	..	71	..	33	4
Non-metallic mineral products	18	20	67	27	..	49	..	51	9
Primary metals	14	28	82	31	..	55	..	54	6
Transportation equipment	21	25	69	51	..	69	..	56	9
Pipeline transportation [5]	25	25	58	33	..	92	..	75	0
Other manufacturing [2]	15	20	56	31	..	39	..	35	20

See footnotes at the end of the table.

Pollution prevention methods by industry – continued

	Product design or reformulation	Equipment or process modifications	Recirculation, recovery, reuse or recycling	Materials, feedstock or solvent substitution	Improved management or purchasing techniques	Prevention of leaks and spills	Good operating practices or training	Energy conservation	Other
					percent [1]				
2000 [6]	**24**	**48**	**67**	**34**	**42**	**73**	**79**	..	**14**
Logging	0	24	46	20	35	79	78	..	28
Oil and gas extraction	18	86	76	36	58	96	91	..	26
Mining	10	40	84	33	51	92	92	..	18
Electric power generation, transmission and distribution	21	40	62	39	55	79	84	..	19
Natural gas distribution	25	78	56	0	56	100	82	..	0
Food	22	46	61	26	36	65	72	..	12
Beverage and tobacco products	6	41	52	11	33	76	80	..	10
Wood products [3]	24	47	70	27	42	67	75	..	17
Pulp, paper and paperboard mills	17	68	83	36	34	87	89	..	16
Petroleum and coal products	48	54	76	34	44	91	94	..	6
Chemicals	40	54	77	40	45	82	88	..	15
Non-metallic mineral products	22	48	73	31	40	66	76	..	22
Primary metals	16	57	76	34	33	78	80	..	10
Fabricated metal products [7]	13	39	60	29	34	68	77	..	15
Transportation equipment	33	59	69	53	58	82	88	..	22
Pipeline transportation [5]	40	49	49	35	55	98	95	..	11
Other manufacturing [2]	26	40	56	37	41	55	67	..	11
2002 [6]	**22**	**49**	**65**	**31**	**37**	**70**	**74**	..	**16**
Logging	5	25	61	9	34	84	85	..	19
Oil and gas extraction	30	77	71	42	48	92	91	..	16
Mining	9	35	77	32	39	82	79	..	34
Electric power generation, transmission and distribution	14	38	63	36	34	80	78	..	16
Natural gas distribution	11	44	82	22	82	100	100	..	33
Food	16	16	55	21	25	66	69	..	17
Beverage and tobacco products	8	31	40	15	17	46	50	..	9
Wood products [3]	16	40	63	19	37	63	74	..	22
Pulp, paper and paperboard mills	10	70	81	30	30	85	90	..	21
Petroleum and coal products	39	63	72	47	43	85	84	..	0
Chemicals	16	40	63	25	35	78	79	..	13
Non-metallic mineral products	23	49	64	29	30	54	62	..	16
Primary metals	12	51	73	32	25	70	70	..	16
Fabricated metal products [7]	14	49	64	33	41	66	73	..	10
Transportation equipment	32	52	61	48	51	71	69	..	24
Pipeline transportation [5]	42	70	54	35	58	100	98	..	0
Other manufacturing [2]	29	48	62	38	43	59	66	..	11
2004 [6]	**20**	**47**	**62**	**28**	**36**	**67**	**69**	..	**19**
Logging	5	28	54	10	30	74	81	..	12
Oil and gas extraction	23	71	71	25	39	88	86	..	32
Mining	13	43	70	26	43	84	75	..	25
Electric power generation, transmission and distribution	16	37	59	38	48	73	70	..	25
Natural gas distribution	13	53	40	20	27	67	67	..	11
Food	14	45	51	18	31	58	68	..	12
Beverage and tobacco products	5	42	52	5	47	79	70	..	36
Wood products [3]	15	41	60	18	30	52	64	..	13
Pulp, paper and paperboard mills	11	56	71	26	26	74	76	..	28
Petroleum and coal products	48	69	79	36	52	93	89	..	0
Chemicals	30	55	66	27	38	78	78	..	10
Non-metallic mineral products	16	32	61	22	15	57	59	..	8
Primary metals	10	47	68	25	35	72	67	..	23
Fabricated metal products [7]	17	45	60	28	43	54	63	..	10
Transportation equipment	22	57	71	49	38	72	77	..	27
Pipeline transportation [5]	25	56	44	21	35	75	86	..	23
Other manufacturing [2]	26	45	59	37	38	56	59	..	25

1. Number of establishments indicating they used the pollution prevention method as a percentage of all establishments that provided a response.
2. Includes all other manufacturing industries not already specified.
3. Before 1997 the wood products industry was included with "other manufacturing".
4. Before the 1998 reference year, establishments were selected based on the 1980 Standard Industrial Classification System (SIC). However, beginning with reference year 1998, industry selection was based on the North American Industry Classification System (NAICS). For further information, see Statistics Canada, 2001, Environmental Protection Expenditures in the Business Sector 1998, catalogue no. 16F0006X.
5. Before the 1998 reference year, pipeline transportation was included with gas distribution systems.
6. As of reference year 1998, the Survey of Environmental Protection Expenditures is conducted every two years.
7. Before 2000 the fabricated metal products industry was included with "other manufacturing".

Note(s): This table includes reported data only. The question on pollution prevention methods differed in reference years 1995 and 1996. Therefore, comparisons from 1995 to 1998 provide a general view but should be treated with caution.

Source(s): Statistics Canada, Environment Accounts and Statistics Division, Environmental Protection Expenditures in the Business Sector, catalogue no. 16F0006X.

Pollution prevention methods by industry and province or territory, 2006

	Product design or reformulation	Equipment or process modifications	Recirculation, on-site recycling, reuse or recovery	Materials, feedstock or solvent substitution	Improved management or purchasing techniques	Prevention of leaks and spills	Good operating practices or training	Other	Total[1]
	percent								
Industry									
Logging	9	19	35	9	20	65	61	9	71
Oil and gas extraction	20	53	48	23	26	77	73	9	87
Mining	16	31	63	23	37	66	65	9	88
Electric power generation, transmission and distribution	23	19	67	28	45	75	75	6	86
Natural gas distribution	10	41	42	20	37	82	85	25	87
Food	9	28	26	4	18	38	42	8	59
Beverage and tobacco products	11	30	76	16	24	66	63	4	94
Wood products	7	7	33	10	17	32	36	5	61
Paper manufacturing	21	32	56	25	30	41	49	2	81
Petroleum and coal products	33	43	58	19	10	61	47	3	87
Chemicals	24	32	52	17	29	59	55	8	76
Non-metallic mineral products	11	19	47	12	24	45	38	10	78
Primary metals	18	46	70	23	28	63	74	5	92
Fabricated metal products	10	18	35	13	24	42	33	5	63
Transportation equipment	18	32	54	32	39	63	55	1	84
Other manufacturing	16	17	40	19	25	32	37	8	65
Pipeline transportation	26	60	58	7	37	95	95	7	95
Total	**14**	**21**	**41**	**16**	**25**	**41**	**42**	**7**	**68**
Province or territory									
Newfoundland and Labrador	10	13	26	12	18	25	29	7	45
Prince Edward Island	6	15	33	9	17	30	37	x	52
Nova Scotia	20	23	24	15	32	32	33	3	57
New Brunswick	13	13	37	11	23	52	46	5	69
Quebec	10	16	39	16	26	33	33	4	62
Ontario	18	25	44	18	25	43	44	8	73
Manitoba	13	21	41	18	22	41	43	8	66
Saskatchewan	8	19	28	15	19	41	34	4	61
Alberta	14	23	45	15	21	49	52	10	73
British Columbia	9	16	35	12	25	48	46	9	63
Yukon, Northwest Territories and Nunavut	15	26	40	29	25	44	46	x	70
Total	**14**	**21**	**41**	**16**	**25**	**41**	**42**	**7**	**68**

1. Percentage of establishments that used at least one pollution prevention method.
Source(s): Statistics Canada, Environment Accounts and Statistics Division.

Distribution of pollution prevention methods by establishment size, 2006

	Number of employees per establishment				
	Fewer than 50	50 to 99	100 to 499	500 to 999	More than 999
	percent				
Product design or reformulation	11	17	17	13	25
Equipment or process modifications	17	20	26	40	63
Recirculation, on-site recycling, reuse or recovery	33	46	49	64	74
Materials, feedstock or solvent substitution	13	16	20	29	50
Improved management or purchasing techniques	22	27	27	23	46
Prevention of leaks and spills	36	39	53	52	83
Good operating practices or training	37	38	55	52	82
Other	6	6	11	6	11
Total [1]	**63**	**68**	**76**	**86**	**97**

1. Percentage of establishments that used at least one pollution prevention method.
Note(s): This table excludes the 'pipeline transportation' industry category.
Source(s): Statistics Canada, Environment Accounts and Statistics Division.

Materials prepared for recycling by type and by province and territory, 2004[1]

	Canada	Newfoundland and Labrador	Prince Edward Island	Nova Scotia	New Brunswick	Quebec[2]	Ontario	Manitoba	Saskatchewan	Alberta	British Columbia	Yukon Territory, Northwest Territories and Nunavut
						tonnes						
Total	7,864,647	35,308	x	220,316	143,804	2,130,100	2,905,953	234,549	132,763	755,908	1,251,667	x
Newsprint	1,349,683	x	x	29,072	8,287	516,000	500,952	27,871	23,839	99,083	135,414	x
Cardboard and boxboard	1,367,011	x	x	12,510	13,758	402,000	540,791	51,214	26,265	99,515	193,045	x
Mixed paper	570,154	x	x	3,187	6,929	113,000	187,551	25,261	10,240	33,935	189,345	x
Glass	399,290	x	x	2,181	x	94,000	198,861	7,813	x	49,739	35,991	x
Ferrous metals	675,818	x	x	3,267	1,540	119,100	260,315	85,433	x	95,916	85,471	x
Copper and aluminum	49,289	x	x	x	x	11,000	22,140	x	x	x	5,870	x
Mixed metals	195,639	x	x	6,105	2,422	0	69,780	4,535	1,961	11,447	93,530	x
White Goods	236,786	x	x	4,584	x	183,000	26,178	x	x	12,108	x	0
Electronics	10,245	0	0	x	x	3,000	5,259	x	x	x	x	0
Plastics	188,307	x	x	4,234	1,111	72,000	54,306	4,255	3,082	10,372	38,623	x
Tires	139,331	0	x	x	x	62,000	6,441	3,569	16,467	8,602	38,508	x
Construction, renovation and demolition	848,197	x	x	59,355	14,984	288,000	303,277	x	13,234	27,926	140,514	x
Organics	1,669,145	0	x	93,458	90,585	225,000	644,586	20,995	x	290,959	265,514	x
Other materials	165,755	x	0	1,792	1,963	42,000	85,514	x	x	x	24,088	x

1. This information covers only those companies and local waste management organizations that reported non-hazardous recyclable material preparation activities and refers only to that material entering the waste stream and do not cover any waste that may be managed on-site by a company or household. Additionally, these data do not include those materials transported by the generator directly to secondary processors such as pulp and paper mills while bypassing entirely any firm or local government involved in waste management activities.
2. Waste diversion data are derived from a survey administered by RECYC-QUÉBEC.

Note(s): Figures may not add up to totals due to rounding.
Source(s): Statistics Canada, Environment Accounts and Statistics Division, Waste Management Industry Survey: Business and Government Sectors, catalogue no. 16F0023X.

Household participation in backyard composting and curbside organics collection, 2006

	Total households composting[1]	Kitchen waste composting[2]	Bin, pile or garden[3]	Collected curbside[3]	Yard waste composting[4]	Bin, pile or garden[5]	Collected curbside[5]
				%			
Newfoundland and Labrador	21	88	90	F	75	92	F
Prince Edward Island	91	95	24	89	61	30	78
Nova Scotia	69	95	41	73	71	48	63
New Brunswick	32	87	53	55	70	62	44
Quebec	13	76	85	11 [E]	84	74	26
Ontario	34	85	67	36	81	55	50
Manitoba	23	76	93	F	77	83	F
Saskatchewan	27	79	94	F	76	84	14 [E]
Alberta	22	71	90	7 [E]	84	72	22
British Columbia	30	76	94	6	87	79	20
Canada	**27**	**82**	**73**	**30**	**81**	**64**	**38**

1. Includes all households
2. As a percentage of the households composting.
3. As a percentage of the households composting kitchen waste.
4. As a percentage of the households composting. Only includes households that were not apartment building dwellers and that had a lawn or garden.
5. As a percentage of the households composting yard waste.

Source:
Environment Accounts and Statistics Division, Households and the Environment Survey, 2006.

Disposal of waste, by source and by province and territory, 2002, 2004 and 2006

	Residential sources [1]			Non-residential sources [2]			All sources		
	2002	2004	2006	2002	2004	2006	2002	2004	2006
	tonnes								
Canada	8,446,766	8,961,583	9,238,376	15,634,606	16,265,183	18,010,801	24,081,371	25,226,766	27,249,178
Newfoundland and Labrador	216,218	228,004	227,618	160,376	172,044	180,110	376,594	400,048	407,728
Prince Edward Island	x	x	x	x	x	x	x	x	x
Nova Scotia	169,649	179,262	169,337	219,546	220,705	232,333	389,194	399,967	401,670
New Brunswick	203,506	208,120	216,357	210,100	234,053	233,881	413,606	442,173	450,238
Quebec [3]	1,875,235	2,209,000	2,183,788	3,971,225	4,245,000	4,624,653	5,846,459	6,454,000	6,808,440
Ontario	3,438,408	3,489,917	3,705,235	6,207,225	6,319,347	6,732,545	9,645,633	9,809,264	10,437,780
Manitoba	412,612	450,658	455,304	483,944	477,459	568,968	896,556	928,117	1,024,272
Saskatchewan	278,692	279,420	296,062	516,432	515,513	537,691	795,124	794,933	833,753
Alberta	866,398	943,420	973,683	2,023,896	2,133,890	2,846,189	2,890,294	3,077,311	3,819,872
British Columbia	929,101	919,323	956,968	1,758,781	1,848,335	1,960,113	2,687,882	2,767,657	2,917,080
Yukon, Northwest Territories and Nunavut	x	x	x	x	x	x	x	x	x

1. Residential non-hazardous wastes disposed includes solid waste produced by all residences and includes waste that is picked up by the municipality (either using its own staff or through contracting firms), and waste from residential sources that is self-hauled to depots, transfer stations and disposal facilities.
2. Non-residential non-hazardous solid wastes are those wastes generated by all sources excluding the residential waste stream. These include: industrial materials, which are generated by manufacturing, and primary and secondary industries, and is managed off-site from the manufacturing operation; commercial materials, which are generated by commercial operations, such as, shopping centres, restaurants, offices, and others; and institutional materials which are generated by institutional facilities, such as, schools, hospitals, government facilities, seniors homes, universities, and others. These wastes also include construction, renovation and demolition non-hazardous waste, also referred to as DLC (demolition, land clearing and construction waste). These refer to wastes generated by construction, renovation and demolition activities. It generally includes materials, such as, wood, drywall, certain metals, cardboard, doors, windows, wiring, and others. It excludes materials from land clearing on areas not previously developed as well as materials that include asphalt, concrete, bricks and clean sand or gravel.
3. The waste disposal data prior to 2006 were derived from a survey administered by RECYC-QUÉBEC.

Note(s): Total amount of non-hazardous waste disposed of in public and private waste disposal facilities includes waste that is exported out of the source province or out of the country for disposal. This does not include wastes disposed in hazardous waste disposal facilities or wastes managed by the waste generator on site.

Source(s): Statistics Canada, CANSIM table 153-0041.

Treatment of unwanted computers or communication devices, by province, 2005

	Newfoundland and Labrador	Prince Edward Island	Nova Scotia	New Brunswick	Quebec	Ontario	Manitoba	Saskatchewan	Alberta	British Columbia	Canada
	%										
Households with unwanted computers or communication devices[1]	12	13	16	15	15	19	16	18	23	21	**18**
Donated or gave away, returned to a depot, drop-off centre or the supplier[2]	37	F	46	41	40	48	41	33	57	48	**47**
Put into the garbage[2]	F	F	23	F	16	18	19	14	7[E]	14	**16**
Still have it / did not know what to do with it[2]	40	F	28	36	41	31	39	48	34	37	**35**
Other[2,3]	F	F	F	F	5[E]	6	F	F	F	F	**5**

1. As a percentage of all households.
2. As a percentage of all households who reported having unwanted computers or communication devices in 2005. Respondents could indicate all that applied, therefore totals may exceed 100%.
3. Used a non-specified disposal method.

Source: Environment Accounts and Statistics Division, Households and the Environment Survey, 2006.

Disposal and diversion of waste, by province and territory
(Total waste disposal)

	2006	2008	2006 to 2008
	Total waste disposal[1]		
	tonnes		% change
Canada	**25,925,964**[r]	**25,871,310**	**-0.2**
Newfoundland and Labrador	428,809[r]	410,590	-4.2
Prince Edward Island	x	x	x
Nova Scotia	359,105[r]	354,231	-1.4
New Brunswick	511,706[r]	479,461	-6.3
Quebec	6,317,393[r]	6,158,152	-2.5
Ontario	9,710,459[r]	9,631,559	-0.8
Manitoba	904,272[r]	966,199	6.8
Saskatchewan	833,753	902,943	8.3
Alberta	3,819,872	4,029,435	5.5
British Columbia	2,917,080	2,811,568	-3.6
Yukon, Northwest Territories and Nunavut	x	x	x

x : suppressed to meet the confidentiality requirements of the *Statistics Act*
[r] : revised.
Note:
1. Total amount of non-hazardous waste disposal in public and private waste disposal facilities includes waste that is exported out of the source province or out of the country for disposal. This does not include waste disposal in hazardous waste disposal facilities or waste managed by the waste generator on site.
Source: Statistics Canada, Environment Accounts and Statistics Division, CANSIM table (for fee) 153-0041, Catalogue no. 16F0023X.
Last modified: 2010-12-22.

Disposal and diversion of waste, by province and territory
(Total materials diverted)

	2006	2008	2006 to 2008
	Total materials diverted[1]		
	tonnes		% change
Canada	7,727,030[r]	8,473,257	9.7
Newfoundland and Labrador	x	x	x
Prince Edward Island	x	x	x
Nova Scotia	275,983	289,950	5.1
New Brunswick	252,174	267,467	6.1
Quebec[2]	2,434,300[r]	2,463,600	1.2
Ontario	2,396,856	2,810,900	17.3
Manitoba	152,799	170,377	11.5
Saskatchewan	106,868	149,619	40.0
Alberta	652,637	728,536	11.6
British Columbia	1,366,191	1,505,112	10.2
Yukon, Northwest Territories and Nunavut	x	x	x

x : suppressed to meet the confidentiality requirements of the *Statistics Act*
[r] : revised.

Notes:
1. This information covers only those companies and local waste management organizations that reported non-hazardous recyclable material preparation activities and refers only to that material entering the waste stream and does not cover any waste that may be managed on-site by a company or household. Additionally, these data do not include those materials transported by the generator directly to secondary processors, such as, pulp and paper mills while bypassing entirely any firm or local government involved in waste management activities.
2. Waste diversion data are derived from a survey administered by RECYC-QUÉBEC.
Source: Statistics Canada, Environment Accounts and Statistics Division, CANSIM table (for fee) 153-0043, Catalogue no. 16F0023X.
Last modified: 2010-12-22.

Sample Tipping Fees by Province

Municipality	Tipping Fees (2010)	Landfill Site Capacity
Alberta		
City of Airdrie	Transfer site fee $20/ truckload(1/2 tonne)	n/a
City of Calgary	$64/tonne (basic sanitary waste, dry disposal waste); $86/tonne (industrial waste)	45 years
City of Camrose	$31.50/tonne	n/a
Town of Canmore	Varies	n/a
City of Cold Lake	$50/tonne (household/commercial waste); $50/tonne (mixed demolition waste)	2.5 years
City of Drumheller	$32.50/tonne (refuse); $37.50/tonne (demolition & industrial waste)	n/a
City of Edmonton	$46/tonne for Cloverbar Landfill; $60/ tonne Waste Management Landfill	5 years each, Cloverbar Landfill (city), Waste Management Landfill (private)
Foothills No. 31 Municipal District	$48/tonne (over 200 kg); $65/tonne (bulky waste)	n/a
Foothills Regional Services	$33/tonne	80 years
Grande Prairie No. 1 Municipal District	$52/tonne (county commercial & non-county)	n/a
Lacombe County Municipal District	$20/tonne (dry rubble)	n/a
Leduc County Municipal District	$27/tonne (regular residential waste)	14+ years
City of Lethbridge	$44.50-$57.50/tonne	23 years
City of Lloydminster	$10/tonne	n/a
City of Medicine Hat	$25/tonne	15-30 years
Mountain View County Municipal District	$100/tonne	n/a
Roseridge Waste Management Svcs Commission	$38.50/tonne	n/a
Sturgeon County Municipal District	Varies	100 years
City of Wetaskiwin	$53/tonne for residents, $95/tonne for non-residents	n/a
Wetaskiwin County No. 10 Municipal District	$85/tonne	100 years
Regional Municipality of Wood Buffalo	$43.11/tonne (household refuse & commercial waste); $52.06/tonne (waste requiring special handling)	4-10 years
British Columbia		
Alberni-Clayoquot Regional District	$95/tonne (domestic waste); $120/tonne (construction & demolition waste)	n/a
City of Burnaby	$71/tonne	n/a
City of Campbell River	Schedule depending on type of waste (from no fee to $350/tonne)	n/a
Capital Regional District	$95/tonne (general refuse)	n/a
Central Okanagan Regional District	$55/tonne	n/a
City of Chilliwack	$73/tonne; $125/tonne (for gypsum)	n/a
Columbia-Shuswap Regional District	$60/tonne	n/a
Comox-Strathcona Regional District	$65/tonne; $150/tonne (loads containing recyclables)	n/a
City of Coquitlam	$71/tonne	n/a
Cowichan Valley Regional District	$110/tonne	n/a
East Kootenay Regional District	No charge for household refuse; User fees apply at staffed facilities on most other loads	n/a
Fraser-Fort George Regional District	$46/tonne	n/a
Fraser Valley Regional District	$163.50/tonne (residents outside Electoral Area A)	n/a
Greater Vancouver Regional District	$65/tonne	5-10 & 30+ years
City of Kamloops	$25/tonne (loads greater than 250 kg)	n/a
City of Kelowna	$55/tonne	n/a
Kitimat-Stikine Regional District	$12.50 - $50 (truck volume)	5-30 years
Kootenay Boundary Regional District	$80/tonne (mixed refuse); $130/tonne (mixed demolition & construction waste)	n/a
Township of Langley	$71/tonne	n/a
District Municipality of Mission	$68/tonne	n/a
Mount Waddington Regional District	$2/can or bag (residential), $100/tonne (construction, 20 years demolition, wood waste)	n/a
Nanaimo Regional District	$105/tonne (solid waste); $210/tonne (controlled waste)	n/a
North Okanagan Regional District	$62/tonne	n/a
Okanagan-Similkameen Regional District	$55/tonne (general refuse); $200/tonne (demolition waste)	n/a
Town of Oliver	$55/tonne (general refuse); $75/tonne (demolition waste)	n/a
Peace River Regional District	$30/tonne or $2/cubic metre	8 years
City of Prince Rupert	$92/tonne	n/a
City of Quesnel	$15/1-ton truck	n/a
City of Richmond	$71/tonne	25 years; private site, owned by Ecowaste Industries
District Municipality of Squamish	$80/tonne	n/a
Squamish-Lillooet Regional District	$65.50/tonne & $12/cubic metre	n/a
District Municipality of Summerland	$55/tonne	n/a
Sunshine Coast Regional District	$95/tonne (residential & commercial waste); $140-$265 (construction waste)	n/a
City of Surrey	$71/tonne	n/a

Environmental Statistics / Waste

Municipality	Tipping Fees (2010)	Landfill Site Capacity
Thompson-Nicola Regional District	Varies, depending on size of load (demolition & land clearing debris only)	n/a
City of Vancouver	$71/tonne	40 years
City of Victoria	$82/tonne	44 years, Hartland Landfill
Manitoba		
City of Brandon	$42/tonne	50 years
Town of Carman	$60/1-ton truck	n/a
City of Portage La Prairie	$25/tonne	40 years
Rural Municipality of Springfield	$22.50/tonne	n/a
City of Winnipeg	$33.50/tonne	n/a
New Brunswick		
Cogerno Northwest	$55/tonne (household); $25/tonne (construction & demolition waste)	n/a
City of Fredericton	$66/tonne (household, ICI); $32/tonne (segregated construction & demolition waste)	n/a
Fredericton Region Solid Waste Commission	$66/tonne (residential/ICI); $32/tonne (construction/demolition material)	n/a
Fundy Region Solid Waste Commission	$108/tonne (municipal & commercial waste); $28/tonne (construction & demolition waste); $35/tonne (compostable material)	n/a
City of Moncton	$55.88/tonne (general mixed waste)	100 years
South West Solid Waste Commission	$68.50/tonne (household waste); $20/tonne (construction/demolition material)	n/a
Westmorland-Albert Solid Waste Corporation	$61.75/tonne (mixed waste); $23/tonne (construction & demolition waste)	n/a
Newfoundland & Labrador		
City of Corner Brook	Schedule as per type of vehicle & cubic meters	11 years
Northwest Territories		
City of Yellowknife	$15/tonne (regular domestic waste); $40/tonne (construction & demolition waste)	n/a
Nova Scotia		
Rural Municipality of Antigonish County	$100/tonne (refuse/garbage); $75/tonne (construction & demolition waste)	n/a
Rural Municipality of Colchester County	$75/tonne (mixed garbage)	70 years (Regional Balefill & Composting Facility, Kemptown)
Regional Municipality of Halifax	$115/tonne	22 years
Rural Municipality of Hants West District	$40/tonne	.5 year
Rural Municipality of Inverness County	$75/tonne	n/a
Rural Municipality of Lunenburg District	$110/tonne	n/a
Rural Municipality of Pictou County	$75/metric tonne; $55/tonne organics	n/a
Rural Municipality of Richmond County	$35/tonne (sorted material); $70/tonne (unsorted material)	
Town of Truro	$75/tonne (mixed garbage)	35 years
Rural Municipality of Yarmouth District	$110/tonne; $91.67/tonne for compost	n/a
Nunavut		
City of Iqaluit	$5/half-ton pick-up truck	n/a
Ontario		
City of Barrie	$155/tonne; $55.70/tonne (commercial brush and yard waste)	10 years
City of Belleville	$99/tonne	n/a
County of Brant	$74/tonne	n/a
City of Brantford	$65/tonne; $140/tonne for mixed loads of wood, metal, cardboard	60 years
City of Chatham-Kent, Municipality of	$60/tonne (Ridge Landfill); $55/tonne (Blenheim Landfill)	n/a
City of Clarence-Rockland	$70/1-7-ton truck	n/a
City of Cornwall	$55/tonne (regular waste, scrap metal & white goods)	35 years
Regional Municipality of Durham	$120/tonne for garbage & mixed loads; no charge for source-separated blue box materials & HHW	25 years
Township of Elizabethtown-Kitley	$25/quarter- to half-ton truck or 8 foot trailer	n/a
Essex County	$53/tonne (industrial, commercial & institutional); $41/tonne (yard waste)	n/a
Township of Georgian Bluffs	$75/tonne (sorted domestic, commercial & industrial materials); $100/tonne (unsorted)	n/a
Town of Greater Napanee	$10/utility trailers, cars, half & three-quarter-ton trucks	n/a
City of Greater Sudbury	$60/tonne	n/a
City of Guelph	$70/tonne; $74/tonne (yard waste - large/commercial vehicles)	n/a
Town of Haldimand, County of	$80/tonne	n/a
Regional Municipality of Halton	13.4 cents per kg (more than 150 kg)	38 years
City of Kawartha Lakes	$85/tonne	25 years
Township of King	$95/tonne	n/a
City of Kingston	$110/tonne	2 years
Lambton County	$45/tonne	county contracts with 2 active private landfills
Loyalist Township	$105/tonne	n/a

Environmental Statistics / Waste

Municipality	Tipping Fees (2010)	Landfill Site Capacity
Town of Meaford, Municipality of	$48-78/tonne	.9 years
Town of Mississippi Mills	$100/tonne	n/a
District Municipality of Muskoka	$115/tonne	n/a
Regional Municipality of Niagara	$80/tonne	6-25 years, various sites
Norfolk County	$80/tonne	12 years
City of North Bay	$65/tonne (Industrial/commercial/institutional)	n/a
Township of North Dundas	$10/cubic yard; $20/compacted yard	n/a
Township of North Glengarry	$50/ton, commercial & industrial waste	n/a
Municipality of North Perth	$65/1-ton truck, household waste	n/a
Northumberland County	$95/tonne (garbage/mixed loads)	n/a
Town of Orangeville	$85/tonne	n/a
City of Ottawa	$90/tonne	30 years
City of Owen Sound	$47.50/tonne, domestic waste; $70/tonne, commercial or industrial general waste	n/a
County of Oxford	61.32/tonne	18 years
City of Pembroke	$72.50/tonne	n/a
City of Peterborough	$85/tonne	25 years
Township of Rideau Lakes	$198/tonne	
Township of Russell	$12.50/cu metre	20 years
City of Sault Ste. Marie	$65/tonne	n/a
Township of South Dundas	$15/half or 3/4-ton pick-up; $55/construction material	n/a
Township of South Glengarry	$10/van, pickup truck, private car, utility trailer; $50/1-ton vehicle	n/a
Town of South Huron, Municipality of	$82/tonne	100 years
Township of South Stormont	$6/car; $8/van; $16/pick up truck; $23/1-ton truck; $28/hay wagon; $16/utility trailer	n/a
City of Stratford	$65.50/tonne	n/a
Township of Tay Valley	$50/cubic yard (construction & demolition)	n/a
Municipality of Thames Centre	$100/tonne, oversized non-recyclable waste; $20/recyclable waste	n/a
City of Thunder Bay	$42.12/tonne; $43.85/ tonne (contaminated soil)	n/a
City of Timmins	$50/5-ton truck; $150/tandem truck; $30/tonne (industrial, commercial, institutional)	n/a
Regional Municipality of Waterloo	$6.80/100 kg (general refuse); $13.60/100 kg (surcharge loads)	30 years (Waterloo), 8 years (Cambridge Waste Management Centre)
Wellington County	$70/tonne	n/a
City of Windsor	$58/tonne (garbage & household waste); $41/tonne (yard waste)	n/a
Regional Municipality of York	$80/tonne (residential); $95/tonne (industrial, commercial & institutional); $65/tonne (yard waste)	n/a
Municipality of The Nation	$4/car; $10/van; $35/farm wagon; $50/1-5 ton vehicle;	50 years
Québec		
Ville d'Amos	$60	n/a
Coaticook	n/a	30 years
Ville de Laval	$90/tonne	n/a
Régie intermunicipale des déchets de la Rouge	$80/tonne	5 years
Régie intermunicipale du comté de Beauce-Sud	$97/tonne	n/a
Ville de Rimouski	$30/tonne (industrial, commercial & institutional)	50 years
Ville de Rivière-du-Loup	$43.50/tonne	50 years
Ville de Rosemère	$23/tonne	n/a
Ville de Saguenay	$66/tonne	n/a
Ville de St-Eustache	$23/tonne	n/a
Saskatchewan		
Rural Municipality of Lumsden No. 189	$30/load (1-ton truck)	n/a
City of North Battleford	$40/tonne	50 years
City of Prince Albert	$30/tonne (residual waste); $42/tonne (non-reusable construction & demolition materials)	100 years
City of Regina	$38/tonne	30-40 years
City of Saskatoon	$50/tonne (solid waste); $58/tonne (special waste)	n/a
City of Swift Current	$22/tonne (regular waste)	n/a
Yukon		
City of Whitehorse	$5/pick-up truckload	n/a

Indoor water conservation practices, by province

	Had a low-volume toilet [1]	Had a low-flow shower head [1]	Municipal water supply		Non-municipal water supply	
			Had a low-volume toilet [2]	Had a low-flow shower head [2]	Had a low-volume toilet [3]	Had a low-flow shower head [3]
			percent			
Canada	**42**	**63**	**42**	**62**	**48**	**65**
Newfoundland and Labrador	30	59	30	56	F	79
Prince Edward Island	31	60	29	59	35	62
Nova Scotia	39	66	37	61	43	75
New Brunswick	38	67	36	66	40	69
Quebec	34	64	33	65	45	61
Ontario	48	65	48	65	54	67
Manitoba	39	49	39	48	44	61
Saskatchewan	42	51	42	51	43 E	48
Alberta	46	58	46	59	46	57
British Columbia	40	60	39	59	54	67

1. As a percentage of all households.
2. As a percentage of households that had a municipal water supply.
3. As a percentage of households that had a non-municipal water supply.

Source(s): Statistics Canada, Environment Accounts and Statistics Division, Households and the Environment Survey, 2009 (survey number 3881).

Trade Shows, Conferences and Seminars

Conferences, seminars, & trade shows are listed by year, month, & day for 2011 and beyond. In cases where specific dates were not provided, the entry appears at the beginning of the month; in cases where only a year was provided, the entry appears at the end of that year. Listings include association annual general meetings, government-sponsored events, industry trade shows, & international meetings. Changes do occur; you are encouraged to verify dates & locations before planning to attend.

Listings may include:
- date
- name of event
- location (facility, city, province, country)
- sponsor / host organization
- scope of the meeting
- description of the event, if available
- contact for the event

Full details on Canadian organizations sponsoring events or conferences may be found in Section 3.

2011

June

Air & Waste Management Association 104th Annual Conference & Exhibition
Date: June 21-24, 2011
Location: Orlando, FL USA
Sponsor/Contact: Air & Waste Management Association
One Gateway Center
420 Fort Duquesne Blvd., 3rd Fl.
Pittsburgh, PA USA
412-232-3444 Fax: 412-232-3450
E-mail: info@awma.org
URL: www.awma.org
Scope: International

Alberta Irrigation Projects Association 2011 Irrigation Technical Conference
Date: June 9, 2011
Location: Lethbridge Lodge Hotel
Lethbridge, AB
Sponsor/Contact: Alberta Irrigation Projects Association
#909, 400 - 4 Ave. South
Lethbridge, AB T1K 7H5
403-328-3063 Fax: 403-327-1043
E-mail: info@aipa.org
URL: www.aipa.org
Scope: Provincial
Contact Information: Administrator: Vicky Kress, Phone: 403-328-3063, E-mail: vicky.kress@aipa.org

American Society of Mechanical Engineers 2011 Annual Meeting
Date: June 10-15, 2011
Location: The Intercontinental Dallas
Dallas, TX USA
Sponsor/Contact: American Society of Mechanical Engineers
3 Park Ave.
New York, NY USA
800-843-2763
E-mail: infocentral@asme.org
URL: www.asme.org
Scope: International
Purpose: An opportunity for engineering professionals to exchange infomation about common challegnes & to learn about developments for the future of the profession
Contact Information: 2011 Annual Meeting Contact: Melissa Torees, Phone: 212-591-8257, E-mail: Torresm@asme.org

American Society of Mechanical Engineers 2011 Emergency Operations & Hoistway Committee Meetings
Date: June 7-9, 2011
Location: Courtyard Marriott Québec
Québec, QC
Sponsor/Contact: American Society of Mechanical Engineers
3 Park Ave.
New York, NY USA
800-843-2763
E-mail: infocentral@asme.org
URL: www.asme.org
Scope: International
Contact Information: Meeting Contact: Allysob Byk, E-mail: BykA@asme.org

American Society of Mechanical Engineers 2011 Escalator & Moving Walk Committee Meeting
Date: June 15, 2011
Location: Marriott Chateau Champlain
Montréal, QC
Sponsor/Contact: American Society of Mechanical Engineers
3 Park Ave.
New York, NY USA
800-843-2763
E-mail: infocentral@asme.org
URL: www.asme.org
Scope: International
Contact Information: Meeting Contact: Riad Mohamed, E-mail: mohamedr@asme.org

American Society of Mechanical Engineers 2011 Gas Transmission & Distribution Piping System Meeting
Date: June 7-9, 2011
Location: St. Louis Union Station Marriott
St. Louis, MO USA
Sponsor/Contact: American Society of Mechanical Engineers
3 Park Ave.
New York, NY USA
800-843-2763
E-mail: infocentral@asme.org
URL: www.asme.org
Scope: International
Contact Information: Meeting Contact: Robert Horvath, E-mail: HorvathR@asme.org

American Society of Mechanical Engineers 2011 Summer Bioengineering Conference
Date: June 21-26, 2011
Sponsor/Contact: American Society of Mechanical Engineers
3 Park Ave.
New York, NY USA
800-843-2763
E-mail: infocentral@asme.org
URL: www.asme.org
Scope: International

American Society of Mechanical Engineers 2011 Turbo Expo
Date: June 6-10, 2011
Location: Vancouver Convention & Exhibition Centre
Vancouver, BC
Sponsor/Contact: American Society of Mechanical Engineers
3 Park Ave.
New York, NY USA
800-843-2763
E-mail: infocentral@asme.org
URL: www.asme.org
Scope: International
Purpose: A technical conference & exhibition of turbine products & services for turbomachinery colleagues from around the globe
Anticipated Attendance: 3000
Contact Information: Program Contact: Stephanie (Sears) Partain, E-mail: Partains@asme.org; Exposition & Sponsoship Contact: Kristin Barranger, E-mail: barrangerk@asme.org

American Society of Mechanical Engineers 2011 Wind Turbine Project Team Meeting
Date: June 14-16, 2011
Location: Holiday Inn Toronto Downtown
Toronto, ON
Sponsor/Contact: American Society of Mechanical Engineers
3 Park Ave.
New York, NY USA
800-843-2763
E-mail: infocentral@asme.org
URL: www.asme.org
Scope: International
Contact Information: Meeting Contact: Geraldine Burdeshaw, E-mail: burdeshawg@asme.org

American Water Works Association 2011 130th Annual Conference & Exposition
Date: June 12-16, 2011
Location: Walter E. Washington Convention Center
Washington, DC USA
Sponsor/Contact: American Water Works Association
6666 West Quincy Ave.
Denver, CO USA
303-794-7711 Fax: 303-347-0804
E-mail: custsvc@awwa.org
URL: www.awwa.org
Scope: International
Purpose: Information about water for association members & associated professionals, featuring sustainability events, technical programs, workshops, presentations by experts, poster sessions, continuing education units, facility tours, & exhibits
Contact Information: Director of Conferences & Events: April DeBaker, E-mail: adebaker@awwa.org; Manager, Conference & Exhibits: Lynn Lyons, E-mail: llyons@awwa.org; Conference & Promotion Manager: Joanne Gaglia, E-mail: jgaglia@awwa.org; Event Operations Supervisor: Lisa Star, E-mail: lstar@awwa.org

Association of Professional Engineers & Geoscientists of British Columbia Seminar: Hydraulic Network Modeling of Sanitary Sewer Collection Systems
Date: June 17, 2011
Location: Vancouver, BC
Sponsor/Contact: Association of Professional Engineers & Geoscientists of British Columbia
#200, 4010 Regent St.
Burnaby, BC V5C 6N2
604-430-8035 Fax: 604-430-8085
E-mail: apeginfo@apeg.bc.ca; communication@apeg.bc.ca
URL: www.apeg.bc.ca
Scope: Provincial
Purpose: A training session about hydraulic modeling to assist utilities
Contact Information: Professional Development Coordinator: Sabine Just, Phone: 604-412-4861, E-mail: sjust@apeg.bc.ca

British Columbia Food Technolgists Meeting: Banquet & Golf Tournament
Date: June 2, 2011
Location: Greenacres Golf Course
Richmond, BC
Sponsor/Contact: British Columbia Food Technolgists
c/o Nealanders International Inc.
#201, 7950 Huston Rd.
Delta, BC V4G 1C2

Trade Shows, Conferences and Seminars

604-940-4181
E-mail: info@bcft.ca; membership@bcft.ca; newsletter@bcft.ca
URL: www.bcft.ca
Scope: Provincial
Purpose: A networking opportunity for technologists & quality assurance providers in British Columbia's food industry
Contact Information: Chair, Banquet & Program Committee: Nancy Ross, E-mail: info@foodquality.ca; Event Registration Contact: Christine Scaman, E-mail: christine.scaman@ubc.ca

British Columbia Nature (Federation of British Columbia Naturalists) 2011 Manning Park Bird Blitz
Date: June 17-19, 2011
Location: British Columbia
Sponsor/Contact: British Columbia Nature (Federation of British Columbia Naturalists)
c/o Parks Heritage Centre
1620 Mount Seymour Rd.
North Vancouver, BC V7G 2R9
604-985-3057
E-mail: manager@bcnature.ca
URL: www.bcnature.ca
Scope: Provincial
Purpose: An event co-sponsored by the Hope Mountain Centre for Outdoor Learning
Contact Information: Office Manager: Betty Davison, E-mail: manager@bcnature.ca

British Columbia Recreation & Parks Association 2011 37th Leisure Development Course
Date: June 8-12, 2011
Location: British Columbia
Sponsor/Contact: British Columbia Recreation & Parks Association
#101, 4664 Lougheed Hwy.
Burnaby, BC V5C 5T5
604-629-0965 Fax: 604-629-2651
E-mail: bcrpa@bcrpa.bc.ca; registration@bcrpa.bc.ca
URL: www.bcrpa.bc.ca
Scope: Provincial
Purpose: Professional development learning for park, recreation, culture, & community development personnel
Anticipated Attendance: 40
Contact Information: E-mail: cnelson48@shaw.ca

Canada - Ontario Environmental Farm Plan Program 2011 Bruce County Workshop
Date: June 1 & 8, 2011
Location: Bruce County, ON
Sponsor/Contact: Ontario Soil & Crop Improvement Association
1 Stone Rd. West
Guelph, ON N1G 4Y2
519-826-4214 Fax: 519-826-4224
E-mail: oscia@ontariosoilcrop.org
URL: www.ontariosoilcrop.org
Scope: Local
Purpose: A voluntary education program
Contact Information: Ontario Soil & Crop Improvement Association Program Representative: Jayne Dietrich, Phone: 519-367-5930, E-mail: bruce@ontariosoilcrop.org

Canada - Ontario Environmental Farm Plan Program 2011 Grenville Area Workshop
Date: June 7 & 14, 2011
Location: Kemptville, ON
Sponsor/Contact: Ontario Soil & Crop Improvement Association
1 Stone Rd. West
Guelph, ON N1G 4Y2
519-826-4214 Fax: 519-826-4224
E-mail: oscia@ontariosoilcrop.org
URL: www.ontariosoilcrop.org
Scope: Local
Purpose: A workshop for farm families
Contact Information: Ontario Soil & Crop Improvement Association Program Representative: Arlene Ross, Phone: 613-821-3900, E-mail: grenville@ontariosoilcrop.org

Canada - Ontario Environmental Farm Plan Program 2011 Grey County Workshop
Date: June 13 & 20, 2011
Location: Markdale, ON
Sponsor/Contact: Ontario Soil & Crop Improvement Association
1 Stone Rd. West
Guelph, ON N1G 4Y2
519-826-4214 Fax: 519-826-4224
E-mail: oscia@ontariosoilcrop.org
URL: www.ontariosoilcrop.org
Scope: Local
Purpose: The Risk Assessment & Action Plan provides the opportunity to rate the level of environmental concern in up to 23 different areas of a farm
Contact Information: Ontario Soil & Crop Improvement Association Program Representative: Ray Robertson, Phone: 519-986-3756, E-mail: grey@ontariosoilcrop.org

Canada - Ontario Environmental Farm Plan Program 2011 Perth Area Workshop
Date: June 7 & 14, 2011
Location: Milverton, ON
Sponsor/Contact: Ontario Soil & Crop Improvement Association
1 Stone Rd. West
Guelph, ON N1G 4Y2
519-826-4214 Fax: 519-826-4224
E-mail: oscia@ontariosoilcrop.org
URL: www.ontariosoilcrop.org
Scope: Local
Purpose: Instruction on how to progress through the Risk Assessment & Action Plan development in the third edition of the Environmental Farm Plan workbook
Contact Information: Ontario Soil & Crop Improvement Association Program Representative: Sharon Diehl, Phone: 519-595-4896, E-mail: perth@ontariosoilcrop.org

Canada Green Building Council 2011 Annual General Meeting
Date: June 2, 2011
Location: Pantages Hotel Toronto Centre
Toronto, ON
Sponsor/Contact: Canada Green Building Council
#202, 47 Clarence St.
Ottawa, ON K1N 9K1
613-241-1184 Fax: 613-241-4782
E-mail: info@cagbc.org; education@cagbc.org
URL: www.cagbc.org
Scope: National
Purpose: Featuring the financial report, the president's report, governance review, question period, the appointment of auditors, & guest speaker Peter Wilson, the Vice-President of Project Delivery for Infrastructure Ontario
Contact Information: E-mail: info@cagbc.org

Canada Green Building Council 2011 Building Tour
Date: June 8, 2011
Location: Oxfam Canada Headquarters
Ottawa, ON
Sponsor/Contact: Canada Green Building Council
#202, 47 Clarence St.
Ottawa, ON K1N 9K1
613-241-1184 Fax: 613-241-4782
E-mail: info@cagbc.org; education@cagbc.org
URL: www.cagbc.org
Scope: Provincial
Purpose: A tour of the Oxfam National Headquarters, a building that achieved LEED-CI Gold, followed by an opportunity to meet the CaGBC board of directors, fellow green building professionals, & clients at Dow's Lake Pavillion
Contact Information: E-mail: Teresa@livearchitecture.ca

Canada Green Building Council 2011 Course: Design Installation & Management of Rainwater Harvesting Systems
Date: June 7, 2011
Location: Earth Rangers' Centre (Theatre)
Woodbridge, ON
Sponsor/Contact: Canada Green Building Council
#202, 47 Clarence St.
Ottawa, ON K1N 9K1
613-241-1184 Fax: 613-241-4782
E-mail: info@cagbc.org; education@cagbc.org
URL: www.cagbc.org
Scope: Provincial
Purpose: A course of interest to builders, designers, architects, contractors, regulators, & anyone interested in learning about the regulatory & technical aspects of rainwater harvesting systems for residential & industrial, commercial, & institutional buildings
Contact Information: E-mail: mrochon@cagbc.org; info@cagbc.org

Canada Green Building Council 2011 Green Associate Study Course
Date: June 1-2, 2011
Location: Blackfoot Inn
Calgary, AB
Sponsor/Contact: Canada Green Building Council
#202, 47 Clarence St.
Ottawa, ON K1N 9K1
613-241-1184 Fax: 613-241-4782
E-mail: info@cagbc.org; education@cagbc.org
URL: www.cagbc.org
Scope: Provincial
Purpose: A workshop with lectures & group activities
Contact Information: E-mail: mrochon@cagbc.org; info@cagbc.ca

Canada Green Building Council 2011 Green Associate Study Course
Date: June 2-3, 2011
Location: Delta Beausejour
Moncton, NB
Sponsor/Contact: Canada Green Building Council
#202, 47 Clarence St.
Ottawa, ON K1N 9K1
613-241-1184 Fax: 613-241-4782
E-mail: info@cagbc.org; education@cagbc.org
URL: www.cagbc.org
Scope: Provincial
Purpose: An educational program in preparation for the Green Associate exam
Contact Information: E-mail: mrochon@cagbc.org; info@cagbc.org

Canada Green Building Council 2011 Green Associate Study Course
Date: June 14-15, 2011
Location: Telsec Business Centre
Toronto, ON
Sponsor/Contact: Canada Green Building Council
#202, 47 Clarence St.
Ottawa, ON K1N 9K1
613-241-1184 Fax: 613-241-4782
E-mail: info@cagbc.org; education@cagbc.org
URL: www.cagbc.org
Scope: Provincial
Purpose: Lectures, group activities, & practice test questions
Contact Information: E-mail: mrochon@cagbc.org; info@cagbc.ca

Canada Green Building Council 2011 Green Associate Study Course
Date: June 15-16, 2011
Location: Vancouver Island Technology Park
Victoria, BC
Sponsor/Contact: Canada Green Building Council
#202, 47 Clarence St.
Ottawa, ON K1N 9K1
613-241-1184 Fax: 613-241-4782
E-mail: info@cagbc.org; education@cagbc.org
URL: www.cagbc.org
Scope: Provincial
Purpose: An educational program meetings eligibility requirements for the Green Associate exam
Contact Information: E-mail: mrochon@cagbc.org; info@cagbc.ca

Trade Shows, Conferences and Seminars

Canada Green Building Council 2011 LEED Canada Documentation Course
Date: June 7, 2011
Location: Ottawa, ON
Sponsor/Contact: Canada Green Building Council
#202, 47 Clarence St.
Ottawa, ON K1N 9K1
613-241-1184 Fax: 613-241-4782
E-mail: info@cagbc.org; education@cagbc.org
URL: www.cagbc.org
Scope: Provincial
Purpose: An interactive workshop for applicants seeking the CaGBC LEED project certification for New Construction
Contact Information: E-mail: mrochon@cagbc.org; info@cagbc.org

Canada Green Building Council 2011 Living Building Challenge
Date: June 23, 2011
Location: Edmonton, AB
Sponsor/Contact: Canada Green Building Council
#202, 47 Clarence St.
Ottawa, ON K1N 9K1
613-241-1184 Fax: 613-241-4782
E-mail: info@cagbc.org; education@cagbc.org
URL: www.cagbc.org
Scope: Provincial
Purpose: An introductory presentation about the Living Building Challenge program for advanced practitioners
Contact Information: E-mail: mrochon@cagbc.org; info@cagbc.ca

Canada Green Building Council 2011 Workshop: LEED Canada for Existing Buildings, Operations & Maintenance
Date: June 9, 2011
Location: Granville Island Hotel
Vancouver, BC
Sponsor/Contact: Canada Green Building Council
#202, 47 Clarence St.
Ottawa, ON K1N 9K1
613-241-1184 Fax: 613-241-4782
E-mail: info@cagbc.org; education@cagbc.org
URL: www.cagbc.org
Scope: Provincial
Purpose: A technical review of the LEED Canada for Existing Buildings, Operations & Maintenance Rating System
Contact Information: E-mail: mrochon@cagbc.org; info@cagbc.ca

Canada Green Building Council 2011 Workshop: LEED Canada for New Construction 2009, Technical Review
Date: June 9, 2011
Location: Sutton Place Hotel
Edmonton, AB
Sponsor/Contact: Canada Green Building Council
#202, 47 Clarence St.
Ottawa, ON K1N 9K1
613-241-1184 Fax: 613-241-4782
E-mail: info@cagbc.org; education@cagbc.org
URL: www.cagbc.org
Scope: Provincial
Purpose: An interactive workshop featuring case studies
Contact Information: E-mail: mrochon@cagbc.org; info@cagbc.ca

Canada Green Building Council 2011 Workshop: Solar Energy, Best Practices for Residential Buildings
Date: June 28, 2011
Location: Earth Rangers' Centre (Theatre)
Woodbridge, ON
Sponsor/Contact: Canada Green Building Council
#202, 47 Clarence St.
Ottawa, ON K1N 9K1
613-241-1184 Fax: 613-241-4782
E-mail: info@cagbc.org; education@cagbc.org
URL: www.cagbc.org
Scope: Provincial
Purpose: Best practices for designing & installing residential solar water heating & photovoltaic systems.
Contact Information: E-mail: mrochon@cagbc.org; info@cagbc.ca

Canadian Association of Chemical Distributors 2011 25th Annual General Meeting
Date: June 15-17, 2011
Location: Delta St. John's
St. John's, NL
Sponsor/Contact: Canadian Association of Chemical Distributors
349 Davis Rd., #A
Oakville, ON L6J 2X2
905-844-9140 Fax: 905-844-5706
URL: www.cacd.ca
Scope: National
Contact Information: Manager, Communications & Member Services: Catherine Wieckowska, Phone: 905-844-9140, E-mail: catherine@cacd.ca

Canadian Association of Recycling Industries (CARI) 2011 70th Annual General Meeting & Convention: Beyond North America
Date: June 23-25, 2011
Location: Fairmont Chateau Whistler
Whistler, BC
Sponsor/Contact: Canadian Association of Recycling Industries
#1, 682 Monarch Ave.
Ajax, ON L1S 4S2
905-426-9313 Fax: 905-426-9314
URL: www.cari-acir.org
Scope: National
Purpose: A convention to explore the theme of global scrap export, with information about new world trading markets, a consumers' panel on the state of the copper, aluminum, & ferrous industries, a keynote speaker on economics, & networking opportunities
Contact Information: President: Bertrand Van Dorpe, Phone: 450-658-2183, Fax: 450-658-1461, E-mail: rouvillestation@videotron.ca

Canadian College of Health Leaders & the Canadian Healthcare Association's 2011 National Healthcare Leadership Conference
Date: June 6-7, 2011
Location: Whistler, BC
Sponsor/Contact: Canadian College of Health Leaders
292 Somerset St. West
Ottawa, ON K2P 0J6
613-235-7218 Fax: 613-235-5451
E-mail: info@cchl-ccls.ca; communications@cchse.org
URL: www.cchl-ccls.ca
Scope: National
Purpose: "Rising to the Challenge - Resources, Realities, & Relationships": A conference for Canada's health system decision-makers, such as directors, trustees, chief executive officers, managers, & department heads, from health regions, hospitals, long-term care organizations, community care organizations, & public health agencies
Contact Information: Coordinator, Conference Services, Canadian College of Health Leaders: Laurie Oman, Phone: 613-235-7218, Toll-Free Phone: 1-800-363-9056, ext. 37, E-mail: loman@cchl-ccls.ca; Manager, Conference Services, Cdn College of Health Leaders: Francine St-Martin, Phone: 613-235-7218, Toll-Free Phone: 1-800-363-9056, ext. 12, E-mail: fst-martin@cchl-ccls.ca

Canadian College of Health Leaders 2011 Annual General Meeting
Date: June 5, 2011
Location: Whistler, BC
Sponsor/Contact: Canadian College of Health Leaders
292 Somerset St. West
Ottawa, ON K2P 0J6
613-235-7218 Fax: 613-235-5451
E-mail: info@cchl-ccls.ca; communications@cchse.org
URL: www.cchl-ccls.ca
Scope: National
Purpose: A business meeting & awards ceremony to recognize recipients of the College's Honorary Life Member Award, the Chair's Award for Distinguished Service, the Chapter Awards for Distinguished Service, the President's Award for Outstanding Corporate Membership in the College, & the CHE Self-directed Learning Paper Award
Contact Information: Manager, Awards & Sponsorships, Canadian College of Health Leaders: Cindy MacBride, Phone: 613-235-7218, ext. 13, Toll-Free Phone: 1-800-363-9056, Fax: 613-235-5451, E-mail: cmacbride@cchl-ccls.ca

Canadian College of Health Leaders 2011 National Awards Gala
Date: June 5, 2011
Location: Whistler, BC
Sponsor/Contact: Canadian College of Health Leaders
292 Somerset St. West
Ottawa, ON K2P 0J6
613-235-7218 Fax: 613-235-5451
E-mail: info@cchl-ccls.ca; communications@cchse.org
URL: www.cchl-ccls.ca
Scope: National
Purpose: A ceremony to honour winners of the the Energy & Environmental Stewardship Award, the Health Care Safety Award, the Innovation Award for Health Care Leadership, the Mentorship Award, the Nursing Leadership Award, the Quality of Life Award, & the Robert Zed Young Health Leader Award
Contact Information: Manager, Awards & Sponsorships, Canadian College of Health Leaders: Cindy MacBride, Phone: 613-235-7218, ext. 13, Toll-Free Phone: 1-800-363-9056, Fax: 613-235-5451, E-mail: cmacbride@cchl-ccls.ca

Canadian Gas Association 2011 Gas Measurement School
Date: June 5-8, 2011
Location: Fairmont Winnipeg
Winnipeg, MB
Sponsor/Contact: Canadian Gas Association
#809, 350 Sparks St.
Ottawa, ON K1R 7S8
613-748-0057 Fax: 613-748-9078
E-mail: info@cga.ca
URL: www.cga.ca
Scope: National
Purpose: Presentations, technical papers, & panel discussions by industry experts, as well as manufactuer exhibits & a new product showcase
Contact Information: E-mail: help@canavents.com

Canadian Heavy Oil Association Technical Event: Drilling & Completions
Date: June 14, 2011
Location: Calgary, AB
Sponsor/Contact: Canadian Heavy Oil Association
#400, 500 - 5th Ave. SW
Calgary, AB T2P 3L5
403-269-1755 Fax: 403-453-0179
E-mail: office@choa.ab.ca
URL: www.choa.ab.ca
Scope: National
Purpose: A technical meeting featuring a guest speaker
Contact Information: Event Coordinator: Georgia A. Hasapes, Phone: 403-269-1755, Fax: 403-453-0179, E-mail: office@choa.ab.ca

Canadian Institute of Chartered Accountants 2011 Financial Services Course
Date: June 20-21, 2011
Location: CICA Offices
Toronto, ON
Sponsor/Contact: Canadian Institute of Chartered Accountants
277 Wellington St. West
Toronto, ON M5V 3H2
416-977-3222 Fax: 416-977-8585
URL: www.cica.ca

Trade Shows, Conferences and Seminars

Scope: National
Purpose: Topics include definitions, GST compliance for financial institutions, & special rules for seizures & repossessions
Contact Information: Principal, Conferences & Courses, Continuing Education: Steve Johnston, Phone: 416-204-3332, E-mail: steve.johnston@cica.ca; Manager, Conferences & Courses, Continuing Ed.: Kieran Murphy, Phone: 416-204-3337, E-mail: kieran.murphy@cica.ca; Registrar, Conferences & Courses, Continuing Ed.: Liza Cruz, Phone: 416-204-3263, E-mail: liza.cruz@cica.ca

Canadian Institute of Chartered Accountants 2011 In-depth Course on GHG Emissions - Risk, Reporting, & Assurance
Date: June 6-8, 2011
Location: Calgary Telus Convention Centre
Calgary, AB
Sponsor/Contact: Canadian Institute of Chartered Accountants
277 Wellington St. West
Toronto, ON M5V 3H2
416-977-3222 Fax: 416-977-8585
URL: www.cica.ca
Scope: National
Purpose: Issues pertaining to Green House Gas (GHG) emissions & related environmental matters, of interest to chartered accountants, engineers, & other professionals who provide consulting services in the area of GHG / carbon emissions
Contact Information: Manager, Conferences & Courses, Continuing Education: Jennifer McEdwards, Phone: 416-204-3338, E-mail: jennifer.mcedwards@cica.ca; Registrar, Conferences & Courses, Continuing Education: Liza Cruz, Phone: 416-204-3263, E-mail: liza.cruz@cica.ca

Canadian Institute of Chartered Accountants 2011 In-depth GST/HST Course
Date: June 5-10, 2011
Location: Pillar & Post Inn
Niagara-on-the-Lake, ON
Sponsor/Contact: Canadian Institute of Chartered Accountants
277 Wellington St. West
Toronto, ON M5V 3H2
416-977-3222 Fax: 416-977-8585
URL: www.cica.ca
Scope: National
Purpose: A course of interest to novice GST advisors in practice or manager in industry or government
Contact Information: Principal, Conferences & Courses, Continuing Education: Steve Johnston, Phone: 416-204-3332, E-mail: steve.johnston@cica.ca; Manager, Conferences & Courses, Continuing Ed.: Kieran Murphy, Phone: 416-204-3337, E-mail: kieran.murphy@cica.ca; Registrar, Conferences & Courses, Continuing Ed.: Liza Cruz, Phone: 416-204-3263, E-mail: liza.cruz@cica.ca

Canadian Institute of Chartered Accountants 2011 Income Tax Brief: The Changing Tax Landscape Faced By High Net Worth Individuals
Date: June 2, 2011
Location: Toronto Board of Trade
Toronto, ON
Sponsor/Contact: Canadian Institute of Chartered Accountants
277 Wellington St. West
Toronto, ON M5V 3H2
416-977-3222 Fax: 416-977-8585
URL: www.cica.ca
Scope: National
Purpose: A presentation, panel discussion, & question & answer session
Contact Information: Principal, Conferences & Courses, Continuing Education: Vivian Leung, Phone: 416-204-3332, E-mail: vivan.leung@cica.ca; Manager, Conferences & Courses, Continuing Education: Kieran Murphy, Phone: 416-204-3337, E-mail: kieran.murphy@cica.ca; Registrar, Conferences & Courses, Continuing Ed.: Liza Cruz, Phone: 416-204-3263; E-mail: liza.cruz@cica.ca

Canadian Institute of Chartered Accountants 2011 Workshop: IFRS Implementation for the Mining Industry
Date: June 15-16, 2011
Location: Segal Graduate School of Business, SFU
Vancouver, BC
Sponsor/Contact: Canadian Institute of Chartered Accountants
277 Wellington St. West
Toronto, ON M5V 3H2
416-977-3222 Fax: 416-977-8585
URL: www.cica.ca
Scope: National
Purpose: Information for accounting professionals about IFRS transition issues for small to medium sized mining companies
Contact Information: Principal, Conferences & Courses, Continuing Education: Pam Robertson, Phone: 416-204-3296, E-mail: pam.robertson@cica.ca; Manager, Conferences & Courses, Continuing Education: Sheri Price, Phone: 416-204-3425, E-mail: sheri.price@cica.ca; Registrar, Conferences & Courses, Continuing Ed.: Liza Cruz, Phone: 416-204-3263, E-mail: liza.cruz@cica.ca

Canadian Institute of Plumbing & Heating 2011 Annual Business Conference
Date: June 26-29, 2011
Location: Victoria Conference Centre
Victoria, BC
Sponsor/Contact: Canadian Institute of Plumbing & Heating
#330, 295 The West Mall
Toronto, ON M9C 4Z4
416-695-0447 Fax: 416-695-0450
E-mail: info@ciph.com
URL: ww.ciph.com
Scope: National
Purpose: An annual gathering of the plumbing & heating industry, featuring business meetings, guest speakers, & opportunities to share best practices
Contact Information: CIPH Phone: 416-695-0447, Toll-Free: 1-800-639-2474; Chair, Conference Planning Committee: John Hammill

Canadian Institute of Public Health Inspectors 77th Annual Educational Conference: Strengthening Collaboration, Strengthening the Profession
Date: June 26-29, 2011
Location: Halifax Marriott Harbourfront Hotel
Halifax, NS
Sponsor/Contact: Canadian Institute of Public Health Inspectors
#720, 999 West Broadway Ave.
Vancouver, BC V5Z 1K5
604-739-8180 Fax: 604-738-4080
E-mail: questions@ciphi.ca; office@ciphi.ca
URL: www.ciphi.ca
Scope: National
Contact Information: Conference Co-Chair: Doreen MacKley, E-mail: mackledm@gov.ns.ca; Conference Co-Chair: Gary O'Toole, E-mail: Gary.OToole@gov.ns.ca

Canadian Medical & Biological Engineering Society 2011 34th Annual National Conference
Date: June 5-8, 2011
Location: Sheraton Centre Toronto Hotel
Toronto, ON
Sponsor/Contact: Canadian Medical & Biological Engineering Society
1485 Laperrière Ave.
Ottawa, ON K1Z 7S8
613-728-1759
E-mail: secretariat@cmbes.ca
URL: www.cmbes.ca
Scope: National
Purpose: A joint conference within the Festival of Conferences on Caregiving, Disabilities, Aging, & Technology (FICCDAT); Some topics within the continuing education program include medical device safety, the covergence of information technology & medical devices, human factors assessmemt for improving patient safety, laser fundamentals, new equipment, hospital network & information systems, renal dialysis, & preparent for the BMET certification exam
Contact Information: Canadian Medical & Biological Engineering Society, Phone: 613-728-1759; Chair, Organizing Committee: Dave Gretzinger; Exhibits, Sponsorships, & Marketing Contact: Tidimogo Gaamangwe; Clinical Engineering Program Contact: Mario Ramirez; Scientific Program Contact: Donald Russell; FICCDAT Secretariat, E-mail: info@ficcdat.ca

Canadian Medical Association Physician Management Institute 2011 Course: Strategic Influence - Advocacy, Alliances, & Accountability
Date: June 24-26, 2011
Location: The Waterside Inn
Mississauga, ON
Sponsor/Contact: Canadian Medical Association
1867 Alta Vista Dr.
Ottawa, ON K1G 5W8
613-731-8610 Fax: 613-236-8864
E-mail: cmamsc@cma.ca; cmatechsupport@cma.ca (technical support)
URL: www.cma.ca
Scope: National
Purpose: Sessions include the health care envionnment & factors that affect the health of Canadians & their health care system, the governance of health care, influencing strategies, & media skills
Anticipated Attendance: 25
Contact Information: Canadian Medical Association Physician Management Institute, Phone: 800-663-7336, ext. 2319, Fax: 613-521-1268, E-mail: pmi@cma.ca

Canadian Meteorological & Oceanographic Society Congress 2011 45th Annual Congress: Ocean, Atmosphere & The Changing Pacific
Date: June 5-9, 2011
Location: Victoria Conference Centre
Victoria, BC
Sponsor/Contact: Canadian Meteorological & Oceanographic Society
P.O. Box 3211 Stn. D
Ottawa, ON K1P 6H7 Canada
613-990-0300 Fax: 613-990-1617
E-mail: communications@cmos.ca; accounts@cmos.ca; publications@cmos.ca
URL: www.cmos.ca
Scope: National
Purpose: Scientific & plenary sessions, as well as business meetings, exhibits, & a social program
Contact Information: Chair, Scientific Program Committee for the Victoria 2011 Congress: Bill Merryfield, E-mail: cccma_cmos2011@ec.gc.ca

Canadian Nuclear Society 2011 2nd Annual Workshop on Nuclear Education & Outreach: Lighting Our Way to The Future
Date: June 8-9, 2011
Location: Sheraton on the Falls
Niagara Falls, ON
Sponsor/Contact: Canadian Nuclear Society
655 Bay St., 17th Fl.
Toronto, ON M5G 2K4
416-977-7620 Fax: 416-977-8131
E-mail: cns-snc@on.aibn.com
URL: www.cns-snc.ca
Scope: National
Purpose: Program includes speakers, demonstrations, a panel discussions about social media & education issues, as well as education & outreach presentations
Contact Information: Canadian Nuclear Society Office: Phone: 416-977-7620, E-mail: cns-snc@on.aibn.com; Technical Program Chair: Brad Moore, E-mail: moorebg@aecl.ca; Workshop Director: John Krasznai, E-mail: john.krasznai@kinectrics.com; Contact, Sponsorship Inquiries: Cherie Ferrari, E-mail: Cherie.Ferrari@kinectrics.com

Canadian Nuclear Society 2011 32nd Annual Conference & 35th Annual CNS / CNA Student Conference

Date: June 5-8, 2011
Location: Sheraton on the Falls
Niagara Falls, ON
Sponsor/Contact: Canadian Nuclear Society
655 Bay St., 17th Fl.
Toronto, ON M5G 2K4
416-977-7620 Fax: 416-977-8131
E-mail: cns-snc@on.aibn.com
URL: www.cns-snc.ca
Scope: National
Purpose: Penary sessions on the following topics: Canadian & Global Energy & Environmental Developments; Communicating the Nuclear Message; Isotopes & Nuclear Medicine; Alternative Energy Technologies; & New Nuclear Technologies
Contact Information: Executive Chair: Frank Doyle, E-mail: fdoyle@rogers.com; Technical Co-Chair: John Roberts, E-mail: cns2011@mcmaster.ca; Plenary Chair: Murray J. Stewart, E-mail: murray.stewart@energy.ca; Contact, Student Conference: Cherie Ferrari, E-mail: cherie.ferrari@kinectrics.com; Contact, Exhibition & Sponsorships: Anne Greve, E-mail: ragreve@sympatico.ca

Canadian Society for Civil Engineering 2011 Annual General Meeting & Conference: Engineers - Advocates for Future Policy
Date: June 14-17, 2011
Location: Westin Hotel
Ottawa, ON
Sponsor/Contact: Canadian Society for Civil Engineering
4877, rue Sherbrooke ouest
Montréal, QC H3Z 1G9
514-933-2634 Fax: 514-933-3504
E-mail: info@csce.ca; membership@csce.ca
URL: www.csce.ca
Scope: National
Purpose: Featuring the 2nd International Engineering Mechanics & Materials Specialty Conference; the 3rd International / 9th Construction Specialty Conference; & the 20th Canadian Hydrotechnical Conference
Contact Information: Chair, Local Organizing Committee: Linda Newton, CD, Ph.D. MCSCE, Phone: 613-949-5861, E-mail: linda.newton@dcc-cdc.gc.ca; Chair, Technical Program: Dr. Roberto M. Narbaitz, Phone: 613-562-5800, ext. 6142, E-mail: narbaitz@uottawa.ca; Registrar: Dr. David Lau, P.Eng., E-mail: david_t_lau@carleton.ca

Canadian Society for Civil Engineering 2011 Executives / Board Workshop
Date: June 15, 2011
Location: Ottawa, ON
Sponsor/Contact: Canadian Society for Civil Engineering
4877, rue Sherbrooke ouest
Montréal, QC H3Z 1G9
514-933-2634 Fax: 514-933-3504
E-mail: info@csce.ca; membership@csce.ca
URL: www.csce.ca
Scope: National
Purpose: A workshop for all society board members & executives to review the new busines plan for the society

Canadian Society for Mechanical Engineering 2011 23rd Biennial Canadian Congress of Applied Mechanics (CANCAM)
Date: June 5-9, 2011
Location: Dept. of Mechanical Engineering, UBC
Vancouver, BC
Sponsor/Contact: Canadian Society for Mechanical Engineering
1295 Hwy. 2 East
Kingston, ON K7L 4V1
613-547-5989 Fax: 613-547-0195
E-mail: csme@cogeco.ca
URL: www.csme-scgm.ca
Scope: National
Purpose: Highlights include the Royal Society of Canada lecture, plenary addresses, workshops, panel discussions, tutorials, a student design competition, technical tours, the presentation of awards, & a social program

Contact Information: General Chair: Clarence W. de Silva, Phone: 604-822-6291, Fax: 604-822-2403, E-mail: desilva@mech.ubc.ca; Program Chair: Jason Gu, Phone: 902-494-3163, Fax: 902-422-7535, E-mail: jason.gu@dal.ca; Student Activities Chair: Peter Ostafichuk, E-mail: ostafich@mech.ubc.ca; Treasurer: Leslie Fernandez. E-mail: leslie.fernandez@ubc.ca

Canadian Standards Association 2011 Annual Conference & Committee Week
Date: June 12-17, 2011
Location: Victoria Conference Centre
Victoria, BC
Sponsor/Contact: Canadian Standards Association
#100, 5060 Spectrum Way
Mississauga, ON L4W 5N6
416-747-4000 Fax: 416-747-2473
E-mail: member@csa.ca; sales@csa.ca; seminars@csa.ca; elearning@csa.ca
URL: www.csa.ca
Scope: National
Purpose: Educational, interactive sessions, speaker presentations, networking opportunities, plus committee meetings
Anticipated Attendance: 500+
Contact Information: E-mail: conference@csa.ca

Canadian Urban Transit Association Training Course: Transit Planning
Date: June 12-17, 2011
Location: Best Western Regency Inn
Abbotsford, BC
Sponsor/Contact: Canadian Urban Transit Association
#1401, 55 York St.
Toronto, ON M5J 1R7
416-365-9800 Fax: 416-365-1295
E-mail: transit@cutaactu.ca
URL: www.cutaactu.ca
Scope: Provincial
Purpose: Case studies, group exercises, simulations, workshops, & presentations about transit planning
Contact Information: Course Contact: John Moudakis, Phone: 416-365-9800, ext. 102, Fax: 416-365-1295, E-mail: moudakis@cutaactu.ca

Canadian Water Resources Association 2011 64th National Conference: Our Water, Our Life - The Most Valuable Resource
Date: June 27-30, 2011
Location: Delta St. John's Hotel & Conference Ctr.
St. John's, NL
Sponsor/Contact: Canadian Water Resources Association
c/o Membership Office
9 Covus Crt.
Ottawa, ON K2E 7Z4
613-237-9363 Fax: 613-594-5190
E-mail: services@aic.ca
URL: www.cwra.org
Scope: National
Purpose: A conference program, featuring keynote speakers, exhibitions, technical training & tours
Contact Information: Canadian Water Resource Association, Newfoundland & Labrador Branch, E-mail: cwra2011nl@gmail.com

Canadian Water Resources Association 2011 Ontario Branch Symposium & Annual General Meeting
Date: June 2, 2011
Location: Black Creek Pioneer Village
Toronto, ON
Sponsor/Contact: Canadian Water Resources Association
c/o Membership Office
9 Covus Crt.
Ottawa, ON K2E 7Z4
613-237-9363 Fax: 613-594-5190
E-mail: services@aic.ca
URL: www.cwra.org
Scope: Provincial
Purpose: "Exploring Ontario's Water Opportunities: Innovative Technologies for Sustainable Resource Management"
Contact Information: Ontario Branch Director: Bob Metcalfe, Phone: 905-668-6195, E-mail: cwraont@rogers.com

Canadian Water Resources Association 2011 Water, Agriculture, & the Environment Conference: Supply, Quality, Management
Date: June 1, 2011
Location: Lethbridge Lodge Hotel & Conference Ctr.
Lethbridge, ON
Sponsor/Contact: Canadian Water Resources Association
c/o Membership Office
9 Covus Crt.
Ottawa, ON K2E 7Z4
613-237-9363 Fax: 613-594-5190
E-mail: services@aic.ca
URL: www.cwra.org
Scope: National
Purpose: Organized by the Alberta Branch of the Canadian Water Resources Association, Alberta Agriculture & Rural Development, & the Canadian National Committee on Irrigation & Drainage
Contact Information: 2011 Conference Contact: Shelley Woods, Phone: 403-381-5839, E-mail: Shelley.A.Woods@gov.ab.ca

Canadian Water Resources Association, Alberta Branch, 2011 Future of Water Workshop Series: Developing Better Leaders
Date: June 17-19, 2011
Location: The Hostel Bear
Canmore, AB
Sponsor/Contact: Canadian Water Resources Association
c/o Membership Office
9 Covus Crt.
Ottawa, ON K2E 7Z4
613-237-9363 Fax: 613-594-5190
E-mail: services@aic.ca
URL: www.cwra.org
Scope: Provincial
Purpose: Dialogue experiences & field trips surrounding the topic of innovative water leadership, designed for multi-sectoral professionals
Contact Information: E-mail: nathalie@waterlution.org

Climate Change & the Implications for Plant Science 2011 Symposium (hosted by CropLife Canada & the University of Guelph)
Date: June 7-8, 2011
Location: University of Guelph
Guelph, ON
Sponsor/Contact: CropLife Canada
#627, 21 Four Seasons Pl.
Toronto, ON M9B 6J8
416-622-9771
URL: www.croplife.ca
Scope: National
Purpose: Topics include projected future climates; climate change impacts; climate change strategies for agriculture; agricultural productivity; the phenology, distribution, & abundance of native pests; the invasion & colonization potential of alien pests; weed / crop interactions & crop losses; farmland biodiversity; biodiversity opportunities & threats; sustainable crop protection; agroecosystems; & improving crop productivity for food security
Contact Information: Office of Open Learning, University of Guelph, Phone: 519-767-5000, Fax: 519-767-1114, E-mail: info@open.uoguelph.ca; Sponsorship Contact: Pat Shaver, Phone: 519-824-4120, ext. 54098, E-mail: pshaver@open.uoguelph.ca

Consulting Engineers of Alberta 2011 Business Professional Development for Engineers Program: Information Technology Risk Management
Date: June 20, 2011
Location: University of Alberta, Downtown Campus
Edmonton, AB
Sponsor/Contact: Consulting Engineers of Alberta

Trade Shows, Conferences and Seminars

Phipps-McKinnon Building
#870, 10020 - 101A Ave.
Edmonton, AB T5J 3G2
780-421-1852 Fax: 780-424-5225
E-mail: info@cea.ca
URL: www.cea.ca
Scope: Provincial
Purpose: A business development education program in the context of the consulting engineering sector
Contact Information: Manager, Events & Communications: Hiju Song, E-mail: hsong@cea.ca

Consulting Engineers of Alberta 2011 Business Professional Development for Engineers Program: Engage Everyone - Project Leadership
Date: June 20-21, 2011
Location: University of Alberta, Downtown Campus
Edmonton, AB
Sponsor/Contact: Consulting Engineers of Alberta
Phipps-McKinnon Building
#870, 10020 - 101A Ave.
Edmonton, AB T5J 3G2
780-421-1852 Fax: 780-424-5225
E-mail: info@cea.ca
URL: www.cea.ca
Scope: Provincial
Purpose: A course designed for engineers who work in large consulting firms & enterprises
Contact Information: Manager, Events & Communications: Hiju Song, E-mail: hsong@cea.ca

Consulting Engineers of Alberta 2011 Business Professional Development for Engineers Program: Building an Effective Client Consultant Team
Date: June 21, 2011
Location: University of Alberta, Downtown Campus
Edmonton, AB
Sponsor/Contact: Consulting Engineers of Alberta
Phipps-McKinnon Building
#870, 10020 - 101A Ave.
Edmonton, AB T5J 3G2
780-421-1852 Fax: 780-424-5225
E-mail: info@cea.ca
URL: www.cea.ca
Scope: Provincial
Purpose: A course designed for engineers who work in small to medium sized enterprises
Contact Information: Manager, Events & Communications: Hiju Song, E-mail: hsong@cea.ca

Consulting Engineers of Alberta Young Professionals' Group 2011 Speaker Series: Liability 101 for YPs
Date: June 9, 2011
Location: Associated Engineering, Jasper Ave.
Edmonton, AB
Sponsor/Contact: Consulting Engineers of Alberta
Phipps-McKinnon Building
#870, 10020 - 101A Ave.
Edmonton, AB T5J 3G2
780-421-1852 Fax: 780-424-5225
E-mail: info@cea.ca
URL: www.cea.ca
Scope: Provincial
Purpose: A session focussing on professional liability, with a speaker from Quadrant Insurance Services
Anticipated Attendance: 40
Contact Information: Manager, Events & Communications: Hiju Song, E-mail: hsong@cea.ca

Consulting Engineers of British Columbia 2011 Annual General Meeting
Date: June 9, 2011
Location: Coast Plaza Stanley Park Hotel
Vancouver, BC
Sponsor/Contact: Consulting Engineers of British Columbia
#1258, 409 Granville St.
Vancouver, BC V6C 1T2
604-687-2811 Fax: 604-688-7110
E-mail: info@cebc.org
URL: www.cebc.org
Scope: Provincial
Purpose: Keynote speaker is Sarah Clark, Chief Executive Officer of Partnerships BC
Contact Information: Phone: 604-687-2811; E-mail: events@cebc.org, info@cebc.org

Electric Vehicle Society of Canada 2011 Meeting
Date: June 16, 2011
Location: Ashtonbee Campus, Centennial College
Toronto, ON
Sponsor/Contact: Electric Vehicle Society of Canada
21 Burritt Rd.
Toronto, ON M1R 3S5
416-755-4324 Fax: 416-755-4324
E-mail: info@evsociety.ca
URL: www.evsociety.ca
Scope: National
Contact Information: E-mail: info@evsociety.ca

Federation of Canadian Municipalities 2011 74th Annual Conference & Municipal Expo
Date: June 3-6, 2011
Location: Halifax, NS
Sponsor/Contact: Federation of Canadian Municipalities
24 Clarence St.
Ottawa, ON K1N 5P3 Canada
613-241-5221 Fax: 613-241-7440
E-mail: federation@fcm.ca
URL: www.fcm.ca
Scope: National
Contact Information: Manager, Membership & Events: Seán Kelly, Phone: 613-244-6045, E-mail: skelly@fcm.ca

Food & Consumer Products of Canada 2011 Giant Tiger Executive Trade Breakfast
Date: June 29, 2011
Location: Toronto Congress Centre
Toronto, ON
Sponsor/Contact: Food & Consumer Products of Canada
#301, 885 Don Mills Rd.
Toronto, ON M3C 1V9
416-510-8024 Fax: 416-510-8043
E-mail: info@fcpc.ca
URL: www.fcpc.ca
Scope: National
Purpose: Subjects include strategy, growth plans, & communication with vendors
Contact Information: Coordinator, Member Services: Heather Spencer, E-mail: Heather.Spencer@fcpc.ca

Food & Consumer Products of Canada 2011 Sodexo Executive Foodservice Breakfast
Date: June 17, 2011
Location: Mississauga Convention Centre
Mississauga, ON
Sponsor/Contact: Food & Consumer Products of Canada
#301, 885 Don Mills Rd.
Toronto, ON M3C 1V9
416-510-8024 Fax: 416-510-8043
E-mail: info@fcpc.ca
URL: www.fcpc.ca
Scope: National
Purpose: Topics include business transformation, culture shift, & the role of supplier partnerships
Contact Information: Coordinator, Member Services: Heather Spencer, E-mail: Heather.Spencer@fcpc.ca

GLOBE Costa Rica 2011: Accelerating the Shift Towards a Low Carbon Economy in Latin America
Date: June 14-16, 2011
Location: Hotel Real InterContinental & Club Tower
San Jose, Costa Rica
Sponsor/Contact: GLOBE Foundation
World Trade Centre
#578, 999 Canada Pl.
Vancouver, BC V6C 3E1
604-695-5001 Fax: 604-695-5019
E-mail: info@globe.ca
URL: www.globe.ca
Scope: International
Purpose: A meeting of business & government leaders, environmental managers, & sustainability practitioners from Latin America, as well as members of the international sustainable business community, for conference sessions & panels on topics such as corporate sustainability, clean energy, energy efficiency, the Smart Grid, water, natural resources & carbon management, sustainable urban development, clean transportation, responsible investment, & finance
Contact Information: General Information (GLOBE Foundation): Social Media: www.twitter.com/GLOBE_Series, events.linkedin.com/GLOBE-Costa-Rica-2011/pub/513234; Vice-Presidnet, Marketing: Nancy Wright, Phone: 604-695-5000, E-mail: nancy.wright@globe.ca; Registration Manager: Zahida Kanani, Phone: 905-841-1688, E-mail: zahida.kanani@globe.ca

Goldschmidt Conference 2011
Date: June 2011
Location: Prague, Czech Republic
Sponsor/Contact: Geochemical Society
c/o Earth & Planetary Sciences Department, Washington University
#CB 11691, Brookings Dr.
St. Louis, MO USA
314-935-4131 Fax: 314-935-4121
E-mail: gsoffice@geochemsoc.org
URL: www.geochemsoc.org
Scope: International
Purpose: An international conference on geochemistry

Growing Your Farm Profits 2011 Bruce County Workshop
Date: June 3 & 10, 2011
Location: Bruce County, ON
Sponsor/Contact: Ontario Soil & Crop Improvement Association
1 Stone Rd. West
Guelph, ON N1G 4Y2
519-826-4214 Fax: 519-826-4224
E-mail: oscia@ontariosoilcrop.org
URL: www.ontariosoilcrop.org
Scope: Local
Purpose: An entry point to potential cost-share opportunities available through Growing Forward Business Development for Farm Businesses
Contact Information: Ontario Soil & Crop Improvement Association Program Representative: Jayne Dietrich, Phone: 519-367-5930, E-mail: bruce@ontariosoilcrop.org

Growing Your Farm Profits 2011 Durham Region & City of Kawartha Lakes Workshop
Date: June 6 & 13, 2011
Location: Goodwood Community Centre
Goodwood, ON
Sponsor/Contact: Ontario Soil & Crop Improvement Association
1 Stone Rd. West
Guelph, ON N1G 4Y2
519-826-4214 Fax: 519-826-4224
E-mail: oscia@ontariosoilcrop.org
URL: www.ontariosoilcrop.org
Scope: Local
Purpose: An opportunity to assess one's business, identify priorities, begin the planning process, develop action plans, & interact with other farmers
Contact Information: Ontario Soil & Crop Improvement Association Program Representative: Robin Brown, Phone: 705-374-4975, E-mail: durham@ontariosoilcrop.org

Growing Your Farm Profits 2011 Durham Region & City of Kawartha Lakes Workshop
Date: June 20 & 27, 2011
Location: Sunderland Co-op
Sunderland, ON
Sponsor/Contact: Ontario Soil & Crop Improvement Association
1 Stone Rd. West
Guelph, ON N1G 4Y2
519-826-4214 Fax: 519-826-4224
E-mail: oscia@ontariosoilcrop.org
URL: www.ontariosoilcrop.org

Scope: Local
Purpose: A point of entry to possible cost-share opportunities available through Growing Forward Business Development for Farm Businesses
Contact Information: Ontario Soil & Crop Improvement Association Program Representative: Robin Brown, Phone: 705-374-4975, E-mail: durham@ontariosoilcrop.org

Growing Your Farm Profits 2011 Grey County Workshop
Date: June 9 & 16, 2011
Location: Markdale, ON
Sponsor/Contact: Ontario Soil & Crop Improvement Association
1 Stone Rd. West
Guelph, ON N1G 4Y2
519-826-4214 Fax: 519-826-4224
E-mail: oscia@ontariosoilcrop.org
URL: www.ontariosoilcrop.org
Scope: Local
Purpose: An event to learn how to plan & manage farm business success
Contact Information: Ontario Soil & Crop Improvement Association Program Representative: Ray Robertson, Phone: 519-986-3756 E-mail: grey@ontariosoilcrop.org

Growing Your Farm Profits 2011 Lennox & Addington & Hastings County Workshop
Date: June 10 & 17, 2011
Location: Ontario
Sponsor/Contact: Ontario Soil & Crop Improvement Association
1 Stone Rd. West
Guelph, ON N1G 4Y2
519-826-4214 Fax: 519-826-4224
E-mail: oscia@ontariosoilcrop.org
URL: www.ontariosoilcrop.org
Scope: Local
Purpose: An interactive workshop for local farmers
Contact Information: Ontario Soil & Crop Improvement Association Program Representative: Stan Meeks, Phone: 613-478-5472, E-mail: hastings@ontariosoilcrop.org

Growing Your Farm Profits 2011 Waterloo Region Workshop
Date: June 7 & 14, 2011
Location: Linwood Community Centre
Linwood, ON
Sponsor/Contact: Ontario Soil & Crop Improvement Association
1 Stone Rd. West
Guelph, ON N1G 4Y2
519-826-4214 Fax: 519-826-4224
E-mail: oscia@ontariosoilcrop.org
URL: www.ontariosoilcrop.org
Scope: Local
Purpose: A workshop for farmers to identify priorities & to develop action plans
Contact Information: Ontario Soil & Crop Improvement Association Program Representative: Liz Samis, Phone: 519-638-3268, E-mail: waterlooGYFP@ontariosoilcrop.org

Growing Your Farm Profits 2011 Wellington County Workshop
Date: June 17 & 24, 2011
Location: Elora OMAFRA Office
Elora, ON
Sponsor/Contact: Ontario Soil & Crop Improvement Association
1 Stone Rd. West
Guelph, ON N1G 4Y2
519-826-4214 Fax: 519-826-4224
E-mail: oscia@ontariosoilcrop.org
URL: www.ontariosoilcrop.org
Scope: Local
Purpose: An event for participants to evaluate their present business management practices, develop action plans, & ensure they are set to implement their plans

Contact Information: Ontario Soil & Crop Improvement Association Program Representative: John Benham: 519-846-0941, E-mail: wellington@ontariosoilcrop.org

Health Sciences Association of Alberta 2011 40th Annual General Meeting
Date: June 2-3, 2011
Location: Edmonton, AB
Sponsor/Contact: Health Sciences Association of Alberta
10212 - 112 St.
Edmonton, AB T5K 1M4
780-488-0168 Fax: 780-488-0534
URL: www.hsaa.ca
Scope: Provincial
Purpose: Featuring presentations from guest speakers
Contact Information: Communications Officer: Scott Pattison, E-mail: scottpat@hsaa.ca

Health Sciences Association of Alberta Board / Governance Session, Board & Staff Golf Retreat, & Board Meeting
Date: June 23-24, 2011
Location: Edmonton, AB
Sponsor/Contact: Health Sciences Association of Alberta
10212 - 112 St.
Edmonton, AB T5K 1M4
780-488-0168 Fax: 780-488-0534
URL: www.hsaa.ca
Scope: Provincial
Contact Information: Communications Officer: Scott Pattison, E-mail: scottpat@hsaa.ca

Health Sciences Association of Alberta Executive Meeting & Retirement Dinner
Date: June 22, 2011
Location: Edmonton, AB
Sponsor/Contact: Health Sciences Association of Alberta
10212 - 112 St.
Edmonton, AB T5K 1M4
780-488-0168 Fax: 780-488-0534
URL: www.hsaa.ca
Scope: Provincial
Contact Information: Communications Officer: Scott Pattison, E-mail: scottpat@hsaa.ca

Indoor Air 2011
Date: June 5-10, 2011
Location: University of Texas at Austin
Austin, TX USA
Sponsor/Contact: International Society of Indoor Air Quality & Climate
c/o Gina Bendy
2548 Empire Grade
Santa Cruz, CA USA
831-426-0148 Fax: 831-426-6522
E-mail: info@isiaq.org
URL: www.isiaq.org
Scope: International
Purpose: Challenges for the indoor air community, including emerging contaminants, the implications of green building design on indoor air quality, & indoor air quality & climate change
Contact Information: General Information, E-mail: indoor@engr.utexas.edu; Conference President: Richard Corsi, Phone: 512-471-3611, E-mail: corsi@mail.utexas.edu; Conference Technical Chair: Glenn Morrison, E-mail: gcm@mst.edu

Institute of Food Technologists 2011 Annual Meeting & Food Expo
Date: June 11-14, 2011
Location: New Orleans Morial Convention Center
New Orleans, LA USA
Sponsor/Contact: Institute of Food Technologists
#1000, 525 West Van Buren
Chicago, IL
312-782-8424 Fax: 312-782-8348
E-mail: info@ift.org; sales@ift.org
URL: www.ift.org
Scope: International
Purpose: Scientific & educational programming for the international food science profession, plus the food industry's largest collection of equipment, ingredient, & packaging suppliers at the IFT Food Expo
Anticipated Attendance: 21,500+
Contact Information: Vice-President, Meetings & Events: Heidi Voorhees, CAE, E-mail: havoorhees@ift.org; Media Inquiries, E-mail: media@ift.org

Institute of Food Technologists 2011 Pre-Annual Meeting Short Courses
Date: June 10-11, 2011
Location: New Orleans, LA USA
Sponsor/Contact: Institute of Food Technologists
#1000, 525 West Van Buren
Chicago, IL
312-782-8424 Fax: 312-782-8348
E-mail: info@ift.org; sales@ift.org
URL: www.ift.org
Scope: International
Purpose: Eight to ten short educational courses, covering topics such as ingredient applications for product innovation & consumer health, safety & vulnerabilities of domestic & imported ingredients, microencapsulation in food applications, & food science for the non-food scientist
Contact Information: Vice-President, Meetings & Events: Heidi Voorhees, CAE, E-mail: havoorhees@ift.org; Media Inquiries, E-mail: media@ift.org

International Heavy Haul Association 2011 Specialist Technical Session: Railroading in Extreme Environments
Date: June 19-22, 2011
Location: Westin Hotel
Calgary, AB
Sponsor/Contact: International Heavy Haul Association
2808 Forest Hills Crt.
Virginia Beach, USA
URL: www.ihha.net
Scope: International
Purpose: A meeting featuring technical sessions & tours, on topics such as vehicle & track interaction, rail performance, rail maintenance, track geometry, rail metallurgy, heat impact on tracks, cold impact on tracks, extending axle loads, wheel performance, emerging technologies, service reliability, safety, the environment, construction in extreme environments, tunnels, & energy
Anticipated Attendance: 350-400
Contact Information: Conference Manager: Marie Lanouette, Phone: 613-993-0414, Fax: 613-993-7250, E-mail: ihha2011@nrc-cnrc.gc.ca

International Union of Food Science & Technology 12th ASEAN Food Conference 2011: Food Innovation - Key to Creative Economy
Date: June 16-18, 2011
Location: Bitek, Bangkok, Thailand
Sponsor/Contact: International Union of Food Science & Technology
International Union of Food Science & Technology Secretariat
P.O. Box 61021
#19, 511 Maple Grove Dr.
Oakville, ON L6J 6X0
905-815-1926 Fax: 905-815-1574
E-mail: secretariat@iufost.org; Newslinks@iufost.org (Newsline)
URL: www.iufost.org
Scope: International

Local Government Management Association of BC Professional Development Program: Municipal Administration Training Institute - Leadership Program
Date: June 12-17, 2011
Location: Quest University
Squamish, BC
Sponsor/Contact: Local Government Management Association of British Columbia
Central Building
620 View St., 7th Fl.
Victoria, BC V8W 1J6

Trade Shows, Conferences and Seminars

250-383-7032 Fax: 250-384-4879
E-mail: office@lgma.ca; editor@lgma.ca (magazine); ads@lgma.ca
URL: www.lgma.ca
Scope: Provincial
Purpose: A 5.5 day residential program for persons in leadership roles in local government in British Columbia
Contact Information: Program Coordinator: Ana Fuller, Phone: 250-383-7032, ext. 227, Fax: 250-383-4879, E-mail: afuller@lgma.ca

National Environmental Health Association 2011 75th Annual Conference & Exhibition
Date: June 15-18, 2011
Location: Columbus, OH USA
Sponsor/Contact: National Environmental Health Association
#1000N, 720 South Colorado Blvd.
Denver, CO USA
303-756-9090 Fax: 303-691-9490
E-mail: staff@neha.org
URL: www.neha.org
Scope: International
Contact Information: Toll-Free Phone: 866-956-2258; Fax: 303-691-9490; E-mail: staff@neha.org

Nature Canada 2011 Annual General Meeting
Date: June 22, 2011
Location: Oak Hammock Marsh Interpretive Centre
Oak Hammock Marsh, MB
Sponsor/Contact: Nature Canada
#300, 75 Albert St.
Ottawa, ON K1P 5E7
613-562-3447 Fax: 613-562-3371
E-mail: info@naturecanada.ca
URL: www.naturecanada.ca
Scope: National
Purpose: Featuring the election of the Board of Directors
Contact Information: Nature Canada Executive Assistant & Office Manager: Sue Robertson, E-mail: srobertson@naturecanada.ca

Nature Manitoba Habitat Committee's 2011 Annual Spurge Purge & Plant Walk
Date: June 25, 2011
Location: Loewen Prairie
Manitoba
Sponsor/Contact: Nature Manitoba
Hammond Building
#401, 63 Albert St.
Winnipeg, MB R3B 1G4
204-943-9029 Fax: 204-943-9029
E-mail: info@naturemanitoba.ca; editor@naturemanitoba.ca (Newsletter)
URL: www.naturemanitoba.ca
Scope: Provincial
Purpose: Work of Nature Manitoba's Habitat Committee on study plots, to preserve the tall grass prairie & to learn more about native plants of the prairie
Contact Information: Event Contact: Marilyn Latta, Phone: 204-253-9245

Nature Manitoba's Birding for Beginners
Date: June 1, 2011
Location: Henteleff Park
Manitoba
Sponsor/Contact: Nature Manitoba
Hammond Building
#401, 63 Albert St.
Winnipeg, MB R3B 1G4
204-943-9029 Fax: 204-943-9029
E-mail: info@naturemanitoba.ca; editor@naturemanitoba.ca (Newsletter)
URL: www.naturemanitoba.ca
Scope: Provincial
Contact Information: Event Contact: Brad Carey, Phone: 204-832-5758

Nature Manitoba's Mantario Wilderness Education Centre 2011 Training
Date: June 20-27, 2011
Location: Mantario Wilderness Education Centre
Whiteshell Prov. Park, MB
Sponsor/Contact: Nature Manitoba
Hammond Building
#401, 63 Albert St.
Winnipeg, MB R3B 1G4
204-943-9029 Fax: 204-943-9029
E-mail: info@naturemanitoba.ca; editor@naturemanitoba.ca (Newsletter)
URL: www.naturemanitoba.ca
Scope: Provincial
Purpose: Preparation for Mantario Wilderness Education Centre's summer educational & recreational programs & field trips, located in the Mantario Wilderness Zone in Whiteshell Provincial Park, Manitoba
Contact Information: Event Contact: Marc Leclair, Phone: 204-233-9054, E-mail: mleclair@mts.net

Nature Nova Scotia 2011 Annual General Meeting & Conference (in partnership with the Bras d'Or Stewardship Society)
Date: June 3-5, 2011
Location: Gaelic College of Celtic Arts & Crafts
St. Anne's, Cape Breton, NS
Sponsor/Contact: Nature Nova Scotia (Federation of Nova Scotia Naturalists)
c/o Nova Scotia Museum of Natural History
1747 Summer St.
Halifax, NS B3H 3A6
902-582-7176
E-mail: doug@fundymud.com
URL: www.naturens.ca
Scope: Provincial
Purpose: Educational presentations & field trips focussing upon the natural history of Cape Breton
Contact Information: Registrar: Jean Gibson, Phone: 902-678-4725, E-mail: ejgibson@ns.sympatico.ca

Nova Scotia Environmental Network 2011 Workshop: Fundraising 101
Date: June 2, 2011
Location: Veith House
Halifax, NS
Sponsor/Contact: Nova Scotia Environmental Network
3115 Veith St.
Halifax, NS B3K 3G9
902-454-6846 Fax: 902-453-3633
E-mail: nsen@cen-rce.org; board_nsen@cen-rce.org
URL: www.nsen.ca
Scope: Provincial
Purpose: Insights on philanthropic trends
Contact Information: Executive Director: Janelle Frail, Phone: 902-454-6846, Fax: 902-453-3633, E-mail: nsen@cen-rce.org

Nova Scotia Environmental Network 2011 Workshop: Moving Water
Date: June 3-5, 2011
Location: Windhorse Farm
New Germany, NS
Sponsor/Contact: Nova Scotia Environmental Network
3115 Veith St.
Halifax, NS B3K 3G9
902-454-6846 Fax: 902-453-3633
E-mail: nsen@cen-rce.org; board_nsen@cen-rce.org
URL: www.nsen.ca
Scope: Provincial
Contact Information: Executive Director: Janelle Frail, Phone: 902-454-6846, Fax: 902-453-3633, E-mail: nsen@cen-rce.org

Ocean, Offshore, & Arctic Engineering 2011 30th International Conference
Date: June 19-24, 2011
Location: Rotterdam, The Netherlands
Sponsor/Contact: American Society of Mechanical Engineers
3 Park Ave.
New York, NY USA
800-843-2763
E-mail: infocentral@asme.org
URL: www.asme.org
Scope: International
Purpose: Subjects include the following: Offshore Technology; Structures, Safety, & Reliability; Materials Technology; Pipeline & Riser Technology; Ocean Space Utilization; Ocean Engineering; Polar & Arctic Sciences & Technology; CFD & VIV; Ocean Renewable Energy; Offshore Geotechnics; Design Methodology of Offshore Structures; Second Order Wave Drift Forces on Floating Structures; & Mooring of Floating Structures in Waves
Contact Information: Conference Chair: Bas Buchner, E-mail: B.Buchner@marin.nl; Technical Program Chair: H.R. Riggs, E-mail: riggs@hawaii.edu; Registration & Hotel Information, E-mail: omae2011@kiviniria.nl

Ontario Soil & Crop Improvement Association 2011 Soil & Water Management Workshop
Date: June 22, 2011
Location: Simcoe County, ON
Sponsor/Contact: Ontario Soil & Crop Improvement Association
1 Stone Rd. West
Guelph, ON N1G 4Y2
519-826-4214 Fax: 519-826-4224
E-mail: oscia@ontariosoilcrop.org
URL: www.ontariosoilcrop.org
Scope: Provincial
Contact Information: Woodstock OMAFRA Resource Centre, Phone: 519-537-6621

Ontario Tire Dealers Association 2011 Annual General Meeting
Date: June 14, 2011
Location: Four Points by Sheraton
Gatineau, QC
Sponsor/Contact: Ontario Tire Dealers Association
P.O. Box 516
34 Edward St.
Drayton, ON N0G 1P0
888-207-9059 Fax: 866-375-6832
URL: www.otda.com
Scope: Provincial
Purpose: A meeting featuring reports, statements, the election of directors, & the appointment of the accountant
Contact Information: Executive Director: Robert Bignell, Phone: 888-207-9059, E-mail: bbignell@otda.com

Petroleum Services Association of Canada 2011 Petroleum Services Investment Symposium
Date: June 16-17, 2011
Location: Hyatt Regency Calgary
Calgary, AB
Sponsor/Contact: Petroleum Services Association of Canada
#1150, 800 - 6 Ave. SW
Calgary, AB T2P 3G3
403-264-4195 Fax: 403-263-7174
E-mail: info@psac.ca
URL: www.psac.ca
Scope: National
Purpose: A chance to learn about new technologies & innovative companies in the Canadian oil & gas service industry
Contact Information: Manager, Meetings & Events: Heather Doyle, Phone: 403-213-2796, E-mail: hdoyle@psac.ca

Radioecology & Environmental Radioactivity International Conference: Environment & Nuclear Renaissance (Sponsored by the Canadian Nuclear Society)
Date: June 19-24, 2011
Location: McMaster University
Hamilton, ON
Sponsor/Contact: Canadian Nuclear Society
655 Bay St., 17th Fl.
Toronto, ON M5G 2K4
416-977-7620 Fax: 416-977-8131
E-mail: cns-snc@on.aibn.com
URL: www.cns-snc.ca

Scope: International
Purpose: Topics include emergency preparedness, radioecological sensitivity (including Arctic & Antarctic environments), environmental protection, radioactive waste management & disposal, environmental aspects of nuclear endeavours, & tritium in the environment
Contact Information: Contact, Sponsorship Information: Peter Ernst, E-mail: peter.ernst@candu.org

Real-Time Measurement, Instrumentation & Control 2011 2nd International Workshop (Sponsored by the Canadian Nuclear Society)
Date: June 2-3, 2011
Location: University of ON Institute of Technology
Oshawa, ON
Sponsor/Contact: Canadian Nuclear Society
655 Bay St., 17th Fl.
Toronto, ON M5G 2K4
416-977-7620 Fax: 416-977-8131
E-mail: cns-snc@on.aibn.com
URL: www.cns-snc.ca
Scope: International
Purpose: Topics include the following: energy & power systems measurement, instrumentation, & control; real time measurement techniques; advanced instrumentation technologies; control system design & analysis; advanced reactor / power plant control; applications on radiation detection & protection; monitoring & diagnosis; plant inspection & maintenance; applications on health physics; applications on space; & applications on oil & gas
Contact Information: Canadian Nuclear Society: Phone: 416-977-7620, E-mail: cns-snc@on.aibn.com; Workshop Co-Chair: Anthony Waker, E-mail: anthony.waker@uoit.ca; Workshop Co-Chair: Hossam A.Gabbar, E-mail: hossam.gabbar@uoit.ca

Recycling Council of British Columbia 2011 37th Annual General Meeting & Zero Waste Conference: The Green Economy - Ready, Set, Grow!
Date: June 8-10, 2011
Location: Whistler Westin Resort & Spa
Whistler, BC
Sponsor/Contact: Recycling Council of British Columbia
#10, 119 West Pender St.
Vancouver, BC V6B 1S5
604-683-6009 Fax: 604-683-7255
E-mail: rcbc@rcbc.bc.ca; hotline@rcbc.bc.ca
URL: www.rcbc.bc.ca
Scope: Provincial
Purpose: Featuring the keynote speaker, Sam Harrington, Environmental Director of Ecovative Design, a company engaged in packaging alternatives, plus a social media workshop with Jan Enns Communications
Contact Information: Executive Director (inquiries about sponsorship opportunities): Brock MacDonald, Phone: 604-683-6009, ext. 307, E-mail: brock@rcbc.bc.ca; Manager, Member & Technology Services (general conference inquiries: Ben Ramos, Phone: 604-683-6009, ext. 314, E-mail: conference@rcbc.bc.ca

Saskatchewan Wildlife Federation 2011 Plant Identification Workshop
Date: June 11, 2011
Location: SWF Habitat Trust Lands
Candiac, SK
Sponsor/Contact: Saskatchewan Wildlife Federation
9 Lancaster Rd.
Moose Jaw, SK S6J 1M8
306-692-8812 Fax: 306-692-4370
E-mail: sask.wildlife@sasktel.net
URL: www.swf.sk.ca
Scope: Provincial
Purpose: Information about Saskatchewan's flora
Contact Information: Education Program Coordinator: JeanAnne Prysliak, Phone: 306-692-8812, E-mail: jprysliak.swf@sasktel.net

Smart Grid Interoperability 2011 2nd Annual Summit
Date: June 7-8, 2011
Location: Woodbine Convention Center
Toronto, ON
Sponsor/Contact: Canadian Electricity Association
#1100, 350 Sparks St.
Ottawa, ON K1R 7S8 Canada
613-230-9263 Fax: 613-230-9326
E-mail: info@electricity.ca
URL: www.electricity.ca
Scope: National
Purpose: A conference for Canada's power industry, regulators, policy makers, & stakeholders, featuring updates, strategies, & lessons learned to improve smart grid interactions
Contact Information: Strategy Institute: Toll-Free Phone: 1-866-298-9343, E-mail: registrations@strategyinstitute.com

Society for Environmental Graphic Design 2011 Conference & Expo
Date: June 1-4, 2011
Location: Palais des congrès (Convention Centre)
Montréal, QC
Sponsor/Contact: Society for Environmental Graphic Design
#400, 1000 Vermont Ave., NW
Washington, DC USA
202-638-5555 Fax: 202-638-0891
E-mail: segd@segd.org
URL: www.segd.org
Scope: International
Purpose: Information for professionals involved with planning, designing, & creating graphics in the built environment
Contact Information: Director, Conference & Meetings: Nazie Dana, Phone: 215-753-0720, E-mail: nazie@segd.org

SustainaBUILD 2011 2nd Annual Conference
Date: June 2, 2011
Location: BMO Centre
Calgary, AB
Sponsor/Contact: Consulting Engineers of Alberta
Phipps-McKinnon Building
#870, 10020 - 101A Ave.
Edmonton, AB T5J 3G2
780-421-1852 Fax: 780-424-5225
E-mail: info@cea.ca
URL: www.cea.ca
Scope: Provincial
Purpose: Conference highlights include net-zero communities & campuses, sustainable oil & gas development, green buildings, energy planning, & net-zero emissions
Contact Information: General & Sponsorship Information Contact: Lucy Leng, Phone: 403-290-1080, ext. 192063, E-mail: lleng@mmart.com; Registration Information Contact: Gillian Wright, Phone: 403-290-1080, ext. 192058, E-mail: gwright@mmart.com

Water Environment Association of Ontario 2011 Specialty Seminar: Whole WWTP Modeling - Overview, Tools, & Future Needs
Date: June 23, 2011
Location: Best Western Hotel
Milton, ON
Sponsor/Contact: Water Environment Association of Ontario
P.O. Box 176
Milton, ON L9T 4N9
416-410-6933 Fax: 416-410-1626
E-mail: julie.vincent@weao.org
URL: www.weao.org
Scope: Provincial
Purpose: An interactive workshop to provide an overview of whole WWTP modeling
Contact Information: Chair, Promotions & Event Planning: Anthony Abbruscato, Phone: 416-499-0090, ext. 73605, E-mail: anthony.abbruscato@ch2m.com

Water Environment Federation 2011 Collection Systems Conference: Rehab or Roulette? Is our Environment at Risk?
Date: June 12-15, 2011
Location: Raleigh Convention Center
Raleigh, NC USA
Sponsor/Contact: Water Environment Federation
601 Wythe St.
Alexandria, VA USA
703-684-2400 Fax: 703-684-2492
E-mail: csc@wef.org
URL: www.wef.org
Scope: International
Purpose: A conference & exhibition held in cooperation with the North Carolina Water Environment Association
Contact Information: Manager, Exhibition Operations: Stefanie Walter, E-mail: swalter@wef.org; Coordinator, Exhibition Sales: Sarah Evans, E-mail: sevans@wef.org; Registration Information, E-mail: registration@wef.org; Technical Program Information, E-mail: CS2011@wef.org

Western Canada Water 2011 Young Professionals Networking Event
Date: June 23, 2011
Location: Metropolitan Billiards
Edmonton, AB
Sponsor/Contact: Western Canada Water
P.O. Box 1708
126 - 3rd Ave. West
Cochrane, AB T4C 1B6
403-709-0064 Fax: 403-709-0068
E-mail: member@wcwwa.ca
URL: www.wcwwa.ca
Scope: Regional
Purpose: A networking opportunity for young professionals in the water & wastewater
Contact Information: Phone: 1-877-283-2003; Fax: 1-877-283-2007

Wildlife Preservation Canada Stories from the Field
Date: June 1, 2011
Location: University of Guelph Faculty Club
Guelph, ON
Sponsor/Contact: Wildlife Preservation Canada
RR#5, 5420 Hwy. 6 North
Guelph, ON N1H 6J2
519-836-9314 Fax: 519-836-8840
E-mail: admin@wildlifepreservation.ca
URL: www.wildlifepreservation.ca
Scope: National
Purpose: Stories about conservation biologists' work on the island of Mauritius

Wildlife Rescue Association of British Columbia 2011 Annual General Meeting
Date: June 15, 2011
Location: Wildlife Rescue Association of BC
Burnaby, BC
Sponsor/Contact: Wildlife Rescue Association of British Columbia
5216 Glencarin Dr.
Burnaby, BC V5B 3C1
604-526-2747 Fax: 604-524-2890
E-mail: info@wildliferescue.ca
URL: www.wildliferescue.ca
Scope: Provincial
Contact Information: Communications Coordinator: Yolanda Brooks, Phone: 604-526-2747, E-mail: yolanda@wildliferescue.ca

Yukon Fish & Game Association 2011 Outdoor Woman Program
Date: June 3-5, 2011
Location: Vista Outdoor Learning Centre
Whitehorse, YT
Sponsor/Contact: Yukon Fish & Game Association
509 Strickland St.
Whitehorse, YT Y1A 2K5
867-667-4263 Fax: 867-667-4237
URL: www.yukonfga.ca
Purpose: Workshop options include bear awareness, hunting ethics & field techniques, northern bushcraft, firearms safety & marksmanship, an introduction to angling & fly fishing, environmental education, waterfowl, ATV & motor boat travel & safety, tackle & techniques at Jackson Lake, & hunt preparation
Contact Information: Phone: 867-667-4263; E-mail: yfga@klondiker.com

Trade Shows, Conferences and Seminars

July

American Society of Mechanical Engineers 2011 Pressure Vessels & Piping Conference: Pressure Vessel Technologies - A Look Ahead into the Next Decade
Date: July 17-21, 2011
Location: Baltimore Marriott Waterfront Hotel
Baltimore, MD USA
Sponsor/Contact: American Society of Mechanical Engineers
3 Park Ave.
New York, NY USA
800-843-2763
E-mail: infocentral@asme.org
URL: www.asme.org
Scope: International
Purpose: Topics related to pressure vessel & piping technologies for power & process industries, such as codes & standards, design & analysis, high pressure technology, & nuclear engineering
Contact Information: Conference Chair: Ronald S. Hafner, E-mail: hafner2@asme.org; Technical Program Chair: Michael E. Nitzel, E-mail: gmnitzel@msn.com; Sponsorship Contact: Carl E. Jaske, E-mail: Carl.Jaske@dnv.com

American Society of Mechanical Engineers Power 2011
Date: July 12-14, 2011
Location: Denver Marriott City Center
Denver, CO USA
Sponsor/Contact: American Society of Mechanical Engineers
3 Park Ave.
New York, NY USA
800-843-2763
E-mail: infocentral@asme.org
URL: www.asme.org
Scope: International
Purpose: Information about the latest technology to improve the operation of power plants
Contact Information: Program Contact: Vince Dilworth, E-mail: dilworthv@asme.org; Registration Contact: Stephen Crane, E-mail: cranes@asme.org

British Columbia Nature (Federation of British Columbia Naturalists) 2011 Exploratory Trip
Date: July 2-9, 2011
Location: Nuit Range, BC
Sponsor/Contact: British Columbia Nature (Federation of British Columbia Naturalists)
c/o Parks Heritage Centre
1620 Mount Seymour Rd.
North Vancouver, BC V7G 2R9
604-985-3057
E-mail: manager@bcnature.ca
URL: www.bcnature.ca
Scope: Provincial
Purpose: A trip east of Tatlayoka Lake
Contact Information: Office Manager: Betty Davison, E-mail: manager@bcnature.ca

British Columbia Nature (Federation of British Columbia Naturalists) 2011 Exploratory Trip
Date: July 16-23, 2011
Location: South Chilcotins, BC
Sponsor/Contact: British Columbia Nature (Federation of British Columbia Naturalists)
c/o Parks Heritage Centre
1620 Mount Seymour Rd.
North Vancouver, BC V7G 2R9
604-985-3057
E-mail: manager@bcnature.ca
URL: www.bcnature.ca
Scope: Provincial
Purpose: A nature trip from Tyaughton Creek to Fortress Ridge & Castle Peak to learn about the area
Contact Information: Office Manager: Betty Davison, E-mail: manager@bcnature.ca

British Columbia Nature (Federation of British Columbia Naturalists) 2011 Summer Camp (in cooperation with the Comox Valley Naturalists)
Date: July 15-19, 2011
Location: Strathcona Park Lodge
Strathcona Park, BC
Sponsor/Contact: British Columbia Nature (Federation of British Columbia Naturalists)
c/o Parks Heritage Centre
1620 Mount Seymour Rd.
North Vancouver, BC V7G 2R9
604-985-3057
E-mail: manager@bcnature.ca
URL: www.bcnature.ca
Scope: Provincial
Purpose: Held at Strathcona Park on Vancouver Island, the oldest park in the British Columbia Parks system, the camp includes educational sessions about the region, as well as trips based on the topics of birds, geology, & botany
Anticipated Attendance: 24
Contact Information: Camp Contact: Pat Munroe, Phone: 250-338-0187, E-mail: dpmunroe@telus.net

Canada - Ontario Environmental Farm Plan Program 2011 Huron County Workshop
Date: July 21 & 28, 2011
Location: Clinton, ON
Sponsor/Contact: Ontario Soil & Crop Improvement Association
1 Stone Rd. West
Guelph, ON N1G 4Y2
519-826-4214 Fax: 519-826-4224
E-mail: oscia@ontariosoilcrop.org
URL: www.ontariosoilcrop.org
Scope: Local
Purpose: Information about protecting soil & water resources, enhancing production benefits, showing due diligence, minimizing environmental risk, & accessing cost-share dollars
Contact Information: Ontario Soil & Crop Improvement Association Program Representative: Lois Sinclair, Phone: 519-357-3146, E-mail: huron@ontariosoilcrop.org

Canada - Ontario Environmental Farm Plan Program 2011 Prescott United Counties Workshop
Date: July 5 & 12, 2011
Location: St Isidore, ON
Sponsor/Contact: Ontario Soil & Crop Improvement Association
1 Stone Rd. West
Guelph, ON N1G 4Y2
519-826-4214 Fax: 519-826-4224
E-mail: oscia@ontariosoilcrop.org
URL: www.ontariosoilcrop.org
Scope: Local
Purpose: A bilingual workshop
Contact Information: Ontario Soil & Crop Improvement Association Program Representative: Micheline Begin, Phone: 613-679-8867, E-mail: russell@ontariosoilcrop.org

Canadian Association of Animal Health Technologists & Technicians 2011 22nd Annual General Meeting: Best Medicine Practices - Timely Topics
Date: July 6-9, 2011
Location: World Trade & Convention Centre
Halifax, NS
Sponsor/Contact: Canadian Association of Animal Health Technologists & Technicians
339 Booth St.
Ottawa, ON K1R 7K1
800-567-2862
E-mail: info@caahtt-acttsa.ca
URL: www.caahtt-acttsa.ca
Scope: National
Purpose: A meeting of Canadian Association of Animal Health Technologists & Technicians members, held in conjunction with the 63rd Canadian Veterinary Medical Association Convention & in partnership with the Eastern Veterinary Technician Association
Contact Information: Conventions & Special Programs Assistant: Sarah M. Cunningham, Phone: 613-236-1162, ext. 121, Fax: 613-236-9681, E-mail: scunningham@cvma-acmv.org

Canadian Institute of Chartered Accountants 2011 Practice Management Workshop for SME Advisors
Date: July 25-27, 2011
Location: Westin Trillium House
Blue Mountains, ON
Sponsor/Contact: Canadian Institute of Chartered Accountants
277 Wellington St. West
Toronto, ON M5V 3H2
416-977-3222 Fax: 416-977-8585
URL: www.cica.ca
Scope: National
Purpose: A workshop for partners of small to medium-sized CA firms
Contact Information: Director, Continuing Education: Frank Colantonio, CA, Phone: 416-204-3328, E-mail: frank.colantonio@cica.ca; Manager, Conferences & Courses, Continuing Education: Jennifer McEdwards, Phone: 416-204-3338, E-mail: jennifer.mcedwards@cica.ca; Registrar, Conferences & Courses, Continuing Ed.: Liza Cruz, Phone: 416-204-3263, E-mail: liza.cruz@cica.ca

Canadian Institute of Chartered Accountants 2011 Workshop: IFRS Implementation for the Mining Industry
Date: July 27-28, 2011
Location: CICA Offices
Toronto, ON
Sponsor/Contact: Canadian Institute of Chartered Accountants
277 Wellington St. West
Toronto, ON M5V 3H2
416-977-3222 Fax: 416-977-8585
URL: www.cica.ca
Scope: National
Purpose: Practical information about accounting policy issues encountered by small to medium sized mining companies transitioning to IFRS
Contact Information: Principal, Conferences & Courses, Continuing Education: Pam Robertson, Phone: 416-204-3296, E-mail: pam.robertson@cica.ca; Manager, Conferences & Courses, Continuing Education: Sheri Price, Phone: 416-204-3425, E-mail: sheri.price@cica.ca; Registrar, Conferences & Courses, Continuing Ed.: Liza Cruz, Phone: 416-204-3263, E-mail: liza.cruz@cica.ca

Canadian Phytopathological Society 2011 Joint Annual Meeting & Conference with Plant Canada
Date: July 17-21, 2011
Location: Nova Scotia
Sponsor/Contact: Canadian Phytopathological Society
c/o Crop Protection & Food Research Ctr Agriculture & Agri-Food Canada
1391 Sandford St.
London, ON N5V 4T3
E-mail: connk@agr.gc.ca
URL: www.cps-scp.ca
Scope: National

Ed-Ventures 2011 for Kids
Date: July - August 2011
Location: Yukon Conservation Society
Whitehorse, YK
Sponsor/Contact: Yukon Conservation Society
302 Hawkins St.
Whitehorse, YT Y1A 1X6 Canada
867-668-5678 Fax: 867-668-6637
E-mail: ycs@ycs.yk.ca
URL: www.yukonconservation.org
Scope: Regional
Purpose: Outdoor education programs for children from ages 4 to 6 & from 7 to 10; Programs are designed to teach scientific study, analytical thinking, conservation, nature appreciation, sustainability, recycling, composting, energy conservation, & the reduction of ecological footprints

Contact Information: Program Contact: Andrea Routley, Phone: 867-668-5678, E-mail: volunteer@ycs.yk.ca

Growing Your Farm Profits 2011 Huron County Workshop
Date: July 8 & 15, 2011
Location: Clinton, ON
Sponsor/Contact: Ontario Soil & Crop Improvement Association
1 Stone Rd. West
Guelph, ON N1G 4Y2
519-826-4214 Fax: 519-826-4224
E-mail: oscia@ontariosoilcrop.org
URL: www.ontariosoilcrop.org
Scope: Local
Purpose: Topics include the assessment of a business, the identifichtion of priorities, & the development of action plans
Contact Information: Ontario Soil & Crop Improvement Association Program Representative: Lois Sinclair, Phone: 519-357-3146, E-mail: huron@ontariosoilcrop.org

Growing Your Farm Profits 2011 Kent & Lambton Areas Workshop
Date: July 5 & 12, 2011
Location: Wilson Hall
Ridgetown, ON
Sponsor/Contact: Ontario Soil & Crop Improvement Association
1 Stone Rd. West
Guelph, ON N1G 4Y2
519-826-4214 Fax: 519-826-4224
E-mail: oscia@ontariosoilcrop.org
URL: www.ontariosoilcrop.org
Scope: Local
Purpose: A workshop of interest to farmers who wish to improve their record keeping, expand their businesss, or plan for succession
Contact Information: Ontario Soil & Crop Improvement Association Program Representative: Joanne Sanderson, Phone: 519-695-3980, E-mail: joanne.sanderson@ontariosoilcrop.org

Growing Your Farm Profits 2011 Middlesex County Workshop
Date: July 6 & 14, 2011
Location: Ontario
Sponsor/Contact: Ontario Soil & Crop Improvement Association
1 Stone Rd. West
Guelph, ON N1G 4Y2
519-826-4214 Fax: 519-826-4224
E-mail: oscia@ontariosoilcrop.org
URL: www.ontariosoilcrop.org
Scope: Local
Purpose: A two day workshop with the opportunity to interact with other farmers from the area
Contact Information: Ontario Soil & Crop Improvement Association Program Representative: Margaret May, Phone: 519-287-5334, E-mail: middlesex@ontariosoilcrop.org

International Association for Bear Research & Management 2011 International Conference & Exhibition
Date: July 17-23, 2011
Location: Westin Ottawa Hotel
Ottawa, ON
Sponsor/Contact: International Association for Bear Research & Management
c/o Terry White, USGS-SAFL, University of Tennessee
274 Ellington Hall
Knoxville, TN USA
Fax: 865-974-3555
E-mail: tdwhite@utk.edu
URL: www.bearbiology.com
Scope: International
Purpose: A conference, for anyone interested in bears, featuring the following sessions: bear specialist group session; bears & climate change; conservation case studies; collaborative projects in bear studies; ecology & behaviour of polar bears; Aboriginal & traditional knowledge of bears; bear behaviour; physiology of bears; population estimation; population ecology of bears; bear feeding; human - bear conflict; & issues & techniques for handling bears
Contact Information: Principle Organizer: Dr. M. Obbard, Phone: 705-755-1549, Fax: 705-755-1559. E-mail: martyn.obbard@ontario.ca; Sponsorship Information, E-mail: iba2011@wildliferesearch.ca

National Association for Environmental Management 2011 Conference: EHS Compliance Excellence & Best Practices
Date: July 27-28, 2011
Location: Hilton Minneapolis / Bloomington
Minneapolis, MN USA
Sponsor/Contact: National Association for Environmental Management
#1002, 1612 K St. NW
Washington, DC USA
202-986-6616 Fax: 202-530-4408
E-mail: programs@naem.org
URL: www.naem.org
Scope: International
Purpose: An opportunity for environmental, health & safety, & sustainability managers to share best practices to ensure compliance, with programs such as communicating EHS risk as a strategic business risk, navigating the maze of product focused regulations, moving your GHG management program forward in an uncertain regulatory environment, auditing best practices, & integrating EHS processes & culture after a merger or acquisition
Contact Information: Program Manager: Mike Mahanna, E-mail: mike@naem.org; Marketing & Sales Manager: Brent Hendrix, E-mail: brent@naem.org

National Solid Wastes Management Association 2011 Safety Seminar
Date: July 26, 2011
Location: Courtyard Marriot
Independence, OH USA
Sponsor/Contact: National Solid Wastes Management Association
#300, 4301 Connecticut Ave. NW
Washington, DC USA
202-244-4700 Fax: 202-966-4824
URL: www.nswma.org
Scope: International
Contact Information: Meetings Manager: Catherine Maimon, E-mail: cmaimon@nswma.org

Nature Manitoba 2011 Natural Garden Tour
Date: July 23, 2011
Location: Manitoba
Sponsor/Contact: Nature Manitoba
Hammond Building
#401, 63 Albert St.
Winnipeg, MB R3B 1G4
204-943-9029 Fax: 204-943-9029
E-mail: info@naturemanitoba.ca; editor@naturemanitoba.ca (Newsletter)
URL: www.naturemanitoba.ca
Scope: Provincial
Contact Information: E-mail: info@naturemanitoba.ca

Ontario Soil & Crop Improvement Association 2011 FarmSmart Expo
Date: July 14-15, 2011
Location: Elora Research Station
Elora, ON
Sponsor/Contact: Ontario Soil & Crop Improvement Association
1 Stone Rd. West
Guelph, ON N1G 4Y2
519-826-4214 Fax: 519-826-4224
E-mail: oscia@ontariosoilcrop.org
URL: www.ontariosoilcrop.org
Scope: Provincial
Purpose: The 4H / Youth Day will take place on July 15
Contact Information: Ontario Soil & Crop Improvement Association, E-mail: oscia@ontariosoilcrop.org

Ontario Soil & Crop Improvement Association 2011 Ontario Forage Expo
Date: July 13, 2011
Location: Elora Research Station
Elora, ON
Sponsor/Contact: Ontario Soil & Crop Improvement Association
1 Stone Rd. West
Guelph, ON N1G 4Y2
519-826-4214 Fax: 519-826-4224
E-mail: oscia@ontariosoilcrop.org
URL: www.ontariosoilcrop.org
Scope: Provincial
Contact Information: Ontario Soil & Crop Improvement Association, E-mail: oscia@ontariosoilcrop.org

Ontario Soil & Crop Improvement Association 2011 Southwest Crop Diagnostic Day
Date: July 2011
Location: University of Guelph
Ridgetown, ON
Sponsor/Contact: Ontario Soil & Crop Improvement Association
1 Stone Rd. West
Guelph, ON N1G 4Y2
519-826-4214 Fax: 519-826-4224
E-mail: oscia@ontariosoilcrop.org
URL: www.ontariosoilcrop.org
Scope: Local
Contact Information: Ontario Soil & Crop Improvement Association, E-mail: oscia@ontariosoilcrop.org

Ontario Soil & Crop Improvement Association 2011 Sprayer Clinic
Date: July 11, 2011
Location: Lindsay, ON
Sponsor/Contact: Ontario Soil & Crop Improvement Association
1 Stone Rd. West
Guelph, ON N1G 4Y2
519-826-4214 Fax: 519-826-4224
E-mail: oscia@ontariosoilcrop.org
URL: www.ontariosoilcrop.org
Scope: Provincial
Contact Information: Ontario Soil & Crop Improvement Association, E-mail: oscia@ontariosoilcrop.org

Water Environment Federation 2011 Energy & Water Conference: Efficiency, Generation, Management, & Climate Impacts
Date: July 31 - August 3, 2011
Location: Hyatt Regency McCormick Place
Chicago, IL USA
Sponsor/Contact: Water Environment Federation
601 Wythe St.
Alexandria, VA USA
703-684-2400 Fax: 703-684-2492
E-mail: csc@wef.org
URL: www.wef.org
Scope: International
Purpose: Information about the water-energy nexus of interest to researchers, designers, technology developers, facility managers & operators, municipal utilities, & other environmental professionals from around the world
Contact Information: Manager, Exhibition Operations: Stefanie Walter, E-mail: swalter@wef.org; Coordinator, Exhibition Sales: Sarah Evans, E-mail: sevans@wef.org; Registration Information, E-mail: registration@wef.org; Technical Program Information, E-mail: EnergyWater2011@wef.org

Yukon Conservation Society Interpretive Guided Nature Hikes (Canyon City historical nature hikes, special hikes with guest naturalists & family walks)
Date: July 2 - August 18, 2011
Location: YK
Sponsor/Contact: Yukon Conservation Society
302 Hawkins St.
Whitehorse, YT Y1A 1X6 Canada
867-668-5678 Fax: 867-668-6637
E-mail: ycs@ycs.yk.ca
URL: www.yukonconservation.org

Trade Shows, Conferences and Seminars

Scope: Regional
Purpose: Featuring environmental education for the public with the goal to foster environmental responsibility
Contact Information: Phone: 867-668-5678; E-mail: ycshikes@ycs.yk.ca

Yukon Fish & Game Association Outdoor Education Camp
Date: July 2-9, 2011
Location: Vista Outdoor Learning Centre
Whitehorse, YT
Sponsor/Contact: Yukon Fish & Game Association
509 Strickland St.
Whitehorse, YT Y1A 2K5
867-667-4263 Fax: 867-667-4237
URL: www.yukonfga.ca
Purpose: An educational opportunity for youth from ages 13 to 16
Contact Information: Camp Director: Clayton White, Phone: 867-633-5526; Yukon Fish & Game Association Office, Phone: 867-667-4263

August

American Society of Mechanical Engineers / NRC 2011 Pump & Valve Symposium
Date: August 14-20, 2011
Location: Hilton DC/Rockville Hotel & Meeting Ctr.
Rockville, MD USA
Sponsor/Contact: American Society of Mechanical Engineers
3 Park Ave.
New York, NY USA
800-843-2763
E-mail: infocentral@asme.org
URL: www.asme.org
Scope: International
Contact Information: Symposium Contact: Robert Horvath, E-mail: HorvathR@asme.org

American Society of Mechanical Engineers 2011 5th International Conference on Energy Sustainability
Date: August 7-10, 2011
Location: Grand Hyatt Washington
Washington, DC USA
Sponsor/Contact: American Society of Mechanical Engineers
3 Park Ave.
New York, NY USA
800-843-2763
E-mail: infocentral@asme.org
URL: www.asme.org
Scope: International
Purpose: Topics include wind energy systems & technologies, concentrating solar power, advances in solar buildings & conservation, the economic & environmental aspects of alternate energy, & sustainable communities
Contact Information: Program Contact: Vince Dilworth, E-mail: dilworthv@asme.org; Registration Contact: Stephen Crane, E-mail: cranes@asme.org

American Society of Mechanical Engineers 2011 9th Fuel Cell Science, Engineering, & Technology Conference
Date: August 7-10, 2011
Location: Grand Hyatt Washington
Washington, DC USA
Sponsor/Contact: American Society of Mechanical Engineers
3 Park Ave.
New York, NY USA
800-843-2763
E-mail: infocentral@asme.org
URL: www.asme.org
Scope: International
Purpose: A conference for educators & students, researchers in the fuel cell community, manufacturers of fuel cells & fuel cell components, utility staff, decision makers, plus members of the business & investment community

Contact Information: Program Contact: Vince Dilworth, E-mail: dilworthv@asme.org; Registration Contact: Stephen Crane, E-mail: cranes@asme.org

American Society of Mechanical Engineers 2011 Computers & Information in Engineering Conference
Date: August 28-31, 2011
Location: Hyatt Regency on Capitol Hill
Washington, DC USA
Sponsor/Contact: American Society of Mechanical Engineers
3 Park Ave.
New York, NY USA
800-843-2763
E-mail: infocentral@asme.org
URL: www.asme.org
Scope: International
Purpose: Plenary sessions, tutorials, keynote lectures, exhibits, & the sharing of research results related to computers in engineering
Contact Information: 2011 General Conference Chair: Nader Jalili, E-mail: n.jalili@neu.edu; Technical Program Co-Chair: Bogdan Epureanu, E-mail: epureanu@umich.edu; Technical Program Co-Chair: Harry Dankowicz, E-mail: danko@illinois.edu; Contact, Meeting Logistics & Registration Information: Erin Dolan, E-mail: dolane@asme.org

American Society of Mechanical Engineers 2011 International Design Engineering Technical Conference
Date: August 28-31, 2011
Location: Hyatt Regency on Capitol Hill
Washington, DC USA
Sponsor/Contact: American Society of Mechanical Engineers
3 Park Ave.
New York, NY USA
800-843-2763
E-mail: infocentral@asme.org
URL: www.asme.org
Scope: International
Purpose: Technical papers explaining research results related to engineering design, as well as lectures, plenary sessions, workshops, & networking opportunities between the research & industrial communities
Contact Information: 2011 General Conference Chair: Nader Jalili, E-mail: n.jalili@neu.edu; Technical Program Co-Chair: Bogdan Epureanu, E-mail: epureanu@umich.edu; Technical Program Co-Chair: Harry Dankowicz, E-mail: danko@illinois.edu; Contact, Meeting Logistics & Registration Information: Erin Dolan, E-mail: dolane@asme.org

Association of Municipalities of Ontario 2011 Annual Conference
Date: August 21-24, 2011
Location: London Convention Centre; Hilton London
London, ON
Sponsor/Contact: Association of Municipalities of Ontario
#801, 200 University Ave.
Toronto, ON M5H 3C6
416-971-9856 Fax: 416-971-6191
E-mail: amo@amo.on.ca; municom@amo.on.ca; policy@amo.on.ca
URL: www.amo.on.ca
Scope: Provincial
Purpose: A conference hosted by the City of London & the County of Middlesex, taking place at the London Convention Centre, the Hilton London, & the Delta London Armouries
Contact Information: Special Events, Phone: 416-971-9856, ext. 330, E-mail: events@amo.on.ca; Coordinator, Special Events & Business Development: Navneet Dhaliwal, E-mail: NDhaliwal@amo.on.ca

Association of Municipalities of Ontario 2011 Heads of Council Forum
Date: August 21, 2011
Location: London, ON
Sponsor/Contact: Association of Municipalities of Ontario

#801, 200 University Ave.
Toronto, ON M5H 3C6
416-971-9856 Fax: 416-971-6191
E-mail: amo@amo.on.ca; municom@amo.on.ca; policy@amo.on.ca
URL: www.amo.on.ca
Scope: Provincial
Purpose: A leadership forum, presenting current issues such as strategic financial subjects
Contact Information: Association of Municipalities of Ontario Events, Phone: 416-971-9856, E-mail: events@amo.on.ca; Coordinator, Special Events & Business Development: Navneet Dhaliwal, E-mail: NDhaliwal@amo.on.ca; Accounts Receivable & Special Events Clerk: Anita Surujdeo, E-mail: ASurujdeo@amo.on.ca

Association of Municipalities of Ontario 2011 Heads of Council Training
Date: August 20, 2011
Location: London, ON
Sponsor/Contact: Association of Municipalities of Ontario
#801, 200 University Ave.
Toronto, ON M5H 3C6
416-971-9856 Fax: 416-971-6191
E-mail: amo@amo.on.ca; municom@amo.on.ca; policy@amo.on.ca
URL: www.amo.on.ca
Scope: Provincial
Purpose: A one day training session for Heads of Council, examining topics such as leadership styles, situational management, leading from influence rather than authority, media relationship management, intergovernmental relations, effective public speaking techniques, & networking
Contact Information: Association of Municipalities of Ontario Events, Phone: 416-971-9856, E-mail: events@amo.on.ca; Coordinator, Special Events & Business Development: Navneet Dhaliwal, E-mail: NDhaliwal@amo.on.ca; Accounts Receivable & Special Events Clerk: Anita Surujdeo, E-mail: ASurujdeo@amo.on.ca

CIVICUS: World Alliance for Citizen Participatio 10th World Assembly - Acting Together for a Just World
Date: August 26-29, 2011
Location: Palais des congrès (Convention Centre)
Montréal, QC
Sponsor/Contact: CIVICUS: World Alliance for Citizen Participation
Stn. 933
24 Gwigwi Mrwebi St.
Johannesburg, South Africa
E-mail: info@civicus.org; membership@civicus.org
URL: www.civicus.org
Scope: International

Canada - Ontario Environmental Farm Plan Program 2011 Carleton Area Workshop
Date: August 24 & 31, 2011
Location: Richmond, ON
Sponsor/Contact: Ontario Soil & Crop Improvement Association
1 Stone Rd. West
Guelph, ON N1G 4Y2
519-826-4214 Fax: 519-826-4224
E-mail: oscia@ontariosoilcrop.org
URL: www.ontariosoilcrop.org
Scope: Local
Purpose: Topics include the reduction of environmental risk, the protection of water & soil resources, & the enhancement of production benefits
Contact Information: Ontario Soil & Crop Improvement Association Program Representative: Arlene Ross, Phone: 613-821-3900, E-mail: carleton@ontariosoilcrop.org

Canada - Ontario Environmental Farm Plan Program 2011 Huron County Workshop
Date: August 25 & September 1, 2011
Location: Clinton, ON

Sponsor/Contact: Ontario Soil & Crop Improvement Association
1 Stone Rd. West
Guelph, ON N1G 4Y2
519-826-4214 Fax: 519-826-4224
E-mail: oscia@ontariosoilcrop.org
URL: www.ontariosoilcrop.org
Scope: Local
Purpose: An educational program for farm families
Contact Information: Ontario Soil & Crop Improvement Association Program Representative: Lois Sinclair, Phone: 519-357-3146, E-mail: huron@ontariosoilcrop.org

Canadian Bar Association Canadian Legal Conference & Expo 2011
Date: August 14-16, 2011
Location: Halifax, NS
Sponsor/Contact: Canadian Bar Association
#500, 865 Carling Ave.
Ottawa, ON K1S 5S8 Canada
613-237-2925 Fax: 613-237-0185
E-mail: info@cba.org
URL: www.cba.org
Scope: National
Purpose: Continuing legal education programs, sessions, & networking opportunities for legal professionals in Canada

Canadian Cattlemen's Association 2011 Semi-Annual Meeting & Convention
Date: August 9-12, 2011
Location: Deerfoot Inn & Casino
Calgary, AB
Sponsor/Contact: Canadian Cattlemen's Association
#310, 6715 - 8 St. NE
Calgary, AB T2E 7H7
403-275-8558 Fax: 403-274-5686
E-mail: feedback@cattle.ca
URL: www.cattle.ca
Scope: National
Purpose: A gathering of producers & industry affiliates
Contact Information: Communications Manager: Gina Teel, Phone: 403-275-8558, ext. 406, E-mail: teelg@cattle.ca

Canadian Institute of Chartered Accountants 2011 IFRS Immersion 2 Course
Date: August 15-18, 2011
Location: Delta Barrington
Halifax, NS
Sponsor/Contact: Canadian Institute of Chartered Accountants
277 Wellington St. West
Toronto, ON M5V 3H2
416-977-3222 Fax: 416-977-8585
URL: www.cica.ca
Scope: National
Purpose: Topics include standards, consolidations, foreign exchange, stock compensation, debt & equity, & derivatives & hedging
Contact Information: Principal, Conferences & Courses, Continuing Education: Pam Robertson, Phone: 416-204-3296, E-mail: pam.robertson@cica.ca; Manager, Conferences & Courses, Continuing Education: Sheri Price, Phone: 416-204-3425, E-mail: sheri.price@cica.ca; Registrar, Conferences & Courses, Continuing Ed.: Liza Cruz, Phone: 416-204-3263, E-mail: liza.cruz@cica.ca

Canadian Institute of Chartered Accountants 2011 In-depth Tax Course (Part 3)
Date: August 20-24, 2011
Location: Westin Whistler Resort & Spa
Whistler, BC
Sponsor/Contact: Canadian Institute of Chartered Accountants
277 Wellington St. West
Toronto, ON M5V 3H2
416-977-3222 Fax: 416-977-8585
URL: www.cica.ca
Scope: National
Purpose: Topics include amalgamations & wind-up transactions, debt restructuring, tax loss planning, stock options, & financing structures
Contact Information: Principal, Conferences & Courses, Continuing Education: Steve Johnston, Phone: 416-204-3332, E-mail: steve.johnston@cica.ca; Manager, Conferences & Courses, Continuing Ed.: Kieran Murphy, Phone: 416-204-3337, E-mail: kieran.murphy@cica.ca; Registrar, Conferences & Courses, Continuing Ed.: Liza Cruz, Phone: 416-204-3263, E-mail: liza.cruz@cica.ca

Canadian Institute of Chartered Accountants 2011 Practice Management Workshop for SME Advisors
Date: August 3-5, 2011
Location: Westin Whistler Resort
Whistler, BC
Sponsor/Contact: Canadian Institute of Chartered Accountants
277 Wellington St. West
Toronto, ON M5V 3H2
416-977-3222 Fax: 416-977-8585
URL: www.cica.ca
Scope: National
Purpose: Workshop topics include effective human resource practices, business development, IT opportunities, & performance metrics
Contact Information: Director, Continuing Education: Frank Colantonio, CA, Phone: 416-204-3328, E-mail: frank.colantonio@cica.ca; Manager, Conferences & Courses, Continuing Education: Jennifer McEdwards, Phone: 416-204-3338, E-mail: jennifer.mcedwards@cica.ca; Registrar, Conferences & Courses, Continuing Ed.: Liza Cruz, Phone: 416-204-3263, E-mail: liza.cruz@cica.ca

Canadian Medical Association 2011 144th Annual Meeting
Date: August 21-24, 2011
Location: St. John's Convention Centre
St. John's, NL
Sponsor/Contact: Canadian Medical Association
1867 Alta Vista Dr.
Ottawa, ON K1G 5W8
613-731-8610 Fax: 613-236-8864
E-mail: cmamsc@cma.ca; cmatechsupport@cma.ca (technical support)
URL: www.cma.ca
Scope: National
Purpose: Education sessions, the annual meeting, the installation & awards ceremony, & networking opportunities
Contact Information: Registration Officer, Phone: 1-800-663-7336, ext. 2383, E-mail: gcregistrations@cma.ca

Canadian Water Resources Association, Alberta Branch, 2011 Course: Applied Fluvial Geomorphology, Level 1
Date: August 15-19, 2011
Location: Golder Associates Conference Facilities
Calgary, AB
Sponsor/Contact: Canadian Water Resources Association
c/o Membership Office
9 Covus Crt.
Ottawa, ON K2E 7Z4
613-237-9363 Fax: 613-594-5190
E-mail: services@aic.ca
URL: www.cwra.org
Scope: Provincial
Purpose: Topics include the fundamentals of river behaviour, sedimentation, fluvial geomorphology, streambank erosion, restoration, fish habitat improvement, & riparian grazing management
Contact Information: Presenter: Dave Rosgen, P.H., Ph.D., Phone: 970-568-0002, Fax: 970-568=0014

Growing Your Farm Profits 2011 Bruce County Workshop
Date: August 11 & 18, 2011
Location: Bruce County, ON
Sponsor/Contact: Ontario Soil & Crop Improvement Association
1 Stone Rd. West
Guelph, ON N1G 4Y2
519-826-4214 Fax: 519-826-4224
E-mail: oscia@ontariosoilcrop.org
URL: www.ontariosoilcrop.org
Scope: Local
Purpose: A workshop & discussion about the main planning principles relevant to Ontario farms
Contact Information: Ontario Soil & Crop Improvement Association Program Representative: Jayne Dietrich, Phone: 519-367-5930, E-mail: bruce@ontariosoilcrop.org

Growing Your Farm Profits 2011 Huron County Workshop
Date: August 2 & 9, 2011
Location: Clinton, ON
Sponsor/Contact: Ontario Soil & Crop Improvement Association
1 Stone Rd. West
Guelph, ON N1G 4Y2
519-826-4214 Fax: 519-826-4224
E-mail: oscia@ontariosoilcrop.org
URL: www.ontariosoilcrop.org
Scope: Local
Purpose: A workshop for farm management teams to learn to plan for & manage farm business success
Contact Information: Ontario Soil & Crop Improvement Association Program Representative: Lois Sinclair, Phone: 519-357-3146, E-mail: huron@ontariosoilcrop.org

Institute of Transportation Engineers 2011 Annual Meeting & Exhibit
Date: August 13-26, 2011
Location: America's Center
St. Louis, MO USA
Sponsor/Contact: Institute of Transportation Engineers
#300, 1099 - 14th St. NW
Washington, DC USA
202-289-0222 Fax: 202-289-7722
E-mail: ite_staff@ite.org
URL: www.ite.org
Scope: International
Contact Information: Contact, Registration Information: Sallie C. Dollins, E-mail: sdollins@ite.org; Contact, Technical Program: Aliyah N. Horton, E-mail: ahorton@ite.org; Contact, Exhibits: Christina Garneski, E-mail: cgarneski@ite.org; Contact, Paper Submittals: Eunice Chege, E-mail: echege@ite.org

Local Government Management Association of BC Professional Development Program: Municipal Administration Training Institute - Foundations Program
Date: August 7-12, 2011
Location: University of Victoria
Victoria, BC
Sponsor/Contact: Local Government Management Association of British Columbia
Central Building
620 View St., 7th Fl.
Victoria, BC V8W 1J6
250-383-7032 Fax: 250-384-4879
E-mail: office@lgma.ca; editor@lgma.ca (magazine); ads@lgma.ca
URL: www.lgma.ca
Scope: Provincial
Purpose: A week long residential program, providing an overview of local government administration
Contact Information: Phone: 250-383-7032; Fax: 250-383-4879; E-mail: office@lgma.ca

Plant Biology 2011
Date: August 6-10, 2011
Location: Palais des congrès (Convention Centre)
Minneapolis, MN
Sponsor/Contact: American Society of Plant Biologists
15501 Monona Dr.
Rockville, MD USA
301-251-0560 Fax: 301-279-2996
E-mail: info@aspb.org
URL: www.aspb.org
Scope: International

Contact Information: Director of Meetings, Marketing, & Membership: Jean Rosenberg, E-mail: jean@aspb.org

SER 4th International World Conference on Ecological Restoration: Re-establishing the Link between Nature & Culture
Date: August 21-25, 2011
Location: Mérida, Yucatán, México
Sponsor/Contact: Society for Ecological Restoration International
#1, 285 West 18th St.
Tucson, AZ USA
520-622-5485 Fax: 520-626-5485
URL: www.ser.org
Scope: International
Purpose: Featuring symposia, keynote & plenary speakers, training workshops, scientific sessions, & field trips to examine the challenges of climate change, habitat loss, biodiversity, & sustainable development
Contact Information: E-mail, General Information: info@ser2011.org; E-mail, Exhibiting & Advertising: exhibitors@ser2011.org; E-mail, Sponsorship Opportunities: sponsors@ser2011.org

September

Alberta Forest Products Association 2011 69th Annual General Meeting & Conference
Date: September 28-30, 2011
Location: Fairmont Jasper Park Lodge
Jasper, AB
Sponsor/Contact: Alberta Forest Products Association
#500, 10709 Jasper Ave.
Edmonton, AB T5J 3N3
780-452-2841 Fax: 780-455-0505
E-mail: info@albertforestproducts.ca
URL: www.albertaforestproducts.ca
Scope: Provincial
Purpose: The annual general meeting, committee meeetings, panel sessions on government & industry perspectives, an awards presentation, & a social program
Contact Information: Director, Communications: Brock Mulligan, Phone: 780-452-2841, ext. 229

Alberta Irrigation Projects Association 2011 Directors' Meeting
Date: September 19, 2011
Location: Magrath Seniors' Centre
Magrath, AB
Sponsor/Contact: Alberta Irrigation Projects Association
#909, 400 - 4 Ave. South
Lethbridge, AB T1K 7H5
403-328-3063 Fax: 403-327-1043
E-mail: info@aipa.org
URL: www.aipa.org
Scope: Provincial
Contact Information: Administrator: Vicky Kress, E-mail: vicky.kress@aipa.org

Alberta Urban Municipalities Association 2011 Annual Convention
Date: September 27 - October 1, 2011
Location: Calgary, AB
Sponsor/Contact: Alberta Urban Municipalities Association
10507 Saskatchewan Dr. NW
Edmonton, AB T6E 4S1 Canada
780-433-4431 Fax: 780-433-4454
E-mail: main@auma.ca
URL: www.auma.ca

American Society of Mechanical Engineers 2011 14th International Conference on Environmental Remediation & Radioactive Waste Management
Date: September 25-29, 2011
Location: Centre des congrès
Reims, France
Sponsor/Contact: American Society of Mechanical Engineers
3 Park Ave.
New York, NY USA
800-843-2763
E-mail: infocentral@asme.org
URL: www.asme.org
Scope: International
Purpose: The following technical areas will be addressed at the conference: Low/Intermediate-Level Radioactive Waste Management; Spent Fuel, Fissile Material, Transuranic; Facility Decontamination & Decommissioning; Environmental Remediation; Environmental Management / Public Involvement / Crosscutting Issues / Global Partnering; & General or Unassigned Abstracts
Contact Information: Contact: Programs & Events: Vince Dilworth, E-mail: dilworthv@asme.org

American Society of Mechanical Engineers 2011 6th Frontiers in Biomedical Devices Conference & Exhibition
Date: September 26-27, 2011
Location: Hyatt Regency Irvine
Irvine, CA USA
Sponsor/Contact: American Society of Mechanical Engineers
3 Park Ave.
New York, NY USA
800-843-2763
E-mail: infocentral@asme.org
URL: www.asme.org
Scope: International
Purpose: Technical papers, talks, & posters about developments in biomedical devices and clinical practices presented by experts in the clinical, academic, & commercial sectors
Contact Information: Contact, Programs & Events: Lee Hawkins, E-mail: hawkinsl@asme.org

American Society of Mechanical Engineers 2011 Conference on Smart Materials, Adaptive Structures, & Intelligent Systems
Date: September 18-21, 2011
Location: Firesky Resort & Spa
Scottsdale, AZ USA
Sponsor/Contact: American Society of Mechanical Engineers
3 Park Ave.
New York, NY USA
800-843-2763
E-mail: infocentral@asme.org
URL: www.asme.org
Scope: International
Purpose: Featuring the following symposia: Multifunctional Materials; Active Materials, Mechanics, & Behavior; Modeling, Simulation, & Control; Enabling Technologies & Integrated System Design; Structural Health Monitoring / NDE; Bio-inspired Smart Materials & Structures; & A Guest Symposium on Sustainability
Contact Information: Contact, Events & Meetings: Mary Jakubowski, E-mail: JakubowskiM@asme.org

American Society of Mechanical Engineers 2011 Small Modular Reactors Symposium
Date: September 28-30, 2011
Location: Hyatt Regency Washington on Capitol Hill
Washington, DC USA
Sponsor/Contact: American Society of Mechanical Engineers
3 Park Ave.
New York, NY USA
800-843-2763
E-mail: infocentral@asme.org
URL: www.asme.org
Scope: International
Purpose: The following technical tracks will be presented: Plant Applications, Engineering & Design; Systems, Structures, Components, & Materials; Fuel & Fuel Cycles; Nuclear Engineering & Analysis (Reactor Physics, Concepts, Thermal Hydraulics); Instrumentation & Controls; Risk Assessment Methods; Safety, Codes & Standards, Regulatory Issues, & Licensing; Advanced Manufacturing, Modular Fabrication & Plant Construction; Supply Chain Mgmt; Plant Economics
Contact Information: Contact, Programs & Events: Mary Jakubowski, E-mail: jakubowski@asme.org

American Water Works Association 2011 Distribution Systems Symposium & Exposition & Water Security Conference
Date: September 11-14, 2011
Location: Nashville, TN USA
Sponsor/Contact: American Water Works Association
6666 West Quincy Ave.
Denver, CO USA
303-794-7711 Fax: 303-347-0804
E-mail: custsvc@awwa.org
URL: www.awwa.org
Scope: International
Purpose: A symposium for distribution engineering & operations professionals & a security conference about emergency preparedness in the water sector
Contact Information: Manager, Conference & Exhibits: Lynn Lyons, E-mail: llyons@awwa.org; Specialty Conference Coordinator: Sarah Abeyta, E-mail: smejia@awwa.org; Exhibits Coordinator: Chris Collins, E-mail: ccollins@awwa.org; Senior Secretary: Theresa Redinger, E-mail: tredinger@awwa.org

American Water Works Association 2011 Financial Management Seminar: The Cost of Service Rate Making
Date: September 21-23, 2011
Location: Planet Hollywood Resort & Casino
Las Vegas, NV USA
Sponsor/Contact: American Water Works Association
6666 West Quincy Ave.
Denver, CO USA
303-794-7711 Fax: 303-347-0804
E-mail: custsvc@awwa.org
URL: www.awwa.org
Scope: International
Purpose: A three day course of interest to rate designers & analysts, accounting professionals, water utility managers, water resources professionals, conservation officers, & municipal & regional government officials
Contact Information: American Water Works Association Customer Service Department, Phone: 800-926-7337, E-mail: custsvc@awwa.org

British Columbia Nature (Federation of British Columbia Naturalists) 2011 Nature Conference & Fall General Meeting
Date: September 29 - October 2, 2011
Location: Delta, BC
Sponsor/Contact: British Columbia Nature (Federation of British Columbia Naturalists)
c/o Parks Heritage Centre
1620 Mount Seymour Rd.
North Vancouver, BC V7G 2R9
604-985-3057
E-mail: manager@bcnature.ca
URL: www.bcnature.ca
Scope: Provincial
Purpose: A gathering of British Columbia natural history groups & local nature clubs, hosted by the Delta Naturalists' Society
Contact Information: Office Manager: Betty Davison, E-mail: manager@bcnature.ca

Canada - Ontario Environmental Farm Plan Program 2011 Bruce County Workshop
Date: September 13 & 20, 2011
Location: Bruce County, ON
Sponsor/Contact: Ontario Soil & Crop Improvement Association
1 Stone Rd. West
Guelph, ON N1G 4Y2
519-826-4214 Fax: 519-826-4224
E-mail: oscia@ontariosoilcrop.org
URL: www.ontariosoilcrop.org
Scope: Local
Purpose: A local workshop with information about the Risk Assessment & Action Plan

Contact Information: Ontario Soil & Crop Improvement Association Program Representative: Jayne Dietrich, Phone: 519-367-5930, E-mail: bruce@ontariosoilcrop.org

Canadian Association of Zoos & Aquariums 2011 Annual Conference
Date: September 28 - October 1, 2011
Location: Kicking Horse Grizzly Bear Refuge
Golden, BC
Sponsor/Contact: Canadian Association of Zoos & Aquariums
#400, 280 Metcalfe St.
Ottawa, ON K2P 1R7
613-567-0099 Fax: 613-233-5438
E-mail: info@caza.ca
URL: www.caza.ca
Scope: National
Purpose: An opportunity to make contacts & exchange information with other zoo & aquarium professionals
Contact Information: Chair, Conference Committee: Denise Prefontaine, E-mail: info@caza.ca

Canadian Avalanche Association 2011 Course: Advanced Weather Skills for Avalanche Workers
Date: September 26-28, 2011
Location: British Columbia
Sponsor/Contact: Canadian Avalanche Association
P.O. Box 2759
110 MacKenzie Ave.
Revelstoke, BC V0E 2S0
250-837-2435 Fax: 250-837-4624
E-mail: info@avalanche.ca
URL: www.avalanche.ca
Scope: National
Purpose: The influence of meteorological parameters on snowpack stability, & how changes in those parameters can be detected in advance
Contact Information: Manager, Industry Training Program: Emily Grady, Phone: 250-837-2435, ext. 223, E-mail: egrady@avalanche.ca

Canadian Avalanche Association 2011 Course: Introduction to Snow Avalanche Mapping
Date: September 12-17, 2011
Location: Golden, BC
Sponsor/Contact: Canadian Avalanche Association
P.O. Box 2759
110 MacKenzie Ave.
Revelstoke, BC V0E 2S0
250-837-2435 Fax: 250-837-4624
E-mail: info@avalanche.ca
URL: www.avalanche.ca
Scope: National
Purpose: An introduction to snow avalanche mapping for persons working or interested in working in the avalanche risk management industry
Contact Information: Manager, Industry Training Program: Emily Grady, Phone: 250-837-2435, ext. 223, E-mail: egrady@avalanche.ca

Canadian Avalanche Association 2011 Course: Introduction to Snow Avalanche Mapping
Date: September 25-30, 2011
Location: Nelson, BC
Sponsor/Contact: Canadian Avalanche Association
P.O. Box 2759
110 MacKenzie Ave.
Revelstoke, BC V0E 2S0
250-837-2435 Fax: 250-837-4624
E-mail: info@avalanche.ca
URL: www.avalanche.ca
Scope: National
Purpose: Skills learned include analyzing climate data, conducting air photograph interpretation, determining the location of avalanche paths, estimating the size & frequency of avalanche occurrences, collecting & recording observations, & presenting data according to industry standards
Contact Information: Manager, Industry Training Program: Emily Grady, Phone: 250-837-2435, ext. 223, E-mail: egrady@avalanche.ca

Canadian Avalanche Association 2011 Course: Introduction to Weather Skills for Avalanche Workers
Date: September 24-25, 2011
Location: British Columbia
Sponsor/Contact: Canadian Avalanche Association
P.O. Box 2759
110 MacKenzie Ave.
Revelstoke, BC V0E 2S0
250-837-2435 Fax: 250-837-4624
E-mail: info@avalanche.ca
URL: www.avalanche.ca
Scope: National
Purpose: A course for persons interested in learning more about weather, its behaviour in mountainous regions, & its interaction with snowpacks
Contact Information: Manager, Industry Training Program: Emily Grady, Phone: 250-837-2435, ext. 223, E-mail: egrady@avalanche.ca

Canadian Biosolids & Residuals 2011 6th Joint Conference & The 34th Québec Symposium on Wastewater: Biosolids Beneficial Use Trends - Here & There
Date: September 25-27, 2011
Location: Centre des Congrès de Québec
Québec, QC
Sponsor/Contact: Water Environment Association of Ontario
P.O. Box 176
Milton, ON L9T 4N9
416-410-6933 Fax: 416-410-1626
E-mail: julie.vincent@weao.org
URL: www.weao.org
Scope: Provincial
Purpose: Organized by Réseau environnement, in collaboration with the Water Environment Association of Ontario, the British Columbia Water & Waste Association, & the Atlantic Canada Water Works Association
Contact Information: Contact, Abstract Information: Philippe Kouadio, E-mail: pkouadio@reseau-environnement.com

Canadian Institute of Chartered Accountants 2011 Annual Financial Reporting & Accounting Conference (IFRS & ASPE)
Date: September 26-27, 2011
Location: Metro Toronto Convention Centre
Toronto, ON
Sponsor/Contact: Canadian Institute of Chartered Accountants
277 Wellington St. West
Toronto, ON M5V 3H2
416-977-3222 Fax: 416-977-8585
URL: www.cica.ca
Scope: National
Purpose: A financial reporting & accounting event focussing upon emerging issues encountered by Canadian private corporations & publicly traded companies
Contact Information: Principal, Conferences & Courses, Continuing Education: Valerie Leach, Phone: 416-204-3451, E-mail: valerie.leach@cica.ca; Manager, Conferences & Courses, Continuing Education: Sheri Price, Phone: 416-204-3425, E-mail: sheri.price@cica.ca

Canadian Institute of Chartered Accountants 2011 Commodity Tax Symposium
Date: September 26-27, 2011
Location: Westin Ottawa Hotel
Ottawa, ON
Sponsor/Contact: Canadian Institute of Chartered Accountants
277 Wellington St. West
Toronto, ON M5V 3H2
416-977-3222 Fax: 416-977-8585
URL: www.cica.ca
Scope: National
Purpose: Information for professionals working in or advising businesses in the area of indirect taxation
Contact Information: Principal, Conferences & Courses, Continuing Education: Steve Johnston, Phone: 416-204-3332, E-mail: steve.johnston@cica.ca; Manager, Conferences & Courses, Continuing Ed.: Kieran Murphy, Phone: 416-204-3337, E-mail: kieran.murphy@cica.ca; Registrar, Conferences & Courses, Continuing Ed.: Liza Cruz, Phone: 416-204-3263, E-mail: liza.cruz@cica.ca

Canadian Institute of Chartered Accountants 2011 IFRS Immersion 1 Course
Date: September 19-22, 2011
Location: Hilton Toronto Hotel
Toronto, ON
Sponsor/Contact: Canadian Institute of Chartered Accountants
277 Wellington St. West
Toronto, ON M5V 3H2
416-977-3222 Fax: 416-977-8585
URL: www.cica.ca
Scope: National
Purpose: Topics covered include standards, financial statement presentation, provisions & contingent liabilities, revenue recognition, & fair value measurement
Contact Information: Principal, Conferences & Courses, Continuing Education: Pam Robertson, Phone: 416-204-3296, E-mail: pam.robertson@cica.ca; Manager, Conferences & Courses, Continuing Ed.: Sheri Price, Phone: 416-204-3425, E-mail: sheri.price@cica.ca; Registrar, Conferences & Courses, Continuing Ed.: Liza Cruz, Phone: 416-204-3263, E-mail: liza.cruz@cica.ca

Canadian Institute of Chartered Accountants 2011 In-depth Brokers & Investment Dealers Course
Date: September 7-9, 2011
Location: St. Andrew's Club & Conference Centre
Toronto, ON
Sponsor/Contact: Canadian Institute of Chartered Accountants
277 Wellington St. West
Toronto, ON M5V 3H2
416-977-3222 Fax: 416-977-8585
URL: www.cica.ca
Scope: National
Purpose: A course presented in cooperation with the Investment Industry Regulatory Organization of Canada
Contact Information: Principal, Continuing Education: Barry Novak, Phone: 416-204-3377, E-mail: barry.novak@cica.ca; Manager, Continuing Education: Jennifer McEdwards, Phone: 416-204-3338, E-mail: Jennifer.mcedwards@cica.ca

Canadian Institute of Forestry / Institut forestier du Canada 2011 103rd Annual General Meeting & Conference
Date: September 18-21, 2011
Location: Deerhurst Resort
Huntsville, ON
Sponsor/Contact: Canadian Institute of Forestry
c/o The Canadian Ecology Centre
P.O. Box 430
6905 Hwy. 17 West
Mattawa, ON P0H 1V0
705-744-1715 Fax: 705-744-1716
E-mail: admin@cif-ifc.org; questions@cif-ifc.org
URL: www.cif-ifc.org
Scope: National
Purpose: Presentations, a research poster session, commercial displays, & field trips in Algonquin Provincial Park, related to topics such as biomass economics & sustainability, international forestry ethnobotany, urban forestry, emulating natural disturbances, stock production, silviculture of declining tree species, & forest inventory
Contact Information: Sponsorship Contact: Krysta Souliere, E-mail: ksouliere@cif-ifc.org

Canadian Institute of Mining, Metallurgy & Petroleum 2011 Smart Learning Seminar: Health Safety Mining Innovations - People & Practice
Date: September 23-24, 2011
Location: University of AB, Lyster Conference Ctr.
Sponsor/Contact: Canadian Institute of Mining, Metallurgy & Petroleum
CIM National Office
#1250, 3500, boul de Maisonneuve ouest
Westmount, QC H3Z 3C1

Trade Shows, Conferences and Seminars

514-939-2710 Fax: 514-939-2714
E-mail: cim@cim.org
URL: www.cim.org
Scope: National
Contact Information: Seminar Chair: Tim Joseph, P.Eng, FCIM, Phone: 780-492-3810, E-mail: tim.joseph@ualberta.ca

Canadian Medical Association Physician Management Institute 2011 Course: Disruptive Behaviour - Resolving Personalized Conflict
Date: September 28-30, 2011
Location: Delta Vancouver Suites
Vancouver, BC
Sponsor/Contact: Canadian Medical Association
1867 Alta Vista Dr.
Ottawa, ON K1G 5W8
613-731-8610 Fax: 613-236-8864
E-mail: cmamsc@cma.ca; cmatechsupport@cma.ca (technical support)
URL: www.cma.ca
Scope: National
Purpose: A course developed in collaboration with the Canadian Medical Association Centre for Physician Health & Well-being to assist physician leaders handle distressed physicians
Anticipated Attendance: 40
Contact Information: Canadian Medical Association Physician Management Institute, Phone: 800-663-7336, ext. 2319, Fax: 613-521-1268, E-mail: pmi@cma.ca

Canadian Medical Association Physician Management Institute 2011 Course: Dollars & Sense - Finance & Economics for the Health Care Leader
Date: September 16-18, 2011
Location: Fairmont Le Château Montebello
Montebello, QC
Sponsor/Contact: Canadian Medical Association
1867 Alta Vista Dr.
Ottawa, ON K1G 5W8
613-731-8610 Fax: 613-236-8864
E-mail: cmamsc@cma.ca; cmatechsupport@cma.ca (technical support)
URL: www.cma.ca
Scope: National
Purpose: Participants learn to resolve fundamental economic dilemmas in health care
Anticipated Attendance: 25
Contact Information: Canadian Medical Association Physician Management Institute, Phone: 800-663-7336, ext. 2319, Fax: 613-521-1268, E-mail: pmi@cma.ca

Canadian Medical Association Physician Management Institute 2011 Course: Negotiation & Conflict Management - Vital Skills for Success
Date: September 25-27, 2011
Location: Delta Vancouver Suites
Vancouver, BC
Sponsor/Contact: Canadian Medical Association
1867 Alta Vista Dr.
Ottawa, ON K1G 5W8
613-731-8610 Fax: 613-236-8864
E-mail: cmamsc@cma.ca; cmatechsupport@cma.ca (technical support)
URL: www.cma.ca
Scope: National
Purpose: Topics covered include managing conflicts within organizations, preventing conflict & influencing escalating conflicts, enhancing collaboration & consensus, principles of negotiation, & dealing with difference & difficulty
Anticipated Attendance: 40
Contact Information: Canadian Medical Association Physician Management Institute, Phone: 800-663-7336, ext. 2319, Fax: 613-521-1268, E-mail: pmi@cma.ca

Canadian Urban Transit Association Training Course: SmartDRIVER Train the Trainer
Date: September 7-9, 2011
Location: Burlington Transit
Burlington, ON
Sponsor/Contact: Canadian Urban Transit Association
#1401, 55 York St.
Toronto, ON M5J 1R7
416-365-9800 Fax: 416-365-1295
E-mail: transit@cutaactu.ca
URL: www.cutaactu.ca
Scope: Provincial
Purpose: Defensive driving
Contact Information: Course Contact: John Moudakis, Phone: 416-365-9800, ext. 102, Fax: 416-365-1295, E-mail: moudakis@cutaactu.ca

Canadian Urban Transit Association Training Course: Transit Ambassador Train the Trainer
Date: September 12-16, 2011
Location: Langford Facility, BC Transit
Victoria, BC
Sponsor/Contact: Canadian Urban Transit Association
#1401, 55 York St.
Toronto, ON M5J 1R7
416-365-9800 Fax: 416-365-1295
E-mail: transit@cutaactu.ca
URL: www.cutaactu.ca
Scope: Provincial
Purpose: A course that recognizes the importance of excellent customer service for all transit employees & management
Contact Information: Course Contact: John Moudakis, Phone: 416-365-9800, ext. 102, Fax: 416-365-1295, E-mail: moudakis@cutaactu.ca

Canadian Urban Transit Association Training Course: Transit Scheduling & Runcutting
Date: September 25-30, 2011
Location: Tigh-Na-Mara Resort & Conference Centre
Parksville, BC
Sponsor/Contact: Canadian Urban Transit Association
#1401, 55 York St.
Toronto, ON M5J 1R7
416-365-9800 Fax: 416-365-1295
E-mail: transit@cutaactu.ca
URL: www.cutaactu.ca
Scope: Provincial
Purpose: Workshops, case studies, presentations, projects, & simulations
Contact Information: Course Contact: John Moudakis, Phone: 416-365-9800, ext. 102, Fax: 416-365-1295, E-mail: moudakis@cutaactu.ca

Centre for Land Reclamation & the Australian Centre for Geomechanics 2011 6th Annual International Conference on Mine Closure
Date: September 18-21, 2011
Location: Lake Louise, AB
Sponsor/Contact: Canadian Land Reclamation Association
PO Box 61047, RPO Kensington
Calgary, AB T2N 4S6
403-289-9435 Fax: 403-289-9435
E-mail: clra@telusplanet.net; aquila7@telusplanet.net (Magazine)
URL: www.clra.ca
Scope: International
Purpose: Research findings & best practices related to mine closure for reclamation scientists, tailings cappings specialists, engineers, & economists from around the world
Contact Information: Golder Associates Ltd., Address: #102, 2535 - 3rd Ave. SE, Calgary, AB T2A 7W5

Council of Forest Industries 2011 Annual Convention
Date: September 15-16, 2011
Location: Prince George, BC
Sponsor/Contact: Council of Forest Industries
Pender Place I Business Building
#1501, 700 Pender St. West
Vancouver, BC V6C 1G8
604-684-0211 Fax: 604-687-4930
E-mail: info@cofi.org
URL: www.cofi.org
Scope: National
Purpose: Presentations & panels addressing forstry issues in British Columbia
Contact Information: Phone: 250-564-5136; Fax: 250-564-3588; E-mail: ac2011@cofi.org

Electric Vehicle Society of Canada 2011 Meeting
Date: September 15, 2011
Location: Ashtonbee Campus, Centennial College
Toronto, ON
Sponsor/Contact: Electric Vehicle Society of Canada
21 Burritt Rd.
Toronto, ON M1R 3S5
416-755-4324 Fax: 416-755-4324
E-mail: info@evsociety.ca
URL: www.evsociety.ca
Scope: National
Contact Information: E-mail: info@evsociety.ca

Global 2011: Innovative Nuclear Energy Systems Toward 2030 & Beyond
Date: September 2011
Location: , Japan
Sponsor/Contact: Canadian Nuclear Society
655 Bay St., 17th Fl.
Toronto, ON M5G 2K4
416-977-7620 Fax: 416-977-8131
E-mail: cns-snc@on.aibn.com
URL: www.cns-snc.ca
Scope: International
Purpose: An event co-sponsored by the Canadian Nuclear Society
Contact Information: Canadian Nuclear Society Office: Phone: 416-977-7620, E-mail: cns-snc@on.aibn.com

Growing Your Farm Profits 2011 Huron County Workshop
Date: September 30 & October 7, 2011
Location: Clinton, ON
Sponsor/Contact: Ontario Soil & Crop Improvement Association
1 Stone Rd. West
Guelph, ON N1G 4Y2
519-826-4214 Fax: 519-826-4224
E-mail: oscia@ontariosoilcrop.org
URL: www.ontariosoilcrop.org
Scope: Local
Purpose: A starting step towards potential cost-share opportunities available through Growing Forward Business Development for Farm Businesses
Contact Information: Ontario Soil & Crop Improvement Association Program Representative: Lois Sinclair, Phone: 519-357-3146, E-mail: huron@ontariosoilcrop.org

Growing Your Farm Profits 2011 Leeds Area Workshop
Date: September 13 & 20, 2011
Location: Kemptville, ON
Sponsor/Contact: Ontario Soil & Crop Improvement Association
1 Stone Rd. West
Guelph, ON N1G 4Y2
519-826-4214 Fax: 519-826-4224
E-mail: oscia@ontariosoilcrop.org
URL: www.ontariosoilcrop.org
Scope: Local
Purpose: An educational program, with opportunities to network with other local Ontario farmers
Contact Information: Ontario Soil & Crop Improvement Association Program Representative: Rita Vogel, Phone: 613-275-1753, E-mail: leeds@ontariosoilcrop.org

Growing Your Farm Profits 2011 Ottawa Carleton, Dundas, Lanark, & Grenville Areas Workshop
Date: September 13 & 20, 2011
Location: Kemptville, ON
Sponsor/Contact: Ontario Soil & Crop Improvement Association
1 Stone Rd. West
Guelph, ON N1G 4Y2
519-826-4214 Fax: 519-826-4224
E-mail: oscia@ontariosoilcrop.org
URL: www.ontariosoilcrop.org

Scope: Local
Purpose: A two day workshop to help farmers reach their goals of farm business success
Contact Information: Ontario Soil & Crop Improvement Association Program Representative: Shelley McPhail, Phone: 613-256-4011, E-mail: dundasGYFP@ontariosoilcrop.org, grenvilleGYFP@ontariosoilcrop.org, lanarkGYFP@ontariosoilcrop.org, carletonGYFP@ontariosoilcrop.org

Growing Your Farm Profits 2011 Renfrew County Workshop
Date: September 13 & 20, 2011
Location: Kemptville, ON
Sponsor/Contact: Ontario Soil & Crop Improvement Association
1 Stone Rd. West
Guelph, ON N1G 4Y2
519-826-4214 Fax: 519-826-4224
E-mail: oscia@ontariosoilcrop.org
URL: www.ontariosoilcrop.org
Scope: Local
Purpose: A practical workshop to assist participants in evaluating their current management practices, developing action plans, & implementing those plans
Contact Information: Ontario Soil & Crop Improvement Association Program Representative: Glen Smith, Phone: 613-628-2987, E-mail: renfrew@ontariosoilcrop.org

Growing Your Farm Profits 2011 Wellington County Workshop
Date: September 9 & 16, 2011
Location: Elora OMAFRA Office
Elora, ON
Sponsor/Contact: Ontario Soil & Crop Improvement Association
1 Stone Rd. West
Guelph, ON N1G 4Y2
519-826-4214 Fax: 519-826-4224
E-mail: oscia@ontariosoilcrop.org
URL: www.ontariosoilcrop.org
Scope: Local
Purpose: An educational program about assessing one's business, identifying priorities, & developing action plans
Contact Information: Ontario Soil & Crop Improvement Association Program Representative: John Benham, Phone: 519-846-0941, E-mail: wellington@ontariosoilcrop.org

Health Sciences Association of Alberta Board Retreat & Stategic Planning
Date: September 12-14, 2011
Location: Alberta
Sponsor/Contact: Health Sciences Association of Alberta
10212 - 112 St.
Edmonton, AB T5K 1M4
780-488-0168 Fax: 780-488-0534
URL: www.hsaa.ca
Scope: Provincial
Contact Information: Communications Officer: Scott Pattison, E-mail: scottpat@hsaa.ca

Health Sciences Association of Alberta Chairs Conference
Date: September 15-16, 2011
Location: Edmonton, AB
Sponsor/Contact: Health Sciences Association of Alberta
10212 - 112 St.
Edmonton, AB T5K 1M4
780-488-0168 Fax: 780-488-0534
URL: www.hsaa.ca
Scope: Provincial
Contact Information: Communications Officer: Scott Pattison, E-mail: scottpat@hsaa.ca

International Union of Microbiological Societies Congress 2011
Date: September 6-16, 2011
Location: Sapporo, Japan
Sponsor/Contact: International Union of Microbiological Societies
Centralbureau voor Schimmelcultures
P.O. Box 85167
Utrecht, Netherlands
E-mail: samson@cbs.knaw.nl
URL: www.iums.org
Scope: International
Purpose: Mycology & bacteriology & applied microbiology (BAM) meetings will take place from September 6-10, & virology meetings will take place from September 11 to 16.

Metallurgy & Materials Society of the Canadian Institute of Mining, Metallurgy & Petroleum World Gold 2011 3rd International Conference
Date: September 30 - October 3, 2011
Location: Montréal Bonaventure Hotel
Montréal, QC
Sponsor/Contact: Metallurgy & Materials Society of the Canadian Institute of Mining, Metallurgy & Petroleum
#1250, 3500, boul de Maisonneuve ouest
Montréal, QC H3Z 3C1
514-939-2710
URL: www.metsoc.org
Scope: International
Purpose: Topics include the following: geology; applied & theoretical rock mechanics; management & economics; maintenance & engineering in mining; MES gold 2011 economics; environment; & mineral processing & the environment
Contact Information: World Gold Chair: Guy Deschenes, Phone: 613-992-0415, E-mail: Guy.Deschenes@NRCan-RNCan.gc.ca

National Solid Wastes Management Association 2011 Heartland Annual Conference
Date: September 27-28, 2011
Location: Quartz Mountain Resort
Lone Wolf, OK USA
Sponsor/Contact: National Solid Wastes Management Association
#300, 4301 Connecticut Ave. NW
Washington, DC USA
202-244-4700 Fax: 202-966-4824
URL: www.nswma.org
Scope: International
Contact Information: Meetings Manager: Catherine Maimon, E-mail: cmaimon@nswma.org

National Solid Wastes Management Association 2011 South Central Annual Conference
Date: September 21-22, 2011
Location: Hyatt Regency Hill Country Resort
San Antonio, TX USA
Sponsor/Contact: National Solid Wastes Management Association
#300, 4301 Connecticut Ave. NW
Washington, DC USA
202-244-4700 Fax: 202-966-4824
URL: www.nswma.org
Scope: International
Contact Information: Meetings Manager: Catherine Maimon, E-mail: cmaimon@nswma.org

National Solid Wastes Management Association 2011 Southeast Annual Conference
Date: September 13-14, 2011
Location: Omni - Amelia Island Plantation
Amelia Island, FL USA
Sponsor/Contact: National Solid Wastes Management Association
#300, 4301 Connecticut Ave. NW
Washington, DC USA
202-244-4700 Fax: 202-966-4824
URL: www.nswma.org
Scope: International
Contact Information: Meetings Manager: Catherine Maimon, E-mail: cmaimon@nswma.org

Northwestern Ontario Municipal Association 2011 Annual Regional Conference
Date: September 21-23, 2011
Location: Ontario
Sponsor/Contact: Northwestern Ontario Municipal Association
P.O. Box 10308
Thunder Bay, ON P7B 6T8
807-683-6662
E-mail: admin@noma.on.ca
URL: www.noma.on.ca
Scope: Local
Purpose: A meeting for both full & associate members of the Northwestern Ontario Municipal Association
Contact Information: Executive Director: Charla Robinson, Phone: 807-683-6662, E-mail: admin@noma.on.ca

Nuclear Reactor Thermalhydraulics 14th International Topical Meeting: Helping the Environment with Advances in Thermalhydraulics
Date: September 25-29, 2011
Location: Hilton Toronto Hotel
Toronto, ON
Sponsor/Contact: Canadian Nuclear Society
655 Bay St., 17th Fl.
Toronto, ON M5G 2K4
416-977-7620 Fax: 416-977-8131
E-mail: cns-snc@on.aibn.com
URL: www.cns-snc.ca
Scope: International
Purpose: A gathering of international academic & industry researchers & practitioners involved in engineering & scientific work focused on nuclear reactor thermalhydraulics
Contact Information: NURETH-14 Organizing Committee: E-mail: Nureth14@cns-snc.ca; Contact, Technical Program: Jovica Riznic, Phone: 613-943-0132, Fax: 613-943-1292, E-mail: jovica.riznic@cnsc-ccsn.gc.ca; Exhibition Information: E-mail: benjamin.rouben@sympatico.ca; Sponsorship Information: E-mail: luxatj@mcmaster.ca

Ontario Good Roads Association Snow School 2011
Date: September 26-28, 2011
Location: Nottawasaga Inn Resort
Alliston, ON
Sponsor/Contact: Ontario Good Roads Association
#2, 6355 Kennedy Rd.
Mississauga, ON L5T 2L5
905-795-2555 Fax: 905-795-2660
E-mail: info@ogra.org
URL: www.ogra.org
Scope: Provincial
Purpose: An overview of winter maintenance materials, equipment, & practices
Anticipated Attendance: 100
Contact Information: Administrative Assistant: Teresa Cabral-Travassos, Phone: 905-795-2555, Fax: 905-795-2660

Ontario Parks Association 2011 Registered Playground Practitioner Program
Date: September 26-30, 2011
Location: Ontario Parks Association
Milton, ON
Sponsor/Contact: Ontario Parks Association
7856 - 5th Line South, RR#4
Milton, ON L9T 2X8
905-864-6182 Fax: 905-864-6184
E-mail: opa@ontarioparksassociation.ca
URL: www.ontarioparksassociation.ca
Scope: Provincial
Purpose: Completing this program & achieving passing grades in the written examinations allows participants to be registered by the Ontario Playground Academy as playground practitioners so that they can inspect playgrounds
Contact Information: Ontario Parks Association, Fax: 905-864-6184, E-mail: opa@ontarioparksassociation.ca

Radiation Safety Institute of Canada 2011 Radiation Safety Officer Professional Certificate Course
Date: September 19-23, 2011
Location: Sutton Place Toronto
Toronto, ON
Sponsor/Contact: Radiation Safety Institute of Canada

Trade Shows, Conferences and Seminars

Head Office & National Education Centre
#300, 165 Avenue Rd.
Toronto, ON M5R 3S4
416-650-9090 Fax: 416-650-9920
E-mail: info@radiationsafety.ca
URL: www.radiationsafety.ca
Scope: National
Contact Information: Scientist & Training Coordinator: Tara Hargreaves, E-mail: th@radiationsafety.ca; General Inquiries, E-mail: info@radiationsafety.ca

Recycling Council of Alberta 2011 Waste Reduction Conference
Date: September 28-30, 2011
Location: Edmonton, AB
Sponsor/Contact: Recycling Council of Alberta
P.O. Box 23
Bluffton, AB T0C 0M0 Canada
403-843-6563 Fax: 403-843-4156
E-mail: info@recycle.ab.ca
URL: www.recycle.ab.ca
Scope: Provincial
Purpose: Presentations on waste reduction topics
Contact Information: Phone: 403-843-6563; E-mail: info@recycle.ab.ca

Sustainable Forestry Initiative 2011 Annual Conference: The Bigger Picture - Conservation, Integrity, Community
Date: September 13-15, 2011
Location: Hilton Burlington
Burlington, VA USA
Sponsor/Contact: Sustainable Forestry Initiative
#700, 900 - 17th St. NW
Washington, DC 20006 USA
E-mail: info@sfiprogram.org
URL: www.sfiprogram.org
Scope: International
Purpose: Business meetings, general sessions, the presentation of annual SFI awards, & networking opportunities
Contact Information: Conference Contact: Amy Doty, Phone: 202-596-3458, E-mail: Amy.Doty@sfiprogram.org

The American Association of Bovine Practitioners 2011 Annual Conference
Date: September 22-24, 2011
Location: St. Louis, MO USA
Sponsor/Contact: American Association of Bovine Practitioners
P.O. Box 3610
#802, 3320 Skyway Dr.
Auburn, AL USA
334-821-0442 Fax: 334-821-9532
E-mail: aabphq@aabp.org
URL: www.aabp.org
Scope: International

Toronto Field Naturalists 2011 Monthly Talk
Date: September 2011
Location: Emmanuel College
Toronto, ON
Sponsor/Contact: Toronto Field Naturalists
#1519, 2 Carlton St.
Toronto, ON M5B 1J3
416-593-2656
E-mail: office@torontofieldnaturalists.org
URL: www.torontofieldnaturalists.org
Scope: Local
Purpose: A Sunday meeting for members of Toronto Field Naturalists & visitors to learn from illustrated talks by experts on natural history
Contact Information: E-mail: office@torontofieldnaturalists.org

Union of British Columbia Municipalities 2011 Annual Convention
Date: September 26-30, 2011
Location: Vancouver Convention Centre
Vancouver, BC
Sponsor/Contact: Union of British Columbia Municipalities
#60, 10551 Shellbridge Way
Richmond, BC V6X 2W9 Canada
604-270-8226 Fax: 604-270-9116
E-mail: ubcm@civicnet.bc.ca
URL: www.civicnet.bc.ca
Scope: Provincial

Waste Management, Decommissioning, & Environmental Restoration for Canada's Nuclear Activities: Current Practices & Future Needs
Date: September 11-14, 2011
Location: Marriott Toronto Downtown Eaton Centre
Toronto, ON
Sponsor/Contact: Canadian Nuclear Society
655 Bay St., 17th Fl.
Toronto, ON M5G 2K4
416-977-7620 Fax: 416-977-8131
E-mail: cns-snc@on.aibn.com
URL: www.cns-snc.ca
Scope: National
Purpose: Featuring an equipment & services exhibition & post-conference technical tours to Canadian nuclear facilities
Contact Information: Conference Administrator: Elizabeth Muckle-Jeffs, Phone: 613-732-7068, Toll-Free Phone: 1-800-868-8776, E-mail: elizabeth@theprofessionaledge.com; Conference Registrar: Denise Rouben, Phone: 416-977-7620, E-mail: cns-snc@on.aibn.com

Western Canada Water 2011 63rd Annual Conference & Exhibition: Cycles - Challenges & Opportunities
Date: September 20-23, 2011
Location: TCU Place
Saskatoon, SK
Sponsor/Contact: Western Canada Water
P.O. Box 1708
126 - 3rd Ave. West
Cochrane, AB T4C 1B6
403-709-0064 Fax: 403-709-0068
E-mail: member@wcwwa.ca
URL: www.wcwwa.ca
Scope: Regional
Purpose: Topics include the support of aging infrastructure, the funding of new infrastructure, employee demographics, & the treatment processes for water & wastewater
Anticipated Attendance: 500+
Contact Information: Member, Western Canada Water 2011 Conference Planning Committee: Bert Munro, Phone: 403-971-4317, E-mail: munrob@ae.ca

October

Advancing Bear Care 2011
Date: October 6-11, 2011
Location: Banff Park Lodge
Banff, AB
Sponsor/Contact: International Association for Bear Research & Management
c/o Terry While, USGS-SAFL, University of Tennessee
274 Ellington Hall
Knoxville, TN USA
Fax: 865-974-3555
E-mail: tdwhite@utk.edu
URL: www.bearbiology.com
Scope: International
Purpose: Highlights of the conference include the following activities: bear species specific workshops; guest speakers who are wild & captive bear experts; hikes into bear habitat led by bear biologists & naturalists; poster presentations about bear care at zoos, sanctuaries, & rehabilitation facilities throughout the world; a bear book & art den; & a silent auction
Contact Information: E-mail: info@bearcaregroup.org, embpoulsen@hotmail.com; Contact, Poster Presentations: Gail Hedberg, E-mail: gail.hedberg@bearcaregroup.org; Bear Book & Art Den Coordinator: Judy Willard, E-mail: jdywillard@yahoo.com; Silent Auction Coordinator: Lory Palmer, E-mail: lory.palmer@bearcaregroup.org

Alberta Recreation & Parks Association 2011 Annual Conference & Energize Workshop: Recreation & Parks - Bringing Quality to Life
Date: October 27-29, 2011
Location: Fairmont Chateau Lake Louise
Lake Louise, AB
Sponsor/Contact: Alberta Recreation & Parks Association
11759 Groat Rd.
Edmonton, AB T5M 3K6 Canada
780-415-1745 Fax: 780-451-7915
E-mail: arpa@arpaonline.ca
URL: www.arpaonline.ca
Scope: Regional
Purpose: Examples of conference sub-themes are as follows: designing for healthy communities; building a culture of stewardship; harmonizing with nature; balancing work with healthy lifestyle choices; investing in wellness; & fostering social innovation & social growth
Anticipated Attendance: 400+
Contact Information: Event Planner: Brenda Hanson, Phone: 780-643-1255, E-mail: bhanson@arpaonline.ca

Alberta Recreation & Parks Association 2011 National Recreation Summit (co-hosted by Alberta Tourism, Parks & Recreation)
Date: October 23-25, 2011
Location: Fairmont Chateau Lake Louise
Lake Louise, AB
Sponsor/Contact: Alberta Recreation & Parks Association
11759 Groat Rd.
Edmonton, AB T5M 3K6 Canada
780-415-1745 Fax: 780-451-7915
E-mail: arpa@arpaonline.ca
URL: www.arpaonline.ca
Scope: National
Purpose: An event for leaders in governmental affairs, recreation development, & public policy analyses
Contact Information: Event Planner: Brenda Hanson, Phone: 780-643-1255, E-mail: bhanson@arpaonline.ca

American Society of Mechanical Engineers 2011 Committee on Fiber-Reinforced Plastic Pressure Vessels Meeting
Date: October 24-27, 2011
Location: Rio All Suite Hotel & Casino
Las Vegas, NV USA
Sponsor/Contact: American Society of Mechanical Engineers
3 Park Ave.
New York, NY USA
800-843-2763
E-mail: infocentral@asme.org
URL: www.asme.org
Scope: International
Purpose: A meeting with the Reinforced Thermoset Plastic Corrosion Resistant Equipment Committee, & the Process Piping Taskgroups
Contact Information: Meeting Contact: Paul Stumpf, E-mail: stumpfpa@asme.org

American Society of Mechanical Engineers 2011 International Offshore Pipeline Forum
Date: October 19-20, 2011
Location: Norris Conference Center
Houston, TX USA
Sponsor/Contact: American Society of Mechanical Engineers
3 Park Ave.
New York, NY USA
800-843-2763
E-mail: infocentral@asme.org
URL: www.asme.org
Scope: International
Contact Information: Event Coordinator: Celeste Torkay, E-mail: micelik@asme.or; Event Contact: Kimberly Miceli, E-mail: micelik@asme.org

American Society of Mechanical Engineers 2011 Nuclear Quality Assurance Meeting

Date: October 18-20, 2011
Location: St. Petersburg Marriott
St. Petersburg, FL USA
Sponsor/Contact: American Society of Mechanical Engineers
3 Park Ave.
New York, NY USA
800-843-2763
E-mail: infocentral@asme.org
URL: www.asme.org
Scope: International
Contact Information: Meeting Contact: Oliver Martinez, E-mail: martinezo@asme.org

American Society of Mechanical Engineers 2011 Program

Date: October 24-28, 2011
Location: Omni Houston Hotel at Westside
Houston, TX USA
Sponsor/Contact: American Society of Mechanical Engineers
3 Park Ave.
New York, NY USA
800-843-2763
E-mail: infocentral@asme.org
URL: www.asme.org
Scope: International
Purpose: Examples of programs include the following: Dynamic Loads in Industrial Facilities due to Terror Blasts & Vapor Cloud Explosions; Design Codes, Standards, & Regulations for Nuclear Power Plant Construction; Rules for Construction of Nuclear Facility Components; Inservice Inspection of Nuclear Power Plant Components; Piping Design; Two-Phase Flow & Heat Transfer; Centrifugal Pump Design & Applications; & Shock & Vibration Analysis

Association of Local Public Health Agencies 2011 Fall Symposium

Date: October 2011
Location: Ontario
Sponsor/Contact: Association of Local Public Health Agencies
#1306, 2 Carlton St.
Toronto, ON M5G 1T6
416-595-0006 Fax: 416-595-0030
E-mail: info@alphaweb.org
URL: www.alphaweb.org
Scope: Provincial
Contact Information: Registration contact: Karen Reece, Phone: 416-595-0006, ext. 25; Fax: 416-595-0030, E-mail: karen@alphaweb.org

Association of Professional Engineers & Geoscientists of British Columbia 2011 Conference & Annual General Meeting: Growing the Professional Community

Date: October 13-15, 2011
Location: Delta Grand Okanagan Conference Centre
Kelowna, BC
Sponsor/Contact: Association of Professional Engineers & Geoscientists of British Columbia
#200, 4010 Regent St.
Burnaby, BC V5C 6N2
604-430-8035 Fax: 604-430-8085
E-mail: apeginfo@apeg.bc.ca; communication@apeg.bc.ca
URL: www.apeg.bc.ca
Scope: Provincial
Purpose: Technical & business sessions, a trade exhibition, a technical tour for members of the Division of Environmental Professionals, & social events of interest to professional engineers, geoscientists, industry leaders, consultants, & government representatives
Anticipated Attendance: 700+
Contact Information: Sponsorship Contact: Shelley Bruins, Phone: 604-412-4860, E-mail: sbruins@apeg.bc.ca

British Columbia Recreation & Parks Association 2011 Ripple Effects Provincial Aquatics Conference

Date: October 20-21, 2011
Location: British Columbia
Sponsor/Contact: British Columbia Recreation & Parks Association
#101, 4664 Lougheed Hwy.
Burnaby, BC V5C 5T5
604-629-0965 Fax: 604-629-2651
E-mail: bcrpa@bcrpa.bc.ca; registration@bcrpa.bc.ca
URL: www.bcrpa.bc.ca
Scope: Provincial
Purpose: An event for aquatics professionals, featuring the fundamentals of training & workplace issues, taking place in the Lower Mainland
Contact Information: Parks & Recreation Program Coordinator: Heather Muter, Phone: 604-629-0965, ext. 229; E-mail: hmuter@bcrpa.bc.ca

CIPHEX Roadshow

Date: October - November, 2011
Sponsor/Contact: Canadian Institute of Plumbing & Heating
#330, 295 The West Mall
Toronto, ON M9C 4Z4
416-695-0447 Fax: 416-695-0450
E-mail: info@ciph.com
URL: ww.ciph.com
Scope: International
Purpose: A trade show, produced by the Canadian Institute of Plumbing & Heating in support of its regions, to present new products & technologies to the plumbing, hydronics, HVACR, electrical pipe, water treatment, & valves & fittings industries
Anticipated Attendance: 1300
Contact Information: General Manager, Trade Shows: Elizabeth McCullough, Phone: 416-695-0447, Toll-Free Phone: 1-888-275-2474, E-mail: e.mccullough@ciph.com; Coordinator: Marian Speelman, E-mail: m.speelman@ciph.com

Canadian Association of Chemical Distributors 2011 Semi Annual Meeting

Date: October 25-26, 2011
Sponsor/Contact: Canadian Association of Chemical Distributors
349 Davis Rd., #A
Oakville, ON L6J 2X2
905-844-9140 Fax: 905-844-5706
URL: www.cacd.ca
Scope: National
Contact Information: Manager, Communications & Member Services: Catherine Wieckowska, Phone: 905-844-9140, E-mail: catherine@cacd.ca

Canadian Association of Recycling Industries (CARI) 2011 14th Annual Consumers' Night

Date: October 24, 2011
Location: Fairmont Royal York
Toronto, ON
Sponsor/Contact: Canadian Association of Recycling Industries
#1, 682 Monarch Ave.
Ajax, ON L1S 4S2
905-426-9313 Fax: 905-426-9314
URL: www.cari-acir.org
Scope: National
Contact Information: Association Manager: Donna Turner, Phone: 905-426-9313, Fax: 905-426-9314, E-mail: donna@cari-acir.org; Manager, Communications & Membership: Tracy Shaw, E-mail: tracy@cari-acir.org

Canadian Conference on Physician Health 2011

Date: October 28-29, 2011
Location: Hilton Toronto Hotel
Toronto, ON
Sponsor/Contact: Canadian Medical Association
1867 Alta Vista Dr.
Ottawa, ON K1G 5W8
613-731-8610 Fax: 613-236-8864
E-mail: cmamsc@cma.ca; cmatechsupport@cma.ca (technical support)
URL: www.cma.ca
Scope: National
Purpose: Co-hosted by the Canadian Medical Association & the Ontario Medical Association Physician Health Program, in collaboration with the Canadian Medical Foundation
Contact Information: E-mail: physicianhealthconference@cma.ca

Canadian Council of Grocery Distributors, 2011 Québec Region Conference

Date: October 2011
Location: Quebec
Sponsor/Contact: Canadian Council of Grocery Distributors
#402, 6455, rue Jean-Talon est
Montréal, QC H1S 3E8
514-982-0267
URL: www.ccgd.ca
Scope: Provincial
Purpose: Speakers, briefing presentations, & networking opportunities for Canadian Council of Grocery Distributors members & non-members from across Québec
Contact Information: Conference Contact: Isabelle Gagné, Phone: 514-982-0267, ext. 229, Fax: 514-982-0659, E-mail: igagne@ccgd.ca

Canadian Dam Association 2011 Annual Conference

Date: October 15-20, 2011
Location: Delta Fredericton Hotel; Convention Ctr.
Fredericton, NB
Sponsor/Contact: Canadian Dam Association
P.O. Box 2281
Moose Jaw, SK S6TH 7W6
URL: www.cda.ca
Scope: National
Purpose: Topics include regulations & dam safety management, surveillance & instrumentation, decommissioning & restoration, long term monitoring of mining dam closures, safety of small dams, public safety management systems, & emergency preparedness
Contact Information: Conference Contact: Tony Chislett, Phone: 709-754-6933; E-mail: 2011conference@cda.ca

Canadian Gas Association 2011 Biennial Technical Symposium: Industrial Application of Gas Turbines

Date: October 17-19, 2011
Location: Fairmont Banff Springs Hotel
Banff, AB
Sponsor/Contact: Canadian Gas Association
#809, 350 Sparks St.
Ottawa, ON K1R 7S8
613-748-0057 Fax: 613-748-9078
E-mail: info@cga.ca
URL: www.cga.ca
Scope: National
Purpose: Discussion panels & the presentation of technical papers about industrial gas turbine operation
Contact Information: E-mail: help@canavents.com

Canadian Health Food Association (CHFA) Expo East 2011

Date: October 13-16, 2011
Location: Metro Toronto Convention Centre
Toronto, ON
Sponsor/Contact: Canadian Health Food Association
#302, 235 Yorkland Blvd.
Toronto, ON M2J 4Y8
416-497-6939 Fax: 905-479-3214
E-mail: info@chfa.ca
URL: www.chfa.ca
Scope: Regional
Purpose: A conference & trade show offering people who work in the natural products or organic industries the opportunity to meet with the industry's leading manufacturers, brokers, & distributors
Contact Information: Director, Trade Show & Conferences: Judy Sharpe, Toll-Free Phone: 1-800-661-4510

Canadian Institute of Chartered Accountants 2011 Conference on Environmental, Social, & Governance Issues

Trade Shows, Conferences and Seminars

Date: October 3-4, 2011
Location: Hyatt Regency
Vancouver, BC
Sponsor/Contact: Canadian Institute of Chartered Accountants
277 Wellington St. West
Toronto, ON M5V 3H2
416-977-3222 Fax: 416-977-8585
URL: www.cica.ca
Scope: National
Purpose: Environmental business risks, opportunities, & strategies
Contact Information: Principal, Continuing Education (for inquiries about technical details: Gord Beal, Phone: 416-204-3432, E-mail: gord.beal@cica.ca; Manager, Continuing Education (for general information): Jennifer McEdwards, Phone: 416-204-3338, E-mail: jennifer.mcedwards@cica.ca; Social Media: www.facebook.com/event.php?eid=137178846340745&index=1

Canadian Institute of Chartered Accountants 2011 IFRS Immersion 1 Course
Date: October 17-20, 2011
Location: Calgary Telus Convention Centre
Calgary, AB
Sponsor/Contact: Canadian Institute of Chartered Accountants
277 Wellington St. West
Toronto, ON M5V 3H2
416-977-3222 Fax: 416-977-8585
URL: www.cica.ca
Scope: National
Purpose: Coverage of the core IFRS standards, for senior accounting professionals in public practice & industry
Contact Information: Principal, Conferences & Courses, Continuing Education: Pam Robertson, Phone: 416-204-3296, E-mail: pam.robertson@cica.ca; Manager, Conferences & Courses, Continuing Ed.: Sheri Price, Phone: 416-204-3425, E-mail: sheri.price@cica.ca; Registrar, Conferences & Courses, Continuing Ed.: Liza Cruz, Phone: 416-204-3263, E-mail: liza.cruz@cica.ca

Canadian Institute of Chartered Accountants 2011 Investigative & Forensic Accounting
Date: October 26-28, 2011
Location: Le Westin Montréal
Montréal, QC
Sponsor/Contact: Canadian Institute of Chartered Accountants
277 Wellington St. West
Toronto, ON M5V 3H2
416-977-3222 Fax: 416-977-8585
URL: www.cica.ca
Scope: National
Purpose: Education on fraud investigations, risk management, dispute resolution, & insurance matters
Contact Information: Manager, Continuing Education: Anne-Marie Laderoute, Phone: 416-204-3329, E-mail: anne-marie.laderoute@cica.ca

Canadian Institute of Chartered Accountants 2011 National Conference on Income Taxes
Date: October 12-13, 2011
Location: Metro Toronto Convention Centre
Toronto, ON
Sponsor/Contact: Canadian Institute of Chartered Accountants
277 Wellington St. West
Toronto, ON M5V 3H2
416-977-3222 Fax: 416-977-8585
URL: www.cica.ca
Scope: National
Purpose: Major tax issues & strategies, plus recent court decisions & pending cases & chanages proposed for the future
Contact Information: Principal, Conferences & Courses, Continuing Education: Steve Johnson, Phone: 416-204-3332, E-mail: steve.johnston@cica.ca; Manager, Conferences & Courses, Continuing Ed.: Kieran Murphy, Phone: 416-204-3337, E-mail: kieran.murphy@cica.ca; Registrar, Conferences & Courses, Continuing Ed.: Liza Cruz, Phone: 416-204-3263, E-mail: liza.cruz@cica.ca

Canadian Institute of Chartered Accountants 2011 Public Sector & Not-for-Profit Financial Reporting Conference
Date: October 5-6, 2011
Location: Ottawa Convention Centre
Ottawa, ON
Sponsor/Contact: Canadian Institute of Chartered Accountants
277 Wellington St. West
Toronto, ON M5V 3H2
416-977-3222 Fax: 416-977-8585
URL: www.cica.ca
Scope: National
Purpose: Subjects cover financial & performance reporting for the public & not-for-profit sectors
Contact Information: Principal, Conferences & Courses, Continuing Education: Pam Robertson, Phone: 416-204-3296, E-mail: pam.robertson@cica.ca; Manager, Conferences & Courses, Continuing Education: Sheri Price, Phone: 416-204-3425, E-mail: sheri.price@cica.ca

Canadian Medical Association Physician Management Institute 2011 Course: Engaging Others
Date: October 19-21, 2011
Location: Le Meridien King Edward Hotel
Toronto, ON
Sponsor/Contact: Canadian Medical Association
1867 Alta Vista Dr.
Ottawa, ON K1G 5W8
613-731-8610 Fax: 613-236-8864
E-mail: cmamsc@cma.ca; cmatechsupport@cma.ca (technical support)
URL: www.cma.ca
Scope: National
Purpose: Topics addressed include motivating others, engaging with dialogue, coaching for optimal performance, & promoting high-performing teams
Anticipated Attendance: 40
Contact Information: Canadian Medical Association Physician Management Institute, Phone: 800-663-7336, ext. 2319, Fax: 613-521-1268, E-mail: pmi@cma.ca

Canadian Medical Association Physician Management Institute 2011 Course: Self-Awareness & Effective Leadership
Date: October 16-18, 2011
Location: Le Meridien King Edward Hotel
Toronto, ON
Sponsor/Contact: Canadian Medical Association
1867 Alta Vista Dr.
Ottawa, ON K1G 5W8
613-731-8610 Fax: 613-236-8864
E-mail: cmamsc@cma.ca; cmatechsupport@cma.ca (technical support)
URL: www.cma.ca
Scope: National
Purpose: Examples of topics are as follows: understanding the challenges & satisfactions of physician leadership; leading with emotional intelligence; insights into personal effectiveness; & applying self-awareness to enhance one's personal leadership
Anticipated Attendance: 40
Contact Information: Canadian Medical Association Physician Management Institute, Phone: 800-663-7336, ext. 2319, Fax: 613-521-1268, E-mail: pmi@cma.ca

Canadian Urban Transit Association Training Course: SmartDRIVER Train the Trainer
Date: October 4-6, 2011
Location: Ragged Lake Transit Ctr., Metro Transit
Halifax, NS
Sponsor/Contact: Canadian Urban Transit Association
#1401, 55 York St.
Toronto, ON M5J 1R7
416-365-9800 Fax: 416-365-1295
E-mail: transit@cutaactu.ca
URL: www.cutaactu.ca
Scope: Provincial
Purpose: A defensive driving course
Contact Information: Course Contact: John Moudakis, Phone: 416-365-9800, ext. 102, Fax: 416-365-1295, E-mail: moudakis@cutaactu.ca

Canadian Urban Transit Association Training Course: Transit Ambassador Train the Trainer
Date: October 17-21, 2011
Location: Calgary Transit
Calgary, AB
Sponsor/Contact: Canadian Urban Transit Association
#1401, 55 York St.
Toronto, ON M5J 1R7
416-365-9800 Fax: 416-365-1295
E-mail: transit@cutaactu.ca
URL: www.cutaactu.ca
Scope: Provincial
Purpose: A course focussing on effective training styles & excellent customer service
Contact Information: Course Contact: John Moudakis, Phone: 416-365-9800, ext. 102, Fax: 416-365-1295, E-mail: moudakis@cutaactu.ca

Canadian Urban Transit Association Training Course: Transit Maintenance & Asset Management
Date: October 23-28, 2011
Location: Red Deer Lodge
Red Deer, AB
Sponsor/Contact: Canadian Urban Transit Association
#1401, 55 York St.
Toronto, ON M5J 1R7
416-365-9800 Fax: 416-365-1295
E-mail: transit@cutaactu.ca
URL: www.cutaactu.ca
Scope: Provincial
Purpose: Effective planning for maintenance operations
Contact Information: Course Contact: John Moudakis, Phone: 416-365-9800, ext. 102, Fax: 416-365-1295, E-mail: moudakis@cutaactu.ca

Electric Vehicle Society of Canada 2011 Meeting
Date: October 20, 2011
Location: Ashtonbee Campus, Centennial College
Toronto, ON
Sponsor/Contact: Electric Vehicle Society of Canada
21 Burritt Rd.
Toronto, ON M1R 3S5
416-755-4324 Fax: 416-755-4324
E-mail: info@evsociety.ca
URL: www.evsociety.ca
Scope: National
Contact Information: E-mail: info@evsociety.ca

Food & Consumer Products of Canada 2011 CEO Executive Conference: Growing in a Changing World
Date: October 6-7, 2011
Location: The Rosseau, a JW Marriott Resort & Spa
Rosseau, ON
Sponsor/Contact: Food & Consumer Products of Canada
#301, 885 Don Mills Rd.
Toronto, ON M3C 1V9
416-510-8024 Fax: 416-510-8043
E-mail: info@fcpc.ca
URL: www.fcpc.ca
Scope: National
Purpose: Topics include the global food crisis, international retailer trends, societ change, the ethnic consumer, the retail scene in Canada, & social media
Contact Information: Coordinator, Member Services: Heather Spencer, E-mail: Heather.Spencer@fcpc.ca

Greenbuild 2011 International Conference & Expo (hosted by the Canada Green Building Council)
Date: October 4-7, 2011
Location: Metro Toronto Convention Centre
Toronto, ON
Sponsor/Contact: Canada Green Building Council
#202, 47 Clarence St.
Ottawa, ON K1N 9K1
613-241-1184 Fax: 613-241-4782
E-mail: info@cagbc.org; education@cagbc.org
URL: www.cagbc.org

Scope: International
Purpose: A learning opportunity featuring industry experts speaking about topics that affect the future of green building
Contact Information: Show Manager: Noreen Burke, E-mail: noreen@corcexpo.com; Director, Communications: Taryn Holowka, E-mail: tholowka@usgbc.org; General Inquiries, E-mail: info@greenbuildexpo.org; Registration Inquiries, E-mail: support@register.greenbuildexpo.org; Housing Customer Svs., E-mail: support@housinggrbld.org; Exhibiting Inquiries, E-mail: expo@usgbc.org

Hike Ontario 2011 Annual Summit
Date: October 2011
Location: Ontario
Sponsor/Contact: Hike Ontario
#400, 165 Dundas St. West
Mississauga, ON L5B 2N6 Canada
905-277-4453
E-mail: info@hikeontario.com
URL: www.hikeontario.com

International Society for Rock Mechanics 12th International Congress on Rock Mechanics: Harmonising Rock Mechanics & the Environment
Date: October 16-21, 2011
Location: Beijing International Convention Center
Beijing, China
Sponsor/Contact: International Society for Rock Mechanics
c/o Laboratório Nacional de Engenharia Civil
101 Av. do Brasil
Lisbon, Portugal
E-mail: secretariat.isrm@lnec.pt
URL: www.isrm.net
Scope: International

International Solid Waste Association 2011 Annual Congress
Date: October 17-20, 2011
Location: Daegu City, South Korea
Sponsor/Contact: International Solid Waste Association
Auerspergstrasse 15, Top 41
Vienna, Austria
E-mail: iswa@iswa.dk
URL: www.iswa.org
Scope: International
Purpose: The presentation of research, information from the world's largest companies in the waste sector, & networking opportunities
Contact Information: Managing Director: Hermann Koller, E-mail: hkoller@iswa.org

International Titanium Association's 27th Annual Conference & Exhibition
Date: October 2-5, 2011
Location: Sheraton San Diego Hotel & Marina
San Diego, CA
Sponsor/Contact: International Titanium Association
#300, 2655 West Midway Blvd.
Broomfield, CO USA
303-404-2221 Fax: 303-404-9111
E-mail: ita@titanium.org
URL: www.titanium.org
Scope: International
Contact Information: Phone: 303-404-2221; Fax: 303-404-9111; E-mail: conference@titanium.org

Local Government Management Association of BC Professional Development Program: Municipal Administration Training Institute - Community Planning
Date: October 2-7, 2011
Location: Lake Okanagan Resort
Kelowna, BC
Sponsor/Contact: Local Government Management Association of British Columbia
Central Building
620 View St., 7th Fl.
Victoria, BC V8W 1J6
250-383-7032 Fax: 250-384-4879
E-mail: office@lgma.ca; editor@lgma.ca (magazine); ads@lgma.ca
URL: www.lgma.ca
Scope: Provincial
Purpose: A week long residential course about community planning & development issues, featuring topics such as bylaws, land use permits, & subdivision processes
Contact Information: Program Coordinator: Ana Fuller, Phone: 250-383-7032, ext. 227, Fax: 250-383-4879, E-mail: afuller@lgma.ca

Local Government Management Association of British Columbia 2011 Clerks & Corporate Officers Forum
Date: October 2011
Location: British Columbia
Sponsor/Contact: Local Government Management Association of British Columbia
Central Building
620 View St., 7th Fl.
Victoria, BC V8W 1J6
250-383-7032 Fax: 250-384-4879
E-mail: office@lgma.ca; editor@lgma.ca (magazine); ads@lgma.ca
URL: www.lgma.ca
Scope: Provincial
Purpose: A 2.5 day program, focussing on best practices & innovations to assist clerks & corporate officers
Contact Information: Program Coordinator: Ana Fuller, Phone: 250-383-7032, ext. 227, Fax: 250-383-4879, E-mail: afuller@lgma.ca

Metallurgy & Materials Society of the Canadian Institute of Mining, Metallurgy & Petroleum COM 2011: 50th Annual Conference of Metallurgists
Date: October 2-5, 2011
Location: Montréal Bonaventure Hotel
Montréal, QC
Sponsor/Contact: Metallurgy & Materials Society of the Canadian Institute of Mining, Metallurgy & Petroleum
#1250, 3500, boul de Maisonneuve ouest
Montréal, QC H3Z 3C1
514-939-2710
URL: www.metsoc.org
Scope: International
Purpose: Featuring historical presentation from industry experts & pioneers plus plenary sessions to highlight the future of metallurgy & materials technology
Contact Information: Manager, Administration & Meetings: Brigitte Farah, Phone: 514-939-2710, ext. 1329, Fax: 514-939-2714, E-mail: bfarah@cim.org

National Association for Environmental Management 2011 19th Annual EHS Management Forum: EHS & Sustainability Success in the New Economic Era
Date: October 19-20, 2011
Location: The Westin La Paloma Resort & Spa
Tuscon, AZ USA
Sponsor/Contact: National Association for Environmental Management
#1002, 1612 K St. NW
Washington, DC USA
202-986-6616 Fax: 202-530-4408
E-mail: programs@naem.org
URL: www.naem.org
Scope: International
Purpose: Interactive sessions, keynote presentations, & exhibits about trends & challenges for the environmental, health & safety profession, including defining & delivering sustainability, supply chain strategies, 21st century leaderships, & foundational EHS excellence
Anticipated Attendance: 500+
Contact Information: Exposition Manager, NAEM EHS Management Forum: Mary Sanchez-Quigg, E-mail: mary.quigg@conferencedirect.com; Deputy Director (inquiries about abstracts): Virginia Hoekenga, E-mail: Virginia@naem.org

National Solid Wastes Management Association 2011 Executive Roundtable Conference
Date: October 17-20, 2011
Location: The Ritz-Carlton, Naples
Naples, FL USA
Sponsor/Contact: National Solid Wastes Management Association
#300, 4301 Connecticut Ave. NW
Washington, DC USA
202-244-4700 Fax: 202-966-4824
URL: www.nswma.org
Scope: International
Contact Information: Meetings Manager: Catherine Maimon, E-mail: cmaimon@nswma.org

National Solid Wastes Management Association 2011 Mid-Atlantic Annual Conference
Date: October 4-5, 2011
Location: The Grove Park Inn Resort & Spa
Asheville, NC USA
Sponsor/Contact: National Solid Wastes Management Association
#300, 4301 Connecticut Ave. NW
Washington, DC USA
202-244-4700 Fax: 202-966-4824
URL: www.nswma.org
Scope: International
Contact Information: Meetings Manager: Catherine Maimon, E-mail: cmaimon@nswma.org

Nova Scotia Environmental Network 2011 20th Anniversary Annual Gathering
Date: October 14-16, 2011
Location: Tatamagouche Centre
Tatamagouche, NS
Sponsor/Contact: Nova Scotia Environmental Network
3115 Veith St.
Halifax, NS B3K 3G9
902-454-6846 Fax: 902-453-3633
E-mail: nsen@cen-rce.org; board_nsen@cen-rce.org
URL: www.nsen.ca
Scope: Provincial
Contact Information: E-mail: nsen@cen-rce.org

Ontario Good Roads Association Environmentally Friendly Road Salt Storage Workshop
Date: October 11, 2011
Location: Mississauga Convention Centre
Mississauga, ON
Sponsor/Contact: Ontario Good Roads Association
#2, 6355 Kennedy Rd.
Mississauga, ON L5T 2L5
905-795-2555 Fax: 905-795-2660
E-mail: info@ogra.org
URL: www.ogra.org
Scope: Provincial
Purpose: Best practices for the safe & proper storage of winter maintenance materials to enhance stewardship of the environment
Anticipated Attendance: 30
Contact Information: Administrative Assistant: Tifanie Lakhan, Phone: 905-795-2555, Fax: 905-795-2660

Radiation Safety Institute of Canada 2011 Radiation Safety Officer Professional Certificate Course
Date: October 4-5, 2011
Location: Sutton Place Toronto
Toronto, ON
Sponsor/Contact: Radiation Safety Institute of Canada Head Office & National Education Centre
#300, 165 Avenue Rd.
Toronto, ON M5R 3S4
416-650-9090 Fax: 416-650-9920
E-mail: info@radiationsafety.ca
URL: www.radiationsafety.ca
Scope: National
Contact Information: Scientist & Training Coordinator: Tara Hargreaves, E-mail: th@radiationsafety.ca; General Inquiries, E-mail: info@radiationsafety.ca

The Future of Heavy Water Reactors 2011 International Conference (HWR - Future)

Trade Shows, Conferences and Seminars

Date: October 2-5, 2011
Location: Ottawa Marriott Hotel
Ottawa, ON Japan
Sponsor/Contact: Canadian Nuclear Society
655 Bay St., 17th Fl.
Toronto, ON M5G 2K4
416-977-7620 Fax: 416-977-8131
E-mail: cns-snc@on.aibn.com
URL: www.cns-snc.ca
Scope: International
Purpose: Organized by the Canadian Nuclear Society, in cooperation with the International Atomic Energy Agency, the conference will address the following topics: current developments & challenges in HWR physics analyses; material & chemistry; reactor core & fuel design; advanced fuel cycle & reactor physics; establishing future collaboration on reactor design; steam generators; thermal-hydraulics & safety; & operating & maintenance experience for HWRs
Contact Information: Conference Contact: L.K.H. Leung, Phone: 613-584-8811, E-mail: leungl@aecl.ca

Toronto Field Naturalists 2011 Monthly Talk
Date: October 2011
Location: Emmanuel College
Toronto, ON
Sponsor/Contact: Toronto Field Naturalists
#1519, 2 Carlton St.
Toronto, ON M5B 1J3
416-593-2656
E-mail: office@torontofieldnaturalists.org
URL: www.torontofieldnaturalists.org
Scope: Local
Purpose: Topics of past monthy meetings have included the need for conservation of freshwater ecosystems & the savanna habitats & tallgrass prairies of southern Ontario
Contact Information: E-mail: office@torontofieldnaturalists.org

Water Environment Federation WEFTEC 2011: 84th Annual Water Environment Federation Technical Exhibition & Conference
Date: October 15-19, 2011
Location: Los Angeles Convention Center
Los Angeles, CA USA
Sponsor/Contact: Water Environment Federation
601 Wythe St.
Alexandria, VA USA
703-684-2400 Fax: 703-684-2492
E-mail: csc@wef.org
URL: www.wef.org
Scope: International
Purpose: Featuring more than 800 presentations & posters, 114 technical sessions, 27 workshops, continuing education, professional development, networking opportunities, & exhibition space
Anticipated Attendance: 18,000
Contact Information: Registration Services, Phone: 708-486-0724, Toll-Free Phone: 1-877-303-0724; Conference Information, Phone: 703-684-2441, Toll-Free Phone: 1-877-933-4734; Exhibiting Information, Phone: 703-684-2443, Toll-Free Phoone: 1-877-677-3976; Membership Information, Phone: 571-830-1545, Toll-Free Phone: 1-800-666-0206

November

Air Transport Association of Canada 2011 77th Annual General Meeting & Trade Show
Date: November 13-15, 2011
Location: Fairmont Queen Elizabeth Hotel
Montréal, QC
Sponsor/Contact: Air Transport Association of Canada
#700, 255 Albert St.
Ottawa, ON K1P 6A9
613-233-7727 Fax: 613-230-8648
E-mail: atac@atac.ca
URL: www.atac.ca
Scope: National
Purpose: An event for major stakeholders from the Canadian commercial aviation industry & delegates from government agencies, manufacturers, & suppliers
Contact Information: Trade Show Coordinator: Debbie Simpson, Phone: 613-233-7727, ext. 312, E-mail: tradeshow@atac.ca

Alberta Association of Municipal Districts & Counties Fall 2011 Convention
Date: November 21-24, 2011
Location: Alberta
Sponsor/Contact: Alberta Association of Municipal Districts & Counties
2510 Sparrow Dr.
Nisku, AB T9E 8N5
780-955-3639 Fax: 780-955-3615
E-mail: aamdc@aamdc.com
URL: www.aamdc.com

Alberta Forest Products Association 2011 Lumber Grading School
Date: November 28, 2011 - December 2, 2011
Location: Calder Hall
Edmonton, AB
Sponsor/Contact: Alberta Forest Products Association
#500, 10709 Jasper Ave.
Edmonton, AB T5J 3N3
780-452-2841 Fax: 780-455-0505
E-mail: info@albertforestproducts.ca
URL: www.albertaforestproducts.ca
Scope: Provincial
Contact Information: Director, Grade Bureau: Norm Dupuis, Phone: 780-452-2841, ext. 235

Alberta Health & Safety 2011 10th Annual Conference & Trade Fair
Date: November 7-9, 2011
Location: Telus Convention Centre
Calgary, AB
Sponsor/Contact: Health & Safety Conference Society of Alberta
P.O. Box 38009
Calgary, AB T3K 5G9 Canada
403-236-2225 Fax: 403-206-7099
E-mail: info@hsconference.com
URL: www.hsconference.com
Scope: Provincial
Contact Information: Conference Coordinator: Carrie Kleppe, Phone: 403-236-2225, Fax: 403-206-7099, E-mail, General Information: info@hsconference.com, Trade Fair Information: tradefair@hsconference.com

Alberta Irrigation Projects Association 2011 Conference
Date: November 28-30, 2011
Location: Lethbridge, AB
Sponsor/Contact: Alberta Irrigation Projects Association
#909, 400 - 4 Ave. South
Lethbridge, AB T1K 7H5
403-328-3063 Fax: 403-327-1043
E-mail: info@aipa.org
URL: www.aipa.org
Scope: Provincial
Purpose: An educational events of interest to members of irrigation districts in Alberta
Contact Information: Administrator: Vicky Kress, E-mail: vicky.kress@aipa.org

American Society of Mechanical Engineers 2011 International Mechanical Engineering Congress & Exposition: Energy & Water Scarcity
Date: November 11-17, 2011
Location: Hyatt Regency & Colorado Covention Ctr.
Denver, CO USA
Sponsor/Contact: American Society of Mechanical Engineers
3 Park Ave.
New York, NY USA
800-843-2763
E-mail: infocentral@asme.org
URL: www.asme.org
Scope: International
Purpose: Examples of congress tracks are as follows: Energy Water Nexus; Energy Systems Analysis, Thermodynamics, & Sustainability; NanoEngineering for Energy; Transportation Systems; Safety Engineering, Risk Analysis, & Reliability Methods; Combustion Science & Engineering; & Heat & Mass Transport Processes
Contact Information: Registration Contact: Erin Dolan, E-mail: dolane@asme.org; Meeting Logistics Contact: Stephen Crane, E-mail: cranes@asme.org

American Society of Mechanical Engineers 2011 Program
Date: November 14-18, 2011
Location: Wyndham Orlando Resort
Orlando, FL USA
Sponsor/Contact: American Society of Mechanical Engineers
3 Park Ave.
New York, NY USA
800-843-2763
E-mail: infocentral@asme.org
URL: www.asme.org
Scope: International
Purpose: Examples of sessions are as follows: Overview of Codes & Standards for Nuclear Power Plant Construction; HAZOP Studies, Other Hazard Evaluation Procedures, & Advanced Concepts for Process Hazard Analysis Combo Course; Heating, Ventilating & Air-Conditioning Systems - Sizing & Design; Advanced Concepts for Process Hazard Analysis; & Comparison of Global Quality Assurance & Management System Standards used for Nuclear Applications

American Water Works Association 2011 Water Quality Technology Conference & Exposition
Date: November 13-17, 2011
Location: Phoenix, AZ USA
Sponsor/Contact: American Water Works Association
6666 West Quincy Ave.
Denver, CO USA
303-794-7711 Fax: 303-347-0804
E-mail: custsvc@awwa.org
URL: www.awwa.org
Scope: International
Purpose: Technical session topics include the following: climate change impacts, source protection, corrosion control, biological treatment, disinfection practices & by-products, inorganic contaminants, distribution system issues, taste & odour issues, residuals, & disposals
Contact Information: Exposition Inquiries, E-mail: jjohnson@awwa.org; American Water Works Association, Customer Service, Phone: 1-800-926-7337, E-mail: awwamktg@awwa.org

Association of Power Producers of Ontario 2011: 23rd Annual Canadian Power Conference & Power Networking Centre
Date: November 15-16, 2011
Location: Metro Toronto Convention Centre
Toronto, ON
Sponsor/Contact: Association of Power Producers of Ontario
P.O. Box 1084 Stn. F
#1602, 25 Adelaide St. East
Toronto, ON M5C 3A1
416-322-6549 Fax: 416-481-5785
E-mail: appro@appro.org; marketing@appro.org
URL: www.appro.org
Scope: Provincial
Purpose: Speakers, conference sessions, exhibits, a student program for Ontario post-secondary students interested in a career in the energy sector, & a banquet
Anticipated Attendance: 1500+
Contact Information: Executive Director: Jake Brooks, E-mail: jake.brooks@appro.org; Marketing Manager: Carole Kielly, Phone: 416-322-6549, ext. 222, E-mail: carole.kielly@appro.org; Manager, Registration & Data: Soraya Rivera, E-mail: soraya.rivera@appro.org; Office Manager: Karla Martinez, E-mail: karla.martinez@appro.org

Canadian Avalanche Association 2011 Course: AvSAR Response
Date: November 25-27, 2011
Location: Revelstoke, BC

Sponsor/Contact: Canadian Avalanche Association
P.O. Box 2759
110 MacKenzie Ave.
Revelstoke, BC V0E 2S0
250-837-2435 Fax: 250-837-4624
E-mail: info@avalanche.ca
URL: www.avalanche.ca
Scope: National
Purpose: A seminar, taught by emergency physicians & avalanche search & rescue specialists, covering the best practices for organized avalanche search & rescue in Canada & emergency medical care for avalanche victims
Contact Information: Manager, Industry Training Program: Emily Grady, Phone: 250-837-2435, ext. 223, E-mail: egrady@avalanche.ca

Canadian Avalanche Association 2011 Course: Avalanche Control Blasting
Date: November 26-27, 2011
Location: Fernie, BC
Sponsor/Contact: Canadian Avalanche Association
P.O. Box 2759
110 MacKenzie Ave.
Revelstoke, BC V0E 2S0
250-837-2435 Fax: 250-837-4624
E-mail: info@avalanche.ca
URL: www.avalanche.ca
Scope: National
Purpose: Training in the safe application of explosives for avalanche control, with coverage of federal & provincial explosives regulations & helicopter delivery methods
Contact Information: Manager, Industry Training Program: Emily Grady, Phone: 250-837-2435, ext. 223, E-mail: egrady@avalanche.ca

Canadian Heavy Oil Association 2011 Fall Conference
Date: November 2011
Sponsor/Contact: Canadian Heavy Oil Association
#400, 500 - 5th Ave. SW
Calgary, AB T2P 3L5
403-269-1755 Fax: 403-453-0179
E-mail: office@choa.ab.ca
URL: www.choa.ab.ca
Scope: National
Contact Information: Event Coordinator: Georgia A. Hasapes, Phone: 403-269-1755, Fax: 403-453-0179, E-mail: office@choa.ab.ca

Canadian Institute of Chartered Accountants 2011 Advanced Personal Financial Planning Conference & Showcase
Date: November 7-8, 2011
Location: Sheraton Centre Hotel
Toronto, ON
Sponsor/Contact: Canadian Institute of Chartered Accountants
277 Wellington St. West
Toronto, ON M5V 3H2
416-977-3222 Fax: 416-977-8585
URL: www.cica.ca
Scope: National
Purpose: Technical sessions on current topics, plus a showcase of financial product & service providers
Contact Information: Manager, Conferences & Courses, Continuing Education: Jennifer McEdwards, Phone: 416-204-3338, E-mail: jennifer.mcedwards@cica.ca

Canadian Institute of Chartered Accountants 2011 Advanced Tax Course: Corporate Reorganizations
Date: November 5-9, 2011
Location: Westin Resort & Spa
Whistler, BC
Sponsor/Contact: Canadian Institute of Chartered Accountants
277 Wellington St. West
Toronto, ON M5V 3H2
416-977-3222 Fax: 416-977-8585
URL: www.cica.ca
Scope: National
Purpose: Topics addressed include interest deductibility, spin-offs, amalgamations, & wind-ups

Contact Information: Principal, Conferences & Courses, Continuing Education: Steve Johnston, Phone: 416-204-3332, E-mail: steve.johnston@cica.ca; Manager, Conferences & Courses, Continuing Ed.: Kieran Murphy, Phone: 416-204-3337, E-mail: kieran.murphy@cica.ca; Registrar, Conferences & Courses, Continuing Ed.: Liza Cruz, Phone: 416-204-3263, E-mail: liza.cruz@cica.ca

Canadian Institute of Chartered Accountants 2011 Advanced Tax Issues for the Owner-managed Business Tax Course
Date: November 19-23, 2011
Location: Queen's Landing Inn
Niagara-on-the-Lake, ON
Sponsor/Contact: Canadian Institute of Chartered Accountants
277 Wellington St. West
Toronto, ON M5V 3H2
416-977-3222 Fax: 416-977-8585
URL: www.cica.ca
Scope: National
Purpose: Information about business succession planning, trusts, owner-manager remuneration, & post mortem tax planning for private company shares
Contact Information: Principal, Conferences & Courses, Continuing Education: Steve Johnston, Phone: 416-204-3332, E-mail: steve.johnston@cica.ca; Manager, Conferences & Courses, Continuing Ed.: Kieran Murphy, Phone: 416-204-3337, E-mail: kieran.murphy@cica.ca; Registrar, Conferences & Courses, Continuing Ed.: Liza Cruz, Phone: 416-204-3263, E-mail: liza.cruz@cica.ca

Canadian Institute of Chartered Accountants 2011 Business & Industry Conference
Date: November 29-30, 2011
Location: Sheraton Centre Toronto Hotel
Toronto, ON
Sponsor/Contact: Canadian Institute of Chartered Accountants
277 Wellington St. West
Toronto, ON M5V 3H2
416-977-3222 Fax: 416-977-8585
URL: www.cica.ca
Scope: National
Purpose: Subjects covered include strategic planning, organizational development, effective risk management, economic trends, & financing opportunities
Contact Information: Manager, Conferences & Courses, Continuing Education: Jennifer McEdwards, Phone: 416-204-3338, E-mail: jennifer.mcedwards@cica.ca; Registrar, Conferences & Courses, Continuing Education: Liza Cruz, Phone: 416-204-3263, E-mail: liza.cruz@cica.ca

Canadian Institute of Chartered Accountants 2011 Conference for Audit Committees
Date: November 21-22, 2011
Location: Toronto, ON
Sponsor/Contact: Canadian Institute of Chartered Accountants
277 Wellington St. West
Toronto, ON M5V 3H2
416-977-3222 Fax: 416-977-8585
URL: www.cica.ca
Scope: National
Purpose: A conference featuring technical sessions, panel discussions, & keynote addresses aimed toward the professional development of audit committee members
Contact Information: Principal, Conferences & Courses, Continuing Ed.: Valerie Leach, Phone: 416-204-3451, E-mail: valerie.leach@cica.ca; Event Coordinator, Conferences & Courses, Continuing Ed.: Marianne So, Phone: 416-204-3331, E-mail: marianne.so@cica.ca; Registrar, Conferences & Courses, Continuing Ed.: Liza Cruz, Phone: 416-204-3263, E-mail: liza.cruz@cica.ca

Canadian Institute of Chartered Accountants 2011 Course: Income Tax Practice
Date: November 19-25, 2011
Location: Blue Mountain Resort
Collingwood, ON

Sponsor/Contact: Canadian Institute of Chartered Accountants
277 Wellington St. West
Toronto, ON M5V 3H2
416-977-3222 Fax: 416-977-8585
URL: www.cica.ca
Scope: National
Purpose: A course to increase understanding of the Income Tax Act, current legislation, & proposed changes for the future
Contact Information: Principal, Conferences & Courses, Continuing Education: Steve Johnston, Phone: 416-204-3332, E-mail: steve.johnston@cica.ca; Manager, Conferences & Courses, Continuing Ed.: Kieran Murphy, Phone: 416-204-3337, E-mail: kieran.murphy@cica.ca; Registrar, Conferences & Courses, Continuing Ed.: Liza Cruz, Phone: 416-204-3263, E-mail: liza.cruz@cica.ca

Canadian Institute of Food Science & Technology, Toronto Section, Table Top Exhibition
Date: November 2011
Location: Toronto, ON
Sponsor/Contact: Canadian Institute of Food Science & Technology
c/o Christine Baily, Toronto Section Administrator
5 Fenwook Circle
Peterborough, ON K9J 6M4
866-437-6030 Fax: 866-719-5396
E-mail: TorontoSection@cifst.ca
URL: www.cifst.ca
Scope: Local
Purpose: An opportunity for suppliers to the food industry to exhibit at a trade show in Toronto
Contact Information: Table Top Director: Melissa Beausoleil, Phone: 905-625-1813, Fax: 905-625-1824, E-mail: melissa@bdflavours.com

Canadian Medical Association Physician Management Institute 2011 Course: Leading Change & Innovation
Date: November 22-24, 2011
Location: Delta Vancouver Suites
Vancouver, BC
Sponsor/Contact: Canadian Medical Association
1867 Alta Vista Dr.
Ottawa, ON K1G 5W8
613-731-8610 Fax: 613-236-8864
E-mail: cmamsc@cma.ca; cmatechsupport@cma.ca (technical support)
URL: www.cma.ca
Scope: National
Purpose: Topics covered include the changing environment, negotiating change, & the change process
Anticipated Attendance: 40
Contact Information: Canadian Medical Association Physician Management Institute, Phone: 800-663-7336, ext. 2319, Fax: 613-521-1268, E-mail: pmi@cma.ca

Canadian Medical Association Physician Management Institute 2011 Course: Management Dynamics - Understanding Hospital Performance
Date: November 20-21, 2011
Location: Delta Vancouver Suites
Vancouver, BC
Sponsor/Contact: Canadian Medical Association
1867 Alta Vista Dr.
Ottawa, ON K1G 5W8
613-731-8610 Fax: 613-236-8864
E-mail: cmamsc@cma.ca; cmatechsupport@cma.ca (technical support)
URL: www.cma.ca
Scope: National
Purpose: A course to help physicians as managers to make decisions about allocating resources, to establish sustainable practices, & to contibute to an effective health care system
Anticipated Attendance: 40
Contact Information: Canadian Medical Association Physician Management Institute, Phone: 800-663-7336, ext. 2319, Fax: 613-521-1268, E-mail: pmi@cma.ca

Trade Shows, Conferences and Seminars

Canadian Medical Association Physician Management Institute 2011 Course: Strategic Planning - From Vision to Action
Date: November 4-6, 2011
Location: The Fairmont Waterfront Vancouver
Vancouver, BC
Sponsor/Contact: Canadian Medical Association
1867 Alta Vista Dr.
Ottawa, ON K1G 5W8
613-731-8610 Fax: 613-236-8864
E-mail: cmamsc@cma.ca; cmatechsupport@cma.ca (technical support)
URL: www.cma.ca
Scope: National
Purpose: A program to help health care leaders monitor & evaluate the impact of a strategic plan on the quality of service delivery
Anticipated Attendance: 25
Contact Information: Canadian Medical Association Physician Management Institute, Phone: 800-663-7336, ext. 2319, Fax: 613-521-1268, E-mail: pmi@cma.ca

Canadian Parks & Wilderness Society 2011 Annual General Meeting
Date: November 5, 2011
Sponsor/Contact: Canadian Parks & Wilderness Society
#506, 250 City Centre Ave.
Ottawa, ON K1R 6K7
613-569-7226 Fax: 613-569-7098
E-mail: info@cpaws.org
URL: www.cpaws.org
Scope: National
Purpose: A meeting to take place in the National Capital Region

Canadian Renewable Fuels 2011 8th Annual Summit: Growing Our Energy Diversity
Date: November 28-30, 2011
Location: The Westin Hotel
Calgary, AB
Sponsor/Contact: Canadian Renewable Fuels Association
#605, 350 Sparks St.
Ottawa, ON K1R 7S8
613-594-5528 Fax: 613-594-3076
URL: www.greenfuels.org
Scope: International
Purpose: Information for biodiesel producers & grain & cellulose ethanol producers, as well as petroleum companies & agricultural associations
Contact Information: Director, Member Relations & Industry Promotions: Deborah Elson, Phone: 613-594-5528, ext 223, E-mail: d.elson@greenfuels.org

Canadian Urban Transit Association 2011 Fall Conference & Trans-Expo
Date: November 5-9, 2011
Location: Toronto, ON
Sponsor/Contact: Canadian Urban Transit Association
#1401, 55 York St.
Toronto, ON M5J 1R7
416-365-9800 Fax: 416-365-1295
E-mail: transit@cutaactu.ca
URL: www.cutaactu.ca
Scope: National
Purpose: An annual technical conference for members of the transit industry
Contact Information: Conference Specialist: Anna Maria Schell, Phone: 416-365-9800, ext. 116

Canadian Urban Transit Association Training Course: Advanced Scheduling & Runcutting
Date: November 29-30, 2011
Location: Oakville Transit
Oakville, ON
Sponsor/Contact: Canadian Urban Transit Association
#1401, 55 York St.
Toronto, ON M5J 1R7
416-365-9800 Fax: 416-365-1295
E-mail: transit@cutaactu.ca
URL: www.cutaactu.ca
Scope: Provincial
Purpose: Innovative ways to keep costs down
Contact Information: Course Contact: John Moudakis, Phone: 416-365-9800, ext. 102, Fax: 416-365-1295, E-mail: moudakis@cutaactu.ca

Canadian Urban Transit Association Training Course: Transit Ambassador Advanced Train the Trainer - Using the Additional Customer Service Modules
Date: November 29 - December 1, 2011
Location: Grand River Transit
Kitchener, ON
Sponsor/Contact: Canadian Urban Transit Association
#1401, 55 York St.
Toronto, ON M5J 1R7
416-365-9800 Fax: 416-365-1295
E-mail: transit@cutaactu.ca
URL: www.cutaactu.ca
Scope: Provincial
Purpose: Advanced modules for CUTA certified transit ambassador trainers
Contact Information: Course Contact: John Moudakis, Phone: 416-365-9800, ext. 102, Fax: 416-365-1295, E-mail: moudakis@cutaactu.ca

Canadian Urban Transit Association Training Course: Transit Ambassador Train the Trainer
Date: November 14-18, 2011
Location: Brampton Transit
Brampton, ON
Sponsor/Contact: Canadian Urban Transit Association
#1401, 55 York St.
Toronto, ON M5J 1R7
416-365-9800 Fax: 416-365-1295
E-mail: transit@cutaactu.ca
URL: www.cutaactu.ca
Scope: Provincial
Purpose: A course where transit system employees are trained by CUTA master trainers to become trainers themselves
Contact Information: Course Contact: John Moudakis, Phone: 416-365-9800, ext. 102, Fax: 416-365-1295, E-mail: moudakis@cutaactu.ca

Consulting Engineers of Alberta 2011 Infrastructure Partners Conference
Date: November 13-15, 2011
Location: Edmonton EXPO Centre, Alberta Ballroom
Edmonton, AB
Sponsor/Contact: Consulting Engineers of Alberta
Phipps-McKinnon Building
#870, 10020 - 101A Ave.
Edmonton, AB T5J 3G2
780-421-1852 Fax: 780-424-5225
E-mail: info@cea.ca
URL: www.cea.ca
Scope: Provincial
Purpose: Alberta infrastructure updates, workshops, keynote speakers, forums, & plenary presentations
Contact Information: Manager, Events & Communications: Hiju Song, Phone: 780-421-1852, E-mail: hsong@cea.ca

Electric Vehicle Society of Canada 2011 Meeting
Date: November 17, 2011
Location: Ashtonbee Campus, Centennial College
Toronto, ON
Sponsor/Contact: Electric Vehicle Society of Canada
21 Burritt Rd.
Toronto, ON M1R 3S5
416-755-4324 Fax: 416-755-4324
E-mail: info@evsociety.ca
URL: www.evsociety.ca
Scope: National
Contact Information: E-mail: info@evsociety.ca

Grow Canada 2011 Conference: Invested, Innovative
Date: November 29 - December 1, 2011
Location: Winnipeg Convention Centre
Winnipeg, MB
Sponsor/Contact: CropLife Canada
#627, 21 Four Seasons Pl.
Toronto, ON M9B 6J8
416-622-9771
URL: www.croplife.ca
Scope: National
Purpose: An examination of how innovation in agriculture drives economic growth
Contact Information: Manager, Member Services: Kim Timmer, Phone: 416-622-9771, ext. 2229, E-mail: timmerk@croplife.ca

Growing Your Farm Profits 2011 Dundas Area Workshop
Date: November 10 & 17, 2011
Location: Ontario
Sponsor/Contact: Ontario Soil & Crop Improvement Association
1 Stone Rd. West
Guelph, ON N1G 4Y2
519-826-4214 Fax: 519-826-4224
E-mail: oscia@ontariosoilcrop.org
URL: www.ontariosoilcrop.org
Scope: Local
Purpose: An event to learn to plan & manage farm business success
Contact Information: Ontario Soil & Crop Improvement Association Program Representative: Shelley McPhail, Phone: 613-256-4011, E-mail: dundasGYFP@ontariosoilcrop.org

Growing Your Farm Profits 2011 Lanark Area Workshop
Date: November 8 & 15, 2011
Location: Ontario
Sponsor/Contact: Ontario Soil & Crop Improvement Association
1 Stone Rd. West
Guelph, ON N1G 4Y2
519-826-4214 Fax: 519-826-4224
E-mail: oscia@ontariosoilcrop.org
URL: www.ontariosoilcrop.org
Scope: Local
Purpose: Subjects covered include the assessment of one's farm business, the identification of priorities, the development of action plans, & the commencement of the planning process toward farm business success
Contact Information: Ontario Soil & Crop Improvement Association Program Representative: Shelley McPhail, Phone: 613-256-4011, E-mail: lanarkGYFP@ontariosoilcrop.org

Growing Your Farm Profits 2011 Renfrew County Workshop
Date: November 29 & December 6, 2011
Location: Ontario
Sponsor/Contact: Ontario Soil & Crop Improvement Association
1 Stone Rd. West
Guelph, ON N1G 4Y2
519-826-4214 Fax: 519-826-4224
E-mail: oscia@ontariosoilcrop.org
URL: www.ontariosoilcrop.org
Scope: Local
Purpose: An entry point to potential cost-share opportunities available through Growing Forward Business Development for Farm Businesses
Contact Information: Ontario Soil & Crop Improvement Association Program Representative: Glen Smith, Phone: 613-628-2987, E-mail: renfrew@ontariosoilcrop.org

Growing Your Farm Profits 2011 Waterloo Region Workshop
Date: November 8 & 15, 2011
Location: Linwood Community Centre
Linwood, ON
Sponsor/Contact: Ontario Soil & Crop Improvement Association
1 Stone Rd. West
Guelph, ON N1G 4Y2
519-826-4214 Fax: 519-826-4224
E-mail: oscia@ontariosoilcrop.org
URL: www.ontariosoilcrop.org

Scope: Local
Purpose: An opportunity for local area farmers to network while learning to plan for farm business success
Contact Information: Ontario Soil & Crop Improvement Association Program Representative: Liz Samis, Phone: 519-638-3268, E-mail: waterlooGYFP@ontariosoilcrop.org

Growing Your Farm Profits 2011 Wellington County Workshop
Date: November 3 & 10, 2011
Location: Elora OMAFRA Office
Elora, ON
Sponsor/Contact: Ontario Soil & Crop Improvement Association
1 Stone Rd. West
Guelph, ON N1G 4Y2
519-826-4214 Fax: 519-826-4224
E-mail: oscia@ontariosoilcrop.org
URL: www.ontariosoilcrop.org
Scope: Local
Purpose: Topics include assessing one's business, identifying priorities, developing action plans, & starting the planning process
Contact Information: Ontario Soil & Crop Improvement Association Program Representative: John Benham, Phone: 519-846-0941, E-mail: wellington@ontariosoilcrop.org

Maintenance & Engineering Society of The Canadian Institute of Mining, Metallurgy & Petroleum 2011 Maintenance Engineering/Mine Operators' Conference
Date: November 6-9, 2011
Location: TCU Place
Saskatoon, SK
Sponsor/Contact: Maintenance & Engineering Society of The Canadian Institute of Mining, Metallurgy & Petroleum c/o Chair, Brad Kingston, Wardrop Engineering Inc.
725 Hewitson St.
Thunder Bay, ON P7B 6B5
807-345-5453
E-mail: brad.kingston@wardrop.com
URL: www.cim.org/med
Scope: National
Purpose: A conference & trade show on the theme of mining in society, featuring a technical program, plenary sessions, field trips, & a social program
Contact Information: Senior Director, Business Management & Strategic Development, Phone: 514-939-2710, ext. 1314, E-mail: jmdemers@cim.org; Director, Conferences & Exhibitions, Phone: 514-939-2710, ext. 1308, E-mail: lbujold@cim.org; Meetings Coordinator: Chantal Murphy, E-mail: cmurphy@cim.org; Exhibition Sales Manager: Martin Bell, E-mail: mbell@cim.org

Municipal Engineers Association 2011 Annual General Meeting & Workshop
Date: November 2011
Sponsor/Contact: Municipal Engineers Association
#2, 6355 Kennedy Rd.
Mississauga, ON L5T 2L5
905-795-2555 Fax: 905-795-2660
E-mail: info@municipalengineers.on.ca
URL: www.municipalengineers.on.ca
Scope: Provincial
Purpose: Workshop registration is open to all members of the Municipal Engineers Association, the Ontario Good Roads Association, the Consulting Engineers of Ontario, & the Ontario Public Works Association
Contact Information: Office of the President, Phone: 905-795-2555, Fax: 905-795-2660

Ontario Good Roads Association Advanced Contract Law Training
Date: November 23, 2011
Location: Ontario
Sponsor/Contact: Ontario Good Roads Association
#2, 6355 Kennedy Rd.
Mississauga, ON L5T 2L5
905-795-2555 Fax: 905-795-2660
E-mail: info@ogra.org
URL: www.ogra.org
Scope: Provincial
Purpose: A workshop to examine administrative issues related to the performance of a contract & variation of a contract
Anticipated Attendance: 40
Contact Information: Office Manager: Carmen Sousa, Phone: 905-795-2555, Fax: 905-795-2660

Ontario Good Roads Association Contract Dispute Resolution Training
Date: November 24, 2011
Location: Ontario
Sponsor/Contact: Ontario Good Roads Association
#2, 6355 Kennedy Rd.
Mississauga, ON L5T 2L5
905-795-2555 Fax: 905-795-2660
E-mail: info@ogra.org
URL: www.ogra.org
Scope: Provincial
Purpose: Content of the course includes the nature & politics of conflict, negotiation strategies, & building long-term relationships in order to achieve more win / win settlements
Anticipated Attendance: 30
Contact Information: Office Manager: Carmen Sousa, Phone: 905-795-2555, Fax: 905-795-2660

Ontario Good Roads Association Introduction to Contract Law Training
Date: November 22, 2011
Location: Ontario
Sponsor/Contact: Ontario Good Roads Association
#2, 6355 Kennedy Rd.
Mississauga, ON L5T 2L5
905-795-2555 Fax: 905-795-2660
E-mail: info@ogra.org
URL: www.ogra.org
Scope: Provincial
Purpose: Information about the laws governing municipal construction & rehabilitation projects, liens, claims, & the risks, liabilities, & consequences of substandard performance
Anticipated Attendance: 40
Contact Information: Office Manager: Carmen Sousa, Phone: 905-795-2555, Fax: 905-795-2660, E-mail: info@ogra.org

Ontario Professional Fire Fighters Association 2011 Annual Legislative Conference
Date: November 2011
Location: Ontario
Sponsor/Contact: Ontario Professional Fire Fighters Association
292 Plains Rd. East
Burlington, ON L7T 2C6
905-681-7111 Fax: 905-681-1489
URL: www.opffa.org
Scope: Provincial
Purpose: An opportunity for representatives from across Ontario to meet with Members of Provincial Parliament to advocate issues of concern

Ontario Sustainable Energy Association 2011 3rd Annual Community Power Conference & Power Networking Centre Trade Show
Date: November 14-15, 2011
Location: Metro Toronto Convention Centre
Toronto, ON
Sponsor/Contact: Ontario Sustainable Energy Association
#201, 156 Front St. West
Toronto, ON M5J 2L6
416-977-4441 Fax: 416-977-4441
E-mail: info@ontario-sea.org; employment@ontario-sea.org
URL: www.ontario-sea.org
Scope: Provincial
Purpose: A conference with community power experts, enablers, supporters, & proponents of interest to community leaders, First Nations & Metis, commercial developers, small & medium sized business owners, & farmers
Contact Information: Coordinator, Tradeshow, Events & Logistics: Nicole Risse, Phone: 416-977-4441, ext. 223, E-mail: Nicole@ontario-sea.org

Radiation Safety Institute of Canada 2011 Radiation Safety Officer Professional Certificate Course
Date: November 28 - December 2, 2011
Location: Sutton Place Toronto
Toronto, ON
Sponsor/Contact: Radiation Safety Institute of Canada Head Office & National Education Centre
#300, 165 Avenue Rd.
Toronto, ON M5R 3S4
416-650-9090 Fax: 416-650-9920
E-mail: info@radiationsafety.ca
URL: www.radiationsafety.ca
Scope: National
Contact Information: Scientist & Training Coordinator: Tara Hargreaves, E-mail: th@radiationsafety.ca; General Inquiries, E-mail: info@radiationsafety.ca

Radiation Safety Institute of Canada 2011 X-Ray Safety Officer Professional Certificate Course
Date: November 15-17, 2011
Location: Sutton Place Toronto
Toronto, ON
Sponsor/Contact: Radiation Safety Institute of Canada Head Office & National Education Centre
#300, 165 Avenue Rd.
Toronto, ON M5R 3S4
416-650-9090 Fax: 416-650-9920
E-mail: info@radiationsafety.ca
URL: www.radiationsafety.ca
Scope: National
Contact Information: Scientist & Training Coordinator: Tara Hargreaves, E-mail: th@radiationsafety.ca; General Inquiries, E-mail: info@radiationsafety.ca

Saskatchewan Association of Rural Municipalities 2011 Midterm Convention
Date: November 9-10, 2011
Location: Conexus Arts Centre
Regina, SK
Sponsor/Contact: Saskatchewan Association of Rural Municipalities
2075 Hamilton St.
Regina, SK S4P 2E1 Canada
306-757-3577 Fax: 306-565-2141
E-mail: sarm@sarm.ca
URL: www.sarm.ca
Scope: Provincial

Society of Environmental Toxicology & Chemistry North America 32nd Annual Meeting
Date: November 13-17, 2011
Location: Hynes Convention Center
Boston, MA USA
Sponsor/Contact: Society of Environmental Toxicology & Chemistry
SETAC Asia / Pacific, SETAC Latin America, & SETAC North America
1010 - 12th Ave. North
Pensacola, FL USA
850-469-1500 Fax: 850-469-9778
E-mail: setac@setac.org
URL: www.setac.org
Scope: International
Anticipated Attendance: 2500

The Royal Canadian Geographical Society 2011 Annual General Meeting & Annual Dinner of the College of Fellows
Date: November 2011
Sponsor/Contact: The Royal Canadian Geographical Society
39 McArthur Ave.
Ottawa, ON K1L 8L7

Trade Shows, Conferences and Seminars

613-745-4629 Fax: 613-744-0947
E-mail: rcgs@rcgs.org
URL: www.rcgs.org
Scope: National
Purpose: Featuring the presentation of the Society's awards at the Annual Dinner

Toronto Field Naturalists 2011 Monthly Talk
Date: November 2011
Location: Emmanuel College
Toronto, ON
Sponsor/Contact: Toronto Field Naturalists
#1519, 2 Carlton St.
Toronto, ON M5B 1J3
416-593-2656
E-mail: office@torontofieldnaturalists.org
URL: www.torontofieldnaturalists.org
Scope: Local
Purpose: Members of Toronto Field Naturalists, as well as visitors, are welcome for a series of illustrated lectures held each month from September to May
Contact Information: E-mail: office@torontofieldnaturalists.org

Toronto Field Naturalists 2011 Monthly Talk
Date: December 2011
Location: Emmanuel College
Toronto, ON
Sponsor/Contact: Toronto Field Naturalists
#1519, 2 Carlton St.
Toronto, ON M5B 1J3
416-593-2656
E-mail: office@torontofieldnaturalists.org
URL: www.torontofieldnaturalists.org
Scope: Local
Purpose: A Sunday meeting on topics of natural history
Contact Information: E-mail: office@torontofieldnaturalists.org

December

Alberta Irrigation Projects Association 2011 Annual General Meeting
Date: December 5, 2011
Location: Lethbridge, AB
Sponsor/Contact: Alberta Irrigation Projects Association
#909, 400 - 4 Ave. South
Lethbridge, AB T1K 7H5
403-328-3063 Fax: 403-327-1043
E-mail: info@aipa.org
URL: www.aipa.org
Scope: Provincial
Purpose: A yearly review of the association's business
Contact Information: Administrator: Vicky Kress, E-mail: vicky.kress@aipa.org

American Society of Mechanical Engineers 2011 Committee on Operation and Maintenance of Nuclear Power Plants Meeting
Date: December 5-9, 2011
Location: Sheraton Sand Key
Clearwater, FL USA
Sponsor/Contact: American Society of Mechanical Engineers
3 Park Ave.
New York, NY USA
800-843-2763
E-mail: infocentral@asme.org
URL: www.asme.org
Scope: International
Contact Information: Meeting Contact: Robert Horvath, E-mail: HorvathR@asme.org

Canadian Institute of Chartered Accountants 2011 IFRS Immersion 2 Course
Date: December 2011
Location: Toronto, ON
Sponsor/Contact: Canadian Institute of Chartered Accountants
277 Wellington St. West
Toronto, ON M5V 3H2
416-977-3222 Fax: 416-977-8585
URL: www.cica.ca
Scope: National
Purpose: Technical lectures & facilitated workshops providing comprehensive coverage of IFRS standards
Contact Information: Director, Continuing Education: Frank Colantonio, CA, Phone: 416-204-3328, E-mail: frank.colantonio@cica.ca

Canadian Nuclear Society 2011 9th International Conference on CANDU Maintenance: Industry Performance - Getting a Grip
Date: December 4-6, 2011
Location: Metro Toronto Convention Centre
Toronto, ON
Sponsor/Contact: Canadian Nuclear Society
655 Bay St., 17th Fl.
Toronto, ON M5G 2K4
416-977-7620 Fax: 416-977-8131
E-mail: cns-snc@on.aibn.com
URL: www.cns-snc.ca
Scope: National
Purpose: A trade show exhibition & working conference focussing on the following topics: short, tightly-managed outages in reliable, well-run, optimally-staffed plants; competent program planning mechanisms; essential tools for rigorous task execution; & "refurb" projects - hugely complex & very scope-expansion prone
Contact Information: Event Administrator: Elizabeth Muckle-Jeffs, Phone: 613-732-7068, Fax: 613-732-3386, E-mail: Elizabeth@theprofessionaledge.com; Conference Registrar, The Canadian Nuclear Society, Phone: 416-977-7620, Fax: 416-663-3504, E-mail: cns-snc@on.aibn.com

Growing Your Farm Profits 2011 Leeds Area Workshop
Date: December 1 & 8, 2011
Location: Athens, ON
Sponsor/Contact: Ontario Soil & Crop Improvement Association
1 Stone Rd. West
Guelph, ON N1G 4Y2
519-826-4214 Fax: 519-826-4224
E-mail: oscia@ontariosoilcrop.org
URL: www.ontariosoilcrop.org
Scope: Local
Purpose: A workshop for farmers who wish to improve their record keeping system, expand their business, or plan for succession
Contact Information: Ontario Soil & Crop Improvement Association Program Representative: Rita Vogel, Phone: 613-275-1753, E-mail: leeds@ontariosoilcrop.org

Other Conferences in 2011

Association of Municipalities of Ontario 2011 Counties, Regions, & Single Tiers Conference

Location: Ontario
Sponsor/Contact: Association of Municipalities of Ontario
#801, 200 University Ave.
Toronto, ON M5H 3C6
416-971-9856 Fax: 416-971-6191
E-mail: amo@amo.on.ca; municom@amo.on.ca; policy@amo.on.ca
URL: www.amo.on.ca
Scope: Provincial
Purpose: A yearly gathering occurring each fall
Contact Information: Special Events, Phone: 416-971-9856, ext. 330, E-mail: events@amo.on.ca; Coordinator, Special Events & Business Development: Navneet Dhaliwal, E-mail: NDhaliwal@amo.on.ca

Electric Vehicle Society of Canada & Toronto Hybrid Group 2011 EV Festival

Location: Toronto, ON
Sponsor/Contact: Electric Vehicle Society of Canada
21 Burritt Rd.
Toronto, ON M1R 3S5
416-755-4324 Fax: 416-755-4324
E-mail: info@evsociety.ca
URL: www.evsociety.ca
Scope: National
Purpose: Information about electric vehicles, hybrids, & plug-in hybrids, as well as displays of electric cars, trucks, motorbikes, ebikes, trikes, & scooters, presented with the assistance of the Durham Electric Vehicle Association & the Electric Vehicle Council of Ottawa
Anticipated Attendance: 500+
Contact Information: E-mail: info@evsociety.ca

Federation of Ontario Cottagers' Associations 2011 Fall Seminar

Location: Ontario
Sponsor/Contact: Federation of Ontario Cottagers' Associations
#201, 159 King St.
Peterborough, ON K9J 2R8
705-749-3622 Fax: 705-749-6522
E-mail: info@foca.on.ca
URL: www.foca.on.ca
Scope: Provincial
Contact Information: Phone: 705-749-3622, ext. 5; E-mail: communications@foca.on.ca

Field Botanists of Ontario 2011 Annual General Meeting

Location: Ontario
Sponsor/Contact: Field Botanists of Ontario
c/o W.D. McIlveen
RR#1
Acton, ON L7J 2L7
E-mail: wmcilveen@sympatico.ca
URL: aww.trentu.ca/fbo
Scope: Provincial
Purpose: Featuring field trips & a guest speaker
Contact Information: 2011 Meeting Contact: Bill Crowley, E-mail: fisheye@eagle.ca

Fisheries Council of Canada 2011 66th Annual Conference

Sponsor/Contact: Fisheries Council of Canada
#900, 170 Laurier Ave. West
Ottawa, ON K1P 5V5
613-727-7450 Fax: 613-727-7453
E-mail: info@fisheriescouncil.org
URL: www.fisheriescouncil.ca
Scope: National
Purpose: Informative meetings, networking opportunities, & social events
Contact Information: E-mail: info@fisheriescouncil.org

Grocery Innovations Canada 2011

Sponsor/Contact: Canadian Federation of Independent Grocers
#902, 2235 Sheppard Ave. East
Toronto, ON M2J 5B5
416-492-2311 Fax: 416-492-2347
E-mail: info@cfig.ca
URL: www.cfig.ca
Scope: National
Contact Information: Director, Events: Eden Minty, Phone: 416-492-2311, ext. 224, E-mail: eminty@cfig.ca; Operations Manager, Expositions, Tradeshow Logistics, & Floor Feature Areas: Irina Costachescu, Phone: 416-492-2311, ext. 234, E-mail: icostachescu@cfig.ca; Coordinator, Events: Phone: 416-492-2311, ext. 231, E-mail: vferguson@cfig.ca

Grocery Showcase West 2011

Sponsor/Contact: Canadian Federation of Independent Grocers
#902, 2235 Sheppard Ave. East
Toronto, ON M2J 5B5

416-492-2311 Fax: 416-492-2347
E-mail: info@cfig.ca
URL: www.cfig.ca
Scope: Regional
Contact Information: Director, Events: Eden Minty, Phone: 416-492-2311, ext. 224, E-mail: eminty@cfig.ca; Operations Manager, Expositions, Tradeshow Logistics, & Floor Feature Areas: Irina Costachescu, Phone: 416-492-2311, ext. 234; Account Rpresentative, Sales (Exhibiting information): Rolster Taylor, Toll-Free Phone: 1-800-661-2344, ext. 223, E-mail: rtaylor@cfig.ca

Local Government Management Association of British Columbia, North Central Chapter, 2011 Annual Fall Conference

Location: British Columbia
Sponsor/Contact: Local Government Management Association of British Columbia
c/o Ron Bowles, North Central Municipal Officers' Association
3215 Eby St.
Terrace, BC V8G 2X8
Scope: Local
Purpose: Educational sessions & networking opportunities for local government managers from the north central region of British Columbia
Contact Information: Conference Information Contact: Ron Bowles, Phone: 250-638-4725, E-mail: rbowles@terrace.ca

Manitoba Environmental Certification & Regulation Awareness 2011 Training Course

Location: Manitoba
Sponsor/Contact: Manitoba Ozone Protection Industry Association
1980B Main St.
Winnipeg, MB R2V 2B6 Canada
204-338-0804 Fax: 204-338-0810
E-mail: mopia@mts.net
URL: www.mopia.ca
Scope: Provincial
Purpose: The Ozone Depleting Substances Act & Regulation in Manitoba requires that any person working on refrigeration or air conditioning equipment that contains a regulated substance must be certified
Contact Information: Manitoba Ozone Protection Industry Association: Phone: 204-338-0804, Toll-Free Phone: 1-888-667-4203, E-mail: mopia@mts.net

Manitoba Water Well Association 2011 Annual General Meeting

Location: Manitoba
Sponsor/Contact: Manitoba Water Well Association
P.O. Box 1648
Winnipeg, MB R3C 2Z6
204-479-3777
E-mail: info@mwwa.ca
URL: www.mwwa.ca
Scope: Provincial
Purpose: An opportunity to provide an update on association activities & to address business & issues, such as by-law changes
Contact Information: Business Manager: Lynn Giersch, E-mail: info@mwwa.ca

Nature Saskatchewan 2011 Fall Meeting

Location: Saskatchewan
Sponsor/Contact: Nature Saskatchewan
#206, 1860 Lorne St.
Regina, SK S4P 2L7
306-780-9273 Fax: 306-780-9263
E-mail: info@naturesask.ca
URL: www.naturesask.ca
Scope: Provincial
Contact Information: Phone: 306-244-0189; E-mail: sasknature@gmail.com

Ontario Association for Geographic & Environmental Education 2011 Fall Conference

Location: Ontario
Sponsor/Contact: Ontario Association for Geographic & Environmental Education
#202, 10 Morrow Ave.
Toronto, ON M6R 2J1
URL: www.oagee.org
Scope: Provincial
Purpose: Recent information & resources of interest to geographers

Ontario Field Ornithologists 2011 Annual Convention
Date: September 17-18, 2011
Location: Point Pelee, ON
Sponsor/Contact: Ontario Field Ornithologists
P.O. Box 455 Stn. R
Toronto, ON M4G 4E1
E-mail: membership@ofo.ca
URL: www.ofo.ca
Scope: Provincial
Purpose: A fall birding trip to see a variety of habitats & bird species, to participate in the evening monarch roost count, & to hear a guest speaker at the banquet
Contact Information: 2011 Convention Contacts: Lynne Freeman, Phone: 416-463-9540, E-mail: lynnef@interlog.com; Brian Gibbon, Phone: 705-726-8969, E-mail: bwg@backland.net; Wendy Hunter, E-mail: sales@ofo.ca

Ontario Municipal Human Resources Association 2011 Fall Conference

Location: Ontario
Sponsor/Contact: Ontario Municipal Human Resources Association
#307, 1235 Fairview St.
Burlington, ON L7S 2K9
905-525-4000 Fax: 905-525-9833
E-mail: admin@omhra.ca
URL: www.omhra.ca
Scope: Provincial
Contact Information: E-mail: admin@omhra.ca

Ontario Professional Fire Fighters Association Annual Fall 2011 Dr. Eric Taylor Labour Educational Seminar

Location: Ontario
Sponsor/Contact: Ontario Professional Fire Fighters Association
292 Plains Rd. East
Burlington, ON L7T 2C6
905-681-7111 Fax: 905-681-1489
URL: www.opffa.org
Scope: Provincial
Purpose: Topics include negotiations, collective bargaining, government lobbying, grievances, & arbitrations
Contact Information: Ontario Professional Fire Fighters Association Education Committee Chair: Ed Kennedy, E-mail: kennedy@torontofirefighters.org

Ontario Refrigeration & Air Conditioning Contractors Association 2011 44th Annual General Meeting & President's Dinner Celebration

Location: Ontario
Sponsor/Contact: Ontario Refrigeration & Air Conditioning Contractors Association
#43, 6770 Davand Dr.
Mississauga, ON L5T 2G3
905-670-0010 Fax: 905-670-0474
E-mail: info@orac.ca
URL: www.orac.ca
Scope: Provincial
Purpose: Featuring education seminars, guest speakers, & group activities

Petroleum Services Association of Canada 2011 Annual General Meeting, Canadian Drilling Activity Forecast Session, & Industry Dinner

Sponsor/Contact: Petroleum Services Association of Canada
#1150, 800 - 6 Ave. SW
Calgary, AB T2P 3G3
403-264-4195 Fax: 403-263-7174
E-mail: info@psac.ca
URL: www.psac.ca
Scope: National
Purpose: The presentation of forecasts for 2012
Contact Information: Manager, Meetings & Events: Heather Doyle, Phone: 403-213-2796, E-mail: hdoyle@psac.ca

2012

January

American Water Works Association & The Water Environment Federation 2012 Utility Management Conference
Date: January 30 - February 2, 2012
Location: Hyatt Regency Miami
Miami, FL USA
Sponsor/Contact: American Water Works Association
6666 West Quincy Ave.
Denver, CO USA
303-794-7711 Fax: 303-347-0804
E-mail: custsvc@awwa.org
URL: www.awwa.org
Scope: International
Purpose: A conference, held in cooperation with the Florida Water Environment Association, for water & wastewater managers & professionals
Contact Information: Exhibition Sales Coordinator: Sarah Evans, Phone: 703-684-2400, ext. 7739, Registration Information, Phone: 703-684-2441, Technical Program & Abstract Information, Phone: 703-684-2400, ext. 7010

Canadian Avalanche Association 2012 Course: Resource & Transportation Avalanche Management
Date: January 23-27, 2012
Location: Nelson, BC
Sponsor/Contact: Canadian Avalanche Association
P.O. Box 2759
110 MacKenzie Ave.
Revelstoke, BC V0E 2S0
250-837-2435 Fax: 250-837-4624
E-mail: info@avalanche.ca
URL: www.avalanche.ca
Scope: National
Purpose: An introduction for technicians & supervisors from transportation & utility & resource sectors, such as forestry, mining, & railways, who manage winter operations & avalanche hazard programs
Contact Information: Manager, Industry Training Program: Emily Grady, Phone: 250-837-2435, ext. 223, E-mail: egrady@avalanche.ca

Fraser Valley Labour Council 2012 Annual General Meeting
Date: January 2012
Location: British Columbia
Sponsor/Contact: Fraser Valley Labour Council
#202, 9292 - 200th St.
Langley, BC V1M 3A6
604-314-9867 Fax: 604-430-6762
E-mail: bharder@usw.ca
URL: www.fvlc.ca
Scope: Local
Contact Information: Secretary: Pamela Willingshofer, E-mail: kidogo@shaw.ca

Growing Your Farm Profits 2012 Grenville Area Workshop
Date: January 12 & 19, 2012
Location: Ontario
Sponsor/Contact: Ontario Soil & Crop Improvement Association

1 Stone Rd. West
Guelph, ON N1G 4Y2
519-826-4214 Fax: 519-826-4224
E-mail: oscia@ontariosoilcrop.org
URL: www.ontariosoilcrop.org
Scope: Local
Purpose: A two day workshop to help farmers assess their businesses, identify priorities, & develop action plans
Contact Information: Ontario Soil & Crop Improvement Association Program Representative: Shelley McPhail, Phone: 613-256-4011, E-mail: grenvilleGYFP@ontariosoilcrop.org

Growing Your Farm Profits 2012 Ottawa Carleton Area Workshop
Date: January 17 & 24, 2012
Location: Ontario
Sponsor/Contact: Ontario Soil & Crop Improvement Association
1 Stone Rd. West
Guelph, ON N1G 4Y2
519-826-4214 Fax: 519-826-4224
E-mail: oscia@ontariosoilcrop.org
URL: www.ontariosoilcrop.org
Scope: Local
Purpose: Participants learn to plan for & manage farm business success
Contact Information: Ontario Soil & Crop Improvement Association Program Representative: Shelley McPhail, Phone: 613-256-4011, E-mail: carletonGYFP@ontariosoilcrop.org

Water Environment Federation 2012 Utility Management Conference
Date: January 30 - February 2, 2012
Location: Hyatt Regency Miami
Miami, FL USA
Sponsor/Contact: Water Environment Federation
601 Wythe St.
Alexandria, VA USA
703-684-2400 Fax: 703-684-2492
E-mail: csc@wef.org
URL: www.wef.org
Scope: International
Purpose: Topics include water resource adequacy, infrastructure stability, community sustainability, product quality, & customer satisfaction
Contact Information: Coordinator, Exhibition Sales: Sarah Evans, E-mail: sevans@wef.org; Registration Information, Phone: 703-684-2441; Technical Program Information, Phone: 703-684-2400, ext. 7010

Western Retail Lumber Association 2012 Prairie Showcase Buying Show & Convention
Date: January 19-21, 2012
Location: Saskatoon, SK
Sponsor/Contact: Western Retail Lumber Association
Western Retail Lumber Association Inc.
#1004, 213 Notre Dame Ave.
Winnipeg, MB R3B 1N3
204-957-1077 Fax: 204-947-5195
E-mail: wrla@wrla.org
URL: www.wrla.org

February

American Association for the Advancement of Science 2012 Annual Meeting
Date: February 16-20, 2012
Location: Vancouver, BC
Sponsor/Contact: American Association for the Advancement of Science
1200 New York Ave. NW
Washington, DC USA
202-326-6440
E-mail: membership@aaas.org; media@aaas.org; development@aaas.org
URL: www.aaas.org
Scope: International
Purpose: Information for scientists, engineers, educators, & policy-makers

Contact Information: Phone: 202-326-6450; Fax: 202-289-4021; E-mail: meetings.aaas.org; Director, Annual Meeting: Barbara Rice, E-mail: brice.aaas.org; Manager, Marketing, Exhibits, & Sponsors: Jill Perla, E-mail: jperla.aaas.org; Meetings Manager: Nicole Maylett, E-mail: nmaylett.aaas.org

American Water Works Association & The American Membrane Technology Association 2012 Membrane Technology Joint Conference & Exposition
Date: February 27 - March 1, 2012
Location: Renaissance Hotel
Glendale, AZ
Sponsor/Contact: American Water Works Association
6666 West Quincy Ave.
Denver, CO USA
303-794-7711 Fax: 303-347-0804
E-mail: custsvc@awwa.org
URL: www.awwa.org
Scope: International
Purpose: A meeting of membrane technology professionals & experts from across North America for a showcase of membrane developments & applications that help to improve water quality & protect public health
Contact Information: American Membrane Technology Association, E-mail: admin@amtaorg.com

Association of Local Public Health Agencies 2012 Winter Symposium
Date: February 2012
Location: Ontario
Sponsor/Contact: Association of Local Public Health Agencies
#1306, 2 Carlton St.
Toronto, ON M5G 1T6
416-595-0006 Fax: 416-595-0030
E-mail: info@alphaweb.org
URL: www.alphaweb.org
Scope: Provincial
Contact Information: Registration contact: Karen Reece, Phone: 416-595-0006, ext. 25; Fax: 416-595-0030, E-mail: karen@alphaweb.org

Canada East Equipment Dealers' Association 2012 Annual Meeting & Convention
Date: February 2012
Sponsor/Contact: Canada East Equipment Dealers' Association
64 Temperance St.
Aurora, ON L4G 2P8
905-841-6888 Fax: 905-841-1214
E-mail: info@orfeda.com
URL: www.orfeda.com
Scope: Regional

Canadian Bar Association Mid-Winter Meeting of Council 2012
Date: February 11-13, 2012
Location: Fairmont Mayakoba
Mayan Riviera, Mexico
Sponsor/Contact: Canadian Bar Association
#500, 865 Carling Ave.
Ottawa, ON K1S 5S8 Canada
613-237-2925 Fax: 613-237-0185
E-mail: info@cba.org
URL: www.cba.org
Scope: National

Geological Association of Canada, Newfoundland & Labrador Section 2012 Technicl Conference
Date: February 2012
Location: Newfoundland & Labrador
Sponsor/Contact: Geological Association of Canada
c/o Heather Rafuse, Department of Natural Resources, Geological Survey
P.O. Box 8700
St. John's, NL A1B 4J6
URL: gac.esd.mun.ca/nl/nfsection.htm
Scope: Provincial
Purpose: An annual meeting featuring guest speakers & a general session for the presentation of papers

Contact Information: Technical Program Chair: Andrew Kerr, E-mail: andykerr@gov.nl.ca; Education Chair: Keith Moore, E-mail: Keith.Moore@geocentre.ca

Ontario Good Roads Association / Rural Ontario Municipal Association 2012 Combined Conference
Date: February 26-29, 2012
Location: Ontario
Sponsor/Contact: Ontario Good Roads Association
#2, 6355 Kennedy Rd.
Mississauga, ON L5T 2L5
905-795-2555 Fax: 905-795-2660
E-mail: info@ogra.org
URL: www.ogra.org
Scope: Provincial
Purpose: Featuring addresses, workshops, information rooms on current municipal issues & innovation, a trade show, & networking opportunities
Anticipated Attendance: 1500+
Contact Information: Ontario Good Roads Association, Phone: 905-795-2555; Fax: 905-795-2660

Ontario Soil & Crop Improvement Association 2012 Provincial Annual Meeting
Date: February 7-8, 2012
Location: Lamplighter Inn
London, ON
Sponsor/Contact: Ontario Soil & Crop Improvement Association
1 Stone Rd. West
Guelph, ON N1G 4Y2
519-826-4214 Fax: 519-826-4224
E-mail: oscia@ontariosoilcrop.org
URL: www.ontariosoilcrop.org
Scope: Provincial
Purpose: Presentations & resolutions
Contact Information: Ontario Soil & Crop Improvement Association President: Max Kaiser, Phone: 613-354-0100

Toronto Field Naturalists 2012 Monthly Talk
Date: February 2012
Location: Emmanuel College
Toronto, ON
Sponsor/Contact: Toronto Field Naturalists
#1519, 2 Carlton St.
Toronto, ON M5B 1J3
416-593-2656
E-mail: office@torontofieldnaturalists.org
URL: www.torontofieldnaturalists.org
Scope: Local
Purpose: Sunday meetings in past months have featured appearances by professionals working with Fisheries & Oceans Canada & Tallgrass Ontario
Contact Information: E-mail: office@torontofieldnaturalists.org

March

Alberta Association of Municipal Districts & Counties Spring 2012 Convention & Trade Show
Date: March 19-21, 2012
Location: Alberta
Sponsor/Contact: Alberta Association of Municipal Districts & Counties
2510 Sparrow Dr.
Nisku, AB T9E 8N5
780-955-3639 Fax: 780-955-3615
E-mail: aamdc@aamdc.com
URL: www.aamdc.com

American Water Works Association 2012 Customer Service & Information Management Conference & Exposition
Date: March 4-6, 2012
Location: Omni Hotel at CNN Center
Atlanta, GA
Sponsor/Contact: American Water Works Association
6666 West Quincy Ave.
Denver, CO USA
303-794-7711 Fax: 303-347-0804
E-mail: custsvc@awwa.org
URL: www.awwa.org

Scope: International
Purpose: Subjects include the following: metering of today, intelligent infrastructure, automated reading management, customer information systems, maintenance management, & best business practices
Contact Information: Education Services, E-mail: educationservices@awwa.org; Customer Services, Phone: 800-926-7337, E-mail: custsvc@awwa.org

American Water Works Association 2012 Sustainable Water Management Conference & Exposition
Date: March 18-21, 2012
Location: Portland, OR USA
Sponsor/Contact: American Water Works Association
6666 West Quincy Ave.
Denver, CO USA
303-794-7711 Fax: 303-347-0804
E-mail: custsvc@awwa.org
URL: www.awwa.org
Scope: International
Purpose: The following topics will be addressed: water conservation program development & management, water resources conflict & collaboration, aquatic & riparian habitat, sustainable utilities & infrastructure, urban planning design & construction, & community sustainability
Contact Information: Manager, Conference & Exhibits: Lynn Lyons, E-mail: llyons@awwa.org; Contact, Conference Coordination: Sarah Mejia, E-mail: smejia@awwa.org

CMX CIPHEX 2012
Date: March 22-24, 2012
Location: Toronto, ON
Sponsor/Contact: Canadian Institute of Plumbing & Heating
#330, 295 The West Mall
Toronto, ON M9C 4Z4
416-695-0447 Fax: 416-695-0450
E-mail: info@ciph.com
URL: ww.ciph.com
Scope: International
Purpose: A trade show & learning forum for the air conditioning, heating, hearth, plumbing, piping, refrigeration, & ventilation industries
Contact Information: General Manager, Trade Shows: Elizabeth McCullough, Phone: 416-695-0447, Toll-Free Phone: 1-888-275-2474, E-mail: e.mccullough@ciph.com

Canadian International Turfgrass 2012 45th Annual Conference & Trade Show
Date: March 2012
Sponsor/Contact: Canadian Golf Superintendents Association
#205, 5520 Explorer Dr.
Mississauga, ON L4W 5L1
905-602-8873 Fax: 905-602-1958
E-mail: cgsa@golfsupers.com
URL: www.golfsupers.com
Scope: International
Purpose: An international confernce & trade show featuring over 100 exhibitors
Anticipated Attendance: 2000
Contact Information: Executive Director, Canadian Golf Superintendents Association: Ken Cousineau, Phone: 905-602-8873, ext. 222, E-mail: kcousineau@golfsupers.com

GLOBE 2012 12th Biennial Conference & Trade Fair on Business & the Environment: Driving Economic Performance Through Sustainability
Date: March 14-16, 2012
Location: Vancouver Convention Centre
Vancouver, BC
Sponsor/Contact: GLOBE Foundation
World Trade Centre
#578, 999 Canada Pl.
Vancouver, BC V6C 3E1
604-695-5001 Fax: 604-695-5019
E-mail: info@globe.ca
URL: www.globe.ca

Scope: International
Purpose: Over 100 speakers with presentations on themes such as corporate sustainability, the future of energy, investment, climate change, carbon management, & green cities, plus an international environmental trade show with more than 400 exhibits highlighting environmental technologies & business opportunities, & the opportunity to network with decision-makers from developed economies & emerging markets
Anticipated Attendance: 10,000+
Contact Information: General Information: Phone: 604-695-5001, Toll-Free Phone: 1-800-274-6097, E-mail: info@globeseries.com, Social Media: www.twitter.com/Globe_Series; Exhibiting Information, E-mail: sales@globeseries.com

Institute of Food Technologists 2012 Annual Wellness Conference
Date: March 2012
Location: , USA
Sponsor/Contact: Institute of Food Technologists
#1000, 525 West Van Buren
Chicago, IL
312-782-8424 Fax: 312-782-8348
E-mail: info@ift.org; sales@ift.org
URL: www.ift.org
Scope: International
Purpose: An annual educational & networking event for dieticians, product developers, & brand managers involved in the development & sale of foods that contribute to health & wellness
Anticipated Attendance: 300+
Contact Information: Manager, Knowledge & Learning Experiences: George Miller, Phone: 312.604.0263, Fax: 312.596.5663, E-mail: wellness@ift.org

Institute of Transportation Engineers 2012 Technical Conference & Exhibit
Date: March 4-7, 2012
Location: Pasadena Convention Center
Pasadena, CA USA
Sponsor/Contact: Institute of Transportation Engineers
#300, 1099 - 14th St. NW
Washington, DC USA
202-289-0222 Fax: 202-289-7722
E-mail: ite_staff@ite.org
URL: www.ite.org
Scope: International
Contact Information: Contact, Registration Information: Sallie C. Dollins, E-mail: sdollins@ite.org; Contact, Technical Program: Aliyah N. Horton, E-mail: ahorton@ite.org; Contact, Exhibits: Christina Garneski, E-mail: cgarneski@ite.org; Contact, Paper Submittals: Eunice Chege, E-mail: echege@ite.org

Manitoba Ozone Protection Industry Association 2012 18th Annual General Meeting
Date: March 19, 2012
Location: Manitoba
Sponsor/Contact: Manitoba Ozone Protection Industry Association
1980B Main St.
Winnipeg, MB R2V 2B6 Canada
204-338-0804 Fax: 204-338-0810
E-mail: mopia@mts.net
URL: www.mopia.ca
Scope: Provincial
Purpose: Election of members to the Board of Directors & the presentation of the annual report to the membership

Pest Management Canada 2012
Date: March 8-10, 2012
Location: Fairmont Waterfront Vancouver
Vancouver, BC
Sponsor/Contact: Canadian Pest Management Association
P.O. Box 1748
Moncton, NB E1C 9X5
Fax: 866-957-7378
E-mail: cpma@pestworld.org
URL: www.pestworldcanada.org

Scope: National
Purpose: Educational sessions, networking opportunities, & exhibits of products, services & techniques
Contact Information: E-mail: cpma@pestworld.org

Saskatchewan Association of Rural Municipalities 2012 Annual Convention
Date: March 12-15, 2012
Location: Ipsco Place
Regina, SK
Sponsor/Contact: Saskatchewan Association of Rural Municipalities
2075 Hamilton St.
Regina, SK S4P 2E1 Canada
306-757-3577 Fax: 306-565-2141
E-mail: sarm@sarm.ca
URL: www.sarm.ca
Scope: Provincial

Society of Toxicology 51st Annual Meeting & ToxExpo
Date: March 11-15, 2012
Location: Moscone Center
San Francisco, CA USA
Sponsor/Contact: Society of Toxicology
#300, 1821 Michael Faraday Dr.
Reston, VA USA
703-438-3115 Fax: 703-438-3113
E-mail: sothq@toxicology.org
URL: www.toxicology.org
Scope: International
Purpose: Toxicology meeting & exhibition
Anticipated Attendance: 6500
Contact Information: Phone: 703-438-3115; Fax: 703-438-3113; E-mail: sothq@toxicology.org

Toronto Field Naturalists 2012 Monthly Talk
Date: March 2012
Location: Emmanuel College
Toronto, ON
Sponsor/Contact: Toronto Field Naturalists
#1519, 2 Carlton St.
Toronto, ON M5B 1J3
416-593-2656
E-mail: office@torontofieldnaturalists.org
URL: www.torontofieldnaturalists.org
Scope: Local
Purpose: Naturalists & geologists are among the experts who have spoken to members of Toronto Field Naturalists & visitors
Contact Information: E-mail: office@torontofieldnaturalists.org

Water Environment Federation 2012 Residuals & Biosolids Conference: Advancing Residuals Management - Technologies & Applications
Date: March 25-28, 2012
Location: Raleigh Convention Center
Raleigh, NC USA
Sponsor/Contact: Water Environment Federation
601 Wythe St.
Alexandria, VA USA
703-684-2400 Fax: 703-684-2492
E-mail: csc@wef.org
URL: www.wef.org
Scope: International
Purpose: A conference held in cooperation with the North Carolina Water Environment Association, featuring topics such as the following: agricultural & industrial residuals management, climate change & greenhouse gas issues, environmental management systems, emerging technologies, odour & pathogen control, thermal processes, sustainability, bioenergy from residuals, marketing of biosolids & residuals products, & biosolids land application
Contact Information: Coordinator, Exhibition Sales: Sarah Evans, E-mail: sevans@wef.org; Registration Information, Phone: 703-684-2441; Technical Program Information, Phone: 703-684-2400, ext. 7010

Trade Shows, Conferences and Seminars

April

Association of Professional Engineers, Geologists & Geophysicists of Alberta 2012 Annual Conference & Annual General Meeting
Date: April 2012
Location: Alberta
Sponsor/Contact: Association of Professional Engineers, Geologists & Geophysicists of Alberta
Scotia One
#1500, 10060 Jasper Ave. NW
Edmonton, AB T5J 4A2
780-426-3990 Fax: 780-426-1877
E-mail: email@apegga.org
URL: www.apegga.org
Scope: Provincial
Purpose: A meeting held each April in Edmonton or Calgary, featuring professional development seminars & other conference events
Contact Information: Manager, Communications: Philip Mulder, Phone: 780-426-3990, ext. 2809, Fax: 780-425-1722, E-mail: pmulder@apegga.org; Manager, Human Resources & Professional Development: Nancy Toth, Phone: 780-426-3990, ext. 2811, Fax: 780-425-1722, E-mail: ntoth@apegga.org

Canadian Health Food Association (CHFA) Expo West 2012
Date: April 20-22, 2012
Location: Vancouver Convention Centre
Vancouver, BC
Sponsor/Contact: Canadian Health Food Association
#302, 235 Yorkland Blvd.
Toronto, ON M2J 4Y8
416-497-6939 Fax: 905-479-3214
E-mail: info@chfa.ca
URL: www.chfa.ca
Scope: Regional
Purpose: Seminars & a trade show for members of the natural products & organics industry
Contact Information: E-mail: info@chfa.ca

Canadian Respiratory Conference 2012
Date: April 26-28, 2012
Location: Westin Bayshore Hotel
Vancouver, BC
Sponsor/Contact: Canadian Lung Association
#300, 1750 Courtwood Cres.
Ottawa, ON K2C 2B5
613-569-6411 Fax: 613-569-8860
E-mail: info@lung.ca
URL: www.lung.ca
Scope: National
Purpose: Jointly organized by the Canadian Lung Association, the Canadian Thoracic Society, the Canadian COPD Alliance, & the Canadian Respiratory Health Professionals
Contact Information: Manager, Marketing & Fundraising: Jennifer Oakley, E-mail: joakley@lung.ca

Local Government Management Association of BC Professional Development Program: Municipal Administration Training Institute - Advanced Communications
Date: April 2012
Location: Bowen Island, BC
Sponsor/Contact: Local Government Management Association of British Columbia
Central Building
620 View St., 7th Fl.
Victoria, BC V8W 1J6
250-383-7032 Fax: 250-384-4879
E-mail: office@lgma.ca; editor@lgma.ca (magazine); ads@lgma.ca
URL: www.lgma.ca
Scope: Provincial
Purpose: A 5.5 day course held each year to share strategies for improved communication skills
Contact Information: Program Coordinator: Ana Fuller, Phone: 250-383-7032, ext. 227, Fax: 250-383-4879, E-mail: afuller@lgma.ca

Municipal Officials Seminar & MTCML Trade Show 2012
Date: April 11-12, 2012
Location: Brandon Keystone Centre
Brandon, MB
Sponsor/Contact: Association of Manitoba Municipalities
1910 Saskatchewan Ave. West
Portage la Prairie, MB R1N 0P1 Canada
204-857-8666 Fax: 204-856-2370
E-mail: amm@amm.mb.ca
URL: www.amm.mb.ca

Northwestern Ontario Municipal Association 2012 Annual General Meeting
Date: April 2012
Location: Ontario
Sponsor/Contact: Northwestern Ontario Municipal Association
P.O. Box 10308
Thunder Bay, ON P7B 6T8
807-683-6662
E-mail: admin@noma.on.ca
URL: www.noma.on.ca
Scope: Local
Purpose: A yearly gathering, which takes place during the last week in April, unless changed by the Board of Directors, offering delegates the opportunity to debate policy resolution related to issues that affect the association's forthcoming advocacy activities
Anticipated Attendance: 180
Contact Information: Executive Director: Charla Robinson, Phone: 807-683-6662, E-mail: admin@noma.on.ca

Petroleum Services Association of Canada 2012 Annual Spring Conference
Date: April 2012
Location: Red Deer, AB
Sponsor/Contact: Petroleum Services Association of Canada
#1150, 800 - 6 Ave. SW
Calgary, AB T2P 3G3
403-264-4195 Fax: 403-263-7174
E-mail: info@psac.ca
URL: www.psac.ca
Scope: National
Purpose: A conference to address issues such as transportation, human capital, & management
Contact Information: Manager, Meetings & Events: Heather Doyle, Phone: 403-213-2796, E-mail: hdoyle@psac.ca

Toronto Field Naturalists 2012 Monthly Talk
Date: April 2012
Location: Emmanuel College
Toronto, ON
Sponsor/Contact: Toronto Field Naturalists
#1519, 2 Carlton St.
Toronto, ON M5B 1J3
416-593-2656
E-mail: office@torontofieldnaturalists.org
URL: www.torontofieldnaturalists.org
Scope: Local
Purpose: A Sunday gathering of members of Toronto Field Naturalists & visitors, occurring each month except June, July, & August
Contact Information: E-mail: office@torontofieldnaturalists.org

WasteExpo 2012 44th Conference & Tradeshow
Date: April 30 - May 3, 2012
Location: Las Vegas Convention Center
Las Vegas, NV USA
Sponsor/Contact: National Solid Wastes Management Association
#300, 4301 Connecticut Ave. NW
Washington, DC USA
202-244-4700 Fax: 202-966-4824
URL: www.nswma.org
Scope: International
Purpose: A solid waste & recycling tradeshow that serve both the public & private sectors
Contact Information: Show Director: Rita Ugianskis-Fishman, E-mail: rita.ugianskis@penton.com; Operations Director: MaryAnn Troiano, E-mail: maryann.troiano@penton.com; Customer Service & Registration Information, E-mail: registration@penton.com

Water Environment Association of Ontario 2012 41st Annual Technical Symposium & OPCEA Exhibition: One World . . . One Water Environment
Date: April 22-24, 2012
Location: Ottawa Convention Centre
Ottawa, ON
Sponsor/Contact: Water Environment Association of Ontario
P.O. Box 176
Milton, ON L9T 4N9
416-410-6933 Fax: 416-410-1626
E-mail: julie.vincent@weao.org
URL: www.weao.org
Scope: Provincial
Purpose: Technical sessions, a keynote speaker, a facility tour, the Ontario Pollution Control Equipment Association exhibition, the annual meeting, & an awards presentation
Contact Information: Chair, Conference Committee: Rob Anderson, Phone: 905-660-9775, ext. 29, E-mail: rob@h2flow.com; Chair, Promotions & Event Planning: Anthony Abbruscato, Phone: 416-499-0090, ext. 73605, E-mail: anthony.abbruscato@ch2m.com

May

Aquaculture Canada 2012: The Aquaculture Association of Canada's Annual Conference & General Meeting
Date: May 27-30, 2012
Location: Rodd Charlottetown
Charlottetown, PE
Sponsor/Contact: Aquaculture Association of Canada
16 Lobster Lane
St. Andrews, NB E5B 3T6
506-529-4766 Fax: 506-529-4609
E-mail: aac@dfo-mpo.gc.ca
URL: www.aquacultureassociation.ca
Scope: National
Purpose: New Frontiers: Bridging Technology & Economic Growth
Contact Information: Association Office Manager: Susan Waddy, Phone: 506-529-4766, E-mail: Susan.Waddy@dfo-mpo.gc.ca

British Columbia Recreation & Parks Association 2012 Symposium
Date: May 9-11, 2012
Location: Victoria Conference Centre
Victoria, BC
Sponsor/Contact: British Columbia Recreation & Parks Association
#101, 4664 Lougheed Hwy.
Burnaby, BC V5C 5T5
604-629-0965 Fax: 604-629-2651
E-mail: bcrpa@bcrpa.bc.ca; registration@bcrpa.bc.ca
URL: www.bcrpa.bc.ca
Scope: Provincial
Purpose: An annual event featuring educational sessions for delegates from British Columbia's park & recreation sector
Anticipated Attendance: 400+

Canadian Council of Grocery Distributors 2012 National Grocery Conference
Date: May 2012
Sponsor/Contact: Canadian Council of Grocery Distributors
#402, 6455, rue Jean-Talon est
Montréal, QC H1S 3E8
514-982-0267
URL: www.ccgd.ca
Scope: National
Purpose: Business meetings, information about the industry's current issues & trends, as well as social activities for delegates, usually held in late May

Contact Information: Conference Contact: Jeanette Lee, Phone: 416-922-6228, ext. 331, Fax: 416-922-5909, E-mail: jlee@ccgd.ca

Canadian Ground Water Association CanWell 2012: Canada's National Ground Water Symposium
Date: May 23-26, 2012
Location: Hamilton Convention Center
Hamilton, ON
Sponsor/Contact: Canadian Ground Water Association
#100-409, 1600 Bedford Hwy.
Bedford, NS B4A 1E8
902-845-1885 Fax: 902-845-1886
E-mail: info@cgwa.org
URL: www.cgwa.org
Scope: International
Purpose: A convention & trade show for professionals from the geothermal & ground water industries, featuring technical sessions, outdoor demonstrations, the annual general meeting of the Canadian Ground Water Association & the Ontario Ground Water Association, as well as a social program & networking opportunities
Anticipated Attendance: 650+
Contact Information: Registration Information, Address: CanWell 2012, 3519 - 5th Line, Bradford, ON, L3Z 2A4

Canadian Institute of Mining, Metallurgy & Petroleum 2012 Annual Conference & Exhibition (in conjunction with the Canadian Rock Mechanics Symposium)
Date: May 6-9, 2012
Location: Shaw Conference Centre
Edmonton, AB
Sponsor/Contact: Canadian Institute of Mining, Metallurgy & Petroleum
CIM National Office
#1250, 3500, boul de Maisonneuve ouest
Westmount, QC H3Z 3C1
514-939-2710 Fax: 514-939-2714
E-mail: cim@cim.org
URL: www.cim.org
Scope: National
Purpose: A mining event, featuring a technical program, workshops, field trips, a student program, & a social program
Contact Information: Meeting Coordinator: Chantal Murphy, Phone: 514-939-2710, E-mail: cmurphy@cim.org

Canadian Urban Transit Association 2012 Annual Conference
Date: May 27-30, 2012
Location: Victoria, BC
Sponsor/Contact: Canadian Urban Transit Association
#1401, 55 York St.
Toronto, ON M5J 1R7
416-365-9800 Fax: 416-365-1295
E-mail: transit@cutaactu.ca
URL: www.cutaactu.ca
Scope: National
Purpose: An opportunity for delegates in the transit industry from across Canada to exchange experiences & ideas
Contact Information: Conference Specialist: Anna Maria Schell, Phone: 416-365-9800, ext. 116

Geological Association of Canada (GAC) & the Mineralogical Association of Canada (MAC) 2012 Joint Annual Meeting: At The Geoscience Edge
Date: May 27-29, 2012
Location: Delta Hotel
St. John's, NL
Sponsor/Contact: Geological Association of Canada
Department of Earth Sciences, Memorial University of Newfoundland
#ER4063, Alexander Murray Bldg.
St. John's, NL A1B 3X5
709-737-7660 Fax: 709-737-2532
E-mail: gac@mun.ca; gacpublications@mun.ca (GEOLOG newsmagazine)
URL: www.gac.ca
Scope: National
Purpose: Featuring a varied technical program, exhibits, field trips, & social events designed for delegates from across Canada
Contact Information: Technical Program Chair: Andrew Kerr, E-mail: andykerr@gov.nl.ca; Communications Chair: Tim Corkery, Phone: 204-945-6554, Fax: 204-945-1406; Finance & Administration Manager: Karen Johnston, Phone: 709-864-2399, E-mail: kajohnston@mun.ca

Health Sciences Association of Alberta 2012 41st Annual General Meeting
Date: May 31 - June 1, 2010
Location: Alberta
Sponsor/Contact: Health Sciences Association of Alberta
10212 - 112 St.
Edmonton, AB T5K 1M4
780-488-0168 Fax: 780-488-0534
URL: www.hsaa.ca
Scope: Provincial
Contact Information: Communications Officer: Scott Pattison, E-mail: scottpat@hsaa.ca

Local Government Management Association of BC Professional Development Program: Municipal Administration Training Institute - Managing People
Date: May 2012
Location: Bowen Island, BC
Sponsor/Contact: Local Government Management Association of British Columbia
Central Building
620 View St., 7th Fl.
Victoria, BC V8W 1J6
250-383-7032 Fax: 250-384-4879
E-mail: office@lgma.ca; editor@lgma.ca (magazine); ads@lgma.ca
URL: www.lgma.ca
Scope: Provincial
Purpose: An annual 5.5 day residential program presenting topics such as collective bargaining, contract administration, occupational health & safety, training, & performance appraisal systems
Contact Information: Program Coordinator: Ana Fuller, Phone: 250-383-7032, ext. 227, Fax: 250-383-4879, E-mail: afuller@lgma.ca

Local Government Management Association of British Columbia 2012 Annual General Meeting & Conference
Date: May 14-17, 2012
Location: Victoria Conference Centre
Victoria, BC
Sponsor/Contact: Local Government Management Association of British Columbia
Central Building
620 View St., 7th Fl.
Victoria, BC V8W 1J6
250-383-7032 Fax: 250-384-4879
E-mail: office@lgma.ca; editor@lgma.ca (magazine); ads@lgma.ca
URL: www.lgma.ca
Scope: Provincial
Purpose: Educational sessions on current issues, keynote speakers, & networking opportunities for members of the Local Government Management Association of British Columbia
Anticipated Attendance: 400-500
Contact Information: Program Coordinator: Ana Fuller, Phone: 250-383-7032, ext. 227, Fax: 250-383-4879, E-mail: afuller@lgma.ca

Local Government Management Association of British Columbia 2012 Women in Leadership Forum
Date: May 2012
Location: British Columbia
Sponsor/Contact: Local Government Management Association of British Columbia
Central Building
620 View St., 7th Fl.
Victoria, BC V8W 1J6
250-383-7032 Fax: 250-384-4879
E-mail: office@lgma.ca; editor@lgma.ca (magazine); ads@lgma.ca
URL: www.lgma.ca
Scope: Provincial
Purpose: Interactive discussions around the topic of leadership for both emerging & executive women leaders
Contact Information: Program Coordinator: Ana Fuller, Phone: 250-383-7032, ext. 227, Fax: 250-383-4879, E-mail: afuller@lgma.ca

Ontario Small Urban Municipalities 2012 59th Annual Conference & Trade Show
Date: May 2-4, 2012
Location: Huntsville, ON
Sponsor/Contact: Ontario Small Urban Municipalities c/o Association of Municipalities of Ontario
#801, 200 University Ave.
Toronto, ON M5H 3C6
416-971-9856 Fax: 416-971-6191
E-mail: amo@amo.on.ca
URL: www.amo.on.ca//AM/Template.cfm?Section=What_s_New7
Scope: Provincial
Purpose: A gathering of Ontario's municipal decision makers for educational sessions, an exhibitor program, & networking events
Anticipated Attendance: 175
Contact Information: OSUM Annual Conference & Trade Show Coordinator: Ted Blowes, Phone: 519-271-0250, ext. 241, E-mail: ted.b@quadro.net

Ontario Water Works Association / Ontario Municipal Water Association 2012 Annual Joint Conference & Trade Show
Date: May 2012
Location: Ontario
Sponsor/Contact: Ontario Municipal Water Association c/o Doug Parker
43 Chelsea Cres.
Belleville, ON K8N 4Z5
613-966-1100 Fax: 613-966-3024
E-mail: dparker@omwa.org
URL: www.omwa.org
Scope: Provincial
Purpose: A conference featuring a plenary session, technical sessions, a trade show, & networking opportunities

Toronto Field Naturalists 2012 Monthly Talk
Date: May 2012
Location: Emmanuel College
Toronto, ON
Sponsor/Contact: Toronto Field Naturalists
#1519, 2 Carlton St.
Toronto, ON M5B 1J3
416-593-2656
E-mail: office@torontofieldnaturalists.org
URL: www.torontofieldnaturalists.org
Scope: Local
Purpose: Emmanuel College is the venue for talks about natural history from September to May
Contact Information: E-mail: office@torontofieldnaturalists.org

Yukon Conservation Society 2012 Annual Bird-a-thon
Date: May 2012
Location: YK
Sponsor/Contact: Yukon Conservation Society
302 Hawkins St.
Whitehorse, YT Y1A 1X6 Canada
867-668-5678 Fax: 867-668-6637
E-mail: ycs@ycs.yk.ca
URL: www.yukonconservation.org
Scope: Regional

June

Air & Waste Management Association 105th Annual Conference & Exhibition
Date: June 19-22, 2012
Location: San Antonio, TX USA
Sponsor/Contact: Air & Waste Management Association

Trade Shows, Conferences and Seminars

One Gateway Center
420 Fort Duquesne Blvd., 3rd Fl.
Pittsburgh, PA USA
412-232-3444 Fax: 412-232-3450
E-mail: info@awma.org
URL: www.awma.org
Scope: International

American Society of Mechanical Engineers 2012 57th Turbo Expo

Date: June 11-15, 2012
Location: Bella Center
Copenhagen, Denmark
Sponsor/Contact: American Society of Mechanical Engineers
3 Park Ave.
New York, NY USA
800-843-2763
E-mail: infocentral@asme.org
URL: www.asme.org
Scope: International
Purpose: Related topics to address the global energy challenge include wind turbines, steam turbines, fans & blowers, & solar brayton & rankine cycle
Anticipated Attendance: 3000
Contact Information: Turbo Expo Contact: Martha Quinlin, E-mail: igti@asme.org; Program Contact: Stephanie (Sears) Partain: Partains@asme.org; Exposition & Sponsorship Contact: Kristin Barranger, E-mail: barrangerk@asme.org; Social Media: www.facebook.com/ASMEIGTI, www.twitter.com/#!/IGTI, www.linkedin.com/company/asme-international-gas-turbine-institute

American Society of Mechanical Engineers 2012 Annual Meeting

Date: June 2-6, 2012
Location: Hilton Montréal Bonaventure
Montréal, QC
Sponsor/Contact: American Society of Mechanical Engineers
3 Park Ave.
New York, NY USA
800-843-2763
E-mail: infocentral@asme.org
URL: www.asme.org
Scope: International
Contact Information: 2012 Annual Meeting Contact: Melissa Torres, E-mail: TorresM@asme.org

American Water Works Association 2012 131st Annual Conference & Exposition

Date: June 10-14, 2012
Location: Dallas, TX USA
Sponsor/Contact: American Water Works Association
6666 West Quincy Ave.
Denver, CO USA
303-794-7711 Fax: 303-347-0804
E-mail: custsvc@awwa.org
URL: www.awwa.org
Scope: International
Purpose: Information for water professionals from around the world
Contact Information: Director of Conferences & Events: April DeBaker, E-mail: adebaker@awwa.org; Manager, Conference & Exhibits: Lynn Lyons, E-mail: llyons@awwa.org; Conference & Promotion Manager: Joanne Gaglia, E-mail: jgaglia@awwa.org; Event Operations Supervisor: Lisa Star, E-mail: lstar@awwa.org

Association of Local Public Health Agencies 2012 Annual Conference

Date: June 2012
Location: Ontario
Sponsor/Contact: Association of Local Public Health Agencies
#1306, 2 Carlton St.
Toronto, ON M5G 1T6
416-595-0006 Fax: 416-595-0030
E-mail: info@alphaweb.org
URL: www.alphaweb.org
Scope: Provincial
Purpose: A meeting for medical officers of health, board of health members, senior public health managers, & community medicine residents
Contact Information: ALPHA Administrative Assistant: Karen Reece, Phone: 416-595-0006, ext. 24; Fax: 416-595-0030, E-mail: karen@alphaweb.org

Canadian Association of Chemical Distributors 2012 26th Annual General Meeting

Date: June 6-8, 2012
Location: Fairmont Chateau Whistler
Whistler, BC
Sponsor/Contact: Canadian Association of Chemical Distributors
349 Davis Rd., #A
Oakville, ON L6J 2X2
905-844-9140 Fax: 905-844-5706
URL: www.cacd.ca
Scope: National
Contact Information: Manager, Communications & Member Services: Catherine Wieckowska, Phone: 905-844-9140, E-mail: catherine@cacd.ca

Canadian Institute of Mining, Metallurgy & Petroleum MASSMIN 2012: 6th Intl Conference & Exhibition on Mass Mining: Advancing the State-of-the-Art

Date: June 11-13, 2012
Location: Laurentian University Fraser Building
Sudbury, ON
Sponsor/Contact: Canadian Institute of Mining, Metallurgy & Petroleum
CIM National Office
#1250, 3500, boul de Maisonneuve ouest
Westmount, QC H3Z 3C1
514-939-2710 Fax: 514-939-2714
E-mail: cim@cim.org
URL: www.cim.org
Scope: International
Purpose: Topics include mine design, rock flow modeling & prediction, mine automation, & mining methods
Contact Information: Conference Co-Chair: Dr. Greg Baiden, Phone: 705-692-8748, E-mail: info@massmin2012.com; Conference Co-Chair: Dr. Yassiah Bissiri, Phone: 705-692-8743, ext. 203, E-mail: ybissiri@penguinasi.com

Canadian Institute of Plumbing & Heating 2012 Annual General Meeting

Date: June 26, 2012
Location: Fairmont Chateau
Montebello, QC
Sponsor/Contact: Canadian Institute of Plumbing & Heating
#330, 295 The West Mall
Toronto, ON M9C 4Z4
416-695-0447 Fax: 416-695-0450
E-mail: info@ciph.com
URL: ww.ciph.com
Scope: National
Purpose: A business meeting for members of the CIPH from across Canada, featuring reports, nominations of officers, reviews of bylaws, & announcements of awards
Contact Information: CIPH Phone: 416-695-0447, Toll-Free: 1-800-639-2474

Canadian Meteorological & Oceanographic Society Congress 2012 46th Annual Congress

Sponsor/Contact: Canadian Meteorological & Oceanographic Society
P.O. Box 3211 Stn. D
Ottawa, ON K1P 6H7 Canada
613-990-0300 Fax: 613-990-1617
E-mail: communications@cmos.ca; accounts@cmos.ca; publications@cmos.ca
URL: www.cmos.ca
Scope: National
Purpose: Scientific & plenary sessions, as well as business meetings, exhibits, & networking opportunities
Contact Information: E-mail: lac@cmos.ca

Canadian Nuclear Society 2012 33rd Annual Conference & 36th Annual CNS / CNA Student Conference

Date: June 10-13, 2012
Location: TCU Place
Saskatoon, SK
Sponsor/Contact: Canadian Nuclear Society
655 Bay St., 17th Fl.
Toronto, ON M5G 2K4
416-977-7620 Fax: 416-977-8131
E-mail: cns-snc@on.aibn.com
URL: www.cns-snc.ca
Scope: National
Purpose: A forum for the exchange of views from scientists, technologists, engineers, & students, plus the presentation of Canadian Nuclear Society awards
Contact Information: Canadian Nuclear Society Office: Phone: 416-977-7620, E-mail: cns-snc@on.aibn.com

Canadian Society for Civil Engineering 2012 Annual General Meeting & Conference

Date: June 6-9, 2012
Location: Edmonton, AB
Sponsor/Contact: Canadian Society for Civil Engineering
4877, rue Sherbrooke ouest
Montréal, QC H3Z 1G9
514-933-2634 Fax: 514-933-3504
E-mail: info@csce.ca; membership@csce.ca
URL: www.csce.ca
Scope: National
Purpose: A conference featuring keynote speakers on subjects relevant to civil engineers
Contact Information: Manager, Communications: Louise Newman, E-mail: louise@csce.ca

Federation of Canadian Municipalities 2012 75th Annual Conference & Municipal Expo

Date: June 1-4, 2012
Location: Saskatoon, SK
Sponsor/Contact: Federation of Canadian Municipalities
24 Clarence St.
Ottawa, ON K1N 5P3 Canada
613-241-5221 Fax: 613-241-7440
E-mail: federation@fcm.ca
URL: www.fcm.ca
Scope: National
Contact Information: Manager, Membership & Events: Seán Kelly, Phone: 613-244-6045, E-mail: skelly@fcm.ca

Goldschmidt Conference 2012

Date: June 24-29, 2012
Location: Palais des congrès (Convention Centre)
Montréal, QC
Sponsor/Contact: Geochemical Society
c/o Earth & Planetary Sciences Department, Washington University
#CB 11691, Brookings Dr.
St. Louis, MO USA
314-935-4131 Fax: 314-935-4121
E-mail: gsoffice@geochemsoc.org
URL: www.geochemsoc.org
Scope: International
Purpose: An international conference on geochemistry

Institute of Food Technologists 2012 Annual Meeting & Food Expo

Date: June 25-28, 2012
Location: Las Vegas, NV USA
Sponsor/Contact: Institute of Food Technologists
#1000, 525 West Van Buren
Chicago, IL
312-782-8424 Fax: 312-782-8348
E-mail: info@ift.org; sales@ift.org
URL: www.ift.org
Scope: International
Purpose: More than 100 scientific sessions, plus approximately 1,900 technical presentations are offered to help participants make decisions about development, safety, nutrient value, quality, packaging, sales, & marketing of foods
Anticipated Attendance: 21,500+

Contact Information: Vice-President, Meetings & Events: Heidi Voorhees, CAE, E-mail: havoorhees@ift.org; Media Inquiries, E-mail: media@ift.org

Peatlands in Balance: 14th International Peat Congress
Date: June 3-8, 2012
Location: Stockholm, Sweden
Sponsor/Contact: International Peat Society
Vapaudenkatu 12
Jyväskylä, Finland
E-mail: ips@peatsociety.org
URL: www.peatsociety.org
Scope: International

Permafrost: 10th International Conference
Date: June 25-29, 2012
Location: Tyumen, Russia
Sponsor/Contact: International Permafrost Association
c/o H. Lantuit, Alfred Wegener Institute for Polar & Marine Research
Telefrafenberg A43
Potsdam, Germany
E-mail: contact@ipa-permafrost.org
URL: ipa.arcticportal.org
Scope: International
Purpose: Organized by the Tyumen Oil & Gas University
Contact Information: E-mail: contact@ipa-permafrost.org

July

American Society of Mechanical Engineers 2012 Pressure Vessels & Piping Conference
Date: July 15-19, 2012
Location: Sheraton Centre Toronto
Toronto, ON
Sponsor/Contact: American Society of Mechanical Engineers
3 Park Ave.
New York, NY USA
800-843-2763
E-mail: infocentral@asme.org
URL: www.asme.org
Scope: International
Contact Information: Conference Contact: Melissa Torres, E-mail: TorresM@asme.org

Healthy Buildings 2012
Date: July 8-12, 2012
Location: Brisbane, Australia
Sponsor/Contact: International Society of Indoor Air Quality & Climate
c/o Gina Bendy
2548 Empire Grade
Santa Cruz, CA USA
831-426-0148 Fax: 831-426-6522
E-mail: info@isiaq.org
URL: www.isiaq.org
Scope: International
Contact Information: President: Professor Lidia Morawska, Queensland University of Technology, E-mail: l.morawska@qut.edu.au

International Commission of Agricultural & Biosystems Engineering 3rd International Conference of Agricultural Engineering
Date: July 8-12, 2012
Location: Valencia, Spain
Sponsor/Contact: International Commission of Agricultural & Biosystems Engineering
c/o Dr. Takaaki Maekawa, School of Life & Environmental Sciences
1-1-1 Tennodai, University of Tsukuba
Tsukuba, Ibaraki, Japan
E-mail: biopro@sakura.cc.tsukuba.ac.jp
URL: www.cigr.org
Scope: International

Yukon Conservation Society 2012 Ed-Ventures for Kids
Date: July - August 2012
Location: Yukon Conservation Society
Whitehorse, YK
Sponsor/Contact: Yukon Conservation Society
302 Hawkins St.
Whitehorse, YT Y1A 1X6 Canada
867-668-5678 Fax: 867-668-6637
E-mail: ycs@ycs.yk.ca
URL: www.yukonconservation.org
Scope: Regional
Purpose: Outdoor educational programs for children from ages 4 to 6 & from 7 to 10; Topics include the Yukon River Watershed, stream sense, ponds, fish, bugs, birds, beavers, & other river dwellers
Contact Information: Program Contact: Andrea Routley, Phone: 867-668-5678, E-mail: volunteer@ycs.yk.ca

Yukon Conservation Society Interpretive Guided Nature Hikes (Canyon City historical nature hikes, special hikes with guest naturalists & family walks)
Date: July 2 - August 18, 2012
Location: YK
Sponsor/Contact: Yukon Conservation Society
302 Hawkins St.
Whitehorse, YT Y1A 1X6 Canada
867-668-5678 Fax: 867-668-6637
E-mail: ycs@ycs.yk.ca
URL: www.yukonconservation.org
Scope: Regional
Purpose: Featuring natural & historical interpretation for the public to develop an appreciation & understanding of the natural world; Special hikes features guest biologists, naturalists, bird specialists, anthropologists, or historians)
Contact Information: Phone: 867-668-5678; E-mail: ycshikes@ycs.yk.ca

August

Association of Municipalities of Ontario 2012 Annual Conference
Date: August 19-22, 2012
Location: Ontario
Sponsor/Contact: Association of Municipalities of Ontario
#801, 200 University Ave.
Toronto, ON M5H 3C6
416-971-9856 Fax: 416-971-6191
E-mail: amo@amo.on.ca; municom@amo.on.ca; policy@amo.on.ca
URL: www.amo.on.ca
Scope: Provincial
Purpose: A meeting of municipal government officials from across the province to discuss current & emerging issues & to elect the association's Board of Directors
Contact Information: Special Events, Phone: 416-971-9856, ext. 330, E-mail: events@amo.on.ca; Coordinator, Special Events & Business Development: Navneet Dhaliwal, E-mail: NDhaliwal@amo.on.ca

CIVICUS: World Alliance for Citizen Participation 11th World Assembly - Acting Together for a Just World
Date: August 23-27, 2012
Location: Palais des congrès (Convention Centre)
Montréal, QC
Sponsor/Contact: CIVICUS: World Alliance for Citizen Participation
Stn. 933
24 Gwigwi Mrwebi St.
Johannesburg, South Africa
E-mail: info@civicus.org; membership@civicus.org
URL: www.civicus.org
Scope: International

Canadian Bar Association Canadian Legal Conference & Expo 2012
Date: August 12-14, 2012
Location: Vancouver Convention Centre
Vancouver, BC
Sponsor/Contact: Canadian Bar Association
#500, 865 Carling Ave.
Ottawa, ON K1S 5S8 Canada
613-237-2925 Fax: 613-237-0185
E-mail: info@cba.org
URL: www.cba.org
Scope: National
Purpose: Continuing legal education programs, sessions, & networking opportunities for legal professionals in Canada

Canadian Medical Association 2012 145th Annual Meeting
Date: August 12-15, 2012
Location: Yellowknife, NT
Sponsor/Contact: Canadian Medical Association
1867 Alta Vista Dr.
Ottawa, ON K1G 5W8
613-731-8610 Fax: 613-236-8864
E-mail: cmamsc@cma.ca; cmatechsupport@cma.ca (technical support)
URL: www.cma.ca
Scope: National
Purpose: A business session, open to all Canadian Medical Association members, plus a ceremonial session for the installation of officers & the presentation of awards
Contact Information: Registration Officer, Phone: 1-800-663-7336, ext. 2383, E-mail: gcregistrations@cma.ca

Institute of Transportation Engineers 2012 Annual Meeting & Exhibit
Date: August 12-15, 2012
Location: Westin Peachtree Plaza
Atlanta, GA USA
Sponsor/Contact: Institute of Transportation Engineers
#300, 1099 - 14th St. NW
Washington, DC USA
202-289-0222 Fax: 202-289-7722
E-mail: ite_staff@ite.org
URL: www.ite.org
Scope: International
Contact Information: Contact, Registration Information: Sallie C. Dollins, E-mail: sdollins@ite.org; Contact, Technical Program: Aliyah N. Horton, E-mail: ahorton@ite.org; Contact, Exhibits: Christina Garneski, E-mail: cgarneski@ite.org; Contact, Paper Submittals: Eunice Chege, E-mail: echege@ite.org

Local Government Management Association of BC Professional Development Program: Municipal Administration Training Institute - Foundations Program
Date: August 2012
Location: University of Victoria
Victoria, BC
Sponsor/Contact: Local Government Management Association of British Columbia
Central Building
620 View St., 7th Fl.
Victoria, BC V8W 1J6
250-383-7032 Fax: 250-384-4879
E-mail: office@lgma.ca; editor@lgma.ca (magazine); ads@lgma.ca
URL: www.lgma.ca
Scope: Provincial
Purpose: A 5.5 day course providing an overview of the roles & responsibilities within local government
Contact Information: Phone: 250-383-7032; Fax: 250-383-4879; E-mail: office@lgma.ca

September

Compost Council of Canada 2011 21st Annual National Compost Conference
Date: September 19-21, 2011
Location: Charlottetown's Delta Prince Edward
Charlottetown, PE
Sponsor/Contact: Compost Council of Canada
16 Northumberland St.
Toronto, ON M6H 1P7
416-535-0240 Fax: 416-536-9892
E-mail: info@compost.org
URL: www.compost.org

Scope: National
Purpose: Presentations, exhibits, facility tours, & networking opportunities for compost, environmental, & organics recycling advocates
Contact Information: 2011 Conference Contact: Danielle Buklis, Phone: 877-571-4769, Fax: 866-902-7272, E-mail: info@compost.org

International Solid Waste Association 2012 Annual Congress
Date: September 17-19, 2012
Location: Palazzo dei Congressi
Florence, Italy
Sponsor/Contact: International Solid Waste Association
Auerspergstrasse 15, Top 41
Vienna, Austria
E-mail: iswa@iswa.dk
URL: www.iswa.org
Scope: International
Purpose: Congress themes include climate change & waste management, zero waste & waste prevention policies, international waste trade, economically developing countries, specific waste crises, recycling of specific waste streams & final residue management, & management & impact of urban hygiene in cities
Contact Information: Managing Director: Hermann Koller, E-mail: hkoller@iswa.org

International Union for Conservation of Nature World Conservation Congress 2012
Date: September 6-15, 2012
Location: International Convention Center (ICC)
Jeju, Republic of Korea
Sponsor/Contact: International Union for Conservation of Nature
28, rue Mauverney
Gland, Switzerland
E-mail: mail@iucn.org.
URL: www.iucn.org
Scope: International
Purpose: Information on methods to improve the management of the natural environment for human, social, & economic development
Contact Information: Congress Manager: Enrique Lahmann; Congress Officer: Pamela Grasemann; Phone: +41 22 999 0336; Fax: +41 22 9990002; E-mail: congress@iucn.org

Metallurgy & Materials Society of the Canadian Institute of Mining, Metallurgy & Petroleum COM 2012: 51st Annual Conference of Metallurgists
Date: September 30 - October 3, 2012
Location: Sheraton on the Falls
Niagara Falls, ON
Sponsor/Contact: Metallurgy & Materials Society of the Canadian Institute of Mining, Metallurgy & Petroleum
#1250, 3500, boul de Maisonneuve ouest
Montréal, QC H3Z 3C1
514-939-2710
URL: www.metsoc.org
Scope: International
Purpose: "Metallurgy & Materials Impact on Society", held in conjunction with Pressure Hydrometallurgy
Contact Information: Publication, Web, & Marketing Contact: Ronona Saunders, Phone: 514-939-2710, ext. 1327, Fax: 514-939-2714, E-mail: rsaunders@cim.org, metsoc@cim.org

Sustainable Forestry Initiative 2012 Annual Conference

Sponsor/Contact: Sustainable Forestry Initiative
#700, 900 - 17th St. NW
Washington, DC 20006 USA
E-mail: info@sfiprogram.org
URL: www.sfiprogram.org
Scope: International
Purpose: Educational sessions, business meetings, the presentation of annual SFI awards, & networking opportunities

Contact Information: Director, Conservation Partnerships & Communications: Allison Welde, E-mail: Allison.Welde@sfiprogram.org

The American Association of Bovine Practitioners 2012 Annual Conference
Date: September 20-22, 2012
Location: Palais des congrès (Convention Centre)
Montréal, QC
Sponsor/Contact: American Association of Bovine Practitioners
P.O. Box 3610
#802, 3320 Skyway Dr.
Auburn, AL USA
334-821-0442 Fax: 334-821-9532
E-mail: aabphq@aabp.org
URL: www.aabp.org
Scope: International

Union of British Columbia Municipalities 2012 Annual Convention
Date: September 23-28, 2012
Location: Kelowna, BC
Sponsor/Contact: Union of British Columbia Municipalities
#60, 10551 Shellbridge Way
Richmond, BC V6X 2W9 Canada
604-270-8226 Fax: 604-270-9116
E-mail: ubcm@civicnet.bc.ca
URL: www.civicnet.bc.ca
Scope: Provincial

Water Environment Federation WEFTEC 2012: 85th Annual Water Environment Federation Technical Exhibition & Conference
Date: September 29 - October 3, 2012
Location: New Orleans Morial Convention Center
New Orleans, LA USA
Sponsor/Contact: Water Environment Federation
601 Wythe St.
Alexandria, VA USA
703-684-2400 Fax: 703-684-2492
E-mail: csc@wef.org
URL: www.wef.org
Scope: International
Purpose: The largest annual water quality event in the world, offering technical sessions, workshops, continuing education, speakers, & the opportunity to network with attendees from over 70 countries
Anticipated Attendance: 18,000
Contact Information: Membership Information, Toll-Free Phone: 1-800-666-0206, International Phone: +44 120-679-6351 or 571-830-1545

Western Canada Water 2012 64th Annual Conference & Exhibition
Date: September 18-21, 2012
Location: Winnipeg, MB
Sponsor/Contact: Western Canada Water
P.O. Box 1708
126 - 3rd Ave. West
Cochrane, AB T4C 1B6
403-709-0064 Fax: 403-709-0068
E-mail: member@wcwwa.ca
URL: www.wcwwa.ca
Scope: Regional
Purpose: Workshops, a technical program, exhibits, an awards presentation, tours, & a social program of interest to utility managers & operators, consulting engineers, & municipal & provincial government representatives
Anticipated Attendance: 500+
Contact Information: Executive Director: Audrey Arisman, E-mail: aarisman@wcwwa.ca

October

Association of Local Public Health Agencies 2012 Fall Symposium
Date: October 2012
Location: Ontario
Sponsor/Contact: Association of Local Public Health Agencies

#1306, 2 Carlton St.
Toronto, ON M5G 1T6
416-595-0006 Fax: 416-595-0030
E-mail: info@alphaweb.org
URL: www.alphaweb.org
Scope: Provincial
Contact Information: Registration contact: Karen Reece, Phone: 416-595-0006, ext. 25; Fax: 416-595-0030, E-mail: karen@alphaweb.org

Canadian Council of Grocery Distributors, 2012 Québec Region Conference
Date: October 2012
Location: Quebec
Sponsor/Contact: Canadian Council of Grocery Distributors
#402, 6455, rue Jean-Talon est
Montréal, QC H1S 3E8
514-982-0267
URL: www.ccgd.ca
Scope: Provincial
Purpose: A conference held each October for Québec members & non-members of the Canadian Council of Grocery Distributors
Contact Information: Conference Contact: Isabelle Gagné, Phone: 514-982-0267, ext. 229, Fax: 514-982-0659, E-mail: igagne@ccgd.ca

Communciation, Energy & Paperworkers Union of Canada 2012 Convention
Date: October 11-18, 2012
Location: Centre des congrès de Québec
Québec, QC
Sponsor/Contact: Communications, Energy & Paperworkers Union of Canada
301 Laurier Ave. West
Ottawa, ON K1P 6M6 Canada
613-230-5200 Fax: 613-230-5801
E-mail: info@cep.ca
URL: www.cep.ca
Scope: National
Anticipated Attendance: 2200

Local Government Management Association of British Columbia 2012 Clerks & Corporate Officers Forum
Date: October 2012
Location: British Columbia
Sponsor/Contact: Local Government Management Association of British Columbia
Central Building
620 View St., 7th Fl.
Victoria, BC V8W 1J6
250-383-7032 Fax: 250-384-4879
E-mail: office@lgma.ca; editor@lgma.ca (magazine); ads@lgma.ca
URL: www.lgma.ca
Scope: Provincial
Purpose: An annual 2.5 day program, presenting best practices & innovations for statuory clerks & corporate officers, & their deputies in British Columbia
Contact Information: Program Coordinator: Ana Fuller, Phone: 250-383-7032, ext. 227, Fax: 250-383-4879, E-mail: afuller@lgma.ca

National Association for Environmental Management 2012 20th Annual EHS Management Forum
Date: October 17-19, 2012
Location: The Ritz-Carlton Naples
Naples, FL USA
Sponsor/Contact: National Association for Environmental Management
#1002, 1612 K St. NW
Washington, DC USA
202-986-6616 Fax: 202-530-4408
E-mail: programs@naem.org
URL: www.naem.org
Scope: International
Purpose: An opportunity for best-practice sharing, benchmarking, & professional networking for environmental, health & safety professionals
Anticipated Attendance: 500+

Contact Information: Exposition Manager, NAEM EHS Management Forum: Mary Sanchez-Quigg, E-mail: mary.quigg@conferencedirect.com; Deputy Director: Virginia Hoekenga, E-mail: Virginia@naem.org

Recycling Council of Alberta 2012 Waste Reduction Conference
Date: October 3-5, 2012
Location: Jasper, AB
Sponsor/Contact: Recycling Council of Alberta
P.O. Box 23
Bluffton, AB T0C 0M0 Canada
403-843-6563 Fax: 403-843-4156
E-mail: info@recycle.ab.ca
URL: www.recycle.ab.ca
Scope: Provincial
Purpose: Information about innovative waste reduction programs & technologies
Contact Information: Phone: 403-843-6563; E-mail: info@recycle.ab.ca

November

Alberta Association of Municipal Districts & Counties Fall 2012 Convention
Date: November 19-22, 2012
Location: Alberta
Sponsor/Contact: Alberta Association of Municipal Districts & Counties
2510 Sparrow Dr.
Nisku, AB T9E 8N5
780-955-3639 Fax: 780-955-3615
E-mail: aamdc@aamdc.com
URL: www.aamdc.com

Alberta Health & Safety 2012 11th Annual Conference & Trade Fair
Date: November 19-21, 2012
Location: Shaw Conference Centre
Edmonton, AB
Sponsor/Contact: Health & Safety Conference Society of Alberta
P.O. Box 38009
Calgary, AB T3K 5G9 Canada
403-236-2225 Fax: 403-206-7099
E-mail: info@hsconference.com
URL: www.hsconference.com
Scope: Provincial
Contact Information: Conference Coordinator: Carrie Kleppe, Phone: 403-236-2225, Fax: 403-206-7099, E-mail, General Information: info@hsconference.com, Trade Fair Information: tradefair@hsconference.com

American Society of Mechanical Engineers 2012 International Mechanical Engineering Congress & Exposition
Date: November 9-15, 2012
Location: Hilton Americas
Houston, TX USA
Sponsor/Contact: American Society of Mechanical Engineers
3 Park Ave.
New York, NY USA
800-843-2763
E-mail: infocentral@asme.org
URL: www.asme.org
Scope: International
Contact Information: 2012 Congress & Exposition Contact: Stephen Crane, E-mail: CraneS@asme.org

Canadian Urban Transit Association 2012 Fall Conference & Trans-Expo
Date: November 2012
Location: Québec, QC
Sponsor/Contact: Canadian Urban Transit Association
#1401, 55 York St.
Toronto, ON M5J 1R7
416-365-9800 Fax: 416-365-1295
E-mail: transit@cutaactu.ca
URL: www.cutaactu.ca

Scope: National
Purpose: A technical conference which covers topics such as maintenance concerns & priority measures
Contact Information: Conference Specialist: Anna Maria Schell, Phone: 416-365-9800, ext. 116

Greenbuild 2012 International Conference & Expo
Date: November 14-16, 2012
Location: San Francisco, CA USA
Sponsor/Contact: Canada Green Building Council
#202, 47 Clarence St.
Ottawa, ON K1N 9K1
613-241-1184 Fax: 613-241-4782
E-mail: info@cagbc.org; education@cagbc.org
URL: www.cagbc.org
Scope: International
Purpose: An opportunity to network with green building colleagues & industry professionals from around the globe
Contact Information: General Inquiries, E-mail: info@greenbuildexpo.org

Municipal Engineers Association 2012 Annual General Meeting & Workshop
Date: November 2012
Sponsor/Contact: Municipal Engineers Association
#2, 6355 Kennedy Rd.
Mississauga, ON L5T 2L5
905-795-2555 Fax: 905-795-2660
E-mail: info@municipalengineers.on.ca
URL: www.municipalengineers.on.ca
Scope: Provincial
Purpose: A learning & networking opportunity for municipal engineers, featuring speakers, tours, & the annual general meeting of the association
Contact Information: Office of the President, Phone: 905-795-2555, Fax: 905-795-2660

Ontario Professional Fire Fighters Association 2012 Annual Legislative Conference
Date: November 2012
Location: Ontario
Sponsor/Contact: Ontario Professional Fire Fighters Association
292 Plains Rd. East
Burlington, ON L7T 2C6
905-681-7111 Fax: 905-681-1489
URL: www.opffa.org
Scope: Provincial
Purpose: An opportunity for representatives from across Ontario to meet with Members of Provincial Parliament to advocate issues of concern

Saskatchewan Association of Rural Municipalities 2012 Midterm Convention
Date: November 14-15, 2012
Location: Saskatoon, SK
Sponsor/Contact: Saskatchewan Association of Rural Municipalities
2075 Hamilton St.
Regina, SK S4P 2E1 Canada
306-757-3577 Fax: 306-565-2141
E-mail: sarm@sarm.ca
URL: www.sarm.ca
Scope: Provincial

Society of Environmental Toxicology & Chemistry North America 33rd Annual Meeting
Date: November 11-15, 2012
Location: Long Beach, CA USA
Sponsor/Contact: Society of Environmental Toxicology & Chemistry
SETAC Asia / Pacific, SETAC Latin America, & SETAC North America
1010 - 12th Ave. North
Pensacola, FL USA
850-469-1500 Fax: 850-469-9778
E-mail: setac@setac.org
URL: www.setac.org
Scope: International
Anticipated Attendance: 2500

The Royal Canadian Geographical Society 2012 Annual General Meeting & Annual Dinner of the College of Fellows
Date: November 2012
Sponsor/Contact: The Royal Canadian Geographical Society
39 McArthur Ave.
Ottawa, ON K1L 8L7
613-745-4629 Fax: 613-744-0947
E-mail: rcgs@rcgs.org
URL: www.rcgs.org
Scope: National
Purpose: A gathering of Society members, featuring the approval of the audited financial statement, a guest speaker, & the presentation of awards

January

Toronto Field Naturalists 2012 Monthly Talk
Date: January 2012
Location: Emmanuel College
Toronto, ON
Sponsor/Contact: Toronto Field Naturalists
#1519, 2 Carlton St.
Toronto, ON M5B 1J3
416-593-2656
E-mail: office@torontofieldnaturalists.org
URL: www.torontofieldnaturalists.org
Scope: Local
Purpose: Subjects of past talks have ranged from Toronto's landscape formation & the building stone used throughout the city to the flora & fauna of the Arctic & Sub-Arctic
Contact Information: E-mail: office@torontofieldnaturalists.org

Other Conferences in 2012

Air Transport Association of Canada 2012 78th Annual General Meeting & Trade Show

Sponsor/Contact: Air Transport Association of Canada
#700, 255 Albert St.
Ottawa, ON K1P 6A9
613-233-7727 Fax: 613-230-8648
E-mail: atac@atac.ca
URL: www.atac.ca
Scope: National
Purpose: A business meeting, the presentation of awards, the chance to view exhibits, & networking opportunities for manufacturers, service providers, flying club & school presidents, operation directors, directors of maintenance, program & procurement managers, chief pilots, & government representatives
Contact Information: Trade Show & Sponsorship Contact: Debbie Simpson, Phone: 613-233-7727, ext. 312, E-mail: tradeshow@atac.ca

Air Transport Association of Canada 2012 Annual Spring Event

Sponsor/Contact: Air Transport Association of Canada
#700, 255 Albert St.
Ottawa, ON K1P 6A9
613-233-7727 Fax: 613-230-8648
E-mail: atac@atac.ca
URL: www.atac.ca
Scope: National
Purpose: An industry symposium, committee meetings, & networking opportunities

Alberta & Northwest Territories Lung Association 2012 3rd Annual Tobacco Stakeholders Workshop

Sponsor/Contact: Alberta & Northwest Territories Lung Association
P.O. Box 4500 Stn. South
#208, 17420 Stony Plain Rd.
Edmonton, AB T5E 6K2
780-488-6819 Fax: 780-488-7195
E-mail: info@ab.lung.ca
URL: www.ab.lung.ca

Trade Shows, Conferences and Seminars

Scope: Regional
Purpose: An event to provide information about tobacco control issues
Contact Information: Alberta & Northwest Territories Lung Association Tobacco Control Regional Manager: Kristin Matthews, Phone: 403-981-8586, E-mail: kmatthews@ab.lung.ca

Alberta & Northwest Territories Lung Association 2012 8th Annual Alberta Sleep Forum

Sponsor/Contact: Alberta & Northwest Territories Lung Association
P.O. Box 4500 Stn. South
#208, 17420 Stony Plain Rd.
Edmonton, AB T5E 6K2
780-488-6819 Fax: 780-488-7195
E-mail: info@ab.lung.ca
URL: www.ab.lung.ca
Scope: Regional
Contact Information: Forum Contact: Cheryl Tonn, Phone: 780-488-6995, ext. 2253, E-mail: ctonn@ab.lung.ca

Alberta & Northwest Territories Lung Association 2012 Annual General Meeting

Sponsor/Contact: Alberta & Northwest Territories Lung Association
P.O. Box 4500 Stn. South
#208, 17420 Stony Plain Rd.
Edmonton, AB T5E 6K2
780-488-6819 Fax: 780-488-7195
E-mail: info@ab.lung.ca
URL: www.ab.lung.ca
Scope: Regional
Purpose: A yearly business meeting for members of the association

Alberta Association of Agricultural Societies 2012 Annual Meeting & Convention

Location: Alberta
Sponsor/Contact: Alberta Association of Agricultural Societies
J.G. O'Donoghue Building
#200, 7000 - 113 St.
Edmonton, AB T6H 5T6
780-427-2174 Fax: 780-422-7755
E-mail: aaas@gov.ab.ca
URL: www.albertaagsocieties.ca
Scope: Provincial
Purpose: An event attended by members of the Alberta Association of Agricultural Societies, where agricultural societies can submit resolutions to the annual general meeting & vote
Contact Information: E-mail: aaas@gov.ab.ca

Alberta Association of Agricultural Societies 2012 Regional Meetings

Location: Alberta
Sponsor/Contact: Alberta Association of Agricultural Societies
J.G. O'Donoghue Building
#200, 7000 - 113 St.
Edmonton, AB T6H 5T6
780-427-2174 Fax: 780-422-7755
E-mail: aaas@gov.ab.ca
URL: www.albertaagsocieties.ca
Scope: Provincial
Purpose: Meetings held throughout the year to provide up-to-date information on industry issues, to present guest speakers, & to facilitate networking
Contact Information: E-mail: aaas@gov.ab.ca

Alberta Association of Landscape Architects 2012 12th Annual Erosion & Sediment Control Course

Location: Alberta
Sponsor/Contact: Alberta Association of Landscape Architects
P.O. Box 21052
Edmonton, AB T6R 2V4
780-435-9902 Fax: 780-413-0076
E-mail: aala@aala.ab.ca
URL: www.aala.ab.ca
Scope: Provincial
Purpose: Information about land development practices & environmental construction for the sustainability of water resources
Contact Information: Course Contact: Amber Toivanen, Phone: 403-268-5271

Alberta Association of Landscape Architects 2012 Annual General Meeting

Location: Alberta
Sponsor/Contact: Alberta Association of Landscape Architects
P.O. Box 21052
Edmonton, AB T6R 2V4
780-435-9902 Fax: 780-413-0076
E-mail: aala@aala.ab.ca
URL: www.aala.ab.ca
Scope: Provincial
Contact Information: AGM Contact: Peter Alexander, E-mail: aala@aala.ab.ca

Alberta Fish & Game Association 2012 Annual General Meeting

Location: Alberta
Sponsor/Contact: Alberta Fish & Game Association
6924 - 104 St.
Edmonton, AB T6H 2L7
780-437-2342 Fax: 780-438-6872
E-mail: office@afga.org
URL: www.afga.org
Scope: Provincial
Purpose: Voting on resolutions

Alberta Forest Products Association 2012 70th Annual General Meeting & Conference

Location: Alberta
Sponsor/Contact: Alberta Forest Products Association
#500, 10709 Jasper Ave.
Edmonton, AB T5J 3N3
780-452-2841 Fax: 780-455-0505
E-mail: info@albertforestproducts.ca
URL: www.albertaforestproducts.ca
Scope: Provincial
Purpose: A business meeting, sessions on topics relevant to the industry, networking opportunities, & a recognition dinner
Contact Information: Director, Communications: Brock Mulligan, Phone: 780-452-2841, ext. 229

Alberta Recreation & Parks Association 2012 Annual Conference & Energize Workshop

Location: Alberta
Sponsor/Contact: Alberta Recreation & Parks Association
11759 Groat Rd.
Edmonton, AB T5M 3K6 Canada
780-415-1745 Fax: 780-451-7915
E-mail: arpa@arpaonline.ca
URL: www.arpaonline.ca
Scope: Regional
Purpose: A conference of interest to parks & recreation directors & managers, facility programmers, municipal & provincial elected officials, community planners, landscape architects, arborists, public health promotion practitioners, researchers, academics, & professionals from related industries such as tourism, agricultural societies, & outdoor education
Anticipated Attendance: 400+
Contact Information: Event Planner: Brenda Hanson, Phone: 780-643-1255, E-mail: bhanson@arpaonline.ca

Alberta Recreation & Parks Association 2012 Biennial Youth Development Through Recreation Services Symposium

Location: The Banff Centre
Banff, AB
Sponsor/Contact: Alberta Recreation & Parks Association
11759 Groat Rd.
Edmonton, AB T5M 3K6 Canada
780-415-1745 Fax: 780-451-7915
E-mail: arpa@arpaonline.ca
URL: www.arpaonline.ca
Scope: Provincial
Purpose: A three day educational event, featuring presentations of interest to practitioners of youth programs
Contact Information: Manager, Children & Youth Programs: Lisa Tink, Phone: 780-644-4794, E-mail: ltink@arpaonline.ca

Alberta Recreation & Parks Association 2012 Provincial Dialogue

Location: Alberta
Sponsor/Contact: Alberta Recreation & Parks Association
11759 Groat Rd.
Edmonton, AB T5M 3K6 Canada
780-415-1745 Fax: 780-451-7915
E-mail: arpa@arpaonline.ca
URL: www.arpaonline.ca
Scope: Provincial
Purpose: Discussion around topics of shared interest to parks & recreation stakeholders

Alberta Society of Professional Biologists 2012 Annual Conference & General Meeting

Location: Alberta
Sponsor/Contact: Alberta Society of Professional Biologists
P.O. Box 21104
Edmonton, AB T6R 2V4
780-434-5765 Fax: 780-413-0076
E-mail: pbiol@aspb.ab.ca
URL: www.aspb.ab.ca
Scope: Provincial
Contact Information: Association & Event Coordinator: Joy Sager, Phone: 780-434-5765, E-mail: joy@managewise.ca; Membership & Communications Coordinator: Shauna Prokopchuk, Phone: 780-434-5765, E-mail: shauna@managewise.ca

Alberta Water & Wastewater Operators Association 2012 37th Annual Operators Seminar

Location: Alberta
Sponsor/Contact: Alberta Water & Wastewater Operators Association
11810 Kingsway Ave.
Edmonton, AB T5G 0X5
780-454-7745 Fax: 780-451-6451
E-mail: awwoa@telus.net
URL: www.awwoa.ab.ca
Scope: Provincial
Purpose: Featuring speakers, a trade show, & networking opportunities for person in Alberta's water & wastewater industry
Contact Information: Phone: 780-454-7745; E-mail: awwoa@telus.net

AllerGen NCE Inc. 2012 7th Annual Conference

Sponsor/Contact: AllerGen NCE Inc.
Michael DeGroote Centre for Learning & Discovery, McMaster University
#3120, 1200 Main St. West
Hamilton, ON L8N 2A5
905-525-9140 Fax: 905-524-0611
E-mail: info@allergen-nce.ca
URL: www.allergen-nce.ca

Scope: National
Purpose: Keynote speakers, discussion panels, research presentations, poster viewing, the presentation of awards, networking opportunities, & a social program
Contact Information: Coordinator, Highly Qualified Personnel & Events: Michelle Harkness, Phone: 905-525-9140, ext. 26633

Association of British Columbia Land Surveyors 2012 Annual General Meeting

Location: British Columbia
Sponsor/Contact: Association of British Columbia Land Surveyors
#301, 2400 Bevan Ave.
Sidney, BC V8L 1W1
250-655-7222 Fax: 250-655-7223
E-mail: office@abcls.ca
URL: www.abcls.ca
Scope: Provincial
Contact Information: Executive Assistant: Vicki Pettigrew, E-mail: office@abcls.ca; Administrative Assistant: Denise Brethour, E-mail: dbrethour@abcls.ca

Association of Consulting Engineering Companies - New Brunswick 2012 15th Annual General Meeting, Trade Show, Conference, & Awards Gala

Location: New Brunswick
Sponsor/Contact: Association of Consulting Engineering Companies - New Brunswick
183 Hanwell Rd.
Fredericton, NB E3B 2R2
506-470-9211 Fax: 506-451-9629
E-mail: info@acec-nb.ca
URL: www.cenb.nb.ca
Scope: Provincial
Purpose: Featuring a business meeting, speakers, conference seminars, exhibits, & the presentation of awards
Contact Information: Executive Director: John Fudge, E-mail: info@acec-nb.ca

Association of Consulting Engineering Companies - New Brunswick 2012 5th Annual Deputy Ministers' Dinner & Information Session

Location: New Brunswick
Sponsor/Contact: Association of Consulting Engineering Companies - New Brunswick
183 Hanwell Rd.
Fredericton, NB E3B 2R2
506-470-9211 Fax: 506-451-9629
E-mail: info@acec-nb.ca
URL: www.cenb.nb.ca
Scope: Provincial
Purpose: An opportunity to network with leaders in New Brunswick's provincial government & colleagues in the field
Contact Information: E-mail: info@acec-nb.ca

Association of Municipalities of Ontario 2012 Counties, Regions, & Single Tiers Conference

Location: Ontario
Sponsor/Contact: Association of Municipalities of Ontario
#801, 200 University Ave.
Toronto, ON M5H 3C6
416-971-9856 Fax: 416-971-6191
E-mail: amo@amo.on.ca; municom@amo.on.ca; policy@amo.on.ca
URL: www.amo.on.ca
Scope: Provincial
Purpose: An annual autumn event
Contact Information: Special Events, Phone: 416-971-9856, ext. 330, E-mail: events@amo.on.ca; Coordinator, Special Events & Business Development: Navneet Dhaliwal, E-mail: NDhaliwal@amo.on.ca

Association of Power Producers of Ontario 2012: 24th Annual Canadian Power Conference

Location: Ontario
Sponsor/Contact: Association of Power Producers of Ontario
P.O. Box 1084 Stn. F
#1602, 25 Adelaide St. East
Toronto, ON M5C 3A1
416-322-6549 Fax: 416-481-5785
E-mail: appro@appro.org; marketing@appro.org
URL: www.appro.org
Scope: Provincial
Purpose: An annual fall event for professionals from the energy industry, government, & regulatory agencies
Contact Information: Executive Director: Jake Brooks, E-mail: jake.brooks@appro.org; Marketing Manager: Carole Kielly, Phone: 416-322-6549, ext. 222, E-mail: carole.kielly@appro.org; Manager, Registration & Data: Soraya Rivera, E-mail: soraya.rivera@appro.org; Office Manager: Karla Martinez, E-mail: karla.martinez@appro.org

Association of Professional Biology 2012 Annual Applied Biology Conference & Trade Show & Annual General Meeting

Location: British Columbia
Sponsor/Contact: Association of Professional Biology
#300, 1095 McKenzie Ave.
Victoria, BC V8P 2L5
250-483-4283 Fax: 250-483-3439
E-mail: apbbc@apbbc.bc.ca
URL: www.apbbc.bc.ca
Scope: Provincial
Purpose: Presentations, guest speakers, workshops, question periods, tours, the presentation of awards, & networking opportunities
Contact Information: Managing Director & Registrar: Megan Hanacek, E-mail: managingdirector@apbbc.bc.ca; Co-Chair, Conference Committee: Al Peatt; Co-Chair, Conference Committee: Dave Polster

Association of Professional Engineers & Geoscientists of British Columbia 2012 Conference & Annual General Meeting

Location: British Columbia
Sponsor/Contact: Association of Professional Engineers & Geoscientists of British Columbia
#200, 4010 Regent St.
Burnaby, BC V5C 6N2
604-430-8035 Fax: 604-430-8085
E-mail: apeginfo@apeg.bc.ca; communication@apeg.bc.ca
URL: www.apeg.bc.ca
Scope: Provincial
Purpose: An opportunity for professional engineers & geoscientists, industry leaders, consultants, & government representatives to discuss current issues & events during a comprehensive program of professional development activities
Anticipated Attendance: 700+
Contact Information: Marketing Specialist: Shelley Bruins, Phone: 604-412-4860, ext. 4860, E-mail: sbruins@apeg.bc.ca

Atlantic Canada Water & Wastewater Association 2012 65th Annual Conference

Location: Charlottetown, PE
Sponsor/Contact: Atlantic Canada Water & Wastewater Association
P.O. Box 41002
Dartmouth, NS B2Y 4P7 Canada
902-434-6002 Fax: 902-435-7796
E-mail: acwwa@hfx.andara.com
URL: www.acwwa.ca
Scope: Regional
Purpose: Educational events, a trade show, election of the ACWWA Executive Committee, & networking opportunities
Anticipated Attendance: 260-340

Contact Information: Technical Director: Margaret Walsh, PhD., P.Eng., E-mail: mwalsh2@dal.ca

British Columbia Lung Association 2012 9th Annual Air Quality & Health Workshop

Location: British Columbia
Sponsor/Contact: British Columbia Lung Association
2675 Oak St.
Vancouver, BC V6H 2K2
604-731-5864 Fax: 604-731-5810
E-mail: info@bc.lung.ca
URL: www.bc.lung.ca
Scope: Provincial
Contact Information: Phone: 604-731-5864; Toll-Free Phone: 1-800-665-5864

British Columbia Lung Association 2012 Annual General Meeting

Location: British Columbia
Sponsor/Contact: British Columbia Lung Association
2675 Oak St.
Vancouver, BC V6H 2K2
604-731-5864 Fax: 604-731-5810
E-mail: info@bc.lung.ca
URL: www.bc.lung.ca
Scope: Provincial
Purpose: An annual meeting to determine the association's direction during the coming year
Contact Information: Phone: 604-731-5864; Toll-Free Phone: 1-800-665-5864

British Columbia Nature (Federation of British Columbia Naturalists) 2012 Nature Conference & Annual General Meeting

Location: British Columbia
Sponsor/Contact: British Columbia Nature (Federation of British Columbia Naturalists)
c/o Parks Heritage Centre
1620 Mount Seymour Rd.
North Vancouver, BC V7G 2R9
604-985-3057
E-mail: manager@bcnature.ca
URL: www.bcnature.ca
Scope: Provincial
Purpose: Field trips, conference presentations, a social program, plus the annual meeting of the federation
Contact Information: Office Manager: Betty Davison, E-mail: manager@bcnature.ca

British Columbia Recreation & Parks Association 2012 35th Annual ProvincialParks & Grounds Spring Training Conference

Location: British Columbia
Sponsor/Contact: British Columbia Recreation & Parks Association
#101, 4664 Lougheed Hwy.
Burnaby, BC V5C 5T5
604-629-0965 Fax: 604-629-2651
E-mail: bcrpa@bcrpa.bc.ca; registration@bcrpa.bc.ca
URL: www.bcrpa.bc.ca
Scope: Provincial
Purpose: An annual conference for parks & grounds professionals that addresses current topics in the industry
Contact Information: Parks & Recreation Program Coordinator: Heather Muter, Phone: 604-629-0965, ext. 229. E-mail: hmuter@bcrpa.bc.ca

British Columbia Water & Waste Association 2012 40th Annual Conference & Trade Show

Location: British Columbia
Sponsor/Contact: British Columbia Water & Waste Association
#221, 8678 Greenall Ave.
Burnaby, BC V5J 3M6
604-433-4389 Fax: 604-433-9859
E-mail: contact@bcwwa.org
URL: www.bcwwa.org

Trade Shows, Conferences and Seminars

Scope: Provincial
Purpose: A four day event, featuring technical sessions & the opportunity to see the latest products at the trade show
Anticipated Attendance: 1000
Contact Information: Event Coordinator: Winnie Tsang, Phone: 604-433-4389, ext. 232, E-mail: wtsang@bcwwa.org

Calgary Zoological Society 2012 Annual General Meeting

Location: Alberta
Sponsor/Contact: Calgary Zoological Society
1300 Zoo Rd. NE
Calgary, AB T2E 7V6
403-232-9300 Fax: 403-237-7582
E-mail: comments@calgaryzoo.ab.ca; guestrelations@calgaryzoo.ab.ca
URL: www.calgaryzoo.org
Scope: Provincial
Purpose: Members of the society receive voting rights at the annual meeting
Contact Information: Manager, Communications: Laurie Skene, E-mail: lauries@calgaryzoo.ab.ca

Canada Green Building Council 2012 Annual General Meeting

Sponsor/Contact: Canada Green Building Council
#202, 47 Clarence St.
Ottawa, ON K1N 9K1
613-241-1184 Fax: 613-241-4782
E-mail: info@cagbc.org; education@cagbc.org
URL: www.cagbc.org
Scope: National
Purpose: Presentations of the financial report & the president's report, & a guest speaker
Contact Information: E-mail: info@cagbc.org

Canada Green Building Council 2012 National Symposium

Sponsor/Contact: Canada Green Building Council
#202, 47 Clarence St.
Ottawa, ON K1N 9K1
613-241-1184 Fax: 613-241-4782
E-mail: info@cagbc.org; education@cagbc.org
URL: www.cagbc.org
Scope: National
Purpose: A continuing education event, including the presentation of achievement awards
Anticipated Attendance: 375+
Contact Information: E-mail: education@cagbc.org

Canadian Association of Agri-Retailers 2012 17th Annual Convention & Trade Show

Sponsor/Contact: Canadian Association of Agri-Retailers
#107, 1090 Waverley St.
Winnipeg, MB R3T 0P4
204-989-9300 Fax: 204-989-9306
E-mail: info@caar.org
URL: www.caar.org
Scope: National
Contact Information: E-mail: info@caar.org

Canadian Association of Animal Health Technologists & Technicians 2012 23rd Annual General Meeting

Location: Fairmont, The Queen Elizabeth
Montréal, QC
Sponsor/Contact: Canadian Association of Animal Health Technologists & Technicians
339 Booth St.
Ottawa, ON K1R 7K1
800-567-2862
E-mail: info@caahtt-acttsa.ca
URL: www.caahtt-acttsa.ca
Scope: National
Purpose: A yearly summer meeting, held in partnership with the 64th Canadian Veterinary Medical Association Convention
Contact Information: Conventions & Special Programs Assistant: Sarah M. Cunningham, Phone: 613-236-1162, ext. 121, Fax: 613-236-9681, E-mail: scunningham@cvma-acmv.org

Canadian Association of Geographers 2012 Annual Meeting & Conference (with the Canadian Federation for the Humanities & Social Sciences)

Location: Wilfrid Laurier U. & U. of Waterloo
Waterloo, ON
Sponsor/Contact: Canadian Association of Geographers
Department of Geography, McGill University
#425, 805, rue Sherbrooke ouest
Montréal, QC H3A 2K6
514-398-4946 Fax: 514-398-7437
E-mail: valerie.shoffey@cag-acg.ca (Executive Secretary)
URL: www.cag-acg.ca
Scope: National
Purpose: A meeting of geographers from across Canada, featuring special sessions, workshops, exhibits, & field trips
Contact Information: Wilfrid Laurier University CAG Representative: Doreen Dassen, E-mail: ddassen@wlu.ca; University of Waterloo CAG Representative: Jean Andrey, E-mail: jandrey@uwaterloo.ca

Canadian Association of Geographers Western Division 2012 54th Annual Conference Meeting

Sponsor/Contact: Canadian Association of Geographers
c/o H. Jiskoot, Water & Environmental Science Bldg., U. of Lethbridge
4401 University Dr.
Lethbridge, AB T1K 3M4
URL: www.geog.uvic.ca/dept/wcag
Scope: Regional
Contact Information: Western Division Vice-President: Theresa Garvin, E-mail: Theresa.Garvin@ualberta.ca

Canadian Association of Geographers, Atlantic Division 2012 24th Annual Meeting

Sponsor/Contact: Canadian Association of Geographers
c/o James Boxall, GIS Centre, Killam Library, Dalhousie University
6225 University Ave.
Halifax, NS B3H 4H8
URL: www.smu.ca/academic/arts/geography/acag
Scope: Regional
Purpose: Paper & poster presentations, plenary addresses, lectures, the presentation of awards, a field trip, social activities, & opportunities to network with other geographers & students from across Canada

Canadian Association of Geographers, Prairie Division 2012 Annual Meeting & Conference

Sponsor/Contact: Canadian Association of Geographers
c/o D. Eberts, J.R. Brodie Science Ctr., Dept of Geography, Brandon U.
#4-09, 270 - 18th St.
Brandon, MB R7A 6A9
URL: pcag.uwinnipeg.ca
Scope: Regional
Purpose: The business meeting of the division, plus paper & poster presentations & a field trip

Canadian Association of Recycling Industries (CARI) 2012 15th Annual Consumers' Night

Sponsor/Contact: Canadian Association of Recycling Industries
#1, 682 Monarch Ave.
Ajax, ON L1S 4S2
905-426-9313 Fax: 905-426-9314
URL: www.cari-acir.org
Scope: National
Contact Information: Association Manager: Donna Turner, Phone: 905-426-9313, Fax: 905-426-9314, E-mail: donna@cari-acir.org; Manager, Communications & Membership: Tracy Shaw, E-mail: tracy@cari-acir.org

Canadian Association of Recycling Industries (CARI) 2012 71st Annual General Meeting & Convention

Sponsor/Contact: Canadian Association of Recycling Industries
#1, 682 Monarch Ave.
Ajax, ON L1S 4S2
905-426-9313 Fax: 905-426-9314
URL: www.cari-acir.org
Scope: National
Purpose: Featuring the annual general meeting, speakers, & exhibits
Contact Information: Association Manager: Donna Turner, Phone: 905-426-9313, Fax: 905-426-9314, E-mail: donna@cari-acir.org; Manager, Communications & Membership: Tracy Shaw, E-mail: tracy@cari-acir.org

Canadian Association of Zoos & Aquariums 2012 Annual Conference

Sponsor/Contact: Canadian Association of Zoos & Aquariums
#400, 280 Metcalfe St.
Ottawa, ON K2P 1R7
613-567-0099 Fax: 613-233-5438
E-mail: info@caza.ca
URL: www.caza.ca
Scope: National
Purpose: A meeting of members to vote on the business of the association
Contact Information: Chair, Conference Committee: Denise Prefontaine, E-mail: info@caza.ca

Canadian Cattlemen's Association 2012 Annual General Meeting

Sponsor/Contact: Canadian Cattlemen's Association
#310, 6715 - 8 St. NE
Calgary, AB T2E 7H7
403-275-8558 Fax: 403-274-5686
E-mail: feedback@cattle.ca
URL: www.cattle.ca
Scope: National
Purpose: An opportunity for members to address industry issues & to elect officers
Contact Information: Communications Manager: Gina Teel, Phone: 403-275-8558, ext. 406, E-mail: teelg@cattle.ca

Canadian Cattlemen's Association 2012 Semi-Annual Meeting & Convention

Sponsor/Contact: Canadian Cattlemen's Association
#310, 6715 - 8 St. NE
Calgary, AB T2E 7H7
403-275-8558 Fax: 403-274-5686
E-mail: feedback@cattle.ca
URL: www.cattle.ca
Scope: National
Purpose: Information sessions, policy setting, networking opportunities, & a social program
Contact Information: Communications Manager: Gina Teel, Phone: 403-275-8558, ext. 406, E-mail: teelg@cattle.ca

Canadian Dam Association 2012 Annual Conference

Sponsor/Contact: Canadian Dam Association
P.O. Box 2281
Moose Jaw, SK S6TH 7W6
URL: www.cda.ca
Scope: National
Purpose: A forum for dam owners & operators, engineers, geoscientists, & stakeholders from throughout Canada to meet for the exchange of information & ideas re;ated to the design, construction, & remedial works of conventional water dams & mining dams

Canadian Environmental Network / Réseau canadien de l'environnement 2012 Annual Conference on the Environment

Sponsor/Contact: Canadian Environmental Network
39 McArthur Ave., Level 1-1
Ottawa, ON K1L 8L7
613-728-9810 Fax: 613-728-2963
E-mail: info@cen-rce.org
URL: www.cen-rce.org
Scope: National
Contact Information: RCEN Office & Events Administrator: Joséphine Hénault, Phone: 613-728-9810, ext. 221; Fax: 613-728-2963; E-mail: josephine@cen-rce.org

Canadian Health Food Association (CHFA) Québec 2012

Sponsor/Contact: Canadian Health Food Association
#302, 235 Yorkland Blvd.
Toronto, ON M2J 4Y8
416-497-6939 Fax: 905-479-3214
E-mail: info@chfa.ca
URL: www.chfa.ca
Scope: Provincial
Purpose: A conference & trade show for individuals who presently work in the natural products or organic products industries
Contact Information: E-mail: info@chfa.ca

Canadian Health Libraries Association (CHLA) / Association des bibliothèques de la santé du Canada (ABSC) 2012 36th Annual Conference

Location: Hamilton, ON
Sponsor/Contact: Canadian Health Libraries Association
39 River St.
Toronto, ON M5A 3P1
416-646-1600 Fax: 416-646-9460
E-mail: info@chla-absc.ca; pr@chla-absc.ca (Public Relations)
URL: www.chla-absc.ca
Scope: National
Purpose: An annual May or June forum for health science librarians to share ideas & to view an exhibit of products & services related to their profession
Contact Information: Continuing Education, E-mail: ce@chla-absc.ca; Public Relations, E-mail: pr@chla-absc.ca

Canadian Institute of Food Science & Technology, Manitoba Section, 2012 Annual General Meeting

Location: Manitoba
Sponsor/Contact: Canadian Institute of Food Science & Technology
c/o A. Tezcucano, Manitoba Agriculture, Food & Rural Initiatives
P.O. Box 100
229 Main St. South
Morris, MB R0G 1K0
E-mail: manitobasection@cifst.ca
URL: www.cifst.ca
Scope: Provincial
Contact Information: Program & Vice-Chair: Ketie Sandhu, E-mail: ksandhu@gourmetbaker.com

Canadian Institute of Forestry / Institut forestier du Canada 2012 104th Annual General Meeting & Conference

Sponsor/Contact: Canadian Institute of Forestry
c/o The Canadian Ecology Centre
P.O. Box 430
6905 Hwy. 17 West
Mattawa, ON P0H 1V0
705-744-1715 Fax: 705-744-1716
E-mail: admin@cif-ifc.org; questions@cif-ifc.org
URL: www.cif-ifc.org
Scope: National
Purpose: Meetings, presentations, poster sessions, displays, & field trips

Canadian Institute of Plumbing & Heating, British Columbia Region, 2012 Annual General Meeting

Location: British Columbia
Sponsor/Contact: Canadian Institute of Plumbing & Heating
c/o Kathryn Fallis
15316 Sequoia Dr.
Surrey, BC V3S 8N4
778-867-5956 Fax: 604-594-5091
E-mail: ciphbc@shaw.ca
URL: www.ciph.com
Scope: Provincial
Contact Information: BC Region Coordinator: Kathryn Fallis, Phone: 778-867-5956, Fax: 604-594-5091, E-mail: ciphbc@shaw.ca

Canadian Institute of Plumbing & Heating, Calgary Alberta Region, 2012 Annual General Meeting

Location: Calgary, AB
Sponsor/Contact: Canadian Institute of Plumbing & Heating
P.O. Box 4520 Stn. C
Calgary, AB T2T 5N3
403-244-4487 Fax: 403-244-2340
URL: www.ciph.com
Scope: Local
Purpose: An update on the Canadian Institute of Plumbing & Heating, featuring guest speakers
Contact Information: Region Coordinator: Connie Pruden, Phone: 403-244-4487, Fax: 403-244-2340, E-mail: conniep@associationsplus.ca

Canadian Institute of Plumbing & Heating, Ontario Region, 2012 Annual General Meeting

Location: Ontario
Sponsor/Contact: Canadian Institute of Plumbing & Heating
c/o Nancy Barden
5827 - 6th Line, RR#1
Hillsburgh, ON N0B 1Z0
519-855-6474 Fax: 519-855-1747
URL: www.ciph.com
Scope: Provincial
Contact Information: Ontario Region Coordinator: Nancy Barden, E-mail: barden@sympatico.ca

Canadian Institute of Public Health Inspectors 2012 78th Annual Educational Conference

Sponsor/Contact: Canadian Institute of Public Health Inspectors
#720, 999 West Broadway Ave.
Vancouver, BC V5Z 1K5
604-739-8180 Fax: 604-738-4080
E-mail: questions@ciphi.ca; office@ciphi.ca
URL: www.ciphi.ca
Scope: National
Purpose: Featuring the presentation of Institute awards

Canadian Medical & Biological Engineering Society 2012 35th Annual National Conference

Location: Halifax, NS
Sponsor/Contact: Canadian Medical & Biological Engineering Society
1485 Laperrière Ave.
Ottawa, ON K1Z 7S8
613-728-1759
E-mail: secretariat@cmbes.ca
URL: www.cmbes.ca
Scope: National
Purpose: A yearly opportunity for Canadian biomedical engineering professionals to learn of recent research, technologies, & trends, & to network with colleagues
Contact Information: Chair, Long-Term Conference Planning: Sarah Kelso, E-mail: skelso@hsc.mb.ca

Canadian Nuclear Society 2012 3rd Annual Workshop on Nuclear Education & Outreach

Sponsor/Contact: Canadian Nuclear Society
655 Bay St., 17th Fl.
Toronto, ON M5G 2K4
416-977-7620 Fax: 416-977-8131
E-mail: cns-snc@on.aibn.com
URL: www.cns-snc.ca
Scope: National
Purpose: An exploration of best practices in the field of nuclear education & outreach, of interest to educators & outreach workers in the nuclear field & anyone else interested in this topic
Contact Information: Canadian Nuclear Society Office: Phone: 416-977-7620, E-mail: 416-977-7620

Canadian Physiological Society 2012 Annual Winter Meeting

Sponsor/Contact: Canadian Physiological Society
c/o Dr. Melanie Woodin, Dept. of Cell & Systems Biology, U. of Toronto
25 Harbord St.
Toronto, ON M5S 3G5
URL: www.cpsscp.ca
Scope: National
Purpose: Featuring guest speakers & networking opportunities
Contact Information: Canadian Physiological Society President: Dr. Douglas L. Jones, Phone: 519-661-2111, ext. 83480, E-mail: doug.jones@schulich.uwo.ca

Canadian Pollution Prevention 2012 16th Annual Roundtable

Sponsor/Contact: Canadian Centre for Pollution Prevention
#134, 215 Spadina Ave.
Toronto, ON M5T 2C7
905-822-4133 Fax: 416-979-3936
E-mail: info@c2p2online.com
URL: www.c2p2online.com
Scope: National
Purpose: A meeting of pollution prevention experts & practitioners to examines environmental challenges

Canadian Renewable Fuels 2012 9th Annual Summit: Growing Our Energy Diversity

Sponsor/Contact: Canadian Renewable Fuels Association
#605, 350 Sparks St.
Ottawa, ON K1R 7S8
613-594-5528 Fax: 613-594-3076
URL: www.greenfuels.org
Scope: International
Purpose: A conference of interest to representatives from the ethanol & biodiesel industries, plus agricultural associations & petroleum companies
Contact Information: Director, Member Relations & Industry Promotions: Deborah Elson, E-mail: d.elson@greenfuels.org

Canadian Respiratory Health Professionals 2012 Annual General Meeting

Sponsor/Contact: Canadian Respiratory Health Professionals
#300, 1750 Courtwood Cres.
Ottawa, ON K2C 2B5
613-569-6411 Fax: 613-569-8860
E-mail: crhpinfo@lung.ca
URL: www.lung.ca/crhp
Scope: National
Purpose: A gathering of members, held each year in conjunction with the Canadian Respiratory Conference

Canadian Society for Mechanical Engineering 2012 Forum

Sponsor/Contact: Canadian Society for Mechanical Engineering

Trade Shows, Conferences and Seminars

1295 Hwy. 2 East
Kingston, ON K7L 4V1
613-547-5989 Fax: 613-547-0195
E-mail: csme@cogeco.ca
URL: www.csme-scgm.ca
Scope: National
Purpose: A meeting held during even years in a Canadian city for mechanical engineers to exchange ideas to to discuss recent research & issues
Contact Information: Canadian Society for Mechanical Engineering, E-mail: csme@cogeco.ca

Canadian Society of Exploration Geophysicists, Canadian Society of Petroleum Geologists & Canadian Well Logging Society 2012 Joint Annual Convention

Sponsor/Contact: Canadian Society of Exploration Geophysicists
#600, 640 - 8th Ave. SW
Calgary, AB T2P 1G7
403-262-0015
E-mail: cseg.office@shaw.ca
URL: www.cseg.ca
Scope: National
Purpose: A technical program, with oral sessions & technical poster presentations, plus an exhibition & networking opportunities
Contact Information: Chair, Joint Annual Convention Committee: Laurie Ross, E-mail: laurie.ross@divestco.com

Canadian Standards Association 2012 Annual Conference & Committee Week

Sponsor/Contact: Canadian Standards Association
#100, 5060 Spectrum Way
Mississauga, ON L4W 5N6
416-747-4000 Fax: 416-747-2473
E-mail: member@csa.ca; sales@csa.ca; seminars@csa.ca; elearning@csa.ca
URL: www.csa.ca
Scope: National
Purpose: Educational sessions, speaker presentations, networking opportunities, as well as committee meetings
Anticipated Attendance: 500+
Contact Information: E-mail: conference@csa.ca

Compost Council of Canada 2012 22nd Annual National Compost Conference

Sponsor/Contact: Compost Council of Canada
16 Northumberland St.
Toronto, ON M6H 1P7
416-535-0240 Fax: 416-536-9892
E-mail: info@compost.org
URL: www.compost.org
Scope: National
Purpose: A meeting for the composting community, including members of government, industry, & academia
Contact Information: E-mail: info@compost.org

Compost Council of Canada 2012 Compost Garden Party

Sponsor/Contact: Compost Council of Canada
16 Northumberland St.
Toronto, ON M6H 1P7
416-535-0240 Fax: 416-536-9892
E-mail: info@compost.org
URL: www.compost.org
Scope: National
Purpose: A gathering to teach the value of composting, edible gardening, & sharing the harvest with those in need
Contact Information: E-mail: info@compost.org

Compost Council of Canada 2012 Regional Workshop: Compost Matters!

Sponsor/Contact: Compost Council of Canada
16 Northumberland St.
Toronto, ON M6H 1P7
416-535-0240 Fax: 416-536-9892
E-mail: info@compost.org
URL: www.compost.org
Scope: National
Purpose: A workshop for persons interested in organics recycling & composting
Contact Information: E-mail: info@compost.org

Conservation Agriculture 2012 Annual Conference

Location: Saskatchewan
Sponsor/Contact: Saskatchewan Soil Conservation Association
P.O. Box 1360
Indian Head, SK S0G 2K0
306-695-4233 Fax: 306-695-4236
E-mail: info@ssca.ca
URL: www.ssca.ca
Scope: Provincial
Purpose: Information about soil conservation technology
Anticipated Attendance: 350+
Contact Information: Executive Manager: Blair McClinton, PAg, Phone: 306-695-4235, E-mail: bmcclinton@ssca.ca; Office Manager: Marilyn Martens, Phone: 306-695-4233

Consulting Engineers of Alberta 2012 15th Annual Transportation Conference & Trade Show

Location: Alberta
Sponsor/Contact: Consulting Engineers of Alberta
Phipps-McKinnon Building
#870, 10020 - 101A Ave.
Edmonton, AB T5J 3G2
780-421-1852 Fax: 780-424-5225
E-mail: info@cea.ca
URL: www.cea.ca
Scope: Provincial
Purpose: An event of interest to design engineering & construction professionals in transportation infrastructure
Anticipated Attendance: 700+
Contact Information: Manager, Events & Communications: Hiju Song, E-mail: hsong@cea.ca

Consulting Engineers of Alberta 2012 34th Annual General Meeting

Location: Alberta
Sponsor/Contact: Consulting Engineers of Alberta
Phipps-McKinnon Building
#870, 10020 - 101A Ave.
Edmonton, AB T5J 3G2
780-421-1852 Fax: 780-424-5225
E-mail: info@cea.ca
URL: www.cea.ca
Scope: Provincial
Purpose: A keynote presentation, a business meeting, & the opportunity to network with peers & clients
Contact Information: Manager, Events & Communications: Hiju Song, E-mail: hsong@cea.ca

Consulting Engineers of Alberta 2012 4th Annual Young Professionals' Forum

Location: Alberta
Sponsor/Contact: Consulting Engineers of Alberta
Phipps-McKinnon Building
#870, 10020 - 101A Ave.
Edmonton, AB T5J 3G2
780-421-1852 Fax: 780-424-5225
E-mail: info@cea.ca
URL: www.cea.ca
Scope: Provincial
Purpose: An informative session for members of the Consulting Engineers of Alberta's Young Professionals' Group
Contact Information: Manager, Events & Communications: Hiju Song, Phone: 780-421-1852, E-mail: hsong@cea.ca

Consulting Engineers of Alberta 2012 Annual Luncheon with the City of Edmonton Council

Location: Alberta
Sponsor/Contact: Consulting Engineers of Alberta
Phipps-McKinnon Building
#870, 10020 - 101A Ave.
Edmonton, AB T5J 3G2
780-421-1852 Fax: 780-424-5225
E-mail: info@cea.ca
URL: www.cea.ca
Scope: Provincial
Purpose: An opportunity for members of Consulting Engineers of Alberta to discuss areas of mutual interest & concern with Edmonton's mayor, council, & senior administration
Contact Information: Manager, Events & Communications: Hiju Song, Phone: 780-421-1852, E-mail: hsong@cea.ca

Consulting Engineers of Alberta 2012 Infrastructure Partners Conference

Location: Alberta
Sponsor/Contact: Consulting Engineers of Alberta
Phipps-McKinnon Building
#870, 10020 - 101A Ave.
Edmonton, AB T5J 3G2
780-421-1852 Fax: 780-424-5225
E-mail: info@cea.ca
URL: www.cea.ca
Scope: Provincial
Purpose: Presentations of interest to design consultants & contractors & updates on Alberta infrastructure
Contact Information: Manager, Events & Communications: Hiju Song, Phone: 780-421-1852, E-mail: hsong@cea.ca

Consulting Engineers of British Columbia 2012 Annual General Meeting

Location: British Columbia
Sponsor/Contact: Consulting Engineers of British Columbia
#1258, 409 Granville St.
Vancouver, BC V6C 1T2
604-687-2811 Fax: 604-688-7110
E-mail: info@cebc.org
URL: www.cebc.org
Scope: Provincial
Purpose: A summary of Consulting Engineers of British Columbia's activities & issues during the past year & plans for the coming year
Contact Information: Phone: 604-687-2811; E-mail: events@cebc.org, info@cebc.org

Consulting Engineers of British Columbia 2012 Annual Transportation Conference

Location: British Columbia
Sponsor/Contact: Consulting Engineers of British Columbia
#1258, 409 Granville St.
Vancouver, BC V6C 1T2
604-687-2811 Fax: 604-688-7110
E-mail: info@cebc.org
URL: www.cebc.org
Scope: Provincial
Purpose: An event planned with groups such as the Ministry of Transportation & Infrastructure & TransLink
Contact Information: Coordinator, Accounting & Events: Alla Samusevich, E-mail: alla@cebc.org, events@cebc.org

Consulting Engineers of British Columbia 2012 Awards Gala

Location: British Columbia
Sponsor/Contact: Consulting Engineers of British Columbia
#1258, 409 Granville St.
Vancouver, BC V6C 1T2

604-687-2811 Fax: 604-688-7110
E-mail: info@cebc.org
URL: www.cebc.org
Scope: Provincial
Purpose: The presentation of the Awards for Engineering Excellence & a showcase of innovation & excellence in engineering design, attended by industry leaders, politicians, & key clients
Contact Information: Coordinator, Accounting & Events: Alla Samusevich, E-mail: alla@cebc.org, events@cebc.org

Consulting Engineers of British Columbia 2012 Client Mixers

Location: British Columbia
Sponsor/Contact: Consulting Engineers of British Columbia
#1258, 409 Granville St.
Vancouver, BC V6C 1T2
604-687-2811 Fax: 604-688-7110
E-mail: info@cebc.org
URL: www.cebc.org
Scope: Provincial
Purpose: A networking event with peers & clients & the chance to learn of forthcoming capital plans & client projects
Contact Information: Coordinator, Accounting & Events: Alla Samusevich, E-mail: alla@cebc.org, events@cebc.org

Consulting Engineers of British Columbia 2012 Government Relations Day

Location: British Columbia
Sponsor/Contact: Consulting Engineers of British Columbia
#1258, 409 Granville St.
Vancouver, BC V6C 1T2
604-687-2811 Fax: 604-688-7110
E-mail: info@cebc.org
URL: www.cebc.org
Scope: Provincial
Purpose: An opportunity for members of the Consulting Engineers of British Columbia to network with government decision makers during a breakfast meeting with British Columbia's Members of the Legislative Assembly & lunch with Deputy Ministers & Assistant Deputy Ministers
Contact Information: Coordinator, Accounting & Events: Alla Samusevich, E-mail: alla@cebc.org, events@cebc.org

Consulting Engineers of British Columbia 2012 Member / Industry Dinner

Location: British Columbia
Sponsor/Contact: Consulting Engineers of British Columbia
#1258, 409 Granville St.
Vancouver, BC V6C 1T2
604-687-2811 Fax: 604-688-7110
E-mail: info@cebc.org
URL: www.cebc.org
Scope: Provincial
Purpose: An educational event for members to learn about the most recent developments in the industry, such as budget & fee guidelines
Contact Information: Coordinator, Accounting & Events: Alla Samusevich, E-mail: alla@cebc.org, events@cebc.org

Consulting Engineers of British Columbia 2012 Young Professionals' Group Seminar

Location: British Columbia
Sponsor/Contact: Consulting Engineers of British Columbia
#1258, 409 Granville St.
Vancouver, BC V6C 1T2
604-687-2811 Fax: 604-688-7110
E-mail: info@cebc.org
URL: www.cebc.org
Scope: Provincial
Purpose: Breakfast seminars held for young professionals in the engineering sector
Contact Information: Coordinator, Accounting & Events: Alla Samusevich, E-mail: alla@cebc.org, events@cebc.org

Consulting Engineers of British Columbia 2013 Awards Gala

Location: British Columbia
Sponsor/Contact: Consulting Engineers of British Columbia
#1258, 409 Granville St.
Vancouver, BC V6C 1T2
604-687-2811 Fax: 604-688-7110
E-mail: info@cebc.org
URL: www.cebc.org
Scope: Provincial
Purpose: The presentation of the Awards for Engineering Excellence in categories such as buildings, municipal, transportation, natural resources, energy & industry, & soft engineering
Contact Information: Coordinator, Accounting & Events: Alla Samusevich, E-mail: alla@cebc.org, events@cebc.org

Council of Forest Industries 2012 Annual Convention

Location: British Columbia
Sponsor/Contact: Council of Forest Industries
Pender Place I Business Building
#1501, 700 Pender St. West
Vancouver, BC V6C 1G8
604-684-0211 Fax: 604-687-4930
E-mail: info@cofi.org
URL: www.cofi.org
Scope: National
Purpose: A meeting about issues affecting the forestry industries of British Columbia
Contact Information: Phone: 250-564-5136; Fax: 250-564-3588; E-mail: ac2011@cofi.org

Drinking Water 2012 15th Biennial Canadian National Conference

Sponsor/Contact: Canadian Water & Wastewater Association
#11, 1010 Polytek Rd.
Ottawa, ON K1J 9H9
613-747-0524 Fax: 613-747-0523
E-mail: tdellison@cwwa.ca
URL: www.cwwa.ca
Scope: National
Purpose: A meeting of Canadian regulators, utility managers, researchers, & other stakeholders in Canadian drinking water
Contact Information: Phone: 613-747-0524; Fax: 613-747-0523, E-mail: admin@cwwa.ca

Federation of Northern Ontario Municipalities 2012 52nd Annual Conference

Location: Ontario
Sponsor/Contact: Federation of Northern Ontario Municipalities
P.O. Box 2175 Stn. A
Sudbury, ON P3A 4S1
705-586-9120 Fax: 705-586-9195
E-mail: fonom@eastlink.ca
URL: www.fonom.org
Scope: Local
Purpose: A meeting for northern Ontario's municipal decision makers, featuring exhibits by suppliers, vendors, & professionals who provide services to municipalities
Anticipated Attendance: 111
Contact Information: FONOM Executive Director: Lynne Reynolds, Phone: 705-586-9120, E-mail: fonom@eastlink.ca

Federation of Ontario Cottagers' Associations 2012 Spring Annual General Meeting

Location: Ontario
Sponsor/Contact: Federation of Ontario Cottagers' Associations
#201, 159 King St.
Peterborough, ON K9J 2R8
705-749-3622 Fax: 705-749-6522
E-mail: info@foca.on.ca
URL: www.foca.on.ca
Scope: Provincial
Contact Information: Phone: 705-749-3622, ext. 5; E-mail: communications@foca.on.ca

Fisheries Council of Canada 2012 67th Annual Conference

Sponsor/Contact: Fisheries Council of Canada
#900, 170 Laurier Ave. West
Ottawa, ON K1P 5V5
613-727-7450 Fax: 613-727-7453
E-mail: info@fisheriescouncil.org
URL: www.fisheriescouncil.ca
Scope: National
Purpose: Educational sessions, opportunities to network, & social programs
Contact Information: E-mail: info@fisheriescouncil.org

Forest Products Association of Nova Scotia 2012 Annual Meeting

Location: Nova Scotia
Sponsor/Contact: Forest Products Association of Nova Scotia
P.O. Box 696
Truro, NS B2N 5E5
902-895-1179 Fax: 902-893-1197
URL: www.fpans.ca
Scope: Provincial
Purpose: A yearly gathering of association members
Contact Information: Coordinator, Communications: Jeff Bishop, E-mail: jbishop@fpans.ca

GLOBE Foundation 2012 6th Annual EPIC Sustainable Living Expo

Sponsor/Contact: GLOBE Foundation
World Trade Centre
#578, 999 Canada Pl.
Vancouver, BC V6C 3E1
604-695-5001 Fax: 604-695-5019
E-mail: info@globe.ca
URL: www.globe.ca
Scope: Regional
Purpose: An event, with over 200 exhibitors, to introduce the public to new environmentally-friendly products & services
Anticipated Attendance: 16,000+
Contact Information: General Information: Phone: 604-695-5001, Toll-Free Phone: 1-800-274-6097, E-mail: info@epicexpo.com; Operations Information: Phone: 604-695-5008, E-mail: operations@epicexpo.com; Exhibit Sales Information: Phone: 604-695-5010, E-mail: exhibits@epicexpo.com; Sponsorship Information: Phone: 604-695-5000, E-mail: sponsor@epicexpo.com

Growing Your Farm Profits 2012 Cochrane Area Workshop

Location: Ontario
Sponsor/Contact: Ontario Soil & Crop Improvement Association
1 Stone Rd. West
Guelph, ON N1G 4Y2
519-826-4214 Fax: 519-826-4224
E-mail: oscia@ontariosoilcrop.org
URL: www.ontariosoilcrop.org
Scope: Local
Purpose: Information about assessing a farm business, identifying priorities, & developing plans
Contact Information: Ontario Soil & Crop Improvement Association Program Representative: Claire Venne,

Trade Shows, Conferences and Seminars

Phone: 705-594-9194, E-mail: cochrane@ontariosoilcrop.org

Local Government Management Association of British Columbia 2012 Administrative Professionals Conference

Location: British Columbia
Sponsor/Contact: Local Government Management Association of British Columbia
Central Building
620 View St., 7th Fl.
Victoria, BC V8W 1J6
250-383-7032 Fax: 250-384-4879
E-mail: office@lgma.ca; editor@lgma.ca (magazine); ads@lgma.ca
URL: www.lgma.ca
Scope: Provincial
Purpose: An annual conference, featuring speakers, professionals, & practitioners, of interest to all level of administrative staff who work in local government offices in British Columbia
Contact Information: Program Coordinator: Ana Fuller, Phone: 250-383-7032, ext. 227, Fax: 250-383-4879, E-mail: afuller@lgma.ca

Local Government Management Association of British Columbia 2012 Annual CAO (Chief Administrative Officers) Forum

Location: British Columbia
Sponsor/Contact: Local Government Management Association of British Columbia
Central Building
620 View St., 7th Fl.
Victoria, BC V8W 1J6
250-383-7032 Fax: 250-384-4879
E-mail: office@lgma.ca; editor@lgma.ca (magazine); ads@lgma.ca
URL: www.lgma.ca
Scope: Provincial
Purpose: A meeting for local government chief administrative officers to discuss issues of concern
Contact Information: Program Coordinator: Ana Fuller, Phone: 250-383-7032, ext. 227, Fax: 250-383-4879, E-mail: afuller@lgma.ca

Manitoba Environmental Industries Association Inc. 2012 Annual General Meeting

Location: Manitoba
Sponsor/Contact: Manitoba Environmental Industries Association Inc.
#100, 62 Albert St.
Winnipeg, MB R3B 1E9
204-783-7090 Fax: 204-783-6501
E-mail: admin@meia.mb.ca
URL: www.meia.mb.ca
Scope: Provincial
Purpose: A gathering of members to address the business of the association & to provide networking opportunities
Contact Information: Executive Director: John Fjeldsted, Phone: 204-783-7090

Manitoba Environmental Industries Association Inc. 2012 Conference: Emerging Issues

Location: Manitoba
Sponsor/Contact: Manitoba Environmental Industries Association Inc.
#100, 62 Albert St.
Winnipeg, MB R3B 1E9
204-783-7090 Fax: 204-783-6501
E-mail: admin@meia.mb.ca
URL: www.meia.mb.ca
Scope: Provincial
Purpose: An annual one day conference to inform participants about recent environmental legislation & regulatory affairs at the provincial & federal levels
Contact Information: Coordinator, Education & Training: Rosemary Deans, Phone: 204-783-7090

Manitoba Environmental Industries Association Inc. 2012 Conference: Remediation & Prevention

Location: Manitoba
Sponsor/Contact: Manitoba Environmental Industries Association Inc.
#100, 62 Albert St.
Winnipeg, MB R3B 1E9
204-783-7090 Fax: 204-783-6501
E-mail: admin@meia.mb.ca
URL: www.meia.mb.ca
Scope: Provincial
Purpose: An annual one day conference with information about recent changes in provincial & federal environmental legislation & regulatory affairs
Contact Information: Coordinator, Education & Training: Rosemary Deans, Phone: 204-783-7090

Manitoba Water Well Association 2012 Annual General Meeting

Location: Manitoba
Sponsor/Contact: Manitoba Water Well Association
P.O. Box 1648
Winnipeg, MB R3C 2Z6
204-479-3777
E-mail: info@mwwa.ca
URL: www.mwwa.ca
Scope: Provincial
Purpose: A review of the year's highlights & an opportunity to address new business
Contact Information: Business Manager: Lynn Giersch, E-mail: info@mwwa.ca

National Environmental Health Association 2012 76th Annual Conference & Exhibition

Sponsor/Contact: National Environmental Health Association
#1000N, 720 South Colorado Blvd.
Denver, CO USA
303-756-9090 Fax: 303-691-9490
E-mail: staff@neha.org
URL: www.neha.org
Scope: International
Contact Information: Toll-Free Phone: 866-956-2258; Fax: 303-691-9490; E-mail: staff@neha.org

Nature Canada 2012 Annual General Meeting

Sponsor/Contact: Nature Canada
#300, 75 Albert St.
Ottawa, ON K1P 5E7
613-562-3447 Fax: 613-562-3371
E-mail: info@naturecanada.ca
URL: www.naturecanada.ca
Scope: National
Purpose: The annual meeting usually features the election of the Board of Directors, the presentation of Nature Canada awards, & the adoption of resolutions
Contact Information: Nature Canada Executive Assistant & Office Manager: Sue Robertson, E-mail: srobertson@naturecanada.ca

Nature Manitoba 2012 Annual General Meeting

Location: Manitoba
Sponsor/Contact: Nature Manitoba
Hammond Building
#401, 63 Albert St.
Winnipeg, MB R3B 1G4
204-943-9029 Fax: 204-943-9029
E-mail: info@naturemanitoba.ca; editor@naturemanitoba.ca (Newsletter)
URL: www.naturemanitoba.ca
Scope: Provincial
Purpose: An opportunity for Nature Manitoba members to discuss & advance policy positions about nature in Manitoba
Contact Information: E-mail: info@naturemanitoba.ca

Nature Nova Scotia 2012 Annual General Meeting & Conference

Location: Nova Scotia
Sponsor/Contact: Nature Nova Scotia (Federation of Nova Scotia Naturalists)
c/o Nova Scotia Museum of Natural History
1747 Summer St.
Halifax, NS B3H 3A6
902-582-7176
E-mail: doug@fundymud.com
URL: www.naturens.ca
Scope: Provincial
Purpose: A 2.5 day event, with an annual meeting featuring reports on the past year's activities to the membership, plus educational talks & field trips
Contact Information: Treasurer: Jean Gibson, Phone: 902-678-4725

New Brunswick Environmental Network 2012 Annual General Meeting

Location: New Brunswick
Sponsor/Contact: New Brunswick Environmental Network
167 Creek Rd.
Waterford, NB E4E 4L7
506-433-6101 Fax: 506-433-6111
E-mail: nben@nben.ca
URL: www.nben.ca
Scope: Provincial
Purpose: Featuring the election of a Steering Committee by member groups
Contact Information: E-mail: nben@nben.ca

Newfoundland & Labrador Construction Association 2012 2nd Annual Construction Career Expo & Opportunities Fair

Location: Newfoundland & Labrador
Sponsor/Contact: Newfoundland & Labrador Construction Association
#201, 333 Pippy Pl.
St. John's, NL A1B 3X2
709-753-8920 Fax: 709-754-3968
E-mail: info@nfld.com
URL: www.nlca.ca
Scope: Provincial
Purpose: An interactive & instructive environment for students, workers, training providers, & prospective employers
Contact Information: Coordinator, Events: Susan Casey, E-mail: scasey@nlca.ca

Newfoundland & Labrador Construction Association 2012 Annual Awards Gala

Location: Newfoundland & Labrador
Sponsor/Contact: Newfoundland & Labrador Construction Association
#201, 333 Pippy Pl.
St. John's, NL A1B 3X2
709-753-8920 Fax: 709-754-3968
E-mail: info@nfld.com
URL: www.nlca.ca
Scope: Provincial
Purpose: An awards presentation to honour industry professionals, featuring a keynote address to delegates
Contact Information: Coordinator, Member Services: Adelle Connors, Phone: 709-753-8920, E-mail: accounting@nlca.ca

Newfoundland & Labrador Construction Association 2012 Annual Conference & Annual General Meeting

Sponsor/Contact: Newfoundland & Labrador Construction Association
#201, 333 Pippy Pl.
St. John's, NL A1B 3X2
709-753-8920 Fax: 709-754-3968
E-mail: info@nfld.com
URL: www.nlca.ca

Scope: Provincial
Purpose: Sessions & keynote addresses of interest to persons such as general, electrical, & mechanical contractors, manufacturers, suppliers, safety professionals, engineers, training providers, LEED accredited professionals, & municipalities
Contact Information: Chair, Conference 2012 Planning Committee: Kevin McEvoy, Phone: 709-368-3134, Fax: 709-368-7477, E-mail: kmcevoy@guildfords.com; Coordinator, Events: Susan Casey, E-mail: scasey@nlca.ca

Newfoundland & Labrador Construction Association 2012 General Membership Meeting

Location: Newfoundland & Labrador
Sponsor/Contact: Newfoundland & Labrador Construction Association
#201, 333 Pippy Pl.
St. John's, NL A1B 3X2
709-753-8920 Fax: 709-754-3968
E-mail: info@nfld.com
URL: www.nlca.ca
Scope: Provincial
Purpose: A presentation of recent association activities & updates on current issues in the construction industry in Newfoundland & Labrador
Contact Information: Coordinator, Member Services: Adelle Connors, E-mail: accounting@nlca.ca

Newfoundland & Labrador Federation of Agriculture 2012 Annual General Meeting

Location: Newfoundland & Labrador
Sponsor/Contact: Newfoundland & Labrador Federation of Agriculture
P.O. Box 1045
308 Brookfield Rd., Bldg. 4
Mount Pearl, NL A1N 3C9
709-747-4874 Fax: 709-747-8827
E-mail: info@nlfa.ca
URL: www.nlfa.ca
Scope: Provincial
Purpose: An opportunity for members in good standing to vote & hold office
Contact Information: Phone: 709-747-4874; E-mail: info@nlfa.ca

Northwestern Ontario Municipal Association 2012 Annual Regional Conference

Location: Ontario
Sponsor/Contact: Northwestern Ontario Municipal Association
P.O. Box 10308
Thunder Bay, ON P7B 6T8
807-683-6662
E-mail: admin@noma.on.ca
URL: www.noma.on.ca
Scope: Local
Purpose: An annual meeting, which takes place in September or October, featuring a variety of presentations on issues of interest to members of the Northwestern Ontario Municipal Association
Contact Information: Executive Director: Charla Robinson, Phone: 807-683-6662, E-mail: admin@noma.on.ca

Nova Scotia Environmental Network 2012 Annual Book Club

Location: Nova Scotia
Sponsor/Contact: Nova Scotia Environmental Network
3115 Veith St.
Halifax, NS B3K 3G9
902-454-6846 Fax: 902-453-3633
E-mail: nsen@cen-rce.org; board_nsen@cen-rce.org
URL: www.nsen.ca
Scope: Provincial
Purpose: A dialogue organized by the Nova Scotia Environmental Network & SENSE: Sustainability Education in Nova Scotia for Everyone
Contact Information: E-mail: nsen@cen-rce.org

Nova Scotia Environmental Network 2012 Annual General Meeting

Location: Nova Scotia
Sponsor/Contact: Nova Scotia Environmental Network
3115 Veith St.
Halifax, NS B3K 3G9
902-454-6846 Fax: 902-453-3633
E-mail: nsen@cen-rce.org; board_nsen@cen-rce.org
URL: www.nsen.ca
Scope: Provincial
Purpose: Featuring the minutes of the preceding general meeting, the annual report of the directors, the executive director's report, consideration of the financial report, the approval of the budget for the ensuing year, the election of directors, & the appointment of auditors
Contact Information: E-mail: nsen@cen-rce.org

Nova Scotia Environmental Network 2012 Annual Roundtable

Location: Nova Scotia
Sponsor/Contact: Nova Scotia Environmental Network
3115 Veith St.
Halifax, NS B3K 3G9
902-454-6846 Fax: 902-453-3633
E-mail: nsen@cen-rce.org; board_nsen@cen-rce.org
URL: www.nsen.ca
Scope: Provincial
Purpose: An annual meeting to strategize about environmental priorities & fundraising
Contact Information: E-mail: nsen@cen-rce.org

Ocean, Offshore, & Arctic Engineering 2012 31st International Conference

Location: Rio de Janeiro, Brazil
Sponsor/Contact: American Society of Mechanical Engineers
3 Park Ave.
New York, NY USA
800-843-2763
E-mail: infocentral@asme.org
URL: www.asme.org
Scope: International

Ontario Cattlemen's Association 2012 Annual Convention

Location: Ontario
Sponsor/Contact: Ontario Cattlemen's Association
130 Malcolm Rd.
Guelph, ON N1K 1B1
519-824-0334 Fax: 519-824-9101
E-mail: ontbeef@cattle.guelph.on.ca
URL: www.cattle.guelph.on.ca
Scope: Provincial
Purpose: An opportunity for Ontario Cattlemen's Association members to help set policy direction on cattle industry issues
Contact Information: Communications Manager: Lianne Appleby, E-mail: lianne@cattle.guelph.on.ca

Ontario Environmental Network 2012 Annual General Meeting

Location: Ontario
Sponsor/Contact: Ontario Environmental Network
P.O. Box 1412 Stn. Main
North Bay, ON P1B 8K6
705-840-2888 Fax: 705-840-5862
E-mail: oen@oen.ca
URL: www.oen.ca
Scope: Provincial
Purpose: Members of the Ontario Environment Network receive voting privileges, plus the right to run for election for the Steering Committee
Contact Information: Ontario Environmental Network Coordinator: Phillip Penna, Phone: 705-840-2888

Ontario Federation of Agriculture 2012 Convention

Location: Ontario
Sponsor/Contact: Ontario Federation of Agriculture
Ontario AgriCentre
#206, 100 Stone Rd. West
London, ON N1G 5L3
519-821-8883 Fax: 519-821-8810
E-mail: info@ofa.on.ca
URL: www.ofa.on.ca
Scope: Provincial
Purpose: Workshops, exhibits, elections, a guest speaker, & networking opportunities
Contact Information: E-mail: info@ofa.on.ca

Ontario Field Ornithologists 2012 Annual Convention

Location: Ontario
Sponsor/Contact: Ontario Field Ornithologists
P.O. Box 455 Stn. R
Toronto, ON M4G 4E1
E-mail: membership@ofo.ca
URL: www.ofo.ca
Scope: Provincial
Purpose: Activities include guest speakers, birding displays, field trips, & a social event
Contact Information: Convention Contacts: John Black, Phone: 905-684-0143, E-mail: jblack3@brocku.ca; Robert Maciver, Phone: 519-260-0729, E-mail: robert.maciver@gmail.com; Chris Escott, Phone: 416-444-8055, E-mail: chris.escott@ofo.ca

Ontario Ground Water Association 2012 60th Annual Convention & Trade Show

Location: Ontario
Sponsor/Contact: Ontario Ground Water Association
48 Front St. East
Strathroy, ON N7G 1Y6
519-245-7194 Fax: 519-245-7196
URL: www.ogwa.ca
Scope: Provincial
Purpose: Meetings, seminars, networking opportunities, & a social program
Contact Information: Office Manager: Anne Gammage, Phone: 519-245-7194, Fax: 519-245-7196

Ontario Medical Association, Sport Medicine Section 2012 Annual Symposium: Sport Med

Location: Ontario
Sponsor/Contact: Ontario Medical Association
#900, 150 Bloor St. West
Toronto, ON M5S 3C1
416-599-2580 Fax: 416-340-2944
E-mail: info@oma.org; membership@oma.org
URL: www.oma.org
Scope: Provincial
Purpose: A symposium of interest to physicians, physiotherapists, exercise physiologists, athletic therapists, residents, & students
Contact Information: Ontario Medical Association, Conference Planning, Toll-Free Phone: 1-800-268-7215, ext. 3461, Fax: 416-340-2244, E-mail: jennifer.csamer@oma.org

Ontario Parks Association 2012 56th Annual Educational Forum

Location: Ontario
Sponsor/Contact: Ontario Parks Association
7856 - 5th Line South, RR#4
Milton, ON L9T 2X8
905-864-6182 Fax: 905-864-6184
E-mail: opa@ontarioparksassociation.ca
URL: www.ontarioparksassociation.ca
Scope: Provincial
Purpose: Educational presentations of interest to park & green space managers & operational staff
Contact Information: Coordinator, Operations & Administration: Shelley May, E-mail: opa@ontarioparksassociation.ca

Trade Shows, Conferences and Seminars

Ontario Parks Association 2012 Accident / Incident Investigation Program

Location: Ontario
Sponsor/Contact: Ontario Parks Association
7856 - 5th Line South, RR#4
Milton, ON L9T 2X8
905-864-6182 Fax: 905-864-6184
E-mail: opa@ontarioparksassociation.ca
URL: www.ontarioparksassociation.ca
Scope: Provincial
Purpose: Education for Ontario Parks Association members & potential members
Contact Information: Coordinator, Operations & Administration: Shelley May, E-mail: opa@ontarioparksassociation.ca

Ontario Parks Association 2012 Ball Diamond Maintenance & Best Practices Workshop

Location: Ontario
Sponsor/Contact: Ontario Parks Association
7856 - 5th Line South, RR#4
Milton, ON L9T 2X8
905-864-6182 Fax: 905-864-6184
E-mail: opa@ontarioparksassociation.ca
URL: www.ontarioparksassociation.ca
Scope: Provincial
Purpose: Maintenance standards & best practices for front line staff
Contact Information: Coordinator, Operations & Administration: Shelley May, E-mail: opa@ontarioparksassociation.ca

Ontario Parks Association 2012 Congress & Trade Show

Location: Ontario
Sponsor/Contact: Ontario Parks Association
7856 - 5th Line South, RR#4
Milton, ON L9T 2X8
905-864-6182 Fax: 905-864-6184
E-mail: opa@ontarioparksassociation.ca
URL: www.ontarioparksassociation.ca
Scope: Provincial
Purpose: Featuring hundreds of vendors with products & services for municipal park & green space managers & operational staff
Contact Information: Coordinator, Operations & Administration: Shelley May, E-mail: opa@ontarioparksassociation.ca

Ontario Parks Association 2012 Municipal Integrated Pest Management Accreditation Workshop

Location: Ontario
Sponsor/Contact: Ontario Parks Association
7856 - 5th Line South, RR#4
Milton, ON L9T 2X8
905-864-6182 Fax: 905-864-6184
E-mail: opa@ontarioparksassociation.ca
URL: www.ontarioparksassociation.ca
Scope: Provincial
Purpose: A course for municipalities that want to be integrated pest management accredited
Contact Information: Coordinator, Operations & Administration: Shelley May, E-mail: opa@ontarioparksassociation.ca

Ontario Parks Association 2012 Parks & Landscaping Equipment Safety Operations Program

Location: Ontario
Sponsor/Contact: Ontario Parks Association
7856 - 5th Line South, RR#4
Milton, ON L9T 2X8
905-864-6182 Fax: 905-864-6184
E-mail: opa@ontarioparksassociation.ca
URL: www.ontarioparksassociation.ca
Scope: Provincial
Purpose: One of three components in the Parks & Open Space Professional training program
Contact Information: Coordinator, Operations & Administration: Shelley May, E-mail: opa@ontarioparksassociation.ca

Ontario Parks Association 2012 Parks Confined Spaces Program

Location: Ontario
Sponsor/Contact: Ontario Parks Association
7856 - 5th Line South, RR#4
Milton, ON L9T 2X8
905-864-6182 Fax: 905-864-6184
E-mail: opa@ontarioparksassociation.ca
URL: www.ontarioparksassociation.ca
Scope: Provincial
Purpose: A parks operation & management related educational program for Ontario Parks Association members & potential members
Contact Information: Coordinator, Operations & Administration: Shelley May, E-mail: opa@ontarioparksassociation.ca

Ontario Parks Association 2012 Parks Equipment Safety Training & Train the Trainer Program

Location: Ontario
Sponsor/Contact: Ontario Parks Association
7856 - 5th Line South, RR#4
Milton, ON L9T 2X8
905-864-6182 Fax: 905-864-6184
E-mail: opa@ontarioparksassociation.ca
URL: www.ontarioparksassociation.ca
Scope: Provincial
Purpose: An introduction to the skills needed for safe operation of park equipment & industry best practices
Contact Information: Coordinator, Operations & Administration: Shelley May, E-mail: opa@ontarioparksassociation.ca

Ontario Parks Association 2012 Parks Oriented Chainsaw Safety Awareness & Basic Chipper Operations & Handling Course

Location: Ontario
Sponsor/Contact: Ontario Parks Association
7856 - 5th Line South, RR#4
Milton, ON L9T 2X8
905-864-6182 Fax: 905-864-6184
E-mail: opa@ontarioparksassociation.ca
URL: www.ontarioparksassociation.ca
Scope: Provincial
Purpose: A requirement from the Department of Labour is for all parks professionals who use chainsaws on the job to receive training in the safe operation of chainsaws
Contact Information: Coordinator, Operations & Administration: Shelley May, E-mail: opa@ontarioparksassociation.ca

Ontario Parks Association 2012 Playground Introductory Compliance & Hazard Analysis Workshop

Location: Ontario
Sponsor/Contact: Ontario Parks Association
7856 - 5th Line South, RR#4
Milton, ON L9T 2X8
905-864-6182 Fax: 905-864-6184
E-mail: opa@ontarioparksassociation.ca
URL: www.ontarioparksassociation.ca
Scope: Provincial
Purpose: Participants will learn about the regulations that apply to playgrounds in Ontario
Contact Information: Coordinator, Operations & Administration: Shelley May, E-mail: opa@ontarioparksassociation.ca

Ontario Parks Association 2012 Supervisor Competency Program

Location: Ontario
Sponsor/Contact: Ontario Parks Association
7856 - 5th Line South, RR#4
Milton, ON L9T 2X8
905-864-6182 Fax: 905-864-6184
E-mail: opa@ontarioparksassociation.ca
URL: www.ontarioparksassociation.ca
Scope: Provincial
Purpose: Participants learns their responsibilities under the Occupational Health & Safety Act & Regulations
Contact Information: Coordinator, Operations & Administration: Shelley May, E-mail: opa@ontarioparksassociation.ca

Ontario Parks Association 2012 Trails Specialist Workshop

Location: Ontario
Sponsor/Contact: Ontario Parks Association
7856 - 5th Line South, RR#4
Milton, ON L9T 2X8
905-864-6182 Fax: 905-864-6184
E-mail: opa@ontarioparksassociation.ca
URL: www.ontarioparksassociation.ca
Scope: Provincial
Purpose: A workshop about constructing sustainable trail systems for municipal park managers, supervisors, architects, planners, & volunteers
Contact Information: Coordinator, Operations & Administration: Shelley May, E-mail: opa@ontarioparksassociation.ca

Ontario Professional Fire Fighters Association 2012 15th Annual Convention

Location: Ontario
Sponsor/Contact: Ontario Professional Fire Fighters Association
292 Plains Rd. East
Burlington, ON L7T 2C6
905-681-7111 Fax: 905-681-1489
URL: www.opffa.org
Scope: Provincial

Ontario Professional Fire Fighters Association 2012 Annual Health & Safety Seminar

Location: Ontario
Sponsor/Contact: Ontario Professional Fire Fighters Association
292 Plains Rd. East
Burlington, ON L7T 2C6
905-681-7111 Fax: 905-681-1489
URL: www.opffa.org
Scope: Provincial
Purpose: A three day seminar to review recent advancements in fire fighter health & safety, attended by fire fighters & fire chiefs from locals which authorize their participation
Contact Information: Health and Safety Committee Chair: Ellard Beaven, E-mail: beavenopffa@ntl.sympatico.ca

Ontario Public Health Association 2012 Annual General Meeting

Location: Ontario
Sponsor/Contact: Ontario Public Health Association
Lawrence Square
#310, 700 Lawrence Ave. West
Toronto, ON M6B 3B4
416-367-3313 Fax: 416-367-2844
E-mail: info@opha.on.ca
URL: www.opha.on.ca
Scope: Provincial

Ontario Respiratory Care Society 2012 Annual Better Breathing Conference

Location: Ontario
Sponsor/Contact: Ontario Respiratory Care Society
#201, 573 King St. East
Toronto, ON M5A 4L3

416-864-9911 Fax: 416-864-9916
E-mail: orcs@on.lung.ca
URL: www.on.lung.ca
Scope: Provincial
Purpose: Presented by The Lung Association's two societies, the Ontario Respiratory Care Society & the Ontario Thoracic Society
Contact Information: Ontario Respiratory Care Society Education Committee Chair: Michael Keim, RRT

Ontario Sustainable Energy Association 2012 4th Annual Community Power Conference & Power Networking Centre Trade Show

Location: Ontario
Sponsor/Contact: Ontario Sustainable Energy Association
#201, 156 Front St. West
Toronto, ON M5J 2L6
416-977-4441 Fax: 416-977-4441
E-mail: info@ontario-sea.org; employment@ontario-sea.org
URL: www.ontario-sea.org
Scope: Provincial
Purpose: Information about becoming a renewable energy entrepreneur, financing projects, forming a community power group, & reaping the benefits from natural resources
Contact Information: Coordinator, Tradeshow, Events & Logistics: Nicole Risse, Phone: 416-977-4441, ext. 223, E-mail: Nicole@ontario-sea.org

Ontario Sustainable Energy Association 2012 Annual General Meeting

Location: Toronto, ON
Sponsor/Contact: Ontario Sustainable Energy Association
#201, 156 Front St. West
Toronto, ON M5J 2L6
416-977-4441 Fax: 416-977-4441
E-mail: info@ontario-sea.org; employment@ontario-sea.org
URL: www.ontario-sea.org
Scope: Provincial
Anticipated Attendance: 2950
Contact Information: Coordinator, Tradeshow, Events & Logistics: Nicole Risse, Phone: 416-977-4441, ext. 223, E-mail: Nicole@ontario-sea.org

Ontario Tire Dealers Association 2012 Annual General Meeting

Sponsor/Contact: Ontario Tire Dealers Association
P.O. Box 516
34 Edward St.
Drayton, ON N0G 1P0
888-207-9059 Fax: 866-375-6832
URL: www.otda.com
Scope: Provincial
Purpose: The presentation of reports & statements, the election of directors, & the appointment of the accountant
Contact Information: Executive Director: Robert Bignell, Phone: 888-207-9059, E-mail: bbignell@otda.com

Petroleum Services Association of Canada 2012 Annual General Meeting, Canadian Drilling Activity Forecast Session, & Industry Dinner

Sponsor/Contact: Petroleum Services Association of Canada
#1150, 800 - 6 Ave. SW
Calgary, AB T2P 3G3
403-264-4195 Fax: 403-263-7174
E-mail: info@psac.ca
URL: www.psac.ca
Scope: National
Purpose: An event held later in the year to provide the drilling activity forecast for 2013
Contact Information: Manager, Meetings & Events: Heather Doyle, Phone: 403-213-2796, E-mail: hdoyle@psac.ca

Petroleum Services Association of Canada 2012 Annual Mid-Year Update

Sponsor/Contact: Petroleum Services Association of Canada
#1150, 800 - 6 Ave. SW
Calgary, AB T2P 3G3
403-264-4195 Fax: 403-263-7174
E-mail: info@psac.ca
URL: www.psac.ca
Scope: National
Purpose: The update of the Canadian Drilling Activity Forecast
Contact Information: Manager, Meetings & Events: Heather Doyle, Phone: 403-213-2796, E-mail: hdoyle@psac.ca

Photovoltaics Industry 2012 5th Annual Workshop

Sponsor/Contact: Solar & Sustainable Energy Society of Canada Inc.
c/o Frederic Pouyot
#173, 207 Bank St.
Ottawa, ON k2P 2N2
613-686-4474 Fax: 613-533-6550
E-mail: bruce@techonfoot.com
URL: www.sesci.ca
Scope: National
Purpose: Subjects include industry developments, policy, financing, trends, & international perspectives

Prospectors & Developers Association of Canada (PDAC) 2012 International Convention, Trade Show, & Investors Exchange Mining Investment Show

Sponsor/Contact: Prospectors & Developers Association of Canada
135 King St. East
Toronto, ON M5C 1G6
416-362-1969 Fax: 416-362-0101
E-mail: info@pdac.ca
URL: www.pdac.ca
Scope: International
Purpose: An international convention, featuring presentations, workshops, technical sessions, a trade show, & investors exchange
Anticipated Attendance: 22,000
Contact Information: Director, Convention: Nicole Sampson, E-mail: nsampson@pdac.ca; PDAC Membership Coordinator: Florence MacLeod, Phone: 416-362-1969, ext. 221, Fax: 416-362-0101, E-mail: fmacleod@pdac.ca, convention@pdac.ca

Radiation Safety Institute of Canada 2012 All About Radiation Safety Employee Training Course

Location: Radiation Safety National Education Ctr. Toronto, ON
Sponsor/Contact: Radiation Safety Institute of Canada Head Office & National Education Centre
#300, 165 Avenue Rd.
Toronto, ON M5R 3S4
416-650-9090 Fax: 416-650-9920
E-mail: info@radiationsafety.ca
URL: www.radiationsafety.ca
Scope: National
Contact Information: Scientist & Training Coordinator: Tara Hargreaves, E-mail: th@radiationsafety.ca; General Inquiries, E-mail: info@radiationsafety.ca

Radiation Safety Institute of Canada 2012 All About X-ray Safety Employee Training Course

Location: Radiation Safety National Education Ctr. Toronto, ON
Sponsor/Contact: Radiation Safety Institute of Canada Head Office & National Education Centre
#300, 165 Avenue Rd.
Toronto, ON M5R 3S4
416-650-9090 Fax: 416-650-9920
E-mail: info@radiationsafety.ca
URL: www.radiationsafety.ca
Scope: National
Contact Information: Scientist & Training Coordinator: Tara Hargreaves, E-mail: th@radiationsafety.ca; General Inquiries, E-mail: info@radiationsafety.ca

Radiation Safety Institute of Canada 2012 Radiation Safety Awareness Education

Sponsor/Contact: Radiation Safety Institute of Canada Head Office & National Education Centre
#300, 165 Avenue Rd.
Toronto, ON M5R 3S4
416-650-9090 Fax: 416-650-9920
E-mail: info@radiationsafety.ca
URL: www.radiationsafety.ca
Scope: National
Purpose: Topics include understanding radiation, radiation protection regulations, controlling exposure to radiation, & health effects of exposure to radiation
Contact Information: Scientist & Training Coordinator: Tara Hargreaves, E-mail: th@radiationsafety.ca; General Inquiries, E-mail: info@radiationsafety.ca

Radiation Safety Institute of Canada 2012 X-ray Safety Awareness Education

Sponsor/Contact: Radiation Safety Institute of Canada Head Office & National Education Centre
#300, 165 Avenue Rd.
Toronto, ON M5R 3S4
416-650-9090 Fax: 416-650-9920
E-mail: info@radiationsafety.ca
URL: www.radiationsafety.ca
Scope: National
Purpose: Subjects include radiation made by machine, radiation protection, the Ontario Ministry of Labour X-ray Safety Regulations, & health effects of exposure to radiation
Contact Information: Scientist & Training Coordinator: Tara Hargreaves, E-mail: th@radiationsafety.ca; General Inquiries, E-mail: info@radiationsafety.ca

Recycling Council of British Columbia 2012 38th Annual General Meeting & Conference

Location: British Columbia
Sponsor/Contact: Recycling Council of British Columbia
#10, 119 West Pender St.
Vancouver, BC V6B 1S5
604-683-6009 Fax: 604-683-7255
E-mail: rcbc@rcbc.bc.ca; hotline@rcbc.bc.ca
URL: www.rcbc.bc.ca
Scope: Provincial
Purpose: The event also features the presentation of the RCBC Environmental Awards to recognize the contributions made by individuals & organizations towards the preservation & protection of British Columbia's environment
Contact Information: Executive Director: Brock MacDonald, Phone: 604-683-6009, ext. 307, E-mail: brock@rcbc.bc.ca

Recycling Council of Ontario 2012 Annual General Meeting

Sponsor/Contact: Recycling Council of Ontario
#225, 215 Spadina Ave.
Toronto, ON M5T 2C7
416-657-2797
E-mail: rco@rco.on.ca
URL: www.rco.on.ca
Scope: Provincial
Purpose: Voting by members for the Board of Directors
Contact Information: Manager, Events: Diane Blackburn: Phone: 416-657-2797, ext. 4, E-mail: events@rco.on.ca; diane@rco.on.ca

Registered Professional Foresters Association of Nova Scotia 2012 Annual General Meeting

Location: Nova Scotia

Trade Shows, Conferences and Seminars

Sponsor/Contact: Registered Professional Foresters Association of Nova Scotia
P.O. Box 1031
Truro, NS B2N 5G9
902-893-0099
E-mail: contact@rpfans.ca
URL: www.rpfans.ca
Scope: Provincial
Purpose: A business meeting for Nova Scotia's professional foresters
Contact Information: Member, Annual General Meeting Planning Committee: Tim O'Brien; Member, Annual General Meeting Planning Committee: Liz Cogan; E-mail: contact@rpfans.ca

Remediation Technologies 2012 Symposium

Location: Banff, AB
Sponsor/Contact: Environmental Services Association of Alberta
#102, 2528 Ellwood Dr. SW
Edmonton, AB T6X 0A9
780-429-6363 Fax: 780-429-4249
E-mail: info@esaa.org
URL: www.esaa.org
Scope: Provincial
Purpose: Remediation technology information for environmental professionals, such as engineering firms, pipeline companies, drill companies, energy marketers, natural gas producers, oil & gase services companies, environmental consulting firms, & mining companies
Contact Information: Director, Program & Event Development: Joe Chowaniec, Phone: 780-429-6363, ext. 223, E-mail: chowaniec@esaa.org; Exhibit Information, E-mail: exhibits@esaa-events.com; Sponsorship Information, E-mail: sponsors@esaa-events.com

Rubber Recycling 2012 Biennial Symposium

Sponsor/Contact: Rubber Manufacturers Association
#900, 1400 K St. NW
Washington, DC USA
202-682-4800
E-mail: info@rma.org
URL: www.rma.org
Scope: International
Contact Information: Phone: 202-682-4800; E-mail: www.rma.org

Saskatchewan Beef Industry 2012 3rd Annual Conference

Location: Saskatchewan
Sponsor/Contact: Saskatchewan Livestock Association
Canada Center Building, Evraz Place
P.O. Box 3771
Regina, SK S4P 3N8
306-757-6133 Fax: 306-525-5852
E-mail: sla@accesscomm.ca
URL: www.sasklivestock.com
Scope: Provincial
Purpose: An event organized by the Saskatchewan Livestock Association, Saskatchewan Cattlemen's Association, Saskatchewan Cattle Feeders Association, Saskatchewan Beef & Forage Symposium Committee, & the Saskatchewan Stock Growers Association
Contact Information: Project Coordinator: Tammy Forrester, Phone: 306-384-6044, Fax: 306-384-4585, E-mail: tammy@rsvpeventdesign.ca

Saskatchewan Camping Association 2012 Annual General Meeting

Location: Saskatchewan
Sponsor/Contact: Saskatchewan Camping Association
3950 Castle Rd.
Regina, SK S4S 6A4
306-586-4026 Fax: 306-790-8634
E-mail: info@saskcamping.ca
URL: www.saskcamping.ca
Scope: Provincial
Purpose: Agenda items, notices, motions, or changes to the constitution or bylaws must be presented to the Board of Directors thirty days in advance of the meeting
Contact Information: Executive Director: Donna Wilkinson, Phone: 306-586-4026, E-mail: donnaw@sasktel.net

Saskatchewan Camping Association 2012 Education Day

Location: Saskatchewan
Sponsor/Contact: Saskatchewan Camping Association
3950 Castle Rd.
Regina, SK S4S 6A4
306-586-4026 Fax: 306-790-8634
E-mail: info@saskcamping.ca
URL: www.saskcamping.ca
Scope: Provincial
Purpose: Featuring a speaker & educational sessions
Contact Information: Executive Director: Donna Wilkinson, Phone: 306-586-4026, E-mail: donnaw@sasktel.net

Saskatchewan Forestry Association 2012 Annual General Meeting

Location: Saskatchewan
Sponsor/Contact: Saskatchewan Forestry Association
#139, 1061 Central Ave.
Prince Albert, SK S6V 4V4
306-763-2189 Fax: 306-763-6456
E-mail: info@whitebirch.ca
URL: www.whitebirch.ca
Scope: Provincial
Purpose: An event featuring a guest speaker
Contact Information: Meeting Contact: Keith Dodge, E-mail: info@whitebirch.ca

Saskatchewan Soil Conservation Association 2012 Annual Crop Advisor Workshop

Location: Saskatchewan
Sponsor/Contact: Saskatchewan Soil Conservation Association
P.O. Box 1360
Indian Head, SK S0G 2K0
306-695-4233 Fax: 306-695-4236
E-mail: info@ssca.ca
URL: www.ssca.ca
Scope: Provincial
Purpose: Professional development training on sustainable soil management systems for crop advisors & agrologists
Contact Information: Executive Manager: Blair McClinton, PAg, Phone: 306-695-4235, E-mail: bmcclinton@ssca.ca; Office Manager: Marilyn Martens, Phone: 306-695-4233

Saskatchewan Wildlife Federation 2012 83rd Annual Convention

Location: Saskatchewan
Sponsor/Contact: Saskatchewan Wildlife Federation
9 Lancaster Rd.
Moose Jaw, SK S6J 1M8
306-692-8812 Fax: 306-692-4370
E-mail: sask.wildlife@sasktel.net
URL: www.swf.sk.ca
Scope: Provincial
Purpose: A yearly gathering of members, featuring the presentation of awards
Contact Information: Coordinator, Communications: Maureen Horrocks, E-mail: maureenhorrocks@gmail.com, sask.wildlife@sasktel.net

Smart Grid Interoperability 2012 3rd Annual Summit

Sponsor/Contact: Canadian Electricity Association
#1100, 350 Sparks St.
Ottawa, ON K1R 7S8 Canada
613-230-9263 Fax: 613-230-9326
E-mail: info@electricity.ca
URL: www.electricity.ca
Scope: National
Purpose: An opportunity for attendees to gain critical insights from small & large utilities, research labs, & regulators from across North America

Society of Canadian Ornithologists / Société des ornithologistes du Canada 2012 30th Annual Meeting

Sponsor/Contact: Society of Canadian Ornithologists
a/s Thérèse Beaudet, SCO Membership Secretary
1281, ch des Lièges
St-Jean de l'Ile d'Orléans, QC G0A 3W0
E-mail: beaudet.lamothe@sympatico.ca
URL: www.sco-soc.ca
Scope: National

Solar & Sustainable Energy Society of Canada Inc. 2012 Annual Conference

Sponsor/Contact: Solar & Sustainable Energy Society of Canada Inc.
c/o Frederic Pouyot
#173, 207 Bank St.
Ottawa, ON k2P 2N2
613-686-4474 Fax: 613-533-6550
E-mail: bruce@techonfoot.com
URL: www.sesci.ca
Scope: National
Purpose: A meeting to learn about new products & applications, & to network in the renewable energy community
Contact Information: E-mail: president@sesci.ca

SustainaBUILD 2012 3rd Annual Conference

Location: Alberta
Sponsor/Contact: Consulting Engineers of Alberta
Phipps-McKinnon Building
#870, 10020 - 101A Ave.
Edmonton, AB T5J 3G2
780-421-1852 Fax: 780-424-5225
E-mail: info@cea.ca
URL: www.cea.ca
Scope: Provincial
Purpose: Information & a showcase of materials & products for all types of healthy & sustainable buildings
Contact Information: General Information Contact: Lucy Leng, Phone: 403-290-1080, ext. 192063, E-mail: lleng@mmart.com

Westcoast Building & Hardware Show 2012

Location: British Columbia
Sponsor/Contact: Building Supply Industry Association of British Columbia
#2, 19299 - 94th Ave.
Surrey, BC V4N 4E6
604-513-2205 Fax: 604-513-2206
URL: www.bsiabc.ca
Scope: Provincial
Purpose: A trade show, featuring new & innovative products & services, for members of the building supply industry
Contact Information: Registration & Sponsorship Information, Phone: 604-513-2205, E-mail: info@bsiabc.ca

Yukon Conservation Society 2012 Annual General Meeting

Location: YK
Sponsor/Contact: Yukon Conservation Society
302 Hawkins St.
Whitehorse, YT Y1A 1X6 Canada
867-668-5678 Fax: 867-668-6637
E-mail: ycs@ycs.yk.ca
URL: www.yukonconservation.org
Scope: Regional
Contact Information: Phone: 867-668-5678

Yukon Fish & Game Association 2012 Annual Meeting, Banquet, & Awards

Location: Yukon Territory
Sponsor/Contact: Yukon Fish & Game Association
509 Strickland St.
Whitehorse, YT Y1A 2K5
867-667-4263 Fax: 867-667-4237
URL: www.yukonfga.ca
Contact Information: Yukon Fish & Game Association Office, Phone: 867-667-4263, E-mail: yfga@klondiker.com

2013

January

Fraser Valley Labour Council 2013 Annual General Meeting
Date: January 2013
Location: British Columbia
Sponsor/Contact: Fraser Valley Labour Council
#202, 9292 - 200th St.
Langley, BC V1M 3A6
604-314-9867 Fax: 604-430-6762
E-mail: bharder@usw.ca
URL: www.fvlc.ca
Scope: Local
Contact Information: Secretary: Pamela Willingshofer, E-mail: kidogo@shaw.ca

February

American Association for the Advancement of Science 2013 Annual Meeting
Date: February 14-18, 2013
Location: Boston, MA USA
Sponsor/Contact: American Association for the Advancement of Science
1200 New York Ave. NW
Washington, DC USA
202-326-6440
E-mail: membership@aaas.org; media@aaas.org; development@aaas.org
URL: www.aaas.org
Scope: International
Purpose: Information for scientists, engineers, educators, & policy-makers
Contact Information: Phone: 202-326-6450; Fax: 202-289-4021; E-mail: meetings.aaas.org; Director, Annual Meeting: Barbara Rice, E-mail: brice.aaas.org; Manager, Marketing, Exhibits, & Sponsors: Jill Perla, E-mail: jperla.aaas.org; Meetings Manager: Nicole Maylett, E-mail: nmaylett.aaas.org

Ontario Good Roads Association / Rural Ontario Municipal Association 2013 Combined Conference
Date: February 24-27, 2013
Location: Ontario
Sponsor/Contact: Ontario Good Roads Association
#2, 6355 Kennedy Rd.
Mississauga, ON L5T 2L5
905-795-2555 Fax: 905-795-2660
E-mail: info@ogra.org
URL: www.ogra.org
Scope: Provincial
Purpose: Information about current municipal issues, business meetings, workshops, a trade show, & networking events
Anticipated Attendance: 1500+
Contact Information: Ontario Good Roads Association, Phone: 905-795-2555; Fax: 905-795-2660

March

Institute of Food Technologists 2013 Annual Wellness Conference
Date: March 2013
Location: , USA
Sponsor/Contact: Institute of Food Technologists
#1000, 525 West Van Buren
Chicago, IL
312-782-8424 Fax: 312-782-8348
E-mail: info@ift.org; sales@ift.org
URL: www.ift.org
Scope: International
Purpose: Information about emerging trends in the food industry & the health & wellness sector
Anticipated Attendance: 300+
Contact Information: Manager, Knowledge & Learning Experiences: George Miller, Phone: 312.604.0263, Fax: 312.596.5663, E-mail: wellness@ift.org

Saskatchewan Association of Rural Municipalities 2013 Annual Convention
Date: March 11-13, 2013
Location: Saskatoon, SK
Sponsor/Contact: Saskatchewan Association of Rural Municipalities
2075 Hamilton St.
Regina, SK S4P 2E1 Canada
306-757-3577 Fax: 306-565-2141
E-mail: sarm@sarm.ca
URL: www.sarm.ca
Scope: Provincial

Society of Toxicology 52nd Annual Meeting & ToxExpo
Date: March 10-14, 2013
Location: Henry B. Gonzalez Convention Center
San Antonio, TX USA
Sponsor/Contact: Society of Toxicology
#300, 1821 Michael Faraday Dr.
Reston, VA USA
703-438-3115 Fax: 703-438-3113
E-mail: sothq@toxicology.org
URL: www.toxicology.org
Scope: International
Purpose: Toxicology meeting & exhibition
Anticipated Attendance: 6500
Contact Information: Phone: 703-438-3115; Fax: 703-438-3113; E-mail: sothq@toxicology.org

April

Association of Professional Engineers, Geologists & Geophysicists of Alberta 2013 Annual Conference & Annual General Meeting
Date: April 2013
Location: Alberta
Sponsor/Contact: Association of Professional Engineers, Geologists & Geophysicists of Alberta
Scotia One
#1500, 10060 Jasper Ave. NW
Edmonton, AB T5J 4A2
780-426-3990 Fax: 780-426-1877
E-mail: email@apegga.org
URL: www.apegga.org
Scope: Provincial
Purpose: An annual gathering in Calgary or Edmonton, featuring professional development activities & other conference events
Contact Information: Manager, Communications: Philip Mulder, Phone: 780-426-3990, ext. 2809, Fax: 780-425-1722, E-mail: pmulder@apegga.org; Manager, Human Resources & Professional Development: Nancy Toth, Phone: 780-426-3990, ext. 2811, Fax: 780-425-1722, E-mail: ntoth@apegga.org

Northwestern Ontario Municipal Association 2013 Annual General Meeting & Conference
Date: April 2013
Location: Ontario
Sponsor/Contact: Northwestern Ontario Municipal Association
P.O. Box 10308
Thunder Bay, ON P7B 6T8
807-683-6662
E-mail: admin@noma.on.ca
URL: www.noma.on.ca
Scope: Local
Purpose: A meeting which is held alternatively in the association's three districts (Kenora, Rain River, or Thunder Bay), featuring informative presentations & networking opportunities
Anticipated Attendance: 180
Contact Information: NOMA Executive Director, Phone: 807-683-6662, E-mail: admin@noma.on.ca

Petroleum Services Association of Canada 2013 Annual Spring Conference
Date: April 2013
Location: Red Deer, AB
Sponsor/Contact: Petroleum Services Association of Canada
#1150, 800 - 6 Ave. SW
Calgary, AB T2P 3G3
403-264-4195 Fax: 403-263-7174
E-mail: info@psac.ca
URL: www.psac.ca
Scope: National
Purpose: A meeting for petroleum service industry workers
Contact Information: Manager, Meetings & Events: Heather Doyle, Phone: 403-213-2796, E-mail: hdoyle@psac.ca

May

American Industrial Hygiene Conference & Exposition 2013
Date: May 18-23, 2013
Location: Palais des congrès (Convention Centre)
Montréal, QC
Sponsor/Contact: American Industrial Hygiene Association
#250, 2700 Prosperity Ave.
Fairfax, VA USA
703-849-8888 Fax: 703-207-3561
E-mail: infonet@aiha.org
URL: www.aiha.org
Scope: International
Contact Information: Manager, Meetings: Susan Dunbar, Phone: 703-846-0746, E-mail: sdunbar@aiha.org; Coordinator, Meetings: Stephanie Vichness, Phone: 703-846-0754, E-mail: svichness@aiha.org; Manager, Exposition: Caroline Lacey, Phone: 703-846-0748, E-mail: clacey@aiha.org

Canadian Society for Civil Engineering 2013 Annual General Meeting & Conference
Date: May 29 - June 1, 2013
Location: Montréal, QC
Sponsor/Contact: Canadian Society for Civil Engineering
4877, rue Sherbrooke ouest
Montréal, QC H3Z 1G9
514-933-2634 Fax: 514-933-3504
E-mail: info@csce.ca; membership@csce.ca
URL: www.csce.ca
Scope: National

Geological Association of Canada (GAC) & the Mineralogical Association of Canada (MAC) 2013 Joint Annual Meeting
Date: May 22-24, 2013
Location: Winnipeg, MB
Sponsor/Contact: Geological Association of Canada
Department of Earth Sciences, Memorial University of Newfoundland
#ER4063, Alexander Murray Bldg.
St. John's, NL A1B 3X5
709-737-7660 Fax: 709-737-2532
E-mail: gac@mun.ca; gacpublications@mun.ca (GEOLOG newsmagazine)
URL: www.gac.ca
Scope: National
Purpose: An annual gathering with a technical program, exhibits, & special events
Contact Information: Communications Chair: Tim Corkery, Phone: 204-945-6554, Fax: 204-945-1406; Finance & Administration Manager: Karen Johnston, Phone: 709-864-2399, E-mail: kajohnston@mun.ca

Trade Shows, Conferences and Seminars

June

American Water Works Association 2013 132nd Annual Conference & Exposition
Date: June 9-13, 2013
Location: Denver, CO USA
Sponsor/Contact: American Water Works Association
6666 West Quincy Ave.
Denver, CO USA
303-794-7711 Fax: 303-347-0804
E-mail: custsvc@awwa.org
URL: www.awwa.org
Scope: International
Purpose: Education & an exposition for water professionals
Contact Information: Director of Conferences & Events: April DeBaker, E-mail: adebaker@awwa.org; Manager, Conference & Exhibits: Lynn Lyons, E-mail: llyons@awwa.org; Conference & Promotion Manager: Joanne Gaglia, E-mail: jgaglia@awwa.org; Event Operations Supervisor: Lisa Star, E-mail: lstar@awwa.org

Canadian Society for Mechanical Engineering 2013 24th Biennial Canadian Congress of Applied Mechanics (CANCAM)

Sponsor/Contact: Canadian Society for Mechanical Engineering
1295 Hwy. 2 East
Kingston, ON K7L 4V1
613-547-5989 Fax: 613-547-0195
E-mail: csme@cogeco.ca
URL: www.csme-scgm.ca
Scope: National
Purpose: A conference for researchers in mechanical, electro-mechanical, civil, manufacturing, & aerospace engineering, as well as applied mathematics
Contact Information: Canadian Society for Mechanical Engineering, E-mail: csme@cogeco.ca

Local Government Management Association of British Columbia 2013 Annual General Meeting & Conference
Date: June 10-14, 2013
Location: Delta Grand Okanagan
Kelowna, BC
Sponsor/Contact: Local Government Management Association of British Columbia
Central Building
620 View St., 7th Fl.
Victoria, BC V8W 1J6
250-383-7032 Fax: 250-384-4879
E-mail: office@lgma.ca; editor@lgma.ca (magazine); ads@lgma.ca
URL: www.lgma.ca
Scope: Provincial
Purpose: A conference plus a tradeshow, featuring suppliers providing products & services to the local government sector in British Columbia
Anticipated Attendance: 400-500
Contact Information: Program Coordinator: Ana Fuller, Phone: 250-383-7032, ext. 227, Fax: 250-383-4879, E-mail: afuller@lgma.ca

July

Canadian Association of Animal Health Technologists & Technicians 2013 24th Annual General Meeting
Date: July 11-14, 2013
Location: The Fairmont Empress Hotel
Victoria, BC
Sponsor/Contact: Canadian Association of Animal Health Technologists & Technicians
339 Booth St.
Ottawa, ON K1R 7K1
800-567-2862
E-mail: info@caahtt-acttsa.ca
URL: www.caahtt-acttsa.ca
Scope: National
Purpose: A meeting usually held in partnership with the Canadian Veterinary Medical Association Convention, featuring full inclusion of technicians in the scientific program
Contact Information: Conventions & Special Programs Assistant: Sarah M. Cunningham, Phone: 613-236-1162, ext. 121, Fax: 613-236-9681, E-mail: scunningham@cvma-acmv.org

Institute of Food Technologists 2013 Annual Meeting & Food Expo
Date: July 13-16, 2013
Location: Chicago, IL USA
Sponsor/Contact: Institute of Food Technologists
#1000, 525 West Van Buren
Chicago, IL
312-782-8424 Fax: 312-782-8348
E-mail: info@ift.org; sales@ift.org
URL: www.ift.org
Scope: International
Purpose: An event featuring the IFT Food Expo, where more than 900 exhibitors showcase new products, tools, techniques, & trends for professionals involved in food science & technology
Anticipated Attendance: 21,500+
Contact Information: Vice-President, Meetings & Events: Heidi Voorhees, CAE, E-mail: havoorhees@ift.org; Media Inquiries, E-mail: media@ift.org

August

Association of Municipalities of Ontario 2013 Annual Conference
Date: August 18-21, 2013
Location: Ontario
Sponsor/Contact: Association of Municipalities of Ontario
#801, 200 University Ave.
Toronto, ON M5H 3C6
416-971-9856 Fax: 416-971-6191
E-mail: amo@amo.on.ca; municom@amo.on.ca; policy@amo.on.ca
URL: www.amo.on.ca
Scope: Provincial
Purpose: A yearly gathering of municipal government officials to discuss current issues
Contact Information: Special Events, Phone: 416-971-9856, ext. 330, E-mail: events@amo.on.ca

Canadian Medical Association 2013 146th Annual Meeting
Date: August 18-21, 2013
Location: Calgary, AB
Sponsor/Contact: Canadian Medical Association
1867 Alta Vista Dr.
Ottawa, ON K1G 5W8
613-731-8610 Fax: 613-236-8864
E-mail: cmamsc@cma.ca; cmatechsupport@cma.ca (technical support)
URL: www.cma.ca
Scope: National
Purpose: Featuring scientific & educational sessions to promote the medical & related arts
Contact Information: Registration Officer, Phone: 1-800-663-7336, ext. 2383, E-mail: gcregistrations@cma.ca

Institute of Transportation Engineers 2013 Annual Meeting & Exhibit
Date: August 4-7, 2013
Location: Sheraton Boston & Hynes Convention Ctr.
Boston, MA USA
Sponsor/Contact: Institute of Transportation Engineers
#300, 1099 - 14th St. NW
Washington, DC USA
202-289-0222 Fax: 202-289-7722
E-mail: ite_staff@ite.org
URL: www.ite.org
Scope: International
Contact Information: Contact, Registration Information: Sallie C. Dollins, E-mail: sdollins@ite.org; Contact, Technical Program: Aliyah N. Horton, E-mail: ahorton@ite.org; Contact, Exhibits: Christina Garneski, E-mail: cgarneski@ite.org; Contact, Paper Submittals: Eunice Chege, E-mail: echege@ite.org

September

The American Association of Bovine Practitioners 2013 Annual Conference
Date: September 19-21, 2013
Location: Milwaukee, WI USA
Sponsor/Contact: American Association of Bovine Practitioners
P.O. Box 3610
#802, 3320 Skyway Dr.
Auburn, AL USA
334-821-0442 Fax: 334-821-9532
E-mail: aabphq@aabp.org
URL: www.aabp.org
Scope: International

Union of British Columbia Municipalities 2013 Annual Convention
Date: September 16-20, 2013
Location: Vancouver Convention Centre
Vancouver, BC
Sponsor/Contact: Union of British Columbia Municipalities
#60, 10551 Shellbridge Way
Richmond, BC V6X 2W9 Canada
604-270-8226 Fax: 604-270-9116
E-mail: ubcm@civicnet.bc.ca
URL: www.civicnet.bc.ca
Scope: Provincial

Western Canada Water 2013 65th Annual Conference & Exhibition
Date: September 17-20, 2013
Location: Edmonton, AB
Sponsor/Contact: Western Canada Water
P.O. Box 1708
126 - 3rd Ave. West
Cochrane, AB T4C 1B6
403-709-0064 Fax: 403-709-0068
E-mail: member@wcwwa.ca
URL: www.wcwwa.ca
Scope: Regional
Purpose: A technical program, a keynote speaker, a trade show, & opportunities to network for utility managers & operators, municipal & provincial government representatives, consulting engineers
Anticipated Attendance: 500+
Contact Information: Western Canada Water, Toll-Free Phone: 1-877-283-2003, Toll-Free Fax: 1-877-283-2007, E-mail: member@wcwwa.ca

October

Metallurgy & Materials Society of the Canadian Institute of Mining, Metallurgy & Petroleum COM 2013: 52nd Annual Conference of Metallurgists
Date: October 27-31, 2013
Location: Palais des congrès de Montréal, Québec
Montréal, QC
Sponsor/Contact: Metallurgy & Materials Society of the Canadian Institute of Mining, Metallurgy & Petroleum
#1250, 3500, boul de Maisonneuve ouest
Montréal, QC H3Z 3C1
514-939-2710
URL: www.metsoc.org
Scope: International
Purpose: A materials science & technology conference & exhibition, combined with annual meeting
Contact Information: Manager, Administration & Meetings: Brigitte Farah, Phone: 514-939-2710, ext. 1329, Fax: 514-939-2714, E-mail: bfarah@cim.org

National Association for Environmental Management 2013 21st Annual EHS Management Forum
Date: October 23-25, 2013
Location: Fairmont Queen Elizabeth
Montréal, QC
Sponsor/Contact: National Association for Environmental Management
#1002, 1612 K St. NW
Washington, DC USA

202-986-6616 Fax: 202-530-4408
E-mail: programs@naem.org
URL: www.naem.org
Scope: International
Purpose: An international gathering of environmental, health & safety, & sustainability practitioners, with opportunities for benchmarking, best-practice sharing, & networking
Anticipated Attendance: 500+
Contact Information: E-mail: programs@naem.org

Water Environment Federation WEFTEC 2013: 86th Annual Water Environment Federation Technical Exhibition & Conference
Date: October 5-9, 2013
Location: McCormick Place
Chicago, IL USA
Sponsor/Contact: Water Environment Federation
601 Wythe St.
Alexandria, VA USA
703-684-2400 Fax: 703-684-2492
E-mail: csc@wef.org
URL: www.wef.org
Scope: International
Purpose: A learning & networking opportunity for water & wastewater professionals from around the world
Anticipated Attendance: 18,000
Contact Information: Membership Information, Toll-Free Phone: 1-800-666-0206, International Phone: +44 120-679-6351 or 571-830-1545

November

Canadian Urban Transit Association 2013 Fall Conference & Trans-Expo
Date: November 2013
Location: Calgary, AB
Sponsor/Contact: Canadian Urban Transit Association
#1401, 55 York St.
Toronto, ON M5J 1R7
416-365-9800 Fax: 416-365-1295
E-mail: transit@cutaactu.ca
URL: www.cutaactu.ca
Scope: National
Purpose: A technical meeting which features subjects such as emission standards & new technologies
Contact Information: Conference Specialist: Anna Maria Schell, Phone: 416-365-9800, ext. 116

Greenbuild 2013 International Conference & Expo
Date: November 20-22, 2013
Location: Philadelphia, PA USA
Sponsor/Contact: Canada Green Building Council
#202, 47 Clarence St.
Ottawa, ON K1N 9K1
613-241-1184 Fax: 613-241-4782
E-mail: info@cagbc.org; education@cagbc.org
URL: www.cagbc.org
Scope: International
Purpose: An educational event, featuring a showcase of new & innovative products & services for the green building industry
Contact Information: General Inquiries, E-mail: info@greenbuildexpo.org

Municipal Engineers Association 2013 Annual General Meeting & Workshop
Date: November 2013
Sponsor/Contact: Municipal Engineers Association
#2, 6355 Kennedy Rd.
Mississauga, ON L5T 2L5
905-795-2555 Fax: 905-795-2660
E-mail: info@municipalengineers.on.ca
URL: www.municipalengineers.on.ca
Scope: Provincial
Purpose: A workshop & business meeting during three days each November
Contact Information: Office of the President, Phone: 905-795-2555, Fax: 905-795-2660

Saskatchewan Association of Rural Municipalities 2013 Midterm Convention
Date: November 6-7, 2013
Location: Regina, SK
Sponsor/Contact: Saskatchewan Association of Rural Municipalities
2075 Hamilton St.
Regina, SK S4P 2E1 Canada
306-757-3577 Fax: 306-565-2141
E-mail: sarm@sarm.ca
URL: www.sarm.ca
Scope: Provincial

Other Conferences in 2013

Air Transport Association of Canada 2013 Annual Spring Event

Sponsor/Contact: Air Transport Association of Canada
#700, 255 Albert St.
Ottawa, ON K1P 6A9
613-233-7727 Fax: 613-230-8648
E-mail: atac@atac.ca
URL: www.atac.ca
Scope: National
Purpose: An industry symposium, committee meetings, & a reception with other ATAC members & invited industry & government guests

Alberta Recreation & Parks Association 2013 Annual Conference & Energize Workshop

Location: Alberta
Sponsor/Contact: Alberta Recreation & Parks Association
11759 Groat Rd.
Edmonton, AB T5M 3K6 Canada
780-415-1745 Fax: 780-451-7915
E-mail: arpa@arpaonline.ca
URL: www.arpaonline.ca
Scope: Regional
Purpose: An educational events for both rural & urban professionals from Alberta & western Canada
Anticipated Attendance: 400+
Contact Information: Event Planner: Brenda Hanson, Phone: 780-643-1255, E-mail: bhanson@arpaonline.ca

Alberta Recreation & Parks Association 2013 Parks Forum

Location: Alberta
Sponsor/Contact: Alberta Recreation & Parks Association
11759 Groat Rd.
Edmonton, AB T5M 3K6 Canada
780-415-1745 Fax: 780-451-7915
E-mail: arpa@arpaonline.ca
URL: www.arpaonline.ca
Scope: Regional
Purpose: An event exploring issues & opportunities for municipal & provincial government parks & open space practitioners & their stakeholders
Contact Information: Forum Contact: Dan Chambers, E-mail: dchambers@arpaonline.ca

Alberta Society of Professional Biologists 2013 Annual Conference & General Meeting

Location: Alberta
Sponsor/Contact: Alberta Society of Professional Biologists
P.O. Box 21104
Edmonton, AB T6R 2V4
780-434-5765 Fax: 780-413-0076
E-mail: pbiol@aspb.ab.ca
URL: www.aspb.ab.ca
Scope: Provincial
Contact Information: Association & Event Coordinator: Joy Sager, Phone: 780-434-5765, E-mail: joy@managewise.ca; Membership & Communications Coordinator: Shauna Prokopchuk, Phone: 780-434-5765, E-mail: shauna@managewise.ca

American Society of Mechanical Engineers 2013 58th Turbo Expo

Sponsor/Contact: American Society of Mechanical Engineers
3 Park Ave.
New York, NY USA
800-843-2763
E-mail: infocentral@asme.org
URL: www.asme.org
Scope: International
Purpose: An international gas turbine technical conference & exposition for turbomachinery professionals to share information about gas turbine technology, research & development, & application
Anticipated Attendance: 3000
Contact Information: Turbo Expo Contact: Martha Quinlin, E-mail: igti@asme.org; Program Contact: Stephanie (Sears) Partain: Partains@asme.org; Exposition & Sponsoship Contact: Kristin Barranger, E-mail: barrangerk@asme.org

Annual Smart Grid Interoperability 2013 4th Annual Summit

Sponsor/Contact: Canadian Electricity Association
#1100, 350 Sparks St.
Ottawa, ON K1R 7S8 Canada
613-230-9263 Fax: 613-230-9326
E-mail: info@electricity.ca
URL: www.electricity.ca
Scope: National
Purpose: An event for attendees to collaborate with regulators, to network with representatives from utilities throughout North America, & to learn from guest speakers contributing & implementing grid interop

Aquaculture Canada 2013: The Aquaculture Association of Canada's Annual Conference & General Meeting

Sponsor/Contact: Aquaculture Association of Canada
16 Lobster Lane
St. Andrews, NB E5B 3T6
506-529-4766 Fax: 506-529-4609
E-mail: aac@dfo-mpo.gc.ca
URL: www.aquacultureassociation.ca
Scope: National
Purpose: An opportunity to learn about recent developments in all aspects of aquaculture
Contact Information: Association Office Manager: Susan Waddy, Phone: 506-529-4766, E-mail: Susan.Waddy@dfo-mpo.gc.ca

Association of Power Producers of Ontario 2013: 25th Annual Canadian Power

Location: Ontario
Sponsor/Contact: Association of Power Producers of Ontario
P.O. Box 1084 Stn. F
#1602, 25 Adelaide St. East
Toronto, ON M5C 3A1
416-322-6549 Fax: 416-481-5785
E-mail: appro@appro.org; marketing@appro.org
URL: www.appro.org
Scope: Provincial
Purpose: An annual autumn conference to discuss recent issues in the energy sector
Contact Information: E-mail: appro@appro.org

Association of Professional Biology 2013 Annual Applied Biology Conference & Trade Show & Annual General Meeting

Location: British Columbia
Sponsor/Contact: Association of Professional Biology
#300, 1095 McKenzie Ave.
Victoria, BC V8P 2L5
250-483-4283 Fax: 250-483-3439
E-mail: apbbc@apbbc.bc.ca
URL: www.apbbc.bc.ca

Trade Shows, Conferences and Seminars

Scope: Provincial
Purpose: Part of the event is the annual general meeting, featuring reports from the association executive & committee chairs, the auditor's report & financial statement, resolutions, & new business
Contact Information: Managing Director & Registrar: Megan Hanacek, E-mail: managingdirector@apbbc.bc.ca

Association of Professional Engineers & Geoscientists of British Columbia 2013 Conference & Annual General Meeting

Location: British Columbia
Sponsor/Contact: Association of Professional Engineers & Geoscientists of British Columbia
#200, 4010 Regent St.
Burnaby, BC V5C 6N2
604-430-8035 Fax: 604-430-8085
E-mail: apeginfo@apeg.bc.ca; communication@apeg.bc.ca
URL: www.apeg.bc.ca
Scope: Provincial
Purpose: A chance to learn & network with colleagues & suppliers during business & technical sessions, a trade exhibition, & social events
Anticipated Attendance: 700+
Contact Information: Marketing Information, Phone: 604-412-4860, ext. 4860

Atlantic Canada Water & Wastewater Association 2013 66th Annual Conference

Location: Halifax, NS
Sponsor/Contact: Atlantic Canada Water & Wastewater Association
P.O. Box 41002
Dartmouth, NS B2Y 4P7 Canada
902-434-6002 Fax: 902-435-7796
E-mail: acwwa@hfx.andara.com
URL: www.acwwa.ca
Scope: Regional
Purpose: Featuring a trade show, educational opportunities, & networking events for water professionals from Atlantic Canada
Anticipated Attendance: 260-340
Contact Information: Technical Director: Margaret Walsh, PhD., P.Eng., E-mail: mwalsh2@dal.ca

British Columbia Nature (Federation of British Columbia Naturalists) 2013 Nature Conference & Annual General Meeting

Location: British Columbia
Sponsor/Contact: British Columbia Nature (Federation of British Columbia Naturalists)
c/o Parks Heritage Centre
1620 Mount Seymour Rd.
North Vancouver, BC V7G 2R9
604-985-3057
E-mail: manager@bcnature.ca
URL: www.bcnature.ca
Scope: Provincial
Purpose: Conference sessions, a keynote speaker, field trips, social events, & annual meetings
Contact Information: Office Manager: Betty Davison, E-mail: manager@bcnature.ca

British Columbia Recreation & Parks Association 2013 36th Annual ProvincialParks & Grounds Spring Training Conference

Location: British Columbia
Sponsor/Contact: British Columbia Recreation & Parks Association
#101, 4664 Lougheed Hwy.
Burnaby, BC V5C 5T5
604-629-0965 Fax: 604-629-2651
E-mail: bcrpa@bcrpa.bc.ca; registration@bcrpa.bc.ca
URL: www.bcrpa.bc.ca
Scope: Provincial
Purpose: Continuing education sessions that cover a wide range of interests for parks & grounds professionals

Contact Information: Parks & Recreation Program Coordinator: Heather Muter, Phone: 604-629-0965, ext. 229. E-mail: hmuter@bcrpa.bc.ca

British Columbia Recreation & Parks Association 2013 Provincial Aquatics Conference

Location: British Columbia
Sponsor/Contact: British Columbia Recreation & Parks Association
#101, 4664 Lougheed Hwy.
Burnaby, BC V5C 5T5
604-629-0965 Fax: 604-629-2651
E-mail: bcrpa@bcrpa.bc.ca; registration@bcrpa.bc.ca
URL: www.bcrpa.bc.ca
Scope: Provincial
Purpose: A two-day conference which occurs every two years, presenting operations, programming, & best practices for aquatics professionals
Contact Information: Parks & Recreation Program Coordinator: Heather Muter, Phone: 604-629-0965, ext. 229; E-mail: hmuter@bcrpa.bc.ca

British Columbia Recreation & Parks Association 2013 Symposium

Location: British Columbia
Sponsor/Contact: British Columbia Recreation & Parks Association
#101, 4664 Lougheed Hwy.
Burnaby, BC V5C 5T5
604-629-0965 Fax: 604-629-2651
E-mail: bcrpa@bcrpa.bc.ca; registration@bcrpa.bc.ca
URL: www.bcrpa.bc.ca
Scope: Provincial
Purpose: An annual meeting of interest to parks & recreation professionals & volunteers, as well as elected officials from across British Columbia
Anticipated Attendance: 400+

British Columbia Water & Waste Association 2013 41st Annual Conference & Trade Show

Location: British Columbia
Sponsor/Contact: British Columbia Water & Waste Association
#221, 8678 Greenall Ave.
Burnaby, BC V5J 3M6
604-433-4389 Fax: 604-433-9859
E-mail: contact@bcwwa.org
URL: www.bcwwa.org
Scope: Provincial
Purpose: Featuring technical presentations & the chance to view the latest products in the water & waste fields
Anticipated Attendance: 1000
Contact Information: Event Coordinator: Winnie Tsang, Phone: 604-433-4389, ext. 232, E-mail: wtsang@bcwwa.org

Canadian Association of Chemical Distributors 2013 27th Annual General Meeting

Sponsor/Contact: Canadian Association of Chemical Distributors
349 Davis Rd., #A
Oakville, ON L6J 2X2
905-844-9140 Fax: 905-844-5706
URL: www.cacd.ca
Scope: National
Contact Information: Manager, Communications & Member Services: Catherine Wieckowska, Phone: 905-844-9140, E-mail: catherine@cacd.ca

Canadian Association of Geographers 2013 Annual Meeting & Conference

Location: Whitehorse, YK
Sponsor/Contact: Canadian Association of Geographers Department of Geography, McGill University
#425, 805, rue Sherbrooke ouest
Montréal, QC H3A 2K6

514-398-4946 Fax: 514-398-7437
E-mail: valerie.shoffey@cag-acg.ca (Executive Secretary)
URL: www.cag-acg.ca
Scope: National
Purpose: A business meeting & an educational programs, including the presentation of research, the exchange of ideas, exhibits, & field trips

Canadian Dam Association 2013 Annual Conference

Sponsor/Contact: Canadian Dam Association
P.O. Box 2281
Moose Jaw, SK S6TH 7W6
URL: www.cda.ca
Scope: National
Purpose: Information about the management, operations, & maintenance of conventional water dams & mining dams

Canadian Gas Association 2013 Biennial Technical Symposium

Sponsor/Contact: Canadian Gas Association
#809, 350 Sparks St.
Ottawa, ON K1R 7S8
613-748-0057 Fax: 613-748-9078
E-mail: info@cga.ca
URL: www.cga.ca
Scope: National
Purpose: A technical symposium organized by the Industrial Application of Gas Turbines Committee
Contact Information: E-mail: help@canavents.com

Canadian Health Libraries Association (CHLA) / Association des bibliothèques de la santé du Canada (ABSC) 2013 37th Annual Conference

Location: Saskatoon, SK
Sponsor/Contact: Canadian Health Libraries Association
39 River St.
Toronto, ON M5A 3P1
416-646-1600 Fax: 416-646-9460
E-mail: info@chla-absc.ca; pr@chla-absc.ca (Public Relations)
URL: www.chla-absc.ca
Scope: National
Purpose: A yearly May or June conference, featuring continuing education courses, lectures, a forum for health science librarians to share ideas, & an exhibit of products & services of interest to participants
Contact Information: Continuing Education, E-mail: ce@chla-absc.ca; Public Relations, E-mail: pr@chla-absc.ca

Canadian Institute of Mining, Metallurgy & Petroleum 2013 Annual Conference & Exhibition

Sponsor/Contact: Canadian Institute of Mining, Metallurgy & Petroleum
CIM National Office
#1250, 3500, boul de Maisonneuve ouest
Westmount, QC H3Z 3C1
514-939-2710 Fax: 514-939-2714
E-mail: cim@cim.org
URL: www.cim.org
Scope: National
Purpose: A mining event, featuring a technical program, workshops, field trips, a student program, & a social program
Contact Information: Meeting Coordinator: Chantal Murphy, Phone: 514-939-2710, E-mail: cmurphy@cim.org

Canadian Institute of Plumbing & Heating 2013 Annual Business Conference

Sponsor/Contact: Canadian Institute of Plumbing & Heating
#330, 295 The West Mall
Toronto, ON M9C 4Z4
416-695-0447 Fax: 416-695-0450
E-mail: info@ciph.com
URL: ww.ciph.com

Scope: National
Purpose: A business meeting for CIPH members, including manufacturers, distributors, wholesalers, manufacturers' agents, & associate service members
Contact Information: CIPH Phone: 416-695-0447, Toll-Free: 1-800-639-2474

Canadian Medical & Biological Engineering Society 2013 36th Annual National Conference

Sponsor/Contact: Canadian Medical & Biological Engineering Society
1485 Laperrière Ave.
Ottawa, ON K1Z 7S8
613-728-1759
E-mail: secretariat@cmbes.ca
URL: www.cmbes.ca
Scope: National
Purpose: An annual gathering of Canadian biomedical engineering professionals for continuing education & networking opportunities
Contact Information: Chair, Long-Term Conference Planning: Sarah Kelso, E-mail: skelso@hsc.mb.ca

Canadian Nuclear Society 2013 34th Annual Conference & 37th Annual CNS / CNA Student Conference

Sponsor/Contact: Canadian Nuclear Society
655 Bay St., 17th Fl.
Toronto, ON M5G 2K4
416-977-7620 Fax: 416-977-8131
E-mail: cns-snc@on.aibn.com
URL: www.cns-snc.ca
Scope: National
Purpose: A discussion of technical developments in subjects related to nuclear technology & its potential
Contact Information: Canadian Nuclear Society Office: Phone: 416-977-7620, E-mail: cns-snc@on.aibn.com

Canadian Physiological Society 2013 Annual Winter Meeting

Sponsor/Contact: Canadian Physiological Society
c/o Dr. Melanie Woodin, Dept. of Cell & Systems Biology, U. of Toronto
25 Harbord St.
Toronto, ON M5S 3G5
URL: www.cpsscp.ca
Scope: National
Purpose: An annual event with lectures & exhibits
Contact Information: Canadian Physiological Society Vice-President: Dr. Stephen M. Sims, Phone: 519-661-2111, ext. 83768, E-mail: stephen.sims@schulich.uwo.ca

Canadian Society of Exploration Geophysicists, Canadian Society of Petroleum Geologists & Canadian Well Logging Society 2013 Joint Annual Convention

Sponsor/Contact: Canadian Society of Exploration Geophysicists
#600, 640 - 8th Ave. SW
Calgary, AB T2P 1G7
403-262-0015
E-mail: cseg.office@shaw.ca
URL: www.cseg.ca
Scope: National
Purpose: Technical sessions & an exhibition, featuring new techologies & innovations in earth sciences
Contact Information: Chair, Joint Annual Convention Committee: Laurie Ross, E-mail: laurie.ross@divestco.com

Canadian Standards Association 2013 Annual Conference & Committee Week

Sponsor/Contact: Canadian Standards Association
#100, 5060 Spectrum Way
Mississauga, ON L4W 5N6
416-747-4000 Fax: 416-747-2473
E-mail: member@csa.ca; sales@csa.ca; seminars@csa.ca; elearning@csa.ca
URL: www.csa.ca
Scope: National
Purpose: Educational presentations & committee meetings
Anticipated Attendance: 500+
Contact Information: E-mail: conference@csa.ca

Canadian Urban Transit Association 2013 Annual Conference

Location: St. John's, NL
Sponsor/Contact: Canadian Urban Transit Association
#1401, 55 York St.
Toronto, ON M5J 1R7
416-365-9800 Fax: 416-365-1295
E-mail: transit@cutaactu.ca
URL: www.cutaactu.ca
Scope: National
Purpose: A yearly policy & management event held in May or June, of interest to transit managers, elected officials, & suppliers
Contact Information: Conference Specialist: Anna Maria Schell, Phone: 416-365-9800, ext. 116

Compost Council of Canada 2013 23rd Annual National Compost Conference

Sponsor/Contact: Compost Council of Canada
16 Northumberland St.
Toronto, ON M6H 1P7
416-535-0240 Fax: 416-536-9892
E-mail: info@compost.org
URL: www.compost.org
Scope: National
Purpose: Current developments in the composting industry, such as research, processing improvements, & community developments
Contact Information: E-mail: info@compost.org

Consulting Engineers of Alberta 2013 16th Annual Transportation Conference & Trade Show

Location: Alberta
Sponsor/Contact: Consulting Engineers of Alberta
Phipps-McKinnon Building
#870, 10020 - 101A Ave.
Edmonton, AB T5J 3G2
780-421-1852 Fax: 780-424-5225
E-mail: info@cea.ca
URL: www.cea.ca
Scope: Provincial
Purpose: Keynote speakers, forums, & workshops about transportation infrastructure in Alberta
Anticipated Attendance: 700+
Contact Information: Manager, Events & Communications: Hiju Song, E-mail: hsong@cea.ca

Consulting Engineers of Alberta 2013 35th Annual General Meeting

Location: Alberta
Sponsor/Contact: Consulting Engineers of Alberta
Phipps-McKinnon Building
#870, 10020 - 101A Ave.
Edmonton, AB T5J 3G2
780-421-1852 Fax: 780-424-5225
E-mail: info@cea.ca
URL: www.cea.ca
Scope: Provincial
Purpose: Presentations by guest speakers plus the business meeting for consulting engineers in Alberta
Contact Information: Manager, Events & Communications: Hiju Song, E-mail: hsong@cea.ca

Consulting Engineers of Alberta 2013 Annual Luncheon with the City of Edmonton Council

Location: Alberta
Sponsor/Contact: Consulting Engineers of Alberta
Phipps-McKinnon Building
#870, 10020 - 101A Ave.
Edmonton, AB T5J 3G2
780-421-1852 Fax: 780-424-5225
E-mail: info@cea.ca
URL: www.cea.ca
Scope: Provincial
Purpose: A meeting of Edmonton's mayor, city council, & senior administration with members of Consulting Engineers of Alberta to address interests & issues
Contact Information: Manager, Events & Communications: Hiju Song, Phone: 780-421-1852, E-mail: hsong@cea.ca

Consulting Engineers of British Columbia 2013 Annual General Meeting

Location: British Columbia
Sponsor/Contact: Consulting Engineers of British Columbia
#1258, 409 Granville St.
Vancouver, BC V6C 1T2
604-687-2811 Fax: 604-688-7110
E-mail: info@cebc.org
URL: www.cebc.org
Scope: Provincial
Purpose: Educational seminars, on issues affecting members, have included topics such as the Harmonized Sales Tax & its effects on project management as well as information about the Site C Dam Project
Contact Information: Phone: 604-687-2811; E-mail: events@cebc.org, info@cebc.org

Consulting Engineers of British Columbia 2013 Annual Transportation Conference

Location: British Columbia
Sponsor/Contact: Consulting Engineers of British Columbia
#1258, 409 Granville St.
Vancouver, BC V6C 1T2
604-687-2811 Fax: 604-688-7110
E-mail: info@cebc.org
URL: www.cebc.org
Scope: Provincial
Purpose: An event presenting educational & networking opportunities to enhance business development
Contact Information: Coordinator, Accounting & Events: Alla Samusevich, E-mail: alla@cebc.org, events@cebc.org

GLOBE Foundation 2013 7th Annual EPIC Sustainable Living Expo

Sponsor/Contact: GLOBE Foundation
World Trade Centre
#578, 999 Canada Pl.
Vancouver, BC V6C 3E1
604-695-5001 Fax: 604-695-5019
E-mail: info@globe.ca
URL: www.globe.ca
Scope: Regional
Purpose: A show for the general public, highlighting information, education, & shopping opportunities related to the most recent styles & advances in sustainable living
Anticipated Attendance: 16,000+
Contact Information: General Information: Phone: 604-695-5001, E-mail: info@epicexpo.com; Operations Information: Phone: 604-695-5008, E-mail: operations@epicexpo.com; Exhibit Sales Information: Phone: 604-695-5010, E-mail: exhibits@epicexpo.com; Sponsorship Information: E-mail: sponsor@epicexpo.com; Volunteer Information, E-mail: volunteers@epicexpo.com

Health Sciences Association of Alberta 2013 42nd Annual General Meeting

Location: Alberta
Sponsor/Contact: Health Sciences Association of Alberta
10212 - 112 St.
Edmonton, AB T5K 1M4

Trade Shows, Conferences and Seminars

780-488-0168 Fax: 780-488-0534
URL: www.hsaa.ca
Scope: Provincial
Contact Information: Communications Officer: Scott Pattison, E-mail: scottpat@hsaa.ca

International Heavy Haul Association 2013 International Conference

Sponsor/Contact: International Heavy Haul Association
2808 Forest Hills Crt.
Virginia Beach, USA
URL: www.ihha.net
Scope: International
Purpose: An international conference, occurring every four years, for delegates from around the world, where long & heavy trains operate, such as researchers in bulk haul railroading, engineering practitioners, & railway operations managers

Local Government Management Association of British Columbia 2013 Administrative Professionals Conference

Location: British Columbia
Sponsor/Contact: Local Government Management Association of British Columbia
Central Building
620 View St., 7th Fl.
Victoria, BC V8W 1J6
250-383-7032 Fax: 250-384-4879
E-mail: office@lgma.ca; editor@lgma.ca (magazine); ads@lgma.ca
URL: www.lgma.ca
Scope: Provincial
Purpose: Information sharing opportunities & networking events for administrative staff who work for local governments in British Columbia
Contact Information: Program Coordinator: Ana Fuller, Phone: 250-383-7032, ext. 227, Fax: 250-383-4879, E-mail: afuller@lgma.ca

Local Government Management Association of British Columbia 2013 CAO (Chief Administrative Officers) Forum

Location: British Columbia
Sponsor/Contact: Local Government Management Association of British Columbia
Central Building
620 View St., 7th Fl.
Victoria, BC V8W 1J6
250-383-7032 Fax: 250-384-4879
E-mail: office@lgma.ca; editor@lgma.ca (magazine); ads@lgma.ca
URL: www.lgma.ca
Scope: Provincial
Purpose: A yearly gathering of local government chief administrative officers from British Columbia for the chance to engage in interactive discussions with speakers & to talk with other chief administrative officers about topics of mutual concern
Contact Information: Program Coordinator: Ana Fuller, Phone: 250-383-7032, ext. 227, Fax: 250-383-4879, E-mail: afuller@lgma.ca

Maintenance & Engineering Society of The Canadian Institute of Mining, Metallurgy & Petroleum 2013 Maintenance Engineering/Mine Operators' Conference

Sponsor/Contact: Maintenance & Engineering Society of The Canadian Institute of Mining, Metallurgy & Petroleum
c/o Chair, Brad Kingston, Wardrop Engineering Inc.
725 Hewitson St.
Thunder Bay, ON P7B 6B5
807-345-5453
E-mail: brad.kingston@wardrop.com
URL: www.cim.org/med
Scope: National
Purpose: A bi-annual operators' conference for persons interested in discussing maintenance & engineering issues
Contact Information: Director, Conferences & Exhibitions, Phone: 514-939-2710, ext. 1308, E-mail: lbujold@cim.org; Meetings Coordinator: Chantal Murphy, Phone: 514-939-2710, ext. 1309, E-mail: cmurphy@cim.org

Manitoba Ozone Protection Industry Association 2013 19th Annual General Meeting

Location: Manitoba
Sponsor/Contact: Manitoba Ozone Protection Industry Association
1980B Main St.
Winnipeg, MB R2V 2B6 Canada
204-338-0804 Fax: 204-338-0810
E-mail: mopia@mts.net
URL: www.mopia.ca
Scope: Provincial
Purpose: The presentation of the annual report, featuring financial & executive reports

Metallurgy & Materials Society of the Canadian Institute of Mining, Metallurgy & Petroleum World Gold 2013 4th International Conference

Sponsor/Contact: Metallurgy & Materials Society of the Canadian Institute of Mining, Metallurgy & Petroleum
#1250, 3500, boul de Maisonneuve ouest
Montréal, QC H3Z 3C1
514-939-2710
URL: www.metsoc.org
Scope: International
Purpose: A conference held every two years, convened by the Canadian Institute of Mining, Metallurgy & Petroleum (CIM), the Australasian Institute of Mining & Metallurgy (AusIMM), & the Southern African Institute of Mining & Metallurgy (SAIMM)

Northwestern Ontario Municipal Association 2013 Annual Regional Conference

Location: Ontario
Sponsor/Contact: Northwestern Ontario Municipal Association
P.O. Box 10308
Thunder Bay, ON P7B 6T8
807-683-6662
E-mail: admin@noma.on.ca
URL: www.noma.on.ca
Scope: Local
Purpose: A meeting, held each September or October, for both full & associate members of the Northwestern Ontario Municipal Association
Contact Information: NOMA Executive Director, Phone: 807-683-6662, E-mail: admin@noma.on.ca

Ocean, Offshore, & Arctic Engineering 2013 32nd International Conference

Location: Nantes, France
Sponsor/Contact: American Society of Mechanical Engineers
3 Park Ave.
New York, NY USA
800-843-2763
E-mail: infocentral@asme.org
URL: www.asme.org
Scope: International

Ontario Environmental Network 2013 Annual General Meeting

Location: Ontario
Sponsor/Contact: Ontario Environmental Network
P.O. Box 1412 Stn. Main
North Bay, ON P1B 8K6
705-840-2888 Fax: 705-840-5862
E-mail: oen@oen.ca
URL: www.oen.ca
Scope: Provincial
Purpose: A gathering for members of the Ontario Environmental Network to cast votes
Contact Information: Ontario Environmental Network Coordinator: Phillip Penna, Phone: 705-840-2888

Ontario Medical Association, Sport Medicine Section 2013 Annual Symposium: Sport Med

Location: Ontario
Sponsor/Contact: Ontario Medical Association
#900, 150 Bloor St. West
Toronto, ON M5S 3C1
416-599-2580 Fax: 416-340-2944
E-mail: info@oma.org; membership@oma.org
URL: www.oma.org
Scope: Provincial
Purpose: Presentation of papers & the awarding of the J.C. Kennedy Award for the person who presents the best paper to combine orignality & scientific research
Contact Information: OMA Public Affairs & Communications Department Contact: Catherine Flaman, Phone: 416-340-2915

Ontario Small Urban Municipalities 2013 60th Annual Conference & Trade Show

Location: Ontario
Sponsor/Contact: Ontario Small Urban Municipalities c/o Association of Municipalities of Ontario
#801, 200 University Ave.
Toronto, ON M5H 3C6
416-971-9856 Fax: 416-971-6191
E-mail: amo@amo.on.ca
URL: www.amo.on.ca//AM/Template.cfm?Section=What_s_New7
Scope: Provincial
Anticipated Attendance: 175
Contact Information: OSUM Annual Conference & Trade Show Coordinator: Ted Blowes, Phone: 519-271-0250, ext. 241, E-mail: ted.b@quadro.net

Ontario Soil & Crop Improvement Association 2013 Provincial Annual Meeting

Location: Ontario
Sponsor/Contact: Ontario Soil & Crop Improvement Association
1 Stone Rd. West
Guelph, ON N1G 4Y2
519-826-4214 Fax: 519-826-4224
E-mail: oscia@ontariosoilcrop.org
URL: www.ontariosoilcrop.org
Scope: Provincial
Purpose: A yearly gathering for farmers & persons involved in agriculture in Ontario
Contact Information: Ontario Soil & Crop Improvement Association, E-mail: oscia@ontariosoilcrop.org

Ontario Sustainable Energy Association 2013 Annual General Meeting

Location: Ontario
Sponsor/Contact: Ontario Sustainable Energy Association
#201, 156 Front St. West
Toronto, ON M5J 2L6
416-977-4441 Fax: 416-977-4441
E-mail: info@ontario-sea.org; employment@ontario-sea.org
URL: www.ontario-sea.org
Scope: Provincial
Anticipated Attendance: 2950
Contact Information: Coordinator, Tradeshow, Events & Logistics: Nicole Risse, Phone: 416-977-4441, ext. 223, E-mail: Nicole@ontario-sea.org

Petroleum Services Association of Canada 2013 Annual General Meeting, Canadian Drilling Activity Forecast Session, & Industry Dinner

Sponsor/Contact: Petroleum Services Association of Canada
#1150, 800 - 6 Ave. SW
Calgary, AB T2P 3G3
403-264-4195 Fax: 403-263-7174
E-mail: info@psac.ca
URL: www.psac.ca
Scope: National
Purpose: A review of the association's year of activities & a drilling forecast for 2014
Contact Information: Manager, Meetings & Events: Heather Doyle, Phone: 403-213-2796, E-mail: hdoyle@psac.ca

Petroleum Services Association of Canada 2013 Annual Mid-Year Update

Sponsor/Contact: Petroleum Services Association of Canada
#1150, 800 - 6 Ave. SW
Calgary, AB T2P 3G3
403-264-4195 Fax: 403-263-7174
E-mail: info@psac.ca
URL: www.psac.ca
Scope: National
Purpose: An update of the Canadian Drilling Activity Forecast, provided by the Petroleum Services Association of Canada
Contact Information: Manager, Meetings & Events: Heather Doyle, Phone: 403-213-2796, E-mail: hdoyle@psac.ca

Photovoltaics Industry 2013 6th Annual Workshop

Sponsor/Contact: Solar & Sustainable Energy Society of Canada Inc.
c/o Frederic Pouyot
#173, 207 Bank St.
Ottawa, ON k2P 2N2
613-686-4474 Fax: 613-533-6550
E-mail: bruce@techonfoot.com
URL: www.sesci.ca
Scope: National
Purpose: Information about how to make photovoltaics happen in Canada, of interst to researchers, government representatives, industry representatives, & students

Recycling Council of Alberta Waste Reduction 2013 Conference

Location: Alberta
Sponsor/Contact: Recycling Council of Alberta
P.O. Box 23
Bluffton, AB T0C 0M0 Canada
403-843-6563 Fax: 403-843-4156
E-mail: info@recycle.ab.ca
URL: www.recycle.ab.ca
Scope: Provincial
Purpose: Sessions & speakers on waste reduction topics
Contact Information: Phone: 403-843-6563; E-mail: info@recycle.ab.ca

Saskatchewan Camping Association 2013 Annual General Meeting

Location: Saskatchewan
Sponsor/Contact: Saskatchewan Camping Association
3950 Castle Rd.
Regina, SK S4S 6A4
306-586-4026 Fax: 306-790-8634
E-mail: info@saskcamping.ca
URL: www.saskcamping.ca
Scope: Provincial
Purpose: Featuring the election of the board of directors of the association
Contact Information: Executive Director: Donna Wilkinson, Phone: 306-586-4026, E-mail: donnaw@sasktel.net

Society of Environmental Toxicology & Chemistry North America 2013 34th Annual Meeting

Sponsor/Contact: Society of Environmental Toxicology & Chemistry
SETAC Asia / Pacific, SETAC Latin America, & SETAC North America
1010 - 12th Ave. North
Pensacola, FL USA
850-469-1500 Fax: 850-469-9778
E-mail: setac@setac.org
URL: www.setac.org
Scope: International
Anticipated Attendance: 2500

Wastewater Management 2013 5th Biennial Canadian National Conference

Sponsor/Contact: Canadian Water & Wastewater Association
#11, 1010 Polytek Rd.
Ottawa, ON K1J 9H9
613-747-0524 Fax: 613-747-0523
E-mail: tdellison@cwwa.ca
URL: www.cwwa.ca
Scope: National
Purpose: An informative event for provincial, territorial, & federal departmental officials responsible for related policies & regulations; wastewater collection or treatment system managers & operators; consultants involved in wastewater engineering or management projects; academics; industrial, commercial, & institutional customers of water & wastewater services; & environmental stakeholder groups
Contact Information: Phone: 613-747-0524; Fax: 613-747-0523; E-mail: admin@cwwa.ca

Water Efficiency & Conservation 2013 5th Biennial Conference

Sponsor/Contact: Canadian Water & Wastewater Association
#11, 1010 Polytek Rd.
Ottawa, ON K1J 9H9
613-747-0524 Fax: 613-747-0523
E-mail: tdellison@cwwa.ca
URL: www.cwwa.ca
Scope: National
Purpose: An exchange of news & views from Canadian utility conservation specialists
Contact Information: Phone: 613-747-0524; Fax: 613-747-0523; E-mail: admin@cwwa.ca

Water Environment Association of Ontario 2013 42nd Annual Technical Symposium & Exhibition

Location: Ontario
Sponsor/Contact: Water Environment Association of Ontario
P.O. Box 176
Milton, ON L9T 4N9
416-410-6933 Fax: 416-410-1626
E-mail: julie.vincent@weao.org
URL: www.weao.org
Scope: Provincial
Purpose: A conference featuring technical sessions, a keynote speaker, a student program, an awards presentation, & networking opportunities
Contact Information: Chair, Conference Committee: Rob Anderson, Phone: 905-660-9775, ext. 29, E-mail: rob@h2flow.com; Chair, Promotions & Event Planning: Anthony Abbruscato, Phone: 416-499-0090, ext. 73605, E-mail: anthony.abbruscato@ch2m.com

Westcoast Building & Hardware Show 2013

Location: British Columbia
Sponsor/Contact: Building Supply Industry Association of British Columbia
#2, 19299 - 94th Ave.
Surrey, BC V4N 4E6
604-513-2205 Fax: 604-513-2206
URL: www.bsiabc.ca
Scope: Provincial
Purpose: A trade show for members of the building supply industry, presenting educational opportunities & new & innovative products & services
Contact Information: Registration & Sponsorship Information, Phone: 604-513-2205, E-mail: info@bsiabc.ca

World Energy 2013 22nd Congress

Location: Daegu City, Republic of Korea
Sponsor/Contact: World Energy Council
Regency House
1-4 Warwick St., 5th Fl.
London, United Kingdom
E-mail: info@worldenergy.org
URL: www.worldenergy.org
Scope: International
Purpose: An international multi-energy forum
Anticipated Attendance: 4000+

2014

January

Western Retail Lumber Association 2014 Prairie Showcase Buying Show & Convention

Date: January 23-25, 2014
Location: Saskatoon, SK
Sponsor/Contact: Western Retail Lumber Association
Western Retail Lumber Association Inc.
#1004, 213 Notre Dame Ave.
Winnipeg, MB R3B 1N3
204-957-1077 Fax: 204-947-5195
E-mail: wrla@wrla.org
URL: www.wrla.org

February

Ontario Good Roads Association / Rural Ontario Municipal Association 2014 Combined Conference

Date: February 23-26, 2014
Location: Ontario
Sponsor/Contact: Ontario Good Roads Association
#2, 6355 Kennedy Rd.
Mississauga, ON L5T 2L5
905-795-2555 Fax: 905-795-2660
E-mail: info@ogra.org
URL: www.ogra.org
Scope: Provincial
Purpose: Workshops, information about current municipal issues, a trade show, & social events
Anticipated Attendance: 1500+
Contact Information: Ontario Good Roads Association, Phone: 905-795-2555; Fax: 905-795-2660

Other Conferences in 2014

GLOBE 2014 13th Biennial Conference & Trade Fair on Business & the Environment

Sponsor/Contact: GLOBE Foundation
World Trade Centre
#578, 999 Canada Pl.
Vancouver, BC V6C 3E1
604-695-5001 Fax: 604-695-5019
E-mail: info@globe.ca
URL: www.globe.ca
Scope: International
Purpose: A global gathering of government leaders, senior executives, & NGO representatives, from more than seventy countries, to share experiences & explore new opportunities during conference sessions & interactive networking opportunities, & to see the most recent environmental & clean technologies at the international trade show
Anticipated Attendance: 10,000+
Contact Information: General Information: Phone: 604-695-5001, Toll-Free Phone: 1-800-274-6097, E-mail: info@globeseries.com; Exhibiting Information, E-mail: sales@globeseries.com

Trade Shows, Conferences and Seminars

Institute of Food Technologists 2014 Annual Wellness Conference
Date: March 2014
Location: , USA
Sponsor/Contact: Institute of Food Technologists
#1000, 525 West Van Buren
Chicago, IL
312-782-8424 Fax: 312-782-8348
E-mail: info@ift.org; sales@ift.org
URL: www.ift.org
Scope: International
Purpose: Informative presentations plus exhibits of interest to food industry professionals in product development, brand management, & marketing
Anticipated Attendance: 300+
Contact Information: General Inquiries: info@ift.org; Conference Information, E-mail: wellness@ift.org

Society of Toxicology 53rd Annual Meeting & ToxExpo
Date: March 23-27, 2014
Location: Boston Convention & Exhibition Center
Boston, MA USA
Sponsor/Contact: Society of Toxicology
#300, 1821 Michael Faraday Dr.
Reston, VA USA
703-438-3115 Fax: 703-438-3113
E-mail: sothq@toxicology.org
URL: www.toxicology.org
Scope: International
Purpose: Toxicology meeting & exhibition
Anticipated Attendance: 6500
Contact Information: Phone: 703-438-3115; Fax: 703-438-3113; E-mail: sothq@toxicology.org

April

Petroleum Services Association of Canada 2014 Annual Spring Conference
Date: April 2014
Location: Red Deer, AB
Sponsor/Contact: Petroleum Services Association of Canada
#1150, 800 - 6 Ave. SW
Calgary, AB T2P 3G3
403-264-4195 Fax: 403-263-7174
E-mail: info@psac.ca
URL: www.psac.ca
Scope: National
Purpose: A gathering of petroleum service industry workers
Contact Information: Manager, Meetings & Events: Heather Doyle, Phone: 403-213-2796, E-mail: hdoyle@psac.ca

May

Canadian Labour Congress 2014 National Convention
Date: May 2014
Sponsor/Contact: Canadian Labour Congress
National Headquarters
2841 Riverside Dr.
Ottawa, ON K1V 8X7
613-521-3400 Fax: 613-521-4655
URL: www.canadianlabour.ca
Scope: National
Purpose: A convention for members of the labour movement to develop an Action Plan, based on committee reports, resolutions, & the discussion of policies

June

American Water Works Association 2014 133rd Annual Conference & Exposition
Date: June 8-12, 2014
Location: Boston, MA USA
Sponsor/Contact: American Water Works Association
6666 West Quincy Ave.
Denver, CO USA
303-794-7711 Fax: 303-347-0804
E-mail: custsvc@awwa.org
URL: www.awwa.org
Scope: International
Purpose: Information about water research & best practices for water professionals from around the globe
Contact Information: American Water Works Association, Phone: 800-926-7337, Fax: 303-347-0804, E-mail: awwamktg@awwa.org

Institute of Food Technologists 2014 Annual Meeting & Food Expo
Date: June 21-24, 2014
Location: New Orleans, LA USA
Sponsor/Contact: Institute of Food Technologists
#1000, 525 West Van Buren
Chicago, IL
312-782-8424 Fax: 312-782-8348
E-mail: info@ift.org; sales@ift.org
URL: www.ift.org
Scope: International
Purpose: An annual gathering of thousands of food professionals from around the world to participate in scientific sessions, poster sessions, the IFT Food Expo, an awards celebration, & networking events
Anticipated Attendance: 21,500+
Contact Information: General Inquiries: info@ift.org; Media Inquiries, E-mail: media@ift.org

July

International Union of Microbiological Societies 2014 XIV Congress
Date: July 27 - August 1, 2014
Location: Palais des congrès (Convention Centre)
Montréal, QC
Sponsor/Contact: International Union of Microbiological Societies
Centralbureau voor Schimmelcultures
P.O. Box 85167
Utrecht, Netherlands
E-mail: samson@cbs.knaw.nl
URL: www.iums.org
Scope: International
Purpose: Meetings of the three divisions of the International Union of Microbiological Societies

August

Canadian Medical Association 2014 147th Annual Meeting
Date: August 17-20, 2014
Location: Ottawa, ON
Sponsor/Contact: Canadian Medical Association
1867 Alta Vista Dr.
Ottawa, ON K1G 5W8
613-731-8610 Fax: 613-236-8864
E-mail: cmamsc@cma.ca; cmatechsupport@cma.ca (technical support)
URL: www.cma.ca
Scope: National
Purpose: A meeting, featuring a business session to consider business & matters referred by the General Council
Contact Information: Registration Officer, Phone: 1-800-663-7336, ext. 2383, E-mail: gcregistrations@cma.ca

Institute of Transportation Engineers 2014 Annual Meeting & Exhibit
Date: August 3-6, 2014
Location: Washington State Convention & Trade Ctr.
Seattle, WA USA
Sponsor/Contact: Institute of Transportation Engineers
#300, 1099 - 14th St. NW
Washington, DC USA
202-289-0222 Fax: 202-289-7722
E-mail: ite_staff@ite.org
URL: www.ite.org
Scope: International
Contact Information: Contact, Registration Information: Sallie C. Dollins, E-mail: sdollins@ite.org; Contact, Technical Program: Aliyah N. Horton, E-mail: ahorton@ite.org; Contact, Exhibits: Christina Garneski, E-mail: cgarneski@ite.org; Contact, Paper Submittals: Eunice Chege, E-mail: echege@ite.org

September

International Commission of Agricultural & Biosystems Engineering XVIII 2014 World Congress
Date: September 16-19, 2014
Location: Beijing, China
Sponsor/Contact: International Commission of Agricultural & Biosystems Engineering
c/o Dr. Takaaki Maekawa, School of Life & Environmental Sciences
1-1-1 Tennodai, University of Tsukuba
Tsukuba, Ibaraki, Japan
E-mail: biopro@sakura.cc.tsukuba.ac.jp
URL: www.cigr.org
Scope: International
Purpose: Agricultural & Biosystems Engineering - Upgrading Our Quality of Life
Contact Information: Congress Contact: Prof. Lanfang Zhang, Phone: 0086-10-64882358, E-mail: cigrwc2014@yahoo.cn

The American Association of Bovine Practitioners 2014 Annual Conference
Date: September 18-20, 2014
Location: Albuquerque, NM USA
Sponsor/Contact: American Association of Bovine Practitioners
P.O. Box 3610
#802, 3320 Skyway Dr.
Auburn, AL USA
334-821-0442 Fax: 334-821-9532
E-mail: aabphq@aabp.org
URL: www.aabp.org
Scope: International

Western Canada Water 2014 66th Annual Conference & Exhibition
Date: September 23-26, 2014
Location: Regina, SK
Sponsor/Contact: Western Canada Water
P.O. Box 1708
126 - 3rd Ave. West
Cochrane, AB T4C 1B6
403-709-0064 Fax: 403-709-0068
E-mail: member@wcwwa.ca
URL: www.wcwwa.ca
Scope: Regional
Purpose: A gathering of utility managers & operators, consulting engineers, & municipal & provincial government representatives for workshops, tours, a trade show, & the chance to network
Anticipated Attendance: 500+
Contact Information: Western Canada Water, Toll-Free Phone: 1-877-283-2003, Toll-Free Fax: 1-877-283-2007, E-mail: member@wcwwa.ca

October

National Association for Environmental Management 2014 22nd Annual EHS Management Forum
Date: October 22-24, 2014
Location: Hilton Austin
Austin, TX USA
Sponsor/Contact: National Association for Environmental Management
#1002, 1612 K St. NW
Washington, DC USA
202-986-6616 Fax: 202-530-4408
E-mail: programs@naem.org
URL: www.naem.org
Scope: International
Purpose: Environmental, health & safety, & sustainability practitioners gain the opportunity to exchange ideas, participate in interactive sessions, & hear timely keynote presentations
Anticipated Attendance: 500+
Contact Information: E-mail: programs@naem.org

Union of British Columbia Municipalities 2014 Annual Convention

Date: October 20-24, 2014
Location: Victoria Conference Centre
Victoria, BC
Sponsor/Contact: Union of British Columbia Municipalities
#60, 10551 Shellbridge Way
Richmond, BC V6X 2W9 Canada
604-270-8226 Fax: 604-270-9116
E-mail: ubcm@civicnet.bc.ca
URL: www.civicnet.bc.ca
Scope: Provincial

Water Environment Federation WEFTEC 2014: 87th Annual Water Environment Federation Technical Exhibition & Conference

Date: October 18-22, 2014
Location: New Orleans Morial Convention Center
New Orleans, LA USA
Sponsor/Contact: Water Environment Federation
601 Wythe St.
Alexandria, VA USA
703-684-2400 Fax: 703-684-2492
E-mail: csc@wef.org
URL: www.wef.org
Scope: International
Purpose: A technical program & a showcase of new products & services of interest to water & wastewater professionals
Anticipated Attendance: 18,000
Contact Information: Membership Information, Toll-Free Phone: 1-800-666-0206, International Phone: +44 120-679-6351 or 571-830-1545

November

Canadian Urban Transit Association 2014 Fall Conference & Trans-Expo

Date: November 2014
Sponsor/Contact: Canadian Urban Transit Association
#1401, 55 York St.
Toronto, ON M5J 1R7
416-365-9800 Fax: 416-365-1295
E-mail: transit@cutaactu.ca
URL: www.cutaactu.ca
Scope: National
Purpose: A technical conference which includes Trans-Expo, a national transit & bus exhibition

Greenbuild 2014 International Conference & Expo

Date: November 8-10, 2013
Location: New Orleans, LA USA
Sponsor/Contact: Canada Green Building Council
#202, 47 Clarence St.
Ottawa, ON K1N 9K1
613-241-1184 Fax: 613-241-4782
E-mail: info@cagbc.org; education@cagbc.org
URL: www.cagbc.org
Scope: International
Purpose: Educational sessions & exhibits devoted to green building
Contact Information: General Inquiries, E-mail: info@greenbuildexpo.org

Greenbuild 2015 International Conference & Expo

Date: November 18-22, 2013
Location: Washington, DC USA
Sponsor/Contact: Canada Green Building Council
#202, 47 Clarence St.
Ottawa, ON K1N 9K1
613-241-1184 Fax: 613-241-4782
E-mail: info@cagbc.org; education@cagbc.org
URL: www.cagbc.org
Scope: International
Purpose: A learning event, featuring opportunities to network with green building colleagues & industry professionals from North America & around the world
Contact Information: General Inquiries, E-mail: info@greenbuildexpo.org

Other Conferences in 2014

Alberta Recreation & Parks Association 2014 Biennial Youth Development Through Recreation Services Symposium

Location: The Banff Centre
Banff, AB
Sponsor/Contact: Alberta Recreation & Parks Association
11759 Groat Rd.
Edmonton, AB T5M 3K6 Canada
780-415-1745 Fax: 780-451-7915
E-mail: arpa@arpaonline.ca
URL: www.arpaonline.ca
Scope: Provincial
Purpose: A three day educational forum, featuring presenters ranging from frontline staff involved in youth programs to youth policy makers
Contact Information: Manager, Children & Youth Programs: Lisa Tink, Phone: 780-644-4794, E-mail: ltink@arpaonline.ca

Aquaculture Canada 2014: The Aquaculture Association of Canada's Annual Conference & General Meeting

Sponsor/Contact: Aquaculture Association of Canada
16 Lobster Lane
St. Andrews, NB E5B 3T6
506-529-4766 Fax: 506-529-4609
E-mail: aac@dfo-mpo.gc.ca
URL: www.aquacultureassociation.ca
Scope: National
Purpose: Presentations on topics relevant to aquaculture, such as government regulations & scientific advancements
Contact Information: Association Office Manager: Susan Waddy, Phone: 506-529-4766, E-mail: Susan.Waddy@dfo-mpo.gc.ca

Association of Power Producers of Ontario 2014: 26th Annual Canadian Power Conference & Power Networking Centre

Location: Ontario
Sponsor/Contact: Association of Power Producers of Ontario
P.O. Box 1084 Stn. F
#1602, 25 Adelaide St. East
Toronto, ON M5C 3A1
416-322-6549 Fax: 416-481-5785
E-mail: appro@appro.org; marketing@appro.org
URL: www.appro.org
Scope: Provincial
Purpose: An annual event held in the autumn, featuring speakers, educational sessions, exhibits, & a student program
Contact Information: E-mail: appro@appro.org

Atlantic Canada Water & Wastewater Association 2014 67th Annual Conference

Location: New Brunswick
Sponsor/Contact: Atlantic Canada Water & Wastewater Association
P.O. Box 41002
Dartmouth, NS B2Y 4P7 Canada
902-434-6002 Fax: 902-435-7796
E-mail: acwwa@hfx.andara.com
URL: www.acwwa.ca
Scope: Regional
Purpose: A trade show, plus educational sessions & networking opportunities for Atlantic Canada's water professionals
Anticipated Attendance: 260-340
Contact Information: Technical Director: Margaret Walsh, PhD., P.Eng., E-mail: mwalsh2@dal.ca

British Columbia Nature (Federation of British Columbia Naturalists) 2014 Nature Conference & Fall General Meeting

Location: British Columbia
Sponsor/Contact: British Columbia Nature (Federation of British Columbia Naturalists)
c/o Parks Heritage Centre
1620 Mount Seymour Rd.
North Vancouver, BC V7G 2R9
604-985-3057
E-mail: manager@bcnature.ca
URL: www.bcnature.ca
Scope: Provincial
Purpose: An annual meeting of naturalists, environmentalists, biologists, & academics who are members of British Columbia Nature
Contact Information: Office Manager: Betty Davison, E-mail: manager@bcnature.ca

British Columbia Water & Waste Association 2014 42nd Annual Conference & Trade Show

Location: British Columbia
Sponsor/Contact: British Columbia Water & Waste Association
#221, 8678 Greenall Ave.
Burnaby, BC V5J 3M6
604-433-4389 Fax: 604-433-9859
E-mail: contact@bcwwa.org
URL: www.bcwwa.org
Scope: Provincial
Purpose: The largest meeting in British Columbia dedicated to the water & waste fields
Anticipated Attendance: 1000
Contact Information: Event Coordinator: Winnie Tsang, Phone: 604-433-4389, ext. 232, E-mail: wtsang@bcwwa.org

Canadian Association of Geographers 2014 Annual Meeting & Conference

Location: York University
Toronto, ON
Sponsor/Contact: Canadian Association of Geographers
Department of Geography, McGill University
#425, 805, rue Sherbrooke ouest
Montréal, QC H3A 2K6
514-398-4946 Fax: 514-398-7437
E-mail: valerie.shoffey@cag-acg.ca (Executive Secretary)
URL: www.cag-acg.ca
Scope: National
Purpose: Educational sessions, workshops, exhibits, field trips, & networking opportunities for geographers from across Canada

Canadian Dam Association 2014 Annual Conference

Sponsor/Contact: Canadian Dam Association
P.O. Box 2281
Moose Jaw, SK S6TH 7W6
URL: www.cda.ca
Scope: National
Purpose: Featuring technical paper presentations, workshops, tours, exhibitor presentations, & a social program

Canadian Ground Water Association CanWell 2014: Canada's National Ground Water Symposium

Sponsor/Contact: Canadian Ground Water Association
#100-409, 1600 Bedford Hwy.
Bedford, NS B4A 1E8
902-845-1885 Fax: 902-845-1886
E-mail: info@cgwa.org
URL: www.cgwa.org
Scope: International
Purpose: A biennial convention of interest to professionals from the geothermal & ground water industries, featuring a trade show with manufacturers, suppliers, & industry representatives displaying new & innovative products
Anticipated Attendance: 650+
Contact Information: E-mail: info@cgwa.org

Trade Shows, Conferences and Seminars

Canadian Health Libraries Association (CHLA) / Association des bibliothèques de la santé du Canada (ABSC) 2014 38th Annual Conference

Sponsor/Contact: Canadian Health Libraries Association
39 River St.
Toronto, ON M5A 3P1
416-646-1600 Fax: 416-646-9460
E-mail: info@chla-absc.ca; pr@chla-absc.ca (Public Relations)
URL: www.chla-absc.ca
Scope: National
Purpose: An annual May or June gathering of health science librarians to participate in continuing education courses & lectures, & to view products & services related to their work
Contact Information: Continuing Education, E-mail: ce@chla-absc.ca; Public Relations, E-mail: pr@chla-absc.ca

Canadian Nuclear Society 2014 35th Annual Conference & 38th Annual CNS / CNA Student Conference

Sponsor/Contact: Canadian Nuclear Society
655 Bay St., 17th Fl.
Toronto, ON M5G 2K4
416-977-7620 Fax: 416-977-8131
E-mail: cns-snc@on.aibn.com
URL: www.cns-snc.ca
Scope: National
Purpose: A meeting open to all persons interested in nuclear science, nuclear engineering, & technology, featuring the presentation of Canadian Nuclear Society awards
Contact Information: Canadian Nuclear Society Office: Phone: 416-977-7620, E-mail: cns-snc@on.aibn.com

Canadian Society for Mechanical Engineering 2014 Forum

Sponsor/Contact: Canadian Society for Mechanical Engineering
1295 Hwy. 2 East
Kingston, ON K7L 4V1
613-547-5989 Fax: 613-547-0195
E-mail: csme@cogeco.ca
URL: www.csme-scgm.ca
Scope: National
Purpose: A meeting of mechanical engineers, held every other year in a Canadian city, for discussion of research & issues important to the profession & related fields
Contact Information: Canadian Society for Mechanical Engineering, E-mail: csme@cogeco.ca

Canadian Society of Exploration Geophysicists, Canadian Society of Petroleum Geologists & Canadian Well Logging Society 2014 Joint Annual Convention

Sponsor/Contact: Canadian Society of Exploration Geophysicists
#600, 640 - 8th Ave. SW
Calgary, AB T2P 1G7
403-262-0015
E-mail: cseg.office@shaw.ca
URL: www.cseg.ca
Scope: National
Purpose: Technical information for persons involved in earth sciences, from geologists to reservoir engineers, & managers
Contact Information: Chair, Joint Annual Convention Committee: Laurie Ross, E-mail: laurie.ross@divestco.com

Canadian Urban Transit Association 2014 Annual Conference

Sponsor/Contact: Canadian Urban Transit Association
#1401, 55 York St.
Toronto, ON M5J 1R7
416-365-9800 Fax: 416-365-1295
E-mail: transit@cutaactu.ca
URL: www.cutaactu.ca
Scope: National
Purpose: A policy & management meeting occurring in May or June each year, featuring the presentation of Corporate Awards to members of the Canadian Urban Transit Association in categories such as transit systems, business members, & affiliate members

Drinking Water 2014 16th Biennial Canadian National Conference

Sponsor/Contact: Canadian Water & Wastewater Association
#11, 1010 Polytek Rd.
Ottawa, ON K1J 9H9
613-747-0524 Fax: 613-747-0523
E-mail: tdellison@cwwa.ca
URL: www.cwwa.ca
Scope: National
Purpose: A conference organized by the Canadian Water & Wastewater Association for the Federal-Provincial-Territorial Committee on Drinking Water
Contact Information: Phone: 613-747-0524; Fax: 613-747-0523, E-mail: admin@cwwa.ca

Geological Association of Canada (GAC) & the Mineralogical Association of Canada (MAC) 2014 Joint Annual Meeting

Sponsor/Contact: Geological Association of Canada
Department of Earth Sciences, Memorial University of Newfoundland
#ER4063, Alexander Murray Bldg.
St. John's, NL A1B 3X5
709-737-7660 Fax: 709-737-2532
E-mail: gac@mun.ca; gacpublications@mun.ca (GEOLOG newsmagazine)
URL: www.gac.ca
Scope: National
Purpose: Featuring exhibits, a technical program, & special events
Contact Information: Communications Chair: Tim Corkery, Phone: 204-945-6554, Fax: 204-945-1406; Finance & Administration Manager: Karen Johnston, Phone: 709-864-2399, E-mail: kajohnston@mun.ca

Indoor Air 2014: The Triennial Conference of the International Society of Indoor Air Quality and Climate (ISIAQ)

Sponsor/Contact: International Society of Indoor Air Quality & Climate
c/o Gina Bendy
2548 Empire Grade
Santa Cruz, CA USA
831-426-0148 Fax: 831-426-6522
E-mail: info@isiaq.org
URL: www.isiaq.org
Scope: International
Purpose: Future challenges for the indoor air community

Local Government Management Association of British Columbia 2014 Annual General Meeting & Conference

Location: Vancouver, BC
Sponsor/Contact: Local Government Management Association of British Columbia
Central Building
620 View St., 7th Fl.
Victoria, BC V8W 1J6
250-383-7032 Fax: 250-384-4879
E-mail: office@lgma.ca; editor@lgma.ca (magazine); ads@lgma.ca
URL: www.lgma.ca
Scope: Provincial
Purpose: A conference & tradeshow held in May or June each year for members of the Local Government Management Association of British Columbia
Anticipated Attendance: 400-500
Contact Information: Program Coordinator: Ana Fuller, Phone: 250-383-7032, ext. 227, Fax: 250-383-4879, E-mail: afuller@lgma.ca

Metallurgy & Materials Society of the Canadian Institute of Mining, Metallurgy & Petroleum COM 2014: 53rd Annual Conference of Metallurgists

Sponsor/Contact: Metallurgy & Materials Society of the Canadian Institute of Mining, Metallurgy & Petroleum
#1250, 3500, boul de Maisonneuve ouest
Montréal, QC H3Z 3C1
514-939-2710
URL: www.metsoc.org
Scope: International
Purpose: A conference featuring short courses, industrial tours, a metals trade show, a poster session, plenary sessions, & student activities
Contact Information: E-mail: metsoc@cim.org

Ontario Soil & Crop Improvement Association 2014 Provincial Annual Meeting

Location: Ontario
Sponsor/Contact: Ontario Soil & Crop Improvement Association
1 Stone Rd. West
Guelph, ON N1G 4Y2
519-826-4214 Fax: 519-826-4224
E-mail: oscia@ontariosoilcrop.org
URL: www.ontariosoilcrop.org
Scope: Provincial
Purpose: An opportunity for farmers & persons involved in agriculture in Ontario to bring local views to give direction to the association
Contact Information: Ontario Soil & Crop Improvement Association, E-mail: oscia@ontariosoilcrop.org

Petroleum Services Association of Canada 2014 Annual General Meeting, Canadian Drilling Activity Forecast Session, & Industry Dinner

Sponsor/Contact: Petroleum Services Association of Canada
#1150, 800 - 6 Ave. SW
Calgary, AB T2P 3G3
403-264-4195 Fax: 403-263-7174
E-mail: info@psac.ca
URL: www.psac.ca
Scope: National
Purpose: At the end of October each year, the Petroleum Services Association of Canada Annual Report is released, in conjunction with the Annual General Meeting & the Canadian Drilling Activity Forecast
Contact Information: Manager, Meetings & Events: Heather Doyle, Phone: 403-213-2796, E-mail: hdoyle@psac.ca

Petroleum Services Association of Canada 2014 Annual Mid-Year Update

Sponsor/Contact: Petroleum Services Association of Canada
#1150, 800 - 6 Ave. SW
Calgary, AB T2P 3G3
403-264-4195 Fax: 403-263-7174
E-mail: info@psac.ca
URL: www.psac.ca
Scope: National
Purpose: A respected petroleum industry event to update the Canadian Drilling Activity Forecast
Contact Information: Manager, Meetings & Events: Heather Doyle, Phone: 403-213-2796, E-mail: hdoyle@psac.ca

2015

March

Institute of Transportation Engineers 2015 Technical Conference & Exhibit
Date: March 29 - April 1, 2015
Location: Westin La Paloma
Tucson, AZ USA
Sponsor/Contact: Institute of Transportation Engineers
#300, 1099 - 14th St. NW
Washington, DC USA
202-289-0222 Fax: 202-289-7722
E-mail: ite_staff@ite.org
URL: www.ite.org
Scope: International
Contact Information: Contact, Registration Information: Sallie C. Dollins, E-mail: sdollins@ite.org; Contact, Technical Program: Aliyah N. Horton, E-mail: ahorton@ite.org; Contact, Exhibits: Christina Garneski, E-mail: cgarneski@ite.org; Contact, Paper Submittals: Eunice Chege, E-mail: echege@ite.org

June

American Water Works Association 2015 134th Annual Conference & Exposition
Date: June 7-11, 2015
Location: Anaheim, CA USA
Sponsor/Contact: American Water Works Association
6666 West Quincy Ave.
Denver, CO USA
303-794-7711 Fax: 303-347-0804
E-mail: custsvc@awwa.org
URL: www.awwa.org
Scope: International
Purpose: An annual meeting providing technical sessions, an exhibit hall, & networking opportunities for water professionals
Contact Information: American Water Works Association, Phone: 800-926-7337, Fax: 303-347-0804, E-mail: awwamktg@awwa.org

July

Institute of Food Technologists 2015 Annual Meeting & Food Expo
Date: July 11-14, 2015
Location: Chicago, IL USA
Sponsor/Contact: Institute of Food Technologists
#1000, 525 West Van Buren
Chicago, IL
312-782-8424 Fax: 312-782-8348
E-mail: info@ift.org; sales@ift.org
URL: www.ift.org
Scope: International
Purpose: The largest annual food science forum & exposition, featuring presentation from experts of research institutions, government agencies, & companies, of interest to food scientists, suppliers, & marketers from around the globe
Anticipated Attendance: 21,500+
Contact Information: General Inquiries: info@ift.org; Media Inquiries, E-mail: media@ift.org

August

Institute of Transportation Engineers 2015 Annual Meeting & Exhibit
Date: August 2-5, 2015
Location: Westin Diplomat
Hollywood, FL USA
Sponsor/Contact: Institute of Transportation Engineers
#300, 1099 - 14th St. NW
Washington, DC USA
202-289-0222 Fax: 202-289-7722
E-mail: ite_staff@ite.org
URL: www.ite.org
Scope: International
Contact Information: Contact, Registration Information: Sallie C. Dollins, E-mail: sdollins@ite.org; Contact, Technical Program: Aliyah N. Horton, E-mail: ahorton@ite.org; Contact, Exhibits: Christina Garneski, E-mail: cgarneski@ite.org; Contact, Paper Submittals: Eunice Chege, E-mail: echege@ite.org

September

Union of British Columbia Municipalities 2015 Annual Convention
Date: September 21-25, 2015
Location: Vancouver Convention Centre
Vancouver, BC
Sponsor/Contact: Union of British Columbia Municipalities
#60, 10551 Shellbridge Way
Richmond, BC V6X 2W9 Canada
604-270-8226 Fax: 604-270-9116
E-mail: ubcm@civicnet.bc.ca
URL: www.civicnet.bc.ca
Scope: Provincial

Water Environment Federation WEFTEC 2015: 88th Annual Water Environment Federation Technical Exhibition & Conference
Date: September 26-30, 2015
Location: McCormick Place
Chicago, IL USA
Sponsor/Contact: Water Environment Federation
601 Wythe St.
Alexandria, VA USA
703-684-2400 Fax: 703-684-2492
E-mail: csc@wef.org
URL: www.wef.org
Scope: International
Purpose: Educational & training opportunities, plus an exhibition by more than 750 companies
Anticipated Attendance: 18,000
Contact Information: Membership Information, Toll-Free Phone: 1-800-666-0206, International Phone: +44 120-679-6351 or 571-830-1545

Western Canada Water 2015 67th Annual Conference & Exhibition
Date: September 22-25, 2015
Location: Winnipeg, MB
Sponsor/Contact: Western Canada Water
P.O. Box 1708
126 - 3rd Ave. West
Cochrane, AB T4C 1B6
403-709-0064 Fax: 403-709-0068
E-mail: member@wcwwa.ca
URL: www.wcwwa.ca
Scope: Regional
Purpose: Information & a showcase of products & services for delegates from the Western Canada Water marketplace, such as utility managers & operators, municipal & provincial government representatives, & consulting engineers
Anticipated Attendance: 500+
Contact Information: Western Canada Water, Toll-Free Phone: 1-877-283-2003, Toll-Free Fax: 1-877-283-2007, E-mail: member@wcwwa.ca

November

Canadian Urban Transit Association 2015 Fall Conference & Trans-Expo
Date: November 2015
Sponsor/Contact: Canadian Urban Transit Association
#1401, 55 York St.
Toronto, ON M5J 1R7
416-365-9800 Fax: 416-365-1295
E-mail: transit@cutaactu.ca
URL: www.cutaactu.ca
Scope: National
Purpose: An annual technical meeting which also features a display of products & services for sales opportunities & business to business marketing

Other Conferences in 2015

Alberta Recreation & Parks Association 2015 Parks Forum

Location: Alberta
Sponsor/Contact: Alberta Recreation & Parks Association
11759 Groat Rd.
Edmonton, AB T5M 3K6 Canada
780-415-1745 Fax: 780-451-7915
E-mail: arpa@arpaonline.ca
URL: www.arpaonline.ca
Scope: Regional
Purpose: A staff development event, with keynote speakers, plenary workshops, & presentations, of interest to practitioners at municipal, provincial, & national parks, allied stakeholders, teachers, & students
Contact Information: E-mail: arpa@arpaonline.ca

Aquaculture Canada 2015: The Aquaculture Association of Canada's Annual Conference & General Meeting

Sponsor/Contact: Aquaculture Association of Canada
16 Lobster Lane
St. Andrews, NB E5B 3T6
506-529-4766 Fax: 506-529-4609
E-mail: aac@dfo-mpo.gc.ca
URL: www.aquacultureassociation.ca
Scope: National
Purpose: Featuring presentations, special sessions, workshops, & posters
Contact Information: Association Office, Phone: 506-529-4766

Atlantic Canada Water & Wastewater Association 2015 68th Annual Conference

Sponsor/Contact: Atlantic Canada Water & Wastewater Association
P.O. Box 41002
Dartmouth, NS B2Y 4P7 Canada
902-434-6002 Fax: 902-435-7796
E-mail: acwwa@hfx.andara.com
URL: www.acwwa.ca
Scope: Regional
Purpose: The association's annual general meeting & the election of its executive committee, plus a trade show, educational events, & networking occasions
Anticipated Attendance: 260-340
Contact Information: Technical Director: Margaret Walsh, PhD., P.Eng., E-mail: mwalsh2@dal.ca

British Columbia Water & Waste Association 2015 43rd Annual Conference & Trade Show

Location: British Columbia
Sponsor/Contact: British Columbia Water & Waste Association
#221, 8678 Greenall Ave.
Burnaby, BC V5J 3M6
604-433-4389 Fax: 604-433-9859
E-mail: contact@bcwwa.org
URL: www.bcwwa.org
Scope: Provincial
Purpose: A four day conference, including technical sessions & the chance to view current products at the trade show
Anticipated Attendance: 1000
Contact Information: Event Coordinator: Winnie Tsang, Phone: 604-433-4389, ext. 232, E-mail: wtsang@bcwwa.org

Canadian Association of Geographers 2015 Annual Meeting & Conference

Sponsor/Contact: Canadian Association of Geographers
Department of Geography, McGill University
#425, 805, rue Sherbrooke ouest
Montréal, QC H3A 2K6
514-398-4946 Fax: 514-398-7437
E-mail: valerie.shoffey@cag-acg.ca (Executive Secretary)
URL: www.cag-acg.ca
Scope: National
Purpose: A business meeting & educational conference

for geographers & students, featuring the presentation of papers & posters, plus exhibits, & social activities

Canadian Health Libraries Association (CHLA) / Association des bibliothèques de la santé du Canada (ABSC) 2015 39th Annual Conference

Location: Vancouver, BC
Sponsor/Contact: Canadian Health Libraries Association
39 River St.
Toronto, ON M5A 3P1
416-646-1600 Fax: 416-646-9460
E-mail: info@chla-absc.ca; pr@chla-absc.ca (Public Relations)
URL: www.chla-absc.ca
Scope: National
Purpose: A joint conference with the Medical Library Association
Contact Information: Continuing Education, E-mail: ce@chla-absc.ca; Public Relations, E-mail: pr@chla-absc.ca

Canadian Medical Association 2015 148th Annual Meeting

Sponsor/Contact: Canadian Medical Association
1867 Alta Vista Dr.
Ottawa, ON K1G 5W8
613-731-8610 Fax: 613-236-8864
E-mail: cmamsc@cma.ca; cmatechsupport@cma.ca (technical support)
URL: www.cma.ca
Scope: National
Purpose: General Council is open to delegates & observers who must be Canadian Medical Association members or invited guests
Contact Information: Registration Officer, Phone: 1-800-663-7336, ext. 2383, E-mail: gcregistrations@cma.ca

Canadian Society for Mechanical Engineering 2015 25th Biennial Canadian Congress of Applied Mechanics (CANCAM)

Sponsor/Contact: Canadian Society for Mechanical Engineering
1295 Hwy. 2 East
Kingston, ON K7L 4V1
613-547-5989 Fax: 613-547-0195
E-mail: csme@cogeco.ca
URL: www.csme-scgm.ca
Scope: National
Purpose: Tech tracks at past conferences have included civil engineering, computational mechanics, dynamics & vibration, education in applied mechanics, fluid mechanics, manufacturing, mechatronics, micro-electro-mechanical systems, solid mechanics & materials, & thermodynamics & heat transfer
Contact Information: Canadian Society for Mechanical Engineering, E-mail: csme@cogeco.ca

Canadian Urban Transit Association 2015 Annual Conference

Sponsor/Contact: Canadian Urban Transit Association
#1401, 55 York St.
Toronto, ON M5J 1R7
416-365-9800 Fax: 416-365-1295
E-mail: transit@cutaactu.ca
URL: www.cutaactu.ca
Scope: National
Purpose: Professional development activities & networking opportunities, held in May or June each year

International Heavy Haul Association 2015 Specialist Technical Session

Sponsor/Contact: International Heavy Haul Association
2808 Forest Hills Crt.
Virginia Beach, USA
URL: www.ihha.net

Scope: International
Purpose: A conference offered every four years to examine heavy haul operation issues

Local Government Management Association of British Columbia 2015 Annual General Meeting & Conference

Location: British Columbia
Sponsor/Contact: Local Government Management Association of British Columbia
Central Building
620 View St., 7th Fl.
Victoria, BC V8W 1J6
250-383-7032 Fax: 250-384-4879
E-mail: office@lgma.ca; editor@lgma.ca (magazine); ads@lgma.ca
URL: www.lgma.ca
Scope: Provincial
Purpose: A meeting & tradeshow held each year in May or June in British Columbia for members of the Local Government Management Association of British Columbia
Anticipated Attendance: 400-500
Contact Information: Program Coordinator: Ana Fuller, Phone: 250-383-7032, ext. 227, Fax: 250-383-4879, E-mail: afuller@lgma.ca

Maintenance & Engineering Society of The Canadian Institute of Mining, Metallurgy & Petroleum 2015 Maintenance Engineering/Mine Operators' Conference

Sponsor/Contact: Maintenance & Engineering Society of The Canadian Institute of Mining, Metallurgy & Petroleum c/o Chair, Brad Kingston, Wardrop Engineering Inc.
725 Hewitson St.
Thunder Bay, ON P7B 6B5
807-345-5453
E-mail: brad.kingston@wardrop.com
URL: www.cim.org/med
Scope: National
Purpose: A technical conference of interest to persons involved in maintenance & engineering in the mining industry

Metallurgy & Materials Society of the Canadian Institute of Mining, Metallurgy & Petroleum COM 2015: 54th Annual Conference of Metallurgists

Sponsor/Contact: Metallurgy & Materials Society of the Canadian Institute of Mining, Metallurgy & Petroleum
#1250, 3500, boul de Maisonneuve ouest
Montréal, QC H3Z 3C1
514-939-2710
URL: www.metsoc.org
Scope: International
Purpose: A technical program, with short courses & industrial tours, plus a metals trade show, the poster session, plenary sessions, & student activities
Contact Information: E-mail: metsoc@cim.org

Metallurgy & Materials Society of the Canadian Institute of Mining, Metallurgy & Petroleum World Gold 2015 5th International Conference

Sponsor/Contact: Metallurgy & Materials Society of the Canadian Institute of Mining, Metallurgy & Petroleum
#1250, 3500, boul de Maisonneuve ouest
Montréal, QC H3Z 3C1
514-939-2710
URL: www.metsoc.org
Scope: International
Purpose: Jointly convened by the Canadian Institute of Mining, Metallurgy & Petroleum (CIM), the Australasian Institute of Mining & Metallurgy (AusIMM), & the Southern African Institute of Mining & Metallurgy (SAIMM)

Wastewater Management 2015 6th Biennial Canadian National Conference

Sponsor/Contact: Canadian Water & Wastewater Association
#11, 1010 Polytek Rd.
Ottawa, ON K1J 9H9
613-747-0524 Fax: 613-747-0523
E-mail: tdellison@cwwa.ca
URL: www.cwwa.ca
Scope: National
Purpose: A meeting to provide insights & solutions to challenges encountered by wastewater managers
Contact Information: Phone: 613-747-0524; Fax: 613-747-0523; E-mail: admin@cwwa.ca

Water Efficiency & Conservation 2015 6th Biennial Conference

Sponsor/Contact: Canadian Water & Wastewater Association
#11, 1010 Polytek Rd.
Ottawa, ON K1J 9H9
613-747-0524 Fax: 613-747-0523
E-mail: tdellison@cwwa.ca
URL: www.cwwa.ca
Scope: National
Purpose: Information for Canadian utility conservation specialists, featuring discussions of policy, best management practices, technology, & education programs
Anticipated Attendance: 85
Contact Information: Phone: 613-747-0524; Fax: 613-747-0523; E-mail: admin@cwwa.ca

2016

June

American Water Works Association 2016 135th Annual Conference & Exposition

Date: June 12-16, 2016
Location: Chicago, IL USA
Sponsor/Contact: American Water Works Association
6666 West Quincy Ave.
Denver, CO USA
303-794-7711 Fax: 303-347-0804
E-mail: custsvc@awwa.org
URL: www.awwa.org
Scope: International
Purpose: Offering a technical program, professional development activities, & exhibitors for the worldwide water community
Contact Information: American Water Works Association, Phone: 800-926-7337, Fax: 303-347-0804, E-mail: awwamktg@awwa.org

August

Institute of Transportation Engineers 2016 Annual Meeting & Exhibit

Date: August 14-17, 2016
Location: Anaheim Convention Center
Anaheim, CA USA
Sponsor/Contact: Institute of Transportation Engineers
#300, 1099 - 14th St. NW
Washington, DC USA
202-289-0222 Fax: 202-289-7722
E-mail: ite_staff@ite.org
URL: www.ite.org
Scope: International
Contact Information: Contact, Registration Information: Sallie C. Dollins, E-mail: sdollins@ite.org; Contact, Technical Program: Aliyah N. Horton, E-mail: ahorton@ite.org; Contact, Exhibits: Christina Garneski, E-mail: cgarneski@ite.org; Contact, Paper Submittals: Eunice Chege, E-mail: echege@ite.org

September

Union of British Columbia Municipalities 2016 Annual Convention

Date: September 26-30, 2016
Location: Penticton Trade & Convention Centre
Penticton, BC
Sponsor/Contact: Union of British Columbia Municipalities
#60, 10551 Shellbridge Way
Richmond, BC V6X 2W9 Canada
604-270-8226 Fax: 604-270-9116
E-mail: ubcm@civicnet.bc.ca
URL: www.civicnet.bc.ca
Scope: Provincial

November

Canadian Urban Transit Association 2016 Fall Conference & Trans-Expo

Date: November 2016
Sponsor/Contact: Canadian Urban Transit Association
#1401, 55 York St.
Toronto, ON M5J 1R7
416-365-9800 Fax: 416-365-1295
E-mail: transit@cutaactu.ca
URL: www.cutaactu.ca
Scope: National
Purpose: A yearly technical conference, which also includes the presentation of Employee Awards based on accomplishments in areas such as attendance, safety, & acts of heroism

Other Conferences in 2016

Canadian Ground Water Association CanWell 2016: Canada's National Ground Water Symposium

Sponsor/Contact: Canadian Ground Water Association
#100-409, 1600 Bedford Hwy.
Bedford, NS B4A 1E8
902-845-1885 Fax: 902-845-1886
E-mail: info@cgwa.org
URL: www.cgwa.org
Scope: International
Purpose: A biennial convention, featuring technical sessions, demonstrations, & a trade show with North America's leading manufacturers & suppliers serving the ground water & geothermal industries
Anticipated Attendance: 650+
Contact Information: E-mail: info@cgwa.org

Canadian Urban Transit Association 2016 Annual Conference

Sponsor/Contact: Canadian Urban Transit Association
#1401, 55 York St.
Toronto, ON M5J 1R7
416-365-9800 Fax: 416-365-1295
E-mail: transit@cutaactu.ca
URL: www.cutaactu.ca
Scope: National
Purpose: Professional development sessions & the presentation of Corporate Awards, held in May or June each year

Water Environment Federation WEFTEC 2016: 89th Annual Water Environment Federation Technical Exhibition & Conference

Location: New Orleans, LA USA
Sponsor/Contact: Water Environment Federation
601 Wythe St.
Alexandria, VA USA
703-684-2400 Fax: 703-684-2492
E-mail: csc@wef.org
URL: www.wef.org
Scope: International
Purpose: An annual educational & networking event drawing water quality experts from around the world
Anticipated Attendance: 18,000
Contact Information: Membership Information, Toll-Free Phone: 1-800-666-0206, International Phone: +44 120-679-6351 or 571-830-1545

Western Canada Water 2016 68th Annual Conference & Exhibition

Location: Calgary, AB
Sponsor/Contact: Western Canada Water
P.O. Box 1708
126 - 3rd Ave. West
Cochrane, AB T4C 1B6
403-709-0064 Fax: 403-709-0068
E-mail: member@wcwwa.ca
URL: www.wcwwa.ca
Scope: Regional
Purpose: Informative sessions, an exhibition, & networking opportunities for utility managers & operators, consulting engineers, & municipal & provincial government representatives
Anticipated Attendance: 500+
Contact Information: Western Canada Water, Toll-Free Phone: 1-877-283-2003, Toll-Free Fax: 1-877-283-2007, E-mail: member@wcwwa.ca

2017

June

American Water Works Association 2017 136th Annual Conference & Exposition

Date: June 11-15, 2017
Location: Philadelphia, PA USA
Sponsor/Contact: American Water Works Association
6666 West Quincy Ave.
Denver, CO USA
303-794-7711 Fax: 303-347-0804
E-mail: custsvc@awwa.org
URL: www.awwa.org
Scope: International
Purpose: A technical program & exhibits for association members & associated professionals
Contact Information: American Water Works Association, Phone: 800-926-7337, Fax: 303-347-0804, E-mail: awwamktg@awwa.org

July

Institute of Transportation Engineers 2017 Annual Meeting & Exhibit

Date: July 30 - August 2, 2017
Location: Sheraton Centre Toronto
Toronto, ON
Sponsor/Contact: Institute of Transportation Engineers
#300, 1099 - 14th St. NW
Washington, DC USA
202-289-0222 Fax: 202-289-7722
E-mail: ite_staff@ite.org
URL: www.ite.org
Scope: International
Contact Information: Contact, Registration Information: Sallie C. Dollins, E-mail: sdollins@ite.org; Contact, Technical Program: Aliyah N. Horton, E-mail: ahorton@ite.org; Contact, Exhibits: Christina Garneski, E-mail: cgarneski@ite.org; Contact, Paper Submittals: Eunice Chege, E-mail: echege@ite.org

September

Union of British Columbia Municipalities 2017 Annual Convention

Date: September 25-29, 2017
Location: Vancouver Convention Centre
Vancouver, BC
Sponsor/Contact: Union of British Columbia Municipalities
#60, 10551 Shellbridge Way
Richmond, BC V6X 2W9 Canada
604-270-8226 Fax: 604-270-9116
E-mail: ubcm@civicnet.bc.ca
URL: www.civicnet.bc.ca
Scope: Provincial

Other Conferences in 2017

International Heavy Haul Association 2017 International Conference

Sponsor/Contact: International Heavy Haul Association
2808 Forest Hills Crt.
Virginia Beach, USA
URL: www.ihha.net
Scope: International
Purpose: An international conference, scheduled every four years, featuring meetings covering the complete spectrum of heavy haul subjects, as well as technical tours

Water Environment Federation WEFTEC 2017: 90th Annual Water Environment Federation Technical Exhibition & Conference

Location: , USA
Sponsor/Contact: Water Environment Federation
601 Wythe St.
Alexandria, VA USA
703-684-2400 Fax: 703-684-2492
E-mail: csc@wef.org
URL: www.wef.org
Scope: International
Purpose: Highlights of the annual international event for water & wastewater professionals include a technical program, technical & committee meetings, facility tours, the presentation of WEF awards, networking opportunities, & a social program
Anticipated Attendance: 18,000
Contact Information: Membership Information, Toll-Free Phone: 1-800-666-0206, International Phone: +44 120-679-6351 or 571-830-1545

Western Canada Water 2017 69th Annual Conference & Exhibition

Sponsor/Contact: Western Canada Water
P.O. Box 1708
126 - 3rd Ave. West
Cochrane, AB T4C 1B6
403-709-0064 Fax: 403-709-0068
E-mail: member@wcwwa.ca
URL: www.wcwwa.ca
Scope: Regional
Purpose: A technical program, a keynote speaker, & a trade show for delegates from Western Canada Water
Anticipated Attendance: 500+
Contact Information: Western Canada Water, Toll-Free Phone: 1-877-283-2003, Toll-Free Fax: 1-877-283-2007, E-mail: member@wcwwa.ca

2018

June

American Water Works Association 2018 137th Annual Conference & Exposition

Date: June 11-15, 2018
Location: Las Vegas, NV USA
Sponsor/Contact: American Water Works Association
6666 West Quincy Ave.
Denver, CO USA
303-794-7711 Fax: 303-347-0804
E-mail: custsvc@awwa.org
URL: www.awwa.org
Scope: International
Purpose: Technical programs, workshops, poster sessions, seminars, continuing education units, & exhibits for the international water community
Contact Information: American Water Works Association, Phone: 800-926-7337, Fax: 303-347-0804, E-mail: awwamktg@awwa.org

Trade Shows, Conferences and Seminars

2019

June

American Water Works Association 2019 138th Annual Conference & Exposition
Date: June 2019
Location: Denver, CO USA
Sponsor/Contact: American Water Works Association
6666 West Quincy Ave.
Denver, CO USA
303-794-7711 Fax: 303-347-0804
E-mail: custsvc@awwa.org
URL: www.awwa.org
Scope: International
Purpose: Presenting water research & best practices of interest to international water professionals
Contact Information: American Water Works Association, Phone: 800-926-7337, Fax: 303-347-0804, E-mail: awwamktg@awwa.org

September

Union of British Columbia Municipalities 2019 Annual Convention
Date: September 23-27, 2019
Location: Vancouver Convention Centre
Vancouver, BC
Sponsor/Contact: Union of British Columbia Municipalities
#60, 10551 Shellbridge Way
Richmond, BC V6X 2W9 Canada
604-270-8226 Fax: 604-270-9116
E-mail: ubcm@civicnet.bc.ca
URL: www.civicnet.bc.ca
Scope: Provincial

2020

June

American Water Works Association 2020 139th Annual Conference & Exposition
Date: June 2020
Location: Orlando, FL USA
Sponsor/Contact: American Water Works Association
6666 West Quincy Ave.
Denver, CO USA
303-794-7711 Fax: 303-347-0804
E-mail: custsvc@awwa.org
URL: www.awwa.org
Scope: International
Purpose: An annual meeting of water professionals, featuring technical programs & exhibits to foster sustainability
Contact Information: American Water Works Association, Phone: 800-926-7337, Fax: 303-347-0804, E-mail: awwamktg@awwa.org

2021

Other Conferences in 2021

American Water Works Association 2021 140th Annual Conference & Exposition

Sponsor/Contact: American Water Works Association
6666 West Quincy Ave.
Denver, CO USA
303-794-7711 Fax: 303-347-0804
E-mail: custsvc@awwa.org
URL: www.awwa.org
Scope: International
Purpose: An international gathering of thousands of water professionals, featuring a technical program, workshops, seminars, & exhibits
Contact Information: American Water Works Association, Phone: 800-926-7337, Fax: 303-347-0804, E-mail: awwamktg@awwa.org

SECTION 2
Environmental Products & Services Buyer's Guide

Included in this section:
- *Subject Index* 3
- *Geographic Index* 47
- *ISO Index* 59
- *Company Listings* 63

Subject Index

Absorbents & Adsorbents, Liquid Waste
See also **Absorption & Adsorption Equipment, Gas; Waste Management, Liquid/Hazardous**
AF Pollution Abatement Systems Inc., 72
Anco Chemicals Inc., 85
Annapolis Valley Peat Moss Co. Ltd., 86
Avenue Industrial Supply Co. Ltd., 98
Bioforj Environmental Services, 108
BV SORBEX, Inc., 119
Can-Ross Environmental Services Ltd., 123
Clear Environmental Products, 143
CP Environmental Technologies, 153
Diversified Waste Solutions, 164
EnviroGuard Ltd., 184
Gator International, 205
Hercules SLR Inc., 229
Hi-Point Industries (1991) Ltd., 231
Hollimex Products Ltd., 232
Imbibitive Technologies Canada, Inc., 238
Interra Environmental Inc., 246
Loraday Environmental Products Ltd., 274
Masternet Ltd., 282
McClymont & Rak Engineers, Inc., 284
The MEP Environmental Products Ltd., 392
Onyx Chemical Cleaning, 313
Pacesetter Sales & Associates Inc., 316
Pigmalion Environmental Services Group, 323
Quatrex Environnement inc., 338
Sanbec, 356
Services industriels Newalta, 363
Sonepar Canada, 373
SpilKleen, 375
Versatech Products Inc., 412
West Coast Spill Supplies Ltd., 424
WRS Environmental, 434
Zep Manufacturing Company of Canada, 436
Zodiac Fabrics Inc., 437
Zorbit Technologies Inc., 437

Absorption & Adsorption Equipment, Gas
See also **Absorbents & Adsorbents, Liquid Waste; Air Pollution Control Equipment**
A.C. Carbone Canada Inc., 63
AimGlobal Technologies Company, Inc., 74
ALCO Gas & Oil Production Equipment Ltd., 77
BC Air Filter Ltd., 103
Blue-Zone Technologies Ltd., 110
Can-Am Instruments Ltd., 122
Cleartech Industries Inc., 143
Elmridge Engineering Inc., 176
Energy Technology Products Ltd., 179
Enterprise Steel Fabricators Ltd., 181
Fabricated Plastics Ltd., 193
IMP Liquid Meters & Petroleum Services, 239
Industrial Plastics Fabricators Ltd., 240
ISCA Management Ltd., 248
LTS Sales Ltd., 274
Macrotek Inc., 278
Nett Technologies Inc., 300
P.J. Hannah Equipment Sales Corp., 315
Pageau Morel & associés, inc., 317
Pegasus Industrial Specialties Inc., 320
Plasticair Inc., 326
Procedair Industries Inc., 333
R&R Drilling Supply Ltd., 339
Refined Specialty Chemicals Inc., 344
Thermal Technics Corporation, 394
Tiger-Vac International Inc., 396
TurboSonic Inc., 404
Watson Process Systems, 423
Weir Power & Industrial, 424
Westech Industrial Ltd., 429

Accident Prevention Services
See also **Environmental Consulting & Contracting Services (General); Occupational Health & Safety Consulting**
Aercoustics Engineering Limited, 71
Beaulier Inc., 104
Emergex Planning Inc., 176
Gator International, 205
McAtee Safety & Environmental Health Services Ltd., 284
Paramount Emergency Planners Ltd., 318
Pepin Prevention des Pertes Inc., 321
Safety Projects International Inc., 355
Sinanni Inc., 369
WPI Safety & Environmental Consultants, 434

Aggregate Recycling
See also **Recycling Services (General)**
AIM Environmental Group, 74
Countryside Disposal Service Ltd., 153
H. Broer Equipment Sales and Service, 223
Pyrotech Mfg. Corp., 337

Agriculture & Agronomy Management
See also **Horticulture & Vegetation Management; Resource Management Services (General)**
Accutest Laboratories Ltd., 66
Ag-West Bio Inc., 72
Agri-Food Laboratories, 73
ATD Waste Systems Inc., 95
Bayer CropScience, 103
BCL Landview Systems Inc., 103
Bio-Contrôle inc., 107
Cadman Power Equipment, 120
CanHemp Corporation, 126
Coastal BioAgresearch Ltd., 145
Dekka Resins Inc., 159
Ecologistics Research Services, 172
ECOMatters Inc., 172
Ferti-Val Inc., 195
FS Partners, 202
Graecam Incorporated, 216
Halltech Environmental Inc., 224
Hyperspectral Data International Inc., 237
International Irrigation Systems Ltd., 245
KnowTech Environmental Inc., 259
LH - Division of Full Circle Organics Inc., 272
LJM Environmental Consulting, 273
Marbicon Inc., 280
Michael Wall & Sons Enterprises Ltd., 288
Monsanto Canada Inc., 293
Organic Farm Services, 314
Organic Resource Management Inc., 314
PDK Projects Inc., 320
Philom Bios Inc., 323
Plant Products Co. Ltd., 326
Prairie Geomatics Ltd., 330
ProAgri Consulting Limited, 333
PRT Inc., 336
Silo Clean International, 367
Solinov Inc., 373
SOTAR Inc., 374
Sun Prairie Organic, 382
System Ecotechnologies Inc., 385
TerraLink Horticulture Inc., 390
TJ Consulting Ltd., 396
Urgel Delisle & Associés inc., 408
Viterra Inc., 414
Western Bio Resources Consulting Ltd., 429
William Dam Seeds Ltd., 432
Zbeetnoff Agro-Environmental Consulting, 436

Agronomy
See **Agriculture & Agronomy Management**

Air
See **Dust Collection & Control Equipment**

Air Filters
See **Filters & Filter Media, Air**

Air Handling Equipment
See also **Air Pollution Control Equipment**
Aeroflo Inc., 71
Aerzen Canada Surpresseurs Compresseurs inc., 71
Air Trac Corp., 75
Airmaster Sales Ltd., 75
Alcore Fabricating Corp., 77
AMKO Systems Inc., 84
Atlantic Air Cleaning Specialists Ltd., 95
Belfab Inc., 104
Delhi Industries Inc., 115
Broan Canada Ltd., 117
Century Environmental Systems, 136
CML Northern Blower Inc., 144
Cunningham Sheet Metal Works Inc., 154
Eneready Products Ltd., 179
Engine Control Systems, 180
Engineered Air, 180
Enviro-Klean Technologies Inc., 182
Eucania International Inc., 190
F.C. O'Neill, Scriven & Associates Ltd., 193
Fabricated Plastics Ltd., 193
Gasmac Inc., 205
Groupe Stavibel Inc., 221
Hammond Manufacturing, 224
Hygrex-Spehr Industries, 237
Inproheat Industries Ltd., 242
Integrated Metal Products, 244
Island Clean Air Inc., 248
John Thurston Machine Ltd., 253
Kernic Systems Inc., 257
Kongskilde Limited, 259
Lennox Industries (Canada) Ltd., 267
Macrotek Inc., 278
MEC Systems Inc., 286
Miniveil Air Systems, 290
MK Plastics Corp., 291
N.R. Murphy Ltd., 296
Pacific Engineering Inc., 316
Pacwill Environmental, 317
Pelmar Engineering Ltd., 320
Philip Doyle Manufacturing Inc., 323
PlymoVent Canada Inc., 326
Precisioneering Ltd., 330
Preston Phipps Inc., 331
Produits Ferpac Ltée, 333
Q-Air Environmental Controls Ltd., 337
Racan Carrier, 341
Rodrigue Métal Ltée, 350
Semco Systems Limited, 362
Sheldons Engineering Inc., 365
Stork Bronswerk Inc., 380
Straub Tadco Inc., 380
Tech Sales Co., 387
Temprite Industries Ltd., 389
Venmar CES, Inc., 410
Wainbee Limited, 415
Wilcorp Manufacturing, 431
YES Environment Technologies Inc., 435

Air Pollution Control Equipment
See also **Absorption & Adsorption Equipment, Gas; Air Handling Equipment; Air Quality Management (General); Calibration Equipment, Air; Chemicals, Air Treatment; Dust Collection & Control Equipment; Dust Suppression Equipment; Electrostatic Precipitators; Filters & Filter Media, Air; Fume Extraction Equipment; Heating, Ventilation & Air Conditioning Equipment; Measuring & Monitoring Equipment, Air; Odour Control Equipment, Air; Ozone Generation Equipment; Scrubbers, Air**
A.C. Carbone Canada Inc., 63
A.C. Plastiques Canada, 63
Acme Engineering Products Ltd., 66
Air Trac Corp., 75
Aker Chemetics, 76
Alfa Plastics Inc., 78
ALTECH Technology Systems Inc., 81
Amaircare Corporation, 82
Ambio Biofiltration Ltd., 82
AMKO Systems Inc., 84
Apollo Environmental Systems Corporation, 87
Arpi's Industries Canada Ltd., 92
Asbeguard Equipment Inc., 93
ATS Scientific Inc., 97
Azco Industries Ltd., 100
Belfab Inc., 104
BG Controls Ltd., 107
Bigelow-Liptak of Canada, 107
Biothermica, 109

CANADIAN ENVIRONMENTAL RESOURCE GUIDE 2011-2012

Subject Index

BOC Canada Limited, 111
CAHFIL FARR (Canada Inc.), 121
Camatec, 122
Canadian Worcester Controls Ltd., 125
CB Engineering, Ltd., 132
Century Environmental Systems, 136
Cimatec Environmental Engineering Inc., 141
Circul-Aire Inc., 141
Clean Air & Water Centre, 142
CMEL Enterprises Ltd., 144
Coen Canada Inc., 146
Comenco Systems Inc., 147
Con-V-Air Inc., 148
DCL International Inc., 158
DynaMotive Energy Systems Corporation, 167
EFC Control Inc., 173
Electro-Air Canada, 174
Elmridge Engineering Inc., 176
Emco Wheaton Corp., 176
Energy Technology Products Ltd., 179
Engine Control Systems, 180
Enterprise Steel Fabricators Ltd., 181
EnviroMed Detection Services, 184
Envirotech Pollution Controls Ltd., 188
Eucania International Inc., 190
Fabricated Plastics Ltd., 193
Firing Industries Ltd., 195
Five Seasons Comfort Limited, 196
Groupe S.M. International Inc., 220
Henlex Inc., 229
Industrial Plastics Fabricators Ltd., 240
InspecTech, 243
Integrated Explorations, 244
ISCA Management Ltd., 248
Island Clean Air Inc., 248
JKM Custom Fabricating Ltd., 252
KBR Canada, 255
Kraemer Tool & Manufacturing Co. Ltd., 260
Lambert Somec inc., 263
Levitt-Safety Limited, 270
Living Resources Inc., 273
Lockerbie & Hole Contracting Ltd., 273
Mac Industrial Exhaust Shop, 277
Maddocks Industrial Filter Division, 278
Marsulex Inc., 281
Matrix Photocatalytic Inc., 282
Miniveil Air Systems, 290
Monitrex Engineering Ltd., 293
Multitel Inc., 295
MW Metal Spinning & Stamping Ltd., 295
N.R. Murphy Ltd., 296
Nederman Canada Ltd., 299
Nett Technologies Inc., 300
Nova Magnetics Burgmann Ltd., 308
Ocean Steel & Construction Ltd., 311
OMB (Americas) Forged Steel Valves, 312
Ordan Thermal Products Ltd., 314
P.J. Hannah Equipment Sales Corp., 315
Peco Filters Ltd., 320
PerkinElmer Life & Analytical Sciences Canada Inc., 321
Plasticair Inc., 326
PlymoVent Canada Inc., 326
Precisioneering Ltd., 330
Procedair Industries Inc., 333
Process Innovations Canada Inc., 333
Promet Environmental Group Ltd., 334
ProViro Instrumentation Inc., 335
Pylon Electronics Inc., 337
Q-Air Environmental Controls Ltd., 337
Quatrosense Environmental Ltd., 338
QuestAir Technologies Inc., 339
R.A. Kirby Sales Inc., 339
Silex Innovations Inc., 367
Smiths Detection, 371
Sutherland-Schultz Inc., 384
T-G Burgmann, 385
Tekran Canada, 389
Temprite Industries Ltd., 389
Thermal Energy International Inc., 394
TLT Co-Vent, 396
TurboSonic Inc., 404
Venables Machine Works Ltd., 410
Venmar Ventilation Inc., 410
Waterloo Evaporateurs Inc., 422
Watson Process Systems, 423

YES Environment Technologies Inc., 435
Zeton Inc., 437

Air Pollution Control Services
See also **Air Quality Assessment Services; Air Quality Management (General); Air Quality Services, Indoor; Heating, Ventilation & Air Conditioning Services**
A. Lanfranco & Associates Inc., 63
ALTECH Environmental Consulting Ltd., 81
Aqua Terre Solutions Inc., 88
Armstrong Monitoring Corp., 91
BH Engineering Systems Ltd., 107
Blue-Zone Technologies Ltd., 110
C.V. Environmental Services, 120
Canadian Emissions Ltd., 124
Church & Trought Inc., 140
Conor Pacific Environmental Technology Inc., 150
Diagnostic Engineering Inc., 163
DJA Environmental Consultants Inc., 164
E.K. Gillin & Associates Inc., 168
Enviro Clean Ltd., 182
Enviro Rentals, 182
Eucania International Inc., 190
Fluor Canada, 197
Glos Associates Inc., 214
Hatch Ltd., 226
Hazard Control Systems Inc., 227
HLS Ecolo, 232
K-Tech Services Ltd., 254
KGS Group Inc., 257
Levelton Consultants Ltd., 270
Oakhill Environmental, 310
Pacwill Environmental, 317
Pollutech Group of Companies Inc., 327
Poyry (Vancouver) Inc., 329
Rowan Williams Davies & Irwin Inc., 352
RPC, 353
SENES Consultants Limited, 362
Trow Consulting Engineers Ltd., 403

Air Quality Assessment Services
See also **Air Pollution Control Services**
A&A Environmental Consultants Inc., 63
A. Lanfranco & Associates Inc., 63
Airtest Technologies Inc., 76
Airzone One Ltd., 76
ALARA Industrial Hygiene Services Ltd., 76
André Simard et associés ltée, 85
APS Aviation Inc., 87
Avalon Mechanical Consultants Ltd., 98
Barrat & Associates Inc., 101
Canadian Environmental Auditors Inc., 124
Canspect Corporation, 127
Chem Solv, 139
Clean Air Services Inc., 142
Coastal Zones Research Institute Inc., 145
Decommissioning Consulting Services Limited, 159
Diagnostic Engineering Inc., 163
Entech Environmental Consultants Ltd., 181
Entech Laboratories, 181
Enviro Rentals, 182
Envirometrex, 184
Flett Research, 196
George Grant Consulting, 211
Gough Risk Management Ltd., 215
Guelph Chemical Laboratories, 222
Guild Contracting Specialists Inc., 222
Hatfield Group, 226
Healthy Homes Consulting, 228
Integra Environmental Inc., 243
Interior Weather Services Ltd., 245
K-Tech Services Ltd., 254
KGS Group Inc., 257
Kinectrics Inc., 257
Kodiak Environmental Limited, 259
Lakes Environmental Software, 263
LEHDER Environmental Services Ltd., 267
Maxxam Analytics Inc., 283
Maxxam Analytics Ltd., 283
McAtee Safety & Environmental Health Services Ltd., 284
Michael Holliday & Associates, 288
Mirarco Mining Innovation, 290
New Trend Environmental Services, 301
Nexus Solutions Inc., 303
Niagara Environmental Dynamics, 303
North West Environmental Group, 306

OCL Services Ltd., 311
Ontario Building Solutions, 312
OSB Services, 314
Paracel Laboratories Ltd., 318
Procyon Consulting Inc., 333
REDUCT & Lobbe Technologies Inc., 344
RPC, 353
Sols Consultants Ltée, 373
Sonepar Canada, 373
Sutherland-Schultz Inc., 384
Tang G. Lee Architect, 386
Terrapex Environmental Ltd., 390
Theodor D. Sterling & Associates Ltd., 393
Unisearch Associates Inc., 405
Wilcorp Manufacturing, 431

Air Quality Management (General)
See also **Air Pollution Control Equipment; Air Pollution Control Services; Pollution Prevention Services**
AB Mechanical Ltd., 64
ABGG Technologies, Inc., 65
Acer Environmental Services Ltd., 66
Aercoustics Engineering Limited, 71
Aeroflo Inc., 71
Alpha Controls & Instrumentation, 79
AMKO Systems Inc., 84
Atlantic Air Cleaning Specialists Ltd., 95
Atlantic Purification Systems, 97
Biolab Inc., 108
BOMA Environmental & Safety Inc., 113
BP Trading Ltd., 114
CBCL Limited, 132
Church & Trought Inc., 140
Cimatec Environmental Engineering Inc., 141
Clean Air & Water Centre, 142
Climate Change Central, 144
Cole-Parmer Canada Inc., 146
CompreVac Inc., 147
Conestoga-Rovers & Associates, 149
Data Tech Environmental Services, 157
Dessau, Inc., 162
Diagnostic Engineering Inc., 163
ECO Fuel Systems Inc., 170
EEP Engineered & Environmental Products Inc., 173
EMP Environmental Management & Protection Corporation, 177
Enercombustion Ltd., 179
Envirometrex, 184
Explore Plus Duct Cleaning Ltd., 192
Filter Innovations Inc., 195
Golder Associates Ltd., 214
Healthy Homes Consulting, 228
Henlex Inc., 229
HLS Ecolo, 232
Hydro-Com Technologies Ltd., 236
Island Clean Air Inc., 248
Michael Holliday & Associates, 288
New Trend Environmental Services, 301
Ortech Environmental Inc., 314
Pelmar Engineering Ltd., 320
Radiation Environmental Management Systems Inc., 341
Ramsay Machine Works Ltd., 342
Robinson Solutions, 348
Roche ltée, Groupe-conseil, 348
SNC-Lavalin Group Inc., 371
Stantec Inc., 377
Strum Environmental, 381
TetrES Consultants Inc., 391
Venerus International Purification Inc., 410
Wood Laboratory Ltd., 433

Air Quality Services, Indoor
See also **Air Pollution Control Services**
A. Lanfranco & Associates Inc., 63
AA Environmental & Associates, 64
ACM Environmental Corporation, 66
Airtest Technologies Inc., 76
Airzone One Ltd., 76
ALARA Industrial Hygiene Services Ltd., 76
Alpha Controls & Instrumentation, 79
Appin Associates, 87
Armstrong Monitoring Corp., 91
Biolab Inc., 108
Buchan, Lawton, Parent Ltd., 118
Clean Air Services Inc., 142
Con-Test, A Division of Contamination Containment Technology Inc., 148

Subject Index

Dectron Internationale, 159
Diagnostic Engineering Inc., 163
Digicon Building Control Solutions, 163
Eagle Home Inspection Services Inc., 168
ECE Group - a Division of Conestoga-Rovers & Associates, 170
Enermodal Engineering Ltd., 179
Engine Control Systems, 180
Enviro Rentals, 182
Fisher Environmental Ltd., 196
Healthy Homes Consulting, 228
HETEK Solutions Inc., 230
Hi-Q Developments Ltd., 231
Indoor Air Quality Ottawa, 240
Jagger Hims Limited, 250
KBU Environmental Technologies Inc., 255
Kodiak Environmental Limited, 259
L.W. Ward Limited, 261
LEX Scientific Inc., 271
Maritime Testing Ltd., 281
Maxxam Analytics Inc., 283
Maxxam Analytics Ltd., 283
McAtee Safety & Environmental Health Services Ltd., 284
Mold & Bacteria Consulting Laboratories (MBL) Inc., 292
New Trend Environmental Services, 301
Ogilvie Scientific Inc., 311
OSB Services, 314
Paracel Laboratories Ltd., 318
PHH ARC Environmental Ltd., 322
Pinchin Environmental Ltd., 324
Power Suction Services Ltd., 329
Power Vac of Nova Scotia, 329
RPC, 353
Sick Building Solutions, 366
Theodor D. Sterling & Associates Ltd., 393
Thermal Technics Corporation, 394
Venmar CES, Inc., 410
Venmar Ventilation Inc., 410
Vizon SciTec Inc., 414
Wilcorp Manufacturing, 431

Aluminum Recycling
See also Metals Recycling; Recycling Services (General)
C-Max Transportation Equipment, 119
Calgary Metal (1985) Ltd., 121
HMI Industries, 232
Hydro Dyne Inc., 236
John Zubick Ltd. Scrap Metals, 253
Joseph & Co. Inc., 253
Neighborhood Recycling, 299
Recyclage d'Alluminium Québec, 343
Rotblott & Sons Ltd., 352
Traders Metal Company Ltd., 400
Triple M Metal, 402
Western Scrap Metals, 429
Wheatland Regional Centre Inc. & SARCAN Recycling, 431

Analytical Instruments
See Measuring & Monitoring Equipment, Laboratory

Anti-freeze Recycling
See also Recycling Services (General)
Active Chemicals Ltd., 67
Anachem Ltd., 84
Barrington Environmental Services, 102
Barrington Industrial Services Limited, 102
CCR Technologies Ltd., 133
Eastern Environmental Services Ltd., 169
Enviro-Gun Ltd., 182
Inland Technologies Inc., 242
Tri-Arrow Industrial Recovery Inc., 401
WRS Environmental, 434
Wynn's Canada Ltd., 435

Anti-freeze, Recycled
Advanced Coolant Technologies Inc., 69
Wynn's Canada Ltd., 435

Aquaculture
See Fisheries & Aquaculture Management

Aquaculture
See Fisheries & Aquaculture Management

Architectural Services
See also Environmental Consulting & Contracting Services (General); House & Home Design, Energy-Efficient
Acoustic Solutions Ltd., 67

BAE Newplan Group Ltd., 101
Brytex Building Systems Inc., 117
Charles Simon Architect & Planner, 138
Connor Architects & Planners, 150
IBI Group, 238
P.J. Cluff Architect Inc., 315
Richard Kadulski Architect, 346

Arctic/Permafrost Engineering
See also Engineering Consulting Services (General)
Bercha Group, 105
BMT Fleet Technology Ltd., 111
Canatec Consultants Ltd., 125
CCL/IBI, 133
EBA Engineering Consultants Ltd., 169
Ferguson Simek Clark, 194
Groupe Stavibel Inc., 221
J.D. Mollard & Associates Ltd., 249
Mondry Del Zotto et associés inc., 292
Offshore Design Associates Inc., 311
Sandwell Engineering Inc., 356
SEA Engineering Company Inc., 360
SGE Hatch Ltd., 364
Talon Projects Inc., 386
Terratech, 390
Williams Engineering Inc., 432

Asbestos Abatement Services
See also Waste Management (General); Waste Management, Liquid/Hazardous
ACM Environmental Corporation, 66
Aluma Systems Inc., 82
Asbeguard Equipment Inc., 93
Cannington Group, 126
Canwest Pumping Systems Ltd., 127
Dewar Insulations Ltd., 162
Dewar Pacific Projects Ltd., 162
Donalco Inc., 165
DRL Environmental Services, 166
Enviro Clean Ltd., 182
Hazmasters Environmental Controls Inc., 228
International Marine Salvage Inc., 245
Kimco Steel Sales Limited, 257
Medina Construction Limited, 286
Monalt Environmental Inc., 292
Nilfisk-Advance Canada Company, 304
PHH ARC Environmental Ltd., 322
Pinchin Environmental Ltd., 324
Power Vac of Nova Scotia, 329
Priestly Demolition Inc., 332
Quantum Murray LP, 338
Safety Express Ltd., 355
Sealtech Restorations Inc., 361
Sendex Environmental Corp., 362
Servco Environmental Solutions Inc., 363
Sprung Instant Structures Ltd., 376
Sutherland-Schultz Inc., 384
Tiger-Vac International Inc., 396
TriWaste Services Inc., 402
Western Industrial Services Ltd., 429

Audit Services, Energy
See also Energy Services
Air Solutions Inc., 75
Amberg Corp. - Environmental & Regulatory Consultants, 82
Anrep Krieg Desilets Gravelle Ltd., 86
Atlantic Orient Canada Inc., 96
Avalon Mechanical Consultants Ltd., 98
Bowser Technical Inc., 114
Buchan, Lawton, Parent Ltd., 118
COGENCanada, 146
David A. McLean & Associates, 158
Denoco Energy Systems Ltd., 161
Efficiency Engineering Inc., 173
Energy Conservation Contractors Warranty Corporation, 179
Enermodal Engineering Ltd., 179
Everts-Lind Enterprises, 191
Faraci Engineering, 194
KC Environmental Group Ltd., 256
Kinder Morgan Canada Inc., 257
NEDCO, 299
Optimira Controls, 313
Pepper Compressed Air & Gas Ltd., 321
Robb Engineering Ltd., 347
Smith & Andersen Consulting Engineering, 370
Sundog Energy Management, 382

Walter Dow Associates Ltd., 416
Willis Energy Services Ltd., 432
Wind Power Inc., 433

Audit Services, Environmental
See also Environmental Consulting & Contracting Services (General); ISO 14000 Registrar
ACM Environmental Corporation, 66
Aercoustics Engineering Limited, 71
AET Group Inc., 72
Agrosysts Ltée, 73
Airzone One Ltd., 76
Amberg Corp. - Environmental & Regulatory Consultants, 82
Antelope Land Services Inc., 86
Apex Geoscience Ltd., 86
Ark Envirotech Inc., 91
Arrakis Consultants Inc., 92
Avoca-tec Environmental Services Inc., 99
BAE Newplan Group Ltd., 101
Barenco Inc., 101
Barrat & Associates Inc., 101
Biophilia Inc., 109
The Brofield Group, 391
Buchan, Lawton, Parent Ltd., 118
Buckham Transport Ltd., 118
Cactus Environmental Services Ltd., 120
Canadian Environmental Auditors Inc., 124
Canadian Environmental Group, 124
Cascades Inc., 130
Cathy's Crawly Composters, 132
Cecon Limited, 135
CIMA+, 141
CMEL Enterprises Ltd., 144
Coffey Geotechnics Inc., 146
Community Resource Services Ltd., 147
Conestoga-Rovers & Associates, 149
Cyr Engineering Ltd., 155
D.M. Wills Associates Limited, 156
David A. McLean & Associates, 158
Dell Tech Laboratories Ltd., 160
DJA Environmental Consultants Inc., 164
Duerden & Keane Consultants Inc., 167
Earthbound Environmental Inc., 168
Eco-North Laboratories, 171
Eco2 Systems Inc., 171
Ecotech Planners & Advisors Inc., 172
Elford Environmental, 175
Enermodal Engineering Ltd., 179
EnvirInfo, 182
Enviro-Met Engineering, 183
Enviro-RISQUE Inc., 183
Enviroconseil, 183
Environmental Advisory Group, 185
Environmental Allies Inc., 185
Environmental Reporting Systems Limited, 186
Envision Compliance, 188
EthicScan Canada, 190
Experts-Conseils BMST inc., 192
Exploitation Santec Inc., 192
ExTech Environmental Services Inc., 192
Flett Research, 196
G.T. Wood Co. Ltd., 204
Global Engineering & Testing Ltd., 213
GlobalTox International Consultants Inc., 213
Green Key Solutions Inc., 217
Green Plan Ltd., 217
Greenland International Consulting Inc., 218
GreenWare Environmental Systems Inc., 218
Groupe SOLROC, 221
Heritage Research Associates Inc., 230
Hiltz & Seamone Co. Ltd., 232
HSE Integrated, 234
Hydro Vision America, 236
Inspec-Sol Inc., 242
Institute of Environmental Research Inc., 243
Intera Engineering Ltd., 244
Interra Environmental Inc., 246
Investigative Science Inc., 247
J&F Waste Systems Inc., 249
JTU Consulting, 253
KBM Forestry Consultants Inc., 255
KC Environmental Group Ltd., 256
Kent Engineering Ltd., 256
Keystone Environmental Ltd., 257
Les Laboratoires Shermont Inc., 269

CANADIAN ENVIRONMENTAL RESOURCE GUIDE 2011-2012

Subject Index

LEX Scientific Inc., 271
M+A Environmental Consultants, 276
Maratek Environmental Inc., 280
Marbicon Inc., 280
Maritime Testing Ltd., 281
McClymont & Rak Engineers, Inc., 284
MTE Consultants Inc., 294
Multiview Locates Inc., 295
Muskoka Containerized Services Ltd., 295
MWH Canada Inc., 295
New East Consulting Services Ltd., 301
Next Environmental, 303
Niagara Environmental Dynamics, 303
North Shore Management Systems Inc., 306
OCL Services Ltd., 311
Paragon Soil & Environmental Consulting Inc., 318
Paul G. Chénard, 319
Penny & Casson Co., 321
Peter T. Mitches & Associates Limited; Project Managers & Consulting, 321
Peto MacCallum Ltd., 321
Pilot Performance Resources Management Inc., 324
PINTER & Associates Ltd., 324
Pottinger Gaherty Environmental Consultants Ltd., 328
PricewaterhouseCoopers Management Consultants, 332
Pridy Associates, 332
Procyon Consulting Inc., 333
ProSolve Consulting Ltd., 335
Redstone Associates Ltd., 343
Rescan Environmental Services Ltd., 345
Risk Check Environmental Ltd., 347
Robinson Consultants Inc., 348
Ronel Engineering Ltd., 351
Rudiger Enterprises Ltd., 354
Sendex Environmental Corp., 362
Servco Environmental Solutions Inc., 363
Services d'Évaluation Santé/Toxicologie Inc., 363
SGS Canada Inc., 364
SLR Consulting Ltd. (Canada), 370
SMS Engineering Ltd., 371
Specialty Technical Publishers, 375
Spill Management Inc., 376
Stratos Inc., 380
Summerhill Group, 381
T. Harris Environmental Management Inc., 385
Talon Projects Inc., 386
Thurber Engineering Ltd., 395
TriWaste Services Inc., 402
Utility Risk Management Ltd., 408
Waste Logic Inc., 417
Water & Earth Science Associates Ltd., 421
Western Site Technologies Inc., 430
Williams Engineering Inc., 432
Winchurch Environmental Inc., 432
Wotherspoon Environmental Inc., 434

Balers & Compactors, Waste
See also **Waste Collection Services & Equipment, Solid; Waste Management, Solid**
All Waste Removal Inc., 78
Amity Plastics Ltd., 84
Les Bras d'Fer Gingras Inc., 267
The Brofield Group, 391
Canadian Recycling Equipment & Systems Ltd., 125
Caristrap International Inc., 128
Fastco Equipment Corporation, 194
Industries Machinex Inc., 241
Kernic Systems Inc., 257
Machinerie Laurin Inc., 278
Sleegers Engineering Inc., 370

Baseline Studies, Environmental
See also **Environmental Consulting & Contracting Services (General)**
Airzone One Ltd., 76
Archipelago Marine Research Ltd., 90
Biothermica, 109
Brincad Technologies Inc., 116
Cascade Environmental Resource Group. Ltd., 130
Cottonwood Consultants Ltd., 152
East Coast Aquatics, 169
Ecotech Planners & Advisors Inc., 172
Environmental Economics International, 185
Envirosphere Consultants Ltd., 187
Ferguson Simek Clark, 194
Fraser Environmental Services, 201
Geo-Logic Inc., 210
Geographic Dynamics Corp., 211
Geowest Environmental Consultants, 212
Groupe SOLROC, 221
Hatfield Group, 226
Hemmera Envirochem Inc., 229
Hydro Vision America, 236
Icefield Instruments Inc., 238
Interior Weather Services Ltd., 245
Ken Summers Biological Services, 256
Laboratoires d'Expertises de Québec Ltée, 262
Land & Sea Environmental Consultants Ltd., 264
Latimat Inc., 265
Lupien Rosenberg Consultants Inc., 274
Marbicon Inc., 280
Metocean Data Systems Limited, 287
MWH Canada Inc., 295
NAR Environmental Consultants Inc., 297
Nelson Environmental Services, 299
New East Consulting Services Ltd., 301
OCL Services Ltd., 311
Paul F. Wilkinson & Associates Inc., 319
Pisces Environmental Consulting Services Ltd., 325
Planning & Engineering Initiatives Ltd., 325
R.U. Kistritz Consultants Ltd., 341
Rescan Environmental Services Ltd., 345
Services d'Évaluation Santé/Toxicologie Inc., 363
SLR Consulting Ltd. (Canada), 370
SPG Hydro International Inc., 375
Symbion Consultants, 384
Tanknology Canada Inc., 386
Taylor Mazier Associates, 387
Tera Environmental Consultants (Alta) Ltd., 389
Terrapex Environmental Ltd., 390
TJ Consulting Ltd., 396
Unisearch Associates Inc., 405
Wakefield Acoustics Ltd., 416
Western Subsea Technology Ltd., 430
Zbeetnoff Agro-Environmental Consulting, 436

Batteries Recycling
See also **Recycling Services (General)**
The Battery Broker Environmental Services Inc., 391
Calgary Metal (1985) Ltd., 121
HMI Industries, 232
John Zubick Ltd. Scrap Metals, 253
Joseph & Co. Inc., 253
Neighborhood Recycling, 299
Nova PB Inc., 308
Raw Materials Corporation, 342
Rechargeable Battery Recycling Corporation, 343
Rotblott & Sons Ltd., 352
ToxCo Waste Management Ltd., 399
Western Scrap Metals, 429

Biological Management
See also **Resource Management Services (General)**
Avmor Ltd., 99
Beulah Tec Limited, 106
Biorex Inc., 109
Centre de Toxicologie du Québec, 136
East Coast Aquatics, 169
Ecocern Inc., 171
Fraser Environmental Services, 201
Geographic Dynamics Corp., 211
LGL Limited Environmental Research Associates, 271
MacDonnell Group, 277
Precision Identification Biological Consultants, 330
R.H. Loucks Oceanology, 340
Robertson Environmental Services Ltd., 348
Scott Resource Services Inc., 360
SPG Hydro International Inc., 375
Tarandus Associates Limited, 387

Biomedical Waste Treatment & Disposal
See also **Waste Management (General); Waste Management, Liquid/Hazardous**
Infratech Corporation, 241
Ivey International Inc., 249
Sprung Instant Structures Ltd., 376
Trecan Combustion Ltd., 400
Vanport Sterilizers Inc., 409

Bioremediation Services
See also **Engineering Consulting Services (General)**
Adventus Canada Inc., 69
Alpine Environmental Ltd., 80
Arbrux Limited, 89
ARC Geobac Group Inc., 89
Atlantic Soils & Associated Management Ltd., 97
BDM Supply Limited, 103
BECK Drilling and Environmental Services Ltd., 104
Beulah Tec Limited, 106
Biogénie, 108
BIOREM Inc., 109
Biotech Solutions, 109
C3 Environmental Group, 120
Cannington Group, 126
CIMA+, 141
Conor Pacific Environmental Technology Inc., 150
Les Consultants RSA, 268
EBA Engineering Consultants Ltd., 169
EcoEthic Inc., 171
Ecomark Ltd., 172
Entraco, 181
Enviro-Safe Chemicals Canada Inc., 183
Enviroconseil, 183
Environmental Solutions Remediation Services, 186
Envirosoil Ltd., 187
GAP EnviroMicrobial Services Inc., 204
GDG Environnement Ltée, 205
George Grant Consulting, 211
Global Engineering & Testing Ltd., 213
GPEC Global Corp., 215
Green Soils Inc., 217
Horizon Environment Inc., 233
Hydrogéo Plus Inc., 236
Investigative Science Inc., 247
Jagger Hims Limited, 250
Kaizen Environmental Services Inc., 254
KC Environmental Group Ltd., 256
MacDonnell Group, 277
Malroz Engineering Inc., 279
Maritime Microbiologicals Inc., 281
Mikro-Tek Inc., 289
Nelson Environmental Remediation Ltd., 299
Next Environmental, 303
Oakridge Environmental Ltd., 310
R&R Drilling Supply Ltd., 339
Rubicon Environmental Inc., 354
Sanexen Environmental Services Inc., 357
Servco Environmental Solutions Inc., 363
Sinanni Inc., 369
Solaction Inc., 372
Sumas Environmental Services Inc., 381
System Ecotechnologies Inc., 385
TankTek Environmental Services Ltd., 386
Technisol Environnement, 388
Terratechnik Environmental Limited, 391
UNOTEC, 407
Vizon SciTec Inc., 414
W.B. Beatty & Associates, 414

Biotechnology Services
See also **Biotreatment Equipment, Water**
BIOREM Inc., 109
Biotech Solutions, 109
Environmental Waste International, 186
Henry Kortekaas & Associates Inc., 229
Maritime Microbiologicals Inc., 281
Sanexen Environmental Services Inc., 357
Scientific Instrumentation Ltd., 360
Scott Resource Services Inc., 360
Sick Building Solutions, 366
Vizon SciTec Inc., 414

Biotreatment Equipment, Water
See also **Biotechnology Services; Water, Wastewater & Groundwater Equipment**
Advanced Biotechnology Inc., 69
Aerzen Canada Surpresseurs Compresseurs inc., 71
Bacta-Pur, 101
Clean Earth Solutions Ltd., 142
Condor Engineering Ltd., 149
ENV Treatment Systems Inc., 182
Envirogineering, 184
Environmental Waste International, 186
EnviroPower Equipment Marketing Inc., 187
Fair Canada Engineering Ltd., 193
General Filtration, 206
H2O Innovation Inc., 223
Hydroxyl Systems Inc., 237
Ivey International Inc., 249

Mancorp Industrial Sales Ltd., 279
Pacific Metals Recycling International, 316
Premier Tech Environment, 331
Premier Tech Environnement / Division municipale, commerciale et ind, 331
Sanexen Environmental Services Inc., 357
Secural Inc., 361
Simark Controls Ltd., 368
Suimon Engineering Canada Ltd., 381
Sunset Solar Systems Ltd., 382
Tanks-A-Lot Ltd., 386
TPE Technologies Inc., 399

Building Materials Consulting, Hazardous
See also Waste Management, Liquid/Hazardous
Healthy Homes Consulting, 228
Hi-Q Developments Ltd., 231
Kleinfeldt Consultants Limited, 258
Multiview Locates Inc., 295
Priestly Demolition Inc., 332
W.T. McGinn & Associates Ltd., 415

Business Development Services
See also Financial & Marketing Services (General); Marketing Services
Air Liquide Canada Ltée, 74
Cheminfo Services Inc., 139
The Delphi Group, 392
Eco Canada, 170
Environmental Consultants & Engineers, 185
Environmental R&D Capital Corporation, 185
The Impact Group, 392
John McMullen & Associates, 252
Nisymco Inc., 304
Quality Matters Inc., 338
Quorum Growth Inc., 339
Santinel Inc., 357
Stratem Inc., 380
University Technologies International, 406

Calibration Equipment, Air
See also Air Pollution Control Equipment
AMKO Systems Inc., 84
Armstrong Monitoring Corp., 91
CD Nova, 134
Drexan Energy Systems Inc., 166
ITM Instruments, 248
RST Instruments Ltd., 354
Sick Building Solutions, 366
Staveley Services Canada Inc., 380
WJF Instrumentation (1990) Ltd., 433

Calibration Equipment, Water & Wastewater
See also Water, Wastewater & Groundwater Equipment
Chem Action Inc., 139
Environnement ESA Inc., 186
Guildline Instruments Limited, 222
Jetvac Inc., 251
Marsh Instrumentation Inc., 281
Metcon Sales & Engineering Ltd., 287
ODIM Brooke Ocean, 311
ProViro Instrumentation Inc., 335
RST Instruments Ltd., 354
Satlantic, 358

Cardboard Recycling
See also Recycling Services (General)
Can-Cell Industries Inc., 123
Crown Packaging Ltd., 154
Emery International Developments, 177
Hanna Paper Fibres Ltd., 224
Kemel Cartons (1973) Ltd., 256
Kimco Steel Sales Limited, 257
Owen G. Carney Ltd., 315
Sonoco Recycling Ltd., 374
Turcal, 404
Wheatland Regional Centre Inc. & SARCAN Recycling, 431

Cartographic Services
See Mapping & Surveying Services

CFC Recovery
See also Waste Management, Liquid/Hazardous
Aerzen Canada Surpresseurs Compresseurs inc., 71
Fielding Chemical Technologies Inc., 195
Malnar Industries Ltd., 279
Penn Refrigeration Ltd., 321
Ray Electric Ltd., 342

Refrigerant Services Inc., 344
Sutherland-Schultz Inc., 384

Chemical & Physical Waste Plants
See also Waste Treatment & Disposal Facilities
Capital H2O Systems Inc., 128
D. Greenfield Associates Ltd., 156
ELI Eco Chemical Technologies Inc., 175
Miller Environmental Corp., 290
Nemato Inc., 300
Reinforced Plastic Systems Inc., 344
René Gervais Inc., Consultants, 345
Spring Air Silver Services Ltd., 376
Sumas Environmental Services Inc., 381
Summit Structures, 382
Swan Hills Treatment Centre, 384

Chemical Feeding & Mixing Equipment
See also Water, Wastewater & Groundwater Equipment
ACG Technology Ltd., 66
ACO Container Systems Ltd., 67
Apex Industries Inc., 86
Ashland Canada, 93
Auto-Chlor Inc., 98
Canbar Inc., 126
Capital H2O Systems Inc., 128
Charland Thermojet Inc., 138
Chem Action Inc., 139
Con-V-Air Inc., 148
Continental Conveyor Ontario Ltd., 151
Les Contrôles PROVAN Associés Inc., 268
Degussa Canada Inc., 159
Drexan Energy Systems Inc., 166
Ecodyne Ltd., 171
F.E. Myers, 193
Fabco Plastics Wholesale (Ontario) Limited, 193
Firing Industries Ltd., 195
Flowserve Inc., 197
H.E. Bent Services Ltd., 223
Hayward Gordon Ltd., 227
Hike Metal Products Ltd., 231
Indachem Inc., 240
Ingersoll-Rand Canada Inc., 241
J&M Industrial Engineering & Sales Ltd., 249
John Thurston Machine Ltd., 253
L.E. Washington Sales Ltd., 261
Magnor, Division of Magchem, 278
Matco Ltd., 282
Metcon Sales & Engineering Ltd., 287
Nalco Canada Co., 296
National Process Equipment Inc., 298
Nordic Systems Corporation, 305
Nortec S.G.S. Inc., 306
Patterson Industries (Canada) Ltd., 319
Performance Fluid Equipement Inc., 321
Plastics America, 326
Promag Enviro Systems Ltd., 334
ProMinent Fluid Controls Ltd., 334
Resource Systems Inc., 345
Siemens Water Technologies, 367
Smart Turner Pumps, 370
T.D. Rooke Associates Ltd., 385
Triangle Fluid Controls Ltd., 401
VIQUA - A Trojan Technologies Company, 413
Weir Power & Industrial, 424
Windsor Pump Co. Ltd., 433

Chemical Production
See also Laboratory Services (General)
AGAT Laboratories Ltd., 72
Atotech Canada Ltd., 97
Biopacific Diagnostic Inc., 109
Diacon Technologies Ltd., 163
Genzyme Canada Inc., 210
Le Groupe Sani Marc, 265
Megalab Inc., 286
Quatic Industries Inc., 338
Ultra-Chem Industries Ltd., 405

Chemical Recycling
See also Paint/Solvent Recycling; Recycling Services (General)
Alfa Laval Inc., 78
CCR Technologies Ltd., 133
Climate Control Systems Inc., 144
Greenflow Environmental Services Inc., 217
Maratek Environmental Inc., 280

Proline Filter Systems Inc., 334
Refined Specialty Chemicals Inc., 344
Refrigerant Services Inc., 344

Chemicals, Air Treatment
See also Air Pollution Control Equipment
AMKO Systems Inc., 84
Anderson Water Systems, 85
Avmor Ltd., 99
Blue Water Agencies Ltd., 110
Degussa Canada Inc., 159
GPEC Global Corp., 215
Hazelmere Research Ltd., 228
ISCA Management Ltd., 248
Lambton Scientific, 263
Levy's Machine Works Ltd., 271
Nature's Environmental Products Inc., 298
Prism Chemicals Inc., 332
Whisco Ltd., 431

Chemicals, Water Treatment
See also Water, Wastewater & Groundwater Equipment
A&C Produits Chimiques Americains Ltée, 63
Accuworx Inc., 66
Advance Laboratories Ltd., 69
Anco Chemicals Inc., 85
Ashland Canada, 93
Atotech Canada Ltd., 97
Barrington Environmental Services, 102
Baymag Inc., 103
Benson Chemicals Limited, 105
BioSolve of Canada Ltd., 109
Border Chemical Company Ltd., 114
Cartier Chemicals Ltd., 130
Degussa Canada Inc., 159
Diacon Technologies Ltd., 163
Eco-Tec Ltd., 171
Elgin Pure Water Supply, 175
EnviroMetal Technologies Inc., 184
Fanchem Ltd., 193
GPEC Global Corp., 215
Graymont Inc., 216
Hollimex Products Ltd., 232
Hotsy Pressure Washers Ltd., 233
Kam Biotechnology Ltd., 254
Kemira Water Solutions Canada Inc., 256
Lacombe Waste Services, 262
Lambton Scientific, 263
Lavo Inc., 265
Mar Cor Purification, 280
Marsulex Inc., 281
Megalab Inc., 286
Metafix, 287
Monsanto Canada Inc., 293
Nalco Canada Co., 296
Nature's Environmental Products Inc., 298
Niagara Water Conditioning Ltd., 303
Nouvelle Technologie (TEKNO), 308
Produits Chimiques Handy Ltée, 333
Quatic Industries Inc., 338
Qwatro Corporation, 339
RenuWater Centre, 345
Syndel International Inc., 385
Tri-Arrow Industrial Recovery Inc., 401

Clarifiers, Water & Wastewater
See also Water, Wastewater & Groundwater Equipment
ACG Technology Ltd., 66
Anderson Water Systems, 85
Andritz Bird, 85
Arlat Technology, 91
Ashland Canada, 93
Capital H2O Systems Inc., 128
Ecofluid Systems Inc., 171
ENV Treatment Systems Inc., 182
Firing Industries Ltd., 195
FLSmidth Canada Ltd., 197
Frontenac Environmental Ltd., 202
GEA Westfalia Separator Canada, Inc., 205
GL&V - Groupe Laperrière & Verreault Inc., 212
GLM Tanks & Equipment Ltd., 213
Global Dewatering Ltd., 213
Greatario Industrial Storage Systems Ltd., 217
Hike Metal Products Ltd., 231
Hydro-Logic Environmental Inc., 236
Jes-Chem Ltd., 251

Subject Index

Komline-Sanderson Ltd., 259
Lambton Scientific, 263
Mancorp Industrial Sales Ltd., 279
Markland Specialty Engineering Ltd., 281
O'Connor Tanks Ltd., 310
Parkson Corporation, 319
Promag Enviro Systems Ltd., 334
Sunset Solar Systems Ltd., 382
U.S. Filter/Asdor Ltd., 405
Universal Filter Media, 406

Cleaners & Chemicals
See also Industrial Management (General); Industrial Products

Active Chemicals Ltd., 67
Avmor Ltd., 99
Bioforj Environmental Services, 108
BioSolve of Canada Ltd., 109
Border Chemical Company Ltd., 114
Canada Colors & Chemicals Ltd., 123
Cartier Chemicals Ltd., 130
Cascades Resource, 131
Degussa Canada Inc., 159
Dell Tech Laboratories Ltd., 160
EnviroSan Products Ltd./SOLUTION 2000, 187
Envirotec Services Incorporated, 187
GPEC Global Corp., 215
Hollimex Products Ltd., 232
Howard Marten Fluid Technologies Inc., 234
IMP Liquid Meters & Petroleum Services, 239
J. Walter Company Ltd., 249
Kam Biotechnology Ltd., 254
Larose & Fils Ltée, 264
Lord & Partners Ltd., 274
Megalab Inc., 286
Nova Chemicals Corporation, 308
Onyx Chemical Cleaning, 313
Orchid Cellmark ULC, 314
Prism Chemicals Inc., 332
Quatic Industries Inc., 338
Qwatro Corporation, 339
Rayplex Limited, 342
Rochester Midland Ltd., 349
Ross Healthcare, Inc., 351
Sanbec, 356
Sensible Life Products, 362
Tankman, 386
West Penetone Inc., 424
Zorbit Technologies Inc., 437

Cleaning Systems & Services
See also Industrial Management (General)

Accuworx Inc., 66
Active Chemicals Ltd., 67
Allianz Madvac Inc., 79
Avmor Ltd., 99
Bacta-Pur, 101
Barrington Industrial Services Limited, 102
Clean Air Services Inc., 142
Clean Harbors Energy & Industrial Services Corp., 142
Clean Ontario, 143
Clear Environmental Products, 143
DynaMotive Energy Systems Corporation, 167
Le Groupe Sani Marc, 265
J. Walter Company Ltd., 249
Lojen Industrial Cleaning Ltd., 273
Lord & Partners Ltd., 274
Metrovan Hotsy Equipment Ltd., 288
Nilfisk-Advance Canada Company, 304
Omega Recycling Technologies, 312
Power Vac of Nova Scotia, 329
Proceco Ltd., 333
Proline Filter Systems Inc., 334
Sanbec, 356
Sanexen Environmental Services Inc., 357
Sprayaway Marine Services Ltd., 376
3M Canada Company, 395
Thuro Inc., 396
Trimax Residuals Management Inc., 401
Western Industrial Services Ltd., 429
Whisco Ltd., 431

Coastal Management
See Marine Management

Cogeneration, Industrial
See also Energy Services

Air Liquide Canada Ltée, 74
Aldworth Engineering Inc., 77
Altek Power Corporation, 81
Biothermica, 109
Cook Engineering, 151
Groupe RSW inc., 220
Honey Electric Ltd., 233
Hooper Welding Enterprises Ltd., 233
Inproheat Industries Ltd., 242
Pepper Compressed Air & Gas Ltd., 321
Suncurrent Industries Inc., 382
Walker Industries Holdings Ltd., 416
Walter Dow Associates Ltd., 416
Wellons Canada, 424
Willis Energy Services Ltd., 432

Compost Equipment
See also Organic Matter Recycling; Recycling Services (General)

Ag-West Bio Inc., 72
AIM Environmental Group, 74
Anex Distributors Ltd., 86
Aquaterre Inc., 89
Biomax Inc., 108
The Brofield Group, 391
Busch Systems International Inc., 118
Cathy's Crawly Composters, 132
Clivus Multrum Canada Ltd., 144
Compost Management, 147
Consolidated Envirowaste Industries Inc., 150
Double T Equipment Ltd., 165
Ferme R&B Fafard Inc., 194
Global Repair Ltd., 213
IPL Inc., 247
Joe Johnson Equipment Inc., 252
LH - Division of Full Circle Organics Inc., 272
Loewen Welding & Manufacturing Ltd., 273
Mequipco Ltd., 286
Norseman Plastics Ltd., 306
Power Grow Systems Inc., 329
Scepter Manufacturing Co. Ltd., 358
Sittler's Manufacturing, 369
Sleegers Engineering Inc., 370
Sprung Instant Structures Ltd., 376
Techstar Plastics Inc., 388
Transform Compost Systems Ltd., 400
Walinga Inc., 416

Computer Software & Systems
See also Information Technology & Communications (General); Measuring & Monitoring Equipment, Laboratory; Modeling Systems; Process Monitoring & Control Services

A. A. Boscariol and Associates Limited, 63
Air Control Engineering Inc., 74
Aker Chemetics, 76
Alan A. Smith Inc., 76
Altus Capital Planning Inc., 81
ASL Environmental Sciences Inc., 94
Atrion International Inc., 97
BCL Landview Systems Inc., 103
Bio-Software Inc., 108
BMT Fleet Technology Ltd., 111
CadhamHayes Systems Inc., 120
Calta Computer Systems Ltd., 122
Canatec Consultants Ltd., 125
CARIS, 128
CB Engineering, Ltd., 132
CEM Specialties Inc., 135
Cengea Solutions Inc., 136
Chromatographic Specialties Inc., 140
Coast Forest Management Ltd., 145
Cobham Tracking & Locating Ltd., 145
Conformance Check Inc., 149
e3 Solutions Inc., 168
EarthFx Inc., 169
EITNL/Earth Information Technologies (nfld) Limited, 174
Emerge Knowledge Design Inc., 176
EmerGeo Solutions Inc., 176
EnvirInfo, 182
Enviro-Systèmes Inc., 183
EnviroMed Detection Services, 184
Expert Systems Inc., 191
Ferguson Simek Clark, 194
Forest Technology Systems Ltd., 199
G & G Computer Services, 203

GAEA Technologies, 204
Gemcom Software International Inc., 205
Gemteck Environmental Software Ltd., 206
Geodetic Software Systems/Geomatics Information Center, 211
GeoInsight Corporation, 211
Geosoft, 212
Geostat Systems International Inc., 212
Greenland International Consulting Inc., 218
GreenWare Environmental Systems Inc., 218
Hazard Control Systems Inc., 227
Howell-Mayhew Engineering Inc., 234
INDECO Strategic Consulting Inc., 240
Intelex Technologies Inc., 244
iQmetrix, 247
ISOVision, 248
J.D. Mollard & Associates Ltd., 249
Jasco Research Inc., 251
Kaehne Consulting Ltd., 254
Kanotech Information Systems Ltd., 255
KnowTech Environmental Inc., 259
Labtronics, 262
Lakes Environmental Software, 263
Lapp-Hancock Associates Limited, 264
Legaré F., Ing. Forestier Conseil, 266
MacDonald, Dettwiler & Associates Ltd., 277
Medgate Inc., 286
Micrologic Ltd., 289
National Instruments Canada, 297
NetPlus-HazMat Tracker, 300
Northway-Photomap Inc., 307
Ontor Ltd., 312
Parklane Computer Systems, 319
PCI Geomatics Group Inc., 320
PricewaterhouseCoopers Management Consultants, 332
REDUCT & Lobbe Technologies Inc., 344
Robinson Solutions, 348
Rockwell Automation Canada Inc., 349
Russell NDE Systems Inc., 354
Simcoe Engineering Group Limited, 368
Summa Engineering Ltd., 381
SustaiNet Software Solutions Inc., 383
Sutherland-Schultz Inc., 384
Torrie Smith Associates Inc., 398
Training & Development Services, 400
Trihedral Engineering Limited, 401
Trivalent Data Systems Ltd., 402
Trux Route Management Systems Inc., 404
Walker Technologies Corporation, 416
Zephyr North, 437

Construction & Excavation Services
See also Engineering Consulting Services (General); Project Management Services

Aecon Group Inc., 71
Ambler & Co. Inc., 82
Arpi's Industries Canada Ltd., 92
Atlas Polar Company Limited, 97
BOS Engineering & Environmental Services Inc., 114
Cardel Construction Ltd., 128
Carswell Consulting Engineers Ltd., 130
Chatwin Engineering Ltd., 138
Clifton Associates Ltd., 144
Construction Val-d'Or Ltée, 150
Cypher International Ltd., 155
D.M. Wills Associates Limited, 156
D.R. Estey Engineering Ltd., 156
Dewar Pacific Projects Ltd., 162
Divex Marine, 164
Enviroconseil, 183
Environova Planning Group Inc., 186
Envirosoil Ltd., 187
Godfrey Associates Ltd., 214
The Greer Galloway Group Inc., Engineers & Planners, 392
Harry Gamble Shipyard, 226
Hiltz & Seamone Co. Ltd., 232
Kang Construction Ltd., 255
Les Laboratoires S.L. inc., 269
Lantech Drilling Services Inc., 264
Layfield Geosynthetics & Industrial Fabrics Ltd., 265
Lecompte Engineering Ltd., 266
Maitland Engineering, 279
Megasecur Inc., 286
Mondry Del Zotto et associés inc., 292
MTE Consultants Inc., 294
Opus DaytonKnight Consultants Ltd., 313

Subject Index

Petrifond Foundation Co. Ltd., 322
Professional Resources Inc., 334
RICHWAY Environmental Technologies Ltd., 346
Robert Laurin, 348
Ron Robinson Limited, 351
Rose Mechanical Water Systems Inc., 351
Sandwell Engineering Inc., 356
SHAL Consulting Engineers Ltd., 365
Shaw Precast Solutions, 365
Sittler Excavating Ltd., 369
Skelton Brumwell & Associates Inc., 369
Socodec Inc., 371
Solaction Inc., 372
Sumas Environmental Services Inc., 381
Sutherland Excavating Ltd., 384
Terrafix Geosynthetics Inc., 390
Terratech, 390
Terratechnik Environmental Limited, 391
Vanbots Construction Corp., 409
Veolia ES Canada Industrial Services Inc., 411
Vibec International Inc., 413
Voice Construction Ltd., 414
W.T. McGinn & Associates Ltd., 415
Willms Construction Ltd., 432

Consumer, Office & Industry Products
See also **Recycled Products**
Atlantic Packaging Products Ltd., 96
BASF Canada Inc., 103
Bétonel Limitée, 106
Brass Craft Canada Ltd., 115
Caframo Co. Ltd., 121
Chemco Inc., 139
CIBA Spécialités Chimiques Canada inc., 141
Clivus Multrum Canada Ltd., 144
Cloverdale Paint Inc., 144
Comfort King Doors & Windows Ltd., 147
Commercial Solutions Inc., 147
Dashwood Industries Ltd., 157
Dundas-Jafine Inc., 167
DuPont Canada Inc., 167
earthRight Solar Products, 169
Les Engrais Naturels McInnes Inc./McInnes Natural Fertilizers Inc., 268
Enviro-Safe Chemicals Canada Inc., 183
Exova, 191
Fair Canada Engineering Ltd., 193
Flakeboard Company Ltd., 196
Fort Garry Industries Ltd., 199
Gerry Brushett Enterprises Limited, 212
Haley Industries Ltd., 223
Highland Equipment Ltd., 231
Hymopack Ltd., 237
Indaco Manufacturing Limited, 240
Industrial Thermo Polymers Ltd., 241
J. Walter Company Ltd., 249
Jomac Canada Inc., 253
K&D Pratt Group Inc., 254
Kappler Canada, 255
Kyocera Mita Canada Ltd., 261
LaserNetworks Inc., 264
Leon's Insulation, 267
MacEwen Petroleum Inc., 277
Maritime Geothermal Ltd., 280
Masternet Ltd., 282
MF Paints, 288
Northerm Windows, 307
Oetiker Limited, 311
Panasonic Canada Inc., 317
Peintures Denalt, 320
Petro-Canada Lubricants, 322
Polar Bear Health Equipment Supplies, 327
Precision Chemical Manufacturing Ltd., 330
Proctor & Gamble Inc., 333
Puresource Inc., 337
Royalpak Inc., 353
Sears Canada Inc., 361
Seeker Green Products Ltd., 361
SHER-PAC Container Systems Ltd., 365
Sherwin-Williams Canada Inc., 365
Showa-Best Glove, Inc., 366
Solignum, 372
Sonepar Canada, 373
Symplastics Ltd., 385
Teckn-O-Laser, 388

Tekmar Control Systems Ltd., 389
Thermo-Cell Industries Ltd., 394
3M Canada Company, 395
TMK IPSCO Inc., 397
Trivar Inc., 402
UPI Inc., 407
West-Lock Fastener Corp., 425
William Dam Seeds Ltd., 432

Contracting Services
See **Environmental Consulting & Contracting Services (General)**

Corrosion Control/Scale Prevention, Water & Wastewater
See also **Industrial Coatings; Liners, Geosynthetic/Geomembrane; Water, Wastewater & Groundwater Equipment**
Ashland Canada, 93
Aurora Environmental Consulting Ltd., 97
Auto-Chlor Inc., 98
Avoca-tec Environmental Services Inc., 99
Border Chemical Company Ltd., 114
Denso North America Inc., 161
G.I. Russell & Co. Ltd., 203
Guertin Brothers Coatings and Sealants Ltd., 222
Interprovincial Corrosion Control Co. Ltd., 246
Jes-Chem Ltd., 251
Kam Biotechnology Ltd., 254
Lambton Scientific, 263
Magnor, Division of Magchem, 278
Marvin Silbert & Associates, 282
Master Builders Technologies Ltd., 282
Nalco Canada Co., 296
Nemato Inc., 300
Nimbus Water Systems, 304
Quatic Industries Inc., 338
Radiodetection (Canada) Ltd., 341
Reinforced Plastic Systems Inc., 344
Sealcon Liner Systems Inc., 361
StonCor Canada, 379
Western Industrial Services Ltd., 429

Data Acquisition & Analysis
See also **Laboratory Services (General); Measuring & Monitoring Equipment, Laboratory**
Accutest Laboratories Ltd., 66
Activation Laboratories Ltd., 67
AGAT Laboratories Ltd., 72
Agri-Food Laboratories, 73
ALS Environmental, 80
BG Controls Ltd., 107
Biorex Inc., 109
Blackbox Automation Inc., 110
Bubble Technology Industries Inc., 118
C.V. Environmental Services, 120
Caduceon Environmental Laboratories, 120
Canadian Seabed Research Ltd., 125
Canberra Company, 126
Canviro, 127
Chromatographic Specialties Inc., 140
Cobham Tracking & Locating Ltd., 145
Demilec Inc., 160
Dionex Canada Limited, 164
Elemental Research Inc., 175
Elite Technologies Inc., 175
Enviro Scan Technologies Inc., 182
Envirometrex, 184
Envirosphere Consultants Ltd., 187
Envitech Automation Inc., 188
EthicScan Canada, 190
Fraser Environmental Services, 201
G3 Consulting Ltd., 204
Globetron Controls Inc., 214
Griffin Laboratories Corporation, 218
Hoskin Scientific Ltd., 233
Hydro Vision America, 236
Instantel, 243
Invensys Systems Canada Inc., 246
JB Laboratories Ltd., 251
KBU Environmental Technologies Inc., 255
KnowTech Environmental Inc., 259
Labtronics, 262
Lotek Wireless Inc., 274
MacDonald & Fils Inc., 277
Maxxam Analytics Inc., 283

Micrologic Ltd., 289
Mirarco Mining Innovation, 290
Multitel Inc., 295
National Instruments Canada, 297
Niagara Analytical Inc., 303
Oceans Ltd., 311
Pacific Phytometric Consultants, 316
PerkinElmer Life & Analytical Sciences Canada Inc., 321
Powertech Labs Inc., 329
QSDM Inc., 338
Quester Tangent Corp., 339
R.A. Kirby Sales Inc., 339
Rockwell Automation Canada Inc., 349
Rocky Mountain Environmental Ltd., 350
Sick Building Solutions, 366
Stewart Group, 379
Trihedral Engineering Limited, 401
Wind Energy Institute of Canada, 432
Zell Oilfield Service Ltd., 436
Zephyr North, 437

Data Acquisition Equipment
See **Measuring & Monitoring Equipment, Laboratory**

Demolition Materials Recycling
See also **Recycling Services (General)**
All Waste Removal Inc., 78
Banyan Chains Inc., 101
Canadian Eagle Recyclers, Inc., 124
Countryside Disposal Service Ltd., 153
H. Broer Equipment Sales and Service, 223
Neighborhood Recycling, 299
New West Gypsum Recycling Inc., 301
Priestly Demolition Inc., 332
Quantum Murray LP, 338
Renovators Resource Inc., 345
Ron Robinson Limited, 351
Thor Global Enterprises Ltd., 395
Try Recycling Inc., 404

Design & Specification Planning Services
See also **Engineering Consulting Services (General)**
A. A. Boscariol and Associates Limited, 63
Acoustic Solutions Ltd., 67
Aercoustics Engineering Limited, 71
Air Trac Corp., 75
Aker Chemetics, 76
ALCO Gas & Oil Production Equipment Ltd., 77
All-Weld Company Limited, 79
Angus, Butler Engineering Ltd., 86
Anrep Krieg Desilets Gravelle Ltd., 86
Atlantic Engineering Consultants Ltd., 95
Avalon Mechanical Consultants Ltd., 98
Beaulier Inc., 104
BECK Drilling and Environmental Services Ltd., 104
Both Belle Robb Ltd., 114
Boutillette Parizeau et Associés inc., 114
Brian Clark Architect, 116
Buchan, Lawton, Parent Ltd., 118
Canatec Consultants Ltd., 125
Carrier Canada Ltd., 129
Carswell Consulting Engineers Ltd., 130
Catterall & Wright, 132
Cecon Limited, 135
Chisholm, Fleming & Associates, 140
Coast Forest Management Ltd., 145
D. Greenfield Associates Ltd., 156
D.M. Wills Associates Limited, 156
Del-Air Systems Ltd., 160
Delcan Water, 160
Durex Steel & Alloy Industries Ltd., 167
ECE Group - a Division of Conestoga-Rovers & Associates, 170
Ellett Industries, 176
Faraci Engineering, 194
Ferguson Simek Clark, 194
Gas Liquids Engineering Ltd., 205
Gaston Marcil, Consultant, 205
Glenn Group Ltd., 213
Godfrey Associates Ltd., 214
Groupe Conseil Bellefeuille, Samson et Associés, 219
Le Groupe Forces, 265
Groupe GLD Inc., Experts-Conseils, 219
Groupe Sodinco inc., 221
Groupe Stavibel Inc., 221
Gryphon International Engineering Services Inc., 222
Henry Kortekaas & Associates Inc., 229

Subject Index

HGC Engineering, 231
Hiltz & Seamone Co. Ltd., 232
Horner Associates Limited, 233
HurterConsult Inc., 235
Inco Technical Services Limited, 239
Integrated Catalyst Engineering Inc., 244
J.R. Cousin Consultants Ltd., 250
Jenike & Johanson, Ltd., 251
King Metal Fabricators Ltd., 258
Koers & Associates Engineering Ltd., 259
Lecompte Engineering Ltd., 266
Levac Robichaud Leclerc Associates Ltd., 270
LH - Division of Full Circle Organics Inc., 272
Maitland Engineering, 279
Maritime Geothermal Ltd., 280
McElhanney Consulting Services Ltd., 284
Metropolitan Consulting Inc., 288
Mondry Del Zotto et associés inc., 292
MTE Consultants Inc., 294
New East Consulting Services Ltd., 301
Noise Solutions Inc., 305
O'Halloran Campbell Consultants Limited, 310
Opus DaytonKnight Consultants Ltd., 313
Opus International Consultants (Canada) Ltd., 313
P.J. Cluff Architect Inc., 315
Pacific Engineering Inc., 316
Pageau Morel & associés, inc., 317
Powertech Labs Inc., 329
Project Engineering Limited, 334
Robb Engineering Ltd., 347
Robert Laurin, 348
SACO Technologies, Inc., 354
Sandwell Engineering Inc., 356
Schwank Group, 359
SGE Hatch Ltd., 364
SHAL Consulting Engineers Ltd., 365
Sinanni Inc., 369
SMS Engineering Ltd., 371
Strait Engineering Ltd., 380
Surpac Minex (Canada) Inc., 383
Sustainable Energy Technologies Ltd., 383
Tang G. Lee Architect, 386
Terrafix Geosynthetics Inc., 390
Terratech, 390
Thermo Dynamics Ltd., 394
Totten Sims Hubicki Associates Ltd., 399
Triton Engineering Services Ltd., 402
Tyler Research Instruments Corp., 404
Urban Systems Ltd., 407
W.T. McGinn & Associates Ltd., 415
Walter Dow Associates Ltd., 416

Diving Services
See also Waste Management, Liquid/Hazardous
Care First Aid Training Inc., 128
Geocor Engineering Inc., 210
Integrated Explorations, 244
Metafix, 287
MIE Consulting Engineers Ltd., 289

Dredging Equipment
Consolidated Giroux Environment Inc., 150
Inland Aquatics, 241
Nalco Canada Co., 296
ODIM Brooke Ocean, 311
Trimax Residuals Management Inc., 401

Drum Recycling
See also Recycling Services (General)
Anachem Ltd., 84
Calgary Metal (1985) Ltd., 121
Da-Lee Dust Control, 156
Dekka Resins Inc., 159
Great Western Containers Inc., 216
Greif Bros. Canada Inc., 218
Joseph & Co. Inc., 253
Lennox Drum Ltd., 267
MAUSER, 283
Poscor Group, 328
Universal Drum Reconditioning Company, 406
Windsor Barrel & Drum Ltd., 433

Dust Collection & Control Equipment
See also Air Pollution Control Equipment
ACME Vacuum Cleaner Co. Ltd., 67
Air Trac Corp., 75
Atlantic Air Cleaning Specialists Ltd., 95

AZZ Blenkhorn & Sawle Limited, 100
Belfab Inc., 104
Century Environmental Systems, 136
Clean Air & Water Centre, 142
Cunningham Sheet Metal Works Inc., 154
Cypress Sales Partnership, 155
Electro-Air Canada, 174
Energy Technology Products Ltd., 179
Enviro-Klean Technologies Inc., 182
Envirotech Pollution Controls Ltd., 188
Eurovac, 191
F.C. O'Neill, Scriven & Associates Ltd., 193
GLM Tanks & Equipment Ltd., 213
HAMON Custodis-Cottrell Canada, Inc., 224
Henlex Inc., 229
Huntsman Corporation Canada Inc., 235
Integrated Metal Products, 244
Integrated Resource Management, 244
ITM Instruments, 248
Kongskilde Limited, 259
Kraemer Tool & Manufacturing Co. Ltd., 260
Lockerbie & Hole Contracting Ltd., 273
Macrotek Inc., 278
Metacor International Inc., 287
N.R. Murphy Ltd., 296
Nederman Canada Ltd., 299
Nilfisk-Advance Canada Company, 304
O'Connor Tanks Ltd., 310
P.J. Hannah Equipment Sales Corp., 315
Preston Phipps Inc., 331
Procedair Industries Inc., 333
Pyradia Inc., 337
Q-Air Environmental Controls Ltd., 337
Racan Carrier, 341
Rodrigue Métal Ltée, 350
Semco Systems Limited, 362
Shaver Industries Inc., 365
Sheldons Engineering Inc., 365
Tiger-Vac International Inc., 396
TurboSonic Inc., 404
Wheelabrator Canada Co., 431

Dust Suppression Equipment
See also Air Pollution Control Equipment
Atlantic Air Cleaning Specialists Ltd., 95
BEX Engineering Limited, 106
Drexan Energy Systems Inc., 166
Géophysique GPR International Inc., 211
Henlex Inc., 229
Jenike & Johanson, Ltd., 251
MEC Systems Inc., 286
TurboSonic Inc., 404
United Oil Services, 406

EcoLogo Certified Alternative Source Electricity Generation
See also Ecology Certified Products & Services
Argus Telecom International Inc., 90
Bancroft Light & Power Company (2000) Ltd., 101
Bracebridge Generation Ltd., 115
Brookfield Power, 117
Canada Composting Inc., 123
Canadian Hydro Developers, Inc., 124
CHI Canada Inc., 140
Eaton Hydro Developers Inc., 169
Energy Ottawa, 179
ENMAX Corporation, 181
EPCOR Energy Services Inc., 188
Hamilton Community Energy, 224
Huron Wind Ltd. Partnership, 235
Hydro One, 236
Hydro One, 236
Irrigation Canal Power Co-operative Ltd., 248
KW Gaspé Ltd. Partnership, 261
Maritime Electric Company Ltd., 280
Matrix Energy, 282
Maxim Power Corp, 283
McKerlie Solar Systems, 285
Minas Basin Pulp & Power Company Limited, 290
Mississippi River Power Corp., 291
Morgan Falls Power Company, 293
NorthPoint Energy Solutions, 307
Ontario Power Generation, 312
The PEI Energy Corp., 393
Pure Energy Inc., 336
Raging River Power & Mining Inc., 341

Regional Power Inc., 344
St. Catharines Hydro Generation Inc., 356
St. George Power LP, 356
SaskPower, 358
Sky Generation, 369
Société d'énergie de la rivière Ste-Anne/AXOR, 371
SunBridge Wind Power, 382
Toromont Energy Ltd., 398
Twin Falls Limited Partnership, 404
Valerie Falls Limited Partnership, 409
Vestas Canada, 413
Vision Quest Windelectric Inc., 414
Whitecourt Power Limited Partnership, 431

EcoLogo Certified Appliances
See also Ecology Certified Products & Services
In!Flame Fireplaces Inc., 239
Tankless Water Heater Company, 386

EcoLogo Certified Automotive Products & Lubricants
See also Ecology Certified Products & Services
AADCO Automotive Inc., 64
Anticorrosion Materials & Technologies Inc., 86
Corolon Coatings & Corrosion Control Technologies Inc., 152
Forsythe Lubrication Associates Ltd., 199
Le Groupe Pétrolier OLCO Inc., 265
H.L. Blachford Ltd., 223
Home Hardware Stores Ltd., 232
J. Walter Company Ltd., 249
Michelin North America (Canada) Inc., 289
Mr. Gas Ltd., 294
Petro-Canada Lubricants, 322
Prolab Technolub, 334
Safety-Kleen Canada Inc., 355
Suncor Energy Products, 382
UPI Inc., 407

EcoLogo Certified Building, Grounds & Construction
See also Ecology Certified Products & Services
ArcelorMittal Dofasco, 90
Can-Cell Industries Inc., 123
Castle Building Centres Groups Ltd., 131
CBR Products - Canadian Building Restoration Products Inc., 133
Clariant (Canada) Inc., 142
Clear Environmental Products, 143
Climatizer Insulation Inc., 144
Clivus Multrum Canada Ltd., 144
Dashwood Industries Ltd., 157
Demilec Inc., 160
Floorworks Inc., 197
Interface FLOR Commercial, 244
J.R. Tinderblox, 250
Johns Manville Canada Inc., 253
Plasti-Fab Ltd., 326
Quad-Lock Building Systems Ltd., 338
Roxul Inc., 353
Shigawake Organics Ltd., 365
Soleno Inc., 372
SRI Petro Chemical Inc., 376
Thermo-Cell Industries Ltd., 394
Total Comfort Solution Inc., 398
Viessmann Manufacturing Company Inc., 413
Water Pik Canada, 422

EcoLogo Certified Cleaning Products
See also Ecology Certified Products & Services
Acklands-Grainger Inc., 66
Alldec Trading Ltd., 79
Arch Industries, 90
Archer Chemical, 90
Avmor Ltd., 99
Bebbington Industries, 104
BioSource Solutions Inc., 109
Cal's Eco Depot, 121
Cascades Resource, 131
Chemcorp Industries Inc., 139
Chemspec Inc, 140
Clean Earth Solutions Ltd., 142
Clear Environmental Products, 143
Cogent Environmental Solutions Ltd., 146
DEB Canada, 159
EcoEthic Inc., 171
Enviro-Solutions Ltd., 183

Subject Index

Environmental Building Science Inc., 185
Frank T. Ross & Sons Ltd., 201
Le Groupe Sani Marc, 265
Ivey International Inc., 249
J. Walter Company Ltd., 249
Lambton Scientific, 263
Lord & Partners Ltd., 274
Mondo Products Company Limited, 292
Napier Environmental Technology, 296
Nature's Environmental Products Inc., 298
Nature's Mate Distribution Inc., 298
Prism Chemicals Inc., 332
Puresource Inc., 337
Qwatro Corporation, 339
Royalpak Inc., 353
Scicorp Systems Inc., 359
Sensible Life Products, 362
Sunoco Inc., 382
Telamode, 389
Transchem Inc., 400
Ultra-Chem Industries Ltd., 405
Westchem Mfg. Ltd., 429
Worldware Enterprises Ltd., 433
WORX Environmental Products Inc., 434

EcoLogo Certified Consumer Products
See also Ecology Certified Products & Services
Alex Milne Associates Ltd., 77
Alldec Trading Ltd., 79
Boart Longyear Inc., 111
Cascades Resource, 131
Cleanit Greenit Compost System, 143
Clear Environmental Products, 143
Frank T. Ross & Sons Ltd., 201
Gouw Quality Onions Ltd., 215
Merchants of Green Coffee, 286
N-T Enterprise Inc., 296
Oasis Bags, 311
Pioneer Petroleums, 325
Prescott Paper Products Inc., 331
Pure Energy Battery Inc., 336
Puresource Inc., 337
Scicorp Systems Inc., 359
Seeker Green Products Ltd., 361
Transchem Inc., 400
Vegewax Candleworx Ltd., 410
The Westford Group Inc., 393

EcoLogo Certified Marine Products
See also Ecology Certified Products & Services
Alex Milne Associates Ltd., 77
Bebbington Industries, 104
Clear Environmental Products, 143
Royalpak Inc., 353
Scicorp Systems Inc., 359

EcoLogo Certified Mutual Funds
Macquarie Power & Infrastructure Income Fund, 278

EcoLogo Certified Office Products
Avery Dennison Canada Inc., 98
Canon Canada Inc., 126
Cascades Resource, 131
Global Contract Inc., 213
Hewlett Packard (Canada) Co., 230
Konica Minolta Business Solutions (Canada) Ltd., 259
Kyocera Mita Canada Ltd., 261
Lexmark Canada Inc., 271
Rayovac Canada Inc., 342
Ricoh Canada Inc., 347
Sharp Electronics of Canada Ltd., 365
Teknion Corporation, 389
Toshiba of Canada Ltd., 398
West Point Products Canada, 424
Xerox Canada Ltd., 435

EcoLogo Certified Paints & Surface Coatings
Acklands-Grainger Inc., 66
Alex Milne Associates Ltd., 77
Anticorrosion Materials & Technologies Inc., 86
Benjamin Moore & Co. Ltd, 105
Bétonel Limitée, 106
Corolon Coatings & Corrosion Control Technologies Inc., 152
Dural Industries, 167
Dutab, 167
General Paint Ltd., 206
Home Hardware Stores Ltd., 232
ICI Paints (Canada) Inc., 238
K&D Pratt Group Inc., 254
MF Paints, 288
MICCA Paints Inc., 288
Para Paints, 318
Peintures Denalt, 320
Les Peintures Sico inc., 269
PPG Canada, 330
Sears Canada Inc., 361
Sherwin-Williams Canada Inc., 365
Sico, 366
Société Laurentide inc., 371
Solignum Inc., 372
Ventes Techniques Nimatec inc., 411

EcoLogo Certified Paper Products & Printing Services
Alliance Envelope Ltd., 79
Atlantic Newsprint Company, 96
Atlantic Packaging Products Ltd., 96
BPG Graphics Solutions, 114
Cascades Fine Papers Group Inc., 130
Cascades Inc., 130
Cascades Resource, 131
Catalyst Paper Corp., 132
Central Reproductions Ltd., 136
Colour Innovations Print Inc., 146
The DATA Group of Companies, 392
DATA Group of Companies, 157
Domtar Inc., 165
The Lowe-Martin Group, 392
Mansfield & Rodney Printing Ltd., 279
NCR Canada Ltd. - Systemedia Division, 299
Papiers Perkins, 317
Pioneer Envelopes Ltd., 325
Premier Envelope, 331
Prescott Paper Products Inc., 331
Quebecor World Concord, 338
Regional Envelope, 344
Ricoh Canada Inc., 347
Royal Envelope Ltd., 353
RP Graphics Group, 353
Seeker Green Products Ltd., 361
Sterling Press, 379
Supremex Inc., 383
Transcontinental Printing Inc., 400
Warren's Imaging & Dryography Inc., 417
Weyerhaeuser Company Ltd., 430
Xerox Canada Inc., 435

EcoLogo Certified Plastic Products & Plastic Film
See also Ecology Certified Products & Services
Avenue Industrial Supply Co. Ltd., 98
Cascades Resource, 131
Hymopack Ltd., 237
Liqui-Box Canada Inc., 272
Phoenix Biomedical Products Inc., 323
Transco Plastic Industries, 400
W. Ralston (Canada) Inc., 414
West-Lock Fastener Corp., 425

EcoLogo Certified Systems & Technologies
Atlantic Wind Power Corp. Ltd., 97
BC Hydro, 103
The Beer Store, 391
Canada Composting Inc., 123
Careful Hand Laundry & Dry Cleaners Ltd., 128
Climate Change Central, 144
Control Fire Systems, 151
EcoFlame International Inc., 171
GroundTech Solutions, 219
Kyocera Mita Canada Ltd., 261
Mainetti Canada Inc., 278
Mirus International Inc., 290
Powersmiths International Corp., 329
Ricoh Canada Inc., 347

Ecology Certified Products & Services
See also EcoLogo Certified Alternative Source Electricity Generation; EcoLogo Certified Appliances; EcoLogo Certified Automotive Products & Lubricants; EcoLogo Certified Building, Grounds & Construction; EcoLogo Certified Cleaning Products; EcoLogo Certified Consumer Products; EcoLogo Certified Marine Products; EcoLogo Certified Plastic Products & Plastic Film

Economic Analyses
See Market Analyses

Education, Environmental
See Information Technology & Communications (General)

Electronic Databases
See also Information Technology & Communications (General)
Biorex Inc., 109
BMT Fleet Technology Ltd., 111
CadhamHayes Systems Inc., 120
David A. McLean & Associates, 158
e3 Solutions Inc., 168
EarthFx Inc., 169
EITNL/Earth Information Technologies (nfld) Limited, 174
Emerge Knowledge Design Inc., 176
Expert Systems Inc., 191
G & G Computer Services, 203
G3 Consulting Ltd., 204
Gemcom Software International Inc., 205
Gemteck Environmental Software Ltd., 206
GeoInsight Corporation, 211
Geowest Environmental Consultants, 212
Grey House Publishing Canada, 218
Kanotech Information Systems Inc., 255
Lapp-Hancock Associates Limited, 264
MacDonald, Dettwiler & Associates Ltd., 277
Medgate Inc., 286
Northway-Photomap Inc., 307
Ontario Waste Materials Exchange, 312
Praxis Inc., 330
Ricoh Canada Inc., 347

Electrostatic Precipitators
See also Air Pollution Control Equipment
Biothermica, 109
Cimatec Environmental Engineering Inc., 141
Electro-Air Canada, 174
Empire Dynamic Structures Ltd., 177
Energy Technology Products Ltd., 179
Envirotech Pollution Controls Ltd., 188
Five Seasons Comfort Limited, 196
HAMON Custodis-Cottrell Canada, Inc., 224
KBR Canada, 255
Lockerbie & Hole Contracting Ltd., 273
Ocean Steel & Construction Ltd., 311
Q-Air Environmental Controls Ltd., 337
Ray Electric Ltd., 342
Sheldons Engineering Inc., 365
TurboSonic Inc., 404
Wheelabrator Canada Co., 431

Emergency Clean-up
See Emergency Response Planning; Spill Equipment; Spills/Clean-up Planning & Assessment; Waste Management, Liquid/Hazardous

Emergency Response Planning
See also Environmental Consulting & Contracting Services (General); Spills/Clean-up Planning & Assessment
AF Pollution Abatement Systems Inc., 72
Biophilia Inc., 109
Biorex Inc., 109
Can-Ross Environmental Services Ltd., 123
Care First Aid Training Inc., 128
Danatec Educational Services Ltd., 156
Duerden & Keane Consultants Inc., 167
EmerGeo Solutions Inc., 176
Emergex Planning Inc., 176
Environmental Accident Protection Inc., 184
Envirotec Services Incorporated, 187
Envision Planning Solutions Inc., 188
Gator International, 205
Global Engineering & Testing Ltd., 213
Goss Gilroy Inc., 215
Gough Risk Management Ltd., 215
Greenbridge Management Inc., 217
Indoor Air Quality Ottawa, 240
Institute of Environmental Research Inc., 243
J.D. Mollard & Associates Ltd., 249
Kent Engineering Ltd., 256
Miller Environmental Corp., 290
Paladin Environmental Consulting Services Ltd., 317
Paramount Emergency Planners Ltd., 318

Subject Index

Parish Geomorphic Ltd., 318
Penny & Casson Co., 321
Pepin Prevention des Pertes Inc., 321
Pigmalion Environmental Services Group, 323
Seacom International Inc., 361
Servco Environmental Solutions Inc., 363
Services Matrec inc., 363
SL Ross Environmental Research Ltd., 370
SpilKleen, 375
Spill Management Inc., 376
United Safety Ltd., 406
Vizon SciTec Inc., 414

End Markets
See also Materials Brokers; Recycling Services (General)

CanHemp Corporation, 126
DEL Warehousing Inc., 160
Goulbourn Stittsville Sanitation Ltd., 215
MGM Management, 288
O-I Canada Corp., 310
Ontario Waste Materials Exchange, 312
Recyclage PF Inc., 343
Rothsay, 352
Therm-O-Comfort Co. Ltd., 393

Energy
See Energy System Design

Energy Equipment
See also Energy Management (General); Energy Management Equipment; Energy Production Equipment; Energy Recovery Equipment; Energy Systems & Equipment, Alternate; Fuels, Alternative; Heating, Ventilation & Air Conditioning Equipment; Insulation & Sealing Products; Lighting, Energy Efficient; Measuring & Monitoring Equipment, Energy; Motors, Energy Efficient

Air Control Engineering Inc., 74
Alstom Canada Inc., 80
BG Controls Ltd., 107
Blower Engineering Inc., 110
BOC Canada Limited, 111
Brace Centre for Water Resources Management, 115
Bradford White Canada Inc., 115
Brass Craft Canada Ltd., 115
Bruce Sutherland & Associates Ltd., 117
Canada Heat Pumps, 123
Canadian Drives Inc., 124
Canadian Portable Structures (1992) Ltd., 125
Canrom Photovoltaics Inc., 126
Carrier Canada Ltd., 129
CMEL Enterprises Ltd., 144
Combustion & Energy Systems Ltd., 146
Comfort King Doors & Windows Ltd., 147
Crossman Machinery Co. Ltd., 154
Dashwood Industries Ltd., 157
Dectron Internationale, 159
Delta Piping Products Canada Inc., 160
Dimplex North America, 164
E.H. Hanson Engineering Group Ltd., 168
earthRight Solar Products, 169
ECO Fuel Systems Inc., 170
Ecology Products International, 172
Energy Conservation Contractors Warranty Corporation, 179
EnRel Energy Group, 181
Estco Battery Management Inc., 190
FCX NH Valves, 194
Ferguson Simek Clark, 194
Groupe GLD Inc., Experts-Conseils, 219
Hammond Manufacturing, 224
HMI Hoyme Manufacturing Inc., 232
Huron Window Corporation, 235
Industrial Thermo Polymers Ltd., 241
Jubilee Rose Enterprises Ltd., 253
L.E. Washington Sales Ltd., 261
Lennox Industries (Canada) Ltd., 267
Miniveil Air Systems, 290
Newmac Manufacturing Inc., 303
Northerm Windows, 307
Northern Alternate Power Systems, 307
Novitherm Canada Inc., 309
OMB (Americas) Forged Steel Valves, 312
Panama Enterprises (1990) Inc., 317
Conserval Engineering Inc., 318
Petromax Ltd., 322
ProPower Equipment Ltd., 335

Schwank Group, 359
SEW Eurodrive Co. of Canada Ltd., 364
Solarmart, 372
Solcan Ltd., 372
Sundog Energy Management, 382
Sutherland-Schultz Inc., 384
Teleflex Canada Ltd., 389
Thermo Dynamics Ltd., 394
Thermo Electric (Canada) Ltd., 394
Thermotech Windows Ltd., 394
Tremco Ltd., 401
Visionwall Corporation, 414

Energy Management (General)
See also Energy Equipment; Energy Services; Energy, Operations & Maintenance Services

ADI Group Inc., 68
Agricultural Technology Centre, 73
Air Control Engineering Inc., 74
Alexander Boome Consulting Engineering, Ltd., 78
Alpha Controls & Instrumentation, 79
Angus, Butler Engineering Ltd., 86
Appin Associates, 87
ASCO Canada, 93
Automatic Controls Ltd., 98
Avoca-tec Environmental Services Inc., 99
Capricorn Control Technologies Ltd., 128
Cole-Parmer Canada Inc., 146
Comenco Systems Inc., 147
The Conserver Group Inc., 391
Cook Engineering, 151
Les Consultants Eoletech S.Q. Inc., 268
Digicon Building Control Solutions, 163
Earth & Environmental Technologies (ETech), 168
Elecsar Engineering Co. Ltd., 174
Enercombustion Ltd., 179
Enviro-Systèmes Inc., 183
Éocycle Technologies Inc., 188
Estco Battery Management Inc., 190
FPInnovations, 200
GAIA Power Inc., 204
Global Facman Entreprises Inc., 213
Helimax Energy Inc., 228
HMI Construction Inc., 232
ICF International Canada Inc., 238
J.L. Richards & Associates Limited, 250
L.W. Ward Limited, 261
Meo & Associates Inc., 286
Mike Fuller Electric Ltd., 289
Mitsubishi Canada Ltd., 291
NEK Environmental Technologies Inc., 299
New World Generation Inc., 301
Norditrade Inc., 305
Nova Scotia Power, an Emera Company, 308
Pacific Institute for Advanced Study, 316
Piikuni Utilities Corp., 323
RailPower Technologies Corp., 341
Ramsay Machine Works Ltd., 342
Renewable Energy Services Inc., 345
Robinson Solutions, 348
Scientific Instrumentation Ltd., 360
Sinnott Farm Services Ltd., 369
Sustainable Energy Technologies Ltd., 383
Techint Goodfellow Technologies Inc., 387
Temprite Industries Ltd., 389
Transalta Utilities, 400
TransGas Limited, 400
W.T. McGinn & Associates Ltd., 415
Wind Power Inc., 433

Energy Management Equipment
See also Energy Equipment

Arrow Speed Controls Ltd., 93
AZZ Blenkhorn & Sawle Limited, 100
Control Techniques Drives Inc., 151
Cutler-Hammer Canada, 154
Digicon Building Control Solutions, 163
Durmitor Inc., 167
Ecology Products International, 172
Enercorp Instruments Ltd., 179
Energy Conservation Contractors Warranty Corporation, 179
Energy Systems & Design Limited, 179
Estco Battery Management Inc., 190
Greystone Energy Systems Inc., 218
Horton CBI Ltd., 233
Hydrogenics Corporation, 236

International Cooling Systems Inc., 245
JM Science Canada Inc., 252
Kaehne Consulting Ltd., 254
Leeson Canada Ltd., 266
Leviton Canada, 270
Megasecur Inc., 286
NEDCO, 299
Osram Sylvania Ltd., 314
Powersmiths International Corp., 329
Rapid-Eau Technologies, 342
SACO Technologies, Inc., 354
SatCon Power Systems (Canada), 358
Schneider Electric Canada Inc., 359
Scintrex Ltd., 360
Sprecher + Schuh Inc., 376
Sustainable Energy Technologies Ltd., 383
Tekmar Control Systems Ltd., 389
Thermo Electric (Canada) Ltd., 394
Thermon Heat Tracing Services, 394
Thomson & Howe Energy Systems Inc., 395
Thomson Technology Inc., 395
Wind Power Inc., 433

Energy Production Equipment
See also Energy Equipment; Power Generation/Production

ABGG Technologies Inc., 65
Boilersmith Ltd., 113
Eastern Wind Power Inc., 169
Energy Systems & Design Limited, 179
Enviro Vault Ltd., 182
Hammond Manufacturing, 224
Hitachi Canadian Industries Ltd., 232
JM Science Canada Inc., 252
Matrix Energy, 282
Northern Lights Energy Systems, 307
OMB (Americas) Forged Steel Valves, 312
Pat Dwyer Construction Inc., 319
Piikuni Utilities Corp., 323
Sambrabec Inc., 356
Sunmotor International Ltd., 382
Taylor Munro Energy Systems Inc., 387
TeraWind Ltd., 389

Energy Recovery Equipment
See also Energy Equipment

A.H. Lundberg Systems Ltd., 63
ABGG Technologies Inc., 65
Alloy Fab Ltd., 79
Altek Power Corporation, 81
Arpi's Industries Canada Ltd., 92
Ashtead Technology Rentals, 93
Berg Chilling Systems Inc., 105
Boilersmith Ltd., 113
Brace Centre for Water Resources Management, 115
Bruce Sutherland & Associates Ltd., 117
Canada Heat Pumps, 123
Charland Thermojet Inc., 138
Cintube Ltd., 141
Comenco Systems Inc., 147
Del-Air Systems Ltd., 160
Ecology Products International, 172
Electro-Mecanik Inc., 175
Engineered Air, 180
Eucania International Inc., 190
Firwin Corporation, 196
Fulton Engineered Specialties Inc., 203
Gasmac Inc., 205
Industrial Combustion Equipment Ltd., 240
Inproheat Industries Ltd., 242
Integrated Metal Products, 244
Integrated Resource Management, 244
IPAC Inc., 247
KMW Systems Inc., 258
Koch Engineering Co. Ltd., 259
MacLeod & Grant Ltd., 278
Malnar Industries Ltd., 279
Maritime Geothermal Ltd., 280
Matco Ltd., 282
Metacor International Inc., 287
Northern Alternate Power Systems, 307
Novitherm Canada Inc., 309
Nu-Air Ventilation Systems Inc., 309
Pageau Morel & associés, 317
Conserval Engineering Inc., 318
Pepper Compressed Air & Gas Ltd., 321

Subject Index

QuestAir Technologies Inc., 339
Ramsay Machine Works Ltd., 342
Taylor Munro Energy Systems Inc., 387
Tech Sales Co., 387
Temprite Industries Ltd., 389
Thermal Technics Corporation, 394
Toromont Caterpillar, 397
Trent Metals Ltd., 401
Venmar CES, Inc., 410
Venmar Ventilation Inc., 410

Energy Resource Management
See also Mines & Minerals Management; Resource Management Services (General)

Ashtead Technology Rentals, 93
Can-K Artificial Lift Systems Inc., 123
Katch Kan Limited, 255
Petro Laboratories Inc., 322
Torrie Smith Associates Inc., 398

Energy Services
See also Audit Services, Energy; Cogeneration, Industrial; Energy Management (General); Energy System Design; Energy System Design, Alternate; Energy, Operations & Maintenance Services; Energy-from-Waste Services; Heating, Ventilation & Air Conditioning Services; House & Home Design, Energy-Efficient; Pipeline Design Services; Power Generation/Production; Vehicle Design Services

Adkinson & Associates, 68
Alexander Boome Consulting Engineering, Ltd., 78
Appin Associates, 87
Arpi's Industries Canada Ltd., 92
Atlantic Orient Canada Inc., 96
Avalon Mechanical Consultants Ltd., 98
Ballard Power Systems Inc., 101
BP Canada Energy Company, 114
Brosz & Associates, 117
Canadian Drives Inc., 124
Canentec Inc., 126
Capricorn Control Technologies Ltd., 128
Cecon Limited, 135
CH2M Hill Canada Limited, 137
Char Developments Ltd., 138
COGENCanada, 146
Comfort King Doors & Windows Ltd., 147
Les Consultants Eoletech S.Q. Inc., 268
Cook Engineering, 151
Cypress Sales Partnership, 155
Dewar Insulations Ltd., 162
Dillon Consulting Ltd., 163
E.H. Hanson Engineering Group Ltd., 168
ECE Group - a Division of Conestoga-Rovers & Associates, 170
ECO Fuel Systems Inc., 170
Electronic Warfare Associates - Canada, Ltd., 175
Envirotech Associates Limited, 187
Frank's Alternate Energy, 201
GAIA Power Inc., 204
Genivar, 207
Global Facman Entreprises Inc., 213
Glos Associates Inc., 214
Gryphon International Engineering Services Inc., 222
Hooper Welding Enterprises Ltd., 233
Hydromantis Inc., 237
Island Technologies Inc., 248
J&B Engineering Inc., 249
Keywood Entreprises Ltd., 257
Lockerbie & Hole Contracting Ltd., 273
M&E Engineering Ltd., 276
M.S. Thompson & Associates Ltd., 276
Marbek Resource Consultants Ltd., 280
Maritime Geothermal Ltd., 280
Mesh Technologies Inc., 287
MIG Engineering Ltd., 289
Morrison Hershfield, 293
Multitel Inc., 295
Norditrade Inc., 305
Northern Alternate Power Systems, 307
Northern Lights Energy Systems, 307
NorthPoint Energy Solutions, 307
OZZ Corporation, 315
Pacific Institute for Advanced Study, 316
Pageau Morel & associés, inc., 317
Conserval Engineering Inc., 318
Power-Pacific Poles Ltd., 329
R.A. Murray International Limited, 340

REDUCT & Lobbe Technologies Inc., 344
Rowan Williams Davies & Irwin Inc., 352
SAR Engineering, 357
Schneider Electric Canada Inc., 359
Sigma Engineering Ltd., 367
Sinnott Farm Services Ltd., 369
Smith & Andersen Consulting Engineering, 370
Sutherland-Schultz Inc., 384
Tecsult Inc., 388
Thermo Dynamics Ltd., 394
Thompson Engineering Consultants Ltd., 395
Thomson Technology Inc., 395
Transalta Utilities, 400
Troy-Ontor Inc., 404
Wind Energy Institute of Canada, 432

Energy System Design
See also Energy Services

Aldworth Engineering Inc., 77
Algonquin Power Income Fund, 78
Avalon Mechanical Consultants Ltd., 98
Bowser Technical Inc., 114
Canrom Photovoltaics Inc., 126
COGENCanada, 146
The Delphi Group, 392
Digicon Building Control Solutions, 163
Eastern Wind Power Inc., 169
Ecology Products International, 172
Efficiency Engineering Inc., 173
Enercombustion Ltd., 179
Energy Systems & Design Limited, 179
Enermodal Engineering Ltd., 179
EnviroPower Equipment Marketing Inc., 187
Faraci Engineering, 194
Groupe RSW inc., 220
Groupe Sodinco inc., 221
Hamworthy-Peabody Combustion Canada Inc., 224
Hydrogenics Corporation, 236
Kinder Morgan Canada Inc., 257
KMW Systems Inc., 258
Lockerbie & Hole Contracting Ltd., 273
Matrix Energy, 282
NEDCO, 299
Nelson-Superior Consultants Ltd., 300
Northern Alternate Power Systems, 307
Optimira Controls, 313
Robb Engineering Ltd., 347
Schneider Electric Canada Inc., 359
Seaforth Engineering Group Inc., 361
Smith & Andersen Consulting Engineering, 370
Sundog Energy Management, 382
Sustainable EDGE Ltd., 383
Thomson & Howe Energy Systems Inc., 395
Thomson Technology Inc., 395
Torrie Smith Associates Inc., 398
Viessmann Manufacturing Company Inc., 413
W.T. McGinn & Associates Ltd., 415
Wellons Canada, 424
Wenvor Technologies Inc., 424

Energy System Design, Alternate
See also Energy Services; Energy Systems & Equipment, Alternate

Adkinson & Associates, 68
ARISE Technologies Corporation, 90
Brace Centre for Water Resources Management, 115
Camatec, 122
Canrom Photovoltaics Inc., 126
Carmanah Technologies Corp., 129
Cintube Ltd., 141
Coen Canada Inc., 146
Ecology Products International, 172
Energy Systems & Design Limited, 179
Enermodal Engineering Ltd., 179
EnRel Energy Group, 181
Enviro-Systèmes Inc., 183
Envirometrex, 184
Faraci Engineering, 194
Finnex Agencies Ltd., 195
Hitachi Canadian Industries Ltd., 232
Howell-Mayhew Engineering Inc., 234
Kaehne Consulting Inc., 254
Levelton Consultants Ltd., 270
Nevin Sadlier-Brown Goodbrand Ltd., 300
Northern Lights Energy Systems, 307
Ottawa Engineering Ltd., 315

Conserval Engineering Inc., 318
Rapid-Eau Technologies, 342
Richard Kadulski Architect, 346
Sambrabec Inc., 356
Scientific Instrumentation Ltd., 360
Solar Solutions Inc., 372
Solcan Ltd., 372
Sun Ross Energy Systems Ltd., 382
Tang G. Lee Architect, 386
Thermo Dynamics Ltd., 394
Thomson & Howe Energy Systems Inc., 395
Thomson Technology Inc., 395
W.R. Graham Services Ltd., 415
Wenvor Technologies Inc., 424
Westport Innovations Inc., 430
Wind Power Inc., 433
Zephyr North, 437

Energy Systems & Equipment, Alternate
See also Energy Equipment; Energy System Design, Alternate

AB Mechanical Ltd., 64
ABGG Technologies Inc., 65
Alternative Fuel Systems (2004) Inc., 81
Argus Telecom International Inc., 90
ARISE Technologies Corporation, 90
Atlantic Orient Canada Inc., 96
Avalon Mechanical Consultants Ltd., 98
Babcock & Wilcox Canada Ltd., 100
Ballard Power Systems Inc., 101
Boilersmith Ltd., 113
Bradford White Canada Inc., 115
Brian Clark Architect, 116
Camatec, 122
Canrom Photovoltaics Inc., 126
Carmanah Technologies Corp., 129
Cheminées Sécurité Internationale Ltée, 139
Cintube Ltd., 141
City Metal Manufacturing Inc., 141
Coen Canada Inc., 146
Combustion & Energy Systems Ltd., 146
Dependable Turbines Ltd., 161
Eastern Wind Power Inc., 169
ECO Fuel Systems Inc., 170
EDM Environmental Design & Management Ltd., 173
Energy Systems & Design Limited, 179
Enerplan Consultants Ltd., 179
EnRel Energy Group, 181
Entegrity Wind Systems Inc., 181
Enviro-Systèmes Inc., 183
Envirometrex, 184
Estco Battery Management Inc., 190
Faraci Engineering, 194
Finnex Agencies Ltd., 195
Generation PV Inc., 207
Inproheat Industries Ltd., 242
KMW Systems Inc., 258
Light Solar Wind Manufacturing, 272
Micro-Watt Control Devices Ltd., 289
Napoleon Appliance Corp., 297
Nevin Sadlier-Brown Goodbrand Ltd., 300
Newmac Manufacturing Inc., 303
Northern Alternate Power Systems, 307
Northern Lights Energy Systems, 307
Ottawa Engineering Ltd., 315
Conserval Engineering Inc., 318
REDUCT & Lobbe Technologies Inc., 344
Research Electronics (Reselco) Ltd., 345
Ron Wedman Engineering Services, 351
Sambrabec Inc., 356
SatCon Power Systems (Canada), 358
Seaforth Engineering Group Inc., 361
Sedore Stoves Canada, 361
Solar Solutions Inc., 372
Solcan Ltd., 372
Sun Ross Energy Systems Ltd., 382
Sunmotor International Ltd., 382
Sustainable Energy Technologies Ltd., 383
Taylor Munro Energy Systems Inc., 387
Thermo Dynamics Ltd., 394
Thermotech Windows Ltd., 394
Thomson & Howe Energy Systems Inc., 395
Thomson Technology Inc., 395
Toromont Caterpillar, 397
Urgel Delisle & Associés inc., 408

Subject Index

Valley Comfort Systems Inc., 409
Wellons Canada, 424
Wind Energy Institute of Canada, 432
Yugo-Tech, 435
Zephyr Alternative Power, 437
Zephyr North, 437

Energy, Operations & Maintenance Services
See also Energy Management (General); Energy Services
Abandonrite, 64
Algonquin Power Income Fund, 78
Atlantic Orient Canada Inc., 96
Brosz & Associates, 117
Can Ecosse Engineering, 122
Capricorn Control Technologies Ltd., 128
The Conserver Group Inc., 391
Denoco Energy Systems Ltd., 161
Eastern Wind Power Inc., 169
Efficiency Engineering Inc., 173
Frank's Alternate Energy, 201
Hydromega Energy Inc., 237
Light Solar Wind Manufacturing, 272
Lockerbie & Hole Contracting Ltd., 273
Natural Forces Technologies Inc., 298
Nova Scotia Power, an Emera Company, 308
Ontario Building Solutions, 312
Optimira Controls, 313
Piikuni Utilities Corp., 323
Thermo Design Engineering Ltd., 394
Veolia ES Canada Industrial Services Inc., 411
Wind Power Inc., 433

Energy-from-Waste Services
See also Energy Services
Altek Power Corporation, 81
Canentec Inc., 126
DynaMotive Energy Systems Corporation, 167
E.H. Hanson Engineering Group Ltd., 168
Inproheat Industries Ltd., 242
Kam Biotechnology Ltd., 254
KMW Systems Inc., 258
Mabarex inc., 277
Procedair Industries Inc., 333
Research Electronics (Reselco) Ltd., 345
Ron Wedman Engineering Services, 351
Servicestat Ltd., 363
Suncurrent Industries Inc., 382
United Oil Services, 406
Wellons Canada, 424

Engineering Consulting Services (General)
See also Arctic/Permafrost Engineering; Bioremediation Services; Construction & Excavation Services; Design & Specification Planning Services; Environmental Consulting & Contracting Services (General); Erosion Control Services; Feasibility/Pre-feasibility Studies; Geological & Hydrogeological Engineering; Geophysical Survey Services; Plant Retrofit Studies; Process Evaluation & Selection Services; Project Management Services; Site Assessment Studies; Site Reclamation & Remedial Action Services; Soil Remediation Services; Transportation Planning Services; Water & Wastewater Consulting
A. A. Boscariol and Associates Limited, 63
Abandonrite, 64
Acadia Consultants & Inspectors Ltd., 65
Acres & Associated Environmental Ltd., 67
ADI Group Inc., 68
Adventis Technologies, 69
AECOM Canada Ltd., 69
Aercoustics Engineering Limited, 71
Ainley Group, 74
Air Products Canada Ltd., 75
Aker Chemetics, 76
Alexander Boome Consulting Engineering, Ltd., 78
ALL-TECH Environmental Services Ltd., 78
ALTECH Environmental Consulting Ltd., 81
AMEC, 82
AN-GEO Environmental Consultants Ltd., 84
Aqua Terre Solutions Inc., 88
Argo Protective Coatings Inc., 90
Armstrong Engineering & Land Surveying Inc., 91
ASI Group Ltd., 93
ATCO Group, 94
Atkinson, Davies Inc., 95
Atlantic Environmental Training & On-Site Services Inc., 95

Avalon Mechanical Consultants Ltd., 98
AXOR Experts-Conseils Inc., 99
B & R Engineering Co. Ltd., 100
BAE Newplan Group Ltd., 101
Bass Engineering Systems Technology, 103
Beasy Nicoll Engineering Ltd., 104
Bigfoot Systems Inc., 107
Bissett Resource Consultants Ltd., 110
Boutillette Parizeau et Associés inc., 114
BPR, 115
Brian Clark Architect, 116
Brisbin & Sentis Engineering Inc., 116
Brosz & Associates, 117
Bruce A. Brown Associates Limited, 117
C.J. MacLellan & Associates Inc., 120
Can Ecosse Engineering, 122
Canadian Seabed Research Ltd., 125
CanAsia Environmental & Engineering Ltd., 125
Canspect Corporation, 127
Cansult Maunsell Limited, 127
Catterall & Wright, 132
CBCL Limited, 132
Cegerco - GCL Inc., 135
CENSOL Inc., 136
CH2M Hill Canada Limited, 137
CH2M HILL Canada Ltd., 137
Challenger Geomatics Ltd., 138
Chem Solv, 139
CLA Experts-Conseils, 142
Claus Engineering (1986) Ltd., 142
Clearstone Engineering Ltd., 143
Coast Forest Management Ltd., 145
Coffey Geotechnics Inc., 146
Comstock Canada Ltd., 148
Conestoga-Rovers & Associates, 149
Conor Pacific Environmental Technology Inc., 150
The Conserver Group Inc., 391
Consultants Mésar inc., 150
Les Consultants RSA, 268
Cook Engineering, 151
Corrosion Service Company Limited, 152
Corrpro Canada, Inc., 152
Cowater International Inc., 153
Crandall Engineering Ltd., 153
Cypher International Ltd., 155
Cyr Engineering Inc., 155
D. Greenfield Associates Ltd., 156
D.M. Wills Associates Limited, 156
D.R. Estey Engineering Ltd., 156
Dakins Engineering Group Ltd., 156
Daniel Fauteux Environnement inc., 157
Decommissioning Consulting Services Limited, 159
Dessau, Inc., 162
Dillon Consulting Ltd., 163
Direct Separation Solutions, 164
DST Consulting Engineers, 166
E.H. Hanson Engineering Group Ltd., 168
EBA Engineering Consultants Ltd., 169
ECE Group - a Division of Conestoga-Rovers & Associates, 170
Echo Environmental, 170
EDM Environmental Design & Management Ltd., 173
Egmond Associates Ltd., 174
El-Rayes Environmental Corp., 174
Elecsar Engineering Co. Ltd., 174
Electronic Warfare Associates - Canada, Ltd., 175
Elliott & Elliott Limited Consulting Engineers, 176
EMP Environmental Management & Protection Corporation, 177
EnGlobe Corp., 180
Entara Consulting Services Ltd., 181
Entech Environmental Consultants Ltd., 181
Envirochem Services Inc., 183
Envirotech Associates Limited, 187
Éocycle Technologies Inc., 188
EPEC Consulting (Sask) Ltd., 189
Esco Engineering, 189
Exova, 191
Experts-Conseils BMST inc., 192
Experts-Conseils CEP Inc., 192
Fabcon Canada Ltd., 193
Fenco Shawinigan Engineering Limited, 194
Fisher Environmental Ltd., 196
Fluor Canada, 197
Focus Surveys Inc., 198
FPInnovations, 200
Frappier & Génier Conseillers, 201

Frederick Goertz Ltd., 201
Fugro Airborne Surveys, 202
Fugro Jacques GeoSurveys Inc., 203
G & G Computer Services, 203
G.A. Borstad Associates Ltd., 203
GE Ground Engineering Ltd., 205
Génius Conseil Inc., 207
Genivar, 207
Genus Loci Ecological Landscapes Inc., 210
Geo-Logic Inc., 210
Geolab Inc., 211
Global Facman Entreprises Inc., 213
Glos Associates Inc., 214
Godfrey Associates Ltd., 214
Golder Associates Ltd., 214
Green Plan Ltd., 217
Groupe Conseil Bellefeuille, Samson et Associés, 219
Groupe EnvirAqua, 219
Groupe GLD Inc., Experts-Conseils, 219
Groupe Séguin, 220
Groupe SM inc., 220
Groupe Teknika, 221
Groupe-Conseil TDA, 221
Gryphon International Engineering Services Inc., 222
GSI Environnement Inc., 222
Hanna Instruments Canada Inc., 224
Hazard Control Systems Inc., 227
Hazco Environmental Services Ltd., 227
Hi-Country Environmental Services Ltd., 231
HMO Limited, 232
Hunter & Associates, 235
HurterConsult Inc., 235
Hy-Grade Geoscience, 235
Hydromantis, 237
IEG Consultants Ltd., 238
InCoretec Inc., 240
Ininew Project Management Inc., 241
Integrated Explorations, 244
International Marine Salvage Inc., 245
Interprovincial Corrosion Control Co. Ltd., 246
Irving Forest Services Limited, 248
Island Technologies Inc., 248
J&B Engineering Inc., 249
J.K. Engineering Ltd., 249
J.L. Richards & Associates Limited, 250
Jones Group Engineering Ltd., 253
Kaehne Consulting Ltd., 254
Kavanagh & Associates Ltd., 255
Ken Noftell Drilling Services, 256
Kerr Wood Leidal Associates Ltd., 257
KGS Group Inc., 257
Klajnerman Contracting Corp., 258
Koers & Associates Engineering Ltd., 259
L&M Engineering Ltd., 261
L.W. Ward Limited, 261
Labelle, Ryan, Genipro Inc., 261
Les Laboratoires S.L. inc., 269
Lea International Ltd., 266
Levac Robichaud Leclerc Associates Ltd., 270
Lupien Rosenberg Consultants Inc., 274
LVM Inc., 275
M.S. Thompson & Associates Ltd., 276
MacAuley Group Ltd., 277
Maddocks Industrial Filter Division, 278
Maitland Engineering, 279
Malroz Engineering Inc., 279
Maple Reinders Environmental Ltd., 279
Maritime Soil Ltd., 281
Matrix Solutions Inc., 282
McElhanney Consulting Services Ltd., 284
McNamara Construction Company, 285
MCR Environmental Consulting, 285
Meo & Associates Inc., 286
Mesh Technologies Inc., 287
Micrologic Ltd., 289
MIE Consulting Engineers Ltd., 289
MIG Engineering Ltd., 289
MissionHGE inc., 291
MLC Associés Inc., 292
MMM Group, 292
Morrison Hershfield, 293
MWA Consultants, 295
The National Testing Laboratories Ltd., 393
National Waste Services, 298
NCL Envirotek Inc., 299

Subject Index

Newfoundland Design Associates Limited, 302
Nor-Alta Environmental Services Ltd., 305
Noram Engineering & Constructors Ltd., 305
Nova Magnetics Burgmann Ltd., 308
Nove Environnement Inc., 309
Oakhill Environmental, 310
Offshore Design Associates Ltd., 311
Opus International Consultants (Canada) Ltd., 313
P. Machibroda Engineering Inc., 315
Pacific Environmental Consulting & Occupational Hygiene Services, 316
Pacific Institute for Advanced Study, 316
Pageau Morel & associés, inc., 317
Parkvalley Consulting Ltd., 319
Pat Dwyer Construction Inc., 319
Peto MacCallum Ltd., 321
Phoenix Engineering Inc., 323
Pipe Specialties Canada, 325
Piteau Associates, 325
Planning Alliance, 326
Pomeroy Consulting Engineers Limited, 328
Pottinger Gaherty Environmental Consultants Ltd., 328
Precision Assessment Technology Corp., 330
Precision Industrial Ltd., 330
Presentey Engineering Products Ltd., 331
Les Produits Environnementaux Atlas, 270
Professional Resources Inc., 334
Project Engineering Limited, 334
Promens Canada Inc., 334
R.A. Campbell & Associates, 339
R.A. Murray International Limited, 340
R.J. Burnside & Associates Limited, 340
R.V. Anderson Associates Limited, 341
Radiation Environmental Management Systems Inc., 341
Remedy Energy Services Ltd., 344
René Gervais Inc., Consultants, 345
Ridgeline Environment Inc., 347
Robinson Consultants Inc., 348
Roche ltée, Groupe-conseil, 348
Ronel Engineering Ltd., 351
RWDI AIR Inc., 354
Safety Plus Inc., 355
Sanix Incorporated, 357
Sarafinchin Associates Ltd., 358
Schlumberger Water Services, 359
SDS Drilling Ltd., 360
SENES Consultants Limited, 362
The Sernas Group Inc., 393
Sigma Engineering Ltd., 367
Sittler Excavating Ltd., 369
SNC-Lavalin Environment Inc., 371
SNC-Lavalin Group Inc., 371
Socodec Inc., 371
Solinov Inc., 373
Solmax-Texel Geosynthetics Inc., 373
Sols Consultants Ltée, 373
SOTAR Inc., 374
Southwestern Flowtech & Environmental Ltd., 374
Spriet Associates London Ltd., 376
Stantec Inc., 377
Strata Soil Sampling Inc., 380
Strategies for the Environment, 380
Sunergy Systems Ltd., 382
Sutherland-Schultz Inc., 384
Sylvain Léger, 384
Talon Projects Inc., 386
Tansley Associates Environmental Services, 387
Techint Goodfellow Technologies Inc., 387
Tecsult Inc., 388
Terra Experts Conseils Inc., 390
Terracon Geotechnique Ltd., 390
Terrapex Environmental Ltd., 390
Terratec Environmental Ltd., 390
TetrES Consultants Inc., 391
Thompson Engineering Consultants Ltd., 395
Thompson Rosemount Group, 395
Triton Consultants Ltd., 402
Trow Consulting Engineers Ltd., 403
Tyler Research Instruments Corp., 404
UMA Group Ltd., 405
Unies Limited, 405
Urban Systems Ltd., 407
URS Canada Inc., 408
V. Fournier & Associates, 408
Varcon Inc., 409

Venerus International Purification Inc., 410
Voghel Inc., 414
W.F. Baird & Associates Coastal Engineers Ltd., 415
W.G. Shaw & Associates, 415
Wardrop Engineering Inc., 416
Web Engineering Ltd., 423
Whitman Benn Group, 431
WHMIS Inc., 431
Willis Energy Services Ltd., 432
WorleyParsons Canada Ltd., 433

Environmental Accounting Services
See also Financial & Marketing Services (General)
Alan Willis & Associates, 76
Chamard & Associés, 138
Cheminfo Services Inc., 139
ODIM Brooke Ocean, 311
Scitax Advisory Partners LLP, 360

Environmental Assessments
See also Environmental Consulting & Contracting Services (General)
AA Environmental & Associates, 64
Acer Environmental Services Ltd., 66
Agrosysts Ltée, 73
Airzone One Ltd., 76
Amberg Corp. - Environmental & Regulatory Consultants, 82
Antelope Land Services Inc., 86
Archipelago Marine Research Ltd., 90
Ark Envirotech Inc., 91
ASI Group Ltd., 93
ASL Environmental Sciences Inc., 94
Aurora Environmental Consulting Ltd., 97
Barenco Inc., 101
Beckie Hydrogeologists (1990) Ltd., 104
Beulah Tec Limited, 106
Biophilia Inc., 109
Brisbin & Sentis Engineering Inc., 116
Cactus Environmental Services Ltd., 120
Calibre Strategic Services Inc., 121
Canning & Pitt Associates Inc., 126
CanTox Environmental Inc., 127
Carswell Consulting Engineers Ltd., 130
Cascade Environmental Resource Group. Ltd., 130
Cascades Inc., 130
Catherine Berris Associates Inc., 132
CCL/IBI, 133
Charlesworth & Associates, 138
Chartwell Consultants Ltd., 138
CIMA+, 141
Clifton Associates Ltd., 144
Coast River Environmental Services Ltd., 145
Conair Group Inc., 148
Cottonwood Consultants Ltd., 152
Custom Environmental Services Ltd., 154
D.G. Taylor Inc., Consulting Ecologist Division, 156
Delcan Water, 160
Dendron Resource Surveys Inc., 161
Diane Beckett, 163
DJA Environmental Consultants Inc., 164
Ecocern Inc., 171
ECOMatters Inc., 172
Ecotech Planners & Advisors Inc., 172
EDA Collaborative Inc., 173
Elford Environmental, 175
Emergex Planning Inc., 176
Enviro-RISQUE Inc., 183
Environmental Advisory Group, 185
Environmental Consultants & Engineers, 185
Envision Compliance, 188
Envision Planning Solutions Inc., 188
Experts-Conseils BMST inc., 192
Friesen Tokar Architects, Landscape & Interior Designers, 201
Fugro Airborne Surveys, 202
G.A. Borstad Associates Ltd., 203
G3 Consulting Ltd., 204
GAEA Technologies, 204
Gamsby & Mannerow Ltd., 204
GDG Environnement Ltée, 205
Gemini Twins Consulting Ltd., 206
Genilab Environnement Inc., 207
Geo-Logic Inc., 210
Geocor Engineering Inc., 210
Geographic Dynamics Corp., 211
Geomarine Associates Ltd., 211
Gourley Construction Ltd., 215

Green Plan Ltd., 217
GroundTech Solutions, 219
Groupe GLD Inc., Experts-Conseils, 219
Groupe SOLROC, 221
Hatfield Group, 226
Hemmera Envirochem Inc., 229
Heritage Research Associates Inc., 230
IBI Group, 238
Icefield Instruments Inc., 238
Inspec-Sol Inc., 242
Institute of Environmental Research Inc., 243
Intera Engineering Ltd., 244
Kaizen Environmental Services Inc., 254
KBM Forestry Consultants Inc., 255
Ken Summers Biological Services, 256
Kent Engineering Ltd., 256
Keystone Environmental Ltd., 257
Kinectrics Inc., 257
Klohn Crippen Berger Ltd., 258
KMK Consultants Limited, 258
Kodiak Environmental Limited, 259
Land & Sea Environmental Consultants Ltd., 264
Landscope Consulting Corp., 264
Lane Environment Limited, 264
Lecompte Engineering Ltd., 266
LGL Limited Environmental Research Associates, 271
Lotowater Technical Services Ltd., 274
Lupien Rosenberg Consultants Inc., 274
M+A Environmental Consultants, 276
Marbek Resource Consultants Ltd., 280
Morrison Hershfield, 293
MWA Consultants, 295
MWH Canada Inc., 295
Natech Environmental Services, 297
The National Testing Laboratories Ltd., 393
Nature's Friend Environmental, 298
Naylor Engineering Associates Ltd., 298
Nelson Environmental Services, 299
New East Consulting Services Inc., 301
Niagara Environmental Dynamics, 303
Notra Inc., 308
O'Connor Associates Environmental Inc., 310
Oakridge Environmental Ltd., 310
Oceans Ltd., 311
Offshore Design Associates Ltd., 311
Paragon Soil & Environmental Consulting Inc., 318
Parish Geomorphic Ltd., 318
Paul F. Wilkinson & Associates Inc., 319
Paul G. Chénard, 319
Peter T. Mitches & Associates Limited; Project Managers & Consulting, 321
PINTER & Associates Ltd., 324
Pisces Environmental Consulting Services Ltd., 325
Plastichem Consulting, 326
Pottinger Gaherty Environmental Consultants Ltd., 328
Poyry (Vancouver) Inc., 329
Prairie Western Reclamation & Consturction Inc., 330
Pridy Associates, 332
R.G. Robinson & Associates (Barrie) Ltd., 340
R.U. Kistritz Consultants Ltd., 341
Redstone Associates Ltd., 343
Refined Specialty Chemicals Inc., 344
Rescan Environmental Services Ltd., 345
Ridgeline Environment Inc., 347
Robert Hornal & Associates Inc., 348
Robinson Consultants Inc., 348
Ronel Engineering Ltd., 351
SAL Engineering Ltd., 356
Scimus Inc., 360
Scott Resource Services Inc., 360
Sedac Inc., 361
Settlement Surveys Ltd., 364
Silva Forest Foundation, 368
Silvana Import Trading Inc., 368
Simcoe Engineering Group Limited, 368
Simon Fraser University, 368
Sittler's Manufacturing, 369
SL Ross Environmental Research Ltd., 370
SLR Consulting Ltd. (Canada), 370
SPG Hydro International Inc., 375
Symbion Consultants, 384
Symbiose Consultants inc, 385
T. Harris Environmental Management Inc., 385
Talon Projects Inc., 386
Tanknology Canada Inc., 386

Subject Index

Tarandus Associates Limited, 387
Taylor Mazier Associates, 387
Technisol Environnement, 388
Tera Environmental Consultants (Alta) Ltd., 389
Terrapex Environmental Ltd., 390
Thurber Engineering Ltd., 395
Thuro Inc., 396
TPE Technologies Inc., 399
Triton Engineering Services Ltd., 402
Triton Environmental Consultants Ltd., 402
Unterman McPhail Associates, 407
Urgel Delisle & Associés inc., 408
W.B. Beatty & Associates, 414
Wakefield Acoustics Ltd., 416
Wallace, Van Egmond Spankle Inc., 416
Waterline Environmental Inc., 422
Watson & Associates Economists Ltd., 423
Williams Engineering Inc., 432
Winchurch Environmental Inc., 432
Winds & Voices Environmental Services Inc., 433
Wotherspoon Environmental Inc., 434
XCG Consultants Ltd., 435
Zbeetnoff Agro-Environmental Consulting, 436

Environmental Consulting & Contracting Services (General)

See also Accident Prevention Services; Architectural Services; Audit Services, Environmental; Baseline Studies, Environmental; Emergency Response Planning; Engineering Consulting Services (General); Environmental Assessments; Environmental Management Systems (ISO 14000); Historical & Heritage Consulting; Landscape Architecture & Analysis Services; Life Cycle Analyses; Permit, Regulation & Standards Consulting; Pest Management Services; Policy Development Consulting; Pollution Prevention Services; Process Change Consulting; Risk Management Services; Site Reclamation & Remedial Action Services; Socio-Economic Studies; Spills/Clean-up Planning & Assessment; Sustainable Development Strategies; Technology Transfer; Total Quality Environmental Management (TQEM); Toxicology Consulting

Abandonrite, 64
Abbeywood Associates Inc., 64
Acadia Consultants & Inspectors Ltd., 65
Accutest Laboratories Ltd., 66
ACE Vegetation Control Service Ltd., 66
Acorus Restoration Native Plant Nursery, 67
Acres & Associated Environmental Ltd., 67
ADI Group Inc., 68
Adventis Technologies, 69
AECOM Canada Ltd., 69
Ag EnviroTech Inc., 72
Agrodev Canada Inc., 73
Agrosysts Ltée, 73
AIC Sullivan's Environmental Services, 73
Ainley Group, 74
ALL-TECH Environmental Services Ltd., 78
Alpine Environmental Ltd., 80
ALS Environmental, 80
ALTECH Environmental Consulting Ltd., 81
ALTECH Technology Systems Inc., 81
AMEC, 82
AMETEK Process Instruments, 84
AN-GEO Environmental Consultants Ltd., 84
Antelope Land Services Inc., 86
Apex Geoscience Ltd., 86
Appin Associates, 87
Applied Groundwater Research Ltd., 87
APS Aviation Inc., 87
Aqua Terre Solutions Inc., 88
Ark Envirotech Inc., 91
Armstrong Engineering & Land Surveying Inc., 91
ASI Group Ltd., 93
ATCO Group, 94
Atlantic Environmental Training & On-Site Services Inc., 95
Atlantic Industrial Services, 95
AWI, 99
B & R Engineering Co. Ltd., 100
Bass Engineering Systems Technology, 103
The Battery Broker Environmental Services Inc., 391
Birchwood Environment Management Inc., 109
Bissett Resource Consultants Ltd., 110
Bolger and Associates Ltd., 113
BOMA Environmental & Safety Inc., 113

Bowie Environmental Edge Management & Assessment Ltd., 114
BPR, 115
BRI International Inc., 116
Brian Clark Architect, 116
Bruce A. Brown Associates Limited, 117
Buchanan Environmental, 118
Buckham Transport Ltd., 118
C.E. Jones & Associates Ltd., 119
C.J. MacLellan & Associates Inc., 120
C.V. Environmental Services, 120
Cactus Environmental Services Ltd., 120
The Cadmus Group, 391
Cambridge Materials Testing Limited, 122
Canadian Environmental Group, 124
Canadian Seabed Research Ltd., 125
CanadianEnvironmental.com, 125
CanAsia Environmental & Engineering Ltd., 125
Canning & Pitt Associates Inc., 126
CanNorth Environmental Services Inc., 126
Cansult Maunsell Limited, 127
CBCL Limited, 132
CEF Consultants Ltd., 135
CENSOL Inc., 136
CH2M Hill Canada Limited, 137
Chamard & Associés, 138
Charles Simon Architect & Planner, 138
Chem Solv, 139
Chemical Emission Management Services, 139
Church & Trought Inc., 140
Cirrus Environmental Services Inc., 141
Clearstone Engineering Ltd., 143
Climate Change Central, 144
CMEL Enterprises Ltd., 144
Coast River Environmental Services Ltd., 145
Coastal Ocean Associates Inc., 145
Community Resource Services Ltd., 147
Comstock Canada Ltd., 148
Conestoga-Rovers & Associates, 149
Conor Pacific Environmental Technology Inc., 150
Consultants Enviroconseil inc., 150
Consultants Filion, Hansen & Associés Inc., 150
Les Consultants LBCD, 268
Cormorant Ltd., 152
Corrpro Canada, Inc., 152
Cowater International Inc., 153
Cypher International Ltd., 155
D. Besner & Associates Inc., 155
Data Tech Environmental Services, 157
DDH Environnement ltée, 159
Dillon Consulting Ltd., 163
Direct Separation Solutions, 164
DST Consulting Engineers, 166
E.B. Tobe Enterprises, 168
E.H. Hanson Engineering Group Ltd., 168
E.K. Gillin & Associates Inc., 168
E2 Management Corporation, 168
Earth & Environmental Technologies (ETech), 168
EBA Engineering Consultants Ltd., 169
Echo Environmental, 170
Eco-Guide International, 170
Ecocern Inc., 171
Ecologistics Research Services, 172
EDA Collaborative Inc., 173
EDM Environmental Design & Management Ltd., 173
Egmond Associates Ltd., 174
El-Rayes Environmental Corp., 174
Elecsar Engineering Co. Ltd., 174
Electronic Warfare Associates - Canada, Ltd., 175
Elford Environmental, 175
EMP Environmental Management & Protection Corporation, 177
Enermodal Engineering Ltd., 179
EnGlobe Corp., 180
Entara Consulting Services Ltd., 181
Entech Environmental Consultants Ltd., 181
Entraco, 181
Envirochem Services Inc., 183
Enviroconseil, 183
Envirometrex, 184
Environmental Accident Protection Inc., 184
Environmental Advisory Group, 185
Environmental Allies Inc., 185
Environmental Communications Options, 185
Environmental Plastics Advisory Service, 185
Environmental Training Institute, 186

Envirotech Associates Limited, 187
Envirotech Engineering, 187
Envirotray Ltd., 188
Envision Sustainability Tools, 188
ENVision...synergy, 188
ETV Canada, 190
Exova, 191
Experts-Conseils CEP Inc., 192
First Stage Enterprises Inc., 196
Fisher Environmental Ltd., 196
Flowmetrix Technical Services Inc., 197
Fluor Canada, 197
FPInnovations, 200
FWR Ecoresource Consultants Ltd., 203
G3 Consulting Ltd., 204
Gage Environmental Management Inc., 204
Gandalf Consulting Ltd., 204
GE Ground Engineering Ltd., 205
Gemini Twins Consulting Ltd., 206
Genivar, 207
Genus Loci Ecological Landscapes Inc., 210
Geo-Logic Inc., 210
Geolab Inc., 211
Global Facman Entreprises Inc., 213
Global Repair Ltd., 213
Glos Associates Inc., 214
Golder Associates Ltd., 214
Greenwood & Associates, 218
Griffiths Muecke Associates, 218
Groupe EnvirAqua, 219
Le Groupe Leblond & Bouchard/Daniel Arbour et associes, 265
Groupe SM inc., 220
GSI Environnement Inc., 222
Hardy Stevenson & Associates, 225
Hazard Alert Training & Supplies Canada Inc., 227
Hazard Control Systems Inc., 227
Hazco Environmental Services Ltd., 227
HEC Group, 228
Helimax Energy Inc., 228
HETEK Solutions Inc., 230
HMO Limited, 232
Horton Tree Farms, 233
Hunter & Associates, 235
Hydro Vision America, 236
Hydromantis Inc., 237
ICF International Canada Inc., 238
IEG Consultants Ltd., 238
IMTT-Newfoundland Ltd., 239
Industrial Forestry Service Ltd., 240
Ininew Project Management Inc., 241
Integrated Environments Ltd., 244
Integrated Explorations, 244
International Marine Salvage Inc., 245
IRC Integrated Resource Consultants Inc., 247
IRIS Environmental Systems Inc., 248
Irving Forest Services Limited, 248
J&B Engineering Inc., 249
J.L. Richards & Associates Limited, 250
JFA James Floyd Associates Ltd., 252
JFM Environmental Ltd., 252
Ken Summers Biological Services, 256
Kerr Wood Leidal Associates Ltd., 257
KGS Group Inc., 257
Kodiak Oilfield Services, 259
Koers & Associates Engineering Ltd., 259
L&M Engineering Ltd., 261
L.W. Ward Limited, 261
Landscope Consulting Corp., 264
Levac Robichaud Leclerc Associates Ltd., 270
Levelton Consultants Ltd., 270
LGL Limited Environmental Research Associates, 271
Linpro Petroleum Services Ltd., 272
Long Environmental Consultants, 273
Lovell & Associates, 274
Lupien Rosenberg Consultants Inc., 274
LURA Consulting, 275
M.S. Thompson & Associates Ltd., 276
Malroz Engineering Inc., 279
Management Horizons, 279
Maple Reinders Environmental Ltd., 279
Matrix Solutions Inc., 282
Meo & Associates Inc., 286
MIG Engineering Ltd., 289
MissionHGE inc., 291
MMM Group, 292

Subject Index

Morrison Environmental Limited, 293
Mountain Valley Geophysics, 294
Multi Recyclage S.D. Inc., 295
MWA Consultants, 295
The National Testing Laboratories Ltd., 393
National Waste Services, 298
NCL Envirotek Inc., 299
Niblett Environmental, 304
Nichols Environmental (Canada) Ltd., 304
Nisymco Inc., 304
Nor-Alta Environmental Services Ltd., 305
North West Environmental Group, 306
North/South Consultants Inc., 306
Notre Development Corp., 308
Nova Magnetics Burgmann Ltd., 308
Nove Environnement Inc., 309
Oakhill Environmental, 310
Oceans Ltd., 311
Oil Spill Control Services Canada, 311
Ontario Centres of Excellence, 312
Opcon Pacific Recycling Ltd., 313
Organic Farm Services, 314
P. Machibroda Engineering Ltd., 315
P.J.B. Duffy & Associates, 316
Pacific Environmental Consulting & Occupational Hygiene Services, 316
Pacific Institute for Advanced Study, 316
Pam Wight & Associates, 317
Parkvalley Consulting Ltd., 319
Parsons Commercial Technology Group Inc., 319
Paul F. Wilkinson & Associates Inc., 319
PCB Disposal Inc., 319
Peto MacCallum Ltd., 321
Phoenix Engineering Inc., 323
Pigmalion Environmental Services Group, 323
Pisces Environmental Consulting Services Ltd., 325
Piteau Associates, 325
Planning Alliance, 326
Pollutech Group of Companies Inc., 327
Precision Assessment Technology Corp., 330
Precision Identification Biological Consultants, 330
ProAgri Consulting Limited, 333
Project Engineering Limited, 334
Promens Canada Inc., 334
Provincial Airlines Ltd. - Environmental Services Division, 335
Provincial Environmental Services Inc., 335
R Plus Industries Alberta Inc., 339
R.J. Burnside & Associates Limited, 340
R.V. Anderson Associates Limited, 341
Radiation Environmental Management Systems Inc., 341
REDUCT & Lobbe Technologies Inc., 344
Remedy Energy Services Ltd., 344
René Gervais Inc., Consultants, 345
Rescan Environmental Services Ltd., 345
Resource Environmental Associates, 345
Robert J. Redhead Limited, 348
Robinson Consultants Inc., 348
Roche ltée, Groupe-conseil, 348
Ronel Engineering Ltd., 351
Rowan Williams Davies & Irwin Inc., 352
SAIC Canada, 355
SCG Industries Ltd., 358
Schlumberger Water Services, 359
SDS Drilling Ltd., 360
Secter Environmental Resource Consulting, 361
Sedac Inc., 361
Seguro Projects Inc., 362
SENES Consultants Limited, 362
The Sernas Group Inc., 393
ServiceMaster of Canada, 363
Services d'Évaluation Santé/Toxicologie Inc., 363
Settlement Surveys Ltd., 364
Sigma Engineering Ltd., 367
SLR Consulting Ltd. (Canada), 370
SNC-Lavalin Environment Inc., 371
SNC-Lavalin Group Inc., 371
Solinov Inc., 373
Solmax-Texel Geosynthetics Inc., 373
SOTAR Inc., 374
Southwestern Flowtech & Environmental Ltd., 374
Stabilis Environment Inc., 377
Stantec Inc., 377
Strata Soil Sampling Inc., 380
Summerhill Group, 381
Swiss Environment & Safety Inc., 384

Sydney Environmental Resources Ltd., 384
Symbiose Consultants inc, 385
System Ecotechnologies Inc., 385
Talon Projects Inc., 386
Tang G. Lee Architect, 386
Tarandus Associates Limited, 387
TEAM-1 Environmental Services Inc., 387
Tecsult Inc., 388
TerraChoice Environmental Marketing, 390
Terratec Environmental Ltd., 390
TetrES Consultants Inc., 391
Thermal Hydronics Supply Ltd., 394
Toxicology Centre, 399
Tract Consulting Inc., 400
Triton Environmental Consultants Ltd., 402
Trow Consulting Engineers Ltd., 403
2cg Inc., 404
UMA Group Ltd., 405
United Safety Ltd., 406
Université du Québec, 406
University of Saskatchewan, 406
Urban Systems Ltd., 407
URS Canada Inc., 408
Utility Risk Management Ltd., 408
V. Fournier & Associates, 408
Varcon Inc., 409
Venerus International Purification Inc., 410
W.G. Shaw & Associates, 415
Wardrop Engineering Inc., 416
Waste Alternatives Inc., 417
Western Site Technologies Inc., 430
Westland Resource Group Inc., 430
WHMIS Inc., 431
WorleyParsons Canada Ltd., 433
Zephyr Alternative Power, 437

Environmental Management Systems (ISO 14000)
See also **Environmental Consulting & Contracting Services (General); Industrial Management (General); ISO 14000 Registrar; Quality Management Systems (ISO 9000)**

Alan Willis & Associates, 76
Amberg Corp. - Environmental & Regulatory Consultants, 82
AquaTox Testing & Consulting Inc., 89
Aware Learning Technologies, 99
Biophilia Inc., 109
Church & Trought Inc., 140
Coastal Zones Research Institute Inc., 145
DJA Environmental Consultants Inc., 164
Duerden & Keane Consultants Inc., 167
Eco2 Systems Inc., 171
ÉEM inc., 173
Electronic Warfare Associates - Canada, Ltd., 175
Engineering Management Services Croscan, 180
EnvirInfo, 182
Enviroconseil, 183
Environmental Reporting Systems Limited, 186
Gemteck Environmental Software Ltd., 206
Greenbridge Management Inc., 217
GreenWare Environmental Systems Inc., 218
Hazard Alert Training & Supplies Canada Inc., 227
HSE Integrated, 234
INDECO Strategic Consulting Inc., 240
Intelex Technologies Inc., 244
LEHDER Environmental Services Ltd., 267
M+A Environmental Consultants, 276
Marbek Resource Consultants Ltd., 280
Michael Wall & Sons Enterprises Ltd., 288
MWA Consultants, 295
MWH Canada Inc., 295
New East Consulting Services Ltd., 301
North Shore Management Systems Inc., 306
Paul G. Chénard, 319
Pilot Performance Resources Management Inc., 324
Procyon Consulting Inc., 333
ProSolve Consulting Ltd., 335
QMI-SAI Global, 337
R.U. Kistritz Consultants Ltd., 341
Refined Specialty Chemicals Inc., 344
SGS Canada Inc., 364
Spill Management Inc., 376
Stratos Inc., 380
SustaiNet Software Solutions Inc., 383
Tera Environmental Consultants (Alta) Ltd., 389
TTA Technology Training Associates Ltd., 404
Viridis Environmental Inc., 413

Water & Earth Science Associates Ltd., 421
XCG Consultants Ltd., 435

Erosion Control Services
See also **Engineering Consulting Services (General)**

A. A. Boscariol and Associates Limited, 63
AC Environmental Services, 65
Acorus Restoration Native Plant Nursery, 67
Agrosysts Ltée, 73
BOS Engineering & Environmental Services Inc., 114
Cascade Environmental Resource Group. Ltd., 130
Chisholm, Fleming & Associates, 140
Civtech Engineering & Surveying Ltd., 141
Construction Val-d'Or Ltée, 150
Les Consultants RSA, 268
Cramer Nursery Inc., 153
Dol Hydroseeding, 164
ECL Envirowest Consultants Ltd., 170
Glenn Group Ltd., 213
Henry Kortekaas & Associates Inc., 229
Koers & Associates Engineering Ltd., 259
Laboratoires d'Expertises de Québec Ltée, 262
LaCas Consultants Inc., 262
Layfield Geosynthetics & Industrial Fabrics Ltd., 265
Longwood Forestry Services Ltd., 273
Maccaferri Canada Ltd., 277
Metropolitan Consulting Inc., 288
MTE Consultants Inc., 294
Nilex Inc., 304
Parish Geomorphic Ltd., 318
R.H. Loucks Oceanology, 340
Scott Resource Services Inc., 360
SHAL Consulting Engineers Ltd., 365
Skelton Brumwell & Associates Inc., 369
Solmers Internationale Experts-Conseils Inc., 373
Soren Construction Ltd., 374
SOTAR Inc., 374
SRK Consulting (Canada) Inc., 376
Terrafix Geosynthetics, 390
Urgel Delisle & Associés inc., 408
Whitman Benn Group, 431

Excavation
See **Construction & Excavation Services**

Expert Testimony
Airzone One Ltd., 76
AXYS Analytical Services Ltd., 99
Barenco Inc., 101
Beaulier Inc., 104
Biophilia Inc., 109
Ecotech Planners & Advisors Inc., 172
Environmental Consultants & Engineers, 185
Hazelmere Research Ltd., 228
Interwest Property Services (1991) Ltd., 246
Investigative Science Inc., 247
LEX Scientific Inc., 271
P.J. Cluff Architect Inc., 315
Plastichem Consulting, 326
Sciencetech Inc., 359
SL Ross Environmental Research Ltd., 370
SPG Hydro International Inc., 375
Tera Environmental Consultants (Alta) Ltd., 389
Wakefield Acoustics Ltd., 416
Williams Engineering Inc., 432

Feasibility/Pre-feasibility Studies
See also **Engineering Consulting Services (General)**

A.H. Lundberg Systems Ltd., 63
Alpine Environmental Ltd., 80
Angus, Butler Engineering Ltd., 86
Anrep Krieg Desilets Gravelle Ltd., 86
Atlantic Engineering Consultants Ltd., 95
BCL Landview Systems Inc., 103
Biogénie, 108
Boutillette Parizeau et Associés inc., 114
Brosz & Associates, 117
BV SORBEX, Inc., 119
Canadian Fishery Consultants Ltd., 124
Canadian Petroleum Engineering Inc., 124
Canatec Consultants Ltd., 125
Carswell Consulting Engineers Ltd., 130
Cemcorp Ltd. Consulting Engineers, 135
Chatwin Engineering Ltd., 138
Chisholm, Fleming & Associates, 140
Custom Environmental Services Ltd., 154
D. Greenfield Associates Ltd., 156

Subject Index

Decommissioning Consulting Services Limited, 159
ECE Group - a Division of Conestoga-Rovers & Associates, 170
Enerscan Consultants Limited, 179
Engineering Management Services Croscan, 180
EPEC Consulting (Sask) Ltd., 189
Fluor Canada, 197
Gas Liquids Engineering Ltd., 205
Géophysique GPR International Inc., 211
Glenn Group Ltd., 213
Groupe RSW inc., 220
Groupe Sodinco inc., 221
Gryphon International Engineering Services Inc., 222
H. Broer Equipment Sales and Service, 223
Henry Kortekaas & Associates Inc., 229
Heritage Research Associates Inc., 230
Horner Associates Limited, 233
HurterConsult Inc., 235
Integrated Catalyst Engineering Inc., 244
Kinder Morgan Canada Inc., 257
Knight Piésold Ltd., 258
Koers & Associates Engineering Ltd., 259
Lecompte Engineering Ltd., 266
MacDonnell Group, 277
Maitland Engineering, 279
McElhanney Consulting Services Ltd., 284
Metropolitan Consulting Inc., 288
Ottawa Engineering Ltd., 315
P.J. Cluff Architect Inc., 315
Pacific Engineering Inc., 316
Poyry (Vancouver) Inc., 329
Ridgeline Environment Inc., 347
Sandwell Engineering Inc., 356
SEG Engineering Inc., 362
SHAL Consulting Engineers Ltd., 365
Sinanni Inc., 369
SMS Engineering Ltd., 371
SRK Consulting (Canada) Inc., 376
Strait Engineering Ltd., 380
Sultech Consulting Ltd., 381
Sustainable EDGE Ltd., 383
Taylor Munro Energy Systems Inc., 387
Triton Engineering Services Ltd., 402
Trivar Inc., 402
Urban Systems Ltd., 407
Walter Dow Associates Ltd., 416

Fertilizers, Recycled
See also Recycled Products
Organic Resource Management Inc., 314

Filters & Filter Media, Air
See also Air Pollution Control Equipment
A.C. Carbone Canada Inc., 63
Acklands-Grainger Inc., 66
ALCO Gas & Oil Production Equipment Ltd., 77
Ambio Biofiltration Ltd., 82
Asbeguard Equipment Inc., 93
AXYS Analytical Services Ltd., 99
BC Air Filter Ltd., 103
CAHFIL FARR (Canada Inc.), 121
Canwest Pumping Systems Ltd., 127
Century Environmental Systems, 136
Cimatec Environmental Engineering Inc., 141
Cleartech Industries Inc., 143
Con-Test, A Division of Contamination Containment Technology Inc., 148
Cunningham Sheet Metal Works Inc., 154
Cypress Sales Partnership, 155
DCL International Inc., 158
Electro-Air Canada, 174
Enervac Corp., 180
Engine Control Systems, 180
Engineered Air, 180
Enterprise Steel Fabricators Ltd., 181
Enviro-Klean Technologies Inc., 182
H.E. Bent Services Ltd., 223
HAMON Custodis-Cottrell Canada, Inc., 224
Henlex Inc., 229
Integrated Metal Products, 244
IPAC Inc., 247
Island Clean Air Inc., 248
Kraemer Tool & Manufacturing Co. Ltd., 260
Living Resources Inc., 273
Maddocks Industrial Filter Division, 278
Metacor International Inc., 287
Mirus International Inc., 290

N.R. Murphy Ltd., 296
National Process Equipment Inc., 298
Nederman Canada Ltd., 299
Nett Technologies Inc., 300
Nilfisk-Advance Canada Company, 304
O'Connor Tanks Ltd., 310
P.J. Hannah Equipment Sales Corp., 315
Performance Fluid Equipement Inc., 321
Petro Laboratories Inc., 322
Q-Air Environmental Controls Ltd., 337
Rodrigue Métal Ltée, 350
Safety Express Ltd., 355
Semco Systems Limited, 362
3M Canada Company, 395
Trent Metals Ltd., 401
Warco Process Technologies, 416
Weir Power & Industrial, 424
Wheelabrator Canada Co., 431
YES Environment Technologies Inc., 435

Filters & Filter Media, Water & Wastewater
See also Water, Wastewater & Groundwater Equipment
ACG Technology Ltd., 66
Acme Engineering Products Ltd., 66
Anco Chemicals Inc., 85
Anderson Water Systems, 85
Annapolis Valley Peat Moss Co. Ltd., 86
Anthrafilter Media & Coal Ltd., 86
Apex Industries Inc., 86
Avoca-tec Environmental Services Inc., 99
AWI, 99
AXYS Analytical Services Ltd., 99
Blower Engineering Inc., 110
Canadian Water Conditioning Inc., 125
Catterall & Wright, 132
Chromatographic Specialties Inc., 140
Cleartech Industries Inc., 143
Condor Engineering Ltd., 149
Eco-Tec Ltd., 171
Ecodyne Ltd., 171
Ecofluid Systems Inc., 171
Elgin Pure Water Supply, 175
Envirogard Products Ltd., 184
Envirogineering, 184
Environmental Remediation Equipment Inc., 185
Filtration Seco Inc., 195
Flexo Products Ltd., 196
FLSmidth Canada Ltd., 197
Fluidcare Ltd., 197
Frontenac Environmental Ltd., 202
FSI International Services Ltd., 202
GAP EnviroMicrobial Services Inc., 204
GE Water & Process Technologies, 205
General Filtration, 206
H.E. Bent Services Ltd., 223
Hercules SLR Inc., 229
Hike Metal Products Ltd., 231
Imbibitive Technologies Canada, Inc., 238
IMP Liquid Meters & Petroleum Services, 239
IPAC Inc., 247
IPEC Industries Ltd., 247
Komline-Sanderson Ltd., 259
Living Resources Inc., 273
Loomers Pumping Services Ltd., 274
LTS Sales Ltd., 274
MacDonald & Fils Inc., 277
Maddocks Industrial Filter Division, 278
Magnor, Division of Magchem, 278
Mar Cor Purification, 280
Metcon Sales & Engineering Ltd., 287
Mifab Canada, 289
Multi-Stage Filter, 295
Nemato Inc., 300
Niagara Environmental Dynamics, 303
Niagara Water Conditioning Inc., 303
Nimbus Water Systems, 304
Nolar Industries Ltd., 305
Nordic Systems Corporation, 305
O'Connor Tanks Ltd., 310
Ontor Ltd., 312
Pall (Canada) Limited, 317
Parameter Control Ltd., 318
Parkson Corporation, 319
Performance Fluid Equipement Inc., 321
Premier Tech Environment, 331

Proline Filter Systems Inc., 334
ProMinent Fluid Controls Ltd., 334
PWC Pure Water Corporation, 337
Réal Huot Inc., 343
RenuWater Centre, 345
RMS Enviro Solv Inc. Québec, 347
Sanitherm Engineering Limited, 357
SEI Industries Ltd., 362
Seprotech Systems Inc., 363
Sonitec Inc., 374
T.D. Rooke Associates Ltd., 385
Touchie Engineering, 399
Tremcar inc., 401
U.S. Filter/Asdor Ltd., 405
Universal Filter Media, 406
VIQUA - A Trojan Technologies Company, 413
Waterloo Biofilter Systems Inc., 422
Weir Power & Industrial, 424
Wyckomar Inc., 434
Zimmark Inc., 437
Zodiac Fabrics Inc., 437

Financial & Marketing Services (General)
See also Business Development Services; Environmental Accounting Services; Full-Cost Accounting Services; Insurance, Environmental Liability; Market Analyses; Marketing Services; Product Development Services; Show & Conference Management; Venture Capital & Funding Services
Adhawk Communications Inc., 68
Adventis Technologies, 69
BRI International Inc., 116
Cetac-West, 137
Entech Environmental Consultants Ltd., 181
Environmental R&D Capital Corporation, 185
Federated Co-operatives Ltd., 194
Helimax Energy Inc., 228
Industrial Ecology Corp., 240
John McMullen & Associates, 252
NEK Environmental Technologies Inc., 299
Pinch Group, 324
Probyn & Company Inc., 333
Raymond James Financial Inc., 342
Stratem Inc., 380
Tecsult Inc., 388
Vision Quest - TransAlta's Wind Business, 413
Westra & Associates Inc., 430

Financial Analyses
See Market Analyses

Fisheries & Aquaculture Management
See also Resource Management Services (General)
Acer Environmental Services Ltd., 66
ACME Vacuum Cleaner Co. Ltd., 67
Agrodev Canada Inc., 73
Applied Aquatic Research Ltd., 87
Archipelago Marine Research Ltd., 90
Biorex Inc., 109
Canadian Benthic Ltd., 124
Canadian Fishery Consultants Ltd., 124
CCL/IBI, 133
Coastal Ocean Associates Inc., 145
East Coast Aquatics, 169
EnviroMed Detection Services, 184
Fundy Engineering & Consulting Ltd., 203
G3 Consulting Ltd., 204
GDG Environnement Ltée, 205
Hatfield Group, 226
Hyperspectral Data International Inc., 237
Integrated Explorations, 244
Knight Piésold Ltd., 258
KnowTech Environmental Inc., 259
Lane Environment Limited, 264
LGL Limited Environmental Research Associates, 271
Lotek Wireless Inc., 274
NAR Environmental Consultants Inc., 297
Nelson Environmental Services, 299
North/South Consultants Inc., 306
PDK Projects Inc., 320
Pisces Environmental Consulting Services Ltd., 325
R.H. Loucks Oceanology, 340
Robertson Environmental Services Ltd., 348
Scott Resource Services Inc., 360
Silvicon Services Inc., 368
Symbion Consultants, 384

Syndel International Inc., 385
Triton Environmental Consultants Ltd., 402
Vemco Ltd., 410
Western Subsea Technology Ltd., 430

Flow Meters, Water & Wastewater
See also Water, Wastewater & Groundwater Equipment
AIC Associated Industrial Controls Ltd., 73
AquaMetrix Inc., 88
Arjay Engineering Ltd., 91
Armatek Controls Limited, 91
Avensys Inc., 98
Bestobell AquaTronix Limited, 106
C.V. Environmental Services, 120
Cancoppas Limited, 126
Chemline Plastics Ltd., 139
Coastal Ocean Associates Inc., 145
Compteurs Lecomte Ltée, 148
Control Microsystems, 151
Les Contrôles PROVAN Associés Inc., 268
Crompton Technology Inc., 153
Davis Controls Ltd., 158
Drexan Energy Systems Inc., 166
Egetec Enterprises Inc., 174
Elite Technologies Inc., 175
Endress+Hauser Canada Ltd., 178
Enviro-Systèmes Inc., 183
Environnement ESA Inc., 186
Flygt Canada, 198
Focal Technologies Inc., 198
Greyline Instruments Inc., 218
H.E. Bent Services Ltd., 223
ITM Instruments, 248
J&M Industrial Engineering & Sales Ltd., 249
LaCas Consultants Inc., 262
LTS Sales Ltd., 274
MacDonald & Fils Inc., 277
Magnetrol International Ltd., 278
Mandel Scientific Co. Inc., 279
Metcon Sales & Engineering Ltd., 287
Mueller Canada, 295
Muis Controls Ltd., 295
Neo Valves, 300
Nimbus Water Systems, 304
Nortec S.G.S. Inc., 306
Oak Environmental Inc., 310
Pacific Engineering Inc., 316
Pumps & Systems, 336
R.A. Kirby Sales Inc., 339
Roctest Ltée, 350
Rotork Controls (Canada) Ltd., 352
Siemens Milltronics Process Instruments Inc., 366
Siemens Water Technologies, 367
Simark Controls Ltd., 368
Southwell Controls Ltd., 374
Stedtnitz Maritime Technology Ltd., 379
Terasen Waterworks, 389
Testwell Instruments, 391
Thermo Electron Corp., 394
Westech Industrial Ltd., 429

Forestry & Reforestation Management
See also Resource Management Services (General)
Alberta-Pacific Forest Industries Inc., 77
Bass Engineering Systems Technology, 103
C.E. Jones & Associates Ltd., 119
Chartwell Consultants Ltd., 138
Coast Forest Management Ltd., 145
Conair Group Inc., 148
Corner Brook Pulp & Paper Ltd., 152
D.R. Estey Engineering Ltd., 156
Dendron Resource Surveys Inc., 161
Digital Land Resources, 163
Dougan & Associates, 165
Forest Protection Limited, 199
Forest Technology Systems Ltd., 199
Geographic Dynamics Corp., 211
Geowest Environmental Consultants, 212
Groupe S.M. International Inc., 220
Hakmet Ltd., 223
Halltech Environmental Inc., 224
Hatfield Group, 226
Horton Tree Farms, 233
Industrial Forestry Service Ltd., 240
Inform Consulting Services Ltd., 241
Interforest Inc., 244

International Irrigation Systems Ltd., 245
Irving Forest Services Limited, 248
ITRES Research Ltd., 248
KBM Forestry Consultants Inc., 255
Keywood Entreprises Ltd., 257
Lab-Élite limitée, 261
Lakehead University, 263
Legaré F., Ing. Forestier Conseil, 266
Longwood Forestry Services Ltd., 273
Marbicon Inc., 280
Mesa Forestry & Environmental Services Ltd., 287
Mikro-Tek Inc., 289
P.J.B. Duffy & Associates, 316
Pacific Phytometric Consultants, 316
PRT Inc., 336
RAM Forest Products Inc., 342
Robertson Environmental Services Ltd., 348
Scott & Stewart Forestry Consultants, 360
Sea Scan International Inc., 361
Silva Forest Foundation, 368
Spencer-Lemaire Industries Ltd., 375
Sylvametrics Consulting, 384
Vanport Sterilizers Inc., 409

Fuel Recycling
See also Oil Recycling; Recycling Services (General)
Active Chemicals Ltd., 67
EIL Environmental Services, 174
The Recycle Systems Company Inc., 393
Regional Petroleum Products Recycling Ltd., 344
Servicestat Ltd., 363
Sprayaway Marine Services Ltd., 376
United Oil Services, 406
Veolia Water Canada, 412
WRS Environmental, 434

Fuels, Alternative
See also Energy Equipment
Atlantic Wind Power Corp. Ltd., 97
Consolidated Envirowaste Industries Inc., 150
DynaMotive Energy Systems Corporation, 167
ECO Fuel Systems Inc., 170
Encana Corporation, 178
Estco Battery Management Inc., 190
Fuel Maker Corp., 202
Hebco International Inc., 228
Inproheat Industries Ltd., 242
Loomers Pumping Services Ltd., 274
Mabarex inc., 277
MacEwen Petroleum Inc., 277
Network Environmental Services Inc., 300
Petro Laboratories Inc., 322
Pioneer Petroleums, 325
Servicestat Ltd., 363
UPI Inc., 407

Full-Cost Accounting Services
See also Financial & Marketing Services (General)
Alan Willis & Associates, 76
Cheminfo Services Inc., 139
Environmental Advisory Group, 185
GreenWare Environmental Systems Inc., 218
Watson & Associates Economists Ltd., 423

Fume Extraction Equipment
See also Air Pollution Control Equipment
Air Trac Corp., 75
Altus Capital Planning Inc., 81
Atlantic Air Cleaning Specialists Ltd., 95
BEX Engineering Limited, 106
CAHFIL FARR (Canada Inc.), 121
DCL International Inc., 158
Elmridge Engineering Inc., 176
Energy Technology Products Ltd., 179
Engine Control Systems, 180
Envirotech Pollution Controls Ltd., 188
Eurovac, 191
F.C. O'Neill, Scriven & Associates Ltd., 193
Fabricated Plastics Ltd., 193
Five Seasons Comfort Limited, 196
Gasmac Inc., 205
Island Clean Air Inc., 248
Kongskilde Limited, 259
N.R. Murphy Ltd., 296
Nederman Canada Ltd., 299
Nemato Inc., 300
Ordan Thermal Products Ltd., 314

Pyradia Inc., 337
Rodrigue Métal Ltée, 350
Sheldons Engineering Inc., 365
Thermal Technics Corporation, 394
Wheelabrator Canada Co., 431
Wilcorp Manufacturing, 431

Geographic Information Systems
See also Information Technology & Communications (General); Mapping & Surveying Services; Remote Sensing & Image Analysis
AERDE Environmental Research, 71
BCL Landview Systems Inc., 103
CARIS, 128
Cascade Environmental Resource Group. Ltd., 130
Catherine Berris Associates Inc., 132
CEF Consultants Ltd., 135
Cengea Solutions Inc., 136
Cobham Tracking & Locating Ltd., 145
Dendron Resource Surveys Inc., 161
Eastcan Geomatics, 169
EITNL/Earth Information Technologies (nfld) Limited, 174
EmerGeo Solutions Inc., 176
Entraco, 181
ESRI Canada Ltd., 190
FMA Heritage Resources Consultants Inc., 198
Forest Protection Limited, 199
Gemteck Environmental Software Ltd., 206
GeoInsight Corporation, 211
Geosolutions Consulting Inc., 212
Geowest Environmental Consultants, 212
Hatfield Group, 226
Hilderman Thomas Frank Cram & Associates, 232
Hyperspectral Data International Inc., 237
Inform Consulting Services Ltd., 241
IRIS Environmental Systems Inc., 248
Kanotech Information Systems Ltd., 255
KBM Forestry Consultants Inc., 255
Lakehead University, 263
Lakes Environmental Software, 263
MacDonald, Dettwiler & Associates Ltd., 277
Northway-Photomap Inc., 307
Opus International Consultants (Canada) Ltd., 313
PCI Geomatics Group Inc., 320
Peter T. Mitches & Associates Limited; Project Managers & Consulting, 321
Prairie Geomatics Ltd., 330
Robinson Consultants Inc., 348
Silva Forest Foundation, 368
Silvana Import Trading Inc., 368
SOTAR Inc., 374
UMA Group Ltd., 405
W.B. Beatty & Associates, 414
Western Subsea Technology Ltd., 430
Zephyr North, 437

Geological & Hydrogeological Engineering
See also Engineering Consulting Services (General)
Apex Geoscience Ltd., 86
Arrakis Consultants Inc., 92
BAE Newplan Group Ltd., 101
Barenco Inc., 101
Bass Engineering Systems Technology, 103
BOS Engineering & Environmental Services Inc., 114
Canadian Petroleum Engineering Inc., 124
Cascade Environmental Resource Group. Ltd., 130
Charlesworth & Associates, 138
Clifton Associates Ltd., 144
Coast Forest Management Ltd., 145
Conestoga-Rovers & Associates, 149
Conestoga-Rovers & Associates, 149
Curtis Environmental & Engineering Inc., 154
Decommissioning Consulting Services Limited, 159
EarthFx Inc., 169
Enviroconseil, 183
GAEA Technologies, 204
Gamsby & Mannerow Ltd., 204
Geo Environmental Engineering - Geocon SNC-Lavalin, 210
Geo-Logic Inc., 210
Geocor Engineering Inc., 210
Geomarine Associates Ltd., 211
Géophysique GPR International Inc., 211
Geostat Systems International Inc., 212
The Greer Galloway Group Inc., Engineers & Planners, 392
GroundTech Solutions, 219
Groupe Consulteaux Inc., 219

Subject Index

Hydro-Com Technologies Ltd., 236
Hydrogéo Plus Inc., 236
Hydrogéochem Environnement Inc., 236
Hydrogeological Consultants, 236
Inspec-Sol Inc., 242
International Water Supply Ltd., 245
Klohn Crippen Berger Ltd., 258
Laboratoires d'Expertises de Québec Ltée, 262
Les Laboratoires S.L. inc., 269
Les Laboratoires Shermont Inc., 269
Lotowater Technical Services Inc., 274
LVM Inc., 275
McClymont & Rak Engineers, Inc., 284
Mobile Augers & Research Ltd., 292
Naylor Engineering Associates Ltd., 298
Nevin Sadlier-Brown Goodbrand Ltd., 300
Oakridge Environmental Ltd., 310
Pedocan Land Evaluation Ltd., 320
Reliance Geological Services Inc., 344
Schlumberger Oilfield Services, 359
Sendex Environmental Corp., 362
Sonic Soil Sampling Inc., 374
SRK Consulting (Canada) Inc., 376
Technisol Environnement, 388
Terracon Geotechnique Ltd., 390
Terratech, 390
Terratlantic Engineering Ltd., 391
Thurber Engineering Ltd., 395
W. Sodin (Gravity) Ltd., 414
W.B. Beatty & Associates, 414

Geophysical Survey Services
See also Engineering Consulting Services (General)
AGO Environmental Electronics Ltd., 73
ARAM Systems Ltd., 89
Canadian Seabed Research Ltd., 125
ClearView Geophysics Inc., 143
G.A. Borstad Associates Ltd., 203
Geomarine Associates Ltd., 211
Geonics Limited, 211
Géophysique GPR International Inc., 211
Icefield Instruments Inc., 238
Metocean Data Systems Limited, 287
Multiview Locates Inc., 295
Notra Inc., 308
Oakridge Environmental Ltd., 310
ODIM Brooke Ocean, 311
Reliance Geological Services Inc., 344
Seaforth Engineering Group Inc., 361
W. Sodin (Gravity) Ltd., 414

Geosynthetics
See Liners, Geosynthetic/Geomembrane

Glass Recycling
See also Recycling Services (General)
Dartmouth Metals & Bottles Ltd., 157
Guardian Industries Canada Corp., 222
Magnum Industries Ltd., 278
Neighborhood Recycling, 299
O-I Canada Corp., 310
Western Scrap Metals, 429
Wheatland Regional Centre Inc. & SARCAN Recycling, 431

Ground/Surface Water Monitoring
See also Ground/Surface Water Remediation; Water, Wastewater & Groundwater Services
A&A Environmental Consultants Inc., 63
Accutest Laboratories Ltd., 66
Alpine Environmental Ltd., 80
ALS Environmental, 80
ARC Geobac Group Inc., 89
Arjay Engineering Ltd., 91
ASL Environmental Sciences Inc., 94
Beckie Hydrogeologists (1990) Ltd., 104
Bio-Limno Research & Consulting, 107
Bolger and Associates Ltd., 113
Boojum Research Ltd., 113
Buchanan Environmental, 118
CadhamHayes Systems Inc., 120
CanTox Environmental Inc., 127
Cascade Environmental Resource Group. Ltd., 130
Charlesworth & Associates, 138
Chisholm, Fleming & Associates, 140
Comco Manufacturing Ltd., 146
Les Consultants RSA, 268
DJA Environmental Consultants Inc., 164

East Coast Aquatics, 169
Egetec Enterprises Inc., 174
Entech Laboratories, 181
Environmental Biodetection Products Inc., 185
Environnement ESA Inc., 186
Envirosphere Consultants Ltd., 187
Fluorosense Inc., 198
Forest Technology Systems Ltd., 199
Fraser Environmental Services, 201
Fundy Engineering & Consulting Ltd., 203
Gamsby & Mannerow Ltd., 204
GAP EnviroMicrobial Services Inc., 204
GlobalTox International Consultants Inc., 213
Groupe Consulteaux Inc., 219
Guelph Chemical Laboratories, 222
Hoskin Scientific Ltd., 233
Insituform Technologies Ltd. - Edmonton, 242
Intera Engineering Ltd., 244
Interior Weather Services Ltd., 245
JB Laboratories Inc., 251
Jetvac Inc., 251
Kaizen Environmental Services Inc., 254
Ken Noftell Drilling Services, 256
Les Laboratoires Shermont Inc., 269
Lakehead University, 263
Malroz Engineering Inc., 279
Maxxam Analytics Ltd., 283
Metocean Data Systems Limited, 287
MIE Consulting Engineers Ltd., 289
NAR Environmental Consultants Inc., 297
Near North Laboratories Inc., 299
Nove Environnement Inc., 309
Oak Environmental Inc., 310
P. Machibroda Engineering Ltd., 315
PBR Laboratories Inc., 319
Quantum Murray LP, 338
R.A. Kirby Sales Inc., 339
R.A. Murray International Limited, 340
R.J. Burnside & Associates Limited, 340
RBR Ltd., 343
René Gervais Inc., Consultants, 345
Rice Engineering & Operating Ltd., 346
Roctest Ltée, 350
Ron Robinson Limited, 351
Sciencetech, Inc., 359
Sendex Environmental Corp., 362
Testwell Instruments, 391
Via-Sat Data Systems, 413
Wellmaster Pipe & Supply, 424
York Fluid Controls Ltd., 435
Zell Oilfield Service Ltd., 436
Zodiac Fabrics Inc., 437

Ground/Surface Water Remediation
See also Ground/Surface Water Monitoring; Water, Wastewater & Groundwater Services
AiMS Environmental, 74
Alpine Environmental Ltd., 80
Aqua Terre Solutions Inc., 88
Biolab Inc., 108
Boojum Research Ltd., 113
Caduceon Environmental Laboratories, 120
Cannington Group, 126
DRL Environmental Services, 166
Earthworks Technology Inc., 169
EnviroMetal Technologies Inc., 184
Environmental Remediation Equipment Inc., 185
EPA Certified Clean Ltd., 188
GPEC Global Corp., 215
Le Groupe Forces, 265
Hydrogéochem Environnement Inc., 236
Insitu Contractors Inc., 242
Ivey International Inc., 249
Kaizen Environmental Services Inc., 254
Kam Biotechnology Ltd., 254
Kent Engineering Ltd., 256
Keystone Environmental Ltd., 257
MIE Consulting Engineers Ltd., 289
MPI Drilling, 294
N.L. Sobey & Associates Limited, 296
Next Environmental, 303
R.J. Burnside & Associates Limited, 340
Rice Engineering & Operating Ltd., 346
Rochester Midland Company, 349
Terratechnik Environmental Limited, 391

Testwell Instruments, 391
Waterloo Barrier Inc., 422
Worldware Enterprises Inc., 433
XCG Consultants Ltd., 435

Hazardous or Toxic Waste Consulting
See Waste Management Consulting, Liquid & Hazardous

Hazardous Waste Management Consulting
See Waste Management Consulting, Liquid & Hazardous

Heat Exchangers
See Energy Recovery Equipment

Heat Transfer Systems
See Energy Recovery Equipment

Heating, Ventilation & Air Conditioning Equipment
See also Air Pollution Control Equipment; Energy Equipment; Heating, Ventilation & Air Conditioning Services
ACME Vacuum Cleaner Co. Ltd., 67
Advanced Biotechnology Inc., 69
Air Control Engineering Inc., 74
Airmaster Sales Ltd., 75
Airtechni Inc., 76
Anrep Krieg Desilets Gravelle Ltd., 86
Arpi's Industries Canada Ltd., 92
Automatic Controls Ltd., 98
AZZ Blenkhorn & Sawle Limited, 100
Bartle & Gibson Co. Ltd., 102
Boilersmith Ltd., 113
Bradford White Canada Inc., 115
Broan Canada Ltd., 117
Caframo Co. Ltd., 121
Canada Heat Pumps, 123
Carrier Canada Ltd., 129
CCI Thermal Technologies Inc., 133
Clean Air Services Inc., 142
Cunningham Sheet Metal Works Inc., 154
Cypress Sales Partnership, 155
Danfoss Inc. - Electric Floor Heating Division, 157
Dectron Internationale, 159
Del-Air Systems Ltd., 160
Denoco Energy Systems Ltd., 161
Deschênes et Fils Ltée., 161
Dimplex North America, 164
Dundas-Jafine Inc., 167
Electro-Air Canada, 174
Enercombustion Ltd., 179
Enercorp Instruments Ltd., 179
Eneready Products Ltd., 179
Engineered Air, 180
Enmet Canada Ltd., 181
Eucania International Inc., 190
F.C. O'Neill, Scriven & Associates Ltd., 193
FCX NH Valves, 194
Five Seasons Comfort Limited, 196
Gasmac Inc., 205
Groupe Deschênes, 219
Hamworthy-Peabody Combustion Canada Inc., 224
HMI Hoyme Manufacturing Inc., 232
Industrial Thermo Polymers Ltd., 241
Innergy Tech, 242
International Cooling Systems Inc., 245
Lennox Industries (Canada) Ltd., 267
Malnar Industries Ltd., 279
McKerlie Solar Systems, 285
Miniveil Air Systems, 290
MSA: Mine Safety Applicances Company, 294
Napoleon Appliance Corp., 297
Newmac Manufacturing Inc., 303
Novitherm Canada Inc., 309
Nu-Air Ventilation Systems Inc., 309
Ontor Ltd., 312
Ordan Thermal Products Ltd., 314
Pageau Morel & associés, inc., 317
Panasonic Canada Inc., 317
Conserval Engineering Inc., 318
Produits Ferpac Ltée, 333
Quatrosense Environmental Ltd., 338
Ray Electric Ltd., 342
Raypak Canada Ltd., 342
REHAU Industries Inc., 344
S.A. Armstrong Limited, 354
SatCon Power Systems (Canada), 358
Schwank Group, 359

Secural Inc., 361
Sick Building Solutions, 366
Stork Bronswerk Inc., 380
Taylor Munro Energy Systems Inc., 387
Tekmar Control Systems Ltd., 389
Temprite Industries Ltd., 389
Thermal Technics Corporation, 394
Trent Metals Ltd., 401
Valley Comfort Systems Inc., 409
Venmar CES, Inc., 410
Venmar Ventilation Inc., 410
Versatile Measuring Instruments Inc., 412
Viessmann Manufacturing Company Inc., 413
Wilcorp Manufacturing, 431
YES Environment Technologies Inc., 435

Heating, Ventilation & Air Conditioning Services
See also Air Pollution Control Services; Energy Services; Heating, Ventilation & Air Conditioning Equipment

Air Solutions Inc., 75
Appin Associates, 87
AZZ Blenkhorn & Sawle Limited, 100
Buchan, Lawton, Parent Ltd., 118
Carrier Canada Ltd., 129
Clean Air Services Inc., 142
The Conserver Group Inc., 391
Cunningham Sheet Metal Works Inc., 154
Denoco Energy Systems Ltd., 161
Efficiency Engineering Inc., 173
Faraci Engineering, 194
Frank's Alternate Energy, 201
Honey Electric Ltd., 233
Malnar Industries Ltd., 279
Matrix Energy, 282
Northern Lights Energy Systems, 307
Nu-Air Ventilation Systems Inc., 309
Ontario Building Solutions, 312
Penn Refrigeration Ltd., 321
Ray Electric Ltd., 342
Raypak Canada Ltd., 342
Robb Engineering Ltd., 347
Russell NDE Systems Inc., 354
Sheldons Engineering Inc., 365
Smith & Andersen Consulting Engineering, 370
Sustainable EDGE Ltd., 383
Thermal Technics Corporation, 394
Viessmann Manufacturing Company Inc., 413
W.T. McGinn & Associates Ltd., 415
Wilcorp Manufacturing, 431

Heavy Metals Removal Equipment, Water & Wastewater
See also Water, Wastewater & Groundwater Equipment

ACG Technology Ltd., 66
Anco Chemicals Inc., 85
Biotech Solutions, 109
BV SORBEX, Inc., 119
Degussa Canada Inc., 159
EPA Certified Clean Ltd., 188
FLSmidth Canada Ltd., 197
Fluor Canada, 197
Greenflow Environmental Services Inc., 217
Hydro-Logic Environmental Inc., 236
Kemira Water Solutions Canada Inc., 256
Lécuyer et Fils Ltée, 266
Mancorp Industrial Sales Ltd., 279
Mar Cor Purification, 280
Nimbus Water Systems, 304
Outokumpu Technology Ltd., 315
Parkson Corporation, 319
Patterson Industries (Canada) Ltd., 319
Proceco Ltd., 333
Seprotech Systems Inc., 363

Historical & Heritage Consulting
See also Environmental Consulting & Contracting Services (General)

Brian Clark Architect, 116
Friesen Tokar Architects, Landscape & Interior Designers, 201
Geomarine Associates Ltd., 211
Glenn Group Ltd., 213
Groupe S.M. International Inc., 220
Groupe SOLROC, 221
Heritage Research Associates Inc., 230
Historica Research Limited, 232
Mayer Heritage Consultants Inc., 284

Settlement Surveys Ltd., 364
Unterman McPhail Associates, 407
Westra & Associates Inc., 430

Horticulture & Vegetation Management
See also Agriculture & Agronomy Management; Resource Management Services (General)

ACE Vegetation Control Service Ltd., 66
Acorus Restoration Native Plant Nursery, 67
Aquaterre Inc., 89
C.E. Jones & Associates Ltd., 119
Cleanit Greenit Compost System, 143
Clintar Groundskeeping Services, 144
Coastal BioAgresearch Ltd., 145
Cramer Nursery Inc., 153
Dol Hydroseeding Inc., 164
Dougan & Associates, 165
Les Engrais Naturels McInnes Inc./McInnes Natural Fertilizers Inc., 268
Environova Planning Group Inc., 186
GDG Environnement Ltée, 205
Le Groupe Leblond & Bouchard/Daniel Arbour et associes, 265
ITRES Research Ltd., 248
Legaré F., Ing. Forestier Conseil, 266
Michael Wall & Sons Enterprises Ltd., 288
Monsanto Canada Inc., 293
N.A.T.S. Nursery Ltd., 296
Pacific Phytometric Consultants, 316
Philom Bios Inc., 323
Plant Products Co. Ltd., 326
PRT Inc., 336
Spencer-Lemaire Industries Ltd., 375
Thimm Engineering Inc., 395
Viterra Inc., 414

House & Home Design, Energy-Efficient
See also Architectural Services; Energy Services

Appin Associates, 87
Bowser Technical Inc., 114
Brian Clark Architect, 116
Can-Cell Industries Inc., 123
Char Developments Ltd., 138
Charles Simon Architect & Planner, 138
Demilec Inc., 160
Electro-Mecanik Inc., 175
Energy Conservation Contractors Warranty Corporation, 179
Enermodal Engineering Ltd., 179
Everts-Lind Enterprises, 191
Habitat Studio & Workshop Ltd., 223
Healthy Homes Consulting, 228
Howell-Mayhew Engineering Inc., 234
Just Homes, 253
Ray Electric Ltd., 342
Richard Kadulski Architect, 346
SAR Engineering, 357
Sustainable EDGE Ltd., 383
Tang G. Lee Architect, 386

Human Resource Services
See also Industrial Management (General)
Eco Canada, 170

HVAC Products & Services
See Heating, Ventilation & Air Conditioning Services

Incineration Services
See also Waste Treatment & Disposal Facilities

Bennett Environmental Inc., 105
Bestobell AquaTronix Limited, 106
Bigelow-Liptak of Canada, 107
CanTox Environmental Inc., 127
GL&V - Groupe Laperrière & Verreault Inc., 212
Incinolet Products, 239
Infratech Corporation, 241
InterLink Business Management Inc., 245
Kaehne Consulting Ltd., 254
Matco Ltd., 282
Material Resource Recovery Inc., 282
Praxair Canada Inc., 330
Swan Hills Treatment Centre, 384
Total Combustion Inc., 398
Trecan Combustion Ltd., 400

Industrial (Non-Hazardous) Waste Consulting
See Waste Management Consulting, Solid

Industrial Coatings
See also Corrosion Control/Scale Prevention, Water & Wastewater; Liners, Geosynthetic/Geomembrane; Waste Management, Liquid/Hazardous

Aimco Solrec Ltd., 74
Denso North America Inc., 161
Fabricated Plastics Ltd., 193
GLM Tanks & Equipment Ltd., 213
Guertin Brothers Coatings and Sealants Ltd., 222
Guspro Inc., 223
Master Builders Technologies Ltd., 282
Sprayaway Marine Services Ltd., 376
StonCor Canada, 379
Tremco Ltd., 401

Industrial Equipment
See also Industrial Management (General); Industrial Products

Allan Fyfe Equipment Limited, 79
Anderson Water Systems, 85
ARISE Technologies Corporation, 90
Boart Longyear Inc., 111
Caristrap International Inc., 128
CCI Thermal Technologies Inc., 133
Cheiron Resources Ltd., 139
Chem Experts Inc., 139
DCL International Inc., 158
Demesa Inc., 160
EEP Engineered & Environmental Products Inc., 173
Elite Technologies Inc., 175
Fort Garry Industries Ltd., 199
Fred Cressman Sales Inc., 201
Fulton Engineered Specialties Inc., 203
GE Multilin, 205
Globetron Controls Inc., 214
Howard Marten Fluid Technologies Inc., 234
InspecTech, 243
K&D Pratt Group Inc., 254
Maccaferri Canada Ltd., 277
Nelson Environmental Remediation Ltd., 299
Pacific Engineering Inc., 316
Power Ignition & Controls, 329
Pyrotech Mfg. Corp., 337
Radiodetection (Canada) Ltd., 341
Rodrigue Métal Ltée, 350
Shaw Precast Solutions, 365
Siemens Milltronics Process Instruments Inc., 366
Slope Indicator Canada, 370
Stemmer Steel Craft Industries Limited, 379
Terex Ltd., 389
Vancouver Gear Works Ltd., 409

Industrial Management (General)
See also Cleaners & Chemicals; Cleaning Systems & Services; Environmental Management Systems (ISO 14000); Human Resource Services; Industrial Equipment; Industrial Products; Lubricants, Sealants, Oils & Greases; Occupational Health & Safety Consulting; Quality Management Systems (ISO 9000); Safety & Protective Equipment

Acklands-Grainger Inc., 66
Aearo Canada Ltd., 69
Allianz Madvac Inc., 79
ATCO Group, 94
Blue Water Agencies Ltd., 110
Caristrap International Inc., 128
DynaMotive Energy Systems Corporation, 167
Greenland Corporation, 217
K&D Pratt Group Inc., 254
Ross Healthcare, Inc., 351
Soper's, 374
Terratec Environmental Ltd., 390
Venerus International Purification Inc., 410

Industrial Products
See also Consumer, Office & Industry Products; Cleaners & Chemicals; Industrial Equipment; Industrial Management (General); Lubricants, Sealants, Oils & Greases

Information Technology & Communications (General)
See also Computer Software & Systems; Electronic Databases; Geographic Information Systems; Labeling, Environmental; Mapping & Surveying Services; Modeling Systems; Process Monitoring & Control Services; Public Participation, Education & Awareness; Publishing

Subject Index

Services; Remote Sensing & Image Analysis; Telecommunications Services; Training & Seminar Management
Adhawk Communications Inc., 68
Altamar International Inc., 81
AMEC, 82
Array Systems Computing Inc., 93
ATCO Group, 94
Atrion International Inc., 97
Calta Computer Systems Ltd., 122
Canadax Industrial Group Limited, 123
Coast Forest Management Ltd., 145
Communicopia.Net Internet Inc., 147
Compusult Limited, 148
CON-SPACE Communications Ltd., 148
Cowater International Inc., 153
Dakins Engineering Group Ltd., 156
Earthguard Environmental Group Inc., 169
El-Rayes Environmental Corp., 174
Electronic Warfare Associates - Canada, Ltd., 175
Entech Environmental Consultants Ltd., 181
The Enviro-Connect, 392
EOA Scientific System Inc., 188
Experts-Conseils BMST inc., 192
G & G Computer Services, 203
Genus Loci Ecological Landscapes Inc., 210
GeoInsight Corporation, 211
Geosolutions Consulting Inc., 212
Hatch Ltd., 226
Hazardous Materials Management Magazine, 227
Helimax Energy Inc., 228
Hemispheres Environmental Consulting Inc., 229
Henderson Paddon & Associates Ltd., 229
Horizons Systems Group Inc., 233
Hunter & Associates, 235
Hydromantis Inc., 237
InfoMine Inc., 241
Infotech Canada Inc., 241
Intelex Technologies Inc., 244
International Submarine Engineering Ltd., 245
Inuktun Services Ltd., 246
M.S. Thompson & Associates Inc., 276
Martec Ltd., 281
Matrix Solutions Inc., 282
Mesh Technologies Inc., 287
Metocean Data Systems Limited, 287
MIG Engineering Ltd., 289
MMM Group, 292
Nelson-Superior Consultants Ltd., 300
Nertec Design Inc., 300
Oldham Engineers Inc., 312
Polaris Corporate Services Inc., 327
R.V. Anderson Associates Limited, 341
Recyclenet Corporation, 343
Roche ltée, Groupe-conseil, 348
Sarafinchin Associates Ltd., 358
Schlumberger Water Services, 359
Seacom International Inc., 361
Sigma Engineering Ltd., 367
Sylvametrics Consulting, 384
Tecsult Inc., 388
Trux Route Management Systems Inc., 404
Université du Québec, 406
Wardrop Engineering Inc., 416
Westland Resource Group Inc., 430
Westra & Associates Inc., 430
whatIf? Technologies Inc., 431

Ink Recycling
See also Recycling Services (General); Toner Cartridges, Recycled
Teckn-O-Laser, 388

Insulation & Sealing Products
See also Energy Equipment
BASF Canada Inc., 103
Can-Cell Industries Inc., 123
Canadian Technical Tape Ltd., 125
Canwest Pumping Systems Ltd., 127
Celfort Construction Materials Inc., 135
CertainTeed Insulation Canada, Inc., 137
Comfort King Doors & Windows Ltd., 147
Daybar Industries Ltd., 158
Demilec Inc., 160
Drexan Energy Systems Inc., 166
Dundas-Jafine Inc., 167
EEP Engineered & Environmental Products Inc., 173
Les Emballages Polyform inc., 268
Energy Conservation Contractors Warranty Corporation, 179
Firwin Corporation, 196
Fuller Austin Insulation Inc., 203
Gemite Products Inc., 206
Le Groupe Légerlite inc., 265
Guardian Industries Canada Corp., 222
Guertin Brothers Coatings and Sealants Ltd., 222
IMP Liquid Meters & Petroleum Services, 239
Impro, 239
Industrial Thermo Polymers Ltd., 241
K&D Pratt Group Inc., 254
Leon's Insulation, 267
Novitherm Canada Inc., 309
Ordan Thermal Products Ltd., 314
Roxul Inc., 353
Schlegel Canada Inc., 359
Therm-O-Comfort Co. Ltd., 393
Thermo-Cell Industries Ltd., 394
Thermotech Windows Ltd., 394
Tremco Ltd., 401
York Fluid Controls Ltd., 435

Insurance, Environmental Liability
See also Financial & Marketing Services (General)
Chartis Insurance Company of Canada, 138
Cheminfo Services Inc., 139
CMD Insurance Services Inc., 144
Hallmark Insurance Brokers Ltd., 224
In Tech Risk Management Inc., 239
Specialty Technical Publishers, 375

Integrated Special Waste Management/Treatment Facilities
See also Waste Treatment & Disposal Facilities
Abydoz Environmental, 65
Bennett Environmental Inc., 105
BFI Canada Inc., 106
Bioforj Environmental Services, 108
CCS Income Trust, 133
The Cintec Group, 391
Conporec Inc., 150
Dagex Inc., 156
EEP Engineered & Environmental Products Inc., 173
Enviro-Gun Ltd., 182
GEA Barr-Rosin Inc., 205
Genivar, 207
Harris & Roome Supply Limited, 225
Inland Technologies Inc., 242
Material Resource Recovery Inc., 282
Miller Environmental Corp., 290
Newalta Corporation, 301
Normcan, 306
Proeco Enviroservices Ltd., 333
Ridgeline Environment Inc., 347
SCC Environmental, 358
Solinov Inc., 373
Swan Hills Treatment Centre, 384
Tri-Arrow Industrial Recovery Inc., 401
Vanport Sterilizers Inc., 409
Veolia Water Canada, 412
Waterloo Evaporateurs Inc., 422

ISO 14000 Registrar
See also Audit Services, Environmental; Environmental Management Systems (ISO 14000); Registrars - Series
BSI Management Systems Canada Inc., 118
Bureau de Normalisation du Québec, 118
Canadian General Standards Board, 124
Intertek Systems Certification, 246
KPMG Performance Registrar Inc., 260
North Shore Management Systems Inc., 306
NSF-ISR, 309
PricewaterhouseCoopers Management Consultants, 332
QMI-SAI Global, 337

ISO 9000 Registrar
See also Quality Management Systems (ISO 9000); Registrars - Series
BSI Management Systems Canada Inc., 118
Bureau de Normalisation du Québec, 118
Canadian General Standards Board, 124
Intertek Systems Certification, 246
KPMG Performance Registrar Inc., 260
NSF-ISR, 309
QMI-SAI Global, 337
QUASAR, 338
SGS Canada Inc., 364
Underwriters' Laboratories of Canada, 405

ISO 9000/14000 Systems
See Quality Management Systems (ISO 9000)

Labeling, Environmental
See also Information Technology & Communications (General)
Acklands-Grainger Inc., 66
Atrion International Inc., 97
Dell Tech Laboratories Ltd., 160
Systems Plus, 385
TerraChoice Environmental Marketing, 390

Laboratories
See Laboratory Services (General)

Laboratory Equipment
See also Laboratory Services (General)
Alcohol Countermeasure Systems Corp., 77
Armstrong Engineering & Land Surveying Inc., 91
Aurora Instruments Ltd., 98
Caframo Co. Ltd., 121
Chromatographic Specialties Inc., 140
Dalynn Biologicals Inc., 156
Dionex Canada Limited, 164
EFC Control Inc., 173
Fred Cressman Sales Inc., 201
Genzyme Canada Inc., 210
Groupe DHB Inc., 219
Intersciences Inc., 246
JM Science Canada Inc., 252
Lakeland Protective Wear Inc., 263
Levy's Machine Works Ltd., 271
M&L Testing Equipment (1995) Ltd., 276
Mandel Scientific Co. Inc., 279
Parkes Scientific Canada Inc., 318
Pegasus Industrial Specialties Inc., 320
PerkinElmer Life & Analytical Sciences Canada Inc., 321
Systems Plus, 385
Tyler Research Instruments Corp., 404
Vacuum Products Canada Inc., 408
VWR International, LLC, 414
Waters Limited, 423
WJF Instrumentation (1990) Ltd., 433

Laboratory Products
See Measuring & Monitoring Equipment, Laboratory

Laboratory Services (General)
See also Chemical Production; Data Acquisition & Analysis; Laboratory Equipment; Measuring & Monitoring Equipment, Laboratory; Medical Laboratory Services; Research & Development, Contract
Accurassay Laboratories, 65
Accutest Laboratories Ltd., 66
Activation Laboratories Ltd., 67
Advance Laboratories Ltd., 69
AGAT Laboratories Ltd., 72
Agri-Food Laboratories, 73
Agricultural Technology Centre, 73
Air Liquide Canada Ltée, 74
Alaron Instruments Inc., 76
Alpha Controls & Instrumentation, 79
ALS Environmental, 80
AMEC, 82
Anachemia Canada Inc., 85
Anco Chemicals Inc., 85
Applied Groundwater Research Ltd., 87
ARC Geobac Group Inc., 89
Atlantic Purification Systems, 97
ATS Scientific Inc., 97
BDS Laboratories, 104
Becquerel Laboratories Inc., 104
Bercan Environmental Resources Inc., 105
Biolab Inc., 108
BMT Fleet Technology Ltd., 111
Bodycot Analex Inc., 113
Bubble Technology Industries Inc., 118
Caledon Laboratory Chemicals Inc., 121
Can-Am Instruments Ltd., 122
Canberra Company, 126
CanDetec Inc., 126
Cantech Inspections Ltd., 127

Canviro, 127
Cardinal Biologicals Ltd., 128
CENSOL Inc., 136
Chem Solv, 139
Coastal Zones Research Institute Inc., 145
Coffey Geotechnics Inc., 146
Cole-Parmer Canada Inc., 146
Corrosion Service Company Limited, 152
Curtis Environmental & Engineering Inc., 154
Dell Tech Laboratories Ltd., 160
Droycon Bioconcepts Inc., 166
Eco-North Laboratories, 171
Econotech Services Ltd., 172
EFC Control Inc., 173
El-Rayes Environmental Corp., 174
Elemental Research Inc., 175
Entech Environmental Consultants Ltd., 181
Entech Laboratories, 181
Entraco, 181
Les Entreprises Julien Inc., 268
Enviro Scan Technologies Inc., 182
Envirosphere Consultants Ltd., 187
Exova, 191
Fisher Environmental Ltd., 196
Flett Research, 196
G.T. Wood Co. Ltd., 204
G3 Consulting Ltd., 204
Genzyme Canada Inc., 210
Griffin Laboratories Corporation, 218
Guelph Chemical Laboratories, 222
Howell-Mayhew Engineering Inc., 234
Hydro Vision America, 236
Hydroqual Laboratories Ltd., 237
I.G. Micromed Environmental Inc., 237
Impact Microbiology Services, 239
Integrated Explorations, 244
Interior Weather Services Ltd., 245
Intersciences Inc., 246
Invensys Systems Canada Inc., 246
JB Laboratories Ltd., 251
JMB Research Ltd., 252
KBU Environmental Technologies Inc., 255
Klohn Crippen Berger Ltd., 258
Lab-Élite limitée, 261
Labexcel Inc., 262
Laboratoires d'Expertises de Québec Ltée, 262
Les Laboratoires Shermont Inc., 269
Lacombe Waste Services, 262
Land & Sea Environmental Consultants Ltd., 264
Laser Diagnostic Instruments International Inc., 264
LEM Laboratory Inc., 267
Levelton Consultants Ltd., 270
Lucas-Milhaupt Toronto, 274
MacDonald & Fils Inc., 277
Martec Ltd., 281
Maxxam Analytics Inc., 283
Maxxam Analytics Ltd., 283
Memorial University of Newfoundland, 286
The National Testing Laboratories Ltd., 393
Niagara Analytical Inc., 303
Nordic Systems Corporation, 305
Nova Magnetics Burgmann Ltd., 308
Oceans Ltd., 311
OSB Services, 314
P. Machibroda Engineering Ltd., 315
Pacwill Environmental, 317
Paracel Laboratories Ltd., 318
Petro Laboratories Inc., 322
Pollutech Group of Companies Inc., 327
PSC Analytical Services, 336
R.A. Murray International Limited, 340
Radiation Environmental Management Systems Inc., 341
Richmond Specialty Mushroom Farms Ltd., 346
RPC, 353
Russell NDE Systems Inc., 354
Scientific Instrumentation Ltd., 360
Silliker JR Laboratories, ULC, 367
SOTAR Inc., 374
Stewart Group, 379
Stuart Hunt & Associates, 381
Terratech, 390
Thermo Electron Corp., 394
2R Services Inc., 404
Unisearch Associates Inc., 405
Université du Québec, 406

Waters Limited, 423
Westra & Associates Inc., 430
Wood Laboratory Ltd., 433
Woodington Systems Inc., 433

Land Use Planning
See also **Resource Management Services (General); Soil Remediation Services**
BCL Landview Systems Inc., 103
C.E. Jones & Associates Ltd., 119
Canadian Environmental Auditors Inc., 124
Cascade Environmental Resource Group. Ltd., 130
Catherine Berris Associates Inc., 132
Clintar Groundskeeping Services, 144
Coast River Environmental Services Ltd., 145
Cottonwood Consultants Ltd., 152
EDA Collaborative Inc., 173
FMA Heritage Resources Consultants Inc., 198
Friesen Tokar Architects, Landscape & Interior Designers, 201
The Greer Galloway Group Inc., Engineers & Planners, 392
Hilderman Thomas Frank Cram & Associates, 232
Interforest Inc., 244
Interwest Property Services (1991) Ltd., 246
Kerr Wood Leidal Associates Ltd., 257
Kleinfeldt Consultants Limited, 258
Landscope Consulting Corp., 264
Long Environmental Consultants, 273
McNair & Marshall Planning & Development Consultants, 285
Meo & Associates Inc., 286
MMM Group, 292
N.A.T.S. Nursery Ltd., 296
Oakridge Environmental Ltd., 310
P.J.B. Duffy & Associates, 316
Progress Land Services Ltd., 334
R.G. Robinson & Associates (Barrie) Ltd., 340
Robert Hornal & Associates Ltd., 348
Secter Environmental Resource Consulting, 361
SENES Consultants Limited, 362
Silva Forest Foundation, 368
Skelton Brumwell & Associates Inc., 369
Symbion Consultants, 384
TJ Consulting Ltd., 396
Tract Consulting Inc., 400
Unterman McPhail Associates, 407
Whitman Benn Group, 431
Zbeetnoff Agro-Environmental Consulting, 436

Landfills & Dump Sites
See also **Waste Treatment & Disposal Facilities**
Abydoz Environmental, 65
Acadia Consultants & Inspectors Ltd., 65
AN-GEO Environmental Consultants Ltd., 84
BFI Canada Inc., 106
CanTox Environmental Inc., 127
Coffey Geotechnics Inc., 146
E.H. Hanson Engineering Group Ltd., 168
Fusionex inc., 203
Gamsby & Mannerow Ltd., 204
Green Soils Inc., 217
GSI Environnement Inc., 222
Lafarge Dundas Quarry, 262
MacDonnell Group, 277
National Waste Services, 298
Northeastern Resource Recovery Ltd., 307
Sani Gestion ONYX, 357
SEG Engineering Inc., 362
Sumas Environmental Services Inc., 381
Walker Industries Holdings Ltd., 416
Waste Services (CA) Inc., 420
Waterloo Evaporateurs Inc., 422
Wellmaster Pipe & Supply, 424

Landscape Architecture & Analysis Services
See also **Environmental Consulting & Contracting Services (General)**
Brian Clark Architect, 116
Catherine Berris Associates Inc., 132
Connor Architects & Planners, 150
ECL Envirowest Consultants Ltd., 170
EDA Collaborative Inc., 173
Elliott & Elliott Limited Consulting Engineers, 176
Environova Planning Group Inc., 186
Henry Kortekaas & Associates Inc., 229
Hilderman Thomas Frank Cram & Associates, 232
IBI Group, 238
J.D. Mollard & Associates Ltd., 249

Legaré F., Ing. Forestier Conseil, 266
Westra & Associates Inc., 430

Leachate Pumping Equipment/Systems
See also **Pumps, Water & Wastewater; Water, Wastewater & Groundwater Equipment**
Brim Pumps & Systems Ltd., 116
Campbell's Concrete Ltd., 122
FLSmidth Canada Ltd., 197
Fusionex inc., 203
Gorman-Rupp of Canada Ltd., 215
L.E. Washington Sales Ltd., 261
Metcon Sales & Engineering Inc., 287
National Process Equipment Inc., 298
Oetiker Limited, 311
Owen G. Carney Ltd., 315
Pompaction Inc., 328
Windsor Pump Co. Ltd., 433

Lead Recycling
See also **Metals Recycling; Recycling Services (General)**
Calgary Metal (1985) Ltd., 121
HMI Industries, 232
John Zubick Ltd. Scrap Metals, 253
Joseph & Co. Inc., 253
Neighborhood Recycling, 299
Nova PB Inc., 308
Raw Materials Corporation, 342
Rotblott & Sons Ltd., 352
Western Scrap Metals, 429

Life Cycle Analyses
See also **Environmental Consulting & Contracting Services (General)**
Altus Capital Planning Inc., 81
AquaTox Testing & Consulting Inc., 89
Carswell Consulting Engineers Ltd., 130
Cemcorp Ltd. Consulting Engineers, 135
The Delphi Group, 392
Environmental Advisory Group, 185
Kaehne Consulting Ltd., 254
Kinectrics Inc., 257
MWA Consultants, 295
N. Vandenassem & Associate, 296
SPG Hydro International Inc., 375
TerraChoice Environmental Marketing, 390
Watson & Associates Economists Ltd., 423

Lighting, Energy Efficient
See also **Energy Equipment**
Acklands-Grainger Inc., 66
Advanced Environmental Water Technologies Inc., 69
Argus Telecom International Inc., 90
Bartle & Gibson Co. Ltd., 102
Dewar Insulations Ltd., 162
ECE Group - a Division of Conestoga-Rovers & Associates, 170
Energy Conservation Contractors Warranty Corporation, 179
EnRel Energy Group, 181
Exploitation Santec Inc., 192
Gentec Inc., 210
Honey Electric Ltd., 233
Leviton Canada, 270
Micro-Watt Control Devices Ltd., 289
NEDCO, 299
Northern Alternate Power Systems, 307
Osram Sylvania Ltd., 314
Panasonic Canada Inc., 317
Parameter Control Ltd., 318
Research Electronics (Reselco) Ltd., 345
Solar Solutions Inc., 372
Terex Ltd., 389
TIR Systems Ltd., 396
Wellons Canada, 424

Liners, Geosynthetic/Geomembrane
See also **Corrosion Control/Scale Prevention, Water & Wastewater; Industrial Coatings; Waste Management, Liquid/Hazardous**
André Simard et associés ltée, 85
Armtec Construction Products, 91
Atlantic Poly Liners Inc., 97
Bémalux Inc., 105
Bentofix Technologies Inc., 105
Bristar Containment Industries Ltd., 117
Century Environmental Services, 136
Fred Cressman Sales Inc., 201
Hercules SLR Inc., 229

Subject Index

HQN Industrial Fabrics Inc., 234
Inscan Contractors (Ontario) Inc., 242
J.W. Bird & Company Ltd., 250
Kentain Products Ltd., 256
Layfield Geosynthetics & Industrial Fabrics Ltd., 265
Lea-Der Coatings (614248 Alberta Ltd.), 266
Lexcan Industrial Supply Ltd., 271
Link-Pipe Inc., 272
Logiball Inc., 273
Membrex Ltée, 286
National Energy Equipment Inc., 297
Nilex Inc., 304
Plastics America, 326
Products BCM Ltée BCM, 333
RAM Lining Systems Inc., 342
SEI Industries Ltd., 362
Solmax International Inc., 373
Solmax-Texel Geosynthetics Inc., 373
Solmers Internationale Experts-Conseils Inc., 373
Terrafix Geosynthetics Inc., 390
Texel Géomembrane Inc., 391
West Coast Spill Supplies Ltd., 424
Western Industrial Services Ltd., 429

Liquid/Hazardous Waste Management
See Waste Management, Liquid/Hazardous

Liquid/Hazardous Waste Management Consulting
See Waste Management Consulting, Liquid & Hazardous

Lubricants, Sealants, Oils & Greases
See also Industrial Management (General); Industrial Products
Active Chemicals Ltd., 67
Genics Inc., 207
Greenland Corporation, 217
Kafko Manufacturing Ltd., 254
Lubrication Engineers of Canada Ltd., 274
Near North Laboratories Inc., 299
Prolab Technolub, 334
Silvana Import Trading Inc., 368
Stork Bronswerk Inc., 380
West Penetone Inc., 424
Zorbit Technologies Inc., 437

Mapping & Surveying Services
See also Geographic Information Systems; Information Technology & Communications (General)
Agrosysts Ltée, 73
Canadian Seabed Research Ltd., 125
CARIS, 128
Cengea Solutions Inc., 136
Conair Group Inc., 148
D.M. Wills Associates Limited, 156
Delta Aerial Surveys Ltd., 160
Dendron Resource Surveys Inc., 161
Eastcan Geomatics, 169
EITNL/Earth Information Technologies (nfld) Limited, 174
ESRI Canada Ltd., 190
Fugro Airborne Surveys, 202
G.A. Borstad Associates Ltd., 203
GeoInsight Corporation, 211
Geosoft, 212
Geosolutions Consulting Inc., 212
Geowest Environmental Consultants, 212
Hyperspectral Data International Inc., 237
Inform Consulting Services Ltd., 241
IRIS Environmental Systems Inc., 248
J.D. Mollard & Associates Ltd., 249
Kanotech Information Systems Ltd., 255
Keywood Enterprises Ltd., 257
MacDonald, Dettwiler & Associates Ltd., 277
Malroz Engineering Inc., 279
Northway-Photomap Inc., 307
Opus International Consultants (Canada) Ltd., 313
Prairie Geomatics Ltd., 330
Radiodetection (Canada) Ltd., 341
Seaforth Engineering Group Inc., 361
Silva Forest Foundation, 368
SOTAR Inc., 374
TJ Consulting Ltd., 396
UMA Group Ltd., 405
Western Subsea Technology Ltd., 430

Marine Management
See Waterways & Wetlands Management

Market Analyses
See also Financial & Marketing Services (General)
AquaTox Testing & Consulting Inc., 89
Calibre Strategic Services Inc., 121
Cheminfo Services Inc., 139
Clayton Research Associates Ltd., 142
CMEL Enterprises Ltd., 144
The Delphi Group, 392
Enerscan Consultants Limited, 179
Engineering Management Services Croscan, 180
Environmental Advisory Group, 185
Goss Gilroy Inc., 215
HurterConsult Inc., 235
Interwest Property Services (1991) Ltd., 246
John McMullen & Associates, 252
Nichols Applied Management, 304
Pam Wight & Associates, 317
PricewaterhouseCoopers Management Consultants, 332
Refined Specialty Chemicals Inc., 344
Stratem Inc., 380
University Technologies International, 406
Watson & Associates Economists Ltd., 423

Marketing Services
See also Business Development Services; Financial & Marketing Services (General)
Adhawk Communications Inc., 68
Cheminfo Services Inc., 139
Environmental R&D Capital Corporation, 185
The Impact Group, 392
Municipal Affairs Consulting, 295
Nisymco Inc., 304
Pam Wight & Associates, 317
Promosalons Canada, 334
University Technologies International, 406
Vision Quest - TransAlta's Wind Business, 413

Material Recycling Facilities
See also Recycling Services (General)
Bema Co. Ltd., 104
BFI Canada Inc., 106
Canadian Fibre, 124
Cramer Nursery Inc., 153
Crown Packaging Ltd., 154
Dagex Inc., 156
Dekka Resins Inc., 159
Emery International Developments, 177
Entropex, 182
Halford Pallet Recyclers Ltd., 224
Industries Machinex Inc., 241
KGS Group Inc., 257
Kimco Steel Sales Limited, 257
Niagara Recycling, 303
Northeastern Resource Recovery Ltd., 307
Owen G. Carney Ltd., 315
Polychem Products Ltd., 328
Raw Materials Corporation, 342
Recyclage Alexandria Recycline (Équipe), 343
The Recycle Systems Company Inc., 393
Roger LaRue Enterprises Ltd., 350
Ron Wedman Engineering Services, 351
Sleegers Engineering Inc., 370
Sprung Instant Structures Ltd., 376
Thor Global Enterprises Ltd., 395
Wittmann Canada, Inc., 433

Material Separation Equipment
See also Recycling Equipment; Recycling Services (General); Shredding & Grinding Equipment
BDR Machinery Ltd., 103
Canadian Fibre, 124
Clean Ontario, 143
Double T Equipment Ltd., 165
Ecotainer Sales Inc., 172
Finnex Agencies Ltd., 195
General Scrap Partnership, 206
Gensco Equipment (1990) Ltd., 210
Hydro Dyne Inc., 236
Industries Machinex Inc., 241
IPL Inc., 247
Kernic Systems Inc., 257
Kongskilde Limited, 259
Machine Knife Co., 278
Mowat Fabrication Ltd., 294
ProSep Inc., 335
R.B. Intermark Inc., 340
Sani Gestion ONYX, 357
Sonoco Recycling Ltd., 374
Techstar Plastics Inc., 388
Wittmann Canada, Inc., 433

Materials Brokers
See also End Markets; Recycling Services (General)
Double Industries & Trading, 165
Hagersville Recycling & Auto Wrecking Ltd., 223
Joseph & Co. Inc., 253
Monster Polymers Inc., 293
Polyland Industries Ltd., 328
STOBEC Inc., 379

Materials Recovery
See Recycling Services (General)

Measuring & Monitoring Equipment, Air
See also Air Pollution Control Equipment; Measuring & Monitoring Equipment, Laboratory
ABB Inc. (Canada), 64
Acme Engineering Products Ltd., 66
Aeroflo Inc., 71
Airtest Technologies Inc., 76
AlphaNuclear Company, 80
AMETEK Process Instruments, 84
AMKO Systems Inc., 84
Aquatic Life Ltd., 89
Arjay Engineering Ltd., 91
Armatek Controls Limited, 91
Armstrong Monitoring Corp., 91
Ashtead Technology Rentals, 93
Avensys Inc., 98
AZZ Blenkhorn & Sawle Limited, 100
Biomation, 108
BW Technologies by Honeywell, 119
CadhamHayes Systems Inc., 120
Campbell Scientific (Canada) Corp., 122
CD Nova, 134
CEM Specialties Inc., 135
Control Microsystems, 151
Crompton Technology Inc., 153
Draeger Safety Canada Ltd., 166
Drexan Energy Systems Inc., 166
Durmitor Inc., 167
Emerson Electric Canada Limited, 177
Enercorp Instruments Ltd., 179
Enmet Canada Ltd., 181
Enviro Rentals, 182
Environmental Remediation Equipment Inc., 185
Forest Protection Limited, 199
GENEQ Inc., 206
HAMON Custodis-Cottrell Canada, Inc., 224
HETEK Solutions Inc., 230
Hoskin Scientific Ltd., 233
Industrial Scientific Corporation, 241
InspecTech, 243
Integra Technologies Ltd., 243
Levy's Machine Works Ltd., 271
M&L Testing Equipment (1995) Ltd., 276
Météoglobe Canada Inc., 287
Metocean Data Systems Limited, 287
Micro-Watt Control Devices Ltd., 289
Muis Controls Ltd., 295
National Instruments Canada, 297
Net Safety Monitoring Inc., 300
New Trend Environmental Services, 301
Novatech Controls, Inc., 309
Ontario Building Solutions, 312
OSB Services, 314
Pacific Engineering Inc., 316
Pacwill Environmental, 317
Promet Environmental Group Ltd., 334
ProViro Instrumentation Inc., 335
Quatrosense Environmental Ltd., 338
Rockwell Automation Canada Inc., 349
Romatec Incorporated, 350
Sciencetech Inc., 359
Scientific Instrumentation Ltd., 360
Sick Building Solutions, 366
Simark Controls Ltd., 368
Sinanni Inc., 369
Smiths Detection, 371
Tekran Canada, 389
Unisearch Associates Inc., 405
Vacuum Products Canada Inc., 408

Subject Index

Via-Sat Data Systems, 413
Westech Industrial Ltd., 429
WJF Instrumentation (1990) Ltd., 433
YES Environment Technologies Inc., 435
York Fluid Controls Ltd., 435

Measuring & Monitoring Equipment, Energy
See also Energy Equipment
A. Lanfranco & Associates Inc., 63
Armatek Controls Limited, 91
Campbell Scientific (Canada) Corp., 122
Capricorn Control Technologies Ltd., 128
CD Nova, 134
Control Microsystems, 151
Eastern Wind Power Inc., 169
Electro-Mecanik Inc., 175
Enercorp Instruments Ltd., 179
F.C. O'Neill, Scriven & Associates Ltd., 193
FLIR Systems, Inc., 197
GE Multilin, 205
Greystone Energy Systems Inc., 218
Honey Electric Ltd., 233
ITM Instruments, 248
Micro-Watt Control Devices Ltd., 289
Muis Controls Ltd., 295
Multitel Inc., 295
Northern Lights Energy Systems, 307
Novatech Controls, Inc., 309
Optimira Controls, 313
Panama Enterprises (1990) Inc., 317
PerkinElmer Life & Analytical Sciences Canada Inc., 321
Research Electronics (Reselco) Ltd., 345
Robinson Solutions, 348
Roctest Ltée, 350
SACO Technologies, Inc., 354
Thermo Electric (Canada) Ltd., 394

Measuring & Monitoring Equipment, Groundwater
See also Water, Wastewater & Groundwater Equipment
Aquatic Life Ltd., 89
Avensys Inc., 98
Bytown Marine Ltd., 119
CCL/IBI, 133
Environmental Remediation Equipment Inc., 185
Fluorosense Inc., 198
GENEQ Inc., 206
ITM Instruments, 248
Metcon Sales & Engineering Ltd., 287
Metocean Data Systems Limited, 287
Satlantic, 358
Solinst Canada Ltd., 373
Sonic Soil Sampling Inc., 374
Waters Limited, 423

Measuring & Monitoring Equipment, Laboratory
See also Computer Software & Systems; Data Acquisition & Analysis; Laboratory Services (General); Measuring & Monitoring Equipment, Air; Measuring & Monitoring Equipment, Water & Wastewater
ABB Inc. (Canada), 64
ABL Environmental Consultants, 65
AGAT Laboratories Ltd., 72
AGO Environmental Electronics Ltd., 73
AimGlobal Technologies Company, Inc., 74
AiMS Environmental, 74
All-Weld Company Limited, 79
Aquatic Life Ltd., 89
Arrow Speed Controls Ltd., 93
ATS Scientific Inc., 97
Aurora Instruments Ltd., 98
Axion Technologies, 99
BG Controls Ltd., 107
BMT Fleet Technology Ltd., 111
BW Technologies by Honeywell, 119
Campbell Scientific (Canada) Corp., 122
Campbell Scientific (Canada) Corp., 122
Can-Am Instruments Ltd., 122
Canadian Safety Equipment Inc., 125
Canadian Worcester Controls Ltd., 125
Canberra Company, 126
CB Engineering, Ltd., 132
Chem Action Inc., 139
Chromatographic Specialties Inc., 140
Compteurs Lecomte Ltée, 148
Cues Canada, 154
Dell Tech Laboratories Ltd., 160

Diagnostix Ltd., 163
Dionex Canada Limited, 164
Eagle Home Inspection Services Inc., 168
Elmec Engineering Ltd., 176
Emerson Electric Canada Limited, 177
EMS Technologies, 178
Enterprise Steel Fabricators Ltd., 181
Les Entreprises Julien Inc., 268
EnviroMed Detection Services, 184
EPA Certified Clean Ltd., 188
Farris Industries Canada, 194
Fisher Scientific Ltd., 196
FLIR Systems, Inc., 197
Flowserve Canada Corp. - Pump Division, 197
Focal Technologies Inc., 198
Folio Instruments Inc., 199
Gentec Inc., 210
George Kelk Corporation, 211
Griffin Laboratories Corporation, 218
Hanna Instruments Canada Inc., 224
Honeywell Ltd., 233
Howell-Mayhew Engineering Inc., 234
Icefield Instruments Inc., 238
Industrial Marine Power Engineering Group, 240
Instantel, 243
International Road Dynamics Inc., 245
Intersciences Inc., 246
Invensys Systems Canada Inc., 246
Jenike & Johanson, Ltd., 251
JM Science Canada Inc., 252
Kinetics Noise Control Inc., 257
Labexcel Inc., 262
Labtronics, 262
Lambton Scientific, 263
Levy's Machine Works Ltd., 271
Logan Geotech Inc., 273
Lotek Wireless Inc., 274
M&L Testing Equipment (1995) Ltd., 276
Magnetrol International Ltd., 278
Mandel Scientific Co. Inc., 279
MDS Sciex, 285
Metcon Sales & Engineering Ltd., 287
Metex Corp. Ltd., 287
Micrologic Ltd., 289
Monsanto Canada Inc., 293
MSA: Mine Safety Applicances Company, 294
Muis Controls Ltd., 295
National Instruments Canada, 297
Niagara Energy Products Limited, 303
Optech Inc., 313
Optikon Corp. Ltd., 313
Pacwill Environmental, 317
Paracel Laboratories Ltd., 318
Parkes Scientific Canada Inc., 318
PDK Projects Inc., 320
Performance Fluid Equipement Inc., 321
PerkinElmer Life & Analytical Sciences Canada Inc., 321
Phason Electronics, 322
Piteau Associates, 325
Les Plastiques Simport Ltée, 270
Point Four Systems Inc., 326
Precision Industrial Ltd., 330
Presentey Engineering Products Ltd., 331
Pro-Lab Diagnostics, 333
Proto Manufacturing Ltd., 335
Pylon Electronics, 337
Pyradia Inc., 337
QSDM Inc., 338
R.A. Kirby Sales Inc., 339
RBR Ltd., 343
Refrigerant Services Inc., 344
Research Electronics (Reselco) Ltd., 345
Rice Engineering & Operating Ltd., 346
RMS Instruments Ltd., 347
Rockwell Automation Canada Inc., 349
Roctest Ltée, 350
RST Instruments Ltd., 354
Scintrex Ltd., 360
Services industriels Newalta, 363
Siemens Building Technologies, Ltd., 366
Sinclair Technologies, 369
Slope Indicator Canada, 370
Sonepar Canada, 373
Southwell Controls Ltd., 374
Sprecher + Schuh Inc., 376

SRB Controls Inc., 376
SRP Control Systems Inc., 377
Startco Engineering Ltd., 378
Staveley Services Canada Inc., 380
Stuart Hunt & Associates, 381
Survalent Technology Corporation, 383
Talkie Tooter Canada Ltd., 386
Tekran Canada, 389
Tertec Enterprises Inc., 391
Thermo Electron Corp., 394
TOR Geoscience Corp., 397
Tyler Research Instruments Corp., 404
Vacuum Products Canada Inc., 408
Vansco Electronics Ltd., 409
Versatile Measuring Instruments Inc., 412
VWR International, LLC, 414
Wainbee Limited, 415
Waters Limited, 423
Williams Milton Roy, 432
Willowglen Systems Inc., 432
WJF Instrumentation (1990) Ltd., 433

Measuring & Monitoring Equipment, Water & Wastewater
See also Measuring & Monitoring Equipment, Laboratory; Water, Wastewater & Groundwater Equipment
AeroTek Manufacturing Ltd., 71
AquaMetrix Inc., 88
Aquatic Life Ltd., 89
Arjay Engineering Ltd., 91
ASL Environmental Sciences Inc., 94
ATS Scientific Inc., 97
Aurora Instruments Ltd., 98
Avensys Inc., 98
Bytown Marine Ltd., 119
CadhamHayes Systems Inc., 120
Campbell Scientific (Canada) Corp., 122
Cancoppas Limited, 126
Carlo Gavazzi (Canada) Inc., 128
CEM Specialties Inc., 135
Chemline Plastics Ltd., 139
Comco Manufacturing Ltd., 146
Control Microsystems, 151
Les Contrôles PROVAN Associés Inc., 268
Crompton Technology Inc., 153
Diagnostix Ltd., 163
Dionex Canada Limited, 164
Endress+Hauser Canada Ltd., 178
Enviro-Systèmes Inc., 183
Environmental Biodetection Products Inc., 185
Environnement ESA Inc., 186
Enviroservices Inc., 187
ESI Environmental Sensors Inc., 189
Exploitation Santec Inc., 192
Focal Technologies Inc., 198
GENEQ Inc., 206
Geonics Limited, 211
Greenland International Consulting Inc., 218
Greyline Instruments Inc., 218
Halltech Environmental Inc., 224
Hanna Instruments Canada Inc., 224
Heron Instruments, 230
IMO Pump Inc., 239
J&M Industrial Engineering & Sales Ltd., 249
John Meunier Inc., 253
Kleinfeldt Consultants Limited, 258
LaCas Consultants Inc., 262
Levitt-Safety Limited, 270
M&L Testing Equipment (1995) Ltd., 276
Mandel Scientific Co. Inc., 279
Markland Specialty Engineering Ltd., 281
Marsh Instrumentation Inc., 281
Metcon Sales & Engineering Ltd., 287
MSA: Mine Safety Applicances Company, 294
Muis Controls Ltd., 295
Neo Valves, 300
Novatech Controls, Inc., 309
Oak Environmental Inc., 310
ODIM Brooke Ocean, 311
Phoenix Contact Ltd., 323
Pompaction inc., 328
ProMinent Fluid Controls Ltd., 334
ProViro Instrumentation Inc., 335
Pylon Electronics, 337
Quatrosense Environmental Ltd., 338

Subject Index

RBR Ltd., 343
Rockwell Automation Canada Inc., 349
Roctest Ltée, 350
Russell NDE Systems Inc., 354
Sabatini Earth Technologies Inc., 354
Sciencetech Inc., 359
Siemens Milltronics Process Instruments Inc., 366
Siemens Water Technologies, 367
Simark Controls Ltd., 368
Solinst Canada Ltd., 373
Southwell Controls Ltd., 374
Systems Plus, 385
Technel Engineering Inc., 387
Terrapex Environmental Ltd., 390
Titan Logix Corp., 396
Waters Limited, 423
Westech Industrial Ltd., 429

Measuring & Monitoring Services, Groundwater
See also Water, Wastewater & Groundwater Services
Clifton Associates Ltd., 144
E.K. Gillin & Associates Inc., 168
Fluorosense Inc., 198
Lambton Scientific, 263
MPI Drilling, 294
Oak Environmental Inc., 310
Pinchin Environmental Ltd., 324
Summa Engineering Ltd., 381
Water Matrix, 421
Wellmaster Pipe & Supply, 424

Mechanical Contractors, Water & Wastewater
See also Water, Wastewater & Groundwater Services
Aqua-Rehab Inc., 88
Arpi's Industries Canada Ltd., 92
Dalco Wastewater Specialists Inc., 156
Filtrum Inc., 195
Fusionex inc., 203
Gevity Group Inc., 212
Hike Metal Products Ltd., 231
Hyprescon Inc., 237
Insituform Technologies Ltd. - Edmonton, 242
Lambert Somec inc., 263
Noel Rochette et Fils Inc., 305
Terminal City Iron Works Ltd., 389

Medical Laboratory Services
See also Laboratory Services (General); Research & Development, Contract
Centre de Toxicologie du Québec, 136
Elemental Research Inc., 175

Metals Recycling
See also Aluminum Recycling; Lead Recycling; Recycling Services (General); Silver Recycling
Alnor Industries Ltd., 79
Calgary Metal (1985) Ltd., 121
Canadian Eagle Recyclers, Inc., 124
Capital Environmental Resource Inc., 127
Countryside Disposal Service Ltd., 153
Cyanide Destruct Systems Inc., 155
Dartmouth Metals & Bottles Ltd., 157
Dominion Recycling Ltd., 165
General Scrap Partnership, 206
Hagersville Recycling & Auto Wrecking Ltd., 223
Harbour Metal Recycling Ltd., 225
HMI Industries, 232
Hydro Dyne Inc., 236
Integrated Resource Management, 244
Jenike & Johanson, Ltd., 251
John Zubick Ltd. Scrap Metals, 253
Joseph & Co. Inc., 253
Kamloops Scrap Iron Ltd., 254
Kimco Steel Sales Limited, 257
Lake Charlotte Sanitation, 263
Lakehead Scrap Metal, 263
Lennox Drum Ltd., 267
Lindsay Iron & Metal Inc., 272
MCC Industrial Services Ltd, 284
Metro Recycling, 287
MGM Management, 288
Municipal Recyclers Ltd., 295
Muskoka Containerized Services Ltd., 295
Navajo Metals, 298
Northwest Metal Recycling, 307
Nova PB Inc., 308
Poscor Group, 328
Raw Materials Corporation, 342
Rotblott & Sons Ltd., 352
Samco Resources & By-Products, 356
Strasser Alloy Steels Ltd., 380
Traders Metal Company Ltd., 400
Triple M Metal, 402
Wascana Recycling & Resource Recovery Corp., 417
Wesman Salvage, 425
Woznuk Brothers Ltd., 434

Mine Tailings Disposal
See also Waste Management, Liquid/Hazardous
Ambler & Co. Inc., 82
Bolger and Associates Ltd., 113
DST Consulting Engineers, 166
ENPAR Technologies Inc., 181
Enviro-Met Engineering, 183
Inco Technical Services Limited, 239
Knight Piésold Ltd., 258
KWH Pipe, 261
Land & Sea Environmental Consultants Ltd., 264
M.J. Labelle Co. Ltd., 276
NAR Environmental Consultants Inc., 297
Nevin Sadlier-Brown Goodbrand Ltd., 300
P. Machibroda Engineering Ltd., 315
Rescan Environmental Services Ltd., 345
Scimus Inc., 360
Sprung Instant Structures Ltd., 376
Terralog Technologies Inc., 390

Mines & Minerals Management
See also Energy Resource Management; Resource Management Services (General)
Aker Metals (Toronto), 76
Boart Longyear Inc., 111
Bolger and Associates Ltd., 113
C.E. Jones & Associates Ltd., 119
Conestoga-Rovers & Associates, 149
ENPAR Technologies Inc., 181
Geostat Systems International Inc., 212
Halltech Environmental Inc., 224
Iron Ore Company of Canada, 248
MacDonnell Group, 277
NB Coal Limited, 299
SENES Consultants Limited, 362
Sonic Soil Sampling Inc., 374
W.G. Shaw & Associates, 415

Modeling Systems
See also Computer Software & Systems; Information Technology & Communications (General); Process Monitoring & Control Services
Beckie Hydrogeologists (1990) Ltd., 104
CanTox Environmental Inc., 127
Cengea Solutions Inc., 136
Chartwell Consultants Ltd., 138
Coastal Ocean Associates Inc., 145
Cobham Tracking & Locating Ltd., 145
EarthFx Inc., 169
EITNL/Earth Information Technologies (nfld) Limited, 174
EmerGeo Solutions Inc., 176
Enermodal Engineering Inc., 179
ESRI Canada Ltd., 190
GAEA Technologies, 204
GeoInsight Corporation, 211
Geosoft, 212
Geosolutions Consulting Inc., 212
Geostat Systems International Inc., 212
Greenland International Consulting Inc., 218
Hickling Arthurs Low Corp., 231
Hydrogéochem Environnement Inc., 236
Jasco Research Ltd., 251
Lakehead University, 263
Lakes Environmental Software, 263
Malroz Engineering Inc., 279
Mirarco Mining Innovation, 290
Natech Environmental Services, 297
Northway-Photomap, 307
REDUCT & Lobbe Technologies Inc., 344
Synex International Inc., 385
Triton Consultants Ltd., 402
Unisearch Associates Inc., 405
whatIf? Technologies Inc., 431
Zephyr North, 437

Monitoring Equipment
See Measuring & Monitoring Equipment, Laboratory

Motors, Energy Efficient
See also Energy Equipment
Canadian Drives Inc., 124
Del-Air Systems Ltd., 160
Energy Conservation Contractors Warranty Corporation, 179
F.C. O'Neill, Scriven & Associates Ltd., 193
Honey Electric Ltd., 233
Simark Controls Ltd., 368
Sterling Power Systems, 379

Mulch
See Organic Matter Recycling

Municipal Solid Waste Consulting
See Waste Management Consulting, Solid

Noise Assessment Services
See also Noise Management (General)
Aercoustics Engineering Limited, 71
ALARA Industrial Hygiene Services Ltd., 76
APS Aviation Inc., 87
ATCO Power, 95
Atlantic Acoustical Associates, 95
Brown Strachan Associates, 117
Chem Solv, 139
Coastal Zones Research Institute Inc., 145
Donald Olynyk, Acoustical Engineer, 165
Enviro-RISQUE Inc., 183
Faszer Farquharson & Associates Ltd., 194
Gough Risk Management Ltd., 215
HFP Acoustical Consultants Corp., 231
HGC Engineering, 231
Integra Environmental Inc., 243
Interior Weather Services Ltd., 245
J.E. Coulter Associates Ltd., 249
Jasco Research Ltd., 251
Latimat Inc., 265
LEX Scientific Inc., 271
McAtee Safety & Environmental Health Services Ltd., 284
The National Testing Laboratories Ltd., 393
Ogilvie Scientific Inc., 311
The Sernas Group Inc., 393
T. Harris Environmental Management Inc., 385
Theodor D. Sterling & Associates Ltd., 393
Wakefield Acoustics Ltd., 416
Westest, 430
WPI Safety & Environmental Consultants, 434

Noise Control Consulting
See also Noise Management (General)
Aercoustics Engineering Limited, 71
ATCO Power, 95
Atlantic Acoustical Associates, 95
Decibel Consultants Inc., 159
Donald Olynyk, Acoustical Engineer, 165
Enviro-RISQUE Inc., 183
Exova, 191
Faszer Farquharson & Associates Ltd., 194
HFP Acoustical Consultants Corp., 231
J.E. Coulter Associates Ltd., 249
Kinetics Noise Control Inc., 257
L.W. Ward Limited, 261
Latimat Inc., 265
McAtee Safety & Environmental Health Services Ltd., 284
PHH ARC Environmental Ltd., 322
The Sernas Group Inc., 393
Theodor D. Sterling & Associates Ltd., 393
Wakefield Acoustics Ltd., 416
Westest, 430

Noise Control Equipment
See also Noise Management (General)
Aercoustics Engineering Limited, 71
Aerzen Canada Surpresseurs Compresseurs inc., 71
Airmaster Sales Ltd., 75
Ashtead Technology Rentals, 93
ATCO Power, 95
Blower Engineering Inc., 110
BVA Systems Ltd./Vibro-Acoustics, 119
Cole-Parmer Canada Inc., 146
Decibel Consultants Inc., 159
Drexan Energy Systems Inc., 166
Eckel Industries, 170
Enviro Rentals, 182
Génie Audio inc., 207
H.E. Bent Services Ltd., 223
HGC Engineering, 231

Subject Index

Hiltz & Seamone Co. Ltd., 232
Instantel, 243
Latimat Inc., 265
Mac Industrial Exhaust Shop, 277
Metso Automation Canada Ltd., 288
MSA: Mine Safety Applicances Company, 294
Multitel Inc., 295
Racan Carrier, 341
Shaver Industries Inc., 365

Noise Deadening Materials
See also Noise Management (General)

Arpi's Industries Canada Ltd., 92
ATCO Power, 95
BVA Systems Ltd./Vibro-Acoustics, 119
Can-Cell Industries Inc., 123
CertainTeed Insulation Canada, Inc., 137
Cunningham Sheet Metal Works Inc., 154
Decibel Consultants Inc., 159
Eckel Industries, 170
Elasto Valve Rubber Products Inc., 174
Firwin Corporation, 196
Groupe Tremca inc., 221
Guardian Industries Canada Corp., 222
Impro, 239
Industrial Thermo Polymers Ltd., 241
Latimat Inc., 265
Leon's Insulation, 267
Shaver Industries Inc., 365
T-G Burgmann, 385
Visionwall Corporation, 414

Noise Management (General)
See also Noise Assessment Services; Noise Control Consulting; Noise Control Equipment; Noise Deadening Materials; Vibration Control Equipment

Acoustic Solutions Ltd., 67
ATCO Power, 95
Atlantic Acoustical Associates, 95
Eckel Industries, 170
Groupe Tremca inc., 221
HFP Acoustical Consultants Corp., 231
J.E. Coulter Associates Ltd., 249
Latimat Inc., 265
Maple Reinders Environmental Ltd., 279
Mesh Technologies Inc., 287
Noise Solutions Inc., 305
Pacific Environmental Consulting & Occupational Hygiene Services, 316
Rowan Williams Davies & Irwin Inc., 352
SENES Consultants Limited, 362
The Sernas Group Inc., 393
Shaver Industries Inc., 365
Soper's, 374

Nuclear Waste Management
See also Waste Management, Liquid/Hazardous

AA Environmental & Associates, 64
Bubble Technology Industries Inc., 118
ECOMatters Inc., 172
Enviropac Inc., 186
Hardy Stevenson & Associates, 225
Indoor Air Quality Ottawa, 240
Kinectrics Inc., 257
Monserco Ltd., 293
Normcan, 306
Notra Inc., 308
Terralog Technologies Inc., 390

Occupational Health & Safety Consulting
See also Accident Prevention Services; Industrial Management (General)

Acoustic Solutions Ltd., 67
AiMS Environmental, 74
Airzone One Ltd., 76
ALARA Industrial Hygiene Services Ltd., 76
ALL-TECH Environmental Services Ltd., 78
ALS Environmental, 80
Aware Learning Technologies, 99
BW Technologies by Honeywell, 119
C5 Plus Ltd., 120
Canadian Safety Equipment Inc., 125
CanTox Environmental Inc., 127
Care First Aid Training Inc., 128
Cemcorp Ltd. Consulting Engineers, 135
Chemical Emission Management Services, 139
Coffey Geotechnics Inc., 146

Danatec Educational Services Ltd., 156
David A. McLean & Associates, 158
Ecotech Planners & Advisors Inc., 172
ÉEM inc., 173
Enviro-RISQUE Inc., 183
Environmental Accident Protection Inc., 184
Environmental Training Institute, 186
Envirotest Inc., 188
Envision Compliance, 188
Epistream Consulting Inc, 189
George Grant Consulting, 211
Global Sensor Systems Inc., 213
Gough Risk Management Ltd., 215
Groupe Consulteaux Inc., 219
H. Pickard & Associates, 223
Hazard Alert Training & Supplies Canada Inc., 227
HSE Integrated, 234
ICC The Compliance Center Inc., 238
ICC The Compliance Centre Inc., 238
Integra Environmental Inc., 243
KBU Environmental Technologies Inc., 255
Kemic Bioresearch Laboratories Ltd., 256
KPS & Associates, 260
LEX Scientific Inc., 271
Lotowater Technical Services Inc., 274
Lovell & Associates, 274
Maxxam Analytics Ltd., 283
McAtee Safety & Environmental Health Services Ltd., 284
Medgate Inc., 286
Michael Holliday & Associates, 288
Mold & Bacteria Consulting Laboratories (MBL) Inc., 292
MSA: Mine Safety Applicances Company, 294
New Trend Environmental Services, 301
North Safety Products Canada, 306
North West Environmental Group, 306
Ogilvie Scientific Inc., 311
Pacesetter Sales & Associates Inc., 316
Paramount Emergency Planners Ltd., 318
Paul G. Chénard, 319
PBR Laboratories Inc., 319
PHH ARC Environmental Ltd., 322
Pilot Performance Resources Management Inc., 324
Pinchin Environmental Ltd., 324
Provincial Airlines Ltd. - Environmental Services Division, 335
Risk Check Environmental Ltd., 347
Scimus Inc., 360
Specialty Technical Publishers, 375
Spill Management Inc., 376
Stratos Inc., 380
Stuart Hunt & Associates, 381
T. Harris Environmental Management Inc., 385
Talkie Tooter Canada Ltd., 386
Toxprobe Inc., 399
Vizon SciTec Inc., 414
WorkLab Inc., 433
WPI Safety & Environmental Consultants, 434

Ocean Dredging
See Diving Services

Odour Control Equipment, Air
See also Air Pollution Control Equipment

A.C. Carbone Canada Inc., 63
A.H. Lundberg Systems Inc., 63
ALTECH Technology Systems Inc., 81
Ambio Biofiltration Ltd., 82
Arbrux Limited, 89
BC Air Filter Ltd., 103
Bigelow-Liptak of Canada, 107
BIOREM Inc., 109
BioSolve of Canada Ltd., 109
Biothermica, 109
CAHFIL FARR (Canada Inc.), 121
Canada Water Supply Ltd., 123
Canbar Inc., 126
Cascades Resource, 131
Cimatec Environmental Engineering Inc., 141
Clean Air & Water Centre, 142
Cleartech Industries Inc., 143
Comenco Systems Inc., 147
E.H. Hanson Engineering Group Ltd., 168
Energy Technology Products Ltd., 179
Engine Control Systems, 180
ENV Treatment Systems Inc., 182
Enviro-Safe Chemicals Canada Inc., 183
Fabricated Plastics Ltd., 193

Fastco Equipment Corporation, 194
Gasmac Inc., 205
HAMON Custodis-Cottrell Canada, Inc., 224
Henlex Inc., 229
Indachem Inc., 240
Infratech Corporation, 241
Inproheat Industries Ltd., 242
InspecTech, 243
Macrotek Inc., 278
MEC Systems Inc., 286
Mequipco Ltd., 286
Météoglobe Canada Inc., 287
Nature's Environmental Products Inc., 298
Nett Technologies Inc., 300
Pacific Environmental Consulting & Occupational Hygiene Services, 316
Pacific Institute for Advanced Study, 316
Plasticair Inc., 326
Prism Chemicals Inc., 332
Scintrex Ltd., 360
T.D. Rooke Associates Ltd., 385
Tiger-Vac International Inc., 396
Total Combustion Inc., 398
Triple M Fiberglass Mfg. Ltd., 401
TurboSonic Inc., 404
Viessmann Manufacturing Company Inc., 413
Warco Process Technologies, 416
Weir Power & Industrial, 424
Whisco Inc., 431
WJF Instrumentation (1990) Ltd., 433

Odour Control Equipment, Water & Wastewater
See also Water, Wastewater & Groundwater Equipment

Accuworx Inc., 66
Bacta-Pur, 101
BIOREM Inc., 109
Canadian Drives Inc., 124
Fabricated Plastics Ltd., 193
HLS Ecolo, 232
Indachem Inc., 240
Kemira Water Solutions Canada Inc., 256
Mancorp Industrial Sales Ltd., 279
Scicorp Systems Inc., 359
Sunset Solar Systems Ltd., 382

Office Products
See Consumer, Office & Industry Products

Oil & Water Separation Equipment
See also Water, Wastewater & Groundwater Equipment

ACG Technology Ltd., 66
Active Chemicals Ltd., 67
AF Pollution Abatement Systems Inc., 72
AIC Associated Industrial Controls Ltd., 73
Aircraft Appliances & Equipment Ltd., 75
Alfa Laval Inc., 78
Andritz Bird, 85
Arjay Engineering Ltd., 91
Brooklin Concrete Products Ltd., 117
Burnaby Bag & Burlap Ltd., 118
C.J. Pink Ltd., 120
Campbell's Concrete Ltd., 122
Can-Am Instruments Ltd., 122
CCS Income Trust, 133
Chem Action Inc., 139
Clean Ontario, 143
Clemmer Technologies Inc., 143
Davis Controls Ltd., 158
Ecodyne Ltd., 171
Enterprise Steel Fabricators Ltd., 181
Environmental Remediation Equipment Inc., 185
Envirotech Pollution Controls Inc., 188
Fair Canada Engineering Ltd., 193
Firing Industries Ltd., 195
Flexo Products Ltd., 196
GE Water & Process Technologies, 205
GEA Westfalia Separator Canada, Inc., 205
General Filtration, 206
GILFAB, 212
Global Dewatering Ltd., 213
Green Turtle Technologies Ltd. (Canada), 217
Hi-Point Industries (1991) Ltd., 231
Hotsy Pressure Washers Ltd., 233
Howard Marten Fluid Technologies Inc., 234
Hydro-Logic Environmental Inc., 236
Indachem Inc., 240

Subject Index

Industrial Marine Power Engineering Group, 240
IPAC Inc., 247
Jetvac Inc., 251
John Meunier Inc., 253
Katch Kan Limited, 255
Komline-Sanderson Ltd., 259
L.E. Washington Sales Ltd., 261
Lafarge Canada Inc., 262
Lécuyer et Fils Ltée, 266
LTS Sales Ltd., 274
MacPherson Brown Ltd., 278
Mancorp Industrial Sales Ltd., 279
Mar Cor Purification, 280
The MEP Environmental Products Ltd., 392
Metrovan Hotsy Equipment Ltd., 288
National Energy Equipment Inc., 297
Nusco Supply & Manufacturing Inc., 309
Pacific Metals Recycling International, 316
Parkson Corporation, 319
Pepper Compressed Air & Gas Ltd., 321
Pipe Specialties Canada, 325
Proceco Ltd., 333
ProViro Instrumentation Inc., 335
Sanitherm Engineering Limited, 357
Seprotech Systems Inc., 363
Stormceptor Canada Inc., 380
Tanks-A-Lot Ltd., 386
Tech Sales Co., 387
Trellcan Rubber Ltd., 401
Triangle Fluid Controls Ltd., 401
Triple M Fiberglass Mfg. Ltd., 401
Wilkinson Heavy Precast Ltd., 431
ZCL Composites Inc., 436
Zimmark Inc., 437

Oil Recycling
See also Fuel Recycling; Recycling Services (General)

Active Chemicals Ltd., 67
Aevitas Inc., 72
Alfa Laval Inc., 78
Amity Plastics Ltd., 84
Barrington Environmental Services, 102
Barrington Industrial Services Limited, 102
Crosbie Industrial Services Ltd., 153
Da-Lee Dust Control, 156
Doherty's Hydraulic Oil Recycling, 164
Eastern Environmental Services Ltd., 169
EIL Environmental Services, 174
Enviro-Gun Ltd., 182
Envirotec Services Incorporated, 187
Inland Technologies Inc., 242
Metrovan Hotsy Equipment Ltd., 288
Niagara Recycling, 303
Par Excellence Developments, Inc., 318
Petro Laboratories Inc., 322
Pyrotech Mfg. Corp., 337
Servicestat Ltd., 363
Sprayaway Marine Services Ltd., 376
Veolia Water Canada, 412
WRS Environmental, 434
Zimmark Inc., 437

Organic Matter Recycling
See also Compost Equipment; Recycling Services (General); Wood Recycling

Anachem Ltd., 84
Aquaterre Inc., 89
B.J. Bear Grain Company Ltd., 100
Biomax Inc., 108
Canada Composting Inc., 123
CanHemp Corporation, 126
Cathy's Crawly Composters, 132
Coastal BioAgresearch Ltd., 145
Compost Management, 147
Consolidated Envirowaste Industries Inc., 150
Cramer Nursery Inc., 153
DynaMotive Energy Systems Corporation, 167
Les Engrais Naturels McInnes Inc./McInnes Natural Fertilizers Inc., 268
Fundy Compost Inc., 203
Gro-Bark (Ontario) Ltd., 218
KC Environmental Group Ltd., 256
MacDonnell Group, 277
Maritime Microbiologicals Inc., 281
N.S. Bauman Inc., 296
Organic Resource Management Inc., 314

Power Grow Systems Inc., 329
Rothsay, 352
Thor Global Enterprises Ltd., 395
Waterloo Evaporateurs Inc., 422

Ozone Generation Equipment
See also Air Pollution Control Equipment

Aerzen Canada Surpresseurs Compresseurs inc., 71
Air Liquide Canada Ltée, 74
Arbrux Limited, 89
Azco Industries Ltd., 100
BOC Canada Limited, 111
Clean Air & Water Centre, 142
Energy Technology Products Ltd., 179
GENEQ Inc., 206
Metropolitan Consulting Inc., 288
T.D. Rooke Associates Ltd., 385

Paint/Solvent Recycling
See also Chemical Recycling; Recycling Services (General)

Aimco Solrec Ltd., 74
Anachem Ltd., 84
Chemrec, 140
Hotz Environmental Services Inc., 233
Howard Marten Fluid Technologies Inc., 234
MCC Industrial Services Ltd, 284
Monalt Environmental Inc., 292
Oakside Chemicals Ltd., 311
The Paint Recycling Company, 393
Parkes Scientific Canada Inc., 318
Raw Materials Corporation, 342
Rawdon Industries Ltd., 342
RMS Enviro Solv Inc. Québec, 347
Société Laurentide inc., 371
Waterloo Evaporateurs Inc., 422

Paper & Paper Products, Recycled
See also Recycled Products

Abitibi-Consolidated Inc., 65
Alliance Envelope Ltd., 79
Atlantic Newsprint Company, 96
Blue Water Agencies Ltd., 110
Bowater Canadian Forest Products Inc., 114
Can-Cell Industries Inc., 123
Canadian Fibre, 124
CanHemp Corporation, 126
Cascades Fine Papers Group Inc., 130
Clearview Packaging Inc., 143
Coast Paper Ltd., 145
Crown Packaging Ltd., 154
Emery International Developments, 177
Hanna Paper Fibres Ltd., 224
Kemel Cartons (1973) Ltd., 256
Kruger Inc., 260
Lyreco Office Products, 276
Maritime Paper Products Ltd., 281
Nestlé Purina PetCare, 300
Niagara Recycling, 303
Norampac Inc., 305
Northeastern Resource Recovery Ltd., 307
Seeker Green Products Ltd., 361
Shred-It, 366
SunOpta, 382
Therm-O-Comfort Co. Ltd., 393
Turtle Island Recycling Co., 404

Paper Recycling
See also Recycling Services (General)

Abitibi-Consolidated Inc., 65
Bowater Canadian Forest Products Inc., 114
Can-Cell Industries Inc., 123
Canadian Paper Recyclers, 124
Capital Environmental Resource Inc., 127
Cascades Inc., 130
Crown Packaging Ltd., 154
Crown Shred & Recycling, 154
Emery International Developments, 177
Hanna Paper Fibres Ltd., 224
IG Machine & Fibers Ltd., 238
Kemel Cartons (1973) Ltd., 256
Kimco Steel Sales Limited, 257
Kongskilde Limited, 259
Lake Charlotte Sanitation, 263
Nestlé Purina PetCare, 300
Proshred Security, 335
Recyclage Alexandria Recycline (Équipe), 343

Seeker Green Products Ltd., 361
Shred-It, 366
Smith-Way Ltd., 371
Sonoco Recycling Ltd., 374
Therm-O-Comfort Co. Ltd., 393
Turcal, 404
Verdyol Mulch of Canada Ltd., 412
Wascana Recycling & Resource Recovery Corp., 417
Wheatland Regional Centre Inc. & SARCAN Recycling, 431

PCB Destruction & Disposal
See also Waste Management, Liquid/Hazardous

Aevitas Inc., 72
Bennett Environmental Inc., 105
BIOREM Inc., 109
Biotech Solutions, 109
Canadian Eagle Recyclers, Inc., 124
The Cintec Group, 391
Conterm Inc., 151
Donalco Inc., 165
ELI Eco Chemical Technologies Inc., 175
Ivey International Inc., 249
Monalt Environmental Inc., 292
PCB Disposal Inc., 319
Plasma Environmental Technologies Inc., 326
Power Vac of Nova Scotia, 329
Powertech Labs Inc., 329
Priestly Demolition Inc., 332
Proeco Enviroservices Ltd., 333
R&R Drilling Supply Ltd., 339
Rondar Inc., 351
Sanexen Environmental Services Inc., 357
SCC Environmental, 358
Sonic Technology Solutions Inc., 374
Swan Hills Treatment Centre, 384

Permit, Regulation & Standards Consulting
See also Environmental Consulting & Contracting Services (General)

Accuworx Inc., 66
Airzone One Ltd., 76
Amberg Corp. - Environmental & Regulatory Consultants, 82
Appin Associates, 87
Biophilia Inc., 109
Calibre Strategic Services Inc., 121
CanTox Environmental Inc., 127
Cascades Inc., 130
CEM Specialties Inc., 135
Danatec Educational Services Ltd., 156
Dougan & Associates, 165
ÉEM inc., 173
EnvirInfo, 182
Environmental Reporting Systems Limited, 186
GlobalTox International Consultants Inc., 213
Goss Gilroy Inc., 215
Groupe Consulteaux Inc., 219
Groupe SOLROC, 221
JTU Consulting, 253
Kaizen Environmental Services Inc., 254
LEHDER Environmental Services Ltd., 267
LJM Environmental Consulting, 273
MWH Canada Inc., 295
NAR Environmental Consultants Inc., 297
Noise Solutions Inc., 305
O'Halloran Campbell Consultants Limited, 310
OSB Services, 314
P.J.B. Duffy & Associates, 316
Petro Laboratories Inc., 322
Poyry (Vancouver) Inc., 329
Procyon Consulting Inc., 333
Rescan Environmental Services Ltd., 345
Risk Check Environmental Ltd., 347
Robert Hornal & Associates Ltd., 348
Safety Projects International Inc., 355
Settlement Surveys Ltd., 364
Tera Environmental Consultants (Alta) Ltd., 389
Tomark Compliance Centre, 397
Trivalent Data Systems Ltd., 402
Vancouver Fraser Port Authority, 409
Water & Earth Science Associates Ltd., 421
William Alexander & Associates Ltd., 432
Winchurch Environmental Inc., 432

Pest Management Services
See also Environmental Consulting & Contracting Services (General)

ACE Vegetation Control Service Ltd., 66
Ag-West Bio Inc., 72
AGRI-SX, 73
Bio-Contrôle inc., 107
Conair Group Inc., 148
Eco-North Laboratories, 171
GDG Environnement Ltée, 205
Marbicon Inc., 280
ProAgri Consulting Limited, 333
Spectrum Resource Group Inc., 375
SPG Hydro International Inc., 375
TerraLink Horticulture Inc., 390

Pipeline Design Services
See also Energy Services; Vehicle Design Services

Cintube Ltd., 141
G.I. Russell & Co. Ltd., 203
Interprovincial Corrosion Control Co. Ltd., 246
Mondry Del Zotto et associés inc., 292
Robb Engineering Ltd., 347
Robertson Environmental Services Ltd., 348
Straub Tadco Inc., 380
Thuro Inc., 396
UMA Group Ltd., 405
Watson Petroleum Services Ltd., 423

Plant Retrofit Studies
See also Engineering Consulting Services (General)

Anrep Krieg Desilets Gravelle Ltd., 86
Babcock & Wilcox Canada Ltd., 100
Canadian Recycling Equipment & Systems Ltd., 125
Cemcorp Ltd. Consulting Engineers, 135
The Conserver Group Inc., 391
Faraci Engineering, 194
Friesen Tokar Architects, Landscape & Interior Designers, 201
Gas Liquids Engineering Ltd., 205
Henry Kortekaas & Associates Inc., 229
Integrated Catalyst Engineering Inc., 244
Noise Solutions Inc., 305
Pepper Compressed Air & Gas Ltd., 321
Semco Systems Limited, 362

Plastic Products, Recycled
See also Recycled Products

Accuworx Inc., 66
Aqua-Pak Styro Containers Ltd., 88
Avenue Industrial Supply Co. Ltd., 98
Blowmoulding Technologies Inc., 110
Buckhorn Canada Inc., 118
Busch Systems International Inc., 118
Canadian Fibre, 124
Dekka Resins Inc., 159
Del-Air Systems Ltd., 160
Double Industries & Trading, 165
Entropex, 182
Fabco Plastics Wholesale (Ontario) Limited, 193
Fabricated Plastics Ltd., 193
IPL Inc., 247
Konica Minolta Business Solutions (Canada) Inc., 259
Lennox Drum Ltd., 267
Masternet Ltd., 282
MAUSER, 283
Monster Polymers Inc., 293
Morval, 294
Niagara Recycling, 303
Northeastern Resource Recovery Ltd., 307
Nova PB Inc., 308
Plast-Ex International Inc., 326
Plastichem Consulting, 326
Plastiglas Industries Limited, 326
Pol-E-Mar Inc., 327
REHAU Industries Inc., 344
Scotia Plastics, 360
SHER-PAC Container Systems Ltd., 365
Shred-It, 366
Simcoe Plastics Ltd., 368
SPI Industries Inc., 375
Symplastics Ltd., 385
Terinex International Ltd., 389
Versatech Industries Inc., 412
Vitafoam Products Canada Ltd., 414

Plastics Recycling
See also Recycling Services (General)

Amity Plastics Ltd., 84
BASF Canada Inc., 103
Blowmoulding Technologies Inc., 110
Bradex Industrial Services Ltd., 115
Brampton Engineering Inc., 115
Cascades Inc., 130
Dekka Resins Inc., 159
Double Industries & Trading, 165
Entropex, 182
Kimco Steel Sales Limited, 257
Kongskilde Limited, 259
Konica Minolta Business Solutions (Canada) Inc., 259
Lennox Drum Ltd., 267
Magnum Industries Ltd., 278
MAUSER, 283
MCC Industrial Services Ltd, 284
Merlin Plastics Supply Inc., 287
MGM Management, 288
Monster Polymers Inc., 293
Neighborhood Recycling, 299
Nu-Plast Polymers International, 309
Plast-Ex International Inc., 326
Plastichem Consulting, 326
Plastiglas Industries Limited, 326
Plastrec Inc., 326
Polychem Products Ltd., 328
Polyland Industries Ltd., 328
SHER-PAC Container Systems Ltd., 365
Shred-It, 366
Simcoe Plastics Ltd., 368
Terinex International Ltd., 389
Universal Drum Reconditioning Company, 406
Ventax Robot Inc., 410
Vitafoam Products Canada Ltd., 414
Wascana Recycling & Resource Recovery Corp., 417
Western Scrap Metals, 429
Wheatland Regional Centre Inc. & SARCAN Recycling, 431
Wittmann Canada, Inc., 433

Policy Development Consulting
See also Environmental Consulting & Contracting Services (General)

Alan Willis & Associates, 76
AquaTox Testing & Consulting Inc., 89
Biophilia Inc., 109
Cottonwood Consultants Inc., 152
Diane Beckett, 163
Global Change Strategies International Co., 213
Hazard Alert Training & Supplies Canada Inc., 227
Hickling Arthurs Low Corp., 231
The Impact Group, 392
INDECO Strategic Consulting Inc., 240
justenvironment, 254
LJM Environmental Consulting, 273
Michael Holliday & Associates, 288
P.J.B. Duffy & Associates, 316
Parish Geomorphic Ltd., 318
Paul F. Wilkinson & Associates Inc., 319
Robert Hornal & Associates Ltd., 348
Robert J. Redhead Limited, 348
Stratos Inc., 380
Summerhill Group, 381
TerraChoice Environmental Marketing, 390
Torrie Smith Associates Inc., 398
Toxprobe Inc., 399
Unterman McPhail Associates, 407
Viridis Environmental Inc., 413
William Alexander & Associates Ltd., 432
WPI Safety & Environmental Consultants, 434

Pollution Prevention Services
See also Air Quality Management (General); Environmental Consulting & Contracting Services (General); Waste Management (General); Water, Wastewater & Groundwater Management (General)

Annapolis Valley Peat Moss Co. Ltd., 86
AquaTox Testing & Consulting Inc., 89
Aware Learning Technologies, 99
Beaulier Inc., 104
Blue-Zone Technologies Ltd., 110
BMT Fleet Technology Ltd., 111
Eco2 Systems Inc., 171
Enviro Vault Ltd., 182
Environmental Economics International, 185
Envision Compliance, 188
Gator International, 205
Greenbridge Management Inc., 217
Groupe Consulteaux Inc., 219
Hiltz & Seamone Co. Ltd., 232
HSE Integrated, 234
Imbibitive Technologies Canada, Inc., 238
IPAC Inc., 247
Kent Engineering Ltd., 256
Lord & Partners Ltd., 274
MacDonnell Group, 277
Maratek Environmental Inc., 280
Marbek Resource Consultants Ltd., 280
Metrovan Hotsy Equipment Ltd., 288
Natech Environmental Services, 297
Noise Solutions Inc., 305
Thimm Engineering Inc., 395
Tiger-Vac International Inc., 396
TPE Technologies Inc., 399
Versatech Products Inc., 412
Vizon SciTec Inc., 414
Zimmark Inc., 437

Polystyrene Recycling
See also Recycling Services (General)

BASF Canada Inc., 103
Dekka Resins Inc., 159
Les Emballages Polyform inc., 268
Le Groupe Légerlite inc., 265
MCC Industrial Services Ltd, 284
Monster Polymers Inc., 293
Plast-Ex International Inc., 326
Polychem Products Ltd., 328
Simcoe Plastics Ltd., 368

Potable/Process Water Treatment Equipment
See also Water, Wastewater & Groundwater Equipment

Aqua-Rehab Inc., 88
AquaMetrix Inc., 88
Campbell's Concrete Ltd., 122
Canadian Water Conditioning Inc., 125
Canbar Inc., 126
Chemline Plastics Ltd., 139
CLA Experts-Conseils, 142
Cleartech Industries Inc., 143
Clemmer Technologies Inc., 143
Davis Controls Ltd., 158
Envirogard Products Ltd., 184
EnviroPower Equipment Marketing Inc., 187
Envitech Automation Inc., 188
Firing Industries Ltd., 195
Flexo Products Ltd., 196
FLSmidth Canada Ltd., 197
GE Water & Process Technologies, 205
General Filtration, 206
H2O Innovation Inc., 223
Hayward Gordon Ltd., 227
Hotsy Pressure Washers Ltd., 233
Hyprescon Inc., 237
J&M Industrial Engineering & Sales Ltd., 249
J.R. Cousin Consultants Ltd., 250
John Meunier Inc., 253
Kentain Products Ltd., 256
Komline-Sanderson Ltd., 259
L.E. Washington Sales Ltd., 261
Layfield Geosynthetics & Industrial Fabrics Ltd., 265
Magnor, Division of Magchem, 278
Maratek Environmental Inc., 280
Markland Specialty Engineering Ltd., 281
Metcon Sales & Engineering Ltd., 287
MSU Mississauga Ltd., 294
Mueller Canada, 295
Napier-Reid Ltd., 297
Niagara Environmental Dynamics, 303
Niagara Water Conditioning Ltd., 303
Nimbus Water Systems, 304
Ontor Ltd., 312
Ozogram Inc., 315
Parameter Control Ltd., 318
Parkson Corporation, 319
Power Plant Supply Co., 329
Promag Enviro Systems Ltd., 334
ProViro Instrumentation Inc., 335
Pumps & Systems, 336
Purifics ES Inc., 337
RAM Lining Systems Inc., 342
REHAU Industries Inc., 344
RenuWater Centre, 345
Rotork Controls (Canada) Ltd., 352
Seprotech Systems Inc., 363
Siemens Water Technologies, 367

Subject Index

Sonitec Inc., 374
Terasen Waterworks, 389
Triangle Fluid Controls Ltd., 401
VIQUA - A Trojan Technologies Company, 413
Waterloo Biofilter Systems Inc., 422
Wilkinson Heavy Precast Ltd., 431
Wyckomar Inc., 434

Power Generation/Production
See also Energy Production Equipment; Energy Services
Adkinson & Associates, 68
Algonquin Power Income Fund, 78
Alstom Canada Inc., 80
ARISE Technologies Corporation, 90
Atlantic Wind Power Corp. Ltd., 97
Babcock & Wilcox Canada Ltd., 100
Brosz & Associates, 117
Can Ecosse Engineering, 122
Cintube Ltd., 141
David A. McLean & Associates, 158
EnRel Energy Group, 181
Enviro-Systèmes Inc., 183
Firwin Corporation, 196
Greenwind Power Corp., 218
Groupe RSW inc., 220
Hooper Welding Enterprises Ltd., 233
Howell-Mayhew Engineering Inc., 234
Hydrogenics Corporation, 236
Hydromega Energy Inc., 237
Industrial Marine Power Engineering Group, 240
Kerr Wood Leidal Associates Ltd., 257
KGS Group Inc., 257
Kinectrics Inc., 257
Mississippi River Power Corp., 291
Natural Forces Technologies Inc., 298
Northern Alternate Power Systems, 307
Nova Scotia Power, an Emera Company, 308
Ramsay Machine Works Ltd., 342
REDUCT & Lobbe Technologies Inc., 344
Renewable Energy Services Inc., 345
Research Electronics (Reselco) Ltd., 345
Sambrabec Inc., 356
Seaforth Engineering Group Inc., 361
Suncurrent Industries Inc., 382
Thomson & Howe Energy Systems Inc., 395
Thomson Technology Inc., 395
Toromont Caterpillar, 397
Transalta Utilities, 400
UMA Group Ltd., 405
Veolia ES Canada Industrial Services Inc., 411
Walter Dow Associates Ltd., 416
Zephyr North, 437

Process Change Consulting
See also Environmental Consulting & Contracting Services (General)
Environmental Advisory Group, 185
Environmental Economics International, 185
Robert J. Redhead Limited, 348
Summerhill Group, 381
Techint Goodfellow Technologies Inc., 387

Process Evaluation & Selection Services
See also Engineering Consulting Services (General)
A. Lanfranco & Associates Inc., 63
A.H. Lundberg Systems Ltd., 63
ALCO Gas & Oil Production Equipment Ltd., 77
BV SORBEX, Inc., 119
Cemcorp Ltd. Consulting Engineers, 135
CMEL Enterprises Ltd., 144
Dalco Wastewater Specialists Inc., 156
Enviro-Met Engineering, 183
Gas Liquids Engineering Ltd., 205
Groupe GLD Inc., Experts-Conseils, 219
H. Broer Equipment Sales and Service, 223
Hickling Arthurs Low Corp., 231
HurterConsult Inc., 235
Integrated Catalyst Engineering Inc., 244
Integrated Resource Management, 244
Jenike & Johanson, Ltd., 251
LEHDER Environmental Services Ltd., 267
Marsh Instrumentation Inc., 281
Nusco Supply & Manufacturing Inc., 309
PAP Engineering Services, 317
Ron Wedman Engineering Services, 351
Sandwell Engineering Inc., 356

Sinanni Inc., 369
Sultech Consulting Ltd., 381
Trihedral Engineering Limited, 401
Watson Process Systems, 423

Process Monitoring & Control Services
See also Computer Software & Systems; Information Technology & Communications (General); Modeling Systems
AeroTek Manufacturing Ltd., 71
Aker Chemetics, 76
Blackbox Automation Inc., 110
CEM Specialties Inc., 135
DPL Group, 166
Genzyme Canada Inc., 210
Harris Industrial Testing, 226
JM Science Canada Inc., 252
KnowTech Environmental Inc., 259
LH - Division of Full Circle Organics Inc., 272
Marsh Instrumentation Inc., 281
Metcon Sales & Engineering Ltd., 287
National Instruments Canada, 297
Orchid Cellmark ULC, 314
Parklane Computer Systems, 319

Product Development Services
See also Financial & Marketing Services (General)
Cheminfo Services Inc., 139
Del-Air Systems Ltd., 160
Fair Canada Engineering Ltd., 193
Kyocera Mita Canada Ltd., 261
Lennox Industries (Canada) Ltd., 267
Prism Chemicals Inc., 332
Sultech Consulting Ltd., 381

Project Management Services
See also Construction & Excavation Services; Engineering Consulting Services (General)
Adventus Canada Inc., 69
ALL-TECH Environmental Services Ltd., 78
Alpine Environmental Ltd., 80
Altus Capital Planning Inc., 81
Angus, Butler Engineering Ltd., 86
Both Belle Robb Ltd., 114
Can Ecosse Engineering, 122
Canadian Petroleum Engineering Inc., 124
Canatec Consultants Ltd., 125
Cardel Construction Ltd., 128
Carswell Consulting Engineers Ltd., 130
CCL/IBI, 133
Cemcorp Ltd. Consulting Engineers, 135
Char Developments Ltd., 138
Chatwin Engineering Ltd., 138
Connections Research, 150
The Cord Group Ltd., 392
Custom Environmental Services Ltd., 154
Decommissioning Consulting Services Limited, 159
Efficiency Engineering Inc., 173
Electronic Warfare Associates - Canada, Ltd., 175
Engineering Management Services Croscan, 180
Environmental Consultants & Engineers, 185
Envirosoil Ltd., 187
Esco Engineering, 189
Fabcon Canada Ltd., 193
G3 Consulting Ltd., 204
Gas Liquids Engineering Ltd., 205
Godfrey Associates Ltd., 214
Greenland International Consulting Inc., 218
Groupe RSW inc., 220
Groupe Sodinco inc., 221
Horner Associates Limited, 233
IBI Group, 238
Integrated Catalyst Engineering Inc., 244
Interior Weather Services Ltd., 245
Island Technologies Inc., 248
Jones Group Engineering Ltd., 253
Kinder Morgan Canada Inc., 257
Lecompte Engineering Ltd., 266
Long Environmental Consultants, 273
M.R. Gordon Consulting Inc., 276
Marsh Instrumentation Inc., 281
McElhanney Consulting Services Ltd., 284
Mondry Del Zotto et associés inc., 292
MTE Consultants Inc., 294
Natural Forces Technologies Inc., 298
NEK Environmental Technologies Inc., 299

O'Halloran Campbell Consultants Limited, 310
Ontario Building Solutions, 312
Opus DaytonKnight Consultants Ltd., 313
Ottawa Engineering Inc., 315
Pacific Engineering Inc., 316
Parkvalley Consulting Ltd., 319
Paul F. Wilkinson & Associates Inc., 319
PINTER & Associates Ltd., 324
Poyry (Vancouver) Inc., 329
ProSolve Consulting Ltd., 335
Reliance Geological Services Inc., 344
Risk Check Environmental Ltd., 347
Robb Engineering Ltd., 347
SAL Engineering Ltd., 356
Sanix Incorporated, 357
Sea Scan International Inc., 361
SGE Hatch Ltd., 364
SHAL Consulting Engineers Ltd., 365
Simcoe Engineering Group Limited, 368
Sinanni Inc., 369
Skelton Brumwell & Associates Inc., 369
SMS Engineering Ltd., 371
SRK Consulting (Canada) Inc., 376
Walker Industries Holdings Ltd., 416
Winds & Voices Environmental Services Inc., 433
Wittmann Canada, Inc., 433

Public Participation, Education & Awareness
See also Information Technology & Communications (General)
Adhawk Communications Inc., 68
AERDE Environmental Research, 71
Aqua-Tex Scientific Consulting Ltd., 88
Barrat & Associates Inc., 101
Bowser Technical Inc., 114
CanTox Environmental Inc., 127
Care First Aid Training Inc., 128
Cascades Inc., 130
CEF Consultants Ltd., 135
Chamard & Associés, 138
Environmental Economics International, 185
Environmental Training Institute, 186
Epistream Consulting Inc, 189
George Grant Consulting, 211
Goss Gilroy Inc., 215
Hazard Alert Training & Supplies Canada Inc., 227
Hazardous Materials Management Magazine, 227
Hilderman Thomas Frank Cram & Associates, 232
Interior Weather Services Ltd., 245
John McMullen & Associates, 252
KC Environmental Group Ltd., 256
Kemic Bioresearch Laboratories Ltd., 256
L&K International Training, 261
Landscope Consulting Corp., 264
Municipal Affairs Consulting, 295
Ogilvie Scientific Inc., 311
Pam Wight & Associates, 317
Paramount Emergency Planners Ltd., 318
Parsons Commercial Technology Group Inc., 319
Praxis Inc., 330
Progress Land Services Ltd., 334
sonnevera international corp., 374
Stuart Hunt & Associates, 381
Suimon Engineering Canada Ltd., 381
SustaiNet Software Solutions Inc., 383
Training & Development Services, 400

Publishing Services
See also Information Technology & Communications (General)
Brincad Technologies Inc., 116
Danatec Educational Services Ltd., 156
The DATA Group of Companies, 392
EnviroLine, 184
EthicScan Canada, 190
GreenWare Environmental Systems Inc., 218
Grey House Publishing Canada, 218
Hazardous Materials Management Magazine, 227
Metrographic Green Print, 287
Port of Entry Inc., 328
Ricoh Canada Inc., 347
Specialty Technical Publishers, 375
Viterra Inc., 414

Pumps, Water & Wastewater
See also Leachate Pumping Equipment/Systems; Water, Wastewater & Groundwater Equipment

Accuworx Inc., 66
Aldworth Engineering Inc., 77
Alfa Laval Inc., 78
Alpine Environmental Ltd., 80
Aquateck Ltd., 89
Blackbox Automation Inc., 110
Bowie Pumps of Canada Ltd., 114
Brim Pumps & Systems Ltd., 116
Busch Vacuum Technics Inc., 119
C.G. Industrial Specialties, Ltd., 119
Cancoppas Limited, 126
Chem Action Inc., 139
CLA Experts-Conseils, 142
Comco Manufacturing Ltd., 146
Consolidated Giroux Environment Inc., 150
Crandall Engineering Ltd., 153
Electric Motor Service (1979) Ltd., 174
F.E. Myers, 193
Filtration Seco Inc., 195
Flowserve Canada Corp. - Pump Division, 197
Flowserve Inc., 197
Flygt Canada, 198
Frontenac Environmental Ltd., 202
GENEQ Inc., 206
Gorman-Rupp of Canada Ltd., 215
Grundfos Canada Inc., 221
H. Broer Equipment Sales and Service, 223
H.E. Bent Services Ltd., 223
Hayward Gordon Ltd., 227
Hibon Inc., 231
Indachem Inc., 240
Ingersoll-Rand Canada Inc., 241
International Water Supply Ltd., 245
Jetvac Inc., 251
KSB Pumps Inc., 261
Logiball Inc., 273
Lotowater Technical Services Inc., 274
MacDonald & Fils Inc., 277
Mandel Scientific Co. Inc., 279
Metex Corp. Ltd., 287
Nardei Fabricators Ltd., 297
National Process Equipment Inc., 298
Niagara Water Conditioning Ltd., 303
Nimbus Water Systems, 304
Oak Environmental Inc., 310
Omega Public Works, 312
Ontor Ltd., 312
Option Environnement Inc., 313
Pencon Equipment Co., 321
Performance Fluid Equipement Inc., 321
Plad Équipement Ltée, 325
Pompaction inc., 328
Pompco Inc., 328
Pompex Inc., 328
Premier Tech Environment, 331
ProMinent Fluid Controls Ltd., 334
Pumps & Systems, 336
R.J. Lévesque et Fils Ltée, 341
RMS Enviro Solv Inc. Québec, 347
S.A. Armstrong Limited, 354
SEI Industries Ltd., 362
Solar Solutions Inc., 372
Sunmotor International Ltd., 382
Taco Canada Ltd., 386
Thuro Inc., 396
Touchie Engineering, 399
Ventes Techniques Nimatec inc., 411
Waterra Pumps Limited, 423
Wellmaster Pipe & Supply, 424

QS 9000 Registrar
See also Quality Management Systems (ISO 9000); Registrars - Series

Bureau de Normalisation du Québec, 118
Intertek Systems Certification, 246
Metafix, 287
NSF-ISR, 309
PricewaterhouseCoopers Management Consultants, 332

Quality Management Systems (ISO 9000)
See also Environmental Management Systems (ISO 14000); Industrial Management (General); ISO 9000 Registrar; QS 9000 Registrar

Groupe SOLROC, 221
North Shore Management Systems Inc., 306
Pilot Performance Resources Management Inc., 324
ProSolve Consulting Ltd., 335
Safety Projects International Inc., 355
SGS Canada Inc., 364

Radioactive Waste Management Consulting
See Waste Management Consulting, Liquid & Hazardous

Recycled Products
See also Consumer, Office & Industry Products; Fertilizers, Recycled; Paper & Paper Products, Recycled; Plastic Products, Recycled; Recycling Services (General); Rubber Products, Recycled; Solvents & Solvent Products, Recycled; Toner Cartridges, Recycled; Waste Exchanges; Wood & Wood Products, Recycled

DEL Warehousing Inc., 160
earthRight Solar Products, 169
Harbour Metal Recycling Ltd., 225
Iogen Corp., 247
Kimco Steel Sales Limited, 257
National Waste Services, 298
NRI Industries, 309
Verdyol Mulch of Canada Ltd., 412
Versatech Industries Inc., 412

Recycling Depot
See also Recycling Services (General); Waste Treatment & Disposal Facilities

The Battery Broker Environmental Services Inc., 391
Canadian Fibre, 124
Ever Green Recycling, 191
Haul-All Equipment Ltd., 227
Recyclage Alexandria Recycline (Équipe), 343
Sonoco Recycling Ltd., 374
Spring Air Silver Services Ltd., 376

Recycling Equipment
See also Material Separation Equipment; Recycling Services (General); Shredding & Grinding Equipment

Allan Fyfe Equipment Limited, 79
Amity Plastics Ltd., 84
Anex Distributors Ltd., 86
Banyan Chains Inc., 101
BDR Machinery Ltd., 103
Blowmoulding Technologies Inc., 110
Buckhorn Canada Inc., 118
Busch Systems International Inc., 118
C-Max Transportation Equipment, 119
Canwest Pumping Systems Ltd., 127
Chem Solv, 139
Clean Ontario, 143
Conway Disposal Ltd., 151
Ecolad Corp., 172
Ecotainer Sales Inc., 172
Enervac Corp., 180
EnviroMed Detection Services, 184
Equipement Labrie Ltee, 189
Extox Industries Inc., 192
Fastco Equipment Corporation, 194
Gensco Equipment (1990) Ltd., 210
Greenflow Environmental Services Inc., 217
Hanna Paper Fibres Ltd., 224
Haul-All Equipment Ltd., 227
Hydro Dyne Inc., 236
Industries de Moules et Plastiques VIF, 241
Industries Machinex Inc., 241
Joe Johnson Equipment Inc., 252
Kason, 255
Kernic Systems Inc., 257
King Metal Fabricators Ltd., 258
Machine Knife Co., 278
MakLoc Buildings Inc., 279
Metafix, 287
Mowat Fabrication Ltd., 294
Norseman Plastics Ltd., 306
Omega Recycling Technologies, 312
Owen G. Carney Ltd., 315
PAP Engineering Services, 317
Parkes Scientific Canada Inc., 318
Plastiglas Industries Limited, 326
Primex Packaging Services, 332
Pyrotech Mfg. Corp., 337
Rawdon Industries Ltd., 342
Recyclage Alexandria Recycline (Équipe), 343
Refrigerant Services Inc., 344

Roger LaRue Enterprises Ltd., 350
Ron Wedman Engineering Services, 351
Sanexen Environmental Services Inc., 357
Scepter Manufacturing Co. Ltd., 358
Skylark Controls, 370
Sleegers Engineering Inc., 370
Sonoco Recycling Ltd., 374
Spring Air Silver Services Ltd., 376
Target Recycling Inc., 387
Thor Global Enterprises Ltd., 395
Universal Handling Equipment Company Limited, 406
Versatech Industries Inc., 412
VQUIP Inc., 414
Walinga Inc., 416
Wasteco, 421
Zimmark Inc., 437

Recycling Services (General)
See also Aggregate Recycling; Aluminum Recycling; Anti-freeze Recycling; Batteries Recycling; Cardboard Recycling; Chemical Recycling; Compost Equipment; Demolition Materials Recycling; Drum Recycling; End Markets; Fuel Recycling; Glass Recycling; Ink Recycling; Lead Recycling; Material Recycling Facilities; Material Separation Equipment; Materials Brokers; Metals Recycling; Oil Recycling; Organic Matter Recycling; Paint/Solvent Recycling; Paper Recycling; Plastics Recycling; Polystyrene Recycling; Recycled Products; Recycling Depot; Recycling Equipment; Shredding & Grinding Equipment; Waste Exchanges; Waste Management Consulting, Solid; Waste Management, Solid; Wood Recycling

A.C. Carbone Canada Inc., 63
ACDEG International Inc., 66
Advanced Coolant Technologies Inc., 69
Aevitas Inc., 72
Aimco Solrec Ltd., 74
Air Products Canada Ltd., 75
Alberta Environmental Rubber Products Inc., 77
All Treat Farms Limited, 78
Alnor Industries Ltd., 79
B.J. Bear Grain Company Ltd., 100
The Battery Broker Environmental Services Inc., 391
Bayer Inc., 103
Bema Co. Ltd., 104
BFI Canada Inc., 106
Brantford Disposal Service, 115
Bruce A. Brown Associates Limited, 117
Cadman Power Equipment, 120
Canadian Eagle Recyclers, Inc., 124
Canadian Recycling Equipment & Systems Ltd., 125
Caster-Rack Systems Ltd., 131
Chamard & Associés, 138
Chemrec, 140
Compost Management, 147
Cosmopolitan Industries Limited, 152
Crown Shred & Recycling, 154
Custom Environmental Services Ltd., 154
Cypher International Ltd., 155
Dartmouth Metals & Bottles Ltd., 157
DEL Warehousing Inc., 160
Deuce Disposal Ltd., 162
Eastern Environmental Services Ltd., 169
Ecocern Inc., 171
Electronics-recycling.com, 175
Enviro Wood Recovery Systems Ltd., 182
EnviroMed Detection Services, 184
Les Équipements Vibrotech Inc., 268
Fort Storage Warehousing & Distribution, 200
FPInnovations, 200
Gary Steacy Dismantling Limited, 204
Genor Recycling Services, 209
Glos Associates Inc., 214
Goulbourn Stittsville Sanitation Ltd., 215
Great Northern Recycling Inc., 216
Griffiths Muecke Associates, 218
GSI Environnement Inc., 222
Hagersville Recycling & Auto Wrecking Ltd., 223
Halifax C&D Recycling, 224
Harbour Metal Recycling Ltd., 225
Hydraulic Systems Ltd., 235
J&F Waste Systems Inc., 249
John Zubick Ltd. Scrap Metals, 253
Knowaste LLC, 259
L.W. Ward Limited, 261

Subject Index

Lake Charlotte Sanitation, 263
Lakeshore Recycling, 263
Lennox Drum Ltd., 267
LINPAC Ropak Packaging, 272
Lucas-Milhaupt Toronto, 274
LURA Consulting, 275
Magnum Industries Ltd., 278
Maritime Ultrasonic Cleaning Inc., 281
Menart S.L. Inc., 286
Metafix, 287
MGM Management, 288
Muskoka Containerized Services Ltd., 295
National Waste Services, 298
Network Environmental Services Inc., 300
Newalta Corporation, 301
NIM Disposals Limited, 304
Norditrade Inc., 305
Norfolk Disposal Services Limited, 305
Norm Shropshall & Sons Ltd., 305
Northwest Metal Recycling, 307
NRI Industries, 309
Omega Recycling Technologies, 312
Ontario Waste Materials Exchange, 312
Pacific Metals Recycling International, 316
The Paint Recycling Company, 393
Petro Sep Membrane Technologies Inc., 322
Pneus Métro Inc., 326
Powerscreen of Canada Ltd., 329
Proline Filter Systems Inc., 334
Proshred Security, 335
Provincial Environmental Services Inc., 335
Ramsay Machine Works Ltd., 342
Récupération Nord-Ben Inc., 343
Recyclage PF Inc., 343
The Recycle Systems Company Inc., 393
Ridgeline Environment Inc., 347
Roger LaRue Enterprises Ltd., 350
Ron Robinson Limited, 351
Rothsay, 352
Sandhill Disposal & Recycling Inc., 356
SARCAN Recycling, 358
SEW Eurodrive Co. of Canada Ltd., 364
Sittler Environmental, 369
Solid Waste Reclamation Inc., 372
Southern Ontario Waste Inc., 374
Spring Air Silver Services Ltd., 376
Sunergy Systems Ltd., 382
SunOpta, 382
Tomlinson Environmental Services, 397
ToxCo Waste Management Ltd., 399
Triple M Metal, 402
Turcal, 404
Turtle Island Recycling Co., 404
Urban Impact Recycling Ltd., 407
Venerus International Purification Inc., 410
Verdyol Mulch of Canada Ltd., 412
Via Disposal Services Ltd., 413
W.J. Sheldrick Sanitation Ltd., 415
Walker Industries Holdings Inc., 416
Wascana Recycling & Resource Recovery Corp., 417
Westra & Associates Inc., 430
York Disposal Service Ltd., 435

Reforestation
See Forestry & Reforestation Management

Registrars - Series
See also ISO 14000 Registrar; ISO 9000 Registrar; QS 9000 Registrar
Control Microsystems, 151

Remedial Action Planning
See Engineering Consulting Services (General)

Remote Sensing & Image Analysis
See also Geographic Information Systems; Information Technology & Communications (General)
AERDE Environmental Research, 71
Agrosysts Ltée, 73
Air Control Engineering Inc., 74
Ashtead Technology Rentals, 93
ASL Environmental Sciences Inc., 94
Avensys Inc., 98
Blackbox Automation Inc., 110
Canadian Seabed Research Ltd., 125
CARIS, 128
Cascade Environmental Resource Group. Ltd., 130

Chartwell Consultants Ltd., 138
Cobham Tracking & Locating Ltd., 145
Conair Group Inc., 148
Delta Aerial Surveys Ltd., 160
Dendron Resource Surveys Inc., 161
EITNL/Earth Information Technologies (nfld) Limited, 174
EnviroMed Detection Services, 184
G.A. Borstad Associates Ltd., 203
Genivar, 207
GeoInsight Corporation, 211
Geosoft, 212
Geosolutions Consulting Inc., 212
Globetron Controls Inc., 214
Hatfield Group, 226
Hyperspectral Data International Inc., 237
Invensys Systems Canada Inc., 246
Jasco Research Ltd., 251
Keywood Entreprises Ltd., 257
Lapp-Hancock Associates Limited, 264
Lotek Wireless Inc., 274
MacDonald, Dettwiler & Associates Ltd., 277
Montrose Technologies Inc., 293
Northway-Photomap Inc., 307
PCI Geomatics Group Inc., 320
Prairie Geomatics Ltd., 330
Pylon Electronics, 337
RBR Ltd., 343
Satlantic, 358
Sea Scan International Inc., 361
Siemens Milltronics Process Instruments Inc., 366
Silva Forest Foundation, 368
Silvana Import Trading Inc., 368
Smiths Detection, 371
Via-Sat Data Systems, 413

Rendering Services, Hazardous Waste
See also Waste Management, Liquid/Hazardous
Environnement Godin Inc., 186
ExTech Environmental Services Inc., 192
Power Vac of Nova Scotia, 329
Proeco Enviroservices Ltd., 333
Veolia Water Canada, 412

Research & Development, Contract
See also Laboratory Services (General); Medical Laboratory Services
Accutest Laboratories Ltd., 66
AGAT Laboratories Ltd., 72
APS Aviation Inc., 87
AXYS Analytical Services Ltd., 99
Bacon Donaldson & Associates Ltd., 101
Bacta-Pur, 101
Barrat & Associates Inc., 101
Bubble Technology Industries Inc., 118
Cambridge Materials Testing Limited, 122
Canviro, 127
Centre de Toxicologie du Québec, 136
Coastal Ocean Associates Inc., 145
Coastal Zones Research Institute Inc., 145
The Cord Group Ltd., 392
Dalynn Biologicals Inc., 156
Ecologistics Research Services, 172
Elemental Research Inc., 175
Envirosphere Consultants Ltd., 187
GAP EnviroMicrobial Services Inc., 204
Genzyme Canada Inc., 210
Griffin Laboratories Corporation, 218
Hazelmere Research Ltd., 228
HGC Engineering, 231
Inco Technical Services Limited, 239
Investigative Science Inc., 247
Lambton Scientific, 263
Maritime Microbiologicals Inc., 281
Maxxam Analytics Inc., 283
Memorial University of Newfoundland, 286
Micrologic Ltd., 289
Mirarco Mining Innovation, 290
Mitsubishi Canada Inc., 291
Oceans Ltd., 311
Offshore Design Associates Ltd., 311
Ontario Centres of Excellence, 312
Pacific Phytometric Consultants, 316
Paracel Laboratories Inc., 318
PBR Laboratories Inc., 319
PDK Projects Inc., 320
Philom Bios Inc., 323

Pildysh Technologies Inc., 323
Powertech Labs Inc., 329
PRT Inc., 336
Pylon Electronics, 337
QCA Laboratories Inc., 337
Quatic Industries Inc., 338
RBR Ltd., 343
Richmond Specialty Mushroom Farms Ltd., 346
RPC, 353
Russell NDE Systems Inc., 354
Shell Canada Limited, 365
Silliker JR Laboratories, ULC, 367
Smiths Detection, 371
Sphere Research Corp., 375
Sultech Consulting Ltd., 381
Toxicology Centre, 399
Tyler Research Instruments Corp., 404
Unisearch Associates Inc., 405
Vizon SciTec Inc., 414

Resource Management Services (General)
See also Agriculture & Agronomy Management; Biological Management; Energy Resource Management; Fisheries & Aquaculture Management; Forestry & Reforestation Management; Horticulture & Vegetation Management; Land Use Planning; Mines & Minerals Management; Waterways & Wetlands Management; Wildlife & Game Management
Acres & Associated Environmental Ltd., 67
AECOM Canada Ltd., 69
AERDE Environmental Research, 71
Agrodev Canada Inc., 73
Agrosysts Ltée, 73
Bissett Resource Consultants Ltd., 110
BRI International Inc., 116
Burden Management & Design Ltd., 118
C.J. MacLellan & Associates Inc., 120
Canadian Benthic Ltd., 124
Catherine Berris Associates Inc., 132
CEF Consultants Ltd., 135
Corner Brook Pulp & Paper Ltd., 152
Cottonwood Consultants Ltd., 152
Cowater International Inc., 153
Dessau, Inc., 162
Dillon Consulting Ltd., 163
Dougan & Associates, 165
Earth & Environmental Technologies (ETech), 168
Ecocern Inc., 171
EDA Collaborative Inc., 173
Entech Environmental Consultants Ltd., 181
Envirosphere Consultants Ltd., 187
FPInnovations, 200
Fugro Airborne Surveys, 202
FWR Ecoresource Consultants Ltd., 203
Genivar, 207
Geosolutions Consulting Inc., 212
Griffiths Muecke Associates, 218
Groupe S.M. International Inc., 220
Hilderman Thomas Frank Cram & Associates, 232
Hunter & Associates, 235
IEG Consultants Ltd., 238
IMTT-Newfoundland Ltd., 239
Interforest Inc., 244
Landscope Consulting Corp., 264
Matrix Solutions Inc., 282
MMM Group, 292
Network Environmental Services Inc., 300
Niblett Environmental, 304
North/South Consultants Inc., 306
Nove Environnement Inc., 309
P.J.B. Duffy & Associates, 316
Paragon Soil & Environmental Consulting Inc., 318
Paul F. Wilkinson & Associates Inc., 319
Pisces Environmental Consulting Services Ltd., 325
Piteau Associates, 325
Planning & Engineering Initiatives Ltd., 325
Pottinger Gaherty Environmental Consultants Ltd., 328
Resource Environmental Associates, 345
Roche ltée, Groupe-conseil, 348
Sanders Resource Manage Inc., 356
Sarafinchin Associates Ltd., 358
Schlumberger Oilfield Services, 359
Secter Environmental Resource Consulting, 361
Sigma Engineering Ltd., 367
Spencer-Lemaire Industries Ltd., 375

Tarandus Associates Limited, 387
Tecsult Inc., 388
TetrES Consultants Inc., 391
Tinari Energy Management Services Inc., 396
Triton Environmental Consultants Ltd., 402
UMA Group Ltd., 405
Université du Québec, 406
W.G. Shaw & Associates, 415
Westland Resource Group Inc., 430
Westra & Associates Inc., 430

Risk Management Services
See also **Environmental Consulting & Contracting Services (General)**
Aercoustics Engineering Limited, 71
Aurora Environmental Consulting Ltd., 97
Biophilia Inc., 109
Can-Ross Environmental Services Ltd., 123
CanTox Environmental Inc., 127
CMEL Enterprises Ltd., 144
Conor Pacific Environmental Technology Inc., 150
Danatec Educational Services Ltd., 156
DST Consulting Engineers, 166
Eco2 Systems Inc., 171
ECOMatters Inc., 172
Emergex Planning Inc., 176
Environmental Accident Protection Inc., 184
Envision Planning Solutions Inc., 188
Global Change Strategies International Co., 213
GlobalTox International Consultants Inc., 213
Goss Gilroy Inc., 215
GPEC International Ltd., 215
Greenbridge Management Inc., 217
GroundTech Solutions, 219
Hemmera Envirochem Inc., 229
Hickling Arthurs Low Corp., 231
HSE Integrated, 234
Intera Engineering Ltd., 244
Keystone Environmental Ltd., 257
LJM Environmental Consulting, 273
Maritime Testing Ltd., 281
Naylor Engineering Associates Ltd., 298
Next Environmental, 303
Notra Inc., 308
O'Connor Associates Environmental Inc., 310
Ogilvie Scientific Inc., 311
Penny & Casson Co., 321
Peter T. Mitches & Associates Limited; Project Managers & Consulting, 321
Provincial Airlines Ltd. - Environmental Services Division, 335
Rescan Environmental Services Ltd., 345
SL Ross Environmental Research Ltd., 370
Specialty Technical Publishers, 375
Strum Environmental, 381
Tanknology Canada Inc., 386
Toxprobe Inc., 399
W.B. Beatty & Associates, 414
WorkLab Inc., 433
WPI Safety & Environmental Consultants, 434

Rubber Products, Recycled
See also **Recycled Products**
Buckhorn Canada Inc., 118
Business Funding Group Inc., 119
DINOFLEX Manufacturing Ltd., 164
Entropex, 182
Magnum Industries Ltd., 278
NRI Industries, 309
Pneus Métro Inc., 326
Target Recycling Inc., 387
TRACC (NB), 400

Safety & Protective Equipment
See also **Industrial Management (General)**
Acoustic Solutions Ltd., 67
Aearo Canada Ltd., 69
Asbeguard Equipment Inc., 93
Blue Water Agencies Ltd., 110
Canadian Safety Equipment Inc., 125
Care First Aid Training Inc., 128
Caristrap International Inc., 128
CCI Thermal Technologies Inc., 133
CenturyVallen, 136
CON-SPACE Communications Ltd., 148
Control Fire Systems, 151
Decibel Consultants Inc., 159

Diversified Waste Solutions, 164
Draeger Safety Canada Ltd., 166
Edwards, 173
Elecsar Engineering Co. Ltd., 174
Electro-Mecanik Inc., 175
EnviroGuard Ltd., 184
Firwin Corporation, 196
Fisher Scientific Ltd., 196
Fred Cressman Sales Inc., 201
GE Multilin, 205
Global Sensor Systems Inc., 213
Globetron Controls Inc., 214
Great Lakes Safety Products Inc., 216
Howard Marten Fluid Technologies Inc., 234
Imbibitive Technologies Canada, Inc., 238
IMP Liquid Meters & Petroleum Services, 239
InspecTech, 243
Katch Kan Limited, 255
KPS & Associates, 260
Lakeland Protective Wear Inc., 263
Levitt-Safety Limited, 270
Matrix Solutions Inc., 282
McAtee Safety & Environmental Health Services Ltd., 284
Megasecur Inc., 286
The MEP Environmental Products Ltd., 392
Micro-Watt Control Devices Ltd., 289
Net Safety Monitoring Inc., 300
Pacesetter Sales & Associates Inc., 316
Pacific Engineering Inc., 316
Pan Tec Inc., 317
Quatrex Environnement inc., 338
Quatrosense Environmental Ltd., 338
Racal Protection Canada, 341
Rocky Mountain Environmental Ltd., 350
Ronco Protective Products, 351
Safety Projects International Inc., 355
The St. George Co. Ltd., 393
Sanbec, 356
Shaver Industries Inc., 365
Showa-Best Glove, Inc., 366
SimplexGrinnell, 368
TEAM-1 Environmental Services Inc., 387
Theodor D. Sterling & Associates Inc., 393
3M Canada Company, 395
Valley Associates Inc., 409
VWR International, LLC, 414
Whisco Ltd., 431
Worldware Enterprises Ltd., 433

Sampling, Monitoring & Measuring (Air, Soil, Water, etc.)
See **Laboratory Services (General)**

Screening Kits, Liquid & Hazardous Waste
See also **Waste Management, Liquid/Hazardous**
Diagnostix Inc., 163
Powerscreen of Canada Ltd., 329

Screens & Strainers, Water & Wastewater
See also **Water, Wastewater & Groundwater Equipment**
Acme Engineering Products Ltd., 66
Arlat Technology, 91
Banyan Chains Inc., 101
Boutillette Parizeau et Associés inc., 114
Buchanan Environmental, 118
Burnaby Bag & Burlap Inc., 118
Capital H2O Systems Inc., 128
Chem Action Inc., 139
Deschênes Drilling Ltd., 161
Double T Equipment Ltd., 165
Drilling Fluids Treatment Systems Inc., 166
GL&V - Groupe Laperrière & Verreault Inc., 212
Hike Metal Products Ltd., 231
Hydro-Logic Environmental Inc., 236
IPEC Industries Ltd., 247
John Meunier Inc., 253
Kason, 255
Maddocks Industrial Filter Division, 278
Napier-Reid Ltd., 297
Parkson Corporation, 319
Power Plant Supply Co., 329
Precision Industrial Ltd., 330
Premier Tech Environnement / Division municipale, commerciale et ind, 331
Pumps & Systems, 336
Sanitherm Engineering Limited, 357

U.S. Filter/Asdor Ltd., 405
Wainbee Limited, 415
Weir Power & Industrial, 424
Wellmaster Pipe & Supply, 424

Scrubbers, Air
See also **Air Pollution Control Equipment**
A.C. Carbone Canada Inc., 63
A.H. Lundberg Systems Ltd., 63
Air Trac Corp., 75
ALCO Gas & Oil Production Equipment Ltd., 77
Alcore Fabricating Corp., 77
All-Weld Company Limited, 79
Apollo Environmental Systems Corporation, 87
Babcock & Wilcox Canada Ltd., 100
BEX Engineering Limited, 106
Century Environmental Systems, 136
Circul-Aire Inc., 141
Condor Engineering Ltd., 149
Elmridge Engineering Inc., 176
Energy Technology Products Ltd., 179
Engine Control Systems, 180
Enterprise Steel Fabricators Ltd., 181
Enviro-Klean Technologies Inc., 182
Esco Engineering, 189
Eurovac, 191
Fair Canada Engineering Ltd., 193
Industrial Plastics Fabricators Ltd., 240
ISCA Management Ltd., 248
KBR Canada, 255
Lockerbie & Hole Contracting Ltd., 273
Mac Industrial Exhaust Shop, 277
MacLeod & Grant Ltd., 278
Macrotek Inc., 278
MEC Systems Inc., 286
Metacor International Inc., 287
Nemato Inc., 300
Nett Technologies Inc., 300
O'Connor Tanks Ltd., 310
Ocean Steel & Construction Ltd., 311
Penn Refrigeration Ltd., 321
Plasticair Inc., 326
Procedair Industries Inc., 333
Process Innovations Canada Inc., 333
Q-Air Environmental Controls Ltd., 337
R&R Drilling Supply Ltd., 339
Reinforced Plastic Systems Inc., 344
T.D. Rooke Associates Ltd., 385
Triple M Fiberglass Mfg. Ltd., 401
TurboSonic Inc., 404
Watson Process Systems, 423
Wheelabrator Canada Co., 431

Septic Tank Maintenance
See also **Waste Management, Liquid/Hazardous**
A1 Sewage Services (1989) Limited, 64
Arbrux Limited, 89
CEDA International Corporation, 135
Crosbie Industrial Services Ltd., 153
Environnement Godin Inc., 186
Geo Environmental Engineering - Geocon SNC-Lavalin, 210
Gerry Brushett Enterprises Limited, 212
Herby Enterprises Ltd., 229
Nature's Mate Distribution Inc., 298
Owen G. Carney Ltd., 315
Septo-Clean Co. Ltd., 363
Souris Valley Industries Ltd., 374
Tanks-A-Lot Ltd., 386
Telamode, 389
Tornatech, 397

Sewage Treatment Equipment
See also **Water, Wastewater & Groundwater Equipment**
Abydoz Environmental, 65
ACME Vacuum Cleaner Co. Ltd., 67
Active Chemicals Ltd., 67
Advanced Environmental Water Technologies Inc., 69
AeroTek Manufacturing Ltd., 71
AIC Associated Industrial Controls Ltd., 73
Anthrafilter Media & Coal Ltd., 86
Apex Industries Inc., 86
AquaMetrix Inc., 88
Arbrux Limited, 89
Arlat Technology, 91
Babcock Supply Ltd., 100
Bacta-Pur, 101

Subject Index

Banyan Chains Inc., 101
Bernard Darveau Ingénieur, 105
Boucher Precast Concrete Ltd., 114
C.J. Pink Ltd., 120
Campbell's Concrete Ltd., 122
Canbar Inc., 126
Capital H2O Systems Inc., 128
Chemline Plastics Ltd., 139
Civtech Engineering & Surveying Ltd., 141
Condor Engineering Ltd., 149
Dalco Wastewater Specialists Inc., 156
EDM Environmental Design & Management Ltd., 173
Elasto Valve Rubber Products Inc., 174
Ellett Industries, 176
Empire Dynamic Structures Ltd., 177
ENV Treatment Systems Inc., 182
Envitech Automation Inc., 188
F.E. Myers, 193
Fair Canada Engineering Ltd., 193
Farris Industries Canada, 194
Filtration Seco Inc., 195
Flexo Products Ltd., 196
GE Water & Process Technologies, 205
GEA Barr-Rosin Inc., 205
GEA Westfalia Separator Canada, Inc., 205
GILFAB, 212
GL&V - Groupe Laperrière & Verreault Inc., 212
Global Dewatering Ltd., 213
Gorman-Rupp of Canada Ltd., 215
Greatario Industrial Storage Systems Ltd., 217
H.E. Bent Services Ltd., 223
Huntsman Corporation Canada Inc., 235
Hydro-Logic Environmental Inc., 236
Hydroxyl Systems Inc., 237
Indachem Inc., 240
Les Industries Fournier Inc., 269
J.R. Cousin Consultants Ltd., 250
Jetvac Inc., 251
Joe Johnson Equipment Inc., 252
John Meunier Inc., 253
John Thurston Machine Ltd., 253
Komline-Sanderson Ltd., 259
L.E. Washington Sales Ltd., 261
Link-Pipe Inc., 272
Markland Specialty Engineering Ltd., 281
Merley Chains Ltd., 287
Metso Automation Canada Ltd., 288
Millar-Williams Hydronics Ltd., 290
Napier-Reid Ltd., 297
Nortec S.G.S. Inc., 306
O'Connor Tanks Ltd., 310
Omega Public Works, 312
Option Environnement Inc., 313
Parkson Corporation, 319
Pencon Equipment Co., 321
Pompaction inc., 328
Pompco inc., 328
Power Plant Supply Co., 329
Premier Plastics Ltd., 331
Premier Tech Environnement / Division municipale, commerciale et ind, 331
Preston Phipps Inc., 331
Promag Enviro Systems Ltd., 334
Quality Fabricating & Supply Limited, 338
Rawdon Technologies Ltd., 342
REHAU Industries Inc., 344
Rotork Controls (Canada) Ltd., 352
SAL Engineering Ltd., 356
Sanitherm Engineering Limited, 357
Scicorp Systems Inc., 359
SEG Engineering Inc., 362
Smart Turner Pumps, 370
Straub Tadco Inc., 380
Suimon Engineering Canada Ltd., 381
System Ecotechnologies Inc., 385
Tank-Craft Ltd., 386
Tanks-A-Lot Ltd., 386
Terasen Waterworks, 389
Terminal City Iron Works Ltd., 389
Tremcar inc., 401
Trojan Technologies Inc., 402
U.S. Filter/Asdor Ltd., 405
Universal Filter Media, 406
V.J. Rice Concrete Ltd., 408
Wainbee Limited, 415

Waterloo Biofilter Systems Inc., 422
Whitman Benn Group, 431
Wilkinson Heavy Precast Ltd., 431
Windsor Pump Co. Ltd., 433
ZCL Composites Inc., 436

Show & Conference Management
See also Financial & Marketing Services (General); Training & Seminar Management

Dekka Resins Inc., 159
dmg world media (Canada) Inc., 164
John McMullen & Associates, 252
Organic Farm Services, 314
Promosalons Canada, 334

Shredding & Grinding Equipment
See also Material Separation Equipment; Recycling Equipment; Recycling Services (General)

Allan Fyfe Equipment Limited, 79
Anex Distributors Ltd., 86
BDR Machinery Ltd., 103
Fastco Equipment Corporation, 194
General Scrap Partnership, 206
Hanna Paper Fibres Ltd., 224
Joe Johnson Equipment Inc., 252
Kernic Systems Inc., 257
Shred-It, 366
Wittmann Canada, Inc., 433

Silver Recycling
See also Metals Recycling

Bartley Silver Co. Inc., 102
Degussa Canada Inc., 159
Greenflow Environmental Services Inc., 217
Lucas-Milhaupt Toronto, 274
R.B. Intermark Inc., 340
Rotblott & Sons Ltd., 352
Western Scrap Metals, 429

Site Assessment Studies
See also Engineering Consulting Services (General)

A&A Environmental Consultants Inc., 63
Adventus Canada Inc., 69
AiMS Environmental, 74
ALL-TECH Environmental Services Ltd., 78
Alpine Environmental Ltd., 80
Apex Geoscience Ltd., 86
ARISE Technologies Corporation, 90
Arrakis Consultants Inc., 92
Atkinson, Davies Inc., 95
Atlantic Engineering Consultants Ltd., 95
Aurora Environmental Consulting Ltd., 97
Biogénie, 108
Biophilia Inc., 109
Biorex Inc., 109
BOMA Environmental & Safety Inc., 113
Burden Management & Design Ltd., 118
Canadian Fishery Consultants Ltd., 124
Carswell Consulting Engineers Ltd., 130
Cheiron Resources Ltd., 139
Craig Hydrogeologic Inc., 153
Decommissioning Consulting Services Limited, 159
Ecologistics Research Services, 172
ÉEM inc., 173
Emergex Planning Inc., 176
ENPAR Technologies Inc., 181
Enviro Scan Technologies Inc., 182
Enviroconseil, 183
Enviroservices Inc., 187
Ferguson Simek Clark, 194
Fundy Engineering & Consulting Ltd., 203
Gemini Twins Consulting Ltd., 206
Geo Environmental Engineering - Geocon SNC-Lavalin, 210
Geo-Logic Inc., 210
Geomarine Associates Ltd., 211
Glenn Group Ltd., 213
GPEC International Ltd., 215
The Greer Galloway Group Inc., Engineers & Planners, 392
Groupe Consulteaux Inc., 219
Hemmera Envirochem Inc., 229
Heritage Research Associates Inc., 230
Horner Associates Limited, 233
HurterConsult Inc., 235
Hydrogéo Plus Inc., 236
Impact Environmental Services Ltd., 239
Intera Engineering Ltd., 244
Investigative Science Inc., 247

Keywood Entreprises Ltd., 257
Kodiak Environmental Limited, 259
Laboratoires d'Expertises de Québec Ltée, 262
Les Laboratoires S.L. inc., 269
LaCas Consultants Inc., 262
Latimat Inc., 265
LEHDER Environmental Services Ltd., 267
Long Environmental Consultants, 273
Longwood Forestry Services Ltd., 273
LVM Inc., 275
Maritime Testing Ltd., 281
MCR Environmental Consulting, 285
Metropolitan Consulting Inc., 288
MTE Consultants Inc., 294
O'Connor Associates Environmental Inc., 310
O'Halloran Campbell Consultants Limited, 310
Oakridge Environmental Ltd., 310
Ottawa Engineering Ltd., 315
P.J.B. Duffy & Associates, 316
Parish Geomorphic Ltd., 318
Pedocan Land Evaluation Ltd., 320
Peter T. Mitches & Associates Limited; Project Managers & Consulting, 321
Peto MacCallum Ltd., 321
Pottinger Gaherty Environmental Consultants Ltd., 328
Pridy Associates, 332
QCA Laboratories Inc., 337
R.A. Murray International Limited, 340
R.G. Robinson & Associates (Barrie) Ltd., 340
Radiodetection (Canada) Ltd., 341
Reliance Geological Services Inc., 344
Roy Northern Environmental Inc., 353
Rubicon Environmental Inc., 354
Sandwell Engineering Inc., 356
Sendex Environmental Corp., 362
SGE Hatch Ltd., 364
Sinanni Inc., 369
Skelton Brumwell & Associates Inc., 369
SRK Consulting (Canada) Inc., 376
Strata Environmental Ltd., 380
Strum Environmental, 381
T. Harris Environmental Management Inc., 385
Technisol Environnement, 388
Thermo Electron Corp., 394
Thurber Engineering Ltd., 395
Totten Sims Hubicki Associates Ltd., 399
Versatech Products Inc., 412
Vizon SciTec Inc., 414
W.L. Whelan Environmental Consultants Ltd., 415
Walter Dow Associates Ltd., 416
Western Bio Resources Consulting Ltd., 429
Wiebe Environmental Services Inc., 431
Wind Energy Institute of Canada, 432

Site Reclamation & Remedial Action Services
See also Engineering Consulting Services (General); Environmental Consulting & Contracting Services (General)

A&A Environmental Consultants Inc., 63
ACE Vegetation Control Service Ltd., 66
Acorus Restoration Native Plant Nursery, 67
Adventus Canada Inc., 69
Aecon Group Inc., 71
Aker Metals (Toronto), 76
Ambler & Co. Inc., 82
Az-Tec Reclaim Ltd., 100
Barenco Inc., 101
Beulah Tec Limited, 106
BG Controls Ltd., 107
Biantco Environmental Services Inc., 107
Bio-Software Inc., 108
Biogénie, 108
Biotech Solutions, 109
Bluewater Environmental Inc., 110
Boojum Research Ltd., 113
C F Reclamation & Fresh Water Services, 119
C3 Environmental Group, 120
Cannington Group, 126
Chatwin Engineering Ltd., 138
Cheiron Resources Ltd., 139
Clifton Associates Ltd., 144
Coast Forest Management Ltd., 145
Coffey Geotechnics Inc., 146
Conestoga-Rovers & Associates, 149
Conestoga-Rovers & Associates, 149

Subject Index

Cook Engineering, 151
Cramer Nursery Inc., 153
Curtis Reclamation Service Ltd., 154
Custom Environmental Services Ltd., 154
Decommissioning Consulting Services Limited, 159
Dove Environmental Services Inc., 165
Elmtree Environmental Ltd., 176
ENPAR Technologies Inc., 181
Entraco, 181
Enviroconseil, 183
Frey & Associates Engineering Ltd., 201
Gamsby & Mannerow Ltd., 204
Gemini Twins Consulting Ltd., 206
Global Engineering & Testing Ltd., 213
Gourley Construction Ltd., 215
Le Groupe Leblond & Bouchard/Daniel Arbour et associes, 265
Hi-Country Environmental Services Ltd., 231
Hydrogéo Plus Inc., 236
Indoor Air Quality Ottawa, 240
Inspec-Sol Inc., 242
Jagger Hims Limited, 250
Jodek Industries Ltd., 252
Kang Construction Ltd., 255
KBL Land Use Consulting Ltd., 255
Keneco Environmental Services Inc., 256
Legaré F., Ing. Forestier Conseil, 266
Longwood Forestry Services Ltd., 273
LVM Inc., 275
McClymont & Rak Engineers, Inc., 284
Naylor Engineering Associates Ltd., 298
Nelson Environmental Remediation Ltd., 299
Newpark Environmental Services, 303
Next Environmental, 303
Notra Inc., 308
O'Connor Associates Environmental Inc., 310
O'Halloran Campbell Consultants Limited, 310
Oakridge Environmental Ltd., 310
Paragon Soil & Environmental Consulting Inc., 318
Penny & Casson Co., 321
Peto MacCallum Ltd., 321
PHH ARC Environmental Ltd., 322
Planning & Engineering Initiatives Ltd., 325
Pottinger Gaherty Environmental Consultants Ltd., 328
Prairie Western Reclamation & Consturction Inc., 330
Pridy Associates, 332
Quantum Murray LP, 338
R&R Drilling Supply Ltd., 339
Red Oak Industries Inc., 343
Risk Check Environmental Ltd., 347
Scott Tank Cleaning Co. Ltd., 360
Servco Environmental Solutions Inc., 363
Sinanni Inc., 369
SLR Consulting Ltd. (Canada), 370
Spanach Construction Ltd., 375
SRK Consulting (Canada) Inc., 376
Strum Environmental, 381
Stuart Hunt & Associates, 381
Sumas Environmental Services Inc., 381
TankTek Environmental Services Ltd., 386
Tansley Associates Environmental Services, 387
Technisol Environnement, 388
Terrapex Environmental Ltd., 390
Thurber Engineering Ltd., 395
Treeline Well Abandonment & Reclamation Ltd., 401
Tri-Arrow Industrial Recovery Inc., 401
TriWaste Services Inc., 402
United Oil Services, 406
W.T. McGinn & Associates Ltd., 415
Ward Chemical, 416
Waterloo Barrier Inc., 422
Western Bio Resources Consulting Ltd., 429
Wiebe Environmental Services Inc., 431
Zell Oilfield Service Ltd., 436

Sludge Processing & Treatment
See also Water, Wastewater & Groundwater Services

AeroTek Manufacturing Ltd., 71
Alfa Laval Inc., 78
Alpha Industrial Services, 79
Associated Engineering Group Ltd., 94
AXOR Experts-Conseils Inc., 99
Bestobell AquaTronix Limited, 106
Burnaby Bag & Burlap Ltd., 118
Capital H2O Systems Inc., 128
Consolidated Giroux Environment Inc., 150
Crosbie Industrial Services Ltd., 153
Dagex Inc., 156
Davis Controls Ltd., 158
Double T Equipment Ltd., 165
EcoEthic Inc., 171
Ecofluid Systems Inc., 171
Endress+Hauser Canada Ltd., 178
Envirogineering, 184
Extox Industries Inc., 192
Fundy Compost Inc., 203
GEA Barr-Rosin Inc., 205
Global Dewatering Ltd., 213
Graymont Inc., 216
Greatario Industrial Storage Systems Ltd., 217
H.E. Bent Services Ltd., 223
IPEC Industries Ltd., 247
John Brooks Company Ltd., 252
KMK Consultants Limited, 258
Komline-Sanderson Ltd., 259
Lacombe Waste Services, 262
Lambton Scientific, 263
Mabarex inc., 277
Markland Specialty Engineering Ltd., 281
Nouvelle Technologie (TEKNO) Inc., 308
Petrozyme Technologies Inc., 322
Produits Chimiques Handy Ltée, 333
Summa Engineering Ltd., 381
Terralog Technologies Inc., 390
Trimax Residuals Management Inc., 401
Waterford Group, 422

Socio-Economic Studies
See also Environmental Consulting & Contracting Services (General)

Adhawk Communications Inc., 68
Calibre Strategic Services Inc., 121
Canning & Pitt Associates Inc., 126
Clayton Research Associates Ltd., 142
Ecocern Inc., 171
Goss Gilroy Inc., 215
Hardy Stevenson & Associates, 225
Hickling Arthurs Low Corp., 231
Nichols Applied Management, 304
P.J. Cluff Architect Inc., 315
Pam Wight & Associates, 317
Paul F. Wilkinson & Associates Inc., 319
Robert Hornal & Associates Ltd., 348
Simon Fraser University, 368
Stratem Inc., 380
Symbion Consultants, 384
Watson & Associates Economists Ltd., 423

Soil Remediation Services
See also Engineering Consulting Services (General); Land Use Planning

A&A Environmental Consultants Inc., 63
AA Environmental & Associates, 64
AC Environmental Services, 65
ACE Vegetation Control Service Ltd., 66
ACM Environmental Corporation, 66
Adventus Canada Inc., 69
Agri-Food Laboratories, 73
AimGlobal Technologies Company, Inc., 74
Ambler & Co. Inc., 82
ARC Geobac Group Inc., 89
Arrakis Consultants Inc., 92
Atlantic Soils & Associated Management Ltd., 97
Beulah Tec Limited, 106
Bioforj Environmental Services, 108
Biogénie, 108
BIOREM Inc., 109
Buckham Transport Ltd., 118
C3 Environmental Group, 120
Canadian Eagle Recyclers, Inc., 124
Cannington Group, 126
Cheiron Resources Ltd., 139
CIMA+, 141
The Cintec Group, 391
Cleanit Greenit Compost System, 143
Comenco Systems Inc., 147
Custom Environmental Services Ltd., 154
D.M. Wills Associates Limited, 156
Degussa Canada Inc., 159
Dewar Pacific Projects Ltd., 162
Dove Environmental Services Inc., 165
DRL Environmental Services, 166
DST Consulting Engineers, 166
DSS Marine Inc., 167
Ecologistics Research Services, 172
Elmtree Environmental Ltd., 176
ENPAR Technologies Inc., 181
Entraco, 181
Enviroconseil, 183
Environmental Solutions Remediation Services, 186
Environnement Godin Inc., 186
Envirosoil Ltd., 187
ESRS Environmental Solution, 190
GAEA Technologies, 204
Geocor Engineering Inc., 210
Global Engineering & Testing Ltd., 213
GPEC Global Corp., 215
GPEC International Ltd., 215
Green Plan Ltd., 217
Green Soils Inc., 217
Harbour Remediation & Transfer Inc., 225
Horizon Environment Inc., 233
Inspec-Sol Inc., 242
InterLink Business Management Inc., 245
Kang Construction Ltd., 255
Klohn Crippen Berger Ltd., 258
Kodiak Environmental Limited, 259
Les Laboratoires S.L. inc., 269
Layfield Geosynthetics & Industrial Fabrics Ltd., 265
Maccaferri Canada Inc., 277
Maritime Testing Ltd., 281
Nelson Environmental Remediation Ltd., 299
Newpark Environmental Services, 303
Next Environmental, 303
North West Environmental Group, 306
Northern Petroleum Services, 307
Oakridge Environmental Ltd., 310
Octagon Environmental Services, 311
Onyx Chemical Cleaning, 313
Paragon Soil & Environmental Consulting Inc., 318
Pinchin Environmental Ltd., 324
Pioneer Petroleums, 325
Roley Construction, 350
ROMOR Atlantic Limited, 351
Ronel Engineering Ltd., 351
Rose Mechanical Water Systems Inc., 351
Roy Northern Environmental Ltd., 353
Sandwell Engineering Inc., 356
Sanexen Environmental Services Inc., 357
SCC Environmental, 358
Sendex Environmental Corp., 362
Sinanni Inc., 369
Solaction Inc., 372
Solid Waste Reclamation Inc., 372
Soren Construction Ltd., 374
SRT Soil Remediation Technologies, 377
Strata Environmental Ltd., 380
Strata Soil Sampling Inc., 380
Sumas Environmental Services Inc., 381
T.D. ThermoDesign, 386
Tansley Associates Environmental Services, 387
TEAM-1 Environmental Services Inc., 387
Terrapex Environmental Ltd., 390
Terratechnik Environmental Limited, 391
Thermo Design Engineering Inc., 394
TJ Consulting Ltd., 396
Waterloo Barrier Inc., 422
WDA Consultants Inc., 423
WHMIS Inc., 431
Williams Engineering Inc., 432
XCG Consultants Ltd., 435

Soil Stabilization
See Erosion Control Services

Solar Energy Conversion
See Energy Systems & Equipment, Alternate

Solid Waste Management
See Waste Management, Solid

Solid Waste Management Consulting
See Waste Management Consulting, Solid

Solvents & Solvent Products, Recycled
See also Recycled Products

Aimco Solrec Ltd., 74
Anachem Ltd., 84
Canwest Pumping Systems Ltd., 127

Subject Index

Chemrec, 140
Fielding Chemical Technologies Inc., 195
Oakside Chemicals Ltd., 311
Refined Specialty Chemicals Inc., 344
Solid Waste Reclamation Inc., 372
STOBEC Inc., 379

Spill Equipment
See also **Emergency Clean-up; Waste Management, Liquid/Hazardous**

A1 Sewage Services (1989) Limited, 64
ACO Container Systems Ltd., 67
Active Chemicals Ltd., 67
Advance Engineered Products Ltd., 68
AF Pollution Abatement Systems Inc., 72
Annapolis Valley Peat Moss Co. Ltd., 86
Aqua Dam & Diversion Ltd., 87
Aqua-Guard Spill Response Inc., 88
Asbeguard Equipment Inc., 93
Avenue Industrial Supply Co. Ltd., 98
BECK Drilling and Environmental Services Ltd., 104
BioSolve of Canada Ltd., 109
Can-Am Instruments Ltd., 122
Can-Ross Environmental Services Ltd., 123
Cartier Chemicals Ltd., 130
Counterspil Research Inc., 153
CP Environmental Technologies, 153
Diversified Waste Solutions, 164
EnviroGuard Ltd., 184
Environnement Godin Inc., 186
Envirotech Nisku Inc., 188
GILFAB, 212
Hassco Industries Inc., 226
Hazmark Inc., 228
Hazmasters Environmental Controls Inc., 228
Hercules SLR Inc., 229
Hi-Point Industries (1991) Ltd., 231
HQN Industrial Fabrics Inc., 234
Interra Environmental Inc., 246
Katch Kan Limited, 255
Lakeland Protective Wear Inc., 263
Levitt-Safety Limited, 270
Lister Industries Ltd., 273
M.J. Labelle Co. Ltd., 276
The MEP Environmental Products Ltd., 392
Penny & Casson Co., 321
Pigmalion Environmental Services Group, 323
Pol-E-Mar Inc., 327
Precisioneering Ltd., 330
Quatrex Environnement inc., 338
Rocky Mountain Environmental Ltd., 350
Rocvent Inc., 350
Sanbec, 356
SEI Industries Ltd., 362
Sonepar Canada, 373
Sphag Sorb (Canada) Inc., 375
SpilKleen, 375
Stormceptor Canada Inc., 380
Tornatech, 397
Versatech Products Inc., 412
VQUIP Inc., 414
West Coast Spill Supplies Ltd., 424
Westeel, 429
Western Canadian Spill Services Ltd., 429
Zodiac Fabrics Inc., 437
Zorbit Technologies Inc., 437

Spills/Clean-up Planning & Assessment
See also **Emergency Clean-up; Emergency Response Planning; Environmental Consulting & Contracting Services (General)**

A1 Sewage Services (1989) Limited, 64
Accurassay Laboratories, 65
Advance Engineered Products Ltd., 68
Alpha Industrial Services, 79
Annapolis Valley Peat Moss Co. Ltd., 86
Aqua-Guard Spill Response Inc., 88
BECK Drilling and Environmental Services Ltd., 104
Beulah Tec Limited, 106
Blue Water Agencies Ltd., 110
BMT Fleet Technology Ltd., 111
Border Chemical Company Ltd., 114
Brosz & Associates, 117
Buckham Transport Ltd., 118
Cactus Environmental Services Ltd., 120
Can-Ross Environmental Services Ltd., 123

Canadian Environmental Auditors Inc., 124
Care First Aid Training Inc., 128
Cartier Chemicals Ltd., 130
CEDA International Corporation, 135
Cheiron Resources Ltd., 139
CIMA+, 141
Clear Environmental Products, 143
Coffey Geotechnics Inc., 146
Conestoga-Rovers & Associates, 149
Cormorant Ltd., 152
Counterspil Research Inc., 153
Crosbie Industrial Services Ltd., 153
Custom Environmental Services Ltd., 154
David A. McLean & Associates, 158
Duerden & Keane Consultants Inc., 167
Ecotech Planners & Advisors Inc., 172
EmerGeo Solutions Inc., 176
EnviroGuard Ltd., 184
Environmental Accident Protection Inc., 184
Envirotec Services Incorporated, 187
Envirotech Nisku Inc., 188
Envirotray Ltd., 188
Envision Planning Solutions Inc., 188
Fabcon Canada Ltd., 193
G.T. Wood Co. Ltd., 204
Gator International, 205
Global Engineering & Testing Ltd., 213
GroundTech Solutions, 219
Harbour Remediation & Transfer Inc., 225
Hazmasters Environmental Controls Inc., 228
Imbitive Technologies Canada, Inc., 238
Institute of Environmental Research Inc., 243
Integrated Explorations, 244
Intera Engineering Ltd., 244
International Submarine Engineering Ltd., 245
Inuktun Services Ltd., 246
KC Environmental Group Ltd., 256
Kent Engineering Ltd., 256
Loraday Environmental Products Ltd., 274
LVM Inc., 275
M.J. Labelle Co. Ltd., 276
McClymont & Rak Engineers, Inc., 284
Megasecur Inc., 286
The MEP Environmental Products Ltd., 392
Muddy River Technologies Inc., 294
Multiview Locates Inc., 295
N. Vandenassem & Associate, 296
Next Environmental, 303
Nilfisk-Advance Canada Company, 304
Northern Petroleum Services, 307
Norvac Industrial Services, 307
O'Connor Associates Environmental Inc., 310
Oil Spill Control Services Canada, 311
Paramount Emergency Planners Ltd., 318
Penny & Casson Co., 321
PHH ARC Environmental Ltd., 322
Pigmalion Environmental Services Group, 323
PINTER & Associates Ltd., 324
Pol-E-Mar Inc., 327
Rocky Mountain Environmental Ltd., 350
Roley Construction, 350
Rudiger Enterprises Ltd., 354
Scott Tank Cleaning Co. Ltd., 360
Servco Environmental Solutions Inc., 363
SL Ross Environmental Research Ltd., 370
SMS Engineering Ltd., 371
Spencer-Lemaire Industries Ltd., 375
Sphag Sorb (Canada) Inc., 375
SpilKleen, 375
Spill Management Inc., 376
Sprayaway Marine Services Ltd., 376
Sutherland Excavating Ltd., 384
TEAM-1 Environmental Services Inc., 387
Thermo Design Engineering Ltd., 394
Thimm Engineering Inc., 395
Toxprobe Inc., 399
Trellcan Rubber Ltd., 401
United Oil Services, 406
Utility Risk Management Ltd., 408
Versatech Products Inc., 412
VQUIP Inc., 414
Waterline Environmental Inc., 422
Western Canadian Spill Services Ltd., 429
Winchurch Environmental Inc., 432
Wotherspoon Environmental Inc., 434

York Fluid Controls Ltd., 435

Storage Tanks & Systems
See also **Waste Management, Liquid/Hazardous**

AAA Petroleum Contracting Ltd., 64
ACO Container Systems Ltd., 67
AeroTek Manufacturing Ltd., 71
AF Pollution Abatement Systems Inc., 72
AGM Steel Industries Ltd., 73
André Simard et associés ltée, 85
Aqua Dam & Diversion Ltd., 87
Avenue Industrial Supply Co. Ltd., 98
Brooklin Concrete Products Ltd., 117
Campbell's Concrete Ltd., 122
Clemmer Technologies Inc., 143
Comptank Corp., 147
Crosbie Industrial Services Ltd., 153
Cyntech Corporation, 155
Cypress Sales Partnership, 155
Da-Lee Dust Control, 156
Dedicated Plastic Tanks Inc., 159
Demers MetalFab Inc., 160
Dewar Pacific Projects Ltd., 162
DTE Industries Ltd., 167
Durex Steel & Alloy Industries Ltd., 167
Ellett Industries, 176
Enterprise Steel Fabricators Ltd., 181
Enviro Vault Ltd., 182
EnviroGuard Ltd., 184
Fabco Plastics Wholesale (Ontario) Limited, 193
Fabricated Plastics Ltd., 193
Flexahopper Plastics Ltd., 196
Focus Industries, 198
Fort Storage Warehousing & Distribution, 200
Fred Cressman Sales Inc., 201
Fundy Engineering & Consulting Ltd., 203
GILFAB, 212
GLM Tanks & Equipment Ltd., 213
Greatario Industrial Storage Systems Ltd., 217
Greif Bros. Canada Inc., 218
Groupe Berlie-Falco Inc., 219
H2Flow Equipment Inc., 223
Hassco Industries Inc., 226
Herby Enterprises Ltd., 229
Hiltz & Seamone Co. Ltd., 232
Hy-Grade Precast Concrete, 235
IMP Liquid Meters & Petroleum Services, 239
Interprovincial Corrosion Control Co. Ltd., 246
Kentain Products Ltd., 256
King Metal Fabricators Ltd., 258
LADEN Steel Fabricators Inc., 262
Lexcan Industrial Supply Ltd., 271
LTS Sales Ltd., 274
M.J. Labelle Co. Ltd., 276
MakLoc Buildings Inc., 279
Multiview Locates Inc., 295
National Energy Equipment Inc., 297
Nemato Inc., 300
Northern Steel Industries, 307
Norwesco Canada Ltd., 308
Nusco Supply & Manufacturing Inc., 309
O'Connor Tanks Ltd., 310
Ocean Steel & Construction Ltd., 311
P. Machibroda Engineering Ltd., 315
Penny & Casson Co., 321
Plastics America, 326
Polyrama Plastics (1987) Ltd., 328
Porta-Mini Systems, 328
Premier Plastics Ltd., 331
Priestly Demolition Inc., 332
Provincial Partitions Ltd., 335
Quality Fabricating & Supply Limited, 338
Quantum Murray LP, 338
Quatrex Environnement inc., 338
Reinforced Plastic Systems Inc., 344
Rocvent Inc., 350
St. Marys Cement Inc., 356
SEI Industries Ltd., 362
Semco Systems Limited, 362
Sleegers Engineering Inc., 370
Solmers Internationale Experts-Conseils Inc., 373
Sprung Instant Structures Ltd., 379
Stemmer Steel Craft Industries Limited, 379
Stormceptor Canada Inc., 380
Tanknology Canada Inc., 386

Subject Index

Tanks-A-Lot Ltd., 386
Tremcar inc., 401
Triple M Fiberglass Mfg. Ltd., 401
TriWaste Services Inc., 402
United Oil Services, 406
Universal Industries, 406
Waterline Environmental Inc., 422
Waterloo Concrete Products, 422
West Coast Spill Supplies Ltd., 424
Westeel, 429
Western Solutions 2000 Ltd., 430
Westland Plastics Ltd., 430
Winchurch Environmental Inc., 432
XCG Consultants Ltd., 435
ZCL Composites Inc., 436

Stormwater Consulting
See also Stormwater Management; Water & Wastewater Consulting; Water, Wastewater & Groundwater Services

Armtec Construction Products, 91
Beasy Nicoll Engineering Ltd., 104
Burnaby Bag & Burlap Ltd., 118
CLA Experts-Conseils, 142
El-Rayes Environmental Corp., 174
Enviroservices Inc., 187
EPEC Consulting (Sask) Ltd., 189
Greenland International Consulting Inc., 218
John Meunier Inc., 253
L.W. Ward Limited, 261
N.L. Sobey & Associates Limited, 296
Pomeroy Consulting Engineers Limited, 328
The Sernas Group Inc., 393
Skelton Brumwell & Associates Inc., 369
Stormceptor Canada Inc., 380
Strait Engineering Ltd., 380
Triton Engineering Services Ltd., 402
Wallace, Van Egmond Spankie Inc., 416
Wilkinson Heavy Precast Ltd., 431

Stormwater Management
See also Stormwater Consulting; Water & Wastewater Consulting; Water, Wastewater & Groundwater Services

Arlat Technology, 91
Armtec Construction Products, 91
Delcan Water, 160
ENV Treatment Systems Inc., 182
Enviroservices Inc., 187
Lafarge Canada Inc., 262
Niblett Environmental, 304
Pomeroy Consulting Engineers Limited, 328
R.U. Kistritz Consultants Ltd., 341
Rocky Mountain Environmental Ltd., 350
The Sernas Group Inc., 393
Sigma Engineering Ltd., 367
Totten Sims Hubicki Associates Ltd., 399
Touchie Engineering, 399
TPE Technologies Inc., 399
Urban Systems Ltd., 407
Wallace, Van Egmond Spankie Inc., 416
West Coast Spill Supplies Ltd., 424

Sustainable Development Strategies
See also Environmental Consulting & Contracting Services (General)

AET Group Inc., 72
Alan Willis & Associates, 76
Brincad Technologies Inc., 116
C.D. Sonter Ltd., 119
Canadian Fishery Consultants Ltd., 124
Charles Simon Architect & Planner, 138
The Delphi Group, 392
Diane Beckett, 163
Environmental Economics International, 185
Envirosphere Consultants Ltd., 187
Geographic Dynamics Corp., 211
Global Change Strategies International Co., 213
Hatfield Group, 226
Hemmera Envirochem Inc., 229
Historica Research Limited, 232
Hydrogéo Plus Inc., 236
IBI Group, 238
INDECO Strategic Consulting Inc., 240
JTU Consulting, 253
justenvironment, 254
KBM Forestry Consultants Inc., 255
LJM Environmental Consulting, 273

M+A Environmental Consultants, 276
Marbek Resource Consultants Ltd., 280
N. Vandenassem & Associate, 296
Optimira Controls, 313
Pam Wight & Associates, 317
Paul G. Chénard, 319
Pilot Performance Resources Management Inc., 324
Purifics ES Inc., 337
R.U. Kistritz Consultants Ltd., 341
Stratos Inc., 380
Summerhill Group, 381
Suncurrent Industries Inc., 382
TankTek Environmental Services Ltd., 386
TerraChoice Environmental Marketing, 390
Torrie Smith Associates Inc., 398
Viridis Environmental Inc., 413
Western Subsea Technology Ltd., 430

Technology Transfer
See also Environmental Consulting & Contracting Services (General)

Ag-West Bio Inc., 72
Bio-Software Inc., 108
Blue-Zone Technologies Ltd., 110
Boojum Research Ltd., 113
Bowser Technical Inc., 114
Canatec Consultants Ltd., 125
Environmental Consultants & Engineers, 185
The Impact Group, 392
Inco Technical Services Limited, 239
InterLink Business Management Inc., 245
ISCA Management Ltd., 248
JTU Consulting, 253
Kaehne Consulting Ltd., 254
N. Vandenassem & Associate, 296
Suimon Engineering Canada Ltd., 381
Suncurrent Industries Inc., 382
Symbion Consultants, 384
Tanks-A-Lot Ltd., 386
Techint Goodfellow Technologies Inc., 387
Western Site Technologies Inc., 430

Telecommunications Services
See also Information Technology & Communications (General)

Blackbox Automation Inc., 110
Boutillette Parizeau et Associés inc., 114
Cobham Tracking & Locating Ltd., 145
DPL Group, 166
Elite Technologies Inc., 175
Honey Electric Ltd., 233
Net Safety Monitoring Inc., 300

Testing
See Laboratory Services (General)

Textiles Recycling
Double Industries & Trading, 165
Life Rhythm Corporation, 272
Vitafoam Products Canada Ltd., 414

Tires Recycling
Alberta Environmental Rubber Products Inc., 77
Bayer Inc., 103
Blowmoulding Technologies Inc., 110
Business Funding Group Inc., 119
Capital Environmental Resource Inc., 127
Environmental Waste International, 186
Hebco International Inc., 228
LOB Blasting Mat, 273
Magnum Industries Ltd., 278
MCC Industrial Services Ltd, 284
NRI Industries, 309
Recovery Technologies Inc., 343
Rubber Rock Resources, 354
Sultech Consulting Ltd., 381
Target Recycling Inc., 387
TRACC (NB), 400

Toner Cartridges Recycling
CanHemp Corporation, 126
Canon Canada Inc., 126
Cartridge Care Canada, 130
Datarite, 157
LaserNetworks Inc., 264
Laserworks Computer Services, 264
MKG Imaging Solutions Inc., 291

Sharp Electronics of Canada Ltd., 365
Teckn-O-Laser, 388

Toner Cartridges, Recycled
See also Ink Recycling; Recycled Products

Cartridge Care Canada, 130
Konica Minolta Business Solutions (Canada) Inc., 259
LaserNetworks Inc., 264
Sharp Electronics of Canada Ltd., 365
Teckn-O-Laser, 388

Total Quality Environmental Management (TQEM)
See also Environmental Consulting & Contracting Services (General)

ACM Environmental Corporation, 66
Enviro-Met Engineering, 183
EthicScan Canada, 190
Gemcom Software International Inc., 205
Hazard Alert Training & Supplies Canada Inc., 227
JTU Consulting, 253
Lupien Rosenberg Consultants Inc., 274
M+A Environmental Consultants, 276
N. Vandenassem & Associate, 296
Paul G. Chénard, 319
ProSolve Consulting Ltd., 335
Refined Specialty Chemicals Inc., 344
Tanknology Canada Inc., 386
Utility Risk Management Ltd., 408

Toxicology Consulting
See also Environmental Consulting & Contracting Services (General)

A&A Environmental Consultants Inc., 63
CanTox Environmental Inc., 127
Centre de Toxicologie du Québec, 136
Entech Laboratories, 181
Genivar, 207
George Grant Consulting, 211
GlobalTox International Consultants Inc., 213
Harris Industrial Testing, 226
Hydroqual Laboratories Ltd., 237
Kemic Bioresearch Laboratories Ltd., 256
Maxxam Analytics Ltd., 283
Michael Holliday & Associates, 288
Ogilvie Scientific Inc., 311
PBR Laboratories Inc., 319
Services d'Évaluation Santé/Toxicologie Inc., 363
Taylor Mazier Associates, 387
Toxicology Centre, 399
Toxprobe Inc., 399
University of Saskatchewan, 406
Vizon SciTec Inc., 414
Wardrop Engineering Inc., 416

Training & Seminar Management
See also Information Technology & Communications (General); Show & Conference Management

ALARA Industrial Hygiene Services Ltd., 76
Brincad Technologies Inc., 116
Danatec Educational Services Ltd., 156
E.K. Gillin & Associates Inc., 168
EITNL/Earth Information Technologies (nfld) Limited, 174
Elecsar Engineering Co. Ltd., 174
Engineering Management Services Croscan, 180
Environmental Accident Protection Inc., 184
Envision Planning Solutions Inc., 188
ESRI Canada Ltd., 190
G & G Computer Services, 203
Geosoft, 212
Gough Risk Management Ltd., 215
Greenbridge Management Inc., 217
Hardy Stevenson & Associates, 225
Hot Zone Training Consultants Inc., 233
INDECO Strategic Consulting Inc., 240
Interra Environmental Inc., 246
Kanotech Information Systems Ltd., 255
Kinder Morgan Canada Inc., 257
L&K International Training, 261
Ontario Environmental Training Consortium, 312
Paul G. Chénard, 319
Pilot Performance Resources Management Inc., 324
Praxis Inc., 330
R&R Drilling Supply Ltd., 339
Safety Projects International Inc., 355
Spill Management Inc., 376
TTA Technology Training Associates Ltd., 404

Subject Index

Transportation Planning Services
See also Engineering Consulting Services (General)
Alchemist Transport Inc., 77
Both Belle Robb Ltd., 114
The Greer Galloway Group Inc., Engineers & Planners, 392
Groupe Conseil Bellefeuille, Samson et Associés, 219
Harold Marcus Ltd., 225
IBI Group, 238
Lea International Ltd., 266
McElhanney Consulting Services Ltd., 284
MMM Group, 292
Opus International Consultants (Canada) Ltd., 313
R.G. Robinson & Associates (Barrie) Ltd., 340
Sandwell Engineering Inc., 356
Sandwell Engineering Inc., 356
Veolia ES Canada Industrial Services Inc., 411

Turnkey Plants, Water & Wastewater
See also Water & Wastewater Operations & Maintenance; Water, Wastewater & Groundwater Services
Apex Industries Inc., 86
AQUASOL EnviroTech Ltd., 89
BSM North America, 118
Chem Solv, 139
Cunningham Sheet Metal Works Inc., 154
Dalco Wastewater Specialists Inc., 156
Delcan Water, 160
ECO-TEK Ecological Technologies Inc., 171
FLSmidth Canada Ltd., 197
Global Dewatering Ltd., 213
H2O Innovation Inc., 223
Hyprescon Inc., 237
Industrial Plastics Fabricators Ltd., 240
Mabarex inc., 277
Napier-Reid Ltd., 297
Option Environnement Inc., 313
Power Plant Supply Co., 329
Rawdon Technologies Ltd., 342
Sanix Incorporated, 357
Tanks-A-Lot Ltd., 386
TPE Technologies Inc., 399
Zeton Inc., 437

Vehicle Design Services
See also Energy Services; Pipeline Design Services
Atlas Polar Company Limited, 97
D.M. Wills Associates Limited, 156

Venture Capital & Funding Services
See also Financial & Marketing Services (General)
Business Funding Group Inc., 119
Environmental R&D Capital Corporation, 185
EthicScan Canada, 190
The Impact Group, 392
Integrated Resource Management, 244
University Technologies International, 406
Watson & Associates Economists Ltd., 423

Vibration Control Equipment
See also Noise Management (General)
Aercoustics Engineering Limited, 71
Airmaster Sales Ltd., 75
Arpi's Industries Canada Ltd., 92
BVA Systems Ltd./Vibro-Acoustics, 119
Cypress Sales Partnership, 155
Decibel Consultants Inc., 159
DPL Group, 166
Elasto Valve Rubber Products Inc., 174
Géophysique GPR International Inc., 211
HGC Engineering, 231
Industrial Marine Power Engineering Group, 240
Instantel, 244
J.E. Coulter Associates Ltd., 249
Kinetics Noise Control Inc., 257
Latimat Inc., 265
Optikon Corp. Ltd., 313
Rockwell Automation Canada Inc., 349
Siemens Milltronics Process Instruments Inc., 366
Skylark Controls, 370

Waste Collection Services & Equipment, Liquid & Hazardous
See also Waste Management, Liquid/Hazardous
A1 Sewage Services (1989) Limited, 64
Aevitas Inc., 72
Barrington Industrial Services Limited, 102
Big Bear Pumping Inc., 107

Les Bras d'Fer Gingras Inc., 267
Brendar Environmental Inc., 116
Busch Vacuum Technics Inc., 119
Canadian Eagle Recyclers, Inc., 124
Caster-Rack Systems Ltd., 131
CEDA International Corporation, 135
Comptank Corp., 147
Cowater International Inc., 153
Cyanide Destruct Systems Inc., 155
DBS Environmental, 158
Envirotec Services Incorporated, 187
Extox Industries Inc., 192
Fastco Equipment Corporation, 194
Goulbourn Stittsville Sanitation Ltd., 215
Groupe Chagnon International, 219
Herby Enterprises Ltd., 229
Hotz Environmental Services Inc., 233
HQN Industrial Fabrics Inc., 234
Insituform Technologies Ltd. - Edmonton, 242
IPL Inc., 247
John Thurston Machine Ltd., 253
King Metal Fabricators Ltd., 258
Lacombe Waste Services, 262
Loewen Welding & Manufacturing Ltd., 273
Miller Environmental Corp., 290
Movac Mobile Vacuum Services Ltd., 294
Newalta Corporation, 301
Niagara Waste Systems Ltd., 303
Norjohn Transfer System Limited, 305
Northern Bridge and Mat Rentals Ltd., 307
Panther Environmental IInc., 317
PCB Disposal Inc., 319
Pebblestone Multi-Services Inc., 320
Photech Environmental Solutions, 323
R.V. Anderson Associates Limited, 341
Roger LaRue Enterprises Ltd., 350
Rose Mechanical Water Systems Inc., 351
RPR Environmental Inc., 353
St. Marys Cement Inc., 356
Scott Tank Cleaning Co. Ltd., 360
Services industriels Newalta, 363
Services Matrec inc., 363
Sonic Technology Solutions Inc., 374
Sprung Instant Structures Ltd., 376
Sumas Environmental Services Inc., 381
T-G Burgmann, 385
Tansley Associates Environmental Services, 387
Tri-Arrow Industrial Recovery Inc., 401
Veolia Water Canada, 412
VQUIP Inc., 414
Walinga Inc., 416
Westeel, 429
Western Industrial Services Ltd., 429

Waste Collection Services & Equipment, Solid
See also Balers & Compactors, Waste; Waste Management, Solid
All Waste Removal Inc., 78
Allianz Madvac Inc., 79
B.D. Rae Waste Management, 100
Barrington Industrial Services Limited, 102
Big Bear Pumping Inc., 107
Les Bras d'Fer Gingras Inc., 267
Busch Vacuum Technics Inc., 119
C-Max Transportation Equipment, 119
Canadian Portable Structures (1992) Ltd., 125
Canbar Inc., 126
Cascades Recovery Inc., 130
Caster-Rack Systems Ltd., 131
Century Plastics Ltd., 136
Countryside Disposal Service Ltd., 153
Cyanide Destruct Systems Inc., 155
DBS Environmental, 158
Ecotater Sales Inc., 172
Ellett Industries, 176
Enviro-Care Services, 182
Equipement Labrie Ltee, 189
Fero Waste & Recycling Inc., 195
Gensco Equipment (1990) Ltd., 210
Goulbourn Stittsville Sanitation Ltd., 215
IPL Inc., 247
Jetvac Inc., 251
Kalyn Siebert Canada Inc., 254
Labrie Environmental Group, 262
MCC Industrial Services Ltd., 284

Niagara Waste Systems Ltd., 303
Norjohn Transfer System Limited, 305
Ontario Sawdust Supplies, 312
Onyx Chemical Cleaning, 313
Organic Resource Management Inc., 314
Owen G. Carney Ltd., 315
Peel Scrap Metal Recycling Ltd., 320
Photech Environmental Solutions, 323
Precision Industrial Ltd., 330
R.D. Cookson Disposal Ltd., 340
Recyclage Alexandria Recycline (Équipe), 343
Roger LaRue Enterprises Ltd., 350
St. Marys Cement Inc., 356
Sandhill Disposal & Recycling Inc., 356
Sani Gestion ONYX, 357
Services Matrec inc., 363
Sittler Environmental, 369
Smith-Way Ltd., 371
Solid Waste Reclamation Inc., 372
Solmers Internationale Experts-Conseils Inc., 373
Thuro Inc., 396
Universal Handling Equipment Company Limited, 406
VQUIP Inc., 414
W.J. Sheldrick Sanitation Ltd., 415

Waste Disposal Equipment, Liquid & Hazardous
See also Waste Management, Liquid/Hazardous
Aevitas Inc., 72
Brendar Environmental Inc., 116
Cyanide Destruct Systems Inc., 155
DBS Environmental, 158
Eco Waste Solutions, 170
ELI Eco Chemical Technologies Inc., 175
Fanchem Ltd., 193
Groupe Chagnon International, 219
Guspro Inc., 223
HQN Industrial Fabrics Inc., 234
Infratech Corporation, 241
Loewen Welding & Manufacturing Ltd., 273
Ordan Thermal Products Ltd., 314
Quatrex Environnement inc., 338
Services Matrec inc., 363
Servicestat Ltd., 363
Tornatech, 397
Transway Systems Inc., 400
Trecan Combustion Ltd., 400
Vanport Sterilizers Inc., 409

Waste Disposal Equipment, Solid
See also Waste Management, Solid
Advance Engineered Products Ltd., 68
Advanced Biotechnology Inc., 69
All Waste Removal Inc., 78
B.D. Rae Waste Management, 100
Banyan Chains Inc., 101
Les Bras d'Fer Gingras Inc., 267
Buckhorn Canada Inc., 118
Champion Moyer Diebel, 138
The Cintec Group, 391
Contor Terminals Inc., 151
Eco Waste Solutions, 170
Fastco Equipment Corporation, 194
Gensco Equipment (1990) Ltd., 210
Gorman-Rupp of Canada Ltd., 215
Goulbourn Stittsville Sanitation Ltd., 215
Haul-All Equipment Ltd., 227
Industries de Moules et Plastiques VIF, 241
Infratech Corporation, 241
Joe Johnson Equipment Inc., 252
Mowat Fabrication Ltd., 294
Ordan Thermal Products Ltd., 314
Orwak Waste Systems Inc. - Canada, 314
Precision Industrial Ltd., 330
R.D. Cookson Disposal Ltd., 340
RemedX Remediation Services Inc., 344
RICHWAY Environmental Technologies Ltd., 346
Services Matrec inc., 363
SSI Schaefer Systems International Ltd., 377
Terralog Technologies Inc., 390
Toromont Caterpillar, 397
Universal Handling Equipment Company Limited, 406
Walinga Inc., 416
Wasteco, 421
Woodington Systems Inc., 433
York Disposal Service Ltd., 435

Subject Index

Waste Exchanges
See also Recycled Products; Recycling Services (General)
Ontario Waste Materials Exchange, 312
STOBEC Inc., 379

Waste Management (General)
See also Asbestos Abatement Services; Biomedical Waste Treatment & Disposal; Pollution Prevention Services; Waste Management Consulting, Solid; Waste Management, Liquid/Hazardous; Waste Management, Solid; Waste Treatment & Disposal Facilities; Waste Treatment Equipment, Liquid & Hazardous
Accurate Industrial Waste Limited, 66
Acres & Associated Environmental Ltd., 67
ADI Group Inc., 68
Advance Laboratories Ltd., 69
AECOM Canada Ltd., 69
AGRECOM inc., 73
AIM Environmental Group, 74
Alrange Container Services, 80
Altek Power Corporation, 81
AN-GEO Environmental Consultants Ltd., 84
ATCO Group, 94
ATD Waste Systems Inc., 95
Atlantic Purification Systems, 97
Atlas Polar Company Limited, 97
Bancroft Western Sales Ltd., 101
Barrington Environmental Services, 102
The Battery Broker Environmental Services Inc., 391
Bennett Environmental Inc., 105
Beulah Tec Limited, 106
BOMA Environmental & Safety Inc., 113
BPR, 115
Bruce A. Brown Associates Limited, 117
Bryco Environmental, 117
Cathy's Crawly Composters, 132
CBCL Limited, 132
CCR Technologies Ltd., 133
CCS Income Trust, 133
Challenger Geomatics Ltd., 138
Chem Solv, 139
Con-Tank Installations Ltd., 148
Convoyeurs B.M.G. inc., 151
Conway Disposal Ltd., 151
Custom Environmental Services Ltd., 154
Cypress Sales Partnership, 155
Data Tech Environmental Services, 157
Dessau, Inc., 162
EFR Disposal, 173
EMP Environmental Management & Protection Corporation, 177
Entretien M. Perron inc. (SANI-TRI), 181
Envirem Technologies Inc., 182
Enviro Waste Management Services Ltd., 182
Enviro-Gun Ltd., 182
Envirochem Services Inc., 183
EnviroMed Detection Services, 184
EnviroSORT Inc., 187
Epsilon Chemicals Ltd., 189
Exova, 191
Fluor Canada, 197
Genor Recycling Services, 209
Glos Associates Inc., 214
Golder Associates Ltd., 214
Graymont Inc., 216
Griffiths Muecke Associates, 218
Le Groupe Sani Marc, 265
Hazco Environmental Services Ltd., 227
HLS Ecolo, 232
Hotz Environmental Services Inc., 233
Inland Technologies Inc., 242
Inproheat Industries Ltd., 242
International Marine Salvage Inc., 245
J.L. Richards & Associates Limited, 250
L.W. Ward Limited, 261
Lake Charlotte Sanitation, 263
Lakeland Protective Wear Inc., 263
Leferink Transfer Ltd., 266
Lupien Rosenberg Consultants Inc., 274
M.J. International Inc., 276
M.S. Thompson & Associates Ltd., 276
MacMillan & Associates, 278
Maple Engineering & Construction Canada Ltd., 279
Maple Reinders Environmental Ltd., 279
MCR Environmental Consulting, 285

Muskoka Containerized Services Ltd., 295
National Waste Services, 298
NCL Envirotek Inc., 299
New Trend Environmental Services, 301
Newalta Corporation, 301
NIM Disposals Limited, 304
Norfolk Disposal Services Limited, 305
Northern Bridge and Mat Rentals Ltd., 307
Nove Environnement Inc., 309
Omega Recycling Technologies, 312
Onyx Chemical Cleaning, 313
P. Machibroda Engineering Ltd., 315
Pacific Environmental Consulting & Occupational Hygiene Services, 316
Pebblestone Multi-Services Inc., 320
Pepi Sewage Disposal Service, 321
Peter T. Mitches & Associates Limited; Project Managers & Consulting, 321
Piteau Associates, 325
Plein Disposal, 326
Pribusin Inc., 332
Proeco Enviroservices Ltd., 333
Proline Filter Systems Inc., 334
Provincial Environmental Services Inc., 335
R.D. Cookson Disposal Ltd., 340
Radiation Environmental Management Systems Inc., 341
Ramsay Machine Works Ltd., 342
Récupération Nord-Ben Inc., 343
Recyc-Haul Waste Management Inc., 343
Rexdale Disposal Ltd., 346
Roche ltée, Groupe-conseil, 348
Roger LaRue Enterprises Ltd., 350
Romatec Incorporated, 350
Sarafinchin Associates Ltd., 358
SENES Consultants Limited, 362
Septo-Clean Co. Ltd., 363
Service de rebuts Soulanges inc., 363
SmithBrook Waste Management Services Inc., 371
SNC-Lavalin Group Inc., 371
Solmax International Inc., 373
Southern Ontario Waste Inc., 374
Supervac 2000, 383
System Ecotechnologies Inc., 385
Tarandus Associates Limited, 387
TEAM-1 Environmental Services Inc., 387
Terratec Environmental Ltd., 390
Tinari Energy Management Services Inc., 396
ToxCo Waste Management Ltd., 399
TriWaste Services Inc., 402
Trow Consulting Engineers Ltd., 403
U-pak Disposal Ltd., 405
United Oil Services, 406
UNOTEC, 407
V. Fournier & Associates, 408
Varian Canada Inc., 410
Via Disposal Services Ltd., 413
W.D. Cookson Ltd., 415
W.J. Sheldrick Sanitation Ltd., 415
Waste Alternatives Inc., 417
Waste Logic Inc., 417
Waste Services (CA) Inc., 420
Wastequip Cusco, 421
Western Site Technologies Inc., 430
WHMIS Inc., 431
WorleyParsons Canada Ltd., 433
York Disposal Service Ltd., 435

Waste Management Consulting, Liquid & Hazardous
See also Waste Management, Liquid/Hazardous
Bennett Environmental Inc., 105
Brendar Environmental Inc., 116
Enervac Corp., 180
Entech Environmental Consultants Ltd., 181
Entraco, 181
Enviro-Met Engineering, 183
ExTech Environmental Services Inc., 192
G.T. Wood Co. Ltd., 204
GlobalTox International Consultants Inc., 213
Groupe Sodinco inc., 221
Historica Research Limited, 232
Institute of Environmental Research Inc., 243
InterLink Business Management Inc., 245
Kleinfeldt Consultants Limited, 258
L&M Engineering Ltd., 261
Maritime Microbiologicals Inc., 281

McElhanney Consulting Services Ltd., 284
NetPlus-HazMat Tracker, 300
Nor-Alta Environmental Services Ltd., 305
Notre Development Corp., 308
Nova Magnetics Burgmann Ltd., 308
PDK Projects Inc., 320
Photech Environmental Solutions, 323
PWC Pure Water Corporation, 337
Quester Tangent Corp., 339
Robert J. Redhead Limited, 348
Scimus Inc., 360
Sendex Environmental Corp., 362
Tecsult Inc., 388
Waste Logic Inc., 417
Water & Earth Science Associates Ltd., 421
Westra & Associates Inc., 430
Woodington Systems Inc., 433
York Fluid Controls Ltd., 435

Waste Management Consulting, Solid
See also Recycling Services (General); Waste Management (General); Waste Management, Solid
AET Group Inc., 72
All Waste Removal Inc., 78
André Simard et associés ltée, 85
Associated Engineering Group Ltd., 94
C.D. Sonter Ltd., 119
Canspect Corporation, 127
Cathy's Crawly Composters, 132
CEF Consultants Ltd., 135
Coastal BioAgresearch Ltd., 145
Comcor Environmental Limited, 146
Conestoga-Rovers & Associates, 149
Conporec Inc., 150
Earthbound Environmental Inc., 168
Ecocern Inc., 171
Entech Environmental Consultants Ltd., 181
Environmental Reporting Systems Limited, 186
Envirotech Associates Limited, 187
EPEC Consulting (Sask) Ltd., 189
G.T. Wood Co. Ltd., 204
Haul-All Equipment Ltd., 227
Indoor Air Quality Ottawa, 240
Integrated Environments Ltd., 244
Interior Weather Services Ltd., 245
InterLink Business Management Inc., 245
J.R. Cousin Consultants Ltd., 250
Knight Piésold Ltd., 258
L&M Engineering Ltd., 261
Laboratoires d'Expertises de Québec Ltée, 262
Lacombe Waste Services, 262
MacDonnell Group, 277
North West Environmental Group, 306
Northeastern Resource Recovery Ltd., 307
René Gervais Inc., Consultants, 345
Robinson Consultants Inc., 348
Services Matrec inc., 363
Solinov Inc., 373
Sols Consultants Ltée, 373
sonnevera international corp., 374
Tecsult Inc., 388
Totten Sims Hubicki Associates Ltd., 399
UMA Group Ltd., 405
Viridis Environmental Inc., 413
Waste Logic Inc., 417
Wasteco, 421
Western Bio Resources Consulting Inc., 429

Waste Management Systems, Liquid & Hazardous
See also Waste Management, Liquid/Hazardous
AIC Associated Industrial Controls Ltd., 73
Aldworth Engineering Inc., 77
Atrion International Inc., 97
Bioforj Environmental Services, 108
Brendar Environmental Inc., 116
Bristar Containment Industries Ltd., 117
Caster-Rack Systems Ltd., 131
Da-Lee Dust Control, 156
Eco Waste Solutions, 170
Enervac Corp., 180
GreenWare Environmental Systems Inc., 218
Hotz Environmental Services Inc., 233
M.J. Labelle Co. Ltd., 276
Millar Western Forest Products Ltd., 290
Pebblestone Multi-Services Inc., 320
Photech Environmental Solutions, 323

Subject Index

Raw Materials Corporation, 342

Waste Management Systems, Solid
See also **Waste Management, Solid**
AET Group Inc., 72
All Waste Removal Inc., 78
Aware Learning Technologies, 99
Bioforj Environmental Services, 108
Les Bras d'Fer Gingras Inc., 267
C.D. Sonter Ltd., 119
Conporec Inc., 150
Earthbound Environmental Inc., 168
Eco Waste Solutions, 170
Eco-Tec Ltd., 171
Ecotainer Sales Inc., 172
Exploitation Santec Inc., 192
Gallason Industrial Cleaning Services Inc., 204
Goulbourn Stittsville Sanitation Ltd., 215
Griffiths Muecke Associates, 218
Groupe Sodinco inc., 221
Haul-All Equipment Ltd., 227
Industries Machinex Inc., 241
Labrie Environmental Group, 262
Loewen Welding & Manufacturing Ltd., 273
MCC Industrial Services Ltd, 284
Norm Shropshall & Sons Ltd., 305
Numet Engineering Ltd., 309
Peel Scrap Metal Recycling Ltd., 320
Photech Environmental Solutions, 323
Southern Ontario Waste Inc., 374
Waste Management of Canada, 417

Waste Management, Liquid/Hazardous
See also **Absorbents & Adsorbents, Liquid Waste; Asbestos Abatement Services; Biomedical Waste Treatment & Disposal; Building Materials Consulting, Hazardous; CFC Recovery; Diving Services; Emergency Clean-up; Industrial Coatings; Liners, Geosynthetic/Geomembrane; Mine Tailings Disposal; Nuclear Waste Management; PCB Destruction & Disposal; Rendering Services, Hazardous Waste; Screening Kits, Liquid & Hazardous Waste; Septic Tank Maintenance; Spill Equipment; Storage Tanks & Systems; Waste Collection Services & Equipment, Liquid & Hazardous; Waste Disposal Equipment, Liquid & Hazardous; Waste Management (General); Waste Management Consulting, Liquid & Hazardous; Waste Management Systems, Liquid & Hazardous; Waste Treatment Equipment, Liquid & Hazardous**
A1 Sewage Services (1989) Limited, 64
Advance Engineered Products Ltd., 68
Aimco Solrec Ltd., 74
Alpha Industrial Services, 79
AMETEK Process Instruments, 84
Anachem Ltd., 84
Argo Protective Coatings Inc., 90
Atlantic Industrial Services, 95
Atrion International Inc., 97
Blue Water Agencies Ltd., 110
Buckham Transport Ltd., 118
C.J. MacLellan & Associates Inc., 120
CAHFIL FARR (Canada Inc.), 121
Canspect Corporation, 127
Cat Tech Canada Company, 131
Chemical Safety Training Associates, 139
Cirrus Environmental Services Inc., 141
Coffey Geotechnics Inc., 146
Comptank Corp., 147
CP Environmental Technologies, 153
Crosbie Industrial Services Ltd., 153
Custom Environmental Services Ltd., 154
Da-Lee Dust Control, 156
DBC Environmental Services Ltd., 158
DSS Marine Inc., 167
Edwards, 173
EIL Environmental Services, 174
ELI Eco Chemical Technologies Inc., 175
Environmental Disposal Concepts Inc., 185
Exova, 191
Fielding Chemical Technologies Inc., 195
Flowmatic Holdings Inc., 197
Global Facman Entreprises Inc., 213
Hotz Environmental Services Inc., 233
Hy-Grade Precast Concrete, 235
ICC The Compliance Centre Inc., 238
Inco Technical Services Limited, 239

International Submarine Engineering Ltd., 245
L&M Engineering Ltd., 261
Levelton Consultants Ltd., 270
Lupien Rosenberg Consultants Inc., 274
Maratek Environmental Inc., 280
McClymont & Rak Engineers, Inc., 284
McCordick Glove & Safety Inc., 284
Medina Construction Limited, 286
Miller Environmental Corp., 290
Monalt Environmental Inc., 292
National Waste Services, 298
Network Environmental Services Inc., 300
Norditrade Inc., 305
Ontario Waste Materials Exchange, 312
Pharmatox Inc., 322
Plasma Environmental Technologies Inc., 326
Proeco Enviroservices Ltd., 333
Provincial Environmental Services Inc., 335
PWC Pure Water Corporation, 337
Quantum Murray LP, 338
Rowan Williams Davies & Irwin Inc., 352
RPR Environmental Inc., 353
Safety Express Ltd., 355
Scimus Inc., 360
SEW Eurodrive Co. of Canada Ltd., 364
Solid Waste Reclamation Inc., 372
Stuart Hunt & Associates, 381
Sunergy Systems Ltd., 382
Swan Hills Treatment Centre, 384
2R Services Inc., 404
UMA Group Ltd., 405
VWR International, LLC, 414
Walker Industries Holdings Ltd., 416
Waterloo Concrete Products, 422
Woodington Systems Inc., 433

Waste Management, Solid
See also **Balers & Compactors, Waste; Recycling Services (General); Waste Collection Services & Equipment, Solid; Waste Disposal Equipment, Solid; Waste Management (General); Waste Management Consulting, Solid; Waste Management Systems, Solid; Waste Minimization Strategies, Solid; Waste Quality Assessment, Solid; Waste Treatment Equipment, Solid**
A.H. Roy & Associates Ltd., 64
ABCO Industries Ltd., 64
Acadia Consultants & Inspectors Ltd., 65
Activation Laboratories Ltd., 67
Advance Engineered Products Ltd., 68
AIM Environmental Group, 74
All Waste Removal Inc., 78
The Battery Broker Environmental Services Inc., 391
BFI Canada Inc., 106
BGR Oilfield Services Incorporated, 107
Les Bras d'Fer Gingras Inc., 267
Buckham Transport Ltd., 118
Burden Management & Design Ltd., 118
C.J. MacLellan & Associates, 120
Canadian Liquids Processors Limited, 124
Caristrap International Inc., 128
CH2M Hill Canada Limited, 137
Challenger Geomatics Ltd., 138
Chamard & Associés, 138
Champion Moyer Diebel, 138
Coffey Geotechnics Inc., 146
Crown Fibre Tube Inc., 154
Cypher International Ltd., 155
Cyr Engineering Ltd., 155
Dartmouth Appliance Repair, 157
DBC Environmental Services Ltd., 158
E.H. Hanson Engineering Group Ltd., 168
Eneco Industries Ltd., 178
EnGlobe Corp., 180
Enviro Waste Ltd., 182
Environmental Disposal Concepts Inc., 185
EPS Wood Products Ltd., 189
Fero Waste & Recycling Inc., 195
Flowmatic Holdings Inc., 197
GPEC International Ltd., 215
Green Island Recycling Ltd., 217
Griffiths Muecke Associates, 218
Groupe GLD Inc., Experts-Conseils, 219
Happy Harry's Used Building Material, 225
J&F Waste Systems Inc., 249
Jagger Hims Limited, 250

Kimco Steel Sales Limited, 257
Loewen Welding & Manufacturing Ltd., 273
Malroz Engineering Inc., 279
Maple Engineering & Construction Canada Ltd., 279
Maritime Auto Salvage, 280
Marriotts Container Rental Ltd., 281
Miller Waste Systems, 290
Minas Basin Pulp & Power Company Limited, 290
MR2-McDonald & Associates, 294
Muskoka Containerized Services Ltd., 295
Network Environmental Services Inc., 300
Niagara Analytical Inc., 303
Niagara Waste Systems Ltd., 303
Norditrade Inc., 305
Norjohn Transfer System Limited, 305
Nova Magnetics Burgmann Ltd., 308
Ontario Waste Materials Exchange, 312
Opus DaytonKnight Consultants Ltd., 313
Pacific Metals Recycling International, 316
Renovators Resource Inc., 345
RICHWAY Environmental Technologies Ltd., 346
SAL Engineering Ltd., 356
Sarafinchin Associates Ltd., 358
Scotia Recycling Ltd., 360
SDS Drilling Ltd., 360
SEW Eurodrive Co. of Canada Ltd., 364
SNC-Lavalin Environment Inc., 371
ToxCo Waste Management Ltd., 399
Transform Compost Systems Ltd., 400
2R Services Inc., 404
Urgel Delisle & Associés inc., 408
Valley Waste Resource Management, 409
Waste Logic Inc., 417
Waste Resource Containers, 420
Wastequip Cusco, 421
Western Site Technologies Inc., 430
WorleyParsons Canada Ltd., 433

Waste Minimization Strategies, Solid
See also **Waste Management, Solid**
AET Group Inc., 72
Annapolis Valley Peat Moss Co. Ltd., 86
AXOR Experts-Conseils Inc., 99
C.D. Sonter Ltd., 119
Caster-Rack Systems Ltd., 131
Endress+Hauser Canada Ltd., 178
Interra Environmental Inc., 246
Lotowater Technical Services Inc., 274
Sanexen Environmental Services Inc., 357
sonnevera international corp., 374
Southern Ontario Waste Inc., 374
Tinari Energy Management Services Inc., 396
Viridis Environmental Inc., 413

Waste Quality Assessment, Solid
See also **Waste Management, Solid**
C.D. Sonter Ltd., 119
Caduceon Environmental Laboratories, 120
Coastal BioAgresearch Ltd., 145
Hoskin Scientific Ltd., 233
MR2-McDonald & Associates, 294
Niagara Analytical Inc., 303
Scimus Inc., 360
Summa Engineering Ltd., 381

Waste Transport
See **Waste Collection Services & Equipment, Liquid & Hazardous**

Waste Treatment & Disposal Facilities
See also **Chemical & Physical Waste Plants; Incineration Services; Integrated Special Waste Management/Treatment Facilities; Landfills & Dump Sites; Recycling Depot; Waste Management (General)**
Acadia Consultants & Inspectors Ltd., 65
Activation Laboratories Ltd., 67
ALTECH Environmental Consulting Ltd., 81
AMETEK Process Instruments, 84
AN-GEO Environmental Consultants Ltd., 84
Bennett Environmental Inc., 105
Brantford Disposal Service, 115
Byram Industrial Services Ltd., 119
C.J. MacLellan & Associates Inc., 120
Canadian Liquids Processors Limited, 124
Catterall & Wright, 132
CCS Income Trust, 133
Custom Environmental Services Ltd., 154

Cyr Engineering Ltd., 155
EnGlobe Corp., 180
Enviro Waste Ltd., 182
EnviroCare Environmental Services Ltd., 183
Hazco Environmental Services Ltd., 227
Incinolet Products, 239
Kerr Wood Leidal Associates Ltd., 257
Maple Engineering & Construction Canada Ltd., 279
Mequipco Ltd., 286
Newalta Corporation, 301
Opus DaytonKnight Consultants Ltd., 313
PCB Disposal Inc., 319
Pebblestone Multi-Services Inc., 320
Plains Environmental Inc., 325
Praxair Canada Inc., 330
Proline Filter Systems Inc., 334
SEW Eurodrive Co. of Canada Ltd., 364
Stablex Canada Inc., 377
Tinari Energy Management Services Inc., 396
Tiru Canada Inc., 396
Tomlinson Environmental Services, 397
ToxCo Waste Management Ltd., 399
2R Services Inc., 404
Western Site Technologies Inc., 430
Zeton Inc., 437

Waste Treatment Equipment, Liquid & Hazardous
See also Waste Management (General); Waste Management, Liquid/Hazardous

Abydoz Environmental, 65
ACO Container Systems Ltd., 67
AIC Associated Industrial Controls Ltd., 73
Alcore Fabricating Corp., 77
All-Weld Company Limited, 79
AMETEK Process Instruments, 84
Apex Industries Inc., 86
Bestobell AquaTronix Limited, 106
BEX Engineering Limited, 106
Campbell's Concrete Ltd., 122
Can-Am Instruments Ltd., 122
Canada Water Supply Ltd., 123
Century Environmental Services, 136
Clean Earth Solutions Ltd., 142
Clean Ontario, 143
Cyanide Destruct Systems Inc., 155
Ecodyne Ltd., 171
Enviro Wood Recovery Systems Ltd., 182
Envirogineering, 184
Environmental Waste International, 186
FLSmidth Canada Ltd., 197
Gensco Equipment (1990) Ltd., 210
GILFAB, 212
Harold Marcus Ltd., 225
Hotsy Pressure Washers Ltd., 233
HQN Industrial Fabrics Inc., 234
Infratech Corporation, 241
Ingersoll-Rand Canada Inc., 241
Inland Technologies Inc., 242
Insituform Technologies Ltd. - Edmonton, 242
Integra Environmental Inc., 243
IPEC Industries Ltd., 247
Kason, 255
Komline-Sanderson Ltd., 259
L.E. Washington Sales Ltd., 261
Loewen Welding & Manufacturing Ltd., 273
Matrix Photocatalytic Inc., 282
McCordick Glove & Safety Inc., 284
Millar-Williams Hydronics Ltd., 290
OMB (Americas) Forged Steel Valves, 312
Orwak Waste Systems Inc. - Canada, 314
Plasma Environmental Technologies Inc., 326
Plastics America, 326
Proline Filter Systems Inc., 334
PWC Pure Water Corporation, 337
Pyradia Inc., 337
Radiodetection (Canada) Ltd., 341
Regional Petroleum Products Recycling Ltd., 344
Resource Systems Inc., 345
Rose Mechanical Water Systems Inc., 351
Rotork Controls (Canada) Ltd., 352
SCC Environmental, 358
SCG Industries Ltd., 358
Services Matrec inc., 363
Stablex Canada Inc., 377
T.D. ThermoDesign, 386

Tremcar inc., 401
Warco Process Technologies, 416
Waterloo Evaporateurs Inc., 422
Westech Industrial Ltd., 429
Windsor Pump Co. Ltd., 433
Zeton Inc., 437

Waste Treatment Equipment, Solid
See also Waste Management, Solid

ACME Vacuum Cleaner Co. Ltd., 67
B.D. Rae Waste Management, 100
Brantford Disposal Service, 115
C.J. Pink Ltd., 120
Canada Water Supply Ltd., 123
Century Environmental Services, 136
Clean Earth Solutions Ltd., 142
Covertech Fabricating Inc., 153
Dagex Inc., 156
Double T Equipment Ltd., 165
Eneco Industries Ltd., 178
Enviro Wood Recovery Systems Ltd., 182
Environmental Waste International, 186
EnviroPower Equipment Marketing Inc., 187
Fair Canada Engineering Ltd., 193
Hayward Gordon Ltd., 227
Hygrex-Spehr Industries, 237
Infratech Corporation, 241
Jetvac Inc., 251
Metacor International Inc., 287
Metafix, 287
Millar-Williams Hydronics Ltd., 290
Orwak Waste Systems Inc. - Canada, 314
Pencon Equipment Co., 321
Pyradia Inc., 337
T.D. ThermoDesign, 386
Tomlinson Environmental Services, 397
Tremcar inc., 401
Windsor Pump Co. Ltd., 433

Wastewater Treatment
See Water, Wastewater & Groundwater Management (General)

Water
See Ground/Surface Water Monitoring

Water & Wastewater Assessment
See also Water, Wastewater & Groundwater Services

Aqua Data Inc., 87
ASI Group Ltd., 93
Associated Engineering Group Ltd., 94
AXYS Analytical Services Ltd., 99
Bio-Limno Research & Consulting, 107
Boojum Research Ltd., 113
BOS Engineering & Environmental Services Inc., 114
Buchanan Environmental, 118
Burden Management & Design Ltd., 118
Caduceon Environmental Laboratories, 120
Canspect Corporation, 127
Canviro, 127
Cyr Engineering Ltd., 155
D. Greenfield Associates Ltd., 156
Enervac Corp., 180
EPEC Consulting (Sask) Ltd., 189
eWaterTek Inc., 191
Fraser Environmental Services, 201
Godfrey Associates Ltd., 214
International Water Supply Ltd., 245
L&M Engineering Ltd., 261
Laboratoire de Canalisation Souterraines Inc., 262
Land & Sea Environmental Consultants Ltd., 264
Lecompte Engineering Ltd., 266
MIE Consulting Engineers Inc., 289
MR2-McDonald & Associates, 294
N.L. Sobey & Associates Limited, 296
Near North Laboratories Inc., 299
Niagara Analytical Inc., 303
Niblett Environmental, 304
Nordic Systems Corporation, 305
Nouvelle Technologie (TEKNO) Inc., 308
PINTER & Associates Ltd., 324
Point Four Systems Inc., 326
Produits Chimiques Handy Ltée, 333
René Gervais Inc., Consultants, 345
Robinson Consultants Inc., 348
Sanix Incorporated, 357
Stewart Group, 379

Urban Systems Ltd., 407
WSH Laboratories Ltd., 434

Water & Wastewater Consulting
See also Engineering Consulting Services (General); Stormwater Consulting; Stormwater Management; Water & Wastewater System Design; Water, Wastewater & Groundwater Services

AA Environmental & Associates, 64
Alan A. Smith Inc., 76
André Simard et associés ltée, 85
Aqua Data Inc., 87
AQUASOL EnviroTech Ltd., 89
Atlantic Engineering Consultants Ltd., 95
AXOR Experts-Conseils Inc., 99
Beasy Nicoll Engineering Ltd., 104
Bio-Limno Research & Consulting, 107
Biolab Inc., 108
Biorex Inc., 109
Bolger and Associates Ltd., 113
BOS Engineering & Environmental Services Inc., 114
Buchanan Environmental, 118
BV SORBEX, Inc., 119
C.J. MacLellan & Associates Inc., 120
Canadian Fishery Consultants Ltd., 124
Challenger Geomatics Ltd., 138
CIMA+, 141
CLA Experts-Conseils, 142
D. Greenfield Associates Ltd., 156
Delcan Water, 160
E.H. Hanson Engineering Group Ltd., 168
EarthFx Inc., 169
Environnement ESA Inc., 186
Enviroservices Inc., 187
Envirotech Associates Limited, 187
Envitech Automation Inc., 188
EPEC Consulting (Sask) Ltd., 189
Esco Engineering, 189
Fusionex inc., 203
GAP EnviroMicrobial Services Inc., 204
Geo Environmental Engineering - Geocon SNC-Lavalin, 210
Geocor Engineering Inc., 210
Godfrey Associates Ltd., 214
Gough Risk Management Ltd., 215
Greenland International Consulting Inc., 218
Le Groupe Forces, 265
Groupe Sodinco inc., 221
Groupe Stavibel inc., 221
Guelph Chemical Laboratories, 222
Hydrogéochem Environnement Inc., 236
International Water Supply Ltd., 245
J.D. Mollard & Associates Ltd., 249
Kerr Wood Leidal Associates Ltd., 257
Keystone Environmental Ltd., 257
Kleinfeldt Consultants Limited, 258
Klohn Crippen Berger Ltd., 258
KMK Consultants Limited, 258
Knight Piésold Ltd., 258
Lambton Scientific, 263
Levelton Consultants Ltd., 270
M.S. Thompson & Associates Ltd., 276
MGM Management, 288
MR2-McDonald & Associates, 294
N.L. Sobey & Associates Limited, 296
Natech Environmental Services, 297
Naylor Engineering Associates Ltd., 298
Niblett Environmental, 304
Opus DaytonKnight Consultants Ltd., 313
Pomeroy Consulting Engineers Limited, 328
Produits Chimiques Handy Ltée, 333
PWC Pure Water Corporation, 337
Robert Laurin, 348
Robinson Consultants Inc., 348
Sanix Incorporated, 357
SDS Drilling Ltd., 360
The Sernas Group Inc., 393
Simcoe Engineering Group Limited, 368
Skelton Brumwell & Associates Inc., 369
Strait Engineering Ltd., 380
Taylor Mazier Associates, 387
Totten Sims Hubicki Associates Ltd., 399
Touchie Engineering, 399
Triton Engineering Services Ltd., 402
UMA Group Ltd., 405
Water & Earth Science Associates Ltd., 421

Subject Index

Water Matrix, 421
Western Bio Resources Consulting Ltd., 429

Water & Wastewater Equipment Installation
See also Water, Wastewater & Groundwater Services

Anderson Water Systems, 85
Birks Co., 110
Bytown Marine Ltd., 119
Canadian Water Conditioning Inc., 125
Dalco Wastewater Specialists Inc., 156
Deschênes Drilling Ltd., 161
ECO-TEK Ecological Technologies Inc., 171
Eriksson Sediment Systems Inc., 189
G.I. Russell & Co. Ltd., 203
Gamsby & Mannerow Ltd., 204
Gaston Marcil, Consultant, 205
Global Dewatering Ltd., 213
Green Turtle Technologies Ltd. (Canada), 217
Horton CBI Ltd., 233
Logiball Inc., 273
Momentum Conveyors, 292
Nalco Canada Co., 296
Neptune Technology Group (Canada) Ltd., 300
Noel Rochette et Fils Inc., 305
Parameter Control Ltd., 318
Pipe Specialties Canada, 325
Premier Plastics Ltd., 331
Premier Tech Environment, 331
RenuWater Centre, 345
Sanix Incorporated, 357
Scicorp Systems Inc., 359
Seprotech Systems Inc., 363
Sonitec Inc., 374
Sutherland-Schultz Inc., 384
Water Matrix, 421
Waterloo Evaporateurs Inc., 422

Water & Wastewater Operations & Maintenance
See also Turnkey Plants, Water & Wastewater; Water, Wastewater & Groundwater Services

Aqua Data Inc., 87
Boart Longyear Inc., 111
Boojum Research Ltd., 113
Burnaby Bag & Burlap Ltd., 118
D. Greenfield Associates Ltd., 156
ECO-TEK Ecological Technologies Inc., 171
EcoEthic Inc., 171
Ecofluid Systems Inc., 171
Elasto Valve Rubber Products Inc., 174
Exploitation Santec Inc., 192
Filtrum Inc., 195
Godfrey Associates Ltd., 214
Green Turtle Technologies Ltd. (Canada), 217
Groupe S.M. International Inc., 220
International Water Supply Ltd., 245
J.R. Cousin Consultants Ltd., 250
John Brooks Company Ltd., 252
KMK Consultants Limited, 258
Laboratoire de Canalisation Souterraines Inc., 262
Logiball Inc., 273
Noel Rochette et Fils Inc., 305
Nordic Systems Corporation, 305
Nouvelle Technologie (TEKNO) Inc., 308
Ontor Ltd., 312
Parameter Control Ltd., 318
Produits Chimiques Handy Ltée, 333
Proserco Inc., 335
PWC Pure Water Corporation, 337
Secural Inc., 361
Terasen Waterworks, 389
Warco Process Technologies, 416
Zodiac Fabrics Inc., 437

Water & Wastewater System Design
See also Water & Wastewater Consulting; Water, Wastewater & Groundwater Services

ALCO Gas & Oil Production Equipment Ltd., 77
Apex Industries Inc., 86
AQUASOL EnviroTech Ltd., 89
Associated Engineering Group Ltd., 94
Atlantic Engineering Consultants Ltd., 95
Azco Industries Ltd., 100
Beasy Nicoll Engineering Ltd., 104
Cancoppas Limited, 126
CIMA+, 141
CLA Experts-Conseils, 142

Les Consultants RSA, 268
Cunningham Sheet Metal Works Inc., 154
Delcan Water, 160
ECO-TEK Ecological Technologies Inc., 171
Ecofluid Systems Inc., 171
EDM Consultants Ltd., 173
Elite Technologies Inc., 175
Envitech Automation Inc., 188
EPEC Consulting (Sask) Ltd., 189
Fusionex inc., 203
Gaston Marcil, Consultant, 205
GE Water & Process Technologies, 205
Gevity Group Inc., 212
Green Turtle Technologies Ltd. (Canada), 217
Le Groupe Forces, 265
Groupe Stavibel Inc., 221
H2O Innovation Inc., 223
Hike Metal Products Ltd., 231
Industrial Plastics Fabricators Ltd., 240
John Brooks Company Ltd., 252
KMK Consultants Limited, 258
MacDonald & Fils Inc., 277
Mesh Technologies Inc., 287
MR2-McDonald & Associates, 294
N.L. Sobey & Associates Limited, 296
Napier-Reid Ltd., 297
Natech Environmental Services, 297
Nordic Systems Corporation, 305
Option Environnement Inc., 313
Pelmar Engineering Ltd., 320
Power Plant Supply Co., 329
PWC Pure Water Corporation, 337
René Gervais Inc., Consultants, 345
Robert Laurin, 348
RPR Environmental Inc., 353
Sanix Incorporated, 357
SEG Engineering Inc., 362
Seprotech Systems Inc., 363
Simcoe Engineering Group Limited, 368
Strait Engineering Ltd., 380
Summa Engineering Ltd., 381
Sustainable EDGE Ltd., 383
Tanks-A-Lot Ltd., 386
Urban Systems Ltd., 407
Water Matrix, 421

Water Conservation Products & Systems
See also Water, Wastewater & Groundwater Equipment

ACG Technology Ltd., 66
AQUASOL EnviroTech Ltd., 89
Brass Craft Canada Ltd., 115
Burnaby Bag & Burlap Ltd., 118
Bytown Marine Ltd., 119
Interbath of Canada Ltd., 244
MSU Mississauga Ltd., 294
Pepper Compressed Air & Gas Ltd., 321
Satlantic, 358
Technel Engineering Inc., 387
Terasen Waterworks, 389
Transcontinental Energy Saving Products Inc., 400
Water Conservation Company Ltd., 421
Water Matrix, 421
Water Pik Canada, 422

Water Handling Equipment
See also Water, Wastewater & Groundwater Equipment

Acme Engineering Products Ltd., 66
ACO Container Systems Ltd., 67
Alcore Fabricating Corp., 77
Aquateck Ltd., 89
Babcock Supply Ltd., 100
Berg Chilling Systems Inc., 105
BEX Engineering Limited, 106
Bradford White Canada Inc., 115
Campbell's Concrete Ltd., 122
Carlo Gavazzi (Canada) Inc., 128
Century Plastics Ltd., 136
Chemline Plastics Ltd., 139
Les Contrôles PROVAN Associés Inc., 268
Crandall Engineering Ltd., 153
Crane Energy Flow Solutions, 153
Deschênes Drilling Ltd., 161
Douglas, Barwick Inc., 165
Elmridge Engineering Inc., 176
Emco, 176
EnviroPower Equipment Marketing Inc., 187

Envitech Automation Inc., 188
Expocrete Concrete Products Ltd., 192
F.E. Myers, 193
Fabco Plastics Wholesale (Ontario) Limited, 193
FCX NH Valves, 194
Flowserve Inc., 197
Flygt Canada, 198
Fortier 2000 Ltée, 200
Fred Cressman Sales Inc., 201
GLM Tanks & Equipment Ltd., 213
Gorman-Rupp of Canada Ltd., 215
Hanson Pressure Pipe, 225
Hotsy Pressure Washers Ltd., 233
Hyprescon Inc., 237
International Cooling Systems Inc., 245
J&M Industrial Engineering & Sales Ltd., 249
LTS Sales Ltd., 274
Metso Automation Canada Ltd., 288
National Process Equipment Inc., 298
Neo Valves, 300
Neptune Technology Group (Canada) Ltd., 300
Nortec S.G.S. Inc., 306
Owen G. Carney Ltd., 315
Phoenix Contact Ltd., 323
Plad Équipement Ltée, 325
Pompaction inc., 328
Power Plant Supply Co., 329
Premier Plastics Ltd., 331
REHAU Industries Inc., 344
Reinforced Plastic Systems Inc., 344
Rotork Controls (Canada) Ltd., 352
S.A. Armstrong Limited, 354
Smart Turner Pumps, 370
Straub Tadco Inc., 380
T-G Burgmann, 385
Taco Canada Ltd., 386
Tank-Craft Ltd., 386
Technel Engineering Inc., 387
Terminal City Iron Works Ltd., 389
Triangle Fluid Controls Ltd., 401
Wilkinson Heavy Precast Ltd., 431
Windsor Pump Co. Ltd., 433
York Fluid Controls Ltd., 435

Water Purification Equipment
See also Water, Wastewater & Groundwater Equipment

ACG Technology Ltd., 66
Acme Engineering Products Ltd., 66
Air Liquide Canada Ltée, 74
Aircraft Appliances & Equipment Ltd., 75
Anthrafilter Media & Coal Ltd., 86
Auto-Chlor Inc., 98
Avani Oxygen Water Corporation, 98
Avoca-tec Environmental Services Inc., 99
Azco Industries Ltd., 100
Babcock Supply Ltd., 100
Bartle & Gibson Co. Ltd., 102
Behrick Enterprises Inc., 104
BV SORBEX, Inc., 119
Canadian Water Conditioning Inc., 125
Condor Engineering Ltd., 149
Eco-Tec Ltd., 171
Emco, 176
Enervac Corp., 180
Envirogard Products Ltd., 184
Envitech Automation Inc., 188
Eriksson Sediment Systems Inc., 189
F.E. Myers, 193
Fair Canada Engineering Ltd., 193
Flexo Products Ltd., 196
Flowserve Inc., 197
General Filtration, 206
H2O Innovation Inc., 223
Hotsy Pressure Washers Ltd., 233
Indachem Inc., 240
Integra Environmental Inc., 243
Living Resources Inc., 273
MacDonald & Fils Inc., 277
Magnor, Division of Magchem, 278
Malroz Engineering Inc., 279
Mar Cor Purification, 280
MSU Mississauga Ltd., 294
Nimbus Water Systems, 304
Nordic Systems Corporation, 305
Nortec S.G.S. Inc., 306

Subject Index

Ontor Ltd., 312
Pencon Equipment Co., 321
Polar Bear Health Equipment Supplies, 327
Proceco Ltd., 333
ProViro Instrumentation Inc., 335
Purifics ES Inc., 337
Rawdon Technologies Ltd., 342
REHAU Industries Inc., 344
RenuWater Centre, 345
Resource Systems Inc., 345
Sabatini Earth Technologies Inc., 354
Sanexen Environmental Services Inc., 357
Seprotech Systems Inc., 363
Sika Canada Inc., 367
Sonitec Inc., 374
Suimon Engineering Canada Ltd., 381
T.D. Rooke Associates Ltd., 385
Trivar Inc., 402
Trojan Technologies Inc., 402
VIQUA - A Trojan Technologies Company, 413
Wyckomar Inc., 434

Water, Wastewater & Groundwater Equipment
See also Biotreatment Equipment, Water; Calibration Equipment, Water & Wastewater; Chemical Feeding & Mixing Equipment; Chemicals, Water Treatment; Clarifiers, Water & Wastewater; Corrosion Control/Scale Prevention, Water & Wastewater; Filters & Filter Media, Water & Wastewater; Flow Meters, Water & Wastewater; Heavy Metals Removal Equipment, Water & Wastewater; Leachate Pumping Equipment/Systems; Measuring & Monitoring Equipment, Groundwater; Measuring & Monitoring Equipment, Water & Wastewater; Odour Control Equipment, Water & Wastewater; Oil & Water Separation Equipment; Potable/Process Water Treatment Equipment; Pumps, Water & Wastewater; Screens & Strainers, Water & Wastewater; Sewage Treatment Equipment; Water Conservation Products & Systems; Water Handling Equipment; Water Purification Equipment; Water, Wastewater & Groundwater Management (General)

A.C. Plastiques Canada, 63
Advanced Environmental Water Technologies Inc., 69
ALCO Gas & Oil Production Equipment Ltd., 77
Alfa Plastics Inc., 78
All-Weld Company Limited, 79
ALTECH Technology Systems Inc., 81
Apex Industries Inc., 86
Applied Oxidation Technologies Inc., 87
Aqua Tech Sales & Marketing Inc., 88
Aqua-Plus, 88
Aqua-Rehab Inc., 88
Aquateck Ltd., 89
Associated Tube Industries, 94
Asta Sales & Marketing Ltd., 94
Atlantic Industries Ltd., 95
AWI, 99
Axford Agencies BC Ltd., 99
Bancroft Western Sales Ltd., 101
Barrett Sales Ltd., 102
Barrington Environmental Services, 102
Béton Provincial Ltée, 106
BG Controls Ltd., 107
Birks Co., 110
Blower Engineering Inc., 110
Boucher Precast Concrete Ltd., 114
Bowie Pumps of Canada Ltd., 114
Brunet Ltée, Tuyaux de béton, 117
C.J. Pink Ltd., 120
Calgon Carbon Corp., 121
Can-Am Instruments Ltd., 122
Can-Aqua Inc., 123
Can-Aqua International Ltée, 123
Canada Water Supply Ltd., 123
Canadian Drives Inc., 124
Canadian Water Conditioning Inc., 125
Cancoppas Limited, 126
Catterall & Wright, 132
CENSOL Inc., 136
Con Cast Pipe, 148
Consolidated Giroux Environment Inc., 150
Construction Val-d'Or Ltée, 150
CPC Tuyauteries Canada Ltée, 153
Crandall Engineering Ltd., 153
Crane Energy Flow Solutions, 153

Dalco Wastewater Specialists Inc., 156
Danfoss Inc. - Hydronic Heating Division, 157
Darke Marketing Inc., 157
Daubois Inc., 158
Dave Vallieres & Associates Inc., 158
Deschênes Drilling Ltd., 161
Diacon Technologies Ltd., 163
Dionex Canada Limited, 164
Domaine Label & Trim Inc., 164
Douglas Brothers, 165
DTE Industries Ltd., 167
Ecodyne Ltd., 171
EDM Consultants Ltd., 173
Endress+Hauser Canada Ltd., 178
Enmet Canada Ltd., 181
Envirogineering, 184
EnviroMed Detection Services, 184
Eriksson Sediment Systems Inc., 189
Expocrete Concrete Products Ltd., 192
Flowmatic Holdings Inc., 197
Flowserve Inc., 197
Flush Quip, 198
Flygt Canada, 198
Fontaine International Corp., 199
Foresteel Industries Inc., 199
Gerry Brushett Enterprises Limited, 212
GET Industries Inc., 212
GL&V - Groupe Laperrière & Verreault Inc., 212
Gratec Inc., 216
Groupe Berlie-Falco Inc., 219
H.E. Bent Services Ltd., 223
Hanson Pressure Pipe, 225
Hercules SLR Inc., 229
Hibon Inc., 231
Hike Metal Products Ltd., 231
HLS Ecolo, 232
Horton CBI Ltd., 233
Hydro-Logic Environmental Inc., 236
Hydro-Mechanical Sales Ltd., 236
Hyprescon Inc., 237
Inland Aquatics, 241
IPEC Industries Ltd., 247
Ipex Inc., 247
J.M. Turcotte ltée, 250
Jetvac Inc., 251
John Meunier Inc., 253
KSB Pumps Inc., 261
KWH Pipe, 261
Lambert Somec inc., 263
Lécuyer et Fils Ltée, 266
MacDonald & Fils Inc., 277
Magotteaux Ltée, 278
Marcel Baril Ltée, 280
Material Resource Recovery Inc., 282
McKell Marketing Ltd., 285
Métropolitain Valve Inc., 288
Metrovan Hotsy Equipment Ltd., 288
Miceli & Frères Ltée, 288
MPI Drilling, 294
Mueller Canada, 295
Murray Krovats Agency Ltd., 295
Nardei Fabricators Ltd., 297
Neilson Excavation, 299
Neo Valves, 300
NORDIKeau Inc., 305
Opus DaytonKnight Consultants Ltd., 313
Ozocan Corporation, 315
P.J. Hannah Equipment Sales Corp., 315
Pall (Canada) Limited, 317
Parkson Corporation, 319
Pencon Equipment Co., 321
Phoenix Contact Ltd., 323
Pipe Specialties Canada, 325
Point Four Systems Inc., 326
Pompco Inc., 328
Precisioneering Ltd., 330
Pretal, 332
Products BCM Ltée BCM, 333
Promag Enviro Systems Ltd., 334
Pumps & Systems, 336
PWC Pure Water Corporation, 337
QuestAir Technologies Inc., 339
R&R Drilling Supply Ltd., 339
Radiodetection (Canada) Ltd., 341
Ramsay Machine Works Ltd., 342

Réal Huot Inc., 343
Resource Systems Inc., 345
Robar, 347
Sanexen Environmental Services Inc., 357
Sanitherm Engineering Limited, 357
SEW Eurodrive Co. of Canada Ltd., 364
Siemens Building Technologies, Ltd., 366
Siemens Water Technologies, 367
Sintra Inc., 369
Solinst Canada Ltd., 373
Stormceptor Canada Inc., 380
Sunergy Systems Ltd., 382
Sutherland-Schultz Inc., 384
Tank-Craft Ltd., 386
Technel Engineering Inc., 387
Teleflex Canada Ltd., 389
TLT Co-Vent, 396
TPE Technologies Inc., 399
Triangle Fluid Controls Ltd., 401
Urecon Ltée, 408
UV Pure Technologies, 408
V.J. Rice Concrete Ltd., 408
Val Temp Sales Ltd., 409
Velan Inc., 410
Venables Machine Works Ltd., 410
Victaulic Co. of Canada Ltd., 413
VIQUA - A Trojan Technologies Company, 413
Wastequip Cusco, 421
Water Conservation Company Ltd., 421
The Water Shed, 393
Waterloo Evaporateurs Inc., 422
Westburne Canada, 425
Westra & Associates Inc., 430
WSH Laboratories Ltd., 434
Wyckomar Inc., 434
York Fluid Controls Ltd., 435
Zazula Process Equipment Ltd., 436
Zurn Industries Limited, 437

Water, Wastewater & Groundwater Management (General)
See also Pollution Prevention Services; Water, Wastewater & Groundwater Equipment; Water, Wastewater & Groundwater Services; Waterways & Wetlands Management

ABBA Pump Parts & Service, 64
ABCO Industries Ltd., 64
Acres & Associated Environmental Ltd., 67
Activation Laboratories Ltd., 67
ADI Group Inc., 68
Advance Laboratories Ltd., 69
Advanced Environmental Water Technologies Inc., 69
AGRECOM inc., 73
AIM Environmental Group, 74
Air Products Canada Ltd., 75
Aker Metals (Toronto), 76
Aldworth Engineering Inc., 77
Alexander Boome Consulting Engineering, Ltd., 78
Alpha Controls & Instrumentation, 79
Applied Oxidation Technologies Inc., 87
Aqua Dam & Diversion Ltd., 87
Aqua-Plus, 88
Aqua-Tex Scientific Consulting Ltd., 88
Argo Protective Coatings Inc., 90
Armstrong Engineering & Land Surveying Inc., 91
Associated Engineering Group Inc., 94
Atlantic Purification Systems, 97
AWI, 99
AXOR Experts-Conseils Inc., 99
Beasy Nicoll Engineering Ltd., 104
Bernard Darveau Ingénieur, 105
BPR, 115
BRI International Inc., 116
Brisbin & Sentis Engineering Inc., 116
Bruce A. Brown Associates Limited, 117
Canadian Clay Products Inc., 124
Cansult Maunsell Limited, 127
Cartier Chemicals Ltd., 130
CBCL Limited, 132
CCS Income Trust, 133
Cecon Limited, 135
Century Environmental Services, 136
Clamex Environnement Inc., 142
Climate Control Systems Inc., 144
Cole-Parmer Canada Inc., 146

Subject Index

Conestoga-Rovers & Associates, 149
Conor Pacific Environmental Technology Inc., 150
Constant America Inc., 150
Cowater International Inc., 153
Dagex Inc., 156
Data Tech Environmental Services, 157
Decommissioning Consulting Services Limited, 159
Deschênes et Fils Ltée., 161
Dessau, Inc., 162
Dillon Consulting Ltd., 163
Droycon Bioconcepts Inc., 166
Eco-Guide International, 170
EEP Engineered & Environmental Products Inc., 173
Egmond Associates Ltd., 174
Electronic Warfare Associates - Canada, Ltd., 175
EMP Environmental Management & Protection Corporation, 177
Les Entreprises Forlam, 268
Environmental Training Institute, 186
Equipements Lapierre Inc., 189
Eriksson Sediment Systems Inc., 189
Experts-Conseils BMST inc., 192
Filter Innovations Inc., 195
FPInnovations, 200
Frontenac Environmental Ltd., 202
Global Facman Entreprises Inc., 213
Glos Associates Inc., 214
Golder Associates Ltd., 214
Graymont Inc., 216
Groupe Berlie-Falco Inc., 219
Groupe Deschênes, 219
Groupe GLD Inc., Experts-Conseils, 219
Le Groupe Sani Marc, 265
Groupe Stavibel Inc., 221
Hatch Ltd., 226
Hazard Control Systems Inc., 227
Hercules SLR Inc., 229
HETEK Solutions Inc., 230
Hydro Vision America, 236
Hydroxyl Systems Inc., 237
Integrated Explorations, 244
J.L. Richards & Associates Limited, 250
KGS Group Inc., 257
Levac Robichaud Leclerc Associates Ltd., 270
Loomers Pumping Services Ltd., 274
Mabarex inc., 277
Maple Engineering & Construction Canada Ltd., 279
Maple Reinders Environmental Ltd., 279
Meo & Associates Inc., 286
Mequipco Ltd., 286
MIE Consulting Engineers Ltd., 289
MIG Engineering Ltd., 289
MissionHGE inc., 291
NCL Envirotek Inc., 299
Nelson Environmental Inc., 299
Neo Valves, 300
Niagara Environmental Dynamics, 303
Niagara Water Conditioning Ltd., 303
Nova Magnetics Burgmann Ltd., 308
Nu-West Services Ltd., 309
Oakhill Environmental, 310
Omega Recycling Technologies, 312
Parkson Corporation, 319
Pelmar Engineering Ltd., 320
Phoenix Contact Ltd., 323
Piteau Associates, 325
Pollutech Group of Companies Inc., 327
Premier Tech Environnement / Division municipale, commerciale et ind, 331
Project Engineering Limited, 334
Provincial Environmental Services Inc., 335
Purifics ES Inc., 337
Pyradia Inc., 337
R.A. Murray International Limited, 340
R.J. Burnside & Associates Limited, 340
R.V. Anderson Associates Limited, 341
Roche ltée, Groupe-conseil, 348
RPR Environmental Inc., 353
SCG Industries Ltd., 358
Services industriels Newalta, 363
SNC-Lavalin Environment Inc., 371
SNC-Lavalin Group Inc., 371
Solmax International Inc., 373
Soper's, 374
Stantec Inc., 377
Statiflo Inc., 379

Sunset Solar Systems Ltd., 382
System Ecotechnologies Inc., 385
Terratec Environmental Ltd., 390
TetrES Consultants Inc., 391
Tinari Energy Management Services Inc., 396
Université du Québec, 406
URS Canada Inc., 408
UV Pure Technologies, 408
V. Fournier & Associates, 408
Warco Process Technologies, 416
Westhoff Engineering Resources Inc., 430
Whitman Benn Group, 431
WJF Instrumentation (1990) Ltd., 433
Wood Laboratory Ltd., 433
WorleyParsons Canada Ltd., 433
Zurn Industries Limited, 437

Water, Wastewater & Groundwater Services
See also Ground/Surface Water Monitoring; Ground/Surface Water Remediation; Measuring & Monitoring Services, Groundwater; Mechanical Contractors, Water & Wastewater; Sludge Processing & Treatment; Stormwater Consulting; Stormwater Management; Turnkey Plants, Water & Wastewater; Water & Wastewater Assessment; Water & Wastewater Consulting; Water & Wastewater Equipment Installation; Water & Wastewater Operations & Maintenance; Water & Wastewater System Design; Water, Wastewater & Groundwater Management (General)

A.C. Carbone Canada Inc., 63
Abydoz Environmental, 65
Acadia Consultants & Inspectors Ltd., 65
Active Chemicals Ltd., 67
AECOM Canada Ltd., 69
AIM Environmental Group, 74
Alexander Boome Consulting Engineering, Ltd., 78
Alpha Controls & Instrumentation, 79
ALTECH Environmental Consulting Ltd., 81
ALTECH Technology Systems Inc., 81
Altus Capital Planning Inc., 81
AMEC, 82
Apex Geoscience Ltd., 86
Aqua Terre Solutions Inc., 88
Aqua-Plus, 88
Aqua-Tex Scientific Consulting Ltd., 88
Armstrong Engineering & Land Surveying Inc., 91
Armtec Construction Products, 91
Associated Engineering Group Ltd., 94
Atlantic Purification Systems, 97
Baymag Inc., 103
BOMA Environmental & Safety Inc., 113
BPR, 115
BRI International Inc., 116
Brisbin & Sentis Engineering Inc., 116
Buchanan Environmental, 118
C.V. Environmental Services, 120
Cadman Power Equipment, 120
Cansult Maunsell Limited, 127
Catterall & Wright, 132
CENSOL Inc., 136
CH2M Hill Canada Limited, 137
Church & Trought Inc., 140
Conestoga-Rovers & Associates, 149
Conor Pacific Environmental Technology Inc., 150
Consolidated Giroux Environment Inc., 150
Consultants Mésar inc., 150
Craig Hydrogeologic Inc., 153
Deschênes Drilling Ltd., 161
Direct Separation Solutions, 164
EBA Engineering Consultants Ltd., 169
Egmond Associates Ltd., 174
El-Rayes Environmental Corp., 174
Elemental Research Inc., 175
EnGlobe Corp., 180
Entech Environmental Consultants Ltd., 181
Les Entreprises Forlam, 268
Envirochem Services Inc., 183
EnviroMetal Technologies Inc., 184
Eriksson Sediment Systems Inc., 189
eWaterTek Inc., 191
Experts-Conseils BMST inc., 192
Ferguson Simek Clark, 194
Filter Innovations Inc., 195
Fisher Environmental Ltd., 196
Flowmetrix Technical Services Inc., 197

Frappier & Génier Conseillers, 201
Fugro Airborne Surveys, 202
Fundy Engineering & Consulting Ltd., 203
GEA Westfalia Separator Canada, Inc., 205
Gemteck Environmental Software Ltd., 206
Genivar, 207
GPEC International Ltd., 215
Graymont Inc., 216
Groupe Séguin, 220
Groupe Teknika, 221
Hanna Instruments Canada Inc., 224
Hardy Stevenson & Associates, 225
HETEK Solutions Inc., 230
Hydromantis Inc., 237
IEG Consultants Ltd., 238
KGS Group Inc., 257
L&M Engineering Ltd., 261
Lupien Rosenberg Consultants Inc., 274
Maple Engineering & Construction Canada Ltd., 279
Matrix Solutions Inc., 282
Mequipco Ltd., 286
MIG Engineering Ltd., 289
Millennium Water Management Ltd., 290
Morrison Hershfield, 293
MR2-McDonald & Associates, 294
NCL Envirotek Inc., 299
Niagara Analytical Inc., 303
Niagara Water Conditioning Ltd., 303
Nouvelle Technologie (TEKNO) Inc., 308
Oakhill Environmental, 310
Piteau Associates, 325
Pomeroy Consulting Engineers Limited, 328
Precision Assessment Technology Corp., 330
Project Engineering Limited, 334
Proserco Inc., 335
PWC Pure Water Corporation, 337
R.V. Anderson Associates Limited, 341
Robicheau's Pumping Service, 348
ROMOR Atlantic Limited, 351
Sabatini Earth Technologies Inc., 354
SCC Environmental, 358
SCG Industries Ltd., 358
Schlumberger Water Services, 359
SENES Consultants Limited, 362
The Sernas Group Inc., 393
Simcoe Engineering Group Limited, 368
SNC-Lavalin Environment Inc., 371
Solinst Canada Ltd., 373
Stantec Inc., 377
Sunset Solar Systems Ltd., 382
Tecsult Inc., 388
Testwell Instruments, 391
Trimax Residuals Management Inc., 401
Trow Consulting Engineers Ltd., 403
UV Pure Technologies, 408
V. Fournier & Associates, 408
W.G. Shaw & Associates, 415
W.T. McGinn & Associates Ltd., 415
Wallace, Van Egmond Spankle Inc., 416
Wardrop Engineering Inc., 416
Westland Resource Group Inc., 430
Wood Laboratory Ltd., 433

Waterways & Wetlands Management
See also Resource Management Services (General); Water, Wastewater & Groundwater Management (General)

Acorus Restoration Native Plant Nursery, 67
AGO Environmental Electronics Ltd., 73
Aqua Dam & Diversion Ltd., 87
Archipelago Marine Research Ltd., 90
Bercan Environmental Resources Inc., 105
Brace Centre for Water Resources Management, 115
Canadian Benthic Ltd., 124
Canning & Pitt Associates Inc., 126
Cascade Environmental Resource Group. Ltd., 130
Cegerco - GCL Inc., 135
Chisholm, Fleming & Associates, 140
Coastal Ocean Associates Inc., 145
The Cord Group Ltd., 392
East Coast Aquatics, 169
ECL Envirowest Consultants Ltd., 170
Eco-Guide International, 170
Ecocern Inc., 171
Forest Technology Systems Ltd., 199

Subject Index

Harry Gamble Shipyard, 226
Hatfield Group, 226
Hiltz & Seamone Co. Ltd., 232
Hydro Vision America, 236
International Marine Salvage Inc., 245
KGS Group Inc., 257
LaCas Consultants Inc., 262
LGL Limited Environmental Research Associates, 271
Maccaferri Canada Ltd., 277
Nelson Environmental Services, 299
Oceans Ltd., 311
Offshore Design Associates Ltd., 311
Pol-E-Mar Inc., 327
Robertson Environmental Services Ltd., 348
Snowcap Waters Ltd., 371
Stedtnitz Maritime Technology Ltd., 379
Synex International Inc., 385
System Ecotechnologies Inc., 385
Taylor Mazier Associates, 387
Terminal City Iron Works Ltd., 389
Triton Consultants Ltd., 402
Vancouver Fraser Port Authority, 409
Via-Sat Data Systems, 413
Zbeetnoff Agro-Environmental Consulting, 436

Wildlife & Game Management
See also **Resource Management Services (General)**

Biorex Inc., 109
Cascade Environmental Resource Group. Ltd., 130
Cottonwood Consultants Ltd., 152
Dendron Resource Surveys Inc., 161
ECL Envirowest Consultants Ltd., 170
Ecocern Inc., 171
Geowest Environmental Consultants, 212
Le Groupe Leblond & Bouchard/Daniel Arbour et associes, 265
Halltech Environmental Inc., 224
Lane Environment Limited, 264
Lotek Wireless Inc., 274
Nelson Environmental Services, 299
Paul F. Wilkinson & Associates Inc., 319
Silvicon Services Inc., 368
SPG Hydro International Inc., 375
Symbion Consultants, 384
Triton Environmental Consultants Ltd., 402

Wind Energy Conversion
See **Energy Systems & Equipment, Alternate**

Wood & Wood Products, Recycled
See also **Recycled Products**

AIM Environmental Group, 74
CHEP Canada, 140
Eco Wood Products, 170
Gro-Bark (Ontario) Ltd., 218

Halford Pallet Recyclers Ltd., 224
Longwood Forestry Services Ltd., 273
Millar Western Forest Products Ltd., 290

Wood Conversion
See **Energy Systems & Equipment, Alternate**

Wood Recycling
See also **Organic Matter Recycling; Recycling Services (General)**

Andrews' Scenic Acres, 85
B.J. Bear Grain Company Ltd., 100
Canadian Eagle Recyclers, Inc., 124
Capital Environmental Resource Inc., 127
Eco Wood Products, 170
Galaxy Pallets Ltd., 204
Gro-Bark (Ontario) Ltd., 218
H. Broer Equipment Sales and Service, 223
Halford Pallet Recyclers Ltd., 224
Lake Charlotte Sanitation, 263
Northland Power, 307
Ontario Sawdust Supplies, 312
Priestly Demolition Inc., 332
Primex Packaging Services, 332
Waterloo Evaporateurs Inc., 422
Woodington Systems Inc., 433

Geographic Index

Alberta

Airdrie
Advanced Biotechnology Inc., 69
Double T Equipment Ltd., 165
United Safety Ltd., 406

Athabasca
West-Lock Fastener Corp., 425

Big Valley
Nature's Friend Environmental, 298

Bluffton
sonnevera international corp., 374

Bonnyville
Panther Environmental IInc., 317

Boyle
Alberta-Pacific Forest Industries Inc., 77
C F Reclamation & Fresh Water Services, 119

Brocket
Piikuni Utilities Corp., 323

Brooks
SmithBrook Waste Management Services Inc., 371

Bruderheim
Red Oak Industries Inc., 343

Calgary
AAA Petroleum Contracting Ltd., 64
Abandonrite, 64
Addy Environmental Services Inc., 68
AGAT Laboratories Ltd., 72
Alpine Environmental Ltd., 80
Alternative Fuel Systems (2004) Inc., 81
Amberg Corp. - Environmental & Regulatory Consultants, 82
AMEC, 82
AMETEK Process Instruments, 84
Antelope Land Services Inc., 86
Applied Aquatic Research Ltd., 87
ARAM Systems Ltd., 89
Ark Envirotech Inc., 91
Arpi's Industries Canada Ltd., 92
ATCO Group, 94
ATCO Power, 95
Aurora Environmental Consulting Ltd., 97
AWI, 99
Bayer CropScience, 103
Baymag Inc., 103
BECK Drilling and Environmental Services Ltd., 104
Bercha Group, 105
Biophilia Inc., 109
BioSolve of Canada Ltd., 109
Bissett Resource Consultants Ltd., 110
BP Canada Energy Company, 114
Brisbin & Sentis Engineering Inc., 116
BW Technologies by Honeywell, 119
C5 Plus Ltd., 120
Calgary Metal (1985) Ltd., 121
Calta Computer Systems Ltd., 122
Canadian Emissions Ltd., 124
Canadian Hydro Developers, Inc., 124
Canadian Petroleum Engineering Inc., 124
Canatec Consultants Ltd., 125
CanHemp Corporation, 126
Canwest Pumping Systems Ltd., 127
Capital H2O Systems Inc., 128
Capricorn Control Technologies Ltd., 128
Cardel Construction Ltd., 128
Carswell Consulting Engineers Ltd., 130
CB Engineering, Ltd., 132
CCR Technologies Ltd., 133
CCS Income Trust, 133
CEDA International Corporation, 135
Cetac-West, 137
CH2M HILL Canada Ltd., 137
Cheiron Resources Ltd., 139
Cirrus Environmental Services Inc., 141
Clean Air Services Inc., 142
Clearstone Engineering Ltd., 143

Climate Change Central, 144
Concept Controls Inc., 148
Cottonwood Consultants Ltd., 152
Curtis Environmental & Engineering Inc., 154
Cyntech Corporation, 155
Dalynn Biologicals Inc., 156
Danatec Educational Services Ltd., 156
Demers MetalFab Inc., 160
Diagnostic Engineering Inc., 163
dmg world media (Canada) Inc., 164
Dove Environmental Services Inc., 165
Drilling Fluids Treatment Systems Inc., 166
Eco Canada, 170
Elford Environmental, 175
Encana Corporation, 178
Engineered Air, 180
ENMAX Corporation, 181
Enviro Rentals, 182
EnviroGuard Ltd., 184
EnviroLine, 184
EnviroSORT Inc., 187
Envirotech Engineering, 187
Envision Planning Solutions Inc., 188
Fair Canada Engineering Ltd., 193
Faszer Farquharson & Associates Ltd., 194
Fluor Canada, 197
FMA Heritage Resources Consultants Inc., 198
FSI International Services Ltd., 202
Gas Liquids Engineering Ltd., 205
Global Engineering & Testing Ltd., 213
Graecam Incorporated, 216
Great Western Containers Inc., 216
Green Key Solutions Inc., 217
Greenland Corporation, 217
Hazco Environmental Services Ltd., 227
HFP Acoustical Consultants Corp., 231
Horton CBI Ltd., 233
HSE Integrated, 234
Hydroqual Laboratories Ltd., 237
Integrated Environments Ltd., 244
Interra Environmental Inc., 246
IRIS Environmental Systems Inc., 248
ITRES Research Ltd., 248
J.K. Engineering Inc., 249
Kaizen Environmental Services Inc., 254
Kang Construction Ltd., 255
KBL Land Use Consulting Ltd., 255
Keneco Environmental Services Inc., 256
Kinder Morgan Canada Inc., 257
Levy's Machine Works Ltd., 271
Matrix Solutions Inc., 282
Maxim Power Corp, 283
McAtee Safety & Environmental Health Services Ltd., 284
Mequipco Ltd., 286
Micro-Watt Control Devices Ltd., 289
Micrologic Inc., 289
Monitrex Engineering Ltd., 293
Movac Mobile Vacuum Services Ltd., 294
MWH Canada Inc., 295
N. Vandenassem & Associate, 296
Nardei Fabricators Ltd., 297
National Process Equipment Inc., 298
Navajo Metals, 298
Net Safety Monitoring Inc., 300
Newalta Corporation, 301
Newpark Environmental Services, 303
Noise Solutions Inc., 305
Normcan, 306
Nova Chemicals Corporation, 308
Nusco Supply & Manufacturing Inc., 309
O'Connor Associates Environmental Inc., 310
Oak Environmental Inc., 310
Paramount Emergency Planners Ltd., 318
Parkvalley Consulting Ltd., 319
Peco Filters Ltd., 320
Phoenix Engineering Inc., 323
Pildysh Technologies Inc., 323
Plasti-Fab Ltd., 326

Praxis Inc., 330
Promet Environmental Group Ltd., 334
ProPower Equipment Ltd., 335
R Plus Industries Alberta Inc., 339
Recyc-Haul Waste Management Inc., 343
RemedX Remediation Services Inc., 344
Remedy Energy Services Ltd., 344
Ridgeline Environment Inc., 347
Rotork Controls (Canada) Ltd., 352
Sabatini Earth Technologies Inc., 354
Schlumberger Oilfield Services, 359
SDS Drilling Ltd., 360
Sealtech Restorations Inc., 361
Shell Canada Limited, 365
Simark Controls Ltd., 368
Spring Air Silver Services Ltd., 376
Sprung Instant Structures Ltd., 376
SunBridge Wind Power, 382
Suncurrent Industries Inc., 382
Sustainable Energy Technologies Ltd., 383
Swiss Environment & Safety Inc., 384
Tang G. Lee Architect, 386
Tankman, 386
Tansley Associates Environmental Services, 387
Tera Environmental Consultants (Alta) Ltd., 389
Terasen Waterworks, 389
Terracon Geotechnique Ltd., 390
Terralog Technologies Inc., 390
Thimm Engineering Inc., 395
Thuro Inc., 396
TMK IPSCO Inc., 397
Tomark Compliance Centre, 397
TOR Geoscience Corp., 397
Total Combustion Inc., 398
Transalta Utilities, 400
Treeline Well Abandonment & Reclamation Ltd., 401
University Technologies International, 406
UNOTEC, 407
Val Temp Sales Ltd., 409
Vision Quest - TransAlta's Wind Business, 413
Vision Quest Windelectric Inc., 414
WDA Consultants Inc., 423
Well To Wire Emissions Control Inc., 424
Westech Industrial Ltd., 429
Western Canadian Spill Services Ltd., 429
Western Site Technologies Inc., 430
Westhoff Engineering Resources Inc., 430
Wiebe Environmental Services Inc., 431
WJF Instrumentation (1990) Ltd., 433
WorleyParsons Canada Ltd., 433
WORX Environmental Products Inc., 434
Wotherspoon Environmental Inc., 434
WSH Laboratories Ltd., 434
Zazula Process Equipment Ltd., 436

Camrose
HMI Hoyme Manufacturing Inc., 232

Cardston
Total Comfort Solution Inc., 398

Carseland
Gemini Twins Consulting Ltd., 206

Clyde
Amity Plastics Ltd., 84

Coaldale
MCR Environmental Consulting, 285

Cremona
Sunergy Systems Ltd., 382

Didsbury
Canadian Worcester Controls Ltd., 125

Drayton Valley
Byram Industrial Services Ltd., 119
Frey & Associates Engineering Ltd., 201
Western Solutions 2000 Ltd., 430

Edmonton
Acoustic Solutions Ltd., 67
Alberta Environmental Rubber Products Inc., 77
ALCO Gas & Oil Production Equipment Ltd., 77

Altamar International Inc., 81
AN-GEO Environmental Consultants Ltd., 84
Apex Geoscience Ltd., 86
Aquateck Ltd., 89
Associated Engineering Group Ltd., 94
Automatic Controls Ltd., 98
Bartle & Gibson Co. Ltd., 102
BCL Landview Systems Inc., 103
BDM Supply Limited, 103
Beulah Tec Limited, 106
Bowie Pumps of Canada Ltd., 114
Brytex Building Systems Inc., 117
Campbell Scientific (Canada) Corp., 122
Can-Cell Industries Inc., 123
Canadian Environmental Group, 124
Cat Tech Canada Company, 131
CCI Thermal Technologies Inc., 133
CenturyVallen, 136
Challenger Geomatics Ltd., 138
Clean Harbors Energy & Industrial Services Corp., 142
Cleanit Greenit Compost System, 143
Commercial Solutions Inc., 147
Corrpro Canada, Inc., 152
Custom Environmental Services Ltd., 154
Doherty's Hydraulic Oil Recycling, 164
Donald Olynyk, Acoustical Engineer, 165
Durex Steel & Alloy Industries Ltd., 167
Ecomark Ltd., 172
EDA Collaborative Inc., 173
EIL Environmental Services, 174
Enviro Scan Technologies Inc., 182
Enviropac Inc., 186
EnviroPower Equipment Marketing Inc., 187
EPA Certified Clean Ltd., 188
EPCOR Energy Services Inc., 188
Epsilon Chemicals Ltd., 189
ExTech Environmental Services Inc., 192
FCX NH Valves, 194
Fuller Austin Insulation Inc., 203
Geographic Dynamics Corp., 211
Geowest Environmental Consultants, 212
Global Dewatering Ltd., 213
Green Plan Ltd., 217
Habitat Studio & Workshop Ltd., 223
Halford Pallet Recyclers Ltd., 224
Hazard Alert Training & Supplies Canada Inc., 227
Hollimex Products Ltd., 232
Howell-Mayhew Engineering Inc., 234
Hydrogeological Consultants, 236
Insituform Technologies Ltd. - Edmonton, 242
Katch Kan Limited, 255
KBR Canada, 255
KC Environmental Group Ltd., 256
KPS & Associates, 260
Layfield Geosynthetics & Industrial Fabrics Ltd., 265
Lister Industries Ltd., 273
Lockerbie & Hole Contracting Ltd., 273
Lojen Industrial Cleaning Ltd., 273
McKell Marketing Ltd., 285
Millar Western Forest Products Ltd., 290
Mobile Augers & Research Ltd., 292
Nichols Applied Management, 304
Nichols Environmental (Canada) Ltd., 304
Nilex Inc., 304
Nor-Alta Environmental Services Ltd., 305
Norwesco Canada Ltd., 308
Pam Wight & Associates, 317
Panama Enterprises (1990) Inc., 317
Paragon Soil & Environmental Consulting Inc., 318
Parkes Scientific Canada Inc., 318
PBR Laboratories, 319
Pedocan Land Evaluation Ltd., 320
Petroleum Enviro Services, 322
Polar Bear Health Equipment Supplies, 327
Polyrama Plastics (1987) Ltd., 328
Power Ignition & Controls, 329

CANADIAN ENVIRONMENTAL RESOURCE GUIDE 2011-2012

Geographic Index

Precision Chemical Manufacturing Ltd., 330
Proeco Enviroservices Ltd., 333
Progress Land Services Ltd., 334
ProSolve Consulting Ltd., 335
Quality Fabricating & Supply Limited, 338
Research Electronics (Reselco) Ltd., 345
Rice Engineering & Operating Ltd., 346
Ronel Engineering Ltd., 351
Russell NDE Systems Inc., 354
Safety Plus Inc., 355
Spanach Construction Ltd., 375
Spencer-Lemaire Industries Ltd., 375
Sphag Sorb (Canada) Inc., 375
Stantec Inc., 377
T.D. ThermoDesign, 386
Tanks-A-Lot Ltd., 386
Thermo Design Engineering Ltd., 394
Titan Logix Corp., 396
Trimax Residuals Management Inc., 401
Triple M Fiberglass Mfg. Ltd., 401
Tyler Research Instruments Corp., 404
Visionwall Corporation, 414
Voice Construction Ltd., 414
Ward Chemical, 416
Waste Logic Inc., 417
Waterous Power Systems, 422
Wavefront Technology Solutions Inc., 423
Westworth Associates Environmental Ltd., 430
WHMIS Inc., 431
Williams Engineering Inc., 432
Williams Milton Roy, 432
Willowglen Systems Inc., 432
ZCL Composites Inc., 436
Zep Manufacturing Company of Canada, 436

Fairview
Northern Alternate Power Systems, 307
Roy Northern Environmental Ltd., 353

Fort Saskatchewan
Gallason Industrial Cleaning Services Inc., 204

Fox Creek
Kodiak Oilfield Services, 259

Grande Prairie
Northern Bridge and Mat Rentals Ltd., 307

High River
Jones Group Engineering Ltd., 253
Proline Filter Systems Inc., 334

Innisfail
Johns Manville Canada Inc., 253
LADEN Steel Fabricators Inc., 262

Irma
Az-Tec Reclaim Ltd., 100

Lethbridge
Agricultural Technology Centre, 73
Biantco Environmental Services Inc., 107
DBS Environmental, 158
Flexahopper Plastics Ltd., 196
Haul-All Equipment Ltd., 227
Irrigation Canal Power Co-operative Ltd., 248

Lloydminster
Universal Industries, 406

Lundbreck
Pat Dwyer Construction Inc., 319

Marwayne
Rubber Rock Resources, 354

Medicine Hat
Echo Environmental, 170

Nanton
Sun Prairie Organic, 382

Nisku
ACE Vegetation Control Service Ltd., 66
Alta-Fab Structures Ltd., 81
Can-K Artificial Lift Systems Inc., 123
GLM Tanks & Equipment Ltd., 213
MakLoc Buildings Inc., 279
The Recycle Systems Company Inc., 393

Olds
Sunmotor International Ltd., 382

Peace River
Enviro Waste Management Services Ltd., 182

Pincher Creek
Hi-Country Environmental Services Ltd., 231

Sinnott Farm Services Ltd., 369
Willms Construction Ltd., 432
Wind Power Inc., 433

Red Deer
Fluidcare Ltd., 197
HMI Industries, 232
Impact Environmental Services Ltd., 239
Pisces Environmental Consulting Services Ltd., 325

Rochester
Westra & Associates Inc., 430

Rocky Mountain House
Curtis Reclamation Service Ltd., 154
Sultech Consulting Ltd., 381

Sherwood Park
AC Environmental Services, 65
Digital Land Resources, 163
Paladin Environmental Consulting Services Ltd., 317

Slave Lake
Deuce Disposal Ltd., 162

Spruce Grove
Genics Inc., 207
Kanotech Information Systems Ltd., 255
Lea-Der Coatings (614248 Alberta Ltd.), 266
Michael Wall & Sons Enterprises Ltd., 288
Nelson Environmental Remediation Ltd., 299
Zell Oilfield Service Ltd., 436

Spruce View
Jodek Industries Ltd., 252

St Albert
Focus Industries, 198

St. Albert
Advanced Coolant Technologies Inc., 69
Muis Controls Ltd., 295

Swan Hills
Swan Hills Treatment Centre, 384

Taber
Gouw Quality Onions Ltd., 215

Thorhild
CP Environmental Technologies, 153

Torrington
Braymo Energy Corporation, 116

Vermilion
Gourley Construction Ltd., 215
Strata Environmental Ltd., 380

Water Valley
Frickie Creek Consulting Corp., 201

Wembley
Plan-it Environmental Consulting Ltd., 325

Wetaskiwin
Envirotech Nisku Inc., 188

Whitecourt
Infratech Corporation, 241
Mesa Forestry & Environmental Services Ltd., 287

Wimborne
Bristar Containment Industries Ltd., 117

British Columbia

Abbotsford
Conair Group Inc., 148
Condor Engineering Ltd., 149
Consolidated Envirowaste Industries Inc., 150
TerraLink Horticulture Inc., 390
Transform Compost Systems Ltd., 400
Westchem Mfg. Ltd., 429

Aldergrove
Ken Summers Biological Services, 256
Richmond Specialty Mushroom Farms Ltd., 346
Sealcon Liner Systems Inc., 361
Southwestern Flowtech & Environmental Ltd., 374

Bamfield
Canadian Benthic Ltd., 124

Blue River
Interior Weather Services Ltd., 245

Brentwood Bay
West Coast Spill Supplies Ltd., 424

Burnaby
AECOM Canada Ltd., 69
ALS Environmental, 80
Axford Agencies BC Ltd., 99
Ballard Power Systems Inc., 101
BC Air Filter Ltd., 103
BC Hydro, 103
Burnaby Bag & Burlap Ltd., 118
Cantech Inspections Ltd., 127
CD Nova, 134
Drexan Energy Systems Inc., 166
ECL Envirowest Consultants Ltd., 170
Ecofluid Systems Inc., 171
Eneready Products Ltd., 179
Energy Technology Products Ltd., 179
Finnex Agencies Ltd., 195
IPEC Industries Ltd., 247
Kerr Wood Leidal Associates Ltd., 257
Keystone Environmental Ltd., 257
Legend Power Systems Inc., 266
Maxxam Analytics Ltd., 283
MWA Consultants, 295
Next Environmental, 303
Pomeroy Consulting Engineers Limited, 328
Promag Enviro Systems Ltd., 334
QuestAir Technologies Inc., 339
SAR Engineering, 357
Silliker JR Laboratories, ULC, 367
Simon Fraser University, 368
Sprayaway Marine Services Ltd., 376
Sumas Environmental Services Inc., 381
TIR Systems Ltd., 396
Versatech Products Inc., 412
Web Engineering Ltd., 423
Wood Laboratory Ltd., 433

Campbell River
Coast Forest Management Ltd., 145
Ivey International Inc., 249

Castlegar
Western Bio Resources Consulting Ltd., 429

Chemainus
Target Recycling Inc., 387

Chilliwack
MEC Systems Inc., 286

Cobble Hill
Entara Consulting Services Ltd., 181

Coquitlam
Empire Dynamic Structures Ltd., 177
FWR Ecoresource Consultants Ltd., 203
Pacific Institute for Advanced Study, 316
RST Instruments Ltd., 354
Tinari Energy Management Services Inc., 396
Vanport Sterilizers Inc., 409

Courtenay
Walker Technologies Corporation, 416

Cranbrook
Armstrong Engineering & Land Surveying Inc., 91

Delta
Active Chemicals Ltd., 67
Airtest Technologies Inc., 76
E.H. Hanson Engineering Group Ltd., 168
Econotech Services Ltd., 172
Envirotech Pollution Controls Ltd., 188
MacPherson Brown Ltd., 278
Merlin Plastics Supply Inc., 287
Muddy River Technologies Inc., 294
Napier Environmental Technology, 296
P.J. Hannah Equipment Sales Corp., 315
Positive Results Environmental Management Ltd., 328
Premier Plastics Ltd., 331
Ross Healthcare, Inc., 351
SEI Industries Ltd., 362
Sinclair Technologies, 369
Talkie Tooter Canada Ltd., 386
Taylor Munro Energy Systems Inc., 387
Transcontinental Printing Inc., 400
Ultra-Chem Industries Ltd., 405
YES Environment Technologies Inc., 435

Enfield
Enfield, CT, USA, 110

Fanny Bay
Snowcap Waters Ltd., 371

Fort St John
Rudiger Enterprises Ltd., 354

Garibaldi Highlands
Nelson Environmental Services, 299

Kamloops
Kamloops Scrap Iron Ltd., 254
Northwest Metal Recycling, 307
Pyrotech Mfg. Corp., 337
Stewart Group, 379
Tankless Water Heater Company, 386
Urban Systems Ltd., 407
Weyerhaeuser Company Ltd., 430

Kelowna
Altek Power Corporation, 81
Enterprise Steel Fabricators Ltd., 181
Griffin Laboratories Corporation, 218
Happy Harry's Used Building Material, 225
Sphere Research Corp., 375

Kimberley
Aqua-Tex Scientific Consulting Ltd., 88
Thomson & Howe Energy Systems Inc., 395

Ladysmith
Applied Oxidation Technologies Inc., 87

Lake Country
Offshore Design Associates Ltd., 311

Langley
Alchemist Transport Inc., 77
Azco Industries Ltd., 100
Claus Engineering (1986) Ltd., 142
ECO Fuel Systems Inc., 170
ECO-TEK Ecological Technologies Inc., 171
KEDCO Constructors Ltd., 256
Mac Industrial Exhaust Shop, 277
N.A.T.S. Nursery Ltd., 296
New West Gypsum Recycling Inc., 301
Pioneer Envelopes Ltd., 325
Robertson Environmental Services Inc., 348
Thomson Technology Inc., 395

Lantzville
Bercan Environmental Resources Inc., 105

Lillooet
Landscope Consulting Corp., 264

Madeira Park
R.A. Campbell & Associates, 339

Maple Ridge
Ag EnviroTech Inc., 72
Mancorp Industrial Sales Inc., 279

Matsqui
Loewen Welding & Manufacturing Ltd., 273

Mission
Scott Resource Services Inc., 360

Nanaimo
Chatwin Engineering Ltd., 138
Inuktun Services Ltd., 246
PDK Projects Inc., 320

New Westminster
Interwest Property Services (1991) Ltd., 246
Orchid Cellmark ULC, 314

North Vancouver
Aqua-Guard Spill Response Inc., 88
Bancroft Western Sales Ltd., 101
Biopacific Diagnostic Inc., 109
Chartwell Consultants Ltd., 138
Counterspil Research Inc., 153
Elemental Research Inc., 175
Elmec Engineering Ltd., 176
Envirochem Services Inc., 183
International Bio-Recovery Corp., 245
JMB Research Ltd., 252
K-Tech Services Ltd., 254
Kaehne Consulting Ltd., 254
Northwest Occupational Health & Safety, 307
Opus DaytonKnight Consultants Ltd., 313
Pacific Environmental Consulting & Occupational Hygiene Services, 316
Piteau Associates, 325
Reliance Geological Services Inc., 344
Sanitherm Engineering Limited, 357
Seguro Projects Inc., 362
Southwell Controls Ltd., 374
Specialty Technical Publishers, 375
Via-Sat Data Systems, 413

Osoyoos
MGM Management, 288
Parksville
Koers & Associates Engineering Ltd., 259
Penticton
Gator International, 205
Valley Comfort Systems Inc., 409
Port Coquitlam
British Columbia, 88
BG Controls Ltd., 107
Dewar Pacific Projects Ltd., 162
Ellett Industries, 176
International Submarine Engineering Ltd., 245
Prince George
All-Wood Fibre Ltd., 79
D.R. Estey Engineering Ltd., 156
Environmental Dynamics Inc., 185
Industrial Forestry Service Ltd., 240
L&M Engineering Ltd., 261
Spectrum Resource Group Inc., 375
Richmond
AimGlobal Technologies Company, Inc., 74
Bacon Donaldson & Associates Ltd., 101
Canadian Fibre, 124
Catalyst Paper Corp., 132
Century Plastics Ltd., 136
CON-SPACE Communications Ltd., 148
Crown Packaging Ltd., 154
Delta Aerial Surveys Ltd., 160
Diacon Technologies Ltd., 163
DynaMotive Energy Systems Corporation, 167
Emergex Planning Inc., 176
Environmental Building Science Inc., 185
Graymont Inc., 216
Greenwind Power Corp., 218
I.G. Micromed Environmental Inc., 237
Industrial Marine Power Engineering Group, 240
IRC Integrated Resource Consultants Inc., 247
Levelton Consultants Ltd., 270
MacDonald, Dettwiler & Associates Ltd., 277
PHH ARC Environmental Ltd., 322
Point Four Systems Inc., 326
Polyland Industries Ltd., 328
Premier Envelope, 331
REDUCT & Lobbe Technologies Inc., 344
RICHWAY Environmental Technologies Ltd., 346
Rocky Mountain Environmental Ltd., 350
Slope Indicator Canada, 370
Teleflex Canada Ltd., 389
Triton Environmental Consultants Ltd., 402
Urban Impact Recycling Ltd., 407
Vancouver Gear Works Ltd., 409
Salmon Arm
Aqua Dam & Diversion Ltd., 87
DINOFLEX Manufacturing Ltd., 164
Ron Wedman Engineering Services, 351
Sidney
ASL Environmental Sciences Inc., 94
AXYS Analytical Services Ltd., 99
BCHazman Management Ltd., 103
ESI Environmental Sensors Inc., 189
G.A. Borstad Associates Ltd., 203
Quester Tangent Corp., 339
Ramsay Machine Works Ltd., 342
Slocan Park
Silva Forest Foundation, 368
Smithers
Silvicon Services Inc., 368
Squamish
Bass Engineering Systems Technology, 103
E.B. Tobe Enterprises, 168
Owen G. Carney Ltd., 315
Power-Pacific Poles Ltd., 329
Surrey
A. Lanfranco & Associates Inc., 63
Air Control Engineering Inc., 74
Air Phaser Environmental Ltd., 75
Alldec Trading Ltd., 79
Anex Distributors Ltd., 86
Aqua-Pak Styro Containers Ltd., 88
CanAsia Environmental & Engineering Ltd., 125
Cloverdale Paint Inc., 144
Dependable Turbines Ltd., 161
Ecotainer Sales Inc., 172
Electronics-recycling.com, 175
Fraser Environmental Services, 201
G3 Consulting Ltd., 204
Gough Risk Management Ltd., 215
Hazelmere Research Ltd., 228
Jubilee Rose Enterprises Ltd., 253
Kam Biotechnology Ltd., 254
Metrovan Hotsy Equipment Ltd., 288
New East Consulting Services Ltd., 301
Opcon Pacific Recycling Ltd., 313
Pacific Phytometric Consultants, 316
Polaris Corporate Services Inc., 327
Powertech Labs Inc., 329
Quad-Lock Building Systems Ltd., 338
Terminal City Iron Works Ltd., 389
Tri-Arrow Industrial Recovery Inc., 401
United Oil Services, 406
Wellons Canada, 424
Trail
ToxCo Waste Management Ltd., 399
Union Bay
Enviro Vault Ltd., 182
Vancouver
A.H. Lundberg Systems Ltd., 63
ACM Environmental Corporation, 66
Alexander Boome Consulting Engineering, Ltd., 78
AQUASOL EnviroTech Ltd., 89
Arrow Speed Controls Ltd., 93
ATD Waste Systems Inc., 95
Aurora Instruments Ltd., 98
Brown Strachan Associates, 117
C.G. Industrial Specialties, Inc., 119
Care First Aid Training Inc., 128
Catherine Berris Associates Inc., 132
CBR Products - Canadian Building Restoration Products Inc., 133
Coast Paper Ltd., 145
Coast River Environmental Services Ltd., 145
Communicopia.Net Internet Inc., 147
Conor Pacific Environmental Technology Inc., 150
Crossman Machinery Co. Ltd., 154
Dynamotive Energy Systems Corporation, 168
Earthcycle, 169
Eaton Hydro Developers Inc., 169
EBA Engineering Consultants Ltd., 169
El-Rayes Environmental Corp., 174
EmerGeo Solutions Inc., 176
Eneco Industries Ltd., 178
Envision Sustainability Tools, 188
EPI Environmental Products Inc., 189
Frederick Goertz Ltd., 201
Gandalf Consulting Ltd., 204
Gemcom Software International Inc., 205
Gemteck Environmental Software Ltd., 206
General Paint Ltd., 206
Hemmera Envirochem Inc., 229
InfoMine Inc., 241
Inproheat Industries Ltd., 242
InterLink Business Management Inc., 245
ISCA Management Ltd., 248
Island Clean Air Inc., 248
Klohn Crippen Berger Ltd., 258
Knight Piésold Ltd., 258
KPMG Performance Registrar Inc., 260
LaCas Consultants Inc., 262
Lea International Ltd., 266
McElhanney Consulting Services Ltd., 284
Mitsubishi Canada Ltd., 291
Nevin Sadlier-Brown Goodbrand Ltd., 300
Noram Engineering & Constructors Ltd., 305
Pacific Metals Recycling International, 316
Paradigm Environmental Technologies Inc., 318
Pottinger Gaherty Environmental Consultants Ltd., 328
Power Suction Services Ltd., 329
Poyry (Vancouver) Inc., 329
Precision Assessment Technology Corp., 330
Precision Identification Biological Consultants, 330
PricewaterhouseCoopers Management Consultants, 332
PWC Pure Water Corporation, 337
Raymond James Financial Inc., 342
Rescan Environmental Services Ltd., 345
Richard Kadulski Architect, 346
Robert Hornal & Associates Ltd., 348
Sandwell Engineering Inc., 356
Sanix Incorporated, 357
Sigma Engineering Ltd., 367
SLR Consulting Ltd. (Canada), 370
Sonic Environmental Solutions Inc., 373
Sonic Technology Solutions Inc., 374
SRK Consulting (Canada) Inc., 376
Suimon Engineering Canada Ltd., 381
Surpac Minex (Canada) Ltd., 383
SustaiNet Software Solutions Inc., 383
Syndel International Inc., 385
Synex International Inc., 385
Theodor D. Sterling & Associates Ltd., 393
Thurber Engineering Ltd., 395
Training & Development Services, 400
Triton Consultants Ltd., 402
TTA Technology Training Associates Ltd., 404
UMA Group Ltd., 405
URS Canada Inc., 408
Vancouver Fraser Port Authority, 409
Vizon SciTec Inc., 414
Westport Innovations Inc., 430
Willis Energy Services Ltd., 432
Xylon Biotechnologies Ltd., 435
Vernon
Behrick Enterprises Inc., 104
Tekmar Control Systems Ltd., 389
Victoria
Abbott Strategies, 64
AGO Environmental Electronics Ltd., 73
Archipelago Marine Research Ltd., 90
Avalon Mechanical Consultants Ltd., 98
C.E. Jones & Associates Ltd., 119
Carmanah Technologies Corp., 129
Forest Technology Systems Ltd., 199
Hydroxyl Systems Inc., 237
Jasco Research Ltd., 251
JB Laboratories Ltd., 251
North West Environmental Group, 306
Pinch Group, 324
Plastichem Consulting, 326
PRT Inc., 336
Secter Environmental Resource Consulting, 361
Sundog Energy Management, 382
Sylvametrics Consulting, 384
Wakefield Acoustics Ltd., 416
Western Subsea Technology Ltd., 430
Westland Resource Group Inc., 430
West Vancouver
ACDEG International Inc., 66
Avani Oxygen Water Corporation, 98
Barrat & Associates Inc., 101
Entech Environmental Consultants Ltd., 181
Environmental Plastics Advisory Service, 185
Hatfield Group, 226
Kent Engineering Inc., 256
P.J.B. Duffy & Associates, 316
Raging River Power & Mining Inc., 341
Whistler
Cascade Environmental Resource Group. Ltd., 130
White Rock
Entropic Energy Inc., 182
Enviro-Klean Technologies Inc., 182
Environmental Consultants & Engineers, 185
R.U. Kistritz Consultants Ltd., 341
Zbeetnoff Agro-Environmental Consulting, 436
Williams Lake
earthRight Solar Products, 169
Winfield
AGM Steel Industries Ltd., 73

Manitoba

Brandon
Wesman Salvage, 425
Dufresne
Talon Projects Inc., 386
Gimli
Kraftur Engineering Inc., 260
Minnedosa
Prairie Geomatics Ltd., 330
Morden
Huron Window Corporation, 235
Pinawa
Acsion Industries Inc., 67
Aquatic Life Ltd., 89
ECOMatters Inc., 172
Portage la Prairie
Westest, 430
Selkirk
K.T. Enviro Clean Inc., 254
St. Andrews
DGH Engineering, 162
Steinbach
Earthbound Environmental Inc., 168
Winnipeg
Air Movement Services Ltd., 75
Airmaster Sales Ltd., 75
Appin Associates, 87
BOMA Environmental & Safety Inc., 113
Border Chemical Company Ltd., 114
Cengea Solutions Inc., 136
CML Northern Blower Inc., 144
The Conserver Group Inc., 391
Cypher International Ltd., 155
Dalco Wastewater Specialists Inc., 156
Emerge Knowledge Design Inc., 176
Energy Conservation Contractors Warranty Corporation, 179
Expert Systems Inc., 191
Faraci Engineering, 194
FEMCO International, 194
FIRETAK Manufacturing Ltd., 195
Flett Research, 196
Flush Quip, 198
Fort Garry Industries Ltd., 199
Fort Storage Warehousing & Distribution, 200
Friesen Tokar Architects, Landscape & Interior Designers, 201
General Scrap Partnership, 206
Guertin Brothers Coatings and Sealants Ltd., 222
Hilderman Thomas Frank Cram & Associates, 232
Ininew Project Management Inc., 241
J.R. Cousin Consultants Ltd., 250
Kemel Cartons (1973) Ltd., 256
KGS Group Inc., 257
Kraus Global Inc., 260
Malnar Industries Ltd., 279
The MEP Environmental Products Ltd., 392
MEP Environmental Products Ltd., 286
Mesh Technologies Inc., 287
Miller Environmental Corp., 290
Monsanto Canada Inc., 293
Murray Krovats Agency Inc., 295
The National Testing Laboratories Ltd., 393
Nelson Environmental Inc., 299
Nordevco Associates Ltd., 305
North/South Consultants Inc., 306
NSF-ISR, 309
Phason Electronics, 322
SEG Engineering Inc., 362
SMS Engineering Ltd., 371
Solar Solutions Inc., 372
Symbion Consultants, 384
TetrES Consultants Inc., 391
Unies Limited, 405
Vansco Electronics Ltd., 409
Westeel, 429
Western Industrial Services Ltd., 429
Western Scrap Metals, 429
Westland Plastics Ltd., 430
Winds & Voices Environmental Services Inc., 433
WRS Environmental, 434

New Brunswick

Charlo
Consolidated Giroux Environment Inc., 150
Dieppe
Lantech Drilling Services Inc., 264
R&R Drilling Supply Ltd., 339
Dipper Harbour

Geographic Index

Craig Hydrogeologic Inc., 153
Dorchester
Atlantic Industries Ltd., 95
Fredericton
Acer Environmental Services Ltd., 66
ADI Group Inc., 68
ARC Geobac Group Inc., 89
Buchanan Environmental, 118
CARIS, 128
Conestoga-Rovers & Associates, 149
D. Besner & Associates Inc., 155
Electric Motor Service (1979) Ltd., 174
Elmtree Environmental Ltd., 176
Envirem Technologies Inc., 182
Fenco Shawinigan Engineering Limited, 194
Glenn Group Ltd., 213
H. Pickard & Associates, 223
Hydro-Com Technologies Ltd., 236
Impact Microbiology Services, 239
J.W. Bird & Company Ltd., 250
Keywood Entreprises Ltd., 257
Maritime Microbiologicals Inc., 281
Opus International Consultants (Canada) Ltd., 313
Project Engineering Limited, 334
RPC, 353
Terratlantic Engineering Ltd., 391
Varcon Inc., 409
Whisco Ltd., 431
Hanwell
Birchwood Environment Management Inc., 109
Redstone Associates Ltd., 343
Harvey York Co
Natech Environmental Services, 297
Knowlesville
TeraWind Ltd., 389
Lincoln
Forest Protection Limited, 199
McLeods
Cyr Engineering Ltd., 155
Minto
NB Coal Limited, 299
TRACC (NB), 400
Miramichi
Sutherland Excavating Ltd., 384
Moncton
Acadia Consultants & Inspectors Ltd., 65
Apex Industries Inc., 86
Atlantic Industrial Services, 95
Crandall Engineering Ltd., 153
Enerplan Consultants Ltd., 179
Fero Waste & Recycling Inc., 195
Gevity Group Inc., 212
Greystone Energy Systems Inc., 218
N-T Enterprise Inc., 296
Neighborhood Recycling, 299
Nestlé Purina PetCare, 300
Touchie Engineering, 399
Petitcodiac
Maritime Geothermal Ltd., 280
Quispamsis
DPL Group, 166
Eastern Wind Power Inc., 169
Richibucto
The Paint Recycling Company, 393
Riverview
Maritime Ultrasonic Cleaning Inc., 281
Rothesay
Atlantic Air Cleaning Specialists Ltd., 95
Rusagonis
Ken Noftell Drilling Services, 256
Saint John
Barrett Sales Ltd., 102
Barrington Industrial Services Limited, 102
Canada Water Supply Ltd., 123
Fundy Engineering & Consulting Ltd., 203
Godfrey Associates Ltd., 214
Irving Forest Services Limited, 248
Maritime Soil Ltd., 281
MDI Waste Management Inc., 285
Ocean Steel & Construction Ltd., 311
Promens Canada Inc., 334
Regional Petroleum Products Recycling Ltd., 344
St. George Power LP, 356
SCG Industries Ltd., 358
Saint-Quentin
Deschênes Drilling Ltd., 161
Sainte-Marie-de-Kent
Explore Plus Duct Cleaning Ltd., 192
Shediac Bridge
Major Water Treatment Tech Ltd., 279
Shippagan
Coastal Zones Research Institute Inc., 145
St Stephen
Flakeboard Company Ltd., 196
Sussex
Eastern Environmental Services Ltd., 169
Energy Systems & Design Limited, 179

Newfoundland & Labrador

Arnolds Cove
IMTT-Newfoundland Ltd., 239
Bauline
Connections Research, 150
Bishop's Falls
Hi-Point Industries (1991) Ltd., 231
Conception Bay South
D.G. Taylor Inc., Consulting Ecologist Division, 156
Corner Brook
Atlantic Engineering Consultants Ltd., 95
Burden Management & Design Ltd., 118
Corner Brook Pulp & Paper Ltd., 152
Deer Lake
EDM Consultants Ltd., 173
Gander
Cecon Limited, 135
Labrador City
Iron Ore Company of Canada, 248
Mount Pearl
Abydoz Environmental, 65
ASCO Canada, 93
BAE Newplan Group Ltd., 101
BSM North America, 118
Compusult Limited, 148
EnviroMed Detection Services, 184
Municipal Recyclers Ltd., 295
Watson Petroleum Services Ltd., 423
St. John's
Canning & Pitt Associates Inc., 126
Community Resource Services Ltd., 147
Cormorant Ltd., 152
Crosbie Industrial Services Ltd., 153
Dominion Recycling Ltd., 165
EITNL/Earth Information Technologies (nfld) Limited, 174
Elliott & Elliott Limited Consulting Engineers, 176
Ever Green Recycling, 191
Fabcon Canada Ltd., 193
Fugro Jacques GeoSurveys Inc., 203
InCoretec Inc., 240
Infotech Canada Inc., 241
JFA James Floyd Associates Ltd., 252
Kavanagh & Associates Ltd., 255
LEM Laboratory Inc., 267
McNamara Construction Company, 285
Medina Construction Limited, 286
Memorial University of Newfoundland, 286
Newfoundland Design Associates Limited, 302
Oceans Ltd., 311
Provincial Airlines Ltd. - Environmental Services Division, 335
PSC Analytical Services, 336
Quality Matters Inc., 338
Roley Construction, 350
SCC Environmental, 358
Seacom International Inc., 361
Servco Environmental Solutions Inc., 363
SGE Hatch Ltd., 364
Sterling Press, 379
Tract Consulting Inc., 400

Northwest Territories

Inuvik
IEG Consultants Ltd., 238
Yellowknife
Char Developments Ltd., 138
Ferguson Simek Clark, 194

Nova Scotia

Amherst
DRL Environmental Services, 166
Jack Atkinson & Associates, 250
Novapet Inc., 308
Antigonish
A.H. Roy & Associates Ltd., 64
C.J. MacLellan & Associates Inc., 120
W.G. Shaw & Associates, 415
Beaverbank
Gerry Brushett Enterprises Limited, 212
Bedford
ALL-TECH Environmental Services Ltd., 78
Atlantic Wind Power Corp. Ltd., 97
BGR Oilfield Services Incorporated, 107
Envirosoil Ltd., 187
Kel-Ann Organics, 256
Pridy Associates, 332
Strum Environmental, 381
Trihedral Engineering Limited, 401
Berwick
Annapolis Valley Peat Moss Co. Ltd., 86
EFR Disposal, 173
Marbicon Inc., 280
Boutiliers Point
Coastal BioAgresearch Ltd., 145
Bridgetown
East Coast Aquatics, 169
H.E. Bent Services Ltd., 223
V.J. Rice Concrete Ltd., 408
Bridgewater
Everts-Lind Enterprises, 191
Brookfield
Fundy Compost Inc., 203
Chezzetcook
Advance Laboratories Ltd., 69
Cleveland
Sun Ross Energy Systems Ltd., 382
Coldbrook
Hiltz & Seamone Co. Ltd., 232
Dartmouth
ABL Environmental Consultants, 65
Aluma Systems Inc., 82
Argo Protective Coatings Inc., 90
Atlantic Orient Canada Inc., 96
Atlantic Purification Systems, 97
Barrington Environmental Services, 102
Beasy Nicoll Engineering Inc., 104
Bebbington Industries, 104
Blue Water Agencies Ltd., 110
Bruce Sutherland & Associates Ltd., 117
Caster-Rack Systems Ltd., 131
Civtech Engineering & Surveying Ltd., 141
Coastal Ocean Associates Inc., 145
Cobham Tracking & Locating Ltd., 145
Connor Architects & Planners, 150
The Cord Group Ltd., 392
Dartmouth Appliance Repair, 157
Dartmouth Metals & Bottles Ltd., 157
Datarite, 157
Digicon Building Control Solutions, 163
DSS Marine Inc., 167
Duerden & Keane Consultants Inc., 167
Environmental Disposal Concepts Inc., 185
Envirosystems Inc., 187
Focal Technologies Inc., 198
FracFlow Consultants Inc., 201
Great Northern Recycling Inc., 216
Guild Contracting Specialists Inc., 222
Harbour Metal Recycling Ltd., 225
Hercules SLR Inc., 229
Horizons Systems Group Inc., 233
Hydraulic Systems Inc., 235
Hydro Dyne Inc., 236
IMP Liquid Meters & Petroleum Services, 239
K&D Pratt Group Inc., 254
King Metal Fabricators Ltd., 258
Land & Sea Environmental Consultants Ltd., 264
Laserworks Computer Services, 264
Maritime Paper Products Ltd., 281
Maritime Testing Ltd., 281
Metocean Data Systems Limited, 287
Metrographic Green Print, 287
Millennium Water Management Ltd., 290
Morgan Falls Power Company, 293
New Trend Environmental Services, 301
Nova Magnetics Burgmann Ltd., 308
OCL Services Ltd., 311
ODIM Brooke Ocean, 311
Oldham Engineers Inc., 312
Petromax Ltd., 322
Pharmatox Inc., 322
Pylon Electronics, 337
Refrigerant Services Inc., 344
Ribbons Recycled Inc., 346
ROMOR Atlantic Limited, 351
Scotia Recycling Ltd., 358
SEA Engineering Company Inc., 360
Seaforth Engineering Group Inc., 361
SRT Soil Remediation Technologies, 377
Thermo Dynamics Ltd., 394
Waste Resource Containers, 420
The Water Shed, 393
Debert
Lasec Enterprises Ltd., 264
Newmac Manufacturing Inc., 303
Dutch Brook
G. Landry Vacuum Services Ltd., 203
Edwardsville
Green Island Recycling Ltd., 217
Elmsdale
Atlantic Poly Liners Inc., 97
BioSource Solutions Inc., 109
Hy-Grade Geoscience, 235
Fall River
Chemical Safety Training Associates, 139
Resource Systems Inc., 345
Falmouth
Environova Planning Group Inc., 186
Glace Bay
Pembroke Environmental Services Ltd., 320
Goodwood
Halifax C&D Recycling, 224
New Era Farms Ltd., 301
Halifax
AERDE Environmental Research, 71
Atlantic Acoustical Associates, 95
B.D. Rae Waste Management, 100
BH Engineering Systems Ltd., 107
Bio-Limno Research & Consulting, 107
Canadax Industrial Group Limited, 123
Canadian Fishery Consultants Ltd., 124
CBCL Limited, 132
CEF Consultants Ltd., 135
Clean Air & Water Centre, 142
Eagle Home Inspection Services Inc., 168
Eastcan Geomatics, 169
EDM Environmental Design & Management Ltd., 173
Enerscan Consultants Limited, 179
Enviro-Care Services, 182
EOA Scientific System Inc., 188
F.C. O'Neill, Scriven & Associates Ltd., 193
G.R. Kelly Environmental Services, 203
Geomarine Associates Ltd., 211
Greenfield Research Inc., 217
Griffiths Muecke Associates, 218
Harris & Roome Supply Limited, 225
Hydro-Mechanical Sales Ltd., 236
Hyperspectral Data International Inc., 237
Lane Environment Limited, 264
MacDonnell Group, 277
MacMillan & Associates, 278
Marriotts Container Rental Ltd., 281
Martec, 281
Natural Forces Technologies Inc., 298
Nova Scotia Power, an Emera Company, 308

Geographic Index

O'Halloran Campbell Consultants Limited, 310
Praxis Environmental, 330
R.A. Murray International Limited, 340
R.H. Loucks Oceanology, 340
Renovators Resource Inc., 345
Sable Offshore Energy Inc., 354
Sanders Resource Manage Inc., 356
Satlantic, 358
Scales Bioresource Consulting Ltd., 358
Vemco Ltd., 410
Whitman Benn Group, 431
William Alexander & Associates Ltd., 432

Hantsport
Minas Basin Pulp & Power Company Limited, 290

Hubley
Trecan Combustion Ltd., 400

Kemptown
Northeastern Resource Recovery Ltd., 307

Kentville
Crown Fibre Tube Inc., 154
Kemic Bioresearch Laboratories Ltd., 256
Valley Waste Resource Management, 409

Kingston
Loomers Pumping Services Ltd., 274

Lake Charlotte
Lake Charlotte Sanitation, 263

Lakeside
Atlantic Environmental Training & On-Site Services Inc., 95

Lantz
Shaw Precast Solutions, 365

Lower Sackville
Enviro Waste Ltd., 182
Healthy Homes Consulting, 228
Hi-Q Developments Ltd., 231

Lunenburg
ABCO Industries Ltd., 64

Mahone Bay
Bigfoot Systems Inc., 107
Reinforced Plastic Systems Inc., 344

Merigomish
Atlantic Soils & Associated Management Ltd., 97

Mount Uniacke
Harris Industrial Testing, 226

New Glasgow
W.R. Graham Services Ltd., 415

Port Hawkesbury
Stora Enso North America, 379
Strait Engineering Ltd., 380

Porters Lake
Canadian Seabed Research Ltd., 125

Shubenacadie
Scotia Plastics, 360

St Andrews
Scott & Stewart Forestry Consultants, 360
Taylor Mazier Associates, 387

Stellarton
MacLeod & Grant Ltd., 278

Stewiacke
EPS Wood Products Ltd., 189
Logan Geotech Inc., 273

Sydney
AB Mechanical Ltd., 64
AIC Sullivan's Environmental Services, 73
Conway Disposal Ltd., 151
Linpro Petroleum Services Ltd., 272
Lynk Electric Ltd., 276
Rawdon Technologies Ltd., 342
Seaboard Industrial Supply Co. Ltd., 361
Sydney Environmental Resources Ltd., 384

Tatamagouche
Environmental Structures, 186
Inform Consulting Services Ltd., 241

Thorburn
Red Devil Drain Service, 343

Truro
BP Trading Ltd., 114
The Enviro-Connect, 392
Horner Associates Limited, 233
Inland Technologies Inc., 242

Interforest Inc., 244
KnowTech Environmental Inc., 259
L&M Feed Services, 261
Maritime Auto Salvage, 280
N.L. Sobey & Associates Limited, 296
RenuWater Centre, 345
Thompson Engineering Consultants Ltd., 395

Tusket
Robicheau's Pumping Service, 348

Waverley
Enviro Clean Ltd., 182
Power Vac of Nova Scotia, 329

Whycocomagh
Envirotray Ltd., 188

Windsor
EEP Engineered & Environmental Products Inc., 173
Envirosphere Consultants Ltd., 187
Nu-Air Ventilation Systems Inc., 309
ProAgri Consulting Limited, 333
Renewable Energy Services Inc., 345

Wolfville
EnvironChem Engineering Consultants, 184
LJM Environmental Consulting, 273

Yarmouth
Hurlburt Construction Limited, 235

Nunavut

Lewiston
Lewiston, NY, USA, 110

Niagara Falls
Canrom Photovoltaics Inc., 126

Ontario

Acton
EcoTec Environmental Consultants Inc., 172
TankTek Environmental Services Ltd., 386

Ajax
Ashland Canada, 93
Con-Test, A Division of Contamination Containment Technology Inc., 148
Dagex Inc., 156
Eco-Tec Ltd., 171
Environmental Waste International, 186
Henry Kortekaas & Associates Inc., 229
J&F Waste Systems Inc., 249
Lennox Drum Ltd., 267
Mondo Products Company Limited, 292
National Waste Services, 298
Ontario Building Solutions, 312
PCB Disposal Inc., 319
Plastiglas Industries Limited, 326
Septo-Clean Co. Ltd., 363

Alexandria
Recyclage Alexandria Recycline (Équipe), 343

Alliston
Oetiker Limited, 311

Almonte
Biomation, 108
Mississippi River Power Corp., 291

Ancaster
Activation Laboratories Ltd., 67
Envirotech Associates Limited, 187
INCOM Manufacturing Group, 240
Integra Environmental Inc., 243

Arnprior
Utility Risk Management Ltd., 408

Arthur
All Treat Farms Limited, 78

Aurora
Blower Engineering Inc., 110
Industrial Scientific Corporation, 241
Universal Filter Media, 406
Winchurch Environmental Inc., 432

Aylmer
H. Broer Equipment Sales and Service, 223

Ayr
Aevitas Inc., 72
Aevitas Inc., 72

Ventax Robot Inc., 410

Baden
Living Resources Inc., 273
Systems Plus, 385

Barrie
Arbrux Limited, 89
Bentofix Technologies Inc., 105
Busch Systems International Inc., 118
Egetec Enterprises Inc., 174
Environmental Reporting Systems Limited, 186
International Water Supply Ltd., 245
Joe Johnson Equipment Inc., 252
Loraday Environmental Products Ltd., 274
McNair & Marshall Planning & Development Consultants, 285
Mueller Canada, 295
Napoleon Appliance Corp., 297
Northway-Photomap Inc., 307
Procyon Consulting Inc., 333
QCA Laboratories Inc., 337
R.G. Robinson & Associates (Barrie) Ltd., 340
Scicorp Systems Inc., 359
Skelton Brumwell & Associates Inc., 369
Troy-Ontor Inc., 404
2R Services Inc., 404
Versatech Industries Inc., 412

Bayfield
RAM Lining Systems Inc., 342

Beamsville
Adkinson & Associates, 68
Pacwill Environmental, 317

Belleville
Interface FLOR Commercial, 244
SEAL-OGIC Innovations Corp., 361
Triangle Fluid Controls Ltd., 401

Bethany
Niblett Environmental, 304

Bolton
Maratek Environmental Inc., 280
W.B. Beatty & Associates, 414

Bothwell
Comptank Corp., 147
Harold Marcus Ltd., 225
Lovell & Associates, 274

Bowmanville
Ron Robinson Limited, 351

Bracebridge
Bracebridge Generation Ltd., 115
Muskoka Containerized Services Ltd., 295

Bradford
Cathy's Crawly Composters, 132

Brampton
AADCO Automotive Inc., 64
Accuworx Inc., 66
Aircraft Appliances & Equipment Ltd., 75
Alfa Plastics Inc., 78
Alpha Industrial Services, 79
Brampton Engineering Inc., 115
Buckhorn Canada Inc., 118
Canadian Eagle Recyclers, Inc., 124
Clear Environmental Products, 143
ClearView Geophysics Inc., 143
The DATA Group of Companies, 392
Daybar Industries Ltd., 158
Degussa Canada Inc., 159
Dundas-Jafine Inc., 167
EMP Environmental Management & Protection Corporation, 177
Frontenac Environmental Ltd., 202
GET Industries Inc., 212
IG Machine & Fibers Ltd., 238
Industrial Plastics Fabricators Ltd., 240
Industrial Thermo Polymers Ltd., 241
Integrated Catalyst Engineering Inc., 244
John Thurston Machine Ltd., 253
KMK Consultants Limited, 258
Komline-Sanderson Ltd., 259
Kraemer Tool & Manufacturing Co. Ltd., 260
Lennox Industries (Canada) Ltd., 267
Lexcan Industrial Supply Ltd., 271
Maple Engineering & Construction Canada Ltd., 279

Master Builders Technologies Ltd., 282
Mirus International Inc., 290
Monserco Ltd., 293
Nu-Plast Polymers International, 309
Ogilvie Scientific Inc., 311
Ontario Environmental Training Consortium, 312
Para Paints, 318
Pilot Performance Resources Management Inc., 324
Plant Products Co. Ltd., 326
Plast-Ex International Inc., 326
Powersmiths International Corp., 329
PPG Canada, Inc., 330
SEW Eurodrive Co. of Canada Ltd., 364
SHAL Consulting Engineers Ltd., 365
SSI Schaefer Systems International Ltd., 377
SunOpta, 382
Tarandus Associates Limited, 387
Terex Ltd., 389
Thermo Electric (Canada) Ltd., 394
Triple M Metal, 402
Trivar Inc., 402
Trow Consulting Engineers Ltd., 403
Venture Foam Products Inc., 411
Waste Management of Canada, 417
York Fluid Controls Ltd., 435

Brantford
Abcott Construction Ltd., 65
Anthrafilter Media & Coal Ltd., 86
Bowser Technical Inc., 114
Brantford Disposal Service, 115
Capital Environmental Resource Inc., 127
Crane Energy Flow Solutions, 153
Dekka Resins Inc., 159
Farris Industries Canada, 194
Flowserve Canada Corp. - Pump Division, 197
Genor Recycling Services, 209
Lakeland Protective Wear Inc., 263
Rawdon Industries Ltd., 342
Smart Turner Pumps, 370
Waterford Group, 422

Breslau
C3 Environmental Group, 120
Canbar Inc., 126
Safety-Kleen Canada Inc., 355

Brockville
Bowie Environmental Edge Management & Assessment Ltd., 114
Chromatographic Specialties Inc., 140
Douglas, Barwick Inc., 165
Outokumpu Technology Ltd., 315
Racal Protection Canada, 341

Brooklin
Brooklin Concrete Products Ltd., 117

Burford
Home Hardware Stores Ltd., 232

Burlington
ABBA Pump Parts & Service, 64
Aqua Tech Sales & Marketing Inc., 88
Atotech Canada Ltd., 97
ATS Scientific Inc., 97
Canadian Portable Structures (1992) Ltd., 125
Career Advancement Employment, 128
Century Environmental Systems, 136
Comstock Canada Ltd., 148
Cutler-Hammer Canada, 154
D. Greenfield Associates Ltd., 156
Dedicated Plastic Tanks Inc., 159
DJA Environmental Consultants Inc., 164
Eco Waste Solutions, 170
Ecodyne Ltd., 171
Endress+Hauser Canada Ltd., 178
Fanchem Ltd., 193
FLIR Systems, Inc., 197
Focus Environmental Group Inc., 198
G & G Computer Services, 203
G.I. Russell & Co. Ltd., 203
GEA Westfalia Separator Canada, Inc., 205
Greenflow Environmental Services Inc., 217
Heron Instruments, 230
Hoskin Scientific Ltd., 233
Interprovincial Corrosion Control Co. Ltd., 246
Investigative Science Inc., 247
Jetvac Inc., 251

Geographic Index

Kernic Systems Inc., 257
Leon's Insulation, 267
M.R. Gordon Consulting Inc., 276
Mar Cor Purification, 280
Marsh Instrumentation Inc., 281
MAUSER, 283
Metropolitan Consulting Inc., 288
Millar-Williams Hydronics Ltd., 290
Nalco Canada Co., 296
Norjohn Transfer System Limited, 305
Overwatch Consulting, 315
Pioneer Petroleums, 325
Plasma Environmental Technologies Inc., 326
Robert J. Redhead Limited, 348
SatCon Power Systems (Canada), 358
Staveley Services Canada Inc., 380
Strasser Alloy Steels Ltd., 380
T-G Burgmann, 385
Tanknology Canada Inc., 386
360 Energy Inc., 395
Transcontinental Energy Saving Products Inc., 400
VQUIP Inc., 414
Waste Services (CA) Inc., 420
Waterline Environmental Inc., 422
Zephyr North, 437
Zeton Inc., 437
Zimmark Inc., 437

Caledon
Fulton Engineered Specialties Inc., 203
RSP International Inc., 354

Caledon East
Sandhill Disposal & Recycling Inc., 356
Sea Scan International Inc., 361

Cambridge
Air Solutions Inc., 75
Babcock & Wilcox Canada Ltd., 100
Cambridge Materials Testing Limited, 122
Comcor Environmental Limited, 146
Dimplex North America, 164
Ecotech Planners & Advisors Inc., 172
Efficiency Engineering Inc., 173
Enervac Corp., 180
Hot Zone Training Consultants Inc., 233
Hotsy Pressure Washers Ltd., 233
JKM Custom Fabricating Ltd., 252
Maccaferri Canada Ltd., 277
MCC Industrial Services Ltd, 284
McCordick Glove & Safety Inc., 284
N.R. Murphy Ltd., 296
Pegasus Industrial Specialties Inc., 320
Rapid-Eau Technologies, 342
Ray Electric Ltd., 342
Recovery Technologies Inc., 343
Rockwell Automation Canada Inc., 349
Sutherland-Schultz Inc., 384
Transchem Inc., 400
Trux Route Management Systems Inc., 404
Twin Falls Limited Partnership, 404
Waterloo Concrete Products, 422
Worldware Enterprises Ltd., 433
Woznuk Brothers Ltd., 434

Camlachie
Omega Public Works, 312

Campbellville
CanDetec Inc., 126
justenvironment, 254

Carp
GeoInsight Corporation, 211
Goulbourn Stittsville Sanitation Ltd., 215
Water & Earth Science Associates Ltd., 421

Cayuga
Norm Shropshall & Sons Ltd., 305

Centralia
Dashwood Industries Ltd., 157

Chalk River
Bubble Technology Industries Inc., 118

Chatham
Cunningham Sheet Metal Works Inc., 154
David A. McLean & Associates, 158
Guspro Inc., 223
Honey Electric Ltd., 233
Veolia ES Canada Industrial Services Inc., 411

Cobourg
Torrie Smith Associates Inc., 398

Cochrane
M.J. Labelle Co. Ltd., 276

Colborne
Gary Steacy Dismantling Limited, 204

Collingwood
Ainley Group, 74
Greenland International Consulting Inc., 218
Organic Farm Services, 314

Concord
Accurate Industrial Waste Limited, 66
All Waste Removal Inc., 78
Allan Fyfe Equipment Limited, 79
Alliance Envelope Ltd., 79
Blue-Zone Technologies Inc., 110
Canadian Drives Inc., 124
Canberra Company, 126
Clean Earth Solutions Ltd., 142
Comenco Systems Inc., 147
DCL International Inc., 158
Eco Wood Products, 170
Electro-Air Canada, 174
Envision Compliance, 188
Eurovac, 191
Five Seasons Comfort Limited, 196
General Filtration, 206
Gratec Ltd., 216
H2Flow Equipment Inc., 223
ICI Paints (Canada) Inc., 238
Institute of Environmental Research Inc., 243
M.J. International Inc., 276
Magnetrol International Ltd., 278
MDS Sciex, 285
Metcon Sales & Engineering Ltd., 287
Nolar Industries Ltd., 305
Optech Inc., 313
OZZ Corporation, 315
Pribusin Inc., 332
Quebecor World Concord, 338
R.A. Kirby Sales Inc., 339
Radiodetection (Canada) Ltd., 341
Ronco Protective Products, 351
Royal Envelope Ltd., 353
Scintrex Ltd., 360
Smith-Way Ltd., 371
Sonic Soil Sampling Inc., 374
T.D. Rooke Associates Ltd., 385
Toromont Caterpillar, 397
Toromont Energy Ltd., 398
Unisearch Associates Inc., 405
York Disposal Service Ltd., 435

Cookstown
Dol Hydroseeding Inc., 164
Verdyol Mulch of Canada Ltd., 412

Cornwall
M.S. Thompson & Associates Ltd., 276
Material Resource Recovery Inc., 282
Thompson Rosemount Group, 395

Courtland
Cadman Power Equipment, 120

Delaware
Historica Research Limited, 232

Delhi
Delhi Industries Inc., 115

Dresden
Babcock Supply Ltd., 100

Dundalk
Rubicon Environmental Inc., 354

Dundas
Alan A. Smith Inc., 76
Anderson Water Systems, 85
M&L Testing Equipment (1995) Ltd., 276
Rothsay, 352
Wilkinson Heavy Precast Ltd., 431
William Dam Seeds Ltd., 432

Eden Mills
Charles Simon Architect & Planner, 138

Eganville
Stedtnitz Maritime Technology Ltd., 379

Elmira
B.J. Bear Grain Company Ltd., 100

NextEnergy Inc., 303
Plein Disposal, 326
Sittler Environmental, 369
Sittler Excavating Ltd., 369

Elora
Compost Management, 147

Erin
Southern Ontario Waste Inc., 374

Fergus
Integrated Resource Management, 244

Fisherville
CIAL Group, 141

Flamborough
Sensible Life Products, 362

Fonthill
Environmental Training Institute, 186

Fort Erie
Niagara Environmental Dynamics, 303
Sherwin-Williams Canada Inc., 365

Frankford
Flowmetrix Technical Services Inc., 197

Freelton
Benson Chemicals Limited, 105

Gananoque
West Point Products Canada, 424

Georgetown
Caledon Laboratory Chemicals Inc., 121
E2 Management Corporation, 168
Egmond Associates Ltd., 174
Hamworthy-Peabody Combustion Canada Inc., 224
Leferink Transfer Ltd., 266
Markland Specialty Engineering Ltd., 281
Parish Geomorphic Ltd., 318
Solinst Canada Ltd., 373
Testwell Instruments, 391
Wallace, Van Egmond Spankle, 416

Gilford
Canadian Environmental Auditors Inc., 124

Glen Williams
Blackbox Automation Inc., 110

Gloucester
Archer Chemical, 90
Boucher Precast Concrete Ltd., 114
Comfort King Doors & Windows Ltd., 147
Lacombe Waste Services, 262
Presentey Engineering Products Ltd., 331

Gormley
Barenco Inc., 101
Cannington Group, 126
J.R. Tinderblox, 250
RAM Forest Products Inc., 342
Restoration Environmental Contractors - Restoration Consultants, 346
Thermo Electron Corp., 394

Guelph
Agri-Food Laboratories, 73
AquaTox Testing & Consulting Inc., 89
Armtec Construction Products, 91
Bioforj Environmental Services, 108
BIOREM Inc., 109
Con Cast Pipe, 148
Cyanide Destruct Systems Inc., 155
Dougan & Associates, 165
ENPAR Technologies Inc., 181
Gamsby & Mannerow Ltd., 204
Gasmac Inc., 205
GlobalTox International Consultants Inc., 213
Guelph Chemical Laboratories, 222
Halltech Environmental Inc., 224
Hammond Manufacturing, 224
Huntsman Corporation Canada Inc., 235
Insitu Contractors Inc., 242
Integrated Explorations, 244
Integrated Metal Products, 244
Jes-Chem Ltd., 251
JTU Consulting, 253
Labtronics, 262
LEX Scientific Inc., 271
Mandel Scientific Co. Inc., 279
Pan Tec Inc., 317

Petrozyme Technologies Inc., 322
Process Innovations Canada Inc., 333
ProMinent Fluid Controls Ltd., 334
Puresource Inc., 337
Quatic Industries Inc., 338
Recyclenet Corporation, 343
Rowan Williams Davies & Irwin Inc., 352
RWDI AIR Inc., 354
UPI Inc., 407
Venerus International Purification Inc., 410
VIQUA - A Trojan Technologies Company, 413
Walinga Inc., 416
Wenvor Technologies Inc., 424
Wyckomar Inc., 434

Hagersville
Hagersville Recycling & Auto Wrecking Ltd., 223

Haley
Haley Industries Ltd., 223

Halton Hills
Andrews' Scenic Acres, 85
Hayward Gordon Ltd., 227

Hamilton
Advanced Environmental Water Technologies Inc., 69
ArcelorMittal Dofasco, 90
Bio-Software Inc., 108
C V Environmental Services, 119
C.V. Environmental Services, 120
Canadian Liquids Processors Limited, 124
Forsythe Lubrication Associates Ltd., 199
Hamilton Community Energy, 224
HEC Group, 228
Hotz Environmental Services Inc., 233
Hydro-Logic Environmental Inc., 236
Hydromantis Inc., 237
Insituform Technologies Ltd. - Hamilton, 242
JNE Consulting Ltd., 252
KBU Environmental Technologies Inc., 255
Lafarge Dundas Quarry, 262
Life Rhythm Corporation, 272
LURA Consulting, 275
M+A Environmental Consultants, 276
Machine Knife Co., 278
Maddocks Industrial Filter Division, 278
McKerlie Solar Systems, 285
Octagon Environmental Services, 311
Onyx Chemical Cleaning, 313
Philip Doyle Manufacturing Inc., 323
Poscor Group, 328
Provincial Environmental Services Inc., 335
Rondar Inc., 351
Samco Resources & By-Products, 356
Solid Waste Reclamation Inc., 372
Soper's, 374
Spill Management Inc., 376
Sterling Power Systems, 379
TEAM-1 Environmental Services Inc., 387
Terratec Environmental Ltd., 390
Transway Systems Inc., 400
UniFold Shelters Ltd., 405
Universal Handling Equipment Company Limited, 406

Holland Landing
Ontario Sawdust Supplies, 312

Honey Harbour
Monster Polymers Inc., 293

Huntsville
Lord & Partners Ltd., 274

Ingleside
DBC Environmental Services Ltd., 158
Telamode, 389

Innerkip
Greatario Industrial Storage Systems Ltd., 217

Jordan Station
Champion Moyer Diebel, 138

Kanata
BMT Fleet Technology Ltd., 111
Control Microsystems, 151
Robinson Consultants Inc., 348
Safety Projects International Inc., 355

Keswick
Bryco Environmental, 117

Geographic Index

Kettleby
Priestly Demolition Inc., 332
Kincardine
Canadian Soil & Climate Protection Corp., 125
Vestas Canada, 413
King City
Durmitor Inc., 167
eWaterTek Inc., 191
LGL Limited Environmental Research Associates, 271
Zephyr Alternative Power, 437
Kingston
Brendar Environmental Inc., 116
Caduceon Environmental Laboratories, 120
Clean Ontario, 143
Earthworks Technology Inc., 169
GAIA Power Inc., 204
Geocor Engineering Inc., 210
Kimco Steel Sales Limited, 257
Malroz Engineering Inc., 279
Pipe Specialties Canada, 325
Robinson Solutions, 348
Kingsville
Esco Engineering, 189
Kitchener
AET Group Inc., 72
Canadian Water Conditioning Inc., 125
Eco2 Systems Inc., 171
Enermodal Engineering Ltd., 179
F.E. Myers, 193
Folio Instruments Inc., 199
FS Partners, 202
Joseph & Co. Inc., 253
Kentain Products Ltd., 256
Morval, 294
MTE Consultants Inc., 294
Naylor Engineering Associates Ltd., 298
Optikon Corp. Ltd., 313
Parameter Control Ltd., 318
Planning & Engineering Initiatives Ltd., 325
Shaver Industries Inc., 365
LaSalle
Meo & Associates Inc., 286
Leamington
Climate Control Systems Inc., 144
Lindsay
Lindsay Iron & Metal Inc., 272
Lions Head
Sky Generation, 369
Little Britain
DEL Warehousing Inc., 160
Lively
Rocvent Inc., 350
London
Atkinson, Davies Inc., 95
Aware Learning Technologies, 99
Bartley Silver Co. Inc., 102
BOS Engineering & Environmental Services Inc., 114
C.J. Pink Ltd., 120
CEM Specialties Inc., 135
Dell Tech Laboratories Ltd., 160
Emco, 176
Enviro-Met Engineering, 183
GAP EnviroMicrobial Services Inc., 204
Hassco Industries Inc., 226
Hazard Control Systems Inc., 227
HETEK Solutions Inc., 230
John Zubick Ltd. Scrap Metals, 253
KMW Systems Inc., 258
Matrix Photocatalytic Inc., 282
Mayer Heritage Consultants Inc., 284
Nexus Solutions Inc., 303
Nimbus Water Systems, 304
Oakside Chemicals Ltd., 311
Parklane Computer Systems, 319
Pepper Compressed Air & Gas Ltd., 321
Peter T. Mitches & Associates Limited; Project Managers & Consulting, 321
Purifics ES Inc., 337
Sciencetech Inc., 359
Sendex Environmental Corp., 362

Sleegers Engineering Inc., 370
Solcan Ltd., 372
Spriet Associates London Ltd., 376
Tank-Craft Ltd., 386
3M Canada Company, 395
Trojan Technologies Inc., 402
Try Recycling Inc., 404
2cg Inc., 404
Zodiac Fabrics Inc., 437
Long Sault
Greyline Instruments Inc., 218
Mansfield
Cogent Environmental Solutions Ltd., 146
Maple
Anco Chemicals Inc., 85
Fabco Plastics Wholesale (Ontario) Limited, 193
Fabricated Plastics Ltd., 193
Markham
AiMS Environmental, 74
Alpha Controls & Instrumentation, 79
Associated Tube Industries, 94
BPG Graphics Solutions, 114
Brosz & Associates, 117
Can-Aqua Inc., 123
Cansult Maunsell Limited, 127
Cheminfo Services Inc., 139
Chisholm, Fleming & Associates, 140
Clintar Groundskeeping Services, 144
Combustion & Energy Systems Ltd., 146
Control Techniques Drives Inc., 151
Corrosion Service Company Limited, 152
Delcan Water, 160
Double Industries & Trading, 165
Emerson Electric Canada Limited, 177
Emery International Developments, 177
Fisher Environmental Ltd., 196
Frank T. Ross & Sons Ltd., 201
GE Multilin, 205
Generation PV Inc., 207
Hanna Paper Fibres Ltd., 224
Intersciences Inc., 246
Macrotek Inc., 278
Miller Waste Systems, 290
Napier-Reid Ltd., 297
Ordan Thermal Products Ltd., 314
Parsons Commercial Technology Group Inc., 319
Seeker Green Products Ltd., 361
Siemens Water Technologies, 367
Silliker Canada Co., 367
SRB Controls Inc., 376
Tertec Enterprises Inc., 391
Toshiba of Canada Ltd., 398
U.S. Filter/Asdor Ltd., 405
Vanbots Construction Corp., 409
Water Pik Canada, 422
Maxville
MacEwen Petroleum Inc., 277
McGregor
Countryside Disposal Service Ltd., 153
North Shore Management Systems Inc., 306
Meaford
WPI Safety & Environmental Consultants, 434
Merrickville
Professional Resources Inc., 334
Millgrove
Rose Mechanical Water Systems Inc., 351
Milton
Aimco Solrec Ltd., 74
CENSOL Inc., 136
Roxul Inc., 353
Semco Systems Limited, 362
Wheelabrator Canada Co., 431
Mississauga
Adventus Canada Inc., 69
Aearo Canada Ltd., 69
Aeroflo Inc., 71
Air Products Canada Ltd., 75
Airzone One Ltd., 76
AKZO Nobel Chemicals Ltd., 76
Alan Willis & Associates, 76
Alnor Industries Ltd., 79
Amaircare Corporation, 82
Ambler & Co. Inc., 82

Applied Groundwater Research Ltd., 87
Ashtead Technology Rentals, 93
Auto-Chlor Inc., 98
Aysix Technologies, 100
BASF Canada Inc., 103
BDR Machinery Ltd., 103
Becquerel Laboratories Inc., 104
The Beer Store, 391
BEX Engineering Limited, 106
Blowmoulding Technologies Inc., 110
BOC Canada Limited, 111
Boojum Research Ltd., 113
Bradford White Canada Inc., 115
BRI International Inc., 116
Brim Pumps & Systems Ltd., 116
Brincad Technologies Inc., 116
Broan Canada Ltd., 117
BSI Management Systems Canada Inc., 118
Canadian Paper Recyclers, 124
Canadian Safety Equipment Inc., 125
Cancoppas Limited, 126
Canon Canada Inc., 126
CanTox Environmental Inc., 127
Carlo Gavazzi (Canada) Inc., 128
Carrier Canada Ltd., 129
Cascades Resource, 131
Castle Building Centres Groups Ltd., 131
Cemcorp Ltd. Consulting Engineers, 135
Central Reproductions Ltd., 136
Chemcorp Industries Inc., 139
Chemical Emission Management Services, 139
Chemspec Inc, 140
CHEP Canada, 140
Cleartech Industries Inc., 143
CMD Insurance Services Inc., 144
CompreVac Inc., 147
Contor Terminals Inc., 151
Crompton Technology Inc., 153
Cues Canada, 154
Dakins Engineering Group Ltd., 156
Danfoss Inc. - Hydronic Heating Division, 157
Diagnostix Ltd., 163
Draeger Safety Canada Ltd., 166
DuPont Canada Inc., 167
e3 Solutions Inc., 168
Educational Program Innovations Centre, 173
Entech Laboratories, 181
Enviro Wood Recovery Systems Ltd., 182
Environmental Advisory Group, 185
Environmental Biodetection Products Inc., 185
Environmental Solutions Remediation Services, 186
ESRS Environmental Solution, 190
ETV Canada, 190
Exova, 191
Extox Industries Inc., 192
Fielding Chemical Technologies Inc., 195
Franz Environmental Inc., 201
Fugro Airborne Surveys, 202
G.T. Wood Co. Ltd., 204
Gemite Products Inc., 206
Genzyme Canada Inc., 210
Geodetic Software Systems/Geomatics Information Center, 211
Geonics Limited, 211
Global Sensor Systems Inc., 213
Golder Associates Ltd., 214
Green Turtle Technologies Ltd. (Canada), 217
Greenbridge Management Inc., 217
Guardian Industries Canada Corp., 222
H.L. Blachford Ltd., 223
Hatch Ltd., 226
Hewlett Packard (Canada) Co., 230
HGC Engineering, 231
Honeywell Ltd., 233
Hunter & Associates, 235
Hydrogenics Corporation, 236
ICC The Compliance Center Inc., 238
ICC The Compliance Centre Inc., 238
IMO Pump Inc., 239
Impro, 239
Inco Technical Services Limited, 239
Interbath of Canada Ltd., 244
IPAC Inc., 247
Jenike & Johanson, Ltd., 251

JFM Environmental Ltd., 252
John Brooks Company Ltd., 252
John McMullen & Associates, 252
Kafko Manufacturing Ltd., 254
Kinetics Noise Control Inc., 257
Kleinfeldt Consultants Limited, 258
Knowaste LLC, 259
Konica Minolta Business Solutions (Canada) Inc., 259
Konica Minolta Business Solutions (Canada) Ltd., 259
KSB Pumps Inc., 261
KWH Pipe, 261
Kyocera Mita Canada Ltd., 261
L&K International Training, 261
L.W. Ward Limited, 261
Leeson Canada Inc., 266
LTS Sales Ltd., 274
MacAuley Group Ltd., 277
Maple Reinders Environmental Ltd., 279
Masternet Ltd., 282
Maxxam Analytics Inc., 283
Merley Chains Ltd., 287
Metro Recycling, 287
MKG Imaging Solutions Inc., 291
Mold & Bacteria Consulting Laboratories (MBL) Inc., 292
Morrison Environmental Limited, 293
MSU Mississauga Ltd., 294
Multiview Locates Inc., 295
National Energy Equipment Inc., 297
Nature's Environmental Products Inc., 298
NCR Canada Ltd. - Systemedia Division, 299
NEDCO, 299
Nederman Canada Inc., 299
Neo Valves, 300
Neptune Technology Group (Canada) Ltd., 300
Nett Technologies, 300
Nilfisk-Advance Canada Company, 304
Nordic Systems Corporation, 305
Ontario Waste Materials Exchange, 312
Optimira Controls, 313
Ortech Environmental Inc., 314
OSB Services, 314
Osram Sylvania Ltd., 314
Pall (Canada) Limited, 317
Panasonic Canada Inc., 317
Peel Scrap Metal Recycling Ltd., 320
Petro Laboratories Inc., 322
Petro-Canada Lubricants, 322
Phoenix Biomedical Products Inc., 323
Phoenix Contact Ltd., 323
Pigmalion Environmental Services Group, 323
Pinchin Environmental Ltd., 324
Plasticair Inc., 326
PlymoVent Canada Inc., 326
Praxair Canada Inc., 330
Primex Packaging Services, 332
Provincial Partitions Ltd., 335
QSDM Inc., 338
QUASAR, 338
Rayovac Canada Inc., 342
Raypak Canada Ltd., 342
Refined Specialty Chemicals Inc., 344
Ricoh Canada Inc., 347
RMS Instruments Ltd., 347
RP Graphics Group, 353
Safety Express Ltd., 355
Schneider Electric Canada Inc., 359
Schwank Group, 359
Scott Tank Cleaning Co. Ltd., 360
ServiceMaster of Canada, 363
Servicestat Ltd., 363
SGS Canada Inc., 364
Sharp Electronics of Canada Ltd., 365
Sheldons Engineering Inc., 365
Siemens Building Technologies Ltd., 366
Silex Innovations Inc., 367
SimplexGrinnell, 368
Smiths Detection, 371
Sonepar Canada, 373
Soren Construction Ltd., 374
SPD Sales Ltd., 375
SpilKleen, 375
Sprecher + Schuh Inc., 376

Geographic Index

SRP Control Systems Ltd., 377
Straub Tadco Inc., 380
Summa Engineering Ltd., 381
Survalent Technology Corporation, 383
Taco Canada Ltd., 386
Techint Goodfellow Technologies Inc., 387
Temprite Industries Ltd., 389
Terratechnik Environmental Limited, 391
Thermal Technics Corporation, 394
Thor Global Enterprises Ltd., 395
Total Safety Canada Inc., 399
Trellcan Rubber Ltd., 401
Trivalent Data Systems Ltd., 402
Universal Drum Reconditioning Company, 406
Vacuum Products Canada Inc., 408
Varian Canada Inc., 410
VWR International, LLC, 414
Wainbee Limited, 415
Wardrop Engineering Inc., 416
Waterra Pumps Limited, 423
Waters Limited, 423
Watson & Associates Economists Ltd., 423
Watson Process Systems, 423
Weir Power & Industrial, 424
Westburne Canada, 425
Wynn's Canada Ltd., 435
Yugo-Tech, 435
Zorbit Technologies Inc., 437
Zurn Industries Limited, 437

Moffat
Birks Co., 110

Morrisburg
Eckel Industries, 170

Napanee
Continental Conveyor Ontario Ltd., 151
Prescott Paper Products Inc., 331

Neebing
Frank's Alternate Energy, 201

Nepean
Estco Battery Management Inc., 190
Fluorosense Inc., 198
Lapp-Hancock Associates Limited, 264
Mike Fuller Electric Ltd., 289
Pol-E-Mar Inc., 327
Thermal Energy International Inc., 394
Thermotech Windows Ltd., 394

New Liskeard
Settlement Surveys Ltd., 364

Newmarket
Alaron Instruments Inc., 76
AquaMetrix Inc., 88
Canada Composting Inc., 123
Envirogineering, 184
HMO Limited, 232
ITM Instruments, 248
Jagger Hims Limited, 250
Lotek Wireless Inc., 274
Management Horizons, 279
Momentum Conveyors, 292
Multi-Stage Filter, 295
Romatec Incorporated, 350
Veolia Water Canada, 412
Versatile Measuring Instruments Inc., 412

Niagara Falls
Business Funding Group Inc., 119
Flexo Products Ltd., 196
Greif Bros. Canada Inc., 218
Niagara Analytical Inc., 303
Niagara Energy Products Limited, 303
Niagara Recycling, 303
Niagara Water Conditioning Ltd., 303
Power Grow Systems Inc., 329

Niagara on the Lake
Firing Industries Ltd., 195

North Bay
Anrep Krieg Desilets Gravelle Ltd., 86
Boart Longyear Inc., 111
Bolger and Associates Ltd., 113
Near North Laboratories Inc., 299
Notre Development Corp., 308

Oakville
Algonquin Power Income Fund, 78
Arjay Engineering Ltd., 91
Bennett Environmental Inc., 105
Bigelow-Liptak of Canada, 107
Can-Am Instruments Ltd., 122
Can-Ross Environmental Services Ltd., 123
CanadianEnvironmental.com, 125
Davis Controls Ltd., 158
Demesa Inc., 160
Dionex Canada Limited, 164
Emco Wheaton Corp., 176
Enmet Canada Inc., 181
Enviro-Sol Plus, 183
GE Water & Process Technologies, 205
Globetron Controls Inc., 214
GPEC Global Corp., 215
Grundfos Canada Inc., 221
Hooper Welding Enterprises Ltd., 233
Inscan Contractors (Ontario) Inc., 242
JM Science Canada Inc., 252
Kodiak Environmental Limited, 259
L.E. Washington Sales Ltd., 261
LaserNetworks Inc., 264
Levitt-Safety Limited, 270
Light Solar Wind Manufacturing, 272
LINPAC Ropak Packaging, 272
Lubrication Engineers of Canada Ltd., 274
Novitherm Canada Inc., 309
Orwak Waste Systems Inc. - Canada, 314
Pencon Equipment Co., 321
Petro Sep Membrane Technologies Inc., 322
Plastics America, 326
Pollutech Group of Companies Inc., 327
Power Plant Supply Co., 329
Prism Chemicals Inc., 332
Rochester Midland Ltd., 349
Schlegel Canada Inc., 359
Shred-It, 366
Solarmart, 372
XCG Consultants Ltd., 435

Oldcastle
Proto Manufacturing Ltd., 335

Orangeville
Long Environmental Consultants, 273
R.J. Burnside & Associates Limited, 340
Symplastics Ltd., 385
Triton Engineering Services Ltd., 402

Orillia
FLSmidth Canada Ltd., 197
Performance Fluid Equipement Inc., 321

Orleans
Mr. Gas Ltd., 294
Thermo-Cell Industries Ltd., 394
Valley Associates Inc., 409
Viridis Environmental Inc., 413

Orono
Cimatec Environmental Engineering Inc., 141

Osgoode
Canada Heat Pumps, 123

Oshawa
Callrich Eco Services Inc., 122
Powerscreen of Canada Ltd., 329
Rayplex Limited, 342

Ottawa
Accutest Laboratories Ltd., 66
Adhawk Communications Inc., 68
Agrodev Canada Inc., 73
Aqua Terre Solutions Inc., 88
Armstrong Monitoring Corp., 91
Assaynet Canada Inc., 94
Buchan, Lawton, Parent Ltd., 118
Dytown Marine Ltd., 110
CadhamHayes Systems Inc., 120
The Cadmus Group, 391
Cal's Eco Depot, 121
Canspect Corporation, 127
CertainTeed Insulation Canada, Inc., 137
COGENCanada, 146
Cowater International Inc., 153
DB Geoservices Inc., 158
The Delphi Group, 392
Dendron Resource Surveys Inc., 161
Diane Beckett, 163
EcoVu Analytics, 173
Electronic Warfare Associates - Canada, Ltd., 175
EMS Technologies, 178
Energy Ottawa, 179
EnRel Energy Group, 181
Epistream Consulting Inc., 189
Export Development Canada, 192
Fisher Scientific Ltd., 196
Geosolutions Consulting Inc., 212
Global Change Strategies International Co., 213
Goss Gilroy Inc., 215
GPEC International Ltd., 215
Heritage Research Associates Inc., 230
Hickling Arthurs Low Corp., 231
HurterConsult Inc., 235
Indoor Air Quality Ottawa, 240
Instantel, 243
Intera Engineering Inc., 244
Iogen Corp., 247
J.L. Richards & Associates Limited, 250
Laser Diagnostic Instruments International Inc., 264
Lecompte Engineering Ltd., 266
The Lowe-Martin Group, 392
Mansfield & Rodney Printing Ltd., 279
Marbek Resource Consultants Ltd., 280
Michael Holliday & Associates, 288
Montrose Technologies Inc., 293
NEK Environmental Technologies Inc., 299
Notra Inc., 308
Ottawa Engineering Ltd., 315
Paracel Laboratories Ltd., 318
Pylon Electronics Inc., 337
Quatrosense Environmental Ltd., 338
RBR Ltd., 343
SAIC Canada, 355
Seprotech Systems Inc., 363
SL Ross Environmental Research Ltd., 370
Stratos Inc., 380
TerraChoice Environmental Marketing, 390
Tomlinson Environmental Services, 397
W.F. Baird & Associates Coastal Engineers Ltd., 415
whatIf? Technologies Inc., 431

Owen Sound
Edwards, 173
Henderson Paddon & Associates Ltd., 229
Incinolet Products, 239
Nature's Mate Distribution Inc., 298
New World Generation Inc., 301

Paris
Kappler Canada, 255
Lotowater Technical Services Inc., 274
The St. George Co. Ltd., 393

Peterborough
Buckham Transport Ltd., 118
D.M. Wills Associates Limited, 156
Enviro-Pack Material Handling, 183
Enviro-Solutions Ltd., 183
Geo-Logic Inc., 210
The Greer Galloway Group Inc., Engineers & Planners, 392
Numet Engineering Ltd., 309
Oakridge Environmental Ltd., 310
Siemens Milltronics Process Instruments Inc., 366
Swish Maintenance Ltd., 384
Trent Metals Ltd., 401

Petrolia
Environmental Accident Protection Inc., 184

Pickering
ACO Container Systems Ltd., 67
Aker Chemetics, 76
Asbeguard Equipment Inc., 93
Avery Dennison Canada Inc., 98
Dewar Insulations Ltd., 162
Hazmasters Environmental Controls Inc., 228
Howard Marten Fluid Technologies Inc., 234
Indaco Manufacturing Limited, 240
Pacific Engineering Inc., 316
Simcoe Engineering Group Limited, 368

Picton
Brian Clark Architect, 116
MPI Drilling, 294

Point Edward
Bluewater Environmental Inc., 110
Hazmark Inc., 228
LEHDER Environmental Services Ltd., 267

Port Colborne
International Marine Salvage Inc., 245
Raw Materials Corporation, 342
SRI Petro Chemical Inc., 376

Port Dover
Harry Gamble Shipyard, 226

Port Hope
Eriksson Sediment Systems Inc., 189
Miniveil Air Systems, 290

Port Perry
Techstar Plastics Inc., 388

Port Severn
Pepi Sewage Disposal Service, 321

Putnam
Lakeshore Recycling, 263

Queensville
Roger LaRue Enterprises Ltd., 350

Richards Landing
Northern Lights Energy Systems, 307

Richmond
AF Pollution Abatement Systems Inc., 72

Richmond Hill
AA Environmental & Associates, 64
Acklands-Grainger Inc., 66
Alcore Fabricating Corp., 77
Altus Capital Planning Inc., 81
AMKO Systems Inc., 84
Avenue Industrial Supply Co. Ltd., 98
Black & Decker Canada Inc., 110
Calgon Carbon Corp., 121
CCL/IBI, 133
CMS: Crisis Management Specialists Inc., 145
Decommissioning Consulting Services Limited, 159
Envirogard Products Ltd., 184
George Grant Consulting, 211
HAMON Custodis-Cottrell Canada, Inc., 224
Hydro Vision America, 236
International Cooling Systems Inc., 245
Klajnerman Contracting Corp., 258
Lexmark Canada Inc., 271
Link-Pipe Inc., 272
Oil Spill Control Services Canada, 311
PCI Geomatics Group Inc., 320
Pro-Lab Diagnostics, 333
Pure Energy Battery Inc., 336
Pure Energy Inc., 336
Risk Check Environmental Ltd., 347
SENES Consultants Limited, 362
Strata Soil Sampling Inc., 380
Tech Sales Co., 387
Victaulic Co. of Canada Ltd., 413
W. Sodin (Gravity) Ltd., 414
Wastequip Cusco, 421
Wittmann Canada, Inc., 433

Rockland
Ambio Biofiltration Ltd., 82
Levac Robichaud Leclerc Associates Ltd., 270

Rockwood
ELI Eco Chemical Technologies Inc., 175
Waterloo Barrier Inc., 422
Waterloo Biofilter Systems Inc., 422

Rosseau
Eco-North Laboratories, 171

Sarnia
Alloy Fab Ltd., 79
Elecsar Engineering Co. Ltd., 174
Entropex, 182
HQN Industrial Fabrics Inc., 234
Integra Technologies Ltd., 243
Lambton Scientific, 263
MIG Engineering Ltd., 289
Thermon Heat Tracing Services, 394

Sault Ste Marie
Traders Metal Company Ltd., 400

Schomberg
Genus Loci Ecological Landscapes Inc., 210

Seaforth
Boilersmith Ltd., 113

Shallow Lake
SPI Industries Inc., 375
Sharon
Pacesetter Sales & Associates Inc., 316
Simcoe
R.D. Cookson Disposal Ltd., 340
W.D. Cookson Ltd., 415
Smiths Falls
Denoco Energy Systems Ltd., 161
Guildline Instruments Limited, 222
Smithville
Galaxy Pallets Ltd., 204
Wind Energy Solutions Canada, 432
Spencerville
CMEL Enterprises Ltd., 144
Spring Bay
Sedore Stoves Canada, 361
St Catharines
ASI Group Ltd., 93
AZZ Blenkhorn & Sawle Limited, 100
Bema Co. Ltd., 104
Can Ecosse Engineering, 122
Gryphon International Engineering Services Inc., 222
Hemispheres Environmental Consulting Inc., 229
Hy-Grade Precast Concrete, 235
Imbibitive Technologies Canada, Inc., 238
International Irrigation Systems Ltd., 245
Oakhill Environmental, 310
Penn Refrigeration Ltd., 321
Photech Environmental Solutions, 323
St. Catharines Hydro Generation Inc., 356
St Jacobs
C-Max Transportation Equipment, 119
St Thomas
Brass Craft Canada Ltd., 115
Elgin Pure Water Supply, 175
Therm-O-Comfort Co. Ltd., 393
St. Thomas
Gorman-Rupp of Canada Ltd., 215
Stoney Creek
AIM Environmental Group, 74
Backup-Power.ca, 101
The Brofield Group, 391
Da-Lee Dust Control, 156
Q-Air Environmental Controls Ltd., 337
RPR Environmental Inc., 353
Stouffville
Hanson Pressure Pipe, 225
Horton Tree Farms, 233
Stratford
E.K. Gillin & Associates Inc., 168
Stemmer Steel Craft Industries Limited, 379
Strathroy
Kongskilde Limited, 259
Sturgeon Falls
LOB Blasting Mat, 273
Sudbury
Elasto Valve Rubber Products Inc., 174
Mirarco Mining Innovation, 290
NAR Environmental Consultants Inc., 297
NIM Disposals Limited, 304
Par Excellence Developments, Inc., 318
Sunderland
EcoEthic Inc., 171
Sutton West
Chem Solv, 139
Thorndale
Ecologistics Research Services, 172
Thornhill
Aquareal Water Systems Inc., 88
Canentec Inc., 126
Chemline Plastics Ltd., 139
Data Tech Environmental Services, 157
Engine Control Systems, 180
MMM Group, 292
Nisymco Inc., 304
Porta-Mini Systems, 328
Silo Clean International, 367
Simcoe Plastics Ltd., 368

Thorold
Niagara Waste Systems Ltd., 303
Walker Industries Holdings Ltd., 416
Woodington Systems Inc., 433
Thunder Bay
A1 Sewage Services (1989) Limited, 64
Accurassay Laboratories, 65
Bowater Canadian Forest Products Inc., 114
Cartridge Care Canada, 130
Cook Engineering, 151
DST Consulting Engineers, 166
Hydro One, 236
KBM Forestry Consultants Inc., 255
Lakehead Scrap Metal, 263
Lakehead University, 263
Nelson-Superior Consultants Ltd., 300
Pumps & Systems, 336
Tillsonburg
Wellmaster Pipe & Supply, 424
Timmins
Mikro-Tek Inc., 289
Tiverton
Huron Wind Ltd. Partnership, 235
Toronto
Abbeywood Associates Inc., 64
Acres & Associated Environmental Ltd., 67
Adventis Technologies, 69
Aecon Group Inc., 71
Aercoustics Engineering Limited, 71
Aercoustics Engineering Limited, 71
AIC Associated Industrial Controls Inc., 73
Ainsworth Inc., 74
Aker Metals (Toronto), 76
ALARA Industrial Hygiene Services Ltd., 76
Alcohol Countermeasure Systems Corp., 77
Aldworth Engineering Inc., 77
Alex Milne Associates Ltd., 77
Alfa Laval Inc., 78
All-Weld Company Limited, 79
Alrange Container Services, 80
ALTECH Environmental Consulting Ltd., 81
ALTECH Technology Systems Inc., 81
Anticorrosion Materials & Technologies Inc., 86
Apollo Environmental Systems Corporation, 87
Arch Industries, 90
Armatek Controls Limited, 91
Array Systems Computing Inc., 93
Atlantic Packaging Products Ltd., 96
Atlas Polar Company Limited, 97
B & R Engineering Co. Ltd., 100
Bancroft Light & Power Company (2000) Ltd., 101
The Battery Broker Environmental Services Inc., 391
Bayer Inc., 103
Benjamin Moore & Co. Ltd, 105
Berg Chilling Systems Inc., 105
Bestobell AquaTronix Limited, 106
BFI Canada Inc., 106
Bradex Industrial Services Ltd., 115
Brenntag Canada Inc., 116
Brookfield Power, 117
Bruce A. Brown Associates Limited, 117
BVA Systems Ltd./Vibro-Acoustics, 119
C.D. Sonter Ltd., 119
Canada Colors & Chemicals Ltd., 123
Cardinal Biologicals Ltd., 128
Careful Hand Laundry & Dry Cleaners Ltd., 128
Carole Burnham Consulting, 129
Cascades Recovery Inc., 130
CH2M Hill Canada Limited, 137
Charlesworth & Associates, 138
Chartis Insurance Company of Canada, 138
ChemiGreen Inc., 139
Church & Trought Inc., 140
City Metal Manufacturing Inc., 141
Clayton Research Associates Ltd., 142
Clearview Packaging Inc., 143
Climatizer Insulation Inc., 144
Clivus Multrum Canada Inc., 144
Coffey Geotechnics Inc., 146
Colour Innovations Print Inc., 146
Conformance Check Inc., 149
Control Fire Systems, 151

Corolon Coatings & Corrosion Control Technologies Inc., 152
Covertech Fabricating Inc., 153
Danfoss Inc. - Electric Floor Heating Division, 157
Denso North America Inc., 161
Dillon Consulting Ltd., 163
Direct Separation Solutions, 164
Diversified Waste Solutions, 164
Donalco Inc., 165
DTE Industries Ltd., 167
Earth & Environmental Technologies (ETech), 168
EarthFx Inc., 169
Eastwest Synergies Inc., 169
ECE Group - a Division of Conestoga-Rovers & Associates, 170
Ecocern Inc., 171
EcoFlame International Inc., 171
EcoLog Information Resources Group, 172
Elmridge Engineering Inc., 176
Enercorp Instruments Ltd., 179
ENV Treatment Systems Inc., 182
Envirometrex, 184
Environmental Allies Inc., 185
Environmental Communications Options, 185
Environmental Economics International, 185
Environmental R&D Capital Corporation, 185
EnviroSan Products Ltd./SOLUTION 2000, 187
Envirotest Inc., 188
ENVision...synergy, 188
ESRI Canada Ltd., 190
EthicScan Canada, 190
Fastco Equipment Corporation, 194
Filter Innovations Inc., 195
First Stage Enterprises Inc., 196
Firwin Corporation, 196
Floorworks Inc., 197
Flowmatic Holdings Inc., 197
Fuel Maker Corp., 202
Gensco Equipment (1990) Ltd., 210
Geo Environmental Engineering - Geocon SNC-Lavalin, 210
George Kelk Corporation, 211
Geosoft, 212
Global Contract Inc., 213
Global Repair Ltd., 213
Green Soils Inc., 217
GreenWare Environmental Systems Inc., 218
Greenwood & Associates, 218
Grey House Publishing Canada, 218
GroundTech Solutions, 219
Hallmark Insurance Brokers Ltd., 224
Harbour Remediation & Transfer Inc., 225
Hardy Stevenson & Associates, 225
Hazardous Materials Management Magazine, 227
Hibon Inc., 231
Highland Equipment Ltd., 231
HLS Ecolo, 232
Hydralogic Systems Inc., 235
Hydro One, 236
Hygrex-Spehr Industries, 237
Hymopack Ltd., 237
IBI Group, 238
ICF International Canada Inc., 238
The Impact Group, 392
In Tech Risk Management Inc., 239
In!Flame Fireplaces Inc., 239
Indachem Inc., 240
INDECO Strategic Consulting Inc., 240
Industrial Ecology Corp., 240
Ingersoll-Rand Canada Inc., 241
InspecTech, 243
Integran Technologies Inc., 243
Intelex Technologies Inc., 244
Ipex Inc., 247
J&B Engineering Inc., 249
J&M Industrial Engineering & Sales Inc., 249
J.E. Coulter Associates Ltd., 249
Just Homes, 253
Kason, 255
Kinectrics Inc., 257
Koch Engineering Co. Ltd., 259
Latimat Inc., 265
Lineman's Testing Laboratories of Canada Limited, 272
Lucas-Milhaupt Toronto, 274

Lyreco Office Products, 276
Macquarie Power & Infrastructure Income Fund, 278
Marsulex Inc., 281
Marvin Silbert & Associates, 282
McClymont & Rak Engineers, Inc., 284
MCW Custom Energy Solutions, 285
Medgate Inc., 286
Merchants of Green Coffee, 286
Metex Corp. Ltd., 287
MIE Consulting Engineers Ltd., 289
Mifab Canada, 289
Monalt Environmental Inc., 292
Morrison Hershfield, 293
Mountain Valley Geophysics, 294
MSA: Mine Safety Appliances Company, 294
Municipal Affairs Consulting, 295
MW Metal Spinning & Stamping Ltd., 295
Network Environmental Services Inc., 300
Norditrade Inc., 305
Norseman Plastics Ltd., 306
North Safety Products Canada, 306
Northland Power, 307
NRI Industries, 309
O'Connor Tanks Ltd., 310
O-I Canada Corp., 310
Ontario Centres of Excellence, 312
Ontario Power Generation, 312
Ontor Ltd., 312
Oxegen Inc., 315
Ozocan Corporation, 315
P.J. Cluff Architect Inc., 315
PAP Engineering Services, 317
Conserval Engineering Inc., 318
Patterson Industries (Canada) Ltd., 319
Pelmar Engineering Ltd., 320
Penny & Casson Co., 321
Peto MacCallum Ltd., 321
Planning Alliance, 326
Port of Entry Inc., 328
Precisioneering Ltd., 330
Probyn & Company Inc., 333
Proctor & Gamble Inc., 333
Proshred Security, 335
QMI-SAI Global, 337
Quantum Murray LP, 338
Quorum Growth Inc., 339
Qwatro Corporation, 339
R.V. Anderson Associates Limited, 341
Rechargeable Battery Recycling Corporation, 343
Regional Envelope, 344
Regional Power Inc., 344
Resource Environmental Associates, 345
Rexdale Disposal Ltd., 346
Rotblott & Sons Ltd., 352
Royalpak Inc., 353
S.A. Armstrong Limited, 354
St. Marys Cement Inc., 356
Sarafinchin Associates Ltd., 358
Scepter Manufacturing Co. Ltd., 358
Scimus Inc., 360
Scitax Advisory Partners LLP, 360
Sears Canada Inc., 361
SHER-PAC Container Systems Ltd., 365
Sick Building Solutions, 366
Sittler's Manufacturing, 369
Skylark Controls, 370
Smith & Andersen Consulting Engineering, 370
Softrisk Technologies Ltd., 372
Sonoco Recycling Ltd., 374
Statiflo Inc., 379
Stormceptor Canada Inc., 380
Strategies for the Environment, 380
Stuart Hunt & Associates, 381
SUBBOR, 381
Summerhill Group, 381
Suncor Energy Products, 382
Sunoco Inc., 382
Sustainable EDGE Ltd., 383
Sustainable Resources Management Group, 383
T. Harris Environmental Management Inc., 385
Teknion Corporation, 389
Tekran Canada, 389
Terrafix Geosynthetics Inc., 390
Terrapex Environmental Ltd., 390

Geographic Index

Toxprobe Inc., 399
Tremco Ltd., 401
TriWaste Services Inc., 402
Turtle Island Recycling Co., 404
U-pak Disposal Ltd., 405
Underwriters' Laboratories of Canada, 405
Unterman McPhail Associates, 407
UV Pure Technologies, 408
Via Disposal Services Ltd., 413
Vitafoam Products Canada Ltd., 414
Walter Dow Associates Ltd., 416
Warren's Imaging & Dryography Inc., 417
Waste Alternatives Inc., 417
Waste Opportunities Inc., 420
Wasteco, 421
Water Conservation Company Ltd., 421
The Westford Group Inc., 393
Whitecourt Power Limited Partnership, 431
Wilcorp Manufacturing, 431
WorkLab Inc., 433
Xeneca Power Development Inc., 435
Xerox Canada Ltd., 435
Trenton
Mowat Fabrication Ltd., 294
Trout Creek
Longwood Forestry Services Ltd., 273
Troy
Big Bear Pumping Inc., 107
Unionville
Earthguard Environmental Group Inc., 169
Uxbridge
Inland Aquatics, 241
Val Caron
Herby Enterprises Ltd., 229
Vaughan
M&E Engineering Ltd., 276
Metso Automation Canada Ltd., 288
Metso Automation Canada Ltd., 288
Secural Inc., 361
Vegewax Candleworx Ltd., 410
Walden
Norvac Industrial Services, 307
Walkerton
Arlat Technology, 91
Wallenstein
N.S. Bauman Ltd., 296
Walsingham
Acorus Restoration Native Plant Nursery, 67
Walton
LH - Division of Full Circle Organics Inc., 272
Waterford
DEB Canada, 159
Norfolk Disposal Services Limited, 305
Waterloo
AGRECOM inc., 73
ARISE Technologies Corporation, 90
Canadian Recycling Equipment & Systems Ltd., 125
Canviro, 127
Clemmer Technologies Inc., 143
Conestoga-Rovers & Associates, 149
EnviroMetal Technologies Inc., 184
Fred Cressman Sales Inc., 201
Gro-Bark (Ontario) Ltd., 218
Lakes Environmental Software, 263
Radiation Environmental Management Systems Inc., 341
Robb Engineering Ltd., 347
Schlumberger Water Services, 359
TurboSonic Inc., 404
Viessmann Manufacturing Company Inc., 413
Wawa
Valerie Falls Limited Partnership, 409
West Lincoln
W.J. Sheldrick Sanitation Ltd., 415
Weston
Solignum Inc., 372
Wheatley
Hike Metal Products Ltd., 231
Whitby
AeroTek Manufacturing Ltd., 71

Atlantic Newsprint Company, 96
Delta Piping Products Canada Inc., 160
GAEA Technologies, 204
Liqui-Box Canada Inc., 272
Nemato Inc., 300
Pebblestone Multi-Services Inc., 320
The Sernas Group Inc., 393
StonCor Canada, 379
Totten Sims Hubicki Associates Ltd., 399
Wiarton
Caframo Co. Ltd., 121
Windsor
A. A. Boscariol and Associates Limited, 63
Ecolad Corp., 172
Glos Associates Inc., 214
Great Lakes Safety Products Inc., 216
Windsor Barrel & Drum Ltd., 433
Windsor Pump Co. Ltd., 433
Wingham
Maitland Engineering, 279
Winona
Air Trac Corp., 75
Woodbridge
ACG Technology Ltd., 66
Con-Tank Installations Ltd., 148
Flowserve Inc., 197
Organic Resource Management Inc., 314
PerkinElmer Life & Analytical Sciences Canada Inc., 321
Technel Engineering Inc., 387
Thermal Hydronics Supply Ltd., 394
Water Matrix, 421
Woodstock
A&A Environmental Consultants Inc., 63

Prince Edward Island

Charlottetown
Campbell's Concrete Ltd., 122
Entegrity Wind Systems Inc., 181
Island Technologies Inc., 248
Maritime Electric Company Ltd., 280
The PEI Energy Corp., 393
North Cape
Wind Energy Institute of Canada, 432

Québec

Alma
Les Consultants RSA, 268
Anjou
Pol R Enterprises Inc., 327
Baie-Comeau
Groupe-Conseil TDA, 221
Baie-Saint-Paul
Consultants Filion, Hansen & Associés Inc., 150
Baie-d'Urfé
Nouvelle Technologie (TEKNO) Inc., 308
OMB (Americas) Forged Steel Valves, 312
REHAU Industries Inc., 344
Solignum, 372
Beauport
Aqua-Plus, 88
Beloeil
Les Plastiques Simport Ltée, 270
Voghel Inc., 414
Blainville
Geostat Systems International Inc., 212
Stablex Canada Inc., 377
Bois-des-Filion
Plad Équipement Ltée, 325
Boisbriand
Busch Vacuum Technics Inc., 119
Demilec Inc., 160
Les Entreprises Forlam, 268
GEA Barr-Rosin Inc., 205
Z-Tech/Geogard Inc., 435
Bon-Conseil
Sintra Inc., 369
Boucherville
Allianz Madvac Inc., 79

DATA Group of Companies, 157
Groupe Bau-Val, 219
HMI Construction Inc., 232
Magnor, Division of Magchem, 278
Produits Ferpac Ltée, 333
Robar, 347
Services Matrec inc., 363
Brossard
RailPower Technologies Corp., 341
Stork Bronswerk Inc., 380
Brownsburg-Chatham
Eco-Guide International, 170
Bécancour
Recyclage d'Alluminium Québec, 343
Candiac
Produits Chimiques Handy Ltée, 333
Cap-de-la-Madeleine
Daniel Fauteux Environnement inc., 157
R.J. Lévesque et Fils Ltée, 341
Carignan
Enviro-Systèmes Inc., 183
Charlesbourg
ABGG Technologies Inc., 65
Biotech Solutions, 109
Chertsey
Compo Recycle, 147
Chicoutimi
Cegerco - GCL Inc., 135
Cegertec Experts-Conseils, 135
Environnement Godin Inc., 186
Le Groupe Leblond & Bouchard/Daniel Arbour et associes, 265
Menart S.L. Inc., 286
Pompe Saguenay Enr., 328
Products BCM Ltée BCM, 333
Sedac Inc., 361
Services industriels Newalta, 363
Chomedey
MICCA Paints Inc., 288
Châteauguay
Banyan Chains Inc., 101
Coaticook
Showa-Best Glove, Inc., 366
Cowansville
Chemrec, 140
Pompex Inc., 328
Delson
Pompage Express M.D. Inc., 328
Dollard-des-Ormeaux
Invensys Systems Canada Inc., 246
Dorval
Eucania International Inc., 190
Drummondville
Geolab Inc., 211
Innergy Tech, 242
Venmar Ventilation Inc., 410
Gatineau
Canadian General Standards Board, 124
CIMA+, 141
Paul G. Chénard, 319
Granby
Les Emballages Polyform inc., 268
Nertec Design Inc., 300
Grandes-Piles
Horizon Environment Inc., 233
Grenville
Hakmet Ltd., 223
Hudson
Service de rebuts Soulanges inc., 363
Terinex International Ltd., 389
Iberville
Groupe Tremca inc., 221
Joliette
Aquasolution Technologies Inc., 89
DGM Inc., 163
Le Groupe Forces, 265
Labexcel Inc., 262
NORDIKeau Inc., 305
Plastrec Inc., 326
Récupération Nord-Ben Inc., 343

Jonquière
Solution 3R, 373
Kingsey Falls
Cascades Inc., 130
Cascades Inc., 130
Norampac Inc., 305
Papiers Perkins, 317
Kirkland
AIRCOM Technologies Inc., 75
La Baie
Les Laboratoires S.L. inc., 269
La Pocatière
Axion Technologies, 99
La Prairie
Groupe Berlie-Falco, 219
Solenco Environnement inc., 372
LaSalle
Supremex Inc., 383
Lasalle
The Cintec Group, 391
Laval
Aqua-Rehab Inc., 88
Avmor Ltd., 99
Bodycot Analex Inc., 113
C.R. Wall Co. Inc., 120
CAHFIL FARR (Canada Inc.), 121
Can-Aqua International Ltée, 123
Caristrap International Inc., 128
Cheminées Sécurité Internationale Ltée, 139
CPC Tuyauteries Canada Ltée, 153
Dessau, Inc., 162
Experts-Conseils CEP, 192
Fusionex, Inc., 203
Hanna Instruments Canada Inc., 224
Larose & Fils Ltée, 264
LVM Inc., 275
Machinerie Laurin Inc., 278
Megalab Inc., 286
Membrex Ltée, 286
Métropolitain Valve Inc., 288
MF Paints, 288
Michelin North America (Canada) Inc., 289
MLC Associés Inc., 292
Multi Recyclage S.D. Inc., 295
Ozogram Inc., 315
Proserco Inc., 335
Quatrex Environnement inc., 338
Racan Carrier, 341
Sanbec, 356
SOTAR Inc., 374
Sunarc of Canada Inc., 382
Tiger-Vac International Inc., 396
Les Cèdres
A.C. Plastiques Canada, 63
AC Plastiques Canada Inc., 65
Cramer Nursery Inc., 153
Longueuil
Belfab Inc., 104
Géophysique GPR International Inc., 211
Pyradia Inc., 337
Santinel Inc., 357
Sico, 366
SNC-Lavalin Environment Inc., 371
Lévis
Elite Technologies Inc., 175
Éocycle Technologies Inc., 188
Magog
Fontaine International Corp., 199
Magotteaux Ltée, 278
Mascouche
GILFAB, 212
Miceli & Frères Ltée, 288
Masonville
Both Belle Robb Ltd., 114
Matane
Béton Provincial Ltée, 106
Groupe Bouffard, 219
Mercier
Ventes Techniques Nimatec inc., 411
Mont-Laurier
Labelle, Ryan, Genipro Inc., 261

Geographic Index

Mont-Tremblant
Robert Laurin, 348

Montréal
A&C Produits Chimiques Americains Ltée, 63
ABB Inc. (Canada), 64
Abitibi-Consolidated Inc., 65
Acme Engineering Products Ltd., 66
ACME Vacuum Cleaner Co. Ltd., 67
AESL Instrumentation inc., 72
Agrosysts Ltée, 73
Air Liquide Canada Ltée, 74
AirScience Inc., 76
Airtechni Inc., 76
Alstom Canada Inc., 80
Anachem Ltd., 84
Anachemia Canada Inc., 85
APS Aviation Inc., 87
Argus Telecom International Inc., 90
Atrion International Inc., 97
Avensys Inc., 98
AXOR Experts-Conseils Inc., 99
Bedard Tankers Inc., 104
Bémalux Inc., 105
Bétonel Limitée, 106
Biothermica, 109
Boutillette Parizeau et Associés inc., 114
Montréal, 118
Canadian Technical Tape Ltd., 125
Cartier Chemicals Ltd., 130
Charland Thermojet Inc., 138
Chem Action Inc., 139
Chem Experts Inc., 139
CHI Canada Inc., 140
Cintube Ltd., 141
Circul-Aire Inc., 141
Clariant (Canada) Inc., 142
Cole-Parmer Canada Inc., 146
Constant America Inc., 150
Les Consultants Eoletech S.Q. Inc., 268
Les Consultants LBCD, 268
Conterm Inc., 151
Les Contrôles PROVAN Associés Inc., 268
Daubois Inc., 158
DDH Environnement ltée, 159
Decibel Consultants Inc., 159
Dectron Internationale, 159
Deschênes et Fils Ltée., 161
Domaine Label & Trim Inc., 164
Domtar Inc., 165
Douglas Brothers, 165
Dural Industries, 167
Dutab, 167
Dynapompe Inc., 168
ÉEM inc., 173
EFC Control Inc., 173
Enercombustion Ltd., 179
Entraco, 181
Environmental Remediation Equipment Inc., 185
Enviroplast inc, 187
Fiducie Desjardins, 195
Flygt Canada, 198
Foresteel Industries Inc., 199
FPInnovations, 200
Gaston Marcil, Consultant, 205
GENEQ Inc., 206
Génie Audio inc., 207
Génius Conseil Inc., 207
Genivar, 207
GL&V - Groupe Laperrière & Verreault Inc., 212
Global Facman Entreprises Inc., 213
Groupe Deschênes, 219
Le Groupe Pétrolier OLCO Inc., 265
Groupe RSW inc., 220
Groupe S.M. International Inc., 220
Groupe Séguin, 220
Groupe SOLROC, 221
Groupe Teknika, 221
Helimax Energy Inc., 228
Henlex Inc., 229
Hydrogéo Plus Inc., 236
Hydromega Energy Inc., 237
Imalog Inc., 238
Industrial Combustion Equipment Ltd., 240
Inspec-Sol Inc., 242
Intertek Systems Certification, 246

J. Walter Company Ltd., 249
Janin Atlas Inc., 251
Kruger Inc., 260
KW Gaspé Ltd. Partnership, 261
Lab-Élite limitée, 261
Lafarge Canada Inc., 262
Lavo Inc., 265
Lupien Rosenberg Consultants Inc., 274
Mabarex inc., 277
MacDonald & Fils Inc., 277
Mainetti Canada Inc., 278
Marie Rousseau, ING, 280
Matco Ltd., 282
Metafix, 287
Météoglobe Canada Inc., 287
MK Plastics Corp., 291
NCL Envirotek Inc., 299
NetPlus-HazMat Tracker, 300
NI Plastique Inc., 303
Nortec S.G.S. Inc., 306
Novatech Controls, Inc., 309
Omega Recycling Technologies, 312
Option Environnement Inc., 313
Pageau Morel & associés, inc., 317
Parkson Corporation, 319
Paul F. Wilkinson & Associates Inc., 319
Peintures Denalt, 320
Les Peintures Sico inc., 269
Petrifond Foundation Co. Ltd., 322
Pneus Métro Inc., 326
Pompaction inc., 328
Preston Phipps Inc., 331
Pretal, 332
Proceco Ltd., 333
Procedair Industries Inc., 333
Promosalons Canada, 334
ProSep Inc., 335
ProViro Instrumentation Inc., 335
R.B. Intermark Inc., 340
Rebuts Solides Canadiens Inc., 343
Recubec Inc., 343
RMS Enviro Solv Inc. Québec, 347
SACO Technologies, Inc., 354
Sambrabec Inc., 356
Services d'Évaluation Santé/Toxicologie Inc., 363
Silvana Import Trading Inc., 368
Sinanni Inc., 369
SNC-Lavalin Group Inc., 371
Société d'énergie de la rivière Ste-Anne/AXOR, 371
Socodec Inc., 371
Sonitec Inc., 374
Stabilis Environment Inc., 377
Stratem Inc., 380
Tecsult Inc., 388
Terratech, 390
TLT Co-Vent, 396
TPE Technologies Inc., 399
Transco Plastic Industries, 400
Turcal, 404
Urban Ecology Centre of Montréal, 407
Velan Inc., 410
W. Ralston (Canada) Inc., 414
Warco Process Technologies, 416
West Penetone Inc., 424

North Hatley
Bacta-Pur, 101

Pincourt
Aqua Data Inc., 87

Pintendre
Clamex Environnement Inc., 142

Plessisville
Convoyeurs B.M.G. inc., 151
Les Équipements Vibrotech Inc., 268
Industries Machinex Inc., 241

Point Claire
Matrix Energy, 282

Pointe-Claire
Dave Vallieres & Associates Inc., 158
Enviro-RISQUE Inc., 183
Envitech Automation Inc., 188
Le Groupe Légerlite inc., 265
Leviton Canada, 270
Sika Canada Inc., 367

Sols Consultants Ltée, 373

Port-Cartier
Recyclage PF Inc., 343

Quebec
Electro-Mecanik Inc., 175

Québec
André Simard et associés ltée, 85
Arrakis Consultants Inc., 92
Bio-Contrôle in., 107
Biogénie, 108
Biomax Inc., 108
Biorex Inc., 109
BPR, 115
Bureau de Normalisation du Québec, 118
Chamard & Associés, 138
CO2 Solution, 145
Consultants Enviroconseil Inc., 150
EnGlobe Corp., 180
Les Entreprises Julien Inc., 268
Enviroconseil, 183
Filtrum Inc., 195
H2O Innovation Inc., 223
Hydrogéochem Environnement Inc., 236
IMTT-Québec Ltd., 239
Laboratoire de Canalisation Souterraines Inc., 262
Laboratoires d'Expertises de Québec Ltée, 262
Lambert Somec inc., 263
Legaré F., Ing. Forestier Conseil, 266
Logiball Inc., 273
MissionHGE inc., 291
Multitel Inc., 295
Noel Rochette et Fils Inc., 305
Roche ltée, Groupe-conseil, 348
Solaction Inc., 372
Symbiose Consultants inc, 385
Technisol Environnement, 388
Tiru Canada Inc., 396
Université du Québec, 406

Repentigny
CLA Experts-Conseils, 142
Filtration Seco Inc., 195

Rimouski
Genilab Environnement Inc., 207

Rivière-du-Loup
Premier Tech Environment, 331
Premier Tech Environnement / Division municipale, commerciale et ind, 331

Rouyn-Noranda
Entretien M. Perron inc. (SANI-TRI), 181
Groupe Stavibel Inc., 221
Marcel Baril Ltée, 280

Saint-Anselme
Groupe DHB Inc., 219

Saint-Basile-le-Grand
Ferme R&B Fafard Inc., 194

Saint-Bruno
Divex Marine, 164
EnvirInfo, 182

Saint-Charles-Borromée
Michel Lavallée, 289

Saint-Damien-de-Buckland
IPL Inc., 247

Saint-Elzéar
Texel Géomembrane Inc., 391

Saint-Eustache
Coen Canada Inc., 146
Groupe Conseil Bellefeuille, Samson et Associés, 219
Hyprescon Inc., 237

Saint-Fabien
Aquaterre Inc., 89

Saint-Georges-de-Windsor
E.A.I. Technologies Inc., 168

Saint-Henri-de-Lévis
Les Composts du Québec inc., 268
Fortier 2000 Ltée, 200

Saint-Hubert
Con-V-Air Inc., 148
Groupe Sodinco inc., 221

Saint-Hyacinthe
Compteurs Lecomte Ltée, 148

Consumaj, 151
Groupe EnvirAqua, 219
Industries de Moules et Plastiques VIF, 241

Saint-Jean-Chrysostome
Supervac 2000, 383

Saint-Jean-sur-Richelieu
A.C. Carbone Canada Inc., 63
Compo-Haut-Richelieu inc., 147
Experts-Conseils BMST inc., 192
Polychem Products Ltd., 328
Soleno Inc., 372
Solinov Inc., 373
Tremcar Inc., 401

Saint-Jérôme
Cascades Fine Papers Group Inc., 130

Saint-Lambert
BV SORBEX, Inc., 119
Mondry Del Zotto et associés Inc., 292
Roctest Ltée, 350

Saint-Laurent
Insituform Technologies Ltd. - Montréal, 242
John Meunier Inc., 253
Tornatech, 397

Saint-Lazare
Urecon Ltée, 408

Saint-Luc
Gestion Eaux Richelieu Inc., 212

Saint-Ludger
Equipements Lapierre Inc., 189

Saint-Nicolas
Saint-Nicolas, 99
Envir'eau Puits Inc., 182
Equipement Labrie Ltee, 189
Labrie Environmental Group, 262
Neilson Excavation, 299

Saint-Romuald
Envirogain Inc., 184
Rodrigue Métal Ltée, 350

Saint-Rémi
Lécuyer et Fils Ltée, 266

Saint-Ubalde
Les Bras d'Fer Gingras Inc., 267

Sainte-Adèle
STOBEC Inc., 379

Sainte-Catherine
Nova PB Inc., 308

Sainte-Foy
Bernard Darveau Ingénieur, 105
Centre de Toxicologie du Québec, 136
Gentec Inc., 210
Réal Huot Inc., 343
Sani Gestion ONYX, 357
Solmax-Texel Geosynthetics Inc., 373
V. Fournier & Associates, 408

Sainte-Julie
SPG Hydro International Inc., 375
Sylvain Léger, 384
Teckn-O-Laser, 388

Sainte-Martine
AGRI-SX, 73

Salaberry-de-Valleyfield
Brunet Ltée, Tuyaux de béton, 117
Celfort Construction Materials Inc., 135
Frappier & Génier Conseillers, 201

Shawinigan
Consultants Mésar inc., 150
Société Laurentide inc., 371

Sherbrooke
Bio-Terre Systems Inc., 108
Environment ESA Inc., 186
Ferti-Val Inc., 195
Groupe SM inc., 220
Les Laboratoires Shermont Inc., 269
Nova Envirocom, 308
Les Produits Environnementaux Atlas, 270

Shigawake
Shigawake Organics Ltd., 365

Sillery
Terra Experts Conseils Inc., 390

Sorel-Tracy

Geographic Index

Conporec Inc., 150
Hebco International Inc., 228
St-Augustin-de-Desmaures
Chemco Inc., 139
St-Bruno-de-Montarville
Beaulier Inc., 104
St-Charles-sur-Richelieu
Urgel Delisle & Associés inc., 408
St-Georges
Groupe GLD Inc., Experts-Conseils, 219
Stanstead
Les Engrais Naturels McInnes Inc./McInnes Natural Fertilizers Inc., 268
Jomac Canada Inc., 253
Ste-Hélène-de-Bagot
Camatec, 122
Ste. Anne de Bellevue
Brace Centre for Water Resources Management, 115
Sutton
Gage Environmental Management Inc., 204
Terrebonne
Enviroservices Inc., 187
M.S.D.A. Inc., 277
Metacor International Inc., 287
Thetford Mines
Biolab Inc., 108
Les Industries Fournier Inc., 269
Prolab Technolub, 334
Trois-Pistoles
J.M. Turcotte ltée, 250
Trois-Rivières
Exploitation Santec Inc., 192
GDG Environnement Ltée, 205
Hardy Filtration, 225
ISOVision, 248
Kalyn Siebert Canada Inc., 254
Nove Environnement Inc., 309
Pepin Prevention des Pertes Inc., 321
René Gervais Inc., Consultants, 345
Trois-Rivières-Ouest

CIBA Spécialités Chimiques Canada inc., 141
Val-d'Or
Construction Val-d'Or Ltée, 150
Varennes
Groupe Chagnon International, 219
GSI Environnement Inc., 222
Kemira Water Solutions Canada Inc., 256
Sanexen Environmental Services Inc., 357
Solmax International Inc., 373
Solmers Internationale Experts-Conseils Inc., 373
Vaudreuil-Dorion
Aerzen Canada Surpresseurs Compresseurs inc., 71
Groupe Consulteaux Inc., 219
National Instruments Canada, 297
Oasis Bags, 311
Victoriaville
Le Groupe Sani Marc, 265
Megasecur Inc., 286
Pompco inc., 328
Vibec International Inc., 413
Waterloo
Waterloo Evaporateurs Inc., 422

Saskatchewan

Assiniboia
Sunset Solar Systems Ltd., 382
Bienfait
Prairie Western Reclamation & Consturction Inc., 330
Fort Qu'appelle
Darke Marketing Inc., 157
Humboldt
Del-Air Systems Ltd., 160
Lampman
Carson Safety & Environmental Services, 130
Macklin
TJ Consulting Ltd., 396
Melville
Plains Environmental Inc., 325
Neilburg

Cactus Environmental Services Ltd., 120
North Battleford
Enviro-Safe Chemicals Canada Inc., 183
Northern Petroleum Services, 307
Pilot Butte
Ecology Products International, 172
Prince Albert
Precision Industrial Ltd., 330
Qu'Appelle
BDS Laboratories, 104
Regina
Advance Engineered Products Ltd., 68
Beckie Hydrogeologists (1990) Ltd., 104
Clifton Associates Ltd., 144
Crown Shred & Recycling, 154
Droycon Bioconcepts Inc., 166
Enviro-Gun Ltd., 182
EnviroCare Environmental Services Ltd., 183
EPEC Consulting (Sask) Ltd., 189
Erin Consulting Ltd., 189
Focus Surveys Inc., 198
GE Ground Engineering Ltd., 205
Genex Swine Group, 207
iQmetrix, 247
J.D. Mollard & Associates Ltd., 249
Magnum Industries Ltd., 278
MR2-McDonald & Associates, 294
NorthPoint Energy Solutions, 307
Saskferco Products Inc., 358
SaskPower, 358
TransGas Limited, 400
Viterra Inc., 414
W.L. Whelan Environmental Consultants Ltd., 415
W.T. McGinn & Associates Ltd., 415
Wascana Recycling & Resource Recovery Corp., 417
Water Resource Consultants Ltd., 422
Rosetown
Wheatland Regional Centre Inc. & SARCAN Recycling, 431
Saskatoon
Ag-West Bio Inc., 72
AlphaNuclear Company, 80

Andritz Bird, 85
Angus, Butler Engineering Ltd., 86
Asta Sales & Marketing Ltd., 94
Calibre Strategic Services Inc., 121
CanNorth Environmental Services Inc., 126
Catterall & Wright, 132
Century Environmental Services, 136
Comco Manufacturing Ltd., 146
Cosmopolitan Industries Limited, 152
Cypress Sales Partnership, 155
Engineering Management Services Croscan, 180
Envirotec Services Incorporated, 187
Expocrete Concrete Products Ltd., 192
Federated Co-operatives Ltd., 194
Hitachi Canadian Industries Ltd., 232
International Road Dynamics Inc., 245
Nu-West Services Ltd., 309
P. Machibroda Engineering Ltd., 315
Philom Bios Inc., 323
PINTER & Associates Ltd., 324
SAL Engineering Ltd., 356
SARCAN Recycling, 358
Scientific Instrumentation Ltd., 360
Startco Engineering Ltd., 378
Summit Structures, 382
System Ecotechnologies Inc., 385
Toxicology Centre, 399
University of Saskatchewan, 406
Venables Machine Works Ltd., 410
Venmar CES, Inc., 410
Tisdale
Northern Steel Industries, 307
Weyburn
Souris Valley Industries Ltd., 374
Wilcox
Canadian Clay Products Inc., 124

Yukon Territory

Whitehorse
Icefield Instruments Inc., 238
Northerm Windows, 307

ISO Index

14000
Envirotech Associates Limited, 187

14000; 9000
SGS Canada Inc., 364

14001
Alberta-Pacific Forest Industries Inc., 77
ALTECH Environmental Consulting Ltd., 81
ArcelorMittal Dofasco, 90
Barrington Environmental Services, 102
Barrington Industrial Services Limited, 102
Benson Chemicals Limited, 105
Bowater Canadian Forest Products Inc., 114
DJA Environmental Consultants Inc., 164
Eco2 Systems Inc., 171
Global Contract Inc., 213
Lord & Partners Ltd., 274
M+A Environmental Consultants, 276
Millar Western Forest Products Ltd., 290
Nova Scotia Power, an Emera Company, 308
Panasonic Canada Inc., 317
QCA Laboratories Inc., 337
Raw Materials Corporation, 342
SENES Consultants Limited, 362
Sonic Environmental Solutions Inc., 373
TEAM-1 Environmental Services Inc., 387
United Safety Ltd., 406
URS Canada Inc., 408
Venerus International Purification Inc., 410
Warren's Imaging & Dryography Inc., 417

14001:2004
Bennett Environmental Inc., 105
Sandwell Engineering Inc., 356

14001; BS 18001
Oxegen Inc., 315

14001; 27001; 9002
Ricoh Canada Inc., 347

14001; 9001
CertainTeed Insulation Canada, Inc., 137
Envirosoil Ltd., 187
RPR Environmental Inc., 353

14064
Drexan Energy Systems Inc., 166

16949:2002
Associated Tube Industries, 94

17025
AXYS Analytical Services Ltd., 99
Becquerel Laboratories Inc., 104
Biolab Inc., 108
Caduceon Environmental Laboratories, 120
I.G. Micromed Environmental Inc., 237
Kaizen Environmental Services Inc., 254
Orchid Cellmark ULC, 314

17025; 9001
Kinectrics Inc., 257
RPC, 353
Staveley Services Canada Inc., 380

2858; 5199
Flowserve Canada Corp. - Pump Division, 197

9000
DSS Marine Inc., 167
Insituform Technologies Ltd. - Edmonton, 242
Insituform Technologies Ltd. - Hamilton, 242
Insituform Technologies Ltd. - Montréal, 242
Leviton Canada, 270
North Safety Products Canada, 306

9000; 14001
Danfoss Inc. - Electric Floor Heating Division, 157
Danfoss Inc. - Hydronic Heating Division, 157

9000; 9002:1994
Crown Fibre Tube Inc., 154

9001
ABB Inc. (Canada), 64
AC Plastiques Canada Inc., 65
Acme Engineering Products Ltd., 66
Acsion Industries Inc., 67
AGAT Laboratories Ltd., 72
Alfa Laval Inc., 78
Axion Technologies, 99
Babcock & Wilcox Canada Ltd., 100
BAE Newplan Group Ltd., 101
Ballard Power Systems Inc., 101
Baymag Inc., 103
Bebbington Industries, 104
Blue Water Agencies Ltd., 110
BOC Canada Limited, 111
Boutillette Parizeau et Associés inc., 114
BSM North America, 118
CAHFIL FARR (Canada Inc.), 121
Campbell Scientific (Canada) Corp., 122
Canadian Worcester Controls Ltd., 125
CARIS, 128
Cascades Inc., 130
CBCL Limited, 132
CEM Specialties Inc., 135
Cemcorp Ltd. Consulting Engineers, 135
CIMA+, 141
Cloverdale Paint Inc., 144
Connor Architects & Planners, 150
Crandall Engineering Ltd., 153
The DATA Group of Companies, 392
DEB Canada, 159
Degussa Canada Inc., 159
DPL Group, 166
Eco Waste Solutions, 170
Ecodyne Ltd., 171
Electro-Mecanik Inc., 175
Elemental Research Inc., 175
EMS Technologies, 178
Enervac Corp., 180
Engine Control Systems, 180
Enviroconseil, 183
Environnement ESA Inc., 186
Fisher Scientific Ltd., 196
FLSmidth Canada Ltd., 197
FMA Heritage Resources Consultants Inc., 198
Fontaine International Corp., 199
Forest Technology Systems Ltd., 199
Fort Garry Industries Ltd., 199
GDG Environnement Ltée, 205
GE Multilin, 205
Gentec Inc., 210
Geo Environmental Engineering - Geocon SNC-Lavalin, 210
Géophysique GPR International Inc., 211
Godfrey Associates Ltd., 214
Groupe Conseil Bellefeuille, Samson et Associés, 219
Groupe EnvirAqua, 219
Groupe RSW inc., 220
Le Groupe Sani Marc, 265
Groupe Teknika, 221
Groupe-Conseil TDA, 221
Guertin Brothers Coatings and Sealants Ltd., 222
Hamworthy-Peabody Combustion Canada Inc., 224
Harris & Roome Supply Limited, 225
Hatch Ltd., 226
Hitachi Canadian Industries Ltd., 232
Honeywell Ltd., 233
Impro, 239
Industrial Scientific Corporation, 241
Infratech Corporation, 241
Innergy Tech, 242
Instantel, 243
Integra Technologies Ltd., 243
International Road Dynamics Inc., 245
Investigative Science Inc., 247
IPL Inc., 247
ISOVision, 248
Janin Atlas Inc., 251
K&D Pratt Group Inc., 254
Knight Piésold Ltd., 258
Kraus Global Inc., 260
Kyocera Mita Canada Ltd., 261
Labelle, Ryan, Genipro Inc., 261
Laboratoires d'Expertises de Québec Ltée, 262
Labrie Environmental Group, 262
Lakeland Protective Wear Inc., 263
The Lowe-Martin Group, 392
Lucas-Milhaupt Toronto, 274
LVM Inc., 275
MDS Sciex, 285
Metocean Data Systems Limited, 287
Metso Automation Canada Ltd., 288
MICCA Paints Inc., 288
Mifab Canada, 289
MKG Imaging Solutions Inc., 291
Multitel Inc., 295
NCL Envirotek Inc., 299
Newmac Manufacturing Inc., 303
Notra Inc., 308
O-I Canada Corp., 310
Oakside Chemicals Ltd., 311
Oetiker Limited, 311
Ontor Ltd., 312
Opus International Consultants (Canada) Ltd., 313
Para Paints, 318
Petro-Canada Lubricants, 322
Phason Electronics, 322
Premier Tech Environnement / Division municipale, commerciale et ind, 331
Proceco Ltd., 333
Procyon Consulting Inc., 333
Prolab Technolub, 334
Pure Energy Battery Inc., 336
Pyradia Inc., 337
Quatic Industries Inc., 338
Quester Tangent Corp., 339
Radiodetection (Canada) Ltd., 341
René Gervais Inc., Consultants, 345
Roche ltée, Groupe-conseil, 348
Rochester Midland Ltd., 349
RST Instruments Ltd., 354
Schlegel Canada Inc., 359

ISO Index

Schwank Group, 359
Scientific Instrumentation Ltd., 360
Scintrex Ltd., 360
Sedac Inc., 361
Sherwin-Williams Canada Inc., 365
Simark Controls Ltd., 368
Smiths Detection, 371
Stemmer Steel Craft Industries Limited, 379
Sterling Press, 379
T-G Burgmann, 385
Taco Canada Ltd., 386
Techstar Plastics Inc., 388
Tecsult Inc., 388
Texel Géomembrane Inc., 391
Thomson Technology Inc., 395
TLT Co-Vent, 396
Training & Development Services, 400
Tremco Ltd., 401
Triangle Fluid Controls Ltd., 401
Ultra-Chem Industries Ltd., 405
Urgel Delisle & Associés inc., 408
V. Fournier & Associates, 408
Vansco Electronics Ltd., 409
Velan Inc., 410
Versatech Industries Inc., 412
Victaulic Co. of Canada Ltd., 413
Viterra Inc., 414
Wardrop Engineering Inc., 416
Westeel, 429
Western Industrial Services Ltd., 429
Zeton Inc., 437
Zodiac Fabrics Inc., 437

9001:1994

BEX Engineering Limited, 106
Endress+Hauser Canada Ltd., 178
Hibon Inc., 231
Invensys Systems Canada Inc., 246

9001:1994; 9001:2000

Levitt-Safety Limited, 270

9001:2000

ADI Group Inc., 68
AeroTek Manufacturing Ltd., 71
AGM Steel Industries Ltd., 73
Aircraft Appliances & Equipment Ltd., 75
All-Weld Company Limited, 79
AMKO Systems Inc., 84
Anachemia Canada Inc., 85
Aqua-Guard Spill Response Inc., 88
Aqua-Pak Styro Containers Ltd., 88
Argus Telecom International Inc., 90
Arjay Engineering Ltd., 91
Armtec Construction Products, 91
Array Systems Computing Inc., 93
Ashtead Technology Rentals, 93
Aurora Instruments Ltd., 98
AZZ Blenkhorn & Sawle Limited, 100
Belfab Inc., 104
Berg Chilling Systems Inc., 105
Brampton Engineering Inc., 115
Bruce Sutherland & Associates Ltd., 117
Can-Am Instruments Ltd., 122
Cansult Maunsell Limited, 127
Chemrec, 140
Cobham Tracking & Locating Ltd., 145
Conestoga-Rovers & Associates, 149
Elasto Valve Rubber Products Inc., 174
Enviro Rentals, 182
EnviroMed Detection Services, 184
GE Water & Process Technologies, 205
Genivar, 207
Groupe SOLROC, 221

Hercules SLR Inc., 229
Hydro Vision America, 236
Industries de Moules et Plastiques VIF, 241
Integrated Metal Products, 244
ITM Instruments, 248
John Meunier Inc., 253
Jomac Canada Inc., 253
Kavanagh & Associates Ltd., 255
Klohn Crippen Berger Ltd., 258
LINPAC Ropak Packaging, 272
Master Builders Technologies Ltd., 282
MSA: Mine Safety Applicances Company, 294
Northern Steel Industries, 307
Northway-Photomap Inc., 307
Nove Environnement Inc., 309
Products BCM Ltée BCM, 333
QSDM Inc., 338
Quad-Lock Building Systems Ltd., 338
Racan Carrier, 341
REHAU Industries Inc., 344
Romatec Incorporated, 350
Ronco Protective Products, 351
S.A. Armstrong Limited, 354
Shaw Precast Solutions, 365
Siemens Milltronics Process Instruments Inc., 366
Stantec Inc., 377
Trojan Technologies Inc., 402
Westest, 430

9001:2000; 9001:2008

CCI Thermal Technologies Inc., 133

9001; 14001

Anticorrosion Materials & Technologies Inc., 86
Avmor Ltd., 99
Boart Longyear Inc., 111
Clariant (Canada) Inc., 142
Davis Controls Ltd., 158
Fielding Chemical Technologies Inc., 195
Katch Kan Limited, 255
Magotteaux Ltée, 278
Management Horizons, 279
Marsh Instrumentation Inc., 281
Miller Environmental Corp., 290
Osram Sylvania Ltd., 314
Powersmiths International Corp., 329
Powertech Labs Inc., 329
Rockwell Automation Canada Inc., 349
Safety Projects International Inc., 355
Sika Canada Inc., 367
SNC-Lavalin Group Inc., 371
Stablex Canada Inc., 377
Zep Manufacturing Company of Canada, 436

9001:2000; 14001

GEA Westfalia Separator Canada, Inc., 205

9001:2000; TS 16949

Forsythe Lubrication Associates Ltd., 199

9001:2000; 17025

Silliker Canada Co., 367
Silliker JR Laboratories, ULC, 367

9001:2001

International Submarine Engineering Ltd., 245
Link-Pipe Inc., 272

9001:2008

ACO Container Systems Ltd., 67
Alpha Controls & Instrumentation, 79
AMETEK Process Instruments, 84
Armstrong Monitoring Corp., 91

BW Technologies by Honeywell, 119
CenturyVallen, 136
Commercial Solutions Inc., 147
Crosbie Industrial Services Ltd., 153
Electronic Warfare Associates - Canada, Ltd., 175
Geo-Logic Inc., 210
Inspec-Sol Inc., 242
JNE Consulting Ltd., 252
Nordic Systems Corporation, 305
ROMOR Atlantic Limited, 351
Symbiose Consultants inc, 385
VIQUA - A Trojan Technologies Company, 413

9001:2008; 14001

Iron Ore Company of Canada, 248

9001; 14000

Dessau, Inc., 162
Weir Power & Industrial, 424

9001; 9002

Caristrap International Inc., 128
Eco-Tec Ltd., 171
IMO Pump Inc., 239
Lennox Industries (Canada) Ltd., 267
Leeson Canada Ltd., 266
Nalco Canada Co., 296
Pan Tec Inc., 317
Stork Bronswerk Inc., 380

9001; 9002:1994

Emerson Electric Canada Limited, 177
Industrial Thermo Polymers Ltd., 241

9001; 9002; 14001

BASF Canada Inc., 103

9001; 9003:1994

Pol R Enterprises Inc., 327

9001; TS 16949

H.L. Blachford Ltd., 223

9002

Acklands-Grainger Inc., 66
Aearo Canada Ltd., 69
Aerzen Canada Surpresseurs Compresseurs inc., 71
Aqua-Rehab Inc., 88
Argo Protective Coatings Inc., 90
Atlas Polar Company Limited, 97
Atotech Canada Ltd., 97
Canon Canada Inc., 126
Cascades Fine Papers Group Inc., 130
Cascades Inc., 130
Climatizer Insulation Inc., 144
Con-Test, A Division of Contamination Containment Technology Inc., 148
Constant America Inc., 150
Divex Marine, 164
Eastcan Geomatics, 169
Edwards, 173
Emco, 176
Les Entreprises Julien Inc., 268
Environnement Godin Inc., 186
Flexahopper Plastics Ltd., 196
Flowserve Inc., 197
Focal Technologies Inc., 198
Galaxy Pallets Ltd., 204
General Paint Ltd., 206
Geolab Inc., 211
George Kelk Corporation, 211
Globetron Controls Inc., 214

ISO Index

Gorman-Rupp of Canada Ltd., 215
Graymont Inc., 216
Greystone Energy Systems Inc., 218
Haley Industries Ltd., 223
Hammond Manufacturing, 224
Howard Marten Fluid Technologies Inc., 234
Huntsman Corporation Canada Inc., 235
Les Industries Fournier Inc., 269
Intertek Systems Certification, 246
Irving Forest Services Limited, 248
KWH Pipe, 261
Les Laboratoires S.L. inc., 269
Les Laboratoires Shermont Inc., 269
Lambert Somec inc., 263
Layfield Geosynthetics & Industrial Fabrics Ltd., 265
Lubrication Engineers of Canada Ltd., 274
Lyreco Office Products, 276
Metafix, 287
Napoleon Appliance Corp., 297
NCR Canada Ltd. - Systemedia Division, 299
Nestlé Purina PetCare, 300
Peintures Denalt, 320

Phoenix Biomedical Products Inc., 323
Phoenix Contact Ltd., 323
Produits Chimiques Handy Ltée, 333
Provincial Partitions Ltd., 335
Puresource Inc., 337
Pylon Electronics, 337
Pylon Electronics Inc., 337
Scepter Manufacturing Co. Ltd., 358
SEW Eurodrive Co. of Canada Ltd., 364
Sintra Inc., 369
Société Laurentide inc., 371
Sonitec Inc., 374
StonCor Canada, 379
Sutherland-Schultz Inc., 384
Swish Maintenance Ltd., 384
Teckn-O-Laser, 388
Terminal City Iron Works Ltd., 389
Thermo-Cell Industries Ltd., 394
Tiger-Vac International Inc., 396
Wainbee Limited, 415
Waterloo Concrete Products, 422
Wilcorp Manufacturing, 431

Worldware Enterprises Ltd., 433

9002:1994
Apex Industries Inc., 86
Draeger Safety Canada Ltd., 166
Empire Dynamic Structures Ltd., 177
TMK IPSCO Inc., 397

9002; 14001
Corolon Coatings & Corrosion Control Technologies Inc., 152
Kruger Inc., 260

9002; 9004
Plad Équipement Ltée, 325

9003
Atlantic Industries Ltd., 95
Avery Dennison Canada Inc., 98
SEA Engineering Company Inc., 360

Products & Services Buyer's Guide

A&A Environmental Consultants Inc.
Formerly: A&A Environmental Services Inc.
#2, 513 Adelaide St.
Woodstock, ON N4S 4B5
519-266-4680
Fax: 519-652-8638
www.aaenvironmental.ca
Firm Type: Management Consulting, Engineering, Scientific/Technical Services
Founded: 1992
Staff: 15
Products/Services/Areas of Expertise: A multi-disciplinary environmental consulting firm active in site assessments and cleanups (ESA Phase I-IV), water resoresource studies, air quality studies, and landfill design and monitoring
Recently Completed / Ongoing Projects: Study of used tire sites, in advance of potential improvements to tire recycling programs in the Province of Ontario (Dec. 2008)
Financial Information:
Type of Ownership: Private
Revenue Sources: 10% nationwide; 10% Provincial; 20% Municipals; 60% Private Contracts
Domestic Markets:
Ontario
Contact(s):
George Duncan, Ph.D, President
H. Robert Jones, Vice-President

Canadian Branches:
Kirkland Lake
P.O. Box 17
5226 Hwy. 112
Tarzwell, ON P0K 1V0
705-642-9811
Fax: 705-642-3137
Peter Crawford, DipT., Contact

London
#126, 4026 Meadowbrook Dr.
London, ON N6L 1C7
519-266-4680
Fax: 519-652-8638
rduncan@aaenvironmental.ca
Rob Duncan, CMA, Contact

North Bay
P.O. Box 237
160 Pinewood Park Dr.
North Bay, ON P1B 8H2
705-476-2076
Fax: 705-495-1750
Elizabeth Fournier, CESA, Contact

Toronto
#311, 50 Eccleston Dr.
Toronto, ON M4A 1K8
416-615-0635
Fax: 416-615-2933
Al Robiaee, M.Sc., Contact

Winnipeg
#203, 2621 Portage Ave.
Winnipeg, MB R3J 0P7
204-889-5275
Fax: 204-889-2348
Dinko Tuhtar, Ph.D, Contact

A&C Produits Chimiques Americains Ltée
A&C American Chemicals Ltd.
3010, rue de Baene
Montréal, QC H4S 1L2
514-336-1493
Fax: 514-336-1768
800-361-9234
custserv@acamchem.com
www.acamchem.com
Firm Type: Distributing, Manufacturing
Founded: 1966
Staff: 20
Products/Services/Areas of Expertise: Solvent purification product development; high purity acids & bases; high purity salts, organics, inorganics; spill cleaning products; analytical reagents; trace element chemicals

Financial Information:
Type of Ownership: Private
Revenue Sources: 10% nationwide; 15% Provincial; 75% Private Contracts
Domestic Markets:
Alberta, British Columbia, Manitoba, New Brunswick, Newfoundland & Labrador, Nova Scotia, Ontario, Prince Edward Island, Québec, Saskatchewan
Foreign Activity:
China, Central Europe, Eastern Europe, USA, Vietnam
Contact(s):
Ken McCracken, President
ken@acamchem.com
Luc Miron, Vice President Sales and Marketing
luc@acamchem.com

A. A. Boscariol and Associates Limited
#214, 2825 Lauzon Rd.
Windsor, ON N8T 3H5
519-966-4006
Fax: 519-974-1017
boscario1@bellnet.ca
Firm Type: Engineering, Waste Management
Founded: 1966
Staff: 12
Products/Services/Areas of Expertise: Municipal engineering, land development & structual services; design; construction inspection; contract administration; damage & failure investigation; structure evaluation; construction & repair cost estimating; other services include solid & hazardous waste management, mitigation & disposal; projects have included solid waste transfer stations, material recovery facilities, sewer rehabilitation, & landfill inspection
Recently Completed / Ongoing Projects: Environmental Inspectors for Landfill No. 3, Maidstone, ON; Sanitary Sewer Rehabilitation Program, St. Clair Beach; Canadian Waste Services Inc. new maintenance facility, Windsor, ON; Waste Management Solid Waste Wentworth Court Transfer Station, Brampton, ON; Essex Windsor Solid Waste Authority, Windsor New Material Recovery Facility
Financial Information:
Type of Ownership: Private
Domestic Markets:
Ontario
Contact(s):
A.A. Boscariol, P.Eng., MA.Sc., Principal

A. Lanfranco & Associates Inc.
#101, 9488 - 189th St.
Surrey, BC V4N 4W7
604-881-2582
Fax: 604-881-2581
877-533-2584
lanfranco@telus.net
www.alanfranco.com
Firm Type: Management Consulting, Scientific/Technical Services
Founded: 1983
Staff: 8
Products/Services/Areas of Expertise: The firm specializes in air pollution sciences and is internationally recognized for its expertise in Dioxin/Furan emission measurements. Services include emissions monitoring, ambient air monitoring, special waste studies, industrial hygiene, & emission testing of marine vessels & diesel engines
Financial Information:
Type of Ownership: Private
Revenue: Greater than $5 Million
Revenue Sources: 5% nationwide; 95% Private Contracts
Domestic Markets:
Alberta, British Columbia, Manitoba
Foreign Activity:
Asia, Caribbean, South America, USA
Markets Sought:
Australia/New Zealand, Central America, China, Central Europe, Eastern Europe, Western Europe, The Pacific Rim, South America, Vietnam
Contact(s):
Alan M. Lanfranco, Principal
Lanfranco@Telus.net

A.C. Carbone Canada Inc.
Formerly: Barnebey-Sutcliffe Corp.; Barnebey-Cheney Ltd.
300, rue Brosseau
Saint-Jean-sur-Richelieu, QC J3B 2E9
450-348-1807
Fax: 450-348-3311
accarbon@accarbone.com
Firm Type: Distributing, Manufacturing
Founded: 1979
Staff: 15
Products/Services/Areas of Expertise: Activated carbon for air & water purification; a range of products providing solutions for any water, wastewater, gas & air contamination problem; non-hazardous carbon recycling service; re-activation services; air filters; solvent recovery systems
Financial Information:
Type of Ownership: Private
Revenue: $500,000 - $1.5 Million
Revenue Sources: 1% nationwide; 1% Provincial; 3% Municipals; 95% Private Contracts
Domestic Markets:
National
Foreign Activity:
Western Europe, South America, USA
Markets Sought:
Central America, South America, Mexico, USA
Contact(s):
Karl Mertn, Sr., President/CEO
Karl Mertn, Jr., General Manager, Sales & Technical
Rudolf Mertn, Vice-President

A.C. Plastiques Canada / ACP
1395, montée Chénier
Les Cèdres, QC J7T 1L9
450-455-3311
Fax: 450-452-2037
info@acplastiques.com
www.acplastiques.com
Firm Type: Manufacturing
Founded: 1968
Staff: 75
Products/Services/Areas of Expertise: Air pollution control products & systems; water & wastewater management equipment

A.H. Lundberg Systems Ltd.
Formerly: Lundberg A.H. Equipment Ltd.
#300, 5055 Joyce St.
Vancouver, BC V5R 4G7
604-629-5599
Fax: 604-629-5199
info@ahlundberg.com; sales@ahlundberg.com
www.ahlundberg.com
Firm Type: Engineering
Founded: 1954
Staff: 18
Products/Services/Areas of Expertise: Systems engineering; equipment design; equipment supply, erection & commissioning; gas collection, scrubbing, stripping, distillation, evaporation, incineration, heat recovery, oxidation (black & white), liquor heaters
Domestic Markets:
National
Foreign Activity:
Australia/New Zealand, The Pacific Rim
Contact(s):
Bruce Der, P.Eng., M.B.A., President
Allan Jensen, P.Eng., Ph.D, Technical Manager

International Branch(es):
A.H. Lundberg Associates Inc.
13201 Bel-Red Rd.
Bellevue, WA USA
425-283-5070
Fax: 425-283-5081
sales@lundbergassociates.com
www.lundbergassociates.com
Bruce Beckstrom

CANADIAN ENVIRONMENTAL RESOURCE GUIDE 2011-2012

Products & Services Buyer's Guide

A.H. Roy & Associates Ltd.
P.O. Box 1775
Antigonish, NS B2G 2M5
902-863-2955
Fax: 902-863-2214
www.ahroy.ca
Firm Type: Engineering
Founded: 1965
Products/Services/Areas of Expertise: Engineering services; incineration & power generation facilities; development of solid waste incinerators; office is located at 275 Main St. Suite 100 Antigonish, Nova Scotia
Domestic Markets:
New Brunswick, Newfoundland & Labrador, Nova Scotia, Prince Edward Island
Contact(s):
V.J. Belliveau, President

A1 Sewage Services (1989) Limited
519 Pole Line Rd., RR#5
Thunder Bay, ON P7C 5M9
807-473-9480
Fax: 807-473-9099
a1sewage@tbaytel.net
www.a1sewage.com
Firm Type: Waste Management
Founded: 1989
Products/Services/Areas of Expertise: Pumping services & liquid waste removal for industrial, commercial & residential clients; septic tank maintenance; portable toilet rentals; non-destructive excavation services. Site address: 144 Barrie Dr., Thunder Bay.
Financial Information:
Type of Ownership: Private
Domestic Markets:
Ontario

AA Environmental & Associates / AAE
#173, 138 Yorkland St.
Richmond Hill, ON L4S 1J1
905-770-5696
Fax: 905-770-4040
contact@aaenvironmental.net
www.aaenvironmentalandassociates.com
Firm Type: Engineering
Founded: 1989
Staff: 8
Member of: Professional Engineers of Ontario
Products/Services/Areas of Expertise: Provides engineering services to the corporate & public sectors; the scope of practice in the environmental field includes: research & investigation; detailed regulatory compliance review; laboratory design & training; project management; pragmatic assessment of remedial options
Recently Completed / Ongoing Projects: Brownfields development; custom-designed in-site closed loop bioremediation system was installed to treat the surface contamination & sub-surface soil contamination underneath the residence & garage
Financial Information:
Type of Ownership: Private
Domestic Markets:
Ontario
Contact(s):
Ahmad Al-Hashimi, P.Eng., Ph.D., Chief Executive Officer
Flora Nadati, Manager, Marketing

AAA Petroleum Contracting Ltd.
163 Scenic Park Cres. NW
Calgary, AB T3L 1R5
403-547-8440
Products/Services/Areas of Expertise: Certified petroleum tank contractor; installs underground or above ground fuel storage tanks, piping & pumps; environmental retrofitting of existing sites & tank removal; remediation
Contact(s):
Gary Smith, President

AADCO Automotive Inc.
38 Hansen Rd.
Brampton, ON L6W 3H4
905-789-9313
Fax: 905-789-9311
866-283-7278
info@aadco.ca
www.aadco.ca
Firm Type: Distributing
Staff: 57
EcoLogo Certified Products & Services: Recycled automotive parts
Products/Services/Areas of Expertise: Canada's only auto recycler endorsed by Environment Canada's EcoLogo; is the first choice supplier of quality recycled automotive parts to the automotive repair industry; 100% dismantling & recycling; goal is zero to landfill
Ecological Note: Recycled automotive parts
Financial Information:
Type of Ownership: Publicly Traded
Contact(s):
Charlie Hodgkinson, CEO
Vince Bulbrook, Vice-President/CFO, Finance and Administration
Don Fraser, Vice-President, Operations

AB Mechanical Ltd.
P.O. Box 1326
Sydney, NS B1P 6K3
902-567-3897
Fax: 902-564-9397
office@abmechanical.ns.ca
www.abmechanical.ca
Firm Type: Manufacturing
Staff: 75
Products/Services/Areas of Expertise: Mechanical installations; hot water, heating, plumbing, ventilation systems; office is located at 35 Rudderham Rd., Point Edward, NS, B2A 4V4
Domestic Markets:
Nova Scotia
Contact(s):
Jim Wilkie, President

Abandonrite
A Division of Nabors Canada
#2800, 500 - 4th Ave. SW
Calgary, AB T2P 2V6
403-237-8000
Fax: 403-237-8001
www.nabors.com/canada/abandonrite.asp
Firm Type: Engineering
Founded: 1988
Staff: 30
Member of: Association of Professional Engineers, Geologists & Geophysicists of Alberta
Products/Services/Areas of Expertise: Complete services to abandoned oil & gas wells, pipelines & facilities; reclamation of oil & gas leases & facilities; pre-drilling site assessments, liabilities assessments of oil & gas wells, leases & facilities
Recently Completed / Ongoing Projects: Well suspensions & abandonments, well site reclamations, pipeline abandonments
Financial Information:
Type of Ownership: Publicly Traded
Revenue: Greater than $5 Million
Revenue Sources: 100% Private Contracts
Domestic Markets:
Alberta, British Columbia, Northwest Territories, Saskatchewan
Markets Sought:
Asia, Australia/New Zealand, South America, Mexico
Contact(s):
Malcolm McKean, General Manager, 403-263-6777
malcolm.mckean@nabors.com
Josh Reed, Contact, Domestic Sales & Marketing
josh.reed@nabors.com
Ken Bax, Manager
ken.bax@nabors.com

ABB Inc. (Canada)
Formerly: Bomem Inc.
8585, rte Transcanadienne
Montréal, QC H4S 1Z6
514-856-6222
Fax: 514-856-6299
800-905-0222
www.abb.ca
Firm Type: Engineering, Manufacturing
Founded: 1973
Quality Environmental Management System(s): 9001
Products/Services/Areas of Expertise: A technology-based provider of power & automation products, systems, solutions & services; offers a range of products & solutions to help clients utilize electrical power effectively & increase productivity in a sustainable way. ABB in Canada employs over 2,500 people in 43 locations. Headquartered in Zurich, Switzerland, with locations worldwide
Domestic Markets:
National
Foreign Activity:
Asia, Australia/New Zealand, Central America, Eastern Europe, Western Europe, The Middle East, The Pacific Rim, USA
Contact(s):
Daniel Assandri, Country Manager, Canada

ABBA Pump Parts & Service
Dracay Management Inc.
5370 Munro Ct.
Burlington, ON L7L 5N8
905-333-2720
Fax: 905-333-0973
800-268-5142
info@abbaparts.com
www.abbaparts.com
Firm Type: Distributing, Manufacturing
Staff: 7
Products/Services/Areas of Expertise: Manufacturer & distributor of high quality parts & assemblies for centrifugal pumps used in water & wastewater treatment facilities
Contact(s):
Jim Miller, Manager
jim_m@abbaparts.com

Abbeywood Associates Inc.
128 Abbeywood Trail
Toronto, ON M3B 3B5
416-445-5306
Fax: 416-383-0353
gordreed@sympatico.ca
Products/Services/Areas of Expertise: A single person firm specializing in Phase 1 Environmental Site Assessments, & consultation on environmental issues for owners
Contact(s):
Gordon A.D. Reed, Principal

Abbott Strategies
5178 Agate Lane
Victoria, BC V8Y 2L9
250-888-9406
rob.abbott@shaw.ca
www.abbottstrategies.com
Firm Type: Management Consulting
Founded: 1997
Member of: Strategic Leadership Forum; Canadian Association of Management Consultants
Products/Services/Areas of Expertise: Mission is to help clients understand how environmental, social & economic choices influence strategic positions & decisions in business, & to demonstrate how more sustainable approaches can improve business performance
Recently Completed / Ongoing Projects: Managing for sustainability framework, Seattle, WA
Financial Information:
Type of Ownership: Private
Domestic Markets:
National
Foreign Activity:
Australia/New Zealand, Western Europe, USA
Contact(s):
Rob Abbott, Founder
Canadian Branches:
Mayne
Comp. 16, Site 221, 502 Dalton Dr.
Mayne, BC V0N 2J0

ABCO Industries Ltd.
P.O. Box 1120
81 Tannery Rd.
Lunenburg, NS B0J 2C0
902-634-8821
Fax: 902-634-8583
866-634-8821
info@abco.ca
www.abco.ca
Firm Type: Manufacturing
Founded: 1947
Staff: 60
Products/Services/Areas of Expertise: Supplier and manufacturer of engineered metal products to processing and marine industries
Contact(s):
J.D. Eisenhauer, CEO

Abcott Construction Ltd.
124 Garden Ave.
Brantford, ON N3S 7W4
519-756-4350
Fax: 519-756-8721
877-558-5584
info@abcott.ca
www.abcott.ca
Firm Type: Engineering
Founded: 1972
Staff: 40
Products/Services/Areas of Expertise: Design-Build construction & environmental projects, abatement, demolition & remediation
Recently Completed / Ongoing Projects: Brantford Golf & Country Club; Nelson Steel; Dana Manufacturing
Financial Information:
Type of Ownership: Private
Revenue: Greater than $5 Million
Revenue Sources: 10% Municipals; 90% Private Contracts
Domestic Markets:
Ontario
Contact(s):
Don Bremner, President
dbremner@abcott.ca
Vic Benson, Senior Project Manager
vbenson@abcott.ca
Patrick Hayes, Senior Project Manager
phayes@abcott.ca
Darryl Lawrie, Construction Manager
dlawrie@abcott.ca

ABGG Technologies Inc.
#500, 9145, boul Mathieu
Charlesbourg, QC G1G 6J9
418-621-8890
Fax: 418-621-8891
info@abgg.ca
www.abgg.ca
Firm Type: Engineering, Manufacturing
Founded: 2001
Staff: 6
Member of: Réseau Environnement
Products/Services/Areas of Expertise: Air pollution control equipment; thermal systems
Recently Completed / Ongoing Projects: 300,000 m3/h electrostatic precipitates; 4-16 dryers for waterbased plants
Financial Information:
Type of Ownership: Private
Revenue: $1.5 Million - $3 Million
Revenue Sources: 100% Private Contracts
Domestic Markets:
New Brunswick, Newfoundland & Labrador, Nova Scotia, Ontario, Prince Edward Island, Québec
Contact(s):
Gérard Gosselin, Président
Benoît Gosselin, Technical Support
Aline Audet, Administrative Assistant

Abitibi-Consolidated Inc.
Formerly: Donohue Inc.
#800, 1155 Metcalfe St.
Montréal, QC H3B 5H2
514-875-2160
info@abitibiconsolidated.com
www.abitibiconsolidated.com
Firm Type: Manufacturing
Founded: 1912
Member of: Canadian Pulp & Paper Association; Ontario Forest Association; Québec Forest Industries Association
Products/Services/Areas of Expertise: Newsprint & uncoated groundwood (value-added groundwood) papers; paper recycling; wood products; woodlands operations; electricity production
Financial Information:
Type of Ownership: Publicly Traded
Domestic Markets:
National
Foreign Activity:
Asia, Caribbean, Eastern Europe, Western Europe, The Middle East, The Pacific Rim, South America, USA
Contact(s):
David J. Paterson, President & CEO
Alain Grandmont, Executive Vice-President, Human Resources
Yves Laflamme, Sr. Vice-President, Wood Products

Canadian Branches:
Vancouver
1401 - 1130 Pender St. West
Vancouver, BC V6E 4A4
604-891-3206
Fax: 250-997-5133
rick_hundel@abicom.com

ABL Environmental Consultants
102 Portland St.
Dartmouth, NS B2Y 1H8
902-466-0050
Fax: 902-469-4399
abl@ablenvironmental.com
www.ablenvironmental.com
Firm Type: Engineering, Waste Management
Founded: 1994
Products/Services/Areas of Expertise: Specializes in wastewater collection & treatment; water treatment & distribution; plant operations & optimization; bench & pilot testing; solid waste management; impact assessment; municipal infrastructure engineering; construction administration & project management; design build & turnkey projects; innovative & alternate technologies; second office located at 43 Webster St., Dartmouth, Nova Scotia, B2Y 1H8
Contact(s):
Thomas P. Austin, M.Sc., P.Eng., President
John C. Lam, P.Eng., Vice-President

Abydoz Environmental
48 Glencoe Dr.
Mount Pearl, NL A1N 4S9
709-895-2120
Fax: 709-895-2911
877-542-5884
info@abydoz.com
www.abydoz.com
Firm Type: Engineering
Founded: 1997
Member of: Association of Professional Engineers of Newfoundland
Products/Services/Areas of Expertise: Water & wastewater treatment; water, wastewater & groundwater equipment; sludge treatment; glycol treatment; landfill leuchute treatment
Recently Completed / Ongoing Projects: Sewage treatment for IOCC, Labrador City, NL; Sewage treatment, Appletree & Glenwood, NL; Sludge treatment system, Stephenville, NL
Financial Information:
Type of Ownership: Private
Revenue: $250,000 - $500,000
Revenue Sources: 100% Private Contracts
Domestic Markets:
New Brunswick, Newfoundland & Labrador, Nova Scotia, Ontario, Prince Edward Island
Foreign Activity:
Central America, USA
Markets Sought:
Caribbean, Mexico
Contact(s):
Eric Cook, President
Glenn Sharp, P.Eng., Engineer

AC Environmental Services
A division of Enertia Engineering Ltd.
#109, 117 Pembina Rd.
Sherwood Park, AB T8H 0J4
780-467-0303
Fax: 780-401-3519
866-796-0303
www.ac-environmental.com
Firm Type: Distributing, Engineering, Waste Management

Products/Services/Areas of Expertise: Bioremediation & spill containment products & services; specializes in oil spill containment, spill clean-up, microbial remediation, heavy metal removal, & hazardous chemical handling; distributor for JNJ Smart-Bond remediation products; green cleaning products for industrial settings. The company is 20% Native-owned. Branch office located at #203, 7 Cedar St., Sudbury, ON - contact 1-877-693-4829
Financial Information:
Type of Ownership: Private
Domestic Markets:
Alberta, Ontario
Contact(s):
Darcy Braun, PEng., M.Sc., Principal Engineer
Darin Hucul, PEng., PEC, Principal Engineer

AC Plastiques Canada Inc.
1395 montée Chénier
Les Cèdres, QC J7T 1L9
450-455-3311
Fax: 450-452-2037
info@acplastiques.com, sales@acplastiques.com
www.acplastiques.com
Firm Type: Distributing, Manufacturing
Quality Environmental Management System(s): 9001
Products/Services/Areas of Expertise: Manufacturer of Dual Laminate & FRP Process equipments such as vessels and piping systems; plastic products and containers
Financial Information:
Type of Ownership: Private
Domestic Markets:
National
Foreign Activity:
China, Eastern Europe, South Africa, USA

Acadia Consultants & Inspectors Ltd. / ACI
Division of ADI Group Inc.
40 Henri Dunant St.
Moncton, NB E1E 1E5
506-857-8313
Fax: 506-857-8315
moncton@adi.ca
www.adi.ca
Firm Type: Engineering, Scientific/Technical Services, Waste Management
Founded: 1973
Staff: 20
Products/Services/Areas of Expertise: Solid waste management; contaminant engineering; site remediation; construction supervision; management consulting; water supply; wastewater treatment; field & laboratory testing; erosion control; feasibility studies
Financial Information:
Type of Ownership: Private
Revenue Sources: 10% nationwide; 15% Provincial; 35% Municipals; 10% Private Contracts
Domestic Markets:
New Brunswick, Prince Edward Island
Foreign Activity:
Eastern Europe, The Middle East, South America
Contact(s):
Roland LeBlanc, P.Eng., President
rleblanc@adi.ca
Hollis Cole, Chief Executive Officer
hbc@adi.ca
Paul Morrison, Vice-President
pdm@adi.ca
David Crandall, Vice-President
ddc@adi.ca

Accurassay Laboratories
1046 Gorham St.
Thunder Bay, ON P7B 5X5
807-626-1630
Fax: 807-622-7571
assay@accurassay.com
www.accurassay.com
Firm Type: Scientific/Technical Services
Member of: Canadian Association of Environmental Analytical Laboratories
Products/Services/Areas of Expertise: Environmental analysis laboratory; geotechnical analysis; emergency spills analysis; sample collection; industrial hygiene analysis; environmental site assessment & clean-up. Main facility located in Thunder Bay, with corporate office in London, ON. Sample preparation facilities are located in Gambo, NL; Sudbury, ON; & Yellowknife, NT
Financial Information:
Revenue: $500,000 - $1.5 Million
Domestic Markets:
Manitoba, Ontario, Québec
Contact(s):
Jason Moore, Contact

Canadian Branches:
Corporate Office
#115, 4096 Meadowbrook Dr.
London, ON N6L 1G4
Fax: 519-652-8638
888-652-8174
assay-ld@accurassay.com
Rob Duncan, Contact

Products & Services Buyer's Guide

Accurate Industrial Waste Limited
100 Bass Pro Mills Dr.
Concord, ON L4K 5X1
905-738-5053
Fax: 905-660-9944
888-596-3960
Firm Type: Waste Management
Founded: 1939
Staff: 4
Member of: Ontario Trucking Association
Products/Services/Areas of Expertise: Liquid waste hauling, including waste oily water & oils, septic services, tank cleaning
Financial Information:
Type of Ownership: Private
Revenue Sources: 15% Municipals; 85% Private Contracts
Domestic Markets:
Ontario
Contact(s):
Ron Passer, President
Mike McCall, Manager, Marketing

Accutest Laboratories Ltd.
#8, 146 Colonnade Rd.
Ottawa, ON K2E 7Y1
613-727-5692
Fax: 613-727-5222
888-271-8378
info@accutestlabs.com
www.accutestlabs.com
Firm Type: Engineering, Scientific/Technical Services
Founded: 1987
Staff: 15
Member of: Canadian Spectroscopy Society; Canadian Association of Environmental Analytical Laboratories; Canadian Institute of Chemistry
Products/Services/Areas of Expertise: Environmental analysis of soil & water; analysis of agricultural soils & animal feeds
Financial Information:
Type of Ownership: Private
Domestic Markets:
National
Foreign Activity:
Asia, South America
Contact(s):
Peter Haulena, Analytical Services Manager
phaulena@accutestlabs.com
Timothy McCooeye, Quality Control Manager
tmccooeye@accutestlabs.com
Robert Walker, Client Services Manager
rwalker@accutestlabs.com

Canadian Branches:
Kingston
608 Norris Ct.
Kingston, ON K7P 2G5
613-634-9307
Fax: 613-634-9308
jonesj@accutestlabs.com
Jeff Jones, C.E.T., Branch Manager

Accuworx Inc.
40 Advance Blvd.
Brampton, ON L6T 4J4
416-410-7222
Fax: 416-410-7405
info@accuworx.ca
www.accuworx.ca
Firm Type: Engineering, Scientific/Technical Services
Founded: 1989
Products/Services/Areas of Expertise: Industrial & commercial cleaning, including pressure washing, soda blasting & industrial vacuuming services
Domestic Markets:
Ontario
Contact(s):
Jason Rosset, President

ACDEG International Inc.
3784 Southridge Ave.
West Vancouver, BC V7V 3J1
604-230-0668
Fax: 604-922-7650
dtfung@axion.net
Firm Type: Distributing, Manufacturing, Waste Management
Founded: 1989
Products/Services/Areas of Expertise: The company has interests in manufacturing (custom manufacturing of electronic components), technology development (waste recycling technologies), marketing & distribution (pulp & paper products), & infrastructure projects; other concerns include electrical power cogeneration, renewable energy, environmental protection, specialty chemicals
Financial Information:
Type of Ownership: Private
Domestic Markets:
National
Foreign Activity:
Asia, China, Vietnam
Contact(s):
David T. Fung, CEO

ACE Vegetation Control Service Ltd.
2001 - 8th St.
Nisku, AB T9E 7Z1
780-955-8980
Fax: 780-955-9426
800-292-6917
acemail@acevegetation.com
www.acevegetation.com
Firm Type: Scientific/Technical Services
Founded: 1980
Products/Services/Areas of Expertise: Vegetation management services, with a client focus on the oil & gas industry, pipeline projects, & utilities; design & implementation of cost-effective, efficient programs to manage vegetation safely
Recently Completed / Ongoing Projects: Pipeline spray program for brush control
Financial Information:
Type of Ownership: Private
Revenue: Greater than $5 Million
Domestic Markets:
Alberta, British Columbia, Manitoba, Northwest Territories, Ontario, Saskatchewan, Yukon Territory
Contact(s):
Richard Law, President

Acer Environmental Services Ltd.
183 Talisman Crescent
Fredericton, NB E3C 1M1
506-206-1379
Fax: 506-460-6323
gpelkey@acerenvironmental.com
www.acerenvironmental.com
Products/Services/Areas of Expertise: Environmental services; risk assessment; impact assessments; waste management services; air quality assesments; environmental auditing
Domestic Markets:
New Brunswick
Contact(s):
Gerald Pelkey, MSc. P.Eng, President, 506-260-0234

ACG Technology Ltd.
#13, 131 Whitmore Rd.
Woodbridge, ON L4L 6E4
905-856-1414
Fax: 905-856-6401
sales@acgtechnology.com
www.acgtechnology.com
Firm Type: Manufacturing, Scientific/Technical Services
Founded: 1981
Staff: 6
Member of: Canadian Environment Industry Association; Association of Professional Engineers of Ontario
Products/Services/Areas of Expertise: Wastewater treatment systems & equipment; recovery systems; oil coalescers, oil/water separators, waste treatment systems & equipment
Financial Information:
Type of Ownership: Private
Revenue Sources: 100% Private Contracts
Domestic Markets:
National
Foreign Activity:
USA
Markets Sought:
The Pacific Rim
Contact(s):
Greg Jackson, President
Blake Tonogai, P.Eng., Partner/Owner, Product Management
Dale Jackson, Technical Sales Representative

Acklands-Grainger Inc. / AGI
Engineered Products Div.
90 West Beaver Creek Rd.
Richmond Hill, ON L4B 1E7
905-731-5516
contact@agi.ca
www.acklandsgrainger.com
Firm Type: Distributing
Founded: 1889
Staff: 2200
Member of: Industrial Suppliers Association
Quality Environmental Management System(s): 9002
Products/Services/Areas of Expertise: Distributor of industrial, safety & fastener supplies with 165 branches across Canada
Financial Information:
Type of Ownership: Foreign-owned
Revenue: Greater than $5 Million
Domestic Markets:
National
Contact(s):
Sean O'Brien, President
Henry Buckley, Vice-President / General Manager, Marketing
Yolanda Daniel, Vice-President, Finance

Canadian Branches:
Edmonton Branch
15986 - 118 Avenue
Edmonton, AB T5V 1C4
780-453-3071
Fax: 780-454-6548
robertss@agi.ca
Wally Ponich, Director

Markham Branch
#1, 30 Shields Court
Markham, ON L3R 9T5
905-940-5535
Fax: 905-940-5537
jamest@agi.ca
John Brand, Business Manager

ACM Environmental Corporation
#217, 2323 Québec St.
Vancouver, BC V5T 4S7
604-873-8599
Fax: 604-873-5956
info@acmenvironmental.com
www.acmenvironmental.com
Firm Type: Management Consulting, Engineering, Scientific/Technical Services, Waste Management
Founded: 1989
Staff: 6
Products/Services/Areas of Expertise: Industrial & environmental health & safety consultants, with expertise in asbestos abatement, lead abatement, mold remediation, site assessments, soil remediation, indoor air quality, grow-op & illegal drug manufacturing facility remediation; lab services offered through associated facilities
Domestic Markets:
Alberta, British Columbia, Manitoba, Saskatchewan, Yukon Territory
Foreign Activity:
Asia, Australia/New Zealand
Markets Sought:
Eastern Europe
Contact(s):
Jari E. Saarela, C.E.I.; R.H.I., President

Acme Engineering Products Ltd.
Acme Produits d'Ingénierie Ltée
5706, av Royalmount
Montréal, QC H4P 1K5
514-342-5656
Fax: 514-342-3131
info@acmeprod.com
www.acmeprod.com
Firm Type: Distributing, Manufacturing
Founded: 1956
Staff: 20
Member of: American Society of Heating, Refrigeration & Air Conditioning Engineers
Quality Environmental Management System(s): 9001
Products/Services/Areas of Expertise: Manufactures & distributes gas detection equipment for building ventilation control; automatic strainers for intake process & effluent filtration; electric & high voltage electronic boilers for process heating; GRS & electric steam superheaters. US office located in

Mooers, NY (518-236-5659)
Recently Completed / Ongoing Projects: Automatic strainers for mine water filtration at Codelco El-Teniente mine, Chile; Gas detection system at Kennedy Centre, Washington, DC; Gas detection panel, Canadian Forces Base, ON; furnace, water strainer, Cominco, BC; 8 automatic strainers, Hydro Québec
Financial Information:
Type of Ownership: Private
Revenue: $1.5 Million - $3 Million
Revenue Sources: 10% nationwide; 20% Provincial; 70% Private Contracts
Domestic Markets:
National
Foreign Activity:
Worldwide
Markets Sought:
Eastern Europe, Mexico
Contact(s):
G.S. Presser, President
Robert Presser, Vice-President
Michael McKee, Manager, Sales

ACME Vacuum Cleaner Co. Ltd.
ACME Vacuum Compagnie Ltée
3000, rue Sartelon
Montréal, QC H4R 1E3
514-336-8852
Fax: 514-336-8225
acme@acme-vacuum.com
www.acme-vacuum.com
Firm Type: Distributing, Manufacturing
Founded: 1909
Staff: 7
Member of: Association québécoise des techniques de l'eau
Products/Services/Areas of Expertise: Design, sale & installation of central vacuum cleaning systems; sale of blowers, dust collectors; industrial mobile vacuums; gas boosters; tube & fittings for central vacuum systems; hoses & tools for vacuums
Domestic Markets:
New Brunswick, Newfoundland & Labrador, Nova Scotia, Ontario, Prince Edward Island, Québec
Contact(s):
Paul Laplante, Contact

ACO Container Systems Ltd.
794 McKay Rd.
Pickering, ON L1W 2Y4
905-683-8222
Fax: 905-683-2969
800-542-9942
www.acotainers.com
Firm Type: Distributing, Manufacturing
Founded: 1974
Staff: 35
Quality Environmental Management System(s): 9001:2008
Products/Services/Areas of Expertise: Bulk liquid storage tanks; intermediate bulk containers; containers range in size from 5 to 10,000 gallons; containment basins; chemical dispensing systems
Domestic Markets:
National
Foreign Activity:
Africa, Mexico, USA
Markets Sought:
Asia, Central America, China, The Pacific Rim, Mexico, USA, Former USSR
Contact(s):
Stephen Assmann, President
Robert Glover, Manager, Export Sales & Marketing

Canadian Branches:
Alberta
121 Schooner Landing NW
Calgary, AB T3L 1X5
403-547-3261
Fax: 403-547-3261
Sid Copperthwaite, Alberta Representative

JGK Solutions
63, rue Grenier
Saint-Luc, QC J2W 1P6
450-359-9578
Fax: 450-398-4488
John Knight, Québec Representative

Ontario
28 Broadmoor Ave.
Barrie, ON L4N 3M9

705-722-3891
Fax: 705-739-7039
Bruce Sticklee, Northern Ontario Representative

Acorus Restoration Native Plant Nursery
#722 6th Concession Rd., RR#1
Walsingham, ON N0E 1X0
519-586-2603
Fax: 519-586-2447
info@ecologyart.com
www.ecologyart.com
Firm Type: Scientific/Technical Services
Founded: 1995
Staff: 8
Products/Services/Areas of Expertise: Ecological restoration; grows local source native plants; ecological consulting; landscaping; installation; ecoparks, green roofs; tree planting; habitat restoration; landfill leachate; mine reclamation; wastewater treatment; storm water management ponds
Financial Information:
Revenue: $250,000 - $500,000
Revenue Sources: 50% Municipals; 50% Private Contracts
Domestic Markets:
National
Foreign Activity:
USA
Contact(s):
Paul Morris, B.Sc., M.Sc., Principal
Catherine Riley-Arenburg, Office Manager

Acoustic Solutions Ltd.
11602 - 119 St.
Edmonton, AB T5G 2X7
780-423-2119
Fax: 780-426-0325
800-661-7241
info@acousticsolutions.com
www.acousticsolutions.com
Firm Type: Management Consulting, Distributing, Manufacturing
Founded: 1974
Staff: 8
Member of: Western Noise Control; Industrial Noise Control
Products/Services/Areas of Expertise: Sound absorbing masonry blocks; noise barrier products; Echotrol baffles & panels; vibration mounts; masking equipment; noise problem analysis; installantion; retro-fit projects
Recently Completed / Ongoing Projects: Skytrain Stations, Vancouver, BC; Esplanade, Medicine Hat, AB; Molson Centre, Montréal; ACT Recreation Centre, Edmonton; North Peace Leisure Pool, Fort St John; Collicutt Centre, Red Deer; U of A Engineering Bldg.
Financial Information:
Type of Ownership: Private
Revenue: $500,000 - $1.5 Million
Revenue Sources: 5% nationwide; 10% Provincial; 10% Municipals; 75% Private Contracts
Domestic Markets:
National
Foreign Activity:
USA
Contact(s):
Isidor Gliener, President
izzy@acousticsolutions.com
John Stepovy, Sales
john@acousticsolutions.com

Acres & Associated Environmental Ltd.
#525, 21 Four Seasons Place
Toronto, ON M9B 6J8
416-622-9502
Fax: 416-622-6249
Firm Type: Management Consulting, Engineering, Scientific/Technical Services, Waste Management
Founded: 1996
Staff: 50
Products/Services/Areas of Expertise: Water resources planning; water treatment, storage & transmission; wastewater treatment; computerized control systems; municipal infrastructure; municipal solid waste management; hazardous materials management & site remediation; environmental health & safety; watershed & natural resource management; environmental assessments, audits & monitoring; environmental permits & approvals
Financial Information:
Type of Ownership: Private
Domestic Markets:
Ontario

Foreign Activity:
Africa, Asia, Caribbean, South America
Contact(s):
Bill Chisholm, President

Canadian Branches:
Niagara Falls
P.O. Box 1001
4342 Queen St.
Niagara Falls, ON L2E 6W1
905-374-4470
Fax: 905-374-8365
admin@niagarafalls.aae.on.ca
Bruce Bennett

Acsion Industries Inc.
P.O. Box 429
402 Ara Mooradian Way
Pinawa, MB R0E 1L0
204-753-2255
Fax: 204-753-8466
acsion@acsion.com
www.acsion.com
Firm Type: Engineering, Manufacturing
Founded: 1998
Staff: 12
Quality Environmental Management System(s): 9001
Products/Services/Areas of Expertise: Developer and provider of electron beam (E-beam) treated products and services in North America; Develops and markets E-beam-based products and services for aerospace, healthcare, and agri-food customers
Financial Information:
Type of Ownership: Private
Domestic Markets:
National
Foreign Activity:
USA
Contact(s):
John Barnard, Director, Research and Technology
barnard@acsion.com

Activation Laboratories Ltd. / ACTLABS
Member company of The Actlabs Group of Companies
1336 Sandhill Dr.
Ancaster, ON L9G 4V5
905-648-9611
Fax: 905-648-9613
888-228-5227
ancaster@actlabs.com
www.actlabs.com
Firm Type: Scientific/Technical Services
Founded: 1987
Staff: 92
Products/Services/Areas of Expertise: Laboratory services & water analysis; custom analytical services; geochemistry & geochronology; pharmaceuticals; environmental; industrial minerals; petroleum; agriculture; forensics; materials testing. Labs located in Ancaster, Timmins, Thunder Bay, Goose Bay & Fredericton
Financial Information:
Type of Ownership: Private
Revenue Sources: 10% nationwide; 10% Provincial; 80% Private Contracts
Domestic Markets:
National
Foreign Activity:
Asia, Australia/New Zealand, Caribbean, South America, Worldwide
Contact(s):
Eric Hoffman, General Manager

Active Chemicals Ltd.
#1, 7157 Honeyman St.
Delta, BC V4G 1E2
604-946-0361
Fax: 604-946-3901
800-663-6090
www.activechemicalsltd.com
Firm Type: Distributing, Manufacturing
Founded: 1968
Staff: 20
Products/Services/Areas of Expertise: Manufacturer of cleaning chemicals, lubricants, additives; treatment of wastewater & oil; contract cleaning systems & services; biodegradable products

Products & Services Buyer's Guide

Financial Information:
Type of Ownership: Private
Revenue Sources: 10% Provincial; 2% Municipals; 88% Private Contracts
Domestic Markets:
National
Foreign Activity:
USA
Markets Sought:
The Pacific Rim
Contact(s):
James C. Wilson, President
Mike Melenka, General Manager

Addy Environmental Services Inc. / AES
#201, 45-2000 Airport Road NE
Calgary, AB T2E 6W5
403-701-4051
jaddy@aes-inc.ca
www.aes-inc.ca
Firm Type: Management Consulting
Founded: 1997
Products/Services/Areas of Expertise: Consulting services for the oil & gas industry, assisting with maintaining environmental, health and safety regulatory compliance
Contact(s):
John Addy, President

Adhawk Communications Inc.
#109, 21 Antares Dr.
Ottawa, ON K2E 7T8
613-723-8516
adhawk@adhawk.ca
www.adhawk.ca
Firm Type: Information Technology
Staff: 8
Products/Services/Areas of Expertise: Communications design & social marketing for health, environmental & urban issues
Contact(s):
Chris Mercer, President

ADI Group Inc.
#300, 1133 Regent St.
Fredericton, NB E3B 3Z2
506-452-9000
Fax: 506-451-7451
adigroup@adi.ca
www.adi.ca
Firm Type: Management Consulting, Engineering, Scientific/Technical Services
Founded: 1945
Staff: 250
Member of: American Water Works Association; Association of Consulting Engineers of Canada; Canadian Water & Wastewater Association; Canadian Environment Industry Association; Maine Rural Water Association; Maine Water Utility Association; Consulting Engineers of New Brunswick; Consulting Engineers of Nova Scotia; Canadian Council of Professional Engineers
Quality Environmental Management System(s): 9001:2000
Products/Services/Areas of Expertise: An employee-owned firm with a focus on contaminant hydrogeology, environmental site assessment, risk assessment, petroleum contamination evaluation & remediation, indoor air quality monitoring, mining & metallurgical services (including reclamation), water & wastewater treatment, solid waste services (sanitary landfills, recycling & composting). Operating companies: ADI Limited, ADI International, ADI Systems Inc., & Geomembrane Technologies Inc. Office locations throughout the Maritimes, as well as Alberta & the U.S. See the website for a complete listing
Activities: Emergency Response: emergency response planning, contingency planning, product management planning, spill response; Environmental Engineering: air pollution control, wastewater treatment systems, solid waste management; Environmental Management: environmental impact assessment, environmental permitting, regulatory liaison, environmental compliance audits, environmental management system to follow ISO 14000 standard
Recently Completed / Ongoing Projects: Power plant wastewater treatment, (Coleson Cove); leachate plume delineation & design of a leachate & methane collection upgrade at Hwy. 101 landfill in Halifax, NS; waste treatment plant Village of New Maryland
Financial Information:
Type of Ownership: Private
Revenue: Greater than $5 Million
Revenue Sources: 5% nationwide; 15% Provincial; 25% Municipals; 55% Private Contracts
Domestic Markets:
National
Foreign Activity:
Worldwide
Contact(s):
Hollis B. Cole, P.Eng., President/CEO
Paul Morrison, P.Eng., President/COO
Graham Brown, M.S.C.E., P.Eng., President, ADI Systems Inc.
David Beattie, P.Eng., Vice President, ADI International Inc.
Brian MacLean, P.Eng., Director, Geomembrane Technologies Inc.

Canadian Branches:
Charlottetown - ADI Limited
P.O. Box 2800
49 Pownal St.
Charlottetown, PE C1A 8C4
902-892-0086
Fax: 902-628-1807
pei@adi.ca
Darrell Fisher, P.Eng.
dfisher@adi.ca

Fredericton - ADI Limited, Head Office
#300, 1133 Regent St.
Fredericton, NB E3B 3Z2
506-452-9000
Fax: 506-459-3954
adigroup@adi.ca
Paul Morrison, P.Eng., President/COO
pdm@adi.ca

Fredericton - ADI Limited, Architectural Services Division
#300, 1133 Regent St.
Fredericton, NB E3B 3Z2
506-452-9000
Fax: 506-452-7303
Thomas Horrocks, AANB, MCIP
tdh@adi.ca

Fredericton - Geomembrane Technologies Inc.
#300, 1133 Regent St.
Fredericton, NB E3B 3Z2
506-452-7304
Fax: 506-459-3954
covers@gticovers.com
Brian MacLean, P.Eng.
rbm@gti.ca

Halifax - ADI Limited
#252, 7071 Bayers Rd.
Halifax, NS B3L 2C2
902-453-5555
Fax: 902-453-6325
halifax@adi.ca
Tim Murphy, P.Eng.
tmurphy@adi.ca

Moncton - ADI Limited/Acadia Consultants & Inspectors Limited
40 Henri Dunant St.
Moncton, NB E1E 1E5
506-857-8889
Fax: 506-857-8315
moncton@adi.ca
Member of: Enerplan Consultants Ltd. located at the same address
Roland LeBlanc, P.Eng.
rleblanc@adi.ca

Oromocto - Geomembane Technologies Inc. Fabrication Plant
6 Lewis St.
Oromocto, NB E2V 2X5
506-357-3077
Fax: 506-357-3070
Darin Evans, P.Eng.
dre@gti.ca

Port Hawkesbury - ADI Limited
P.O. Box 1688
77 Kings Rd.
Sydney, NS B1S 1A2
902-625-5745
Fax: 902-625-5746
porthawkesbury@adi.ca
Gary Landry, P.Eng.
glandry@adi.ca

Saint John - ADI Limited
520 Somerset St.
Saint John, NB E2K 2Y7
506-646-8020
Fax: 506-646-8025
saintjohn@adi.ca
Richard Smith, P.Eng.
rns@adi.ca

St. John's - ADI Limited
60 Pippy Place
St. John's, NL A1B 4H7
709-579-2027
Fax: 709-579-7115
nfld@adi.ca
Member of: Newfoundland and Labrador Consulting Engineers Ltd. located at the same address
William Melendy, P.Eng
wmelendy@adi.ca

Sydney - ADI Limited
P.O. Box 1688
77 Kings Rd.
Sydney, NS B1S 1A2
902-562-2394
Fax: 902-564-5660
sydney@adi.ca
Omar Roach, CET
oroach@adi.ca

International Branch(es):
Wolfeboro, NH - ADI Systems Inc.
P.O. Box 397
7 Pointe Sewall Rd.
Wolfeboro, NH USA
603-569-0955
Fax: 603-569-0957
Albert Cocci, Ph.D, P.E.
acocci@adi.ca

Adkinson & Associates
4044 Aberdeen Rd., SS3
Beamsville, ON L0R 1B6
905-563-0539
Fax: 905-563-0539
don_adkinson@canada.com
Firm Type: Management Consulting, Information Technology, Scientific/Technical Services
Founded: 1979
Staff: 2
Products/Services/Areas of Expertise: Consultants specializing in photovoltaic technology; related system design feasiblity studies, product sourcing, marketing, production, & research assistance
Financial Information:
Type of Ownership: Private
Revenue Sources: 100% Private Contracts
Domestic Markets:
National
Foreign Activity:
Caribbean, USA
Contact(s):
Donald Adkinson, President/CEO

Advance Engineered Products Ltd.
144 Henderson Dr.
Regina, SK S4N 5P7
306-721-5678
Fax: 306-721-5010
www.advanceengineeredproducts.com
Firm Type: Distributing, Manufacturing
Founded: 1984
Staff: 720
Products/Services/Areas of Expertise: Manufacturer of steel/aluminum petroleum & chemical tanks & trailers; vacuum loading equipment
Activities: Waste transportation & cleanup research
Domestic Markets:
National
Foreign Activity:
Asia, The Pacific Rim, Mexico, USA
Contact(s):
Gerry van Wachem, President
Bill Pietz, Sales, Vacuum Truck Division (Edmonton Branch)

Canadian Branches:
Calgary Office
5502 - 56 Ave. SE
Calgary, AB T2C 4M6
403-720-4888
Fax: 403-720-4850
Dave Carrier

Edmonton Office
10498 - 17 St.
Edmonton, AB T6P 1V8
780-467-8891
Fax: 780-467-0950
Earl Mitty

Advance Laboratories Ltd.
A subsidary of Epsilon Chemicals Ltd.
Eastern Shore Industrial Park
30 Colford Dr.
Chezzetcook, NS B0J 1N0
902-827-3339
Fax: 902-827-3773
800-499-3773
labs@advancelabs.com
www.advancelabs.com
Firm Type: Engineering, Manufacturing, Scientific/Technical Services
Founded: 1987
Staff: 11
Member of: Epsilon Chemicals Ltd.
Products/Services/Areas of Expertise: The firm is engaged in the manufacture of environmentally friendly, biodegradable chemicals used in food processing, sanitation, & transportation. Eg.: cleaning chemicals; pollution control chemicals; environmentally correct solvent & non-solvent degreasers & detergents
Domestic Markets:
New Brunswick, Newfoundland & Labrador
Foreign Activity:
Central America, Eastern Europe, Western Europe
Contact(s):
Colm O'Carroll, President/CEO
Stephen Landry, COO
stephen@advancelabs.com

Advanced Biotechnology Inc. / ABT
P.O. Box 3637
2 East Lake Way
Airdrie, AB T4B 2B8
403-912-7424
Fax: 403-948-4780
info@abtinc.ca
www.gomixer.com
Firm Type: Distributing, Manufacturing, Waste Management
Founded: 2003
Staff: 2
Member of: Double T Equipment Ltd.
Products/Services/Areas of Expertise: Manufacturer & distributor of the GOMIXER complete organic waste disposal system; wood gasifier heating systems
Financial Information:
Type of Ownership: Private
Domestic Markets:
National
Foreign Activity:
USA, Worldwide
Contact(s):
Thomas Thomas, President
Rey Rawlins, Sales

Advanced Coolant Technologies Inc.
RR#2
St. Albert, AB T8N 1M9
780-460-0777
Fax: 780-973-4706
Firm Type: Waste Management
Founded: 2000
Staff: 6
Financial Information:
Type of Ownership: Private
Revenue: $1.5 Million - $3 Million
Revenue Sources: 100% Private Contracts
Domestic Markets:
Alberta, British Columbia, Manitoba, Saskatchewan
Contact(s):
Cam Watt, Owner
Darrin Zachow, Manager, Sales

Rob Okerman, General Manager
Contact(s):
Damion

Canadian Branches:
Red Deer
#2, 6841 - 52 Ave.
Red Deer, AB T4N 4L2
403-346-0777
Fax: 403-346-0779

Advanced Environmental Water Technologies Inc.
Formerly: Aubin Corporation
#A1, 423 King St. West
Hamilton, ON L8P 4Y1
905-527-8417
Fax: 905-527-8293
888-928-3754
sales@aewt.com
www.aewt.com
Products/Services/Areas of Expertise: Residential & commercial water/wastewater equipment & services; distributor of the Water-King environmentally friendly water conditioner
Domestic Markets:
National
Foreign Activity:
USA

Adventis Technologies
a division of Adventis Capital Inc.
#1015, 77 King St. West
Toronto, ON M5K 1P2
905-901-4791
Fax: 905-469-4959
info@adventiscaptial.com
www.adventiscapital.com
Firm Type: Management Consulting, Engineering, Manufacturing
Member of: JNE Chemicals; H2Point On-Site Hydrogen Generators
Products/Services/Areas of Expertise: Custom manufacture of small hydrogen generators for use in industry or for small fleet owners; advantages include small footprint, compressed storage & low cost of power generation. Turnkey renewable power solutions, project management & engineering
Contact(s):
Lucy Casacia, Managing Partner

Adventus Canada Inc.
Formerly: Adventus Remediation Technologies
1345 Fewster Dr.
Mississauga, ON L4W 2A5
905-273-5374
Fax: 905-273-4367
1-888-295-8661
info@adventusgroup.com
www.adventusgroup.com
Firm Type: Engineering, Manufacturing, Scientific/Technical Services
Founded: 2002
Staff: 23
Member of: Canadian Environment Industry Association
Products/Services/Areas of Expertise: Remediation of soils & wastes containing high levels of chlorinated phenols, polyaromatic hydrocarbons, chlorinated pesticides, heavy oils & waxes to below CCME criteria for industrial soils
Recently Completed / Ongoing Projects: Bioremediation for industrial wood preserving site; manufactured a gas plant site; organo-chlorine pesticide plant site
Financial Information:
Type of Ownership: Private
Domestic Markets:
National
Foreign Activity:
USA
Markets Sought:
Eastern Europe, Western Europe
Contact(s):
Jim Mueller, Ph.D., President/Director, Remedial Solutions & Strategies
Alan G. Seech, Ph.D., CEO/Director, Technology
Kerry Bolanos-Shaw, M.Sc., Vice-President, Operations

Canadian Branches:
Penticton
#367, 113 - 437 Martin St.
Penticton, BC V2A 5L1

250-496-5527
Fax: 905-273-4367

Aearo Canada Ltd.
Formerly: Cabot Safety Canada
#8-9, 6889 Rexwood Rd.
Mississauga, ON L4V 1R2
905-795-0700
Fax: 905-564-5250
888-387-9681
www.aearo.com
Products/Services/Areas of Expertise: Manufacturer of eye & face protection, hearing & respiratory protection & prescription safety eyewear
Domestic Markets:
National
Foreign Activity:
Worldwide
Contact(s):
David Savage, Vice-President

AECOM Canada Ltd.
Also Known As: AECOM
AECOM Technology Corporation
Formerly: Gartner Lee Ltd.#275, 3001 Wayburne Dr.
Burnaby, BC V5G 4W3
604-689-3431
Fax: 604-685-1035
canadacommunications@aecom.com
www.aecom.com
Firm Type: Engineering, Scientific/Technical Services
Staff: 1600
Member of: Association of Consulting Engineering Companies, Canada; Canadian Council for Aboriginal Business
Products/Services/Areas of Expertise: Included in the comprehensive range of engineering & consultation services offered by AECOM are: environmental management services & planning; onsite impact assessment & remediation; compliance monitoring; decommissioning.
Financial Information:
Type of Ownership: Foreign-owned
Revenue: Greater than $5 Million
Domestic Markets:
National
Contact(s):
John L. Kinley, CEO, North America, AECOM
askamericas@aecom.com
Doug Allingham, P.Eng, Exec. VP, Canada Central
doug.allingham@aecom.com
Pierre Asselin, Exec. VP, Canada East
pierre.asselin@aecom.com
Robert Johnston, Exec. VP, Canada West
rob.johnston@aecom.com

Canadian Branches:
Baie-Comeau
231, boul LaSalle
Baie-Comeau, QC G4Z 1S7
418-296-2345
Fax: 418-296-2333

Barrie
10 Checkley St.
Barrie, ON L4N 1W1
705-721-9222
Fax: 705-734-0764

Beloeil
#205, 545 Sir Wilfrid-Laurier
Beloeil, QC J3G 4H8
450-467-0206
Fax: 450-467-5554

Bracebridge
345 Ecclestone Dr.
Bracebridge, ON P1L 1R1
705-645-5992
Fax: 705-645-1841

Burnaby
3292 Production Way, 4th Fl.
Burnaby, BC V5A 4R4
604-444-6400
Fax: 604-294-8597

Calgary - Kensington
2540 Kensington Rd. NW
Calgary, AB T2N 3S3

Products & Services Buyer's Guide

403-270-9200
Fax: 403-270-0399

Calgary - Railway
#200, 6807 Railway St. SE
Calgary, AB T2H 2V6
403-254-3301
Fax: 403-270-9196

Chicoutimi
#520, 255, rue Racine est
Chicoutimi, QC G7H 7L2
418-615-0596
Fax: 418-615-0597

Cobalt
P.O. Box 736
#2, 1 Station Rd.
Cobalt, ON P0J 1C0
705-679-5979
Fax: 705-679-5750

Cobourg
513 Division St.
Cobourg, ON K9A 5G6
905-372-2121
Fax: 905-372-3621

Edmonton - 103rd
17203 - 103rd Ave.
Edmonton, AB T5S 1J4
780-488-6800
Fax: 780-488-2121

Edmonton - 107th
17007 - 107th Ave.
Edmonton, AB T5S 1G3
780-486-7000
Fax: 780-486-7070

Fort McMurray
10216 Centennial Dr.
Fort McMurray, AB T9H 1Y5
780-715-1655

Gatineau
#303, 228, boul Saint-Joseph
Gatineau, QC J8Y 3X4
819-777-1630
Fax: 819-777-2047

Guelph
#2, 512 Woolwich St.
Guelph, ON N1H 3X7
519-763-7783
Fax: 519-763-7783

Halifax
P.O. Box 576 CRO
#SH400, 1701 Hollis St.
Halifax, NS B3J 3M8
902-428-2021
Fax: 902-428-2031

Hamilton
#201, 45 Goderich Rd.
Hamilton, ON L8E 4W8
905-578-3040
Fax: 905-578-4129

Hinton
217 Pembina Ave.
Hinton, AB T7V 2B3
780-865-4363
Fax: 780-865-5812

Kelowna
#201, 3275 Lakeshore Rd.
Kelowna, BC V1W 3S9
250-762-3727
Fax: 250-762-7789

Kingston
654 Norris Ct.
Kingston, ON K7P 2R9
613-389-3703
Fax: 613-389-6729

Kitchener
#290, 50 Sportsworld Crossing Rd.
Kitchener, ON N2P 0A4
519-650-5313
Fax: 519-650-3424

Laval
#200, 1, place Laval
Laval, QC H7N 1A1
450-967-1260
Fax: 450-629-8737

Lethbridge
514 Stafford Dr. North
Lethbridge, AB T1H 2B2
403-329-4822
Fax: 403-329-1678

London
Citi Plaza
#410, 250 York St.
London, ON N6A 6K2
519-673-0510
Fax: 519-673-5975

Longueuil
450, boul Sainte-Foy
Longueuil, QC J4J 5G5
450-651-4120
Fax: 450-651-4856

Lévis
#100, 1120, boul de la Rive-Sud
Saint-Romuald, QC G6W 5M6
418-834-7878
Fax: 418-834-7997

Markham - Commerce Valley
105 Commerce Valley Dr. West, 7th Fl.
Markham, ON L3T 7W3
905-886-7022
Fax: 905-886-9494

Markham - Town Centre
#300, 300 Town Centre Blvd.
Markham, ON L3R 5Z6
905-477-8400
Fax: 905-477-1456

Medicine Hat
#101, 552 - 18 St. SW
Medicine Hat, AB T1A 8A7
403-527-3183
Fax: 403-526-0403

Mississauga - Cancross
#A, 5600 Cancross Ct.
Mississauga, ON L5R 3E9
905-501-0641
Fax: 905-501-0181

Mississauga - Commerce
5080 Commerce Blvd.
Mississauga, ON L4W 4P2
905-238-0007
Fax: 905-238-0038

Montréal - Gauchetière ouest
Place du Canada
#1400, 1010, rue de la Gauchetière ouest
Montréal, QC H3B 2N2
514-287-8500
Fax: 514-287-8600

Montréal - Sainte-Catherine ouest
85, rue Sainte-Catherine ouest
Montréal, QC H2X 3P4
514-287-8500
Fax: 514-287-8600

North Bay
#103, 189 Wyld St.
North Bay, ON P1B 1Z2
705-472-7520
Fax: 705-476-9722

Ottawa
#302, 1150 Morrison Dr.
Ottawa, ON K2H 8S9
613-820-8282
Fax: 613-820-8338

Québec - Franquet
350, rue Franquet
Sainte-Foy, QC G1P 4P3
418-871-2444
Fax: 418-871-5868

Québec - Galeries
#500, 5600, boul des Galeries
Québec, QC G2K 2H6
418-648-9512
Fax: 418-648-1011

Québec - Wilfrid-Hamel
4700, boul Wilfrid-Hamel
Québec, QC G1P 2J9
418-871-2444
Fax: 418-871-5868

Red Deer
#206, 4807 - 50 Ave.
Red Deer, AB T4N 4A5
403-342-1141
Fax: 403-342-6863

Regina
#183, 1621 Albert St.
Regina, SK S4P 2S5
306-522-3266
Fax: 306-522-3277

Rivière-du-Loup
2, rue de la Cour
Rivière-du-Loup, QC G5R 1J2
418-863-6457
Fax: 418-863-4253

Rouyn-Noranda
436, av Larivière
Rouyn-Noranda, QC J9X 4J1
819-797-0608
Fax: 819-763-7824

Saint-Bruno-de-Montarville
#101, 1430, rue Hocquart
St-Bruno-de-Montarville, QC J3V 6E1
450-461-1616
Fax: 450-461-3297

Saint-Jérôme
480, rue Saint-Georges
Saint-Jérôme, QC J7Z 5B3
450-431-1261
Fax: 450-431-1225

Saskatoon
539
#200, 2100 - 8th St.
Saskatoon, SK S7H 0V1
306-955-3300
Fax: 306-955-0044

Sault Ste. Marie
523 Wellington St. East
Sault Ste. Marie, ON P6A 2M4
705-942-2612
Fax: 705-942-3642

Sparwood
125 Elk Valley Industrial Rd. #3
Sparwood, BC V0B 2G0
250-425-2167
Fax: 250-425-2577

St. Catharines
#3, 30 Hannover Drive
St. Catharines, ON L2W 0A1
905-682-0212
Fax: 905-682-4495

Sudbury
#1, 1040 Lorne St. South
Sudbury, ON P3C 4R9
705-674-8343
Fax: 705-674-1694

Swan Hills
P.O. Box 1500
Swan Hills, AB T0G 2C0
780-333-4197
Fax: 780-333-4196

Sydney
#2B, 164 Charlotte St.
Sydney, NS B1P 1C3
902-595-6000
Fax: 902-595-6020

Trois-Rivieres
2, rue Fusey
Trois-Rivieres, QC G8T 2T1
819-373-6820
Fax: 819-373-7573

Vancouver
#970, 789 West Pender
Vancouver, BC V6C 1H2
604-444-6400
Fax: 604-685-2624

Vaudreuil-Dorion
401, boul Harwood
Vaudreuil-Dorion, QC J7V 7W1
450-455-4491
Fax: 450-455-4898

Victoria
#200, 415 Gorge Rd. East
Victoria, BC V8T 2W1
250-475-6355
Fax: 250-475-6388

Whitby
300 Water St.
Whitby, ON L1N 9J2
905-668-9363
Fax: 905-668-0221

Whitehorse
2251 - 2nd Ave.
Whitehorse, YT Y1A 5W1
867-633-6474
Fax: 867-633-6321

Windsor
#4, 350 Cabana Rd. East
Windsor, ON N9G 1A3
519-969-8449
Fax: 519-969-9420

Winnipeg
99 Commerce Dr.
Winnipeg, MB R3P 0Y7
204-477-5381
Fax: 204-284-2040

Yellowknife
GoGa Cho Bldg.
P.O. Box 1259
4916 - 47th St., 3rd Fl.
Yellowknife, NT X1A 2N9
867-873-6316
Fax: 867-873-6407

Aecon Group Inc.
#800, 20 Carlson Ct.
Toronto, ON M9W 7K6
416-293-7004
Fax: 416-754-8736
877-232-2677
aecon@aecon.com
www.aecon.com
Firm Type: Engineering, Manufacturing, Scientific/Technical Services
Founded: 1957
Staff: 3000
Products/Services/Areas of Expertise: Development & project financing; design & engineering; procurement & construction; operation & facility management; manufacturing & fabrication
Domestic Markets:
National
Foreign Activity:
USA
Contact(s):
John M. Beck, Chairman/CEO, Management Executive, 416-754-8735Fax: 416-754-8736
Scott C. Balfour, President & Chief Financial Officer
Paul D. Koenderman, Exec. Vice-President & CEO, Aecon Industrial Group
L. Brian Swartz, Sr. Vice-President, Legal and Commercial Services

Aercoustics Engineering Limited
#165, 50 Ronson Dr.
Toronto, ON M9W 1B3
416-249-3361
Fax: 416-249-3613
aercoustics@aercoustics.com
www.aercoustics.com
Firm Type: Engineering
Founded: 1971
Staff: 25
Member of: Consulting Engineers of Ontario
Products/Services/Areas of Expertise: Consulting services in acoustics, noise control & vibration; environmental audits & assessment; active noise control system design; integration & management; acoustic performance verification tests, gas turbine noise control design; sound power measurement methods in accordance with ISO 9000 standards, machinery vibration, product design, testing, expert testimony & preparation of test protocols
Recently Completed / Ongoing Projects: Renovation & noise control, Vancouver Orpheum; acoustic audits & assessment, Trans-Canada Pipeline
Domestic Markets:
Alberta, British Columbia, Manitoba, New Brunswick, Northwest Territories, Ontario, Prince Edward Island, Québec
Foreign Activity:
Asia, Australia/New Zealand, The Middle East, The Pacific Rim, South America, Mexico, USA
Markets Sought:
Central America, Eastern Europe, Western Europe
Contact(s):
Vince Gambino, P.Eng., President, 416-249-3361Fax: 416-249-3613
vgambino@aercoustics.com
John O'Keefe, M.Sc., P.Eng., Principal

Aercoustics Engineering Limited
#165, 50 Ronson Dr.
Toronto, ON M9W 1B3
416-249-3361
Fax: 416-249-3613
aercoustics@aerocoustics.com
www.aercoustics.com
Firm Type: Engineering
Founded: 1971
Member of: AMPC Consultants; Buttcon Limited; Commonwealth Historic Resource Management; Doug Welch Design; Ellis Don Construction; Fisher Dachs Associates; Glotman Simpson Architects; Merber Corporation Consulting Engineers; Novita; Peter Sheffield Associates; Theatre Consultants Collaborative; TMP Engineering; Vanbots
Products/Services/Areas of Expertise: Engineering consultants in acoustics design, noise & vibration control; custom solutions, & research & development
Recently Completed / Ongoing Projects: Acoustics for Queen Elizabeth Theatre, Esplanade Arts & Heritage Centre, Simon Fraser University, Young Centre for the Performing Arts, Four Seasons Centre for the Performing Arts, Filmport Studios, Art Gallery of Ontario, CBC Broadcasting Centre, Manitoba Hydro Place; noise control for Aylmer Ethanol Plant, Acton Aggregate Quarry, Kingsbridge Wind Plant; vibration control for Royal Conservatory of Music/Telus Centre, Art Gallery of Ontario, Twenty Gothic. Current projects include: TEDCO Corus Quay, Sick Kids Research Tower, Aga Khan Museum
Domestic Markets:
National
Foreign Activity:
USA
Contact(s):
John O'Keefe, B.A.Sc., M.Sc., P.Eng., M, Principal

AERDE Environmental Research
P.O. Box 1002 Central
Halifax, NS B3J 2X1
902-423-2211
Fax: 902-484-3027
dwerle@ca.inter.net
Firm Type: Management Consulting, Information Technology, Scientific/Technical Services
Founded: 1988
Products/Services/Areas of Expertise: Environmental monitoring & natural resource analysis; remote sensing & satellite-based Earth observation technology; radar (SAR) research & development, technology transfer; aerial photography & mapping; data processing; training programs & workshops; consulting services; wetland conservation. Office located at 19 Forward Ave., Halifax
Recently Completed / Ongoing Projects: Development of radar remote sensing CD-ROM training packages; scientific evaluation of satellite radar images; design & implementation of radar remote sensing applications; evaluation of wetlands for environmental impact assessments; remote sensing & GIS technology transfer for environmental monitoring & natural resource analysis
Domestic Markets:
National
Foreign Activity:
Asia, Western Europe, South America, USA
Contact(s):
Dirk Werle, Partner & Geoscientist

Aeroflo Inc.
Formerly: Aerovent Canada Inc.
#12, 205 Matheson Blvd. East
Mississauga, ON L4Z 3E3
905-890-6192
Fax: 905-890-6193
800-779-4021
aeroflo@aeroflo.com
www.aeroflo.com
Firm Type: Distributing, Manufacturing
Founded: 1986
Member of: American Society of Heating, Refrigerating & Air Conditioning Engineers; Association of Professional Engineers of Ontario
Products/Services/Areas of Expertise: Ventilation solutions for industrial, commercial & residential environments; industrial centrifugal fans & blowers; fan blades; blower wheels; exhaust fans; fiberglass fans; in-line fans; motorized impellers. Continental Fan Manufacturing Inc. is a sister company
Domestic Markets:
National
Foreign Activity:
South America, USA,
Contact(s):
Victor B. Afanasiev, P.Eng., President/CEO

AeroTek Manufacturing Ltd.
Formerly: Cametoid Ltd.; Industrial Measurements
1449 Hopkins St.
Whitby, ON L1N 2C2
905-666-3400
Fax: 905-666-3413
www.aerotekmfg.com
Firm Type: Manufacturing
Founded: 1950
Member of: Water Environment Association of Ontario; Ontario Pollution Control Equipment Association
Quality Environmental Management System(s): 9001:2000
Products/Services/Areas of Expertise: Corrosion protection without pollution for aerospace & industry; specializing in aerospace coatings, vacuum coatings, anodizing, electroplating, & painting; Ion Vapour Deposition (IVD) is an environmentally friendly alternative to tradition corrosion-resistant coatings, using no hazardous materials & producing no hazardous waste; processing service is RoHS & OSHA-compliant
Domestic Markets:
Nova Scotia, Northwest Territories, Ontario, Québec, Yukon Territory
Foreign Activity:
Central America, USA
Contact(s):
Jonathan Schofield, President
David Pile, Operations Manager

Aerzen Canada Surpresseurs Compresseurs inc.
Aerzen Canada Blowers Compressors Inc.
1995, Montée Labossière
Vaudreuil-Dorion, QC J7V 8P2
450-424-3966
Fax: 450-424-3985
800-779-0057
info@aerzen.ca
www.aerzen.ca
Firm Type: Distributing, Engineering, Manufacturing
Founded: 1987
Member of: German-Canadian Chamber of Commerce; Association québécoise des techniques
Quality Environmental Management System(s): 9002
Products/Services/Areas of Expertise: Positive displacement blowers & oil-free screw compressor packages for air & gas handling applications; aviation, ozomation, bio-gas
Financial Information:
Type of Ownership: Private
Revenue: $3 Million - $5 Million
Revenue Sources: 20% Provincial; 5% Municipals; 75% Private Contracts

Products & Services Buyer's Guide

Domestic Markets:
National
Foreign Activity:
Central America, South America
Contact(s):
Alaric Haerens, General Manager; Marketing Manager, Marketing
Alaric.Haerens@aerzen.ca
Paul Birdi, P.Eng., Sr. Project Engineer
Paul.Birdi@aerzen.ca
Scott McLeod, Sales and Project Engineer
Scott.McLeod@aerzen.ca

AESL Instrumentation inc.
18504, rue Larocque
Montréal, QC H9K 1N2
514-620-1547
Fax: 514-620-5155
info@aesl.ca
www.aesl.ca
Products/Services/Areas of Expertise: Offers a wide range of products related to process, instrumentation & control as applied to the water industry. Services include sales, installation & repair, & technical advice. Clients include water filtration facilities, waste water plants, governments & municipalities, as well as pharmaceutical & chemical companies

AET Group Inc.
531 Wellington St. North
Kitchener, ON N2H 5L6
519-570-9723
Fax: 519-576-9589
info@aet-group.com
www.aetconsultants.com
Firm Type: Management Consulting, Waste Management
Founded: 1997
Staff: 8
Member of: Ontario Waste Management Association; Recycling Council of Ontario; Canadian Green Building Council; Ontario Environment Industry Association; Municipal Waste Integration Network; Association of Municipal Recyclers
Products/Services/Areas of Expertise: AET Consultants Inc., EcoServices, Integrated Green Building Concepts, & Eco2 Systems Inc. merged in Aug., 2008 to form AET Group Inc. AET Group Inc. is a multidisciplinary, employee-owned environmental consulting firm providing solutions in the areas of waste management, building sciences, ecology, energy & environmental management. AET Group's clients are found in industry, government & private organizations across North America
Recently Completed / Ongoing Projects: Single stream blue box waste composition study, Reg. Mun. of York; single family waste composition studies, Reg. Mun. of York, Simcoe County, Town of Blue Mountains, Wellington County; multi-family waste composition study, City of Toronto, Peel Region; public street bin litter/recycling waste composition study, City of Toronto; mrf waste composition study & optimization strategy, City of Hamilton; ici waste audits & waste reduction workplans, Linamar Corp., GE Canada, Dana Canada, CompX Waterloo, Blount Canada, BonL Canada, Teleflex GFI; construction solid waste management plans, Mattamy Homes, Monarch Construction, Churchill Homes, Cook Homes, Reid's Heritage Group
Financial Information:
Type of Ownership: Private
Revenue: $250,000 - $500,000
Revenue Sources: 75% Municipals; 25% Private Contracts
Domestic Markets:
Ontario
Markets Sought:
Asia, Central America, Central Europe, Eastern Europe, Western Europe, Mexico, USA
Contact(s):
Scott Freiburger, BES, CEA, CCEP, EMS(A), President/CEO
Larry Freiburger, DCT, LEED AP, COO

Aevitas Inc.
Formerly: A.F. White Ltd.;PCB Containment Technology Inc.;Fluorescent Lamp Recyclers
75 Wanless Court
Ayr, ON N0B 1E0
519-740-1333
Fax: 519-740-2320
877-448-5900
www.aevitas.ca

Firm Type: Waste Management
Founded: 1974
Staff: 10
Products/Services/Areas of Expertise: Recycling & supply of mineral insulating oils; upgrade oil in transformers; lamps recycling; PCB waste containment
Recently Completed / Ongoing Projects: Upgrade oil in transformers for public utilities, manufacturers & service companies
Financial Information:
Type of Ownership: Private
Revenue Sources: 100% Private Contracts
Domestic Markets:
National
Foreign Activity:
USA
Contact(s):
Byron Day, President
Judie White, General Manager

Canadian Branches:
Brantford
46 Adams Blvd.
Brantford, ON N3S 7V2
519-752-7646
Fax: 519-752-5235
877-448-5900

Cornwall
P.O. Box 683
2425 Industrial Park Dr.
Cornwall, ON K6H 7M4
613-938-7575
Fax: 613-938-0660
800-244-6812

Kirkland Lake
455 Archer Dr.
Kirkland Lake, ON P2N 3J5
705-567-9997
Fax: 705-567-9979
887-791-9997

Québec
725 Meloche Ave.
Dorval, QC H9P 2S4
514-637-3111
Fax: 514-637-3222

Aevitas Inc.
Formerly: Fluorescent Lamp Recyclers Inc.
75 Wanless Cr.
Ayr, ON N0B 1E0
519-740-1333
Fax: 519-740-2320
800-324-8997
www.aevitas.ca
Firm Type: Waste Management
Founded: 1995
Staff: 8
Member of: Ontario Waste Management Association
Products/Services/Areas of Expertise: Recycling of mercury bearing lamps; treatment of all mercury waste; treatment & disposal of PCB waste; hazardous waste disposal
Financial Information:
Type of Ownership: Private
Revenue: $500,000 - $1.5 Million
Revenue Sources: 10% nationwide; 10% Provincial; 80% Private Contracts
Domestic Markets:
Alberta, Manitoba, New Brunswick, Newfoundland & Labrador, Nova Scotia, Ontario, Prince Edward Island, Québec, Saskatchewan
Contact(s):
Tom Maxwell, Vice President
Byron Day, Vice-President

AF Pollution Abatement Systems Inc.
3570 Twin Elm Rd., RR#2
Richmond, ON K0A 2Z0
613-838-9300
Fax: 613-838-9919
800-465-7672
info@afpollution.com
www.afpollution.com
Firm Type: Distributing
Founded: 1981
Staff: 6

Products/Services/Areas of Expertise: Oil spill response stations & spill cleanup kits; oil & chemical spill booms, absorbents for absorbing & containing spills; skimmers, extractors; spill contingency planning; waste oil storage systems
Domestic Markets:
New Brunswick, Newfoundland & Labrador, Nova Scotia, Québec
Foreign Activity:
USA
Contact(s):
Ronald Myers, President/CEO
Joanne Myers-Gerrits, Manager

Ag EnviroTech Inc.
#8, 11435 - 201A St. A
Maple Ridge, BC V2X 0Y3
604-465-1557
Fax: 604-465-2316
Firm Type: Scientific/Technical Services, Waste Management
Member of: Greenflow Environmental Services Inc.
Products/Services/Areas of Expertise: Silver recovery
Contact(s):
Henry Koch, President

Ag-West Bio Inc. / AWB
#101, 111 Research Dr.
Saskatoon, SK S7N 3R2
306-975-1939
Fax: 306-975-1966
agwest@agwest.sk.ca
www.agwest.sk.ca
Firm Type: Scientific/Technical Services
Founded: 2004
Staff: 12
Member of: Agrology Institute of Canada; Industrial Biotechnology Association
Products/Services/Areas of Expertise: Ag-West Bio is membership-based organization for Saskatchewan's bio-economy; works as a catalyst for partnerships & industry growth through investments, strategic alliances, providing regulatory advice & communications; memberships includes over 90 corporations, associations & individuals representing natural health products
Financial Information:
Type of Ownership: Non Profit
Revenue Sources: 100% Provincial
Domestic Markets:
Alberta, British Columbia, Manitoba, Ontario, Saskatchewan
Foreign Activity:
Asia, Australia/New Zealand, The Pacific Rim, USA
Contact(s):
Ian McPhadden, President/CEO
ian.mcphadden@agwest.sk.ca
Muriel Adams, Acting General Manager
muriel.adams@agwest.sk.ca
Jackie Robin, Director, Communications
jackie.robin@agwest.sk.ca

AGAT Laboratories Ltd.
2910 - 12 St. NE
Calgary, AB T2E 7P7
403-735-2005
Fax: 403-735-2771
866-764-7554
info@agatlabs.com
www.agatlabs.com
Firm Type: Scientific/Technical Services
Founded: 1979
Staff: 300
Member of: Canadian Association of Environmental Analytical Laboratories; American Industrial Hygiene Association; Standards Council of Canada, Canadian Council of Independent Laboratories
Quality Environmental Management System(s): 9001
Products/Services/Areas of Expertise: A full service, accredited laboratory & science company operating globally. Environmental analytical services; inorganic, organic & microbiological testing for soil, water, air & other samples. Divisions include food, geology & petrology, reservoir engineering, mining, tribology, oil sands, oil & gas chemistry, & agriculture. E-services include online reports & data for consultation. Branch locations in Calgary, Mississauga, Montréal, Québec City, Dartmouth, Burnaby, Whitehorse, & in Ville Hermosa, Mexico
Activities: Environmental analysis & treatment; instrumentation & controls; laboratory instruments, apparatus & facilities; medical diagnostic equipment; physical properties testing & inspection

equipment; atmospheric research equipment parts; geological evaluations
Financial Information:
Type of Ownership: Private
Domestic Markets:
National
Foreign Activity:
Mexico,
Contact(s):
Gordon Nelson, B.Sc., Vice President, Environmental & Quality Assurance
Derek Fraser, Manager, Business Development

Canadian Branches:
Ontario Region Main Office - Mississauga
5835 Coopers Ave.
Mississauga, ON L4Z 1Y2
905-712-5100
Fax: 905-712-5122
Staff: 250
Brian Brunetti, B.Eng.Mgt., P.Eng., Exec. Vice President, AGAT Laboratories Ltd.

AGM Steel Industries Ltd.
Formerly: AGM Specialty Fabricators; AGM Agricultural Growers Machinery
11850 Oceola Rd.
Winfield, BC V4V 1H1
250-766-2424
Fax: 250-766-2255
877-766-2424
dwayne@agmsteel.com
Firm Type: Manufacturing
Founded: 1956
Staff: 20
Quality Environmental Management System(s): 9001:2000
Products/Services/Areas of Expertise: Manufacture, re-manufacture & testing of intermediate bulk containers (IBC's) for the storage & transport of dangerous/non-dangerous goods (liquids, solids, powders, gels, etc.); custom tanks for non-controlled shipping of solids or liquids; ISO 9001:2000/Transport Canada
Financial Information:
Type of Ownership: Private
Revenue: $500,000 - $1.5 Million
Revenue Sources: 100% Private Contracts
Domestic Markets:
National
Foreign Activity:
Australia/New Zealand, Caribbean, Central America, The Pacific Rim, South America, Mexico, USA
Markets Sought:
Central America, Eastern Europe, The Pacific Rim, South America, Mexico
Contact(s):
Dwayne Armeneau, President/CEO
Eric Patrick, Manager, Quality Control
Denise Patrick, Accounts Manager

AGO Environmental Electronics Ltd.
#10, 626 Esquimalt Rd.
Victoria, BC V9A 3L4
250-386-4015
Fax: 250-386-4016
info@agoenvironmental.com
www.agoenvironmental.com
Firm Type: Distributing, Manufacturing, Scientific/Technical Services
Founded: 1986
Staff: 8
Products/Services/Areas of Expertise: Instrument winches & wire payout systems for oceanographics, geophysics & environmental services; water samplers; subsea connectors; subsea video systems; pipeline video cameras; seabed terminal impact naval gauge for rapid determination of sea floor characteristics
Financial Information:
Type of Ownership: Private
Domestic Markets:
National
Foreign Activity:
Australia/New Zealand, Western Europe, The Pacific Rim, Mexico, USA, Former USSR
Markets Sought:
Asia, Australia/New Zealand, Western Europe, The Pacific Rim, USA, Former USSR, United Kingdom
Contact(s):
James R. Harrington, President

AGRECOM inc.
312 Karen Pl.
Waterloo, ON N2L 6K8
519-746-3651
Fax: 519-746-3826
info@agrecomconsult.com
www.agrecomconsult.com
Products/Services/Areas of Expertise: AGRECOM inc. is an environmental consulting company serving the Canadian & U. S. markets in waste management & groundwater protection services; sells hydrogeologic & environmental software; provides information technology services for the hydrogeologic & environmental industry; experience in the development of on-line active map database applications
Contact(s):
Mikhail Gogolev
mgogolev@agrecomconsult.com
Ernst Zaltsberg, P.Geo.
Paul Pitman, P.Geo.
Ondrej Sracek, Ph.D.

Agri-Food Laboratories
#1, 503 Imperial Rd. North
Guelph, ON N1H 6T9
519-837-1600
Fax: 519-837-1242
800-265-7175
lab@agtest.com
www.agtest.com
Firm Type: Scientific/Technical Services
Founded: 1984
Products/Services/Areas of Expertise: Analytical services for feed, soil & water; quality control testing for agricultural manufacturing of feed & fertilizer; GIS mapping center
Contact(s):
Trish Kelly, General Manager

AGRI-SX
P.O. Box 1
Sainte-Martine, QC J0S 1V0
514-943-2901
Fax: 450-691-4054
agri-sx.com
Products/Services/Areas of Expertise: The company is engaged in dislodging undesirable birds & animals from areas of human traffic & relocating them to their natural habitats. Research & technology manufacturing centres located in Chateauguay
Recently Completed / Ongoing Projects: Removal of 500 gulls from the Québec Int'l Airport; removal of gulls & geese from beaches in Montréal, Québec & Magog
Contact(s):
Jacques Pueyo, Contact

Agricultural Technology Centre
Formerly: Alberta Farm Machinery Research Centre
Also Known As: AgTech Centre
3000 College Dr. South
Lethbridge, AB T1K 1L6
403-329-1212
Fax: 403-328-5562
www1.agric.gov.ab.ca
Firm Type: Management Consulting, Scientific/Technical Services
Founded: 1988
Staff: 25
Products/Services/Areas of Expertise: The Centre is primarily a research facility which provides expertise & assistance in the design & development of farm equipment; evaluation & testing; research into new technologies & their environmental, economic & agronomic effects on farming operations; & education in the form of presentations & demonstrations
Contact(s):
Rick Atkins, Manager
rick.atkins@gov.ab.ca

Agrodev Canada Inc.
#100, 150 Isabella St.
Ottawa, ON K1S 1V7
613-234-3300
Fax: 613-234-6601
www.agrodev.ca
Firm Type: Management Consulting, Scientific/Technical Services, Waste Management
Founded: 1976
Products/Services/Areas of Expertise: An employee-owned firm which provides professional & management expertise to private & public sector clients engaged in international development. Areas of focus include social development, organizational development & training, natural resources management, environmental management, & fisheries & aquaculture development. Agrodev has completed more than 300 projects in 75 countries around the world
Recently Completed / Ongoing Projects: Assisted the Government of Nepal in developing EIA guidelines & procedures; assisted the Palestinian Authority in developing & implementing environmental planning & assessment
Financial Information:
Type of Ownership: Private
Domestic Markets:
National
Foreign Activity:
Africa, Asia, Worldwide
Contact(s):
Jack S. Baker, President
jbaker@agrodev.ca

Agrosysts Ltée
Agrosysts Ltd.
442, ch Cherrier
Montréal, QC H9C 1G2
514-696-7443
Fax: 514-696-4661
Firm Type: Management Consulting, Engineering, Scientific/Technical Services
Founded: 1978
Member of: Canadian Land Reclamation Association; International Society for Photogrammetry & Remote Sensing; Canadian Environmental Auditing Association
Products/Services/Areas of Expertise: Environmental analysis; resource-use planning; computer-assisted mapping & geographical information systems; monitoring of vegetation coverage, forestry, crops, soil degradation; environmental impact studies & urban development studies
Domestic Markets:
National
Foreign Activity:
Africa, Asia, Central America, South America, USA
Contact(s):
Martin van Lierop, President/CEO

AIC Associated Industrial Controls Ltd. / AIC
#507, 500 Duplex Ave.
Toronto, ON M4R 1V6
416-440-4194
amblard.aic@sympatico.ca
Firm Type: Distributing, Engineering
Founded: 1995
Staff: 3
Products/Services/Areas of Expertise: Flow measurement instrumentation; supplier & consultant in specialized instrumentation for difficult flow measurement challenges; municipal wastewater treatment plants & combined sewer overflow infrastructure for full pipes as well as partially-filled conduits containing fluids with high solids content
Recently Completed / Ongoing Projects: Waste treatment plant, Gatineau-Hull; collector system; Montréal-Laval; collection system & wastewater treatment plants, Québec City
Financial Information:
Type of Ownership: Private
Revenue Sources: 80% Municipals; 20% Private Contracts
Domestic Markets:
Alberta, New Brunswick, Newfoundland & Labrador, Nova Scotia, Ontario, Québec
Markets Sought:
China, South America, Mexico, Vietnam
Contact(s):
Jody Amblard, President

AIC Sullivan's Environmental Services
A Division of Envirosystems Inc.
675 Keltic Dr.
Sydney, NS B1L 1B6
902-564-0578
Fax: 902-564-6333
www.enviro-systems.com
Products/Services/Areas of Expertise: A full solution service provider for sewer, plumbing, municipal, residential or environmental problems; 24 hour emergency response to environmental & oil spill emergencies; services include municipal pipe cleaning, residential septic services & special cleaning in tank & chemical

Products & Services Buyer's Guide

Contact(s):
Doug Hill, Contact

AIM Environmental Group
Also Known As: Aim Waste Management Inc.
400 Jones Rd.
Stoney Creek, ON L8E 5P4
905-560-0090
Fax: 905-560-0099
inquire@aimgroup.ca
www.aimgroup.ca
Firm Type: Waste Management
Founded: 1989
Products/Services/Areas of Expertise: Civil services: potable water & sewage pump & treatment facilities; Environmental: facility decommissioning, demolition & abatement services; remediation: soil & groundwater treatment & disposal; waste handling transportation & disposal; facility management: in-vessel compost facility operations
Recently Completed / Ongoing Projects: Removed concrete rink slab & bleachers for renovations, June/02, Burlington Arena, ON
Contact(s):
Theo Van Wely, President
theo@aimgroup.ca
Frank Peters, Business Unit Manager, Composting
fpeters@aimgroup.ca
Dennis Perlotto, General Manager, Remediation Services
dennis@aimgroup.ca

Aimco Solrec Ltd.
425 Morobel Dr.
Milton, ON L9T 4N6
905-878-2627
Fax: 905-878-4728
info@aimcosolrec.com
www.aimcosolrec.com
Firm Type: Distributing, Waste Management
Founded: 1974
Staff: 20
Products/Services/Areas of Expertise: Collection, transport, disposal & recycling of waste solvents, including caustics, oils, oily waters, paint, inks, & other solvents
Financial Information:
Type of Ownership: Private
Revenue Sources: 100% Private Contracts
Domestic Markets:
National
Contact(s):
Wahid Mohammed, Sales Manager
wmohammed@aimcosolrec.com

AimGlobal Technologies Company, Inc.
#170, 13151 Vanier Pl.
Richmond, BC V6V 2J1
604-244-7272
Fax: 604-244-7258
sales@aimglobaltech.com
Firm Type: Distributing, Manufacturing

Products/Services/Areas of Expertise: Portable, hand-held gas detection equipment & accessories for fire, confined space, leak detection, & emergency response applications
Financial Information:
Type of Ownership: Publicly Traded
Domestic Markets:
National
Foreign Activity:
Mexico, USA
Contact(s):
Mel Gould, President/COO

AiMS Environmental
#111, 1020 Denison St.
Markham, ON L3R 3W5
905-474-0058
Fax: 905-474-0601
mmjagani@aimsconsulting.com
www.aimsconsulting.com
Firm Type: Management Consulting, Engineering
Founded: 1993
Staff: 10
Member of: Professional Engineers of Ontario; International Association of Hydrogeologists; Canadian Geotechnical Society
Member of: International Association of Hydrogeologists
Products/Services/Areas of Expertise: Phase I & II environmental site assessments; site remediation; environmental inspection & testing; contaminated soil removal; storage tank removal; asbestos surveys & abatement inspections; brownfields, soil & groundwater investigations; site & building decommissioning; air emmissions & waste management solutions; & special projects consulting
Recently Completed / Ongoing Projects: Ottawa Street landfill, Kitchener; Lincoln Mall, St. Catharines; Ford Dealership, Richmond Hill
Financial Information:
Type of Ownership: Private
Revenue: $500,000 - $1.5 Million
Revenue Sources: 5% Municipals; 95% Private Contracts
Domestic Markets:
Ontario
Foreign Activity:
USA
Contact(s):
Mohamed Jagani, P.Eng., P.E., President, Civil & Environmental Engineer
Sidney Joseph, C.Chem., P.Eng., CEO
Forry Fong, P.Eng., Manager, Project

Ainley Group
280 Pretty River Pkwy.
Collingwood, ON L9Y 4J5
705-445-3451
Fax: 705-445-0968
collingwood@ainleygroup.com
www.ainleygroup.com
Firm Type: Management Consulting, Engineering
Staff: 100
Products/Services/Areas of Expertise: Multi-disciplinary engineering & planning services in a wide environmental, municipal & transportation, services include asset management, systems optimization, building services, computer modelling & gis; provides project management, detailed design, construction services & plant commissioning
Domestic Markets:
Ontario
Contact(s):
Joe Mullan, P.Eng., President & CEO
mullan@ainleygroup.com
Simon Ainley, P.Eng., Chairman
ainley.s@ainleygroup.com
Bill Hugget, CGA, Vice-President, Finance and Administration
huggett@ainleygroup.com
Mike P. Ainsley, P.Eng., Vice-President, Environmental
ainley.m@ainleygroup.com
Canadian Branches:
Barrie
550 Welham Rd.
Barrie, ON L4N 8Z7
705-726-3371
Fax: 705-726-4391
barrie@ainleygroup.com
Joe Mullan, P.Eng

Belleville
45 South Front St.
Belleville, ON K8N 2Y5
613-966-4243
Fax: 613-966-1168
belleville@ainleygroup.com
Brent Barnes, P.Eng.

Ottawa
2724 Fenton Rd.
Ottawa, ON K1T 3T7
613-822-1052
Fax: 613-822-1573
ottawa@ainleygroup.com
James Swanson, P.Eng.

Ainsworth Inc.
131 Bermondsey Rd.
Toronto, ON M4A 1X4
416-751-4420
Fax: 416-751-9031
800-387-6056
helpdesk@ainsworth.com
www.ainsworth.com
Firm Type: Engineering
Founded: 1937
Staff: 525
Products/Services/Areas of Expertise: Comprehensive energy management program; single source responsibility for the identification, design, installation, metering & monitoring of energy efficient measures
Domestic Markets:
National
Contact(s):
Albert Renaud, President/CEO
albert_renaud@ainsworth.com

Canadian Branches:
Calgary
#102, 7304 - 30 St. SE
Calgary, AB T2C 1W2
403-265-6750
Fax: 403-265-6751

Edmonton
4003 - 76 Avenue NW
Edmonton, AB T6B 2S8
780-463-1305
Fax: 780-466-4080

Halifax
57 Crane Lake Dr.
Halifax, NS B3S 1B5
902-450-5651
Fax: 902-450-5300

Regina
1141 - 8th Ave.
Regina, SK S4R 1E1
306-721-7777
Fax: 306-721-7788

Stoney Creek
442 Millen Rd.
Stoney Creek, ON L8E 6H2
905-664-8546
Fax: 905-664-0943

Vancouver
#104, 17741 - 65A Ave.
Surrey, BC V3S 1Z8
604-576-1355
Fax: 604-576-2713

Winnipeg
8 - 1201 Grassmere Rd.
Winnipeg, MB R4A 1C4
204-654-6100
Fax: 204-654-6101

Air Control Engineering Inc.
#105, 19415 56th Ave.
Surrey, BC V3S 6K2
604-530-5066
Fax: 604-530-5086
866-530-5066
info@aircontroleng.com
www.aircontroleng.com
Products/Services/Areas of Expertise: Manufacturer & distributor of advanced design dust collection equipment; representative for the JHM Moldow Company's line of filter systems & related equipment; services include professional evaluation of existing systems, upgrading & installation
Domestic Markets:
Alberta, British Columbia

Air Liquide Canada Ltée
Canada Liquid Air
#1700, 1250, boul René-Lévesque ouest
Montréal, QC H3B 5E6
514-933-0303
Fax: 514-846-7700
800-817-7697
info.alc@airliquide.com
www.ca.airliquide.com
Firm Type: Engineering, Manufacturing, Scientific/Technical Services, Waste Management
Founded: 1911
Staff: 1385
Member of: Association québécoise des techniques de l'eau; Water Environment Federation; Water Environment Association of Ontario; Centre patronal de l'environnement du Québec; Association pour la prévention de la contamination de l'air et du sol; Air & Waste Management Association - Québec Section; Canadian Environment Industry Association
Products/Services/Areas of Expertise: Bulk supply of oxygen, hydrogen, nitrogen, argon & carbon dioxide; on-site supply of ozone, nitrogen & oxygen; supply of ozone generators & technology (automatic control panels & apparatus for gas

dissolution in wastewater); applications: oxygen enrichment of activated sludge wastewater systems (for BOD reduction), carbon dioxide for pH control of alkaline effluents, ozone for COD, colour reduction & disinfection, nitrogen oxide reduction by oxygen enrichment, sulphur dioxide emissions reduction, wastewater organics removal, pulp & paper bleaching, enhance metal recovery, cyanide destruction & effluent treatment
Domestic Markets:
National
Contact(s):
Luc Doyon, Chairman & CEO
Julie Brouard, Communications Manager, 514-846-7735

Canadian Branches:
Atlantic
180 Akerley Blvd.
Dartmouth, NS B3B 2B7
902-468-5152
Fax: 902-468-5783
Neil O'Connor

Ontario
5315 North Service Rd.
Burlington, ON L7L 6C1
905-335-4877
Fax: 905-335-0301
Stu Younger

Québec
11201, boul. Ray-Lawson
Anjou, QC H1J 1M6
514-356-7600
Fax: 514-351-0531
Tim Phaneuf

Western
10020 - 56 Ave.
Edmonton, AB T6E 5Z2
780-438-5600
Fax: 780-438-2801
Roger Perreault

Air Movement Services Ltd.
51-B Speers Rd.
Winnipeg, MB R2J 1M2
204-233-7456
Fax: 204-237-4789
airmove@ilos.net
Products/Services/Areas of Expertise: Heating, Ventilating, and Air Conditioning testing & balancing; building commissioning; Indoor air quality assessment & mitigation
Domestic Markets:
Manitoba

Air Phaser Environmental Ltd.
6667 - 194th St.
Surrey, BC V4N 0C2
604-308-7435
Fax: 604-533-7134
info@airphaser.com
www.airphaser.com
Firm Type: Engineering

Products/Services/Areas of Expertise: Treatment of industrial air emissions by neutralizing pollutants using only electricity; non-thermal plasma technology to control/neutralize odours; H2S removal; applications include VOC abatement (i.e. automotive paint, solvent VOC emissions), odour control for animal feed, compost, sewage, & wastewater
Financial Information:
Type of Ownership: Private
Contact(s):
Douglas Lanz, President

Air Products Canada Ltd.
#102, 989 Derry Rd. East
Mississauga, ON L5T 2J8
905-364-3064
Fax: 905-364-3024
www.airproducts.com/canada
Products/Services/Areas of Expertise: Measuring & Monitoring Equipment, Laboratory; Toner Cartridges Recycling; Tires Recycling; Sewage Treatment Equipment
Domestic Markets:
National

Canadian Branches:
Calgary
Petro Canada Centre, West Tower
#3000, 150 - 6th Ave. SW
Calgary, AB Y2P 3Y7
403-539-5157

Corunna
150 St. Clair Parkway
Corunna, ON N0N 1G0
519-862-4243

Edmonton
720 Petroleum Way
Edmonton, AB T6S 1H5
780-417-1957
Fax: 780-417-9306

LaSalle
#311, 7475, boul Newman
Lasalle, QC H8N 2X3
514-363-4331
Fax: 514-365-2527
800-361-5256

Nanticoke
Lake Erie Industrial Park
RR#3
Nanticoke, ON N0A 1L0
519-587-2401
Fax: 519-587-5106

Sarnia
P.O. Box 1059
20 Indian Rd. South
Sarnia, ON N7T 7K2
519-332-1500
Fax: 519-332-6844
800-565-5795

St. Augustin
185, rue de Grand Lacs
St. Augustin, QC G3A 2K8
418-878-1400
Fax: 418-878-3235
800-363-3572

Air Solutions Inc.
#K, 240 Holiday Inn Dr.
Cambridge, ON N3C 1X4
519-658-6232
Fax: 519-658-6103
800-267-6830
info@airsolutions.ca
www.airsolutions.ca
Firm Type: Distributing, Scientific/Technical Services
Founded: 1986
Member of: Canadian Home Builders' Association; Heating, Refrigeration & Air Conditioning Institute of Canada; Professional Engineers Ontario
Products/Services/Areas of Expertise: Training & technical services related to energy efficient building design, mechanical systems, indoor air quality
Recently Completed / Ongoing Projects: Co-authored a Domestic Energy Advisor training program for salespeople at a large facility; completed a mold investigation for a northern community of 250 homes
Financial Information:
Type of Ownership: Private
Revenue: $500,000 - $1.5 Million
Revenue Sources: 10% nationwide; 90% Private Contracts
Domestic Markets:
National
Foreign Activity:
USA
Contact(s):
Gord Cooke, President
gcooke@airsolutions.ca

Air Trac Corp.
583 Barton St.
Winona, ON L8E 5S2
905-643-4446
info@airtraccorp.com
www.airtraccorp.com
Firm Type: Distributing, Engineering, Manufacturing
Founded: 1986
Staff: 6

Products/Services/Areas of Expertise: With its head office in Niagara Falls, NY, Air Trac is a leading provider of innovative solutions in air flow technology to the automotive, ceramic, chemical, food, mining, & pharmaceutical industries worldwide. Products & services include air pollution control equipment, fresh air supply & exhaust systems, & pneumatic conveying of bulk solids; fabrication, installation, start-up, maintenance, parts, & testing
Financial Information:
Type of Ownership: Private
Revenue Sources: 100% Private Contracts
Domestic Markets:
National, Ontario, Québec
Foreign Activity:
Central America, China, The Middle East, USA, United Kingdom, Worldwide
Contact(s):
Ron Kalka, President

AIRCOM Technologies Inc.
16781, boul. Hymus
Kirkland, QC H9H 3L4
514-695-4740
Fax: 514-695-0581
info@aircom.ca
www.aircom.ca
Firm Type: Engineering, Manufacturing

Products/Services/Areas of Expertise: Distributes air & gas rotating machinery for pressure and vacuum applications; in-house and field repair services; project engineering
Financial Information:
Type of Ownership: Private
Domestic Markets:
New Brunswick, Newfoundland & Labrador, Nova Scotia, Ontario, Prince Edward Island, Québec
Contact(s):
Marc Lafleur, General Manager
marcl@aircom.ca
Denis Lemoing, Director, Sales - Machines & Projects
denisl@aircom.ca

Aircraft Appliances & Equipment Ltd.
150 East Dr.
Brampton, ON L6T 1C1
905-791-1666
Fax: 905-791-1863
info@aaeltd.com
www.aaeltd.com
Firm Type: Distributing, Manufacturing
Founded: 1949
Quality Environmental Management System(s): 9001:2000
Products/Services/Areas of Expertise: Reverse osmosis water treatment systems; oily water separators; filtration & purification systems
Domestic Markets:
National
Foreign Activity:
Australia/New Zealand, Western Europe, The Pacific Rim, South America, Mexico, USA
Contact(s):
Bryan T. Dawson, President/CEO
bdawson@aaeltd.com
Andrew Willnecker, Director, Export Sales and Marketing
awillnecker@aaeltd.com

Airmaster Sales Ltd.
400 Keewatin St.
Winnipeg, MB R2X 2R9
204-944-7446
Fax: 204-632-9747
800-788-6805
mac@airmastersales.com
www.airmastersales.com
Firm Type: Distributing, Manufacturing
Founded: 1960
Member of: American Society of Heating, Refrigerating & Air Conditioning Engineers
Products/Services/Areas of Expertise: Ventilation equipment & accessories; traffic signs & accessories
Domestic Markets:
National
Foreign Activity:
USA
Contact(s):
Quentin MacCharles, President

Products & Services Buyer's Guide

AirScience Inc.
#3525, 1751 rue Richardson
Montréal, QC H3K 1G6
514-937-4614
Fax: 514-937-4820
sales@airscience.net
www.airscience.net
Firm Type: Distributing, Scientific/Technical Services
Founded: 1993
Products/Services/Areas of Expertise: Research and Development in producing biofuels; supply of air emission and pollution control systems
Financial Information:
Type of Ownership: Private
Domestic Markets:
National
Foreign Activity:
Asia, The Middle East, Mexico
Contact(s):
Gérard Magnin, President

Airtechni Inc.
1555, rue Chabanel ouest
Montréal, QC H4N 2W3
514-382-3560
Fax: 514-383-4587
info@airtechni.com
www.airtechni.com
Firm Type: Distributing
Founded: 1975
Staff: 16
Member of: American Society of Heating, Ventilation & Air Conditioning
Products/Services/Areas of Expertise: Energy saving geothermal heating & air conditioning systems
Recently Completed / Ongoing Projects: Stores, schools, libraries, offices
Financial Information:
Type of Ownership: Private
Revenue: Greater than $5 Million
Revenue Sources: 10% nationwide; 10% Provincial; 8% Municipals; 72% Private Contracts
Domestic Markets:
Québec
Contact(s):
Bernard Gravel, President

Airtest Technologies Inc.
#9, 1520 Clivedon Ave.
Delta, BC V3M 6J8
604-517-3888
Fax: 604-517-3900
888-855-8880
info@airtesttechnologies.com
www.airtest.com
Firm Type: Distributing, Manufacturing
Founded: 1996
Staff: 10
Products/Services/Areas of Expertise: Gas monitoring & detecting equipment; stand-alone monitors & sensor transmitters
Financial Information:
Type of Ownership: Publicly Traded
Revenue Sources: 5% nationwide; 95% Private Contracts
Domestic Markets:
National
Foreign Activity:
Asia, USA
Contact(s):
George Graham, President

Airzone One Ltd.
222 Matheson Blvd. East
Mississauga, ON L4Z 1X1
905-890-6957
Fax: 905-890-8629
www.airzoneone.com
Firm Type: Management Consulting, Scientific/Technical Services
Founded: 2000
Staff: 10
Products/Services/Areas of Expertise: An employee-owned firm specializing in air quality monitoring & analysis, noise assessments, & occupational health & safety (audits, remedial measures, training, etc.)
Recently Completed / Ongoing Projects: Industrial hygiene & air monitoring for high tech firms; air quality audits for school boards; monitoring of personal breathing zones of subjects exposed to diesel & ethanol bus emissions in Winnipeg, Medicine Hat, Windsor & Toronto; investigation of airborne fungal contamination in downtown Toronto office buildings
Contact(s):
Ron McMahan, President/CEO
Phil Fellin, Vice-President/Manager, Air Monitoring & Analysis
Franco Di-Giovanni, Sr. Air Quality Manager

Aker Chemetics
Aker Solutions Canada Inc.
Formerly: Aker Kvaerner Chemetics; Kvaerner Chemetics - Kvaerner Canada 2001 Clements Rd.
Pickering, ON L1W 4C2
905-619-5200
Fax: 905-619-5345
www.akersolutions.com
Firm Type: Engineering, Scientific/Technical Services
Founded: 1971
Member of: Canadian Pulp & Paper Association
Products/Services/Areas of Expertise: Engineered systems, proprietary equipment & turnkey plants to customers in the pulp & paper, chemical & metal smelting industries; a division of Aker Solutions Canada Inc. which delivers a range of products and services to the oil & gas, construction, metals and mining industries
Foreign Activity:
Australia/New Zealand, China, Western Europe, The Pacific Rim, South Africa, United Kingdom, Vietnam
Canadian Branches:
Vancouver
#400, 1818 Cornwall Ave.
Vancouver, BC V6J 1C7
604-734-1200
Fax: 604-734-0340

Aker Metals (Toronto)
Aker Solutions Canada Inc.
Formerly: Aker Kvaerner Metals (Toronto); Kvaerner Metals Davisville Centre
#301, 1920 Yonge St.
Toronto, ON M4S 3E2
416-340-1145
Fax: 416-343-9300
www.akersolutions.com
Firm Type: Engineering

Products/Services/Areas of Expertise: Metals engineering technology; mining & handling of primary raw materials to metals processing & forming; site remediation; water treatment & engineering; a division of Aker Solutions Canada Inc. which delivers a range of products and services to the oil & gas, construction, metals and mining industries
Recently Completed / Ongoing Projects: Olympic Dam Project, Western Mining Co.; Baley Gold Project, Armada Gold Corp.; metallurgical technical centre pilot plant, Falconbridge Ltd.
Financial Information:
Type of Ownership: Private
Revenue Sources: 10% nationwide; 90% Private Contracts
Domestic Markets:
National
Foreign Activity:
Worldwide
Contact(s):
Ian McColl, Executive Vice-President
Michael Smallwood, Vice-President

AKZO Nobel Chemicals Ltd.
#318, 1 City Centre Dr.
Mississauga, ON L5B 1M2
905-273-5959
Fax: 905-273-7339
csrcan@sc.akzonobel.com
www.surface.akzonobelusa.com
Firm Type: Distributing, Manufacturing
Founded: 1994
Products/Services/Areas of Expertise: Manufacturers & suppliers of agricultural, mining & industrial organic chemicals
Foreign Activity:
Western Europe, The Pacific Rim, South America, USA
Contact(s):
Jeanne Lalach, Contact, Mining & Fertilizer Additives

Alan A. Smith Inc.
17 Lynndale Dr.
Dundas, ON L9H 3L4
905-628-4682
Fax: 905-628-1364
info@alanasmith.com
www.alanasmith.com
Firm Type: Engineering, Information Technology
Founded: 1978
Staff: 3
Products/Services/Areas of Expertise: Software for urban drainage, hydrology & hydraulic in civil municipal engineering; specialty studies in urban hydrology; stormwater management
Recently Completed / Ongoing Projects: Expert witness at several stormwater management disputes; specialist sub-consultant
Financial Information:
Type of Ownership: Private
Domestic Markets:
National
Foreign Activity:
USA,
Contact(s):
Alan A. Smith, President/CEO
alan@alanasmith.com

Alan Willis & Associates
1889 Truscott Dr.
Mississauga, ON L5J 2A1
905-822-0171
Firm Type: Management Consulting
Founded: 1991
Products/Services/Areas of Expertise: Environmental performance measurement, accounting, management strategy & systems, & environmental auditing
Financial Information:
Type of Ownership: Private
Domestic Markets:
National
Foreign Activity:
Western Europe, USA
Contact(s):
Alan D. Willis, President

ALARA Industrial Hygiene Services Ltd.
103 Parkview Hill Cres.
Toronto, ON M4B 1R5
416-759-9579
Fax: 416-759-0372
info@alara.ca
www.alara.ca
Firm Type: Management Consulting, Scientific/Technical Services
Founded: 1987
Staff: 2
Member of: American Industrial Hygiene Association; American Conference of Governmental Industrial Hygienists; Association of the Chemistry Profession of Ontario
Products/Services/Areas of Expertise: Air monitoring; noise exposure evaluation; hazard control strategies; health & safety audits; industrial hygiene; indoor air quality; health & safety training; professional seminars; hazard control strategies
Recently Completed / Ongoing Projects: Air sampling for toxic dusts & organic vapours; evaluation of industrial ventilation systems; indoor environmental quality & indoor air quality in offices & hospital; evaluation of mold contamination in buildings; professional training workshop
Financial Information:
Type of Ownership: Private
Revenue: $250,000 - $500,000
Revenue Sources: 5% nationwide; 10% Provincial; 10% Municipals; 75% Private Contracts
Domestic Markets:
National
Foreign Activity:
USA
Markets Sought:
Caribbean, Central America, Mexico
Contact(s):
Charles Pilger, CIH, ROH, CChem., Sr. Occupational Hygienist
Marguerite Pilger, CIH, ROH, Sr. Occupational Hygienist/Project Manager

Alaron Instruments Inc.
Unit 1, Suite 402, 1111 Davis Dr.
Newmarket, ON L3Y 9E5
Fax: 800-576-7886
800-559-6238
sales@alaron.ca
www.alaron.ca
Products/Services/Areas of Expertise: Distributors of control instruments & monitoring equipment, including environmental

Products & Services Buyer's Guide

instruments, materials testing equipment, & water analysis meters

Alberta Environmental Rubber Products Inc. / AERP
13500 - 156 St. NW
Edmonton, AB T5V 1L3
780-447-1994
Fax: 780-447-5405
800-761-8473
admin@aerpi.com
www.aerpi.com
Firm Type: Distributing, Manufacturing
Founded: 1993
Staff: 70
Products/Services/Areas of Expertise: The firm is engaged in the collection & processing of scrap tires & the sale of the recycled tire product - eg. rubberized roofing & track material, playground material
Financial Information:
Type of Ownership: Private
Domestic Markets:
National
Contact(s):
Glenn Cohen, President
glenn.cohen@aerpi.com

Alberta-Pacific Forest Industries Inc.
P.O. Box 8000
Hwy.63 North
Boyle, AB T0A 0M0
780-525-8148
Fax: 780-525-8423
800-661-5210 ext 8334
info@alpac.ca
www.alpac.ca
Firm Type: Manufacturing
Founded: 1989
Staff: 1100
Quality Environmental Management System(s): 14001
EcoLogo Certified Products & Services: Systems & technologies
Ecological Note: Systems & technologies
Financial Information:
Type of Ownership: Publicly Traded
Contact(s):
Al Ward, President/COO

Alchemist Transport Inc.
23720 - 72 Ave.
Langley, BC V1M 3K9
604-882-1518
Fax: 604-882-1399
888-255-6311
gary@alchemisttransport.com
www.alchemisttransport.com
Firm Type: Waste Management
Founded: 1968
Products/Services/Areas of Expertise: Transportation of hazardaus and non-hazardous waste
Domestic Markets:
Alberta, British Columbia, Manitoba, Ontario, Québec, Saskatchewan
Foreign Activity:
USA
Contact(s):
Gary Zappone, President, 604-787-9222

ALCO Gas & Oil Production Equipment Ltd.
5203 - 75th St.
Edmonton, AB T6E 5S5
780-465-9061
Fax: 780-466-8110
plant@alcogasoil.com
www.alcogasoil.com
Firm Type: Engineering, Manufacturing, Scientific/Technical Services
Founded: 1972
Staff: 175
Products/Services/Areas of Expertise: Design & manufacture of oil & gas processing equipment & water treatment materials
Financial Information:
Type of Ownership: Private
Revenue: Greater than $5 Million
Revenue Sources: 2.5% nationwide; 2.5% Provincial; 95% Private Contracts
Domestic Markets:
Alberta, British Columbia, Saskatchewan

Foreign Activity:
Asia, Australia/New Zealand, The Middle East, South America, Mexico, Former USSR
Contact(s):
Ken Pelletier, Vice-President, Sales (Calgary), 403-243-5055
kenp@alcogasoil.com
Canadian Branches:
Calgary Branch
Sales & Marketing
#310, 4014 MacLeod Trail SE
Calgary, AB T2G 2R7
403-243-5055
Fax: 403-287-1562
sales@alcogasoil.com
Ken Pelletier, Vice-President

Alcohol Countermeasure Systems Corp. / ACS
60 International Blvd.
Toronto, ON M9W 6J2
416-619-3500
Fax: 416-619-3501
info@acs-corp.com
www.acs-corp.com
Firm Type: Manufacturing
Founded: 1976
Staff: 270
Member of: Alliance of Manufacturers & Exporters Canada
Products/Services/Areas of Expertise: Manufacturer of laboratory equipment & breath alcohol testers
Recently Completed / Ongoing Projects: Florida Ignition Interlock Program; New Mexico Ignition Interlock Program
Financial Information:
Type of Ownership: Private
Domestic Markets:
National
Foreign Activity:
Worldwide
Contact(s):
Felix J.E. Comeau, Chairman and CEO
Christopher J. Wilson, Director, BreathTest Products
Contact(s):
Ian R. Marples, President
Canadian Branch:
Mississauga/Guardian Interlock Systems Corp.
#14, 975 Midway Blvd.
Mississauga, ON L5T 2C6
905-670-2288
Fax: 905-670-8211
International Branch(es):
Australia
#8, 11 Packard Ave.
Castle Hill, NSW Australi
612-8853-6200
Fax: 612-8850-1296
enquiries@guardianinterlock.com.au
Sweden
Larjungevagen 6
Haninge Sweden
8-776-1805
USA
#903, 5818 Hoffner Ave.
Orlando, FL USA
407-207-3337
Fax: 407-207-3314
877-227-7112
info@acs-corp.com
Jessica Hayes

Alcore Fabricating Corp.
65 Newkirk Rd.
Richmond Hill, ON L4C 3G4
905-770-6565
Fax: 905-737-1296
alcoref@aol.com
www.alcorefabricating.com
Firm Type: Manufacturing
Founded: 1960
Products/Services/Areas of Expertise: Waste storage containers; laboratory equipment; design & fabrication of corrosion-resistant equipment for the containment & conveyance of chemicals, including tanks, pipe, exhaust systems with scrubbers & stacks; fabrication of engineered plastics, dual laminates

Domestic Markets:
National
Foreign Activity:
Asia, Mexico, USA
Contact(s):
Manfred Junkert, President
Peter Ton, Marketing & Sales Manager

Aldworth Engineering Inc.
#103, 85 Curlew Dr.
Toronto, ON M3A 2P8
416-446-6300
Fax: 416-446-6303
staff@aldwortheng.com
www.aldwortheng.com
Firm Type: Engineering
Founded: 1989
Staff: 6
Products/Services/Areas of Expertise: Municipal projects: water & wastewater, solid wastes, air pollution, etc.; energy conservation: energy audits, small power plants; parks & recreation: hockey arenas & swimming pools; building services: mechanical (hvac, etc.) & electrical (power/controls, etc.)
Recently Completed / Ongoing Projects: Toronto: Humber, ventilation upgrade; Ashbridges Bay, plant wide heating; Western Arena - rink & post upgrades
Financial Information:
Type of Ownership: Private
Revenue Sources: 10% Provincial; 65% Municipals; 25% Private Contracts
Domestic Markets:
Ontario
Markets Sought:
China, Vietnam,
Contact(s):
George Aldworth, P.Eng., President
george@aldwortheng.com
Richard J. Saab, B.E.Sc., Project Engineer
David J. Moon, P.Eng., Electrical Engineering Associate
dave@aldwortheng.com

Alenag Brokers
360, ch St-Roch nord
Rock Forest, QC J1N 2T3
819-864-7943
Fax: 819-864-7954
Contact(s):
Lawrence W. Perry, President
Canadian Branches:
Québec Branch
#404, 764, St-Joseph est
Québec, QC G1K 3C4
418-647-4587
Fax: 418-647-0256
Jean Louis Chamard, Vice-President
Sherbrooke Branch
#300, 855, rue Pepin
Sherbrooke, QC J1L 2P8
819-829-0101
Fax: 819-829-2717

Alenag Brokers
360, ch St-Roch nord
Rock Forest, QC J1N 2T3
819-864-7943
Fax: 819-864-7954

Alex Milne Associates Ltd.
#3, 1870 Albion Rd.
Toronto, ON M9W 5T2
416-742-4911
Fax: 416-742-6005
800-563-5947
alexmiln@idirect.com
www.alexmilne.com
Firm Type: Distributing, Manufacturing
Founded: 1967
Staff: 2
Member of: Ontario Marine Operators Association; Ontario Federation of Anglers & Hunters; Ontario Cottage Association; Ontario Sailing Association
EcoLogo Certified Products & Services: Natural Marine Aluminum Boat Performance Wax; Natural Marine Outdrive Spray; Natural Marine Fender Protector
Products/Services/Areas of Expertise: Manufactures & distributes non-toxic Natural Marine Foul-Release underwater

coatings for military, marine police, racing & recreational craft; Zebra mussel control products for boaters & cottagers; EcoLogo marine care products; battery equalizer; equine care products
Recently Completed / Ongoing Projects: Occusafe Lubricants
Ecological Note: Natural Marine Aluminum Boat Performance Wax; Natural Marine Outdrive Spray; Natural Marine Fender Protector
Financial Information:
Type of Ownership: Private
Revenue: $500,000 - $1.5 Million
Revenue Sources: 2% nationwide; 2% Provincial; 6% Municipals; 90% Private Contracts
Domestic Markets:
National
Foreign Activity:
Australia/New Zealand, Eastern Europe, USA
Markets Sought:
China, Vietnam
Contact(s):
Bill Milne, President
Ellen Koch

Alexander Boome Consulting Engineering, Ltd. / ABCELTD
#702, 1625 Hornby St.
Vancouver, BC V6Z 2M2
604-290-6194
aboome@abceltd.com
www.abceltd.com
Firm Type: Engineering
Founded: 1978
Staff: 6
Member of: Consulting Engineers of BC; Association of Consulting Engineers of Canada
Products/Services/Areas of Expertise: Consulting engineers providing project management services, environmental & energy analyses, air & water flow testing & verification, smoke control testing & verification; areas of practice include HVAC, energy & green buildings, aqua culture plants, pumping stations, & municipal piping & drainage systems. Branch office located at 1122 Boucher Lake Rd., Moberly Lake, BC - contact (250) 788-7896
Recently Completed / Ongoing Projects: Elkview Coal Silo venting; paint spray booth for Dept. of National Defense jet hangar, Comox; HVAC & plumbing for Air Canada Office HQ in Richmond; Pulp warehouse storm upgrade for Vancouver Wharves; Abbotsford Int'l Airport building & HVAC; Gibbsons Park Plaza Mall storm water system, fire & domestic water mains, HVAC & plumbing
Financial Information:
Type of Ownership: Private
Revenue: $500,000 - $1.5 Million
Revenue Sources: 10% Provincial; 5% Municipals; 85% Private Contracts
Domestic Markets:
Alberta, British Columbia
Foreign Activity:
Asia, USA
Contact(s):
Alexander J. Boome, P.Eng., PE, President
aboome@abceltd.com

Alfa Laval Inc.
101 Milner Ave.
Toronto, ON M1S 4S6
416-299-6101
Fax: 416-297-8690
888-253-2226
alfacan.info@alfalaval.com
www.alfalaval.ca
Firm Type: Manufacturing
Founded: 1883
Staff: 400
Member of: Water Environment Federation; Water Environment Association of Ontario; Western Canada Water & Wastewater Association; Association québécoise des techniques de l'eau
Quality Environmental Management System(s): 9001
Products/Services/Areas of Expertise: Suppliers of heat exchangers, pumps, valves, high-speed separators for power, marine, industrial, chemical, municipal, & pulp & paper applications
Financial Information:
Type of Ownership: Foreign-owned
Revenue: Greater than $5 Million
Revenue Sources: 5% nationwide; 5% Provincial; 25% Municipals; 65% Private Contracts
Domestic Markets:
National
Contact(s):
Ashley Davis, President, 416-297-3417Fax: 416-299-5476
ashley.davis@alfalaval.com
Goswell John, General Manager, Equipment Division, 416-297-3410Fax: 416-299-6476
john.goswell@alfalaval.com
Hazel Baptista, Executive Assistant, 416-299-6101Fax: 416-267-8690
Canadian Branches:
Calgary
#305, 2912 Memorial Drive SE
Calgary, AB T2A 6R1
403-269-5300
Fax: 403-569-7727

Edmonton
6344 Roper Rd.
Edmonton, AB T6B 3P9
780-413-6349
Fax: 780-450-6747

Montréal
B
#B101, 7900 boul. Taschereau ouest
Brossard, QC J4X 1C2
450-466-0111
Fax: 450-466-0005

Vancouver
#334, 1275 West 6th Ave.
Vancouver, BC V6H 1A6
604-734-2225
Fax: 604-734-2265

Alfa Plastics Inc.
2 Baker Rd.
Brampton, ON L6T 4E3
905-792-8005
Fax: 905-792-6667
info@alfaplastics.com
www.alfaplastics.com
Firm Type: Distributing, Manufacturing
Founded: 1976
Staff: 35
Products/Services/Areas of Expertise: Manufacturer, wholesaler & distributor of custom thermo-plastic articles for all industries; pipe fittings, valves, sheets, tubing & rod, pipe headers, process control systems, fusion spooling; also, exhaust fans & air purification machinery
Financial Information:
Type of Ownership: Private
Domestic Markets:
National
Foreign Activity:
USA
Contact(s):
Gert Jungeblut, General Manager
gert@alfaplastics.com
Robert Woolcott, Manager, Sales
Cathy Brown, Agent, Inside Sales

Algonquin Power Income Fund
Formerly: Algonquin Power Corporation Inc.
2845 Bristol Circle
Oakville, ON L6H 7H7
905-465-4500
Fax: 905-465-4514
www.algonquinpower.com
Firm Type: Management Consulting, Engineering
Founded: 1989
Products/Services/Areas of Expertise: Manages, operates & develops hydro-electric generating product or facilities
Financial Information:
Type of Ownership: Publicly Traded
Domestic Markets:
National
Foreign Activity:
USA
Contact(s):
Kenneth Moore, Chairman, Board of Directors
Ian Robertson, CEO
David Bronicheski, CFO, Managing Director
George Steeves, Director

All Treat Farms Limited
#109, 7963 Wellington Rd.
Arthur, ON N0G 1A0
519-848-3145
Fax: 519-848-2598
alltreat@alltreat.com
www.alltreat.com
Firm Type: Manufacturing, Waste Management
Founded: 1956
Member of: Compost Council of Canada
Products/Services/Areas of Expertise: Composting facility, licenced for organic materials; bird feed; wood recycling; gold & sports turf; horticultural products
Domestic Markets:
Ontario
Markets Sought:
USA
Contact(s):
George H. White, President
Rod Kidnie, Manager, National Sales

All Waste Removal Inc.
20 Freshway Dr.
Concord, ON L4K 1R9
905-669-4340
Fax: 905-669-9945
www.ecowood-products.com
Firm Type: Waste Management
Founded: 1972
Member of: Ontario Waste Management Association; Recycling Council of Ontario; Canadian Wood Pallet & Container Association
Products/Services/Areas of Expertise: Roll-off containers for removal of commercial & industrial waste & recyclables; front-end service for generators with space restrictions; sanitized trucks for produce & food waste; industrial commercial waste collection & recycling services
Contact(s):
Brian Ainscough, Contact
Fred Bernard, Operations Manager
Mike Thomas, Manager

ALL-TECH Environmental Services Ltd.
#202, 20 Duke St.
Bedford, NS B4A 2Z5
902-835-3727
Fax: 902-835-5266
email@toalltech.com
www.toalltech.com
Firm Type: Management Consulting, Scientific/Technical Services

Products/Services/Areas of Expertise: Asbestos inspection & air monitoring; occupational hygiene audits & assessments; confined space auditing & testing; building inspection for decommissioning; indoor air quality; lead paint testing & consulting
Recently Completed / Ongoing Projects: Asbestos abatement, Halifax Airport
Financial Information:
Type of Ownership: Private
Revenue Sources: 50% nationwide; 10% Provincial; 40% Private Contracts
Domestic Markets:
New Brunswick, Newfoundland & Labrador, Nova Scotia, Prince Edward Island
Contact(s):
Terry Smith, General Manager

Canadian Branches:
Bathurst Satellite
506-544-6611

Charlottetown
53 Queen St.
Charlottetown, PE C1A 4T5
902-569-0172
Fax: 902-569-5453

Moncton Satellite Office
506-384-7246

Saint John
185 Old Black River Rd.
Saint John, NB E2R 1A3
506-658-1058
Fax: 506-652-7998

St. John's
#402, 151 Crosbie Rd.
St. John's, NL A1B 4B4
709-754-4146
Fax: 709-754-4194

Sydney
#101, 1 Inglis St.
Sydney, NS B1P 6H4
902-565-8243
Fax: 902-539-3381

All-Weld Company Limited
49 Passmore Ave.
Toronto, ON M1V 4T1
416-299-3311
Fax: 416-299-3387
888-368-8884
mail@allweld.ca
www.allweld.ca
Firm Type: Engineering, Manufacturing
Founded: 1920
Staff: 55
Quality Environmental Management System(s): 9001:2000
Products/Services/Areas of Expertise: Design, engineering & manufacture of specialty alloy process equipment serving the chemical (light & heavy), petrochemical, environmental, nuclear, mining, pharmaceutical & laboratory industries. Aurora Filters, a subsidary company specializing in nutsche filters for the pharaceutical & chemical industries, is located at the same address
Domestic Markets:
National
Foreign Activity:
Africa, Asia, Australia/New Zealand, Caribbean, Eastern Europe, Western Europe, The Pacific Rim, South America, Mexico, USA
Contact(s):
W.A. Dunsmoor, P.Eng., President & General Manager
A.D. (Tony) Grist, Sales Manager

All-Wood Fibre Ltd.
P.O. Box 2250
3645 - 18th Ave.
Prince George, BC V2N 1A8
250-563-1770
Fax: 250-563-1880
info@all-woodfibre.com
www.all-woodfibre.com
Firm Type: Scientific/Technical Services, Waste Management
Founded: 1994
Products/Services/Areas of Expertise: Industry leader in portable wood chipping for the pulp industry; extraction of wood from old log yards and landfills; identification of logs for chipping; related services
Financial Information:
Type of Ownership: Private
Domestic Markets:
Alberta, British Columbia
Contact(s):
Leonard Legault, President & Co-Founder
Wendy Legault, Managing Director
Gerald Kutney, Ph.D., COO

Allan Fyfe Equipment Limited
266 North Rivermede Rd.
Concord, ON L4K 3N6
905-669-1313
Fax: 905-669-9802
info@allanfyfe.com
www.allanfyfe.com
Firm Type: Distributing
Founded: 1948
Products/Services/Areas of Expertise: Grinders; chippers; hydraulic tools
Domestic Markets:
New Brunswick, Nova Scotia, Ontario, Québec
Contact(s):
Alastair Fyfe, Vice-President
afyfe@allanfyfe.com
Harold Isenberg, Sales Manager, Sales
harold@allanfyfe.com

Alldec Trading Ltd.
Division of TCS Management Ltd.
#108, 19329 Enterprise Way
Surrey, BC V3S 6J8
604-534-3688
Fax: 604-534-0166

866-633-7788
info@alldec.com
www.alldec.com
Firm Type: Distributing
Founded: 1988
Products/Services/Areas of Expertise: Environmentally safe skin care products for industry, home & hobby; industrial tools, automotive products, hardware & lumberyard products; Eco Green Solutions - environmentally friendly auto degreaser, oil buster, household cleaner, window cleaner, aluminum cleaner, vehicle wash
Financial Information:
Type of Ownership: Private
Revenue: $250,000 - $500,000
Revenue Sources: 100% Private Contracts
Domestic Markets:
Alberta, British Columbia, Manitoba, Nova Scotia, Ontario, Québec, Saskatchewan
Foreign Activity:
Mexico, USA
Contact(s):
Jan Vincent, Vice-President, Marketing
Robert Jones, Manager, Sales

Alliance Envelope Ltd.
111 Jacob Keffer Pky.
Concord, ON L4K 4V1
905-879-0000
Fax: 905-879-0156
800-567-6925
info@royalenvelope.com
www.royalenvelope.com
Firm Type: Manufacturing
Founded: 1989
EcoLogo Certified Products & Services: Customized & stock envelopes
Products/Services/Areas of Expertise: Offers a range of envelope-related products and services, including an environmentally friendly product line and direct mail designs
Ecological Note: Customized & stock envelopes
Contact(s):
Bob Barless, Vice-President

Allianz Madvac Inc.
Formerly: Madvac Inc.
1690, rue Eiffel
Boucherville, QC J4B 7W1
450-616-8100
Fax: 450-616-8103
800-862-3822
sales@madvac.com
www.madvac.com; www.allianzmadvac.com
Firm Type: Distributing, Manufacturing
Founded: 1986
Staff: 150
Member of: National Solid Waste Management Association, Inc.
Products/Services/Areas of Expertise: Complete line of patented litter collection systems, including street sweepers, designed to eliminate the disadvantages associated with manual litter collection; provides a cost-efficient, highly productive & virtually maintenance-free method of litter removal; ideal for municipal, industrial, commercial litter management
Financial Information:
Type of Ownership: Publicly Traded
Revenue: Greater than $5 Million
Revenue Sources: 25% nationwide; 25% Provincial; 25% Municipals; 25% Private Contracts
Domestic Markets:
National
Foreign Activity:
Asia, South America, Mexico, USA, United Kingdom, Worldwide
Markets Sought:
Eastern Europe, Former USSR
Contact(s):
Gabriel Charky, CEO
Andreas Pollmueller, Vice President, Export Sales & Marketing

International Branch(es):
California
4651 Schaefer Ave.
Chino, CA USA
909-613-5600
Al Paganucci

Alloy Fab Ltd.
763 Chester St.
Sarnia, ON N7S 5N2

519-336-4363
Fax: 519-336-8903
info@alloyfab.on.ca
www.alloyfab.com
Firm Type: Engineering, Manufacturing
Founded: 1987
Staff: 25
Products/Services/Areas of Expertise: Heat exchangers; waste heat boilers; pressure vessels; process equipment; equipment for refinery desulfurization, hydrotreating projects; feed/effluent exchangers
Domestic Markets:
National
Foreign Activity:
USA, Worldwide
Contact(s):
Brant Jacklin, General Manager

Alnor Industries Ltd.
1566 Bonhill Rd.
Mississauga, ON L5T 1C7
905-362-1029
Fax: 905-326-0805
877-322-1121
info@alnorindustries.com
www.alnorindustries.com
Founded: 1995
Staff: 5
Products/Services/Areas of Expertise: Dealers & suppliers of high quality segregated scrap, including ferrous, & nonferrous new production scrap metal; collection equipment; cable recycling; metal processing, selling, buying & recycling
Financial Information:
Type of Ownership: Private
Revenue: $3 Million - $5 Million
Revenue Sources: 100% Private Contracts
Domestic Markets:
Ontario
Foreign Activity:
Asia, Central Europe, Eastern Europe
Contact(s):
Al Bauer, President
Christian Bauer, Vice-President

Alpha Controls & Instrumentation
#6, 361 Steelcase Rd. West
Markham, ON L3R 3V8
905-477-2133
Fax: 905-477-4219
800-567-8686
alphasales@alphacontrols.com
www.alphacontrols.com
Firm Type: Distributing
Founded: 1980
Member of: Canadian Process Control Association
Quality Environmental Management System(s): 9001:2008
Products/Services/Areas of Expertise: Distributes a range of measuring, testing & controlling instruments to the Canadian pharmaceutical, automotive, food & beverage, waste & water treatment, aerospace, chemical & petrochemical, power, & HVAC industries. Products include instrumentation, controllers, transmitters, transducers, recorders, temperature controllers. On-site calibration lab services (ISO/IEC 17025). Branch locations in Montréal & Ottawa
Financial Information:
Type of Ownership: Private
Domestic Markets:
National
Contact(s):
Jerry Sand, President/CEO
Marc Brand, Sales Manager

Canadian Branches:
Montréal
280, rue Frenette
Rosemère, QC J7A 2Z3
450-621-3626
Fax: 450-261-4089
888-621-3626

Alpha Industrial Services
Also Known As: Optima Industrial Services
#3A, 55 Selby Rd.
Brampton, ON L6W 1K5
416-731-5435
ed@alphaservices.ca
alphaservice.ca

Products & Services Buyer's Guide

Products/Services/Areas of Expertise: Leasing, sales (new & used), parts & service of a variety of products including: lab equipment, dryers, grinders, cooling & heating equipment, material handing equipment, leak detectors; parts for servo valves, air valves, temperature controllers, timers & counters, transformers; complete automation: robotics, pickers, packaging, conveying systems, quality control, custom machinery; industrial installations; reconditioning, retrofit, & repairs

AlphaNuclear Company
2100 Dudley St.
Saskatoon, SK S7M 5W3
306-956-6678
Fax: 306-956-6661
info@alphanuclear.com
www.alphanuclear.com
Firm Type: Manufacturing
Founded: 1975
Staff: 6
Products/Services/Areas of Expertise: Monitoring equipment for environmental, mining & geoscience applications; measuring instruments for radon
Domestic Markets:
British Columbia, Manitoba, New Brunswick, Nova Scotia, Québec, Saskatchewan
Foreign Activity:
Worldwide
Contact(s):
Andre Boucher, Manager

Alpine Environmental Ltd.
#119, 1440 Aviation Park NE
Calgary, AB T2E 7E2
403-291-1081
Fax: 403-291-3537
800-610-7849
info@alpine-env.com
www.alpine-env.com
Firm Type: Scientific/Technical Services
Founded: 1979
Staff: 180
Products/Services/Areas of Expertise: Oilfield & drilling waste management; land reclamation & site remediation; environmental audits; wastewater treatment; emergency spill response & clean-up; groundwater investigation & supply
Recently Completed / Ongoing Projects: Impact assessment of pipeline; investigation of underground storage tank sites; environmental assessment of decommissioned sour gas plant; emergency clean-up of train derailment
Financial Information:
Type of Ownership: Private
Domestic Markets:
Alberta, British Columbia, Saskatchewan
Foreign Activity:
Asia
Contact(s):
Troy Bulbuck, President/CEO
Kathy Reich, CFO
Ranju Shergill, CAO

Canadian Branches:
Drayton Valley, AB
780-542-5780

Edmonton, AB
780-436-2740

Estevan, SK
306-634-0024

Fort Liard, NT
867-770-4571

Fort Nelson, BC
250-774-3626

Fort St John, BC
250-787-0010

Grande Prairie, AB
780-538-0050

Vermilion, AB
780-853-2082

Alrange Container Services / ACS
44 Medulla Ave.
Toronto, ON M8Z 5L9
416-239-9559
Fax: 416-239-7535
866-455-7455
sales@alrange.com
www.alrange.com
Products/Services/Areas of Expertise: Manufacture, repair, and sale of shipping containers
Domestic Markets:
National
Foreign Activity:
USA
Contact(s):
Chris Cornwall, President
cornwall@alrange.com

ALS Environmental
Formerly: ALS Analytical Service Laboratories Ltd.
#100, 8081 Lougheed Highway
Burnaby, BC V5A 1W9
604-253-4188
Fax: 604-253-6700
800-665-0243
vancouver@alsenviro.com
www.alsenviro.com
Firm Type: Scientific/Technical Services
Founded: 1982
Staff: 90
Member of: Canadian Association for Environmental Analytical Laboratories; Air & Waste Management Association; Canadian Environment Industry Association; Standards Council of Canada
Products/Services/Areas of Expertise: Chemical testing, research & consultation laboratory specializing in organic & inorganic environmental chemistry; environmental testing & monitoring; waste characterization services; mobile lab services; site assessment; drinking water & industrial hygiene analysis; parameters include metals, BTEX, hydrocarbons, phenolics, PAH, PCB, VOC, pesticides & other environmental contaminants; international consulting services for design & development of laboratories, including technical training; company has 15 foreign offices, see website for details
Recently Completed / Ongoing Projects: Laboratory analysis for environmental studies, site assessment & permit monitoring; occupational hygiene consulting & analysis; international consulting & training for the development of environmental laboratories
Financial Information:
Type of Ownership: Foreign-owned
Revenue Sources: 5% nationwide; 2% Provincial; 3% Municipals; 90% Private Contracts
Domestic Markets:
National
Foreign Activity:
Asia, Australia/New Zealand, Central America, China, The Pacific Rim, South America, Mexico, USA, Vietnam
Contact(s):
Rob Deverall, President
Scott Hannam,, Executive Manager

Canadian Branches:
Burlington
#5, 5420 Mainway Dr.
Burlington, ON L7L 6A4
905-331-3111
Fax: 905-331-4567

Calgary
1313 - 44 Ave. NE
Calgary, AB T2E 6L5
403-291-9897
Fax: 403-291-0298
calgary@alsenviro.com

Edmonton
9936 - 67 Ave.
Edmonton, AB T6E 0P5
780-413-5227
Fax: 780-437-2311

Fort McMurray
Bay 1, 245 Macdonald Cr.
Fort McMurray, AB T9H 4B5
780-791-1524
Fax: 780-791-1586

Fort St. John
P.O. Box 256
9420 - 93rd Ave.
Fort St John, BC V1J 6W7
250-261-5517
Fax: 250-261-5587
FortStJohn@alsenviro.com

Grande Prairie
9505 - 111 St.
Grande Prairie, AB T8V 5W1
780-539-5196
Fax: 780-513-2191

London
#29, 309 Exeter Rd.
London, ON N6L 1C1
519-652-6044
Fax: 519-652-0671

Mississauga
#26, 5730 Coopers Ave.
Mississauga, ON L4Z 2E9
905-507-6910
Fax: 905-507-6927

Richmond Hill
#1, 95 West Beaver Creek Rd.
Richmond Hill, ON L4B 1H2
905-881-9887
Fax: 905-881-8062

Saskatoon
819 - 58 St. East
Saskatoon, ON S7K 6X5
306-668-8370
Fax: 306-668-8383

Thunder Bay
1081 Barton St.
Thunder Bay, ON P7B 5N3
807-623-6463
Fax: 807-623-7598

Waterloo
#1, 60 Northland Rd.
Waterloo, ON N2V 2B8
519-886-6910
Fax: 519-886-9047

Winnipeg
#12, 1329 Niakwa Rd. East
Winnipeg, MB R2J 3T4
204-255-9720
Fax: 204-255-9721

Yellowknife
75 Con Rd.
Yellowknife, NT X1A 2R2
867-873-5593
Fax: 867-920-4238

Alstom Canada Inc.
#2320, 1010, rue Sherbrooke ouest
Montréal, QC H3A 2R7
514-281-6200
Fax: 514-281-6300
www.alstom.com
Products/Services/Areas of Expertise: Service & maintenance of power generation equipment, as well as environmental control systems, with related after sales services; rolling stock remanufacture & overhauling
Recently Completed / Ongoing Projects: Mica, GM Shrum, Peribonka, Eastmain 1, Chief Joseph (U.S.); TransAlta, Nova Scotia Power; City of Calgary, Railpower; Control Centre for metro system (Montréal)
Domestic Markets:
National
Contact(s):
Pierre Gauthier, President/CEO

Canadian Branches:
Brossard - Alstom Power Service
7-B, Place du Commerce
Brossard, QC J4W 3K3
450-465-9795
Fax: 450-465-4403

Burlington - Alstom Power Service
845 Harrington Court
Burlington, ON L7N 3P3

905-333-3667
Fax: 905-333-4911

Calgary - Alstom Power Service
Executive Tower
#850, 11012 Macleod Trail SE
Calgary, AB T2J 6A5
403-225-5526
Fax: 403-278-9483

Calgary - Alstom Transport Service
7550 Ogdendale Rd. SE
Calgary, AB T2C 4X9
403-236-6933
Fax: 403-236-6914
866-365-3107

Edmonton - Alstom Power Service
14440 - 123rd Ave.
Edmonton, AB T5L 2Y3
780-447-4660
Fax: 780-447-3910

Hull - Alstom Power Service
60, rue Jean-Proulx
Hull, QC J8Z 1W1
613-747-5116
Fax: 613-747-5883

Ottawa - Alstom Power Service
#600, 1430 Blair Pl.
Ottawa, ON K1J 9N2
613-747-5222
Fax: 613-747-5888
Products/Services/Areas of Expertise: Ottawa is the main location for Alstom Power Service

Richmond - Alstom Power Service
#193 - 21300 Gordon Way
Richmond, BC V6W 1M2
604-232-5527
Fax: 604-232-5569

Sorel-Tracy - Alstom Canada Inc., Power Hydro
1350, ch St-Roch
Sorel-Tracy, QC J3R 5P9
450-746-6500
Fax: 450-746-6590

Alta-Fab Structures Ltd.
504 - 13 Ave.
Nisku, AB T9E 7P6
780-955-7733
Fax: 780-955-7851
800-252-7990
hvw@altafab.com
www.altafab.com
Firm Type: Manufacturing, Scientific/Technical Services
Founded: 1973
Staff: 450
Products/Services/Areas of Expertise: Provides pre-fabricated, modular buildings; produces floor plans, & working spaces for custom buildings, wellsites, office complexes & camps for various industries & companies
Contact(s):
Hank Van Weelden, Vice-President, Sales/Marketing

Altamar International Inc.
Also Known As: Altamar Translation & Interpretation
#203, 10275 Jasper Ave.
Edmonton, AB T5J 1X8
780-428-1400
Fax: 780-444-6444
877-477-1400
altamar@altamarinternational.com
www.altamarinternational.com
Founded: 1992
Products/Services/Areas of Expertise: Translators & interpreters available in the following areas: law, engineering, medicine, oil & gas, mining, construction, aeronautics, international trade & NAFTA; services include translations/interpretations in : contracts & agreements; import/export documents; business correspondence; multilingual websites; legal documents; transcriptions; technical manuals; voice-overs; on-site translation & interpretation services; proofreading, printing & formatting; teleconferencing
Domestic Markets:
Alberta, British Columbia, Ontario
Foreign Activity:
Mexico

Contact(s):
Margarita Hansen, President
Russell Gilles, Co-ordinator
Eugene Erlor, Secretary
Canadian Branches:
Calgary
5905 - 11 St. SE, Bay 6
Calgary, AB T2H 2A6
403-262-5906
Fax: 403-262-1092
877-477-1400
altamar@altamarinternational.com

Ottawa
877-477-1400
altamar@altamarinternational.com

Toronto
877-477-1400
altamar@altamarinternational.com

Vancouver
877-477-1400
altamar@altamarinternational.com

Yellowknife
877-477-1400
altamar@altamarinternational.com

ALTECH Environmental Consulting Ltd.
A member firm of the ALTECH Group
12 Banigan Dr.
Toronto, ON M4H 1E9
416-467-5555
Fax: 416-467-9824
800-323-4937
aecl@altech-group.com
www.altech-group.com
Firm Type: Management Consulting, Engineering, Scientific/Technical Services
Founded: 1986
Staff: 16
Member of: Ontario Environment Industry Association; Canadian Environmental Auditing Association; Air & Waste Management Association
Quality Environmental Management System(s): 14001
Products/Services/Areas of Expertise: A multi-disciplinary, full service environmental engineering firm, specializing in: environmental management & audit services (ISO 14000 standards), site assessments & remediation, waste management services, wastewater studies & treatment, energy management, health & safety, air monitoring & assessment, noise assessment, technical & business analysis, project management, groundwater & soil investigations & installations; Phase I, II, III services & cleanup. ALTECH Technology Systems Inc. is a sister company
Recently Completed / Ongoing Projects: Energy efficiency audits with follow-up installations, designed & built 4 industrial wastewater treatment plants; conducted 500 Phase I & II investigations & completed many industrial cleanups
Financial Information:
Type of Ownership: Private
Revenue: $3 Million - $5 Million
Revenue Sources: 5% nationwide; 5% Provincial; 90% Private Contracts
Domestic Markets:
National
Foreign Activity:
Asia, Caribbean, Central America, South America, Mexico, USA
Contact(s):
Brian Bobbie, President

ALTECH Technology Systems Inc.
A member firm of the ALTECH Group
12 Banigan Dr.
Toronto, ON M4H 1E9
416-467-5555
Fax: 416-467-9824
866-734-8437
ats@altech-group.com
www.altech-group.com
Firm Type: Engineering, Manufacturing, Waste Management
Founded: 1987
Staff: 8
Member of: Canadian Environment Industry Association
Products/Services/Areas of Expertise: Proprietary & patented air pollution abatement & wastewater treatment technologies; featuring System REITHER, a patented air scrubbing system & System HydroKleen, a membrane bioreaction for industrial wastewaters; conduct bench scale treatability tests & design commercially available treatment systems for industrial laundry, textile & dying plants, food, meat & dairy processing, chemical manufacturing, pulp & paper manufacturing, petroleum refining, electroplating operations, water recycling & management in the photo processing industry; installation of fixed base thermal desorber for contaminated soils; sludge drying & solidification system for waste management
Domestic Markets:
National
Foreign Activity:
Asia, Australia/New Zealand, Caribbean, Central America, Central Europe, Eastern Europe, Western Europe, South America, Mexico, USA
Contact(s):
Alex R. Keen, President

Altek Power Corporation
#1004, 1708 Dolphin Ave.
Kelowna, BC V1Y 9S4
250-717-3707
Fax: 250-717-3708
888-717-3707
Firm Type: Distributing, Manufacturing, Scientific/Technical Services
Founded: 1979
Staff: 3
Products/Services/Areas of Expertise: An independent power producer & manufacturer of distributed generation plants, with emphasis on environmentally responsible energy solutions; areas of business focus include power turbine manufacturing & sales, biomass sales, power projects & patents
Financial Information:
Type of Ownership: Publicly Traded
Domestic Markets:
National
Foreign Activity:
Eastern Europe, The Middle East, USA
Markets Sought:
South America, Mexico, USA,
Contact(s):
Rod Reum, President
rreum@altekpower.com

Alternative Fuel Systems (2004) Inc.
Formerly: AFS Environmental Solutions Inc..
#1, 4321 - 14th St. NE
Calgary, AB T2E 7A9
403-262-1833
Fax: 403-237-7441
info@afsglobal.com; sales@afsglobal.com
www.afsglobal.com
Firm Type: Distributing, Manufacturing, Scientific/Technical Services
Founded: 2004
Staff: 12
Products/Services/Areas of Expertise: The firm designs, develops & manufactures core components for the international automotive sector, with emphasis on the alternative fuel market. Products include: electronic engine management controllers, & natural gas handling components & associated software, ignition systems, fuel enjectors, engine control modules, natural gas pressure regulators, & interfacing tools. Services include custom design & engineering, software & calibration
Financial Information:
Type of Ownership: Publicly Traded
Domestic Markets:
National
Foreign Activity:
Eastern Europe, The Pacific Rim, USA
Contact(s):
Jim F. Perry, President/CEO

Altus Capital Planning Inc. / ACPI
Altus Group
1595 - 16th Ave. 4th Fl.
Richmond Hill, ON L4B 3N9
905-764-2440
Fax: 905-764-2445
info@altuscapitalplanning.com
www.capitalplanningsolutions.com
Firm Type: Management Consulting, Information Technology
Founded: 1996
Member of: American Water Works Association, Water Environmental Federation, American Public Works Association, Réseau Environnement

Products/Services/Areas of Expertise: Integrated decision support system, HIMA, is a 5-step process that produces multiyear capital plans for multiple types of asset categories using precise multicriteria analysis to enhance strategic planning
Recently Completed / Ongoing Projects: City of Newark, Ohio, USA; City of Hamilton, ON; Québec City, QC; National Defense of Canada; City of Moncton, NB
Financial Information:
Type of Ownership: Private
Revenue Sources: 5% nationwide; 5% Provincial; 85% Municipals; 5% Private Contracts
Domestic Markets:
National
Foreign Activity:
USA
Markets Sought:
Australia/New Zealand, Central Europe, Western Europe
Contact(s):
Alan Gordon, President & CEO

Canadian Branches:
Québec
Formerly: Harfan Technologies inc.
#200, 2014, rue Cyrille-Duquet
Québec, QC G1N 4N6
418-873-5200
Fax: 418-873-5201
www.harfan.com

Aluma Systems Inc.
a Brand Energy & Infrastructure Services company
40 Simmonds Dr.
Dartmouth, NS B3B 1R3
902-468-9533
Fax: 902-468-5040
www.aluma.com; www.beis.com
Products/Services/Areas of Expertise: Infrastructure services including concrete formwork & shoring, engineering design of aluminum & steel shoring solutions & scaffolding, project management & site technical direction, custom aluminum concrete forming systems; services to the construction & infrastructure industries, offshore oil industry & Canadian Oil Sands, & the petrochemical industry
Domestic Markets:
National
Contact(s):
Ken Seaward, Manager
Mike Batchelor, Regional Operating Vice-President, Canada

Amaircare Corporation
770 Gana Ct.
Mississauga, ON L5S 1P1
905-565-9488
Fax: 905-565-9866
800-268-7732
info@amaircare.com
www.amaircare.com
Firm Type: Manufacturing
Founded: 1994
Products/Services/Areas of Expertise: Hepa air filtration systems & replacement products
Contact(s):
Jim Woods, President
jimwoods@amaircare.com

Amberg Corp. - Environmental & Regulatory Consultants
#600, 440 - 10816 MacLeod Trail South
Calgary, AB T2J 5N8
403-547-4956
contact@amberg.ca
www.amberg.ca
Firm Type: Management Consulting
Founded: 1995
Member of: Canadian Environmental Auditing Association
Products/Services/Areas of Expertise: Develops & implements environmental, health & safety & quality management systems; emissions assessment; environmental assessment; training programs; supports environmental sustainability in agriculture
Domestic Markets:
Alberta, British Columbia, Manitoba, Saskatchewan
Contact(s):
Frank W. Kloiber, Principal
fkloiber@amberg.ca

Canadian Branches:
Edmonton Office
#604, 10025 - 106th St.
Edmonton, AB T5J 1G4
780-990-0911

Ambio Biofiltration Ltd.
P.O. Box 644
Rockland, ON K4K 1L4
613-446-0274
Fax: 613-446-0275
pride@ambio.ca
www.ambio.ca
Firm Type: Engineering, Manufacturing, Scientific/Technical Services
Founded: 1993
Products/Services/Areas of Expertise: Designs, constructs & maintains biofilters for odour, BTEX & VOC control in sewage treatment plants, composting & recycling facilities, sludge drying operations, food processing companies, chemical industries, surface coatings operations (lacquering & spray painting), manufacturing & industrial plants & printing operations
Domestic Markets:
National
Foreign Activity:
The Middle East, USA
Contact(s):
Calvin Pride, President, 613-277-2084
Shan B. Shanchayan, Project Engineer, 613-355-3385Fax: 613-446-0275
shan@ambio.ca

Ambler & Co. Inc.
5804 Datsun Rd.
Mississauga, ON L5A 2Y9
905-677-4574
Fax: 905-677-4818
ambler@on.aibn.com
Firm Type: Engineering
Founded: 1994
Staff: 22
Products/Services/Areas of Expertise: Contaminated soil excavation
Financial Information:
Revenue: $500,000 - $1.5 Million
Domestic Markets:
Ontario
Contact(s):
Brian Ambler, President
Dave Carson, Construction Manager

AMEC
900 AMEC Place
801 - 6 Ave. SW
Calgary, AB T2P 3W3
403-298-4170
Fax: 403-298-4125
www.amec.com
Firm Type: Management Consulting, Engineering, Information Technology, Scientific/Technical Services, Waste Management
Founded: 1951
Staff: 2200
Member of: Association of Consulting Engineers of Canada; Canadian Association of Environmental Analytical Labs; Canadian Standards Association
Products/Services/Areas of Expertise: Geotechnical & materials engineering; ground improvement services; engineering; scientific & contracting services to industrial, resource, commercial industry & government clients in North America & strategic international markets; air, water, soil, & groundwater assessment, testing & monitoring; remediation services; habitat restoration; industrial wastewater systems & water resources engineering; pipeline construction; container recovery & recycling; laboratory services; materials testing & water resource services; mine design; mine waste (tailings) management; permafrost engineering. With main offices in Oakville, Toronto, Vancouver & Calgary, AMEC also operates across the U.S., as well as in China, Germany, Russia, Japan & the UK
Recently Completed / Ongoing Projects: Little Bow River Project, Dam & Reservoir, AB; Chase Creek Stream Channel Restoration, BC; Urban Water Management, Regina, SK; Site assessments for a major oil company & a major petrochemical plant in AB; Suncor Oil Sands Project, Fort McMurray, AB; Hospital Water Supply, Canmore, AB; Sewage Plant, Annacis Isl., BC; Farm Soil & Water Management Project, Kafr El Sheikh, Egypt

Financial Information:
Type of Ownership: Publicly Traded
Revenue: Greater than $5 Million
Revenue Sources: 5% nationwide; 10% Provincial; 20% Municipals; 65% Private Contracts
Domestic Markets:
National
Foreign Activity:
Africa, Asia, Caribbean, Central America, China, Central Europe, Eastern Europe, The Pacific Rim, South America, Mexico, USA, Former USSR, Vietnam, Worldwide
Markets Sought:
Asia, Australia/New Zealand
Contact(s):
Roger Jinks, President
Gary Walters, CFO & Exec. Vice-President
Ian Darrach, Exec. Vice-President
Laurie Davidson, Exec. Vice-President, Eastern Canada
Jim Beechinor, Exec. Vice-President, Corporate Development
David Rowney, Director, Marketing & Communications
Les Panek, Sr. Vice-President
les.panek@amec.com
Contact(s):
Don Nicol, Manager

Canadian Branches:
Abbotsford
31899 Mercantile Way
Abbotsford, BC V2T 4C3
604-864-9971
Fax: 604-864-4276
john.laxdal@amec.com
Founded: 1994
John Laxdal, Regional Manager

Bonnyville
5506 - 50 Ave., Bay 1
Bonnyville, AB T9N 2K8
780-826-4759
Fax: 780-826-7044
kristy.tetreau@amec.com
Kristy Tetreau, Supervisor

Burnaby
2227 Douglas Rd.
Burnaby, BC V5C 5A9
604-294-3811
Fax: 604-294-4664
peter.lighthall@amec.com
Peter Lighthall, Vice-President

Calgary
140 Quarry Park Blvd. SE
Calgary, AB T2C 3G3
403-248-4331
Fax: 403-248-2188
Staff: 200
Products/Services/Areas of Expertise: This location is one of several in the Earth & Environmental division; consulting services include environmental management, science & engineering services, geotechnical engineering, materials engineering & testing, mining services, human environment services, water resources management, & environmental management information systems. Materials Laboratory located at 1003 53 Ave NE in Calgary
Les Panek, Sr. Vice-President

Dartmouth
#301, 32 Troop Ave.
Dartmouth, NS B3B 1Z1
902-468-2848
Fax: 902-468-1314
yvette.hughes@amec.com
Yvette Hughes, Unit Manager

Edmonton
5681 - 70 St.
Edmonton, AB T6B 3P6
780-436-2152
Fax: 780-435-8425
fred.apon@amec.com
Fred Apon, Unit Manager

Fort McMurray
10204 Centennial Dr.
Fort McMurray, AB T9H 1Y5
780-791-0848
Fax: 780-790-1194
zobayur.rahman@amec.com

Zobayur Rahman, Unit Manager

Fort St. John
11007 Alaska Rd.
Fort St John, BC V1J 6P3
250-785-5982
Fax: 250-785-3122
janine.wolff@amec.com
Founded: 1997
Products/Services/Areas of Expertise: The office houses a testing lab for soils, aggregates, asphalt & concrete
Janine Wolff, Administrative Assistant

Fredericton
25 Waggoners Lane
Fredericton, NB E3B 2L2
506-458-1000
Fax: 506-450-0829
david.parkinson@amec.com
Staff: 33
David Parkinson, Unit Manager

Hamilton
#1, 505 Woodward Ave.
Hamilton, ON L8H 6N6
905-312-0700
Fax: 905-312-0771
ivan.severinsky@amec.com
Staff: 15
Products/Services/Areas of Expertise: Testing of concrete, asphalt, soils, & aggregate
Ivan Severinsky, Manager

Kamloops
#1293, 913 Laval Cres.
Kamloops, BC V2C 5P4
250-374-1347
Fax: 250-374-2944
bradley.jackman@amec.com
Bradley Jackman, Supervisor

Lethbridge
1430B - 31 St. North
Lethbridge, AB T1H 5J8
403-327-7474
Fax: 403-327-7682
michael.edmonds@amec.com
Founded: 1965
Products/Services/Areas of Expertise: Focus is on geotechnical assessment for roadway design & construction, as well as a range of development projects. A 2nd Lethbridge office is located at 740 4th Ave. S., contact 403-329-1467
Michael Edmonds, Unit Manager

Lloydminster
5406 - 52 Ave.
Lloydminster, AB T9V 2T5
780-875-8975
Fax: 780-875-1970
jay.jaber@amec.com
Products/Services/Areas of Expertise: The office houses a testing lab for soils, aggregates, asphalt & concrete
Jay Jaber, Unit Manager

London
#2, 1398 Wellington Rd. South
London, ON N6E 3N6
519-681-2400
Fax: 519-668-1754
bob.dufton@amec.com
Staff: 20
Products/Services/Areas of Expertise: Expertise in occupational hygiene, as well as environmental engineering applications (Phase I-II site assessments, remediation) & building & materials science
Bob Dufton, Group Leader

Medicine Hat
964A - 23 St. SW
Medicine Hat, AB T1A 8G3
403-527-5871
Fax: 403-528-3860
michael.edmonds@amec.com
Founded: 1980
Michael Edmonds, Unit Manager

Mississauga
#110, 160 Traders Blvd. East
Mississauga, ON L4Z 3K7
905-568-2929
Fax: 905-568-1686
colin.macleod@amec.com
Founded: 1990
Staff: 50
Products/Services/Areas of Expertise: Specialists in environmental assessments, site remediation, facility decommissioning, groundwater development, air quality services, landfill engineering
Colin MacLeod, Unit Manager

Moncton
#350, 1133 St. George Blvd.
Moncton, NB E1E 4E1
506-855-5542
Fax: 506-857-9974
paul.belyea@amec.com
Products/Services/Areas of Expertise: This office serves the Earth & Environmental Div., as well as the Power & Process Div.
Paul Belyea, Sr. Engineer

Nanaimo
4385 Boban Dr.
Nanaimo, BC V9T 5V9
250-758-1887
Fax: 250-758-1899
john.laxdal@amec.com
Staff: 15
Products/Services/Areas of Expertise: A materials testing lab is housed at this office
John Laxdal, Unit Manager

Oshawa
#4-5, 1240 Phillip Murray Ave.
Oshawa, ON L1J 6Z9
905-720-4100
Fax: 905-720-4628
stephen.chong@amec.com
Founded: 1999
Staff: 9
Products/Services/Areas of Expertise: Lab services, hydrogeological services, materials testing
Stephen Chong, Area Manager

Ottawa
#300, 210 Colonnade Rd. S
Ottawa, ON K2E 7L5
613-727-0658
Fax: 613-727-9465
Products/Services/Areas of Expertise: Specialists in environmental & building sciences
Leigh Knegt, Area Supervisor

Prince George
3456 Opie Cres.
Prince George, BC V2N 2P9
250-564-3243
Fax: 250-562-7045
nick.polysou@amec.com
Staff: 16
Products/Services/Areas of Expertise: A full service materials testing lab is housed at this office. A satellite office is maintained in Smithers, BC
Nick Polysou, Manager

Red Deer
#4, 5551 - 45th St.
Red Deer, AB T4N 1L2
403-343-8566
Fax: 403-342-5850
paul.vanderraadt@amec.com
Staff: 20
Paulie Van Der Raadt, Unit Manager

Regina
608 McLeod St.
Regina, SK S4N 4Y1
306-721-7100
Fax: 306-721-2626
gene.froc@amec.com
Staff: 15
Products/Services/Areas of Expertise: Geotechnical engineering & environmental services, materials testing, construction monitoring & supervision
Gene Froc, Manager

Saint John
Hilyard Place, Bldg. B
#110, 580 Main St.
Saint John, NB E2K 1J5
506-652-9497
Fax: 506-652-9517
david.parkinson@amec.com
Products/Services/Areas of Expertise: This office provides environmental services for aquaculture, as well as environmental effects monitoring, site assessments & remediation
David Parkinson, Unit Manager

Sarnia
870 Confederation St.
Sarnia, ON N7T 2E5
519-337-5409
Fax: 519-337-2514
brian.fogg@amec.com
Staff: 10
Brian Fogg, Group Leader

Saskatoon
3017 Faithful Ave.
Saskatoon, SK S7K 8B3
306-975-0444
Fax: 306-955-2446
mark.humbert@amec.com
Staff: 30
Products/Services/Areas of Expertise: Site assessment & remediation, materials testing. Offices also located at #301, 121 Research Dr., 121 - 105th St. E., Saskatoon
Mark Humbert, Manager

Scarborough
104 Crockford Blvd.
Toronto, ON M1R 3C3
416-751-6565
Fax: 416-751-7592
george.chow@amec.com
George Chow, Unit Manager

Smithers
P.O. Box 3966
#3, 3167 Tatlow Rd.
Smithers, BC V0J 2N0
250-847-8783
Fax: 250-847-9049
nick.polysou@amec.com
Founded: 1997
Nick Polysou, Unit Manager

St. John's
P.O. Box 13216 C
St. John's, NL A1B 4A5
709-722-7023
Fax: 709-722-7353
rod.winsor@amec.com
Products/Services/Areas of Expertise: Office location: #202, 133 Crosbie Rd.
Rod Winsor, Unit Manager

Sudbury
131 Fielding Rd.
Lively, ON P3Y 1L7
705-682-2632
Fax: 705-682-2260
dan.cacciotti@amec.com
Staff: 18
Products/Services/Areas of Expertise: Satellite offices in Timmins & Thunder Bay
Dan Cacciotti, Area Supervisor

Sydney
Cabot House
#208, 500 Kings Rd.
Sydney, NS B1S 1B1
902-564-1110
Fax: 902-564-6318
yvette.hughes@amec.com
Founded: 1987
Products/Services/Areas of Expertise: This office specializes in site assessments, remediation, air quality assessment, occupational health & safety, and geophysical surveys
Yvette Hughes, Unit Manager

Thorold
#5, 3300 Merrittville Hwy.
Thorold, ON L2V 4Y6
905-687-6616
Fax: 905-687-6620
ivan.severinsky@amec.com
Ivan Severinsky, Unit Manager

Thunder Bay
777 Red River Rd.
Thunder Bay, ON P7B 1J9
807-344-7218
Fax: 807-344-6211
monica.anthony@amec.com
Products/Services/Areas of Expertise: Specialists in geotechnical engineering applications, materials testing Phase I-III ESAs, asbestos audits, landfill works, air quality, water studies, and dam safety
Monica Anthony, Office Manager

Windsor
#30, 3096 Devon Dr.
Windsor, ON N8X 4L2
519-969-7530
Fax: 519-969-0160
curling.ellsworth@amec.com
Curling Ellsworth, Group Leader

Winnipeg
440 Dovercourt Dr.
Winnipeg, MB R3Y 1N4
204-488-2997
Fax: 204-489-8261
harley.pankratz@amec.com
Founded: 1987
Staff: 25
Products/Services/Areas of Expertise: Specializes in geotechnical engineering, environmental sciences & materials testing
Harley Pankratz, Manager

Yellowknife
P.O. Box 2245
Yellowknife, NT X1A 2P7
867-920-4140
Fax: 867-920-4402
paul.cavanagh@amec.com
Founded: 1988
Products/Services/Areas of Expertise: Office location: #6, 5102 50th Ave., Yellowknife. Provides geotechnical & environmental services, with a focus on construction support, to clients in NWT & Nunavut
Paul Cavanagh, Unit Manager

Markham
#305, 3190 Steeles Ave. East
Markham, ON L3R 1G9
905-415-2632
Fax: 905-415-1686

Mississauga Analytical Laboratory
#4, 160 Traders Blvd. East
Mississauga, ON L4Z 3K7
905-890-0785
Fax: 905-890-1141
suman.punani@amec.com
Staff: 17
Products/Services/Areas of Expertise: State of the art laboratory facility to test soil/sludge, water, air, asbestos, cement & metals for industrial, resource, commercial & government clients

Oakville
#700, 2020 Winston Park Dr.
Oakville, ON L6H 6X7
905-829-5400
Fax: 905-829-5401
Staff: 600
Quality Environmental Management System(s): 9001:2008
Products/Services/Areas of Expertise: One of AMEC's main offices, the Oakville location provides services to the mining, power & process industry sectors

AMETEK Process Instruments
A business unit of AMETEK, Inc., Process & Analytical Instruments Div.
2876 Sunridge Way NE
Calgary, AB T1Y 7H9
403-235-8400
Fax: 403-248-3550
800-661-9198
debbylato@ametek.com
www.ametekpi.com
Firm Type: Manufacturing, Scientific/Technical Services
Founded: 1965
Staff: 60
Member of: Chandler Engineering, Tulsa OK; LAND Instruments, Dronfield UK; Solartron ISA, Shildon, UK
Quality Environmental Management System(s): 9001:2008
Products/Services/Areas of Expertise: Research & development of instruments for air emission monitoring; industrial process control; problem-solving expertise; products include: continuous on-line photometric analyzers, moisture analyzers, quadrupole mass spectrometers, trace oxygen analyzers. In addition to its U.S. offices, the company has 8 international locations, including Canada, China (3), India, Singapore, Germany, & France
Financial Information:
Type of Ownership: Publicly Traded
Revenue Sources: 100% Private Contracts
Domestic Markets:
National
Foreign Activity:
Worldwide

International Branch(es):
China - AMETEK Beijing
CITIC Bldg., Rm. 2305
19, Jianguomenwai Dajie
Beijing China
86-10-8526-2111
Fax: 86-10-8526-2141
Products/Services/Areas of Expertise: Other China offices in Chegdu (Sichuan), and Shanghai
Rubin Huang

France - AMETEK Precision Instruments SAS
Rond point de l'epine des champs
Buroplus, Batiment D
Elancourt France
33-130-688-920
Fax: 33-130-688-929

Germany - AMETEK GmbH
Rudolf-Diesel Str. 16
Meerbusch Germany
49-2159-9136-0
Fax: 49-2159-9136-39
Jochen Geiger

USA
455 Corporate Blvd.
Newark, DE USA
302-456-4400
Fax: 302-456-4444
Products/Services/Areas of Expertise: U.S. offices located in Delaware, DE; Broken Arrow, OK; Houston, TX; Austin, TX; & Pittsburgh, PA
Doug Stakern

Amity Plastics Ltd.
P.O. Box 59
Clyde, AB T0G 0P0
780-348-5355
Fax: 780-348-5275
800-270-4344
Firm Type: Distributing, Manufacturing
Founded: 1996
Staff: 6
Member of: Amity Ag-Enterprises Inc.; Amity Welding & Fabricating Inc.; Alberta Research Council; Crop Protection Institute of Canada
Member of: Canadian Federation of Independent Business
Products/Services/Areas of Expertise: Distributor of 100% recycled plastic & rubber products, including highway guardrail posts, parking curbs, landscape ties, water splash pads, speed bumps & curb ramps, corral posts, round bale feeders; clients include Alberta contractors, construction companies, school divisions, small business & the Alberta Dept. of Highways
Financial Information:
Type of Ownership: Private
Domestic Markets:
Alberta, British Columbia, Saskatchewan

AMKO Systems Inc. / ASI
#6, 250 West Beaver Creek Rd.
Richmond Hill, ON L4B 1C7
905-771-1444
Fax: 905-771-1616
800-267-2656
cems@amkosystems.com
www.amkosystems.com
Firm Type: Distributing, Engineering, Manufacturing, Scientific/Technical Services
Founded: 1980
Staff: 9
Member of: Instruments Society of America
Quality Environmental Management System(s): 9001:2000
Products/Services/Areas of Expertise: Turn-key solutions provider for process & continuous emission monitoring systems (CEMS), systems engineering, certification RATA testing; monitors gas particulates, flow, mass emissions; sample-conditions systems; in-situ & extractive dust & gas analysis & measurement; liquid analyzers; process control & monitoring
Recently Completed / Ongoing Projects: Installed CEMS into the majority of Co-Gen, HRSG & simple-cycle gas-fired power plants & coal-fired generating stations in Canada. Cement, pulp & paper, EFW, steel, pharmaceutical, etc.
Financial Information:
Type of Ownership: Private
Revenue Sources: 5% nationwide; 5% Provincial; 5% Municipals; 85% Private Contracts
Domestic Markets:
Alberta, British Columbia, Manitoba, New Brunswick, Nova Scotia, Ontario, Prince Edward Island, Québec, Saskatchewan
Foreign Activity:
Asia, Australia/New Zealand, Western Europe, The Pacific Rim, Mexico, USA
Markets Sought:
Caribbean
Contact(s):
John Kosch, President/CEO
Paul Jedynak, Sales
Jason Loroway, Sales

AN-GEO Environmental Consultants Ltd.
#204, 8708 - 48 Ave. NW
Edmonton, AB T6E 5L1
780-450-3377
Fax: 780-450-3232
angeo@sprynet.com
www.an-geo.com
Firm Type: Management Consulting
Founded: 1992
Products/Services/Areas of Expertise: Environmental site assessment; expert testimony; landfill siting; design & monitoring; risk assessment & management
Financial Information:
Type of Ownership: Private
Domestic Markets:
National
Foreign Activity:
Asia, USA
Contact(s):
David Y.F. Ho, P.Eng., Principal

Anachem Ltd.
Anachem Ltée
255, rue Norman
Montréal, QC H8R 1A3
514-481-8010
Fax: 514-481-6340
info@anachem.ca
www.anachem.ca
Firm Type: Waste Management
Founded: 1942
Staff: 25
Products/Services/Areas of Expertise: Halogenated & non-halogenated solvent recycling; hazardous & organic waste recycling; waste management consulting; blending & disposal; brokers in recycled & virgin chemicals for all industrial purposes
Financial Information:
Type of Ownership: Private
Domestic Markets:
New Brunswick, Nova Scotia, Ontario, Québec
Foreign Activity:
USA
Contact(s):
Richard Zieba, President
rzieba@anachem.ca
Robert Mainville, Manager, Sales
rmainville@anachem.ca

Canadian Branches:
Ottawa
613-834-6749
Fax: 613-834-8302
terri@anachem.ca
Terri Sokolowski

Anachemia Canada Inc.
Also Known As: Anachemia Science
255, rue Norman
Montréal, QC H8R 1A3
514-489-5711
Fax: 514-363-5281
800-361-0209
info@anachemia.com
www.anachemia.com
Firm Type: Distributing, Scientific/Technical Services
Founded: 1942
Staff: 180
Quality Environmental Management System(s): 9001:2000
Products/Services/Areas of Expertise: Laboratory supply house; reagent chemical manufacturer; supplier of mining, analytical & sample prep equipment; products for chemical warfare defense; hazardous waste recycling (Anachemia Ltd.); products for precious metal analysis
Financial Information:
Type of Ownership: Private
Revenue: Greater than $5 Million
Revenue Sources: 10% nationwide; 90% Private Contracts
Domestic Markets:
Alberta, British Columbia, Manitoba, Ontario, Québec
Foreign Activity:
South America, USA
Contact(s):
Martin Robinson, President
Carol Haley, Vice President, Sales & Marketing
Michel Belanger, Vice President, Chemical Products
Irene Holloway, Vice President, Supply Management
Bill Clifford, Director, Mining Products & International Sales

Canadian Branches:
Edmonton
Alberta, Northeast BC & NWT Sales & Customer Support
15006 - 116 Ave.
Edmonton, AB T5M 3T4
780-451-0665
Fax: 780-452-2478
800-361-0209
edmonton@anachemia.com
Amanda Thompson, Sales Coordinator

Kirkland Lake Mines Assay Supplies
Northern Ontario & Québec Sales & Customer Support
P.O. Box 850
953 Government Rd. West
Kirkland Lake, ON P2N 3K5
705-567-3346
Fax: 705-567-3613
800-361-0209
mas@anachemia.com
Fernande Cambray, Branch Manager

Montréal
Eastern Sales & Customer Support
255, rue Norman
Lachine, QC H8R 1A3
514-489-5711
Fax: 514-483-6407
800-361-0209
montreal@anachemia.com
Philippe Lachance, Sales Coordinator

Toronto
Southern Ontario Sales & Customer Support
#65, 6535 Millcreek Dr.
Mississauga, ON L5N 2M2
905-567-8292
Fax: 905-567-5939
800-361-0209
toronto@anachemia.com
Diane Roy, Regional Sales Manager

Vancouver
BC & Yukon Sales & Customer Support
#10, 3571 Viking Way
Richmond, BC V6V 1W1
604-270-2152
Fax: 604-270-2826
800-361-0209
intsales@anachemia.com
Products/Services/Areas of Expertise: The Vancouver office also provides chemicals, equipment & supplies to the international mining industry. Contact Bill Clifford, Mining Services Support, 888-438-7577, or email intsales@anachemia.com

Sean Murry, Vice-President, Anachemia Science, Vancouver

Winnipeg
Manitoba, Saskatchewan & NW Ontario Sales & Customer Support
#4, 214 DeBaets St.
Winnipeg, MB R2J 3W6
204-661-6734
Fax: 204-663-3421
800-361-0209
winnipeg@anachemia.com
Myrna Law, Sales Coordinator

International Branch(es):
Chile - Anachemia Science S.A.
South America Sales & Customer Support
Parque Industrial Estrella de Sur
Av. San Eugenio 12112
San Bernardo, Santiago Chile
56-2-655-1410
Fax: 56-2-655-1422
ventas@anachemia.cl
Miguel Valdes, Branch Manager

Sparks, NV
Nevada & Western U.S. Sales & Customer Support
738 Spice Island Dr.
Sparks, NV USA
775-331-2300
Fax: 775-331-2646
800-724-3620
reno@anachemia.com
Peter Cavender, Branch Manager/Director of Mining, North America

Anco Chemicals Inc.
85 Malmo Ct.
Maple, ON L6A 1R4
905-832-2276
Fax: 905-832-3701
888-268-2626
info@ancochemicals.com
www.ancochemicals.com
Firm Type: Distributing
Founded: 1962
Member of: Canadian Association of Chemical Distributors; International Institute of Ammonia Refrigeration
Products/Services/Areas of Expertise: Refrigeration chemicals; secondary heat transfer chemicals; inhibited propylene/ethylene glycol; silicon fluid; high-temperature oils & other specialty fluids; hydrocarbon absorption system; booms, pads, recovery drums; calcium chloride for process, industrial & ice melt uses
Financial Information:
Type of Ownership: Private
Revenue Sources: 5% Municipals; 95% Private Contracts
Domestic Markets:
National
Foreign Activity:
South America, USA
Markets Sought:
Western Europe
Contact(s):
Stephen Earle, President
Ian Dowding, CEO

Canadian Branches:
Montréal
6905, boul. Hébert
Sainte-Catherine, QC J5C 1B5
450-632-0950
Fax: 450-632-1856
Ken Marsland

Anderson Water Systems
Ondeo Degremont Inc.
44 Head St.
Dundas, ON L9H 3H3
905-627-9233
Fax: 905-628-6623
info-anderson@degtec.com
www.degremont-technologies.com
Firm Type: Manufacturing
Founded: 1952
Staff: 85
Products/Services/Areas of Expertise: Supplier of water treatment systems & equipment to cogeneration plants, petrochemical plants, pulp & paper plants & other industries

Financial Information:
Type of Ownership: Foreign-owned
Revenue: Greater than $5 Million
Revenue Sources: 10% Provincial; 90% Private Contracts
Domestic Markets:
Ontario
Foreign Activity:
Worldwide
Contact(s):
Philippe Lhussier, CEO

André Simard et associés ltée
Div. of Le Groupe ASA
#204, 2500, rue Jean Perrin
Québec, QC G2C 1X1
418-845-8889
Fax: 418-845-5559
888-628-8221
andre.simard@asimard.com
Firm Type: Engineering
Founded: 1997
Staff: 50
Member of: Solid Waste Association of North America
Products/Services/Areas of Expertise: Landfill design, biogas & leachate treatment & management, quality assurance, bioreactor design & operation, municipal engineering
Recently Completed / Ongoing Projects: Landfill & bioreactor, Ste-Sophie QC; Sanitary landfill, Wendake infrastructure redevelopment
Financial Information:
Revenue: $3 Million - $5 Million
Revenue Sources: 50% Municipals; 50% Private Contracts
Domestic Markets:
Québec
Foreign Activity:
South America
Markets Sought:
Caribbean
Contact(s):
André Simard, President

Andrews' Scenic Acres
9365 #10 Sideroad, RR#5
Halton Hills, ON L9T 2X9
905-878-5807
Fax: 905-878-4997
farm@andrewsscenicacres.com
www.andrewsscenicacres.com
Firm Type: Distributing, Waste Management, AGRICULTURE
Founded: 1980
Member of: Scotch Block Winery
Member of: Ontario Farm Fresh Marketing Association; Escarpment County; Ontario Berry Growers Association
Products/Services/Areas of Expertise: Pick-your-own fruits & vegetables; Green Energy Tour; recycling of clean sawdust, wood shavings, woodchips, chipped Christmas trees for mulch; agri-education program

Andritz Bird
A Division of Andritz Ltd.
Formerly: Bird Machine of Canada-Div. of Baker Hughes Canada Inc.
2600 Wentz Ave.
Saskatoon, SK S7K 2L1
306-931-0801
Fax: 306-931-2442
separation.ca@andritz.com
www.andritz.com
Firm Type: Distributing, Manufacturing
Founded: 1968
Staff: 35
Member of: Andritz AG
Products/Services/Areas of Expertise: Industrial centrifuges & filtering equipment; solid/liquid separation technologies
Financial Information:
Type of Ownership: Foreign-owned
Revenue: Greater than $5 Million
Foreign Activity:
Africa, China, The Middle East, USA
Contact(s):
Herb Hargrove, General Manager
Steve Pidduck, Contact, Domestic Sales & Marketing
Darryl Pahlke, Contact, Customer Service
darryl.pahlke@andritz.com

Products & Services Buyer's Guide

Anex Distributors Ltd.
Ecotainer Sales Inc.
2253 Harbourgreene Dr.
Surrey, BC V4A 5J3
604-535-7293
Fax: 604-535-7967
800-561-6525
info@ecotainer.ca
www.ecotainer-anex.com
Firm Type: Distributing
Founded: 1987
Staff: 2
Member of: Recycling Council of Alberta
Products/Services/Areas of Expertise: Industrial equipment for waste recycling & reduction; heavy duty plastic containers for recycling & materials handling
Financial Information:
Type of Ownership: Private
Revenue Sources: 10% Municipals; 90% Private Contracts
Domestic Markets:
Alberta, British Columbia, Manitoba, Northwest Territories, Saskatchewan, Yukon Territory
Contact(s):
Tom Button, Contact

Angus, Butler Engineering Ltd.
#1, 2225 Northridge Dr.
Saskatoon, SK S7L 6X6
306-477-1113
Fax: 306-373-5045
abel@the.link.ca
Firm Type: Engineering
Founded: 1956
Staff: 8
Products/Services/Areas of Expertise: Feasibility studies & program development; architectural, engineering, interior design, landscape drawings, specifications & contract administration; engineering & project management for air quality, hot & cold fluid pumping & piping; agricultural materials handling systems; instrumentation & controls; electrical power generation & distribution; lighting; communications; alarm & industrial computer programming; preventative maintenance management; energy management; harmonic content reduction & power factor correction
Recently Completed / Ongoing Projects: Royal University Hospital, Saskatoon; administration/shop complex, McArthur River; Saskatoon & Prince Albert correctional centre studies; crop services building, Agriculture Canada
Financial Information:
Type of Ownership: Private
Revenue Sources: 10% nationwide; 10% Provincial; 10% Municipals; 70% Private Contracts
Domestic Markets:
Alberta, Manitoba, Saskatchewan
Foreign Activity:
Africa
Contact(s):
Jerry Helfrich, President

Annapolis Valley Peat Moss Co. Ltd. / AVPM
Formerly: AVP Cansorb Ltd.
3647 Hwy. #1
Berwick, NS B0P 1E0
902-538-8022
Fax: 902-538-9609
800-565-1410
avpeat@istar.ca
www.avpeat.com
Firm Type: Distributing, Manufacturing
Founded: 1949
Staff: 50
Products/Services/Areas of Expertise: Distributor of Canadian spagnum peat moss & other professional growing mediums; manufacturer & distributor of Cansorb organic oil absorbent, made from peat moss; retail customer products such as potting soils, manures, mulches. Gulf Island Peat Moss Co. Inc., is a wholly-owned subsidiary; Miscouche Peat Ltd., & Northern Peat Ltd. are other locations, all in Prince Edward Island
Financial Information:
Type of Ownership: Private
Revenue: Greater than $5 Million
Revenue Sources: 100% Private Contracts
Domestic Markets:
Nova Scotia, Ontario, Prince Edward Island
Foreign Activity:
Africa, Asia, Australia/New Zealand, Caribbean, Central Europe, Western Europe, The Middle East, Mexico, USA
Contact(s):
Henry Endres, President
Kyle Endres, Managing Director
Dawn Morton, Manager, Overseas Sales/Cansorb Sales

Anrep Krieg Desilets Gravelle Ltd.
Formerly: Anrep Krieg Desilets & Associates
#204, 101 Worthington St. East
North Bay, ON P1B 1G5
705-474-7000
Fax: 705-474-7362
akdg@on.aibn.com
Firm Type: Management Consulting, Engineering
Founded: 1993
Staff: 10
Products/Services/Areas of Expertise: Consulting engineers in the areas of structural, mechanical, electrical & civil; services include feasibility & pre-feasibility studies; design & specification planning services; plant retrofit studies; energy audit services; HVAC equipment
Financial Information:
Type of Ownership: Private
Domestic Markets:
Ontario
Contact(s):
John Krieg, Partner/President
Canadian Branches:
Sudbury Office
#206a, 109 Elm St.
Sudbury, ON P3C 1T4
705-674-7500
Fax: 705-674-7501

Antelope Land Services Inc.
Formerly: Enviro-Field Services Inc.
#200, 1210 - 8 St. SW
Calgary, AB T2R 1L3
403-265-2855
Fax: 403-266-4389
800-432-1846
info@antelopeland.com
www.antelopeland.com
Firm Type: Scientific/Technical Services
Founded: 1978
Products/Services/Areas of Expertise: Soil analysis for oil & gas industry; acquisitions and administration of land assets in western Canada
Financial Information:
Type of Ownership: Private
Revenue: $250,000 - $500,000
Revenue Sources: 100% Private Contracts
Domestic Markets:
Alberta, British Columbia, Saskatchewan
Contact(s):
Paula Anderson, Land Administrator
panderson@antelopeland.com

Anthrafilter Media & Coal Ltd.
20 Sharp Rd.
Brantford, ON N3T 5L8
519-751-1080
Fax: 519-751-0617
swildey@anthrafilter.net
www.anthrafilter.net
Firm Type: Distributing, Engineering
Founded: 1976
Staff: 5
Member of: American Water Works Association - Ontario Section
Products/Services/Areas of Expertise: Removal, disposal, supply & installation of filter media for water & wastewater treatment plants; supply of coal & coke products
Financial Information:
Type of Ownership: Private
Domestic Markets:
National
Foreign Activity:
South America, Mexico, USA
Contact(s):
J. David Loney, President
Steve Wildey, General Manager
International Branch(es):
Anthrafilter (U.S.) Inc.
4992 Sweet Home Rd.
Niagara Falls, NY USA
Anthrafilter (U.S.) Inc.
#201, 5700 Escondida Blvd.
St. Petersburg, FL USA

Anticorrosion Materials & Technologies Inc.
Also Known As: AMT Inc.
2 Haas Rd.
Toronto, ON M9W 3A2
416-401-8855
Fax: 416-401-8878
info@corolon.com
www.corolon.com; www.ruststop.ca
Firm Type: Distributing, Manufacturing
Founded: 1992
Staff: 10
Member of: Canadian Association of Mining Equipment & Services for Export
Quality Environmental Management System(s): 9001; ISO
Products/Services/Areas of Expertise: Complete lines of protective coatings & corrosion control products for protecting steel, metal & concrete, smoke stacks, industrial & petroleum tanks, swimming pools, automobiles, motorcycles, farm equipment, & other mobile equipment; Rust Stop product line; Corolon Coatings & Corrosion Control Technologies Inc. is a sister company
Financial Information:
Type of Ownership: Private
Revenue: $500,000 - $1.5 Million
Revenue Sources: 100% Private Contracts
Domestic Markets:
Ontario, Québec
Foreign Activity:
Eastern Europe, South America, Former USSR
Markets Sought:
China, The Pacific Rim, Mexico, USA, Vietnam
Contact(s):
Stan E. Buchowski, P.Eng., President

Apex Geoscience Ltd.
#200, 9797 - 45th Ave.
Edmonton, AB T6E 5V8
780-439-5380
Fax: 780-433-1336
apexgeo@apexgeoscience.com
www.apexgeoscience.com
Products/Services/Areas of Expertise: Environmental & geological consulting services; resource evaluation studies; environmental audits & assessments, soil & water sampling & analysis, remediation services, & project management
Domestic Markets:
Alberta, British Columbia
Foreign Activity:
Australia/New Zealand
Contact(s):
Dean Besserer, Vice-President
dbesserer@apexgeoscience.com
Canadian Branches:
Vancouver
#1212 - 9797 - 45th Ave.
Vancouver, BC V6C 1T2
604-696-9628
Fax: 604-696-9648

Apex Industries Inc.
100 Millennium Blvd.
Moncton, NB E1E 2G8
506-857-1620
Fax: 506-857-7563
800-268-3331
fabrication_sales@apexindustries.com
www.apexindustries.com
Firm Type: Manufacturing
Founded: 1961
Staff: 225
Quality Environmental Management System(s): 9002:1994
Products/Services/Areas of Expertise: Technologies, including precision components for aircraft, space, communication & defense vehicle industries; machine works, such as bins, building trusses, cranes, girders, loading & pedestrian bridges, pressure vessels, tanks & weldments; custom door systems, including security & fire doors

Domestic Markets:
Newfoundland & Labrador, Nova Scotia, Prince Edward Island
Foreign Activity:
Central America, USA
Contact(s):
Keith Donaldson, Director, Sales and Business Development, 506-857-7544
kmdonaldson@apexindustries.com

Canadian Branches:
Dartmouth
#12, 60 Thornhill Dr.
Dartmouth, NS B3B 1S1
902-468-2739
Fax: 902-468-2902
Tim Fraser, Manager

Fredericton
1149 Smythe St.
Fredericton, NB E3B 3H4
506-454-1600

Apollo Environmental Systems Corporation
#150, 270 Yorkland Blvd.
Toronto, ON M2J 5C9
416-491-1441
Fax: 416-491-5343
Firm Type: Manufacturing
Founded: 1988
Staff: 4
Member of: Canadian Environment Industry Association - Ontario; Water Environment Federation
Products/Services/Areas of Expertise: Markets patented scrubbers for the removal of hydrogen sulphide from biogas & waste air streams; developing other applications of the gas-liquid contactor & a new sulphur recovery process for natural gas sweetening
Recently Completed / Ongoing Projects: Ongoing Biogas scrummer in Australia
Financial Information:
Type of Ownership: Private
Domestic Markets:
National
Foreign Activity:
USA
Markets Sought:
Australia/New Zealand, Western Europe, Mexico, USA
Contact(s):
James W. Smith, President

Appin Associates
1384 Spruce St.
Winnipeg, MB R3E 2V7
204-925-1450
Fax: 204-925-1459
appin@appin.com
www.appin.com
Firm Type: Engineering
Founded: 1980
Member of: Association of Professional Engineers of Manitoba; Professional Engineers Association of Ontario
Products/Services/Areas of Expertise: Mechanical design; energy management systems; indoor air quality; HVAC systems design/trouble shooting; DDC system design (DVCL Bacnet); independent HVAC commissioning agents
Financial Information:
Type of Ownership: Private
Revenue Sources: 40% nationwide; 10% Municipals; 50% Private Contracts
Domestic Markets:
Alberta, British Columbia, Manitoba, Northwest Territories, Ontario, Saskatchewan, Yukon Territory
Foreign Activity:
USA
Contact(s):
Grant Wichenko, P.Eng., President/CEO

Applied Aquatic Research Ltd.
1929 - 10th Ave. SW
Calgary, AB T3C 0K3
403-294-0488
Fax: 403-266-7520
info@appliedaquatic.com
www.appliedaquatic.com
Firm Type: Management Consulting, Scientific/Technical Services
Founded: 1996
Staff: 23
Products/Services/Areas of Expertise: Specialized solutions & research focusing on fisheries management, disturbance & development concerns of aquatic ecosystems; services include study design & implementation, freshwater & marine pipeline construction, crossing design, mitigation & habitat restoration, wetlands investigations & restoration, emergency response planning & mitigation, water quality monitoring, & training courses for environmental & oilfield professionals
Recently Completed / Ongoing Projects: TMX Project, AB & BC; Athabasca River Pipeline installation, AB; Enbridge-Southern Lights Project, SK & MB; QAES Audit of the Battle River, AB; Corridor Pipeline Project, AB
Financial Information:
Type of Ownership: Private
Revenue: $500,000 - $1.5 Million
Revenue Sources: 5% Provincial; 95% Private Contracts
Domestic Markets:
Alberta, British Columbia, Manitoba, Saskatchewan, Yukon Territory
Contact(s):
Thomas Boag, M.Sc., P.Biol., President & Sr. Fish Biologist

Applied Groundwater Research Ltd.
2550 Argentia Rd.
Mississauga, ON L5N 5R1
905-858-1914
Fax: 905-542-2954
Products/Services/Areas of Expertise: Environmental consulting services; laboratory services
Contact(s):
Stan Feenstra, P.Geo., President

Applied Oxidation Technologies Inc. / AOT
P.O. Box 818
#1, 13136 Thomas Rd.
Ladysmith, BC V0R 2E0
250-245-4484
Fax: 250-245-8849
llambert@island.net
Firm Type: Engineering
Founded: 1997
Staff: 4
Products/Services/Areas of Expertise: Designer, builder & manufacturer of industrial & municipal wastewater remediation technology & drinking water technology; on-site household sewage treatment plants for small footprint or difficult terrain & septage process plants
Recently Completed / Ongoing Projects: Wastewater technology plant & drinking water technology plant, Ladysmith, BC; NSF certification of household sewage treatment plant; septage process plant
Financial Information:
Type of Ownership: Private
Revenue Sources: 5% nationwide; 60% Municipals; 35% Private Contracts
Domestic Markets:
British Columbia
Markets Sought:
Australia/New Zealand, Central America, South America, Mexico
Contact(s):
Lawrence A. Lambert, P.Eng., President

APS Aviation Inc.
Also Known As: Aviation Planning Services Ltd.
#105, 6700 Côte-de-Liesse
Montréal, QC H4T 2B5
514-878-4388
Fax: 514-861-6310
services@apsaviation.ca
www.adga.ca
Firm Type: Engineering, Scientific/Technical Services
Founded: 1967
Staff: 15
Products/Services/Areas of Expertise: Consulting services to all sectors of aviation industry; study of dispersal of atmospheric pollutants from aircraft; assessment of overflight noise on communities; noise exposure forecasts & alleviation; R&D on aircraft ground de-icing; airport operations
Recently Completed / Ongoing Projects: Glycol recovery program, Montréal airports; environmental impact of de-icing & anti-icing fluids
Financial Information:
Type of Ownership: Private
Revenue Sources: 75% nationwide; 25% Private Contracts
Domestic Markets:
Ontario, Québec
Foreign Activity:
Africa, Asia, The Middle East
Markets Sought:
Africa, Asia, Central America, The Middle East
Contact(s):
Jacques Lyrette, CEO

Aqua Dam & Diversion Ltd.
6970 - 10th Ave. SE
Salmon Arm, BC V1E 1X8
250-832-1332
Fax: 250-832-1332
aquadam@sunwave.net
www.aquadam.com
Firm Type: Distributing
Founded: 1991
Products/Services/Areas of Expertise: Site containment; coffer dams; emergency response; instream construction
Financial Information:
Type of Ownership: Private
Revenue: $500,000 - $1.5 Million
Revenue Sources: 15% nationwide; 20% Provincial; 20% Municipals; 45% Private Contracts
Domestic Markets:
National
Foreign Activity:
The Pacific Rim, USA
Markets Sought:
Australia/New Zealand
Contact(s):
Vince Meraw, President

Aqua Data Inc.
95 - 5th Ave.
Pincourt, QC J7V 5K8
514-425-1010
Fax: 514-425-3506
800-567-9003
info@aquadata.com
www.aquadata.com
Firm Type: Management Consulting, Engineering, Information Technology
Founded: 1987
Staff: 60
Member of: American Water Works Association; Water Environment Federation; Réseau environnement
Products/Services/Areas of Expertise: Specializes in the computerized diagnosis of water distribution & wastewater collection systems in municipal, industrial & commercial settings. The firm conducts studies on water systems, & prepares plans for interventions, maintenance & water savings. Branch & affiliate offices in Montréal, Laval, Sainte-Thérèse, Longueuil, Beauceville, Dartmouth (NS), Rockland (ON), & Tampa, Florida
Financial Information:
Type of Ownership: Private
Revenue: Greater than $5 Million
Revenue Sources: 95% Municipals; 5% Private Contracts
Domestic Markets:
New Brunswick, Nova Scotia, Ontario, Prince Edward Island, Québec
Foreign Activity:
Africa, USA
Contact(s):
Francis Lebuis, President/COO
Nathalie Periche, P.Eng., Technical Director, Business Development

Canadian Branches:
Dartmouth - Aqua Data Atlantic
64 Trider Cres.
Dartmouth, NS B3B 1R6
902-468-9447
Fax: 902-468-2090
aquadata.jean@ns.sympatico.ca
Jean Harrison, M.Sc.A., President

Longueuil - Aquatech Water Management Services Inc.
#110, 101, boul Roland-Therrien
Longueuil, QC J4H 4B9
450-646-5270
Fax: 450-646-7977
jgcadorette@aquatech-inc.com
Products/Services/Areas of Expertise: Head office location for this affiliated company; a branch office is located in Beauceville, QC - contact 418-774-6454 or email: ssauvageau@aquatech-inc.com

Products & Services Buyer's Guide

Rockland - Aqua Data Inc.
3213 Old Hwy. 17
Rockland, ON K4K 1W1
613-446-1992
Fax: 613-446-0504
mguibord@aquadata.com
Marcel Guibord, Representative, Eastern Ontario

Sainte-Thérèse - Aqua Data Rive Nord
366, rue des Muguets
Sainte-Thérèse, QC J7E 5T4
450-430-0800
Fax: 450-971-2067
alain_chabot@videotron.ca
Alain Chabot, President

Aqua Tech Sales & Marketing Inc.
4390 Paletta Ct.
Burlington, ON L7L 5R2
905-631-5815
Fax: 905-637-8655
866-594-0767
franks@aquatech.ws
www.aquatech.ws
Firm Type: Distributing
Founded: 1980
Products/Services/Areas of Expertise: Water & wastewater management & equipment
Contact(s):
Bill Palamar, President
Frank Stempski, Vice-President & General Manager
Darryl Singleton, Vice-President, Sales and Marketing

Canadian Branches:
British Columbia
#106, 1585 Broadway St.
Port Coquitlam, BC V3C 2M7
778-285-9596

Aqua Terre Solutions Inc.
SNC-Lavalin Environment
#110, 20 Colonnade Rd.
Ottawa, ON K2E 7M6
613-226-2456
Fax: 613-226-9980
info@aquaterre.ca
www.aquaterre.ca
Firm Type: Engineering, Scientific/Technical Services
Founded: 1974
Staff: 110
Member of: Association of Professional Engineers of Ontario; Association of Professional Geoscientists of Ontario
Products/Services/Areas of Expertise: Provides complete environmental consulting services including: environmental audits, site investigation, site decommissioning, soil & groundwater remediation systems (e.g. product recovery, vapour extraction, bioremediation, & pump & treat systems), regulatory approvals, hydrogeological studies, exposure & risk assessment, & groundwater modelling
Financial Information:
Type of Ownership: Private
Domestic Markets:
National
Foreign Activity:
Western Europe, The Middle East, USA
Contact(s):
Mark Foerster, Manager

Canadian Branches:
Calgary
909 - 5th Ave. SW, 4th Fl.
Calgary, AB T2P 3G5
403-266-2555
Fax: 403-266-2554
Mike De Luca, Contact

Lethbridge
#8, 2620 - 5th Ave. North
Lethbridge, AB T1H 6J6
403-317-9161
Fax: 403-317-9181
Corey Shilliday, Contact

Saskatoon
#200, 333-25th St. East
Saskatoon, SK S7K 0L4
306-244-8663
Fax: 306-244-8682
T. Fuzakas, Manager

Toronto
#200, 20 DeBoers Dr.
Toronto, ON M3K 2B4
416-635-5882
Fax: 416-635-5353
David McClellan, Manager

Aqua-Guard Spill Response Inc.
#100, 1055 - West 14th St.
North Vancouver, BC V7P 3P2
604-980-4899
Fax: 604-980-9560
sales@aquaguard.com
www.aquaguard.com
Firm Type: Distributing, Manufacturing
Founded: 1992
Quality Environmental Management System(s): 9001:2000
Products/Services/Areas of Expertise: Manufactures multi-functional recovery oil skimmers for plants, rivers & oceans; full range of equipment for the containment & recovery of oil spills in all environments, oil spill containment booms; temporary fabric storage tanks
Activities: Oil spill prevention & control; development of new methods to reduce complacency, boost awareness & increase response capability; spill control software to track & monitor equipment, increase the speed of response, manage response & track spills, monitor environmental, social & industrial concerns, & incorporate Geographic Information System (GIS) software to analyse & display sensitive areas or areas at risk
Financial Information:
Type of Ownership: Private
Revenue: Greater than $5 Million
Revenue Sources: 15% nationwide; 85% Private Contracts
Domestic Markets:
National
Foreign Activity:
Africa, Asia, Caribbean, Central America, Eastern Europe, The Middle East, The Pacific Rim, South America, Mexico, USA
Contact(s):
Lawrence Pertile, President
lawrence@aquaguard.com
Cameron Janz, Chief Operating Officer
cameronj@aquaguard.com

Aqua-Pak Styro Containers Ltd.
7398 - 132nd St.
Surrey, BC V3W 4M7
604-590-2886
Fax: 604-590-8412
tim@aquapak.com
www.aquapak.com
Firm Type: Manufacturing
Founded: 1986
Quality Environmental Management System(s): 9001:2000
Products/Services/Areas of Expertise: Designs & manufactures packaging systems, with a focus on expanded polystyrene packaging (no CFCs) for the seafood/acquaculture industry. The company also produces the Quad-Lock Insulating Concrete Forms building system, with clients throughout Europe, Latin America & the Caribbean. In addition to the Surrey plant, Noboco Styro Containers Ltd., located in Campbell River, BC, provides additional manufacturing capacity
Contact(s):
Tim Dayton, General Manager

Aqua-Plus
45, rue Dumoncel
Beauport, QC G1E 5M9
418-667-0782
Products/Services/Areas of Expertise: Water, wastewater & groundwater management, services & equipment
Contact(s):
C. Dupont, Consultant

Aqua-Rehab Inc.
2145, rue Michelin
Laval, QC H7L 5B8
450-687-3472
Fax: 450-687-4570
800-661-3472
aqua@aquarehab.com
www.aquarehab.com
Firm Type: Distributing
Founded: 1988
Member of: Gaz Métro; Canadian Public Works Association; Québec Municipal Engineers
Quality Environmental Management System(s): 9002
Products/Services/Areas of Expertise: Water & wastewater pipe rehabilitation; cathodic protection
Recently Completed / Ongoing Projects: Rehabilitation of watermains for several municipalities, Québec
Financial Information:
Type of Ownership: Private
Domestic Markets:
British Columbia, New Brunswick, Nova Scotia, Ontario, Québec
Foreign Activity:
USA
Contact(s):
Luc Danis, Director, Finances
ldanis@aquarehab.com

Aqua-Tex Scientific Consulting Ltd.
390 - 7th Ave.
Kimberley, BC V1A 2Z7
250-427-0260
Fax: 250-427-0280
aqua-tex@islandnet.com
www.aqua-tex.ca
Firm Type: Engineering, Scientific/Technical Services
Founded: 1993
Products/Services/Areas of Expertise: Specializes in freshwater ecology & watershed management, assessment & pro-active planning; experienced in urban stream rehabilitation, drinking water supply protection & management; training & education
Financial Information:
Type of Ownership: Private
Domestic Markets:
British Columbia
Markets Sought:
USA
Contact(s):
William Patrick Lucey, President & Sr. Aquatic Ecologist
Cori L. Barraclough, Freshwater Ecologist

Canadian Branches:
Victoria
#201, 3690 Shelbourne St.
Victoria, BC V8P 4H2
250-598-0266
Fax: 250-598-0263
Domestic Markets:
British Columbia

AquaMetrix Inc.
A subsidiary of The Amidyne Group
#7, 1245 Maple Hill Ct.
Newmarket, ON L3Y 9E8
905-954-0841
Fax: 905-954-0415
800-742-1413
info@amidyne.com
www.amidyne.com
Firm Type: Distributing, Manufacturing
Founded: 1955
Staff: 30
Member of: American Water Works Association, Water Environment Federation; Instrument Society of America; Canadian Process Control Association
Products/Services/Areas of Expertise: Manufacturer of instrumentation & sensors for nuclear power, water, wastewater & industrial applications. Production includes on-line & hand-held instrumentation for ORP, pH, conductivity, resistivity, dissolved oxygen & flow. Versatile Measuring Instruments Inc. is a sister company
Financial Information:
Type of Ownership: Private
Domestic Markets:
National
Foreign Activity:
Worldwide
Contact(s):
Charles Johnson, President
David Gerry, Head, Marketing
Brett Hodge, Head, Sales

Aquareal Water Systems Inc.
#17, 390 Steeles Ave. West
Thornhill, ON L4J 6X2
905-771-5092
Fax: 905-771-5094
info@aquareal.com
www.aquareal.com

Products/Services/Areas of Expertise: Offers purified water to communities & also retails in water purification systems
Domestic Markets:
Ontario

Canadian Branches:
North York
240 Willowdale Ave.
North York, ON M2N 4Z5
416-221-1107
Fax: 416-221-5988

AQUASOL EnviroTech Ltd.
2772-1055 Georgia St West
Vancouver, BC V6E 4H8
604-688-8002
Fax: 604-688-8030
888-288-8288
info@aquasoltech.com
Firm Type: Scientific/Technical Services
Founded: 1996
Products/Services/Areas of Expertise: Wastewater treatment
Financial Information:
Type of Ownership: Private
Domestic Markets:
Alberta, British Columbia
Foreign Activity:
Asia, China, The Pacific Rim, Vietnam
Contact(s):
Jeff Yenyou Zheng, Ph.D., President, CFO & Director

Aquasolution Technologies Inc.
414, rue Dollard
Joliette, QC J6E 4M4
450-755-1555
Fax: 450-759-3212
admin@aquasolution.com
www.aquasolution.com
Firm Type: Manufacturing
Founded: 1985
Products/Services/Areas of Expertise: Specializes in the manufacturing of custom-made potable water systems
Contact(s):
Pierre-Félix Brisson, President

Aquateck Ltd.
Also Known As: Aquateck West Ltd.
9842 - 60 Ave.
Edmonton, AB T6E 0C5
780-435-5919
Fax: 780-435-6019
866-435-3366
edmonton@aquateck.com
www.aquateck.com
Firm Type: Distributing
Founded: 1990
Products/Services/Areas of Expertise: Distributor of quality pumps manufactured by Goulds Pumps; products include pumps for water handling/water treatment, sump/effluent/sewage pumps, irrigation pumps, turbine pumps, G & L pumps, water well casing & accessories
Domestic Markets:
National
Contact(s):
Les Brubacher

Canadian Branches:
Calgary
2410A - 2 Ave. SE
Calgary, AB T2E 6J9
403-272-0052
Fax: 403-272-0998
866-272-3311
calgary@aquateck.com
Jim Burke

Guelph
#124 & 128 - 355 Elmira Rd. North
Guelph, ON N1K 1S5
519-826-9888
Fax: 519-826-7586
800-839-5358
guelph@aquateck.com
Perry Leifso

Lethbridge
3612 - 14 Ave. North
Lethbridge, AB T1H 6E7
403-380-2552
Fax: 403-380-2650
877-380-2556
lethbridge@aquateck.com
Larry Kundrik

Montréal
2485, rue Guenette
Montréal, QC H4R 2E9
514-633-0999
Fax: 514-633-9374
877-633-0999
montreal@aquateck.com
Mike Ward

Ottawa
#116, 2700 Lancaster Rd.
Ottawa, ON K1B 4T7
613-526-4613
Fax: 613-526-0560
800-839-5358
ottawa@aquateck.com
Perry Leifso

Québec
2800, av Dalton, Local 2
Québec, QC G1P 3F4
418-651-0171
Fax: 418-651-6160
877-799-2178
quebec@aquateck.com
Christian Boivin

Aquaterre Inc.
209, route 132 est
Saint-Fabien, QC G0L 2Z0
418-869-3197
Fax: 418-869-2215
Firm Type: Manufacturing
Founded: 1983
Staff: 9
Member of: Fédération interdisciplinaire de l'horticulture ornementale; Association québécoise des industries du compostage
Products/Services/Areas of Expertise: Organic fertilizers for horticultural market; feasibility studies, project implementation studies, impact studies on the use of organic matter in agriculture & horticulture
Activities: Biotechnology; agriculture, fisheries; natural fertilizers & fertilizer materials
Domestic Markets:
New Brunswick, Ontario
Foreign Activity:
Asia
Markets Sought:
USA
Contact(s):
Denys Trépanier, General Manager
Hugues Thériault, Marketing & Sales

Aquatic Life Ltd.
34 Alexander Ave.
Pinawa, MB R0E 1L0
204-753-5270
Fax: 204-753-2082
800-409-8378
aquatic@aquaticlife.ca
www.aquaticlife.ca
Firm Type: Distributing
Founded: 1986
Staff: 5
Products/Services/Areas of Expertise: Distribution of environmental testing products including water, soil, air monitoring systems (water testing equipment, equipment for groundwater contamination, noise pollution, air pollution equipment)
Financial Information:
Type of Ownership: Private
Domestic Markets:
National
Foreign Activity:
Worldwide
Contact(s):
Jeff Simpson, President

Canadian Branches:
Alberta
403-774-4071
Finley Myskiw, Contact
fmyskiw@aquaticlife.ca

AquaTox Testing & Consulting Inc.
11B Nicholas Beaver Rd., RR3
Guelph, ON N1H 6H9
519-763-4412
Fax: 519-763-4419
mrendas@aquatox.ca
www.aquatox.ca
Firm Type: Scientific/Technical Services
Founded: 2007
Products/Services/Areas of Expertise: Freshwater and marine aquatic toxicity testing, monitoring and consulting services have been provided to more than 300 organizations involved in the mining, pulp and paper, municipal wastewater, iron and steel, electrical power, chemical manufacturing, food and beverage and petrochemical sectors.
Contact(s):
Keith Holtze, President
kholtze@aquatox.ca
Lesley Novak, Vice-President
lnovak@aquatox.ca

Canadian Branches:
Toronto Branch
#705, 100 Adelaide St. West
Toronto, ON M5H 1S3
416-410-0432
Fax: 416-632-5231
cial@inforamp.net
Heide Ciplin, Information Analyst

ARAM Systems Ltd.
Formerly: Geo-X Systems Ltd.
7236 - 10 St. NE
Calgary, AB T2E 8X3
403-537-2100
Fax: 403-537-2101
www.inovageo.com
Firm Type: Distributing, Scientific/Technical Services
Staff: 11
Products/Services/Areas of Expertise: Provider of cable-based land seismic recording systems. Acquired by ION Geophysical Corporation, Houston, TX, in 2008. The Canadian location provides sales, rentals, repairs, customer support, R&D, & training
Contact(s):
Chris Chamberlain, President/CEO, ARAM Systems Ltd.

Arbrux Limited
#6, 33 Alliance Blvd.
Barrie, ON L4M 5K2
705-739-7878
Fax: 705-739-7826
888-211-3548
www.arbrux.com
Firm Type: Distributing, Manufacturing
Founded: 1979
Staff: 3
Member of: Water Environment Federation; Water Environment Association of Ontario; Ontario Pollution Control Equipment Association
Products/Services/Areas of Expertise: Aerators; fountains; de-icers; mixers; aspirators; high output alternators; battery isolators; voltage regulators; converters; equalizers; chargers; transfer switches; power inverters
Domestic Markets:
National
Contact(s):
Peter Barbe, President

ARC Geobac Group Inc.
Formerly: Geobac Technology Group Inc.
380 Smythe St.
Fredericton, NB E3B 3E4
506-451-1991
Fax: 506-457-2100
geobacnb@nbnet.nb.ca
www.geobac.ca
Firm Type: Management Consulting, Engineering
Founded: 1991
Staff: 4
Member of: Canadian Environment Industry Association
Products/Services/Areas of Expertise: Brownfield assessment & reclamation; in situ & ex situ remediation; risk assessment for active & decommissioned lands; environmental site assessment

(Ph. I-IV); wetlands engineering; water supply development, protection & quality; forensic investigation; mediation & cost analysis; salt water supply; salt water intrusion
Activities: Research & development
Financial Information:
Type of Ownership: Private
Revenue Sources: 25% Municipals; 75% Private Contracts
Domestic Markets:
New Brunswick, Newfoundland & Labrador, Nova Scotia, Prince Edward Island
Foreign Activity:
Central Europe
Contact(s):
Victor K. Nowicki, President
Anne E. Bertrand, General Manager

ArcelorMittal Dofasco
Also Known As: Dofasco Inc.
P.O. Box 2460
1330 Burlington St. East
Hamilton, ON L8N 3J5
905-544-3761
800-363-2726
customer_inquiries@dofasco.ca;
purchasing_logistics@dofasco.ca
www.dofasco.ca
Firm Type: Distributing, Manufacturing
Founded: 1912
Quality Environmental Management System(s): 14001
Products/Services/Areas of Expertise: Manufacturer & distributor of flat rolled steels; Certificates of Approval, required for facilities that release emissions to the atmosphere, cover all of ArcelorMittal Dofasco's appropriate facilities
Domestic Markets:
National
Foreign Activity:
Mexico, USA
Contact(s):
Juergen G. Schachler, President/CEO
Graham Browne, Vice-President, Human Resources & General Administration
Brad Davey, Vice-President, Sales & Marketing
Sean Donnelly, Vice-President, Technology & Continuous Improvement
Daniel Janczak, Vice-President, Manufacturing
Robert W. Nuttall, Vice-President, Finance
Jim Stirling, General Manager, Environment

Arch Industries
200 Bartor Rd.
Toronto, ON M9M 2W6
416-741-7247
Fax: 416-741-7400
sales@archindustries.com
www.archindustries.com
Firm Type: Distributing
Founded: 1983
Products/Services/Areas of Expertise: Industrial wiping products; reclaimed wipers
Contact(s):
Arthur Falkenstein, President

Archer Chemical
#1, 4090 Belgreen Dr.
Gloucester, ON K1G 3N2
613-737-5332
Fax: 613-737-3329
877-737-5332
jean@archerchemical.com
www.archerchemical.com
Firm Type: Distributing, Manufacturing
Founded: 1991
EcoLogo Certified Products & Services: General purpose cleaners & industrial/commercial cleaners: Green Unikleen & Green 4 Kleen
Products/Services/Areas of Expertise: Offers an environmentally friendly line of cleaning products; also carries environmentally friendly glass washers and dish machines; services food service industry as well as health institutions
Ecological Note: General purpose cleaners & industrial/commercial cleaners: Green Unikleen & Green 4 Kleen
Domestic Markets:
Ontario, Québec
Contact(s):
Jean Plante, Principal

Archipelago Marine Research Ltd.
525 Head St.
Victoria, BC V9A 5S1
250-383-4535
Fax: 250-383-0103
amr@archipelago.ca
www.archipelago.ca
Firm Type: Engineering, Scientific/Technical Services
Founded: 1978
Staff: 175
Products/Services/Areas of Expertise: Near-shore habitat inventory; assessment; environmental impact analysis; fishery monitoring; resource management
Domestic Markets:
National, British Columbia
Foreign Activity:
Australia/New Zealand
Contact(s):
Shawn Stebbins, Co-founder
Howard McElderry, Co-founder
howardm@archipelago.ca
Brian Emmett, Vice-President, Marine Environmental Services
briane@archipelago.bc.ca

Canadian Branches:
Port Hardy
P.O. Box 1592
#203, 8755 Granville St.
Port Hardy, BC V0N 2P0
250-949-7150
Fax: 250-949-7151

Prince Rupert
#14, 342 Third Ave. West
Prince Rupert, BC V8J 1L5
250-627-1167
Fax: 250-627-1316

Ucluelet
P.O. Box 406
1672 Cedar Rd. Main Floor
Ucluelet, BC V0R 3A0
250-726-2724
Fax: 250-726-2725

Argo Protective Coatings Inc.
Formerly: Galvatech Inc.
160 Joseph Zatzman Dr.
Dartmouth, NS B3B 1P1
902-468-1040
Fax: 902-468-2643
Products/Services/Areas of Expertise: With locations in Burnside & Woodside, NS, the company is engaged in the application of protective coatings to steel structures (hot dipped galvanizing, metalizing/thermal spraying, blasting & painting). Chemicals used in the coating provess are either recycled back to the manufacturer or are distilled for re-use on-site
Contact(s):
David Langlois, President

Argus Telecom International Inc.
2505, rue Guenette
Montréal, QC H4R 2E9
514-331-0840
Fax: 514-331-0843
800-363-1888
argus@argustel.com
www.argustel.com
Firm Type: Distributing
Founded: 1985
Staff: 86
Quality Environmental Management System(s): 9001:2000
Products/Services/Areas of Expertise: Photovoltaic telecommunications systems; consulting & system monitoring services; remote solar powered sites for telecommunication industry; offices across Canada & in Hong Kong, Taiwan, the Philippines, Sri Lanka, Malaysia & Indonesia
Financial Information:
Type of Ownership: Private
Revenue: Greater than $5 Million
Domestic Markets:
National
Foreign Activity:
Asia, The Pacific Rim, Worldwide
Contact(s):
John McCabe, President/CEO
jmccabe@argustel.com
Diane Boisvert, Vice President, Operations
dboisvert@argustel.com
Elaine Boisvert, Marketing Administrator
eboisvert@argustel.com

Canadian Branches:
Edmonton
3936 - 47th St.
Edmonton, AB T6L 4B8
780-468-5968
Fax: 780-490-4764
ggardiner@argustel.com
Products/Services/Areas of Expertise: This office serves Alberta & the Northwest Territories
George Gardiner, Area Sales Manager

Halifax
5 Carter Cres.
Antigonish, NS B2G 2S7
902-835-1875
cmasters@argustel.com
Products/Services/Areas of Expertise: This office serves Nova Scotia, Newfoundland & Labrador, New Brunswick & Prince Edward Island
Charles (Alfie) Masters, Vice President, Training & Standardization

Saskatoon
34 Churchill Dr.
Saskatoon, SK S7K 3X4
306-352-3999
Fax: 306-934-1037
hheshka@argustel.com
Products/Services/Areas of Expertise: This office serves Saskatchewan
Harvey Heshka, Area Sales Manager

Toronto
#300, 1370 Don Mills Rd.
Toronto, ON M3B 3N7
416-510-8310
Products/Services/Areas of Expertise: This office serves Ontario

Vancouver
#12, 1730 Broadway St.
Port Coquitlam, BC V3C 2M8
604-530-2223
Fax: 604-939-7840
nswan@argustel.com
Products/Services/Areas of Expertise: This office serves British Columbia, & the Yukon
Neal Swan, Area Sales Manager

Winnipeg
#609, 428 Portage Ave.
Winnipeg, MB R3C 0E2
204-943-7343
Products/Services/Areas of Expertise: This office serves Manitoba

ARISE Technologies Corporation
65 Northland Rd.
Waterloo, ON N2V 1Y8
519-725-2244
Fax: 519-725-8907
877-274-7383
info@arisetech.com
www.arisetech.com
Firm Type: Distributing, Manufacturing
Founded: 1979
Staff: 12
Member of: Solar Energy Society of Canada Inc., Energy Action Council of Toronto, Canadian Solar Industries Association
Products/Services/Areas of Expertise: Operates through 3 divisions: PV Cell Division (Germany), manufacturing photovoltaic cells; PV Silicon Division, producing silicon for PV cell applications; & PV Systems Division, providing turnkey solutions for rooftops & solar farms
Financial Information:
Type of Ownership: Publicly Traded
Revenue Sources: 5% nationwide; 5% Provincial; 5% Municipals; 85% Private Contracts
Domestic Markets:
National
Foreign Activity:
Central America, The Pacific Rim, South America, Mexico
Contact(s):
Daniel (Dan) P. Shea, B.ASc., President/CEO

Arjay Engineering Ltd.
2851 Brighton Rd.
Oakville, ON L6H 6C9
905-829-2418
Fax: 905-829-4701
800-387-9487
arjay@arjayeng.com
www.arjayeng.com
Firm Type: Distributing, Manufacturing
Founded: 1982
Staff: 12
Member of: Ontario Pollution Control Equipment Association; Alliance of Manufacturers & Exporters Canada; Canadian Environment Industry Association; Professional Engineers Ontario; Oakville Chamber of Commerce
Quality Environmental Management System(s): 9001:2000
Products/Services/Areas of Expertise: Designs & manufactures process & environmental controls: level monitors & controls, ppm oil in water monitors, liquid detectors & alarms, open channel flow monitors, plugged chute detectors, gas detection systems; custom design & engineering services & control panel assembly. Manufacturing facilities located in Oakville, Vancouver & Beijing, China
Domestic Markets:
National
Foreign Activity:
Asia, Central America, China, The Middle East, Mexico, USA
Contact(s):
Rick Reeves, President & CEO
Greg Reeves, General Manager

Ark Envirotech Inc.
#102, 1439 - 17 St. SE
Calgary, AB T2G 1J9
403-335-3655
info@arkenvirotech.ca
www.arkenvirotech.ca
Firm Type: Scientific/Technical Services
Founded: 1993
Member of: Canadian Environmental Auditing Association; Association of Environmental Site Assessors of Canada
Member of: Canadian Assoc. of Petroleum Producers
Products/Services/Areas of Expertise: Environmental services dealing with soil, water & groundwater
Recently Completed / Ongoing Projects: Landfarm industrial waste to reclaim soils. Reclaim salt contaminated land with drainage tile system, Phase I & II Environmental Assessments
Financial Information:
Type of Ownership: Private
Revenue: $500,000 - $1.5 Million
Revenue Sources: 100% Private Contracts
Domestic Markets:
Alberta, British Columbia, Saskatchewan,
Contact(s):
George Neely, Training Program
george@arkenvirontech.ca

Arlat Technology
Price Schonstrom Inc.
P.O. Box 249
35 Elm St.
Walkerton, ON N0G 2V0
519-881-0262
Fax: 519-881-3573
800-485-7101
info@arlat.com
www.arlat.com
Firm Type: Manufacturing
Founded: 1982
Member of: Water Environment Federation; American Water Works Association; Canadian Pulp & Paper Technical Association
Products/Services/Areas of Expertise: Wastewater treatment equipment including mechanical bar screens, filter screens, grit classifiers, screenings dewatering presses, chain & flight clarifier equipment, grit separators
Recently Completed / Ongoing Projects: Provided bar screens for: water pollution control facility, Ashbridges Bay, Toronto; wastewater treatment plant, Keen Mountain, Red Onion, Fluvanna Jails in Virginia
Financial Information:
Type of Ownership: Private
Revenue Sources: 80% Municipals; 20% Private Contracts
Domestic Markets:
Alberta, British Columbia, New Brunswick, Newfoundland & Labrador, Nova Scotia, Ontario, Prince Edward Island, Québec, Saskatchewan
Foreign Activity:
Eastern Europe, The Pacific Rim, South Africa, USA, United Kingdom
Markets Sought:
Australia/New Zealand, Western Europe, Mexico
Contact(s):
Richard Grubb, President
Jay Craddock, Manager

Armatek Controls Limited
55 Judson St.
Toronto, ON M8Z 1A4
416-251-3111
Fax: 416-251-1951
sales@armatek.com
www.armatek.com
Firm Type: Distributing
Founded: 1966
Staff: 19
Products/Services/Areas of Expertise: Distributes instruments & industrial controls, including orifice plates, custom panels, temperature assemblies, pressure & flow instruments & systems, process instrumentation, concentration analyzers, interface detectors, flowmeters, signal conditioners, alarms, corrosion monitoring instruments, flame & fire detectors, & fire suppression systems; services include installation, service & repair
Financial Information:
Type of Ownership: Private
Revenue: Greater than $5 Million
Domestic Markets:
New Brunswick, Newfoundland & Labrador, Nova Scotia, Ontario, Prince Edward Island, Québec
Contact(s):
Jon Charette, Office Manager

Canadian Branches:
Montréal
#205, 970, Montee de Liesse
Montréal, QC H4T 1W7
514-332-5200
Fax: 514-332-2530
ventes@armatek.com
René Petitclerk, Manager

Sarnia
260 Tecumseh St.
Sarnia, ON N7T 2K9
519-332-0100
Fax: 519-332-8821
jlivings@armatek.com
John Livings

Armstrong Engineering & Land Surveying Inc.
34 - 11th Ave. South
Cranbrook, BC V1C 2P1
250-489-3013
Fax: 250-489-4522
www.aels.bc.ca
Firm Type: Engineering, Scientific/Technical Services
Founded: 1980
Member of: Association of Professional Engineers of British Columbia; Corporation of Land Surveyors of British Columbia
Products/Services/Areas of Expertise: Engineering consulting services; environmental consulting services; environmental audits
Financial Information:
Type of Ownership: Private
Revenue: $500,000 - $1.5 Million
Revenue Sources: 10% Provincial; 10% Municipals; 80% Private Contracts
Domestic Markets:
British Columbia
Contact(s):
John F. Armstrong, P.Eng., B.C.L.S., General Manager

Armstrong Monitoring Corp.
215 Colonnade Rd. South
Ottawa, ON K2E 7K3
613-225-9531
Fax: 613-225-6965
800-465-5777
info@armstrongmonitoring.com
www.armstrongmonitoring.com

Firm Type: Manufacturing
Founded: 1981
Quality Environmental Management System(s): 9001:2008
Products/Services/Areas of Expertise: Hazardous gas monitoring & petroleum leak detection systems; air quality monitoring systems; liquid/vapour/materials management
Activities: Sensors for hazardous gas sensing & detection; leak detection for petroleum industry
Financial Information:
Type of Ownership: Private
Domestic Markets:
National
Foreign Activity:
Worldwide
Contact(s):
Scott Dudley, President/CEO
Scott Bissett, Director, Sales & Marketing
Don Smordin, Head, Field Service

Armtec Construction Products
P.O. Box 3000
#3, 370 Speedvale Ave. West
Guelph, ON N1H 7M7
519-763-2360
Fax: 519-763-0437
800-265-9391
sales@armtec.com
www.armtec.com
Firm Type: Distributing, Manufacturing
Founded: 1908
Staff: 300
Member of: Corrugated Steel Pipe Institute; Polyethylene Pipe Institute
Quality Environmental Management System(s): 9001:2000
Products/Services/Areas of Expertise: With 21 plants & 22 sales offices, Armtec is Canada's oldest & largest manufacturer & distributor of corrugated steel products & corrugated HDPE pipe used in infrastructure & natural resource environments. Products include fabricated steel & plastic drainage products, retaining walls, storm sewers, culverts, water control gates, geosynthetic products, erosion control, soil reinforcement, separation & filtration. Armtec owns the assets of Brooklin Concrete Products Ltd., as well as Boucher Precast Concrete Ltd., and has acquired Durisol Inc. of Hamilton, and Bruce Tile of Walkerton. This is the sales office location, with the plant facility at 41 George St., Guelph - contact 519-822-0046
Financial Information:
Type of Ownership: Publicly Traded
Revenue: Greater than $5 Million
Domestic Markets:
National
Foreign Activity:
Africa, Australia/New Zealand, Caribbean, Central America, South Africa, South America, USA, Former USSR, United Kingdom, Worldwide
Contact(s):
Kevin Young, President
kyoung@armtec.com
Doug Leitch, Manager, International Sales
dleitch@armtec.com
Ceri Howell, Vice President, Sales & Marketing

Canadian Branches:
Atlantic Region - Bishop's Falls
P.O. Box 40
Exploits Ave.
Bishop's Falls, NL A0H 1C0
709-258-5357
Fax: 709-258-5241
800-258-5258
Products/Services/Areas of Expertise: Sales office & plant/warehouse facility
Roger Goobie, Area Supervisor
rgoobie@armtec.com

Atlantic Region - Sackville
21 Crescent St.
Sackville, NB E4L 3V1
506-536-1920
Fax: 506-536-1926
Products/Services/Areas of Expertise: Sales office & plant/warehouse facility. In the Atlantic Canada region, a plant/warehouse facility & sales office is located at 283 Main St., Bible Hill, NS - contact 902-843-3157; & in PEI, a plant/warehouse is located in Summerside, with a sales office in Slemon Park - contact 902-436-1523

Robert Sams, Senior Sales Manager, Atlantic Canada
rsams@armtec.com

Atlantic Region - St. John's
10 Forbes St.
St. John's, NL A1E 3L5
709-754-3553
Fax: 709-754-3555
Products/Services/Areas of Expertise: Sales office, with a plant facility located in Bishop's Falls, NF
Glen Smith, Sales Representative
gsmith@armtec.com

Ontario Region - Comber
P.O. Box 28
7010 Windsor Ave., Tilbury West Twp.
Comber, ON N0P 1J0
519-687-2338
Fax: 519-687-2132
Products/Services/Areas of Expertise: Sales office
Dave Groot, Sales Representative
dgroot@armtec.com

Ontario Region - Dresden
Dresden Yard, RR#2
Dresden, ON N0P 1M0
519-683-6231
Products/Services/Areas of Expertise: Sales office & plant/warehouse facility
Larry Mansfield, Sales Representative, 519-849-6150
lmansfield@armtec.com

Ontario Region - Forest
P.O. Box 143
5996 Townsend Line
Forest, ON N0N 1J0
519-786-5742
Fax: 519-786-2370
800-265-1447
Products/Services/Areas of Expertise: Plant/warehouse facility

Ontario Region - Guelph
41 George St.
Guelph, ON N1H 1S5
519-822-0046
Products/Services/Areas of Expertise: Plant/warehouse facility; sales office located at #3, 370 Speedvale Ave. W. - contact 800-265-9391. For the Woodstock plant/warehouse facility (ISO 9001:2000), located at 901 Pattullo Ave. W, contact 519-421-1102. For the Bruce Tile plant at RR#3 Walkerton, contact 519-392-6929
Brett Graham, Sales Manager Infrastructure
bgraham@armtec.com

Ontario Region - Orangeville
33 Centennial Rd.
Orangeville, ON L9W 1R1
519-942-2643
Fax: 519-942-9587
Products/Services/Areas of Expertise: Sales office & plant/warehouse facility
Ken MacDougall, Sales Manager, Building Trades North America
kmacdougall@armtec.com

Ontario Region - Peterborough
975 Hwy. 7, RR#7
Peterborough, ON K9J 6X7
705-743-2101
Fax: 705-743-2142
800-363-5047
Products/Services/Areas of Expertise: Sales office & plant/warehouse facility. For the Chesterville facility, located off Old Hwy. #43 & Smith Rd., Chesterville, contact 613-448-2314
Simon Perdue, Senior Sales Representative
sperdue@armtec.com

Ontario Region - Sudbury
40 Vagnini Ct.
Lively, ON P3Y 1K8
705-692-7007
Fax: 705-692-7227
800-315-2720
Products/Services/Areas of Expertise: Sales office
Mark Hannaberg, Sales Representative
mhannaberg@armtec.com

Ontario Region - Thunder Bay
P.O. Box 10009
2 Cooper Rd., Hwy. 11/17 West
Thunder Bay, ON P7C 4V1
807-939-2601
Fax: 807-939-1282
Products/Services/Areas of Expertise: Sales office & plant/warehouse facility
Garry Michaluk, Area Supervisor
gmichaluk@armtec.com

Ontario Region - Toronto
116 Corstate Ave.
Concord, ON L4K 4X2
905-738-3172
Fax: 905-738-3175
Products/Services/Areas of Expertise: Sales office & plant/warehouse facility
Frank Mandarin, Sales Manager
fmandarin@armtec.com

Pacific Region - Langley
Airport Executive Park
#100, 10185 - 199B St.
Richmond, BC V1M 3W9
604-881-4430
Fax: 604-881-4319
Products/Services/Areas of Expertise: Sales office & plant/warehouse facility
Kim Molby, Vice President, Western Region
kmolby@armtec.com

Pacific Region - Nanaimo
1848 Schoolhouse Rd.
Nanaimo, BC V9X 1T4
250-754-1238
Fax: 250-754-3699
Products/Services/Areas of Expertise: Sales office & plant/warehouse facility
Chuck Baynham

Pacific Region - Prince George
2001 Industrial Way
Prince George, BC V2N 5S6
250-561-0017
Fax: 250-561-1240
Products/Services/Areas of Expertise: Sales office & plant/warehouse facility

Prairie Region - Calgary
8715 - 48 St. SE
Calgary, AB T2C 2P8
403-258-0255
Fax: 403-255-8657
Products/Services/Areas of Expertise: Sales office & plant/warehouse facility
Cody Kibala, Site Supervisor
ckibala@armtec.com

Prairie Region - Edmonton
#202, 10464 Mayfield Rd. NW
Edmonton, AB T5P 4P4
780-444-1560
Fax: 780-444-1790
Products/Services/Areas of Expertise: Sales office
Don Descotes, Sales Manager
ddescotes@armtec.com

Prairie Region - Lethbridge
2210 - 39 St. North
Lethbridge, AB T1H 5J2
403-320-2888
Fax: 403-320-2034
Products/Services/Areas of Expertise: Sales office & plant/warehouse facility
Chad Shaw, Sales Representative
cshaw@armtec.com

Prairie Region - Saskatoon
2902 Jasper Ave.
Saskatoon, SK S7J 4L7
306-242-5741
Fax: 306-931-3235
Products/Services/Areas of Expertise: Sales office & plant/warehouse facility
Jim McGeary, Area Supervisor
jmcgeary@armtec.com

Prairie Region - Winnipeg
2455 Dugald Rd.
Winnipeg, MB R2C 5H5
204-957-7787
Fax: 204-956-4229
Products/Services/Areas of Expertise: Sales office & plant/warehouse facility
Ron Prychitko, Sales Manager, Manitoba & Saskatchewan
rprychitko@armtec.com

Québec Region - Montréal
#201, 1430, rue Hocquart
St-Bruno-de-Montarville, QC J3V 6E1
450-441-3525
Fax: 450-441-3520
877-554-8556
Products/Services/Areas of Expertise: Sales office
Yvon Lesperance, Vice President & Region Manager, Eastern Canada
ylesperance@armtec.com

Québec Region - Québec City
85, rue de Rotterdam
St-Augustin-de-Desmaures, QC G3A 1T1
418-878-3630
Fax: 418-878-3672
Products/Services/Areas of Expertise: Sales office & plant/warehouse facility
Christian Gilbert, Sales Representative

Québec Region - St-Clet
669, rte 201
Saint-Clet, QC J0P 1S0
450-456-3366
Fax: 450-456-3137
Products/Services/Areas of Expertise: Sales office & plant/warehouse facility
François Paradis, Sales Representative
fparadis@armtec.com

Prairie Region - Redwater
P.O. Box 27
58 St. South
Redwater, AB T0A 2W0
780-942-3813
Fax: 780-942-2352
Products/Services/Areas of Expertise: Plant/warehouse facility

Arpi's Industries Canada Ltd.
6815 - 40 St. SE
Calgary, AB T2C 2W7
403-236-2444
Fax: 403-236-8345
888-239-2774
arpiscal@arpis.com
www.arpis.com
Firm Type: Engineering, Manufacturing, Scientific/Technical Services
Founded: 1963
Products/Services/Areas of Expertise: Mechanical contractors; supply & service of plumbing items; retrofitting & renovating service for heating, ventilation, airconditioning & fireplaces; manufactured sheet metal products
Domestic Markets:
British Columbia, Saskatchewan
Contact(s):
Julie Berdin, President/General Manager
Barry Cousins, Vice-President

Arrakis Consultants Inc.
#470, 7050, boul Wilfrid-Hamel ouest
Québec, QC G2G 1B5
418-877-6168
Fax: 418-877-0388
800-267-6168
arrakis@arrakis-consultants.ca
Firm Type: Engineering, Scientific/Technical Services
Founded: 1990
Staff: 5
Member of: Association québécoise des techniques de l'eau; International Association of Hydrogeologists; National Groundwater Association; Association provincial des constructeurs d'habitations du Québec; Association des eaux souterraines du Québec
Products/Services/Areas of Expertise: Groundwater consultants; environmental geology; contamination investigation & cleanup

Domestic Markets:
New Brunswick, Québec
Foreign Activity:
Africa
Markets Sought:
Mexico
Contact(s):
Dominique Proulx, President

Array Systems Computing Inc.
1120 Finch Ave. West, 7th Fl.
Toronto, ON M3J 3H7
416-736-0900
Fax: 416-736-4715
866-214-4044
marketing@array.ca
www.array.ca
Firm Type: Engineering, Scientific/Technical Services
Founded: 1981
Quality Environmental Management System(s): 9001:2000
Products/Services/Areas of Expertise: Design, development, installation & integration of meteorological satellite ground stations, including antenna, hardware, software; feasibility studies, system design & programming in real-time image/processing technology areas
Activities: Remote sensing; computer vision; satellite & radar systems; RADARSAT studies; synthetic aperture radar; signal processing
Contact(s):
Stuart J. Berkowitz, President/CEO
Benjamin Hung, Chief Technology Officer

Arrow Speed Controls Ltd.
#111, 8410 Ontario St.
Vancouver, BC V5X 3E7
604-321-4033
Fax: 604-321-9415
arrowinfo@arrowspeed.com
www.arrowspeed.com
Firm Type: Distributing, Manufacturing
Founded: 1979
Products/Services/Areas of Expertise: Variable frequency drive integrator with design, manufacturing, start-up & service; designer of PLS control systems; applications for soft starts, dynamic brakes, DC motors & controls
Domestic Markets:
National
Foreign Activity:
USA
Contact(s):
John Oldham, President
joldham@arrowspeed.com

Canadian Branches:
Barrie
705-734-4170
Fax: 705-527-0446
wmazzer@arrowspeed.comm

Edmonton
#205, 6030 - 88 St.
Edmonton, AB T6E 6G4
780-414-1266
Fax: 780-414-1269
Gordon Kosmenko, Contact

Montréal
#500, 7575, rte Transcanadienne
Ville St-Laurent, QC H4T 1V6
514-336-1441
Fax: 514-337-3989

Prince George
250-964-7210
Fax: 250-964-7213
kconnell@arrowspeed.com

Toronto
7855 Tranmere Dr.
Mississauga, ON L5S 1V5
905-673-7400
Fax: 905-673-7800
info@arrowspeed.com
Dragan Vasic, Contact

Vernon
250-542-8229
Fax: 250-542-8219
cnielsen@arrowspeed.com

Asbeguard Equipment Inc.
#2, 1915 Clements Rd.
Pickering, ON L1W 3V1
905-427-9290
Fax: 905-427-3769
800-727-2144
Firm Type: Distributing, Manufacturing
Founded: 1982
Staff: 6
Products/Services/Areas of Expertise: Asbestos removal equipment
Domestic Markets:
National
Contact(s):
Barrie Nichols, President
Brian Strawn, Sales Manager
Ian Henderson, Inside Sales

ASCO Canada
10 Corisande Dr.
Mount Pearl, NL A1N 5A4
709-748-7800
www.ascocanada.com
Firm Type: Management Consulting
Founded: 1995
Products/Services/Areas of Expertise: Oil & gas logistics company, with services including running supply bases, providing marine management, waste management and industrial cleaning
Domestic Markets:
Alberta, Newfoundland & Labrador, Nova Scotia
Foreign Activity:
Asia, Caribbean, Western Europe, USA, United Kingdom

Canadian Branches:
Balzac
262111, R.R. 10
Balzac, AB T0M 0E0
403-567-1664

Calgary
#300, 400 - 5th Ave. SW
Calgary, AB T2P 0L6
403-206-4707

Dartmouth
161 Williams Ave.
Dartmouth, NS B3B 0B4
902-468-6123
Fax: 902-481-0957

Edmonton/Nisku
404 - 22nd Ave.
Nisku, AB T9E 7W8
780-955-9700

Ashland Canada
525 Finley Ave.
Ajax, ON L1S 2E5
905-683-0150
Fax: 905-427-0688
800-263-2058
www.ashland.com
Firm Type: Distributing, Manufacturing
Founded: 1964
Products/Services/Areas of Expertise: Among other product lines, Ashland offers process, utility-water & functional chemistries used to improve operational efficiencies, enhance product quality, & minimize environmental impact. Clients are found in the pulp & paper industry, food & beverage industry, mining, chemical processing & general manufacturing. The Ajax location houses administration, a production facility for the Ashland Hercules Water Technologies Unit (water treatment chemicals such as biocides, cleaners, coagulants & flocculants, converting additives, defoamers, deposit & scale inhibitors, internal & surface size agents, membrane treatments, odor inhibitors & neutralizers, oxygen scavengers, pulp mill additives, tissue-making additives, wet & dry strength additives, & wood adhesives)eed equipment), & a warehouse
Financial Information:
Type of Ownership: Foreign-owned
Domestic Markets:
National
Foreign Activity:
USA

Canadian Branches:
Saint-Jean
Ashland Hercules Water Technologies Unit
310, rue Brosseau
Saint-Jean, QC J3B 2E9
450-348-4967
Fax: 450-348-7129

Montréal
Ashland Performance Materials & Consumer Markets Units
10515, rue Notre-Dame est
Montréal, QC H1B 2M1
514-650-3950
Fax: 514-650-3959

Kelowna
Ashland Performance Materials Unit
9750 McCarthy Rd.
Kelowna, BC V4V 1S5
250-766-2933
Fax: 250-766-3435
Products/Services/Areas of Expertise: Ashland Performance Materials manufactures composite & specialty polymer technologies for the manufacturing, building & construction, packaging, coating, & converting industries; our solutions are: corrosion resistant; fire retardant; ultraviolet, water & chemical resistant; heat & moisture resistant; low hazardous air pollutant; impact resistant & scratch-proof

Mississauga
Ashland Hercules Water Technologies Unit
#700, 55 City Centre Dr.
Mississauga, ON L5B 1M3
905-279-3338
Fax: 905-279-4949

Mississauga
Ashland Performance Materials & Consumer Markets Units
905 Winston Churchill Blvd.
Mississauga, ON L5J 4E7
905-823-1800
Fax: 905-823-5293
Products/Services/Areas of Expertise: Ashland's Consumer Markets Unit offers the Valvoline brand of automotive & industrial lubricants, automotive chemicals, & car care products; the Valvoline brand provides enhanced fuel economy, & advanced soot & carbon-deposit control

Ashtead Technology Rentals
#18, 3505 Laird Rd.
Mississauga, ON L5L 5Y7
905-607-9639
Fax: 905-607-8592
800-242-3910
www.ashtead-technology.com
Firm Type: Distributing
Founded: 2000
Staff: 4
Member of: Ontario Environmental Industry Association; Canadian Institute for NDE
Quality Environmental Management System(s): 9001:2000
Products/Services/Areas of Expertise: Rentals of environmental monitoring equipment: IAQ monitors, PID's/FID's, toxic gas monitors, industrial hygiene equipment; non-destructive testing (NDT) equipment & remote visual inspection equipment (video probes)
Financial Information:
Type of Ownership: Publicly Traded
Domestic Markets:
National
Foreign Activity:
Worldwide
Contact(s):
Jean Mario Tanyan, Sales Manager, Key Accounts Manager

ASI Group Ltd.
Formerly: Aquatic Sciences Inc.
250 Martindale Rd.
St Catharines, ON L2R 6P9
905-641-0941
Fax: 905-641-1825
info@asi-group.com
www.asi-group.com
Firm Type: Engineering
Founded: 1987
Staff: 100
Member of: Association of Professional Engineers; American Water Works Association; North American Benthological

Society; Canadian Environment Industry Association; Institute of Space & Terrestrial Sciences
Products/Services/Areas of Expertise: Engineering (water & waste water treatment), design, build, operate turnkey plants; Ecological services: EEM's, aquatic biology, environmental audits, aquatic toxicity laboratory, odour control for landfill leachate; Marine services: civil engineering inspections & underwater structures, zebra mussel control, biofilm control
Financial Information:
Type of Ownership: Private
Revenue: Greater than $5 Million
Revenue Sources: 30% Provincial; 20% Municipals; 50% Private Contracts
Domestic Markets:
National
Foreign Activity:
Asia, Australia/New Zealand, Central America, Eastern Europe, South America, Mexico, USA
Contact(s):
Carmen Sferrazza, President
carmen@asi-group.com
Andrew Vitaterna, Manager, Engineering
Barb Laurens, Manager, Sales & Marketing
blaurens@asi-group.com

Canadian Branches:
Sarnia
120 Seaway Rd.
Sarnia, ON N7T 8A5
519-383-7822
Fax: 519-383-7870
Bob Tyre, Regional Manager

ASL Environmental Sciences Inc.
1986 Mills Rd.
Sidney, BC V8L 5Y3
250-656-0177
Fax: 250-656-2162
877-656-0177
asl@aslenv.com
www.aslenv.com
Firm Type: Manufacturing, Scientific/Technical Services
Founded: 1977
Staff: 28
Member of: Vancouver Island Advance of Technology Centre
Products/Services/Areas of Expertise: River flow surveys for defining sturgeon habitat on Columbia River - Columbia Power; Ocean current surveys for siting & monitoring of fish farms; thermal effects study of cooling water effluents in Port Moody Arm
Recently Completed / Ongoing Projects: Oceanographic program in Equitorial Guinea for Marathon Oil; conducting ice studies in northern Canada and Russia
Financial Information:
Type of Ownership: Private
Revenue Sources: 10% nationwide; 90% Private Contracts
Domestic Markets:
National
Foreign Activity:
Worldwide
Contact(s):
Colleen McQuade, Marketing Coordinator
cmcquade@aslenv.com
Rick Birch, Equipment Rental Manager
rbirch@aslenv.com

Assaynet Canada Inc.
#330, 384 Bank St.
Ottawa, ON K2P 1Y4
613-231-8444
Fax: 613-231-5552
sales@assaynet.com
www.assaynet.com
Products/Services/Areas of Expertise: Builds LIMS, industry-specific, state-of-the-art data management solutions for the environmental & mining industries
Contact(s):
Tania Orduz, General Manager

Associated Engineering Group Ltd.
#1000, 10909 Jasper Ave.
Edmonton, AB T5J 5B9
780-451-7666
Fax: 780-454-7698
inquiries@ae.ca
www.ae.ca

Firm Type: Engineering, Scientific/Technical Services
Founded: 1946
Staff: 700
Member of: Association of Consulting Engineers of Canada; Association of Professional Engineers & Geoscientists of B.C.; Association of Professional Engineers of Alberta, Saskatchewan & Ontario
Products/Services/Areas of Expertise: Water supply & treatment, wastewater treatment & disposal, water resources, solid waste management, transportation, urban development, industrial services
Recently Completed / Ongoing Projects: Annacis & Lulu Island wastewater treatment plants secondary upgrades
Financial Information:
Type of Ownership: Private
Domestic Markets:
National
Foreign Activity:
Africa, Asia, Caribbean, China, USA, Vietnam
Contact(s):
Kerry Rudd, P.Eng., President/CEO
Steve Croxford, P.Eng., Manager, Water and Wastewater

Canadian Branches:
Calgary
#400, 600 Crowfoot Cres. NW
Calgary, AB T3G 0B4
403-262-4500
Fax: 403-269-7640

Comox
1994 Comox Ave.
Comox, BC V9M 3M7
250-339-9896
Fax: 250-339-5855

Fort McMurray
#211, 9912 Franklin Ave.
Fort McMurray, AB T9H 2K5
780-715-3850
Fax: 780-715-3851

Fort McMurray
#211, 9912 Franklin Ave.
Fort McMurray, BC T9H 2K5
780-715-3850
Fax: 780-715-3851

Kelowna
#610, 1632 Dickson Ave.
Kelowna, BC V1Y 7T2
250-763-3638
Fax: 250-763-8880

Langley
#301 - 9440 202nd St.
Langley, AB V1M 4A6
604-888-3572

Lethbridge
#1001, 400 - 4th Ave. South
Lethbridge, AB T1J 4E1
403-329-1404
Fax: 403-329-4745

Medicine Hat
840 Kingsway Ave. SE
Medicine Hat, AB T1A 8G5
403-528-3771
Fax: 403-528-9701

Red Deer
#303, 5913 - 50th Ave.
Red Deer, AB T4N 4C4
403-314-5327
Fax: 403-314-4968

Regina
199 Leonard St. North
Regina, SK S4N 5X5
306-721-2466
Fax: 306-721-2474

Saskatoon
#1, 2225 Northridge Dr.
Saskatoon, SK S7L 6X6
306-653-4969
Fax: 306-242-4904

St. Catharines
#208, 110A Hannover Dr.
St Catharines, ON L2W 1A4

905-348-0990
Fax: 905-346-0992

Toronto
#800, 304 The East Mall
Toronto, ON M9B 6E2
416-622-9502
Fax: 416-622-6249

Vancouver
#300, 4940 Canada Way
Burnaby, BC V5G 4M5
604-293-1411
Fax: 604-291-6163

Associated Tube Industries
Division of Samuel Manu-Tech Inc.
7455 Woodbine Ave.
Markham, ON L3R 1A7
905-475-6464
Fax: 905-475-5202
800-387-4217
stainlesscda@associatedtube.com
www.associatedtube.com
Firm Type: Manufacturing
Quality Environmental Management System(s): 16949:2002
Products/Services/Areas of Expertise: Manufacturers of welded stainless steel & high nickel alloy pipe & tubing
Financial Information:
Type of Ownership: Publicly Traded
Domestic Markets:
National
Foreign Activity:
Australia/New Zealand, The Pacific Rim, USA
Contact(s):
Mark Winkler, President
mwinkler@associatedtube.com
Peter Neilas, Vice-President, Finance
pneilas@associatedtube.com
Paul Evers, Director, Technology
pevers@associatedtube.com
Mike Hawkins, Director, Operations
mhawkins@associatedtube.com
Mark Kowall, Director, Sales
mkowall@associatedtube.com

Asta Sales & Marketing Ltd.
#4, 510 - 44th St. East
Saskatoon, SK S7K 0W1
306-933-4125
Fax: 306-933-4145
Products/Services/Areas of Expertise: Water & wastewater management & equipment
Contact(s):
Al Howitt

ATCO Group
#1600, 909 - 11 Ave. SW
Calgary, AB T2R 1N6
403-292-7500
Fax: 403-292-7532
www.atco.com
Firm Type: Management Consulting, Engineering, Information Technology
Founded: 1947
Staff: 7700
Products/Services/Areas of Expertise: ATCO Group (ATCO Ltd.) is an Alberta-based company that provides innovative business solutions in a number of areas including pipelines, natural gas & electricity transmission & distribution, power generation, natural gas gathering/processing/storage/liquids extraction, structures & logisitics, & noise abatement. ATCO Group comprises the following companies: ATCO Gas, ATCO Electic, ATCO Pipelines, ATCO EnergySense, ATCO Blue Flame Kitchen, Northland Utilities, Yukon Electic Company, ATCO Power, ASHCOR Technologies, ATCO Energy Solutions, ATCO Midstream, ATCO Water, ATCO Structures & Logistics, ATCO I-Tek, & Canadian Utilities Limited
Financial Information:
Type of Ownership: Publicly Traded
Revenue: Greater than $5 Million
Domestic Markets:
National
Foreign Activity:
Worldwide
Contact(s):
Nancy C. Southern, President/CEO
Ronald D. Southern, Chairman

Canadian Branches:
Kingston
#W21, 4 Cataraqui St.
Kingston, ON K7K 1Z7
613-507-2826
Fax: 613-507-2832
Doug Wood, General Manager

Ottawa
#100, 170 Laurier Ave. West
Ottawa, ON K1P 5V5
613-787-9696
Fax: 613-238-7314
Michael Gervair, Sr. Vice-President, Business Develop

ATCO Power
Member company of the ATCO Group
#900, 919 - 11th Ave. SW
Calgary, AB T2R 1P3
403-209-6900
Fax: 403-209-6920
www.atcopower.com; www.atco.com
Firm Type: Distributing, POWER
Products/Services/Areas of Expertise: ATCO Power develops, constructs, owns & operates environmentally progressive independent power generation plants; 16 plants in Canada & the U.K., 3 plants in Australia, operated by ATCO Australia
Financial Information:
Type of Ownership: Publicly Traded
Revenue: Greater than $5 Million
Domestic Markets:
National
Foreign Activity:
Australia/New Zealand, United Kingdom, Worldwide
Markets Sought:
Australia/New Zealand, United Kingdom
Contact(s):
John Ell, President

Canadian Branches:
Brazil Office - ATCO Acústica do Brasil Ltda.
Av. Sete de Setembro, 5388 CJ 1006, 100 Andar-Batel
Curitiba, PR Brazil
55-41-3369-3435
www.atcoacustica.com.br

International Branch(es):
US Office
#105, 800 Wilcrest Dr.
Houston, TX USA
866-452-2604
Products/Services/Areas of Expertise: A 2nd office is located at #207, 8 West Dry Creek Circle, Denver, CO

United Kingdom Office
P.O. Box 672
Whitley Bay UK
44(0)-191-237-1867
, Jerry

ATD Waste Systems Inc.
3095 - 24 Ave. West
Vancouver, BC V6L 1R7
604-736-4474
Fax: 604-736-4493
1cleanfarm@hogmanure.com
www.hogmanure.com
Firm Type: Manufacturing, Scientific/Technical Services, Waste Management
Founded: 1993
Products/Services/Areas of Expertise: Hog manure management systems designed to minimize impacts on the environment, while providing a saleable byproduct in the form of organic fertilizer
Financial Information:
Type of Ownership: Private
Domestic Markets:
Alberta, British Columbia, Manitoba, New Brunswick, Nova Scotia, Ontario, Prince Edward Island, Québec, Saskatchewan
Foreign Activity:
USA
Markets Sought:
Western Europe
Contact(s):
Victor Van Slyke, President

Atkinson, Davies Inc.
#12, 60 Meg Dr.
London, ON N6E 3T6
519-685-6400
Fax: 519-685-0943
atkinsondavies@atkinsondavies.com
www.atkinsondavies.com
Firm Type: Engineering
Founded: 1980
Products/Services/Areas of Expertise: Geotechnical & construction materials testing; environmental site assessments; Phase I & II environmental remediation & site enclosures
Recently Completed / Ongoing Projects: Robarts Research Centre (University Hospital) London, ON; Springbank Drive widening, London, ON; Woodstock Regional Hospital, Woodstock, ON
Financial Information:
Type of Ownership: Private
Revenue: $500,000 - $1.5 Million
Revenue Sources: 2% nationwide; 8% Provincial; 40% Municipals; 50% Private Contracts
Domestic Markets:
Ontario
Contact(s):
Colin J.W. Atkinson, President
atkinsondavies@atkinsondavies.com

Atlantic Acoustical Associates
P.O. Box 96 M
Halifax, NS B3J 2L4
902-425-3096
Fax: 902-425-0044
Firm Type: Scientific/Technical Services
Founded: 1984
Staff: 2
Member of: Acoustical Society of America; Canadian Acoustical Association; American Society of Heating, Refrigerating & Air Conditioning Engineers; Royal Architectural Institute of Canada; Audio Engineering Society; Nova Scotia Association of Architects
Products/Services/Areas of Expertise: Environmental impact assessment; site remediation; noise quality assessment; laboratory analysis
Domestic Markets:
New Brunswick, Newfoundland & Labrador, Nova Scotia, Prince Edward Island
Contact(s):
Peter Terroux, Principal Consultant

Atlantic Air Cleaning Specialists Ltd.
P.O. Box 4407
Rothesay, NB E2E 5X8
506-849-1044
Fax: 506-849-1045
800-561-5766
info@aircleaning.ca
www.aircleaning.ca
Firm Type: Manufacturing, Scientific/Technical Services
Founded: 1988
Products/Services/Areas of Expertise: Air cleaning & collection system design & installation; dust suppression, fume extraction, air testing & analysis
Domestic Markets:
New Brunswick, Newfoundland & Labrador, Nova Scotia, Prince Edward Island, Québec
Contact(s):
Bob Milne, General Manager, Sales, 506-848-9067
bob@aircleaning.ca

Atlantic Engineering Consultants Ltd.
34 Main St.
Corner Brook, NL A2H 1C3
709-634-3612
Fax: 709-634-4628
djdicesare@aecl.nfld.net
Firm Type: Management Consulting, Engineering
Founded: 1971
Staff: 16
Products/Services/Areas of Expertise: Municipal planning & engineering, civil, structural, electrical & mechanical consulting engineering, marine structures, environmental studies, & feasibility studies
Financial Information:
Type of Ownership: Private
Revenue: $500,000 - $1.5 Million
Revenue Sources: 15% nationwide; 10% Provincial; 60% Municipals; 15% Private Contracts
Domestic Markets:
Newfoundland & Labrador
Contact(s):
D.J. DiCesare, P.Eng., President/CEO
M.C. Gorman, P.Eng., Vice-President

Atlantic Environmental Training & On-Site Services Inc.
#4, 2 Lakeside Dr.
Lakeside, NS B3T 1L7
902-453-1226
Fax: 902-453-5838
fwc@atlenv.ca
www.atlenv.ca
Firm Type: Management Consulting
Founded: 1998
Staff: 2
Member of: Environmental Auditing Association; Society of Certified Technicians & Technologists of Nova Scotia
Products/Services/Areas of Expertise: The firm is engaged in environmental training & project management, with emphasis on environmental health & safety. Training courses focus on hazardous waste operations, emergency response training, biological testing, environmental assessment training, chemical & biological spill response, transportation of dangerous goods, & Workplace Hazardous Material Information System (WHMIS) - to name a few areas. Expertise also includes environmental auditing (ISO 14000), health & safety planning, pollution prevention & sustainable development, & developing household hazardous waste collection programs
Recently Completed / Ongoing Projects: HAZMAT audits & environmental reviews, DND
Financial Information:
Type of Ownership: Private
Revenue: $100,000 - $250,000
Revenue Sources: 30% nationwide; 70% Private Contracts
Domestic Markets:
British Columbia, New Brunswick, Newfoundland & Labrador, Nova Scotia, Ontario, Prince Edward Island
Contact(s):
Bill Laurette, CET, President

Atlantic Industrial Services
A Division of Envirosystems Inc.
2024, Rte 28 Berry Mills Rd.
Moncton, NB E1C 8L4
506-862-2750
Fax: 506-862-2760
800-565-4383
www.enviro-systems.com
Products/Services/Areas of Expertise: One of Atlantic Canada's largest handlers of hazardous waste, the firm provides a comprehensive range of disposal options for industrial and transportation sectors, among others, as well as households
Contact(s):
Adrian Saunders, Contact

Atlantic Industries Ltd.
P.O. Box 1006
3155 Rte. 935
Dorchester, NB E4K 3V5
506-379-2455
Fax: 506-379-2290
877-245-7473
info@ail.ca
www.ail.ca
Firm Type: Manufacturing
Founded: 1965
Quality Environmental Management System(s): 9003
Products/Services/Areas of Expertise: Manufacturers of corrugated metal products, such as culverts, sewers, tunnels, bridges & stream enclosures
Domestic Markets:
National
Contact(s):
L. Michael Wilson, President/CEO
mike@ail.ca
Wade Abbott, General Manager, Eastern Canada
wade@ail.ca

Canadian Branches:
Armstrong
4155 Crozier Rd.
Armstrong, BC V0E 1B0
250-546-9479
Fax: 250-546-9411
bc@ail.ca

Products & Services Buyer's Guide

Ayr
560 Waydom Dr.
Ayr, ON N0B 1E0
519-622-8600
Fax: 519-622-1372
ontsales@ail.ca

Calgary
#220, 5925 - 12th St., SE
Calgary, AB T2H 2M3
403-730-6980
Fax: 403-730-6981
calgary@ail.ca

Carp
P.O. Box 118
Carp, ON K0A 1L0
613-839-3431
Fax: 613-839-1201
ontsales@ail.ca

Deer Lake
34 South Main St.
Deer Lake, NL A8A 2B7
709-635-2159
Fax: 709-635-2733
nf@ail.ca

Louiseville
109, av Dalcourt
Louiseville, QC J5V 2A6
819-228-2751
Fax: 819-228-4367
qc@ail.ca

Mount Pearl/St. John's
388 Kenmount Rd.
Mount Pearl/St. John's, NL A1B 3R2
709-738-2772
Fax: 709-738-2773
nf@ail.ca

Pitt Meadows
19400 Park Rd.
Pitt Meadows, BC V3Y 1C8
604-460-8334
Fax: 604-460-8117
bc@ail.ca

Prince George
8485 Willow Cale Rd.
Prince George, BC
250-561-1755
Fax: 250-561-1851
princegeorge@ail.ca

Westlock
P.O. Box 5058
1237 Old Pickardville Rd.
Westlock, AB T7P 2P4
780-349-5430
Fax: 780-349-5445
ab@ail.ca

Atlantic Newsprint Company
1900 Thickson Rd. S
Whitby, ON L1N 9E1
905-686-5957
Fax: 905-686-5900
www.atlantic.ca
Firm Type: Manufacturing
Founded: 1991
EcoLogo Certified Products & Services: Recycled newsprint
Products/Services/Areas of Expertise: Manufactures recycled newsprint
Ecological Note: Recycled newsprint
Contact(s):
Sean Curran, Manager, Sales
Michael Booth, Manager, Sales
mmbooth@computan.on.ca

Atlantic Orient Canada Inc.
#200, 300 Prince Albert Rd.
Dartmouth, NS B2Y 4J2
902-468-1621
Fax: 902-468-6865
ppynn@aocwind.ca
www.atlanticorientcanada.ca
Firm Type: Distributing, Engineering, Scientific/Technical Services
Founded: 1995
Products/Services/Areas of Expertise: Developers of wind energy projects in Canada & abroad; focus is on the supply & installation of the AOC 15/50 wind turbine, which produces energy at competitive rates for distributed generation, village electrification, diesel-based utilities & purchased power displacement for agriculture, industry & municipalities; services include project engineering & feasibility studies, project management, installation, commissioning & service work
Recently Completed / Ongoing Projects: Wind energy projects in Big Trout Lake, ON; Rankin Inlet, NU; Blind River, ON; Sachs Harbour NT; North Cape, PE; USA, Morocco, Northern Ireland, India & England
Contact(s):
Stan Mason, P.Eng., Co-owner
Paul Pynn, P.Eng., Project Manager/Engineer

Atlantic Packaging Products Ltd.
111 Progress Ave.
Toronto, ON M1P 2Y9
416-298-8101
Fax: 416-297-2218
800-268-5620
www.atlantic.ca
Firm Type: Distributing, Manufacturing
Founded: 1945
Staff: 2000
Products/Services/Areas of Expertise: Business units include: Add Ink division (graphic & structural design, point of purchase displays, etc.); Corrugated division products for private & commercial use; Color Pak division (pre-printed linerboard); Consumer Products; Newsprint company; Flexible Packaging; Supply Chain division; Atlantic Fibres division; Containerboard Mills division; the Recycling division (in 2010, its recycled newsprint plant in Whitby closed); & Mitchel-Lincoln Packaging Ltd. is a sister company. Services include distribution, recycling programs. The company is recognized for its commitment to sustainable practices, & to recycling & the reduction of pollutants & waste in its manufacturing processes
Financial Information:
Type of Ownership: Private
Domestic Markets:
National
Foreign Activity:
Caribbean, Central Europe, Eastern Europe, USA
Contact(s):
John Cherry, President
Contact(s):
Diane Roy, Sales Manager, Corrugated Div., Drummondville
diane.roy@ml-group.com
Contact(s):
Russ Stuart, Sales Manager, Corrugated Div., Montréal
russ.stuart@ml-group.com

Canadian Branches:
Agincourt - Consumer Products Div. - Paper Towel, Tissue & Napkins
55 Milliken Blvd.
Toronto, ON M1V 1V4
416-298-5542
800-268-5620 X5542

Brampton - Corrugated Division
195 Walker Dr.
Brampton, ON L6T 3Z9
905-799-7510
886-718-8951

Don Mills - Atlantic Decorative & Display Division - Add Ink
36 Overlea Blvd.
Toronto, ON M4H 1B7
416-421-3636
Fax: 416-421-1996
Dahra Granovsky, Vice President, Add Ink & Color Pak

Ingersoll - Corrugated Division
45 Chisholm Dr.
Ingersoll, ON N5C 2C7
519-485-4921
800-265-9905

London - Supply Chain Mgmt. Div.
327 Sovereign Rd.
London, ON N6M 1A6
519-438-6153
Fax: 519-438-6401
800-265-4767

Mississauga - Corrugated Division
5711 Atlantic Dr.
Mississauga, ON L4W 1H3
905-670-0301
800-668-5457

Montréal - Recycling Division - Atlantic Fibres
#205, 8300, Côte-de-Liesse
Montréal, QC H4T 1G7
514-735-3300
Fax: 514-735-9444
800-378-2426
Products/Services/Areas of Expertise: This is the head office of Atlantic Fibres. Product line includes baled waste paper fibres, newsprint, linerboard rolls, various grades of tissue rolls

Ottawa - Supply Chain Mgmt. Div.
2764A Sheffield Rd.
Ottawa, ON K1B 3V9
613-745-9955
Fax: 613-745-5294
800-267-7079

Scarborough - Corrugated Division
350 Midwest Rd.
Toronto, ON M1P 3A9
416-298-5314
800-268-5620 X5314
Bob Hagan, Vice President/General Manager, Corrugated

Scarborough - Flexible Packaging Division - Paper Bags
80 Progress Ave.
Toronto, ON M1P 2Z1
416-609-5890
800-268-5620 X5890
Products/Services/Areas of Expertise: For the Flexible Packaging division, a 2nd Scarborough location at 255 Brimley Rd. produces plastic film & bags - contact 416-609-5890
Andy Tocchet, Vice President/General Manager, Consumer Prods., Flexible Pkging., Supply Chain Mgmt.

Scarborough - Recycling Division - Canes Recycling
333 Progress Rd.
Toronto, ON M1P 2Z7
416-298-3274

Scarborough - Recycling Division - Atlantic Recycling
111 Progress Rd.
Toronto, ON M1P 2Y9
416-298-5307
800-268-5620 X5307

Sudbury - Supply Chain Mgmt. Div.
1474 Fairburn St.
Sudbury, ON P3A 1N7
705-566-2844
Fax: 705-566-9280
800-461-7000
Products/Services/Areas of Expertise: Provides solutions to sourcing, supply & logistics needs for Canadian organizations

Whitby - Newsprint Division - Atlantic Newsprint Company
1900 Thickson Rd. South
Whitby, ON L1B 5R5
905-428-3020
866-285-7378
Founded: 1991
Products/Services/Areas of Expertise: Canada's first 100% recycled newsprint plant processes 200,000 tonnes annually using state-of-the-art technology

Drummondville - Corrugated Div. - Mitchel-Lincoln Packaging Ltd.
925, rue Rocheleau
Drummondville, QC J2C 6L8
819-477-9700
800-567-2547
www.ml-group.com

Saint-Laurent - Corrugated Div. - Mitchel-Lincoln Packaging Ltd.
3737, boul Thimens
Montréal, QC H4R 1V1
514-332-3480
800-361-5727
www.ml-group.com

Saint-Laurent - Supply Chain Mgmt. Div. - Festival Packaging Inc.
An operating unit of Mitchel-Lincoln Packaging Ltd.
Festival Store

8310, Côte-de-Liesse
Montréal, QC H4T 1G7
514-340-1119
Fax: 514-340-1678
www.festival.ca
Products/Services/Areas of Expertise: Festival provides boxes, packaging materials & moving kits for moving & storage requirements

International Branch(es):
Buffalo, NY - Recycling Division - Atlantic Fibres (USA) Inc.
18 C Tracy St.
Buffalo, NY USA
716-852-0911
866-852-0911

Atlantic Poly Liners Inc.
103 Park Rd.
Elmsdale, NS B2S 2L3
902-860-0085
Fax: 902-883-8900
dale@aplinc.catico.ca
www.atlanticpolyliners.ca
Firm Type: Engineering, Manufacturing
Founded: 1991
Member of: International Association of Geosynthetic Installers
Products/Services/Areas of Expertise: High density polyethylene & bentonite clay containment liners for holding ponds
Domestic Markets:
New Brunswick, Newfoundland & Labrador, Nova Scotia, Prince Edward Island
Contact(s):
Scott Haverstock, President

Atlantic Purification Systems
P.O. Box 877
10 Ferguson Rd.
Dartmouth, NS B2Y 3Z5
902-469-2806
Fax: 902-463-3529
sales@aps.ns.ca
www.aps.ns.ca
Firm Type: Distributing
Founded: 1970
Staff: 22
Member of: Association of Professional Engineers & Geophysicists of Nova Scotia; American Water Works Association; Water Environment Association of Ontario; Water Environment Federation
Products/Services/Areas of Expertise: Environmental water & waste treatment equipment; chlorination; ozonation; ultra-violet disinfection equipment; RO, UF, MF filtration, separation, ion exchange; fluid handling, pumps, pipes, valves; control & metering; ultrasonic flowmeters; process analyzers; air pollution & odour control systems; sludge processing
Recently Completed / Ongoing Projects: Duplex lift station, pumps, Dieppe; water recirculation system, filters, Shippigan; grit collectors, Fredericton
Financial Information:
Type of Ownership: Private
Revenue Sources: 20% nationwide; 20% Provincial; 40% Municipals; 20% Private Contracts
Domestic Markets:
New Brunswick, Newfoundland & Labrador, Nova Scotia, Prince Edward Island
Markets Sought:
Central America, The Middle East, South America, Mexico,
Contact(s):
Kenneth V. Reardon, P.Eng., President & General Manager
kvr@aps.ns.ca
Terry D. Reardon, Vice-President, Sales & Marketing
terry@aps.ns.ca
Hettie Sacre, Manager, Environmental Systems
hettie@aps.ns.ca

Atlantic Soils & Associated Management Ltd. / ASAM
RR#1, Pictou County
Merigomish, NS B0K 1G0
902-396-4110
Fax: 902-396-1810
ashleycameron@ns.aliantzinc.ca
www.atlanticsoils.ca
Firm Type: Engineering, Waste Management
Founded: 1994
Staff: 4
Member of: NS Construction Safety Association; NS Environmental Industry Association
Products/Services/Areas of Expertise: Acceptance & bioremediation of petroleum-impacted soils
Recently Completed / Ongoing Projects: Clean up of various petroleum contaminated sites for Town of Truro, County of Colchester
Financial Information:
Type of Ownership: Private
Revenue Sources: 10% nationwide; 10% Provincial; 20% Municipals; 60% Private Contracts
Domestic Markets:
Nova Scotia
Contact(s):
Ashley Cameron, Contact, 902-396-6974

Atlantic Wind Power Corp. Ltd.
P.O. Box 48155
Bedford, NS B4A 3Z2
902-835-3352
Fax: 902-484-7075
info@awpc.com
www.awpc.com
Firm Type: Engineering, Manufacturing
Founded: 2005
EcoLogo Certified Products & Services: Develops windpower
Products/Services/Areas of Expertise: Developers and installers of wind farms and single wind turbines in Atlantic Canada
Recently Completed / Ongoing Projects: In process are two Vestas 1.8 MW turbines,30 MW, at Pubnico Point project in Nova Scotia & five more at 3Ci's 54 MW Mount Copper project in Quebec
Ecological Note: Develops windpower
Domestic Markets:
New Brunswick, Newfoundland & Labrador, Nova Scotia, Prince Edward Island
Contact(s):
Charles Demond, President

Atlas Polar Company Limited
60 Northline Rd.
Toronto, ON M4B 3E5
416-751-7740
Fax: 416-751-6475
888-799-4422
info@atlaspolar.com
www.atlaspolar.com
Firm Type: Waste Management
Founded: 1938
Staff: 55
Quality Environmental Management System(s): 9002
Products/Services/Areas of Expertise: Distributors and suppliers of material handling equipment: articulated cranes; truck-mounted forklifts; hooklift systems; remote control and automated trashraking systems
Contact(s):
R. Parr, President

Atotech Canada Ltd.
Formerly: M&T Harshaw Canada
1180 Corporate Dr.
Burlington, ON L7L 5R6
905-332-0111
Fax: 905-332-0841
800-387-8368
andrew.vecchiarelli@atotech.com
www.atotech.com
Firm Type: Manufacturing
Founded: 1991
Quality Environmental Management System(s): 9002
Products/Services/Areas of Expertise: Proprietary products, chemicals & equipment used in the metal finishing industry
Domestic Markets:
Alberta, British Columbia, Manitoba, Ontario, Québec
Foreign Activity:
Western Europe, Mexico, USA
Contact(s):
Gene Torcoletti, President
Gene.Torcoletti@Atotech.com
Andy Vecchiarelli, Manager, Domestic Sales & Marketing

Atrion International Inc.
Formerly: ClearCross
4777, rue Levy
Montréal, QC H4R 2P9
514-337-2114
Fax: 514-337-2115
888-828-7466
www.atrionintl.com
Firm Type: Information Technology, Scientific/Technical Services
Founded: 1989
Staff: 8
Products/Services/Areas of Expertise: With branch locations in France & The Netherlands, Atrion develops software solutions to assist companies with governance, risk & compliance efforts, with a focus on the regulatory environment regarding Environment, Health & Safety. Atrion's versatile Product Compliance Solution is compatible with every major ERP & PLM solution. Clients include companies in the chemical, petrochemical, industrial gas, coatings & inks, flavours & fragrances, & consumer products industries
Financial Information:
Type of Ownership: Private
Revenue Sources: 100% Private Contracts
Domestic Markets:
National
Foreign Activity:
Worldwide
Contact(s):
Patrick J. Lavoie, President/CEO

ATS Scientific Inc.
4030 Mainway
Burlington, ON L7M 4B9
905-332-1251
Fax: 905-332-1394
800-661-6700
sales@ats-scientific.com
www.ats-scientific.com
Firm Type: Distributing, Scientific/Technical Services
Founded: 1989
Staff: 15
Products/Services/Areas of Expertise: Distributor of scientific instrumentation and supplies
Domestic Markets:
National
Contact(s):
Alex Heino, President
Gilles Groulx, National Sales Manager

Aurora Environmental Consulting Ltd.
Also Known As: Aurora Corrosion Control
3773 - 19 St. NE
Calgary, AB T2E 6S8
403-291-4495
Fax: 403-250-5872
aurora@auroracorrosion.ca
www.auroracorrosion.ca
Firm Type: Engineering, Scientific/Technical Services
Founded: 1987
Member of: NACE International
Products/Services/Areas of Expertise: Corrosion control - cathodic protection systems, design, evaluation, maintenance, material supply, installation; environmental services - consultation, audits, assessments, testing (soil conductivity/resistivity)
Recently Completed / Ongoing Projects: Assess corrosion status of buried storage tanks; design process plant protection system for buried pressure lines & fire water systems; service station site remediation program
Financial Information:
Type of Ownership: Private
Revenue Sources: 10% Municipals; 90% Private Contracts
Domestic Markets:
Alberta, British Columbia, Manitoba, Ontario, Saskatchewan
Contact(s):
Clarke N. Cherniwchan, President
clarke@auroracorrosion.ca
Robert J. Maynard, P.Eng., Principal Engineer
bobm@auroracorrosion.ca

Canadian Branches:
Grande Prairie
P.O. Box 22093
9323 - 67 Ave.
Grande Prairie, AB T8V 6X1
780-402-8447

Swift Current
P.O. Box 2346
Macoun Dr.
Swift Current, SK S9H 4V2

306-741-2978
Fax: 306-778-7696

Aurora Instruments Ltd.
1001 East Pender St.
Vancouver, BC V6A 1W2
604-215-8700
Fax: 604-215-9700
800-883-2918
info@aurora-instr.com
www.aurora-instr.com
Firm Type: Distributing, Manufacturing, Scientific/Technical Services
Founded: 1989
Quality Environmental Management System(s): 9001:2000
Products/Services/Areas of Expertise: The firm is engaged in the design, manufacture & servicing of scientific instruments for use in research in elemental analysis, genomics, proteomics & drug discovery. Products include the Atomic Absorption Spectrometer, Atomic Fluorescence Spectrometer, UV/Vis Spectrophotometers, Microwave Digestion systems, & VERSA liquid handling systems
Financial Information:
Type of Ownership: Private
Domestic Markets:
National
Foreign Activity:
Africa, Asia, Eastern Europe, Western Europe, The Middle East, The Pacific Rim, South America, USA
Markets Sought:
Caribbean, Central America, Mexico
Contact(s):
Dong C. Liang, Ph.D., President
Fay Liang, General Manager

Auto-Chlor Inc.
5161 Tomken Rd.
Mississauga, ON L4W 1P1
905-624-0919
Fax: 905-624-0937
Firm Type: Manufacturing
Founded: 1974
Staff: 6
Member of: Association of Condominium Managers
Products/Services/Areas of Expertise: Water treatment systems specializing in chlorinated water for swimming pools, spas & wells; all chemicals required for water balancing & sanitizing pools & spas; neutralizing cyanide; bacteria control for boilers; all filtering equipment for pools & spas; all accessories for pools & spas
Financial Information:
Type of Ownership: Private
Domestic Markets:
Ontario
Contact(s):
Robert James, President

Automatic Controls Ltd.
9010 - 20 St. NW
Edmonton, AB T6P 1K8
780-417-7000
Fax: 780-417-7001
888-255-5454
info@automatic-controls.com
www.automatic-controls.com
Firm Type: Distributing, Engineering, Information Technology
Founded: 1980
Staff: 50
Products/Services/Areas of Expertise: Designs, supplies, installs & services heating, ventilation & air-conditioning equipment throughout Alberta, the Yukon, & Northwest Territories; the official supplier of Invensys Building Systems, & carrier of the SIEBE, Barber-Colman, & Robertshaw product lines; focus is on energy-efficient solutions & state-of-the-art technologies
Financial Information:
Type of Ownership: Private
Revenue Sources: 100% Private Contracts
Domestic Markets:
Alberta, Northwest Territories, Yukon Territory
Contact(s):
Jim Leahy, CEO
Canadian Branches:
Calgary
#200, 1550 - 8 St. SW
Calgary, AB T2R 1K1

403-508-7797

Avalon Mechanical Consultants Ltd.
#300, 1245 Esquimalt Rd.
Victoria, BC V9A 3P2
250-384-4128
Fax: 250-384-4134
avalon@avalonmechanical.com
www.avalonmechanical.com
Firm Type: Management Consulting, Engineering, Scientific/Technical Services
Founded: 1984
Staff: 12
Member of: American Society of Heating, Refrigerating & Air Conditioning Engineers
Products/Services/Areas of Expertise: Mechanical design for buildings; energy management; indoor air quality; environmental research; energy audits; renewable energy system design. The firm is LEED certified by the U.S. Green Building Counsel. Avalon Energy Management operates as a division
Recently Completed / Ongoing Projects: Defence Construction Canada LEED Design Review (Western Canada); Upper Harbour Place Interiors Project; University of Victoria Engineering Computer Science Building; St. Margaret's School Addition; École Victor Brodeur; The Tillicum Library; Pacific Sport Institute; Nanaimo Fire Station No. 4
Domestic Markets:
British Columbia
Contact(s):
Bob Landell, A.Sc.T., LEED AP, Principal
bob@avalonmechanical.com
Mirek Demidow, M.Sc., P.Eng., Principal

Avani Oxygen Water Corporation
Formerly: Avani Water Corp.
#108, 2419 Bellevue Ave.
West Vancouver, BC V7V 4T4
604-913-2386
Fax: 604-913-2398
marketing@avaniwater.com
www.avaniwater.com
Firm Type: Distributing, Manufacturing
Staff: 50
Products/Services/Areas of Expertise: Water purification process & extra oxygen purified bottled water
Financial Information:
Type of Ownership: Private
Domestic Markets:
Alberta, British Columbia
Foreign Activity:
Asia, China, The Pacific Rim, USA, Vietnam
Markets Sought:
Caribbean, Central America, Western Europe, Mexico

Avensys Inc.
A wholly-owned subsidiary of Avensys Corporation
400, boul Montpellier
Montréal, QC H4N 2G7
514-428-6766
Fax: 514-428-8999
888-965-4700
info@avensys.com
www.avensys.com
Firm Type: Distributing, Manufacturing, Scientific/Technical Services
Founded: 1974
Staff: 115
Products/Services/Areas of Expertise: Leading Canadian distributor of instrumentation & systems for the environmental industry; offers equipment for water, wastewater, groundwater, air quality, atmospheric emission, gas detection, hydrology & meteorology applications; provides cost-effective, customer-driven solutions, high quality products from single instrument to fully integrated & customized systems. Avensys Solutions provides environmental monitoring services (air, water, soil), Avensys Tech is the manufacturing division, & ITF Optical Technologies Inc. is engaged in research & development
Financial Information:
Type of Ownership: Publicly Traded
Revenue: Greater than $5 Million
Domestic Markets:
National
Foreign Activity:
Worldwide
Contact(s):
John G. Fraser, President
Hassan Kassi, M.Sc., Ph.D, COO/President, ITF Labs

Canadian Branches:
Central Canada - Avensys Solutions
422 Consumers Rd.
Toronto, ON M2J 1P8
416-499-4421
Fax: 416-499-0816
888-965-4700
info@avensys.com
Products/Services/Areas of Expertise: Avensys Solutions incorporates Willer Engineering Ltd., which merged with Avensys in March, 2008. Offices in Toronto, Sarnia, Calgary, Abbotsford, & Dartmouth. For the Sarnia office, located at 373 Vidal St., contact David Wheatley, Branch Manager at 888-965-4700 or dweatley@avensys.com
Anup Jain, Area Manager
ajain@avensys.com

Eastern Canada - Avensys Inc.
400, boul Montpellier
Montréal, QC H4N 2G7
514-428-6766
Fax: 514-428-8999
888-965-4700
info@avensys.com
Products/Services/Areas of Expertise: The Montréal office houses Avensys Solutions & Avensys Tech/ITF Labs. For Avensys Tech, contact 888-922-1044. In Atlantic Canada, the Dartmouth office is located at #207, 175 Main St. - contact Jack Daigle, Field Sales Representative, at 888-965-4700 or jdaigle@avensys.com
Pierre Michaud, Vice President, Sales & Marketing
pmichaud@avensys.com

Western Canada - Avensys Solutions
5810 - 2nd St. SW
Calgary, AB T2H 0H2
403-266-1960
Fax: 403-242-6168
888-965-4700
info@avensys.com
Products/Services/Areas of Expertise: For the Abbotsford, BC office located at 33043 Caithness Place, contact John Andersen, Sr. Sales Consultant for BC/Yukon/NWT at 888-965-4700 or jandersent@avensys.com
Tyler Cooper, Sales Representative
tcooper@avensys.com

Avenue Industrial Supply Co. Ltd.
#110, 35 Staples Ave.
Richmond Hill, ON L3B 4W6
905-946-8174
Fax: 800-332-4432
800-267-0588
info@avenuesupply.com
www.avenuesupply.com
Firm Type: Distributing
Founded: 1989
Member of: Canadian Marketing Association; BALPEX
Products/Services/Areas of Expertise: Materials handling, materials storage, spill cleanup & containment, packaging/shipping, shop equipment, dock equipment, safety products, janitorial & maintenance products
Financial Information:
Type of Ownership: Foreign-owned
Revenue: Greater than $5 Million
Domestic Markets:
National
Contact(s):
Nelson Rivers, President
Canadian Branches:
Calgary
110 - 52 Aero Dr. NE
Calgary, AB T2E 8Z9
403-207-3322

Avery Dennison Canada Inc.
Avery Dennison Corporation
1840 Clements Rd.
Pickering, ON L1W 3R8
905-837-4700
Fax: 800-831-2494
800-462-8379
communications@averydennison.com
www.avery.ca
Products/Services/Areas of Expertise: Office and Consumer Products; Pressure sensitive materials; graphic materials;

self-adhesive materials
Ecological Note: Avery paper tags for shipping & identification

Avmor Ltd.
950 rue Michelin
Laval, QC H7L 5C1
450-629-8074
Fax: 450-629-4512
800-387-8074
info@avmor.com
www.avmor.com
Firm Type: Manufacturing
Founded: 1948
Staff: 100
Quality Environmental Management System(s): 9001; ISO
Products/Services/Areas of Expertise: Chemical specialties with emphasis on cleaning & maintenance products; neutralizing & masking agents for water treatment facilities & waste disposal centres
Financial Information:
Type of Ownership: Private
Revenue: Greater than $5 Million
Domestic Markets:
National
Foreign Activity:
Worldwide
Contact(s):
Mattie Chinks, President
mattie@avmor.com
Matt Del Vecchio, Vice-President, Food Service Sales
mdelvecchio@avmor.com

Avoca-tec Environmental Services Inc.
Also Known As: Avoca-tec Energy Management
416-701-1148
avoca@avoca-tec.com
www.avoca-tec.com
Firm Type: Management Consulting, Distributing
Founded: 1993
Staff: 7
Products/Services/Areas of Expertise: The firm assists businesses in finding solutions to critical energy issues, including the reduction of greenhouse gases, & oil & gas consumption; also provides cooling system solutions, & is a technical agent for Scalewatcher (electric de-scaling) & Orival automatic self-cleaning water filters
Recently Completed / Ongoing Projects: Church & Dwight, Canvar Inc., Ville de Montréal; Inco, Sudbury; Enercombustion, Cornwall; Casco Inc., Energy Management Office, Carleton University, Ottawa; Drinking water treatment, Montreal, QC; water treatment lime seal, Granicor Inc.; natural gas reduction, Inco, Sudbury, ON
Financial Information:
Type of Ownership: Private
Revenue: $500,000 - $1.5 Million
Revenue Sources: 10% Provincial; 10% Municipals; 80% Private Contracts
Domestic Markets:
New Brunswick, Nova Scotia, Ontario, Prince Edward Island, Québec
Foreign Activity:
USA
Markets Sought:
Caribbean
Contact(s):
Brent Baiden, President
bbaiden@sympatico.ca
Roger Drouin, P.Eng., Technical Sales
Kami Panahi, B.Sc. (Eng.), Director, Engineering

Canadian Branches:
Ottawa-Carleton, Brockville, Belleville & Guelph
c/o ERM (Energy Resource Management)
665 Poitras St.
Rockland, ON K4K 1M8
Fax: 800-579-1590
877-763-5236
info@erm-gre.com

Aware Learning Technologies
Occu-Med
#1, 75 Bessemer Rd.
London, ON N6E 1P9
519-668-1693
Fax: 519-686-2024
877-552-9273
info@awarelearning.com
awarelearning.com
Firm Type: Management Consulting
Member of: Canadian Society of Safety Engineering; London Chamber of Commerce; Environmental Management Resource for Business
Products/Services/Areas of Expertise: Developer of computer-based training for health & safety; worker's compensation claims management; job/task analysis; accident analysis; WHMIS audits & compliance; TDG compliance; training needs assessments; training in accident prevention for managers & supervisors; joint health & safety committee effectiveness; workplace inspections; accident investigations; self guided kits; hazardous waste management; pollution control/prevention; emergency response planning; customized environmental seminars & workshops
Financial Information:
Type of Ownership: Private
Domestic Markets:
National

AWI
Also Known As: AWI Filter
4450 - 46 Ave. SE
Calgary, AB T2B 3N7
403-255-7377
Fax: 403-255-3129
866-755-7377
info@awifilter.com
www.awifilter.com
Firm Type: Management Consulting, Distributing, Scientific/Technical Services
Founded: 1977
Products/Services/Areas of Expertise: AWI is a leader in water filter optimization, providing cost-effective water filtration services for the water treatment industry to optimize & upgrade their filtration systems; AWI has developed the technical expertise & patented the underdrain systems & components required to economically upgrade municipal & industrial water filtration systems in North America & world-wide. U.S. office located in Sandy, UT

Axford Agencies BC Ltd.
3115 Underhill Ave.
Burnaby, BC V5A 3C8
604-421-7335
Firm Type: Distributing
Founded: 1980
Staff: 10
Products/Services/Areas of Expertise: Water & wastewater management & equipment
Contact(s):
Don Axford

Axion Technologies
Formerly: Pocatec
151, rue du Parc-de-l'Innovation
La Pocatière, QC G0R 1Z0
418-856-1454
Fax: 418-856-5978
www.pocatec.com
Firm Type: Manufacturing
Founded: 1974
Quality Environmental Management System(s): 9001
Products/Services/Areas of Expertise: Measuring & monitoring equipment; communication system for transit service (train, metro, bus, etc); fiberoptics teaching module; traffic light controller; battery charger
Recently Completed / Ongoing Projects: Complete information and entertainment system for Amtrak; Integrated computerized control system for all Walt Disney Monorail train and car operations
Domestic Markets:
National
Foreign Activity:
Western Europe, Mexico, USA
Contact(s):
Carl Cassista, President & CEO
c.cassista@axiontech.ca

Canadian Branches:
Saint-Nicolas
1074, chemin Industriel
Saint-Nicolas, QC G7A 1B3
418-836-0037
Domestic Markets:
National
Foreign Activity:
Western Europe, USA

AXOR Experts-Conseils Inc.
A wholly-owned subsidiary of AXOR Group inc.
1950, rue Sherbrooke ouest, 4e étage
Montréal, QC H3H 1E7
514-846-4000
Fax: 514-846-4005
axor@axor.com
www.axor.com
Firm Type: Engineering
Founded: 1972
Staff: 300
Member of: Association des ingénieurs conseils du Québec; Association of Consulting Engineers of Canada
Products/Services/Areas of Expertise: As the principal subsidary of AXOR Group inc., the firm is engaged in consulting engineering services, principally to the construction industry. With offices in Québec, Western Canada & the UAE, divisions include Côte-Nord region, Environment, Urban Infrastructures, Mechanical & Electrical, Structure & Civil Engineering, Transport & Management/Construction. Expertise in energy, real estate (development, acquisition, financing), & project management. Services in all engineering fields, with consulting in areas such as wastewater treatment, sludge handling & disposal, public works & municpal projects, bridges & viaducts, roads, lighting & hydroelectic power, fire protection, building mechanics, energy efficiency, & process optimization & audits
Recently Completed / Ongoing Projects: Hotel, Pierre-Elliott-Trudeau Int'l Airport; Head Office, Aéroports de Montréal; Lassonde Buildings, École Polytechnique; U.S. Embassy; Le Nordais Wind Farm; Théâtre du Nouveau Monde; Port de Sept-xles; Cairo, Egypt: Gabal el Asfar Wastewater Treatment Plant, Stage 2, Phase 1
Financial Information:
Type of Ownership: Private
Revenue: Greater than $5 Million
Domestic Markets:
Alberta, British Columbia, Québec
Foreign Activity:
Central America, The Middle East, Mexico
Markets Sought:
Africa, The Middle East
Contact(s):
Jacques Grenier, B.eng., M.eng., CEO
Marc-André Desjardins, Ph.D., Vice President, Environment
Yvan Dupont, P.Eng., Chairman

Canadian Branches:
Candiac
#3, 18, rue Papineau
Candiac, QC J5R 5S8
450-444-5384

Sept-xles
#105, 660, boul Laure
Sept-Iles, QC G4R 1X9
418-968-1320
Fax: 418-968-5027
Products/Services/Areas of Expertise: AXOR began in Sept-xles, & this office provides services to the entire Côte-Nord region
Denis Cadaret, Vice President, Côte-Nord

Vancouver
#303, 1847 Broadway St. West
Vancouver, BC V6J 1Y6
604-734-7878
Fax: 604-734-7877

Vaudreuil-Dorion
#100, 155, av St-Charles
Vaudreuil, QC J7V 2K9
450-424-3868

International Branch(es):
Edmonton
James Curry Jefferson Bldg.
11630 - 109th St.
Edmonton, AB T5G 2T8
780-471-3911
Fax: 780-479-8204

AXYS Analytical Services Ltd.
A member company of the AXYS Group of Companies
2045 Mills Rd. W
Sidney, BC V8L 5X2

250-655-5800
Fax: 250-655-5811
888-373-0881
askaxys@axysanalytical.com
www.axysanalytical.com
Firm Type: Scientific/Technical Services
Founded: 1974
Staff: 80
Member of: Seastar Chemicals Inc. (AXYS Group); AXYS Technologies Inc.; AXYS VARILAB s.r.o.
Quality Environmental Management System(s): 17025
Products/Services/Areas of Expertise: A world leader in ultra trace analysis of persistent organic pollutants & emerging organic contaminants, AXYS offers expertise & analysis in a wide range of biological & human matrices, as well as specialty analysis of pesticides, alkanes & hopanes, retinoids & pyrethroids
Recently Completed / Ongoing Projects: Large scale analysis of human blood for organochlorine contamination; analysis of fish tissues for PCB & PBDE concentrations; development of analytical methodology for current use pesticides in collaboration with public research; PPOA/PFOS
Financial Information:
Type of Ownership: Private
Revenue Sources: 10% nationwide; 25% Provincial; 20% Municipals; 45% Private Contracts
Domestic Markets:
National
Foreign Activity:
Australia/New Zealand, China, Central Europe, Western Europe, The Pacific Rim, USA, Vietnam
Markets Sought:
Central America, Mexico,
Contact(s):
Richard Grace, President
rgrace@axys.com
Laurie Phillips, Sales, 250/655-5804
lphillips@axys.com
Coreen Hamilton, Sr. Scientist, 250/655-5802
chamilton@axys.com

Aysix Technologies
#2, 2595 Dunwin Dr.
Mississauga, ON L5L 3N9
Fax: 905-569-6244
800-595-0514
info@aysix.com
www.aysix.com
Products/Services/Areas of Expertise: Water & waste water analytical instrumentation monitoring instruments: dissolved oxygen, total suspended solids, interface level, filter backwash, wastewater samplers, residual chlorine, conductivity, turbidity, dentisy, pH/ORP

Az-Tec Reclaim Ltd.
4901 - 48th St.
Irma, AB T0B 2H0
780-754-2605
Fax: 780-754-2592
az-tec@telus.net
Firm Type: Management Consulting, OTHER
Founded: 1998
Staff: 3
Products/Services/Areas of Expertise: Heavy equipment operators for oil field leases; services include roto splicing, tilling, rock picking, land leveling, mowing, discing, cultivating, reclamation, leased fencing, seeding
Recently Completed / Ongoing Projects: Reclamation of remote sumps; pipeline right of way restoration; lease building
Contact(s):
Larry R. Mark
lrmark@telus.net

Azco Industries Ltd.
#1, 19696 Telegraph Trail
Langley, BC V1M 3E5
604-882-2996
Fax: 604-455-0607
azco@azcozon.com
www.azcozon.com
Firm Type: Engineering, Manufacturing
Founded: 1975
Member of: International Ozone Association; Professional Engineers Association
Products/Services/Areas of Expertise: Discharge ozone generators & support equipment; potable & wastewater treatment; treatment systems for swimming pools, fish farms, municipal drinking water, bottling industries, food processing, medical, air treatment
Financial Information:
Type of Ownership: Private
Domestic Markets:
National
Foreign Activity:
Worldwide
Contact(s):
Leonard Girard, B.Sc., General Manager
Vladimir Stuchlik, M.Sc., P.Eng, Manager

AZZ Blenkhorn & Sawle Limited
A member company of AZZ incorporated
100 Grantham Ave. South
St Catharines, ON L2R 7B9
905-684-9251
Fax: 905-684-3336
800-263-6570
BSLSales@azz.com
www.azz-bsl.com
Firm Type: Distributing, Engineering, Manufacturing
Founded: 1948
Staff: 50
Quality Environmental Management System(s): 9001:2000
Products/Services/Areas of Expertise: Core product lines include: switchgear & controls; modular buildings; & protective relay panels. Solutions for wind energy collector & interconnect substations; integrated power solutions; custom control solutions for nuclear power. Services include: custom fabrication of enclosures (for electrical substations, pumping stations, monitoring stations, generators, water treatment); turnkey electrical equipment solutions incorporating third party equipment; & complete electrical, structural & mechanical engineering services
Domestic Markets:
National
Foreign Activity:
Africa, Asia, Eastern Europe, The Middle East, The Pacific Rim, South America, Mexico, USA, United Kingdom
Contact(s):
Balachandran Ramamoorthy, Manager

B & R Engineering Co. Ltd.
#200, 14 Haas Rd.
Toronto, ON M9W 3A2
416-742-5144
Fax: 416-742-5488
barenco@on.aibn.com
Firm Type: Engineering, Scientific/Technical Services
Founded: 1977
Staff: 16
Products/Services/Areas of Expertise: Engineering consulting services; environmental consulting services
Contact(s):
Bruno Hockmann, P.Eng., President

B.D. Rae Waste Management
#123, 301 Lacewood Dr.
Halifax, NS B3M 4L1
902-452-8181
Fax: 902-445-0126
866-683-7937
info@bdrae.ca
www.bdrae.ca
Firm Type: Engineering, Waste Management
Founded: 1997
Staff: 7
Products/Services/Areas of Expertise: The firm provides recycling services to the restaurant industry in Atlantic Canada; specific focus on fryer oil, donair fat, lard, salad oils, grill grease, bacon fat, rotisserie grease, & margarine & butter
Financial Information:
Type of Ownership: Private
Domestic Markets:
New Brunswick, Newfoundland & Labrador, Nova Scotia, Prince Edward Island
Contact(s):
Brian Doiron, Owner

B.J. Bear Grain Company Ltd.
25 Earl Martin Dr.
Elmira, ON N3B 3L4
519-669-1750
Fax: 519-669-3818
800-545-2736
kgrundy@bjbear.ca
www.bjbear.ca
Products/Services/Areas of Expertise: Food & plant waste for animal feed
Contact(s):
Kyle Grundy, President

Babcock & Wilcox Canada Ltd.
581 Coronation Blvd.
Cambridge, ON N1R 5V3
519-621-2130
Fax: 519-621-9681
www.babcock.com/bwc
Firm Type: Manufacturing
Founded: 1968
Quality Environmental Management System(s): 9001
Products/Services/Areas of Expertise: Scrubbers, alternate energy systems (biomass, wood), power generation, plant retrofits, energy recovery systems
Financial Information:
Type of Ownership: Foreign-owned
Revenue: Greater than $5 Million
Revenue Sources: 100% Private Contracts
Domestic Markets:
National
Foreign Activity:
South America
Contact(s):
Mike Lees, President
Jun Tang, Director, Nuclear Power Sales
jtang@babcock.com
Trevor Reid, Director, Thermal Power Marketing & Sales
ttreid@babcock.com

Canadian Branches:
Calgary
#1020, 444 - 5th Avenue SW
Calgary, AB T2P 2T8
403-461-9719

Melville
P.O. Box 2320
222 Service St., Highway 10 E
Melville, SK S0A 2P0
306-728-3373
Fax: 306-728-3424

Edmonton
17611 - 105 Ave., 1st Fl.
Edmonton, AB T5S 1T1
403-461-9719
Mark Cerny, Regional Manager

Montréal
5592, boul des Rossignols
Laval, QC H7L 5Z1
450-681-3100
Fax: 450-681-8996
Charles Gilbert, District Sales Manager

Saint John
479 Rothesay Ave.
Saint John, NB E2J 2C6
506-633-2880
Fax: 506-633-1353
Tim Hicks, District Sales Manager

Vancouver
#225, 13091 Vanier Place
Richmond, BC V6V 2J1
604-275-4777
Fax: 604-275-6488

Babcock Supply Ltd.
10357 Base Line Road, RR#5
Dresden, ON N0P 1M0
519-683-2696
Fax: 519-683-2548
800-463-7163
bsl@bellnet.ca
www.users.sitewaves.com/index.cfm?page=1090
Firm Type: Distributing, Manufacturing
Founded: 1962
Staff: 5
Member of: Porter's Quality Precast Concrete & Accessories
Products/Services/Areas of Expertise: Tanks; catchbasins; manholes; well tile; septic sewage systems; hydro vaults & transfer pads; custom precast concrete
Contact(s):

Sue Cleland, Contact

Backup-Power.ca
Griffin Chapman Environmental Inc.
#1, 530 Seaman St.
Stoney Creek, ON L8E 3X7
905-257-1119
Fax: 905-257-0119
866-485-4199
info@backup-power.ca
www.backup-power.ca
Firm Type: Manufacturing, Scientific/Technical Services
Founded: 2001
Products/Services/Areas of Expertise: Backup-Power.ca specializes in solar & backup power needs for home & business, including such products as grid-tied, solar power systems & portable backup systems.
Domestic Markets:
National
Foreign Activity:
USA

Bacon Donaldson & Associates Ltd.
12271 Horseshoe Way
Richmond, BC V7A 4V4
604-275-3800
Fax: 604-275-3821
hshoe@comspec.com
Firm Type: Management Consulting, Engineering
Founded: 1972
Staff: 20
Products/Services/Areas of Expertise: Contract research & development; consultation; testing & analysis; collection of reagents: ores, metals, minerals; machinery for extracting precious metals from waste; detoxification of cyanide waste solutions; research & testing in acid mine drainage
Contact(s):
Gerry Sieben, General Manager

Bacta-Pur
Also Known As: IET-Aquaresearch Ltd.
CP 2680
27 Route 143 South
North Hatley, QC J0B 2C0
819-842-2494
Fax: 819-842-2414
877-222-8278
info@bactapur.com
www.bactapur.com
Firm Type: Manufacturing
Founded: 1984
Products/Services/Areas of Expertise: Wastewater treatment, optimization, grease reduction (restaurant & sewage); water body restoration; sludge digestion; ammonia control; hydrocarbon biodegradation.
Recently Completed / Ongoing Projects: Bacta-Pur System of bioaugumentation products & ecological engineering equipment: biofilters Bacta-Pur Ecofiltres & Bacta-Pur Bactivators; ongoing grease control in sewers, restaurants/hotels; reduction of sludge in average lagoons; the Bacta-Pur System has been used for water filtering by the Giant Panda Institue, Chengdu, China, by the Karachi Golf Club, Pakistan, and by a certified environmental farm in British Columbia
Financial Information:
Type of Ownership: Private
Revenue: $1.5 Million - $3 Million
Revenue Sources: 5% Municipals; 95% Private Contracts
Domestic Markets:
British Columbia, Manitoba, New Brunswick, Nova Scotia, Ontario, Québec
Foreign Activity:
Africa, Asia, China, Western Europe, USA, Vietnam
Contact(s):
Marie-Claude Cantin, Ph.D., President/CEO
Karl F. Ehrlich, Ph.D., Vice-President

International Branch(es):
Pakistan Office
International Water Associates Pakistan
138 G1 Block Johar Town
Lahore Pakistan
42-529-0859-60
sales@bactapur.com.pk

BAE Newplan Group Ltd.
A division of SNC-Lavalin Inc.
1133 Topsail Rd.
Mount Pearl, NL A1N 5G2
709-368-0118
Fax: 709-368-3541
bassem.eid@snclavalin.com
www.snclavalin.com
Firm Type: Engineering
Staff: 40
Quality Environmental Management System(s): 9001
Products/Services/Areas of Expertise: Full service environmental engineering firm; specializes in environmental auditing & engineering, impact assessments, coastal zone management, waste management. Services in municipal infrastructure, ports & marine environments, fisheries, civil engineering, structural engineering, mechanical & electrical, mining, oil & gas, hydroelectric power development, & project/construction management
Recently Completed / Ongoing Projects: Mine/mill project, Voisey's Bay; environmental services & engineering, Town of Stephenville; flood, emergency assessment (environmental & engineering) Town of Conception Bay; south waste water treatment plant (2-year program)
Financial Information:
Type of Ownership: Publicly Traded
Revenue: Greater than $5 Million
Revenue Sources: 10% nationwide; 30% Provincial; 30% Municipals; 30% Private Contracts
Domestic Markets:
National
Contact(s):
Albert Williams, CEO
albert.williams@snclavalin.com
Bassem Eid, Vice President, Ports/Marine & Environment
bassem.eid@snclavalin.com
Rennie Hypes, Manager, Environmental
rennie.hypes@snclavalin.com

Ballard Power Systems Inc.
9000 Glenlyon Pkwy.
Burnaby, BC V5J 5J8
604-454-0900
Fax: 604-412-4700
marketing@ballard.com
www.ballard.com
Firm Type: Manufacturing
Founded: 1979
Quality Environmental Management System(s): 9001
Products/Services/Areas of Expertise: Developing, manufacturing & marketing zero-emission proton exchange membrane (PEM) fuel cells for use in transportation application & fuel cell systems for portable & stationary products ranging from 1 kilowatt to 250 kilowatts; commercializes electric drives for fuel cell & other electric vehicles, power conversion products for fuel cells, natural gas & hydrogen generator sets & other distributed generation products; is a Tier 1 automotive supplier of friction materials for power train components; proprietary technology is enabling automobile, bus, electrical equipment, portable power & stationary product manufacturers to develop environmentally clean products for sale; has manufacutring facilities in Burnaby, BC and Lowell, MA, USA
Financial Information:
Type of Ownership: Publicly Traded
Revenue: Greater than $5 Million
Revenue Sources: 21% nationwide; 79% Private Contracts
Domestic Markets:
British Columbia
Foreign Activity:
Asia, Central Europe, Western Europe, The Pacific Rim, USA
Contact(s):
John Sheridan, President/CEO
Paul Cass, Vice-President, Operations
Bruce Cousins, Vice-President/CFO

Bancroft Light & Power Company (2000) Ltd.
#18, 156 Duncan Mill Rd.
Toronto, ON M3B 3N2
416-386-0299
Fax: 416-386-0620
michael.mcleod@rcscanada.ca
Products/Services/Areas of Expertise: Company is engaged in a project to bring hydroelectric power to the Bancroft area
Ecological Note: Power producer
Domestic Markets:
Ontario

Contact(s):
Michael McLeod, President

Bancroft Western Sales Ltd.
1038 West 3rd St.
North Vancouver, BC V7P 3J6
604-984-4558
Fax: 604-984-6892
bws@bancroftwestern.com
www.bancroftwestern.com
Firm Type: Distributing
Founded: 1971
Products/Services/Areas of Expertise: Distributor of manufacturing machinery & parts to the mining, & pulp & paper industries
Contact(s):
Lee G. Bancroft, Executive Manager

Banyan Chains Inc.
Banyan Chaînes
350, boul Ford, Local 140-150
Châteauguay, QC J6J 4Z2
450-692-7337
Fax: 450-692-5778
877-366-2550
banyanchaines.qc.aira.com
www.banyanchaines.com
Firm Type: Distributing, Manufacturing
Founded: 1982
Staff: 11
Member of: Ontario Pollution Control Equipment Association
Products/Services/Areas of Expertise: Distributor of chains in various materials for diverse uses, and crushers, solid waste shredders, wood hogs, vibrating feeders & conveyors, new & rebuilt, along with parts & service; manufacturer of fabricated steel chain sprockets in a variety of styles
Domestic Markets:
New Brunswick, Newfoundland & Labrador, Nova Scotia, Ontario, Prince Edward Island, Québec
Contact(s):
A.R. Smith, President/CEO
Gerry Moriarty, Sales

Barenco Inc.
P.O. Box 295
#202, 2561 Stouffville Rd.
Gormley, ON L0H 1G0
905-887-6661
Fax: 905-887-1999
barenco@barenco.ca
www.barenco.ca
Firm Type: Management Consulting, Engineering, Scientific/Technical Services
Founded: 1987
Staff: 30
Member of: Professional Engineers of Ontario; Association of Professional Geoscientists of Ontario
Products/Services/Areas of Expertise: Environmental site assessment, risk assessment & audits; soil & groundwater sampling; underground storage tank testing & removal; site remediation & decommissioning; waste disposal & treatment; indoor/ambient air sampling; pollution control systems; advice & consulting; liaison with regulatory agencies; environmental contracting; environmental forensics; research & development
Recently Completed / Ongoing Projects: Site remediation, bioremediation, oil company; tank farm upgrade, chemical manufacturer; risk assessment, former retail petroleum site; decommissioning, former pharmaceutical manufacturer's property for residential re-development; site specific risk assessment, Brownfield redevelopment, former manufacturing facilities
Financial Information:
Type of Ownership: Private
Domestic Markets:
Manitoba, New Brunswick, Newfoundland & Labrador, Nova Scotia, Northwest Territories, Ontario, Prince Edward Island, Yukon Territory
Contact(s):
Jim Phimister, President/CEO

Barrat & Associates Inc.
#207, 1425 Marine Dr.
West Vancouver, BC V7T 1B9
604-922-4061
Fax: 604-987-3394

Firm Type: Management Consulting, Scientific/Technical Services
Member of: Canadian Environment Industry Association
Products/Services/Areas of Expertise: Provides air quality assessment services, environmental audits, public participation, education & awareness, & R&D; curriculum development for environmental sciences programs
Contact(s):
Olga Barrat, Ph.D., Principal

Barrett Sales Ltd.
96 Stanley St.
Saint John, NB E2K 3Y4
506-693-8630
Fax: 506-642-6499
Products/Services/Areas of Expertise: Plumbing equipment
Contact(s):
Fred Barrett, Contact

Canadian Branches:
Dieppe
357, rue Grande Vallée
Dieppe, NB E1A 6G5
506-854-3401

Barrington Environmental Services
An operating division of J.D. Irving, Limited
Formerly: Quantex Technologies Inc.25 Akerley Blvd.
Dartmouth, NS B3B 1J7
902-468-8848
Fax: 902-468-8767
lachevrotiere.andre@barringtonis.com
www.jdirving.com
Firm Type: Waste Management
Founded: 1991
Staff: 20
Quality Environmental Management System(s): 14001
Products/Services/Areas of Expertise: The firm offers industrial waste disposal solutions, specialty chemicals & technical consultation. Services include waste collection & management, & related transportation, recycling & disposal of liquid & solid industrial waste & used oil; waste water treatment, tanker cleaning, environmental monitoring, lab services, Frac Tank rentals, & hazardous waste management. Facilities located in Saint John & Halifax. Barrington Industrial Services Ltd. is a sister company
Financial Information:
Type of Ownership: Private
Revenue Sources: 30% nationwide; 10% Provincial; 60% Private Contracts
Domestic Markets:
New Brunswick, Newfoundland & Labrador, Nova Scotia, Prince Edward Island
Contact(s):
Sid Hales, Manager, Marketing

Barrington Industrial Services Limited
An operating unit of J.D. Irving, Limited
Formerly: Irving EquipmentP.O. Box 3400 B
720 Grandview Ave.
Saint John, NB E2M 4X9
506-635-5600
Fax: 506-632-4474
stewart.clint@barringtonis.com
www.jdirving.com
Firm Type: Waste Management
Founded: 1985
Staff: 120
Member of: Water Jet Technology Association; National Oil Recyclers Association
Quality Environmental Management System(s): 14001
Products/Services/Areas of Expertise: Broad range of industrial cleaning, pumping & waste management services in used oil, oily wastes & solid waste; technical consulting; solid waste management; hazardous waste management; diving/dredging; emergency response. Barrington Environmental Services is a sister company
Financial Information:
Type of Ownership: Private
Revenue Sources: 5% Provincial; 5% Municipals; 90% Private Contracts
Domestic Markets:
New Brunswick, Newfoundland & Labrador, Nova Scotia, Prince Edward Island, Québec,
Contact(s):
Clint Stewart, P.Eng., General Manager
Roger N. Cyr, General Manager, Equipment Division

Ron Roy, P.Eng., Operations Manager
Canadian Branches:
Halifax
P.O. Box 8684 A
Halifax, NS B3K 5M4
902-494-5890
Fax: 902-494-5224
André Lachevrotière, Operations Manager

Newcastle
P.O. Box 128
119 King George Hwy.
Miramichi, NB E1V 3M3
506-622-3310
Fax: 506-622-0978
Darwin Vickers, Operations Supervisor

International Branch(es):
Maine
Operations
154 Hildreth St. North
Bangor, ME USA
207-945-3299
Fax: 207-945-4099
Tracy Cook, Manager

Bartle & Gibson Co. Ltd.
13475 Fort Rd. NW
Edmonton, AB T5A 1C6
780-472-2850
Fax: 780-476-6686
800-661-5615
bartle@bartlegibson.com
www.bartlegibson.com
Firm Type: Distributing
Founded: 1946
Staff: 350
Products/Services/Areas of Expertise: Water treatment systems & equipment; water purification systems & equipment; water conservation equipment; energy-efficient equipment
Financial Information:
Type of Ownership: Private
Domestic Markets:
British Columbia, Northwest Territories, Yukon Territory
Contact(s):
Robert Whitty, President, Alberta
Reg Wong, Manager, Edmonton - North Side

Canadian Branches:
Airdrie
Bay #4, 220 East Lake Blvd.
Airdrie, AB T4A 2G2
403-945-9481
Fax: 403-945-9487
Andrea Bird, Manager

Barrhead
P.O. Box 4439
6128 - 46 St.
Barrhead, AB T7N 1A3
780-674-4255
Fax: 780-674-2833
Jordan Tiggelaar, Manager

Calgary
4300 - 21st St. NE
Calgary, AB T2E 9A6
403-291-1099
Fax: 403-291-2849
David Descoteau, Manager

Calgary - South Side
5729 - Burbank Rd. SE
Calgary, AB T2H 1Z5
403-216-6717
Fax: 403-252-6881
Rick March, Manager

Edmonton - Jasper Place
10045 - 158 St.
Edmonton, AB T5P 0H8
780-483-1411
Fax: 780-486-0814
Barry Smereka, Manager

Edmonton - South Side
6724 - 59th St. NW
Edmonton, AB T6B 3N6
780-437-7767
Fax: 780-437-6319

Shane Edwards, Manager
Edson
4508 - 2nd Ave.
Edson, AB T7E 1C1
780-723-6180
Fax: 780-723-7493
Dwight Cooke, Manager

Fort McMurray
8224 Fraser Ave.
Fort McMurray, AB T9H 1W8
780-743-4476
Fax: 780-791-6616
Sean Powers, Manager

Hinton
P.O. Box 6008
121 Scott St.
Hinton, AB T4V 1H2
780-865-4800
Fax: 780-865-7900
Ken Alexander, Manager

Lethbridge
3760 - 18th Ave. North
Lethbridge, AB T1H 5S7
403-320-0411
Fax: 403-320-7313
Bruce Topolnisky, Manager

Lloydminster
5203 - 62nd St.
Lloydminster, AB T9V 2E3
780-875-2683
Fax: 780-875-8978
Greg Mynzak, Manager

Medicine Hat
2021 - 10 Ave. SW
Medicine Hat, AB T1A 8B7
403-527-3565
Fax: 403-526-8164
John Langill, Manager

Peace River
9909 - 96 Ave.
Peace River, AB T8S 1H5
780-624-4050
Fax: 780-624-1110
Jim Picard, Manager

Spruce Grove
P.O. Box 4281
50 Oswald Dr.
Spruce Grove, AB T7X 3B4
780-962-4891
Fax: 780-962-0878
Scott Leishman, Manager

Wetaskiwin
#102, 4509 - 49 St.
Wetaskiwin, AB T9A 1H1
780-352-3722
Fax: 780-352-8407
Matt Keating, Manager

Yellowknife
4003 School Draw Ave.
Yellowknife, NT X1A 2T9
867-920-2248
Fax: 867-873-5730
salesywk@bartlegibson.com
Wade Makaro, Manager

Bartley Silver Co. Inc.
104 Westbury Ave.
London, ON N6J 3G1
519-686-0321
Firm Type: Manufacturing, Scientific/Technical Services
Founded: 1969
Staff: 4
Products/Services/Areas of Expertise: Electrolytic silver recovery equipment; silver recovery from photographic solutions
Financial Information:
Type of Ownership: Private
Revenue Sources: 100% Private Contracts
Domestic Markets:
Ontario
Contact(s):
Peter C. Bartley, President/CEO

BASF Canada Inc.
a subsidiary of BASF SE
100 Milverton Dr., 5th Fl.
Mississauga, ON L5R 4H1
289-360-1300
Fax: 289-360-6000
866-485-2273
www2.basf.us/basf-canada
Firm Type: Distributing, Manufacturing, Waste Management
Staff: 500
Member of: BASF Corporation
Quality Environmental Management System(s): 9001; 9002
Products/Services/Areas of Expertise: With sales offices across Canada & plant facilities in Blackie, Nisku, Brampton, Cornwall, Toronto, Smith Falls, Windsor, Saint-Léonard & Montréal, the firm provides solutions & quality products which include agricultural & nutrition products, chemicals, plastics, performance products & fine chemicals. Sustainable practices, such as management of wastes, & health & safety are emphasized; the company supports the Chemistry Industry Association of Canada's Responsible Care initiative, a program which ensures ecology & safety values as a priority in operations
Financial Information:
Type of Ownership: Publicly Traded
Contact(s):
Laurent Tainturier, President

Bass Engineering Systems Technology
P.O. Box 1123
Squamish, BC V8B 0A8
604-898-9395
basshome@uniserve.com
Products/Services/Areas of Expertise: Offers services in the following areas: forestry planning, terrain stability, hydrology, road design & environmental issues
Contact(s):
Jim Bass, President

Bayer CropScience / BCS
#200, 160 Quarry Park Blvd. SE
Calgary, AB T2C 3G3
403-723-7400
888-283-6847
askUS@Bayercropscience.ca
www.bayercropscience.ca
Firm Type: Scientific/Technical Services
Member of: CropLife Canada
Products/Services/Areas of Expertise: Markets and develops fungicides, herbicides, insecticides and seed treatment; markets hybrid canola; locations include seed-processing, seed-breeding and formulation facilities
Domestic Markets:
Alberta, British Columbia, Ontario, Saskatchewan
Contact(s):
Derrick Rozdeba, Manager, Integrated Communications, 403-723-7432
derrick.rozdeba@bayercropscience.com

Canadian Branches:
Abbotsford
6 - 2303 Windsor St.
Abbotsford, BC V2T 6M1
604-859-3187

Airdrie
1419 Thorburn Dr. SE
Airdrie, AB T4A 2C4
403-948-0680

Guelph
160 Research Lane
Guelph, ON N1G 5B2
519-767-3366

Kamloops
912 Laval Cres.
Kamloops, BC V2C 5P5
250-377-4159

Lethbridge
3106 - 9 Ave. N
Lethbridge, AB T1H 5E5
403-329-0706

Lethbridge, Seed Plant
2-3904 - 62 Ave. N
Lethbridge, AB T1H 6P3
403-331-3377

Ottawa
1125 Colonel By Dr.
Ottawa, ON K1S 5B6
613-722-8111

Saskatoon
334 Packham Ave.
Saskatoon, SK S7N 2T1
306-373-0701

Winnipeg
430B Dovercourt Dr.
Winnipeg, MB R3Y 1N4
204-989-5432

Bayer Inc.
77 Belfield Rd.
Toronto, ON M9W 1G6
416-248-0771
800-622-2937
contactbayer@bayer.com
www.bayer.ca
Firm Type: Waste Management
Staff: 1000
Products/Services/Areas of Expertise: Develops and manufacutres a variety of products related to human and animal health; markets pharmaceuticals and self-test diagnostic devices and monitors
Contact(s):
Phil Blake, President/CEO
Ute Bockstegers, Chief Financial Officer/Head, Business Administration and Partnering
Shurjeel Choudhri, Senior Vice-Presdient/Head, Medical and Scientific Affairs
Stefan Freeman, Head, Animal Health

Baymag Inc.
A member company of The Refratechnik Group
#800, 10655 Southport Rd. SW
Calgary, AB T2W 4Y1
403-271-9400
Fax: 403-271-0010
sales@baymag.com
www.baymag.com
Firm Type: Distributing, Manufacturing
Founded: 1982
Staff: 80
Quality Environmental Management System(s): 9001
Products/Services/Areas of Expertise: The firm is a leading producer of high grade magnesium oxide, used in a variety of industrial, agricultural & environmental applications, including waste & waste water treatment, soil remediation, solids settling & sludge reduction, heavy metals removal, & flue gas desulphurization
Domestic Markets:
National
Foreign Activity:
Africa, Asia, Australia/New Zealand, Western Europe, South America, USA
Markets Sought:
The Pacific Rim
Canadian Branches:
Exshaw II
Gap Lake
Exshaw, AB T0L 2C0
403-673-3790
Fax: 403-673-3825

BC Air Filter Ltd.
2809 Norland Ave.
Burnaby, BC V5B 3A9
604-291-2544
Fax: 888-291-2510
888-291-2546
sales@bcairfilter.com
www.bcairfilter.com
Firm Type: Distributing, Manufacturing
Founded: 1967
Member of: National Air Filter Association
Products/Services/Areas of Expertise: Heating; ventilation, air conditioning; filtration materials
Financial Information:
Type of Ownership: Private
Revenue Sources: 10% nationwide; 10% Provincial; 10% Municipals; 70% Private Contracts
Domestic Markets:
Alberta, British Columbia
Contact(s):
Ray Riopel, Director, Sales and Marketing, 604-671-5808
John Bishop, Branch Manager, 250-718-0841
Canadian Branches:
Kelowna
#106, 2955 Acland Rd.
Kelowna, BC V1X 7X2
250-765-6980
Fax: 250-765-6981
bcakelowna@bcairfilter.com
Domestic Markets:
Alberta, British Columbia

BC Hydro
Environmental Strategy
6911 Southpoint Dr.
Burnaby, BC V3N 4X8
604-224-9376
Fax: 604-528-3137
800-224-9376
www.bchydro.com/environment
Products/Services/Areas of Expertise: BC Hydro aims to become a leading sustainable energy company by producing & delivering electricity in environmentally & socially responsible ways
Ecological Note: Hydro & wind energy producer
Domestic Markets:
British Columbia
Contact(s):
Brenda Goehring, Manager, Environmental Strategy
Ray Stewart, Chief Officer, Safety, Health, and Environment

BCHazman Management Ltd.
9357 Maryland Dr.
Sidney, BC V8L 2R4
250-656-4619
Fax: 250-656-3382
877-326-2832
info@bchazmat.com
www.bchazmat.com
Products/Services/Areas of Expertise: Consulting services; Hazardous materials handling & storage; safety consulting services & training; ISO 14000 Auditing
Domestic Markets:
British Columbia
Contact(s):
David Rogers, President/Founder

BCL Landview Systems Inc. / BCL
Also Known As: Landview Systems
Barlott Consulting Ltd.
#600, 10665 Jasper Ave.
Edmonton, AB T5J 3S9
780-448-7476
Fax: 780-421-1270
800-616-9401
mail@landview.com
www.landview.com
Firm Type: Scientific/Technical Services
Founded: 1989
Products/Services/Areas of Expertise: Soil conservation; water management; agricultural engineering; energy; environmental studies; project management; feasibility studies; program development; strategic & operation planning program; policy evaluation; research technology; mapping & decision support systems
Contact(s):
Paul J. Barlott, President

BDM Supply Limited
6810 - 68 Ave. NW
Edmonton, AB T6B 3C5
780-465-2200
Fax: 780-465-5318
888-434-6113

BDR Machinery Ltd.
4580 Eastgate Pkwy.
Mississauga, ON L4W 4K4
905-625-9236
Fax: 905-625-6437
sales@bdrmachinery.com
www.brunetteindustries.com
Firm Type: Distributing
Founded: 1980
Staff: 5

Products & Services Buyer's Guide

Products/Services/Areas of Expertise: This is the Eastern Canada Office of Brunette Industries Ltd., manufactuer & distributor of equipment for the forestry industry: wood & bark equipment: chipping, grinding & screening equipment, debarkers, electronic log sweeps, reclaimers, uni-log feeders, singulators; Brunette also offers a machine shop, & parts & service
Financial Information:
Type of Ownership: Private
Revenue Sources: 100% Private Contracts
Domestic Markets:
Manitoba, New Brunswick, Newfoundland & Labrador, Nova Scotia, Ontario, Prince Edward Island, Québec
Contact(s):
Christer Eyram, President
christer@bdrmachinery.com

BDS Laboratories
Northern Bank Bldg.
P.O. Box 363
13 Qu'Appelle St.
Qu'Appelle, SK S0G 4A0
306-699-2679
Fax: 306-699-7190
888-237-5227
bds.laboratories@sasktel.net
www.bdslabs.com
Firm Type: Scientific/Technical Services
Member of: AOAC International, American Society for Microbiology (ASM), Society of Industrial Microbiology (SIM), Mycological Society of America (MSA), Saskatchewan Food Processors Association, Saskatchewan Meat Processors Association and the Saskatchewan Environmental & Industrial Managers Association (SEIMA)
Products/Services/Areas of Expertise: Offers analytical services, including microbial, toxin, biochemical and testing
Domestic Markets:
Saskatchewan
Contact(s):
John Blachford, Manager, Chemistry

Beasy Nicoll Engineering Ltd.
80 Eileen Stubbs Ave.
Dartmouth, NS B3B 1Y6
902-468-4740
Fax: 902-468-1908
Firm Type: Engineering, Scientific/Technical Services
Founded: 1976
Staff: 18
Products/Services/Areas of Expertise: Environmental & municipal services, including environmental protection, site development, sludge handling, solid & hazardous waste management & water & pollution control facilities; industrial services, including plans & designs for industrial parks, building modifications & structural investigations
Contact(s):
Murray Nicoll, P.Eng., Contact

Beaulier Inc.
#203, 1400, rue Marie-Victorin
St-Bruno-de-Montarville, QC J3V 6B9
450-441-9100, poste 2206
Fax: 450-441-9113
info@beaulier.qc.ca
www.beaulier.qc.ca
Firm Type: Engineering
Founded: 1978
Staff: 15
Products/Services/Areas of Expertise: A consulting engineering firm in the fields of industrial ventilation,, dust control, fire and explosion prevention in such industrial sectors as metallurgy, mines, quarries, composite materials, flexography, rubber transformation, sawmills, etc.
Financial Information:
Type of Ownership: Private
Revenue: $500,000 - $1.5 Million
Revenue Sources: 10% Provincial; 90% Private Contracts
Domestic Markets:
Québec
Foreign Activity:
USA
Markets Sought:
Central America, South America, Mexico
Contact(s):
Hugues Châteauneuf, ing., President
Maurice Beaudet, Sr. Group Engineer
m.beaudet@beaulier.qc.ca

Bebbington Industries
44 Wright Ave.
Dartmouth, NS B3B 1G6
902-468-8180
Fax: 902-468-8559
800-280-6667
info@bebbingtonindustries.com
www.bebbingtonindustries.com
Firm Type: Distributing, Manufacturing
Founded: 1992
Staff: 11
Quality Environmental Management System(s): 9001
EcoLogo Certified Products & Services: Down East home cleaning products: All Purpose Cleaner; Liquid Laundry Detergent; marine products: Bilge Cleaner; General Purpose Marine Cleaner; Green Knight cleaning products for janitorial, marine & industrial applications: Degreaser; Degreaser GK-501
Products/Services/Areas of Expertise: The firm manufactures & distributes environmentally friendly cleaning products for residential, industrial, healthcare & commercial settings; products include the Down East, & Green Knight lines
Ecological Note: Down East home cleaning products: All Purpose Cleaner; Liquid Laundry Detergent; marine products: Bilge Cleaner; General Purpose Marine Cleaner; Green Knight cleaning products for janitorial, marine & industrial applications: Degreaser; Degreaser GK-501
Contact(s):
Tony Bebbington, CEO

BECK Drilling and Environmental Services Ltd.
A subsidiary of HAZCO Environmental & Decommissioning Services
9919 Shepard Rd. SE
Calgary, AB T2C 3C5
403-297-1399
Fax: 403-297-1390
800-561-3482
beck@beckdrill.com
www.beckdrill.com
Firm Type: Engineering, Scientific/Technical Services
Founded: 1977
Staff: 100
Products/Services/Areas of Expertise: Provides geotechnical, environmental & geological coring services to clients in the environmental consulting, mining, engineering, property development & oil & gas industries
Domestic Markets:
Alberta, British Columbia, Ontario, Yukon Territory
Contact(s):
Garry Wegleitner, President
garry@beckdrill.com

Canadian Branches:
Edmonton
12311 - 17th St. NE
Edmonton, AB T6S 1A7
780-443-6272
Brian Louden, Edmonton Area Manager
blouden@hazco.com

Vancouver Corporate Office
13511 Vulcan Way.
Richmond, BC V6V 1K4
604-214-7007
Fax: 604-214-7017
Scott Pretty, Operations Manager
spretty@hazco.com

Beckie Hydrogeologists (1990) Ltd.
381B Park St.
Regina, SK S4N 5B2
306-721-0846
Fax: 306-721-7729
Firm Type: Engineering, Scientific/Technical Services
Founded: 1976
Products/Services/Areas of Expertise: Environmental audits & impact statements; disposal wells; modelling systems

Becquerel Laboratories Inc.
#4, 6790 Kitimat Rd.
Mississauga, ON L5N 5L9
905-826-3080
Fax: 905-826-4151
877-726-3080
info@becquerellabs.com
www.becquerellabs.com
Firm Type: Scientific/Technical Services
Founded: 1982
Staff: 7
Quality Environmental Management System(s): 17025
Products/Services/Areas of Expertise: Expertise in neutron activation analysis & radiological analysis; customized analysis for high-purity quartz, coal, diamonds & plasticsd; laboratory analysis for radionuclides; trace element analysis; analysis for naturally occurring radioactive material (NORM)
Financial Information:
Type of Ownership: Private
Domestic Markets:
National
Foreign Activity:
USA,
Contact(s):
Steven Simpson, B.Sc., MBA, President/Quality Assurance Manager
ssimpson@becquerellabs.com
D. Craig Stuart, Ph.D., Senior Scientist, Neutron Activcation Analysis
cstuart@becquerellabs.com

Bedard Tankers Inc.
Compagnie Citernes Bedard Inc.
Formerly: Eco Kool Technologies Inc.
5785, Place Turcot
Montréal, QC H4C 1V9
514-937-1670
Fax: 514-937-2190
btinc@aei.org
www.bedardtankers.com
Firm Type: Manufacturing
Founded: 1966
Products/Services/Areas of Expertise: Manufacturer & distributor of liquid, dry bulk, liquified compressed gases, & cryogenic tanker trailers; services include complete repair, testing & parts service; state-of-the-art facilities & the highest manufacturing standards
Financial Information:
Type of Ownership: Private
Contact(s):
Nabil Attirgi, President
nattirgi@bedardtankers.com

Behrick Enterprises Inc.
4215 - 24 Ave.
Vernon, BC V1T 1M1
250-549-1497
Fax: 250-549-7272
behrick@telus.net
Firm Type: Distributing, Manufacturing
Founded: 1977
Staff: 4
Products/Services/Areas of Expertise: Self-regenerating air dryers for ozonators; ultraviolet water sterilizers of polyvinyl chloride; water & air treatment equipment
Financial Information:
Type of Ownership: Private
Revenue Sources: 10% Municipals; 90% Private Contracts
Domestic Markets:
Alberta, British Columbia, Ontario, Québec, Saskatchewan, Yukon Territory
Foreign Activity:
South Africa, USA, United Kingdom
Contact(s):
David A. Behrick, President

Belfab Inc.
Pyradia Inc.
430, boul Guimond
Longueuil, QC J4G 1P8
450-463-3344
Fax: 450-463-3252
sales@belfab.net
www.belfab.net
Firm Type: Manufacturing
Founded: 1973
Quality Environmental Management System(s): 9001:2000
Products/Services/Areas of Expertise: Designs and manufactures air filtration equipment; air pollution control equipment; dust collectors
Contact(s):
Mario Bouthillier, Vice-President

Bema Co. Ltd.
Also Known As: 277033 Ontario
#200, 20 Lake St.
St Catharines, ON L2R 5W7

905-984-6677
Fax: 905-984-6684
Firm Type: Waste Management
Staff: 4
Products/Services/Areas of Expertise: Chemical brokering of industrial by-products; the firm handles petroleum coke, coal tar, oxides, glycols, fumed silica, & heat transfer fluids
Foreign Activity:
USA
Contact(s):
Michael Bates, President
J. Bates, Vice President
Y. MacNamara, Sales Coordinator
G. Lodick, Environment Coordinator

Bémalux Inc.
3080, rue de Baene
Montréal, QC H4S 1K7
514-337-2770
Fax: 514-332-0132
800-361-1939
Products/Services/Areas of Expertise: Geosynthetic liners
Contact(s):
Jules Blais, President

Canadian Branches:
Environmental Division
#27, 35 Waterman Ave.
London, ON N6C 5T3
519-680-2054
Fax: 519-680-2054
1-800-361-1939
John Jory, Contact

International Branch(es):
Colloid Environmental Technologies Company
1500 West Shure Dr.
Arlington Heights, IL USA
708-392-5800
Fax: 708-506-6150

Benjamin Moore & Co. Ltd
#100, 7070 Mississauga Rd.
Toronto, ON L5N 5M8
905-813-3700
Fax: 905-813-3704
800-387-8790
info@benjaminmoore.ca
www.benjaminmoore.ca
Firm Type: Distributing, Manufacturing
Founded: 1906
Staff: 275
EcoLogo Certified Products & Services: Complete range of interior & exterior paints
Products/Services/Areas of Expertise: Develops and markets EcoLogo-certified paints & surface coatings with low volatile organic compound (VOC) formulation; retailers can be found across the country
Ecological Note: Complete range of interior & exterior paints
Domestic Markets:
National,
Contact(s):
Mike Kolind, General Manager, Central Canada, Marketing
Mark Hodge, General Manager, Western Canada, Marketing
Richard Tremblay, General Manager, Eastern Canada, Marketing

Bennett Environmental Inc. / BEI
#208, 1540 Cornwall Rd.
Oakville, ON L6J 7W5
905-339-1540
Fax: 905-339-0016
800-386-1388
info@bennettenv.com
www.bennettenv.com
Firm Type: Waste Management
Founded: 1991
Member of: Canadian Environment Industry Association
Quality Environmental Management System(s): 14001:2004
Products/Services/Areas of Expertise: High temperature treatment services for the remediation of contaminated soil; thermal solutions to contamination problems in Canada & U.S.
Recently Completed / Ongoing Projects: Canada federal remediation projects; US EPA remediation projects; private responsible partied remediation projects
Financial Information:
Type of Ownership: Publicly Traded
Revenue: Greater than $5 Million
Revenue Sources: 35% nationwide; 35% Provincial; 30% Private Contracts
Domestic Markets:
National
Foreign Activity:
Caribbean, Central America, Mexico, USA
Contact(s):
Jack Shaw, President & CEO
Fred Cranston, Chief Financial Officer
Wendy Ford, Corporate Controller
Contact(s):
Jean Pierre Bouchard, Plant Manager

Canadian Branches:
St-Ambroise
Also Known As: Récupère Sol Inc. (RCI)
80, rue des Mélèzes
Saint-Ambroise, QC G7P 2N4
418-695-3302
Fax: 418-695-3303
rsi@videotron.com

Benson Chemicals Limited
RR#1
Freelton, ON L0R 1K0
905-659-3351
Fax: 905-659-1689
800-265-0014
info@bensonchemicals.ca
www.bensonchemicals.ca
Firm Type: Distributing
Founded: 1956
Staff: 22
Member of: Canadian Association of Chemical Distributors; Ontario Trucking Association
Quality Environmental Management System(s): 14001
Products/Services/Areas of Expertise: A distributor of acids & alkalines: hydrochloric acid, muriatic acid, nitric acid, potassium hydroxide, sodium hydroxide, sulphuric acid, & phosphoric acid. Market includes industrial & commercial clients. Services include intallation, maintenance & monitoring of clients' storage tank systems, seminars on safe chemical handling & storage, & emergency response to chemical events/spills
Financial Information:
Type of Ownership: Private
Revenue Sources: 100% Private Contracts
Domestic Markets:
Ontario
Contact(s):
Randy Wagenaar, Sales Representative
r.wagenaar@bensonchemicals.ca

Bentofix Technologies Inc.
Formerly: GSE Lining Technology (Canada) Ltd.)
23 Truman Rd.
Barrie, ON L4M 3V7
705-725-1938
Fax: 705-725-8860
eenglish@gseworld.com
www.gseworld.com
Firm Type: Manufacturing
Founded: 1973
Staff: 40
Products/Services/Areas of Expertise: Manufactures & installs liner products including geomembranes, geosynthetic clay liners, geonets, geocomposites & concrete protection products
Financial Information:
Type of Ownership: Foreign-owned
Revenue Sources: 5% nationwide; 5% Provincial; 10% Municipals; 80% Private Contracts
Domestic Markets:
National
Foreign Activity:
Worldwide
Contact(s):
Ernest C. English, President
Scott Lucas, Vice-President

Bercan Environmental Resources Inc.
Formerly: Canber Industries Ltd.
P.O. Box 238
6645 Elm Rd.
Lantzville, BC V0R 2H0
250-390-3113
Fax: 250-390-2312
candlshb@cadvision.com
Firm Type: Manufacturing
Founded: 1979
Staff: 2
Products/Services/Areas of Expertise: Develops anaerobic & aerobic facultative bio-remediation technology, anarobic with facultative processing of organic matter, sewage sludge waste, water purification, animal wastes, will produce with new formulative, methane gas, hydrogen gas, removing carbon dioxide & sulfides; manufactures environmentally safe bio-chemical cleaners
Contact(s):
Allan J. McInnes, President

Bercha Group
Formerly: Bercha Engineering Limited
P.O. Box 61105 Kensington
Calgary, AB T2N 4S6
403-270-2221
Fax: 403-270-2014
bgroup@berchagroup.com
www.berchagroup.com
Firm Type: Engineering
Founded: 1976
Products/Services/Areas of Expertise: Risk analysis; environmental risk assessment; engineering, operational & environmental simulation; remote sensing & GIS; digital image analysis; structural mechanics & dynamics; ice & iceberg mechanics; polar & frontier engineering; made up of three companies Bercha Engineering responsible for services in Canada, Bercha International deals with all international work & Bercha (Malaysia) Sdn. Bhd. responsible for services in Malaysia
Domestic Markets:
National
Foreign Activity:
Asia, Central America, The Middle East, South America, USA,
Contact(s):
F.G. Bercha, President

Berg Chilling Systems Inc.
51 Nantucket Blvd.
Toronto, ON M1P 2N5
416-755-2221
Fax: 416-755-3874
bergsales@berg-group.com
www.berg-group.com
Firm Type: Distributing, Engineering, Manufacturing
Founded: 1972
Staff: 90
Quality Environmental Management System(s): 9001:2000
Products/Services/Areas of Expertise: Refrigerated cooling & pumping systems for industrial process cooling; fiberglass cooling towers for industrial process cooling & city water conservation; industrial ice makers
Domestic Markets:
National
Foreign Activity:
Africa, Asia, Australia/New Zealand, Central America, The Pacific Rim, South America, Mexico, USA
Contact(s):
R. Lorne Berggren, Chair & CEO
Don Berggren, President
Mike Walsh, Manager
mwalsh@berg-group.com

Bernard Darveau Ingénieur / BDI
3027, rue de Boulogne
Sainte-Foy, QC G1W 2C4
418-651-3939
Fax: 418-651-6650
bernard.darveau@videotron.qc.ca
Firm Type: Engineering
Founded: 1989
Staff: 2
Products/Services/Areas of Expertise: Civil engineering; palatable water drainage & water supply, sewer treatment
Financial Information:
Type of Ownership: Private
Revenue: $100,000 - $250,000
Revenue Sources: 12% nationwide; 13% Provincial; 50% Municipals; 25% Private Contracts
Domestic Markets:
Québec
Contact(s):
Bernard Darveau, President

Bestobell AquaTronix Limited
Formerly: BEP Bestobell Engineering Products
241 Norseman St.
Toronto, ON M8Z 2R5
416-231-9216
Fax: 416-231-9121
800-668-3979
salesdesk@bestobell.com
www.bestobell.com
Firm Type: Distributing
Founded: 1953
Staff: 10
Products/Services/Areas of Expertise: Analytical Instruments (sensors & systems for measurement & control of municipal & industrial water-based processes); Level Switches; Level Transmitters & Indicators; Flow Measurement Instruments; Temperature Measurement Instruments; Wireless Monitoring Systems; Pressure Measurement Instruments; Process Indicators; Boiler Controls; Steam Traps; Slurry Valves; & Safety Valves. We provide technical support, repair & calibration service, start-up/commissioning assistance, custom solutions, steam trap surveys & energy analysis, & in-house training seminars.
Domestic Markets:
National
Contact(s):
Herb Kershaw, Managing Director

Béton Provincial Ltée
P.O. Box 160
1825, av du Phare ouest
Matane, QC G4W 3N1
418-562-0074
Fax: 418-562-0081
ventes@betonprovincial.com
www.betonprovincial.com
Products/Services/Areas of Expertise: Water & wastewater management equipment
Contact(s):
Walter Bélanger

Bétonel Limitée
8600, de l'Épée
Montréal, QC H3N 2G6
514-273-8855
Fax: 514-273-7391
888-238-6635
info@betonel.com
www.betonel.com
Firm Type: Distributing, Manufacturing
Founded: 1959
EcoLogo Certified Products & Services: VIP 100% acrylic; Club 20; Latex; Climate 100% acrylic exterior; commercial water paint products
Products/Services/Areas of Expertise: Manufacturer & distributor of consumer, office & industry products; Ecologo certified paints & surface coatings
Ecological Note: VIP 100% acrylic; Club 20; Latex; Climate 100% acrylic exterior; commercial water paint products
Contact(s):
Martin Rivard, Director, General Operations
mrivart@betonel.com

Beulah Tec Limited
#110, 10525 - 170 St. NW
Edmonton, AB T5P 4W2
708-484-6368
Fax: 708-481-2431
btecedm@telusplanet.net
Firm Type: Scientific/Technical Services, Waste Management
Staff: 11
Member of: Alberta Society of Professional Biologists; Environmental Services Association of Alberta
Products/Services/Areas of Expertise: Waste management & waste minimization technologies; development of waste management projects & facilities to improve market share; facility operation; waste treatment & recycling; phase I, II & III assessments & clean-up
Recently Completed / Ongoing Projects: Operates PRRC - Paintearth Resource Recovery Centre in Coronation, AB
Financial Information:
Type of Ownership: Private
Revenue: $250,000 - $500,000
Revenue Sources: 30% Municipals; 70% Private Contracts
Domestic Markets:
Alberta, British Columbia, Manitoba, Saskatchewan
Contact(s):
Mark Polet, President
Terri Polet, CEO

BEX Engineering Limited
5115 Timberlea Blvd.
Mississauga, ON L4W 2S3
905-238-8920
Fax: 905-238-8955
info@bex.com
www.bex.com
Firm Type: Manufacturing
Founded: 1962
Quality Environmental Management System(s): 9001:1994
Products/Services/Areas of Expertise: Spray nozzles; tank mixing eductors
Financial Information:
Type of Ownership: Private
Domestic Markets:
National
Foreign Activity:
Asia, China, Central Europe, Eastern Europe, The Pacific Rim, South America, Mexico, USA, Vietnam
Contact(s):
Derek Bowen, President

International Branch(es):
Germany
Siemensring 44P
Willich Germany
49 2154/88 70 06
Fax: 49 2154/88 7009
deutschland@bex.com

USA
836 Phoenix Dr.
Ann Arbor, MI USA
734-389-0464
Fax: 734-389-0470
sales@bex.com

BFI Canada Inc.
Formerly: Browning-Ferris Industries Ltd.
#300, 135 Queens Plate Dr.
Toronto, ON M9W 6V1
416-741-5221
Fax: 416-741-4565
corporate.communications@bficanada.com
www.bficanada.com
Firm Type: Waste Management
Member of: Ontario Waste Management Association
Products/Services/Areas of Expertise: Solid non-hazardous waste management company; provides residential, commercial & industrial waste collection, recycling & disposal services serving 19 markets in Québec, Ontario, Manitoba, Alberta & BC; operates four transfer collection stations, seven material facilities, owns &/or operates landfill sites serving the Calgary, Winnipeg, Lethbridge & Montréal markets
Financial Information:
Type of Ownership: Publicly Traded
Revenue: $500,000 - $1.5 Million
Domestic Markets:
Alberta, British Columbia, Manitoba, Ontario, Québec
Foreign Activity:
USA
Contact(s):
Keith A. Carrigan, CEO & Vice-Chairman
Charles F. Flood, President
Joseph H. Wright, Non-Executive Chairman
Daniel M. Dickinson, Director
Contact(s):
Yves Normandin, Vice-President

Canadian Branches:
Barrie
21 Bertram Industrial Pkwy.
Midhurst, ON L0L 1X0
705-721-9930
Fax: 705-739-6227
barrie@bficanada.com
Bryan Carrigan, District Manager

Blenheim, Ridge Landfill
P.O. Box 1871
20262 Eriau Rd.
Blenheim, ON N0P 1A0
519-676-5000
Fax: 519-676-4967
ridgelandfill@bficanada.com
Robert Lang

Calgary
5566 - 54 Ave. SE
Calgary, AB T2C 3A5
403-236-3883
Fax: 403-279-0317
calgary@bficanada.com
Harold Richardson, District Manager

Calgary Landfill
201 - 194 Ave. South East & McLeod Trail
Calgary, AB T2W 2C4
403-201-5075
Fax: 403-201-5087
calgary@bficanada.com
James Moore, District Manager

Chatham
91 Sass Rd.
Chatham, ON N7M 5J4
519-360-9435
Fax: 519-360-9839
chatham@bficanada.com
Michael Pare, District Manager

Edmonton
3410 - 74 Ave.
Edmonton, AB T6B 2P7
780-468-6801
Fax: 780-468-3197
edmonton@bficanada.com
David Martens, District Manager

Hamilton
464 Rennie St.
Hamilton, ON L8H 3P5
905-312-9222
Fax: 905-312-1428
hamilton@bficanada.com
Brad Mandryk, District Manager

Kelowna
#4, 150 Campion Rd.
Kelowna, BC V1X 7S8
250-765-0565
Fax: 250-765-9428
kelowna@bficanada.com
Tom Loewen, District Manager

Kingston
Also Known As: Kingston Area Recycling
196 Lappan's Lane
Kingston, ON K7K 6Z4
613-546-5012
Fax: 613-546-1259
kingston@bficanada.com
Mark Siydock, Facility Manager

Lethbridge
722 - 30 St. North
Lethbridge, AB T1H 5G7
403-327-4842
Fax: 403-327-6160
lethbridge@bficanada.com
Colin Harms, District Manager

London
4695 Wellington Rd. South
London, ON N6E 0A6
519-681-4040
Fax: 519-681-7920
london@bficanada.com
Dave Raney, District Manager

Medicine Hat
Bay #5, 1735 Brier Park Rd. NW
Medicine Hat, AB T1C 1V5
403-527-1942
Fax: 403-529-0912
medicinehat@bficanada.com
Lois Rissling, District Manager

Montréal
Also Known As: Entreprise Sanitaire F.A. Ltée
4900 Chemin St-Elzear
Laval, QC H7E 4P2

450-661-5080
Fax: 450-661-8079
laval@bficanada.com
Claude Forget, District Manager

Ottawa
132 Willowlea Rd.
Carp, ON K0A 1L0
613-836-6900
Fax: 613-836-4792
ottawa@bficanada.com
Keith McIntosh, District Manager

Thunder Bay
Site 13, Comp. #2
122 Cooper Rd.
Thunder Bay, ON P7C 4V1
807-939-2000
Fax: 807-939-4142
thunderbay@bficanada.com
Tammy Holtzman, District Manager

Toronto
10 Freshway Dr.
Concord, ON L4K 1S3
905-669-0288
Fax: 905-669-5944
toronto@bficanada.com
Lou Berardicurti, District Manager

Vancouver
25 Fawcett Rd.
Coquitlam, BC V3K 6V2
604-525-2072
Fax: 604-525-5762
800-372-0282
vancouver@bficanada.com
Joe Rajotte, District Manager

Victoria
2240 Keating X Rd.
Saanichton, BC V8M 2Z6
250-652-4414
Fax: 250-652-5172
victoria@bficanada.com
Michael Tripp, District Manager

Windsor
826 Felix Ave.
Windsor, ON N9C 3K8
519-258-2334
Fax: 519-258-3375
1-800-265-0861
windsor@bficanada.com
Michael Pare, District Manager

Winnipeg
375 Oak Point Hwy.
Winnipeg, MB R2R 1T9
204-633-9730
Fax: 204-694-5017
winnipeg@bficanada.com
Frank McKeown, District Manager

Winnipeg Landfill
Also Known As: Prairie Green Landfill
P.O. Box 1590
Winnipeg, MB R3C 2Z6
204-694-7615
Fax: 204-694-5017
winnipeg@bficanada.com
Clifford Lechow, District Manager

Lachenaie
Also Known As: Usine de triage Lachenaie ltée
3779, chemin des 40-Arpents
Terrebonne, QC J6V 9T6
450-474-2423
lachenaie@bficanada.com

BG Controls Ltd.
#115, 1551 Broadway St.
Port Coquitlam, BC V3C 6N9
604-942-0288
Fax: 604-942-5858
info@bgcontrols.com
www.bgcontrols.com
Firm Type: Distributing
Founded: 1982
Member of: Instrument Society of America; British Columbia Water & Waste Association

Products/Services/Areas of Expertise: Air/liquid analyzers; hazardous gas detectors; wastewater samplers; level monitors; pressure switches; telemetering & data acquisition; valve actuators
Contact(s):
Dom Sacco, General Manager
dsacco@bgcontrols.com

BGR Oilfield Services Incorporated
#201, 2 Bluewater Rd.
Bedford, NS B4B 1G7
902-456-0530
bgr@bgr.ca
www.bgr.ca
Firm Type: Scientific/Technical Services, Waste Management

Products/Services/Areas of Expertise: An offshoot of B.G. Roberts Chemicals (water treatment solutions for the mining, & pulp & paper industries, & municipalities), this firm is engaged in the development of environmentally friendly & cost effective solutions for the oil industry. The focus is on technologies to remove oil contamination from well bore cuttings, processed oil sands, tank bottoms, drilling muds & hydrocarbon contaminated solids
Financial Information:
Type of Ownership: Private
Contact(s):
Brian G. Roberts, President
broberts@bgr.ca

BH Engineering Systems Ltd. / BHESL
P.O. Box 25041
Halifax, NS B3M 4H4
902-443-2400
Fax: 902-445-5110
www.navnet.net/~bhes/index.htm
Firm Type: Engineering

Products/Services/Areas of Expertise: Provides studies & services in: oceans/offshore engineering, electric power systems engineering, & environmental systems. Company divisions include: Advanced Research, Advanced Technical Training, Advanced Technical Publications, & Software Development. The company partners with other private sector players with expertise in the areas of interest
Financial Information:
Type of Ownership: Private
Domestic Markets:
National
Foreign Activity:
Worldwide
Contact(s):
Ferial El-Hawary, President

Biantco Environmental Services Inc. / BESI
1812 - 21 Ave. North
Lethbridge, AB T1H 4B6
403-327-8170
Fax: 403-327-5104
888-327-8194
www.biantco.com
Products/Services/Areas of Expertise: Reclamation projects for the oil industry, & for other industrial, commercial & agricultural clients; services include project management, environmental drilling, land fill services, excavating & segregating contaminated soil, vapour barrier & vapour extraction system installation, soil remediation & allu treatment, certified UST decommissioning, & demolitions
Domestic Markets:
Alberta
Contact(s):
Barny Knelsen, Contact

Big Bear Pumping Inc.
Formerly: Big Bear Services
2036 Hwy 5 West, RR#1
Troy, ON L0R 2B0
519-647-2230
Firm Type: Waste Management
Staff: 3
Products/Services/Areas of Expertise: Septic & Sewage Service; Waste Transport; Portable Outhouses
Contact(s):
Randy Hunt, Owner/Operator

Bigelow-Liptak of Canada
2384 Speers Rd.
Oakville, ON L6L 5M2
905-825-1800
Fax: 905-825-2292
bigelow@bigelow-liptak.com
www.bigelow-liptak.com
Firm Type: Manufacturing
Founded: 1940
Staff: 20
Products/Services/Areas of Expertise: Incinerators, hot-air furnaces, gas, oil, coal, wood-fired; liquid wastes, off gases & fume incinerators, ovens, melting furnaces
Financial Information:
Type of Ownership: Private
Revenue: Greater than $5 Million
Domestic Markets:
National
Foreign Activity:
Worldwide
Contact(s):
John Williams, Division Manager
Frank Morrison, Sales Manager

International Branch(es):
Pittsburgh
Ave. B - Buncher Industrial Park
Leetsdale, PA USA
412-741-3850
Fax: 412-741-6646
bigelow@nauticom.net
Jim Roz

Bigfoot Systems Inc.
Formerly: F&S Manufacturing
6750 Hwy. 3, Martins Point
Mahone Bay, NS B0J 2E0
902-627-1600
Fax: 902-627-1700
800-934-0393
info@bigfootsystems.com
www.bigfootsystems.com
Firm Type: Distributing, Manufacturing
Founded: 1996
Staff: 5
Products/Services/Areas of Expertise: Concrete & sonotube footing forms; decktools software
Contact(s):
Jack Fickes, President/CEO
jack@bigfootsystems.com

Bio-Contrôle inc.
4715, av. des Replats
Québec, QC G2J 1B8
418-653-3101
Fax: 418-653-3096
800-663-3101
biocontrole@bio-controle.com
www.atmtech.biz/bio-controle
Firm Type: Distributing, Scientific/Technical Services
Founded: 1985
Staff: 20
Products/Services/Areas of Expertise: Services include food safety inspection & integrated audit, audit & accreditation of suppliers, consultation & support for quality systems management to HACCP standards & GFSI program requirements, training for food handlers & managers, online training, food testing, & water testing; products include SystemSURE Plus ATP Hygiene Monitoring System, Ultrasnap surface testing system, Aquasnap ATP water testing device, PRO-Clean proteins detection agent, SpotCheck & SpotCheck Plus lactose/glucose detection agents, & Insite pathogen test for Listeria
Contact(s):
Serge Sévigny, President/CEO

Canadian Branches:
Montréal
#400, 2300, rue Sherbrooke ouest
Montréal, QC H2K 1E5
514-528-9232
Fax: 514-528-6849

Bio-Limno Research & Consulting
28 Stone Gate Dr.
Halifax, NS B3N 3J2

902-425-8989
Fax: 902-425-8989
info@bio-limno.com
www.bio-limno.com
Firm Type: Scientific/Technical Services
Founded: 1995
Staff: 2
Member of: North American Lake Management Society; American Society of Limnology and Oceanography; Society of Canadian Limnologists; Society of International Limnologists; International Society for Diatom Research; Environmental Services Association of Alberta
Member of: Nova Scotia Environmental Industry Association
Products/Services/Areas of Expertise: Analysis (identification & enumeration) of algae, zooplankton & macroinvertabrates; water quality assessments; report writing on water quality data
Recently Completed / Ongoing Projects: Analysis of phytoplankton in North American Great Lakes
Financial Information:
Type of Ownership: Private
Revenue: $50,000 - $100,000
Revenue Sources: 10% Provincial; 90% Private Contracts
Domestic Markets:
Alberta, British Columbia, Northwest Territories, Ontario, Québec, Yukon Territory
Foreign Activity:
USA
Contact(s):
Michael Agbeti, Ph.D., Principal

Bio-Software Inc.
#299, 762 Upper James St.
Hamilton, ON L9C 3A2
905-308-7821
Fax: 905-308-8468
info@bio-software.com
www.bio-software.com
Firm Type: Information Technology, Scientific/Technical Services
Founded: 1982
Staff: 4
Member of: Canadian Society of Environmental Biologists; Canadian Environment Industry Association
Products/Services/Areas of Expertise: Database management systems for environmental applications; developers of environmental data analysis & management system (EDAMS); modelling & simulation of air, water, groundwater & biota for environmental & industrial systems; data acquisition & analysis; statistical analysis & design for environmental assessments, audits, remedial action plans & industrial processes
Financial Information:
Type of Ownership: Private
Domestic Markets:
National
Foreign Activity:
USA
Contact(s):
Fraser Gorrie, President

Bio-Terre Systems Inc.
150, rue de Vimy
Sherbrooke, QC J1J 3M7
819-562-3871
Fax: 819-563-8984
info@bioterre.com
www.bioterre.com
Firm Type: Engineering
Founded: 1998
Products/Services/Areas of Expertise: Low temperature anaerobic digestion technology; high net energy livestock waste digestion technology for recycling waste into sources of energy and fertilizer
Recently Completed / Ongoing Projects: 2 hog farms in Quebec, one in Manitoba
Financial Information:
Type of Ownership: Private
Domestic Markets:
Manitoba, Québec
Contact(s):
Dennis Hodgkinson, P.Eng., President
dgheng@mb.sympatico.ca
Canadian Branches:
Manitoba
12 Aviation Blvd.
St. Andrews, MB R1A 3N5

204-334-8846
Fax: 204-334-6965

Bioforj Environmental Services
Also Known As: Bioforj Ontario Limited
P.O. Box 156
16 Strathmere Pl.
Guelph, ON N1H 6J9
519-767-9854
Fax: 519-821-8030
info@bioforj.com
www.bioforj.com
Firm Type: Management Consulting, Distributing, Manufacturing
Founded: 1987
Staff: 6
Products/Services/Areas of Expertise: Environmental contractor for spill response products, site remediation, soil & groundwater, waste management, including nutrient management; Bentonite linder & drill products supply
Financial Information:
Type of Ownership: Private
Revenue Sources: 100% Private Contracts
Domestic Markets:
New Brunswick, Newfoundland & Labrador, Nova Scotia, Ontario, Prince Edward Island, Québec
Contact(s):
Robert Johnson, B.S., President/Microbiologist
robertj@bioforj.com

Biogénie
Also Known As: Biogénie S.R.D.C. inc.
#200, 4495 Wilfrid-Hamel Blvd.
Québec, QC G1P 2J7
418-653-4422
Fax: 418-653-3583
800-267-4422
info@biogenie-env.com
www.biogenie-env.com
Firm Type: Engineering
Founded: 1986
Staff: 160
Member of: Canadian Association of Petroleum Producers; Réseau Environnement; American Petroleum Institute
Products/Services/Areas of Expertise: Site remediation solutions for the petroleum, petrochemical & utility industries.
Recently Completed / Ongoing Projects: Treatment of PCP-contaminated soil on a Superfund site; remediation of a PCP-impacted former radar station; remediation of a battery site (oil production facility) in Alberta
Financial Information:
Type of Ownership: Private
Revenue: Greater than $5 Million
Revenue Sources: 10% nationwide; 15% Provincial; 75% Private Contracts
Domestic Markets:
Alberta, New Brunswick, Northwest Territories, Nunavut, Ontario, Québec
Foreign Activity:
Western Europe, USA
Contact(s):
François Gagnon, General Manager
quebec@biogenie-env.com

Canadian Branches:
Edmonton
#136, 2301 Premier Way
Sherwood Park, AB T8H 2K8
780-416-0414
Fax: 780-416-0417
1-877-347-4505
alberta@biogenie-env.com
Jeff Dirks, General Manager

Guelph
236 Glasgow St. North
Guelph, ON N1H 4X2
519-763-2227
Fax: 519-763-9887
nryan@biogenie-env.com
Neil Ryan, Director, Business Development

Iqaluit
1229
1809 Kakivak Ct.
Iqualit, NU X0A 0H0
867-979-5980
Fax: 867-979-5985
northern@biogenie-env.com

Michel Pouliot, Vice-President, SAR Canada & USA

Montréal
1140, rue Levis
Lachenaie, QC J6W 5S6
450-961-3535
Fax: 450-961-0220
1-866-961-3695
montreal@biogenie-env.com
Claude Deschambault, General Manager

International Branch(es):
Yellowknife
P.O. Box 2691
Yellowknife, NT X1A 2R1

Biolab Inc.
3401, boul Frontenac
Thetford Mines, QC G6H 4G3
418-338-2193
Fax: 418-338-6579
800-250-1516
info@groupebiolab.ca
www.groupebiolab.ca
Firm Type: Scientific/Technical Services
Founded: 1984
Quality Environmental Management System(s): 17025
Products/Services/Areas of Expertise: Laboratory analysis, microbiology, chemistry for water, wastewater, soil, vegetation; fertilizers, pesticides; hazardous waste management; environmental assessments
Domestic Markets:
Québec
Contact(s):
Renée Émond, President/CEO
Serge Vallée, Vice-President, Operations
Martin Vézina, Director, Sales and Marketing

Biomation
P.O. Box 156
335 Perth St.
Almonte, ON K0A 1A0
613-256-2821
Fax: 613-256-5872
888-667-2324
dh@biomation.com
www.biomation.com
Firm Type: Distributing
Founded: 1989
Staff: 3
Products/Services/Areas of Expertise: Sales, service & support for radon monitoring equipment used by engineering contractors; source of clean conductive polypropylene waste
Financial Information:
Type of Ownership: Private
Revenue: $250,000 - $500,000
Revenue Sources: 10% nationwide; 15% Provincial; 75% Private Contracts
Domestic Markets:
National
Contact(s):
Dave Hanneson, President

Biomax Inc.
A subsidiary of Conporec Inc.
#133, 820, boul. Charest est
Québec, QC G1K 8H8
418-529-2585
Fax: 418-529-9413
www.conporec.com
Firm Type: Engineering, Manufacturing, Waste Management
Founded: 1986
Staff: 12
Member of: Canadian Composting Council
Products/Services/Areas of Expertise: Design, manufacture & distribution of composting equipment & systems
Recently Completed / Ongoing Projects: 30,000 tonnes/year pulp & paper sludge composting plant near Ottawa
Financial Information:
Type of Ownership: Private
Revenue Sources: 50% Municipals; 50% Private Contracts
Domestic Markets:
Québec
Markets Sought:
USA
Contact(s):
Jean Beaudoin, President, Conporec Inc.

Biopacific Diagnostic Inc.
#114, 828 Harbourside Dr.
North Vancouver, BC V7P 3R9
604-985-7000
Fax: 604-985-3366
800-267-5800
biopacific@telus.net
www.biopacific.net
Firm Type: Distributing, Manufacturing
Founded: 1983
Products/Services/Areas of Expertise: Distributor for Diagnostic Chemicals Ltd., Evergreen Scientific, Simport, Thrmo Orion, Barnstead International & other companies supplying biochemistry reagents & plastic disposables
Domestic Markets:
National
Foreign Activity:
USA

Biophilia Inc.
236 Coachwood Cres. SW
Calgary, AB T3H 1E8
403-246-1986
Fax: 403-686-2012
wthorne@biophilia.com
www.biophilia.com
Firm Type: Management Consulting
Founded: 1994
Products/Services/Areas of Expertise: An environmental consulting firm specializing in tailored, client-focused solutions to environmental management; services include strategic planning, needs indentification, assessment, & mitigation of environmental impacts; project management; environmental audits; site assessments (Ph. I & II); spill response planning; air, surface water & groundwater monitoring; training; research
Contact(s):
Wendy E. Roberts Thorne, M.E.Des., P.Eng., President
wthorne@biophilia.com

BIOREM Inc.
Also Known As: BIOREM Technologies Inc.
7496 Wellington Rd. 34, RR#3
Guelph, ON N1H 6H9
519-767-9100
Fax: 519-767-1824
800-353-2087
info@biorem.biz
www.biorem.biz
Firm Type: Distributing, Manufacturing
Founded: 1991
Member of: Canadian Environment Industry Association
Products/Services/Areas of Expertise: A leader in air pollution control; manufactures & distributes a range of biofilter products & technologies for odour removal, H2S, VOCs & hazardous air pollutants
Recently Completed / Ongoing Projects: 250,000 cfm custom design Biofiltair(tm) biofilter system for rendering, Dundas, ON.; 30,000 cfm 6X Basystem modular biofilter system for municipal wastewater, Jefferson County, Alabama; Biofilter for sludge loadout, Toronto, ON.
Financial Information:
Type of Ownership: Publicly Traded
Revenue: $3 Million - $5 Million
Revenue Sources: 70% Municipals; 30% Private Contracts
Domestic Markets:
National
Foreign Activity:
China, USA
Contact(s):
Peter Brujins, President/CEO
Robert Wood, MBA, CMA, CFO
rwood@biorem.biz
Ian H. Borrell, Vice-President, Sales and Marketing
Mark K. Hawley, P.Eng., Vice-President, Operations

Biorex Inc.
295, ch Ste-Foy
Québec, QC G1R 1T5
418-522-4945
Fax: 418-522-5218
info@biorex.com
www.biorex.com
Firm Type: Scientific/Technical Services
Founded: 1978
Products/Services/Areas of Expertise: Marine biology; contaminated sediments; data acquisition & analysis; emergency response planning; electronic databases; environmental assessment; fisheries & aquaculture management; site assessment studies; water & wastewater consulting; waterways & wetlands management; wildlife & game management
Financial Information:
Type of Ownership: Private
Domestic Markets:
New Brunswick, Nova Scotia, Prince Edward Island, Québec
Foreign Activity:
Eastern Europe
Contact(s):
Marc Gagnon, President

Canadian Branches:
Eastern Québec
#102, 198, boul de Gaspé
Gaspé, QC G4X 1B1
418-368-5597
Fax: 418-368-1372
biorex@globetrotter.qc.ca
France Henry, Director

Maritimes
#13, 111, boul St-Pierre
Caraquet, NB E1W 1B9
506-727-7635
Fax: 506-727-7338
biorexnb@nbnet.nb.ca
Maurice Jean, Director

BioSolve of Canada Ltd.
499 Canterbury Dr. SW
Calgary, AB T2W 1J4
403-238-4228
Fax: 403-238-5822
800-282-3254
biosolve@telusplanet.net
Firm Type: Distributing
Founded: 1955
Staff: 4
Member of: Environmental Services Association of Alberta
Products/Services/Areas of Expertise: Clean-up/mitigation agent for hydrocarbon products, soil remediation, fuel tank cleaning, sludge reduction, vapor suppression, spill clean-up & fighting class A & B fires
Financial Information:
Type of Ownership: Private
Revenue Sources: 100% Private Contracts
Domestic Markets:
National
Markets Sought:
Eastern Europe, Former USSR

BioSource Solutions Inc.
Formerly: Leading Chemical Mfg. Inc.
#3, 32 Park Rd.
Elmsdale, NS B2S 2L2
902-883-8090
Fax: 902-883-8226
877-883-8226
biosource@ns.aliantzinc.ca
www.biosourcesolutionsinc.com
Firm Type: Manufacturing
Founded: 1992
Staff: 7
EcoLogo Certified Products & Services: Zymo family of biological cleaning & odour products
Products/Services/Areas of Expertise: Environmental cleaning & odour products
Ecological Note: Zymo family of biological cleaning & odour products
Domestic Markets:
National
Markets Sought:
USA
Contact(s):
Bob Pieroway, Contact

Biotech Solutions
2328 chemin de la Grande Ligne
Charlesbourg, QC G2N 2G3
Fax: 418-841-1079
888-841-0957
portamax@sympatico.ca
Firm Type: Scientific/Technical Services
Founded: 2002
Staff: 8
Products/Services/Areas of Expertise: Biotech products can remediate hydrocarbons (PHA's), chlorinated solvents, herbicides, pesticides, PCP/Dioxins & PCB's as well as heavy metal technology that treats lead, chrome, cadmium, arsenic &other heavy metals; provides expertise & technology to render hazardous heavy metals, impacted soils, sludge, ashes & sediment non-hazardous
Financial Information:
Type of Ownership: Private
Domestic Markets:
National
Foreign Activity:
China, Vietnam
Contact(s):
Yvon Cloutier, President/Director of Engineering
ycloutier@biotechsolutions.ca

Canadian Branches:
Montreal
Microbiologist/Chemist
8097 rue Nicolet
Brossard, QC J4Y 2S6
514-792-0957
Fax: 514-678-6026
dowens@biotechsolutions.ca
Dennis C. Owens, Vice-President

Toronto
Whitby, ON L1N 7X3
416-460-5285
Fax: 416-668-8361
fthompson@biotechsolutions.ca
Frank Thompson, General Manager

Biothermica
426, Sherbrooke est
Montréal, QC H2L 1J6
514-488-3881
Fax: 514-488-3125
biothermica@biothermica.com
www.biothermica.com
Firm Type: Management Consulting, Engineering, Scientific/Technical Services
Founded: 1987
Staff: 20
Member of: Air & Waste Management Association; Ordre des Ingénieurs du Québec
Products/Services/Areas of Expertise: Design & development of solutions for the control of air pollution, & the reduction of methane emissions from landfill sites & underground coal mines; turnkey projects for gaseous pollutant emissions control, landfill gas recovery, & coal mine methane oxidation.
Recently Completed / Ongoing Projects: McCain, RTO project; Landfill Gas project; preliminary enginering, biomas power plant
Financial Information:
Type of Ownership: Private
Revenue: Greater than $5 Million
Revenue Sources: 10% nationwide; 90% Private Contracts
Domestic Markets:
Ontario, Québec
Foreign Activity:
Africa, Caribbean, Western Europe, USA
Markets Sought:
South America, Mexico, USA
Contact(s):
Guy Drouin, P.Eng., MBA, President
guy.drouin@biothermica.com

Birchwood Environment Management Inc.
33 Lloyd St.
Hanwell, NB E3C 1M4
506-440-0064
info@birchwoodenv.ca
www.birchwoodenv.ca
Products/Services/Areas of Expertise: Provides legal/consulting services in: Environmental Management System (EMS) development & implementation; system integration (quality, health & safety, existing environmental programs); training programs (ISO systems, general awareness, due diligence, regulatory issue, emerging trends); specialized consulting services (environmental legal tracking, sustainable forest management, pollution prevention, climate change, regulatory affairs); & EMS & regulatory compliance auditing
Contact(s):
Glenn Keays, President
Sharon Keays, Financial Officer

Products & Services Buyer's Guide

Birks Co.
Also Known As: The Birks Company, Birksco
2132 - 15 Side Rd.
Moffat, ON L0P 1J0
905-854-9875
Fax: 905-854-0180
sales@birksco.com
www.birksco.com
Firm Type: Manufacturing
Founded: 1949
Products/Services/Areas of Expertise: Sales, engineering & technical support for products & packaged systems, servicing the municipal sewer & water, plumbing, irrigation & fire protection market; source for SMART CARD truckfill staions & sewer/wastewater dump stations; backflow prevention devices for use in potable water distribution systems; for point of use or premise isolation; prevents reverse flow of contaminated water into the potable water system
Domestic Markets:
National
Markets Sought:
Eastern Europe, Western Europe
Contact(s):
Michael Birks, President
mbirks@birksco.com

Bissett Resource Consultants Ltd.
#250, 839 - 5 Ave. SW
Calgary, AB T2P 3C8
403-294-1888
Fax: 403-263-0073
mail@bissettres.com
www.bissettres.com
Firm Type: Management Consulting, Engineering
Founded: 1984
Staff: 100
Member of: Canadian Association of Petroleum Producers; Canadian Federation of Independent Business; Petroleum Services Association of Canada
Products/Services/Areas of Expertise: Petroleum engineering & operating services in drilling, completions & well servicing; emergency response planning; safety planning & audits; location & access construction; environmental assessment & reclamation; project management & field supervision
Financial Information:
Type of Ownership: Private
Domestic Markets:
Alberta, British Columbia, Nova Scotia, Northwest Territories, Québec, Saskatchewan, Yukon Territory
Foreign Activity:
Worldwide
Contact(s):
K.R. (Dick) Bissett, President
dick@bissettres.com
Russ J. Brown, General Manager, Management Executive
russ_b@bissettres.com
Dan Belczewski, P.Eng., Sr. Engineer, Drilling
dan@bissettres.com

Black & Decker Canada Inc.
#300, 125 Mural St.
Richmond Hill, ON L4B 1M4
905-886-9511
Fax: 905-764-4630
www.blackanddecker.com
Firm Type: Distributing, Manufacturing
Staff: 600
Products/Services/Areas of Expertise: Ecologo certified equipment, machinery & automotive products

Blackbox Automation Inc.
586 Main St.
Glen Williams, ON L7G 3T6
905-873-0141
Fax: 905-877-1809
800-873-0141
Firm Type: Distributing, Manufacturing
Founded: 1976
Staff: 8
Products/Services/Areas of Expertise: Radio remote control of heavy equipment for operation in hazardous locations; radio control of fixed equipment by wireless LAN (CANBUS)
Recently Completed / Ongoing Projects: Radio Control R/C of wheel loader working at Highwall, R/C of locomotives & trackmobiles, R/C of 125' condor aerial platform, R/C of trackside equipment along 8 miles of railway right of way

Financial Information:
Type of Ownership: Private
Revenue: $500,000 - $1.5 Million
Revenue Sources: 100% Private Contracts
Domestic Markets:
Alberta, British Columbia, Manitoba, New Brunswick, Newfoundland & Labrador, Nova Scotia, Northwest Territories, Ontario, Québec, Saskatchewan, Yukon Territory
Foreign Activity:
Central America, The Middle East, South America, USA
Markets Sought:
Asia, Western Europe
Contact(s):
Malcolm Black, President

Blower Engineering Inc.
40 Industrial Pkwy. North
Aurora, ON L4G 4C2
905-841-2215
Fax: 905-841-3360
800-388-1339
Canada@BlowerEngineering.com
www.blowerengineering.com
Firm Type: Manufacturing
Member of: Water Environment Association of Ontario; Mushroom Growers Association; Ready Mix Association; Precast Concrete Association
Products/Services/Areas of Expertise: Blower packages for sewage aeration; vacuum pump packages for sewage filtering operation; energy-efficiency steam generators; methane gas boosters
Financial Information:
Type of Ownership: Private
Revenue Sources: 10% Municipals; 90% Private Contracts
Domestic Markets:
National
Foreign Activity:
Australia/New Zealand, China, Mexico, USA, Former USSR, Vietnam
Contact(s):
Thomas S. Byrnes. Sr., P.Eng., President/CEO
tomsr@blowerengineering.com
Robyn L. Byrnes, Accounting
William O.R. Byrnes, Plant Manager
Tom Byrnes, Jr., Vice-President, Marketing
International Branch(es):
Enfield, CT, USA
9 Cora St.
Enfield, CT USA
Fax: 860-749-7431
860-749-7461
Mail@BlowerEngineering.com
Lewiston, NY, USA
210 South 8th St.
Lewiston, NY USA
Fax: 800-523-8808
800-388-1339
Mail@BlowerEngineering.com

Blowmoulding Technologies Inc.
#20, 1210 Midway Blvd.
Mississauga, ON L5T 2B8
905-670-1705
Fax: 905-670-9387
ausbti@allstream.net
Firm Type: Distributing, Engineering, Manufacturing, Scientific/Technical Services
Founded: 1989
Staff: 6
Products/Services/Areas of Expertise: Equipment, engineering services & consulting for the blowmoulding industry; recycling & general plastic processing
Financial Information:
Type of Ownership: Private
Revenue Sources: 100% Private Contracts
Domestic Markets:
National
Foreign Activity:
USA
Markets Sought:
Western Europe

Blue Water Agencies Ltd.
40 Topple Dr.
Dartmouth, NS B3B 1L6

902-468-4900
Fax: 902-468-4901
shipstores@bluewateragencies.ca
www.bluewateragencies.ca
Firm Type: Distributing
Founded: 1975
Member of: NS Environmental Industry Association
Quality Environmental Management System(s): 9001
Products/Services/Areas of Expertise: Oil & chemical absorbents; spill cleanup equipment, response kits; waste handling equipment, balers, shredders; waste management handling; currently services 27 ports and harbours
Domestic Markets:
New Brunswick, Newfoundland & Labrador, Nova Scotia, Prince Edward Island, Québec
Contact(s):
Patrick Wilson, President

Canadian Branches:
New Brunswick
#804, 1216 Sand Cove Rd.
Saint John, NB E2M 5V8
506-672-1700
Fax: 506-672-1704

Newfoundland
127 Clyde Ave.
Mount Pearl, NL A1N 4R9
709-754-8900
Fax: 709-754-8901

Québec
3400, rue St. Patrick
Montréal, QC H4E 1A2
514-798-8566
Fax: 514-798-8565

Blue-Zone Technologies Ltd.
Also Known As: Deltasorb Anesthetic Collection Service
#14, 84 Citation Dr.
Concord, ON L4K 3C1
905-761-1224
Fax: 905-761-3371
health@bluezone.ca
www.bluezone.ca
Firm Type: Scientific/Technical Services, Waste Management
Founded: 1996
Staff: 7
Member of: Canadian Anesthesiologists Society; Canadian Environment Industry Association - Ontario
Products/Services/Areas of Expertise: Offers hospitals a cost effective, environmentally friendly alternative to venting toxic anesthetics; services include delivery & canister exchange service, installation of the Deltasorb system in operating rooms, & staff training. Pending approval, the company plans to provide the medical community with a viable alternative source for anesthetics, as well as a full-scale anesthetic waste collection, recovery, reconstitution & reuse program
Financial Information:
Type of Ownership: Private
Revenue Sources: 0% nationwide; 0% Provincial
Domestic Markets:
British Columbia, Ontario, Québec
Markets Sought:
Asia, Western Europe, USA
Contact(s):
Vaughn Goettler, CEO
Dusanka Filipovic, President
Laurence Whitby, Vice-President, Operations

Canadian Branches:
Ottawa
37 Linden Terrace
Ottawa, ON K1S 1Z1
613-563-3292
Fax: 613-563-2676
rbower@bluezone.ca
Richard Bower

Bluewater Environmental Inc.
Also Known As: Bluewater Environmental (Western Canada) Inc.
#201, 704 Mara St.
Point Edward, ON N7V 1X4
519-337-0228
Fax: 519-337-9178
888-808-9782

eng@blueh2o.ca
www.blueh2o.ca
Firm Type: Engineering, Scientific/Technical Services, Waste Management
Founded: 1986
Products/Services/Areas of Expertise: Environment consultants and engineering company; offers expertise from Phase I Site Assessments to sophisticated remediation analyses, strategies and cleanups for a wide range of sectors, including industrial, commercial, residential, and food & beverage

BMT Fleet Technology Ltd.
BMT Group Ltd.
Formerly: Fleet Technology Ltd. 311 Legget Dr.
Kanata, ON K2K 1Z8
613-592-2830
Fax: 613-592-4950
fleet@fleetech.com
www.fleetech.com
Firm Type: Scientific/Technical Services
Founded: 1973
Staff: 22
Products/Services/Areas of Expertise: The company offers engineering support for design, construction, & eventual disposal stages in sectors including: civil & industrial infrastructure, defense, energy, marine & transport industry. Expertise extends to environmental & cold region engineering services.
Recently Completed / Ongoing Projects: Collaboration with University of Victoria to design & deliver North America's first ever "green" ship, a hybrid, electric research vessel to investigate changing coastal ecosystems
Domestic Markets:
National
Foreign Activity:
USA, United Kingdom,
Contact(s):
Gary Smith, BMT Group, Regional Director, Americas
Aaron Dinovitzer, President
adinovitzer@fleetech.com
David Stocks, Vice-President, Pacific Region
dstocks@fleetech.com

Canadian Branches:
St. John's
25 Kenmount Rd.
St. John's, NL A1B 1W1
709-753-5690
Fax: 709-753-5694
nl@fleetech.com

Vancouver
#412, 611 Alexander St.
Vancouver, BC V6A 1E1
604-253-0955
Fax: 604-253-5023
west@fleetech.com
Tyler Greenberg, Architect Contact
tyler@relative-space.com

Victoria
Shoal Point
#101, 19 Dallas Rd.
Victoria, BC V8V 5A6
250-598-5150
Fax: 250-598-5160
west@fleetech.com

International Branch(es):
Loughborough, UK
The Point
Granite Way, Mountsorrel
Loughborough, Leics UK
44-0-1509-621814
uk@fleetech.com
Alan Smith, Contact
alan.s@fortstorage.com

Boart Longyear Inc.
111 Main St. West
North Bay, ON P1B 2W4
705-474-2800
Fax: 705-474-2373
info@boartlongyear.com
www.boartlongyear.com
Products/Services/Areas of Expertise: Supplies products, systems & services to the natural resource industry (minerals, energy & water), the construction & quarrying industries & industrial markets worldwide.
Domestic Markets:
National
Foreign Activity:
Worldwide
Contact(s):
Brenda Hassard, Administrator, Marketing

Canadian Branches:
Calgary
4025 - 96 Ave. SE
Calgary, AB T2C 4T7
403-287-1460
Fax: 403-243-0580

Cochenour
Box 280, Hwy. 125
Cochenour, ON P0V 1L0
807-662-6191
Fax: 807-662-6281
info@boartlongyear.com

Flin Flon
4 Timber Lane
Flin Flon, MB R8A 1S3
204-687-7379
Fax: 204-896-3714
info@boartlongyear.com

Haileybury
310 Niven St.
Haileybury, ON P0J 1K0
705-672-3800
Fax: 705-672-3729
info@boartlongyear.com

Marathon
Race Track Industrial Park
P.O. Box 1165
Old Heron Bay Rd.
Marathon, ON P0T 2E0
807-229-1313
Fax: 807-229-1644
info@boartlongyear.com

Mississauga
2442 South Sheridan Way
Mississauga, ON L5J 2M7
905-822-7922
Fax: 905-822-7232
info@boartlongyear.com

Moncton
2088 Salisbury Rd.
Moncton, NB E1C 8J5
506-858-9977
Fax: 506-857-8456
info@boartlongyear.com

Saskatoon
403 - 47th St.
Saskatoon, SK S7K 5H4
306-931-4466
Fax: 306-931-1150
info@boartlongyear.com

Val d'Or
155, rue des Distributeurs
Val-d'Or, QC J9P 6Y1
819-825-6131
Fax: 819-825-2897
info@boartlongyear.com

Vancouver
7930 Huston Rd.
Delta, BC V4G 1C2
604-946-6590
Fax: 604-946-6594
info@boartlongyear.com

BOC Canada Limited
A company of The Linde Group
Formerly: Canadian Oxygen Ltd. 5860 Chedworth Way
Mississauga, ON L5R 0A2
905-501-1700
Fax: 905-501-1717
888-256-7359
info@lindecanada.com
www.lindecanada.com; www.boc-gases.com
Firm Type: Distributing, Manufacturing
Founded: 1949
Staff: 1000
Quality Environmental Management System(s): 9001
Products/Services/Areas of Expertise: Compressed gases for industrial, medical, scientific & hospitality settings: bulk sales of atmospheric gases, hydrogen, helium; bulk sales of carbon dioxide; gaseous chemicals, such as ammonia, chlorine, sulphur hexafluoride; refrigerants: ammonia, HFCs, HCFCs; & welding equipment & consumables. Services include safety training, audits & risk management services
Financial Information:
Type of Ownership: Foreign-owned
Domestic Markets:
National
Foreign Activity:
Western Europe, USA, Worldwide
Contact(s):
Lisa Michaels, Marketing Services
lisa.michaels@boccanada.com

Canadian Branches:
Amos
532, rue Principale sud
Amos, QC J9 3K5
819-732-7585
Fax: 819-732-5913
amos.lg.ca@linde.com

Barrie
#5 & #6, 30 Saunders Rd.
Barrie, ON L4N 9A8
705-734-1337
Fax: 705-734-0720
barrie.lg.ca@linde.com

Bathurst
#4, 2010 Industrial Ave.
Bathurst, NB E2A 4W7
506-548-9842
Fax: 506-546-7771
bathurst.lg.ca@linde.com

Belleville
340 Bell Blvd.
Belleville, ON K8P 5H7
613-962-3481
Fax: 613-962-3627
belleville.lg.ca@linde.com

Bois-des-Filion
201, rue Henry-Bessemer
Bois-des-Filion, QC J6Z 4S9
450-686-0202
Fax: 450-965-7645
terrebonne.lg.ca@linde.com

Bracebridge
14 Monica Lane
Bracebridge, ON P1L 1V3
705-645-8761
Fax: 705-645-1697
bracebridge.lg.ca@linde.com

Brampton
2090 Steeles Ave. East
Brampton, ON L6T 1A7
905-790-3679
Fax: 905-790-1667
brampton.lg.ca@linde.com

Brockville
1450 California Ave.
Brockville, ON K6V 5V5
613-342-3974
Fax: 613-342-1384
brockville.lg.ca@linde.com

Calgary
4610 - 80th Ave. SE
Calgary, AB T2C 3A3
403-279-7581
Fax: 403-236-8720
calgary.lg.ca@linde.com

Cambridge
45 Raglin Pl.
Cambridge, ON N1R 7J2
519-740-1740
Fax: 519-740-1233
cambridge.lg.ca@linde.com

Products & Services Buyer's Guide

Chatham
940 Richmond St.
Chatham, ON N7M 5K3
519-351-9241
Fax: 519-351-3703
chatham.lg.ca@linde.com

Chicoutimi
1341, rue Manic
Chicoutimi, QC G7K 1G7
418-545-6630
Fax: 418-545-8829
chicoutimi.lg.ca@linde.com

Concord
#1, 11 Creditstone Rd.
Concord, ON L4K 2P1
905-669-1871
Fax: 905-669-1878
concord.lg.ca@linde.com

Cornwall
704 Rosemount Ave.
Cornwall, ON K6J 3E6
613-933-3380
Fax: 613-937-0987
cornwall.lg.ca@linde.com

Dartmouth
Burnside Industrial Park
#12, 10 Thornhill Dr.
Dartmouth, NS B3B 1S1
902-468-6595
Fax: 902-468-6596
halifax.lg.ca@linde.com

Drummondville
560, rue Cormier
Québec, QC J2C 5C4
819-478-4216
Fax: 819-478-5867
drummondville.lg.ca@linde.com

Edmonton
6569 Gateway Blvd.
Edmonton, AB T6H 2J1
780-989-5995
Fax: 780-437-3168
edmonton.lg.ca@linde.com

Fort McMurray
196 MacDonald Cres.
Fort McMurray, AB T9H 4B2
780-743-8622
Fax: 780-790-1321
fortmcmurray.lg.ca@linde.com

Granby
37, rue Carrier
Granby, QC J2J 2M6
450-378-5930
Fax: 450-378-1022
granby.lg.ca@linde.com

Grande Prairie
10915 - 86 Ave.
Grande Prairie, AB T8V 8K2
780-538-8200
Fax: 780-538-3292
grandprairie.lg.ca@linde.com

Guelph
404 Elizabeth St.
Guelph, ON N1H 6J6
519-822-6490
Fax: 519-822-0651
guelph.lg.ca@linde.com

Hull
1025, boul de la Carrière
Hull, QC J8Y 6W5
819-777-7375
Fax: 819-777-7400
hull.lg.ca@linde.com

Joliette
989, rue Raoul-Charette
Joliette, QC J6E 8S4
450-759-7878
Fax: 450-759-8239
joliette.lg.ca@linde.com

Kingston
35 Terry Fox Dr.
Kingston, ON K7L 4V8
613-548-4242
Fax: 613-548-8338
kingston.lg.ca@linde.com

Kitimat
331 Enterprise Ave.
Kitimat, BC V8C 2E1
250-639-9188
Fax: 250-632-2700
kitimat.lg.ca@linde.com

Langley
10097 - 201 St.
Langley, BC V1M 3G4
604-882-7642
Fax: 604-882-7645
langley.lg.ca@linde.com

Laval
930, rue Bergar
Laval, QC H7L 5A1
450-663-5570
Fax: 450-663-3399
laval.lg.ca@linde.com

Lloydminster
6201C - 50th Ave.
Lloydminster, SK S9V 2G4
306-825-2222
Fax: 306-825-5608
lloydminster.lg.ca@linde.com

London
20 Towerline Pl.
London, ON N6E 2T1
519-686-4150
Fax: 519-686-8452
london.lg.ca@linde.com

Matagami
16, rue Nottaway
Matagami, QC J0Y 2A0
819-739-4113
Fax: 819-739-4185
matagami.lg.ca@linde.com

Midland
293 Whitfield Cres.
Midland, ON L4R 4K6
705-526-3704
Fax: 705-526-8099
midland.lg.ca@linde.com

Moncton
24 Somers Rd.
Moncton, NB E1H 3C9
506-858-0306
Fax: 506-857-1727
moncton.lg.ca@linde.com

Montréal (Saint-Laurent)
5615, rue Vanden-Abeele
Montréal, QC H4S 1S1
514-335-0455
Fax: 514-335-0249
stlaurent.lg.ca@linde.com

Montréal (St-Léonard)
5555, boul des Grandes Prairies
Montréal, QC H1R 1B4
514-323-4110
Fax: 514-323-7261
stleonard.lg.ca@linde.com

Montréal (St-Patrick)
2720B, rue St-Patrick
Montréal, QC H3K 1B8
514-933-8113
Fax: 514-933-0342
stpatrick.lg.ca@linde.com

Nisku
1309 - 8 St.
Nisku, AB T9E 7M4
780-955-2269
Fax: 780-955-3344
nisku.lg.ca@linde.com

North Bay
1810 Seymour St.
North Bay, ON P1B 8J1
705-472-6430
Fax: 705-472-4573
northbay.lg.ca@linde.com

Oakville
#3, 1410 Speers Rd.
Oakville, ON L6L 5M1
905-469-9680
Fax: 905-469-9682
oakville.lg.ca@linde.com

Ottawa
1101 Parisien St.
Ottawa, ON K1B 3R6
613-745-9455
Fax: 613-744-8786
ottawa.lg.ca@linde.com

Owen Sound
1935 - 17th St. East
Owen Sound, ON N4K 5P5
519-376-4087
Fax: 519-371-6040
owensound.lg.ca@linde.com

Pembroke
#110, 320 Boundary Rd. East
Pembroke, ON K8A 6W5
613-732-3561
Fax: 613-735-3296
pembroke.lg.ca@linde.com

Peterborough
#201, 375 Pido Rd., RR#6
Peterborough, ON K9J 6X7
705-743-0292
866-256-7359

Québec
579, av Godin
Québec, QC G1M 3G7
418-688-0150
Fax: 418-688-3409
quebeccity.lg.ca@linde.com

Regina
665 McDonald St.
Regina, SK S4N 4X1
306-525-6176
Fax: 306-565-3883
regina.lg.ca@linde.com

Rivière-du-Loup
45, rue du Carrefour
Rivière-du-Loup, QC G5R 6B5
418-867-2737
Fax: 418-867-3590
riviereduloup.lg.ca@linde.com

Rouyn-Noranda
305, boul Industriel
Rouyn-Noranda, QC J9X 6P2
819-764-6103
Fax: 819-764-3470
rouyn.lg.ca@linde.com

Saint-Georges-de-Beauce
15550, boul Lacroix
Saint-Georges-de-Beauce, QC G5Y 1R7
418-228-3272
beauce.lg.ca@linde.com

Saint-Jean-sur-Richelieu
720, rue St-Jacques
Saint-Jean-sur-Richelieu, QC J3B 2M7
450-347-5394
Fax: 450-347-2057
stjean.lg.ca@linde.com

Sarnia
#1, 101 Duff Dr.
Sarnia, ON N7W 1A7
519-336-2239
Fax: 519-336-1645
sarnia.lg.ca@linde.com

Saskatoon
#A, 720 - 51 St. East
Saskatoon, SK S7K 4K4

306-394-1183
Fax: 306-931-7822
saskatoon.lg.ca@linde.com

Sherbrooke
1240, rue Galt est
Sherbrooke, QC J1G 1Y5
819-564-7877
Fax: 819-564-0619
sherbrooke.lg.ca@linde.com

St-Hubert
4635, rue Fortier
Saint-Hubert, QC J3Y 7L3
450-676-6224
Fax: 450-676-0877
sthubert.lg.ca@linde.com

St. Catharines
2 Cushman Rd.
St Catharines, ON L2M 6S8
905-684-2364
Fax: 905-684-9164
stcatharines.lg.ca@linde.com

Stoney Creek
4 Commerce Ct.
Stoney Creek, ON L8E 4G3
905-643-6999
Fax: 905-643-3666
stoneycreek.lg.ca@linde.com

Stratford
63 Griffith Rd. West
Stratford, ON N5A 6S4
519-271-2882
Fax: 519-271-9901
stratford.lg.ca@linde.com

Sudbury
#, 1476 Falconbridge Rd.
Sudbury, ON P3A 4S8
705-566-3660
Fax: 705-566-1466
sudbury.lg.ca@linde.com

Timmins
855 Algonquin Blvd. East
Timmins, ON P4N 7H1
705-268-6466
Fax: 705-268-5266
timmins.lg.ca@linde.com

Toronto (Etobicoke)
88 North Queen St.
Toronto, ON M8Z 2C9
416-251-6505
Fax: 416-251-1072
etobicoke.lg.ca@linde.com

Trois-Rivières
2835, rue Sidbec nord
Trois-Rivières, QC G8Z 3X8
819-373-1017
Fax: 819-373-1896
troisrivieres.lg.ca@linde.com

Val d'Or
1450, rue 4e
Val-d'Or, QC J9P 6X2
819-825-6011
Fax: 819-824-6771
valdor.lg.ca@linde.com

Vancouver
54 East 3rd Ave.
Vancouver, BC V5T 1C3
604-255-6531
Fax: 604-707-0812
vancouver.lg.ca@linde.com

Victoria
538 Hillside Ave.
Victoria, BC V8T 1Y9
250-383-4041
Fax: 250-383-8355
victoria.lg.ca@linde.com

Waterloo
#1, 611 Colby Dr.
Waterloo, ON N2V 1A1
519-884-1320
Fax: 519-884-0248
waterloo.lg.ca@linde.com

Whitby
1111 Burns St. East
Whitby, ON L1N 6A6
905-668-6877
Fax: 905-668-0924
whitby.lg.ca@linde.com

Windsor
1935 Provincial Rd.
Windsor, ON N8W 5V7
519-948-6666
Fax: 519-948-5385
windsor.lg.ca@linde.com

Winnipeg
875 King Edward St.
Winnipeg, MB R3H 0P8
204-987-7800
Fax: 204-694-3515
winnipeg.lg.ca@linde.com

Bodycot Analex Inc.
3025, Montée St-Aubin
Laval, QC H7L 4E4
450-682-3240
Fax: 450-682-6995
www.bodycote.ca
Firm Type: Engineering, Scientific/Technical Services
Founded: 1973
Staff: 90
Products/Services/Areas of Expertise: Research, development & quality control in chemistry, biology, biotechnology, toxicology; fate assessment & industrial wastewater treatment; site evaluation; decommissioning; environmental audits; human & environmental risk assessment; laboratory facilities for soil, water, air, sediments & waste analysis
Domestic Markets:
New Brunswick, Newfoundland & Labrador, Ontario
Foreign Activity:
Central America, Western Europe, USA
Contact(s):
Vincent Lenaerts, Ph.D., President

Boilersmith Ltd.
P.O. Box 70
156 Main St. S
Seaforth, ON N0K 1W0
519-527-0600
Fax: 519-527-0150
boilersales@boilersmith.com
www.boilersmith.com
Firm Type: Manufacturing
Founded: 1987
Staff: 20
Products/Services/Areas of Expertise: Manufacturer of firetube boilers for woodwaste burning systems & sewage sludge gas burning
Financial Information:
Type of Ownership: Private
Revenue: $1.5 Million - $3 Million
Domestic Markets:
National
Foreign Activity:
USA
Contact(s):
Charles B. Smith, President
Dan Bennewies, Manager, Marketing
Richard Verberve, Manager, Sales

Bolger and Associates Ltd.
#402, 441 William St.
North Bay, ON P1A 1X6
705-471-8484
Fax: 705-476-0475
pbolger@bolgerandassociates.com
www.bolgerandassociates.com
Firm Type: Management Consulting
Founded: 2001
Staff: 1
Member of: Canadian Environmental Auditing Association
Products/Services/Areas of Expertise: Consulting in environmental health & safety; services include strategic planning, scenario planning, management systems & auditing, risk management, leadership training & coaching, accident prevention & investigation, contingency planning, environmental impact assessment, facilitation, & negotiation/mediation.
Financial Information:
Type of Ownership: Private
Revenue Sources: 100% Private Contracts
Domestic Markets:
Ontario
Markets Sought:
Asia, Australia/New Zealand, Central Europe, Western Europe, South America, USA,
Contact(s):
Pat Bolger, B.Sc., M.Sc., CEA, President

BOMA Environmental & Safety Inc. / BOMA E&S
#203, 2621 Portage Ave.
Winnipeg, MB R3J 0P7
204-889-5275
Fax: 204-889-2348
info@bomaes.ca
www.bomaes.ca
Firm Type: Management Consulting, Engineering, Scientific/Technical Services
Founded: 1996
Staff: 4
Member of: Western Canada Water & Wastewater Association; Association of Professional Engineers of Manitoba; Professional Engineers Ontario; Association of the Chemical Profession of Ontario; Air & Waste Management Association
Products/Services/Areas of Expertise: A consulting firm specializing in environmental management & occupational health & safety concerns. The company provides a range of services: air pollution control, environmental audits, impact assessment, site assessment, risk assessment, permitting & approvals, & solid & hazardous waste management. Other services include development of WHMIS in the workplace, employee training, & fire prevention & safety
Recently Completed / Ongoing Projects: Environmental permitting for various industries (woodworking, commercial printing, metal, etc.); stack testing for an aerospace company; mould & asbestos sampling & remediation
Financial Information:
Type of Ownership: Private
Revenue: $100,000 - $250,000
Revenue Sources: 30% Municipals; 70% Private Contracts
Domestic Markets:
Manitoba, Ontario
Foreign Activity:
Central Europe
Markets Sought:
The Middle East, The Pacific Rim, USA
Contact(s):
Dinko Tuhtar, P.Eng., Sr. Environmental Engineer

Boojum Research Ltd.
1459 Pickwick Dr.
Mississauga, ON L5V 1V7
416-861-1086
Fax: 416-861-0634
margarete.kalin@utoronto.ca
www.boojumresearch.com
Firm Type: Scientific/Technical Services
Founded: 1987
Staff: 2
Products/Services/Areas of Expertise: Ecological engineering for base metal, uranium & coal wastes; decommissioning technology for mining waste management areas
Activities: On-site research & development of wastewater treatment in mining industry; ecological engineering for base metals, uranium & coal waste; biological nitrogen compound removal from wastewater
Recently Completed / Ongoing Projects: Several mine sites in Canada
Financial Information:
Type of Ownership: Private
Revenue: $250,000 - $500,000
Revenue Sources: 100% Private Contracts
Domestic Markets:
Newfoundland & Labrador, Ontario, Saskatchewan
Foreign Activity:
Central Europe
Contact(s):
Margarete Kalin, President & Research Director
Martin Smith, Vice-President, Operations

Border Chemical Company Ltd.
P.O. Box 62037
104 Regent
Winnipeg, MB R2C 5G2
204-222-3276
Fax: 204-224-0562
Firm Type: Manufacturing
Founded: 1959
Staff: 75
Products/Services/Areas of Expertise: Chemical production; cleaners/chemical
Financial Information:
Type of Ownership: Publicly Traded
Domestic Markets:
Manitoba, Ontario, Saskatchewan
Foreign Activity:
USA
Contact(s):
Dennis Smerchanski, General Manager
Jim Moreton, Sales Manager
Egan Godfredson, Plant Superintendent

BOS Engineering & Environmental Services Inc.
46 Donnybrook Rd.
London, ON N5X 3C8
519-850-9987
Fax: 519-663-8057
a.bos@sympatico.ca
Firm Type: Management Consulting, Engineering, Scientific/Technical Services
Founded: 1995
Staff: 5
Products/Services/Areas of Expertise: Soil & water engineering services for waste treatment; erosion control; flood levels; subdivision/severance planning; stormwater management; watershed studies, with a focus on rural non-point source pollution & its control; sediment control & remediation; fisheries habitat management
Recently Completed / Ongoing Projects: Reservoir Rehabilitation Study, Mount Forest, ON; source reduction accounting model to estimate pollutant reduction from implementation of rural non-point source practices on watershed scale; phosphorus effluent trading in Bay of Quinte watershed; case study of phosphorus effluent trading in Kawartha watershed, ON
Financial Information:
Type of Ownership: Private
Revenue Sources: 90% Private Contracts
Domestic Markets:
Ontario
Markets Sought:
Mexico, USA
Contact(s):
Art Bos, President

Both Belle Robb Ltd.
526, route de Masonville
Masonville, QC J0E 1X0
514-396-3314
gcb@bbrl.com
www.bbrl.com
Firm Type: Management Consulting, Engineering, Scientific/Technical Services
Founded: 1973
Staff: 20
Products/Services/Areas of Expertise: Engineering services; construction management; hydro turnkey services
Financial Information:
Type of Ownership: Private
Revenue Sources: 5% nationwide; 10% Provincial; 85% Private Contracts
Domestic Markets:
National
Foreign Activity:
Asia, Central America, South America, USA,
Contact(s):
G. Carlo Belle, President

International Branch(es):
BBRL Inc.
#200, 3500 Eastern Blvd.
Montgomery, AL USA
205-271-4100
Fax: 205-271-4192

Boucher Precast Concrete Ltd.
Armtec Limited Partnership
5598 Power Rd.
Gloucester, ON K1G 3N4
613-822-1488; 613-521-5893
Fax: 613-822-2302
800-344-0151
bpc@storm.ca
www.boucherprecast.com
Firm Type: Manufacturing
Founded: 1954
Products/Services/Areas of Expertise: Manufactures box culverts, median barriers, catch basins & maintenance holes; conducts concrete testing; tests for slump & air entrainment
Financial Information:
Type of Ownership: Private
Domestic Markets:
Québec
Contact(s):
Paul Boucher, President

Boutillette Parizeau et Associés inc.
9825, rue Verville
Montréal, QC H3L 3E1
514-383-3747
Fax: 514-383-8760
info@bpa.ca
www.bpa.ca
Firm Type: Engineering
Founded: 1956
Staff: 125
Member of: Association des Ingénieurs du Québec; Association of Professional Engineers of Ontario
Quality Environmental Management System(s): 9001
Products/Services/Areas of Expertise: Mechanical, electrical, energy, telecommunication, studies & analyses, plans, specifications, supervision, ventilating, air conditioning, heating, piping, refrigerating, plumbing, fire protection, controls, security systems
Recently Completed / Ongoing Projects: Caisse de dépôt et placement du Québec; Complexe Hôtelier du Casino du Lac-Leamy; Complex les Ailes de la Mode
Financial Information:
Type of Ownership: Private
Domestic Markets:
Ontario, Québec
Foreign Activity:
Africa, Former USSR
Contact(s):
Claude Decary, ing., Président/directeur général
cdecary@bpa.ca
Yvan Côté, ing., Project Manager

Bowater Canadian Forest Products Inc.
AbitibiBowater Inc.
Formerly: Bowater Pulp & Paper Canada Inc., Avenor Inc.2001 Neebing Ave.
Thunder Bay, ON P7E 6S3
807-475-2110
Fax: 807-475-8643
info@abitibibowater.com
www.bowater.ca
Firm Type: Manufacturing
Founded: 1998
Staff: 616
Quality Environmental Management System(s): 14001
Products/Services/Areas of Expertise: Paper & magazine stock recycling; pulp & paper manufacturing; northern bleached softwood/hardwood kraft pulp; virgin & recycled newsprint
Domestic Markets:
British Columbia, New Brunswick, Ontario, Québec
Foreign Activity:
USA
Contact(s):
Doug Murray, Manager

Bowie Environmental Edge Management & Assessment Ltd.
240 Ormond St.
Brockville, ON K6V 2L5
613-345-7337
Fax: 613-345-0358
Contact(s):
James S. Bowie, President

Bowie Pumps of Canada Ltd.
9333 - 41st Ave. NW
Edmonton, AB T6E 6R5
780-465-7812
Fax: 780-469-2587
877-862-6943
info@bowiepumps.com
www.bowiepumps.com
Firm Type: Manufacturing
Founded: 1983
Products/Services/Areas of Expertise: Rotary gear pumps
Contact(s):
T.W. Kunyk, President & General Manager, 780/469-2587
S. Stubbard, Sales

Bowser Technical Inc.
200 St. George St.
Brantford, ON N3R 1W4
519-756-9116
Fax: 519-756-9227
dara@bowsertech.com
www.bowsertech.com
Firm Type: Scientific/Technical Services
Founded: 1989
Member of: Solar Energy Society of Canada Inc.; Heating, Refrigeration & Air Conditioning Institute; Canadian Home Builders Association; Ontario Building Officials Association; Association of Architectural Technologists of Ontario
Products/Services/Areas of Expertise: Building ventilation systems; indoor air quality; building energy efficiency
Contact(s):
Dara G. Bowser, President

BP Canada Energy Company
240 - 4th Ave. SW
Calgary, AB T2P 2H8
403-233-1313
Fax: 403-233-1444
www.bp.com
Firm Type: Distributing, Engineering
Staff: 1500
Products/Services/Areas of Expertise: Active in natural gas exploration, development, production, marketing & trading; significant position in the natural gas liquids business; active in marketing & trading petrochemicals, power, crude oil, lubricants & jet fuel; operates pipelines, storage terminals, & gathering & processing facilities
Recently Completed / Ongoing Projects: Mist Mountain Coalbed Gas Project; Noel Major Project (natural gas development)
Financial Information:
Type of Ownership: Foreign-owned
Contact(s):
Brian E. Frank, President & CEO

BP Trading Ltd.
7 Edward St.
Truro, NS B2N 3E2
902-895-2243
Fax: 902-895-5025
866-281-6197
bobbrown@bptrading.ca
www.bptrading.ca
Products/Services/Areas of Expertise: Markets environmental products & services in New England & Atlantic Canada specifically those for dust control & stabilization on unpaved roads & highways & super absorbents to handle industry spill & leak-related problems
Domestic Markets:
New Brunswick, Newfoundland & Labrador, Nova Scotia, Prince Edward Island
Foreign Activity:
USA
Contact(s):
Robert Brown, President

BPG Graphics Solutions
Formerly: Baker Graphics Inc.
800 Cochrane Dr.
Markham, ON L3R 8C9
905-944-9444
Fax: 905-944-9111
877-602-3737
www.bpggraphics.com
Firm Type: Scientific/Technical Services
Founded: 1992

EcoLogo Certified Products & Services: Commercial offset printer
Products/Services/Areas of Expertise: Offset printing; received FSC certification (SCG-COC-004789), promoting responsible management of the world's forests
Ecological Note: Commercial offset printer
Financial Information:
Type of Ownership: Private
Domestic Markets:
National
Markets Sought:
USA
Contact(s):
Steve Trypis, Operating Manager, Sales
strypis@bpggraphics.com

BPR
Formerly: Beaulieu, Poulin et Robitaille, Ingénieurs-conseils; Asseau Inc.
4655, boul Wilfrid-Hamel
Québec, QC G1P 2J7
418-871-8151
Fax: 418-871-9625
pierre.lavallee@groupe-bpr.com
www.groupe-bpr.com
Firm Type: Management Consulting, Engineering
Founded: 1961
Member of: Ordre des ingénieurs du Québec
Products/Services/Areas of Expertise: A multi-disciplinary firm specializing in civil, structural & municipal engineering, with a focus on wastewater treatment, maritime engineering, municipal infrastrucutre projects, & construction management. Clients are from the chemical, petrochemical, & mining industries. Offices throughout Québec, in Ontario & in France
Financial Information:
Type of Ownership: Private
Revenue: $500,000 - $1.5 Million
Domestic Markets:
Québec
Foreign Activity:
Western Europe, USA
Markets Sought:
USA
Contact(s):
Pierre Lavallée, Ph.D. (Water), President/CEO
Paul Lafleur, M.Sc., Chairman
Rino Dumont, Director

Brace Centre for Water Resources Management
McGill University
Formerly: Brace Research InstituteCivil Engineering & Applied Mechanics
Mcdonald Campus
P.O. Box 900
#21, 111 Lakeshore Rd.
Ste. Anne de Bellevue, QC H9X 3V9
514-398-7833
Fax: 514-398-7767
brace@mcgill.ca
www.mcgill.ca/brace
Firm Type: Engineering, Scientific/Technical Services
Founded: 1959
Products/Services/Areas of Expertise: Research & development of methods of eliminating or reducing salt content of sea water for effective economical use for irrigation; water resources development; water delivery systems of arid regions in developing areas of the world & related technology development for increased productivity
Domestic Markets:
National
Foreign Activity:
Africa, Asia, Central America, The Middle East, South America
Contact(s):
V.T.V. Nguyen, P.Eng.; MEng.; PhD, Director, 514-398-6870Fax: 514-398-7361
Edward McKyes, Associate Director, Macdonald Campus
Nathalie Tufenkji, Associate Director, McGill Campus
Suzelle Barrington, Academic Staff, Waste & Water Management; Gender Equity
Carolyne Choquette, Academic Staff, Hydrology Modeling; GIS; Water Policy
Peter G. Brown, Academic Staff, Ethics, government & the environment
Joann Whalen, Academic Staff, Soil ecology & nutrient management in agroecosystems
Chandra A. Madramootoo, Academic Staff, Irrigation & Drainage; Water Quality

Bracebridge Generation Ltd.
196 Taylor Rd.
Bracebridge, ON P1L 1J9
705-646-9014
Fax: 705-645-4667
www.bracebridgegeneration.com
Firm Type: Manufacturing
Founded: 1894
EcoLogo Certified Products & Services: Generates environmentally friendly local electricity
Products/Services/Areas of Expertise: Mission is to generate environmentally friendly local electricity; promote the efficient use of electrical energy; maintain safety and operating standards for electricity generation; provide informative & instructional tours; maintain the historic richness of its 4 facilities
Ecological Note: Generates environmentally friendly local electricity
Contact(s):
Chris Litschko, President/CEO

Bradex Industrial Services Ltd.
Also Known As: Bradex Chemicals for Industry
#201, 904 The East Mall
Toronto, ON M9B 6K2
416-626-8943
Fax: 416-620-5648
bradexchem@bellnet.ca
www.bradexchem.com
Firm Type: Distributing
Founded: 1984
Staff: 5
Products/Services/Areas of Expertise: Brokering surplus materials & chemicals; methanol, formaldehyde, UREA; caustic chemical recycling; waste streams; soil remediation consulting
Financial Information:
Type of Ownership: Private
Revenue: $250,000 - $500,000
Revenue Sources: 100% Private Contracts
Domestic Markets:
Ontario
Contact(s):
Edward Gres, President/CEO
Rob Klimkait, Manager, Marketing
Anni Cvitan, Administration

Bradford White Canada Inc.
1869 Sismet Rd.
Mississauga, ON L4W 1W8
905-238-0100
Fax: 905-238-0105
info@bradfordwhitecanada.com
www.bradfordwhite.com
Firm Type: Manufacturing
Founded: 1940
Member of: Canadian Oil Heat Association
Products/Services/Areas of Expertise: The company offers a wide variety of products related to water heating and storage, including: flame retention oil burners & gas burners; oil-fired water heaters; power gas burners; air handlers; solar water heaters; storage tanks
Financial Information:
Type of Ownership: Private
Revenue: Greater than $5 Million
Revenue Sources: 100% Private Contracts
Domestic Markets:
National
Foreign Activity:
Caribbean, USA
Markets Sought:
Australia/New Zealand, China, Vietnam
Contact(s):
Ian D.M. Brooker, Vice-President/General Manager
Michael Brooker, Vice-President, Manufacturing
Paul McDonald, Contact, Sales
pmcdonald@bradfordwhitecanada.com

Brampton Engineering Inc.
8031 Dixie Rd.
Brampton, ON L6T 3V1
905-793-3000
Fax: 905-793-1753
800-867-9997
salesadmin@be-ca.com
www.be-ca.com
Firm Type: Manufacturing
Founded: 1983
Member of: Society of Plastics; Canadian Manufacturers Association
Quality Environmental Management System(s): 9001:2000
Products/Services/Areas of Expertise: Multilayer blown film systems (air & water quenched); extruders, screws, screen changers, dies, air rings, internal bubble cooling systems, cages, nips, haul-offs, winders, process control systems
Financial Information:
Type of Ownership: Private
Revenue: Greater than $5 Million
Revenue Sources: 100% Private Contracts
Domestic Markets:
National
Foreign Activity:
Worldwide
Contact(s):
R.L. (Bud) Smith, President & Chief Executive Officer
bsmith@be-ca.com
Philip Kwok, Vice-President, Sales - World Wide
pkwok@be-ca.com
Jim Stobie, Vice President, Sales - North America

International Branch(es):
BE (China) Inc.
Zhongyinhuilong Bldg.
#1707, 8 Suhua Road
Suzhou, Jiangsu China
86-512-6295-91887
Fax: 86-512-65226627
be@be-china.cn
Zhang Ai Hue, General Manager

Delhi Industries Inc.
Formerly: Delhi Sheet Metal Works
Manufacturing
523 James St.
Delhi, ON N4B 2Z3
519-582-2440
Fax: 519-582-0581
sales@delhi-industries.com
www.delhi-industries.com
Firm Type: Distributing, Manufacturing
Founded: 1939
Staff: 150
Products/Services/Areas of Expertise: Manufacturer of air moving products, such as blowers & fans; Clients include the heating, ventilation, & air conditioning industry & the original equipment manufacturers furnace & appliance markets
Financial Information:
Type of Ownership: Private
Domestic Markets:
National
Foreign Activity:
USA,
Contact(s):
David Thurgood, President
dthurgood@delhi-industries.com
Jerry VanLeuvenhage, Specialist, Product Development
jvanleuvenhage@delhi-industries.com

Brantford
Sales & Distribution
83 Shaver St.
Brantford, ON N3T 5M1
519-582-2440
Fax: 519-582-0581
sales@delhi-industries.com

Brantford Disposal Service
P.O. Box 271
144 Mohawk St.
Brantford, ON N3T 5M8
519-756-6380
Fax: 519-752-5455
Products/Services/Areas of Expertise: Recycling services; waste treatment facilities & equipment
Contact(s):
Gary Norris, Manager

Brass Craft Canada Ltd.
35 Currah Rd.
St Thomas, ON N5P 3R2
519-633-0340
Fax: 519-633-0777

800-265-4322
www.brasscraft.com
Firm Type: Distributing, Manufacturing
Founded: 1967
Staff: 110
Member of: Canadian Standards Association; Canadian Home & Hardware Manufacturers Association
Products/Services/Areas of Expertise: Water supply & gas appliance connector products for professional plumbing; machining non-ferrous alloys
Financial Information:
Type of Ownership: Publicly Traded
Domestic Markets:
National
Contact(s):
Todd Talbot, President
Doug Kennedy, Manager, Sales (Wholesale)
DKennedy@brasscrafthq.com
Bob Husband, Manager, Sales (OEM)
BHusband@brasscrafthq.com

Braymo Energy Corporation
P.O. Box 123
110 - 2nd Ave.
Torrington, AB T0M 2B0
Fax: 866-327-2966
877-327-2966
info@braymo.com
www.braymo.com
Firm Type: Distributing, Manufacturing
Products/Services/Areas of Expertise: Custom design and supply of heating systems that use alternative fuel sources
Financial Information:
Type of Ownership: Private
Domestic Markets:
National
Foreign Activity:
USA

Brendar Environmental Inc.
Formerly: Brendar Environmental Associates
1220 Rockwood Dr.
Kingston, ON K7P 2L1
613-634-2010
Fax: 613-634-2577
800-440-9744
office@brendar.com
www.brendar.com
Firm Type: Waste Management
Founded: 1994
Staff: 7
Products/Services/Areas of Expertise: Specializes in hazardous waste management services for industrial commercial services & institutional sectors; services household hazardous waste programs for municipalities; transportation & disposal facilities
Recently Completed / Ongoing Projects: Household Hazardous Waste Programs, Ontario municipalities; training sessions
Financial Information:
Type of Ownership: Private
Domestic Markets:
Ontario
Contact(s):
T.B. (Brent) Bolger, President & Technical Director
Gordon Nijboer, Manager, Accounting
gordon@brendar.com

Brenntag Canada Inc.
Formerly: Stanchem Inc.
43 Jutland Rd.
Toronto, ON M8Z 2G6
416-259-8131
Fax: 416-259-6175
800-387-7324
sales@brenntag.ca
www.brenntag.ca
Firm Type: Distributing, Manufacturing
Staff: 150
Member of: The Chlorine Institute Incorporated; American Water Works Association; Canadian Water & Waste Water Association; Water Environment Association of Ontario
Products/Services/Areas of Expertise: Water treatment chemicals; sodium hypochlorite for potable water & wastewater disinfection
Domestic Markets:
National
Canadian Branches:
Calgary
777 - 8th Ave. SW, 19th fl.
Calgary, AB T2P 3R5
Fax: 403-233-7011
877-252-9301

Dartmouth
105 Akerley Blvd., #A
Dartmouth, NS B3B 1R7
902-468-9690
Fax: 902-468-3085

Edmonton
6628 - 45th St.
Leduc, AB T9E 7C9
780-986-4544
Fax: 780-986-1070

Fort St. John
9709 - 78th St.
Fort St John, BC V1J 4J8
250-785-4441
Fax: 250-785-9988

Grande Prairie
#210, 13925 - 99th St.
Grande Prairie, AB T8V 7G2
780-538-1141
Fax: 780-532-9098

Langley
20333 - 102B Ave.
Langley, BC V1M 3H1
604-513-9009
Fax: 604-513-9010

Montréal
2900, rue Jean-Baptiste Deschamps
Lachine, QC H8T 1C8
514-636-9230
Fax: 514-636-8229

Toronto
60 Titan Rd.
Toronto, ON M8Z 2J8
416-259-8231
Fax: 416-233-7706

Winnipeg
681 Plinguet St.
Winnipeg, MB R2J 2X2
204-233-3416
Fax: 204-233-7005

BRI International Inc.
#200, 2595 Skymark Ave.
Mississauga, ON L4W 4L5
905-629-8788
Fax: 905-629-8798
800-661-2948
bri@bri.ca
www.bri.ca
Firm Type: Management Consulting
Founded: 1985
Staff: 7
Member of: Canadian Manufacturers & Exporters Canada, Ontario Chamber of Commerce
Products/Services/Areas of Expertise: Using international best practices & standards as guidelines, provides consulting services & training in change management to organizations. Focus is on sustainable practices & socially responsible corporate behaviours. Services also include consulting in risk management systems for water & wastewater utilities, as well as for food & water safety, the environment, health & safety in the workplace, & managing greenhouse gas emissions (based on ISO 14064-1 & 14064-2). BRI is developing its Aboriginal Centre of Excellence for Sustainable Development, to enable Aboriginal peoples to contribute to sustainability efforts in their communities
Recently Completed / Ongoing Projects: Drinking Water Quality Management Systems in Ontario, water utilities; Implementing CSR & sustainable development in India; Training trainers & management consultants in Brazil, Canada, Costa Rica, India & Jamaica
Financial Information:
Type of Ownership: Private
Revenue: $500,000 - $1.5 Million
Revenue Sources: 40% Municipals; 50% Private Contracts
Domestic Markets:
National
Foreign Activity:
Worldwide
Contact(s):
Robert G. (Bob) White, B.A.Sc., MBA, P.Eng., CMC, President
bob@brc.ca

Brian Clark Architect
525 County Rd. 11
Picton, ON K0K 2T0
613-476-4839
Fax: 613-476-4839
brianc@connect.reach.net
Firm Type: Engineering
Founded: 1986
Staff: 2
Member of: Ontario Association of Architects
Products/Services/Areas of Expertise: Environmental design; architectural design; passive solar design; restorations; ecological design
Recently Completed / Ongoing Projects: Community daycare; private residences; banks
Financial Information:
Type of Ownership: Private
Revenue Sources: 20% Provincial; 20% Municipals; 60% Private Contracts
Domestic Markets:
Ontario
Contact(s):
Brian Clark, President/CEO

Brim Pumps & Systems Ltd.
#38, 1320 Britannia Rd. East
Mississauga, ON L4W 1C8
905-670-0140
Fax: 905-670-8246
877-202-5522
brim@bellnet.ca
Firm Type: Distributing, Manufacturing
Founded: 1977
Products/Services/Areas of Expertise: Pumping viscous, solids & abrasive materials
Financial Information:
Type of Ownership: Private
Domestic Markets:
National
Contact(s):
Brian J. Mulvihill, President
Norm Collier, Sales Manager
Joy Robinson, Office Manager

Brincad Technologies Inc.
#1105, 3400 Riverspray Cres.
Mississauga, ON L4Y 3M5
905-615-0584
Fax: 905-615-9598
sales@brincad.ca
www.brincad.ca
Firm Type: Management Consulting
Founded: 1993
Staff: 1
Products/Services/Areas of Expertise: Brincad Technologies helps minimize change in our global climates & maximize gains in our key resources - by prioritizing knowledge, tools & actions needed to manage the pathways & sustainability of resources
Contact(s):
Brian Davies, President

Brisbin & Sentis Engineering Inc. / BSEI
Centre Eight Ten
#110, 7777 10th St. NE
Calgary, AB T2E 8X2
403-247-2001
Fax: 403-247-2013
bsei@bsei.ca
www.bsei.ca
Firm Type: Engineering
Founded: 1977
Products/Services/Areas of Expertise: Engineering consulting services; water & wastewater management; impact assessments; water & wastewater management services; Municipal consulting engineers
Contact(s):
Richard K. Geleta, P.Eng., President & Director/Senior Engineer
Raymond Bouillet, C.E.T., Vice-President & Director

Bristar Containment Industries Ltd.
P.O. Box 643
119 Railway Ave.
Wimborne, AB T0M 2G0
Fax: 403-631-3454
877-631-3453
info@bristarcontainment.com
www.bristarcontainment.com
Firm Type: Manufacturing
Founded: 1995
Staff: 15
Products/Services/Areas of Expertise: Manufactures secondary containment systems for above ground storage tanks; services include: design, engineering, fabrication & installation; products include steel berms, geomembranes & geotextiles
Recently Completed / Ongoing Projects: Upgrade secondary containment, Imperial Oil, Cynthia; secondary containment installation, Encana; installation secondary containment, Talisman Lakeview
Financial Information:
Type of Ownership: Private
Revenue: Greater than $5 Million
Revenue Sources: 100% Private Contracts
Domestic Markets:
Alberta, British Columbia, Saskatchewan, Yukon Territory
Foreign Activity:
Africa, Caribbean
Contact(s):
Brian Campbell, Project Manager

Broan Canada Ltd.
1140 Tristar Dr.
Mississauga, ON L5T 1H9
905-670-2500
Fax: 905-795-8311
888-882-7626
Products/Services/Areas of Expertise: Manufacturer of range hoods, central vacuum cleaners, bathroom ventilators
Domestic Markets:
National
Contact(s):
Sylvain Fecteau, Vice-President, Operations

Brookfield Power
Formerly: Maclaren Energy Inc.
Brookfield Place
#300, 181 Bay St.
Toronto, ON M5J 2T3
416-363-9491
enquiries@brookfield.com
www.brookfieldpower.com
Products/Services/Areas of Expertise: Producer, transmitter & distributor of hydroelectric power
Ecological Note: Water-powered electricity
Contact(s):
Richard Legault, President & CEO
Donald Tremblay, Exec. Vice-President & CFO

Canadian Branches:
Gatineau Office
480, boul de la Cité
Gatineau, QC J8T 8R3
819-561-2722
Fax: 819-561-7188

Brooklin Concrete Products Ltd.
Armtec Limited Partnership
6760 Baldwin St.
Brooklin, ON L1M 1B5
905-655-3311
Fax: 905-655-3847
800-655-3430
brooklinsales@brooklin.com
www.brooklin.com
Firm Type: Distributing, Manufacturing
Founded: 1952
Products/Services/Areas of Expertise: Markets landscaping products; septic storage tanks/systems; storage buildings/receptors for hazardous materials, electrical equipment, fluids/oils
Financial Information:
Type of Ownership: Private
Domestic Markets:
Ontario

Canadian Branches:
Haliburton
P.O. Box 818
Hwy. 121
Haliburton, ON K0M 1S0
705-457-1395
Fax: 705-457-2587
800-273-9084
haliburtonsales@brooklin.com

Huntsville
P.O. Box 5449
Hwy. 11
Huntsville, ON P1H 3K8
705-789-2338
Fax: 705-789-9829
800-264-3302
huntsvillesales@brooklin.com

Newmarket
18599 Yonge St. North
Newmarket, ON L3Y 4V8
905-895-2373
Fax: 905-895-3264
888-407-6443
newmarketsales@brooklin.com

Brosz & Associates
64 Bullock Dr.
Markham, ON L3P 3P2
905-472-6660
Fax: 905-472-6665
info@brosz.net
www.brosz.net
Firm Type: Engineering, Scientific/Technical Services
Founded: 1970
Member of: AAFS; ANSI; ASTM; CEA; CFAA; CSFS; EDA; IAAI; IAE; IAFS; IEEE; IIFES; NETA; NFPA; OEL; PEO; Ryerson University; University of Toronto
Products/Services/Areas of Expertise: Specializes in forensic investigation services for incidents of an electrical, explosive, fire, flood nature; provides legal, expert witness services
Domestic Markets:
National
Foreign Activity:
USA,
Contact(s):
Helmut G. Brosz, P.Eng, President & CEO

Brown Strachan Associates
#2, 1290 Homer St.
Vancouver, BC V6B 2Y5
604-689-0514
Fax: 604-689-2703
bsa@brownstrachan.com
www.brownstrachan.com
Firm Type: Management Consulting, Engineering
Member of: Association of Canadian Engineering Companies; Consulting Engineers of British Columbia
Products/Services/Areas of Expertise: Consulting engineers specializing in acoustics, noise & vibration
Contact(s):
Robert Strachan, Partner
David Brown, Partner

Bruce A. Brown Associates Limited
Also Known As: Brown Associates
#2, 109 Vanderhoof Ave.
Toronto, ON M4G 2H7
416-424-3355
Fax: 416-424-3350
877-666-3355
bruce@brownassociates.ca
12/98 bk"
Firm Type: Engineering, Scientific/Technical Services
Founded: 1971
Staff: 8
Products/Services/Areas of Expertise: Decommission & demolition monitoring; waste reduction; soil & groundwater contamination assessment & remediation; design of large on-site sewage systems; administration of plans approvals process for redevelopment of industrial lands; site investigations for licensing & rehabilitation of pits & quarries; laboratory services
Financial Information:
Revenue Sources: 5% nationwide; 5% Provincial; 90% Private Contracts
Domestic Markets:
Ontario

Contact(s):
B.A. Brown, P.Eng., President/CEO

Bruce Sutherland & Associates Ltd.
95 Joseph Zatzman Dr.
Dartmouth, NS B3B 1N3
902-455-2405
Fax: 902-466-7175
info@brucesutherlandassoc.com
www.brucesutherlandassoc.com
Firm Type: Distributing
Founded: 1954
Quality Environmental Management System(s): 9001:2000
Products/Services/Areas of Expertise: Boilers & boiler room equipment
Domestic Markets:
New Brunswick, Nova Scotia
Contact(s):
James W. Grant, CEO
Wayne Moore, President
Neil Gordon, Vice-President, Sales
Ross Miller, Vice-President, Parts

Canadian Branches:
Fredericton Sales & Service Office
#180, 527 Beaverbrook Ct.
Fredericton, NB E3B 1X6
506-447-8960
Fax: 506-458-9178
ngordon@brucesutherlandassoc.com

Moncton Parts Branch
145 Millenium Blvd.
Moncton, NB E1E 2G7
506-857-0645
Fax: 506-857-0789
rmiller@brucesutherlandassoc.com

Brunet Ltée, Tuyaux de béton
1625, boul Longlois
Salaberry-de-Valleyfield, QC J6S 1C2
450-373-8262
Fax: 450-373-3360
800-871-1577
info@brunet.cc
www.brunet.cc
Firm Type: Manufacturing
Staff: 30
Member of: Canadian Concrete Pipe Association; Association québécoise des fabricants de tuyaux de béton
Products/Services/Areas of Expertise: Concrete pipe; prefabricated concrete products
Contact(s):
Bernard Brunet, Marketing Manager
brunet@rocler.qc.ca

Bryco Environmental
46 Ivygreen Rd.
Keswick, ON L4P 4B6
905-476-0793
Fax: 905-476-4666
info@brycoenvironmental.ca
www.brycoenvironmental.ca
Firm Type: Waste Management
Founded: 1988
Member of: Ontario Waste Management Association
Products/Services/Areas of Expertise: Specializes in hazardous and non-hazardous industrial waste disposal; waste audits and consultation
Domestic Markets:
Ontario
Contact(s):
John K. Bryant, President

Brytex Building Systems Inc.
5610 - 97 St. NW
Edmonton, AB T6E 3J1
780-437-7970
Fax: 780-437-5022
brytex@brytex.com
www.brytex.com
Firm Type: Manufacturing
Founded: 1987
Member of: Manufacturers Health & Safety Association; Alberta Construction Safety Association; Canadian Chamber of Commerce; Sheet Metal Workers International Association
Products/Services/Areas of Expertise: Company designs, manufactures, and erects metal buildings, including

Products & Services Buyer's Guide

self-supporting, rigid frame and pre-engineered type buildings; CAN/CSA A660 Quality System Certified
Domestic Markets:
Alberta, British Columbia, Manitoba, Ontario, Saskatchewan,
Contact(s):
Al Stix, President
Darrell Stix, Controller

BSI Management Systems Canada Inc.
#102, 6205 Airport Rd.
Mississauga, ON L4V 1E1
416-620-9991
Fax: 416-620-9911
800-862-6752
inquiry.canada@bsigroup.com
www.bsiamericas.com/BSICanada/index.xalter
Products/Services/Areas of Expertise: ISO 14000 & ISO 9000 accredited environmental management systems registrar
Domestic Markets:
National

Canadian Branches:
Montréal
#2001, 1, Place Ville Marie
Montréal, QC H3B 2C4

BSM North America
Formerly: Construction Management Technologies Inc.
P.O. Box 915
19 Old Placentia Rd.
Mount Pearl, NL A1N 3C8
709-747-1444
Fax: 709-747-1430
info@bmsna.com
www.bmsna.com
Firm Type: Manufacturing
Founded: 1997
Staff: 4
Quality Environmental Management System(s): 9001
Products/Services/Areas of Expertise: Products & services for sewage waste disposal
Financial Information:
Revenue: $100,000 - $250,000
Contact(s):
Aloysius Ducey, Owner

Bubble Technology Industries Inc. / BTI
P.O. Box 100
31278 Hwy. 17
Chalk River, ON K0J 1J0
613-589-2456
Fax: 613-589-2763
inquiries@bubbletech.ca
www.bubbletech.ca
Firm Type: Manufacturing, Scientific/Technical Services
Founded: 1988
Staff: 20
Products/Services/Areas of Expertise: Radiation detection & analysis; contract research & development; radiation detectors & laboratory services
Domestic Markets:
National
Foreign Activity:
Worldwide
Contact(s):
Lianne Ing, Vice-President, Business Development
Rob Noulty, Ph.D., Manager, Product Sales
Salah Djeffal, Ph.D., Manager, Radiation Services

Buchan, Lawton, Parent Ltd.
Also Known As: BLP Ltd.
#5, 5370 Canotek Rd.
Ottawa, ON K1J 9E6
613-748-3762
Fax: 613-748-3817
getinfo@blp.ca
www.blpltd.com
Firm Type: Engineering
Founded: 1979
Staff: 15
Member of: Association of Professional Engineers of Ontario
Products/Services/Areas of Expertise: Energy & environmental engineering; energy efficiency in buildings; new building design; building retrofit; environmentally appropriate buildings & products
Financial Information:
Type of Ownership: Private

Domestic Markets:
National
Foreign Activity:
USA
Canadian Branches:
Toronto Office
18 Curity Ave.
Toronto, ON M4B 1X7
416-285-7445
Fax: 416-285-7221
getinfo@blp.ca

Buchanan Environmental
136 Gibson St.
Fredericton, NB E3A 4E2
506-454-3474
Fax: 506-454-3532
buchenv@fundy.net
Firm Type: Scientific/Technical Services
Founded: 1991
Staff: 7
Products/Services/Areas of Expertise: Aquatic toxicity assessment studies; potable water analysis - microbiology coliform, Ecoli
Recently Completed / Ongoing Projects: Contracts with Irving Oil, Irving Forest Products, Irving Pulp & Paper, Fraser Papers, Avenor Maritimes Inc., Royal Oak Mines, PCS Inc. (N.B. Division), Repap New Brunswick, St. Anne-Nackawic Pulp Co. Ltd., Lakeutopia Paper, Caribou Mines, McCain Foods (Canada) Ltd., Jacques Whitford Environment Ltd., SGS (Canada) Inc.
Financial Information:
Type of Ownership: Private
Revenue: $100,000 - $250,000
Revenue Sources: 1% Provincial; 99% Private Contracts
Domestic Markets:
New Brunswick, Newfoundland & Labrador, Nova Scotia, Prince Edward Island
Markets Sought:
USA
Contact(s):
Randy D. Buchanan, M.Sc., President

Buckham Transport Ltd.
P.O. Box 601
Peterborough, ON K9J 6Z8
705-939-6311
Fax: 705-939-6763
800-563-1142
buckhamtransp@nexicom.net
www.buckhamtransport.com
Firm Type: Waste Management
Founded: 1948
Staff: 90
Products/Services/Areas of Expertise: Bulk commodity, freight & environmental company; hazardous & non-hazardous waste transfer facility & transportation; response to emergencies, such as spills or hazardous clean-up
Domestic Markets:
National
Foreign Activity:
USA,
Contact(s):
William A. Buckham, President
Bill Hope, General Manager
David Neilson, Manager, Waste Division
Randy Hie, Chief, Maintenance

Buckhorn Canada Inc.
A Myers Industries company
8032 Torbram Rd.
Brampton, ON L6T 3T2
905-791-6500
Fax: 905-791-9942
800-461-7579
sales@buckhorncanada.com
www.buckhorncanada.com
Firm Type: Distributing, Manufacturing
Founded: 1981
Staff: 16
Member of: Blue Bins Unlimited
Products/Services/Areas of Expertise: Designer & manufacturer of pallets, bulk boxes, totes, trays, & other reusable plastic products; serves a range of markets including automotive, electronics, agriculture, food processing, & pharmaceuticals; environmentally friendly products & processes

Financial Information:
Type of Ownership: Publicly Traded
Revenue: $1.5 Million - $3 Million
Revenue Sources: 10% Provincial; 90% Municipals
Domestic Markets:
National
Foreign Activity:
USA
Contact(s):
Jim Morrison, Vice-President/General Manager

Canadian Branches:
Calgary
Western Canada & the Territories
255 Parkside Way SE
Calgary, AB T2J 3Z3
403-278-9303
Fax: 403-225-1696
mbusby@shaw.ca
Mathew Busby, District Sales Manager

Montréal - Côte Saint-Luc
Québec & Eastern Canada
5795, Sir Walter Scott
Montréal, QC H4W 2T7
514-808-8562 (Cell)
Fax: 514-336-8338
800-461-7579
Julius Janits, District Sales Manager

Burden Management & Design Ltd.
27 Broadway
Corner Brook, NL A2H 4C5
709-639-8442
Fax: 709-639-3024
Products/Services/Areas of Expertise: Solid waste management; noise & vibration assessment; water & wastewater treatment consulting; site assessment; design & specifications; field sampling & monitoring; erosion control; parks, natural resource management
Domestic Markets:
Alberta, British Columbia, Newfoundland & Labrador
Contact(s):
J.C. Gorman

Bureau de Normalisation du Québec / BNQ
333, rue Franquet
Québec, QC G1P 4C7
418-652-2238
Fax: 418-652-2292
800-386-5114
bnqinfo@bnq.qc.ca
www.bnq.qc.ca
Firm Type: Scientific/Technical Services
Founded: 1961
Products/Services/Areas of Expertise: ISO 14000 & ISO 9000 accredited environmental management systems registrars
Domestic Markets:
Québec
Contact(s):
Jacques Girard, Directeur, Normalisation et Certification

Canadian Branches:
Montréal
8475, avenue Christophe-Colomb
Montréal, QC H2M 2N9
Fax: 514-383-3260
800-386-5114

Burnaby Bag & Burlap Ltd.
5291 Imperial St.
Burnaby, BC V5J 1E5
604-434-4725
Fax: 604-435-8466
sales@burnabybag.ca
www.burnabybag.ca
Firm Type: Manufacturing
Founded: 1973
Staff: 6
Products/Services/Areas of Expertise: Consumer office products
Contact(s):
Gary Vanderwell, President

Busch Systems International Inc.
Formerly: Busch-Coskery of Canada Inc.
343 Saunders Rd.
Barrie, ON L4N 9A3

705-722-0806
Fax: 705-722-8972
800-565-9931
busch@buschsystems.com
www.buschsystems.com
Firm Type: Distributing, Manufacturing
Founded: 1985
Staff: 20
Products/Services/Areas of Expertise: Specializes in recycling & composting container solutions; manufacturers over 170 products; programs focused on waste reduction; product line includes centralized containers, classroom/curbside bins, office receptacles, carts, composters, promotional & educational tools
Domestic Markets:
National
Foreign Activity:
Western Europe, Mexico, USA,
Contact(s):
Craig Busch, President/CEO

Busch Vacuum Technics Inc.
Also Known As: Busch Canada
1740, boul Lionel-Bertrand
Boisbriand, QC J7H 1N7
450-435-6899
Fax: 450-430-5132
800-363-6360
info@busch.ca
www.busch.ca
Firm Type: Engineering, Manufacturing, Scientific/Technical Services
Founded: 1963
Staff: 16
Products/Services/Areas of Expertise: High quality vacuum pumps, systems & accessories for industry
Domestic Markets:
National
Contact(s):
Paul M. Weiser, P.Eng., General Manager

Canadian Branches:
Ontario Branch
111 Topflight Rd.
Mississauga, ON L5S 1Y1
905-565-8058
Fax: 905-565-8059
Alex Ross, Sales

Business Funding Group Inc.
Formerly: BF Recycling
4240 Briarwood Ave.
Niagara Falls, ON L2E 5W1
905-356-8822
Fax: 905-356-6266
Firm Type: Waste Management
Founded: 1994
Staff: 2
Member of: North American Recyclers Rubber Association
Products/Services/Areas of Expertise: Rubber & tire recycling
Domestic Markets:
Ontario, Québec
Foreign Activity:
Australia/New Zealand, The Pacific Rim, USA
Contact(s):
Doug Jones, President

BV SORBEX, Inc.
c/o Dr. B. Volesky
471, av. Berkley
Saint-Lambert, QC J4P 3E7
514-502-5388
boya.volesky@mcgill.ca
www.bvsorbex.net
Firm Type: Scientific/Technical Services
Staff: 13
Products/Services/Areas of Expertise: The company offers cost-effective biosorbent products for a number of applications, including water purification, & recovery & recycling of metals from mining, ore-processing, & metalplating processes; design of biosorption process; & consulting services for industrial effluent treatment & decontamination/detoxification
Financial Information:
Type of Ownership: Private
Domestic Markets:
Ontario, Québec
Foreign Activity:
Australia/New Zealand, South America, USA
Contact(s):
Boya Volesky, President

BVA Systems Ltd./Vibro-Acoustics
727 Tapscott Rd.
Toronto, ON M1X 1A2
416-291-7371
Fax: 416-291-8049
info@vibro-acoustics.com
www.vibro-acoustics.com
Firm Type: Distributing, Engineering, Manufacturing
Founded: 1960
Staff: 100
Member of: Canadian Acoustic Society
Products/Services/Areas of Expertise: The firm is engaged in the design, testing & manufacture of noise & vibration control products for air handling systems: HVAC silencers, fan silencers, stack silencers, acoustical panels, plenums & enclosures, floating floor systems, seismic & wind restraint systems, & vibration isolation systems
Domestic Markets:
National
Foreign Activity:
USA
Contact(s):
Douglas Ross, Manager, 647-258-5326
dross@vibro.acoustics.com

BW Technologies by Honeywell
2840 - 2 Ave. SE
Calgary, AB T2A 7X9
403-248-9226
Fax: 403-273-3708
800-663-4164
info@gasmonitors.com
www.bwtnet.com
Firm Type: Manufacturing
Founded: 1987
Quality Environmental Management System(s): 9001:2008
Products/Services/Areas of Expertise: Gas detection instrumentation, personal detectors, multi-gas detectors, wireless multi-point independent systems, solar powered systems; personnel & facility protection for oxygen, combustible & toxic hazards
Recently Completed / Ongoing Projects: Introduction of the new generation wireless gas detection systems
Financial Information:
Type of Ownership: Foreign-owned
Revenue: Greater than $5 Million
Revenue Sources: 10% nationwide; 90% Private Contracts
Domestic Markets:
National
Foreign Activity:
Worldwide
Contact(s):
Cody Slater, President & CEO
Bryan Bates, Exec. Vice-President & COO
Thomas Jones, Sr. Vice-President & CFO
Carl Johnson, Vice-President, Management Executive

Byram Industrial Services Ltd.
P.O. Box 6478
Drayton Valley, AB T7A 1K4
780-542-4733
Fax: 780-542-5092

Bytown Marine Ltd.
Gladwin Business Park
B1-B2, 2212 Gladwin Cres.
Ottawa, ON K1B 5N1
613-723-8424
Fax: 613-723-0212
800-461-6511
info@bml.ca
www.bml.ca
Firm Type: Distributing
Founded: 1986
Staff: 10
Products/Services/Areas of Expertise: Data loggers & sensors for remote collection of hydromet data; solar power systems; air & water temperature sensors
Financial Information:
Type of Ownership: Private
Revenue: $500,000 - $1.5 Million
Revenue Sources: 40% nationwide; 50% Provincial; 10% Private Contracts
Domestic Markets:
National
Contact(s):
R.F.G. Walker, President
Tony J. Mason, Vice-President
tmason@bml.ca

C F Reclamation & Fresh Water Services
P.O. Box 613
Boyle, AB T0A 0M0
780-689-3902
Fax: 780-689-5175

C V Environmental Services
23 East 27th St.
Hamilton, ON L8V 3E6
905-389-2624
Fax: 905-389-1233
Contact(s):
Stephen Toplack, President

C-Max Transportation Equipment
Also Known As: Weber's Fabricating Ltd.
P.O. Box 610
3044 Sawmill Rd.
St Jacobs, ON N0B 2N0
519-664-3796
Fax: 519-664-3624
fireinfo@c-max.ca
www.c-max.ca
Firm Type: Manufacturing
Founded: 1974
Staff: 15
Member of: National Solid Waste Management Association
Products/Services/Areas of Expertise: Recycler trucks; food waste haulers; dump trucks; trailers (dump, flat deck, equipment); specializing in aluminum
Financial Information:
Type of Ownership: Private
Revenue Sources: 25% Municipals; 75% Private Contracts
Domestic Markets:
Alberta, Ontario
Foreign Activity:
USA
Contact(s):
Clare Weber, President

C.D. Sonter Ltd.
#201, 99 Floral Pkwy.
Toronto, ON M6L 2C4
416-248-4881
Fax: 416-248-5447
carmen@cdsonter.com
www.cdsonter.com
Products/Services/Areas of Expertise: Environmental consulting specializing in the analysis & implementation of cost effective waste & 3Rs programs

C.E. Jones & Associates Ltd.
#104, 645 Fort St.
Victoria, BC V8W 1G1
250-383-8375
Fax: 250-383-9354
cjones@jonesassoc.com
Firm Type: Management Consulting
Founded: 1986
Staff: 13
Member of: Canadian Land Reclamation Association
Products/Services/Areas of Expertise: Environmental consulting, specializing in the reclamation of disturbed lands; also grower of native plants
Financial Information:
Type of Ownership: Private
Domestic Markets:
Alberta, British Columbia, Northwest Territories, Yukon Territory
Foreign Activity:
Central Europe, South America
Contact(s):
Carol E. Jones, Principal

C.G. Industrial Specialties, Ltd.
8980 Oak St.
Vancouver, BC V6P 4B7
604-263-1671
Fax: 604-263-0947

Products & Services Buyer's Guide

sales@cgis.ca
www.cgis.ca
Firm Type: Distributing
Founded: 1980
Staff: 41
Products/Services/Areas of Expertise: Distribution of valves, piping & sealing products & environmental spill equipment; consulting services with engineering, oil & gas & mining companies
Contact(s):
Ross Waters, President, Sales

Canadian Branches:
Calgary Branch
#310, 777 - 3rd Ave. SW
Calgary, AB T2P 0G8
403-271-6695
Fax: 403-271-4659
keving@cgis.ca
Kevin Gilbert, Outside Sales Representative

Edmonton Branch
Regional Sales
2812 Ellwood Dr. SW
Edmonton, AB T6X 0A9
780-462-1014
Fax: 780-462-7953
davef@cgis.ca
Dave Friesen, Manager

Prince George Branch
Sales
#1A, 3521 Opie Cres.
Prince George, BC V2N 1B8
250-562-8261
Fax: 250-562-5366
kevinn@cgis.ca
Kevin Niebergall, Branch Manager

C.J. MacLellan & Associates Inc.
Highland Professional Centre
#2, 65 Beech Hill Rd.
Antigonish, NS B2G 2P9
902-863-1220
Fax: 902-863-3225
cjmac@cjmac.ns.ca
www.cjmac.ns.ca
Firm Type: Engineering, Scientific/Technical Services
Founded: 1973
Staff: 25
Products/Services/Areas of Expertise: Environmental consulting; emergency response; environmental audits; environmental impact assessments; risk management; training & education; land use planning; marine coastal management; water resources; water/wastewater treatment; liquid & hazardous waste management
Financial Information:
Type of Ownership: Private
Domestic Markets:
National
Foreign Activity:
Worldwide
Contact(s):
Harry Daemen, P.Eng., Manager
Edwin MacLellan, Ph.D.; P.Eng.; MCIP, Environmental Planner

C.J. Pink Ltd.
138 Clarke Rd.
London, ON N5W 5E1
519-455-6680
Fax: 519-455-2005
888-351-7586
cdnsales@cjpink.com; info@cjpink.com
www.cjpink.com
Firm Type: Manufacturing
Founded: 1932
Staff: 20
Member of: National Precast Concrete Association
Products/Services/Areas of Expertise: Precast concrete products including stair systems for high-rise and multi-level buildings, septic and holding tanks and the Norweco Singulaire class VI sewage treatment system.
Contact(s):
Chris Pink, President
Steve Bundy, Sales Manager

C.R. Wall Co. Inc.
CP 1697 Saint-Martin
Laval, QC H7V 3P9
450-628-6253
Fax: 450-628-2033
877-460-2278
mdesmeules@crwall.com
www.crwall.com
Contact(s):
Michel Desmeules, Contact

C.V. Environmental Services
23 East 27th St.
Hamilton, ON L8V 3E6
905-389-2624
Fax: 905-389-1233
cves@icom.ca
Firm Type: Scientific/Technical Services
Founded: 1995
Staff: 5
Member of: Canadian Environment Industry Association; Air & Waste Management Association; Occupational Hygiene Association of Ontario; Water Environment Association of Ontario; Hamilton/Wentworth Chamber of Commerce
Products/Services/Areas of Expertise: Environmental monitoring & data analysis; environmental management; occupational health & safety
Financial Information:
Type of Ownership: Private
Revenue Sources: 100% Private Contracts
Domestic Markets:
Ontario
Foreign Activity:
USA
Markets Sought:
Caribbean, Central America, Western Europe
Contact(s):
Stephen A. Toplack, President

C3 Environmental Group
350 Woolwich St. South
Breslau, ON N0B 1M0
519-648-3118
Fax: 519-648-3505
c3group@c3group.com
www.c3group.com
Firm Type: Scientific/Technical Services
Founded: 1973
Staff: 45
Products/Services/Areas of Expertise: Contracting & engineering services relating to primary & secondary containment, site remediation & bioremediation
Domestic Markets:
National
Foreign Activity:
USA

Canadian Branches:
Toronto Branch
#7, 181 Rutherford Rd. South
Brampton, ON L6W 3P4
905-451-4901
Fax: 905-451-0101
polymeric@c3groupo.com

C5 Plus Ltd.
828 Cannell Rd. SW
Calgary, AB T2W 1T4
403-215-0040
Fax: 403-294-0959
info@c5plus.com
www.c5plus.com
Products/Services/Areas of Expertise: Occupational health & safety consulting
Contact(s):
John Dean, Principal

Cactus Environmental Services Ltd.
P.O. Box 117
Neilburg, SK S0M 2C0
306-823-4368
Fax: 306-823-4316
Firm Type: Scientific/Technical Services
Founded: 1994
Staff: 3
Products/Services/Areas of Expertise: Environmental consulting; cleaning oil spills; geoprobe soil coring in frozen soil

Financial Information:
Type of Ownership: Private
Revenue Sources: 100% Private Contracts
Domestic Markets:
Alberta, Saskatchewan
Contact(s):
Allen Hewko, President

CadhamHayes Systems Inc.
P.O. Box 74056 Beechwood
Ottawa, ON K1M 2H9
613-789-8649
Fax: 613-789-5207
webinfo@cadhamhayes.ca
www.cadhamhayes.ca
Firm Type: Information Technology
Founded: 1978
Staff: 10
Products/Services/Areas of Expertise: Integrated environmental monitoring software systems to capture & evaluate physical & quality measurements, output from automated continuous sensing equipment & networks
Financial Information:
Type of Ownership: Publicly Traded
Domestic Markets:
National
Contact(s):
John S. Cadham, President
George Prazmowski, Director

Cadman Power Equipment
P.O. Box 100
38 Main St.
Courtland, ON N0J 1E0
519-688-2222
Fax: 519-688-2100
inquiries@cadmanpower.com
www.cadmanpower.com
Firm Type: Engineering, Waste Management
Founded: 1952
Products/Services/Areas of Expertise: Recognized leader in irrigation & nutrient management equipment & design

Caduceon Environmental Laboratories
A division of Caduceon Enterprises Inc.
Formerly: Areco Canada Inc. 285 Dalton Ave
Kingston, ON K7K 6Z1
613-544-2001
Fax: 613-544-2770
www.caduceon.com
Firm Type: Scientific/Technical Services
Founded: 1986
Staff: 70
Member of: Standards Council of Canada; Canadian Association of Environmental Analytical Laboratories
Quality Environmental Management System(s): 17025
Products/Services/Areas of Expertise: Full service environmental laboratory specializing in organic, inorganic & microbiological analyses in air, water, soil, oil & sediments
Recently Completed / Ongoing Projects: Dept. of National Defense & Canadian Forces Bases, remediation, wastewater, drinking water; City of Ottawa, remediation; AMEC, landfill monitoring
Financial Information:
Type of Ownership: Publicly Traded
Domestic Markets:
National
Foreign Activity:
USA
Contact(s):
Richard Hombek, President
Scott Burrows, Laboratory Manager

Canadian Branches:
Ottawa
Laboratory
2378 Holly Lane
Ottawa, ON K1V 7P1
613-228-1145
Greg Clarkin, Manager

Richmond Hill
Laboratory
#14, 110 West Beavercreek Rd.
Richmond Hill, ON L4B 1J9
289-475-5442
Fax: 866-562-1963
cwright@caduceonlabs.com

Christine Wright, Manager

Windsor
Laboratory
#5, 3201 Marentette Ave.
Windsor, ON N8Z 4G3
519-966-9541
Fax: 519-966-9567
Lorina Ferko, Manager

Caframo Co. Ltd.
Airport Rd., RR#2
Wiarton, ON N0H 2T0
519-534-1080
Fax: 519-534-1088
800-223-7266
contactus@caframo.com
www.caframo.com
Firm Type: Distributing, Manufacturing
Founded: 1955
Products/Services/Areas of Expertise: Fans, humidifers, heaters, laboratory equipment, stirrers
Financial Information:
Type of Ownership: Private
Domestic Markets:
National
Foreign Activity:
USA
Markets Sought:
Central America, Western Europe, South America,

CAHFIL FARR (Canada Inc.)
Formerly: Farr Inc.
2785, rue Francis-Hughes
Laval, QC H7L 3J6
450-629-3030
Fax: 450-662-6035
800-976-9382
info@camfilfarr.com
www.camfilfarr.com
Firm Type: Manufacturing
Founded: 1945
Staff: 2
Quality Environmental Management System(s): 9001
Products/Services/Areas of Expertise: Air pollution control equipment; dust collectors; air filters; air control dampers
Domestic Markets:
National
Foreign Activity:
USA
Contact(s):
Dominique Mignacco, President
mignaccod@camfilfarr.com

Canadian Branches:
British Columbia
2431 Canoe Ave.
Coquitlam, BC V3K 6A9
604-468-8990
Fax: 604-468-8991
877-919-3277

Concord
2700 Steeles Ave. West
Concord, ON L4K 3V3
905-415-3030
Fax: 905-415-2020
800-811-8780

Manitoba
#1, 2061 Logan Ave.
Winnipeg, MB R2R 0V1
204-774-2020
Fax: 204-783-3209
866-421-1670

Ottawa
#403, 1230 Old Innes Rd.
Ottawa, ON K1B 3V3
613-521-5555
Fax: 613-741-0830
800-811-8782

Cal's Eco Depot
Formerly: Cal's Pressure Wash
2265 Gladwin Cres.
Ottawa, ON K1B 4K9

613-288-2257
Fax: 613-288-2100
888-673-9274
Firm Type: Manufacturing
Founded: 1995
Staff: 18
Member of: Canadian Federation of Independent Businesses
EcoLogo Certified Products & Services: General purpose, industrial & commercial cleaners
Products/Services/Areas of Expertise: Supplier of parts & cleaning solutions for the pressure wash industry & the environment
Ecological Note: General purpose, industrial & commercial cleaners
Financial Information:
Type of Ownership: Private
Domestic Markets:
National
Contact(s):
Calvin Devlin, President

Caledon Laboratory Chemicals Inc.
Formerly: Caledon Laboratories Ltd.
40 Armstrong Ave.
Georgetown, ON L7G 4R9
905-456-0226
Fax: 905-877-6666
877-225-3366
service@caledonlabs.com
www.caledonlabs.com
Products/Services/Areas of Expertise: Preparation of chemicals for use in research & analysis
Contact(s):
Doug Brock, President

Calgary
Calgary Operations
1313 - 44 Ave. NE, Bay 7
Calgary, AB T2E 6L5
403-291-9897
Fax: 403-291-0298
1-800-667-7645
Contact(s):
Ron Minks, Director
Contact(s):
Warren Greig, Supervisor
Contact(s):
Nicole Bertrand, Director
Contact(s):
Darren Shynkaruk, Manager
Contact(s):
Jim Vukmanich, Supervisor
Contact(s):
D. Levesque, Director
Contact(s):
Luke MacMillan, Representative

Canadian Branches:
Montréal
Technology
2225A, ch Saint-Francois
Dorval, QC H9P 1K3
514-421-2005, ext. 300
Fax: 514-421-4447
Sylvain Laporte, Supervisor

Calgary
Calgary Operations
1313 - 44 Ave. NE, Bay 7
Calgary, AB T2E 6L5
403-291-9897
Fax: 403-291-0298
1-800-667-7645

Edmonton Lab
10158 - 103 St., 2nd Fl.
Edmonton, AB T5J 0X6
780-413-5265
Fax: 780-424-4602

Grande Prairie
Quality Control
9505 - 111 St.
Grande Prairie, AB T8V 5W1
780-539-5196
Fax: 780-513-2191

Ottawa
#13, 210 Colonnade Rd.
Nepean, ON K2E 7L5
613-731-1005
Fax: 613-736-1107

Saskatoon
Business
General Purpose Bldg.
124 Veterinary Rd.
Saskatoon, SK S7N 5E3
306-668-8370
Fax: 306-668-8383
1-800-667-7645

Thunder Bay
Laboratory
181 Barton St.
Thunder Bay, ON P7B 5N3
807-623-6463
Fax: 807-623-7598

Waterloo
#1, 50 Bathurst Dr.
Waterloo, ON N2V 2C5
519-886-6910
Fax: 519-886-9047

Winnipeg
Marketing & Sales
745 Logan Ave.
Winnipeg, MB R3E 3L5
204-945-3705
Fax: 204-945-0763
1-800-607-7555

Calgary Metal (1985) Ltd.
3415 Ogden Rd. SE
Calgary, AB T2G 4N4
403-262-4542
Fax: 403-262-1114
info@calgarymetal.com
www.calgarymetal.com
Firm Type: Waste Management
Founded: 1985
Staff: 45
Member of: Canadian Association of Recycling Industries, Institute of Scrap Recycling Industries, National Association of Steel Pipe Distributors
Products/Services/Areas of Expertise: Scrap metal processor & dealer; provides container service, picker truck for large, bulky metal, & mobile shears to process & remove scrap metal from industrial plants
Financial Information:
Type of Ownership: Private
Revenue: Greater than $5 Million
Domestic Markets:
Alberta, British Columbia, Saskatchewan
Contact(s):
Richard Dvorkin, President
Raymond Girard, Manager, Operations, 403-262-4542

Canadian Branches:
Hat Salvage & Steel
1248 South Railway St. SE
Medicine Hat, AB T1A 2W6
403-527-3800

Calgon Carbon Corp.
#3, 50 Mural St.
Richmond Hill, ON L4B 1E4
905-889-5853
www.calgoncarbon.com
Products/Services/Areas of Expertise: Activated carbon products & systems
Contact(s):
Lynden Maslen, Manager

International Branch(es):
Pittsburg
P.O. Box 717
400 Calgon Carbon Dr.
Pittsburgh, PA USA
412-787-6700

Calibre Strategic Services Inc.
Formerly: Calibre Consultants Inc.
#202, 2750 Faithful Ave.
Saskatoon, SK S7K 6M6

306-931-1129
Fax: 306-242-9827
jmacpherson@calibrestrategic.com
Firm Type: Management Consulting, Scientific/Technical Services
Founded: 1979
Products/Services/Areas of Expertise: Socio-economic impact assessment & public consultation; market research & analysis; feasibility analysis & business plans
Recently Completed / Ongoing Projects: Socio-economic impact assessments to mining & technology investments
Domestic Markets:
Alberta, British Columbia, Saskatchewan
Contact(s):
James C. MacPherson, President

Canadian Branches:
Calgary
#114, 6815 - 8th St. NE
Calgary, AB T2E 7H7
Henri P. Carriere, Manager

Nanaimo
2945 Haliday Cres.
Nanaimo, BC V9T 1B2
James C. MacPherson

Callrich Eco Services Inc.
777 Tarn Crt.
Oshawa, ON L1J 6Y8
905-626-1844
Fax: 905-576-9866
866-412-5064
info@callrichecoservices.com
www.callrichecoservices.com
Firm Type: Distributing
Founded: 1991
Staff: 3
Member of: Zerodraft
EcoLogo Certified Products & Services: Climatizer cellulose insulation
Products/Services/Areas of Expertise: Home performance contracting; solar water heating; water efficiency products; spray foam insulation
Ecological Note: Climatizer cellulose insulation
Financial Information:
Type of Ownership: Private
Revenue Sources: 2% Provincial; 98% Private Contracts
Domestic Markets:
Ontario
Contact(s):
Rich Krechowicz, Owner
rich@callrichecoservices.com

Calta Computer Systems Ltd.
#202, 7003 - 5th Ave. SE
Calgary, AB T2H 2G2
403-252-5094
Fax: 403-252-5102
ccompute@calta.com
www.calta.com
Firm Type: Engineering
Founded: 1981
Staff: 2
Member of: Association of Professional Engineers of Alberta
Products/Services/Areas of Expertise: Provides data transmission products & consulting, H/W PLC09 Arbitrator, S/W Mdbus (Modbus simulator for Windows)
Financial Information:
Type of Ownership: Private
Revenue Sources: 100% Private Contracts
Domestic Markets:
National
Foreign Activity:
Worldwide
Contact(s):
Sydney Deitch, President
Lorne Schneider, Vice-President

Camatec
Affiliate of Coen Burners Canada Inc.
#240, 775 Paul-Lussier
Ste-Hélène-de-Bagot, QC J0H 1M0
450-466-9222
Fax: 450-446-9224
camatec@camatec.ca
www.camatec.ca

Products/Services/Areas of Expertise: Air pollution control equipment; alternate energy system design & equipment
Contact(s):
Pierre Cadorette

Cambridge Materials Testing Limited
1177 Franklin Blvd.
Cambridge, ON N1R 7W4
519-621-6600
Fax: 519-621-6082
customerservice2004@cambridgematerials.com
www.cambridgematerials.com
Products/Services/Areas of Expertise: Environmental consulting services; research & development; Laboratory and testing services
Contact(s):
Peter J. Cooper, President

Canadian Branches:
Cambridge Materials Testing Ltd.
Mississauga Division
#13, 6991 Millcreek Dr.
Mississauga, ON L5N 6B9
905-812-3856
Fax: 905-812-3866

Campbell Scientific (Canada) Corp. / CSC
11564 - 149 St.
Edmonton, AB T5M 1W7
780-454-2505
Fax: 780-454-2655
dataloggers@campbellsci.ca
www.campbellsci.ca
Firm Type: Scientific/Technical Services
Founded: 1978
Staff: 39
Member of: Canadian Meteorological & Oceanographic Society; Canadian Agrometeorological Society
Quality Environmental Management System(s): 9001
Products/Services/Areas of Expertise: Data acquisition/control systems for meteorological/climatological autostations or similar applications
Financial Information:
Type of Ownership: Private
Revenue Sources: 25% nationwide; 10% Provincial; 10% Municipals; 50% Private Contracts
Domestic Markets:
National
Foreign Activity:
Australia/New Zealand, Eastern Europe, The Pacific Rim, USA
Contact(s):
Brian Day, General Manager

Campbell's Concrete Ltd.
P.O. Box 373
402 Mt. Edward Rd.
Charlottetown, PE C1A 7K7
902-368-3442
Fax: 902-894-5581
800-361-3442
info@cclweb.com
www.cclweb.com
Firm Type: Distributing, Manufacturing
Founded: 1974
Staff: 40
Member of: American Water Works Association
Products/Services/Areas of Expertise: Water handling equipment; sewage treatment equipment
Financial Information:
Type of Ownership: Private
Revenue Sources: 10% Provincial; 10% Municipals; 80% Private Contracts
Domestic Markets:
New Brunswick, Nova Scotia, Prince Edward Island
Contact(s):
Kent W. Green, President
Gerard Campbell, General Manager

Camvac Inc.
Parc Industriel #2
2895, rue Jules Vachon
Trois-Rivières, QC G9A 5E1
819-372-0471
Contact(s):
M. Michel Goudreau, President
Contact(s):
M. Pierre-Louis Lavergne, Président
Contact(s):
M. Jean Morissette, Président
Contact(s):
M. Daniel Bonneville, Président
Contact(s):
M. Michel Gagnon, Président
Contact(s):
M. Robyn Labonté, Président

Canadian Branches:
Camvac Inc.
Parc Industriel #2
2895, rue Jules Vachon
Trois-Rivières, QC G9A 5E1
819-372-0471

Saniverne Inc.
P.O. Box 691
810, 8e rue
St-Georges-de-Champlain, QC G9T 5J4
819-538-4531

Servac L.T. Inc.
P.O. Box 788
281, rue St-Joseph
La Tuque, QC G9X 3P6
819-523-4763
Fax: 819-523-8320

Servac O.T. Inc.
24, rue de Bécancour
Gatineau, QC J8P 7G7
819-663-1777
Fax: 819-663-2525

Servac S.H. Inc.
83, rue du Parc Industriel
Windsor, QC J1S 2T2
819-822-1820
Fax: 819-845-2472

Servac S.L. Inc.
Parc Industriel
P.O. Box 755
405, rue Claire-Fontaine
Alma, QC G8B 6H1
418-662-9710
Fax: 418-662-2212

Can Ecosse Engineering
#1A, 612 Welland Ave.
St Catharines, ON L2M 1A2
905-682-5633
Fax: 905-682-0344
mail@canecosse.com
www.canecosse.com
Firm Type: Engineering, Scientific/Technical Services
Founded: 1992
Staff: 10
Products/Services/Areas of Expertise: Consulting engineers; turnkey power plant & cogeneration projects; design, procurement & construction of projects
Contact(s):
Kenneth W. Stewart, P.Eng., President

Can-Am Instruments Ltd.
2851 Brighton Rd.
Oakville, ON L6H 6C9
905-829-0030
Fax: 905-829-4701
800-215-4469
can-am@can-am.net
www.can-am.net
Firm Type: Distributing
Founded: 1963
Staff: 12
Member of: Instrument Society of America; Ontario Pollution Control Equipment Federation
Quality Environmental Management System(s): 9001:2000
Products/Services/Areas of Expertise: Waste water sampling equipment; control & measuring instrumentation
Domestic Markets:
New Brunswick, Newfoundland & Labrador, Nova Scotia, Ontario, Prince Edward Island
Contact(s):
Mark R. Reeves, President
Richard J. Reeves, CEO
Peter Smyth, Technical Representative
Phil Hennebery, Technical Representative
Ken MacDonald, Technical Representative

Can-Aqua Inc.
79 Main St. N
Markham, ON L3P 1X7
905-201-6226
Fax: 905-201-2299
canaqua@on.aibn.ca
Products/Services/Areas of Expertise: Water & wastewater management & equipment

Can-Aqua International Ltée
1955, boul Dagenais ouest
Laval, QC H7L 5V1
450-625-3088
Fax: 450-625-3365
Firm Type: Distributing, Engineering
Founded: 1972
Products/Services/Areas of Expertise: Water & wastewater management & equipment
Financial Information:
Type of Ownership: Private
Revenue Sources: 100% Private Contracts
Domestic Markets:
Québec

Can-Cell Industries Inc.
Formerly: Canadian Cellulose Insulation Ltd.
14735 - 124 Ave.
Edmonton, AB T5L 3B2
780-447-1255
Fax: 780-447-1034
800-661-5031
sales@can-cell.com
www.can-cell.com
Firm Type: Distributing, Manufacturing
Founded: 1976
Staff: 170
Member of: Allied Paper Savers Inc.; Celufibre Industries Inc.
Member of: Cellulose Insulation Manufacturers Association of Canada; Canadian Home Builders' Association
EcoLogo Certified Products & Services: Weathershield loose-fill thermal & acoustical insulation
Products/Services/Areas of Expertise: Building insulation for attics, walls & floors; spray-on insulation for thermal, acoustical or fire prevention control; hydroseeding mulch; distribution of building materials, hardware, energy-saving products; recycling of all grades of paper, as well as plastics & other products
Ecological Note: Weathershield loose-fill thermal & acoustical insulation
Domestic Markets:
Alberta, British Columbia, Manitoba, Northwest Territories, Saskatchewan, Yukon Territory
Contact(s):
Harold Tiemstra, President
Karl Tiemstra, Vice-President, Operations
Warren Tiemstra, Vice-President, Sales & Marketing

Canadian Branches:
Calgary
4649 - 52 Ave. SE
Calgary, AB T2E 6P5
403-275-4133
Fax: 403-295-7774
800-268-8902

Edmonton - Allied Paper Savers Inc.
16820 - 129 Ave.
Edmonton, AB T8V 1L1
780-447-1648
Fax: 780-447-1737
888-680-1648

Edmonton - Celufibre Industries Inc.
16355 - 130 Ave.
Edmonton, AB T5V 1K5
780-447-1274
Fax: 780-447-1034

Kelowna
#14, 730 Stremel Rd.
Kelowna, BC V1X 5E7
250-491-9091
Fax: 250-491-9018
888-739-6014

Langley
#2, 20177 97 Ave.
Langley, BC V3A 7S4
604-513-8830
Fax: 604-513-8802
800-661-7005

Nanaimo
#5, 940 Old Victoria Rd.
Nanaimo, BC V9R 6Z8
250-754-2943
Fax: 250-754-2953
888-739-6015

Regina
365 Maxwell Cres.
Regina, SK S4N 5X9
306-359-1100
Fax: 306-924-5868
888-321-3141

Saskatoon
#4, 846 - 56 St., East
Saskatoon, SK S7K 5Y8
306-934-0033
Fax: 306-934-3034
800-661-0033

Winnipeg
1503 Redwood Ave.
Winnipeg, MB R2X 3B2
204-633-5684
Fax: 204-633-6858
866-319-1467

Can-K Artificial Lift Systems Inc.
401, 18 Ave.
Nisku, AB T9E 7T5
780-426-4800
Fax: 780-462-3044
info@can-k.com
www.can-k.com
Products/Services/Areas of Expertise: Design & custom manufacture different industrial components

Can-Ross Environmental Services Ltd.
2270 South Service Rd. West
Oakville, ON L6L 5M9
905-847-7190
Fax: 905-847-7175
888-847-7190
www.canross.com
Firm Type: Distributing, Manufacturing, Waste Management
Founded: 1985
Staff: 25
Member of: Acklands Grainger; BDI; Kinecor; Guillevin International Co.; Levitt-Safety Limited; Shield Specialized Emergency Services Inc.; Stone Company Ltd.; BLR; Grand River Sales; Hansler Smith Limited; Hollingsworth Supply Services; Northern Safety; Fercomat inc.; Stor-it Systems Ltd.
Products/Services/Areas of Expertise: Sorbents & other spill control products; spill kits; oil containment boom & socks; hazardous materials storage buildings; services include oil spill control & compliance assessment, waste minimization programs, product training; company utilizes recycled materials in its plant when praticable
Domestic Markets:
National
Foreign Activity:
Western Europe, Worldwide
Contact(s):
Ted Edgar, President/CEO

Canada Colors & Chemicals Ltd.
North Tower
#1300, 175 Bloor St. East
Toronto, ON M4W 3R8
416-443-5500
Fax: 416-449-9039
eb-admin@canadacolors.com
www.canadacolors.com
Firm Type: Distributing
Founded: 1920
Products/Services/Areas of Expertise: Provider of over 5,000 commodity & specialty products, supplying businesses in the industrial & solvent sector, food & fine chemicals, coatings & polymer additives, oil & gas, soap & detergent, mining, pulp & paper, environmental & water treatment markets
Domestic Markets:
National

Canadian Branches:
Brampton
238 Glidden Rd.
Brampton, ON L6W 2H8
905-459-1232
Brendan Filby, Regional Manager, Sales
bfilby@dcl-inc.com

Delta
1071 Cliveden Ave., Annacis Island
Delta, BC V3M 5V1
604-525-3326
866-525-3326

Leduc
6610 - 45th St.
Leduc, AB T9E 7C9
780-980-6481

St. Laurent
9999 Trans-Canada Highway
Saint-Laurent, QC H4S 1V1
514-333-7820

Windsor
3280 Jefferson Blvd.
Windsor, ON N8T 2W8
519-252-5776

Canada Composting Inc.
Formerly: Halton Recycling Ltd.
#301, 390 Davis Dr.
Newmarket, ON L3Y 7T8
905-830-1160
Fax: 905-830-0416
www.canadacomposting.com
Firm Type: Manufacturing
Products/Services/Areas of Expertise: Development of organics processing solutions using Anaerobic Digestion; Production of renewable bioenergy
Financial Information:
Type of Ownership: Private
Domestic Markets:
Ontario
Foreign Activity:
Asia, Australia/New Zealand, Central Europe, Eastern Europe, Western Europe, The Pacific Rim
Contact(s):
Kevin Matthews, President, 905-830-1160
kmatthews@canadacomposting.com

Canada Heat Pumps
Formerly: Rocton Energy Systems Ltd.
P.O. Box 219
5488 Main St.
Osgoode, ON K0A 2W0
613-826-0762
Fax: 613-826-0808
Firm Type: Manufacturing
Member of: Canadian Earth Energy Association
Products/Services/Areas of Expertise: Water-to-air, water-to-water heat pumps; customized waste heat recovery systems
Contact(s):
William A. Hamilton, Owner

Canada Water Supply Ltd.
P.O. Box 1225
Saint John, NB E2L 4G7
506-652-5885
Fax: 506-633-0031
www.canadawater.ca
Firm Type: Distributing
Founded: 1975
Products/Services/Areas of Expertise: Water, wastewater & groundwater equipment; odour control equipment; solid, liquid & hazardous waste equipment
Domestic Markets:
New Brunswick, Newfoundland & Labrador, Nova Scotia, Prince Edward Island
Contact(s):
Sandy Robertson, CEO

Canadax Industrial Group Limited
6173 Pepperell St.
Halifax, NS B3H 2P1

Products & Services Buyer's Guide

902-422-0444
Fax: 902-425-1606
canadax@fox.nstn.ca

Canadian Benthic Ltd.
PO Box 97
Bamfield, BC V0R 1B0
250-728-3274
Firm Type: Scientific/Technical Services
Founded: 1975
Staff: 1
Products/Services/Areas of Expertise: Marine, aquaculture & fish nursery studies
Contact(s):
J.G. Lindsay, President

Canadian Clay Products Inc.
P.O. Box 70
Wilcox, SK S0G 5E0
306-732-2085
Fax: 306-732-2100
ccp@canadianclay.com
www.canadianclay.com
Firm Type: Manufacturing
Founded: 1990
Staff: 8
Products/Services/Areas of Expertise: Sodium bentonite for seepage & leachate control, flocculants in water & wastewater treatment
Domestic Markets:
Alberta, British Columbia, Manitoba, Ontario
Foreign Activity:
Western Europe, USA
Markets Sought:
Central America, Eastern Europe, The Middle East

Canadian Drives Inc.
#2, 242 Applerood Cres.
Concord, ON L4K 4E5
905-660-2766
Fax: 905-660-0901
sales@canadiandrives.com
www.canadiandrives.com
Firm Type: Distributing
Founded: 1973
Products/Services/Areas of Expertise: Distributor & integrator of electrical & mechanical power transmission products
Financial Information:
Type of Ownership: Private
Domestic Markets:
National
Contact(s):
Paul Fenton, President
Bondy S. Nair, B.Eng(Mechanical), Manager, Sales & Operations
Joe Chebat, C.E.T., Representative, Technical Service
Ryan Fenton, Contact, Inside Sales

Canadian Eagle Recyclers, Inc.
16 Melanie Dr.
Brampton, ON L6T 4K9
905-792-2209
Fax: 905-458-1702
Firm Type: Management Consulting, Waste Management
Founded: 1989
Products/Services/Areas of Expertise: Waste disposal services; Waste storage bins; Waste management consulting
Domestic Markets:
Ontario
Contact(s):
Michael Card, Contact

Canadian Emissions Ltd.
5329 1A St. SW
Calgary, AB T2H 0E5
403-278-8605
Fax: 403-278-8786
Products/Services/Areas of Expertise: Air pollution control services
Contact(s):
Tony Hansen

Canadian Environmental Auditors Inc.
35 Lakeshore Blvd.
Gilford, ON L0L 1R0
705-456-3318
Fax: 705-456-1255

Firm Type: Management Consulting
Founded: 1987
Products/Services/Areas of Expertise: Environmental consulting
Financial Information:
Type of Ownership: Private

Canadian Environmental Group
1200 - 10665 Jasper Ave. NW
Edmonton, AB T5J 3S9
780-426-2600
Fax: 780-423-6874
cvg@canadianvaluation.com
Firm Type: Engineering
Staff: 3
Products/Services/Areas of Expertise: Environmental audits
Financial Information:
Type of Ownership: Private
Revenue: Less than $50,000
Domestic Markets:
Alberta
Contact(s):
Peter Smith, President

Canadian Fibre
3971 Boundary Rd.
Richmond, BC V6V 1T8
604-524-4627
Fax: 604-524-3946
Firm Type: Waste Management
Founded: 1990
Products/Services/Areas of Expertise: Collects blue boxes & other waste materials; Recycles
Financial Information:
Type of Ownership: Private
Domestic Markets:
National,
Contact(s):
J.J. Song, Manager

Canadian Fishery Consultants Ltd. / CFCL
P.O. Box 606
1489 Hollis St.
Halifax, NS B3J 2R7
902-422-4698
Fax: 902-422-8147
cfcl@canfish.com
www.canfish.com
Firm Type: Management Consulting, Scientific/Technical Services
Founded: 1980
Staff: 6
Member of: Association of Professional Engineers of Nova Scotia; World Aquaculture Association
Products/Services/Areas of Expertise: Fisheries; aquaculture; coastal management; financial analyses; feasibility studies; resource analysis; fish hatchery work; turnkey operations; engineering services; project management
Recently Completed / Ongoing Projects: Hatcheries and Landing Sites in Uganda; Appraisal mission for African Development Bank; viability studies in Namibia, Guatemala
Financial Information:
Type of Ownership: Private
Revenue Sources: 50% nationwide; 15% Provincial; 10% Municipals; 25% Private Contracts
Domestic Markets:
New Brunswick, Newfoundland & Labrador, Nova Scotia, Prince Edward Island
Foreign Activity:
Africa, Caribbean, Central America, The Middle East, The Pacific Rim
Markets Sought:
Africa, Mexico
Contact(s):
Alan Perry, P.Eng., President
Wayne Lewis, Vice-President, International

Canadian General Standards Board / CGSB/ONGC Office des Normes Générales du Canada
Place de Portage, Phase III
#6B1, 11, rue Laurier
Gatineau, QC K1A 1G6
819-956-0425
Fax: 819-956-5740
800-6665-2472
ncr.cgsb-ongc@pwgsc.gc.ca
www.ongc-cgsb.gc.ca

Products/Services/Areas of Expertise: ISO 14000 & ISO 9000 accredited environmental management systems registrars
Domestic Markets:
National
Contact(s):
Terrence Davies, Director
terrence.davies@pwgsc.gc.ca

Canadian Hydro Developers, Inc.
#500, 1324 - 17th Ave. SW
Calgary, AB T2T 5S8
403-269-9379
Fax: 403-244-7388
canhydro@canhydro.com
www.canhydro.com
Firm Type: Manufacturing
Founded: 1990
EcoLogo Certified Products & Services: Owner, developer & operator of 20 EcoLogo facilities, including run-of-river hydroelectric plants, wind plants, & a biomass plant
Products/Services/Areas of Expertise: Green power projects are distributed across rural Canada
Ecological Note: Owner, developer & operator of 20 EcoLogo facilities, including run-of-river hydroelectric plants, wind plants, & a biomass plant
Financial Information:
Type of Ownership: Publicly Traded
Domestic Markets:
National
Contact(s):
John Keating, Chief Executive Officer
Kent Brown, Exec. Vice-President & CFO, 403-269-9379
kbrown@canhydro.com
Lindsey Moen, Coordinator, Communications, 403-802-2099
lmoen@canhydro.com

Canadian Liquids Processors Limited / CLP
15 Biggar Ave.
Hamilton, ON L8L 3Z3
888-312-1000
info@canadianliquids.com
www.canadianliquids.com
Firm Type: Management Consulting, Scientific/Technical Services, Waste Management
Founded: 1980
Products/Services/Areas of Expertise: Provider of environmentally responsible product destruction for various sugar & alcohol based liquid goods; Converter of liquid goods into ethanol, a renewable fuel
Financial Information:
Type of Ownership: Private
Domestic Markets:
British Columbia, Manitoba, Ontario
Contact(s):
Erica Siebert, General Manager
eseibert@canadianliquids.com
Lori Dupont-Freill, Manager, Accounts
ldupontfreill@canadianliquids.com
Sean O'Neill, Manager, Plant
seano@canadianliquids.com
Shelly Coombs, Coordinator, Traffic
shellyc@canadianliquids.com

Canadian Paper Recyclers
7528 Bath Rd.
Mississauga, ON L4T 1L2
905-671-2737
Fax: 905-671-2736
Firm Type: Scientific/Technical Services, Waste Management
Founded: 1989
Products/Services/Areas of Expertise: Recycling of fine paper
Financial Information:
Type of Ownership: Private
Revenue Sources: 100% Private Contracts
Contact(s):
Gregory A. Keenan, President
Charlie Galio, Vice-President, Sales & Marketing

Canadian Petroleum Engineering Inc.
#1900, 717 - 7th Ave. SW
Calgary, AB T2P 0Z3
403-263-0752
Fax: 403-233-0859
cpe09@cpe.ab.ca
www.cpe.ab.ca
Firm Type: Engineering
Founded: 1995

Member of: Association of Professional Engineers, Geologists, Geophysicists of Alberta
Products/Services/Areas of Expertise: Engineering, geology, project management & field supervisory services to the oil & gas industry
Financial Information:
Type of Ownership: Private
Domestic Markets:
Alberta, New Brunswick, Northwest Territories
Foreign Activity:
Mexico, Former USSR, Worldwide
Contact(s):
Ed Fercho, President
efercho96@cpe.ab.ca
Lorne Hammer, Principal
lhammer@cpe.ab.ca

Canadian Portable Structures (1992) Ltd.
4400 Corporate Dr.
Burlington, ON L7L 5R3
905-335-5500
Fax: 905-335-1492
800-526-4277
info@cdnportable.com
www.cdnportable.com
Firm Type: Manufacturing
Founded: 1980
Staff: 13
Products/Services/Areas of Expertise: Portable chemical storage buildings; portable, relocatable, modular buildings
Domestic Markets:
National
Foreign Activity:
USA
Contact(s):
Marty Ryan, President & Sales Manager
marty.ryan@cdnportable.com
Paul Redden, Estimating
paul.redden@cdnportable.com

Canadian Recycling Equipment & Systems Ltd.
#2, 100 Frobisher Dr.
Waterloo, ON N2V 2A1
519-746-0990
Fax: 519-746-8122
Firm Type: Distributing, Manufacturing
Founded: 1988
Products/Services/Areas of Expertise: Equipment distributor & wholesaler of balers, conveyors, crushers, separators, shredders, & other equipment
Financial Information:
Type of Ownership: Private
Domestic Markets:
National
Contact(s):
Gary Barlow, President

Canadian Safety Equipment Inc.
Formerly: Enmet Safety Sales
#114, 2465 Cawthra Rd.
Mississauga, ON L5A 3P2
905-949-2741
Fax: 905-272-1866
800-265-0182
info@cdnsafety.com
www.cdnsafety.com
Firm Type: Distributing
Founded: 1990
Staff: 7
Products/Services/Areas of Expertise: Gas detection equipment; self-contained breathing apparatus; communications equipment; man-hoists; confined space entry equipment
Domestic Markets:
New Brunswick, Newfoundland & Labrador, Nova Scotia, Ontario, Prince Edward Island
Contact(s):
Ross Humphry, President
Tiffany Rittenhouse
Rory Hunt
Steve Rittenhouse

Canadian Branches:
Sudbury
242 Covington St.
Garson, ON P3L 1J9
705-693-5424
Fax: 705-693-7759

Brent Hannah

Canadian Seabed Research Ltd.
341 Myra Rd.
Porters Lake, NS B3E 1G2
902-827-4200
Fax: 902-827-2002
www.csr-marine.com
Firm Type: Engineering, Scientific/Technical Services
Founded: 1985
Staff: 7
Products/Services/Areas of Expertise: Seabed mapping & positioning; contaminated sediments surveys; sewage outfall mapping & monitoring; mine tailings surveys; aquaculture site selection studies; petroleum geo-hazard site surveys; shipwreck search, assessment & recovery; ground geophysics & hydrogeology; groundwater contamination assessment; site audits; archaeological investigations; geomatics & remote sensing services; processing & interpretation of radar data
Domestic Markets:
National
Foreign Activity:
Central America, Eastern Europe, USA
Contact(s):
Glen Gilbert, President
Patric Campbell, General Manager
Blaine Carr, Operations Manager

Canadian Soil & Climate Protection Corp. / SCP
Canadian Agra Complex
P.O. Box 460
2091 Hwy. 21
Kincardine, ON N2Z 2Y9
519-396-9124
Fax: 519-396-9025
inquires@scpcorp.com
www.scpcorp.com
Firm Type: Management Consulting, Scientific/Technical Services

Products/Services/Areas of Expertise: Services include training courses, environmental monitoring, environmental management systems, soil investigations, Phase I, II, & III ESA, hydrogeological studies, litigation support, & decommissioning; Clients include industries such as agriculture, mining, manufacturing, nuclear, & pulp & paper
Financial Information:
Type of Ownership: Private
Domestic Markets:
Ontario
Contact(s):
Hanna Ayyad, President
hayyad@scpcorp.com
Rem Okoli, Manager, Environmental
rokoli@scpcorp.com

Canadian Technical Tape Ltd.
455, boul de la Côte Vertu
Montréal, QC H4N 1E8
Fax: 800-334-1029
800-334-1567
info@cttgroup.com
www.cttgroup.com
Firm Type: Manufacturing
Founded: 1950
Staff: 500
Products/Services/Areas of Expertise: Manufacturer of pressure sensitive tapes, plastic film, & trash, recycling, storage, & compostable bags; Clients include industry, packaging, medical, construction, athletic, food, & hardware
Financial Information:
Type of Ownership: Private
Domestic Markets:
National
Foreign Activity:
USA, Worldwide
Contact(s):
Leonard Cohen, President
Paul Cohen, Vice-President, Sales & Marketing
Serge Binette, Marketing Manager

International Branch(es):
Tennessee
2222 Eddie Williams Rd.
Johnson City, TN USA

423-928-8331
Fax: 423-928-0311
cii@cttgroup.com

Canadian Water Conditioning Inc.
#16, 62 McBrine Pl.
Kitchener, ON N2R 1H3
519-748-4343
Fax: 519-748-6904
800-583-4849
water1@bellnet.ca
www.water1.ca
Firm Type: Distributing, Manufacturing
Founded: 1980
Staff: 16
Member of: Water Quality Association; Better Business Bureau; Kitchener Waterloo Chamber of Commerce
Products/Services/Areas of Expertise: Industrial, commercial, residential & agricultural water treatment & filtration equipment; water softeners; ultraviolet disinfection; reverse osmosis systems; ozone systems
Financial Information:
Type of Ownership: Private
Domestic Markets:
National
Foreign Activity:
Africa
Contact(s):
Terry Willett, President & CEO
David Halbert, Manager, Sales & Marketing

Canadian Worcester Controls Ltd.
General Delivery
Didsbury, AB T0M 0W0
403-335-3319
Fax: 403-335-3591
Products/Services/Areas of Expertise: Ball valves; actuators; control devices including anti-fugitive emission valve
Domestic Markets:
National
Contact(s):
Ronald Kozlowski, Vice-President

CanadianEnvironmental.com
Canadian Environmental Envirojobs Inc.
2342 Munn's Ave.
Oakville, ON L6H 6G9
905-257-1119
Fax: 905-257-0119
admin@canadianenvironmental.com
www.canadianenvironmental.com
Firm Type: Management Consulting
Founded: 2001
Products/Services/Areas of Expertise:
CanadianEnvironmental.com is a free resource allowing environmental professionals across Canada online access to: environmental news, information on legislation, jobs postings, & listings of companies selling environment-related products.
Domestic Markets:
National
Contact(s):
Laura Griffin, President
lgriffin@canadianenvironmental.com

CanAsia Environmental & Engineering Ltd.
#215, 8334 - 128th St.
Surrey, BC V3W 4G2
604-572-5158
Fax: 604-572-4518
Firm Type: Management Consulting, Engineering
Founded: 1997
Staff: 15
Products/Services/Areas of Expertise: Environmental, geotechnical, structural & civil consulting & contracting services; general engineering consulting; project management
Contact(s):
Raj Aujla, Ph.D., MCSc, President

Canatec Consultants Ltd.
Alastair Ross Technology Centre
#122, 3553 - 31st St. NW
Calgary, AB T2L 2K7
403-228-0962
Fax: 403-282-1238
canatec@canatec.ca
www.canatec.ca

Firm Type: Engineering, Scientific/Technical Services
Founded: 1988
Staff: 6
Products/Services/Areas of Expertise: Environmental evaluations, arctic engineering, operations support in arctic; project management, oil spill research; cleanup systems; specialized software development
Financial Information:
Type of Ownership: Private
Domestic Markets:
Alberta, Northwest Territories, Prince Edward Island
Foreign Activity:
USA, Former USSR
Contact(s):
Chris Hill, President

Canbar Inc.
P.O. Box 267
250 Woolwich St. South
Breslau, ON N0B 1M0
519-648-2278
Fax: 519-648-2001
info@canbar.com
www.canbar.com
Firm Type: Manufacturing
Founded: 1872
Staff: 30
Products/Services/Areas of Expertise: Chemical storage tanks; wood stove tanks & pipes (denstocks)
Financial Information:
Type of Ownership: Private
Revenue: Greater than $5 Million
Revenue Sources: 15% Provincial; 85% Private Contracts
Domestic Markets:
National
Foreign Activity:
Australia/New Zealand, Central America, Western Europe, USA
Contact(s):
T.H. Hart, General Manager

Canberra Company / NRD
Formerly: Aptec Engineering Ltd.
West 50B Caldari Rd.
Concord, ON L4K 4N8
905-660-5373
Fax: 905-660-9693
concord.general@canberra.com
www.canberra.com
Firm Type: Manufacturing
Founded: 1967
Staff: 35
Products/Services/Areas of Expertise: Environmental analysis & surface contamination control of radioactive materials
Activities: Multi-channel gamma-ray analyzer development; quantitative software development; radiation monitoring instrumentation
Domestic Markets:
National
Foreign Activity:
Africa, Asia, Australia/New Zealand, Western Europe, The Pacific Rim, USA
Contact(s):
Jim Outos, Contact, Sales and Service
joutos@canberra.com

Cancoppas Limited
#2, 2595 Dunwin Dr.
Mississauga, ON L5L 3N9
905-569-6246
Fax: 905-569-6244
800-595-0514
controls@cancoppas.com
www.cancoppas.com
Firm Type: Distributing, Engineering
Founded: 1973
Staff: 13
Member of: Water Environment Association of Ontario; Ontario Pollution Control Equipment
Products/Services/Areas of Expertise: Marketing, sales & service of process measurement control & environment instrumentation
Financial Information:
Type of Ownership: Private
Domestic Markets:
National
Contact(s):
Jake Alaica, P.Eng., President

Steve Gilligan, Sales Manager
Canadian Branches:
IMC Coppas Québec Ltee.
5681 ch. St. Francois
Saint-Laurent, QC H4S 1V6
514-331-2870
Fax: 514-331-5085
controls@imccoppas.com
www.imccoppas.com
Steve Nucci

CanDetec Inc.
P.O. Box 282
#6A, 35 Crawford Cres.
Campbellville, ON L0P 1B0
905-854-4530
Fax: 905-854-2549
Firm Type: Scientific/Technical Services
Founded: 2001
Staff: 2
Contact(s):
Dennis J. Gregor, President

Canentec Inc.
68 Maxwell Crt.
Thornhill, ON L4J 6X8
905-764-8129
Fax: 905-764-2881
info@canentec.com
www.canentec.com
Products/Services/Areas of Expertise: Assists companies who wish to become a biodiesel manufacturer
Contact(s):
Michael Sills, Ph.D, President
michael.sills@canentec.com

CanHemp Corporation
#190, 1919B - 4th St. SW
Calgary, AB T2S 1W4
403-232-8576
Fax: 403-262-1263
hipnhemp@tcel.com
www.hempworld.com/shop/CanHemp.html
Firm Type: Distributing, Manufacturing
Founded: 1996
Staff: 3
Member of: Canadian Industrial Hemp Council; Promotional Producers of Canada; Calgary Chamber of Commerce
Products/Services/Areas of Expertise: Finished hemp products; unique specialty products
Recently Completed / Ongoing Projects: Custom cedar wine boxes
Financial Information:
Type of Ownership: Private
Revenue: $100,000 - $250,000
Revenue Sources: 100% Private Contracts
Domestic Markets:
Alberta, Manitoba
Foreign Activity:
Eastern Europe, The Pacific Rim, USA
Markets Sought:
Australia/New Zealand, Central America, Western Europe
Contact(s):
Marc Clement, President & CEO

Canning & Pitt Associates Inc.
P.O. Box 21461
St. John's, NL A1A 5G2
709-738-0133
Fax: 709-753-4471
scanning@canpitt.ca
www.canpitt.ca
Firm Type: Scientific/Technical Services
Founded: 1991
Staff: 3
Products/Services/Areas of Expertise: Economic assessment & management consulting firm working in environmental assessment, socio-economic impact evaluation, compensation analysis & strategic planning, particularly for the marine environment & fisheries
Contact(s):
Stratford Canning, Partner
scanning@canpitt.ca
Robert Pitt, Partner
rpitt@canpitt.ca

Cannington Group
Formerly: Cannington Excavating 1989 Limited
#4, 4 Fortecon Dr.
Gormley, ON L0H 1G0
905-841-1848
Fax: 905-841-1062
info@thecanningtongroup.com
www.thecanningtongroup.com
Firm Type: Scientific/Technical Services
Founded: 2005
Staff: 20
Member of: Ontario Waste Management Association; Ontario Petroleum Contractors Association; Recycling Council of Ontario
Products/Services/Areas of Expertise: Full service contractor specializing in providing cost effective solutions for environmental demolition & waste management; on-site soil processing, tank removals & installation, bioremediation, landfill reclamation & construction, custom crushing, exavation & site works & transportation & disposal of all types of soil & liquids
Recently Completed / Ongoing Projects: Wychwood TTC Burns remediation; West Dowlands demolition; Brampton remediation works
Financial Information:
Type of Ownership: Private
Revenue: Greater than $5 Million
Revenue Sources: 20% nationwide; 20% Provincial; 30% Municipals; 30% Private Contracts
Domestic Markets:
Ontario
Contact(s):
David McCrossan, President
dmacrossan@thecanningtongroup.com
Frank Appollinaro, Vice-President

CanNorth Environmental Services Inc.
#4, 130 Robin Cres.
Saskatoon, SK S7L 6M7
306-652-4432
Fax: 306-652-4431
info@cannorth.com
www.cannorth.com
Products/Services/Areas of Expertise: Environmental consulting & contracting services
Contact(s):
Peter Vanriel, General Manager

Canon Canada Inc.
6390 Dixie Rd.
Mississauga, ON L5T 1P7
905-795-2111
Fax: 905-795-2028
www.canon.ca
Firm Type: Distributing
Founded: 1973
Staff: 1500
Quality Environmental Management System(s): 9002
EcoLogo Certified Products & Services: Facsimile machines; photocopiers
Products/Services/Areas of Expertise: Toner cartridge remanufacturing; business, consumer & medical products
Ecological Note: Facsimile machines; photocopiers
Financial Information:
Type of Ownership: Publicly Traded
Domestic Markets:
National
Contact(s):
Tamotsu Nakamura, President
D. Mason Olds, Vice-President & General Manager
Stanley Skorayko, Vice-President, Corporate Communications & Environmental Affairs
Tony Valente, Vice President, Finance & Accounting
Canadian Branches:
Calgary Branch
2828 - 16 St. NE
Calgary, AB T2E 7K7
403-291-4350
Fax: 403-291-3586
Kevin Felker

Canrom Photovoltaics Inc.
1654 Ontario Ave.
Niagara Falls, NY USA
716-282-2975
Fax: 716-285-8508
info@canrom.com
www.canrom.com

Products/Services/Areas of Expertise: Manufacturer of solar cells, solar panes, & systems
Contact(s):
Nick Dalacu
ndalacu@canrom.com

Canspect Corporation
#301, 301 Moodie Dr.
Ottawa, ON K2H 9C4
613-596-0033
Fax: 613-596-0433
info@canspect.com
www.canspect.com
Firm Type: Scientific/Technical Services
Founded: 1980
Staff: 40
Products/Services/Areas of Expertise: Engineering consulting services; liquid/hazardous/solid waste management; air quality assessment; water & wastewater assessment
Domestic Markets:
National
Foreign Activity:
Worldwide
Contact(s):
Taha Qirbi, President

Cansult Maunsell Limited
An AECOM company
Formerly: Cansult Limited105 Commerce Valley Dr. West
Markham, ON L3T 7W3
905-886-7022
Fax: 905-886-9494
www.aecom.com
Firm Type: Engineering
Founded: 2006
Staff: 700
Member of: Professional Engineers of Ontario; Association of Canadian Engineering Consultants
Quality Environmental Management System(s): 9001:2000
Products/Services/Areas of Expertise: Design & specifications; project management; environmental impact assessments; water & wastewater treatment; consulting engineering
Financial Information:
Type of Ownership: Publicly Traded
Revenue: $1.5 Million - $3 Million
Revenue Sources: 25% nationwide; 25% Provincial; 25% Municipals; 25% Private Contracts
Domestic Markets:
Ontario
Foreign Activity:
Caribbean, The Middle East
Contact(s):
James A. Metcalfe, B.A., President & CEO
A.Lorne Atkinson, Chair
David C. Stephen, Sr. Vice-President
R. Lorne Proudlock, Sr. Vice-President & CFO
George H. Horning, Vice-President & Secretary
International Branch(es):
Abu Dhabi
c/o Al Jazira Sports & Cultural Club
P.O. Box 43266
Muroor Rd. (4th St.)
Abu Dhabi UAE
-971-2-414-6000
Fax: -971-2-414-6001
abudhabi@aecom.com
www.aecom.com

Doha
The Pearl Building, 4th Fl.
P.O. Box 6650
Airport Rd.
Umm Ghuwalina Qatar
-974-4-407-9000
Fax: -974-4-437-6782
doha@aecom.com
www.aecom.com

Dubai
Monarch Tower
P.O. Box 51028
1 Sheikh Zayed Rd.
Dubai UAE
-971-4-318-7200
Fax: -971-4-318-7201

dubai@aecom.com
www.aecom.com

Cantech Inspections Ltd.
#106, 3738 North Fraser Way
Burnaby, BC V5J 5G7
604-434-4443
Fax: 604-434-4449
866-434-4443
cantech@cantechinspections.com
www.cantechinspections.com
Firm Type: Scientific/Technical Services
Founded: 1987
Staff: 18
Member of: Mechanical Services Association; Canadian Nuclear Safety Commission
Member of: Canadian Welding Bureau, American Society of Non-Destructive Testing, Transport Canada Airworthiness
Products/Services/Areas of Expertise: Non-destructive testing & inspection; fabrication shops; steel erection inspection; bridge inspection; pipe & station hydrogas, penstocks, co-generation plants; mobile services; results on site; aircraft inspection; aircraft parts, wheels, ground penetrating radar
Recently Completed / Ongoing Projects: Terasen Gas; Canron West (Supreme Steel); Lincoln Centre, Seattle; Lockerbie & Hole; Boiler Tube Fabrication, etc.; Cascade Aerospace; Penta Aviation; Enterprise Steel (Vessel Fabrication); Rapid-Span Structures (Bridge Building); Vancouver Convention Centre; Aircraft inspection
Financial Information:
Type of Ownership: Private
Revenue: $250,000 - $500,000
Revenue Sources: 5% nationwide; 5% Provincial; 5% Municipals; 85% Private Contracts
Domestic Markets:
Alberta, British Columbia, Yukon Territory
Contact(s):
Ethel M. Cook, Administrator
Mike MacDonald, Director
David Ruston, Sales
Mani Nittritz, Director, Aerospace
Blaine Whaley, Director, Operations

CanTox Environmental Inc.
#300, 2233 Argentia Rd.
Mississauga, ON L5N 2X7
905-542-2900
Fax: 905-542-1011
info@cantoxenvironmental.com
www.cantoxenvironmental.com
Firm Type: Scientific/Technical Services
Founded: 1985
Staff: 75
Member of: Society of Toxicology in Canada, American Society of Toxicology
Products/Services/Areas of Expertise: Environmental toxicology; human health risk assessment; safety research programs; product stewardship; development of safety assessment criteria; environmental impact assessments; development of workplace standards
Recently Completed / Ongoing Projects: Human health & ecological risk assessment of several contaminated sites; development of Health Canada guidance document for human health risk assessment of contaminated sites in Canada; aquatic food chain modelling of contaminants in the Northern Rivers Basin, Alberta; human health risk assessment of several landfills, Ontario
Domestic Markets:
National
Foreign Activity:
Caribbean, Central America, South America, Mexico, USA
Contact(s):
J. Shapiro, Chair
Robert J. Willes, President

Canadian Branches:
Calgary Branch
Western Div.
#1800, 840 - 7 Ave. SW
Calgary, AB T2P 3G2
403-237-0275
Fax: 403-237-0291
cantox@cadvision.com
Gordon Brown, Vice-President

Halifax Branch
Sovereign Place
#506, 5121 Sackville St.
Halifax, NS B3J 1K1
902-429-0278
Fax: 902-429-0279
cantoxns@isisnet.com
Christine Moore, Senior Scientist

Ottawa
#204, 411 Roosevelt Ave.
Ottawa, ON K2A 3X9
613-761-1464
Fax: 613-761-7653

Canviro
Division of Maxxam Analytics
#12, 50 Bathurst Dr.
Waterloo, ON N2V 2C5
519-747-2575
Fax: 519-747-3806
Firm Type: Scientific/Technical Services
Founded: 1977
Staff: 32
Member of: Canadian Association for Environmental Analytical Laboratories
Products/Services/Areas of Expertise: Analysis of soil, water, air & biota for trace level organic, inorganic & conventional contaminants; environmental compliance testing for drinking, ground, waste, surface water, hazardous & solid waste, sewer effluent, ambient air & smokestack emissions; on-site field services
Domestic Markets:
National
Foreign Activity:
USA
Contact(s):
Jeff Pike, President
Taras Obal, Manager, Operations
AnnMarie Wright, Customer Service
Frank Muschalla, Technical Sales Representative

Canwest Pumping Systems Ltd.
4405 - 50 Ave. SE
Calgary, AB T2B 3R4
403-259-2201
Fax: 403-259-2512
info@canwestltd.com
www.canwestltd.com
Firm Type: Distributing
Founded: 1960
Staff: 10
Products/Services/Areas of Expertise: Wash pumps, distillers, filters; asbestos abatement equipment; paint & lubrication equipment; solvent recovery; hot melt equipment; coating equipment
Financial Information:
Type of Ownership: Private
Domestic Markets:
Alberta, British Columbia
Contact(s):
Wayne Jones, General Manager
Ken Cook, Sales

Canadian Branches:
Edmonton Branch
4011 - 97th St.
Edmonton, AB T6E 5Y5
780-440-3038
Fax: 780-440-6438
canpump@canwestltd.com
Cheryl Kaczur, Branch Manager

Capital Environmental Resource Inc.
Formerly: Kingswood Waste Systems Ltd.
Powerline Rd.
P.O. Box 1705
Brantford, ON N3T 5V7
519-759-4370
Fax: 519-759-7204
Products/Services/Areas of Expertise: Waste audits; recycling of wood, tires, cardboard, newspaper, metals
Contact(s):
Al Loopstra, President
Glen Kingswood, Vice-President, South Western & Eastern Ontario Operations

Products & Services Buyer's Guide

Capital H2O Systems Inc.
12315 - 17th St. SW
Calgary, AB T2W 4A1
403-251-2438
Fax: 403-251-0428
ch2o@capitalh2o.com
www.capitalh2o.com
Firm Type: Engineering
Founded: 1994
Staff: 2
Member of: Western Canada Water & Wastewater; American Water Works Association; Water Environment Federation
Products/Services/Areas of Expertise: Water & wastewater technologies & equipment; chemical feed & control sludge handling; water quality monitoring
Recently Completed / Ongoing Projects: Nutrient monitoring, Bonnybrook WWTP, Calgary; chlorination for Lamb-Weston WTP, Taber; anaerobic/aerobic treatment for Rogers Sugar, Taber
Financial Information:
Type of Ownership: Private
Revenue: $500,000 - $1.5 Million
Revenue Sources: 50% Municipals; 50% Private Contracts
Domestic Markets:
Alberta, British Columbia, Manitoba, Saskatchewan
Contact(s):
Paul Wong, M.Sc., MBA, President

Capricorn Control Technologies Ltd.
131 Malvern Ct. NE
Calgary, AB T2A 4W2
403-235-0960
Fax: 403-235-0992
wkupila@shaw.ca
Firm Type: Scientific/Technical Services
Staff: 2
Member of: Alberta Society of Engineering Technicians & Technologists; Instrument Society of America
Products/Services/Areas of Expertise: Automated control specialist
Financial Information:
Type of Ownership: Publicly Traded
Revenue Sources: 100% Private Contracts
Domestic Markets:
National
Foreign Activity:
Asia, Caribbean, The Middle East
Contact(s):
Wendell Kupila, President

Cardel Construction Ltd.
180 Quarry Park Blvd. SE
Calgary, AB T2C 3G3
403-258-1511
Fax: 403-252-3376
www.cardelhomes.com
Firm Type: Scientific/Technical Services
Founded: 1973
Staff: 90
Products/Services/Areas of Expertise: Construction & project management; residential/commercial construction
Financial Information:
Type of Ownership: Private
Domestic Markets:
Alberta

Cardinal Biologicals Ltd.
Also Known As: Cardinal Labs
#210 - 40 Wynford Drive
Toronto, ON M3C 1J5
416-447-9126
Fax: 416-444-9524
info@cardinalsite.com
www.cardinalsite.com
Firm Type: Scientific/Technical Services
Founded: 1976
Staff: 8
Products/Services/Areas of Expertise: Laboratory services
Financial Information:
Type of Ownership: Private
Revenue: $500,000 - $1.5 Million
Domestic Markets:
Ontario
Contact(s):
Bill Hullah, President
Nick Cowan, Director, Sales

Gary Dainard, Director, Business Development

Care First Aid Training Inc.
Also Known As: Care Institute
1770 East 18th Ave.
Vancouver, BC V5N 4E8
604-873-6018
Fax: 604-873-4443
800-923-4566
elaine@care-institute.com
www.care-institute.com
Firm Type: Management Consulting, Manufacturing
Staff: 42
Products/Services/Areas of Expertise: First aid training; safety & health training; emergency response team training
Domestic Markets:
Alberta, British Columbia
Foreign Activity:
USA
Contact(s):
Elaine Shigetomi, President
Karin Hauswald, Marketing & Sales Coordintor

Career Advancement Employment / CAES
#200, 522 Burlington Ave.
Burlington, ON L7S 1R8
905-681-8240
Fax: 905-639-4601
info@careeradvancement.on.ca
www.careeradvancement.on.ca
Firm Type: Management Consulting
Founded: 1997
Staff: 4
Member of: Burlington Chamber of Commerce; Water Environment Association of Ontario; Centre for Research in the Environment & Space Technology; Materials & Manufacturing Ontario; Ontario Environmental Industry Association; Ontario Centres of Excellence
Products/Services/Areas of Expertise: Employment recruitment & placement services
Financial Information:
Type of Ownership: Private
Domestic Markets:
National
Foreign Activity:
USA
Contact(s):
Jim Gilchrist, B.E.S., President
Melissa Cherepa, Manager, Administrative Services
Richard Wolfsgruber, P.Eng., Manager, Business Development

Careful Hand Laundry & Dry Cleaners Ltd.
#52/53, 2700 Dufferin St.
Toronto, ON M6B 4J3
416-787-9119
Fax: 416-787-0950
president@carefulhandlaundry.com
www.carefulhandlaundry.com
Firm Type: Scientific/Technical Services
Founded: 1929
EcoLogo Certified Products & Services: Fabric cleaning service
Products/Services/Areas of Expertise: Fabric care, with no loss of solvent to the atmosphere & spill containment around machines to protect soil & groundwater
Ecological Note: Fabric cleaning service
Domestic Markets:
Ontario
Contact(s):
Brian Chelsky, President
brian@carefulhandlaundry.com

CARIS
115 Waggoners Lane
Fredericton, NB E3B 2L4
506-458-8533
Fax: 506-459-3849
infos@caris.com
www.caris.com
Firm Type: Information Technology
Founded: 1979
Staff: 125
Member of: Geomatics Industry Association of Canada
Quality Environmental Management System(s): 9001
Products/Services/Areas of Expertise: Software & systems integration; development, support & marketing of GIS & digital mapping software; research & development projects
Financial Information:
Type of Ownership: Private
Domestic Markets:
National
Foreign Activity:
Worldwide
Markets Sought:
Asia, Central Europe, Eastern Europe, Western Europe, South America, Mexico, USA
Contact(s):
Salem Masry, P.Eng., President/CEO

Canadian Branches:
Ontario
#400, 222 Queen St.
Ottawa, ON K1P 5V9
613-298-8720
Fax: 613-850-8657
solutions@caris.com

Québec
76, ch Stoneridge
Chelsea, QC J9B 1Z2
819-827-4318
Fax: 819-827-5161
solutions@caris.com

International Branch(es):
Netherlands
P.O. Box 47
Mgr. van Oorschotstraat 13
Heeswijk NL
+31-0-413-296-010
Fax: +31-0-413-296-0
sales@caris.nl

USA
415 North Alfred St.
Alexandria, VA USA
703-299-9711
Fax: 703-299-9715
carisusa@caris.com

Caristrap International Inc.
1760, boul Fortin
Laval, QC H7S 1N8
450-667-4700
Fax: 450-663-1520
800-361-9466
akarass@caristrap.com
www.caristrap.com
Firm Type: Manufacturing
Founded: 1954
Staff: 250
Member of: Association of American Railroads
Quality Environmental Management System(s): 9001; ISO
Products/Services/Areas of Expertise: Baling & materials handling systems & equipment; strapping for waste paper, textiles, fibers, scrap metals, plastic bales; repulpable paper strap
Financial Information:
Type of Ownership: Private
Revenue: Greater than $5 Million
Revenue Sources: 30% nationwide; 20% Provincial; 50% Private Contracts
Domestic Markets:
National
Foreign Activity:
Asia, Australia/New Zealand, Central America, Central Europe, Eastern Europe, South America, Mexico, USA
Markets Sought:
The Middle East
Contact(s):
Audrey Karass, President
akarass@caristrap.com
Lyne Sosiak, Sales Coordinator
Tinca Cindea, Quality

Carlo Gavazzi (Canada) Inc.
Formerly: Electromatic Canada Inc.
2660 Meadowvale Blvd.
Mississauga, ON L5N 6M6
905-542-0979
Fax: 905-542-2248
comments@carlogavazzi.com
www.gavazzionline.com
Firm Type: Distributing
Founded: 1977

Products/Services/Areas of Expertise: Wholesale industrial automation components; wastewater level controls; water & wastewater management equipment; oil/water separation equipment; clarifiers; heavy metals removal equipment & systems; stormwater management
Domestic Markets:
National
Foreign Activity:
USA
Contact(s):
Fred Shirzadi, President/CEO
Dennis Pizzardi, Vice-President

Canadian Branches:
Montréal Office
3777, boul du Tricentaire
Montréal, QC H1B 5W3
514-644-2544
Fax: 514-644-2808
888-575-2275

Carmanah Technologies Corp.
Formerly: SPS Energy Solutions; Soltek PowerSource Energy Solutions
Bldg. 4
203 Harbour Rd.
Victoria, BC V9A 3S2
250-380-0052
Fax: 250-380-0062
877-722-8877
info@carmanah.com
www.carmanah.com
Firm Type: Distributing, Engineering
Founded: 1996
Staff: 230
Member of: Canadian Solar Industries Association; Light Up the World Foundation; BC Hydro Power Smart
Products/Services/Areas of Expertise: Manufacturer of renewable & energy-efficient technology solutions; the Company is currently focused on three technology groups; solar-powered LED lighting, solar power systems (off grid & grid tie), & LED illuminated signage
Financial Information:
Type of Ownership: Publicly Traded
Revenue: $1.5 Million - $3 Million
Domestic Markets:
National
Foreign Activity:
Worldwide
Contact(s):
Ted Lattimore, CEO
Andrea Voysey, Marketing Director
Mike Cannon, Vice-President, Sales

Canadian Branches:
Calgary
#5, 6025 - 12th St. SE
Calgary, AB T2H 2K1
403-252-6047
Fax: 403-252-5580
800-665-3749

Carole Burnham Consulting
26 Plateau Cres.
Toronto, ON M3C 1M8
416-445-0500
Fax: 416-445-0160
cburnham@attcanada.ca
Firm Type: Management Consulting
Founded: 1999
Staff: 1
Member of: Ontario Environment Industry Association; Association of Professional Engineers of Ontario; Ordre des Ingénieurs du Québec; Air & Waste Management Association; American Academy of Environmental Engineers
Products/Services/Areas of Expertise: Facilitation, bilateral consultations; environmentally sound management of hazardous waste; resource recovery strategies; climate change analysis & strategies; management of environmental assessments for energy & metallurgy projects; sustainable development reporting
Recently Completed / Ongoing Projects: Analysis of Canada's Climate Change Action Plan; assistance in climate change technologies classification; principles & criteria for environmentally sound management of hazardous waste
Financial Information:
Type of Ownership: Private
Revenue: $50,000 - $100,000
Revenue Sources: 25% nationwide; 75% Private Contracts
Domestic Markets:
Alberta, British Columbia, Northwest Territories, Nunavut, Ontario, Québec
Markets Sought:
USA
Contact(s):
Carole Burnham, Ph.D., P.Eng., Sr. Consultant

Carrier Canada Ltd.
1515 Drew Rd.
Mississauga, ON L5S 1Y8
905-672-0606
Fax: 905-672-7156
800-561-8178
Firm Type: Distributing
Founded: 1934
Staff: 500
Products/Services/Areas of Expertise: HVAC equipment; zoning systems; control systems; parts, service
Domestic Markets:
Alberta, British Columbia, Manitoba, New Brunswick, Nova Scotia, Ontario, Québec, Saskatchewan
Contact(s):
Robert Hunter, President/CEO
Dave Poissant, Director, CMU Products & National Accounts, 905/567-2757
Ron Trautmann, Manager, Environment, Health & Safety

Canadian Branches:
Barrie
35 Morrow Rd.
Barrie, ON L4N 3V7
705-721-1313
S. Kennedy

Burnaby
3819 Still Creek Ave.
Burnaby, BC V5C 4E2
604-291-7788

Calgary North
3440E - 12 St. NE
Calgary, AB T2E 6N1
403-250-9616
D. Preibe

Calgary South
#24, 3636 - 7 St. SE
Calgary, AB T2G 2Y8
403-243-0233
N. Hill

Concord
#5, 18 Killaloe Rd.
Concord, ON L4K 2P2
905-761-1511
J. Young

Dartmouth
#6, 656 Windmill Rd.
Dartmouth, NS B3B 1B8
902-468-8946
C. Gillespie

Edmonton North
11735 - 108 Ave.
Edmonton, AB T5H 1B8
780-452-7434
J. Penney

Edmonton South
5903 - 87A St.
Edmonton, AB T6E 5W6
780-465-5323
F. Woynorowski

Hamilton
18 Brockley Dr.
Hamilton, ON L8E 3P1
905-561-2260
K. Adams

Kelowna
#100, 2250 Acland Rd.
Kelowna, BC V1X 6N6
250-860-3667
T. Hehn

Kitchener Shirley
#2, 260 Shirley Dr.
Kitchener, ON N2B 2E1
519-744-5274
R. Farrell

Kitchener Trillium
#8, 250 Trillium Dr.
Kitchener, ON N2E 1X2
519-895-0110
D. Bowman

Langley
20350 Langley By-Pass
Langley, BC V3A 5E7
604-532-8737
M. Eastwood

London
501 Newbold St.
London, ON N6E 1K4
519-455-7091
P. Blakeman

Longueuil
#2600, 2672 boul Jacques Cartier est
Longueuil, QC J4N 1P8
450-670-6111
Y. Pepin

Mississauga Drew
1515 Drew Rd.
Mississauga, ON L5S 1Y8
905-672-0860
J. Bullen

Mississauga Everest
5118 Everest Dr.
Mississauga, ON L4W 2R4
905-625-1677
C. Soulis

Moncton
191 Henri Durant St.
Moncton, NB E1E 2T4
506-857-0808
I. Sawden

Nanaimo
#C, 2575 McCullough Rd.
Nanaimo, BC V9S 5W5
250-751-3687
S. Siglet

North Bay
44 Venture Cr.
North Bay, ON P1B 8G4
705-474-4260
A. Fiddament

Ottawa Baxter
Baxter Centre
1050 Baxter Rd.
Ottawa, ON K2C 3P1
613-820-4328
D. Taria

Ottawa Lola
#3, 1155 Lola St.
Ottawa, ON K1K 4C1
613-741-6603
M. Suave

Québec/Vanier
595, boul Pierre Bertrand
Québec, QC G1M 3T8
418-872-4222
A. Bilodeau

Regina
1361 Halifax St.
Regina, SK S4R 1T9
306-525-0108
J. Chay

Saskatoon
#409, 38th St.
Saskatoon, SK S7K 0T1
306-652-1842
R. DeBussac

Products & Services Buyer's Guide

St Catharines
#1, 113 Cushman Rd.
St Catharines, ON L2M 6S9
905-622-1600
D. Payne

St. Laurent
5060 Levy St.
Saint-Laurent, QC H4R 2P1
514-856-9811
S. Gauthier

St. Leonard
5135, rue Metropolitan est
St. Leonard, QC H1R 1Z7
514-326-3277
S. Gauthier

Sudbury
945A Cambrian Heights Dr.
Sudbury, ON P3C 5M6
705-566-3174
S. Fransen

Timmins
629 Spruce St. South
Timmins, ON P4N 2P2
705-264-2363
B. Clarke

Toronto
#1-3, 150 Milner Ave.
Toronto, ON M1S 3R3
416-609-0180
C. Ellis

Vancouver
155 - 3 Ave West
Vancouver, BC V5Y 1E6
604-876-9278
R. Isley

Windsor
4550 Rhodes Dr.
Windsor, ON N8W 5J4
519-945-2220
M. Boussey

Winnipeg East
560 Archibald St.
Winnipeg, MB R2J 0X4
204-233-2244
G. Kormylo

Winnipeg West
#7, 1725 St. James St.
Winnipeg, MB R3H 1H3
204-775-2523
T. Lobb

Carson Safety & Environmental Services
P.O. Box 160
Lampman, SK S0C 1N0
306-487-4112
Fax: 306-487-3235
lmartin@cap.lampman.sk.ca
Contact(s):
Lloyd Martin, Environmental Engineer

Carswell Consulting Engineers Ltd.
3415 - 3 Ave. NW
Calgary, AB T2N 0M4
403-283-0791
Fax: 403-270-3970
carswelh@shaw.ca
www.carswell-engineering.com
Firm Type: Engineering, Scientific/Technical Services
Founded: 1956
Staff: 8
Products/Services/Areas of Expertise: Consulting engineers; civil, mechanical, electrical, architectural
Financial Information:
Type of Ownership: Private
Revenue Sources: 20% Municipals; 80% Private Contracts
Domestic Markets:
Alberta, British Columbia, Saskatchewan
Contact(s):
Harry Carswell, P.Eng., President
Robert Carswell, Sec.-Treas.
John Carswell, P.Eng., Vice-President

Cartier Chemicals Ltd.
Produits Chimiques Cartier Ltée
445, av 21E
Montréal, QC H8S 3T8
514-637-4631
Fax: 514-637-8804
800-361-9432
info@cartierchem.com
www.cartierchem.com
Firm Type: Manufacturing
Founded: 1939
Staff: 25
Products/Services/Areas of Expertise: Environmentally safe neutralizers for hazardous chemicals, concentrated acids, formaldehyde, liquid caustic spills; environmentally safe petroleum & petroleum products spill dispersants; environmentally safe cleaners & degreasers; absorbent immobilizers for mercury; oil spill demoussing agents; customized spill response kits
Domestic Markets:
National
Foreign Activity:
Africa, Western Europe, The Pacific Rim, USA
Contact(s):
E.W. Robins, President/CEO

Cartridge Care Canada
215 Red River Rd.
Thunder Bay, ON P7B 1A5
807-345-4050
888-582-0080
sales@cartridgecare.ca
Firm Type: Scientific/Technical Services
Founded: 1985
Staff: 4
Products/Services/Areas of Expertise: Computer printer toner cartridges, ribbons recycling
Contact(s):
Ken Stockla, Contact
Wendy Blackman, President
Canadian Branches:
Marathon
P.O. Box 704
Marathon, ON P0T 2E0
807-229-3006

Cascade Environmental Resource Group. Ltd.
Formerly: GeoAlpine Environmental Consulting Ltd.
#3, 1005 Alpha Lake Rd.
Whistler, BC V0N 1G1
604-938-1949
Fax: 604-938-1247
info@cascade-environmental.ca
www.cascade-environmental.ca
Firm Type: Management Consulting, Scientific/Technical Services
Founded: 1990
Staff: 11
Member of: Canada West Ski Areas Association; Association of Wetland Scientists; Canadian Association of Geographers; International Association for Impact Assessment; Associated Environmental Site Assessors of Canada; Canadian Water Research Association; College of Applied Biology BC
Products/Services/Areas of Expertise: Environmental & land use planning; resource & ecological inventory; ecosystem mapping; impact assessments; environmental audits; environmental assessment (phase I & II); geotechnical & hydrotechnical studies; riparian habitat management; parks & recreation planning
Recently Completed / Ongoing Projects: Environmental planning services, Garibaldi Springs Golf Course; Construction monitoring, Rutherford Creek Power Project; Environmental assessment, Athletes Village 2010 Olympics; Commercial recreation applications, Coast Range Heliskiing; Terrestrial ecosystem mapping, District of Squamish
Financial Information:
Type of Ownership: Private
Revenue Sources: 30% Provincial; 20% Municipals; 50% Private Contracts
Domestic Markets:
British Columbia
Markets Sought:
The Pacific Rim, South America, USA
Contact(s):
Dave Williamson, Principal
dwilliamson@cascade-environmental.ca
Mike Nelson, Principal

Cascades Fine Papers Group Inc.
Formerly: Rolland Inc.
2, av Rolland
Saint-Jérôme, QC J7Z 5S1
450-569-3909
Fax: 450-569-3947
800-567-9872
infofinepaper@cascades.com
www.environmentalbychoice.com
Firm Type: Manufacturing
Founded: 1982
Staff: 400
Quality Environmental Management System(s): 9002
EcoLogo Certified Products & Services: New Life, Rolland Enviro, Rolland Inspiration, Rolland Opaque, Rolland Higtech, 8T GenerationII, Rockland, New Life DP100
Products/Services/Areas of Expertise: Post-consumer fine papers, coated & uncoated
Recently Completed / Ongoing Projects: 100% post-consumer paper (uncoated), New Life DP100, Rolland Enviro, Rolland Inspiro, Ecofiber accredited EcoLogo & PCF
Ecological Note: New Life, Rolland Enviro, Rolland Inspiration, Rolland Opaque, Rolland Higtech, 8T GenerationII, Rockland, New Life DP100
Contact(s):
Mario Plourde, President/CEO

Cascades Inc.
Environment Department
CP 30
404, rue Marie-Victorin
Kingsey Falls, QC J0A 1B0
819-363-5100
Fax: 819-363-5155
Firm Type: Engineering, Manufacturing, Scientific/Technical Services
Staff: 27
Quality Environmental Management System(s): 9001
Products/Services/Areas of Expertise: Recycling of paper, plastics; environmental audits; training & education
Domestic Markets:
Alberta, Newfoundland & Labrador, Ontario, Québec
Foreign Activity:
Western Europe, USA
Contact(s):
Leon Marineau, Vice-President, Environment

Cascades Inc.
P.O. Box 30
404, boul Marie-Victorin
Kingsey Falls, QC J0A 1B0
819-363-5100
Fax: 819-363-5155
info@cascades.com
www.cascades.com
Firm Type: Distributing, Manufacturing
Founded: 1964
Quality Environmental Management System(s): 9002
EcoLogo Certified Products & Services: Jumbo rolls of paper for envelopes other packaging applications
Products/Services/Areas of Expertise: Manufacturer of papers with virgin & recycled fibres
Ecological Note: Jumbo rolls of paper for envelopes other packaging applications
Domestic Markets:
New Brunswick, Ontario, Prince Edward Island, Québec
Foreign Activity:
Caribbean, Western Europe, Mexico, USA
Contact(s):
Alain Lemaire, President/CEO
Léon Marineau, Vice-President, Environment
Claude Cosette, Vice-President, Organizational Development

Cascades Recovery Inc.
A member company of Cascades Specialty Products Group, Cascades Inc.
Formerly: Metro Waste Paper Recovery Inc.66 Shorncliffe Rd.
Toronto, ON M8Z 5K1
416-231-2525
Fax: 416-232-8820
866-345-3322
toronto@metrowaste.com

Firm Type: Waste Management
Founded: 1964
Member of: Paper & Paperboard Packaging Environmental Council
Products/Services/Areas of Expertise: Waste transport
Domestic Markets:
Alberta, British Columbia, Manitoba, Ontario
Contact(s):
Al Metauro, Chief Executive Officer
Contact(s):
Barry Pitcher
Contact(s):
Tami Urzada
Contact(s):
Deanne Stevenson
Contact(s):
Laurie Sweig
Contact(s):
Darren Wahl
Contact(s):
Mike Sullivan
Contact(s):
Shelley Rouse
Contact(s):
Todd Gillard
Canadian Branches:
Calgary
10351 - 46th St. SE
Calgary, AB T2G 2X9
403-243-5700
calgary@metrowaste.com

Edmonton
2015 - 87th Ave.
Sherwood Park, AB T6P 1L5
780-464-4761
edmonton@metrowaste.com

Kelowna
144 Cambro Rd.
Kelowna, BC V1X 7T3
250-491-2242
kelowna@metrowaste.com

Ottawa
2811 Sheffield Rd.
Ottawa, ON K1B 3V8
613-742-1222
ottawa@metrowaste.com

Prince George
8545 Willow Cale Rd.
Prince George, BC V2N 6Z9
250-563-0233
princegeorge@metrowaste.com

Surrey
12345 - 104th Ave.
Surrey, BC V3V 3H2
604-589-4385
surrey@metrowaste.com

Toronto - Commander
Scarborough
45 Commander Blvd.
Toronto, ON M1S 3E7
416-292-5149
toronto@metrowaste.com

Toronto - Thornmount
Scarborough
45 Thornmount Dr.
Toronto, ON M1B 5P5
416-292-5149
toronto@metrowaste.com

Vancouver
8325 Main St.
Vancouver, BC V5X 3M3
604-327-5272
vancouver@metrowaste.com

Victoria
2800 Bridge St.
Victoria, BC V8T 4T3
250-480-1274
victoria@metrowaste.com

Winnipeg
100 Omands Creek Blvd.
Winnipeg, MB R2R 1V7
204-632-4457
winnipeg@metrowaste.com

Cascades Resource
Division of Cascades Fine Papers Group Inc.
Formerly: Graphic Papers3190 Caravelle Dr.
Mississauga, ON L4V 1K9
416-674-2335
Fax: 416-674-7613
877-790-2335
www.cascades.com
Firm Type: Distributing
Staff: 496
Member of: Canadian Paper Trade Association; Packaging Association of Canada
Products/Services/Areas of Expertise: Printing papers; graphic arts; sanitation; maintenance; health; safety; business imaging; packaging & shipping; supplies & systems
Financial Information:
Type of Ownership: Publicly Traded
Revenue Sources: 1% nationwide; 2% Provincial; 3% Municipals; 94% Private Contracts
Domestic Markets:
National, Alberta, British Columbia, Manitoba, New Brunswick, Newfoundland & Labrador, Nova Scotia, Ontario, Prince Edward Island, Québec, Saskatchewan
Contact(s):
Alain Lemaire, President & CEO
Alain Ducharme, Corporate Vice President

Canadian Branches:
Belleville
95 Hanna Ct., Group Box 5
Belleville, ON K1P 5H2
613-968-3460
Fax: 613-968-3446

Calgary
950 - 64th Ave. NE
Calgary, AB T2E 8S8
403-730-9393
Fax: 403-730-9394

Dartmouth
19-29 Gurholt Dr.
Dartmouth, NS B3B 1J8
902-468-5585
Fax: 902-468-5434

Edmonton
18070 - 109 Ave.
Edmonton, AB T5S 2K2
780-486-7500
Fax: 780-486-9452

Kitchener
1460 Strasburg Rd.
Kitchener, ON N2R 1K1
519-748-5111
Fax: 519-748-0981

Mississauga (Caravelle)
3190 Caravelle Dr.
Mississauga, ON L4V 1K9
416-674-2335
Fax: 416-764-7613

Mississauga (Orland)
3300 Orland Dr.
Mississauga, ON L4V 1C6
905-671-4222
Fax: 905-671-4528

Montréal
10 000, boul Ray Lawson
Montréal, QC H1J 1L8
514-351-3520
Fax: 514-351-4036

Newfoundland
Donovan's Industrial Park
126 Clyde Ave.
Mount Pearl, NL A1N 4S3
709-747-5959
Fax: 709-682-8634

Ottawa
1250 Leeds Ave.
Ottawa, ON K1B 3W3
613-741-9655
Fax: 613-741-7623

Québec
2893, rue Kepler
Sainte-Foy, QC G1X 3V4
418-858-0116
Fax: 418-658-3884

Sudbury
1350 Kelly Lake Rd.
Sudbury, ON P3E 5P4
705-673-1500
Fax: 705-673-5471

Toronto
345 Passmore Ave.
Toronto, ON M1V 3N8
416-298-4440
Fax: 416-412-9213

Vancouver
8999 Fraserton Ct.
Burnaby, BC V5J 5H8
604-412-4810
Fax: 604-438-2355
1-800-336-7933

Winnipeg
2260 Logan Ave.
Winnipeg, MB R2R 0J2
204-633-3705
Fax: 204-694-0874

Caster-Rack Systems Ltd.
109 Ilsley Ave.
Dartmouth, NS B3B 1S8
902-468-1880
Fax: 902-468-2589
800-565-1880
www.caster-rack.com
Firm Type: Distributing
Founded: 1989
Staff: 7
Member of: Compost Council of Canada
Products/Services/Areas of Expertise: Curbside collection cart systems for municipal & commercial recyclables & compost
Recently Completed / Ongoing Projects: Residential curbside organic collection systems, Halifax, Truro, Lunenburg, N.S. & East Prince, P.E.I.
Financial Information:
Type of Ownership: Private
Revenue Sources: 70% Municipals; 30% Private Contracts
Domestic Markets:
New Brunswick, Newfoundland & Labrador, Nova Scotia, Prince Edward Island
Foreign Activity:
Caribbean, USA
Contact(s):
Michael Matthews, President
Mark Martell, General Manager, Caster & Roller Sales

Castle Building Centres Groups Ltd.
#400, 6375 Dixie Rd.
Mississauga, ON L5T 2S1
905-564-3307
Fax: 905-564-6592
www.castle.ca
Firm Type: Distributing
Founded: 1963
EcoLogo Certified Products & Services: Surface coatings
Products/Services/Areas of Expertise: Is the largest national group of independently owned & operated lumber & building material stores, represented in over 250 communities across Canada, every location is operated by the individual owners & ensures that customers are participating in the growth of their community
Ecological Note: Surface coatings
Contact(s):
James Jones, Manager, Business Development
jjones@castle.ca

Cat Tech Canada Company
Formerly: Catalyst Technology Canada
4403 - 84th Ave.
Edmonton, AB T6B 2S6

780-468-4544
Fax: 780-463-6355
CTISales@cat-tech.com
www.cat-tech.com
Firm Type: Scientific/Technical Services
Staff: 30
Products/Services/Areas of Expertise: Providing all phases of catalyst changeout to petroleum & chemical companies
Financial Information:
Type of Ownership: Private
Revenue Sources: 100% Private Contracts
Domestic Markets:
National
Foreign Activity:
Worldwide
Contact(s):
Terry Tyler, President
Stephen Brennom, Vice-President, Technical Services

Canadian Branches:
Eastern Region Branch
282 Tecumseh St.
Sarnia, ON N7T 2K9
519-339-9855
Fax: 519-339-0153

Catalyst Paper Corp.
Formerly: Norske Canada Ltd.
2nd Floor, 3600 Lysander Lane
Richmond, BC V7B 1C3
604-247-4400
Fax: 604-247-0512
contactus@catalystpaper.com
www.catalystpaper.com
Firm Type: Manufacturing
Staff: 3500
EcoLogo Certified Products & Services: Pulp
Products/Services/Areas of Expertise: Paper and pulp paper products
Ecological Note: Pulp
Financial Information:
Type of Ownership: Publicly Traded
Domestic Markets:
National
Foreign Activity:
Worldwide
Contact(s):
Lyn Brown, Director, Corporate Relations & Social Responsibility, 604-257-4713
Graham Kissack, Environment, 604-220-9482
environment@catalystpaper.com

Canadian Branches:
Coquitlam - Paper Recycling
1050 United Boulevard
Coquitlam, BC V3K 6V4
604-525-5734

Crofton
P.O. Box 70
Crofton, BC V0R 1R0
250-246-6100

Elk Falls
P.O. Box 2000
Campbell River, BC V9W 5C9
250-287-5200

Port Alberni
4000 Stamp Ave.
Port Alberni, BC V9Y 5J7
250-724-7089

Powell River Office
5775 Ash Ave.
Powell River, BC V8A 4K3
604-483-3722

Catherine Berris Associates Inc.
#420, 1639 - 2 Ave. West
Vancouver, BC V6J 1H3
604-736-6336
Fax: 604-736-2338
office@cbainc.bc.ca
www.cbainc.bc.ca
Firm Type: Management Consulting
Founded: 1985
Staff: 4
Products/Services/Areas of Expertise: Environmental & land use planning; geographic information systems; coastal planning; conflict resolution; visual impact assessment & simulations; landscape restoration
Contact(s):
Catherine Berris, MCIP, FCSLA, President/CEO

Cathy's Crawly Composters
P.O. Box 13013
Bradford, ON L3Z 1A1
905-775-9495
888-775-9495
cathy@cathyscomposters.com
www.cathyscomposters.com
Firm Type: Management Consulting, Distributing, Manufacturing
Founded: 2002
Staff: 4
Products/Services/Areas of Expertise: Vermiculture business supplying red wiggler worms, vermicomposting bins, castings & books; conducts workshops & demonstrations; raises awareness about the environment & encourages sustainable practices; future directions include manure management
Contact(s):
Cathy Nesbitt, Founder
, President

Catterall & Wright
1221 - 8th St. East
Saskatoon, SK S7H 0S5
306-343-7280
Fax: 306-956-3199
cw@cwce.ca
www.cwce.ca
Firm Type: Engineering
Founded: 1965
Staff: 12
Products/Services/Areas of Expertise: Engineering services; preliminary investigations, design, construction inspection, project management for municipal infrastructure including subdivision servicing, water & sewage pumping & treatment, sidewalk, curb & road construction, storm sewers & drainage, recreation & other municipal buildings, small municipal airports
Recently Completed / Ongoing Projects: Upgrading filters, water plant, Saskatoon; main sewage pumphouse, Humboldt; municipal airport upgrade, Melfort
Financial Information:
Revenue Sources: 15% nationwide; 15% Provincial; 60% Municipals; 10% Private Contracts
Domestic Markets:
Saskatchewan
Contact(s):
W. Wright, Principal
A. Mickelson, Principal
N. McLeod, Principal

CB Engineering, Ltd.
#20, 1220 - 59 Ave SE
Calgary, AB T2H 2M4
403-259-6220
Fax: 403-259-3377
800-992-2364
info@cbeng.com
www.cbeng.com
Firm Type: Distributing
Founded: 1974
Staff: 100
Products/Services/Areas of Expertise: Measuring & monitoring equipment
Financial Information:
Type of Ownership: Private
Domestic Markets:
National
Contact(s):
Craig Bowyer, President

Canadian Branches:
Edmonton
#515, 9945 - 50 St.
Edmonton, AB T6A 0L4
780-465-9370
Fax: 780-469-9217

Halifax
P.O. Box 22040
7071 Bayers Rd.
Halifax, NS B3L 4T7
902-229-8175

Montréal
2315, Halpern
Montréal, QC H4S 1S3
514-332-3230
Fax: 514-332-3552

Sarnia
#411G, 265 North Front St.
Sarnia, ON N7T 7X1
519-336-4482
Fax: 519-344-1666

Toronto
#2, 110 Snow Blvd.
Vaughan, ON L4K 4B8
905-760-9399
Fax: 905-760-9319

Vancouver
#211, 3030 Lincoln Ave.
Coquitlam, BC V3B 6B4
604-472-9037
Fax: 888-259-1666

Winnipeg
P.O. Box 154
99 Scurfield Blvd.
Winnipeg, MB R3Y 1Y1
204-953-2470
Fax: 888-259-1666

International Branch(es):
Anchorage
#103, 750 West 2nd Ave.
Anchorage, AK USA
907-279-2799
Fax: 907-279-2820

Portland
#325B, 101 East 8th St.
Vancouver, WA USA
360-693-1520
Fax: 360-693-1449

Seattle
#201, 909 - 7th Ave.
Kirkland, WA USA
425-822-1702
Fax: 425-822-5442

CBCL Limited
Formerly: Canadian-British Consultants Limited
P.O. Box 606
1489 Hollis St.
Halifax, NS B3J 2R7
902-421-7241
Fax: 902-423-3938
info@cbcl.ca
www.cbcl.ca
Firm Type: Engineering, Scientific/Technical Services
Founded: 1955
Staff: 22
Member of: Canadian Society of Civil Engineers; Association of Consulting Engineers of Canada; Nova Scotia Environmental Industry Association; Aquaculture Association of Canada
Quality Environmental Management System(s): 9001
Products/Services/Areas of Expertise: Multidiscipline services in sustainable development; fisheries management; coastal zone management; water & wastewater treatment; waste management; aquaculture & environmental assessments
Recently Completed / Ongoing Projects: Muggah Creek Watershed, phase I site assessment; Port Hawkesbury water treatment plant; closure of Bowater industrial landfill; Shrimp Aquaculture Project in Gujarat
Financial Information:
Type of Ownership: Private
Revenue: Greater than $5 Million
Revenue Sources: 5% nationwide; 15% Provincial; 30% Municipals; 50% Private Contracts
Domestic Markets:
New Brunswick, Newfoundland & Labrador, Nova Scotia, Prince Edward Island
Foreign Activity:
Africa, Asia, Caribbean, Central America, South America
Markets Sought:
The Pacific Rim, Mexico, USA
Contact(s):
Alan Perry, M.Sc., P.Eng., President/CEO
Mike Murphy, Vice-President
Ann Wilkie, Vice-President, Environmental Services

Canadian Branches:
Charlottetown
P.O. Box 1659
#201, 135 St. Peters Rd.
Charlottetown, PE C1A 7N4
902-892-0303
Fax: 902-368-3444
Jody MacLeod, Manager

Corner Brook
P.O. Box 428
38 Main St.
Corner Brook, NL A2H 6E3
709-639-4225
Fax: 709-639-4220
Dean Reid, Sr. Project Manager

Fredericton
P.O. Box 451 A
#110, 77 Westmorland St.
Fredericton, NB E3B 4Z9
506-450-9441
Fax: 506-450-4199
Jonathan Fullarton, Manager

Happy Valley-Goose Bay
P.O. Box 1989 B
350 Hamilton River Rd.
Happy Valley-Goose Bay, NL A0P 1E0
709-896-9707
Fax: 709-896-9708
Brian Johnson, Sr. Technologist

Saint John
P.O. Box 20040
22 King St.
Saint John, NB E2L 5B2
506-633-6650
Fax: 506-633-6659
John Flewelling, Manager

St. John's
ICON Building
187 Kenmount Rd.
St. John's, NL A1B 3P9
709-364-8623
Fax: 709-364-8627
Bob Walsh, Manager

Sydney
P.O. Box 567
164A Charlotte St.
Sydney, NS B1P 6H4
902-539-1330
Fax: 902-539-4406
Lorne Martin, Manager

CBR Products - Canadian Building Restoration Products Inc.
#102, 876 Cordova DVSN
Vancouver, BC V6A 3R3
604-254-3325
Fax: 604-215-2278
888-311-5339
info@cbrproducts.com
www.cbrproducts.com
Firm Type: Manufacturing
Founded: 1991
EcoLogo Certified Products & Services: Broda stains, finishes & anti-grafitti coatings
Products/Services/Areas of Expertise: Manufactures a comprehensive line of high-performance, non-toxic & environmentally responsible restoration & preservation coatings for residential & commercial applications; formulated with the highest quality ingredients, CBR coatings withstand rigorous wear while protecting & enhancing properties of wood, concrete & masonry surfaces
Ecological Note: Broda stains, finishes & anti-grafitti coatings
Contact(s):
Bill Willis, Owner

CCI Thermal Technologies Inc.
5918 Roper Rd.
Edmonton, AB T6B 3E1
780-466-3178
Fax: 780-468-5904
800-661-8529
info@ccithermal.com
www.ccithermal.com
Firm Type: Manufacturing
Founded: 1964
Quality Environmental Management System(s): 9001:2008;
Products/Services/Areas of Expertise: CCI Thermal Technologies Inc., one of Canada's best managed companies & a leader in the design & manufacture of industrial heating & filtration equipment, is the result of a merger between Ciscan Industries Ltd., Ruffneck Heaters, DriQuik Inc., Calorítech Inc., Wellman Thermal Systems, Flo-Dri Inc., & 3L Filters. We manufacture & service Cata-Dyne explosion-proof flameless, infrated catalytic gas heaters & accessories, Ruffneck & Norseman explosion-proof heaters & thermosats, Calorítech electric heaters & tubular elements, DriQuik oven systems, & 3L filter products. Edmonton plant location also houses the corporate head office; branch plants in Oakville, Orillia, & Greensburg, Indiana.
Financial Information:
Type of Ownership: Private
Revenue Sources: 100% Private Contracts
Domestic Markets:
Alberta, British Columbia, Manitoba, Ontario, Québec, Saskatchewan
Foreign Activity:
Worldwide
Contact(s):
Harold A. Roozen, Chairman/CEO

Canadian Branches:
Oakville
2721 Plymouth Dr.
Oakville, ON L6H 5R5
905-829-4422
Fax: 905-829-4430
1-800-410-3131

Orillia
1 Hunter Valley Rd.
Orillia, ON L3V 6H2
705-325-3473
Fax: 705-325-2106
1-877-325-3473

International Branch(es):
Indiana
P.O. Box 146
1420 West Main St.
Greensburg, IN USA
812-663-4141
Fax: 812-663-4202
1-800-473-2402

CCL/IBI
IBI Group
Formerly: Cumming Cockburn Limited#200, 9133 Leslie St.
Richmond Hill, ON L4B 4N1
905-763-2322
Fax: 905-763-9983
877-601-7397
www.ibigroup.com
Firm Type: Engineering
Founded: 1960
Staff: 90
Products/Services/Areas of Expertise: Urban planning & development; traffic & roadways; sewage & drainage systems; water supply & distribution; water resources engineering & hydrologic modelling; flood management; stormwater management; stream & shoreline erosion; hydraulics & marine structures; water & wind power engineering; environmental impact assessment & mitigation planning; environmental approvals & monitoring; peer review; 6 other international locations
Financial Information:
Type of Ownership: Private
Domestic Markets:
National
Foreign Activity:
Africa, Central Europe, Eastern Europe, Western Europe, The Middle East, USA
Contact(s):
John Bolen, General Manager
jbolen@ibigroup.com
Harold Bolone, Director, Environmental Sciences
hbolone@ibigroup.com

Canadian Branches:
Calgary
Kensington House
#400, 1167 Kensington Cres. NW
Calgary, AB T2N 1X7
403-270-5600
Fax: 403-270-5610
ksallaway@ibigroup.com

Edmonton
Standard Life Building
10405 Jasper Ave.
Edmonton, AB T5J 3N4
780-428-4000
Fax: 780-426-3256
pmoore@ibigroup.com

Kingston
#110, 650 Dalton Ave.
Kingston, ON K7M 8N7
613-531-4440
Fax: 613-531-7789

Richmond
#130, 7360 Westminster Hwy.
Richmond, BC V6X 1A1
604-232-1100
Fax: 604-232-1177
gandrishak@ibigroup.com

Vancouver
#700, 1285 West Pender St.
Vancouver, BC V6E 4B1
604-683-8797
Fax: 604-683-0492
ibivan@ibigroup.com

CCR Technologies Ltd.
Formerly: Canadian Chemical Reclaiming Ltd.
#300, 5 Richard Way SW
Calgary, AB T3E 7M8
403-543-6699
Fax: 403-262-2941
800-820-4682
info@reclaim.com
www.reclaim.com
Firm Type: Engineering, Scientific/Technical Services
Founded: 1987
Staff: 25
Products/Services/Areas of Expertise: Refining, recycling or reducing industrial waste; mobile reclaiming service for refiners & gas processors; technology licensing & solutions mainly to off-shore gas processors; recycling of antifreeze
Financial Information:
Type of Ownership: Publicly Traded
Revenue Sources: 100% Private Contracts
Domestic Markets:
Alberta, British Columbia, Ontario
Foreign Activity:
Western Europe, USA, Worldwide
Contact(s):
Pete Graham, President/CEO

International Branch(es):
Houston
#550, 1500 CityWest Blvd.
Houston, TX USA
281-988-5800
Fax: 281-988-5858
jsczesny@reclaim.com
John Sczesny, Contact

CCS Income Trust / CCS
Formerly: Canadian Crude Seperators Inc.
Also Known As: Oilfield Waste Processing & Disposal
#2400, 530 - 8th Ave. SW
Calgary, AB T2P 3S8
403-233-7565
Fax: 403-261-5612
info@ccsincometrust.com
www.ccsincometrust.com
Firm Type: Scientific/Technical Services, Waste Management
Founded: 1985
Staff: 2500
Products/Services/Areas of Expertise: Oil treating; oilfield waste management & processing, disposal & transportation; soil reclamation; thermal treating; remediation technology; NORM disposal

Products & Services Buyer's Guide

Domestic Markets:
Alberta, British Columbia, Saskatchewan
Contact(s):
Dave Werklund, President/CEO/Chair
Marshall McRae, CFO/Secretary/Vice-President, Finance
John Bean, Vice-President, Corporate Finance
Jim McMahon, Vice-President, Business Development
Rick Wise, Vice-President, Engineering, Regulatory & Midstream Development
Gordon Vivian, President, Concord Well Servicing
David Mattinson, President, Hazco
Contact(s):
Brian Huseby, Plant Manager
Contact(s):
Mike Ollenberger, Plant Manager
Contact(s):
Gary Edwards, Plant Manager
Contact(s):
Mike Ollenberger, Plant Manager
Contact(s):
Brian Huseby, Plant Manager
Contact(s):
Mike Ollenberger, Plant Manager
Contact(s):
Tyler Fittes, Plant Manager
Contact(s):
Rick Good, Plant Manager
Contact(s):
Chris Bye, Plant Manager
Contact(s):
Chris Bye, Plant Manager
Contact(s):
Todd Baumgartner, Plant Manager
Contact(s):
Marty Payne, Manager
Contact(s):
Allen Douglas, Plant Manager
Contact(s):
Charlie Schell, Plant Manager
Contact(s):
Tim Dalgleish, Plant Manager
Contact(s):
Martin Dean, Plant Manager
Contact(s):
Clark Sittler, Plant Manager
Contact(s):
Richard Newby, Plant Manager
Contact(s):
Ray Juneau, Plant Manager
Contact(s):
Ray Juneau, Plant Manager
Contact(s):
Mike Johnson, Plant Manager
Contact(s):
Mike Johnson, Plant Manager
Contact(s):
Robert Menzies, Plant Manager
Contact(s):
Joe Look, Plant Manager
Contact(s):
Chris Whitford, Plant Manager
Contact(s):
Dale Fittes, Plant Manager
Contact(s):
Tim Froot, Plant Manager
Contact(s):
Jim Grove, Plant Manager
Canadian Branches:
Fort Nelson/Sierra TRD
9940 - 102 Ave.
Fort St John, BC V1J 2E1
250-775-1266
Fax: 250-262-0151
Michael Voight, Plant Manager

Lomond Landfill
80A - 18 St.
Weyburn, SK S4H 2W4
306-456-2212
Fax: 306-456-2236
Mark Hill, Landfill Manager

Northern Rockies Landfill
Mile 285, Alaska Hwy.
Fort Nelson, BC V0C 1R0
250-774-3027
Fax: 250-774-3028
Mike Blades, Landfill Manger

Spirit River Landfill
P.O. Box 501
Rycroft, AB T0H 3A0
780-765-3745
Fax: 780-765-3751
Louis Bunron, Landfill Manager

Spirit River TRD
P.O. Box 159
Spirit River, AB T0H 3G0
750-832-1648
Joe Look, Plant Manager

Tower Road Landfill
P.O. Box 526
Carrot Creek, AB T0E 0G0
403-795-2467
Fax: 403-795-2542
Luke Van Dyk, Landfill Manager

Big Valley
P.O. Box 221
Big Valley, AB T0J 0G0
403-876-2636
Fax: 403-876-2248

Boundary Lake TRD
250-262-9930
Fax: 250-262-7578

Brazeau TRD
780-894-2291
Fax: 780-894-2296

Cecil Lake Well
250-787-8866
Fax: 250-787-7411

Coronation
c/o Coronation Tire
4901 Victoria Ave.
Coronation, AB T0C 1C0
403-575-3911
Fax: 403-575-3927

Flatrock Well
250-262-1943

Fox Creek Landfill
780-622-2981
Fax: 780-622-2361

Fox Creek TRD
780-622-3355
Fax: 780-622-3664

Gull Lake Landfill
306-672-3300
Fax: 306-672-4252

Gull Lake TRD
P.O. Box 390
Gull Lake, SK S0N 1A0
306-672-3300
Fax: 306-682-4252

Hardisty Caverns, Blending & Terminal
780-888-3565
Fax: 780-888-3978

High Prairie TRD
P.O. Box 1454
High Prairie, AB T0G 1E0
780-523-5890
Fax: 780-523-3220

Judy Creek TRD
P.O. Box 687
Whitecourt, AB T7S 1S1
780-778-1970
Fax: 780-778-6957

Kindersley TRD
P.O. Box 390
Kindersley, SK S0L 1S0
306-463-6220
Fax: 306-463-3479

La Glace Landfill
780-356-0007
Fax: 780-356-2159

La Glace TRD
11434 - 94 Ave. SW
Grande Prairie, AB T8V 5Z5
780-766-3111
Fax: 780-766-2959

Lindberg Cavern
780-724-3002
Fax: 780-724-4961

Marshall Landfill
306-387-6507
Fax: 306-387-6188

Mitsue Landfill
780-849-3327
Fax: 780-849-3866

Mitsue TRD
P.O. Box 1730
Slave Lake, AB T0G 2A0
780-849-3319
Fax: 780-849-3866

Rainbow Lake Landfill
780-956-5650
Fax: 780-956-5630

Rainbow Lake TRD
780-956-5650
Fax: 780-956-5630

Rocky Mountain House Landfill
403-845-7894
Fax: 403-845-7896

Silberberry Landfill
250-827-6834
Fax: 250-827-6836

Silberberry TRD
250-827-6834
Fax: 250-827-6836

Unity Cavern
306-228-3001
Fax: 306-228-4290

Valleyview
c/o Concord Well Servicing
P.O. Box 1528
Valleyview, AB T0H 3N0
780-524-3336
Fax: 780-524-3957

West Edson TRD
780-723-1912
Fax: 780-723-5561

CD Nova
5330 Imperial St.
Burnaby, BC V5J 1E6
604-430-5612
Fax: 604-437-1036
800-663-0615
sales@cdnova.com
www.cdnova.com
Firm Type: Distributing, Manufacturing
Founded: 1977
Staff: 22
Member of: Air & Waste Management Association
Products/Services/Areas of Expertise: Measuring & monitoring equipment; ambient & source-level analyzers & samplers; data acquisition & telemetry systems; complete systems engineered & installed
Domestic Markets:
National
Foreign Activity:
The Pacific Rim
Contact(s):
D.F. Bealle, President
W.B. Fleming, Vice-President, Marketing
Allan W. Fleming, Environmental Sales, Burnaby

Canadian Branches:
CD Nova Instruments Ltd.
#117, 1144 - 29 Ave. NE
Calgary, AB T2E 7P1
403-250-5600
Fax: 403-250-5625
1-800-263-2684
instruments@cdnova.com
Jim Shorey, Technical Services

CD Nova Tech Inc. - Ontario
#3, 2800 - 14th Ave.
Markham, ON L3R 0E4
905-940-8338
Fax: 905-940-6659
1-800-561-4245
tech@cdnova.com
Steve Bonser, Manager, Environmental Division

CD Nova Tech Inc. - Québec
Ventes Environnement
#205, 2152 boul. Lapiniere
Brossard, QC J4W 1L9
450-656-6620
Fax: 450-656-1242
Stéphane Mercure, Directeur

Cecon Limited
Also Known As: Central Engineering Consultants of Newfoundland
93 Edinburgh Ave., 2nd Fl.
Gander, NL A1V 1C9
709-256-7112
Fax: 709-256-8324
cecon.ltd@nfld.net
www.cecon.ca
Firm Type: Engineering, Scientific/Technical Services
Founded: 1979
Staff: 25
Products/Services/Areas of Expertise: Feasibility studies; engineering design; environmental site assessment services; solid waste disposal & management
Contact(s):
Barry Thomson, P. Eng., President/CEO
Junior Colbourne, Vice-President
Paul Sceviour, Environmental Engineer

Canadian Branches:
St. John's
#108, 49 - 55 Elizabeth Ave.
St. John's, NL A1A 1W9
709-754-7112
Fax: 709-754-7112
cecon@nf.aibn.com

CEDA International Corporation
#500, 11012 Macleod Trail South
Calgary, AB T2J 6A5
403-253-3233
Fax: 403-252-6700
info@cedagroup.com
www.cedagroup.com
Firm Type: Engineering, Scientific/Technical Services
Member of: Alberta Special Waste Services Association
Products/Services/Areas of Expertise: Hazardous waste treatment & disposal; site cleanup; lab packs; emergency response; volume reduction, soil reclamation; effluent pond maintenance; catalyst handling/disposal, tank cleaning
Contact(s):
Derek Martin, Executive Vice-President

Canadian Branches:
Coquitlam
1564 Booth Ave.
Coquitlam, BC V3K 1B7
604-540-4100
Fax: 604-540-4200

Fort Saskatchewan
11208 - 84 Ave.
Fort Saskatchewan, AB T8L 3V7
780-992-9365
Fax: 780-992-7241

Mattawa
P.O. Box 308
78 Taggart Lake Rd.
Mattawa, ON P0H 1V0
705-744-7014
Fax: 705-744-7015

Sarnia
1369 Lougar Ave.
Sarnia, ON N7S 5N5
519-337-7104
Fax: 519-332-4652

Stoney Creek
390 Dewitt Rd.
Stoney Creek, ON L8E 4P6
905-662-7921
Fax: 905-662-2429

CEF Consultants Ltd.
#801, 5885 Cunard St.
Halifax, NS B3K 1E3
902-425-4802
Fax: 902-425-4807
cef@cefconsultants.ns.ca
www.cefconsultants.ns.ca
Firm Type: Management Consulting, Scientific/Technical Services
Founded: 1983
Products/Services/Areas of Expertise: Environmental & fisheries planning; Environmental monitoring; Impact risk assessment; Marine seismic survey reviews; Environmental communications
Financial Information:
Type of Ownership: Private
Domestic Markets:
National, Alberta, New Brunswick, Nova Scotia
Foreign Activity:
Caribbean, Central America, Central Europe, Eastern Europe, United Kingdom
Contact(s):
Norval Collins, President & Founder
ncollins@cefconsultants.ns.ca

Cegerco - GCL Inc.
Also Known As: Cegertec Inc.
930, rue Jacques-Cartier est
Chicoutimi, QC G7H 7K9
418-549-6680
Fax: 418-549-7105
Products/Services/Areas of Expertise: Engineering consulting services; marine management
Contact(s):
François Laperrière, Vice-President, Travaux Publiques

Cegertec Experts-Conseils
CP 1000
255, rue Racine est
Chicoutimi, QC G7H 5G4
418-549-6680
Fax: 418-549-7105
chicoutimi@cegertec.qc.ca
www.cegertec.qc.ca

Canadian Branches:
Alma
#7, 200, av de Pont sud
Alma, QC G8B 2T6
418-668-5236
Fax: 418-668-0931
alma@cegertec.qc.ca

Montréal
630 boul. René-Lévesque Ouest
Montréal, QC H3B 1S6
514-393-0707
montreal@cegertec.qc.ca

Québec
#211, 2500 rue Jean-Perrin
Québec, QC G2C 1X1
418-847-8049
Fax: 418-847-1361
quebec@cegertec.qc.ca

Roberval
883 boul. St-Joseph
Roberval, QC G8H 2L8
418-275-6989
Fax: 418-275-5971
roberval@cegertec.qc.ca

Celfort Construction Materials Inc.
Formerly: Celfortec Inc.
P.O. Box 310
Salaberry-de-Valleyfield, QC J6S 4V6
450-377-1725
Fax: 450-377-2973
800-667-0450
Firm Type: Manufacturing
Founded: 1986
Staff: 90
Products/Services/Areas of Expertise: Extruded polystyrene insulation for the construction industry; non-asbestos fibre reinforced cement product for use in humid or corrosive manufacturing environments
Domestic Markets:
National
Foreign Activity:
USA
Contact(s):
John Zacharias, President
Stephen Buckle, Director, Marketing
Jean-Claude Leclerc, Vice-President, Sales
Errill O'Hara, Regional Sales Manager

Canadian Branches:
Calgary Branch
413 Deerview Dr.
Calgary, AB T2J 6X2

Halifax Branch
#100, 800 Sackville Dr.
Lower Sackville, NS B4E 1R8

Toronto Branch
116 Galaxy Blvd.
Etobicoke, ON M9W 4Y6
416-798-0303

CEM Specialties Inc. / CEMSI
#11, 1100 Dearness Dr.
London, ON N6E 1N9
519-681-9595
Fax: 519-681-8799
866-236-7732
admin@cemsi.on.ca
www.cemsi.on.ca
Firm Type: Manufacturing
Founded: 1992
Staff: 16
Member of: Air & Waste Management Association; Air Pollution Control Association; Independent Power Producers Association; Instrument Society of America; American Society for Quality Control
Quality Environmental Management System(s): 9001
Products/Services/Areas of Expertise: Design & manufacture of continuous emission monitoring systems; air pollution emissions monitoring; service & repair; consulting in systems application; ambient monitoring stations; gas analyzers; sampling system components
Recently Completed / Ongoing Projects: Design, installation & commissioning of CEM system for: Laidlaw, Peel Resource, 3M Canada, DuPont Canada Inc., Kerala State Electricity Board, Essroc Cement, Weyerhaeuser Inc., Ontario Hydro, SaskPower, Safety Kleen
Financial Information:
Type of Ownership: Private
Revenue: Greater than $5 Million
Revenue Sources: 100% Private Contracts
Domestic Markets:
National
Foreign Activity:
Worldwide
Markets Sought:
Central America, China, The Middle East, The Pacific Rim, South America, Vietnam
Contact(s):
Henry C. Vergeer, President, Operations
vergeer@cemsi.on.ca
Brad King, Manager, Marketing
king@cemsi.on.ca
Neil Holt, Vice-President, Operations
holt@cemsi.on.ca

Cemcorp Ltd. Consulting Engineers
2158 Fowler Lane
Mississauga, ON L5K 1B8
905-566-7227
Fax: 905-566-7228
888-672-2739
cemcorp@cemcorp.com
www.cemcorp.com
Firm Type: Engineering
Founded: 1984
Staff: 6
Member of: Association of Consulting Engineers of Canada; Consulting Engineers of Ontario; Canadian Heat Exchanger & Vessel Manufacturers Association
Quality Environmental Management System(s): 9001
Products/Services/Areas of Expertise: Plant retrofit studies; pre-feasibility/feasibility studies; process evaluation & selection;

Products & Services Buyer's Guide

project management; PC-based process computer systems; pre-start reviews
Recently Completed / Ongoing Projects: Dust collection feasibility study & engineering & implementation - Redpath Sugars, Toronto
Financial Information:
Type of Ownership: Private
Revenue: $500,000 - $1.5 Million
Revenue Sources: 100% Private Contracts
Domestic Markets:
National
Foreign Activity:
Worldwide
Contact(s):
J.C. Coulter, President
M.A. Coulter, Managing Director

Cengea Solutions Inc.
Formerly: Linnet Geomatics International Inc.
#700, 259 Portage Ave.
Winnipeg, MB R3B 2A9
204-957-7566
Fax: 204-957-7568
866-546-6381
contact-me@cengea.com
www.linnet.ca
Firm Type: Information Technology
Founded: 1988
Staff: 4
Member of: Canadian-US Environmental Technology Association
Products/Services/Areas of Expertise: GIS integrated systems for environmental management organizations; soil & waste conservation; watershed management; biodiversity information management; supply chain management software for forestry & agriculture; application development; systems integration; feasibility studies; data conversion
Financial Information:
Type of Ownership: Private
Revenue: Greater than $5 Million
Domestic Markets:
National
Foreign Activity:
Worldwide
Contact(s):
Bruce Graham, President
Vivek Beijal, Vice-President, Consulting

CENSOL Inc.
Formerly: Pollutech International Limited
582 Hawthorne Cres.
Milton, ON L9T 4N8
905-878-8775
Fax: 905-878-8775
contact@censol.ca
www.censol.ca
Firm Type: Management Consulting, Engineering
Founded: 1994
Staff: 1500
Products/Services/Areas of Expertise: Canadian bidding cluster of some of the country's premier environmental companies; original member companies include Maxxam, Pollutech, Marshall Macklin Monaghan, Seprotech, Trojan & Norbert W. Schmidtke; working on markets in Mexico, Latin America, China, S.E. Asia, & the Middle East; provides environmental technologies, equipment, consulting engineering services, laboratory services in water pollution control, air pollution & site remediation services; combined expertise in 44 industrial sectors
Recently Completed / Ongoing Projects: Retained to develop a total environmental solution for contaminated drinking water in 00 communities, Uruguay; completed projects in 19 countries & is capable of providing services in 31 languages
Financial Information:
Type of Ownership: Private
Revenue: Greater than $5 Million
Revenue Sources: 100% Private Contracts
Foreign Activity:
Asia, Central America, Eastern Europe, Western Europe, The Middle East, The Pacific Rim, South America, Mexico
Markets Sought:
USA
Contact(s):
Richard Laughton, President

Central Reproductions Ltd.
4524 Eastgate Pkwy.
Mississauga, ON L4W 3W6
905-238-1250
Fax: 905-238-4994
888-236-4759
support@central-repro.com
www.central-repro.com
Firm Type: Scientific/Technical Services
Founded: 1983
EcoLogo Certified Products & Services: Lithographic printing services
Products/Services/Areas of Expertise: Lithographic Printing Services
Ecological Note: Lithographic printing services

Centre de Toxicologie du Québec / CTQ Québec Toxicology Centre
945, av Wolfe
Sainte-Foy, QC G1V 5B3
418-650-5115
Fax: 418-654-2148
ctq@inspq.qc.ca
www.inspq.qc.ca/ctq
Firm Type: Scientific/Technical Services
Founded: 1973
Staff: 35
Member of: Canadian Association of Environmental Analytical Laboratories
Products/Services/Areas of Expertise: Laboratory services & research & development services; biological monitoring of workers & other individuals exposed to environmentally toxic substances such as pesticides, heavy metals, PCBs & solvents
Financial Information:
Type of Ownership: Non Profit
Domestic Markets:
National
Foreign Activity:
Worldwide
Contact(s):
Claude Thellen, Scientific Director

Century Environmental Services
A Wolseley company
Formerly: Perma Engineered Sales (1983) Ltd.Engineered Pipe Group
3422 Millar Ave.
Saskatoon, SK S7K 5Y7
306-934-4549
Fax: 306-244-1715
800-268-5111
www.wolseleyinc.ca; www.hdpe.ca
Firm Type: Distributing
Founded: 1983
Staff: 25
Member of: International Erosion Control Association; Western Canada Water & Wastewater Association; American Water Works Association
Products/Services/Areas of Expertise: Distributes geomembranes & geosynthetics to the heavy construction industry; water & wastewater treatment systems & accessories; Engineered Pipe Group has offices across Canada
Financial Information:
Type of Ownership: Publicly Traded
Domestic Markets:
National
Contact(s):
Glen Cotton, Regional Manager
glen.cotton@wolseleyinc.ca

Century Environmental Systems
2249 Sussex Ct.
Burlington, ON L7P 3R8
905-336-3702
Fax: 905-332-5956
Firm Type: Manufacturing
Founded: 1981
Staff: 6
Member of: Air & Waste Management Association
Products/Services/Areas of Expertise: Industrial dust control products; reverse-jet cartridge dust collectors; bag house dust collectors; high efficiency scrubbers; replacement parts for most popular brands of dust collectors
Domestic Markets:
National
Contact(s):
Bruce Stronach, President

Century Plastics Ltd.
12291 Horseshoe Way
Richmond, BC V7A 4V5
604-271-1324
Fax: 604-271-2999
century@centuryplastics.ca
www.centuryplastics.ca
Firm Type: Manufacturing
Founded: 1975
Staff: 12
Products/Services/Areas of Expertise: Waste storage containers; water storage tanks
Contact(s):
Dale Moskovitch, Sales

CenturyVallen
Also Known As: Hagemeyer Canada, Inc.
A Sonepar Canada company
4810 - 92nd Ave. NW
Edmonton, AB T6B 2X4
780-468-3366
www.centuryvallen.com; www.soneparcanada.com
Firm Type: Distributing
Founded: 1937
Quality Environmental Management System(s): 9001-2008
Products/Services/Areas of Expertise: B2B distributor of industrial MRO & safety products & services; hazmat & spill control personal protection; industrial safety products; respiratory equipment; medical first aid, gas detection & monitoring; fire protection; electrical lighting shop equipment; janitorial chemicals & supplies; hand tools; fastening & fittings; welding equipment
Activities: Launched Six Sigma in 2004
Financial Information:
Type of Ownership: Publicly Traded
Domestic Markets:
Alberta, British Columbia, Manitoba, Nova Scotia, Ontario, Québec, Saskatchewan
Contact(s):
Guy Mersereau, Vice-President/General Manager
Deanna Smith, Branch Manager

Canadian Branches:
Bonnyville
6402 - 50 Ave.
Bonnyville, AB T9N 2M1
780-826-3131
Fax: 780-826-6167
Wayne Rogers, Branch Manager

Calgary
#10, 5451 - 48 Ave. SE
Calgary, AB T2B 3S2
403-287-1690
Fax: 403-287-3526
Jason Venus, Branch Manager

Cambridge
#1, 650 Jamieson Pkwy.
Cambridge, ON N3C 0A5
519-658-4182
Fax: 519-658-2150
800-387-5490
Scott Fleming, Branch Manager

Edmonton - 149 St.
11619 - 149 St.
Edmonton, AB T5M 1X1
780-454-0471
Fax: 780-452-2092
Jason Mandrusiak, Branch Manager

Edmonton - 39 Ave.
9410 - 39 Ave.
Edmonton, AB T6E 5T3
780-430-4000
Fax: 780-430-0200
Andy Leroux, Branch Manager

Elkford
2 Front St.
Elkford, BC V0B 1H0
250-865-7555
Fax: 250-865-7559
Steven Patmore, Branch Manager

Fort McMurray
#3, 431 MacKenzie Blvd.
Fort McMurray, AB T9H 4C5

780-743-4336
Fax: 780-791-6212
Jim Ferguson, Branch Manager

Grande Prairie
10203 - 123 St.
Grande Prairie, AB T8V 2B8
780-532-0843
Fax: 780-532-0819
Wade Crantz, Branch Manager

Lethbridge
3004 - 9 Ave.
Lethbridge, AB T1H 5E5
403-329-4747
Fax: 403-329-1718
Roland Peters, Branch Manager

Medicine Hat
1366 Brier Park Dr. NW
Medicine Hat, AB T1C 1Z7
403-526-6461
Fax: 403-527-8423
Steve Greene, Branch Manager

Mississauga
#7, 6710 Maritz Dr.
Mississauga, ON L5W 0A1
905-565-1686
Fax: 905-565-0390
Wes Delnea, Branch Manager

Nisku
#302, 3912 - 84 Ave.
Leduc, AB T9E 8M6
780-986-1525
Fax: 780-986-6272
Cory Jones, Branch Manager

Red Deer
7948 Edgar Industrial Way
Red Deer, AB T4P 3R2
403-343-6671
Fax: 403-346-3133
Dale Rotenburger, Branch Manager

Regina
563 McDonald St.
Regina, SK S4N 4X1
306-721-2223
Fax: 306-721-2344
800-667-2223
John Powell, Branch Manager

Saskatoon
2631 Faithfull Ave.
Saskatoon, SK S7K 5W2
306-242-1166
Fax: 306-242-0015
800-664-1128
Jason Roberge, Branch Manager

St. Catharines
#1, 27 Seapark Dr.
St. Catharines, ON L2M 6S5
905-688-1866
Fax: 905-688-5020
Angelo Procopio, Branch Manager

Trail
1608 Bay Ave.
Trail, BC V1R 4B4
250-364-2573
Fax: 250-364-2393
Jeff Burtwell, Branch Manager

Winnipeg
#1, 16 Mazenod Rd.
Winnipeg, MB R2J 4H2
204-668-8886
Fax: 204-668-3260
888-668-8858
Ross Robertson, Branch Manager

CertainTeed Insulation Canada, Inc.
Formerly: Ottawa Fibre Inc.
1365 Johnston Rd.
Ottawa, ON K1V 8Z1
613-247-7116
Fax: 613-736-7281
www.certainteed.com

Firm Type: Manufacturing
Founded: 2009
Quality Environmental Management System(s): 14001; 900
Products/Services/Areas of Expertise: Fibreglass insulation, residential, commercial, industrial; ceiling tiles
Financial Information:
Type of Ownership: Foreign-owned
Domestic Markets:
Ontario
Foreign Activity:
USA

Canadian Branches:
Oakville
1540 Cornwall Rd.
Oakville, ON L6J 7W5
905-815-1429
Sandra Basic, Manager, 905-403-2815

Cetac-West
#420, 715 - 5th Ave. SW
Calgary, AB T2P 2X6
403-777-9595
Fax: 403-777-9599
cetac@cetacwest.com
www.cetacwest.com
Firm Type: Financial
Founded: 1994
Products/Services/Areas of Expertise: A private sector, not-for-profit corporation committed to helping small-sized & medium-sized enterprises to commercialize environmental technologies
Financial Information:
Type of Ownership: Non Profit
Domestic Markets:
Alberta, British Columbia, Manitoba, Saskatchewan
Contact(s):
Joe Lukacs, President/CEO
jlukacs@cetacwest.com

CH2M Hill Canada Limited
Formerly: CH2M Hill Engineering Ltd. & Gore & Storrie Limited; CH2M Gore & Storrie
255 Consumers Rd.
Toronto, ON M2J 5B6
416-499-9000
Fax: 416-499-4687
askch2m@ch2m.com
www.ch2mhillcanada.com
Firm Type: Engineering, Scientific/Technical Services
Staff: 310
Member of: Canadian Environment Industry Association
Products/Services/Areas of Expertise: Wastewater collection, treatment & disposal; water treatment, supply & distribution; urban drainage & stormwater management; solid & hazardous waste management; energy management; air pollution & odour control; water resources engineering; environmental planning; environmental audits; systems analysis & data processing; site assessment & decommissioning
Financial Information:
Revenue Sources: 1% nationwide; 7% Provincial; 81% Municipals; 11% Private Contracts
Domestic Markets:
National
Foreign Activity:
The Pacific Rim, USA
Contact(s):
Andrew Phillip, President
Drew Dresher, Sr. Vice-President, Design & Construction
Bill Hayes, Sr. Vice-President, Environment, Energy & Systems
Peter Nicol, Sr. Vice-President, Water
peter.nicol@ch2m.com

Canadian Branches:
Barrie
#303, 126th Wellington St.
Barrie, ON L4N 1K9
705-722-8800
Fax: 705-722-6516
Norman D. Huggins

Burnaby
2100 Metrotower II
4720 Kingsway
Burnaby, BC V5H 4N2
604-684-3282
Fax: 604-684-3292
Bill Hayes

Calgary
1100, 1st St. SE
Calgary, AB T2G 1B1
403-407-6000
Fax: 403-407-6001
Ken McWhinnie

Edmonton
Highfield Place
#800, 10010 - 106 St.
Edmonton, AB T5J 3L8
780-409-9298
Fax: 780-409-9302
Gary Kriviak

Kamloops
#330, 301 Victoria St.
Kamloops, BC V2C 2A3
250-314-6599
Fax: 250-314-6563
Mike Baker

London
#107, Adelaide St. North
London, ON N5Y 5K7
519-679-0992
Fax: 519-858-1535

Ottawa
#330, 1101 Prince of Wales Dr.
Ottawa, ON K2C 3W7
613-723-8700
Fax: 613-723-7489
J. Shawn Gibbons

St. Catharines
P.O. Box 758
4 Queen St.
St Catharines, ON L2R 6Y3
905-684-7425
Fax: 905-684-2400
Jack Hellinga

Toronto
255 Consumers Rd.
North York, ON M2J 5B6
416-499-9000
Fax: 416-499-4687
Andrew Philip

Victoria
#205, 4420 Chatterton Way
Victoria, BC V8X 5J2
250-658-7000
Fax: 250-658-7001
Art Hibbs

Waterloo
72 Victoria St., 3rd Fl.
Kitchener, ON N2G 4Y9
519-579-3500
Fax: 519-579-8986
Diana Vengelisti

Winnipeg
211 Bannatyne Ave., 4th Fl.
Winnipeg, MB R3B 3P2
204-488-2214
Fax: 204-488-2245
Carmine Militano

CH2M HILL Canada Ltd.
Formerly: Veco Canada Ltd.
Energy Operations
#1200, 401 - 9th Ave. SW
Calgary, AB T2P 3C5
403-232-9800
Fax: 403-232-9840
www.ch2m.com
Firm Type: Engineering, Scientific/Technical Services
Staff: 1500
Products/Services/Areas of Expertise: Project management, engineering, procurement, construction, operations & maintenance to the energy, resource, process industries & to the public sector; environmental & regulatory services; program management; compliance reviews; permitting applications; provision of dispersion & emission data
Domestic Markets:
National
Foreign Activity:
Worldwide

Contact(s):
Rene Massinon, Director

Canadian Branches:
Burnaby
CH2M HILL Energy Operations
4599 Tillicum St.
Burnaby, BC V5J 3J9
604-659-3335
Fax: 604-659-3345

Challenger Geomatics Ltd.
Capilano Centre
#200, 9945 - 50th St.
Edmonton, AB T6A 0L4
780-424-5511
Fax: 780-424-3837
edmonton@chalgeo.com
www.chalgeo.com
Firm Type: Engineering, Scientific/Technical Services
Founded: 1984
Products/Services/Areas of Expertise: Geomatic & engineering services to government & private industry, including the oil & gas sector; services include surveying; civil & municipal engineering services in the areas of land development, traffic & transportation, building development; aerial mapping; GIS applications; marine & hydrographic surveys; control surveys; custom mapping; software development. Offices in Calgary, Fort McMurray, & Whitehorse
Domestic Markets:
Alberta, British Columbia, Manitoba, Saskatchewan, Yukon Territory
Foreign Activity:
Africa, The Pacific Rim
Contact(s):
David R. Thomson, President

Canadian Branches:
Calgary
#300, 6940 Fisher Rd. SE
Calgary, AB
403-253-8101
Fax: 403-253-1985
1-888-253-8102
calgary@challengergeomatics.com

Fort McMurray
#164, 101 Signal Rd.
Fort McMurray, AB T9H 4N6
780-743-8697
Fax: 780-743-9786
mcmurray@challengergeomatics.com

Inukshuk
Bag Service #7
Inukshuk, NT X0E 0T0
867-777-7820
Fax: 867-777-3256
inquiries@inukshukgeomatics.com

Whitehorse
302 Jarvis St.
Whitehorse, YT Y1A 2H2
867-668-6940
Fax: 867-668-6950
whitehorse@challengergeomatics.com

Chamard & Associés
1046, rue du Domaine
Québec, QC G1Y 2C6
418-658-3362
Fax: 418-657-6261
877-844-7111
www.chamardetassocies.com
Firm Type: Management Consulting, Engineering
Founded: 1997
Staff: 4
Member of: Réseau environnement
Products/Services/Areas of Expertise: Waste management; environmental strategic planification; environmental audit
Recently Completed / Ongoing Projects: Hydro-Québec waste management plan; Ville Montréal waste management
Financial Information:
Type of Ownership: Private
Revenue: $250,000 - $500,000
Revenue Sources: 10% nationwide; 10% Provincial; 30% Municipals; 50% Private Contracts
Domestic Markets:
Québec

Contact(s):
Jean-Louis Chamard, President
jlchamard@chamardetassocies.com
N. Desgagnes, Engineer, 514/844-7111
n.desgagnes@chamardetassocies.com

Champion Moyer Diebel
Also Known As: Moyer Diebel Ltd.
P.O. Box 301
2674 North Service Rd.
Jordan Station, ON L0R 1S0
905-562-4195
Fax: 905-562-4618
800-263-5978
info@moyerdiebellimited.com
www.championindustries.com/canada/index.php
Firm Type: Manufacturing
Founded: 1945
Products/Services/Areas of Expertise: Washers; waste handling systems
Domestic Markets:
National

Char Developments Ltd.
902 Williams Ave.
Yellowknife, NT X1A 3J3
867-873-2410
Fax: 867-920-2490
Firm Type: Engineering
Founded: 1976
Staff: 8
Products/Services/Areas of Expertise: Energy-efficient design; air leakage control; project management; low energy housing
Contact(s):
Doug Ashby, President

Charland Thermojet Inc.
30, rue Robert
Montréal, QC H9C 1H4
514-624-4772
Fax: 514-624-4776
800-624-4709
Firm Type: Distributing, Manufacturing
Founded: 1988
Staff: 5
Products/Services/Areas of Expertise: Water & waste treatment plants; foods processing plants; pharmaceuticals; refiners
Domestic Markets:
New Brunswick, Newfoundland & Labrador, Nova Scotia, Ontario, Prince Edward Island, Québec, Saskatchewan
Foreign Activity:
The Pacific Rim, USA
Contact(s):
Claude Charland, General Manager

Charles Simon Architect & Planner
Formerly: Charles Simon Architect Inc.
221 Barden St.
Eden Mills, ON N0B 1P0
519-856-9921
Fax: 519-856-9921
simon.edenmills@everus.ca
www.simon-archplan.com
Firm Type: Management Consulting, Engineering
Founded: 1970
Member of: Ontario Association of Architects; Town Planning Institute of Canada; Ontario Association of Landscape Architects (Honouraty)
EcoLogo Certified Products & Services: 1
Products/Services/Areas of Expertise: Architectural services, planning, consulting; emphasis on green design at every scale; from small buildings to neighbourhoods
Ecological Note: 1
Financial Information:
Type of Ownership: X
Revenue: $100,000 - $250,000
Foreign Activity:
The Pacific Rim
Contact(s):
Charles Simon, Principal

Charlesworth & Associates
Also Known As: David L. Charlesworth & Associates Inc.
56 Hunter St.
Toronto, ON M4J 1C2
416-462-0400
Fax: 416-462-9005
info@charlesworth.cc
www.charlesworth.cc
Firm Type: Scientific/Technical Services
Founded: 1987
Staff: 4
Products/Services/Areas of Expertise: Hydrogeology; geology; landfill investigations; groundwater protection; water resources evaluation; groundwater monitoring; environmental impact assessment; expert testimony; terrain analysis & air photo interpretation
Recently Completed / Ongoing Projects: Groundwater Resources Study, Hamilton, ON; water resources study, Barbados; groundwater component of several Caribbean solid waste studies
Domestic Markets:
National
Foreign Activity:
Africa, Caribbean, South America
Contact(s):
David L. Charlesworth, President
David Ruttan, Senior Associate

Chartis Insurance Company of Canada
Formerly: AIG Environmental of Canada
145 Wellington St. West
Toronto, ON M5J 1H8
416-596-3000
Fax: 416-596-3584
800-387-4481
askChartisCanada@chartisinsurance.com
www.chartisinsurance.com
Firm Type: Financial

Products/Services/Areas of Expertise: Commercial insurance products & services, including Environmental/Pollution Liability Insurance, Industry focused Environmental Insurance, & Marine & Energy Insurance. Offices in Toronto, Montréal & Vancouver
Financial Information:
Type of Ownership: Publicly Traded
Revenue Sources: 100% Private Contracts
Contact(s):
Peter Hancock, CEO, Chartis Inc.
Peter J. Eastwood, President, Chartis U.S./Canada

Chartwell Consultants Ltd.
#210, 275 Fell Ave.
North Vancouver, BC V7P 3R5
604-980-5061
Fax: 604-986-0361
info@chartwell-consultants.com
www.chartwell-consultants.com
Firm Type: Scientific/Technical Services
Founded: 2000
Staff: 24
Products/Services/Areas of Expertise: Forestry; environmental impact studies; soil & site sensitivity studies; silviculture services; aerial photography; mapping, GIS, remote sensing; surface modelling
Contact(s):
Cliff Roberts, General Manager, 604-980-5061
croberts@chartwell-consultants.com

Chatwin Engineering Ltd.
1614 Morey Rd.
Nanaimo, BC V9S 1J7
250-753-9171
Fax: 250-754-4459
866-753-9171
info@chatwinengineering.com
www.chatwinengineering.com
Firm Type: Engineering, Scientific/Technical Services
Founded: 1982
Staff: 2
Products/Services/Areas of Expertise: Water resources; solid waste management; sewage treatment; transportation; soil remediation
Contact(s):
Brian Chatwin, P.Eng., President/CEO

Canadian Branches:
Victoria Office
#130, 1555 McKezie Ave.
Victoria, BC V8N 1A4
250-370-9171
Fax: 250-370-9197
victoria@chatwinengineering.com

Cheiron Resources Ltd.
#124, 919 Centre St. NW
Calgary, AB T2H 0G3
403-241-3276
Fax: 403-398-0705
info@cheiron-resources.com
www.cheiron-resources.com
Firm Type: Manufacturing
Founded: 1995
Products/Services/Areas of Expertise: Suppliers of the \OilScreen\"" Line of \""instant\"" disposable oil screening test kits for identifying the presence of LNAPL's & DNAPL's in soil or on water or solid surfaces""
Financial Information:
Type of Ownership: Private
Revenue Sources: 100% Private Contracts
Domestic Markets:
Alberta, Ontario, Saskatchewan
Foreign Activity:
Australia/New Zealand, Western Europe, USA
Markets Sought:
Western Europe
Contact(s):
Carol Blakey, Principal

Chem Action Inc.
4559, boul Métropolitain Est
Montréal, QC H1R 1Z4
514-593-1515
Fax: 514-593-1313
administration@chemaction.com
www.chemaction.com
Firm Type: Distributing
Founded: 1987
Staff: 8
Products/Services/Areas of Expertise: Specialized fluid handling equipment: prominent metering pumps, vanton transfer pumps, progressive cavity pumps, mechanical & in-line static mixers, high shear clay mixers, water analysis instrumentation, submersible aerators gravity systems
Financial Information:
Type of Ownership: Private
Revenue Sources: 100% Private Contracts
Domestic Markets:
Québec
Contact(s):
Louis Cantin, Manager, Sales
lcantin@chemaction.com

Chem Experts Inc.
Division Provan
2315 Halpern St.
Montréal, QC H4S 1S3
514-332-3230
Fax: 514-332-3552
info@provan.ca
www.provan.ca
Firm Type: Distributing
Founded: 1976
Staff: 25
Contact(s):
Jean-Luc Paradis, Contact

Chem Solv
20848 Dalton Rd.
Sutton West, ON L0E 1R0
905-722-6035
Fax: 905-722-5195
chemsolv@rogers.com
Firm Type: Management Consulting, Engineering, Information Technology, Scientific/Technical Services, Waste Management
Founded: 1985
Staff: 7
Member of: Canadian Environmental Auditing Association; Environmental Information Association; American Industrial Hygiene Association; Air & Waste Management Association; Canadian Society of Safety Engineering; National Asbestos Council-Canadian Chapter
Products/Services/Areas of Expertise: Environmental auditing; soils & water investigation & analysis; air quality assessments; emission testing
Financial Information:
Revenue Sources: 5% Provincial; 5% Municipals; 90% Private Contracts
Domestic Markets:
Alberta, British Columbia, Nova Scotia, Ontario, Québec
Foreign Activity:
South America, Mexico, USA
Markets Sought:
The Pacific Rim
Contact(s):
Peter Robertson, Principal
Hugh Robertson, Director, Marketing & Training

Chemco Inc.
124, rue de Hambourg
St-Augustin-de-Desmaures, QC G3A 0B3
418-878-5422
Fax: 418-878-5323
800-575-5422
info@chemco-inc.com
www.chemco-inc.com
Firm Type: Manufacturing
Founded: 1988
Products/Services/Areas of Expertise: Water, soil and air treatment products
Contact(s):
Pierre Dessureault, Contact

Chemcorp Industries Inc.
5730 Coopers Ave., #19
Mississauga, ON L4Z 2E8
905-712-8335
Fax: 905-712-8909
888-729-6478
info@odortreatment.com
www.odortreatment.com
Firm Type: Distributing, Manufacturing
EcoLogo Certified Products & Services: Odour control products for waste management, recreation industry, facilities maintainance & sanitation, passenger transportation
Products/Services/Areas of Expertise: Develops, manufactures, packages & distributes a line of unique odor control products; clients operate in industrial, institutional & commercial markets
Ecological Note: Odour control products for waste management, recreation industry, facilities maintenance & sanitation, passenger transportation
Financial Information:
Type of Ownership: Private
Contact(s):
Harry Sarkar, President

Chemical Emission Management Services
Also Known As: CEMS
5211 Preservation Circle
Mississauga, ON L5M 7T3
905-820-6126
Fax: 905-820-1245
tkhan@cems-group.com
www.cems-group.com
Products/Services/Areas of Expertise: CEMS specializes in environmental health, occupational health & safety, manufacturing process solutions & quality management; establishes & reviews safety programs following international standards; provides support for ISO 9001:2000 support for integrating or managing Quality Management Systems

Chemical Safety Training Associates
34 Hunts Brook Rd.
Fall River, NS B2T 1G5
902-861-4060
Fax: 902-861-4060
indesign@eastlink.ca
Contact(s):
Don Waugh, Contact

ChemiGreen Inc.
Unit 70-16, 40 Magnetic Dr.
Toronto, ON M3J 2C4
416-739-9815
Fax: 647-260-0692
888-995-0996
info@chemigreen.com
www.chemigreen.com
Firm Type: Management Consulting, Scientific/Technical Services
Founded: 2007
Staff: 10
Activities: Keeping spills on-site; developer of the Wi-Plug, a wireless solution for chemical spill containment
Financial Information:
Type of Ownership: Private
Revenue: $250,000 - $500,000

Cheminées Sécurité Internationale Ltée
2125, rue Monterey
Laval, QC H7L 3T6
450-973-9999
Fax: 450-687-9569
sales.marketing@securitychimneys.com
www.securitychimneys.com
Products/Services/Areas of Expertise: High-efficiency wood & gas fireplaces; insulated chimneys, gas vents, pipes
Contact(s):
Michel Verrier, Vice-President

Cheminfo Services Inc.
#205, 30 Centurian Dr.
Markham, ON L3R 9S7
905-944-1160
Fax: 905-944-1175
info@cheminfoservices.com
www.cheminfoservices.com
Firm Type: Management Consulting
Founded: 1982
Staff: 5
Member of: Association of Professional Engineers of Ontario
Products/Services/Areas of Expertise: Business development & marketing consulting firm; specializes in chemical, plastic & related sectors; conducts studies on behalf of chemical & resin suppliers, plastic processors & government agencies
Recently Completed / Ongoing Projects: Produced a report on new source performance standards for printing; produced a report on the North American pulp & paper bleaching chemicals market outlook to 2000; provided business assessment for a technical/business resource centre serving the Canadian specialty chemicals sector
Domestic Markets:
National
Foreign Activity:
Asia, Central America, Western Europe, Mexico, USA,
Contact(s):
Angelo Proestos, Managing Director
William Palmer, Manager, Sales & Marketing

Chemline Plastics Ltd.
55 Guardsman Rd.
Thornhill, ON L3T 6L2
905-889-7890
Fax: 905-889-8553
request@chemline.com
www.chemline.com
Firm Type: Distributing
Founded: 1968
Staff: 25
Member of: Ontario Pollution Control Equipment Association
Products/Services/Areas of Expertise: Chemline stocks manual & actuated valves, strainers, flowmeters; controls all made of corrosion resistant solid thermoplastics; PP & PVDF pipe, fittings & fusion equipment; Teflon tubing, fittings & valves; flowmeters are variable area & paddle wheel type including instruments; application areas include waste & water treatment plants, landfills, etc.
Financial Information:
Type of Ownership: Private
Revenue Sources: 100% Private Contracts
Domestic Markets:
National
Foreign Activity:
Worldwide
Contact(s):
Richard Ruddock, President
rruddock@chemline.com
Rob Parish, Manager, Sales
rparish@chemline.com

Canadian Branches:
Québec
#500, 7575, rte Transcanadienne
Saint-Laurent, QC H4T 1V6

514-331-0115
Fax: 514-337-3989
ftremblay@chemline.com
Frederic Tremblay

Chemrec
190, rue Brosseau
Cowansville, QC J2K 3G6
450-266-0333
Fax: 450-266-0330
info@chemrec.com
www.chemrec.com
Firm Type: Manufacturing, Waste Management
Founded: 1990
Staff: 36
Quality Environmental Management System(s): 9001:2000
Products/Services/Areas of Expertise: Waste solvent recycling
Financial Information:
Type of Ownership: Private
Revenue Sources: 100% Private Contracts
Domestic Markets:
Ontario, Québec
Foreign Activity:
USA
Contact(s):
Joe Michel, P.Eng., Président
Marc Boisvenue, Sales & Marketing

Chemspec Inc
1260 Lakeshore Rd. East
Mississauga, ON L5E 3B8
416-421-5212
Fax: 416-421-9884
800-268-6093
info@chemspec-canada.com
www.chemspec-canada.com
Firm Type: Distributing, Manufacturing
Founded: 1968
EcoLogo Certified Products & Services: ECOgent General Purpose Cleaner is certified under PRC-097 (Environment Canada's Environmental Choice Program for cleaning products)
Products/Services/Areas of Expertise: Manufacturer of detergent free carpet & upholstery cleaning products & products for fire & water damage restoration
Ecological Note: ECOgent General Purpose Cleaner is certified under PRC-097 (Environment Canada's Environmental Choice Program for cleaning products)

CHEP Canada
7400 Danbro Cres. East
Mississauga, ON L5N 8C6
905-790-2437
Fax: 905-789-4279
chepcanada@chep.com
www.chep.com
Firm Type: Scientific/Technical Services
Founded: 1979
Staff: 200
Products/Services/Areas of Expertise: Issues, collects, conditions & reissues pallets & containers
Domestic Markets:
National
Foreign Activity:
Africa, Asia, Central Europe, Western Europe, The Pacific Rim, Mexico, USA
Contact(s):
Michael F. Dimond, President, CHEP Canada
Brian S. Beattie, Sr. Vice-President, Marketing
Donna Slyster, Sr. Vice-President & Chief Information Officer

Canadian Branches:
Boucherville
331, ch du Tremblay
Boucherville, QC J4B 7M1
450-449-2374
Fax: 450-449-1207

Brampton
76 Wentworth Ct.
Brampton, ON L6T 5M7
905-790-2437 x4243
Fax: 905-790-6546

Burlington
c/o Newcastle Group
1500 Corporate Dr.
Burlington, ON L7L 6H4

905-319-1997

Calgary
#134, 4750 - 43rd St. SE
Calgary, AB T2B 3N3
403-236-1633

Edmonton
11263 - 186th St.
Edmonton, AB T5S 2T7
780-486-0237
Fax: 780-486-3781

Kelowna
c/o Columbia Bottling Enterprises Limite
635 Dease Rd.
Kelowna, BC V1X 4A4
250-765-9115

Leamington
c/o Amco Storage
P.O. Box 237
Wilkinson Dr.
Leamington, ON N8H 3W2
519-326-2661

Lethbridge
c/o Decade Distribution
1820 - 31st St. North
Lethbridge, AB T1H 5K8
403-329-9347

London
c/o Trisec Warehousing
1040 Wilton Grove Rd.
London, ON N6A 4L6
519-668-0423

Moncton
145 English Dr.
Moncton, NB E1E 3X3
506-858-8393
Fax: 506-858-0372

Québec
c/o Robert Transport
2800, boul Hamel
Québec, QC G1P 2J1
1-888-286-4828

Regina
c/o PMK Logistics Inc.
P.O. Box 7290
310 - 4th Ave. East
Regina, SK S4N 5Z6
306-751-8100

Saskatoon
c/o Aero Delivery (1982) Ltd.
1502 Quebec St.
Saskatoon, SK S7K 1V7
306-651-2437

St-Laurent
3805, rue Sartelon
Montréal, QC H4S 2A6
514-745-5208
Fax: 514-745-8069

Vancouver
#2, 559 Annance Court
Vancouver, BC V3M 6Y7
604-520-2583
Fax: 604-520-6174

Whitby
c/o Durham Pallet Services
202 South Blair St.
Whitby, ON L1N 8X9
905-668-6062

Winnipeg
2240 Logan Ave.
Winnipeg, MB R2R 0J2
204-633-2456
Fax: 204-633-6349

CHI Canada Inc.
#1204, 1255, rue University
Montréal, QC H3B 3N9
514-397-0463
Fax: 514-397-0284
www.chienergy.com
Products/Services/Areas of Expertise: Energy management & conservation consultants
Recently Completed / Ongoing Projects: Under the Star Lake Hydro Partnership formed with Abitibi-Consolidated Inc., has developed & operates the 15 MW Star Lake Hydroelectric Generating Station in West Central Newfoundland. The remotely operated facility integrates environmentally friendly products & equipment such as biodegradable hydraulic oil for its intake gate system & anoil-less hydrostatic bearing for the turbine unit. The Star Lake Hydroelectric Generating Station is a baseload facility which allows for the reduction of greenhouse gas emissions from the Holyrood oil-fired generating plant
Ecological Note: Green Choice Generation
Domestic Markets:
Québec
Contact(s):
Pascal J. Brun, President

Chisholm, Fleming & Associates
#301, 317 Renfrew Dr.
Markham, ON L3R 9S8
905-474-1458
Fax: 905-474-1910
888-241-4149
cfa@ChisholmFleming.com
www.chisholmfleming.com
Firm Type: Engineering, Scientific/Technical Services
Founded: 1956
Staff: 15
Products/Services/Areas of Expertise: Engineering design of municipal water, sewage & stormwater systems; flood & erosion control works; bank stabilization works; roads, traffic & transportation facilities & structures
Recently Completed / Ongoing Projects: Projects for 14 Ontario municipalities
Contact(s):
Bob Chisholm, Director, Sales & Marketing
William Chisholm, Managing Director

Chromatographic Specialties Inc.
300 Laurier Blvd., PO Bag 1150
Brockville, ON K6V 5W1
613-342-4678
Fax: 613-342-1144
800-267-8103
sales@chromspec.com
www.chromspec.com
Firm Type: Scientific/Technical Services
Founded: 1963
Staff: 25
Products/Services/Areas of Expertise: Manufacture of packed columns for GC analysis with distribution of fused silica capillary columns; distribution of supplies for GC & HPLC including columns, valves, reagents, vials, standards, autosamplers, liquid handling systems, inlet systems, filter systems; gas chromatographs; GC & HPLC data systems & software
Contact(s):
Michael McKend, President
Ken Jordan, Sales & Technical Marketing Manager

Church & Trought Inc. / CTI
#106, 885 Don Mills Rd.
Toronto, ON M3C 1V9
416-391-2527
Fax: 416-391-1931
www.churchandtrought.com
Firm Type: Engineering
Founded: 1990
Products/Services/Areas of Expertise: Air emission, noise, odour, indoor air quality, & environmental site assessments; Industrial hygiene & surface water monitoring; Wastewater & solid & liquid industria waste management; Site remediation; Environmental regulatory compliance audits; Design & installation of ventilation & air pollution control systems; Health, safety, & environmental education programs
Domestic Markets:
National
Foreign Activity:
Africa, Australia/New Zealand, South America, Mexico, USA, Former USSR
Contact(s):
John Trought, P.Eng., Contact, 416-391-2527
jtrought@churchandtrought.com
Lou Locatelli, C.E.T., CCEP, CEAS, P.Geo, Contact, 416-391-2527
llocatelli@churchandtrought.com

Gary Markotich, B.A.Sc., P.Eng., Contact, 416-391-2527
gmarkotich@churchandtrought.com

CIAL Group
119 Concession Rd. 6
Fisherville, ON L0A 1G0
416-410-0432
Fax: 416-362-5231
info@cialgroup.com
www.cialgroup.com
Firm Type: Management Consulting
Founded: 1989
Products/Services/Areas of Expertise: An independent environmental policy & program consulting firm experienced in design & implementation of pollution prevention, lifecycle management & sustainable development projects in the private sector; clients include major corporations in the food, consumer products, energy, transportation sectors, trade associations & government departments.

CIBA Spécialités Chimiques Canada inc.
#202, 2200, rue Sidbec-Sud
Trois-Rivières-Ouest, QC G8Z 4H1
819-373-4973
customerservice.ca@cibasc.com
www.cibasc.com
Contact(s):
Michael Heinz, Chief Executive Officer
Martin Riediker, Chief Technology Officer

CIMA+
Formerly: Stantec Experts Conseils Ltee.
#201, 420, boul Maloney est
Gatineau, QC J8P 1E7
819-663-9294
Fax: 819-663-0084
info@cima.ca
www.cima.ca
Firm Type: Engineering
Founded: 1969
Staff: 100
Member of: American Water Works Association; Water Environment Federation; Réseau Environnement
Quality Environmental Management System(s): 9001
Products/Services/Areas of Expertise: Water treatment; wastewater collection & treatment; evaluation & rehabilitation of contaminated sites; solid waste disposal; leachate treatment
Recently Completed / Ongoing Projects: Septic sludge treatment & composting site, Kazabazua, QC; water treatment plant, Maniwaki, QC; various water distribution & treatment projects Western Québec
Financial Information:
Type of Ownership: Private
Revenue: $500,000 - $1.5 Million
Revenue Sources: 5% nationwide; 20% Provincial; 50% Municipals; 25% Private Contracts
Domestic Markets:
Ontario, Québec
Foreign Activity:
Africa, Central America
Contact(s):
Andre Mathieu, P.Eng., Director, Environment
Canadian Branches:
Laval
#600, 3400, boul du Souvenir
Laval, QC H7V 3Z2
514-337-2462
Fax: 450-682-1013

Longueuil
2147, rue de la Province
Longueuil, QC J4G 1Y6
514-337-2462
Fax: 450-646-0805

Montréal
#900, 740, rue Notre-Dame ouest
Montréal, QC H3C 3X6
514-337-2462
Fax: 514-281-1632

Ottawa
#110, 240 Catherine St.
Ottawa, ON K2P 2G8
613-860-2462
Fax: 613-860-1870

Québec
#300, 1145, boul Lebourgneuf
Québec, QC G2K 2K8
418-623-3373
Fax: 418-623-3321

Rivière-du-Loup
37, rue Delage
Rivière-du-Loup, QC G5R 3Z1
418-862-8217
Fax: 418-862-8252

Sherbrooke
3385, rue King ouest
Sherbrooke, QC J1L 1P8
819-565-3385
Fax: 819-821-4283

St-Jérôme
#200, 300, rue Longpré
Saint-Jérôme, QC J7Y 3B9
450-436-2174
Fax: 450-436-2179

St-Romuald/Lévis
#201, 2030, boul de la Rive-Sud
Saint-Romuald, QC G6W 2S8
418-834-2273
Fax: 418-834-3356

International Branch(es):
Algeria
Les Sources
38, rue Guy de Maupassant, Bir Mourad Rais,
Alger DZA
213-21-56-54-12
Fax: 213-213-21-56-5
infoalger@cima.ca

Congo
P.O. Box 3635
av de la Mongala
Kinshasa, Ngaliema COD
Fax: 243-81-59-94-60
infocongo@cima.ca

Niger
P.O. Box 688
Sis, Mali Béro Blvd.
Niamey NER
227-72-52-34
Fax: 227-72-52-97
infoniger@cima.ca

Cimatec Environmental Engineering Inc.
P.O. Box 268
Orono, ON L0B 1M0
416-289-8882
Fax: 416-289-4185
800-565-5326
sales@cimatec.com
www.cimatec.com
Firm Type: Manufacturing
Founded: 1987
Staff: 30
Member of: Ontario Long Term Care Association; Heating Refrigeration & Air Conditioning Institute of Canada - Manufacturers Division
Products/Services/Areas of Expertise: Home of the Airscreen Air Cleaner, the original developer of the electronic air filter, unique in its ability to kill live airborne contaminants as well as effectively trap & remove pollutants; researches & develops adorned electronic air filtration technology for the IAQ market place, distributed throughout the U.S., Canada & Mexico
Recently Completed / Ongoing Projects: Hospital Angeles del Pedregal, Mexico; Bronco Billy's Casino, Cripple Creek, Co.; Imago Restaurants, Toronto
Financial Information:
Type of Ownership: Publicly Traded
Revenue: $3 Million - $5 Million
Revenue Sources: 10% nationwide; 90% Private Contracts
Domestic Markets:
National
Foreign Activity:
Western Europe, The Middle East, Mexico, USA
Contact(s):
Andrew Roblin, President/CEO
Andrew@cimatec.com
Robert Cudney, Director
Jeff Chesebrough, Chief Operating Officer

Gary Sills, Executive Director, Commercial Division

Cintube Ltd.
Formerly: Canadian Boilers Ltd.
Also Known As: Tube Bend
333, boul St-Joseph
Montréal, QC H8S 2K9
514-634-3592
Fax: 514-636-3336
www.cintube.com
Firm Type: Manufacturing
Founded: 1957
Staff: 100
Products/Services/Areas of Expertise: Power boilers; custom pipe & tube bending; thermal fluid heaters; heat exchangers; bends, angles & beams; all metals & alloys
Domestic Markets:
National
Foreign Activity:
Asia, USA
Canadian Branches:
Mississauga
1250 Matheson Blvd. East
Mississauga, ON L4W 1R2
905-625-1900
Fax: 905-625-1500
bart.martindale@cintube.ca

Montréal Rail
1546, ch Gladstone
Montréal, QC H4E 1C4
514-767-3200
Fax: 514-767-5696
m.guernon@cintube.ca

Prescott
River Rd. East
Prescott, ON K0E 1T0
613-925-4277
Fax: 613-925-1256
pwm@bellnet.ca

Circul-Aire Inc.
3999, Côte Vertu
Montréal, QC H4R 1R2
514-336-3330
Fax: 514-337-3336
800-800-1868
info@circul-aire.com
www.circul-aire.com
Products/Services/Areas of Expertise: Designer & manufacturer of indoor air treatment solutions to maximize health, such as air purification systems & energy recovery systems

Cirrus Environmental Services Inc.
#10, 1916 - 30th Ave. NE
Calgary, AB T2E 7B2
403-291-6442
Fax: 403-735-1971
800-661-0047
cirrus@cirrusenviro.com; employment@cirrusenviro.com
www.cirrusenviro.com
Firm Type: Management Consulting, Engineering
Founded: 1995
Products/Services/Areas of Expertise: An environmental consulting & engineering company involved in the integration of health, safety, & environmental requirements for businesses

City Metal Manufacturing Inc.
565 Canarctic Dr.
Toronto, ON M3J 2P9
416-663-2620
Fax: 416-663-2717
citymetal@bellnet.ca
Products/Services/Areas of Expertise: Energy-efficient wood stoves, Metal stampings
Contact(s):
Andrea Rapallo, President

Civtech Engineering & Surveying Ltd.
P.O. Box 3239
Dartmouth, NS B2W 5G2
902-434-4600
Fax: 902-434-9856
800-210-1227

Firm Type: Management Consulting, Waste Management
Founded: 1986
Member of: NS Environmental Industry Association
Products/Services/Areas of Expertise: Performs sewage disposal services, drainage studies, erosion & sedimentation control operations
Contact(s):
Thomas F. Giovannetti, P.Eng., Engineer

CLA Experts-Conseils
629, rue Notre-Dame
Repentigny, QC J6A 2V5
450-581-8070
Fax: 450-581-0861
www.claing.com
Firm Type: Engineering
Founded: 1973
Staff: 11
Products/Services/Areas of Expertise: Engineering services with structural & environmental specialties
Recently Completed / Ongoing Projects: Design & survey construction for upgrading water treatment plant & wastewater treatment for municipalities, QC
Financial Information:
Type of Ownership: Private
Revenue Sources: 40% Provincial; 50% Municipals; 10% Private Contracts
Domestic Markets:
Québec
Contact(s):
Pierre Chartrand, Environmental Department

Clamex Environnement Inc.
CP 44
340, ave du Marechal
Pintendre, QC G6C 1R8
418-837-1444
Fax: 418-837-7723
clamex@qc.aira.com
www.clamex.qc.ca
Firm Type: Engineering, Scientific/Technical Services
Founded: 1985
Contact(s):
Joel Deschênes, Contact

Clariant (Canada) Inc.
4600, rue Cousens
Montréal, QC H4S 1X3
514-334-1117
Fax: 514-334-6182
media.relations@clariant.com
www.clariant.com
Firm Type: Manufacturing
Quality Environmental Management System(s): 9001, ISO
Products/Services/Areas of Expertise: Manufacturer of specialty chemicals; Monitoring of resource consumption, waste management, emissions, & safety take place at all facilities
Financial Information:
Type of Ownership: Foreign-owned
Contact(s):
Hariolf Kottmann, Chief Executive Officer, Clariant
Jonathan Wylde, Head, Clariant Oil Services, Canada

Canadian Branches:
Delta
1081 Cliveden Ave.
Delta, BC V3M 5V1
604-526-1717
Fax: 604-515-3955

Drummondville
3025, rue Power
Drummondville, QC J2B 6X1
819-475-0006
Fax: 819-475-4363

Lachine
2300 - 46 Ave.
Lachine, QC H8T 2P3
514-420-0770
Fax: 514-420-0208

Markham
#7, 421 Bentley St.
Markham, ON L3R 9T2
905-479-4700
Fax: 905-479-3558

Toronto
2 Lone Oak Ct.
Toronto, ON M9C 5R9
416-847-7000
Fax: 416-847-7001

Calgary - Clariant Oil Services
#950, 717 - 7th Ave. SW
Calgary, AB T2P 0Z3
403-262-7846
Fax: 403-262-9355

Lloydminster - Clariant Oil Services
5710 - 44 St.
Lloydminster, AB T9V 0B6
780-871-0700
Fax: 780-871-0867

Slave Lake - Clariant Oil Services
701 - 12th Ave. NE
Slave Lake, AB T0G 2A0
780-849-4722
Fax: 780-849-4732

Claus Engineering (1986) Ltd.
6620 - 248 St.
Langley, BC V4W 1C1
604-607-0218
Fax: 604-607-0183
Firm Type: Engineering
Founded: 1986
Member of: Professional Engineers & Geoscientists of British Columbia
Products/Services/Areas of Expertise: Consulting engineering services to forest, mineral, manufacturing, transportation & waste management industries
Contact(s):
D. Roy Ellis, President

Clayton Research Associates Ltd. / CRAL
1580 Kingston Rd.
Toronto, ON M1N 1S2
416-699-5645
Fax: 416-699-2252
clayton@clayton-research.com
www.altusgroup.com/Clayton
Firm Type: Management Consulting
Founded: 1972
Staff: 15
Products/Services/Areas of Expertise: Impact assessments (socio-economic, economic) of proposed environmental projects; formulation of compensation packages to deal with impacts; design assessment of environmental proposed policies from vantage of effectiveness & cost
Domestic Markets:
National
Contact(s):
Frank A. Clayton, PhD, President
Patricia Arsenault, Sr. Vice-President
Jeannette Gillezeau, Vice-President

Clean Air & Water Centre
Formerly: Atlantic Enertech Ltd.
Also Known As: The Clean Air Centre
P.O. Box 2466 Central
6041 North St.
Halifax, NS B3J 3E4
902-429-4354
Fax: 902-429-4364
800-474-0770
cleanair@cleanaircentre.com; breatheeasy@cleanaircentre.com
www.cleanaircentre.com
Firm Type: Distributing
Founded: 1972
Products/Services/Areas of Expertise: Products for personal, residential, commercial, industrial, agricultural, & institutional use include electronic air purifiers; dust, odour, & infection control equipment; & chemical-free air & water sterilization technology
Financial Information:
Type of Ownership: Private
Domestic Markets:
National
Contact(s):
D.M. Murray, President

Clean Air Services Inc.
7017 Farrell Rd. SE, #C
Calgary, AB T2H 0T3
403-254-2714
Fax: 403-243-8149
www.cleanairservicesinc.com
Firm Type: Engineering, Scientific/Technical Services
Member of: COR Safety Program
Products/Services/Areas of Expertise: Management of the safe abatement of asbestos, mould, lead, PCB, & mercury, including the removal, encapsulation, enclosure, & disposal
Financial Information:
Type of Ownership: Private
Contact(s):
Phil Crook, Managing Director
phil@cleanairservicesinc.com
Andrew Crook, Project Manager
andrew@cleanairservicesinc.com
Graham Graham Crook, Project Manager
graham@cleanairservicesinc.com

Canadian Branches:
Lethbridge
3015B - 12th Ave. North
Lethbridge, AB T1H 5K9
403-327-5997
Fax: 403-327-6147
Danny Dalton, Project Manager
danny@cleanairservicesinc.com

Clean Earth Solutions Ltd.
#4, 178 Pennsylvania Ave.
Concord, ON L4K 4B1
905-482-2149
Fax: 905-482-2149
866-885-2706
info@cleanearthltd.com
www.cleanearthltd.com
Products/Services/Areas of Expertise: Manufacturer of environmentally responsible products, including industrial cleaning solutions, fire foam concentrates, & enhanced in situ aerobic hydrocarbon bioremediation solutions

Clean Harbors Energy & Industrial Services Corp.
A Clean Harbors Inc. company
Formerly: Eveready Industrial Services Ltd.15817 - 121A Ave.
Edmonton, AB T5V 1B1
780-451-6969
Fax: 780-451-6990
800-661-6689
info@evereadyindustrial.com
www.evereadyindustrial.com
Firm Type: Waste Management

Products/Services/Areas of Expertise: The Clean Harbors group of companies is a leading provider of environmental & hazardous waste management services, with service centres across Canada; hazardous & non-hazardous waste recycling, treatment & disposal; CleanPack laboratory chemical packing; household hazardous waste management services; field services; industrial waste & cleaning services; vacuum services; emergency response & disaster recovery; transformer services; tank cleaning & decontamination
Financial Information:
Type of Ownership: Foreign-owned; Publicly Traded
Domestic Markets:
Alberta, British Columbia, Manitoba, Nova Scotia, Ontario, Québec, Saskatchewan

Canadian Branches:
Fort McMurray
230A Mackay Cres.
Fort McMurray, AB T9H 5C6
780-743-0222
Fax: 780-791-3242
fortmcmurray@evereadyindustrial.com

Fort Nelson
4803 48 Ave.
Fort Nelson, BC V0C 1R0
250-233-8811
fortnelson@evereadyindustrial.com

Grande Prairie
8003 - 110th St.
Grande Prairie, AB T8W 6T2
780-532-4331
Fax: 780-532-4405
grandeprairie@evereadyindustrial.com

Nanaimo
#111, 1 - 5765 Turner Rd.
Nanaimo, BC V9T 6M4
250-729-8844
Fax: 250-729-8144
nanaimo@evereadyindustrial.com

Peace River
P.O. Box 7170
Peace River, AB T8S 1S8
780-624-1440
Fax: 780-624-1443
peaceriver@evereadyindustrial.com

Regina
525 E Dewdney Ave.
Regina, SK S4N 4E9
306-546-3322
Fax: 306-546-3321
regina@evereadyindustrial.com

Swift Current
P.O. Box 696
Swift Current, SK S9H 2B1
306-741-4268
swiftcurrent@evereadyindustrial.com

Wainwright
1902 - 15 Ave.
Wainwright, AB T9W 1S8
780-842-2841
wainwright@evereadyindustrial.com

Winnipeg
P.O. Box 9 GRP 582
325 Transport Rd., RR#5
Winnipeg, MB R3C 2Z2
204-669-7867
Fax: 204-654-4679
winnipeg@evereadyindustrial.com

Clean Ontario
#6, 598 Cataraqui Woods Dr.
Kingston, ON K7P 1T8
613-384-7500
Fax: 613-384-7525
800-472-3890
custserv@kos.net
www.cleanontario.com
Firm Type: Distributing
Founded: 1986
Products/Services/Areas of Expertise: High pressure cleaning equipment; washers; oil/water separators; wastewater evaporators
Financial Information:
Type of Ownership: Private
Domestic Markets:
Ontario
Canadian Branches:
Barrie Office
#8, 43 Morrow Rd.
Barrie, ON L4N 3V7
705-734-0560
Fax: 705-737-5020
jgroot@on.aibn.com

Cleanit Greenit Compost System
15619 - 112 Ave.
Edmonton, AB T5M 2V8
780-488-7926
Fax: 780-452-8284
877-774-5678
www.cleanitgreenit.net
Products/Services/Areas of Expertise: Produces organic soil from compost
Ecological Note: Produces organic soil
Contact(s):
Kirsten Castro-Wunsch, Managing Director
kirsten@cleanitgreenit.net

Clear Environmental Products
#7, 170 Wilkinson Rd.
Brampton, ON L6T 4Z5
905-452-7827
Fax: 905-452-5042
clear.environmental@hotmail.com
Firm Type: Distributing
Founded: 1999
Member of: Ontario Marine Operators Association
EcoLogo Certified Products & Services: Marine oil absorbents include AquaFend Filter, Outdoors Super Absorbent, Select Super Absorbent, Universal Super Absorbent, & Universal Super Neutralizing Absorbent
Products/Services/Areas of Expertise: Environmental products include bilge absorbent & containment booms
Ecological Note: Marine oil absorbents include AquaFend Filter, Outdoors Super Absorbent, Select Super Absorbent, Universal Super Absorbent, & Universal Super Neutralizing Absorbent
Financial Information:
Type of Ownership: Private
Contact(s):
Mike King, Sales Agent

Clearstone Engineering Ltd.
#700, 900 - 6th Ave. SW
Calgary, AB T2P 3K2
403-266-8820
Fax: 403-266-8871
www.clearstone.ca
Products/Services/Areas of Expertise: Full service environmental engineering firm; specializes in air emission assessment & industrial air pollution management
Contact(s):
David Picard, Principal

Cleartech Industries Inc.
Formerly: Carbon & Filtration Products Co.
7480 Bath Rd.
Mississauga, ON L4T 1L2
Fax: 888-281-8109
800-387-7503
orders@cleartech.ca
www.cleartech.ca
Firm Type: Distributing
Founded: 1979
Staff: 12
Products/Services/Areas of Expertise: Distributor of chemicals, chemical feed equipment, process equipment, instrumentation and laboratory products.
Domestic Markets:
National
Canadian Branches:
Calgary Branch
5516 - 40th St. SE
Calgary, AB T2C 2A1
1-800-387-7503
orders@cleartech.ca
Edmonton Branch
12020 - 142 St. NW
Edmonton, AB T5L 2G8
1-800-387-7503
orders@cleartech.ca
Regina Branch
555 Henderson Dr.
Regina, SK S4N 5X2
Fax: 888-281-8109
1-800-387-7503
saskatchewan@cleartech.ca; orders@cleartech.ca
Richmond Branch
12431 Horseshoe Way
Richmond, BC V7A 4X6
1-800-387-7503
orders@cleartech.ca
Winnipeg Branch
340 Saulteaux Cres.
Winnipeg, MB R3J 3T2
Fax: 888-281-8109
1-800-387-7503
orders@cleartech.ca
Saskatoon Plant
North Corman Industrial Park
2302 Hanselman Ave.
Saskatoon, SK S7L 5Z3
306-664-2522
1-800-387-7503
saskatchewan@cleartech.ca; orders@cleartech.ca
Saskatoon Plant
2302 Hanselman Ave.
Saskatoon, SK S7L 5Z3
1-800-387-7503
saskatchewan@cleartech.ca; orders@cleartech.ca

ClearView Geophysics Inc.
12 Twisted Oak St.
Brampton, ON L6R 1T1
905-458-1883
Fax: 905-792-1884
general@geophysics.ca
www.geophysics.ca
Firm Type: Engineering, Scientific/Technical Services
Founded: 1996
Staff: 3
Member of: Prospectors & Developers Association of Canada; Professional Engineers of Ontario; Engineers & Environmental Geophysics Society; Environment Assessment Association
Products/Services/Areas of Expertise: Non-intrusive ground investigations; geophysical survey services & consulting
Recently Completed / Ongoing Projects: Site assessments, geophysics component to locate buried metal, Toronto; navigable - DGPS system to survey large areas, Northwest Territories; Utility locates
Financial Information:
Type of Ownership: Private
Revenue Sources: 10% nationwide; 10% Provincial; 80% Private Contracts
Domestic Markets:
National
Foreign Activity:
Central Europe, Eastern Europe, Western Europe, The Middle East, USA
Contact(s):
Joe Mihelcic, President/Geophysicist

Clearview Packaging Inc.
Formerly: EcoLogical Recycled Paper
38 Thornmount Dr.
Toronto, ON M1B 5P2
416-283-1831
Fax: 416-283-0246
Firm Type: Manufacturing
Founded: 1978
Products/Services/Areas of Expertise: Manufacturer of boxes for giftware, cometics, confectioneries, & novelties
Contact(s):
Rocco Rossi, Manager
Contact(s):
Wendy Gamble, Contact
Canadian Branches:
Ecologic Recycled Paper Products - Scarborough
Bldg. 4
#1, 3600 Danforth Ave
Scarborough, ON M1N 4C5

Clemmer Technologies Inc.
Formerly: Mocoat Industrial
446 Albert St.
Waterloo, ON N2L 3V3
519-884-4320
Fax: 519-884-6623
800-265-8840
www.clemmertech.com
Firm Type: Manufacturing
Staff: 11
Products/Services/Areas of Expertise: Fiberglass & steel tanks for the oil & gas industry, water & sewer; custom liquid containment from 500 gallons (2,270 liters) to 11,000 gallons (50,000 liters) in both single & double wall
Financial Information:
Type of Ownership: Private
Domestic Markets:
Alberta, British Columbia, Northwest Territories, Saskatchewan
Foreign Activity:
The Middle East, USA
Contact(s):
Cliff Arcand, Contact, Pressure Vessels
carcand@clemmersteelcraft.com
Doug Scheifley, Contact, Liquid Storage
dscheifley@clemmersteelcraft.com
Canadian Branches:
Eastern Region
#4, 297 Collishaw St.
Moncton, NB E1C 9R2
506-388-3888
Fax: 506-877-1648
1-888-258-8166
Scott Oickle, Contact, Sales
soickle@clemmersteelcraft.com

Products & Services Buyer's Guide

Western Region
4006 60th Ave.
Innisfail, AB T4G 1S7
403-227-1861
Fax: 403-227-0318
bjack@clemmersteelcraft.com
Brian Jack

Clifton Associates Ltd.
340 Maxwell Cres.
Regina, SK S4N 5Y5
306-721-7611
Fax: 306-721-8128
info@clifton.ca
www.clifton.ca
Firm Type: Engineering
Founded: 1978
Products/Services/Areas of Expertise: Provider of technical solutions for problems involving soil, rock, air & water; Environmental engineering services include site assessments, baseline studies, compliance monitoring, environmental audits, permits & licensing, spill control & remediation, decommissioning & reclamation, & waste management
Domestic Markets:
National
Contact(s):
Wayne Clifton, Founder & President
Canadian Branches:
Battleford
10015 Thatcher Ave.
Battleford, SK S0M 0E0
306-445-1621
Fax: 306-937-3731

Calgary
2222 - 30th Ave. NE
Calgary, AB T2E 7K9
403-263-2556
Fax: 403-234-9033

Edmonton
4409 - 94th St.
Edmonton, AB T6E 6T7
780-432-6441
Fax: 780-432-6271

Lloydminster
#10, 6309 - 43rd St. West
Lloydminster, AB T9V 2W9
780-872-5980
Fax: 780-872-5983

Regina
340 Maxwell Cres.
Regina, SK S4N 5Y5
306-721-7611
Fax: 306-721-8128

Saskatoon
#4, 1925 - 1st Ave. North
Saskatoon, SK S7K 6W1
306-975-0401
Fax: 306-975-1076

Edmonton
#930, 10303 Jasper Ave.
Edmonton, AB T5J 3N6
780-408-4580
Fax: 780-408-4585

Climate Change Central / C3
#100, 999 - 8th St. SW
Calgary, AB T2R 1J5
403-517-2700
Fax: 403-517-2727
866-609-2700
contact@climatechangecentral.com
www.climatechangecentral.com
Firm Type: Management Consulting
Founded: 2000
Products/Services/Areas of Expertise: Encourages action on climate change through education, demonstration projects, & consumer rebate programs
Recently Completed / Ongoing Projects: Alberta Renewable Diesel Demonstration (ARDD); Hail a Hybrid; Retire Your Ride, a vehicle recycling program
Financial Information:
Type of Ownership: Non Profit

Domestic Markets:
Alberta
Contact(s):
Simon Knight, President/CEO
Lynn Sveinson, Chief Operating Officer
John Rilett, Vice-President
Helen Corbett, Director, Communications

Climate Control Systems Inc.
Also Known As: Labbate Climate Control Systems Inc.
408 Mersea Rd. 3, RR#2
Leamington, ON N8H 3V5
519-322-2515
Fax: 519-322-3031
climate@mnsi.net
www.climatecontrol.com
Firm Type: Distributing, Manufacturing
Founded: 1985
Products/Services/Areas of Expertise: Designer, manufacturer, & distributor of fertilizer & irrigation systems to improve the health of greenhouse crops
Domestic Markets:
National
Foreign Activity:
Worldwide
Contact(s):
Eric Labbate, Founder & President
Antonio Gomez, Director, Sales & Marketing
mrantoniogomez@bellnet.ca
Eric Labatte, Contact, Engineering & Technical Support
Tina Labatte, Contact, Customer Service
tmlabbate@gmail.com

Climatizer Insulation Inc.
120 Claireville Dr.
Toronto, ON M9W 5Y3
416-798-1235
Fax: 416-798-1311
info@climatizerinsulation.com
www.climatizerinsulation.com
Firm Type: Manufacturing
Founded: 1977
Staff: 20
Member of: Greater Toronto Home Builders Association; Ontario Home Builders Association
Quality Environmental Management System(s): 9002
EcoLogo Certified Products & Services: Climatizer cellulose loose-fill insulation
Products/Services/Areas of Expertise: Manufacturer of cellulose loose-fill insulation
Recently Completed / Ongoing Projects: Developed Enviro-Batt(TM), a sprayed cellulose batting
Ecological Note: Climatizer cellulose loose-fill insulation
Financial Information:
Type of Ownership: Private
Revenue: $3 Million - $5 Million
Revenue Sources: 10% Provincial; 10% Municipals; 80% Private Contracts
Domestic Markets:
Ontario
Markets Sought:
The Pacific Rim
Contact(s):
Karl Molcar, President
Breen Carson, Manager, Sales
breenc@climatizerinsulation.com

Clintar Groundskeeping Services
#1, 70 Esna Park
Markham, ON L3R 1E3
905-943-9530
Fax: 905-943-9529
800-361-3542
info@clintar.com
www.clintar.com
Firm Type: Scientific/Technical Services
Founded: 1973
Products/Services/Areas of Expertise: Landscaping, groundskeeping, horticultural technique
Financial Information:
Type of Ownership: Private
Domestic Markets:
Ontario
Contact(s):
Robert C. Wilton, President

Canadian Branches:
Toronto Branch
1051 Martin Grove Rd.
Toronto, ON M9W 4W6
416-245-3140
Fax: 416-245-6009
akousik@clintar.com

Clivus Multrum Canada Ltd.
1558 Queen St. East
Toronto, ON M4L 1E8
416-466-0635
Fax: 416-466-0635
800-645-4767
www.clivusmultrum.com
Products/Services/Areas of Expertise: Consumer, office & industry products; compost equipment; Ecologo certified building, grounds & construction
Ecological Note: Clivus Multrum Compost Toilet
Domestic Markets:
National
Foreign Activity:
USA
Contact(s):
Laurence H. Scott, Managing Director

Cloverdale Paint Inc.
6950 King George Hwy.
Surrey, BC V3W 4Z1
604-596-6261
Fax: 604-597-2677
helpdesk@cloverdalepaint.com
www.cloverdalepaint.com
Firm Type: Manufacturing
Founded: 1938
Staff: 520
Quality Environmental Management System(s): 9001
Products/Services/Areas of Expertise: Paint & surface coatings; 57 stores in Canada
Financial Information:
Type of Ownership: Private
Domestic Markets:
Alberta, British Columbia, Saskatchewan
Foreign Activity:
USA
Contact(s):
Ed Linton, Officer, Environment and Safety Compliance

CMD Insurance Services Inc.
#215, 1945 Dundas St. East
Mississauga, ON L4X 2T8
905-624-4866
Fax: 905-624-8238
800-665-3406
response@cmdenvironmental.com
www.cmdenvironmental.com
Firm Type: Financial
Founded: 1910
Products/Services/Areas of Expertise: Financial & marketing services
Contact(s):
Richard Drescher, Vice-President

CMEL Enterprises Ltd.
P.O. Box 220
RR#4
Spencerville, ON K0E 1X0
613-658-3099
Fax: 613-658-2897
Firm Type: Engineering, Scientific/Technical Services
Founded: 1979
Staff: 2
Products/Services/Areas of Expertise: Research & development & engineering design; assessment of regulations & guidelines; impact & compliance; process evaluation & audits; risk analysis
Contact(s):
R.W. Marcellus, President

CML Northern Blower Inc.
901 Regent Ave. West
Winnipeg, MB R2C 2Z8
204-222-4216
Fax: 204-222-7601
info@northernblower.com
www.northernblower.com

Firm Type: Manufacturing
Founded: 1982
Staff: 150
Products/Services/Areas of Expertise: Industrial fan equipment
Financial Information:
Type of Ownership: Private
Domestic Markets:
National
Foreign Activity:
Australia/New Zealand, The Pacific Rim, South America, Mexico, USA
Contact(s):
Vern Campbell, General Manager
Mark Windeatt, Sales

CMS: Crisis Management Specialists Inc.
40 Castle Rock Dr.
Richmond Hill, ON L4C 5H5
905-780-6140
Fax: 905-780-8714
info@crisisspecialists.com
www.crisisspecialists.com
Products/Services/Areas of Expertise: High-profile, executive crisis management: evaluations, training, operational support; customized software programs; international experience
Contact(s):
D. Brian Hay, Principal
bhay@crisisspecialists.com

CO2 Solution
2300 rue Jean-Perrin
Québec, QC G2C 1T9
418-842-3456
Fax: 418-842-1732
877-884-3456
info@co2solution.com
www.co2solution.com
Products/Services/Areas of Expertise: Recycling of Carbon Dioxide into an environmentally friendly material
Contact(s):
Glenn Kelly, President & CEO

Coast Forest Management Ltd.
#203, 2005 Eagle Dr.
Campbell River, BC V9H 1V8
250-287-2077
Fax: 250-287-2076
info@cfm.bc.ca
www.cfm.bc.ca/index.htm
Firm Type: Management Consulting, Engineering
Founded: 1982
Products/Services/Areas of Expertise: Consulting services for forest resource management & timber development; timber search; harvest planning; government liaison; policy briefs & proposals; logging engineering & supervision; silviculture prescription & integrated management
Recently Completed / Ongoing Projects: Ongoing forest land management in British Columbia for companies, government & First Nations
Financial Information:
Type of Ownership: Private
Revenue: $1.5 Million - $3 Million
Contact(s):
Keith Atkinson, General Manager
keithatkinson@cfm.bc.ca

Canadian Branches:
Port Alberni
7000 B Pacific Rim Hwy
Port Alberni, BC V9Y 8Y3
250-724-4425
Fax: 250-724-4426

Coast Paper Ltd.
Papier Coast
850 West Kent Ave.
Vancouver, BC V6P 3G1
604-321-8511
Fax: 604-321-4771
www.coastpaper.com
Firm Type: Distributing
Founded: 1941
Staff: 95
Products/Services/Areas of Expertise: Marketer & distributor of fine, high-performance printing & office paper, graphic arts supplies & equipment, & industrial products, such as health & safety equipment, packaging solutions, & janitorial supplies; Services include Coast Custom Converting to reduce waste
Financial Information:
Type of Ownership: Publicly Traded
Domestic Markets:
National
Foreign Activity:
Worldwide
Contact(s):
Greg Bodnar, Director, Canada West
Gunther Sturhahn, General Manager, British Columbia
Steve Ingham, Manager, Training & Development

Canadian Branches:
Calgary
2820 - 37th Ave. NE
Calgary, AB T1Y 5T3
403-291-1030
Fax: 403-250-5443
Steve Groshak, Manager

Edmonton
17808 - 116th Ave.
Edmonton, AB T5S 1V1
780-452-1275
Fax: 780-451-3527
Founded: 1976
Dave Murray, Manager

Lachine
1600, 32e av
Lachine, QC H8T 3R1
514-856-0350
Fax: 514-856-0359
Guido Amato, General Manager, Québec Region

Regina
707D MacDonald St.
Regina, SK S4N 5M2
306-522-6600
Fax: 306-545-3066
Founded: 1998
Shawn Murray, Manager

Saskatoon
807 - 60th St. East
Saskatoon, SK S7K 5Z7
306-931-6600
Fax: 306-931-0114
Founded: 1986
Shawn Murray, Manager

Vaughan
200 Galcat Dr.
Vaughan, ON L4L 0B9
905-850-1170
Fax: 905-264-4848
Founded: 1986
Staff: 115
Products/Services/Areas of Expertise: Coast Paper Toronto is PEFC certified
James Tovell, General Manager, Ontario Region

Winnipeg
88 Terracon Pl.
Winnipeg, MB R2J 4G7
204-987-9700
Fax: 204-987-9705
Founded: 1997
Tom Daeninck, Manager

Coast River Environmental Services Ltd.
1672 - 75th Ave. West
Vancouver, BC V6P 6G2
604-264-7522
Fax: 604-264-9152
mail@coastriver.com
www.coastriver.com
Firm Type: Management Consulting
Founded: 1991
Products/Services/Areas of Expertise: Provider of environmental consulting services in the areas of environmental planning, aquatic & terrestrial biology, & ecology
Activities: Environmental monitoring; Environmentally sensitive areas studies; Environmental impact assessment; Watershed assessment & management; Marine & coastal zone management; Watercourse classification; Fisheries management & inventory; Environmental & land development planning; Habitat restoration & enhancement; Environmental permitting & approvals
Recently Completed / Ongoing Projects: Fisheries & marine assessment for the Lions Gate Upgrade Project, including development of habitat compensation & enhancement works in Burrard Inlet; Environmental planning & monitoring for South Okanagan Natural Gas Pipeline Project; City of Surrey environmental sensitive areas study update & recommendations for improved environmental values in parks plan; Stoney Creek bioengineering assessment study; Overview assessment of the Indian River Watershed; Development of a comprehensive coastal zone management program for the Government of Barbados; Environmental scoping of a proposed port development at Thai Vai, for the Government of Vietnam, Asian Development Bank, & World Bank
Financial Information:
Type of Ownership: Private
Domestic Markets:
National
Foreign Activity:
Worldwide
Contact(s):
John Millar, R.P.Bio, Principal

Coastal BioAgresearch Ltd. / CBA
268 Boutiliers Point Rd.
Boutiliers Point, NS B3Z 1V1
902-826-2931
Firm Type: Management Consulting, Scientific/Technical Services
Founded: 1984
Products/Services/Areas of Expertise: A research & development company with expertise in composting systems
Financial Information:
Type of Ownership: Private
Foreign Activity:
Worldwide
Contact(s):
Philip R. Warman, PhD, PAg, President/CEO
prwarman@eastlink.ca

Coastal Ocean Associates Inc. / COA
7 Canal St., 2nd Fl.
Dartmouth, NS B2Y 2W1
902-463-7677
Fax: 902-463-5696
coa@coainc.ns.ca
Firm Type: Scientific/Technical Services
Founded: 1994
Staff: 12
Products/Services/Areas of Expertise: Environmental consulting & contracting services; emergency response planning; environmental baseline studies; environmental assessments; expert testimony; oceanography; numerical modelling
Financial Information:
Type of Ownership: Private
Domestic Markets:
British Columbia, New Brunswick, Newfoundland & Labrador, Nova Scotia, Prince Edward Island

Coastal Zones Research Institute Inc. / CZRI/IRZC
Institut de recherche sur les zones côtiéres inc.
Formerly: Peat Research & Development Centre Inc.
232 - B, ave de l'Église
Shippagan, NB E8S 1J2
506-336-6600
Fax: 506-336-6601
www.irzc.umcs.ca
Firm Type: Engineering, Scientific/Technical Services
Founded: 2002
Member of: Université de Moncton
Products/Services/Areas of Expertise: Research in the areas of fishery & marine products, aquaculture, peat & peatlands, & sustainable development of coastal zones
Financial Information:
Type of Ownership: Non Profit
Domestic Markets:
National
Foreign Activity:
USA
Contact(s):
Gastien Godin, General Director
gastien.godin@irzc.umcs.ca

Cobham Tracking & Locating Ltd.
Formerly: Seimac Ltd.; Orion Electronics Ltd.
#300, 120 Eileen Stubbs Ave.
Dartmouth, NS B3B 1Y1

902-468-3007
Fax: 902-468-3009
888-473-4622
employment@cobhamtl.com
www.cobhamtl.com
Firm Type: Engineering, Information Technology, Manufacturing, Scientific/Technical Services
Founded: 2007
Quality Environmental Management System(s): 9001:2000
Products/Services/Areas of Expertise: Part of Cobham Surveillance, Cobham Tracking & Locating Ltd. is engaged in the development of electronic tracking & locating equipment. The company designs, manufactures, distributes, & supports radio positioning & telemetry tags which are used in search & rescue & law enforcement situations.
Financial Information:
Type of Ownership: Private
Domestic Markets:
National
Foreign Activity:
Worldwide
Contact(s):
Paul Steward, Program Director, Search & Rescue Products
paul.steward@cobham.com

Coen Canada Inc.
226, rue Roy
Saint-Eustache, QC J7R 5R6
450-472-7922
Fax: 450-472-3350
coencanada@coen.com
www.coen.com
Firm Type: Manufacturing
Founded: 1982
Products/Services/Areas of Expertise: Burners; kiln burners; duct burners; air heaters; combustion systems for industrial applications; burner management systems
Financial Information:
Type of Ownership: Foreign-owned
Contact(s):
José Perez, Director
Dominique Rancourt, Controller

Coffey Geotechnics Inc.
Formerly: Shaheen & Peaker; S&P Geo-Engineering; Geo-Canada
20 Meteor Dr.
Toronto, ON M9W 1A4
416-213-1255
Fax: 416-213-1260
www.coffey.com
Firm Type: Management Consulting, Engineering
Founded: 1957
Products/Services/Areas of Expertise: Part of Coffey International Limited, Coffey Geotechnics Inc. provides information & recommendations in the following areas: environmental engineering, geotechnical engineering, & inspection & testing services. Operations are conducted in areas such as hydrogeology, the oil & gas sector, nearshore structures, & tunnelling
Activities: Conducting environmental soil & groundwater engineering services; providing transportation & pipeline services; offering specialized services for infrastructure projects, such as roads, bridges, rail, & tunnels
Recently Completed / Ongoing Projects: Lester B. Pearson International Airport expansion project; Toronto Transit City program; Trent Rapids hydroelectric project
Financial Information:
Type of Ownership: Foreign-owned
Domestic Markets:
Alberta, Ontario
Contact(s):
John Douglas, Managing Director/CEO, Coffey International Limited
Mark Croudace, Group Executive, Business Development
Urs Meyerhans, Group Executive, Finance
Bob Simpson, Group Executive, Corporate Strategy
Mark Newton, Group Executive, People & Culture

Canadian Branches:
Burlington
#8, 5040 Mainway
Burlington, ON L7L 5R9
905-633-8100
Fax: 905-633-8102
www.coffey.com

Domestic Markets:
Ontario,

Calgary
#21, 3030 Sunridge Way NE
Calgary, AB T1Y 7K4
403-250-8850
Fax: 403-291-0186
www.coffey.com
Recently Completed / Ongoing Projects: Keystone Pipeline, to transport crude oil from Hardisty, Alberta to the markets in the USA Midwest
Domestic Markets:
Alberta

Markham
#10, 351 Steelcase Rd. West
Markham, ON L3R 4H9
905-474-9255
Fax: 905-474-9267
www.coffey.com
Domestic Markets:
Ontario

COGENCanada
Formerly: Thermoshare Energy Consultants
481 Valade Cres.
Ottawa, ON K1A 3K1
613-731-6783
Fax: 613-523-7249
info@cogencanada.org
www.cogencanada.org
Products/Services/Areas of Expertise: Energy consulting; energy management system & design, congeneration studies
Contact(s):
Gordon Robb, President
gordon.robb@sympatico.ca

Cogent Environmental Solutions Ltd.
13 Adrian Ave.
Mansfield, ON L0N 1M0
705-434-4489
Fax: 705-434-9675
877-994-9908
cogentenvironmental@ecogent.ca
www.ecogent.ca
Products/Services/Areas of Expertise: Distributor of sustainable, healthy cleaning solutions, such as detergent free cleaners, oxidizing cleaners, & ECOgent general purpose cleaner
Ecological Note: ECOgent & ECOgent2 general purpose cleaners
Contact(s):
Michael Rochon, Principal

Cole-Parmer Canada Inc.
Formerly: Labcor Technical Sales Inc.
#210 - 5101 Buchan St.
Montréal, QC H4P 2R9
514-355-6100
Fax: 514-355-7119
800-363-5900
info@coleparmer.ca; catalogs@coleparmer.ca;
hr@coleparmer.ca
www.coleparmer.ca
Firm Type: Distributing
Founded: 1988
Products/Services/Areas of Expertise: Distributor of instruments & services for the scientific & engineering communities, such as aerators, airflow measurement instruments, steam generators, chloride analyzers, thermo scientific melting point apparatuses, cleaning equipment, environmental chambers, evaporators, water purification & testing equipment, refractometers, furnaces, turbidity meters, hydrometers, pressure & vacuum instruments, ultraviolet equipment, various types of pumps, plus material handling services & calibration services
Domestic Markets:
National

Colour Innovations Print Inc.
161 Norfinch Dr.
Toronto, ON M3N 1Y2
416-663-6703
Fax: 416-663-3918
877-302-9777
general@colourinnovations.com
www.colourinnovations.com

Firm Type: Scientific/Technical Services
Founded: 1988
Staff: 55
EcoLogo Certified Products & Services: Pre-press & commercial printing
Products/Services/Areas of Expertise: Ecologo certified paper products & printing services
Ecological Note: Pre-press & commercial printing
Financial Information:
Type of Ownership: Private
Revenue: $3 Million - $5 Million
Domestic Markets:
Ontario
Markets Sought:
Caribbean, Western Europe, USA
Contact(s):
Matthew Alexander, President
John Bradley, Manager, Sales

Combustion & Energy Systems Ltd.
Formerly: KV Combustion & Energy Systems Ltd.
#110, 25 Royal Crest Ct.
Markham, ON L3R 9X4
905-415-9400
Fax: 905-415-9482
info@combustionandenergy.com
www.combustionandenergy.com
Products/Services/Areas of Expertise: Manufacturer and designer of heat recovery and combustion systems
Contact(s):
Keith Veitch

Comco Manufacturing Ltd.
811A - 58th St. East
Saskatoon, SK S7K 6X5
306-652-5005
Fax: 306-652-5099
800-225-4417
info@comco-controls.com
www.comco-controls.com
Firm Type: Engineering, Information Technology, Manufacturing
Founded: 1986
Staff: 20
Member of: Saskatchewan Trade & Export Partnership; Grain Elevator & Processing Society
Products/Services/Areas of Expertise: Engineering services; software development (PLC programming, Hml design); manufacturing (CSA/US approved panels); post-pellet liquid applicators & automatic packages; batching software; milling software
Financial Information:
Type of Ownership: Private
Domestic Markets:
National, Alberta, Manitoba, Saskatchewan
Foreign Activity:
Asia, USA
Contact(s):
Darrell Deck, General Manager
Willie M. Unger, President

Comcor Environmental Limited
#12, 320 Pinebush Rd.
Cambridge, ON N1T 1Z6
519-621-6669
Fax: 519-621-9944
www.comcor.com
Firm Type: Engineering, Scientific/Technical Services, Waste Management
Founded: 1985
Member of: Integrated Gas Recovery Services Inc.
Member of: Consulting Engineers of Ontario
Products/Services/Areas of Expertise: Specialist in landfill gas management, waste purification, & environmental engineering
Financial Information:
Type of Ownership: Private
Domestic Markets:
National
Contact(s):
Edward Crosby, B.A. (Econ), Chief Executive Officer
Walter Graziani, P. Eng., President
Paul Bulla, P. Eng., Vice-President, Operations
Alexander Magditsch, M.A.Sc., P. Eng., Vice-President, Engineering
Kim Vince, B. Sc., Coordinator, Environmental Compliance & Health & Safety

Canadian Branches:
Mississauga
Britannia Facility
950 Plymouth Rd.
Mississauga, ON L5V 3Y8

Ottawa
Trail Road Facility
4475 Trail Rd., RR#2
Ottawa, ON K0A 2Z0

Thorold
East Quarry Facility
2800 Thorold Townline Rd.
Thorold, ON L2V 3Y8

Comenco Systems Inc.
#46, 60 Pippin Rd.
Concord, ON L4K 4M8
905-738-6118
Fax: 905-738-8868
800-421-6488
comenco@comenco.com
www.comenco.com
Firm Type: Manufacturing
Founded: 1991
Staff: 10
Products/Services/Areas of Expertise: Mobile & stationary soil remediation & vapour abatement systems; air pollution control; thermal & catalytic oxidizers for volatile organic contaminants; heating & combustion equipment; high temperature heat recovery
Financial Information:
Type of Ownership: Private
Revenue Sources: 100% Private Contracts
Domestic Markets:
National
Foreign Activity:
Worldwide
Markets Sought:
Western Europe, The Middle East, South America
Contact(s):
Raymond Hsu, P.Eng., President
hsu@comenco.com
Eric Watson, Sales and Marketing Consultant, Sales
ewatson@comenco.com

Canadian Branches:
Concord Branch
#46, 60 Pippin Rd.
Concord, ON L4K 4M8
905-738-6118
Fax: 905-738-8868
wlucas@comenco.com

Comfort King Doors & Windows Ltd.
Formerly: Carleton Doors
1521 Sieveright Rd.
Gloucester, ON K1T 1M5
613-526-4550
Fax: 613-526-3957
comfortking@comfortking.ca
www.comfortking.ca
Firm Type: Distributing
Founded: 1976
Member of: Building Owners & Managers Association of Ottawa-Carleton
Products/Services/Areas of Expertise: Home energy consultants; energy-efficient windows
Domestic Markets:
Northwest Territories, Ontario, Québec
Foreign Activity:
The Pacific Rim, South America
Contact(s):
Pat G. Hunter, President
Norm Boyer, Sales Manager

Commercial Solutions Inc.
Formerly: Canadian Forestry Equipment Ltd.
4203 - 95th St.
Edmonton, AB T6E 5R6
780-432-1611
Fax: 780-433-5176
888-522-9822
www.cfe.ca
Firm Type: Distributing
Founded: 1966

Staff: 5
Quality Environmental Management System(s): 9001:2008
Products/Services/Areas of Expertise: Soil sampling products; power transmission products & services; industrial products; resource management products & services; safety products; mining products.
Financial Information:
Type of Ownership: Private
Domestic Markets:
National
Contact(s):
Jim Barker, President/CEO

Canadian Branches:
Mississauga Office
#4 1540 Trinity Dr.
Mississauga, ON L5T 1L6
905-795-1610
Fax: 905-795-1632
1-800-387-4940
Burk Urmetzer

Pointe Claire Office
Unit E, 100 boul. Hymus
Pointe-Claire, QC H9R 1E4
514-697-1100
Fax: 514-630-8090
1-800-361-5572
Steve Rooney

Communicopia.Net Internet Inc.
Also Known As: Communicopia
#601, 134 Abbott St.
Vancouver, BC V6B 2K4
604-844-7672
info@communicopia.net
www.communicopia.net
Firm Type: Scientific/Technical Services
Founded: 1993
Staff: 10
Member of: Canadian Environment Industry Association
Products/Services/Areas of Expertise: Retrieval of environmental information for preparation of promotional campaigns, issues & events; information distribution systems & databases; internet web page development
Financial Information:
Type of Ownership: Private
Revenue Sources: 20% Provincial; 80% Private Contracts
Domestic Markets:
National
Foreign Activity:
USA
Contact(s):
Jason Mogus, President & CEO
Christopher Roy, Senior Strategist

Community Resource Services Ltd.
P.O. Box 5936
St. John's, NL A1C 5X4
709-576-6946
Fax: 709-576-6946
crs_ltd@ns.sympatico.ca
Contact(s):
Mark Shrimpton, Principal

Compo Recycle
225, rue Du Progès
Chertsey, QC J0K 3K0
450-753-3765
Fax: 450-882-3693
888-482-6676
information@comporecycle.com
www.comporecycle.com
Firm Type: Waste Management
Founded: 1997
Staff: 70
Products/Services/Areas of Expertise: Amélioration de la qualité de l'environnement; gestion intégrée de la Collecte-à-3Voies (Recyclage Compostage et Enfouissement)
Contact(s):
Sylvain Lafortune, Président/Directeur général

Canadian Branches:
Saint-Ambroise-de-Kildare
4e Rang
Saint-Ambroise-de-Kildare, QC J0K 1C0

Compo-Haut-Richelieu inc.
Administrative Centre & Ecocentre
825, rue Lucien-Beaudin
Saint-Jean-sur-Richelieu, QC J2X 5L2
450-347-0299
Fax: 450-347-7859
800-324-0299
info@compo.qc.ca
www.compo.qc.ca
Products/Services/Areas of Expertise: Operator of ecocentre facilities, including container rental, waste collection, & education
Domestic Markets:
Québec

Canadian Branches:
Lacolle
Ecocentre
8, rue du Parc Industriel
Lacolle, QC J0J 1J0
450-246-2521

Saint-Jean-sur-Richelieu - Gaudette
Ecocentre
950, rue Gaudette
Saint-Jean-sur-Richelieu, QC J2W 3G1
450-349-6809

Compost Management
165 Geddes St.
Elora, ON N0B 1S0
519-846-8317
Fax: 519-846-8319
Firm Type: Management Consulting, Scientific/Technical Services, Waste Management
Founded: 1988
Staff: 20
Products/Services/Areas of Expertise: Field operation & management of centralized composting facilities & related consulting
Domestic Markets:
National
Contact(s):
Paul Taylor, President

Composite Manufacturing Corp.
16 Fisherman Dr.
Brampton, ON L7A 1G2

Canadian Branches:
Composite Manufacturing Corp.
16 Fisherman Dr.
Brampton, ON L7A 1G2

Gentech Engineering
P.O. Box 813
3195 Third Ave. East
Owen Sound, ON N4K 5P7

CompreVac Inc.
3067 Jarrow Ave.
Mississauga, ON L4X 2C6
905-924-4096
Fax: 905-624-4099
888-603-6172
sales@comprevac.com
www.comprevac.com
Firm Type: Distributing
Founded: 1975
Products/Services/Areas of Expertise: Provides vacuum pumps & air compressors, air pumps and related services.

Comptank Corp.
RR#2
Bothwell, ON N0P 1C0
519-695-2915
Fax: 519-695-2114
888-695-2915
comptank@ciaccess.com
www.comptank.com
Firm Type: Manufacturing
Founded: 1986
Staff: 15
Member of: Society of the Plastics Industry of Canada
Products/Services/Areas of Expertise: Tanks for corrosive hazardous waste; vacuum tank semi-trailers for corrosive liquids
Financial Information:
Revenue: $1.5 Million - $3 Million
Domestic Markets:
National

Products & Services Buyer's Guide

Foreign Activity:
USA
Contact(s):
Denis Marcos, Vice-President

Compteurs Lecomte Ltée
2925, rue Cartier
Saint-Hyacinthe, QC J2S 1L4
450-774-3406
Fax: 450-773-0759
800-263-3406
flecomte@lecomte.ca
www.lecomte.ca
Products/Services/Areas of Expertise: Water meters & accessories
Contact(s):
François Lecomte, President/CEO

Compusult Limited
P.O. Box 1000
40 Banister St.
Mount Pearl, NL A1N 3C9
709-745-7914
Fax: 709-745-7927
888-307-7707
info@compusult.net
www.compusult.net
Firm Type: Scientific/Technical Services
Founded: 1985
Products/Services/Areas of Expertise: Computer consulting firm focusing on the development of scientific applications to support environmental data acquisition & management
Contact(s):
Barry O'Rourke, President

Hamilton
400 Parkdale Ave. North
Hamilton, ON L8H 5Y2
905-549-3559

Comstock Canada Ltd.
3455 Landmark Rd.
Burlington, ON L7M 1T4
905-335-3333
Fax: 905-335-0304
www.comstockcanada.com
Firm Type: Engineering
Founded: 1904
Products/Services/Areas of Expertise: Mechanical, electrical, & high voltage underground contractor, with services including planning, constructing, operations, & maintenance
Contact(s):
Geoffrey Birkbeck, Chief Executive Officer
Robert Quinn, President/COO
Aldo Morabito, Chief Financial Officer
Brian Rielly, Executive Vice-President, Operations, Eastern Canada
Pete Semmens, Executive Vice President, Procurement & Special Projects, Western Canada
Bryan Tyers, Manager, Corporate Safety, ISO, & MSR

Canadian Branches:
Edmonton
10180 - 101st St.
Edmonton, AB T5J 3S4
780-732-1899
Dale Belter, Contact

London
1200 Trafalgar St.
London, ON N5Z 1H5
519-451-6450
Tim White, General Manager

Mississauga
3182 Orlando Dr.
Mississauga, ON L4V 1R5
905-678-0004
Keith Tuffrey, Vice-President

Val Caron
2736 Belisle Dr.
Val Caron, ON P3H 1N4
705-897-3333
Denis Gareau, Sr. Vice-President

Winnipeg
#1860, 2116 Logan Ave.
Winnipeg, MB R2R 0J2
204-633-7907

Andy Tremorin, Contact

Con Cast Pipe
229 Brock Rd South, R.R.#3
Guelph, ON N1H 6H9
519-763-8655
Fax: 519-763-1956
800-668-7473
sales@concastpipe.com
www.concastpipe.com
Firm Type: Manufacturing
Founded: 1989
Staff: 100
Member of: Ontario Concrete Products
Products/Services/Areas of Expertise: Water & wastewater management equipment; precast products: reinforced concrete pipe, manholes, catchbasins, box units, retaining wall gravity wall system; culvert system; oil separator
Financial Information:
Type of Ownership: Private
Revenue Sources: 10% Provincial; 20% Municipals; 70% Private Contracts
Contact(s):
Brian Wood, President
Derek Guberney, Sales Manager

CON-SPACE Communications Ltd.
Corporate Headquarters
#505, 5600 Parkwood Way
Richmond, BC V6V 2M2
604-244-9323
Fax: 604-270-2138
800-546-3405
info@con-space.com
www.con-space.com
Firm Type: Engineering, Manufacturing
Founded: 1991
Staff: 40
Products/Services/Areas of Expertise: Manufacturer of technical rescue equipment for first responders, such as the SearchCam line, CON-SPACE Hardline, CON-SPACE Radio Accessories, & Delsar Life Detectors
Financial Information:
Type of Ownership: Publicly Traded
Revenue Sources: 2% Private Contracts
Domestic Markets:
National
Foreign Activity:
Worldwide
Contact(s):
Paulin Laberge, Chair
Renee Magnusson, Contact, Inside Sales & Customer Service
rmagnusson@con-space.com

International Branch(es):
Newark, Nottinghamshire, United Kingdom
#2, Stephenson Crt., Brunel Park
Newark, Nottinghamshire UK
+44 (0) 1636 642484
ukinfo@con-space.com
www.con-space.com/eurindex.html
Nick White, Contact, Sales

Con-Tank Installations Ltd.
#6, 1 Ashbridge Cir.
Woodbridge, ON L4L 3R5
905-850-2112
Fax: 905-850-9065
Products/Services/Areas of Expertise: waste management
Contact(s):
Stefano Magliozzi, Sr. Project Manager

Con-Test, A Division of Contamination Containment Technology Inc.
#15, 520 Westney Rd. South
Ajax, ON L1S 6W5
905-428-6671
Fax: 905-428-7703
800-321-3816
rene.soetens@con-test.com
www.con-test.com
Firm Type: Scientific/Technical Services
Founded: 1978
Quality Environmental Management System(s): 9002
Products/Services/Areas of Expertise: Specialist in biological contamination control & cleanroom evaluation; Services include pressure testing, air quality assessment, decontamination, & containment laboratory commissioning for clients such as hospitals, pharmaceutical & research companies, laboratories, & universities
Financial Information:
Type of Ownership: Private
Domestic Markets:
National
Contact(s):
René Soetens, President

Con-V-Air Inc.
#3500, rue 1re
Saint-Hubert, QC J3Y 8Y5
450-462-5959
Fax: 450-462-0756
info@con-v-air.com
www.con-v-air.com
Firm Type: Distributing
Founded: 1991
Products/Services/Areas of Expertise: Specialist in solids handling, with products such as screw conveyors, spill free railcar connectors, hydrated lime & quick lime storage, handling, & solution preparation systems, rotary air locks, storage tanks, pneumatic conveying systems for bulk handling, mixers for dry solids, bulks bag unloaders, & sludge spreaders

Canadian Branches:
Mississauga
#32, 6800 Kitimat Rd.
Mississauga, ON L5N 5M1
905-285-9934
Fax: 905-285-9935

Conair Group Inc.
Formerly: Conair Aviation Ltd.
1510 Tower Rd.
Abbotsford, BC V2T 6H5
604-855-1171
Fax: 604-855-1017
info@conair.ca
www.conair.ca
Firm Type: Engineering
Founded: 1969
Staff: 10
Products/Services/Areas of Expertise: Design, manufacture & operation of aircraft, helicopter systems & other specialty aviation equipment for forest fire control, forest fertilization, oil spill control, coastal surveillance, mapping, remote sensing, environmental impact assessment
Domestic Markets:
National
Foreign Activity:
Asia, Western Europe, The Pacific Rim, South America, Mexico, USA
Contact(s):
David Schellenberg, President & CEO
dschellenberg@conair.ca
Rick Pedersen, Vice-President & General Manager
rpedersen@conair.ca

Concept Controls Inc.
#1, 2315 - 30th Ave. NE
Calgary, AB T2E 7C7
403-208-1065
Fax: 403-250-1011
888-207-2212
sales@conceptcontrols.com
www.conceptcontrols.com
Firm Type: Distributing

Products/Services/Areas of Expertise: Gas calibration and detection products; industrial hygeine products; fiberglass grating; passive samplers and water quality products; Calibration and rental of products
Financial Information:
Type of Ownership: Private
Domestic Markets:
National
Foreign Activity:
USA
Contact(s):
Brent Yaschuk, Contact
brenty@conceptcontrols.com

Canadian Branches:
Eastern Canada
#14, 2283 Argentia Rd.
Mississauga, ON L5N 5Z2

905-567-3651
Fax: 905-567-3652
800-793-9548

Northern Alberta
6031 - 103A St.
Edmonton, AB T6H 2J7
780-423-3881
Fax: 780-436-0063
888-438-3225

Québec
2598 Place du Boléro
Saint-Lazare, QC J7T 3Z8
Fax: 905-567-3652
800-793-9548

International Branch(es):
USA
#300, 7702 East Doubletree Ranch Rd.
Scottsdale, AZ USA
480-945-0052
Fax: 480-348-3999

Condor Engineering Ltd.
32539 Verdon Way
Abbotsford, BC V2T 7Y3
604-576-1387
Fax: 604-576-9467
condoreg@telus.net
Firm Type: Manufacturing
Founded: 1961
Staff: 8
Products/Services/Areas of Expertise: Custom fiberglass
Financial Information:
Type of Ownership: Private
Revenue: $500,000 - $1.5 Million
Revenue Sources: 10% Provincial; 10% Municipals; 80% Private Contracts
Domestic Markets:
Alberta, British Columbia
Foreign Activity:
USA
Contact(s):
Brian Ellerman, President

Conestoga-Rovers & Associates / CRA
651 Colby Dr.
Waterloo, ON N2V 1C2
519-884-0510
Fax: 519-884-0525
hr@CRAworld.com (employment inquiries)
www.craworld.com
Firm Type: Management Consulting, Engineering
Founded: 1976
Quality Environmental Management System(s): 9001:2000
Products/Services/Areas of Expertise: Provider of engineering & construction services, environmental consulting, & information technology services, such as environmental site assessment & remediation, air quality services, solid waste management, noise & vibration consulting, sediment management, & sustainability services
Financial Information:
Type of Ownership: Private
Domestic Markets:
National
Foreign Activity:
South America, Mexico, USA, United Kingdom
Contact(s):
Ed Roberts, B.A.Sc., P.Eng., President
Ian Richardson, M.A.Sc., P.E., P. Eng., Executive Vice-President
Glenn Turchan, M.A.Sc., P.Eng., Executive Vice-President
Steve Quigley, B. Tech, P. Eng., P.E., Secretary
Tony Ying, MBA, B.Sc., Treasurer

Canadian Branches:
Brossard
#220, 9955, av de Catania
Brossard, QC J4Z 3V6
450-618-0510
Fax: 450-678-6306
Jocelyn Theberge, Contact

Calgary
#601, 5920 - 1A St. SW
Calgary, AB T2H 0G3
403-271-2000
Fax: 403-271-3013
Stephen Ball, Contact

Charlottetown
60 St. Peters Rd.
Charlottetown, PE C1S 5N5
902-368-8858
Fax: 902-368-8625
Richard MacEwen, Contact

Dartmouth
45 Akerley Blvd.
Dartmouth, NS B3B 1J7
902-468-1248
Fax: 902-468-2207
Kevin Emenau, Contact

Fredericton
466 Hodgson Rd.
Fredericton, NB E3C 2G5
506-458-1248
Fax: 506-462-7646
Roger Poirer, Contact

Mississauga
#200, 111 Brunel Rd.
Mississauga, ON L4Z 1X3
905-712-0510
Fax: 905-712-0515
Tom Guoth, Contact

Montréal
4610, boul de la Cote-Vertu
Montréal, QC H4S 1C7
514-336-0510
Fax: 514-336-9434
Jocelyn Theberge, Contact

Ottawa
#400, 179 Colonnade Rd.
Ottawa, ON K2E 7J4
613-727-0510
Fax: 613-727-0704
Michael A. Benson, Contact

Owen Sound
1852 - 3rd Ave. East
Owen Sound, ON N4K 2M5
519-371-3311
Fax: 519-371-9587
Klaus Schmidtke, Contact

Richmond
#121, 10551 Shellbridge Way
Richmond, BC V6X 2W9
604-214-0510
Fax: 604-214-0525
Deacon Liddy, Contact

Sault Ste Marie
96 White Oak Dr. East
Sault Ste Marie, ON P6B 4J8
705-254-2438
Fax: 705-254-2430
Robert Bressan, Contact

St Catharines
#3, 261 Martindale Rd.
St Catharines, ON L2W 1A2
905-682-0510
Fax: 905-682-8818
Marc Gaudet, Contact

St. John's
1118 Topsail Rd.
St. John's, NL A1B 3N7
709-364-5353
Fax: 709-364-5368
James O'Neill, Contact

Sydney
270 Charlotte St.
Sydney, NS B1P 6J9
902-564-3313
Fax: 902-564-4681
Walter Van Veen, Contact

Toronto
205 Lesmill Rd.
Toronto, ON M3B 2V1
416-449-1030
Fax: 416-449-2876
Tom Guoth

Windsor
#200, 1880 Assumption St.
Windsor, ON N8Y 1C4
519-966-9886
Fax: 519-966-3894
Gavin O'Neill, Contact

Conestoga-Rovers & Associates
Formerly: MGI Limited
466 Hodgson Rd.
Fredericton, NB E3C 2G5
506-458-1248
Fax: 506-462-7646
infofredericton@craworld.com
www.craworld.com
Firm Type: Scientific/Technical Services
Founded: 1986
Staff: 85
Member of: National Groundwater Association; International Association of Hydrogeologists; Association of Groundwater Scientists & Engineers; Association of Professional Engineers of New Brunswick; Prospectors & Developers Association; Canadian Institute of Mining, Metallurgy & Petroleum; Geological Association of Canada; Canadian Federation of Independent Bu
Products/Services/Areas of Expertise: Air quality evaluations; air pollution control services; engineering consulting services; environmental consulting; resource management; water & wastewater treatment services; waste management; sampling monitoring; groundwater studies; contaminant assessment & remediation; geoscientific investigations; environmental audits; geotechnical engineering; forest & watershed management; erosion & sedimentation; GIS & IT services. Amaglamated with Conestoga-Rovers & Associates in 2005.
Financial Information:
Type of Ownership: Private
Domestic Markets:
New Brunswick, Newfoundland & Labrador, Nova Scotia, Prince Edward Island
Contact(s):
John Hart, Senior Technical Advisor
Roger Poirier, Vice-President
Peter Oram, Vice-President

Canadian Branches:
Corner Brook
355 O'Connell Dr.
Corner Brook, NL A2H 7E4
709-364-5353
Fax: 709-785-2086
Sheldon Adey

Newfoundland
P.O. Box 8353 A
1118 Topsail Rd.
St. John's, NL A1B 3N7
709-364-5353
Fax: 709-364-5368
David Bourden

Nova Scotia
Operations
45 Akerly Blvd.
Dartmouth, NS B3B 1J7
902-468-1248
Fax: 902-468-2207
Jim Fraser, Director

Prince Edward Island
60 St. Peters Rd.
Charlottetown, PE C1A 5N5
902-368-8858
Fax: 902-368-8625
Scott Llewellyn

Sydney
P.O. Box 1234
270 Charlotte St.
Sydney, NS B1P 1C7
902-564-3313
Fax: 902-564-4681
Walter VanVeen

Conformance Check Inc.
Formerly: Environmental Software Associates Ltd.
52 Harrop Ave.
Toronto, ON M9B 2G9
416-620-0846
Fax: 866-306-5084

info@conformancecheck.com
www.conformancecheck.com
Firm Type: Scientific/Technical Services
Founded: 1992
Staff: 7
Products/Services/Areas of Expertise: CD-ROM training package; environmental compliance software
Domestic Markets:
National
Foreign Activity:
USA
Markets Sought:
China, Vietnam
Contact(s):
John David Phyper, P.Eng., Principal
John Wolfe, Manager, Marketing

Connections Research
1 Westerpoint Lane
Bauline, NL A1K 1E9
709-335-8272
Fax: 709-335-2086
info@connectionsresearch.com
Firm Type: Manufacturing
Founded: 1991
Staff: 2
Products/Services/Areas of Expertise: Works with resource-based organizations to assess, prioritize & plan the environmental resources of their operations
Foreign Activity:
Worldwide
Contact(s):
Colleen O'Toole, Principal

Connor Architects & Planners
Affiliate of CBCL Limited
Formerly: Connor Preston Architects200 Portland St.
Dartmouth, NS B2Y 1J4
902-465-7227
Fax: 902-465-7228
info@cap.ns.ca
www.cap.ns.ca
Firm Type: Scientific/Technical Services
Member of: Nova Scotia Association of Architects; Royal Architectural Institute of Canada
Quality Environmental Management System(s): 9001
Products/Services/Areas of Expertise: Architecture; land use planning; architectural programming; building science; condition assessments
Recently Completed / Ongoing Projects: Amherst town planning; development agreements, Pine Grove Estates; commercial developments, Cambridge Shopping Centres
Financial Information:
Type of Ownership: Private
Revenue: $500,000 - $1.5 Million
Revenue Sources: 5% nationwide; 15% Provincial; 30% Municipals; 50% Private Contracts
Domestic Markets:
National
Markets Sought:
Caribbean, The Pacific Rim, Mexico, USA
Contact(s):
Peter Connor, Architect & Sr. Consultant
Mike O'Neil, Operations Manager

Conor Pacific Environmental Technology Inc.
P.O. Box 49224
1055 Dunsmuir St.
Vancouver, BC V7X 1L2
604-669-3373
Fax: 604-669-3353
bob.nowack@conorpacific.com; info@precisiontecha.com
www.conorpacific.com
Firm Type: Engineering, Scientific/Technical Services
Founded: 1988
Products/Services/Areas of Expertise: Wholly owned subsidiary of Precision Assessment Technology Corp.; Environmental specialists in contaminated site assessment and remediation, water and wastewater treatment, air quality modelling and monitoring
Financial Information:
Type of Ownership: Publicly Traded
Domestic Markets:
National
Foreign Activity:
USA
Markets Sought:
Asia, The Pacific Rim
Contact(s):
R.E. (Bob) Nowack, Chairman & Chief Executive Officer

Conporec Inc.
3125, rue Joseph-Simard
Sorel-Tracy, QC J3P 5N3
450-746-9996
Fax: 450-746-7587
info@conporec.com
www.conporec.com
Firm Type: Waste Management
Founded: 1987
Member of: Canadian Composting Council; Association of Composting Industries in Québec
Products/Services/Areas of Expertise: The firm's focus is on the ecological treatment of household waste using a patented biological technology that offers an alternative to landfilling; services include a variety of composting technologies for municipal solid waste, as well as organic wastes; research & development; engineering; procurement; construction management; operation & maintenance; training; financing. Offices in Sorel-Tracy, Québec, & Croissy-Beauborg, France. Biomax Inc. is a subsidiary.
Recently Completed / Ongoing Projects: A 3-year contract with the city of Toronto for the transport & processing of organic waste
Financial Information:
Type of Ownership: Private
Revenue: $3 Million - $5 Million
Revenue Sources: 85% Municipals; 15% Private Contracts
Domestic Markets:
Québec
Foreign Activity:
Worldwide
Contact(s):
Jean Beaudouin, President
Claude Marmen, Sr. Vice-President
Denis Potvin, Vice-President, Research & Development

Consolidated Envirowaste Industries Inc.
Formerly: Biowaste Management Ltd.
27715 Huntington Rd.
Abbotsford, BC V4X 1B6
604-856-6836
Fax: 604-856-5644
800-667-1942
dhalward@telus.net
Firm Type: Waste Management
Founded: 1989
Staff: 110
Member of: Composting Council of Canada
Products/Services/Areas of Expertise: Organic waste processing plants; composting facilities; soil amendments; potting soils; fertilizers; biomass processing; leachate processing & treatment
Financial Information:
Type of Ownership: Publicly Traded
Revenue: Greater than $5 Million
Foreign Activity:
USA
Contact(s):
Rick Chase, Vice-President
Doug Halward, CEO

Consolidated Giroux Environment Inc.
Also Known As: Consolidated Dewatering Inc.
P.O. Box 2043
11 Reid St.
Charlo, NB E8E 2W8
506-684-5821
Fax: 506-684-1915
cgiroux@girouxinc.com
www.girouxinc.com
Firm Type: Waste Management
Founded: 1975
Staff: 30
Products/Services/Areas of Expertise: Sludge dewatering; environmental dredging
Recently Completed / Ongoing Projects: Pulp & paper sludge dewatering in New Brunswick; dredging of lagoons, Noranda Mining
Financial Information:
Type of Ownership: Private
Revenue Sources: 10% nationwide; 10% Provincial; 20% Municipals; 60% Private Contracts
Domestic Markets:
New Brunswick, Newfoundland & Labrador, Nova Scotia, Ontario, Prince Edward Island, Québec
Contact(s):
Malcolm Wilson, General Manager
Marc Hebert, Manager
Eugene Rousselle, Manager, Manufacturing

Constant America Inc.
Formerly: Constant Laboratories Inc.
2120, rue Cabot
Montréal, QC H4E 1E4
514-761-3339
Fax: 514-761-1117
800-565-7888
constant@constantamerica.com; specialist@constantamerica.com
www.constantamerica.com
Firm Type: Distributing, Manufacturing
Founded: 1982
Quality Environmental Management System(s): 9002
Products/Services/Areas of Expertise: Manufacturer & distributor of specialty, environmentally friendly chemicals for the water treatment, pulp & paper, transportation, food & beverage, & industrial, & institutional industries
Domestic Markets:
National
Foreign Activity:
Worldwide

Construction Val-d'Or Ltée
CP 173
1935, 3e av
Val-d'Or, QC J9P 4P3
819-874-7272
Fax: 819-874-8569
const.valdor@cablevision.qc.ca
Firm Type: Engineering, Waste Management
Founded: 1945
Staff: 100
Member of: Association Constructeurs Routes & Grands Travaux du Québec
Products/Services/Areas of Expertise: Erosion control, land & soil stabilization; construction, excavation & construction management; water & wastewater management equipment
Recently Completed / Ongoing Projects: Water & wastewater works, Ville de Malartic, municipalité de Trécesson
Financial Information:
Type of Ownership: Private
Revenue Sources: 10% nationwide; 20% Provincial; 60% Municipals; 10% Private Contracts
Domestic Markets:
Québec
Contact(s):
Robert Drapeau, President
Steven Drapeau, Administrator, Marketing
Angelo Dumas, Project Manager

Consultants Enviroconseil inc.
#200, 5214, boul Hamel
Québec, QC G2E 2G9
418-877-8182
Fax: 418-877-8846
enviroconseil@enviroconseil.com; rh@enviroconseil.com (HR)
www.enviroconseil.com
Products/Services/Areas of Expertise: Consulting engineering company, with expertise in solid waste management, water management, & the environment
Recently Completed / Ongoing Projects: Alterations to landfill techniques at Frampton & Val d'Or, Québec
Domestic Markets:
Québec

Consultants Filion, Hansen & Associés Inc.
22, rue Leclerc
Baie-Saint-Paul, QC G3Z 3B6
418-435-5536
Contact(s):
Gilles Filion, Contact

Consultants Mésar inc.
P.O. Box 218
776, 5e rue
Shawinigan, QC G9N 6T9

819-537-5771
Fax: 819-537-4985
mauricie@mesar.qc.ca
www.mesar.qc.ca
Firm Type: Engineering, Scientific/Technical Services
Founded: 1980
Staff: 175
Products/Services/Areas of Expertise: Engineering consulting services; water & wastewater management services
Financial Information:
Revenue: Greater than $5 Million
Contact(s):
Bertrand Proulx, Président
Yvan Massé, Executive Vice President
Jean St-Onge, Executive Vice President

Consumaj
#201, 3271, boul Laframboise
Saint-Hyacinthe, QC J2S 4Z6
450-773-6155
Fax: 450-773-3373
consumaj@consumaj.com
www.consumaj.com
Firm Type: Management Consulting
Founded: 1991
Staff: 15
Products/Services/Areas of Expertise: Civil engineering; environmental engineering; odor evaluation; bio-socio treatment; construction service; agronomist; fertilization plans; agricultural general manager
Contact(s):
Jean-Denis Major, Président

Conterm Inc.
220, av Labrosse
Montréal, QC H9R 1A1
514-694-2164
Fax: 514-694-1640
info@conterm.ca
www.conterm.ca
Firm Type: Distributing, Manufacturing
Founded: 1972
Products/Services/Areas of Expertise: Manufacturer of portable steel buildings & structures; Distributor of containers; Provider of depot & repair services to container leasing & steamship companies; Operator of a domestic container warehousing & storage leasing fleet
Financial Information:
Type of Ownership: Private
Domestic Markets:
Ontario, Québec
Contact(s):
Richard Pagani, President
richard@conterm.ca
Ted Blaize, Manager, Operations
ted@conterm.ca
Ara Aghjayan, Comptroller
ara@conterm.ca
Franco De Ciccio, Contact, Leasing & Sales

Continental Conveyor Ontario Ltd.
100 Richmond St.
Napanee, ON K7R 3S3
613-354-3318
Fax: 613-354-5789
SalesNap@continentalconveyor.ca
www.continentalconveyor.ca
Firm Type: Manufacturing
Founded: 1963
Staff: 35
Products/Services/Areas of Expertise: Belt conveyors, screw conveyors, bucket elevators, vibratory conveyors
Financial Information:
Revenue: $1.5 Million - $3 Million
Domestic Markets:
National
Contact(s):
David Lynn, President/CEO
B.R. Lynn, Marketing
W.D. Lynn, Sales

Contor Terminals Inc.
1611 Britannia Rd. East
Mississauga, ON L4W 1S5
905-670-7771
Fax: 905-670-8721
info@contor.com
www.contor.com
Firm Type: Manufacturing
Founded: 1976
Products/Services/Areas of Expertise: Containment systems for PCB & hazardous material storage
Financial Information:
Type of Ownership: Private
Domestic Markets:
National
Foreign Activity:
Central America, Mexico, USA
Contact(s):
Gordon Box, President
gordb@contor.com
Lily Mancuso, Container Sales & Service
lilym@contor.com
Tony Virdo, General Manager

Control Fire Systems
63 Advance Rd.
Toronto, ON M8Z 2S6
416-236-2371
Fax: 416-233-6814
info@controlfiresystems.com
www.controlfiresystems.com
Firm Type: Distributing
Founded: 1978
EcoLogo Certified Products & Services: Environmentally Friendly, (non-global warming, non ozone depleting) fire suppression system; UL/ULC approved system for both occupied and non-occupied spaces; Argotec fire suppression system
Products/Services/Areas of Expertise: Manufacture of fire protection products; Fire protection services
Ecological Note: Environmentally Friendly, (non-global warming, non ozone depleting) fire suppression system; UL/ULC approved system for both occupied and non-occupied spaces; Argotec fire suppression system
Contact(s):
Darren McCaw, President
dmccaw@controlfiresystems.com

Control Microsystems
Corporate Headquarters
48 Steacie Dr.
Kanata, ON K2K 2A9
613-591-1943
Fax: 613-591-1022
888-267-2232
sales@controlmicrosystems.com
www.controlmicrosystems.com
Firm Type: Distributing
Founded: 1980
Products/Services/Areas of Expertise: Supplier of Supervisory Control & Data Acquisition (SCADA) hardware & software to a variety of utility markets
Financial Information:
Type of Ownership: Private
Domestic Markets:
National
Foreign Activity:
Asia, Australia/New Zealand, Central Europe, Eastern Europe, Western Europe, USA

Canadian Branches:
Calgary
Western Canada Regional Operations
6109 - 6th St. SE
Calgary, AB T2H 1L9
403-243-8955
Fax: 403-287-3248
888-246-8287
sales@controlmicrosystems.com

International Branch(es):
Denver, USA
USA Operations
#600, 90 Madison St.
Denver, CO USA
303-455-2022
Fax: 303-309-9692
866-446-1965
sales@controlmicrosystems.com

East Kew, Victoria, Australia
Asia Pacific Operations
#103, 832 High St.
East Kew, Australia
11 61 (3) 9249 9562
cmap@controlmicrosystems.com

Leiden, The Netherlands
European Operations
Delftse Jaagpad 1B, 2324AA
Leiden, The Netherlands
+31 (0) 71 5791650
Fax: +31(0)715324539
eurosales@controlmicrosystems.com

Control Techniques Drives Inc. / CT
Division of Emerson Electric Canada Limited
Formerly: Emerson Industrial Controls (1993)306 Town Centre Blvd.
Markham, ON L3R 0Y6
905-948-3402
Fax: 905-942-3418
800-893-2321
www.controltechniques.com
Firm Type: Manufacturing
Founded: 1960
Staff: 7
Member of: American Society of Heating, Refrigerating & Air Conditioning Engineers; Water Environment Federation
Products/Services/Areas of Expertise: Reduced energy consumption for fan, pump, chiller & blower systems using adjustable frequency AC drive controls; upgrade of industrial variable speed applications with DC drive controls & motor; flux vector AC drives
Financial Information:
Type of Ownership: Publicly Traded
Domestic Markets:
National
Foreign Activity:
Worldwide
Contact(s):
Frederic Lambert, President
Gary Coleman, Manager, Sales

Convoyeurs B.M.G. inc.
2250, rue St-Jean
Plessisville, QC G6L 2Y4
819-362-6317
Fax: 819-362-6166
info@convoyeursbmg.com
www.convoyeursbmg.com
Products/Services/Areas of Expertise: Construit de nombreux équipements destinés à l'industrie de la récupération, d'usine d'épuration des eaux usées, d'usine oeuvrant dans le domaine du bois ainsi qu'aux usines de pâtes et papier.
Contact(s):
Léo Campbell, Président
leo.campbell@carbotech-intl.com
Jean-Paul Bergeron, Directeur général
jpbergeron@convoyeursbmg.com

Conway Disposal Ltd.
320 Frederick St.
Sydney, NS B1P 6J9
902-539-2909
Products/Services/Areas of Expertise: Provider of waste management services
Domestic Markets:
Nova Scotia

Cook Engineering
740 South Syndicate Ave.
Thunder Bay, ON P7E 1E9
807-625-6700
Fax: 807-623-4491
cook@cookeng.com
www.cookeng.com
Firm Type: Engineering, Scientific/Technical Services
Founded: 1962
Staff: 110
Member of: Air & Waste Management Association; Canadian Pulp & Paper Association; Canadian Institute of Mining
Products/Services/Areas of Expertise: Consulting engineering services; boiler air pollution control; paper mill sludge processing & incineration; mine closures; water treatment
Financial Information:
Type of Ownership: Private
Revenue: Greater than $5 Million

Revenue Sources: 10% nationwide; 10% Provincial; 10% Municipals; 70% Private Contracts
Domestic Markets:
Ontario
Foreign Activity:
USA
Contact(s):
D.E. Knutsen, P.Eng., President, 807/625-6721
Primo A. Scalzo, P.Eng., Manager, Transportation, 807/625-6700
pscalzo@cookeng.com
Barry Brooks, Manager, Pulp & Paper, 807-625-6728
bbrooks@cookeng.com
Dave Butler, P.Eng., Manager, Mining, 807-625-6720
dbutler@cookeng.com

Cormorant Ltd.
280 B Water St.
St. John's, NL A1C 1B7
709-739-5858
Fax: 709-739-0002
cormorant@cormorant.nf.net
www.cormorant-ltd.com
Products/Services/Areas of Expertise: Consulting company with expertise in the operational side of marine environmental issues; Clients include government & offshore oil & gas, petroleum distribution, mining, & pulp & paper industries
Recently Completed / Ongoing Projects: Hibernia Environmental Effects Monitoring Program Field Surveys, Grand Banks; Stephenville Tank Spill Response, Western Coast of Newfoundland & Labrador; Voisey's Bay Shoreline Geomorphology, Northern Coast of Labrador; Voisey's Bay Ice Monitoring, Northern Coast of Labrador; Newfoundland Oil Handling Facility Site Assessment; Oil Handling Facility Oil Spill Response Training, Newfoundland & Labrador; Environmental Assessment Program Coordination, Northern Coast of Labrador; Terra Nova Environmental Effects Monitoring Program - Baseline Field Surveys, Grand Banks; Single Vessel Sidesweep Oil Recovery System Development, Newfoundland & Labrador; Wellsite Meteorological and Oceanographic Monitoring, Grand Banks; Seabed Habitat Mapping, Newfoundland & Labrador
Domestic Markets:
Newfoundland & Labrador
Contact(s):
James B. Dempsey, B.Sc, Specialist, Marine Environmental Operations
Randy G. Norman, Marine Environmental Technologist
Kevin O. Price, Technical Consultant

Corner Brook Pulp & Paper Ltd.
P.O. Box 2001
1 Mill Rd.
Corner Brook, NL A2H 6J4
709-637-3104
Fax: 709-637-3469
woodlandsinfo@cb.kruger.com
www.cbppl.com
Firm Type: Manufacturing
Founded: 1925
Staff: 1500
Products/Services/Areas of Expertise: Recycled paper & paper products
Financial Information:
Revenue: Greater than $5 Million
Domestic Markets:
Newfoundland & Labrador
Contact(s):
George Van Dusen, Forest Management Superintendent

Corolon Coatings & Corrosion Control Technologies Inc.
2 Haas Rd.
Toronto, ON M9W 3A2
416-401-8855
Fax: 416-401-8878
info@corolon.com
www.corolon.com
Firm Type: Distributing, Manufacturing
Founded: 1994
Staff: 10
Quality Environmental Management System(s): 9002; ISO
Products/Services/Areas of Expertise: Manufacturer & distributor of paints, sealants, coatings & corrosion control products for protecting steel, metal & concrete, smoke stacks, industrial & petroleum tanks, swimming pools, automobiles, farm equipment; Anticorrosion Materials & Technologies Inc. is a sister company

Financial Information:
Type of Ownership: Private
Revenue: $500,000 - $1.5 Million
Contact(s):
Stan Buchowski, President

Corrosion Service Company Limited
205 Riviera Dr.
Markham, ON L3R 5J8
416-630-2600
Fax: 416-630-2393
www.corrosionservice.com
Firm Type: Scientific/Technical Services
Founded: 1950
Products/Services/Areas of Expertise: Services related to the science of corrosion prevention, such as the development of the anodic & cathodic protection systems to provide corrosion control
Activities: External corrosion direct assessment (ECDA); Tank bottom cathodic protection; Close interval survey; AC mitigation; Reinforced concrete cathodic protection; Supply of air & oil cooled transformer rectifiers & state-of-the-art remote monitoring systems

Canadian Branches:
Calgary
Bay A
2916 - 19th St. NE
Calgary, AB T2E 6Y9
403-233-2601
Fax: 403-233-2658

Dartmouth
#41, 10 Akerley Blvd.
Dartmouth, NS B3B 1J4
902-468-7878
Fax: 902-468-2187

Edmonton
#101, 18020 - 105th Ave.
Edmonton, AB T5S 2P1
780-465-2600
Fax: 780-444-3384

Montréal
1250, rue Graham-Bell
Boucherville, QC J4B 6H5
450-449-2600
Fax: 450-449-6353

Sarnia
373 South Vidal St., #F
Sarnia, ON N7T 2V3
519-336-0740
Fax: 519-336-5934

International Branch(es):
Riyadh, Saudi Arabia
Corrosion Service Saudi Arabian LLC
P.O. Box 230888
Riyadh, Saudi Arabia
+966 1 211 8184
Fax: 416-630-2393

Wilmington, USA
Corrosion Service Company Inc.
Wilmington, DE USA
800-676-4984
Fax: 905-474-2539

Corrpro Canada, Inc.
10848 - 214 St.
Edmonton, AB T5S 2A7
750-447-4565
Fax: 750-447-3215
engineering_info@corrpro.ca; materials_info@corrpro.ca
www.corrpro.ca
Products/Services/Areas of Expertise: Provider of total corrosion services to the petrochemical, oil & gas, marine, & municipal markets; Products include rectifiers, CP materials, corrosion monitoring products, junction boxes, instruments, coatings, & battery chargers
Activities: Corrosion engineering services; corrosion field survey services; Cathodic protection construction services; Internal corrosion monitoring services; Pipeline services; Non-destructive testing services; Leak detection services; Educational services

Canadian Branches:
Calgary
#200, 807 Manning Rd. NE
Calgary, AB T2E 7M8
403-235-6400
Fax: 403-272-9508
calgary@corrpro.ca

Estevan
P.O. Box 430
318 Superior Ave.
Estevan, SK S4A 2A4
306-634-5629
Fax: 306-634-7047
estevan@corrpro.ca

Fort St. John
8607 - 101 St.
Fort St John, BC V1J 5K4
250-787-9100
Fax: 250-787-9122
bc@corrpro.ca

Grande Prairie
109, 11281 - 89th Ave.
Grande Prairie, AB T8V 5X3
780-513-4108
Fax: 780-513-8208
BC@corrpro.ca

Lloydminster
P.O. Box 692
#1, 5106 - 62nd St.
Lloydminster, AB T9V 2E4
780-875-8225
Fax: 780-875-8410
lloydminster@corrpro.ca

Mississauga
#3, 7895 Tranmere Dr.
Mississauga, ON L5S 1V9
905-677-2700
Fax: 905-677-2432
ontario@corrpro.ca

Montréal
1985, 55e av
Dorval, QC H9P 1G9
514-636-0085
Fax: 514-636-8671
montreal@corrpro.ca

Regina
P.O. Box 4614
1555H McDonald St.
Regina, SK S4P 3Y3
306-757-3335
Fax: 306-757-0717
regina@corrpro.ca

Cosmopolitan Industries Limited
28 - 34th St. East
Saskatoon, SK S7K 3Y2
306-664-3158
Fax: 306-244-5509
info@cosmoindustries.com
members.shaw.ca/cosmoind/cosmo.htm
Firm Type: Waste Management
Founded: 1971
Products/Services/Areas of Expertise: Provider of waste management services, including the waste paper program
Activities: Collection & sortation of old office paper, newspapers, magazines, cardboard, used beverage containers; Confidential document destruction
Contact(s):
Peter Gerrard, Executive Director
pgerrard@cosmogolf.ca
Ed Schille, Manager, Contracts, Sales & Marketing
Ed Steckler, Production Manager, Waste Reduction Division

Cottonwood Consultants Ltd.
615 Deercroft Way SE
Calgary, AB T2J 5V4
403-271-1408
Firm Type: Management Consulting, Scientific/Technical Services
Founded: 1978
Products/Services/Areas of Expertise: Environmental & technical services consultants; Physical & biological researchers

Activities: Wildlife status reports; Study of environmentally significant areas; Environmental assessments
Financial Information:
Type of Ownership: Private
Domestic Markets:
Alberta
Contact(s):
Cliff Wallis, Botanist

Counterspil Research Inc.
#205, 1075 West First St.
North Vancouver, BC V7P 3T4
604-990-6944
Fax: 604-990-6945
mail@counterspil.com
www.counterspil.com
Firm Type: Scientific/Technical Services
Founded: 1986
Products/Services/Areas of Expertise: Company with expertise in the control of oil & chemical spills, through prevention, preparedness, & response
Activities: Risk assessment; Sensitivity mapping; Contingency planning; Spill modelling; Training; Equipment testing; Cleanup advice
Recently Completed / Ongoing Projects: Oil-in-ice response guide development & testing of skimmers, Norway; Best available technology & in situ burning assessment, BP Exploration (Alaska) Inc.; Response training, Western Forest Products Inc. & BC Hydro; Spill response exercises, Tennessee Valley Authority
Financial Information:
Type of Ownership: Private
Domestic Markets:
National
Foreign Activity:
Africa, Caribbean, Central America, China, Western Europe, The Pacific Rim, South America, Mexico, USA, Former USSR

Countryside Disposal Service Ltd.
7865 Howard Ave., RR#1
McGregor, ON N0R 1J0
519-726-6071
Fax: 519-726-6776
888-227-7701
Firm Type: Waste Management
Founded: 1973
Staff: 10
Member of: Essex Windsor Waste Management Committee
Products/Services/Areas of Expertise: White goods & associated metals recycling; collection of household waste; ICI waste
Financial Information:
Type of Ownership: Private
Revenue Sources: 60% Municipals; 40% Private Contracts
Domestic Markets:
Ontario
Contact(s):
Lawrence Lucier, Director
Pat Lucier, Director
Chris Lucier, Manager
Contact(s):
Chris or Pat Lucier

Canadian Branches:
Countryside Freight Forwarders
7013 Smith Industrial
McGregor, ON N0R 1J0
519-726-4777
Fax: 519-726-6776

Covertech Fabricating Inc.
279 Humberline Dr.
Toronto, ON M9W 5T6
416-798-1340
Fax: 416-798-1342
800-837-8961
info@covertechfab.com; sales@covertechfab.com
www.covertechfab.com
Firm Type: Manufacturing
Founded: 1990
Staff: 45
Products/Services/Areas of Expertise: Daily landfill covers; temporary covers; geosynthetic liners
Financial Information:
Type of Ownership: Private
Revenue: $250,000 - $500,000

Domestic Markets:
National
Foreign Activity:
USA,
Contact(s):
John Starr, Vice-President

Cowater International Inc.
#400, 411 Roosevelt Ave.
Ottawa, ON K2A 3X9
613-722-6434
Fax: 613-722-5893
general@cowater.com; jobs@cowater.com
www.cowater.com
Firm Type: Management Consulting, Scientific/Technical Services
Founded: 1985
Member of: Cowater Consultores Lda., Maputo, Mozambique; Cowater CRG South Africa, Cape Town, South Africa; Cowater Alaska Inc., Alaska, USA; Cowater Accountability Group Inc., Ottawa, ON
Products/Services/Areas of Expertise: Management consulting firm specializing in international development
Activities: Water, sanitation, & envionmental services; Social development; Municipal services & enterprise development; Financial management, audit, & accounting
Financial Information:
Type of Ownership: Private
Domestic Markets:
National
Foreign Activity:
Africa, Asia, Central America, The Pacific Rim, USA
Contact(s):
Mark Baron, M.P.A., M.S., P.Eng., President
Norman Looker, M.A.Sc., P.Eng, Vice-President, Water, Sanitation, & Environment Group
Mike McGarry, Sr. Engineer, Water & Sanitation
David Baron, M.B.A., B.A., General Manager

CP Environmental Technologies
P.O. Box 364
Thorhild, AB T0A 3J0
780-448-1784
Fax: 780-398-2629
Products/Services/Areas of Expertise: Distributes hydrocarbon absorbents; spill & cleanup equipment eliminates leaching; used on land & water; capable of in-situ bioremediation of hydrocarbon contaminated soils
Contact(s):
Ken Pollard, President

CPC Tuyauteries Canada Ltée
#200, 400, boul St-Martin ouest
Laval, QC H7M 3Y2
450-668-5600
Fax: 450-668-1209
Products/Services/Areas of Expertise: Water & wastewater management equipment
Contact(s):
Jean-Claude Leblanc, Représentant

Craig Hydrogeologic Inc.
140 Meadow Cove Rd.
Dipper Harbour, NB E5J 2S9
506-659-3064
Fax: 506-659-9002
craig@xplornet.com
www.craighydrogeologic.ca
Firm Type: Scientific/Technical Services, Waste Management
Founded: 1993
Domestic Markets:
New Brunswick
Contact(s):
H. Douglas Craig, Contact

Cramer Nursery Inc.
Pepinière Cramer inc.
1002, ch St-Dominique
Les Cèdres, QC J7T 3A1
450-452-2121
Fax: 450-452-4053
1-888-827-2637
info@cramer.ca
Firm Type: Distributing
Founded: 1965

Products/Services/Areas of Expertise: Producer of ornamental plants, such as trees, shrubs, perennials, indigenous plants, & water plants
Financial Information:
Type of Ownership: Private
Contact(s):
Walter Cramerstetter, Contact

Canadian Branches:
Dollard-des-Ormeaux
3000, rue du Marché
Dollard-des-Ormeaux, QC H9B 2Y3
514-421-6665

L'Ile-Perrot
1101, boul Don Quichotte
L'Ile-Perrot, QC J7V 5V6

Crandall Engineering Ltd.
#400, 1077 St. George Blvd.
Moncton, NB E1E 4C9
506-857-2777
Fax: 506-857-2753
866-857-2777
info@crandallnb.com
www.crandallnb.com
Firm Type: Engineering
Founded: 1952
Quality Environmental Management System(s): 9001
Products/Services/Areas of Expertise: Engineering/consulting operations; water & wastewater treatment & management; water supply services; transportation; project management
Contact(s):
Joseph J. Kileel, P.Eng., President
Michel Cormier, P.Eng., Vice-President

Crane Energy Flow Solutions
Division of Crane Canada Inc.
Formerly: Crane Valves354 Elgin St.
Brantford, ON N3S 7P9
519-759-3911
Fax: 519-759-7970
800-563-6302
www.cranevalve.com
Firm Type: Distributing, Manufacturing
Member of: Canadian Standards Association; Canadian Nuclear Association
Products/Services/Areas of Expertise: Valves for control of fluid flow in critical applications
Domestic Markets:
National
Contact(s):
Fred Koch, Manager, Manufacturing, Production, Operations
Tim Butcher, Manager, Sales & Marketing
tim_butcher@cranevalve.com

Crompton Technology Inc.
7544 Bath Rd.
Mississauga, ON L4T 1L2
905-671-2304
Fax: 905-671-3661
info@crompton-canadaeast.com;
sales@crompton-canadaeast.com
www.crompton-canadaeast.com
Firm Type: Distributing, Scientific/Technical Services
Founded: 2002
Products/Services/Areas of Expertise: Distributor of products, such as measuring instruments, control instruments, protection instruments, programmable digital panel meters, bar graph meters, volt transducers, Watt transducers, current transducers, DC Shunts, Control Electrical Transformers, Control Switches, counters, timers, & datalogging systems
Activities: Initial calibration; Maintenance & repairs
Contact(s):
Paul Gerardi, English Language Contact, Customer Service,
905-671-2304
pgerardi@crompton-canadaeast.com
Dave Jadoo, French Language Contact, Customer Service,
905-671-2304

Crosbie Industrial Services Ltd.
P.O. Box 8338
St. John's, NL A1B 3N7
709-722-8212
Fax: 709-739-0602
spower@crosbiegroup.com
www.crosbieindustrial.com

Firm Type: Waste Management
Founded: 1982
Member of: Newfoundland Environmental Services Limited
Quality Environmental Management System(s): 9001:2008
Products/Services/Areas of Expertise: Septic waste removal; industrial sludge removal; pit & sump cleaning; petroleum tank cleaning; wet/dry vacuum truck services; water blasting; underground storage tank removal & disposal; emergency spill response; oil spill clean-up; general industrial cleaning; used oil collection & recycling; pumping of lubricating & hydraulic oils; marine oil spill containment & clean-up; hazardous waste disposal
Contact(s):
Steve Power, COO

Crossman Machinery Co. Ltd.
8284 Sherbrooke St.
Vancouver, BC V5X 4E8
604-325-3262
Fax: 604-325-6191
cmcvcr@telus.net
Firm Type: Manufacturing
Staff: 14
Products/Services/Areas of Expertise: Designer & manufacturer of electro-mechanical drive systems, including gearboxes, couplings & braking systems for all sizes of wind turbines
Contact(s):
Don MacLeod

Crown Fibre Tube Inc.
P.O. Box 10
705 Park St., RR#1
Kentville, NS B4N 3V9
902-678-8901
Fax: 902-679-1104
crown@crownfibretube.com
Products/Services/Areas of Expertise: Manufacturer of converted paper, such as newsprint, mailing tubes, & die cut items
Foreign Activity:
The Pacific Rim, USA
Contact(s):
Lloyd M. Anderson, Manager
Andrew Hardman, Manager, Production

Crown Packaging Ltd.
P.O. Box 94188
13911 South Foot of Garden, City Rd.
Richmond, BC V6Y 2A4
604-277-7111
Fax: 604-275-1684
info@crownpackaging.com
www.crownpackaging.com
Products/Services/Areas of Expertise: Collection & processing of recyclable paper products; produces recycled paperboard & paper packaging products
Contact(s):
Ron London, Vice-President, Sales

Canadian Branches:
Calgary
#101, 5555 - 69th Ave. SE
Calgary, AB T2C 4Y7
403-225-3800
Fax: 403-225-3888

Kelwona Branch
2092 Enterprise Way
Kelowna, BC V1Y 6H7
250-860-2274
Fax: 250-860-0345

Crown Publications, Inc.
106 Ontario St.
Victoria, BC V8V 1M9
250-386-4636
Fax: 250-386-0221
crown@crownpub.bc.ca
www.crownpub.bc.ca
Products/Services/Areas of Expertise: Offers BC Government publications and legislation and Federal Government code books, nautical charts, topographical, road, street, and world wall maps, as well as a wide selection of BC specific books. For provincial statutes & regulations see: www.leg.bc.ca

Crown Shred & Recycling
P.O. Box 1303
225 6th Ave. East
Regina, SK S4P 3B8
306-545-5454
Fax: 306-545-6125
1-877-545-5999
csrelmer@sasktel.net
www.crownshredandrecycling.com
Firm Type: Waste Management
Founded: 1988
Products/Services/Areas of Expertise: Collector, processor, & marketer of recyclable material from municipal recycling programs, individual residents, industrial institutions, & commercial establishments
Activities: Residential curbside program; Office recycling & document destruction service
Financial Information:
Type of Ownership: Private
Domestic Markets:
Saskatchewan
Contact(s):
Jack Shaw, President/CEO
Elmer Epp, Manager, Residential Sales
Rick Haddad, Manager, Commercial Business

Canadian Branches:
Prince Albert
#201, 460 - 40th St. East, RR#2
Prince Albert, SK S4V 5P9
306-763-9292
Fax: 306-763-9293
Cory Shaw, Manager

Cues Canada
Formerly: Knopafex Ltd.
#2, 1675 Sismet Rd.
Mississauga, ON L4W 1P9
905-238-9178
Fax: 905-238-5018
larryc@cuesinc.com
www.cuesinc.com
Firm Type: Distributing
Founded: 1983
Staff: 17
Products/Services/Areas of Expertise: Computerized closed circuit television sewer inspection reporting system
Financial Information:
Type of Ownership: Publicly Traded
Revenue Sources: 50% Municipals; 50% Private Contracts
Domestic Markets:
National
Foreign Activity:
Australia/New Zealand, Central America, Central Europe, USA, Worldwide
Markets Sought:
South America
Contact(s):
Larry Corkill, Sales Manager

Cunningham Sheet Metal Works Inc.
62 Byng Ave.
Chatham, ON N7M 3E2
519-351-2252
Fax: 519-351-2253
csmwinc.@ciaccess.com
www.cunninghamsheetmetalchatham.com
Firm Type: Manufacturing
Founded: 1908
Products/Services/Areas of Expertise: Manufacturer of sheet, plate, structural, round, & square tube, in mild steel, stainless steel, & aluminum
Activities: Air system design; Design, fabrication & installation; Plant shutdown services; Emergency repairs
Financial Information:
Type of Ownership: Private

Curtis Environmental & Engineering Inc.
Formerly: Curtis Engineering and Testing Ltd.
#1A, 820 - 28th St. NE
Calgary, AB T2A 5K1
403-273-4980
Fax: 403-273-5957
environmental@curtisengeering.ca
www.curtisengineering.ca
Firm Type: Engineering, Scientific/Technical Services
Founded: 1984
Products/Services/Areas of Expertise: Provider of environmental engineering, & geotechnical & materials testing (E-mail: geotechnical@curtisengineering.ca; Phone: 403-273-5868); Clients include government & industry
Activities: Soils testing; Materials testing; Quality control on materials during construction; Foundation & slope stability studies; Streets & roads engineering
Financial Information:
Type of Ownership: Private
Domestic Markets:
Alberta
Contact(s):
William E. Curtis, M.Sc., P.Eng., President & General Manager

Curtis Reclamation Service Ltd.
P.O. Box 490
Rocky Mountain House, AB T0M 1T0
403-845-4774
Fax: 403-845-4774

Custom Environmental Services Ltd.
Also Known As: Proeco Corporation
7722 - 9th St.
Edmonton, AB T6P 1L6
780-440-1825
Fax: 780-440-2428
800-661-5792
gerrygerke@proeco.com
www.proeco.com
Firm Type: Waste Management
Founded: 1985
Staff: 25
Products/Services/Areas of Expertise: Full-service hazardous waste management, including field investigations, remediation, design & contracting; risk assessment & audits; regulatory compliance; waste recycling & disposal; PCB management; emergency response; spill control & cleanup; environmental insurance coverage; treatment & transfer sites in Canada; oilfield waste management services
Financial Information:
Type of Ownership: Private
Revenue: Greater than $5 Million
Revenue Sources: 20% nationwide; 10% Provincial; 10% Municipals; 60% Private Contracts
Domestic Markets:
National
Foreign Activity:
Caribbean, Central America, South America, Mexico, USA, Worldwide
Contact(s):
Vacant, President/CEO
Gerry Gerke, Manager, Sales
Gavin Scott, General Manager, Site Facilities

Cutler-Hammer Canada
Formerly: Eaton Yale Ltd.
5050 Mainway
Burlington, ON L7L 5Z1
905-333-6442
Fax: 905-333-2724
800-268-3578
www.eatoncanada.ca
Firm Type: Manufacturing
Founded: 1960
Staff: 70
Products/Services/Areas of Expertise: Control equipment for electric motors including speed control, motor protection & soft starting; range of sensors, limit switches, push buttons & pilot lights
Domestic Markets:
National
Contact(s):
Paul Tlustos, Contact

Canadian Branches:
Calgary
#133, 2611 Hopewell Pl. NE
Calgary, AB T1Y 7J7
403-252-3324
Fax: 403-640-1876

Connaught
1109 Connaught Rd.
Connaught, ON P0N 1A0
705-363-2001
Fax: 705-363-2002

Dartmouth
#100, 32 Troop Ave.
Dartmouth, NS B3B 1Z1
902-481-3400
Fax: 902-481-3410

Delta
1693 Cliveden Ave.
Delta, BC V3M 6V5
604-519-1250
Fax: 604-519-1260

Edmonton
12465 - 153rd St.
Edmonton, AB T5V 1E4
780-490-3280
Fax: 780-450-1750

Kitchener
975 Bleams Rd., #1
Kitchener, ON N2E 3Z5
519-893-9033
Fax: 519-893-3114

Lachine
1410, 55e av
Lachine, QC H8T 3J8
516-633-9316
Fax: 516-420-6151

London
697 Consortium Ct.
London, ON N6E 2S8
519-649-2383
Fax: 519-649-1220

Midland
624 Randles Cres.
Midland, ON L4R 4V4
705-526-6957
Fax: 705-526-7088

Mississauga
4120 Sladeview Cr., #B
Mississauga, ON L5L 5Z3
902-820-0108
Fax: 902-820-0220

Moncton
#3, 245 Collishaw St.
Moncton, NB E1C 9P9
506-853-3311
Fax: 506-856-5999

Oshawa
#2, 1333 Thorton Rd. South
Oshawa, ON L1J 8M8
905-443-0981
Fax: 905-443-0986

Ottawa
2615 Lancaster Rd., #26
Ottawa, ON K1B 5N2
613-739-1115
Fax: 613-739-7339

Regina
#203, 2222 Albert St.
Regina, SK S4P 2V2
306-546-2121
Fax: 306-546-2120

Saskatoon
#217, 116 Research Dr.
Saskatoon, SK S7N 3R3
306-244-1082
Fax: 306-244-1083

St. John's
15 Hallett Cres.
St. John's, NL A1B 4C4
709-726-2800
Fax: 709-726-2818

Stoney Creek
#2B, 745 South Service Rd.
Stoney Creek, ON L8E 5Z2
800-928-3260

Sudbury
#4, 1349 Kelly Lake Rd.
Sudbury, ON P3E 5P5

705-524-7955
Fax: 705-524-9761

Thunder Bay
#1200, 1184 Roland St.
Thunder Bay, ON P7B 5M4
807-623-0966
Fax: 807-623-0961

Vanier
#240, 900, Pierre-Bertrand
Vanier, QC G1M 3K2
418-681-1371
Fax: 418-681-3790

Windsor
4525 Rhodes Dr., #100
Windsor, ON N8W 5R8
519-944-7002
Fax: 519-944-0242

Winnipeg
#13, 1650 Notre Dame Ave.
Winnipeg, MB R3H 1H6
204-694-0569
Fax: 204-633-2450

Cyanide Destruct Systems Inc.
Also Known As: CDS Inc.
135 Dimson Ave.
Guelph, ON N1G 3C5
519-837-1899
Fax: 519-837-8329
hrobey@cyanidedestruct.com
www.cyanidedestruct.com
Firm Type: Distributing, Manufacturing
Founded: 1986
Products/Services/Areas of Expertise: Designer, manufacturer & marketer of cyanide waste treatment systems; Clients include pharmaceutical, agricultural, plating, & hi-tech industries
Activities: Precious metal recovery; Cyanide waste transportation; Cyanide treatment & disposal
Domestic Markets:
National
Foreign Activity:
Worldwide
Contact(s):
Herbert L. Robey, P.Eng., Contact
hrobey@cyanidedestruct.com
Contact(s):
Andrew Harvey, Contact
aharvey@cyanidedestruct.com

Canadian Branches:
Barrie
CDS Environmental Services
293 Saunders Rd.
Barrie, ON L4N 9A3
705-725-6262
Fax: 705-725-0036
1-888-886-9022

Cyntech Corporation
235061 Wrangler Link SE
Calgary, AB T2P 2G6
403-228-1767
Fax: 403-245-6632
info@cyntechcorp.com
www.cyntechcorp.com
Firm Type: Manufacturing, Scientific/Technical Services
Founded: 1981
Products/Services/Areas of Expertise: Provider of solutions to the energy & petro-chemical industry, including tank services, pipeline stabilization products, & foundation solutions
Financial Information:
Type of Ownership: Private
Domestic Markets:
Alberta, Saskatchewan

Cypher International Ltd.
Also Known As: Cypher Environmental Ltd.
391 Campbell St.
Winnipeg, MB R3N 1B6
204-489-1214
Fax: 204-489-7372
admin@cypherltd.com
www.cypherltd.com; www.cypherenvironmental.com

Firm Type: Distributing, Manufacturing, Scientific/Technical Services
Founded: 1998
Products/Services/Areas of Expertise: Researcher of environmental technologies
Activities: Road dust suppression; Soil stabilization; Waste water remediation; Algae reduction; Organic bioremediation; Bod & cod removal; Effluent odour control, with environmental agricultural & infrastructure products
Financial Information:
Type of Ownership: Private
Domestic Markets:
National
Foreign Activity:
Worldwide

Cypress Sales Partnership
Formerly: Mecon Sales Inc.
2615 Wentz Ave.
Saskatoon, SK S7K 5J1
306-242-3333
Fax: 306-242-3373
866-242-3393
sales@cypresssales.com
www.cypresssales.com
Firm Type: Distributing
Founded: 1991
Staff: 14
Products/Services/Areas of Expertise: Heat recovery products; air handling equipment; dust collectors; filters, HVAC products & systems; vibration control systems & equipment; waste storage; underground tanks; control valves
Contact(s):
Bernard Kaminski, Partner
Gordon Nagus, Partner

Canadian Branches:
Regina Branch
1145 - 8 Ave.
Regina, SK S4R 1E1
306-757-5656
Fax: 306-757-8024
Keith Goosen, Industrial Sales
k.goosen@cypresssales.com

Cyr Engineering Ltd.
Cyr Ingénierie Ltée
30651 Rte. 134
McLeods, NB E3N 5V4
506-753-6176
Fax: 506-753-5715
Firm Type: Engineering, Scientific/Technical Services
Founded: 1987
Staff: 6
Member of: Association of Professional Engineers of New Brunswick; Association of Professional Engineers of Canada; Consulting Engineers of Canada
Member of: Association of Consulting Engineering Companies
Products/Services/Areas of Expertise: Environmental audits; construction & project management; feasibility studies; site assessment; process evaluation & selection; solid waste management; water & wastewater treatment consulting; sewage pumping stations
Financial Information:
Type of Ownership: Private
Revenue: $100,000 - $250,000
Revenue Sources: 20% Provincial; 65% Municipals; 15% Private Contracts
Domestic Markets:
New Brunswick
Contact(s):
Roger E. Cyr, P.Eng., President

D. Besner & Associates Inc.
Also Known As: DIB Consulting
20 Oxford Ct.
Fredericton, NB E3B 2W8
506-454-3812
Fax: 506-455-3599
dbesner@nbnet.nb.ca
Firm Type: Management Consulting
Founded: 2001
Member of: New Brunswick Environmental Industries Association; New Brunswick Association of Professional Engineers; Canadian Federation of Independent Business
Products/Services/Areas of Expertise: Environmental consulting & contracting services

Products & Services Buyer's Guide

Recently Completed / Ongoing Projects: Ambient air quality report, Saint John, NB; business plan development, NB Lung Association; environmental impact assessment - policy review, NB Dept. of the Environmental & Local Government
Financial Information:
Type of Ownership: Private
Domestic Markets:
New Brunswick, Newfoundland & Labrador, Nova Scotia, Prince Edward Island
Markets Sought:
Caribbean, USA
Contact(s):
Dave Besner, President

D. Greenfield Associates Ltd.
4020 Derry Rd. West, RR#2
Burlington, ON L9T 2X6
905-335-3911
Fax: 905-335-3963
Firm Type: Management Consulting, Waste Management
Founded: 1974
Products/Services/Areas of Expertise: Environmental consultant, with expertise in the sewage & industrial waste fields; Clients include the iron & steel processing industry, utilities, & governent agencies
Financial Information:
Type of Ownership: Private
Domestic Markets:
Ontario
Foreign Activity:
Central America
Contact(s):
D. Greenfield, President

D.G. Taylor Inc., Consulting Ecologist Division
74 Swansea St.
Conception Bay South, NL A1W 4S5
709-834-2461
Fax: 709-834-7158
dtaylor@nfld.com
Products/Services/Areas of Expertise: Provider of ecological & regulatory management services; Clients include both public & private organizations
Contact(s):
D.G. Taylor, Consulting Ecologist
dtaylor@nfld.com

D.M. Wills Associates Limited
452 Charlotte St.
Peterborough, ON K9J 2W3
705-742-2297
Fax: 705-741-3568
wills@dmwills.com
www.dmwills.com
Firm Type: Engineering
Founded: 1988
Staff: 30
Products/Services/Areas of Expertise: Civil & environmental, transportation, municipal, structural surveys, construction administration, site supervision, consulting engineering
Financial Information:
Type of Ownership: Private
Revenue Sources: 10% nationwide; 40% Provincial; 20% Municipals; 30% Private Contracts
Domestic Markets:
Ontario
Markets Sought:
Western Europe, The Pacific Rim
Contact(s):
Bruce Bonner, P.Eng., President
Dani Buck, Controller
dbuck@dmwills.com
Canadian Branches:
Cobourg Office
#102, Lower Mall, 257 Division St.
Cobourg, ON K9A 3P9
905-377-8150
Fax: 705-741-3568
wills@dmwills.com
Bruce Bonner, P.Eng.

North Bay
#4, 955 Stockdale Rd.
North Bay, ON P1B 9G3
705-474-6031
Fax: 705-474-8453
d.m.wills@bellnet.ca

Ottawa
160 MacLaren St.
Ottawa, ON K2P 0K9
613-231-5222
Fax: 613-231-4866
awilkins@dmwills.com

D.R. Estey Engineering Ltd.
4722 Continental Way
Prince George, BC V2N 5S5
250-561-2574
Fax: 250-562-7614
Firm Type: Engineering
Founded: 1988
Products/Services/Areas of Expertise: Provider of structural, civil, & forestry engineering services
Financial Information:
Type of Ownership: Private
Contact(s):
D.R. Estey, P.Eng., President

Da-Lee Dust Control
50 Jones Rd.
Stoney Creek, ON L8E 5N2
905-643-1135
Fax: 905-643-2299
1-800-268-4490
info@daleedustcontrol.com; sales@daleedustcontrol.com
www.daleedustcontrol.com
Firm Type: Scientific/Technical Services
Founded: 1978
Products/Services/Areas of Expertise: Provider of professional dust control & ice management solutions for municipalities, industries, indoor riding arenas, & outdoor rings; Company also specializes in water treatment applications of calcium chloride & concrete accelerant applications
Activities: Use of calcium chloride for treatment of oily wastes & wastewater
Recently Completed / Ongoing Projects: Applications of calcium chloride in wastewater treatment at the folowing types of industries: steel, aluminum, metal finishing, fertilizers, commercial laundries, glass & ceramics, television tubes, & municipal wastewater
Domestic Markets:
Ontario
Contact(s):
Dave Rogers, General Manager
Canadian Branches:
Goderich
421 MacEwan St.
Goderich, ON N7A 4M1
519-524-5903
info@daleedustcontrol.com; sales@daleedustcontrol.com

Dagex Inc.
21 Parkes Dr.
Ajax, ON L1S 4W4
905-427-2666
Fax: 905-427-6366
info@dagex.ca
www.dagex.ca
Firm Type: Distributing, Manufacturing
Founded: 1984
Staff: 4
Member of: Ontario Pollution Control Equipment Association; Canadian Association of Metal Finishers; Wastewater Environmental Association of Ontario
Products/Services/Areas of Expertise: Separation equipment & water/wastewater treatment systems: self-cleaning step screen & bar screen, static screening & dewatering systems, filter presses & dryers, in-line filters, continuous sand wash filters, custom settlers & container plants, design services; grit recovery & washing
Recently Completed / Ongoing Projects: Rothsay Recycling, filter press; City of Orillia, step screen, wash press; Cotrell Paper, step screen; Zenon Environmental, wash press; Industrial Press Machinery, sandfilter; Municipality of Port Hope, step screen, wash press
Financial Information:
Type of Ownership: Private
Revenue: $1.5 Million - $3 Million
Revenue Sources: 40% Municipals; 60% Private Contracts
Domestic Markets:
National
Contact(s):
David A. Griffiths, President

Monique Bates, Managing Director

Dakins Engineering Group Ltd.
#1, 4161 Sladeview Cres.
Mississauga, ON L5L 5R3
905-814-6024
Fax: 905-814-6029
info@dakins.ca
www.dakins.ca
Firm Type: Distributing, Engineering
Founded: 2001
Products/Services/Areas of Expertise: The systems integrator firm also resells control equipment & instrumentation to the water & wastewater industry
Activities: Designing, selling, commissioning, & servicing SCADA systems; Building all styles of control panels; PLC & HMI programming; Training

Dalco Wastewater Specialists Inc.
1848 Portage Ave.
Winnipeg, MB R3J 0G9
204-831-9773
Fax: 204-889-0720
dalco@mb.sympatico.ca
Firm Type: Distributing, Engineering, Scientific/Technical Services
Founded: 1989
Staff: 4
Member of: Water Environment Federation, Western Canada Water & Wastewater Association, Manitoba Water & Wastewater Association
Products/Services/Areas of Expertise: Water pollution control; design, mechanical & electrical supply, upgrade & contracting for wastewater treatment plants
Recently Completed / Ongoing Projects: Design/build sewage treatment plant, Shamattawa & Wasagamack, MB; upgrade of sewage treatment plant, Poplar Hill School, ON & Berens River nursing station, MB
Financial Information:
Type of Ownership: Private
Revenue Sources: 80% Municipals; 20% Private Contracts
Domestic Markets:
Manitoba, Ontario
Foreign Activity:
USA

Dalynn Biologicals Inc.
Formerly: Dalynn Laboratory Products
3253 - 34 St. NE
Calgary, AB T1Y 6X2
403-291-0067
Fax: 403-250-9010
888-404-4045
info@dalynn.com
www.dalynn.com
Firm Type: Manufacturing
Founded: 1985
Staff: 12
Products/Services/Areas of Expertise: A manufacturer & distributor of in-vitro diagnostic products for clinical & industrial microbiology labs
Financial Information:
Type of Ownership: Private
Revenue: $1.5 Million - $3 Million
Domestic Markets:
Alberta, British Columbia, Manitoba, Northwest Territories, Ontario, Saskatchewan, Yukon Territory
Foreign Activity:
Central Europe, Western Europe, The Pacific Rim, USA,
Contact(s):
David J. O'Connell, President
Michael Chan, Technical Representative

Danatec Educational Services Ltd.
#201, 11450 - 29th St. SE
Calgary, AB T2Z 3V5
403-232-6950
Fax: 403-232-6952
1-800-465-3366
info@danatec.com; sales@danatec.com; support@danatec.com
www.danatec.com
Firm Type: Management Consulting, Distributing, Information Technology
Founded: 1985
Products/Services/Areas of Expertise: Administrator of workplace safety training solutions; Provider of general safety training publications & programs for the health & safety industry;

Distributor of reference & training materials for Transportation of Dangerous Goods (TDG), to meet Transport Canada's standards; Designer of Workplace Hazardous Materials Information System (WHMIS) products, including WHMIS Online Training, WHMIS Self-Teach, & the "WHMIS - Tell Me Your Story" DVD
Financial Information:
Type of Ownership: Private
Domestic Markets:
National
Contact(s):
Ronald J.E. Martin, President

Canadian Branches:
Calgary
#201, 11450 - 29th St. SE
Calgary, AB T2Z 3V5
403-723-3281
Fax: 403-232-6952
1-800-465-3366
Chris Plante, Sales Agent
chris@danatec.com

Cornwall
RR#2
Cornwall, ON K6H 5R6
613-931-2494
Fax: 613-931-2748
Bruce Elderbroom, Sales Agent

Dartmouth
30 Smith Ave.
Dartmouth, NS B2V 1M4
902-434-0141
Fax: 902-434-2319
1-800-565-3571
Dusty Miller, Sales Agent
dusty@danatec.com

Edmonton
8919 - 162 St.
Edmonton, AB T5R 2M5
780-484-2090
Fax: 780-481-7872
1-877-537-3505
Bill Smith, Sales Agent
b.smith@danatec.com

Langley
#423, 8840 - 210th St.
Langley, BC V1M 2Y2
604-882-4999
Fax: 604-882-4980
1-877-326-2832
Kevin Swinden, Sales Agent
kevin@danatec.com

Montréal
CFT Canada
701, av Meloche
Montréal, QC H9P 2S4
514-631-0273
Fax: 514-631-7250
1-800-361-0283

Prince Albert
Prince Albert, SK
306-960-2261
Fax: 306-922-5553
Jim Barbondy, Sales Agent

Winnipeg
#20, 360 Keewatin St.
Winnipeg, MB R2X 2Y3
204-694-2566
Fax: 204-633-0044
1-888-877-1077
Rick Taraschuk, Sales Agent
rick@danatec.com

Danfoss Inc. - Electric Floor Heating Division
#410, 6711 Mississauga Rd.
Toronto, ON L5N 2W3
905-285-2050
Fax: 905-285-2055
866-676-8062
www.danfoss.ca; www.devi.danfoss.com/north_america
Firm Type: Distributing, Manufacturing
Founded: 2003
Quality Environmental Management System(s): 9000; ISO

Products/Services/Areas of Expertise: Manufacturer of floor heating equipment with low energy consumption
Financial Information:
Type of Ownership: Foreign-owned
Contact(s):
Lise Belec, Sales Representative
lise_belec@danfoss.com

Danfoss Inc. - Hydronic Heating Division
#410, 6711 Mississauga Rd.
Mississauga, ON L5N 2W3
905-285-2050
Fax: 905-285-2055
1-866-375-4822
heatingsales@danfoss.com
www.danfoss.ca; www.na.heating.danfoss.com
Firm Type: Manufacturing
Quality Environmental Management System(s): 9000; ISO
Products/Services/Areas of Expertise: Manufacturer of components for the generation, distribution, & use of heat in homes & buildings
Financial Information:
Type of Ownership: Foreign-owned
Contact(s):
Dave Mason, Regional Manager, 905-285-2062Fax: 905-285-2056

Daniel Fauteux Environnement inc.
40, rue D'Ailleboust
Cap-de-la-Madeleine, QC G8T 1K2
819-379-8111
Fax: 819-375-4777
dfauteux.environnement@qc.aira.com
Contact(s):
Daniel Fauteux, Directeur

Darke Marketing Inc.
P.O. Box 188
52 Bence Beach,
Fort Qu'appelle, SK S0G 1S0
306-332-5577
Fax: 306-332-6145
darke.mkg@sasktel.net
Products/Services/Areas of Expertise: Distributor of water & wastewater products, such as Zurn acid neutralizing tanks, backflow preventors, floor, trench, & roof drains, & strainers, as well as water-saving toilets
Contact(s):
Frank Darke, Contact

Dartmouth Appliance Repair
196 Windmill Rd.
Dartmouth, NS B3A 1E9
902-469-2037
Fax: 902-464-1349
Products/Services/Areas of Expertise: Repair firm for appliances, including CFC removal
Domestic Markets:
Nova Scotia

Dartmouth Metals & Bottles Ltd.
P.O. Box 41 Main
14 Dawn Dr.
Dartmouth, NS B2Y 3Y2
902-468-1995
Fax: 902-468-2242
dartmouthmetals@ns.aliantzinc.ca
www.dartmouthmetals.ca
Firm Type: Waste Management
Founded: 1979
Products/Services/Areas of Expertise: Collector, processor, & recycler of ferrous & non-ferrous metals
Activities: Demolition, including the dismantling of buildings, bridges, locomotives, & ships; Site clean-up; Roll-off container service
Domestic Markets:
Nova Scotia
Contact(s):
Peter Giberson, Owner

Dashwood Industries Ltd.
Hwy. 4
Centralia, ON N0M 1K0
Fax: 519-228-2083
800-265-4284
www.dashwood.com
Firm Type: Distributing, Manufacturing
Founded: 1928

Member of: Canadian Window & Door Manufacturers Association (CWDMA)
Products/Services/Areas of Expertise: Manufacturer of windows, skylights, & doors, with product testing to Energy Star specifications; Distributor of window & door products to the building industry
Financial Information:
Type of Ownership: Foreign-owned
Domestic Markets:
Ontario

DATA Group of Companies
Formerly: Relizon Canada Inc.
1570, rue Ampère
Boucherville, QC J4B 7L4
450-449-7171
Fax: 450-449-8700
www.datagroup.ca
Products/Services/Areas of Expertise: Offers environmental friendly solutions including computer forms, continuous, cut sheet, unit sets, stock, envelopes, labels & commercial printing
Ecological Note: Business forms & documents
Contact(s):
David M. Odell, President/CEO
Paul O'Shea, CFO

Canadian Branches:
Brampton
9195 Torbram Rd.
Brampton, ON L6S 6H2
905-791-3151
Fax: 905-791-3277
800-268-0128

Edmonton
9503 - 12th Ave. SW
Edmonton, AB T6X 0C3
780-462-9700
Fax: 780-450-2621

Data Tech Environmental Services
A Division of 1003369 Ontario Inc.
34 Framingham Dr.
Thornhill, ON L3T 4H3
905-886-0963
Fax: 905-764-5158
tbranny@datatechenvironmental.com
www.datatechenvironmental.com
Firm Type: Scientific/Technical Services

Products/Services/Areas of Expertise: Provider of site assessments & environmental audits for undeveloped, industrial, commercial, & residential properties
Activities: Air quality sampling; Assisting in the development & implementation of remedial projects for contaminated sites; Asbestos & urea formaldehyde foam insulation removal; Chemical clean-up; Underground storage tank removal
Recently Completed / Ongoing Projects: Construction of biopile soil treatment facility, Greater Toronto Airports Authority; Excavation & treatment of contaminated soil in Greenwood, Nova Scotia, Federal Government
Financial Information:
Type of Ownership: Private
Domestic Markets:
Ontario

Canadian Branches:
Glen Cameron
81 Glen Cameron Rd.
Thornhill, ON L3T 1N8
905-881-1215

Datarite
30 Troop Ave.
Dartmouth, NS B3B 1Z1
902-468-2600
Fax: 902-468-8679
800-565-5922
dcoley@datarite.com
www.datarite.com
Firm Type: Distributing, Waste Management
Founded: 1983
Products/Services/Areas of Expertise: Provider of office supplies, business equipment, & technical services
Activities: Providing free empty cartridge pick-up; Offering the environmentally friendly Imagerite brand of copier, fax & printer ink, plus recycled & remanufactured imaging cartridges

Products & Services Buyer's Guide

Domestic Markets:
New Brunswick, Newfoundland & Labrador, Nova Scotia, Prince Edward Island
Canadian Branches:
Charlottetown
64 St. Peters Rd.
Charlottetown, PE C1A 5N8
902-892-5811
Fax: 902-566-4978
ltremere@datarite.com

Moncton
115 Harrisville Blvd.
Moncton, NB E1H 3T3
506-855-1852
Fax: 506-859-7904
rphillips@datarite.com

Saint John
1216 Sand Cove Rd.
Saint John, NB E2M 5V8
506-674-1121
Fax: 506-674-1435

St. John's
21 Mews Pl.
St. John's, NL A1B 4N2
709-722-3400
Fax: 709-576-6418
jmason@datarite.com

Daubois Inc.
6155, boul des Grandes-Prairies
Montréal, QC H1P 1A5
514-328-1253
Fax: 514-328-7694
800-561-2664
info@daubois.com
www.daubois.com
Firm Type: Distributing, Manufacturing
Founded: 1960
Products/Services/Areas of Expertise: Developer, manufacturer, & distributor of specialized mortars & pre-mixed concretes for the restoration of historic buildings & for the construction industry
Activities: Providing technical support, including worksite follow-up
Canadian Branches:
Toronto
1150 Caledonia Rd.
Toronto, ON M6A 2W5
416-787-4917
Fax: 416-787-7803
800-263-9408

Dave Vallieres & Associates Inc.
101 Columbus
Pointe-Claire, QC H9R 4K3
514-630-6848
Fax: 514-630-6322
info@davevallieres.com
www.davevallieres.com
Products/Services/Areas of Expertise: Water & wastewater management & equipment
Canadian Branches:
Loretteville
9200 rue Vérone
Québec, QC G2B 0N1
418-842-0119
Fax: 418-842-7416
Fernand Poirier

David A. McLean & Associates
#200, 330 Richmond St.
Chatham, ON N7M 1P7
519-351-8155
Fax: 519-351-8183
866-651-6711
dma@dmatechnical.com
www.dmatechnical.com
Firm Type: Management Consulting
Founded: 1991
Staff: 21
Products/Services/Areas of Expertise: Energy management, conservation & automated monitoring; environmental site assessment; occupational health & safety audits & training; mercury spill clean-up

Domestic Markets:
Ontario
Contact(s):
Dave McLean, President
Al Davidson, Partner

Davis Controls Ltd.
2200 Bristol Circle
Oakville, ON L6H 5R3
905-829-2000
Fax: 905-829-2630
800-701-7460
info@daviscontrols.com
www.daviscontrols.com
Firm Type: Distributing, Manufacturing
Founded: 1933
Quality Environmental Management System(s): 9001; ISO
Products/Services/Areas of Expertise: Manufacturer & distributor of the following types of instruments & controls: level measurement & contol gauges; flow measurement & control sensors & meters; pressure temperature & moisture controllers; & signal conditioning transmitters & alarms
Activities: Assisting the water & wastewater market by distributing instruments for the following purposes: energy & water quality monitoring; containment spills, toxic, combustible & oxygen gas detection; & water flow applications
Financial Information:
Type of Ownership: Private
Canadian Branches:
Calgary
Calgary, AB
403-255-5035
Fax: 403-255-5077
info@daviscontrols.com

London
London, ON
519-641-8953
Fax: 519-641-0081
info@daviscontrols.com

Montréal
#406, 6700, Côte de Liesse
Montréal, QC H4T 2B5
514-737-4817
Fax: 514-737-9948
infomtl@daviscontrols.com

New Glasgow
New Glasgow, NS
902-755-1831
Fax: 902-755-1832
info@daviscontrols.com

Québec
Québec, QC
418-564-5068
Fax: 514-737-9948
infomtl@daviscontrols.com

Vancouver
Vancouver, BC
604-298-9101
Fax: 604-298-9102
info@daviscontrols.com

Daybar Industries Ltd.
50 West Dr.
Brampton, ON L6T 2J4
905-625-8000
Fax: 905-625-4204
888-332-9227
sales@daybar.com
www.daybar.com
Firm Type: Manufacturing
Founded: 1964
Staff: 50
Member of: Door & Hardware Institute; Canadian Steel Door & Frame Manufactuters Association
Products/Services/Areas of Expertise: Commercial duty hollow metal steel doors & hollow metal steel door frames
Financial Information:
Type of Ownership: Private
Domestic Markets:
National
Foreign Activity:
Western Europe, USA
Contact(s):
Mark Dodson, Executive Vice President
Americo (Mike) Iannucci, Sales Manager
Christine Barrett, Administrator/ Account Representative

DB Geoservices Inc.
Formerly: Geoservices
18 Springdale Cres.
Ottawa, ON K2H 5T8
613-820-1439
Fax: 613-820-0832
don.ball@rogers.com
Firm Type: Management Consulting
Founded: 1998
Staff: 2
Member of: Project Management Institute; Geomatics Industry Association of Canada; Alliance for Marine Remote Sensing
Products/Services/Areas of Expertise: Project management services for environmentally related projects; Project Management training and mentoring
Recently Completed / Ongoing Projects: Study of User Needs for a new Satellite Imagery Product of entire Canadian Land Mass in the Sustainable Development Community; Strategic Plan for the Earth Observation Application Development Program of the Canadian Space Agency; Study of Commercialization Best Practices in the Public Sector and Not-for-profit Sector in Canada
Financial Information:
Type of Ownership: Private
Revenue: $250,000 - $500,000
Revenue Sources: 60% nationwide; 40% Private Contracts
Domestic Markets:
British Columbia, Nova Scotia, Ontario, Québec
Foreign Activity:
Asia, Western Europe
Contact(s):
Donald Ball, President

DBC Environmental Services Ltd.
P.O. Box 490
14855 Dafoe Rd.
Ingleside, ON K0C 1M0
613-537-2255
Fax: 613-537-8561
info@davidbrownconstruction.ca
www.davidbrownconstruction.ca
Firm Type: Scientific/Technical Services, Waste Management
Staff: 6
Products/Services/Areas of Expertise: Hazardous or non-hazardous, liquid or solid waste disposal; site decommissioning
Domestic Markets:
Ontario
Contact(s):
Gary MacLeod, General Manager

DBS Environmental
1430 - 33 St. North
Lethbridge, AB T1H 5H3
403-328-4833
Fax: 403-328-4729
888-328-4833
info@dbsenvironmental.com
dbsenvironmental.com
Firm Type: Waste Management
Founded: 1977
Staff: 3
Products/Services/Areas of Expertise: Licensed waste management facility; provides transportation of special wastes; mobile transfer site; waste broker & disposal consulting; emergency response services; floating oil skimmers for oil & chemical spills
Financial Information:
Revenue: $250,000 - $500,000
Contact(s):
Carole Neilsen, President

DCL International Inc.
P.O. Box 90
Concord, ON L4K 1B2
905-660-6450
Fax: 905-660-6435
800-872-1968
sales@dcl-inc.com
www.dcl-inc.com
Products/Services/Areas of Expertise: Specialize in the purification of engine emissions; manufacture exhaust conditioners: diesel particle filters, catalytic converters, silencers

& fume diluters designed to address the air quality problems caused by industrial vehicles & equipment
Foreign Activity:
Asia, Western Europe, South America,
Contact(s):
George Swiatek, President

Canadian Branches:
British Columbia Office
Industrial Catalyst Division
#3105 - 1288 W. Georgia St.
Vancouver, BC V6E 4R3
778-999-0883

DDH Environnement ltée
505, boul René-Lévesque ouest, 8e étage
Montréal, QC H2Z 1Y7
514-398-0544
Fax: 514-398-0545
info@ddh-env.com
www.ddh-env.com
Firm Type: Management Consulting, Waste Management
Founded: 1989
Staff: 20
Foreign Activity:
Africa, Central America, Western Europe, USA
Contact(s):
Jean Halde, Contact

DEB Canada
P.O. Box 730
42 Thompson Rd.
Waterford, ON N0E 1Y0
519-443-8697
Fax: 519-443-5160
800-567-1652
debcanada@debcanada.com
www.debcanada.com
Firm Type: Distributing, Manufacturing
Founded: 1964
Quality Environmental Management System(s): 9001
EcoLogo Certified Products & Services: Industrial Hand Cleaners, Sunflower heavy duty hand cleanser; Deb Naturelle Hair & Body Shampoo Product
Products/Services/Areas of Expertise: Development and manufacture of skin cleansers, protective & conditioning creams, showering, bathing products & dispensing systems for all occupational skin hygiene markets
Ecological Note: Industrial Hand Cleaners, Sunflower heavy duty hand cleanser; Deb Naturelle Hair & Body Shampoo Product
Contact(s):
Ashgar Ali
ali@debcanada.com
Marvin Mauer
marvin@debcanada.com

Decibel Consultants Inc.
#2500, 265, boul Hymus
Montréal, QC H9R 1G6
514-630-4855
Fax: 514-630-4595
800-363-4855
decibel@decibel-consultants.com
www.decibel-consultants.com
Firm Type: Engineering
Founded: 1986
Staff: 10
Member of: Canadian Acoustical Association; Vibration Institute; Institute of Noise Control Engineering
Products/Services/Areas of Expertise: Noise measurements; noise source identification; implementation of corrective measures
Recently Completed / Ongoing Projects: Noise forecast, windmill project, Matane; noise study & supply of four silencers, Alcan, Laterriere; noise reduction, Kimberly Clark
Financial Information:
Type of Ownership: Private
Revenue: $500,000 - $1.5 Million
Revenue Sources: 20% Municipals; 80% Private Contracts
Domestic Markets:
New Brunswick, Newfoundland & Labrador, Nova Scotia, Ontario, Prince Edward Island, Québec
Contact(s):
Gilles Leroux, President, Business Development
Serge Berube, Technical Specialist

Canadian Branches:
Acoustock Inc.
#2800, 265, boul Hymus
Pointe-Claire, QC H9R 1G6
514-630-7104
Fax: 514-630-8198
acoustc@ibm.net

Decommissioning Consulting Services Limited / DCS
#11, 121 Granton Dr.
Richmond Hill, ON L4B 3N4
905-882-5984
Fax: 905-882-8962
engineers@dcsltd.ca
www.dcsltd.ca
Firm Type: Engineering, Scientific/Technical Services
Founded: 1990
Staff: 45
Products/Services/Areas of Expertise: Phase I property & facility assessments; phase II & III site assessments; asbestos management programs; remedial options feasibility studies; risk assessment studies; site decommissioning & remediation design; plant deactivation & demolition design; waste management engineering; geotechnical engineering; industrial hygiene & air quality studies; water & wastewater management engineering; environmental project management services; environmental monitoring services
Financial Information:
Type of Ownership: Private
Revenue Sources: 20% nationwide; 10% Provincial; 30% Municipals; 40% Private Contracts
Domestic Markets:
British Columbia, Ontario
Foreign Activity:
Asia, South America, USA
Contact(s):
Richard B. German, P.Eng., Sr. Principal
John N. Hilton, M.A.Sc., O.Eng., President
Ted. Chart, P.Eng., Project Director

Dectron Internationale
4300, boul Poirier
Montréal, QC H4R 2C5
514-334-9609
Fax: 514-334-9184
info@dectron.com
www.dectron.com
Firm Type: Manufacturing
Founded: 1976
Staff: 102
Products/Services/Areas of Expertise: Manufactures dehumidification equipment; offers engineering expertise & quality products for applications requiring humidity control; for use in residential, industrial & commercial applications (indoor swimming pool areas, health spas, schools, community centres, hotels-motels, factories, ice rinks & any applications where humidity needs to be controlled); eliminates building damage & reduces operating & maintenance costs; provides a comfortable & healthy environment
Domestic Markets:
National
Foreign Activity:
Worldwide
Contact(s):
Aurelio Useche, Vice-President
Mauro Parissi, Chief Financial Officer

Dedicated Plastic Tanks Inc.
#5B, 5109 Harvester Rd.
Burlington, ON L7L 5Y9
905-333-8625
Fax: 905-333-8260
800-685-3174
tanksales@plastictanks.ca
www.plastictanks.ca
Firm Type: Distributing

Products/Services/Areas of Expertise: Distributor of plastic liquid storage tanks & liquid transfer products, such as closed top tanks, open top tanks, septic tanks, transport tanks, underground tanks, well manager tank systems, & intermediate bulk containers
Financial Information:
Type of Ownership: Private
Domestic Markets:
National

Degussa Canada Inc.
Also Known As: Evonik North America
235 Orenda Rd.
Brampton, ON L6T 1E6
905-451-3810
Fax: 905-451-4469
800-387-5680
www.degussa-nafta.com
Firm Type: Distributing, Manufacturing
Founded: 1979
Staff: 198
Quality Environmental Management System(s): 9001
Products/Services/Areas of Expertise: Manufactures & distributes hydrogen peroxide, which is used in the pulp & mining industries & for environmental applications
Financial Information:
Type of Ownership: Foreign-owned
Revenue Sources: 100% Private Contracts
Domestic Markets:
Alberta, British Columbia, New Brunswick, Ontario, Québec, Saskatchewan
Foreign Activity:
Mexico, USA, Worldwide
Contact(s):
Richard Boettcher, Manager, Operations
Contact(s):
Dieter Hollmann, Manager

Canadian Branches:
Burlington
P.O. Box 5057
3380 South Service Rd.
Burlington, ON L7N 3J5
905-336-3423
Fax: 905-332-5632
Gary Mitchell, Manager

Cadillac Terminal
33, rue Dumont
Cadillac, QC J0Y 1C0
819-759-4665
Fax: 819-759-4670
Benoit Pitre

Québec
#235, 325 du Marais
Québec, QC G1M 3R3
418-524-0606
Fax: 418-524-3211
Huguette Ferland

Gibbons
Plant
P.O. Box 1000
Hwy. 643 East
Gibbons, AB T0A 1N0
780-992-3300
Fax: 780-992-3380

Dekka Resins Inc.
P.O. Box 20004
55 Plant Farm Blvd.
Brantford, ON N3P 2A4
519-753-1888
Fax: 519-753-7678
sales@dekkaresins.com
www.dekkaresins.com
Firm Type: Distributing, Manufacturing
Founded: 1989
Staff: 100
Products/Services/Areas of Expertise: Plastics recycling; plastic raw material blending; custom sheet, custom sheet grinding, densifying
Financial Information:
Type of Ownership: Private
Revenue: Greater than $5 Million
Revenue Sources: 100% Private Contracts
Domestic Markets:
National
Foreign Activity:
Asia, Eastern Europe, Western Europe, The Middle East, South America, Mexico, USA
Contact(s):
Roy Keighley, General Manager
Martin Craig, Manager, Sales
Phil Hensen, Manager, Purchasing

Products & Services Buyer's Guide

International Branch(es):
Dekka Resins USA
501 Percision Dr.
Waco, TX USA
817-772-4000
Fax: 817-751-7599

DEL Warehousing Inc.
P.O. Box 119
413 Eldon Rd.
Little Britain, ON K0M 2C0
705-786-1572
Fax: 705-786-0471
Products/Services/Areas of Expertise: Provider of warehousing services

Del-Air Systems Ltd.
P.O. Box 2500
1704 - 4th Ave.
Humboldt, SK S0K 2A0
306-682-5011
Fax: 306-682-5559
800-667-1722
sales@del-air.com
www.del-air.com
Firm Type: Manufacturing
Founded: 1980
Staff: 60
Member of: Prairie Implement Manufacturers Association
Products/Services/Areas of Expertise: Product & technology for a complete environment control system for confinement barns; complete ventilation designs
Financial Information:
Revenue: Greater than $5 Million
Revenue Sources: 100% Private Contracts
Domestic Markets:
National
Foreign Activity:
Worldwide
Contact(s):
Robert Hawkins, President
Lloyd Crawford, General Manager
Eric von Doellen, Manager, Sales

Delcan Water
Formerly: Deleuw, Cather & Company of Canada Ltd.
#500, 625 Cochrane Dr.
Markham, ON L3R R9R
905-943-0500
Fax: 905-943-0400
info@delcan.com
www.delcan.com
Firm Type: Engineering
Founded: 1953
Products/Services/Areas of Expertise: Municipal & industrial wastewater collection & treatment; water treatment & supply; environmental audits & planning & environmental management systems including pollution prevention
Recently Completed / Ongoing Projects: Walkerton Inquiry Papers on Water Quality; R.O. Pickard Environmental Qtr. Screen & Degrit Bypass; San Salvador Airport WWTP, El Salvador; wastewater treatment plants in Venzuela
Financial Information:
Type of Ownership: Private
Domestic Markets:
National
Foreign Activity:
Central America, The Pacific Rim, South Africa, United Kingdom
Contact(s):
Jim Kerr, CEO
j.kerr@delcan.com
Jack Powers, CFO
finance@delcan.com
W. Victor Anderson, Executive Vice-President, Structures
structures@delcan.com
Douglas G. Langley, B.Sc., Executive Vice-President, Corporate Development
d.langley@delcan.com
Canadian Branches:
Hamilton
Hamilton Operations
#201, 154 Main St. East
Hamilton, ON L8N 1G9
905-525-2554
Fax: 905-525-5710
hamilton@delcan.com
Robert J. Bower, P.Eng., Manager

London
Water Division
1069 Wellington Rd. South
London, ON N6E 2H6
519-681-8771
Fax: 519-681-4995
london@delcan.com
Ken W. Hodges, P.Eng., Manager

Niagara Falls
Niagara Falls Operations
4056 Dorchester Rd.
Niagara Falls, ON L2E 6M9
905-356-7003
Fax: 905-356-7008
niagarafalls@delcan.com
Steve Brant, P.Eng., Manager

Ottawa
Water Division
#100, 1223 Michael St.
Ottawa, ON K1J 7T2
613-738-4160
Fax: 613-739-7105
ottawa@delcan.com
Greg Ashley, P.Eng., Manager

Vancouver
Water Division
#300, 604 Columbia St. West
New Westminster, BC V3M 1A6
604-525-9333
Fax: 604-525-9458
vancouver@delcan.com
Pram Kashyap, P.Eng., Manager

Victoria
Water Division
4082 Shelburne St.
Victoria, BC V8N 4P6
250-477-2206
Fax: 250-441-2207
victoria@delcan.com
Pram Kashyap, P.Eng., Manager

Dell Tech Laboratories Ltd.
UWO Research Park
#200, 100 Collip Circle
London, ON N6G 4X8
519-858-5021
Fax: 519-858-5026
trose@delltech.com
www.delltech.com
Firm Type: Scientific/Technical Services
Founded: 1980
Staff: 11
Member of: International Sanitary Supply Association; Canadian Sanitary Supply Association; Canadian Cosmetic, Toiletry & Fragrance Association; Canadian Consumer Specialty Products Association
Products/Services/Areas of Expertise: Contract laboratory services; Canadian chemical regulations; WHMIS, TDG product registration; new substances notification
Financial Information:
Type of Ownership: Private
Domestic Markets:
National
Foreign Activity:
Australia/New Zealand, Western Europe, USA,
Contact(s):
Stephen Chambers, President
schambers@delltech.com

Delta Aerial Surveys Ltd. / DAS
#2121, 11871 Horseshoe Way
Richmond, BC V7A 4V4
604-275-3505
Fax: 604-275-6685
mail@deltamap.com
www.deltamap.com
Firm Type: Scientific/Technical Services
Founded: 1979
Staff: 7
Member of: Canadian Institute of Geomatics; Urban & Regional Information Systems Association
Products/Services/Areas of Expertise: GIS, mapping, remote sensing & image analysis, aerial photography; orthophotos

Financial Information:
Type of Ownership: Private
Revenue: $500,000 - $1.5 Million
Revenue Sources: 40% Provincial; 30% Municipals; 30% Private Contracts
Domestic Markets:
Alberta, British Columbia, Newfoundland & Labrador, Northwest Territories, Ontario, Yukon Territory
Foreign Activity:
USA
Contact(s):
Ken Douglas, President

Delta Piping Products Canada Inc. / DPPI
Also Known As: Delta Pipe
#3, 2020 Wentworth St. West
Whitby, ON L1N 9A8
905-433-8918
Fax: 905-433-1958
Brian.Thomas@deltapipingproducts.ca
www.deltapipingproducts.ca
Firm Type: Distributing
Founded: 1980
Products/Services/Areas of Expertise: Canadian distributor for Perma-Pipe Inc. & Advance Products & Systems, Inc.; Products include pre-insulated piping systems, moulded rubber pipe, wall sleeves, wall mechanical seals, end seals, isolation flange gasket kits, flange protectors, Radolid protection caps, & safety spray shields; Clients include governmental agencies, institutions, industrial chemical & petroleum producers, & heating & cooling companies
Activities: Offering front end design assistance, such as the provision of thermal heat loss data; Providing field technical assistance for pre-insulated piping products; Offering inspection services of buried insulated piping runs
Financial Information:
Type of Ownership: Private
Domestic Markets:
National
Contact(s):
Brian Thomas, President
Ian Thomas, Manager, Marketing
Canadian Branches:
Ottawa
Ottawa, ON
613-337-5300
Fax: 613-337-5530
Ian.Thomas@deltapipingproducts.ca

Demers MetalFab Inc.
Formerly: Demers Maier Metfab Inc.
4632 - 1 St. SE
Calgary, AB T2G 2L3
403-777-1060
Fax: 403-243-7106
demers3@telus.net
www.demersmetalfab.com
Firm Type: Waste Management
Staff: 16
Products/Services/Areas of Expertise: Hazardous materials storage shelters
Contact(s):
Lloyd Ross, President

Demesa Inc.
458 Morden Rd.
Oakville, ON L6K 3W4
905-842-6985
Fax: 905-842-0226
info@demesa.ca
www.demesa.ca
Firm Type: Distributing
Founded: 2001
Products/Services/Areas of Expertise: Distributor of instruments, such as photo-ionization detectors, gas detection instruments, air sampling equipment, water quality monitors, landfill monitors, & industrial hygiene equipment; Clients include industrial & environmental industries
Activities: Offering training, repair service, & calibration services

Demilec Inc.
870, Curé Boivin
Boisbriand, QC J7G 2A7
450-437-0123
Fax: 450-437-2338
866-437-0223

demilec@demilec.com
www.demilec.com
Firm Type: Manufacturing
Founded: 1983
Staff: 35
EcoLogo Certified Products & Services: Sealection 500 thermal insulation
Products/Services/Areas of Expertise: Polyurethane system's house; rigid, flexible & integral skin foam, coatings, adhesives, flagstones, binders & sealants; company has 9 foreign offices,
Ecological Note: Sealection 500 thermal insulation
Financial Information:
Type of Ownership: Private
Revenue Sources: 5% nationwide; 5% Provincial; 5% Municipals; 85% Private Contracts
Domestic Markets:
Alberta, British Columbia, Manitoba, New Brunswick, Northwest Territories, Ontario, Québec, Saskatchewan, Yukon Territory
Foreign Activity:
Mexico, USA, Former USSR
Contact(s):
Jacques Larivière, President
François Lalande, Marketing Specialist
Serge Pomerleau, Sales Director
Mario Charlebois, Technical Director

Dendron Resource Surveys Inc.
#G2, 880 Lady Ellen Place
Ottawa, ON K1Z 5L9
613-725-2971
Fax: 613-725-1716
info@dendron.com
www.dendron.com
Firm Type: Scientific/Technical Services
Founded: 1978
Staff: 20
Member of: Geomatics Industry Association of Canada
Products/Services/Areas of Expertise: Collection, manipulation & analysis of data for natural resource management & appraisal; aerial photography interpretation; remote sensing technologies; GIS; simulation models
Recently Completed / Ongoing Projects: Mapping damage/flood caused by hurricane Mitch in Honduras; forest mapping in Eastern US; applying airborne lasers for precise topographic mapping
Financial Information:
Type of Ownership: Private
Revenue: $1.5 Million - $3 Million
Revenue Sources: 30% nationwide; 35% Provincial; 2% Municipals; 33% Private Contracts
Domestic Markets:
National
Foreign Activity:
Central America, South America, USA
Contact(s):
Udo Nielsen, President
Andy Welch, Marketing Manager

Denoco Energy Systems Ltd.
2 Victoria Ave.
Smiths Falls, ON K7A 2P1
613-283-0574
Fax: 613-283-3593
dennis@denoco.com
www.denoco.com
Firm Type: Engineering, Scientific/Technical Services
Founded: 1982
Products/Services/Areas of Expertise: Design, contracting & installation of ground & water source heat pumps
Contact(s):
Dennis O'Connor, President

Denso North America Inc.
#12, 90 Ironside Cres.
Toronto, ON M1X 1M3
416-291-3435
Fax: 416-291-0898
sales@densona.com
www.densona.com
Firm Type: Distributing
Founded: 1985
Staff: 16
Products/Services/Areas of Expertise: Anti-corrosion coatings
Financial Information:
Type of Ownership: Private
Domestic Markets:
National
Foreign Activity:
Mexico, USA
Contact(s):
Andrew Clark, Sales Coordinator
Joel Pepin, General Manager
Canadian Branches:
Edmonton
12210, 45 St.
Edmonton, AB T5W 2V3
780-449-4060
Fax: 780-449-5300
jaru@densona.com
International Branch(es):
Houston
9747 Whithorn Drive
Houston, TX USA
281-821-3355
Fax: 281-821-0304
info@densona.com

Department of Justice
P.O. Box 1320
Yellowknife, NT X1A 2L9
867-920-6418
communications_advisor@gov.nt.ca
www.justice.gov.nt.ca/legislation/searchleg&reg.htm
Products/Services/Areas of Expertise: Consolidations of Statutes and Regulations can be viewed in either PDF or WordPerfect

Department of Justice Canada
Communications Branch
Consolidated Statutes and Regulations
Legislative Services Branch
284 Wellington St., SAT-4
Ottawa, ON K1A 0H8
613-957-4222
Fax: 613-954-0811
webadmin@justice.gc.ca
http://laws.justice.gc.ca/en/contact/contact_laws.html
Products/Services/Areas of Expertise: The documents comprising the Consolidated Statutes & Regulations are reproduced in HTML only & are not available in PDF. Documents can be reproduced in accordance with the Reproduction of Federal Law Order, see:
laws.justice.gc.ca/en/otherreg/SI-97-5/index.html. For federal statutes & regulations see: laws.justice.gc.ca/

Dependable Turbines Ltd. / DTL
17930 Roan Pl.
Surrey, BC V3S 5K1
604-576-3175
Fax: 604-576-3183
sales@dtlhydro.com
www.dtlhydro.com
Firm Type: Engineering, Manufacturing, Scientific/Technical Services
Founded: 1978
Products/Services/Areas of Expertise: Designer & manufacturer of hydro-electric turbines
Activities: Site assessments; After sales service; Refurbishing Turbines
Recently Completed / Ongoing Projects: Klemtu Reserve, British Columbia; Tunnel Hill, California; Tapjeong & Cheongcheon, Korea
Domestic Markets:
National
Foreign Activity:
Africa, Asia, South America, USA

Deschênes Drilling Ltd.
Les Forages Deschênes Ltée
245, Mgr-Martin West
Saint-Quentin, NB E8A 2E6
506-235-2829
Fax: 506-235-2670
rogerdescdril@nb.aibn.com
deschenesdrilling.com
Firm Type: Distributing
Founded: 1965
Staff: 14
Member of: New Brunswick Water Well Association; Canadian Water Well Association
Products/Services/Areas of Expertise: Water well drilling; submersible pump installation; environmental drilling; P.U.C. & stainless steel screens, environmental products
Financial Information:
Type of Ownership: Private
Domestic Markets:
New Brunswick, Nova Scotia, Prince Edward Island, Québec,
Contact(s):
Gilles Deschênes, President
Roger Roy, Controller
Canadian Branches:
Bathurst
P.O. Box 146
Pointe-Verte, NB E0B 2H0
506-783-8256
Alphé Valcourt, Sales Representative

Deschênes et Fils Ltée.
#100, 3901, rue Jarry est
Montréal, QC H1Z 2G1
514-374-3110
Fax: 514-374-5141
800-361-1784
ventes@deschenes.ca
www.deschenes.ca
Products/Services/Areas of Expertise: Distributor of plumbing & heating materials, as well as fire protection equipment; Products include pumps, piping & fittings, water heaters, plumbing fixtures, & fire extinguishers
Canadian Branches:
Joliette
230, boul de l'Industrie
Joliette, QC J6E 8V1
450-759-8880
Fax: 450-759-8033
1-877-759-5565

Laval
3155, boul Industriel
Laval, QC H7L 4P8
450-629-3939
Fax: 450-629-4580

Montréal - Plateau
5, rue Plateau
Montréal, QC H9R 5W1
514-630-6330
Fax: 514-630-3627
1-800-298-6330

Montréal - Saint-Michel
Salle d'exposition
8335, boul Saint-Michel
Montréal, QC H1Z 3E6
514-374-3110
Fax: 514-374-5141
1-800-361-1784

Montréal - St-Patrick
2020, rue St-Patrick
Montréal, QC H3K 1A9
514-932-3191
Fax: 514-933-4198

Saint-Hubert
4545, boul Sir Wilfrid Laurier
Saint-Hubert, QC J3Y 3X3
450-656-2223
Fax: 450-656-6213
1-800-361-3619

Saint-Hyacinthe
6400, av Choquette
Saint-Hyacinthe, QC J2S 8L1
450-773-4450
Fax: 450-773-0339
1-800-263-6032

Saint-Jérôme
600, rue Prince
Saint-Jérôme, QC J7Y 4E3
450-432-5550
Fax: 450-432-9990
1-877-432-5550

Sherbrooke
2325, rue Hertel
Sherbrooke, QC J1J 2J1
819-823-1000
Fax: 819-823-6991
1-800-567-3551

Products & Services Buyer's Guide

Montréal - Acadie
Doraco-Noiseux
9150, boul, de l'Acadie
Montréal, QC H4N 2T2
514-385-1212
Fax: 514-385-6262
acadie@doraco-noiseux.com

Montréal - Bélanger
Doraco-Noiseux
1452, rue Bélanger
Montréal, QC H2G 1A7
514-729-1821
Fax: 514-729-2941
belanger@doraco-noiseux.com

Montréal - Jarry est
Industries C.F.H.
#100, 3901, rue Jarry est
Montréal, QC H1Z 2G1
514-374-3110
Fax: 514-374-5141
1-800-361-1784
Products/Services/Areas of Expertise: Distributor of fire prevention equipment

Dessau, Inc.
Formerly: Dessau-Soprin
#300, 1200, boul St-Martin ouest
Laval, QC H7S 2E4
514-281-1010
Fax: 450-668-8232
laval@dessausoprin.com
www.dessausoprin.com
Firm Type: Management Consulting, Engineering
Founded: 1957
Staff: 4000
Member of: Water Environment Federation; Association québécoise des techniques de l'eau; Association des conseillers en environnement du Québec
Member of: Canadian Consulting Engineer; Professional Engineers of Ontario
Quality Environmental Management System(s): 9001; ISO
Products/Services/Areas of Expertise: Firm provides multidisciplinary services in engineering, environmental & construction management, with specialities in: energy, telecom, transportation, environment, geotechnique, materials & quality, building engineering, management & construction, urban development, program management, geology & mining engineering; services offered: studies for opportunity, investment & feasibility; market & utility rate analyses; economic, financial & cost; structural rehabilitation & restoration; preliminary & final design; geotechnical; digital modelling analyses; construction supervision & commissioning of facilities, construction management, project management, quality assurance, training & transfer of technology, laboratory inspection, testing & analyses of materials, legal & investigative expertise services, turnkey projects, Build-Own-Transfer (BOT) & Build-Own-Operate-Transfer (BOOT) projects
Recently Completed / Ongoing Projects: Lapinière wastewater treatment plant, Laval, QC; Waste management project, Burkina Faso, Africa; Environmental action program, Jamaica; Characterization & rehabilitation program, ESSO; Environmental impact studies, roads, powerlines, dams, etc.
Financial Information:
Type of Ownership: Private
Revenue: Greater than $5 Million
Revenue Sources: 7% nationwide; 25% Provincial; 31% Municipals; 37% Private Contracts
Domestic Markets:
Newfoundland & Labrador, Ontario, Québec
Foreign Activity:
Africa, Caribbean, China, Vietnam, Worldwide
Contact(s):
Jean-Pierre Sauriol, P.Eng., President
Denis Guindon, Vice-President, Sales & Marketing
Martin Laroche, Vice-President

Canadian Branches:
Gatineau
#110, 885, boul de la Carrière
Gatineau, QC J8Y 6S6
819-778-3143
Fax: 819-770-1373
lab.gatineau@dessausoprin.com

Laval
#300, 1200, St-Martin ouest
Laval, QC H7S 2E4
514-281-1010
laval@dessausoprin.com

Longueuil
#300, 375, boul Roland-Therrien
Longueuil, QC J4H 4A6
514-281-1010
longueuil@dessausoprin.com

Longueuil
883, rue Bériault
Longueuil, QC J4G 1X7
514-281-5151
fondatec@dessausoprin.com

Montréal
#600, 1060, University
Montréal, QC H3B 4V3
514-281-1010
Fax: 514-281-1060
enviro@dessausoprin.com

Québec
#300, 1220, boul Lebourgneuf
Québec, QC G2K 2G4
418-626-1688
Fax: 418-626-5464
quebec@dessausoprin.com

Rouyn-Noranda
#101, 405, rue Murdoch
Rouyn-Noranda, QC J9X 1G7
819-764-9508
Fax: 819-764-4431
rouyn@dessausoprin.com

Rouyn-Noranda
P.O. Box 638
768, rue Lord
Rouyn-Noranda, QC J9X 5C6
819-762-5119
Fax: 819-762-6253
lvmrouyn@sympatico.ca

Sorel-Tracy
#100, 148, rue George
Sorel-Tracy, QC J3P 1C6
514-746-1200
Fax: 514-746-1201
monteregie@dessausoprin.com

St-Jérôme
#900, 16, boul J.-F. Kennedy
Saint-Jérôme, QC J7Y 4B6
450-432-3436
Fax: 450-432-8598
fondatec2@dessausoprin.com

St-Romuald
#210, 1112, boul de la Rive-Sud
Saint-Romuald, QC G6W 5M6
418-839-6447
Fax: 418-839-1419
sromuald@dessausoprin.com

Val-d'Or
1032, 3e av ouest
Val-d'Or, QC J9P 1T6
819-825-1353
Fax: 819-825-1130
val-dor@dessausoprin.com

International Branch(es):
Algeria
28B Said Hamdine, Hydra 16035
Alger Algeria
-213-21-54-93-64
Fax: -213-21-54-93-6

Chile
Providencia 2237
Santiago Chile
-56-2-335-8090
Fax: -56-2-335-8091

Dominican Republic
Abraham Lincoln esq. José a Soler, Edifi
Progressus Local 4D 40 Piso
Santo Domingo Dominica

809-563-1409
Fax: 809-565-5484

Venezuela
Ave. Intercomunal Andrés Bello, Sector L
Centro Comercial CMT, Planta Baja, Local 24, Lecher
Estado Anzoategui Venezuel
-58-281-286-2132
Fax: -58-281-286-694

Deuce Disposal Ltd.
P.O. Box 362
240 Balsam Rd. NE
Slave Lake, AB T0G 2A0
780-849-3334
Fax: 780-849-3266
Products/Services/Areas of Expertise: Collector of residential waste, recyclables, & organics; Manager of a recycling depot; Supplier of portable toilets & sewage systems to the oil industry
Domestic Markets:
Alberta

Canadian Branches:
High Prairie
General Delivery
High Prairie, AB T0G 1E0
888-849-3125

Red Earth Creek
General Delivery
Red Earth Creek, AB T0G 1X0
888-849-3125

Dewar Insulations Ltd.
#13, 1815 Ironstone Manor
Pickering, ON L1W 3W9
905-831-7729
Fax: 905-831-1656
info@dewargroup.com
www.dewargroup.ca
Firm Type: Engineering, Scientific/Technical Services
Founded: 1957
Staff: 20
Member of: Ontario Asbestos Removal Contractors Association
Products/Services/Areas of Expertise: Asbestos removal; consultation & retrofit of industrial & commercial insulation
Financial Information:
Type of Ownership: Private
Contact(s):
Scott Dewar, President
Bob Young, Estimator

Dewar Pacific Projects Ltd.
11580 Mitchell Rd.
Port Coquitlam, BC V3B 1A5
604-945-7791
Fax: 604-945-7721
dewarpacific@telus.net
Firm Type: Scientific/Technical Services, Waste Management
Founded: 1957
Staff: 15
Member of: Canadian Environment Industry Association
Products/Services/Areas of Expertise: Services include asbestos abatement & removal, storage tank removal, decommissioning & remediation services, & demolition projects
Financial Information:
Type of Ownership: Private
Domestic Markets:
British Columbia
Contact(s):
R.M. Butler, President

DGH Engineering
12 Aviation Blvd.
St. Andrews, MB R1A 3N5
204-334-8846
Fax: 204-334-8846
dgh@dghengineering.com
www.dghengineering.com
Firm Type: Engineering
Founded: 1989
Staff: 21
Products/Services/Areas of Expertise: Engineering services for the agriculture sector; mechanical control systems; structural designs; pollution control systems; waste and wastewater handling
Domestic Markets:
Manitoba
Contact(s):

Dennis Hodgkinson, President

DGM Inc.
Formerly: Gestion LV
751 Marion St.
Joliette, QC J6E 8S3
450-752-1152
Fax: 450-752-1162
800-299-8986
gestlv@bellnet.ca
www.gestlv.com
Firm Type: Manufacturing
Founded: 1988
Products/Services/Areas of Expertise: Reconditioning service for mechanical seals on pumps in wastewater treatment plants; sale & fabrication on new mechanical seals, including tungsten carbide & silicon carbide
Financial Information:
Type of Ownership: Private
Domestic Markets:
National
Contact(s):
Jean-Paul Vigneault, Mechanical Seal Consultant

Diacon Technologies Ltd.
#135, 11960 Hammersmith Way
Richmond, BC V7A 5C9
604-271-8855
Fax: 604-271-4266
888-290-2299
cservice@dicon.com
www.diacon.com
Firm Type: Distributing, Manufacturing
Staff: 13
Products/Services/Areas of Expertise: Water & wastewater management equipment; water treatment chemicals; wood treatment chemicals; chemical production
Contact(s):
Konrad R. Tittler, President

Diagnostic Engineering Inc.
#111, 616 - 71 Ave. SE
Calgary, AB T2H 2R1
403-253-4856
Fax: 403-253-4873
info@diagnosticgroup.ca
www.diagnosticgroup.ca
Firm Type: Distributing, Engineering, Scientific/Technical Services
Founded: 1989
Staff: 10
Member of: Association of Professional Engineers; Geologists & Geophysicists of Alberta
Products/Services/Areas of Expertise: Ambient air monitoring & emissions diagnostics; urban areas monitoring & assessment; indoor air quality assessment; air quality monitoring, dispersion modeling; odour control engineering; odour reduction & elimination; air monitoring & meteorological monitoring instruments; equipment & custom built monitoring stations & trailers; urban area monitoring mini stations; diagnostic air patrol
Recently Completed / Ongoing Projects: Mobile air monitoring for sour wells drilling & completion operations, gas plants & odour assessment; meteorological monitoring for oil & gas industry; stand alone SO2 & H2S monitoring networks for gas flare impact assessment; indoor air quality assessments including extensive mould assessments
Financial Information:
Type of Ownership: Private
Revenue: $500,000 - $1.5 Million
Revenue Sources: 5% Municipals; 95% Private Contracts
Domestic Markets:
Alberta, British Columbia, Saskatchewan
Foreign Activity:
USA
Contact(s):
Thomas Vyskocil, P.Eng., President
thomasv@diagnosticgroup.ca
Patrick Roelofsen, Vice-President

Diagnostix Ltd.
#5, 2845 Argentia Rd.
Mississauga, ON L5N 8G6
905-286-4290
Fax: 905-286-5260
800-282-4075
customerservice@diagnostix.ca
www.diagnostix.ca
Firm Type: Distributing
Founded: 1989
Staff: 9
Products/Services/Areas of Expertise: Immunoassay diagnostic kits for PCBs, PCPs, BTX, TPH & PAH, 15 different pesticides & herbicides, mycotoxins, bacteria, antibiotics, steroids, vitamins, therapeutic drugs & drugs of abuse; solid phase extraction columns for environmental analysis
Financial Information:
Type of Ownership: Private
Domestic Markets:
National
Foreign Activity:
Asia
Contact(s):
Howard Lee, President
Bob Robertson, Vice-President

Diane Beckett
353 Chapel St.
Ottawa, ON K1N 7Z5
613-231-6274
Firm Type: Management Consulting
Founded: 1987
Staff: 1
Products/Services/Areas of Expertise: Environment & development planning & management including policy analysis; institutional strengthening; project identification; monitoring & evaluation; social/environmental impact assessments; program/project management
Financial Information:
Type of Ownership: Private
Domestic Markets:
National
Foreign Activity:
Africa, Asia, South America
Contact(s):
Diane Beckett, President/CEO

Digicon Building Control Solutions
#11, 201 Brownlow Ave.
Dartmouth, NS B3B 1W2
902-468-2633
Fax: 902-468-5187
sales@digiconcontrols.com
www.digiconcontrols.com
Firm Type: Scientific/Technical Services
Founded: 1990
Staff: 9
Products/Services/Areas of Expertise: Building automation; energy conservation; air quality; plant management; lighting & security systems
Domestic Markets:
New Brunswick, Nova Scotia, Prince Edward Island
Contact(s):
Les Beal, Contact

Digital Land Resources
103 Main Terrace
Sherwood Park, AB T8A 0R7
780-975-9407
Fax: 780-464-2287
Products/Services/Areas of Expertise: A geomatics firm

Dillon Consulting Ltd.
Dillon Groupe Conseil Limitée
Formerly: M.M. Dillon Ltd.
#800, 235 Yorkland Blvd.
Toronto, ON M2J 4Y8
416-229-4646
Fax: 416-229-4692
www.dillon.ca
Firm Type: Management Consulting, Engineering, Scientific/Technical Services
Founded: 1946
Staff: 600
Products/Services/Areas of Expertise: Provider of consulting services related to environmental sciences, planning, engineering, & management; Specific areas of practice include natural environment management, environment, health, & safety, waste management & remediation design, water & wastewater systems design, municipal engineering, transportation engineering & systems planning, building & facilities design, & water resources; Clients include goverments, industries, resource organizations, & real estate businesses
Financial Information:
Type of Ownership: Private
Domestic Markets:
National
Foreign Activity:
Africa, Asia, Caribbean, Central America, Central Europe, Eastern Europe, Western Europe, South America
Contact(s):
Jim Balfour, President
Allan Mitchell, Chief Financial Officer
Paul Acquaah, Manager, Toronto Office
pacquaah@dillon.ca

Canadian Branches:
Brossard
Édifice E
#200, 7900, boul Taschereau ouest
Brossard, QC J4X 1C2
450-465-0404
Fax: 450-465-3232
Claude David, Manager, Montréal Office
cdavid@dillon.ca

Calgary
#200, 334 - 11th Ave. SE
Calgary, AB T2G 0Y2
403-215-8880
Fax: 403-215-8889
Dave Poole, Manager, Calgary Office

Cambridge
#1, 5 Cherry Blossom Rd.
Cambridge, ON N3H 4R7
519-650-9833
Fax: 519-650-7424
Tom Jones, Manager, Cambridge Office
tjones@dillon.ca

Chatham
202 King St. West
Chatham, ON N7M 1E5
519-354-7802
Fax: 519-354-2050
Larry Oulds, Manager, Chatham Office
loulds@dillon.ca

Fredericton
#200, 1149 Smythe St.
Fredericton, NB E3B 3H4
506-444-8820
Fax: 506-444-8821
Jeff Braun, Manager, Fredericton Office
JBraun@dillon.ca

Gloucester
#200, 5335 Canotek Rd.
Gloucester, ON K1J 9L4
613-745-2213
Fax: 613-745-3491
Robert Vastag, Manager, Gloucester Office
rvastag@dillon.ca

Halifax
#100, 137 Chain Lake Dr.
Halifax, NS B3S 1B3
902-450-4000
Fax: 902-450-2008
Mick Williams, Manager, Halifax Office
mwilliams@dillon.ca

London
#1400, 130 Dufferin Ave.
London, ON N6A 5R2
519-438-6192
Fax: 519-672-8209
Rob Kell, Manager, London Office
RKell@dillon.ca

Nelson
812 Vernon St.
Nelson, BC V1L 4G4
250-505-5470
Fax: 250-505-5472
Julia Roberts, Manager, Nelson Office
jroberts@dillon.ca

Oakville
#14, 1155 North Service Rd. West
Oakville, ON L6M 3E3
905-901-2912
Fax: 905-901-2918
Mark Brobbel, Manager, Oakville Office
mbrobbel@dillon.ca

Products & Services Buyer's Guide

Richmond
#130, 10691 Shellbridge Way
Richmond, BC V6X 2W8
604-278-7847
Fax: 604-278-7894
Richard Pope, Manager, Richmond Office
rpope@dillon.ca

Saint John
Bldg. C, Hilyard Place
#201C, 600 Main St.
Saint John, NB E2K 1J5
506-633-5000
Fax: 506-633-5110
David Creber, Manager, Saint John Office
dcreber@dillon.ca

St Catharines
#1, 235 Martindale Rd.
St Catharines, ON L2W 1A5
905-685-0293
Fax: 905-685-3952
Mark Brobbel, Manager, St Catharines Office, 905-901-2912Fax: 905-901-2918
mbrobbel@dillon.ca

Sydney
275 Charlotte St.
Sydney, NS B1P 1C6
902-562-9880
Fax: 902-562-9890
Mary White, Manager, Sydney Office
mwhite@dillon.ca

Windsor
#608, 3200 Deziel Dr.
Windsor, ON N8W 5K8
519-948-5000
Fax: 519-948-5054
Shannon Belleau, Manager, Windsor Office
sbelleau@dillon.ca

Winnipeg
#200, 895 Waverley St.
Winnipeg, MB R3T 5P4
204-453-2301
Fax: 204-452-4412
Founded: 1964
Ray Carter, Manager, Winnipeg Office
RCarter@dillon.ca

Yellowknife
P.O. Box 1409
#303, 4920 - 47 St.
Yellowknife, NT X1A 2P1
867-920-4555
Fax: 867-873-3328
Brad Mueller, Manager, Yellowknife Office
bmueller@dillon.ca

Dimplex North America
Formerly: Chromolox
1367 Industrial Rd.
Cambridge, ON N1R 7G8
519-650-3630
Fax: 519-650-3651
800-668-6663
www.dimplex.com
Firm Type: Manufacturing
Staff: 250
Products/Services/Areas of Expertise: Manufactures electric heating products & electric fireplace inserts
Domestic Markets:
National
Foreign Activity:
USA
Contact(s):
Martyn Champ, President
Judy Tutkaluk, Marketing Executive

DINOFLEX Manufacturing Ltd.
P.O. Box 3309
5590 - 46 Ave. SE
Salmon Arm, BC V1E 4S1
250-832-7780
Fax: 250-832-7788
877-713-1899
sales@dinoflex.com
www.dinoflex.com
Firm Type: Manufacturing
Founded: 1989
Staff: 30
Products/Services/Areas of Expertise: Waste tire rubber into rubber tile flooring; rubber pavers; playground surfacing; wheel chocks; weed guards for trees & posts
Domestic Markets:
National
Foreign Activity:
Asia, Central America, Central Europe, Mexico, USA
Contact(s):
Sabine Presch, President

Dionex Canada Limited
#204, 1540 Cornwall Rd.
Oakville, ON L6J 7W5
905-844-9650
Fax: 905-844-6134
www.dionex.com
Domestic Markets:
National
Foreign Activity:
Worldwide

Direct Separation Solutions
24 Thirty Sixth St.
Toronto, ON M8W 3K9
647-343-6595
Fax: 647-345-6543
info@directseparation.ca
www.directseparation.ca
Firm Type: Distributing

Products/Services/Areas of Expertise: Provides a complete selection of environmentally friendly, affordable and time-tested Oil/Water separation products for all applications
Financial Information:
Type of Ownership: Private
Domestic Markets:
National
Contact(s):
Brent Cotter, Sales and Marketing Manager
brent@directseparation.ca

Diversified Waste Solutions
#406, 1 Eva Rd.
Toronto, ON M9C 4Z5
416-621-1779
Fax: 416-622-4130
Products/Services/Areas of Expertise: Sorbent products; spill response kit; containment & extraction system dikes; plugs & covers; safety supplies, training & consulting
Domestic Markets:
National
Contact(s):
Don Wright, Marketing

Divex Marine
#102, 525, rue Savard
Saint-Bruno, QC J3V 6C1
450-441-2974
Fax: 450-441-3791
877-441-7676
divex@divexmarine.com
www.divexmarine.com
Firm Type: Scientific/Technical Services
Founded: 1963
Quality Environmental Management System(s): 9002
Products/Services/Areas of Expertise: Construction & excavation services; underwater works
Domestic Markets:
National
Contact(s):
Michel Bies, Contact

DJA Environmental Consultants Inc.
Also Known As: DJA
#5, 5100 South Service Rd.
Burlington, ON L7L 6A5
905-681-6899
Fax: 905-681-6855
888-681-6899
dja@djaenv.com
www.djaenv.com
Firm Type: Management Consulting, Engineering
Founded: 1995
Quality Environmental Management System(s): 14001
Products/Services/Areas of Expertise: Environmental & consulting firm
Activities: Designing & installing engineered pollution control systems; Wastewater treatment & permitting; Hazardous waste management; Environmental audits & assessments; Acoustic assessments; Site investigation & remediation; Environmental compliance
Financial Information:
Type of Ownership: Private
Domestic Markets:
National,

dmg world media (Canada) Inc.
#302, 1333 - 8 St. SW
Calgary, AB T2R 1M6
403-209-3555
Fax: 403-245-8649
888-799-2545
wesscott@ca.dmgworldmedia.com
www.dmgworldmedia.com
Firm Type: Management Consulting
Founded: 1989
Staff: 10
Products/Services/Areas of Expertise: International exhibition & publishing company, producing more than 300 market-leading trade exhibitions, consumer shows & fairs; produces 45 related trade & consumer magazines, newspapers, directories & market reports; more than 30 offices worldwide; 9 business groups: Consumer Events, North America, Consumer, UK, Art & Antiquities, Technology, Gift, Business Media International, Surg, Australasia, Dubai
Recently Completed / Ongoing Projects: Responsible for the organization of the Fort McMurray Oil Sands Tradeshow & Conference, Global Petroleum Show, Go-Expo: Gas & Oil Expo, Offshore Newfoundland Petroleum Show; International Pipeline Exposition
Domestic Markets:
National
Foreign Activity:
Worldwide
Contact(s):
Pat Atkinson, Operations Manager
Wes Scott, Group Sales Manager
Paula Arnold, Marketing Manager

Doherty's Hydraulic Oil Recycling
5951 - 92 St. NW
Edmonton, AB T6E 3A5
780-435-0134
Fax: 780-437-6445
Products/Services/Areas of Expertise: Provider of oil waste recycling services

Dol Hydroseeding Inc.
RR#4
Cookstown, ON L0L 1L0
705-458-4353
Fax: 705-458-1047
800-661-7078
info@dolhydroseeding.com
www.dolhydroseeding.com
Firm Type: Manufacturing
Staff: 15
Products/Services/Areas of Expertise: Hydroseeding & sodding; contractors specializing in erosion control & revegetation
Domestic Markets:
Ontario, Québec
Foreign Activity:
USA
Contact(s):
Joe Dol, President
Peter Davy, Administrative Manager
Roger Dol, Seeding Manager

Domaine Label & Trim Inc.
Étiquettes & Accessoires Domaine
1130, rue Beaulac
Montréal, QC H4R 1R7
514-633-5686
Fax: 514-908-5687
info@domainelabel.com
www.domainelabel.com
Products/Services/Areas of Expertise: Distributor of identification & decorative products; Products include woven labels, rubber patches, heat transfers, zipper pulls, & plastic relief patches; Clients include the clothing & footwear industries

Contact(s):
Rosie Palermo, Contact
rosie@domainelabel.com

Dominion Recycling Ltd.
P.O. Box 1143
St. John's, NL A1C 5M5
709-753-6158
Fax: 709-753-6136
domrec@nf.aibn.com
Firm Type: Waste Management
Founded: 1992
Staff: 6
Products/Services/Areas of Expertise: Recycling of non-ferrous metals
Domestic Markets:
National
Contact(s):
Derm Power, President

Domtar Inc.
CP 7210 A
395, boul de Maisonneuve ouest
Montréal, QC H3A 1L6
514-848-5400
Fax: 514-848-6850
information@domtar.com
www.domtar.com
Firm Type: Engineering, Manufacturing, Scientific/Technical Services
Staff: 7000
EcoLogo Certified Products & Services: Recycled fine papers: Encore Kraft Envelope; Naturals Text & Cover; Recycled File Folders; Sandpiper Text, Cover & Writing
Products/Services/Areas of Expertise: Environmental analysis & treatment; paper producer specializing in recycled writing & printing papers; 12 paper mills & 4 pulp mills across North America
Ecological Note: Recycled fine papers: Encore Kraft Envelope; Naturals Text & Cover; Recycled File Folders; Sandpiper Text, Cover & Writing
Financial Information:
Type of Ownership: Publicly Traded
Domestic Markets:
National
Foreign Activity:
USA

Donalco Inc.
#10, 20 Melford Dr.
Toronto, ON M1B 2X6
416-292-7118
Fax: 416-292-5745
877-726-6920
donalcotoronto@donalco.com
www.donalco.com
Products/Services/Areas of Expertise: An industry leader in supplying & installing industrial, commercial & institutional fireproofing, intumescent fireproofing, & firestopping; services also include hazmat waste removal & remediation of asbestos, mould, PCB's, lead, & mercury
Financial Information:
Type of Ownership: Private
Revenue Sources: 0% Provincial
Domestic Markets:
Alberta, Ontario,
Contact(s):
Mike Barker, President
mbarker@donalco.com
Bill Shannon, Senior Estimator
bshannon@donalco.com
Brad Hart, Senior Estimator
bhart@donalco.com
John Watson, Project Estimator
jwatson@donalco.com
Contact(s):
Edward Brennan, Division Manager
edwardrennan@donalcoottawa.com

Canadian Branches:
Calgary
535 Cleveland Cres. SE
Calgary, AB T2G 4R8
403-275-1418
Fax: 403-275-1433
888-894-6704
donalcocgy@donalco.com

Edmonton
8218 McIntyre Rd.
Edmonton, AB T6E 5C4
780-448-1660
Fax: 780-448-0102
888-894-6704
donalcoedm@donalco.com

Ottawa - Donalco Inc.
#2, 17 Grenfell Cres.
Ottawa, ON K2G 0G3
613-216-7678
Fax: 613-216-7679
donalco@donalcoottawa.com

Donald Olynyk, Acoustical Engineer
9224 - 90 St. NW
Edmonton, AB T6C 3M1
780-465-4125
Fax: 780-465-4169
don.olynyk@shaw.ca
Firm Type: Engineering, Scientific/Technical Services
Founded: 1973
Member of: Association of Professional Engineers; Geologists & Geophysicists of Alberta; American Society of Testing & Materials; Canadian Acoustical Association; Association of Professional Engineers & Geoscientists of Saskatchewan
Products/Services/Areas of Expertise: Noise assessment & control consulting
Recently Completed / Ongoing Projects: Acoustical design of Winston Knoll Collegiate, Regina, SK; acoustical design of Canada Games Arena, Grande Prairie, AB; acoustical remediation of Londonderry Pool, Edmonton, AB; Noise impact of electric furnace at Alta Steel, Edmonton, AB.; acoustical remediation of Al Ritchie Arena, Regina, SK
Domestic Markets:
Northwest Territories
Contact(s):
Donald Olynyk

Double Industries & Trading
25 Royal Ct.
Markham, ON L3R 9X4
905-470-7331
Firm Type: Engineering, Scientific/Technical Services
Founded: 1992
Staff: 4
Member of: Association of Professional Engineers of Manitoba
Domestic Markets:
Ontario
Foreign Activity:
Asia, USA
Contact(s):
Ander Lam, President

Double T Equipment Ltd. / DTE
P.O. Box 3637
2 East Lake Way
Airdrie, AB T4B 2B8
403-948-5618
Fax: 403-948-4780
800-661-9195
www.doubletequipment.com
Firm Type: Manufacturing
Founded: 1976
Staff: 20
Member of: Advanced Biotechnology Inc.; Biowatt (Germany)
Products/Services/Areas of Expertise: Custom equipment solutions: mushroom growing systems, composting solutions, bulk materials handling, fertilizer systems, self-propelled windrow turners
Financial Information:
Type of Ownership: Private
Domestic Markets:
National
Foreign Activity:
Worldwide
Contact(s):
Thomas Thomas, President
Rey Rawlins, Sales Representative

Dougan & Associates
Also Known As: D&A
77 Wyndham St. S
Guelph, ON N1E 5R3
519-822-1609
Fax: 519-822-5389
info@dougan.ca
www.dougan.ca
Firm Type: Scientific/Technical Services
Founded: 1981
Staff: 14
Member of: Society for Ecological Restoration; International Society of Arboriculture; Ontario Nature; Federation of Ontario Botanists
Products/Services/Areas of Expertise: Ecological consulting services; wildlife biology; natural heritage planning; habitat design, assessment & management; urban tree & forest management; ecological monitoring & restoration; ecological landscape design; peer review & expert witness testimony
Recently Completed / Ongoing Projects: Species at risk & ecological land classification, Point Pelee National Park, ON; northwest Brampton Open Space Management Plan, ON; City of Toronto environmentally sensitive areas inventories & mapping
Financial Information:
Type of Ownership: Private
Revenue Sources: 5% nationwide; 5% Provincial; 50% Municipals; 40% Private Contracts
Domestic Markets:
Ontario
Contact(s):
James Dougan, Principal & Sr. Ecologist
jdougan@dougan.ca
Margy de Gruchy, Ecologist
mdegruchy@dougan.ca
Todd Fell, Manager, Ecological Design
tfell@dougan.ca

Douglas Brothers
350, boul Décarie
Montréal, QC H4L 4W5
514-747-2471
Fax: 514-747-3124
800-361-1688
Products/Services/Areas of Expertise: Sewage treatment equipment & systems; stainless, carbon & alloy steel pipe & fittings; process & pressure piping; sheet metal; petrochemical & nuclear products; pressure vessels, towers, heat exchangers, tanks; sheet metal & plate custom products in carbon & stainless steels, aluminum, nickel, lead & other alloys
Contact(s):
George H. Holland, President/CEO
Paul E. Dostie, Vice-President, Sales & Marketing

Douglas, Barwick Inc.
P.O. Box 756
150 California Ave.
Brockville, ON K6V 5W1
613-342-8471
Fax: 613-342-4432
dbi@douglasbarwick.com
www.douglasbarwick.com
Firm Type: Manufacturing
Founded: 1922
Staff: 100
Products/Services/Areas of Expertise: Stainless steel pipes & fittings for water treatment, sewage & pumping stations; stainless steel tanks & custom metal fabrication
Financial Information:
Type of Ownership: Private
Domestic Markets:
Alberta, Ontario, Québec
Foreign Activity:
USA
Contact(s):
George Martin, President
Lorne Raycroft, Manager, Quality Control

Dove Environmental Services Inc.
P.O. Box 20331 Calgary Pl.
505, 4 Ave. SW
Calgary, AB T2P 0J8
403-266-3845
Fax: 403-269-6684
888-266-3845
ldove@accesscom.ca
Firm Type: Management Consulting, Manufacturing
Founded: 1991
Products/Services/Areas of Expertise: Clean-up products with environmental purposes; spill response; site remediation
Financial Information:
Type of Ownership: Private
Revenue: $500,000 - $1.5 Million

Domestic Markets:
Alberta, Manitoba, Saskatchewan
Foreign Activity:
USA
Contact(s):
Larry J. Dove, President

DPL Group
11 William Court
Quispamsis, NB E2E 4B1
506-847-2347
Fax: 506-847-2348
800-561-8880
info@dplcore.com; sales@dplcore.com
www.dpl.ca
Firm Type: Engineering, Information Technology, Manufacturing, Scientific/Technical Services
Founded: 1974
Staff: 76
Quality Environmental Management System(s): 9001
Products/Services/Areas of Expertise: Control systems design; electrical system design; software development; cellemetry monitoring
Recently Completed / Ongoing Projects: Moncton sewage treatment system; McCain Foods plant controls
Financial Information:
Type of Ownership: Private
Revenue: $1.5 Million - $3 Million
Revenue Sources: 5% Municipals; 95% Private Contracts
Domestic Markets:
Alberta, British Columbia, Manitoba, New Brunswick, Newfoundland & Labrador, Nova Scotia, Ontario, Prince Edward Island, Québec, Saskatchewan
Foreign Activity:
Central Europe, USA
Contact(s):
Will Kelly, Director
Ray Crowdis, Director
Alan DesRoches, Marketing Manager

Canadian Branches:
Nova Scotia Branch
2 Bluewater Rd.
Bedford, NS B4B 1G7
902-835-9937
Fax: 902-835-9938
gillisj@dpl.ca
Jim Gillis

Draeger Safety Canada Ltd.
An operating company of Drägerwerk AG & Co. KGaA
7555 Danbro Cres.
Mississauga, ON L5N 6P9
905-821-8988
Fax: 905-821-2565
877-372-4371
sales.canada@draeger.com
www.draeger.com
Firm Type: Distributing
Founded: 1988
Staff: 17
Quality Environmental Management System(s): 9002:1994
Products/Services/Areas of Expertise: Draeger Safety is a leading manufacturer of gas detection & respiratory protection products, including Draeger tubes, CMS, portable monitors, fixed gas detection systems, cartridge respirators; a complete line of breathing protection products from 5-minute escape systems to disposable air purifying products, SCBA's & 4-hour rebreathers; Simulation & Training products, such as the Confined Space Training Trailer, Live Fire Training Systems, Swede Survival Flashover Systems & Submarine escape devices
Financial Information:
Type of Ownership: Foreign-owned
Domestic Markets:
National
Foreign Activity:
Worldwide
Contact(s):
Wes Kenneweg, President/CEO
wes.kenneweg@draeger.com
Lynn Scharfe, Representative, Domestic Sales & Marketing
lynn.scharfe@draeger.com
Kent Armstrong, Canadian Divisional Sales Manager,
905/821-8988
kent.armstrong@draeger.com
Kevin Christian, Regional Sales Manager

Shelli Cosmides, Manager, Marketing & Communications
shelli.cosmides@draeger.com
Canadian Branches:
Edmonton
5203 - 86 St. NW
Edmonton, AB T6E 6T1
780-461-5775
Fax: 780-461-5808

Halifax
10 Thornhill Dr.
Halifax, NS B3B 1R9
902-481-7605

Sudbury
1300 Lorne St.
Sudbury, ON P3C 5N1
705-674-0437
Fax: 705-674-0756

Drexan Energy Systems Inc.
8676 Commerce Court
Burnaby, BC V5A 4N7
604-421-8406
Fax: 888-448-6560
info@drexanenergy.com
www.drexanenergy.com
Firm Type: Management Consulting, Distributing
Member of: Branick Industries
Quality Environmental Management System(s): 14064
Products/Services/Areas of Expertise: A leader in quality carbon offset market solutions for the transportation industry; nitrogen tire inflation systems; turnkey solutions to harvest carbon emissions
Financial Information:
Type of Ownership: Private
Revenue: Greater than $5 Million
Domestic Markets:
National
Contact(s):
Konrad Mech, Co-Founder & Vice-President

Canadian Branches:
Calgary
#205, 259 Midpark Way SE
Calgary, AB T2X 1M2
403-225-7772
Fax: 403-258-2527

Edmonton
4140 - 97th St. NW
Edmonton, AB T6E 5Y6
780-413-1774
Fax: 780-413-1776

Drilling Fluids Treatment Systems Inc. / DFTS
7530 - 114th Ave. SE
Calgary, AB T2C 4T3
403-279-0123
Fax: 403-279-2233
888-844-3387
info@dfts.com
www.dfts.com
Firm Type: Manufacturing
Founded: 1988
Staff: 9
Products/Services/Areas of Expertise: Screening systems; screens; strainers; shale shakers; pressure gauges & chokes.
Financial Information:
Type of Ownership: Private
Domestic Markets:
Alberta, British Columbia, Manitoba, Saskatchewan
Foreign Activity:
USA
Contact(s):
E.A. Kutryk, President

Canadian Branches:
Edmonton Branch
#6, 4407 - 66 Ave.
Leduc, AB T9E 7E2
780-980-9299
Fax: 780-986-4477
1-866-490-3387

DRL Environmental Services
21339 Hwy. 2, RR#7
Amherst, NS B4H 3Y5

902-661-6890
Fax: 902-661-6892
jmorrissey@drlservices.com
www.drlservices.com
Products/Services/Areas of Expertise: Asbestos abatement services; ground/surface water remediation; soil remediation services
Contact(s):
John Morrissey, President

Droycon Bioconcepts Inc.
315 Dewdney Ave.
Regina, SK S4N 0E7
306-585-1762
Fax: 306-585-3000
sales@dbi.ca
www.dbi.sk.ca
Firm Type: Manufacturing
Founded: 1987
Staff: 9
Products/Services/Areas of Expertise: Biodetectors for the determination of specific bacterial groups in water
Domestic Markets:
Alberta, Manitoba, Ontario, Saskatchewan
Foreign Activity:
Africa, Asia, USA
Markets Sought:
Western Europe
Contact(s):
D. Roy Cullimore, President

DST Consulting Engineers
605 Hewitson St.
Thunder Bay, ON P7B 5V5
807-623-2929
Fax: 807-623-1792
800-668-4201
thunderbay@dstgroup.com
www.dstgroup.com
Firm Type: Engineering
Founded: 1971
Products/Services/Areas of Expertise: Specializes in site characterization; environmental assessments; alternative risk-based solutions for sites too costly to clean-up; clean-up of contaminated sites
Recently Completed / Ongoing Projects: NOWPARC, complete solution for $9.3 million creasote contaminated sediment clean-up on Lake Superior, including environmental assessment, design, construction supervision & water treatment
Financial Information:
Type of Ownership: Private
Domestic Markets:
National
Foreign Activity:
The Middle East, USA
Markets Sought:
South America
Contact(s):
Scott Tozer, Contact

Canadian Branches:
Dryden
34A Hearst Ave.
Dryden, ON P8N 2K4
807-223-7055
Fax: 807-221-2064
1-807-286-5309
jpeterson@dstgroup.com
Jeff Peterson, Contact

Kenora
P.O. Box 51
Kenora, ON P9N 3X1
807-548-2383
Fax: 807-548-1967
1-800-286-5309
kenora@dstgroup.com
Jeff Peterson, Contact

Ottawa
#203 - 2150 Thurston Drive
Ottawa, ON K1G 5T9
613-748-1415
Fax: 613-748-1356
1-877-378-3745
ottawa@dstgroup.com
Brendan Harrigan, Contact

Sudbury
#4, 1351E Kelly Lake Rd.
Sudbury, ON P3E 5P5
705-523-6680
Fax: 705-523-6690
866-432-5554
sudbury@dstgroup.com
Ray Jambakhsh, Contact

Toronto
C/O - Ottawa Branch
toronto@dstgroup.com
Brendan Harrigan, Contact

International Branch(es):
Beirut Office
Lastra Bldg., 3rd Fl.
Al Midan St.
Dekwaneh Lebanon
0-961-1-688-789
dst.agi@inco.com.lb
Robert Edde

Minneapolis Office
#832 - 801 Twelve Oaks Center Dr.
Wayzata, MN USA
952-473-7193
Fax: 952-473-1492
smg@gale-tec.com
Steve Gale, Contact

DSS Marine Inc.
71 Wright Ave.
Dartmouth, NS B3B 1H4
902-835-4848
Fax: 902-835-6269
sales@dssmarine.com
www.dssmarine.com
Firm Type: Scientific/Technical Services
Staff: 9
Quality Environmental Management System(s): 9000
Products/Services/Areas of Expertise: Soil remediation services; liquid/hazardous waste management
Contact(s):
Darren Trites, President

DTE Industries Ltd.
69 Comstock Rd.
Toronto, ON M1L 2G9
416-757-6278
Fax: 416-757-5579
800-385-1400
sales@dteindustries.com
www.dteindustries.com
Firm Type: Manufacturing
Founded: 1952
Products/Services/Areas of Expertise: Sewage treatment equipment; waste storage containers; aboveground, underground steel storage tanks
Domestic Markets:
National
Foreign Activity:
USA
Contact(s):
Robert Hawn, Sales Representative

Duerden & Keane Consultants Inc.
26 Forest Dr.
Dartmouth, NS B3A 2M3
902-435-7562
Fax: 902-484-7639
colinduerden@duerdenandkeane.com
www.duerdenandkeane.com
Firm Type: Management Consulting
Founded: 1994
Member of: Canadian Environmental Auditing Association; Association of Professional Environmental Auditors
Products/Services/Areas of Expertise: Environmental management consulting; environmental auditing
Financial Information:
Type of Ownership: Private
Domestic Markets:
National, New Brunswick, Newfoundland & Labrador, Nova Scotia, Ontario
Foreign Activity:
Worldwide
Contact(s):
Colin Duerden, Manager
colinduerden@duerdenandkeane.com

Dundas-Jafine Inc.
80 West Dr.
Brampton, ON L6T 3T6
905-450-7200
Fax: 905-450-7207
800-387-2578
sales@dundasjafine.com
www.dundasjafine.com
Firm Type: Manufacturing
Founded: 1934
Staff: 35
Member of: Canadian Home & Hardware Manufacturers Association
Products/Services/Areas of Expertise: Air ventilation products
Domestic Markets:
National
Foreign Activity:
Worldwide
Contact(s):
Jin Juhasz, Director, Marketing
Allen Haybarger, National Sales Manager
Ed McLaren, Director, Sales

DuPont Canada Inc.
P.O. Box 2200 Streetsville
Mississauga, ON L5M 2H3
905-821-5193
Fax: 905-821-5057
800-387-2122
information@can.dupont.com
ca.dupont.com
Firm Type: Manufacturing
Founded: 1877
Staff: 300
Member of: Canadian Chemical Producers Association
Products/Services/Areas of Expertise: Nylon industrial yarn; synthetic fibres; polymer resins; packaging films; automotive finishes; crop products; industrial chemicals
Domestic Markets:
National
Contact(s):
William B. White, President
Glen Wood, Director, Operations
David E. Yake, Director, Research & Business Development
Michael J. Oxley, Vice-President & CFO, Finance

Canadian Branches:
Ajax Branch
408 Fairall St.
Ajax, ON L1S 1R6
905-683-5500
Fax: 905-618-6016

Corunna
291 Albert St.
Corunna, ON N0N 1G0
519-862-5700
Fax: 519-862-5880
James A. O'Connor, Regional Manager & Sarnia Site Manag

Kingston Branch
P.O. Box 2100
455 Front Rd.
Kingston, ON K7L 4Z6
613-544-6000
Fax: 613-548-5201

Maitland Branch
P.O. Box 611
1400 County Rd. #2
Maitland, ON K0E 1P0
613-348-3611
Fax: 613-348-4200

Thetford Mines
1045, rue Monfette nord
Thetford Mines, QC G6G 5T1
418-338-8567
Fax: 418-338-0433

Whitby
201 South Blair St.
Whitby, ON L1N 5S8
905-668-5811
Fax: 905-666-7005

Dural Industries
A division of Multibond Inc.
550, av Marshall
Montréal, QC H9P 1C9
514-636-6230
Fax: 514-631-7737
800-561-2340
dural@ifscos.com
www.dural.ca
Firm Type: Manufacturing
Founded: 1974
EcoLogo Certified Products & Services: Durakote Ultraplus; Durakote Ultra; Durakote Professional; DuraPro & Protector Plus
Products/Services/Areas of Expertise: Offers a wide range of adhesives, coatings, emulsion polymers & refractories to diverse markets
Ecological Note: Durakote Ultraplus; Durakote Ultra; Durakote Professional; DuraPro & Protector Plus

Durex Steel & Alloy Industries Ltd.
Also Known As: Duragreen Tanks
3912 - 69 Ave.
Edmonton, AB T6B 2V2
780-465-9834
Fax: 780-469-0586
888-661-8265
tanks1@telusplanet.net
www.durex-tanks.com
Firm Type: Manufacturing
Founded: 1965
Products/Services/Areas of Expertise: Storage tanks, double-wall tanks for all liquids: jet fuel, waste oil, gas, diesel, acids & custom fabricating
Financial Information:
Type of Ownership: Private
Revenue Sources: 10% Provincial; 20% Municipals; 70% Private Contracts
Domestic Markets:
Alberta, British Columbia, Manitoba, Northwest Territories, Ontario, Saskatchewan, Yukon Territory
Contact(s):
John Berge, President
David Scott, Operations Manager

Durmitor Inc.
23 Crossley Ct.
King City, ON L7B 1H4
905-833-3148
Fax: 905-833-2112
mugray@aol.com
Firm Type: Manufacturing
Founded: 1974
Staff: 6
Products/Services/Areas of Expertise: Measuring & monitoring equipment for HVAC; energy management systems
Domestic Markets:
National
Foreign Activity:
Australia/New Zealand, Eastern Europe, Western Europe, South America, USA

International Branch(es):
Branmag Inc.
Wurlitzer Industrial Park
908 Niagara Falls Blvd.
North Tonawanda, NY USA
716-693-5994
T. Chirico

Dutab
2670 rue Paulus
Montréal, QC H4S 1G1
514-337-5345
Fax: 514-745-2969
800-567-2658
www.dutab.com
Products/Services/Areas of Expertise: Manufacturers & distributors of adhesives for consumer & industrial use
Ecological Note: Adhesives
Contact(s):
Mirelle Dandurand
mdandurand@adfastcorp.com

DynaMotive Energy Systems Corporation
Formerly: Dynamotive Technologies Corporation
#140, 13091 Vanier Place
Richmond, BC V6V 2J1

604-295-6800
Fax: 604-295-6805
877-863-2268
info@dynamotive.com
www.dynamotive.com
Firm Type: Manufacturing
Founded: 1991
Staff: 25
Member of: Canadian Environment Industry Association; Taiwan Chamber of Commerce in British Columbia
Products/Services/Areas of Expertise: Bio-fuel production (BioOil & Char); provides alternative, sustainable & environmental friendly energy solutions
Recently Completed / Ongoing Projects: Complete construction & commission of the ten tonnes per day pilot plant, Vancouver
Financial Information:
Type of Ownership: Publicly Traded
Revenue: $500,000 - $1.5 Million
Revenue Sources: 10% nationwide; 90% Private Contracts
Domestic Markets:
Alberta, British Columbia, Ontario, Saskatchewan
Foreign Activity:
Asia, Western Europe, South America, USA
Markets Sought:
Western Europe, The Pacific Rim, South America, USA
Contact(s):
K. Andrew Kingston, President/CEO
Richard Lin, Chair
Jeffrey Lin, Vice-President, Business Development

Dynamotive Energy Systems Corporation
Angus Corporate Centre
#230 - 1700 West 75th Ave.
Vancouver, BC V6P 6G2
604-267-6000
Fax: 604-267-6005
877-863-2268
info@dynamotive.com
www.dynamotive.com
Firm Type: Scientific/Technical Services, Waste Management
Products/Services/Areas of Expertise: Development of energy solutions through converting biomass into environmentally friendly BioOil
Recently Completed / Ongoing Projects: Commercial demonstration BioOil plant located in West Lorne, ON.
Financial Information:
Type of Ownership: Publicly Traded
Contact(s):
Nathan Neumer, Director, Communications

Dynapompe Inc.
Industries Garanties Ltée
5420, rue Paré
Montréal, QC H4P 1R3
514-342-3030
Fax: 514-342-3421
Contact(s):
Michel Gaudette, Contact

E.A.I. Technologies Inc.
341, ch Brouillard
Saint-Georges-de-Windsor, QC J0A 1J0
819-823-3318
Fax: 819-828-0146
gaetan.brouillard@sympatico.ca
Contact(s):
Gaétan Brouillard, Contact

E.B. Tobe Enterprises
P.O. Box 1791
Squamish, BC V8B 0B3
604-898-9171
Fax: 604-898-9161
tobe@shaw.ca
Products/Services/Areas of Expertise: Watershed restoration & public education
Contact(s):
Edith B. Tobe, B.Sc., AScT, Environmental Consultant

E.H. Hanson Engineering Group Ltd.
#4, 7551 Vantage Way
Delta, BC V4G 1C9
604-946-0111
Fax: 604-946-6359
ehanson@direct.ca
Firm Type: Engineering, Scientific/Technical Services
Founded: 1980
Staff: 8
Member of: Association of Professional Engineers & Geoscientists of British Columbia; Association of Professional Engineers of Manitoba; American Public Works Association; Air & Waste Management Association
Products/Services/Areas of Expertise: Landfill design, odour control; landfill gas utilization; recycling, incineration, composting; water treatment; contaminated soil investigation & remediation; digester gas utilization
Domestic Markets:
National
Foreign Activity:
Western Europe, USA
Contact(s):
Elson H. Hanson, P.Eng., President/CEO

E.K. Gillin & Associates Inc.
Also Known As: EKGINC
#362, 356 Ontario St.
Stratford, ON N5A 7X6
519-662-3819
Fax: 519-662-6595
888-771-6754
ekginc@ekginc.com
www.ekginc.com
Firm Type: Management Consulting
Founded: 1990
Staff: 7
Member of: Environmental Management Resource Centre for Business; Canadian Centre for Occupational Health Services
Member of: Air & Waste Management Association
Products/Services/Areas of Expertise: Consulting & training services specializing in strategic management services
Recently Completed / Ongoing Projects: ISO 14000 implementation; mould testing; asbestos testing; NPRI preparation; Certificate of Approval (Air); air & noise testing
Financial Information:
Type of Ownership: Private
Revenue: $500,000 - $1.5 Million
Revenue Sources: 15% nationwide; 10% Provincial; 5% Municipals; 70% Private Contracts
Domestic Markets:
National
Foreign Activity:
USA
Markets Sought:
USA
Contact(s):
Patrick Smale, President
patrick.smale@ekginc.com
Christine Friel, Office Administration

E2 Management Corporation
113 Mountainview Rd. South
Georgetown, ON L7G 4K2
905-873-9484
Fax: 905-873-3054
etwom@e2management.com
www.e2management.com
Firm Type: Management Consulting
Founded: 1987
Member of: Canadian Environment Industry Association
Products/Services/Areas of Expertise: Specializes in environmental management systems, alignment to ISO 14000, using proven quality management systems, tools & principles; high-end training, Internet-based communication & learning programs; strategic planning for sustainability; business development plans; product stewardship programs; utilizes a multi-disciplinary approach to improve international competitiveness for clients
Recently Completed / Ongoing Projects: Enviro-Ready
Contact(s):
Lynn Johannson, President
Brandon Smith, Manager, Marketing

E2D Laboratory
15 Columbia Dr.
Amherst, NH USA
Canadian Branches:
E2D Laboratory
15 Columbia Dr.
Amherst, NH USA

e3 Solutions Inc.
East Tower
#703, 2700 Matheson Blvd. E
Mississauga, ON L4W 4V9
905-629-8885
Fax: 905-629-8844
888-819-0014
contact@e3solutionsinc.com
www.e3solutionsinc.com
Firm Type: Information Technology
Founded: 1997
Staff: 22
Member of: VerdantIS; Sustainable Waterloo; Direct Energy; Sustainable Insights Group, LLC; Carbonzero; WireIE; XCG Consultants Ltd.; Niagara Sustainability Initiative
Products/Services/Areas of Expertise: Provides software solutions for measuring, monitoring & verifying greenhouse gas emissions; clients include small business, educational institutions, climat action groups, government agencies
Recently Completed / Ongoing Projects: Pilot project for Chrysler Corp.; implementation for Nortel; corporate network installation for General Mills, Bell Canada; additional systems for US Army, Cdn. Coast Guard, Magna Automotive, Cadillac Fairview & others
Financial Information:
Type of Ownership: Private
Revenue Sources: 100% Private Contracts
Domestic Markets:
National
Foreign Activity:
China, Western Europe, South America, Mexico, USA, Vietnam,
Contact(s):
Kevin Coyne, President/CEO
Les Gower, CFO/Corporate Secretary
Julian Moffatt, Vice-President, Client Solutions

International Branch(es):
Alabama
138 South Gay St.
Auburn, AL USA
334-887-22411, ext.11

North Carolina
#325, 2505 Meridian Pkwy.
Durham, NC 27713 USA
919-806-2440
Fax: 919-806-8609

Eagle Home Inspection Services Inc.
6422 Berlin St.
Halifax, NS B3L 1T6
902-455-3377
Fax: 902-455-1333
ehis@istar.ca
Firm Type: Manufacturing
Founded: 1996
Staff: 10
Contact(s):
Doug Leahy, President

Earth & Environmental Technologies (ETech)
Formerly: CRESTech.
4850 Keele St., 2nd Fl.
Toronto, ON M3J 3K1
416-665-3311
Fax: 416-665-2032
richard.worsfold@oce-ontario.org
www.crestech.ca
Products/Services/Areas of Expertise: Clean Water Technologies; Resource Management; Sustainable Agriculture and Agri-Food; Sustainable Energy Solutions; Sustainable Infrastructure
Contact(s):
Richard D. Worsfold, Director, 416-665-5473

Canadian Branches:
Waterloo
Research Program
BFG Bldg
200 University Ave. West
Waterloo, ON N2L 3G1
519-885-5466
Fax: 519-885-5466
Karen Ford, Manager

Earthbound Environmental Inc.
P.O. Box 143
Steinbach, MB R5G 1M1

204-346-1534
Fax: 204-326-5059
mailbox@earthbound.mb.ca
www.earthbound.mb.ca
Firm Type: Management Consulting, Engineering
Founded: 1991
Staff: 2
Member of: Manitoba Environmental Industries Association
Products/Services/Areas of Expertise: Integrated waste management services
Recently Completed / Ongoing Projects: Scrap metal recycling in northern communities; regional recycling system design
Financial Information:
Type of Ownership: Private
Revenue: $250,000 - $500,000
Domestic Markets:
Manitoba, Nunavut
Foreign Activity:
Mexico
Contact(s):
Stu Clark
Ken Friesen, Vice-President, 204/346-1534

Earthcycle
#1100, 1166 Alberni St.
Vancouver, BC V6E 3Z3
604-899-0928
Fax: 604-682-4133
info@earthcycle.com
www.earthcycle.com
Founded: 2003
Products/Services/Areas of Expertise: Manufacturer of biodegradable and compostable packaging
Financial Information:
Type of Ownership: Private
Contact(s):
Shannon Boase, Founder & President

EarthFx Inc.
3363 Yonge St.
Toronto, ON M4N 2M6
416-410-4260
Fax: 416-481-6026
info@earthfx.com
www.earthfx.com
Firm Type: Scientific/Technical Services
Staff: 10
Products/Services/Areas of Expertise: Earth science data management services; custom applications; groundwater modelling
Financial Information:
Type of Ownership: Private
Domestic Markets:
Alberta, Northwest Territories, Ontario, Québec
Contact(s):
Lawrence Davidson

Earthguard Environmental Group Inc.
178 Main St.
Unionville, ON L3R 2G9
905-415-1200
info@earthguard.ca
www.earthguard.ca
Products/Services/Areas of Expertise: Environmental consulting services; ISO 14001 certification
Contact(s):
Joseph Pilarski, Chairman/CEO

earthRight Solar Products
Earthright Store
79F North 3rd Ave.
Williams Lake, BC V2G 2A5
250-392-7119
Fax: 250-392-7129
877-925-2929
sales@solareagle.com
www.solareagle.com
Firm Type: Distributing
Founded: 1990
Staff: 3
Products/Services/Areas of Expertise: Environmental products, including solar, alternate energy, finishing & cleaning products
Domestic Markets:
National
Contact(s):
Ron Young, President
Pat Young, Vice-President

Earthworks Technology Inc.
650 Cataraqui Woods Dr.
Kingston, ON K7P 2Y4
613-634-0307
Contact(s):
David McTurk, President

East Coast Aquatics
P.O. Box 129
Bridgetown, NS B0S 1C0
902-665-4682
Fax: 902-665-4375
mike@eastcoastaquatics.ca
www.eastcoastaquatics.ca
Firm Type: Scientific/Technical Services
Founded: 1999
Products/Services/Areas of Expertise: Freshwater fish & fish habitat assessment & restoration; stream restoration; sedimentation/erosion control; bioengineering; watershed management planning; water quality monitoring
Recently Completed / Ongoing Projects: Integrated watershed management plans; fish surveys for population density & distribution; sediment control planning & related water testing for construction sites; natural resources inventories, Parks Canada; trout surveys & tagging
Financial Information:
Type of Ownership: Private
Revenue: $50,000 - $100,000
Revenue Sources: 75% nationwide; 15% Provincial; 10% Municipals
Domestic Markets:
New Brunswick, Newfoundland & Labrador, Nova Scotia, Prince Edward Island
Markets Sought:
USA
Contact(s):
Michael Parker, Principal/Sr. Fisheries Biologist

Eastcan Geomatics
3597 Dutch Village Rd.
Halifax, NS B3N 2T1
902-429-7901
Fax: 902-454-4700
info@eastcan.ca
www.eastcan.ca
Firm Type: Scientific/Technical Services
Founded: 1959
Staff: 20
Quality Environmental Management System(s): 9002
Products/Services/Areas of Expertise: Digital photogrammetric mapping; navigation & sounding equipment
Financial Information:
Type of Ownership: Private
Revenue Sources: 5% Provincial; 5% Municipals; 90% Private Contracts
Domestic Markets:
National
Foreign Activity:
Worldwide
Contact(s):
John P. Duff, CEO

Eastern Environmental Services Ltd.
17 Jones Ct.
Sussex, NB E4E 2S2
506-432-9500
Fax: 506-432-9595
800-933-5959
eesl@nbnet.nb.ca
www.easternenvironmental.ca
Firm Type: Waste Management
Member of: New Brunswick Environment Industry Association
Products/Services/Areas of Expertise: Processes include recycling of waste solvents, used oil filters, treating sludge & other petroleum derived waste; fully environmentally licensed by the Federal & Provincial Environmental Departments to transport, store & operate a recycling facility in Sussex N.B.
Contact(s):
Brad Howland, Vice-President

Eastern Wind Power Inc.
A subsidiary of Western Wind Energy Inc.
29 Reynar Dr.
Quispamsis, NB E2G 1J9
506-650-8038
jhaar@easternwindpower.us
www.easternwindpower.com
Firm Type: Scientific/Technical Services
Staff: 3
Products/Services/Areas of Expertise: Primary goal is the development of commercial wind farms; provides site evaluation, wind analysis services, meteorological study tower installation; for viable sites EWP will build & operate wind turbines to generate electricity; is a wholly owned subsidiary of Western Wind Energy Corporation of BC
Recently Completed / Ongoing Projects: 60 metre meteorological study tower
Contact(s):
Jonathan Haar, President & CEO

Eastwest Synergies Inc.
#1607, 25 The Esplanade
Toronto, ON M5E 1W5
416-360-8056
Fax: 416-360-0156
Contact(s):
Fernando R. Talavera, Director

Eaton Hydro Developers Inc.
Formerly: Furry Creek Power Ltd.
1790 The Grosvenor
1040 Georgia St. West
Vancouver, BC V6E 4H8
604-642-5700
Fax: 604-642-5706
woronuik@eatonpower.com
www.eatonpower.com
Products/Services/Areas of Expertise: Developing a run-of-river hydroelectric project on the Upper Furry Creek, which will divert a portion of the creek's water flow into a water pipe that will be used to generate electricity; estimated to be 6.2 to 9.8 mw in size with an annual output of 30 to 40 gigawatt hours, enough energy for 6,000 to 9,000 homes
Ecological Note: Water-powered renewable low-impact electricity
Contact(s):
Don Swoboda, President/COO, Eaton Power Corp.
swoboda@eatonpower.com

EBA Engineering Consultants Ltd.
Formerly: Stewart EBA
Oceanic Plaza
1066 West Hastings, 9th Fl.
Vancouver, BC V6E 3X2
604-685-0275
Fax: 604-684-6241
eba@eba.ca
www.eba.ca
Firm Type: Management Consulting, Scientific/Technical Services
Founded: 1958
Staff: 350
Member of: BC Environmental Information Institute; Mining Association of BC; Urban Development Institute; ICI Environmental Managers Association
Products/Services/Areas of Expertise: Environmental site audits; site assessments; contamination studies; groundwater & UST assessments; site remediation; risk analysis & assessment; solid waste characterization studies; landfill design; waste minimization audits; hazardous waste planning; environmental compliance; environmental impact assessments
Recently Completed / Ongoing Projects: Investigation & design of remediation for Place des Amis townhouse complex in Coquitlam for CMHC & Red Door Housing; design of debris flood protection berms, Horstman Creek, Whistler for Intrawest; Roger's Pass Shaughnessy Rail Tunnel Design (6,000 ft.), for CP Rail; BC Roster Reviews
Domestic Markets:
Alberta, British Columbia, Manitoba, Northwest Territories, Saskatchewan, Yukon Territory
Foreign Activity:
Western Europe, USA
Markets Sought:
Asia
Contact(s):
Paul Ruffel, President
Ian Stewart, P.Eng., Vice-President

Products & Services Buyer's Guide

Canadian Branches:
Calgary
Riverbend Atrium One
#115, 200 Rivercrest Drive SE
Calgary, AB T2C 2X5
403-203-3355
Fax: 403-203-3301
P.A. (Paul) Evans, Contact

Edmonton
14940 - 123 Ave. NW
Edmonton, AB T5L 1B4
780-451-2121
Fax: 780-454-5688
J.P. (Paul) Ruffell, Contact

Kelowna
#150, 1715 Dickson Ave.
Kelowna, BC V1Y 9G6
250-862-4832
Fax: 250-862-2941
Scott Martin, Contact

Lethbridge
442 - 10 St. North
Lethbridge, AB T1H 2C7
403-329-9009
Fax: 403-328-8817
M.J. (Marc) Sabourin, Contact

Nanaimo
#1, 4376 Boban Dr.
Nanaimo, BC V9T 5V1
250-756-2256
Fax: 250-756-2686
Jerry Schmidt, Contact

Northwest Territories
P.O. Box 2244
#201, 4916 - 49 St.
Yellowknife, NT X1A 2P7
867-920-2287
Fax: 867-873-3324
Ed Hoeve, Contact

Yukon
#6, 151 Industrial Rd.
Whitehorse, YT Y1A 2V3
867-668-3068
Fax: 867-668-4349
J.R. (Richard) Trimble, Contact

ECE Group - a Division of Conestoga-Rovers & Associates
205 Lesmill Rd.
Toronto, ON M3B 2V1
416-449-1040
Fax: 416-449-2876
ece@craworld.com
www.craworld.com
Firm Type: Engineering
Founded: 1955
Staff: 55
Member of: Toronto Construction Association
Products/Services/Areas of Expertise: Environmental engineering & design services for building systems: mechanical, electrical, communications, life safety & security; energy management; forensic investigative expertise; feasibility studies, reports & surveys; systems design; project management
Financial Information:
Type of Ownership: Private
Domestic Markets:
National
Foreign Activity:
Worldwide
Contact(s):
Gunnar Heissler, Sr. Technical Consultant
Michael Kern, Business Development
Richard Pilliounis, Engineering Manager

Echo Environmental
#50, 419 - 3 St. SE
Medicine Hat, AB T1A 0G9
403-504-4078
Fax: 403-504-4085
Firm Type: Management Consulting, Scientific/Technical Services
Founded: 1996
Products/Services/Areas of Expertise: Environmental services for oil & gas industry
Financial Information:
Type of Ownership: Private
Revenue Sources: 100% Private Contracts
Domestic Markets:
Alberta
Contact(s):
Jim Fairgrieve, President

Eckel Industries
P.O. Box 776
15 Allison Ave.
Morrisburg, ON K0C 1X0
613-543-2967
Fax: 613-543-4173
800-563-3574
eckel@eckel.ca
www.eckel.ca
Firm Type: Manufacturing
Founded: 1960
Staff: 5
Products/Services/Areas of Expertise: Noise control products; machinery enclosures & control booths, architectural noise control panels, noise dampening & absorbing materials, audiometric testing booths
Recently Completed / Ongoing Projects: Greens Creek pollution control facility, Ottawa; noise control, Ashbridges Bay water treatment plant, Toronto; audiometric rooms, Costco & Hearx
Financial Information:
Type of Ownership: Private
Revenue: Greater than $5 Million
Revenue Sources: 25% nationwide; 10% Provincial; 5% Municipals; 60% Private Contracts
Domestic Markets:
National
Foreign Activity:
Western Europe, Mexico, USA
Markets Sought:
Asia, Central America, South America
Contact(s):
Alan Eckel, President
Blake Noon, Vice-President & General Manager

ECL Envirowest Consultants Ltd.
Formerly: Envirowest Consultants Ltd.
#130, 3700 North Fraser Way
Burnaby, BC V5J 5H4
604-451-0505
Fax: 604-451-0557
admin@ecl-envirowest.bc.ca
www.ecl-envirowest.bc.ca
Firm Type: Engineering, Scientific/Technical Services
Founded: 1984
Staff: 16
Products/Services/Areas of Expertise: Environmental monitoring; fish/wildlife inventories & studies; habitat creation/enhancement; sediment & erosion control; environmental design; ecological landscaping; hydrology & water resources; creel surveys; underwater videos & photography; technical studies & on-site supervision
Contact(s):
Ian W. Whyte, President/CEO
Mark A. Adams, Sr. Project Manager

Eco Canada
#200, 308 - 11th Ave. SE
Calgary, AB T2G 0Y2
403-233-0748
Fax: 403-269-9544
info@eco.ca
www.eco.ca
Firm Type: Management Consulting
Staff: 29
Products/Services/Areas of Expertise: Job board & other recruitment services; business & career services for the environmental industry & profession
Contact(s):
Grant Trump, President & CEO
Fung Ling Ma, Director, Finance & Administration

ECO Fuel Systems Inc.
#2, 20043 - 92A Ave.
Langley, BC V1M 3A5
604-888-8384
Fax: 604-888-6607
800-663-1980
info@ecofuel.com
www.ecofuel.com
Firm Type: Distributing, Engineering, Information Technology, Manufacturing, Scientific/Technical Services
Founded: 1982
Staff: 7
Member of: Natural Gas Industry Alliance of Canada
Products/Services/Areas of Expertise: Natural gas vehicle conversion kits, systems; energy consulting; alternative fuel conversion systems for vehicles; air quality management
Financial Information:
Type of Ownership: Private
Domestic Markets:
National
Foreign Activity:
Worldwide

Eco Waste Solutions
#14, 5195 Harvester Rd.
Burlington, ON L7L 6E9
905-634-7022
Fax: 905-634-0831
866-326-2876
info@ecosolutions.com
www.ecosolutions.com
Firm Type: Manufacturing
Founded: 1994
Staff: 11
Member of: Canadian Environment Industry Association
Quality Environmental Management System(s): 9001
Products/Services/Areas of Expertise: Point-of-need waste management solutions; pioneered thermal treatment technologies for solid & liquid wastes, yielding practical & patented solutions that reduce expenses while providing environmentally responsible waste management alternatives
Financial Information:
Type of Ownership: Private
Revenue: $500,000 - $1.5 Million
Domestic Markets:
National
Foreign Activity:
Caribbean, Central America, South America, Mexico, USA
Contact(s):
Steve Meldrum, CEO
Tracey J. Goldberg, Director, Marketing & Sales Support
Jean Lucas, Director, Business Development

Eco Wood Products
20 Freshway Dr.
Concord, ON L4K 1S3
905-669-4340
Fax: 905-669-9945
sales@ecowood-products.com
www.ecowood-products.com
Firm Type: Distributing, Manufacturing, Waste Management
Founded: 1972
Staff: 25
Member of: Ontario Waste Management Association; Recycling Council of Ontario; Canadian Wood Pallet & Container Association
Products/Services/Areas of Expertise: Produces animal bedding materials & landscape mulch; wood recycling & chipping services, sawdust production & wood waste haulage; provides animal bedding & landscaping materials
Financial Information:
Type of Ownership: Private
Domestic Markets:
Ontario
Contact(s):
Mike Thomas, Manager, Marketing
Fred Bernard, Operations Manager

Eco-Guide International
Also Known As: Aquago
146, ch Dalesville
Brownsburg-Chatham, QC J8G 1H4
450-533-9191
Fax: 450-533-9175
866-411-9191
info@lake2000.com
www.lake2000.com; www.aquago.com
Products/Services/Areas of Expertise: Eco-Guide works in the field of lake protection restoration; offers specialized products that are related to lake restoration and general waste water applications; committed to finding the right solution to specific environmental problems; customers are individuals,

municipalities, lake associations, law & engineering firms & recreational sites.
Recently Completed / Ongoing Projects: Constant growth in the lake management field; have worked on over 100 lakes

Eco-North Laboratories
RR#1
Rosseau, ON P0C 1J0
705-732-1805
Fax: 705-732-1804
Firm Type: Engineering, Scientific/Technical Services
Founded: 1991
Staff: 3
Products/Services/Areas of Expertise: Waste management, composting; water quality guidelines documentation; pesticide residues in organic fruit; alternative agriculture; environmental monitoring; laboratory analysis
Contact(s):
John E. Warner, Manager

Eco-Tec Ltd.
1145 Squires Beach Rd.
Ajax, ON L1W 3T9
905-427-0077
Fax: 905-427-4477
800-478-5517
ecotec@eco-tec.com
www.eco-tec.com
Firm Type: Manufacturing, Scientific/Technical Services
Founded: 1970
Staff: 75
Member of: American Electroplating & Surface Finishers Society; American Institute of Iron & Steel Engineers; Architectural Anodizers Council
Quality Environmental Management System(s): 9001; ISO
Products/Services/Areas of Expertise: Chemical purification & recycling equipment for process chemicals; chromic acid & nickel salt recovery units; copper recovery & various acid purification systems
Financial Information:
Type of Ownership: Private
Domestic Markets:
National
Foreign Activity:
Worldwide
Contact(s):
Kevin Munns, Marketing
Mike Dejak, Sales

International Branch(es):
Eco-Tec Europe Ltd.
Burntwood Business Park
#29C Ring Road, Zone 3
Staffordshire GBR
44-15436-83086
Fax: 44-15436-74117
ete@eco-tec.com
Bill Anderson, Managing Director

ECO-TEK Ecological Technologies Inc.
Formerly: ECO-TEK Wastewater Treatments Inc
#10, 20543 - 96 Ave.
Langley, BC V1M 3W3
778-298-6835
Fax: 778-298-6836
kimron@ecotek.ca
www.ecotek.ca
Firm Type: Engineering
Founded: 1993
Staff: 3
Products/Services/Areas of Expertise: Design, build, operate ecologically engineered waste to resource systems where wastewater is transformed in a greenhouse protected ecosystem into plants, compost & clean water
Recently Completed / Ongoing Projects: Water reclamation for organic urban agriculture facility in Havana; Yarrow Ecovillage cooperative solar aquatics, planning stage
Financial Information:
Type of Ownership: Private
Revenue: $100,000 - $250,000
Revenue Sources: 50% nationwide; 25% Municipals; 25% Private Contracts
Domestic Markets:
Alberta, British Columbia, Saskatchewan
Foreign Activity:
Asia, Caribbean, Central America, China, The Middle East, Mexico, Vietnam

Markets Sought:
Australia/New Zealand, Central Europe,
Contact(s):
Kimron D. Rink, President
Ann Sheridan, Business Manager
Perry Rink, Project Manager

Eco2 Systems Inc.
an AET Group Inc. member company
531 Wellington St. North
Kitchener, ON N2H 5L6
519-576-9723
Fax: 519-570-9589
info@aet-group.com
www.aetconsultants.com
Firm Type: Management Consulting
Founded: 2001
Staff: 2
Member of: Canadian Environmental Certification Approvals Board
Quality Environmental Management System(s): 14001
Products/Services/Areas of Expertise: Environmental, health & safety professionals providing consulting, auditing & training services including environmental management systems (ISO 14001), occupational health & safety management systems (OHSAS 18001), regulatory compliance, pollution prevention, specialized communication & government reporting consultation, training & project management; the firm offers turnkey programs with expertise in a variety of industries
Recently Completed / Ongoing Projects: Ottawa Hydro NPRI/O.Reg 127 Reporting; Project Managment Northstar Serospace (Canada) Inc.; ISO 14001 EMS Audit - Blovata Canada, Danada Canada, Envrinmental Compliance Audot - Teleflex GFI; OHSAS 18001 Training Workshop
Financial Information:
Type of Ownership: Private
Revenue: $100,000 - $250,000
Revenue Sources: 10% Municipals; 90% Private Contracts
Domestic Markets:
National, Ontario
Foreign Activity:
Worldwide
Markets Sought:
Western Europe, The Middle East, South America, Mexico
Contact(s):
Scott Freiburger, President/CEO
Janet McKenzie, Vice President

Ecocern Inc.
4 Nursewood Rd.
Toronto, ON M4E 3R8
416-699-6045
info@ecocern.ca
www.ecocern.ca
Firm Type: Distributing, Scientific/Technical Services
Founded: 1978
Staff: 4
Member of: Ontario Association for Impact Assessment; Society for Ecological Restoration
Products/Services/Areas of Expertise: Solid waste management; fisheries, aquaculture; wildlife & habitats management; environmental audits, impact assessments; field sampling & monitoring; distribution of non-harmful degreasing products
Financial Information:
Type of Ownership: Private
Domestic Markets:
Ontario
Contact(s):
David H. Lewis, President

Ecodyne Ltd.
4475 Corporate Dr.
Burlington, ON L7J 5T9
905-332-1404
Fax: 905-332-6726
888-326-3963
info@ecodyne.com
www.ecodyne.com
Firm Type: Manufacturing
Founded: 1958
Staff: 80
Quality Environmental Management System(s): 9001
Products/Services/Areas of Expertise: Water & waste treatment equipment; cooling towers
Domestic Markets:
National

Foreign Activity:
Africa, Asia, Central America, Eastern Europe, Western Europe, The Middle East, South America, USA
Contact(s):
Gregory O. Allemano, President/CEO
Paul Kitchen, General Sales Manager

EcoEthic Inc.
P.O. Box 566
23 Thompson Rd.
Sunderland, ON L0C 1H0
705-357-9978
Fax: 705-357-9971
888-436-3996
ecoinfo@ecoethic.ca
www.ecoethic.ca
Firm Type: Distributing, Manufacturing
Founded: 1997
Staff: 4
Member of: Ontario Association Sewage Industry Services; Ontario Private Campground Association
EcoLogo Certified Products & Services: RV & marine holding tank additives
Products/Services/Areas of Expertise: On-site wastewater treatment; bacterial waste treatment of septage, lagoons & municipal wastewater; EcoLogo certified odour control of wastewater systems; EcoLogo certified non-toxic cleaning products; distributor of Multtoa Composting Toilets
Ecological Note: RV & marine holding tank additives
Financial Information:
Type of Ownership: Private
Revenue: $250,000 - $500,000
Domestic Markets:
National
Foreign Activity:
Australia/New Zealand, USA
Markets Sought:
Australia/New Zealand, Caribbean, China, South Africa, Mexico, United Kingdom, Vietnam
Contact(s):
Rob Davis

EcoFlame International Inc.
#300, 2120 Queen St. East
Toronto, ON M4E 1E2
416-694-7587
Fax: 416-694-1793
westford@ecogel.com
www.ecogel.com
Products/Services/Areas of Expertise: EcoFlame markets an ethanol, sugar cane based & non toxic heating gel for use in the hospitality, restaurant & catering industries; it is energy efficient, reduces carbon dioxide emissions by at least 50%, burns cleanly & eliminates all other poisonous greenhouse gases, including carbon monoxide; all other heating fuel products are poisonous & derivatives of petroleum & coal, each of which are a finite resource; sugar cane is a renewable resource; is a socially responsible company committed to the research, development & marketing of environmentally responsible products to the hospitality industry & to the private consumer
Ecological Note: EcoFlame gel for consumer & hospitality industry
Contact(s):
Don Haldenby, President
Janice Perkins, 416/694-7587

Ecofluid Systems Inc.
Also Known As: Ecofluid USBF
#209, 5589 Byrne Rd.
Burnaby, BC V5J 3J1
604-662-4544
Fax: 604-662-4564
info@ecofluid.com
www.ecofluid.com
Firm Type: Engineering, Manufacturing
Founded: 1995
Staff: 5
Member of: Canadian Environmental Industry Association
Products/Services/Areas of Expertise: Manufactures & supplies activated sludge biological wastewater treatment & water reclamation plants; provides municipal, industrial, institutional & residential wastewater treatment systems; upgrades existing systems; processes animal manure to humus fertilizer
Recently Completed / Ongoing Projects: Tertiary WWTP Nanoose Bay,BC; Saltspring cottages tertiarry WWTP, Saltspring Island, BC; Cowan Point WWTP, Bowen Island, BC

Products & Services Buyer's Guide

Financial Information:
Type of Ownership: Private
Revenue: $500,000 - $1.5 Million
Revenue Sources: 30% nationwide; 70% Private Contracts
Domestic Markets:
National
Foreign Activity:
Caribbean, Central America, Mexico, USA
Contact(s):
Karel Galland, P.Eng., President

Ecolad Corp.
2539 Dougall Ave.
Windsor, ON N8X 1T5
519-250-0366
Fax: 519-250-0160
800-665-6263
ecolad@ecolad.com
www.ecolad.com
Firm Type: Manufacturing
Founded: 1972
Staff: 6
Member of: Canadian Buy Recycled Alliance
Products/Services/Areas of Expertise: Recycling containers & litter receptacles
Recently Completed / Ongoing Projects: Presently supplying municipalities, campgrounds, golf courses, shopping centres, industrial complexes, colleges, hospitals & medical centres
Financial Information:
Revenue Sources: 50% Municipals; 50% Private Contracts
Domestic Markets:
National
Foreign Activity:
USA
Contact(s):
Mitchell Awad, President

International Branch(es):
USA
#350, 243 W. Congress
Detroit, MI USA

EcoLog Information Resources Group
Formerly: Southam Environmental Group
#800, 12 Concorde Pl.
Toronto, ON M3C 4J2
416-442-5600
Fax: 416-510-5133
800-668-2374
customercare@bizinfogroup.ca
www.ecolog.com
Firm Type: Information Technology
Founded: 1983
Products/Services/Areas of Expertise: Environment & occupational health, safety & worker's compensation legislation in print, CD & online; various weekly & monthly newsletters
Financial Information:
Type of Ownership: Private
Revenue: $1.5 Million - $3 Million
Domestic Markets:
National
Foreign Activity:
USA, Worldwide
Contact(s):
Carol Bell-LeNoury, General Manager
c.bell-lenoury@bizinfogroup.ca
Lidia Lubka, Publisher/Editor
llubka@ecolog.com

Ecologistics Research Services
21599 Cherry Hill Rd.
Thorndale, ON N0M 2P0
519-461-1167
Fax: 519-461-1151
bkerr@ecologistics.com
www.ecologistics.com
Firm Type: Management Consulting, Scientific/Technical Services
Founded: 2000
Staff: 5
Activities: Soil & water conservation; bio-monitoring systems; environmental fate
Financial Information:
Type of Ownership: Private
Contact(s):
Brian Kerr, President
bkerr@ecologistics.com

Sarah Neals-Bolinger, Archivist/Research Technician
Sneals@ecologistics.com
Lyndsay Meadows, Research Technician
lmeadows@ecologistics.com

Ecology Products International
Formerly: ECI Energy Concepts Inc.
P.O. Box 510
514 Railway Ave.
Pilot Butte, SK S0G 3Z0
306-781-4561
Fax: 306-781-4858
radiant@sasktel.net
Firm Type: Scientific/Technical Services
Founded: 1988
Products/Services/Areas of Expertise: Solar heating & drying systems; radiant floor heating; low grade energy heating & cooling systems
Domestic Markets:
Alberta, Manitoba, Saskatchewan
Contact(s):
Vic Ellis, President
Allan Ramsey, Business Manager

Ecomark Ltd.
#100, 16812 - 114 Ave. NW
Edmonton, AB T5M 3S2
780-444-0706
Fax: 780-337-8631
ecomark@ecomarkenv.com
www.ecomarkenv.com
Products/Services/Areas of Expertise: Environmental liability & risk management consulting; remediation & reclamation project management; corporate environmental management services
Contact(s):
Mark Polet, P.Biol., President
Terri Polet, B.Sc., CEO

Canadian Branches:
Calgary
#200, 638 - 11 Ave. SW
Calgary, AB T2R 0E2
403-410-3863

Edson Office
General Delivery #6
Edson, AB T7E 1T1
780-728-7397

ECOMatters Inc.
P.O. Box 430
24 Aberdeen Ave.
Pinawa, MB R0E 1L0
204-753-2747
Fax: 204-753-8478
sheppard@ecomatters.com
www.ecomatters.com
Firm Type: Management Consulting, Scientific/Technical Services
Founded: 1998

Econotech Services Ltd.
852 Derwent Way
Delta, BC V3M 5R1
604-526-4221
Fax: 604-526-1898
800-463-5700
info@econotech.com
www.econotech.com
Firm Type: Scientific/Technical Services
Founded: 1972
Staff: 30
Member of: Canadian Association of Environmental Analytical Laboratories
Products/Services/Areas of Expertise: Research, technical consulting & environmental/process testing with special expertise in the pulp & paper industry; pilot plant & laboratory facilities; AOX testing
Financial Information:
Type of Ownership: Private
Revenue Sources: 99% Private Contracts
Domestic Markets:
National
Foreign Activity:
Australia/New Zealand, Central America, The Middle East, The Pacific Rim, South America, Mexico, USA
Contact(s):

Keith Becker, Vice-President
Thomas Yuen, Coordinator, Analytical Department

Ecotainer Sales Inc.
Also Known As: ANEX Recycling Equipment
2253 Harbourgreene Dr.
Surrey, BC V4A 5J3
604-535-7293
Fax: 604-535-7967
800-561-6525
tom@ecotainer.ca
www.ecotainer.ca
Firm Type: Distributing
Founded: 1991
Staff: 1
Products/Services/Areas of Expertise: Recycling & waste management containers, home composters; compactors; balers; shredders; granulaters
Contact(s):
Tom Button, Sales Manager

Canadian Branches:
St. Catharines
7 South Dr.
St Catharines, ON L2R 4T9
905-932-9242
mike@ecotainer.ca
Mike Damore, Sales Manager

EcoTec Environmental Consultants Inc.
11537 Town Line Rd., RR#1
Acton, ON L7J 2L7
519-853-4914
Fax: 519-853-5013
dclark@ecotecenvironmental.com
www.ecotecenvironmental.com
Firm Type: Scientific/Technical Services
Founded: 1991
Member of: American Fisheries Society; Asian Fisheries Society; World Aquaculture Society; Aquaculture Association of Canada; Canadian Golf Course Superintendents Association; Canadian Water Resources Association
Products/Services/Areas of Expertise: Aquatic & terrestrial habitat design/construction; environmental impact assessment; waste management; aquaculture, fisheries, wildlife & vegetation inventories; natural channel design; water & soil assessment; coastal zone management; research diving; environmental inspection; & Phase I & II site assessments
Financial Information:
Type of Ownership: Private
Contact(s):
Doug Clark, Principal

Canadian Branches:
Merrickville Branch
3301 Country Rd. 16
Merrickville, ON K0G 1N0
613-269-2826
Fax: 613-269-2827
Marten Doomekamp, Eastern Branch Manager

Ecotech Planners & Advisors Inc.
15 Sofron Dr.
Cambridge, ON N3C 4G5
519-664-9823
Fax: 519-654-0328
www.ecotechplanners.com
Firm Type: Management Consulting, Scientific/Technical Services
Founded: 1987
Staff: 3
Member of: Environmental Assessment Association
Products/Services/Areas of Expertise: Environmental consulting; site remediation; environmental audits; waste management; waste stabilization/solidification; emergency response & spill contingency regulatory liaison; expert testimony; training & seminars; groundwater treatment for removal of dissolved & free hydrocarbons & fuels solvents
Financial Information:
Type of Ownership: Private
Domestic Markets:
Ontario,
Contact(s):
Jim Dochstader, President/CEO
Scott Bielaczyk, Operations Manager

EcoVu Analytics
105 Schneider Rd.
Ottawa, ON K2K 1Y3
613-592-0025
Fax: 613-592-5254
info@ecovuanalytics.com
www.ecovuanalytics.com
Firm Type: Scientific/Technical Services
Founded: 2002
Staff: 4
Products/Services/Areas of Expertise: Water remediation; Proprietary technology for removing hydrophobic chemical contaminants from source & industrial waters
Contact(s):
Ray Novokowski, President/CEO

EDA Collaborative Inc.
One Eleven Court
10212 - 111 St.
Edmonton, AB T5K 1K9
780-423-4990
Fax: 780-425-0393
info@eda.ca
www.eda.ca
Firm Type: Engineering
Founded: 1979
Staff: 20
Member of: Canadian Society of Landscape Architects; Canadian Association of Landscape Architects; American Association of Landscape Architects
Products/Services/Areas of Expertise: Environmental planning & design; waste management & end-use planning; public consultation
Domestic Markets:
National
Foreign Activity:
Africa, Asia, The Middle East, USA
Contact(s):
Ted Muller, Principal

Canadian Branches:
Toronto Office
26 Dalhousie St.
Toronto, ON M5B 2A5
416-362-2228
Fax: 416-362-7542
eda@eda-inc.com
Bruce Cudmore

EDM Consultants Ltd.
P.O. Box 3802 Main
Deer Lake, NL A8A 3M1
709-635-8271
Fax: 709-635-5334
Firm Type: Engineering, Scientific/Technical Services
Founded: 1982
Products/Services/Areas of Expertise: Highway & road design & construction; site design; wastewater treatment; water system treatment
Contact(s):
Brad Chaulk, President

EDM Environmental Design & Management Ltd. / EDM
The Maitland Terrace
#300, 2085 Maitland St.
Halifax, NS B3K 2Z8
902-425-7900
Fax: 902-425-7990
info@edm.ca
www.edm.ca
Firm Type: Management Consulting, Engineering
Founded: 1993
Staff: 10
Products/Services/Areas of Expertise: Landscape ecology, land reclamation, geomatics applications, visual/visibility analysis, parks planning & design, ecological engineering for waste treatment, including solar aquatics systems design, ecological planning, community economic development, waterfront planning & design, aquaculture facilites design
Recently Completed / Ongoing Projects: Bear River Solar Aquatics Sewage Treatment plant design; Voisey's Bay mine/mill visual impact assessment; Gander Lake watershed management strategy; design of the Halifax Grand Parade upgrade; Black River fish farm design; Borden/Carleton landscape management plan

Financial Information:
Type of Ownership: Private
Revenue Sources: 10% nationwide; 30% Provincial; 30% Municipals; 30% Private Contracts
Domestic Markets:
New Brunswick, Newfoundland & Labrador, Nova Scotia, Prince Edward Island
Markets Sought:
Central America, USA
Contact(s):
Margot Young, MLA, CSLA, Senior Planner
Trevor Hume, GIS Manager

Educational Program Innovations Centre / EPIC
Coopers Business Centre
5759 Coopers Ave.
Mississauga, ON L4Z 1R9
905-361-1901
Fax: 905-361-1906
888-374-2338
epic@epic-edu.com
www.epic-edu.com
Products/Services/Areas of Expertise: One of the leading providers of engineering continuing education in North America, offers continuing engineering education via engineering courses, in-house training, engineering distance education, PEO Professional Engineers Ontario exams preparation courses, operating engineer program, engineering resources, mailing list & more on topics of importance to engineers, scientists & technologists
Contact(s):
Hira Ahuja, President

Canadian Branches:
Halifax
#B10, 3034 Windsor St.
Halifax, NS B3K 5G1
902-455-5100

Edwards
Unit of SPX Canada
625 - 6 St. East
Owen Sound, ON N4K 5P8
519-376-2430
Fax: 519-371-0940
Firm Type: Distributing, Manufacturing
Founded: 1929
Staff: 1800
Quality Environmental Management System(s): 9002
Products/Services/Areas of Expertise: Audio & visual signals for indoor, outdoor & hazardous locations; wide area emergency warning systems; fire alarm equipment; security equipment; nursecall communications; sprinkler systems; photobadging
Contact(s):
Susan Quiquero, Manager, National Promotions
susan.quiquero@edwards.spx.com

ÉEM inc.
6104, rue Sherbrooke ouest
Montréal, QC H4A 2P1
514-481-3401
Fax: 514-481-4679
info@eem.ca
www.eem.ca
Firm Type: Management Consulting
Founded: 1988
Staff: 10
Products/Services/Areas of Expertise: Environmental management system review, design, development & auditing; regulatory interpretation & permitting; NPRI reporting; training material design & preparation; training delivery; environmental site assessment
Financial Information:
Type of Ownership: Private
Domestic Markets:
National
Foreign Activity:
Africa, The Pacific Rim, South America, Mexico
Contact(s):
Paul MacLean, M.Sc., CEA, EMA (LA), President

Canadian Branches:
Ontario Office
#210, 130 Bridgeland Ave.
Toronto, ON M6A 1Z4

EEP Engineered & Environmental Products Inc. / EEP
P.O. Box 2698
44 Albert St.
Windsor, NS B0N 2T0
902-798-0300
Fax: 902-798-0633
mail@eep.ca
www.eep.ca
Firm Type: Distributing
Founded: 1992
Staff: 4
Products/Services/Areas of Expertise: Pumps; grinders; values; heat exchanges; dust collectors; dewatering screens; air pollution control
Domestic Markets:
New Brunswick, Newfoundland & Labrador, Nova Scotia, Prince Edward Island

Canadian Branches:
New Brunswick
150 Bessie's Garden Lane
Harvey York Co, NB E6K 2J7
506-366-2912
Fax: 506-366-2908
Rob Burtt, Sales Engineer

EFC Control Inc.
Les Laboratoires Quelab Inc.
2331, rue Dandurand
Montréal, QC H2G 3C5
514-277-2558
Fax: 514-277-4714
800-361-1434
info@quelab.com
Firm Type: Manufacturing
Founded: 1974
Staff: 52
Products/Services/Areas of Expertise: Self-contained recirculating hood for laboratory applications
Financial Information:
Type of Ownership: Private
Revenue: Less than $50,000
Revenue Sources: 20% nationwide; 80% Provincial
Domestic Markets:
Ontario, Québec
Foreign Activity:
Western Europe
Markets Sought:
Caribbean, Central America, South America
Contact(s):
Roger Boulais, President
roger.boulais@quelab.qc.ca
Michel Éthier, Sales/Marketing Director

Efficiency Engineering Inc.
#203, 420 Sheldon Dr.
Cambridge, ON N1T 2H9
519-624-9965
Fax: 519-624-9316
www.ee-solutions.com
Firm Type: Engineering, Scientific/Technical Services
Founded: 1990
Staff: 8
Member of: Association of Heating, Refrigeration & Air Conditioning Engineers; Association of Professional Engineers of Ontario; Illuminating Engineering Society of North America
Products/Services/Areas of Expertise: Program planning, assessment & engineering for energy & water conservation projects; operating cost savings & carbon dioxide emission reductions; specialize in commercial & institutional building portfolios
Financial Information:
Type of Ownership: Private
Domestic Markets:
Ontario
Foreign Activity:
USA

EFR Disposal
P.O. Box 260
1440 Hwy. 360
Berwick, NS B0P 1E0
902-538-8474
Fax: 902-538-8249
info@efrdisposal.com
www.efrdisposal.com

Products & Services Buyer's Guide

Contact(s):
Michael Grady, Manager

Egetec Enterprises Inc.
Formerly: MSE Engineering Systems Ltd.
25 Moore Pl.
Barrie, ON L4N 6N8
705-734-1090
Fax: 705-734-1083
888-745-1671
egetec@egetec.ca
www.egetec.ca
Firm Type: Distributing
Founded: 1974
Products/Services/Areas of Expertise: Measuring & monitoring equipment; field aquatic samplers; temperature indicators; marine science & oceanographic instruments; underwater tow & instrument cables, special cable harnesses, underwater electrical connectors & terminations, underwater solenoids, switches
Recently Completed / Ongoing Projects: Special cable harness/connectors for Depts. of National Defence, Fisheries & Oceans
Financial Information:
Type of Ownership: Private
Revenue: $250,000 - $500,000
Revenue Sources: 60% nationwide; 2% Provincial; 1% Municipals; 37% Private Contracts
Domestic Markets:
National,
Contact(s):
Alfred Egerton, President
aegerton@egetec.ca

Egmond Associates Ltd. / EAL
27 Hall Rd.
Georgetown, ON L7G SY7
905-877-6496
Fax: 905-877-6821
800-267-4797
info@egmondassociates.com
www.egmondassociates.com
Firm Type: Engineering, Manufacturing
Founded: 1987
Staff: 4
Member of: Association of Professional Engineers; Canadian Society for Civil Engineering; Canadian Geotechnical Society; Association of Professional Engineers of Ontario
Products/Services/Areas of Expertise: Phase 1 - 3 environmental engineering site assessments; water & water wells (GVOL); contaminated lands
Recently Completed / Ongoing Projects: Phase 1 - 2 investigation of strip mall, infiltration of rainwater
Financial Information:
Type of Ownership: Private
Revenue Sources: 90% Private Contracts
Domestic Markets:
Ontario
Foreign Activity:
USA
Contact(s):
John Van Egmond, P.Eng., President
john_van_egmond@egmondassociates.com

International Branch(es):
Minneapolis
#500, 701 - 4 Ave. South
Minneapolis, MN USA

EIL Environmental Services
16041 - 132 Ave.
Edmonton, AB T5V 1H8
780-448-0866
Fax: 780-482-5750
gary.michalchuk@eilenvironmental.com
www.eilenvironmental.com
Firm Type: Waste Management
Founded: 1991
Staff: 17
Member of: Environmental Services Association of Alberta
Products/Services/Areas of Expertise: Hazardous waste management & disposal services
Financial Information:
Type of Ownership: Private
Revenue: $100,000 - $250,000
Domestic Markets:
Alberta, British Columbia, Northwest Territories, Saskatchewan

Contact(s):
Gary Michalchuk, President
Gary Demeriez, Sales Manager

EITNL/Earth Information Technologies (nfld) Limited / EITNL
20 Mercer's Dr.
St. John's, NL A1A 2X1
709-738-1638
www.eitnl.ca
Firm Type: Management Consulting, Engineering, Information Technology
Founded: 1996
Products/Services/Areas of Expertise: Geomatics consulting, including land & marine settings; GIS design & implementation, web mapping systems; GIS website hosting; geomatics training programs, seminars
Recently Completed / Ongoing Projects: Town of Gander; Town of Conception Bay South; NL Seabed Atlas; Eastern School District, NL; MapsNL - NL Surveys & Mapping; SmartBay - Placentia Bay, NL; NL Dept. of Transportation & Works
Financial Information:
Type of Ownership: Private
Revenue Sources: 0% nationwide; 0% Provincial; 0% Municipals; 0% Private Contracts
Domestic Markets:
New Brunswick, Newfoundland & Labrador, Nova Scotia, Prince Edward Island
Contact(s):
Robert Leeman, P.Eng., NLS, NBLS, President

El-Rayes Environmental Corp.
2601 East Mall
Vancouver, BC V6T 1Z4
604-222-2387
Firm Type: Management Consulting, Engineering, Information Technology, Scientific/Technical Services
Founded: 1992
Staff: 5
Products/Services/Areas of Expertise: Environmental consulting firm that provides services to municipal, provincial, & federal governments & industry; services include consulting, research & development, & transfer of state-of-the-art technologies; areas of environmental services include municipal & industrial wastewater treatment, water treatment, solid & hazardous waste management, leachate treatment, environmental audits & site assessment, regulatory compliance, permitting, monitoring, remediation of contaminated sites, & treatability studies
Recently Completed / Ongoing Projects: Development of pollution prevention guide for the brewing & wine-making, auto-recycling & wood preservation industries
Financial Information:
Type of Ownership: Private
Revenue Sources: 30% nationwide; 10% Provincial; 30% Municipals; 30% Private Contracts
Domestic Markets:
Alberta, British Columbia
Foreign Activity:
Africa, USA
Markets Sought:
Asia, The Middle East
Contact(s):
Hamdy El-Rayes, Ph.D., P.Eng., M.B.A., President

Elasto Valve Rubber Products Inc. / EVR
Also Known As: Elasto-Valve
1691 Pioneer Rd.
Sudbury, ON P3G 1B2
705-523-2026
Fax: 705-523-2033
800-461-6331
sales@evrproducts.com
www.evrproducts.com
Firm Type: Manufacturing
Founded: 1984
Staff: 35
Quality Environmental Management System(s): 9001:2000
Products/Services/Areas of Expertise: Vibration & expansion control; connectors for pipe & ducting; pinch valves for slurries & sludge; in line diaphragm seals for pressure instruments
Financial Information:
Type of Ownership: Publicly Traded
Domestic Markets:
National

Foreign Activity:
Asia, Australia/New Zealand, Western Europe, The Middle East, South America, USA
Markets Sought:
Central America, Eastern Europe, Mexico,
Contact(s):
Peter Sucharda, Engineer, Sales & Marketing

Elecsar Engineering Co. Ltd.
P.O. Box 2009
Sarnia, ON N7T 7K2
519-337-6580
Fax: 519-332-6198
sarnia@elecsar.com
www.elecsar.com
Firm Type: Engineering
Founded: 1980
Staff: 15
Member of: Association of Professional Engineers of Ontario; Municipal Engineers Association; Ontario Chamber of Commerce; Independent Power Producers' Society of Ontario; Ontario Association of Engineering Technicians & Technologists
Products/Services/Areas of Expertise: Solid waste transport & disposal; recycling of paint, solvents, plastics; noise & vibration assessment; energy consulting; risk assessment; site assessment; design & specifications; bulk electrical power engineering
Recently Completed / Ongoing Projects: Addition of a 100MWA standby transformer in an industrial transformer station; transformer fire fighting training; new 230kV transformer station at a petrochemical refinery & car plant
Financial Information:
Type of Ownership: Private
Revenue: $1.5 Million - $3 Million
Revenue Sources: 30% Municipals; 70% Private Contracts
Domestic Markets:
National
Foreign Activity:
Asia, The Pacific Rim, USA
Contact(s):
David McGarry, C.E.T., President/Operations Manager
Gord Roberts, P.Eng., Vice-President/Engineering Manager
Bob Thompson, C.E.T., Project Manager
Mark Sopel, P.Eng., Project Manager

Canadian Branches:
Toronto Office
#19, 7330 Yonge St.
Thornhill, ON L4J 7Y7
905-881-8961
Fax: 905-881-8962
toronto@elecsar.com
Gord Roberts, P.Eng.

Electric Motor Service (1979) Ltd.
129 Westmorland St.
Fredericton, NB E3B 3L4
506-458-8770
Fax: 506-458-8771
800-561-3089
www.electricmotorservice.ca
Products/Services/Areas of Expertise: Water pumps; water treatment equipment

Electro-Air Canada
351 North Rivermede Rd.
Concord, ON L4K 3N2
416-213-5636
Fax: 416-213-5593
800-267-8305
info@fiveseasonsaircleaners.com
www.fiveseasonsaircleaners.com
Firm Type: Manufacturing
Founded: 1962
Member of: Clean Air Device Manufacturers Association
Products/Services/Areas of Expertise: Air purification equipment for residential, commercial & industrial use
Financial Information:
Type of Ownership: Private
Domestic Markets:
National
Foreign Activity:
Worldwide
Markets Sought:
Asia, Central America, Eastern Europe, South America, Mexico, USA
Contact(s):

Beverly David, President/CEO
Caroline David, Marketing & Sales Manager
Robert Crowe, Product Manager

Electro-Mecanik Inc.
Franklin Empire Inc.
215, rue Fortin
Quebec, QC G1M 3M2
418-683-1725
Fax: 418-683-1726
888-683-1724
emecan@feinc.com
www.feinc.com
Firm Type: Manufacturing
Founded: 1962
Staff: 53
Quality Environmental Management System(s): 9001
Products/Services/Areas of Expertise: Laboratory equipment
Domestic Markets:
Québec
Contact(s):
Gilles Roy, Président
Guy Plamondon, Directeur des ventes & marketing
Jean-Noel Bégin, Vice-Président

Canadian Branches:
Alma Branch
167, Claire-Fontaine
Alma, QC G8B 6G9
418-480-1950
Fax: 418-480-3555
800-361-5044
alma@feinc.com
Bernard St-Gelais, Manager

Montréal Branch
8421, rue Darnley
Mont-Royal, QC G7H 5B2
514-341-3720
Fax: 514-340-1240
800-361-5044
shop@feinc.com

Electronic Warfare Associates - Canada, Ltd.
#1600, 55 Metcalfe St.
Ottawa, ON K1P 6L5
613-230-6067
Fax: 613-230-4933
ewainfo@ewa-canada.com
www.ewa-canada.com
Firm Type: Engineering, Information Technology, Scientific/Technical Services
Founded: 1988
Staff: 28
Member of: FIRST.Org, Inc. (Forum of Incident Response & Security Teams)
Quality Environmental Management System(s): 9001:2008
Products/Services/Areas of Expertise: Specializes in providing systems & software engineering services & project management support for complex systems to various government departments including the Department of National Defence, other agencies & to industry; provides preparation of procurement approval documentation; preparation of statements of operational requirement, operational concept documents & project implementation plans; performance of pre-definition & definition studies, including feasibility & technology studies; preparation of system development & installation specifications including corresponding statement of work; preparation & execution of structured proposal evaluation plans for contractors' proposals; independent verification & validation of contractor hardware & software deliverables; design & implementation of software & hardware systems
Financial Information:
Type of Ownership: Private
Revenue Sources: 90% nationwide; 5% Municipals; 5% Private Contracts
Domestic Markets:
National
Foreign Activity:
Australia/New Zealand, USA
Markets Sought:
Asia, Central America, Western Europe, South America, Mexico
Contact(s):
Jim Robbins, President

Canadian Branches:
Atlantic Office
#601, 139 Water St.
St. John's, NL A1C 1B2
709-726-0667
Fax: 709-726-0668
Joe Dawson, Regional Manager
jdawson@ewa-canada.com

British Columbia Office
6090 Sperling Ave.
Burnaby, BC V5E 2T9
604-524-8141
Dave Squires, Regional Manager
dsquires@ewa-canada.com

Electronics-recycling.com
#120, 13065 - 84th Ave.
Surrey, BC V3W 1B3
604-599-8078
Fax: 866-482-7478
info@electronics-recycling.com
www.electronics-recycling.com
Firm Type: Waste Management
Staff: 3
Products/Services/Areas of Expertise: Management of e-waste for manufacturers, business, government offices, hospitals, educational & other organizations; drop-off & pick-up collection; one-stop recycling services; refurbishing of electronic equipment; CRT tube recycling; certificate of environmental responsiblity; R&D protection, certificate of destruction; logistics support; consulting; solutions for other waste
Financial Information:
Revenue: Less than $50,000
Contact(s):
Edward Wu, President
Derers Mange, Marketing
derers@electronics-recycling.com
Christian Hunt, Sales
chris@electronics-recycling.com
Karen Zhang, Accounting
karen@electronics-recycling.com

Elemental Research Inc. / ERI
#309, 267 Esplanade West
North Vancouver, BC V7M 1A5
604-986-0445
Fax: 604-986-0071
eri@elementalresearch.com
Firm Type: Scientific/Technical Services
Founded: 1987
Staff: 25
Quality Environmental Management System(s): 9001
Products/Services/Areas of Expertise: Contract research & advanced analytical services including method development & validation; expertise & applications based on mass spectrometry (ICPMS, GCMS, LCMS, LC-ICPMS, etc.)
Recently Completed / Ongoing Projects: Speciation of metals in biota (e.g., As III vs As V) by Lc-ICPMS, trace metals, including heavy metals, analysis on biological matrices as well as soils & waters
Financial Information:
Type of Ownership: Private
Revenue: $1.5 Million - $3 Million
Revenue Sources: 3% nationwide; 3% Provincial; 94% Private Contracts
Domestic Markets:
National
Foreign Activity:
Worldwide
Contact(s):
David J. Gray, President
Sheri Watson, Sales & Marketing Correspondent

Elford Environmental
Also Known As: Elford Appraisal & Consulting Services
#355, 3132 - 26 St. NE
Calgary, AB T1Y 6Z1
403-292-9191
Fax: 403-230-8103
elford.environmental@shawlink.ca
Firm Type: Management Consulting
Founded: 1981
Staff: 6
Member of: Appraisal Institute of Canada
Products/Services/Areas of Expertise: Environmental audit services & assessments; General environmental consulting & contracting services
Financial Information:
Type of Ownership: Private
Revenue Sources: 100% Private Contracts
Domestic Markets:
Alberta, British Columbia, Saskatchewan
Contact(s):
Robin K. Elford, Contact

Elgin Pure Water Supply
22 Spackman Blvd.
St Thomas, ON N5P 4A3
519-633-1861
Fax: 519-633-1910
lakes@execulink.com
Firm Type: Distributing
Founded: 1981
Staff: 6
Member of: Canadian Water Quality Association; Pollution Probe; Greenpeace
Products/Services/Areas of Expertise: Bottled water delivery, water coolers, drinking water products; water treatment equipment; pressure systems, pumps, chlorination systems, iron removers, softeners
Financial Information:
Type of Ownership: Private
Domestic Markets:
Ontario
Contact(s):
Harold Lake, President/CEO
Bonnie Lake, Owner

ELI Eco Chemical Technologies Inc.
Formerly: ELI Eco Logic International Inc
Also Known As: Eco Logic
143 Dennis St.
Rockwood, ON N0B 2K0
519-856-9591
Fax: 519-856-9235
beth.kummling@ecologic.ca
Firm Type: Engineering
Founded: 1986
Staff: 11
Products/Services/Areas of Expertise: Eco Logic is a viable alternative to incineration for the treatment of highly hazardous organic contaminants; a patented, closed-loop process which chemically breaks down organic contaminants into product gas (primarily methane & hydrogen), water vapour & carbon monoxide; various feed mechanisms are employed for the treatment of liquids, soils & bulk solids, such as electrical equipment
Recently Completed / Ongoing Projects: Chemical weapons destruction testing
Financial Information:
Type of Ownership: Publicly Traded
Revenue: Greater than $5 Million
Domestic Markets:
Ontario
Foreign Activity:
Australia/New Zealand, The Pacific Rim, USA
Markets Sought:
Asia, Eastern Europe, Western Europe
Contact(s):
Fred T. Arnold, Ph.D., CEO
Garry DeCudlo, Vice-President, Business Development
Beth Kummling, M.Sc., Director of Business Development

International Branch(es):
Harwood
835 Cumberstone Rd.
Harwood, MD USA
301-261-5381
Fred T. Arnold

Elite Technologies Inc.
51, rue du Bel-Air
Lévis, QC G6V 6K9
418-834-3001
Fax: 418-834-2651
800-263-3134
info@elitetechnologie.com
www.elitetechnologie.com
Firm Type: Engineering
Founded: 1980
Staff: 50

Member of: Instrumentation Systems & Automation; Ordre des technologue du Québec; Ordre des ingenieurs du Québec
Products/Services/Areas of Expertise: Services in instrumentation, automation & process control fields; engineering, construction & maintenance; CEMS & specialized equipment
Recently Completed / Ongoing Projects: Modernization of instrumentation & process control, central thermal plant; designed & fabricated 3 CEMS for Pratt & Whitney
Financial Information:
Type of Ownership: Private
Revenue Sources: 1% nationwide; 3% Provincial; 12% Municipals; 84% Private Contracts
Domestic Markets:
Alberta, Manitoba, New Brunswick, Newfoundland & Labrador, Nova Scotia, Ontario, Québec
Foreign Activity:
USA
Contact(s):
Michel Ruel, President
Canadian Branches:
Montréal
227-D, boul Brunswick
Pointe-Claire, QC H9R 4X5
514-695-7001
Fax: 514-695-2665
866-654-5001

Ellett Industries
1575 Kingsway Ave.
Port Coquitlam, BC V3C 4E5
604-941-8211
Fax: 604-941-6854
ellett@ellett.ca
www.ellett.ca
Firm Type: Manufacturing
Founded: 1921
Staff: 150
Member of: National Association of Corrosion Engineers; Titanium Development Association; American Society of Mechanical Engineers
Products/Services/Areas of Expertise: Sewage treatment equipment; waste storage containers; design & fabrication of equipment using corrosion-resistant material; heat exchangers, tanks & pipes; evaporators
Financial Information:
Type of Ownership: Private
Revenue: Greater than $5 Million
Domestic Markets:
Alberta, British Columbia
Foreign Activity:
Asia, Australia/New Zealand, The Pacific Rim, South America
Contact(s):
John S. Ellett, President
Lyle Osberg, Sales Manager

Elliott & Elliott Limited Consulting Engineers
28 Cochrane St.
St. John's, NL A1C 3L3
709-753-6570
Fax: 709-753-9323
Contact(s):
Cy Elliott, Manager

Elmec Engineering Ltd.
1410 Crown St.
North Vancouver, BC V7J 1G5
604-985-4721
Fax: 604-985-3687
elmecengineering@ivancouver.com
www.elmecengineering.com
Firm Type: Engineering, Manufacturing
Founded: 1972
Staff: 7
Member of: Association of Professional Engineers & Geologists of BC
Products/Services/Areas of Expertise: Gas turbine fuel conversion, distillate fuel to natural gas
Recently Completed / Ongoing Projects: Natural gas conversion gas turbine power plant 2004, Indonesia; Polymer treatment system, sediment & coal mine, 2005, BC, Canada
Financial Information:
Type of Ownership: Private
Revenue: $500,000 - $1.5 Million
Revenue Sources: 100% Private Contracts

Domestic Markets:
British Columbia
Foreign Activity:
Australia/New Zealand, South Africa, South America, USA, United Kingdom
Contact(s):
Steve Gyabronka, President
Leo Vanderby, Controller

Elmridge Engineering Inc.
Also Known As: Elmridge Jet Apparatus
#15, 3625 Weston Rd.
Toronto, ON M9L 1V9
416-749-7730
Fax: 416-749-2550
888-338-2867
sales@elmridge.org
www.elmridge.org
Firm Type: Manufacturing
Staff: 25
Products/Services/Areas of Expertise: Jet apparatus for pumping, mixing, evacuation
Domestic Markets:
National
Foreign Activity:
Western Europe, Mexico, USA
Contact(s):
Strachan Bowen, President
International Branch(es):
USA
39111 West Six Mile Rd.
Livonia, MI USA

Elmtree Environmental Ltd.
P.O. Box 444 A
Fredericton, NB E3B 4Z9
506-444-0133
Fax: 506-452-2108
elmtree@nbnet.nb.ca
www.elmtree.ca
Firm Type: Scientific/Technical Services, Waste Management
Founded: 1994
Products/Services/Areas of Expertise: Site reclamation & remedial action services; soil remediation services
Contact(s):
Darren Chamberlain, Manager

Emco
1108 Dundas St. East
London, ON N5W 3A7
519-453-9600
Fax: 519-645-2465
www.emcoltd.com
Firm Type: Distributing
Founded: 1906
Staff: 3000
Quality Environmental Management System(s): 9002
Products/Services/Areas of Expertise: Distributes plumbing, heating, including fire protection, ventilation, air conditioning, water works
Financial Information:
Type of Ownership: Private
Revenue: Greater than $5 Million
Domestic Markets:
National
Contact(s):
Rick Fanthome, President

Emco Wheaton Corp.
A dvision of Gardner Denver, Inc.
2480 Bristol Circle
Oakville, ON L6H 5S1
905-829-8619
Fax: 905-829-8620
webassist@emcowheaton.com
www.emcowheaton.com
Firm Type: Manufacturing
Products/Services/Areas of Expertise: Manufacture & supply of centrifugal blowers & related accessories for wastewater aeration requirements
Financial Information:
Type of Ownership: Foreign-owned
Domestic Markets:
Ontario

Foreign Activity:
USA
Contact(s):
Stan R. Elsdon, President
Darren Sabino, Manager, Domestic Sales & Marketing Export Sales & Marketing
darren.sabino@emcowheaton.com
Canadian Branches:
Mississauga - Blower Division
2425 Matheson Blvd. East, 8th Fl.
Mississauga, ON L4W 5K4
416-763-4681
Fax: 416-763-0440

Emerge Knowledge Design Inc.
Also Known As: Emerge Environmental Information Solutions
#305, 250 McDermot Ave.
Winnipeg, MB R3B 0S5
204-772-7239
Fax: 204-775-7946
888-600-3907
info@emergeknowledge.com
www.emergeknowledge.com
Firm Type: Information Technology
Founded: 2001
Staff: 4
Products/Services/Areas of Expertise: Environmental information services
Financial Information:
Type of Ownership: Private
Revenue: $100,000 - $250,000
Domestic Markets:
Alberta, British Columbia, Manitoba, Ontario
Foreign Activity:
USA

EmerGeo Solutions Inc.
#1001, 1166 Alberni St.
Vancouver, BC V6E 3Z3
604-681-0989
Fax: 604-681-0079
888-577-0911
sales@emergeo.com
www.emergeo.com
Firm Type: Management Consulting, Distributing, Information Technology
Founded: 1998
Products/Services/Areas of Expertise: EM2000; ILP; emergency management; EHS
Financial Information:
Type of Ownership: Private
Domestic Markets:
National
Foreign Activity:
Australia/New Zealand, Caribbean, Western Europe, The Pacific Rim, USA, Worldwide
Contact(s):
Mike Morrow, President
Tony M. Ricci, Chief Financial Officer

Emergex Planning Inc.
#265, 3580 Moncton St.
Richmond, BC V7E 3A4
604-303-8803
Fax: 604-303-7743
888-992-0888
info@emergexplanning.com
www.emergexplanning.com
Firm Type: Management Consulting
Founded: 1992
Member of: College of Applied Biologists of BC
Products/Services/Areas of Expertise: Identification of environmental impacts in various media (soil, sediment, water), as a result of environmental emergencies (natural or anthropogenic); design of environmental remediation/mitigation measures to reduce long-term effects of emergency; environmental remediation measures incorporated into recovery plans
Recently Completed / Ongoing Projects: Environmental management flood recovery plans: Squamish, Province of BC
Financial Information:
Type of Ownership: Private
Revenue: $500,000 - $1.5 Million
Revenue Sources: 10% nationwide; 40% Provincial; 20% Municipals; 30% Private Contracts

Domestic Markets:
National
Foreign Activity:
USA
Markets Sought:
Asia, Australia/New Zealand, Caribbean, The Pacific Rim
Contact(s):
Tully Waisman, President/CEO
tully@emergexplanning.com
Chessy Langford, Environmental Scientist
chessy@emergexplanning.com

Emerson Electric Canada Limited
Also Known As: Emerson Canada
An operating company of Emerson Electic Co.
306 Town Centre Blvd.
Markham, ON L3R 0Y6
905-948-3400
Fax: 905-948-3414
info@emersonelectric.ca; InfoCanada@Emerson.com
www.emersoncanada.ca
Firm Type: Distributing, Manufacturing
Founded: 1957
Staff: 2000
Quality Environmental Management System(s): 9002:1994;
Products/Services/Areas of Expertise: Emerson is a global company offering a diverse range of products & services to meet the needs of various sectors including the chemical, food & beverage, life sciences, oil & gas, power, pulp & paper, refining, & waste & wastewater industries. Emerson Canada manufactures electrical & electronic products & systems, & through its operating subsidiaries products including valves, switches & industrial controls, compressors & condensors, process controls, measuring & monitoring devices, commercial & industrial cleaners, & electronic components
Financial Information:
Type of Ownership: Foreign-owned; Publicly Traded
Domestic Markets:
National
Foreign Activity:
Worldwide
Markets Sought:
China, The Pacific Rim, South America
Contact(s):
Larry C. Barrett, President
Contact(s):
Tom Adkins, Director
tom.adkins@kenonic.com
Contact(s):
Hugh Flesher, Manager, Export Sales & Marketing
hugh.flesher@emersonprocess.com

Canadian Branches:
Hamilton - Emerson Process Management
Asset Optimization Division - East
Fisher Valves & Instruments
#2, 20 Depew St.
Hamilton, ON L8L 7H8
905-548-6698
Fax: 905-548-6396
Products/Services/Areas of Expertise: Instrument & valve service for Fisher Valves & Instruments; Fisher products include actuators, control valves, digital valve controllers, field instrumentation, nuclear valves & controllers, positioners, & wireless products

Brantford - ASCO Numatics / ASCO
Also Known As: ASCO Valve Canada
P.O. Box 160
17 Airport Rd.
Brantford, ON N3T 5M8
519-758-2700
Fax: 519-758-5540
ascomail@asco.ca
www.ascovalve.ca
Products/Services/Areas of Expertise: Solenoid valves & other quality precision products for the automation of equipment & the control of air, liquids, & gases; client sectors include the automotive, biofuels, petroleum & chemical pharmaceutical, nuclear power, & pulp & paper industries

Calgary - Daniel Industries Canada Inc.
Also Known As: Daniel Measurement & Control
4215 - 72 Ave. SE
Calgary, AB T2C 2G5
403-279-1879
Fax: 403-236-1337
www.emersonprocess.com
Products/Services/Areas of Expertise: Fiscal flow & energy measurement products & systems, with a focus on the oil & gas sector; flow meters & metering systems; analyzers; control valves

Calgary - Emerson Process Management
Kenonic Controls Limited
110 Quarry Park Blvd.
Calgary, AB T2C 3G3
403-258-6200
Fax: 403-258-6201
emerson.reception@emerson.com
www.emersonprocess.com
Firm Type: Management Consulting, Distributing, Engineering, Information Technology, Manufacturing
Founded: 1972
Staff: 350
Products/Services/Areas of Expertise: Automation & automation engineering; plant control systems (engineering, installation & service); information technology; consulting & training. Client sectors include the petroleum, oil & gas industries, natural resources & environmental sectors, power generation facilities, & telecommunications
Foreign Activity:
Africa, Caribbean, Eastern Europe, The Middle East, The Pacific Rim, South America, USA, Former USSR

Dorval - Emerson Energy Systems
#303, 455, boul. Fenelon
Montréal, QC H9S 5T8
514-422-8884
Fax: 514-422-8887
www.emersonnetworkpower.com
Products/Services/Areas of Expertise: DC power, distribution, control & monitoring systems; enclosures, cabinets & other shelter solutions; infrastructure monitoring solutions; renewable & hybrid energy solutions including high-efficiency rectifiers, fuel cell solutions for telecom networks, & remote management solutions that minimize energy use

Edmonton - Bettis Canada Ltd.
4112 - 91A St.
Edmonton, AB T6E 5V2
780-450-3600
Fax: 780-450-1400
800-383-1988
www.emersonvalveautomation.com
Firm Type: Distributing, Manufacturing
Founded: 1970
Staff: 95
Quality Environmental Management System(s): 9001
Products/Services/Areas of Expertise: Valve actuators & controls; pneumatic & hydraulic valve actuators; relays, pressure pilots & limit switches for valve actuators & control systems. Client focus on the oil & gas, pipeline, & production sectors as well as the pulp & paper industry
Foreign Activity:
Africa, Asia, Australia/New Zealand, China, Central Europe, Eastern Europe, The Middle East, The Pacific Rim, South America, USA, Former USSR, United Kingdom
Markets Sought:
The Middle East

London - Numatics Limited
363 Sovereign Rd.
London, ON N6B 1A4
519-452-1777
Fax: 519-452-3995
Products/Services/Areas of Expertise: Pneumatics & motion control products; valves; vacuum products; power clamps; filers; drying systems; gripper products; actuators. Client sectors include the automotive, food & beverage, biofuels, pulp & paper, water & wastewater, & nuclear power industries

Mississauga - Liebert Canada
#1, 3580 Laird Rd.
Mississauga, ON L5L 5Z7
905-569-8282
Fax: 905-569-9418
www.emersonnetworkpower.com
Products/Services/Areas of Expertise: Integrated data centre solutions that optimize infrastructure efficiency & capacity; uninterruptible power, power distribution & enclosure solutions; precision cooling solutions; infrastructure monitoring systems; data centre storage; surge protection solutions

Montréal - Leroy-Somer
#201, 8518, Place Devonshire
Montréal, QC H4P 2K1
514-332-1880
Fax: 514-332-5912
canada@leroy-somer.com
www.leroy-somer.com
Products/Services/Areas of Expertise: Alternators & drive systems, with a focus on hydraulic turbine drive systems for hydroelectric power faciilities; auxiliary drive systems for wind turbines; solutions for solar trackers; marine sector applications; IE2 efficiency motors, variable speed drives, & synchronous drive mechanisms that save energy & reduce the ecological footprint

Emery International Developments
Formerly: Roy W. Emery Limited
#1, 340 Ferrier St.
Markham, ON L3R 2Z5
905-470-6066
Fax: 905-470-6505
info@emeryinternational.com
www.emeryinternational.com
Firm Type: Engineering, Manufacturing, Waste Management
Founded: 1974
Staff: 20
Member of: Canadian Pulp & Paper Association
Member of: Markham Board of Trade
Products/Services/Areas of Expertise: Design & manufacture of turnkey pulp moulding plants for production of packaging materials from recycled waste; reuse of paper sludges & other wastes
Financial Information:
Type of Ownership: Private
Revenue Sources: 100% Private Contracts
Domestic Markets:
National
Foreign Activity:
Worldwide
Markets Sought:
Eastern Europe, South America
Contact(s):
James Emery, CEO
Alan Emery, CFO
John Emery, Chair
Brian Lemire, COO
Barb Hughes, Director, Sales & Marketing
barbara@emeryinternational.com

EMP Environmental Management & Protection Corporation
Formerly: ERM-Ontario, Inc.
#404, 21 Queen St. East
Brampton, ON L6W 3P1
905-796-1199
Fax: 905-796-2526
post@empcanada.com
Firm Type: Management Consulting, Engineering
Founded: 1990
Staff: 6
Products/Services/Areas of Expertise: Environmental, health & safety consulting firm; site assessments & auditing; air & water quality; site remediation; health & safety programs; waste management; third party services; training & seminars
Domestic Markets:
National
Foreign Activity:
Worldwide
Contact(s):
Kevin Ridley, President

Empire Dynamic Structures Ltd.
Formerly: Coast Steel Fabricators Ltd; AGRA Coast Ltd; AMEC Dynamic Structures Ltd
Also Known As: Dynamic Structures
78 Fawcett Rd.
Coquitlam, BC V3K 6V5
604-639-8200
Fax: 604-294-4550
www.amecds.com
Firm Type: Manufacturing
Founded: 1926
Staff: 110
Quality Environmental Management System(s): 9002:1994
Products/Services/Areas of Expertise: Designer & manufacturer of complex structures for the steel fabrication market, the amusement ride industry, & the telescope observatory market; Management system based on standards contained in Occupational Health & Safety Management

Products & Services Buyer's Guide

Systems 18001 & ISO 14001, "Environmental Management Systems"
Domestic Markets:
Alberta, British Columbia, Manitoba, Saskatchewan
Foreign Activity:
Worldwide

EMS Technologies
Formerly: CAL Corporation
400 Maple Grove Rd.
Ottawa, ON K2V 1B8
613-591-9064
Fax: 613-591-9120
800-600-9759
info@emssatcom.com
www.ems-t.com
Firm Type: Manufacturing
Founded: 1974
Quality Environmental Management System(s): 9001
Products/Services/Areas of Expertise: Aerospace & communications; electro-optical space science instruments, antennas, electronic systems; mobile satellite communication terminals, search-&-rescue satellite ground stations
Contact(s):
Paul Domorski, President/CEO

Encana Corporation
P.O. Box 2850
#1800, 855 - 2nd St. SW
Calgary, AB T2P 2S5
403-645-2000
Fax: 403-645-3400
888-568-6322
www.encana.com
Firm Type: Manufacturing, X
Products/Services/Areas of Expertise: Exploration & development of natural gas, including shale & tight gas resources plays; processes take into consideration worker health & safety, as well as environmental impacts, with a focus on reducing energy use & emissions; operations in Canada & the U.S.
Recently Completed / Ongoing Projects: Bighorn; Cutbank Ridge (AB & BC); Greater Sierra (BC); Coalbed Methane (Horseshoe Canyon); Deep Panuke (NS)
Financial Information:
Type of Ownership: Publicly Traded
Domestic Markets:
Alberta, British Columbia, Nova Scotia
Foreign Activity:
USA
Contact(s):
Randy Eresman, President/CEO
Sherri Brillon, Exec. Vice-President/CFO
Mike Graham, Exec. Vice-President/President, Canadian Division

Canadian Branches:
Calgary - Dome Tower
Dome Tower
P.O. Box 2850
333 - 7 Ave. SW
Calgary, AB T2P 2S5
888-568-6322

Calgary - Encana Place
Encana Place
P.O. Box 2850
150 - 9th Ave. SW
Calgary, AB T2P 2S5
403-645-2000
Fax: 403-645-2950
888-568-6322

Calgary - One Palliser Square
P.O. Box 2850
125 - 9th Ave. SE
Calgary, AB T2P 2S5
888-568-6322

Calgary - Scotia Centre
Scotia Centre
P.O. Box 2850
700 - 2 St. SW
Calgary, AB T2P 2S5
888-568-6322

Calgary - Telus House
Telus House
P.O. Box 2850
411 - 1 St. SE
Calgary, AB T2P 2S5
888-568-6322

Calgary - Tower Centre
P.O. Box 2850
115 - 9th Ave. SE
Calgary, AB T2P 2S5
888-568-6322

Dawson Creek
#4, 12008 - 8 St.
Dawson Creek, BC V1G 4Y5
888-568-6322

Drumheller
P.O. Box 2409
900 South Railway Ave.
Drumheller, AB T0J 0Y0
888-568-6322

Edson
4731 - 2 Ave.
Edson, AB T7E 1C1
888-568-6322

Fort Nelson
P.O. Box 2380
4404 - 55 St.
Fort Nelson, AB V06 1R0
888-568-6322

Grande Cache
P.O. Box 1260
10017 - 99 St.
Grande Cache, AB T0E 0Y0
888-568-6322

Grande Prairie
11040 - 78 Ave.
Grande Prairie, AB T8W 2M2
888-568-6322

Halifax
Founders Square
#700, 1701 Hollis St.
Halifax, NS B3J 3M8
902-422-4500
Fax: 902-425-2766
888-568-6322
dpinfo@encana.com

Hythe
P.O. Box 155
Hythe, AB T0H 2C0
888-568-6322

Nisku
Nisku Module Yard
1107 - 11 St.
Nisku, AB T9E 0C6
888-568-6322

Pine Lake
P.O. Box 69
Pine Lake, AB T0M 1S0
888-568-6322

Ponoka
4205, Hwy. 2A
Ponoka, AB T4J 1V9
888-568-6322

Rocky Mountain House
#2, 4419 - 45 Ave.
Rocky Mountain House, AB T4T 1B4
888-568-6322

Sexsmith
P.O. Box 540
Sexsmith, AB T0H 3C0
888-568-6322

Strathmore
601 Westmount Dr.
Strathmore, AB T1P 1W8
888-568-6322

Endress+Hauser Canada Ltd.
Endress+Hauser Canada Ltée
An independent affiliate of The Endress+Hauser Group
1075 Sutton Dr.
Burlington, ON L7L 5Z8
905-681-9292
Fax: 905-681-9444
800-668-3199
info@ca.endress.com
www.ca.endress.com
Firm Type: Distributing, Manufacturing
Founded: 1990
Staff: 60
Member of: Honeywell; Metso Automation; Rockwell Automation; Bayer Technology Services
Quality Environmental Management System(s): 9001:1994
Products/Services/Areas of Expertise: Flow meters; measuring & monitoring systems; potable/process water treatment equipment; water analysis devices; on-line analyzers
Financial Information:
Type of Ownership: Foreign-owned; Private
Domestic Markets:
National
Foreign Activity:
Worldwide
Contact(s):
Richard Lewandowski, General Manager
Piero Giansante, Marketing Manager

Canadian Branches:
Calgary
#245, 7326 - 10 St. NE
Calgary, AB T2R 8W1
403-777-2252
Fax: 403-777-2253
888-918-5049
Shawn Dietrich, Calgary Sales Manager

Edmonton
#318, 8925 - 51st Ave.
Edmonton, AB T6E 5J3
780-486-3222
Fax: 780-486-3466
888-918-5049
Tom Osborn, Alberta & BC Sales Manager

Montréal
#100, 6800, Côte de Liesse
Montréal, QC H4T 2A7
514-733-0254
Fax: 514-733-2924

Vancouver
P.O. Box 91044
West Vancouver, BC V7V 3N3
604-925-7600
Fax: 604-925-7601
Lorne Maclean, Contact
lorne.maclean@ca.endress.com

Eneco Industries Ltd.
#600, 666 Burrard St.
Vancouver, BC V6C 2X8
604-649-4518
Fax: 604-649-3480
eneco@eneco.ca
www.eneco.ca
Firm Type: Manufacturing
Founded: 1989
Staff: 8
Products/Services/Areas of Expertise: Produces solid waste gasifiers designed to reduce volumes by 95% & recover glass, metals & latent energy for recycling; energy by-products include electricity, purified water, air conditioning & process steam; systems feature low capital & operating costs
Recently Completed / Ongoing Projects: TOPS Catalyst recovery plant & solid waste destruction system - 20 tonnes/day, Malaysia; CORE municipal waste to energy plant - 300 tonnes/day with 6MW continous electrical output, China; TOPS navy base waste processing plan - 20 tonnes/day, USA
Financial Information:
Type of Ownership: Private
Domestic Markets:
National
Foreign Activity:
Caribbean, The Pacific Rim, USA
Markets Sought:
South America
Contact(s):
Ross Dickinson, President

Enercombustion Ltd.
525, av Lepine
Montréal, QC H9P 2S9
514-636-0710
Fax: 514-636-6632
sales@enercombustion.com
www.enercombustion.com
Firm Type: Distributing, Engineering
Founded: 1979
Staff: 19
Products/Services/Areas of Expertise: Fuel-fired equipment, such as high-efficiency gas or oil burners, night setback systems, no-heat air replacement units, stack economizers; high-efficiency heating equipment
Financial Information:
Type of Ownership: Private
Revenue Sources: 2% nationwide; 2% Provincial; 2% Municipals; 94% Private Contracts
Domestic Markets:
National
Contact(s):
Karl Schmidt, President/CEO

Canadian Branches:
Cornwall - Ontario
1657 Birmingham St.
Cornwall, ON K6H 2Z5
613-938-6148
Fax: 613-932-9794
sales@enercombustion.com
Greg Murray

Kingston - Ontario
28 Steve Fonyo Dr.
Kingston, ON K7M 8N9
613-544-2799
Fax: 613-544-8639
1-888-544-2799

Enercorp Instruments Ltd.
25 Shorncliffe Rd.
Toronto, ON M9B 3S4
416-231-5335
Fax: 416-231-7662
800-363-7263
sales@enercorp.com
www.enercorp.com
Firm Type: Manufacturing
Founded: 1977
Staff: 13
Products/Services/Areas of Expertise: Air quality monitoring equipment; measuring & monitoring equipment; meteorological instruments for wind, precipitation, pressure, temperature, humidity; process controls; sensors, controllers, recorders & indicators
Financial Information:
Type of Ownership: Private
Revenue: $1.5 Million - $3 Million
Revenue Sources: 1% nationwide, 2% Provincial; 1% Municipals; 96% Private Contracts
Domestic Markets:
National
Foreign Activity:
Australia/New Zealand, South America, Mexico, USA
Contact(s):
Gary McNally, Sales Manager

Eneready Products Ltd.
#4, 6420 Beresford St.
Burnaby, BC V5E 1B6
604-433-5697
Fax: 604-438-8906
Firm Type: Distributing
Founded: 1980
Products/Services/Areas of Expertise: Residential & small commercial ventilation, heat recovery ventilation equipment & accessories
Domestic Markets:
National
Foreign Activity:
USA
Contact(s):
David Hill, President/CEO

Energy Conservation Contractors Warranty Corporation / CWC
#410, 250 McDermot Ave.
Winnipeg, MB R3B 0S5
204-956-5888
Fax: 204-956-5819
800-263-5974
neca@neca.ca
www.neca.ca
Firm Type: Management Consulting
Founded: 1983
Staff: 6
Member of: Manitoba Ozone Protection Industry Association; National Energy Conservation Association
Products/Services/Areas of Expertise: Energy conservation
Activities: Energy conservation in business
Recently Completed / Ongoing Projects: National Energy Conservation Association; Eco Network
Domestic Markets:
National
Foreign Activity:
USA
Markets Sought:
Eastern Europe, Mexico
Contact(s):
Laverne Dalgleish, CEO
Trevor Anderson, Publication Manager

Energy Ottawa
#220, 1145 Hunt Club Rd.
Ottawa, ON K1V 0Y3
613-225-0418
Fax: 613-738-6406
info@energyottawa.com
www.energyottawa.com
Products/Services/Areas of Expertise: Generates EcoLogo-certified green power
Contact(s):
Rosemarie Leclair, President/CEO
Greg Clarke, COO
Chris Whitehead, Director, Generation
Geoff Simpson, Director, Finance

Energy Systems & Design Limited / ES&D
P.O. Box 4557
Sussex, NB E4E 5L7
506-433-3151
Fax: 506-433-6151
hydropow@microhydropower.com
www.microhydropower.com
Firm Type: Distributing, Manufacturing, Scientific/Technical Services
Founded: 1980
Staff: 5
Products/Services/Areas of Expertise: Research, design & manufacture micro-hydro-electric generation systems & related components, including turbine wheels
Financial Information:
Type of Ownership: Private
Revenue Sources: 2.5% nationwide; 2.5% Provincial; 95% Private Contracts
Domestic Markets:
National
Foreign Activity:
Worldwide
Contact(s):
Paul Cunningham, CEO
Vernon Woolsey, Sales
Kent McNeilly, Manager, Marketing & Export

Energy Technology Products Ltd.
#104, 3060 Norland Ave.
Burnaby, BC V5B 3A6
604-291-6851
Fax: 604-291-6855
etpvan@navigata.net
Firm Type: Distributing
Founded: 1981
Staff: 4
Products/Services/Areas of Expertise: Commercial & industrial HVAC equipment; gas detection & air pollution control devices; fans/air curtains; dust collection; vacuum systems; garage exhaust, shop exhaust; fume/smoke extraction
Domestic Markets:
Alberta, British Columbia, Manitoba, Northwest Territories, Nunavut, Saskatchewan, Yukon Territory

Contact(s):
W.D. Payne, President/CEO
R. Klassen, Sales Representative

Enermodal Engineering Ltd.
A member of MMM Group
650 Riverbend Dr.
Kitchener, ON N2K 3S2
519-743-8777
Fax: 519-743-8778
kitchener@enermodal.com
www.enermodal.com
Firm Type: Engineering, Information Technology
Founded: 1980
Staff: 28
Member of: Solar Energy Society of Canada Inc., Professional Engineers of Ontario, National Fenestration Rating Council; American Society of Heating & Refrigeration Engineers
Products/Services/Areas of Expertise: Energy-efficient consulting including energy audits & conservation studies; evaluation of energy-saving products; evaluation of environmental cost of energy; computer prediction of building energy use & indoor air contaminants; energy analysis software; demand side management program analysis & development; sustainable building design; mechanical & electrical engineering services
Recently Completed / Ongoing Projects: Waterloo Greenhome; Green on the Grand; Niigon Technologies; Mountain Equipment Co-Op; Bloorview Children's Centre; E'Terra Ecolodge; Earth Rangers Wildlife Centre; Univ. of Ottawa Biology Bldg.; Stratus Winery
Financial Information:
Type of Ownership: Private
Revenue: $500,000 - $1.5 Million
Revenue Sources: 50% nationwide; 10% Provincial; 40% Private Contracts
Domestic Markets:
New Brunswick, Nova Scotia, Ontario, Saskatchewan
Foreign Activity:
USA
Contact(s):
Stephen Carpenter, P.Eng., President/CEO
John Kokko, P.Eng.
LauraLee Fletcher, Office Manager

International Branch(es):
Calgary
#602, 2303 - 4th St. SW
Calgary, AB T2S 2S7
403-244-0474
Fax: 403-244-0475
calgary@enermodal.com

Denver Branch
1325, 16th Ave. E
Denver, CO USA
303-861-2070
Fax: 303-830-2016
denver@enermodal.com
Sue Reilly, P.E.

Enerplan Consultants Ltd.
40 Henri Dunant St.
Moncton, NB E1E 1E5
506-858-1300
Fax: 506-858-1906
866-363-7752
info@enerplan.com
www.enerplan.com
Contact(s):
Kirk Bavis, P.Eng., President

Canadian Branches:
St. John's
239 Major's Path
St. John's, NL A1A 5A1
709-722-2028
Fax: 709-722-1136

Enerscan Consultants Limited
22 Julie's Walk
Halifax, NS B3M 2Z7
902-445-4433
Fax: 902-457-3283
info@enerscan.ca
www.enerscan.ca

Products & Services Buyer's Guide

Firm Type: Management Consulting
Founded: 1981
Staff: 8
Products/Services/Areas of Expertise: Energy management consultants; Clients include governments, institutions, industries, manufacturers, processors, & multi-unit residential buildings
Activities: Energy audits; Retrofit design, Feasibility studies; Energy consumption monitoring; Project planning & implementation; Building inspections; Training
Recently Completed / Ongoing Projects: Demand management studies, Ontario Hydro
Domestic Markets:
National
Foreign Activity:
Worldwide
Contact(s):
Dale Robertson, P.Eng., President
dale@enerscan.ca

Enervac Corp.
Environmental Technology Group
700 Franklin Blvd.
Cambridge, ON N1R 5S9
519-623-9890
Fax: 519-623-8250
sales@enervac.com
www.enervac.com
Firm Type: Manufacturing, Waste Management
Founded: 1978
Staff: 40
Quality Environmental Management System(s): 9001
Products/Services/Areas of Expertise: Removal of oil from water by coalescence & ultrafiltration & flocculation; removal of water from oil by vacuum processing
Financial Information:
Revenue Sources: 100% Private Contracts
Domestic Markets:
Alberta, British Columbia, Manitoba, New Brunswick, Nova Scotia, Ontario, Québec
Foreign Activity:
Australia/New Zealand, Central America, The Pacific Rim, Mexico, USA
Contact(s):
Anthony Guglielmi, President
Scott Allen, Vice President
Paul Hodgson, Sales Manager, Domestic Sales & Marketing
Y.B. Metha, Manager, Research/Development/Engineering
Scott Allen, Engineer, Research/Development/Engineering
V. Prakash, Int'l Sales Manager, Export Sales & Marketing

Engine Control Systems / ECS
83 Commerce Valley Dr. E
Thornhill, ON L3T 7T3
905-707-7746
Fax: 905-707-7686
800-661-9963
ecs@enginecontrolsystems.com
www.enginecontrolsystems.com
Firm Type: Manufacturing
Founded: 1980
Staff: 73
Quality Environmental Management System(s): 9001
Products/Services/Areas of Expertise: Emission control & diesel engine exhaust aftertreatment systems for on-road trucks & buses, mining, construction & materials handling equipment
Domestic Markets:
National
Foreign Activity:
Africa, Australia/New Zealand, Central Europe, Western Europe, South Africa, South America, Mexico, USA, United Kingdom
Markets Sought:
The Pacific Rim, South America
Contact(s):
Ed Richards, President
Dana Brewster, Manager, North American Sales
Neville Montague, Manager, Export & Sales

International Branch(es):
Nevada Office
#103, 4910 Longley Lane
Reno, NV USA
775-827-3400
Fax: 775-827-1670
800-331-9421
Wayne Cochrane

Sweden Office
Box 9015, 5-200 39 Malmö
Sweden, Agnesfridsvägen Sweden
-46-40-6701550
Fax: -46-40-210335
ecseu@enginecontrolsystems.com
Lars Hergart

Engineered Air / EngA
1401 Hastings Cres. SE
Calgary, AB T2G 4C8
403-287-2590
Fax: 403-243-5059
www.engineeredair.com
Firm Type: Distributing, Manufacturing
Founded: 1966
Staff: 780
Products/Services/Areas of Expertise: Design & manufacture of heating, ventilating & air conditioning units
Financial Information:
Type of Ownership: Private
Revenue: Greater than $5 Million
Domestic Markets:
National
Foreign Activity:
USA
Contact(s):
Brian Neufeld, General Manager
Contact(s):
David Kukkonen, Plant Manager
Contact(s):
Ken Miller, Plant Manager
Contact(s):
Trevor Chiasson, Plant Manager
Contact(s):
David Kukkonen, Plant Manager

Canadian Branches:
Burnaby Office
#303, 8988 Fraserton Ct.
Burnaby, BC V5J 5H8
604-736-2420
Fax: 604-736-3197
Bob Cornfield, Manager

Edmonton Office
4266 - 91A St.
Edmonton, AB T6E 5V2
780-462-4101
Fax: 780-450-0641
Perry Zapernick, Manager

Halifax - Atlantic Provinces Office
#54, 10 Akerley Blvd.
Dartmouth, NS B3B 1J4
902-835-2242
Fax: 902-835-6259
Peter Melnyk, Manager

Hamilton Office
#12, 100 Lancing Dr.
Hamilton, ON L8W 3A1
905-572-1111
Fax: 905-572-1115
Chris McClelland, Manager

Laval Office
1450, rue Cunard
Laval, QC H7S 2B7
450-662-1210
Fax: 450-662-2455
John Deuel, Manager

London Office
#11, 60 Meg Dr.
London, ON N6E 3T6
519-649-1700
Fax: 519-649-1707
Phil Bracewell, Manager

Mississauga Office
#32, 5155 Spectrum Way
Mississauga, ON L4W 5A1
905-602-4430
Fax: 905-602-4546
Bill Reynolds, Division Business Manager
Bob Rochefort, Division Sales Manager

Ottawa Office
20 Gurdwara Rd., Bay 11
Nepean, ON K2E 8B5
613-723-1661
Fax: 613-723-0818
Glenn MacLean, Manager

Regina Office
845 Broad St.
Regina, SK S4R 8G9
306-569-8588
Fax: 306-525-6889
Mel Bachman, Manager

Saskatoon Office
#102, 2366 Ave. C North
Saskatoon, SK S7L 5X5
306-653-5291
Fax: 306-955-2737
Rod Fehr, Manager

Winnipeg Office
#74, 1313 Border St.
Winnipeg, MB R3H 0X4
204-632-8535
Fax: 204-632-8534
Jim Shuturma, Manager

Calgary Sales Office
#5, 6120 - 11th St. SE
Calgary, AB T2H 2L7
403-444-4095
Fax: 403-287-4765
Bob Lounsberry, Manager

Barrie Plant
#14, 511 Wellham Rd.
Barrie, ON L4N 8Z6
705-725-1096
Fax: 705-725-8863

Calgary Heat Transfer Plant
6324 - 10 St. SE
Calgary, AB T2H 2K7
403-279-2282
Fax: 403-279-8481

Edmonton Plant
6130 - 97 St.
Edmonton, AB T6E 3J4
780-430-0310
Fax: 780-434-6272

Newmarket Plant
1175 Twinney Dr.
Newmarket, ON L3Y 9C8
905-898-1114
Fax: 905-898-7244

Engineering Management Services Croscan
Also Known As: EMS Croscan
P.O. Box 4042
323 - 6 Ave. North
Saskatoon, SK S7K 3T1
306-665-9098
Fax: 306-653-4489
dan@emscroscan.ca
www.emscroscan.ca
Firm Type: Management Consulting, Engineering
Founded: 1971
Staff: 3
Products/Services/Areas of Expertise: Market assessment; pre-feasibility/feasibility studies; pre-investment studies; project management economic analysis; operations planning; training; forensic engineering
Domestic Markets:
National
Foreign Activity:
Western Europe
Contact(s):
Boris Kishchuk, President
Daniel Kishchuk, Vice-President

EnGlobe Corp.
#100, 4495, boul Wilfrid-Hamel
Québec, QC G1P 2J7
418-781-0191
Fax: 418-653-3583
info@englobecorp.com
www.englobecorp.com

Firm Type: Engineering, Scientific/Technical Services, Waste Management
Staff: 450
Products/Services/Areas of Expertise: EnGlobe is an integrated environmental services company specializing in the management of organic-based waste streams & contaminated soils, & their beneficial reuse. Its subsidiaries include: Biogénie, Celtic Technologies Ltd., GSI Environnement Inc., & Tanknology Canada.
Activities: Site assessment & remediation; organic waste management; tank testing & calibration
Financial Information:
Type of Ownership: Private
Revenue: Greater than $5 Million
Domestic Markets:
National
Foreign Activity:
Western Europe, USA
Contact(s):
Michael Harris, Chair
André Héroux, President & CEO
Mario Saucier, CFO
msaucier@englobecorp.com
Georges Szaraz, Sr. VP, Organic Waste

ENMAX Corporation
141 - 50th Ave. SE
Calgary, AB T2G 4S7
403-514-3000
Fax: 403-514-3365
877-310-2010
www.enmax.com
Firm Type: Distributing
Founded: 1998
Products/Services/Areas of Expertise: Energy distribution, supply & service
Financial Information:
Type of Ownership: Private
Revenue: Greater than $5 Million
Domestic Markets:
Alberta
Contact(s):
Gary Holden, President/CEO

Canadian Branches:
ENMAX Envision
141, 50th Ave SE
Calgary, AB T2G 4S7
403-514-3900

Red Deer
#100, Red Deer Professional Bldg.
4808 Ross St.
Red Deer, AB T4N 1X5

Enmet Canada Ltd.
2851 Brighton Rd.
Oakville, ON L6H 6C9
905-829-4700
Fax: 905-829-4701
800-367-4706
enmet@enmetgasdetection.com
www.enmetgasdetection.com
Firm Type: Distributing, Manufacturing, Scientific/Technical Services
Founded: 1978
Staff: 12
Products/Services/Areas of Expertise: Toxic & combustible gas detection
Financial Information:
Type of Ownership: Private
Revenue Sources: 2% nationwide; 4% Provincial; 20% Municipals; 74% Private Contracts
Domestic Markets:
National
Foreign Activity:
USA
Contact(s):
Greg Reeves, Sales Manager
greeves@arjayeng.com

ENPAR Technologies Inc.
#12, 449 Laird Rd.
Guelph, ON N1G 4W1
519-836-6155
Fax: 519-836-5683
info@enpar-tech.com
www.enpar-tech.com
Firm Type: Engineering, Scientific/Technical Services
Founded: 1996
Staff: 6
Products/Services/Areas of Expertise: Remediation of acid mine drainage; treatment of nitrate & ammonia contaminated groundwater; geochemical consulting; site assessment; aggregate assessment
Financial Information:
Type of Ownership: Publicly Traded
Revenue: $250,000 - $500,000
Revenue Sources: 50% nationwide; 50% Private Contracts
Domestic Markets:
British Columbia, Manitoba, Nova Scotia, Ontario, Québec
Foreign Activity:
The Pacific Rim, USA
Markets Sought:
South America
Contact(s):
Gene Shelp, President/CEO
Leonard Seed, M.Sc., P.Eng., Sr. Lab Scientist
Karl Reimer, M.Sc., P.Eng., Project Engineer

EnRel Energy Group
2350 Blackstone Cres.
Ottawa, ON K1B 4H2
613-748-1809
Fax: 613-748-1809
nismail0423@rogers.com
Firm Type: Engineering, Manufacturing
Founded: 1995
Products/Services/Areas of Expertise: Solar street lights; 12V compact fluorescent lights; solar essential power; wind generator power
Recently Completed / Ongoing Projects: Solar lights for Turkish factory, Malta airport warehouse, Bahamas resorts, Canadian embassies offshore
Financial Information:
Type of Ownership: Private
Domestic Markets:
Ontario
Foreign Activity:
Africa, Caribbean, The Middle East
Markets Sought:
Caribbean, Central America, USA
Contact(s):
Nae Ismail, Director
Shahid Aziz, Engineering

Entara Consulting Services Ltd.
1065 Braithwaite Dr.
Cobble Hill, BC V0R 1L0
250-743-5302
Fax: 250-743-5302
hugoentara@aol.com
Products/Services/Areas of Expertise: Engineering consulting services
Contact(s):
J. Francis Hugo, Principal

Entech Environmental Consultants Ltd.
3187 Thompson Pl.
West Vancouver, BC V7V 3E3
604-921-1932
Fax: 604-921-1934
info@entech.ws
www.entech.ws
Firm Type: Management Consulting, Manufacturing
Founded: 1973
Staff: 30
Products/Services/Areas of Expertise: Oldest environmental consultancy company in BC with expertise in environmental impact assessments, biophysical inventory work, Phase I & II assessments & remediation; aquaculture planning, development & project management; rehabilitation of historical structures; feasibility studies & business plans & marketing studies for the natural resource industry
Financial Information:
Type of Ownership: Private

International Branch(es):
Bellingham
109E Chestnut St.
Bellingham, WA USA
604-921-1932

Entech Laboratories
Affiliate of CanTest Laboratories Ltd.
#4, 6820 Kitimat Rd.
Mississauga, ON L5N 5M3
905-821-1112
Fax: 905-821-2095
Contact(s):
Mickey Misra

Entegrity Wind Systems Inc. / EWSI
34B Belmont St.
Charlottetown, PE C1A 5H1
902-368-7171
Fax: 902-368-7139
info@entegritywind.com
www.entegritywind.com
Firm Type: Manufacturing

Products/Services/Areas of Expertise: Manufactures the EWSI wind turbine, 50kw, 50/60hz, asynchronous, 400-600V, ideal for use at schools, municipal services, industrial complexes, remote isolated grids & farms; 150-200,000 kw/hr annual production in good wind regime
Recently Completed / Ongoing Projects: Working on single phase compatable version for 2006-2007
Financial Information:
Type of Ownership: Private
Revenue Sources: 10% nationwide; 10% Provincial; 10% Municipals; 70% Private Contracts
Domestic Markets:
National
Foreign Activity:
The Pacific Rim, South America, USA
Contact(s):
Malcolm Lodge, Chief Technical Officer

International Branch(es):
US Sales Office
#100, 4855 Riverbend Rd.
Boulder, CO USA
304-440-8799
Fax: 304-577-9775
info@westernwindsystems.com
Shelby Walton

Enterprise Steel Fabricators Ltd.
1655 Dilworth Dr.
Kelowna, BC V1Y 8M4
250-762-3131
Fax: 250-860-6618
mail@entsf.ca
www.entsf.ca
Firm Type: Manufacturing
Founded: 1981
Staff: 50
Products/Services/Areas of Expertise: Air pollution treatment equipment; measuring & monitoring equipment; industrial chemical waste treatment equipment; design & fabrication of pressure vessels
Domestic Markets:
National
Foreign Activity:
Africa, Asia, The Middle East, The Pacific Rim, South America, Mexico, USA

Entraco
#200, 1075, Côte du Beaver Hall
Montréal, QC H2Z 1S5
514-954-8800
Fax: 514-954-8818
info@entraco.ca
www.entraco.ca
Firm Type: Engineering, Scientific/Technical Services
Founded: 1982
Staff: 14
Products/Services/Areas of Expertise: Site reclamation; hazardous waste management; field sampling & monitoring; environmental audits, impact assessments; mapping, remote sensing & image analysis; training & education
Contact(s):
Louis Archambault, Président

Entretien M. Perron inc. (SANI-TRI)
220, av Marcel Baril
Rouyn-Noranda, QC J9X 7C1
819-797-4040
Fax: 819-797-8441

Contact(s):
Claude Perron

Entropex
1271 Lougar Ave.
Sarnia, ON N7S 5N5
519-332-0430
Fax: 519-332-8220
800-665-5076
jsharpe@entropex.com
www.entropex.com
Firm Type: Waste Management
Founded: 1978
Products/Services/Areas of Expertise: Plastics recycling
Contact(s):
Carl Yates, Manager

Entropic Energy Inc.
#189, 106 - 1656 Martin Dr.
White Rock, BC V4A 6E7
604-538-3033
Fax: 604-538-3553
info@entropicenergy.com
www.entropicenergy.com
Products/Services/Areas of Expertise: Producers of a tachnology that can economically convert heat into electricity on a small scale
Financial Information:
Type of Ownership: Private
Contact(s):
Doug Smith, President

ENV Treatment Systems Inc.
70 High St.
Toronto, ON M8Y 3N9
416-503-7639
Fax: 416-503-8925
envinc@interlog.com
Firm Type: Distributing, Manufacturing
Founded: 1997
Staff: 6
Member of: Water Environment Federation; Ontario Pollution Control Equipment Association; Professional Engineers of Ontario; Canadian Radiation Protection Association
Products/Services/Areas of Expertise: Supplier, manufacturer of water, wastewater treatment equipment including screenings handling, aeration, grit removal; sludge handling; filtration; clarifiers, process systems
Recently Completed / Ongoing Projects: Ashbridge's Bay, WPCP, Woodward Ave. WPCP, Burlington Skyway WWTP, Niagra Falls WPCP, Highland Creek WPCP
Financial Information:
Type of Ownership: Private
Revenue Sources: 15% nationwide; 30% Provincial; 45% Municipals; 10% Private Contracts
Domestic Markets:
British Columbia, New Brunswick, Newfoundland & Labrador, Nova Scotia, Ontario, Prince Edward Island
Foreign Activity:
South America, Mexico, USA
Markets Sought:
Central Europe, Eastern Europe, Western Europe,
Contact(s):
Edward Pivonik, President

Envir'eau Puits Inc.
904, rue du Belvédère
Saint-Nicolas, QC G7A 3V3
418-831-8987
Fax: 418-831-7288
envireau@videotron.ca
Products/Services/Areas of Expertise: Hydrogeology consultants
Contact(s):
Renald McCormack, Contact

Envirem Technologies Inc.
180 Hodgson Rd.
Fredericton, NB E3C 2G4
506-459-3464
Fax: 506-453-1332
800-524-9111
sales@envirem.com
www.envirem.com/envirem_tech/index/index.cfm
Products/Services/Areas of Expertise: Waste management; organic and horticultural products; Organic residue management

EnvirInfo
15, Sabrevois
Saint-Bruno, QC J3V 1G9
450-653-9254
Fax: 450-653-1124
info@envirinfo.qc.ca
www.envirinfo.qc.ca
Firm Type: Management Consulting
Founded: 1994
Products/Services/Areas of Expertise: Environmental auditing; environmental permitting & management; database management; software development
Financial Information:
Type of Ownership: Private
Revenue Sources: 100% Private Contracts
Domestic Markets:
Ontario, Québec
Contact(s):
Claude Lalumière, eng.

Enviro Clean Ltd.
P.O. Box 100
933 Cobequid Rd.
Waverley, NS B0N 2S0
902-860-3282
Fax: 902-860-2629
Products/Services/Areas of Expertise: Indoor air quality; asbestos removal; microbiological cleanup

Enviro Rentals
Formerly: Gasonic Instruments Inc.
#8, 823 - 41st Ave. NE
Calgary, AB T2E 6Y3
403-276-2532
Fax: 403-276-2668
800-668-7368
info@envirorentals.com
www.envirorentals.com
Firm Type: Distributing
Founded: 1993
Staff: 8
Quality Environmental Management System(s): 9001-2000
Products/Services/Areas of Expertise: Equipment rental for industrial hygiene, safety & environmental purposes
Financial Information:
Type of Ownership: Private
Domestic Markets:
Alberta, British Columbia, Manitoba, Newfoundland & Labrador, Ontario, Québec, Saskatchewan

Enviro Scan Technologies Inc.
7723 - 157th St.
Edmonton, AB T5R 2A1
780-436-8430
Fax: 780-437-1306
Products/Services/Areas of Expertise: Sampling, monitoring, surveys services
Contact(s):
Lana Buoy

Enviro Vault Ltd.
P.O. Box 129
6448 South Island Hwy.
Union Bay, BC V0R 3B0
250-335-9048
Fax: 250-335-9068
888-945-0172
russ@envirovault.com
www.envirovault.com
Firm Type: Manufacturing
Founded: 1996
Staff: 5
Products/Services/Areas of Expertise: Installation of a chamber to the inside of an oil storage tank; valves, sample taps, etc. normally mounted externally are installed inside this chamber & accessed through a door cut in the tank shell
Recently Completed / Ongoing Projects: Installation of Enviro Vaults into new & existing oil storage tanks in Alberta & Saskatchewan
Financial Information:
Type of Ownership: Private
Revenue: $100,000 - $250,000
Revenue Sources: 100% Private Contracts
Domestic Markets:
Alberta, British Columbia, Northwest Territories, Saskatchewan
Markets Sought:
USA

Contact(s):
Russ Hebblethwaite, President/CEO
Janice Swanson, Office Manager
Canadian Branches:
Calgary Office
#503, 10 Discovery Ridge Hill
Calgary, AB T3H 5X2
403-263-4433
Fax: 403-263-4431
Tyler Hebblethwaite, Field Sales

Enviro Waste Ltd.
P.O. Box 125
Lower Sackville, NS B4C 2S8
902-864-4213
Fax: 902-864-1404
Contact(s):
Stephen Taylor, Contact

Enviro Waste Management Services Ltd.
P.O. Box 7200
Peace River, AB T8S 1S8
780-624-4613
Fax: 780-624-4186
888-866-3855

Enviro Wood Recovery Systems Ltd.
6710 Columbus Rd.
Mississauga, ON L5T 2G1
905-564-2952
enviro-wood@sympatico.ca; a_hussain@sympatico.ca
Products/Services/Areas of Expertise: Recycling services; waste treatment equipment
Contact(s):
Tammi Zaidi, Contact
kzaidi@sympatico.ca

Enviro-Care Services
HRDA Enterprises Ltd.
5557 Cunard St.
Halifax, NS B3K 1C5
902-454-6231
Fax: 902-454-6231
enviro-care@ns.sympatico.ca
Firm Type: Waste Management
Founded: 1989
Member of: The Nova Scotia Environmental Industry Association
Products/Services/Areas of Expertise: Residential waste collections, compost & recyclables collection
Financial Information:
Type of Ownership: Non Profit
Revenue Sources: 100% Municipals
Contact(s):
Josef Kvitek, Contact

Enviro-Gun Ltd.
P.O. Box 1069
8850 General Rd.
Regina, SK S4P 3B2
306-775-0131
Fax: 306-775-1128
gunner@accesscomm.ca
Firm Type: Waste Management
Founded: 1995
Staff: 6
Products/Services/Areas of Expertise: Collection of used oil, filters & plastics; lab packing; hazardous waste handling & transfer site; solvent distillation; anti-freeze recycling
Financial Information:
Type of Ownership: Private
Revenue: $100,000 - $250,000
Revenue Sources: 25% Provincial; 65% Municipals; 10% Private Contracts
Domestic Markets:
Saskatchewan
Contact(s):
Clint Kimery, Facility Manager

Enviro-Klean Technologies Inc. / EKTI
#200, 1812 - 152nd St.
White Rock, BC V4B 5L5
604-535-0427
Fax: 604-535-0424
866-882-8020
sales@enviroklean.com
www.enviroklean.com

Firm Type: Manufacturing
Founded: 1997
Products/Services/Areas of Expertise: Soil remediation equipment
Recently Completed / Ongoing Projects: Korean military bases
Financial Information:
Type of Ownership: Private
Domestic Markets:
National
Foreign Activity:
Australia/New Zealand, Central Europe, Eastern Europe, Western Europe, The Middle East, The Pacific Rim, South America, Mexico, USA
Contact(s):
Lawrence Hamilton, President

Enviro-Met Engineering
334 Edmonton St.
London, ON N5W 4Y2
519-659-7864
viky@sympatico.ca; broadpeng@hotmail.com
Firm Type: Management Consulting, Engineering, Information Technology, Scientific/Technical Services
Founded: 1994
Staff: 1
Products/Services/Areas of Expertise: Risk analysis; site inspection/referral; supervision of MOE work orders; public awareness hearings; expert witness
Recently Completed / Ongoing Projects: Site inspection & supervised alteration of operating procedures at tailings site, Costa Rica; development of gold recovery plant at zero discharge, Zimbabwe, Africa
Domestic Markets:
Manitoba, Ontario
Foreign Activity:
Africa, Central America
Markets Sought:
Asia, Eastern Europe
Contact(s):
Peter Broad, P.Eng., President

Enviro-Pack Material Handling
320 McKellar St.
Peterborough, ON K9J 1P7
705-876-9251
Fax: 705-876-9287
info@enviro-pack.biz
www.enviro-pack.biz
Firm Type: Distributing
Founded: 1994
Staff: 6
Products/Services/Areas of Expertise: Reusable/returnable packaging; plastic pallets & containers
Financial Information:
Type of Ownership: Private
Revenue: $1.5 Million - $3 Million
Revenue Sources: 100% Private Contracts
Domestic Markets:
National,

Enviro-RISQUE Inc.
#3, 78 Lucerne Ave.
Pointe-Claire, QC H9R 2V2
514-426-8720
Fax: 514-426-8719
cwsherry@aol.com
Firm Type: Management Consulting
Founded: 1991
Staff: 2
Products/Services/Areas of Expertise: Environmental audits, surveys, assessments & corrective recommendations; research; management; occupational health & safety; compliance; noise; hygiene; MSDS service; asbestos; indoor air quality; air & dust sampling; ergonomics; architectural acoustics; engineering design; expert witness; radiation; research & development; respiratory protection; training/instruction; ventilation
Financial Information:
Type of Ownership: Private
Domestic Markets:
National
Foreign Activity:
USA
Contact(s):
Cameron W. Sherry, President
Winnifred Sherry, Vice-President

Enviro-Safe Chemicals Canada Inc.
Also Known As: Enviro-Safe Canada
10011 Thatcher Ave.
North Battleford, SK S9A 3W8
306-446-0505
Fax: 306-446-0515
info@envirosafechem.com
www.envirosafechem.com
Firm Type: Manufacturing
Founded: 1989
Staff: 6
Products/Services/Areas of Expertise: Aerosol packaging & bulk packaging; formulation of specialty chemicals i.e., degreasers, hand protectors; will formulate individual formulations & package for individual companies; biodegradable industrial products, ice melt, orange oils, oilfield degreasers
Recently Completed / Ongoing Projects: Automotive products (AutoAssist); citrus scent biodegradable odour suppressant in pump container; hotel & restaurant industry; oil field chemicals
Financial Information:
Type of Ownership: Private
Revenue: $250,000 - $500,000
Revenue Sources: 10% nationwide; 25% Provincial; 50% Municipals; 15% Private Contracts
Domestic Markets:
National
Markets Sought:
Asia, Mexico
Contact(s):
James R. Davey, President

Enviro-Sol Plus
#333, 466 Speers Rd.
Oakville, ON L6K 3W9
Fax: 905-844-6953
888-767-2268
www.enviro-sol.com

Enviro-Solutions Ltd.
2060 Fisher Dr.
Peterborough, ON K0J 8N4
705-745-3070
Fax: 705-745-7358
877-674-4373
info@enviro-solution.com
www.enviro-solution.com
Firm Type: Manufacturing
Founded: 1993
EcoLogo Certified Products & Services: Institutional & industrial cleaning chemicals: spot & stain remover; washroom cleaner; cream cleanser; bowl & urinal cleanser; envirocide odour eliminator; general purpose cleaner; heavy duty degreaser; glass cleaner; deodorant lotion soap; carpet extrac
Ecological Note: Institutional & industrial cleaning chemicals: spot & stain remover; washroom cleaner; cream cleanser; bowl & urinal cleanser; envirocide odour eliminator; general purpose cleaner; heavy duty degreaser; glass cleaner; deodorant lotion soap; carpet extrac
Contact(s):
Mike Sawchuk
sawchuk@enviro-solution.com

Enviro-Systèmes Inc.
2945, ch Sainte-Thérèse
Carignan, QC J3L 2B1
450-658-6910
Fax: 450-658-2275
Firm Type: Distributing
Founded: 1977
Staff: 3
Member of: Association québécoise des techniques de l'eau
Products/Services/Areas of Expertise: Instrumentation & control equipment & distributed control systems for measurement of level, pressure, flow, temperature & water quality anaylsis in municipal water & wastewater treatment plants
Financial Information:
Type of Ownership: Private
Revenue Sources: 50% Municipals; 50% Private Contracts
Contact(s):
Daniel Arcouette, President/CEO

EnviroCare Environmental Services Ltd.
19 McNaughton Ave.
Regina, SK S4R SL9
306-545-1021
Fax: 306-545-3411
www.envirocare.tv

Envirochem Services Inc.
Formerly: Envirochem Consultants Ltd.
310 East Esplanade
North Vancouver, BC V7L 1A4
604-986-0233
Fax: 604-986-8583
866-321-3311
response@envirochem.com
www.envirochem.com
Firm Type: Engineering, Scientific/Technical Services
Founded: 1984
Staff: 10
Member of: Air & Waste Management Association
Products/Services/Areas of Expertise: Toxic chemical management; spill cleanup verification; risk assessment; environmental audits; pollution prevention; ISO 14001 compliance; compliance monitoring & development & customization of EMS software
Recently Completed / Ongoing Projects: Air quality testing of shipping terminals, dry docks, shipyards & wharves; emergency spill response; continued auditing; compliance monitoring; health & safety; ISO 14001 auditing
Financial Information:
Type of Ownership: Private
Revenue: $500,000 - $1.5 Million
Revenue Sources: 5% nationwide; 5% Provincial; 5% Municipals; 85% Private Contracts
Domestic Markets:
Alberta, British Columbia
Foreign Activity:
USA
Contact(s):
Thomas Finnbogason, President/Partner
Paul Beauchemin, Vice-President/Partner
Canadian Branches:
Toronto Office
422 Clendenan Ave.
Toronto, ON M6P 2X6
416-767-5567
Fax: 416-767-5567
Tony Dinino

Enviroconseil
2320, rue de Celles
Québec, QC G2C 1X8
418-843-3838
Fax: 418-843-3737
disabel@enviroconseil.qc.ca
Firm Type: Engineering
Founded: 1988
Staff: 15
Quality Environmental Management System(s): 9001
Products/Services/Areas of Expertise: Phase I environmental site assessments; site characterization studies; restoration of contaminated sites; risk assessments; hydrogeological studies; environmental management systems & diagnostic; waste management; emergency plans & management; bioremediation services; geological & hydrogeological engineering; site reclamation & remedial action services; soil remediation services; environmental audits; EMS audits; environmental management systems; ISO 14000 support; policy development consulting; risk management; training & seminar management; liners; geosynthetic & geomembrane; waste management consulting; landfills & dump sites (conception, design, evaluation); biotreatment of water; measuring & monitoring equipment groundwater; assessment & consulting for water & wastewater
Recently Completed / Ongoing Projects: EMS implementation & wastewater & soil treatment, Hydro-Québec
Financial Information:
Type of Ownership: Private
Revenue: $500,000 - $1.5 Million
Revenue Sources: 10% nationwide; 5% Provincial; 5% Municipals; 80% Private Contracts
Domestic Markets:
Québec
Contact(s):
Denis Isabel, President
Denis Bernier, Director

Canadian Branches:
Montréal
10531, boul L.-H. Lafontaine
Anjou, QC H1J 2E8
514-345-1494
Fax: 514-345-1269

Envirogain Inc.
#220 - 1112, boul. de la Rive-Sud
Saint-Romuald, QC G6W 5M6
418-834-2640
Fax: 418-839-1419
envirogain@envirogain.com
www.envirogain.com
Products/Services/Areas of Expertise: Technologies for organic material treatment & reuse; animal manure reuse and treatment; municipal and residential sludge treatment; agrifood and pulp & paper industries waste reuse and treatment
Financial Information:
Type of Ownership: Private
Domestic Markets:
National
Contact(s):
Camil Dutil, President/CEO, 418-834-2640
camil.dutil@envirogain.com
Rock Chabot, Vice-President, 418-834-2640
rock.chabot@envirogain.com

Envirogard Products Ltd.
Also Known As: Rainfresh
#6, 446 Major Mackenzie Dr. East
Richmond Hill, ON L4C 1J2
905-884-9388
Fax: 905-884-3532
800-667-8072
info@rainfresh.ca
www.rainfresh.ca
Firm Type: Manufacturing
Founded: 1970
Staff: 19
Products/Services/Areas of Expertise: Domestic, commercial water filtration & purification products
Domestic Markets:
National
Foreign Activity:
Central America, Eastern Europe, Western Europe, The Middle East, The Pacific Rim, South America, Mexico, USA
Contact(s):
Scott Macdonald, President/General Manager
Bryan Gilbart, Vice-President, Marketing & Sales

Envirogineering
Division of Filchem
#22, 1225 Gorham St.
Newmarket, ON L3Y 7V1
905-853-1363
800-263-7427
info@filchem.com
www.filchem.com
Firm Type: Waste Management
Founded: 1981
Staff: 3
Products/Services/Areas of Expertise: Erosion control products; floating row cover products designed for the agricultural industry
Activities: Landfill covers; Spill Containment; Sludge Dewatering/Filter Presses
Financial Information:
Type of Ownership: Private
Revenue: $1.5 Million - $3 Million
Revenue Sources: 15% Municipals; 85% Private Contracts
Domestic Markets:
National
Contact(s):
Steve Benner, President

EnviroGuard Ltd.
Formerly: Enviro Guard Products Ltd
2410M - 2nd Ave. SE
Calgary, AB T2E 6J9
403-235-6011
Fax: 403-235-6068
800-486-5215
info@enviroguard.net
www.enviroguard.net
Firm Type: Distributing
Founded: 1993
Staff: 5
Member of: Environmental Services Association of Alberta
Products/Services/Areas of Expertise:
Absorbents/adsorbents; emergency response; spill equipment; storage tanks systems; safety products
Financial Information:
Type of Ownership: Private
Revenue: $500,000 - $1.5 Million
Revenue Sources: 10% nationwide; 5% Provincial; 5% Municipals; 80% Private Contracts
Domestic Markets:
National
Foreign Activity:
USA
Markets Sought:
Eastern Europe, Western Europe, South America,
Contact(s):
Dan Dramalis, President

EnviroLine
4905 - 23rd Ave. NW
Calgary, AB T3B 5A8
403-263-3272
Fax: 403-263-3280
enviroline@shaw.ca
Firm Type: Information Technology
Founded: 1989
Staff: 1
Member of: Canadian Science Writers Association; Canadian Association of Journalists; Alberta Writers' Guild
Products/Services/Areas of Expertise: Business newsletter for the environmental industry; communications, public relations consulting; editing services; freelance writing
Recently Completed / Ongoing Projects: Communications consulting: National Institute of Technology, University of Calgary, Alberta Heritage Foundation for Medical Research
Financial Information:
Type of Ownership: Private
Revenue: $50,000 - $100,000
Revenue Sources: 5% nationwide; 5% Provincial; 90% Private Contracts
Domestic Markets:
Alberta, British Columbia
Markets Sought:
USA
Contact(s):
Mark Lowey, Editor

EnviroMed Detection Services
Formerly: EnviroMed Analytical Inc.
26 Glencoe Dr.
Mount Pearl, NL A1N 4S8
709-368-9000
Fax: 709-368-1256
800-561-0043
enviromed@enviromed.ca
www.enviromed.ca
Firm Type: Distributing, Scientific/Technical Services
Founded: 1991
Staff: 5
Member of: Newfoundland Environmental Industries Association
Quality Environmental Management System(s): 9001-2000
Products/Services/Areas of Expertise: Sales, service & rentals of testing, monitoring, analytical, field & laboratory instrumentation equipment; applications include environmental, industrial hygiene, air quality, safety, electrical, non-destructive testing hydrology & hazardous waste
Financial Information:
Type of Ownership: Private
Revenue Sources: 5% nationwide; 10% Provincial; 10% Municipals; 75% Private Contracts
Domestic Markets:
New Brunswick, Newfoundland & Labrador, Nova Scotia, Prince Edward Island
Contact(s):
Lee Parimeter, President

EnviroMetal Technologies Inc. / ETI
#7, 745 Bridge St. West
Waterloo, ON N2V 2G6
519-746-2204
Fax: 519-746-2209
info@eti.ca
www.eti.ca
Firm Type: Scientific/Technical Services
Founded: 1993
Staff: 5
Member of: CRestech
Products/Services/Areas of Expertise: Technology for removing hazardous volatile organic compounds from groundwater
Recently Completed / Ongoing Projects: Field installations at 150 sites in the USA, Europe, Canada, Japan, Australia, UK
Financial Information:
Type of Ownership: Private
Revenue Sources: 30% nationwide; 70% Private Contracts
Domestic Markets:
National
Foreign Activity:
Australia/New Zealand, Central Europe, Eastern Europe, Western Europe, USA
Markets Sought:
Asia, The Pacific Rim
Contact(s):
John Vogan, President
Michael Duchene, Project Director

Envirometrex
#302, 14A Hazelton Ave.
Toronto, ON M5R 2E2
416-928-0917
Fax: 416-928-0714
r.kolomeychuk@envirometrex.ca
www.envirometrex.ca
Firm Type: Scientific/Technical Services
Founded: 1992
Member of: Ontario Environmental Industry Association; Air & Waste Management Association; Canadian Meteorological & Oceanographic Society; Canadian Wind Energy Association
Products/Services/Areas of Expertise: Air quality/emission monitoring; emission inventories; dispersion modelling; compliance assessments; environmental & meteorological instrumentation system & development; applied meteorology; meteorological data & measurements; wind energy & small hydro resource management; atmospheric icing of structures
Financial Information:
Revenue Sources: 15% nationwide; 10% Municipals; 75% Private Contracts
Domestic Markets:
National
Markets Sought:
Eastern Europe
Contact(s):
Richard Kolomeychuk, President

EnvironChem Engineering Consultants
2 Alline St.
Wolfville, NS B0P 1X0
902-542-9891
Fax: 902-542-0213
ece@istar.ca
pages.istar.ca/~ece
Products/Services/Areas of Expertise: Consulting services in areas of environmental engineering & management; air pollution control; emission inventory; performance analysis of air & water pollution control equipment; public consultation, training & education
Contact(s):
Richard Palczynski, Ph.D., P.Eng., President

Environmental Accident Protection Inc.
Also Known As: EAP Inc.
P.O. Box 929
4156 Petrolia St.
Petrolia, ON N0N 1R0
519-882-3542
Fax: 519-882-3562
information@eap-inc.com
www.eap-inc.com
Firm Type: Management Consulting
Founded: 1993
Staff: 2
Member of: Municipal Fire Services Instructors' Association; Ontario Propane Association; National Fire Protection Association; Chemical Valley Emergency Coordinating Organization
Products/Services/Areas of Expertise: Regulatory compliance training & consulting services; hazardous material handling in emergency situations; safety, environmental, transportation regulations
Recently Completed / Ongoing Projects: HazMat training, clean harbours; confined space entry/rescue, Union Gas

Financial Information:
Type of Ownership: Private
Revenue: $250,000 - $500,000
Revenue Sources: 10% nationwide; 15% Provincial; 5% Municipals; 70% Private Contracts
Domestic Markets:
National
Foreign Activity:
Western Europe, USA
Markets Sought:
Asia, Australia/New Zealand, Central America, Eastern Europe, The Pacific Rim, South America, Mexico
Contact(s):
Mark S. Braet, President, Marketing & Sales

Environmental Advisory Group / EAG
#43, 2205 South Millway
Mississauga, ON L5L 3T2
905-569-0620
Fax: 905-569-2637
info@enviroadvisory.com
www.enviroadvisory.com
Firm Type: Management Consulting
Founded: 1990
Staff: 3
Products/Services/Areas of Expertise: Multidisciplinary environmental consulting firm; assists healthcare companies to plan & execute management strategies; services include waste audits, packaging assessments, market research projects, leadership of in-house environmental teams, education & data consultation/management
Recently Completed / Ongoing Projects: Experience in the pharmaceutical industry; monitoring current & pending legislation & regulations concerning environmental issues; joint market research project (Starch), captured & quantified many of the opinions held by Canadian community pharmacists & physicians about environmental issues & the pharmaceutical industry; projects completed for Astra Pharma, Glaxo Wellcome, SmithKline Beecham, Janssen-Ortho; Pfizer; Genpharm
Domestic Markets:
Ontario, Québec
Markets Sought:
USA
Contact(s):
Lisa J. James, President
Sue Watt, Project Engineer

Environmental Allies Inc.
#2801, 7 Jackes Ave.
Toronto, ON M4T 1E3
416-968-9178
Fax: 416-968-9178
allies@bellnet.ca
Products/Services/Areas of Expertise: Environmental audits services
Financial Information:
Revenue Sources: 100% Private Contracts
Domestic Markets:
Ontario

Environmental Biodetection Products Inc. / EBPI
6800 Campobello Rd.
Mississauga, ON L5N 2L8
905-487-7359
Fax: 905-794-2338
800-361-2325
ebpi@ebpi-kits.com
www.ebpi-kits.com
Firm Type: Manufacturing, Scientific/Technical Services
Founded: 1992
Staff: 4
Products/Services/Areas of Expertise: Analytical test kits for water & wastewater toxicity, genotoxicity, mutagenicity, coliforms, E. coli; educational & training workshops for assessment & monitoring water quality in remote towns & communities
Financial Information:
Type of Ownership: Private
Domestic Markets:
National
Foreign Activity:
Worldwide

Environmental Building Science Inc.
#100, 9200 Van Horne Way
Richmond, BC V6Z 1W3
604-279-9994 ext. 100
Fax: 604-279-9934
866-543-8645
info@oillift.net
www.oillift.net
Ecological Note: General purpose, commercial & industrial cleaning products
Contact(s):
Kevin Daum, Contact

Environmental Communications Options
Also Known As: ECO
154 Davenport Rd.
Toronto, ON M5R 1J2
416-972-7401
Fax: 416-972-7434
inquiries@huffstrategy.com
www.huffstrategy.com
Contact(s):
Donald W. Huff, President

Canadian Branches:
Sudbury
#604, 128 Larch St.
Sudbury, ON P3E 5J8
Fax: 1-800-641-7366
1-800-494-4199
inquiries@huffstrategy.com

Environmental Consultants & Engineers
#109, 1341 George St.
White Rock, BC V4B 4A1
604-542-2524
Firm Type: Engineering, Scientific/Technical Services
Founded: 1993
Staff: 1
Member of: Association of Professional Engineers of BC
Products/Services/Areas of Expertise: Environmental training programs; air pollution control
Financial Information:
Type of Ownership: Private
Revenue: $50,000 - $100,000
Revenue Sources: 100% Private Contracts
Domestic Markets:
National
Foreign Activity:
Caribbean, Central America, South America, Mexico, Worldwide
Contact(s):
Grant Frame, President

Environmental Disposal Concepts Inc.
#6, 101 Ilsley Ave.
Dartmouth, NS B3B 1S8
902-468-5658
Fax: 902-468-4623
Firm Type: Manufacturing
Founded: 1995
Products/Services/Areas of Expertise: Registered owner of a patented operational system engineered for the safe crushing of spent fluorescent light tubes
Contact(s):
Dana Emmerson, President/CEO

Environmental Dynamics Inc.
#201, 1110 - 6th Ave.
Prince George, BC V2L 3M6
250-562-5412
Fax: 250-562-5413
bredden@edynamics.com
www.edynamics.com
Firm Type: Management Consulting
Founded: 1994
Products/Services/Areas of Expertise: Specializes in fish & wildlife biology & ecology; erosion & sediment control; environmental impact assessments; environmental planning; habitat mitigation, compensation & rehabilitation; project permitting & management; training
Contact(s):
Bob Redden, President

Canadian Branches:
Alberta Branch
#108, 9840 - 97th Ave.
Grande Prairie, AB T8V 7K2
780-532-5375
Fax: 780-538-2079
dalbright@edynamics.com
Rob VanSchubert, General Manager

Yukon Branch
402 Hawkins St.
Whitehorse, YT Y1A 1X8
867-393-4882
Fax: 867-393-4883
ptobler@edynamics.com
Patrick Tobler, Branch Manager

Environmental Economics International / EEI
317 Adelaide St. West
Toronto, ON M5V 1P9
416-972-7400
srang@enveel.com
Firm Type: Management Consulting
Founded: 1990
Staff: 1
Products/Services/Areas of Expertise: Strategic planning; environment program implementation & policy development; environmental assessment; expertise in air & water quality; chemical management
Financial Information:
Type of Ownership: Private
Domestic Markets:
National
Foreign Activity:
Mexico, USA
Contact(s):
Sarah Rang, Partner

Environmental Plastics Advisory Service / EPAS
#101, 2165 Argyle Ave.
West Vancouver, BC V7V 1A5
604-922-7899
Fax: 604-922-4595
jimcairns@telus.net
Products/Services/Areas of Expertise: Environmental consulting services
Contact(s):
Jim Cairns, Contact

Environmental R&D Capital Corporation
P.O. Box 19
#806, 1 Toronto St.
Toronto, ON M5C 2V6
416-777-0530
Fax: 416-368-0430
erd@web.net
Firm Type: Financial
Founded: 1994
Staff: 3
Member of: Canadian Venture Capital Association
Products/Services/Areas of Expertise: Venture capital company interested in investment opportunities relating to the environmental industry
Financial Information:
Type of Ownership: Private
Domestic Markets:
National
Foreign Activity:
USA
Contact(s):
Derrick Rolfe, Managing Director

Environmental Remediation Equipment Inc. / ERE
Équipement de réhabilitation Environnemental inc.
Also Known As: ERE Inc.
8605, Champ d'Eau
Montréal, QC H1P 3B8
514-326-8852
Fax: 514-326-8961
888-287-3732
sales@ereinc.com
www.ereinc.com
Firm Type: Distributing, Manufacturing
Founded: 1994
Staff: 12
Member of: Réseau environnement; Association des entrepreneurs de services en environnement du Québec
Member of: Canadian Federation of Independent Business
Products/Services/Areas of Expertise: Puresample: equipment, instruments & accessories for sampling & monitoring of air, water & soil; Remediation: equipment for collection & treatment of floating hydrocarbons, volatile organic compounds, dense non aqueous phase liquids & contaminated soils; Filtration & Separation: specializing in wastewater treatment; & Rental: various equipment for monitoring & remediation

Recently Completed / Ongoing Projects: Design, fabrication of on-site, mobile treatment unit
Financial Information:
Type of Ownership: Private
Revenue Sources: 20% nationwide; 10% Provincial; 5% Municipals; 65% Private Contracts
Domestic Markets:
National
Foreign Activity:
Western Europe, South America, Mexico, USA
Markets Sought:
Eastern Europe, The Middle East, South Africa, United Kingdom
Contact(s):
Angelo Diadelfo, President
angelod@ereinc.com
Diana Trasente, Director
dianat@ereinc.com

Environmental Reporting Systems Limited
Formerly: Alexander Environmental Consulting Services
#819, 80 Bradford St.
Barrie, ON L4N 6S7
705-728-2457
Fax: 705-728-4415
webmail@erslimited.com
Firm Type: Management Consulting, Engineering, Scientific/Technical Services
Founded: 1994
Staff: 3
Products/Services/Areas of Expertise: Waste auditing & reduction planning; resource recovery; compliance audits; C. of A.: applications, emissions reporting
Domestic Markets:
Ontario
Contact(s):
Grahaem H. Capaldi, President

Environmental Solutions Remediation Services / ESRS
#1102, 50 Burnhamthorpe Rd. W
Mississauga, ON L5B 3C2
905-896-8181
Fax: 905-896-3485
info@esrs.info
www.esrs.info
Firm Type: Waste Management
Staff: 48
Products/Services/Areas of Expertise: Provides environmental science services for events impacting air, land & water resources; all opinions & workmanship are verifiable, scientifically sound & insured
Contact(s):
Mark Samis, M.Sc., MBA, P.Geo., Vice-President

Canadian Branches:
Alberta
#100, 807 Manning Rd. NE
Calgary, AB T2E 7M8
403-215-6041
Fax: 403-269-4326

New Brunswick
#101, 14 King St.
Saint John, NB E2L 1G2
506-642-3777
Fax: 506-634-3144

Nova Scotia
#200, 11 Morris Dr.
Dartmouth, NS B3B 1M2
902-468-3777
Fax: 902-421-1015

Ontario - Hamilton
67 Frid St., #5
Hamilton, ON L8P 4M3
905-524-1523
Fax: 905-524-2536

Ontario - Ottawa
#15, 190 Colonnade Rd.
Ottawa, ON K2E 7J5
613-728-9153
Fax: 613-224-5700

Québec - Gatineau
258, boul St-Joseph
Gatineau, QC J8Y 3X8
819-776-3171
Fax: 819-776-6075

Québec - Montréal
#1000, 1250, rue Guy
Montréal, QC H3H 2T4
514-932-0499
Fax: 514-938-5445

Environmental Structures
King Lothar Dr.
Tatamagouche, NS B0K 1V0
902-657-9187
Fax: 902-657-9187
biosolar@istar.ca
Contact(s):
Jorn Schroder, Contact

Environmental Training Institute / ETI
14 Milburn Dr.
Fonthill, ON L0S 1E4
905-892-1177
Fax: 905-892-1177
etivc@iaw.on.ca
www.etivc.org
Firm Type: Information Technology
Founded: 1987
Member of: American Water Works Association; Water Environment Federation; National Environmental Trainers Association
Products/Services/Areas of Expertise: Training for operators of water/wastewater treatment facilities
Financial Information:
Type of Ownership: Private

Environmental Waste International
283 Station St.
Ajax, ON L1S 1S3
905-686-8689
Fax: 905-428-8730
800-399-2366
info@ewmc.com
www.ewmc.com
Firm Type: Waste Management
Founded: 1992
Staff: 10
Products/Services/Areas of Expertise: General waste management
Recently Completed / Ongoing Projects: USDA biological wastewater sterilization system; UK Royal Navy food waste sterilization system
Financial Information:
Type of Ownership: Publicly Traded
Revenue: $250,000 - $500,000
Revenue Sources: 100% nationwide
Foreign Activity:
Worldwide
Contact(s):
Stephen Simms, President/CEO
Robert Maier, Vice-President, Operations & Manufacturing
Michael G. Vocilka, Marketing & Sales
Doug Norton, Vice-President, Engineering

Environnement ESA Inc.
ESA Environment Inc.
205, rue Léger
Sherbrooke, QC J1L 2H4
819-566-4020
Fax: 819-566-2389
866-566-4020
info@esa.ca
www.esa.qc.ca
Firm Type: Engineering, Waste Management
Founded: 1992
Member of: Ordre des ingénieurs du Québec; Ordre des technologues professionnels du Québec
Quality Environmental Management System(s): 9001
Products/Services/Areas of Expertise: Wastewater characterization & flow measurement
Financial Information:
Type of Ownership: Private
Revenue: $1.5 Million - $3 Million
Contact(s):
Germain Thibault, President/CEO

Canadian Branches:
Laval
1740, rue Berlier
Laval, QC H7L 4A1
450-681-3601
Fax: 450-681-5190

Environnement Godin Inc.
Formerly: Pompes Sanitaires Godin et fils inc.
Also Known As: Godin Inc.
150, des Routiers
Chicoutimi, QC G7H 5B1
418-543-4057
Fax: 418-543-9783
clermont.gilbert@fgilbert.com
www.groupegilbert.com
Firm Type: Scientific/Technical Services
Founded: 1969
Staff: 125
Quality Environmental Management System(s): 9002
Products/Services/Areas of Expertise: Waste treatment; spills waste clean-up services; hazardous waste transport & disposal
Financial Information:
Type of Ownership: Private
Domestic Markets:
Québec
Contact(s):
Clermont Gilbert, President/CEO

Environova Planning Group Inc.
Formerly: Horticultural & Recreation Consultants Ltd.
P.O. Box 99
12 Curry Lane
Falmouth, NS B0P 1L0
902-798-4798
Fax: 902-798-5411
environ@eastlink.ca
www.environova.ca
Firm Type: Scientific/Technical Services
Founded: 1973
Member of: Atlantic Planners Institute, Nova Scotia Chapter; American Planning Association; American Society of Consulting Arborists; International Society of Arboriculture, Atlantic Chapter; Landscape Nova Scotia; Recreation Association of Nova Scotia; Recreation Nova Scotia
Products/Services/Areas of Expertise: Landscape architecture design & consulting for public, institutional, commercial & residential projects; facility development planning for parks & recreational sites; arboricultural consulting & forensic expert witness services; tree management & preservation plans & studies; urban & rural planning; tourism development strategies; landscape lighting & water feature design; specialized garden design & horticultural management
Financial Information:
Type of Ownership: Private
Revenue: $100,000 - $250,000
Domestic Markets:
New Brunswick, Nova Scotia, Prince Edward Island
Contact(s):
Stan Kochanoff, President
Peggy Kochanoff, Illustrator & Graphic Designer
Heather Cannon, Environmental Planner

Canadian Branches:
Maritime Landscape Services Limited
P.O. Box 99
RR#2
Falmouth, NS B0P 1L0
902-798-4798
Fax: 902-798-5411
environ@eastlink.ca

Enviropac Inc.
2236 - 80 Ave. NW
Edmonton, AB T6P 1N2
780-440-1942
Fax: 780-440-1952
enviropac@shaw.ca
Firm Type: Scientific/Technical Services
Founded: 1993
Products/Services/Areas of Expertise: Deals with all types of radiation regulation, meter calibration, etc.
Contact(s):
Bob Masnyk, President

Enviroplast inc
11060, boul Parkway
Montréal, QC H1J 1R6
514-352-6060
Fax: 514-352-9177
sales@enviroplast.com
www.enviroplast.com
Products/Services/Areas of Expertise: Plastic, film, polypropylene & PVC recycling, granulating, densifying, & reprocessing services; energy cost reduction services; research & project development; project partnerships, import & export development
Domestic Markets:
National
Foreign Activity:
Asia, USA
Markets Sought:
South America
Contact(s):
Michel Charlebois, President
Renata Cerilli, Director, Sales & Purchasing

EnviroPower Equipment Marketing Inc.
#222, 6030 - 88 St.
Edmonton, AB T6E 6G4
780-490-4995
Fax: 780-490-4970
www.enviropower.ca
Firm Type: Distributing
Founded: 1997
Products/Services/Areas of Expertise: Energy & waste/heat recovery equipment; air pollution control & gas handling equipment; water treatment & wastewater treatment equipment; solid fuel & ash handling equipment
Recently Completed / Ongoing Projects: Cariboo Pulp & Paper, Quesnel, BC; NorskeCanada, Pt. Alberni, BC; EPCOR/Hamon G3 Project, Genesee, AB; SaskPower, Estevan, SK; Suncor Millennium/Bantrel, Fort McMurray, AB; Canfor/Temec, Prince George, BC
Financial Information:
Type of Ownership: Private
Domestic Markets:
Alberta, British Columbia
Contact(s):
John M. Giles, President
Peter Kociolek, Contact
pkociolek@enviropower.ca

Canadian Branches:
Calgary Office
#911, 1919 - 4th St. SW
Calgary, AB T2S 1W4
403-293-3995
Fax: 780-490-4970
Glen Johnson, Contact
gjohnson@enviropower.ca

EnviroSan Products Ltd./SOLUTION 2000
170 Alexandra Blvd.
Toronto, ON M4R 1M4
416-483-5580
Fax: 416-483-5539
www.envirosan.com
Firm Type: Manufacturing
Founded: 1975
Products/Services/Areas of Expertise: Cleaners & chemicals
Domestic Markets:
National
Foreign Activity:
Worldwide
Contact(s):
Paul Marks, President

Enviroservices Inc.
589, St-Jean-Baptiste
Terrebonne, QC J6W 4R2
450-471-0552
Fax: 450-471-6038
info@enviroservices.qc.ca
www.enviroservices.qc.ca
Firm Type: Engineering, Scientific/Technical Services
Founded: 1979
Staff: 25
Products/Services/Areas of Expertise: Water pollution control; flow monitoring & wastewater sampling; dye testing for pulp & paper mills; sewer overflow monitoring & sampling; soil investigation; ISO 14000 training
Recently Completed / Ongoing Projects: Flow monitoring at 24 sites over 4-month period, Edmonton; wastewater sampling for 30 paper mills & 25 industries; dye testing for 11 paper mills; storm runoff sampling nuclear plants, Darlington, Pickering, Bruce
Financial Information:
Type of Ownership: Private
Revenue Sources: 10% nationwide; 20% Provincial; 20% Municipals; 50% Private Contracts
Domestic Markets:
Alberta, New Brunswick, Nova Scotia, Ontario, Québec
Contact(s):
Serge Coderre, President
Jean Marie Lizotte, Marketing Contact
Benoit Dagenais, Director, Environmental Department

Envirosoil Ltd.
P.O. Box 48100
Bedford, NS B4A 4Z2
902-835-3381
Fax: 902-835-7300
dmonk@dexter.ca
www.envirosoil.com
Firm Type: Waste Management
Quality Environmental Management System(s): 14001; ISO
Products/Services/Areas of Expertise: Soil recycling, bio-remediation, low temperature thermal desorption
Financial Information:
Type of Ownership: Private
Domestic Markets:
Nova Scotia
Contact(s):
Dan Monk, Manager

EnviroSORT Inc.
A wholly owned subsidiary of Clean Harbors Canada, Inc.
#700, 540 - 5th Ave. SW
Calgary, AB T2P 0M2
403-509-2150
Fax: 403-509-2155
888-571-1747
www.cleanharbors.com
Products/Services/Areas of Expertise: Specialized container management; vacuum services; waste management & recycling; household hazardous waste services. Facilities in Grande Prairie & Red Deer County
Domestic Markets:
Alberta

Canadian Branches:
Grande Prairie Facility
14020 - 97 St.
Grande Prairie, AB T8V 7B7
Fax: 780-532-9306
1-800-567-4209
grandeprairie@envirosort.com

Red Deer Facility
#4415, 39139 Hwy. 2A
Red Deer, AB T4S 2A8
403-342-7823
Fax: 403-343-4209
1-800-567-4209
reddeer@envirosort.com

Envirosphere Consultants Ltd.
P.O. Box 2906
#5, 120 Morrison Dr.
Windsor, NS B0N 2T0
902-798-4022
Fax: 902-798-4022
888-545-0553
enviroco@ns.sympatico.ca
www.envirosphere.ca
Firm Type: Scientific/Technical Services
Founded: 1990
Staff: 5
Products/Services/Areas of Expertise: Sampling & analysis; databases; ecotourism; water resources consulting; biological sampling & analysis; environmental communications
Contact(s):
Patrick L. Stewart, President

Envirosystems Inc.
11 Brown Ave.
Dartmouth, NS B3B 1Z7
902-481-8008
Fax: 902-481-8019
866-288-8008
www.enviro-systems.com
Firm Type: Distributing, Manufacturing, Waste Management
Founded: 1995
Staff: 500
Products/Services/Areas of Expertise: Products & services include industrial cleaning (tank cleaning, vacuum services, chemical cleaning, high pressure cleaning, hydro excavation); waste recycling & reduction (including industrial & household hazardous waste); robotic services; other environmental & project management services. Operating divisions include: Atlantic Industrial Cleaners, Atlantic Industrial Services, AIC Sullivan's Environmental Services, Hotz Environmental, Hydrovac Industrial Services, & Quadra Industrial Services
Contact(s):
Phil Leverman, President

Envirotec Services Incorporated
Formerly: Envirotec Waste Management Ltd.
P.O. Box 25055
100 Cory Rd.
Saskatoon, SK S7K 8B7
306-244-9500
Fax: 306-244-9501
main@envirotec.ca
www.envirotec.ca
Firm Type: Management Consulting, Waste Management
Founded: 1989
Staff: 70
Member of: Saskatchewan Environmental Industry & Managers Association; Saskatchewan Association for Resource Recovery Corporation; Saskatchewan Association for Conservation Officers; Saskatchewan Volunteer Fire Fighter's Association; Saskatchewan Waste Reduction Council; Saskatchewan Safety Council; Saskatchewan Construction Safety Association
Products/Services/Areas of Expertise: The company provides integrated environmental & industrial services to Saskatchewan & Western Canada, with a focus on: hazardous waste disposal & recycling; emergency spill response; environmental remediation, decontamination & decommissioning; vacuum truck services & specialized transportation; confined space entry & industrial services; industrial cleaning services; automotive fluids recovery & recycling; & specialized products & supplies. Branch office located in Regina.
Financial Information:
Type of Ownership: Private
Domestic Markets:
Alberta, Manitoba, Saskatchewan
Contact(s):
Lyle Clouatre, General Manager

Envirotech Associates Limited
Formerly: IDG Environmental Solutions Inc.
100280-027 Legend Ct.
Ancaster, ON L9K 1P2
905-304-4666
Fax: 905-304-1073
henryv@envirotechbiz.com
www.envirotechbiz.com
Firm Type: Engineering
Founded: 1988
Staff: 3
Member of: Canadian Environmental Auditing Association; Canadian Environment Industry Association
Quality Environmental Management System(s): 14000
Products/Services/Areas of Expertise: Environmental audits; regulatory compliance issues; air quality; pollution control; waste & hazardous waste management; wastewater analysis; decommissioning & remediation; energy audits
Domestic Markets:
National
Foreign Activity:
Asia, Mexico
Contact(s):
Henry A. Vens, President

Envirotech Engineering
Formerly: Envirotech Solutions Inc., Hart Environmental Management Systems
#10B, 1235 - 64th Ave. SE
Calgary, AB T2H 2J7
403-225-8755
Fax: 403-225-8756
info@envirotecheng.com
www.envirotecheng.com

Firm Type: Management Consulting
Founded: 2001
Staff: 3
Products/Services/Areas of Expertise: Full-service engineering consulting firm; environmental assessment and remediation services
Contact(s):
Dan Bulat, P.Geol., Partner, Assessment & Remediation Services
Ted Hart, P.Eng, Partner, Environmental Management

Envirotech Nisku Inc.
P.O. Box 6414 Main
Wetaskiwin, AB T9A 2G1
780-352-5132
Fax: 780-352-1774
lenbrown@xplornet.com
Firm Type: Waste Management
Founded: 1988
Staff: 3
Products/Services/Areas of Expertise: Oil containment & recovery equipment for both emergency & non-emergency situations
Financial Information:
Revenue: $250,000 - $500,000
Domestic Markets:
Alberta
Contact(s):
L.G. Brown, President
klbrown@telusplanet.net

Envirotech Pollution Controls Ltd.
#9, 8207 Swenson Way
Delta, BC V4G 1J5
604-951-2330
Fax: 604-951-2335
800-932-5096
enviropc@telus.net
www.envirotechbc.com
Firm Type: Distributing
Founded: 1989
Staff: 6
Products/Services/Areas of Expertise: Sales & service of air pollution equipment & waste water equipment
Activities: Sell, design, install & repair pollution-control equipment & systems
Recently Completed / Ongoing Projects: Catamaran Ferries International; BC Ferry Corp.; AVCORP; ACRO AEROSPACE
Financial Information:
Type of Ownership: Private
Revenue: $3 Million - $5 Million
Revenue Sources: 2% Provincial; 2% Municipals; 96% Private Contracts
Domestic Markets:
British Columbia
Contact(s):
George Daschko, President

Envirotest Inc.
#900, 45 Sheppard Ave. East
Toronto, ON M2N 5W9
416-222-8487
Fax: 416-221-1686
800-667-3884
mjmorris@envirotest-ont.com
www.envirotest-ont.com
Firm Type: Scientific/Technical Services
Founded: 1981
Staff: 4
Products/Services/Areas of Expertise: Occupational health & hygiene surveys & testing
Contact(s):
Malcolm Morris, Director, Professional Services

Envirotray Ltd.
46 Milford Rd.
Whycocomagh, NS B0E 3M0
902-756-2336
Firm Type: Manufacturing
Founded: 1998
Staff: 2
Products/Services/Areas of Expertise: Manufacturing of spill containment systems for oil tanks
Financial Information:
Type of Ownership: Private
Revenue: Less than $50,000
Revenue Sources: 100% Private Contracts

Domestic Markets:
Nova Scotia
Contact(s):
Fred Morrison, President

Envision Compliance
#1, 124 Connie Cres.
Concord, ON L4K 1C7
905-760-1638
Fax: 905-760-1642
800-318-7090
tom@envisioncompliance.com
www.envisioncompliance.com
Firm Type: Management Consulting
Founded: 1990
Staff: 4
Member of: Ontario Printing & Imaging Association; Specialty Graphics & imaging Association
Products/Services/Areas of Expertise: Environmental audits; certificates of Approval-Air; health & safety audits; pre-stat reviews; fire audits; TDG & WHMIS training; waste management products; health & safety products; occupational health & safety consulting
Financial Information:
Type of Ownership: Private
Revenue: $500,000 - $1.5 Million
Revenue Sources: 15% nationwide; 85% Private Contracts
Domestic Markets:
National
Foreign Activity:
USA
Contact(s):
Thomas Gorham, President & Managing Partner

Envision Planning Solutions Inc.
Formerly: Peter Devenis & Associates
131 Scenic Hill Close NW
Calgary, AB T3L 1R1
403-241-8883
Fax: 403-241-3883
envision@shaw.ca
Firm Type: Management Consulting, Scientific/Technical Services
Founded: 1993
Staff: 2
Products/Services/Areas of Expertise: Emergency management & proactive planning specialists for the resource industry (spill response, emergency preparedness, crisis management, environmental compliance)
Recently Completed / Ongoing Projects: Environmental audit, Kazakhstan; emergency response simulation & tabletop exercise, contingency planning, pipeline spill risk assessment, training programs
Domestic Markets:
National
Foreign Activity:
Asia, Eastern Europe, South America, USA
Markets Sought:
South America
Contact(s):
Peter Devenis, President

Envision Sustainability Tools
#300 - 1 Alexander St.
Vancouver, BC V6A 1B2
604-225-2000
Fax: 604-225-2001
info@envisiontools.com
www.envisiontools.com
Firm Type: Scientific/Technical Services
Founded: 1997
Products/Services/Areas of Expertise: Consultants in environmental sustainabilities technology; Urban and regional planning software
Contact(s):
Mike Walsh, President

ENVision...synergy
120 Dewhurst Blvd.
Toronto, ON M4J 3J6
416-778-4713
Fax: 416-778-1956
info@envision-synergy.net
www.envision-synergy.com
Firm Type: Management Consulting
Founded: 2001
Staff: 5

Products/Services/Areas of Expertise: Facilitation & Mediation services; Environmental assessment & evaluation; Organizational development
Contact(s):
Charlotte Young, Ph.D, Director of Practice

Envitech Automation Inc.
180 Brunswick Ave.
Pointe-Claire, QC H9R 5P9
514-426-4430
Fax: 514-426-4435
envitech@envitech.com
www.envitech.com
Firm Type: Engineering, Manufacturing
Founded: 1989
Staff: 15
Products/Services/Areas of Expertise: Water & wastewater treatment, design, engineering, equipment
Domestic Markets:
Ontario, Québec
Foreign Activity:
Western Europe, USA
Contact(s):
Réjean Larouche, General Manager

EOA Scientific System Inc.
Captain Spry Centre
10 Kidston Rd.
Halifax, NS B3R 2J7
902-477-2464
Fax: 902-477-6834
888-666-6362
info@eoascientific.com
www.eoascientific.com
Products/Services/Areas of Expertise: Designs science education software & resources that are pedagogically correct with a mix of instructive & constructive components
Contact(s):
Robert Paul, President/CEO

Éocycle Technologies Inc.
#106, 49 rue du Bel-Air
Lévis, QC G6V 6K9
418-833-0926
Fax: 418-833-8152
info@eocycle.com
www.eocycle.com
Firm Type: Engineering, Manufacturing
Founded: 2000
Staff: 10
Products/Services/Areas of Expertise: Manufacturers of permanent magnet generators & power converters for direct-drive wind turbines
Contact(s):
Maxine Dubois

EPA Certified Clean Ltd.
6748 - 99 St.
Edmonton, AB T6E 5B8
780-433-9270
epa@telusplanet.net
Firm Type: Distributing, Manufacturing

Products/Services/Areas of Expertise: Certified clean environment sample containers for the environmental testing labs
Financial Information:
Type of Ownership: Private
Revenue Sources: 100% Private Contracts
Domestic Markets:
Alberta, British Columbia, Manitoba, Ontario, Saskatchewan
Foreign Activity:
The Pacific Rim
Markets Sought:
USA
Contact(s):
Russ Reeves, President

EPCOR Energy Services Inc.
10065 Jasper Ave.
Edmonton, AB T5J 3B1
780-412-3028
Fax: 780-412-3808
mnoble@epcor.com
www.epcor.com
Products/Services/Areas of Expertise: Green Power program to its residential customers, allows customers to purchase

Environmental Choice certified energy which is added to the provincial power grid & make the future more environmentally sustainable
Ecological Note: EPCOR Eco-Packs: 4 packages of environmentally sustainable energy for residential electricity consumption
Contact(s):
Karen Slobogan
ksloboga@epcor.ca
Cheryl Atkinson, Policy Specialist, Sustainable Development
catkison@epcor.com
Jonathan Matt, Utilites

EPEC Consulting (Sask) Ltd. / EPEC
1601A - 4 Ave.
Regina, SK S4R 8P9
306-757-8694
Fax: 306-757-4202
epec@epec-consulting.com
Firm Type: Engineering
Founded: 1984
Staff: 6
Products/Services/Areas of Expertise: Engineering consulting services primarily focused on municipal projects including water supply, transmission, treatment, storage & distribution; sewage collection, treatment & disposal; storm drainage systems; urban roadways; solid waste disposal
Domestic Markets:
Saskatchewan
Contact(s):
James W. Campbell, P.Eng., President/CEO

EPI Environmental Products Inc.
802 - 1788 W Broadway
Vancouver, BC V6J 1Y1
604-738-6281
Fax: 604-738-7839
info@epi-global.com
www.epi-global.com
Products/Services/Areas of Expertise: Develops, manufactures, distributes and sells degradable and biodegradable chamical additives to manufacturers of plastic products in the packaging, agriclulural and composting industries; Plastic products with these additives become biodegradable with exposure to sunlight, heat or other stress
Domestic Markets:
National
Foreign Activity:
Worldwide
Contact(s):
Joseph G. Gho, Chairman & CEO
jgho@epi-global.com

Epistream Consulting Inc
573 Edison Ave.
Ottawa, ON K2A 1V5
613-729-5447
Fax: 613-798-5304
paul.villeneuve@epistream.ca
www.epistream.ca
Firm Type: Management Consulting, Scientific/Technical Services
Founded: 2002
Products/Services/Areas of Expertise: Epistream provides consulting in the areas of epidemiology, biostatistics & health survey research; serves private industry & government agencies, who are faced with challenges that demand statistical & environmental experience; technical staff, includes epidemiologists, statisticians, toxicologists & biochemists
Contact(s):
Paul Villeneuve
paul.villeneuve@epistream.ca

EPS Wood Products Ltd.
5 Willow Lake
Stewiacke, NS B0N 2J0
902-897-0939
Fax: 902-897-0476
Contact(s):
Ernie Snow, Owner

Epsilon Chemicals Ltd. / E-CHEM
Edmonton Research Park
1926 - 94th St.
Edmonton, AB T6N 1J3
780-438-3040
Fax: 780-438-3033
800-361-6348
epsilon@echem.ca
www.echem.ca
Firm Type: Management Consulting, Scientific/Technical Services
Founded: 1990
Staff: 10
Member of: Advance Laboratories Limited; Atlantic Systems Inc.
Products/Services/Areas of Expertise: Solutions for sanitation, wastewater & maintenance problems for the food, industrial & environmental industries. Consultion services & comprehensive line of chemical cleaners & sanitizers; equipment; training; turnkey wastewater treatment plants
Domestic Markets:
National
Contact(s):
Colm O'Carroll, President
Contact(s):
Stephen Landry, Operations Manager
stephen@advancelabs.com
Contact(s):
Fred Roy, Technical Sales Manager, Ontario
froy@echem.ca
Joe Kuropas, Sales Manager, Eastern Region, Atlantic Systems Inc.
jkuropas@echem.ca

Canadian Branches:
Calgary
#199, 1919B - 4th St. NW
Calgary, AB T2S 1W4
403-250-0956
Fax: 403-264-5664
David Nicholls, Sales Manager
dnicholls@echem.ca

Halifax - Advance Laboratories Ltd.
Eastern Shore Industrial Park
30 Colford Dr.
Chezzetcook, NS B0J 1N0
902-827-3339
Fax: 902-827-3773
800-499-3773
labs@advancelabs.com
www.advancelabs.com

Mississauga - Atlantic Systems Inc.
#214, 2550 Argentia Rd.
Mississauga, ON L5N 5R1
905-821-1922

Equipement Labrie Ltee
175, rte du Pont
Saint-Nicolas, QC G7A 2T3
418-831-8250
Fax: 418-831-5255
800-463-6638
sales@labriegroup.com
www.labriegroup.com
Firm Type: Manufacturing
Founded: 1971
Staff: 450
Member of: National Solid Waste Management Association; Solid Waste Association of North America; Réseau Environnement
Products/Services/Areas of Expertise: Manual, semi-automated & automated side loading collection vehicles, recycling collection vehicles, front loading & rear loading collection vehicles & liquid waste collection vehicles
Financial Information:
Type of Ownership: Private
Domestic Markets:
National
Foreign Activity:
Eastern Europe, USA
Contact(s):
Claude Boivin, President
Jean Bourgeois, CEO
Eric Tremblay, Vice-President, Sales & Marketing
Victor Berg, National Sales Manager

Equipements Lapierre Inc.
99, rue de l'Escale
Saint-Ludger, QC G0M 1W0
819-548-5454
Fax: 819-548-5460
info@equipementslapierre.com
www.equipementslapierre.com
Firm Type: Manufacturing
Founded: 1945
Products/Services/Areas of Expertise: Manufactures waster-water treatment systems
Contact(s):
Donald Lapierre, President

Eriksson Sediment Systems Inc.
50 Walton St.
Port Hope, ON L1A 1N1
905-885-6664
Fax: 905-885-7471
carr@eagle.ca
Firm Type: Scientific/Technical Services
Founded: 1994
Products/Services/Areas of Expertise: New technologies providing full-service, integrated marine sediment remediation; services include sampling, sediment removal & sediment pre-treatment (including dewatering & water purification)
Domestic Markets:
National
Foreign Activity:
USA
Contact(s):
Lars Eriksson, President
Roger Carr, Vice-President

Erin Consulting Ltd.
#200, 2825 Saskatchewan Dr.
Regina, SK S4T 1H3
306-789-9799
Fax: 306-789-9490
erin@sasktel.net
erincon.sasktelwebhosting.com
Firm Type: Management Consulting
Founded: 1995
Staff: 14
Products/Services/Areas of Expertise: Various environmental management services including: phytoremediation; bioremediation; environmental information management
Contact(s):
Lloyd Saul, President

Esco Engineering
179 Lansdowne Ave.
Kingsville, ON N9Y 1Y1
519-733-3122
Fax: 519-733-6094
pas@esco-engineering.ca
www.esco-engineering.ca
Firm Type: Engineering
Founded: 1989
Staff: 7
Products/Services/Areas of Expertise: Water & air pollution control system design & evaluation; fume exhaust systems; low water usage plate-type scrubbers; pollution control for pickling & metal processing
Financial Information:
Type of Ownership: Private
Revenue Sources: 100% Private Contracts
Domestic Markets:
British Columbia, Ontario, Québec
Foreign Activity:
USA
Contact(s):
Neil Stone, Chief Engineer
nstone@esco-engineering.ca
Peter Blokker, Project Manager, Sales
pblokker@esco-engineering.ca

ESI Environmental Sensors Inc.
#2071C Malaview Ave.
Sidney, BC V8L 5X6
250-655-3211
Fax: 250-655-3299
800-799-6324
info@esica.com
www.esica.com
Firm Type: Manufacturing
Founded: 1973
Staff: 20
Products/Services/Areas of Expertise: Manufacture, sales, technical support & service for moisture sensing instrument; marine, meteorological & soils focused environmental products;

Products & Services Buyer's Guide

complete calibration facilities for pressure, salinity, temperature; service centre for instrumentation products
Financial Information:
Type of Ownership: Publicly Traded
Domestic Markets:
National
Foreign Activity:
Worldwide
Markets Sought:
The Middle East, Mexico, Former USSR
Contact(s):
Matthew Watson, Chief Executive Officer

ESRI Canada Ltd. / ESRI
Formerly: Environmental Systems Research Institute, Inc
#900, 12 Concorde Pl.
Toronto, ON M3C 3R8
416-441-6035
Fax: 416-441-6838
800-447-9778
info@esricanada.com
www.esricanada.com
Firm Type: Scientific/Technical Services
Founded: 1985
Staff: 230
Products/Services/Areas of Expertise: Distributes Geographic Information Systems (GIS) products & services; also provides consulting, training & technical support for GIS
Contact(s):
Alex Miller, President

Canadian Branches:
Toronto
#900, 12 Concorde Pl.
Toronto, ON M3C 3R8
416-441-6035
Fax: 416-441-2106
ontariosales@esricanada.com
Heather Milnes, Regional Manager

Atlantic
#606, 1496 Bedford Hwy.
Bedford, NS B4A 1E5
902-423-5199
Fax: 902-492-3912
atlanticsales@esricanada.com
Eric Melanson, Regional Manager

Calgary
Prairies
Sierra Place
#250, 706 - 7th Ave. SW
Calgary, AB T2P 0Z1
403-262-3774
Fax: 403-263-4023
prairiesales@esricanada.com
Tim Walker, Regional Manager

Edmonton
Sterling Place
#200, 9940 - 106 St.
Edmonton, AB T5K 2N2
780-424-3774
Fax: 780-424-6110
prairiesales@esricanada.com
Neil Cory, District Sales Manager

Kelowna
#406, 1708 Dolphin Ave.
Kelowna, BC V1Y 9S4
250-861-3794
Fax: 250-861-3732
Myron Doherty, Pacific Regional Manager

Montréal
#1110, 1425, boul René-Lévesque ouest
Montréal, QC H3G 1T7
514-875-8568
Fax: 514-875-9362
infoquebec@esricanada.com
Alain Dombrowski, Directeur régional

Ottawa
National Capital
#430, 1600 Carling Ave.
Ottawa, ON K1Z 1G3
613-234-2103
Fax: 613-234-6288
nationalcapitalsales@esricanada.com
Neil Spooner, District Manager

Québec
#1140, 1265, boul Charest Ouest
Québec, QC G1N 2C9
418-654-9597
Fax: 418-654-2001
infoquebec@esricanada.com
Alain Dombrowski, Directeur régional

Vancouver
#614, 1130 West Pender St.
Vancouver, BC V6E 4A4
604-682-4562
Fax: 604-682-5692
pacificsales@esricanada.com
Myron Doherty, Regional Manager

Victoria
#505, 1207 Douglas St.
Victoria, BC V8W 2E7
250-383-8330
Fax: 250-383-3846
pacificsales@esricanada.com
Scott Stafford-Veale, Account Manager

Winnipeg
177 Lombard Ave., 7th Fl.
Winnipeg, MB R3B 0W5
204-943-3774
Fax: 204-949-0921
prairiesales@esricanada.com
David Carpenter, Account Manager

ESRS Environmental Solution / ESRS
A division of Cunningham Lindsey
50 Burmanthorpe Rd. W
Mississauga, ON L5B 3C2
905-896-8181
Fax: 905-896-3585
info@esrs.info
www.esrs.ca
Firm Type: Management Consulting, Financial
Staff: 28
Products/Services/Areas of Expertise: Offers insurers comprehensive, professional environmental services for any type of event that has environmental implications; investigates incidents that can potentially affect the environment; makes scientific, legal & economic recommendations & manages all aspects of risk communication, cleanup, remediation & disposal of environmental hazards
Contact(s):
Mark Samis, Vice-President, Operations, ESRS Environmental Solutions

Estco Battery Management Inc.
Also Known As: Electricity Storage & Conversion R&D
#100, 19 Grenfell Cres.
Nepean, ON K2G 0G3
613-290-2556
www.estco.ca
Firm Type: Engineering, Manufacturing, Scientific/Technical Services
Founded: 1995
Staff: 10
Products/Services/Areas of Expertise: Research & development of battery & fuel cell management systems
Financial Information:
Type of Ownership: Private
Domestic Markets:
British Columbia, Ontario, Québec
Foreign Activity:
Asia, Western Europe, South America, Mexico, Former USSR
Contact(s):
William Adams, Ph.D., President
Bob Melville, P.Eng, MBA, Executive Vice-President, Strategic Alliances

EthicScan Canada
P.O. Box 54034 Lawrence Plaza
Toronto, ON M6A 3B7
416-783-6776
Fax: 416-783-7386
info@ethicscan.ca
www.ethicscan.ca
Firm Type: Management Consulting
Founded: 1987
Staff: 8
Member of: Ethics Practitioners Association of Canada
Products/Services/Areas of Expertise: Environmental ethics; multi-stakeholder facilitation research service on environmental & social performance of Canadian companies, benchmark of social & environmental performance
Domestic Markets:
British Columbia, Ontario, Québec
Foreign Activity:
Western Europe, USA
Contact(s):
David Nitkin, President/CEO

Canadian Branches:
Canadian Clearinghouse for Consumer & Corporate Ethics Research
64 Brookview Dr.
Toronto, ON M6A 2K2
david@ethicscan.ca

ETV Canada
Also Known As: Environmental Technology Verification
#201A, 2070 Hadwen Rd.
Mississauga, ON L5K 2C9
905-822-4133
Fax: 905-822-3558
etv@etvcanada.ca
www.etvcanada.ca
Firm Type: Scientific/Technical Services
Founded: 1997
Staff: 5
Member of: Canadian Environmental Industry Association
Products/Services/Areas of Expertise: Environmental technology verification program - third party, credible verification of vendors' performance claims regarding their environmental technologies, owned by the Ontario Centre for Environmental Technology Advancement (OCETA)
Financial Information:
Type of Ownership: Private
Revenue: $250,000 - $500,000
Revenue Sources: 100% Private Contracts
Domestic Markets:
National
Foreign Activity:
Worldwide
Contact(s):
John H. Neate, Senior Associate
Mona El-Hallak, Senior Technical Director
Deborah McNairn, Development Analyst
Contact(s):
Joe Lukacs
Contact(s):
Manon Laporte
Contact(s):
Ed Mallett, President & CEO

Canadian Branches:
CETAC-West
Norcen Tower
#420, 715 - 5th Ave. SW
Calgary, AB T2P 2X6
403-777-9595
Fax: 403-777-9599
mkelly@cetacwest.com
www.cetacwest.com

Enviro Accès
#150, 85, rue Belvédère nord
Sherbrooke, QC J1H 4A7
819-823-2230
Fax: 819-823-6632
mlaporte@enviroaccess.ca
www.enviroaccess.ca

OCETA
2070 Hadwen Rd., #201A
Toronto, ON L5K 2C9
905-822-4133
Fax: 905-822-3558
oceta@oceta.on.ca
www.oceta.on.ca

Eucania International Inc.
563, av Lepine
Dorval, QC H9P 2R2

514-631-1669
Fax: 514-631-0867
877-631-1669
info@eucania.com; la@eucania.com
www.eucania.com
Firm Type: Manufacturing
Founded: 1975
Staff: 20
Products/Services/Areas of Expertise: Aluminum blower wheels for wood stoves, fire places, air-purifiers, air conditioners, refrigeration & lasers
Domestic Markets:
Ontario, Québec
Foreign Activity:
USA
Markets Sought:
Australia/New Zealand, Western Europe, South America
Contact(s):
Christian Gachignard, President & Chief Executive Officer
Lauria Avon, Vice-President

Eurovac
116 Buttermill Ave.
Concord, ON L4K 3X7
905-738-9255
Fax: 905-738-4603
800-265-3878
info@eurovac.com
www.eurovac.com
Firm Type: Manufacturing
Staff: 30
Products/Services/Areas of Expertise: Dust collection equipment; high vacuum systems for removal of dust &/or fumes at the source; installation & conversion of tools
Financial Information:
Type of Ownership: Private
Revenue Sources: 10% Municipals; 90% Private Contracts
Domestic Markets:
Alberta, British Columbia, Manitoba, Ontario, Saskatchewan
Foreign Activity:
Central America, The Pacific Rim, South America, Mexico, USA
Contact(s):
Burt Reiter, President
breiter@eurovac.com
Charlie Reiter, Manager, Sales
creiter@eurovac.com
Bert Retter, Manager, Sales
bretter@eurovac.com
Eric Epema, Manager, Plant
eepema@eurovac.com

Ever Green Recycling
292 Waterford Bridge Rd.
St. John's, NL A1E 1E6
709-777-3596
Fax: 709-777-3315
hcc.barcathe@hccsj.nf.ca
www.waterfordfoundation.nf.ca
Firm Type: Waste Management
Member of: Newfoundland Environmental Industry Association
Products/Services/Areas of Expertise: Recycling depot
Financial Information:
Type of Ownership: Non Profit
Domestic Markets:
Newfoundland & Labrador
Contact(s):
Catherine Barrett, Executive Director

Everts-Lind Enterprises
5722 Hwy 332, Middle LaHave
Bridgewater, NS B4V 2Y5
902-766-4533
Fax: 902-766-4533
richard@evertslindcustomhomes.com
www.evertslindcustomhomes.com
Firm Type: Scientific/Technical Services
Founded: 1972
Member of: Heating, Refrigerating & Air Conditioning Institute of Canada; Canadian Home Builders Association; Canadian Home Builders Association
Products/Services/Areas of Expertise: Residential energy conservation & ventilation systems
Domestic Markets:
Nova Scotia
Contact(s):
Richard Lind, President/CEO

eWaterTek Inc.
115 Watch Hill Rd., R.R. #4
King City, ON L7B 1K1
905-508-0200
Fax: 905-508-0065
hirschel@ewatertek.ca
www.ewatertek.ca
Firm Type: Management Consulting
Founded: 1999
Products/Services/Areas of Expertise: eWaterTek is focused on R&D; has developed patented technologies to provide municipalities & utilities clients with automated water monitoring services & reports; eWaterTek's technology allows access to online information about drinking water quality with a full array of chlorine & heavy metal contaminant analysis; system may also be used to satisfy the need for water security
Financial Information:
Type of Ownership: Private
Contact(s):
Hirschel Moskoff, CIO

Exova
Formerly: Bodycote Materials Testing Canada Inc.; Technitrol Eco Inc.
2395 Speakman Dr.
Mississauga, ON L5K 1B3
905-822-4111
Fax: 905-823-1446
866-263-9268
sales@exova.com
www.exova.ca
Firm Type: Engineering, Scientific/Technical Services
Founded: 1963
Products/Services/Areas of Expertise: Quality control in areas of chemistry, biology, product testing & environment, ecotoxicology; environmental engineering; risk assessment; failure analysis; site characterization; impact studies; industrial hygiene; audits; laboratory analysis for soil, water, air; product testing; forensic science investigations; expert testimony
Domestic Markets:
National
Foreign Activity:
Central America, USA
Canadian Branches:
Burlington
#9, 1440 Graham's Lane
Burlington, ON L7S 1W3
905-631-7785
Fax: 905-631-7786

Calgary
#5, 2712 - 37th Ave. NE
Calgary, AB T1Y 5L3
403-291-2022
Fax: 403-291-2021

Calgary
4605 - 12 St. NE
Calgary, AB T2E 4R3
403-291-3024
Fax: 403-291-2819

Cambridge
15 High Ridge Ct.
Cambridge, ON N1R 7L3
519-621-8191
Fax: 519-621-7700

Drayton Valley
7407 - 485 Township Rd.
Drayton Valley, AB T7A 1S8
780-542-6812
Fax: 780-542-4844

Edmonton
7217 Roper Rd. NW
Edmonton, AB T6B 3J4
780-438-5522
Fax: 780-434-8586

Fort McMurray Depot
10208 Centennial Dr.
Fort McMurray, AB T9H 1Y5

Fort St. John
10624 - 101 Ave.
Fort St. John, BC V1J 2B9
250-785-2731
Fax: 250-785-7092

Grande Prairie
11301 - 96 Ave.
Grande Prairie, AB T8V 5M3
780-532-8709
Fax: 780-539-0611

Kingston
608 Norris Ct.
Kingston, ON K7P 2R9
613-634-9307
Fax: 613-634-9308

Lloydminster
6203B - 43 St.
Lloydminster, AB T9V 2W9
780-874-9245
Fax: 780-874-9248

Niagara Falls/St. Catharines
#630, 380 Vansickle Rd.
St. Catharines, ON L2R 6P7
905-680-8887
Fax: 905-680-4256

Ottawa
#8, 146 Colonnade Rd.
Ottawa, ON K2E 7Y1
613-727-5692
Fax: 613-727-5222

Pointe-Claire
121, boul Hymus
Pointe-Claire, QC H9R 1E6
514-697-3273
Fax: 514-697-2090

Québec
1818, rte de l'Aéroport
Québec, QC G2G 2P8
418-871-8722
Fax: 418-871-9556
866-365-2310

St-Bruno
1390 rue Hocquart
St-Bruno-de-Montarville, QC J3V 6E1
450-441-5880
Fax: 450-441-4316

Surrey
#104, 19575 - 55A Ave.
Surrey, BC V3S 8P8
604-514-3322
Fax: 604-514-3323

Experimental Fusion Facility
Centre canadien de fusion magnétique
1804, Montée Ste-Julie
Varennes, QC J3X 1S1
450-652-8701
Fax: 450-652-8625
Contact(s):
I. Shkazofsky, Director, Fusion
Contact(s):
A. Ghosh, Director, Space & Photonics
Canadian Branches:
Experimental Fusion Facility
Centre canadien de fusion magnétique
1804, Montée Ste-Julie
Varennes, QC J3X 1S1
450-652-8701
Fax: 450-652-8625

Pointe-Claire Laboratory
151, boul Hymus
Pointe-Claire, QC H9R 1E9
514-694-8751
Fax: 514-695-7492

Expert Systems Inc.
#200, 32 Balmoral St.
Winnipeg, MB R3C 1X4
204-786-1069
expert@expertsystems.com
www.expertsystems.com
Firm Type: Information Technology
Founded: 1986
Products/Services/Areas of Expertise: Software development & consulting; information management; custom database management systems

Contact(s):
Gregg Garychuk, President

Experts-Conseils BMST inc.
Also Known As: BMST Experts-conseils inc.
#203, 200, rue MacDonald
Saint-Jean-sur-Richelieu, QC J3B 8J6
450-359-7070
Fax: 450-359-7066
Firm Type: Engineering
Founded: 1984
Staff: 20
Member of: American Water & Wastewater Association; Association québécoise des techniques de l'eau; Association québécoise du transport et des routes inc.; Association des ingénieurs-conseils du Québec
Products/Services/Areas of Expertise: Engineering consulting services; information technology/communications; water & wastewater management; environmental audits
Domestic Markets:
Québec
Contact(s):
Bernard Rousseau, Ingénieur Associé
Michel Deslauriers, Ingénieur
Yves Fallu, Ingénieur Associé
Nicolas Théberge, Ingénieur Associé
Daniel Donais, Ingénieur

Experts-Conseils CEP Inc.
1980, rue Michelin
Laval, QC H7L 5C2
450-686-0240
Fax: 450-686-1440
877-686-0240
info@expcep.com
www.expcep.com
Firm Type: Management Consulting, Scientific/Technical Services
Founded: 1973
Staff: 45
Contact(s):
Jean-René Dumont, Contact

Exploitation Santec Inc.
1455, rue Champlain
Trois-Rivières, QC G9A 5X4
819-379-3379
Firm Type: Engineering
Founded: 1986
Staff: 20
Products/Services/Areas of Expertise: Soil & water management & treatment; environmental monitoring; equipment operation; engineering services
Financial Information:
Type of Ownership: Private
Domestic Markets:
Ontario, Québec
Contact(s):
Jean-Marc Girouard, Président
François McMurray, Chargé de projet

Explore Plus Duct Cleaning Ltd.
836 Coates Mills Rd. S
Sainte-Marie-de-Kent, NB E4S 1R4
506-388-8900
epdc@nb.aibn.com
Products/Services/Areas of Expertise: Air quality management
Contact(s):
Robert Nuttall, President

Expocrete Concrete Products Ltd.
1800 - 11th St. West
Saskatoon, SK S7M 1H9
306-652-7232
Fax: 306-665-3211
www.expocrete.com
Firm Type: Manufacturing
Founded: 1979
Products/Services/Areas of Expertise: Expocrete Concrete Products manufactures & markets concrete hardscape, industrial precast, & masonry products.
Financial Information:
Type of Ownership: Private
Domestic Markets:
Alberta, British Columbia, Saskatchewan

Foreign Activity:
USA
Contact(s):
Martin Bates, Chief Executive Officer
Brad Taylor, Chief Financial Officer
Bruce Dick, Vice-President, Commercial Sales
Mike Mclean, Vice-President, Retail & Dealer Sales
Canadian Branches:
Acheson
#38, 53016 Hwy. 60
Acheson, AB T7X 5A7
780-962-4010
Fax: 780-962-3230
800-232-9443
sales_edmont@expocrete.com
www.expocrete.com

Balzac
P.O. Box 40
260032 Range Rd. 291
Balzac, AB T0M 0E0
403-279-0404
Fax: 403-279-4191
800-279-3728
sales_calgar@expocrete.com
www.expocrete.com

Export Development Canada / EDC
151 O'Connor St.
Ottawa, ON K1A 1K3
613-598-2500
Fax: 613-237-0451
866-574-0451
www.edc.ca
Products/Services/Areas of Expertise: Crown corporation that offers financing, insurance, and risk management solutions to help Canadian exporters expand their international business
Domestic Markets:
National
Canadian Branches:
Atlantic Region - Halifax
Tower 1
#1406, 1959 Upper Water St.
Halifax, NS B3J 3N2
902-442-5205
Fax: 902-442-5204
contactatlantic@edc.ca
David Surette, Vice-President, Atlantic Region

Atlantic Region - Moncton
#400, 735 Main St.
Moncton, NB E1C 1E5
506-851-6066
Fax: 506-851-6406
contactatlantic@edc.ca

Atlantic Region - St. John's
90 O'Leary Ave.
St. John's, NL A1B 2C7
709-772-8808
Fax: 709-772-8693
contactatlantic@edc.ca

Ontario Region - London
#1512, 148 Fullarton St.
London, ON N6A 5P3
519-963-5400
Fax: 519-963-5407
contactontario@edc.ca

Ontario Region - Mississauga
#805, 1 City Centre Drive
Mississauga, ON L5B 1M2
905-366-0300
Fax: 905-366-0332
contacteast@edc.ca

Ontario Region - Toronto
P.O. Box 810
#810, 150 York St.
Toronto, ON M5H 3S5
416-640-7600
Fax: 416-862-1267
contactontario@edc.ca
Dan Mancuso, Vice-President, Ontario Region

Québec Region - Montréal
P.O. Box 124 de la Bourse
#4520, 800 Victoria Sq.
Montréal, QC H4Z 1C3
514-908-9200
Fax: 514-878-9891
contactquebec@edc.ca
Diane Dubé, Vice-President, Québec Region

Québec Region - Québec City
#1340 - 2875 boul. Laurier
Sainte-Foy, QC G1V 2M2
418-266-6130
Fax: 418-266-6131
contactquebec@edc.ca

Western Region - Calgary
Home Oil Tower
#606, 324 - 8th Ave. SW
Calgary, AB T2P 2Z2
403-537-9800
Fax: 403-537-9811
contactwest@edc.ca
Linda Niro, Vice-President, Western Region

Western Region - Edmonton
#1000, 10180 - 101st St.
Edmonton, AB T5J 3S4
780-702-5233
Fax: 780-702-5235
contactwest@edc.ca

Western Region - Vancouver
One Bentall Centre
P.O. Box 58
#1030 - 505 Burrard St.
Vancouver, BC V7X 1M5
604-638-6950
Fax: 604-638-6955
contactwest@edc.ca

Western Region - Winnipeg
Commodity Exchange Tower
#2075 - 360 Main St.
Winnipeg, MB R3C 3Z3
204-975-5090
Fax: 204-975-5094
contactwest@edc.ca

ExTech Environmental Services Inc.
15227 - 124 St. NW
Edmonton, AB T5X 1Z4
780-457-5140
Fax: 780-456-6736
jrmoses@compuserve.com
Firm Type: Scientific/Technical Services
Founded: 1989
Staff: 5
Products/Services/Areas of Expertise: Packaging, transportation & disposal of special & hazardous wastes
Financial Information:
Type of Ownership: Private
Revenue Sources: 15% Provincial; 65% Municipals; 20% Private Contracts
Domestic Markets:
Alberta
Foreign Activity:
USA
Contact(s):
Jim Moses, General Manager

Extox Industries Inc.
6419 Netherhart Rd.
Mississauga, ON L5T 1C3
905-670-7738
Fax: 905-670-5617
800-501-8601
info@extox.com
www.extox.com
Firm Type: Waste Management
Founded: 1993
Staff: 4
Products/Services/Areas of Expertise: Chlorinated wastes recycling facility; transportation & processing of waste filters & liquids/sludge
Recently Completed / Ongoing Projects: Granted delisting permit from the Ontario Ministry of Environment & Energy
Financial Information:
Type of Ownership: Private

Revenue: $500,000 - $1.5 Million
Revenue Sources: 100% Private Contracts
Domestic Markets:
National
Foreign Activity:
USA
Contact(s):
Artur J. Keyes, Director
artur@extox.com

F.C. O'Neill, Scriven & Associates Ltd.
5450 Cornwallis St.
Halifax, NS B3K 1A9
902-429-0701
Fax: 902-429-9729
gendel@onsa.ns.ca
www.onsa.ns.ca
Firm Type: Engineering
Founded: 1954
Staff: 28
Products/Services/Areas of Expertise: Residential, commercial, institutional & light industrial building services; energy conservation consulting; biomedical waste disposal; HVAC; fire protection; plumbing; lighting; communications; power distribution
Financial Information:
Type of Ownership: Private
Revenue Sources: 15% nationwide; 20% Provincial; 5% Municipals; 60% Private Contracts
Domestic Markets:
New Brunswick, Nova Scotia, Ontario, Prince Edward Island
Foreign Activity:
Caribbean, Central Europe
Contact(s):
Lloyd Schofield, P.Eng., President
Glenn Brunt, P.Eng., Vice-President

Canadian Branches:
Sydney Branch
Electrical
341 Townsend St.
Sydney, NS B1P 5G1
902-562-8090
Fax: 902-562-6621
bobr@onsa.ca
Staff: 3
Robert Rudderham, P.Eng., Head

F.E. Myers
Division of Pentair Canada Inc.
P.O. Box 9138
269 Trillium Dr.
Kitchener, ON N2G 4W5
519-748-5470
Fax: 519-748-2553
www.femyers.com
Firm Type: Distributing, Engineering, Manufacturing
Founded: 1870
Staff: 600
Member of: Canadian Institute of Plumbing & Heating; Canadian Association of Pump Manufacturers
Products/Services/Areas of Expertise: Sewage treatment equipment; water treatment systems & equipment; jet pumps, submersible pumps, metering pumps, sump & sewage pumps, non-clog grinder pumps, water tanks, water treatment equipment, swimming pool pumps, lawn sprinkler pumps, industrial pumps
Domestic Markets:
National
Foreign Activity:
Asia, Central America, The Middle East, South America, Mexico, USA
Contact(s):
Ian MacKinnon, General Manager
Ken Shane, National Sales Manager, Residential Products
Al W. Noble, National Sales Manager, Industrial & Wastewater
Ernie Kovaks, Director, Engineering

International Branch(es):
F.E. Myers - USA
1101 Myers Pkwy.
Ashland, OH USA
419-289-1144
Fax: 419-281-9980
Tom Pakes

Fabco Plastics Wholesale (Ontario) Limited
2175A Teston Rd.
Maple, ON L6A 1T3
905-832-0600
Fax: 905-832-0992
800-668-8415
info@fabcoplastics.com
www.fabcoplastics.com
Firm Type: Distributing
Founded: 1962
Staff: 100
Member of: International Association of Plastics Distributors
Products/Services/Areas of Expertise: Plastic products for industry; pipe, valves, tanks, fittings, pumps, containers, sheet, rod, tube, welding equipment, teflon, nylon, acetate, fiberglass
Financial Information:
Type of Ownership: Private
Domestic Markets:
National
Foreign Activity:
Asia, Australia/New Zealand, China, The Middle East, The Pacific Rim, Mexico, USA, Vietnam
Contact(s):
Bill Kehren, President
Claus Dieners, Operations Manager

Canadian Branches:
Edmonton
12938 - 148 St.
Edmonton, AB T5L 2H8
780-451-0238
Fax: 780-455-4816
1-800-661-7926
edmonton@fabcoplastics.com
John Shrum, Branch Manager

Laval
5000, autoroute 440, Laval ouest
Chomedey, QC H7T 2Z8
450-687-2721
Fax: 450-687-3635
1-888-637-5278
montreal@fabcoplastics.com
Martin Gjerek, Sales Manager

Surrey
9511 - 194A St.
Surrey, BC V4N 4G4
604-882-1564
Fax: 604-882-1432
1-800-232-2422
surrey@fabcoplastics.com
Wes Stewart, Sales Manager

Fabcon Canada Ltd.
Atlantic Place
P.O. Box 69
#606, 215 Water St.
St. John's, NL A1C 6C9
709-754-2145
Fax: 709-754-2412
fabcon.canada@fabcon.nf.ca
www.fabcon.net
Firm Type: Management Consulting, Engineering, Scientific/Technical Services
Founded: 1991
Products/Services/Areas of Expertise: Construction management & environmental services to offshore oil & gas companies, both operating & engineering projects
Recently Completed / Ongoing Projects: Terra Nova, Hibernia & Sable Island Projects
Domestic Markets:
Newfoundland & Labrador, Nova Scotia, Prince Edward Island

Fabricated Plastics Ltd. / FABCO
2175 Teston Rd.
Maple, ON L6A 1T3
905-832-8161
Fax: 905-832-2111
info@fabricatedplastics.com
www.fabricatedplastics.com
Firm Type: Manufacturing
Founded: 1962
Staff: 150
Member of: Society of the Plastics Industry; Water Environment Association of Ontario; National Association of Corrosion Engineers
Products/Services/Areas of Expertise: Design, engineer & custom fabrication of pollution control & chemical processing equipment from FRP or thermoplastic lined FRP materials for the chemical processing & pollution control industries; products include: pipe, tanks, vessels, scrubbers, mist eliminators, columns, hoods, stacks, launders, cooling towers & ducting
Financial Information:
Type of Ownership: Private
Domestic Markets:
National
Foreign Activity:
Worldwide
Contact(s):
D.L. Sablinskas, President
Greg Landry, Vice-President, Marketing
L.Y. Woo, Vice-President, Engineering

Canadian Branches:
Edmonton
12938 - 148 St.
Edmonton, AB T5L 2H8
780-451-0238
Fax: 780-455-4816
edmonton@fabcoplastics.com
John Shrum, Branch Manager

Vancouver
9511 - 194A St.
Surrey, BC V4N 4G4
604-882-1564
Fax: 604-882-1432
surrey@fabcoplastics.com
Wes Stewart, Branch Manager

Fair Canada Engineering Ltd.
#205, 259 Midpark Way SE
Calgary, AB T2X 1M2
403-269-5311
Fax: 403-265-5559
services@faircan.com
www.faircan.com
Firm Type: Distributing, Engineering
Founded: 1984
Staff: 3
Member of: Association of Professional Engineers, Geologists & Geophysicists of Alberta
Products/Services/Areas of Expertise: Application engineering & process systems/packages; design, fabrication & assembly of integrated systems; start-up supervision, commissioning & project management services; training services; site inspections to assess the condition of all components of clarifiers, filters; entire packaged water treatment plants
Recently Completed / Ongoing Projects: Beverage plant water treatment system upgrade; Syncrude: demineralization system, deaeration system & pre-cast filter; AEC: induced gas flotation systems (oil removal)
Financial Information:
Type of Ownership: Private
Revenue: Greater than $5 Million
Revenue Sources: 100% Provincial
Domestic Markets:
Alberta, British Columbia, Saskatchewan,
Contact(s):
John E. Fair, President

Fanchem Ltd.
#207, 3228 South Service Rd.
Burlington, ON L7N 3H8
905-637-7034
Fax: 905-637-7037
Firm Type: Manufacturing, Waste Management
Founded: 1975
Staff: 3
Member of: Canadian Association of Chemical Distributors
Products/Services/Areas of Expertise: Supplier of water/wastewater chemicals (iron salts) & heavy industrial chemicals; liquid hazardous & non-hazardous waste management disposal & transport
Financial Information:
Type of Ownership: Private
Revenue: $1.5 Million - $3 Million
Revenue Sources: 25% Municipals; 75% Private Contracts
Domestic Markets:
Alberta, Ontario, Québec
Foreign Activity:
USA

Contact(s):
Tina Pelton, Office Manager
tpelton@pvschemicals.com
Brian Malcolm, Sales Manager

Faraci Engineering
Formerly: E.J. Faraci and Associates
19 Mager Dr. West
Winnipeg, MB R2M 0R9
204-949-1000
Fax: 204-235-0877
faraciengineering@ibm; faraciengineering@attglobal.net
Firm Type: Engineering, Scientific/Technical Services
Founded: 1991
Products/Services/Areas of Expertise: Renewable energy engineering; energy conservation evaluation
Domestic Markets:
National
Foreign Activity:
Eastern Europe, The Pacific Rim, USA
Contact(s):
E.J. Faraci, President

Farris Industries Canada
P.O. Box 1210
15 Shaver St.
Brantford, ON N3T 5T3
519-756-4800
Fax: 519-756-4016
800-265-8420
Firm Type: Manufacturing
Founded: 1955
Staff: 70
Products/Services/Areas of Expertise: Sewage treatment equipment; power boilers; measuring & monitoring equipment; pressure relief valves; sewage treatment venting equipment
Contact(s):
P.M. Whitton, Sales Manager
Bob Enlund, Sales Representative

Canadian Branches:
Calgary
Calgary, AB
403-221-8475
Fax: 403-265-6646
Bob Callander

Edmonton
Edmonton, AB
780-440-1811
Fax: 780-440-2216
Tom Andrew

Sarnia
Sarnia, ON
519-862-5384
Fax: 519-862-3592
P.M. Whitton, Sales Manager

Fastco Equipment Corporation
P.O. Box 161 U
Toronto, ON M8Z 5P1
905-562-1547
800-366-1325
dfast@fastcoequipment.com
Firm Type: Distributing
Founded: 1993
Member of: Ontario Waste Management Association
Products/Services/Areas of Expertise: Sales & service on compactors, balers, shredders & on-board truck scales for the solid waste & recycling industries; transfer trailers & sludge containers; intermodal containers
Domestic Markets:
National
Contact(s):
Duane Fast, President

Faszer Farquharson & Associates Ltd.
#304, 605 - 1 St. SW
Calgary, AB T1P 3S9
403-508-4996
Fax: 403-508-4998
Firm Type: Engineering
Staff: 11
Products/Services/Areas of Expertise: Noise control, noise surveys, noise impact assessments
Financial Information:
Type of Ownership: Private
Domestic Markets:
Alberta, British Columbia, Ontario, Saskatchewan
Foreign Activity:
USA,
Contact(s):
Clifford Faszer, P.Eng., President
James Farquharson, CET, Principal

FCX NH Valves
Formerly: Newman Hender; Newman Hattersley Ltd.
9423 - 41 Ave. NW
Edmonton, AB T6E 5X7
780-434-8521
Fax: 780-434-4289
800-661-3813
newhat@netcom.ca
Firm Type: Distributing
Founded: 1955
Staff: 23
Member of: Canadian Gas Processor Suppliers Association
Products/Services/Areas of Expertise: Valves & anti-corrosion tapes & mastics
Domestic Markets:
National
Foreign Activity:
The Middle East, South America, USA
Contact(s):
Lorne Nakonechny, President
Geoff Robertson, QA/ISO
Larry Lastiwka, Inside Sales
Joel Gorr, Inside Sales

Canadian Branches:
Calgary
#205, 259 Midpark Way SE
Calgary, AB T2X 1M2
403-254-9666
Fax: 403-256-2440
1-800-661-3813
Dan Stephenson

Guelph
40 Waxwing Cres.
Guelph, ON N1C 1E3
519-763-5039
Fax: 519-763-4297
1-800-263-6145
Carol Bard

Lachenaie
352, rue de Tilly
Lachenaie, QC J6V 1G3
450-585-8541
Fax: 450-585-2112
Mario Dupuis

Mississauga
#2, 2430 Lucknow Dr.
Mississauga, ON L5S 1V3
905-678-2870
Fax: 905-678-1275
1-800-263-6145
Wendy Bertrand, Operations Manager

Ste-Anne-des-Plaines
Québec
88, rue Dugas
Sainte-Anne-des-Plaines, QC J0N 1H0
450-478-0027
Fax: 450-478-4889
Claude Perry, Regional Manager

Federated Co-operatives Ltd.
Also Known As: The Co-op Connection
P.O. Box 1050
401 - 22nd St. East
Saskatoon, SK S7K 3M9
306-244-3311
Fax: 306-244-3403
inquiries@fcl.ca
www.coopconnection.ca
Contact(s):
Kris Bradshaw, Coordinator, Environmental & Product Services

FEMCO International
727 Somerset Ave.
Winnipeg, MB R3T 1E3
204-940-3551
Fax: 204-940-3555

Fenco Shawinigan Engineering Limited
Also Known As: SNC-Lavalin Inc.
500 Beaverbrook Ct., 5th Fl.
Fredericton, NB E3B 5X4
506-459-2645
Fax: 506-444-9419
brian.decoste@snclavalin.com
Firm Type: Engineering
Founded: 1962
Staff: 75
Products/Services/Areas of Expertise: Engineering consulting services
Contact(s):
David C. Preston, Manager, Domestic Sales
david.preston@snclavalin.com

Ferguson Simek Clark
P.O. Box 1777
4910 - 53 St.
Yellowknife, NT X1A 2P4
867-920-2882
Fax: 867-920-4319
fscnorth@fsc.ca
www.fsc.ca
Firm Type: Engineering
Founded: 1976
Staff: 50
Products/Services/Areas of Expertise: Consulting engineers & architects specializing in cold regions technology, design & construction; municipal & industrial waste treatment; water supply & treatment; water resources engineering; waste site remediation; impact assessment; remote monitoring; project management
Financial Information:
Type of Ownership: Private
Domestic Markets:
Alberta, Northwest Territories, Ontario, Yukon Territory
Foreign Activity:
Eastern Europe, The Pacific Rim, Former USSR,
Contact(s):
Stefan Simek, President
stefans@fsc.ca
Robert Maddigan, Principal Civil Engineer
Garry Karst, Vice-President
garryk@fsc.ca

Canadian Branches:
Edmonton
#200, 10835 - 124 St.
Edmonton, AB T5M 0H4
780-439-0090
Fax: 780-439-1158
fscalta@fsc.ca
Ross Addurahman, Manager

Iqaluit
Noble House 1088C
P.O. Box 1779
Iqaluit, NU X0A 0H0
867-979-0555
Fax: 867-979-5711
fsc@fsc.ca
Terry Gray, Manager

Whitehorse
#202, 107 Main St.
Whitehorse, YT Y1A 2A7
867-633-2400
Fax: 867-633-2481
fscyukon@fsc.ca
Timothy Turner-Davis, Manager

International Branch(es):
Russia
#117, 57 Kryukova St.
Yuzhno-Sakhalinsk Russia
11-7-4242-72-10-06

Ferme R&B Fafard Inc.
26, rue Principale
Saint-Basile-le-Grand, QC J3N 1M3
450-441-1167
Fax: 450-441-0277
Firm Type: Waste Management
Founded: 1987
Products/Services/Areas of Expertise: Agricultural composting systems
Contact(s):

Real Fafard, Associate

Fero Waste & Recycling Inc.
1300 Berry Mills Rd.
Moncton, NB E1E 4R8
506-855-3376
Fax: 506-855-3322
800-668-3376
info@fero.ca
www.fero.ca
Firm Type: Waste Management
Founded: 1993
Staff: 31
Products/Services/Areas of Expertise: Waste hauling & construction; Demolition hauling
Financial Information:
Type of Ownership: Private
Revenue Sources: 5% Provincial; 95% Private Contracts
Domestic Markets:
New Brunswick, Nova Scotia, Prince Edward Island
Contact(s):
Albino Pisciutta, Owner

Canadian Branches:
Fredericton, NB
Fax: 506-472-3376

Saint John, NB
506-652-3376

Moncton, NB
Fax: 506-855-3376

Dieppe, NB
506-855-3376

Bathurst, NB
506-546-8016

Richibucto, NB
Fax: 506-523-8135

Campbellton, NB
506-753-3373

Miramichi, NB
506-773-3376

Rexton, NB
506-876-2791

Shediac, NB
506-388-0992

Ferti-Val Inc.
800, rue de l'Ardoise
Sherbrooke, QC J0B 1H0
819-566-5103
Fax: 819-566-7903
877-566-5103
info@ferti-val.com
www.ferti-val.com
Firm Type: Waste Management
Founded: 1993
Products/Services/Areas of Expertise: Recycling and conversion of residual materials
Domestic Markets:
Québec
Contact(s):
Sebastien Hue, Projects Manager

Fiducie Desjardins
CP 34 Desjardins
1, Complexe Desjardins
Montréal, QC H5B 1E4
514-286-3498
Fax: 514-844-3545
denis.chevrette@fid.desjardins.com
Contact(s):
Denis Chevrette, Contact

Fielding Chemical Technologies Inc.
3575 Mavis Rd.
Mississauga, ON L5C 1T7
905-279-5122
Fax: 905-279-4130
888-873-2524
info@fieldchem.com
www.fieldchem.com
Firm Type: Manufacturing, Waste Management
Founded: 1957
Staff: 80
Member of: Canadian Environment Industry Association; National Association of Chemical Recyclers
Quality Environmental Management System(s): 9001; ISO
Products/Services/Areas of Expertise: Solvent recycling & disposal; fuel blending; recycling of liquid & gaseous chlorofluorocarbons; hazardous liquid waste disposal
Domestic Markets:
Ontario, Québec
Foreign Activity:
USA
Contact(s):
Ellen McGregor, President

Canadian Branches:
Mississauga Plant
3549 Mavis Rd.
Mississauga, ON L5C 1T7
905-279-5123
Fax: 905-279-9277
1-888-873-2524

Filter Innovations Inc.
744 Gordon Baker Rd.
Toronto, ON M2H 3B4
416-490-7848
Fax: 416-490-0974
inquiries@filterinnovations.com
www.filterinnovations.com
Firm Type: Engineering, Manufacturing, Scientific/Technical Services
Founded: 1992
Staff: 8
Member of: North York Board of Commerce
Products/Services/Areas of Expertise: Treatment of groundwater, process water & wastewater utilizing a variety of products; self-cleaning back-flushing filters for particulate removal (algae, dirt, zebra mussels, etc.); bag filters (1-800 micron filtration); oil/water separators, ultrafiltration; absorption media; adsorption medias for large molecular weight organics (oil/grease); low temperature distillation; activated carbon; zeta rods; non-chemical water treatment to control scale, biofilm & corrosion
Recently Completed / Ongoing Projects: Turn key waste water treatment system for removal of oil from water using ultrafiltration; ground water remediation removing oils, solvents & heavy metals; use of non-chemical treatment to control biological growth & biofilm at pulp & paper plants; eliminate use of chemicals for prevention of scale & biofilm in cooling towers using self-cleaning filters
Financial Information:
Type of Ownership: Private
Revenue: $1.5 Million - $3 Million
Revenue Sources: 5% nationwide; 3% Provincial; 3% Municipals; 89% Private Contracts
Domestic Markets:
National
Foreign Activity:
Africa, Western Europe, USA
Markets Sought:
Australia/New Zealand, Central Europe, The Pacific Rim, Mexico
Contact(s):
John Dragasevich, President
Maureen Dragasevich, Manager, Operations

Filtration Seco Inc.
Affiliate of U.S. Filter/Asdor Ltd.
#210, 243, boul Brien
Repentigny, QC J6A 6M4
450-582-4266
Fax: 450-585-5464
Products/Services/Areas of Expertise: Equipment for transport, dewatering & storage of sewer sludge

Filtrum Inc.
430, rue des Entrepreneurs
Québec, QC G1M 1B3
418-687-0628
Fax: 418-687-3687
info@filtrum.qc.ca
www.filtrum.qc.ca
Firm Type: Scientific/Technical Services
Founded: 1980
Staff: 40
Member of: Association québécoise des techniques de l'eau
Products/Services/Areas of Expertise: Mechanical contracting
Financial Information:
Type of Ownership: Private
Revenue Sources: 80% Municipals; 20% Private Contracts
Domestic Markets:
Québec,
Contact(s):
Isabelle Boucher, Directrice administrative
François Noël, President

Canadian Branches:
St-Hubert Branch
3500 - 1re rue
Saint-Hubert, QC J3Y 8Y5
450-676-8558
Fax: 450-676-1399

Finnex Agencies Ltd.
5180 Still Creek Ave.
Burnaby, BC V5C 4E4
604-299-9702
Fax: 604-299-0475
Firm Type: Distributing, Manufacturing
Founded: 1970
Staff: 6
Member of: Pulp & Paper Technologists Association of Canada
Products/Services/Areas of Expertise: Biomass energy products & services; bark dewatering; pulp mill sludge dewatering; Bark Hogs - vertical drop & horizontal feed
Recently Completed / Ongoing Projects: Supplied 4 Saalasti Bark Master Bark Dewatering Presses, Norske Canada, Crofton, B.C.
Financial Information:
Type of Ownership: Private
Revenue: $3 Million - $5 Million
Revenue Sources: 100% Private Contracts
Domestic Markets:
National
Foreign Activity:
USA
Contact(s):
Mauri Skogster, Manager
mauri@finnex.com
Larry Kramer, Manager, Sales

FIRETAK Manufacturing Ltd.
1497 Dublin Ave.
Winnipeg, MB R3E 3G8
204-975-0334
Fax: 204-975-0431
866-326-4412
info@firetak.com
www.firetak.com
Firm Type: Distributing, Manufacturing
Founded: 1990
Products/Services/Areas of Expertise: Manufacturer and distributor of collabsible liquid containers for emergency response teams, fire departments, forestry, industrial, and military
Financial Information:
Type of Ownership: Private
Contact(s):
Donaghy, Manager

Firing Industries Ltd.
#301, 509 Glendale Ave. East
Niagara on the Lake, ON L0S 1J0
905-688-0962
Fax: 905-688-6643
firing@firing.com
www.firing.com
Firm Type: Distributing
Founded: 1973
Staff: 3
Products/Services/Areas of Expertise: Environmental process equipment; baghouse dust monitors; centrifuges; dryers, spray, flash, fluid bed; bulk chemicals handling systems; screens; feeders for lime, polymer
Financial Information:
Type of Ownership: Private
Domestic Markets:
National
Contact(s):
Michel DuBuc, President
David Feasby, Applications Specialist

Products & Services Buyer's Guide

Debbie Barnes, Marketing Manager
Canadian Branches:
Montréal Office
#750, 6600, rte TransCanada
Pointe-Claire, QC H9R 4S2
514-848-9191
Fax: 514-848-0692
firing@firing.com
Michel DuBuc

First Stage Enterprises Inc.
#104, 1185 Eglinton Ave. East
Toronto, ON M2J 1Y8
416-426-7234
info.nhsru@firststageinc.com
www.firststageinc.com
Products/Services/Areas of Expertise: Association and Event Management
Domestic Markets:
Ontario
Contact(s):
Doug Rosser, President
drosser@firststageinc.com

Firwin Corporation
1685 Flint Rd.
Toronto, ON M3J 3W8
416-745-9389
Fax: 416-745-0782
firwin@firwin.com
www.firwin.com
Firm Type: Manufacturing
Founded: 1982
Staff: 20
Member of: Thermal Insulation Association of Canada; Institute of Diesel & Gas Turbine Engineeress
Products/Services/Areas of Expertise: Exhaust removable/reusable insulation blankets, engines, exhaust pipe systems; removable/reusable valves, strainers, flanges, expansion joint insulation energy-saving blankets for production & process equipment; sound reduction removable blankets for equipment, pipes, etc.; spray shields
Recently Completed / Ongoing Projects: Washigton Convention Centre; Mississauga Waste Dump Power Plant Fire Pumps
Financial Information:
Type of Ownership: Private
Revenue: $3 Million - $5 Million
Revenue Sources: 40% nationwide; 60% Private Contracts
Domestic Markets:
National
Foreign Activity:
Australia/New Zealand, Caribbean, Central America, Western Europe, The Middle East, The Pacific Rim, Mexico, USA
Markets Sought:
South America,
Contact(s):
Paul Herman, President
pherman@total.net
Jon Miles, Designer
Brett Herman, Vice-President, Sales & Sutomer Service
bherman@firwin.com
Miriam Herman, Vice-President
mherman@firwin.com

Canadian Branches:
Boulden Energy
550 Shoemaker Rd.
King of Prussia, PA USA
610-992-9030
Fax: 610-992-9034
marc@bouldenenergy.com
Ted Karas

Diesel Injection Services
#2, 25 Radall Ave.
Dartmouth, NS B3B 1L4
902-668-4736
Fax: 902-468-4738
larry.perrin@diss.cc
Larry Perrin

Henery et Fils
87, rue Aurora
Pointe-Claire, QC H9R 3G5

514-697-4197
Fax: 514-697-0411
hprahenery@qc.aira.com
Pascal Rimbaud

Tom Reich
585 Coldstream Crt
Atlanta, GA USA
404-255-4816
Fax: 404-255-4816
tomreich@bellsouth.net

Fisher Environmental Ltd.
#15, 400 Esna Park Dr.
Markham, ON L3R 3K2
905-475-7755
Fax: 905-475-7718
fisher@fisherenvironmental.com
www.fisherenvironmental.com
Firm Type: Engineering, Scientific/Technical Services
Founded: 1989
Staff: 12
Products/Services/Areas of Expertise: A full-service, environmental engineering & consulting company, Fisher Environmental offers: laboratory services; environmental site assessments & remediation; compliance audits; wastewater treatments; air quality monitoring; PCB management & removal; PCB lighting ballast recycling; asbestos testing; Underground Storage Tank Management programs.
Recently Completed / Ongoing Projects: Effluent treatment study for Culinar Foods Inc.; decommissioning of US Air Force Base; indoor air quality study for Kelloggs Canada Inc.
Domestic Markets:
Ontario
Foreign Activity:
USA
Contact(s):
David A. Fisher, P.Eng, Founder & President

Fisher Scientific Ltd.
Thermo Fisher Scientific
P.O. Box 9200 Terminal
112 Colonnade Rd.
Ottawa, ON K2E 7L6
613-226-3273
Fax: 613-226-7658
800-234-7437
help@fishersci.ca
www.fishersci.ca
Firm Type: Distributing
Founded: 1926
Quality Environmental Management System(s): 9001
Products/Services/Areas of Expertise: Distributor of science laboratory products & industrial safety & protective equipment
Domestic Markets:
National
Contact(s):
George Angus, President

Five Seasons Comfort Limited
351 North Rivermede Rd.
Concord, ON L4K 3N2
416-213-5636
Fax: 416-213-5593
800-267-8305
info@fiveseasonsaircleaners.com
www.fiveseasonsaircleaners.com
Firm Type: Manufacturing
Founded: 1970
Member of: Clean Air Device Manufacturers Association
Products/Services/Areas of Expertise: Air purification equipment for residential, commercial & industrial use
Financial Information:
Type of Ownership: Private
Domestic Markets:
National
Foreign Activity:
Asia, The Middle East, The Pacific Rim, Former USSR
Markets Sought:
Eastern Europe, Western Europe, The Middle East, South America, Mexico
Contact(s):
Beverly David, President
Caroline David, Marketing & Sales Manager

Flakeboard Company Ltd.
P.O. Box 490
St Stephen, NB E3L 3A6

506-466-2370
Fax: 506-466-7113
Contact(s):
Dave Moffatt, Contact

Flett Research
440 de Salaberry Ave.
Winnipeg, MB R2L 0Y7
204-667-2505
Fax: 204-667-2505
flett@flettresearch.ca
www.flettresearch.ca
Firm Type: Scientific/Technical Services
Founded: 1978
Staff: 5
Member of: Canadian Society of Limnologists, International Society of Limnologists, Association of Official Analytical Chemists; American Chemical Society
Products/Services/Areas of Expertise: Measurement of environmental contaminants in air, water & soils; low-level determinations of radioactivity sediment core dating by Pb-210 & Cs-137 & ultra-trace mercury levels; environmental audits & impact assessments
Domestic Markets:
National
Foreign Activity:
Worldwide
Contact(s):
Robert Flett, President/CEO

Flexahopper Plastics Ltd.
Spenceley Group
2530 - 39 St. North
Lethbridge, AB T1H 5J2
403-328-8146
Fax: 403-328-8476
888-328-8176
info@flexahopper.com
www.flexahopper.com
Products/Services/Areas of Expertise: The company is a plastics processor, specialising in rotational molding & thermoforming.
Domestic Markets:
National
Foreign Activity:
Australia/New Zealand, USA
Contact(s):
Bill Spenceley, President & CEO
bspenceley@flexahopper.com
Robert Kennedy, Sales & Marketing
rkennedy@flexahopper.com
Rob Steeves, Sales, West Coast Office
rsteeves@flexahopper.com

Canadian Branches:
West Coast Sales Office
#12, 7157 Honeyman St.
Delta, BC V4G 1E2
604-946-8783
Fax: 604-946-8784

Flexo Products Ltd.
4777 Kent Ave.
Niagara Falls, ON L2H 1J5
905-354-2723
Fax: 905-354-1301
800-263-2540
sales@flexoproducts.com
www.flexoproducts.com
Firm Type: Manufacturing
Founded: 1918
EcoLogo Certified Products & Services: Industrial & commercial cleaners
Products/Services/Areas of Expertise: Flexo manufactures a full line of cleaning compounds, for carpet care, floor finishes, industrial degreasing, washroom maintenance, health care, skin care, & deodorizing. It also sells used & demo cleaning equipment.
Activities: It has a policy to reduce waste & levels of environmental impact, to conserve energy, & to explore opportunities for re-use & recycling.
Ecological Note: Industrial & commercial cleaners
Domestic Markets:
Ontario
Contact(s):
Steve Parker, P.Eng., President & CEO
sparker@flexoproducts.com

Canadian Branches:
Cambridge
100 Sheldon Dr.
Cambridge, ON N1R 7S7
519-740-0770
Fax: 519-740-0534

Toronto
19 Bessemer Ct.
Concord, ON L4K 3E1
416-667-8875
Fax: 416-667-0869

FLIR Systems, Inc.
Formerly: Agema Infrared Systems Ltd.
920 Sheldon Court
Burlington, ON L7L 5K6
905-637-5696
Fax: 905-639-5488
800-613-0507
rob.milner@flir.com
www.flirthermography.com
Firm Type: Distributing, Manufacturing, Scientific/Technical Services
Founded: 1965
Staff: 8
Member of: Canadian Institute of Non-Destructive Engineering; Electrical Contractors Association
Products/Services/Areas of Expertise: Designs, manufactures & markets thermal imaging infrared cameras; product line includes aerial broadcast cameras & machine vision systems; the equipment is useful in a range of settings including non-destructive testing, condition monitoring, temperature measurement & thermal testing, manufacturing process control, & research & development
Financial Information:
Type of Ownership: Publicly Traded
Revenue: Greater than $5 Million
Revenue Sources: 10% nationwide; 5% Provincial; 80% Private Contracts
Domestic Markets:
National
Foreign Activity:
Central America, Eastern Europe, Western Europe, USA
Contact(s):
Greg Bork, President
Contact(s):
Dave Ross, Contact
dross@ctsales.ca
Contact(s):
Keith Ledwell, Contact
kledwell@ctsales.ca
Canadian Branches:
Bathurst - Canadian Technical Services
P.O. Box 938
1250 Rte 430
Bathurst, NB E2A 4H7
506-545-8320
Fax: 506-549-3831

St. John's - Canadian Technical Services
#283, 38 Pearson St.
St. John's, NL A1A 3R1
709-693-2366
Fax: 709-437-7201

Floorworks Inc.
365 Dupont St. West
Toronto, ON M5R 1W3
416-961-6891
Fax: 416-961-3881
info@floorworks.ca
www.floorworks.ca
Products/Services/Areas of Expertise: Natural prefinished &/or site-finished flooring for floating, gluing or nailing, for residential, commercial, industrial, residential & computer flooring; products include stained & unstained northern hardwoods, sustainably harvested and/or plantation grown tropical woods & bamboo
Activities: The company has a policy to minimize its impact on the environment, & to avoid artificial materials & chemicals wherever possible; Relative Space is a concept retail showroom designed & facilitated by Floorworks, & located at the Toronto site & in NY.
Ecological Note: Engineered plank &/or parquet wood or bamboo floor covering; TEKA Styles include: line, Line multi, Line computer floor, Bamboo Deck, Industrial Floor, Dur 2 Strip, Quatro
Contact(s):
Brian Greenberg
briangreenberg@floorworks.ca
International Branch(es):
Relative Space
2 Bond St.
New York, NY USA
212-353-3370
bond@relative-space.com
www.relative-space.com

Flowmatic Holdings Inc.
#22, 2300 Finch Ave. West
Toronto, ON M9M 2Y3
416-749-7200
Fax: 416-749-4739
800-800-9017
sales@flowmatic.ca
www.flowmatic.ca
Products/Services/Areas of Expertise: High pressure washing systems & parts; material waste management; on-site solvent reclamation
Contact(s):
Rick Arnold, President/CEO

Flowmetrix Technical Services Inc.
127 Zion Rd.
Frankford, ON K0K 2C0
613-398-0296
Fax: 613-398-0294
service@flowmetrix.ca
www.flowmetrix.ca
Products/Services/Areas of Expertise: Flowmetrix provides a full range of high quality, specialized, cost effective liquid flow monitoring & flow meter calibration services to professional engineering firms, municipalities & corporations.
Canadian Branches:
Western Ontario
212 Terrence Ave.
Dorchester, ON N0L 1G3
Fax: 519-268-3459

Flowserve Canada Corp. - Pump Division
Flowserve Corp.
Formerly: Ingersoll-Dresser Pumps Canada Inc.P.O. Box 40
15 Worthington Dr.
Brantford, ON N3T 5M5
519-753-7381
Fax: 519-753-0845
800-563-4320
Firm Type: Manufacturing
Staff: 100
Quality Environmental Management System(s): 2858-5199
Products/Services/Areas of Expertise: Pumping equipment for water, wastewater, pollution control
Domestic Markets:
National
Foreign Activity:
Worldwide
Contact(s):
Fred Koch, Site Leader, 519-896-1161
fkoch@flowserve.com
Ignacio Villalobos, Corporate Controller
ivillalobos@flowserve.com
Canadian Branches:
Calgary Branch
#15, 2221 - 41 Ave., NE
Calgary, AB T2E 6P2
403-212-3811
Duncan McMillan, Sales Contact

Flowserve Inc.
Formerly: Duriron Canada Inc.
120 Vinyl Ct.
Woodbridge, ON L4L 4A3
905-856-0701
Fax: 905-856-6990
dcation@flowserve.com
www.flowserve.com
Firm Type: Manufacturing
Founded: 1964
Staff: 57
Quality Environmental Management System(s): 9002
Products/Services/Areas of Expertise: Pumps, valves for chemical industry, pulp & paper, water treatment, wastewater; pumps, seal, valves repair
Financial Information:
Type of Ownership: Publicly Traded
Domestic Markets:
National
Contact(s):
Doug Richards, General Manager
Canadian Branches:
Calgary
#106, 5920 - 1A St. SW
Calgary, AB T2H 0G3
403-212-3811
Fax: 403-212-3846

Edmonton
9044 - 18 St., #1
Edmonton, AB T6P 1K6
780-464-1188
Fax: 780-464-1801

Nova Scotia
West Gore, NS
902-632-2411
Fax: 902-632-2406

Ontario
#8, 5736 Finch Ave. East
Toronto, ON M1B 5R1
416-292-2877
Fax: 416-292-5190

FLSmidth Canada Ltd.
Formerly: FLSmidth Dorr-Oliver Eimco; Eimco Process Equipment Inc
174 West St. South
Orillia, ON L3V 6L4
705-325-6181
Fax: 705-325-3363
info.doecanada@flsmith.com
www.flsmidth.com
Firm Type: Manufacturing
Founded: 1953
Member of: Canadian Pulp & Paper Association; Water Environment Federation; Association québécoise des techniques de l'eau
Quality Environmental Management System(s): 9001
Products/Services/Areas of Expertise: Solids-liquids separation equipment in water & wastewater markets
Domestic Markets:
National
Foreign Activity:
Asia, Australia/New Zealand, The Pacific Rim, South America, Mexico, USA
Markets Sought:
Western Europe
Contact(s):
Dennis McGillivray, Sales

Fluidcare Ltd.
#4038E, 39139 Hwy. 2A
Red Deer, AB T4S 2A8
403-346-6476
Fax: 403-346-5152

Fluor Canada
Formerly: Fluor Daniel Wright Ltd.
55 Sunpark Plaza SE
Calgary, AB T2X 3R4
403-537-4000
Fax: 403-537-4222
www.fluor.com/canada
Firm Type: Engineering
Founded: 1988
Products/Services/Areas of Expertise: Project management; consulting engineering services; environmental engineering
Domestic Markets:
National
Foreign Activity:
Worldwide
Markets Sought:
Worldwide
Contact(s):
Eva Wyszkowski-Hartman, CEO

Products & Services Buyer's Guide

Canadian Branches:
Vancouver
#700, 1075 West Georgia St.
Vancouver, BC V6E 4M7
604-488-2000
Fax: 604-488-0582

Fluor Constructors International Inc.
403-537-4030
Fax: 403-537-4601

Canadian Branches:
Fluor Constructors International Inc.
403-537-4030
Fax: 403-537-4601

Fluorosense Inc.
#101, 1948 Merivale Rd.
Nepean, ON K2G 1E9
613-224-1192
Fax: 613-224-0256
Firm Type: Engineering, Manufacturing
Founded: 1995
Staff: 5
Products/Services/Areas of Expertise: Research & development of electro optic equipment; manufactures fluorosense monitors & breath analysis medical device
Recently Completed / Ongoing Projects: Bio-Alloy research/demonstration instrument; Breath analyzer (human breath bacteria detection)
Financial Information:
Type of Ownership: Private
Revenue Sources: 100% Private Contracts
Domestic Markets:
Alberta, Ontario
Foreign Activity:
Asia, China, Western Europe, The Middle East, USA, Vietnam
Markets Sought:
Australia/New Zealand, South America, Mexico
Contact(s):
William J. Sinclair, Founder & Director

Flush Quip
1900 Brookside Blvd.
Winnipeg, MB R3C 2E6
204-694-3318
Fax: 204-697-4790
ubaziuk@mts.net
www.flushquip.com
Firm Type: Distributing, Manufacturing
Founded: 1984
Staff: 3
Products/Services/Areas of Expertise: Sewer cleaning accessories, nozzles, hoses; confined space entry equipment
Domestic Markets:
National
Foreign Activity:
Australia/New Zealand, Western Europe, Mexico, USA
Contact(s):
Morris Baziuk, President/CEO
Ursula Baziuk, Sales

Flygt Canada
ITT Industries Company
Formerly: ITT Canada Ltd.300, av Labrosse
Montréal, QC H9R 4V5
514-695-0100
Fax: 514-697-0602
www.ittflygt.ca
Firm Type: Distributing, Manufacturing
Founded: 1955
Staff: 3800
Member of: Canadian Manufacturers Association
Products/Services/Areas of Expertise: Water handling systems & equipment; distributor pumps, valves; measuring & monitoring equipment; processing industry & municipal applications
Domestic Markets:
National
Contact(s):
Raymond Simond, Communications Manager

Canadian Branches:
Calgary
6704 - 30th St. SE
Calgary, AB T2C 1N9
403-279-8371
Fax: 403-279-0948

Carl Barg, Director
Edmonton
10554 - 169th St.
Edmonton, AB T5P 3X6
780-489-1961
Fax: 780-486-5530
Derrick Chaulk, Manager
Halifax
15 McQuade Lake Cres.
Halifax, NS B3S 1C4
902-450-1177
Fax: 902-450-1170
Jim Paris, Manager
Moncton
P.O. Box 158
189 Collishaw Rd.
Moncton, NB E1C 8J3
506-857-2244
Fax: 506-859-8612
David W. Nurse, Manager
Montréal
300, av Labrosse
Montréal, QC H9R 4V5
514-695-0100
Fax: 514-697-0602
Louis Dumoulin, Manager
Ottawa
21 Bentley Ave.
Nepean, ON K2E 6T7
613-225-9600
Fax: 613-225-5496
Éric Benoit, Manager
Québec
609, rue Adanac
Beauport, QC G1C 7G6
418-667-1694
Fax: 418-666-9593
Daniel Bastein, Manager
Saskatoon
#10, 3111 Millar Ave.
Saskatoon, SK S7K 6N3
306-933-4849
Fax: 306-931-0051
Donald Campbell, Manager
St. John's
Vanguard Court
P.O. Box 7
St. John's, NL A1C 5H5
709-722-6717
Fax: 709-722-9832
David Mitchell, Manager
Sudbury
1086 Elisabella Rd.
Sudbury, ON P3A 4R7
705-560-2141
Fax: 705-560-8260
Bruce McFadden, Manager
Toronto
93 Claireville Dr.
Toronto, ON M9W 6K9
416-679-1199
Fax: 416-679-0406
Timothy Sansom, Manager
Val-d'Or
1070, rue de l'Écho
Val-d'Or, QC J9P 5Y8
819-825-0792
Fax: 819-825-5677
Guy Lefebvre, Manager
Vancouver
74 Glacier Rd.
Coquitlam, BC V3K 5Y9
604-941-6664
Fax: 604-941-3659
Mark Brady, Manager
Winnipeg
55 Terracon Place
Winnipeg, MB R2J 4B3

204-235-0050
Fax: 204-235-0066
Doug Lemon, Manager

FMA Heritage Resources Consultants Inc.
Formerly: Fedirchuk McCullough & Associates Ltd.
#200, 1719 - 10 Ave. SW
Calgary, AB T3C 0K1
403-245-5661
Fax: 403-244-4701
fma@fmaheritage.com
www.fma-heritage.com
Firm Type: Scientific/Technical Services
Founded: 1981
Quality Environmental Management System(s): 9001
Products/Services/Areas of Expertise: Pre-development services; impact assessment & mitigation; post-impact assessment studies; public education programs; long-term management programs; traditional land use studies; cumulative effects & environmental impact assessments; legal testimony; geographic information systems modelling & data management
Contact(s):
Gloria Fedirchuk, Ph.D., Managing Principal

Canadian Branches:
British Columbia Branch
13 - 6782 Veyaness Rd.
Victoria, BC V8M 2C2
250-652-4652
Fax: 250-652-2377
irw@irwilson.com

Focal Technologies Inc.
Formerly: Focal Marine Ltd.
Also Known As: Moog Components Group
77 Frazee Ave.
Dartmouth, NS B3B 1Z4
902-468-2263
Fax: 902-468-2249
888-302-2263
mcg@moog.com
www.polysci.com
Firm Type: Manufacturing
Founded: 1983
Staff: 85
Quality Environmental Management System(s): 9002
Products/Services/Areas of Expertise: Electrical slip rings; fibre optic rotary joints; fluid rotary unions; optical plankton counters; multiplexers
Financial Information:
Type of Ownership: Private
Revenue Sources: 1% nationwide; 99% Private Contracts
Domestic Markets:
National
Foreign Activity:
Worldwide
Contact(s):
John Purdy, Manager, Sales
Dan Gibson, Manager, Business Development

Focus Environmental Group Inc.
5360 South Service Rd.
Burlington, ON L7L 5L1
905-690-7638
Fax: 905-690-7639

Focus Industries
Formerly: Versa Fibreglass Products Ltd.
17A Rayborn Cr.
St Albert, AB T8N 5C3
780-459-5599
Fax: 780-459-4401
866-688-6257
info@focusindustries.ca
www.focusindustries.ca
Products/Services/Areas of Expertise: Nationally recognized leader in the manufacture & distribution of fiberglass tanks & specialty fiberglass products for farming & the oil industry; Versa Fibreglass products & The Handler are brands belonging to Focus Industries
Contact(s):
Brian Bateman, Manager, Marketing
bateman@focusindustries.ca

Focus Surveys Inc.
#210, 1230 Blackfoot Dr.
Regina, SK S4S 7G4

306-586-0837
Fax: 306-586-3105
regina@focus.ca
www.focus.ca
Firm Type: Engineering, Scientific/Technical Services
Founded: 1986
Staff: 15
Products/Services/Areas of Expertise: Legal & engineering surveys, cadastral mapping
Contact(s):
John Holmlund, Executive Chair

Folio Instruments Inc.
#A, 277 Manitou Dr.
Kitchener, ON N2C 1L4
519-748-4612
Fax: 519-748-1535
800-683-6546
102456.242@compuserve.com
www.folioinstruments.com
Products/Services/Areas of Expertise: Measuring & monitoring equipment
Contact(s):
Gordon Howes, President

Canadian Branches:
Calgary
4620 Manilla Rd. SE
Calgary, AB T2G 4B7
403-291-6685
Fax: 403-735-1047
Tim Thorpe, Sales Engineer

Kitchener
#1, 277 Manitou Dr.
Kitchener, ON N2C 1L4
519-748-4612
Fax: 519-748-1535
Gordon Howes, President

Montréal
Sales & Marketing
1645, rue St-Patrick
Montréal, QC H3K 3G9
514-937-7931
Fax: 514-937-4533
1-800-767-9695
Rhett Barriere, Vice-President

Ottawa
111 Oriole Ave.
Kanata, ON K2L 1E6
613-836-5497
Fax: 613-836-3900
Bob Blackmore, Sales Engineer

Sarnia
777 - 1st St.
Wyoming, ON N0N 1T0
519-383-5724
Fax: 519-845-0253
Ron Richardson, Service Engineer

Fontaine International Corp.
Formerly: M. Fontaine Ltd.
1295, Sherbrooke
Magog, QC J1X 2T2
819-843-3068
Fax: 819-843-1006
info@hfontaine.com
www.hfontaine.com
Firm Type: Manufacturing
Founded: 1964
Staff: 180
Quality Environmental Management System(s): 9001
Products/Services/Areas of Expertise: Industry leader in the design & manufacture of water flow control gates for water & wastewater treatment facilites as well as energy, irrigation & flood control
Financial Information:
Type of Ownership: Private
Revenue: Greater than $5 Million
Revenue Sources: 20% Provincial; 60% Municipals; 20% Private Contracts
Domestic Markets:
National
Foreign Activity:
Worldwide
Contact(s):

François Fontaine, Vice-President, Sales
Canadian Branches:
Ottawa
18 Mannington Ct.
Ottawa, ON K2J 4A1
613-843-0283
Fax: 613-843-0284

International Branch(es):

3 Executive Park Dr.
Bedford, NH USA
603-626-6680
Fax: 603-626-6689

Brazil
252 - Conj 104, rua Iguatemi
Sao Paulo, SP Brazil
-55-11-3167-7020
Fax: -55-11-3167-703

Europe
P.O. Box 9001
11 avenue Charles de Gaulle
Roissy-en-France France
-33-1-34-29-47-69
Fax: -33-1-34-29-47-

Ireland
Donabate Business Centre
Block 2, Ballisk Ct.
Donabate, CO Ireland
-353-1-808-5375
Fax: -353-1-808-5376

U.K.
6 Wistowgate
Cawood UK
-44-1-757-269-331
Fax: -44-1-757-269-3

Forest Protection Limited / FPL
Fredericton International Airport
2502 Route 102 Hwy.
Lincoln, NB E3B 7E6
506-446-6930
Fax: 506-446-6934
info@forestprotectionlimited.com
www.forestprotectionlimited.com
Firm Type: Information Technology, Scientific/Technical Services
Founded: 1952
Staff: 50
Member of: Canadian Aerial Applicators Association; National Aerial Applicators Association; New Brunswick Environmental Industry Association
Products/Services/Areas of Expertise: Transport Canada licensed aerial operator; own & operate aircraft used for fire management, pest management, vegetation management, aerial surveys, GIS, GPS, mapping
Financial Information:
Type of Ownership: Private
Revenue: Greater than $5 Million
Domestic Markets:
National
Foreign Activity:
USA
Markets Sought:
Caribbean, South America, Mexico
Contact(s):
David Davies, Contact

Forest Technology Systems Ltd. / FTS
1065 Henry Eng Pl.
Victoria, BC V9B 6B2
250-478-5561
Fax: 250-905-7004
800-548-4264
sales@ftshydrology.com
www.ftshydrology.com
Firm Type: Engineering, Manufacturing
Founded: 1980
Staff: 32
Member of: Canadian Manufacturers & Exporters
Quality Environmental Management System(s): 9001
Products/Services/Areas of Expertise: Environmental automated monitoring solutions for weather & water parameters designed for remote installations
Recently Completed / Ongoing Projects: Remote fire weather networks in Canada & the US; surface weather monitoring network in Mexico; sediment transfer studies in US
Financial Information:
Type of Ownership: Private
Revenue: Greater than $5 Million
Revenue Sources: 50% nationwide; 50% Provincial
Domestic Markets:
National
Foreign Activity:
Asia, Australia/New Zealand, China, Western Europe, South America, Mexico, USA, Vietnam,
Contact(s):
David Illing, CEO
dilling@ftsinc.com

Foresteel Industries Inc.
Lefebvre Frères Ltd.
Formerly: Foresteel (1988) Inc.13500, boul Métropolitain est
Montréal, QC H1A 3W1
514-645-9251
Fax: 514-645-2436
info@lffabrication.com
www.lffabrication.com
Firm Type: Manufacturing
Founded: 1914
Staff: 175
Products/Services/Areas of Expertise: Reactors; heat exchangers; pressure vessels; heavy fabrication; machinery testing
Contact(s):
François Gamache, President
fgamache@lffabrication.com

Forsythe Lubrication Associates Ltd.
120 Chatham St.
Hamilton, ON L8P 2B5
905-525-7192
Fax: 905-525-7024
800-363-2759
www.forsythe.on.ca
Firm Type: Manufacturing
Founded: 1911
Staff: 25
Quality Environmental Management System(s): 9001:2000;
EcoLogo Certified Products & Services: No Fire Glycol HPWG 46B - fire resistant hydraulic fluid
Products/Services/Areas of Expertise: Water glycol/high pressure water glycol; misting oil; heat transfer fluid; custom compounding; toll blending
Ecological Note: No Fire Glycol HPWG 46B - fire resistant hydraulic fluid
Financial Information:
Type of Ownership: Private
Contact(s):
Bob Forsythe, President
rgf@forsythe.on.ca
Dee Forsyth-Arbour, CEO
darbour@forsythe.on.ca

Fort Garry Industries Ltd.
2525 Inkster Blvd., RR#2
Winnipeg, MB R3C 2E6
204-632-8261
Fax: 204-956-1786
800-282-8044
headoffice@fgiltd.com
www.fgiltd.com
Firm Type: Distributing, Manufacturing
Founded: 1919
Staff: 360
Member of: CBS Parts Ltd., with branches in Abbotsford, Burnaby, Kamloops, Prince George, & Surrey, BC
Quality Environmental Management System(s): 9001
Products/Services/Areas of Expertise: Supplying truck & trailer parts & equipment; remanufacturing brake shoes, fan clutches & hydraulic brake components (SuperStopr brand); manufacturing fire trucks & fire-fighting equipment (Fort Garry Fire Trucks); manufacturing rubber products, including recovering & re-manufacturing press rollers & installing rubber liners in tanks
Domestic Markets:
National
Contact(s):
Richard Spitzke, President
Jeff Carriere, VP, Finance
jcarriere@fgiltd.com

Products & Services Buyer's Guide

Robyn Spitzke-Kent, Executive VP
rskent@fgiltd.com
Liza Fontaine, Purchasing Manager
lfontaine@fgiltd.com
David Lippoway, Regional Manager, MB, NW, ON
dlippoway@fgiltd.com
Ron Hansen, Regional Manager, Alberta
rhansen@fgiltd.com
Barry Burton, Regional Manager, Saskatchewan
bburton@fgiltd.com

Canadian Branches:
Brandon Branch
1440 Highland Ave.
Brandon, MB R7C 1A7
204-571-5980
Fax: 204-571-5982
866-883-6120
Tyler Cybulsky, Branch Manager

Calgary - Truck Installation Centre
9625 - 48 St. SE
Calgary, AB T2C 2R1
403-236-5502
Fax: 403-236-5668
800-661-3126
Lyle Malinowski, Service Manager

Calgary Branch
5350 - 72 Ave. SE
Calgary, AB T2C 4X5
403-236-9712
Fax: 403-236-7249
800-661-3126
Wayne Shutiak, Branch Manager

Edmonton - Truck Installation Centre
11434 - 154 St. NW
Edmonton, AB T5M 3R4
780-454-4880
Fax: 780-488-7880
Glenn Bornes, Branch Manager

Edmonton Branch
16230 - 118th Ave.
Edmonton, AB T5V 1C6
780-447-4422
Fax: 780-447-3289
800-663-9366
Greg Israel, Regional Sales Manager, Alberta

Grande Prairie Branch
10610 - 82nd Ave.
Clairmont, AB T0H 0W0
780-402-9864
Fax: 780-402-8659
866-424-5479
Troy White, Branch Manager

Langley Branch
Canadian Truck & Trailer Repair
5733 - 198th St.
Langley, BC V3A 1G5
604-533-5005
Fax: 604-533-5754
Bob Carlyle, OE Sales Manager

Lethbridge - Equipment Sales Office
1110 - 39th St. North
Lethbridge, AB T1H 5L8
403-331-6315
Fax: 403-331-6317
866-865-3962
Mark Dyck, Sales Representative

Lloydminster Branch
P.O. Box 1530
5701 - 63 Ave.
Lloydminster, SK T9V 3B8
780-875-9115
Fax: 780-875-1403
800-661-9709
Brad Schoettler, Branch Manager

Mississauga Branch
731 Gana Crt.
Mississauga, ON L5S 1P2
905-564-5404
Fax: 905-564-8455
888-456-6567
Guido Groppini, Branch Manager

Oak Bluff Branch
Super Stop Rebuilding Division
160 Oakland Rd.
Oak Bluff, MB R0G 1N0
204-895-4515
Fax: 204-895-4306
Doug Martens, Branch Manager

Red Deer Branch
7947 Edgar Industrial Dr.
Red Deer, AB T4P 3R2
403-343-1383
Fax: 403-347-8275
866-297-0022
Brent Kreese, Branch Manager

Regina Branch
1523 Ross Ave. East
Regina, SK S4N 7E5
306-757-5606
Fax: 306-781-7926
800-552-8044
Richard Kazakoff, Branch Manager

Saskatoon Branch
P.O. Box 1848
3445 Miners Ave.
Saskatoon, SK S7K 7K9
306-242-3465
Fax: 306-933-4850
800-772-4599
Craig Cardell, Branch Manager

Surrey - Equipment Sales Office
9515 - 195 St.
Surrey, BC V4N 4G3
604-888-5522
Fax: 604-888-2007
800-663-4115
Bob Carlyle, Branch Manager

Thunder Bay Branch
915 Walsh St. West
Thunder Bay, ON P7E 4X5
807-577-5724
Fax: 807-475-9033
800-465-5044
Randy Joyce, Branch Manager

Fort Storage Warehousing & Distribution
Univar Company
169 Lowson Cr.
Winnipeg, MB R3P 1A6
204-488-9774
Fax: 204-488-9867
webinquiry@fortstorage.com
www.fortstorage.com
Firm Type: Distributing
Founded: 1974
Staff: 34
Member of: Industrial Warehouse Logistics Association (IWLA); Warehousing Education & Research Council (WERC)
Products/Services/Areas of Expertise: Chemical warehousing & logistics; certified by the Agricultural Warehousing Standards Association (AWSA) for the storage of Agrichemicals for resale purposes
Financial Information:
Type of Ownership: Private
Domestic Markets:
Alberta, Manitoba, Ontario, Saskatchewan
Contact(s):
Alan Smith, Business Manager, 204-488-5860
alan.s@fortstorage.com

Canadian Branches:
Airdrie
P.O. Box 3304
35 East Lake Circle NE
Airdrie, AB T4A 2J9
403-948-9777
Fax: 403-948-9785
Kirk Moffat, Contact
kirkm@fortstorage.com

Guelph
555 Southgate Dr.
Guelph, ON N1G 3W6

Saskatoon
4115 Thatcher Ave.
Saskatoon, SK S7K 3J7
306-653-8101
Fax: 306-653-4996
Kirk Moffat, Contact
kirkm@fortstorage.com

Fortier 2000 Ltée
Groupe Riverin
146, rue Commerciale
Saint-Henri-de-Lévis, QC G0R 3E0
418-882-0696
Fax: 418-882-2067
info@fortier2000.ca
www.fortier2000.com
Firm Type: Manufacturing
Founded: 1985
Staff: 180
Products/Services/Areas of Expertise: Fabrication de produits de béton
Domestic Markets:
Québec
Contact(s):
Guy Turcotte, Ing., Directeur général, 418-540-1695
g.turcotte@fortier2000.com
Mario Villeneuve, Directeur des ventes, 418-929-7597
m.villeneuve@fortier2000.com

FPInnovations
Formerly: Forintek Canada Corp. & Pulp & Paper Research Institute (Paprican)
570, boul. Saint-Jean
Montréal, QC H9R 3J9
514-630-4100
Fax: 514-630-4134
info@fpinnovations.ca
www.fpinnovations.ca
Firm Type: Scientific/Technical Services, RESEARCH
Founded: 2007
Staff: 600
Member of: NSERC Forest Sector R&D Initiative; ArboraNano (Canadian Forest NanoProducts Network); CRIBE (Centre for Research & Innovation in the Bio-economy); NEWBuilds (Network for Engineered Wood-based Building Systems)
Products/Services/Areas of Expertise: The world's largest private, not-for-profit forest research institute, with a mandate to strengthen Canada's forest sector through research, innovation & knowledge transfer; provides leadership in the R&D process, works towards optimizing the forest sector value chain, & develops new products & market opportunities within a framework of environmental sustainability
Financial Information:
Type of Ownership: Non Profit
Domestic Markets:
National
Contact(s):
Pierre Lapointe, President/CEO
Nathalie Guilbault, Director, Corporate Communications
nathalie.guilbault@fpinnovations.ca

Canadian Branches:
Pointe-Claire - Forest Operations
580, boul. Saint-Jean
Montréal, QC H9R 3J9
514-696-1140
Fax: 515-694-4351

Pointe-Claire - Pulp & Paper Research
570, boul. Saint-Jean
Montréal, QC H9R 3J9
514-630-4100
Fax: 514-630-4134

Québec - Wood Products Research
319, rue Franquet
Québec, QC G1P 4R4
418-659-2647
Fax: 418-659-2922

Vancouver - Forest Operations
2601 East Mall
Vancouver, BC V6T 1Z4
604-228-1555
Fax: 604-228-0999

Vancouver - Pulp & Paper Research
3800 Westbrook Mall
Vancouver, BC V6S 2L9

604-222-3200
Fax: 604-222-3207

Vancouver - Wood Products Research
2665 East Mall
Vancouver, BC V6T 1W5
604-224-3221
Fax: 604-222-5690

FracFlow Consultants Inc.
2 Fielding Ave., #D
Dartmouth, NS B3B 1E1
902-468-1317
Fax: 902-468-4704
866-295-4704
fracflow@ns.sympatico.ca
www.nfld.net/fracflow
Contact(s):
G. Glenn Bursey, Vice-President

Frank T. Ross & Sons Ltd.
#14, 70 Esna Park Dr.
Markham, ON L3R 6E7
416-282-1107
Fax: 416-282-8150
info@franktross.com
www.franktross.com
Firm Type: Manufacturing
Founded: 1927
Member of: Corus Entertainment Inc. (Treehouse TV)
EcoLogo Certified Products & Services: A comprehensive array of household cleaners; air fresheners; furniture polish; hygiene products & body lotion
Products/Services/Areas of Expertise: The company offers EcoLogo-certified, cleaning & home products. Its main brands are Weldbond, NatureClean & Treehouse products for children. Ecological Note: A comprehensive array of household cleaners; air fresheners; furniture polish; hygiene products & body lotion
Financial Information:
Type of Ownership: Private
Revenue Sources: 100% Private Contracts
Domestic Markets:
Alberta, British Columbia, Manitoba, New Brunswick, Newfoundland & Labrador, Nova Scotia, Ontario, Prince Edward Island, Québec, Saskatchewan, Yukon Territory
Foreign Activity:
Australia/New Zealand, China, The Middle East, The Pacific Rim, USA, United Kingdom
Contact(s):
Blake Ross, President
blake@franktross.com
Bernie Ross, CEO

Frank's Alternate Energy
396 Copper Cliff Rd. East
Neebing, ON P7L 0B6
807-964-2050
888-786-9463
sunwind@tbaytel.net
www.sunwindwater.com
Firm Type: Distributing, Scientific/Technical Services
Founded: 1994
Staff: 3
Member of: Canadian Solar Industries Association (CanSIA); Canadian Wind Energy Association (CanWEA)
Products/Services/Areas of Expertise: The company provides renewable energy systems for off-grid cottages & homes; specializes in consultation, system design, installation, including tower erection for wind machines & custom fabrication; promotes renewable energy technologies to school groups & campers' associations.
Domestic Markets:
Ontario
Contact(s):
Frank Ilczyszyn, Owner/Manager
Jane Olddale, System Design/Marketing
Don Sopotiuck, Electronics Technician

Franz Environmental Inc.
4005 Hickory Dr.
Mississauga, ON L4W 1L1
905-614-1978
Fax: 905-614-1981
www.franzenvironmental.ca
Firm Type: Management Consulting, Engineering

Products/Services/Areas of Expertise: The company is an environmental & engineering consulting firm, specializing in contaminant risk assessment, environmental monitoring & remediation. Senior professionals provide technical support for hearings & litigation.
Financial Information:
Type of Ownership: Private
Domestic Markets:
National
Foreign Activity:
Western Europe, USA
Contact(s):
Thomas Franz, President
tfranz@franzenvironmental.com
Steve Livingstone, Vice-President
slivingstone@franzenvironmental.com

Canadian Branches:
Montréal
#120, 825, boul Guimond
Longueuil, QC J4G 2M7
450-674-2207
Fax: 450-674-2217

Ottawa
#200, 329 Churchill Ave. North
Ottawa, ON K1Z 5B8
613-721-0555
Fax: 613-721-0029

Vancouver
#308, 1080 Mainland St.
Vancouver, BC V6B 2T4
604-632-9941
Fax: 604-632-9942

Victoria
#104, 4430 Chatterton Way
Victoria, BC V8X 5J2
250-479-5103
Fax: 250-479-5134

Whitehorse
P.O. Box 10277
Whitehorse, YT Y1A 7A1
867-456-7714

Frappier & Génier Conseillers
30, ave du Centenaire
Salaberry-de-Valleyfield, QC J6S 5X4
450-373-3330
Fax: 450-373-5831
Products/Services/Areas of Expertise: Engineering consulting services; water & wastewater management services
Contact(s):
Pierre Frappier, President

Fraser Environmental Services / FES
Formerly: Linde Looy Aquatic Biology
9358 Cinnamon Dr.
Surrey, BC V3V 1V2
604-588-9738
Fax: 604-588-9738
lindelooy@shaw.ca
Firm Type: Scientific/Technical Services
Founded: 1992
Staff: 6
Member of: Association of Professional Biologists of BC; American Society of Limnology & Oceanography; International Phycological Society; College of Applied Biology
Products/Services/Areas of Expertise: Taxonomic identification of plankton, periphyton & benthic invertebrates
Recently Completed / Ongoing Projects: Biological analyses, BC Ministry of Water, Land & Air Protection, private companies
Financial Information:
Revenue Sources: 30% Provincial; 70% Private Contracts
Domestic Markets:
National
Foreign Activity:
The Pacific Rim, USA, Worldwide
Markets Sought:
Asia, Australia/New Zealand, Caribbean, China, South America, Mexico, Vietnam
Contact(s):
Linde Looy, Aquatic Biologist
Linda Currie, Aquatic Biologist
Cris Baldazzi, Aquatic Biologist
Sue Salter, Aquatic Biologist

Fred Cressman Sales Inc.
264 Sunview St.
Waterloo, ON N2L 3V9
519-884-3225
Fax: 519-884-1326
Firm Type: Distributing
Founded: 1982
Staff: 3
Products/Services/Areas of Expertise: Firefighing equipment; storage equipment
Financial Information:
Type of Ownership: Private
Revenue: Less than $50,000
Revenue Sources: 10% nationwide; 90% Private Contracts
Domestic Markets:
National
Foreign Activity:
USA
Contact(s):
Fred Cressman, President

Frederick Goertz Ltd.
314 East 5th Ave.
Vancouver, BC V5T 1H4
604-871-9066
Fax: 604-871-9067
800-663-1952
fgoertz@sprint.ca
Firm Type: Scientific/Technical Services
Founded: 1910
Staff: 10
Products/Services/Areas of Expertise: Survey & construction instruments; meteorological equipment; canadian manufacturer of filing (document) systems
Financial Information:
Type of Ownership: Private
Domestic Markets:
Alberta, British Columbia
Foreign Activity:
USA
Markets Sought:
The Pacific Rim
Contact(s):
James Goodlet, Vice-President & Manager, Sales

Frey & Associates Engineering Ltd.
P.O. Box 7866
5408 - 53rd Avenue
Drayton Valley, AB T7A 1S9
780-542-3096
Fax: 780-542-6405
Products/Services/Areas of Expertise: Engineering services
Domestic Markets:
National
Foreign Activity:
The Middle East

Frickie Creek Consulting Corp.
P.O. Box 387
Water Valley, AB T2M 2E0
403-637-2630

Friesen Tokar Architects, Landscape & Interior Designers / FT3
#200, 300 Waterfront Dr.
Winnipeg, MB R3B 0G5
204-885-9323
Fax: 204-837-7235
ft@ft3.ca
www.friesentokar.com
Firm Type: Management Consulting
Founded: 1975
Staff: 25
Products/Services/Areas of Expertise: Environmental studies & impact assessments; energy conservation analysis; building retrofit design; building investigations & assessment; heritage building preservation; visual impact analysis; land use management & master planning; site selection, analysis & planning
Recently Completed / Ongoing Projects: Canadian Wheat Board office building, retrofit, Winnipeg; Solar panels installation, lower Fort Garry Visitors Centre; Restoration of former girls school, Molochansk, Ukraine
Financial Information:
Revenue: $3 Million - $5 Million
Revenue Sources: 15% nationwide; 25% Provincial; 20% Municipals; 40% Private Contracts

Products & Services Buyer's Guide

Domestic Markets:
Alberta, Manitoba, Ontario, Saskatchewan
Foreign Activity:
Eastern Europe, USA
Contact(s):
Rudy P. Friesen, Principal
friesen@friesentokar.com
Brian W. Torkar, Principal
torkar@friesentokar.com
Jerald D. Peters, Principal
peters@friesentokar.com

Frontenac Environmental Ltd.
6 Bram Crt.
Brampton, ON L6W 3R6
905-457-5145
Fax: 905-457-1730
Firm Type: Distributing
Staff: 5
Member of: Water Environment Association of Ontario
Products/Services/Areas of Expertise: Wastewater/water treatment equipment
Financial Information:
Type of Ownership: Private
Domestic Markets:
Ontario
Contact(s):
Rick Mills, Technical Sales Representative
George Bennett, Technical Sales Representative

FS Partners
Growmark Inc. - Canada
#7, 1 Chandaria Pl.
Kitchener, ON N2C 2S3
519-895-5300
Fax: 519-895-3598
info@fspartners.ca
www.fspartners.ca
Firm Type: Scientific/Technical Services
Staff: 150
Products/Services/Areas of Expertise: FS Partners is the retail division of Growmark Inc, Canada. It is an organization of cooperatives that market grain & agronomy/energy products throughout southwestern & central Ontario.
Domestic Markets:
Ontario
Foreign Activity:
USA
Contact(s):
Jayne Atkins, CEO

Canadian Branches:
Alliston
55 Tupper St.
Alliston, ON L9R 1E4
705-435-6235
888-513-1111
Don Campbell, Manager
dcampbell@fspartners.ca

Aylmer
220 Elm St.
Aylmer, ON N5H 2M8
519-765-1620
Morley Friesen, Manager
mfriesen@fspartners.ca

Ayr
1107 Northumberland St.
Ayr, ON N0B 1E0
519-632-7900
877-297-3378
Kevin Stumpf, Manager
kstumpf@fspartners.ca

Beeton Elevator
P.O. Box 747
2697 Tottenham Rd. 10
Beeton, ON L0G 1A0
905-729-2047
800-263-1261
Pete Anderson, Manager
panderson@fspartners.ca

Courtland
19 North St.
Courtland, ON N0J 1E0
519-688-3157

Morley Friesen, Manager
mfriesen@fspartners.ca

Drayton
44 Main St. West
Drayton, ON N0G 1P0
519-638-3026
800-265-2284
Marilyn McQueen, Manager
mmcqueen@fspartners.ca

Elmvale
P.O. Box 3041
1091 Concession 8 Flos/Hwy 27
Elmvale, ON L0L 1P0
705-322-3041
877-388-5988

Flesherton - Lube Center
774317 Highway 10 North
Flesherton, ON N0C 1E0
519-924-0033

Grand Valley
202350 County Rd. 109
Grand Valley, ON L0N 1G0
519-928-2100
866-928-2101

Harmony
2945 CR-26, RR2
Harmony, ON N0B 2R0
519-273-2121
877-613-2121
Anne O'Hearn, Contact

Milverton
6433 Road 131, RR1
Milverton, ON N0K 1M0
519-595-7820
888-595-7820
Greg Ryan, Manager
gryan@fspartners.ca

Mitchell
P.O. Box 370
3956 Rd. 160
Mitchell, ON N0K 1N0
519-348-8441
877-748-8441
Larry Hale, Manager
lhale@fspartners.ca

Monkton Grain
190 Mill St.
Monkton, ON N0K 1P0
519-347-2232
Andrew Troyer, Manager
atroyer@fspartners.ca

Norwich
136 Main St.
Norwich, ON N0J 1P0
519-863-2700
800-265-4034
Morley Friesen, Manager
mfriesen@fspartners.ca

Simcoe - Delhi Agronomy
1161 Fertilizer Rd., RR7
Simcoe, ON N3Y 4K6
519-582-0444
800-265-8024
Morley Friesen, Manager
mfriesen@fspartners.ca

Simcoe - Delhi Grain
184 Windham Rd. 14, RR7
Simcoe, ON N3Y 4K6
519-582-3370
800-265-8024
Devin Homick, Manager
dhomick@fspartners.ca

Staffordville
55720 Jackson Line
Staffordville, ON N0J 1Y0
519-866-5872

Stayner
P.O. Box 360
212 Huron St.
Stayner, ON L0M 1S0
705-428-2840
800-373-4471

FSI International Services Ltd.
4635 - 8A St. NE
Calgary, AB T2E 4J6
403-571-4225
Fax: 403-230-3106
888-571-4225
www.fsi-international.com

Fuel Maker Corp.
70 Worcester Rd.
Toronto, ON M9W 5X2
416-674-3034
Fax: 416-674-3042
877-383-5625
cdninfo@fuelmaker.com
www.fuelmaker.com
Firm Type: Scientific/Technical Services
Founded: 1989
Products/Services/Areas of Expertise: Manufacturers, distributes, installs & services vehicle refueling appliances & accessories for fueling vehicles powered by CNG

Fugro Airborne Surveys
Fugro N.V.
Formerly: Geoterrex-Dighem 2505 Meadowvale Blvd.
Mississauga, ON L5N 5S2
905-812-0212
Fax: 905-812-1504
bbrown@fugroairborne.com
www.fugroairborne.com
Firm Type: Information Technology, Scientific/Technical Services
Founded: 1967
Staff: 500
Member of: Society of Exploration Geophysicists; Canadian Exploration Geophysical Society; Association of Professional Engineers; European Association of Exploration Geophysicists
Products/Services/Areas of Expertise: Airborne geological surveys with fixed wing or helicopter platforms around the world; the systems, electromagnetic & magnetic, map subsurface changes in the earth's geology, soil types & thickness, man-made buried metallic objects, & detect the presence of fresh, salt or contaminated water in otherwise dry ground; provides turnkey services which includes all flying & processing of geophysical data
Recently Completed / Ongoing Projects: Location/detection of buried radioactive sources, U.S. military base; mapping contaminant plumes from an abandoned mine, California; salt water encroachment, Florida Everglades; mapping bedrock for a planned pipeline, Québec; mapping Acid Mine drainage
Financial Information:
Type of Ownership: Publicly Traded
Revenue Sources: 90% Private Contracts
Domestic Markets:
National
Foreign Activity:
Worldwide
Contact(s):
Bill Brown, Business Development

Canadian Branches:
Ottawa, Ontario
2191 Thurston Dr.
Ottawa, ON K1G 6C9
613-731-9575
Fax: 613-731-0453
groberts@fugroairborne.com
Gord Roberts, Geophysicist

International Branch(es):
Lima, Peru
Ignacio Merino 711
Miraflores, Lima Peru
-511-221-3610
Fax: -511-421-8217
Steve Wardlaw, General Manager

Paris, France
1, rue Léon Migaux
Massy Cedex France
-331-6447-3000
Fax: -331-6447-3970

Dominique Boitier, Sales & Marketing

Rio de Janero, Brazil
Rua Conde de Lages
Avenida Ayrton Senna, 2541 - Rua F1. Lote 04
Rio de Janeiro Brazil
-5521-3501-7700
Fax: -5521-3501-7701
geomag@geomag.com.br

Sydney, Australia
Sydney NSW
7-9 George Pl.
Artarmon Australi
-612-9481-8077
Fax: -612-9481-8581
postmaster@geoterrex.com.au
Paul Strandberg, General Manager

Fugro Jacques GeoSurveys Inc.
25 Pippy Place
St. John's, NL A1B 3X2
709-726-4252
Fax: 709-726-5007
mcole@fjg.ca
Contact(s):
Mike Cole, President

Fuller Austin Insulation Inc.
8525 Davies Rd.
Edmonton, AB T6E 4N3
780-481-9600
Fax: 780-468-3136
www.fulleraustin.com
Products/Services/Areas of Expertise: Industrial insulation contracting specialist
Contact(s):
Ron Martineau, President & COO
Randy Brodeur, Vice-President, Alberta Operations
Perry Pugh, Vice-President, Saskatchewan & Manitoba Operations

Fulton Engineered Specialties Inc.
Formerly: Fulton Enterprises Inc
13908 Hurontario St.
Caledon, ON L7C 2B8
905-838-0303
Fax: 905-838-0301
info@fultonengineeredspecialties.com
www.fultonengineeredspecialties.com
Firm Type: Manufacturing
Founded: 1975
Staff: 40
Member of: Canadian Heat Exchange & Vessel Manufacturers Association
Products/Services/Areas of Expertise: Waste storage containers; power boiler shells; heating boiler shells; heat exchangers; custom pressure vessels, custom storage tanks, vacuum vessels, hot water boiler shells, steam boiler shells, aluminum pressure vessels, stainless steel pressure vessels, manways for waste handling; truck mounted tanks; pressure manways; cryogenic systems
Financial Information:
Type of Ownership: Private
Revenue: Greater than $5 Million
Revenue Sources: 100% Private Contracts
Domestic Markets:
National
Foreign Activity:
Caribbean, USA
Contact(s):
Walter Widla, President

Fundy Compost Inc. / ICI
RR#2
Brookfield, NS B0N 1C0
902-673-3020
Fax: 902-673-3020
fundycompost@ns.sympatico.ca
Firm Type: Manufacturing
Founded: 1995
Staff: 2
Member of: Composting Council of Canada
Products/Services/Areas of Expertise: Organic wastes processing; treatment of effluent; organic wastes management consulting; soil erosion control; land reclamation; production of compost products

Financial Information:
Type of Ownership: Private
Revenue: $500,000 - $1.5 Million
Revenue Sources: 55% Municipals; 45% Private Contracts
Domestic Markets:
Nova Scotia
Contact(s):
Walter Termeer, P.Ag., CAC, CEO
Donna Emin, Administration

Fundy Engineering & Consulting Ltd.
27 Wellington Row
Saint John, NB E2L 3H4
506-635-1566
Fax: 506-635-0206
877-635-1566
fundy@fundyeng.com
www.fundyeng.com
Firm Type: Engineering
Founded: 1989
Staff: 35
Member of: NB Environmental Industries Association
Products/Services/Areas of Expertise: Land use studies; contamination investigations; groundwater contamination; underground storage tanks; environmental site assessments; geotechnical services; blasting control; earthwork inspection; electrical & mechanical engineering
Financial Information:
Type of Ownership: Private
Domestic Markets:
New Brunswick, Nova Scotia, Prince Edward Island
Contact(s):
Peter McKelvey, P.Eng., President

Fusionex inc.
A Wolseley company
Formerly: Les Plastiques Fusionex Inc.2855, rue Étienne-Lenoir
Laval, QC H7R 6J4
450-963-3010
Fax: 450-963-6811
www.fusionex.com; www.hdpe.ca
Firm Type: Distributing
Founded: 1983
Products/Services/Areas of Expertise: Fusionex se spécialise dans la distribution et la fusion de tuyaux et raccords en Polyéthylène Haute Densité (PEHD); oeuvre dans plusieurs secteurs d'activités tels que: infrastructures urbaines, industrielles, minières, environnementales, télécommunications, électriques, gazières (naturel), captage des bio-gaz et des eaux de lixiviation, irrigation, aquaculture, acériculture, etc.
Financial Information:
Type of Ownership: Publicly Traded
Domestic Markets:
Québec
Contact(s):
Guylaine Lefebvre, Directrice régionale
guylaine.lefebvre@wolseleyinc.ca

FWR Ecoresource Consultants Ltd.
1291 White Pine Place
Coquitlam, BC V3B 6Y5
604-945-5183
Fax: 604-945-5189
fwr@fwr-ecoresource.ca
www.fwr-ecoresource.ca
Firm Type: Scientific/Technical Services

Products/Services/Areas of Expertise: Environmental consulting & habitat enhancement services
Financial Information:
Type of Ownership: Publicly Traded
Contact(s):
Clayton Anderson, Principal

G & G Computer Services
3071 Centennial Dr.
Burlington, ON L7M 1B5
905-332-1510
guzy1@sympatico.ca
Firm Type: Information Technology, Scientific/Technical Services
Founded: 1990
Staff: 1
Products/Services/Areas of Expertise: Business process engineering; database design & programming; network installation & support; data conversions & transfers; process automation; power & data back-up implementation; training; refurbishing lead acid batteries; DC systems design

Recently Completed / Ongoing Projects: Medical study financial control systems; equipment rental tracking system; quotation system for electrical components manufacturer; production floor flow control program
Financial Information:
Type of Ownership: Private
Revenue: $50,000 - $100,000
Revenue Sources: 100% Private Contracts
Domestic Markets:
Ontario
Contact(s):
Janusz Guzy, Owner

G. Landry Vacuum Services Ltd.
885 Front Lake Rd.
Dutch Brook, NS B1M 1B4
902-564-8413
Fax: 902-562-2508
Contact(s):
Joe Landry, Owner

G.A. Borstad Associates Ltd.
Also Known As: Borstad Associates Ltd.
#114, 9865 West Saanich Rd.
Sidney, BC V8L 5Y8
250-656-5633
Fax: 250-656-3646
gary@borstad.com
www.borstad.com
Firm Type: Scientific/Technical Services
Founded: 1983
Staff: 7
Member of: International Society for Optical Engineering; American Society of Limnology & Oceanography
Products/Services/Areas of Expertise: Remote sensing of environment from aircraft & satellites, especially hyperspectral; pollution; water quality; animals; fish; aquatic vegetation; wetlands; land use; forests; vegetation classification & detection of disease/stress; mineral exploration
Recently Completed / Ongoing Projects: Mapping of tropical coral reefs & lagoons; historical land use & changes; mine reclamation monitoring; water quality monitoring in coastal rivers; satellite oceanography; remote sensing training; mineral, oil & gas exploation
Financial Information:
Type of Ownership: Private
Revenue Sources: 30% nationwide; 30% Provincial; 5% Municipals; 35% Private Contracts
Domestic Markets:
National
Foreign Activity:
Worldwide
Contact(s):
Gary Borstad, President
Randy Kerr, Senior Systems Analyst

G.I. Russell & Co. Ltd.
3380 South Service Rd.
Burlington, ON L7N 358
905-634-5509
Fax: 905-634-3187
preservesteel@on.aibn.com
Firm Type: Engineering, Scientific/Technical Services
Founded: 1956
Staff: 5
Member of: Association of Consulting Engineers of Canada; Consulting Engineers of Ontario; Association of Professional Engineers of Ontario; National Association of Consulting Engineers
Products/Services/Areas of Expertise: Pipeline systems for design applications; cathodic isolation & protection system designs to secure safe electrical grounding & corrosion prevention for underground storage tanks & pipelines, piling & wharves; plant process equipment
Domestic Markets:
National
Foreign Activity:
Asia, Australia/New Zealand, USA
Contact(s):
Gordon I. Russell, P.Eng., President

G.R. Kelly Environmental Services
738 Hammonds Plains Rd.
Halifax, NS B4B 1B1
902-835-4655
Fax: 902-835-8318
grkellyent@ns.sympatico.ca

Contact(s):
Greg Kelly, Contact

G.T. Wood Co. Ltd.
3354 Mavis Rd.
Mississauga, ON L5C 1T8
905-272-1696
Fax: 905-272-1425
800-305-2036
sales@gtwood.com
www.gtwood.com
Firm Type: Management Consulting, Engineering, Waste Management
Founded: 1972
Staff: 50
Products/Services/Areas of Expertise: Hazardous waste transport & disposal; facility management; environmental audits; laboratory services; high voltage electrical & engineering services
Recently Completed / Ongoing Projects: Decontamination, Trenton
Financial Information:
Type of Ownership: Private
Revenue Sources: 100% Private Contracts
Domestic Markets:
National
Foreign Activity:
USA,
Contact(s):
Larry Snow, President

G3 Consulting Ltd.
#206, 8501 - 162nd St.
Surrey, BC V4N 1B2
604-598-8501
Fax: 604-598-8525
info@g3consulting.com
www.g3consulting.com
Firm Type: Scientific/Technical Services
Founded: 1992
Member of: Professional Biologists of BC; Society of Environmental Toxicology & Chemistry; American Institute of Chemists; Vancouver Board of Trade; American Fisheries Society
Products/Services/Areas of Expertise: Environmental assessments; project management; watershed restoration; field & laboratory work; data quality control & analysis; custom database design & report production; environmental effects monitoring - EEM; environmental impact assessments; pollution monitoring; water quality & fisheries assessments; GIS & mapping; bioethic & periphyton taxomony; Species at Risk & streamside assessments
Recently Completed / Ongoing Projects: Environmental effects monitoring studies on behalf of pulp & paper & mining industry; organochlorine assessment studies on behalf of federal & provincial governments & the pulp & paper industry; large scale watershed restoration & fisheries assessments, environmental monitoring systems & risk assessments conducted on behalf of government & industry
Contact(s):
Gregory P. Thomas, President
Robin Bellisle, Manager

GAEA Technologies
87 Garden St.
Whitby, ON L1N 9E7
905-666-7527
Fax: 416-853-1565
sales@gaea.ca
www.gaea.ca
Firm Type: Distributing, Information Technology, Scientific/Technical Services
Founded: 1994
Staff: 5
Products/Services/Areas of Expertise: Software for civil engineering & geology
Recently Completed / Ongoing Projects: Pocket ESA for collecting & reporting environmental assessment data
Financial Information:
Type of Ownership: Private
Domestic Markets:
National
Contact(s):
Mike Fraser, President
mfraser@gaea.ca

Gage Environmental Management Inc.
117, des Pignons
Sutton, QC J0E 2K0
450-538-5151
Fax: 450-538-5454

GAIA Power Inc.
Formerly: GAIA Power Consulting
41 Durham St.
Kingston, ON K7L 1J2
613-530-2100
Fax: 613-530-3555
info@gaiapower.com
www.gaiapower.com
Products/Services/Areas of Expertise: Specializes in the development of renewable energy sources across Canada; offers a modular wind power solution including sales & consulting services for wind power financing, marketing, community consultation & education, regulatory & land acquisition, technical & construction engineering, & wind farm operation
Contact(s):
Samit Sharma, P.Eng. MBA
Paula Major

Galaxy Pallets Ltd.
P.O. Box 68
124 Erie St.
Smithville, ON L0R 2A0
905-957-3392
Fax: 905-957-2199
Firm Type: Manufacturing, Waste Management
Founded: 1966
Staff: 20
Quality Environmental Management System(s): 9002
Products/Services/Areas of Expertise: Recycling of wooden pallets; manufacture of wood products including pallets, boxes & special products
Domestic Markets:
Ontario
Foreign Activity:
USA
Contact(s):
Bruce McFarlane, President/CEO

Gallason Industrial Cleaning Services Inc.
11222D - 87 Ave.
Fort Saskatchewan, AB T8L 2T2
780-998-7773
Fax: 780-998-7774
Firm Type: Waste Management
Founded: 1985
Staff: 12
Products/Services/Areas of Expertise: Waste materials handling; industrial vacuuming; catalyst handling; hydro blasting; materials transportation; tank cleaning; steam cleaning; portable toilet rentals; emergency response services
Contact(s):
Mark Johnson, Owner/Sales Manager
Gregg Gallaway, Owner/Operations Manager

Gamsby & Mannerow Ltd. / G&M
Block C
#2, 650 Woodlawn Rd. West
Guelph, ON N1K 1B8
519-824-8150
Fax: 519-824-8089
info@gamsby.com
www.gamsby.com
Firm Type: Engineering
Founded: 1966
Staff: 7
Products/Services/Areas of Expertise: Environmental impact assessments & audits; industrial/commercial site decommissioning, remediation & cleanup; hydrogeologic investigations, groundwater supply/development; aquifer detailing, evaluation & protection; sanitary landfill site selection, design & monitoring; municipal wastewater treatment plant facilities
Domestic Markets:
Ontario,
Contact(s):
Dave Hicknell, President
dhicknell@gamsby.com
Glenn Anderson, Vice-President
ganderson@gamsby.com
John Slocombe, Treasurer
jslocombe@gamsby.com
Paul McLennan, Guelph Branch Manager
pmclennan@gamsby.com
Canadian Branches:
Exeter
#4, 145 Thames Rd. West
Exeter, ON N0M 1S3
519-235-2539
exeter@gamsby.com
Brad Bunke, Branch Manager
bbunke@gamsby.com

Kitchener
#D, 330 Trillium Dr.
Kitchener, ON N2E 2K6
519-291-9339
kitchener@gamsby.com
Glenn Anderson, Branch manager
ganderson@gamsby.com

Listowel
975 Wallace Ave. North
Listowel, ON N4W 1M6
519-291-9339
Fax: 519-291-5172
listowel@gamsby.com
David Hicknell, Branch Manager
bhicknell@gamsby.com

Owen Sound
#1, 1260 - 2nd St.
Owen Sound, ON N4K 2J3
519-376-1805
Fax: 519-376-8977
owensound@gamsby.com
John Slocombe, Branch Manager
jslocombe@gamsby.com

Gandalf Consulting Ltd.
P.O. Box 48806
#517, 1190 Melville St.
Vancouver, BC V7X 1A6
604-633-2750
Fax: 604-633-2755
response@gandalfconsulting.bc.ca
www.gandalfconsulting.bc.ca
Products/Services/Areas of Expertise: Environmental consulting & contracting services
Contact(s):
Robert Symington, Hydrogeologist
symington@gandalfconsulting.bc.ca

GAP EnviroMicrobial Services Inc.
#14, 1020 Hargrieve Rd.
London, ON N6E 1P5
519-681-0571
Fax: 519-681-7150
info@gapenviromic.com
www.gapenviromic.com
Firm Type: Scientific/Technical Services
Founded: 1996
Staff: 20
Products/Services/Areas of Expertise: Microbiology laboratory specializing in potable water & wastewater analysis: detection & identification of microorganisms, field studies, expert witness, identification & isolation of cryptosporadium & giardia

Gary Steacy Dismantling Limited
P.O. Box 188
Colborne, ON K0K 1S0
905-355-3046
Fax: 905-355-5480
info@steacydismantling.com
www.steacydismantling.com
Firm Type: Waste Management
Founded: 1984
Products/Services/Areas of Expertise: Hazardous waste destruction; recycling of metals & transformer oils
Financial Information:
Type of Ownership: Private
Domestic Markets:
National
Contact(s):
Gary Steacy, President

Gas Liquids Engineering Ltd.
#300, 2749 - 39 Ave. NE
Calgary, AB T1Y 4T8
403-250-2950
Fax: 403-291-9730
gasliquids@gasliquids.com
www.gasliquids.com
Firm Type: Engineering
Founded: 1987
Staff: 70
Member of: Environmental Services Association of Alberta; Canadian Gas Processors Suppliers Association
Products/Services/Areas of Expertise: Offers engineering & project management services in natural gas purification & liquids recovery, process & facilities design, process simulation, optimization, debottlenecking & retrofitting, upgrading facilities & expansions, & effluent & emissions management as relevant to oil & gas facilities
Recently Completed / Ongoing Projects: Design equipment specifications & project management for an expanded CO_2 recovery facility
Financial Information:
Type of Ownership: Private
Domestic Markets:
Alberta, British Columbia, Manitoba, New Brunswick, Nova Scotia, Ontario, Saskatchewan
Foreign Activity:
Asia, Caribbean, Central Europe, Eastern Europe, The Middle East, South America, USA
Contact(s):
D. Mackenzie, President
P. Marshall, Manager, Business Development
P. Griffin, Vice-President, International Projects & Business Operations
A. Toews, Vice-President, Facilities
J. Maddocks, Vice-President, Engineering

Gasmac Inc.
509 Clair Rd. West
Guelph, ON N1H 6H9
519-836-5362
Fax: 519-836-4242
Firm Type: Manufacturing
Founded: 1923
Products/Services/Areas of Expertise: Heat exchangers; incinerators
Financial Information:
Type of Ownership: Private
Domestic Markets:
National
Foreign Activity:
Worldwide

Gaston Marcil, Consultant
#202, 110, boul Crémazie ouest
Montréal, QC H2P 1B9
514-384-4220
Fax: 514-383-6017
Firm Type: Engineering
Founded: 1981
Staff: 2
Member of: American Water Works Association; Water Environment Federation; Réseau Environment
Products/Services/Areas of Expertise: Design of water & wastewater treatment plants
Domestic Markets:
Québec
Contact(s):
Gaston Marcil, Consultant

Gator International
#212, 113 - 237 Martin St.
Penticton, BC V2A 5L1
250-493-3635
Fax: 250-493-9347
sales@gatorinternational.com
www.gatorinternational.com
Firm Type: Distributing
Founded: 1988
Products/Services/Areas of Expertise: Hydrocarbon bioremediation & absorption
Financial Information:
Type of Ownership: Private
Revenue Sources: 95% Private Contracts
Domestic Markets:
National
Foreign Activity:
Asia, Australia/New Zealand, South America
Contact(s):
W.N. Cary, CEO.

GDG Environnement Ltée
430, rue St-Laurent, 2e étage
Trois-Rivières, QC G8T 6H3
819-373-3097
Fax: 819-373-6832
gdg.environnement@gdg.ca
www.gdg.ca
Firm Type: Engineering, Scientific/Technical Services
Founded: 1980
Member of: Spécialistes en extermination de Québec, Association des conseillers en environnement de Québec
Quality Environmental Management System(s): 9001
Products/Services/Areas of Expertise: Aquaculture, environmental & ecological impact studies; biting fly & pest control, fish & vegetation management; environmentally safe pesticides & herbicides; biodigestion of contaminants; aquatic studies; toxicology; bioassays
Domestic Markets:
New Brunswick, Newfoundland & Labrador, Nova Scotia, Prince Edward Island, Québec
Contact(s):
Jean-Sébastien Bérubé, President & CEO
Isabelle Martin, Vice-President, Operations
Christian Beck, Vice-President, Development of Science & Technology
Martin Lord, Vice-President, Marketing & International Development

GE Ground Engineering Ltd.
415 - 7th Ave.
Regina, SK S4N 4P1
306-569-9075
Fax: 306-565-3677
geground@accesscom.ca
Firm Type: Engineering
Founded: 1972
Staff: 20
Member of: Association of Soil & Foundation Engineers
Products/Services/Areas of Expertise: Environmental & geotechnical consulting
Financial Information:
Type of Ownership: Private
Domestic Markets:
Saskatchewan
Contact(s):
Tim Edelman, President & CEO
timadelman@accesscomm.ca
Steven J. Harty, P.Eng, Senior Engineer

GE Multilin
Formerly: GE Power Management; Multilin
215 Anderson Ave.
Markham, ON L6E 1B3
905-294-6222
Fax: 905-201-2098
gemultilin@ge.com
www.gedigitalenergy.com
Firm Type: Manufacturing
Founded: 1978
Staff: 235
Quality Environmental Management System(s): 9001
Products/Services/Areas of Expertise: Complete range of products & services from components to turnkey projects; generator protection; line protection; transformer protection; motor & feeder protection; digital & electromechanical products; equipment for control, metering & systems for generating plants, substations & industrial operations
Financial Information:
Type of Ownership: Publicly Traded
Domestic Markets:
National
Foreign Activity:
Worldwide
Contact(s):
Norris Woodruff, General Manager
Marilyn Thrasher, Marketing Manager
marilyn.thrasher@indsys.ge.com
Delia Stewart, Inside Sales Manager

GE Water & Process Technologies
A Unit of GE Infrastructure
Formerly: Zenon Environmental Inc. 3239 Dundas St. West
Oakville, ON L6M 4B2
905-465-3030
Fax: 905-465-3050
866-439-2837
www.zenon.com; www.gewater.com
Firm Type: Distributing, Engineering, Manufacturing
Founded: 1980
Quality Environmental Management System(s): 9001:2000
Products/Services/Areas of Expertise: Developer & supplier of membranes for water purification, wastewater treatment, & water reuse for both municipal & industrial customers
Financial Information:
Type of Ownership: Foreign-owned
Domestic Markets:
National
Foreign Activity:
Asia, Australia/New Zealand, China, Central Europe, The Pacific Rim, South America, Mexico, Worldwide

GEA Barr-Rosin Inc.
Formerly: Barr-Rosin Inc.
92, boul Prevost
Boisbriand, QC J7G 2S2
450-437-5252
Fax: 450-437-6740
800-561-8305
sales.barr-rosin.ca@geagroup.com
www.barr-rosin.ca
Firm Type: Engineering, Manufacturing
Founded: 1996
Products/Services/Areas of Expertise: specializing in custom-engineered industrial drying technology; air dispersion dryers, coolers and calciners for wet materials in food, chemical and polymer industries
Domestic Markets:
National
Foreign Activity:
USA, United Kingdom, Worldwide
Contact(s):
Guy Lonergan, President
Contact(s):
Shachar Parran, CEO
Gideon Vardi, Vice-President

GEA Westfalia Separator Canada, Inc.
835 Harrington Ct.
Burlington, ON L7N 3P3
905-319-3900
Fax: 905-319-3903
info@gea-westfalia.ca
www.gea-westfalia.ca
Firm Type: Manufacturing
Founded: 1993
Quality Environmental Management System(s): 9001:2000;
Products/Services/Areas of Expertise: Manufacturer of separators, decanters, & ceramic membrane filter elements; Markets include the food sector, industry, the marine sector, & environmental technology
Financial Information:
Type of Ownership: Foreign-owned
Domestic Markets:
National

Gemcom Software International Inc.
#1100, 1066 West Hastings St.
Vancouver, BC V6E 3X1
604-684-6550
Fax: 604-684-3541
info@gemcomsoftware.com
www.gemcomsoftware.com
Firm Type: Distributing, Information Technology, Scientific/Technical Services
Founded: 1985
Products/Services/Areas of Expertise: Mining software; business solutions for mining; training; consulting services; analysis & review; company has 8 foreign offices, see website for details
Financial Information:
Type of Ownership: Publicly Traded
Revenue: Greater than $5 Million
Domestic Markets:
National

Foreign Activity:
Worldwide
Contact(s):
Rick Moignard, President/CEO
Garth A. Albright, CFO & Corporate Secretary
Robert W. Selzler, Vice-President, Marketing
Steve Carter, Vice President, Research & Development

Canadian Branches:
Toronto
#1801, 145 King St. W
Toronto, ON M5H 1J8
416-866-8244
Fax: 416-866-8539
1-866-560-5846
sales-na@gemcomsoftware.com

Gemini Twins Consulting Ltd.
P.O. Box 368
Carseland, AB T0J 0M0
403-934-7247
Fax: 403-901-2005
Firm Type: Management Consulting
Founded: 1994
Member of: Alberta Institute of Agrologists
Products/Services/Areas of Expertise: Environmental site assessments; site reclamation; decontamination
Financial Information:
Type of Ownership: Private
Revenue Sources: 100% Private Contracts
Domestic Markets:
Alberta
Contact(s):
Colette Cloutier, President

Gemite Products Inc.
1787 Drew Rd.
Mississauga, ON L5S 1J5
905-672-2020
Fax: 905-672-6780
888-443-6483
techinfo@gemite.com
www.gemite.com
Firm Type: Manufacturing
Founded: 1978
Products/Services/Areas of Expertise: Exterior wall insulating systems for new construction & retrofit; industrial coatings; secondary containment
Domestic Markets:
National
Foreign Activity:
Asia, Eastern Europe, The Middle East, South America, Mexico, USA
Contact(s):
Igor Nikolajev, P.Eng., President
igor@gemite.com

International Branch(es):
Gemite (USA)
888-443-6483
Fax: 888-443-6329
1-888-4-GEMITE
sales@gemite.com
Paul Novak

Gemteck Environmental Software Ltd.
#1010, 409 Granville St.
Vancouver, BC V6C 1T2
604-669-5554
Fax: 604-669-5154
info@gemteck.com
www.gemteck.com
Firm Type: Information Technology
Founded: 1998
Member of: National Ground Water Association
Products/Services/Areas of Expertise: Development of environmental information management software & marketing of such products worldwide
Financial Information:
Type of Ownership: Private
Domestic Markets:
National
Foreign Activity:
Worldwide
Contact(s):
Howard Adam, President

GENEQ Inc.
8047, rue Jarry est
Montréal, QC H1J 1H6
514-354-2511
Fax: 514-354-6948
800-463-4363
info@geneq.com
www.geneq.com
Firm Type: Distributing
Founded: 1972
Staff: 28
Member of: Water Environment Association of Ontario; Association québécoise des techniques de l'eau; Water Environment Federation; Canadian Meteorology & Oceanology Society
Products/Services/Areas of Expertise: Supplier of scientific instruments for the environment, civil & mining engineering, meteorology, geomatics, materials testing & for the lab; groundwater remediation equipment, water quality meters, weather stations, data-loggers, water level recorders, wind speed indicators, soil moisture meters, rain gauges
Financial Information:
Type of Ownership: Private
Revenue: Greater than $5 Million
Domestic Markets:
National
Foreign Activity:
Worldwide
Contact(s):
Maurice Parisé, President/CEO
Rene Parisé, Vice-President
Claude Germain, Sales Representative
Norman MacDonald, Manager, Sales
Hicham El Ktaibi, Sales Representative

General Filtration
Division of Lee Chemicals Ltd.
441A Applewood Cres.
Concord, ON L4K 4J3
905-761-9000
Fax: 905-761-9001
888-233-1969
info@generalfiltration.com
www.generalfiltration.com
Firm Type: Distributing
Founded: 1955
Staff: 12
Products/Services/Areas of Expertise: Liquid filter media for all purposes; filter aids, filter cartridges, filter pads, filter vessels, activated carbon
Financial Information:
Type of Ownership: Private
Revenue: Greater than $5 Million
Revenue Sources: 2% Municipals; 98% Private Contracts
Domestic Markets:
National
Contact(s):
Ed Bridge, Marketing
Paul Lawrence, President

General Paint Ltd.
950 Raymur Ave.
Vancouver, BC V4A 3M5
604-253-3131
Fax: 604-253-3136
888-301-4454
gpinfo@generalpaint.com
www.generalpaint.com
Firm Type: Manufacturing
Founded: 1911
Staff: 500
Quality Environmental Management System(s): 9002
EcoLogo Certified Products & Services: General Paint products
Products/Services/Areas of Expertise: Paint & related materials (decorative & protective)
Ecological Note: General Paint products
Financial Information:
Type of Ownership: Foreign-owned
Revenue: Greater than $5 Million
Contact(s):
Rolph Alden, President

Canadian Branches:
Calgary Branch
7291 - 11 St. SE
Calgary, AB T2H 2S1
403-531-3454
Fax: 403-531-3449

Edmonton Branch
14510 - 111 Ave.
Edmonton, AB T5M 2P4
403-452-9940
Fax: 403-447-5660

Okanagan Branch
#101, 1990 Cooper Rd.
Kelowna, BC V1K 8K5
250-762-4320
Fax: 250-762-8848

Ontario Branch
172 Belfield Rd.
Toronto, ON M9W 1H1
416-243-7578
Fax: 416-243-1886

Saskatoon Branch
28 - 33rd St. East
Saskatoon, SK S7K 0R9
306-652-8066
Fax: 306-653-4807

Victoria Branch
3026 Jutland Rd.
Victoria, BC V8T 2T2
250-385-4455
Fax: 250-385-4478

Winnipeg Branch
1045 St. James St.
Winnipeg, MB R3H 1B1
204-982-6300
Fax: 204-982-6311

General Scrap Partnership
#200, 233 Portage Ave.
Winnipeg, MB R3B 2A7
204-943-0563
Fax: 204-944-1593
Firm Type: Waste Management
Founded: 1967
Staff: 200
Member of: Canadian Association of Recycling Industries; Institute of Scrap Recycling Industries, Inc.; International Bureau of Recycling Industries
Products/Services/Areas of Expertise: Scrap metal processing
Financial Information:
Type of Ownership: Publicly Traded
Revenue Sources: 100% Private Contracts
Domestic Markets:
Alberta, Manitoba, Ontario, Saskatchewan
Foreign Activity:
USA
Contact(s):
Blair Waldvogel, President/CEO
bwaldvogel@genscrap.com
Sebastian Lau, Manager, Environment, Quality & Safety

Canadian Branches:
Bucks Auto Parts Calgary
P.O. Box 129 T
5857 - 12th St. SE
Calgary, AB T2H 2G7
403-276-2825
Fax: 403-253-3151

Bucks Auto Parts Regina
P.O. Box 860
3081 Pasqua St. North
Regina, SK S4P 3B1
306-721-7283
Fax: 306-721-7280

Bucks Auto Parts Saskatoon
P.O. Box 20036
Saskatoon, SK S7L 7K9
306-249-7278
Fax: 306-249-2660

Bucks Auto Parts Thunder Bay
P.O. Box 10099
305 - 104th St.
Thunder Bay, ON P7B 6T6
807-623-5222
Fax: 807-623-8098

Bucks Auto Parts Winnipeg
P.O. Box 67
1550 Springfield Rd.
Winnipeg, MB R2H 3B4
204-925-7278

Genalta Recycling Inc.
P.O. Box 3120
9301 - 34th St.
Edmonton, AB T8A 2A6
780-466-9010
Fax: 780-461-2369

General Scrap
P.O. Box 67
Winnipeg, MB R2H 3B4
204-222-4221
Fax: 204-224-0561

Kar Basher Manitoba Ltd.
#855, 49 St. East
Brandon, MB R7A 7R2
204-726-8080
Fax: 204-726-8654

Kar Basher of Alberta Ltd.
P.O. Box 3196
231 Range Rd.
Sherwood Park, AB T8A 2A6
780-464-6922
Fax: 780-449-4312

Lakehead Scrap Metal
Mission Island
P.O. Box 1009
Thunder Bay, ON P7B 6T6
807-623-4559
Fax: 807-623-8093

Navajo Metals
P.O. Box 129 T
5857 - 12th St. SE
Calgary, AB T2H 2G7
403-252-7787
Fax: 403-253-3151
1-800-267-1606

Springfield Salvage
P.O. Box 67
Winnipeg, MB R2H 3B4
204-224-4184
Fax: 204-224-0561

Wheat City Metals
P.O. Box 860
2881 Pasqua St. North
Regina, SK S4P 3B1
306-775-3611
Fax: 306-775-3663
1-800-363-3611

International Branch(es):
Continental Metal Products - Minot
P.O. Box 308
3101 Valley St.
Minot, ND USA
701-839-4803
Fax: 701-852-6829
1-800-735-4945
Del Lougheed, General Manager

Continental Metal Products - Dickinson
P.O. Box 1201
Dickinson, ND USA
701-227-4947
Fax: 701-227-3933
1-800-227-4947
Tim Major, General Manager

Generation PV Inc.
#9, 158 Anderson Ave.
Markham, ON L6E 31A9
905-294-8600
Fax: 905-294-8302
800-311-4286
info@generationpv.com
www.generationpv.com
Firm Type: Distributing
Staff: 6
Member of: Canadian Solar Industries Association; Canadian Wind Energy Association; Canadian Federation of Independent Businesses; Durham Strategic Alliance
Products/Services/Areas of Expertise: Provides professional power systems to North American & international industrial & commercial clients; services OEM accounts & supports selective distribution through a qualified VAR network; solar & wind generated power, DC power & battery back-up systems; offers solar modules, solar systems, batteries, controllers & other balance-of-system components, as well as custom system design services
Recently Completed / Ongoing Projects: Designed & supplied over 35,000 renewable power systems in more than 60 countries
Financial Information:
Type of Ownership: Private
Domestic Markets:
National
Foreign Activity:
Worldwide
Contact(s):
Eric Kalmbach, President
ekalmbach@generationpv.com
Dave Kalmbach, Manager, Distribution Sales
dkalmbach@generationpv.com
Jason Kalmbach, Manager, Industrial Sales
jkalmbach@generationpv.com

Genex Swine Group
633 Park St.
Regina, SK S4N 5N1
306-721-9498
Fax: 306-721-2528
Contact(s):
Ted Bass, Vice-President, Production

Genics Inc.
Formerly: Genics-Can Inc
Acheson Industrial Park
53016 Hwy. 60, 561 Acheson Rd.
Spruce Grove, AB T7X 3G7
780-962-1000
Fax: 780-962-1052
877-943-6427
sales@genicsinc.com
www.genicsinc.com
Firm Type: Manufacturing
Founded: 1989
Staff: 3
Products/Services/Areas of Expertise: Development & manufacturer of environmentally friendly, worker safe products to preserve wood & extend in-service life of wood assets
Domestic Markets:
Alberta, British Columbia, Manitoba, Québec, Saskatchewan
Contact(s):
Wesley Wall P.Ag., President
Calvin Wall, Vice-President

Génie Audio inc.
#102, 125, rue Gagnon
Montréal, QC H4N 1T1
514-856-9212
Fax: 514-856-9002
800-363-0793
info@genieaudio.com
www.genieaudio.com
Firm Type: Distributing, Manufacturing
Founded: 1962
Staff: 7
Products/Services/Areas of Expertise: Environmental chambers & rooms; noise control systems & equipment
Contact(s):
Yvan Croteau, President/CEO
Robert Lapenseé, Marketing

Genilab Environnement Inc.
P.O. Box 1236
Rimouski, QC G5M 1A5
418-724-7030
Fax: 418-724-7057
genilab@quebectel.com
Firm Type: Engineering, Scientific/Technical Services
Staff: 24
Products/Services/Areas of Expertise: Environmental studies; impact assessments; Geomatics
Domestic Markets:
New Brunswick, Québec
Foreign Activity:
USA
Contact(s):
Acène Kouicem, President

Génius Conseil Inc.
Formerly: Groupe Séguin Experts-Conseil Inc.
13200, boul Métropolitain est
Montréal, QC H1A 5K8
514-642-8422
Fax: 514-642-4912
info@geniusconseil.com
www.geniusconseil.com
Firm Type: Engineering
Founded: 1980
Products/Services/Areas of Expertise: Une firme d'ingénieurs-conseils
Contact(s):
Michel Lalonde, Président
Gino Lanni, Directeur, Structure
Yvon Côté, Directeur, Infrastructures, transport et environnement
Serge Desmarais, Directeur, Administration et finances
André Prieur, Directeur, Gestion et surveillance
Alain Deroy, Technologue senior

Canadian Branches:
Candiac
#2, 23, ch Haendel
Candiac, QC J5R 1R7
450-635-0099
Fax: 450-635-0087

Mirabel
#401, 17660, rue Charles, 2e étage
Mirabel, QC J7J 0C3
450-433-6060
Fax: 450-433-2111

Genivar
1600, boul René-Lévesque ouest, 16e étage
Montréal, QC H3H 1P9
514-340-0046
Fax: 514-340-1337
info.environment@genivar.com
www.genivar.com
Firm Type: Engineering, Scientific/Technical Services
Founded: 1959
Staff: 3500
Quality Environmental Management System(s): 9001:2000
Products/Services/Areas of Expertise: Consulting engineering & project services in areas such as the environment, development of technical landfill sites, energy efficiency, wind energy, power, hydraulics, municipal infrastructure, transportation, telecommunications, mining & mineral processing, chemical & oil services, & pulp & paper, & wood Products
Recently Completed / Ongoing Projects: Water & wastewater master plan for Montreal; Erie Shores wind farm, Port Burwell; Magpie hydroelectric project, Minganie, Quebec; Ethanol plant, Belle Plaine, Saskatchewan; Wastewater rehabilitation project, Trinidad & Tobago; Airport road reservoir & pumping station, Brampton, Ontario; South Peel water & wastewater treatment plants expansion, Region of Peel, Ontario; Biogas capture, Saint-Tite-des-Caps, Quebec; Salmon restoration project in the Betsiamites River, North Shore region, Quebec; Bank stabilization program, Québec side of the Ottawa River
Financial Information:
Type of Ownership: Publicly Traded
Domestic Markets:
National
Foreign Activity:
Worldwide
Contact(s):
Pierre Shoiry, President/CEO
pierre.shoiry@genivar.com
Marc Rivard, Exec. Vice-President, Canadian Operations
marc.rivard@genivar.com
Marcel Boucher, Chief Financial Officer
marcel.boucher@genivar.com
Robert Dandurand, Vice-President, Administration
robert.dandurand@genivar.com
Jacques Angers, Director, Health & Safety
jacques.angers@genivar.com
Ginette Bourbonnais, Director, Procurement & Facilities Management
ginette.bourbonnais@genivar.com
Marlène Casciaro, Director, Communications
marlene.casciaro@genivar.com

Products & Services Buyer's Guide

Marcel Comtois, Director, Quality
marcel.comtois@genivar.com

Canadian Branches:
Amos
#200, 3, rue Principale nord
Amos, QC J9T 2K5
819-732-0457
Fax: 819-732-0458

Baie-Comeau
31, rue Marquette
Baie-Comeau, QC G4Z 1K4
418-296-8911
Fax: 418-296-2889

Bancroft
P.O. Box 187
69 Cleak Ave.
Bancroft, ON K0L 1C0
613-332-2841
Fax: 613-332-5718

Beloeil
#200, 545, boul Sir Wilfrid-Laurier
Beloeil, QC J3G 4H8
450-467-0353
Fax: 450-467-4442

Burlington
777C Walkers Line
Burlington, ON L7N 2G1
905-632-6500
Fax: 905-632-3883

Burnaby
#308, 4211 Kingsway
Burnaby, BC V5H 1Z6
604-294-5800
Fax: 604-294-0400

Calgary - 3rd Ave. NE
#103, 2710 - 3rd Ave. NE
Calgary, AB T2A 2L5
403-248-9463
Fax: 403-250-7811

Calgary - 58th Ave. SE
1212 - 58th Ave. SE
Calgary, AB T2H 2C9
403-271-4442
Fax: 403-271-4489

Chibougamau
#23, 553 - 3e av
Chibougamau, QC G8P 1R4
418-748-8141
Fax: 418-748-8145

Clarksburg
P.O. Box 308
103 Hillcrest Dr.
Clarksburg, ON N0H 1J0
519-599-3793
Fax: 519-599-2878

Drummondville
#101, 1001, rue Bernier
Drummondville, QC J2C 6T5
819-477-3609
Fax: 819-477-3297

Edmonton
11446 Winterburn Rd.
Edmonton, AB T5S 2C4
780-452-5453
Fax: 780-452-6873

Edson
Centennial Industrial Park
#131, 135 - 27 St.
Edson, AB T7E 1N9
780-712-5000
Fax: 780-712-4339

Fort McMurray
P.O. Box 5388
#100, 9905 Sutherland St.
Fort McMurray, AB T9H 1V3
780-743-3969
Fax: 780-743-3923

Gaspé
#1, 43, boul York est, 2e étage
Gaspé, QC G4X 2L1
418-368-6069
Fax: 418-368-8871

Gatineau
500, boul Gréber, 3e étage
Gatineau, QC J8T 7W3
819-243-2827
Fax: 819-243-2019

Grande Prairie
10070 - 117th Ave.
Grande Prairie, AB T8V 7S4
780-538-2667
Fax: 780-538-2951

Grimsby
#201, 12 Ontario St.
Grimsby, ON L3M 3G9
905-309-6466
Fax: 905-309-7043

Grimshaw
P.O. Box 1159
4411 - 51st St.
Grimshaw, AB T0H 1W0
780-332-1000
Fax: 780-332-1100

Hanover
101 - 14th Ave.
Hanover, ON N4N 3W1
519-364-5700
Fax: 519-364-6937

Kuujjuaq
P.O. Box 459
1600, rue Akianut
Kuujjuaq, QC J0M 1C0
819-964-0491
Fax: 819-964-0615

Kuujjuarapik
P.O. Box 329
av Henri-Jamet
Kuujjuarapik, QC J0M 1G0
819-929-3028
Fax: 819-929-3800

L'Ile-Perrot
#9, 89, boul Don Quichotte
L'Ile-Perrot, QC J7V 6X2
514-453-1621
Fax: 514-453-9305

La Crete
P.O. Box 349
La Crete, AB T0H 2H0
780-928-4461
Fax: 780-928-4465

La Tuque
323, rue Saint-François
La Tuque, QC G9X 1S2
819-523-9469
Fax: 819-523-8770

Lac La Biche
10 Nipewon Rd.
Lac La Biche, AB T0A 2C1
780-623-2526
Fax: 780-623-3312

Lac-Mégantic
4152, rue Laval
Lac-Mégantic, QC G6D 1B3
819-583-5110
Fax: 819-583-5991

Laval
#525, 2525, boul Daniel-Johnson
Laval, QC H7T 1S9
450-686-0980
Fax: 450-686-0987

Lethbridge
4303 - 8th Ave. North
Lethbridge, AB T1H 6N2
403-327-7746
Fax: 403-380-2825

Longueuil
#101, 2405, boul Fernand-Lafontaine
Longueuil, QC J4N 1N7
450-679-7220
Fax: 450-670-9076

Lévis
Complexe des deux Rives
#401, 1300, boul de la Rive-Sud
Lévis, QC G6W 5M6
418-839-1430
Fax: 418-839-8407

Malartic
1060, rue LaSalle
Malartic, QC J0Y 1Z0
819-757-3111
Fax: 819-757-4111

Markham - 14th Ave.
#206, 2800 - 14th Ave.
Markham, ON L3R 0E4
905-940-4567
Fax: 905-940-4566

Markham - 14th Ave..
#210, 2800 - 14th Ave.
Markham, ON L3R 0E4
905-946-8900
Fax: 905-946-8966

Markham - Cochrane St.
600 Cochrane St., 5th Fl.
Markham, ON L3R 5K3
905-475-7270
Fax: 905-475-5994

Medicine Hat
#110, 1222 Brier Park Rd. NW
Medicine Hat, AB T1C 0B7
403-528-8818
Fax: 403-528-8917

Mont-Laurier
#3, 436, rue de la Madone
Mont-Laurier, QC J9L 1S3
819-623-3302
Fax: 819-623-7616

Mont-Tremblant
#1, 386, rue Saint-Jovite
Mont-Tremblant, QC J8E 2Z9
819-425-3483
Fax: 819-425-9181

Montréal - Henri-Bourassa
#320, 1600, boul Henri-Bourassa ouest
Montréal, QC H3M 3E2
514-382-0590
Fax: 514-382-0593
Ali Ettehadieh

Montréal - René-Lévesque
504, boul René-Lévesque ouest, 8e étage
Montréal, QC H2Z 1Y7
514-398-0544
Fax: 514-398-0545

Montréal - Saint-Hubert
5154, rue Saint-Hubert
Montréal, QC H2J 2Y3
514-273-3147
Fax: 514-273-3854

Ottawa - Fitzgerald Rd.
15 Fitzgerald Rd.
Ottawa, ON K2H 9G1
613-829-2800
Fax: 613-829-8299

Ottawa - Kirkwood Ave.
356 Kirkwood Ave.
Ottawa, ON K1Z 8P1
613-729-2818
Fax: 613-729-2138

Ottawa - Robertson Rd.
#221, 39 Robertson Rd.
Ottawa, ON K2H 8R2
613-828-4445
Fax: 613-828-4077

Owen Sound
#212, 945 - 3rd Ave East,
Owen Sound, ON N4K 2K8
519-376-7612
Fax: 519-376-8008

Prescott
P.O. Box 449
235 Water St. West
Prescott, ON K0E 1T0
613-925-0990
Fax: 613-925-9909

Québec - Gradins
5355, boul des Gradins
Québec, QC G2J 1C8
418-623-2254
Fax: 418-624-1857

Québec - Lebourgneuf
#300, 1175, boul Lebourgneuf
Québec, QC G2K 0B4
418-780-0878
Fax: 418-780-4182

Québec - Église
#440, 1000, rte de l'Église
Québec, QC G1V 3V9
418-653-6404
Fax: 418-653-6414

Red Deer
7710 Edgar Industrial Crt.
Red Deer, AB T4P 4E2
403-342-7650
Fax: 403-342-7691

Regina
#200 - 438 Victoria Ave. East
Regina, SK S4N 0N7
306-585-1990
Fax: 306-586-9113

Rivière-du-Loup
35, rue Saint-Louis, #D
Rivière-du-Loup, QC G5R 2V3
418-862-6636
Fax: 418-862-6425

Rocky Mountain House
#204, 4407 - 45A Ave.
Rocky Mountain House, AB T4T 1A3
403-845-5662
Fax: 403-845-5663

Rouyn-Noranda
152, av Murdoch
Rouyn-Noranda, QC J9X 1E1
819-797-3222
Fax: 819-762-6640

Saguenay
125, rue Racine est
Saguenay, QC G7H 1R5
418-698-4488
Fax: 418-698-6677

Saint-Charles-Borromée
#402, 28, ch du Golf est
Saint-Charles-Borromée, QC J6E 2B4
450-759-7190
Fax: 450-759-1324

Saint-Félicien
#202, 1125, boul Sacré-Coeur
Saint-Félicien, QC G8K 1P6
418-679-2151
Fax: 418-679-9245

Saint-Georges
#200, 11505 - 1re av est
St-Georges, QC G5Y 7X3
418-228-8041
Fax: 418-228-8045

Saint-Jean-sur-Richelieu
#203, 200, rue MacDonald
Saint-Jean-sur-Richelieu, QC J3B 8J6
450-359-7070
Fax: 450-359-7066

Saint-Jérôme
482, rue Laviolette
Saint-Jérôme, QC J7Y 2T9
450-431-0309
Fax: 450-431-5441

Sainte-Marie
#103, 1017, boul Vachon nord
Sainte-Marie, QC G6E 1M3
418-387-8191
Fax: 418-386-2967

Saskatoon
#210, 15 Innovation Blvd.
Saskatoon, SK S7N 2X8
306-665-6223
Fax: 306-665-8589

Sept-Îles
1166, boul Laure
Sept-Îles, QC G4S 1C4
418-962-2241
Fax: 418-962-3641

Sherbrooke - Léger
171A, rue Léger
Sherbrooke, QC J1L 1M2
819-340-6124
Fax: 819-340-6124

Sherbrooke - Léger
171B, rue Léger
Sherbrooke, QC J1L 1M2
819-562-8888
Fax: 819-562-7888

Sherwood Park
#132, 2693 Broadmoor Blvd.
Sherwood Park, AB T8H 0G1
780-410-6740
Fax: 780-449-4050

Slave Lake
Plaza 2000
207 - 2nd Ave. NW
Slave Lake, AB T0G 2A1
780-849-3205
Fax: 780-849-5762

Timmins
P.O. Box 120
834 Mountjoy St. South
Timmins, ON P4N 7C5
705-264-9413
Fax: 705-267-2725

Toronto - Harbour St.
60 Harbour St., 4th Fl.
Toronto, ON M5J 1B7
416-977-9666
Fax: 416-977-9662

Toronto - Merton St.
#306, 250 Merton St.
Toronto, ON M4S 1B1
416-484-4200
Fax: 416-484-8260

Trois-Rivières
#300, 3450, boul Gene-H.-Kruger
Trois-Rivières, QC G9A 4M3
819-375-1292
Fax: 819-375-1217

Val-d'Or - 3e
1075 - 3e av est
Val-d'Or, QC J9P 6M1
819-825-4711
Fax: 819-825-4715

Val-d'Or - Québécoise
1462, rue de la Québécoise
Val-d'Or, QC J9P 5H4
819-825-4274
Fax: 819-825-1514

Val-d'Or - Québécoise
1450, rue de la Québécoise
Val-d'Or, QC J9P 5H4
819-825-4274
Fax: 819-824-1514

Valleyview
#206, 4803 - 50th Ave.
Valleyview, AB T0H 3N0
780-891-2704
Fax: 780-891-2182

Vancouver - West Broadway
#200, 1985 West Broadway
Vancouver, BC V6J 4Y3
604-736-5421
Fax: 604-736-1519

Victoria - Bastion Sq.
#303, 45 Bastion Sq.
Victoria, BC V8W 1J1
250-388-5312
Fax: 250-388-6543

Victoria - Chatterton Way
#202, 4430 Chatterton Way
Victoria, BC V8X 5J2
250-386-2521
Fax: 250-381-1865

Victoria - West Saanich Rd.
#130, 4396 West Saanich Rd.
Victoria, BC V8Z 3E9
250-386-6721
Fax: 250-386-2844

Wabasca
P.O. Box 147
Wabasca, AB T0G 2K0
780-891-2704
Fax: 780-891-2182

Wetaskiwin
5731 - 40th Ave.
Wetaskiwin, AB T9A 2Z1
780-361-2280
Fax: 780-361-2290

Winnipeg
10 Prairie Way
Winnipeg, MB R2J 3J8
204-477-6650
Fax: 204-474-2864

Vancouver - Cornwall Ave. - PBK Architects Inc.
#220, 1818 Cornwall Ave.
Vancouver, BC V6J 1C7
604-736-5329
Fax: 604-736-1519

International Branch(es):
Bamako, Mali
P.O. Box 2786
Bamako Mali
11 223 675 9573

Belgrade, Serbia
Bulevar Kralja Aleksandra 43/5, 11000
Belgrade Serbia
+381 11 3034 859
Fax: 381 11 3034 869

Maraval, Trinidad & Tobago
1A-6A Ellerslie Plaza
Maraval Trinidad
868-628-0068
Fax: 868-628-0073

Port of Spain, Trinidad & Tobago
Nicholas Tower
63-64, Independence Sq. South
Port of Spain Trinidad
868-624-8039
Fax: 868-623-7170

Sarajevo, Bosnie-Herzegovine
Obala Kulina Bana 12/1, 71000
Sarajevo Bosnie
+387 33 554 235
Fax: +387 33 554 236

Genor Recycling Services
Formerly: Genor Services Ltd.
434 Henry St.
Brantford, ON N3T 5M1
519-756-5264
Fax: 519-756-2323
recycling@genor.ca

Products & Services Buyer's Guide

Firm Type: Scientific/Technical Services, Waste Management
Founded: 1943
Staff: 20
Products/Services/Areas of Expertise: Recycling of boxboard, fine paper, aluminum, newspapers, corrugated containers & steel, office paper; confidential shredding
Domestic Markets:
Ontario, Québec
Foreign Activity:
USA
Contact(s):
Norman Haac, President
Peter Katadotis, Manager
Mark Moffat, Sales Manager
Contact(s):
Ken Finucan

Canadian Branches:
Putnam
101 Beam Rd.
Putnam, ON N0L 2E0
519-485-0621
Fax: 519-485-6143

Gensco Equipment (1990) Ltd.
53 Carlaw Ave.
Toronto, ON M4M 2R6
416-465-7521
Fax: 416-465-4489
800-268-6797
info@genscoequip.com
www.genscoequip.com
Firm Type: Distributing, Manufacturing
Founded: 1919
Staff: 12
Member of: Canadian Association of Recycling Industries; Institute of Scrap Recycling Industries; National Association of Demolition Contractors
Products/Services/Areas of Expertise: Scrap handling & recycling equipment
Domestic Markets:
National
Foreign Activity:
Central America, South America, Mexico, USA,
Contact(s):
David Zelunka, General Manager

International Branch(es):
Gensco America Inc.
5307 Dividend Dr.
Decatur, GA USA
770-808-8711
Fax: 770-808-8739

Gentec Inc.
2625, rue Dalton
Sainte-Foy, QC G1P 3S9
418-651-8000
Fax: 418-651-6695
800-463-4480
info@gentec.ca
www.gentec.ca
Firm Type: Manufacturing
Founded: 1959
Quality Environmental Management System(s): 9001
Products/Services/Areas of Expertise: Measuring & monitoring equipment; lighting control systems, centralized energy management systems
Contact(s):
François Giroux, President
Marc Laliberte, Vice-President, Marketing

Canadian Branches:
Western Canada
614 Elm St.
St Thomas, ON N5R 1K7
519-637-0217
Fax: 519-637-1237
1-866-651-8002

International Branch(es):
US
#201, 35 Gateway Dr.
Plattsburgh, NY USA
Fax: 518-793-2687
1-888-235-7506

Genus Loci Ecological Landscapes Inc.
Formerly: Ecological Outlook
P.O. Box 341
270 Main St.
Schomberg, ON L0G 1T0
905-939-8498
Fax: 905-939-7044
877-476-2079
info@genus-loci.ca
www.genus-loci.ca
Firm Type: Information Technology, Scientific/Technical Services
Founded: 1990
Staff: 6
Member of: Ecovillage Network of Canada; Institute of Cultural Affairs Canada
Member of: Canadian Environmental Education & Communications Network; Ontario Association of Landscape Architects; Society for Ecological Restoration
Products/Services/Areas of Expertise: Ecological landscape planning & architecture; landscape construction; ecological restoration; naturalization; erosion control; ecological surveys & monitoring; landscape management plans; environmental education & communication; interpretive planning; facilitation
Recently Completed / Ongoing Projects: Ecological restoration and/or landscape projects; Oak Ridges Moraine Natural Heritage Evaluations; Strategic Plan for Managing Invasive Plants in Southern Ontario; City of Guelph Natural Heritage Strategy Phase One, team member; Creditview Wetland Conservation Plan, City of Mississauga, team member
Financial Information:
Type of Ownership: Private
Domestic Markets:
National
Contact(s):
Jean-Marc Daigle, B.L.Arch., M.E.S., Partner
Simon C. Ackles-Dold, B.Sc., MLA, OALA, Associate

Genzyme Canada Inc.
West Tower
#800, 2700 Matheson Blvd. East
Mississauga, ON L4W 4V9
905-625-0011
Fax: 905-625-7811
877-220-8918
www.genzyme.ca
Firm Type: Scientific/Technical Services
Founded: 1996
Products/Services/Areas of Expertise: A biotechnology & health care products company; Developer of products & services for therapeutics & biosurgery operations
Recently Completed / Ongoing Projects: Following the approval of Health Canada in 2009, Synvisc-OneT (Hylan GF-20), a viscosupplement for osteoarthritis of the knee, became available
Financial Information:
Type of Ownership: Foreign-owned
Contact(s):
Brian Lewis, General Manager, Genzyme Canada
Patrick van Gelder, Business Unit Director, Biosurgery

Canadian Branches:
Charlottetown
Formerly: Diagnostic Chemicals Ltd.
Genzyme Diagnostics
70 Watts Ave.
Charlottetown, PE C1E 2B9
902-566-1396
Fax: 902-628-6504
800-565-0265
www.genzymediagnostics.com

Geo Environmental Engineering - Geocon SNC-Lavalin
2200 Lake Shore Blvd. West
Toronto, ON M8V 1A4
416-252-5311
Fax: 416-231-5356
www.snclavalin.com
Firm Type: Engineering, Scientific/Technical Services
Staff: 15
Quality Environmental Management System(s): 9001
Products/Services/Areas of Expertise: Geo-environmental engineering for mine-related geotechnical & hydrological works; foundation design for plant sites; design for waste rock & tailings disposal facilities & operations; safety audits & dam inspections; contaminated site remediation; due diligence reviews; feasibility & detailed studies, water management studies; closure planning
Financial Information:
Type of Ownership: Publicly Traded
Revenue: $3 Million - $5 Million
Revenue Sources: 2% nationwide; 10% Provincial; 10% Municipals; 78% Private Contracts
Domestic Markets:
British Columbia, New Brunswick, Newfoundland & Labrador, Ontario
Contact(s):
Karlis Janson, General Manager, Geocon Division
karlis.jansons@snclavalin.com

Geo-Logic Inc.
#29, 347 Pido Rd.
Peterborough, ON K9J 6X7
705-749-3317
Fax: 705-749-9248
general@geo-logic.ca
www.geo-logic.ca
Firm Type: Engineering
Founded: 1988
Staff: 30
Member of: Canadian Testing Association; Canadian Standards Association; Canadian Geotechnical Society; National Groundwater Association; Canadian Welding Bureau; Environmental Assessment Association
Quality Environmental Management System(s): 9001:2008
Products/Services/Areas of Expertise: Environmental site assessments; ground engineering; hydrogeology; geotechnical; materials testing; inspection services; majority of shares owned by Inspec-Sol Inc.
Financial Information:
Type of Ownership: Private
Revenue Sources: 10% nationwide; 30% Provincial; 10% Municipals; 50% Private Contracts
Domestic Markets:
Ontario
Contact(s):
George K. Gunther, President
John T. Tewsley, Vice-President
Nyle C. McIlveen, Vice-President

Canadian Branches:
Oshawa Office
#102, 1143 Wentworth St. West
Oshawa, ON L1J 8P7
905-728-1500
Fax: 905-728-9800

Pembroke Office
#1, 330 Boundary Rd.
Pembroke, ON K8A 6W5
613-735-8361
Fax: 613-735-4278

Geocor Engineering Inc.
120 Lappans Lane
Kingston, ON K7L 6Z4
613-531-1855
Fax: 613-507-1857
877-807-1855
geocor@geocorengineering.com
www.geocorengineering.com
Firm Type: Engineering
Founded: 1985
Staff: 5
Member of: Professional Engineers of Ontario
Products/Services/Areas of Expertise: Engineering consulting services; geotechnical, geoenvironmental, coastal, materials testing & inspection; sewage systems
Recently Completed / Ongoing Projects: UST investigation & removal; Phases I-III ESA including abatement & risk assessment for regional lab
Financial Information:
Type of Ownership: Private
Revenue Sources: 30% nationwide; 10% Provincial; 10% Municipals; 50% Private Contracts
Domestic Markets:
Ontario
Foreign Activity:
USA
Contact(s):
Scott H. Cordell, P.Eng., President
Tyson W. Wright, B.Eng., Project Engineer
Matthew K. Pedlar, Civil Engineer Technologist

Fraser Armstrong, Site Engineer

Geodetic Software Systems/Geomatics Information Center
4156 Sunflower Dr.
Mississauga, ON L5L 2L5
905-820-4224
Fax: 905-820-0897
PASteeves@GSSGeomatics.com
www.gssgeomatics.com
Firm Type: Scientific/Technical Services
Founded: 1982
Products/Services/Areas of Expertise: Develops computer software for geodetic & land surveying calculations
Contact(s):
Peter Steeves, Contact

Geographic Dynamics Corp. / GDC
9762 - 54 Ave.
Edmonton, AB T6E 0A9
780-436-1217
Fax: 780-436-4348
888-216-4616
info@gdc-online.com
www.gdc-online.com
Firm Type: Management Consulting
Founded: 1990
Staff: 20
Member of: Alberta Society of Professional Biologists; Canadian Institute of Forestry; Canadian Land Reclamation Association
Products/Services/Areas of Expertise: Forest management surveys
Financial Information:
Type of Ownership: Private
Revenue: $3 Million - $5 Million
Revenue Sources: 10% Provincial; 90% Private Contracts
Domestic Markets:
Alberta, British Columbia, Northwest Territories, Saskatchewan
Contact(s):
John D. Beckingham, CEO & Sr. Ecologist
jbeckingham@gdc_online.com

GeoInsight Corporation
Formerly: Gregory Geoscience Ltd.
106 Huntley Manor Dr.
Carp, ON K0A 1L0
613-831-6434
Fax: 613-831-6435
hmoore-gg@cyberus.ca
www.cyberus.ca/~hmoore-gg/GeoInsight.htm
Firm Type: Information Technology, Scientific/Technical Services
Founded: 1973
Staff: 1
Products/Services/Areas of Expertise: Application of remote sensing & GIS technologies to the mapping, analysis & monitoring of the environment; software to aid in geomatics analysis; remote sensing products
Domestic Markets:
National
Contact(s):
Harold Moore, President

Geolab Inc.
1430, boul Lemire
Drummondville, QC J2C 5A4
819-475-6688
Fax: 819-475-6695
info@geolab.ca
www.geolab.ca
Firm Type: Engineering
Founded: 1996
Member of: Réseau Environnement; Association of Professional Engineers Ontario; Ordre des ingénieurs du Québec; Association Québécoise de vérifcations environnemental
Quality Environmental Management System(s): 9002
Products/Services/Areas of Expertise: Soils investigation (geotechnical); materials quality controls (laboratory & site analysis for concrete, soils & asphalt); environmental site assessment phases 1, 2, 3; non destructive tests on site (auscultation of concrete structures); groundwater monitoring (contained); soil remediation services
Financial Information:
Type of Ownership: Private
Revenue: $1.5 Million - $3 Million

Canadian Branches:
Sherbrooke
4234, rue King ouest
Sherbrooke, QC J1L 1W6
819-563-3372
Fax: 819-563-3326
infosh@geolab.ca

Victoriaville
285, boul. des Bois-Francs S
Victoriaville, QC G6P 4T2
819-751-2220
Fax: 819-751-2228
infovc@geolab.ca

Geomarine Associates Ltd.
P.O. Box 41 M
202 Fergusons Cove Rd.
Halifax, NS B3J 2L4
902-422-6482
Fax: 902-442-6483
Firm Type: Management Consulting
Founded: 1973
Staff: 2
Products/Services/Areas of Expertise: Environmental assessments; geological & hydrogeological engineering; geophysical survey services; historical & heritage consulting; site assessment studies
Recently Completed / Ongoing Projects: A report documenting the farfield parameters of the November 1, 1755 Lisbon Tsunami in the western Atlantic presented at the 32nd colloquium and annual general meeting of the Atlantic Geoscience Society in February 2006
Financial Information:
Type of Ownership: Private
Revenue: $50,000 - $100,000
Revenue Sources: 25% nationwide; 75% Private Contracts
Domestic Markets:
New Brunswick, Newfoundland & Labrador, Nova Scotia, Northwest Territories, Nunavut, Prince Edward Island
Foreign Activity:
Central America
Markets Sought:
USA
Contact(s):
Alan Ruffman, President

Geonics Limited
#8, 1745 Meyerside Dr.
Mississauga, ON L5T 1C6
905-670-9580
Fax: 905-670-9204
geonics@geonics.com
www.geonics.com
Firm Type: Manufacturing
Founded: 1962
Staff: 30
Member of: Society of Engineering Geophysicists; Association of Ground Water Sciences Engineers; National Groundwater Association; Environmental & Engineering Geophysical Society
Products/Services/Areas of Expertise: Electromagnetic instruments for geoscience applications
Financial Information:
Type of Ownership: Private
Revenue Sources: 25% nationwide; 25% Provincial; 5% Municipals; 45% Private Contracts
Domestic Markets:
National
Foreign Activity:
Worldwide
Contact(s):
Miro Bosnar, President
Simon Boniwell, Sales Manager, North America
Mike Catalano, Technical Sales

Géophysique GPR International Inc.
2545, rue Delorimier
Longueuil, QC J4K 3P7
450-679-2400
Fax: 514-521-4128
800-672-4774
info@gprmtl.com
www.gprmtl.com
Firm Type: Engineering
Founded: 1974
Staff: 19
Member of: Ordre des ingénieurs du Québec; Canadian Society of Exploration Geophysicists
Quality Environmental Management System(s): 9001
Products/Services/Areas of Expertise: Offers services in engineering geology; underground tanks & pipes localization; site characterization; soil, sediments & water sampling; hydrogeology; marine surveys & hydrology; environmental impact assessments; civil engineering; aquifer localization; remote sensing studies; roadbase & pavement assessments; Heli-borne Electromagnetic
Recently Completed / Ongoing Projects: Retraction seismic & vibrations: risk analysis, design & studies; Reflection Seismic & Georadan; Heliborne Electromagnetic & Marine geophysics & Hydrography
Financial Information:
Type of Ownership: Private
Revenue: $1.5 Million - $3 Million
Revenue Sources: 10% nationwide; 10% Provincial; 10% Municipals; 70% Private Contracts
Domestic Markets:
British Columbia, Manitoba, New Brunswick, Ontario, Québec
Foreign Activity:
Africa, Caribbean, Central America, South Africa, South America, USA, United Kingdom
Contact(s):
Réjean Paul, P.Eng., President & CEO
rejean.paul@gprmtl.com
Robert Turcotte, Business Development
robert.turcotte@gprmtl.com
Jean-Luc Arsenault, P.Eng., Quality Control
jean-luc.arsenault@gprmtl.com

Canadian Branches:
Toronto Branch
#103, 6741 Columbus Rd.
Mississauga, ON L5T 2G9
905-696-0656
Fax: 905-696-0570
gprtor@on.aibn.com
Milan Situm, P.Geophysicist

International Branch(es):
Geophysics GPR International - Zimbabwe
P.O. Box Al590
30 East Rd., Belgravia
Avondale Zimbabwe
-(2634) 790763
Fax: -(2634) 790763
harare@gprzim.icon.co.zw
Penias Mpofo

George Grant Consulting
17 Waterhouse Way
Richmond Hill, ON L4C 9H8
905-737-1788
Fax: 905-737-0424
drgrant@rogers.com
www.academyofwellness.com
Firm Type: Scientific/Technical Services
Founded: 1988
Staff: 6
Products/Services/Areas of Expertise: Air quality; tight building syndrome; toxicological, microbiological & chemical testing & results interpretation; seminars on wellness in the workplace & occupational stress; lunch & learn wellness lectures
Domestic Markets:
National
Foreign Activity:
Caribbean, Western Europe, USA
Contact(s):
George Grant, President

George Kelk Corporation
Also Known As: KELK
48 Lesmill Rd.
Toronto, ON M3B 2T5
416-445-5850
Fax: 416-445-5972
888-275-5355
kelkcorp@kelk.com
www.kelk.com
Firm Type: Manufacturing
Founded: 1953
Staff: 115
Quality Environmental Management System(s): 9002
Products/Services/Areas of Expertise: Measuring & monitoring equipment

Products & Services Buyer's Guide

Domestic Markets:
National
Foreign Activity:
Worldwide
Contact(s):
Peter Kelk, President

Geosoft
85 Richmond St. West, 8th Fl.
Toronto, ON M5H 2C9
416-369-0111
Fax: 416-369-9599
800-363-6277
info@geosoft.com
www.geosoft.com
Firm Type: Information Technology
Founded: 1986
Staff: 35
Products/Services/Areas of Expertise: Software & related services for processing/analysing large volume earth science spatial data
Activities: Groundwater & environmental mapping/GIS technology development
Financial Information:
Type of Ownership: Private
Revenue: Greater than $5 Million
Domestic Markets:
National
Foreign Activity:
Worldwide
Contact(s):
Tim Dobush, CEO
tim.dobush@geosoft.com
Michelene Lewis, Marketing Specialist
michelene.lewis@geosoft.com
Rina Hartmann, Account Manager
rina.hartmann@geosoft.com

International Branch(es):
Geosoft Africa Ltd.
Buren Bldg.
2nd Fl., Kasteelpark Office Park, c/o Nossob & Joch
Erasmuskloof X3, Pretoria ZAF
-27-12-347-4519
Fax: -27-12-347-6936
info.za@geosoft.com

Geosoft Australia Pty. Ltd.
#14, 100 Railway Road
Subiaco, WA AUS
-61-8-9382-1900
Fax: -61-8-9382-1911
info.au@geosoft.com

Geosoft Europe Ltd.
Wallingford
20/21 Market Place, 1st Fl.
Oxfordshire GBR
-44-1491-835-231
Fax: -44-1491-835-28
info@geosofteurope.co.uk

Geosoft Latinoamerica Ltda.
Praca Floriano, 51/19 Andar
Rio de Janeiro Brazil
-55-21-2111-8150
Fax: -55-21-2111-818
geosoft.latino@openlink.com.br

Geosolutions Consulting Inc.
6367 McCordick Rd.
Ottawa, ON K0a 2T0
613-489-0550
Fax: 613-727-7563
info@geosolutions.com
www.geosolutions.com
Firm Type: Information Technology
Founded: 1994
Staff: 6
Member of: Geomatics Industry Association of Canada
Products/Services/Areas of Expertise: Geographic information systems consulting; map production; systems development; data conversion; training
Financial Information:
Type of Ownership: Private
Revenue: $500,000 - $1.5 Million
Domestic Markets:
National

Foreign Activity:
Caribbean, South America
Contact(s):
Dave Branson, President

Canadian Branches:
Victoria
931 Craigflower Rd.
Victoria, BC V9A 2X7
250-382-7316
talbert@geosolutions.com

Geostat Systems International Inc.
Systèmes Géostat International inc.
#203, 10, boul de la Seigneurie est
Blainville, QC J7C 3V5
450-433-1050
Fax: 450-433-1048
800-474-6561
info@geostat.com
www.geostat.com
Firm Type: Engineering, Scientific/Technical Services
Founded: 1981
Staff: 14
Products/Services/Areas of Expertise: Consulting, computerized orebody modeling & mine planning, geostatical analysis, independent auditing; consulting in environment (waste site characterization), petroleum & gas (reservoir characterization), hydrography (bathymetric surrey design) & forestry
Domestic Markets:
National
Foreign Activity:
Asia, Australia/New Zealand, Central America, Eastern Europe, South America, USA
Markets Sought:
Eastern Europe
Contact(s):
Claude Du Plessis, Président

Geowest Environmental Consultants
#203, 4208 - 97 St.
Edmonton, AB T6E 5Z9
780-461-5000
Fax: 780-461-5036
Firm Type: Scientific/Technical Services
Founded: 1991
Staff: 30
Products/Services/Areas of Expertise: Natural resource & environmental consulting services; resource analysis; GIS, remote sensing; biophysical & ecological inventory; GIS/environmental modelling; forestry & resource appraisal; natural resource training
Domestic Markets:
Alberta, British Columbia, Manitoba, Northwest Territories, Nunavut, Ontario, Yukon Territory
Contact(s):
Dennis O'Leary, President & Sr. Quaternary Geologist

Gerry Brushett Enterprises Limited
94 Mayflower Ave.
Beaverbank, NS B4G 1C1
902-864-4751
Fax: 902-865-4732
Firm Type: Distributing
Founded: 1982
Staff: 2
Products/Services/Areas of Expertise: Bio-additives for use in wastewater treatment plants, processing plants, dairies, commercial & public institutions
Domestic Markets:
National
Contact(s):
G. Brushett, President

Gestion Eaux Richelieu Inc.
400, av du Parc
Saint-Luc, QC J2W 2S7
450-348-2667
Fax: 450-348-1677
Contact(s):
Robin Duchesne, Contact

GET Industries Inc.
Also Known As: Grind Hog
P.O. Box 640
Brampton, ON L6V 2L6

905-451-9900
Fax: 519-927-9315
877-213-7418
get@grindhog.com
www.grindhog.com
Firm Type: Manufacturing
Founded: 1975
Products/Services/Areas of Expertise: Sewage shredding & screening devices for the preliminary treatment of domestic wastewaters
Contact(s):
David Martin, Owner

Gevity Group Inc.
P.O. Box 23178
#A15, 270 Baig Blvd.
Moncton, NB E1A 6S8
506-855-7081
Fax: 506-855-7087

GILFAB
625, boul Industrial
Mascouche, QC J7K 3G6
450-474-7400
Fax: 450-474-7404
877-826-5274
www.asi-tank.com
Firm Type: Manufacturing
Founded: 1930
Products/Services/Areas of Expertise: Sewage treatment equipment; storage tanks; oil/water separation equipment; oil spill equipment
Financial Information:
Type of Ownership: Private
Domestic Markets:
New Brunswick, Newfoundland & Labrador, Nova Scotia, Ontario, Prince Edward Island, Québec
Foreign Activity:
USA
Contact(s):
Normand Rousseau, President
Angele Levasseur, Contact, Sales & Marketing
Laurent Brunet, Contact, Technical Services

GL&V - Groupe Laperrière & Verreault Inc.
Formerly: Dorr-Oliver Canada
#2100, 2001 McGill College, 21st fl.
Montréal, QC H3A 1G1
514-284-2224
Fax: 514-284-2225
courriermtl@glv.com
www.glv.com
Firm Type: Manufacturing
Staff: 300
Member of: Water Environment Federation
Products/Services/Areas of Expertise: Sewage treatment equipment & systems; air pollution treatment equipment; water treatment systems & equipment; industrial solid waste treatment equipment; industrial chemical waste treatment equipment
Financial Information:
Revenue Sources: 20% Provincial; 80% Municipals
Domestic Markets:
National
Foreign Activity:
Central America, South America, USA
Contact(s):
Laurent Verreault, CEO

Canadian Branches:
Montréal Branch
Metcalfe Tower
#600, 1500, rue Metcalfe
Montréal, QC H3A 1X6
514-284-2224
Fax: 514-284-2225
courriermtl@glv.com

Oakville Branch
#300, 2010 Winston Park
Oakville, ON L6H 5R7
905-491-2750
Fax: 905-491-2790
info.ewtca@glv.com

Trois-Rivières - Manufacturing
227, St-Maurice
Trois-Rivières, QC G9A 5E5

819-371-8227
Fax: 819-378-0535
info.fabrication@glv.com
Trois-Rivières Branch
#2, 3100, Westinghouse
Trois-Rivières, QC G9A 5E1
819-371-8282
Fax: 819-373-3527
info.fabrication@glv.com

Glenn Group Ltd.
Formerly: Daniel K. Glenn Ltd.
P.O. Box 624
Fredericton, NB E3B 5A6
506-455-2473
Fax: 506-459-2685
sleblanc@glenngroup.ca
www.glenngroup.ca
Firm Type: Engineering
Founded: 1983
Member of: Atlantic Provinces Association of Landscape Architects; Canadian Society of Landscape Architects; Landscape New Brunswick; American Society of Landscape Architects; New Brunswick Environment Industry Association
Products/Services/Areas of Expertise: A full service landscape architectural design firm with a commitment to environmentally sensitive design
Activities: Architectural landscaping; Park planning
Recently Completed / Ongoing Projects: St. Thomas University, Fredericton, NB; Water Street Cruise Terminal, Saint John, NB
Financial Information:
Type of Ownership: Private
Contact(s):
Daniel K. Glenn, BLA, FCSLA, APALA, ASLA, Principal
dkg@glenngroup.ca
Ron Hanna, P.Tech., Senior Technologist
rhanna@glenngroup.ca
Brian Parker, MLA, BFA, CSLA, Senior Landscape Architect
bparker@glenngroup.ca

GLM Tanks & Equipment Ltd.
Industrial Park
1508 - 8 St.
Nisku, AB T9E 7S6
780-955-2233
Fax: 780-955-2241
800-661-9828
nisku@glmtanks.com
www.glmtanks.com
Firm Type: Manufacturing
Founded: 1979
Staff: 250
Products/Services/Areas of Expertise: Storage tanks (carbon & stainless steel) & treating equipment; double wall secondary containment tanks; aboveground/underground tanks
Domestic Markets:
Alberta, British Columbia, Manitoba, Ontario, Saskatchewan
Foreign Activity:
Central America, USA
Contact(s):
Lee Gottschlich, President & General Manager

Canadian Branches:
Calgary Branch
Sales
#900, 706 - 7th Ave. SW
Calgary, AB T2P 0Z1
403-231-2730
Fax: 403-234-8274
1-800-661-9446
calgary@glmtanks.com
Owen Gilbert, Manager

Battleford Branch
P.O. Box 1229
14 St. & 5 Ave.
Battleford, SK S0M 0E0
306-937-7785
Fax: 306-937-7788
1-800-663-7785
battleford@glmtanks.com

Camrose Branch
3812 - 42nd Ave.
Camrose, AB T4V 4B9

780-672-0777
Fax: 780-672-1088
1-866-672-0777
glm@glmtanks.com

Grande Prairie
9101 - 150 Ave.
Grande Prairie, AB T8X 0B1
780-830-1474
Fax: 780-830-1478
1-888-830-1474
gprairie@glmtanks.com

Global Change Strategies International Co. / GCSI
#305, 150 Isabella St.
Ottawa, ON K1S 1V7
613-232-7979
Fax: 613-232-3993
Firm Type: Management Consulting
Founded: 1996
Products/Services/Areas of Expertise: Environmental consulting & contracting services; its parent company is Natsource LLC, NY.
Financial Information:
Type of Ownership: Foreign-owned
Contact(s):
James P. Bruce, Senior Associate

Global Contract Inc.
1350 Flint Rd.
Toronto, ON M3J 2J7
416-661-3660
Fax: 416-736-6685
www.globalcontract.com
Firm Type: Distributing, Manufacturing
Founded: 1993
Quality Environmental Management System(s): 14001
EcoLogo Certified Products & Services: Boulevard & Evolve Systems are certified to GREENGUARD, which indicates good indoor air quality to contribute to a favorable productive environment & enable building occupants to experience a level of comfort
Products/Services/Areas of Expertise: Global Contract offers a line of office furniture, while aiming to be environmentally responsible. Showrooms are located across the country.
Ecological Note: Boulevard & Evolve Systems are certified to GREENGUARD, which indicates good indoor air quality to contribute to a favorable productive environment & enable building occupants to experience a level of comfort
Domestic Markets:
National
Foreign Activity:
Australia/New Zealand, Caribbean, Central America, Western Europe, The Middle East, South America, United Kingdom
Contact(s):
Chanoch Friedel, President
Lonna Yorg-Turner, Director, Marketing
lonna@globaltotaloffice.com

Global Dewatering Ltd.
P.O. Box 1
16831 - 128A Ave.
Edmonton, AB T5V 1K9
780-440-4848
Fax: 780-440-1391
info@globaldewater.com
www.globaldewater.com
Products/Services/Areas of Expertise: Mobile mechanical dewatering, dredging & sludge conditioning
Contact(s):
Fred Pheasey, President

Global Engineering & Testing Ltd.
#15, 3500 - 27 St. NE
Calgary, AB T1Y 5E2
403-291-5091
Fax: 403-291-9729
global.engineering@shaw.ca
www.goglobalfirst.com
Firm Type: Engineering
Founded: 1985
Staff: 12
Member of: Professional Association of Alberta & British Columbia
Member of: Association of Professional Engineers, Geologists, and Geophysicists of Alberta
Products/Services/Areas of Expertise: Provide environmental consultant services; perform remediaton of the Investigations for

Industrial contamination, garstation on the subsoil groundwater; province phase I, II & III environmental site assessments, etc.
Recently Completed / Ongoing Projects: Environmental investigation, design & inspection of the remedial work, Muller Trucking, High River, AB; investigation & clean-up of vapour extraction system, Alberta Treasury, Calgary, AB
Financial Information:
Type of Ownership: Private
Revenue: $500,000 - $1.5 Million
Revenue Sources: 10% Provincial; 25% Municipals; 65% Private Contracts
Domestic Markets:
Alberta, British Columbia
Contact(s):
Jack Kao, President

Global Facman Entreprises Inc.
12180, ch du Golf
Montréal, QC H4K 1S5
514-338-3745
Fax: 514-338-3738
800-746-1568
accounting@globalmvo.com
www.globalmvo.com
Firm Type: Management Consulting
Founded: 1991
Staff: 6
Products/Services/Areas of Expertise: Environmental consulting & contracting services
Recently Completed / Ongoing Projects: Reduction in greenhouse gas emissions, Brazil; water sewer study, Rio de Janeiro
Financial Information:
Type of Ownership: Private
Revenue: $500,000 - $1.5 Million
Revenue Sources: 45% nationwide; 55% Private Contracts
Contact(s):
Frédérick T. Day, Contact

Global Repair Ltd.
33 Bellefair Ave.
Toronto, ON M4L 3T7
416-686-3690
Fax: 416-686-1744
866-271-0719
sales@globalrepair.ca
www.globalrepair.ca
Products/Services/Areas of Expertise: Global Repair provides compost equipment for soil regeneration & educational material, innovative, ecological farm, garden & landscape soil amendments; we help growers 'Utilize resources and Maximize Profits' TM; applicable for farms, large animal operations, forests, mushrooms, orchards, vineyards, forages, gardens, lawns, parks, golf courses, all types of composting & more.

Global Sensor Systems Inc.
400 Brunel Rd.
Mississauga, ON L4Z 2C2
905-507-0007
Fax: 905-507-4177
www.globalsensorsystems.com
Firm Type: Manufacturing
Founded: 1977
Staff: 8
Products/Services/Areas of Expertise: Electronic back up safety devices for vehicles; CCTV cameras & monitors
Financial Information:
Type of Ownership: Private
Revenue: $500,000 - $1.5 Million
Revenue Sources: 80% Municipals; 20% Private Contracts
Domestic Markets:
Alberta, British Columbia, Manitoba, Ontario, Québec, Saskatchewan
Foreign Activity:
USA,
Contact(s):
Ray H. Glenn, General Manager
rayglenn@globalsensorsystems.com

GlobalTox International Consultants Inc.
#6, 367 Woodlawn Rd. West
Guelph, ON N1H 7K9
519-766-1000
Fax: 519-766-1100
info@globaltox.ca
www.globaltox.ca

Products & Services Buyer's Guide

Firm Type: Scientific/Technical Services
Founded: 1992
Staff: 15
Member of: Society of Toxicology of Canada; Society of Toxicology (USA); Society for Risk Analysis
Products/Services/Areas of Expertise: Consulting company specializing in all aspects of toxicology; environmental services include site-specific risk assessment for the cleanup of contaminated sites & risk communication; offers legal support in all areas of human & environmental toxicology; provides expertise in the derivation & interpretation of health-based guidelines for chemicals in water, air & soil; serves clients in both the public & private sectors, as well as non-government organizations; services also include: risk assessment, product testing & registration
Recently Completed / Ongoing Projects: Completed projects for Marshall Macklin Monaghan, Environment & Energy, City of Edmonton, City of Toronto, Health Canada in areas of toxicology
Domestic Markets:
National
Foreign Activity:
Western Europe, The Pacific Rim, USA
Contact(s):
Ronald Brecher, Principal
rbrecher@globaltox.ca

Globetron Controls Inc.
Formerly: Globetron Electronics Corporation
Also Known As: Globetron
3185 Dundas St. West
Oakville, ON L6M 4J4
905-825-1335
Fax: 905-825-0475
800-800-4606
sales@globetron.com
www.globetron.com
Firm Type: Distributing
Founded: 1988
Staff: 5
Quality Environmental Management System(s): 9002
Products/Services/Areas of Expertise: Distributor of components for automation applications; air & liquid flow installations; energy-saving, motor control applications
Financial Information:
Type of Ownership: Private
Domestic Markets:
National
Foreign Activity:
USA
Contact(s):
Craig Brown, General Manager
cbrown@globetron.com

Glos Associates Inc.
Formerly: Glos Engineering Ltd.
3535 North Service Rd. East
Windsor, ON N8W 5R7
519-966-6750
Fax: 519-966-6753
www.glosassociates.com
Firm Type: Engineering
Founded: 1966
Staff: 20
Products/Services/Areas of Expertise: Architectural & engineering services
Financial Information:
Type of Ownership: Private
Domestic Markets:
Ontario
Contact(s):
C. Glos, P.Eng., President & Chief Engineer
J.L. Glos, Vice-President
Martin Glos, Vice-President

Godfrey Associates Ltd.
186 Adelaide St.
Saint John, NB E2K 1X1
506-632-9010
Fax: 506-633-7093
godfrey@nbnet.nb.ca
Firm Type: Engineering, Scientific/Technical Services
Founded: 1965
Staff: 18
Quality Environmental Management System(s): 9001
Products/Services/Areas of Expertise: Design & construction supervision of water & wastewater facilities

Contact(s):
Grant W. Godfrey, P.Eng., President/CEO
K.W. Hannah, P.Eng., Vice-President

Golden Maple Leaf (Hangzhou) Technology Consulting Co. L
#601, 107 Hangzhou Xin Cun, Wen San Xi Lu
Hangzhou Zhejiang Provinc PR China
-(86) (571) 8989629
Fax: -(86) (571) 898
Contact(s):
George Lu, Dr., General Manager
Canadian Branches:
Golden Maple Leaf (Hangzhou) Technology Consulting Co. L
#601, 107 Hangzhou Xin Cun, Wen San Xi Lu
Hangzhou Zhejiang Provinc PR China
-(86) (571) 8989629
Fax: -(86) (571) 898

Golder Associates Ltd.
2390 Argentia Rd.
Mississauga, ON L5N 5Z7
905-567-4444
Fax: 905-567-6561
800-414-8314
solutions@golder.com
www.golder.com
Firm Type: Engineering, Scientific/Technical Services
Founded: 1960
Staff: 1400
Products/Services/Areas of Expertise: Specialising in ground engineering & environmental services
Domestic Markets:
National
Foreign Activity:
Worldwide
Contact(s):
Frederick W. Firlotte, President
John Westland, Office Manager
Susan DeRyck, Manager, Marketing
Brian Conlin, Principal
Ron G. Barsi, P.Geo., Principal
Pierre Beaudry, P.Geo., Principal
Peter M. Chapman, Ph.D., R.P.Bio., Principal
Ty Garde, P.Eng., Principal
Pierre Harnois, ing, Principal
Michael (Max) Maxwell, Ph.D.,P.Geo, Principal
J.Scott McKenzie, Principal
W.Douglas Pelly, P.Eng., Principal
R.Michael Raine, Principal
Stephen G. Simmering, P.Eng., Principal
Mark J. Telesnicki, P.Eng., Principal
Robert van Wyngaarden, Principal
M. (Yogi) Yogendrakumar, Ph.D., P.Eng., Principal
Andreas Wagner, Principal

Canadian Branches:
Abbotsford
#202, 2790 Gladwin Rd.
Abbotsford, BC V2T 4S8
604-850-8786
Fax: 604-850-8756
Mark Goldbach, Office Manager

Burnaby
#500, 4260 Still Creek Dr.
Burnaby, BC V5C 6C6
604-296-4200
Fax: 604-298-5253
Ateesh Roop, Office Manager

Calgary
#102, 2535 - 3rd Ave. SE
Calgary, AB T2A 7W5
403-299-5600
Fax: 403-299-5606
Louise Menard, Office Manager

Castlegar
195, Place Frontenac
Pointe-Claire, QC H9R 4Z7
514-694-0474
Fax: 514-694-3436
Rick Firlotte, President

Don Mills
#110, 85 Curlew Dr.
Toronto, ON M3A 2P8
416-383-1760
Fax: 416-383-1762
Anthony O'Brien, Contact

Edmonton
#300, 10525 - 170 St.
Edmonton, AB T5P 4W2
780-483-3499
Fax: 780-483-1574
Greg Herasymuik, Office Manager

Fort McMurray
340 MacLennan Cres.
Fort McMurray, AB T9H 5C8
780-743-4040
Fax: 780-743-4237
Debbie Smilar, Office Manager

Fort St. John
10628 Peck Lane Rd.
Fort St John, BC V1J 4M7
250-785-9281
Fax: 250-785-7287
Kurtis Saker, Contact

Kamloops
#100, 388 First Ave.
Kamloops, BC V2C 6W3
250-828-6116
Fax: 250-828-1215
Duncan Hendricks, Office Manager

Kelowna
#220, 1755 Springfield Rd.
Kelowna, BC V1Y 5V5
250-860-8424
Fax: 250-860-9874
Rick Peleshytyk, Office Manager

London
#1, 309 Exeter Rd.
London, ON N6L 1C1
519-652-0099
Fax: 519-652-6299
Phillip M. Moddle, Office Manager

Mississauga
2390 Argentia Rd.
Mississauga, ON L6N 5Z7
905-567-4444
Fax: 905-567-6561
Sean McFarland, Office Manager

Montréal
#10, 9200, boul de l'Acadie
Montréal, QC H4N 2T2
514-630-0990
Fax: 514-630-1178
Martin Kelly, Office Manager

Ottawa
32 Steacie Dr.
Ottawa, ON K2K 2A9
613-592-9600
Fax: 613-592-9601
Rick Branchaud, Office Manager

Prince George
2272 South Nicholson St.
Prince George, BC V2N 1V6
250-563-5866
Fax: 250-563-3814
Dave Hamilton, Contact

Québec
#206, 2500, Jean-Perin
Québec, QC G2C 1H1
418-842-0686
Fax: 418-842-9964
Marc Houde, Manager

Red Deer EH&S
#1A, 7887 - 49 Ave.
Red Deer, AB T4P 2B4
403-309-7309
Fax: 403-403-0013
Michelle Kutz, Contact

Saskatoon
1721, 8th St. E
Saskatoon, SK S7H 0T4

306-665-7989
Fax: 306-665-3342
Laurent F. Gareau, Office Manager

Sudbury
1010 Lorne St.
Sudbury, ON P3C 4R9
705-524-6861
Fax: 705-524-1984
Kevin Beauchamp, Office Manager

Surrey
12388-B - 88th Ave.
Surrey, BC V3W 3J6
604-591-6616
Fax: 604-591-6608
Emily Kwok, Contact

Toronto
#1220, 141 Adelaide St. W
Toronto, ON M5H 3L5
416-366-6999
Fax: 416-366-6777
Kirk Rodgers, Office Manager

Val-d'Or
375, av Centrale
Val-d'Or, QC J9P 1P4
819-825-5665
Fax: 819-825-6888
François Chabot, Contact

Victoria
2640 Douglas St.
Victoria, BC V8T 4M1
250-881-7372
Fax: 250-881-7470
Jeffrey D. Bailey, Office Manager

Whitby
100 Scotia Ct.
Whitby, ON L1N 8Y6
905-723-2727
Fax: 905-723-2182
Steve D. Keenan, Office Manager

Windsor
#100, 2465 McDougall St.
Windsor, ON N6X 3N9
519-250-3733
Fax: 519-250-6452
Phil Moodle, Office Manager

Winnipeg
#1, 25 Scurfield Blvd.
Winnipeg, MB R3Y 1G4
204-489-9100
Fax: 204-489-9339
Timothy J. Garde, Office Manager

Yellowknife
#9, 4905 - 48th St.
Yellowknife, NT X1A 3S3
867-873-6319
Fax: 867-873-6379
Grant Clarke, Office Manager

Gorman-Rupp of Canada Ltd.
70 Burwell Rd.
St. Thomas, ON N5P 3R7
519-631-2870
Fax: 519-631-4624
grcanada@gormanrupp.com
www.grcanada.com
Firm Type: Manufacturing
Founded: 1960
Staff: 41
Member of: Water Environment Association of Ontario
Member of: Canadian Chamber of Commerce
Quality Environmental Management System(s): 9002
Products/Services/Areas of Expertise: Self-priming & standard centrifugal pumps; rotary gear pumps; diaphragm sludge pumps
Financial Information:
Type of Ownership: Foreign-owned
Domestic Markets:
National
Contact(s):
Gary Creeden, VP & General Manager
gcreeden@grcanada.com

Michel Boyer, Manager
mboyer@grcanada.com
Mike Cosgrove, Manager
mcosgrove@grcanada.com
International Branch(es):
Mansfield, Ohio
P.O. Box 1217
305 Bowman St.
Mansfield, OH USA
419-755-1011
Fax: 419-755-1251
grsales@gormanrupp.com

Goss Gilroy Inc. / GGI
#900, 150 Metcalfe St.
Ottawa, ON K2P 1P1
613-230-5577
Fax: 613-235-9592
800-611-0511
ggi@ggi.ca
www.ggi.ca
Firm Type: Management Consulting
Founded: 1982
Staff: 30
Products/Services/Areas of Expertise: Organizational analysis for environmental programs & activities; evaluation of public sector environment programs & activities; management audits of programs with scientific/technical environmental components; marine emergency response planning; public health surveys on environment-related issues
Financial Information:
Type of Ownership: Private
Domestic Markets:
National
Foreign Activity:
Africa, Asia, South America
Contact(s):
Celine Pinsent, Ph.D., Partner

Canadian Branches:
St. John's
401 Empire Ave.
St. John's, NL A1E 1W6
709-754-2065
Fax: 709-754-6303
1-800-289-1407
gginfld@ggi.ca
Ken Organ, Partner

Gough Risk Management Ltd.
12292 Gilley St.
Surrey, BC V4A 3E1
604-535-3211
gough@interchange.ubc.ca
Firm Type: Management Consulting
Founded: 1991
Staff: 1
Member of: American Industrial Hygiene Association; Registered Professional Biologists Association of British Columbia
Products/Services/Areas of Expertise: Occupational & environmental health & safety monitoring, assessment & training
Financial Information:
Type of Ownership: Private
Revenue Sources: 20% nationwide; 20% Provincial; 5% Municipals; 55% Private Contracts
Domestic Markets:
British Columbia
Contact(s):
George Gough, President

Goulbourn Stittsville Sanitation Ltd.
106 Westhunt Dr.
Carp, ON K0A 1L0
613-836-6069
Fax: 613-836-6072
david.graham@goulbournsanitation.ca
www.goulbournsanitation.ca
Firm Type: Waste Management
Founded: 1975
Staff: 27
Member of: Recycling Council of Ontario; Ontario Waste Management Association
Products/Services/Areas of Expertise: Collection & recycling of glass, newspapers, PET, OCC, metal & organics

Financial Information:
Type of Ownership: Private
Revenue Sources: % Private Contracts
Domestic Markets:
Ontario,

Gourley Construction Ltd.
4606, 49 Ave.
Vermilion, AB T9X 1R6
780-853-5087
Fax: 780-853-2604
Firm Type: Management Consulting, Scientific/Technical Services
Staff: 5
Products/Services/Areas of Expertise: Oil field well site reclamation; environmental abandonments
Financial Information:
Type of Ownership: Private
Domestic Markets:
Alberta, Saskatchewan
Contact(s):
Tim Gourley, President

Gouw Quality Onions Ltd.
5801 - 54 Ave.
Taber, AB T1G 1X4
403-223-1440
Fax: 403-223-2036
gqo@gqo.ca
www.gouwqualityonions.com
Firm Type: Manufacturing
Founded: 1987
EcoLogo Certified Products & Services: Gouw Quality Onions
Products/Services/Areas of Expertise: Onion growers
Ecological Note: Gouw Quality Onions
Contact(s):
Casey Gouw Jr., Sales & Controller
Kyle Gouw, Farm Manager

Government Publications
P.O. Box 637
Halifax, NS B3J 2T3
902-424-5200
Fax: 902-424-0516
800-670-4357
www.gov.ns.ca/snsmr/publications
Products/Services/Areas of Expertise: Government Publications operates as an electronic and mail order service for the distribution of government books, reports, manuals, directories, Acts, and Statutes. Generally, any publication issued by Government of Nova Scotia departments or agencies can be ordered through this service Government departments may also distribute publications directly through departmental websites or ordering processes. For provincial statutes & regulations see: www.gov.ns.ca/legislature/legc/index.htm

GPEC Global Corp.
Formerly: Hobbs Miller Maat Inc
#104, 2295 Bristol Circle
Oakville, ON L6H 6P8
905-829-1197
Fax: 905-829-1135
info@gpecglobal.com
www.gpecglobal.com
Firm Type: Engineering, Scientific/Technical Services
Founded: 1994
Staff: 15
Products/Services/Areas of Expertise: Waste Management technology, green power technology and services
Financial Information:
Type of Ownership: Private
Revenue Sources: 100% Private Contracts
Domestic Markets:
Alberta, British Columbia, Manitoba, Nova Scotia, Ontario, Québec
Foreign Activity:
Australia/New Zealand, Mexico, USA
Contact(s):
Paul Davis, President
Derk Z. Maat, Vice-President, Engineering

GPEC International Ltd. / GPEC
Formerly: Green Plan Environmental Corp.
#3, 2880 Sheffield Rd.
Ottawa, ON K1B 1A4

613-747-1788
Fax: 613-747-0520
gpec@gpecinternational.com
Firm Type: Management Consulting, Engineering, Waste Management
Founded: 1992
Member of: Association of Professional Engineers of Ontario; Association of Professional Engineers of New Brunswick
Products/Services/Areas of Expertise: Site assessment; site remediation & restoration; storage tank management & services; pollution prevention & compliance promotion; waste management; wastewater & groundwater treatment; risk assessment & management; environmental impact assessment
Recently Completed / Ongoing Projects: Multi-million dollar cleanups of former industrial & military sites involving contaminants; landfill design & construction; well water studies; thermal treatment of hydrocarbon contaminated soil & debris; bioremediation on-site at an airport facility; development of the national hazardous waste management program for a middle-east nation
Financial Information:
Type of Ownership: Private
Domestic Markets:
National
Foreign Activity:
Africa, Asia, The Middle East, South America, Mexico, USA
Contact(s):
Noel Perera, President

Graecam Incorporated
56 Glacier Dr. SW
Calgary, AB T3C 5A1
403-244-3556
Fax: 403-228-9794
graecam@cadvision.com
Contact(s):
Ron Emerson, B.Sc., P.Ag

Gratec Ltd.
Formerly: Greey/BIF
#1, 30 Ritin Lane
Concord, ON L4K 4C5
905-738-0021
www.gratecservice.com
Firm Type: Manufacturing, Scientific/Technical Services
Founded: 1874
Staff: 2
Member of: Machinery & Equipment Manufacturers' Association of Canada; Canadian Pulp & Paper Association; Ontario Pollution Control Equipment Association; Canadian Institute of Mining, Metallurgy & Petroleum
Products/Services/Areas of Expertise: Manufacturing of wastewater pollution control systems; service & repair centre for mixers & BIF pumps
Financial Information:
Type of Ownership: Private
Domestic Markets:
National,

Graymont Inc.
Formerly: Graybec Inc.
#200, 10991 Shellbridge Way
Richmond, BC V6X 3C6
604-207-4292
Fax: 604-207-9014
866-207-4292
www.graymont.com
Firm Type: Manufacturing
Founded: 1948
Staff: 352
Member of: Grupo Calidra
Quality Environmental Management System(s): 9002
Products/Services/Areas of Expertise: Lime & limestone production
Domestic Markets:
New Brunswick, Ontario, Québec
Foreign Activity:
USA
Contact(s):
J. Graham Weir, Chair
gweir1@graymont.com
William Dodge, President & CEO
bdodge1@graymont.com
Stéphane Godin, Exec. VP & COO
sgodin1@graymont.com

Kenneth J. Lahti, Vice-Pres. & CFO
klahti1@graymont.com
Canadian Branches:
Eastern Canada Regional Office
#25, 206, rue de Lauzon
Boucherville, QC J4B 1E7
450-449-2262
Fax: 450-449-2256

Western Canada Regional Office
#260, 4311 - 12th St. NE
Calgary, AB T2E 4P9
403-250-9100
Fax: 403-291-1303

Bedford Lime Plant
1015, ch de la Carrière
Bedford, QC J0J 1A0
450-248-3307
Fax: 450-248-7272

Exshaw Lime Plant
P.O. Box 130
Exshaw, AB R0L 2C0
403-673-3595

Faulkner Lime Plant
P.O. Box 1
Faulkner, MB R0C 0Y0
204-449-2078

Havelock Lime Plant
4634 Rte 880
Havelock, NB E4Z 5K8
506-534-2311
Fax: 506-534-8241

Joliette Lime Plant
P.O. Box 380
1300, rue Notre-Dame
Joliette, QC J6E 3Z9
450-759-8195
Fax: 450-759-8376

Marbleton Lime Plant
303, rue Principale ouest
Marbleton, QC J0B 2L0
819-887-6381
Fax: 819-887-6857

Pavilion Lime Plant
P.O. Box 187
Cache Creek, BC V0K 1H0
250-457-6291

Summit Lime Plant
P.O. Box 40
2018 - 9th St.
Coleman, AB T0K 0M0
403-563-3374

Great Lakes Safety Products Inc.
3303 Walker Rd.
Windsor, ON N8W 3R9
519-972-6605
glspi@wincom.net
www.greatlakessafetyproducts.com
Firm Type: Distributing
Founded: 1989
Staff: 7
Products/Services/Areas of Expertise: Safety/protective products
Domestic Markets:
National
Foreign Activity:
USA
Contact(s):
Tom Diemer, President

Great Northern Recycling Inc.
41 Gurholt Dr.
Dartmouth, NS B3B 1J8
902-468-8128
Fax: 902-468-8129
Contact(s):
Terri Kaulback, General Manager

Great Western Containers Inc.
3220 - 118th Ave. SE, 3rd Fl.
Calgary, AB T2Z 3X1

403-705-0760
Fax: 403-236-6237
info@gwcontainers.com
www.gwcontainers.com
Firm Type: Distributing, Waste Management
Founded: 1979
Staff: 135
Member of: Alberta Special Waste Services Association
Products/Services/Areas of Expertise: As well as manufacturing new container drums, the company repairs & conditions old drums for reuse. Its product inventory includes steel & polyethylene containers for the food & petrochemical sectors.
Domestic Markets:
Alberta, British Columbia, Manitoba, Northwest Territories, Saskatchewan, Yukon Territory
Contact(s):
Nils Bodtker, President & CEO
Gary Yamada, CFO & VP, Finance
gyamada@gwcontainers.com
Marc Proulx, VP, Operations
mproulx@gwcontainers.com
Ken Chisholm, VP, Sales & Marketing
kchisholm@gwcontainers.com
Contact(s):
Rosa Estrela, Manager
restrela@gwcontainers.com
Contact(s):
George Tourigny, Manager
gtourigny@gwcontainers.com
Contact(s):
Gary Thiessen, Manager
gthiessen@gwcontainers.com
Contact(s):
Jason Jack, Manager
jjack@gwcontainers.com

Canadian Branches:
Montréal Warehouse
#134, 5695 boul des Grandes-Prairies
St-Leonard, QC H1R 1B3
514-326-5940
Fax: 514-326-7072
Jordan Arshinoff-Foss, Sales Contact
jarshinoff-foss@gwcontainers.com

Regina Warehouse
125 Dewdney Ave. East
Regina, SK S4N 4G3
306-352-3644
Fax: 306-522-5877
Shawn Kerr, Manager
skerr@gwcontainers.com

Toronto Warehouse
#8, 35 Royal Group Cres.
Vaughan, ON L4H 1X9
289-371-0211
Fax: 289-371-0214
Todd Harner, Manager
tharner@gwcontainers.com

Vancouver Warehouse
8219 River Way
Delta, BC V4G 1L1
604-946-7244
Fax: 604-946-8100
800-898-7887
Rick Rudichuk, Manager
rrudichuk@gwcontainers.com

Calgary Reconditioning Plant
7905 - 46 St. SE
Calgary, AB T2C 2Y6
403-279-2090
Fax: 403-203-4649

Edmonton Reconditioning Plant
1912 - 66th Ave.
Edmonton, AB T6P 1M4
780-440-2222
Fax: 780-440-4763

Lloydminster Manufacturing Plant
5408 - 52 Ave.
Lloydminster, AB T9V 1P8
780-875-4421
Fax: 780-875-6010
866-875-4421

Winnipeg Reconditioning Plant
328 Dawson Rd. North
Winnipeg, MB R2J 0S7
204-233-3333
Fax: 204-237-1551

Greatario Industrial Storage Systems Ltd.
P.O. Box 399
715647 County Road #4
Innerkip, ON N0J 1M0
519-469-8169
Fax: 519-469-8157
sales@greatarioengsys.com
www.greatarioengsys.com
Firm Type: Distributing
Founded: 1987
Staff: 10
Member of: American Water Works Association
Products/Services/Areas of Expertise: Glass fused-to-steel storage tanks (above ground); potable water storage tanks; dry bulk storage; sludge mining systems; aluminum domes & covers
Financial Information:
Type of Ownership: Private
Revenue Sources: 95% Provincial; 5% Private Contracts
Domestic Markets:
New Brunswick, Newfoundland & Labrador, Nova Scotia, Ontario, Prince Edward Island, Québec
Contact(s):
Glen Gregory

Canadian Branches:
Aquabec
#230-6, 15, rue Buteau
Gatineau, QC J8Z 1V4
819-772-2080
Fax: 819-772-2066
aquabec@istar.ca
Michael Arnkvarn

Green Island Recycling Ltd.
345 Gulf Cres.
Edwardsville, NS B2A 4V2
902-564-8104
Fax: 902-564-8095
greenisland@ns.sympatico.ca
Firm Type: Waste Management
Founded: 1999
Staff: 12
Products/Services/Areas of Expertise: Recycling processing & marketing
Financial Information:
Type of Ownership: Private
Contact(s):
Tom MacMillan, President

Green Key Solutions Inc.
#8, 400 1B - 19 St. NE
Calgary, AB T2E 6X8
403-442-3834
Fax: 403-442-3101
info@greenkeysolutions.com
www.greenkeysolutions.com
Firm Type: Management Consulting, Scientific/Technical Services
Founded: 1995
Staff: 8
Member of: Midwest Laboratories Canada; Canadian Association Agriculture Retailers; Alberta Food Processors Association
Member of: Alberta Institute of Agrology; Saskatchewan Institute of Agrology; Manitoba Institute of Agrology
EcoLogo Certified Products & Services: 1
Products/Services/Areas of Expertise: Agrological consulting services
Recently Completed / Ongoing Projects: Manure management projects for several cattle, swine, poultry & dairy operations within the three Prairie provinces
Ecological Note: 1
Financial Information:
Revenue: $500,000 - $1.5 Million
Revenue Sources: 100% Private Contracts
Domestic Markets:
Alberta, British Columbia, Manitoba
Contact(s):
Troy LaForge
troy@greenkeysolutions.com

Errol Schimke
errol@greenkeysolutions.com

Green Plan Ltd.
#101, 5104 - 82 Ave. NW
Edmonton, AB T6H 0E6
780-455-4292
Fax: 780-451-6787
gpmail@green-plan.com
www.green-plan.com
Firm Type: Scientific/Technical Services
Founded: 1989
Products/Services/Areas of Expertise: Green Plan is an environmental consultant firm with services including: site assessment; environmental impact assessment; site remediation.
Financial Information:
Type of Ownership: Private
Domestic Markets:
Alberta, British Columbia
Contact(s):
Grant Potolicki, Founder & President

Green Soils Inc.
39 Fenmar Dr.
Toronto, ON M9L 1M1
416-745-8080
Fax: 416-745-3478
gsi@primus.ca
Firm Type: Waste Management
Founded: 1993
Staff: 10
Products/Services/Areas of Expertise:
Hydrocarbon-contaminated soil remediation
Financial Information:
Type of Ownership: Private
Domestic Markets:
Ontario
Contact(s):
Ashley Herman, Site Manager

Green Turtle Technologies Ltd. (Canada)
Monteco Ltd.
2596 Dunwin Dr.
Mississauga, ON L5L 1J5
416-966-9444
Fax: 416-966-3439
877-966-9444
infoca@greenturtletech.com
www.greenturtletech.com
Firm Type: Management Consulting, Distributing
Founded: 1974
Products/Services/Areas of Expertise: Green Turtle provides business, institutions & industry with cost-efficient wastewater treatment solutions that ensure regulatory compliance, including Proceptor oil & grease separators & PHIS Neutralization Systems.
Financial Information:
Type of Ownership: Private
Domestic Markets:
National
Foreign Activity:
Worldwide
Contact(s):
John Walker, Territory Manager, Ontario & Eastern Canada,
416-294-6092
jwalker@greenturtletech.com
Chantal Boisson, Territory Manager, Eastern Ont. & Québec,
514-449-4128
cboisson@greenturtletech.com
Trevor Burns, Territory Manager, Western Canada,
403-390-0803
tburns@greenturtletech.com

Greenbridge Management Inc.
838 Caldwell Ave.
Mississauga, ON L5H 1Y9
905-271-6262
info@greenbridge.com
www.greenbridge.com
Firm Type: Management Consulting
Founded: 1986
Staff: 8
Products/Services/Areas of Expertise: Environmental management systems (ISO 14000) including gap analysis & implementation consulting; training programs; risk assessment; policy development

Financial Information:
Type of Ownership: Private
Revenue Sources: 100% Private Contracts
Domestic Markets:
Alberta, British Columbia, Manitoba, New Brunswick, Newfoundland & Labrador, Nova Scotia, Ontario, Québec
Foreign Activity:
Western Europe, USA,
Contact(s):
Philip E.J. Green, President

Greenfield Research Inc.
P.O. Box 25018
Halifax, NS B3M 4H4
902-422-9426
Fax: 902-443-6424
greenfield@greenfieldresearch.ca
www.greenfieldresearch.ca
Products/Services/Areas of Expertise: Research & development on process & product; manpower & training; re-vamping of old-boilers; software development

Greenflow Environmental Services Inc.
#2, 4151 Morris Dr.
Burlington, ON L7L 5L5
905-333-3004
Fax: 905-333-1306
800-287-5416
sales@greenflow.com
www.greenflow.com
Firm Type: Distributing, Waste Management
Founded: 1992
Staff: 4
Member of: Ag Envirotech Inc.
Member of: Canadian Environmental Industry Ass'n; Canadian Society for Non Destructive Testing; Ontario Printing & Imaging Ass'n; Canadian Federation of Independent Business; Recycling Council of Ontario; Photo Marketing Ass'n; Council of Medical Imaging; Burlington Chamber of Commerce; Better Business Bureau
Products/Services/Areas of Expertise: Serving clients in the graphic arts, printing, photo, NDT, medical, dental, veterinary, auto body, industrial & other manufacturing industries, Greenflow Environmental is licensed to transport hazardous & non-hazardous liquid & solid wastes. Waste transfer site. Services include waste disposal, chemical recycling & disposal; sales, service & installation of related products & waste systemsin several lines & brands
Domestic Markets:
Ontario
Contact(s):
Allan J. Pettman, President/Partner
al@greenflow.com
Brian Selfe, Partner
brian@greenflow.com

Greenland Corporation
7016 - 30 St. SE
Calgary, AB T2C 1N9
403-720-7049
Fax: 403-720-4951
800-598-7636
info@greenpluslubes.com
www.greenpluslubes.com
Firm Type: Manufacturing
Founded: 1994
Staff: 10
Member of: Environmental Services Association of Alberta
Member of: American Ground Water Trust
EcoLogo Certified Products & Services: Environmentally safe, vegetable oil-based lubricants; environmentally safe hydraulic fluids, chain saw bar oil, wire rope lubricant, gear oils, greases & saw guide oil
Products/Services/Areas of Expertise: Greenland Corp. manufactures vegetable oil-based industrial lubricants that provide high performance lubricant characteristics while minimizing both the risk of damage to the environment from leaks & spills, & the chemical hazard posed to equipment operators & mechanics.
Ecological Note: Environmentally safe, vegetable oil-based lubricants; environmentally safe hydraulic fluids, chain saw bar oil, wire rope lubricant, gear oils, greases & saw guide oil
Domestic Markets:
National
Foreign Activity:
USA

Products & Services Buyer's Guide

Markets Sought:
Western Europe, The Pacific Rim, Mexico
Contact(s):
Philip F. Chatters, President
Robert Coak, Director, Domestic Sales & Marketing

Greenland International Consulting Inc.
Formerly: Greenland Engineering Group
120 Hume St.
Collingwood, ON L9Y 1V5
705-444-8805
Fax: 705-444-5482
greenland@grnland.com
www.grnland.com
Firm Type: Engineering, Scientific/Technical Services
Founded: 1994
Staff: 8
Products/Services/Areas of Expertise: Water resource & environmental consulting; flood control, stormwater management services; water quality control; environmental & ecologic studies; software research & development
Financial Information:
Revenue Sources: 10% nationwide; 40% Provincial; 30% Municipals; 20% Private Contracts
Domestic Markets:
Ontario
Foreign Activity:
Asia, Eastern Europe, The Pacific Rim, USA
Canadian Branches:
Greater Toronto
#304, 15995 Airport Rd.
Caledon East, ON L7C 1H9
905-584-1458
Fax: 905-584-1461

GreenWare Environmental Systems Inc.
#200, 469 King St. West
Toronto, ON M5V 1K4
416-867-9504
Fax: 416-367-2653
800-474-0627
greeninfo@greenware.ca
www.greenware.ca
Firm Type: Information Technology
Founded: 1991
Staff: 6
Member of: Canadian Environment Industry Association; Canadian Environmental Auditing Association
Products/Services/Areas of Expertise: Specializes in environmental management information systems; software for ISO 14000 environmental audits & environmental performance monitoring & reporting; consulting & training on ISO 14000 & information systems, environmental auditing & worldwide web services; areas of expertise include environmental management, information systems, environmental law, accounting, auditing
Financial Information:
Type of Ownership: Private
Domestic Markets:
National
Foreign Activity:
Australia/New Zealand, Caribbean, Western Europe, South America, USA

Greenwind Power Corp.
#30, 11151 Horseshoe Way
Richmond, BC V7A 4S5
604-275-2700
Fax: 604-275-2708
866-789-9463
info@greenwindpower.com
www.greenwindpower.com
Firm Type: Manufacturing
Staff: 5
Products/Services/Areas of Expertise: Specializes in providing power to remote communities & isolated industry through the integration of wind energy, battery storage & diesel generators.
Contact(s):
Ron Knoedler

Greenwood & Associates
280 Inglewood Dr.
Toronto, ON M4T 1J1
416-322-7174
Fax: 416-322-0418
ellengreenwood@rogers.com

Contact(s):
Ellen Greenwood, President

Greif Bros. Canada Inc.
Formerly: Greif Containers Inc.
4219 Park St.
Niagara Falls, ON L2E 2P2
905-358-3271
Fax: 905-356-2603
www.greif.com
Firm Type: Manufacturing
Founded: 1926
Staff: 250
Member of: Canadian Manufacturers of Chemical Specialties; Canadian Packaging Association; Canadian Manufacturers' Association
Products/Services/Areas of Expertise: Steel & fibre drums for collection, storage, transport & disposal of hazardous materials
Domestic Markets:
National
Canadian Branches:
Belleville
300 University Ave.
Belleville, ON K8N 5T6
613-968-6429
Fax: 613-968-2849

LaSalle
7000, rue Allard
Montréal, QC H8N 1Y7
514-363-0721
Fax: 514-363-9467

Lloydminster
5408 - 52 Ave.
Lloydminster, SK T9V 2T5
780-875-4421
Fax: 780-875-6010

Maple-Grove
211C Maple Grove Rd.
Maple Grove, QC J6N 1L4
450-429-1179
Fax: 450-429-3300

Milton
383 Main St.
Milton, ON L9T 1P7
905-878-9641
Fax: 905-878-5057

Oakville
165 Wyecroft Rd.
Oakville, ON L6K 3N8
905-842-1473
Fax: 905-842-0116

Stoney Creek
370 Millen Rd.
Stoney Creek, ON L8E 2H5
905-664-4433
Fax: 905-664-4491

Winona
725 Arvin Ave.
Stoney Creek, ON L8E 5R3
905-643-4241
Fax: 905-643-4427

Grey House Publishing Canada
#301, 555 Richmond St. W.
Toronto, ON M5V 3B1
Fax: 416-644-1904
866-433-4739
info@greyhouse.ca
www.greyhouse.ca
Firm Type: Distributing, Information Technology
Founded: 2007
Staff: 11
Products/Services/Areas of Expertise: Publishes & distributes the Canadian Environmental Resource Guide & associated mailing lists based on information in the directory; full text environmental reports from federal & provincial environment ministries; access to US federal agency environmental reportage
Financial Information:
Type of Ownership: Private
Domestic Markets:
National

Foreign Activity:
Worldwide

Greyline Instruments Inc.
16456 Sixsmith Dr.
Long Sault, ON K0C 1P0
613-938-8956
Fax: 613-938-4857
888-473-9546
info@greyline.com
www.greyline.com
Firm Type: Manufacturing
Founded: 1986
Staff: 3
Products/Services/Areas of Expertise: Measuring & monitoring equipment; flow & level monitoring/control instruments; products feature non-contacting sensors
Domestic Markets:
National
Foreign Activity:
Worldwide
International Branch(es):
Greyline Instruments Inc.
105 Water St.
Massena, NY USA
315-788-9500
Fax: 315-764-0419
info@greyline.com
E. Higginson

Greystone Energy Systems Inc.
150 English Dr.
Moncton, NB E1E 4G7
506-853-3057
Fax: 506-853-6014
800-561-5611
mail@greystoneenergy.com
www.greystoneenergy.com
Firm Type: Distributing, Manufacturing
Founded: 1983
Quality Environmental Management System(s): 9002
Products/Services/Areas of Expertise: Energy management systems
Financial Information:
Type of Ownership: Private
Contact(s):
William Robblee, President
robblee@greystoneenergy.com
Scott MacKinnon, Vice-President, Sales & Marketing
mackinnon.s@greystone.com
Lucas Steeves, Manager, Engineering

Griffin Laboratories Corporation
#2, 2550 Acland Rd.
Kelowna, BC V1X 7L4
250-765-3399
Products/Services/Areas of Expertise: Laboratory services; measuring & monitoring equipment; research & development

Griffiths Muecke Associates
5539B Young St.
Halifax, NS B3K 1Z7
902-423-8629
Fax: 902-421-1990
Firm Type: Management Consulting
Staff: 3
Products/Services/Areas of Expertise: Environmental & community planning, resources management, public consultation, mediation & public information; areas of expertise include waste management, tourism & recreation development, community economic development & socio-economic impact assessment
Domestic Markets:
New Brunswick, Newfoundland & Labrador, Nova Scotia, Prince Edward Island
Contact(s):
Lesley Griffiths, Partner

Gro-Bark (Ontario) Ltd.
Formerly: Scott's Composting Farm Inc.
#220F, 155 Frobisher Dr.
Waterloo, ON N2V 2E1
519-885-3411
Fax: 519-885-6742
888-476-2275
www.gro-bark.com

Firm Type: Scientific/Technical Services
Founded: 1981
Staff: 9
Products/Services/Areas of Expertise: Commercial & industrial composting in the Hamilton & Toronto areas
Financial Information:
Type of Ownership: Private
Revenue Sources: 100% Private Contracts
Domestic Markets:
Ontario
Contact(s):
William G. McKague, President

Canadian Branches:
Georgetown Branch
816 Mayfield Rd. West
Caledon, ON L7C 0Y6
905-846-1515

GroundTech Solutions
P.O. Box 1271 K
Toronto, ON M4P 3E5
416-410-3130
Fax: 416-410-1249
877-877-1862
info@groundtechsolutions.com
www.groundtechsolutions.com
Firm Type: Distributing

Products/Services/Areas of Expertise: Exclusive Canadian distributor for Geoprobe Systems, innovative drilling & soil sampling products for working with contaminants in soil; groundwater monitoring, prepack well screens, sludge testing, mechanical bladder pump, soil conductivity & CPT computers
Financial Information:
Type of Ownership: Private
Revenue Sources: 100% Private Contracts
Domestic Markets:
National
Contact(s):
Sven Dean, President
svendean@groundtechsolutions.com

Groupe Bau-Val
#2006, 210, boul Montarville
Boucherville, QC J4B 6T3
514-875-4270
legroupe@bauval.com
www.bauval.com
Firm Type: Manufacturing
Founded: 1954
Staff: 250
Products/Services/Areas of Expertise: Construction & road maintenance: crushing, paving, bagging, construction material, snow removal & recycling, construction material
Contact(s):
Jean-Luc Goyer, Contact

Groupe Berlie-Falco Inc.
Formerly: Berlie-Falco Technologies Inc.
1245, rue Industrielle
La Prairie, QC J5R 2E4
450-444-0566
Fax: 450-444-2227
turnkey@berliefalco.com
www.berliefalco.com
Firm Type: Engineering, Manufacturing
Founded: 1975
Staff: 75
Member of: Berlie Technologies Inc.; Falco Technologies Inc.
Products/Services/Areas of Expertise: Custom-built, skid-mounted process systems for a variety of applications; our systems are suitable in a variety of industries & settings including food & beverage, biotechnology, chemical, cosmetic, mining, municipal wastewater, pulp & paper, & pharmaceutical. We have expertise in automation & control, bulk solids handling, dewatering, fluid transport (pumps, fans, blowers, & compressors), heat exchanger systems, material storage (silos, hoppers, tanks), mixing, rotary drum drying, solid/gas & solid/liquid separation; & stirred tank reactors.
Recently Completed / Ongoing Projects: 600 USGM water filtration & PH dosing system for a beer plant in Nova Scotia; sludge dryer of 3,500 kg/hr near Washington, DC; fabrication & erection of a 500,000 USG biobed tank in Ontario
Financial Information:
Type of Ownership: Private
Revenue: Greater than $5 Million
Revenue Sources: 10% Municipals; 90% Private Contracts
Domestic Markets:
National
Foreign Activity:
South America, USA
Markets Sought:
Central America, South America,
Contact(s):
Marc Regnaud, Co-President
mregnaud@berliefalco.com
Bertrand Blanchette, Co-President
bblanchette@berliefalco.com
Thierry Simon, Vice-President, Sales & Marketing/Falco Technologies Inc.
tsimon@berliefalco.com
Stéphane Audy, Vice-President, Engineering/Berlie Technologies Inc.
saudy@berliefalco.com

Groupe Bouffard
Sanitaire et récupération
CP 114
75, rue Savard
Matane, QC G4W 3M9
418-562-3706
Fax: 418-562-6564
Contact(s):
Norbert Bouffard, Contact

Groupe Chagnon International
Formerly: Chagnon Ltd.
580, boul Lionel-Boulet
Varennes, QC J3X 1S5
450-652-9847
Fax: 450-652-7326
888-652-9847
sales@chagnon.qc.ca
www.chagnon.qc.ca
Firm Type: Manufacturing, Waste Management
Founded: 1961
Products/Services/Areas of Expertise: Roll-off trucks & tankers, rear-end & containers
Financial Information:
Type of Ownership: Private
Domestic Markets:
Alberta, British Columbia, Manitoba, New Brunswick, Nova Scotia, Ontario, Québec
Foreign Activity:
Africa, Asia, Central America, Mexico
Contact(s):
Roger Savard, President & CEO

Groupe Conseil Bellefeuille, Samson et Associés / BSA
107, rue St-Louis
Saint-Eustache, QC J7R 1X8
450-472-6020
Fax: 450-472-9716
bsaing@allstream.net
Firm Type: Engineering
Founded: 1984
Staff: 20
Quality Environmental Management System(s): 9001
Products/Services/Areas of Expertise: Engineering consulting services
Recently Completed / Ongoing Projects: Services to municipalities; building condominiums
Financial Information:
Type of Ownership: Private
Revenue: $1.5 Million - $3 Million
Revenue Sources: 50% Municipals; 50% Private Contracts
Domestic Markets:
Québec
Contact(s):
Bertrand Samson

Groupe Consulteaux Inc.
203, rue St-Charles
Vaudreuil-Dorion, QC J7V 2L4
450-455-1921
Fax: 450-455-1922
888-455-1921
groupeconsulteaux@consulteaux.com
www.consulteaux.com

Firm Type: Engineering, Scientific/Technical Services
Founded: 1986
Staff: 10
Products/Services/Areas of Expertise:
Geological/hydrogeological engineering; ground/surface water monitoring, treatment & operation
Financial Information:
Type of Ownership: Private
Domestic Markets:
National
Contact(s):
Ronald Piché, President & General Director

Canadian Branches:
Ste-Agathe-des-Monts
102, boul Morin
Sainte-Agathe-des-Monts, QC J8C 3K8
819-324-2000
Fax: 819-324-0319

Groupe Deschênes
#250, 3901, rue Jarry est
Montréal, QC H1Z 2G1
514-253-3110
Fax: 514-253-3666
info@groupedeschenes.com
www.groupedeschenes.com
Products/Services/Areas of Expertise: Distribution of plumbing & heating products, electrical & industrial supplies, fire protection products, refrigeration, air-conditioning, ventilation products, heating controls & related products; waterworks & sewer systems
Contact(s):
Jacques Deschênes, Chair
Martin Deschênes, President & CEO

Groupe DHB Inc.
651, boul Bégin
Saint-Anselme, QC G0R 2N0
418-885-9595
Fax: 418-885-4957
info@groupedhb.com
www.groupedhb.com
Products/Services/Areas of Expertise: Manufactures custom built tools or equipment for research programs

Groupe EnvirAqua
1925, rue Girouard ouest
Saint-Hyacinthe, QC J2S 3A5
450-773-5942
Fax: 450-773-9789
Products/Services/Areas of Expertise: Engineering consulting services; environmental consulting services
Contact(s):
Réal D'Anjou

Groupe GLD Inc., Experts-Conseils
Also Known As: GLD Inc.
#200, 11505, 1re av est
St-Georges, QC G5Y 7X3
418-228-8041
Fax: 418-228-8045
groupegld@gld.qc.ca
www.gld.qc.ca
Firm Type: Engineering, Scientific/Technical Services
Founded: 1960
Staff: 33
Products/Services/Areas of Expertise: Engineering consulting services; design & specifications; feasibility studies; process evaluation & selection; environmental baseline studies & impact assessments; environmental permitting, regulations & standards; energy recovery technology; HVAC products & systems; municipal solid waste consulting; waste disposal systems & equipment; waste quality assessment & treatment equipment; water & wastewater treatment
Financial Information:
Type of Ownership: Private
Revenue Sources: 15% Provincial; 60% Municipals; 25% Private Contracts
Domestic Markets:
Québec
Foreign Activity:
USA

Canadian Branches:
Beauce
#103, 1068, boul Vachon nord
Sainte-Marie, QC G6E 1M3

418-387-8191
Fax: 418-386-2967

Lac-Mégantic
4152, rue Laval
Lac-Mégantic, QC G6B 1B3
819-583-5110
Fax: 819-583-5991

Sainte-Marie
#103, 1017, boul Vachon nord
Sainte-Marie, QC G6E 1M3
418-387-8191
Fax: 418-386-2967
gldstm@gld.qc.ca

Groupe RSW inc. / RSW
Formerly: Rousseau Sauvé Warren Inc.
#500, 1010, de la Gauchetière ouest
Montréal, QC H3B 0A1
514-878-2621
Fax: 514-397-0085
rsw@rswinc.com
www.rswinc.com
Firm Type: Engineering
Founded: 1970
Staff: 300
Member of: Ordre des ingénieurs-consuls du Québec; Ordre des ingénieurs-consuls du Canada
Quality Environmental Management System(s): 9001
Products/Services/Areas of Expertise: Consulting engineering firms offering multidisciplinary professional services in the energy, environment, mining & infrastructure sectors; offers services specific to the hydroelectric & transmission line sectors
Financial Information:
Type of Ownership: Private
Domestic Markets:
British Columbia, Newfoundland & Labrador, Ontario, Québec
Foreign Activity:
Africa, Asia, Caribbean, Central America, China, Mexico, Former USSR, Vietnam
Contact(s):
Georges P. Dick, President/CEO
Jacques Mercier, Vice-President, Marketing & Business Development

Groupe S.M. International Inc.
Also Known As: SMi
433, rue Chabanel ouest, 12e étage
Montréal, QC H2N 2J8
514-982-6001
Fax: 514-982-6106
infosm@groupesm.com
www.groupesm.com
Firm Type: Engineering, Information Technology, Scientific/Technical Services
Founded: 1972
Staff: 400
Products/Services/Areas of Expertise: SMi integrates land planning management, sustainable development, resource protection & responsible management. Its services include: regional & urban planning; environmental management & planning; impact assessments; information systems; industrial siting; forest management & planning; water treatment & distribution; wastewater collection & treatment; irrigation & drainage systems; watershed management; solid & hazardous waste management; soil restoration; air pollution monitoring & control; remote sensing.
Foreign Activity:
Worldwide
Contact(s):
Bernard Poulin, President & CEO
bpoulin@groupesm.com
Guy Charbonneau, VP, Finance & Administration
gcharbonneau@groupesm.com
Lison Benarroch, VP, Strategic Development
lbenarroch@groupesm.com
Richard Breault, VP, Energy, Industry, Buildings
rbreault@groupesm.com
Gerard Fiot, VP, Middle East Operations
gfiot@groupesm.com

Canadian Branches:
Bécancour
3075, rue Nicolas-Perrot
Bécanour, QC G9H 3C1
819-294-1444
Fax: 819-294-1888

Drummondville
1175, rue Janelle
Drummondville, QC J2C 3E2
819-475-0550
Fax: 819-475-6930

Gatineau - Carrière
#101, 885, boul de la Carrière
Gatineau, QC J8Y 3Y7
819-779-5555
Fax: 819-775-9336

Gatineau - St-Joseph
#402, 490, boul St-Joseph
Gatineau, QC J8Y 3Y7
819-779-5555
Fax: 819-779-5550

Granby - Dufferin
#100, 35, rue Dufferin
Granby, QC J2G 4W5
450-372-6607
Fax: 450-372-8546

Granby - St-Jude sud
1, 34, rue St-Jude sud
Granby, QC J2J 2N4
450-360-0667
Fax: 450-360-0500

Laval
#480, 500, boul St-Martin
Laval, QC H7M 3Y2
450-662-6002
Fax: 450-662-9304

Longueil - Lac
2350, ch du Lac
Longueil, QC J4N 1G8
514-332-6001
Fax: 514-332-5066

Longueuil - Fernand-Lafontaine
2111, boul Fernand-Lafontaine
Longueil, QC J4G 2J4
450-651-0981
Fax: 450-651-9542

Lévis
#210, 1120, boul de la Rive-Sud
Lévis, QC G6W 5M6
418-839-6001

Montréal
6209, rue Marivaux
Montréal, QC H1P 3H6
514-789-2440
Fax: 514-789-2441

Québec
#116, 1200, av St-Jean-Baptiste
Québec, QC G2E 5E8
418-871-9330
Fax: 418-871-9343

Rigaud
268, ch de l'Anse, RR2
Rigaud, QC G2E 5E8
418-451-4255
Fax: 418-451-4255

Sainte-Agathe-des-Monts
1065, rue Principale est
Sainte-Agathe-des-Monts, QC J8C 1L7
819-326-8274
Fax: 819-326-8275

Shawinigan
#200, 612, 5e rue
Shawinigan, QC G9N 1E9
819-534-0404
Fax: 819-534-0034

Sherbrooke - Galt
740, rue Galt ouest, 2e étage
Sherbrooke, QC J1H 1Z3
819-566-8855
Fax: 819-566-0224

Sorel-Tracy
Édifice 69
1800, rue Émile-Bernard, 100e étage
Sorel-Tracy, QC J3R 0A6

450-743-1921
Fax: 450-743-8771

St-Jean-sur-Richelieu
#100, 109, rue Richelieu
St-Jean-sur-Richelieu, QC J3B 6X2
450-347-7888
Fax: 450-347-4444

St-Mathieu-de-Beloeil
3225, rue de l'Industrie
St-Mathieu-de-Beloeil, QC J3G 4S5
450-464-6806
Fax: 450-464-6806

Toronto
#205, 6205B Airport Rd.
Mississauga, ON L4V 1E3
905-677-9009
Fax: 905-677-9014

Trois-Rivières
#700, 500, Côte Richelieu
Trois-Rivières, QC G9A 2Z1
819-375-4401
Fax: 819-375-6294

Valleyfield
#225, 30, avenue du Centenaire
Valleyfield, QC J6S 5X4
450-373-3330
Fax: 450-373-5831

International Branch(es):
Algérie
5, rue Kaddouche Abdelkader, 3e étage, Ben-Aknoun
Alger Algérie
213-21-92-81-15
Fax: 213-21-92-82-08

Luxembourg
560, rue de Neudorf
Luxembourg Luxembou
352-451-451
Fax: 352-451-452-401

Saudi Arabia
ABT Building, 2nd Fl.
Al-Dammam Highway
Al-Khobar S Arabia
966-38876399
Fax: 966-38876388

Suisse
69, rue du Rhône, ch 1207
Genève Suisse
4122 700-3802
Fax: 4122 700-3803

USA
One Aventura Executive Center
#914, 209000 - 30th Ave. NE
Aventura, Florida USA
305-792-0015
Fax: 305-931-0279

United Arab Emirates
Building 295, Mezzanine 2
P.O. Box 91777
M. Bin Zayed, Mussaffah Shabiya Khalifa, ME-11
Abu Dhabi U.A.E.

Groupe Séguin
13200, boul Métropolitain est
Montréal, QC H1A 5K8
514-642-8422
Fax: 514-642-4912
info@groupeseguin.com
www.groupeseguin.com
Firm Type: Engineering, Scientific/Technical Services
Staff: 80
Products/Services/Areas of Expertise: Engineering consulting services; water & wastewater management services
Contact(s):
Michel Lalonde, President

Groupe SM inc.
Division de Groupe SM International inc.
740, rue Galt ouest, 2e étage
Sherbrooke, QC J1H 1Z3
819-566-8855
Fax: 819-566-0224

gfouquet@groupesm.com
www.groupesm.com
Firm Type: Engineering, Scientific/Technical Services
Staff: 550
Products/Services/Areas of Expertise: Engineering consulting services; environmental consulting services
Contact(s):
Guy Fouquet

Groupe Sodinco inc.
Formerly: Sodinco Experts Conseils inc.
#200, 3981, rue Mont-Royal
Saint-Hubert, QC J4T 2H4
450-926-1331
Fax: 450-926-1561
mecano@francomedia.qc.ca
Firm Type: Management Consulting, Engineering, Scientific/Technical Services, Waste Management
Founded: 1985
Staff: 7
Products/Services/Areas of Expertise: Site reclamation & remedial action; feasibility studies; construction management; water & wastewater consulting engineering; municipal engineering; process pumping & piping
Activities: Alternative method for small community sewage treatment & sludge drying bed
Recently Completed / Ongoing Projects: Waste treatment, Poland; water work, Guatemala
Financial Information:
Type of Ownership: Private
Revenue Sources: 5% nationwide; 10% Provincial; 60% Municipals; 25% Private Contracts
Domestic Markets:
Québec
Foreign Activity:
Central America, Eastern Europe, The Middle East, South America
Contact(s):
Claude Leduc, P.Eng., President
Jean-Louis Breton, P.Eng., Vice-President
Luc Lemay, Engineer

Groupe SOLROC
#100, 8225, rue Mayrand
Montréal, QC H4P 2C7
514-342-5855
Fax: 514-737-6541
www.solroc.com
Firm Type: Management Consulting, Engineering, Waste Management
Founded: 1981
Staff: 50
Quality Environmental Management System(s): 9001:2000
Products/Services/Areas of Expertise: With clients in Québec, Ontario, the Eastern U.S., & abroad, Le Groupe SOLROC provides multidisciplinary engineering & consulting services, including geotechnical studies, geological & hydro-geological assessments, civil engineering services, inspection & assessment of industrial, residential & commercial buildings, Phase I, II & III environmental assessments, remediation, solid & hazardous waste management & treatment, environmental compliance audits, materials testing & sampling, & laboratory services
Domestic Markets:
Ontario, Québec
Foreign Activity:
USA, Worldwide
Markets Sought:
USA
Contact(s):
Aimé Bensoussan, CEO

Groupe Stavibel Inc.
Formerly: JPL Consultant Inc.
150, rue Gamble ouest
Rouyn-Noranda, QC J9X 2R7
819-764-5181
Fax: 819-797-0158
stavibel-rn@stavibel.qc.ca
www.stavibel.qc.ca
Firm Type: Engineering
Founded: 1959
Products/Services/Areas of Expertise: Engineering; municipal foundation structure; mechanical & electrical engineering
Financial Information:
Type of Ownership: Private

Domestic Markets:
Québec
Foreign Activity:
USA
Canadian Branches:
Amos
762, de l'Industrie
Amos, QC J9T 4L9
819-732-8355
Fax: 819-732-0165
stavibel-am@stavibel.qc.ca

La Sarre
649-A, 2e rue est
La Sarre, QC J9Z 2Y9
819-333-1257
Fax: 819-333-1258
stavibel-ls@stavibel.qc.ca

Montréal
#510, 550, rue Sherbrooke ouest
Montréal, QC H3A 1B9
514-849-2432
Fax: 514-843-6561
stavibel-mtl@stavibel.qc.ca

Val-d'Or
1271, 7e rue
Val-d'Or, QC J9P 3S1
819-825-2233
Fax: 819-825-1322
stavibel-vd@stavibel.qc.ca
Gilles Brisson, Associé

Groupe Teknika
Formerly: Teknika HBA, Groupe HBA, Experts-Conseils
#200, 1441, boul René-Lévesque
Montréal, QC H3G 1T7
514-931-1080
Fax: 514-935-1645
877-283-5364
marketing@groupeteknika.com
www.groupeteknikahba.com
Firm Type: Engineering
Founded: 1928
Staff: 625
Quality Environmental Management System(s): 9001
Products/Services/Areas of Expertise: Engineering consulting services; policy implementation assistance; environmental impact assessment
Financial Information:
Type of Ownership: Private
Domestic Markets:
Québec
Foreign Activity:
Africa, Asia, South America
Canadian Branches:
Asbestos
601 boul Simoneau
Asbestos, QC J1T 4G7
819-879-6129
Fax: 819-879-6331
asbestos@hba.qc.ca

Drummondville
2555, rue Saint-Pierre
Drummondville, QC J2C 7Y2
819-471-3775
Fax: 819-478-8436
1-888-423-9118

Granby
30, rue Dufferin
Granby, QC J2G 4W6
450-378-3322
Fax: 450-378-6281

Montréal
4890, 5e Ave
Montréal, QC H2L 4C6
514-521-4290
Fax: 514-521-4637

Québec
#205, 5400, boul des Galeries
Québec, QC G2K 2B4
418-623-0598
Fax: 418-623-1636
hbaque@hba.qc.ca

Saint-Hyacinthe
5505, rue Trudeau, Local A
Saint-Hyacinthe, QC J2S 1H5
450-774-5280
Fax: 450-774-4498
1-800-665-5280

Saint-Jean-sur-Richelieu
#245, 100, rue Richelieu
Québec, QC J3B 6X3
450-346-8449
Fax: 450-346-9249

Sherbrooke
150, rue de Vimy
Sherbrooke, QC J1J 3M7
819-562-3871
Fax: 819-563-3663
1-800-567-6927

Sherbrooke (Shermont)
2605, rue Bonin
Sherbrooke, QC J1K 1C5
819-821-4373
Fax: 819-564-3938
1-800-567-6032

Trois-Rivières
3120, rue Bellefeuille
Trois-Rivières, QC G9A 5R5
819-379-9021
Fax: 819-376-1580
trois-rivieres@hba.qc.ca

Trois-Rivières (Shermont)
3120, rue Bellefeuille
Trois-Rivières, QC G9Z 5R5
819-376-1526
Fax: 819-376-1580
1-866-376-1526

Victoriaville
50, route de la Grande-Ligne
Victoriaville, QC G9P 6R9
819-758-8265
Fax: 819-758-6492

Groupe Tremca inc.
800, boul Pierre Tremblay
Iberville, QC J2X 4W8
450-346-4481
Fax: 450-346-7447
800-363-1458
info@tremca.com
www.tremca.com
Firm Type: Manufacturing
Staff: 100
Products/Services/Areas of Expertise: Manufactures landscaping products, precast concrete steps & slabs, site amenities, concrete pipes; noise absorptive wall system & architectural & structural elements
Financial Information:
Type of Ownership: Private
Domestic Markets:
Québec
Contact(s):
Michel Caron, Chair
Eric Caron, President & CEO

Groupe-Conseil TDA
26, boul Comeau
Baie-Comeau, QC G4Z 3A8
418-296-6711
Fax: 418-296-8971
gctda@globetrotter.qc.ca
www.gctda.ca
Firm Type: Engineering, Scientific/Technical Services
Founded: 1959
Staff: 40
Quality Environmental Management System(s): 9001
Products/Services/Areas of Expertise: Engineering consulting services

Grundfos Canada Inc.
2941 Brighton Rd.
Oakville, ON L6H 6C9
905-829-9533
Fax: 905-829-9512
800-644-9599

canada@grundfos.com
www.grundfos.ca
Firm Type: Distributing, Manufacturing
Founded: 1992
Staff: 51
Member of: Canadian Association of Pump Manufacturers, Canadian Institute of Plumbing & Heating, Hydronics Marketing Group
Products/Services/Areas of Expertise: Environmental pumps; groundwater pumps; hot water circulation pumps
Domestic Markets:
National
Foreign Activity:
Worldwide
Contact(s):
Simon Feddema, President, 905-491-6607
sfeddema@grundfos.com
Lew Parps, VP, Operations, 905-491-6608
lparps@grundfos.com
Grace D'Addio, Finance Manager, 905-491-6614
gdaddio@grundfos.com

Gryphon International Engineering Services Inc.
#404, 80 King St.
St Catharines, ON L2R 7G1
905-984-8383
Fax: 905-984-8394
gryphon@gryphoneng.com
www.gryphoneng.com
Firm Type: Engineering
Founded: 1990
Staff: 35
Products/Services/Areas of Expertise: Gryphon is an employee-owned firm that offers engineering design & consulting services in the thermal power & energy industry. Areas of expertise include: Power Generation & Cogeneration; Boilers & Steam Plants; Chilled-Water & Hot-Water Production; Electrical & Instrumentaion Systems; Utility Distribution Systems.
Domestic Markets:
Ontario
Foreign Activity:
Africa, The Middle East, USA
Contact(s):
Paul Durkin, P.Eng, President
pjdurkin@gryphoneng.com
Jim Noordermeer, P.Eng, Principal & Manager, Business Development & Projects
jnoord@gryphoneng.com
Dominic Au, P.Eng, Principal & Manager, Engineering
dau@gryphoneng.com

GSI Environnement Inc.
EnGlobe Corp.
1501, boul Lionel-Boulet
Varennes, QC J3X 1P7
450-929-4949
Fax: 450-929-1659
montreal@gsienv.ca
www.gsienv.ca
Firm Type: Engineering, Scientific/Technical Services, Waste Management
Founded: 1987
Staff: 209
Member of: Réseau Environnement; Environmental Regional Council of Estrie, Conseil régional de l'environnement de Montréal, Federation of Quebec Chambers of Commerce; Association Québecoise des industriels du Compostage
Products/Services/Areas of Expertise: Integrated management of solid & liquid waste, soil & contaminated water; restoration of contaminated sites, composting & beneficial reuse, leachate treatment systems, landfill management, sludge conditioning & dehydration, laboratory analysis, environmental management
Recently Completed / Ongoing Projects: Oily sludge treatment centres; wastewater treatment systems for communities & industries; biogas treatment system
Financial Information:
Type of Ownership: Private
Revenue: Greater than $5 Million
Domestic Markets:
National
Foreign Activity:
USA
Contact(s):
Emanuelle Landry, Contact
Alain Boisvert, Business Development Director

Canadian Branches:
Amos
213, 1ère avenue ouest
Amos, QC J9T 1V1
819-732-5675
Fax: 819-732-5648
amos@gsienv.ca

Québec
#100, 4495, boul Wilfrid-Hamel
Québec, QC G1P 2J7
418-872-4227
Fax: 418-872-0149
quebec@gsienv.ca

Saint-Henri - Les Composts du Québec
P.O. Box 488
415, ch Plaisance
St-Henri, QC G0R 3E0
418-822-2736
Fax: 418-882-2255
800-463-1030
composts@composts.com
www.gsienv.ca/en/services/products-category.php?cat=93

Guardian Industries Canada Corp.
Guardian Industries Corp.
Distribution Center
#100, 3380 Airway Dr.
Mississauga, ON L4V 1N7
905-677-4545
Fax: 905-677-4568
guardianbranding@guardian.com
www.guardian.com
Firm Type: Manufacturing
Founded: 1979
Staff: 110
Products/Services/Areas of Expertise: Glass fibre insulation
Domestic Markets:
Manitoba, New Brunswick, Nova Scotia, Ontario, Prince Edward Island, Québec
Foreign Activity:
USA

Canadian Branches:
Baie-St-Paul
Glass Fabrication Plant
63, ch St-Laurent
Baie-St-Paul, QC G3Z 2L5
418-435-6820

Rexdale
Glass Fabrication Plant
355 Attwell Drive
Rexdale, ON M9W 5C2
416-674-6945
Fax: 416-674-8576

Saint-Agapit
Glass Fabrication Plant
1236 rue Principal
Saint-Agapit, QC G0S 1Z0
418-888-5305

Saint-Apollinaire
Glass Fabrication Plant
288, rue Laurier
Saint-Apollinaire, QC G0S 2E0
418-881-2303
Fax: 418-881-2315

Shippagan - Vitrerie Novy Glass Ltee
Glass Fabrication Plant
P.O. Box 3293
415, rue 1ère
Shippagan, NB E8S 3H9
506-336-8202

Terrbonne - Thermos Rive Nord Inc.
Glass Fabrication Plant
835, boul Industriel
Terrbonne, QC J6Y 1V7
450-621-1333

Trois-Rivières - Industries Cover Inc.
Glass Fabrication Plant
2400, boul des Récollets
Trois-Rivières, QC G8Z 3X7
819-375-0835

Ville d'Anjou - Industries Cover Inc.
Glass Fabrication Plant
9300, boul Ray Lawson
Ville d'Anjou, QC H1J 1Y6
800-353-4460

Guelph Chemical Laboratories
Technology Centre
24 Corporate Ct.
Guelph, ON N1G 5G5
519-836-2313
Fax: 519-836-3273
info@chemisar.com
www.chemisar.com
Firm Type: Management Consulting, Scientific/Technical Services
Founded: 1978
Products/Services/Areas of Expertise: Comprehensive environmental testing, including: water, wastewater & soils testing by Ministry of Environment & EPA methods; all aspects of MISA testing & hazardous waste management; all aspects of air pollution measurement & compliance assessment; coal, coke & petroleum product analysis; research & development in support of services & technology development
Contact(s):
R.N. Pandey

Guertin Brothers Coatings and Sealants Ltd.
50 Panet Rd.
Winnipeg, MB R2J 0R9
204-237-0241
Fax: 204-233-5051
800-665-0340
pguertin@guertincoatings.com
www.guertinbros.com
Firm Type: Manufacturing
Founded: 1947
Staff: 55
Quality Environmental Management System(s): 9001
Products/Services/Areas of Expertise: Polymer: castable prepolymers; film laminating adhesives; industrial coatings: epoxies, polyurethanes, alkyas, acrylics, high solids, water reducible; sealants & caulking compounds: acrylic latex, butyl, thermoplastic rubber; moisture curepolyurethanes
Domestic Markets:
Alberta, British Columbia, Manitoba, Ontario, Québec, Saskatchewan
Foreign Activity:
Australia/New Zealand, Western Europe, USA
Contact(s):
Phil Guertin, President
Charles Guertin, Vice-President

Guild Contracting Specialists Inc.
21 McCurdy Ave.
Dartmouth, NS B2Y 3Z2
902-481-7933
Fax: 902-468-5052
Contact(s):
Joseph Josey, Manager

Guildline Instruments Limited / GIL
21 Gilroy St.
Smiths Falls, ON K7A 4S9
613-283-3000
Fax: 613-283-6082
800-310-8104
sales@guildline.ca
www.guildline.ca
Firm Type: Manufacturing
Founded: 1956
Staff: 25
Products/Services/Areas of Expertise: Precision electronic instruments for measuring electrical properties/temperature; temperature-controlled precision immersion baths; salinity
Recently Completed / Ongoing Projects: Delivered 80+ automated resistance measuring systems to the USAF
Financial Information:
Type of Ownership: Private
Revenue: $3 Million - $5 Million
Revenue Sources: 10% nationwide; 90% Private Contracts
Domestic Markets:
National
Foreign Activity:
Australia/New Zealand, Caribbean, Central America, China, Central Europe, Eastern Europe, Western Europe, The Middle

East, The Pacific Rim, South Africa, South America, Mexico, USA, Former USSR, United Kingdom, Vietnam
Contact(s):
Richard Timmons, President/CEO
Leona Peters, Coordinator, Sales
Andre Perras, Manager, Production

Guspro Inc.
280 Grand Ave. East
Chatham, ON N7L 4K1
519-352-4550
Fax: 519-352-7676
888-648-7776
guspro@guspro.com
www.guspro.com
Firm Type: Engineering, Manufacturing
Founded: 1932
Staff: 60
Products/Services/Areas of Expertise: Ovens for burning off waste product; paint removal; waste management
Financial Information:
Type of Ownership: Private
Revenue Sources: 10% Provincial; 90% Private Contracts
Domestic Markets:
National
Foreign Activity:
Central Europe, South America, Worldwide
Markets Sought:
China, South America, Vietnam
Contact(s):
Paul Sunnen, President
pauls@guspro.com
Les Herman, Manager, Finance & Administration
lesh@guspro.com
Dennis Pook, Manager, Domestic Sales & Marketing Export Sales
dennisp@guspro.com

H. Broer Equipment Sales and Service / BSL
Formerly: Broer Services Ltd.
702 Talbot St. West
Aylmer, ON N5H 2V1
519-773-3100
Fax: 519-773-2040
info@hbi.on.ca
www.hbi.on.ca
Products/Services/Areas of Expertise: Specializes in generators, rail equipment, compact construction equipment, diesel engines, industrial equipment parts & service
Domestic Markets:
Ontario
Contact(s):
Marcel Broer, General Manager
marcel@hbi.on.ca
S.D. Broer, Vice-President

H. Pickard & Associates
#106, 259 Brunswick St.
Fredericton, NB E3B 1G8
506-455-1574
Fax: 506-454-4593
888-892-7888
pickardh@nbnet.nb.ca
www.ashcat.com
Firm Type: Management Consulting
Founded: 1997
Staff: 2
Products/Services/Areas of Expertise: Health & safety consulting
Domestic Markets:
New Brunswick, Nova Scotia, Prince Edward Island
Contact(s):
Hubert E. Pickard, Owner

H.E. Bent Services Ltd.
Formerly: Eco Systems Limited
Bridgetown Development Centre
P.O. Box 670
#200, 16 Queen St.
Bridgetown, NS B0S 1C0
902-665-4200
800-565-2828
Firm Type: Distributing
Founded: 1992
Staff: 2
Member of: American Water Works Association; Water Environment Federation

Products/Services/Areas of Expertise: Water & wastewater treatment equipment & supplies; solid waste treatment equipment; computer software; laboratory products
Recently Completed / Ongoing Projects: Aeration systems, grinder; clarifier, mixers, blowers, polymer
Financial Information:
Revenue: $1.5 Million - $3 Million
Domestic Markets:
New Brunswick, Newfoundland & Labrador, Nova Scotia, Prince Edward Island
Foreign Activity:
Caribbean, Central America, South America, Mexico
Contact(s):
Henry Everett Bent, P.Eng., President/CEO

H.L. Blachford Ltd.
2323 Royal Windsor Dr.
Mississauga, ON L5J 1K5
905-823-3200
Fax: 905-823-9290
800-388-1857
www.blachford.ca
Firm Type: Manufacturing
Founded: 1921
Staff: 200
Member of: Chemistry Industry Association of Canada's
Member of: CCPA Responsible Care
Quality Environmental Management System(s): 9001; TS 1
EcoLogo Certified Products & Services: Quaker Quintolubric 822 fire resistant hydraulic fluid
Products/Services/Areas of Expertise: The company's products include: lubricants; specialty chemicals; rubber floor systems; acoustic & thermal insulation.
Ecological Note: Quaker Quintolubric 822 fire resistant hydraulic fluid
Financial Information:
Type of Ownership: Private
Domestic Markets:
National
Contact(s):
John Blachford, President
Karen Prapavessis, Manager, Finance & Administration
Dan Franson, Director, Sales & Marketing

H2Flow Equipment Inc.
#7, 470 North Rivermede Rd.
Concord, ON L4K 3R8
905-660-9775
Fax: 905-660-9744
info@h2flow.com
www.h2flow.com
Firm Type: Distributing
Founded: 2006
Staff: 4
Member of: Ontario Waterworks Association; Water Environment Association of Ontario
Member of: Ontario Pollution Control Equipment Association
Products/Services/Areas of Expertise: Sales, installation & service of Permastore glass-fused-to-steel tanks & covers; applications include aerobic & anaerobic reactors, digestecs, water storage tanks, towers, wastewater, slurry, leachate, clarifiers, etc.
Financial Information:
Type of Ownership: Private
Revenue Sources: 5% nationwide; 25% Provincial; 25% Municipals; 45% Private Contracts
Domestic Markets:
National
Contact(s):
Michael Albanese, P.Eng., President, Engineering Sales
michael@h2flow.com
Albert Wakim, Vice-President, Sales & Engineering
albert@h2flow.com
Darrin Hopper, Manager, National Sales
darrin@h2flow.com

H2O Innovation Inc.
#240, 420, boul Charest est
Québec, QC G1K 8M4
418-688-0170
Fax: 418-688-9259
888-688-0170
info@h2oinnovation.com
www.h2oinnovation.com
Firm Type: Scientific/Technical Services
Founded: 2000
Staff: 50

Products/Services/Areas of Expertise: Drinking water, desalination, water for manufacturing processes, wastewater treatment, maple products industry; piloting, sales, post sales services
Domestic Markets:
National
Contact(s):
Frédéric Dugré, President/CEO
Olivia Dion, Coordinator, Marketing
Jacques Labreque, Director, Sales

Habitat Studio & Workshop Ltd.
Formerly: Amerongen & Caverhill Builders Ltd.
#102, 10033 - 80 Ave.
Edmonton, AB T6E 2A2
780-433-1107
Fax: 780-432-0894
habitats@habitat-studio.com
www.habitat-studio.com
Firm Type: Manufacturing
Founded: 1993
Products/Services/Areas of Expertise: Conservation & environmentally friendly houses
Contact(s):
Peter Amerongen, President

Hagersville Recycling & Auto Wrecking Ltd.
P.O. Box 609
Indian Line Rd., RR#2
Hagersville, ON N0A 1H0
905-768-1116
Fax: 905-768-1339
surety@compuserve.com
Products/Services/Areas of Expertise: Handling & processing all types of ferrous & non-ferrous materials; brokerage of steel & metal items
Recently Completed / Ongoing Projects: Established auto salvage yard for parts & vehicles
Domestic Markets:
National
Foreign Activity:
USA
Markets Sought:
Eastern Europe, Western Europe
Contact(s):
Harold Goldblatt, President
Jerry Goldblatt, Non Ferrous Manager
Ed Gaspar, Yard Manager

Hakmet Ltd.
41, rue du Moulin
Grenville, QC J0V 1J0
819-242-2400
Fax: 819-242-4066
800-361-2288
hakmet@hakmet.com
www.hakmet.com
Firm Type: Distributing, Manufacturing
Founded: 1976
Staff: 20
Products/Services/Areas of Expertise: Wood chippers; firewood processors; crushers; sawmills; harvesters; loaders; trailers
Financial Information:
Type of Ownership: Private
Domestic Markets:
National
Foreign Activity:
South America, USA,
Contact(s):
Mika Hakala, President

Haley Industries Ltd.
634 Magnesium Rd.
Haley, ON K0J 1Y0
613-432-8841
Fax: 613-432-0743
www.haley.on.ca
Firm Type: Manufacturing
Founded: 1952
Quality Environmental Management System(s): 9002
Products/Services/Areas of Expertise: Magnesium, aluminum metal coating for the aerospace industry
Financial Information:
Type of Ownership: Publicly Traded
Domestic Markets:
National

Products & Services Buyer's Guide

Foreign Activity:
Worldwide
Contact(s):
Peter Clark, Vice-President & General Manager
Randy Joe, Director, Sales & Marketing

Halford Pallet Recyclers Ltd.
8629 - 126 Ave.
Edmonton, AB T5B 1G8
780-474-4989
Fax: 780-477-3489
Firm Type: Distributing, Manufacturing
Founded: 1997
Staff: 3
Products/Services/Areas of Expertise: Reconditioned & used wooden pallets
Financial Information:
Type of Ownership: Private
Revenue: Less than $50,000
Revenue Sources: 100% Private Contracts
Domestic Markets:
Alberta
Contact(s):
Jeff McNish, Manager

Halifax C&D Recycling
16 Mills Dr.
Goodwood, NS B3T 1P3
902-876-8644
Fax: 902-876-1878
www.halifaxcdrecycling.ca
Firm Type: Waste Management
Founded: 1995
Staff: 25
Products/Services/Areas of Expertise: The company accepts construction debris materials for transfer processing & disposal.
Domestic Markets:
Nova Scotia
Contact(s):
Dan Chassie, President
Lee-Anne Chassie, General Manager
lchassie@halifaxcdrecycling.ca
Chris Lawrence, Yard Supervisor, Halifax
Ken Jagoe, Yard Supervisor, Dartmouth

Hallmark Insurance Brokers Ltd.
#100, 4 Lansing Sq.
Toronto, ON M2J 5A2
416-492-4070
Fax: 416-492-4321
800-492-4070
hib@hallmarkins.com
www.hallmarkins.com
Firm Type: Financial
Founded: 1948
Staff: 75
Products/Services/Areas of Expertise: Insurance brokers in the business of protecting those involved in waste management services
Contact(s):
Gordon C. McCauley, Chair
John Walters, President
john.walters@hallmarkins.com
James Broad, CEO
jbroad@hallmarkins.com
Ubey Sangarapillai, Manager, Finance
ubey@hallmarkins.com

Halltech Environmental Inc.
129 Watson Rd. South
Guelph, ON N1L 1E4
519-766-4568
Fax: 519-766-0729
sales@htex.com
www.htex.com
Firm Type: Distributing, Manufacturing, Scientific/Technical Services
Founded: 1991
Staff: 6
Products/Services/Areas of Expertise: Halltech is a manufacturer & distributor of products for environmental research. Services & products include: standard & customized limnology equipment; soil, water & air sampling, monitoring & analysis instrumentation; sales, training & support of Global Positioning Systems; chromatography & laboratory supplies; absorbents & remediation products. Other operating divisions of the company are: Exploration Outfitters, Halltech Atmospheric Systems, Halltech Agricultural GPS, & Halltech Aquatic Research Inc.
Domestic Markets:
National
Foreign Activity:
Worldwide
Contact(s):
Murray K. Hall, President

Hamilton Community Energy / HCE
Hamilton Hydro Services Inc.
79 Bay St. North
Hamilton, ON L8R 3P8
905-317-4595
Fax: 905-317-4775
contact@hamiltonce.com
www.hamiltonce.com
Products/Services/Areas of Expertise: HCE is a utilities company operating a district heating plant that uses cogeneration heat & power technology to produce & supply thermal energy.
Recently Completed / Ongoing Projects: Geo exchange & solar thermal technologies
Ecological Note: Energy efficiency heating/cooling systems for building(s)
Domestic Markets:
Ontario
Contact(s):
Robert Desnoyers, President, 905-317-4722
rdesnoyers@hamiltonce.com
Ron Harten, General Manager, 905-521-4903
ron.harten@hamiltonce.com

Hammond Manufacturing
394 Edinburgh Rd. North
Guelph, ON N1H 1E5
519-822-2960
Fax: 519-822-0715
ca-info@hammondmfg.com
www.hammondmfg.com
Firm Type: Manufacturing
Founded: 1917
Staff: 500
Quality Environmental Management System(s): 9002
Products/Services/Areas of Expertise: Electrical enclosures & electronic racks
Contact(s):
Robert F. Hammond, Chair & CEO
D.R. Williams, Vice-President, Finance

HAMON Custodis-Cottrell Canada, Inc.
Formerly: Research-Cottrell (Canada) Ltd.
#2, 23 West Beaver Creek Rd.
Richmond Hill, ON L4B 1K4
905-771-0234
Fax: 905-771-9730
800-423-9011
services.hccanada@hamonusa.com
www.hamon.com
Products/Services/Areas of Expertise: Air pollution control
Contact(s):
Andre Grondin, Region Manager

Hamworthy-Peabody Combustion Canada Inc.
Formerly: Peabody Engineering Canada
#36B, 360 Guelph St.
Georgetown, ON L7G 4B5
905-877-2222
Fax: 905-877-1985
sales@hamworthy-peabody.com
www.hamworthy-peabody.com
Firm Type: Manufacturing
Founded: 1963
Staff: 2
Member of: Canadian Boiler Society; Canadian Institute of Energy
Quality Environmental Management System(s): 9001
Products/Services/Areas of Expertise: Combustion & related solutions for the industrial & utility markets
Financial Information:
Type of Ownership: Foreign-owned
Revenue: Greater than $5 Million
Domestic Markets:
National
Foreign Activity:
Central America, South America, USA
Contact(s):
Lawrence Berry, President
lberry@hamworthy-peabody.com
International Branch(es):
Hamworthy Peabody Combustion Inc.
70 Shelton Technology Centre
Shelton, CT USA
203-922-1199
Fax: 203-922-8866
1-877-732-2639
sales@hamworthy-peabody.com

Hanna Instruments Canada Inc.
3156, boul Industriel
Laval, QC H7L 4P7
450-629-1444
Fax: 450-629-3335
800-842-6629
info@hannacan.com
www.hannacan.com
Firm Type: Distributing, Manufacturing
Founded: 1991
Staff: 12
Products/Services/Areas of Expertise: Analyses of water, hydroponic aquaculture, food, greenhouse, maple syrup, municipal environment, pool & spas, laboratory waste water, water purification
Financial Information:
Type of Ownership: Private
Revenue: $3 Million - $5 Million
Contact(s):
Alexander Bernier-Monzon, Assistant, Marketing, 450/649-1444
marketing@hannacan.com

Hanna Paper Fibres Ltd.
70 Addiscott Ct.
Markham, ON L3R 9Y8
905-475-9844
Fax: 905-475-5537
markham@hannapaper.com
www.hannapaper.com
Firm Type: Waste Management
Founded: 1977
Staff: 75
Products/Services/Areas of Expertise: Recycling of fine paper; confidential document destruction service
Financial Information:
Type of Ownership: Private
Domestic Markets:
Nova Scotia, Ontario
Foreign Activity:
Western Europe, USA

Canadian Branches:
Mississauga
#1, 1111 Tristar Dr.
Mississauga, ON L5T 1W5
905-564-7260
Fax: 905-564-7454
mississauga@hannapaper.com

St-Joseph-De-Beauce
760, av Guy-Poulin
Saint-Joseph-de-Beauce, QC G0S 2V0
514-397-5859
Fax: 514-397-6047

St-Laurent
7500, Côte-de-Liesse est
Montréal, QC H4T 1E7
514-739-4446
Fax: 514-731-3846

International Branch(es):
Connecticut
718 North Colony Rd.
Wallingford, CT USA
203-265-2644
Fax: 203-265-2676
jkiernan@hannapaper.com
Jim Kiernan

Massachusetts
31 Suffolk Rd.
Mansfield, MA USA
508-339-3210
Fax: 508-337-3355
jjnelson@hannapaper.com
Joe Jelson

New York
475 Ludwig Ave.
Buffalo, NY USA
716-891-9312
Fax: 716-891-4710
buffalo@hannapaper.com

Ohio
4287 Dues Dr.
Cincinnati, OH USA
513-860-5060
Fax: 513-860-2010

Hanson Pressure Pipe
Formerly: Lafarge Pressure Pipe
5337 Bethesda
Stouffville, ON L4A 7X3
905-640-5151
Fax: 905-640-5154
info@hansonpipeandprecast.com
www.hansonpipeandprecast.com
Products/Services/Areas of Expertise: Water handling equipment
Contact(s):
Bob Hoppe, General Manager
Martin Doran, Sales Manager

Happy Harry's Used Building Material
1639B Cary Ave.
Kelowna, BC V1X 2C1
250-862-3204
Fax: 250-862-3215
info@happyharry.com
www.happyharry.com
Products/Services/Areas of Expertise: Recycler of building material
Contact(s):
Tom Bohna, CEO, Operations/Sales

Canadian Branches:
Burlington
4128 South Service Rd.
Burlington, ON L7L 4X5

Digby
366 Hwy. 303
Digby, NS B0V 1A0

Mississauga
110 Derry Rd. West
Mississauga, ON L5M 2E5

Sackville
20 Bulmer Lane
Sackville, NB E4L 3R4

Vernon
5201 - 27th St.
Vernon, BC V1T 6L2
250-717-7488
Fax: 250-769-1290

Westville
5430 Hwy. 104
Westville, NS B0K 2A0

Harbour Metal Recycling Ltd.
191 Joseph Zatzman Dr.
Dartmouth, NS B3B 1M5
902-468-6787
Fax: 902-468-1347
recycle@ns.aliantzinc.ca
Firm Type: Waste Management
Founded: 1991
Staff: 4
Products/Services/Areas of Expertise: Metals recycling
Domestic Markets:
Nova Scotia
Contact(s):
Doug Conrad, Manager

Harbour Remediation & Transfer Inc.
97 Commissioners St.
Toronto, ON M5A 3V9
416-406-0987
Fax: 416-406-0476
info@hrandt.com
www.hrandt.com
Products/Services/Areas of Expertise: Spills/clean-up planning; soil remediation

Hardy Filtration
Formerly: Filt-Mes Inc.
3360, boul Royal
Trois-Rivières, QC G9A 4M3
819-373-7400
Fax: 819-373-7341
info@hardyfiltration.com
www.hardyfiltration.com
Contact(s):
Réjean Hardy, Contact

Hardy Stevenson & Associates / HSA
364 Davenport Rd.
Toronto, ON M5R 1K6
416-944-8444
Fax: 416-944-0900
877-267-7794
hsa@hardystevenson.com
www.hardystevenson.com
Firm Type: Management Consulting
Founded: 1990
Staff: 45
Member of: Economic Developers Council; Canadian Standards Association; Professional Engineers of Ontario; Association of Business Communicators
Products/Services/Areas of Expertise: Environmental facilitation, assists clients involved in project approvals, particularly public approvals that have the potential for public concern; assesses potential socio-economic impacts, facilitates meetings; completes land-use & environmental planning studies & designs; implements public consultation programs; familiar with projects in various sectors including forestry, landfills, highways, roadway expansions, nuclear energy & waste, natural gas, transmission lines, commercial & housing development
Recently Completed / Ongoing Projects: Successful approval of Conservation Plan, Oak Ridges Moraine, ON; 2010 Olympic Bid Social Impact Assessment, Vancouver, BC; Peer review of nuclear waste remediation project, Port Granby, Port Hope; Wastewater treatment plant public consultation & communication, Lakeview
Financial Information:
Type of Ownership: Private
Revenue: $500,000 - $1.5 Million
Revenue Sources: 10% nationwide; 10% Provincial; 50% Municipals; 30% Private Contracts
Domestic Markets:
Ontario, Yukon Territory
Foreign Activity:
The Pacific Rim
Markets Sought:
South America
Contact(s):
David R. Hardy, Principal
Mark Stevens, Senior Associate
Charlotte Young, Senior Associate
Dave Schulman, Senior Associate
Ron Corbett, Senior Associate
John Murray, Senior Associate

Harold Marcus Ltd.
15124 Longwoods Rd. (Hwy. 2)
Bothwell, ON N0P 1C0
519-695-3734
Fax: 519-695-2249
www.haroldmarcus.com
Firm Type: Waste Management
Founded: 1946
Staff: 150
Products/Services/Areas of Expertise: With its fleet of 230 trailers & 130 power units, the company transports waste & recyclable products throughout North America in tank, box van, roll off, dump trailers. It also provides assistance in external emergency situations for industrial & government services.
Financial Information:
Type of Ownership: Private
Domestic Markets:
National
Foreign Activity:
USA
Contact(s):
Denis Marcus, President
John Scott, Sales Manager
Randy Badiuk, Manager, Compliance & Safety

Canadian Branches:
Montréal Office
529, boul du Curé-Boivin
Boisbriand, QC J7G 2A8
450-430-1770
Fax: 450-430-5456
Kevin Healey, Directeur régional

Sarnia Office
30 Indian Rd. South
Sarnia, ON N7T 3W1
519-337-5979

International Branch(es):
USA Office
14040 South Parnell Ave.
Riverdale, IL USA
708-201-7733
Fax: 708-201-1133

Harris & Roome Supply Limited
P.O. Box 9078 A
3600 Joseph Howe Dr.
Halifax, NS B3K 5M7
902-457-8730
Fax: 902-457-1558
www.graybarcanada.com
Firm Type: Distributing
Founded: 1920
Staff: 275
Quality Environmental Management System(s): 9001
Products/Services/Areas of Expertise: Measuring & monitoring equipment; energy-efficient lighting; recycling of batteries; remote sensing & image analysis; computer systems
Financial Information:
Type of Ownership: Private
Domestic Markets:
New Brunswick, Newfoundland & Labrador, Nova Scotia, Prince Edward Island
Contact(s):
John Moore, Vice-President & General Manager

Canadian Branches:
Bathurst
P.O. Box 776
1765 Connolly Ave.
Bathurst, NB E2A 3Z6
506-548-2922
Fax: 506-546-1517
bmazerolle@graybarcanada.com
Robert Mazerolle, Manager

Bridgewater
P.O. Box 356
108 Logan Rd.
Bridgewater, NS B4V 2W9
902-543-9155
Fax: 902-543-5137
cboutilier@graybarcanada.com
Cecil Boutilier, Manager

Charlottetown
13 Walker Dr.
Charlottetown, PE C1A 8S5
902-566-1404
Fax: 902-566-4065
pherritt@graybarcanada.com
Perry Herritt, Manager

Corner Brook
P.O. Box 762
356 O'Connell Dr.
Corner Brook, NL A2H 6G7
709-632-7315
Fax: 709-632-2451
aparsons@graybarcanada.com
Albert Parsons, Manager

Dartmouth
P.O. Box 935
260 Brownlow Ave.
Dartmouth, NS B2Y 3Z6
902-468-6665
Fax: 902-468-2696
omcloughlin@graybarcanada.com
O'Shein McLoughlin, Manager

Products & Services Buyer's Guide

Florenceville
P.O. Box 432
16647 Rte. 2
Florenceville, NB E7L 1Y9
506-392-6084
Fax: 506-392-8314
cbasque@graybarcanada.com
Peter Horncastle, Manager

Fredericton
P.O. Box 396 A
668 Prospect St. West
Fredericton, NB E3B 4Z9
506-458-8265
Fax: 506-452-9753
djustason@graybarcanada.com
Don Justason, Manager

Grand Falls-Windsor
P.O. Box 417
4 Bayley St.
Grand Falls-Windsor, NL A2A 2J8
709-489-4161
Fax: 709-489-4424
gsmith@graybarcanada.com
Gordon Smith, Manager

Halifax
P.O. Box 9078 A
3600 Joseph Howe Dr.
Halifax, NS B3K 5M7
902-443-8311
Fax: 902-443-5171
mmiller@graybarcanada.com
Mike Miller, Manager

Kentville
9 Roscoe Dr.
Kentville, NS B4N 3V7
902-678-2800
Fax: 902-679-1997
mmalley@graybarcanada.com
Mark Malley, Manager

Moncton
385 Edinburgh Dr.
Moncton, NB E1E 2L2
506-853-8188
Fax: 506-859-8109
jcrozier@graybarcanada.com
Jim Crozier

New Glasgow
P.O. Box 695
136 Terra Cotta Dr.
New Glasgow, NS B2H 5G2
902-755-4673
Fax: 902-752-3881
trichardson@graybarcanada.com
Terry Richardson, Manager

Saint John
P.O. Box 2480
300 Charlotte St.
Saint John, NB E2L 3V9
506-634-2094
Fax: 506-634-8018
iallen@graybarcanada.com
Ian Allen, Manager

St. John's Branch
P.O. Box 8626 A
47 Pippy Pl.
St. John's, NL A1B 3T1
709-722-6161
Fax: 709-722-8886
abarrett@harrisroome.com
Alvin Barrett, Manager

Sydney
P.O. Box 159
1100 Upper Prince St.
Sydney, NS B1P 5P6
902-564-5504
Fax: 902-562-4536
drose@graybarcanada.com
Dave Rose, Manager

Truro
45 Polymer Rd.
Truro, NS B2N 6T8
902-893-4251
Fax: 902-893-4806
bthompson@graybarcanada.com
Brycen Thompson, Manager

Wabush Branch
P.O. Box 1049
4 First St.
Wabush, NL A0R 1B0
709-282-3555
Fax: 709-282-3554
fcritch@graybarcanada.com
Felix Critch, Manager

Yarmouth
P.O. Box 247
6 Industry Ave.
Yarmouth, NS B5A 4B2
902-742-6771
Fax: 902-742-0246
scleveland@graybarcanada.com
Scott Cleveland, Manager

Harris Industrial Testing
1320 Ashdale Rd., RR#1
Mount Uniacke, NS B0N 1Z0
902-757-0232
Fax: 902-757-0973
hits@ns.sympatico.ca
www3.ns.sympatico.ca/hits
Firm Type: Scientific/Technical Services
Founded: 1990
Staff: 3
Products/Services/Areas of Expertise: Aquatic toxicity testing
Recently Completed / Ongoing Projects: Compliance monitoring
Financial Information:
Type of Ownership: Private
Revenue Sources: 1% nationwide; 1% Provincial; 98% Private Contracts
Domestic Markets:
New Brunswick, Newfoundland & Labrador, Nova Scotia, Ontario, Prince Edward Island
Foreign Activity:
USA
Contact(s):
Gary Harris, President
hits@ns.sympatico.ca

Harry Gamble Shipyard
Also Known As: Gamble Shipyard
10 Patterson St.
Port Dover, ON N0A 1N0
519-583-2111
Firm Type: Manufacturing
Founded: 1924
Staff: 7
Products/Services/Areas of Expertise: Hydraulic suction dredges; marine contracting; rebuilding Detroit diesel engines
Domestic Markets:
Ontario
Foreign Activity:
USA
Markets Sought:
Western Europe, South America
Contact(s):
Harry Gamble, Owner
Peggy Gamble Scruton, OFC Manager

Hassco Industries Inc.
Formerly: Hassan Steel Fabricators Ltd.
223 Ashland Ave.
London, ON N5W 4E3
519-451-3100
Fax: 519-451-3102
800-668-0814
info@hassco.ca
Firm Type: Manufacturing
Founded: 1947
Staff: 18
Products/Services/Areas of Expertise: Steel above & below ground storage tanks & containment units for petroleum products, chemicals & waste products, single & double wall; oil/water separators
Financial Information:
Type of Ownership: Private
Revenue Sources: 2% nationwide; 2% Provincial; 1% Municipals; 95% Private Contracts
Domestic Markets:
National
Foreign Activity:
USA
Contact(s):
David A. Hassan, President
Ahmed Hassan, Manager, Marketing

Hatch Ltd.
Formerly: Hatch Associates Ltd.
2800 Speakman Dr.
Mississauga, ON L5K 2R7
905-855-7600
Fax: 905-855-8270
www.hatch.ca
Firm Type: Management Consulting, Engineering
Founded: 1955
Staff: 4000
Quality Environmental Management System(s): 9001
Products/Services/Areas of Expertise: Secondary resource processing; environmental regulations & standards; environmental audits; hazardous & non-hazardous wastewater treatment; mine tailings; plant retrofit consulting; noise & vibration studies; field sampling & monitoring; soil remediation; environmental strategy & management; gas handling/clean-up systems
Domestic Markets:
National
Foreign Activity:
Africa, Asia, Australia/New Zealand, Western Europe, South America, USA
Contact(s):
Kurt A. Strobele, President & CEO

Canadian Branches:
Hamilton
500 Sherman Ave. North
Hamilton, ON L8L 8J6
905-543-8555
Fax: 905-312-6465

Montréal
#200, 5, Place Ville-Marie
Montréal, QC H3B 2G2
514-861-0583
Fax: 514-397-1651
Roger Urquhart

Sorel-Tracy
3220, boul St-Louis
Sorel-Tracy, QC J3R 5P8
450-743-2763
Fax: 450-743-1480

Sudbury
Notre Dame Business Complex
#ND 255, 40 Elm St.
Sudbury, ON P3C 1S8
705-688-0250
Fax: 705-688-0244

Vancouver
Oceanic Plaza
#400, 1066 West Hastings St.
Vancouver, BC V6E 3X2
604-689-5767
Fax: 604-689-3918

Hatfield Group
Also Known As: Hatfield Consultants Ltd.
#201, 1571 Bellevue Ave.
West Vancouver, BC V7V 1A6
604-926-3261
Fax: 604-926-5389
hcp@hatfieldgroup.com
www.hatfieldgroup.com
Firm Type: Scientific/Technical Services
Founded: 1974
Staff: 28
Member of: Canadian Environmental Industry Association; World Aquaculture Society; Aquaculture Association of Canada; Association of Professional Biologists of BC
Products/Services/Areas of Expertise: Fisheries, aquaculture; agriculture; environmental impact assessments; feasibility studies; project management; pollution control; marine/coastal management; human resource development institutional strengthening; GIS/remote sensing

Financial Information:
Type of Ownership: Private
Revenue Sources: 40% nationwide; 15% Provincial; 5% Municipals; 40% Private Contracts
Domestic Markets:
Alberta, British Columbia, Northwest Territories, Yukon Territory
Foreign Activity:
Asia, South America, USA
Markets Sought:
Asia
Contact(s):
Thomas Boivin, President/Senior Environmental Biologist
Grant Bruce, Vice-President/Senior Chemist

Canadian Branches:
Fort McMurray
8542B Franklin Ave.
Fort McMurray, AB T9H 2J4
780-743-4290
Fax: 780-715-1164

International Branch(es):
Bangkok
66Q House, Asoke Bldg., 12th Fl.
Sukhumvit 21 Rd., 12th Fl., Klongtoey
Bangkok Thailand
-662-264-2064
Fax: -662-264-2074

Indonesia
LIPI Building, 3rd Floor
Jl. Ir. H. Juanda No. 18
Bogor IDN
-(62 251)-8324-487
Fax: -(62 251)-8340-

Santiago
IICL-Puma
Marchant Pereira No. 668 Providencia
Santiago Chile
-(56 2) 204 1900
Fax: -(56 2) 204 765

Haul-All Equipment Ltd.
4115 - 18th Ave. North
Lethbridge, AB T1H 5G1
403-328-7788
Fax: 403-328-9956
888-428-5255
sales@haulall.com
www.haulall.com
Firm Type: Manufacturing
Member of: National Recycling Coalition; Solid Waste Association of North America
Products/Services/Areas of Expertise: Designs & manufactures recycling containers, collection vehicles & transfer stations; develops waste management & recycling systems
Financial Information:
Type of Ownership: Private
Domestic Markets:
National
Foreign Activity:
Australia/New Zealand, Central America, China, The Pacific Rim, South America, USA, Vietnam
Contact(s):
Dennis Neufeldt, President
Susan Bailey, Marketing Director

Hayward Gordon Ltd.
5 Brigden Gate
Halton Hills, ON L7G 0A3
905-693-8595
Fax: 905-693-1452
info@haywardgordon.com
www.haywardgordon.com
Firm Type: Distributing, Manufacturing
Founded: 1952
Staff: 80
Member of: Water Environment Federation, Canadian Association of Mining Equipment &Services for Export, Pulp & Paper Technical Association of Canada, Ontario Pollution Control Equipment Association, American Water Works Association
Products/Services/Areas of Expertise: Solids handling pumps including: vortex, screw centrifugal, chopper; Process mixers including: statics, portable, top entry, side entry; Systems: polymer, chemical feed, volumetric feeders, starch cookers, pump/mixer & tank, filtration metering systems, mineral dispersion & wetting systtems; Hayward Gordon provides single-source design, manufacture & start-up for custom engineered pumping systems; based on process & applications specifications will produce P&ID's, design the system & source all components, you will receive a skidded, tested & functional system, custom designed to specific applications; requirements completed with pumps, piping, controls & instrumentation; serving Water & Wastewater (municipal/industrial), Food & Beverage, Pharmaceutical, Mining, Pulp & Paper, Automotive, Steel, Oil & Petroleum, Chemical & related industries, Worldwide
Financial Information:
Type of Ownership: Private
Domestic Markets:
National
Foreign Activity:
Worldwide
Contact(s):
John Hayward, President
Susan Schumacher, Marketing Specialist
Brent McConomy, Sales Director, National

Canadian Branches:
Calgary
#8, 6143 - 4th St. SE
Calgary, AB T2H 2H9
403-253-2737
Fax: 403-253-1353
calgary@haywardgordon.com
Tom Stiles

Montréal
Blackburn
16755, boul Hymus
Kirkland, QC H9H 3L4
514-697-6445
Fax: 514-697-1164
montreal@haywardgordon.com
, Cliff

Vancouver
166 Riverside Dr.
North Vancouver, BC V7H 1T9
604-986-8764
Fax: 604-986-8794
pacific@haywardgordon.com
Steve Evans

Hazard Alert Training & Supplies Canada Inc. / HATSCAN
4940 - 87th St.
Edmonton, AB T6E 5W3
780-466-6960
Fax: 780-466-6048
800-561-2319
contact@hatscan.com
www.hatscan.com
Firm Type: Information Technology
Founded: 1988
Staff: 8
Products/Services/Areas of Expertise: The company offers a suite of published products in areas of: OH&S & EHS training; customized training programs for WHMIS, TDG; environmental compliance; spill response; waste management; accident investigation; due diligence; safety inspections; WHMIS computer-assisted training program; EHS compliance; OH&S & WCB claims management. In May 2009, the company was acquired & is now published by Carswell, www.carswell.com.
Financial Information:
Type of Ownership: Private
Domestic Markets:
National
Contact(s):
Reg Ferguson, President

Hazard Control Systems Inc.
34 Orkney Cres.
London, ON N5X 3R7
519-433-9843
Fax: 519-433-9922
wayne.macleod@sympatico.ca
Firm Type: Management Consulting
Founded: 1991
Staff: 1
Products/Services/Areas of Expertise: Compliance management consultant, auditor & trainer for environmental health & safety subjects including Transportation of Dangerous Goods & ISO 14000, OHSAS 18001
Domestic Markets:
National
Foreign Activity:
USA
Contact(s):
Wayne MacLeod, M.Eng,CET,CTM,CEA,EMS,OHS, President

Hazardous Materials Management Magazine
Also Known As: CHMM Inc.
#800, 12 Concorde Pl.
Toronto, ON M3C 4J2
416-442-5600
Fax: 416-510-5133
sales@hazmag.com
www.hazmatmag.com
Firm Type: Information Technology
Founded: 1989
Staff: 10
Member of: Canadian Business Press; Environmental Services Association of Alberta
Products/Services/Areas of Expertise: Magazine publishers focusing on North American pollution prevention & control in Canada; information technology & communications services; database management; marketing services; internet services; Solid Waste & Recycling Magazine; direct mail post cards
Financial Information:
Type of Ownership: Private
Domestic Markets:
National
Foreign Activity:
Mexico, USA
Contact(s):
Brad O'Brien, Publisher
Guy Crittenden, Editor

Hazco Environmental Services Ltd.
#103, 3355 - 114th Ave. SE
Calgary, AB T2Z 0K7
403-297-0444
Fax: 403-253-3188
800-667-0444
info@hazco.com
www.hazco.com
Firm Type: Waste Management
Founded: 1989
Staff: 175
Products/Services/Areas of Expertise: Environmental contracting; site remediation; spill clean-up; hazardous & special waste management; transportation; construction & material handling expertise
Recently Completed / Ongoing Projects: Removal, transport & disposal of spill impacted soils from various locations, Manitoba; construction of new bio-remediation pad & disposal cell, Cowley, AB; decontamination of a warehouse through the detailed removal of free mercury, Winnipeg, MB
Financial Information:
Type of Ownership: Private
Domestic Markets:
Alberta, British Columbia, Manitoba, Northwest Territories, Saskatchewan
Contact(s):
David Mattinson, President
John Thompson, CEO
Gregory Campbell, Executive Vice-President

Canadian Branches:
Beaverlodge Branch
P.O. Box 95
302 - 3 Ave. West
Beaverlodge, AB T0H 0C0
780-354-3279
Fax: 780-354-3495
beaverlodge@hazco.com

Edmonton Branch
12311 - 17th St. NE
Edmonton, AB T6S 1A7
780-456-1444
Fax: 780-456-9696
edmonton@hazco.com

Fort McMurray
P.O. Box 23009
Fort McMurray, AB T9H 5B7
780-714-3372
Fax: 780-714-3392
lburke@hazco.com

Products & Services Buyer's Guide

Fort St. John Branch
Bay 1
8820 - 100 St.
Fort St John, BC V1J 3W9
250-785-9001
Fax: 250-785-9449
fortstjohn@hazco.com

Kelowna Branch
3334 Sexsmith Rd.
Kelowna, BC V1X 7S5
250-765-5740
Fax: 250-765-5743
gallan@hazco.com

Kitchener Branch
#15, 500 Trillium Dr.
Kitchener, ON N2R 1K3
519-886-2972
Fax: 519-886-3078
pbauer@hazco.com

Manitoba Branch
1199 St. James St.
Winnipeg, MB R3H 0K8
204-832-4561
Fax: 204-832-3203
winnipeg@hazco.com

Northern Branch
Bldg. 1057
P.O. Box 686
Iqaluit, NU X0A 0H0
867-979-5252
Fax: 867-979-5251
gsanderson@hazco.com

Northern Region Head Office
Spirit River Waste Management Facility
P.O. Box 501
Rycroft, AB T0H 3A0
780-765-3745
Fax: 780-765-3751
grandeprairie@hazco.com

Saskatchewan Branch
P.O. Box 93
Weyburn, SK S4H 2J9
306-861-8294
dbradley@hazco.com

Thunder Bay Branch
866A, Alloy Place
Thunder Bay, ON P7B 6E6
807-622-2313
Fax: 807-622-2322
gpower@hazco.com

Vancouver Branch
13511 Vulcan Way
Richmond, BC V6V 1K4
604-214-7000
Fax: 604-214-7017
reception-van@hazco.com

International Branch(es):
Lima, Peru
Av Camino Real 348, Edificio Torre El Pilar, Oficin
Lima Peru
511-221-8157
Fax: 511-221-8157
info@hazcoperu.com

Seattle, WA
#2100, 1700 Seventh Ave.
Seattle, WA USA
206-903-0516
Fax: 206-652-2430
seattle@hazco.com

Hazelmere Research Ltd.
1940 - 180 St., RR#3
Surrey, BC V4P 1M6
604-541-0589
Fax: 604-541-0109
oehr@shaw.ca
Firm Type: Management Consulting, Scientific/Technical Services
Founded: 1988
Staff: 2
Member of: BC Inventors Society; Toastmasters International
Products/Services/Areas of Expertise: Intellectual property managment including experimental & patent design, expert witness, electrochemical engineering, hydrogen fromation inhibitor, mercuty pollution control, heavy oil upgrading
Recently Completed / Ongoing Projects: Mercury capture in coal fired electric power plants, hydrogen inhibitors for zinc electrowinning, heavy oil upgrading, expert witness
Financial Information:
Type of Ownership: Private
Revenue: $50,000 - $100,000
Revenue Sources: 100% Private Contracts
Domestic Markets:
British Columbia
Foreign Activity:
USA
Contact(s):
Klaus Oehr, President
oehr@shaw.ca

Hazmark Inc.
P.O. Box 25021
Riverfront Rd.
Point Edward, ON N7V 4K1
519-344-1884
Fax: 519-332-1580
800-265-5085
info@hazmark.com
www.hazmark.com
Products/Services/Areas of Expertise: In addition to custom & standard truck markings & workplace signs, the company manufactures placards & markings for the transportation of dangerous goods, in compliance with regulations in Canada, USA & Mexico.

Hazmasters Environmental Controls Inc.
#1, 1915 Clements Rd.
Pickering, ON L1W 3V1
905-427-0220
Fax: 905-427-9901
877-747-7117
connect@hazmasters.com
www.hazmasters.com
Firm Type: Distributing
Founded: 1989
Staff: 16
Member of: Canadian Environment Industry Association
Products/Services/Areas of Expertise: The company provides safety equipment & products for personal protection used in a range of hazardous situations, including: asbestos removal, emergency response & spill cleanup, lead abatement; fall protection & rescue.
Domestic Markets:
National
Contact(s):
Randy Myers, President
randymyers@hazmasters.com

Canadian Branches:
Burnaby
3103 Thunderbird Cres.
Burnaby, BC V5A 3G1
604-420-0025
Fax: 604-420-5282

Calgary
Bay D
1135 - 44th Ave. SE
Calgary, AB T2G 4X4
403-247-1100
Fax: 403-247-1121
, Manager

Dartmouth
#5, 60 Thornhill Dr.
Dartmouth, NS B3B 1S1
902-468-8467
Fax: 902-468-8134

Edmonton
16632 - 117 Ave.
Edmonton, AB T5M 3W2
780-481-1300
Fax: 780-481-3900

Montréal
126, av Lindsay
Dorval, QC H9P 2T8
514-633-8533
Fax: 514-633-5737
877-244-8533

Mount Pearl
22 Sagona Ave.
Mount Pearl, NL A1N 4R2
709-747-7117
Fax: 709-747-7118

Ottawa
51 Capital Dr.
Ottawa, ON K2G 0E7
613-224-5447
Fax: 613-224-1341
888-287-7831

Victoria
575 Hillside Ave.
Victoria, BC V8T 1Y8
250-384-0025
Fax: 250-384-0065

Winnipeg
1226 Sherwin Rd.
Winnipeg, MB R3H 0V3
204-694-4500
Fax: 204-633-4035

Healthy Homes Consulting
20 Maplewood Ct.
Lower Sackville, NS B4G 1B6
902-864-1955
Fax: 902-865-7000
Firm Type: Management Consulting, Scientific/Technical Services

Products/Services/Areas of Expertise: Indoor air quality consulting; materials research; testing; equipment rental; trouble-shooting; building evaluations; training & consultations
Financial Information:
Type of Ownership: Private
Contact(s):
Robin Barrett, Chief Consultant

Hebco International Inc.
151, av De L'Hotel-Dieu
Sorel-Tracy, QC J3P 1M2
450-780-1051
Fax: 450-780-0291
Products/Services/Areas of Expertise: Pyrolysis technology for tires & other organic wastes recycling
Domestic Markets:
Québec
Contact(s):
Jean-Pierre Bernier, Engineer

HEC Group
Formerly: Hamilton Executive Consultants
#400, 69 John St. South
Hamilton, ON L8N 2B9
905-527-7761
Fax: 905-527-9937
hec@hec-group.com
www.hec-group.com
Firm Type: Scientific/Technical Services
Founded: 1976
Staff: 12
Member of: National Environmental Network
Products/Services/Areas of Expertise: Technical recruiting services specializing in environment
Domestic Markets:
National
Foreign Activity:
USA

Helimax Energy Inc.
Hélimax Énergie inc.
#100, 4100, rue Molson
Montréal, QC H1Y 3L1
514-272-2175
Fax: 514-272-0410
info@helimax.com
www.helimax.com
Firm Type: Management Consulting
Founded: 1998
Staff: 50
Member of: Canadian Wind Energy Association, American Wind Energy Association, Association of Power Producers of Ontario

Products/Services/Areas of Expertise: Wind energy consulting; site prospecting, wind resource & environmental assessment, wind project technical & financial feasibility studies, market strategies, forecasting, assessment of legislative & regulatory framework & due diligence financial evaluation; serves various sectors, including IPPs, power utilities, governmental agencies & the financial community
Contact(s):
Adina Mihai

Hemispheres Environmental Consulting Inc.
Formerly: Two Hemispheres Environmental Consulting Inc.
47 Hillcrest Ave.
St Catharines, ON L2R 4Y3
905-682-1278
nmartin@niagara.com
Products/Services/Areas of Expertise: Environmental consultant & writer
Contact(s):
Narelle Martin, Consultant

Hemmera Envirochem Inc. / HEI
#250, 1380 Burrard St.
Vancouver, BC V6Z 2H3
604-669-0424
Fax: 604-669-0430
office@hemmera.com
www.hemmera.com
Firm Type: Management Consulting, Engineering, Scientific/Technical Services
Founded: 1994
Staff: 57
Products/Services/Areas of Expertise: Environmental impact assessment; preliminary & detailed site investigations; site decommissioning & reclamation; risk assessment; baseline quality studies; water quality monitoring; water supply systems; federal & provincial environmental assessments
Recently Completed / Ongoing Projects: Numerical modeling of groundwater, Environment Canada; detailed site investigation; human health & ecological site assessment, Transport Canada
Financial Information:
Type of Ownership: Private
Revenue: Greater than $5 Million
Revenue Sources: 35% nationwide; 3% Municipals; 57% Private Contracts
Domestic Markets:
Alberta, British Columbia, Yukon Territory
Contact(s):
Paul Hemsley, President
Eric K. Pringle, Vice-President, Operations

Canadian Branches:
Burnaby
#505, 3292 Production Way
Burnaby, BC V5A 4R4
604-669-0424
Fax: 604-669-0430

Victoria
19 Bastion Sq., 4th fl.
Victoria, BC V8W 1J1
250-388-3584
Fax: 250-388-3517

Hemmera Envirochem Inc. (North Van Lab)
310 East Esplanade
North Vancouver, BC V7L 1A4
604-986-7393
Fax: 604-980-1197

Henderson Paddon & Associates Ltd. / HPA
#212, 945 - 3rd Ave. East
Owen Sound, ON N4K 2K8
519-376-7612
Fax: 519-376-8008
888-376-7612
hpa@hp.on.ca
www.hp.on.ca
Firm Type: Engineering
Founded: 1972
Staff: 60
Member of: National Groundwater Association; Consulting Engineers of Ontario; Association of Professional Geoscientists of Ontario
Products/Services/Areas of Expertise: Solid waste management; hydrogeology; environmental site assessment, site investigation & remediation; underground storage tank management; groundwater resource development; PCB clean-up; Aboriginal environmental & civil engineering services; water treatment plant design; communal water system assessment & feasibility; transportation construction administration; air quality management
Recently Completed / Ongoing Projects: Phase III Environmental Issues Inventory for 5 First Nations communities on James Bay design, development & operations reports for 750,000 tonnes/year landfill; hydrogeologic modelling for quarry expansion approval; GUDI hydrogeologic assessments, Municipal; well specifications & perennial yield evaluations
Financial Information:
Type of Ownership: Private
Revenue Sources: 10% nationwide; 10% Provincial; 40% Municipals; 50% Private Contracts
Domestic Markets:
Alberta, Ontario
Contact(s):
Jeffrey T. Graham, P.Eng., President
Norman A. Bell, P.Geo., Vice-President
nabell@hp.on.ca
Rakesh Sharma, P.Eng., Water Treatment Engineer
Jeff E. Armstrong, Secretary
Sudhakar Kurli, M.Sc., M.Tech., Hydrogeologist
Rod D. Peters, B.Sc., P.Eng., First Nations Manager
Wayne Carmichael, Manager, Water Operations

Canadian Branches:
Clarksburg Branch
P.O. Box 308
103 Hillcrest Dr.
Clarksburg, ON N0H 1J0
519-599-3793
Fax: 519-519-2878
hpa3@hp.on.ca
John S. West

Grimsby
#201, 12 Ontario St.
Grimsby, ON L3M 3G9
905-309-6466
Fax: 905-309-7043
rklodnicki@hp.on.ca

Hanover
101 - 14th Ave.
Hanover, ON N4N 3W1
519-364-5700
Fax: 519-364-6937
hpahanover@hp.on.ca

Henlex Inc.
2600, rue Diab
Montréal, QC H4S 1E8
514-339-2522
Fax: 514-339-2526
800-922-2522
info@henlex.com
www.henlex.com
Firm Type: Manufacturing
Founded: 1954
Staff: 12
Member of: Association hygiéne industriel du Québec
Products/Services/Areas of Expertise: Industrial air hygiene through source capture, specializing in low-volume high-velocity technology, blower turbine dust collector, source capture wing micro-captor, welding smoke extraction
Financial Information:
Type of Ownership: Private
Revenue: $1.5 Million - $3 Million
Revenue Sources: 5% Provincial; 2% Municipals; 93% Private Contracts
Domestic Markets:
British Columbia, New Brunswick, Newfoundland & Labrador, Nova Scotia, Ontario, Prince Edward Island, Québec
Foreign Activity:
USA
Contact(s):
Michel Gagnon, President & CEO
michelgagnon@henlex.com

Henry Kortekaas & Associates Inc.
82 Sherwood Rd. East
Ajax, ON L1T 2Z2
905-427-2782
Fax: 905-427-9964
866-959-9997
hkortek@sympatico.ca
www.hklandarch.com
Firm Type: Scientific/Technical Services
Founded: 1983
Staff: 6
Member of: Ontario Association of Landscape Architects; Canadian Society of Landscape Architects
Products/Services/Areas of Expertise: Landscape architecture, environmental planning, natural space preservation, restoration, & site planning & design
Financial Information:
Revenue: $100,000 - $250,000
Domestic Markets:
Ontario
Contact(s):
Henry Kortekaas, Principal

Herby Enterprises Ltd.
Valley East Industrial Park
2870 White St.
Val Caron, ON P3N 1B2
705-897-5425
Fax: 705-897-6992
800-267-4372
herbyenterprises.com
Firm Type: Engineering, Scientific/Technical Services
Founded: 1965
Staff: 16
Member of: Ontario Association of Sewage Industry Services; Portable Toilet Association International
Products/Services/Areas of Expertise: The company offers a variety of waste treatment services & products: special waste transport; special waste from laboratory chemicals to tanker loads; video sewer & pipe line inspection; sewer cleaning & pumping; distributing of spills absorbent, drain cleaner, sewer cleaning equipment, aquarobic sewage treatment systems, polyethylene tanks; sewer smoke testing.
Domestic Markets:
Ontario
Contact(s):
Herbert J. Lindsay, President
herby@herbyenterprises.com
Suzanne Pelletier, Officer Manager
spelletier@herbyenterprises.com
Nicole Brosseau, Account Inquiries & Billing
nbrosseau@herbyenterprises.com

Hercules SLR Inc. / CMI
Formerly: Bridgeport Wire Rope & Chain Ltd.; Bridport Industries Ltd.
520 Windmill Rd.
Dartmouth, NS B3B 1B3
902-482-3125
Fax: 902-468-8948
www.herculesslr.com
Firm Type: Distributing, Manufacturing
Founded: 2006
Staff: 200
Member of: AWRF, DNV, QMI
Quality Environmental Management System(s): 9001:2000
Products/Services/Areas of Expertise: Markets, rents, repairs, inspects & tests lifting gear and rigging products; offers courses on fall protection and equipment use, including forklifts, overhead cranes, steel cable installation and manipulation
Financial Information:
Type of Ownership: Private
Revenue Sources: 10% nationwide; 10% Provincial; 10% Municipals; 70% Private Contracts
Domestic Markets:
New Brunswick, Newfoundland & Labrador, Nova Scotia, Ontario, Québec
Contact(s):
Chris Giannou, President
cgiannou@herculesslr.com
Dwayne Fader, Sales Manager, Sales, Atlantic Canada
dfader@herculesslr.com

Canadian Branches:
Dartmouth
70 Akerley Blvd.
Dartmouth, NS B3B 1R1
902-468-0300
Fax: 902-468-0303
866-651-3147

Labrador City
50 Avalon Dr.
Labrador City, NL A2V 2K6
709-944-3691
Fax: 709-944-7932

Mississauga
280 Superior Blvd.
Mississauga, ON L5T 2L2
905-564-3387
Fax: 905-564-7239

Moncton
520 Edinburgh Dr.
Moncton, NB E1E 4C6
506-382-7770
Fax: 506-856-5131
800-734-9111

Mount Pearl
173 Glencoe Dr., Donovan's Industrial Park
Mount Pearl, NL A1N 4P6
709-747-7960
Fax: 709-747-7964

Pointe-Claire
3800, route Transcanadienne
Pointe-Claire, QC H9R 1B1
514-428-5511
Fax: 514-428-5555
800-361-2147

Québec
#104, 2930, rue Watt
Québec, QC G1X 4G3
418-650-1444
Fax: 418-653-7397

St. John
9 Dedication St.
St. John, NB E2R 1A7
506-696-3707
Fax: 506-652-4505

Heritage Research Associates Inc.
962 Blythdale Rd.
Ottawa, ON K2A 3N7
613-722-1949
Fax: 613-722-1949
hra@magma.ca
www.magma.ca/~hra
Firm Type: Scientific/Technical Services
Founded: 1982
Staff: 10
Products/Services/Areas of Expertise: Provides historians with extensive land & technology-oriented archival research skills; performs the cultural heritage component of environmental assessment; offers secure site specific archival information to support hazardous waste research
Recently Completed / Ongoing Projects: Harvey Barracks, site history, special subject investigation, Cultural Heritage component of Ontario Realty Corporation's Class EA Renewal; many Federal Heritage Building Review Office cultural assessments; planning & policy review in preparation for Canadian Register of Historic Places
Financial Information:
Type of Ownership: Private
Revenue: $250,000 - $500,000
Revenue Sources: 45% nationwide; 20% Provincial; 5% Municipals; 30% Private Contracts
Domestic Markets:
National
Contact(s):
Margaret Carter, Principal
Robert J. Burns, Associate

Heron Instruments
2031 James St.
Burlington, ON L7R 1H2
905-634-4449
Fax: 905-634-9657
800-331-2032
info@heroninstruments.com
www.heroninstruments.com
Firm Type: Manufacturing
Founded: 1995
Staff: 9
Products/Services/Areas of Expertise: The company designs & manufactures groundwater monitoring instumentation.

Domestic Markets:
National
Foreign Activity:
Australia/New Zealand, Central Europe, Western Europe, South America, USA, United Kingdom
Contact(s):
Donald Toon, Owner

HETEK Solutions Inc.
Formerly: Heath Consultants Ltd.
2085 Piper Lane
London, ON N5V 3S5
519-659-1144
Fax: 519-453-2182
888-432-8422
sales@hetek.com
www.hetek.com
Firm Type: Engineering, Scientific/Technical Services
Founded: 1956
Staff: 50
Member of: Water Environment Federation, American Water Works Association, Ontario Energy Association
Products/Services/Areas of Expertise: Water leakage detection program; portable water flow monitoring; sewer flow monitoring (1 & 1); C value testing; hydrostatic test failure detection; gas leakage control program; environmental site assessments; heavy hydrocarbon evaluations; industrial inspection; instrument repair & maintenance; mobile calibration service; air quality monitoring; pipe & cable locate service; safety & education seminars; Meters & AMR systems; water leak detectors; water leak correlation units; insertion flow meters; ultrasonic flow meters; data loggers - universal; chemical products; gas alarm systems; gas leak detectors; combustible & toxic gas alarms; confined space retrieval systems; underground tank testing systems; training & educational program; water treatment systems; pipe & cable locators; helium tracer gas detector; rain gauges; portable & fixed site flow meters
Financial Information:
Revenue Sources: 5% nationwide; 5% Provincial; 20% Municipals; 70% Private Contracts
Domestic Markets:
Alberta
Foreign Activity:
Africa, Caribbean, Central America, The Pacific Rim, USA
Contact(s):
David Keeling, P.Eng., President
G. Wayne Hennigar, Director & CEO
wayne.hennigar@hetek.com
Andrew Pauley, VP & General Manager
andy.pauley@hetek.com
Brice Brown, Contact, Domestic Sales & Marketing
andy.pauley@hetek.com
Gary Fricke, Sales Contact, USA
gary.fricke@hetek.com
Canadian Branches:
Alberta
#5, 10820 - 27th St. SE
Calgary, AB T2K 3R6
403-273-5033
Fax: 403-273-5481
sales@hetek.com
www.hetek.com

Hewlett Packard (Canada) Co.
5150 Spectrum Way
Mississauga, ON L4W 5G1
905-206-4725
Fax: 905-206-4739
888-447-4636
www.hp.ca
Products/Services/Areas of Expertise: HP has printer products, R&D investments have resulted in innovations in printing & imaging technologies with over 7,000 patents; has earned the position of a market leader across all computer printing categories including inkjet, laser, designjet, print servers, scanners & supplies
Ecological Note: Laser jet/desk top printers

Canadian Branches:
Calgary
#3600, Petro Canada Tower
150 - 6th Ave. SW
Calgary, AB T2P 3Y7
Fax: 403-237-9309

Calgary
#3000, 715 - 5th Ave.
Calgary, AB T2P 2X6
403-295-4400
Fax: 403-295-4450

Edmonton
#2100, Commerce Place
10155 - 102nd St.
Edmonton, AB T5J 4G8
Fax: 780-420-4550

Gatineau
200, boul de la Technologie
Gatineau, QC J8Z 3H6
819-772-7000
Fax: 819-772-7036

Halifax
#420, 1718 Argyle St.
Halifax, NS B3J 3N6
Fax: 902-481-2811

Kanata
100 Hertzberg Rd.
Kanata, ON K2K 2A6
613-591-5111
Fax: 613-591-4375

Kingston
656 Progress Ave.
Kingston, ON K7M 4S9
Fax: 613-384-5953

Kirkland
17500, Trans Canada Hwy., South Service Rd.
Kirkland, QC H9J 2X8
514-697-4232
Fax: 514-697-6941

London
#15, 1100 Dearness Dr.
London, ON N6E 1N9
Fax: 519-690-5222

Markham
675 Cochrane Dr.
Markham, ON L3R 0Y7
905-948-3000
Fax: 905-948-3070

Moncton
#101, 1133 St. George Blvd.
Moncton, NB E1E 4E1
506-857-3860
Fax: 506-857-3872

Pembroke
215 - 217 Pembroke St. East
Pembroke, ON K8A 3J8
613-735-3677
Fax: 613-435-7858

Québec
#350, 1165, boul LeBourgneuf
Québec, QC G2K 2C9
Fax: 418-624-1223

Regina
492V Hoffer Dr.
Regina, SK S4N 7A1
Fax: 306-791-0012

Richmond
#150, 13571 Commerce Pkwy.
Richmond, BC V6V 2L1
Fax: 604-270-0859

St. John's
#105, 20 Crosbie Pl.
St. John's, NL A1B 3Y8
709-722-1164
Fax: 709-722-1183

Sudbury
128 Pine St.
Sudbury, ON P3C 1X3
705-671-2624
Fax: 705-668-1043

Toronto
#1216, 120 Adelaide St. W
Toronto, ON M5H 1T1
Fax: 416-862-7382

Victoria
#508, 1175 Douglas St.
Victoria, BC V8W 2E2

Winnipeg
#810, 200 Graham Ave.
Winnipeg, MB R3C 4L5
204-989-3515
Fax: 204-989-3553

HFP Acoustical Consultants Corp.
#1140, 10201 Southport Rd. SW
Calgary, AB T2W 4X9
403-259-6600
Fax: 403-259-6611
888-259-3600
info@hfpacoustical.com
www.hfpacoustical.com
Firm Type: Engineering
Founded: 1979
Staff: 17
Member of: Association of Professional Engineers of Alberta; Association of Professional Engineers of Saskatchewan; Association of Professional Engineers of Texas; Institute of Noise Control Engineers; Canadian Acoustical Association; Accoustical Society of America; National Council of Acoustical Consultants
Products/Services/Areas of Expertise: Noise control engineering for the oil & gas industry
Financial Information:
Type of Ownership: Private
Revenue: $500,000 - $1.5 Million
Revenue Sources: 100% Private Contracts
Domestic Markets:
Alberta, British Columbia, Manitoba, Northwest Territories, Nunavut, Ontario, Saskatchewan, Yukon Territory
Foreign Activity:
Australia/New Zealand, Central America, Central Europe, Western Europe, The Pacific Rim, South America, Mexico, USA
Contact(s):
Leslie Frank, P. Eng.

International Branch(es):
Houston
#115, 6001 Savoy
Houston, TX USA
713-789-9400
Fax: 713-789-5493
1-888-789-9400
info@hpacoustical.com
Ron Spillman, P.E.

HGC Engineering / HGC
Also Known As: Howe Gastmeier Chapnik Limited
Plaza 1
#203, 2000 Argentia Rd
Mississauga, ON L5N 1P7
905-826-4044
Fax: 905-826-4940
info@hgcengineering.com
www.hgcengineering.com
Firm Type: Engineering
Founded: 1994
Staff: 15
Products/Services/Areas of Expertise: Noise & vibration; field measurement & assessments; impact studies; design & specification of noise control measures for retrofit installations or the operation of new facilities
Domestic Markets:
National
Foreign Activity:
Worldwide
Contact(s):
Brian Howe, President

Hi-Country Environmental Services Ltd.
P.O. Box 73
Pincher Creek, AB T0K 1W0
403-627-5429
Fax: 403-627-2446
hcesl@telusplanet.net
Founded: 1991
Staff: 1
Products/Services/Areas of Expertise: Land reclamation
Financial Information:
Type of Ownership: Private
Domestic Markets:
Alberta

Contact(s):
Rudy Zalesak, President

Hi-Point Industries (1991) Ltd.
P.O. Box 779
141 Sunset Dr.
Bishop's Falls, NL A0H 1C0
709-258-6274
Fax: 709-258-5905
800-661-1675
oclansorb@nf.sympatico.ca
www.oilabsorbents.ca
Firm Type: Manufacturing
Founded: 1984
Staff: 30
Member of: American Society for Quality Control; Newfoundland Environment Industries Association
Products/Services/Areas of Expertise: Oil absorbents from peat moss; spill kits & emergency response stations; oil/water separators; containment booms; remediation services; oil containment berms; flex-tanks; turbidity curtains
Financial Information:
Type of Ownership: Private
Revenue: $3 Million - $5 Million
Domestic Markets:
National
Foreign Activity:
Asia, Australia/New Zealand, Central America, Western Europe, The Middle East, The Pacific Rim, South America, Mexico, USA
Contact(s):
Bill Butler, President
Jeff Roberts, Manager, Sales
Glenn Janes, Marketing, 709/634-9080
Brian Mercer, Manager, Containment Products, 709/258-6370
hi_point@nf.sympatico.ca

Hi-Q Developments Ltd.
20 Maplewood Ct.
Lower Sackville, NS B4G 1B6
902-864-1955
Fax: 902-865-7000
hiq@eastlink.ca
Firm Type: Management Consulting

Products/Services/Areas of Expertise: Indoor air quality consulting; materials research, testing, equipment rental, building evaluations, training, consultations. It has an A+ rating from the Better Business Bureau.
Recently Completed / Ongoing Projects: Consulting for Nova Scotia Environmental Health Centre
Financial Information:
Type of Ownership: Private
Revenue Sources: 10% nationwide; 10% Provincial; 10% Municipals; 70% Private Contracts
Domestic Markets:
New Brunswick, Nova Scotia, Ontario, Prince Edward Island, Québec
Foreign Activity:
USA,
Contact(s):
Robin Barrett, Chief Consultant

Hibon Inc.
Ingersoll Rand Industrial Technologies
51 Worcester Rd.
Toronto, ON M8W 4K2
416-460-9651
Fax: 866-686-2804
www.hibon.com
Firm Type: Manufacturing
Founded: 1975
Staff: 30
Quality Environmental Management System(s): 9001:1994
Products/Services/Areas of Expertise: Blowers; vacuum pumps
Domestic Markets:
National
Foreign Activity:
Mexico, USA
Contact(s):
David Cherry, Regional Sales Manager
david_cherry@irco.com

Canadian Branches:
Montréal - Service & Parts
Ingersoll Rand Industrial Technologies
12055, Côte de Liesse
Dorval, QC H9P 1B4
514-631-3501
Fax: 514-631-3502
John Harkness, Service Manager
john_harkness@irco.com
Christian St. Amand, Service Québec
christian-st-amand@irco.com

Hickling Arthurs Low Corp. / HAL
#1300, 150 Isabella St.
Ottawa, ON K1S 1V7
613-237-2220
Fax: 613-237-7347
hal@hal.ca
www.hal.ca
Firm Type: Management Consulting
Founded: 1975
Staff: 50
Products/Services/Areas of Expertise: A consultancy specializing in: technology assessment & technology impact; group decision support systems; modelling; policy, economic analysis; management of technology
Domestic Markets:
National
Foreign Activity:
USA
Contact(s):
David R. Low, Chair
David Arthurs, President

Highland Equipment Ltd.
136 The East Mall
Toronto, ON M8Z 5V5
416-236-9610
Fax: 416-236-9611
800-956-5630
helcan@highlandequip.com
www.highlandequip.com
Firm Type: Manufacturing
Founded: 1973
Staff: 65
Products/Services/Areas of Expertise: Sanitary stainless steel; process equipment for food, dairy, beverage & pharmaceutical industries
Financial Information:
Type of Ownership: Private
Revenue: Greater than $5 Million
Domestic Markets:
National
Foreign Activity:
Western Europe, USA
Contact(s):
David Smith, President
smithd@highlandequip.com
D. Mamon, Co-Chair, Sales
mamond@highlandquip.com

International Branch(es):
Twinsburg, OH
Sales
2146 Enterprise Pkwy., #E
Twinsburg, OH USA
330-425-2721
Fax: 330-425-2724
coopera@highlandequip.com
A. Cooper, Vice-President

Hike Metal Products Ltd.
Also Known As: Hike Metal
P.O. Box 698
Wheatley, ON N0P 2P0
519-825-4691
Fax: 519-825-7572
sales@hikemetal.com
www.hikemetal.com
Firm Type: Manufacturing
Founded: 1958
Staff: 25
Products/Services/Areas of Expertise: Sewage treatment equipment; steel & aluminum welding
Financial Information:
Type of Ownership: Private

Products & Services Buyer's Guide

Revenue Sources: 70% nationwide; 10% Provincial; 5% Municipals; 15% Private Contracts
Domestic Markets:
Ontario
Foreign Activity:
Caribbean, Central America, South America, USA, Worldwide
Markets Sought:
Mexico
Contact(s):
Andy Stanton, President
Alan Borret, Design/Engineering

Hilderman Thomas Frank Cram & Associates
Formerly: Hilderman Witty Crosby Hanna & Associates
#500, 115 Bannatyne Ave. East
Winnipeg, MB R3B 0R3
204-944-9907
Fax: 204-957-1467
info@htfc.mb.ca
www.htfc.mb.ca
Firm Type: Management Consulting, Scientific/Technical Services
Founded: 1970
Staff: 12
Member of: Canadian Institute of Planners; Canadian Society of Landscape Architects; Canadian Society for Landscape Ecology & Management
Products/Services/Areas of Expertise: Landscape architects & planners; site planning & design; environmental & social impact assessment; landscape restoration; landfill (sanitary) planning & design
Recently Completed / Ongoing Projects: Site development for Manitoba Hazardous Waste Corp.; environmental research initiative feasibility study & development plan, Atikokan; post-project initial environmental evaluation, Winnipeg River
Domestic Markets:
National
Foreign Activity:
Mexico, USA,
Contact(s):
James C. Thomas, Principal
Garry Hilderman, Principal
Jeffrey Frank, Principal
Heather Cram, Principal

Hiltz & Seamone Co. Ltd.
76 Coldbrook Village Park Dr.
Coldbrook, NS B4R 1B9
902-678-2774
Fax: 902-678-6990
hiltzsea@hiltzsea.ns.ca
www.hiltzsea.ns.ca
Firm Type: Management Consulting, Engineering
Founded: 1959
Staff: 12
Products/Services/Areas of Expertise: Engineering & environmental audits & impact studies; site remediation; wastewater studies; energy conservation
Domestic Markets:
Nova Scotia
Contact(s):
D.A. Seamone, Principal

Historica Research Limited
P.O. Box 145
Delaware, ON N0L 1E0
519-264-1852
Fax: 519-264-3005
history@golden.net
Firm Type: Scientific/Technical Services
Founded: 1980
Staff: 1
Member of: Society for Industrial Archeology; Society for Historical Archeology
Products/Services/Areas of Expertise: Industrial archaeology; historic hazardous waste assessments; environmental assessments of historically sensitive structures & landscapes
Recently Completed / Ongoing Projects: Historic hazardous assessment, Gooderham & Worts Distillery, Toronto; historic hazardous assessment, Regional Municipality of Waterloo; mitigation archaeology, Regional Municipality of Hamilton-Wentworth
Domestic Markets:
National
Foreign Activity:
USA
Contact(s):

Christopher Andreae, President

Hitachi Canadian Industries Ltd.
826 - 58th St. East
Saskatoon, SK S7K 5Z4
306-242-9222
Fax: 306-242-9211
www.hitachi.sk.ca
Firm Type: Manufacturing
Staff: 300
Quality Environmental Management System(s): 9001
Products/Services/Areas of Expertise: Wind tower manufacturing
Financial Information:
Type of Ownership: Private
Domestic Markets:
National
Foreign Activity:
USA
Contact(s):
Denise Frey, Manager, Sales & Marketing
dfrey@hitachi.sk.ca

HLS Ecolo
Formerly: Ecolo Worldwide
59 Penn Dr.
Toronto, ON M9L 2A6
416-740-3900
Fax: 416-740-3800
info@ecolo.com
www.hlsecolo.com
Firm Type: Manufacturing
Founded: 1981
Member of: Water Environment Federation
Member of: Solid Waste Association of North America, Building Owners and Managers Association, Air & Waste Management Association
Products/Services/Areas of Expertise: Odor control equipment; oder control chemicals; odor control services; air quality equipment; air pollution control equipment; waste water treatment; solid waste treatment
Activities: Odour control research & development
Financial Information:
Type of Ownership: Publicly Traded
Revenue: Greater than $5 Million
Revenue Sources: 20% Municipals; 80% Private Contracts
Domestic Markets:
National
Foreign Activity:
Worldwide
Contact(s):
Michael Beckley, President & CEO
mbeckley@chlsecolo.com
Paul Chapple, Vice-President, Marketing
pchapple@hlsecho.com

HMI Construction Inc.
1451, rue Graham Bell
Boucherville, QC J4B 6A1
450-449-3999
Fax: 450-449-3988
hmimtl@hmic.qc.ca
www.hmiconstruction.ca
Firm Type: Scientific/Technical Services
Founded: 1956
Staff: 80
Products/Services/Areas of Expertise: Industrial contractors involved in electricity, mechanical & automation work; projects oriented towards energy & environment
Financial Information:
Type of Ownership: Private
Contact(s):
Pierre Marquis
Canadian Branches:
Québec
6275, boul l'Ormière
Québec, QC G2B 3W7
418-842-3232
Fax: 418-842-0075

HMI Hoyme Manufacturing Inc.
4512 - 39th St.
Camrose, AB T4V 2N5
780-672-6553
Fax: 780-672-6554
800-661-7382

hoyme@hoyme.com
www.hoyme.com
Firm Type: Manufacturing
Founded: 1984
Staff: 12
Products/Services/Areas of Expertise: Energy conservation equipment; ventilation equipment; automatic combustion air dampers; zone air & replacement air dampers; motorless air exchanger (HRV)
Domestic Markets:
National
Foreign Activity:
USA
Contact(s):
Clifford Hoyme, President & General Mgr.
Marla Sandberg, Sales/Order Desk

HMI Industries
Formerly: Harpers Metals Ltd.
8149 Edgar Industrial Close
Red Deer, AB T4P 3R4
403-346-4185
Fax: 403-346-3953
800-313-5535
info@hmiindustries.com
www.hmiindustries.com
Firm Type: Engineering, Scientific/Technical Services
Founded: 1951
Staff: 28
Products/Services/Areas of Expertise: The company provides a variety of services with a focus on scrap metal recycling. Other services include: oilfield demolition & clean-up; waste bin pick-up; emergency demolition response for derailment.
Financial Information:
Type of Ownership: Private
Domestic Markets:
Alberta
Contact(s):
Shady Vida, President
Curtis Slater, Director, Finance
Dallas Schwanke, Controller

HMO Limited
#9, 350 Harry Walker Parkway
Newmarket, ON L3Y 8L3
905-895-6078
Fax: 905-895-0171
Products/Services/Areas of Expertise: Engineering consulting services; water supply & treatment
Contact(s):
Bert Ofoha, Prof.Eng., Consultant

Hollimex Products Ltd.
8750 - 53 Ave.
Edmonton, AB T6E 5G2
780-468-1137
Fax: 780-469-1899
www.hollimex.com
Products/Services/Areas of Expertise: Drilling fluids, food additives, mining reagents

Home Hardware Stores Ltd.
Paint & Home Products Div.
P.O. Box 250
6 Brian Dr.
Burford, ON N0E 1A0
519-664-2252
Fax: 519-664-3717
www.homehardware.com
Firm Type: Distributing, Manufacturing
Founded: 1979
Staff: 95
EcoLogo Certified Products & Services: Retailers for: Easy Spray Boat Buttom Cleaner, Hand Foam Gojo Soap, Mr. Green Litter Box Deodorizer; Paints & surface coatings: Beauti-Tone; Home Painter; Painters Paint; Super Beauti-Tone; Wood Shield
Products/Services/Areas of Expertise: Cleaning products; paints & surface coatings
Ecological Note: Retailers for: Easy Spray Boat Buttom Cleaner, Hand Foam Gojo Soap, Mr. Green Litter Box Deodorizer; Paints & surface coatings: Beauti-Tone; Home Painter; Painters Paint; Super Beauti-Tone; Wood Shield
Contact(s):
Paul Straus, President & CEO
Rob Wallace, Media Contact
rob.wallace@homehardware.ca

Honey Electric Ltd.
400 Park Ave. West
Chatham, ON N7M 1W9
519-351-0484
Fax: 519-351-8710
800-265-2166
corporate@honeyelectric.com
www.honeyelectric.com
Firm Type: Scientific/Technical Services
Founded: 1978
Staff: 20
Member of: Solar Energy Society of Canada Inc., Canadian Photovoltaic Association; Solar Energy Society of Canada
Products/Services/Areas of Expertise: Solar pool & hot water heating; solar electrical systems; batteries; sales, service, installation & repairs; window treatments & transparent window insulation
Financial Information:
Type of Ownership: Private
Domestic Markets:
Ontario
Contact(s):
Reg MacDonald, Owner

Honeywell Ltd.
3333 Unity Dr.
Mississauga, ON L5L 3S6
905-608-6000
Fax: 905-608-6001
Products/Services/Areas of Expertise: Measuring & monitoring equipment

Hooper Welding Enterprises Ltd.
1390 Advance Rd.
Oakville, ON L6L 6L6
905-827-2600
Fax: 905-827-1600
888-252-6179
www.hooperwelding.com
Firm Type: Engineering, Manufacturing
Founded: 1952
Products/Services/Areas of Expertise: Pressure vessels, heat exchangers, power boilers, nuclear vessels, petro-chemical vessel & towers, skid systems, (ASME & PED codes)
Financial Information:
Type of Ownership: Private
Revenue: $1.5 Million - $3 Million
Revenue Sources: 100% Private Contracts
Domestic Markets:
National
Foreign Activity:
Worldwide
Contact(s):
Ross Hooper, President
ross.hooper@hooperwelding.com
Jim Wright, General Manager
Chris Hooper, Sales Manager

Horizon Environment Inc.
120, rte 155
Grandes-Piles, QC G0X 1H0
819-538-3921
Fax: 819-538-0889
800-545-7657
info@horizonenviro.com
www.horizonenviro.com
Firm Type: Waste Management
Staff: 18
Member of: Ontario Waste Management Association
Products/Services/Areas of Expertise: Thermal treatment; bioremediation; secure landfilling; treatment of contaminated soil & sediment
Financial Information:
Type of Ownership: Private
Revenue Sources: 13% nationwide; 13% Provincial; 13% Municipals; 61% Private Contracts
Domestic Markets:
New Brunswick, Newfoundland & Labrador, Nova Scotia, Ontario, Prince Edward Island, Québec
Foreign Activity:
USA
Contact(s):
Alnoor Manji, President/CEO
amanji@horizonenviro.com
Éric Paquin, Vice-President, Marketing
epaquin@horizonenviro.com
Antonio Pingue, Vice-President, Business Development
apingue@horizonenviro.com
Claude Fournier, Vice-President, Environment
cfournier@horizonenviro.com

Horizons Systems Group Inc.
P.O. Box 537
#301, 11 Portland St.
Dartmouth, NS B2Y 1H1
902-463-8308
Fax: 902-463-8951
866-606-8308
info@horizoncanada.com
www.horizoncanada.com
Firm Type: Information Technology
Founded: 1993
Products/Services/Areas of Expertise: Software developers for use in areas of environmental concern, especially about offshore oil exploration
Contact(s):
Sean McDermott, Director

Horner Associates Limited
89 Queen St.
Truro, NS B2N 2B2
902-895-1507
Fax: 902-893-2152
horner@adi.ca
Firm Type: Engineering, Scientific/Technical Services
Founded: 1963
Staff: 12
Products/Services/Areas of Expertise: Engineering consulting services; environmental consulting; waste management; solid waste management; water & wastewater systems, treatment & services
Recently Completed / Ongoing Projects: Nova Scotia: Barrington, Louisbourg, Millbrook, Antigonish
Financial Information:
Type of Ownership: Private
Revenue Sources: 95% Municipals; 5% Private Contracts
Domestic Markets:
New Brunswick, Newfoundland & Labrador, Nova Scotia, Prince Edward Island
Markets Sought:
South America
Contact(s):
Michael G. Topley, P.Eng., Principal Engineer & President

Horton CBI Ltd.
Bow Valley Sq. II
#600, 205 - 5th Ave. SW
Calgary, AB T2P 2V7
403-264-1333
Fax: 403-264-2453
Firm Type: Manufacturing
Founded: 1914
Staff: 300
Products/Services/Areas of Expertise: Stratified water tanks for thermal energy storage; water & wastewater treatment systems; egg-shaped anaerobic sewage digesters; solids contact clarifiers for potable & wastewater treatment
Domestic Markets:
National
Contact(s):
Ken East, Vice-President & Director of Sales
Canadian Branches:
Niagara Falls
4342 Queen St., 3rd Fl.
Niagara Falls, ON L2E 7J7
905-371-1500
Fax: 905-371-3930

Horton Tree Farms
Formerly: Horton Forestry Services Ltd.
14844 Warden Ave.
Stouffville, ON L4A 7X5
905-888-1738
Fax: 905-888-1887
800-420-7385
www.hortontreefarms.com
Firm Type: Scientific/Technical Services
Founded: 1966
Staff: 9
Member of: Ontario Professional Foresters Association; Landscape Ontario; Christmas Tree Growers Association of Ontario
Products/Services/Areas of Expertise: Christmas trees, maple sugar bush, education centre
Domestic Markets:
Ontario
Contact(s):
Harold Horton, General Manager

Hoskin Scientific Ltd.
4210 Morris Dr.
Burlington, ON L7L 5L6
905-333-5510
Fax: 905-333-4976
salesb@hoskin.ca
www.hoskin.ca
Firm Type: Distributing
Staff: 20
Member of: Canadian & Ontario Water Well Associations
Products/Services/Areas of Expertise: Engineering test equipment; soil, asphalt, concrete, environmental & industrial instrumentation
Domestic Markets:
National

Canadian Branches:
Montréal Branch
300, rue Stinson
Saint-Laurent, QC H4N 2E7
514-735-5267
Fax: 514-735-3454
salesm@hoskin.ca

Vancouver Branch
3735 Myrtle St.
Burnaby, BC V5C 4E7
604-872-7894
Fax: 604-872-0281
salesb@hoskin.ca

Hot Zone Training Consultants Inc.
#3, 250 Thompson Dr.
Cambridge, ON N1T 2E3
519-622-5801
Fax: 519-622-4632
888-898-8966
info@hotzonetraining.com
www.hotzonetraining.com
Products/Services/Areas of Expertise: Seminar & training management
Contact(s):
Peter A. White, President

Hotsy Pressure Washers Ltd.
Also Known As: Hotsy Cleaning Systems
#2, Shearson Cres.
Cambridge, ON N1T 1J6
519-740-1331
Fax: 519-740-7317
800-265-7146
info@hotsyontario.ca
www.hotsyontario.ca
Firm Type: Distributing, Engineering
Founded: 1984
Staff: 10
Products/Services/Areas of Expertise: Custom built washer systems; wash water recycle systems
Contact(s):
Richard Arnold, President

Hotz Environmental Services Inc.
A division of Envirosystems, Inc.
239 Lottridge St.
Hamilton, ON L8L 6W1
905-545-2665
Fax: 905-545-7822
888-333-4680
info@hotzenvironmental.com
www.hotzenvironmental.com
Firm Type: Waste Management
Founded: 1928
Staff: 75
Products/Services/Areas of Expertise: Hazardous waste management; household hazardous waste services; hazardous waste consulting, collection, recycling/disposal; risk audits; remediation, decommissioning; emergency response/spill cleanup; small quantity waste service; paint recycling & exporting recycled paint worldwide
Domestic Markets:
Ontario

Foreign Activity:
Caribbean, Eastern Europe, South Africa, USA, United Kingdom
Contact(s):
Pamela McCauley, Vice-President, Business Development
pamela@hotzenvironmental.com
Don Harber, General Manager

Howard Marten Fluid Technologies Inc.
The distribution division of Howard Marten Company
Formerly: Malcolm Campbell & Son Ltd. 902 Dillingham Rd.
Pickering, ON L1W 1Z6
905-831-2901
Fax: 905-831-9369
800-628-5823
sales@howardmarten.com
www.howardmarten.ca
Firm Type: Distributing
Founded: 2010
Quality Environmental Management System(s): 9002
Products/Services/Areas of Expertise: Industrial finishing equipment, fluid handling & lubrication equipment; solvent recovery systems; pressure cleaning equipment; air compressors
Domestic Markets:
Alberta, British Columbia, Manitoba, Saskatchewan
Foreign Activity:
Africa, Asia, USA

Canadian Branches:
Calgary
4450 - 50th Ave.
Calgary, AB T2B 3R4
403-259-2201
Fax: 403-259-2512
Roy Gilmet
roy.gilmet@howardmarten.com

Cambridge
190 Turnbull Ct.
Cambridge, ON N1T 1J1
519- 740-1124
Fax: 519-740- 8568

Coquitlam
#4, 68 Schooner St.
Coquitlam, BC V3K 7B1
604-525-8499
Fax: 604-525-8395
800-563-1248
Jason Plate
jason.plate@howardmarten.com

Edmonton
10315 - 65th Ave.
Edmonton, AB T6H 1V1
Fax: 780-435-8718
800-405-0148
John Kehoe
john.kehoe@howardmarten.com

Saint-Laurent
670 McCaffrey St.
Saint-Laurent, QC V3K 7B1
514-733-1600
Fax: 514-733-5803
Wayne Lanteigne
wayne.lanteigne@howardmarten.com

Saskatoon
#7, 3040 Miners Ave.
Saskatoon, SK S7K 5V1
306-931-1164
Fax: 306-931-9270
888-931-1164
Howard Lowe
howard.lowe@howardmarten.com

Winnipeg
1153 Sanford St.
Winnipeg, MB R3A 3A1
204-582-4965
Fax: 204-589-2567
888-462-3331
Cyrus Ross
cyrus.ross@howardmarten.com

Howell-Mayhew Engineering Inc.
15006 - 103 Ave.
Edmonton, AB T5P 0N8
780-484-0476
Fax: 780-484-3956
www.hme.ca
Firm Type: Engineering, Scientific/Technical Services
Founded: 1985
Staff: 2
Member of: Solar Energy Society of Alberta; Association of Professional Engineers, Geologists & Geophysicists of Alberta
Member of: Canadian Solar Industries Association
Products/Services/Areas of Expertise: Consulting, field performance testing & evaluation of energy-efficient residential buildings; photovoltaic systems; solar PV system; project development
Financial Information:
Type of Ownership: Private
Revenue: $100,000 - $250,000
Revenue Sources: 50% nationwide; 25% Provincial; 25% Municipals
Domestic Markets:
Alberta, British Columbia, Northwest Territories, Saskatchewan, Yukon Territory
Foreign Activity:
Australia/New Zealand, Western Europe, USA
Markets Sought:
Australia/New Zealand, Central Europe
Contact(s):
D. Gordon Howell, President
ghowell@hme.ca
William J. Mayhew, Vice-President

HQN Industrial Fabrics Inc.
760 Chester St.
Sarnia, ON N7S 5N1
519-344-9050
Fax: 519-344-5511
800-361-7068
info@hqnfabrics.com
www.hqnfabrics.com
Firm Type: Manufacturing
Founded: 1987
Staff: 18
Products/Services/Areas of Expertise: The company manufactures & distributes: waste container bags/liners; tarpaulins - plastic, vinyl, canvas, hypalon; covers & barriers - flame & weather proof; oil spill containment boom & spill berms.
Financial Information:
Type of Ownership: Private
Revenue: $1.5 Million - $3 Million
Revenue Sources: 3% Municipals; 97% Private Contracts
Domestic Markets:
National
Foreign Activity:
USA
Contact(s):
Paul Hardy, President
phardy@hqnfabrics.com
Mike Nottley, Secretary-Treasurer

HSE Integrated
Formerly: SDS Group Inc
#1000, 630 - 5 Ave. SW
Calgary, AB T2P 0S8
403-266-1833
Fax: 403-266-1834
888-346-8260
info@hseintegrated.com
www.hseintegrated.com
Products/Services/Areas of Expertise: Fire safety company offering fire/shower equipment & expertise, safety audits, emergency response plans, safety programs & standby assistance for plant construction & turnaround projects
Contact(s):
David Yagerter, Chair/CEO
James Hill, President
Lori McLeod-Hill, CFO

Canadian Branches:
Bonnyville
P.O. Box 6679
5615 - 50th Ave.
Bonnyville, AB T9N 2K9
780-826-5300
Fax: 780-826-4772

Brooks
P.O. Box 1217
315 - 6th St. East
Brooks, AB T1R 1C1
403-362-7867
Fax: 403-362-4660

Dartmouth
95 Isley Ave.
Dartmouth, NS B3B 1L5
902-468-6490
Fax: 902-468-6491

Edmonton
3120 - 93rd St.
Edmonton, AB T6N 1C6
780-463-9078
Fax: 780-450-3790

Fort McMurray
Bay 1, 350 MacAlpine Cres.
Fort McMurray, AB T9H 4A8
780-715-2088
Fax: 780-715-3684

Fort Saskatchewan
#1, 8306 - 13th St.
Fort Saskatchewan, AB T8L 3T8
780-998-2266
Fax: 780-998-0954

Fort St John
Site 1, Comp 18, 7912 Alaska Rd., RR#1, Stn M
Fort St John, BC V1J 4M6
250-785-6333
Fax: 250-785-6301

Grande Prairie
9645 - 116th St.
Grande Prairie, AB T8V 5W3
780-532-2088
Fax: 780-532-6688

High Level
#2, 10908 - 97th St.
High Level, AB T0H 1Z0
780-926-2088
Fax: 780-926-3254

Medicine Hat
2139 - 10th Ave. SW
Medicine Hat, AB T1A 8B7
403-527-1505
Fax: 403-527-1520

Pincher Creek
P.O. Box 1839
1116 MacLeod St.
Pincher Creek, AB T0K 1W0
403-627-2087
Fax: 403-627-2085

Prescott
P.O. Box 203
North Augusta, ON K0G 1R0
613-926-1772
Fax: 613-926-1773

Red Deer
8148 Edgar Industrial Close
Red Deer, AB T4P 3R4
403-342-2088
Fax: 403-342-0342

Rocky Mountain House
P.O. Box 2047
4316 - 49th Ave.
Rocky Mountain House, AB T4T 1B5
403-845-3005
Fax: 403-845-3014

Saint John
McAllister Industrial Park
28 McIliveen Dr.
Saint John, NB E2L 4Y7
506-637-9050
Fax: 506-637-9051

Sarnia
1190 Michener St.
Sarnia, ON N7S 4B1
519-332-0044
Fax: 519-332-5955

Slave Lake
P.O. Box 66
404 Birch Rd. NE
Slave Lake, AB T0G 2A0
780-849-2078
Fax: 780-849-2087

Sylvan Lake
3 Industrial Dr.
Sylvan Lake, AB T4S 1P4
403-887-1111
Fax: 403-887-3339

Whitecourt
3404 - 34th Ave.
Whitecourt, AB T7X 1X3
780-778-2088
Fax: 780-778-1966

Windsor
1333 College Ave.
Windsor, ON N9B 1M8
519-988-1895
Fax: 519-988-1673

International Branch(es):
Taylor, MI
26401 Northline Rd.
Taylor, MI USA
734-947-9111
Fax: 734-947-9428

Hunter & Associates
Also Known As: Hunter GIS
#18, 2285 Dunwin Dr.
Mississauga, ON L5L 3S3
905-607-4120
Fax: 905-607-1132
gisinfo@hunter-gis.com
www.hunter-gis.com
Firm Type: Information Technology, Scientific/Technical Services
Founded: 1977
Staff: 10
Products/Services/Areas of Expertise: Remote sensing & image analysis; engineering geology/hydrogeology; forestry & environmental management; watershed planning; Geographic Information Systems (GIS); pipeline route selection; environmental assessments; coastal zone management; GIS software development; corporate intranets
Financial Information:
Type of Ownership: Private
Revenue Sources: 10% nationwide; 10% Provincial; 10% Municipals; 70% Private Contracts
Domestic Markets:
National
Foreign Activity:
Caribbean, The Pacific Rim
Contact(s):
Garry T. Hunter, President
Scott MacPhee, Manager, GIS Applications

Huntsman Corporation Canada Inc.
Also Known As: Huntsman Performance Products
256 Victoria Rd. South
Guelph, ON N1E 5R1
519-824-3280
www.huntsman.com
Firm Type: Manufacturing
Founded: 1975
Quality Environmental Management System(s): 9002
Products/Services/Areas of Expertise: Water treatment chemicals; dust collectors
Financial Information:
Type of Ownership: Private
Domestic Markets:
National
Foreign Activity:
Worldwide
Contact(s):
Ralph Shapiro, President
Jeanette Hull, Environmental Contact

Hurlburt Construction Limited
P.O. Box 233
Yarmouth, NS B5A 4B2
902-742-5848
Fax: 902-742-9718
800-565-5848
mark@hurlburtconstruction.com
www.hurlburtconstruction.com
Firm Type: Engineering

Products/Services/Areas of Expertise: Engaged in industrial, commercial & residential civil contracting & construction; excavation; wells & septic systems; demolition; snow removal; top soil, sand & gravel; road construction
Financial Information:
Type of Ownership: Private
Domestic Markets:
Nova Scotia
Contact(s):
Mark Hurlburt, President

Huron Wind Ltd. Partnership
P.O. Box 1540
Tiverton, ON N0G 2T0
519-361-7777
enquiries@huronwind.com
www.huronwind.com
Firm Type: Engineering
Founded: 2002
Member of: Cameco Corporation; TransCanada PipeLines; OMERS
EcoLogo Certified Products & Services: Renewable, low-impact, wind-powered electricity
Products/Services/Areas of Expertise: Producer of wind electricity
Ecological Note: Renewable, low-impact, wind-powered electricity
Financial Information:
Type of Ownership: Private
Domestic Markets:
Ontario
Contact(s):
Murray Paterson, Vice-President

Huron Window Corporation
345 Mountain St. South
Morden, MB R6M 1J5
204-822-6281
Fax: 204-822-6343
800-565-3491
huron@huronwin.com
www.huronwin.com
Firm Type: Manufacturing
Founded: 1980
Staff: 25
Member of: Canadian Home Builders' Association; Manitoba Home Builders' Association; Insulating Glass Manufacturers Alliance (IGMA)
Products/Services/Areas of Expertise: Insulated steel doors & PVC windows manufacturing
Financial Information:
Type of Ownership: Private
Domestic Markets:
Manitoba, Ontario, Saskatchewan
Markets Sought:
USA
Contact(s):
Victor Fehr, General Manager
victor@huronwin.com
Brodie Fehr, Corporate Sales
Brodief@huronwin.com

HurterConsult Inc.
#4, 5330 Canotek Rd.
Ottawa, ON K1J 9C1
613-749-2181
Fax: 613-749-1382
info@hurterconsult.com
www.hurterconsult.com
Firm Type: Engineering
Founded: 1978
Staff: 3
Member of: Technical Association of the Pulp & Paper Industry; Pulp & Paper Technical Association of Canada; Professional Engineers Of Ontario
Products/Services/Areas of Expertise: Independent consulting engineering firm providing services internationally for the design & implementation of all types of pulp, paper & fibreboard mills based on wood & non-wood raw materials including straw, bamboo, reeds, grasses, hemp, sisal, flax & other agricultural residues
Recently Completed / Ongoing Projects: Prefeasibility study for nonwood pulp & paper mill in Manitoba; pulp, paper & fibreboard section of study for Agriculture & Agri-Food Canada on new market opportunities
Domestic Markets:
National
Foreign Activity:
Worldwide
Contact(s):
Robert W. Hurter, President/CEO
bobhurter@hurterconsult.com

Hy-Grade Geoscience
181 Hescott St.
Elmsdale, NS B2S 1L9
902-883-7415
info@hy-gradegeoscience.com
www.hy-gradegeoscience.com
Firm Type: Management Consulting, Engineering
Founded: 1996
Member of: Pinchin LeBlanc Environmental Ltd.
Products/Services/Areas of Expertise: Environmental & Earth Science investigations; environmental assessments
Domestic Markets:
New Brunswick, Newfoundland & Labrador, Nova Scotia, Prince Edward Island
Contact(s):
David C. Carter, P.Geo, President & Sr. Geologist
dcarter@hy-gradegeoscience.com

Hy-Grade Precast Concrete
2411 First St. South
St Catharines, ON L2R 6P7
905-684-8568
Fax: 905-684-8560
800-229-8568
hg@precast.on.ca
www.precast.on.ca
Firm Type: Manufacturing
Founded: 1948
Member of: National Precast Concrete Association; Toronto Construction Association
Products/Services/Areas of Expertise: Pre-engineered, precast, concrete structures for hazardous materials; electrical equipment; pump systems
Financial Information:
Type of Ownership: Private
Domestic Markets:
Ontario
Foreign Activity:
USA
Contact(s):
Dominic Girotti, President & Owner
dg@hygradeprecast.com
Gina Lathan, Sales Manager, North America
glathan@hygradeprecast.com
Peter Belanger, Account Manager
pb@hygradeprecast.com

Hydralogic Systems Inc.
59 Penn Dr.
Toronto, ON M9L 2A6
416-740-3900
Fax: 416-740-3800
800-667-6355
info@hydralogic.ca
www.hydralogic.ca
Firm Type: Manufacturing
Founded: 2003
Products/Services/Areas of Expertise: Manufactures & markets custom micronutrient formulations & odour control products to wastewater, solid waste & agricultural industries under BioStreme & AirStreme brands
Contact(s):
Michael Beckley, C.E.T., President/CEO
Bruce Clark, CFO

Hydraulic Systems Ltd.
41 Ilsey Ave.
Dartmouth, NS B3B 1K9
902-468-6640
Fax: 902-468-3212
800-648-7706
admin@hydraulic-systems.com
www.hydraulic-systems.com
Products/Services/Areas of Expertise: Turn-key projects incorporating centralized hydraulic power systems, hydrostatic drives, deck machinery, pneumatic & mechanical systems,

filtration systems, integrated control systems & complete pipework services
Canadian Branches:
Newfoundland
2 Maverick Place
St. John's, NL A1L 0H6
709-726-3490
Fax: 709-726-3729
1-877-926-3490
nfld@hydraulic-systems.com
Eddy Knox, Manager

Hydro Dyne Inc.
P.O. Box 41061
Dartmouth, NS B2Y 4P7
902-465-2873
Fax: 902-469-4786
Firm Type: Manufacturing
Founded: 1993
Staff: 2
Products/Services/Areas of Expertise: Provides service & systems for removing paint, adhesives & plastic sheeting from aluminum & steel panels on highway road signs; process performed without removing the chromate of galvonized coatings
Financial Information:
Type of Ownership: Private
Revenue Sources: 5% Provincial; 1% Municipals; 4% Private Contracts
Domestic Markets:
Manitoba, New Brunswick, Newfoundland & Labrador, Nova Scotia, Ontario, Saskatchewan
Foreign Activity:
USA
Contact(s):
Tim MacDonald, Owner

Hydro One
North Tower
483 Bay St., 15th Fl. Reception
Toronto, ON M5G 2P5
416-345-5000
877-955-1155
www.hydroone.com
Products/Services/Areas of Expertise: Alternative source electricity distribution.
Contact(s):
Sandra Struthers, Chief Financial Officer
sandy.struthers@hydroone.com

Hydro One
Remote Communities
680 Beaverhall Pl.
Thunder Bay, ON P7E 6G9
416-474-3870
remotes@hydroone.com
Products/Services/Areas of Expertise: Generates & distributes electricty to 18 remote communities across northern Ontario, not connected to the provincial energy grid
Ecological Note: Renewable low-impact electricity
Contact(s):
Rick Rhodes

Hydro Vision America
An operating unit of Hydro Vision GmbH
10520 Yonge St., Unit 35B, Suite 212
Richmond Hill, ON L4C 3C7
905-833-0885
Fax: 905-833-0823
info@hydrovision.us
www.hydrovision.us
Products/Services/Areas of Expertise: With headquarters in Kaufbeuren, Germany, Hydro Vision is an independent manufacturer of products for flow monitoring used in water resource & wastewater systems. Clients are located in over 30 countries & include environmental organizations, governments & consulting engineers. In Canada, D'Aqua Technologies Inc., located in Oakville, ON is a 2nd operating unit - contact Sylvia Silva at 905-465-9261 or sylvia.silva@daquatech.com
Domestic Markets:
National
Contact(s):
Sylvia Silva, National Sales Manager, North America
sylvia.silva@daquatech.com

Hydro-Com Technologies Ltd.
A division of R.V. Anderson Associates Ltd.
445 Urquhart Cres.
Fredericton, NB E3B 8K4
506-455-2888
Fax: 506-455-0193
fredericton@rvanderson.com
www.rvanderson.com/contact/map-hydro-com.shtml
Products/Services/Areas of Expertise: Hydrotechnical engineering; inflow & infiltration studies

Hydro-Logic Environmental Inc.
#250, 762 Upper James St.
Hamilton, ON L9C 3A2
905-777-9494
Fax: 905-777-8678
info@hydrologic.ca
www.hydrologic.ca
Products/Services/Areas of Expertise: Wastewater treatment equipment
Contact(s):
George S. Pastoric

Hydro-Mechanical Sales Ltd.
#1, 3700 Joseph Howe Dr.
Halifax, NS B3L 4H4
902-443-2274
Fax: 902-443-2275
www.hydromechanical.ca
Firm Type: Distributing
Staff: 7
Products/Services/Areas of Expertise: Water & wastewater management & equipment
Domestic Markets:
New Brunswick, Newfoundland & Labrador, Nova Scotia, Prince Edward Island
Contact(s):
Jim Bell, President
jim@hydromechanical.ca
Canadian Branches:
Moncton
#13, 297 Collishaw St.
Moncton, NB E1C 9R2
506-859-1107
Fax: 506-859-2424
Mark Kenny, Manager

St. John's
85 Tolt Rd.
St. John's, NL A1E 5W6
709-895-0090
Fax: 709-368-6887
Dennis Burt

Hydrogenics Corporation
5985 McLaughlin Rd.
Mississauga, ON L5R 1B8
905-361-3660
Fax: 905-361-3626
sales@hydrogenics.com
www.hydrogenics.com
Firm Type: Engineering, Manufacturing
Founded: 1995
Staff: 4
Products/Services/Areas of Expertise: Develops, manufactures & supplies proton exchange membrane (PEM) fuel cell stacks; power sources; generators; offices located in USA, China, India, & Russia
Financial Information:
Type of Ownership: Private
Revenue Sources: 25% nationwide; 75% Private Contracts
Domestic Markets:
Alberta, Ontario, Québec
Foreign Activity:
USA
Markets Sought:
Asia, Western Europe
Contact(s):
Daryl Wilson, President/CEO
Jennifer Barber, Vice-President, Finance & Corporate Controller
Joseph Cargnelli, Chief Technology Officer
Canadian Branches:
Hydrogenics Test Systems
4242 Phillips Ave., #C
Burnaby, BC V5A 2X2
604-676-4000
Fax: 604-676-4111
International Branch(es):
Hydrogenics Corporation - Japan
Naruse Akihabara Bldg. 5F
22 Matsunaga-cho, Kanda, Chiyoka-ku
Tokyo Japan
-81-3-3526-6557
Fax: -81-3-3526-6558

Hydrogenics GmbH
Am Wiesenbusch 2 - Halle 5
Gladbeck Germany
-49-2043-944-133
Fax: -49-2043-944-14

Hydrogenics Onsite Generation
Nijverheidsstraat 48c
Oevel Belgium
-32-0-14-46-21-10
Fax: -32-0-14-46-21-

Hydrogéo Plus Inc.
#10, 9200, boul de l'Acadie
Montréal, QC H4N 2T2
514-383-5651
Fax: 514-383-5332
info@hydrogeoplus.com
www.hydrogeoplus.com
Firm Type: Engineering, Scientific/Technical Services
Founded: 2000
Staff: 12
Member of: Ordre des ingénieurs du Québec; Reseau Environnement
Products/Services/Areas of Expertise: Site remediation; hydrogeology
Financial Information:
Type of Ownership: Private
Revenue: $500,000 - $1.5 Million
Domestic Markets:
British Columbia, New Brunswick, Newfoundland & Labrador, Québec
Foreign Activity:
Central Europe, Western Europe, The Middle East, South America, Worldwide
Contact(s):
Denis Millette, Eng., Ph.D., President

Hydrogéochem Environnement Inc.
#1, 1184, av Cartier
Québec, QC G1R 2S7
418-647-6814
info@hydrogeochem.qc.ca
www.hydrogeochem.qc.ca
Firm Type: Engineering
Founded: 1996
Staff: 1
Member of: Ordre des ingénieur(e)s du Québec
Products/Services/Areas of Expertise: Hydrogeology; geochemistry, in particular related to mine activities; geochemical simulations; numerical modeling of groundwater & contaminant migration
Recently Completed / Ongoing Projects: Rehabilitation of mine tailings impoundment, East Sullivan site, Québec; design & follow up of the acid mine drainage treatment system, East Sullivan site, Québec; hydrogeological characterization of a site for municipal waste deposit, Rouyn site, Québec; hydrogelological & geochemical characterizations & groundwater modelling, Manitou site, Québec
Financial Information:
Type of Ownership: Private
Revenue: $50,000 - $100,000
Revenue Sources: 10% nationwide; 80% Provincial; 10% Private Contracts
Domestic Markets:
Québec
Markets Sought:
Central America, Central Europe, South America
Contact(s):
Diane Germain, President

Hydrogeological Consultants
17740 - 118 St. NW
Edmonton, AB T5S 2W3
780-483-7240
Fax: 780-484-9413
800-661-7972

info@hcl.ca
www.hcl.ca
Firm Type: Management Consulting
Founded: 1969
Products/Services/Areas of Expertise: Groundwater consulting; environmental assessments
Financial Information:
Type of Ownership: Private

Hydromantis Inc.
#1601, 1 James St. S
Hamilton, ON L8P 4R5
905-522-0012
Fax: 905-522-0031
info@hydromantis.com
www.hydromantis.com
Firm Type: Engineering
Founded: 1985
Staff: 35
Member of: Professional Engineers of Ontario; Water Environment Association; Consulting Engineers of Ontario; Water Environment Research Foundation
Products/Services/Areas of Expertise: Provides consulting engineering services for optimization & design of water & wastewater treatment plants; provides training & technology transfer in the areas of water & wastewater treatment, plant process control & instrumentation; provides customized software & programming for SCADA; specializes in the development of software for the simulation & modelling of wastewater treatment plants
Recently Completed / Ongoing Projects: City of Hamilton biosolids master plan; Halton Region Milton WWTP UV disinfection design; Ontario Ministry of the Environment water & sewage design guidelines; Haldimand County Caledonia wastewater treatment plan design; Waterloo Region Wells 34/36 water plant designs; City of Cornwall water treatment plant; City of Windsor wastewater disinfection design; Pima County, Arizona wastewater treatment modelling with GPS-X
Financial Information:
Type of Ownership: Private
Revenue: $3 Million - $5 Million
Revenue Sources: 10% nationwide; 10% Provincial; 60% Municipals; 20% Private Contracts
Domestic Markets:
Ontario
Foreign Activity:
China, Central Europe, Western Europe, The Pacific Rim, Mexico, USA, Vietnam
Contact(s):
Mike Newbigging, President
Brian Monaghan, Marketing
Chris Mroczek, Director, Design
Jeff Mullin, Director, Design

Canadian Branches:
Cambridge Branch
420 Sheldon Dr.
Cambridge, ON N1T 2H9
519-624-7223
Fax: 519-624-7224
Mike Newbigging

Hydromega Energy Inc.
1134, rue Sainte-Catherine ouest, 12e étage
Montréal, QC H3B 1H4X9
514-392-9266
Fax: 514-392-1466
Firm Type: Management Consulting, Engineering, Manufacturing
Founded: 1985
Staff: 16
Member of: Québec Hydroelectric Association
Products/Services/Areas of Expertise: Hydroelectric power producer, developer & operator
Financial Information:
Type of Ownership: Private
Revenue Sources: 100% Provincial
Domestic Markets:
Québec
Foreign Activity:
USA
Markets Sought:
Central America, Eastern Europe, South America, Mexico,
Contact(s):
Philip Lawee, Contact

Hydroqual Laboratories Ltd.
#4, 6125 - 12 St. SE
Calgary, AB T2H 2K1
403-253-7121
Fax: 403-252-9363
info@hydroqual.ca
www.hydroqual.ca
Firm Type: Scientific/Technical Services
Staff: 12
Member of: Water Environment Federation; Canadian Association of Environmental Analytical Laboratories
Products/Services/Areas of Expertise: Toxicity testing of effluents, products (CEPA, DECA, FIFRA, TSCA, GLP); contaminated site investigations; toxicity identification evaluations; testing for ecological & environmental risk assessments; biotreatability testing; microbial characterizations; custom testing services
Financial Information:
Type of Ownership: Private
Revenue Sources: 10% nationwide; 10% Provincial; 10% Municipals; 70% Private Contracts
Domestic Markets:
National
Foreign Activity:
Western Europe, The Pacific Rim, USA
Contact(s):
Stephen Goudey, President

Hydroxyl Systems Inc.
#202, 26 Bastion Sq.
Victoria, BC V8W 1H9
250-381-8850
Fax: 250-381-8870
888-655-3348
info@hydroxyl.com
Firm Type: Manufacturing
Founded: 1993
Staff: 30
Products/Services/Areas of Expertise: Packaged wastewater treatment systems for residential & commercial use
Financial Information:
Type of Ownership: Private
Revenue: Greater than $5 Million
Domestic Markets:
National
Foreign Activity:
USA
Contact(s):
Carolyn Rogers, President & CEO
crogers@hydroxyl.com
Greg Kazakoff, Vice-President, Finance & Accounting
gkazakoff@hydroxyl.com

Hygrex-Spehr Industries
#18, 1040 Martin Grove Rd.
Toronto, ON M9W 4W4
416-916-9014
Fax: 647-439-6615
info@hygrex.com
www.hygrex.com
Firm Type: Distributing, Manufacturing
Founded: 1982
Staff: 20
Products/Services/Areas of Expertise: Dry air generator, for drying of filter cake sludges, water based paints, water-washed components, retrofit gas/heat ovens, elimination of humidity in plant environments
Financial Information:
Type of Ownership: Private
Domestic Markets:
National
Contact(s):
Clayton Claveau, COO
Erwin Spehr, President
Tanya Shepley, Marketing Director
Honey Felske, Sales Director

Hymopack Ltd.
41 Medulla Ave.
Toronto, ON M8Z 5L6
416-232-1733
Fax: 416-232-2194
877-594-4966
custserv@hymopack.com
www.hymopack.com
Ecological Note: Eco-Sacs plastic bags
Contact(s):

Gerry Maldoff, President
Carry Weiss, Sales Executive

Hyperspectral Data International Inc. / HDI
#119, 7071 Bayers Rd.
Halifax, NS B3L 2C2
902-461-2161
Fax: 902-453-6325
info@hdi.ns.ca
www.hdi.ns.ca
Firm Type: Scientific/Technical Services
Founded: 1997
Staff: 6
Products/Services/Areas of Expertise: Hyperspectral surveys including data collection, analysis & mapping services
Recently Completed / Ongoing Projects: River quality monitoring for USEPA; land use study in Ohio for USEPA
Financial Information:
Type of Ownership: Private
Revenue: $500,000 - $1.5 Million
Domestic Markets:
New Brunswick, Nova Scotia, Prince Edward Island
Foreign Activity:
Africa, Caribbean, Central Europe, Western Europe, South America, USA
Contact(s):
Paul Morrison, CEO
Herb Ripley, President
Bill Jones, Manager, Applications

Hyprescon Inc.
A subsidiary of Hanson Pipe & Precast Inc.
699, boul Industriel
Saint-Eustache, QC J7R 6C3
450-623-2200
Fax: 450-623-3308
888-497-7371
sales@hyprescon.com
Firm Type: Manufacturing
Founded: 1990
Member of: American Waterworks Association; American Concrete Pressure Pipe Association
Products/Services/Areas of Expertise: Manufacture & sales of concrete pressure pipe & fittings from 350mm to 2800mm diameters to AWWA C-303, C-301 & C-304 specifications
Financial Information:
Type of Ownership: Private
Domestic Markets:
National
Foreign Activity:
USA
Contact(s):
Guy Laflamme, Facility Manager
Contact(s):
Rick Bayard, Facility Manager
Contact(s):
Steve Gates, Facility Manager

Canadian Branches:
Stouffville Plant
5387 Bethesda Rd.
Stouffville, ON L4A 7X3
905-640-5151
Fax: 905-640-5154
800-679-1163

Uxbridge Plant
102 Prouse Rd.
Uxbridge, ON L4A 7X4
905-642-4380

I.G. Micromed Environmental Inc.
#190, 12860 Clarke Pl.
Richmond, BC V6V 2H1
604-279-0666
Fax: 604-279-0663
info@igmicromed.com
www.igmicromed.com
Firm Type: Scientific/Technical Services
Quality Environmental Management System(s): 17025
Products/Services/Areas of Expertise: Microbiological testing laboratory; product shelf life evaluations; HACCP implementation; plant & equipment inspection; on-site consulting; air quality testing
Financial Information:
Type of Ownership: Private
Contact(s):
Richard Geere

Products & Services Buyer's Guide

IBI Group
230 Richmond St. West, 5th Fl.
Toronto, ON M5V 1V6
416-596-1930
Fax: 416-596-0644
nirwin@ibigroup.com
www.ibigroup.com
Firm Type: Engineering, Scientific/Technical Services
Founded: 1974
Staff: 1200
Products/Services/Areas of Expertise: Consulting & design services in transportation/systems; land planning & urban/regional development planning; facilities planning, programming & design
Recently Completed / Ongoing Projects: Highway preliminary design studies; Ontario Ministry of Transportation; Halton waste landfill site; Credit Valley water quality study
Domestic Markets:
National
Foreign Activity:
Worldwide
Contact(s):
N.A. Irwin, P.Eng., Chair/Director
Ewen S. Fisher, Director, Environmental Group
Trevor McIntyre, Director, Urban Design
Don Drackley, Associate, Transportation/Environmental Group
Canadian Branches:
Calgary
#400, 1167 Kensington Cres. NW
Calgary, AB T2N 1X7
403-270-5600
Fax: 403-270-5610
S.W. Shawcross

Edmonton
Standard Life Bldg.
#1050, 10405 Jasper Ave.
Edmonton, AB T5J 5N4
780-428-4000
Fax: 780-426-3256
P.J. Moore

Montréal
460, rue McGill
Montréal, QC H2Y 2H2
514-954-5300
Fax: 514-954-5345
Daniel Paré

Vancouver
#700, 1285 West Pender St.
Vancouver, BC V6E 4B1
604-683-8797
Fax: 604-683-0492
R. Andy McNally

International Branch(es):
Boston, MA
77 Franklin St., 7th Fl.
Boston, MA USA
617-450-0701
Fax: 617-450-0702

Denver, CO
#610, 1401 - 17th St.
Denver, CO USA
303-713-1013
Fax: 303-713-1014
denver@ibigroup.com
Peter Zurawel

Irvine, CA
#110, 18401 Von Karman Ave.
Irvine, CA USA
714-833-5588
Fax: 714-833-5511
A.W. Baillie

London, UK
Kemp House
152 - 160 City Rd., 1st Fl.
London GBR
-44-2070-171-850
Fax: -44-2072-518-33
enquiriesuk@ibigroup.com
David Kamnitzer

Seattle, WA
#1400, 801 Second Ave.
Seattle, WA USA
206-521-9091
Fax: 206-521-9095
P.P. Lavallee

ICC The Compliance Center Inc.
#7, 205 Matheson Blvd. East
Mississauga, ON L4Z 1X8
905-890-7227
www.thecompliancecenter.com

ICC The Compliance Centre Inc.
Also Known As: International Compliance Centre
#7, 205 Matheson Blvd. East
Mississauga, ON L4Z 1X8
905-890-7227
Fax: 905-890-7070
888-977-4834
www.thecompliancecenter.com
Products/Services/Areas of Expertise: Services & products to assist compliance with hazardous materials & transportation legislation; WHMIS regulations
Domestic Markets:
National
Foreign Activity:
Mexico, USA
Contact(s):
Wally Heaps, Branch Manager
Dan Albert, Systems Sales Director
Canadian Branches:
Montréal
88, av Lindsay
Montréal, QC H9P 2T8
514-636-8146
Fax: 514-636-3522
1-888-977-4834
Kate Morris, Branch Manager

Icefield Instruments Inc.
P.O. Box 30036
#300 - 116 Galena Rd.
Whitehorse, YT Y1A 5M2
867-633-4264
Fax: 867-633-4217
877-423-3435
information@icefield.yk.ca
www.icefield.yk.ca
Firm Type: Scientific/Technical Services
Founded: 1990
Products/Services/Areas of Expertise: Geophysical consulting services with emphasis on hydrology & glaciology; design & manufacture of custom geophysical/environmental instrumentation; data acquisition platforms for demanding field applications; custom geophysical software; baseline geoscience & environmental impact studies; contract research
Domestic Markets:
Alberta, British Columbia, Northwest Territories, Yukon Territory
Foreign Activity:
Asia, Western Europe
Contact(s):
Erik Blake, Ph.D., P.Geo., P.Geoph., President
erik@icefield.yk.ca

ICF International Canada Inc.
#808, 277 Wellington St. West
Toronto, ON M5V 3E4
416-341-0990
Fax: 416-341-0383
info@icfi.com
www.icfi.com
Firm Type: Management Consulting
Founded: 1995
Staff: 15
Member of: Ontario Environment Industry Association
Products/Services/Areas of Expertise: General energy management; general environmental consulting & contracting services
Financial Information:
Type of Ownership: Private
Revenue Sources: 15% nationwide; 15% Provincial; 70% Private Contracts
Domestic Markets:
Alberta, British Columbia, Manitoba, New Brunswick, Nova Scotia, Ontario, Québec, Saskatchewan

Foreign Activity:
Worldwide
Contact(s):
Duncan Rotherham, Vice-President, Canadian Operations
Canadian Branches:
Oakville - Toronto Area Office
1301 Golden Meadow Trail
Oakville, ON L6H 3H1
905-844-9510
Fax: 905-844-9510

Ottawa - ICF Marbek
#300, 222 Somerset St. West
Ottawa, ON K2P 2G3
613-523-0784
Fax: 613-523-0717
info@marbek.ca
www.marbek.ca

ICI Paints (Canada) Inc.
Also Known As: Color Your World
A brand of Akzo Nobel Canada Inc.
8200 Keele St.
Concord, ON L4K 2A5
905-669-1020
Fax: 905-669-3433
800-387-7311
cilpaint@ici.com
www.icipaints.ca
Ecological Note: CIL, Dulux, Glidden, ICI, Fast & Easy, Color Your World, Painters Choice, Spred, Ultra-Hide products
Foreign Activity:
USA
Contact(s):
David Hamill, Chief Executive Officer, Akzo Nobel Decorative Paints
Pierre Dufresne, General Manager, Decorative Paints, Canada
Brad Elkins, Media Contact, 905-669-3464
brad.elkins@akzonobel.com

IEG Consultants Ltd. / IEG
Formerly: Hycal Environmental Sciences Ltd.
Dowland Bldg.
Inuvik, NT X0E 0T0
867-777-8520
Fax: 867-777-2747
info@ieg.ca
www.ieg.ca
Firm Type: Engineering, Scientific/Technical Services
Founded: 1998
Staff: 35
Products/Services/Areas of Expertise: Environmental & socio-economic planning; contaminated site & waste management services; environmental health & safety management; engineering services; Northern & Aboriginal training
Financial Information:
Type of Ownership: Private
Domestic Markets:
National
Foreign Activity:
South America
Markets Sought:
Former USSR

IG Machine & Fibers Ltd.
87 Orenda Rd.
Brampton, ON L6W 1V7
905-457-0745
Fax: 905-457-9923
Firm Type: Manufacturing
Staff: 44
Products/Services/Areas of Expertise: Paper broker; roofing manufacturer

Imalog Inc.
#100, 5940, boul Thimens
Montréal, QC H4R 2K9
514-337-7979
Fax: 514-337-7589
Contact(s):
Tony Dischiavi

Imbibitive Technologies Canada, Inc.
Also Known As: Imtech Canada Inc.
#1, 8 Hiscott St.
St Catharines, ON L2R 1C6

905-641-2323
Fax: 905-641-3601
888-843-2323
imtech@imbiberbeads.com
www.imbiberbeads.com
Firm Type: Manufacturing
Founded: 1994
Staff: 14
Products/Services/Areas of Expertise: Manufacturer of absorbent polymer, imbiber beads engineered to capture & contain a broad cross-section of organic chemical spectrum, including BTEX, chlorinated solvents, PCB's, crude oil, jet fuel, diesel, MEK, MIBK, etc.; spill response & pollution prevention applications
Recently Completed / Ongoing Projects: Performance certified by Environment Canada ETV programme, June '97; nominated by US Air Force for White House Closing the Circle award, P2 Environmental Innovation '98; recommended by USAF MEEP Report for emergency spill response & P2; Tech museum awards, Laurzate 2003
Financial Information:
Type of Ownership: Private
Revenue: $500,000 - $1.5 Million
Revenue Sources: 5% nationwide; 95% Private Contracts
Domestic Markets:
National
Foreign Activity:
Asia, Australia/New Zealand, Western Europe, USA
Contact(s):
John S. Brinkman, President/CEO
Nick Flor, Vice-President
J. Chris Polis, Corporate Product Manager

IMO Pump Inc.
A division of Colfax Corp.
Formerly: IMO Industries (Canada) Inc.6750 Davand Dr.
Mississauga, ON L5T 1L8
905-564-3344
Fax: 905-564-3577
customercare-americas@colfaxcorp.com
www.imo-pump.com
Products/Services/Areas of Expertise: Sale of pumps for hydrocarbon & chemical processing, power generation, pulp & paper, crude oil transport & general industrial machinery
Contact(s):
Julius Toth, Contact

Canadian Branches:
Calgary Branch
#8A, 4620 Manilla Rd. SE
Calgary, AB T2G 4B7
403-253-7491
Fax: 403-252-9833
Miles Chaykowski, Contact
miles.chaykowski@colfaxcorp.com

Edmonton Branch
5103 - 123rd St.
Edmonton, AB T6H 3S9
780-439-0226
Fax: 780-439-6222
Leo Barry, Contact
leo.barry@colfaxcorp.com

IMP Liquid Meters & Petroleum Services
A division of IMP Group Ltd.
Burnside Industrial Park
19 Alkerley Blvd.
Dartmouth, NS B3B 1J6
902-468-3958
Fax: 902-468-2261
www.impgroup.com
Firm Type: Distributing, Manufacturing
Founded: 1980
Staff: 5
Products/Services/Areas of Expertise: Filters, gas absorption/adsorption systems; chemical feeding, mixing equipment; screens & strainers; water handling products & equipment
Domestic Markets:
New Brunswick, Newfoundland & Labrador, Nova Scotia, Prince Edward Island
Contact(s):
Kenneth C. Rowe, Executive Chair, IMP Group
Stephen Plummer, President & CEO, IMP Group
Raymond P. Mccormick, Sr. VP & CFO, IMP Group
Contact(s):

Terry White, Branch Manager
terry.white@impmarine.com
Canadian Branches:
IMP Group Ltd. (Marine Div.) - St. John's
P.O. Box 8560
5-7 Pippy Pl.
St. John's, NL A1B 3P4
709-722-4221
Fax: 709-722-9763
info@impmarine.com
www.impmarine.com

IMP Group Ltd. (Marine Div.) - Dartmouth
120 Thornhill Dr.
Dartmouth, NS B3B 1S3
902-468-2111
Fax: 902-468-3077
info@impmarine.com
www.impmarine.com

Impact Environmental Services Ltd.
Box 29, Site 10, RR#1
Red Deer, AB T4N 5E1
403-346-1180
Fax: 403-346-9720

Impact Microbiology Services
Formerly: Connors Microbiological Consulting
2 Garland Ct.
Fredericton, NB E3B 6C2
506-459-7033
Fax: 506-460-8315
www.impactmicrobiology.com
Contact(s):
Elena Connors, Director, Microbiology
econnors@impactmicrobiology.com

Impro
Affiliate of Georges Nadeau Inc.
5265 General Rd.
Mississauga, ON L4W 2K4
905-602-4300
Fax: 905-602-8166
800-954-6776
csimpro@polrnet.com
www.polrnet.com/impro.htm
Contact(s):
Bob Fellows

IMTT-Newfoundland Ltd.
A partnership of IMTT & Newfoundland Transshipment Ltd.
P.O. Box 451
201 Whiffen Head Rd.
Arnolds Cove, NL A0B 1A0
709-463-4688
Fax: 709-463-4752
www.imtt.com; www.ntl.net
Firm Type: Engineering
Member of: Newfoundland & Labrador Environmental Industry Association
Products/Services/Areas of Expertise: Marine terminal includes an approach causeway, tug basin, trestle, & two jetties, with berthing & marine topside facilities (crude transfer & control system); onshore facilities include a tank farm, tank heating system, interconnecting flowlines, supporting facilities, storm water handling system & fire protection system
Contact(s):
Howard Kelly, Terminal Manager
hgkelly@imtt.nf.ca
Maurice Baker, Manager, Operation Maintenance

IMTT-Québec Ltd.
A partnership of IMTT, Dan Odfjell Group, Port de Québec
P.O. Box 53010
Quai 50
Québec, QC G1J 5K3
418-667-8641
Fax: 418-667-9551
www.imttque.com; www.imtt.com
Firm Type: Engineering
Staff: 25
Products/Services/Areas of Expertise: Marine terminal handling petroleum products, biodiesel, bulk goods, & chemicals; has 53 tanks (steel, lined, insulated, heated, refrigerated, online monitoring); 24-hr. deep-water connection; 2 docks; 9 piggable dock lines; rail connections; truck fleets nearby; truck scale
Contact(s):

Marc Dulude, Exec. Vice-President
marc.dulude@imttque.com

In Tech Risk Management Inc.
#400, 480 University Ave.
Toronto, ON M5G 1V2
416-348-9111
Fax: 416-348-9121
800-947-9666
info@intechrisk.com
www.intechrisk.com
Products/Services/Areas of Expertise: Canada's largest independent pure insurance risk management company; for over 20 years, In Tech has been providing reliable consultation & timely financial insurance risk management services to clients with a variety of risks; provide expertise in financial risk management, consulting & document tracking
Contact(s):
Rory M. Roberts, President

In!Flame Fireplaces Inc.
#310, 99 Atlantic Ave.
Toronto, ON M6K 3J8
416-530-0555
Fax: 416-530-9895
888-396-9219
www.inflame.ca
Firm Type: Distributing
Member of: Environmental Choice Program; Ontatio Camping Association; Greater Toronto Home Builders' Association; Canadian Home Builders Association
EcoLogo Certified Products & Services: Sunjel Premium is a remarkable renewable resource, derived from natural sugar cane or corn, & each 369g canister burns for 2-3 hours
Products/Services/Areas of Expertise: Is a leader in Alcohol Gel development, being the first & only Canadian Company certified to carry the EcoLogo for Simulated Gel Fireplaces for unvented fireplace use.
Ecological Note: Sunjel Premium is a remarkable renewable resource, derived from natural sugar cane or corn, & each 369g canister burns for 2-3 hours
Contact(s):
Tim Petrullo
tpetrullo@inflame.ca

Incinolet Products
2022 - 7th Ave. East
Owen Sound, ON N4K 6R9
519-938-9108
Fax: 519-938-9214
800-263-0379
incinolet@on.aibn.com
www.incinolet.ca
Firm Type: Distributing
Founded: 1995
Staff: 4
Products/Services/Areas of Expertise: Canadian distributor of Incinolet incinerating electric toilets
Domestic Markets:
National
Contact(s):
Joanne Whyte

Inco Technical Services Limited / ITSL
Inco Ltd.
2060 Flavelle Blvd.
Mississauga, ON L5K 1Z9
905-403-2406
Fax: 905-403-2402
robbins@inco.com
www.inco.com
Firm Type: Engineering, Scientific/Technical Services
Founded: 1980
Staff: 10
Products/Services/Areas of Expertise: Sulphur dioxide, air, cyanide destruction process; complete technical services including: laboratory testwork, engineering, plant commissioning
Domestic Markets:
National
Foreign Activity:
Africa, Australia/New Zealand, Central America, China, Eastern Europe, Western Europe, The Pacific Rim, Mexico, USA, Former USSR, Vietnam
Contact(s):
G.H. Robbins, Director, Business Development

Products & Services Buyer's Guide

INCOM Manufacturing Group
1259 Sandhill Dr.
Ancaster, ON L9G 4V5
905-648-6811
Fax: 905-648-7188
800-263-6238
cwd@incomdirect.com
www.incomdirect.com

InCoretec Inc.
Formerly: Coretec Inc.
Baine Johnston Center
#804, 10 Fort William Pl.
St. John's, NL A1C 1K4
709-739-7770
Fax: 709-739-7780
Firm Type: Engineering
Founded: 1988
Staff: 7
Products/Services/Areas of Expertise: Predictive Artificial Intelligence, utilized in various applications, ranging from icebergs & their drift trajectories to marine vessels & their intended courses; Advanced Ship Autopilot System to predict friction encountered in robotic motion control applications
Contact(s):
Mona El-Tahan, President/CEO

Indachem Inc.
#3, 1040 Martin Grove Rd.
Toronto, ON M4W 4W4
416-743-3751
Fax: 416-743-2038
ballen@keddco.com
www.indachem.com
Firm Type: Distributing
Founded: 1978
Staff: 4
Products/Services/Areas of Expertise: Polymer activation & feed systems; chlorination/dechlorination control; odour control; centrifuges; oily water separators; metering pumps; high pressure pumps & non-clog centrifugal pumps; chemical induction & mixing systems; emergency valve actuators; arsenic removal
Financial Information:
Type of Ownership: Private
Domestic Markets:
National
Contact(s):
Brian Allen, Contact

Indaco Manufacturing Limited
#11, 813 Brock Rd.
Pickering, ON L1W 3L8
905-839-0422
Fax: 905-839-0200
800-433-7334
info@indaco.ca
www.indaco.ca
Firm Type: Manufacturing
Founded: 1991
Staff: 5
Products/Services/Areas of Expertise: Manufacturer of bags made with a compostable, patented polymer; degradation is activated by heat & oxygen rather than bacteria; bags are used for the collection of leaf & yard waste; bags & liners are ideal for wet waste/organic collection in both residential & commercial applications, & are available to fit any container size; also manufactures films which can be dry degraded, to further minimize landfill disposal; all products are non-toxic, non polluting & have been developed as the environmental solution for the collection of compostables through years of research & development
Financial Information:
Type of Ownership: Private
Domestic Markets:
National
Foreign Activity:
Asia, Australia/New Zealand, Central Europe, The Middle East, USA,

INDECO Strategic Consulting Inc.
#412, 77 Mowat Ave.
Toronto, ON M6K 3E3
416-532-4333
888-463-3121
info@indeco.com
www.indeco.com

Firm Type: Management Consulting, Scientific/Technical Services
Founded: 1994
Staff: 6
Member of: Ontario Environmental Industry Association; Canadian Energy Efficiency Alliance; Electricity Distributors Association
Products/Services/Areas of Expertise: Assist clients in the development of strategic planning processes that integrate environmental considerations into the corporate planning process; design & implementation of environmental, health & safety management information systems; services include measuring & reporting on corporate performance in environmental management, developing strategies to anticipate & respond to public policy, assessing technology & market opportunities, obtaining environmental & energy regulatory approvals, communication & training in technical & organizational issues, attaining corporate client accreditation for environmental initiatives & design & evaluation of policy measures & programs to promote technological innovation & reduce environmental impacts
Recently Completed / Ongoing Projects: Assisting an industrial association in assessing & reporting their emissions; assisting energy distribution companies in developing & implementing demand side management plans & programs
Financial Information:
Type of Ownership: Private
Revenue Sources: 10% Municipals; 90% Private Contracts
Domestic Markets:
National
Foreign Activity:
Asia, Central America, South America, USA
Contact(s):
David Heeney, President, 416/204-0356
dheeney@indeco.com
Judy Simon, Vice-President, 416/204-0357
jsimon@indeco.com
Heather Davidson-Meyn, Sr. Consultant, 416/204-0361
hdavidson-meyn@indeco.com
Shona Adamson, Sr. Consultant, 416/204-0359
sadamson@indeco.com

Indoor Air Quality Ottawa
Building C
#10, 2285 St. Laurent Blvd.
Ottawa, ON K1G 4Z6
613-237-8381
Fax: 613-237-1269
rankin@magma.ca
www.iaqottawa.com
Firm Type: Management Consulting, Scientific/Technical Services
Founded: 2004
Member of: Armstrong Monitoring Corporation, Better Business Bureau, Canada Green Building Council, Indoor Air Quality Association
Products/Services/Areas of Expertise: The firm investigates radon, lead, asbestos & mold in residential & commercial settings. Services include building durability & sustainability reports, school profiles, arena/pool profiles, designated substance surveys, consultation & testing re Grow Ops, home inspections, insurance clearance testing, lectures & training. Air quality monitors & data loggers available for lease
Financial Information:
Type of Ownership: Private
Revenue: Less than $50,000
Revenue Sources: 100% Private Contracts
Domestic Markets:
Ontario
Contact(s):
Shawn Rankin, Principal

Industrial Combustion Equipment Ltd.
525, av Edward VII
Montréal, QC H9P 1E7
514-631-2020
Fax: 514-636-0608
Products/Services/Areas of Expertise: Heat transfer systems, for processing, heating, cooling, waste heat recovery
Contact(s):
Phillip Cowie, Directeur, Marketing

Industrial Ecology Corp. / IEC
#205, 55 St. Clair Ave. West
Toronto, ON M4V 2Y7
416-362-5890
Fax: 416-362-1218

Firm Type: Financial
Founded: 1991
Staff: 5
Products/Services/Areas of Expertise: Specializes in the commercialization & development of new technologies & businesses in the recycling, environmental, waste & energy sectors; acts as a merchant bank for those opportunities which qualify & meet the firm's investment criteria & also assists new enterprises to source start-up, development & expansion capital
Financial Information:
Type of Ownership: Private
Domestic Markets:
National
Jim Buckler, Vice-President & CFO

Industrial Forestry Service Ltd. / IFS
1595 Fifth Ave.
Prince George, BC V2L 3L9
250-564-4115
Fax: 250-563-9679
ifs@indforserv.bc.ca
www.indforserv.bc.ca
Firm Type: Scientific/Technical Services
Founded: 1952
Staff: 130
Products/Services/Areas of Expertise: Forestry consulting
Domestic Markets:
Alberta, British Columbia

Canadian Branches:
Dawson Creek Office
11613 - 7th St.
Dawson Creek, BC V1G 4S4
250-784-1987
Fax: 250-784-1986
ifsdc@indforserv.bc.ca

Prince George Office
22135 Ness Lake Rd.
Prince George, BC V2K 5L9
250-697-4545
Fax: 250-967-4691
nurserv@indforserv.bc.ca

Industrial Marine Power Engineering Group / IMPEG
Div. of Mechtronics Technology Inc.
#2110, 1851 Savage Rd.
Richmond, BC V6V 2R6
604-276-8188
Fax: 604-276-2790
impeg@impeg.com
www.impeg.com
Firm Type: Engineering, Manufacturing
Founded: 1974
Staff: 10
Products/Services/Areas of Expertise: Measuring & monitoring equipment; laboratory equipment; oil recovery vessel; propulsions & controls for oil skimmer
Financial Information:
Type of Ownership: Private
Domestic Markets:
Alberta, British Columbia, Manitoba, New Brunswick, Newfoundland & Labrador, Ontario
Foreign Activity:
Asia, Australia/New Zealand, Central America, USA
Contact(s):
Stephen Hui, President
Rodney Ng, Vice-President, Sales

Industrial Plastics Fabricators Ltd.
75 Selby Rd.
Brampton, ON L6W 1K5
905-454-7632
Fax: 905-454-7363
866-694-9381
frank@ipflimited.com
www.ipflimited.com
Firm Type: Manufacturing
Founded: 1982
Staff: 14
Products/Services/Areas of Expertise: Exhaust fans; mist eliminators; scrubbers; ventilation systems; chemical storage tanks; custom built fiberglass fittings & pipe; process tanks; plating saddles; air agitation coils; pipe headers; mine launders; exhaust stacks; plating & anodizing systems; wastewater treatment systems

Financial Information:
Type of Ownership: Private
Revenue: $1.5 Million - $3 Million
Domestic Markets:
National
Foreign Activity:
Mexico, USA
Contact(s):
Frank S. Pereira, President
Tom Wong, Vice-President

Industrial Scientific Corporation
#197, 14845 - 6 Yonge St.
Aurora, ON L4G 6H8
905-727-5595
Fax: 905-727-1594
800-338-3287
www.indsci.com
Firm Type: Manufacturing
Quality Environmental Management System(s): 9001
Products/Services/Areas of Expertise: Portable/fixed gas monitors; calibration; rentals; service
Financial Information:
Type of Ownership: Publicly Traded
Revenue Sources: 10% nationwide; 10% Provincial; 10% Municipals; 70% Private Contracts
Domestic Markets:
National

Industrial Thermo Polymers Ltd. / ITP
153 Van Kirk Dr.
Brampton, ON L7A 1A4
905-846-3666
Fax: 905-846-0363
800-387-3847
info@tundrafoam.com
www.tundrafoam.com
Firm Type: Manufacturing
Founded: 1980
Staff: 60
Member of: MasterNet Ltd.; Venture Foam Products
Quality Environmental Management System(s): 9001; 9002
Products/Services/Areas of Expertise: Foam pipe insulation; backer rod insulation; attic rafter insulation; custom PE foam profiles
Domestic Markets:
National
Foreign Activity:
Asia, Australia/New Zealand, Eastern Europe, The Middle East, The Pacific Rim, USA
Contact(s):
Steve Hartman, President
Art Cyr, Vice-President

Industries de Moules et Plastiques VIF
VIF Mould & Plastics Industries Ltd.
Also Known As: VIF Industries
4000, boul Casavant ouest
Saint-Hyacinthe, QC J2S 9E3
450-774-6953
Fax: 450-774-4970
info@vifplastics.com
www.vifplastics.com
Firm Type: Manufacturing
Founded: 1973
Staff: 60
Member of: Society of Plastic Engineers; l'Association canadienne de l'industrie des plastiques au Québec
Quality Environmental Management System(s): 9001:2000
Products/Services/Areas of Expertise: Équipement médical; systèmes de contrôle du climat
Financial Information:
Type of Ownership: Private
Revenue: Greater than $5 Million
Domestic Markets:
British Columbia, Nova Scotia, Ontario, Québec
Foreign Activity:
USA
Contact(s):
Thierry Carrière, Owner & President

Industries Machinex Inc.
Machinex Industries Inc.
Parc Industriel
2121, rue Olivier
Plessisville, QC G6L 3G9
819-362-3281
Fax: 819-362-2280
info@machinex.ca
www.machinex.ca
Firm Type: Manufacturing
Founded: 1970
Staff: 100
Products/Services/Areas of Expertise: Complete engineering design, fabrication & installation of MRF & MSW equipment; provides turnkey project for the recycling industry: single stream, front-end processing, waste handling, C&C, etc.
Recently Completed / Ongoing Projects: MRF: Disposal, Escondido, CA; MRF: Canada Fibers, Toronto, ON; C&D: Waterway, Chesapeake, VA; Material recycling facility: California Waste, Oakland, CA; Canadian Waste, Edmonton, AB; Ottawa Valley Waste Recovery, Pembroke, ON; front-end processing & composting facility, FWMC, Brookfield, PE; OCC processing line, TRI-R, Denver, CO
Financial Information:
Type of Ownership: Private
Revenue Sources: 25% Municipals; 75% Private Contracts
Domestic Markets:
National
Foreign Activity:
Asia, China, Western Europe, USA, Vietnam
Markets Sought:
South America,
Contact(s):
Pierre Paré, President

Canadian Branches:
Pickering
#11, 817 Brock St. South
Pickering, ON L1W 3L9
905-420-0466
Fax: 905-420-0319
sales@machinexrt.ca

International Branch(es):
Chicago
#1300, 8770 Bryn Mawr Ave. West
Chicago, IL USA
773-867-8801
Fax: 773-867-8802
info@mti.machinex.ca
Nicholas Belanger

InfoMine Inc.
Formerly: Enviromine Inc.
#900, 580 Hornby St.
Vancouver, BC V6C 3B6
604-683-2037
Fax: 604-681-4166
info-ca@infomine.com
www.infomine.com
Firm Type: Information Technology
Founded: 1989
Products/Services/Areas of Expertise: Provides comprehensive & in-depth, online information on mining & mineral exploration worldwide
Financial Information:
Type of Ownership: Private
Domestic Markets:
National
Foreign Activity:
Australia/New Zealand, South Africa, South America, USA
Contact(s):
Andy Robertson, Ph.D, Exec. Chair, President & CEO
andyr@infomine.com
Julian Houlding, COO & Chief Technical Officer
jhoulding@infomine.com
Graham Baldwin, Director, Business Development
gbaldwin@infomine.com

Inform Consulting Services Ltd.
140 Brule Point Rd., RR1
Tatamagouche, NS B0K 1V0
902-657-3023
Fax: 902-657-7303
Products/Services/Areas of Expertise: Forestry, reforestation; GIS, mapping
Contact(s):
Gerald Linfield

Infotech Canada Inc.
P.O. Box 8431
570 Newfoundland Dr.
St. John's, NL A1B 3N9
709-726-4736
Fax: 709-757-0301
800-974-1241
support@infotechsolutions.com
www.infotechsolutions.com
Firm Type: Information Technology
Founded: 1994
Products/Services/Areas of Expertise: Helps facilitate information management & communications
Domestic Markets:
National
Contact(s):
Victor Bonnah, Co-Founder, President & CEO
Steve Clarke, Co-Founder & CIO
Amanda Murphy, Vice-President, Operations

Canadian Branches:
Ottawa Branch
25 Gatesbury St.
Ottawa, ON K2J 4X5
613-482-1873
Fax: 613-482-1874

Infratech Corporation
P.O. Box 2099
3415 - 35th Ave.
Whitecourt, AB T7S 1P7
780-778-4226
Fax: 780-778-4220
888-377-5432
sales@infratech.cc
www.infratech.cc
Firm Type: Manufacturing
Founded: 1987
Staff: 35
Member of: Environment Services Association of Alberta
Quality Environmental Management System(s): 9001
Products/Services/Areas of Expertise: Design & manufacture of incineration equipment; solid/liquid/gaseous waste incinerators & thermal oxidizers - low emission flares, process burners; IR inspection services; combustion equipment optimization services
Financial Information:
Type of Ownership: Private
Revenue Sources: 100% Private Contracts
Domestic Markets:
Alberta, British Columbia, New Brunswick, Newfoundland & Labrador, Nova Scotia, Northwest Territories, Nunavut, Ontario, Saskatchewan
Foreign Activity:
Africa, Asia, Caribbean, Eastern Europe, The Middle East, South America, Mexico, USA, Former USSR

Ingersoll-Rand Canada Inc.
Production Equipment Group
51 Worcester Rd.
Toronto, ON M9W 4K2
416-213-4500
Fax: 416-213-4616
www.ingersoll-rand.com
Products/Services/Areas of Expertise: Complete line of air-operator diaphragm or reciprocating pumps to handle liquid wastes in plant, transportation & remediation stages
Contact(s):
G.P. Webb, General Manager
Agako Nouch, Vice-President, Finance & Administration
A. Trudelle, Product Sales & Marketing Manager
E. Galbraith, Engineering

Ininew Project Management Inc.
owned & operated by three Manitoba First Nations
#700, 294 Portage Ave.
Winnipeg, MB R3C 0B9
204-956-0900
Fax: 204-956-4766
ininew@ininew.com
www.ininew.com
Firm Type: Management Consulting, Engineering
Founded: 1990
Products/Services/Areas of Expertise: Project management, architectural services, engineering, environmental services, & community planning in First Nations communities

Inland Aquatics
P.O. Box 156
67 Brock St. West
Uxbridge, ON L9P 1R3

905-852-0204
Fax: 905-852-0657
foxton@allstream.net
www.inlandaquatics.ca
Firm Type: Engineering
Founded: 1995
Staff: 13
Products/Services/Areas of Expertise: Inland Aquatics has extensive experience in aquatic weed control through the use of commercial mechanical weed harvesters & dredging operations; provides environmental assistance in areas where aquatic vegetation growth & erosion control of shoreline & river banks is needed; field services
Contact(s):
Bruce Foxton, Operations Manager

Inland Technologies Inc.
Formerly: Inland Oil Limited (1993)
P.O. Box 253
14 Queen St.
Truro, NS B2N 5C1
902-895-6346
Fax: 902-895-6349
877-633-5263
marketing@inlandgroup.ca
www.inlandgroup.ca
Firm Type: Scientific/Technical Services, Waste Management
Founded: 1981
Staff: 50
Member of: Offshore Trade Association of Nova Scotia; Nova Scotia Environmental Industry Association
Products/Services/Areas of Expertise: Glycol collection & recycling, primarily at airports; site remediation, primarily for hydrocarbon impacted soils
Recently Completed / Ongoing Projects: Construction of oily waste treatment plant in Brunei, SE Asia; construction of glycol recycling facility in Minneapolis, MN; service all major national airports from Vancouver to Halifax
Financial Information:
Type of Ownership: Private
Domestic Markets:
British Columbia, Manitoba, New Brunswick, Newfoundland & Labrador, Nova Scotia, Ontario, Prince Edward Island, Québec
Foreign Activity:
The Pacific Rim, USA
Markets Sought:
Caribbean, China, Eastern Europe, The Pacific Rim, Mexico, Vietnam
Contact(s):
James G. Bagnell, President
Roger Langille, Vice President, Operations
Teresa Lush, Manager, Sales & Marketing

Innergy Tech
605, rue Rocheleau
Drummondville, QC J2C 6L8
819-475-2666
Fax: 819-475-9541
800-203-9015
info@innergytech.com
www.innergytech.com
Firm Type: Manufacturing
Founded: 1995
Staff: 40
Member of: Air Conditioning & Refrigeration Institute
Quality Environmental Management System(s): 9001
Products/Services/Areas of Expertise: Manufacturer of enthalpic core, polypropylene core, heat pipes, residential thermal wheels, aluminium core, energy & heat recovery components
Recently Completed / Ongoing Projects: New heat wheel & enthalp coves; high pressure aluminum cores
Financial Information:
Type of Ownership: Private
Revenue: $1.5 Million - $3 Million
Revenue Sources: 100% Private Contracts
Domestic Markets:
Alberta, British Columbia, Manitoba, New Brunswick, Newfoundland & Labrador, Nova Scotia, Ontario, Québec, Saskatchewan
Foreign Activity:
Central Europe, The Pacific Rim, USA
Contact(s):
Jean-Francois Lalande, General Manager

Inproheat Industries Ltd.
Affiliate of Coen Burners Canada Inc.
680 Raymur Ave.
Vancouver, BC V6A 2R1
604-254-0461
Fax: 604-254-6377
888-684-6776
info@inproheat.com
www.inproheat.com
Firm Type: Engineering, Manufacturing, Scientific/Technical Services
Founded: 1958
Staff: 30
Products/Services/Areas of Expertise: Energy-efficient, environmentally responsible natural gas equipment; direct contact solution heating systems; combustion products and services
Financial Information:
Type of Ownership: Private
Revenue Sources: 5% nationwide; 5% Provincial; 90% Private Contracts
Domestic Markets:
Alberta, British Columbia, Manitoba, Northwest Territories, Saskatchewan
Foreign Activity:
Africa, Asia, Central America, China, The Pacific Rim, South Africa, South America, Mexico, United Kingdom, Vietnam
Contact(s):
Eric Panz, P.Eng., President
epanz@inproheat.com
Steven Panz, P.Eng., Vice-President, Energy Systems Group
spanz@inproheat.com
Gus Panz, Exec. Vice-President
gpanz@inproheat.com

Canadian Branches:
Calgary
#207, 4999 - 43rd St. SE
Calgary, AB T2B 3N4
403-253-2228
Fax: 403-253-4049
Ken Wright

Edmonton
1305 - 77th Ave.
Edmonton, AB T6P 1M8
780-440-2930
Fax: 780-440-4852
1-800-363-8563
ddunbar@inproheat.com
David Dunbar

Winnipeg
10 Hutchings St.
Winnipeg, MB R2X 2X1
204-694-2691
Fax: 204-632-8427
1-800-424-2152
hfox@inproheat.com
Harold Fox

Inscan Contractors (Ontario) Inc.
#33, 212 Wyecroft Rd.
Oakville, ON L6K 3T9
905-842-5075
Fax: 905-842-5895
general@inscancontractors.com
www.inscancontractors.com
Products/Services/Areas of Expertise: Manufacturer of various Insulation and Aabatement products
Contact(s):
Brent Chaston, General Manager

Insitu Contractors Inc.
150 Stevenson St. South
Guelph, ON N1E 5N7
519-763-0700
Fax: 519-763-6684
general@insitucontractors.com
www.insitucontractors.com
Firm Type: Scientific/Technical Services
Founded: 1992
Staff: 6
Member of: Canadian Geotechnical Society; National Ground Water Association; Professional Engineers Ontario
Products/Services/Areas of Expertise: Groundwater control for environmental & construction works
Financial Information:
Type of Ownership: Private
Revenue: $1.5 Million - $3 Million
Revenue Sources: 100% Private Contracts
Domestic Markets:
Ontario
Contact(s):
Harry Oussoren, P.Eng., President

Insituform Technologies Ltd. - Edmonton
Formerly: Insituform Mar-Tech Ltd.
7605 - 18th St. NW
Edmonton, AB T6P 1N9
780-413-0200
Fax: 780-413-0777
800-234-2992
www.insituform.com
Firm Type: Engineering, Scientific/Technical Services
Founded: 1971
Staff: 22
Quality Environmental Management System(s): 9000
Products/Services/Areas of Expertise: Technologies & services for rehabilitating sewer, water, energy & mining pipelines; corrosion protection; sliplining, microtunneling, pipe jacking, service lateral rehabilitation; cured-in-place pipes
Financial Information:
Type of Ownership: Foreign-owned
Domestic Markets:
National
Foreign Activity:
Worldwide
Contact(s):
Ken Foster, Vice-President, Canada

Insituform Technologies Ltd. - Hamilton
3 Burford Rd.
Hamilton, ON L8E 3C6
905-561-1778
Fax: 905-561-5379
www.insituform.com
Firm Type: Engineering, Scientific/Technical Services
Quality Environmental Management System(s): 9000
Financial Information:
Type of Ownership: Foreign-owned
Contact(s):
Dave Runge, District Manager
drunge@insituform.com

Insituform Technologies Ltd. - Montréal
Also Known As: Insituform Québec
139, rue Barr
Saint-Laurent, QC H4T 1W6
514-739-9999
Fax: 514-739-9988
www.insituform.com/content/518/quebec.aspx
Firm Type: Engineering, Scientific/Technical Services
Quality Environmental Management System(s): 9000
Products/Services/Areas of Expertise: Réhabilitation des conduites d'égouts sanitaires et pluviaux et des conduites de refoulement
Financial Information:
Type of Ownership: Foreign-owned
Domestic Markets:
Québec
Foreign Activity:
Worldwide
Contact(s):
Manon Ringuette
mringuette@insituform.com

Inspec-Sol Inc.
#200, 4600, boul côte Vertu
Montréal, QC H4S 1C7
514-333-5151
Fax: 514-333-4674
inspecsl@inspecsol.com
www.inspecsol.com
Firm Type: Engineering
Founded: 1972
Staff: 600
Member of: Conestoga-Rovers & Associates; Canadian Environmental Auditing Association (CEAA); Quebec Association of Environmental Auditing (AQVE)
Quality Environmental Management System(s): 9001:2008
Products/Services/Areas of Expertise: Multidisciplinary engineering & consulting services in the areas of civil engineering, geotechnical engineering, materials engineering,

building science, environment, & metallurgy. With over 600 employees located in 28 offices across Eastern Canada & the U.S., the firm provides project consulting & assistance to the highest standards
Financial Information:
Type of Ownership: Private
Domestic Markets:
National
Foreign Activity:
Africa, Asia, Central America, Central Europe, USA
Contact(s):
Salvatore Oppedisano, ing., P.Eng., President
soppedisano@inspecsol.com

Canadian Branches:
Detroit - Plymouth, MI
#200, 14496 Sheldon Rd.
Plymouth, MI USA
734-453-5123
Fax: 734-453-5201

Kingston
#104, 1225 Gardiners Rd.
Kingston, ON K7P 0G3
613-389-9812
Fax: 613-389-5287

Laval
3061, rue Joseph-A-Bombardier
Laval, QC H7P 6C5
450-973-4165
Fax: 450-973-9040
Products/Services/Areas of Expertise: Other Québec offices include Mont-Tremblant, Brossard, Beauharnois, Thetford Mines, Québec, Lévis (St-Romuald), Saguenay (Chicoutimi), Alma, Saint-Félicien, Rimouski, Matane, Gaspé, Iles-de-la-Madeleine, New Richmond, & Sept-Iles. Maritimes offices in Fredericton, & Dartmouth. Please see company website for contact details

Ottawa
#400, 179 Colonnade Rd.
Nepean, ON K2E 7J4
613-727-0895
Fax: 613-727-0581

Québec
#390, 445, av. St-Jean-Baptiste
Québec, QC G2E 5N7
418-658-0112
Fax: 418-658-2144

Thetford Mines
128, rue Notre-Dame est
Thetford Mines, QC G6G 2J8
418-338-0636
Fax: 418-338-4882

Toronto - Mississauga
#200, 111 Brunel Rd.
Mississauga, ON L4Z 1X3
905-712-4771
Fax: 905-712-0515
Products/Services/Areas of Expertise: Other Ontario locations include Waterloo, St. Catharines, Peterborough, Pembroke, Durham Region (Oshawa), Kingston, & Ottawa. Please see company website for contact details

Waterloo
651 Colby Dr.
Waterloo, ON N2V 1C2
519-725-9328
Fax: 519-884-5256

InspecTech
A division of InspecTech Analygas Group. Inc.
Formerly: Analygas Systems 450 Midwest Rd.
Toronto, ON M1P 3A9
416-757-1179
Fax: 416-757-8096
group@inspectech.ca
www.inspectech.ca
Firm Type: Engineering, Manufacturing
Founded: 1991
Products/Services/Areas of Expertise: Gas analysis & detection equipment for emissions; environmental monitoring & control; multigas analyzers; automotive emission test systems
Financial Information:
Revenue Sources: 2% nationwide; 2% Provincial; 10% Municipals; 86% Private Contracts
Domestic Markets:
National
Foreign Activity:
Asia, Australia/New Zealand, Mexico, USA
Markets Sought:
Central America, Central Europe, Eastern Europe, Western Europe, South America
Contact(s):
A.C. Richardson, President
Zbigniew Kaminski, Vice-President, Engineering
zkaminski@inspectech.ca
Martin Plut, Sales
mplut@inspectech.ca

Instantel
309 Legget Dr.
Ottawa, ON K2K 3A3
613-592-4642
Fax: 613-592-4296
800-267-9111
sales@instantel.com
www.instantel.com
Firm Type: Manufacturing
Founded: 1982
Quality Environmental Management System(s): 9001
Products/Services/Areas of Expertise: Noise & vibration monitoring equipment
Activities: Noise & vibration research & development
Financial Information:
Type of Ownership: Private
Domestic Markets:
National
Foreign Activity:
Worldwide

Institute of Environmental Research Inc.
Also Known As: DPRA Canada
#300, 7501 Keele St.
Concord, ON L4K 1Y2
905-660-1060
Fax: 905-660-7812
800-661-8437
ier@dpra.com
www.dpracanada.com
Firm Type: Management Consulting
Founded: 1972
Member of: International Association for Impact Assessment, Ontario Society for Environmental Management, Canadian Institute of Planning
Products/Services/Areas of Expertise: Social impact assessment; strategic planning; environmental assessment; environmental strategic planning; environmental assessment coordination; public consultation; expert testimony; emergency response planning & management consulting; conflict resolution
Domestic Markets:
British Columbia
Foreign Activity:
Asia, Mexico, USA
Markets Sought:
South America, Mexico
Contact(s):
James Micak, Sr. Vice-President
Peter Homenuck, Sr. Principal

Canadian Branches:
British Columbia Office
2487 Plumer St.
Victoria, BC V8S 5G9
Fax: 250-598-3105
1-800-661-8437

Integra Environmental Inc.
1430 Cormorant Rd.
Ancaster, ON L9G 4V5
905-304-3713
Fax: 905-304-5742
800-661-6678
dans@integraenv.com
www.integraenv.com
Firm Type: Distributing, Manufacturing
Founded: 1983
Staff: 3
Member of: Water Quality Association
Products/Services/Areas of Expertise: International distribution of water purification equipment & air sampling products; designs, engineers & manufactures high-purity water systems
Financial Information:
Type of Ownership: Private
Revenue Sources: 5% nationwide; 10% Provincial; 85% Private Contracts
Domestic Markets:
National
Foreign Activity:
USA
Markets Sought:
South America, Mexico
Contact(s):
Dan Scruton, President
Marc Bajzik, Vice-President, Sales
Bob Stephens, Application Specialist

Canadian Branches:
Richmond Office
#1159, 11871 Horseshoe Way
Richmond, BC V7A 5H5
604-275-7933
Fax: 604-275-7943
Turner Carol

Integra Technologies Ltd.
P.O. Box 592
#1, 1355 Confederation St.
Sarnia, ON N7S 4T2
519-332-1100
Fax: 519-332-1134
800-779-2658
sarnia@integratechnologies.com
www.integratechnologies.com
Firm Type: Distributing, Engineering
Staff: 40
Quality Environmental Management System(s): 9001
Products/Services/Areas of Expertise: On-site flange bolting & machining services; products for oil & gas, petrochemical, & power generation markets; offshore platform removal; ocean floor cleaning
Domestic Markets:
National
Foreign Activity:
Caribbean, Mexico, USA
Contact(s):
Wayne McCarver, General Manager, Canada

Canadian Branches:
Alberta
8121 - 43rd St. NW
Edmonton, AB T6B 2M3
780-413-6872
Fax: 780-413-6873
edmonton@integratechnologies.com

Nova Scotia
#6, 50 Raddall Ave.
Dartmouth, NS B3B 1T2
902-481-3986
Fax: 902-481-3987
novascotia@integratechnologies.com
Gisèle Brewer, Coordinator, 506-453-8372 Fax: 506-457-7899
gisele.brewer@gnb.ca

Integran Technologies Inc.
1 Meridian Rd.
Toronto, ON M9W 4Z6
416-675-6266
Fax: 416-675-1666
crm@integran.com
www.integran.com
Firm Type: Distributing, Manufacturing, Scientific/Technical Services
Founded: 1999
Staff: 47
Member of: US National Defense Industrial Association
Products/Services/Areas of Expertise: Developer/supplier of metallurgical, nano-structured products & technologies
Recently Completed / Ongoing Projects: Researching replacement of toxic cadmium coatings with non-toxic materials; developing safer alternative to hard chrome for coating high-strength steel fasteners
Financial Information:
Type of Ownership: Private
Domestic Markets:
National
Foreign Activity:
USA
Contact(s):

Gino Palumbo, President & CEO
palumbo@integran.com
Nancy Lavignasse, Chief Financial & Admin. Officer
Francisco Gonzalez, VP, Process Development
gonzalez@integran.com

Canadian Branches:
Toronto Business Development
93 Skyway Ave.
Toronto, ON M9W 6N6

Toronto Prototyping
136 Skyway Ave.
Toronto, ON M9W 4Y9

Integrated Catalyst Engineering Inc.
Also Known As: ICE Inc.
14 Dunn Pl.
Brampton, ON L6T 1S1
905-458-5424
Fax: 905-793-3578
aouellet@icecanada.com
www.icecanada.com
Firm Type: Management Consulting, Engineering, Scientific/Technical Services
Founded: 1993
Staff: 10
Member of: Professional Engineers Ontario; Ordre des ingenieurs du Québec
Products/Services/Areas of Expertise: Project management; mechanical, electrical; process control & automation
Financial Information:
Type of Ownership: Private
Revenue: $250,000 - $500,000
Revenue Sources: 100% Private Contracts
Domestic Markets:
Ontario, Québec
Foreign Activity:
USA
Contact(s):
Alain Ouellet, P.Eng., President

Integrated Environments Ltd.
Currie Barracks, Bldg. B6
#110, 2451 Dieppe Ave. SW
Calgary, AB T3E 7J9
403-685-8390
Fax: 403-686-8965
thom.stubbs@int-env.ca
www.integrated-environments.com
Contact(s):
Joseph F. Wells, Principal
Miles Scott-Brown, Principal

Integrated Explorations
P.O. Box 1385
#1, 67 Watson Rd. South
Guelph, ON N1H 6N8
519-822-2608
Fax: 519-822-3076
info@iebiolab.com
www.iebiolab.com
Firm Type: Management Consulting, Engineering, Manufacturing, Scientific/Technical Services
Founded: 1977
Staff: 8
Products/Services/Areas of Expertise: Underwater contaminant mapping & cleanup; lake restoration; biotechnical waste treatment development; air biofilters; bioremediation services; environmental microbiology & chemistry lab services
Recently Completed / Ongoing Projects: 2 completed & 2 ongoing bioremediation projects; U.V. water sterilizer evaluations 2001, 2002, 2003
Financial Information:
Type of Ownership: Private
Revenue: $500,000 - $1.5 Million
Revenue Sources: 5% nationwide; 5% Provincial; 10% Municipals; 80% Private Contracts
Domestic Markets:
New Brunswick, Nova Scotia, Ontario, Prince Edward Island
Foreign Activity:
USA
Markets Sought:
Eastern Europe, Western Europe, South America
Contact(s):
Al Melkic, President & Research Director
Todd Henry, Vice-President, Marketing
Stan Taylor, General Manager

Angela Williams, Lab Manager

Integrated Metal Products
355 Michener Rd.
Guelph, ON N1K 1E8
519-836-9062
Fax: 519-836-2962
sales@integrated-metal.com
integrated-metal.com
Firm Type: Manufacturing
Founded: 1987
Staff: 15
Quality Environmental Management System(s): 9001-2000
Products/Services/Areas of Expertise: Contract, high-precision, metal fabrication company; solar panels; alternative energy products; wind power tower components; bio-solids dryer components; electrical cabinetry for inverter power conditioning
Domestic Markets:
Ontario, Québec
Foreign Activity:
USA
Contact(s):
Keith Billings, President
kb@integrated-metal.com

Integrated Resource Management
935 Scotland St., RR#4, Stn Main
Fergus, ON N1M 2W5
519-843-4156
Fax: 519-843-5475
intres@sympatico.ca
www.drzno.ca
Firm Type: Scientific/Technical Services
Founded: 1991
Staff: 3
Member of: Iron & Steel Society
Products/Services/Areas of Expertise: Environmental consulting services; metal recycling consultancy; steel industry zinc metal recycling; electric arc furnace dust recovery
Recently Completed / Ongoing Projects: Engineering design of plants to manufacture zinc oxide; evaluation of lead & zinc recovery technology, India; evaluation of metal recovery projects for venture capital
Financial Information:
Type of Ownership: Private
Revenue: $50,000 - $100,000
Revenue Sources: 10% nationwide; 90% Private Contracts
Domestic Markets:
National
Foreign Activity:
Worldwide
Contact(s):
Peter J. Robinson, President & CEO

Intelex Technologies Inc. / ILX
#100, 366 Adelaide St. West
Toronto, ON M5V 1R9
416-599-6009
Fax: 416-599-6867
877-932-3747
intelex@intelex.com
www.intelex.com
Firm Type: Information Technology
Founded: 1992
Staff: 30
Products/Services/Areas of Expertise: A leading provider of business performance management (BPM) solutions which help clients continually improve in environmental, quality, health & safety enterprise performance; clients achieve accelerated performance while maximizing efficiencies, minimizing costs, realizing customer satisfaction & ensuring regulatory compliance.
Financial Information:
Type of Ownership: Private
Domestic Markets:
National
Foreign Activity:
Asia, Australia/New Zealand, Central Europe, Eastern Europe, Western Europe, The Pacific Rim, South America, USA,
Contact(s):
Ted Grunau, Chair
Mark Jaine, Executive-Vice-President

International Branch(es):
Compliance Management Pty Ltd.
526 The Esplanade
Warners Bay Australi
-6149-657-289
Fax: -6149-657-389
dfdjd@hunterlink.net.au
Dennis Debney

Eco Practice
via Francesco Massi 12, pal D, 00152
Rome Italy
-0039-06-5894759
Fax: -0039-06-583579
intelex@ecopractice.com
Dario Tripiciano

Intera Engineering Ltd.
Formerly: Duke Engineering & Services (Canada) Inc.; Raven Beck Environmental
#200, 1 Raymond St.
Ottawa, ON K1R 1A2
613-232-2525
Fax: 613-232-7149
www.interaeng.ca
Firm Type: Engineering, Scientific/Technical Services
Founded: 1991
Staff: 23
Products/Services/Areas of Expertise: Environmental audits/assessments; site investigations/remediation; regional hydrogeology & water resource evaluation; hydrogeologic modeling; risk assessment
Contact(s):
Ken Raven, Manager

Interbath of Canada Ltd.
5556 Tomken Rd.
Mississauga, ON L4W 1P4
905-624-3009
Fax: 905-624-0796
800-661-5361
Firm Type: Manufacturing
Founded: 1975
Products/Services/Areas of Expertise: Water conservation products & systems

Interface FLOR Commercial
Formerly: Interface Flooring Systems (Canada) Inc.
233 Lahr Dr.
Belleville, ON K8N 5S2
613-966-8090
Fax: 613-966-8817
800-267-2149
www.interfaceflor.ca
Products/Services/Areas of Expertise: Canada's only manufacturer of stabilized back commercial carpet in 50 cm tiles & 2 metre performance broadloom. Carpet tile is modular, allows easy access to under-floor wiring/cabling & allows changing one tile at a time to repair areas with excessive wear or damage rather than removing an entire floor of carpet; tiles can be easily removed & replaced with no employee down-time or cost & very little environmental impact
Ecological Note: Commercial carpet

Interforest Inc.
519 Prince St.
Truro, NS B2N 1E8
902-893-4342
Fax: 902-893-4959
Firm Type: Management Consulting
Founded: 1987
Staff: 7
Member of: Registered Professional Foresters Association of Nova Scotia
Products/Services/Areas of Expertise: Environmental consulting; resource/land mapping operations; remote sensing & image analysis; integrated resource management; forestry management
Domestic Markets:
New Brunswick, Nova Scotia, Prince Edward Island
Contact(s):
Michael A. Brown, B.Sc.F.
frcmike@eastlink.ca

Interior Weather Services Ltd.
P.O. Box 19
1246 Yellowhead Hwy.
Blue River, BC V0E 1J0
250-673-8448
cycp@mercuryspeed.com
Firm Type: Scientific/Technical Services
Founded: 1969
Staff: 3
Member of: BC Aviation Council
Products/Services/Areas of Expertise: Field sampling & monitoring; meteorology & climatology; meteorological data acquisition
Domestic Markets:
Alberta, British Columbia
Foreign Activity:
USA
Contact(s):
Stephen Quinn, President/CEO

Canadian Branches:
Blue River Weather Station
P.O. Box 19
Blue River, BC V0E 1J0
250-673-8448
Fax: 250-673-8315
cycp@mercuryspeed.com

InterLink Business Management Inc. / ILBM
#1803, 1075 Comox St.
Vancouver, BC V6E 1K2
604-671-0244
Fax: 604-689-7507
877-567-7955
sonia@ilbm.net
Firm Type: Management Consulting, Financial, Waste Management
Founded: 1995
Staff: 4
Member of: Canadian Environmental Industry Association; National Trade Union Of Banks, Insurance & Financial Affairs
Products/Services/Areas of Expertise: Consulting company that links international opportunities with domestic capabilities in hazardous waste management, soil remediation, air pollution control, oil & gas, oil pollution equipment, incinerators; assists in obtaining financial aid from government
Recently Completed / Ongoing Projects: Soil remediation, USA/EPA; Oil pollution remediation in Eastern Europe
Financial Information:
Type of Ownership: Private
Revenue Sources: 40% nationwide; 10% Provincial; 50% Private Contracts
Domestic Markets:
British Columbia, Ontario, Québec
Foreign Activity:
Africa, Eastern Europe, Western Europe, The Middle East, USA
Markets Sought:
Australia/New Zealand, Central America, South America,
Contact(s):
Sonia Shoukry, President

International Bio-Recovery Corp. / IBR
52 Riverside Dr.
North Vancouver, BC V7H 1T4
604-924-1023
Fax: 604-924-1043
info@ibrcorp.com
www.ibrcorp.com
Firm Type: Manufacturing, Waste Management
Founded: 1993
Staff: 15
Products/Services/Areas of Expertise: Sells & markets technology that manufactures biological fertility products from organic waste materials
Financial Information:
Type of Ownership: Publicly Traded
Revenue: $3 Million - $5 Million
Revenue Sources: 100% Private Contracts
Domestic Markets:
British Columbia, Ontario
Foreign Activity:
China, Central Europe, Western Europe, The Middle East, The Pacific Rim, Mexico, USA, Vietnam
Markets Sought:
Asia
Contact(s):
Steve Leptick, P.Eng., Interim President/CEO

International Cooling Systems Inc.
300 Granton Dr.
Richmond Hill, ON L4B 1H7
416-213-5566
Fax: 416-213-5577
888-213-5566
info@intlcoolingsystems.com
www.intlcoolingsystems.com
Firm Type: Manufacturing
Founded: 1990
Products/Services/Areas of Expertise: Water cooling, water recirculation systems; chillers, temperature controllers
Financial Information:
Type of Ownership: Private
Revenue: $3 Million - $5 Million
Revenue Sources: 100% Private Contracts
Domestic Markets:
Alberta, British Columbia, Manitoba, New Brunswick, Newfoundland & Labrador, Nova Scotia, Northwest Territories, Ontario, Prince Edward Island, Québec
Foreign Activity:
Mexico, USA

International Branch(es):
Dallas
330 Cochran Ridge Rd.
Dallas, GA USA
770-712-6031

International Irrigation Systems Ltd.
291 Riverview Blvd.
St Catharines, ON L2T 3N3
905-688-4090
Fax: 905-688-4093
877-477-4476
info@irrigro.com
www.irrigro.com
Firm Type: Manufacturing
Founded: 1975
Staff: 5
Products/Services/Areas of Expertise: Irrigro micro-porous drip irrigation systems
Financial Information:
Type of Ownership: Private
Domestic Markets:
National
Foreign Activity:
Worldwide
Contact(s):
Robert L. Neff, President

International Branch(es):
Niagara Falls, NY
P.O. Box 163
1755 Factory Outlet Blvd.
Niagara Falls, NY USA

International Marine Salvage Inc.
P.O. Box 6
17 Invertose Dr.
Port Colborne, ON L3K 5V7
905-835-1203
Fax: 905-835-6824
888-937-3382
admin@rawmaterials.com
www.rawmaterials.com
Firm Type: Manufacturing, Waste Management
Founded: 1985
Staff: 20
Products/Services/Areas of Expertise: Battery recycling & disposal; recycling of ferrous & non-ferrous metals; seawall construction (piers, docks, shore protection); environmental consulting; waste treatment, recycling processes
Domestic Markets:
Ontario, Québec
Foreign Activity:
Asia, The Pacific Rim, USA
Contact(s):
Wayne Elliott, President
Contact(s):
K.W. Elliott, President

Canadian Branches:
Port Colborne
P.O. Box 6
Port Colborne, ON L3K 5V7

905-835-1203
Fax: 905-835-5945
admin@rawmaterials.com

International Road Dynamics Inc. / IRD
702 - 43rd St. East
Saskatoon, SK S7K 3T9
306-653-6600
Fax: 306-242-5599
info@irdinc.com
www.irdinc.com
Firm Type: Distributing, Engineering, Information Technology, Manufacturing
Founded: 1980
Quality Environmental Management System(s): 9001
Products/Services/Areas of Expertise: Multi-discipline, intelligent transportation technology; traffic data collection systems; pollution data collection systems
Financial Information:
Type of Ownership: Publicly Traded
Domestic Markets:
National
Foreign Activity:
Worldwide
Contact(s):
Terry Bergan, President & CEO
Randy Hanson, Exec. VP & COO
Mel Karakochuk, CFO & VP, Finance
Sharon Parker, Vice-President, Corporate Resources
Rod Klashinsky, Vice-President, Sales

International Submarine Engineering Ltd.
1734 Broadway St.
Port Coquitlam, BC V3C 2M8
604-942-5223
Fax: 604-942-7577
info@ise.bc.ca
www.ise.bc.ca
Firm Type: Engineering, Manufacturing, Scientific/Technical Services
Founded: 1974
Quality Environmental Management System(s): 9001:2001
Products/Services/Areas of Expertise: Subsea equipment; remote-operated vehicles; international remote traffic systems; remote radar display digitizers
Domestic Markets:
National
Foreign Activity:
Worldwide
Contact(s):
James McFarlane, President
rovs@ise.bc.ca

International Water Supply Ltd. / IWS
Compagnie Internationale des Eaux de Québec Ltée
P.O. Box 310
342 Bayview Dr.
Barrie, ON L4M 4T5
705-733-0111
Fax: 705-721-0138
800-461-9636
iws@iws.ca
www.iws.ca
Firm Type: Engineering
Founded: 1933
Staff: 40
Member of: American Water Works Association; National Ground Water Association; Canadian Public Works Association; Canadian Ground Water Association
Products/Services/Areas of Expertise: IWS specializes in groundwater supply, development & engineering, hydrogeology; groundwater exploration; well construction & maintenance; mineshaft pump sales, installation & maintenance
Recently Completed / Ongoing Projects: Municipality of Pickle Lake, groundwater management study; Oxford County, Norwich water supply investigation; Regional Municipality of Waterloo, well/pump maintenance program
Financial Information:
Type of Ownership: Private
Revenue Sources: 3% nationwide; 12% Provincial; 55% Municipals; 30% Private Contracts
Domestic Markets:
National
Contact(s):
J.A. Harris, P.Eng, President
Gary A. Kuehl, P.Geo.
Mike R. Fairbanks, P.Geo.

Products & Services Buyer's Guide

Canadian Branches:
Saskatoon
317 - 103rd St.
Saskatoon, SK S7N 1Y9
306-373-7070
Fax: 306-373-1922
saskatoon@iwc.ca
Bruce Wilson, P.Eng.

Interprovincial Corrosion Control Co. Ltd. / ICCC
930 Sheldon Ct.
Burlington, ON L7L 5K6
905-634-7751
Fax: 905-333-4313
800-699-8771
info@rustrol.com
www.rustrol.com
Firm Type: Manufacturing
Founded: 1957
Member of: National Association of Corrosion Engineers; Ontario Sewer & Watermain Contractor's Association; Association of Professional Engineers of Ontario; American Water Works Association
Products/Services/Areas of Expertise: Cathodic protection engineering design/services; corrosion protection materials; protection of buried or immersed steel structures; cathodic protection materials including zinc, magnesium & other sacrificial anodes; cast iron & graphite impressed current anodes; rectifiers; low resistivity backfills for deep anode beds; coating holiday detectors; pipeline pigs; flange insulation kits
Financial Information:
Type of Ownership: Private
Domestic Markets:
National
Foreign Activity:
Worldwide

Interra Environmental Inc.
Formerly: Interra Industrial Products Ltd.
Also Known As: Safe Earth
#12, 2180 Pegasus Way NE
Calgary, AB T2E 2H5
403-236-4901
Fax: 403-236-1759
866-249-7583
interra@telus.net
www.envirospill.com
Firm Type: Distributing, Manufacturing
Founded: 1993
Staff: 5
Products/Services/Areas of Expertise: Emergency spill response products & services, spill kits; training; emergency spill response; consulting: Phase 1, 2, 3; analysis; environmental compliance analysis
Recently Completed / Ongoing Projects: Soil remediation, Phase III; on-going 24-hr spill response
Financial Information:
Type of Ownership: Private
Domestic Markets:
Alberta, British Columbia, Manitoba, Northwest Territories, Nunavut, Saskatchewan
Foreign Activity:
Central America, The Middle East, USA
Markets Sought:
Australia/New Zealand, Eastern Europe, Mexico, Former USSR
Contact(s):
Barry Lesiuk, President

Intersciences Inc.
169 Idema Rd.
Markham, ON L3R 1A9
905-940-1831
Fax: 905-940-1832
800-661-6431
marketing@interscience.com
www.interscience.com
Firm Type: Distributing, Manufacturing
Founded: 1991
Staff: 22
Member of: Canadian Laboratory Suppliers Association
Products/Services/Areas of Expertise: Molecular biology, cell biology, immunobiology, pharmaceutical tablet testing, & general lab products & instruments
Financial Information:
Type of Ownership: Private

Domestic Markets:
National
Foreign Activity:
Western Europe, USA
Markets Sought:
Asia, Australia/New Zealand, Central America,
Contact(s):
Leon G. Guluzian, President & General Manager
lguluzian@interscience.com
Suzanne Guluzian, Controller & VP, Finance
sguluzian@interscience.com
Adam Richardson, Technical Marketing Manager
arichardson@interscience.com

Intertek Systems Certification
Formerly: Intertek Testing Services; Intertek Testing Certification
1829, 32 av
Montréal, QC H8T 3J1
514-631-3100
Fax: 514-631-1133
800-561-5051
intertek-sc@intertek-sc.com
www.intertek-sc.com
Firm Type: Scientific/Technical Services
Founded: 1999
Staff: 2500
Member of: Standard Council of Canada; Canadian Institute of Plumbing & Heating; International Association of Electrical Inspectors
Quality Environmental Management System(s): 9002
Products/Services/Areas of Expertise: Leading management systems registrar, offering certification to internationally recognzied standards including ISO 9001 & 14001
Financial Information:
Type of Ownership: Publicly Traded
Domestic Markets:
National
Foreign Activity:
Worldwide
Contact(s):
Jose De Olivia
Bill Vosburg, Vice-President

Canadian Branches:
Coquitlam Office
1500 Brigantine Dr.
Coquitlam, BC V3K 7C1
604-520-3321
Fax: 604-524-9186
kevin.nakamoto@intertek.com
Kevin Nakamoto

Mississauga
6225 Kenway Dr.
Mississauga, ON L5T 2L3
905-678-7820
Fax: 905-678-7131
www.intertek-sc.com
Richard Nicholas

Interwest Property Services (1991) Ltd.
Formerly: Ronald O. Grant & Sons
650 Columbia St.
New Westminster, BC V3M 1A9
604-522-1621
Fax: 604-522-5624
dannygrant@interwest.info
www.interwest.info
Firm Type: Scientific/Technical Services
Founded: 1950
Staff: 6
Member of: B.C. Institute of Agrologists; Canadian Consulting Aerologists; Appraisal Institute of Canada
Products/Services/Areas of Expertise: Agricultural appraisals; cranberry & livestock operations management; right of way acquisition; surplus land disposal; land use studies; environmental impact assessment; appraisals of damages to real estate from all causes
Recently Completed / Ongoing Projects: Sea to Sky Hwy. acquisition & appraisal; Sky Train acquisition & appraisal
Financial Information:
Type of Ownership: Private
Revenue Sources: 10% nationwide; 50% Provincial; 10% Municipals; 30% Private Contracts
Domestic Markets:
British Columbia

Contact(s):
Danny Grant, Partner

Inuktun Services Ltd. / ISL
#C, 2569 Kenworth Rd.
Nanaimo, BC V9T 3M4
250-729-8080
Fax: 250-729-8077
877-468-5886
info@inuktun.com
www.inuktun.com
Firm Type: Scientific/Technical Services
Founded: 1989
Staff: 44
Products/Services/Areas of Expertise: Manufacturer & designer of remotely operated robotic systems & modular robotic components for use in confined spaces & hazardous environments: pipe & duct inspection, cleaning, search & rescue, underwater cameras & equipment
Financial Information:
Type of Ownership: Private
Revenue Sources: 20% nationwide; 10% Provincial; 10% Municipals; 60% Private Contracts
Domestic Markets:
Alberta, British Columbia, New Brunswick, Ontario, Québec
Foreign Activity:
Asia, Western Europe, The Middle East, USA
Contact(s):
Colin Dobell, President
Mike Southwell, Manager, Sales & Marketing

Invensys Systems Canada Inc.
Formerly: Foxboro Canada Inc.
4, rue Lake
Dollard-des-Ormeaux, QC H9B 3H9
514-421-4210
Fax: 514-421-8057
www.invensys.com
Firm Type: Management Consulting, Distributing, Engineering, Manufacturing, Scientific/Technical Services
Founded: 1933
Quality Environmental Management System(s): 9001:1994
Products/Services/Areas of Expertise: Technology for oil refineries, fossil fuel & nuclear power generation plants, & petrochemical works; communication & control systems for rail transit; components, systems & services for energy-saving appliances, commercial & residential; uses reduced-energy manufacturing processes
Financial Information:
Type of Ownership: Foreign-owned
Contact(s):
Chris Relton, Director, Sales
Ralph Tozzi, Manager, Marketing Analysis/Communications

Canadian Branches:
Burlington
880 Laurentian Dr.
Burlington, ON L7N 3V6
905-333-3774
Fax: 905-333-2600

Burnaby
8555 Commerce Crt.
Burnaby, BC V5A 4N4
604-293-1631
Fax: 604-293-1098

Calgary
4540 - 104th St. SE
Calgary, AB T2C 1R7
403-777-1150
Fax: 403-274-8651

Edmonton
#117, 8905 - 51 Ave. NW
Edmonton, AB T6E 5J3
780-448-0522
Fax: 780-463-6405

Mississauga - Invensys Controls
#14, 3505 Laird Rd.
Mississauga, ON L5L 5Y7
905-828-7294
Fax: 905-828-1265

Moncton
567 St. George St.
Moncton, NB E1E 2B9

506-857-4174
Fax: 506-859-8091

Montréal
#670, 3300, boul Cavendish
Montréal, QC H4B 2M8
514-485-6611
Fax: 514-485-6617

Sudbury - Invensys Rail
1349 Kelly Lake Rd.
Sudbury, ON P3E 5P5
705-523-1331

Thunder Bay - Invensys Operations Management
1135 Roland St.
Thunder Bay, ON P7B 5M5
807-622-3746
Fax: 807-622-3533

Investigative Science Inc. / ISI
#2, 1050 Cooke Blvd.
Burlington, ON L7T 4A8
905-634-4200
Fax: 905-634-1966
mail@investigativescience.com
www.investigativescience.com
Firm Type: Management Consulting
Founded: 1991
Member of: Chemical Institute of Canada; Canadian Society of Forensic Science; Air & Waste Management Association
Quality Environmental Management System(s): 9001
Products/Services/Areas of Expertise: Environmental support for insurance, legal & forensic science; sensitive site management, bioremediation, custom analysis & expert interpretation of laboratory results; accredited verifier for Canadian ETV program
Financial Information:
Type of Ownership: Private
Revenue Sources: 100% Private Contracts
Domestic Markets:
National, Manitoba, Ontario
Foreign Activity:
Africa, The Pacific Rim, USA
Markets Sought:
Australia/New Zealand, Caribbean, Central Europe, Western Europe
Contact(s):
Peter Child, Co-founder

Iogen Corp.
310 Hunt Club Rd. East
Ottawa, ON K1V 1C1
613-733-9830
Fax: 613-733-0781
info@iogen.ca
www.iogen.ca
Firm Type: Scientific/Technical Services
Founded: 1985
Staff: 18
Products/Services/Areas of Expertise: Cellulose ethanol, a renewable transportation fuel that reduces greenhouse gas emissions, used in today's cars; Enzyme treatment programs for pulp mills designed to maximize cost savings & bleaching enzymes; enzyme products used in the textile industry & as an animal feed additive
Financial Information:
Type of Ownership: Private

IPAC Inc.
Formerly: Hiross Canada Inc. (1993)
#7, 2180 Dunwin Dr.
Mississauga, ON L5L 5M8
905-828-5530
Fax: 905-828-5018
Firm Type: Distributing
Founded: 1972
Staff: 5
Products/Services/Areas of Expertise: Heat exchangers; water treatment systems & equipment; water/oil separators
Financial Information:
Revenue Sources: 10% Provincial; 90% Private Contracts
Domestic Markets:
National

IPEC Industries Ltd.
2889 Norland Ave.
Burnaby, BC V5B 3A9
604-291-7150
Fax: 604-291-7190
800-663-8409
sales@ipec.ca
www.ipec.ca
Firm Type: Manufacturing
Founded: 1979
Staff: 25
Products/Services/Areas of Expertise: Wastewater treatment & filtration
Recently Completed / Ongoing Projects: Water & waste treatment plants: Adelaide WWTP (London, ON), Durango WWTP, Cargill, IBP, Tyson, McCains, Weyerhauser, Ralston Foods, Maple Leaf
Financial Information:
Type of Ownership: Private
Revenue Sources: 20% Municipals; 80% Private Contracts
Domestic Markets:
National
Foreign Activity:
Worldwide
Markets Sought:
The Pacific Rim,
Contact(s):
Albert Irwin, President
bart@ipec.ca
Mike Malec, Sales Manager
mike@ipec.ca

Ipex Inc.
Formerly: Scepter/Canron Inc.
50 Valleybrook Dr.
Toronto, ON M3B 2S9
416-445-3400
Fax: 416-445-4461
866-473-9462
www.ipexinc.com
Firm Type: Manufacturing
Founded: 1992
Member of: American Water Works Association
Products/Services/Areas of Expertise: Non-corrosive polyvinyl chloride pipes & fittings for sewerlines, watermains, plumbing & electrical conduct

Canadian Branches:
Calgary
7710 - 40th St. SE
Calgary, AB T2C 3S4
403-236-8333
Fax: 403-279-8443

Edmonton
4225 - 92 Ave.
Edmonton, AB T6B 3M7
780-415-5300
Fax: 780-415-5358

Langley
20460 Duncan Way
Langley, BC V3A 7A3
604-534-8631
Fax: 604-534-7616

Mississauga
6810 Invader Rd.
Mississauga, ON L5T 2B6
905-670-7676
Fax: 905-670-5295

Montréal
6665, ch St-François
Saint-Laurent, QC H4S 1B6
514-337-2624
Fax: 514-337-7886

Montréal Administrative Office
#101, 3, Place du Commerce, Iles-des-Soeurs
Verdun, QC H3E 1H7
514-769-2200
Fax: 514-769-1672

Saint John
Grandview Industrial Park
P.O. Box 127
Saint John, NB E2L 3X8
506-633-7473
Fax: 506-633-8720

Saskatoon
611, 47th St. E
Saskatoon, SK S7K 5G5
306-933-4664
Fax: 306-934-2020

St. John's
P.O. Box 13247 A
27 Clyde St.
St. John's, NL A1B 4A5
709-747-7472
Fax: 709-368-9111

Winnipeg
2081 Logan Ave. West
Winnipeg, MB R2R 0J1
204-633-3111
Fax: 204-633-3075

IPL Inc.
140, rue Commerciale
Saint-Damien-de-Buckland, QC G0R 2Y0
418-789-2880
Fax: 418-789-3153
800-463-7083
info-ipl@ipl-plastics.com
www.ipl-plastics.com
Firm Type: Manufacturing
Founded: 1939
Staff: 675
Quality Environmental Management System(s): 9001
Products/Services/Areas of Expertise: Plastics products for recycling industries; recycling curbside containers, bottle & can collectors
Domestic Markets:
National
Foreign Activity:
USA

Canadian Branches:
Mississauga
#305, 350 Burnhamthorpe
Mississauga, ON L5B 3J1
905-791-5895
Fax: 905-791-2500

iQmetrix
#500, 2221 Cornwall St.
Regina, SK S4P 2L1
Fax: 306-569-0183
866-476-3874
sales@iqmetrix.com
www.iqmetrix.com
Firm Type: Information Technology
Founded: 1999
Products/Services/Areas of Expertise: Software development
Contact(s):
Chris Krywulak, President/CEO

International Branch(es):

#500, 6300 South Syracuse Way
Centennial, CO 80111
303-996-5920
Fax: 303-996-5926

IRC Integrated Resource Consultants Inc.
#160, 14480 River Rd.
Richmond, BC V6V 1L4
604-278-7714
Fax: 604-278-7741
irc@mindlink.bc.ca
Firm Type: Management Consulting
Founded: 1987
Staff: 10
Products/Services/Areas of Expertise: Environmental Assessment studies; stormwater management; outfall investigations; water quality modelling; site assessments; investigations & remediation plans; effluent treatment studies & investigations
Recently Completed / Ongoing Projects: Greater Vancouver Iona outfall deep sea monitoring studies 1987-97; Gold River Mill organochlorine monitoring 1989-97; Toxicity lab CAEL certified
Financial Information:
Type of Ownership: Private
Revenue Sources: 5% Provincial; 10% Municipals; 85% Private Contracts
Domestic Markets:
British Columbia

Foreign Activity:
South America
Markets Sought:
Central America, South America, USA

IRIS Environmental Systems Inc.
635 - 36 Ave. NE
Calgary, AB T2E 2L8
403-543-4455
Fax: 403-543-4459
calgary@irisenvironmental.ca
www.irisenvironmental.ca
Firm Type: Scientific/Technical Services
Founded: 1987
Staff: 30
Member of: Harmony Walkers Inc.
Products/Services/Areas of Expertise: Environmental consulting & CAD/GIS services; impact assessment, mitigation & monitoring; expertise in geomorphology, hydrology, limnology, fisheries, wildlife, climatology & atmosphere
Recently Completed / Ongoing Projects: Plastun Independent Biomass Power Station Project
Domestic Markets:
National
Foreign Activity:
Worldwide
Contact(s):
Rob Lothian, Co-Owner
rob_lothian@irisenvironmental.ca
Anouk Kendall, Vice-President
anouk_kendall@irisenvironmental.ca

Canadian Branches:
Montréal Office
#202, 3575 boul St-Laurent
Montréal, QC H2X 2T7
514-844-8448
anouk_kendall@irisenvironmental.ca

Ottawa Office
Project Services International Inc.
#101, 260 St. Patrick St.
Ottawa, ON K1P 5R2
613-244-1050
Fax: 613-244-8315
pamela@psi-spi.com

Victoria Office
2761 Margate Ave.
Victoria, BC V8S 3A8
250-598-4415
Fax: 250-598-4450
james_ramsay@irisenvironmental.ca

Iron Ore Company of Canada / IOC
A member of the Rio Tinto Group
P.O. Box 1000
Labrador City, NL A2V 2L8
709-944-8349
Fax: 709-944-8079
www.ironore.ca
Firm Type: Engineering, Manufacturing
Founded: 1955
Staff: 1900
Quality Environmental Management System(s): 9001:2008
Products/Services/Areas of Expertise: Producer of iron ore; supplier of iron ore pellets & concentrates; mine, concentrator & pelletizing plant; Environment, Safety & Health (ESH) Policy
Domestic Markets:
National
Foreign Activity:
Worldwide
Contact(s):
Zoë Yujnovich, President & CEO
Rolland Morier, VP, Fniance & Strategy
Manon Beauchemin, VP, External Relations & Corporate Affairs
Heather Bruce-Veitch, Director, External Relations
heather.bruce-veitch@ironore.ca

Canadian Branches:
Port Facilities
1, rue Retty
Sept-Iles, QC G4R 3C7
418-968-7400
Fax: 418-968-7109

Irrigation Canal Power Co-operative Ltd.
P.O. Box 278
1210 - 36 St. North
Lethbridge, AB T1J 3Y7
403-328-4401
Fax: 403-328-4460
smrid@smrid.ab.ca
www.smrid.ab.ca
Products/Services/Areas of Expertise: Owned & operation by three irrigation districts located in Southern Alberta: the St. Mary River, the Taber & the Raymond; plants are located on irrigation canals; power can only be produced when irrigation water is available, as irrigation demand takes precedence over power production
Recently Completed / Ongoing Projects: Presently investigating future hydroelectric sites on existing water conveyance infrastructures as well as wind sites within Southern Alberta for future power development
Ecological Note: Hydro-electric power
Contact(s):
Ron L. Renwick, P.Eng., General Manager

Irving Forest Services Limited
P.O. Box 5777
300 Union St.
Saint John, NB E2L 4M3
506-632-7777
Fax: 506-648-2205
info@jdirving.com
www.jdirving.com
Products/Services/Areas of Expertise: Engineering consulting services; environmental consulting services; forestry consulting

ISCA Management Ltd.
#505, 2320 - 40 Ave. West
Vancouver, BC V6M 4H6
604-266-1838
dougcaldwell@compuserve.com
Firm Type: Distributing
Founded: 1979
Products/Services/Areas of Expertise: Sulphur oxide, nitrogen oxide, heavy metal systems for industrial flue systems; technology development
Domestic Markets:
National
Foreign Activity:
Eastern Europe, Western Europe, USA
Contact(s):
Douglas Caldwell, President
B. Mueller, Vice-President

Island Clean Air Inc.
8793 Cambie St.
Vancouver, BC V6P 3J9
604-322-2979
Fax: 604-322-8674
800-661-6211
info@islandcleanair.com
www.islandcleanair.com
Firm Type: Manufacturing
Founded: 1992
Staff: 16
Member of: Automotive Industries Association of Canada; Better Business Bureau
Member of: Vancouver Board of Trade
Products/Services/Areas of Expertise: Duster series, mobile air filtration systems; Duster 3000 Downdraft mobile prep station for autobody shops; dusters for print shops, (graphics & industrial), woodworking
Financial Information:
Type of Ownership: Private
Domestic Markets:
National
Foreign Activity:
Worldwide
Contact(s):
Joe Lim, President
joe@islandcleanair.com
Nikki Abutaleb, Office Administrator
nikki@islandcleanair.com

Canadian Branches:
Toronto
#1107, 30 Elm Dr. East
Mississauga, ON L5A 4C3

905-366-1414
Fax: 905-366-1415
bob@islandcleanair.com
Bob Beattie

Island Technologies Inc. / ITI
201 Water St.
Charlottetown, PE C1A 1B1
902-626-3393
islandtechnologiesinc.com
Firm Type: Management Consulting, Engineering
Staff: 1
Member of: Canadian Wind Energy Association
Products/Services/Areas of Expertise: Specializes in engineering & project management for wind energy & applications; provides services in research & development, design, specification & construction supervision for wind turbine installations; provides design assistance to utilities & energy end users for remote small grid wind-diesel & autonomous wind energy systems
Contact(s):
Malcolm A. Lodge, Founder & President
mlodge@islandtechnologiesinc.com

ISOVision
3550, boul Gene-H-Kruger
Trois-Rivières, QC G9A 4M3
819-374-6777
Fax: 819-379-3449
www.isovision.com
Firm Type: Management Consulting
Founded: 2000
Quality Environmental Management System(s): 9001

ITM Instruments
Formerly: Airflow Developments (Canada) Ltd.
16975 Leslie St.
Newmarket, ON L3Y 9A1
905-947-1771
Fax: 905-947-1551
800-561-8187
information@itm.com
www.itm.com
Firm Type: Distributing
Founded: 1961
Staff: 6
Member of: Ontario Pollution Control Equipment Federation; Canadian Meteorological & Oceanographic Society; Mechanical Contractors Association of Canada
Quality Environmental Management System(s): 9001:2000
Products/Services/Areas of Expertise: Airflow monitoring equipment for fanned HVAC systems & weather stations; data acquisition systems designed & supplied for all environmental parameters; distributor of test & measurment instruments & controls
Financial Information:
Type of Ownership: Private
Domestic Markets:
National
Foreign Activity:
USA
Contact(s):
David Reed, President/CEO
Steve Arsenault, Marketing
Maurice Parent, Sales

Canadian Branches:
Edmonton
7043, 68th Ave. NW
Edmonton, AB T6B 3E3
780-409-9278
Fax: 780-409-9279
jpo@itm.com
Pat Olson

Montréal
20800, boul. Industriel
Montréal, QC H9X 0A1
514-457-7280
Fax: 514-457-4329
mfp@itm.com
Maurice Patent

ITRES Research Ltd.
#110, 3553 - 31 St. NW
Calgary, AB T2L 2K7
403-250-9944
Fax: 403-250-9916

info@itres.com
www.itres.com
Firm Type: Engineering, Manufacturing, Scientific/Technical Services
Founded: 1979
Staff: 33
Products/Services/Areas of Expertise: Airborne optical remote sensing services & information products, including sensors; design & manufacture of custom-built electro-optical instrumentation; contract research; compact airborne visible & near infra-red imaging spectrograph for purchase or lease
Financial Information:
Type of Ownership: Private
Domestic Markets:
National
Foreign Activity:
Asia, Australia/New Zealand, Western Europe, The Pacific Rim, South America, USA
Contact(s):
Doug Davison, President/CEO

Ivey International Inc.
Also Known As: Ivey-Sol
P.O. Box 706
Campbell River, BC V9W 6J3
250-923-6326
Fax: 250-923-0718
800-246-2744
www.iveyinternational.com
Firm Type: Engineering, Scientific/Technical Services, Waste Management
Founded: 1983
Staff: 4
Member of: Canada Colors & Chemicals
Member of: National Groundwater Association; Environmental Assessment Association; Environmental Services Association of Alberta
Products/Services/Areas of Expertise: Ivey-sol surfactant, soil & water remediation for contaminants that include: TPH (gasoline, diesel, bunkerc), PAH, BCP, chlorinated solvents & heavy metals
Recently Completed / Ongoing Projects: Several soil & groundwater remediation sites, Canada, USA & Spain; PAH, PCB, DAPL waste oil disposal; planning projects in Japan & Taiwan
Financial Information:
Type of Ownership: Private
Domestic Markets:
National
Foreign Activity:
Worldwide
Markets Sought:
Africa, Eastern Europe, Western Europe, The Pacific Rim, South America, Mexico
Contact(s):
George A. Ivey, President & CEO, Senior Remedial Specialist
budivey@iveyinternational.com

J&B Engineering Inc.
#501, 5734 Yonge St.
Toronto, ON M2M 4E7
416-229-2636
Fax: 416-229-6965
info@jandb-engineering.com
www.jandb-engineering.com
Firm Type: Engineering, Scientific/Technical Services
Founded: 1979
Staff: 16
Products/Services/Areas of Expertise: Engineering consulting services; environmental consulting services; energy consulting
Recently Completed / Ongoing Projects: Service station, upgrades, bulk plant & distribution, terminal upgrades, Petro-Canada, Shell Canada, Ontario Hydro
Domestic Markets:
Alberta, British Columbia, Newfoundland & Labrador, Nova Scotia, Ontario
Contact(s):
James L. Machan, President

J&F Waste Systems Inc.
375 Clements Rd. West
Ajax, ON L1S 7R2
905-427-8064
Fax: 905-683-9492
800-263-9318
www.jfwaste.com

Firm Type: Waste Management
Founded: 1983
Staff: 38
Member of: Ontario Waste Management Association
Products/Services/Areas of Expertise: Waste haulers; collection of fine & mixed paper, corrugated containers, glass bottles, metal cans; comprehensive recycling for industrial, commercial, institutional & residential sectors
Contact(s):
Lenny Campitelli, President
Barry Henderson, Diversion & Recycling Programs

J&M Industrial Engineering & Sales Ltd.
#11, 5320 Finch Ave. East
Toronto, ON M1S 5G3
416-665-2300
Fax: 416-665-7530
sales@jandmengineering.com
www.jandmengineering.com
Firm Type: Distributing
Founded: 1975
Staff: 5
Products/Services/Areas of Expertise: Specialists in flowmeters, liquid level products, pH, ORP, D.O. products, signal conditioning, lime slakers, tank gauging
Domestic Markets:
National

J. Walter Company Ltd.
5977 aut Transcanadienne
Montréal, QC H9R 1C1
514-630-2800
Fax: 514-630-2828
888-592-5837
walter@walter.com
www.walter.com
Firm Type: Manufacturing
Founded: 1952
Staff: 120
Member of: Industrial Supply Association, Canadian Welding Association Gases & Welding Distributors Association
EcoLogo Certified Products & Services: Bio-Circle L is a bioremediating cleaner/degreaser, biodegradable, non-toxic, non-flammable, free of V.O.C., maintains a constant cleaning power & eliminates waste disposal problems; Bio-Circle parts cleaning system, combining the solution Bio-Circle L w
Products/Services/Areas of Expertise: Walter's offers innovative abrasives, power tools, tooling & chemical tools Ecological Note: Bio-Circle L is a bioremediating cleaner/degreaser, biodegradable, non-toxic, non-flammable, free of V.O.C., maintains a constant cleaning power & eliminates waste disposal problems; Bio-Circle parts cleaning system, combining the solution Bio-Circle L w
Financial Information:
Type of Ownership: Private
Revenue: Greater than $5 Million
Revenue Sources: 5% nationwide; 5% Provincial; 5% Municipals; 85% Private Contracts
Domestic Markets:
National
Foreign Activity:
Worldwide
Contact(s):
B. Amiel, President, 514/630-2812
bamiel@jwalter.ca
P. Martel, Manager, Marketing, 514/630-2837
pmartel@jwalter.ca
C. Collier, Vice-President, Sales, 514/630-2840
ccollier@jwalter.ca
P. Lavallee, Manager, PDT, 514/630-2810
plavallee@jwalter.ca
J.M. Maayoufi, SDM, 514/630-2821
jmmaayoufi@jwalter.ca

Canadian Branches:
Mississauga
#12, 151 Superior Blvd.
Mississauga, ON L5T 2L1
905-795-8555
Fax: 905-795-8558
eporter@jwalter.ca
Eric Porter

Vancouver
#1, 1595 Cliveden Ave. West
Vancouver, BC V3M 6M2

604-540-4777
Fax: 604-540-4778
rjones@jwalter.ca
Rich Jones, Manager, Sales

J.D. Mollard & Associates Ltd.
Avord Tower
#810, 2002 Victoria Ave.
Regina, SK S4P 0R7
306-352-8811
Fax: 306-352-8820
mollard@jdmollard.com
www.jdmollard.com
Firm Type: Engineering, Scientific/Technical Services
Founded: 1956
Staff: 6
Member of: Association of Professional Engineers, Geologists & Geoscientists of Alberta; Association of Professional Engineers & Geoscientists of Saskatchewan; Consulting Engineers of Canada
Products/Services/Areas of Expertise: Specialists in applied multidisciplinary remote sensing; route location & terrain analysis; aggregate location & quantity & quality appraisal; natural hazard mapping & analysis; mine, mineral & petroleum exploration & development; site selection & terrain assessment; land use & environmental studies; water resource studies; soil, geology & geotechnical studies; geomatics
Recently Completed / Ongoing Projects: Studies carried out for over 5,000 consulting assignments in various areas including government, oil & gas, pipelines, railways, mining, power, contractors, construction material suppliers & consulting engineering firms
Financial Information:
Type of Ownership: Private
Revenue Sources: 25% nationwide; 15% Provincial; 10% Municipals; 50% Private Contracts
Domestic Markets:
Alberta, Manitoba, Ontario, Saskatchewan
Contact(s):
J.D. Mollard, P.Eng, Ph.D., LLD., FCAE,, President

J.E. Coulter Associates Ltd.
#211, 1210 Sheppard Ave. East
Toronto, ON M2K 1E3
416-502-8598
Fax: 416-502-3473
www.jecoulterassoc.com
Firm Type: Management Consulting, Engineering
Founded: 1986
Staff: 7
Member of: Canadian Acoustical Association; Professional Engineers Ontario
Products/Services/Areas of Expertise: Acoustical consulting engineers; noise & vibration consulting; environmental noise impact assessment
Recently Completed / Ongoing Projects: Did noise impact assessment of Canadian National Exhibition; Molson Amphitheatre; Go Transit, Hamilton; Hwy. 401; Cayuga Raceway; Mosport Park
Financial Information:
Type of Ownership: Private
Domestic Markets:
Ontario
Contact(s):
John E. Coulter, P.Eng, President
jcoulter@on.aibn.com
Howard R. Patlik, Vice-President

J.K. Engineering Ltd. / JEKL
#320, 7930 Bowness Rd. NW
Calgary, AB T3B 0H3
403-247-1777
Fax: 403-286-9895
jkeng@telus.net
www.jkeng.ca
Firm Type: Engineering, Manufacturing
Founded: 1987
Staff: 10
Member of: Association of Professional Engineers of Alberta; Association of Professional Engineers of BC; Association of Professional Engineers of Ontario; American Water Works Association
Products/Services/Areas of Expertise: Water & wastewater treatment design; construction supervision & supply of package plants; groundwater development; monitoring, fabrication & supply of groundwater level monitoring equipment
Recently Completed / Ongoing Projects: Water treatment

Products & Services Buyer's Guide

plants in Weagomow Lake, Bearskin Lake, Blue Mountain Ridge, Cut Lake, Kananaskis Guest Ranch, Sachigo Lake; groundwater investigation & testing & water treatment plant, Goldeye Centre; Groundwater Development, Valiant Ranches; processed (oil) water treatment in Iran & Mexico
Financial Information:
Type of Ownership: Private
Revenue: $500,000 - $1.5 Million
Revenue Sources: 20% nationwide; 30% Municipals; 50% Private Contracts
Domestic Markets:
Alberta, British Columbia, Ontario
Foreign Activity:
Eastern Europe, The Middle East, Mexico
Contact(s):
Jan Korzeniowski, President

J.L. Richards & Associates Limited
864 Lady Ellen Pl.
Ottawa, ON K1Z 5M2
613-728-3571
Fax: 613-728-6012
mail@jlrichards.ca
www.jlrichards.ca
Firm Type: Engineering
Founded: 1955
Staff: 170
Products/Services/Areas of Expertise: Consulting engineering; architecture; energy management; planning; noise control consulting; waste management consulting; cogeneration; stormwater management
Recently Completed / Ongoing Projects: Optimization study, design & operational management services, Trail Rd. Landfill, City of Ottawa
Financial Information:
Type of Ownership: Private
Domestic Markets:
Northwest Territories, Ontario, Québec
Foreign Activity:
Africa, Central America, The Pacific Rim, South America,
Contact(s):
George T. McCaffrey, President
Fay A. Cormier, Chief Civil Engineer

Canadian Branches:
Kingston
#206, 863 Princess St.
Kingston, ON K7L 5N4
613-544-1424
Fax: 613-544-5679
David Hunter, Branch Manager

North Bay
#200, 175 Progress Rd.
North Bay, ON P1B 8G4
705-495-7597
Fax: 705-495-6692
Bryan Parkinson, Manager

Sudbury
#217, 469 Bouchard St.
Sudbury, ON P3E 2K8
705-522-8174
Fax: 705-522-1512
Steven Langille, Branch Manager

Timmins
#201, 150 Algonquin Blvd. E
Timmins, ON P4N 1A7
705-360-1899
Fax: 705-360-1788
Georges Quirion, Manager

J.M. Turcotte ltée
34, Route 132
Trois-Pistoles, QC G0L 4K0
418-851-3612
Fax: 418-851-4576
800-263-3612
Firm Type: Distributing
Founded: 1961
Staff: 25
Products/Services/Areas of Expertise: Water & wastewater management equipment
Contact(s):
Denis Turcotte, President

J.R. Cousin Consultants Ltd. / JRCC
91A Scurfield Blvd.
Winnipeg, MB R3Y 1G4
204-489-0474
Fax: 204-489-0487
info@jrcc.ca
www.jrcc.ca
Firm Type: Engineering
Founded: 1981
Staff: 15
Products/Services/Areas of Expertise: Water treatment & distribution; community planning & development; survey, design & landscaping; environmental, geotechnical & geohydrology engineering; municipal & civil; project management; transportation; sewage collection & treatment
Financial Information:
Type of Ownership: Private
Domestic Markets:
Manitoba, Ontario
Contact(s):
Jerry Cousin, P.Eng., President
Tim Lasuik, CET, Vice-President

J.R. Tinderblox
#13, 11 Cardico Dr.
Gormley, ON L0H 1G0
905-888-8820
Fax: 905-888-8821
tinderblox@sympatico.ca
www.tinderblox.com
Products/Services/Areas of Expertise: Diverts wood waste through recycling, by manufacturing an alternative firewood product for use in fireplaces, woodstoves, campsites, pizza ovens etc.
Ecological Note: Compressed firewood, Tinderblox Firewood is manufactured from 100% clean, low pollution wood waste for efficient energy consumption; no chemicals or bonding agents are used in the process; it burns clean & efficient with minimal ash residue
Contact(s):
Lorraine Munro, Contact

J.W. Bird & Company Ltd.
670 Wilsey Rd.
Fredericton, NB E3B 5C6
506-453-9915
Fax: 506-453-0513
const.nb@birdstairs.ca
www.birdstairs.ca
Firm Type: Distributing
Founded: 1958
Staff: 75
Products/Services/Areas of Expertise: Distributor of construction products
Recently Completed / Ongoing Projects: Crane Mountain landfill; Maritime Road Development (Moncton to Fredericton Hwy.); Shippagan Lagoon
Financial Information:
Type of Ownership: Private
Revenue: $1.5 Million - $3 Million
Revenue Sources: 15% nationwide; 15% Provincial; 15% Municipals; 55% Private Contracts
Domestic Markets:
New Brunswick, Newfoundland & Labrador, Nova Scotia, Prince Edward Island
Foreign Activity:
USA
Contact(s):
Geoff Munn, President
Ernie Lean, Manager, Sales

Canadian Branches:
Dartmouth
102 John Savage Ave.
Dartmouth, NS B3B 0C9
902-468-2884
Fax: 902-468-2846
1-800-565-3166
admin.ns@birdstairs.ca

Fredericton
670 Wilsey Rd.
Fredericton, NB E3B 7K4
506-453-9915
Fax: 506-453-0513
1-800-263-4995
birds@nbnet.nb.ca

Geoff Munn
Moncton
530 McNaughton
Moncton, NB E1H 2K1
506-384-2200
Fax: 506-388-4200
gjohannesen@birdstairs.ca
Greg Johannesen

Newfoundland
153 Glencoe Dr.
Mount Pearl, NL A1N 4S7
709-747-0040
Fax: 709-747-0051
dseaward@nfld.net
Dennis Seaward

Saint John
90 Paradise Row
Saint John, NB E2K 3H6
506-652-6034
Fax: 506-652-7044
saintjohn@birdstairs.ca
Barrie Younker

Jack Atkinson & Associates
P.O. Box 22 Main
Amherst, NS B4H 3Y6
902-667-9985
Fax: 902-667-0485
Founded: 1973
Staff: 1
Member of: Agricultural & Industrial Manufacturers Representatives Association
Products/Services/Areas of Expertise: Tub grinders, compost screeners, turners, mixers, soil contamination clean-up products
Financial Information:
Type of Ownership: Private
Domestic Markets:
New Brunswick, Newfoundland & Labrador, Nova Scotia, Prince Edward Island
Contact(s):
John Atkinson, Owner

Jagger Hims Limited / JHL
#301, 1091 Gorham St.
Newmarket, ON L3Y 8X7
905-853-3303
Fax: 905-853-1759
800-263-7419
www.jaggerhims.com
Firm Type: Engineering
Founded: 1988
Staff: 32
Member of: Aggregate Producers Association; Association of Professional Engineers of Ontario; Canadian Consulting Engineers; Consulting Engineers of Ontario
Products/Services/Areas of Expertise: Site audits & remediation; solid waste disposal; solid & liquid containment systems; groundwater contamination studies; wastewater disposal; water supply; contaminated groundwater recovery; cleanup feasibility studies & cleanup supervision; engineering geology; aggregate resource inventories; geotechnical engineering; biosolids management; oil & gas well decommissioning; in-site bioremediation; indoor air quality management
Domestic Markets:
Ontario
Foreign Activity:
USA
Contact(s):
Brian D. Jagger, Branch Manager
Andrew G. Hims, Principal
ahims@jaggerhims.com
Douglas E. Jagger, Principal
djagger@jaggerhims.com
Daniel S. Mohr, P.Eng., Project Engineer
dmohr@jaggerhims.com
Gary R. Hendy, P.Eng., Project Engineer
ghendy@jaggerhims.com

Canadian Branches:
Collingwood
#5, 101 Pretty River Parkway S
Collingwood, ON L9Y 4M8
705-444-2788
Fax: 705-444-0081

1-888-285-1272
ahims@jaggerhims.com
Andrew G. Hims, P.Eng, Branch Manager

Peterborough: Site Investigation Services
#103, 294 Rink St.
Peterborough, ON K9J 2K2
705-743-6850
Fax: 705-743-6854
1-866-818-8366
sash@jaggerhims.com
J.Stephen Ash, P.Eng, Branch Manager

St Catharines
#601, 1 St. Paul St.
St Catharines, ON L2R 7L2
905-687-1771
Fax: 905-687-1773
1-800-668-2598
dmohr@jaggerhims.com
Dan Mohr, P.Eng., Branch Manager

Windsor
#720, 4510 Rhodes Dr.
Windsor, ON N8W 5K5
519-974-5887
Fax: 519-974-5175
1-800-545-5406
Jason Balsdon, MA (Sc); P.Eng, Branch Manager

International Branch(es):
Northville, Mi
#C, 126 North Center
Northville, MI USA
248-449-4051
Fax: 248-449-8251
1-800-545-5406
Jason Balsdon, Branch Manager

Janin Atlas Inc.
#200, 8200, boul Décarie
Montréal, QC H4P 2P5
514-739-3291
Fax: 514-341-3060
janin@janin.ca
www.janin.ca
Firm Type: Management Consulting, Engineering
Founded: 1997
Member of: VINCI Concessions Canada Inc., Construction DJL; Advitam Solutions; Freyssinet Technologies
Quality Environmental Management System(s): 9001
Products/Services/Areas of Expertise: The firm is a leader in the field of heavy construction, with a focus on design-build & turnkey projects, & infrastructure inspection & repair. Along with its affiliates, Janin Atlas supports a sustainable approach to regional infrastructure development
Recently Completed / Ongoing Projects: Saint John & Jemseg Bridges; Beauharnois Bridge; Royal Victoria Hospital; St-Eustache Hospital; Toulnustouc Hydroelectric Development; New York City Water Tunnel No. 3; Eastmain-1 Hydroelectric Development
Domestic Markets:
Québec
Foreign Activity:
USA
Contact(s):
Thierry Portafaix, President

Jannock Steel Fabricating Co.
#19, 89 Galaxy Blvd.
Etobicoke, ON M9W 1B7
416-674-4787

Canadian Branches:
Westeel Alberta
P.O. Box 550
407 - 22 Ave.
Nisku, AB T0C 2G0
780-955-2500

Westeel Regina
P.O. Box 500
540 - 10 Ave. East
Regina, SK S4P 3A2
306-525-5481

Westeel Saskatoon
North Corman Industrial Park
P.O. Box 1370
Saskatoon, SK S7K 3P5
306-931-0066

Westeel St-Hyacinthe
820, Marineau
Saint-Hyacinthe, QC J2S 7A9
450-796-2677

Westeel Winnipeg
P.O. Box 792
Winnipeg, MB R3C 2N5
204-233-7133

Jannock Steel Fabricating Co.
#19, 89 Galaxy Blvd.
Etobicoke, ON M9W 1B7
416-674-4787

Marclin-Westeel Ltd. Nisku
P.O. Box 223
1608 - 8 St.
Nisku, AB T0C 2G0
780-955-2514

Marclin-Westeel Ltd. Calgary
#600, 11012 MacLeod Trail South
Calgary, AB T2J 6A5
403-278-4500

Jasco Research Ltd.
#2101, 4464 Markham St.
Victoria, BC V8Z 7X8
250-483-3300
Fax: 250-483-3301
info@jasco.com
www.jasco.com
Firm Type: Information Technology, Scientific/Technical Services
Founded: 1981
Staff: 21
Member of: National Marine Electronics Association
Products/Services/Areas of Expertise: Applied research in the areas of environmental noise assessments, physical oceanography, underwater acoustics, scientific data analysis, operations-research, geophysics & development of computing systems; acoustic monitoring for environmental regulation adherence, image analysis software development services
Recently Completed / Ongoing Projects: Monitoring & modelling of underwater noise levels at port construction projects, LNG deep water ports, underwater pipeline & cable installation projects, & for siesmic surveys worldwide
Financial Information:
Type of Ownership: Private
Domestic Markets:
National, Alberta, British Columbia, Nova Scotia, Northwest Territories, Ontario
Foreign Activity:
Asia, Australia/New Zealand, China, Western Europe, USA, Vietnam, Worldwide
Markets Sought:
Central America, Central Europe, The Pacific Rim, South America
Contact(s):
Scott Carr, Chief Executive Officer
Roberto Racca, Chief Communications Officer
rob@jasco.com
Dave Hannay, Chief Science Officer
Holly Sneddon-Ingeberg, Project Manager

Canadian Branches:
Halifax
#301, 32 Troop Ave.
Halifax, NS B3B 1Z1
902-405-3336
Fax: 902-405-3337
halifax@jasco.com
Scott Carr, Vice-President

JB Laboratories Ltd.
827 Fort St.
Victoria, BC V8W 1H6
250-385-6112
Fax: 250-382-6364
866-385-6112
Firm Type: Scientific/Technical Services
Founded: 1989
Staff: 6
Products/Services/Areas of Expertise: Water & wastewater analysis for sewage treatment plants & water services

Financial Information:
Type of Ownership: Private
Revenue Sources: 40% Municipals; 60% Private Contracts
Domestic Markets:
British Columbia

Jenike & Johanson, Ltd.
#100, 5955 Airport Rd.
Mississauga, ON L4V 1R9
905-694-9769
Fax: 905-694-9809
mailcan11@jenike.com
www.jenike.com
Firm Type: Engineering, Scientific/Technical Services
Founded: 1975
Staff: 5
Products/Services/Areas of Expertise: Bulk material handling systems; dust minimization, supression & collection; hazardous material handling; conditioning vessels & purge silos
Recently Completed / Ongoing Projects: Functional recommendations & flow property testing for loading titanium dioxide onto ships & for stockpiling ground clinker; conditioning vessel for plastic pellets; handling systems for refuse
Financial Information:
Type of Ownership: Private
Revenue Sources: 100% Private Contracts
Domestic Markets:
National
Foreign Activity:
Central America, The Middle East, South America, Mexico, USA, Former USSR
Contact(s):
Mike Rulff, President
Tracy Holmes, Vice-President

International Branch(es):
Chile
Av. Libertad 798, Of. 501
Vina del Mar Chile
56-32-2690596
Fax: 56-32-2690596
jenike-chile@entelchile.net

USA - California
3485 Empresa Dr.
San Luis Obispo, CA USA
805-541-0901
Fax: 805-541-4680
mail10@slo.jenike.com

USA - Massachusetts
400 Business Park Dr.
Tyngsboro, MA USA
978-649-3300
Fax: 978-649-3399
mail11@jenike.com

Jes-Chem Ltd.
3 Berkley Pl.
Guelph, ON N1E 1E5
519-821-9061
Fax: 519-767-0981
Firm Type: Waste Management
Founded: 1978
Member of: Water Environment Association of Ontario
Products/Services/Areas of Expertise: Flocculants & water clarifiers for solids removal & sludge conditioning for municipalities, oil refineries, mining companies, pulp & paper industry; scale control agents
Domestic Markets:
National
Foreign Activity:
The Pacific Rim, USA
Contact(s):
Jack Schill, President/CEO
jackschill@rogers.com

Jetvac Inc.
#15 & 16, 4280 Harvester Rd.
Burlington, ON L7L 5Z5
905-639-8240
Fax: 905-639-8245
800-420-8240
info@jetvac.ca
www.jetvac.ca
Firm Type: Distributing
Founded: 1988

Staff: 5
Member of: Water Environment Association of Ontario
Products/Services/Areas of Expertise: Manufactures oil/water separators, vacuum toilets, sewage treatment systems & vacuum collection systems
Recently Completed / Ongoing Projects: Condensate Collection by Vacuum, sold 20 systems, US supermarkets; sewage systems, Algoma Central Marine & Canada Steamship Lines; oil water treatment, Halifax Shipyard Ltd.
Financial Information:
Type of Ownership: Private
Revenue: $1.5 Million - $3 Million
Revenue Sources: 10% nationwide; 40% Provincial; 50% Private Contracts
Domestic Markets:
British Columbia, New Brunswick, Nova Scotia, Ontario
Foreign Activity:
USA
Contact(s):
Alan Russell, President

JFA James Floyd Associates Ltd.
77 Gower St.
St. John's, NL A1C 1N66L2
709-579-7744
Fax: 709-726-6307
Contact(s):
James Floyd, Owner

JFM Environmental Ltd.
183 Glenn Hawthorne Blvd.
Mississauga, ON L5R 2K8
905-712-1500
Fax: 905-712-1555
www.jfmel.com
Firm Type: Management Consulting
Founded: 1993
Products/Services/Areas of Expertise: Provides a range of remediation solutions, management & assessment
Contact(s):
J. Frank Marcoccia, Principal

Canadian Branches:
London Office
#114, 1673 Richmond St.
London, ON N6G 2N3
519-858-9191
Fax: 519-452-3089

JKM Custom Fabricating Ltd.
280 Sheldon Dr.
Cambridge, ON N1T 1A8
519-623-6850
Fax: 519-623-3413
www.jkmfabricating.com
Firm Type: Manufacturing
Founded: 1974
Staff: 25
Products/Services/Areas of Expertise: Air pollution control equipment
Financial Information:
Type of Ownership: Private
Contact(s):
Allan F. Barber, President
allan@jkmfabricating.com

JM Science Canada Inc.
#3, 1230 Rushbrooke Dr.
Oakville, ON L6M 1K9
905-825-3438
Fax: 905-847-1695
800-495-1678
www.jmscience.com
Firm Type: Distributing
Founded: 1986
Staff: 4
Products/Services/Areas of Expertise: Equipment for environmental laboratories, HPLC columns, titrators, detectors & accessories for liquid chromatography; process control equipment for power plants, relay/transducer products
Financial Information:
Type of Ownership: Private
Domestic Markets:
National
Foreign Activity:
USA
Contact(s):
John D. MacFarlane
john@jmscience.com

JMB Research Ltd.
3219 Allan Rd., 2nd Fl.
North Vancouver, BC V7J 3C6
604-985-1837
Fax: 604-985-3219
admin@jmbresearch.ca
www.jmbresearch.ca
Firm Type: Management Consulting, Engineering, Scientific/Technical Services, Waste Management
Staff: 3
Products/Services/Areas of Expertise: Indoor air quality testing; phase I & II site assessment; contaminated site remediation; storage tank removal; environmental training; applied research
Recently Completed / Ongoing Projects: Will test levels of chemical & microbiological contamination in homes or buildings used for marijuana grow operations
Financial Information:
Type of Ownership: Private
Contact(s):
Joffre Berry, President

JNE Consulting Ltd.
A company of the Joe Ng Group
176 Shaw St.
Hamilton, ON L8L 3P7
905-529-5122
Fax: 905-529-1974
info@jne.ca
www.jneconsulting.ca
Firm Type: Management Consulting, Engineering, Scientific/Technical Services, Waste Management
Founded: 1980
Staff: 350
Member of: Daqo Group Co. Ltd.; Mitsubishi Canada
Quality Environmental Management System(s): 9001:2008
Products/Services/Areas of Expertise: Multi-disciplinary, consulting engineering services; experience in industrial wastewater issues; control systems integration; manufactures & distributes valued-added antibiotics & nutritional products
Recently Completed / Ongoing Projects: JNE Power division manufactures, markets, services photovoltaic module for solar power usage; provides turnkey design & construction services for development of wind power plants
Financial Information:
Type of Ownership: Private
Domestic Markets:
National
Foreign Activity:
USA
Contact(s):
Joe Ng, President
jng@jne.ca
George A. MacCuish, Vice-President
gmaccuish@jnepeng.com

Canadian Branches:
Burlington
3370 South Service Rd.
Burlington, ON L7N 3M6
905-681-3905
Fax: 905-681-9857

Sault Ste. Marie
#202, 550 Queen St. W
Sault Ste Marie, ON P6A 1A6
705-759-0250
Fax: 705-759-2639

Jodek Industries Ltd.
P.O. Box 111
Spruce View, AB T0M 1V0
403-728-3966
Fax: 403-728-3806

Joe Johnson Equipment Inc.
2521 Bowman St.
Barrie, ON L9S 3V6
705-733-7700
Fax: 705-733-8800
800-263-1262
joe@jjei.com
www.jjei.com
Firm Type: Distributing
Founded: 1988
Staff: 12
Member of: National Solid Waste Management Association
Products/Services/Areas of Expertise: Contractors & municipal equipment distributor of wood chippers, recycling vehicles, compost turners, street & sidewalk sweepers, sewer cleaning equipment, asphalt patchers
Domestic Markets:
New Brunswick, Newfoundland & Labrador, Nova Scotia, Ontario, Prince Edward Island, Québec
Contact(s):
Joe Johnson, President/CEO
Joe Johnson Jr., Vice-President
Jeff Johnson, Sales Manager
Brian Knight, Regional Sales Manager
Scott Tyler, Regional Sales Manager

John Brooks Company Ltd.
Also Known As: Fluid Handling Solutions
1260 Kamato Rd.
Mississauga, ON L4W 1Y1
905-624-4200
Fax: 905-624-6379
877-624-5757
ontariosales@johnbrooks.ca
www.fluidhandlingsolutions.com
Firm Type: Management Consulting, Distributing
Founded: 1938
Staff: 250
Products/Services/Areas of Expertise: Provides complete solutions for a wide variety of fluid filtration problems, strainers, bag filters, housings, filter cartridge, high efficiencey (HE) filter systems

Canadian Branches:
Calgary
403-219-0939
Fax: 403-250-1440
albertasales@johnbrooks.ca

Dartmouth
902-832-3935
Fax: 902-832-4567
quebecmaritimessales@johnbrooks.ca

Edmonton
780-468-4499
Fax: 780-468-5143
albertasales@johnbrooks.ca

Mississauga
905-624-4200
Fax: 905-624-6379
ontariosales@johnbrooks.ca

Montréal
514-636-6400
Fax: 514-636-6433
quebecmaritimessales@johnbrooks.ca

Sudbury
705-521-1184
Fax: 705-521-0926
ontariosales@johnbooks.ca

Vancouver
604-942-7622
Fax: 604-942-9429
bcsales@johnbrooks.ca

Winnipeg
204-786-5529
Fax: 204-783-4453
manitobasales@johnbrooks.ca

John McMullen & Associates
#40, 3420 South Millway
Mississauga, ON L5L 3V4
905-608-1127
Fax: 905-820-0953
john.mcmullen@sympatico.ca
Firm Type: Management Consulting
Member of: Ontario Environment Industry Association
Products/Services/Areas of Expertise: Strategic marketing services for the commercialization of new technologies, processes & services, special event planning, communications & stakeholder relations
Recently Completed / Ongoing Projects: Investment roadmapping for clean technologies; identification of priority opportunities in environmental monitoring & control technologies;

national conference on integrated solutions to manure management
Financial Information:
Type of Ownership: Private
Revenue: $100,000 - $250,000
Revenue Sources: 100% Private Contracts
Domestic Markets:
National
Markets Sought:
USA
Contact(s):
John McMullen, President
john.mcmullen@sympatico.ca

John Meunier Inc.
A subsidiary of Veolia Water Solutions & Technologies
4105, rue Sartelon
Saint-Laurent, QC H4S 2B3
514-334-7230
Fax: 514-334-5070
sales@johnmeunier.com
www.johnmeunier.com
Firm Type: Engineering, Waste Management
Founded: 1948
Staff: 130
Member of: Association québécoise des techniques de l'eau; Water Environment Federation; American Water Works Association
Quality Environmental Management System(s): 9001:2000
Products/Services/Areas of Expertise: The company provides treatment solutions for drinking & process water, as well as municipal & industrial effluents: potable & wastewater treatment systems; industrial wastewater treatment; sludge treatment; odour treatment; water recycling & reuse; instrumentation: flow monitoring, process instruments, metering pumps, sampling instruments; consultation & expertise in the management of construction projects for turnkey plants & facilities for industry; green-field projects, treatment systems & remediation. Offices in Mississauga, ON & Glenside, Pennsylvania
Recently Completed / Ongoing Projects: Potable water plant upgrades, QC; WWTP pretreatment, Mexico, USA & Canada; dried sludge pumps, USA
Financial Information:
Type of Ownership: Foreign-owned
Revenue: Greater than $5 Million
Domestic Markets:
National
Foreign Activity:
Mexico, USA,
Contact(s):
Gilles Filion, Chairman
Yvan Liegey, President

Canadian Branches:
Mississauga
Plaza IV
#430, 2000 Argentia Rd.
Mississauga, ON L5N 1W1
905-286-4846
Fax: 905-286-0488
Products/Services/Areas of Expertise: For the U.S. office in Glenside, PA contact 215-885-4740

John Thurston Machine Ltd.
26 Westwyn Ct.
Brampton, ON L6T 4T5
905-451-4221
Fax: 905-451-4490
www.johnthurstonmachine.com
Products/Services/Areas of Expertise: Waste storage containers; sewage treatment equipment; air handling equipment; chemical feeding & mixing equipment
Contact(s):
Jim Yule, Sales

John Zubick Ltd. Scrap Metals
105 Clarke Rd.
London, ON N5W 5C9
519-451-5470
Fax: 519-451-4245
800-263-3294
info@zubick.com
www.zubick.com
Firm Type: Waste Management
Founded: 1945
Staff: 55
Member of: Canadian Association of Recycling Industries
Products/Services/Areas of Expertise: Dealers of scrap metals; hauling service for London & area; mobile crews for scrap metal removal from landfill sites, plants, auto wrecker yards, demolition sites
Recently Completed / Ongoing Projects: Removal of obsolete rail cars; railway emergency response team equipped with cranes (shears, magnets, grapples), loaders & trucks; cleanup of car bodies & metal piles from auto wreckers & collectors
Domestic Markets:
Ontario
Contact(s):
George Zubick, President
Bruce Zubick, Vice-President

Johns Manville Canada Inc.
4704 - 58 St.
Innisfail, AB T4G 1A2
403-227-7100
Fax: 403-227-7112
www.jm.com
Firm Type: Manufacturing
EcoLogo Certified Products & Services: Fiberglass insulation including: Johns Manville Goldline (batts & rolls) & Rich-R Gold Blowing Wool
Products/Services/Areas of Expertise: Fiberglass building insulation production; Johns Manville insulation is the first insulation devised from post-consumer glass & has received dual certification by the Canadian government & a U.S. agency for its recycled content
Ecological Note: Fiberglass insulation including: Johns Manville Goldline (batts & rolls) & Rich-R Gold Blowing Wool
Financial Information:
Type of Ownership: Publicly Traded
Revenue Sources: 100% Private Contracts
Domestic Markets:
National
Foreign Activity:
USA
Contact(s):
Dennis Fehr, Coordinator, Environmental
fehr@jm.com
Terry Sullivan, Marketing, Canadian
sulivat@jm.com

Jomac Canada Inc.
10, rue Bachelder
Stanstead, QC J0B 3E2
819-876-7531
Fax: 819-876-5361
800-567-2765
info@jomaccanada.com
www.jomaccanada.com
Firm Type: Manufacturing
Founded: 1906
Staff: 75
Member of: Wells Lamont Industry Group
Quality Environmental Management System(s): 9001:2000
Products/Services/Areas of Expertise: Manufacturers of industrial safety gloves
Domestic Markets:
National
Contact(s):
Andrew McKnight, Marketing Manager, Canada
amcknight@jomaccanada.com
Dan Pollock, Regional Manager, Ontario
dpollock@jomaccanada.com
Don Vallee, Regional Manager, Western Canada
dvallee@jomaccanada.com

Jones Group Engineering Ltd.
RR#2
High River, AB T1V 1N2
403-395-3869
Firm Type: Engineering
Staff: 2
Products/Services/Areas of Expertise: Specializes in renewable energy developments; services provided include: computer modelling, wind resource monitoring, wind turbine performance testing, project management & public education
Contact(s):
Mary-Ellen Jones, M.Sc., P.Eng.

Joseph & Co. Inc.
Also Known As: Regional Waste Disposal (Kitchener) Ltd.
257 Victoria St. North
Kitchener, ON N2H 5C9
519-743-0205
Fax: 519-743-9341
info@josephco.ca
www.josephco.ca
Firm Type: Waste Management
Founded: 1880
Staff: 20
Member of: Canadian Association of Recycling Industries
Products/Services/Areas of Expertise: Scrap metal & industrial steel; sorting, grading & preparation of ferrous & non-ferrous metals for delivery to foundries, steel mills & smelters; container services for metals & industrial, commercial & residential refuse
Domestic Markets:
Ontario,
Contact(s):
Max Norris, President
Amichai Tsafarti, Controller
David Tsafarti, Operations Manager

JTU Consulting
75 Wimbledon Rd.
Guelph, ON N1H 7V7
519-836-3739
Fax: 519-747-0006
jtu@sentex.net
Firm Type: Management Consulting, Scientific/Technical Services
Founded: 1990
Member of: Canadian Environment Industry Association; Ontario Natural Gas Association; Canadian Gas Association; Ontario Society for Environmental Management
Products/Services/Areas of Expertise: Provides expert advice on applications for environmental approvals, certificates of approval & environmental management; conducts environmental training programs
Recently Completed / Ongoing Projects: Assists clients on an ongoing basis to develop & implement environmental management programs, internal & external environmental audit programs, risk assessment studies, spills prevention & response plans, other environmental protocols & accompanying manuals, & public consultation programs
Domestic Markets:
National
Foreign Activity:
Africa, USA
Contact(s):
Jasmine Urisk, President
Terry Faye, Vice-President, Marketing & Communications

Jubilee Rose Enterprises Ltd.
#69, 15515 - 24th Ave.
Surrey, BC V4A 2J4
604-535-7339
Fax: 604-535-7691
sales@jubileerose.com
www.jubileerose.com
Products/Services/Areas of Expertise: Oil energy-efficient products; distributors of industry-specific calculators & electric measures
Contact(s):
Alannah Hubburmin

Just Homes
11 Audley Ave.
Toronto, ON M4M 1P5
416-466-8480
Fax: 416-466-8165
877-466-8470
roger@justhomes.ca
www.justhomes.ca
Firm Type: Management Consulting, Engineering
Founded: 1985
Products/Services/Areas of Expertise: Architectural, mechanical, electrical design/construction, project management consultant for low energy, indoor air quality (IAQ), environmentally sustainable residential dwellings; renovation; additions
Financial Information:
Type of Ownership: Private
Revenue Sources: 100% Private Contracts
Domestic Markets:
National
Foreign Activity:
USA
Contact(s):
Roger H. Algie, Owner

Products & Services Buyer's Guide

justenvironment
15 Timber Run Court, RR#2
Campbellville, ON L0P 1B0
905-659-4732
Fax: 905-659-4733
mrudolph@justenvironment.com
www.justenvironment.com
Firm Type: Information Technology
Founded: 1995
Staff: 2
Member of: Ontario Environmental Industries Association
Products/Services/Areas of Expertise: Strategic planning; management consulting; government relations; public relations; policy evaluations & analysis; strategic communications; ENGO Relations (Environmental Non-Governmental Organization Relations)
Recently Completed / Ongoing Projects: Ongoing retainer relationships with: Clean Air Renewable Energy Coalition; Suncor Energy Inc.; Inco Ltd.; Walker Industries Holding Ltd.; Nature Conservancy of Canada
Financial Information:
Type of Ownership: Private
Revenue: $250,000 - $500,000
Revenue Sources: 100% Private Contracts
Domestic Markets:
Alberta, British Columbia, Manitoba, Ontario, Québec
Contact(s):
Mark S. Rudolph, President
mrudolph@justenvironment.ca
Jan Whitelaw, Vice-President
jwhitelaw@justenvironment.ca

K&D Pratt Group Inc.
P.O. Box 279
210 John Savage Ave.
Dartmouth, NS B3B 0C9
902-468-1955
Fax: 902-468-6756
800-567-1955
kdinfo@kdpratt.com
www.kdpratt.com
Firm Type: Distributing
Founded: 1922
Staff: 100
Quality Environmental Management System(s): 9001
Products/Services/Areas of Expertise: Distribution & service throughout Atlantic Canada, providing quality products & services for over 80 years; customers are in the construction, contracting fire service, government, manufacutring, mining, oil & gas, telecommunication & utility sectors; communications, industrial, construction, fire & safety, Marine & industrial Coatings, oil & gas, service centre, K&D United Safety Service, Turbcraft Instruments & Control
Financial Information:
Type of Ownership: Private
Revenue: Greater than $5 Million
Domestic Markets:
Alberta, New Brunswick, Newfoundland & Labrador, Nova Scotia, Prince Edward Island
Contact(s):
Leigh Puddester, President, 709/922-5690
Karen Vallise, Marketing Coordinator, 902/468-1955
karen.vallis@kdpratt.com
Darren MacLeod, Managing Director
Melissa English-Barbour, HSEQ Coordinator
Steve McPhee, Industrial Sales Manager, 902/468-1955
steve.mcphee@kdpratt.com

Canadian Branches:
New Brunswick
P.O. Box 36
15 Consumers Dr.
Saint John, NB E2J 4Z7
506-658-1148
Fax: 506-648-9365
kdinfonb@kdpratt.com
Patrick Graves

Newfoundland & Labrador
P.O. Box 3160
73 Blackmarsh Rd.
St. John's, NL A1B 3N3
709-722-5690
Fax: 709-722-6975
kdinfonf@kdpratt.com
Matt Shinkle

Tubcraft Insturments & Controls
P.O. Box 8160
73 Blackmarsh Rd.
St. John's, NL A1B 3N3
709-722-5690
Fax: 709-722-6975
1-800-563-9595
marketing@tubecraft.com

K-Tech Services Ltd.
551 West 20th St.
North Vancouver, BC V7M 1Y8
604-988-6032
Contact(s):
Igor E. Kusec, Specialist, Air Pollution Control

K.T. Enviro Clean Inc.
605 Mercy St.
Selkirk, MB R1A 2B3
204-785-4850
Fax: 204-482-1217
800-461-5666
kgenviro@mb.sympatico.ca
Products/Services/Areas of Expertise: Chemicals supply and distribution; hazardous waste management & recycling/disposal; hazardous waste transport; site remediation; emergency response for chemical and hazardous waste spills
Contact(s):
Tom Screawn

Kaehne Consulting Ltd.
Formerly: J. Kaehne & Associates Ltd.
#7, 3046 Edgemont Blvd.
North Vancouver, BC V7R 2N4
604-904-9101
Fax: 604-904-9102
kcl@kaehne.com
www.kaehne.com
Firm Type: Management Consulting, Engineering
Founded: 1986
Staff: 20
Member of: Association of Consulting Engineers of Canada; Canadian Institute of Mining
Products/Services/Areas of Expertise: Electrical, instrumentation & mechanical engineering; design & project management services for power, mining, materials handling, chemical, & oil & gas industries
Financial Information:
Type of Ownership: Private
Revenue Sources: 100% Private Contracts
Domestic Markets:
Yukon Territory
Foreign Activity:
Caribbean
Contact(s):
Jerry Kaehne, CEO

Kafko Manufacturing Ltd.
1231 Kamato Rd.
Mississauga, ON L4W 2M2
905-624-3000
Fax: 905-624-5234
800-326-3015
www.kafko.com
Products/Services/Areas of Expertise: Lubricants, sealants, oils & greases
Contact(s):
John Gall, Sales Representative

Kaizen Environmental Services Inc. / KESI
333 - 50th Ave. SE
Calgary, AB T2G 2B3
403-297-0411
Fax: 403-297-0830
888-525-5902
kaizen@kaizenenviro.com
Firm Type: Engineering
Founded: 1993
Staff: 35
Member of: Calgary Chamber of Commerce; Canadian Association of Drilling Engineers; Environmental Services Association of Alberta; Canadian Land Reclamation Association; Canadian Association of Drilling Contractors
Quality Environmental Management System(s): 17025
Products/Services/Areas of Expertise: Applied analytical chemistry; accredited laboratory; hydrogeology, engineering, biology, chemistry, agriculture, commercial real estate transactions; industrial remediation
Activities: KaizenLab, www.kaizenlab.ca
Recently Completed / Ongoing Projects: Reclamation of 120 sites in central Alberta; decontamination of chemical bleeding facility; natural attenuation of gas plan hydrocarbons in soils
Financial Information:
Type of Ownership: Private
Domestic Markets:
Alberta, British Columbia, Northwest Territories, Yukon Territory
Foreign Activity:
Caribbean, Central America, South America
Markets Sought:
Western Europe
Contact(s):
Douglas R. De Freitas, President
Koshy Malayil, Analytical Divisions Manager

Canadian Branches:
Grande Prairie
#308, 10104 - 101 Ave.
Grande Prairie, AB T8V 0Y3
780-538-0972
Fax: 780-538-3014
888-538-0972
Ryan Schroeder

International Branch(es):
Trinidad
Rajkumar St.
Freeport Trinidad
868-299-0009
Fax: 868-673-6420
kaizen-tt.com
Doug deFreitas

Kalyn Siebert Canada Inc.
8750, boul Industriel
Trois-Rivières, QC G9A 5E1
819-379-3738
Fax: 819-379-7536
Products/Services/Areas of Expertise: Transfer trailers for solid waste handling

Kam Biotechnology Ltd.
#101, 9710 - 187th St.
Surrey, BC V4N 3N6
604-888-4336
Fax: 604-888-6623
admin@kambiotechnology.com
www.kambiotechnology.com
Firm Type: Manufacturing
Founded: 1989
Staff: 12
Products/Services/Areas of Expertise: Adapted bacterial cultures for use in hazardous & non-hazardous waste remediation
Financial Information:
Type of Ownership: Private
Revenue Sources: 100% Private Contracts
Domestic Markets:
British Columbia, Ontario
Foreign Activity:
Worldwide
Contact(s):
Aline Ferchichi, President
Mongi Ferchichi, CEO
Karim Ferchichi, Vice-President, Operations
George Gil, Sr. Research Scientist, Applied Microbiology
Neil Simpson, Marketing/Sales
Bharat Bhushan, Sr. Research Scientist
Mehrdad Keshmiri, Sr. Research Scientist
Naig Naing Win, Sr. Research Scientist

Kamloops Scrap Iron Ltd.
955 Ord Rd.
Kamloops, BC V2B 7B5
250-554-3491
Fax: 250-554-4200
866-797-2727
scrap@mail.ocis.net
www.kamscrap.com
Firm Type: Waste Management
Founded: 1981
Products/Services/Areas of Expertise: Metals recycling
Contact(s):
Jim Clark, General Manager

Kang Construction Ltd.
#3, 1725 - 30 Ave. NE
Calgary, AB T2E 7P6
403-250-8868
Fax: 403-250-1788
kang@kangconstruction.com
Firm Type: Engineering
Founded: 1982
Member of: Calgary Construction Association; Alberta Home Warranty
Products/Services/Areas of Expertise: Excavation, civil work, environmental clean-up & projects
Recently Completed / Ongoing Projects: Reconstruction & overnight construction,Calgary International Airport; Building foundation & site assessment, Airdrie; Weeping tile, Hull Child Services
Financial Information:
Type of Ownership: Private
Revenue: $1.5 Million - $3 Million
Revenue Sources: 20% Municipals; 80% Private Contracts
Domestic Markets:
Alberta
Contact(s):
Alvin Kang, President/CEO
alvin@kangconstruction.com

Kanotech Information Systems Ltd.
Formerly: Generation 5 Technology Ltd.
#1, 27107 Twp. Rd. 510
Spruce Grove, AB T7Y 1H6
780-906-2888
800-661-9338
questions3@kanotech.com
www.kanotech.com
Firm Type: Information Technology
Founded: 1985
Products/Services/Areas of Expertise: Software development providing GIS to architects, engineers, planners & other professionals in the public & private sectors; supports automated mapping, facilities management, planning, design & spatial analytical requirements
Activities: Research & development relating to the building or integrating of environmental analysis programs
Financial Information:
Type of Ownership: Private
Domestic Markets:
Alberta, British Columbia, Manitoba, Ontario, Saskatchewan
Foreign Activity:
USA
Contact(s):
Dean Whitford, President/CEO
Megan Marrie, Manager, Marketing

Kappler Canada
P.O. Box 555
105 Scott Ave.
Paris, ON N3L 3T6
519-442-4774
Fax: 519-442-7477
866-997-4774
canada@kappler.com
www.kappler.com
Products/Services/Areas of Expertise: Disposable & reusable chemical protective garments & hospital/medical garments
Domestic Markets:
National,

Kason
Division of Separator Engineering Ltd.
#85, 2220 Midland Ave.
Toronto, ON M1P 3E6
416-292-8822
Fax: 416-292-3882
877-694-4441
info@separatorengineering.com;
jbyrnes@separatorengineering.com
www.kason.com
Firm Type: Manufacturing
Founded: 1956
Products/Services/Areas of Expertise: Screening equipment for granular solids & slurries
Financial Information:
Type of Ownership: Private
Revenue Sources: 100% Private Contracts
Domestic Markets:
National

Foreign Activity:
Worldwide
Contact(s):
Laurence Stone, President
International Branch(es):
Millburn, NJ
67 - 71 East Willow St.
Millburn, NJ USA
973-467-8140
Fax: 973-258-9533
info@kason.com
Larry Stone, Chair
United Kingdom
Block 4, Units 12 & 13, Park Business Vi
Park Hall Rd., Longton, Stoke-on-Trent
Staffordshire UK
-782/597-540
Fax: -782/597-549
sales@kasoneurope.co.uk
Mark Blairs

Katch Kan Limited
5606 - 103A St. NW
Edmonton, AB T6H 2J5
780-414-6083
Fax: 780-414-6084
800-840-2877
info@katchkan.com
www.katchkan.com
Firm Type: Manufacturing
Founded: 1994
Staff: 20
Member of: Canadian Association of Petroleum Producers; Canadian Association of Drilling Contractors; Environmental Services Association, Alberta
Quality Environmental Management System(s): 9001; ISO
Products/Services/Areas of Expertise: Katch Kan provides systems & services that maximize personnel safety, environmental stewardship, as well as operational savings for the upstream oil & gas industry
Financial Information:
Type of Ownership: Private
Revenue Sources: 100% Private Contracts
Domestic Markets:
National
Foreign Activity:
Worldwide
Contact(s):
Quinn Holtby, President
Nathan Walters, Marketing Director
mwalters@katchkan.com

Kavanagh & Associates Ltd.
P.O. Box 13039 A
74 O'Leary Ave.
St. John's, NL A1B 3V8
709-722-0024
Fax: 709-722-0345
kavanagh@kavanaghandassociates.ca
www.kavanaghandassociates.ca
Firm Type: Engineering
Founded: 1991
Staff: 12
Quality Environmental Management System(s): 9001:2000
Products/Services/Areas of Expertise: Engineering services
Contact(s):
Sean Kavanagh, President
Kevin Hannon, P.Eng., Project Engineer

KBL Land Use Consulting Ltd.
#230, 323 - 10th Ave. SW
Calgary, AB T2R 0A5
403-262-5505
Fax: 403-265-9552
kim.lee@kblianduse.com
www.kbllanduse.com
Contact(s):
James Thorbourne, President
Canadian Branches:
Grande Prairie
#201, 9625 - 115 St.
Grande Prairie, AB T8V 5Z6
780-831-7311

Lloydminster
#201, 5011 - 47th St.
Lloydminster, AB T9V 0E8
780-871-0711
Fax: 780-571-0722
Swift Current
#205, 1081 Central Ave. North
Swift Current, SK S9H 4Z2
306-773-3009
Fax: 306-773-3109
Weyburn
28 - 4th St. NE
Weyburn, SK S4H 0J7
306-842-2088
Fax: 306-842-3356

KBM Forestry Consultants Inc.
349 Mooney St.
Thunder Bay, ON P7B 5L5
807-345-5445
Fax: 807-345-3440
800-465-3001
hbax@kbm.on.ca
www.kbm.on.ca
Firm Type: Scientific/Technical Services
Founded: 1973
Staff: 25
Member of: Ontario Professional Foresters Association
Products/Services/Areas of Expertise: Silviculture equipment; mechanical site preparation; forest audits including compliance, environmental, forest management & sustainability; forest management plans, forestry research & technical writing; forest system & wildlife habitat supply modelling; forestry negotiation; advice, mediation business planning, negotiations & on-reserve management services to First Nations
Recently Completed / Ongoing Projects: ISO/CSA audits; four independent forest audits; forest management planning; photo interpretation & ecosite labeling; forest inventories; First Nation joint venture
Financial Information:
Type of Ownership: Private
Revenue Sources: 5% nationwide; 5% Provincial; 90% Private Contracts
Domestic Markets:
Alberta, Manitoba, Newfoundland & Labrador, Ontario, Saskatchewan
Foreign Activity:
South America, USA
Contact(s):
Herb Bax, President
Jim Paré, Manager, Sales
jpare@kbm.on.ca
Laird Van Damme, Consulting Forester
Peter Higgelke, Consulting Forester
Cindy Whittington, Comptroller
Brad Chaulk, Technical Services
International Branch(es):
KBM Chile S.A.
Longitudinal 5 Sur km 505.5
Los Angeles Chile
-56-43-369522
Fax: -56-43-369534
kbmchile@mcl.cl
Daniel Hermosilla, Contact

KBR Canada
Formerly: Kellogg, Brown & Root Canada Company; Brown & Root
P.O. Box 5588 South
3300 - 76 Ave.
Edmonton, AB T6E 6P8
780-468-1341
Fax: 780-490-3375
www.kbr.com
Firm Type: Manufacturing
Founded: 1951
Products/Services/Areas of Expertise: General industrial construction; piperack & equipment module fabrication of assembly & pipe spool fabrication; spool fabrication of alloy & exotic materials & welding; module fabrication; assembly & erection

KBU Environmental Technologies Inc.
#2, 1099 - 6 Hwy. North, RR#2
Hamilton, ON L8N 2Z7

905-690-2835
Firm Type: Manufacturing, Scientific/Technical Services
Founded: 1989
Staff: 6
Member of: Air & Waste Management Association
Products/Services/Areas of Expertise: Laboratory analysis of air samples; air quality investigation/consulting; occupational health & safety; sales & rental of vacuum canisters for air sampling
Financial Information:
Type of Ownership: Private
Domestic Markets:
National
Foreign Activity:
China, South America, USA, Vietnam
Contact(s):
Ken Unkerskov, President

KC Environmental Group Ltd.
15619 - 112 Ave.
Edmonton, AB T5M 2V8
780-488-7926
Fax: 780-452-8284
877-774-5678
kcgroup@cleanitgreenit.net
www.cleanitgreenit.net
Firm Type: Engineering, Information Technology, Scientific/Technical Services
Founded: 1990
Products/Services/Areas of Expertise: Composting; ecolabelling; spills & clean-up planning & assessment; audit services; public participation, education & awareness; bioremediation services
Financial Information:
Type of Ownership: Private
Revenue Sources: 10% nationwide; 30% Provincial; 20% Municipals; 40% Private Contracts
Domestic Markets:
Alberta, British Columbia, Saskatchewan
Contact(s):
Kristen Castro-Wunsch, President
Bryan Armstrong, Manager, Business

KEDCO Constructors Ltd.
23238 Mavis Ave.
Langley, BC V1M 2S4
604-882-4992
Fax: 604-882-4993
dkedrosky@telus.net
Contact(s):
Dave Kedrosky, Contact

Kel-Ann Organics
91 Duke St.
Bedford, NS B4A 2Z2
902-835-7645
Fax: 902-835-9803
kel-ann@msn.com
Firm Type: Manufacturing
Founded: 1977
Staff: 18
Member of: Landscape Nova Scotia
Products/Services/Areas of Expertise: Manufacturers of organic soils & bark mulch
Financial Information:
Type of Ownership: Private
Contact(s):
Michael Pink, Contact

Kemel Cartons (1973) Ltd.
684 Dufferin Ave.
Winnipeg, MB R2W 2Z4
204-586-5896
Fax: 204-589-5940
cartons@mts.net
kemelcartons.com
Firm Type: Waste Management
Founded: 1940
Products/Services/Areas of Expertise: Recycling of corrugated containers, cardboard & paper
Domestic Markets:
Alberta, British Columbia, Manitoba, Saskatchewan
Foreign Activity:
USA
Contact(s):
Marvin Kemel, President

Kemic Bioresearch Laboratories Ltd.
P.O. Box 878
70 Exhibition St.
Kentville, NS B4N 4H8
902-678-8195
Fax: 902-678-2839
info@kemic.com
www.kemic.com
Firm Type: Scientific/Technical Services
Founded: 1980
Staff: 4
Products/Services/Areas of Expertise: Toxicology consulting
Domestic Markets:
National
Foreign Activity:
Western Europe, USA
Contact(s):
Peter W. Mullen, President
pmullen@kemic.com

Kemira Water Solutions Canada Inc.
Formerly: Eaglebrook Environmental Corporation
3405, boul Marie-Victorin
Varennes, QC J3X 1T6
450-652-0665
Fax: 450-652-7343
800-465-6171
servicecanada@kemira.com
www.kemirawater.ca
Firm Type: Manufacturing, Waste Management
Founded: 1980
Staff: 60
Member of: Canadian Manufacturers Association
Products/Services/Areas of Expertise: Manufacture, sale & transport of chemicals; ferric chloride, ferric sulphate; ferrous chloride, ferrous sulphate, aluminum sulphate, PHAS, PACI, PASS, ACH, polyaluminum dilatide & polyaluminum sulphate, for use in municipal & industrial wastewater treatment; applications include phosphate & BOD removal, odour control & sludge conditioning, drinking water treatment
Domestic Markets:
National
Foreign Activity:
Africa, Australia/New Zealand, The Pacific Rim, South America, Mexico, USA
Contact(s):
Manuel Moreau, Director, Sales, Municipal, Canada
manuel.moreau@kemira.com

Canadian Branches:
Brantford
626 Oak Park Rd.
Brantford, ON N3T 5L8
519-759-7570
Fax: 519-759-8962

Ottawa
2810 Sheffield Rd.
Ottawa, ON K1B 3V9
613-746-1574
Fax: 613-746-5858

Ken Noftell Drilling Services
Also Known As: Noftell Drillling Services
95 Bryson Rd.
Rusagonis, NB E3B 8E1
506-455-3781
Firm Type: Scientific/Technical Services
Founded: 1994
Staff: 3
Products/Services/Areas of Expertise: Soil investigation; standard penetration test with AW rods; split spoon samples; continuous sampling &/or wash borings; observation wells & piezometer installations; drive well points installed; auger drilling
Financial Information:
Type of Ownership: Private
Revenue Sources: 4% Provincial; 1% Municipals; 95% Private Contracts
Domestic Markets:
New Brunswick, Newfoundland & Labrador, Nova Scotia, Prince Edward Island
Contact(s):
Ken Noftell, Owner/Operator

Ken Summers Biological Services
26848 - 33A Ave.
Aldergrove, BC V3W 3G7

604-856-8687
Firm Type: Scientific/Technical Services
Founded: 1986
Products/Services/Areas of Expertise: Environmental consulting & contracting services; baseline studies; environmental assessments

Keneco Environmental Services Inc.
3333 - 8th Ave. SE, 3rd Fl.
Calgary, AB T2G 3A4
403-237-8137
Fax: 403-770-4003
hr@kenecoenviro.com
www.codeco.com
Products/Services/Areas of Expertise: Site reclamation & remedial action services; part of CODECO Energy Group
Contact(s):
Tom Stevenson, General Manager

Kent Engineering Ltd.
475 Gordon Pl.
West Vancouver, BC V7T 1R7
604-926-8601
Firm Type: Management Consulting, Engineering
Founded: 1971
Staff: 11
Products/Services/Areas of Expertise: Environmental engineering services; environmental audits & assessments; wastewater treatment; air emission control; soil remediation; design & upgrade of petroleum products storage facilities
Recently Completed / Ongoing Projects: Decommissioning of plant, site assessment & design of remediation plan, Wills Oil Co. Ltd.; plant decommissioning & site assessment, Nyes Foundry Ltd.
Financial Information:
Type of Ownership: Private
Revenue Sources: 20% nationwide; 80% Private Contracts
Domestic Markets:
Alberta, British Columbia, Manitoba, Northwest Territories, Saskatchewan, Yukon Territory
Foreign Activity:
USA
Markets Sought:
Asia, South America
Contact(s):
Clarence D. Kent, President
Contact(s):
Harold G. Forsyth

Canadian Branches:
I-Tec Systems Design Ltd.
#9, 12372 - 84 Ave.
Surrey, BC V3W 3G6
604-597-6192
Fax: 604-597-3978
itec@dowco.com

Kentain Products Ltd.
55 Howard Pl.
Kitchener, ON N2K 2Z4
519-576-0994
Fax: 519-576-0919
800-366-0535
info@kentain.com
www.kentain.com
Firm Type: Manufacturing
Founded: 1976
Staff: 5
Member of: Water Environment Association of Ontario; American Electroplaters & Surface Finishers Association
Products/Services/Areas of Expertise: Manufacturer of flexible PVC, bag-type, liners for chemical stroage tank & secondary containment areas
Recently Completed / Ongoing Projects: Glenmore watertreatment plant, Calgary, AB; Sudbury water treatment plant, Sudbury, ON; Edmonton water treatment plant, Edmonton, AB
Financial Information:
Type of Ownership: Private
Revenue: $250,000 - $500,000
Revenue Sources: 35% Municipals; 65% Private Contracts
Domestic Markets:
National
Contact(s):
Glen Lippert, President

Kernic Systems Inc.
Formerly: Kernic Equipment Sales Ltd.
5230 South Service Rd.
Burlington, ON L7L 5K2
905-632-0562
Fax: 905-632-0027
800-678-9516
administration@kernicsystems.com
www.kernicsystems.com
Firm Type: Distributing, Engineering, Manufacturing
Founded: 1978
Staff: 20
Products/Services/Areas of Expertise: Manufacturer of balers, shredders & pneumatic air systems; recycling system for printers, envelope manufacturer, folding carton & corrugated box, industries; waste paper recycling systems
Financial Information:
Type of Ownership: Private
Revenue: Greater than $5 Million
Revenue Sources: 100% Private Contracts
Domestic Markets:
National
Foreign Activity:
Worldwide
Markets Sought:
Asia, Central America, The Pacific Rim
Contact(s):
Derek R. Simons, President
dsimons@kernicservices.com
Kerry McAleese, Marketing Manager
John Jurk, Manager, General Sales
jjurk@kernicservices.com

Canadian Branches:
Maren Engineering Corporation
Sales Dept.
P.O. Box 278
111 West Taft Dr.
South Holland, IL USA
708-333-6250
Fax: 708-333-7507
sales@marenengineering.com

Kerr Wood Leidal Associates Ltd. / KWL
#200, 4185A Still Creek Dr.
Burnaby, BC V5C 6G9
604-294-2088
Fax: 604-294-2090
mail@kwl.ca
www.kwl.ca
Firm Type: Management Consulting, Engineering
Founded: 1975
Staff: 100
Member of: Association of Consulting Engineers of Canada; Association of Consulting Engineers of British Columbia
Products/Services/Areas of Expertise: Plans & designs municipal water systems; water source selection; water treatment evaluations; water audits; seismic assessments
Domestic Markets:
British Columbia
Contact(s):
Mike Currie, M.Eng, P.Eng, President

Canadian Branches:
Okanagan
#202, 3334 - 30th Ave.
Vernon, BC V1T 2C8
250-503-0841
Fax: 250-503-0847
okanagan@kwl.bc.ca

Victoria
#201, 3045 Douglas St.
Victoria, BC V8T 4N2
250-595-4223
Fax: 250-595-4224
victoria@kwl.bc.ca

Keystone Environmental Ltd.
Formerly: Keystone Environmental Resources Ltd.
#320, 4400 Dominion St.
Burnaby, BC V5G 4M7
604-430-0671
Fax: 604-430-0672
keyinfo@keystoneenviro.com
www.keystoneenviro.com

Firm Type: Engineering, Scientific/Technical Services
Founded: 1988
Staff: 50
Member of: Air & Waste Management Association; Association of Professional Engineering of Alberta; Association of Professional Engineers & Geoscientists of BC; Association of Professional Engineers of Ontario
Products/Services/Areas of Expertise: Environmental engineering & sciences including environmental audits, remedial investigations, feasibility studies, risk assessments, site remediation, industrial waste, air emissions, hazardous waste management consulting, regulatory guidance & approvals
Domestic Markets:
Alberta, British Columbia, Saskatchewan, Yukon Territory
Foreign Activity:
USA
Contact(s):
K.A. Evans, Principal
D.L. Bryant, Principal

Keywood Entreprises Ltd.
101A Moss Ave.
Fredericton, NB E3A 2G2
506-458-9366
Fax: 506-450-3706
keywood@keywood-trees.com
www.keywood-trees.com
Firm Type: Scientific/Technical Services
Founded: 1965
Products/Services/Areas of Expertise: Tree farm, specializing in balsam fir Christmas trees
Financial Information:
Type of Ownership: Private
Contact(s):
Gordon B. Young, President

KGS Group Inc.
865 Waverley St.
Winnipeg, MB R3T 5P4
204-896-1209
Fax: 204-896-0754
kgs@kgsgroup.com
www.kgsgroup.com
Firm Type: Management Consulting, Engineering
Founded: 1985
Staff: 120
Products/Services/Areas of Expertise: Multidiscipline engineering: environmental, geotechnical, hydrogeological, civil, structural, hydraulic, mechanical, electrical & instrumentation; environmental site audits, assessments, cleanups, remedial action; hydrogeology; waste management; ground/surface water quality; hydroelectric stations, retrofit; reservoir assessments; impact & risk assessment; water supply & treatment
Financial Information:
Type of Ownership: Private
Revenue: Greater than $5 Million
Domestic Markets:
Alberta, British Columbia, Manitoba, Northwest Territories, Ontario, Saskatchewan
Markets Sought:
Central America, Mexico, USA
Contact(s):
Demetrios Kontzamanis, Chair
Jim Smith, President

Canadian Branches:
Regina Branch
#440, 2365 Albert St.
Regina, SK S4P 4K1
306-757-9681
Fax: 306-757-9684

Thunder Bay Branch
1001 William St.
Thunder Bay, ON P7B 6M1
807-623-2195
Fax: 807-473-5671
kgstbay@kgsgroup.com

Toronto
#402, 4310 Sherwoodtowne Blvd.
Mississauga, ON L4Z 4C4
905-848-2473
Fax: 204-848-9664

Kimco Steel Sales Limited
Formerly: Kingston Iron and Metal Ltd.
P.O. Box 300
1325 John Counter St.
Kingston, ON K7L 4W1
613-544-1822
Fax: 613-548-4653
800-267-0902
www.kimcosteel.com
Firm Type: Waste Management
Founded: 1913
Staff: 60
Products/Services/Areas of Expertise: Recycling of boxboard, corrugated containers, newspapers, fine paper & mixed plastic
Domestic Markets:
Ontario, Québec
Foreign Activity:
USA
Contact(s):
Gregg Rosen, Vice-President

Kinder Morgan Canada Inc.
Formerly: Terasen Inc.;BC Gas International Inc.
#2700, 300 - 5th Avenue SW
Calgary, AB T2P 5J2
403-514-6400
Fax: 403-514-6401
800-535-7219
km_web@kindermorgan.com
www.kindermorgan.com
Products/Services/Areas of Expertise: Is a leader in the petroleum transportation industry. The company transports over 680,000 barrels per day of petroleum products to markets in Canada, the United States and offshore
Foreign Activity:
Asia, Eastern Europe, South America, Mexico, Former USSR
Contact(s):
Ian Anderson, President
Hugh Harden, Vice-President, Operations

Kinectrics Inc.
800 Kipling Ave.
Toronto, ON M8Z 6C4
416-207-6000
Fax: 416-207-6532
info@kinectrics.com
www.kinectrics.com
Firm Type: Engineering, Manufacturing, Scientific/Technical Services
Founded: 2000
Staff: 225
Member of: AEA Technology Group; Professional Engineers of Ontario; CANDU owners group
Quality Environmental Management System(s): 17025; ISO
Products/Services/Areas of Expertise: Engineering & testing services for generation plant (nuclear & non-nuclear) transmission & distribution, environmental technologies products & technologies for the energy industry
Recently Completed / Ongoing Projects: Major oil containment system installation for a nuclear station; Large hydro-electric dam rehabilitation; Various tooling products for nuclear stations
Financial Information:
Type of Ownership: Foreign-owned
Domestic Markets:
Alberta, Manitoba, New Brunswick, Nova Scotia, Northwest Territories, Québec
Foreign Activity:
Western Europe, USA, Former USSR
Contact(s):
David Harris, President/CEO
Shahrokh Eawgeweh, Vice-President, Sales & Marketing
Husain Mehdi, General Manager, Environmental & Nuclear Services
husain.mehdi@kinectrics.com
Young Ngo, General Manager, Environmental Technology Solutions
young.ngo@kinectrics.com

Kinetics Noise Control Inc.
Vibron Products Group
Formerly: Vibron Consulting Engineers3570 Nashua Dr.
Mississauga, ON L4V 1L2
905-670-4922
Fax: 905-670-1698
800-684-2766

Products & Services Buyer's Guide

sales@kineticsnoise.com
www.vibron.com
Products/Services/Areas of Expertise: Mass control products; vibration isolation; seismic restraint; architectural, industrial & heavy industrial noise control solutions
Contact(s):
Richard Anthony, Manager

King Metal Fabricators Ltd.
Also Known As: Myers Waste Oil Storage Systems
219 Waverley Rd.
Dartmouth, NS B2X 2C3
902-434-7110
Fax: 902-434-9478
kingmetal@ns.sympatico.ca
Firm Type: Engineering, Manufacturing
Founded: 1986
Staff: 13
Products/Services/Areas of Expertise: Waste oil storage systems; engineering consulting for design & specifications; pumping systems for waste petroleum products
Domestic Markets:
National
Foreign Activity:
USA
Contact(s):
Don Myers, President
Tom Parsons, Engineer

Klajnerman Contracting Corp.
#30, 70 East Beaver Creek Rd.
Richmond Hill, ON L4B 3B2
905-886-7180
Fax: 905-886-7182
info@kccorp.ca
www.kccorp.ca
Products/Services/Areas of Expertise: Engineering consulting services
Contact(s):
Tracy Graham

Kleinfeldt Consultants Limited
#102, 2400 Meadowpine Blvd.
Mississauga, ON L5N 6S2
905-542-1600
Fax: 905-542-2729
877-493-1600
info@kcl.ca
www.kcl.ca
Firm Type: Engineering
Founded: 1961
Products/Services/Areas of Expertise: Hazardous building materials consulting; land use planning; water & wastewater measuring & monitoring equipment; liquid & hazardous waste management consulting
Contact(s):
Richard Nellis

Klohn Crippen Berger Ltd. / KCBL
Formerly: Klohn Crippen Environmental Services
2955 Virtual Way, 5th Fl.
Vancouver, BC V5M 4X6
604-669-3800
Fax: 604-669-3835
info@klohn.com
www.klohn.com
Firm Type: Engineering
Founded: 1951
Staff: 230
Quality Environmental Management System(s): 9001:2000
Products/Services/Areas of Expertise: Multi-disciplinary engineering & environmental services, including soil treatment, water treatment & management; surface water management; groundwater monitoring; site assessment monitoring & remediation; landfill design & monitoring; environmental baseline studies & impact assessments for a wide range of industrial & municipal clients, GIS; geotechnical lab; environmental lab
Recently Completed / Ongoing Projects: Remediation of metals & hydrocarbon-contaminated soils; stormwater treatment at industrial sites; oily wastewater treatment at a shipyards & coal mine; groundwater modelling & assessment, Barbados; environmental baseline studies at mines; acid rock damage at mines; flood control; watershed assessment; environmental audit; socio-economic assessments
Financial Information:
Type of Ownership: Private
Revenue Sources: 19% nationwide; 14% Provincial; 17% Municipals; 50% Private Contracts
Domestic Markets:
Alberta, British Columbia, Manitoba, Northwest Territories, Ontario, Saskatchewan, Yukon Territory
Foreign Activity:
Australia/New Zealand, Central America, South America
Markets Sought:
Central Europe, Eastern Europe, Mexico
Contact(s):
Bryan Watts, President/CEO
Deborah Chatterton, Director, Marketing

Canadian Branches:
Calgary
500, 2618 Hopewell Place NE
Calgary, AB T2E 7H7
403-274-3424
Fax: 403-274-5349
info@klohn.com
Brian Rogers, P.Eng.

Castlegar
P.O. Box 3686
1451 Columbia Ave.
Castlegar, BC V1N 1H8
250-365-0054
Fax: 250-365-0074
info@klohn.com
Richard Carrington, P.Eng.

Inuvik
Dowland Building
P.O. Box 3178
Inuvik, NT X0E 0T0
867-777-8520
Fax: 867-777-2747
info@klohn.com

Lloydminster
#102, 1724 - 50 Ave.
Lloydminster, AB T9V 0Y1
780-871-0711
Fax: 780-871-0722
info@klohn.com
Doug Seegmiller, District Manager

Sudbury
#7, 1351C Kelly Lake Rd.
Sudbury, ON P3E 5P5
705-522-1367
Fax: 705-523-5670
info@klohn.com
Lawrence Clelland, C.Eng.

Vancouver
2955 Virtual Way, 5th Fl.
Vancouver, BC V5M 4X6
604-669-3800
Fax: 604-669-3835
info@klohn.com
Mark Thorpe, Dr.

KMK Consultants Limited
220 Advance Blvd.
Brampton, ON L6T 4J5
905-459-4780
Fax: 905-459-7869
kmk@kmk.ca
www.kmk.ca
Firm Type: Engineering
Founded: 1959
Staff: 115
Member of: Water Environment Federation; American Water Works Association; National Association of Corrosion Engineers
Products/Services/Areas of Expertise: Consulting civil engineering, planning & landscape architecture services; feasibility studies, reports, functional & detail design, working drawings, specification & contract documentation, contract administration, on-site inspection, project commissioning; specializes in water, wastewater, municipal enineering & land development
Contact(s):
Robert D. Fleeton, P.Eng., President

Canadian Branches:
Cobalt Office
Cobalt Train Stn
P.O. Box 736
#2, 1 Station Rd.
Cobalt, ON P0J 1C0
705-679-5979
Fax: 705-679-5750
cobalt@kmk.ca
Bruce McMullan

Kitchener Office
509 Mill St.
Kitchener, ON N2G 2Y5
519-743-6111
Fax: 519-743-3330
kitchener@kmk.ca
Tom Montgomery

Pickering Office
#200, 1099 Kingston Rd.
Pickering, ON L1V 1B5
905-837-0314
Fax: 905-837-0553
pickering@kmk.ca
Eric Tuson, P.Eng

Windsor
#4, 350 Cabana Rd.
Windsor, ON N9G 1A3
519-969-8449
Fax: 519-969-9420
windsor@kmk.ca
Paolo Eugeni, P.Eng.

KMW Systems Inc.
635 Wilton Grove Rd.
London, ON N6N 1N7
519-686-1771
Fax: 519-686-1132
kmwinfo@kmwgroup.com
www.kmwenergy.com
Firm Type: Manufacturing
Founded: 1987
Staff: 10
Products/Services/Areas of Expertise: Biomass Fired Energy Systems utilizing a variety of bio-fuels such as wet or dry wood waste, mill sludge or processed urban waste
Financial Information:
Type of Ownership: Private
Domestic Markets:
National
Foreign Activity:
Australia/New Zealand, Central America, South America, Mexico, USA
Contact(s):
Eric Bertil Rosen, President
Bengt Jobe, Project Development

Canadian Branches:
Regional Sales & Service
#400, 1133 St. George Blvd.
Moncton, NB E1E 4E1
506-855-5171
Fax: 506-855-5626
Al Hietapakka, Regional Sales & Service Manager

Knight Piésold Ltd.
#1400, 750 Pender St. West
Vancouver, BC V6C 2T8
604-685-0543
Fax: 604-685-0147
kpl@knightpiesold.com
www.knightpiesold.com
Firm Type: Management Consulting, Engineering, Information Technology, Waste Management
Founded: 1975
Staff: 54
Member of: Consulting Engineers of British Columbia; Mining Association of Canada
Quality Environmental Management System(s): 9001
Products/Services/Areas of Expertise: Consulting services in geotechnical, geological, waste management & water resources engineering; environmental services; Knight Piésold Group operates in 18 countries in the field of mining, power, water, transportation & environmental engineering
Recently Completed / Ongoing Projects: Hydroelectric Project EIA, Miller Creek; Hydroelectric Project EIA, Rutherford Creek; Mine Project EIA, Tiberon Nui Phao; Mine Project EIA, Farallon Resources
Financial Information:
Type of Ownership: Private

Revenue: Greater than $5 Million
Revenue Sources: 100% Private Contracts
Domestic Markets:
Alberta, British Columbia, Manitoba, Nunavut, Ontario, Yukon Territory
Foreign Activity:
Africa, Asia, Australia/New Zealand, Caribbean, Central America, The Middle East, South Africa, South America, Mexico, USA, United Kingdom
Contact(s):
Ken Brouwer, P.Eng., Managing Director
Jeremy Haile, President
Chris Brodie, R.P.Bio., Manager, Environmental Services

Canadian Branches:
North Bay Branch
1650 Main St.
North Bay, ON P1B 8G5
705-476-2165
Fax: 705-474-8095
northbay@knightpiesold.com
Ken Embree

Knowaste LLC
5198 Everest Dr.
Mississauga, ON L4W 2R4
905-568-0334
Fax: 905-568-7805
NorthAmerica@knowaste.com
www.knowaste.com
Firm Type: Waste Management
Staff: 30
Products/Services/Areas of Expertise: Disposable diapers & adult incontinence recycling
Recently Completed / Ongoing Projects: Opening of recycling facility in the US
Financial Information:
Type of Ownership: Private
Revenue: $1.5 Million - $3 Million
Revenue Sources: 100% Private Contracts
Domestic Markets:
Ontario
Foreign Activity:
Asia, Central Europe, Eastern Europe, USA
Contact(s):
Juliann Turner, Contact, Industrial, Government & Commercial Contracts

KnowTech Environmental Inc. / KTE
Formerly: Lifeline Software
Also Known As: Shand & Co. Computer Consultants
210 Lyman St.
Truro, NS B2N 4S6
902-893-7138
Fax: 902-893-7640
800-890-8608
more@kteinfo.com
www.kteinfo.com
Firm Type: Scientific/Technical Services
Founded: 2003
Staff: 2
Member of: Software Industry Association of Nova Scotia
Products/Services/Areas of Expertise: The HACCP Minder features automatic monitoring & alarming of free ammonia, total N, dissolved oxygen, pH, salinity, ORP, temperature & water level to lobster ponds & aquaculture operations.
Financial Information:
Type of Ownership: Private
Revenue Sources: 100% Private Contracts
Domestic Markets:
New Brunswick, Newfoundland & Labrador, Nova Scotia, Ontario, Prince Edward Island
Foreign Activity:
USA
Contact(s):
J.A. Shand, President

Koch Engineering Co. Ltd.
Also Known As: Koch Heat Transfer Group
4750 Sheppard Ave. East
Toronto, ON M1S 3V7
416-293-3666
Fax: 416-293-6409
info@khtcan.ca
www.kochheattransfer.com

Firm Type: Manufacturing
Founded: 1964
Staff: 150
Products/Services/Areas of Expertise: Heat exchangers
Contact(s):
Mike Walker, President

Kodiak Environmental Limited
#1A, 871 Equestrian Ct.
Oakville, ON L6L 6L7
905-825-2943
Fax: 905-825-8743
www.kodiak.ca
Products/Services/Areas of Expertise: Environmental consulting services including Phase 1 & 2 environmental site assessments, Phase 3 remediation, air quality testing & environmental drilling services
Domestic Markets:
Ontario
Contact(s):
Randall Goodwin, Environmental Scientist
rgoodwin@kodiak.ca

Kodiak Oilfield Services
P.O. Box 1169
100 - 1st. St.
Fox Creek, AB T0H 1P0
780-622-3787
kodiakos@telusplanet.net
Firm Type: Scientific/Technical Services
Founded: 1980
Products/Services/Areas of Expertise: Oilfield maintenance; environmental consulting & contracting services
Financial Information:
Type of Ownership: Private
Domestic Markets:
Alberta
Contact(s):
Larry Davidson, President
Merv Vaadeland, Supervisor

Koers & Associates Engineering Ltd. / KAEL
P.O. Box 790
194 Memorial Ave.
Parksville, BC V9P 2G8
250-248-3151
Fax: 250-248-5362
kael@koers-eng.com
Firm Type: Engineering
Founded: 1985
Staff: 17
Member of: Water Environment Federation, American Water Works Association; Canadian Water Resources Association, British Columbia Water & Waste Association
Products/Services/Areas of Expertise: Consulting engineering services in civil/municipal engineering; water resource engineering; liquid & solid waste management; land development
Financial Information:
Type of Ownership: Private
Revenue Sources: 5% Provincial; 70% Municipals; 25% Private Contracts
Domestic Markets:
British Columbia
Contact(s):
D.A. Koers, P.Eng., President
Dave Shillabeer, P.Eng., Sec.-Treas.

Komline-Sanderson Ltd.
#4, 75 Rosedale Ave.
Brampton, ON L6X 4H4
905-453-5330
Fax: 905-453-2214
info@komline.com
Firm Type: Manufacturing
Staff: 10
Products/Services/Areas of Expertise: Water treatment systems & equipment; liquid/solid separation equipment, sludge dewatering & thickening, rotary drum vacuum filters, packaged wastewater filtration & treatment systems; sludge plunger pumps & dissolved air flotation for clarification of wastewater
Domestic Markets:
National
Foreign Activity:
Mexico, USA
Contact(s):
Alan Bowser, Vice-President

Kongskilde Limited
710 Wright St.
Strathroy, ON N7G 3H8
519-245-9917
Fax: 519-245-8293
mail@kc.kongskilde.com
www.kongskilde.com
Firm Type: Distributing, Manufacturing
Founded: 1961
Staff: 27
Products/Services/Areas of Expertise: Soil preparation; grain handling systems; pneumatic conveying systems for industry; heaters for agriculture, construction & industry; slurry injection equipment
Financial Information:
Type of Ownership: Private
Revenue Sources: 2% nationwide; 2% Provincial; 98% Private Contracts
Domestic Markets:
Alberta, British Columbia, Manitoba, New Brunswick, Newfoundland & Labrador, Nova Scotia, Ontario, Prince Edward Island, Québec, Saskatchewan
Foreign Activity:
Mexico, USA
Contact(s):
John Lauridsen, CFO
jla@kongskilde.com
Hans Rasmussen, Resident Manager
hr@kongskilde.com

International Branch(es):
Bloomington, IL.
#2, 2439 Main St.
Bloomington, IL USA
309-820-1090
Fax: 309-820-1364
mail@kus.kongskilde.com

Konica Minolta Business Solutions (Canada) Inc.
369 Britannia Rd. East
Mississauga, ON L4Z 2H5
905-890-6600
866-890-6600
www.konicaminolta.ca
Firm Type: Distributing
Founded: 1983
Member of: Photo Marketing Association
EcoLogo Certified Products & Services: Line of both analog & digital photocopiers, which also bear the Energy Star Logo & the Blue Angel Mark
Products/Services/Areas of Expertise: EcoLogo certified line of both analog & digital photocopiers, which also bear the Energy Star Logo, & the Blue Angel Mark; recognizes the importance of ensuring the safety of its copiers & related consumables used worldwide; to help protect the environment, we have created a safety policy that applies to our photocopiers & all consumables
Ecological Note: Line of both analog & digital photocopiers, which also bear the Energy Star Logo & the Blue Angel Mark
Financial Information:
Type of Ownership: Foreign-owned
Revenue Sources: 100% Private Contracts
Domestic Markets:
National
Contact(s):
Kerry Meehan, President/CEO
Tony Rossi, Manager, National Sales & Marketing
Roy Bruckner, Products Specialist
Felicia Palumbo, National Marketing Support Assistant
felicia.palumbo@bt.konicaminolta.ca
Cynthia Arsenault
toronto@bt.konicaminolta.ca

Konica Minolta Business Solutions (Canada) Ltd.
369 Britannia Rd. East
Mississauga, ON L4Z 2H5
905-890-6600
Fax: 905-283-2511
877-890-6600
copier@bt.konicaminolta.ca
www.konicaminolta.ca
Products/Services/Areas of Expertise: Manufacturers of imaging technologies and products; manufacturers of printers and copiers; manufacturers of colour measurement technologies; medical imaging products
Ecological Note: Analog & digital photocopiers

Products & Services Buyer's Guide

Domestic Markets:
National

KPMG Performance Registrar Inc.
P.O. Box 10426 Pacific Centre
777 Dunsmuir St., 9th Fl.
Vancouver, BC V7Y 1K3
604-691-3401
Fax: 604-691-3031
www.kpmg.ca/performanceregistrar
Products/Services/Areas of Expertise: ISO 9001 & ISO 14001 accredited management systems registrar
Contact(s):
Michael Alexander, President
mlalexander@kpmg.ca

KPS & Associates
10305 - 174 St. NW
Edmonton, AB T5S 1H1
780-409-5620
Fax: 780-409-5621
info@kpsa.ca
www.kpsa.ca
Products/Services/Areas of Expertise: Consultation emphasis on human resources & safety in the workplace

Kraemer Tool & Manufacturing Co. Ltd.
75 Devon Rd.
Brampton, ON L6T 5A4
905-458-0400
Fax: 905-458-0688
800-443-6443
info@kraemertool.com
www.kraemertool.com
Firm Type: Manufacturing
Founded: 1967
Staff: 21
Member of: Canadian Manufacturers & Exporters Associations
Products/Services/Areas of Expertise: Dust & fume collection systems
Recently Completed / Ongoing Projects: Wet collectors; down draft tables
Financial Information:
Type of Ownership: Private
Revenue: $1.5 Million - $3 Million
Revenue Sources: 5% nationwide; 95% Private Contracts
Domestic Markets:
National
Foreign Activity:
Caribbean, USA
Contact(s):
Philipp Kraemer, President/CEO
Rosemarie Kraemer, Vice-President, Marketing
Lynda Kraemer, Purchasing

Kraftur Engineering Inc.
P.O. Box 7000
228 Municipal Dr.
Gimli, MB R0C 1B0
204-642-9677
Fax: 204-642-9688
800-665-8326
kraftur@mts.net
www.kraftur.com
Firm Type: Engineering

Products/Services/Areas of Expertise: Energy management services; energy conservation services; energy audits; engineering consulting services
Financial Information:
Type of Ownership: Private
Contact(s):
Loren Gudbjartsson, Contact

Kraus Global Inc.
25 Paquin Rd.
Winnipeg, MB R2J 3V9
204-663-3601
Fax: 204-663-7112
inquiries@krausglobal.com
www.krausglobal.com
Firm Type: Manufacturing
Founded: 1962
Quality Environmental Management System(s): 9001
Products/Services/Areas of Expertise: Provider of transportation refueling systems; equipment and components in the petroleum & alternative fuel industries

Financial Information:
Type of Ownership: Private
Domestic Markets:
National
Foreign Activity:
China
Contact(s):
Jim Kohut, Manager, Marketing Services

Kruger Inc.
3285, ch Bedford
Montréal, QC H3S 1G5
514-737-1131
Fax: 514-343-3124
www.kruger.com
Firm Type: Manufacturing
Founded: 1905
Staff: 1000
Quality Environmental Management System(s): 9002; ISO
Products/Services/Areas of Expertise: Products manufactured from virgin & recycled fibers, such as newsprint, coated & supercalendered paper, linerboard, recovered paper, packaging, lumber, wood panels & tissue
Financial Information:
Type of Ownership: Private
Domestic Markets:
British Columbia, Newfoundland & Labrador, Ontario, Québec
Contact(s):
Joseph Kruger, Chair/CEO
Jean Majeau, Vice-President, Corporate Affairs
Contact(s):
Normand Handfield, Manager

Canadian Branches:
Montréal Paperboard Sales & Mill
Sales
5845, place Turcot
Montréal, QC H4C 1V9
514-934-0845
Fax: 514-934-4972
sdesgagnes@pb.kruger.com
Serge Desgagnés, Manager

Alberta Tissue Sales
#40, 6567 - 48th St. SE
Calgary, AB T2C 3J7
403-252-6060
Fax: 403-252-7339

British Columbia Tissue Sales
1625 - 5th Ave.
New Westminster, BC V3M 1Z7
604-522-7893
Fax: 604-522-0296

Montréal Forest & Wood Products Sales
Marketing & Sales
7777, boul Décarie, 6e étage
Montréal, QC H4P 2H2
514-788-2502
Fax: 514-343-3210
mboily@kruger.com
Martin Boily, Vice-President

Montréal Newsprint Sales
Newsprint Sales
3285, ch Bedford
Montréal, QC H3S 1G5
514-737-1131
Fax: 514-343-3126
lsimpson@kruger.com
L. Simpson, Vice-President

Nova Scotia Tissue Sales
#440, 1600 Bedford Highway
Bedford, NS B4A 1E8
902-466-2448
Fax: 902-464-0486

Ontario Tissue Sales
#200, 1900 Minnesota Ct.
Mississauga, ON L5N 5R5
905-826-5450
Fax: 905-826-8313

Québec Tissue Sales
Tour C
#10, 800, boul Chomedey
Laval, QC H7V 3Y4

450-687-0111
Fax: 450-687-3445

Toronto Newsprint Sales
#510, 111 Gordon Baker Rd.
Toronto, ON M2H 3R1
416-494-2277
Fax: 416-494-3722
gatwell@kruger.com
Gordon Atwell, Sales Representative

Bromptonville Newsprint Mill
220, rte. de Windsor
Sherbrooke, QC J1C 0E6
819-846-2721
Fax: 819-846-7147

Corner Brook Pulp & Paper Mill
P.O. Box 2001
Corner Brook, NL A2H 6J4
709-637-3000
Fax: 709-639-8432

Crabtree Mill
P.O. Box 500
100, 1e av
Crabtree, QC J0K 1B0
450-754-2855
Fax: 450-754-4556

Forestville Mill
P.O. Box 1240
150, rte Maritime
Forestville, QC G0T 1E0
418-587-6008
Fax: 418-587-6074

Gatineau Mill
P.O. Box 3200 B
20, rue Laurier
Gatineau, QC J8X 4H3
819-595-5302
Fax: 819-595-5396

LaSalle Plant
7474, rue Cordner
Lasalle, QC H8N 2W3
514-366-8050
Fax: 514-366-4538

Launay Mill
793, rue Chicobi
Launay, QC J0Y 1W0
819-796-3376
Fax: 819-796-2277

Longlac Customer Service/Mill
Katamaki Rd.
Longlac, ON P0T 2A0
807-876-2220
Fax: 807-876-4604
807-876-2257

Longue-Rive Planing & Drying Mill
856, rte 138
Longue-Rive, QC G0T 1Z0
418-231-2239
Fax: 418-231-2334

Mississauga DRIcore Mill & Panels Sales
2311 Royal Windsor Dr.
Mississauga, ON L5J 1K5
905-403-0425
Fax: 905-403-0426
1-888-566-4522

Montréal Recycling Mill
Mill
5770, rue Notre-Dame ouest
Montréal, QC H4C 1V2
514-937-4255
Fax: 514-937-2275

New Westminster Mill
1625 - 5th Ave.
New Westminster, BC V3M 1Z7
604-522-5711
Fax: 604-520-9200

Parent Mill
P.O. Box 100
Parent, QC G0X 3P0

819-667-2711
Fax: 819-667-2228

Ragueneau Mill
P.O. Box 400
3100, ch d'Auteuil
Ragueneau, QC G0H 1S0
418-567-4114
Fax: 418-567-9559

Sherbrooke Mill
P.O. Box 240 Lennoxville
2888, rue Collège
Sherbrooke, QC J1M 1Z4
819-565-8220
Fax: 819-566-0245

Toronto Plant
280 Belfield Rd.
Toronto, ON M9W 1H6
416-675-7740
Fax: 416-675-6818

Trois-Rivières Mill
P.O. Box 188
Trois-Rivières, QC G9A 5P6
819-375-1691
Fax: 819-375-3163

KSB Pumps Inc.
5885 Kennedy Rd.
Mississauga, ON L4Z 2G3
905-568-9200
Fax: 905-568-3740
ksb@ksbcanada.ca
www.ksb.ca
Products/Services/Areas of Expertise: Water & wastewater management equipment; pumps
Contact(s):
M. Hadavi, Sales Manager

KW Gaspé Ltd. Partnership
1950, rue Sherbrooke ouest, 4e étage
Montréal, QC H3H 1E7
514-846-4000
Fax: 514-846-4020
Products/Services/Areas of Expertise: Owns wind generating facilities producing green renewable electrical power near Cap-Chat & Matane on the Gaspé Peninsula in the Province of Quebec
Ecological Note: Wind turbine generated electricity
Contact(s):
Nicole Lafleur

KWH Pipe
Formerly: Wilk & Hoeglund (Canada) Ltd.
6507 Mississauga Rd.
Mississauga, ON L5N 1A6
905-858-0206
Fax: 905-858-0208
sales@kwhpipe.ca
www.kwhpipe.ca
Firm Type: Manufacturing
Founded: 1967
Staff: 110
Quality Environmental Management System(s): 9002
Products/Services/Areas of Expertise: Polyethylene pipe for municipal water & wastewater systems, marine installations, ground source heat pump applications
Financial Information:
Type of Ownership: Private
Revenue: Greater than $5 Million
Domestic Markets:
National
Foreign Activity:
Central America, South America, Mexico, USA
Contact(s):
Paul van Warmerdam, President & CEO
David Fuerth, Sales & Marketing Manager
Ted Taylor, Senior Accounts

Canadian Branches:
British Columbia Branch
#503B, 17665 - 66A Ave.
Surrey, BC V3S 2A7
604-574-7473
Fax: 604-534-7073
1-800-668-1892

Huntsville Branch
P.O. Box 5435
37 Centre St. North
Huntsville, ON P1H 2K8
705-789-2396
Fax: 705-789-7003

Québec & Maritime Branch
#101, 7333, Place des Roserales
Anjou, QC H1M 2X6
514-352-3540
Fax: 514-352-3290

Saskatoon Branch
P.O. Box 9447
348 Edson St.
Saskatoon, SK S7K 7E9
306-242-0755
Fax: 306-934-8625

Kyocera Mita Canada Ltd. / KMCA Mika CopyStar
6120 Kestrel Rd.
Mississauga, ON L5T 1S8
905-670-4425
Fax: 905-670-8116
877-326-7976
technical@kyoceramita.ca
www.kyocera.ca
Firm Type: Distributing
Founded: 1977
Staff: 49
Member of: Better Business Bureau
Quality Environmental Management System(s): 9001
EcoLogo Certified Products & Services: Certified office products
Products/Services/Areas of Expertise: Assists cmopanies & organizations of all sizes, achieve the smooth & efficient running of their operations by providing document management devices that are simple & easy to use & have the lowest cost of ownership
Recently Completed / Ongoing Projects: Reviewing products with the Environmental Choice program
Ecological Note: Certified office products
Financial Information:
Type of Ownership: Private
Revenue: Greater than $5 Million
Revenue Sources: 7% nationwide; 4% Provincial; 2% Municipals; 87% Private Contracts
Domestic Markets:
Alberta, British Columbia, Manitoba, New Brunswick, Newfoundland & Labrador, Nova Scotia, Ontario, Prince Edward Island, Québec, Saskatchewan
Contact(s):
Raymond Baraya, President
raymond_baraya@kyoceramita.com
Marco Nalli, Manager, National Marketing & Technical
marco_nalli@kyoceramita.com
Ann-Marie Pidgeon, Marketing Department, National Accounts Specialist
annmarie@kyoceramita.com

L&K International Training
Division of 360training
505 Queesnsway E
Mississauga, ON L5A 4B4
905-270-6200
Fax: 905-270-3786
800-668-6064
inquiry@lk-intl.com
www.lk-intl.com
Firm Type: Information Technology
Founded: 1972
Products/Services/Areas of Expertise: Electrical utility technical training; over 1,100 technical training titles focussing on generation, transmission, distribution & safety, available on video, CD-ROM, MPEG, VCD formats & other languages
Domestic Markets:
National
Foreign Activity:
Worldwide
Contact(s):
Earl Robertson, President
Michael Codd, CFO

L&M Engineering Ltd.
#201, 1840 Third Ave.
Prince George, BC V2M 1G4
250-562-1977
Fax: 250-562-1967
www.lmengineering.bc.ca
Firm Type: Engineering
Founded: 1992
Staff: 15
Products/Services/Areas of Expertise: Civil & municipal engineering; liquid industrial waste treatment
Recently Completed / Ongoing Projects: Municipal sewage treatment, Taylor, BC; fire fighting foam treatment, Prince George airport; sludge disposal, Northwood Pulp Mill, Prince George
Financial Information:
Type of Ownership: Private
Revenue Sources: 5% nationwide; 2% Provincial; 25% Municipals; 68% Private Contracts
Contact(s):
Terry Fjellstrom, Principal

L&M Feed Services
84 Fairview Dr.
Truro, NS B2N 1S4
902-899-7827
Fax: 902-893-4197
lmfeeds@tru.eastlink.ca
Contact(s):
Ian MacHattie, General Manager

L.E. Washington Sales Ltd.
2851 Brighton Rd.
Oakville, ON L6H 6C9
905-829-4111
Fax: 905-829-2366
Firm Type: Distributing
Founded: 1986
Staff: 3
Products/Services/Areas of Expertise: Metering pumps; power transmission; progressing cavity pumps & parts
Contact(s):
Larry Washington, President

L.W. Ward Limited
957 Melton Dr.
Mississauga, ON L4Y 1K9
905-277-4881
Fax: 905-279-1121
Firm Type: Engineering
Founded: 1949
Staff: 3
Products/Services/Areas of Expertise: Environmental consulting & engineering; field sampling & monitoring; energy conservation & recovery; agriculture; water conservation; waste reduction & recycling
Domestic Markets:
Ontario
Contact(s):
Lance W. Ward, P.Eng., President

Lab-Élite limitée
P.O. Box 150
5950, ch. de la Côte-de-Liesse
Montréal, QC H4T 1E2
514-866-6664
Fax: 514-866-6373
Products/Services/Areas of Expertise: Chemical analysis, consulting & auditing of scientific research & experimental development for industrial & community sectors in the fields of environment, metallurgy, forestry, pulp & paper, mining, chemical & petroleum
Activities: Consulting & auditing of scientific research & experimental development for industrial & community sectors in the fields of environment, metallurgical, forestry, pulp & paper, mining, chemical & petroleum
Contact(s):
Dominic Ziccardi, President

Labelle, Ryan, Genipro Inc.
Formerly: P. Ryan & associés inc.
436, rue de La Madone
Mont-Laurier, QC J9L 1S3
819-623-3302
Fax: 819-623-7616
p.ryan.ass@sympatico.ca
Firm Type: Engineering
Staff: 12
Quality Environmental Management System(s): 9001

Products & Services Buyer's Guide

Products/Services/Areas of Expertise: Engineering consulting services in water & wastewater treatment
Recently Completed / Ongoing Projects: Contracts completed for municipalities of Mont Tremblant & Lac Des Ecorces
Financial Information:
Type of Ownership: Private
Revenue: $1.5 Million - $3 Million
Revenue Sources: 15% Provincial; 50% Municipals; 35% Private Contracts
Domestic Markets:
Québec
Contact(s):
Patrick Ryan, President
Alain Ryan, Sales Manager

Labexcel Inc.
Parc industriel de Joliette
725, rue Marion
Joliette, QC J6E 8S3
450-755-4404
Fax: 450-755-4792
Products/Services/Areas of Expertise: Laboratory services; measuring & monitoring equipment

Laboratoire de Canalisation Souterraines Inc.
Also Known As: LCS Inc.
255, av St-Sacrement
Québec, QC G1N 3X9
418-651-9306
Fax: 418-651-9597
lcs@labolcs.ca
www.labolcs.ca
Products/Services/Areas of Expertise: Water & wastewater treatment; operations & maintenance; water & wastewater assessment
Contact(s):
Lynda Landry, President

Laboratoires d'Expertises de Québec Ltée / LEQ
2320, rue de Celles
Québec, QC G2C 1X8
418-845-0858
Fax: 418-845-0300
info@leqltech.com
www.leqltech.com
Firm Type: Engineering
Founded: 1979
Quality Environmental Management System(s): 9001
Products/Services/Areas of Expertise: Geotechnics; hydrogeology; quality control for building, concrete, asphalt, steel, rock, soil; environmental assessments; impact studies; vibration control
Domestic Markets:
New Brunswick, Québec
Contact(s):
Raymond Juneau, Vice-President
Yves Tardif, Hydrogeology/Environment

Labrie Environmental Group
Formerly: Labrie Equipment Ltd.
175, route de Pont
Saint-Nicolas, QC G7A 2T3
418-831-8250
Fax: 418-831-5255
800-463-6638
sales@labriegroup.com
www.labriegroup.com
Firm Type: Manufacturing, Waste Management
Founded: 1933
Quality Environmental Management System(s): 9001
Products/Services/Areas of Expertise: Leading designer & manufacturer of highly-productive, semi-automated & automated refust & recycling collection vehicles
Contact(s):
Claude Boivin, President
claude.boivin@labriegroup.com
Pierre Létourneau, CGA, Executive Vice-President, Corporate Affairs & Secretary
pierre.letourneau@labriegroup.com
Jean Bourgeois, MBA, CA, CEO
jean.bourgeois@labriegroup.com

Labtronics
546 Governors Rd.
Guelph, ON N1K 1E3
519-767-1061
Fax: 519-836-4431
info@labtronics.com
www.labtronics.com
Firm Type: Distributing, Manufacturing
Founded: 1986
Products/Services/Areas of Expertise: Laboratory software, data integration & management
Domestic Markets:
National
Foreign Activity:
Eastern Europe, Western Europe, Mexico, USA
Contact(s):
Robert Pavlis, President
Steve Bolton, Manager, Marketing
Darlene Willard, Office Manager
International Branch(es):
The Netherlands
Hanzeweg 10A
Gouda NLD
-310-182-551243
Fax: -310-182-551270
eurosales@labtronics.com

LaCas Consultants Inc.
#200, 1311 Howe St.
Vancouver, BC V6Z 2P3
604-688-2535
info@lacas-consultants.com
www.lacas-consultants.com
Firm Type: Engineering
Founded: 1991
Staff: 2
Member of: Association of Professional Engineers & Geoscientists of British Columbia; Association of Professional Engineers & Geoscientists of Alberta
Products/Services/Areas of Expertise: Engineering consulting services; river & hydrotechnical engineering; fisheries habitat & stream restoration & analysis
Financial Information:
Type of Ownership: Private
Revenue Sources: 25% nationwide; 25% Provincial; 25% Municipals; 25% Private Contracts
Domestic Markets:
Alberta, British Columbia
Foreign Activity:
The Pacific Rim
Contact(s):
Brian LaCas, P.Eng., Senior River Engineer & Hydrologist

Lacombe Waste Services
Formerly: Lacombe Waste Oil
5555 Power Rd.
Gloucester, ON K1G 3N4
613-822-2700
Fax: 613-822-6183
800-263-5048
mail@lacombewaste.ca
www.lacombewaste.ca
Firm Type: Waste Management
Founded: 1972
Staff: 40
Products/Services/Areas of Expertise: Recycling of waste oil, water treatment; non-hazardous & hazardous wastes; solid & liquid, drums & bulk
Financial Information:
Type of Ownership: Private
Domestic Markets:
New Brunswick, Newfoundland & Labrador, Nova Scotia, Ontario, Prince Edward Island, Québec
Contact(s):
George Neilson, President
george.neilson@lacombewaste.ca
Rob Kingsbury, Environmental Manager

LADEN Steel Fabricators Inc.
P.O. Box 6239
3600 - 61 Ave.
Innisfail, AB T4G 1S9
403-227-5400
Fax: 403-227-4073
800-661-3747
info@laden.ca
www.laden.ca
Firm Type: Manufacturing
Staff: 100
Member of: Canadian Welding Bureau
Products/Services/Areas of Expertise: Protec Storage Solutions; ULC listed chemical storage; FM approved, flammable & combustable storage buildings; explosive magazines; mobile emergency shower systems; grain handling systems; skids; steel manufacturing; oilfield skids
Financial Information:
Type of Ownership: Private
Revenue: $1.5 Million - $3 Million
Revenue Sources: 25% nationwide; 25% Provincial; 25% Municipals; 25% Private Contracts
Domestic Markets:
National
Foreign Activity:
USA
Markets Sought:
Australia/New Zealand
Contact(s):
Dennis Wall, President/CEO
Lori Norsworthy, Sales
sales@laden.ca

Lafarge Canada Inc.
#800, 606 Cathcart St.
Montréal, QC H3B 1L7
514-861-1411
Fax: 514-861-1123
www.lafargenorthamerica.com
Firm Type: Manufacturing
Products/Services/Areas of Expertise: Pipe & standard products; Stormceptor system for containment of hydrocarbon/sediment pollutants from stormwater runoff
Financial Information:
Type of Ownership: Publicly Traded
Domestic Markets:
National

Lafarge Dundas Quarry
P.O. Box 2029
Hamilton, ON L8N 3S9
905-527-3671
Fax: 905-628-2100
800-358-6049
Contact(s):
Rich Woodruff, Quarry Manager
Canadian Branches:
Redland Quarries - Queenston Transfer Station
RR#1, Stanley Ave. North
Niagara Falls, ON L2E 6S4
905-262-4270

Laidlaw Carriers Inc. - Van Division
P.O. Box 518
Milton, ON L9T 4Z1
905-875-0875
Fax: 905-875-4380
Contact(s):
Laban Herr, General Manager
Contact(s):
Dave Golton, General Manager
Contact(s):
Dan Matthews, General Manager
Contact(s):
Phil Ralf, General Manager
Contact(s):
Rick Jankura
Contact(s):
Larry Matthews, General Manager
Canadian Branches:
Québec Branch
1900, av 52
Lachine, QC H8T 2X9
514-636-0604
Fax: 514-636-9526
Scott Talbot

Woodstock Branch
P.O. Box 776
605 Athlone Ave.
Woodstock, ON N4S 8A2
519-539-0471
Scott Talbot, General Manager

Sure-Way Carriers Inc.
7215 Torbram Rd.
Mississauga, ON L4T 1G7

905-678-2727
Fax: 905-678-9028
1-800-263-8573

Laidlaw Carriers Inc. - Van Division
P.O. Box 518
Milton, ON L9T 4Z1
905-875-0875
Fax: 905-875-4380

Laidlaw Carriers Inc. - Tank Division
P.O. Box 4
605 Athlone Ave.
Woodstock, ON N4S 7W5
519-539-6103
Fax: 519-539-0177

Laidlaw Carriers Inc. - Flatbed Division
P.O. Box 430
Hagersville, ON N0A 1H0
905-768-3375
Fax: 905-768-5923

Laidlaw Carriers Inc. - Liquid Division
P.O. Box 818
Woodstock, ON N4S 8A3
519-539-2034

Woodstock Driver Services
P.O. Box 1180
240 Universal Dr.
Woodstock, ON N4S 8A3
519-537-3711

Laidlaw Medical Services
63 Medulla Ave.
Etobicoke, ON M8Z 5L6
416-233-3050
Fax: 416-234-1301
Contact(s):
André Martineau, Vice-President, General Manager
Canadian Branches:
Regional Office - Central
#502, 265 North Front St.
Sarnia, ON N7P 7X1
519-332-0720
Fax: 519-332-0369
1-800-265-7549
Eric Hunter, Vice-President

Regional Office - Eastern
#200, 7305, boul Marie-Victorin
Brossard, QC J4W 1A6
450-923-9999
Fax: 450-923-1977
1-800-361-2209
R.J. Desmarais, Vice-President

Regional Office - Maritimes
81 Isley Ave.
Dartmouth, NS B3B 1L5
902-468-2733
Fax: 902-468-6737
Barry Timmins

Regional Office - Western
Canada Trust Tower
#3000, 421 - 7 Ave. SW
Calgary, AB T2P 4K9
403-263-6004
Fax: 403-263-0556
1-800-661-4415
A.P. Cadotte, Vice-President

Laidlaw Medical Services
63 Medulla Ave.
Etobicoke, ON M8Z 5L6
416-233-3050
Fax: 416-234-1301
International Branch(es):
Laidlaw Environmental Services - USA Office
220 Outlet Pointe Blvd.
Columbia, SC USA
803-798-2993
Fax: 803-798-3660
Bill Stilwell, President

Lake Charlotte Sanitation
11470 #7 Hwy
Lake Charlotte, NS B0J 1Y0
902-845-2450
Fax: 902-845-2477
Firm Type: Waste Management
Founded: 1963
Staff: 3
Products/Services/Areas of Expertise: Waste management; materials separation; wood recycling
Financial Information:
Type of Ownership: Private
Revenue Sources: 50% Provincial; 50% Private Contracts
Domestic Markets:
Nova Scotia
Contact(s):
Ford H. Webber, Owner

Lakehead Scrap Metal
Subsidiary of General Scrap & Partnership Ltd.
305, 106th St.
Thunder Bay, ON P7B 6T6
807-623-4559
Fax: 807-623-8093

Lakehead University
Centre for Northern Forest Ecosystem Research
955 Oliver Rd.
Thunder Bay, ON P7B 5E1
807-343-4024
Fax: 807-343-4001
brooke.pilley@mnr.gov.on.ca
cnfer.mnr.gov.on.ca
Firm Type: Scientific/Technical Services
Staff: 27
Products/Services/Areas of Expertise: Cooperative, multi-disciplinary research on forest lands & water of Northern Ontario in order to provide sound science for development, application & review of resource management policy
Activities: Studies effects of timber management on the environment; includes aquatic & terrestrial systems, fisheries & wildlife, nutrient cycling, tourism & cultural resources
Domestic Markets:
Ontario
Contact(s):
Ed Iwachewski, Manager
Brad Allison, Biologist, Moose
Doug Reid, Research Scientist, Boreal Silviculture
Julie Elliott, Research Technician, Spatial Ecology
Blake LaPorte, Senior Technician, Coldwater Lakes
Brooke Pilley, Contact, Communications

Lakeland Protective Wear Inc.
59 Bury Ct.
Brantford, ON N3S 0A9
519-757-0700
Fax: 519-757-0799
800-489-9131
www.lakeland.com
Firm Type: Distributing, Manufacturing
Staff: 10
Quality Environmental Management System(s): 9001
Products/Services/Areas of Expertise: Laboratory equipment; safety & protective equipment; general waste management; provide of heat, fire & chemical protective clothing for use in hazmat remediation & general industry
Financial Information:
Type of Ownership: Publicly Traded
Domestic Markets:
National
Contact(s):
Randy Hillmer, Manager, Sales

Lakes Environmental Software
#3, 419 Phillip St.
Waterloo, ON N2L 3X2
519-746-5995
Fax: 519-746-0793
info@weblakes.com
www.weblakes.com
Firm Type: Engineering, Information Technology, Scientific/Technical Services
Founded: 1995
Staff: 23
Products/Services/Areas of Expertise: Air dispersion modelling; emissions inventory software; risk assessment software
Financial Information:
Type of Ownership: Private
Domestic Markets:
National
Foreign Activity:
Worldwide
Markets Sought:
Asia, The Middle East, The Pacific Rim, Mexico
Contact(s):
Jesse L. Thé, President
jesse@weblakes.com
Michael A. Johnson

Lakeshore Recycling
Affiliate of Genor Services Ltd.
P.O. Box 100
Putnam Rd., RR#1
Putnam, ON N0L 2B0
519-485-0621
Products/Services/Areas of Expertise: Collection & recycling services
Contact(s):
Ken Finucan, Executive Manager

Lambert Somec inc.
1505, rue des Tanneurs
Québec, QC G1N 4S7
418-687-1640
Fax: 418-688-7577
lamsoadm@lambertsomec.com
www.lambertsomec.com
Firm Type: Manufacturing
Founded: 1961
Staff: 350
Quality Environmental Management System(s): 9002
Products/Services/Areas of Expertise: HVAC, plumbing, piping, electricity & mechanical constructor in commercial & industrial sectors
Financial Information:
Type of Ownership: Private
Revenue Sources: 10% nationwide; 30% Provincial; 10% Municipals; 50% Private Contracts
Domestic Markets:
Québec
Foreign Activity:
Africa, South America, Mexico
Markets Sought:
Asia, Central America,
Contact(s):
Denis Linteau, Président
Canadian Branches:
Boucherville Office
1340, rue Volta
Boucherville, QC J4B 6G6
450-641-4650
Fax: 450-641-4671
lamsomtl@lambertsomec.com

International Branch(es):
Senegal Office
International Development
Zone Industrielle Sud
P.O. Box 3844
Rocade Fann Bel-Air
Dakar Senegal
(221) 849-34-94
Fax: (221) 832-42-92
Richard Normand, Vice-President

Lambton Scientific
Division of Technical Chemical Services Inc.
P.O. Box 2020
391 Vidal St. South
Sarnia, ON N7T 7L1
519-344-4747
Fax: 519-344-2350
888-344-8383
info@lambtonscientific.com
www.lambtonscientific.com
Firm Type: Manufacturing, Scientific/Technical Services
Founded: 1972
Staff: 6
Member of: Canadian Association of Environmental Analytical Laboratories
Products/Services/Areas of Expertise: Full environmental laboratory capabilities
Financial Information:
Type of Ownership: Private
Revenue: $1.5 Million - $3 Million

Revenue Sources: 2% Provincial; 3% Municipals; 95% Private Contracts
Domestic Markets:
Ontario
Foreign Activity:
USA
Contact(s):
J. Malcolm James, President
mjames@techchemservices.com
Chris James, General Manager
cjames@techchemservices.com
Andy Schmidtmeyer, Manager, Laboratory
aschmidtmeyer@lambtonscientific.com
Mike Newman, Organics
mnewman@lambtonscientific.com
Mike Scaini, Metals
mscaini@lambtonscientific.com

Land & Sea Environmental Consultants Ltd.
25 Estates Rd.
Dartmouth, NS B2Y 4K3
902-461-2009
Fax: 902-461-0848
ocl@accesscable.net
Firm Type: Scientific/Technical Services
Founded: 1990
Staff: 6
Member of: Western Dredging Association; American Chemical Society
Products/Services/Areas of Expertise: Environmental assessment & monitoring; field sampling & monitoring; mine tailings; water & wastewater assessment; environmental aspects of port, harbour & coastal development; environmental management; environmental audits
Domestic Markets:
National
Foreign Activity:
Asia, Central America, The Pacific Rim
Contact(s):
Scott MacKnight, President

Landscope Consulting Corp.
4015 Moha Rd.
Lillooet, BC V0K 1V0
250-256-0056
Firm Type: Management Consulting, Scientific/Technical Services
Founded: 1984
Staff: 2
Products/Services/Areas of Expertise: Natural resources management; environmental impact studies & assessments; integrated natural resource planning; sustainable agriculture; land use studies; landscape analysis; project assessment & analysis; facilitation & mediation
Contact(s):
Trevor Chandler, Ph.D., P.Ag., President

Canadian Branches:
Vancouver Branch
1860 Grant St.
Vancouver, BC V5L 2Y8
604-250-6836
Fax: 604-255-9150
northrop@direct.ca
Jim Norie, P.Eng., Senior Planner

Lane Environment Limited
Formerly: P. Lane & Associates Ltd.
1663 Oxford St.
Halifax, NS B3H 3Z5
902-423-8197
Fax: 902-429-8089
lane@cs.dal.ca
Firm Type: Scientific/Technical Services
Founded: 1993
Member of: Latin American Study Association
Products/Services/Areas of Expertise: Environmental impact & risk assessments; sustainable development planning & assessment; environmental policy analysis with a Latin American focus
Contact(s):
Patricia A. Lane, Ph.D., President

Lantech Drilling Services Inc.
P.O. Box 4324
398 Dover Rd.
Dieppe, NB E1A 6E9
506-853-9131
Fax: 506-853-7759
lantech@lantechdrilling.com
www.lantechdrilling.com
Firm Type: Scientific/Technical Services
Founded: 1990
Staff: 60
Products/Services/Areas of Expertise: Contract drilling services for environmental, hydrogeological & waste management projects
Domestic Markets:
New Brunswick, Newfoundland & Labrador, Nova Scotia, Ontario, Prince Edward Island, Québec
Foreign Activity:
USA,
Contact(s):
John LeBlanc, President
Mark Bloome, Operations Manager (Atlantic)

Canadian Branches:
Ontario Branch
3661 Mount Albert Rd., RR#1
Sharon, ON L0G 1V0
905-478-2243
Fax: 905-478-2249
mwilliams@lantechdrilling.com
Mark Williams, General Manager (Ontario)

Lapp-Hancock Associates Limited
9 Kane Terrace
Nepean, ON K2J 2A5
613-825-5898
Fax: 613-825-7640
inquiries@lapp-hancock.ca
www.lapp-hancock.ca
Firm Type: Management Consulting
Founded: 1985
Staff: 22
Member of: Institute of Electrical Engineers; Institute of Electrical & Electronics Engineers
Products/Services/Areas of Expertise: Telecommunications & radio frequency management consulting; remote sensing studies
Domestic Markets:
National
Foreign Activity:
Eastern Europe, Western Europe, The Middle East, The Pacific Rim
Contact(s):
Garry Rolston, President & CEO

Larose & Fils Ltée
2255, boul Industriel
Laval, QC H7S 1P8
514-382-7000
877-382-7001
info@larose.ca
www.larose.ca
Firm Type: Distributing, Manufacturing
Founded: 1954
Staff: 60
Member of: Canadian Sanitation Standards Association, International Sanitary Supply Association
Products/Services/Areas of Expertise: Disinfectants & cleaning chemicals
Financial Information:
Type of Ownership: Private
Revenue: Greater than $5 Million
Domestic Markets:
Québec
Contact(s):
Jean LaRose, President
Manon Larose, General Manager

Canadian Branches:
Québec Branch
#160, 275, rue Métivier
Québec, QC G1M 3X8
418-683-7000

Lasec Enterprises Ltd.
P.O. Box 159
424 Dakota Rd.
Debert, NS B0M 1G0
902-662-3360
Fax: 902-662-2420
lasec@sympatico.ca

Products/Services/Areas of Expertise: Manufactures & distributes recycled wood fibre products for absorbant & containment of all petroleum products
Contact(s):
Graham Sweetapple, Contact

Laser Diagnostic Instruments International Inc.
Formerly: LDI International Inc.
Also Known As: LDI3
#1, 146 Colonade Rd. South
Ottawa, ON K2E 7Y1
613-723-7474
Fax: 613-723-2086
866-794-5370
info@ldi3.com
www.ldi3.com
Firm Type: Scientific/Technical Services
Founded: 2001
Staff: 4
Products/Services/Areas of Expertise: Laser-based analysis instrumentation
Contact(s):
Alexandre Vorobiev, President

LaserNetworks Inc.
#1, 2823 Bristol Circle
Oakville, ON L6H 6X5
905-847-5990
800-461-4879
info@lasernetworks.com
www.lasernetworks.com
Firm Type: Distributing, Information Technology, Waste Management
Founded: 1987
Staff: 100
Products/Services/Areas of Expertise: Customized hardware & software solutions for printing & imaging; document capture & workflow; secure confidential printing; forms automation; print compression; job accounting; centralized digital fax; host printing; MICR encoding; COST PER PAGE Program reduces printing & imaging costs by up to 40%; printer supplies for all printer makes & models; recycling of toner cartridges
Domestic Markets:
National
Contact(s):
Brian Stevenson, Controller

Canadian Branches:
Edmonton
11444 - 119 St.
Edmonton, AB T5G 2X6
780-497-7697

Montréal
#2200, 1250, boul René-Lévesque ouest
Montréal, QC H3C 3R2
514-933-3373

Ottawa
#200, 440 Laurier Ave. West
Ottawa, ON K1R 7X6
613-788-2752

Saanichton
L24, 6822 Veyaness Rd.
Saanichton, BC V8M 1W1
250-598-2480

Surrey
#17, 18812 - 96 Ave.
Surrey, BC V4N 3R1
604-882-8854

Toronto
#1307, 69 Yonge St.
Toronto, ON M5E 1K3
416-363-7404

Winnipeg
385 St Mary Ave.
Winnipeg, MB R3C 0N1
204-956-7797

Laserworks Computer Services
75 F Ackerley Blvd.
Dartmouth, NS B3B 1R7
902-468-5430
Fax: 902-468-2186
info@laserworks.ca
www.laserworks.ca

Products/Services/Areas of Expertise: Recovery of toner cartridges
Domestic Markets:
Nova Scotia

Latimat Inc.
Formerly: Environmental Cleaning Systems
#4, 20 Claireport Cres.
Toronto, ON M9W 6P6
416-740-2597
Fax: 416-740-7470
877-528-4637
latimat@ica.net
www.latimat.com
Firm Type: Manufacturing
Founded: 1992
Staff: 6
Member of: Powerwashers of North America; Cleaning Equipment Trade Association; Canadian Carwash Association
Products/Services/Areas of Expertise: Portable wash pads & accessories, minimum discharge mobile wash systems, pressure washers & water treatment systems. Latimat patents acquired by Kyoto Containment Systems Inc.
Recently Completed / Ongoing Projects: US Military, Navy, National Guard - wash mats; Kuwait, Saudi Arabia - aircraft cleaning; CN, CP - railmats; Saturn V Rocket; Home Depot Tool Rental
Financial Information:
Type of Ownership: Private
Domestic Markets:
Alberta, British Columbia, Manitoba, New Brunswick, Nova Scotia, Ontario, Québec, Saskatchewan
Foreign Activity:
Australia/New Zealand, Central Europe, Western Europe
Contact(s):
Doug Latimer, President
Shelly Latimer, National Sales Manager

Lavo Inc.
11900, St-Jean-Baptiste
Montréal, QC H1C 2J3
514-526-7783
Fax: 514-526-8556
800-361-6898
questions@lavo.ca
www.lavo.ca
Firm Type: Distributing
Founded: 1948
Staff: 150
Products/Services/Areas of Expertise: Water treatment chemicals
Financial Information:
Type of Ownership: Private
Domestic Markets:
Ontario, Québec
Foreign Activity:
USA
Contact(s):
Paul Bouthillier, President
pbouthilier@lavo.ca
Alain Proulx, Sales
aproulx@lavo.ca

Law Library
Court of Justice, Arnakallak Bldg. 224
P.O. Box 297
Iqaluit, NU X0A 0H0
867-975-6134
Fax: 867-975-6148
courtlibrary@gov.nu.ca
www.nucj.ca/library/library.htm
Products/Services/Areas of Expertise: Plays a central role in providing effective and innovative access to information resources to a wide range of users within and outside the Justice system in Nunavut. The library's services and collections anticipate and respond to the reference and research needs of the Judiciary, Justice Department staff, the local and national legal community and the general public

Layfield Geosynthetics & Industrial Fabrics Ltd.
Also Known As: Layfield GIF
A division of the Layfield Group of Companies
Formerly: Layfield Plastics Ltd.11603 - 180 St.
Edmonton, AB T6S 2H6
780-453-6731
Fax: 780-455-5218
800-840-2884
edmonton@layfieldgroup.com
www.layfieldgroup.com
Firm Type: Distributing, Engineering, Manufacturing
Founded: 1978
Staff: 250
Member of: Association of Professional Engineers, Geologists & Geophysicists of Alberta
Quality Environmental Management System(s): 9002
Products/Services/Areas of Expertise: Geomembranes, floating covers, geotextiles, erosion control, tarpaulins; Engineers, manufacturers, fabricates, distributes & installs geosynthetics products; manufacturing facility located in Richmond, BC, with fabrication facilities in Edmonton & El Cajon, CA. Branch locations in Calgary & Vaughan. The Layfield Group of Companies operates through 3 divisions: Geosynthetic & Industrial Fabrics, Poly Films, & Environmental Systems. The corporate office is located in Richmond, BC, with branches & facilities in California, the State of Washington, western Canada & Vaughan, Ontario. In October, 2007 Layfield acquired the rights to the Aqua Dam product line from Aqua Dam & Diversion Ltd.
Financial Information:
Type of Ownership: Private
Revenue: Greater than $5 Million
Domestic Markets:
National
Foreign Activity:
Australia/New Zealand, Mexico, USA
Contact(s):
Tom Rose, President/CEO, Layfield Group of Companies
Brian Fraser, MBA, CIM, P.Mgr., Vice President/General Manager, Env. Systems, Geosynthetics, Indust. Fabrics - Canada
Mark Simpson, B.Sc., MBA, P.Eng., General Manager, Env. Systems, Geosynthetics, Indust. Fabrics-E. Canada

Canadian Branches:
Richmond - Layfield Poly Films Ltd.
1120 Silversmith Pl.
Richmond, BC V7A 5E4
604-275-5588
Fax: 604-275-7867
800-558-8275
richmond@layfieldgroup.com
Products/Services/Areas of Expertise: Location of Layfield Poly Films Ltd., and the corporate head office of the Layfield Group of Companies
Mark Rose, General Manager, Poly Films

Vaughan - Layfield Geosynthetics & Industrial Fabrics Ltd.
#9, 20 Staffern Dr.
Vaughan, ON L4K 2Z7
905-761-9123
Fax: 905-761-0035
888-436-4273
toronto@layfieldgroup.com
Mark Simpson, B.Sc., MBA, P.Eng., General Manager, Env. Systems, Geosynthetics, Indust. Fabrics-E. Canada

International Branch(es):
Seattle - Layfield Plastics Inc.
851 Houser Way North
Renton, WA USA
425-254-1075
Fax: 425-254-1575
800-796-6868
seattle@layfieldgroup.com
Pat Sanborn, General Manager, Env. Systems, Geosynthetics, Indust. Fabrics - U.S.

Le Groupe Forces / SENC
#105, 19, rue St-Charles-Borromée
Joliette, QC J6E 4S8
450-756-8040
Fax: 450-756-6559
tfreire@grforces.qc.ca
Firm Type: Engineering
Founded: 1992
Staff: 8
Products/Services/Areas of Expertise: Design & specification planning services; groundwater & surface water remediation; water & wastewater consulting & system design
Financial Information:
Type of Ownership: Private
Revenue: $500,000 - $1.5 Million
Revenue Sources: 20% Provincial; 60% Municipals; 20% Private Contracts
Domestic Markets:
Québec
Contact(s):
Thierry Freire, Contact

Le Groupe Leblond & Bouchard/Daniel Arbour et associes
Formerly: Le Groupe Leblond Tremblay & Bouchard
282, rue Ste-Anne
Chicoutimi, QC G7J 2M4
418-543-7997
Fax: 418-543-5341
saguenay@arbour.ca
www.leblondbouchard.ca
Firm Type: Scientific/Technical Services
Founded: 1976
Staff: 9
Products/Services/Areas of Expertise: Environmental impact studies; site assessments; land use planning; environmental control strategies
Financial Information:
Type of Ownership: Private
Domestic Markets:
Québec
Contact(s):
Jean-Yves Bouchard, Planner Vice President
Robert Leblond, Eng., Planner Vice President

Le Groupe Légerlite inc.
5901, Transcanadienne
Pointe-Claire, QC H9R 1B7
514-694-2493
Fax: 514-694-2501
800-283-2493
plecuyer@legerlite.com
www.legerlite.com
Firm Type: Manufacturing
Founded: 1991
Staff: 50
Products/Services/Areas of Expertise: Insulation; packaging

Canadian Branches:
Toronto
#1B, 480 Tapscott Rd.
Toronto, ON M1B 1W3
416-335-0192
Fax: 416-335-0194
amoreira@foamconcept.com

Le Groupe Pétrolier OLCO Inc.
2775, av George
Montréal, QC H1L 6J7
514-645-6526
Fax: 514-645-8048
800-363-1120
www.olco.ca
Products/Services/Areas of Expertise: Producer of petroleum products including propane, furnace oils, diesel, and gasoline.
Ecological Note: Ethanol-Blended Gasoline

Le Groupe Sani Marc
The Sani Marc Group
42, rue de l'Artisan
Victoriaville, QC G6P 7E3
819-758-1541
Fax: 819-758-5800
www.sanimarc.com
Firm Type: Distributing, Manufacturing
Founded: 1969
Member of: Canadian Sanitation Supply Association; Canadian Meat Council
Quality Environmental Management System(s): 9001
Products/Services/Areas of Expertise: Water treatment chemicals; sanitary products, methods & cleaning chemical products; pool & spa chemical products
Financial Information:
Type of Ownership: Private
Domestic Markets:
Alberta, British Columbia, Manitoba, New Brunswick, Newfoundland & Labrador, Nova Scotia, Ontario, Prince Edward Island, Québec, Saskatchewan
Foreign Activity:
Asia, USA
Contact(s):
Pierre Goudreault, President
Rick Thompson, Vice-President, Pool Division
Michel Plante, Director, Research & Development
Patrick Couture, Vice-President, Business Development

Products & Services Buyer's Guide

Canadian Branches:
Boucherville
35-2, rue de Lauzon
Boucherville, QC J4B 1E7

Oakville
#1, 2910 Brighton Rd.
Oakville, ON L6H 5S3
905-829-5862
Fax: 905-829-2746
Rick Thomson

Québec
#100, 275 av. Saint-Sacrement
Québec, QC G1N 3Y1
Nicole Arsenault

Lea International Ltd.
Formerly: Lea Associates
#802, 595 Howe St.
Vancouver, BC V6C 2T5
604-609-2272
Fax: 604-609-7008
leainternational@lea.ca
www.lea.ca
Firm Type: Management Consulting
Staff: 50
Products/Services/Areas of Expertise: Consulting service with emphasis on transportation, planning, engineering, management & training
Financial Information:
Type of Ownership: Private
Domestic Markets:
British Columbia
Foreign Activity:
Asia
Contact(s):
Dave Saunders, President

Canadian Branches:
Toronto
#900, 625 Cochrane Dr.
Markham, ON L3R 9R9
905-470-0015
Fax: 905-470-0030
leaeast@lea.ca

International Branch(es):
New Delhi
Mohan Cooperative Industrial Estate
B-1/E 27, Mathura Rd.
New Delhi India
-91-11-26973950-55
Fax: -91-11-26971062

Lea-Der Coatings (614248 Alberta Ltd.)
P.O. Box 4086
90 Oswald Dr.
Spruce Grove, AB T7X 3B3
780-962-5060
Fax: 780-962-0501
sales@lea-der.com
www.lea-der.com
Firm Type: Manufacturing
Founded: 1996
Staff: 10
Member of: Edmonton Construction Association; Better Business Bureau
Products/Services/Areas of Expertise: Supply & install non-slip coatings & industrial matting
Financial Information:
Type of Ownership: Private
Revenue: $500,000 - $1.5 Million
Domestic Markets:
Alberta
Contact(s):
Derwin Joelson, President
Leah Joelson, Sec.-Treas.
Darrell Demers, Sales

Lecompte Engineering Ltd.
Bldg. C
#201, 1417 Cyrville Rd.
Ottawa, ON K1B 3C7
613-236-6162
Fax: 613-236-2945
lecompte@trytel.com
Firm Type: Engineering
Founded: 1966

Member of: Association of Professional Engineers of Ontario; American Water Works Association; Ordre des ingénieurs du Québec
Products/Services/Areas of Expertise: Civil, environmental & structural engineering; environmental assessments; feasibility studies; retrofit of existing services; upgrading & implementation of water systems & wastewater plants; project management; preparation of plans & specifications; construction supervision & management
Domestic Markets:
Ontario, Québec
Contact(s):
Jacques Lecompte, President
Gaetan Beauchamp, Engineering Manager
Jean Hébert, Environmental Engineer
Mark Lecompte, Technical Advisor
Contact(s):
Gaetan Beauchesne, Municipal Engineer

Canadian Branches:
J.A. Lecompte & Associés inc.
24, rue Principale
Aylmer, QC J9H 3L1
819-684-0183
Fax: 819-684-1177

Lécuyer et Fils Ltée
17, du Moulin
Saint-Rémi, QC J0L 2L0
450-454-3928
Fax: 450-454-7254
800-561-0970
stormceptor@lecuyerbeton.com
www.lecuyerbeton.com
Firm Type: Distributing, Manufacturing

Products/Services/Areas of Expertise: Water & wastewater management equipment
Financial Information:
Type of Ownership: Private
Domestic Markets:
Québec
Contact(s):
Réjean Tremblay, Vice-président exécutif

Leeson Canada Ltd.
A Regal-Beloit company
320 Superior Blvd.
Mississauga, ON L5T 2N7
905-670-4770
Fax: 905-670-4378
800-563-0949
leeson@leeson.ca; sales@leeson.ca
www.leeson.ca
Firm Type: Distributing, Manufacturing
Founded: 1978
Quality Environmental Management System(s): 9001; 9002
Products/Services/Areas of Expertise: Electric motors; gear reducers & gearmotors; adjustable speed drives; brakes & clutches; industrial control sheaves; capacitors; pumps
Financial Information:
Type of Ownership: Foreign-owned
Domestic Markets:
National
Foreign Activity:
USA
Contact(s):
Glen Peer, Vice-President/General Manager
gpeer@leeson.ca
Dan McKelvie, National Marketing Manager
dmckelvie@leeson.ca
Michael Tough, National Sales Manager
mtough@leeson.ca
Contact(s):
Doug Stafford, Branch Manager
dstafford@leeson.ca

Canadian Branches:
Edmonton - Sales Office & Warehouse
8318 Davies Rd.
Edmonton, AB T6E 4Y5
780-437-3380
Fax: 780-434-3448
Mike Strenkowski, Branch Manager
mstrenkowski@leeson.ca

Langley - Sales Office & Warehouse
9087A - 198 St.
Langley, BC V1M 3B1
Fax: 604-888-0337
888-599-1177
Jeff Male, Branch Manager
jmale@leeson.ca

Moncton - Sales Office & Warehouse
#A13, 270 Baig Blvd.
Moncton, NB E1E 1C8
506-383-8883
Fax: 506-383-8887
877-851-1667
Ken Sheehan, Branch Manager
ksheehan@leeson.ca

Montréal - Sales Office & Warehouse
2467, rue Guenette
Montréal, QC H4R 2E9
514-337-8020
Fax: 514-337-0773
800-967-8020
Ken Sheehan, Branch Manager
ksheehan@leeson.ca

Winnipeg - Sales Office & Warehouse
#19, 1421 St James St.
Winnipeg, MB R3H 0Y9
204-786-6802
Fax: 204-786-6934
Charlie Vogel, Branch Manager
cvogel@leeson.ca

Hanover - Manufacturing Plant
#638 - 14 St.
Hanover, ON N4N 2A1
519-364-6024
Fax: 519-364-3239

Leferink Transfer Ltd.
57 Armstrong Ave.
Georgetown, ON L7G 4S1
905-877-1420
Fax: 905-877-7189
info@leferink.com
www.leferink.com
Firm Type: Waste Management
Founded: 1983
Staff: 6
Member of: Ontario Waste Management Association
Products/Services/Areas of Expertise: Solid, non-hazardous, commercial, institutional, industrial & residential waste transfer to disposal sites in Ontario & USA
Recently Completed / Ongoing Projects: Municipal waste, Orangeville & Shelburne; commercial waste, Collingwood, Milton, Georgetown, Brampton, Guelph; industrial waste, Halton, Peel, Wellington, Simcoe
Financial Information:
Type of Ownership: Private
Revenue Sources: 20% Municipals; 80% Private Contracts
Domestic Markets:
Ontario
Contact(s):
Bert Leferink, President

Legaré F., Ing. Forestier Conseil
831, rue Marguerite-Bourgeoys
Québec, QC G1S 3W5
418-681-8834
Fax: 418-681-5140
Firm Type: Management Consulting, Engineering
Founded: 1990
Products/Services/Areas of Expertise: Consulting & technical services for forestry & wooded urban areas, environmental impact assessments & studies; feasibility studies; project management; site rehabilitation; software system (SIGMA) & inventory services
Markets Sought:
USA
Contact(s):
François Legaré, Executive Director
Denis Rousseau, Forestry Technician

Legend Power Systems Inc.
8618 Commerce Court
Burnaby, BC V5A 4N6

866-772-8797
info@legendpower.com
www.legendpower.com
Products/Services/Areas of Expertise: Manufacturers of the Electrical Harmonizer, which optimizes the power supply of a facility, cutting down on electrical costs
Financial Information:
Type of Ownership: Publicly Traded
Domestic Markets:
National
Contact(s):
Gary Killacky, Chief Technical Officer
gkillacky@legendpower.com

LEHDER Environmental Services Ltd.
#210, 704 Mara St.
Point Edward, ON N7V 1X4
519-336-4101
Fax: 519-336-4311
info@lehder.com
www.lehder.com
Firm Type: Management Consulting, Engineering, Scientific/Technical Services
Founded: 1995
Staff: 25
Products/Services/Areas of Expertise: Air quality management; property liability, phase I & II; hazardous materials, TDG, WHMIS training, MSDS development; environmental management systems; process assessments; odour evaluation & measurement
Financial Information:
Type of Ownership: Private
Revenue Sources: 100% Private Contracts
Domestic Markets:
National
Foreign Activity:
USA
Contact(s):
Sid Lethbridge, Principal
slethbridge@lehder.com
Mike Denomme, Principal
Mark Roehler, Principal
Des Hayles, Principal
Marnie Freer, Principal
Peter Pakalnis, Principal
Daryl Zander, Principal

Canadian Branches:
Western Division
9954 - 67th Ave.
Edmonton, AB T6E 0P5
780-462-4099
Fax: 780-462-4392

LEM Laboratory Inc.
607 Torbay Rd.
St. John's, NL A1A 4Y6
709-576-0308
Fax: 709-576-0008
Firm Type: Scientific/Technical Services
Member of: Newfoundland Environmental Industries Association
Products/Services/Areas of Expertise: Laboratory services; analytical microbiology; feed & food products, water, aquatic toxicology; Rainbow Trout & Daphnia Magna bioassays
Contact(s):
Bevin LeDrew, President
Leann Collins, Marketing Manager
Sandra Whiteway, Laboratory Supervisor

Lennox Drum Ltd.
233 Fuller Rd.
Ajax, ON L1S 2E1
905-427-1441
Fax: 905-427-4986
800-263-7528
info@lennoxdrum.com
www.lennoxdrum.com
Firm Type: Manufacturing, Waste Management
Founded: 1979
Staff: 50
Products/Services/Areas of Expertise: All aspects of container management recycling of steel & poly containers; supply of new & used recycled containers
Financial Information:
Type of Ownership: Private
Revenue: Greater than $5 Million
Revenue Sources: 100% Private Contracts
Domestic Markets:
Ontario, Québec
Foreign Activity:
USA
Contact(s):
Jerry Lennox, President
Ray Lennox, Vice-President, Sales
Ted Kormann, Operations Manager

Lennox Industries (Canada) Ltd.
10 Woodslea Rd.
Brampton, ON L6T 5P2
905-799-2100
Fax: 905-799-9699
800-537-9899
www.lennox.com
Firm Type: Manufacturing
Founded: 1952
Staff: 250
Quality Environmental Management System(s): 9001; ISO
Products/Services/Areas of Expertise: Energy-efficient gas furnaces; cooling units; heat pumps; energy recovery technology
Financial Information:
Type of Ownership: Publicly Traded
Domestic Markets:
National
Contact(s):
Fred Ennamorato, Manager, Residential District
Nick Ennamorato, Manager, Commercial District

Canadian Branches:
Burnaby Branch
2962 Lake City Way
Burnaby, BC V5A 1T9
604-421-5424
Fax: 604-421-6718
Serge Laredo

Calgary Branch
P.O. Box 5460 A
3916 - 70 Ave. SE
Calgary, AB T2C 2K1
403-279-7577
Fax: 403-236-5138
Gary Lemke

Dartmouth Branch
133 Isley Ave., Unit D
Dartmouth, NS B3B 1S9
902-468-5995
Fax: 902-468-5969
Mike Barrett

Edmonton Branch
8103 McIntyre Rd. (58th St.)
Edmonton, AB T6E 5J7
780-440-1555
Fax: 780-440-4328
Troy Saunders

Gloucester Branch
1177 Parisien St.
Gloucester, ON K1B 4W4
613-745-1527
Fax: 613-745-2770
Archie Campbell

Hamilton Branch
#10, 351 Nash Rd. North
Hamilton, ON L8H 7P4
905-560-4200
Fax: 905-560-1550
Jim Joyce

London Branch
#5, 1 Adelaide St. North
London, ON N5B 3P4
519-439-3377
Fax: 519-439-3361
Sam Rizzo

Regina Branch
2110 - 77th Ave.
Regina, SK S4R 1G4
306-757-3636
Fax: 306-352-1828
Rich Raine

Saint-Laurent Branch
3540, rue Poirier
Saint-Laurent, QC H4R 2J5

514-336-8440
Fax: 514-336-1998
Jean Beaudet

Saskatoon Branch
3026 Faithful Ave.
Saskatoon, SK S7K 0B1
306-934-4848
Fax: 306-934-5009
Todd Wheeler

Scarborough Branch
#13, 2010 Ellesmere Rd.
Scarborough, ON M1H 3B1
416-754-4311
Fax: 416-754-4031
Steve Fyfe

Waterloo Branch
#10, 115 Randall Dr.
Waterloo, ON N2V 1C5
519-886-3666
Fax: 519-886-3884
Bruce Hatton

Winnipeg Branch
1653 St. James St.
Winnipeg, MB R3H 0X1
204-633-0299
Fax: 204-694-6896
John Martin

Leon's Insulation
Superior Plus
#3, 1121 Walkers Line
Burlington, ON L7N 2G4
905-335-5012
800-561-3495
general@winroc.com
www.leonsinsulation.com
Firm Type: Distributing
Founded: 1956
Staff: 150
Member of: Toronto Home Builders Association
Products/Services/Areas of Expertise: Residential insulation products; polyethylene vapour barriers; roof vents; basement blanket insulation; foundation drainage systems; drywall & related products
Financial Information:
Type of Ownership: Publicly Traded
Revenue: Greater than $5 Million
Revenue Sources: 100% Private Contracts
Domestic Markets:
Ontario
Contact(s):
Daniel L. Desrochers, General Manager
Tom Scott, Asst. General Manager

Canadian Branches:
Stouffville
East
6 Sangster Rd.
Stouffville, ON L4A 7X4
905-640-6811
Fax: 905-640-0717
generaleast@winroc.com
Chris Foster, Operations Manager

Les Bras d'Fer Gingras Inc.
367, boul Chabot
Saint-Ubalde, QC G0A 4L0
418-277-2690
Fax: 418-277-2692
bdfg@bdfg.qc.ca
www.dbfg.qc.ca
Firm Type: Distributing, Manufacturing
Founded: 1988
Staff: 11
Products/Services/Areas of Expertise: Design, manufacture of lifters for waste removal & management
Financial Information:
Type of Ownership: Private
Revenue Sources: 100% Private Contracts
Domestic Markets:
National
Foreign Activity:
China, Western Europe, The Middle East, Mexico, USA
Markets Sought:
Eastern Europe

Products & Services Buyer's Guide

Contact(s):
Appollinaire Gingras, President
Serge Gingras, Vice-President
Réjean Léveillée, Sales Manager

Les Composts du Québec inc.
CP 448
415, ch Plaisance
Saint-Henri-de-Lévis, QC G0R 3E0
418-882-2736
Fax: 418-882-2255
800-463-1030
composts@composts.com
www.composts.com
Products/Services/Areas of Expertise: Compostage des matières organiques d'origine agricole, forestière, industrielle et municipale; fabrication et commercialisation de terreaux horticoles spécialisés à base de compost
Contact(s):
Isabelle Lessard, Conseillère, Marketing et communications

Les Consultants Eoletech S.Q. Inc.
Formerly: Eoletech Inc.
CP 307
Montréal, QC H9W 5T8
514-697-6313
eoletech@eoletech.com
www.eoletech.com
Products/Services/Areas of Expertise: Energy consultant in: wind energy, alternative energy, energy conservation, industrial, nuclear & thermal power projects
Contact(s):
Saeed Quraeshi

Les Consultants LBCD
Formerly: Sodexen Inc.
#1001, 425, boul de Maisonneuve ouest
Montréal, QC H3A 3G5
514-339-1500
Fax: 514-339-1599
montreal@lbcd.org
www.lbcd.org
Firm Type: Scientific/Technical Services
Founded: 1975
Member of: Association des ingénieurs-conseils du Québec; Association of Consulting Engineers of Canada
Products/Services/Areas of Expertise: LBCD's main fields of activity include structural, mechanical, electrical & environmental engineering, potable water treatment, wastewater treatment, urban infrastructure & materials handling; ISO-9001-2000 certified
Domestic Markets:
New Brunswick, Nova Scotia, Ontario, Québec
Foreign Activity:
Asia, USA
Markets Sought:
China, Vietnam
Contact(s):
Pierre Beauchamp, P.Eng., President & CEO
Jean-Noël Côté, P.Eng., Vice-President & Director of Engineering

Canadian Branches:
Salaberry-de-Valleyfield
40, rue Sainte-Cécile
Salaberry-de-Valleyfield, QC J6T 1L7
450-371-5722
Fax: 450-371-6955
vall@lbcd.org

Vaudreuil-Dorion
#1008, 1000, av St-Charles, 10e étage
Vaudreuil-Dorion, QC J7V 8P5
450-455-6119
Fax: 450-455-6388
vaud@lbcd.org

Les Consultants RSA
925, av du Pont Nord
Alma, QC G8B 7B6
418-668-3373
Fax: 418-668-0274
rsa@mail.digicom.qc.ca
Firm Type: Engineering, Scientific/Technical Services
Founded: 1962
Staff: 30
Member of: Water Environment Federation, Association québécoise des techniques de l'eau, Air & Waste Management Association, American Water Works Association
Products/Services/Areas of Expertise: Water & wastewater treatment systems design; shore protection (lakes, reservoirs, rivers), soil remediation
Contact(s):
Patrice Maltais, Directeur General
Guillaume Massé, Engineer
Réjean Villeneuve, Engineer
Normand Villeneuve, Engineer
Contact(s):
Pierre Bouchard, President

Canadian Branches:
UNIGEC - STAS
1846, rue Outarde
Chicoutimi, QC G7B 5K3
418-696-0074
Fax: 418-545-8335
marketing@stas.biz

Les Contrôles PROVAN Associés Inc.
PROVAN Controls Associates Inc.
2315, rue Halpern
Montréal, QC H4S 1S3
514-332-3230
Fax: 514-332-3552
info@provan.ca
www.provan.ca
Firm Type: Distributing
Founded: 1976
Staff: 20
Member of: Réseau Environnement; CB Engineering Pacific Inc. (U.S.)
Products/Services/Areas of Expertise: Distributor of valves, instrumentation & process controls: process analyzers; process automation, measurement & controls; plant safety & preventative maintenance equipment; water & wastewater treatment equipment; valving. Clients are found in the pulp & paper, mining & metals, chemical & petrochemical, food, pharmaceutical, & the HVAC industries, as well as in muncipalities & electrical utilities. Services include professional diagnostic, repair, start-up/commissioning, & maintenance sevices. For the branch office located in Québec, contact 418-285-3974
Recently Completed / Ongoing Projects: Supply of electric actuators to Québec City; supply of valves & control valves, mag meter, check valves to two major pulp & paper companies for water treatment plans
Financial Information:
Type of Ownership: Private
Revenue: $1.5 Million - $3 Million
Revenue Sources: 70% Municipals; 30% Private Contracts
Domestic Markets:
New Brunswick, Newfoundland & Labrador, Ontario, Prince Edward Island, Québec
Contact(s):
Dan Hoobin, President
Daniel Forest, Vice-President, Sales
René Rocheleau, Inside Sales

Les Emballages Polyform inc.
Also Known As: Polyform Inc.
454, rue Édouard
Granby, QC J2G 3Z3
450-378-9093
Fax: 450-378-3096
800-463-8378
polyform@polyform.com
www.polyform.com
Firm Type: Manufacturing
Founded: 1967
Products/Services/Areas of Expertise: Insulation; packaging; protection equipment; flower boxes, fish boxes, flotation components; dunnage trays
Domestic Markets:
Alberta, British Columbia, New Brunswick, Nova Scotia, Ontario, Québec, Saskatchewan
Foreign Activity:
USA
Contact(s):
Jean-Louis Beliveau, President
Sylvain Bouchard, Representative, Insulation Product Sales
Martin Hébert, Contact, Sales

Les Engrais Naturels McInnes Inc./McInnes Natural Fertilizers Inc.
120, rue Railroad
Stanstead, QC J0B 3E2
819-876-7555
Fax: 819-876-1166
info@biobiz.ca
www.biobiz.ca
Firm Type: Manufacturing
Founded: 1991
Staff: 5
Member of: Nature-Action Inc., Centre d'agriculture biologique
Products/Services/Areas of Expertise: Organic fertilizer & mineral supplements; bio-lawn fertilizing program
Domestic Markets:
New Brunswick, Nova Scotia, Ontario, Québec
Markets Sought:
USA
Contact(s):
Luc Desjardins, President
Terry Shaw, Vice-President

Les Entreprises Forlam
4240, rue Marcel-Lacasse
Boisbriand, QC J7H 1N3
450-430-0441
forlam@gc.aira.com
Contact(s):
Martin Lamarre, Contact

Les Entreprises Julien Inc.
935, rue Lachance
Québec, QC G1P 2H3
418-687-3630
Fax: 418-687-3993
800-461-3377
www.julien.ca
Firm Type: Manufacturing
Founded: 1946
Staff: 400
Member of: National Kitchen and Bath Association; Decorative Plumbing & Hardware Association; American Society of Interior Designers; Canadian Association of Chain Drug Stores
Quality Environmental Management System(s): 9002
Products/Services/Areas of Expertise: Stainless steel fabrication, transport, electrial & household appliances, agrifood, medical & food processing industries
Domestic Markets:
National
Foreign Activity:
Africa, Caribbean, Western Europe, The Middle East, USA
Contact(s):
Gilles St-Pierre, President/General Manager
Contact(s):
Lyndon Hubert
Contact(s):
Don Jessome

Canadian Branches:
Condon Barr Food Equipment Ltd.
14515 - 118 Ave.
Edmonton, AB T5L 2M7
780-454-0432
Fax: 780-455-9229
1-800-661-3378

Jessom Food Equipment Ltd.
8 Ralston Ave.
Dartmouth, NS B3B 1H7
902-468-8778
Fax: 902-468-4597
www.jessomfood.com

Les Équipements Vibrotech Inc.
Also Known As: Vibrotech Inc.
CP 333
2000, av Methot
Plessisville, QC G6L 2Y8
819-362-8871
Fax: 819-362-2930
info@vibrotech-inc.com
www.vibrotech-inc.com
Products/Services/Areas of Expertise: Recycling equipment
Contact(s):
Jean-Claude Faggion, Application Specialist
jfaggion@vibrotech-inc.com

Les Industries Cascades Ltée
404, rue Marie-Victorin
Kingsey Falls, QC J0A 1B0
819-363-2245

Canadian Branches:
Belleville Branch
240 Adam St.
Belleville, ON K8N 5B2
613-968-5205
Fax: 613-968-4012

Calgary Branch
5734 Burbank Cres. SE
Calgary, AB T2H 1Z6
403-255-9200
Fax: 403-255-6868

Edmonton Branch
16210 - 114 Ave. NW
Edmonton, AB T5M 2Z5
780-451-1076
Fax: 780-452-7265

Kitchener Branch
100 Campbell, Unit 10
Kitchener, ON N2H 4X8
519-745-3691
Fax: 519-745-0776

Lachine Branch
1475 - 32e av
Lachine, QC H8T 3J1
514-636-9926
Fax: 514-636-8317

London Branch
1025 Hargrieve Rd., Unit 7
London, ON N6E 1P7
519-681-4809
Fax: 519-681-2543

Moncton Branch
270 Baig Blvd.
Moncton, NB E1E 1C8
506-857-8288
Fax: 506-857-8380

Ottawa Branch
1290 Old Innes Rd.
Ottawa, ON K1B 3V3
613-749-1155
Fax: 613-749-2179

Scarborough Branch
440 Passmore Ave.
Scarborough, ON M1V 5J8
416-609-9268
Fax: 416-609-9698

Sherbrooke Branch
771, rue Longpré
Sherbrooke, QC J1G 4S8
819-564-8386
Fax: 819-821-2614

St Catharines Branch
159 Cushman Rd., Unit 1
St Catharines, ON L2R 6V9
905-688-0262
Fax: 905-688-4709

Ste-Foy Branch
400, rue Volta
Sainte-Foy, QC G1N 4J2
418-683-3660
Fax: 418-683-2265

Sudbury Branch
500 Barrydowne Rd., Unit 5
Sudbury, ON P3A 3T3
705-566-6614
Fax: 705-566-8476

Winnipeg Branch
#1, 1865 Sargent Ave.
Winnipeg, MB R3H 0E4
204-783-2068
Fax: 204-783-1036

Les Industries Cascades Ltée
404, rue Marie-Victorin
Kingsey Falls, QC J0A 1B0
819-363-2245

PHA Industries Ltd.
1725 McPherson Ct.
Pickering, ON L1W 3H9
905-831-2231
Fax: 905-831-3531

Papiers Grande Ville inc.
#200, 1475 - 32e av
Lachine, QC H8T 3J1
514-636-3357
Fax: 514-636-8149

Wyant Chemicals
440 Passmore Ave.
Scarborough, ON M1V 5J8
416-609-9077
Fax: 416-609-9698

Les Industries Fournier Inc.
Fournier Industries Inc.
3787, boul Frontenac ouest
Thetford Mines, QC G6H 2B5
418-423-4241
Fax: 418-423-7366
general@fournierindustries.com
www.fournierindustries.com
Firm Type: Manufacturing
Founded: 1959
Staff: 140
Quality Environmental Management System(s): 9002
Products/Services/Areas of Expertise: Dewatering equipment; rotary press dewaters sludge for municipal & industrial sludge such as pulp & paper sludge
Financial Information:
Type of Ownership: Private
Revenue Sources: 75% Municipals; 25% Private Contracts
Domestic Markets:
British Columbia, New Brunswick, Nunavut, Québec
Foreign Activity:
Asia, Western Europe, USA
Markets Sought:
Asia, Central America, South America

Les Laboratoires S.L. inc.
363, rue Joseph Gagné sud
La Baie, QC G7B 3P6
418-544-6827
Fax: 418-544-1189
labaie@labosl.ca
www.laboratoiressl.com
Firm Type: Engineering
Founded: 1976
Staff: 60
Quality Environmental Management System(s): 9002
Products/Services/Areas of Expertise: Environment, hydrogeology, geotechnics, material inspection; geology, project inspection & supervision; quality control & surveying; roadway management
Financial Information:
Type of Ownership: Private
Revenue: $1.5 Million - $3 Million
Revenue Sources: 10% nationwide; 20% Provincial; 30% Municipals; 40% Private Contracts
Domestic Markets:
Québec
Contact(s):
Joachim Simard, President
Lina Villeneuve, Relationniste
Donald Tremblay, Head, Environment

Les Laboratoires Shermont Inc.
2605, rue Bonin
Sherbrooke, QC J1K 1C5
819-821-4373
Fax: 819-564-3938
800-567-6032
www.labo-shermont.com
Firm Type: Scientific/Technical Services
Founded: 1958
Staff: 60
Member of: Canadian Council of Independent Laboratories
Quality Environmental Management System(s): 9002
Products/Services/Areas of Expertise: Geotechnical engineering services including soil investigations, boring & drilling, environmental audits; quality control for soils, concrete, asphalt, steel & paint; environmental services including flow monitoring, water/wastewater/soil/sediment monitoring; quality control & inspection of roofing; registered in full conformity ISO 9002; accredited ISO CEI Guide 25
Recently Completed / Ongoing Projects: Wastewater surveys, St. Lawrence River; contaminated soil evaluations for petroleum stations, banks, private developers & other industries
Financial Information:
Type of Ownership: Publicly Traded
Revenue Sources: 5% nationwide; 35% Provincial; 30% Municipals; 30% Private Contracts
Domestic Markets:
Québec
Foreign Activity:
USA,
Contact(s):
Eric Charron, President
André Lévesque, P.E., M.Eng., Vice-President & COO
Philippe Savoie, Marketing & Sales Contact
Luc Bertrand, Geotechnical Engineer
Y.G. Prevost, Environmental Engineer

Canadian Branches:
Drummondville
2555, rue Saint-Pierre
Drummondville, QC J2C 7Y2
819-477-3775
Fax: 819-478-8436
1-888-423-9118

Montréal
4890, 5 ave.
Montréal, QC H1Y 2S2
514-521-4290
Fax: 514-521-4637

Saint-Hyacinthe
#A, 5505, av Trudeau
Saint-Hyacinthe, QC J2S 1H5
450-774-5280
Fax: 450-774-4498
1-800-665-5280
Luc Bergeron

Saint-Jean-sur-Richelieu
#245, 100 rue Richelieu
Saint-Jean-sur-Richelieu, QC J3B 6X3
450-346-8449
Fax: 450-346-9249

Trois-Rivières
3120, rue Bellefeuille
Trois-Rivières, QC G9A 5R5
819-376-1526
Fax: 819-376-1580
1-866-376-1526
Bruno Lapointe, Regional Director

Victoriaville
50, de la Grande-Ligne
Victoriaville, QC G6P 6R9
819-758-8265
Fax: 819-755-6492
1-800-567-2526

Les Peintures Sico inc.
Formerly: Le Groupe Ro-na Dismat inc.
47, ch Bates
Montréal, QC H2V 1A6
514-495-5712
Fax: 514-495-1934
brigitte.charpentier@sico.com
www.sico.com
Firm Type: Manufacturing
Founded: 1937
Staff: 1000
Member of: Ordre des chimistes du Québec
EcoLogo Certified Products & Services: Manufactures certified paints, surface coatings & Green Seal certified paints
Ecological Note: Manufactures certified paints, surface coatings & Green Seal certified paints
Financial Information:
Revenue: Greater than $5 Million
Domestic Markets:
Ontario, Québec
Foreign Activity:
Mexico, USA
Contact(s):
Brigitte Charpentier, Contact

Luc Pepin, Chief, Regulatory officer, 514/495-5700
luc.pepin@sico.com

Les Plastiques Simport Ltée
Also Known As: Simport
2588, rue Bernard Pilon
Beloeil, QC J3G 4S5
450-464-1723
Fax: 450-464-3394
info@simport.com
www.simport.com
Firm Type: Manufacturing
Founded: 1975
Products/Services/Areas of Expertise: Manufacturer of disposable plasticware used in hospital, industrial & research laboratories; tubes, containers & bottles for specimen collection, transport & storage, embedding cassettes & accessories for pathology laboratories, cryogenic tubes & storage boxes, etc.
Financial Information:
Type of Ownership: Private
Domestic Markets:
National
Foreign Activity:
Worldwide
Contact(s):
Andre Lafond, President
Ross Charette, Manager, Sales & Marketing
Patrick Auger, Manager, Sales

Les Produits Environnementaux Atlas
53, rue Cate
Sherbrooke, QC J1J 2N9
819-565-9688
Fax: 819-565-5204
atlas@qc.aira.com
Contact(s):
Attiave Toussaint

Les Publications du Québec
#500, 1000, route de l'Église
Québec, QC G1V 3V9
418-643-5150
Fax: 418-643-6177
800-463-2100
service.clientele@cspq.gouv.qc.ca
www.publicationsduquebec.gouv.qc.ca
Products/Services/Areas of Expertise: L'appellation ®Les Publications du Québec⁻ désigne la maison d'édition du gouvernement du Québec. Édite et commercialise une grande variété de produits des ministères et organismes gouvernementaux: livres grand public et spécialisés, cédéroms, produits Internet, etc. Les produits de nature juridique comme la Gazette officielle du Québec, les lois et les règlements, sont publiés par l'Éditeur officiel, qui exerce également ses activités sous la raison sociale ®Les Publications du Québec⁻

Levac Robichaud Leclerc Associates Ltd.
Levac Robichard Leclerc Associés ltée
Formerly: Neil A. Levac Engineering Ltd.
#1, 2884 Chamberland St.
Rockland, ON K4K 1M6
613-446-7777
Fax: 613-446-1427
nlevac@lrl.ca
www.lrl.ca
Firm Type: Engineering, Scientific/Technical Services
Founded: 1984
Staff: 20
Member of: Professional Engineers of Ontario; Association des Ingénieurs du Québec
Products/Services/Areas of Expertise: Multi-disciplinary engineering & project management firm
Financial Information:
Type of Ownership: Private
Domestic Markets:
Ontario, Québec
Contact(s):
Neil Levac, President
Christian Robichaud, Vice-President
Stéphane Leclerc, Treasurer
Canadian Branches:
Gatineau
465, boul. de la Gappe
Gatineau, QC J8T 0A2
819-243-3063

Hawkesbury
P.O. Box 414
#540, 1 Main St.
Hawkesbury, ON K6A 2S2
613-632-5105
Fax: 613-632-6618

Levelton Consultants Ltd.
Formerly: Levelton Engineering Ltd.
Also Known As: B.H. Levelton & Associates Inc.
#150, 12791 Clarke Pl.
Richmond, BC V6V 2H9
604-278-1411
Fax: 604-278-1042
info@levelton.com
www.levelton.com
Firm Type: Management Consulting, Engineering, Scientific/Technical Services
Founded: 1966
Staff: 240
Member of: Canadian Environment Industry Association
Products/Services/Areas of Expertise: Environmental engineering services: environmental impact assessment, regulatory approvals & permits; meteorology/climatology & air quality assessment; greenhouse gas management; emissions analysis & control technology evaluation; emission & ambient air quality testing & monitoring; indoor air quality & occupational hygiene; water quality & wastewater treatment; environmental planning & strategic studies; site assessment & remediation services; environmental & health risk assessment. Geotechnical engineering services: site development & ground improvement; building foundations; marine structures; hydrogeology; slope stability & terrain assessment; excavation, shoring & underpinning; transportation facilities; geotechnical testing & construction supervision; industrial facilities, including storage tanks, materials handling equipment & containment dykes. Building science services: LEED accredited energy efficiency consultation; construction; remediation; design; review & testing
Financial Information:
Type of Ownership: Private
Revenue Sources: 5% nationwide; 5% Provincial; 10% Municipals; 80% Private Contracts
Domestic Markets:
Alberta, British Columbia
Foreign Activity:
Asia, The Pacific Rim
Contact(s):
Neil A. Cumming, Exec. Vice-President
Canadian Branches:
Abbotsford
#110, 34077 Gladys Ave.
Abbotsford, BC V2S 2E8
604-855-0206
Fax: 604-853-1186
abbotsford@levelton.com
www.levelton.com

Calgary
#203, 6919 - 32nd Ave. NW
Calgary, AB T3B 0K6
403-247-1813
Fax: 403-247-1814
calgary@levelton.com
www.levelton.com

Courtenay
#8, 2663 Kilpatrick Ave.
Courtenay, BC V9N 7C8
250-334-9222
Fax: 250-334-3955
courtenay@levelton.com
www.levelton.com

Edmonton
12323 - 67th St.
Edmonton, AB T5B 1N1
780-438-0844
Fax: 780-435-1812
edmonton@levelton.com
www.levelton.com

Kelowna
#108, 3677 Hwy. 97N
Kelowna, BC V1X 5C3
250-491-9778
Fax: 250-491-9729

kelowna@levelton.com
www.levelton.com

Nanaimo
1935 Bollinger Rd.
Nanaimo, BC V9S 5W9
250-753-1077
Fax: 250-753-1203
nanaimo@levelton.com
www.levelton.com

Surrey
#301, 19292 - 60th Ave.
Surrey, BC V3S 3M2
604-533-2992
Fax: 604-533-0768
surrey@levelton.com
www.levelton.com

Victoria
760 Enterprise Cres.
Victoria, BC V8Z 6R4
250-475-1000
Fax: 250-475-2211
victoria@levelton.com
www.levelton.com

Leviton Canada
A member company of Leviton Manufacturing Co., Inc.
165, boul. Hymus
Pointe-Claire, QC H9R 1E9
514-954-1840
Fax: 514-954-1853
800-461-2001
infocanada@leviton.com
www.leviton.com
Firm Type: Distributing, Manufacturing
Founded: 1953
Quality Environmental Management System(s): 9000
Products/Services/Areas of Expertise: Electronic lighting controls; switches, receptacles, connectors; surge protectors; voice/data communication products; energy management products for commercial & residential use; electric vehicle supply equipment & support services
Financial Information:
Type of Ownership: Foreign-owned
Domestic Markets:
National
Contact(s):
Jean Belhumeur, President/COO
Canadian Branches:
Surrey
#2009, 7445 - 132 St.
Surrey, BC V3W 1J8
604-594-8415
Fax: 604-594-3365

Toronto
35 Oak St.
Toronto, ON M9N 1A1
416-443-9300

Levitt-Safety Limited
Levitt-Sécurité ltée
2872 Bristol Circle
Oakville, ON L6H 5T5
905-829-3299
Fax: 905-829-2919
888-453-8488
csr@levitt-safety.com
www.levitt-safety.com
Firm Type: Management Consulting, Distributing
Founded: 1935
Member of: NL Technologies; Gastec; supplyFORCE; HSE Integrated
Quality Environmental Management System(s): 9001:1994;
Products/Services/Areas of Expertise: Distributor of health & safety products & environmental monitoring equipment; EHS training & consultation; EHS instrument solutions; fire & life safety services; fire protection systems; safety prescription eyewear; EHS rentals
Financial Information:
Type of Ownership: Private
Revenue: Greater than $5 Million
Revenue Sources: 10% nationwide; 5% Provincial; 5% Municipals; 80% Private Contracts
Domestic Markets:
National

Contact(s):
Bruce Levitt, President/CEO
blevitt@levitt-safety.com

Canadian Branches:
Calgary
417 - 53rd Ave. SE, Bay 4
Calgary, AB T2H 2E7
403-252-2703
Fax: 403-252-2787

Dorval
659, av. Meloche
Dorval, QC H9P 2T1
514-636-9011
Fax: 514-636-0923

Edmonton
9241 - 48 St.
Edmonton, AB T6B 2R9
780-461-8088
Fax: 780-461-8371

Fort McMurray
#3D, 380 MacKenzie Blvd.
Fort McMurray, AB T9H 4C4
780-743-5032
Fax: 780-743-5034

Kitimat
312B Railway Ave.
Kitimat, BC V8C 2G2
250-632-7766
Fax: 250-632-7752

Moncton
20 Driscoll Cres.
Moncton, NB E1E 3R8
506-853-3810
Fax: 506-859-8297

Ottawa
#115 & 206, 21 Antares Ave.
Ottawa, ON K2E 7T8
613-225-9550
Fax: 613-723-5851

Port Coquitlam
#106, 1611 Broadway St.
Port Coquitlam, BC V3C 2M7
604-464-6332
Fax: 604-464-6055

Regina
644 Henderson Dr.
Regina, SK S4N 5X3
306-721-7455
Fax: 306-721-3323

Sarnia
#3, 396 McGregor Rd. South
Sarnia, ON N7T 7H5
519-336-8530
Fax: 519-336-0533

Sudbury
#4, 1040 Lorne St.
Sudbury, ON P3C 4R9
705-673-0547
Fax: 705-673-9960

Winnipeg
100 Plymouth St.
Winnipeg, MB R2X 2V7
204-633-7228
Fax: 204-633-1268

Yellowknife
c/o Safety North
15 Coronation Dr.
Yellowknife, NT X1A 2N5

International Branch(es):
Brisbane, Australia
c/o NLT Australia PTY Ltd.
22-26 Cessna Dr.
Caboolture, QLD Australi
61-7-5495-2944

Santiago, Chile
c/o NLT Chile Ltda
Espronceda 539, ¥u¤oa
Santiago Chile

56-2-343-0506

Levy's Machine Works Ltd.
3503 - 78th Ave. SE
Calgary, AB T2C 1J7
403-279-2010
Fax: 403-279-0701
levysmac@levysmachineworks.com
www.levysmachineworks.com
Firm Type: Manufacturing
Founded: 1980
Staff: 14
Products/Services/Areas of Expertise: Design & manufacture of custom-made laboratory equipment; repair & redesign of existing equipment; gas monitoring systems
Financial Information:
Type of Ownership: Private
Domestic Markets:
Alberta
Foreign Activity:
China, USA, Vietnam
Contact(s):
Darcy Downs, President
Peter Laity, Sales Manager

LEX Scientific Inc.
#204, 2 Québec St.
Guelph, ON N1H 2T3
519-824-7082
Fax: 519-824-5784
800-824-7082
mhoffbauer@lexscientific.com
www.lexscientific.com
Firm Type: Engineering, Scientific/Technical Services
Founded: 1987
Staff: 12
Products/Services/Areas of Expertise: Technical consulting & laboratory services for industrial hygiene, hazardous materials management & indoor air quality; environmental audits; hazardous materials management consulting; environmental monitoring for asbestos, formaldehyde, radon, dust, noise & VOCs; Forensic analysis & expert witness services
Recently Completed / Ongoing Projects: Industrial hygiene surveys; asbestos survey & hazards assessment; hazardous materials abatement monitoring of a hospital demolition; paper mill decommissioning
Financial Information:
Type of Ownership: Private
Revenue: $500,000 - $1.5 Million
Revenue Sources: 5% Provincial; 5% Municipals; 90% Private Contracts
Domestic Markets:
Ontario
Foreign Activity:
Western Europe, USA
Markets Sought:
Western Europe, USA
Contact(s):
Michael Hoffbauer, Director

Lexcan Industrial Supply Ltd.
52 Bramwin Crt.
Brampton, ON L6T 5G2
905-792-8300
Fax: 905-792-8305
877-792-8308
info@lexcan.com
www.lexcan.com
Firm Type: Distributing, Manufacturing
Founded: 1968
Products/Services/Areas of Expertise: Geomembranes, oil- & chemical-resistant membranes for reservoir, lagoon or tank containment of water, chemicals, wastes; geosynthetic reinforcement membranes for soil stabilization & erosion control
Domestic Markets:
National
Foreign Activity:
Western Europe
Contact(s):
Don Moore, Manager, Containment Systems

Lexmark Canada Inc.
50 Leek Cres.
Richmond Hill, ON L4B 4J3
905-763-5427
Fax: 905-763-0581
800-539-6275
www.lexmark.com/canada
Products/Services/Areas of Expertise: Ecologo certified office products
Ecological Note: Printers
Domestic Markets:
National
Foreign Activity:
Worldwide
Contact(s):
Tracey Doherty, Contact, 905-763-5471
tdoherty@lexmark.com

Canadian Branches:
Brossard
A - 9975 avenue de Catania
Brossard, QC J4Z 3V6

Calgary
Mission Centre
#300, 2303 - 4th St. SW
Calgary, AB T2S 2S7

Edmonton
#210, 12220 Stony Plain Rd.
Edmonton, AB T5N 3Y4

Ottawa
#500, 1900 City Park Dr.
Ottawa, ON K1J 1A3

Sainte-Foy
#332, 2750, rue Einstein
Sainte-Foy, QC G1P 4R1

Vancouver
#315, 1681 Chestnut St.
Vancouver, BC V6J 4M6

LGL Limited Environmental Research Associates
P.O. Box 280
22 Fisher St.
King City, ON L7B 1A6
905-833-1244
kingcity@lgl.com
www.lgl.com
Firm Type: Management Consulting
Founded: 1971
Staff: 80
Products/Services/Areas of Expertise: Ecological research & environmental consulting; marine, wildlife, fisheries, botanical, agricultural, wetland & forestry consulting; environmental impact assessment & planning; mapping/GIS
Financial Information:
Type of Ownership: Private
Domestic Markets:
National
Foreign Activity:
Worldwide
Contact(s):
Rolph A. Davis, Chair
W. John Richardson, Exec. Vice-President
William Cross, Vice-President
Denis Thomson, Vice-President
Liz Speller, Environmental Planner

Canadian Branches:
Burlington
3365 Harvester Rd., Ground Level
Burlington, ON L7N 3N2
905-333-1667
burlington@lgl.com
Brad Bricker, Sr. Environmental Scientist

Cochrane
21 Gleneagles Terrace
Cochrane, AB T4C 1W4
403-932-1918

Nanaimo
2459 Holyrood Dr.
Nanaimo, BC V9S 4K7
250-758-1264
Fax: 250-758-1298
mgaboury@lgl.com
Marc Gaboury, Fisheries Biologist/Restoration Ecol

Sidney
9768 Second St.
Sidney, BC V8L 3Y8

Products & Services Buyer's Guide

250-656-0127
Fax: 250-655-4761
dbaker@lgl.com
Malcolm Foy, Sr. Environmental Scientist

St. John's
Atlantic Region
P.O. Box 13248 A
388 Kenmount Rd.
St. John's, NL A1B 4A5
709-754-1992
Fax: 709-754-7718
rbuchanan@lgl.com
Robert Buchanan, Vice-President

Whitehorse
P.O. Box 33011
Whitehorse, YT Y1A 5Y5
867-393-2330
Fax: 867-393-2331
nmaclean@lgl.com
Norm MacLean, Wildlife Ecologist

International Branch(es):
Anchorage
1101 East 76th Ave.
Anchorage, AL USA
907-562-3339
Fax: 907-562-7223
alaska@lgl.com

Bryan
1410 Cavitt St.
Bryan, TX USA
979-775-2000
Fax: 979-775-2002
cole@lgl.com

Ellensburg
76 Packwood Lane
Ellensburg, WA USA
509-962-8294
bnass@lgl.com

LH - Division of Full Circle Organics Inc.
RR#1
Walton, ON N0K 1Z0
519-887-9378
Fax: 519-887-9011
800-265-9682
Firm Type: Manufacturing, Scientific/Technical Services, Waste Management
Founded: 1979
Staff: 12
Member of: Canadian Composting Council
Products/Services/Areas of Expertise: Large-scale high rate aerobic in-vessel composting systems; facility design assistance; project management; mechanical components
Domestic Markets:
National
Foreign Activity:
USA
Markets Sought:
Australia/New Zealand, The Pacific Rim
Contact(s):
Chris Lee, President
clee@huron.net

Life Rhythm Corporation
#22, 772 Upper Paradise Rd.
Hamilton, ON L9C 2P5
905-575-8695
Fax: 905-383-7770
liferhythmcorp@sympatico.ca
Firm Type: Manufacturing

Products/Services/Areas of Expertise: Manufacture & design recycled cotton/polar fleece apparel
Financial Information:
Type of Ownership: Private
Revenue: $100,000 - $250,000
Revenue Sources: 50% Provincial; 50% Private Contracts
Domestic Markets:
National, Alberta, British Columbia, Manitoba, Nova Scotia, Ontario, Prince Edward Island
Foreign Activity:
Australia/New Zealand, USA, Worldwide

Markets Sought:
Central Europe, Eastern Europe, Western Europe, The Pacific Rim
Contact(s):
J. Morrissey, Manager, Sales & Marketing

Light Solar Wind Manufacturing / LSWM
#3, 461 North Service Rd. West
Oakville, ON L6M 2V5
905-847-8190
bmboyd@cogeco.ca
Firm Type: Distributing
Staff: 4
Products/Services/Areas of Expertise: Provides energy producing equipment for off-grid and grid-tied applications
Financial Information:
Type of Ownership: Private
Revenue Sources: 100% Private Contracts
Domestic Markets:
New Brunswick, Newfoundland & Labrador, Nova Scotia, Ontario
Foreign Activity:
Caribbean, Central America, Central Europe, South America, USA
Contact(s):
Barry Boyd, Marketing
John Sutwin, Sales
Shirley Porter, Accounting

Lindsay Iron & Metal Inc.
4 Needham St.
Lindsay, ON K9V 1L6
705-328-0904
Firm Type: Waste Management
Founded: 1985
Staff: 4
Products/Services/Areas of Expertise: Purchase & sale of scrap metal
Financial Information:
Type of Ownership: Private
Revenue Sources: 100% Private Contracts
Domestic Markets:
Ontario
Contact(s):
Heather Coutu
Aurel Coutu, Owner/Manager

Lineman's Testing Laboratories of Canada Limited
41 Rivalda Rd.
Toronto, ON M9M 2M4
416-742-6911
Fax: 416-748-0290
800-299-9769
main@ltl.ca
www.ltl.ca
Firm Type: Management Consulting
Founded: 1958
Staff: 40
Products/Services/Areas of Expertise: Provides electrical services, specializing in industrial & utility markets in Canada & internationally

Canadian Branches:
Western Canada Distribution & Sales
5825 - 97th St. NW
Edmonton, AB T6E 3J2
780-434-4911
Fax: 780-434-9911
1-800-530-8640
mainab@ltl.ca
Peter D'Sa, Territory Sales Manager

Link-Pipe Inc.
#2, 27 West Beaver Creek Rd.
Richmond Hill, ON L4B 1M8
905-886-0335
Fax: 905-886-7323
800-265-5696
info@linkpipe.com
www.linkpipe.com
Firm Type: Manufacturing
Founded: 1980
Staff: 10
Member of: National Association of Sewer Service Companies; North American Society of Trenchless Technology
Quality Environmental Management System(s): 9001:2001
Products/Services/Areas of Expertise: Stainless steel sleeves for underground pipe repair without excavation

Financial Information:
Type of Ownership: Private
Revenue: $1.5 Million - $3 Million
Revenue Sources: 100% Private Contracts
Domestic Markets:
Alberta, Manitoba, Ontario, Québec, Saskatchewan
Foreign Activity:
China, Western Europe, The Middle East, The Pacific Rim, USA, Vietnam,
Contact(s):
Lembit Maimets, President
Helena Lam, Administrator
Olev Maimets, Sales Engineer

LINPAC Ropak Packaging
A member company of the LINPAC Group
Formerly: Ropak Canada Inc. 2240 Wyecroft Rd.
Oakville, ON L6L 6M1
905-827-9340
Fax: 905-827-8841
info@ropakcorp.com
www.ropakcorp.com
Products/Services/Areas of Expertise: Manufacturer of recyclable/reusable rigid plastic shipping containers, used for packaging consumer, industrial, regulated, food & various non-food products. LINPACK Ropak has locations across N. America, with headquarters in Fountain Valley, California
Domestic Markets:
National
Contact(s):
Mark Gibson, Plant Manager
Fred Gerber, Manager, Divisional Sales
Contact(s):
Jack Smith, Plant Manager
Contact(s):
Donna Ramsay, Associate

Canadian Branches:
Northeast
29 Memorial Cres.
Springhill, NS B0M 1X0
902-597-3787
Fax: 902-597-8318

Northwest
5850 - 272nd St.
Langley, BC V4W 3Z1
604-857-1177
Fax: 604-857-7743

Linpro Petroleum Services Ltd.
2350 Kings Rd.
Sydney, NS B1L 1C1
902-562-2433
linpro@syd.eastlink.ca
www.linpro.ns.ca
Firm Type: Scientific/Technical Services
Founded: 1990
Staff: 10
Products/Services/Areas of Expertise: Removal & disposal as well as installation of above ground & underground tanks; installation & maintenance of equipment relating to the petroleum industry; assemble, install & maintain remediation equipment as well as perform total environmental cleanups
Financial Information:
Type of Ownership: Private
Revenue: $1.5 Million - $3 Million
Revenue Sources: 15% nationwide; 5% Municipals; 80% Private Contracts
Contact(s):
Kevin Everett, Contact

Liqui-Box Canada Inc.
Formerly: Enhance Packaging Technologies
201 Blair St. South
Whitby, ON L1N 5S6
905-668-5811
Fax: 905-666-7005
Products/Services/Areas of Expertise: Liquid packaging systems: form/fill/seal equipment, pumping / metering equipment, downstream packaging & handling equipment, recycling experience & films from for specific needs; technical assistance & support
Ecological Note: Liquid packaging systems
Contact(s):
Harry Akamphuber, Manager, National Sales & Service
harry.k.akamphuber@can.dupont.com

Lister Industries Ltd.
7410 - 68 Ave.
Edmonton, AB T6B 0A1
780-468-2040
Fax: 780-468-3337
info@listerindustries.com
www.listerindustries.com
Firm Type: Manufacturing
Founded: 1968
Staff: 60
Products/Services/Areas of Expertise: Rig matts of wood & steel used as temporary bridges; road mats of wood interlocked to form roadways across swamps & muskeg with a minimum of disturbance to the surrounding topography; large snow melters used for cleaning up oilspills; access matts
Financial Information:
Type of Ownership: Private
Domestic Markets:
Alberta, British Columbia, Manitoba, Northwest Territories, Saskatchewan
Foreign Activity:
Africa, Asia, Eastern Europe, The Middle East, The Pacific Rim, South America, USA
Contact(s):
Peter Ellmann, President

Living Resources Inc.
85 Hillview Dr.
Baden, ON N0B 1G0
519-634-9718
Firm Type: Distributing
Founded: 1978
Staff: 4
Products/Services/Areas of Expertise: Food processing (milling, dehydration, kneading); bread machines; juicers; air & water purification
Domestic Markets:
New Brunswick, Newfoundland & Labrador, Nova Scotia, Northwest Territories, Prince Edward Island, Québec
Foreign Activity:
USA
Contact(s):
Sandra Roth, President

LJM Environmental Consulting
P.O. Box 418
Wolfville, NS B0P 1X0
902-542-7970
Fax: 902-542-7315
lisa.mitchell@ljmenvironmental.ca
www.ljmenvironmental.ca
Firm Type: Management Consulting
Founded: 1995
Member of: Nova Scotia Barristers' Society; Nova Scotia Environmental Industries Association
Products/Services/Areas of Expertise: Environmental & agricultural management consulting; environmental & agricultural law
Recently Completed / Ongoing Projects: Training of loans officers on enviro-legal issues; development of guidebook on federal environmental legislation; advice to farmers on environmental & land use law
Financial Information:
Type of Ownership: Private
Revenue: $50,000 - $100,000
Revenue Sources: 35% nationwide; 40% Provincial; 25% Private Contracts
Domestic Markets:
Alberta, British Columbia, Manitoba, New Brunswick, Newfoundland & Labrador, Nova Scotia, Ontario, Prince Edward Island, Saskatchewan
Contact(s):
Lisa Mitchell, President

LOB Blasting Mat
P.O. Box 1859
RR#1
Sturgeon Falls, ON P0H 2G0
705-753-1588
Products/Services/Areas of Expertise: Manufacturing of used tires into blasting mats

Lockerbie & Hole Contracting Ltd.
A member of the AECON group of companies
14940 - 121A Ave.
Edmonton, AB T5V 1A3
780-452-1250
Fax: 780-452-1284
800-417-2329
mail@lockerbiehole.com
www.lockerbiehole.com
Firm Type: Management Consulting, Engineering
Founded: 1898
Products/Services/Areas of Expertise: Construction services to the commercial, municipal & institutional sectors, with a focus on LEED certified construction; green building projects & complete mechanical services
Financial Information:
Type of Ownership: Publicly Traded
Domestic Markets:
National
Foreign Activity:
USA
Contact(s):
Gordon Panas, President/CEO
Contact(s):
Philip Ward, President/COO
pward@lockerbiehole.com

Canadian Branches:
Calgary
7335 Flint Rd. SE
Calgary, AB T2H 1G3
403-571-2121
Fax: 403-253-5725
Products/Services/Areas of Expertise: This location also houses Lockerbie Stanley Inc.
Bill Clark, Vice-President

New Westminster
401 Salter St.
New Westminster, BC V3M 5Y1
604-777-5950
Fax: 604-777-5945
800-473-6491
Mike Zaine, Vice-President/Regional Manager

Saskatoon
3710 Millar Ave.
Saskatoon, SK S7P 0B1
306-382-6166
Fax: 306-382-2306
Scott Baliski, Sr. Project Manager

Victoria
P.O. Box 48001
3575 Douglas St.
Victoria, BC V8Z 3L0
250-370-2999
Fax: 250-370-5944
Dave Villeneuve, Branch Manager

Brantford - Lockerbie & Hole Eastern Inc.
P.O. Box 875
451 Elgin St.
Brantford, ON N3S 7P5
519-751-8000
Fax: 519-751-9108
800-669-2083

Loewen Welding & Manufacturing Ltd.
P.O. Box 66
33655 Harris Rd.
Matsqui, BC V4X 3R2
604-826-7844
Fax: 604-826-6051
info@loewenwelding.com
www.loewenwelding.com
Firm Type: Manufacturing
Founded: 1969
Staff: 40
Products/Services/Areas of Expertise: Sewage treatment equipment; feed mixers & manure spreaders; industrial self-loading vacuum units; compost handling & turning equipment
Recently Completed / Ongoing Projects: Design & manufacture of compost handling equipment & in-vessel compost turner, Pac-Bio, Oyster River, BC; design & manufacture self-loading tanks, Alberta Oil Fields
Financial Information:
Type of Ownership: Private
Revenue: Greater than $5 Million
Domestic Markets:
Alberta, British Columbia, Manitoba, Saskatchewan
Foreign Activity:
Western Europe, The Middle East, USA
Contact(s):
Ernie Loewen, President
Wayne Raiche, General Manager

Logan Geotech Inc.
P.O. Box 188
Stewiacke, NS B0N 2J0
902-639-2343
Fax: 902-639-9010
800-565-2311
lgi@istar.ca
Firm Type: Engineering
Staff: 20
Products/Services/Areas of Expertise: Supply & operation of auger drills for soil & bedrock sampling
Contact(s):
Gerald Wright, Manager
Fred Logan, Operations

Logiball Inc.
Formerly: American Logiball; Reno Inc.
440, rue Papin
Québec, QC G1P 3T9
418-656-9767
Fax: 418-653-5746
800-246-5988
logiball@logiball.com
www.logiball.com
Firm Type: Manufacturing
Staff: 9
Products/Services/Areas of Expertise: Inflatable pipe plugs (Logiball); test & seal packers, carrier plug F8r spot repair; equipment for sewer lines & low pressure pipes
Financial Information:
Type of Ownership: Private
Revenue Sources: 5% Municipals; 95% Private Contracts
Domestic Markets:
Alberta, British Columbia, Manitoba, New Brunswick, Ontario, Québec
Foreign Activity:
Asia, Australia/New Zealand, Western Europe, USA
Contact(s):
Marc André Anctil, President
Guy Richard, Sales
Nadia Julien, Office Manager

Lojen Industrial Cleaning Ltd.
7140 - 67 St.
Edmonton, AB T6B 3A6
780-466-8151
Fax: 780-465-6032
Contact(s):
Patrick McKeever, President

Long Environmental Consultants
43 Forest Park Rd.
Orangeville, ON L9W 1A1
519-941-3540
Fax: 519-941-8575
Firm Type: Engineering, Scientific/Technical Services
Founded: 1993
Staff: 4
Products/Services/Areas of Expertise: Site audit & evaluation; land development consulting; site plans; environmental management & monitoring & permitting
Recently Completed / Ongoing Projects: Environmental Monitoring Network; subdivision development; gravel pit site planning; quarry management plans & resource evaluation
Financial Information:
Type of Ownership: Private
Revenue Sources: 10% nationwide; 5% Provincial; 5% Municipals; 80% Private Contracts
Domestic Markets:
Ontario
Contact(s):
R.J. Long, P.Eng., President
D.M. Beattie, Senior Environmental Engineer
D.A. Walmsley, Senior Environmental Planner
Todd Laws, CADD/Tech
Jeffrey Rollings, Planning Tech

Longwood Forestry Services Ltd. / LFS
P.O. Box 129
Lindsay Hill Rd.
Trout Creek, ON P0H 2L0

705-723-1108
longwood@vianet.on.ca
Firm Type: Engineering, Scientific/Technical Services
Staff: 5
Products/Services/Areas of Expertise: Forestry & reforestation, mapping, field sampling & monitoring, stand tending, forest surveys & GPS
Domestic Markets:
Ontario
Contact(s):
Steven Mallory, President
Andy Straughan, Vice-President

Loomers Pumping Services Ltd.
14976 Hwy. 1 Wilmot
Kingston, NS B0P 1R0
902-765-2774
Fax: 902-765-0144
loomers@ns.sympatico.ca
Products/Services/Areas of Expertise: Collection of waste oil & filters, pumping of septic tanks, rental of portable toilets
Contact(s):
Garnet Loomer, Contact

Loraday Environmental Products Ltd.
#1, 142 Commerce Park Dr.
Barrie, ON L4N 8W8
705-733-3342
Fax: 705-733-3352
888-853-6600
info@loraday.com
www.loraday.com
Firm Type: Distributing, Manufacturing
Founded: 1994
Products/Services/Areas of Expertise: Absorbents; spill control; spill containment
Financial Information:
Type of Ownership: Private
Domestic Markets:
National
Contact(s):
Peter R. Lorimer, President

Lord & Partners Ltd.
#9, 741 Muskoka Rd. #3 North
Huntsville, ON P1H 2L3
705-788-1966
Fax: 705-788-1969
877-490-6660
info@lordandpartners.com
www.lordandpartners.com
Firm Type: Manufacturing
Founded: 1991
Staff: 15
Quality Environmental Management System(s): 14001
EcoLogo Certified Products & Services: B.K.1 - Brake Parts Cleaner; BRAD G.P.S.; BRAD G.P.S. Heavy Duty; L.P.101 Engine Degreaser & Shampoo; L.P. Gelsol Natural Degreaser; L.P. Parts W.Sol.; Marble Clean 91; Power Wash - Pressure Wash; Skone Bilge Cleaner & Degreaser; Super Green - All Purpos
Products/Services/Areas of Expertise: Environmentally responsible cleaners & degreasers, non-toxic, biodegradable, naturally derived solvents; pollution prevention services
Ecological Note: B.K.1 - Brake Parts Cleaner; BRAD G.P.S.; BRAD G.P.S. Heavy Duty; L.P.101 Engine Degreaser & Shampoo; L.P. Gelsol Natural Degreaser; L.P. Parts W.Sol.; Marble Clean 91; Power Wash - Pressure Wash; Skone Bilge Cleaner & Degreaser; Super Green - All Purpos
Financial Information:
Type of Ownership: Private
Domestic Markets:
Alberta, Manitoba, New Brunswick, Newfoundland & Labrador, Nova Scotia, Northwest Territories, Ontario, Québec
Foreign Activity:
China, USA, Vietnam
Markets Sought:
Asia, Eastern Europe, Western Europe
Contact(s):
Barry Young, President & CEO
Alison Phillips, Environmental Management Representative

Lotek Wireless Inc.
Formerly: Lotek Engineering Inc.
115 Pony Dr.
Newmarket, ON L3Y 7B5
905-836-6680
Fax: 905-836-6455
biotelemetry@lotek.com
www.lotek.com
Firm Type: Manufacturing, Scientific/Technical Services
Founded: 1984
Staff: 120
Products/Services/Areas of Expertise: Designer & manufacturer of fish & wildlife monitoring systems
Domestic Markets:
National
Foreign Activity:
Asia, Australia/New Zealand, South America, USA
Contact(s):
Jim Lotimer, President
Canadian Branches:
St John's Branch
114 Cabot St.
St. John's, NL A1C 1Z8
709-726-3899
Fax: 709-726-5324

Lotowater Technical Services Inc. / LTS
P.O. Box 451
Paris, ON N3L 3T5
519-442-2086
Fax: 519-442-7242
800-923-6923
info@lotowater.com
www.lotowater.com
Firm Type: Engineering
Founded: 1989
Member of: Professional Geoscientists; Professional Engineers of Ontario
Products/Services/Areas of Expertise: Technical services, well contractors; hydrogeological consulting; geophysical logging & video
Financial Information:
Type of Ownership: Private
Revenue: $3 Million - $5 Million
Revenue Sources: 90% Municipals; 10% Private Contracts
Domestic Markets:
Ontario
Contact(s):
Bill Beaton, M.Sc., P. Eng., President

Lovell & Associates
14285 Zone Centre Line
Bothwell, ON N0P 1C0
519-695-2475
Fax: 519-695-2560
admin@lovellassoc.com
www.lovellassoc.com

LTS Sales Ltd.
6592 Davand Dr.
Mississauga, ON L5T 2M3
905-670-2131
Fax: 905-670-8542
Firm Type: Distributing, Engineering, Manufacturing
Staff: 55
Products/Services/Areas of Expertise: Fluid systems; waste treatment, filtration, monitors, spill protection for petro-chemical & propane industries; hydrocarbon vapour collection absorption/adsorption systems
Domestic Markets:
National
Foreign Activity:
The Pacific Rim, USA
Contact(s):
Bill Jones, President/CEO
Wendy Jones, Vice-President
Dick Snider, Engineer
Canadian Branches:
Alberta
7610 - 5 St. SE, #B
Calgary, AB T2H 2L9
403-287-6023
Fax: 403-287-6025
Carl Kedzierski, Manager

British Columbia
8516 Baxter Pl.
Burnaby, BC V5A 4T8
604-944-9733
Fax: 604-944-9718

Tom Scupham, Manager

Manitoba
#2, 765 Marion St.
Winnipeg, MB R2J 0K6
204-231-1938
Fax: 204-231-1816
Mike Wakaluk, Manager

New Brunswick
45 Samantha St., Unit #1, Bldg.#15
Fredericton, NB E3A 6V1
506-458-8603
Fax: 506-458-2849

Newfoundland
Donavan's Industrial Park
51 Sagona Ave.
Mount Pearl, NL A1N 4P9
709-364-9222
Fax: 709-364-1327

Nova Scotia
71 Simmond's Dr.
Dartmouth, NS B3B 1N7
902-468-2480
Fax: 902-468-5704

Ontario
6592 Davand Dr.
Mississauga, ON L5T 2M3
905-564-1817
Fax: 905-564-7097
Bill Maser, Manager

Québec
8010, rue Jarry est
Anjou, QC H1J 1H5
514-355-7430
Fax: 514-355-7497
Walter Baron, Manager

Lubrication Engineers of Canada Ltd.
2200 Bristol Circle
Oakville, ON L6H 5R3
905-829-3833
Fax: 905-829-2630
800-465-8237
info@lubeng.com
www.lubeng.com
Firm Type: Distributing
Staff: 4
Quality Environmental Management System(s): 9002
Products/Services/Areas of Expertise: Reduction in operating temperatures & electricity consumption in aeration blowers, influent pumps, speed reducers & air compressors
Domestic Markets:
National
Contact(s):
N. Montgomery, President

Lucas-Milhaupt Toronto
Handy & Harman of Canada Ltd.
290 Carlingview Dr.
Toronto, ON M9W 5G1
416-675-1860
Fax: 416-675-1956
800-463-1465
www.lucasmilhaupt.com
Firm Type: Manufacturing
Founded: 1936
Staff: 30
Quality Environmental Management System(s): 9001
Products/Services/Areas of Expertise: Precious metals recovery & disposal of associated waste products; gold & silver alloys
Domestic Markets:
National
Foreign Activity:
Western Europe, USA
Contact(s):
Keith McTaggart, General Manager
kmctaggart@handyharmancanada.com

Lupien Rosenberg Consultants Inc.
4600, Côte-Vertu ouest
Montréal, QC H4S 1C7
514-333-5151
Fax: 514-333-4674

flampron@inspecsol.com
www.inspecsol.com
Firm Type: Engineering
Founded: 1976
Products/Services/Areas of Expertise: Environmental services include: environmental policies & procedures, environmental site assessments, environmental audits, soil/groundwater assessments, risk assessments, decommissioning, remediation planning, waste management; geotechnical services include: hydrogeological assessment, monitoring well installation, soil structure interaction, quality control & material testing
Domestic Markets:
Ontario, Québec
Foreign Activity:
South America
Markets Sought:
The Pacific Rim
Contact(s):
Salvatore Oppedisano, President
François Côté, Vice-President

LURA Consulting
Formerly: LURA Group
#601, 36 Hunter St. E
Hamilton, ON L8N 3W8
905-527-0754
Fax: 905-528-4179
800-267-9259
info@lura.ca
www.lura.ca
Firm Type: Scientific/Technical Services
Founded: 1974
Staff: 15
Products/Services/Areas of Expertise: Environmental planning & communications; educational & advertising campaigns for environmental programs/products/services; public consultation; workshop design & facilitation; consensus building; consulting services in waste management & 3Rs, resource management, water resources, training & education
Domestic Markets:
National
Foreign Activity:
Eastern Europe, Western Europe, USA
Contact(s):
Sally Leppard, President/CEO
sleppard@lura.ca
Liz Nield, Consultant, 416/644-1801Fax: 416/533-3453
lnield@lura.ca

LVM Inc.
A subsidiary of Dessau Group
#300, 1200, boul St-Martin ouest
Laval, QC H7S 2E4
514-281-1010
info@lvm.ca
www.dessau.com
Firm Type: Engineering, Scientific/Technical Services
Founded: 2008
Staff: 1200
Member of: National Ground Water Association; Association professionelle des géologues & géophysiciens du Québec
Quality Environmental Management System(s): 9001
Products/Services/Areas of Expertise: Environmental site assessment; site remediation; hydrogeology; toxicological & ecotoxicological risk analysis; asbestos management
Financial Information:
Type of Ownership: Private
Domestic Markets:
Ontario, Québec
Foreign Activity:
Africa, Caribbean, South America
Contact(s):
Jacques Gauthier, President & CEO
Guy Meunier, Senior VP & COO

Canadian Branches:
Boucherville
#100, 85, rue J.-A.-Bombardier
Boucherville, QC J4B 8P1
450-641-1740
Fax: 450-449-0235
boucherville@lvm.ca

Brantford
#3, 440 Hardy Rd.
Brantford, ON N3T 5L8
519-720-0078
Fax: 519-720-0976
brantford@lvm.ca

Chicoutimi
#101, 245, rue Riverin
Chicoutimi, QC G7H 4R6
418-615-0411
Fax: 418-615-0417
chicoutimi@lvm.ca

Dorval
#102, 415, av Bourke
Dorval, QC H9S 3W9
514-636-9292
Fax: 514-631-0910
dorval@lvm.ca

Drummondville
1430, boul Lemire
Drummondville, QC J2C 5A4
819-475-6688
Fax: 819-475-6695
drummondville@lvm.ca

Gatineau
#100, 900, boul de la Carrière
Gatineau, QC J8Y 6T5
819-778-3143
Fax: 819-770-1373
gatineau@lvm.ca

Grande-Rivière
340, Grande-Allée ouest
Grande-Rivière, QC G0C 1V0
418-385-2144
Fax: 418-680-2438

Joliette
803, rue Richard
Joliette, QC J6E 2T9
450-755-3201
Fax: 450-755-3202
joliette@lvm.ca

Kingston
#127, 556 O'Connor Dr.
Kingston, ON K7P 1N3
613-507-4306
Fax: 613-389-1563
kingston@lvm.ca

Kitchener
353 Bridge St. East
Kitchener, ON N2K 2Y5
519-741-1313
Fax: 519-741-5422
kitchener@lvm.ca

La Baie
363, rue Joseph-Gagné sud
La Baie, QC G7B 3P6
418-544-6827
Fax: 418-544-1189
labaie@lvm.ca

London
Atkinson, Davies Inc.
#12, 60 Meg Dr.
London, ON N6E 3T6
519-685-6400
Fax: 519-685-0943
london@lvm.ca

Longueuil - Bériault
883, rue Bériault
Longueuil, QC J4G 1X7
514-281-5151
Fax: 450-670-3390
longueuil@lvm.ca

Longueuil - Roland-Therrien
#400, 375, boul Roland-Therrien
Longeuil, QC J4H 4A6
514-281-5151
Fax: 450-442-9996
longueuil@lvm.ca

Lévis
#400, 425, 3e av
Saint-Romuald, QC G6W 5M6
418-835-9889
Fax: 418-835-5851
levis@lvm.ca

Milton
Premier/Levaque Inc.
#212, 420 Bronte St. South
Milton, ON L9T 0H9
905-819-1600
Fax: 905-819-1800
milton@lvm.ca

Montréal - Anjou
8320, rue Pauline-Vanier
Anjou, QC H1J 3B5
514-355-3512
Fax: 514-355-0108
montreal@lvm.ca

Montréal - Beaver-Hall
#300, 1080, côte du Beaver-Hall
Montréal, QC H2Z 1S8
514-281-5151
Fax: 514-798-8790
montreal@lvm.ca

North Bay
Merlex
120 Progress Ct.
North Bay, ON P1B 8G4
705-476-2550
Fax: 705-476-8882
northbay@lvm.ca

Ottawa
#105, 2625 Queensview Dr.
Ottawa, ON K2B 8K2
613-226-9667
Fax: 613-226-7389
ottawa@lvm.ca

Québec - Espinay
325, rue de l'Espinay
Québec, QC G1L 2J2
418-647-1402
Fax: 418-648-9288
quebec@lvm.ca

Québec - Lebourgneuf
#250, 1260, boul Lebourgneuf
Québec, QC G2K 2G2
418-626-1688
Fax: 418-626-1661
quebec@lvm.ca

Rimouski
331, rue Rivard
Rimouski, QC G5L 7J6
418-723-1144
Fax: 418-722-4691
rimouski@lvm.ca

Rivière-du-Loup
7, rue St-Magloire
Rivière-du-Loup, QC G5R 3G8
418-867-2911
Fax: 418-867-1172
rdl@lvm.ca

Rouyn-Noranda
129, av Marcil-Baril
Rouyn-Noranda, QC J9X 7B9
819-762-5119
Fax: 819-762-6253
rouyn@lvm.ca

Saint-Félicien
999, boul Hammel
Saint-Félicien, QC G8K 1X8
418-679-1281
Fax: 418-679-2728
stfelicien@lvm.ca

Saint-Jean-sur-Richelieu
#204, 315, rue MacDonald
Saint-Jean-sur-Richelieu, QC J3B 8J3
514-281-5151
Fax: 450-359-7458
stjean@lvm.ca

Products & Services Buyer's Guide

Saint-Jérôme
#900, 16, boul J.-F.-Kennedy
Saint-Jérôme, QC J7Y 4B6
450-432-3436
Fax: 450-432-8598
stjerome@lvm.ca

Sainte-Thérèse
201, rue Blainville ouest
Sainte-Thérèse, QC J7E 1Y4
450-435-6159
Fax: 450-435-2407
stetherese@lvm.ca

Salaberry-de-Valleyfield
555, ch Larocque
Salaberry-de-Valleyfield, QC J6T 4C8
450-371-5226
Fax: 450-371-5227
valleyfield@lvm.ca

Sept-Iles
464, av Perreault
Sept-Iles, QC G4R 1K5
418-962-9878
Fax: 418-962-9363
septiles@lvm.ca

Shawinigan
2729, av Saint-Marc
Shawinigan, QC G9N 2K6
819-539-8900
Fax: 819-539-1834
shawinigan@lvm.ca

Sherbrooke
4222, boul Bourque
Sherbrooke, QC J1L 1W6
819-563-3372
Fax: 819-563-3326
sherbrooke@lvm.ca

Stratford
25 Market Pl.
Stratford, ON N5A 1A4
519-273-0101
Fax: 519-273-7188
stratford@lvm.ca

Thetford Mines
1699, boul Frontenac est
Thetford Mines, QC G6G 6P6
418-338-9277
Fax: 418-338-9112
thetford@lvm.ca

Toronto
#7, 1821 Albion Rd.
Toronto, ON M9W 5W8
416-213-1060
Fax: 416-213-1070
toronto@lvm.ca

Victoriaville
285, boul des Bois-Francs sud
Victoriaville, QC G6P 4T2
819-751-2220
Fax: 819-751-2228
victoriaville@lvm.ca

Windsor
1361 Ouellette Ave.
Windsor, ON N8X 1J6
519-946-0352
Fax: 519-741-5422
windsor@lvm.ca

Lynk Electric Ltd.
Also Known As: Lynk Automation
P.O. Box 1174
110 Reeves St.
Sydney, NS B1P 6J9
902-562-1132
Fax: 902-562-1699
lynkautomation@auracom.com
www.linkautomation.com
Products/Services/Areas of Expertise: Environmental IT products for monitoring, analysis & assessment; commercial, industrial & municipal markets
Contact(s):
Barry Kennedy, Vice-President

Lyreco Office Products
Formerly: Today's Business Products Ltd.
875 Middlefield Rd.
Toronto, ON M1V 4Z5
416-754-8485
Fax: 416-292-5308
800-668-9340
contact.canada@lyreco.com
www.lyreco.ca
Firm Type: Manufacturing
Staff: 170
Quality Environmental Management System(s): 9002
Products/Services/Areas of Expertise: Office supplies & furniture made from recovered materials
Domestic Markets:
National
Foreign Activity:
Worldwide
Contact(s):
Eric Bigeard, CEO

M&E Engineering Ltd.
#2002, 1700 Langstaff Rd.
Vaughan, ON L4K 3S3
416-250-7222
Fax: 905-761-9979
info@me-eng.com
www.me-eng.com
Firm Type: Engineering
Founded: 1994
Staff: 17
Products/Services/Areas of Expertise: Energy consulting engineers
Contact(s):
Ed Porasz, P.Eng.

M&L Testing Equipment (1995) Ltd.
31 Dundas St. East
Dundas, ON L9H 7H8
905-689-7327
Fax: 905-689-3978
800-263-9244
info@mltest.com
www.mltest.com
Firm Type: Distributing
Founded: 1960
Staff: 13
Products/Services/Areas of Expertise: Destructive & non-destructive testing equipment for soils, concrete, asphalt, steel & plastic
Contact(s):
Mike Mizener, President, Marketing & Sales
Jennifer Carter, General Manager

Canadian Branches:
Calgary Branch
4530 - 14 St. NE
Calgary, AB T2E 6T7
403-250-6765
Fax: 403-250-6803
1-800-663-4779
calgary@mltest.com; info@mltest.com
Murray Mitchell, Sales Manager

M+A Environmental Consultants
172 Hillcrest Ave.
Hamilton, ON L8P 2X4
905-529-0678
Fax: 905-529-9136
Firm Type: Management Consulting, Scientific/Technical Services
Founded: 1986
Member of: Canadian Environment Industry Association; Canadian Society of Environmental Biologists
Quality Environmental Management System(s): 14001
Products/Services/Areas of Expertise: Specialists in ISO 14000, environmental assessment & institutional strengthening; consulting to industry & all levels of government with experience across Canada & around the world; environmental management, impact assessment & management; auditing; stakeholder participation; sustainable development; marine sciences; ecotourism & training
Recently Completed / Ongoing Projects: ISO 14000 implementation in mining, manufacturing, forestry, pulp & paper, agricultural, municipal government sectors; impact assessments in Canada, India, China, Vietnam, Philippines; institutional strengthening in Indonesia & Trinidad & Tobago
Domestic Markets:
National
Foreign Activity:
Asia, Central America, The Middle East, USA,
Contact(s):
David R. McCallum, President

M.J. International Inc.
#17, 349 Bowes Rd.
Concord, ON L4K 1J3
905-731-8104
Fax: 905-731-8231

M.J. Labelle Co. Ltd.
P.O. Box 610
109 Hwy 11 West
Cochrane, ON P0L 1C0
705-272-4201
Fax: 705-272-6005
posmar@mjlabelle.com
www.mjlabelle.com
Firm Type: Waste Management
Founded: 1955
Staff: 120
Products/Services/Areas of Expertise: Land & water clean-up & disposal; clean-up of petroleum & hazardous chemicals spills; winter clean-up & roads/ice crossings to isolated areas
Recently Completed / Ongoing Projects: Ontario Northland Communications, fuel spill
Financial Information:
Type of Ownership: Private
Revenue Sources: 100% Private Contracts
Domestic Markets:
Ontario
Contact(s):
Marcel J. Labelle, President
Peter Osmar, Vice President
Darcy Labelle, Sales Manager

M.R. Gordon Consulting Inc.
513 Kenmarr Cres.
Burlington, ON L7L 4R6
905-333-5055
Fax: 905-632-4513
Products/Services/Areas of Expertise: Project management services
Contact(s):
Mike Gordon

M.S. Thompson & Associates Ltd.
1345 Rosemount Ave.
Cornwall, ON K6J 3E5
613-933-5602
Fax: 613-936-0335
mail@trg.ca
www.trg.ca
Firm Type: Engineering, Scientific/Technical Services
Founded: 1954
Staff: 75
Products/Services/Areas of Expertise: Engineering services: municipal, environmental, electrical, mechanical, chemical, structural, hydrogeological, architectural
Domestic Markets:
Ontario
Foreign Activity:
Caribbean
Contact(s):
Mark Smelko, President
Lyle Casselman, Environmental Auditor
Rick Eamon, Vice-President
Donald Branch, Vice-President

Canadian Branches:
Guelph
#1, 367 Woodlawn Rd. W
Guelph, ON N1H 7K9
519-827-1453
Fax: 519-827-1483

Kingston
#201, 780 Midpark Dr.
Kingston, ON K7M 7P6
613-634-7373
Fax: 613-634-3523

Ottawa
#300, 2197 Riverside Dr.
Ottawa, ON K1H 7X3

613-749-9685
Fax: 613-749-7918

M.S.D.A. Inc.
589, Saint-Jean-Baptiste
Terrebonne, QC J6W 4R2
514-492-8116
Fax: 514-471-6038
Contact(s):
Dumitrou Murgoi

Mabarex inc.
2021, rue Halpern
Montréal, QC H4S 1S3
514-334-6721
Fax: 514-332-1775
800-636-6721
mabarex@mabarex.com
www.mabarex.com
Firm Type: Distributing, Manufacturing
Founded: 1983
Products/Services/Areas of Expertise: Water, wastewater & sludge treatment equipment
Financial Information:
Type of Ownership: Private
Revenue: Greater than $5 Million
Domestic Markets:
National
Foreign Activity:
Worldwide
Contact(s):
Louis Barré, President
Hoang Van Hoi, Technical Manager
J.P. Raboud, Process Specialist

Mac Industrial Exhaust Shop
19487 - 94th Ave.
Langley, BC V4N 4E6
604-888-0575
Fax: 604-888-6314
macmuffler@telus.net
www.macmuffler.com
Firm Type: Manufacturing
Staff: 7
Products/Services/Areas of Expertise: Manufacturing & distributing exhaust products (mufflers, silencers, spark arrestors) for industrial equipment, marine, trucking & construction equipment
Recently Completed / Ongoing Projects: Design & development of critical grade mufflers for small gas & diesel engines
Financial Information:
Type of Ownership: Private
Domestic Markets:
Alberta, British Columbia, Ontario
Foreign Activity:
USA
Contact(s):
Neil Macaulay, President

MacAuley Group Ltd.
5800 Ambler Dr..
Mississauga, ON L4W 4J4
905-827-2690
Fax: 905-827-1949
Products/Services/Areas of Expertise: Engineering consulting services
Contact(s):
Kenneth M. MacAuley, President

Maccaferri Canada Ltd.
#B, 400 Collier Macmillan Dr.
Cambridge, ON N1R 7H7
519-623-9990
Fax: 519-623-1309
800-668-9396
hq@maccaferri-canada.com
www.maccaferri-northamerica.com
Firm Type: Distributing, Manufacturing
Member of: Canadian Manufacturing Association
Products/Services/Areas of Expertise: Complete solutions for soil erosion, drainage & slope stability: gabions & gabionmats, geogrids, green terramesh for slope stability, retaining walls, cellular confinement, erosion control blankets, geotextiles (woven/nonwoven), rockfall protection, road reinforcement, bioengineering & revegetation

Domestic Markets:
National
Contact(s):
Santino Tersigni, General Manager
stersigni@maccaferri-canada.com

Canadian Branches:
Nova Scotia Branch
#44, 201 Brownlow Ave.
Dartmouth, NS B3B 1J4
902-468-8615
Fax: 902-468-8617
bosmun@maccaferri-canada.com
Barry Osmun

Québec Branch
#202, 1060, Cure Labelle
Blainville, QC J7C 2M6
450-420-1845
Fax: 450-420-1847
cboisson@maccaferri-canada.com
Chantal Boisson

Vancouver Branch
#613, 736 Granville St.
Vancouver, BC V6Z 1G3
604-683-4824
Fax: 604-683-7089
bpeirone@maccaferri-canada.com
Barth Peirone

MacDonald & Fils Inc.
MacDonald & Sons
7995, 14e av
Montréal, QC H1Z 3M1
514-374-0450
Fax: 514-374-5687
800-363-7137
mac@macdonald-fils.ca
www.macdonald-fils.ca
Firm Type: Distributing, Manufacturing
Founded: 1966
Member of: Québec Water Well; Canadian Water Well; Ontario Water Well; Water Quality Association
Products/Services/Areas of Expertise: Potable water treatment & systems; sewage systems
Domestic Markets:
New Brunswick, Newfoundland & Labrador, Nova Scotia, Ontario, Prince Edward Island, Québec
Foreign Activity:
Asia, Central America, USA
Contact(s):
Francine MacDonald, President
Gordon Smith, Vice-President
Robert MacDonald, Vice-President
Melanie Guilbeault, Microbiologist

Canadian Branches:
Kingston
244 Dalton St.
Kingston, ON K7K 6G3
613-544-2024
Fax: 613-544-1375
1-800-578-3013
W.O. Lodge

St-Romuald
1114, boul de la Rive Sud
Saint-Romuald, QC G6W 5M6
418-839-2703
Fax: 418-839-5591
1-888-622-3328
D. Deschenes

MacDonald, Dettwiler & Associates Ltd. / MDA
13800 Commerce Pkwy.
Richmond, BC V6V 2J3
604-244-0400
Fax: 604-231-4938
888-780-6444
clientservices@mdacorporation.com
www.mdacorporation.com
Firm Type: Distributing, Engineering, Information Technology, Scientific/Technical Services
Founded: 1969
Staff: 3000
Products/Services/Areas of Expertise: The company is a leader in satellite information, & through its Geospatial Services operations provides data, information products & services from commercially available radar & optical satellites. The operation of Canada's RADARSAT-1 & RADARSAT-2 satellites is the responsibility of MDA & the exclusive distribution rights are held by the company. Expertise in the following areas is offered: ice monitoring & mapping, monitoring of illegal fishing & oil dumping, airport hazard mapping, urban land classification for commercial, residential & green space zones, marine oil exploration, maritime security monitoring, wetland mapping, natural resource monitoring & management, & terrain mapping & 3-D modeling
Financial Information:
Type of Ownership: Publicly Traded
Revenue: Greater than $5 Million
Domestic Markets:
National
Foreign Activity:
Asia, Central America, South America, USA
Contact(s):
Daniel E. Friedmann, President/CEO

Canadian Branches:
Ottawa
#201, 57 Auriga Dr.
Ottawa, ON K2E 8B2
613-727-1087
Fax: 613-727-5853
800-265-3894

International Branch(es):
Gatineau
75A, ch McClelland
Cantley, QC J8V 2Y8
819-827-3001
Fax: 819-827-1955

MacDonnell Group
Formerly: Vaughan Engineering
P.O. Box 2045 M
#1100, 1505 Barrington St.
Halifax, NS B3J 3K5
902-425-3980
Fax: 902-423-7593
inquiry@macdonnellgroup.com
www.macdonnellgroup.com
Firm Type: Management Consulting, Engineering
Founded: 1959
Products/Services/Areas of Expertise: Management consulting firm, specializing in engineering, security training, & cultural productions
Activities: Providing engineering services, such as corrosion free bridge decks & structural health monitoring; Offering infrastucture planning & design, in the areas of bridges, ports & marines, roads & streets, & municipal infrastructure; Providing risk management, training, & integrated maritime security services; Offering consulting services, in areas such as ports, harbours, & waterfront planning, tourism development projects, & adaptive re-use for built infrastructure
Recently Completed / Ongoing Projects: Mount Royal land development project management; Barrington Business Park site development study
Financial Information:
Type of Ownership: Private
Domestic Markets:
National
Foreign Activity:
Worldwide
Contact(s):
Vidya Limaye, Vice-President, Engineering & Innovation

Canadian Branches:
Toronto
#612, 23 Brant St.
Toronto, ON M5V 2L5
416-364-0865
inquiry@macdonnellgroup.com

International Branch(es):
Portland, Maine, USA
11 Katahdin Rd.
Portland, ME USA
207-799-3400
Fax: 207-799-3401
mirage@maine.rr.com

MacEwen Petroleum Inc.
P.O. Box 100
18 Adelaide St.
Maxville, ON K0C 1T0

613-527-2100
Fax: 613-527-2728
800-267-7175
inquiries@macewen.ca
www.macewen.ca
Products/Services/Areas of Expertise: Automotive products
Contact(s):
Darrell Mooney, Contact

Machine Knife Co.
Also Known As: Central Welding Company Limited
240 Beach Rd.
Hamilton, ON L8L 4B2
905-545-7277
Fax: 905-545-5450
machineknife@on.aibn.com
Firm Type: Manufacturing
Founded: 1942
Staff: 15
Member of: Canadian Association of Recycling Industries
Products/Services/Areas of Expertise: Knives for high-torque low speed shredders used to recycle paper, steel, copper & other precious metals
Contact(s):
Lyle Hoskin, General Manager

Machinerie Laurin Inc.
487, rue Principale
Laval, QC H7X 1C4
450-689-1962
Fax: 450-689-2527
admin@laurin-inc.com
www.laurin-inc.com
Contact(s):
Denis Laurin, President

MacLeod & Grant Ltd.
P.O. Box 809
106 MacKay St.
Stellarton, NS B0K 1S0
902-752-5532
Fax: 902-752-7778
www.macleodandgrant.com
Firm Type: Distributing
Staff: 8
Products/Services/Areas of Expertise: Commercial-industrial heating, domestic hot water & boiler room equipment
Domestic Markets:
New Brunswick, Newfoundland & Labrador, Nova Scotia, Northwest Territories
Contact(s):
Peter Grant, Office Manager

Canadian Branches:
Moncton Office
#213, 451 Paul St.
Moncton, NB E1A 6W8

MacMillan & Associates
46 Gorsebud Close
Halifax, NS B3S 1P6
902-443-6503
Fax: 902-443-6787
tom.macmillan@ns.sympatico.ca
Firm Type: Waste Management
Staff: 2
Products/Services/Areas of Expertise: Waste management services
Contact(s):
Tom MacMillan, Contact

MacPherson Brown Ltd.
8248 River Way
Delta, BC V4G 1C4
604-952-4644
Fax: 604-952-4645
tanks@macphersonbrown.com
www.macphersonbrown.com
Products/Services/Areas of Expertise: Manufacturer of tanks for farming, industrial & residential use; portable tanks; above ground tanks; used oil tanks

Macquarie Power & Infrastructure Income Fund
Formerly: Clean Power Operating Trust
Also Known As: Macquarie Power Management Ltd.
Canadian Pacific Tower, TD Centre
#2200, 100 Wellington St. W
Toronto, ON M5K 1J3
416-607-5009
Fax: 416-607-5073
mpt@macquarie.com
www.macquarie.com
Products/Services/Areas of Expertise: Provides stable, long-term cash flow to investors from the environmentally preferred generation of electricity. The Fund invests only in power generating assets that use renewable energy sources such as water, wind, wood waste & landfill gas. Clean Power is the first income fund to be certified under Canada's Environmental ChoiceM Program.
Ecological Note: Renewable electricity investment funds
Contact(s):
Peter Keskinen
Steven Probyn
sprobyn@probyngroup.com

Macrotek Inc.
Formerly: McCarthy Robinson Engineering Inc.
#4, 400 Bentley St.
Markham, ON L3R 8H6
905-415-1799
Fax: 905-415-1790
888-415-1799
macrob@macrotek.net
www.macrotek.net
Firm Type: Engineering, Manufacturing
Founded: 1930
Staff: 8
Member of: Air & Waste Management Association; Professional Engineers of Ontario
Products/Services/Areas of Expertise: Air & noise pollution control equipment: baghouses, mist eliminators, scrubbers, air filters, silencers; industrial filtration equipment for air, gases; energy conservation; fume scrubbing; dust collection
Recently Completed / Ongoing Projects: Dust collection system, limestone dust, odour scrubber & urea scrubber, ammonia scrubbing, limestone dusk collecter
Financial Information:
Type of Ownership: Private
Revenue: $3 Million - $5 Million
Revenue Sources: 100% Private Contracts
Domestic Markets:
Alberta, British Columbia, Manitoba, New Brunswick, Ontario, Québec, Saskatchewan
Foreign Activity:
Caribbean, Central America, China, South America, USA, Vietnam
Contact(s):
Thomas D. Payne, P.Eng., President
tpayne@macrotek .net

Maddocks Industrial Filter Division
Formerly: Industrial Filter Fabrics Ltd.
663 Woodward Ave.
Hamilton, ON L8H 6P3
905-549-9626
Fax: 905-547-7660
800-263-8660
sales@maddocksgroup.com
www.maddocksgroup.com
Firm Type: Distributing, Engineering, Manufacturing, Scientific/Technical Services
Founded: 1971
Staff: 43
Member of: Air & Waste Management Association; Canadian Institute of Mining & Metallurgy; American Foundrymens Society Inc.; Grain Elevators & Processors Society; Canadian Manufacturers Association
Products/Services/Areas of Expertise: Filter media, bags, cartridges & accessories for dust collection & liquid process systems; cages, venturis, clamps, filter bags, cartridge filters; complete line of filters for press, drum, vacuum & rotary disc filtration
Domestic Markets:
National
Foreign Activity:
USA

Magnetrol International Ltd.
#1 & 2, 145 Jardin Dr.
Concord, ON L4K 1X7
905-738-9600
Fax: 905-738-1306
info@magnetrol.com
www.magnetrol.com
Firm Type: Manufacturing
Founded: 1932
Products/Services/Areas of Expertise: Level & flow control instrumentation; overfill & spill protection
Financial Information:
Type of Ownership: Private
Domestic Markets:
National,

Magnor, Division of Magchem
1271, rue Ampère
Boucherville, QC J4B 5Z5
450-655-1711
Fax: 450-655-5428
800-571-1711
magnor@magnor.ca
www.magnor.ca
Firm Type: Manufacturing
Founded: 1965
Staff: 18
Member of: Association québécoise des techniques de l'eau; American Society of Plumbing Engineers
Products/Services/Areas of Expertise: De-aerating heaters; water softeners; dealkalinizers; demineralizers; pressure filters, anthracite, activated carbon, sand, garnet; chemical feed systems; proportioning pumps; control panels; centralized sample treatment & control station; glycol pressurization systems; cooling tower sediment filters; closed system filters; neutralization systems; reverse osmosis
Domestic Markets:
New Brunswick, Ontario, Québec
Contact(s):
Jacques Pichet, President
André Janelle, Vice-President, Marketing

Canadian Branches:
Burlington
#5, 1440 Graham's Lane
Burlington, ON L7S 1W3
905-681-6558
Fax: 905-668-5497

Burnaby
#263, 141 - 6200 McKay Ave.
Burnaby, BC V5H 4M9
604-616-1233

Magnum Industries Ltd.
190 Hodsman Rd.
Regina, SK S4N 5X4
306-721-2247
Fax: 306-721-3770
Firm Type: Distributing, Manufacturing
Founded: 1988
Staff: 15
Products/Services/Areas of Expertise: Manufacture & distribute landscaping & traffic control products made from tire regrind, recycled glass bottles, plastic, polyethylene
Financial Information:
Type of Ownership: Private
Domestic Markets:
National
Foreign Activity:
The Pacific Rim, USA
Contact(s):
Larry Hesterman, President
Harold Moen, Director

Magotteaux Ltée
P.O. Box 369
601, rue Champlain
Magog, QC J1X 3W9
819-843-0443
Fax: 819-843-7050
pascal.corbusier@magotteaux.com
www.magotteaux.com
Firm Type: Distributing
Founded: 1920
Staff: 135
Quality Environmental Management System(s): 9001; ISO
Products/Services/Areas of Expertise: Water & wastewater management equipment
Contact(s):
Pascal Corbusier

Mainetti Canada Inc.
8272, av 19
Montréal, QC H1Z 4J8

514-376-1876
Fax: 514-376-4296
sales@canada.mainetti.com
Ecological Note: Plastic garment hanger reuse & recovery systems
Contact(s):
Charles Smallhorn, President
John Le Piane, Sales Manager

Maitland Engineering
A Division of R.J. Burnside & Associates Ltd.
Formerly: Maitland Engineering Services Ltd. P.O. Box 10
449 Josephine St.
Wingham, ON N0G 2W0
519-357-1521
Fax: 519-357-3624
888-357-1521
wingham@rjburnside.com
Firm Type: Management Consulting, Engineering
Staff: 8
Member of: Professional Engineers of Ontario
Products/Services/Areas of Expertise: Engineering consulting services; feasibility/pre-feasibility studies; design & specifications engineering; construction, excavation & construction management
Financial Information:
Type of Ownership: Private
Domestic Markets:
Ontario
Contact(s):
Jeff Dickson, Branch Manager

Major Water Treatment Tech Ltd.
24 Leandre Rd.
Shediac Bridge, NB E4R 1M5
506-532-1024
Fax: 506-532-8184
Contact(s):
Rheal Poirer, President

MakLoc Buildings Inc.
Also Known As: Chemloc Buildings
706 - 17 Ave.
Nisku, AB T9E 7T1
780-955-2951
Fax: 780-955-7721
888-774-7792
admin@makloc.com
www.makloc.com
Firm Type: Manufacturing
Founded: 1971
Staff: 100
Products/Services/Areas of Expertise: Aboveground rigid frame storage buildings custom built; chemical storage facilities; paper recycling storage containers; custom built metal buildings for all purposes
Domestic Markets:
Alberta, British Columbia, Northwest Territories, Saskatchewan
Foreign Activity:
USA
Contact(s):
Enio Zanello, President & General Manager
Ken Ross, Sales Manager

Canadian Branches:
Calgary Office
235145 Wrangler Dr. SE
Rocky View, AB T1X 0K3
403-235-0438
Fax: 403-235-0913
makadmin@makloc.com
Larry Clisby, Manager

Malnar Industries Ltd.
Formerly: Johnson Bros. Manufacturing International
903 Marion St.
Winnipeg, MB R2J 0K7
204-237-4881
Fax: 204-233-6936
info@malnar.com
www.malnar.com
Firm Type: Manufacturing
Founded: 1971
Products/Services/Areas of Expertise: Manufacturer of industrial refrigeration equipment
Domestic Markets:
National

Foreign Activity:
The Middle East, South America, USA
Contact(s):
Don Edwards, President
Kelly Roe, Manager, Sales & Marketing

Malroz Engineering Inc.
308 Wellington St., 2nd Fl.
Kingston, ON K7K 7A8
613-548-3446
Fax: 613-548-7975
malroz@malroz.com
www.malroz.com
Firm Type: Engineering, Scientific/Technical Services
Founded: 1989
Staff: 10
Products/Services/Areas of Expertise: Hydrogeology studies; waste management consulting; environmental audits; environmental site assessments; leak/spill cleanup (soil & groundwater remediation); risk assessments; environmental impact studies
Financial Information:
Revenue Sources: 10% nationwide; 5% Provincial; 30% Municipals; 55% Private Contracts
Domestic Markets:
Ontario, Québec
Foreign Activity:
Central America, South America, Mexico, USA
Contact(s):
David Malcolm, P.Eng., President/CEO
Steven Rose, P.Eng., Director

Management Horizons
2779 Herald Rd.
Newmarket, ON L0G 1V0
905-853-4775
Fax: 905-853-5306
866-467-4446
info@mgmthorizons.com
www.mgmthorizons.com
Products/Services/Areas of Expertise: Environmental consulting & contracting services
Contact(s):
John Wolfe, CEO

Mancorp Industrial Sales Ltd.
Formerly: Manark Industrial Sales Ltd.
20186, 113B Ave.
Maple Ridge, BC V2X 0Y9
604-420-4332
Fax: 604-942-4950
800-595-2632
info@mancorp.ca
mancorp.ca
Firm Type: Distributing, Manufacturing
Founded: 1965
Staff: 19
Products/Services/Areas of Expertise: Hot & cold high pressure washers; wash water treatment & recycling systems; evaporation equipment; aqueous parts washers; bioremediation equipment
Domestic Markets:
Alberta, British Columbia, Manitoba, Northwest Territories, Saskatchewan, Yukon Territory
Contact(s):
F.G. Sheffer, President
K.G. Sheffer, Sales Manager
G.N. Sheffer, Operations Manager
Donna Proctor, Inside Sales
M. Hughes, Service Manager

Mandel Scientific Co. Inc.
2 Admiral Pl.
Guelph, ON N1G 4N4
519-763-9292
Fax: 519-763-2005
888-883-3636
info@mandel.ca
www.mandel.ca
Firm Type: Distributing
Founded: 1969
Staff: 90
Member of: Canadian Laboratory Suppliers Association; Canadian Council of Independent Laboratories
Products/Services/Areas of Expertise: Measuring & monitoring equipment

Domestic Markets:
National
Contact(s):
Barbara Humm, Vice-President, Operations, Marketing & Information Technology
Julie Mercure, Marketing Manager
jmercure@mandel.ca

Mansfield & Rodney Printing Ltd. / MRP
861 Boyd Ave.
Ottawa, ON K2A 2C9
613-232-2946
Fax: 613-232-0472
sales@mansfieldrodney.com
www.mansfieldrodney.com
Firm Type: Scientific/Technical Services
Founded: 1962
Staff: 8
EcoLogo Certified Products & Services: Lithographic printing services
Products/Services/Areas of Expertise: Printing/typesetting
Ecological Note: Lithographic printing services
Financial Information:
Type of Ownership: Private
Revenue: $500,000 - $1.5 Million
Domestic Markets:
National
Foreign Activity:
USA
Contact(s):
Steve Rodney, Contact

Maple Engineering & Construction Canada Ltd.
Also Known As: Maple Reinders Inc.
#600, 201 County Court Blvd.
Brampton, ON L6W 4L2
905-457-6444
Firm Type: Engineering, Scientific/Technical Services
Founded: 1967
Staff: 150
Products/Services/Areas of Expertise: Water & wastewater treatment facilities; project management; equipment & mechanical installations
Financial Information:
Type of Ownership: Private
Revenue: Greater than $5 Million
Revenue Sources: 20% nationwide; 40% Provincial; 20% Municipals; 20% Private Contracts
Domestic Markets:
National
Foreign Activity:
Western Europe
Contact(s):
M. Reinders, P.Eng., President
J. Haanstra, Vice-President

Maple Reinders Environmental Ltd. / MRE
Formerly: F.J. Reinders & Associates Canada Ltd.
2660 Argentia Rd.
Mississauga, ON L5N 5V4
905-821-4844
Fax: 905-821-4822
main@maple.ca
www.maple-reinders.com
Firm Type: Engineering
Founded: 1967
Staff: 6
Products/Services/Areas of Expertise: Environmental services, building rehabilitation
Financial Information:
Revenue Sources: 5% nationwide; 10% Provincial; 15% Municipals; 70% Private Contracts
Domestic Markets:
National
Contact(s):
F.J. Reinders, P.Eng., Chairman
Mike Reinders, P.Eng.; MBA, President

International Branch(es):
Pan American Reinders Inc.
#202, 1980 North Atlantic Ave.
Cocoa Beach, FL USA
407-784-9200
Fax: 407-799-1446

Products & Services Buyer's Guide

Mar Cor Purification / MCP
A company owned by Cantel Medical Corp.
Formerly: Biolab Equipment Canada Ltd.#6, 3250 Harvester Rd.
Burlington, ON L7N 3W9
905-639-7025
Fax: 905-639-0425
800-268-5035
info@mcpur.com
www.mcpur.com
Firm Type: Distributing, Manufacturing
Founded: 1969
Member of: Pure Water Confederation of America Filtration Engineering
Products/Services/Areas of Expertise: Water purification system design, including continuous deionization systems, reverse osmosis, ultra-filtration, water analysis, deionized water service exchange cylinders; selective sorbents in skid-mounted portable tanks for the removal of pollutants in wastewater
Domestic Markets:
National
Foreign Activity:
USA
Contact(s):
Darcy McCabe, Operations Manager
dmccabe@mcpur.com

Canadian Branches:
Montréal - Service Center
89, av Lindsay
Dorval, QC H9P 2S6
514-636-0032
Fax: 514-636-8429
1-800-268-0032

Maratek Environmental Inc.
#8-10, 60 Healey St.
Bolton, ON L7E 5A5
905-857-2738
Fax: 905-857-2764
800-667-6272
sales@maratek.com
www.maratek.com
Firm Type: Distributing, Scientific/Technical Services, Waste Management
Founded: 1975
Staff: 50
Products/Services/Areas of Expertise: Silver recovery; environmental product & equipment sales; photographic waste hauling & recycling, photo-chemical waste disposal, & consulting & service; pollution prevention technology development; manufacturing & marketing
Domestic Markets:
National
Contact(s):
Colin Darcel, P.Eng, President
cdarcel@maratek.com

Canadian Branches:
Alberta Office
1003 - 55th Ave. NE, Bay E
Calgary, AB T2E 6W1
403-730-8300
Fax: 403-730-8302

British Columbia Office
P.O. Box 50094
4623 Byrne Rd.
Burnaby, BC V5J 5G3
604-436-1333
Fax: 604-431-9847

Manitoba Office
605 Mercy St.
Selkirk, MB R1A 2B3
204-785-4580
Fax: 204-785-4856

Ontario Office - Kanata
53 Shetland Way
Kanata, ON K2M 1S4
613-599-6970

Ontario Office - Ottawa
P.O. Box 41066 Elmvale
#8, 65 Bentley Ave.
Ottawa, ON K1G 5K9
613-741-9442
Fax: 613-727-1949

Marbek Resource Consultants Ltd.
A subsidiary of ICF International Inc.
#300, 222 Somerset St. West
Ottawa, ON K2P 2G3
613-523-0784
Fax: 613-523-0717
info@marbek.ca
www.marbek.com
Firm Type: Scientific/Technical Services
Founded: 1983
Staff: 12
Member of: Association of Heating, Refrigerating & Conditioning Engineers; Association of Energy Services Professionals; Association of Energy Engineers; Canadian Environment Industry Association; Society for Environmental Toxicology & Chemistry
Products/Services/Areas of Expertise: Consulting services in the related fields of energy & environment: demandside management, energy efficiency, environmental management, environmental life cycle management, global warming & emissions mitigation; environmental impact assessment procedures & policies includes services such as economic, policy & technical analysis, program development, surveys & reviews, communications & stakeholder consultation, & strategic advice
Domestic Markets:
National
Foreign Activity:
Africa, Asia, Central America, The Pacific Rim, Mexico
Contact(s):
Paul Robillard, Principal/Treasurer
George Matheson, Principal
Martin Adelaar, Principal/Secretary
Stephen Hazell, General Counsel & Director of Environmental Assessment

Marbicon Inc.
P.O. Box 280
4287 Brooklyn St.
Berwick, NS B0P 1E0
902-538-7101
Fax: 902-538-8801
marbicon@eastlink.ca
www.marbicon.ca
Firm Type: Engineering, Scientific/Technical Services
Founded: 1984
Staff: 5
Member of: Environmental Assessment Association
Products/Services/Areas of Expertise: Pest management; forestry; parks, resource management; field sampling & monitoring; mapping; training & education; environmental impact assessment
Contact(s):
Jim Jotcham, President

Marcel Baril Ltée
Parc Industriel Noranda
101, av. Marcel-Baril
Rouyn-Noranda, QC J9X 5P5
819-764-3211
Fax: 819-764-9785
800-567-6440
mlb@marcelbaril.qc.ca; info@marcelbaril.qc.ca
marcelbaril.qc.ca
Firm Type: Distributing
Founded: 1955
Staff: 70
Products/Services/Areas of Expertise: Building, materials, plumbing supply, hardware, industrial, water works, HDPE Sclairpipe
Contact(s):
Guy Baril, Contact
Jean-Yves Baril, President
jy.baril@marcelbaril.qc.ca
Robert Baril, Vice-President
rbaril@marcelbaril.qc.ca

Canadian Branches:
Gatineau
780, boul. Greber
Gatineau, QC J8V 3P8
819-243-8903
Fax: 819-243-9809
1-800-567-6440

Mirabel
14130, Boul. Curé Labelle
Mirabel, QC J7J 1L6
450-971-6619
Fax: 450-971-5498

Marie Rousseau, ING
1517, rue Sauvé est
Montréal, QC H2C 2A6
514-304-7418
Contact(s):
Marie Rousseau

Maritime Auto Salvage
P.O. Box 201
Truro, NS B2N 5C1
902-662-2321
Fax: 902-662-4146
mas@maritimeauto.com
www.maritimeauto.com
Firm Type: Waste Management
Founded: 1932
Products/Services/Areas of Expertise: Steel & automotive recycling
Contact(s):
Ed MacDonald, President

Canadian Branches:
The Parts Place
Burnside Industrial Park
61 Raedall Ave.
Dartmouth, NS B3B 1L4
902-468-7179

Maritime Electric Company Ltd. / MECL
P.O. Box 1328
180 Kent St.
Charlottetown, PE C1A 7N2
902-629-3628
Fax: 902-629-3665
800-670-1012
kgriffin@maritimeelectric.com
www.maritimeelectric.com
Firm Type: Manufacturing
Staff: 175
EcoLogo Certified Products & Services: Wind power electricity
Products/Services/Areas of Expertise: Electricity generated by wind power & fossil fuel
Ecological Note: Wind power electricity
Domestic Markets:
Prince Edward Island
Contact(s):
Fred J. O'Brien, President/CEO
Kim Griffin, Manager, Corporate Communications & Public Affairs
John D. Gaudet, Vice-President, Corporate Planning & Energy Supply

Maritime Geothermal Ltd.
P.O. Box 2555
170 Plantation Rd.
Petitcodiac, NB E4Z 6H4
506-756-8135
Fax: 506-756-2988
info@nordicghp.com
www.nordicghp.com/mg
Firm Type: Manufacturing
Founded: 1979
Member of: Canadian Earth Energy Association
Products/Services/Areas of Expertise: Geothermal heat pumps (manufactured in 27 models); complete heat pump testing & rating facility; duct design & layout services; building heat loss calculations; system efficiency monitoring service; sales/installation training
Activities: Natural resource management research; environmentally safe renewable energy forms
Domestic Markets:
British Columbia, New Brunswick, Nova Scotia, Ontario, Prince Edward Island, Québec, Saskatchewan
Foreign Activity:
Eastern Europe, Western Europe, USA
Contact(s):
Glenn Kaye, President
Laura McPhee, Marketing Consultant
Dan Rheault, P.Eng., Engineering & New Product Development

Maritime Microbiologicals Inc. / MMBI
379 Saunders St.
Fredericton, NB E3B 1N9
506-454-9781
dboyle@nbnet.nb.ca
www.marimicro.ca
Firm Type: Manufacturing, Scientific/Technical Services
Founded: 1997
Staff: 5
Member of: Composting Council of Canada; Canadian Mushroom Growers Association
Products/Services/Areas of Expertise: Consulting in the general area of mycology; specialty mushrooms, mycorrhizal fungi, plant pathogens, organopollutant degradation by fungi, composting
Recently Completed / Ongoing Projects: Developed method for inducing white-rot fungi to grow in & degrade organopollutants in soil; developing control methods for green mould (T. harzianum) for the mushroom industry; metal chelation by fungi; land reclamation using mycorrhizal plants; biological control
Financial Information:
Type of Ownership: Private
Revenue: $100,000 - $250,000
Revenue Sources: 25% nationwide; 25% Provincial; 50% Private Contracts
Domestic Markets:
New Brunswick, Nova Scotia, Ontario, Prince Edward Island
Contact(s):
David Boyle, Ph.D., President

Maritime Paper Products Ltd.
Burnside Industrial Park
P.O. Box 668
25 Borden Ave.
Dartmouth, NS B2Y 3Y9
902-468-5353
Fax: 902-468-7314
800-565-5353
sales@maritimepaper.com
www.maritimepaper.com
Firm Type: Manufacturing
Founded: 1931
Products/Services/Areas of Expertise: Recycled paper & paper products
Domestic Markets:
New Brunswick, Newfoundland & Labrador, Nova Scotia, Prince Edward Island, Québec
Foreign Activity:
USA
Contact(s):
Gary Johnson, President
garyj@maritimepaper.com
Steve MacDonald, Vice-President, Finance
stevem@maritimepaper.com
Don MacKenzie, Director, Engineering
donm@maritimepaper.com
Brian Wambolt, Manager, Sales
brianw@maritimepaper.com

Canadian Branches:
Charlesbourg Office
#102, 813, rue des Calcédoines
Charlesbourg, QC G2L 2N8
418-628-4960
Fax: 418-628-4979
Pierre Fortin
pedrofortin@bell.blackberry.net

Saint John Office
730 Dever Rd.
Saint John, NB E2M 4J3
506-635-3150
Fax: 506-635-1882
Brian French
brianf@maritimepaper.com

St. John's Office
Donovans Industrial Park
14 Clyde Ave.
St. John's, NL A1B 4S1
709-368-3369
Fax: 709-368-2410
Jim Whight, Operations
jimw@maritimepaper.com

Summerside Office
192 Greenwood Dr.
Summerside, PE C1N 6G1
902-436-4875
Fax: 902-436-3494
Brian Doucet
briand@maritimepaper.com

International Branch(es):
USA Office - Maine
169A Lewiston Rd.
Gray, ME USA
207-657-5535
Fax: 207-657-4999
Bill Priest
billp@maritimepaper.com

Maritime Soil Ltd.
401 Old Black River Rd.
Saint John, NB E2L 4A5
506-634-8540
Fax: 506-634-8411
Contact(s):
Robert L. Arseneau, Contact

Maritime Testing Ltd.
97 Troop Ave.
Dartmouth, NS B3B 2A7
902-468-6486
Fax: 902-468-4919
888-418-3600
martest@maritimetesting.ca
www.maritimetesting.ca
Firm Type: Engineering, Scientific/Technical Services
Founded: 1985
Staff: 30
Products/Services/Areas of Expertise: Maritime Testing is an engineering, consulting environmental services firm providing environmental site assessments, risk assessments, remediation, erosion & sedimentation control design, wetland assessments, indoor air quality assessments, hazardous material surveys, industrial hygiene monitoring, environmental permitting, etc.
Financial Information:
Type of Ownership: Private
Domestic Markets:
New Brunswick, Newfoundland & Labrador, Nova Scotia, Prince Edward Island
Contact(s):
Kim Strong, President
kstrong@maritimetesting.ca
Doreen Chenard, Manger, Environmental Assessments,
902/468-6486
dchenard@maritimetesting.ca

Maritime Ultrasonic Cleaning Inc.
P.O. Box 7311
213A Pine Glen Rd.
Riverview, NB E1B 1T4
506-386-1750
Fax: 506-386-3732
888-633-5100
musci@nb.aibn.com
Products/Services/Areas of Expertise: Cleaning services
Contact(s):
Brad Jones, President

Markland Specialty Engineering Ltd.
#9, 305 Armstrong Ave
Georgetown, ON L7G 4X6
905-873-7791
Fax: 905-873-6012
markland@sludgecontrols.com
www.sludgecontrols.com
Firm Type: Manufacturing
Founded: 1967
Member of: Water Environment Association of Ontario; Water Environment Federation; Association of Professional Engineers of Ontario; Instrument Society of America
Products/Services/Areas of Expertise: Electronic process control instrumentation for water pollution control; sludge blanket level control; ultrasonic suspended solids measurement; wastewater sampling
Recently Completed / Ongoing Projects: Ships industrial instrumentation all over the world
Financial Information:
Type of Ownership: Private
Domestic Markets:
National

Foreign Activity:
Worldwide
Contact(s):
Reg Tansony, P.Eng., General Manager

Marriotts Container Rental Ltd.
#7388, 4 Glen Baker Dr.
Halifax, NS B3R 2K2
902-876-7388
Fax: 902-876-9044
marriotts@sprint.ca
Contact(s):
Kevin Marriott, Owner

Marsh Instrumentation Inc.
Subsidiary of Marsh Engineering Ltd.
#1, 1016C Sutton Dr.
Burlington, ON L7L 6B8
905-332-1172
Fax: 905-332-1668
800-449-2719
www.marshinst.com
Firm Type: Engineering, Scientific/Technical Services
Founded: 1986
Staff: 35
Quality Environmental Management System(s): 9001; ISO
Products/Services/Areas of Expertise: System integration for process controls; On-site calibration for process instrumentation; Technical manpower & project management services
Financial Information:
Type of Ownership: Private
Revenue Sources: 5% nationwide; 15% Provincial; 20% Municipals; 60% Private Contracts
Domestic Markets:
Ontario
Markets Sought:
USA
Contact(s):
R. Bake

Marsulex Inc.
Formerly: United Chemical Co.
#300, 111 Gordon Baker Rd.
Toronto, ON M2H 3R1
416-496-9655
Fax: 416-496-1874
800-387-5030
www.marsulex.com
Firm Type: Distributing, Manufacturing
Founded: 1989
Member of: American Water Works Association; Western Canada Water & Wastewater Association
Products/Services/Areas of Expertise: Provider of outsourced environmental compliance solutions
Financial Information:
Type of Ownership: Publicly Traded
Revenue: $1.5 Million - $3 Million
Domestic Markets:
Alberta, British Columbia, Saskatchewan
Foreign Activity:
USA
Contact(s):
Laurie Tugman, President & CEO
William Martin, CFO
Robert Cardell, General Manager & Vice-President, Power Generation Group
bcardell@marsulex.com
Brian E. Stasiewicz, Vice-President, Refinery Services Group
bstasiewicz@marsulex.com

Martec Ltd.
#400, 1888 Brunswick St.
Halifax, NS B3J 3J8
902-425-5101
Fax: 902-421-1923
info@martec.com
www.martec.com
Products/Services/Areas of Expertise: Information technology & communications; laboratory services
Contact(s):
Jim Warner, President

Canadian Branches:
Gatineau Office
#101, 717, boul St-Joseph
Gatineau, QC J8Y 4B6

819-595-3526
Fax: 819-595-1739

Medicine Hat Office
55 Vista Pl. SE
Medicine Hat, AB T1B 4V4
403-527-9456

International Branch(es):
Arlington Office
#700, 1655 North Fort Myer Dr.
Arlington, VA USA
703-875-2138
Fax: 703-525-8841

Marvin Silbert & Associates
23 Glenelia Ave.
Toronto, ON M2M 2K6
416-225-0226
Fax: 416-225-2227
marvin@silbert.org
www.silbert.org
Firm Type: Management Consulting, Scientific/Technical Services
Staff: 86
Products/Services/Areas of Expertise: Consulting & training in application or use of water within process, cooling & boiler systems; statistical process control application & training; assisting in the evaluation of Revenue Canada SR & ED claims
Financial Information:
Type of Ownership: Private
Domestic Markets:
Alberta, New Brunswick, Nova Scotia, Ontario, Québec, Saskatchewan
Foreign Activity:
USA
Contact(s):
Marvin D. Silbert, Ph.D, P.Eng., FCIC, President

Master Builders Technologies Ltd.
1800 Clark Blvd.
Brampton, ON L6T 4M7
905-789-0668
Fax: 905-792-0651
800-387-5862
Firm Type: Distributing, Manufacturing
Member of: BASF Canada
Quality Environmental Management System(s): 9001:2000
Products/Services/Areas of Expertise: Manufacturer of concrete additives; fibreglass resin products; chemical reagent; corrosion control coatings & linings. Environmentally safe practices, & health & safety are operational values
Domestic Markets:
National
Foreign Activity:
Worldwide
Contact(s):
Fortunato Sanchioni, Contact, BASF Canada, 905-792-2012

Masternet Ltd.
1236 Cardiff Blvd.
Mississauga, ON L5S 1P6
905-795-9293
Fax: 905-795-9293
800-216-2536
info@masternetltd.com
www.masternetltd.com
Firm Type: Manufacturing
Founded: 1988
Staff: 40
Member of: National Fence Association; National Aquaculture Association
Products/Services/Areas of Expertise: Wattle netting, Vexar Plactic Safety & Snow fence; netting & mesh products for use with oil containment booms & absorbent products; plastic net bag & custom meshes
Recently Completed / Ongoing Projects: Straw wattles; oil sorbet safety booms, safety fence
Financial Information:
Type of Ownership: Private
Domestic Markets:
National
Foreign Activity:
Worldwide
Contact(s):
Linda Duval, President
Mark Baker, Manager, Sales
Brian Sharpe, Vice-President, Sales & Marketing

Matco Ltd.
#200, 10833, av Moisan
Montréal, QC H1G 4N6
514-323-0001
Fax: 514-323-3330
800-387-3551
mcarroll@matcoltee.com; amlacasse@matcoltee.com
www.matcoltee.com
Firm Type: Distributing
Founded: 1951
Member of: American Society of Plumbing Engineers
Products/Services/Areas of Expertise: Power boilers; laboratory equipment; boiler room equipment; incinerators
Financial Information:
Type of Ownership: Private
Revenue: $3 Million - $5 Million
Domestic Markets:
Northwest Territories, Québec
Contact(s):
Maureen Carroll, President

Material Resource Recovery Inc.
Also Known As: MRR
P.O. Box 683 Main
2425 Industrial Park Rd.
Cornwall, ON K6H 5T5
613-938-7575
Fax: 613-938-0660
800-224-6812
info@mrri.com
www.mrri.com
Firm Type: Waste Management
Founded: 1998
Staff: 18
Products/Services/Areas of Expertise: PCB treatment & transfer; odorant tank & equipment treatment; compressed gas cylinder treatment
Financial Information:
Type of Ownership: Publicly Traded
Revenue: $3 Million - $5 Million
Revenue Sources: 2% nationwide; 98% Private Contracts
Domestic Markets:
National
Foreign Activity:
USA
Contact(s):
Steve Flannery, General Manager
Tom Wass, Sales Manager

Matrix Energy
Energie Matrix
296, ave Labrosse
Point Claire, QC H9R 5L8
514-630-5630
Fax: 514-426-9123
866-630-5630
info@matrixenergy.ca
www.matrixenergy.ca
Firm Type: Distributing
Founded: 1985
Staff: 8
Member of: Québec Solar Association, Canadian Solar Industries Association, Solar Energy Society of Canada Inc., International Solar Energy Society; Association québécoise pour la maitrise d'énergie
Products/Services/Areas of Expertise: Autonomous power; grid-tie & net metering solar & wind power products & systems; solar air heating & ventilation; solar thermal, photovoltaic & wind power systems & components
Recently Completed / Ongoing Projects: Solar, air, heating & ventilation systems; solar, electric equipment supplier; solar electric system
Financial Information:
Type of Ownership: Private
Revenue: $3 Million - $5 Million
Revenue Sources: 5% nationwide; 5% Provincial; 90% Private Contracts
Domestic Markets:
National
Foreign Activity:
Caribbean
Contact(s):
B. Wilkinson, President
Marc Magar, Marketing
Patrick Savoie, Sales
Brian Wilkinson, General Manager

Matrix Photocatalytic Inc.
Formerly: Nutech Environmental
22 Pegler St.
London, ON N5Z 2B5
519-660-8669
Fax: 519-660-8525
Firm Type: Engineering, Manufacturing, Scientific/Technical Services
Founded: 1982
Staff: 4
Products/Services/Areas of Expertise: Photocatalytic treatment systems for the removal & destruction of organic pollutants in air or water; applications include soil vapour extraction, plant manufacturing & air stripping emissions, plant process water & groundwater
Domestic Markets:
National
Foreign Activity:
The Pacific Rim, USA
Contact(s):
Bob Henderson, President

Matrix Solutions Inc.
Formerly: E2 Environmental Alliance Inc.
#200, 150 - 13th Ave. SW
Calgary, AB T2P 0V2
403-237-0606
Fax: 403-263-2493
877-774-5525 Emergency
info@matrixsolutions.com
www.matrix-solutions.com
Firm Type: Scientific/Technical Services
Founded: 1984
Staff: 300
EcoLogo Certified Products & Services: 1
Products/Services/Areas of Expertise: Environmental management, water/soil contamination, surface water engineering, EIA/EMS, auditing, regulatory development, training, peer review
Ecological Note: 1
Domestic Markets:
National
Foreign Activity:
Worldwide
Contact(s):
John Feick, Executive Chair
Robert Pockar, P.Eng, President & CEO
Blake Louden, P.Geol, VP, Assessment & Remediation Services
Jonathan Hutt, P.Eng, VP, Saskatchewan Operations
Marim Halat, Chief Financial Officer

Canadian Branches:
Alberta - Drayton Valley
5717 - 50 Ave., Bay B
Drayton Valley, AB T7A 1R8
780-542-2625
Fax: 780-542-5096
Julia O'Shannassy

Alberta - Edmonton
#142, 6325 Gateway Blvd.
Edmonton, AB T6H 5H6
780-490-6830
Fax: 780-465-2973
Tyler Swaren

Alberta - Grande Prairie
#105, 9715 - 105 St.
Grande Prairie, AB T8V 7X7
780-532-9779
Fax: 780-532-9805
Kreg Alde

Alberta - Lloydminster
#1A, 5803 - 63 St.
Lloydminster, AB T9V 3K2
780-875-3312
Fax: 780-871-0927
John Banks

Alberta - Medicine Hat
924 - 16 St. SW
Medicine Hat, AB T1A 8A4
403-526-0650
Fax: 403-526-0679
James Freeman

BC - Fort St. John
10927 Alaska Rd.
Fort St. John, BC V1J 6P3
250-785-7833
Fax: 250-785-7813
Kreg Alde

Manitoba - Virden
#3, 372 - 7 Ave. South
Virden, MB R0M 2C0
204-748-3256
Fax: 204-748-3268

Saskatchewan - Kindersley
1320 - 9 Ave. West, Bay W1
Kindersley, AB S0L 1S0
306-463-2190
Fax: 306-463-2190

Saskatchewan - Oxbow
874 Prospect Ave.
Oxbow, SK T0M 0N0
306-483-2179
Fax: 306-483-2197

Saskatchewan - Regina
34A Great Plains Rd.
Emerald Park, SK S4L 1B7
306-781-7750
Fax: 306-781-7751

Saskatchewan - Swift Current
#10, 1071 Central Ave. North
Swift Current, SK S9H 4Z1
306-773-3009
Fax: 306-773-3109

Saskatchewan - Weyburn
P.O. Box 279
1780 Railway Ave.
Weyburn, SK S4H 2K1
306-842-3088
Fax: 306-842-3356

MAUSER
Formerly: Hunter Drums Ltd.
1121 Pioneer Rd.
Burlington, ON L7M 1K5
905-332-4800
Fax: 905-332-5515
info.ca@mausergroup.com
www.mausergroup.com
Firm Type: Distributing, Manufacturing
Founded: 1963
Member of: Society of the Plastics Industry Inc.; Plastic Drum Institute; Steel Shipping Container Institute; Society of Petroleum Engineers
Products/Services/Areas of Expertise: Plastic & steel recycling drums for cans, glass & paper; tamper-evident containers for medical waste incineration; disposable drum liners; salvage & recovery drums, hazardous waste drums; recycling of steel & plastic drums
Domestic Markets:
National
Canadian Branches:
Bramalea
300 Walker Dr.
Brampton, ON L6T 4B3
905-791-7155
Fax: 905-791-5424
info.ca@mausergroup.ca

Maxim Power Corp
#1210, 715 - 5 Ave. SW
Calgary, AB T2P 2X6
403-263-3021
Fax: 403-263-9125
maxim@maximpowercorp.com
www.maximpowercorp.com
Products/Services/Areas of Expertise: Maxim's mission is to enhance shareholder & customer value by acquiring or developing, owning & operating, innovative & environmentally responsible electric & thermal energy projects
Ecological Note: Is an Independent Power Producer, IPP
Contact(s):
John Babenic, President/CEO
Pat Lucas, Vice-President, Operations

Maxxam Analytics Inc.
#240, 7070 Mississauga Rd.
Mississauga, ON L5N 7G2
905-288-2150
Fax: 905-288-2169
866-611-1118
info@maxxam.ca
www.maxxam.ca
Firm Type: Scientific/Technical Services
Founded: 1996
Staff: 2000
Member of: Canadian Environment Industry Association; Canadian Association of Environmental Analytical Laboratories; International Association of Environmental Testing Laboratories; Canadian Council of Independent Laboratories
Products/Services/Areas of Expertise: Physical, chemical, biological & toxicity testing in all aspects of the environment: ambient air sampling & analysis; stack emission sampling & analysis; landfill gas analysis; water, soil, fish & waste analysis; PCB & dioxin analysis; analysis of congeners by high resolution MS; testing of biological fluids; tissues & biota samples; agrochemical residue testing
Financial Information:
Type of Ownership: Private
Domestic Markets:
National
Foreign Activity:
Asia, Eastern Europe, Mexico
Contact(s):
Jon Hantho, CEO
Pierre Beaumier, Exec. Vice-President
Andrew Masters, Exec. Vice-President, East
Bernie Brassard, Exec. Vice-President, West
Jay Marteniuk, Manager, Marketing Development
Canadian Branches:
Bedford
#105, 200 Bluewater Rd.
Bedford, NS B4B 1G9
902-420-0202
Fax: 902-420-8612
1-800-565-7227

Burlington
5555 North Service Rd.
Burlington, ON L7L 5H7
905-332-8788
Fax: 905-332-9169
1-800-668-0639

Burnaby
8577 Commerce Ct.
Burnaby, BC V5A 4N5
604-444-4808
Fax: 604-444-4511
1-800-440-4808

Calgary
2021 - 41 Ave. NE
Calgary, AB T2E 6P2
403-291-3077
Fax: 403-291-9468
1-800-386-7247

Edmonton
9331 - 48 St.
Edmonton, AB T6B 2R4
780-468-3500
Fax: 780-466-3332
1-800-386-7247

Fort McMurray
300A MacLennan Cr.
Fort McMurray, AB T9H 4G1
780-791-9170
Fax: 780-791-7665

Grande Prairie
#101, 7002 - 98 St.
Grande Prairie, AB T0H 0W0
780-532-0227
Fax: 780-532-0288

London
#101, 4053 Meadowbrook Dr.
London, ON N6L 1E8
519-652-9444
Fax: 519-652-8189
1-800-268-7396

Montréal
889, Montée de Liesse
Saint-Laurent, QC H48T 1P5
514-448-9001
Fax: 514-448-9119

Ottawa
#900, 33 Colonnade Rd.
Nepean, ON K2E 7J6
613-274-0573
Fax: 613-274-0574
1-877-480-7272

St. John's
#101A, 49 - 55 Elizabeth Ave.
St. John's, NL A1A 1W9
709-754-0203
Fax: 709-754-8612
1-888-492-7227

Stettler
4705 - 42 St.
Stettler, AB T0C 2L1
403-742-1107
Fax: 403-742-0170

Sydney
P.O. Box 897
90 Esplanade
Sydney, NS B1P 6J1
902-567-1255
Fax: 902-539-6504
1-888-535-7770

Winnipeg
#F, 1420 Clarence Ave.
Winnipeg, MB R3T 1T6
204-477-8721
Fax: 204-477-8719
1-866-800-6208

Yellowknife
349 Old Airport Rd.
Yellowknife, NT X1A 3X6
867-445-2448

Maxxam Analytics Ltd.
Formerly: CanTest Laboratories Ltd.; CanAm Laboratories Ltd.
4606 Canada Way
Burnaby, BC V5G 1K5
604-734-7276
Fax: 604-731-2386
800-665-8566
info@maxxamanalytics.com
www.maxxam.ca
Firm Type: Scientific/Technical Services
Founded: 1969
Staff: 90
Products/Services/Areas of Expertise: Independent laboratory; environmental audits for real estate transactions; public drinking water quality; assessments of workplace environments; environmental impact studies; contamination of food products; pesticide screening
Domestic Markets:
Alberta, British Columbia, Manitoba, Ontario, Saskatchewan
Foreign Activity:
Western Europe, USA
Markets Sought:
Asia
Contact(s):
Don Enns, President & Chief Executive Officer
Steve Timuss, Director, Business Development
Contact(s):
Steve Timuss, Marketing & Sales Coordinator
Canadian Branches:
Kelowna
915 Ellis St.
Kelowna, BC V1Y 1Y9
250-765-7501
Fax: 250-765-7509
info@maxxamanalytics.com
Glen W. Craig, Project Manager/Technical Sales

Toronto
Business Development, BioPharma Servi
18 Inkpen Lane
Whitby, ON L1R 2H2

Products & Services Buyer's Guide

905-665-5556
Fax: 905-665-2690
1-877-734-7276
llutter@cantest.com
www.cantest.com
Lorelei Lutter, Director

Victoria
Vancouver Island Technology Park
#1104, 4464 Markham St.
Victoria, BC V8Z 7X8
250-385-6112
Fax: 250-382-6364
866-385-6113
info@maxxamanalytics.com
Glen Craig, Laboratory Supervisor

Winnipeg Lab
675 Berry St., #D
Winnipeg, MB R3H 1A7
204-254-1825
Fax: 204-772-2386
866-800-6208
info@maxxamanalytics.com
Marnie Kolach

Maxxam Analytics
4606 Canada Way
Burnaby, BC V5G 1K5
604-734-7276
Fax: 604-731-2386
800-665-8566
International Branch(es):
Eurotest Ltd.
Shirley Ave., Vale Rd.
Windsor
Berkshire UK
-(44 175) 386 7267
Fax: -(44 175) 386 7
Paul Crosby

McKenzie Laboratories Inc.
#1, 3725 East Atlantic Ave.
Phoenix, AZ USA
602-470-0288
Fax: 602-470-0756
Earl Hopper

Mayer Heritage Consultants Inc. / MHCI
Formerly: Mayer, Poulton & Associates Inc.
#5, 1615 North Routledge Park
London, ON N6H 5L6
519-472-8100
Fax: 519-472-1661
800-465-9990
mayerheritage@bellnet.ca
Firm Type: Scientific/Technical Services
Founded: 1983
Staff: 8
Member of: Ontario Archaeological Society
Products/Services/Areas of Expertise: Archaeological & built heritage assessments of development properties subject to provincial & federal planning & environmental conditions
Recently Completed / Ongoing Projects: Ontario Hwy 407, R.M. of Halton; Bluewater Bridge, Sarnia; CN Railway tunnel, Sarnia; SkyDome stadium, Toronto
Financial Information:
Type of Ownership: Private
Domestic Markets:
Manitoba, Ontario, Québec
Foreign Activity:
USA
Contact(s):
Robert G. Mayer, President

McAtee Safety & Environmental Health Services Ltd.
23 Parkwood Rise SE
Calgary, AB T2J 3X7
403-271-9796
Fax: 403-271-9796
mcatee@telusplanet.net
Firm Type: Scientific/Technical Services
Founded: 1995
Staff: 1
Member of: Canadian Society of Engineering - Calgary Chapter; American Industrial Hygiene Association - Alberta Chapter

Products/Services/Areas of Expertise: Safety consulting & occupational hygiene consulting; mould assessments; worker exposure monitoring
Financial Information:
Type of Ownership: Private
Domestic Markets:
Alberta, British Columbia, Saskatchewan
Contact(s):
C. McAtee, President

MCC Industrial Services Ltd
Subsidiary of Mitsui & Co. (Canada) Ltd.
#1, 125 Vondrau Dr.
Cambridge, ON N3E 1A8
519-650-9886
Fax: 519-653-9141
800-311-4622
info@mccindustrial.ca
www.mccindustrial.ca
Firm Type: Management Consulting, Waste Management
Founded: 1988
Staff: 45
Member of: National Solid Waste Management Association; Mississauga Board of Trade; Canadian Polystyrene Recycling Association; Ontario Waste Management Association
Products/Services/Areas of Expertise: Waste reduction; recycling programs; waste audits; waste management services; consulting services
Domestic Markets:
National
Foreign Activity:
USA
Contact(s):
O. Takahashi, President/General Manager
A. Cooper, Manager, Project Development
M. Maher, Controller

McClymont & Rak Engineers, Inc.
117 Disco Rd.
Toronto, ON M9W 1M3
416-675-0160
Fax: 416-675-6371
office@mccrak.com
Firm Type: Management Consulting, Engineering
Founded: 1982
Staff: 20
Member of: Association of Professional Engineers of Ontario
Products/Services/Areas of Expertise: Environmental, geotechnical engineering; material testing
Financial Information:
Type of Ownership: Private
Revenue: $3 Million - $5 Million
Domestic Markets:
Ontario
Foreign Activity:
Worldwide
Markets Sought:
Asia, Eastern Europe, Former USSR
Contact(s):
Lad J. Rak, P.Eng., Vice-President
lrak@mccrak.com
Nayef. Mahgroub, P.Eng., Environmental Engineer
nmahgoup@mccrak.com

McCordick Glove & Safety Inc.
400 Jamieson Pkwy.
Cambridge, ON N3C 4N3
519-651-2233
Fax: 519-651-0508
877-623-4455
info@mccordick.com
www.mccordick.com
Firm Type: Distributing
Founded: 1979
Staff: 12
Products/Services/Areas of Expertise: Hazardous material handling equipment
Domestic Markets:
Alberta, British Columbia, Manitoba, Ontario, Québec,
Contact(s):
John J. Huck, President
Phil Huck, VP, Domestic Sales & Marketing
Steven Kamski, VP, Finance & Accounting

Canadian Branches:
Alberta Office
195 Turbo Dr.
Sherwood Park, AB T8H 2J6
780-466-9660
Fax: 780-468-5886
800-661-5379
Tony Yanew

BC Office
#65, 7789 - 134th St.
Surrey, BC V3W 9E9
604-543-0307
Fax: 604-543-0377
877-543-1133
Tony Yanew

Manitoba Office
#8, 130 Midland St.
Winnipeg, MB R3E 3R3
204-772-2495
Fax: 204-775-2650
800-561-8112
John Malatches

Québec Office
Gants et Securité McCordick Inc.
#804, 1380, rue Joliot-Curie
Boucherville, QC J4B 7L9
450-449-5835
Fax: 450-449-5839
800-465-7439
Ricky Chabot

McElhanney Consulting Services Ltd. / MCSL
A member company of The McElhanney Group
#100, 780 Beatty St.
Vancouver, BC V6B 2M1
604-683-8521
Fax: 604-683-4350
info@mcelhanney.com
www.mcelhanney.com/mcsl
Firm Type: Engineering
Founded: 1910
Staff: 215
Products/Services/Areas of Expertise: Engineering consulting services; liquid/hazardous waste management consulting; feasibility/pre-feasibility studies; design & specifications, engineering
Financial Information:
Type of Ownership: Private
Domestic Markets:
Alberta, British Columbia, Saskatchewan
Foreign Activity:
The Pacific Rim
Contact(s):
Chris Newcomb, P.Eng, President
cnewcomb@mcelhanney.com

Canadian Branches:
Calgary
#500, 999 - 8th St. SW
Calgary, AB T2R 1J5
403-262-5042
Fax: 403-246-3337
Dave McElhanney

Campbell River
1307 Shoppers Row
Campbell River, BC V9W 2C9
250-287-7799
Fax: 250-287-7662
Mark DeGagne, Branch Manager

Canmore
#203, 502 Bow Valley Trail
Canmore, AB T1W 1N9
403-609-3992
Fax: 403-609-3989

Courtenay
495 Sixth St.
Courtenay, BC V9N 6V4
250-338-5495
Fax: 250-338-7700
Ian Whitehead, Branch Manager

Cranbrook
34 - 11th Ave. South
Cranbrook, BC V1C 2P1

250-489-3013
Fax: 250-489-4522

Duncan
#202, 5855 York Rd.
Duncan, BC V9L 3S3
250-748-3335
Fax: 250-748-6279

Edmonton
#138, 14315 - 118th Ave.
Edmonton, AB T5L 4S6
780-461-3420
Fax: 780-452-7033
Henry Devos

Kamloops
293 First Avenue
Kamloops, BC V2C 3J3
250-374-2200
Fax: 250-374-2314

Maple Ridge
#3, 21409 Lougheed Hwy.
Maple Ridge, BC V2X 2R8
604-466-4881
Fax: 604-466-4891

Nanaimo
#1, 1351 Estevan Rd.
Nanaimo, BC V9S 3Y3
250-716-3336
Fax: 250-716-3339
Bob Hoffstrom

Penticton
#102, 130 Nanaimo Ave. West
Penticton, BC V2A 8G1
250-492-7399
Fax: 250-492-5488
Derek Blaszak

Powell River
4507 Manson Ave.
Powell River, BC V8A 3N3
604-485-4203
Fax: 604-485-9287

Prince George
1633 First Ave.
Prince George, BC V2L 2Y8
250-561-2229
Fax: 250-563-1941
Ken Maddox

Prince Rupert
174 - 3rd Ave. East
Prince Rupert, BC V8J 1K5
250-624-1427
Fax: 250-627-8989

Saskatoon
P.O. Box 32024 Erindale
Saskatoon, SK S7N 1N8
306-649-0740
Fax: 306-649-0772

Smithers
P.O. Box 787
3907 - 4th Ave.
Smithers, BC V0J 2N0
250-847-4040
Fax: 250-847-4160
Scott Loptson

Surrey
13160 - 88th Ave.
Surrey, BC V3W 3K3
604-596-0391
Fax: 604-596-8853
Gary Tencha

Terrace
#1, 5008 Pohle Ave.
Terrace, BC V8G 4S8
250-635-7163
Fax: 250-635-9586
Colin Adam, Branch Manager

Victoria
1595 Bay St., Unit B
Victoria, BC V8R 2B5

250-370-9221
Fax: 250-370-9223
International Branch(es):
Indonesia
PT McElhanney Indonesia
Jl. Pejaten Barat II No.20, Unit A
Jakarta, Selatan Indonesi
62 21 7179 3137
Fax: 62 21 7179 0361
www.mcelhanney.com/ptmi
Francisco Goncalves

McKell Marketing Ltd.
14803 - 134th Ave.
Edmonton, AB T5L 4V5
780-453-6687
Fax: 780-451-4283
Products/Services/Areas of Expertise: Water & wastewater management & equipment
Contact(s):
Bruce McKell

McKerlie Solar Systems
Also Known As: Ultra-Sun Solar Industries Inc.
138 Garden Cres.
Hamilton, ON L8V 4T4
905-388-3459
Fax: 905-388-4335
Firm Type: Manufacturing
Member of: Canadian Solar Industries Association, Solar Energy Society of Canada Inc.
Products/Services/Areas of Expertise: Solar heating & solar electric sales, design & installation; passive solar construction (sunrooms, solariums); heat recovery ventilation
Contact(s):
David W. McKerlie, P.Eng., President/CEO

McNair & Marshall Planning & Development Consultants
33 St. Vincent St.
Barrie, ON L4M 3Y3
705-726-9101
Fax: 705-737-5519
mcnairmarshall@rogers.com
Firm Type: Scientific/Technical Services
Founded: 1976
Staff: 2
Products/Services/Areas of Expertise: Land use planning
Domestic Markets:
Ontario
Contact(s):
Alan McNair, Partner
Barbara Marshall, Environmental Contact

McNamara Construction Company
P.O. Box 13095
St. John's, NL A1B 3V8
709-782-3800
cordellr@nfld.net
Firm Type: Engineering
Staff: 50
Products/Services/Areas of Expertise: Heavy civil construction, design build, turnkey, hydroelectric projects
Recently Completed / Ongoing Projects: Granite Canal hydroelectric project, High Falls
Financial Information:
Type of Ownership: Publicly Traded
Revenue Sources: 50% Provincial; 50% Private Contracts
Domestic Markets:
Newfoundland & Labrador, Ontario
Markets Sought:
Asia
Contact(s):
John Mulcahy, General Manager

MCR Environmental Consulting
2239 - 21 Ave.
Coaldale, AB T1M 1J2
403-345-4480
wgajdostik@newpark.ca
Firm Type: Waste Management
Founded: 1994
Products/Services/Areas of Expertise: Disposal of drilling waste; pre-site assessment; soil analysis

Financial Information:
Type of Ownership: Private
Revenue Sources: 100% Private Contracts
Domestic Markets:
Alberta
Contact(s):
Ward Gajdostik, President

MCW Custom Energy Solutions
#600, 156 Front St. West
Toronto, ON M5J 2L6
416-598-2920
Fax: 416-598-5394
mcw_tor@mcw.com
www.mcw-ers.com
Products/Services/Areas of Expertise: Provides services ranging from complete single source performance contracting to individual energy management initiatives; strategic long-term building operations planning; innovative design solutions; cost-effective engineering; environmental code compliance planning; disciplined project management; training needs assessment & energy awareness workshops; energy management manuals & documentation; long-term sustained energy monitoring; project financing
Canadian Branches:
Kelowna Branch
#202, 2323 Hunter Rd.
Kelowna, BC V1X 7C5
250-860-6421
Fax: 250-860-6431
mcw_kel@mcw.com

Ottawa Branch
464 Somerset St. West
Ottawa, ON K1R 5J8
613-231-6755
Fax: 613-231-2480
mcw_ott@mcw.com

Trail Branch
1303 Bay Ave.
Trail, BC V1R 4A7
250-364-3188
Fax: 250-364-3189
mcw_tor@mcw.com

Vancouver Branch
#1400, 1185 West Georgia St.
Vancouver, BC V6E 4E6
604-687-1821
Fax: 604-683-5681
mcw_van@mcw.com

Winnipeg Branch
#210, 1821 Wellington Ave.
Winnipeg, MB R3C 0G4
204-779-7900
Fax: 204-779-1119
mcw_wpg@mcw.com

MDI Waste Management Inc.
P.O. Box 1289
479 Rothesay Ave.
Saint John, NB E2L 4G7
506-634-2220
Fax: 506-634-2236
Contact(s):
Jim Watt, Contact

MDS Sciex
71 Four Valley Dr.
Concord, ON L4K 4V8
416-660-9005
Fax: 416-660-2600
www.mdssciex.com
Firm Type: Engineering, Manufacturing, Scientific/Technical Services
Founded: 1978
Staff: 475
Member of: Analytical & Life Sciences Systems Association
Quality Environmental Management System(s): 9001
Products/Services/Areas of Expertise: Mass spectrometry-based analytical equipment used to measure & monitor air & water
Financial Information:
Type of Ownership: Publicly Traded
Domestic Markets:
National

Foreign Activity:
Worldwide
Contact(s):
Andy Boorn, President
Simon Pitchford, Vice-President, Marketing, Sales & Service
John E. Fulford, Vice-President, Core Research

Canadian Branches:
Singapore
Woodlands Central EST
Blk. 33, #04-06 Marsiling Industrial Estate Rd. 3
Singapor
-65-6586-1110
Fax: -65-6362-3605

USA
#200, 1170 Veterans Blvd.
San Francisco, CA USA
650-635-4380

MEC Systems Inc.
Also Known As: \Mister\" High Pressure Systems"
8409 Lockheed Pl.
Chilliwack, BC V2P 8A7
604-792-7779
Fax: 604-792-7072
mister@mecsystems.com
www.mecsystems.com
Firm Type: Manufacturing
Founded: 1984
Staff: 12
Member of: Canadian Environment Industry Association
Products/Services/Areas of Expertise: Manufacturer of air quality control systems to clean air & deodorize industrial areas; dust suppression equipment, odour control equipment & cooling humidification systems
Financial Information:
Type of Ownership: Private
Domestic Markets:
National
Foreign Activity:
Worldwide
Markets Sought:
Asia, Australia/New Zealand, China, The Pacific Rim, Mexico, Vietnam
Contact(s):
Steve Crawford, CEO
Darryl Klassen, General Sales Manager
Lorraine Ante, Vice-President, Marketing

Medgate Inc.
Also Known As: Medgate OHS&E
#1700, 95 St. Clair Ave. West
Toronto, ON M4V 1N6
416-863-6800
Fax: 416-863-6501
800-276-9120
contactus@medgate.com
www.medgate.com
Firm Type: Information Technology
Founded: 1985
Products/Services/Areas of Expertise: Occupational health & safety; environmental cost control & compliance software
Financial Information:
Type of Ownership: Private
Domestic Markets:
National
Contact(s):
Mark Wallace, President & CEO
Stan Marsden, Sr. Vice-President, Operations
Marni Weiner, Director, Sales

Medina Construction Limited
P.O. Box 21021
St. John's, NL A1A 5B2
709-576-1495
Fax: 709-576-8126
medina@thezone.net
Contact(s):
Owen Crossan, President

Megalab Inc.
905, rue Michelin
Laval, QC H7L 5B6
450-663-1100
Fax: 450-663-1117
cghoche@megalab.ca
www.megalab.ca
Firm Type: Manufacturing
Founded: 1984
Staff: 5
Products/Services/Areas of Expertise: Water treatment chemicals
Financial Information:
Type of Ownership: Private
Revenue: $250,000 - $500,000
Domestic Markets:
Ontario, Québec
Contact(s):
Camille Ghoche, President

Megasecur Inc.
#3, 145, boul Jutras est
Victoriaville, QC G6P 4L8
819-751-0222
Fax: 819-751-5550
888-756-0222
info@megasecur.com
www.megasecur.com
Firm Type: Manufacturing
Founded: 1998
Staff: 2
Member of: Association of State Flood Plain Managers; Réseau environnement
Products/Services/Areas of Expertise: Manufacturer of the Water-Gate; instant water barrier, used to replace sandbags for multiple applications such as temporary flood control, deviate water spills, block water courses, build water reservoirs & contain toxic discharges
Recently Completed / Ongoing Projects: Flood control, 435 feet of barrier protection, Paris, France; Oil spill prevention, 850 feet of barrier protection, Alaska, USA; Hydro Electric Staion, increase water level, Panama
Financial Information:
Type of Ownership: Private
Revenue: $500,000 - $1.5 Million
Revenue Sources: 5% nationwide; 35% Provincial; 40% Municipals; 20% Private Contracts
Domestic Markets:
National
Foreign Activity:
Worldwide
Markets Sought:
South Africa, South America, Mexico, United Kingdom
Contact(s):
Daniel Dery, President
Jacques Lauzon, Director, Sales
jlauzon@megasecur.com
Helen LeMay, Sales Coordinator
hlemay@megasecur.com

Membrex Ltée
5590, boul des Laurentides
Laval, QC H7K 2K2
450-628-3873
Products/Services/Areas of Expertise: Geosynthetic/geomembrane liners
Contact(s):
Réginald Ratle, President

Memorial University of Newfoundland
Also Known As: CERR
Centre for Earth Resources Research
c/o Department of Earth Sciences
St. John's, NL A1B 3X5
709-737-4519
Fax: 709-737-2589
cerr@esd.mun.ca
www.esd.mun.ca/~cerr/
Products/Services/Areas of Expertise: Six areas of interest: petroleum, minerals, geophysics, marine studies, International liaison & professional development; national & international research endeavors; projects completed or underway include, the Canadian Lithoprobe Project, Arctic Ocean Ice Island Project & the international Ocean Drilling Program
Contact(s):
John M. Hanchar, Director

Menart S.L. Inc.
1239, rue de la Manic
Chicoutimi, QC G7K 1A1
418-545-2990
Fax: 418-545-1163
Sept05 MLH (was S)"
Contact(s):
Serge Lamontagne

Meo & Associates Inc.
7200 Disputed Rd.
LaSalle, ON N9A 6Z6
519-250-8088
Fax: 519-250-8070
rmeo@meoassociates.com
www.meogroup.com
Firm Type: Engineering
Founded: 1986
Staff: 10
Products/Services/Areas of Expertise: Engineering consulting services; environmental consulting services; architecture
Domestic Markets:
Ontario
Foreign Activity:
Caribbean, Mexico, USA
Markets Sought:
Mexico
Contact(s):
Raffaele Meo, P.Eng., M.A.Sc., President
Michael Piskovic, O.A.A., A.I.A., Associate, Architectural Services

MEP Environmental Products Ltd.
68 Paramount Rd.
Winnipeg, MB R2X 2W3
204-632-4118
Fax: 204-632-5809
877-632-4118
info@mepenvironmental.com
www.mepenvironmental.com
Products/Services/Areas of Expertise: Distribution of safety equipment and spill supply products; distribution of absorbents; secondary containment products; repair products
Domestic Markets:
National
Contact(s):
Karen Grzenda, General Manager
karen@mepenvironmental.com

Mequipco Ltd.
#101, 5126 - 126 Ave. SE
Calgary, AB T2Z 0H2
403-259-8333
Fax: 403-259-8335
800-663-9035
contactus@mequipco.com
www.mequipco.com
Firm Type: Distributing
Member of: Western Canada Water & Wastewater Association; Manitoba Water & Wastewater Association; Saskatchewan Water & Wastewater Association; Alberta Water & Wastewater Association; British Columbia Water & Wastewater Association
Products/Services/Areas of Expertise: Municipal: drinking-water treatment, wastewater; industrial: water process/potable treatment
Financial Information:
Type of Ownership: Private
Domestic Markets:
Alberta, British Columbia, Manitoba, Northwest Territories, Saskatchewan, Yukon Territory
Contact(s):
Brad Hussack, President
Dave Stephens, Vice-President

Canadian Branches:
Richmond Office
#225, 11020 - #5 Rd.
Richmond, BC V7A 4E7
604-273-0553
Fax: 604-277-8302
Devlin Wing, Branch Manager

Winnipeg Office
#305, 2265 Pembina Hwy.
Winnipeg, MB R3T 5J3
204-982-1040
Fax: 204-982-1045
Dan Landry, Branch Manager

Merchants of Green Coffee
2 Matilda St.
Toronto, ON M4M 1L9
416-741-5369
Fax: 416-778-9796
888-741-5369

merchants@merchantsofgreencoffee.com
www.merchantsofgreencoffee.com
Products/Services/Areas of Expertise: Is an enterprise dedicated to restoring the great taste of fresh coffee to the marketplace through fair trade & sustainable business practices; is comprised of a global network of individuals, businesses & organizations, & established the Sustainable Coffee program, one of the most environmentally & socially sustainable coffee packages the market has ever seen; this program is a combination of traditional growing practices & advanced processing technology that has created a unique & sustainable supply of quality Arabica coffee that supports producers & consumers while reducing carbon emissions
Ecological Note: Organically grown, fair trade coffee
Contact(s):
Brad Zavislake
brad@merchantsofgreencoffee.com

Merley Chains Ltd.
3079 Universal Dr.
Mississauga, ON L4X 2E2
905-625-1972
Fax: 905-625-0190
info@merleychains.ca
www.merleychains.ca
Firm Type: Distributing
Founded: 1975
Staff: 5
Products/Services/Areas of Expertise: Equipment for sludge collection
Contact(s):
Karl Killingbeck, Sales Manager

Merlin Plastics Supply Inc.
#109, 917 Cliveden Ave.
Delta, BC V3M 5R6
604-522-6799
Fax: 604-522-6791
www.merlinplastics.com
Contact(s):
Tony Moucachen, President

Canadian Branches:
Calgary Office
616 - 58th Ave. SE
Calgary, AB T2H 0P8
403-259-6637
Fax: 403-259-6679

Mesa Forestry & Environmental Services Ltd.
5303 - 46 St.
Whitecourt, AB T7S 1A6
780-778-5823
Fax: 780-778-6360
admin@mesa-alberta.com
mesa-alberta.com

Mesh Technologies Inc.
#15, 395 Berry St.
Winnipeg, MB R3J 1N6
204-831-0351
Fax: 204-888-8702
mesh@meshtech.ca
www.meshtech.ca
Firm Type: Engineering
Founded: 1990
Staff: 10
Member of: Manitoba Environmental Industries Association
Products/Services/Areas of Expertise: Multidiscipline engineering & management firm; provides municipal, mechanical, electrical, controls (automation), engineering analysis; building science; machine design; computer modelling & services
Recently Completed / Ongoing Projects: Bioclear technology plant expansion, Winnipeg, MB; HVAC energy study, Winnipeg, MB; several machine design applications, Gateway Bookbirding, Winnipeg, MB; Schwietzer-Mauduit, Carman, MB; national defence, Base Refueling Stn., Shilo, MB; CN engine rebuild department relocation, Transcona, MB; Iguluit biohazard incinerator
Financial Information:
Type of Ownership: Private
Revenue: $250,000 - $500,000
Revenue Sources: 10% nationwide; 5% Municipals; 85% Private Contracts
Domestic Markets:
Manitoba, Ontario, Saskatchewan
Contact(s):

Ron K. Giercke, President

Metacor International Inc.
Formerly: Metacor Steel Products Ltd.
3139, boul des Entreprises
Terrebonne, QC J6X 4J9
450-968-0200
Fax: 450-968-0555
info@metacor.ca
www.metacor.ca
Firm Type: Manufacturing
Founded: 1977
Products/Services/Areas of Expertise: Custom-made plate work fabrication (steel or stainless); cyclones, silos, tanks, vessels, stacks, ducting, conveyors, screw conveyors, dust collectors, filter house structures, water-cooled roofs & ductworks
Markets Sought:
Asia, Western Europe,

Metafix
1925 - 46th Ave.
Montréal, QC H8T 2P1
514-633-8663
Fax: 514-633-1678
800-667-8921
sales@metafix.com
www.metafix.com
Firm Type: Manufacturing
Founded: 1987
Member of: Photo Marketing Association
Quality Environmental Management System(s): 9002
Products/Services/Areas of Expertise: Waste management; water treatment chemicals; heavy metals removal equipment; water, wastewater & groundwater flowmeters & equipment; silver recovery
Financial Information:
Type of Ownership: Private
Revenue Sources: 100% Private Contracts
Domestic Markets:
National
Contact(s):
John L. Riviere, President/CEO
Chris Thorne, Graphics Arts Sales Associate
Gordon Bathurst, Sr. Vice-President

Metcon Sales & Engineering Ltd.
#3, 15 Connie Cres.
Concord, ON L4K 1L3
905-738-2355
Fax: 905-738-5520
metacon@metconeng.com
www.metconeng.com
Firm Type: Distributing, Manufacturing
Founded: 1985
Staff: 45
Products/Services/Areas of Expertise: Measuring & monitoring equipment; water treatment systems & equipment; sewage treatment equipment & systems; chemical feed instrumentation for water & wastewater systems
Financial Information:
Type of Ownership: Private
Revenue: Greater than $5 Million
Revenue Sources: 70% Provincial; 30% Private Contracts
Domestic Markets:
Manitoba, Ontario, Saskatchewan
Contact(s):
Ahron Nahmias, President
David Tidy
Joel Jacobson

Canadian Branches:
Winnipeg
#113, 1555 St. James St.
Winnipeg, MB R3H 1B5
204-774-5552
metcon@metconeng.com

Météoglobe Canada Inc.
11645, boul. Gouin Ouest
Montréal, QC H8Y 1Y4
514-683-0438
info@meteoglobe.ca
www.meteoglobe.ca
Firm Type: Engineering
Founded: 1987
Staff: 3

Products/Services/Areas of Expertise: OEM Technodor Suprathreshold olfactometer, used to measure odor's intensity
Financial Information:
Type of Ownership: Private
Domestic Markets:
National
Foreign Activity:
Worldwide
Contact(s):
Richard Gilbert, President

Metex Corp. Ltd.
#4, 91 Kelfield St.
Toronto, ON M9W 5A3
416-240-1920
Fax: 416-240-7021
www.metexcorporation.com
Products/Services/Areas of Expertise: Cooling tower & boiler controllers; monitors for pH, conductivity, ORP & free chlorine; portable instruments; chemical metering pumps; flow sensors & monitors; signal conditioners; custom manufacturing
Contact(s):
Andrew Toth, President

Canadian Branches:
Buffalo Office
4506 Main St.
Buffalo, NY USA
1-800-730-0302

Metocean Data Systems Limited
21 Thornhill Dr.
Dartmouth, NS B3B 1R9
902-468-2505
Fax: 902-468-4442
800-565-1830
www.metocean.com
Firm Type: Manufacturing
Founded: 1985
Staff: 30
Quality Environmental Management System(s): 9001
Products/Services/Areas of Expertise: Satellite transmission buoys for severe environments; automatic monitoring systems
Financial Information:
Type of Ownership: Private
Domestic Markets:
British Columbia, Newfoundland & Labrador, Nova Scotia, Ontario
Foreign Activity:
Africa, Australia/New Zealand, Eastern Europe, The Middle East, The Pacific Rim, USA
Contact(s):
Tony Chedrawy, President
Greg Connor, Sales Manager

Canadian Branches:
Florida Office
#260, 6538 Collins Ave.
Miami Beach, FL USA
305-968-6050

Metro Recycling
Also Known As: Consolidated Recycling Inc.
3148 Mavis Rd.
Mississauga, ON L5C 1T8
905-277-4711
Fax: 905-279-2115
800-267-9903
trading@metrorecycling.com
www.metrorecycling.com
Firm Type: Waste Management
Founded: 1956
Member of: Institute of Scrap Recycling Industries; Canadian Association of Recycling Industries
Products/Services/Areas of Expertise: Recycling of ferrous & non-ferrous metals
Foreign Activity:
USA
Contact(s):
Hy Ackerman, President
Jake Kafri, Vice-President, Tradings

Metrographic Green Print
Div. of Metrographic Printer Services Ltd.
#4, 80 Raddall Ave.
Dartmouth, NS B3B 1T7
902-468-4644
Fax: 902-468-3935

Products & Services Buyer's Guide

800-367-4644
info@metrographic.ca
www.metrographic.ca
Firm Type: Scientific/Technical Services
Founded: 1975
Products/Services/Areas of Expertise: Printing services, use of environmentally safe products in all aspects of the printing process
Financial Information:
Type of Ownership: Private
Revenue Sources: 1% nationwide; 5% Provincial; 1% Municipals; 93% Private Contracts
Domestic Markets:
New Brunswick, Nova Scotia, Ontario

Métropolitain Valve Inc.
3954, boul Leman
Laval, QC H7E 1A1
514-955-7952
Products/Services/Areas of Expertise: Water & wastewater management equipment
Contact(s):
Pierre Boisseau, President

Metropolitan Consulting Inc.
Formerly: Metropolitan Planning & Engineering Inc.
2290 Queensway Dr.
Burlington, ON L7R 3T2
905-637-2926
Fax: 905-637-3268
kgonnsen@metrocon.ca
www.mpe-psi.com
Firm Type: Engineering
Founded: 1991
Staff: 19
Products/Services/Areas of Expertise: Municipal planning & engineering; project management; feasibility studies; land compensation/expropriation; traffic engineering; environmental approvals; waste management & environmental advice; site assessment; environmental approvals; assimilative capacity; environmental assessments; regulation compliance review
Recently Completed / Ongoing Projects: Permit & take Water, Burlington Springs Gold Course; Phase I, II peer review, City of Burlington; Detroit Bioconversion; Phase I environmental assessment, numerous housing developments
Financial Information:
Type of Ownership: Private
Revenue: $500,000 - $1.5 Million
Revenue Sources: 5% Provincial; 35% Municipals; 60% Private Contracts
Domestic Markets:
Ontario
Contact(s):
Karl Gonnsen, President

Metrovan Hotsy Equipment Ltd.
#1, 9515 - 190th St.
Surrey, BC V4N 3S1
604-882-8202
Fax: 604-882-1631
800-884-6879
Firm Type: Distributing
Staff: 10
Products/Services/Areas of Expertise: Oil water separators; wash water recycling; pressures & parts washers; high pressure; hot water washers; steam cleaners; environment safe detergents; waste oil burners; speed pumps; system design & installation
Domestic Markets:
British Columbia, Yukon Territory
Contact(s):
Dave Johnston, President
Diane Dykhyuzen, Office Manager

Metso Automation Canada Ltd.
A subsidiary of Metso Corp.
Formerly: Neles Jamesbury Ltd.#1, 8161 Keele St.
Vaughan, ON L4K 1Z3
905-532-2000
Fax: 905-532-2001
info.automation@metso.com
www.metso.com
Firm Type: Manufacturing
Founded: 1968
Member of: Valve Manufacturers Association
Quality Environmental Management System(s): 9001
Products/Services/Areas of Expertise: Valves & accessories
Financial Information:
Type of Ownership: Publicly Traded
Domestic Markets:
National
Foreign Activity:
Worldwide
Canadian Branches:
Edmonton Service Center
8319 Roper Rd.
Edmonton, AB T6E 6S4
780-434-7744
Fax: 780-434-7867
Clayton Billey, Manager
clayton.billey@metso.com

Québec Service Center
4716, boul Thimens
Montréal, QC H4R 2B2
514-258-5552
Fax: 514-380-2405
Mike Chenier, Manager
michel.chenier@metso.com

Metso Automation Canada Ltd.
A subsidiary of Metso Corp.
Formerly: Neles Jamesbury Ltd.#1, 8161 Keele St.
Vaughan, ON L4K 1Z3
905-532-2000
Fax: 905-532-2001
info.automation@metso.com
www.metso.com
Firm Type: Manufacturing
Founded: 1968
Member of: Valve Manufacturers Association
Quality Environmental Management System(s): 9001
Products/Services/Areas of Expertise: Valves & accessories
Financial Information:
Type of Ownership: Publicly Traded
Domestic Markets:
National
Foreign Activity:
Worldwide

MF Paints
1605, boul Dagenais ouest
Laval, QC H7L 5A3
450-628-3831
Fax: 450-628-6221
800-363-8034
info@peinturesmf.com
www.peinturesmf.com
Firm Type: Distributing, Manufacturing
Founded: 1967
EcoLogo Certified Products & Services: Iso-Stain Latex; Latex Plus; Portico Latex; Proline Latex; Vogue Latex
Ecological Note: Iso-Stain Latex; Latex Plus; Portico Latex; Proline Latex; Vogue Latex
Contact(s):
Emanuele Morello, Contact

MGM Management
324 Grizzly Pl.
Osoyoos, BC V0H 1V6
250-495-4592
Fax: 250-495-4597
mark@mgm-management.com
www.mgm-management.com
Products/Services/Areas of Expertise: MGM Management provides clients with experience in environmental technical analysis, project management, market development & environmental policy advice.
Contact(s):
Mark McKenney, President

MICCA Paints Inc.
1740, St-Elzéar ouest
Chomedey, QC H7L 3N2
450-686-1740
Fax: 450-686-0477
800-361-3238
info@micca.ca
www.miccapaint.com
Firm Type: Distributing, Manufacturing
Founded: 1985
Staff: 26
Member of: Canadian Paint & Coatings Association; Association des gens d'affaires et professionnels du Québec
Quality Environmental Management System(s): 9001
EcoLogo Certified Products & Services: All latex and acrylic paints manufactured by Micca Paint Inc. are certified; MICCA Moda, Acrylic, Stain, Traffic Paint, Texture, Moda-Pro
Products/Services/Areas of Expertise: Manufacturer of latex, alkyd & acrylic paints, stain, varnish
Ecological Note: All latex and acrylic paints manufactured by Micca Paint Inc. are certified; MICCA Moda, Acrylic, Stain, Traffic Paint, Texture, Moda-Pro
Financial Information:
Type of Ownership: Private
Revenue: Greater than $5 Million
Revenue Sources: 1% nationwide; 2% Municipals; 97% Private Contracts
Domestic Markets:
Ontario, Québec
Foreign Activity:
USA
Markets Sought:
Central Europe, Western Europe
Contact(s):
Michel Cutrone, President
Jennifer Clouston, Manager, Marketing
Jean-Guy Doyle, Controller
George Kahlil, Quality Control
Patrick Rodrique, Director, Operations & ISO

Miceli & Frères Ltée
735, boul Industriel
Mascouche, QC J7K 3G6
450-474-6189
Fax: 450-474-3493
877-474-6189
info@miceli.biz
www.miceli.biz
Products/Services/Areas of Expertise: Water & wastewater management equipment
Contact(s):
Dominic Miceli, Directeur général
domenico@miceli.biz

Michael Holliday & Associates / MH&A
149 Bayswater Ave.
Ottawa, ON K1Y 2G2
613-728-9769
Fax: 613-731-2488
mgh@mh-associates.com
Firm Type: Scientific/Technical Services
Founded: 1978
Staff: 3
Member of: American Industrial Hygiene Association; Air & Waste Management Association; Institute of Professional Environmental Practice
Products/Services/Areas of Expertise: Consultants in environmental & occupational health
Recently Completed / Ongoing Projects: Peer review of environmental assessments; assessment of the internal responsibility system (IRS), recommendations for improvement in underground mines; development of a framework for the periodic review of new substances assessments carried out by Health Canada & Environment Canada; assistance in a cost benefit analysis of a proposed control instrument for 2-butoxyethanol; examination of regulatory programs that undertake risk assessments of polymers for Health Canada; expert advice on the human-exposure component of new-chemical assessments conducted in various OECD countries for Health Canada
Financial Information:
Type of Ownership: Private
Revenue: $50,000 - $100,000
Revenue Sources: 60% nationwide; 25% Provincial; 15% Private Contracts
Domestic Markets:
National
Foreign Activity:
Africa, USA
Markets Sought:
Mexico
Contact(s):
Michael G. Holliday, Q.E.P., Senior Partner

Michael Wall & Sons Enterprises Ltd.
Acheson Industrial Park
53016 Hwy. 60, 561 Acheson Rd.
Spruce Grove, AB T7X 3G7

780-483-9255
Fax: 780-962-1052
walzy@connect.ab.ca
Firm Type: Scientific/Technical Services
Founded: 1981
Staff: 32
Products/Services/Areas of Expertise: Plant science; horticulture; soil science; crop production; environmental management; wood preservation
Financial Information:
Type of Ownership: Private
Revenue Sources: 75% Provincial; 20% Municipals; 5% Private Contracts
Domestic Markets:
Alberta, British Columbia
Contact(s):
Wesley Wall, Director

Michel Lavallée
5 de Normandie St.
Saint-Charles-Borromée, QC J6E 7P2
450-586-2480

Michelin North America (Canada) Inc.
#510, 2540, boul Daniel Johnson
Laval, QC H7T 2T9
450-978-4731
Fax: 450-978-7590
888-871-4444
ralph.beaveridge@ca.michelin.com
www.michelin.ca
Ecological Note: Michelin Energy Passenger Tire; Michelin Fuel Efficient Truck Tires
Contact(s):
Ralph Beaveridge

Micro-Watt Control Devices Ltd.
2721 Hopewell Pl. NE
Calgary, AB T1Y 7J7
403-250-1594
Fax: 403-291-6671
888-388-1592
mwsales@microwattcontrols.com
www.microwattcontrols.com
Firm Type: Distributing
Founded: 1984
Staff: 35
Member of: Instrument Society of America
Products/Services/Areas of Expertise: Distributes products that detect & monitor combustible & toxic levels of gas in industrial & commercial complexes; also products that detect smoke, particulate matter, oilmists, etc., & that instantaneously detect fire; also distributes emergency communications, video monitoring, & solar-powered equipment, as well as process instrumentation, flare stack monitors & industrial horns & strobes
Financial Information:
Type of Ownership: Private
Revenue Sources: 100% Private Contracts
Domestic Markets:
National
Contact(s):
Ken Coffey, Owner
kenc@microwattcontrols.com
Ryan Albizzati, Chief Financial Officer
ryana@microwattcontrols.com

Canadian Branches:
Edmonton
9490 - 51 Ave.
Edmonton, AB T6E 5A6
780-465-3644
Fax: 780-465-6337
Gord Stephenson
gords@microwattcontrols.com

Fort St. John
#118, 10704 - 97 Ave.
Fort St John, BC V1J 6L7
250-785-8876
Fax: 250-785-8788
Aaron Krafczyk
aaronk@microwattcontrols.com

Grande Prairie
#109, 8716-108th St.
Grande Prairie, AB T8V 4C7

780-832-0234
Fax: 780-832-0235
866-256-1688
Brett Billey
brettb@microwattcontrols.com

Micrologic Ltd.
#5, 1323 - 44 Ave. NE
Calgary, AB T2E 6L5
403-250-2911
Fax: 403-250-5009
info@micrologic.ab.ca
www.micrologic.ab.ca/
Firm Type: Engineering
Founded: 1978
Staff: 3
Member of: Association of Professional Engineers, Geologists & Geophysicists of Alberta
Products/Services/Areas of Expertise: Measuring & monitoring equipment; laboratory equipment; electronic instrument design & development services; electronics engineering consultants; microprocessor-based product development
Financial Information:
Type of Ownership: Private
Revenue Sources: 100% Private Contracts
Domestic Markets:
Alberta
Foreign Activity:
USA
Markets Sought:
Australia/New Zealand
Contact(s):
Robert Atkins, P.Eng., President

MIE Consulting Engineers Ltd.
Also Known As: MIE Marine
#306, 146 Laird Dr.
Toronto, ON M4G 3V7
416-424-2675
Fax: 416-424-2683
800-668-0630
Firm Type: Engineering, Scientific/Technical Services
Founded: 1978
Staff: 4
Member of: Association of Professional Engineers of Ontario
Products/Services/Areas of Expertise: Diving services for facilities inspection; bottom sampling for impact assessments; engineering design & evaluation of marine structures; research on corrosion in fresh waters
Recently Completed / Ongoing Projects: Dunnville Dam rehabilitation; impact of zebra mussels on steel structures; condition surveys of Great Lakes harbour facilities; station renovations for GO Transit
Financial Information:
Type of Ownership: Private
Revenue: $250,000 - $500,000
Revenue Sources: 70% nationwide; 20% Provincial; 10% Municipals
Domestic Markets:
National
Foreign Activity:
USA
Markets Sought:
Australia/New Zealand, Caribbean,
Contact(s):
J.D. Jones, P.Eng, MBA, President
Ramon Traballo, B.Sc.Eng., Consultant/Diver

Mifab Canada
#4, 150 Norfinch Dr.
Toronto, ON M3N 1X6
416-679-0380
Fax: 416-679-0350
800-387-3880
headoffice@mifab.com
www.mifab.com
Firm Type: Manufacturing
Founded: 1982
Quality Environmental Management System(s): 9001
Products/Services/Areas of Expertise: Mifab is a manufacturer of engineered commercial plumbing products.
Financial Information:
Type of Ownership: Foreign-owned
Domestic Markets:
National

Foreign Activity:
The Middle East, USA
Contact(s):
Alex Patterson, President
Terry Hanna, Vice-President
Frank Azizi, Representative, Customer Service
Vishnu Nauth, Representative, Customer Service

Canadian Branches:
North Battleford
101 Canola Ave.
North Battleford, SK S9A 2Y3
306-445-7201
Fax: 905-673-2499
800-387-3880
headoffice@mifab.com
www.mifab.com
Randy Abrahamson, Manager, Operations
Lee Hooker, Manager, Production

MIG Engineering Ltd.
453 Christina St. North
Sarnia, ON N7T 5W3
519-337-8000
Fax: 519-337-8001
800-644-3943
sarnia@migeng.com
www.migeng.com
Firm Type: Engineering
Founded: 1959
Staff: 20
Member of: Consulting Engineers of Ontario; Professional Engineers of Ontario
Products/Services/Areas of Expertise: Manages & designs from inception to operation, municipal infrastructure projects, both new & upgrades; specializing in water & wastewater, buildings, industrial parks, transportation (bridges, border crossings); also specializes in linear transmission facilities (water, industrial gases, electricity)
Recently Completed / Ongoing Projects: 4 km high pressure pipeline; buried services relocation, Ontario Hydro; class EA & project implementation of sewage treatment plant upgrade, Ilderton, ON; water EA & implementation, Brooke-Alvinston; sewage treatment facility upgrade, Warwick
Financial Information:
Type of Ownership: Private
Revenue Sources: 10% Provincial; 50% Municipals; 40% Private Contracts
Domestic Markets:
Ontario
Foreign Activity:
USA
Contact(s):
Marty L. Raaymakers, C.S.T., President
Jamie A. Montieth, C.Tech, Director

Canadian Branches:
London
#780, 195 Dufferin Ave.
London, ON N6A 1K7
519-680-1226
Fax: 519-680-1371

Mike Fuller Electric Ltd.
45 Epworth Ave.
Nepean, ON K2G 2L8
613-225-3249
Fax: 613-727-8342
Firm Type: Management Consulting, Engineering

Products/Services/Areas of Expertise: Electricians' services are offered by the residential authorized contractor.
Financial Information:
Type of Ownership: Private
Domestic Markets:
Ontario
Contact(s):
Mike Fuller, Contact

Mikro-Tek Inc.
P.O. Box 2120
115 Sandy Falls Rd.
Timmins, ON P4N 7X8
705-268-3536
Fax: 705-268-7411
mikro-tek@mikro-tek.com
www.mikro-tek.com

Products & Services Buyer's Guide

Firm Type: Manufacturing, Scientific/Technical Services
Founded: 1990
Products/Services/Areas of Expertise: The biotechnology company developed a technology to increase carbon sequestration, resulting in increased plant survival & growth. The need for chemicals & fertilizers is reduced. Aggregated sequestration projects take place in the following sectors: forestry, agriculture, & land reclamation.
Financial Information:
Type of Ownership: Private
Domestic Markets:
National
Foreign Activity:
South America
Contact(s):
Mark Kean, Founder

Millar Western Forest Products Ltd.
16640 - 111 Ave.
Edmonton, AB T5M 2S5
780-486-8200
Fax: 780-486-8282
mwfp@millarwestern.com
www.millarwestern.com
Firm Type: Manufacturing
Quality Environmental Management System(s): 14001
Products/Services/Areas of Expertise: Pulp & lumber facilities are operated by Millar Western. The company meets or surpasses environmental laws & regulations related to its operations. Sustainable forest management is employed in all woodlands operations. The mill & woodlands operations have been certified under FORESTCARE, the Alberta's code of practice governing care of the forest, environment, & communities.
Financial Information:
Type of Ownership: Private
Domestic Markets:
National
Foreign Activity:
Asia, Central Europe, Eastern Europe, Western Europe, USA
Contact(s):
H. MacKenzie Millar, President & Chief Executive Officer
J. Craig Armstrong, Chief Operating Officer & Executive Vice-President
Kevin Edgson, Chief Financial Officer & Vice-President, 780-486-8219
Dave Keir, Vice-President, Human Resources, 780-486-8224
Jack Joys, Director, Energy, 780-486-8263
Janet Millar, Director, Communications, 780-486-8249
Stefan Demharter, General Manager, Wood Products

Millar-Williams Hydronics Ltd.
#12, 4060 Fairview St.
Burlington, ON L7L 4Y8
905-637-9496
Fax: 905-333-5446
800-263-6651
mwhl@idirect.com
www.millarwilliams.on.ca
Firm Type: Distributing, Manufacturing
Founded: 1966
Products/Services/Areas of Expertise: Millar-Williams Hydronics Ltd. is a manufacturer & distributor of pumps, valves, conveyor systems, & related products. It specializes in custom designed systems.
Contact(s):
A.R. Williams, President

Millennium Water Management Ltd.
65 Coventry Lane
Dartmouth, NS B2V 2K5
902-462-3868
Fax: 902-462-2767
Products/Services/Areas of Expertise: Millennium Water Management provides potable, industrial, & wastewater treatment services & equipment.
Domestic Markets:
Nova Scotia
Contact(s):
Bernie Zwicker, President

Miller Environmental Corp.
65 Trottier Bay
Winnipeg, MB R3T 3R3
204-925-9600
Fax: 204-925-9601

Firm Type: Scientific/Technical Services, Waste Management
Founded: 1987
Staff: 25
Member of: Manitoba Environmental Industries Association
Quality Environmental Management System(s): 9001; ISO
Products/Services/Areas of Expertise: Provides comprehensive & environmentally sound industrial waste management services to a wide range of industries; with a modern, fully licensed industrial waste treatment facility; aqueous waste processing; inorganic solids & sludge processing; miscellaneous inorganic chemicals processing; liquid organic waste processing; organic solids & sludge processing; miscellaneous organic chemicals processing
Recently Completed / Ongoing Projects: Operator of the former Manitoba Hazardous Waste Management Corp. (MHWMC), providing commercial consulting services on issues such as waste market characterization, waste management planning, project management for site remediation, & other waste management activities; presently operating a household hazardous waste collection depot in Winnipeg, providing a public service within Manitoba & on a commercial basis for outside Manitoba
Financial Information:
Type of Ownership: Private
Revenue: Greater than $5 Million
Revenue Sources: 10% nationwide; 10% Provincial; 80% Private Contracts
Domestic Markets:
Alberta, Manitoba, Ontario, Saskatchewan
Foreign Activity:
USA
Contact(s):
Joel Carlson, Manager, Sales

Canadian Branches:
St. Jean Baptiste
Operations
P.O. Box 279
St Jean Baptiste, MB R0G 2B0
204-737-2140
Fax: 204-737-2225
Marcel Bissonnette, Manager

Miller Waste Systems
8050 Woodbine Ave.
Markham, ON L3R 2N8
905-475-6356
Fax: 905-475-6396
800-465-5914
millerwaste@millergroup.ca
www.millergroup.ca
Firm Type: Waste Management
Staff: 450
Products/Services/Areas of Expertise: The diverse waste management company operates collection vehicles & designs, constructs, & operates waste diversion facilities.
Activities: Operating transfer stations, waste recovery facilities, & composting facilities; Providing hazardous waste management services; Offering full recycling programs; Providing wood waste recovery services
Financial Information:
Type of Ownership: Private
Domestic Markets:
New Brunswick, Nova Scotia, Ontario
Contact(s):
George South, General Manager

Minas Basin Pulp & Power Company Limited
P.O. Box 401
53 Prince St.
Hantsport, NS B0P 1P0
902-684-1219
Fax: 800-743-1428
800-792-2493
sales@minas.ns.ca
www.minas.ns.ca
Firm Type: Manufacturing
Founded: 1927
Products/Services/Areas of Expertise: Minas Basin Pulp & Power Company Limited produces recycled paperboard, such as linerboard & coreboard. The company uses 100% recycled fibre, & operates in total compliance with all federal Pulp & Paper Effluent Regulations.
Recently Completed / Ongoing Projects: Building a biodiesel plastics processing plant to convert plastic garbage intoa marketable fuel source; Constructing a facility to create electricity from forest byproducts

Contact(s):
Scott Travers, President & Chief Operating Officer
John Woods, Vice-President, Energy Development

Miniveil Air Systems
Formerly: Miniveil Ltd.
340 Ward St.
Port Hope, ON L1A 4A6
905-885-4015
Fax: 905-885-6478
info@miniveil.com
www.miniveil.com
Firm Type: Manufacturing
Founded: 1956
Products/Services/Areas of Expertise: Miniveil Air Systems manufactures air curtains to use on openings where different environments must be kept separate.
Financial Information:
Type of Ownership: Private
Domestic Markets:
National
Foreign Activity:
USA
Contact(s):
J. Larsson, President

Mirarco Mining Innovation
Laurentian University
933 Ramsey Lake Rd.
Sudbury, ON P3E 6B5
705-675-1151
Fax: 705-675-4838
800-461-4030
mirarco@mirarco.org
www.mirarco.org
Firm Type: Scientific/Technical Services
Founded: 1998
Products/Services/Areas of Expertise: Research & development for environmental systems; environmental monitoring & testing (air, soil & water); modelling, eg. wind data, ground water, temperature, GID & satellite imagery data; particulate analysis & chemistry, rehabilitation, waste management
Recently Completed / Ongoing Projects: Novel composter technology testing; environmental sensor network testing & development; drinking water testing, simulation, modelling & analysis; impacts of industrial practice on air quality & ecosystem
Financial Information:
Type of Ownership: Non Profit
Revenue: $1.5 Million - $3 Million
Revenue Sources: 30% nationwide; 20% Provincial; 50% Private Contracts
Domestic Markets:
Ontario, Saskatchewan
Foreign Activity:
China, Western Europe, USA, Vietnam
Markets Sought:
The Pacific Rim, South America
Contact(s):
Steve Hall, President
shall@mirarco.org
Sean Maloney, Vice-President, Operations
smaloney@mirarco.org
Graeme Spiers, Director, Centre for Environmental Monitoring
gspiers@mirarco.org

Mirus International Inc.
31 Sun Pac Blvd.
Brampton, ON L6S 5P6
905-494-1120
Fax: 905-494-1140
888-866-4787
mirus@mirusinternational.com
www.mirusinternational.com
Firm Type: Distributing, Manufacturing
Founded: 1991
Member of: MIRUS Magnetics Inc.
Member of: US Green Building Council
EcoLogo Certified Products & Services: Energy efficient power quality products
Products/Services/Areas of Expertise: MIRUS International Inc. is engaged in the design & manufacture of high efficiency harmonic mitigating products for electrical power distribution systems.
Ecological Note: Energy efficient power quality products

Products & Services Buyer's Guide

Financial Information:
Type of Ownership: Private
Domestic Markets:
National
Foreign Activity:
Worldwide
Contact(s):
Tony Hoevenaars, President & Chief Executive Officer
Michael Levin, Chief Engineer, Research & Development

MissionHGE Inc.
#205, 2800 av St-Jean-Baptiste
Québec, QC G2E 6J5
418-872-1161
Fax: 418-872-5626
quebec@missionhge.qc.ca
www.missionhge.qc.ca
Contact(s):
Michel Caron, Président
Canadian Branches:
Boucherville Office
#716A, 1370, rue Joliot-Curie
Boucherville, QC J4B 7L9
450-449-4511
Fax: 450-449-8966
boucherville@missionhge.qc.ca

Rimouski Office
79, rue de l'Évêché est
Rimouski, QC G5L 1X7
418-721-4040
Fax: 418-721-4004
rimouski@missionhge.qc.ca

Mississauga Laboratory
#4, 160 Traders Blvd.
Mississauga, ON L4Z 3K7
905-890-0785
Fax: 905-890-1141

Canadian Branches:
Bonnyville Branch
P.O. Box 7699
Bonnyville, AB T9N 2J1
780-826-4759

Burnaby Branch
2227 Douglas Rd.
Burnaby, BC V5C 5A9
604-294-3811
Fax: 604-294-4664

Calgary Headquarters
221 - 18 St. SE
Calgary, AB T2E 6J5
403-248-4331
Fax: 403-248-2188
L.A. Panek, Vice-President, Environment

Dawson Creek Branch
10201 - 17 St.
Dawson Creek, BC V1G 4C3
250-782-1883
Fax: 250-782-3430

Edmonton Branch
4810 - 93 St.
Edmonton, AB T6E 5M4
780-436-2152
Fax: 780-435-8425

Kamloops Branch
913 Laval Cres.
Kamloops, BC V2C 5P4
250-374-1347
Fax: 250-374-2944

Lethbridge Branch
1430B - 31 St. North
Lethbridge, AB T1H 5J8
403-327-7474
Fax: 403-327-7682

Lloydminster Branch
P.O. Box 1518
5406 - 52 Ave.
Lloydminster, AB S9V 1K5
780-875-8975
Fax: 780-875-1970

Medicine Hat Branch
964D - 23 St. SW
Medicine Hat, AB T1A 8G3
403-527-5871
Fax: 403-528-3860

Nanaimo Branch
3070 Barons Rd.
Nanaimo, BC V9T 4B5
250-758-1887
Fax: 250-758-1899

Prince Geoge Branch
610 Richard Rd.
Prince George, BC V2K 4L3
250-564-3243
Fax: 250-562-7045

Red Deer Branch
#4, 5551 - 45 St.
Red Deer, AB T4N 1L2
403-343-8566
Fax: 403-342-5850

Regina Branch
608 McLeod St.
Regina, SK S4N 4Y1
306-721-7100
Fax: 306-721-2626

Winnipeg Branch
95B Scurfield Blvd.
Winnipeg, MB R3Y 1G4
204-920-4140
Fax: 204-489-8261

Yellowknife Branch
P.O. Box 2245
135 Enterprise Rd.
Yellowknife, NT X1A 2P7
867-920-4140
Fax: 867-873-2197

Mississauga Laboratory
#4, 160 Traders Blvd.
Mississauga, ON L4Z 3K7
905-890-0785
Fax: 905-890-1141

International Branch(es):
HBT AGRA Limited - Tanzania
P.O. Box 963
New Bagamoyo Rd., Plot 46
Dar es Salaam Tanzania
-011-255-51-72847
Fax: -011-255-51-728

Moore & Taber
1290 North Hancock St.
Anaheim, CA USA
714-779-2591
Fax: 714-779-8377

RZA-AGRA
#100, 11335 NE 122 Way
Kirkland, WA USA
206-820-4669
Fax: 206-821-3914

Sergent, Hauskins & Beckwith
3232 West Virginia Ave.
Pheonix, AZ USA
602-272-6848
Fax: 602-272-7239

Mississippi River Power Corp. / MRPC
Formerly: Almonte Hydro
P.O. Box 179
28 Mill St.
Almonte, ON K0A 1A0
613-256-2403
Fax: 613-256-9593
800-532-1502
info@mississippiriverpower.com
www.mississippiriverpower.com
Firm Type: Manufacturing
Founded: 2000
Products/Services/Areas of Expertise: Mississippi River Power Corp. is the owner & operator of a generating station in Almonte, Ontario. All power generated by the run-of-river generating plant is clean or green power.

Recently Completed / Ongoing Projects: Constructing the Lower Falls Redevelopment Project
Domestic Markets:
Ontario
Contact(s):
Des Houston, President
Scott Newton, Manager, Operations
snewton@mississippiriverpower.com
John Fraser, Secretary-Treasurer

Mitsubishi Canada Ltd. / MCL
#2800, 200 Granville St.
Vancouver, BC V6C 1G6
604-654-8000
Fax: 604-654-8222
www.mitsubishi.ca
Firm Type: Manufacturing, Scientific/Technical Services
Founded: 1965
Staff: 31
Member of: Toyo Tire Canada; Alpac Forest Products; Alpac Pulp Sales; MC Tubular Products Canada; Metal One Canada / Nifast Canada; Iron Ore Company of Canada
Products/Services/Areas of Expertise: Major products include carbon, coal, iron ore, petrochemical products, functional chemicals, materials for synthetic fibres & resins, & food & feed additives
Activities: Developing renewable energy, such as wind power & solar photovoltaic energy; Expanding power stations, power transmission, & steel mill plants
Recently Completed / Ongoing Projects: Infrastructure development, involving iron ore, uranium, coal, & copper; LNG export terminals; Wind power; Carbon Dioxide Capture & Storage (CCS); i-MiEV electric vehicles; Biofuel & fuel cells
Financial Information:
Type of Ownership: Foreign-owned
Foreign Activity:
Central Europe, Eastern Europe, Western Europe
Contact(s):
Yorihiko Kojima, President & Chief Executive Officer

Canadian Branches:
Toronto Office
#715, 55 University Ave.
Toronto, ON M5J 2H7
416-362-6731
Fax: 416-365-1384
Staff: 12

MK Plastics Corp.
4955, av De Courtrai
Montréal, QC H3W 1A6
514-871-9999
Fax: 514-871-1753
mkfans@mkplastics.com
www.mkplastics.com
Firm Type: Manufacturing
Founded: 1963
Products/Services/Areas of Expertise: Fiberglass fans & blowers
Contact(s):
Minel Kupferberg, President
Jeff Roberts, Vice-President, Operations

MKG Imaging Solutions Inc.
Formerly: MKG Cartridge Systems Inc.
1090 Lorimar Dr.
Mississauga, ON L5S 1R8
905-564-9218
Fax: 905-564-9225
800-881-7545
sales@mkg.org
www.mkg.org
Firm Type: Manufacturing
Founded: 1988
Staff: 300
Quality Environmental Management System(s): 9001
Products/Services/Areas of Expertise: Repacking of used laser & fax toner cartridges to distributors & rechargers
Domestic Markets:
National
Foreign Activity:
Worldwide
Contact(s):
Michael Grist, President
gristm@mkg.org
Robert Ellerby, Controller

Products & Services Buyer's Guide

MLC Associés Inc.
#950, 1200, boul Chomedey
Laval, QC H7V 3Z3
450-687-7077
Fax: 450-687-5700
Products/Services/Areas of Expertise: Engineering consulting services
Domestic Markets:
Québec
Contact(s):
Claude Chagnon, Vice-President

MMM Group
Also Known As: Marshall Macklin Monaghan Ltd.
100 Commerce Valley Dr. West
Thornhill, ON L3T 0A1
905-882-1100
Fax: 905-882-0055
mmm@mmm.ca
www.mmm.ca
Firm Type: Engineering
Founded: 1962
Member of: Seawood Solutions & Services Inc.; McCormick Rankin Corp.; MRC McLean Hazel; Delphi-MRC; Ecoplans Ltd.; Site 360 Consulting Inc.; Enermodal Engineering Ltd.
Member of: Association of Professional Engineers; Canadian Institute of Planners
Products/Services/Areas of Expertise: Engineering planning consulting services; environmental consulting services; transportation engineering & planning; municipal engineering & structural engineering; urban & regional planning; environmental management for public & private sector clients
Recently Completed / Ongoing Projects: Site selection studies, Manitoba Hydro; environmental impact assessments, various projects
Financial Information:
Type of Ownership: Private
Revenue: $1.5 Million - $3 Million
Domestic Markets:
National
Foreign Activity:
Worldwide
Contact(s):
D. Hicks, CEO
E. Hicks, Associate

Canadian Branches:
Canmore
#203, 729 - 10th St.
Canmore, AB T1W 2A3
403-678-3500
Fax: 403-678-3501

Edmonton
#200, 10576 - 113 St.
Edmonton, AB T5H 3H5
780-423-4123
Fax: 780-426-0659
edmonton@mmm.ca

Halton-Peel
#106, 2410 Meadowpine Blvd.
Mississauga, ON L5N 6S2
905-826-4770
Fax: 905-826-8007
hpro@mmm.ca

Kelowna
#101, 389 Queensway Ave.
Kelowna, BC V1Y 8E6
250-869-1334
Fax: 250-869-1334

Montréal
Groupe MMM Limitée
#901, 1155 rue University
Montréal, QC H3B 3A7
514-878-1100
Fax: 514-878-9082

Ottawa
#302, 1111 Prince of Wales Dr.
Ottawa, ON K2C 3T2
613-274-3200
Fax: 613-236-2270
williss@mmm.ca

Saskatoon
#4, 1925 - 1st Ave. North
Saskatoon, SK S7K 6W1
306-657-4233
Fax: 306-380-1521

Vancouver
#700, 1045 Howe St.
Vancouver, BC V6Z 2A9
604-685-9381
Fax: 604-683-8655

Whitby
#201, 701 Rossland Rd. East
Whitby, ON L1N 8Y9
905-668-3022
Fax: 905-668-9443
rosec@mmm.ca

Winnipeg
#111, 93 Lombard Ave.
Winnipeg, MB R3B 3B1
204-943-3178
Fax: 204-943-4948
winnipeg@mmm.ca

Mobile Augers & Research Ltd.
5603 - 54 St.
Edmonton, AB T6B 3G8
780-436-3960
Fax: 780-434-7242
800-428-4377
nzacharko@mobile.augers.com
www.mobileaugers.com
Firm Type: Scientific/Technical Services
Founded: 1959
Products/Services/Areas of Expertise: Mobile Augers & Research Ltd. is a geotechnical & environmental site investigation drilling firm. New technology is developed to provide safer drilling programs.
Recently Completed / Ongoing Projects: Runway at Rothera Research Station, Antarctica; Arctic research at Ellesmere Island, Nunavut; LRT tunnel, Edmonton, Alberta; Permafrost stabilizatin, Churchill, Manitoba
Domestic Markets:
Alberta, British Columbia, Manitoba, Northwest Territories, Nunavut, Saskatchewan
Foreign Activity:
Worldwide

Mold & Bacteria Consulting Laboratories (MBL) Inc. / MBL
#1A, 1020 Brevik Pl.
Mississauga, ON L4W 4N7
905-290-9101
Fax: 905-290-0499
866-813-0648
info@moldbacteria.com
www.moldbacteria.com
Firm Type: Management Consulting, Scientific/Technical Services
Founded: 2004
Products/Services/Areas of Expertise: Mold & Bacteria Consulting Laboratories identifies & enumerates mold & bacteria, commonly found in air & fluids. The company also offers a Mold Training Course, which covers processes from recognizing indoor mold to performing mold remediation.
Domestic Markets:
Alberta, British Columbia, Manitoba, Ontario,

Momentum Conveyors
48 Prospect St.
Newmarket, ON L3Y 3S9
905-895-3262
Fax: 905-895-5427
momentum_conveyor@rogers.com
www.momentumconveyor.com
Firm Type: Engineering, Manufacturing
Founded: 1968
Products/Services/Areas of Expertise: Momentum Conveyors is engaged in the design, fabrication, & maintenance of conveyor systems & components.
Activities: Servicing industries such as recycling, forestry, paper, corrugated cardboard, food, & medical
Financial Information:
Type of Ownership: Private
Domestic Markets:
Ontario

Contact(s):
Nick Johnson, Co-Owner & Operator
Jeff Johnson, Co-Owner & Operator

Monalt Environmental Inc.
#4, 73 Railside Rd.
Toronto, ON M3A 1B2
416-391-3241
Fax: 416-391-3815
monaltenv@yahoo.ca
www.monaltenvironmental.com
Firm Type: Scientific/Technical Services
Founded: 1990
Member of: Environmental Abatement Council of Ontario; Toronto Construction Association; Better Bussiness Bureau
Products/Services/Areas of Expertise: Monalt Environmental Inc. is involved in the removal of asbestos for residential, municipal, institutional, commercial, & industrial clients. Other services include lead & mold abatement. The company is in good standing with the Workplace Safety & Insurance Board.
Recently Completed / Ongoing Projects: Toronto District School Board; Peel District School Board; Duham Region School Board; University of Toronto; North York Hospital; Toronto Grace Hospital; Toronto East Hospital; Humber Memorial Hospital; Scarborough General Hospital; Riverdale Hospital; Whitby Psychiatric Hospital; Humber Treatment Plant; Duffin - Creek Waste Water Treatment Plant
Financial Information:
Type of Ownership: Private
Domestic Markets:
Ontario
Contact(s):
John Paduraru, Estimator

Mondo Products Company Limited
#1, 695 Westney Rd.
Ajax, ON L1S 6M9
905-426-9339
Fax: 905-426-5240
800-465-5676
rob@mondo-products.com
www.mondo-products.com
Firm Type: Distributing, Manufacturing
Founded: 1970
Products/Services/Areas of Expertise: Mondo Products Company Limited is a manufacturer & distributor of concentrated chemicals for the car wash industry. MSDS Technical Data Sheets are available for all detergents & specialty products.
Financial Information:
Type of Ownership: Private
Domestic Markets:
National
Contact(s):
Steve Boston, Owner
steve@mondo-products.com
Brad Boston, President
brad@mondo-products.com
Robert Devlin, General Manager
rob@mondo-products.com
Ryan Tasker, Manager, Information Technology
ryan@mondo-products.com

Mondry Del Zotto et associés inc.
8, rue St-Denis
Saint-Lambert, QC J4P 2G2
450-465-1101
Fax: 450-465-1409
mdaine@ergonet.com
Firm Type: Engineering
Founded: 1974
Staff: 5
Products/Services/Areas of Expertise: Petroleum installation design; industrial, commercial & residential projects involving civil, electrical & mechanical design aspects; project budgeting; construction supervision & management; expertise in arctic installation & construction
Domestic Markets:
Alberta, New Brunswick, Newfoundland & Labrador, Northwest Territories, Ontario, Québec
Markets Sought:
Eastern Europe, Western Europe, South America, Mexico, USA
Contact(s):
Ezio Del Zotto, P.Eng., President
Richard V. Mondry, P.Eng., Sec.-Treas.

Monitrex Engineering Ltd.
#7, 4604 - 13th St. NE
Calgary, AB T2E 6P1
403-291-3590
Products/Services/Areas of Expertise: Monitrex Engineering is engaged in air monitoring & air pollution control.
Domestic Markets:
Alberta
Contact(s):
Jim Westlake, Contact

Monsanto Canada Inc.
#900, One Research Rd.
Winnipeg, MB R3T 6E3
204-985-1000
Fax: 888-556-5565
800-667-4944
www.monsanto.ca
Firm Type: Manufacturing
Staff: 300
Products/Services/Areas of Expertise: The agricultural company employs biotechnology to make seeds easier for farmers to grow. Monsanto Canada's seed-based products contribute to the production of healthier foods, better animal feed, crop protection, & a reduction of agriculture's impact on the environment. A range of herbicides is also offered by Monsanto Canada.
Activities: Producing corn, canola, & soybean seed products which are marketed under the DEKALB brand name; Researching products that will benefit farmers, processors, & consumers
Recently Completed / Ongoing Projects: Research on seed & trait development in corn, canola, & soybeans, with a focus on issues such as drought tolerance & nitrogen use efficiency
Financial Information:
Type of Ownership: Foreign-owned
Domestic Markets:
National,
Contact(s):
Ryan Baldwin, President, Seeds & Traits
Cory McArthur, President, Crop Protection
Carolin Chambers, Lead, Customer Operations
John Dossetor, Lead, Government Affairs
Trish Jordan, Lead, Public & Industry Affairs
Mike McGuire, Lead, East Sales & Marketing
Brian Treacy, Lead, Regulatory Affairs

Monserco Ltd.
#2, 190 Wilkinson Rd.
Brampton, ON L6T 4W3
905-450-3507
Fax: 905-450-8523
800-665-7736
vgtathe@energysolutions.com
www.monserco.com
Firm Type: Management Consulting, Waste Management
Founded: 1978
Products/Services/Areas of Expertise: Monserco Limited is a supplier of radiation waste management services, radioanalytical laboratory services, radiological consulting services, nuclear gauge services, & emergency response services. The company's practices & facilities are licensed & approved by the Canadian Nuclear Safety Commission.
Activities: Handling & disposing nuclear waste
Recently Completed / Ongoing Projects: Customers include hospitals, nuclear facilities, universities, pharmaceutical companies, & paper & steel industries
Financial Information:
Type of Ownership: Private
Domestic Markets:
National
Contact(s):
Ron Leblond, Vice-President & General Manager
Chad MacLean, Manager, Operations
Vik Tathe, Manager, Business Development
Tim Ryder, Officer, Radiation Safety
Vivek Manickam, Senior Health Physicist

Canadian Branches:
Brossard - Monserco Limitée
3455, Isabelle, #G
Brossard, QC J4Y 2R2
450-444-1213
Fax: 450-444-1235
800-401-1213
mrfrenette@energysolutions.com
www.monserco.com
Domestic Markets:
Québec
Mathieu Frenette, Health Physicist
Raphael Durocher, Radiation Technician

Monster Polymers Inc.
P.O. Box 145
300 Prisque Rd.
Honey Harbour, ON P0E 1E0
705-792-0222
Fax: 705-756-5673
rod@monsterpolymers.com
www.monsterpolymers.com
Firm Type: Management Consulting, Distributing
Founded: 1990
Products/Services/Areas of Expertise: Monster Polymers Inc. assists customers with their thermoplastic resin purchasing & sales.
Activities: Buying & selling plastic raw materials
Domestic Markets:
National
Foreign Activity:
Worldwide
Contact(s):
Rod Monster, Founder & President
Sterling Monster, Vice-President

Montrose Technologies Inc.
Formerly: Dipix Technologies Inc.
1051 Baxter Rd.
Ottawa, ON K2C 3P2
613-562-1113
Fax: 613-249-7341
info@montrose-tech.com
www.montrose-tech.com
Products/Services/Areas of Expertise: Remote sensing; image hardware & software; microscopic imaging/measurement systems; systems integration; machine vision
Domestic Markets:
National
Foreign Activity:
Eastern Europe, Western Europe, The Middle East, The Pacific Rim, USA
Contact(s):
Anton Kitai, President
Robert Parker, Vice-President, Engineering & Operations

Morgan Falls Power Company
#200, 300 Prince Albert Rd.
Dartmouth, NS B2Y 4J2
902-468-3579
Fax: 902-468-6865
info@seaforthng.ca
www.seaforthengineering.com/morgan.htm
Firm Type: Manufacturing
Founded: 1985
EcoLogo Certified Products & Services: Morgan Falls received EcoLogo certification.
Products/Services/Areas of Expertise: Morgan Falls Power Corporation is the owner & operator of an 850-KW run-of-river hydroelectric facility. The environmentally sustainable, renewable energy project is situated in New Germany, Nova Scotia. The facility features a fish by-pass technology to prevent the entrapment of fish.
Recently Completed / Ongoing Projects: Participating in the Nova Scotia Strategy on Climate Change
Ecological Note: Morgan Falls received EcoLogo certification.
Contact(s):
Stan Mason, Contact

Morrison Environmental Limited
1087 Meyerside Dr.
Mississauga, ON L5T 1M5
905-564-8944
Fax: 905-564-8952
info@morrison-environmental.com
www.morrison-environmental.com
Firm Type: Management Consulting, Engineering
Member of: Canadian Ground Water Associtation; Canadian Water & Wastewater Association; Ontario Ground Water Association; American Water Works Association; National Ground Water Association
Products/Services/Areas of Expertise: The professional engineering firm specializes in groundwater consultations to both private & public sector clients.
Activities: Finding, producing, treating, & controlling groundwater
Domestic Markets:
National
Foreign Activity:
Worldwide

Morrison Hershfield
Formerly: Maxim Engineering Inc.
#600, 25 Yorkland Blvd.
Toronto, ON M2J 1T1
416-499-3110
Fax: 416-499-9658
888-649-4730
toronto@morrisonhershfield.com
www.morrisonhershfield.com
Firm Type: Management Consulting, Engineering
Founded: 1946
Products/Services/Areas of Expertise: Morrison Hershfield provides multidisciplinary engineering services. Engineering solutions are offered in the following areas: energy & industrial, buildings, technology & telecom, transportation, environment, water & wastewater, & land development.
Recently Completed / Ongoing Projects: Niagara tunnel intake works; Hospital link transit corridor environmental assessment, Ottawa; Jefferson Salamander breeding habitat assessment, Ontario; Heritage bridge restoration, Ontario; Darlington B new nuclear build, Ontario; Wasaga Beach residential development environmental impact statement, Ontario; Aquatic & terrestrial ecosystems inventory & impact assessment services, Ontario
Financial Information:
Type of Ownership: Foreign-owned
Domestic Markets:
Alberta, British Columbia, Ontario
Contact(s):
Bruce Miller, P.Eng., President
Catherine Karakatsanis, P.Eng., Senior Vice-President, Buildings & Facilities
Mark Lucuik, P.Eng., LEED AP, Director Sustainability

Canadian Branches:
Burlington
#175, 1005 Skyview Dr.
Burlington, ON L7P 5B1
905-319-6668
Fax: 905-319-5548
burlington@morrisonhershfield.com
www.morrisonhershfield.com
Domestic Markets:
Ontario

Calgary
#300, 6807 Railway St. SE
Calgary, AB T2H 2V6
403-246-4500
Fax: 403-246-4220
calgary@morrisonhershfield.com
www.morrisonhershfield.com
Domestic Markets:
Alberta

Edmonton
#200, 17303 - 102 Ave.
Edmonton, AB T5S 1J8
780-483-5200
Fax: 780-484-3883
edmonton@morrisonhershfield.com
www.morrisonhershfield.com
Domestic Markets:
Alberta

Grande Prairie
P.O. Box 203
10901 - 100 St.
Grande Prairie, AB T8V 1R6
780-532-0600
Fax: 780-532-8669
grandeprairie@morrisonhershfield.com
www.morrisonhershfield.com
Domestic Markets:
Alberta

Ottawa
2440 Don Reid Dr.
Ottawa, ON K1H 1E1
613-739-2910
Fax: 613-739-4926
877-644-7687

ottawa@morrisonhershfield.com
www.morrisonhershfield.com
Domestic Markets:
Ontario

Vancouver
#610, 3585 Graveley St.
Vancouver, BC V5K 5J5
604-454-0402
Fax: 604-454-0403
vancouver@morrisonhershfield.com
www.morrisonhershfield.com
Domestic Markets:
British Columbia

Victoria
536 Broughton St., 2nd Fl.
Victoria, BC V8W 1C6
250-361-1215
Fax: 250-361-1235
victoria@morrisonhershfield.com
www.morrisonhershfield.com
Domestic Markets:
British Columbia

Morval
A Division of Woodbridge Foam Corporation
P.O. Box 878
68 Shirley Ave.
Kitchener, ON N2G 4E1
519-579-6100
Fax: 519-579-1449
packaging@woodbridgegroup.com
www.morval.com
Products/Services/Areas of Expertise: Morval is involved in the custom moulded bead foam plastics business. Products include protective packaging, insulated containers, & material handling totes. The company's markets include consumer electronics, appliances, pharmaceutical, automotive, & construction.

Mountain Valley Geophysics / MVG
#519, 245 Dixon Rd.
Toronto, ON M9P 2M4
416-249-6664
Fax: 416-249-6965
info@mvgcorp.com; inspections@mvgcorp.com
www.mvgcorp.com
Products/Services/Areas of Expertise: Mountain Valley Geophysics offers environmental consulting & onsite field survey services. Investigative environments include water supply & drainage targeting & landfill delineation & leachate monitoring.

Movac Mobile Vacuum Services Ltd.
P.O. Box 76070
#300, 400 - 5th Ave. SW
Calgary, AB T2P OL6
403-201-3710
Fax: 403-201-3684
888-727-7922
info@movac.ca; bward@movac.ca (sales); ops@movac.ca (operations)
www.movac.ca
Products/Services/Areas of Expertise: Movac Mobile Vacuum Services Ltd. serves the oil & gas industry by providing professional drilling waste management & vacuum trucking services.
Domestic Markets:
Alberta, British Columbia, Saskatchewan
Contact(s):
Brad Chacalias, Manager, Domestic Sales & Marketing

Mowat Fabrication Ltd.
P.O. Box 682 Main
166 North Murray St.
Trenton, ON K8V 5W6
613-394-5041
Fax: 613-394-6530
Firm Type: Manufacturing
Founded: 1983
Products/Services/Areas of Expertise: The metal fabricating company manufactures truck trailers, tanks, farm machinery, food products machinery, conveyors, & metal accessories for buildings.
Financial Information:
Type of Ownership: Private
Domestic Markets:
Ontario

Foreign Activity:
Central America, South America, USA
Contact(s):
Kirk Mowat, President
Jason Vanslyke, General Manager

MPI Drilling
Formerly: Meta Probe Inc. (1993)
Comp. 6007
Picton, ON K0K 2T0
613-393-2165
Fax: 613-393-2180
800-413-2581
info@mpidrilling.com
mpidrilling.com
Firm Type: Manufacturing, Scientific/Technical Services
Founded: 1993
Staff: 6
Member of: National Groundwater Association; Ontario Groundwater Association
Products/Services/Areas of Expertise: Products are designed to obtain virtually undisturbed samples of unconsolidated soils, sediments, etc.
Recently Completed / Ongoing Projects: Sampling services provided for Mimico PLC, Zacatecas, Mexico, silver, tailings, exploration; DLS Services, Brighton, ON, oilspill delineation
Financial Information:
Type of Ownership: Private
Revenue: $500,000 - $1.5 Million
Revenue Sources: 15% nationwide; 85% Private Contracts
Domestic Markets:
National
Foreign Activity:
Western Europe, The Pacific Rim, South America, Mexico, USA
Contact(s):
John Clarke, President
Hugh Scott, Vice-President, Operations

Mr. Gas Ltd.
#1, 1420 Youville Dr.
Orleans, ON K1C 7B3
613-824-6777
Fax: 613-824-5235
info@mrgasltd.ca
www.mrgasltd.ca
Firm Type: Distributing
Founded: 1972
Products/Services/Areas of Expertise: Mr. Gas operates gasoline retail stations, car washes, & OOPS convenience stores. The company's fuel contains the detergent AP-58 (Pluredyne) to keep fuel injectors & intake valves clean.
Domestic Markets:
Ontario, Québec

MR2-McDonald & Associates
P.O. Box 4823
#204, 4303 Albert St.
Regina, SK S4S 3R6
306-584-7071
Fax: 306-584-8666
mr2.mcdonald@sasktel.net
Firm Type: Engineering, Scientific/Technical Services
Founded: 1982
Staff: 12
Member of: Water Environment Federation; Association of Professional Engineers & Geoscientists of Saskatchewan; American Water Works Association; Association of Groundwater Scientists & Engineers; Canadian Water Resources Association; Association of Consulting Engineers of Canada; Association of Professional Engineers, Geologists & Geophysicists of Alberta
Products/Services/Areas of Expertise: Water & sewage works; water treatment, water quality (surface, ground, drinking); environmental engineering; waste management; pollution control facilities; aquatic biology; studies, predesign, design; contract administration; training; water quality monitoring & data management; environmental impact reviews
Domestic Markets:
National
Contact(s):
Rodger McDonald, P.Eng., Principal Engineer

MSA: Mine Safety Applicances Company / MSA
#222, 5535 Eglinton Ave. West
Toronto, ON M9C 5K5
416-620-4225
800-672-2222
www.msanet.com

Firm Type: Manufacturing
Founded: 1914
Staff: 5000
Quality Environmental Management System(s): 9001:2000
Products/Services/Areas of Expertise: MSA manufactures safety & instrument products to protect & improve health, safety, & the environment. Products are used by workers in the oil & gas & chemical industries, fire services, the military, & law enforcement. Examples of products include portable & permanent gas detection instruments, hearing protection equipment, body armour, & air purifying respirators.
Financial Information:
Type of Ownership: Publicly Traded
Domestic Markets:
National
Foreign Activity:
Worldwide
Contact(s):
William M. Lambert, President & Chief Executive Officer
Joseph A. Bigler, President, MSA North America
Dennis L. Zeitler, Chief Financial Officer & Senior Vice-President

Canadian Branches:
Edmonton
16435 - 118 Ave.
Edmonton, AB T5V 1H2
780-483-0988

MSU Mississauga Ltd.
#300, 2222 South Sheridan Way
Mississauga, ON L5J 2M4
905-823-4340
Fax: 905-823-4947
800-268-5336
sales@msumississagua.com
www.msumississauga.com
Firm Type: Manufacturing
Founded: 1977
Staff: 20
Member of: Ontario Concrete Pipe Association; Ontario Sewer & Watermain Construction Association; Alliance of Manufacturers; Canadian Welding Bureau
Products/Services/Areas of Expertise: Safety climbing equipment; miscellaneous metal products; access hatches; railings; ladders
Financial Information:
Type of Ownership: Private
Domestic Markets:
National
Foreign Activity:
Worldwide
Contact(s):
Virginia Junkin, President
Nimette Taylor, Office Manager
Steve Junkin, Plant Manager

MTE Consultants Inc.
520 Bingemans Centre Dr.
Kitchener, ON N2K 3S2
519-743-6500
Fax: 519-743-6513
mail@mte85.com
www.mte85.com
Firm Type: Engineering
Founded: 1985
Staff: 100
Member of: Consulting Engineers of Ontario
Products/Services/Areas of Expertise: Site assessment; design & specifications; project management
Contact(s):
Dave J. Wilhelm, Project Manager

Canadian Branches:
Burlington
#315, 3027 Harvester Rd.
Burlington, ON L7N 3G7
905-639-2552
Fax: 905-639-7727
hamilton@mte85.com

Muddy River Technologies Inc.
Formerly: Muddy River Environmental Ltd.
#122, 7198 Vantage Way
Delta, BC V4G 1K7
604-940-9125
Fax: 604-940-9138
info@muddyriv.com
www.muddyriv.com

Products/Services/Areas of Expertise: Muddy River Technologies Inc. is engaged in the research, development, & manufacturing of water & wastewater treatment systems.
Activities: Manufacturing dissolved air flotation equipment, mixers & aerators, oil & water separators, & GAC filters; Purifying & disinfecting potable water; Meeting municipal discharge guidelines for wastewater
Recently Completed / Ongoing Projects: Improving the performance of a wastewater system at a gourmet & specialty meat processing plant; Separating oil, oil-wetted solids, & water in the automotive industry, so that automotive recyclers comply with the Environmental Code of Practice
Contact(s):
Peter Jack, President
Patty Jack, Manager, Business Development
Nels Ladouceur, Manager, Technical Services
Mike Garner, Commissioning Engineer

Mueller Canada
82 Hooper Rd.
Barrie, ON L4N 8Z9
705-719-9965
Fax: 705-719-4959
info@muellercanada.com
www.muellercanada.com
Firm Type: Manufacturing
Founded: 1912
Products/Services/Areas of Expertise: Mueller Canada is a manufacturer of flow control products, which are used for water & waste water treatment, water & gas distribution, oil production, & food & beverage processing.
Domestic Markets:
Alberta, Québec

Canadian Branches:
Calgary
11440 - 54th St. SE
Calgary, AB T2C 4Y6
403-236-2880
Fax: 403-236-2997
www.muellercanada.com
Domestic Markets:
Alberta

Saint-Jérôme
230, av Castonguay
Saint-Jérôme, QC J7Y 2J7
450-436-2288
Fax: 450-436-1379
www.muellercanada.com
Domestic Markets:
Québec,

Muis Controls Ltd.
29 Riel Dr.
St. Albert, AB T8N 5C6
780-459-7080
Fax: 780-459-7085
800-661-8823
info@muiscontrols.com; sales@muiscontrols.com
www.muiscontrols.com
Firm Type: Distributing
Founded: 1981
Products/Services/Areas of Expertise: Muis Controls Ltd. is a supplier of flow measurement & flow control products. The company servces the manufacturing, industrial, commercial, municipal, & O.E.M. markets.
Domestic Markets:
National
Foreign Activity:
USA

Multi Recyclage S.D. Inc.
3030, Montée Saint-François
Laval, QC H7E 4P2
450-625-9191
Fax: 450-625-9628
888-306-5151
info@multirecyclage.com
www.multirecyclage.com
Contact(s):
Michel Fournier

Multi-Stage Filter
#47, 17665 Leslie St.
Newmarket, ON L3Y 3E3
905-853-0164
Fax: 905-853-8807

866-853-0164
info@msfilter.com
Firm Type: Distributing
Founded: 1990
Products/Services/Areas of Expertise: Specializes in slow sand filtration applications for water & sewage treatment; developed & tested a Multi-Stage Filtration process that effectively treats raw water with high turbidity, algae & color without the use of pre-treatment chemicals or complex filter backwash procedures

Multitel Inc.
2905, rue de Celles
Québec, QC G2C 1W7
418-847-2255
Fax: 418-847-1966
888-685-8483
Firm Type: Information Technology, Manufacturing
Founded: 1980
Staff: 40
Quality Environmental Management System(s): 9001
Products/Services/Areas of Expertise: Multitel serves the telecommunication, power, water & wastewater industries by providing remote monitoring systems & power management software & services.
Financial Information:
Type of Ownership: Private
Domestic Markets:
National
Foreign Activity:
USA
Contact(s):
Benoit Methot, President
benoit.methot@multitel.com
Marie-Michèle Caron, Director, Marketing
marie-michele.caron@multitel.com

Multiview Locates Inc.
Formerly: Multiview Geoservices Inc.
325 Matheson Blvd. East
Mississauga, ON L4Z 1X8
905-629-8959
Fax: 905-629-7379
800-363-3116
info@multiview.ca
www.multiview.ca
Firm Type: Engineering, Scientific/Technical Services
Founded: 1989
Member of: Association of Professional Engineers of Ontario; Association of Professional Geoscientists of Ontario; Ontario Regional Common Ground Alliance; Building Owners & Managers Association; Centre for Advancement of Trenchless Technology; Toronto Construction Association; Ottawa Construction Association
Products/Services/Areas of Expertise: multiVIEW Locates Inc. provides subsurface mapping services to support environmental, geotechnical, & engineering projects throughout the world.
Activities: Providing environmental & geotechnical site evaluation, buried utility delineation, & structural assessment
Financial Information:
Type of Ownership: Private
Domestic Markets:
National
Foreign Activity:
Worldwide

Municipal Affairs Consulting
83 Cambridge Ave.
Toronto, ON M4K 2L2
416-471-7355
apotts@munaffairs.com
www.munaffairs.com
Products/Services/Areas of Expertise: Government & media relations services are provided, including council on policy development, administrative processes, & procurement.
Activities: Monitoring & managing clients' issues; Engaging in advocacy activities on behalf of clients
Contact(s):
Arthur Potts, Founder & Principal
apotts@munaffairs.com

Municipal Recyclers Ltd.
82 Clyde Ave.
Mount Pearl, NL A1N 4S2
709-747-1783
Fax: 709-747-3841

Products/Services/Areas of Expertise: Municipal Recyclers Ltd. recycles ferrous & non-ferrous scrap metal.
Domestic Markets:
Newfoundland & Labrador

Murray Krovats Agency Ltd.
1126 Sanford St.
Winnipeg, MB R3E 2Z9
204-786-2747
Fax: 204-775-3186
866-444-0009
Products/Services/Areas of Expertise: Water & wastewater management & equipment

Muskoka Containerized Services Ltd.
Division of Capital Environmental Resources Inc.
P.O. Box 1779
Bracebridge, ON P1L 1V7
705-645-4453
Fax: 705-645-9485
800-461-4448
Firm Type: Waste Management
Founded: 1971
Staff: 85
Member of: Ontario Waste Management Association
Products/Services/Areas of Expertise: Waste transport & recycling; landfill services; transfer station
Domestic Markets:
Ontario
Contact(s):
Al Hussey, District Manager

MW Metal Spinning & Stamping Ltd.
60 Alness St.
Toronto, ON M3J 2G9
416-661-8003
Fax: 416-661-4355
877-904-7134
info@metalspinning.com
Firm Type: Manufacturing
Founded: 1940
Staff: 10
Products/Services/Areas of Expertise: Custom metal spinning
Foreign Activity:
USA
Contact(s):
Annette Goldstein, Vice-President

MWA Consultants
#300, 6388 Marlborough Ave.
Burnaby, BC V5H 4P4
604-431-7998
Fax: 604-431-7218
Firm Type: Management Consulting, Engineering
Founded: 1993
Staff: 5
Member of: Canadian Pulp & Paper Association
Products/Services/Areas of Expertise: Environmental consulting firm specializing in environmental management systems, environmental engineering & research, environmental education & communications services
Recently Completed / Ongoing Projects: Prepared NorskeCanada's 2000-2005 greenhouse gas action plan; Developed GHG Information for BC's Water Use Planning Interagency Management Committee; Life Cycle assessment for Canfor Corp.
Financial Information:
Type of Ownership: Private
Domestic Markets:
National
Contact(s):
David Miller, Business Manager
dmiller@mwaconsultants.com
Lynn Ross, Sr. Consultant
lynnross@mwaconsultants.com

MWH Canada Inc. / MWH
Formerly: Northern EnviroSearch Ltd.
#1010, 600 - 6th Ave. SW
Calgary, AB T2P 0S5
403-543-5353
Fax: 403-233-2513
mwhcorpcomm@mwhglobal.com
www.mwhglobal.com
Firm Type: Scientific/Technical Services
Founded: 2008
Staff: 30

Member of: Canadian Land Reclamation Association; Association of Professional Engineers Geologists & Geophysicists of Alberta; Alberta Institute of Agrologists; Alberta Society of Professional Biologists; Association of Professional Engineers & Geoscientists of Saskatchewan; Northwest Territories of Engineers, Geologists & Geophysicists
Products/Services/Areas of Expertise: Environmental protection planning; operations on First Nations lands; environmental remediation management & reclamation; environmental site assessments; property transfer audits; field services
Recently Completed / Ongoing Projects: Reclamation, remediation, field studies & applications for seismic & drilling exploration in NWT & Yukon
Financial Information:
Type of Ownership: Foreign-owned
Domestic Markets:
Alberta, British Columbia, Saskatchewan
Contact(s):
Bob Raina, Unit Leader, MWH EnviroSearch Business

Canadian Branches:
Estevan
P.O. Box 93
110 Perkins St.
Estevan, SK S4A 2A2
306-636-7004
Fax: 306-636-2143

Lloydminster
#2, 5204 - 63rd St.
Lloydminster, AB T9V 2E6
780-871-0864
Fax: 780-871-0869

Saskatoon
#104, 108 Research Dr.
Saskatoon, SK S7N 3R3
306-373-1110
Fax: 306-373-2444

Vancouver
One Bentall Centre
P.O. Box 17
#1580, 505 Burrard St.
Vancouver, BC V7X 1M5
604-648-6161
Fax: 604-648-6181

N-T Enterprise Inc.
264 High St.
Moncton, NB E1C 6C2
506-857-3107
877-857-0125
nt1@nbnet.nb.ca
Firm Type: Manufacturing
Founded: 1988
Staff: 2
EcoLogo Certified Products & Services: The Reusable & Baby Fit diapers
Ecological Note: The Reusable & Baby Fit diapers
Contact(s):
Nasif Sidhom

N. Vandenassem & Associate
14312 Deer Ridge Dr. SE
Calgary, AB T2J 5W1
403-225-0100
Fax: 403-271-4252
Firm Type: Management Consulting
Founded: 1988
Staff: 2
Products/Services/Areas of Expertise: Environmental clean-up technology; project management of clean-up & remediation tasks; environmentally friendly industrial & transportation technologies
Financial Information:
Revenue Sources: 20% Provincial; 10% Municipals; 70% Private Contracts
Domestic Markets:
National
Foreign Activity:
Africa, Asia, Central America, The Pacific Rim, South America, Mexico, USA, Former USSR
Markets Sought:
China, Vietnam
Contact(s):
Nicholas Vandenassem, President
David J. Vandenassem, Consultant
Tom Prior, Consultant

N.A.T.S. Nursery Ltd.
24555 - 32nd Ave.
Langley, BC V2Z 2J5
604-530-9300
Fax: 604-530-9500
rod@natsnursery.com
www.natsnursery.com
Firm Type: Distributing
Founded: 1985
Products/Services/Areas of Expertise: Northwest native plants, hardy ferns & ground covers
Financial Information:
Type of Ownership: Private
Revenue Sources: 5% Municipals; 95% Private Contracts
Domestic Markets:
National
Foreign Activity:
USA
Contact(s):
Rod Nataros, Owner

N.L. Sobey & Associates Limited
278 Lower Truro Rd.
Truro, NS B2N 1B1
902-895-2790
Fax: 902-893-2966
newton@sobeyandassociates.com
www.sobeyandassociates.com
Firm Type: Engineering
Founded: 1978
Staff: 5
Member of: Consulting Engineers of Nova Scotia
Products/Services/Areas of Expertise: Civil engineering consulting services
Financial Information:
Type of Ownership: Private
Revenue Sources: 5% nationwide; 10% Provincial; 5% Municipals; 80% Private Contracts
Domestic Markets:
New Brunswick, Nova Scotia, Prince Edward Island
Contact(s):
Newton Sobey, M.Eng., P.Eng., President

N.R. Murphy Ltd.
430 Franklin Blvd.
Cambridge, ON N1R 8G6
519-621-6210
Fax: 519-621-2841
4nodust@nrmurphyltd.com
www.nrmurphy.com
Firm Type: Manufacturing
Founded: 1943
Staff: 35
Products/Services/Areas of Expertise: Dry dust collecting equipment; industrial exhausters & related accessories; design & manufacture of air pollution control equipment for industrial use
Financial Information:
Type of Ownership: Private
Revenue: Greater than $5 Million
Domestic Markets:
National
Foreign Activity:
Asia, The Pacific Rim, South America, USA
Contact(s):
Norman Murphy, President/CEO
Craig Moffatt, Sales & Marketing
Ray Johnston, General Manager
Terry Decaro, Production Manager

N.S. Bauman Ltd.
7214 Line 86
Wallenstein, ON N0B 2S0
519-669-5447
Fax: 519-669-3590
Firm Type: Manufacturing
Founded: 1951
Staff: 11
Products/Services/Areas of Expertise: Processing of bakery waste; dehydrating plant
Financial Information:
Type of Ownership: Private
Revenue Sources: 100% Private Contracts
Domestic Markets:
Ontario
Contact(s):
Willard Bauman, President
Wayne Bauman, Plant Manager

Nalco Canada Co.
A division of Nalco Inc.
Formerly: Diversey Water Technologies Ltd.1055 Truman St.
Burlington, ON L7R 3V7
905-632-8791
Fax: 905-632-0849
800-265-5059
www.nalco.com
Firm Type: Engineering, Manufacturing, Scientific/Technical Services
Founded: 1885
Staff: 300
Quality Environmental Management System(s): 9002; 9001
Products/Services/Areas of Expertise: Leading provider of water & wastewater treatment chemicals, chemical feed control equipment, analytical & consulting services for supply, boiler, cooling, process & wastewater applications; serves the industrial, transport, institutional & commercial sectors; technical service representatives are located in major centres
Financial Information:
Type of Ownership: Foreign-owned; Publicly Traded
Foreign Activity:
Worldwide
Contact(s):
Tim Weeger, President

Canadian Branches:
Alberta Energy Services - Nisku
2002 - 4th St., Unit B
Nisku, AB T9E 7W4
780-955-6900
Fax: 780-955-6922

Alberta Energy Services - Calgary
#180, 3553 - 31 St. NW
Calgary, AB T2L 2K7
403-284-6275
Fax: 403-282-2926

Alberta Energy Services - Fort McMurray
#4E, 380 McKenziwe Blvd.
Fort McMurray, AB T9H 4C4
780-743-3777
Fax: 780-743-1819

Ontario Energy Services - Sarnia
#3, 1149 Vanier Rd.
Sarnia, ON N7S 3Y6
877-631-5299
Fax: 519-332-8297

Ontario Water & Process Services
1055 Truman St.
Burlington, ON L7R 3V7
905-632-8791
Fax: 905-632-0849

Québec Water & Process Services
#180, 750, boul Pierre-Bertrand
Québec, QC G1M 3L2
418-683-8000
Fax: 418 681-5377

Napier Environmental Technology
720 Eaton Way
Delta, BC V3M 6J9
604-526-0802
Fax: 604-526-7772
800-663-9274
cservice@napiere.com
www.napiere.com
Products/Services/Areas of Expertise: Paint & varnish remover that contains no methylene chloride, is odourless & will not burn skin; formula is industrial strength & easy to use; works on coatings such as epoxies, urethanes, latex, varnish & laquer; removes multiple layers of paint at a time
Ecological Note: RemovALL paint & varnish remover
Contact(s):
Steve Balmer, President/COO
Drew Gagnier, Vice-President, Marketing
Michael Sloan, Vice President, Sales - Industrial

Napier-Reid Ltd.
#2, 10 Alden Rd.
Markham, ON L3R 2S1
905-475-1545
Fax: 905-475-2021
800-615-4406
info@napier-reid.com
www.napier-reid.com
Firm Type: Engineering, Manufacturing
Founded: 1950
Staff: 17
Member of: Ontario Pollution Control Equipment Association; Water Environment Association of Ontario; American Water Works Association; Water Environment Federation
Products/Services/Areas of Expertise: Engineered systems & equipment for water & wastewater treatment; municipal & industrial markets; packaged water & sewage treatment plants; aeration systems; screening equipment; packaged pump stations; API separators; groundwater remediation equipment; granular activated carbon filters; conventional gravity filters; membrane filters; pressure filters; flocculators; clarifiers; rotating biological contractors; sequencing batch reactors; sludge heat exchangers; dissolved air flotation; aeration systems; classifiers; membrane bio-reactors
Financial Information:
Type of Ownership: Private
Revenue: Greater than $5 Million
Revenue Sources: 75% Municipals; 25% Private Contracts
Domestic Markets:
National
Foreign Activity:
Africa, Caribbean, Central America, China, Eastern Europe, The Middle East, The Pacific Rim, South America, Mexico, Vietnam
Markets Sought:
China, Vietnam
Contact(s):
Tim Otton, President
Frank Li, Manager, Projects
frankli@napier-reid.com
Andrew Hutton, Overseas Sales
andrew@napier-reid.com

Napoleon Appliance Corp. / NAC
Division of Wolf Steel Ltd.
214 Bayview Dr.
Barrie, ON L4N 4Y8
705-726-4278
Fax: 705-725-2564
ask@napoleon.on.ca
www.napoleon.on.ca
Firm Type: Manufacturing
Founded: 1976
Staff: 4
Member of: Hearth Products Association; Canadian Gas Association; American Gas Association
Quality Environmental Management System(s): 9002
Products/Services/Areas of Expertise: High-efficiency wood & gas stoves, fireplaces, fireplace inserts, gas grills
Financial Information:
Type of Ownership: Private
Revenue Sources: 100% Private Contracts
Domestic Markets:
National
Foreign Activity:
Asia, Central Europe, USA
Markets Sought:
Asia, Australia/New Zealand, Central America, South America, Mexico,
Contact(s):
Wolfgang Schroeter, President
Ted Menna, Sales & Marketing Manager
Ingrid Schroeter, Vice-President
Roger Gripton, Vice-President, Sales

International Branch(es):
Wolf Steel USA Inc.
103 Miller Rd.
Crittenden, KY USA

NAR Environmental Consultants Inc.
1130 Southlane Rd.
Sudbury, ON P3G 1N6
705-522-5990
Fax: 705-522-1898
nar@cyberbeach.net
Firm Type: Management Consulting
Founded: 1990
Products/Services/Areas of Expertise: Environmental baseline studies; fisheries & aquaculture management; ground & surface water monitoring; mine tailings disposal; permit, regulation & standards consulting
Contact(s):
Brad Bowman, President

Nardei Fabricators Ltd.
8915 - 44th St. SE
Calgary, AB T2C 2P5
403-279-3301
Fax: 403-279-5871
info@nardei.com
www.nardei.com
Firm Type: Manufacturing
Founded: 1984
Staff: 50
Products/Services/Areas of Expertise: Custom fabricators of pressure piping assemblies, process modules, & pressure vessels; ASME \S\"" & \""U\""""
Domestic Markets:
British Columbia, Manitoba, Québec, Saskatchewan
Contact(s):
Robert Nardei, President
Tom Casey, Vice-President

Natech Environmental Services
109 Patterson Cross Rd.
Harvey York Co, NB E6K 1L9
506-366-1080
Fax: 506-366-1090
natech@nbnet.nb.ca
www.natech.nb.ca
Firm Type: Management Consulting, Engineering, Scientific/Technical Services
Founded: 1993
Staff: 4
Products/Services/Areas of Expertise: Environmental remediation; hydraulic modeling; outfall dispersion studies; estuary remediation; wastewater treatment plant design
Domestic Markets:
New Brunswick, Nova Scotia, Prince Edward Island
Foreign Activity:
Western Europe
Contact(s):
J. Schroer, M.Eng,P.Eng.

National Energy Equipment Inc.
Formerly: RNG Group Inc
1850 Derry Rd. East
Mississauga, ON L5S 1Y6
905-564-2422
Fax: 905-564-9490
info@nee.ca
www.nee.ca
Firm Type: Distributing
Founded: 1947
Staff: 550
Member of: Landi Renzo S.p.A., Italia
Member of: Petroleum Equipment Institute; Propane Gas Association of Canada
Products/Services/Areas of Expertise: Liquid handling equipment, systems & service depot; oil & water separation; secondary containment piping systems; double-walled storage tanks
Domestic Markets:
National
Foreign Activity:
USA
Contact(s):
Tom Ferries, President & CEO
Jack Cloete, Financial Controller
jcloete@nee.ca
Raymond Gouron, VP, Québec
rgouron@nee.ca

Canadian Branches:
Calgary
1350 - 42 Ave. SE, Bay R
Calgary, AB T2G 4V6
403-735-1103
Fax: 403-735-2337
888-287-0074
Art Kirk, Regional Vice-President

Dartmouth
1 Royles Ave.
Dartmouth, NS B3B 2A6
902-468-7342
Fax: 902-468-7341
George Hayman, Service Manager

Edmonton
17107 - 188 Ave. NW
Edmonton, AB T5S 2V3
780-468-4454
Fax: 780-637-8622
888-468-8580
Glen Brotzel, Operations Manager

Moncton
489 Adélard-Savoie Blvd.
Dieppe, NB E1A 7E7
506-861-1010
Fax: 506-861-1013
Ralph Wilson, Branch Manager

Montréal
10801, boul Ray Lawson
Anjou, QC H1J 1M5
514-355-2366
Fax: 514-355-2223
800-363-9960
Max Sentner, Branch Manager

Nanaimo
9583 Bare Point Rd.
Chemainus, BC V0R 1K5
250-246-6543
Fax: 250-246-6586
Gary Don, Territory Sales Manager

Ottawa
26 Capital Dr.
Nepean, ON K2G 0E9
613-224-0685
Fax: 613-224-3606
Dave Webster, Regional Service Manager

Port Coquitlam
1467 Spirfire Pl.
Port Coquitlam, BC V3C 6L4
778-588-7635
Fax: 604-472-7180
Dale Gach, Regional Operations Manager

Regina
1415 Pettigrew Ave. East
Regina, SK S4N 5W1
306-721-1030
Fax: 306-721-1034
Yvon Lachaine, Operations Manager

Saskatoon
3610 Kochar Ave.
Saskatoon, SK S7P 0C2
306-665-0223
Fax: 306-655-1214
Tim Bekolay, Prairie Region Manager

St. John's
18 Dundee Ave.
Mount Pearl, NL A1N 4R7
709-747-0015
Fax: 709-747-0222
Gord Walsh, Branch Manager

Winnipeg
1431 Church Ave.
Winnipeg, MB R2X 1G5
204-632-0043
Fax: 204-694-7520
800-665-7520
John Alksnis, Sales Manager

National Instruments Canada
#812, 1000, av Saint-Charles
Vaudreuil-Dorion, QC J7V 8P5
450-510-3055
Fax: 450-510-3056
800-433-3488
info@ni.com
www.ni.com
Firm Type: Distributing
Founded: 1976
Products/Services/Areas of Expertise: Computer software/systems; measuring & monitoring equipment; data acquisition

Products & Services Buyer's Guide

Financial Information:
Type of Ownership: Foreign-owned
Domestic Markets:
Manitoba, Ontario, Saskatchewan
Contact(s):
Joe Daher, Canada Branch Mgr., Americas Sales Force
joe.daher@ni.com

Canadian Branches:
Alberta, Saskatchewan & Manitoba
Calgary, AB
403-457-1239
Fax: 403-457-1240
Rishi Lukka, District Sales Rep.
rishi.lukka@ni.com

British Columbia, Northwest Territories, Yukon Territory & Nunavut
10531 Gilmore Cres.
Richmond, BC V6X 1X3
604-233-6900
Fax: 604-233-6901
Gurshan Sidhu, District Sales Rep.
gurshan.sidhu@ni.com

Mississauga & Northern Toronto
#801, 111 Peter St.
Toronto, ON M5V 2H1
647-340-4653
Fax: 512-683-0100
Tong Yang, District Sales Rep.
tong.yang@ni.com

Montréal
1905, rue Wolfe
Montréal, QC H2l 3J9
514-288-57221
Fax: 450-510-3056
Denis Tison, District Sales Manager
denys.tison@ni.com
Jean-Claude Rutagengwa, Tenchical Sales Rep
jean-claude.rutagengwa@ni.com

Ottawa, Eastern Ontario & Western Québec
#314, 99 Fifth Ave.
Ottawa, ON K1S 5P5
613-598-0095, ext.4922
Fax: 613-598-0118
Nicola Ricciardi, Field Engineer
nicola.ricciardi@ni.com

Quebec & the Maritimes
1443, rue du Zéphyr
Québec, QC G2G 1N6
418-691-7714
Fax: 450-510-3056
Vincent Carpentier, Field Sales Rep.
vincent.carpentier@ni.com

Southwestern Ontario
#108, 447 Frederick St.
Kitchener, ON N2H 2P4
519-342-1168
Fax: 519-342-1170
David Golembiewski, District Sales Rep.
david.golembiewski@ni.com

Toronto & Southern Ontario
#801, 111 Peter St.
Toronto, ON M5V 2H1
416-466-1107
Fax: 416-977-1818
Dominic Lalli, District Sales Rep.
dominic.lalli@ni.com

National Process Equipment Inc.
Formerly: Wilron Equipment Ltd.; Hydro Dynamics Ltd.
#5, 3401 - 19th St. NE
Calgary, AB T2E 6S8
403-219-0270
Fax: 403-291-4919
800-942-5588
webinquiries@natpro.com
www.natpro.com
Firm Type: Distributing, Waste Management
Founded: 1998
Staff: 160
Products/Services/Areas of Expertise: Wastewater & plant effluent pumps, compressors & related process equipment

Financial Information:
Type of Ownership: Private
Domestic Markets:
National
Foreign Activity:
Worldwide
Contact(s):
Frank Killoran, President & CEO
Dave Harvey, National Sales Manager

Canadian Branches:
Edmonton
10685 - 176 St.
Edmonton, AB T5S 1G5
780-452-4490
Fax: 780-452-9140

Halifax
Burnside Industrial Park
#111, 11 Morris Dr.
Dartmouth, NS B3B 1M2
902-468-7890
Fax: 902-468-3011

Montréal
2650, av André
Dorval, QC H9P 1K6
514-421-0331
Fax: 514-421-0337

Saskatoon
#3, 1540 Alberta Ave.
Saskatoon, SK S7K 7C9
306-242-4611
Fax: 306-242-3837

Toronto
109 Wilkinson Rd.
Brampton, ON L6T 4X1
905-453-2639
Fax: 905-453-9391

Vancouver
#128, 9 Burbidge St.
Coquitlam, BC V3K 7B2
604-521-7867
Fax: 604-521-4967

Winnipeg
1501 St. James St.
Winnipeg, MB R3H 0W9
204-694-9890
Fax: 204-632-7588

National Waste Services / NWS
540 Finley Ave.
Ajax, ON L1S 2E3
905-831-6297
Fax: 905-426-6241
888-681-1174
Firm Type: Waste Management
Founded: 2000
Products/Services/Areas of Expertise: National Waste Services is a regional integrated solid waste services company that provides transfer, collection, disposal and recycling services for industrial, commercial, institutional (ICI) and municipal non-hazardous waste. The company is a Canadian controlled private corporation.
Financial Information:
Type of Ownership: Private
Revenue Sources: 100% Private Contracts
Domestic Markets:
Ontario
Contact(s):
Danny Ardellini, President/COO
dardellini@nwscanada.com
Phil Swigger, Vice-President, Finance
Rob Campitelli, Controller
rcampitelli@nwscanada.com

Natural Forces Technologies Inc.
Cogswell Tower
#502, 2000 Barrington St.
Halifax, NS B3J 3K1
902-423-6094
Fax: 902-422-9780
www.naturalforces.ca
Firm Type: Management Consulting, Manufacturing
Staff: 2

Products/Services/Areas of Expertise: A wind development company with expertise in local issues pertaining to wind farm development; deals with project management & operation
Contact(s):
Robert Apold, Contact, Development
rapold@naturalforces.ca

Nature's Environmental Products Inc.
PDM Group of Companies
#3, 7475 Kimbel St.
Mississauga, ON L5S 1E7
905-795-7749
Fax: 905-795-7744
800-249-9245
pdm@pdmgroup.ca
www.nepdm.com
Products/Services/Areas of Expertise: Environmental company specializing in the development & application of Micro cell Technology is being applied every day in the restoration of soil & groundwater quality to permit reuse, redevelopment and/or risk free rehabilitation; it is also being used to destroy organic liquid/solid wastes & sludge's generated by petrochemical industries on a worldwide scale
Ecological Note: Household, commercial, industrial, automotive/marine & institutional cleaning products
Domestic Markets:
Ontario
Foreign Activity:
Africa, Asia, China, Mexico, USA, Vietnam
Contact(s):
Joanne Torlone, Contact
Paul DeMaleco, CEO

Nature's Friend Environmental
P.O. Box 328
Big Valley, AB T0J 0G0
403-876-2226
Fax: 403-876-2266

Nature's Mate Distribution Inc.
P.O. Box 1059
#2, 2020 - 20 St. East
Owen Sound, ON N4K 6K6
519-372-2065
Fax: 519-372-1143
888-489-8003
info@naturesmate.com
www.naturesmate.com
Products/Services/Areas of Expertise: ACTIZYME is a broad spectrum pellet for sewer systems, sewerage plants, septics, greasetraps, drainlines, pits, treatment plants, boats, ponds, etc.; has five bacterial strains in spore form with four added enzymes for rapid response; special facultative strains are designed to operate in both anaerobic & aerobic conditions; stops odors, liquifies & digests sludge, grease, fats & other solids; reduces pollution levels & solves problems in wastewater treatment
Ecological Note: Septic tank additives
Contact(s):
Josephine Kochany
Joe Kochany

Navajo Metals
5857 - 12th St. SE
Calgary, AB T2H 2X9
403-252-7787
Fax: 403-253-3151
Products/Services/Areas of Expertise: Metal recycling

Naylor Engineering Associates Ltd.
353 Bridge St. East
Kitchener, ON N2K 2Y5
519-741-1313
Fax: 519-741-5422
www.nayloreng.com
Firm Type: Engineering
Founded: 1983
Staff: 55
Member of: Professional Engineers Ontario; Canadian Council of Independent Laboratories; National Ground Water Association; Canadian Geotechnical Society; Canadian Society for Chemical Engineering
Products/Services/Areas of Expertise: Site assessment & environmental management related to land acquisition & property development; risk assessment & management; remediation of soils & groundwater; wastewater treatment systems

Financial Information:
Type of Ownership: Private
Revenue Sources: 5% nationwide; 15% Provincial; 25% Municipals; 55% Private Contracts
Domestic Markets:
Ontario
Foreign Activity:
Caribbean
Contact(s):
Dave Naylor, President
dnaylor@nayloreng.com
Carol Mitchell, Sr. Environmental Engineer
cmitchell@nayloreng.com
Bill Leedham, Sr. Environmental Engineer

Canadian Branches:
Brantford
#3, 440 Hardy Rd.
Brantford, ON N3T 5L8
519-720-0078
Fax: 519-720-0976

Stratford
25 Market Pl.
Stratford, ON N5A 1A4
519-273-0101
Fax: 519-273-7188

NB Coal Limited
12 Tower Rd.
Minto, NB E4B 3V1
506-327-2200
Fax: 506-327-2100
Contact(s):
Michele Coleman, Contact

NCL Envirotek Inc.
138A, rue Isabey
Montréal, QC H4T 1V3
514-737-9139
Fax: 514-737-2526
888-737-9139
information@nclenvirotek.com
www.nclenvirotek.com
Firm Type: Engineering
Founded: 1985
Staff: 9
Quality Environmental Management System(s): 9001
Products/Services/Areas of Expertise: Geotechnical studies for buildings, tunnels, dams, slopes, etc.; Environmental studies, soil characterization, decontamination, landfill conception, etc.; Quality control, concrete, soil
Financial Information:
Type of Ownership: Private
Revenue: $500,000 - $1.5 Million
Revenue Sources: 10% nationwide; 5% Provincial; 15% Municipals; 70% Private Contracts
Domestic Markets:
Québec
Contact(s):
Nicola Capozio, Engineering President
Contact(s):
Luc Hanellin

Canadian Branches:
Soil & Concrete
1154, rue Principale
St-Roche-de-l'Achigan, QC J0K 3H0
450-588-3374
Fax: 450-588-3866

NCR Canada Ltd. - Systemedia Division
6360 Northwest Dr.
Mississauga, ON L4V 1J7
905-677-2223
Fax: 905-677-5048
mark.sammut@canada.ncr.com
www.ncr.com/product/smg
Products/Services/Areas of Expertise: Paper products
Ecological Note: Custom continuous singles, cut sheets, paper rolls, snapset & multipart business forms

Near North Laboratories Inc.
#11, 191 Booth Rd, RR#5
North Bay, ON P1A 4K3
705-497-0550
Fax: 705-497-0549
nnlabs@vianet.ca
www.nearnorthlabs.ca

Firm Type: Scientific/Technical Services
Founded: 1989
Staff: 12
Member of: Canadian Association of Environmental Analytical Laboratories; CCIL
Products/Services/Areas of Expertise: Analytical testing services for water & wastewater, soil analyses, air monitoring, research & product development, sampling, treatability studies
Financial Information:
Type of Ownership: Private
Domestic Markets:
National
Contact(s):
Brenda McLay, Director

NEDCO
Westburne Division
5600 Keaton Cres.
Mississauga, ON L5R 3G3
905-568-2425
Fax: 905-568-2976
bruce.strain@nedco.ca
www.nedco.ca
Products/Services/Areas of Expertise: Energy-efficient products; energy-efficient lighting, energy management controls & systems
Domestic Markets:
National
Contact(s):
R.S. Waterman, Vice-President & General Manager
R. Arbuckle, Marketing Manager
R.F. Ferguson, Industrial Manager

Nederman Canada Ltd.
6675 Millcreek Dr.
Mississauga, ON L5N 5M4
905-542-9296
Fax: 905-542-2206
866-332-2611
info@nedermancanada.com
www.nederman.com
Firm Type: Manufacturing
Staff: 34
Products/Services/Areas of Expertise: Equipment to extract vehicle exhaust from workspace; equipment to capture dust, fumes, vapour, smoke at source; fume & dust extraction equipment to clean polluted air & return clean air back to the industrial workplace; retractable air, water & oil reels
Domestic Markets:
National
Contact(s):
Sven Kristensson, President/CEO
Joseph Collins, National Sales Manager
Ed Jaksetic, National Project Manager

International Branch(es):
AB PH Nederman & Co.
Sydhamnsgatan 2
Helsingborg Sweden
-46-42188700
Fax: -46-42147971

Neighborhood Recycling
1635 Berry Mills Rd.
Moncton, NB E1E 4R7
506-858-1600
Fax: 506-852-9102
Firm Type: Waste Management
Founded: 1988
Staff: 58
Products/Services/Areas of Expertise: Crushing & cleaning of recyclable glass; cutting of steel (scrap) & shipping it to be recycled into steel (new)
Financial Information:
Type of Ownership: Private
Revenue Sources: 100% Private Contracts
Domestic Markets:
New Brunswick, Nova Scotia, Prince Edward Island
Contact(s):
Murray Cruickshank, President

Neilson Excavation
578, ch Olivier
Saint-Nicolas, QC G7A 1A6
418-831-2141
Fax: 418-831-8059
Products/Services/Areas of Expertise: Water & wastewater management equipment

Contact(s):
Jean Fava, President
Germain Pelletier, Environmental Officer

NEK Environmental Technologies Inc.
#107, 1390 Prince of Wales Dr.
Ottawa, ON K2C 3N6
613-224-1594
Fax: 613-224-1642
info@nek.ca
www.nek.ca
Firm Type: Management Consulting
Staff: 10
Products/Services/Areas of Expertise: Provides a highly qualified team of experts in the field of renewable energy systems such as wind energy; assists clients at any phase of the project development, including initial planning & permit applications, feasibility studies, project design, contract management, private-public partnership arrangements; Provides turn-key projects, build-own-operate projects, & explores financing options
Domestic Markets:
National
Foreign Activity:
Central Europe, Western Europe, South America, United Kingdom

Nelson Environmental Inc.
101 Dawson Rd.
Winnipeg, MB R2J 0S6
204-949-7500
888-426-8180
info@nelsonenvironmental.com
www.nelsonenvironmental.com
Products/Services/Areas of Expertise: Provides water & wastewater treatment technology & system design for municipal, industrial & agricultural applications
Contact(s):
Martin Hildebrand, President

Nelson Environmental Remediation Ltd. / NER
52520A Range Rd. 271
Spruce Grove, AB T7X 3M8
780-960-3660
Fax: 780-962-6885
888-960-8222
garlanda@telusplanet.net
Firm Type: Engineering
Founded: 1994
Staff: 30
Member of: Environmental Services Association of Alberta
Products/Services/Areas of Expertise: Mobile, onsite Thermal Desorption service for treatment of hydrocarbon contaminated soil
Recently Completed / Ongoing Projects: ATCO Electric; Celanese Canada Inc.; Enbridge Pipelines; ConocoPhillips; Encana Corp.; Imperial Oil Ltd.
Financial Information:
Type of Ownership: Private
Revenue: $3 Million - $5 Million
Revenue Sources: 100% Private Contracts
Domestic Markets:
Alberta, British Columbia, Northwest Territories, Nunavut, Ontario, Québec, Saskatchewan, Yukon Territory
Foreign Activity:
Central Europe, Western Europe, South America, USA
Markets Sought:
Central Europe, Eastern Europe, Western Europe, The Middle East, South America, USA
Contact(s):
Darryl Nelson, President
Warren Nelson, Vice-President
nelsonw@telusplanet.net
Art Garland, Business Development
garlanda@telusplanet.net
John Tucker, Supervisor, Operations

Nelson Environmental Services
P.O. Box 1043
2135 Ridgeway Cr.
Garibaldi Highlands, BC V0N 1T0
604-898-9859
mnelson@mountain-inter.net
Firm Type: Management Consulting
Staff: 2
Member of: Association of Professional Biologists of BC;

Products & Services Buyer's Guide

Associated Environmental Site Assessors of Canada; North America Lake Management Society
Products/Services/Areas of Expertise: Limnology studies; stream & lake habitat enhancement studies; nutrient modelling; water quality monitoring programs; environmental construction supervision; impact mitigation strategies; environmental impact statement preparation
Domestic Markets:
National
Contact(s):
Mike Nelson, President/CEO

Nelson-Superior Consultants Ltd.
120 Cardinal Ct., RR#1
Thunder Bay, ON P7K 1G1
807-939-2926
hansenbruce@shaw.ca
Firm Type: Management Consulting, Engineering, Information Technology, Scientific/Technical Services
Founded: 1991
Products/Services/Areas of Expertise: Management information system design & application; energy management strategies; activity-based costing systems; business development feasibility & planning
Contact(s):
Bruce Hansen, President

Nemato Inc.
Formerly: Nemato Composites Inc.
1605 McEwen Dr.
Whitby, ON L1N 7L4
905-571-5305
800-361-5025
mail@nemato.com
www.nemato.com
Firm Type: Engineering, Manufacturing
Founded: 1988
Staff: 80
Products/Services/Areas of Expertise: Manufacturers of FRP moulded grating, FRP pipe systems, FRP covers, filtration systems & accessories & track spillage pan systems
Recently Completed / Ongoing Projects: Large sewage & water treatment tank covers, Nova Scotia Power & Brunswick Mining; railway track spillage system, CN
Financial Information:
Type of Ownership: Private
Revenue Sources: 5% nationwide; 15% Municipals; 80% Private Contracts
Domestic Markets:
National
Foreign Activity:
Africa, Australia/New Zealand, Central America, South America, Mexico
Contact(s):
Steve Andrews, President
Duncan Lyon, Vice-President
Rein Aaslepp, Manager

Neo Valves
#6, 1020 Brevik Pl.
Mississauga, ON L4W 4N7
905-624-9090
Fax: 905-624-8020
888-515-8885
valves@neovalves.com
www.neovalves.com
Firm Type: Distributing
Staff: 15
Member of: American Water Works Association; Water Environment Federation; Canadian Gas Association
Products/Services/Areas of Expertise: Valves for wastewater & water treatment applications; sludge valves, plug valves, gate valves, pinch valves, stainless ball valves, actuated valves
Domestic Markets:
National
Foreign Activity:
Mexico, USA
Contact(s):
David Buchanan, General Manager
Robert Moore, Sales
Ken Raymond, Sales
Jim Fox, Sales

Neptune Technology Group (Canada) Ltd. / SLBRMS
Formerly: Schlumberger Resource Management Services
Also Known As: Schlumberger RMS Canada Ltd.
7275 West Credit Ave.
Mississauga, ON L5N 5M9
905-858-4211
Fax: 905-858-0428
800-363-7886
www.neptunetg.com
Firm Type: Distributing
Founded: 1892
Staff: 100
Member of: Canadian Water & Waste Water Association
Products/Services/Areas of Expertise: Residential & commercial/industrial water meters, including meter reading systems, installation, testing & repair services
Domestic Markets:
Alberta, British Columbia, Manitoba, New Brunswick, Newfoundland & Labrador, Nova Scotia, Ontario, Prince Edward Island, Québec, Saskatchewan
Contact(s):
Dave Stoddart, Vice-President & General Manager
Angela Zapp, Manager, Marketing

Nertec Design Inc.
Formerly: Nertec Solutions Inc.
950, rue Cowie
Granby, QC J2J 1P2
450-375-0556
Fax: 450-375-8746
866-663-7832
janet@cyberdata.ca
Firm Type: Information Technology
Founded: 1985
Staff: 30
Contact(s):
Jean-Claude Lauret

Nestlé Purina PetCare
Formerly: Canbrands International Ltd.
Also Known As: Yesterday's News Cat Litter
28 Elizabeth St.
Moncton, NB E1C 9T1
506-859-9118
Fax: 506-859-8013
800-267-5287
www.yesterdaysnews.com
Firm Type: Manufacturing
Founded: 1987
Staff: 50
Quality Environmental Management System(s): 9002
Products/Services/Areas of Expertise: Cat litter & small animal bedding made from recycled newspapers; also manufactures dog litter
Financial Information:
Type of Ownership: Private
Revenue Sources: 100% Private Contracts
Domestic Markets:
National
Foreign Activity:
Asia, Western Europe, USA
Contact(s):
Guy Bourque, Manager, Plant
Monique Duguay, Manager, Quality Assurance

Net Safety Monitoring Inc.
2721 Hopewell Place NE
Calgary, AB T1Y 7J7
403-219-0688
Fax: 403-219-0694
866-347-3427
netsafe@net-safety.com
www.net-safety.com
Firm Type: Manufacturing
Member of: Association of Professional Engineers, Geologists & Geophysicists of Alberta
Products/Services/Areas of Expertise: Manufactures monitoring instrumentation to detect toxic & combustible gases, smoke, particulate mists & flame; also manufactures emergency communications, video monitoring & motion detection equipment; target applications are industrial complexes
Financial Information:
Type of Ownership: Private
Revenue Sources: 100% Private Contracts
Domestic Markets:
National
Foreign Activity:
Caribbean, South America, Mexico, USA
Contact(s):
M. Coffey, President
Larry McGee, Director, Sales

NetPlus-HazMat Tracker
#105, 8750, Côte de Liesse
Montréal, QC H4T 1H2
514-862-8265
Fax: 514-344-7215
netplus@wpglobal.net
www.wpglobal.com
Firm Type: Information Technology
Founded: 1999
Staff: 5
Products/Services/Areas of Expertise: System for tracking hazardous waste material from the generator, with manifest, from generator to transport to a facility; interfaces with the processing module to track receiving, storage, treatment & disposal with bar-code tracking
Domestic Markets:
National
Contact(s):
David Chourke, President
Allan Desgroseillers, Director, Sales

Nett Technologies Inc.
#2, 6707 Goreway Dr.
Mississauga, ON L4V 1P7
905-672-5453
Fax: 905-672-5949
800-361-6388
jpopik@nett.ca
www.nett.ca
Firm Type: Manufacturing
Founded: 1994
Staff: 45
Member of: Canadian Association of Mining Equipment & Services for Export
Products/Services/Areas of Expertise: Manufactures catalytic purifiers, emission control products, catalytic mufflers, diesel filters, fume diluters for the material-handling, construction, mining & stationary industries, engine exhaust systems
Financial Information:
Type of Ownership: Private
Revenue: $3 Million - $5 Million
Revenue Sources: 100% Private Contracts
Domestic Markets:
National
Foreign Activity:
Worldwide
Contact(s):
John Popik, President
Steve McDonald, Marketing Manager
Rich Jones, Sales Manager
Thyson Poehlmann, Engineer

Network Environmental Services Inc.
31 Golden Gate Ct.
Toronto, ON M1P 3A4
416-299-0116
Fax: 416-299-9649
800-272-6118
maston@networkenvironmental.net
www.networkenvironmental.net
Firm Type: Waste Management
Founded: 1989
Staff: 5
Products/Services/Areas of Expertise: Recycling & disposal of all hazardous & non-hazardous liquid & solid wastes
Financial Information:
Type of Ownership: Private
Revenue Sources: 100% Private Contracts
Domestic Markets:
National
Foreign Activity:
USA
Contact(s):
M. Aston, President

Nevin Sadlier-Brown Goodbrand Ltd.
#306, 126E - 12th St. North
Vancouver, BC V7L 2J5
604-990-3622
Fax: 604-683-1270
tlsb@telus.net

Firm Type: Engineering, Scientific/Technical Services
Founded: 1972
Staff: 4
Products/Services/Areas of Expertise: Geological consulting services with emphasis on geothermal resources & metallic & industrial minerals
Contact(s):
Timothy L. Sadlier-Brown, President

New East Consulting Services Ltd.
Also Known As: New East
#203, 12877 - 76th Ave.
Surrey, BC V3W 1E6
604-591-1915
Fax: 604-591-9923
newest@telus.net
Firm Type: Engineering
Founded: 1994
Staff: 20
Member of: Association of Professional Engineers & Geoscientists of BC
Products/Services/Areas of Expertise: Engineering consulting in managing water, wastewater, stormwater & solid waste; environmental management for industries (ISO14000, pollution prevention, greenhouse gas reduction credits); technology transfer negotiation
Recently Completed / Ongoing Projects: Water quality restoration of a lake through wetlands & public education, China; greenhouse gas emission reduction opportunity identification study, Korea; municipal infrastructure design of a large industrial park, Surrey, BC
Financial Information:
Type of Ownership: Private
Revenue: $1.5 Million - $3 Million
Revenue Sources: 5% nationwide; 50% Municipals; 45% Private Contracts
Domestic Markets:
British Columbia
Foreign Activity:
Asia, China, Vietnam
Markets Sought:
South America
Contact(s):
Ken-Beck Lee, President/CEO
kblee@neweast-canada.com
Soomin Yu, Marketing
soominya@neweast-canada.com

New Era Farms Ltd.
61 Evergreen Place
Goodwood, NS B3T 1P2
902-876-5185
Fax: 902-876-5163
newera@ns.sympatico.ca
Contact(s):
Andrew Wort, General Manager

New Trend Environmental Services
P.O. Box 21037
Dartmouth, NS B2W 6B2
902-462-2951
Fax: 902-462-6066
rich@newtrend.ca
www.newtrend.ca
Firm Type: Scientific/Technical Services
Founded: 1990
Staff: 2
Member of: Building Owners & Managers Association
Products/Services/Areas of Expertise: Pioneered the use of Condensation Particle Counters (CPC) for indoor air quality investigations; indoor air quality consultation & training on using CPC technology to track sources of ultrafine particles in buildings
Recently Completed / Ongoing Projects: Trained over 800 professionals throughout North America & Europe on using CPC technology in indoor air quality investgations
Financial Information:
Type of Ownership: Private
Revenue: $100,000 - $250,000
Domestic Markets:
New Brunswick, Newfoundland & Labrador, Nova Scotia, Prince Edward Island
Contact(s):
Richard Fogarty, President
rich@newtrend.ca

New West Gypsum Recycling Inc.
5620 - 198 St.
Langley, BC V3A 7C7
604-534-9925
Fax: 604-534-9688
info@nwgypsum.com
www.nwgypsum.com
Firm Type: Waste Management
Founded: 1986
Staff: 30
Member of: Recycling Council of Ontario; Waste Management Association of British Columbia; Recycling Council of British Columbia
Products/Services/Areas of Expertise: Gypsum waste recycling
Domestic Markets:
British Columbia, Ontario
Contact(s):
John A. McCamley, President/CEO

Canadian Branches:
New Westminster
38 Vulcan St.
New Westminster, BC V3L 5T7
604-520-6647
Fax: 604-534-9688
mccamley@nwgypsum.com
John A. (Tony) McCamley, General Manager

Oakville
Recycling Services
2182 Wyecroft Rd.
Oakville, ON L6L 5V6
905-847-0520
Fax: 905-847-0522
oakville@nwgypsum.com
Shawn Radvanyi, Manager

New World Generation Inc.
P.O. Box 441
232 - 8th St. East
Owen Sound, ON N4K 5P5
519-371-0249
Fax: 519-371-1867
newworldgeneration@msn.com
Products/Services/Areas of Expertise: Operating consultants of the 3e.sustainer enhancement system; patented process is being refined & engineered to service existing intermittent energy sources or future installations making them capable of sustained electrical energy delivery
Contact(s):
Paul Merswolke, President

Newalta Corporation
211 - 11 Ave. SW
Calgary, AB T2R 0C6
403-806-7000
Fax: 403-806-7348
info@newalta.com
www.newalta.com
Firm Type: Waste Management
Founded: 1993
Staff: 1500
Products/Services/Areas of Expertise: Newalta focuses on maximizing the value inherent in industrial waste, through the recovery of saleable products & recycling; also provides environmentally sound disposal of solid, non-hazardous industrial waste
Financial Information:
Type of Ownership: Publicly Traded
Domestic Markets:
Alberta, British Columbia, Manitoba, Ontario, Québec, Saskatchewan,
Contact(s):
Alan P. Cadotte, President & CEO
acadotte@newalta.com
Bill Robertson, Manager, Sales & Marketing, 403/806-7103
brobertson@newalta.com
Dan Pippard, Director, Environment, Health & Safety
dpippard@newalta.com
Craig White, Vice-President, Business Development
Barbara Parry, Lab Services Manager, EH&S
bparry@newalta.com

Canadian Branches:
Abbotsford
31087 Peardonville Rd., RR#7
Abbotsford, BC V2T 6K4

604-855-9100
Fax: 604-855-0306

Airdrie
42 Eastlake Circle
Airdrie, AB T4B 2B9
403-948-1360
Fax: 403-948-1370

Amelia
4811 - 47th St. East
Redwater, AB T0A 2W0
780-942-2240
Fax: 780-942-2018

Barrie
1131 Snow Valley Rd.
Barrie, ON L4M 4S5
705-737-1221
Fax: 705-737-5121
800-742-0842

Beaverlodge
820 - 8th Ave. Industrial Park
Beaverlodge, AB T0H 0C0
780-354-4122
Fax: 780-354-3694

Brantford
112 Adams Rd.
Brantford, ON N3S 7V2
519-756-9770
Fax: 519-756-9950
800-263-5129

Brooks
P.O. Box 577
Brooks, AB T1R 1B5
403-362-4266
Fax: 403-362-2111

Calgary
9611 - 44th St. SE
Calgary, AB T2C 2P7
403-215-6900
Fax: 403-215-6947

Cranbrook
2101 Theatre Rd.
Cranbrook, BC V1C 7G6
250-426-2073
Fax: 250-426-3144

Dartmouth
Formerly: Matrix Environmental
#290, 3 Spectacle Lake Dr.
Dartmouth, NS B3B 1W8
902-720-4002
Fax: 902-720-4003
866-870-2771
Alton Payne, President

Delta
#9, 7492 Progress Way
Delta, BC V4G 1E7
604-952-1220
Fax: 604-940-0376

Drayton Valley
P.O. Box 6180
Drayton Valley, AB T7A 1R7
780-542-4626
Fax: 780-542-3969

Drumheller
P.O. Box 387
Drumheller, AB T0J 0Y0
403-823-2706
Fax: 403-823-4187

Eckville
P.O. Box 600
Eckville, AB T0M 0X0
403-746-2092
Fax: 403-746-2434

Edmonton (Industrial Cleaning)
6024 - 27th St.
Edmonton, AB T6P 1Y5
780-465-1400
Fax: 780-463-7714

Products & Services Buyer's Guide

Edmonton (Process)
6110 - 27 St.
Edmonton, AB T6P 1J9
780-461-8926
Fax: 780-468-0964

Elk Point
P.O. Box 1001
Elk Point, AB T0A 1A0
780-724-4333
Fax: 780-724-3519

Fairview
#106, 10127 - 127 Ave.
Grande Prairie, AB T8V 1A0
780-538-4422
Fax: 780-539-4655

Fort Erie
1731 Pettit Rd.
Fort Erie, ON L2A 5N1
905-994-1900
Fax: 905-994-1777

Fort Saskatchewan
11230 - 88 Ave.
Fort Saskatchewan, AB T8L 3W5
780-998-1459
Fax: 780-465-4655

Fort St. John
P.O. Box 6905
Fort St John, BC V1J 4J3
250-789-3051
Fax: 250-789-3402

Gordondale
P.O. Box 30
Gordondale, AB T0H 1V0
780-353-3770
Fax: 780-353-2100

Grande Prairie
P.O. Box 36
Grande Prairie, AB T8V 5N3
780-539-1845
Fax: 780-539-0260

Green Court
P.O. Box 178
Mayerthorpe, AB T0E 1N0
780-780-0150
Fax: 780-780-0151

Halbrite
P.O. Box 218
Weyburn, SK S4H 2J9
306-458-2419
Fax: 306-458-2274

Hamilton (Brant St.)
235 - 237 Brant St.
Hamilton, ON L8L 4E3
905-548-5789
Fax: 905-548-6447

Hamilton (Imperial St.)
52 Imperial St.
Hamilton, ON L8L 4E3
905-668-9599
Fax: 905-547-3513

Hays
P.O. Box 39
Hays, AB T0K 1BN0
403-725-2244
Fax: 403-725-2256

Hughenden
P.O. Box 28
Hughenden, AB T0B 2E0
780-856-2526
Fax: 780-856-2201

Kitscoty
P.O. Box 93
Kitscoty, AB T0B 2P0
780-847-4727
Fax: 780-847-4728

Leduc
3901 - 84 Ave.
Leduc, AB T9E 8M5
780-980-6474
Fax: 780-980-6699

Leduc Drilling Site
6603 - 44 St.
Leduc, AB T9E 7E5
780-980-6474
Fax: 780-980-2550

Nanaimo
1080 Maughan Rd.
Nanaimo, BC V9X 1J2
250-722-3885
Fax: 250-722-3802

Nisku
405 - 18 Ave.
Nisku, AB T9E 7T5
780-955-2456
Fax: 780-955-3464

Niton Junction
P.O. Box 38
Niton Junction, AB T0E 1S0
780-795-2364
Fax: 780-795-2587

North Vancouver
130 Forester St.
Vancouver, BC V7H 2M9
604-929-1282
Fax: 604-929-8371

Pigeon Lake
RR#1
Westerose, AB T0C 2V0
780-389-4449
Fax: 780-389-3592

Plover Lake
P.O. Box 540
Unity, SK S0K 4L0
306-372-4175
Fax: 306-372-4176

Prince George
9203 Rock Island Rd.
Prince George, BC V2N 5T4
250-960-1404
Fax: 250-960-1405

Raymond
P.O. Box 1040
300 Railway Ave.
Raymond, AB T0K 2S0
403-752-3213
Fax: 403-752-4766

Red Deer
P.O. Box 790
Blackfalds, AB T0M 0J0
403-885-5655
Fax: 403-885-2111

Red Earth Creek
P.O. Box 208
Red Earth Creek, AB T0G 1X0
780-649-3793
Fax: 780-649-3402

Redwater
4811 - 47 St. East
Redwater, AB T0A 2W0
780-942-2240
Fax: 780-942-2018

Regina
2770 Pinkie Rd.
Regina, SK S4T 7X3
360-545-4655
Fax: 360-569-7188

Rexdale
55 Vulcan St.
Toronto, ON M9W 1L3
416-245-8338
Fax: 416-245-8321
800-667-4403

Richmond
P.O. Box 190
Golden Prairie, SK S0N 0Y0

306-662-3899
Fax: 306-662-4930

Sparwood
P.O. Box 1870
631 Douglas Fir
Sparwood, BC V0B 2G0
250-425-0435
Fax: 250-425-0411

Stauffer
P.O. Box 25
Stauffer, AB T0M 1W0
403-746-2266
Fax: 403-746-2268

Stettler
P.O. Box 781
Stettler, AB T0C 2L0
403-742-5414
Fax: 403-742-6300

Stoney Creek
65 Green Mountain Rd.
Stoney Creek, ON L8J 1X5
905-561-0305
Fax: 905-549-4515

Surrey
7720 Anvil Way
Surrey, BC V3W 4H7
604-596-6559
Fax: 604-596-3265

Swift Current
#1, 1081 Central Ave. North
Swift Current, SK S9H 4Z1
306-773-8820
Fax: 306-773-8803
877-773-8820

Taber
P.O. Box 4302
Taber, AB T1G 2C7
403-223-2659
Fax: 403-223-8262

Valleyview
P.O. Box 2154
Valleyview, AB T0H 3N0
780-524-4336
Fax: 780-524-2212

West Stoddart
P.O. Box 6905
Fort St John, BC V1J 4J3
250-789-3051
Fax: 250-789-3402

Williesden Green
P.O. Box 2156
Rocky Mountain House, AB T0M 1T2
403-844-8641
Fax: 403-844-8642

Windsor
4505 - 4 St.
Windsor, ON N9E 4A5
519-265-0822
Fax: 519-250-7757
800-265-0822

Winfield
9595 McCarthy Rd.
Kelowna, BC V4V 1S5
250-766-0964
Fax: 250-766-0965

Zama City
P.O. Box 86
Zama City, AB T0E 4E0
780-683-2231
Fax: 780-683-2334

Newfoundland Design Associates Limited
Bally Rou Place
280 Torbay Rd.
St. John's, NL A1A 3W8
709-726-4490
Fax: 709-726-4499
admin@ndal.com
www.ndal.com
Products/Services/Areas of Expertise: Engineering services

Contact(s):
Reg A. Babstock, CEO

Newmac Manufacturing Inc.
P.O. Box 9
Lancaster Cres.
Debert, NS B0M 1G0
902-662-3840
Fax: 902-662-2581
newmac@fox.nstn.ca
www.newmacfurnaces.com
Firm Type: Manufacturing
Staff: 35
Member of: Heating, Refrigerating & Air Conditioning Institute
Quality Environmental Management System(s): 9001
Products/Services/Areas of Expertise: High-efficiency domestic heating systems, forced air furnaces
Domestic Markets:
British Columbia, Manitoba, Newfoundland & Labrador, Nova Scotia, Ontario, Prince Edward Island, Québec
Foreign Activity:
USA
Contact(s):
Ken Johnson, President

Newpark Environmental Services
#300, 635 - 6 Ave. SW
Calgary, AB T2P OT5
403-266-7383
Fax: 403-263-1760
environment@newpark.ca
www.newpark.ca
Products/Services/Areas of Expertise: Environmental consultants
Domestic Markets:
Alberta, British Columbia, New Brunswick, Northwest Territories, Nunavut, Saskatchewan, Yukon Territory
Foreign Activity:
USA
Contact(s):
Natalie Levak

Canadian Branches:
Antigonish
P.O. Box 962
Antigonish, NS B2G 2S3
902-867-1940
Fax: 902-867-1941

Grande Prairie Service
1137 96 Ave.
Antigonish, NS T8V 5M4
780-831-6849
Fax: 780-842-6794

Next Environmental
#215, 2550 Boundary Rd.
Burnaby, BC V5M 3Z3
604-419-3800
Fax: 604-419-3801
hgross@next.bc.ca
www.next.bc.ca
Firm Type: Management Consulting
Founded: 1998
Staff: 16
Products/Services/Areas of Expertise: Specialists in the investigation & remediation of contaminated sites
Recently Completed / Ongoing Projects: Remediation project in BC (over $10,000,000), involving petroleum hydrocarbon & metals; solvent contamination project; numerous remediation projects resulting in government certification
Financial Information:
Type of Ownership: Private
Revenue Sources: 2% nationwide; 3% Provincial; 5% Municipals; 90% Private Contracts
Domestic Markets:
British Columbia
Contact(s):
H.P. Gross, President

NextEnergy Inc.
35 Earl Martin Dr.
Elmira, ON N3B 3L4
Fax: 877-684-3112
800-367-9810
dhatherton@nextenergy.com
www.nextenergysolutions.com

Firm Type: Distributing
Founded: 2000
Products/Services/Areas of Expertise: Geothermal energy systems; heating/cooling systems for commercial or home use
Domestic Markets:
National
Contact(s):
David Hatherton, President

Nexus Solutions Inc.
#254, 759 Hyde Park Rd.
London, ON N6H 3S2
519-649-6100
Fax: 519-681-8799
sales@cemview.com
www.cemview.com
Firm Type: Information Technology
Founded: 1999
Staff: 7
Products/Services/Areas of Expertise: CEMView data acquisition & reporting software for environmental emission monitoring for compliance applications
Domestic Markets:
National
Foreign Activity:
USA,
Contact(s):
Joe Sue-Tang, President

NI Plastique Inc.
#325-B, 911, rue Jean-Talon est
Montréal, QC H2R 1V5
514-270-1102
Fax: 514-270-1104
Contact(s):
Frédérik Richard

Niagara Analytical Inc.
P.O. Box 205
5805 Progress St.
Niagara Falls, ON L2E 6T3
905-374-5227
Fax: 905-356-9672
labs@bellnet.ca
www.vaxxine.com/labs
Firm Type: Scientific/Technical Services
Founded: 1992
Staff: 13
Member of: Canadian Association for Environmental Analytical Laboratories; Chemical Institute of Canada; Canadian Society of Chemistry; Association of Chemical Professionals of Canada
Products/Services/Areas of Expertise: Environmental analytical laboratory specializing in priority pollutant analysis; water & wastewater analysis; oil, soil & physical testing; industrial hygiene analysis & microbiological analysis; food & dairy
Financial Information:
Type of Ownership: Private
Revenue Sources: 5% nationwide; 15% Provincial; 15% Municipals; 65% Private Contracts
Domestic Markets:
New Brunswick, Ontario, Québec
Foreign Activity:
USA
Contact(s):
Brian I. Johnson, President/Senior Chemist
brian@vaxxine.com
Stephanie A. Johnson, Vice-President

Niagara Energy Products Limited
Formerly: Taylor Forge Limited.
4749 Buttrey St.
Niagara Falls, ON L2E 7K7
905-371-2500
Fax: 905-371-2235
800-633-6743
nepfg@vaxxine.com
www.niagaraenergyproducts.com/home.html
Products/Services/Areas of Expertise: Manufactures: components for the Energy and Petro-Chemical Industries in North America and overseas; pipe fittings and flanges for both the nuclear and industrial markets; transportable Dry Storage Containers (DSC's) for storage of waste nuclear fuel; nuclear and commercial valves

Niagara Environmental Dynamics
PO Box 1406, RPO County Fair 96
Fort Erie, ON L2A 6G2
905-871-8553
Fax: 905-871-7056
ned@niagara-environmental.com
www.niagara-environmental.com
Firm Type: Distributing
Founded: 1990
Staff: 6
Products/Services/Areas of Expertise: Water & wastewater management; air quality assessment; environmental audits; impact assessments; filters/filter media; potable/process water treatment systems; water filters, bacterial filters, medical equipment filters, air filters
Financial Information:
Type of Ownership: Private
Revenue: $500,000 - $1.5 Million
Revenue Sources: 2% Provincial; 15% Municipals; 80% Private Contracts
Domestic Markets:
Ontario
Foreign Activity:
USA
Contact(s):
Michael Mugas, President
David Talley, Project Manager

International Branch(es):
Niagara Environmental Dynamics
1973 Tonawanda Creek Rd.
Amherst, NY USA
716-692-6851
ned@niagara-environmental.com

Niagara Recycling
4935 Kent St.
Niagara Falls, ON L2H 1J6
905-356-4141
Fax: 905-356-3628
800-594-5542
norman.kraft@regional.niagara.on.ca
www.niagararecycling.org
Firm Type: Waste Management
Founded: 1978
Products/Services/Areas of Expertise: Recycling services; collection, processing & marketing of fine paper, glass, aluminum, tin, newspapers, PET, HDPE, tin, steel, polystyrene, boxboard & cardboard
Domestic Markets:
Ontario
Contact(s):
Norman Kraft, General Manager
Elinor King, Commercial Sales
elinor.king@niagararecycling.org

Niagara Waste Systems Ltd.
Also Known As: Walker Environmental Services
Subsidiary of Walker Industries Holdings Ltd.
P.O. Box 100
Thorold, ON L2V 3Y8
905-680-1980
Fax: 905-680-1916
800-263-2526
customerservice@niagarawastesystems.com
www.walkerind.com
Firm Type: Waste Management
Founded: 1876
Staff: 50
Products/Services/Areas of Expertise: Offers waste disposal services & analytical services
Financial Information:
Type of Ownership: Private
Domestic Markets:
Ontario
Contact(s):
Joseph Lyng, Manager, Sales & Marketing

Niagara Water Conditioning Ltd.
P.O. Box 425
5805 Progress St.
Niagara Falls, ON L2E 5T8
905-356-7622
Fax: 905-356-9672
800-387-6337
Firm Type: Distributing
Founded: 1992

Staff: 4
Member of: Canadian Water Quality Association
Products/Services/Areas of Expertise: Dealer of water treatment equipment for residential, commercial & industrial uses; water softeners, chlorinators, reverse-osmosis, charcoal filters, UV sterilization, de-ionization systems, chemicals, acid water neutralizers
Financial Information:
Type of Ownership: Private
Domestic Markets:
Ontario
Foreign Activity:
USA
Contact(s):
Bruce Sennuck, Vice-President

Niblett Environmental / NEA
P.O. Box 160
1484 Hwy. 7A
Bethany, ON L0A 1A0
705-277-1929
Fax: 705-277-1951
general@niblettenvironmental.on.ca
Firm Type: Scientific/Technical Services
Founded: 1985
Staff: 6
Member of: Canadian Society of Environmental Biologists; American Fisheries Society
Products/Services/Areas of Expertise: Natural resource evaluation; consulting inventories & impact assessment of proposals on fish, wildlife, vegetation, water quality & sediment quality; peer review; environmental monitoring
Recently Completed / Ongoing Projects: Environmental assessment of new sewer & water supply systems for a municipality; community design plan for a new neighbourhood in Ottawa
Financial Information:
Type of Ownership: Private
Revenue: $500,000 - $1.5 Million
Revenue Sources: 20% nationwide; 10% Provincial; 30% Municipals; 40% Private Contracts
Domestic Markets:
Nova Scotia, Ontario
Foreign Activity:
South America, USA
Contact(s):
Philip Niblett, President/CEO
Janis Speel, Vice-President, Marine Biology

Nichols Applied Management
#1100, 10130 - 103 St.
Edmonton, AB T5J 3N9
780-424-0091
Fax: 780-428-7644
pnichols@nicholsconsulting.com
www.nicholsconsulting.com
Firm Type: Management Consulting
Founded: 1973
Member of: Canadian Evaluation Society; Institute of Certified Management Consultants
Products/Services/Areas of Expertise: Project economic & cost-benefit studies; infrastructure financing studies; socio-economic impact assessments
Financial Information:
Type of Ownership: Private
Revenue Sources: 25% Provincial; 25% Municipals; 50% Private Contracts
Domestic Markets:
Alberta, Northwest Territories
Foreign Activity:
USA
Markets Sought:
Asia, Caribbean, The Pacific Rim
Contact(s):
Peter Nichols, Partner
info@nicholsappliedmanagement.com

Nichols Environmental (Canada) Ltd.
17331 - 107 Ave.
Edmonton, AB T5S 1E5
780-484-3377
Fax: 780-484-5093
askus@nicholsenvironmental.com
www.nicholsenvironmental.com
Products/Services/Areas of Expertise: Environmental consulting & contracting services
Contact(s):
Rob Dickie, President
Canadian Branches:
Peace Region
10417 - 99 Ave.
Grande Prairie, AB T8V 0S4
780-513-0477
Fax: 780-513-1447

Nilex Inc.
Also Known As: Geosynthetic Products Inc.
9304 - 39 Ave. NW
Edmonton, AB T6E 6L8
780-463-9535
Fax: 780-463-1773
800-667-4811
edmonton@nilex.com; info@nilex.com
www.nilex.com
Firm Type: Distributing, Scientific/Technical Services
Founded: 1977
Staff: 100
Member of: ISNetworld; Alberta Construction Association
Products/Services/Areas of Expertise: Supply & installation of geosynthetics, membrane liners, geotextiles, erosion control, silt fences, geogrids & wickdrains; MSE walls
Domestic Markets:
Alberta, British Columbia, Ontario, Saskatchewan
Foreign Activity:
USA
Contact(s):
Walter van Woudenberg, Founder & CEO
Ian Wilson, President
iwilson@nilex.com

Canadian Branches:
Abbotsford
1781 Clearbrook Rd.
Abbotsford, BC V2T 5X5
604-420-6433
Fax: 604-420-0445
800-663-0478
abbotsford@nilex.com
Ian Corne

Calgary
9222 - 40 St. SE
Calgary, AB T2C 2P3
403-543-5454
Fax: 403-543-5455
888-543-5454
calgary@nilex.com
Jason Luty

Saskatoon
#3, 320 Jessop Ave.
Saskatoon, SK S7N 1Y6
306-956-0088
Fax: 306-956-0055
saskatoon@nilex.com
Lee Jaboeuf

Toronto
130 Yorkland Blvd.
Toronto, ON M2J 1R5
416-640-6002
Fax: 416-640-6006
877-640-6002
toronto@nilex.com

Vancouver
3963 Phillips Ave.
Burnaby, BC V5A 3K4
604-420-6433
Fax: 604-420-0445
800-663-0478
burnaby@nilex.com
Dan MacDonald

Vernon
Vernon, BC
250-260-3300
Fax: 250-260-3520
800-663-0478
vernon@nilex.com

International Branch(es):
USA Head Office - Denver
15171 East Fremont Dr.
Centennial, CO USA
303-766-2000
Fax: 303-766-1110
denver@nilex.com

Nilfisk-Advance Canada Company
Formerly: Nilfisk Ltd.
396 Watline Ave.
Mississauga, ON L4Z 1X2
905-712-3260
Fax: 905-712-3255
800-668-8400
marketing@nilfisk-advance.ca
www.pa.nilfisk-advance.com
Firm Type: Distributing
Founded: 1980
Staff: 20
Member of: Canadian Sanitation Supply Association; International Sanitation Supply Association; National Asbestos Council
Products/Services/Areas of Expertise: Filtered vacuum cleaners, portable dust collectors for collection & control of toxic &/or hazardous substances, such as lead dust, asbestos, silica, mercury, radioactive particulates, beryllium alloy, plant debris, ultra-fine nuisance dust
Domestic Markets:
National
Contact(s):
Bruce Takahashi, President
Joe Johnston, Vice-President, Sales

NIM Disposals Limited
P.O. Box 2421 A
2755 Lasalle Boulevard
Sudbury, ON P3A 4S8
705-566-9363
Fax: 705-566-1498
www.nimdisposals.com
Products/Services/Areas of Expertise: Waste management, recycling services, demolition, scrap metal
Domestic Markets:
Ontario
Contact(s):
Joan Greenspoon, Director

Nimbus Water Systems
509 Commissioners Rd. West
London, ON N6J 1Y5
519-474-0411
Fax: 519-474-2941
888-760-8543
nimbus@odyssey.on.ca
Firm Type: Distributing
Founded: 1987
Staff: 4
Member of: Water Quality Association; London Chamber of Commerce
Products/Services/Areas of Expertise: Reverse osmosis water purification technology & water treatment for industrial, commercial & residential applications; water treatment products; environmentally friendly salt substitute products for water softener regenerate (potassium chloride); water dispensing stations
Domestic Markets:
Ontario
Foreign Activity:
USA
Markets Sought:
Asia, The Middle East
Contact(s):
Russel R. More, President/CEO
Lucy N. More, Marketing/Manager of Operations

Canadian Branches:
Nimbus Water Depot
509 Commissioners Rd. West
London, ON N6J 1Y5
Lucy More, Contact

Nisymco Inc.
812-7 Townsgate Dr.
Thornhill, ON L4J 7Z9
905-597-0094
nisymco@hotmail.com
Firm Type: Management Consulting, Scientific/Technical Services
Founded: 1987
Staff: 5

Products/Services/Areas of Expertise: Environmental consulting & marketing services; engineering services
Contact(s):
Eli Hay, Chief Executive Officer

Noel Rochette et Fils Inc.
3483, boul Mgr-Gauthier
Québec, QC G1E 2W9
418-661-7719
Fax: 418-661-3196
mmercier@noelrochette.com
www.noelrochette.com
Firm Type: Scientific/Technical Services
Staff: 25
Products/Services/Areas of Expertise: Mechanical contractors; water & wastewater treatment
Domestic Markets:
New Brunswick, Québec
Contact(s):
Michel Mercier, President

Noise Solutions Inc.
#301, 206 - 7 Av. SW
Calgary, AB T2P 0W7
403-232-0916
Fax: 403-234-7304
877-666-6473
info@noisesolutions.com
www.noisesolutions.com
Firm Type: Management Consulting
Founded: 1997
Member of: Association of Professional Engineers, Geologists & Geophysicists of Alberta
Products/Services/Areas of Expertise: Provides turnkey, engineered solutions to noise suppression problems faced by industry; provides comprehensive noise assessments, custom design, manufacturing & installation of various noise control equipment
Financial Information:
Type of Ownership: Private
Domestic Markets:
Alberta, British Columbia, Saskatchewan
Foreign Activity:
USA
Contact(s):
Scott MacDonald, President
smacdonald@noisesolutions.com
Rod MacDonald, Vice-President
rmacdonald@noisesolutions.com

Canadian Branches:
Delburne
P.O. Box 9
2101 - 21st Ave.
Delburne, AB T0M 0V0
403-749-2226
Fax: 403-749-2259

International Branch(es):
USA - Denver
P.O. Box 2584
Littleton, CO USA
303-623-1080
Fax: 303-317-5490
denversales@noisesolutions.com

Nolar Industries Ltd.
602 Millway Ave.
Concord, ON L4K 3V3
905-669-5513
Fax: 905-669-6587
800-836-2694
www.nolarindustries.com
Products/Services/Areas of Expertise: Filtration equipment
Contact(s):
Larry Raponi, President
lraponi@nolarindustries.com
Seymour J. Gould, Quality Manager
sgould@nolarindustries.com
Michael Raponi, Sales
mraponi@nolarindustries.com

Nor-Alta Environmental Services Ltd.
#157, 9768 - 170th St.
Edmonton, AB T5T 5L4
780-486-4931
Fax: 780-486-4046
888-524-2012
info@nor-alta.com
www.nor-alta.com
Firm Type: Scientific/Technical Services
Founded: 1983
Staff: 35
Member of: Canadian Land Reclamation Association; American Industrial Hygiene Association
Products/Services/Areas of Expertise: Environmental consulting; drilling waste management; indoor air sampling; remediation & reclamation for the energy sector
Financial Information:
Type of Ownership: Private
Domestic Markets:
Alberta, British Columbia, Northwest Territories, Saskatchewan, Yukon Territory
Foreign Activity:
Africa, The Middle East, USA
Contact(s):
Jim Haeberle, President & General Manager
jhaeberle@nor-alta.com

Noram Engineering & Constructors Ltd.
#1800, 200 Granville St.
Vancouver, BC V6C 1S4
604-681-2030
Fax: 604-683-9164
questions@noram-eng.com
www.noram-eng.com
Firm Type: Engineering, Manufacturing
Staff: 100
Products/Services/Areas of Expertise: Specializes in development, commercialization & supply of leading-edge chemical processes & environmental technologies
Financial Information:
Type of Ownership: Private
Domestic Markets:
British Columbia, Ontario
Foreign Activity:
Asia, Central America, China, Western Europe, The Pacific Rim, Mexico, USA, Vietnam
Contact(s):
Jeff Guild, Manager, Environmental

Norampac Inc.
A division of Cascades Canada Inc.
P.O. Box 30
404, boul Marie-Victorin
Kingsey Falls, QC J0A 1B0
819-363-5100
Fax: 819-363-5155
www.norampac.com
Products/Services/Areas of Expertise: Recycled paper & paper products
Contact(s):
Marc-André Dépin, President/CEO

Nordevco Associates Ltd.
15 Acadia Bay
Winnipeg, MB R3T 3J1
204-269-3340
Fax: 204-269-9097
info@nordevco.net
Firm Type: Management Consulting
Staff: 11
Products/Services/Areas of Expertise: Environmental consulting in agriculture, soil & groundwater, and sewage & wastewater; Developers of BactiDomus Delivery Technology, a treatment for a broad variety of problems caused by contaminated soil & groundwater
Contact(s):
Paul Deprez, President
pdeprez@nordevco.net

Nordic Systems Corporation
1044 Rangeview Rd.
Mississauga, ON L5E 1H3
905-278-3331
Fax: 905-278-5197
800-268-1756
info@nordicsystems.com
Firm Type: Distributing
Founded: 1947
Staff: 50
Member of: Reelcraft Industries
Quality Environmental Management System(s): 9001:2008
Products/Services/Areas of Expertise: Reelcraft hose & cable reels; reels for oil recovery booms

Domestic Markets:
National
Foreign Activity:
Australia/New Zealand, Western Europe, South America, USA
Contact(s):
John Bain, Director, Sales & Marketing

NORDIKeau Inc.
Formerly: Axeau Inc.
603, boul. Base de Roc
Joliette, QC J6E 5P3
450-756-6227
Fax: 450-756-8313
nordikeau@bellnet.ca
www.nordikeau.com
Firm Type: Waste Management
Founded: 1985
Staff: 20
Products/Services/Areas of Expertise: Manages installation equipment for waste water & drinking water; provides training for the employees of the town
Financial Information:
Type of Ownership: Private
Domestic Markets:
Québec
Contact(s):
Jean-François Bergeron, President

Norditrade Inc.
132 Banff Rd.
Toronto, ON M4P 2P5
416-467-8438
Fax: 416-489-4168
info@norditrade.com
www.norditrade.com
Firm Type: Management Consulting, Distributing
Founded: 1991
Staff: 3
Products/Services/Areas of Expertise: Specializes in international trade development & management, particularly between environmental companies in Canada & the Scandinavian countries
Financial Information:
Type of Ownership: Private
Revenue: $250,000 - $500,000
Revenue Sources: 100% Private Contracts
Domestic Markets:
National
Foreign Activity:
Western Europe, USA
Contact(s):
Lars Henriksson, President
lars@norditrade.com

Norfolk Disposal Services Limited
380 Main St. S
Waterford, ON N0E 1Y0
519-443-8022
Fax: 519-443-4504
www.norfolkdisposal.ca
Products/Services/Areas of Expertise: Waste management; recycling services
Contact(s):
Louis Debono, President
Bernie Debono, General Manager

Norjohn Transfer System Limited
Subsidiary of Walker Industries Holdings Limited
5030 Mainway
Burlington, ON L7L 5Z1
905-332-3136
Fax: 905-319-0328
customerservice@norjohntransfersystems.com
www.walkerind.com
Products/Services/Areas of Expertise: Solid, liquid & hazardous waste collection services & equipment; solid waste management
Domestic Markets:
Ontario
Contact(s):
Archie Reynolds, General Manager

Norm Shropshall & Sons Ltd.
1704 Hwy. 3, RR#1
Cayuga, ON N0A 1E0
905-772-5502
Fax: 905-772-0003

Products/Services/Areas of Expertise: Recycling services; waste management
Contact(s):
Don Shropshall, President
Wayne Shropshall, General Manager

Normcan
A division of CCS Corp.
Formerly: Lionhead Engineering & Consulting Ltd.#1800, 140 - 10 Ave. SE
Calgary, AB T2G 0R1
403-233-7565
Fax: 403-261-5612
info@normcan.com
www.normcan.com
Firm Type: Waste Management
Founded: 1987
Staff: 14
Member of: Hazco Waste Services
Member of: Environmental Services Association of Alberta; Alberta Oilfield Treating & Disposal Association
Products/Services/Areas of Expertise: Complete management of naturally occurring radioactive materials (N.O.R.M.) from initial identification to disposal; operates Canada's only licensed N.O.R.M. equipment decontamination & storage facility
Recently Completed / Ongoing Projects: Decontamination of over 2,000 joints of oilfield tubs; site decontamination at a decommissioned industrial facility; facility turnarounds, safety & waste management
Financial Information:
Type of Ownership: Private
Domestic Markets:
Alberta, British Columbia, Newfoundland & Labrador, Saskatchewan
Contact(s):
Cody Cuthill, General Manager
Curtis McKinnon, Manager, Operations

Canadian Branches:
Decontamination & Storage Facility
233 - 2nd Ave.
Standard, AB T0J 3G0
403-644-0002
Fax: 403-644-0003

Norseman Plastics Ltd.
39 Westmore Dr.
Toronto, ON M9V 3Y6
416-745-6980
Fax: 416-745-1874
800-267-4391
sales@norsemanplastics.com
www.norsemanplastics.com
Firm Type: Manufacturing
Founded: 1969
Member of: Recycling Council of Ontario; Association of Municipal Recyclers of Canada; Clean Nova Scotia Foundation
Products/Services/Areas of Expertise: Recycling containers for industry & government, including composters, roll-out carts, fine paper containers for source separation; retrievable reusable containers; injection moulding plastics
Financial Information:
Type of Ownership: Private
Domestic Markets:
National
Foreign Activity:
USA
Markets Sought:
Western Europe, The Pacific Rim, Mexico
Contact(s):
Ben Walton, Inside Sales
BWalton@norsemanplastics.com

Nortec S.G.S. Inc.
#100, 3300, boul Cavendish
Montréal, QC H4B 2M8
514-487-1055
Fax: 514-487-0058
265h@nortecsgs.com
www.nortecsgs.com
Firm Type: Distributing
Founded: 1979
Staff: 8
Member of: Pulp & Paper Association of Canada
Products/Services/Areas of Expertise: Chemical feeding & mixing equipment; sewage treatment equipment systems; waste handling products
Recently Completed / Ongoing Projects: Al Amar gold mine, Saudia Arabia; Diavik Diamond mines, NWT; Venture Platform Sable Gas, NS; Abitibi-Consolidated, Sheldon, TX
Financial Information:
Type of Ownership: Private
Revenue: $3 Million - $5 Million
Revenue Sources: 5% Municipals; 95% Private Contracts
Domestic Markets:
National
Foreign Activity:
Africa, Caribbean, The Middle East, South America
Contact(s):
Syd Smith, CEO
Yves Rochon, Sales Manager
J-F. Ébengué, Manager

North Safety Products Canada
Also Known As: North by Honeywell
26 Dansk Ct.
Toronto, ON M9W 5V8
416-675-2810
Fax: 416-675-6898
800-316-7233
info@northsafety.ca
www.northsafety.ca
Firm Type: Manufacturing
Founded: 1969
Member of: Canadian Standards Association
Quality Environmental Management System(s): 9000
Products/Services/Areas of Expertise: Occupational health & safety products including eye, face, head, respiratory, hearing, hand & fall protection products; self-contained breathing apparatus, instrumentation; controlled environment products; dermatological products & first aid kits & supplies; personal protective equipment & accessories to aviation & aerospace, manufacturing, transportation, mining, utility, construction, consumer, military & other markets
Financial Information:
Type of Ownership: Foreign-owned
Domestic Markets:
National
Foreign Activity:
Western Europe, USA
Contact(s):
Claude L. Roberge, President & CEO
croberge@northsafety.com
Vern Metcalfe, VP & General Manager
John Greer, Vice-President, Marketing

Canadian Branches:
Edmonton
6303 Roper Rd.
Edmonton, AB T6B 3G6
780-437-2641
Fax: 780-436-0048
800-661-3638

Montréal
10550, boul Parkway
Anjou, QC H1J 2K4
514-351-7233
Fax: 514-355-7233
888-212-7233

International Branch(es):
Netherlands
North by Honeywell
Anodeweg 1, 4338 RA
Middelburg Netherla
31(0)118 656400
Fax: 31(0)118 627535
Peter Vaes, Manager
peter.vaes@honeywell.com

USA - Rhode Is.
North by Honeywell
2000 Plainfield Pike
Cranston, RI USA
401-943-4400
Fax: 401-946-9285
800-430-4110
honeywellsafetyproducts@honeywell.com

North Shore Management Systems Inc.
7343 Howard Rd., RR 1
McGregor, ON N0R 1J0
519-726-9669
Fax: 519-726-9668
northshoremanagement.com
Firm Type: Scientific/Technical Services
Founded: 2002
Staff: 8
Products/Services/Areas of Expertise: offers training courses for auditors and management teams on ISO standards
Domestic Markets:
National
Foreign Activity:
Asia, China, Central Europe, The Middle East, South America, Mexico, USA
Contact(s):
Jeff Greaves, RAB QMS Lead Auditor, President
jsgreaves@sympatico.ca

North West Environmental Group
#3, 835 Devonshire Rd.
Victoria, BC V9A 4T5
250-384-9695
Fax: 250-384-9865
northwest@nwest.bc.ca
www.nwest.bc.ca
Firm Type: Management Consulting, Engineering, Scientific/Technical Services

Products/Services/Areas of Expertise: Environmental consulting services; waste management consulting; air quality assessment
Financial Information:
Type of Ownership: Private
Domestic Markets:
Alberta, British Columbia
Contact(s):
William (Bill) Sullivan, Manager

Canadian Branches:
Cobble Hill
3103 Shawnigan Lake Rd.
Cobble Hill, BC V0R 1L0
250-743-3408

Kelowna
951 Pinewood Pl.
Kelowna, BC V1Z 3G7
250-769-2110
Fax: 250-769-2172

Vancouver
3597 - 23rd Ave. West
Vancouver, BC V6S 1K4
604-737-1701
Fax: 604-737-1701

Williams Lake
#80, 500 Wotzke Dr.
Williams Lake, BC V2G 4S9
250-398-8800
Fax: 250-398-8199

North/South Consultants Inc.
83 Scurfield Blvd.
Winnipeg, MB R3Y 1G4
204-284-3366
Fax: 204-477-4173
nscons@nscons.ca
www.nscons.ca
Firm Type: Scientific/Technical Services
Founded: 1981
Staff: 65
Products/Services/Areas of Expertise: Environmental consulting services; environmental impact assessment; fisheries consulting
Domestic Markets:
Alberta, British Columbia, Manitoba, Northwest Territories, Ontario, Québec, Saskatchewan, Yukon Territory
Contact(s):
Stuart Davies, President

Canadian Branches:
Calgary
#440, 1121 Centre St. NW
Calgary, AB T2E 7K6
403-410-4066
Fax: 403-269-5633

Northeastern Resource Recovery Ltd.
185 Mingo Rd.
Kemptown, NS B6L 2K4
902-897-0450
Fax: 902-897-0453
Firm Type: Management Consulting, Waste Management
Founded: 1998
Staff: 30
Products/Services/Areas of Expertise: Recycling, processing & marketing
Financial Information:
Type of Ownership: Private
Domestic Markets:
Nova Scotia
Contact(s):
Tom MacMillan, President

Northerm Windows
A division of RAB Energy Group Inc.
17 Burns Rd.
Whitehorse, YT Y1A 4Z3
867-668-5088
Fax: 867-668-7474
800-661-0442
sales@northerm.yk.ca
www.northerm.yk.ca
Firm Type: Manufacturing
Founded: 1985
Member of: Canadian Window & Door Manufacturers Association
Products/Services/Areas of Expertise: Double, triple, low-emissivity insulating glass; multi-chamber vinyl frames; argon gas in sealed unit
Foreign Activity:
South America, USA
Contact(s):
Dave Borud, President & General Manager

Northern Alternate Power Systems / NAPS
P.O. Box 638
Fairview, AB T0H 1L0
780-835-3032
Firm Type: Distributing, Engineering, Information Technology, Manufacturing, Scientific/Technical Services
Founded: 1985
Staff: 4
Member of: American Solar Energy Society; International Solar Energy Society; Photovoltaic Information & Education Association; American Hydrogen Society
Products/Services/Areas of Expertise: Renewable energy products; solar heating equipment
Domestic Markets:
National
Foreign Activity:
Western Europe, The Middle East, The Pacific Rim, South America, USA
Markets Sought:
Western Europe

Northern Bridge and Mat Rentals Ltd.
Formerly: Rigboss Rentals Ltd.
P.O. Box 18 Site 1
RR3
Grande Prairie, AB T8V 5N3
780-538-4135
800-354-4144
info@northernbridge.ca
www.northernbridge.ca
Firm Type: Waste Management

Products/Services/Areas of Expertise: Oil field surface equipment rentals, oil field waste disposal (used oil & filters); Temporaty bridge and mat rentals
Financial Information:
Type of Ownership: Private
Revenue Sources: 100% Private Contracts
Domestic Markets:
Alberta, British Columbia, Northwest Territories, Saskatchewan, Yukon Territory

Northern Lights Energy Systems
RR#1, Hwy #900
Richards Landing, ON P0R 1J0
705-246-2073
Fax: 705-246-2073
info@northernlightsenergy.com
www.northernlightsenergy.com
Firm Type: Distributing, Manufacturing
Founded: 1986
Staff: 2
Member of: Solar Energy Society of Canada Inc., Canadian Photovoltaic Industries Association, Canadian Wind Energy Association
Products/Services/Areas of Expertise: Design, installation & sales of renewable energy systems including solar water heating & electricity production from solar, wind & hydroelectric systems; uninterruptable power supply
Recently Completed / Ongoing Projects: 2 residential gridtie solar systems; Installation for Algoma Central Railway tour train; solar & hydro electricity, Canyon Park; solar hot water system installation for local motel
Financial Information:
Revenue: $1.5 Million - $3 Million
Revenue Sources: 5% nationwide; 10% Provincial; 85% Private Contracts
Domestic Markets:
Ontario
Markets Sought:
USA
Contact(s):
Laurence McKay, Owner
Diena McKay, Sales

Northern Petroleum Services
P.O. Box 2
North Battleford, SK S9A 2Y6
306-445-8227
Fax: 306-445-4005
Products/Services/Areas of Expertise: Spills/clean-up planning/assessment; soil remediation
Contact(s):
R. Iverson, Manager

Northern Steel Industries
A division of Vicwest Operating Ltd.
P.O. Box 1718
1015 - 112th Ave.
Tisdale, SK S0E 1T0
306-873-4531
Fax: 306-873-2252
888-674-8265
nsi@northern-steel.com
www.northern-steel.com
Firm Type: Manufacturing
Founded: 2006
Staff: 15
Member of: Steel Tank Institute
Quality Environmental Management System(s): 9001:2000
Products/Services/Areas of Expertise: Manufacturer of above & below ground, double-walled, liquid storage tanks
Financial Information:
Type of Ownership: Publicly Traded
Domestic Markets:
National,
Contact(s):
Ernie Martens, General Manager
Brad Warner, Coordinator, Sales & Marketing
brad.warner@northern-steel.com

Northland Power
30 St. Clair Ave. West, 17th Fl.
Toronto, ON M4V 3A2
416-962-6262
Fax: 416-962-6266
environment@northlandpower.ca
www.northlandpower.ca
Products/Services/Areas of Expertise: Cogeneration technology; biomass & natural gas fuels; power generation
Contact(s):
John Brace, Director, Business Development

NorthPoint Energy Solutions
SaskPower
3E, 2025 Victoria Ave.
Regina, SK S4P 0S1
306-566-2103
Fax: 306-566-3364
info@northpointenergy.com
www.northpointenergy.com
Firm Type: Distributing
Founded: 2001
Products/Services/Areas of Expertise: The energy marketing agent for SaskPower
Contact(s):
Grant Ring, President/CEO
gring@northpointenergy.com

Northway-Photomap Inc.
Formerly: Northway Map Technology; Photographic Survey Corp.
Also Known As: Northway/Photomap/Remote Sensing Ltd.
#2, 75 Hooper Rd.
Barrie, ON L4N 9S3
705-730-6694
Fax: 705-730-6805
www.northway-photomap.com
Firm Type: Engineering
Founded: 1998
Staff: 35
Quality Environmental Management System(s): 9001:2000
Products/Services/Areas of Expertise: Laboratory equipment; maps & aerial photographs; GIS consulting; photographic, photogrammetric equipment; mapping & allied services; computer/data processing services & software
Recently Completed / Ongoing Projects: Ontario basic mapping program, Federal Dept. of Natural Resources; database creation & loading for Canadian airports
Financial Information:
Type of Ownership: Private
Domestic Markets:
Ontario
Contact(s):
Fred Mural, President
Paul Francis, Vice-President

Canadian Branches:
Toronto
47 Lesmill Rd.
Toronto, ON M3B 2T8
416-441-6025
Fax: 416-441-2432

Northwest Metal Recycling
717 Carrier St.
Kamloops, BC V2H 1G1
250-374-8522
Fax: 250-374-3610
Firm Type: Waste Management
Founded: 1982
Staff: 4
Products/Services/Areas of Expertise: Metals recycling; BIM service
Financial Information:
Type of Ownership: Private
Revenue Sources: 100% Private Contracts
Domestic Markets:
British Columbia
Contact(s):
Gary Brigden, Manager

Northwest Occupational Health & Safety
A division of Training by Design Inc.
1174 Chamberlain Dr.
North Vancouver, BC V7K 1P3
604-980-5812
Fax: 604-980-8512
nwohs@mdi.ca
www.nwohs.com
Products/Services/Areas of Expertise: Air monitoring; hazard assessments; indoor environmental quality; mould inspections; noise exposure assessment
Recently Completed / Ongoing Projects: Workplace Hazardous Materials Information System
Contact(s):
Neil McManus, Director

Norvac Industrial Services
56 Magill St.
Walden, ON P3Y 1K7
705-692-1333
Fax: 705-692-1334
info@norvac.ca
www.norvac.ca
Products/Services/Areas of Expertise: High pressure cleaning & vacuuming in northern environment
Contact(s):
Leo Kosowan, President

Norwesco Canada Ltd.
Nortco Plastics Division
Formerly: Nortco Plastics Inc. 7520 Yellowhead Trail NW
Edmonton, AB T5B 1G3
780-474-7440
Fax: 780-474-3454
888-474-7441
info@norwescocanada.com
www.norwescocanada.com
Firm Type: Manufacturing
Member of: Association of Rotational Moulders
Products/Services/Areas of Expertise: Storage tanks & systems
Domestic Markets:
National,

Notra Inc.
#200, 2725 Queensview Dr.
Ottawa, ON K2B 0Z1
613-738-0887
Fax: 613-738-4406
www.notra.ca
Firm Type: Scientific/Technical Services
Founded: 1995
Staff: 50
Member of: Association of Professional Engineers of Ontario; Project Management Institute
Quality Environmental Management System(s): 9001
Products/Services/Areas of Expertise: Environmental risk management; unexplored ordnance disposal; radiation safety; geophysics & environmental assessments; marine engineering; combat systems engineering; life cycle material management; engineering studies; shop repair & survey; specification development; technical data & publications management & management system development; implementation & audit; consultant support; project rescue; reviews; assessments; audits; risk management & training
Recently Completed / Ongoing Projects: Partner with Augusta Westland International Ltd for Maritime Helicopter Project; Unexploded ordnance disposal, CFB Petawawa
Financial Information:
Type of Ownership: Private
Revenue: Greater than $5 Million
Revenue Sources: 70% nationwide; 30% Private Contracts
Domestic Markets:
National
Foreign Activity:
USA
Markets Sought:
Central America, South America
Contact(s):
Steven Burns, CEO
sburns@notra.ca
Wolfgang Kaske, Director
wkaske@@notra.ca
Garry Loeper, Sr. Project Manager
gwloeper@notra.ca

Canadian Branches:
Calgary
167 Arbour Ridge Cir. NW
Calgary, AB T3G 3V9

Halifax
#511, 1657 Barrington St.
Halifax, NS B3J 2A1

Victoria
#1, 434 Fraser St.
Victoria, BC V9A 6G9

Notre Development Corp.
160 Pinewood Dr., RR5
North Bay, ON P1B 8Z4
705-495-6411
Fax: 705-495-1750
Firm Type: Management Consulting
Founded: 1989
Staff: 4
Member of: Ontario Waste Management Association, National Solid Wastes Management Association
Products/Services/Areas of Expertise: Consultant for landfill development of abandoned open pit mines; community/public relations; public speaking on waste management/recycling topics
Contact(s):
Gordon E. McGuinty, President
Elizabeth Fournier, Vice-President

Nouvelle Technologie (TEKNO) Inc.
Also Known As: TEKNO Inc.
#200, 20275 Clark Graham
Baie-d'Urfé, QC H9X 3T5
514-457-9991
Fax: 514-457-9922
aide@tekno.ca
www.tekno.ca
Firm Type: Waste Management
Founded: 1985
Staff: 40
Products/Services/Areas of Expertise: Water & wastewater audit, training, operation, management assessment, technical support, bench-scale treatment
Recently Completed / Ongoing Projects: Start up of a wastewater treatment plant & training workforce, Mauricius Island; Operation of reverse osmosis plant in a Fiberford plant, McMillan Bloedel, Pembrooke, ON
Financial Information:
Type of Ownership: Private
Domestic Markets:
Alberta, Newfoundland & Labrador, Ontario, Québec
Foreign Activity:
Africa, Asia, Caribbean, Central America, The Pacific Rim, Mexico, USA
Contact(s):
Jean-Jacques Duval, Président
Réjean Piché, Vice-Président

Nova Chemicals Corporation
P.O. Box 2518 M
1000 Seventh Ave. SW
Calgary, AB T2P 5C6
403-750-3600
Fax: 403-269-7410
public@novachem.com
www.novachem.com
Products/Services/Areas of Expertise: Olefins/polyolefins & styrene/ styrenic polymers
Contact(s):
Christopher D. Pappas, Sr. Vice-President/COO

Canadian Branches:
Mississauga Sales Office
#200, 6711 Mississauga Rd.
Mississauga, ON L5N 2W3
905-542-3338
Fax: 905-542-8075

Sarnia Sales Office
P.O. Box 3054
201 North Front St.
Sarnia, ON N7T 7V1
519-332-1212
Fax: 519-332-0408

Nova Envirocom
140, rue Léger
Sherbrooke, QC J1L 1L9
819-820-0291
Fax: 819-820-2853
866-898-6682
info@novaenvirocom.ca
www.novaenvirocom.ca
Firm Type: Scientific/Technical Services
Founded: 1996
Products/Services/Areas of Expertise: Implantation & management of environmental programs for municipalities

Nova Magnetics Burgmann Ltd. / NMBL
A wholly-owned subsidiary of Burgmann Dichtungswerke GmbH & Co. KG
1 Research Dr.
Dartmouth, NS B2Y 4M9
902-465-6625
Fax: 902-465-6629
800-565-7051
info@novamagnetics.ca
Firm Type: Manufacturing
Founded: 1981
Staff: 15
Products/Services/Areas of Expertise: Zero leakage magnetic couplings; diving life support equipment; specialty blowers; regenerative blowers; hyperbaric blowers; environmental conditioning systems
Activities: Waste management; wastewater treatment, air pollution abatement & solid waste processing; biotechnology; biological fertilizers & biodegradation of pollutants
Financial Information:
Type of Ownership: Foreign-owned
Domestic Markets:
National
Foreign Activity:
Asia, Western Europe, The Pacific Rim, USA
Contact(s):
Tim Sanford, P.Eng., President

International Branch(es):
Feodor Burman GmbH – Western Europe Distributor
Aubere Sauerlacher Str. 6-10
Wolfratshausen Germany
-8171-231-286
Fax: -8171-231-053
scherer@burgmann.com
Hans Scherer

Nova PB Inc.
1200, rue Garnier
Sainte-Catherine, QC J5C 1B4
450-632-9910
Fax: 450-632-9090
mciver@novapb.com; service@novapb.qc.ca
www.novapb.com
Firm Type: Waste Management
Founded: 1984
Products/Services/Areas of Expertise: Plastics, battery & lead recycling; lead-bearing hazardous waste recycling; waste oil consumer; spent oil filter recycling
Recently Completed / Ongoing Projects: Spent oil filter recycling facility
Domestic Markets:
National
Foreign Activity:
Central America, Western Europe, USA
Contact(s):
Robert Lavigne, President/CEO
Brian McIver, Vice-President, Marketing & Sales
Claude Fortin, Vice-President, Operations
Marc Desautels, Marketing & Environment

Nova Scotia Power, an Emera Company
P.O. Box 910
Halifax, NS B3J 2W5
902-428-6230
Fax: 902-428-6108
800-428-6230
www.nspower.ca
Firm Type: Distributing, Manufacturing, Scientific/Technical Services
Founded: 1907
Quality Environmental Management System(s): 14001
Products/Services/Areas of Expertise: Production & distribution of electricity
Financial Information:
Type of Ownership: Publicly Traded
Domestic Markets:
Nova Scotia
Contact(s):
Ralph Tedesco, President/CEO
Dan Muldoon, General Manager, Customer Operations
Rick Janega, General Manager, Power Production

Novapet Inc.
23 Tupper Blvd.
Amherst, NS B4H 4J4
902-667-1398
Fax: 902-667-1492
Firm Type: Manufacturing
Founded: 1998
Staff: 19
Products/Services/Areas of Expertise: Recycling plastics; polyethyleneterephthalate (PET) flakes; HDPE flakes
Financial Information:
Type of Ownership: Private
Revenue Sources: 100% Private Contracts
Domestic Markets:
New Brunswick, Newfoundland & Labrador, Nova Scotia, Ontario, Prince Edward Island, Québec
Foreign Activity:
USA
Contact(s):
Amy Davis, Administration Coordinator

Novatech Controls, Inc.
Les Contrôles Novatech
5600, rue Cypihot
Montréal, QC H4S 1V7
514-339-5374
Fax: 514-339-1550
800-465-5374
info@novatech.ca
www.novatech.ca
Firm Type: Distributing, Manufacturing
Founded: 1986
Staff: 25
Member of: Instrument Society of America
Products/Services/Areas of Expertise: Gas analysis & detection, liquid analysis, physical parameters analysis for process, environment & ambiant air
Recently Completed / Ongoing Projects: Continuous emission monitoring systems & analytical process systems
Financial Information:
Type of Ownership: Private
Domestic Markets:
Manitoba, New Brunswick, Newfoundland & Labrador, Nova Scotia, Ontario, Prince Edward Island, Québec
Foreign Activity:
Asia, Western Europe, USA
Contact(s):
Ed Gardiner, CEO

Canadian Branches:
Sarnia
P.O. Box 253
Sarnia, ON N7T 7H9
519-384-5637
George Noll

Toronto
#25, 4120 Ridgeway Dr.
Mississauga, ON L5N 5S9
905-569-9814
Fax: 905-569-7095
Matt Welland

Nove Environnement Inc.
Formerly: Pluritec Environnement
1650, rue Champlain
Trois-Rivières, QC G9A 4S9
819-371-3481
Fax: 819-371-2616
nove@nove.qc.ca
www.nove.qc.ca
Firm Type: Engineering, Scientific/Technical Services
Founded: 1986
Staff: 30
Member of: International Association of Impact Assessment; Assocation québéoise de vérification environnementale; Association québécoise d'etude d'impact; Réseau environnement
Quality Environmental Management System(s): 9001:2000
Products/Services/Areas of Expertise: Hazardous waste management consulting; air & water quality assessment; planning; forestry; resource management; water resource management; environmental audits, impact assessments, mapping, risk assessment, field sampling & monitoring, toxicology, technology transfer
Recently Completed / Ongoing Projects: Expansion of a solid waste disposal site, Lachenail; public health risk assessment, Magnola Metallurgies Asbestos; gas-steam turbine power plant, Hydro-Québec; hydroelectricity project, Hydro-Québec; northern expansion of sanitary landfill in Lachenaie, BFI; health risk analysis, CP Rail; environmental audit of property, Canadian Coast Guard; air quality modeling
Financial Information:
Type of Ownership: Private
Domestic Markets:
Québec
Contact(s):
Daniel Boisvert, President & Forest Engineer
Yvon Courchesne, Vice-President & Biologist
Martin Anctil, Chemical Engineer

Novitherm Canada Inc.
158 Suffolk Ave.
Oakville, ON L6K 2L6
905-815-0977
Fax: 905-338-5390
800-871-0079
info@novitherm.com
www.novitherm.com
Firm Type: Distributing
Founded: 1994
Member of: Greater Toronto Apartment Association; Fair Rental Policy Organization
Products/Services/Areas of Expertise: Distributor of scientifically designed heat reflector panels; provides an alternative to upgrade the efficiency of both free-standing & convector types of radiator heating in older buildings without major capital cost; Incentive programs with Enbridge Consumers Gas in Ontario, with du Fonds en Efficaite Energetique
Recently Completed / Ongoing Projects: 50+ multi-residential buildings with national property management companies at CFB Borden; University of Ottawa buildings; Quoting schools & hospitals in Québec
Financial Information:
Type of Ownership: Private
Domestic Markets:
National
Foreign Activity:
USA
Contact(s):
Frank Snyder, President & Gen. Mgr.
frank@novitherm.com
Bruce Fulcher, VP, Special Projects, 416-251-1772
bruce@novitherm.com

Canadian Branches:
Collingwood
#206, 74 Hurontario St.
Collingwood, ON L9Y 2L8

NRI Industries
Also Known As: National Rubber Company Inc.
394 Symington Ave.
Toronto, ON M6N 2W3
416-675-1111
Fax: 416-656-1231
info@nriindustries.com
www.nriindustries.com
Firm Type: Waste Management
Staff: 456
Products/Services/Areas of Expertise: North America's largest fully integrated manufacturer of rubber products
Domestic Markets:
Ontario
Foreign Activity:
USA,

NSF-ISR / D&T QRI
Formerly: Deloitte & Touche
#2300, 360 Main St.
Winnipeg, MB R3C 3Z3
204-944-3625
Fax: 204-942-6958
patridge@nsf-isr.org
www.nsf-isr.org
Firm Type: Management Consulting
Staff: 15
Products/Services/Areas of Expertise: Is an internationally credited leader in quality, environmental, health & safety management registration, in an extensive range of industries; have completed registrations to ISO 9001:2000, ISO/TS16949, ISO 14001, ISO 13485, RC14001, RCMS, TL9000, AS9100, AS9120, ISO 22000, HACCP
Domestic Markets:
National
Foreign Activity:
Worldwide
Contact(s):
Irene Seetner, Quality Registrar Inc.
iseetner@deloitte.ca

Canadian Branches:
Kitchener
4210 King St. East
Kitchener, ON N2P 2G5
Fax: 905-426-5499
1-877-435-9001
seetner@nsf-isr.org

Montréal
#300, 1 Place Ville Marie
Montréal, QC H3B 4T9
800-390-4108
kwas@nsf-isr.org

Nu-Air Ventilation Systems Inc.
P.O. Box 2758
16 Nelson St.
Windsor, NS B0N 2T0
902-798-2261
Fax: 902-798-2557
nuair@nu-airventilation.com
www.nu-airventilation.com
Firm Type: Manufacturing
Founded: 1992
Staff: 40
Member of: Home Ventilating Institute; Heating, Refrigeration & Air Conditioning Institute of Canada; Nova Scotia Home Builders Association
Products/Services/Areas of Expertise: Manufactures residential & light commercial ventilation equipment including air to air heat recovery ventilators & air exchange & purification units
Recently Completed / Ongoing Projects: EnerBoss Air Handler; Dalhousie University Eco-Efficiency Award winner
Financial Information:
Type of Ownership: Private
Revenue Sources: 100% Private Contracts
Domestic Markets:
National
Foreign Activity:
Asia, The Pacific Rim, USA
Markets Sought:
Western Europe
Contact(s):
Earl Caldwell, President

Nu-Plast Polymers International
A division of Nexcycle Plastics Inc.
235 Wilkinson Rd.
Brampton, ON L6T 4M2
905-454-2666
Fax: 905-454-2668
800-463-6169
Firm Type: Waste Management
Founded: 1984
Products/Services/Areas of Expertise: Recycling of plastics, primarily PE, PP; custom tolling of industrial scrap; formulation of recycling resins suitable for various manufacturing needs
Domestic Markets:
National
Foreign Activity:
Africa, Asia, Central America, Western Europe, The Middle East, The Pacific Rim, South America, USA
Contact(s):
Joseph Rusinek, Vice-President

Nu-West Services Ltd.
P.O. Box 9461
Saskatoon, SK S7K 7E9
306-244-4092
Fax: 306-242-7746
Firm Type: Scientific/Technical Services
Founded: 1991
Products/Services/Areas of Expertise: Research & development in liquid-liquid separation; Oil Recycling
Contact(s):
Dale Acton, Managing Director

Numet Engineering Ltd. / NEL
P.O. Box 1776
678 Neal Dr.
Peterborough, ON K9J 7X6
705-743-2708
Fax: 705-743-3216
numet@numet.com
www.numet.com
Products/Services/Areas of Expertise: Materials handling & process systems for nuclear waste management
Contact(s):
H. Lowe, P. Eng., President
Robert Beckett, Vice-President

Nusco Supply & Manufacturing Inc.
Formerly: Nusco Manufacturing & Supply Ltd.
#1130, 140 - 4 Ave. SW
Calgary, AB T2P 3N3
403-266-3449
Fax: 403-265-8544
sales@nusco.com
www.nusco.com

Products & Services Buyer's Guide

Firm Type: Distributing, Engineering, Manufacturing
Founded: 1983
Staff: 175
Member of: Association of Professional Engineers, Geologists & Geophysicists of Alberta
Products/Services/Areas of Expertise: Tank & vessel storage equipment; pipe, valve & fittings sales; field erected tanks; wellsite & plant production equipment for oil/gas, petrochemical, mining & forest industries; Steam condensers
Financial Information:
Type of Ownership: Private
Revenue: Greater than $5 Million
Revenue Sources: 100% Private Contracts
Domestic Markets:
Alberta, British Columbia, Saskatchewan, Yukon Territory
Foreign Activity:
USA,
Contact(s):
Fred Moore, President
Norm Denoon, Vice-President, Operations
Mike Rutherford, Vice-President, Tubular
Contact(s):
Rob Hoffman, Superintendant

Canadian Branches:
Manufacturing
1604 - 8th St.
Nisku, AB T9E 7S6
780-955-2051
Fax: 780-955-9402

O'Connor Associates Environmental Inc.
#100, 318 - 11th Ave. SE
Calgary, AB T2G 0Y2
403-294-4200
Fax: 403-294-4240
800-661-8141
info@oconnor-associates.com
www.oconnor-associates.com
Products/Services/Areas of Expertise: Environmental auditing; site remediation; spill response & cleanup; waste management; air quality management; laboratory measuring & monitoring equipment
Domestic Markets:
Alberta, British Columbia, Manitoba, Ontario
Contact(s):
Michael O'Connor, Founder & President

Canadian Branches:
Edmonton
9405 - 63 Ave.
Edmonton, AB T6E 0G2
780-669-4380
Fax: 780-435-9916
866-669-4380

Ottawa
#104, 5420 Canotek Rd.
Ottawa, ON K1J 1E9
613-742-1781
Fax: 613-742-6064

Toronto
#100, 3715 Laird Rd.
Mississauga, ON L5L 0A3
905-820-1210
Fax: 905-820-1221

Vancouver
19890 - 92A Ave.
Langley, BC V1M 3A9
604-513-1000
Fax: 604-513-1040
866-513-7808

Winnipeg
7 Terracon Place
Winnipeg, MB R2J 4B3
204-489-2964
Fax: 204-489-3014
877-489-2964

O'Connor Tanks Ltd.
15 Bermondsey Rd.
Toronto, ON M4B 1Z4
416-751-1140
Fax: 416-751-7181
sales@oconnor-tanks.com
www.oconnor-tanks.com
Firm Type: Manufacturing
Founded: 1949
Products/Services/Areas of Expertise: Sewage treatment equipment; waste storage containers; pressure vessels; tanks; towers; columns
Financial Information:
Type of Ownership: Private
Revenue Sources: 100% Private Contracts
Domestic Markets:
National
Foreign Activity:
Worldwide

O'Halloran Campbell Consultants Limited
#252, 7071 Bayers Rd.
Halifax, NS B3L 2C2
902-429-9826
Fax: 902-429-5457
admin@ohcc.ns.ca
www.ohcc.ns.ca
Firm Type: Engineering
Founded: 1980
Staff: 20
Member of: Association of Professional Engineers of Nova Scotia; Civil Engineers of Nova Scotia
Products/Services/Areas of Expertise: Environmental permitting; regulations & standards; design & specifications; project management; site assessment & reclamation
Financial Information:
Type of Ownership: Private
Domestic Markets:
New Brunswick, Newfoundland & Labrador, Nova Scotia, Prince Edward Island
Contact(s):
Michael W. Martell, 902-429-9826
mmartell@ohcc.ns.ca
Dan O'Halloran, President
Marcel Deveau, Vice-President

O-I Canada Corp.
A subsidiary of Owens Illinois Group Inc.
Formerly: Consumers Glass 777 Kipling Ave.
Toronto, ON M8Z 5Z4
416-232-3000
Fax: 416-232-3059
www.o-i.com
Firm Type: Manufacturing, Waste Management
Founded: 1917
Staff: 1000
Quality Environmental Management System(s): 9001
Products/Services/Areas of Expertise: Glass container recycling & packaging design; end market for recycled glass containers; glass container manufacturer
Financial Information:
Type of Ownership: Publicly Traded; Foreign-owned
Revenue Sources: 100% Private Contracts
Domestic Markets:
National
Foreign Activity:
Worldwide
Contact(s):
Miguel Escobar, President, O-I North America

Canadian Branches:
Brampton
100 West Dr.
Brampton, ON L6T 2J5
905-457-2423

Hawkesbury
1233 Cameron St.
Hawkesbury, ON K6A 2B8
514-939-8500

Milton
100 Chisholm Dr.
Milton, ON L9T 3G9
905-878-1238

Scoudouc
225 Parker Rd.
Scoudouc, NB E4P 3P7
506-532-7200

Stoney Creek
444 Seaman St.
Stoney Creek, ON L8E 2V9
905-664-6161

Oak Environmental Inc.
#103, 4712 - 13 St. NE
Calgary, AB T2E 6P1
403-250-9810
Fax: 403-250-3978
info@oakenviro.com
www.oakenviro.com
Firm Type: Distributing, Manufacturing
Founded: 1985
Staff: 7
Member of: Canadian Water Well Association; Environmental Services Association of Alberta; Better Business Bureau
Products/Services/Areas of Expertise: Vacuum/blower units for on-site vapour extraction, soil remediation, landfill degassing, aeration, radon removal, bioremediation; products & equipment for the ground & groundwater contamination detection & remediation
Financial Information:
Type of Ownership: Private
Domestic Markets:
National
Foreign Activity:
USA
Markets Sought:
The Pacific Rim
Contact(s):
Terry McNeill, President
terry@oakenviro.com
Wesley Hutchen, Operations Manager
wesley@oakenviro.com

Oakhill Environmental
530A Eastchester Ave.
St Catharines, ON L2M 7P3
905-988-1243
Fax: 905-988-1887
888-868-0102
info@oakhillenvironmental.com
www.oakhillenvironmental.com
Firm Type: Engineering, Scientific/Technical Services
Founded: 1994
Staff: 5
Member of: Professional Engineers Ontario; Association of Professional Geoscientists of Ontario; Canadian Environmental Auditing Association; Air & Waste Management Association
Products/Services/Areas of Expertise: Phase I, II, III environmental site assessments; environmental audits; certificates of approval; noise studies; environmental drilling services
Recently Completed / Ongoing Projects: Environmental audits of over 80 federal facilities including Parliament Buildings in Ottawa
Financial Information:
Type of Ownership: Private
Revenue Sources: 40% nationwide; 5% Provincial; 5% Municipals; 50% Private Contracts
Domestic Markets:
Ontario
Markets Sought:
Central Europe, USA

Oakridge Environmental Ltd.
P.O. Box 431
Peterborough, ON K9J 6Z3
705-745-1181
Fax: 705-745-4163
oakridgeenvironmental@bellmet.ca
www3.sympatico.ca/ore/
Firm Type: Engineering, Scientific/Technical Services
Founded: 1992
Staff: 2
Member of: Geological Association of Canada; International Association of Hydrogeologists; Association of Geoscientists of Ontario
Products/Services/Areas of Expertise: Environmental consulting services; geological/hydrogeological engineering; impact assessments; water & wastewater assessment; audits
Financial Information:
Type of Ownership: Private
Domestic Markets:
Ontario
Contact(s):
Brian King, President & Environmental Geologist
Rob West, Senior Environmental Scientist

Oakside Chemicals Ltd.
3300 White Oak Rd.
London, ON N6E 1L8
519-681-1103
Fax: 519-681-4263
Firm Type: Waste Management
Founded: 1975
Staff: 4
Member of: Kelcoatings Ltd.
Quality Environmental Management System(s): 9001
Products/Services/Areas of Expertise: Recycling of spent solvents
Financial Information:
Type of Ownership: Private
Revenue Sources: 100% Private Contracts
Domestic Markets:
Ontario, Québec,
Contact(s):
Ted Kelly, President/CEO
tkelly@oaksidechemicals.com

Oasis Bags
167, rue Joseph-Carrier
Vaudreuil-Dorion, QC J7V 5V5
450-424-1564
Fax: 450-424-4361
877-286-2747
oasisbags@oasisbags.com
www.oasisbags.com
Firm Type: Distributing
Founded: 1989
EcoLogo Certified Products & Services: Reusable cotton utility bags
Products/Services/Areas of Expertise: Specializes in producing environmentally responsible bags using stringent environmental criteria for its reusable cloth shopping bags while offering an inexpensive, promotional choice to specifications
Ecological Note: Reusable cotton utility bags
Financial Information:
Type of Ownership: Private
Revenue Sources: 100% Private Contracts
Domestic Markets:
National
Foreign Activity:
USA
Contact(s):
Laurie Maloni, President
Seema Maloni, Vice-President, Operations

Ocean Steel & Construction Ltd.
400 Chesley Dr.
Saint John, NB E2K 5L6
506-632-2600
Fax: 506-632-7689
sales@oceansteel.com
www.oceansteel.com
Firm Type: Manufacturing
Founded: 1955
Staff: 225
Products/Services/Areas of Expertise: Steel fabrication of tanks & pressure vessels; custom fabrication; marine & materials handling; structures; bridges; building frames; cyclones, casings, hoppers, ductwork, clarifiers, stacks
Domestic Markets:
New Brunswick, Newfoundland & Labrador, Nova Scotia, Prince Edward Island
Foreign Activity:
Africa, USA
Contact(s):
Hans W. Klohn, President
Harrison Wilson, Manager
Bernie Blakely, P.Eng, Business Development

Oceans Ltd.
85 Lemarchant Rd.
St. John's, NL A1C 2H1
709-753-5788
Fax: 709-753-3301
oceans@oceans.nf.net
www.oceans.nf.net
Firm Type: Scientific/Technical Services
Founded: 1981
Staff: 22
Products/Services/Areas of Expertise: Expertise in: meteorology/climate studies, oceanographic field studies, wind & wave extreme analysis, environmental effects biomonitoring, hyperbaric pressure testing & marine search & rescue R&D & iceberg profiling
Recently Completed / Ongoing Projects: Weather forecasting/oceanographic projects off east coast of Canada for major clients - Exxon Mobil (Hibernia & Sable Offshore Energy projects), Petro-Canada, Marathon Canada Ltd.
Financial Information:
Type of Ownership: Private
Revenue: $500,000 - $1.5 Million
Revenue Sources: 20% nationwide; 80% Private Contracts
Domestic Markets:
Newfoundland & Labrador, Nova Scotia
Markets Sought:
Western Europe, USA
Contact(s):
Judith Bobbitt, President
jbobbitt@oceans.nf.net
Nicole Scaplen, Marketing Coordinator
nscaplen@oceans.nf.net

Canadian Branches:
Halifax Office
Purdy's Wharf, Tower 2
#202, 1969 Upper Water St.
Halifax, NS B3J 3R7
902-492-9221
Fax: 902-492-4545
smelsre@oceans.nf.net
Simon Melrose

OCL Services Ltd.
47 North St.
Dartmouth, NS B2Y 1B7
902-463-0114
Fax: 902-466-5743
info@oclgroup.com
www.oclgroup.com
Firm Type: Scientific/Technical Services
Staff: 8
Member of: Air & Waste Management Association; Indoor Air Quality Association
Products/Services/Areas of Expertise: Indoor air & ambient air quality; assessment & remediation of chemicals in environment; environmental auditing; environmental management
Domestic Markets:
New Brunswick, Newfoundland & Labrador, Nova Scotia, Ontario, Prince Edward Island
Contact(s):
Scott MacKnight, President

Octagon Environmental Services
23 Chapple St.
Hamilton, ON L8L 8K7
905-312-0800

ODIM Brooke Ocean / BOT
Formerly: Brooke Ocean Technology Ltd.
#11, 50 Thornhill Dr.
Dartmouth, NS B3B 1S1
902-468-2928
Fax: 902-468-1388
salesg@brooke-ocean.com
www.brooke-ocean.com
Firm Type: Manufacturing
Staff: 23
Products/Services/Areas of Expertise: Water column profiling from moving vessel or mooring; laser optical plankton counter; moving vessel profiler; seattorie ocean profiler; seafloor penetrometer
Financial Information:
Type of Ownership: Private
Revenue Sources: 10% nationwide; 90% Private Contracts
Domestic Markets:
National
Foreign Activity:
Worldwide
Contact(s):
Arnold Furlong, Partner

Oetiker Limited
203 Dufferin St. South
Alliston, ON L9R 1W7
705-435-4394
Fax: 705-435-3155
info@ca.oetiker.com
www.oetiker.com
Firm Type: Manufacturing
Founded: 1943
Quality Environmental Management System(s): 9001
Products/Services/Areas of Expertise: Clamp, safety couplings, accessories, pneumatic systems
Financial Information:
Type of Ownership: Private
Domestic Markets:
National
Foreign Activity:
Central America, China, Central Europe, Eastern Europe, Western Europe, The Pacific Rim, South America, Mexico, USA, Vietnam
Contact(s):
Sam Wyss, General Manager

Offshore Design Associates Ltd. / ODA
16438 Carr's Landing Rd.
Lake Country, BC V4V 1C3
250-766-1023
Firm Type: Engineering, Scientific/Technical Services
Founded: 1980
Staff: 2
Member of: Association of Professional Engineers & Geoscientists of the Province of BC
Products/Services/Areas of Expertise: Wave & ice structure interaction; specification & project management of model test programs; consulting services to offshore industries & government; coastal & ocean engineering research & development; expert testimony for environmental impact statement programs; arctic engineering
Domestic Markets:
British Columbia, Newfoundland & Labrador, Ontario
Foreign Activity:
Western Europe
Contact(s):
Derek Muggeridge, P.Eng., President
dmuggeridge@cablelan.net
H.M. Muggeridge, Secretary

Ogilvie Scientific Inc. / OSI
10 Picadilly Pl.
Brampton, ON L6S 5E2
905-799-2960
Fax: 905-791-1142
Firm Type: Scientific/Technical Services
Founded: 1991
Member of: American Industrial Hygiene Association; American Conference of Governmental Industrial Hygienists; Canadian Registration Board of Occupation Hygienists; Occupational Hygiene Association of Ontario
Products/Services/Areas of Expertise: Occupational health & safety consulting services; legislative compliance, workplace audits, policy & program development, air quality measurements
Financial Information:
Type of Ownership: Private
Domestic Markets:
National
Markets Sought:
USA
Contact(s):
Jim Ogilvie, President
Gerry Saunders, Vice-President, Marketing

Oil Spill Control Services Canada
123 Briggs Ave.
Richmond Hill, ON L4B 1X6
905-764-5663
Fax: 905-764-9219
oilspill@sympatico.ca
Firm Type: Scientific/Technical Services, Waste Management
Founded: 1993
Products/Services/Areas of Expertise: Responds to spills & fires worldwide; emergency preparedness assessment; oil, haz-mat, fire training
Financial Information:
Type of Ownership: Private
Revenue: Greater than $5 Million
Revenue Sources: 100% Private Contracts
Domestic Markets:
National
Foreign Activity:
Worldwide
Contact(s):
Dec Doran, Owner/Operator

Oldham Engineers Inc.
125 Joseph Zatzman Dr.
Dartmouth, NS B3B 1W1
902-468-6998
Fax: 902-468-6577
oei@fox.nstn.ca
www.oei.ns.ca
Firm Type: Management Consulting, Engineering
Founded: 1984
Products/Services/Areas of Expertise: Electronics engineering services
Contact(s):
Eamonn Oldham, President

Canadian Branches:
Oakville
#125, 99 Bronte Rd.
Oakville, ON L6L 3B7
416-365-1877

OMB (Americas) Forged Steel Valves
OMB (Americas) valves en acier forgé
Also Known As: OMB Valves
58, rue Apple Hill
Baie-d'Urfé, QC H9X 3H4
514-457-0813
Fax: 514-457-0814
www.ombvalves.com
Firm Type: Distributing, Manufacturing
Founded: 1991
Products/Services/Areas of Expertise: Forged steel valves; developed a compact bellows seal valve specifically designed to protect the environment from harmful leakage from valve stuffing boxes
Recently Completed / Ongoing Projects: Sable Offshore Energy Project; Nova Chemicals Ethylene Plant Expansion
Financial Information:
Type of Ownership: Foreign-owned
Domestic Markets:
National
Contact(s):
Jack Toyota, General Manager
j.toyota@ombvalves.com

Omega Public Works
Also Known As: Omega Industrial Products
A division of 598056 Ont. Inc.
P.O. Box 70
6722 Camlachie Rd.
Camlachie, ON N0N 1E0
519-899-2530
Fax: 519-899-2531
www.omegapublicworks.ca
Firm Type: Distributing
Founded: 1994
Staff: 6
Products/Services/Areas of Expertise: Pumping equipment
Financial Information:
Type of Ownership: Private
Domestic Markets:
Manitoba, New Brunswick, Newfoundland & Labrador, Nova Scotia, Ontario, Prince Edward Island
Contact(s):
Jeff Mayo
jeff@omegapublicworks.ca

Omega Recycling Technologies
Also Known As: Omega
761, boul Lebeau
Montréal, QC H4N 1S5
514-737-4100
Fax: 514-731-1684
800-361-1194
info@omega-systems.ca
www.omega-systems.ca
Firm Type: Manufacturing
Founded: 1980
Staff: 35
Products/Services/Areas of Expertise: Solvent recycling systems; absorption systems; oil purification systems; oil dehydration systems (oil/water separator); water treatment systems; universal filtration systems
Financial Information:
Type of Ownership: Private
Domestic Markets:
Alberta, British Columbia, Ontario, Québec, Saskatchewan

Foreign Activity:
Asia, Central America, Western Europe, The Middle East, South America, Mexico, USA
Contact(s):
Moshe Suissa, President
Sam Suissa, Vice-President

Ontario Building Solutions
#200, 28 Pollard Cres.
Ajax, ON L1T 3N8
416-268-1092
Fax: 905-427-5572
info@buildingoperation.com
www.buildingoperation.com
Firm Type: Management Consulting, Scientific/Technical Services
Founded: 2004
Staff: 3
Member of: Building Owners & Management Association
Products/Services/Areas of Expertise: Indoor air quality testing & diagnostics; preventative maintenance program, design & implementation; 3rd party consulting on indoor air quality issues
Recently Completed / Ongoing Projects: Air flow balancing Bentall Real Estate; City of Kawartha Lakes, testing of air quality & HVAC system, diagnosis of municipal buildings
Financial Information:
Type of Ownership: Private
Domestic Markets:
Ontario
Contact(s):
Randy Godding, President
randy@buildingoperation.com

Ontario Centres of Excellence
Formerly: ETech
Centre of Excellence for Energy
#200, 156 Front St. W
Toronto, ON M5J 2L6
416-861-1092
Fax: 416-971-7164
866-759-6014
www.oce-ontario.org
Products/Services/Areas of Expertise: ETech engages firms, clients & academic partners in the following market-driven strategic clusters: clean water technologies, resource management, sustainable agriculture & agri-food, sustainable energy solutions, sustainable infrastructure; organizations & academics in these clusters are encouraged to contact ETech to find out how to access the broad range of services available
Domestic Markets:
Ontario
Contact(s):
Dan McGillivray, Managing Director, Centre of Excellence for Energy, 416-861-1092
dan.mcgillivray@oce-ontario.org

Ontario Environmental Training Consortium / OETC
#206, 37 George St. N
Brampton, ON L6X 1R5
905-796-2851
Fax: 905-796-8744
877-796-2851
info@oetc.on.ca
www.oetc.on.ca
Products/Services/Areas of Expertise: Training program for operators of water systems; establishes recognized professional standards for operators; gives greater assurance of good & safe drinking water to the residents of Ontario; provides greater protection of the aquatic environment; assures efficient and safe use of operating facility; provides for optimum utilization of public money spent on water & wastewater utilities; & increases professionalism of an important environmental occupation; Ontario's licensing program is a mandatory program
Domestic Markets:
Ontario
Contact(s):
Doris Find, Receptionist
doris.find@oetc.on.ca

Ontario Power Generation
A company wholly owned by the Province of Ontario
700 University Ave.
Toronto, ON M5G 1X6
416-592-2555
Fax: 416-592-3177
877-592-2555

webmaster@opg.com
www.opg.com
Firm Type: Distributing, Manufacturing
Founded: 1999
Staff: 1200
Quality Environmental Management System(s): ISO 14001:2004
EcoLogo Certified Products & Services: Alternative Source Energy Evergreen (tm) Energy Green Power
Products/Services/Areas of Expertise: OPG's Evergreen (tm) Energy Green Power is environmentally-friendly power generated from renewable energy resources of low-impact hydro, biomass, wind & solar facilities; 31 EcoLogo-certified facilities (29 small hydroelectric, & 2 wind-powered stations) with a combined capacity of 160 megawatts
Ecological Note: Alternative Source Energy Evergreen (tm) Energy Green Power
Financial Information:
Type of Ownership: Publicly Traded
Contact(s):
Jake Epp, Chair
Tom Mitchell, President & CEO
Donn Hanbidge, Sr. Vice-President & CFO

Ontario Sawdust Supplies
48 Sluse Rd.
Holland Landing, ON L9N 1G8
905-836-9356
Fax: 905-836-4010
800-267-5246
www.ontariosawdust.com
Firm Type: Distributing, Manufacturing, Waste Management
Founded: 1954
Staff: 15
Member of: Ontario Independent Meat Processors
Products/Services/Areas of Expertise: Pick-up & recycling of wood chips, sawdust & shearings for recycling; distribution of wood flour
Financial Information:
Type of Ownership: Private
Domestic Markets:
National
Contact(s):
Rosanne Falcone, President
Joe Falcone, Vice-President, Marketing & Sales
joe@ontariosawdust.com

Ontario Waste Materials Exchange / OWME
Ontario Centre for Environmental Technology Advancement (OCETA)
Formerly: OWE - ORTECH c/o OCETA
#201A, 2070 Hadwen Rd.
Mississauga, ON L5K 2C9
905-822-4133
Fax: 905-822-3558
888-845-9038
owe@oceta.on.ca
Firm Type: Scientific/Technical Services
Founded: 1984
Products/Services/Areas of Expertise: Consulting services to Ontario industries in waste management; contacts for potential reuse or raw material substitute opportunities; recycling industry contacts
Financial Information:
Type of Ownership: Non Profit
Domestic Markets:
Ontario
Contact(s):
Stacy Jones, Program Coordinator

Ontor Ltd.
12 Leswyn Rd.
Toronto, ON M6A 1K3
416-781-5286
Fax: 416-781-7680
info@ontor.com
www.ontor.com
Firm Type: Distributing
Founded: 1947
Staff: 100
Member of: Instrument Society of America; Heating, Refrigerating & Air Conditioning Institute; Canadian Oil Heat Association
Quality Environmental Management System(s): 9001
Products/Services/Areas of Expertise: Automation products for the process control & factory automation markets; heating

components, ventilating, air conditioning, refrigeration & plumbing accessories
Contact(s):
Robert Elder, President
Gary Waddell, Vice-President, HVAC

Canadian Branches:
Burlington
#8, 4391 Harvester Rd.
Burlington, ON L7L 4X1
905-592-9858
Fax: 905-639-4600

Calgary & Edmonton
207 Aspen Hills Villas SW
Calgary, AB T3H 0H8
403-585-5339
Fax: 403-206-7502
Tom Groves, Sales Representative

Kitchener
#5, 20 Hanson Ave.
Burlington, ON N2C 2E2
519-579-4259
Fax: 519-576-5071

Mississauga
#13-14, 170 Ambassador Dr.
Mississauga, ON L5T 2H9
905-461-9535
Fax: 905-564-1715
Dennis Barsby, Sales Representative

Montréal
101, rue Louvain ouest
Montréal, QC H2N 1A3
514-733-3375
Fax: 514-733-3442
Benoit Guindon, Division Manager

Québec
#214, 1400, av St-Jean-Baptiste
Québec, QC G2E 5B7
418-527-0227
Fax: 418-527-8710

Onyx Chemical Cleaning
Formerly: Ontario Chemical Cleaning Inc.
80 Birmingham St.
Hamilton, ON L8L 6W5
905-547-5661
Fax: 905-547-0511
william.deboer@veoliase.com
www.onyxindustrial.com
Firm Type: Management Consulting
Founded: 1988
Staff: 10
Products/Services/Areas of Expertise: Industrial chemical cleaning; hazardous materials transport & disposal; site restorations; plant decommissioning; tank & vessel cleaning; pumping services
Financial Information:
Type of Ownership: Private
Revenue: $1.5 Million - $3 Million
Revenue Sources: 100% Private Contracts
Domestic Markets:
National
Foreign Activity:
USA
Contact(s):
William DeBoer, Manager

Opcon Pacific Recycling Ltd.
19341 Zero Ave.
Surrey, BC V3S 9R9
604-538-7535
Firm Type: Scientific/Technical Services
Founded: 1991
Staff: 5
Products/Services/Areas of Expertise: Recycle or reformulate lubricant oils on customers' premises; industrial lubricants which can be processed: metal-working fluids, hydraulic oils, gear oils, transformer oils, turbine oils, heat transfer oils & process oils
Domestic Markets:
Alberta, British Columbia
Foreign Activity:
USA
Contact(s):
Gary Livingstone, President/CEO

Greg Livingstone, General Manager

Optech Inc.
300 Interchange Way
Concord, ON L4K 5Z8
905-606-0808
Fax: 905-660-0829
inquiries@optech.ca
www.optech.ca
Products/Services/Areas of Expertise: Laboratory measuring & monitoring equipment
Contact(s):
Philip Arsenault, Vice-President
philipa@optech.on.ca
Sumona Dalta, Manager
sumona@optech.on.ca

Optikon Corp. Ltd.
1099 Guelph St.
Kitchener, ON N2B 2E4
519-745-4115
Fax: 519-745-6922
info@optikon.ca
www.optikon.ca
Firm Type: Scientific/Technical Services
Founded: 1974
Products/Services/Areas of Expertise: Measuring & monitoring equipment; laboratory equipment; vibration control equipment
Domestic Markets:
National
Foreign Activity:
Eastern Europe, Western Europe, USA
Contact(s):
Steve Daicos, President
Barry Brandon, Operations Manager

Optimira Controls
Formerly: Cinergy Solutions - Demand; VESTAR Ltd.; Rose Technology Group Ltd
3035 Orlando Dr.
Mississauga, ON L4V 1L6
866-797-6497
controls@optimira.com
www.optimira.com
Firm Type: Distributing, Manufacturing
Founded: 1997
Products/Services/Areas of Expertise: Supplier of integrated building automation systems solutions to improve a building's environment by maximizing safety & energy efficiency
Recently Completed / Ongoing Projects: Ice Pavillion, Niagara Falls, Ontario; Efficiency upgrades & GHG reduction, RCMP Training Academy, Regina, Saskatchewan
Financial Information:
Type of Ownership: Foreign-owned
Domestic Markets:
Ontario
Foreign Activity:
USA
Contact(s):
Stephen Clevett, Chief Executive Officer, Optimira Energy Group
Jeff Volkers, General Manager, Optimira Controls

Option Environnement Inc.
#1817, 360 rue Saint-Jacques ouest
Montréal, QC H2Y 1P5
514-257-6380
Fax: 514-257-6382
impacts@opt-env.qc.ca
www.optionenvironnement.com
Firm Type: Engineering, Scientific/Technical Services
Founded: 1997
Staff: 3
Products/Services/Areas of Expertise: Environmental impact assessments; wetland assessments & management, GIS; public participation, education & awareness; biological management & assessment
Financial Information:
Type of Ownership: Publicly Traded
Revenue Sources: 10% Provincial; 40% Municipals; 50% Private Contracts
Domestic Markets:
Québec
Foreign Activity:
Africa, Caribbean, USA
Markets Sought:
Asia, The Pacific Rim, South America,

Contact(s):
Paul Drouin, President
Christiane Roy, Vice-President
Lucie McNeil, Secretary

Opus DaytonKnight Consultants Ltd.
Formerly: Dayton & Knight Ltd.
#210, 889 Harbourside Dr.
North Vancouver, BC V7P 3S1
604-990-4800
Fax: 604-990-4805
dkeng@dayton-knight.com
www.dayton-knight.com
Firm Type: Management Consulting, Engineering, Scientific/Technical Services
Founded: 2010
Staff: 80
Products/Services/Areas of Expertise: Wastewater management, treatment & disposal; water quality supply, treatment & delivery; trenchless technologies; stormwater management; solid waste management; odour management & treatment
Financial Information:
Type of Ownership: Private
Revenue Sources: 5% nationwide; 5% Provincial; 90% Municipals
Domestic Markets:
Alberta, British Columbia
Foreign Activity:
Africa, Australia/New Zealand, The Pacific Rim, USA
Contact(s):
Sean Brophy, P. Eng., President/CEO
Jack Lee, P. Eng., Vice President, Operations
Harlan Kelly, P.E.; P. Eng., Vice President, Technologies

Canadian Branches:
Abbotsford
#305, 2722 Allwood St.
Abbotsford, BC V2T 3R7
604-852-9256
Fax: 604-852-9240
abbotsford@dayton-knight.com

Prince George
#101, 2700 Queensway St.
Prince George, BC V2L 1N2
250-562-0038
Fax: 250-562-0058

Smithers
P.O. Box 939
#1, 3772 - 4th Ave.
Smithers, BC V0J 2N0
250-847-1913
Fax: 250-847-1914
smithers@dayton-knight.com
Paul Wellington, P.Eng.

Opus International Consultants (Canada) Ltd.
Formerly: Geoplan Opus Consultants Inc.; Geoplan Consultants Inc
Also Known As: Opus
80 Bishop Dr.
Fredericton, NB E3C 1B2
506-451-0055
Fax: 506-450-4838
opus@opusinternational.ca
www.opusinternational.ca
Firm Type: Engineering
Founded: 1988
Staff: 20
Member of: Association of Professional Engineers & Geoscientists of New Brunswick; Association of New Brunswick Land Surveyors
Quality Environmental Management System(s): 9001
Products/Services/Areas of Expertise: Transportation planning, economic analysis; highway design, traffic engineering, geographic information systems; survey engineering; road asset management
Financial Information:
Revenue: $1.5 Million - $3 Million
Revenue Sources: 30% nationwide; 50% Provincial; 10% Municipals; 10% Private Contracts
Domestic Markets:
British Columbia, New Brunswick, Newfoundland & Labrador, Nova Scotia, Ontario, Prince Edward Island
Contact(s):

Products & Services Buyer's Guide

Chris Harrison, President, Western Canada
chris.harrison@opusinternational.ca
Shawn Landers, President, Eastern Canada
shawn.landers@opusinternational.ca
Canadian Branches:
Kelowna
#255-1715 Dickson Ave.
Kelowna, BC V1Y 9G6
250-868-4925
Fax: 250-868-4923
Peter Kortegast, Business Manager

Vancouver
#850, 1185 West Georgia St.
Vancouver, BC V6E 4E6
604-684-4488
Fax: 604-684-5908
Sarah Rocchi, VP, Vancouver

Victoria
#401, 707 Fort St.
Victoria, BC V8W 3G3
250-952-5640
Fax: 250-920-5620
Martin Gordon, VP, Victoria

International Branch(es):
USA - Detroit
#110, 6230 Orchard Lake Rd.
West Bloomfield, MI USA
248-539-2222
Fax: 248-539-3670
Jeffrey Bagdade, VP, Detroit

Orchid Cellmark ULC
Formerly: Orchid/Helix Biotech
635 Columbia St.
New Westminster, BC V3M 1A7
604-523-2945
Fax: 604-523-2974
800-563-4363
customersupport@orchidcellmark.ca
www.orchidcellmark.ca
Firm Type: Distributing
Founded: 2005
Staff: 8
Quality Environmental Management System(s): 17025
Products/Services/Areas of Expertise: Organochlorine compounds used by pulp & paper industry; environmental monitoring chemical
Financial Information:
Type of Ownership: Foreign-owned
Domestic Markets:
National
Foreign Activity:
Australia/New Zealand, Western Europe, USA
Contact(s):
Jennifer Clay, Director, Operations

Ordan Thermal Products Ltd.
#9, 21 Amber St.
Markham, ON L3R 4Z3
905-475-9292
Fax: 905-475-3286
866-273-9292
info@ordanthermal.com
www.ordanthermal.com
Firm Type: Distributing, Engineering, Manufacturing
Founded: 1976
Staff: 6
Products/Services/Areas of Expertise: Measuring & monitoring equipment; air treatment equipment & systems; incineration equipment; industrial combustion equipment; gas-fired burners
Financial Information:
Type of Ownership: Private
Revenue Sources: 100% Private Contracts
Domestic Markets:
National
Foreign Activity:
Central Europe, The Middle East, USA
Contact(s):
A. Banks, Manager

Organic Farm Services
P.O. Box 116
Collingwood, ON L9Y 3Z4
705-444-0923
Fax: 705-444-0380
organix@georgian.net
www.guelphorganicconf.ca
Firm Type: Management Consulting
Founded: 1989
Member of: Canadian Organic Growers; Ecological Farmers Association of Ontario; Organic Trade Association; International Federation of Organic Agriculture Movements
Products/Services/Areas of Expertise: Organic market development; product research; trade show marketing/organization; professional consulting for companies & groups; promotion/publicity of ecological & agricultural products; training courses for eco-entrepreneurs
Recently Completed / Ongoing Projects: Organizer of the annual organic conference; writer for Vista Magazine & Canadian Natural Health Retailer Magazine
Domestic Markets:
National
Foreign Activity:
USA
Contact(s):
Tomás L. Nimmo, President

Organic Resource Management Inc. / ORMI
#601, 3700 Steeles Ave. West
Woodbridge, ON L4L 8K8
905-264-7700
Fax: 877-264-7273
866-946-6764
sales@ormi.com
www.ormi.com
Firm Type: Waste Management
Founded: 1984
Staff: 50
Products/Services/Areas of Expertise: Collection of non-hazardous liquid organic residuals from excess organic material separated from wastewater discharges. Residuals are collected by vacuum trucks & taken to processing facilities to remove excess water before being recycled. Services include grease trap cleaning, installation & repair; drain flushing & snaking, inspection & cleaning; food processor service, including pre-treatment residuals & off-spec/destruction; collection & processing of food waste, residuals & feed stock. Head office in Woodbridge, with branch offices in Toronto, Ottawa, & Vancouver
Domestic Markets:
British Columbia, Ontario, Québec
Foreign Activity:
USA
Contact(s):
Charles H. Buehler, Chairman/CEO

Canadian Branches:
Ottawa
#7, 3205 Swansea Cres.
Ottawa, ON K1G 3W5
613-737-5959
Fax: 613-737-9798
Leo Bissonnette

Richmond
17700 River Rd.
Richmond, BC V6V 1L9
604-277-1628
Fax: 604-278-6075
Ron Hnatiuk

Woodbridge
#601, 7200 Steeles Ave. West
Woodbridge, ON L4L 8K8
905-264-7700
Fax: 905-264-7273
1-800-661-4613
John Griffiths

Ortech Environmental Inc.
2395 Speakman Dr.
Mississauga, ON L5K 1B3
905-822-4120
Fax: 905-855-0406
877-774-6560
info@ortech.ca
www.ortech.ca
Products/Services/Areas of Expertise: Provides industrial facility compliance support for air, odour & noise issues, including souce/stack ttesting, ambient air monitoring, odour assessments, emission inventory preparation & permitting, air dispersion modelling, industrial hygiene, effluent monitoring, consulting services, wind resource assessment
Canadian Branches:
Sarnia
1133C Vanier Rd.
Sarnia, ON N7S 3Y6
519-336-3327
Fax: 519-336-8580
ortech@ebtech.net
Rod Brooks

Windsor
#128, 11811 Tecumseh Rd. East
Windsor, ON N8N 4M7
519-739-2220
Fax: 519-739-1647
ortech@mnsi.net
Scott Manser

Orwak Waste Systems Inc. - Canada
Also Known As: Orwak Recycling Systems Ltd.
A subsidiary of Tomra Systems ASA
#8, 2320 Bristol Circle
Oakville, ON L6H 5S2
905-829-5030
Fax: 905-829-3364
800-391-5030
Firm Type: Distributing, Waste Management
Founded: 1989
Staff: 8
Products/Services/Areas of Expertise: Waste compactors, recycling balers & specialty recycling equipment
Financial Information:
Type of Ownership: Foreign-owned
Domestic Markets:
National
Foreign Activity:
USA

OSB Services
2759 Thamesgate Dr.
Mississauga, ON L4T 1G5
905-677-0022
Fax: 905-677-0029
osb@osbservices.com
www.osbservices.com
Firm Type: Scientific/Technical Services
Founded: 1993
Staff: 7
Member of: Association of the Chemical Profession of Ontario; The Canadian Registration Board of Occupational Hygienists
Products/Services/Areas of Expertise: Source & industrial emissions characterization & quantification; emissions audits; air permits & certificates; air quality testing; biogas characterization as an alternative fuel & treatment requirement; custom analysis for VOCs employing sorbent tubes
Financial Information:
Type of Ownership: Private
Domestic Markets:
Ontario
Contact(s):
John Sliwinski, Manager

Osram Sylvania Ltd.
2001 Drew Rd.
Mississauga, ON L5S 1S4
905-673-6171
Fax: 905-671-5584
800-544-4828
www.sylvania.com
Firm Type: Distributing
Founded: 1949
Staff: 850
Member of: Electrical & Electronic Manufacturers Association of Canada
Quality Environmental Management System(s): 9001; ISO
Products/Services/Areas of Expertise: Energy-efficient light sources & electric control gear
Financial Information:
Type of Ownership: Publicly Traded; Foreign-owned
Revenue: Greater than $5 Million
Domestic Markets:
National
Foreign Activity:
Worldwide
Contact(s):
Wayne Steinhoff, President

Patrick Hatzis, Vice-President
Abbas Khan, VP, Domestic Sales & Marketing

Ottawa Engineering Ltd.
2747 Priscilla St.
Ottawa, ON K2B 7E1
613-820-8234
Fax: 613-820-5571
info@ottawengineering.com
www.ottawengineering.com
Firm Type: Management Consulting, Engineering
Founded: 1984
Staff: 4
Member of: Professional Engineers of Ontario
Products/Services/Areas of Expertise: Small-scale hydro power projects; planning, complete engineering & management services
Domestic Markets:
National
Foreign Activity:
Caribbean, Central America, South America
Contact(s):
Kearon J. Bennett, President
Pierre Boulanger, Project Engineer

Outokumpu Technology Ltd.
Formerly: Outokumpu Mintec Canada Inc.
P.O. Box 86
180 Laurier Blvd.
Brockville, ON K6V 5T7
613-345-5502
Fax: 613-345-0160
800-668-2118
www.outokumpu.ca
Firm Type: Distributing, Manufacturing
Staff: 15
Products/Services/Areas of Expertise: Mineral processing
Contact(s):
Lorne Phillips, General Manager
lorne.phillips@outokumpu.com

Overwatch Consulting
2136 Heidi Ave.
Burlington, ON L7M 3X2
905-319-1555
Firm Type: Management Consulting, Scientific/Technical Services

Products/Services/Areas of Expertise: Radiation detection, measurements, protection, nuclear instrumentation; radiation safety training for first responders; technical sales & training; first response to spills of radioactive materials
Recently Completed / Ongoing Projects: Radiation safety training for Ontario Power Generation; Gerdan-Ameristeel, Ministry of Labour of Ontario, Toronto Fire Dept.
Financial Information:
Type of Ownership: Private
Revenue: $100,000 - $250,000
Revenue Sources: 10% Provincial; 20% Municipals; 70% Private Contracts
Domestic Markets:
Ontario
Foreign Activity:
USA
Contact(s):
Don Rickard, President

Owen G. Carney Ltd.
Also Known As: Carney's Waste Systems
Squamish Business Park
38950 Queens Way
Squamish, BC V8B 0K8
604-892-5604
Fax: 604-892-5038
admin@carneyswaste.com
www.carneyswaste.com
Firm Type: Scientific/Technical Services, Waste Management
Founded: 1965
Staff: 40
Member of: National Solid Waste Management Association
Products/Services/Areas of Expertise: Waste removal including recycling; flushing storm drains etc.; pumping septic tanks, portable toilets
Domestic Markets:
British Columbia
Contact(s):
Owen G. Carney, President
owen@carneyswaste.com

Oxegen Inc.
#300, 258 Adelaide St. East
Toronto, ON M5A 1N1
416-686-3180
Fax: 416-686-4184
877-693-4361
Firm Type: Information Technology
Founded: 1999
Staff: 8
Quality Environmental Management System(s): 14001; BS
Products/Services/Areas of Expertise: An international internet-based software solutions company, specializing in the design, development & delivery of low cost Environmental & Occupational Health & Safety Management Systems; the platform is revolutionary in its design & approach, removing the traditional barriers of cost, complexity & time to implement from traditional consultant-based & paper-based management systems
Contact(s):
Ryan Vincent, CEO
Chantal Vaillancourt, VP, Business Development
chantal@oxegen.com

Ozocan Corporation
Also Known As: Hankin Atlas Ozone Systems
#12, 690 Progress Ave.
Toronto, ON M1H 3A6
416-439-7860
Fax: 416-439-6806
800-881-2381
info@ozocan.com
www.ozocan.com
Firm Type: Distributing, Manufacturing
Member of: International Ozone Association
Products/Services/Areas of Expertise: Ozocan is a manufacturer of ozone generating equipment & accessories for water & wastewater treatment, bottled water treatment, odour control, swimming pool water treatment & cooling tower recirculating water treatment. It offers parts & service for all brands of equipment; conducts pilot studies for new applications; rents equipment for emergencies.
Contact(s):
Ronald L. Laroque, President
Canadian Branches:
Calgary Branch
Hankin Water Technologies Ltd.
#1450, 540 - 5th Ave. SW
Calgary, AB T2P 0M2
403-291-0053
Hugh Blair, Contact
International Branch(es):
Thermelek Engineering Services Ltd.
Thermelek House
Peakdale Rd., Glossop
Derbyshire UK
44-1457-863-451
Fax: 44-1457-863-875

Ozogram Inc.
79, rue Comtois
Laval, QC H7Y 1S7
450-998-6661
Fax: 450-969-1888
info@ozogram.com
www.ozogram.com
Products/Services/Areas of Expertise: Filtration catalytique au sable vert; pompes péristaltiques Stenner; réservoirs pour pompes
Contact(s):
Carl Chaput

OZZ Corporation
20 Floral Pkwy.
Concord, ON L4K 4R1
905-669-6223
Fax: 905-660-1341
866-969-6001
info@ozzcorp.com
www.ozzcorp.com
Products/Services/Areas of Expertise: Enhance energy efficiency & lifestyle for our customers by developing & deploying innovative & integrated energy technology & solutions; these solutions include electrical & cabling infrastructure, building comfort systems & energy metering, monitoring & control, designed to meet the needs of customers-homeowners, builders, property managers & utilities across Ontario
Domestic Markets:
National
Canadian Branches:
OZZ Comfort Solutions (Ottawa)
#102, 2141 Thurston Drive
Ottawa, ON K1G 6C9
613-224-0074
Fax: 613-224-0078
ottawa@ozzcorp.com

P. Machibroda Engineering Ltd.
806 - 48th St. East
Saskatoon, SK S7K 3Y4
306-665-8444
Fax: 306-652-2092
pmel.sk@machibroda.ca
www.machibroda.com
Firm Type: Engineering
Founded: 1977
Member of: Associations of Professional Engineers of Saskatchewan, Manitoba, Alberta & British Columbia
Products/Services/Areas of Expertise: Subsurface environmental monitoring installations; test drilling; geophysical logging; stratigraphical analysis; surface & groundwater analysis; contaminant transport; engineering analysis & reports; remedial cleanup management
Recently Completed / Ongoing Projects: Landfill design; hydrogeological studies; SIDS investigation; site remediation
Financial Information:
Type of Ownership: Private
Domestic Markets:
Alberta, British Columbia, Manitoba, Saskatchewan
Contact(s):
Paul Machibroda, P.Eng., President
p.machibroda@machibroda.com
Ray Machibroda, P.Eng., Manager
r.machibroda@machibroda.com
Canadian Branches:
Edmonton
12114A - 163 St. NW
Edmonton, AB T5V 1H4
780-415-5233
Fax: 780-415-5234
pmel.ab@machibroda.com

P.J. Cluff Architect Inc. / APC
Also Known As: Associated Planning Consultants
#202, 1213 Bayview Ave.
Toronto, ON M4G 2Z8
416-482-5212
Fax: 416-482-8183
apc.cluff@rogers.com
Firm Type: Scientific/Technical Services
Founded: 1957
Staff: 5
Products/Services/Areas of Expertise: Architectural, master planning & programming services for hospitals, homes for the aged, disabled persons & seniors housing/behaviour; environment evaluations
Recently Completed / Ongoing Projects: Accessibility audits for City of Toronto & Bell Canada Buildings; St. Joseph Mother House; San Francisco & Toronto Custom Houses; accessibility consulting services to towns of Markham, Richmond Hill, Vaughan, City of Toronto, Niagara Casino, Niagara Falls, On., Regions of Peel, Waterloo & Mohawk Colleges; Dept. of National Defence, new immigration detention centre, Toronto
Financial Information:
Type of Ownership: Private
Revenue: $100,000 - $250,000
Revenue Sources: 10% nationwide; 20% Provincial; 55% Municipals; 15% Private Contracts
Domestic Markets:
Newfoundland & Labrador, Ontario
Foreign Activity:
USA
Contact(s):
Pamela Cluff, President

P.J. Hannah Equipment Sales Corp.
#1 - 1668 Derwent Way
Delta, BC V3M 6R9
604-522-9094
Fax: 604-524-8133

Products & Services Buyer's Guide

800-663-6793
mail@pjhannah.com
www.pjhannah.com
Firm Type: Manufacturing
Founded: 1973
Staff: 20
Products/Services/Areas of Expertise: Design, manufacture & supply packaged wastewater treatment plants; air pollution control equipment; storm water management equipment
Domestic Markets:
National
Foreign Activity:
USA
Contact(s):
Peter Hannah, President
Chris Merritt, Technical Sales

Canadian Branches:
Mississauga Branch
#9, 151 Brunel Rd.
Mississauga, ON L4Z 2H6
905-712-0620
Fax: 905-712-1240
Gary Black

P.J.B. Duffy & Associates / PDA
5839 Eagle Island
West Vancouver, BC V7W 1V6
604-921-6119
Fax: 604-921-6664
pjbduffy@compuserve.com
Firm Type: Management Consulting
Founded: 1978
Staff: 2
Products/Services/Areas of Expertise: Environmental & resource management; forest research & environmental planning; environmental impact assessment; workshop facilitation
Recently Completed / Ongoing Projects: Environment legislation analysis for forest industries, Chile; environment legislation analysis for manufacturing, Peru; environmental assessment, BC; environmental assessment training, Transport Canada, Univ. of BC; urban forestry in Iran & Costa Rica
Financial Information:
Type of Ownership: Private
Domestic Markets:
Alberta, British Columbia, Northwest Territories, Ontario, Yukon Territory
Foreign Activity:
Africa, Asia, Caribbean, Central America, The Middle East, The Pacific Rim, Former USSR
Contact(s):
Patrick Duffy, President

Pacesetter Sales & Associates Inc.
20 Arthur Hall Dr.
Sharon, ON L0G 1V0
905-478-8042, 905-478-8010
clindsay@pacesettersales.com
www.pacesettersales.com
Firm Type: Distributing, Manufacturing, MARKETING
Founded: 1992
Staff: 15
Member of: Canadian Professional Sales Association
Products/Services/Areas of Expertise: Representatives for manufacturers of personal & environmental safety products
Financial Information:
Type of Ownership: Private
Domestic Markets:
National,
Contact(s):
Craig Lindsay, President
Pat Henderson, Western Canada Sales Manager, 780/481-0969
phenderson@pacesettersales.com

Canadian Branches:
Alberta
8310 - 153 St.
Edmonton, AB T5R 1N5
780-481-0969
Fax: 780-481-0969
phenderson@pacesettersales.com
Pat Henderson

Pacific Engineering Inc.
P.O. Box 221
Pickering, ON L1V 2R4

905-831-5025
Fax: 905-831-7401
dlim@pacificranger.com
Firm Type: Manufacturing, Scientific/Technical Services
Founded: 1976
Staff: 8
Member of: Professional Engineers Ontario
Products/Services/Areas of Expertise: Air compressors; centrifugal pumps; ventilators; heat transfer equipment; gas engine-driven equipment; generator set; water/oil separator
Recently Completed / Ongoing Projects: General Motor sub-assembly plant
Financial Information:
Type of Ownership: Private
Revenue Sources: 5% Provincial; 5% Municipals; 90% Private Contracts
Domestic Markets:
National
Foreign Activity:
Africa, Asia, Australia/New Zealand, Caribbean, Central America, The Pacific Rim, South America, USA
Markets Sought:
Central America, Central Europe, Western Europe, South America, Mexico, USA, Former USSR, United Kingdom
Contact(s):
David Lim, P.Eng., President

Pacific Environmental Consulting & Occupational Hygiene Services
Formerly: Hansen & Associates
1336 Main St.
North Vancouver, BC V7J 1C#
604-980-3577
Fax: 604-980-2188
info@pacificenvironmentalbc.com
www.pacificenvironmentalbc.com
Firm Type: Scientific/Technical Services
Founded: 1994
Staff: 18
Member of: Environmental Manager's Association of BC
Products/Services/Areas of Expertise: Environmental: site investigations, remediation plans, certificate of compliance, PCB'S, lead, methane gas, asbestos, hazardous waste, underground storage tanks, chemical spillage; Asbestos & Other Hazardous Materials; Indoor Air Quality & Mould Testing; Occupational Health & Safety; Technical Services; Laboratory Services; Training Programs; Legal Services, expert witness testimony
Recently Completed / Ongoing Projects: Hazardous materials assessment, abatement & disposal projects: Grosvenor Canada, Kitimat Hospital - BC Northern Health Authority, Ocean Falls, Ministry of Agriculture, St. Vincent's Hospital, Marijuana Grow-op/Clandestine Lab Remediation - PWGSC, School District 44 Crawlspaces - North Vancouver, Langley School Surveys, PG Regional Hospital - Northern Health Authority, Coquitz Middle School - Greater Victoria School District
Financial Information:
Type of Ownership: Private
Revenue Sources: 5% nationwide; 10% Provincial; 30% Municipals; 55% Private Contracts
Domestic Markets:
Alberta, British Columbia, Saskatchewan, Yukon Territory
Contact(s):
Peter Hansen, President

Canadian Branches:
Nanaimo
P.O. Box 298
7217 Lanzville Rd., #10
Lantzville, BC V0R 2H0
250-390-1101
Fax: 250-390-1153
Gord Wedman

Prince George Branch
#202, 1940 Third Ave.
Prince George, BC V2M 1G7
250-562-1145
Fax: 250-562-1146
Glenn Wong

Victoria
1933 Lee Ave.
Victoria, BC V8R 4W9
250-380-3911
Fax: 250-380-1123
Tim Salusbury

Pacific Institute for Advanced Study / PIAS
Formerly: TEMS Inc.
936 Thermal Dr.
Coquitlam, BC V3J 6R8
604-469-7946
Fax: 604-469-3552
pacific@imag.net
www.pacificinstitute.com
Firm Type: Engineering
Founded: 1990
Staff: 5
Member of: BC Wastewater Association; World Future Society; Oregon Environmental Association; Canadian Association of Physicists; Canadian Institute for Strategic Studies; Professional Engineers of Ontario; Association of Professional Engineers & Geoscientists of BC
Products/Services/Areas of Expertise: All aspects of advanced green building design, solar engineering, alternate energy, micro-hydro, ocean tidal & current energy, energy management, contaminated site remediation, corporate training programs, trends & futures studies, computational fluid dynamics
Recently Completed / Ongoing Projects: Engineering of a LEED platinum green guilding; CFD modelling of new small turbine engines; use of sonification for the treatment of PCB contaminated soil
Financial Information:
Type of Ownership: Private
Revenue: $500,000 - $1.5 Million
Revenue Sources: 10% nationwide; 20% Provincial; 70% Private Contracts
Domestic Markets:
National
Foreign Activity:
Asia, Australia/New Zealand, Eastern Europe, Western Europe, The Middle East, South America, USA, United Kingdom, Worldwide
Markets Sought:
Asia, Eastern Europe, Mexico, Former USSR
Contact(s):
Paul D. Tinari, President/Director
Nancy Tinari, Sales Director
Jerry Yudelson, Marketing Director

Pacific Metals Recycling International
Also Known As: Pacific Metals Ltd.
8360 Ontario St.
Vancouver, BC V5X 3E5
604-327-1148
Fax: 604-327-3614
mlotzkar@pacificmetals.ca
www.pacificmetals.ca
Firm Type: Waste Management
Founded: 1912
Staff: 35
Products/Services/Areas of Expertise: Scrap metal, paper, plastic, glass & electronics recycling; recyclables; waste handling
Financial Information:
Type of Ownership: Private
Revenue: Greater than $5 Million
Domestic Markets:
National
Foreign Activity:
Asia, China, USA, Worldwide
Markets Sought:
Asia, South America, Mexico
Contact(s):
Mark Lotzkar, President/General Manager

Pacific Phytometric Consultants
1531 - 133B St.
Surrey, BC V4A 6A5
604-531-1948
phytomet@shaw.ca
Firm Type: Scientific/Technical Services
Founded: 1984
Products/Services/Areas of Expertise: Regeneration silviculture, nursery culture, seedling handling & plantation establishment
Domestic Markets:
National
Foreign Activity:
USA
Contact(s):
Rob Scagel, Principal Consultant

Pacwill Environmental
4961 King Street E., Unit T1
Beamsville, ON L0R 1B0
905-563-9097
Fax: 866-425-0015
866-840-0014
sales@pacwill.ca
www.pacwill.ca
Firm Type: Distributing, Scientific/Technical Services
Founded: 1993
Member of: Teledyne Instruments, California Analytical Instrumentation, Apex, Tisch Environmental Inc., Magee Scientific, Nova Analytical Systems Inc., AMP-Cherokee, Met One Instruments, BGI Inc., A.P. Buck Inc., Chromatotec, Environmental Monitor Service Inc.
Products/Services/Areas of Expertise: Regulation-compliant equipment & services for the collection & concentration of air samples; source emission & ambient air monitoring
Financial Information:
Type of Ownership: Private
Domestic Markets:
National
Foreign Activity:
Worldwide
Contact(s):
James D. Packard, President
Eric Cogswell, General Manager

Canadian Branches:
Fredericton
#315 Carleton St.
Fredericton, NB E3B 3T8
506-462-0014
Fax: 506-462-0015
Staff: 7
Thomas Johnsen

Pageau Morel & associés, inc.
#110, 210, boul Crémazie ouest
Montréal, QC H2P 1C6
514-382-5150
Fax: 514-384-9872
info@pageaumorel.com
www.pageaumorel.com
Firm Type: Engineering
Founded: 1956
Staff: 150
Member of: Institute of Environmental Sciences
Products/Services/Areas of Expertise: Consulting engineering services
Domestic Markets:
Ontario, Québec
Contact(s):
Réjean Berthiaume, ing., Président
Roland Charneux, ing., M.Ing., Directeur général et Vice-président, Exploitation

Canadian Branches:
Gatineau Branch
#302, 365, boul Gréber
Gatineau, QC J8T 5R3
819-776-4665
Fax: 819-776-4775

Laval Branch
1695, boul. Laval, bur. 200
Laval, QC H7S 2M2
450-668-8884
Fax: 450-668-6993

Paladin Environmental Consulting Services Ltd.
#155, 51551 Range Rd. 212A
Sherwood Park, AB T8G 1B2
780-922-0072
877-464-5900
palenv@xplornet.com
www.paladinenvironmental.com

Pall (Canada) Limited
Also Known As: Pall Biomedical, Pall Gelman Sciences
3450 Ridgeway Drive, Unit 6
Mississauga, ON L5L 0A2
905-542-0330
Fax: 905-542-0331
800-263-5910
cssrequest@pall.com
www.pall.com

Firm Type: Distributing
Founded: 1945
Staff: 40
Products/Services/Areas of Expertise: Sales & distribution of filters
Domestic Markets:
National

Canadian Branches:
Montréal
2535, de Miniac
Montréal, QC H4S 1E5
514-332-7255
Fax: 514-332-0996
800-435-6268

Pam Wight & Associates
14715 - 82 Ave.
Edmonton, AB T5R 3R7
780-483-7578
Fax: 780-483-7627
pamwight@superiway.net
Firm Type: Management Consulting
Member of: The Ecotourism Society
Products/Services/Areas of Expertise: Provides services in sustainable tourism & ecotourism planning, design, location, operation, feasibility, business planning & development; also provides land use & integrated planning services, resource conservation & environmental & social impact studies, utilizing community planning, capacity building, & public consultation & participation techniques; conducts market research & offers environmental management & planning services
Financial Information:
Type of Ownership: Private
Revenue Sources: 60% nationwide; 20% Provincial; 20% Private Contracts
Domestic Markets:
National
Foreign Activity:
Australia/New Zealand, Caribbean, Eastern Europe
Markets Sought:
Central America, South America
Contact(s):
Pamela A. Wight, President

Pan Tec Inc.
41 Grange St.
Guelph, ON N1E 2T8
519-824-5617
Fax: 519-824-5617
800-361-3079
info@pr88.com
www.pr88.com
Firm Type: Distributing
Staff: 5
Quality Environmental Management System(s): 9001; ISO
Products/Services/Areas of Expertise: Health & safety products; skin protection cream; PR88; water soluble PR99 barrier cream; acid resistant
Financial Information:
Type of Ownership: Private
Domestic Markets:
National
Foreign Activity:
Worldwide
Contact(s):
Thomas Jakob, President

Panama Enterprises (1990) Inc.
11850 - 149 St. NW
Edmonton, AB T5V 1P2
780-452-5757
Fax: 780-452-5767
888-489-2416
panama@compusmart.ab.ca
www.panamawindsocks.com
Firm Type: Distributing, Manufacturing
Staff: 8
Products/Services/Areas of Expertise: Manufacturing of windsocks & frames; distribution of oil field supplies; Canadian distributor of Morgan Chemical Injectors
Financial Information:
Type of Ownership: Private
Revenue Sources: 100% Private Contracts
Domestic Markets:
National
Contact(s):
Jack Read, President
Claire Read, Vice-President

Panasonic Canada Inc.
5770 Ambler Dr.
Mississauga, ON L4W 2T3
905-624-5010
Fax: 905-624-9714
www.panasonic.ca
Firm Type: Distributing, Manufacturing
Founded: 1967
Staff: 620
Quality Environmental Management System(s): 14001
Products/Services/Areas of Expertise: Consumer & industrial electronics
Financial Information:
Type of Ownership: Foreign-owned; Publicly Traded
Revenue: Greater than $5 Million
Domestic Markets:
National
Contact(s):
Ian Vatcher, President, Panasonic Canada Inc.
Sean De Vries, Manager, Environmental

Canadian Branches:
Calgary
6835 - 8th St. NE
Calgary, AB T2E 7H7
403-256-2429
Fax: 403-256-5753

Lachine
3075, rue Louis-A.-Amos
Montréal, QC H8T 1C4
514-633-8684
Fax: 514-633-1086

Richmond
12111 Riverside Way
Richmond, BC V6W 1K8
604-204-3217
Fax: 604-204-3202

St-Laurent
6505 Transcanadienne, Ste 230
Montréal, QC H4T 1S3
514-747-3737
Fax: 514-747-0117

Winnipeg
1349 Dugald Rd.
Winnipeg, MB R2J 0H2
204-231-3000
Fax: 204-231-3030

Panther Environmental IInc.
P.O. Box 7793
Bonnyville, AB T9N 2J1
780-812-2702
Fax: 780-812-2710

PAP Engineering Services
34 Jasmine Rd.
Toronto, ON M9M 2P9
416-743-9601
Fax: 416-747-9058
Firm Type: Engineering, Manufacturing
Founded: 1982
Member of: Professional Engineers of Ontario
Products/Services/Areas of Expertise: Supplies oil solvent recovery distillation units to eliminate pollution & disposal costs; equipment to reclaim both solvents & oil; wastewater evaporators; anti-freeze equipment
Recently Completed / Ongoing Projects: 30 USGPH solvent recovery for USA
Financial Information:
Type of Ownership: Private
Domestic Markets:
National
Foreign Activity:
USA
Contact(s):
Pat Priorello, President/CEO

Papiers Perkins
Div. Cascades Inc.
CP 30
404, boul Marie Victorin
Kingsey Falls, QC J0A 1B0

Products & Services Buyer's Guide

819-363-5601
Fax: 819-363-5655
info@cascades.com
Products/Services/Areas of Expertise: Manufacturer of paper towels
Ecological Note: Paper towels
Contact(s):
Alain Lemaire, President & CEO

Par Excellence Developments, Inc.
P.O. Box 2213 A
Sudbury, ON P3A 4S1
705-669-1870
ped@vianet.on.ca
Products/Services/Areas of Expertise: Markets & licenses use of a proprietary gas oil stabilization & purification process
Contact(s):
Don Kress, President

Para Paints
11 Kenview Blvd.
Brampton, ON L6T 5G5
905-792-0940
Fax: 905-792-1090
800-461-7272
www.para.com
Firm Type: Manufacturing
Founded: 1915
Quality Environmental Management System(s): 9001
EcoLogo Certified Products & Services: PARA's Ultra, Premium, Professional, Primetech & Sceno tintable paints
Products/Services/Areas of Expertise: PARA Paints is a Canadian manufacturer of paints, wood stains & wood care products; the Brampton, Ontario manufacturing & distribution facility is one of the most technologically advanced & environmentally sound paint plants in Canada & the world
Ecological Note: PARA's Ultra, Premium, Professional, Primetech & Sceno tintable paints
Financial Information:
Type of Ownership: Private

Paracel Laboratories Ltd.
2319 St. Laurent Blvd.
Ottawa, ON K1G 4J8
613-731-9577
Fax: 613-731-9064
drobertson@paracellabs.com
www.paracellabs.com
Firm Type: Scientific/Technical Services
Founded: 1985
Member of: Canadian Association of Environmental Laboratories; International Association of Environmental Testing Laboratories
Products/Services/Areas of Expertise: All types of chemical analyses specializing in environmental testing; indoor air quality & all related microbial & bacterial analyses
Domestic Markets:
National
Foreign Activity:
USA
Contact(s):
Dale Robertson, Contact

Paradigm Environmental Technologies Inc.
#200 - 1600 West 6th Ave.
Vancouver, BC V6J 1R3
604-742-0360
Fax: 604-742-0368
info@microsludge.com
www.paradigmenvironmental.com
Firm Type: Engineering, Waste Management
Founded: 1999
Products/Services/Areas of Expertise: Developers of MicroSludge, a sustainable technology for municipal wastewater treatment plants; Wastewater treatment technologies
Recently Completed / Ongoing Projects: MicroSludge is currently in the process of seeking new markets, having just finished a successful 12-month beta test at the Los Angeles County Wastewater Treatment Plant.
Financial Information:
Type of Ownership: Publicly Traded
Domestic Markets:
National
Foreign Activity:
USA
Markets Sought:
USA,

Contact(s):
Gord Skene, President
gskene@microsludge.com
Filipe Figueira, Director, Marketing
ffigueira@microsludge.com
Rob Stephenson, Chief Technical Officer
rstephenson@microsludge.com

Paragon Soil & Environmental Consulting Inc.
Formerly: Can-Ag Enterprises Ltd.
14805 - 119 Ave.
Edmonton, AB T5L 2N9
780-434-0400
Fax: 780-482-1260
info@paragonsoil.com
www.paragonsoil.com/home.html
Firm Type: Scientific/Technical Services
Founded: 2002
Staff: 10
Member of: Canadian Society of Soil Science; Agricultural Institute of Canada; Canadian Land Reclamation Association; Alberta Institute of Agrologists
Products/Services/Areas of Expertise: Soil-related consulting services; land reclamation & remediation; physical land classification; SCC modelling; environmental site assessments; terrestrial assessments & regulatory planning
Financial Information:
Type of Ownership: Private
Revenue Sources: 15% Provincial; 85% Private Contracts
Domestic Markets:
National
Contact(s):
Leonard Leskiw, M.Sc., P.Ag., President

Parameter Control Ltd.
#16, 62 McBrine Pl.
Kitchener, ON N2R 1H3
519-748-6420
Fax: 519-748-6904
water1@bellnet.ca
www.water1.ca
Firm Type: Manufacturing, Scientific/Technical Services
Founded: 1981
Staff: 7
Member of: Kitchener Waterloo Chamber of Commerce; Water Quality Association; Better Business Bureau
Products/Services/Areas of Expertise: Potable & wastewater treatment equipment; pH probes, conductivity meters, chemical metering/dosing pumps, flow meters, water softeners, filters, reverse osmosis, ultraviolet disinfection; commercial, industrial, residential clients
Financial Information:
Type of Ownership: Private
Revenue Sources: 10% nationwide; 10% Provincial; 10% Municipals; 70% Private Contracts
Domestic Markets:
National
Foreign Activity:
Africa
Contact(s):
Terry Willett, President

Paramount Emergency Planners Ltd.
1120 - 29th Ave. NE
Calgary, AB T2E 7P1
403-205-3977
Fax: 403-205-4879
866-207-3977
info@emergencyplanners.com
www.emergencyplanners.com
Firm Type: Management Consulting
Founded: 1996
Staff: 20
Products/Services/Areas of Expertise: Development & implementation of emergency response plans & safety management programs
Financial Information:
Type of Ownership: Private
Domestic Markets:
Alberta, British Columbia, Manitoba, Saskatchewan
Foreign Activity:
USA

Conserval Engineering Inc.
200 Wildcat Rd.
Toronto, ON M3J 2N5

416-661-7057
Fax: 416-661-7146
info@solarwall.com
www.solarwall.com
Firm Type: Distributing, Manufacturing
Founded: 1977
Member of: American Solar Energy Society (ASES); Canadian Solar Industries Association (CanSIA); Solar Energy Industries Association (SEIA); US Green Building Council (USGBC)
Products/Services/Areas of Expertise: Manufacturer & distributor of renewable energy solutions, such as the solar collector known as SolarWall, & the PV/Thermal system
Domestic Markets:
National
Foreign Activity:
China, Central Europe, Eastern Europe, Western Europe, The Pacific Rim, USA
Contact(s):
John Hollick, Chief Executive Officer

Paris, France
66, av des Champs Elysees
Paris France
info@solarwall.eu

Canadian Branches:
Buffalo, USA
#28, 4242 Ridge Lea Rd.
Buffalo, NY USA
716-835-4903
Fax: 716-835-4904
solarwallusa@solarwall.com

Parish Geomorphic Ltd.
#207, 10 Mountainview Rd. South
Georgetown, ON L7G 4J9
905-877-9531
Fax: 905-877-4143
www.parishgeomorphic.com
Firm Type: Management Consulting, Engineering
Founded: 1996
Staff: 15
Member of: Association of Professional Geoscientists of Ontario
Products/Services/Areas of Expertise: Specializes in applications of fluvial geomorphology, natural channel design, stream naturalization; erosion analyses: bank stability, bed scour, aquatic habitat evaluation, channel inventory, monitoring, policy & protocol development
Recently Completed / Ongoing Projects: Urban stream road crossing design guide; regional monitoring program, fluvial geomorphology component; erosion assessments; natural channel designs; bank stabilization
Financial Information:
Type of Ownership: Private
Revenue: $500,000 - $1.5 Million
Revenue Sources: 10% nationwide; 10% Provincial; 20% Municipals; 60% Private Contracts
Domestic Markets:
Ontario
Foreign Activity:
USA,
Contact(s):
John D. Parish, M.A., P.Geo., Director
jparish@parishgeomorphic.com
Rosmarie Fran, Administration
rfran@parishgeomorphic.com

Canadian Branches:
Fredericton
#203, 346 Queen St.
Fredericton, NB E3B 1B2
506-472-8440
Fax: 506-472-6250
Aaron Corr, P.Eng.

Parkes Scientific Canada Inc.
17360 - 108 Ave.
Edmonton, AB T5S 1E8
780-484-1849
Fax: 780-484-0601
info@parkesscientific.com
Firm Type: Distributing, Scientific/Technical Services
Founded: 1985
Staff: 3
Products/Services/Areas of Expertise: Solvent recycling equipment; petroleum testing equipment

Financial Information:
Type of Ownership: Private
Revenue Sources: 30% nationwide; 70% Private Contracts
Domestic Markets:
National
Foreign Activity:
Worldwide
Contact(s):
Lance Parkes, President

Parklane Computer Systems
521 Nottinghill Rd., Unit 10
London, ON N6K 4L4
519-657-3386
Fax: 519-657-3375
information@parklanesys.com
www.parklanesys.com
Products/Services/Areas of Expertise: Occupational health & safety software products; due diligence concerns

Parkson Corporation
#205, 1000, St-Jean
Montréal, QC H9R 5P1
514-636-8712
Fax: 514-636-9718
canada@parkson.com
www.parkson.com
Firm Type: Manufacturing
Founded: 1971
Staff: 150
Member of: Water Environment Association of Ontario; Water Environment Federation; American Waste Water Association; Réseau Environnement; Ontario Pollution Equipment Control Association; British Columbia Water & Waste Association; Western Canada Water & Wastewater Association
Products/Services/Areas of Expertise: Wastewater treatment systems; potable & process water treatment systems; tertiary treatment; biological systems; solids handling systems; aeration; clarification; coarse screening; dewatering; filtration; fine screening; grit separation & washing oil/water separation; screenings washing, conveying, dewatering systems; scum removal; sludge removal; sludge dewatering; sludge thickening; sludge & grit conveying & load-out; solar sludge drying; stormwater/CSO screening; seepage receiving systems
Domestic Markets:
National
Contact(s):
Bill Acton, President/CEO
Michael Miller, Vice-President, Marketing
Jean R. Grenier, Regional Manager
L. Ott, Sales Coordinator

International Branch(es):
Parkson Corporation - Head Office
2727 North West 62 St., PO Box 408399
Fort Lauderdale, FL USA
954-974-6610
Fax: 954-974-6182
technology@parkson.com

Parkvalley Consulting Ltd.
#810, 700 - 4 Ave. SW
Calgary, AB T2P 3J4
403-269-3501
Fax: 403-263-7152
information@parkvalley.net
www.geoffdean.com/parkvalley/about.htm
Firm Type: Management Consulting
Founded: 1977
Staff: 6
Products/Services/Areas of Expertise: Environmental consulting, project management
Financial Information:
Type of Ownership: Private
Revenue Sources: 100% Private Contracts
Domestic Markets:
Alberta, British Columbia

Canadian Branches:
Edmonton
17611 - 105 Ave.
Edmonton, AB T5S 1T1
780-484-6750
Fax: 780-484-6764

Parsons Commercial Technology Group Inc.
Formerly: Parsons Protect Air;Protect Air Company
2751 John St.
Markham, ON L3R 2Y8
905-944-8877
Fax: 905-944-8977
www.parsons.com
Products/Services/Areas of Expertise: Provides design & construction services for many diverse markets such as life sciences, infrastructure, transportation, water, telecommunications, aviation, commercial, environmental, planning, industrial manufacturing, and homeland security
Contact(s):
Marcia Moro, Contact

Pat Dwyer Construction Inc.
P.O. Box 38
Lundbreck, AB T0K 1H0
403-628-2291
Fax: 403-628-2191
dwyerinc@jrtwave.com
Firm Type: Engineering, Scientific/Technical Services
Founded: 1967
Staff: 10
Products/Services/Areas of Expertise: Specialize in heavy earth works, light industrial construction & equipment rentals, design & build civil engineering & construction, helicopter direction & environmental drilling
Contact(s):
Pat Dwyer

Patterson Industries (Canada) Ltd.
250 Danforth Rd.
Toronto, ON M1L 3X4
416-694-3381
Fax: 416-691-2768
800-336-1110
process@pattersonindustries.com
www.pattersonindustries.com
Firm Type: Engineering, Manufacturing
Founded: 1945
Staff: 35
Products/Services/Areas of Expertise: Heat exchangers; custom design, engineering & manufacturing of wastewater treatment systems for the food, feed, steel mills, metal working & chemical industries
Financial Information:
Revenue Sources: 100% Private Contracts
Domestic Markets:
National
Foreign Activity:
Asia, The Pacific Rim, South America, Mexico, USA
Contact(s):
H.W. Haischt, President & General Manager
M.C. Lindsey, Sales Manager

Paul F. Wilkinson & Associates Inc.
5800, av Monkland, 2e étage
Montréal, QC H4A 1G1
514-482-6887
Fax: 514-482-0036
pfw@wilkinson.ca
Firm Type: Scientific/Technical Services
Founded: 1975
Staff: 10
Products/Services/Areas of Expertise: Social sciences; impact assessments; economic development; mediation; negotiation; resource development; resettlement; ISO 14000
Recently Completed / Ongoing Projects: Davis Inlet community relocation project; environmental screening (social) of a dam in India; environmental screening (social & biophysical) of a road in the Philippines
Financial Information:
Revenue Sources: 40% Municipals; 60% Private Contracts
Domestic Markets:
New Brunswick, Newfoundland & Labrador, Northwest Territories, Ontario, Québec
Foreign Activity:
Africa, Asia, USA
Markets Sought:
South America
Contact(s):
Paul F. Wilkinson, President
Brigitte Masella, Manager, Research, Development & Engineering

Paul G. Chénard
38, rue Thérien
Gatineau, QC J8Y 1H8
819-776-0873
Fax: 819-778-3665
verivert@videotron.ca
Firm Type: Management Consulting
Founded: 1996
Member of: Canadian Environmental Auditing Association; Association québécoise de vérification environnementale
Products/Services/Areas of Expertise: Implementation of environmental management systems (EMS); internal & external environmental audits; environmental management training; seminar facilitation
Recently Completed / Ongoing Projects: EMS implementation (ISO 14001), aircraft component manufacturer; registration audits of ISO 14001 EMS; auditor training
Financial Information:
Type of Ownership: Private
Revenue: $50,000 - $100,000
Revenue Sources: 10% nationwide; 90% Private Contracts
Domestic Markets:
Alberta, British Columbia, New Brunswick, Newfoundland & Labrador, Ontario, Québec
Foreign Activity:
The Middle East
Markets Sought:
Central America, Western Europe, The Middle East, South America, USA
Contact(s):
Paul G. Chénard, Contact

PBR Laboratories Inc. / PBR
Also Known As: Prairie Biological Research Ltd
9960 - 67 Ave. NW
Edmonton, AB T6E 0P5
780-450-3957
Fax: 780-450-3960
866-450-3957
pbr@pbr.ca
www.pbr.ca
Firm Type: Management Consulting, Scientific/Technical Services
Founded: 1984
Staff: 9
Member of: Alberta Society of Professional Biologists; Canadian Association of Environmental Analytical Laboratories; Society of Toxicology; BioAlberta; BioteCanada
Products/Services/Areas of Expertise: Water & wastewater analysis; risk assessment; toxicological evaluations; food pathogens & toxins; microbiological analysis; product safety; bioremediation; cyanobacterial toxins
Activities: Bioremediation; development of analytical methods & kits for algal toxins in fresh water & diarrhetic shellfish toxins
Financial Information:
Type of Ownership: Private
Revenue Sources: 18% nationwide; 2% Provincial; 20% Municipals; 60% Private Contracts
Domestic Markets:
Alberta, British Columbia, Northwest Territories, Ontario, Québec, Saskatchewan
Foreign Activity:
USA
Contact(s):
Ram Mehta, President & CEO
Arnold Urbonas, Vice-President, Operations

PCB Disposal Inc.
A division of Sanexen Environmental Services Inc.
72 Lake Driveway West
Ajax, ON L1S 3X1
905-428-6480
Fax: 905-428-6481
800-563-7227
www.pcbdisposalinc.com
Firm Type: Waste Management
Founded: 1987
Staff: 5
Products/Services/Areas of Expertise: Full-service PCB management & destruction company offering transformer replacements, disposal of all PCB wastes, sampling & analysis, site remediation, transformer reclassification & disposal; PCB destruction, water decontamination, PCB & hazardous waste storage facilities, PCB transportation, environmental audits, ballast identification & management, tank decontamination & disposal, multiple generator PCB consolidation & destruction

projects, metal recovery & recycling; educational seminars & E/R training; PCB transfer station equipped with PCB incinerator in Colborne, ON
Financial Information:
Type of Ownership: Private
Domestic Markets:
National
Contact(s):
Eric A.H. Smith, President & CEO
esmith@pcbdisposalinc.com

PCI Geomatics Group Inc.
50 West Wilmot St.
Richmond Hill, ON L4B 1M5
905-764-0614
Fax: 905-764-9604
info@pcigeomatics.com
www.pcigeomatics.com
Firm Type: Manufacturing
Founded: 1982
Products/Services/Areas of Expertise: Geographic management software with capabilities in remote sensing, GIS, terrain analysis, data visualization & image analysis
Domestic Markets:
National
Foreign Activity:
Worldwide
Contact(s):
Terry Moloney, President & CEO
Brad Schmidt, Vice-President, Sales & Marketing
Lynne Brown-Harper, Vice-President, Operations
Robert Lang, Chief Financial Officer

Canadian Branches:
Gatineau
#400, 490, boul St-Joseph
Gatineau, QC J8Y 3Y7
819-770-0022
Fax: 819-770-0098
sales@pcigeomatics.com

International Branch(es):
China - Beijing
Core Plaza, Haidian District
#2-1020, No. 1, ShanYuan St., ZhongGuanCun XiQu
Beijing China
86-010-624167453
Fax: 86-010-62416746
xin@pcigeomatics.com
www.pcigeomatics.cn

UK - Scotland
Westpoint
4 Redheughs Rigg, South Gyle
Edinburgh Scotland
Fax: 44(0)1313386778
International Phone: 44 (0)131 338 6991
sales@pcigeomatics.com

USA - New Mexico
#222, 4848 Tramway Ridge, NE
Albuquerque, NM USA
888-343-0003
Fax: 888-343-0003
ussales@pcigeomatics.com

USA - Virginia
#400, 500 Montgomery St.
Alexandria, VA
412-389-9767
Fax: 888-343-0003
sales@pcigeomatics.com

PDK Projects Inc.
5072 Vista View Cres.
Nanaimo, BC V9V 1L6
250-751-8890
Fax: 250-751-8225
info@pdkprojects.com
www.pdkprojects.com
Firm Type: Scientific/Technical Services
Founded: 1997
Staff: 5
Products/Services/Areas of Expertise: Environmental & agricultural applications of near-infrared spectroscopy
Recently Completed / Ongoing Projects: Analysis of nutrients in hog manure with field portable near-infrared spectrometer to monitor nutrient loading & balance N.P.; rapid method for the measurement of C per unit area in a freshwater coastal wetland for C inventory purposes
Financial Information:
Type of Ownership: Private
Revenue: $100,000 - $250,000
Revenue Sources: 10% nationwide; 30% Provincial; 60% Private Contracts
Domestic Markets:
National, Manitoba
Foreign Activity:
USA
Markets Sought:
Asia, Central America, Eastern Europe, Former USSR
Contact(s):
Diane F. Malley, President
Paul D. Martin, Operations Manager

Pebblestone Multi-Services Inc.
2000 Wentworth St.
Whitby, ON L1N 8W9
905-725-0899
garbage@idirect.ca
Firm Type: Waste Management
Founded: 1984
Member of: Ontario Waste Management Association
Products/Services/Areas of Expertise: Waste management; transfer station operation; industrial, commercial & residential collection; transportation of sludge & special waste
Financial Information:
Type of Ownership: Private
Domestic Markets:
Ontario,
Contact(s):
Brad Harper, Contact

Peco Filters Ltd.
1351 Hastings Cres. SE
Calgary, AB T2G 4C8
403-243-6700
Fax: 403-287-9304
canadasales@perryequipment.com
www.pecousa.com
Firm Type: Manufacturing

Products/Services/Areas of Expertise: Manufacturing of filter vessels & elements for the oil & gas industry
Financial Information:
Type of Ownership: Private
Revenue Sources: 100% Private Contracts
Contact(s):
Norm Hertzberg, General Manager

Pedocan Land Evaluation Ltd.
50th St. Atria
#140, 9405 - 50th St.
Edmonton, AB T2B 2T4
780-462-5123
Fax: 780-922-5650
canadasales@perryequipment.com
Firm Type: Scientific/Technical Services
Founded: 1977
Products/Services/Areas of Expertise: Site assessments; geological/hydrogeological engineering

Canadian Branches:
Calgary Branch
#620, 1010 - 1st St. SW
Calgary, AB T2R 1K4
403-265-8008
Fax: 403-265-8032
general@pedocan.com

Peel Scrap Metal Recycling Ltd.
2301 Anson Dr.
Mississauga, ON L5S 1G6
905-612-1288
Fax: 905-612-1376
Firm Type: Manufacturing, Waste Management
Founded: 1990
Staff: 8
Products/Services/Areas of Expertise: Recycling of ferrous & non-ferrous scrap metals
Financial Information:
Type of Ownership: Private
Domestic Markets:
Ontario
Contact(s):
Gary Dvorkin, President/CEO

Jeff Shaffer

Pegasus Industrial Specialties Inc.
211 Shearson Cres.
Cambridge, ON N1T 1J5
519-620-7991
Fax: 519-620-7992
800-315-0387
sales@pegasus-glass.com
www.pegasus-glass.com
Firm Type: Manufacturing
Founded: 1968
Staff: 12
Member of: Guelph Chamber of Commerce
Products/Services/Areas of Expertise: Manufacture glassware for all method 5 stack sampling monitors; large monitoring systems for federal & provincial governments
Financial Information:
Type of Ownership: Private
Revenue Sources: 10% nationwide; 10% Provincial; 5% Municipals; 85% Private Contracts
Domestic Markets:
National
Foreign Activity:
Central America, USA
Markets Sought:
Central America, South America

Peintures Denalt
Denalt Paints Ltd.
8620, rue Pascal Gagnon
Montréal, QC H1P 1Z1
514-328-2727
Fax: 514-328-9635
800-361-3847
www.denaltpaints.com/index7.htm
Firm Type: Manufacturing
Founded: 1958
Quality Environmental Management System(s): 9002
EcoLogo Certified Products & Services: Denalt & Décor paints
Ecological Note: Denalt & Décor paints

Pelmar Engineering Ltd.
#8, 445 Midwest Rd.
Toronto, ON M1P 4Y9
416-288-1736
Fax: 416-288-0385
888-754-6329
pelmar@pelmareng.com
www.pelmareng.com
Firm Type: Distributing, Engineering, Information Technology, Manufacturing
Founded: 1981
Staff: 6
Member of: American Water Works Association; Ontario Water Works Association; Ontario Municipal Water Association
Products/Services/Areas of Expertise: Water treatment, industrial filtration, potable water systems, compressed air systems for cooling & blow offs, automatic water control, valves, airvalves, pressure regulation, pump control valves
Recently Completed / Ongoing Projects: Municipal water treatment & filtration systems, industrial filtration, industrial cooling systems
Financial Information:
Type of Ownership: Private
Revenue: $500,000 - $1.5 Million
Revenue Sources: 10% Provincial; 10% Municipals; 80% Private Contracts
Domestic Markets:
National
Foreign Activity:
Asia, Australia/New Zealand, Caribbean, Central America, The Middle East, South America, Mexico, USA, Worldwide
Contact(s):
Hanan S. Silbermann, B.Sc., M.Eng., President/Technical Manager
hanran@pelmareng.com
Robert (Bob) Clark, Manager, Sales
sales@pelmareng.com
Leon Tabak, Operations
pelmar@pelmareng.com

Pembroke Environmental Services Ltd.
219 Commercial St.
Glace Bay, NS B1A 3B9
902-849-5587
Fax: 902-842-0542

kpembrok@istar.ca
www.pembrokegroup.com
Products/Services/Areas of Expertise: Environmental assessments; oil spill services; indoor air quality services; fire & flood restoration; occupational health & safety services

Pencon Equipment Co.
109 Thomas St., 2nd Fl.
Oakville, ON L6J 3A7
905-845-1727
Fax: 905-845-1792
Firm Type: Distributing
Founded: 1982
Products/Services/Areas of Expertise: Anaerobic digesters; compressors; rotary positive displacement blowers & multistage & regenerative blowers
Financial Information:
Type of Ownership: Private
Domestic Markets:
National

Penn Refrigeration Ltd.
#5, 18 Seapark Dr.
St Catharines, ON L2M 6S6
905-685-4255
Fax: 905-685-0333
penn.refrigeration@on.aibn.com
www.pennrefrigeration.com/index.html
Firm Type: Manufacturing, Scientific/Technical Services
Founded: 1961
Staff: 8
Member of: Refrigeration Service Engineers Society Canada
Products/Services/Areas of Expertise: HVAC contracting, sales & service; manufacture of carbon dioxide scrubbers & generators; non-cryogenic nitrogen generators for purging/process blanketing; oxygen generation for enhancement of oxygen levels
Domestic Markets:
Nova Scotia, Ontario, Québec
Foreign Activity:
The Pacific Rim, USA
Contact(s):
Robert Galati, President/CEO
Gene Sajur, Sales

Penny & Casson Co.
Formerly: Peel Petro Chemical Services Inc.
3039 Kennedy Rd.
Toronto, ON M1V 1S7
416-298-1144
Fax: 416-298-7984
800-389-5287
pennyandcasson@sympatico.ca
www3.sympatico.ca/pennyandcasson
Firm Type: Engineering, Scientific/Technical Services
Founded: 1940
Products/Services/Areas of Expertise: Emergency response; site assessment; waste management; above & below ground ULC tank testing; tank removal & cleanup; secondary contained aboveground tank ULC; environmental audits; risk management; oil spill equipment; storage; fuel recycling; site remediation
Financial Information:
Type of Ownership: Private
Revenue Sources: 5% nationwide; 5% Provincial; 10% Municipals; 80% Private Contracts
Domestic Markets:
Ontario
Contact(s):
Bill Penny, President
Bruce Carter, Manager, General Construction Operations
Ray Leonard, Manager, General Construction Marketing

Pepi Sewage Disposal Service
78 Evergreen Lane
Port Severn, ON L0K 1S0
705-756-2644
Fax: 705-756-2646
poohbabe60@aol.com
Firm Type: Waste Management
Founded: 1974
Staff: 4
Member of: Ontario Association of Sewage Industry Services
Products/Services/Areas of Expertise: Sewage disposal on land & water; portable toilet rentals, ecoethical products
Financial Information:
Type of Ownership: Private
Domestic Markets:
Ontario
Contact(s):
Robert Murrell, President

Pepin Prevention des Pertes Inc.
4600, rue de Boucherville
Trois-Rivières, QC G8Y 5J1
819-371-3181
Fax: 819-371-0339
micpepin@tr.cgocable.ca
Firm Type: Scientific/Technical Services
Founded: 1992
Staff: 5
Products/Services/Areas of Expertise: Environmental consulting services; spills/clean-up planning, assessment; emergency drill education
Financial Information:
Type of Ownership: Private
Revenue: $250,000 - $500,000
Domestic Markets:
Québec
Contact(s):
Michel Pepin, President
Sylvie Lefebvre, Environmental Consultant

Pepper Compressed Air & Gas Ltd.
376 Sovereign Rd.
London, ON N6A 4C3
519-659-2691
Fax: 519-659-3590
Firm Type: Distributing, Engineering, Manufacturing
Founded: 1978
Staff: 10
Products/Services/Areas of Expertise: Energy-efficient air compressors, vacuum pumps, air dryers
Domestic Markets:
National
Foreign Activity:
The Middle East, USA,
Contact(s):
Don Taylor, President/CEO

Performance Fluid Equipement Inc.
50 Progress Dr.
Orillia, ON L3V 6H1
705-434-9006
Fax: 705-434-9007
866-683-7867
info@performancequip.com
www.performancequip.com
Firm Type: Distributing, Manufacturing
Founded: 2000
Staff: 21
Products/Services/Areas of Expertise: Seepex Progressive Cavity Pumps, AOD Pumps, centrifugal, vertical turbine, split case, metering pumps & systems, sludge pumps, solid handling pumps, filters, macerators
Financial Information:
Type of Ownership: Private
Revenue: $1.5 Million - $3 Million
Revenue Sources: 70% Municipals; 10% Private Contracts
Domestic Markets:
National, Alberta, British Columbia, Manitoba, New Brunswick, Newfoundland & Labrador, Nova Scotia, Ontario, Prince Edward Island, Québec, Saskatchewan
Foreign Activity:
South America, USA
Contact(s):
George Balcerczyk, President
Diane Balcerczyk, Advertising/Marketing Manager
Roger Mayo, Sales Manager
Brian Cameron, Applications Engineer

Canadian Branches:
Québec Region
1325, du Comte
Charlesbourg, QC G2L 1B8
418-626-2801
Fax: 418-626-2788

Western Region
#104, 3424 - 27 St. SE
Calgary, AB T1Y 5E2
403-219-0821
Fax: 403-219-0817
Darryl Hughes

PerkinElmer Life & Analytical Sciences Canada Inc.
Formerly: PerkinElmer Life Sciences Canada
#6, 501 Rowntree Dairy Rd.
Woodbridge, ON L4L 8H1
905-851-4585
Fax: 905-851-1814
800-561-4646
Products/Services/Areas of Expertise: Analytical instruments
Contact(s):
Ian Brown, President
ian.brown@perkinelmer.com

Canadian Branches:
Montréal
#600, 1744, rue William
Montréal, QC H3T 1R4
514-937-9949
Fax: 514-937-0777
1-800-293-4501

St-Laurent
7740, boul Henri-Bourassa ouest
Montréal, QC H4S 1W3
514-745-1500
Fax: 514-745-3891
1-800-267-7241

Peter T. Mitches & Associates Limited; Project Managers & Consulting
Toronto Regional Office
350 Ridout St. S.
London, ON N6C 3Z5
519-663-5550
Fax: 519-663-9770
pmitches@bellnet.ca
Firm Type: Engineering, Scientific/Technical Services
Founded: 1961
Staff: 12
Products/Services/Areas of Expertise: Environmental audits, impact assessments; GIS; risk assessment, site assessment; waste management; civil, structural, mechanical & electrical engineers
Contact(s):
Peter T. Mitches, President & Chief Engineer

Peto MacCallum Ltd.
Formerly: Peto Associates Ltd.
165 Cartwright Ave.
Toronto, ON M6A 1V5
416-785-5110
Fax: 416-785-5120
corporate@petomaccallum.com
www.petomaccallum.com
Firm Type: Management Consulting, Engineering
Founded: 1973
Staff: 170
Member of: Ass'n of Consulting Engineering Companies - Canada; Ass'n of Professional Geoscientists of Ontario; Canadian Homebuilders Ass'n; Canadian Standards Ass'n; Consulting Engineers of Ontario; Professional Engineers of Ontario
Products/Services/Areas of Expertise: Geoenvironmental, hydrogeological & geotechnical engineering services; construction materials engineering; design/build services; quality control & quality assurance inspection & testing; building science services; environmental site assessment including site & facility auditing; preparation of site remediation/clean-up & excess soil & groundwater management plans
Domestic Markets:
Ontario
Foreign Activity:
Asia, The Middle East, South Africa, United Kingdom
Markets Sought:
Asia, The Middle East, South America
Contact(s):
Turney Lee-Bun, P.Eng., President
Andrew I. Injodey, M.B.A., Vice-President/Treasurer
Alnoor (Al) Nathoo, P.Eng, Vice-President, Toronto Operations

Canadian Branches:
Barrie
19 Churchill Dr.
Barrie, ON L4N 8Z5
705-734-3900
Fax: 705-734-9911
barrie@petomaccallum.com
Turney Lee-Bun, P.Eng., Branch Manager

Products & Services Buyer's Guide

Hamilton
45 Burford Rd.
Hamilton, ON L8E 3C6
905-561-2231
Fax: 905-561-6363
hamilton@petomaccallum.com
Wayne Belcourt, CET, Branch Manager

Kitchener
16 Franklin St. South
Kitchener, ON N2C 1R4
519-893-7500
Fax: 519-893-0654
kitchener@petomaccallum.com
Gerry Mitchell, MEng, P.Eng, Branch Manager

Petrifond Foundation Co. Ltd.
8320, boul St-Laurent
Montréal, QC H2P 2M3
514-387-2838
Fax: 514-387-9684
petrifond@petrifond.com
www.petrifond.com
Firm Type: Scientific/Technical Services
Founded: 1961
Staff: 70
Products/Services/Areas of Expertise: Cut-off walls for isolating groundwater pollutants; jet grouting & on-site soil mixing; construction
Domestic Markets:
National
Foreign Activity:
Caribbean, USA
Contact(s):
Peter Paganuzzi, President

Petro Laboratories Inc.
1295 Matheson Blvd. East
Mississauga, ON L4W 1R1
905-361-2388
Fax: 905-361-2411
petrolb@ipoline.com
Firm Type: Scientific/Technical Services
Founded: 1987
Staff: 4
Products/Services/Areas of Expertise: Independent laboratory specializing in petro-chemical products, oil, lube & fuel analysis, properties & specification for lubricant grease, solvent waste composition, typical routine tests are ICP metal scan, flash point, freezing point, BTU heating value, IR scan
Domestic Markets:
Ontario
Foreign Activity:
USA
Contact(s):
James Szeto, Chief Chemist

Petro Sep Membrane Technologies Inc.
2270 Speers Rd.
Oakville, ON L6L 2X8
905-825-3109
Fax: 905-825-3285
sales@petrosepmembrane.com
Firm Type: Engineering
Member of: Professional Engineers of Ontario; Environmental Assessment Association
Products/Services/Areas of Expertise: Custom engineers membrane-based systems to dehydrate, purify & separate or recover solvents to meet-to-new composition; systems can also be used to remove VOC's from contaminated water; solvents can be purified or recovered to 99.5% without chemicals, by-products or the need to regenerate
Financial Information:
Type of Ownership: Foreign-owned
Revenue Sources: 100% Private Contracts
Domestic Markets:
National
Foreign Activity:
Worldwide
Contact(s):
Gerry Van Houdt, Manager, North American Sales
Zaim Ghandi, Director, Marketing

Petro-Canada Lubricants
385 Southdown Rd.
Mississauga, ON L5J 2Y3
905-403-6718
Fax: 905-403-6875

Products/Services/Areas of Expertise: Automotive products
Ecological Note: Re-refined 15W40, 10W30 motor oil

Petroleum Enviro Services
A division of ASM Corrosion Control Ltd.
#2, 10016 - 29A Ave. NW
Edmonton, AB T6N 1A8
780-461-4941
Fax: 780-461-6067
www.petroleumenviro.com
Products/Services/Areas of Expertise: Services include environmental site assessments (ESA Phases I-III), petroleum storage tank installations & removals; soil & groundwater remediation
Contact(s):
Eion MacKeigan, P.Eng., General Manager

Petromax Ltd.
16A Fielding Ave.
Dartmouth, NS B3B 1E1
902-468-3333
Fax: 902-468-8636
info@petromaxltd.com
www.petromax.ca
Products/Services/Areas of Expertise: Energy equipment
Contact(s):
Henry Lopez, Manager

Petrozyme Technologies Inc.
7496 Wellington Rd., RR#3
Guelph, ON N1H 6H9
519-767-2299
sales@petrozyme.ca
www.petrozyme.com
Contact(s):
Bill Mullin, Manager, Business Development

Pharmatox Inc.
#301, 800 Windmill Rd.
Dartmouth, NS B3B 1T3
902-468-1095
Fax: 902-468-1097
info@pharmatox.ca
www.pharmatox.ca
Products/Services/Areas of Expertise: Liquid/hazardous waste management
Contact(s):
Greg Johnstone, President

Phason Electronics
2 Terracon Place
Winnipeg, MB R2J 4G7
204-233-1400
Fax: 204-233-3252
sales@phason.ca
www.phason.ca
Products/Services/Areas of Expertise: Laboratory equipment; measuring & monitoring equipment
Contact(s):
Ed Restau, Sales Manager

PHH ARC Environmental Ltd.
A member company of The Pinchin Group
Formerly: PHH Environmental Ltd.#406, 13251 Delf Pl.
Richmond, BC V6V 2A2
604-244-8101
Fax: 604-244-8491
877-322-4744
info@phharcenv.com
www.phharcenv.com
Firm Type: Engineering, Scientific/Technical Services
Founded: 1981
Member of: American Industrial Hygiene Association; Canadian Registered Board of Industrial Hygienists; National Asbestos Council of Canada; Association of Professional Engineers & Geoscientists of BC; BOMA BC; Association of Professional Engineers & Geoscientists of Saskatchewan; Association of Professional Engineers, Geologists & Geophycists of Alberta
Products/Services/Areas of Expertise: Environmental services: risk management, site assessment, waste management, underground storage tanks, environmental site support, site safety, health & emergency response plans, ozone depleting substances surveys, environmental compliance audits; regulated material management: surveys, action plans & management programs for controlling regulated materials in buildings & industry (asbestos, lead, PCB, UFFI, mercury), abatement projects, laboratory services; occupational hygiene & safety: development & implementation of health & safety programs, contaminants & air quality investigation & remediation, noise evaluation & control, education & training courses
Domestic Markets:
National
Foreign Activity:
Australia/New Zealand, USA
Markets Sought:
Australia/New Zealand
Contact(s):
John Holland, President
Steve Wilk, Regional Manager
Don Jakul, Vice-President, Regional Management

Canadian Branches:

Calgary
#111, 11505 35 St. SE
Calgary, AB T2Z 4B1
403-250-5722
Fax: 403-291-0612
djakul@phharcenv.com
Domestic Markets:
National
Don Jakul

Edmonton
#200, 9707 - 110 St.
Edmonton, AB T5K 2L9
780-425-6600
Fax: 780-425-5126
swilk@phharcenv.com
Domestic Markets:
National
Steve Wilk

Kelowna
#202 - 451 Adams Rd.
Kelowna, BC V1X 7R9
250-491-9111
Fax: 250-491-9167
877-322-4744
info@phharcenv.com
Domestic Markets:
National
S. Cooper

Keremeos
1960 Osprey Lane
Cawston, BC V0X 1C1
250-499-0090
Fax: 250-499-0085
877-322-4744
jbagley@phharcenv.com
Domestic Markets:
National
Jim Bagley

Prince George
P.O. Box 22041
Prince George, BC V2N 4Z8
250-592-9203
Fax: 250-592-9239
kmuirhead@phharcenv.com
Domestic Markets:
National
Kathy Muirhead

Red Deer
Unit 14
7471 Edgar Industrial Bend
Red Deer, AB T4P 3Z5
403-347-0713
Fax: 403-347-8733
877-322-4744
info@pphharcenv.com
Domestic Markets:
National,
Greg Pippus

Regina
605 Park Street
Regina, SK S4N 5N1
306-352-8640
Fax: 306-352-3063
877-322-4744
info@phharcenv.com
Domestic Markets:
National
C. Benoit

Saskatoon
210 Cardinal Crescent
Saskatoon, SK S7L 6H8
306-244-8799
Fax: 306-653-2057
info@phharcenv.com
Domestic Markets:
National
Mark Huston

Victoria
Unit B
4259 Commerce Circle
Victoria, BC V8Z 4M2
250-592-9203
Fax: 250-592-9239
877-322-4744
kmuirhead@phharcenv.com
Domestic Markets:
National
Kathy Muirhead

Nakusp
P.O. Box 160
107 Burton Main Rd.
Burton, BC V0G 1E0
250-265-4232
Fax: 250-265-4235
877-322-4744
info@phharcenv.com
Domestic Markets:
National

Philip Doyle Manufacturing Inc.
75 Covington St.
Hamilton, ON L8E 2Y4
905-561-0545
Fax: 905-561-5858
info@philipdoyle.com
www.philipdoyle.com
Firm Type: Manufacturing
Founded: 1966
Products/Services/Areas of Expertise: Engineered cooling systems & control rooms, including pulpit, mobile, caster cooler & crane HVAC units

Philom Bios Inc.
3935 Thatcher Ave.
Saskatoon, SK S7R 1A3
306-657-8200
Fax: 306-975-1215
888-744-5662
philom@philombios.ca
www.philombios.com
Firm Type: Manufacturing
Founded: 1980
Staff: 68
Member of: Canadian Seed Trade Association
Products/Services/Areas of Expertise: Biological products for plant growing industry, including inoculants & fertility efficiency tools
Activities: Research & development of biological products based on naturally ocurring micro organisms to enhance plant productivity; replacement & reduction of agricultural chemicals
Financial Information:
Type of Ownership: Publicly Traded
Revenue: Greater than $5 Million
Revenue Sources: 100% Private Contracts
Domestic Markets:
National
Foreign Activity:
Australia/New Zealand, USA
Contact(s):
Calvin. Sonntag, President
Sanford Gleddie, Vice-President, Research & Business Development
Trevor Thiessen, Vice-President, Commercial Operations

Canadian Branches:
Australia
Australi
-618-8303-7142
Sandy Gleddie

Phoenix Biomedical Products Inc.
7085 Tomken Rd.
Mississauga, ON L5S 1R7
905-670-8299
Fax: 905-670-0195
stardish@phoenix-biomed.com
www.phoenix-biomed.com
Firm Type: Manufacturing
Founded: 1980
Staff: 50
Member of: Canadian Medical Technologies consortium; Association of Ontario Medical Manufacturers
Quality Environmental Management System(s): 9002
EcoLogo Certified Products & Services: Star Dish, line of petri dishes
Products/Services/Areas of Expertise: Manufactures high-quality sterile Petri dishes; STARTDISH, the only laboratory product to be awarded the EcoLogo, allows up to 35% reduction in the amount of plastic used to manufacture each dish, reducing disposal waste & cost
Ecological Note: Star Dish, line of petri dishes
Financial Information:
Type of Ownership: Private
Foreign Activity:
Worldwide

Phoenix Contact Ltd.
235 Watline Ave.
Mississauga, ON L4Z 1P3
905-890-2820
Fax: 905-890-0180
800-890-2820
Firm Type: Distributing, Manufacturing
Founded: 1983
Staff: 25
Quality Environmental Management System(s): 9002
Products/Services/Areas of Expertise: Water & wastewater management; water & wastewater management equipment; measuring & monitoring equipment; interconnection devices; modules; interface equipment; transient voltage surge; suppression equipment
Financial Information:
Type of Ownership: Private
Domestic Markets:
National,
Contact(s):
A. Sobotta, Co-General Manager, Marketing
asobotta@phoenixcontact.ca
Nick Henry, National Sales Manager

Phoenix Engineering Inc.
#103, 2710 - 3 Ave. NE
Calgary, AB T2A 2L5
403-248-9463
Fax: 403-250-7811
info@phoenixengg.com
www.phoenixengg.com
Firm Type: Engineering
Founded: 1985
Staff: 5
Products/Services/Areas of Expertise: Established to meet the need for applied resource assessments & wind farm array design expertise in the wind industry; Provides turn-key installations of wind monitoring systems & wind resource analysis software
Domestic Markets:
National
Foreign Activity:
Caribbean, Mexico, USA
Contact(s):
David R. Baker, President
Gerard Philpott, Vice-President, Engineering & Operations

Photech Environmental Solutions
600 Read Rd.
St Catharines, ON L2R 7K6
905-938-9465
Fax: 905-938-8978
877-938-9465
sbarlow@photech-env.com
www.photech-env.com
Firm Type: Scientific/Technical Services, Waste Management
Founded: 1997
Staff: 10
Products/Services/Areas of Expertise: Service, transport & disposal of hazardous waste materials; on-site services for smaller generators
Financial Information:
Type of Ownership: Private
Revenue: $500,000 - $1.5 Million
Revenue Sources: 100% Private Contracts
Domestic Markets:
Ontario, Québec
Foreign Activity:
USA
Contact(s):
Fergal J. McDonough, Sales
Shawn Barlow, Operations

Pigmalion Environmental Services Group
Formerly: Pigmalion Environmental Products
5128 Everest Dr.
Mississauga, ON L4W 2R4
905-602-4349
Fax: 905-602-6760
800-387-7581
sales@pigmalion.ca
www.pigmalion.ca
Firm Type: Distributing
Founded: 1986
Staff: 20
Member of: Community Awareness Emergency Response
Products/Services/Areas of Expertise: Handling problems with liquids (respond, absorb, contain, reduce)
Financial Information:
Type of Ownership: Private
Domestic Markets:
Alberta, British Columbia, Ontario, Québec
Foreign Activity:
Western Europe
Contact(s):
Donald Redford, President
donaldr@pygmalion.ca
Rashmi Weila, Vice-President, Sales
rashmiw@pygmalion.ca

Piikuni Utilities Corp.
P.O. Box 70
Brocket, AB T0K 0H0
403-965-3001
Fax: 403-965-3009
peiganut@telusplanet.net
Products/Services/Areas of Expertise: Government agencies independent power producer
Contact(s):
William Big Bull, Project Coordinator

Pildysh Technologies Inc.
Formerly: Pildysh & Associates Consultants Ltd.
Also Known As: Pildysh Engineering Inc.
#288, 200 Rivercrest Dr. SE
Calgary, AB T2C 2X5
403-720-6699
Fax: 403-720-6609
info@pildyshtech.com
www.pildyshtech.com
Firm Type: Engineering
Founded: 1987
Staff: 15
Member of: American Concrete Institute
Products/Services/Areas of Expertise: Engineering & construction services, new products & technologies for construction, oil & gas & other industries; waste management & utilization; building materials & products; environmental containments & liners; specialty concrete works for severe environments
Recently Completed / Ongoing Projects: Utilization of slag in building products; utilization of oil-contaminated sand in building products; development of sulfur binder for hazardous waste stabilization/encapsulation
Financial Information:
Type of Ownership: Private
Revenue Sources: 100% Private Contracts
Domestic Markets:
National
Foreign Activity:
Central Europe, Eastern Europe, Western Europe, USA
Markets Sought:
Mexico, USA
Contact(s):
Mike Pildysh, M.Eng, P.Eng., President
Mark Krahn, Ph.D., Manager
Contact(s):
Richard Bueble, P.Eng.

Products & Services Buyer's Guide

Canadian Branches:
R&D Laboratory
6214 - 90 Ave. SE
Calgary, AB T2C 2T3
403-720-7889
Fax: 403-720-7890

Pilot Performance Resources Management Inc.
Bramalea Woods
P.O. Box 68584
1235 Williams Pkwy. East
Brampton, ON L6S 6A1
905-792-3130
Fax: 905-792-3047
jpilot@pilotiso.com
www.pilotiso.com
Firm Type: Management Consulting
Founded: 1994
Member of: Canadian Environmental Auditing Association; Toronto Board of Trade; Board of Environmental Auditor Certification - U.S.; Algonquin-Power Liaison Committee
Products/Services/Areas of Expertise: ISO training: web-ISO e-learning, on-site; Consulting in management systems ISO; Auditing, international management systems, GAPS
Recently Completed / Ongoing Projects: ISO 14001 & OHSAS 18001 integration implementation with ISO 9001 Quality; ISO e-learning, first in North America
Financial Information:
Type of Ownership: Private
Revenue: $100,000 - $250,000
Revenue Sources: 5% nationwide; 5% Provincial; 5% Municipals; 85% Private Contracts
Domestic Markets:
National
Foreign Activity:
Worldwide
Markets Sought:
Australia/New Zealand, China, The Pacific Rim, Vietnam
Contact(s):
Jayne Pilot, President/CEO

Pinch Group
#1000, 1175 Douglas St.
Victoria, BC V8W 2E1
250-405-2420
Fax: 250-405-2499
877-405-2400
pinchgroup@raymondjames.ca
www.pinchgroup.ca
Firm Type: Financial
Staff: 5
Member of: Social Investment Organization
Products/Services/Areas of Expertise: Offers investment management & financial planning; incorporates ethics into the investment process; the website provides a resource on ethical, socially responsible or environmental/green investing
Domestic Markets:
Alberta, British Columbia, Ontario
Contact(s):
Brian Pinch, Senior Financial Advisor
Frank Arnold, Associate Financial Advisor
Michael Higgins, Associate Financial Advisor

Canadian Branches:
Toronto
Scotia Plaza
P.O. Box 415
#5300, 40 King St. West
Toronto, ON M5H 3Y2
416-777-7000
Fax: 416-777-7020
1-877-363-1024

Vancouver
Cathedral Place
#2100, 925 West Georgia St.
Vancouver, BC V6C 3L2
605-659-8000
Fax: 605-659-8099
1-888-545-6624

Vancouver
#800, 333 Seymour St.
Vancouver, BC V6B 5E2
604-654-1111
Fax: 604-654-0209
1-888-545-6624

Pinchin Environmental Ltd.
A member company of The Pinchin Group
2470 Milltower Crt.
Mississauga, ON L5N 7W5
905-363-0678
Fax: 905-363-0681
855-746-2446
rconnelly@pinchin.com
www.pinchin.com
Firm Type: Management Consulting, Engineering, Scientific/Technical Services
Founded: 1981
Staff: 195
Member of: PHH ARC Environmental Limited; PHH Environmental (U.K.); Pinchin LeBlanc Environmental Ltd.; Le Groupe Gesfor, Poirier, Pinchin inc.
Products/Services/Areas of Expertise: Environmental engineering, & health & safety services; sustainability & building sciences; emissions reduction & compliance; environmental due diligence & remediation; lab services for asbestos, lead, mould & odour; indoor air quality; hazardous materials management; occupational health & safety; training
Financial Information:
Type of Ownership: Private
Revenue: Greater than $5 Million
Domestic Markets:
National
Contact(s):
Don Pinchin, President & Owner
Jeff Grossi, B.A., C.A., COO
Contact(s):
Ron LeBlanc
Contact(s):
Steve Wilk
Contact(s):
Ross O'Keefe
Contact(s):
John Holland
Contact(s):
Jeremy Donovan
Contact(s):
Jo-Ann Costley
Contact(s):
Paul Staeben

Canadian Branches:
Hamilton
#11, 875 Main St. W.
Hamilton, ON L8S 4P9
905-577-6206
Fax: 905-577-6207
rwagner@pinchin.com
Rob Wagner, C.E.T.

Kenora
#A1, 10 Main St.
Kenora, ON P9N 1S7
807-468-4110
Fax: 807-468-7674
dwiebe@pinchin.com
Dale Wiebe

Ottawa
#200, 515 Leggett Dr.
Kanata, ON K2K 3G4
613-592-3387
Fax: 613-592-5897
lbackman@pinchin.com
Larry Backman

Southwestern Ontario
30 Queen St. S.
Tilbury, ON N0P 2L0
519-682-4492
Fax: 519-682-4693
gmanning@MNSI.net
Graham Manning, C.E.T.

Waterloo
#103, 470 Weber St. N.
Waterloo, ON N2L 6J2
519-746-4210
Fax: 519-746-7108
rparker@pinchin.com
Rob Parker, B.Sc., CIH

Winnipeg
54 Terracon Place
Winnipeg, MB R2J 4G7
204-452-0983
Fax: 204-453-0788
dstefanchuk@pinchin.com
Don Stefanchuk, C.E.T.

Dartmouth - Pinchin LeBlanc Environmental Ltd.
42 Dorey Ave.
Dartmouth, NS B3B 0B1
902-461-9999
Fax: 902-461-9932
rleblanc@pinchinleblanc.com
www.pinchinleblanc.com

Edmonton - PHH ARC Environmental Limited
#200, 9707 - 110 St.
Edmonton, AB T5K 2L9
780-425-6600
Fax: 780-425-5126
877-322-4744
swilk@phharcenv.com
www.phharcenv.com

Labrador City - Pinchin LeBlanc Environmental Ltd.
30 Circular Rd.
Labrador City, NL A2V 2K3
709-944-6766
Fax: 709-944-6764
rokeefe@pinchinleblanc.com
www.pinchinleblanc.com

Montréal - Le Groupe Gesfor, Poirier, Pinchin inc.
#211, 6705, rue Jean-Talon est
Montréal, QC H1S 1N2
514-251-1313
Fax: 514-251-1818
800-529-5870
quebec@gesfor.com
www.gesfor.com

Québec - Le Groupe Gesfor, Poirier, Pinchin inc.
#202, 730, rue Godin
Québec, QC G1M 2K4
418-681-1999
Fax: 418-681-5553
866-681-1999
info@gesfor.com
www.gesfor.com

Richmond - PHH ARC Environmental Limited
#406, 13251 Delf Place
Richmond, BC V1X 2A2
604-244-8101
Fax: 604-244-8491
info@phharcenv.com
www.phharcenv.com

Saint John - Pinchin LeBlanc Environmental Ltd.
69-E Marr Rd.
Rothesay, NB E2E 3J9
506-848-1981
Fax: 506-849-8262
jdonovan@pinchinleblanc.com
www.pinchinleblanc.com

Saskatoon - PHH ARC Environmental Limited
210 Cardinal Cres.
Saskatoon, SK S7L 6H8
306-244-8799
Fax: 306-653-2057
877-322-4744
jcostley@phharcenv.com
www.phharcenv.com

St. John's - Pinchin LeBlanc Environmental Ltd.
27 Austin St., 2nd Fl.
St. John's, NL A1B 4C3
709-754-4490
Fax: 709-754-1359
pstaeben@pinchinleblanc.com
www.pinchinleblanc.com

PINTER & Associates Ltd. / PAL
#4, 320 Jessop Ave.
Saskatoon, SK S7N 1Y6
306-244-1710
Fax: 306-933-4986
pintermain@pinter.ca
www.pinter.ca
Firm Type: Management Consulting, Engineering
Founded: 1998
Staff: 14

Member of: Association of Professional Engineers & Geoscientists of Saskatchewan; Saskatchewan Environment Industry Managers Association; Consulting Engineers of Saskatchewan
Products/Services/Areas of Expertise: Consulting services in the areas of environment, safety & geotechnical engineering; environmental services in Phases I, II, III ESAs; water system audits; environmental audits; site remediation, safety programs, safety training, safety audit
Recently Completed / Ongoing Projects: Assessment & remediation in two heavy metal contaminated sites for SK Environment; Environmental screening report for Indian & Northern Affairs Canada; Phase I & II ESA of entire First National reserves; assessments & cleanup of hundreds of contaminated sites of hydrocarbons, metals, dioxins, furans, etc.
Financial Information:
Type of Ownership: Private
Revenue: $500,000 - $1.5 Million
Revenue Sources: 20% nationwide; 10% Provincial; 20% Municipals; 50% Private Contracts
Domestic Markets:
Alberta, British Columbia, Manitoba, Saskatchewan
Contact(s):
Lawrence Pinter, CEO
Henry Dayday, Director, Marketing
Erika Ritchie, Environmental Manager
Dana Fenske, Project Engineer
Sherry Cochran, Project Engineer

Pioneer Envelopes Ltd.
4978 - 275th St.
Langley, BC V4W 0A3
604-607-4441
Fax: 604-607-4442
800-597-6276
raheem@pioneerenvelopes.com
www.pioneerenvelopes.com
Firm Type: Distributing, Manufacturing
Founded: 1922
EcoLogo Certified Products & Services: Envelopes made from recycled paper, brand name Recycleopes
Products/Services/Areas of Expertise: All types of standard & special sized envelopes are produced from Environmental ChoiceM certified recycled paper.
Ecological Note: Envelopes made from recycled paper, brand name Recycleopes
Contact(s):
Raheem Merali, President

Pioneer Petroleums
5360 South Service Rd.
Burlington, ON L7L 5L1
905-633-3424
Fax: 905-639-2490
info@pioneer.ca
www.pioneer.ca
Firm Type: Distributing
Founded: 1956
Staff: 100
EcoLogo Certified Products & Services: Enviroclean gasoline
Products/Services/Areas of Expertise: Ethanol-blended gasoline
Recently Completed / Ongoing Projects: All blends of gasoline having up to 10% ethanol added
Ecological Note: Enviroclean gasoline
Financial Information:
Type of Ownership: Private
Revenue: Greater than $5 Million
Revenue Sources: 100% Private Contracts
Domestic Markets:
Ontario
Foreign Activity:
USA
Contact(s):
Timothy W. Hogarth, President/CEO
Geoff Hogarth, Director, Marketing
Brian Kitchen, Vice-President, Retail Operations

Pipe Specialties Canada
661 Justus Dr.
Kingston, ON K7M 4H5
613-384-2500
Fax: 613-384-2900
888-772-7473
psc@pipespecialties.com
www.pipespecialties.com

Firm Type: Distributing
Founded: 1993
Staff: 13
Member of: NACE International - The Corrosion Society; Canadian Professional Sales Association
Products/Services/Areas of Expertise: Design, distribution, fabrication & installation of fibreglass pipe, fibreglass valves, fibreglass grating & stainless steel couplings
Financial Information:
Type of Ownership: Private
Revenue Sources: 10% nationwide; 10% Provincial; 10% Municipals; 70% Private Contracts
Domestic Markets:
National
Foreign Activity:
Africa, South America, Mexico, USA
Contact(s):
Robert Leonard, President
Carol Anne Leonard, Vice-President
Canadian Branches:
Western
#102, 4910 Builders Rd. SE
Calgary, AB T2G 4C6
403-273-4900
Fax: 403-253-4950

Pisces Environmental Consulting Services Ltd.
#25, 37337 Burnt Lake Trail
Red Deer, AB T4S 2K5
403-347-5418
Fax: 403-347-0681
Firm Type: Scientific/Technical Services
Founded: 1981
Staff: 6
Products/Services/Areas of Expertise: Fisheries resource assessment; environmental impact assessment
Financial Information:
Type of Ownership: Private
Revenue Sources: 30% Provincial; 10% Municipals; 60% Private Contracts
Domestic Markets:
Alberta, British Columbia,

Piteau Associates
Also Known As: Piteau Associates Engineering Ltd.
#215, 260 Esplanade West
North Vancouver, BC V7M 3G7
604-986-8551
Fax: 604-985-7286
info@piteau.com
www.piteau.com
Firm Type: Engineering
Founded: 1977
Member of: Canadian Environment Industry Association; Consulting Engineers of BC
Products/Services/Areas of Expertise: Performs studies in geophysics, economic geology, rock mechanics, open pit slope design, tunnels, dams, highways, mines, hydrogeology, soil & groundwater remediation, tailings, & site reclamation
Financial Information:
Type of Ownership: Private
Domestic Markets:
National
Foreign Activity:
Worldwide
Contact(s):
Alan F. Stewart, President, Geotechnical Engineering
Andrew Holmes, Vice-President, Hydrogeology
International Branch(es):
Peru Office
Calle Jorge Vandorghen 234, Miraflores
Lima 18 Peru
-(51-1) 421-3034
Fax: -(51-1) 440-309
peru@piteau.com

Plad Équipement Ltée
680, de la Sablière
Bois-des-Filion, QC J6Z 4T7
450-965-0224
Fax: 450-965-1571
plad@plad.com
www.plad.com
Firm Type: Distributing, Manufacturing
Founded: 1959

Staff: 65
Quality Environmental Management System(s): 9002; ISO
Products/Services/Areas of Expertise: Pumps & pumping systems
Financial Information:
Revenue Sources: 5% nationwide; 5% Provincial; 5% Municipals; 85% Private Contracts
Domestic Markets:
Alberta, British Columbia, New Brunswick, Newfoundland & Labrador, Nova Scotia, Ontario, Québec, Saskatchewan
Foreign Activity:
USA
Canadian Branches:
British Columbia
#109A, 81 Golden Dr.
Coquitlam, BC V3K 6R2
604-464-1166
Fax: 604-464-3668
Mike Hilton, Branch Manager

Québec
1795, boul Hamel ouest
Québec, QC G1N 3Y9
418-681-7281
Fax: 418-682-5937

Toronto
#8, 1380 Matheson Blvd.
Mississauga, ON L4W 4M1
905-624-8952
Fax: 905-624-5543

Plains Environmental Inc.
P.O. Box 519
Melville, SK S0A 2P0
306-728-3636
Fax: 306-728-3660
pein@sk.sympatico.ca
www.plainsenvironmental.com
Firm Type: Waste Management
Founded: 1992
Staff: 6
Products/Services/Areas of Expertise: Oil field waste disposal & recovery facility
Financial Information:
Type of Ownership: Private
Revenue Sources: 100% Private Contracts
Domestic Markets:
Manitoba, Saskatchewan
Contact(s):
Wad Hillier, General Manager

Plan-it Environmental Consulting Ltd.
P.O. Box 68
Wembley, AB T0H 3S0
780-831-8995
Fax: 780-766-2480
nickw@telusplanet.net
Contact(s):
Nick Kuszniryk, President

Planning & Engineering Initiatives Ltd.
379 Queen St. South
Kitchener, ON N2G 1W6
519-745-9455
Fax: 519-745-7647
www.peil.net
Products/Services/Areas of Expertise: Parks & recreation master plans, environmental & land use studies; site plans; rehabilitation of gravel pits
Contact(s):
Paul Puopolo, President & CEO
John Ariens, Vice President
David R. Sisco, Secretary-Treasurer
John Torrance-Perks, Director
Sergio Manchia, Director
John Perks, Senior Engineer
Canadian Branches:
Hamilton Branch
#200, 360 James St. North, East Wing
Hamilton, ON L8L 1H5
905-546-1010
Fax: 905-546-1011
John Ariens, Director of Development

Products & Services Buyer's Guide

Planning Alliance
Formerly: John Van Nostrand Associates Ltd.
#205, 317 Adelaide St. West
Toronto, ON M5V 1P9
416-593-6499
Fax: 416-593-4911
info@planningalliance.ca
www.planningalliance.ca
Products/Services/Areas of Expertise: Urban planning & environmental engineering services; integrated, community-based urban development & services projects
Domestic Markets:
National
Contact(s):
John van Nostrand, Partner
Graeme Burt, Partner
Anna Dunets Wills, Associate

Plant Products Co. Ltd.
314 Orenda Rd.
Brampton, ON L6T 1G1
905-793-7000
Fax: 905-793-9632
Products/Services/Areas of Expertise: Nitrogenous & phosphatic fertilizers; prepared fertilizer mixtures; pesticides
Activities: Biotechnology; nitrogenous fertilizers; phosphatic fertilizers; prepared fertilizer mixtures; pesticides
Contact(s):
Roger Fisher
Jennifer Hale

Plasma Environmental Technologies Inc.
#300, 1100 Burloak Dr.
Burlington, ON L7L 6B2
905-332-9792
Fax: 905-332-9792
contact@plasmaenvironmental.com
www.plasmaenvironmental.com
Firm Type: Distributing, Manufacturing
Founded: 1994
Products/Services/Areas of Expertise: Transportable plasma arc system for destruction of liquid hazardous wastes
Domestic Markets:
National
Foreign Activity:
Asia, Eastern Europe, South America, Mexico, USA
Contact(s):
Alex Falconer, CFO/Chair
Wayne Maddever, CEO/President
Laszlo Heredy, Chief Scientist

Plast-Ex International Inc.
15 Armthorpe Rd.
Brampton, ON L6T 5M4
905-793-3600
Fax: 905-793-2500
postoffice@plast-ex.com
www.plast-ex.com
Firm Type: Waste Management
Founded: 1988
Staff: 30
Member of: Environment & Plastic Institute of Canada, Society of the Plastics Industry
Products/Services/Areas of Expertise: Recycling/reprocessing of plastic waste materials; marketing, export development of reprocessed material
Domestic Markets:
Ontario
Foreign Activity:
Asia
Contact(s):
Frank Chang, President
Lily Chang, General Manager

Plasti-Fab Ltd.
#270, 3015 - 5 Ave. NE
Calgary, AB T2A 6T8
403-569-4312
Fax: 403-248-9325
jwhalen@plastifab.com
www.plastifab.com
Firm Type: Distributing, Manufacturing
Founded: 1970
EcoLogo Certified Products & Services: PlastiSpan thermal insulation
Products/Services/Areas of Expertise: EPS, expanded polystyrene, product solutions for commercial, residential & geotechnical engineered applications throughout North America.
Ecological Note: PlastiSpan thermal insulation
Contact(s):
Jim Whalen, Manager, Technical Marketing
jwhalen@plastifab.com

Plasticair Inc.
Formerly: Plasticair Systems Inc.
1275 Crestlawn Dr.
Mississauga, ON L4W 1A9
905-625-9164
Fax: 905-625-0147
sales@plasticair.com; info@plasticair.com
www.plasticair.com
Firm Type: Engineering, Manufacturing
Founded: 1980
Staff: 12
Products/Services/Areas of Expertise: Air pollution control equipment for corrosion-resistant environments
Domestic Markets:
Alberta, British Columbia, Manitoba, Nova Scotia, Ontario, Québec, Saskatchewan
Foreign Activity:
Asia, South America, Mexico, USA
Contact(s):
Paul Sixsmith, President/CEO

Plastichem Consulting
3965 Juan de Fuca Terrace
Victoria, BC V8N 5W9
250-721-0732
Fax: 250-472-2546
dmwiles@telus.net
Firm Type: Scientific/Technical Services
Founded: 1990
Staff: 3
Member of: Chemical institute of Canada; American Chemical Society
Products/Services/Areas of Expertise: Consulting on controlled lifetime plastics; degradation; stabilization; compostability of plastics; new product development; expert witness services
Financial Information:
Type of Ownership: Private
Domestic Markets:
British Columbia
Foreign Activity:
USA
Contact(s):
David M. Wiles, President

Plastics America
#21 & 22, 212 Wyecroft Rd.
Oakville, ON L6K 3T9
905-337-7475
Fax: 905-337-7634
sales@plasticsamerica.ca
www.plasticsamerica.ca
Firm Type: Distributing, Engineering, Manufacturing
Founded: 1972
Staff: 25
Products/Services/Areas of Expertise: Industrial plastic piping systems, PVC, HDPE, PP, PVDF; custom machining & fabrication of components for water & air pollution control equipment; tanks from 5 to 10,000 gallons; secondary containment, especially concrete lining
Financial Information:
Type of Ownership: Private
Revenue Sources: 5% nationwide; 95% Private Contracts
Domestic Markets:
National

Plastiglas Industries Limited
403 Clements Rd. West
Ajax, ON L1S 6N3
905-428-2002
Fax: 905-428-1975
customerservice@plastiglas.on.ca
www.plastiglas.on.ca
Firm Type: Manufacturing
Founded: 1971
Staff: 35
Products/Services/Areas of Expertise: Interior/exterior fiberglass furnishings which include waste containers & recyclers, planters, tables seating, displays & cases; architectural cladding, retrofit & restoration; Stratum, a recycled fiberglass composite material use in cladding systems & urban furnishings, table tops
Domestic Markets:
National
Foreign Activity:
Western Europe, The Pacific Rim, USA
Contact(s):
Steve Baker, President/CEO
Rick Baker, Vice-President
Sandy Taylor, Manager, Marketing
Becky Beverage, Office Manager

Canadian Branches:
Versatech
7460, De Chambois
Montréal, QC H3R 3E6
514-738-0188
Fax: 514-738-3804
Danielle Couture

Plastrec Inc.
1461, rue Lépine
Joliette, QC J6E 4B7
450-760-2333
Fax: 450-760-2444
info@plastrec.ca
www.plastrec.ca
Firm Type: Waste Management
Founded: 1992
Products/Services/Areas of Expertise: Plastics recycling
Contact(s):
Louis Robitaille, Contact

Plein Disposal
#1, 84 Howard Ave.
Elmira, ON N3B 2E1
519-669-5136
Fax: 519-669-3405
Firm Type: Waste Management
Staff: 11
Products/Services/Areas of Expertise: Waste management; waste & recycling services
Financial Information:
Type of Ownership: Private
Revenue: $500,000 - $1.5 Million
Revenue Sources: 80% Municipals; 20% Private Contracts
Domestic Markets:
Ontario
Contact(s):
Adolph Plein, President

PlymoVent Canada Inc.
#24, 1200 Aerowood Dr.
Mississauga, ON L5T 1X2
905-564-4748
Fax: 905-564-4609
800-465-0327
info@plymovent.ca
www.plymovent.ca
Firm Type: Distributing
Member of: Canadian Welding Institute
Products/Services/Areas of Expertise: Products & equipment for air pollution control; air handling equipment

Pneus Métro Inc.
6750, rue Léger
Montréal, QC H1G 1L5
514-328-4222
Fax: 514-328-7930
888-685-4222
info@pneusmetro.com
www.pneusmetro.com
Products/Services/Areas of Expertise: Recycling services; recycled rubber products
Contact(s):
Jean Arcand

Point Four Systems Inc.
#100, 13720 Mayfield Pl.
Richmond, BC V6V 2E4
604-273-9939
Fax: 604-273-9937
800-267-9936
info@pointfour.com
www.pointfour.com
Firm Type: Distributing, Engineering, Manufacturing
Founded: 1988
Staff: 15

Member of: BC Salmon Farmers Association; BC Water & Waste Association; Canadian Aquaculture Association; American Fisheries Society; Canadian Environment Industry Association; Aquaculture Suppliers Association; International Ozone Association
Products/Services/Areas of Expertise: Systems for the measurement, control & diffusion of oxygen & other gases in water, such as oxygen injection equipment, portable meters & sensors, monitoring & control systems, oxygen generators & aquaculture equipment
Recently Completed / Ongoing Projects: Wedge-Lock - latest in diffuser technology; Aqua-Net Sensor; total dissolved gas pressure monitor; microbes for pond & lake aeration
Financial Information:
Revenue Sources: 20% nationwide; 5% Provincial; 5% Municipals; 70% Private Contracts
Domestic Markets:
National
Foreign Activity:
Africa, Australia/New Zealand, China, Western Europe, South America, USA, Vietnam
Contact(s):
Brian Hirsch, General Manager
Walter Volberg, Sales

Pointe-Claire Technology Centre
240, boul Hymus
Pointe-Claire, QC H9R 1G5
514-630-9524
Fax: 514-630-9379

Canadian Branches:
Pointe-Claire Technology Centre
240, boul Hymus
Pointe-Claire, QC H9R 1G5
514-630-9524
Fax: 514-630-9379
Contact(s):
Jim Graham, Manager
jgraham@polrnet.com

Pol R Enterprises Inc.
Formerly: Georges Nadeau Inc.
8300, Place Lorraine
Anjou, QC H1J 1E6
514-493-9000
Fax: 514-493-6643
800-361-0489
nadeaum@polrnet.com
www.polrnet.com
Firm Type: Distributing, Information Technology, Manufacturing
Founded: 1962
Member of: Nadeau (QC); IMPRO (ON); Scotia Insulations (Eastern Canada); IMAP Audits Inc. (Sarnia); Artik/OEM Inc. (ON, QC, MB)
Member of: Thermal Insulation Association of Canada
Quality Environmental Management System(s): 9001; 9003
Products/Services/Areas of Expertise: Industrial & commercial insulation products; specialty products & services include fire-stops, sound attenuating materials for the transportation industry, asbestos removal, & acoustical & thermal insulation & components for the OEM sector
Domestic Markets:
New Brunswick, Newfoundland & Labrador, Nova Scotia, Ontario, Prince Edward Island, Québec
Foreign Activity:
Africa, Caribbean, The Pacific Rim, USA, United Kingdom
Markets Sought:
Asia, Central Europe, South America, Mexico

Contact(s):
Dorothy Clark
Contact(s):
Paul Desrochers, Director of Operations

Canadian Branches:
Ajax - Artik/OEM Inc.
560B Finley Ave.
Ajax, ON L1S 2E3
905-428-8728
Fax: 905-428-7066
Products/Services/Areas of Expertise: Specialized insulation systems & products for the transportation sector

Dartmouth - Scotia Insulations
20 Borden Ave.
Dartmouth, NS B3B 1C8

902-468-8333
Fax: 902-468-5805
csns@polrnet.com
Firm Type: Distributing, Manufacturing
Founded: 1974

Mississauga - IMPRO
5265 General Rd.
Mississauga, ON L4W 2K4
905-602-1486
Fax: 905-602-8166
impro@polrnet.com

Mount Pearl - Scotia Insulations
Donavan's Industrial Park
134 Clyde Ave.
Mount Pearl, NL A1N 4S1
709-747-6688
Fax: 709-747-6699
csnf@polrnet.com

Point Edward - IMPRO
#129, 704 Mara St.
Point Edward, ON N7V 1X4
519-383-6977
Fax: 519-383-7874

Québec - Artik/OEM Inc.
5085, rue Rideau
Québec, QC G2E 5P9
418-872-1860
Fax: 418-872-5172
866-412-7845
Products/Services/Areas of Expertise: Specialized insulation systems & products for the transportation sector

Saint John - Scotia Insulations
363 Old Black River Rd.
Saint John, NB E2J 4Y2
506-632-7798
Fax: 506-632-8193
csnb@polrnet.com

Sarnia - IMAP Audits Inc.
#402B, 546 Christina St. N.
Sarnia, ON N7T 5W6
519-333-6869
Fax: 519-333-6855
imapaudits.com
Products/Services/Areas of Expertise: Comprehensive industrial audits in the areas of asbestos management, insulation, fireproofing, coatings, heat tracing, & secondary containment

Winnipeg - Artik/OEM Inc.
2262 Springfield Rd.
Winnipeg, MB R2C 2Z2
204-222-0714
Fax: 204-222-0601
Products/Services/Areas of Expertise: Specialized insulation systems & products for the transportation sector

Pol-E-Mar Inc.
9 Antares Dr.
Nepean, ON K2E 7K5
613-723-1541
Fax: 613-723-8692
800-250-9224
info@polemar.com
www.polemar.com
Firm Type: Distributing, Manufacturing
Founded: 1990
Staff: 10
Products/Services/Areas of Expertise: Oil spill control equipment, including booms, portable storage tanks, power packs, sorbents, pumps, oil/water separators
Domestic Markets:
National
Foreign Activity:
The Middle East, The Pacific Rim, USA
Markets Sought:
Caribbean, South America
Contact(s):
John McKim, General Manager
johnm@polemar.com
Contact(s):
André Leclerc

Canadian Branches:
Dartmouth
11 Frazee Ave.
Dartmouth, NS B3B 0A5
902-466-2151
Fax: 902-466-2264

Polar Bear Health Equipment Supplies
Also Known As: Polar Bear Water Distillers
9342 - 118 Ave.
Edmonton, AB T5G 0N4
780-477-1328
Fax: 780-474-5770
800-661-9954
wanda@polarbearhealth.com
Firm Type: Manufacturing
Founded: 1947
Staff: 10
Member of: Canadian Health Food Association; Better Business Bureau; Edmonton Chamber of Commerce
Products/Services/Areas of Expertise: Water distillers; water dispensers; water filters; health products; vegetable juicers; reverse osmosis water purification; UV water sterilizers
Financial Information:
Type of Ownership: Private
Revenue: $500,000 - $1.5 Million
Revenue Sources: 100% Private Contracts
Domestic Markets:
National
Foreign Activity:
USA
Contact(s):
Wanda Bradbury, Manager

Polaris Corporate Services Inc.
Formerly: Beak Corporate Services Inc.
P.O. Box 106
#106, 1656 Martin Dr.
Surrey, BC V4A 6E7
604-541-1083
tdelaney@polariscorp.ca
www.polariscorp.com
Products/Services/Areas of Expertise: Management consulting; Environmental Auditing services
Contact(s):
Tom Delaney, Contact

Pollutech Group of Companies Inc.
Also Known As: Pollutech Environmental Consultants
#5, 768 Westgate Rd.
Oakville, ON L6L 5N2
905-847-0065
Fax: 905-847-3840
gbrown@pollutechgroup.com
www.pollutechgroup.com
Firm Type: Scientific/Technical Services
Founded: 1969
Staff: 30
Member of: Canadian Association for Environmental Analytical Laboratories; Canadian Environment Industry Association; Canadian Environment Auditing Association; Canadian Manufacturers & Exporters
Products/Services/Areas of Expertise: Member companies include Pollutech Environmental Limited, Pollutech Enviroquatics Limited, Pollutech Geoenvironmental Limited, Pollutech International Limited; provides plant audits, decommissioning studies, environmental risk assessments, expert testimony, corporate consulting & advisory services, process evaluations in effluent & water treatment; atmospheric discharges, hazardous industrial wastes; waste recovery & utilization; testing facilities; natural environment & workplace environment services
Recently Completed / Ongoing Projects: Dept. of Foreign Affairs environmental inspections - 153 properties in 27 countries; biodigester project in Nicaragua - design & project management for large distillery; Ministry of Environment - survey of water treatment facilities at Ontario campgrounds; petrochemical plant - investigation & remediation program for contaminated sediment
Domestic Markets:
National
Foreign Activity:
Africa, Asia, Central America, Western Europe, The Middle East, Mexico, USA
Contact(s):
Tim Moran, President
G.M. Brown, Vice-President, Oakville

Products & Services Buyer's Guide

Canadian Branches:
Point Edward Branch
704 Mara St.
Point Edward, ON N7V 1X4
519-339-8787
Fax: 519-336-6965
tmoran@peql.net
Tim S. Moran, Vice-President (Sarnia)

Polychem Products Ltd.
725, rue Gaudette
Saint-Jean-sur-Richelieu, QC J3B 7S7
450-348-7392
Fax: 450-348-0564
www.polychemproducts.com
Products/Services/Areas of Expertise: Processing of thermoplastic scrap & waste; involved in a pilot project for recycling of post-consumer plastic waste
Domestic Markets:
National
Foreign Activity:
Asia, Western Europe, USA
Contact(s):
Gianni Berloni, General Manager

Polyland Industries Ltd.
#1, 14231 Burrows Rd.
Richmond, BC V6V 1K9
604-270-0811
Fax: 604-270-7897
Firm Type: Manufacturing
Founded: 1986
Products/Services/Areas of Expertise: Reprocessing of factory waste plastic (pelletizing); plastic scrap trader
Domestic Markets:
Alberta
Foreign Activity:
China, USA, Vietnam
Contact(s):
Joe Lam, President
M.A. Butler, Vice-President & General Manager

Polyrama Plastics (1987) Ltd.
12345 - 149 St. NW
Edmonton, AB T5L 2J5
780-545-3202

Pomeroy Consulting Engineers Limited
#400, 6450 Roberts St.
Burnaby, BC V5G 4E1
604-294-5800
Fax: 604-294-0400
info@pomeroy.ca
www.pomeroy.ca
Firm Type: Engineering
Founded: 1965
Staff: 24
Member of: BC Water & Waste Association; American Water Works Association
Products/Services/Areas of Expertise: Engineering consultant for site development, on-site wastewater management & disposal, drainage & grading solutions; environmentally sustainable solutions
Domestic Markets:
British Columbia, Yukon Territory
Markets Sought:
Asia
Contact(s):
John Wallace, P.Eng., President
Yvonne Hartfiel, Business Development
Douglas Sinclair, P.Eng., Manager, Civil Engineering

Pompaction inc.
119, boul Hymus
Montréal, QC H9R 1E5
514-697-8600
Fax: 514-697-0343
action@pompaction.com
www.pompaction.com
Firm Type: Distributing
Founded: 1979
Staff: 25
Member of: Association québécoise des techniques de l'eau; Association des entrepreneurs de services en environnement du Québec; Association de la construction du Québec
Products/Services/Areas of Expertise: Sewage treatment equipment systems; pumps; pump controller; seals; packings; sales; repairs; parts; rental; maintenance; water handling products & equipment; leachate pumping equipment/systems; measuring & monitoring systems
Recently Completed / Ongoing Projects: Supplied pumps for St-Amable, Contrecoeur & Havre St-Pierre
Financial Information:
Revenue Sources: 40% Municipals
Domestic Markets:
National
Contact(s):
Sylvain Gagnier, President & General Manager
Francis Gagnier, Vice-President & Sales Manager
Yannick Beaulé, Asst. Sales Manager

Canadian Branches:
Abitibi
1804, Jean-Jacques Cossette
Val-d'Or, QC J9P 4N9
819-874-5298
Fax: 819-874-5299
cpoirier@pompaction.com

Québec
2409, rue Dalton
Sainte-Foy, QC G1P 3S5
418-657-7775
Fax: 418-657-1861
athiboutot@pompaction.com

Pompage Express M.D. Inc.
121, Industrielle
Delson, QC J0L 1G0
450-632-9467
Fax: 450-632-9410
800-693-3023
info@pompage-express.com
www.pompage-express.com
Firm Type: Scientific/Technical Services
Staff: 18
Products/Services/Areas of Expertise: Environmental remediation; drain, sewer, aqueduct cleaning & rehabilitation; contamination detection; industrial decontamination; recycling, treatment, & disposal of dangerous substances
Contact(s):
Michel Donais

Pompco inc.
345, boul Labbé Nord
Victoriaville, QC G6P 1B1
819-758-1581
Fax: 819-758-4837
800-263-1581
service@pompco.com
www.pompco.com
Firm Type: Manufacturing
Founded: 1978
Staff: 10
Products/Services/Areas of Expertise: Sewage treatment equipment; water pumps for agricultural, residential & light industrial uses
Activities: Water pumps
Financial Information:
Type of Ownership: Private
Revenue Sources: 100% Private Contracts
Domestic Markets:
New Brunswick, Nova Scotia, Ontario, Prince Edward Island, Québec
Foreign Activity:
Mexico, USA
Markets Sought:
Mexico, USA
Contact(s):
Bernard Garand, President
Yves Allard, Controller

Pompe Saguenay Enr.
#108, 1700, boul Saint-Paul
Chicoutimi, QC G7J 4N1
418-545-7605
Fax: 418-545-8690
mroy!@videotron.ca
Contact(s):
Martin Roy

Pompex Inc.
105, rue Dean
Cowansville, QC J2K 3Y2
450-263-1441
Fax: 450-263-9012
pompex@pompex.com
www.pompex.com
Firm Type: Distributing
Founded: 1978
Products/Services/Areas of Expertise: Water & wastewater pumps
Contact(s):
Daniel Couture

Port of Entry Inc.
Medio Ambiente Online
#7, 5 Tyre Ave.
Toronto, ON M9A 1C5
416-234-5057
Fax: 416-234-8030
info@portofentry.com
www.portofentry.com
Products/Services/Areas of Expertise: Bilingual portal for the environmental sector in the Americas, promoting innovation; publishes environmental information; audience is comprised on environment related professionals in consulting companies, industry, universities, government & ngos
Contact(s):
Alejandra Rojo, President

Porta-Mini Systems
10 Cedar Ave.
Thornhill, ON L3T 3V9
416-221-6660
info@portamini.com
www.portamini.com
Products/Services/Areas of Expertise: Storage tanks/systems
Domestic Markets:
Ontario
Contact(s):
Howard Waisglass

Poscor Group
Formerly: Metal Services Group - Division of Philip Services Corp.
P.O. Box 39
670 Strathearne Ave. North
Hamilton, ON L8H 7H7
905-547-8888
Fax: 905-547-9994
866-794-8625
info@poscor.com
www.poscor.com
Firm Type: Waste Management
Founded: 1998
Products/Services/Areas of Expertise: Recycling of ferrous scrap metals
Financial Information:
Type of Ownership: Publicly Traded
Domestic Markets:
National
Foreign Activity:
Western Europe, USA
Contact(s):
Nigel Morgan, Owner

Positive Results Environmental Management Ltd.
P.O. Box 4
Delta, BC V4K 3N5
604-946-6332
Fax: 604-940-6929
Contact(s):
C.F. Askin, President

Pottinger Gaherty Environmental Consultants Ltd.
#1200, 1185 Georgia St. West
Vancouver, BC V6E 4E6
604-682-3707
Fax: 604-682-3497
888-557-5548
info@pggroup.com
www.pggroup.com
Firm Type: Engineering, Scientific/Technical Services
Founded: 1991
Member of: Canadian Environment Industry Association
Products/Services/Areas of Expertise: Site investigations: preliminary 1, 2 & detailed; soil, groundwater & sediment remediation; risk assessment; hazardous building materials; industrial environmental services; strategic advice; environmental impact assessments; environmental inventories;

environmental opinions & reviews; monitoring; land use planning; public consultation; approvals: federal, provincial, municipal approval processes
Recently Completed / Ongoing Projects: Certificate of compliance, Pacific Press Lands, Vancouver; environmental impact assessment of hydroelectric project, Yukon; enviro planning of large urban residential project
Domestic Markets:
British Columbia, Ontario
Foreign Activity:
The Pacific Rim, Mexico, USA
Contact(s):
Edmund L. Pottinger, President
William Gaherty, Vice-President
Susan Wilkins, Vice-President, Environmental Planning

Canadian Branches:
Newmarket
171 Main St.
Newmarket, ON L3Y 3Y9
905-898-5555
Fax: 905-898-5510
1-800-357-8498
info@pggroup.com
Barbara Laskarzewska, E.I.T.

Oshawa
17 Brock St.
Oshawa, ON L1G 1R2
905-579-4908
Fax: 905-579-3207
1-888-888-1395
info@pggroup.com
Staff: 3
John DeWilde, P.Eng.

Power Grow Systems Inc.
8923 Chippawa Creek Rd.
Niagara Falls, ON L2E 6S5
905-357-6421
Firm Type: Waste Management
Founded: 1995
Staff: 4
Products/Services/Areas of Expertise: Organic waste management; compost recycling; organic compost
Contact(s):
C. Pettus, Site Manager
S. Romer, Office Manager

Canadian Branches:
Toronto Branch
C51 Almosa Dr.
North York, ON M2J 2N8
416-222-4138
Fax: 416-222-8578
Ed Ciepiela, Marketing Manager

Power Ignition & Controls
Div. of Spartan Controls
5967 - 103A St. NW
Edmonton, AB T6H 2J7
780-436-9047
Fax: 780-436-5136
info@powerignition.com
www.powerignition.com
Domestic Markets:
Alberta, British Columbia, Saskatchewan

Canadian Branches:
Calgary
305 - 27th St. SE
Calgary, AB T2A 7V2
403-207-0700

Fort St John
10919 Alaska Rd.
Fort St John, BC V1J 6P3
250-785-0285

Grande Prairie
11419 - 98 Ave.
Grande Prairie, AB T8V 5S5
780-539-1161

Power Plant Supply Co.
124 Wilson St.
Oakville, ON L6K 3G8
905-845-7951
Fax: 905-845-6695

Firm Type: Distributing, Manufacturing
Founded: 1956
Staff: 7
Member of: American Water Works Association; Water Environment Federation
Products/Services/Areas of Expertise: Water & wastewater treatment systems & equipment
Recently Completed / Ongoing Projects: Region of Durham Ajax water plant; Humber sewage treatment plant
Financial Information:
Type of Ownership: Private
Revenue Sources: 5% nationwide; 10% Provincial; 55% Municipals; 30% Private Contracts
Domestic Markets:
Ontario,
Contact(s):
Frank Hopkins, Owner

Power Suction Services Ltd. / PSS
1544 Rand Ave.
Vancouver, BC V6P 3G2
604-266-9615
Fax: 604-266-6916
www.psservice.ca
Firm Type: Scientific/Technical Services, Waste Management
Founded: 1958
Staff: 20
Member of: Canadian Environment Industry Association
Member of: National Air Dut Cleaning Association
Products/Services/Areas of Expertise: Supplies high powered equipment for the cleaning of commercial, industrial ventilation & air conditioning systems
Financial Information:
Type of Ownership: Private
Revenue: $500,000 - $1.5 Million
Revenue Sources: 30% nationwide; 30% Provincial; 20% Municipals; 20% Private Contracts
Domestic Markets:
Alberta, British Columbia
Contact(s):
Andrew Perkins, Director, IR Section Manager
Mike McLennan, Director, Account Manager

Power Vac of Nova Scotia
Formerly: Signal Environmental Services Ltd.
933 Cobequid Rd.
Waverley, NS B0N 2S0
902-860-2425
Fax: 902-860-2629
cflynn@enviroclean.ca
www.powervacofns.com
Products/Services/Areas of Expertise: Indoor air quality services; asbestos abatement services; cleaning systems & services; PCB destruction & disposal; hazardous waste rendering services
Contact(s):
Carney Flynn, General Manager

Canadian Branches:
Power Vac of Newfoundland
155 McNamara Dr.
Paradise, NL A1L 0A7
709-781-3264
Fax: 709-781-3265
866-747-3264
hpower@powervacnl.com
www.powervacofnl.com
Henry Power, President/Operator

Power-Pacific Poles Ltd.
P.O. Box 187
39400 Government Rd.
Squamish, BC V0N 3G0
604-898-3884
Fax: 604-898-3886
contact@powerpacificpoles.com
www.powerpacificpoles.com
Products/Services/Areas of Expertise: Manufacturer of steel multi-sided tapered & straight shafts for uses such as transmission towers, cellular communication towers, area lighting, traffic signal structures, sports field lighting & sign support
Contact(s):
Jorma Rauma, Director

Powerscreen of Canada Ltd.
800 Farewell St.
Oshawa, ON L1H 6N5
905-576-0037
Fax: 905-576-0048
psc@powerscreencanada.com
www.powerscreencanada.com
Firm Type: Distributing, Manufacturing
Founded: 1976
Staff: 12
Products/Services/Areas of Expertise: Mobile screening equipment; trommels for production needs in composting, municipal solid waste, wood grinding & landfill mining
Financial Information:
Type of Ownership: Publicly Traded
Domestic Markets:
Ontario, Québec
Contact(s):
Brian Farmer, President
Eddie Mangan, Manager, Marketing

Powersmiths International Corp.
10 Devon Rd.
Brampton, ON L6T 5B5
905-791-1493
Fax: 905-791-8870
800-747-9627
info@powersmiths.com
www.powersmiths.com
Firm Type: Engineering, Manufacturing
Staff: 400
Quality Environmental Management System(s): 9001; ISO
EcoLogo Certified Products & Services: Energy efficient, harmonic filtering transformers & other electrical system technologies
Products/Services/Areas of Expertise: Manufacturers of harmonic filtering transformers which has three-fold energy & cost saving power quality & environmental protection
Ecological Note: Energy efficient, harmonic filtering transformers & other electrical system technologies
Financial Information:
Type of Ownership: Private
Domestic Markets:
National
Foreign Activity:
Worldwide
Contact(s):
Cyril Eldridge, Manager, Marketing Communications

Powertech Labs Inc.
12388 - 88th Ave.
Surrey, BC V3W 7R7
604-590-7500
Fax: 604-590-5347
info@powertechlabs.com
www.powertech.bc.ca
Firm Type: Engineering, Scientific/Technical Services
Founded: 1980
Staff: 100
Member of: Association for Environmental Analytical Laboratories
Quality Environmental Management System(s): 9001; ISO
Products/Services/Areas of Expertise: Electric & magnetic field evaluations; alternate energy systems; vehicle emission assessment; waste treatment; environmental analytical services; energy-efficiency testing of lighting products, electric motors
Financial Information:
Revenue: $1.5 Million - $3 Million
Revenue Sources: 100% Provincial
Domestic Markets:
Alberta, British Columbia, Ontario
Foreign Activity:
USA,
Contact(s):
Prabha Kundur, President
Nick Dominelli, Director, Applied Chemistry

Poyry (Vancouver) Inc.
Formerly: NLK Consultants Inc.
#200, 1550 Alberni St.
Vancouver, BC V6G 1A5
604-689-0344
Fax: 604-443-1000
info@poyry.com
www.poyry.com

Firm Type: Engineering
Founded: 1974
Staff: 50
Products/Services/Areas of Expertise: Environmental impact assessment; effluent treatment engineering; project & construction management; specializes in pulp & paper industry
Recently Completed / Ongoing Projects: Bleach plant upgrade; stress anslysis; North American Kraft Mill relocation; assistance with environmental issues, primary effluent clarifier; CHIP LD chest by-pass; ARC flash study; forest indutry overview; paper machine upgrade; IMP mill debottle necking; washer improvements; caustic addition to the WESP
Financial Information:
Type of Ownership: Publicly Traded
Revenue: Greater than $5 Million
Domestic Markets:
Alberta, British Columbia, Ontario, Québec, Saskatchewan
Foreign Activity:
Worldwide
Contact(s):
James Mason, President
james.mason@poyry.com
Bob Pedersen, Manager, Business Development
bob.pedersen@poyry.com
Bill Gunning, Manager, Environmental
bill.gunning@poyry.com

Canadian Branches:
Montréal
#700, 5250 rue Ferrier
Montréal, QC H4P 1L6
514-341-3221
Fax: 514-341-3278
criros@nlkmtl.nlkeng.com

PPG Canada, Inc.
Architectural Coatings
4 Kenview Blvd.
Brampton, ON L6T 5E4
905-790-5349
www.ppg.com
Firm Type: Distributing
Founded: 1883
Member of: Canadian Paint Manufacturers Association
EcoLogo Certified Products & Services: Lucite, Olympic, Pittsburgh & Manor Hall paints
Products/Services/Areas of Expertise: PPG Canada Inc. supplies paint products that are formulated for maximum performance, while meeting the environmental standards required in the Canadian marketplace.
Ecological Note: Lucite, Olympic, Pittsburgh & Manor Hall paints
Financial Information:
Type of Ownership: Foreign-owned
Domestic Markets:
National
Contact(s):
Robert Fierheller, Manager, Sales
rfierheller.ppg.com

Prairie Geomatics Ltd.
5 Bison Dr.
Minnedosa, MB R0J 1E0
204-867-5725
Fax: 204-867-5722
888-444-0302
sales@gpszone.ca
www.prairie.mb.ca
Firm Type: Scientific/Technical Services
Founded: 1995
Staff: 5
Member of: Canadian Aeronautics & Space Institute; Canadian Remote Sensing Society
Products/Services/Areas of Expertise: GPS sales/service; GIS; mapping/surveying; remote sensing & image analysis; agriculture/precision farming
Domestic Markets:
National
Contact(s):
Art Dalton, Owner/Manager
art@gpszone.ca

Prairie Western Reclamation & Consturction Inc.
P.O. Box 27
Bienfait, SK S0C 0M0
306-388-2652
Fax: 306-388-2345

Praxair Canada Inc.
#1200, 1 City Centre Dr.
Mississauga, ON L5B 1M2
905-803-1600
Fax: 905-803-1698
800-772-9247
www.praxair.com
Products/Services/Areas of Expertise: Incineration & biotreatment technologies

Canadian Branches:
Edmonton
9020 - 24th St.
Edmonton, AB T6B 2X6
780-467-9000
Fax: 780-467-9009

Montréal
3200, boul Pitfield
Montréal, QC H4S 1K6
514-337-6000
Fax: 514-337-0677

Praxis Environmental
2380 Clifton St.
Halifax, NS B3K 4V1
902-422-7537
Contact(s):
Daniel Rainham, Contact

Praxis Inc.
2215 - 19th St. SW
Calgary, AB T2T 4X1
403-245-6404
Fax: 403-249-8983
888-882-1285
praxinc@praxis.ca
www.praxis.ca
Firm Type: Management Consulting
Founded: 1980
Member of: International Association for Impact Assessment; International Association for Public Participation
Products/Services/Areas of Expertise: Socio-economic assessments & management; development & implementation of public consultation programs; survey research; impact assessments; communications; policy development; facilitating corporate change; delivery of conferences & workshops; business planning
Financial Information:
Type of Ownership: Private
Revenue Sources: 20% nationwide; 30% Provincial; 20% Municipals; 30% Private Contracts
Domestic Markets:
National
Foreign Activity:
China, Western Europe, South America, Vietnam
Contact(s):
Richard Roberts, President
roberts@praxis.ca
Ann McNichol, Sr. Associate
David de Lange, Sr. Associate

Canadian Branches:
Praxis Pacific
3848 St. Georges Ave.
North Vancouver, BC V7N 1W5
604-980-2522
Fax: 604-980-9992
praxpacific@praxis.ca

Praxis Research
Bldg. B1
#242, 2451 Dieppe Ave. SW
Calgary, AB T3E 7K1
403-249-8822
Fax: 403-249-8983
praxresearch@praxis.ca

Precision Assessment Technology Corp. / PATC
Four Bentall Centre
P.O. Box 49224
1055 Dunsmuir St.
Vancouver, BC V7X 1L2
604-669-3371
Fax: 604-669-3353
info@precisiontecha.com
www.precisiontecha.com
Firm Type: Engineering, Scientific/Technical Services
Founded: 1987
Products/Services/Areas of Expertise: Drilling equipment & drilling services for site characterization, ground water assessment & remediation; wells monitoring; ground water & soil decontamination; geophysical logging
Contact(s):
Tony Kirschner, Vice-President, Corporate Development
Contact(s):
Gary Bean

Canadian Branches:
Precision Sampling, Inc..
1081 Essex Ave.
Richmond, CA USA
510-237-4575
Fax: 510-237-4574
cary@precisionsampling.com

Precision Chemical Manufacturing Ltd.
16671 - 113 Ave.
Edmonton, AB T5M 2X2
780-484-5641
Fax: 780-484-5714
800-661-3335
info@precision-chemical.com
www.precision-chemical.com
Firm Type: Manufacturing
Founded: 1979
Staff: 7
Products/Services/Areas of Expertise: Industrial & janitorial cleaning chemical; floor finishes; automotive polishes; waxes; cleaners
Domestic Markets:
Alberta, British Columbia, Manitoba, Saskatchewan
Foreign Activity:
Asia, The Pacific Rim
Contact(s):
Bob Warring, Sales Manager

Precision Identification Biological Consultants
3622 - 3rd Ave. West
Vancouver, BC V6R 1L9
604-734-5048
precid@shaw.ca
Firm Type: Management Consulting
Founded: 1986
Staff: 4
Member of: Registered Professional Biologists of British Columbia
Products/Services/Areas of Expertise: Environmental consulting & contracting services; biological management; environmental impact assessments; habitat inventory; habitat restoration; baseline studies; eelgrass restoration & assessment
Financial Information:
Type of Ownership: Private
Revenue Sources: 50% nationwide; 25% Provincial; 12% Municipals; 13% Private Contracts
Domestic Markets:
British Columbia
Foreign Activity:
USA
Markets Sought:
Caribbean, The Pacific Rim
Contact(s):
Cynthia Durance, President

Precision Industrial Ltd.
P.O. Box 1836
1020 - 1st Ave. NW
Prince Albert, SK S6V 6J9
306-763-7471
Fax: 306-763-6565
ross.pi@sasktel.net
www.precisionindustrialltd.com
Products/Services/Areas of Expertise: Measuring & monitoring equipment; engineering services; conveying systems for waste solids (municipal wastes); screening systems; metering bins; reclaim bins
Contact(s):
Ross Brooks, P. Eng., President

Precisioneering Ltd.
303 Nantucket Blvd.
Toronto, ON M1P 2P2
416-751-9200
Fax: 416-751-9382
800-465-1800
sales@precisioneering.com
www.precisioneering.com

Firm Type: Manufacturing
Founded: 1964
Staff: 60
Products/Services/Areas of Expertise: Air handling equipment; air pollution control equipment; water treatment systems & equipment; corrosion-resistant equipment; liquid & gas processes; hazardous spill containment systems; corrugated plate separators; fiberglass grating, stair treads; ladders & structures
Contact(s):
David Richardson, President
Albert Wan, Product Manager

Premier Envelope
6600 McMillan Way
Richmond, BC V6W 1J7
604-273-9500
Fax: 604-273-8007
800-565-2671
www.premierenvelope.com
Products/Services/Areas of Expertise: All types of envelopes stock & specials
Ecological Note: Envelopes
Contact(s):
Ian Gee, President
Jean Brun, Account Manager

Canadian Branches:
Calgary
4620 Manilla Rd. SE
Calgary, AB T2G 4B7
403-243-8933
Fax: 403-287-9056
Erwin Koehn, Sales Manager

Edmonton
11260 - 184th St. NW
Edmonton, AB T5S 2S6
780-465-0006
Fax: 780-465-0151
800-661-5565
Rick Keys, Operations Manager

Premier Plastics Ltd.
8328 River Way
Delta, BC V4G 1C4
604-952-6686
Fax: 604-952-6696
800-661-4473
tanks@premierplastics.com
www.premierplastics.com
Firm Type: Manufacturing
Founded: 1991
Staff: 9
Member of: Canadian Environment Industry Association
Products/Services/Areas of Expertise: Polyethylene water & chemical storage tanks, septic systems; custom rotational molding
Financial Information:
Type of Ownership: Private
Revenue Sources: 100% Private Contracts
Domestic Markets:
Alberta, British Columbia
Foreign Activity:
Central America, USA
Markets Sought:
South America, Mexico
Contact(s):
John L. Richardson, President

Premier Tech Environment
Premier Tech Environnement
Also Known As: Enterprises Premier CDN
1, av Premier
Rivière-du-Loup, QC G5R 6G1
418-867-8883
Fax: 418-862-6642
800-632-6356
ecoflo@premiertech.com
www.ptaqua.com
Firm Type: Distributing, Manufacturing
Founded: 1923
Staff: 150
Products/Services/Areas of Expertise: On-site wastewater treatment solutions for the residential, commercial & industrial sectors

Financial Information:
Type of Ownership: Publicly Traded
Domestic Markets:
Ontario, Québec
Foreign Activity:
Asia, Western Europe, USA
Contact(s):
Marie-Élaine Ladoucer, Marketing Agent, ext. 6643

Premier Tech Environnement / Division municipale, commerciale et ind
Formerly: Eco Process & Equipment International Inc., Eco Équipment inc.
1 av Premier
Rivière-du-Loup, QC G5R 6C1
418-867-8883
Fax: 418-436-3896
800-632-6356
pte@premiertech.com
www.premiertech.com; www.premiertechenv.com
Firm Type: Distributing, Manufacturing
Founded: 1978
Staff: 20
Quality Environmental Management System(s): 9001
Products/Services/Areas of Expertise: Wastewater treatment process & equipment; sequencing batch reactor system; aerated lagoon system
Recently Completed / Ongoing Projects: Wastewater treatment, Juicy Beef Patties, Jamaica; wastewater treatment plant, China
Financial Information:
Type of Ownership: Private
Revenue: $3 Million - $5 Million
Revenue Sources: 12% nationwide; 13% Provincial; 33% Municipals; 33% Private Contracts
Domestic Markets:
Alberta, New Brunswick, Nova Scotia, Québec
Foreign Activity:
Asia, Caribbean, China, The Pacific Rim, Mexico, USA, Vietnam
Contact(s):
André Clermont, Directeur des opérations

Prescott Paper Products Inc.
Sac au Sol Inc.
201 Richmond Blvd.
Napanee, ON K7R 3Z9
613-354-1330
Fax: 613-354-1923
800-366-6812
gcolgan@bagtoearth.com
www.bagtoearth.com
Firm Type: Manufacturing
Founded: 1946
Staff: 60
EcoLogo Certified Products & Services: Products available under the Bag to Earth name; retailer bags available in private label with in-line four colour printing.
Products/Services/Areas of Expertise: Provides flexible packaging solutions to the waste diversion industry in the form of biodegradable & compostable paper bags which are used for the collection of yard waste, wet organics (food waste) from residences & industrial & commercial institutions across North America. Bag to Earth products are successfully used in a number of cities & municipalities. These EcoLogo certified products need no debagging, are completely biodegrade & compost with the organic contents & assist in a very positive way in the diversion process of reducing the demand on landfill & in the conversion of organic waste into a valuable nutrient rich product, which will be returned back to earth
Ecological Note: Products available under the Bag to Earth name; retailer bags available in private label with in-line four colour printing.
Financial Information:
Type of Ownership: Private
Domestic Markets:
National
Contact(s):
George Colgan, President
gcolgan@ppaper.com

Presentey Engineering Products Ltd.
P.O. Box 919
2784 Fenton Rd., RR#5
Gloucester, ON K1T 3T7
613-822-1251
Fax: 613-822-1256

pepl@presentey.com
www.presentey.com
Firm Type: Engineering, Manufacturing
Founded: 1958
Member of: Canadian Air Traffic Control Association
Products/Services/Areas of Expertise: Air handling equipment; measuring & monitoring equipment; laboratory equipment; transmissometer equipment; wind & altimeter digital display systems; visibility monitors; automated weather observation systems; runway visual range systems
Foreign Activity:
Asia, Western Europe, The Pacific Rim, USA
Contact(s):
Nicole Presentey, General Manager

Preston Phipps Inc.
6400, rue Vanden Abeele
Montréal, QC H4S 1R9
514-333-5340
Fax: 514-333-6680
info@prestonphipps.com
www.prestonphipps.com
Firm Type: Distributing
Founded: 1933
Staff: 90
Products/Services/Areas of Expertise: Distributor of a comprehensive range of industrial steam, valve, HVAC & water treatment products & solutions; products include steam specialties, valves & piping accessories, heating & ventilation systems, laboratory ventilation systems, water treatment solutions, & flow measurement & control equipment; services include pre-sale technical support, warranty maintenance, training & engineered solutions
Domestic Markets:
New Brunswick, Newfoundland & Labrador, Nova Scotia, Ontario, Prince Edward Island, Québec
Contact(s):
Jos J. Paulin, President
jpaulin@prestonphipps.com
Mark Paulin, Vice President, Operations
mpaulin@prestonphipps.com

Canadian Branches:
Burnaby
#214, 4259 Canada Way
Burnaby, BC V5G 1H1
778-328-9888
Fax: 778-328-9889
vancouver@prestonphipps.com

Calgary
#106, 809 Manning Rd.NE
Calgary, AB T2E 7M9
403-272-5199
Fax: 403-273-5180
calgary@prestonphipps.com

Dartmouth
Bldg. E
202 Brownlow Ave., Unit E
Dartmouth, NS B3B 1T5
902-468-2004
Fax: 902-468-2109
dartmouth@prestonphipps.com

Edmonton
9357 - 45th Ave.
Edmonton, AB T6E 5Z7
780-437-5199
Fax: 780-437-5303
edmonton@prestonphipps.com

Mississauga
#12, 171 Ambassador Dr.
Mississauga, ON L5T 2J1
905-795-1300
Fax: 905-795-1310
toronto@prestonphipps.com

Ottawa
#204, 200 Tremblay Rd.
Ottawa, ON K1G 3H5
613-244-6334
Fax: 613-244-6335
ottawa@prestonphipps.com

Québec
755, rue des Rocailles
Québec, QC G2J 1A2

Products & Services Buyer's Guide

418-628-6471
Fax: 418-628-8198
quebec@prestonphipps.com
Saint John
North Market Wharf
#N305, 1 Market Sq.
Saint John, NB E2L 4Z6
506-658-0730
Fax: 506-658-0735
st-john@prestonphipps.com
Sarnia
#202, 429 Exmouth St.
Sarnia, ON N7T 5P1
519-344-2824
Fax: 519-336-0387
sarnia@prestonphipps.com
St. John's
11 Hayfield Place
St. John's, NL A1I 0E3
709-781-8793
Fax: 709-781-8792
jgallant@prestonphipps.com

Pretal
Groupe G & G Ltee
Formerly: Pretal 2000 Inc.6245, boul des Grandes Prairies
Montréal, QC H1P 1A5
514-325-3711
Fax: 514-325-3900
pretal@pretal.com
www.pretal.com
Firm Type: Manufacturing
Founded: 1999
Staff: 4
Products/Services/Areas of Expertise: Access hatch for underground room & roof ladder, handrail, safety post, vent, intermediate landing pedestrian bridges
Financial Information:
Type of Ownership: Private
Revenue: $3 Million - $5 Million
Domestic Markets:
New Brunswick, Nova Scotia, Ontario, Prince Edward Island, Québec
Foreign Activity:
USA
Contact(s):
Alain Brouillette, Manager

Pribusin Inc.
#57, 101 Freshway Dr.
Concord, ON L4K 1R9
905-660-5336
Fax: 905-660-4068
www.pribusin.com
Firm Type: Manufacturing
Founded: 1980
Staff: 10
Products/Services/Areas of Expertise: Process control equipment; isolators; integrators; multiplexers; waste management control equipment
Financial Information:
Type of Ownership: Private
Revenue Sources: 10% nationwide; 60% Provincial; 20% Municipals; 10% Private Contracts
Domestic Markets:
National
Foreign Activity:
Asia, Central Europe, USA
Contact(s):
Jackie Price

PricewaterhouseCoopers Management Consultants
#700, 250 Howe St.
Vancouver, BC V6C 3S7
604-806-7000
Fax: 604-806-7806
www.pwc.com/sustainability
Products/Services/Areas of Expertise: Strategic & feasibility studies of environmental programs & projects; advice on public-private partnerships in infrastructure financing; development of financial models; environment function/management systems review; environmental audits; information systems
Contact(s):

Bruce E. McIntyre, Global Forest & Paper Practice
bruce.mcintyre@ca.pwc.com
Canadian Branches:
Calgary
#1200, 425 - 1 St. SW
Calgary, AB T2P 3V7
403-267-1200
Mel Wilson
Edmonton
2401 Toronto-Dominion Tower, Edmonton Ce
Edmonton, AB T5J 2Z1
780-493-8200
Dave Thompson
Halifax
Central Guaranty Tower
#900, 1801 Hollis St.
Halifax, NS B3J 3N4
902-420-1900
Mike Anaka
Hamilton
P.O. Box 1018
4 Hughson St. South
Hamilton, ON L8N 3R1
905-525-9650
Kitchener
#900, 55 King St. West
Kitchener, ON N2G 4W1
519-579-6300
Mike Carty
London
Canada Trust Tower
#1500, 275 Dundas St.
London, ON N6B 3L1
519-679-9160
Mississauga
Mississauga Executive Centre
#1600, 2 Robert Speck Pkwy.
Mississauga, ON L4Z 1H8
905-272-1200
Montréal
1100, boul René-Lévesque ouest
Montréal, QC H3B 2G4
514-879-5600
Carol Emond
Ottawa
Barrister House
#1100, 180 Elgin St.
Ottawa, ON K2P 2K3
613-238-8200
Roxanne Anderson
Québec
Place de la Cité
#870, 2635, boul Hochelaga
Sainte-Foy, QC G1V 4W2
418-658-5782
Daniel Caboret
Saskatoon
#400, 123 - 2 Ave. South
Saskatoon, SK S7K 7E6
306-244-6164
Lyle Pittman
Toronto
Royal Trust Tower, Toronto-Dominion Cent
#3000, 77 King St. West
Toronto, ON M5K 1G8
416-863-1133
Fax: 416-365-8178
Mike Harris
Vancouver
Price Waterhouse Centre
601 West Hastings St.
Vancouver, BC V6B 5A5
604-682-4711
Bruce McIntyre
Windsor
Bank of Commerce Bldg.
#1200, 100 Ouellette Ave.
Windsor, ON N9A 6T3
519-258-6052

Winnipeg
2200 One Lombard Pl.
Winnipeg, MB R3B 0X7
204-943-7321
Gord Webster

Pridy Associates
8 Shore Ave.
Bedford, NS B4A 2C4
902-835-5570
don@pridyassociates.ns.ca
www.pridyassociates.ns.ca
Firm Type: Management Consulting
Founded: 1993
Staff: 3
Products/Services/Areas of Expertise: Consulting engineers in the areas of building science, geotechnical engineering, materials engineering & environmental science
Contact(s):
Donald Pridy, Managing Principal

Priestly Demolition Inc. / PDI
3200 Lloydtown/Aurora Rd.
Kettleby, ON L0G 1J0
905-841-3735
Fax: 905-841-6282
800-263-2076
info@priestly.ca
www.priestly.ca
Firm Type: Management Consulting, Engineering
Founded: 1993
Staff: 120
Products/Services/Areas of Expertise: Demolition: industrial, commercial, residential; brownfield renewal; site remediation; industrial decommissioning; asbestos removal; asset recovery
Contact(s):
Ryan Priestly, President
Alan Percy, Controller
John Phillips, Project Manager

Primex Packaging Services
Formerly: Jubil Material Management Service
6360 Vipond Dr.
Mississauga, ON L5T 1J9
905-564-2020
Fax: 905-564-2727
info@primexlogistics.com
www.primexlogistics.com
Firm Type: Waste Management
Founded: 1990
Staff: 8
Products/Services/Areas of Expertise: Repackaging of products & quality sorting of \held\"" inventories""
Domestic Markets:
Ontario, Québec
Foreign Activity:
USA
Contact(s):
John Holbrook, General Manager
jholbrook@primexpackaging.com

Prism Chemicals Inc.
#3, 1420 Cornwall Rd.
Oakville, ON L6J 7W5
905-337-1874
Fax: 905-337-0328
888-538-3300
fborges@prismchemicals.com
www.prismchemicals.com; www.eco-max.ca
Firm Type: Manufacturing
Founded: 1999
Member of: Canadian Sanitation Supply Association; International Sanitary Supply Association
EcoLogo Certified Products & Services: Eco-Max Brand Products: MPC-100, 200, 201 Ultra Multi-purpose cleaners; Ultra bathroom cleaner; Ultra glass cleaner; heavy duty cleaner; carpet cleaner; Ultra liquid laundry; Ultra odour neutralizer; graffiti remover; Active ingredients are derived from
Products/Services/Areas of Expertise: Manufacturers of environmentally responsible cleaning products, deodorizing products, skin care products, floor care products; bio-technology based products; Manugacturer of Eco-Max brand of EcoLogo certified, non-toxic, natural cleaning products derived from 100% botanical, sustainable actives
Ecological Note: Eco-Max Brand Products: MPC-100, 200, 201 Ultra Multi-purpose cleaners; Ultra bathroom cleaner; Ultra glass cleaner; heavy duty cleaner; carpet cleaner; Ultra liquid laundry;

Ultra odour neutralizer; graffiti remover; Active ingredients are derived from
Financial Information:
Type of Ownership: Private
Domestic Markets:
National
Foreign Activity:
Asia, The Middle East, USA
Markets Sought:
Asia, Australia/New Zealand, Caribbean, Central Europe, Eastern Europe, Western Europe,
Contact(s):
Felix R. Borges, President/CEO

Pro-Lab Diagnostics
20 Mural St.
Richmond Hill, ON L4B 1K3
905-731-0300
Fax: 905-731-0206
800-268-2341
support@pro-lab.com
www.pro-lab.com
Firm Type: Manufacturing
Founded: 1974
Staff: 15
Products/Services/Areas of Expertise: Laboratory equipment
Contact(s):
Mark Reed, General Manager

ProAgri Consulting Limited
501 Gabriel Rd.
Windsor, NS B0N 2T0
902-798-2114
Fax: 902-798-2542
proagri@ns.sympatico.ca
Products/Services/Areas of Expertise: Agriculture & agronomy management; environmental consulting & contracting services; pest management services
Domestic Markets:
New Brunswick, Newfoundland & Labrador, Nova Scotia, Prince Edward Island
Contact(s):
Kent Groves, Specialist, Marketing
Traci Curry, Specialist, Project Management

Probyn & Company Inc.
67 Yonge St., 16th Fl.
Toronto, ON M5E 1J8
416-777-2800
Fax: 416-777-1190
sgs@probyngroup.com
www.probyngroup.com
Products/Services/Areas of Expertise: Specialists of project financing in energy & environmental projects in excess of $5 million; services include developmental, advisory, contract development, financial structuring & institutional syndication, financings to date in Canada over $800 million. Equity funded in excess of $110 million
Contact(s):
Stephen Probyn, President

Proceco Ltd.
7300, rue Tellier
Montréal, QC H1N 3T7
514-254-8494
Fax: 514-254-8184
800-978-6677
cleaning@proceco.com
www.proceco.com
Firm Type: Engineering, Manufacturing
Founded: 1975
Staff: 110
Quality Environmental Management System(s): 9001
Products/Services/Areas of Expertise: Spray washers using water-based solution to replace vapour degreasers, solvent cleaning systems, hot tanks, etc.; design & manufacture of turntable, belt conveyor & immersion washers; parts cleaning machines using water-based solutions replacing ozone-depleting solvents
Financial Information:
Type of Ownership: Private
Revenue Sources: 100% Private Contracts
Domestic Markets:
National
Foreign Activity:
Worldwide
Contact(s):
Helmut Schauer, CEO
hschauer@proceco.com
Robert Burns, President
Robert Daoust, Director, Sales

Procedair Industries Inc.
625, av President Kennedy, 14e étage
Montréal, QC H3A 1K2
514-284-0341
Fax: 514-284-1326
Firm Type: Scientific/Technical Services
Founded: 1982
Staff: 50
Member of: Air & Waste Management Association
Products/Services/Areas of Expertise: Air pollution control systems for acid gas scrubbing; cold & hot gas dedusting
Recently Completed / Ongoing Projects: Aluminum smelters dry scrubbers; dust collection for Cement Kilns
Domestic Markets:
National
Foreign Activity:
Central America, South America, Mexico, USA
Markets Sought:
Asia
Contact(s):
Bernard Cloutier, General Manager
Andrew Haberl, Sales Director

Process Innovations Canada Inc.
#B, 530 Massey Rd.
Guelph, ON N1K 1B4
519-763-1852
process@freespace.net
Firm Type: Distributing
Founded: 1994
Products/Services/Areas of Expertise: Scrubbing equipment wet & dry; particulate emissions monitoring
Financial Information:
Type of Ownership: Private
Revenue Sources: 100% Private Contracts
Domestic Markets:
Ontario, Québec
Contact(s):
Jay Millman, Vice-President
Kim Harrington, Customer Service Representative

Proctor & Gamble Inc.
4711 Yonge St., 15th Fl.
Toronto, ON M2N 5M5
416-730-4711
Fax: 416-730-5950
www.pg.com
Firm Type: Manufacturing
Staff: 100
Products/Services/Areas of Expertise: Chemicals; powder & liquid household detergents; washing & cleaning preparations; polishes, waxes & related preparations; household chemical specialties
Contact(s):
H. Romeike, Manager, Sales & Marketing
Glenn Parker, Manager, Environmental Quality

Procyon Consulting Inc. / PCI
238 Hickling Trail
Barrie, ON L4M 5W5
705-739-9738
Fax: 705-739-8448
admin@procyon.ca
www.procyon.ca
Firm Type: Management Consulting
Founded: 1991
Staff: 5
Member of: Professional Engineers of Ontario; Ontario Environmental Industries Association
Quality Environmental Management System(s): 9001
Products/Services/Areas of Expertise: ISO 9000 & ISO 14000 training & audits
Financial Information:
Type of Ownership: Private
Revenue: $100,000 - $250,000
Revenue Sources: 5% Municipals; 95% Private Contracts
Domestic Markets:
Ontario
Foreign Activity:
Mexico, USA
Markets Sought:
Australia/New Zealand
Contact(s):
George K. Chamberlin, Principal

Products BCM Ltée BCM
Formerly: BCM Limitée, Produits municipaux
340, Émile Couture
Chicoutimi, QC G7H 8B6
418-545-1698
Fax: 418-545-1206
www.produitsbcm.com
Firm Type: Distributing
Founded: 1975
Quality Environmental Management System(s): 9001:2000
Products/Services/Areas of Expertise: Water & wastewater management equipment; liners, geosynthetic/geomembrane
Contact(s):
Martial Bouchard, President & Directeur Général
Denis Gauthier, Vice-President

Produits Chimiques Handy Ltée
Handy Chemicals Ltd.
120, boul de l'Industrie
Candiac, QC J5R 1J2
450-659-9693
Fax: 450-659-0523
800-265-9693
info@handy-chemicals.com
www.handy-chemicals.com
Firm Type: Manufacturing
Founded: 1956
Member of: American Water Works Association; Association québécoise des techniques de l'eau
Quality Environmental Management System(s): 9002
Products/Services/Areas of Expertise: Superplasticizer components, shotcrete accelerators & specialty dispersants for the gypsum, oil well, textile & leather & pulp & paper industries
Domestic Markets:
National
Foreign Activity:
Asia, Central America, Western Europe, USA
Contact(s):
Nelu Spiratos, President/CEO

International Branch(es):
USA Office
#324, 24200 Chagrin Blvd.
Beachwood, OH USA
216-594-0658
Fax: 216-591-0665
1-800-827-1003
info@handy-chemicals.com

Produits Ferpac Ltée
259, D'Alençon RR 61
Boucherville, QC J4B 5E4
450-655-2468
Fax: 450-655-9101
Products/Services/Areas of Expertise: Manufacturer of range hoods & attic ventilators
Contact(s):
Philip Boisaubert, Director

Proeco Enviroservices Ltd.
7722 - 9 St. NW
Edmonton, AB T6P 1L6
780-440-1825
Fax: 780-440-2428
800-661-5792
darrellh@proeco.com
www.proeco.com
Firm Type: Waste Management
Founded: 1997
Products/Services/Areas of Expertise: Total waste management services, hazardous & non-hazardous materials
Financial Information:
Type of Ownership: Private
Revenue: $500,000 - $1.5 Million
Domestic Markets:
National
Foreign Activity:
USA
Contact(s):
Brian Winters, President
Darrell Hener, Vice-President, Operations

Products & Services Buyer's Guide

Professional Resources Inc.
Affiliate of Both Belle Robb Ltd.
P.O. Box 69
329 Main St. West
Merrickville, ON K0G 1N0
613-238-1744
Contact(s):
David Hammonds, P.Eng.
dh@bbrl.com

Progress Land Services Ltd.
#300, 14815 - 119 Ave. NW
Edmonton, AB T5L 2N9
780-454-4717
Fax: 780-454-6172
mail@progressland.com
www.progressland.com
Firm Type: Management Consulting
Founded: 1984
Staff: 31
Products/Services/Areas of Expertise: Surface land services
Financial Information:
Type of Ownership: Private
Domestic Markets:
Alberta, British Columbia, Manitoba, Saskatchewan
Contact(s):
Elliott Friedrich, President/General Manager
elliottf@progressland.com

Project Engineering Limited
778 King St.
Fredericton, NB E3B 1G2
506-450-2930
Fax: 506-451-0415
project@proejectengineering.ca
Firm Type: Engineering
Founded: 1987
Staff: 10
Member of: American Water Works Association; Maritime Provinces Water & Wastewater Association; New Brunswick Environmental Industry Association; Consulting Engineers of New Brunswick
Products/Services/Areas of Expertise: Municipal & environmental engineering; consulting & design services to municipalities, industry & private developers
Recently Completed / Ongoing Projects: Wastewater treatment environmental impact assessment, Town of Oromocto; Hwy 101 upgrade, Wastewater treatment collection & pumping system, Village of New Maryland; Two Nations crossing overpass, city of Fredericton; water & sewer main crossing, Saint John River, City of Fredericton; water reservoir & pumphouse, Woodstock First Nations; Wastewater treatment evaluation, NB Salmon Growers Association
Financial Information:
Type of Ownership: Private
Domestic Markets:
New Brunswick
Contact(s):
John M. McKinney, P.Eng., President
Stephen Pyke, P.Eng., Senior Environmental Engineer

Prolab Technolub / PROLAB
Formerly: Prolab-Bio Inc.
4531, rue Industrielle
Thetford Mines, QC G6H 2J1
418-423-2777
Fax: 418-423-7619
800-795-2777
prolab@minfo.net
www.prolab-technologies.com
Firm Type: Manufacturing
Founded: 1985
Staff: 32
Member of: Society of Tribologists and Lubrication Engineers
Quality Environmental Management System(s): 9001
EcoLogo Certified Products & Services: Biodegradable synthetic hydraulic lubricants for hydraulic, chain & pneumatic applications including Bio-Chain, Hy-Bio & Air-Bio
Products/Services/Areas of Expertise: Manufactures & distributes 150 high quality products dedicated to preventive maintenance for industry & commercial vehicles; lubricants (including biodegradable), bio-lubricants, biodegreaser, cleaners, bio rust-proofing, car care products, after market additives
Recently Completed / Ongoing Projects: Biorustproofing
Ecological Note: Biodegradable synthetic hydraulic lubricants for hydraulic, chain & pneumatic applications including Bio-Chain, Hy-Bio & Air-Bio
Financial Information:
Type of Ownership: Publicly Traded
Revenue: $3 Million - $5 Million
Revenue Sources: 2% nationwide; 2% Provincial; 10% Municipals; 86% Private Contracts
Domestic Markets:
Alberta, British Columbia, Manitoba, New Brunswick, Newfoundland & Labrador, Nova Scotia, Northwest Territories, Ontario, Prince Edward Island, Québec
Foreign Activity:
Central America, Central Europe, Eastern Europe, South America, Mexico
Contact(s):
Jean-Guy Grenier, President
Chantal Grenier, General Manager
Christian Perron, Manager, Sales
Nicole Cadoret, Biologist

Proline Filter Systems Inc.
P.O. Box 5429
High River, AB T1V 1M5
403-652-5124
Firm Type: Waste Management
Founded: 1992
Staff: 3
Products/Services/Areas of Expertise: Mobile fluid filtration & reclamation service; on-site filtration of most contaminated fluids; glycol recycling
Recently Completed / Ongoing Projects: Reclaiming pipeline hydrotest water for surface disposal; reclaiming process solvents (amines & glycols) in gas plants to prevent replacement & disposal
Financial Information:
Type of Ownership: Private
Revenue Sources: 100% Private Contracts
Domestic Markets:
National

Promag Enviro Systems Ltd.
Formerly: H.D. Fowler Co. Ltd.
8042 Winston St.
Burnaby, BC V5A 2H5
604-421-6844
Fax: 604-421-6842
866-449-2781
info@promagenviro.ca
www.promagenviro.ca
Firm Type: Distributing
Founded: 1994
Staff: 3
Member of: British Columbia Water & Waste Association; Water Environment Federation
Products/Services/Areas of Expertise: Manufacturers' representative & distributor of municipal sewage treatment plant equipment, metering pumps & controllers, filters, test kits; water & wastewater treatment equipment & processes; installation & on-site service; in-house repair services; parts & supplies
Recently Completed / Ongoing Projects: Sludge Cake pumps, screenings compactor, Lulu Island, BC; trickling filter media, Annacis Island, BC; sludge dewatering, Montrose & Port McNeill, BC; chemical metering systems, Port Simpson & Kitkatla, BC
Financial Information:
Type of Ownership: Private
Revenue: $500,000 - $1.5 Million
Revenue Sources: 5% nationwide; 10% Provincial; 50% Municipals; 35% Private Contracts
Domestic Markets:
Alberta, British Columbia, Saskatchewan,
Contact(s):
Ken G. Magaw, President
kmagaw@promagenviro.ca
Mike Magaw, Manager, Technical Sales
mike@promagenviro.ca

Promens Canada Inc.
Formerly: Bonar Plastics Corporation, Saeplast Canada, Dynoplast
100 Industrial Dr.
Saint John, NB E2L 3Y5
506-633-0101
Fax: 506-658-0227
800-567-3966
www.bonarplastics.com
Firm Type: Management Consulting, Manufacturing, Waste Management
Founded: 1979
Staff: 80
Products/Services/Areas of Expertise: Manufacturing and distribution of insulated containers, pallets, meat buggies & carts, as well as cylindrical buoys for aquaculture industry and serves Canada, the USA, Mexico, and Central and South Americas.
Domestic Markets:
National
Foreign Activity:
Central America, South America, Mexico, USA
Contact(s):
Mike Kilpatrick, Coordinator, East Coast, Sales
mike.kilpatrick@promens.com
Dolores Vogel, Coordinator, Sales, 604-530-2233Fax: 506-657-7100
dvogel@promens.com

Promet Environmental Group Ltd.
#101, 1120 - 53 Ave. NE
Calgary, AB T2E 6N9
403-275-0414
Fax: 403-295-0699
877-577-6638
sales@promet.ca
www.promet.com
Products/Services/Areas of Expertise: Air pollution control equipment; air measuring & monitoring equipment
Contact(s):
William A. Murray, President

ProMinent Fluid Controls Ltd.
490 Southgate Dr.
Guelph, ON N1G 4P5
519-836-5692
Fax: 519-836-5226
sales@prominent.ca
www.prominent.ca
Firm Type: Manufacturing
Founded: 1960
Staff: 45
Member of: Ontario Pollution Control Equipment Association
Products/Services/Areas of Expertise: Metering pumps; chemical measurement & control equipment/systems; sensors; chlorine dioxide generators; ozone generators; polymer preparation & feed systems; automatic backwash gravity filters; chromate, cyanide & nitrite control systems; zebra mussel control systems; subsidiaries & distributors in 60 countries
Activities: Water, wastewater, phosphate reduction research & development
Financial Information:
Type of Ownership: Private
Revenue Sources: 5% nationwide; 15% Provincial; 20% Municipals; 60% Private Contracts
Domestic Markets:
National
Foreign Activity:
Worldwide
Contact(s):
Garth deBruyn, General Manager
Todd Reeves, Sales
Michael McNulty, Technical Manager

International Branch(es):
USA
RIDC Park West
136 Industry Dr.
Pittsburgh, PA USA
412-787-2484
Fax: 412-787-0704

Promosalons Canada
Also Known As: French Trade Exhibitions
#1120, 1501 av McGill College
Montréal, QC H3A 3M8
514-861-5668
Fax: 514-861-7926
canada.montreal@promosalons.com
www.promosalons.com
Firm Type: Information Technology
Staff: 2
Products/Services/Areas of Expertise: Promotion of international trade exhibitions; Pollutec, the international exhibition of environmental equipment, technology & services, is 1 of approx. 30 shows promoted each year

Financial Information:
Type of Ownership: Non Profit
Foreign Activity:
Worldwide
Contact(s):
Christelle Rey, Contact
crey@promosalons.com

Canadian Branches:
Toronto Office
20 Queen St. West
Toronto, ON M5H 3R3
416-929-3562
800-387-2566
canada.toronto@promosalons.com
Clothilde Meritet, Contact
cmeritet@promosalons.com

ProPower Equipment Ltd.
P.O. Box 42178 PRO Southland
Calgary, AB T2J 7A6
403-255-3888
Fax: 403-255-7445
wordens@telus.net
www.propowerequipment.com
Firm Type: Distributing, Manufacturing
Founded: 1984
Contact(s):
Sean Worden

ProSep Inc.
Formerly: TORR Canada Inc.
1155, rue Wellington
Montréal, QC H3C 1V9
514-522-5550
Fax: 514-522-2643
www.torrcanada.com
Firm Type: Distributing, Manufacturing

Products/Services/Areas of Expertise: The firm provides a comprehensive range of products for oil, gas, & water treatment. ProSep Technologies, Inc., located in Houston, TX, is an affiliate offering water treatment systems, crude oil dehydrators & desalters, internals for scrubbing & demisting, & gas sweetening membranes. ProPure, ProPure ME, & ProSep AP are other affiliates, located in Norway, Bahrain, & Kuala Lumpur
Financial Information:
Type of Ownership: Publicly Traded
Revenue Sources: 100% Private Contracts
Domestic Markets:
Alberta, British Columbia, New Brunswick, Ontario, Québec
Foreign Activity:
Africa, Asia, Australia/New Zealand, Western Europe, The Middle East, The Pacific Rim, South Africa, Mexico, USA, United Kingdom
Contact(s):
Jacques L. Drouin, President/CEO, ProSep Inc.
Lew Mologne, President, ProSep Technologies, Inc.

Proserco Inc.
An operating unit of Dessau, Inc.
#300, 1200, boul Saint-Martin ouest
Laval, QC H7S 2E4
514-281-6500
Fax: 514-668-5532
info@proserco.qc.ca
proserco.qc.ca
Firm Type: Engineering, Scientific/Technical Services
Founded: 1985
Staff: 21
Member of: Dessau, Inc.; LVM-Technisol
Products/Services/Areas of Expertise: Water & wastewater treatment, operations & maintenance
Financial Information:
Type of Ownership: Private
Revenue Sources: 55% Municipals; 45% Private Contracts
Domestic Markets:
Québec
Contact(s):
Gilles Filion, President/CEO

Proshred Security
#100, 245 Yorkland Blvd.
Toronto, ON M2J 4W9
416-297-0875
Fax: 416-297-5618
866-379-5028
proshred@proshred.com
www.proshred.com
Firm Type: Waste Management
Founded: 1986
Products/Services/Areas of Expertise: On-site confidential document destruction
Financial Information:
Type of Ownership: Private
Domestic Markets:
National
Contact(s):
Ron Campbell, CEO
Ken Taylor, CFO

ProSolve Consulting Ltd.
#3, 10012 - 29A Ave. NW
Edmonton, AB T6N 1A8
780-414-1895
Fax: 780-485-3115
info@prosolve.ca
www.prosolve.ca
Firm Type: Management Consulting
Founded: 1987
Staff: 11
Member of: Association of Professional Engineers; Geologists & Geophysicists of Alberta
Products/Services/Areas of Expertise: Operations management consulting services including ISO 14000, ISO 9000, industrial & manufacturing engineering
Recently Completed / Ongoing Projects: Dual ISO 14001 & ISO 9001 for resource company; tank design & engineering for TDG tank manufacturer; industrial plant design & layout
Financial Information:
Type of Ownership: Private
Revenue: $100,000 - $250,000
Revenue Sources: 100% Private Contracts
Domestic Markets:
Alberta, Manitoba, Saskatchewan
Foreign Activity:
USA
Contact(s):
David Hall, President

Proto Manufacturing Ltd.
2175 Solar Cres.
Oldcastle, ON N0R 1L0
519-737-6330
Fax: 519-737-1692
800-965-8378
proto@protoxrd.com
www.protoxrd.com
Firm Type: Manufacturing
Founded: 1967
Products/Services/Areas of Expertise: Measuring & monitoring equipment; residual stress
Financial Information:
Type of Ownership: Private
Domestic Markets:
National
Foreign Activity:
Asia, Western Europe, The Pacific Rim, USA
Contact(s):
Michael Brauss, President

International Branch(es):
American Office
Marquette Bldg.
1980 East Michigan Ave.
Ypsilanti, MI USA
313-965-2900
Fax: 734-485-5732
proto@protoxrd.com

Provincial Airlines Ltd. - Environmental Services Division
Formerly: Provincial Airlines Environmental Services
P.O. Box 29030
St. John's, NL A1A 5B5
709-576-1226
Fax: 709-576-1548
esd@provair.com
www.provair.com/environmental/
Firm Type: Scientific/Technical Services
Founded: 1998
Staff: 19

Products/Services/Areas of Expertise: Environmental consulting & contracting services; occupational health & safety consulting; risk management services
Contact(s):
Pat Barron Jr., Coordinator, Operations

Provincial Environmental Services Inc.
#4, 505 Kenora Ave.
Hamilton, ON L8E 3P2
905-577-0575
Fax: 905-577-0842
800-263-9762
info@provincialenvironmental.com
www.provincialenvironmental.com
Firm Type: Engineering, Scientific/Technical Services
Founded: 1990
Staff: 12
Member of: Chemical Institute of Canada
Products/Services/Areas of Expertise: Transport of industrial hazardous & non-hazardous liquid waste; recycling; reuse & recovery of waste materials; distribution of spill kits, chemical spill & absorbent pads & booms
Activities: Waste management & recycling studies
Domestic Markets:
Ontario
Contact(s):
Vince Gagich, President/CEO
vgagich@provincialenvironmental.com
John Daneliuk, General Manager
jdaneliuk@provincialenvironmental.com

Provincial Partitions Ltd.
6660 Campobello Rd
Mississauga, ON L5N 2L9
905-817-1000
Fax: 905-817-1100
866-551-9256
info@pro-part.com
www.ppimod.com
Firm Type: Manufacturing
Founded: 2005
Member of: The Powder Coating Institute; Modular Building Institute
Quality Environmental Management System(s): 9002
Products/Services/Areas of Expertise: Modular space solutions; full turnkey packages in design, manufacturing, factory trained installations; full product service & support; interior/exterior prefabricated buildings, inplant offices, environmental rooms, custom applications
Recently Completed / Ongoing Projects: Peterborough Regional Health Centre dialysis unit; Sommerset Academy gymnasium; Omron Canada clean room
Financial Information:
Type of Ownership: Private
Revenue: Greater than $5 Million
Domestic Markets:
National
Foreign Activity:
Caribbean, South America, Mexico, USA
Contact(s):
Todd Frankland, President/Owner
Danny Thornhill, Sales Manager

Canadian Branches:
Pointe-Claire Branch
#650, 6600, Transcanada Hwy.
Pointe-Claire, QC H9R 4S2
514-695-5457
Fax: 514-697-0186

International Branch(es):
Orchard Park Branch
PE Engineering Sales
415 Independence Dr.
Orchard Park, NY USA
716-662-0474
Fax: 716-662-0475
paul.enderle@pe-engineering.com
Paul Enderle

ProViro Instrumentation Inc.
3484, Valiquette
Montréal, QC H4S 1X8
514-373-7724
Fax: 514-737-2751
info@proviro.com
www.proviro.com

Products/Services/Areas of Expertise: Distributors of environmental, industrial & process control instrumentation to the water & wastewater treatment, pulp & paper, food, chemical & petrochemical industries
Contact(s):
Chris Castravelli, Founder

PRT Inc. / PRT
Formerly: Pacific Regeneration Technologies Inc.
#101 - 1006 Fort Street
Victoria, BC V8V 3K4
250-546-6713
Fax: 250-381-0252
877-476-9778
customersupportassistants@prt.com
www.prt.com
Firm Type: Management Consulting, Distributing, Scientific/Technical Services
Founded: 1988
Products/Services/Areas of Expertise: Forest seedling production; silviculture operations; horticulture; native plants; conifer seedlings
Financial Information:
Type of Ownership: Publicly Traded
Revenue: Greater than $5 Million
Revenue Sources: 10% Provincial; 90% Private Contracts
Domestic Markets:
Alberta, British Columbia, Ontario, Saskatchewan
Foreign Activity:
USA
Contact(s):
John Kitchen, President/CEO
Rob Miller, CFO & Vice-President, Finance
Herb Markgraf, Vice-President, Business Development

Canadian Branches:
Armstrong
668 St. Anne Rd.
Armstrong, BC V0E 1B5
250-546-6713
Fax: 250-546-8799
armstrong@prtgroup.com
Stewart Haywood-Farmer, Manager

Beaverlodge
P.O. Box 449
Beaverlodge, AB T0H 0C0
780-354-2288
Fax: 780-354-3090
beaverlodge@prtgroup.com
Patrick Graveley, Manager

Campbell River
3820 Snowden Rd.
Campbell River, BC V9H 1P5
250-286-1224
Fax: 250-286-1229
campbellriver@prtgroup.com
Marc Poirier, Manager

Coldstream
10003 Hwy.#6
Vernon, BC V7B 3B6
250-545-0638
coldstream@prtgroup.com
David Chappele, Manager

Dryden
P.O. Box 757
775 Pollard Rd.
Dryden, ON P8N 2Z4
807-937-8360
Fax: 807-937-8361
dryden@prtgroup.com
Scott Carpenter, Manager

Harrop
6320 Harrop - Procter Rd.
Nelson, BC V1L 6P9
250-229-5353, 4344
Fax: 250-229-4154
harrop@prtgroup.com
Dan Livingston

Hybrid
1282 Woolridge Rd.
Pitt Meadows, BC V3Y 1Z1
604-465-6276
Fax: 604-465-9829
hybrid@prtgroup.com

Stewart Howarth, Manager

Kirkland Lake
P.O. Box 20
RR#2, Site 2
Swastika, ON P0K 1T0
705-642-6402
Fax: 705-642-3447
kirklandlake@prtgroup.com
Darcy McElveny, Manager

Prince Albert
P.O. Box 1901
Prince Albert, SK S6V 6J9
306-953-4700
Fax: 306-953-4709
princealbert@prtgroup.com
Grant Harrison, Manager

Red Rock Nursery
18505 Forest Nursery Rd.
Prince George, BC V2N 5Y7
250-963-9199
Fax: 250-963-9230
redrock@prtgroup.com
Mike Thelitz, Manager

Summerland
P.O. Box 1770
Summerland, BC V0H 1Z0
250-494-9899
Fax: 250-494-9844
summerland@prtgroup.com
Ivan Haag, Manager

Summit
4121 Morris Rd.
Telkwa, BC V0J 2X0
250-846-5882
Fax: 250-846-5796
summit@prtgroup.com
Shawn Sponton

Vernon
7501 Bench Rd.
Vernon, BC V1H 1H3
250-542-4100
Fax: 250-542-1200
vernon@prtgroup.com
Chris Mostyn, Manager

International Branch(es):
Nevada
6380 Elizabeth St.
Nevada, NV USA
775-727-4660
Fax: 775-727-4668
nevada@prtgroup.com
Dave McElveny, Manager

Oregon
31783 Meridian Rd. South
Hubbard, OR USA
503-651-3266
Fax: 503-651-3277
oregon@prtgroup.com
Kevin Giles, Manager

PSC Analytical Services
#49, 55 Elizabeth Ave.
St. John's, NL A1A 1W9
709-754-0203
Fax: 709-754-8612
rwhelan@philipinc.com
Contact(s):
Rob Whelan, Laboratory Manager

Publications Ontario
50 Grosvenor St.,
Toronto, ON M7A 1N8
416-326-5300
Fax: 416-325-3407
800-267-8097
www.publications.serviceontario.ca/ecom
Products/Services/Areas of Expertise: Publications Ontario distributes many, but not all, Government of Ontario publications

Pumps & Systems
Division of 1107809 Ontario Ltd.
Formerly: Abaxial Associates Inc.#1 - 1112 Russell St.
Thunder Bay, ON P7B 5N2

807-622-3767
Fax: 807-622-3804
888-690-2203
sales@pumpsandsystems.com
www.pumpsandsystems.com
Firm Type: Distributing
Founded: 1973
Staff: 5
Products/Services/Areas of Expertise: Sewage grinder pumps stations & associated products for low pressure sewer systems; water, wastewater, steam products
Financial Information:
Revenue Sources: 10% Provincial; 30% Municipals; 60% Private Contracts
Domestic Markets:
Ontario
Contact(s):
Bill Horkey, President

Pure Energy Battery Inc.
Formerly: Pure Energy Battery Corp
35 Pollard St.
Richmond Hill, ON L4B 1A8
905-707-9577
Fax: 905-707-7435
800-769-2439
info@pureenergybattery.com
www.pureenergybattery.com
Firm Type: Distributing, Manufacturing
Founded: 1993
Quality Environmental Management System(s): 9001
EcoLogo Certified Products & Services: Pure Energy Rechargeable Alkaline Batteries; Pure Energy Enviro Charger; Pure Energy Charge Pal
Products/Services/Areas of Expertise: Alkaline batteries; Chargers; Electronics
Ecological Note: Pure Energy Rechargeable Alkaline Batteries; Pure Energy Enviro Charger; Pure Energy Charge Pal
Financial Information:
Type of Ownership: Private
Domestic Markets:
National
Foreign Activity:
Worldwide
Contact(s):
Josef Daniel-Ivad, Vice-President, Research & Development
Stephen Meldrum, President & General Manager
Pat Terrio, Vice-President, Operations

Pure Energy Inc.
30 Pollard St.
Richmond Hill, ON L4B 1C3
905-707-9577
Fax: 905-707-7435
800-868-5756
www.pureenergybattery.com
Firm Type: Distributing, Manufacturing
EcoLogo Certified Products & Services: Rechargeable alkaline batteries
Products/Services/Areas of Expertise: Manufacturer & distributor of rechargeable alkaline batteries, battery chargers, & cordless telephones. Pure Energy is to date the world's sole manufacturer of the long-lasting, environmentally superior rechargeable alkaline battery. Manufacturing facility located in Amherst, NS
Ecological Note: Rechargeable alkaline batteries
Financial Information:
Type of Ownership: Publicly Traded
Contact(s):
D. Wayne Hartford, President/CEO
whartford@pevi.ca
Josef Daniel-Ivad, Vice President, Research & Development
josef@pureenergybattery.com
Stephen Meldrum, Director, Business Development
smeldrum@pevi.ca
Jeff Chalmers, Assistant General Manager
jchalmers@pevi.ca
Contact(s):
Pat Terrio, Vice-President

Canadian Branches:
Amherst
Operations
41 Tantramar Cres.
Amherst, NS B4H 4J6

902-667-4100
Fax: 902-667-4684
pterrio@pevi.ca

Puresource Inc.
7018 Wellington Rd. 124 South
Guelph, ON N1H 6J4
519-837-2140
Fax: 519-937-1584
800-265-7245
www.puresource.ca
Firm Type: Distributing
Founded: 1989
Staff: 9
Member of: Canadian Health Food Association
Quality Environmental Management System(s): 9002
Products/Services/Areas of Expertise: A broker & distributor of a broad range of natural products, including herbal, nutritional & sport supplements, herbal & medicinal teas, homeopathics, personal care products, non-dairy beverages & energy bars, & environmentally friendly cleaners for the home
Recently Completed / Ongoing Projects: New Canadian labels to meet new CCR regulations
Financial Information:
Type of Ownership: Private
Revenue: $100,000 - $250,000
Revenue Sources: 100% Private Contracts
Domestic Markets:
National
Contact(s):
Gary Masse, National Sales Manager
gary.masse@puresource.ca
Teresa Egerton, Inside Sales Manager
teresa.egerton@puresource.ca
Joanne Johnson, Eastern Sales Manager
joanne.johnson@puresource.ca

Purifics ES Inc.
340 Sovereign Rd.
London, ON N6M 1A8
519-473-5788
Fax: 519-473-0934
info@purifics.com
www.purifics.com
Firm Type: Engineering, Manufacturing
Founded: 1993
Staff: 7
Products/Services/Areas of Expertise: Unique solutions to purify, condition & control water & air; proprietary technologies to promote sustainable development, dramatically reduce lifecycle costs, eliminate risk & prevent waste. The firm houses production facilities, offices, laboratory & automation department
Financial Information:
Type of Ownership: Private
Revenue Sources: 5% nationwide; 95% Private Contracts
Domestic Markets:
Alberta, New Brunswick, Nova Scotia, Ontario
Foreign Activity:
Australia/New Zealand, The Pacific Rim, USA
Markets Sought:
Western Europe, The Middle East, Mexico
Contact(s):
Brian Butters, P.Eng., President
bbutters@purifics.com
Tony Powell, P.Eng., Applications Manager
tpowell@purifics.com

PWC Pure Water Corporation / PWC
5318 - 4A Ave., Delta
Vancouver, BC V4M 1H5
604-219-7898
Fax: 604-948-9812
william@watercorp.com
www.watercorp.com
Firm Type: Distributing, Manufacturing
Founded: 1993
Member of: American Water Works Association; British Columbia Water & Wastewater Association
Products/Services/Areas of Expertise: Water & wastewater purification, filtration, treatment, disinfection, reuse/recycle equipment
Financial Information:
Type of Ownership: Private
Revenue: $1.5 Million - $3 Million
Revenue Sources: 10% Municipals; 90% Private Contracts
Domestic Markets:
National

Foreign Activity:
Asia, Australia/New Zealand, Central America, China, Eastern Europe, The Middle East, The Pacific Rim, South America, Mexico, USA, Former USSR, Vietnam, Worldwide
Markets Sought:
Africa, Asia, Australia/New Zealand, Caribbean, Central America, China, Central Europe, Eastern Europe, Western Europe, The Middle East, South America, Mexico, USA, Former USSR, United Kingdom, Vietnam
Contact(s):
William Danshin, President

Pylon Electronics
31 Trider Cres.
Dartmouth, NS B3B 1V6
902-468-3344
Fax: 902-468-1203
halifax_csr@pylonelectronics.com
www.pylonelectronics.com
Firm Type: Manufacturing
Quality Environmental Management System(s): 9002
Products/Services/Areas of Expertise: Portable water quality monitors; custom test instrumentation
Financial Information:
Type of Ownership: Private
Revenue Sources: 50% nationwide; 3% Provincial; 1% Municipals; 46% Private Contracts
Domestic Markets:
Nova Scotia
Markets Sought:
Western Europe, South America, USA

Pylon Electronics Inc.
147 Colonnade Rd.
Ottawa, ON K2E 7L9
613-226-7920
Fax: 613-226-8195
800-896-4439
instrument@pylonelectronics.com
www.pylonelectronics.com
Firm Type: Manufacturing
Founded: 1955
Quality Environmental Management System(s): 9002
Products/Services/Areas of Expertise: Ordinance & buried hazards detection; radiation monitoring & measurement; automated chemical analysis detectors; supervisory & control instruments for satellite ground stations & telecommunications maintenance & testing equipment
Activities: Instrumentation & controls; environmental analysis & treatment; gas analysis apparatus; physical properties testing & inspection equipment; nuclear radiation detecting & measuring instruments; signal systems; radon gas detection measurement
Financial Information:
Type of Ownership: Private
Revenue: $500,000 - $1.5 Million
Revenue Sources: 25% nationwide; 25% Provincial; 50% Private Contracts
Foreign Activity:
Worldwide
Markets Sought:
South Africa, South America, Former USSR, United Kingdom
Contact(s):
Ewa Zielinksi, Coordinator, Marketing Sales

Pyradia Inc.
430, rue Guimond
Longueuil, QC J4G 1P8
450-463-3344
Fax: 450-463-3252
888-797-2342
sales@pyradia.com
www.pyradia.com
Firm Type: Distributing, Engineering, Manufacturing
Founded: 1973
Quality Environmental Management System(s): 9001
Products/Services/Areas of Expertise: Supplier of industrial heating equipment (ovens & furnaces); services include repair, maintenance & optimization; upgrades to new or used equipment; resale of parts & control equipment; consultation; design & assembly of controllers, electronic panels & integration of probes. Pyradia also supplies web converting equipment
Domestic Markets:
National
Foreign Activity:
USA,

Pyrotech Mfg. Corp.
An operating unit of Pyrotech Holdings Corp.
681 Athabasca St. West
Kamloops, BC V2H 1C5
250-851-9991
Fax: 250-851-9992
877-851-9991
info@pyropaver.com
www.pyropaver.com
Firm Type: Manufacturing
Founded: 1988
Staff: 25
Products/Services/Areas of Expertise: Hot in-place asphalt recycling systems, notably the PYROPAVER series of equipment. This is an environmentally sound, cost effective solution to restoring road pavement. Pyrotech Holdings also owns/operates Arc Asphalt Recycling Inc., Green Roads Recycling, & Paveover Inc.
Financial Information:
Type of Ownership: Private
Revenue: $1.5 Million - $3 Million
Revenue Sources: 100% Private Contracts
Domestic Markets:
National
Foreign Activity:
Worldwide
Contact(s):
Al Rorison, President

Q-Air Environmental Controls Ltd.
319 Arvin Ave.
Stoney Creek, ON L8E 2M3
905-662-6831
Fax: 905-662-8983
800-265-6861
sales@qair.com
www.qair.com
Firm Type: Distributing, Engineering, Manufacturing
Founded: 1979
Products/Services/Areas of Expertise: Industrial pollution control systems, fans & blowers; all types of air pollution control equipment from direct sales to turnkey applications
Financial Information:
Type of Ownership: Private
Foreign Activity:
USA
Contact(s):
Tony Quirk, President
Sheila Conuny, Sales Manager

QCA Laboratories Inc.
60 Churchill Dr.
Barrie, ON L4N 8Z5
705-733-3500
Fax: 705-733-2772
Firm Type: Scientific/Technical Services
Founded: 1997
Quality Environmental Management System(s): 14001
Products/Services/Areas of Expertise: Analysis & testing of waste water; soil testing
Financial Information:
Type of Ownership: Private
Revenue Sources: 10% nationwide; 10% Provincial; 20% Municipals; 60% Private Contracts
Domestic Markets:
Ontario

QMI-SAI Global
Formerly: QMI
Also Known As: Quality Management Institute
#100, 20 Carlson Ct.
Toronto, ON M9W 7K6
416-401-8700
Fax: 416-401-8650
800-465-3717
qmi@qmi.com
www.qmi.com
Firm Type: Management Consulting
Founded: 1984
Staff: 150
Products/Services/Areas of Expertise: With its headquarters in Toronto & service centres worldwide, QMI-SAI Global is a management systems registrar providing consultation, training & support for organizations attempting or in the process of registration to ISO & other industry standards. This organization is engaged in standards development, information services &

Products & Services Buyer's Guide

other assistance; SAI Global Certification Services certificates are recognized & accepted around the world; accredited by the Standards Council of Canada as a registrar for ISO 9001, ISO/TS 16949, AS9100-Series, ISO 14001, OHAS 18001, RC14001, RCMS, ISO 22000, ISO 29001, ANSI Z10, and other standards
Financial Information:
Type of Ownership: Non Profit
Revenue Sources: 100% Private Contracts
Domestic Markets:
National
Foreign Activity:
Worldwide
Contact(s):
Malcolm Phipps, Director, Corporate Policies

QSDM Inc.
6470 Kestrel Rd.
Mississauga, ON L5T 1Z7
905-565-1800
Fax: 905-565-1801
mail@qsdm.com
www.qsdm.com
Firm Type: Distributing, Manufacturing
Founded: 1984
Member of: Canadian Federation of Independent Business; IPC - Association Connecting Electronics Industries; Ontario Aerospace Council
Quality Environmental Management System(s): 9001:2000
Products/Services/Areas of Expertise: Electronic equipment for aerospace, rail transit & medical markets: screen printers, multi-function high speed placement machines, SMT reflow ovens; services include PCB layout, SMT assembly, PTH assembly, mechanical assembly, In-circuit testing, system testing, environmental testing. For the U.S. & International office, contact International Aerospace Products in Henderson, NV - 702-456-6701 or lgreen@qsdm.com
Financial Information:
Type of Ownership: Private
Domestic Markets:
National
Foreign Activity:
USA
Contact(s):
Conrad Zalai, Marketing Manager
Connie Wilke, Marketing Coordinator

Quad-Lock Building Systems Ltd.
7398 - 132 St.
Surrey, BC V3W 4M7
604-590-3111
Fax: 604-590-8412
888-711-5625
info@quadlock.com
www.quadlock.com
Firm Type: Distributing, Manufacturing
Founded: 1994
Staff: 16
Member of: Aqua-Pak Styro Containers, Ltd.
Quality Environmental Management System(s): 9001:2000
EcoLogo Certified Products & Services: Insulating concrete form contains no harmful substances with R-Values from R-22 to R-40, the highest in the industry
Products/Services/Areas of Expertise: Quad-Lock manufacturers Insulating Concrete Form systems for walls, floors & roofs. With the highest R-Value available, these systems are versatile, environmentally friendly, energy efficient & recyclable. The concrete pannels are made with high density, fire retardant polystyrene beads (EPS) & contain no formaldehyde, HFCs, CFCs, or other harmful substances. Services include training programs for the installer & distribution networks; this network ensures local, on-the-ground support for sales, training & on-site assistance
Ecological Note: Insulating concrete form contains no harmful substances with R-Values from R-22 to R-40, the highest in the industry
Contact(s):
Hubert Max Kusterman, CEO
Rhyne Stinchfield, Director, North American Sales
Karen Bunz, Manager, Customer Care
marketing@quadlock.com

Quality Fabricating & Supply Limited
Supreme Steel
3751 - 76 Ave.
Edmonton, AB T6B 2S8
780-468-6762
Fax: 780-468-0995
qualityfabricating@supremesteel.com
www.supremesteel.com
Firm Type: Manufacturing
Founded: 1975
Staff: 30
Products/Services/Areas of Expertise: Custom fabrication of waste storage containers, sewage treatment equipment, structured steel for pipe & equipment supports
Domestic Markets:
Alberta, British Columbia, Ontario
Foreign Activity:
Africa, South America, USA

Quality Matters Inc.
P.O. Box 26045
St. John's, NL A1C 5T9
709-722-7860
Fax: 709-739-4865
info@qualitymatter.net
Firm Type: Management Consulting
Staff: 6
Contact(s):
Karen Noftall, President

Quantum Murray LP / QMLP
Formerly: Murray Demolition; Quantum Environmental; Thomson Metals & Disposal
#300, 345 Horner Ave.
Toronto, ON M8W 1Z6
416-253-6000
Fax: 416-253-6699
800-251-7773
info@qmlp.ca
www.murraydemolition.com
Firm Type: Scientific/Technical Services
Founded: 2007
Staff: 700
Products/Services/Areas of Expertise: Quantum Murray LP is a decommissioning, environmental contractor, & waste management company. It offers the following services: demolition, salvaging & recycling scrap metal, hazardous materials abatement, remediation, & emergency response & training.
Financial Information:
Type of Ownership: Private
Domestic Markets:
Alberta, British Columbia, Ontario

QUASAR
Also Known As: Quality Systems Assessment Registrar
A division of the CWB Group
7250 West Credit Ave.
Mississauga, ON L5N 5N1
905-542-0547
Fax: 905-542-1318
800-461-9001
quasar@cwbgroup.com
www.quasarquality.org
Products/Services/Areas of Expertise: ISO 9000, 9001 & 14001 accredited quality systems registrar
Contact(s):
Ed Whalen, General Manager
ed.whalen@cwbgroup.com

Quatic Industries Inc.
P.O. Box 952
23 Admiral Place
Guelph, ON N1H 6M6
519-821-7780
Fax: 519-821-7784
800-265-8392
sales@quatic.com
www.quatic.com
Firm Type: Manufacturing, Scientific/Technical Services
Founded: 1970
Staff: 50
Member of: Association of Water Technologies
Quality Environmental Management System(s): 9001
Products/Services/Areas of Expertise: Water treatment chemicals; water treatment systems & equipment
Financial Information:
Type of Ownership: Private
Domestic Markets:
Ontario
Contact(s):
Cal Fair, Sales Manager

Quatrex Environnement inc.
Quatrex Environmental Inc.
2105, rue Monterey
Laval, QC H7L 3T6
450-963-4747
Fax: 450-622-5392
800-967-3002
info@quatrex.ca
www.quatrex.ca
Firm Type: Distributing, Manufacturing
Founded: 1990
Staff: 15
Products/Services/Areas of Expertise: Manufacturer & distributor of hazardous materials containers; spill kits & spill response products; containment products; sorbents: hydroponic, universal, granular, chemical; hazmat buildings; safety cabinets; recycling products; products for flamable substances management; liquid waste solidifiers; facility protection products; bulk bags, drums, pails; drum crushers; stormwater management solutions. Quatrex's Ontario facility is located at #16, 1011 Haultain Court, Mississauga, ON - contact 905-848-1039
Financial Information:
Type of Ownership: Private
Domestic Markets:
National
Markets Sought:
USA
Contact(s):
Patrick Paradis, President

Quatrosense Environmental Ltd. / QEL
P.O. Box 749
5935 Ottawa St.
Ottawa, ON K0A 2Z0
613-838-4005
Fax: 613-838-4018
qel@qelsafety.com
www.qel.dedesco.com
Firm Type: Distributing, Manufacturing
Founded: 1986
Staff: 26
Member of: Instrumentation Systems & Automation Society; American Society of Heating, Refrigerating & Air Conditioning Engineers Inc.; NASA; United Space Alliance (USA)
Products/Services/Areas of Expertise: Manufacturer & distributor of instrumentation for hazardous gas detection, combustion analysis, & flame detection; offers specialized equipment & turnkey solutions for the mining, petrochemical, brewing & landfill industries
Financial Information:
Type of Ownership: Private
Domestic Markets:
National
Foreign Activity:
The Pacific Rim, South America, USA
Markets Sought:
Australia/New Zealand, Central America, The Middle East,
Contact(s):
David Jenkins, President
Stan Conquest, Manager
Simon Warland, Manager, Customer Service

Quebecor World Concord
Div. of Quebecor World
89 Connie Cres.
Concord, ON L4K 1L3
905-669-2386
Fax: 905-669-2378
www.quebecorworldinc.com
Products/Services/Areas of Expertise: Prints high quality flyers & circulars on EcoLogoM recycled newsprint in many page counts & formats
Ecological Note: Flyers printed on recycled newsprint
Contact(s):
Richard Granger, Purchasing Manager
richard.granger@quebecorworld.com

Queen's Printer
Edmonton Bookstore, Main Fl., Park Plaza
10611 - 98 Ave.
Edmonton, AB T5K 2P7
780-427-4952
Fax: 780-452-0668
800-310-0000

qp@gov.ab.ca
www.qp.gov.ab.ca
Products/Services/Areas of Expertise: The official source of Government of Alberta laws and publications since 1906. For provincial statutes & regulations see: www.qp.gov.ab.ca/catalogue/display/cfm?page_id=40. For provincial statutes & regulations see: www.qp.gov.ab.ca/catalogue/display/cfm?page_id=40. The monthly e-Bookmark newsletter is produced by the Alberta Queen's Printer to keep customers informed of changes to Alberta's laws, as well as new and updated products and services via email. To subscribe, send an email or fax as listed above, including your email address

Queen's Printer
#117, 670 King St.
Fredericton, NB E3B 5H1
506-453-2520
Fax: 506-457-7899
queens.printer@gnb.ca
www.gnb.ca/0062/acts/index-e.asp
Products/Services/Areas of Expertise: The Queen's Printer for New Brunswick publishes, distributes and sells New Brunswick's public legislation and The Royal Gazette

Queen's Printer
Dept. of Government Services, Ground Fl.
P.O. Box 8700
St. John's, NL A1B 4J6
709-729-3649
www.gs.gov.nl.ca/gs/oqp
Products/Services/Areas of Expertise: The Queen's Printer Bookstore has been the official source of the Newfoundland and Labrador Government legislation and publications since 1986. The Queen's Printer publishes, distributes and sells Newfoundland and Labrador Consolidated Statutes, Regulations, The Newfoundland and Labrador Gazette and selected departmental publications

Queen's Printer
Walter Scott Building
#B19, 3085 Albert St.
Regina, SK S4S 0B1
306-787-6894
Fax: 306-798-0835
800-226-7302
qprinter@justice.gov.sk.ca
www.qp.gov.sk.ca
Products/Services/Areas of Expertise: The Office of the Queen's Printer publishes and distributes the authoritative versions of all Government of Saskatchewan legislation, regulations and other legislative publications including The Saskatchewan Gazette, the Statutes of Saskatchewan, the Regulations of Saskatchewan, the Tables to Statutes and Regulations of Saskatchewan, the Rules of Court (English / French), and any publications that the Lieutenant Governor in Council may order

Queen's Printer & Document Publishing Centre
Island Information Service
P.O. Box 2000
Charlottetown, PE C1A 7N8
902-368-4000
island@gov.pe.ca
www.gov.pe.ca/publications/index.php3
Products/Services/Areas of Expertise: Information about publications available to the public (reports, brochures, manuals, etc.) from the Government of Prince Edward Island are posted on website as soon as publications are released. Many publications may be read online or printed copies may be delivered by mail. For provincial statutes & regulations see: www.gov.pe.ca/law/index.php3

Queen's Printer Subscriptions
P.O. Box 2703
Whitehorse, YT Y1A 2C6
867-667-8573
Fax: 867-393-6210
800-661-0408
queens.printer@gov.yk.ca
www.hpw.gov.yk.ca/selling/legissubs.html
Products/Services/Areas of Expertise: Provides access to Government of Yukon statutes and regulations, The Yukon Gazette, reports, brochures, manuals, etc. For territorial statutes & regulations see: www.justice.gov.yk.ca/legislation/index.html

QuestAir Technologies Inc.
Formerly: Questor Industries Inc.
6961 Russell Ave.
Burnaby, BC V5J 4R8
604-454-1134
Fax: 604-454-1137
info@questairinc.com
www.questairinc.com
Products/Services/Areas of Expertise: Pressure swing adsorption technologies; gas separation & purification equipment; air purification; vapour recovery; thermal-powered oxygen concentration process; water purification through reverse osmosis; energy recovery technology & hydrogen technology
Activities: Gas separation & purification equipment & analysis; air purification, vapour recovery; thermally powered oxygen concentration process; water purification (reverse osmosis); energy recovery technology; hydrogen technology
Contact(s):
Jonathan Wilkinson, President/CEO
Matt Babicki, Principal Engineer
Andrew G. Hall, Vice-President, Sales & Business
Bowie Keefer, Principal Scientist
Sherry Tryssenaar, CFO & Vice-President, Finance & Administration

Quester Tangent Corp.
#201, 9865 West Saanich Rd.
Sidney, BC V8L 5Y8
250-656-6677
Fax: 250-655-4696
info@questertangent.com
www.questertangent.com
Firm Type: Manufacturing, Scientific/Technical Services
Founded: 1983
Staff: 28
Quality Environmental Management System(s): 9001
Products/Services/Areas of Expertise: Quesler Tangent provides real-time data acquisition systems for seabed classification, hydrographic survey & rapid transit electronics.
Financial Information:
Type of Ownership: Private
Domestic Markets:
National
Foreign Activity:
Asia, Australia/New Zealand, China, Western Europe, The Pacific Rim, USA, Vietnam, Worldwide
Contact(s):
John Neville, CEO
Stephen McKay, President
William Collings, Vice-President
Chris Elliott, Sales Manager

Quorum Growth Inc.
#1720, 70 York St.
Toronto, ON M5J 1S9
416-971-6998
Fax: 416-971-5955
info@quorum.ca
www.quorum.ca
Firm Type: Management Consulting
Founded: 1978
Products/Services/Areas of Expertise: Venture capital financing
Contact(s):
Wanda Dorosz, CEO & Managing Partner

Qwatro Corporation
#6, 110 Claireport Cres.
Toronto, ON M9W 6P3
416-675-2388
Fax: 416-675-0384
866-488-2788
information@qwatro.com
www.qwatro.com
Firm Type: Manufacturing
Founded: 2001
Staff: 15
EcoLogo Certified Products & Services: Industrial cleaning & maintenance products
Products/Services/Areas of Expertise: Manufacturer of environmentally friendly EcoLogo certified industrial maintenance & sanitation products
Ecological Note: Industrial cleaning & maintenance products
Financial Information:
Type of Ownership: Private

Domestic Markets:
British Columbia, New Brunswick, Ontario, Québec
Foreign Activity:
Western Europe
Contact(s):
Robert Wagner, President
Janet Wells, Exec. Vice-President

R Plus Industries Alberta Inc.
Formerly: Blue Sky Environmental Company Ltd
3616 - 14A St. SE
Calgary, AB T2G 3L2
403-265-1700
Fax: 403-233-9145
800-661-0156
rplus@telusplanet.net
www.telusplanet.net/public/rplus
Firm Type: Management Consulting, Waste Management
Founded: 1974
Products/Services/Areas of Expertise: R Plus Industries Inc. is an accredited agency which provides occupational health & safety training for asbestos workers. Its contract services include asbestos abatement, hazardous material remediation, sprayed & loose fibre & polyurethane insulation, & fireproofing. The company also provides protective spray coatings for tanks, pipelines, & roofs. It serves the commercial, industrial, & residential sectors.
Financial Information:
Type of Ownership: Private
Revenue Sources: 0% Private Contracts
Domestic Markets:
Alberta
Contact(s):
Patrick Windle, President

R&R Drilling Supply Ltd.
P.O. Box 4377
479 LeGrand Blvd.
Dieppe, NB E1A 7E7
506-859-8680
Fax: 506-859-7086
800-565-8680
Firm Type: Distributing, Engineering, Manufacturing
Staff: 7
Products/Services/Areas of Expertise: Design of environmental/remediation systems; consulting on waterwell/environmental drilling technologies & procedures; distribution of environmental recovery products & site assessment material
Recently Completed / Ongoing Projects: Environmental material & consulting services (base clean-ups) for National Defence; water supply for municipal projects, industrial power plants, manufacturing facilities; design remediation systems for BTEX spills; consultation on drilling procedures & design for water supply & environmental clean-up
Domestic Markets:
Alberta, Ontario
Markets Sought:
Asia, Australia/New Zealand, Central America, The Middle East, The Pacific Rim
Contact(s):
John Cann, President

R.A. Campbell & Associates
RR#1, Site 2, C#21
Madeira Park, BC V0N 2H0
604-883-9212
Fax: 604-883-9260
800-792-7719
Firm Type: Engineering

Products/Services/Areas of Expertise: Real estate services expertise covers waterfront, moorage, retirement, relocation, recreation, weekend retreat, building lots, acreage & view properties, etc.
Financial Information:
Type of Ownership: Private
Revenue: $250,000 - $500,000
Revenue Sources: 100% Private Contracts
Domestic Markets:
British Columbia
Contact(s):
Ryan Campbell, P.Eng., President

R.A. Kirby Sales Inc.
#16, 200 Viceroy Rd.
Concord, ON L4K 3N8

905-738-6225
Fax: 905-738-4355
sales@kirbysales.com
www.kirbysales.com
Firm Type: Distributing
Founded: 1983
Staff: 5
Member of: Air & Waste Management Association
Products/Services/Areas of Expertise: Portable gas analyzers; oil/water monitors; groundwater monitoring
Financial Information:
Type of Ownership: Private
Revenue Sources: 20% nationwide; 40% Provincial; 40% Private Contracts
Domestic Markets:
National
Contact(s):
Richard Kirby, President
Derrick Wynne, Sales Manager

R.A. Murray International Limited
Formerly: Ramsen Engineering Associates Inc.
1358 Queen St.
Halifax, NS B3J 2H5
902-422-9656
Fax: 902-420-1455
home@ramil.ca
www.ramil.ca
Products/Services/Areas of Expertise: Water supply & sewage treatment material procurement; design of water supply systems; project management
Foreign Activity:
Africa, Caribbean, Central America, South America
Contact(s):
Richard A. Murray, P.Eng., President

R.B. Intermark Inc.
#108, 15, boul Kirkland
Montréal, QC H9J 1N2
514-695-7172
Fax: 514-695-2108
digitron.brimo@simpatico.ca
Firm Type: Distributing, Manufacturing
Products/Services/Areas of Expertise: Manufacture & distribution of digitron silver recovery systems - closed loop recycling electrolytic units that recover silver from photochemistry; expert in the area of pollution control
Financial Information:
Type of Ownership: Private
Revenue Sources: 100% Private Contracts
Domestic Markets:
National
Foreign Activity:
Western Europe, USA
Markets Sought:
Asia, China, Central Europe, South America, Former USSR, Vietnam
Contact(s):
René J. Brimo, President

R.D. Cookson Disposal Ltd.
319 St. John's Rd. East, RR#3
Simcoe, ON N3Y 4K2
519-428-1515
Fax: 519-428-7708
Firm Type: Waste Management
Founded: 1983
Staff: 6
Member of: Ontario Waste Management Association; Canadian Federation of Independent Business
Products/Services/Areas of Expertise: The firm is engaged in recycling services, industrial/commercial & residential waste collection; special services include front loader supply & service & roll-off containers; serves Norfolk, Haldimand & Oxford Counties in Ontario
Financial Information:
Type of Ownership: Private
Revenue: $50,000 - $100,000
Revenue Sources: 10% Provincial; 90% Private Contracts
Domestic Markets:
Ontario
Contact(s):
Robert D. Cookson, President

R.G. Robinson & Associates (Barrie) Ltd.
#200, 10 High St.
Barrie, ON L4N 1W1
705-721-9222
Fax: 705-734-0764
engplan@rgra.on.ca
www.rgra.on.ca
Firm Type: Engineering, Scientific/Technical Services
Founded: 1987
Staff: 30
Products/Services/Areas of Expertise: Offers planning & engineering in all areas of civil/municipal engineering: land use planning; site servicing; utility design; environmental assessments; sewage collection/treatment; water supply treatment
Financial Information:
Type of Ownership: Publicly Traded
Domestic Markets:
Ontario
Contact(s):
Ron Robinson, P.Eng., President

R.H. Loucks Oceanology
24 Clayton Park Dr.
Halifax, NS B3M 1L3
902-443-1113
Firm Type: Scientific/Technical Services
Founded: 1975
Staff: 2
Products/Services/Areas of Expertise: Estuarine & coastal oceanography; environmental impact assessment; coastal zone planning & erosion dynamics; fisheries oceanography
Contact(s):
Ronald H. Loucks, President

R.J. Burnside & Associates Limited
Also Known As: Burnside
15 Townline
Orangeville, ON L9W 3R4
519-941-5331
Fax: 519-941-8120
800-265-9662
info@rjburnside.com
www.rjburnside.com
Firm Type: Management Consulting, Engineering, Waste Management
Founded: 1970
Staff: 275
Member of: Neegan Burnside Ltd.
Member of: American Water Works Ass'n; Water Environment Federation; Ass'n of Consulting Engineers of Canada; Consulting Engineers of Ontario
Products/Services/Areas of Expertise: Infrastructure engineering services & environmental consulting, with a focus on civil engineering, energy efficiency solutions, solid waste management, environmental impact assessment, site remediation, satellite remote sensing & waste resources; water supply development, treatment & distribution; sewage collection & treatment; roads & bridges; reservoirs, water & wastewater treatment plants; & land development; electrical engineering; structural engineering; mechanical engineering; client groups include the private sector, muncipalities, & First Nations groups
Recently Completed / Ongoing Projects: Town of Orangeville water supply; Town of Alliston bypass
Domestic Markets:
Newfoundland & Labrador, Nunavut, Ontario
Foreign Activity:
Africa, Central America, The Pacific Rim, South America,
Contact(s):
John Burnside, P.Eng., M.Sc., MBA, President
Andrew Morris, Vice-President, Operations, Business Planning & Strategy
Dave Bannister, Vice-President, Technical Services
Mark Sheedy, Vice-President, QA/QC Field Services
Contact(s):
Jackie Kay, P.Eng., MBA, Contact
Contact(s):
Mervin Dewasha, P.Eng., CEO
Peter J. Luce, P.Eng., Director, Market & Business Development
peter.luce@neeganburnside.com
Contact(s):
Erik Buus, Contact

Canadian Branches:
Barrie
#301, 128 Wellington St. W.
Barrie, ON L4N 8J6
705-797-2047
Fax: 705-797-2037
don.nicol@rjburnside.com
Don Nicol, B.Sc., P.Geo, Contact

Brampton
#200, 170 Steelwell Rd.
Brampton, ON L6T 5T3
905-793-9239
Fax: 905-793-5018
Dave.Kesler@rjburnside.com
Dave Kesler, P.Eng., Contact

Collingwood
3 Ronell Cres.
Collingwood, ON L9Y 4J6
705-446-0515
Fax: 705-446-2399
Jim.Georgas@rjburnside.com
Jim Georgas, C.E.T., Contact

Newmarket
#200, 16775 Yonge St.
Newmarket, ON L3Y 8J4
905-953-8967
Fax: 905-953-8945
Dave.Scomazzon@rjburnside.com
Dave Scomazzon, P.Eng., Contact

Pickering
#202, 1053 Brock Rd.
Pickering, ON L1W 3T7
905-686-3067
Fax: 905-686-9652
TJ.Rule@rjburnside.com
TJ Rule, P.Eng., Contact

Stratford
332 Lorne Ave. East
Stratford, ON N5A 6S4
519-271-5111
Fax: 519-271-3790
Jeremy.Taylor@rjburnside.com
Jeremy Taylor, P.Eng., Contact

Wingham
P.O. Box 10
449 Josephine St.
Wingham, ON N0G 2W0
519-357-1521
Fax: 519-357-3624
Jeremy.Taylor@rjburnside.com
Jeremy Taylor, P.Eng., Contact

Guelph - Neegan Burnside Engineering Ltd.
292 Speedvale Ave. W., Unit 20
Guelph, ON N1H 1C4
519-823-4995
Fax: 519-836-5477
jackie.kay@rjburnside.com
www.neeganburnside.com; www.rjburnside.com

Iqualuit - Nuna Burnside Engineering & Environmental Ltd.
Building 764
P.O. Box 879
Fred Coman St.
Iqualuit, NU X0A 0H0
867-975-2052
Fax: 867-975-2053
www.nunaburnside.com
Products/Services/Areas of Expertise: Specializes in capacity development; economic development; green power; building engineering services; infrastructure development; environmental services; transportation; housing development; GIS; broadband communications

Orangeville - Neegan Burnside Engineering Ltd.
15 Townline
Orangeville, ON L9W 3R4
519-941-1161
Fax: 519-941-8120
800-595-9149
peter.luce@rjburnside.com
www.neeganburnside.com; www.rjburnside.com

Winnipeg - Neegan Burnside Engineering Ltd.
106B Scurfield Blvd.
Winnipeg, MB R3Y 1G4
204-949-7110
Fax: 204-949-7111

Erik.Buus@rjburnside.com
www.neeganburnside.com; www.rjburnside.com
Founded: 1970
Member of: R.J. Burnside & Associates Limited; Nuna Burnside Engineering & Environmental Ltd.
Products/Services/Areas of Expertise: Land development; site due diligence & assessments; preliminary engineering; design & construction; stormwater water management; traffic management; electrical engineering; environmental services; civil engineering; mechanical engineering; GIS; renewable energy solutions. First Nations majority owned, the firm specializes in consultation with all stakeholder groups, including First Nations, in order to support culture & community values, & protect the environment

R.J. Lévesque et Fils Ltée
890, rue Houssart
Cap-de-la-Madeleine, QC G8T 8P8
819-376-6123
Fax: 819-376-3699
Contact(s):
Maxime Lévesque

R.U. Kistritz Consultants Ltd.
15870 Columbia Ave.
White Rock, BC V4B 5H7
604-536-1357
Fax: 604-275-3260
ron@kistritzconsultants.com
kistritzconsultants.com
Firm Type: Scientific/Technical Services
Founded: 1980
Staff: 2
Products/Services/Areas of Expertise: A consulting company offering services which focus on habitat ecology & water quality of freshwater & coastal marine ecosystems. Services include research, habitat inventories, water quality sampling & analyses, environmental impact assessments, aquatic habitat enhancement, preparation of sediment control plans, environmental monitoring. Clients have included all levels of government, private sector organizations & First Nations groups
Recently Completed / Ongoing Projects: Habitat inventory & management classification of lower Fraser River; environmental protection plan for city of North Vancouver; development of CD-ROM of flora of Pacific Northwest
Financial Information:
Type of Ownership: Private
Revenue Sources: 30% nationwide; 10% Provincial; 30% Municipals; 30% Private Contracts
Domestic Markets:
Alberta, British Columbia, Saskatchewan
Foreign Activity:
South America
Contact(s):
Ron U. Kistritz, M.Sc., R.P.Bio., Principal

R.V. Anderson Associates Limited
#400, 2001 Sheppard Ave. East
Toronto, ON M2J 4Z8
416-497-8600
Fax: 416-497-0342
toronto@rvanderson.com
www.rvanderson.com
Firm Type: Management Consulting, Engineering
Founded: 1948
Staff: 167
Member of: Water Environment Federation; American Water Works Association; Consulting Engineers of Ontario; Association of Consulting Engineers of Canada
Products/Services/Areas of Expertise: An employee-owned, independent consulting practice of engineers, with a focus on water treatment & management, wastewater services, municipal infrastructure, transportation, structures & tunnels, urban development, architecture & building services, environmental management, electrical, SCADA & telecommunications; services include planning, management, design/build, operations & optimization, asset management & all services incorporate sustainability. Offices in Toronto, Ottawa, Niagara, Sudbury, London (ON), Moncton, Fredericton, and St. John's
Financial Information:
Type of Ownership: Private
Domestic Markets:
New Brunswick, Nova Scotia, Ontario, Prince Edward Island
Foreign Activity:
Asia, The Middle East, The Pacific Rim
Contact(s):
Ken A. Morrison, P.Eng., President

Reg J. Andres, P.Eng., Vice-President, Municipal
Gary A. Farrell, C.G.A., Sec.-Treas.
Ken W. Campbell, P.Eng., Vice-President
Canadian Branches:
Fredericton
c/o Hydro-Com Technologies
445 Urquhart Cres.
Fredericton, NB E3B 8K4
506-445-2888
Fax: 506-455-0193
Gary Hachey, Manager
London Branch
320 Adelaide St. South
London, ON N5Z 3L2
519-681-9916
Fax: 519-681-0899
london@rvanderson.com
Robert Kuzyk, Manager
Moncton Branch
c/o Touchie Engineering
#801, 850 Main St. West
Moncton, NB E1C 1G2
506-857-8525
Fax: 506-858-5972
Rodney Hopper, Manager
Ottawa Branch
#200, 1755 Woodward Dr.
Ottawa, ON K2C 0P9
613-226-1844
Fax: 613-226-8930
ottawa@rvanderson.com
Al R. Perks, Regional Manager
Sudbury Branch
c/o Dennis Consultants
#6, 436 Westmount Ave.
Sudbury, ON P3A 5Z8
705-560-5555
Fax: 705-560-5822
sudbury@rvanderson.com
Armand Therrien, Manager
Welland Branch
#304, 76 Division St.
Welland, ON L3B 3Z7
905-735-3659
Fax: 905-735-9299
welland@rvanderson.com
Vaino Raun, Manager

Racal Protection Canada
P.O. Box 665
1175 California Ave.
Brockville, ON K6V 6J4
613-345-1349
Fax: 613-345-0826
800-267-4414
Firm Type: Distributing
Products/Services/Areas of Expertise: Safety protective products; respiratory protection
Financial Information:
Type of Ownership: Foreign-owned
Domestic Markets:
National
Contact(s):
Jamie Price, Director, Sales & Marketing

Racan Carrier
Division of UTC Canada Corporation
2025, boul Dagenais ouest
Laval, QC H7L 5V1
514-324-5050
Fax: 450-625-6818
866-466-8796
racan.customerservice@carrier.utc.com
www.racan-carrier.com
Firm Type: Manufacturing
Founded: 1971
Staff: 160
Quality Environmental Management System(s): 9001:2000
Products/Services/Areas of Expertise: Manufactures & distributes air handling units; filters, fans, heat exchangers, heating, cooling & humidification solutions, controls for AHU equipment

Financial Information:
Type of Ownership: Private
Domestic Markets:
National
Foreign Activity:
USA
Contact(s):
Savio Ricciardi, Vice-President

Radiation Environmental Management Systems Inc.
Also Known As: REMS Inc.
238 Winderheights Pl.
Waterloo, ON N2T 1P1
519-885-2520
Fax: 519-746-0435
hdsharma@golden.net
Firm Type: Engineering, Scientific/Technical Services
Founded: 1981
Staff: 2
Products/Services/Areas of Expertise: Measurement of non-ionizing & ionizing radiation; risk assessment; monitoring of workplace & domestic toxic chemicals; radioactive waste disposal
Financial Information:
Revenue: $100,000 - $250,000
Domestic Markets:
National
Contact(s):
H.D. Sharma, President

Radiodetection (Canada) Ltd.
#34, 344 Edgeley Blvd.
Concord, ON L4K 4B7
905-660-9995
Fax: 905-660-9579
800-665-7953
dave@radiodetection.ca
www.radiodetection.ca
Firm Type: Distributing, Manufacturing
Founded: 1972
Staff: 3
Member of: Municipal Electric Association; Canadian Gas Association
Quality Environmental Management System(s): 9001
Products/Services/Areas of Expertise: Underground locating devices for use on buried utility services; electronic location system for monitoring progress of horizontal boring tools; buried pipe/conduit/tank locating; corrosion assessment; utility fault locating
Financial Information:
Type of Ownership: Publicly Traded
Domestic Markets:
National
Contact(s):
Dave Wulff, National Sales Manager
dave.wulff@radiodetection.spx.com
Scott McPhail, Customer Service
scott.mcphail@radiodetection.spx.com
International Branch(es):
Radiodetection
P.O. Box 756
Bridgton, ME USA
207-647-6495
Fax: 207-647-9496

Raging River Power & Mining Inc.
#216, 545 Clyde Ave.
West Vancouver, BC V7T 1C5
604-925-3377
Fax: 604-925-3394
Products/Services/Areas of Expertise: In charge of the Raging River small hydro project, expected to generate 13GWh of electricity per year.
Ecological Note: Electricity, renewable low-impact
Contact(s):
Steve Stacey
steve@surespan.com

RailPower Technologies Corp.
#105, 9955 av de Catania
Brossard, QC J4Z 3V5
450-678-5277
866-678-5277
info@railpower.com
www.railpower.com

Firm Type: Engineering
Founded: 2001
Staff: 39
Products/Services/Areas of Expertise: Energy technology systems for use in transportation & power generation
Contact(s):
José Mathieu, President/CEO
Frank Donnelly, Chief Technology Officer
Patrice Beaudry, Vice-President, International Business Development & Program Mgmt
Lorraine Potvin, Vice-President/CFO

International Branch(es):
Railpower Hybrid Technologies Corp.
2021 Peninsual Dr.
Erie, PA USA
814-835-2212
Fax: 814-835-2908

RAM Forest Products Inc.
1 Ram Forest Rd.
Gormley, ON L0H 1G0
905-727-1164
Fax: 905-727-7758
sales@ram-forest.com
www.ram-forest.com
Products/Services/Areas of Expertise: Forestry distributor & manufacturer

RAM Lining Systems Inc.
78189 La Vrangue Dr., RR#1
Bayfield, ON N0M 1G0
519-524-1904
Fax: 519-524-6721
ramlining@xplornet.com
www.ramlining.com
Firm Type: Distributing
Founded: 1993
Staff: 7
Member of: International Association of Geosynthetic Installers
Products/Services/Areas of Expertise: Supply & installation of geomembrane liners used as waterproofing membranes, & for containment of leachates, spills, potable water, contaminated soils, hazardous chemicals, sewage, & landfill
Recently Completed / Ongoing Projects: Colchester Regional Balefill Facility - HDPE Landfill, NS; other projects include installation of HDPE for diverse purposes in various Canadian sites: Manitowadge, ON; Chatham Ethanol Plant; Great Lakes Power; Imperial Oil (Sarnia, ON); Dow Chemical (Sarnia, ON); Ontario Hydro; Alcan Aluminum Ltd.; Falconbridge Mines; Pearson International Airport (Toronto, ON)
Financial Information:
Type of Ownership: Private
Revenue Sources: 10% nationwide; 10% Provincial; 30% Municipals; 50% Private Contracts
Domestic Markets:
National
Markets Sought:
Australia/New Zealand, South America, Mexico
Contact(s):
Frank Kunc, President
Yvon St. Onge, Vice President/Project Manager
Gerald De Boer, Vice President/Project Manager
Ray Coletta, Secretary/Project Manager

Ramsay Machine Works Ltd.
2066 Henry Ave.
Sidney, BC V8L 5Y1
250-656-5314
Fax: 250-656-5388
www.ramsaygroup.com
Firm Type: Manufacturing
Founded: 1903
Products/Services/Areas of Expertise: Environmental equipment; air handling equipment; air pollution control systems; scrubbers; demolition materials; plastics recycling; recycling systems & equipment; oil spill equipment; incineration/incinerators
Activities: Soil reclamation research; compaction studies & development
Financial Information:
Revenue Sources: 25% nationwide; 30% Provincial; 25% Municipals; 20% Private Contracts
Domestic Markets:
National
Foreign Activity:
Asia, Western Europe, The Pacific Rim, USA

Markets Sought:
South America
Contact(s):
Gregory H.P. Ramsay, President

Rapid-Eau Technologies
P.O. Box 1113
Cambridge, ON N1R 5Y2
519-740-8786
Fax: 519-740-0422
dave@rapid-eau.com
www.rapid-eau.com
Products/Services/Areas of Expertise: Development of small hydro generating stations
Contact(s):
David De de Montmorency, P.Eng., President

Raw Materials Corporation
Also Known As: RMC
Div. of International Marine Salvage Inc.
P.O. Box 6
17 Invertose Dr.
Port Colborne, ON L3K 5V7
905-835-1203
Fax: 905-835-6824
888-937-3382
admin@rawmaterials.com
www.rawmaterials.com
Firm Type: Management Consulting, Engineering, Waste Management
Founded: 1990
Staff: 40
Member of: Ontario Waste Management Association; Canadian Association of Recycling Industries
Quality Environmental Management System(s): 14001
Products/Services/Areas of Expertise: Process recycling of all secondary materials; battery recycling; design, fabrication of shredder; shipbreaking; metal recovery; ferrous & non-ferrous processing & recycling; computer recycling; fluorescent lamp recycling; mercury & lead recycling
Recently Completed / Ongoing Projects: Client list includes more than half of the Fortune 500
Financial Information:
Type of Ownership: Private
Revenue Sources: 1% nationwide; 1% Provincial; 3% Municipals; 95% Private Contracts
Domestic Markets:
National
Foreign Activity:
Asia, Central America, China, The Pacific Rim, South America, Mexico, USA, Vietnam
Contact(s):
Wayne Elliott, President
James Ewles, General Manager, Hazardous Waste Div.
Richard Unyi, Director, Health, Safety & Environmental
Dylan Elliott, General Manager, Metals Div.

Rawdon Industries Ltd.
58 Easton Rd.
Brantford, ON N3P 1J5
519-756-1740
Fax: 519-759-7592
mail@tampoprintcanada.com
Firm Type: Distributing
Staff: 3
Products/Services/Areas of Expertise: Solvent recyclers for in-house recovery & purification of solvents
Domestic Markets:
National
Markets Sought:
USA
Contact(s):
Kristan Clare, Vice-President, Sales & Marketing

Rawdon Technologies Ltd.
P.O. Box 575
110 Reeves St.
Sydney, NS B1P 6H4
902-562-2106
Fax: 902-562-1699
cbrushett@syd.auracom.com
www.rawdontechnologies.com
Firm Type: Waste Management

Products/Services/Areas of Expertise: Prefabricated water; wastewater treatment facility for small & medium-sized municipalities; dissolved air filtration systems

Recently Completed / Ongoing Projects: Water quality study for community of Coxheath, NS
Financial Information:
Type of Ownership: Private
Revenue: $50,000 - $100,000
Revenue Sources: 40% Provincial; 40% Municipals; 20% Private Contracts
Domestic Markets:
Nova Scotia
Contact(s):
Alan Hawco, President
Rob Spencer, Secretary
Gordon Balcombe, Vice-President

Ray Electric Ltd.
20 Park Hill Rd. East
Cambridge, ON N1R 1P2
519-623-0330
Fax: 519-623-1286
info@rayelectric.com
www.rayelectric.com
Firm Type: Distributing, Manufacturing
Founded: 1909
Staff: 9
Member of: Cambridge Electrical Contractors Association
Products/Services/Areas of Expertise: In addition to manufacturing & distributing its own line of electric heathing solutions (Hydro-Air), Ray Electric carries a full line of Carrier products, including heat pumps, gas furnaces, air conditioners, & ductless air conditioning systems; journeyman electricians, refrigeration mechanics, gas fitters, & heat pump specialists on staff
Domestic Markets:
National
Contact(s):
Larry Ray, President/CEO
Steven Ray, Vice-President
Jules Laurin, Production Foreman

Raymond James Financial Inc.
Formerly: Goepel McDermid Inc.
#2200, 925 West Georgia St.
Vancouver, BC V6C 3L2
604-659-8000
Fax: 604-659-8099
888-545-6624
Products/Services/Areas of Expertise: Financing services; investment dealers

Rayovac Canada Inc.
5448 Timberlea Blvd.
Mississauga, ON L4W 2T7
905-624-4448
Fax: 905-629-2571
www.rayovac.com
Ecological Note: Rayovac Renewal rechargeable alkaline system; Rayovac AA, AAA, C & D batteries
Contact(s):
Bob Falconi, Marketing
falconi@rayovac.com

Raypak Canada Ltd.
2805 Slough St.
Mississauga, ON L4T 1G2
905-677-7999
Fax: 905-677-8036
info@raypakcanada.com
www.raypakcanada.com
Firm Type: Manufacturing
Founded: 1963
Staff: 32
Member of: Canadian Gas Association; American Society of Heating, Refrigerating & Air Conditioning Engineers; Canadian Institute of Plumbing & Heating
Products/Services/Areas of Expertise: Energy-efficient boilers, water heaters; energy control systems
Domestic Markets:
National
Foreign Activity:
China, Western Europe, Vietnam
Contact(s):
Bruce Sunley, Vice-President & General Manager

Rayplex Limited
341 Durham Ct.
Oshawa, ON L1J 1W8

905-579-1433
Fax: 905-579-1431
info@fibreglass.com
www.fibreglass.com
Firm Type: Distributing, Manufacturing
Founded: 1968
Staff: 6
Products/Services/Areas of Expertise: The firm is engaged in the design & manufacture of fibreglass & plastic products, as well as equipment to use, dispense & mould fibreglass & plastic products in the construction & car manufacturing sectors for construction companies & car manufacturers, as well as equipment to dispense & mould fibreglass & plastic products Tanks, resins, fillers, brushes & rollers
Contact(s):
Ray Bilsky

RBR Ltd.
Formerly: Richard Brancker Research Ltd
27 Monk St.
Ottawa, ON K1S 3Y7
613-233-1621
Fax: 613-233-4100
info@rbr-global.com
www.rbr-global.com
Firm Type: Manufacturing
Founded: 1976
Staff: 12
Products/Services/Areas of Expertise: Submersible data recorders for temperature, pressure, conductivity, pH & DO; hydrophobic grid membrane filter (HGMF) equipment for microbiologists; chlorophyll fluorometer for biologists
Recently Completed / Ongoing Projects: Electronics for CORK loggers used in drill holes at the bottom of the Pacific
Domestic Markets:
National
Foreign Activity:
Asia, Australia/New Zealand, Western Europe, The Middle East, The Pacific Rim, Mexico, USA
Contact(s):
F. Johnson, President
richard@rbr-global.com
Kara-Lee Golota, Vice-President
Graham Jones, Manager, R&D
Bart Geleynse, Manager, Marketing

Réal Huot Inc.
(Parc Colbert)
2640, rue Dalton
Sainte-Foy, QC G1P 3S4
418-651-2121
Fax: 418-651-8216
info@realhuot.ca
www.realhuot.ca
Products/Services/Areas of Expertise: Water & wastewater management equipment; filters/filter media; water & wastewater treatment
Contact(s):
Réal Huot, Founder

Rebuts Solides Canadiens Inc.
2240, rue Michel-Jurdant
Montréal, QC H1Z 4N7
514-789-0085
Products/Services/Areas of Expertise: A subsidiary of Groupe Tiru (France), the firm is engaged in waste management & recycling
Domestic Markets:
Québec
Contact(s):
Pierre C. Lemoine

Rechargeable Battery Recycling Corporation / RBRC
La Société de recyclage des piles rechargables
16 Northumberland St.
Toronto, ON M6H 1P7
416-535-9210
Fax: 416-536-9892
888-224-9764
www.rbrc.org
Firm Type: Waste Management
Founded: 1994
Staff: 5
Products/Services/Areas of Expertise: Non-profit public service organization dedicated to the recycling of rechargeable batteries & cellular phones. Corporate headquarters located in Atlanta, GA - contact 678-419-9900

Financial Information:
Type of Ownership: Non Profit
Domestic Markets:
National
Foreign Activity:
USA
Contact(s):
Carl Smith, President/CEO
Susan Antler, Contact, 416-535-9210
santler@rbrc.ca
Tyrone Biljan, Regional Recycling Manager, North Central Region
tbiljan@rbrc.ca

Recovery Technologies Inc. / RTG
1225 Franklin Blvd.
Cambridge, ON N1R 7E5
519-740-6801
Fax: 519-740-2639
sales@rtechcorp.com
www.rtechcorp.com
Firm Type: Manufacturing, Waste Management
Founded: 1989
Staff: 35
Products/Services/Areas of Expertise: Cryogenic tire recycling & sale of cryogenic crumb rubber, used for road building, in artificial turf & other products
Financial Information:
Type of Ownership: Private
Revenue: $3 Million - $5 Million
Domestic Markets:
National
Foreign Activity:
USA
Contact(s):
Jenny Stranges, President/CEO

Recubec Inc.
Recubec inc.
485, av Marien
Montréal, QC H1B 4V8
514-645-9233
Fax: 514-645-2050
info@recubec.ca
www.recubec.ca
Founded: 1982
Products/Services/Areas of Expertise: The firm is engaged in the management & transport of hazardous & non-hazardous industrial waste; services include onsite testing, containment, pumping & cleanup; products include roll-off leakproof or permeable containers
Domestic Markets:
Québec
Contact(s):
Patrick Lalonde

Récupération Nord-Ben Inc.
A division of EBI Group
1481, rue Raoul-Charette
Joliette, QC J6E 8S5
450-759-9007
Fax: 450-759-5369
nordben@groupe-ebi.com
www.groupe-ebi.com
Products/Services/Areas of Expertise: Recycling services; waste management
Domestic Markets:
Québec
Contact(s):
Chantal Frappier

Recyc-Haul Waste Management Inc.
P.O. Box 51011 Beddington
Calgary, AB T3K 3V9
403-272-3138
Fax: 403-274-2018
Products/Services/Areas of Expertise: Waste management
Contact(s):
Dean Fleischhacker, President

Recycle Alexandria Recycline (Équipe) / RARE
Formerly: Equipe Recycling
265 Industrial Blvd.
Alexandria, ON K0C 1A0
613-525-5112
Fax: 613-525-5114

rare@personainternet.com
www.rare-recycling.on.ca
Firm Type: Waste Management
Founded: 1990
Staff: 6
Products/Services/Areas of Expertise: Waste management; recycling services
Financial Information:
Type of Ownership: Private
Domestic Markets:
Ontario
Contact(s):
René Jeaurond

Recyclage d'Alluminium Québec
695, rue Dutord
Bécancour, QC G9H 2Z6
819-294-2020
Fax: 819-294-2666
rcnord@quebectel.com
Products/Services/Areas of Expertise: Recyclade du aluminum
Contact(s):
Pierre Gagnon

Recyclage PF Inc.
CP 262
10, rue de Ruisseau
Port-Cartier, QC G5B 2G8
418-766-6581
Fax: 418-766-6581
recyclepf@bbsi.net
Firm Type: Waste Management
Founded: 1979
Staff: 18
Products/Services/Areas of Expertise: Recycling services for scrap metal, glass, paper, plastics; aluminum, batteries, cardboard, steel/plastic drums, lead, scrap lead, textiles & silver
Domestic Markets:
New Brunswick, Newfoundland & Labrador, Québec
Foreign Activity:
USA
Contact(s):
Claude Paradis, President

Recyclenet Corporation
Also Known As: ALLOYchange.com
P.O. Box 24017
Guelph, ON N1E 6V8
519-767-2913
webmaster@alloychange.com
www.alloychange.com
Firm Type: Information Technology

Products/Services/Areas of Expertise: A worldwide information trading site, established to promote trade in the exotic metal industry
Financial Information:
Type of Ownership: Private
Revenue Sources: 100% Private Contracts
Domestic Markets:
National
Contact(s):
Tom Hattle, Contact

Red Devil Drain Service
P.O. Box 1
Thorburn, NS B0K 1W0
902-396-4011
Fax: 902-396-4754
red.devil@ns.sympatico.ca
Contact(s):
Keith Smith, Contact

Red Oak Industries Inc.
P.O. Box 582
Bruderheim, AB T0B 0S0
780-796-3851
Fax: 780-796-3850
Contact(s):
Gordon Burrell, Manager

Redstone Associates Ltd.
82 Venus Cres.
Hanwell, NB E3C 1N1

Products & Services Buyer's Guide

506-458-1475
Fax: 506-457-4604
keys@brunnet.net
Products/Services/Areas of Expertise: Environmental consultants & services
Contact(s):
David Keys, Contact

REDUCT & Lobbe Technologies Inc.
P.O. Box 800
#186, 8120 No. 2 Rd.
Richmond, BC V7C 5J8
604-275-3711
Fax: 604-275-3715
dispatch@reduct.com
www.reduct.com
Firm Type: Management Consulting, Information Technology
Founded: 1986
Staff: 5
Products/Services/Areas of Expertise: The firm offers expertise in the evaluation, risk assessment & cost analysis of advanced energy & environmental solutions, using Business Intelligence & Process Intelligence approaches, as well as unique technologies to help clients solve complex problems & provide decision support to their processes
Domestic Markets:
National
Foreign Activity:
Asia, Eastern Europe, USA
Contact(s):
Adam J. Szladow, President

Refined Specialty Chemicals Inc.
4420 Guildwood Way East
Mississauga, ON L5R 2B1
905-568-3394
Fax: 905-568-4012
Firm Type: Scientific/Technical Services
Founded: 1994
Staff: 6
Products/Services/Areas of Expertise: Risk management; risk assessment; inventory control & obsolete inventory recovery
Recently Completed / Ongoing Projects: Obsolete inventory recovery, Canada Colors; equipment recommendations & supply, Bayer Canada; surplus inventory recovery, Ontario Hydro
Financial Information:
Type of Ownership: Private
Revenue Sources: 10% nationwide; 10% Provincial; 10% Municipals; 70% Private Contracts
Domestic Markets:
New Brunswick, Newfoundland & Labrador, Nova Scotia, Northwest Territories, Ontario, Prince Edward Island, Québec
Foreign Activity:
Central America, South America, USA
Contact(s):
Stella Bernard, President
Frank Bissoon, General Manager
Devin Bissoon, Sales Manager

Refrigerant Services Inc.
105 Akerley, Unit D
Dartmouth, NS B3B 1R7
902-468-4997
Fax: 902-468-5102
refrigerant@ns.aliantzinc.ca
www3.ns.sympatico.ca/refrigerant
Firm Type: Distributing, Manufacturing
Founded: 1987
Staff: 6
Member of: Heating, Refrigeration & Air Conditioning Institute
Products/Services/Areas of Expertise: Refrigerant processing & disposal, cylinder acquallification
Recently Completed / Ongoing Projects: Joint ventures in USA, England & Australia, refrigerant separation technology & equipment
Financial Information:
Type of Ownership: Private
Revenue Sources: 100% Private Contracts
Domestic Markets:
National
Foreign Activity:
Australia/New Zealand, Western Europe, USA
Markets Sought:
USA
Contact(s):
Jim Thomas, President

Regional Envelope
A Division of SupremeX
400 Humberline Dr.
Toronto, ON M9W 5T3
416-759-9395
Fax: 416-848-8388
Ecological Note: Envelopes

Regional Petroleum Products Recycling Ltd.
P.O. Box 3742 B
Saint John, NB E2M 5C1
506-635-4837
Fax: 506-635-8237
Contact(s):
Rita O'Connor, Contact

Regional Power Inc.
#710, 40 University Ave.
Toronto, ON M5J 1T1
416-593-4717
Fax: 416-593-4925
www.regionalpower.com
Products/Services/Areas of Expertise: Regional owns & operates 5 hydro-electric generating stations & commissioned a sixth station which it operates for the owner. The total capacity of these facilities is 37 MW. They generate enough energy each year to supply a town of 40,000 people.
Recently Completed / Ongoing Projects: Has focused on the development of smaller & medium sized (25 MW to 100 MW), gas fired, co-generation plants, using many of the development skills & expertise acquired through its hydro electric development experience.
Ecological Note: Alternative source electricity
Domestic Markets:
British Columbia, Northwest Territories, Ontario, Québec
Contact(s):
Anna Posavad, Financial Manager
Canadian Branches:
Montréal
#1330, 1010 de la Gauchetiecre Ouest
Montréal, QC H3B 2N2
514-868-9498
Fax: 514-286-7900

REHAU Industries Inc.
An operating company of REHAU Incorporated
625, av Lee
Baie-d'Urfé, QC H9X 3S3
514-457-3345
Fax: 514-457-6990
800-361-0830
info@rehau-na.com
www.rehau-na.com
Firm Type: Distributing, Engineering, Information Technology, Manufacturing
Founded: 1948
Staff: 1000
Quality Environmental Management System(s): 9001:2000
Products/Services/Areas of Expertise: "United Polymer Solutions", with clients in the construction, automotive & industrial sectors; expertise in materials development, systems design & surface technology, with a focus on sustainable practices & designs; products include window & door systems, heating & plumbing, fire protection, automotive components such as bumpers & fenders, water & air management, & thermoplastic sealing systems. Locations worldwide, including sales offices in Vancouver, Winnipeg, Toronto, Montréal, Moncton & St. John's, & plant facilities in Winnipeg, Prescott, & Baie d'Urfé (Montréal)
Financial Information:
Type of Ownership: Foreign-owned
Domestic Markets:
National
Foreign Activity:
Africa, Asia, Australia/New Zealand, Eastern Europe, Western Europe, The Middle East, The Pacific Rim, South America, Mexico, USA
Contact(s):
Jack Anderson, Regional Sales Manager
Antonio Sacco, Manager
antonio.sacco@rehau-na.com

International Branch(es):
North American Headquarters - REHAU Incorporated
1501 Edwards Ferry Rd. NE
Leesburg, VA USA

703-777-5255
Fax: 703-777-3053
rehau.mailbox@rehau.com

Reinforced Plastic Systems Inc.
P.O. Box 299
740 South Main St.
Mahone Bay, NS B0J 2E0
902-624-8383
Fax: 902-624-6395
800-343-9355
www.reinforcedplasticsystems.com
Firm Type: Engineering, Manufacturing
Founded: 1956
Staff: 200
Products/Services/Areas of Expertise: Designer & manufacturer of corrosion & erosion resistant pipe, FRP/GRP ABCO pipe (1-120 inch dia.), tanks & field manufactured vessels (up to 25m dia.); stact liners, towers & custom products; 2nd Canadian facility located at 99 Industrial Park Rd., Minto, NB (Maritime Fibreglass Fabricators)
Recently Completed / Ongoing Projects: Vessel nozzles & precipitator/absorber, Lurgi, Germany; absorber/ME/overflow piping & seal boxes, Babcock & Wilcox, USA; oxidation/absorber/slurry recycle & process piping, Tdreco, Czech Republic
Financial Information:
Type of Ownership: Private
Domestic Markets:
Alberta, British Columbia, Manitoba, New Brunswick, Newfoundland & Labrador, Nova Scotia, Ontario, Québec, Saskatchewan
Foreign Activity:
Worldwide
Markets Sought:
Australia/New Zealand, Caribbean
Contact(s):
Ken Eisner, Assistant Sales Manager

Canadian Branches:
Maritime Fiberglass Fabricators Ltd.
99 Industrial Park Rd.
Minto, NB E4B 3A6
506-327-6505
Fax: 506-327-6755
mffminto@mffnb.ca
Darrel McLean, General Manager

Reliance Geological Services Inc.
418 East 14th St.
North Vancouver, BC V7L 2N8
604-984-3663
Fax: 425-984-9524
admin@reliancegeological.com
www.reliancegeological.com
Firm Type: Engineering, Scientific/Technical Services
Founded: 1989
Products/Services/Areas of Expertise: Provides consulting & contract field services, with a focus on the mining & mineral exploration sectors. Services include research, examination & evaluation; site assessments; technical report preparation; contracting of exploration services; project management; geochemical evaluations; geotechnical field services
Domestic Markets:
National
Foreign Activity:
Mexico, USA
Contact(s):
Peter Leriche, President

RemedX Remediation Services Inc.
#305, 1550 - 5th St. SW
Calgary, AB T2R 1K3
403-209-0004
Fax: 403-244-3154
remedx@telusplanet.net
www.remedx.net
Products/Services/Areas of Expertise: Full-service remediation & reclamation contracting & technical services
Contact(s):
Barrie Flood, President

Remedy Energy Services Ltd.
#255, 720 - 28 St. NE
Calgary, AB T2A 6R3
403-272-0703
Fax: 403-272-0624

info@remedyenergy.com
www.remedyresource.com
Products/Services/Areas of Expertise: Consulting and project management services to the Oil & Gas Industry
Domestic Markets:
Alberta
Contact(s):
Rand Silkie, President

René Gervais Inc., Consultants
Consultants René Gervais Inc
1455, rue Champlain
Trois-Rivières, QC G9A 5X4
819-371-3313
Fax: 819-371-2288
Firm Type: Engineering
Founded: 1984
Staff: 15
Member of: Association québécoise des technologues de l'environnement
Quality Environmental Management System(s): 9001
Products/Services/Areas of Expertise: Water & wastewater treatment; municipal solid waste consulting; engineering consulting services
Financial Information:
Type of Ownership: Private
Revenue: $500,000 - $1.5 Million
Revenue Sources: 10% nationwide; 20% Provincial; 60% Municipals; 10% Private Contracts
Domestic Markets:
Québec
Foreign Activity:
South America, Mexico
Contact(s):
René Gervais, ing., M.Sc.A., President

Renewable Energy Services Inc.
P.O. Box 3610
135 Gerrish St.
Windsor, NS B0N 2T0
902-798-5085
Fax: 902-798-5934
877-798-5085
resl@ns.sympatico.ca
Firm Type: Scientific/Technical Services
Staff: 3
Products/Services/Areas of Expertise: Operating company for the Scotian Windfields
Contact(s):
Brian Watling

Renovators Resource Inc.
6040 Almon St.
Halifax, NS B3K 1T8
902-429-3889
Fax: 902-425-6795
877-230-7700
frontdesk@renovators-resource.com
www.renovators-resource.com
Firm Type: Waste Management
Founded: 1994
Products/Services/Areas of Expertise: Disposal of used building materials; architectural salvage
Contact(s):
Jennifer Corson, President

RenuWater Centre
A Division of Joyron Enterprises Ltd.
#3, 197 Pictou Rd.
Truro, NS B2N 2S7
902-895-4467
Fax: 902-893-6811
800-565-4468
inquiries@renuwater.com
www.renuwater.com
Firm Type: Distributing
Founded: 1987
Staff: 45
Member of: Canadian Water Quality Association
Products/Services/Areas of Expertise: Provides water equipment
Financial Information:
Type of Ownership: Private
Revenue: $500,000 - $1.5 Million
Revenue Sources: 100% Private Contracts
Domestic Markets:
Nova Scotia

Contact(s):
Tammy Slauenwhite, President

Republic Environmental Systems (Fort Erie) Ltd.
P.O. Box 340
1731 Petit Rd.
Fort Erie, ON L2A 5N1
905-994-1900
Fax: 905-994-1777
Contact(s):
Harry Wells
Contact(s):
John Petlic
Contact(s):
Tom Baker, General Manager
Contact(s):
Fraser Cross, General Manager

Canadian Branches:
Republic Environmental Systems (Fort Erie) Ltd.
P.O. Box 340
1731 Petit Rd.
Fort Erie, ON L2A 5N1
905-994-1900
Fax: 905-994-1777

Republic Environmental Systems (Pickering) Ltd.
1070 Toy Ave.
Pickering, ON L1W 3P1
905-686-6287
Fax: 905-686-8642

Republic Environmental Systems (Brantford) Ltd.
P.O. Box 1477
112 Adams Blvd.
Brantford, ON N3T 5V6
519-756-9770
Fax: 519-756-9950

Republic Environmental Systems (Brockville) Ltd.
P.O. Box 845
RR#5
Brockville, ON K6V 5W1
613-342-3703
Fax: 613-342-1621

Rescan Environmental Services Ltd.
Also Known As: Rescan Group Ltd.
1111 West Hastings St., 6th Fl.
Vancouver, BC V6E 2J3
604-689-9460
Fax: 604-687-4277
877-689-9460
rescan@rescan.com
www.rescan.com
Firm Type: Management Consulting, Scientific/Technical Services
Founded: 1981
Member of: Canadian Society of Environmental Biologists
Products/Services/Areas of Expertise: Hazardous waste treatment & control; environmental impact assessments; environmental audits; risk analysis; site investigations; licensing & permitting; oceanographic studies; subaqueous placement of waste material; acid rock drainage; site remediation
Domestic Markets:
British Columbia, Newfoundland & Labrador, Northwest Territories, Yukon Territory
Foreign Activity:
Africa, Asia, Caribbean, Central America, China, The Pacific Rim, South America, Vietnam
Contact(s):
Clem A. Pelletier, President/CEO
George Poling, Sr. Vice-President

Canadian Branches:
Yellowknife
#908, 5201 - 50th Ave.
Yellowknife, NT X1A 3S9
867-920-2090
Fax: 867-920-2015

International Branch(es):
Compania Rescan Peru SA
av Paz Soldan 170, Oficina 401, San Isidro
Lima Peru
-51-1-422-8380
Fax: -51-1-422-7152

Rescan Chile Ltda
Calle Juan Gutemberg 438, Galpon 10
Antofagasta Chile

Rescan Consultants Inc.
#3200, 1001 Fourth Ave. Plaza
Seattle, WA USA
206-726-2145
Fax: 206-382-9648

Research Electronics (Reselco) Ltd.
16302 - 80 Ave.
Edmonton, AB T5R 3M6
780-489-6207
Fax: 780-489-6207
Firm Type: Management Consulting, Scientific/Technical Services
Founded: 1965
Staff: 2
Member of: Association of Professsional Engineers, Geologists & Geophysicists of Alberta
Products/Services/Areas of Expertise: Quantum engineering-based SRET (selective resonance energy transfer) materials
Financial Information:
Type of Ownership: Private
Revenue: Less than $50,000
Revenue Sources: 100% Private Contracts
Domestic Markets:
Alberta
Foreign Activity:
Central Europe

Research Facility
1302 Hwy. #2
Emeryville, ON N0R 1C0

Canadian Branches:
Research Facility
1302 Hwy. #2
Emeryville, ON N0R 1C0

Resource Environmental Associates
#700, 111 Gordon Baker Rd.
Toronto, ON M2H 3R1
416-495-1314
Fax: 416-495-9211
consultants@rea.ca
www.rea4ehs.com
Products/Services/Areas of Expertise: Environmental consulting & contracting services; resource management services

Canadian Branches:
Markham
#110, 11 Allstate Parkway
Markham, ON L3R 9T8
416-495-1314
Fax: 416-495-9211

Ottawa
#110, 30 Concourse Gate
Ottawa, ON K2E 7V7
613-225-5200
Fax: 613-225-5210
ottawaconsultants@rea.ca

Total Environmental Services Contracting Ltd - Vaughan
#2 Rowntree Dairy Rd.
Vaughan, ON L4L 5W4
905-856-1585
Fax: 416-291-9036
vince@rea-contacting.ca

International Branch(es):
REA Envirohealth International - Barbados
Station Hill
St. Michael Barbados
246-228-0634
Fax: 246-427-7541
envirohealth@rea.ca

Resource Systems Inc.
51 Ballathie Cres.
Fall River, NS B2T 1P6
902-861-4710
Fax: 902-861-1366
moakes@resourcesystemsinc.ca
www.resourcesystemsinc.ca

Firm Type: Distributing
Founded: 1986
Staff: 3
Products/Services/Areas of Expertise: Offers a range of water & wastewater disinfection technologies for clients in the municipal & industrial sectors; a complete line of online, hand-held & laboratory process monitoring instruments for water & wastewater; & process equipment solutions for water, wastewater & industrial treatment
Recently Completed / Ongoing Projects: Chlorination of water in Bridgewater, Oxford, Springhill, NS; Shediac, Gagetown, Blacks Harbour, NB (completed); chlorination of water/wastewater, Bouctouche, NB, Glace Bay NS; C02 systems Celaie Bay, Acichat, Springhill, NS
Financial Information:
Type of Ownership: Private
Revenue: $250,000 - $500,000
Revenue Sources: 50% nationwide; 5% Provincial; 25% Municipals; 65% Private Contracts
Domestic Markets:
New Brunswick, Nova Scotia, Prince Edward Island,
Contact(s):
Larry Oakes, Owner/Senior Advisor

Restoration Environmental Contractors - Restoration Consultants / REC
Also Known As: REC Demolition
A Division of 836171 Ontario Inc.
P.O. Box 746
#5, 10 Stalwart Industrial Dr.
Gormley, ON L0H 1G0
905-888-0066
Fax: 905-888-0071
800-894-4924
rec@restorationenvironmental.com
www.environmentalhazards.com
Firm Type: Engineering, Scientific/Technical Services, Waste Management
Founded: 1989
Staff: 62
Member of: Abcott Construction Limited; Consulting Engineers of Ontario; Environmental Abatement Council of Ontario
Products/Services/Areas of Expertise: "Complete Turn-key Operations from Assessment to Remediation". Experts in demolition, asbestos abatement, mould & fungi remediation, hazardous material removal, lead abatement, infectious disease control, UFFI removal, industrial plant cleanups, site remediation & disaster recovery, decommissioning closures, biological hazards, PCB's, soil remediation, underground storage tank removal. Clients in all sectors, including industrial, commercial, government & institutional
Recently Completed / Ongoing Projects: Asbestos abatement project for Mayprop Investment's Old Crown Life Building, Toronto, ON; lead dust & asbestor removal, Bombardier, Thunder Bay, ON; asbestos removal, Toronto Transit Commission
Financial Information:
Type of Ownership: Private
Domestic Markets:
Ontario
Foreign Activity:
USA
Contact(s):
Steven Ball, President
Don Bremner, Vice President, Operations
David Bremner, Sr. Project Manager, Hazardous Materials

Canadian Branches:
Brantford
124 Garden Ave.
Brantford, ON N3S 7W4
519-757-1126
Fax: 519-756-8721
877-781-0246

Florida
c/o Restoration Environmental
#109, Bldg. 1, 106 - 1st St. East
Tierra Verde, FL USA
800-894-4924
800-894-4924

Ottawa
Victoria Memorial Museum
240 McLeod St.
Ottawa, ON K1P 6P4
866-554-3334

Sturgeon Falls
129 Cache Bay Rd.
Sturgeon Falls, ON P0H 2G0
866-854-1115

Toronto
416-543-4719

Rexdale Disposal Ltd.
680 Garyray Rd.
Toronto, ON M9L 1R3
416-744-8114
Fax: 416-744-9109
Products/Services/Areas of Expertise: Waste management
Contact(s):
Mauro Rossi, General Manager

Ribbons Recycled Inc.
81 Wright Ave., Unit H
Dartmouth, NS B3B 1H4
902-468-5622
Fax: 902-468-3232
800-808-5622
info@ribbonsrecycled.com
www.ribbonsrecycled.com
Firm Type: Distributing, Manufacturing, Waste Management
Founded: 1992
Products/Services/Areas of Expertise: Ribbons Recycled Inc. is the head office for Inkjet X-change, & is a re-manufacturer of Inkjet, Dot Matrix & Laser Printer toner cartridges & ribbons; services include on-site or in-house printer service & repair, & sale of reconditioned printers
Domestic Markets:
New Brunswick, Nova Scotia, Ontario
Contact(s):
Don MacKinnon, President

Rice Engineering & Operating Ltd.
Also Known As: RICE
9333 - 41 Ave. NW
Edmonton, AB T6E 6R5
780-469-1356
Fax: 780-469-2587
888-742-3364
info@riceeng.com
www.riceeng.com
Firm Type: Distributing, Manufacturing
Founded: 1952
Staff: 7
Member of: Environmental Services Association of Alberta; BC Groundwater Association; Saskatchewan Groundwater Association
Products/Services/Areas of Expertise: An employee-owned company engaged in supplying products, equipment & expertise to clients in the chemical & industrial processing, geotechnical & environmental, mineral exploration, & petroleum & petrochemical sectors. Operating divisions include Earth Sciences (environmental, waterwell technologies, industrial drilling products, geotechnical instrumentation); Industrial (process piping, fluid transfer, filtration products); & Energy Products (corrosion prevention, piping repair products, Duoline products). Branch offices in Calgary, & Vaughan (ON). For the Vaughan office, located at 147 Citation Dr., contact 905-760-0170
Domestic Markets:
Alberta, British Columbia, Manitoba, Ontario, Saskatchewan
Contact(s):
Terry Kunyk, President
Scott Stubbard, Manager, Operations

Canadian Branches:
Calgary
4511 Manhattan Rd. SE
Calgary, AB T2G 2B3
403-287-2805
Fax: 403-287-3597
Michael Kleespies, Sales Representative

Richard Kadulski Architect
#204, 1037 Broadway West
Vancouver, BC V6H 1E3
604-689-1841
Fax: 604-689-1641
kadulski@direct.ca
Firm Type: Scientific/Technical Services
Member of: Architectural Institute of BC; Canadian Home Builders Association; Solar Energy Society of Canada Inc.
Products/Services/Areas of Expertise: Energy-efficient building design

Contact(s):
Richard Kadulski, President/CEO

Richmond Specialty Mushroom Farms Ltd.
26227 - 62nd Ave.
Aldergrove, BC V4W 1L8
604-857-8959
Fax: 604-857-2726
877-541-3663
rsmf@specialtymushroom.net
www.specialtymushroom.net
Firm Type: Scientific/Technical Services
Founded: 1986
Staff: 7
Products/Services/Areas of Expertise: Builds computer controlled environmental chambers for growing mushrooms
Financial Information:
Type of Ownership: Private
Revenue Sources: 100% Private Contracts
Domestic Markets:
National
Foreign Activity:
USA

RICHWAY Environmental Technologies Ltd.
Formerly: Richway Environmental Preservation Co. Ltd.
#100, 11300 No. 5 Rd.
Richmond, BC V7A 5J7
604-275-2201
Fax: 604-275-2203
info@richway.ca
www.richway.ca
Firm Type: Engineering, Waste Management
Founded: 1995
Staff: 150
Products/Services/Areas of Expertise: The firm provides comprehensive consulting, system design, engineering & project management services to the waste management sector. Services include project planning, design, installation, operation & financing. The primary technology supplied is the RICHWAY Waste-to-Energy System, which converts solid waste to electricity using an advanced combustion technology (Controlled Air Pyrolysis System) & a state-of-the-art emission control system which removes harmful pollutants resulting from the burning of solid waste. Branch offices in China & Thailand
Recently Completed / Ongoing Projects: Industrial waste incineration, Baoding, Hebei Province, China (1997); municipal solid waste processing, Liaoyang, Liaoning Province, China (1998), & in Shenzhen, Guangdong Province (1999)
Financial Information:
Type of Ownership: Private
Revenue: Greater than $5 Million
Revenue Sources: 30% nationwide; 40% Provincial; 2-% Municipals
Domestic Markets:
British Columbia
Foreign Activity:
Asia, China, The Pacific Rim, Vietnam
Contact(s):
Leonard Li, President
Henry Tso, Contact
marketing@richway.ca

International Branch(es):
Beijing
1807/1809 Huibin Bldg.
Chaoyang District
Beijing China
-86 10 84972469
Fax: -85 10 84972467
Michael Yang
michaely@richway.ca

Guangdong
Gonglian District, West Train Station
Huizhou, Guangdong Prov. China
-86 752 2372936
Fax: -86 752 2372932
hzrichway@hzrichway.com
Yanfen Huang

Hong Kong
13F Neich Tower
128 Gloucester Rd.
Wanchai, Hong Kong China
-852 27294328
Fax: -852 21170661
info@richwaygroup.com

David Ng

Installation Co. Ltd.
99 Moo2 Bangkunkong Bangruay
Nonthaburi Thailand
-66 2 887 9163;66 1 824 2159
Fax: -66 2 887 5628
installationcoltd@yahoo.com
Pattiya Chompuech

Shenzhen
611 Haitian Bldg.
Caitian South Rd., Futian District
Shenzhen China
86 755 83460611
Fax: 86 755 83460996
richway@public.szptt.net.cn
Wei Liu

Ricoh Canada Inc.
A wholly-owned subsidiary of Ricoh Corporation
Formerly: Savin Canada; Lanier Canada; Gestetner Canada#300, 5520 Explorer Dr.
Mississauga, ON L4W 5L1
905-795-9659
Fax: 905-795-6926
888-730-9163
customerservice@ricoh.ca
www.ricoh.ca
Firm Type: Distributing, Information Technology, Manufacturing
Founded: 1981
Staff: 800
Quality Environmental Management System(s): 27001; 140
EcoLogo Certified Products & Services: Docunomics; print-on-demand; print & information logistics; lithographic printing; internet & extranet digital document creation & digital distribution; facilities & fleet management; document re-engineering; automated database management
Products/Services/Areas of Expertise: Ricoh manufactures & distributes document & content management solutions, with a focus on computer-networked & digital multifunctional document systems, black & white digital imaging systems, facsimile products, printers, scanners, digital duplicators, document management & wide format engineering systems. Ricoh worldwide is a leader in energy conservation & sustainability practices, with stringent guidelines to prevent pollution, utilize energy & resources efficiently, & reduce & dispose of waste products responsibly. Its Trade-Up Program allows clients to trade in old equipment (regardless of manufacturer) for cash, & there are programs to donate old equipment to non-profit organizations. All equipment & related supplies (eg. toner bottles & cartridges) sold by Ricoh may be recycled. Ricoh Canada has received the Ecologo certification
Ecological Note: Docunomics; print-on-demand; print & information logistics; lithographic printing; internet & extranet digital document creation & digital distribution; facilities & fleet management; document re-engineering; automated database management
Financial Information:
Type of Ownership: Private
Revenue: Greater than $5 Million
Revenue Sources: 10% nationwide; 10% Provincial; 15% Municipals; 65% Private Contracts
Domestic Markets:
National,
Contact(s):
Glenn Laverty, President/CEO
Tony Sutcliffe, Vice-President & General Counsel

Ridgeline Environment Inc.
Formerly: Bio-Synergy Resources Inc.
#200, 3016 - 19th St. NE
Calgary, AB T2E 6Y9
403-806-2380
Fax: 403-806-2381
info@biosynergyresources.com
www.biosynergyresources.com
Firm Type: Scientific/Technical Services
Founded: 1999
Member of: Canadian Association of Petroleum Producers (CAPP); Canadian Land Reclamation Association (CLRA); Environmental Services Association of Alberta (ESAA); Alberta Construction Safety Association (ACSA)
Products/Services/Areas of Expertise: Soil remediation; feasibility & treatability studies; environmental evaluation of sites, centres for recycling, treatment & use of hazardous & special wastes

Financial Information:
Type of Ownership: Private
Domestic Markets:
Alberta
Contact(s):
Tyler Heathcote, President
Tony Ker, CEO, Director
Brad Shybunka, B.Sc., P.Ag, COO/Director

Canadian Branches:
Edmonton
#280, 9766 - 51st St.
Edmonton, AB T6E 0A6
780-988-5455
Fax: 780-988-5462

Grande Prairie
8704 - 99th St., 2nd Fl.
Clairmont, AB T0H 0W0
780-567-3264
Fax: 780-567-3207

Lloydminster
#203 5303 50th Ave.
Lloydminster, SK S9V 0P9
306-825-2324
Fax: 306-825-2343

Red Deer
5571 - 45th St., Bay #2
Red Deer, AB T4N 1L2
403-342-2130
Fax: 403-342-2005

Risk Check Environmental Ltd.
Formerly: Environmental Auditors Ltd.
York Corporate Centre
#240, 100 York Blvd.
Richmond Hill, ON L4B 1J8
905-886-7965
Fax: 905-886-7967
www.riskcheckinc.com
Firm Type: Engineering
Founded: 1989
Staff: 10
Member of: Canadian Environment Industry Association
Products/Services/Areas of Expertise: Engineering, occupational health & safety; site supervision; liaison with regulatory bodies; environmental audits; site characterization; evaluation of plant facility compliance; assessment of waste streams & disposal practices; design of waste containment facilities, decommissioning & clean-up, bioremediation services; owns & operates several soil vapour extraction units for use in soil remediation
Recently Completed / Ongoing Projects: Provided project management & contractor supervision with respect to the removal of two underground gasoline storage tanks, one underground waste oil storage tank, removal of five underground hydraulic hoists & excavation of impaired soil in the vicinity of the underground storage tanks, underground hydraulic hoists & an oil interceptor located onsite; phase III ESA of an automotive dealership, Toronto
Domestic Markets:
National
Foreign Activity:
USA
Contact(s):
Chris Kelson, CEO

RMS Enviro Solv Inc. Québec
Formerly: Mecorsys Inc.
555, ave O'Connell
Montréal, QC H9P 1E4
514-636-6204
Fax: 514-636-0206
800-563-1093
info@rmsenviro.com
www.rmsenviro.com
Firm Type: Distributing, Scientific/Technical Services
Founded: 1993
Products/Services/Areas of Expertise: Municipal/industrial contractor: temporary bypass pumping systems, trash & high head self-priming/run-dry centrifugal pumps, galvanized quick-disconnect & plastic piping, rubber hose, emergency spills response peristaltic hosepumps & skimmers, hydraulic submersible pumps & power units, automated/remote control & manned lagoon dredges & booster pumps, double containment zero leakage pumps, solvent recovery systems, vacuum equipment, replacement cloth & filter plates
Domestic Markets:
National
Contact(s):
Robert M. Spicer, President/General Manager

Canadian Branches:
Toronto Branch
36 Norbett Dr.
Gormley, ON L0H 1G0
877-767-7867

RMS Instruments Ltd.
#6877, 1 Goreway Dr.
Mississauga, ON L4V 1L9
905-677-5533
Fax: 905-677-5030
rms@rmsinst.com
www.rmsinst.com
Firm Type: Engineering, Manufacturing, Scientific/Technical Services
Founded: 1980
Staff: 10
Products/Services/Areas of Expertise: Measuring & monitoring equipment; laboratory equipment; data recording systems, test & measurement instruments: chart recorders, data acquisition systems, various recording media, automatic aeromagnetic digital compensators; power line monitor recorder; airborne geophysical exploration systems & engineering; service & support
Financial Information:
Type of Ownership: Private
Domestic Markets:
National
Foreign Activity:
Africa, Asia, Australia/New Zealand, Central America, Western Europe, South America,
Contact(s):
Onorio Rocca, President
Lynn Tucker, Administration

Robar
Formerly: Robar Industries Ltée
Also Known As: Les Produits Industriels Robar Inc.
1460, Joliot-Curie
Boucherville, QC J4B 7L9
450-641-9525
Fax: 450-641-4894
800-315-9525
dave.brewer@robar.ca
www.robarindustries.com
Products/Services/Areas of Expertise: Water & wastewater management equipment
Contact(s):
Dave Brewer, Sales Manager

Robb Engineering Ltd.
452 Ainsworth Ct.
Waterloo, ON N2T 1H5
519-885-2858
Fax: 519-885-0441
gjrobb@golden.net
www.robb.ca
Firm Type: Engineering
Founded: 1993
Staff: 2
Products/Services/Areas of Expertise: Consulting engineering services to the HVAC & energy management sectors; services include feasibility studies, design, construction support services; certified for work on mechanical & plumbing systems
Recently Completed / Ongoing Projects: Complete HVAC & digital control system, main plant offices of Babcock & Wilcox, Canada; HVAC retrofit for Budd Canada Inc., Kitchener, ON
Financial Information:
Type of Ownership: Private
Revenue: $100,000 - $250,000
Revenue Sources: 10% nationwide; 15% Municipals; 75% Private Contracts
Domestic Markets:
Ontario
Contact(s):
George Robb, P.Eng., President/Project Manager

Products & Services Buyer's Guide

Robert Hornal & Associates Ltd.
Formerly: Hornal Consultants Ltd.
2576 West 7th Ave.
Vancouver, BC V6K 1Y9
604-731-2697
Fax: 604-731-0244
888-412-2697
rhornal@hornal.com
www.hornal.com
Firm Type: Management Consulting
Founded: 1984
Staff: 3
Products/Services/Areas of Expertise: A consulting firm specializing in resource management, Aboriginal, environmental & social-economic issues: environmental assessments of mining, oil & gas development projects; land use planning; land claim administration & dispute resolution; policy development; mines & minerals management
Recently Completed / Ongoing Projects: Training Mackenzie Valley Environmental Impact Review Working Group
Financial Information:
Type of Ownership: Private
Revenue Sources: 30% nationwide; 30% Provincial; 40% Private Contracts
Domestic Markets:
British Columbia, Northwest Territories, Yukon Territory
Contact(s):
Robert Hornal, President
L. McNeil, Senior Researcher

Robert J. Redhead Limited
616 Holly Hill Cres.
Burlington, ON L7L 3Z7
905-631-7573
Fax: 905-631-6708
info@redheadlimited.com
www.redheadlimited.com
Founded: 1978
Member of: Canadian Chamber of Commerce; Ontario Environmental Industry Association
Products/Services/Areas of Expertise: Environmental consulting; policy development; process change; liquid & hazardous waste management consulting
Financial Information:
Type of Ownership: Private
Revenue: $100,000 - $250,000
Revenue Sources: 20% nationwide; 10% Provincial; 70% Private Contracts
Domestic Markets:
National
Foreign Activity:
Western Europe, USA
Contact(s):
Robert J. Redhead, President

Robert Laurin
#201, 1322, rue de Saint-Jovite
Mont-Tremblant, QC J8E 3J9
819-425-8623
Fax: 819-425-7436
robert.laurin@qc.aira.com
Firm Type: Engineering
Staff: 2
Member of: Ordre des ingénieurs du Québec; Association canadienne des Barrages; Réseau Environnement
Products/Services/Areas of Expertise: Consulting engineer
Recently Completed / Ongoing Projects: Muncipalité d'Amherst: poste de pompage et traitement d'eau potable, réservoir gravitaire en béton armé; Municipalité de St-Faustin-Lac-Carré: assainissement et traitement; Scerie Claude Forget inc.; divers projets
Financial Information:
Type of Ownership: Private
Revenue: $100,000 - $250,000
Revenue Sources: 50% Municipals; 50% Private Contracts
Domestic Markets:
Québec
Contact(s):
Robert Laurin, Principal

Robertson Environmental Services Ltd. / RESL
1525 - 200 St.
Langley, BC V2Z 1W5
604-530-9800
Fax: 604-628-9874
info@robertsonenvironmental.com
www.robertsonenvironmental.com
Firm Type: Management Consulting
Founded: 1997
Staff: 18
Products/Services/Areas of Expertise: Provides a broad range of wildlife inventory & environmental management services to public & private sector clients; services include environmental impact assessments, wildlife & vegetation inventories & monitoring, pre-construction salvages for species at risk, project management, environmental program audits, reviews & evaluations, technical report writing & copy editing; clients may come from the hydroelectric, gas, mining, transportation, infrastructure, land development, port development, & forestry sectors, as well as from cities & municipalities, & provincial & federal governments. The firm has taken part in planning inititatives & consultation to projects as diverse as the proposed windfarms on Vancouver Island to the Sea to Sky Highway Improvement Project, & other concerns
Domestic Markets:
British Columbia,
Contact(s):
Ian Robertson, M.Sc., R.P.Bio., Principal
Susanne Sloboda, Assoc.Env.St., Dip.Tech.

Robicheau's Pumping Service
P.O. Box 75A
RR#1
Tusket, NS B0W 3M0
902-648-2227
Fax: 902-742-6315
Products/Services/Areas of Expertise: Septic tank pumping, installations & repair, for residential & commercial clients; licensed storage tank disposal & installation; licensed waste oil removal & pumping; spill cleanup
Domestic Markets:
Nova Scotia
Contact(s):
Wayne Cobbett, Principal
wcobbett@eastlink.ca

Robinson Consultants Inc.
Formerly: A.J. Robinson & Associates Inc.;
Geo-Analysis Inc.
350 Palladium Dr.
Kanata, ON K2V 1A8
613-592-6060
Fax: 613-592-5995
ajrobinson@rcii.com
www.rcii.com
Firm Type: Engineering
Founded: 1977
Staff: 20
Products/Services/Areas of Expertise: Civil engineering firm providing consulting services in the areas of municipal engineering (water & sewage systems, solid waste management, pump stations), transportation (highway design, traffic engineering, bridges & structures), water resources (storm water management, flood plain mapping, groundwater & drainage), municipal drains, environmental services (audits, monitoring, remediation), land development, operational planning (emergency planning, snow removal, etc.), & project development to public & private sector clients. Services include: feasibility studies, environmental studies, reports, design, construction administration & inspection, project management & engineering analysis. Current technologies are used to full advantage
Recently Completed / Ongoing Projects: Master drainage studies for Manotick, Richmond, Stittsville; floodplain mapping projects on Steven Creek & Rideau River; Michael Snow disposal facility, Ottawa; March Rd. drainage strategy, Kanata; Arnprior waste disposal site
Financial Information:
Revenue Sources: 20% nationwide; 20% Provincial; 50% Municipals; 10% Private Contracts
Domestic Markets:
Ontario
Foreign Activity:
The Middle East, The Pacific Rim
Contact(s):
Andy J. Robinson, P.Eng., President
ajrobinson@rcii.com

Robinson Solutions
Formerly: Energy Management Systems
1456 Centennial Dr.
Kingston, ON K7L 4V2
613-389-7611
Fax: 613-634-3783
info@robinsonsolutions.com
www.robinsonsolutions.com
Firm Type: Engineering, Scientific/Technical Services
Founded: 1977
Staff: 15
Member of: Canadian Automated Buildings Association; Canadian Institute of Energy; Building Owners & Managers Association of Canada
Products/Services/Areas of Expertise: Building automation system for industrial, commercial, institutional facilities; computer control web ready monitor control & alarm systems; metering for air quality electrical/gas consumption
Financial Information:
Type of Ownership: Private
Revenue: $3 Million - $5 Million
Revenue Sources: 5% nationwide; 10% Provincial; 5% Municipals; 80% Private Contracts
Domestic Markets:
Alberta, British Columbia, Ontario
Contact(s):
Michael Robinson, President
Dwight Mains, Vice President

Roche ltée, Groupe-conseil
Roche Ltd., Consulting Group
Formerly: Roche International
Also Known As: Roche Consulting Engineers
#300, 3075, ch des Quatre-Bourgeois
Québec, QC G1W 4Y4
418-654-9600
Fax: 418-654-9699
marketing@roche.ca
www.roche.ca
Firm Type: Engineering
Founded: 1963
Staff: 1400
Quality Environmental Management System(s): 9001
Products/Services/Areas of Expertise: Diversified engineering & consulting firm offering scientific & technical services, project management, construction services & resource management strategies to national & international clients. Expertise includes building, construction, energy, environment, forestry, health & safety, industry, mining, real estate, transportation, urban planning & water infrastructures. Practices which enhance sustainability are a focus. Roche provides a French-speaking work environment in its offices in Québec, & services in French to its French-speaking clients. Subsidiaries include Évimbec ltée (property appraisal), Forchemex Ltd. Consulting Group (forest management), Groupe-conseil TDA inc. (an affiliate), & Urbanex (urban planning & landscape architecture). More than 40 offices in Québec, Canada & abroad - for a complete list, please consult www.roche.ca
Recently Completed / Ongoing Projects: Subregional environmental information system, south-east Asia; fisheries development project, Guinea; mining development project, Morocco; design & construction of a waste oil recycling & contaminated soil treatment centre for Shell Brunei Oil Co., Brunei
Financial Information:
Type of Ownership: Private
Revenue: Greater than $5 Million
Revenue Sources: 8% nationwide; 8% Provincial; 12% Municipals; 72% Private Contracts
Domestic Markets:
New Brunswick, Nova Scotia, Ontario, Québec
Foreign Activity:
Africa, Asia, Caribbean, Central America, China, South America, Mexico, USA, Former USSR, Vietnam
Contact(s):
Mario W. Martel, President/CEO
Gaston Déry, Vice President, Sustainable Development
Jacques Thivierge, Vice President, Marketing & Communications

Canadian Branches:
Baie-Comeau
905, rue du Puyjalon
Baie-Comeau, QC G5C 1N1
418-589-7817
Fax: 418-589-8487

Products/Services/Areas of Expertise: This is the Baie-Comeau office for both Roche ltée, Groupe-conseil & subsidiary Évimbec ltée. For the office of Groupe-conseil TDA inc., contact 418-296-6711

Bonaventure
146-E, rue Grand-Pré
Bonaventure, QC G0C 1E0
418-534-3130
Fax: 418-534-4158
Products/Services/Areas of Expertise: This office also houses subsidiary Urbanex

Boucherville
#360, 550 boul de Mortagne
Boucherville, QC J4B 5E4
450-449-6600
Fax: 450-449-2341
Products/Services/Areas of Expertise: This office also houses subsidiary Urbanex

Candiac
201, boul de l'Industrie
Candiac, QC J5R 6A6
450-619-7887
Fax: 450-619-1795
Products/Services/Areas of Expertise: This office also houses subsidiary Urbanex

Caraquet - Groupe Conseil Roche Atlantique ltée
Roche Atlantic Consulting Group Ltd.
#110, 27, boul Industriel
Caraquet, NB E1W 0A2
506-727-1160
Fax: 506-727-1161
Products/Services/Areas of Expertise: Roche Atlantic maintains offices also in Dalhousie & Edmunston, NB

Gaspé
156, rue de la Reine
Gaspé, QC G4X 1T4
418-368-0107
Fax: 418-368-0138
Products/Services/Areas of Expertise: This office also houses subsidiaries Roche Construction inc., & Urbanex

Gatineau
#230, 15, rue Buteau
Hull, QC J8Z 1V4
819-777-8877
Fax: 819-777-4082
Products/Services/Areas of Expertise: This office also houses subsidiary Urbanex

Lac-Mégantic
#101, 5109, rue Frontenac
Lac-Mégantic, QC G6B 1H2
819-583-1170
Fax: 819-583-2280
Products/Services/Areas of Expertise: This office also houses subsidiary Urbanex

Laval
4479, autoroute Laval (440) ouest
Laval, QC H7P 4W6
450-973-9111
Fax: 450-973-9811

Mont-Joli
1798, rue Lechasseur
Mont-Joli, QC G5H 2Z4
418-775-8816
Fax: 418-775-2616
Products/Services/Areas of Expertise: This office also houses subsidiary Urbanex

Montréal
#1500, 630, boul René-Lévesque ouest
Montréal, QC H3B 1S6
514-393-9110
Fax: 514-393-1511
Products/Services/Areas of Expertise: This office also houses subsidiaries Roche Construction inc., & Urbanex. For subsidiary Pasquin St-Jean & associés, contact 514-282-8100

Rivière-du-Loup
186A, rue Lafontaine
Rivière-du-Loup, QC G5T 3A7
418-868-1644
Fax: 418-868-1646

Products/Services/Areas of Expertise: The Rivière-du-Loup office also houses Roche subsidiaries Évimbec Ltd., Roche Construction inc., & Urbanex. Please consult www.roche.ca for contact details

Rouyn-Noranda
#201, 170, av Principale
Rouyn-Noranda, QC J9X 4P7
819-762-4891
Fax: 819-762-9922
Products/Services/Areas of Expertise: This office also houses subsidiaries Évimbec ltée, & Urbanex

Saguenay
159, Côte Salaberry
Saguenay, QC G7H 4K2
418-549-6471
Fax: 418-549-3268
Products/Services/Areas of Expertise: This office also houses subsidiaries Évimbec ltée, Roche Construction inc., & Urbanex

Saint-Raymond
423B, rue Saint-Cyrille
Saint-Raymond, QC G3L 4S6
418-337-9410
Fax: 418-654-9699
Products/Services/Areas of Expertise: This office also houses subsidiary Urbanex

Sept-Iles
#100, 421, av Arnaud
Sept-Iles, QC G4R 3B3
418-968-8873
Fax: 418-962-3260
Products/Services/Areas of Expertise: This office also houses subsidiaries Évimbec ltée, Forchemex Ltd. Consulting Group, Roche Construction inc., & Urbanex

Thetford Mines
183, rue Pie-XI
Thetford Mines, QC G6G 3N3
418-338-8515
Fax: 418-338-6643
Products/Services/Areas of Expertise: This office also houses subsidiaries Roche Construction inc., Évimbec ltée, & Urbanex

Rochester Midland Ltd.
851 Progress Ct.
Oakville, ON L6J 5A8
905-847-3000
Fax: 905-847-1675
800-387-7174
www.rochestermidland.ca
Firm Type: Manufacturing
Founded: 1903
Staff: 95
Member of: Canadian Consumer Specialty Products Association
Quality Environmental Management System(s): 9001
Products/Services/Areas of Expertise: Specialty chemical products & services for boilers, cooling systems (open & closed), wastewater treatment, process water, feed & monitoring equipment
Financial Information:
Type of Ownership: Private
Revenue: Greater than $5 Million
Revenue Sources: 100% Private Contracts
Domestic Markets:
British Columbia, Manitoba, New Brunswick, Nova Scotia, Ontario
Contact(s):
Sue Gazky, Vice-President & Business Manager
Steve Sanford, Product Manager, Water Energy Division
Lynne Scarlett, Lab Supervisor
George Newbery, Operations Manager

Rockwell Automation Canada Inc.
135 Dundas St.
Cambridge, ON N1R 5X1
519-623-1810
Fax: 519-623-8930
www.rockwellautomation.ca
Firm Type: Distributing, Information Technology, Manufacturing
Quality Environmental Management System(s): 9001; ISO
Products/Services/Areas of Expertise: A company in the Rockwell Automation, Inc. family, headquartered in Milwaukee, WI, Rockwell Automation Canada is engaged in providing manufacturers with industrial automation control & information solutions. Products include the Allen-Bradley line of integrated control & information platforms, intelligent motor controls & industrial components. Services include comprehensive customer support (on-site & remote), parts & repair, training. Locations across Canada
Financial Information:
Type of Ownership: Publicly Traded
Revenue: $3 Million - $5 Million
Domestic Markets:
National
Contact(s):
Marion Clyde, Office Manager

Canadian Branches:
Brampton
40 Bramtree Ct.
Brampton, ON L6S 5Z7
905-793-0965
Fax: 905-793-7468

Calgary
#230, 6223 - 2nd St. SE
Calgary, AB T2H 1J5
403-253-1020
Fax: 403-259-5483

Dartmouth
260 Brownlow Ave.
Dartmouth, NS B3B 1V9
902-468-2454
Fax: 902-468-3606

Delta
802 Carleton Crt.
Delta, BC V3M 6Y6
604-520-5976
Fax: 604-520-6235

Edmonton
11510 - 168 St.
Edmonton, AB T5M 3T9
780-444-1101
Fax: 780-486-7887

Laval
3043, rue Joseph-A.-Bombardier
Laval, QC H7P 6C5
450-781-5100
Fax: 450-781-5101

Moncton
93 Ulysse Dr.
Dieppe, NB E1A 7C2
506-855-6542
Fax: 506-855-7287

Nanaimo
201 Selby St.
Nanaimo, BC V9R 2R2
250-741-8226
Fax: 250-741-8227

Prince George
871A - 3rd Ave.
Prince George, BC V2L 3C7
250-564-6422
Fax: 250-564-6462

Saskatoon
Bay C, 203 - 4th St. East
Saskatoon, SK S7K 5H1
306-242-2100
Fax: 306-242-9985

St. Thomas
50 Howard Ave.
St. Thomas, NL A1L 1C1
709-773-0036
Fax: 709-773-0104

Sudbury
49 Lady Ashley Dr.
Sudbury, ON P3E 5Z8
705-522-5121
Fax: 705-522-8914

Thunder Bay
1060 Gorham St.
Thunder Bay, ON P7B 5X5
807-345-3411
Fax: 807-345-4287

Products & Services Buyer's Guide

Windsor
#408, 3200 Deziel Dr.
Windsor, ON N8W 5K8
519-944-2611
Fax: 519-944-4632

Winnipeg
#L, 675 Berry St.
Winnipeg, MB R3H 1A7
204-786-3047
Fax: 204-786-4996

Rocky Mountain Environmental Ltd. / RME
#3155, 21331 Gordon Way
Richmond, BC V6W 1J9
604-275-1346
Fax: 604-241-0995
888-671-4556
sales@spilldepot.com
www.spilldepot.com
Firm Type: Management Consulting, Distributing, Waste Management
Founded: 1996
Staff: 5
Member of: Environmental Managers Association; National Fire Protection Association
Products/Services/Areas of Expertise: Spill response products & services: absorbents, containment, booms, skimmers, oil/water separators, industrial pumps, personal protection equipment, gas monitors; on-site risk assessments, contingency planning, waste removal; training in spill response; environmental & safety consulting
Financial Information:
Type of Ownership: Private
Revenue: $1.5 Million - $3 Million
Revenue Sources: 10% nationwide; 10% Provincial; 20% Municipals; 60% Private Contracts
Domestic Markets:
National
Foreign Activity:
Worldwide
Markets Sought:
China, The Middle East, The Pacific Rim, Vietnam
Contact(s):
Ron MacMillan, President
Gerry Hay, Trainer

Roctest Ltée
665, rue Pine
Saint-Lambert, QC J4P 2P4
450-465-1113
Fax: 450-465-1938
877-762-8378
info@roctest.com
www.roctest.com
Firm Type: Manufacturing
Founded: 1967
Staff: 70
Products/Services/Areas of Expertise: Manufacturer of geotechnical, geomechanical & structural monitoring instruments for measurements of stress, strain, load, pressures, displacement, settlements, inclinations, orientations & temperatures; sales, maintenance, installation, training system integration, in-situ soil & rock testing for civil & mining engineering projects; data acquisition systems; vibrating wire & fiber optic sensors
Activities: Environmental analysis & treatment; construction material testing equipment; water sampling & monitoring systems; physical properties testing & inspection equipement; geophysical & mineral prospecting equipment & parts
Domestic Markets:
National
Foreign Activity:
Worldwide
Contact(s):
Jean Archambault, Vice President, Sales & Marketing
jarchambault@roctest.com

International Branch(es):
Bellingham, WA
#670, 177 Telegraph Rd.
Bellingham, WA USA
206-774-9812
Fax: 206-418-6455
rhardman@roctest.com
Eric Trent

France
10, av Eiffel, 77220
Gretz-Armainvilliers France
-33-1-64-06-40-80
Fax: -33-1-64-06-40-
info@telemac.fr
Jean Vaseux

Rocvent Inc.
Walden Industrial Park
55 Magill St.
Lively, ON P3Y 1K6
705-692-5854
Fax: 705-692-9044
info@rocvent.com
www.rocvent.com
Firm Type: Distributing, Manufacturing
Founded: 1980
Staff: 20
Products/Services/Areas of Expertise: A manufacturer of mine & tunnel ventilation tubing & ducting; comprehensive line of fans, fan silencers & related accessories; design & manufacture of flexible tanks, repair sleeves, pond liner sheets, etc.
Domestic Markets:
National
Foreign Activity:
USA
Contact(s):
Bernt Ivarsson, President

Rodrigue Métal Ltée
Centre Industriel
1890, 1e rue
Saint-Romuald, QC G6W 5M6
418-839-0671
Fax: 418-839-0201
rodair@rodriguemetal.com
www.rodriguemetal.com
Firm Type: Manufacturing
Founded: 1964
Staff: 150
Member of: Association des manufacturiers de bois de sciage du Québec
Products/Services/Areas of Expertise: The company designs, manufactures & installs dust collection & air conveying equipment. Products include structural frameworks, wrought metals, hammer mills, & chippers. Services include custom machining & assembly services
Activities: Structural steel & iron work; industrial air filtration; machine shop
Recently Completed / Ongoing Projects: Louisiana Pacific Corp., Jeld-Wen Portes & Fenêtres, Tafisa Ltee., Airtek Pneumatics Ltd., Industries Maibec Inc., J.D.Irving Ltd., Temlam Inc., Abitibi Consolidated du Canada, Menuiserie des Pins Ltee., Tembec Industries Inc.
Financial Information:
Type of Ownership: Private
Revenue: Greater than $5 Million
Revenue Sources: 10% Municipals; 90% Private Contracts
Domestic Markets:
New Brunswick, Nova Scotia, Ontario, Québec
Foreign Activity:
USA,
Contact(s):
Claude Rodrigue, President
Gilles Beaudry, Director, Sales & Design
Daniel Beaupre, P.Eng., Director, Engineering
Patrick Roy, Engineering Project Director
Contact(s):
Serge Maheux, Production Coordinator

Canadian Branches:
Industrial Air Filtration Division
Centre Industriel
1890, 1e rue
Saint-Romuald, QC G6W 5M6
418-839-0400
Fax: 418-839-0201
rodair@rodriguemetal.com

Roger LaRue Enterprises Ltd.
Also Known As: LaRue's Waste & Recycling
23082 McCowan Rd.
Queensville, ON L4P 3E2
905-478-4988
Fax: 905-478-8789
Firm Type: Waste Management
Founded: 1954
Staff: 56
Member of: Ontario Waste Management Association
Products/Services/Areas of Expertise: Commercial & industrial waste hauling & recycling services & facilities
Contact(s):
Fred LaRue, Vice-President

Roley Construction
P.O. Box 29135
St. John's, NL A1A 5E1
709-739-9381
Fax: 709-753-2741
ches@chespeach.com
Firm Type: Management Consulting, Engineering
Member of: Newfoundland & Labrador Environmental Industry Association
Products/Services/Areas of Expertise: The firm is engaged in spill cleanup services, site remediation & decommissioning
Contact(s):
Ches Peach, Principal

Romatec Incorporated
#3, 250 Harry Walker Pkwy.
Newmarket, ON L3Y 7B4
905-952-0000
Fax: 905-952-2151
800-268-3137
Toronto@romatec.com
www.romatec.com
Firm Type: Distributing
Founded: 1955
Member of: Air & Waste Management Association
Quality Environmental Management System(s): 9001:2000
Products/Services/Areas of Expertise: Romatec's instrumentation division provides quality products for process & emissions monitoring. Products include valves, pumps, instrumentation for various purposes (combustion control analyzers, emission monitors, measuring equipment, gauges, pollution sensors, etc.), specialty products. Romatec Environmental Systems provides a full line of proprietary products & services to the gas, water, industrial process & infrastructure markets, including continuous emission monitoring, particulate/opacity monitoring, combustion control, process analysis & control, & gas analyzers & equipment. Romapharm serves the biopharm sector. Services include installation & start-up, routine calibration & preventative maintenance, emergency services, in-house repair, & training
Domestic Markets:
Alberta, Manitoba, New Brunswick, Nova Scotia, Ontario, Prince Edward Island, Québec
Foreign Activity:
USA
Contact(s):
Steve Dockerty, President
dockertys@romatec.com
Don G. Hewson, P.Eng., Director
hewsond@romatec.com
Frank Spray, Manager, Sales
sprayf@romatec.com

Canadian Branches:
Calgary
Manchester Bldg.
#201/203, 339 - 50th Ave. SE
Calgary, AB T2G 2B3
403-203-2931
Fax: 403-264-3166
877-766-2937
Calgary@romawest.com
Archie Smith, Inside Technical Sales

Edmonton
Valve Automation Centre
7720 - 69th St.
Edmonton, AB T6B 2J7
780-440-6147
Fax: 780-440-6148
Edmonton@romawest.com
Gary Parpinel, Regional Manager

Jonquière
2123, rue Deschenes
Jonquière, QC G7S 4L1
418-548-4658
Fax: 418-548-9022
Jonquiere@romatec.com

Pierre Dufresne, Sales
Maritimes
7940 Hwy. 215, RR#1
Maitland, NS B0N 1T0
902-468-2525
Fax: 902-468-1606
Maritimes@romatec.com
Keith Wallis, Technical Sales

Montréal
9485, Route Transcanadienne
Montréal, QC H4S 1V3
514-332-9302
Fax: 514-332-0578
800-361-9302
Montreal@romatec.com
Tom Mostowy, Director

Northern Ontario
P.O. Box 109
1292 Bay of Island Dr.
Whitefish Falls, ON P0P 2H0
705-285-0911
Fax: 705-285-0912
Northern_Ontario@romatec.com
Al Wingrave, Technical Sales

Sarnia
#1, 1173 Michener Rd.
Sarnia, ON N7S 5G5
519-337-7416
Fax: 519-336-0998
877-337-7416
Sarnia@romatec.com
Bill Reid, Director

ROMOR Atlantic Limited
#10, 51 Raddall Ave.
Dartmouth, NS B3B 1T6
902-466-7000
Fax: 902-466-4880
romor@romor.ca; sales@romor.ca; techsupport@romor.ca
www.romor.ca
Firm Type: Management Consulting, Distributing, Scientific/Technical Services
Founded: 1984
Member of: Offshore Technology Association of Nova Scotia; Newfoundland Offshore Industry Association; Marine Ocean Technology Network; Marine Technology Society
Quality Environmental Management System(s): 9001:2008
Products/Services/Areas of Expertise: The firm distributes oceanographic, offshore oil & gas, geophysical & defense instrumentation & supplies, including custom & hard to locate items. Services include repairs, technical assistance, research & project management consultation
Contact(s):
Darrin Verge, President
dverge@romor.ca

Ron Robinson Limited
3075 Maple Grove Rd.
Bowmanville, ON L1C 3K4
905-697-0400
Fax: 905-697-0581
rrl@ronrobcon.com
www.ronrobcon.com
Firm Type: Engineering
Founded: 1957
Products/Services/Areas of Expertise: This heavy civil construction company specializes in sewer, watermain & road construction, general contracting & project management, undergound hydro, cathodic protection & directional drilling, all with a focus on environmentally sound practices. Services include site development, land clearing, demolition, soil bio-engineering to mitigate soil erosion & improve water quality, & equipment rentals
Domestic Markets:
Ontario
Contact(s):
Ron R. Robinson, President

Ron Wedman Engineering Services
1581 - 13 Ave. SE
Salmon Arm, BC V1E 2G8
250-832-4634
rwedman@jetstream.net
Firm Type: Engineering
Founded: 1992

Staff: 1
Member of: Professional Engineers of BC
Products/Services/Areas of Expertise: Project management; engineering & design
Recently Completed / Ongoing Projects: Material handling & sorting system; project management; engineering design & drafting; specialized equipment in mining & wood industry
Financial Information:
Type of Ownership: Private
Revenue Sources: 100% Private Contracts
Domestic Markets:
Alberta, British Columbia
Contact(s):
Ron Wedman, Owner

Ronco Protective Products
267 Rivermede Rd. North
Concord, ON L4K 3N7
905-660-6700
Fax: 905-660-6903
877-663-7735
ronco@ronco.ca
www.ronco.ca
Firm Type: Distributing, Manufacturing
Founded: 1996
Member of: British Columbia Food Protection Association; Canadian Restaurant and Foodservice Association; Conseil de la transformation agroalimentaire et des produits de consommation; Malaysian Rubber Glove Manufacturers' Association; International Association for Food Protection
Quality Environmental Management System(s): 9001:2000
Products/Services/Areas of Expertise: Manufacturers of gloves & protective apparel; includes disposable vinyl, latex & nitrile gloves, reusable gloves; industrial cotton, leather & dipped gloves; non-woven bouffant caps, masks, shoe covers, aprons & sleeves. Offices in Trois-Rivières, China & Malaysia
Financial Information:
Type of Ownership: Private
Domestic Markets:
Alberta, British Columbia, Manitoba, New Brunswick, Newfoundland & Labrador, Nova Scotia, Ontario, Prince Edward Island, Québec, Saskatchewan
Foreign Activity:
China, The Pacific Rim, USA, Vietnam
Contact(s):
Jo Fleishmann, President, 905/660-6700
Ron Pecchioli, Director, Sales & Marketing, 905/660-6700

Rondar Inc.
333 Centennial Pkwy. North
Hamilton, ON L8E 2X6
905-561-2808
Fax: 905-561-8871
800-263-6884
techserv@rondar.com
www.rondar.com
Firm Type: Engineering, Scientific/Technical Services
Founded: 1970
Staff: 60
Member of: Electrical Utilities Safety Association of Ontario
Products/Services/Areas of Expertise: This independent Canadian company provides a range of essential diagnostic services, including quality analysis, early fault detection & documentation, & solutions to the power systems sector. Services include high voltage management: substation maintenance, transformer testing & repair, relay & meter testing & calibration, circuit breaker inspection, testing, calibration & conversion; power "ON" services: thermographic (infrared) inspections, insulating fluid analysis, relay testing & repair; commissioning/acceptance testing: power systems & co-generation projects, start-up, point to point wiring checks, testing; engineering services: system evaluation, power quality monitoring, system harmonic analysis, arc flash studies, system load flow studies, ground grid design; thermography: distribution & transmission lines, control panels, generators, etc.
Recently Completed / Ongoing Projects: Ongoing industrial & utility transformer reclassification
Financial Information:
Type of Ownership: Private
Revenue: Greater than $5 Million
Revenue Sources: 10% nationwide; 5% Municipals; 85% Private Contracts
Domestic Markets:
Ontario,
Contact(s):
Darvin E. Puhl, President

Canadian Branches:
Kitchener
#13, 31 McBrine Dr.
Kitchener, ON N2R 1J1
519-896-8935
Fax: 519-896-6898
Ken Scott, District Service Manager

Toronto
#9, 20 Venture Dr.
Toronto, ON M1B 3R7
416-286-2444
Fax: 416-286-2445
techserv@rondar.com
Jim Hansen, District Service Manager

Ronel Engineering Ltd.
#200, 8716 - 51 Ave.
Edmonton, AB T6E 5E8
780-466-6888
Fax: 780-466-7117
ronel@telusplanet.net
Firm Type: Management Consulting, Engineering
Founded: 1994
Products/Services/Areas of Expertise: Environmental site assessments; construction & excavation services; erosion control services; soil & groundwater remediation services; mining environmental services; waste dump design
Financial Information:
Type of Ownership: Private
Revenue: $1.5 Million - $3 Million
Revenue Sources: 10% Municipals; 90% Private Contracts
Domestic Markets:
Alberta, British Columbia, Saskatchewan
Contact(s):
Ron Lau, P.Eng., President

Rose Mechanical Water Systems Inc.
General Delivery
Millgrove, ON
905-689-0091
Fax: 905-659-4974
www.rosemechanical.yp.ca
Firm Type: Engineering, Scientific/Technical Services
Founded: 1997
Member of: Ontario Ground Water Association
Products/Services/Areas of Expertise: Licensed by the Ontario Min. of Environment, the company offers pump services, water treatment, & backhoe services; wells, cisterns, pressure & holding tanks; sump pumps, sewage systems; water treatments: softeners, iron & sulfer removal, ultraviolet units; reverse osmosis, in line filters; emergency service
Financial Information:
Type of Ownership: Private
Domestic Markets:
Ontario
Contact(s):
Chris Rose, Principal

Ross Healthcare, Inc.
Also Known As: Ross Chempharma Inc.
Member company of Group Ross, Inc.
#6, 1520 Cliveden Ave.
Delta, BC V3M 6J8
604-521-6626
Fax: 604-521-6695
800-663-8303
lmercier@rosshealthcare.org
www.epsross.com
Firm Type: Manufacturing
Founded: 1996
Staff: 8
Products/Services/Areas of Expertise: Develops & manufactures specialty products for the dental channel of distribution (PCxx dental products) & the environmental safety products market - Mercon mercury decontaminiation solutions (spill kits & clean-up solutions)
Financial Information:
Type of Ownership: Private
Revenue: $500,000 - $1.5 Million
Revenue Sources: 100% Private Contracts
Domestic Markets:
National
Foreign Activity:
Asia, Australia/New Zealand, USA
Markets Sought:
Central Europe, Eastern Europe, Western Europe

Products & Services Buyer's Guide

Contact(s):
Marc Ross, President
mross@epsross.com
Lise T. Mercier, Associate, Marketing & Sales
lmercier@epsross.com
N. Michael Ross, Corporate Contact
mr@epsross.com

International Branch(es):
Ross Healthcare, Inc.
P.O. Box 570
Point Roberts, WA USA
800-663-8303
Lise T. Mercier, Associate, Marketing & Sales

Rotblott & Sons Ltd.
443 Adelaide St. West
Toronto, ON M5V 1S9
416-703-0456
Fax: 416-703-0460
service@rotblotts.com
www.rotblotts.com
Firm Type: Distributing, Waste Management
Founded: 1919
Staff: 6
Products/Services/Areas of Expertise: Rotblott & Sons Ltd. specializes in machinery, scrap metal & plant dismantling. Rotblott's Discount Warehouse Inc., incorporated in 1990, is a sister company which buys & sells all types of surplus merchandise, including scrap metal, machinery, steel, iron, shelving & racking; supplies of special use to the film industry are a specialty
Contact(s):
Howard Rotblott, Principal

Rothsay
Division of Maple Leaf Foods Inc.
Formerly: Ontario Rendering Co. Ltd. P.O. Box 8270
880 Hwy. 5 West
Dundas, ON L9H 5G1
905-628-2258
Fax: 905-628-8577
800-263-0302
rothsay@rothsay.ca
www.rothsay.ca
Firm Type: Manufacturing, Waste Management
Founded: 1952
Staff: 300
Member of: Animal Protein Producers Industry; National Renderers Association; Fats and Proteins Research Foundation; Canadian Restaurant and Foodservices Association; Animal Nutrition Association of Canada
Products/Services/Areas of Expertise: One of Canada's largest rendering operations. The rendering process recycles animal by-products into a range of other products, such as commercial tallow (used in candle & soap making, steel manufacture, glycerine for the chemical industry) & protein products (eg. bone meal, fish meal, used in animal feed). Rothsay collects & converts for further use organic, food waste, bones & fat, waste cooking oil, animal carcasses & by-products. Rothsay Biodiesel, a sister company located in Guelph, ON, produces an environmentally friendly, renewable fuel & is Canada's first commercial biodiesel plant
Domestic Markets:
Manitoba, New Brunswick, Newfoundland & Labrador, Nova Scotia, Ontario, Prince Edward Island, Québec
Contact(s):
Kevin Golding, President, Rothsay & Maple Leaf Agri-Farms Inc.

Canadian Branches:
Foxtrap
P.O. Box 16008 Foxtrap
Foxtrap, NL A1X 2E2
709-834-2181
Fax: 709-834-2303
Scott Henry

Montréal - Rothsay/Laurenco
605, 1re av
Sainte-Catherine, QC J0L 1E0
450-632-3250
Fax: 450-632-4703
montreal@rothsay.ca
Member of: Association québécoise des industries de nutrition animale et céréalière
Guy Lussier

Moorefield
Wellington County Rd. 7, RR#1
Moorefield, ON N0G 2K0
519-638-3081
Fax: 519-638-3410
moorefield@rothsay.ca
Brad Erhardt

Truro
P.O. Box 151
169 Lower Truro Rd.
Truro, NS B2N 5C1
902-895-2801
Fax: 902-893-0176
truro@rothsay.ca
Kurt Cormier

Winnipeg
607 Dawson Rd.
Winnipeg, MB R2J 0T2
204-233-7347
Fax: 204-235-0030
winnipeg@rothsay.ca
Glen Gratton

Rotork Controls (Canada) Ltd.
#6, 820 - 28th St. NE
Calgary, AB T2A 6K1
403-569-9455
Fax: 403-569-9414
800-561-8899
info@rotork.ca
www.rotork.com
Firm Type: Manufacturing
Founded: 1968
Products/Services/Areas of Expertise: Rotork is at the forefront of valve actuation solutions, with products used extensively in the oil & gas, power, water & waste water industries: electric & hydraulic valve actuators & control systems, process control actuators, gearboxes & accessories. The Rotork Group is comprised of Rotork Controls, Rotork Fluid Systems, & Rotork Gears. Locations worldwide
Domestic Markets:
National
Foreign Activity:
Worldwide
Contact(s):
Christopher Bone, President
chris.bone@rotork.ca

Canadian Branches:
Burnaby - NORPAC Automation
A division of NORPAC Controls Ltd.
7500 Winston Ave.
Burnaby, BC V5A 4X5
604-422-3700
Fax: 604-422-3788
www.norpaccontrols.com
Glen Cherepak, Sales Contact
gcherepak@norpaccontrols.com

Calgary - CE Franklin Ltd.
#1900, 300 - 5th Ave. SW
Calgary, AB T2P 3C4
403-531-5600
Fax: 403-265-1968
www.cefranklin.com
Products/Services/Areas of Expertise: CE Franklin distributes pipe, valves, flanges & fittings, & general oilfield supplies to the oil & gas industry, & is a distributor for Rotork in Canada
Tim Ritchie, Sales Contact
tritchie@cefranklin.com

Edmonton
9627 - 41 Ave.
Edmonton, AB T6E 5X7
780-462-8153
Fax: 780-462-0854
info@rotork.ca
www.rotork.com
John Albert, Sales Contact
john.albert@rotork.ca

Mississauga
#4, 2850 Argentia Rd.
Mississauga, ON L5N 8G4
905-363-0313
Fax: 905-363-0320

info@rotork.ca
www.rotork.ca
Jeff Kelley, Sales Contact
jeff.kelley@rotork.ca

Montréal
#208, 7800, boul Metropolitain est
Montréal, QC H1K 1A1
514-355-3003
Fax: 514-355-0024
Yves Tremblay, Sales, Service & Technical Contact,
514-835-3488
yves.tremblay@rotork.ca

Mount Pearl - Eastern Valve & Control Specialties
Donovan's Industrial Park
2 Southern Cross Rd.
Mount Pearl, NL A1N 5A2
709-757-2730
Fax: 709-757-2731
www.easternvalve.ca
Tony Goobie, Sales Contact
tgoobie@easternvalve.ca

Mt. Uniacke - Mobile Valve Repairs Ltd.
P.O. Box 90
140-142 Old Windsor Hwy./Hwy. 1
Mount Uniacke, NS B0N 1Z0
902-866-0719
Fax: 902-866-1091
877-825-8776
www.mobilevalve.com; www.sourceatlantic.ca
Products/Services/Areas of Expertise: For the Mobile Valve location in Saint John, NB, contact Tim Place at 506-634-8646. For the Tracy, NB, location contact Steve Mifflin at 506-368-7311
Graham MacNeil, Sales Contact
macneil.graham@sourceatlantic.ca

Regina - Cypress Sales Partnership
1145 - 8 Ave.
Regina, SK S4R 1E1
306-757-5656
Fax: 306-757-8024
www.cypresssales.com
Keith Goosen, Sales Contact
kgoosen@cypresssales.com

Sarnia
#3, 838 Upper Canada Dr.
Sarnia, ON N7W 1A4
519-337-9190
Fax: 519-337-0017
info@rotork.ca
www.rotork.ca
Rick Cabajsky, Sales Contact
rick.cabajsky@rotork.ca

Saskatoon - Cypress Sales Partnership
2615 Wentz Ave.
Saskatoon, SK SK7 5J1
306-242-3333
Fax: 306-242-3373
www.cypresssales.com
Mihai Radu, Service & Technical Contact
m.radu@cypresssales.com

Rowan Williams Davies & Irwin Inc. / RWDI
650 Woodlawn Rd. West
Guelph, ON N1K 1B8
519-823-1311
Fax: 519-823-1316
info@rwdi.com
www.rwdi.com
Firm Type: Engineering
Founded: 1972
Staff: 350
Member of: Air & Waste Management Association; Canadian Environment Industry Association; American Meteorological Association
Products/Services/Areas of Expertise: A leading Canadian specialty consulting engineering firm with offices worldwide, RWDI offers expertise in the areas of wind engineering, environmental air quality, & noise management. Services include design review, modeling, consultation & planning (notably for sustainable building design), stack & field testing, an asbestos & mould lab, structural monitoring, technical software development, & the provision of expert testimony. Wind tunnel testing, computational fluid dynamics testing & modeling, & water flume testing are many other specialties. RWDI Air Inc.,

RWDI Anemos Limited, Motioneering Inc., & Virtualwind Inc. are member firms of The RWDI Group of companies. RWDI also maintains offices in India & the United Arab Emirates - please consult the website for details
Recently Completed / Ongoing Projects: Urban air quality assessments of major cities in Canada & Hong Kong; air quality, dust, noise & odour issues; air quality for resource & manufacturing industry; determination of indoor ventilation conditions for new laboratory facilities in North America
Financial Information:
Type of Ownership: Private
Revenue: Greater than $5 Million
Revenue Sources: 5% nationwide; 95% Private Contracts
Domestic Markets:
National
Foreign Activity:
Worldwide
Contact(s):
Michael J. Soligo, M.A.Sc., P.Eng., President/CEO
Peter A. Irwin, Ph.D., P.Eng., Senior Consultant
Anton E. Davies, Ph.D., P.Eng., QEP, Vice President

Canadian Branches:
Calgary
#1000, 736 - 8th Ave. SW
Calgary, AB T2P 1H4
403-232-6771
Fax: 403-232-6762
Products/Services/Areas of Expertise: This location also houses RWDI Air Inc.

Vancouver
#830, 999 West Broadway
Vancouver, BC V5Z 1K5
604-730-5688
Fax: 604-730-2915
Products/Services/Areas of Expertise: This location also houses RWDI Air Inc.

International Branch(es):
Dunstable, UK - RWDI Anemos Ltd.
Lawrence Industrial Estate
#4, Lawrence Way
Dunstable, Bedfordshire UK
+44(0)1582-470250
enquiry@rwdi-anemos.com
www.rwdi-anemos.com
Products/Services/Areas of Expertise: Provides wind engineering & environmental services to clients in Europe & the Middle East
Paul Freathy, Managing Director

Miami, FL - RWDI USA LLC
10165 USA Today Way
Miramar, FL USA
954-431-6800
Fax: 954-431-6844
solutions@rwdi.com
Staff: 15
Products/Services/Areas of Expertise: This location houses a boundary layer wind tunnel facility, model shop & offices
Frank Kriksic, General Manager

Roxul Inc.
A subsidiary of Rockwool International A/S
551 Harrop Dr.
Milton, ON L9T 3H3
905-878-8474
Fax: 905-878-8077
800-265-6878
www.roxul.com
Products/Services/Areas of Expertise: Rockwool International is the largest mineral wool insulation producer in the world, with 23 plants in 14 countries. In addition to providing energy efficiencies to residential, commercial & industrial building projects & other applications, the product is fire resistant, water repellent, non-corrosive & resistant to mould, fungi & bacteria growth. Roxul Inc. maintains plant facilties in Milton, ON & Grand Forks, BC & has been recognized for leading the way to reduce energy consumption, air emissions & other production waste at its plants
Recently Completed / Ongoing Projects: Pearson Airport
Ecological Note: High density batt, board & pipe insulation
Domestic Markets:
National
Foreign Activity:
USA
Contact(s):
Trent Ogilvie, President
Dennis Beamish, Vice-President, ICI North America
Paraic Lally, Vice-President, Residential
Leslie McLaren, Marketing Service Manager

Roy Northern Environmental Ltd.
10209 - 109th St.
Fairview, AB T0H 1L0
780-835-2682
Fax: 780-835-2140
droy@roynorthern.com
www.roynorthern.com
Firm Type: Scientific/Technical Services
Member of: Alberta Institute of Agrologists; Alberta Society of Engineering Technologists
Products/Services/Areas of Expertise: Environmental site assessments; soil conservation & reclamation; wellsite/pipeline reclamation & remediation; pre-disturbance planning & assessment
Financial Information:
Type of Ownership: Private
Domestic Markets:
Alberta, British Columbia
Contact(s):
Doug Roy, President, 780/835-7500
Rod Peters, Manager, Operations & Environment, 780-835-7506
rod.peters@roynorthern.com

Canadian Branches:
Fort St. John
#207, 10139 - 100th St.
Fort St John, BC V1J 3Y6
250-261-6644
Fax: 250-261-6915

Royal Envelope Ltd.
111 Jacob Keffer Pkwy.
Concord, ON L4K 4V1
905-879-0000
Fax: 905-879-0156
800-567-6925
ltucci@royalenvelope.com
www.royalenvelope.com
Firm Type: Manufacturing
Founded: 1989
Member of: Envelope Manufacturers Association of America; National Association of Major Mail Users
EcoLogo Certified Products & Services: Enviro-Lope envelopes
Products/Services/Areas of Expertise: Ecologo certified paper products & printing services, with a specialty in custom made envelopes for direct mail, trade & financial customers. Product rationalization, volume discounts, reports, storage & distribution are services offered to clients & suppliers. The company is committed to protecting the environment by its efficient use of materials in production, & its Enviro-lope product is made from FSC certified paper from recycled fibre
Ecological Note: Enviro-Lope envelopes
Financial Information:
Type of Ownership: Private
Revenue: $1.5 Million - $3 Million
Revenue Sources: 1% nationwide; 2% Provincial; 1% Municipals; 96% Private Contracts
Domestic Markets:
National
Foreign Activity:
USA
Contact(s):
Peter Bowles, President
Lou Tucci, Vice President

Royalpak Inc.
#3, 1870 Albion Rd.
Toronto, ON M9W 5T2
416-746-4226
Fax: 416-746-8291
866-746-9900
info@royalpak.com
www.royalpak.com
Firm Type: Distributing, Manufacturing
Founded: 1997
EcoLogo Certified Products & Services: Royalpak line of cleaning products for the janitorial, industrial, institutional, automotive & marine industries
Products/Services/Areas of Expertise: The company manufactures & supplies cleaning products to distributors in the janitorial, industrial & automotive markets across Canada, & now ships to locations in the U.S., South America & Israel as well. A comprehensive line of Ecologo certified products is available, & clients may choose from various label options
Ecological Note: Royalpak line of cleaning products for the janitorial, industrial, institutional, automotive & marine industries
Domestic Markets:
National
Foreign Activity:
The Middle East, South America, USA

RP Graphics Group
5990 Falbourne St.
Mississauga, ON L5R 3S7
905-507-8782
Fax: 905-507-0113
info@rpgraphics.com
www.rpgraphics.com
Firm Type: Manufacturing
Founded: 1960
EcoLogo Certified Products & Services: Lithographic printing services
Ecological Note: Lithographic printing services
Contact(s):
George Mazzaferro, President

RPC
Also Known As: Research and Productivity Council
921 College Hill Rd.
Fredericton, NB E3B 6Z9
506-452-1212
Fax: 506-452-0594
800-563-0844
info@rpc.ca
www.rpc.ca
Firm Type: Engineering, Manufacturing, Scientific/Technical Services
Founded: 1962
Staff: 100
Member of: Canadian Association for Environmental Analytical Laboratories; New Brunswick Environment Industry Association; Nova Scotia Environment Industry Association
Quality Environmental Management System(s): 17025; ISO
Products/Services/Areas of Expertise: An independent contract R&D & technical services organization engaged in analytical chemistry, engineering, prototype design, & manufacture & testing services. Provides services in a number of areas, including analysis & testing, fish health, molecular biology, forensic biology, food development & testing, mineral process development & testing, industrial process development, air quality testing, custom machining & manufacturing, industrial & electronic troubleshooting, NDT inspections & field testing, calibration & equipment repair, ultrasonic measurement devices, & medical gas certifications
Recently Completed / Ongoing Projects: DND/CFB Gagetown Environmental Monitoring; Sydney Tar Ponds/PWGSC Contaminant Assessment; AECL Chalk River Environmental Monitoring; trace metals analysis, USEPA Coastal 2000
Financial Information:
Type of Ownership: Private
Revenue: Greater than $5 Million
Revenue Sources: 13% nationwide; 15% Provincial; 1% Municipals; 71% Private Contracts
Domestic Markets:
National
Foreign Activity:
Australia/New Zealand, Central America, China, Western Europe, The Middle East, South America, USA, Vietnam
Contact(s):
Eric Cook, Executive Director
Joel Hill, Manager, Business Development
Ross Kean, Head, Inorganic Analytical Services, 506/452-1399

RPR Environmental Inc.
#164, 166 South Service Rd.
Stoney Creek, ON L8E 3H6
905-662-0062
Fax: 905-662-3828
800-667-5217
sales@rpr-environmental.com
www.rpr-environmental.com
Firm Type: Scientific/Technical Services, Waste Management
Founded: 1990
Quality Environmental Management System(s): 14001; ISO
Products/Services/Areas of Expertise: Hazardous & non-hazardous liquid & solid waste management; on-site

technical services & compliance training; waste removal: all wastes in any volume
Financial Information:
Type of Ownership: Private
Revenue Sources: 5% nationwide; 5% Provincial; 10% Municipals; 80% Private Contracts
Domestic Markets:
Alberta, Manitoba, Ontario, Québec, Saskatchewan
Foreign Activity:
USA
Contact(s):
Patrick Whitty, General Manager

RST Instruments Ltd.
#200, 2050 Hartley Ave.
Coquitlam, BC V3K 6W5
604-540-1100
Fax: 604-540-1005
800-665-5599
info@rstinstruments.com
www.rstinstruments.com
Firm Type: Distributing, Manufacturing, Scientific/Technical Services
Founded: 1977
Quality Environmental Management System(s): 9001
Products/Services/Areas of Expertise: The firm is engaged in engineering instrumentation, including design of site-specific products, calibration & repair services. Products include: inclinometers & tilt sensors; readouts & dataloggers; borehole packers; grout monitors; load/stress/pressure sensors; extensometers; settlement systems; analysis software; & Carlson Concrete Instruments. Services include technical assistance & field services; customized solutions; rentals for water level meters, data loggers & readouts, load cells, packers, pumps, water quality meters & seismographs
Contact(s):
Rob Taylor, Principal

RSP International Inc.
Also Known As: Render Safe Procedures International
6 Simcoe St.
Caledon, ON L7K 0A4
519-942-3407
Fax: 519-942-3261
rspi@netrover.com
www.rspinternational.com
Firm Type: Management Consulting, Waste Management
Founded: 1990
Staff: 3
Member of: Ontario Environment Industry Association; Society of Explosives Engineers
Products/Services/Areas of Expertise: Transport & disposal of potentially explosive, shock sensitive or reactive chemicals (peroxides, peroxidable chemicals, ethers, acetals, picrates, fulminates, organic nitrates, all chemical explosives); bomb threat procedures training; Render Safe Procedures is an international standard in disposal of explosives. Clients come from educational, industrial, commercial, medical & government fields
Financial Information:
Type of Ownership: Private
Revenue: $50,000 - $100,000
Revenue Sources: 100% Private Contracts
Domestic Markets:
British Columbia, New Brunswick, Newfoundland & Labrador, Nova Scotia, Ontario, Québec
Contact(s):
Fred M. Lemieux, B.Sc., Director

Rubber Rock Resources
P.O. Box 385
Marwayne, AB T0B 2X0
780-847-2670
Fax: 780-875-1377
Firm Type: Waste Management
Founded: 1994
Products/Services/Areas of Expertise: Road mining tires & farm tractor tires recycling
Contact(s):
Allan Brown, Contact

Rubicon Environmental Inc.
RR#4
Dundalk, ON N0C 1B0
519-986-4125
Fax: 519-986-4087
866-778-2426
rubicon@rubiconenvironmental.net
www.rubiconenvironmental.net
Firm Type: Engineering
Staff: 7
Products/Services/Areas of Expertise: Petroleum site assessments & remediation
Domestic Markets:
Ontario,
Contact(s):
Paul Rew, P.Eng., President

Rudiger Enterprises Ltd.
11294 Clairmont Frontage
Fort St John, BC V2J 4H8
250-785-3399
Products/Services/Areas of Expertise: Environmental consultants & services
Contact(s):
Emil Rudiger, Manager

Russell NDE Systems Inc.
Formerly: Cyberscope Industries Inc.; Russell Technologies Inc.
4909 - 75 Ave.
Edmonton, AB T6B 2S3
780-468-6800
Fax: 780-462-9378
800-661-0127
info@russelltech.com
www.russelltech.com
Firm Type: Distributing, Manufacturing, Scientific/Technical Services
Founded: 1972
Products/Services/Areas of Expertise: The company manufactures & distributes instruments & probes for NDE (Non-Destructive Examiniation) & NDT (Non-Destructive Testing) applications; provides NDT training; custom tools for pipeline, boiler water wall & well casing applications; NDT inspection services
Financial Information:
Type of Ownership: Private
Revenue Sources: 100% Private Contracts
Domestic Markets:
Alberta, British Columbia, Manitoba, Saskatchewan
Foreign Activity:
Australia/New Zealand, Western Europe, The Middle East, South America, Mexico, USA
Contact(s):
Dave Russell, President

RWDI AIR Inc.
650 Woodlawn Rd. W
Guelph, ON N1K 1B8
519-823-1311
Fax: 519-823-1316
info@rwdiair.com
www.rwdiair.com
Firm Type: Engineering
Founded: 1972
Products/Services/Areas of Expertise: This member firm of The RWDI Group of companies specializes in solutions to air quality, noise & vibration, & hazard/risk issues for clients in the industrial, commercial & government sectors. Main branch office locations in Vancouver & Calgary, with other branch offices in Thunder Bay, London, Windsor & Ottawa. Please consult www.rwdiair.com for details. See also entry for Rowan Williams Davies & Irwin Inc./RWDI
Domestic Markets:
National
Foreign Activity:
Worldwide
Contact(s):
John Alberico, B.Sc., M.Sc., CCEP, General Manager

Canadian Branches:
Calgary
#1000, 736 - 8th Ave. SW
Calgary, AB T2P 1H4
403-232-6771
Fax: 403-232-6762
Staff: 36
Mike Lepage, Project Director

Vancouver
#830, 999 West Broadway
Vancouver, BC V5Z 1K5
604-730-5688
Fax: 604-730-2915
Staff: 5
Kathy Preston, Project Director

S.A. Armstrong Limited
23 Bertrand Ave.
Toronto, ON M1L 2P3
416-755-2291
Fax: 416-759-9101
Firm Type: Distributing, Engineering, Manufacturing
Founded: 1934
Member of: British Automatic Fire Sprinkler Association; Society of Fire Protection Engineers; American Society of Plumbing Engineers; BOMA; National Fire Protection Association; Mechanical Contractors Association of Canada; American Society of Mechanical Engineers
Quality Environmental Management System(s): 9001:2000
Products/Services/Areas of Expertise: Designers, manufacturers & distributors of high quality, energy & cost efficient fluid flow equipment, pumps, controls, valves; heat exchangers; HVAC; fire pumps; boosters, submersibles & verticle turbines; residential & light commercial hydronics. Clients worldwide in the residential, commercial & industrial sectors. Services include technical assistance, replacement parts & service, interactive consultation; partnering opportunities. Sales representatives across Canada, & company locations in Québec, the U.S., the U.K., Australia, India & China. Consult the company website for contact details
Financial Information:
Type of Ownership: Private
Domestic Markets:
National
Foreign Activity:
Asia, Australia/New Zealand, Eastern Europe, Western Europe, The Middle East, The Pacific Rim, Mexico, USA
Contact(s):
Charles A. Armstrong, President/CEO
James C. Armstrong, Executive Vice President

Sabatini Earth Technologies Inc.
Formerly: Sabatini Geoenvironmental Inc.
#203, 6919 - 32 Ave. NW
Calgary, AB T3B 0K6
403-247-1813
Fax: 403-247-1814
kjhugo@sabatini.ab.ca
www.sabatini.ab.ca
Firm Type: Engineering
Founded: 1993
Staff: 3
Products/Services/Areas of Expertise: Soil & groundwater expertise; groundwater monitoring & remediation; soil clean-up
Recently Completed / Ongoing Projects: Aquifer study, town water supply; in-situ soil & groundwater clean-up, former service station; flare pit remediation & groundwater removal
Domestic Markets:
Alberta,
Contact(s):
Ken Hugo, Hydrogeologist

Sable Offshore Energy Inc.
Founders Sq.
1701 Hollis St., 11th Fl.
Halifax, NS B3J 3M8
902-496-0960
Fax: 902-496-4931
Contact(s):
Mike Coolen, Manager

SACO Technologies, Inc.
Formerly: SACO Smartvision Inc.
7809, rte Transcanadienne
Montréal, QC H4S 1L3
514-745-0310
Fax: 514-745-0315
800-991-7226
www.smartvision.com
Firm Type: Distributing, Manufacturing
Founded: 1986
Member of: Illumivision Inc.; 3M; PRG; Mobil Alliance
Products/Services/Areas of Expertise: The company was acquired by LSI Industries Inc. in 2006 & continues to be a leader in high-performance LED (light emitting diode) technology & products. SACO's proprietary SMARTVISION system is a recognized brand, with video screens located in sports venues & other commercial & industrial facilities. The screens use less

power but have an outstanding life expectancy & can be customized to any size, for multiple applications
Recently Completed / Ongoing Projects: Bon Jovi HAVE A NICE DAY Tour; U2 VERTIGO Tour; Nine Inch Nails North American Tour; Paul McCartney North American Tour; numerous other sports & entertainment venues across North America; Nasdaq-Amex Time Square, New York City
Financial Information:
Type of Ownership: Foreign-owned
Domestic Markets:
Alberta, British Columbia, Manitoba, New Brunswick, Newfoundland & Labrador, Nova Scotia, Northwest Territories, Ontario, Prince Edward Island, Québec, Saskatchewan
Foreign Activity:
Asia, Central America, China, The Middle East, South America, Mexico, Vietnam, Worldwide
Markets Sought:
China, Eastern Europe, Vietnam

Safety Express Ltd.
4190 Sladeview Cres., Units 1 & 2
Mississauga, ON L5L 0A1
905-608-0111
Fax: 905-608-0091
800-465-3898
info@safetyexpress.com
www.safetyexpress.com
Firm Type: Distributing
Founded: 1985
Staff: 12
Member of: Canadian National Asbestos Council
Products/Services/Areas of Expertise: Distributor of a range of safety products & equipment for hazardous environments; thermal imaging cameras; restoration equipment; abatement equipment; protective clothing; fall protection equipment; janitorial products; first aid products; signs & shipping supplies; rentals, service & repair; safety product training
Domestic Markets:
National
Foreign Activity:
USA
Contact(s):
Nak Tsounis, President

Canadian Branches:
Calgary
508 - 42nd Ave. SE
Calgary, AB T2G 1Y6
403-243-8324
Fax: 403-243-7683

Edmonton
10441 - 172 St.
Edmonton, AB T5S 1K9
780-486-4889
Fax: 780-486-4996

Halifax
#22, 100 Wright Ave.
Dartmouth, NS B3B 1L2
902-406-4106

Montréal
754, av. Lajoie
Dorval, QC H9P 1G8
514-422-8886
Fax: 514-422-9911

Ottawa
#110, 2700 Lancaster Rd.
Ottawa, ON K1B 4T7
613-526-5800
Fax: 613-526-5802

Vancouver
#6, 2931 Viking Way
Richmond, BC V6V 1Y1
604-244-8005
Fax: 604-244-8009

Safety Plus Inc.
8820 - 100th St. NW
Edmonton, AB T6E 3Y5
780-413-0037
Fax: 780-413-0170
Firm Type: Engineering
Founded: 1990
Staff: 3
Products/Services/Areas of Expertise: Environmental decommissioning, dismantling & clean-up; real estate transaction audits; underground storage tank management; waste reclamation & recovery audits; hazardous soil & chemical wastes removal; environmental research & development; environmental characterizations; certificates of approval; metals, plastics & by-product recycling; abatement, removals & recovery (asbestos, lead, solvents); safety engineering
Financial Information:
Type of Ownership: Private
Revenue Sources: 15% Municipals; 85% Private Contracts
Domestic Markets:
National
Contact(s):
Paul M. Aumuller, President/Owner
Julie P. Ward, Marketing Rep.
Paolo Accettone, Project Engineer

Safety Projects International Inc.
P.O. Box 13161
Kanata, ON K2K 1X4
613-254-9233
Fax: 613-254-7147
pomfretb@spi5star.com
www.spi5star.com
Firm Type: Management Consulting, Distributing, Information Technology
Founded: 1979
Staff: 78
Member of: Institution of Occupational Safety & Health
Quality Environmental Management System(s): 9001; ISO
Products/Services/Areas of Expertise: Full service OH&S consultancy, providing OHSAS, 18001 audits & training using our proprietary 5 star Health & Safety Management System Canada's Largest Video/DVD Producer in OH&S; over 500 training modules & over 200 DVD's
Recently Completed / Ongoing Projects: N.C.C. Emirate Airlines, ADNDC
Financial Information:
Type of Ownership: Private
Revenue: $100,000 - $250,000
Revenue Sources: 10% nationwide; 15% Provincial; 75% Private Contracts
Domestic Markets:
Alberta, British Columbia, Manitoba, New Brunswick, Newfoundland & Labrador, Northwest Territories, Ontario, Québec, Saskatchewan
Foreign Activity:
Africa, Asia, China, The Middle East, South Africa, USA, United Kingdom, Vietnam
Contact(s):
William Pomfret, President
R. McKinnon, Manager, Marketing
O.Tolentrio, Manager, Sales

Safety-Kleen Canada Inc.
Oil Recovery Division & Lubricants Division
300 Woolwich St. South
Breslau, ON N0B 1M0
519-648-2291
Fax: 519-648-3488
dale.macintyre@safety-kleen.com
www.safety-kleen.com
Firm Type: Manufacturing, Waste Management
Staff: 400
EcoLogo Certified Products & Services: Canada's Choice Engine Oil; Automotive & industrial lubricants
Products/Services/Areas of Expertise: Collects used oils for the purpose of producing re-refined base stocks to be used in the manufacture of automotive & industrial lubricants. The re-refining process includes dehydration, defueling, distillation & hydro treating, removing all additives, polymers, contamination & oxidized molecules, yielding a base stock accepted by industry as being equivalent to virgin stocks. These base stocks are blended with selected new additives & tested to produce approved finished lubricants, meeting current industry, API, military & specific customer specifications & standards
Ecological Note: Canada's Choice Engine Oil; Automotive & industrial lubricants
Financial Information:
Type of Ownership: Publicly Traded
Domestic Markets:
Alberta, British Columbia, Manitoba, New Brunswick, Nova Scotia, Ontario, Québec, Saskatchewan
Foreign Activity:
Australia/New Zealand, Western Europe, USA
Contact(s):
Denis Goulet, Managing Director/Country Manager
Dale MacIntyre, Vice-President, Canadian Refinery Operations
Canadian Branches:
Ancaster
P.O. Box 81270
1574 Hwy. #2, Units 1 & 2
Ancaster, ON L9G 3L3
905-648-3270
Fax: 905-648-7828
Ian Convery, Branch Manager

Brampton
25 Regan Rd.
Brampton, ON L7A 1B2
905-840-0118
Fax: 905-840-9279
Scott Moir, Customer Service Manager

Calgary
3816 - 7th St. SE
Calgary, AB T2G 2Y8
403-243-3877
Fax: 403-243-4010
Jeff Huston, Branch Manager

Chambly
2730, boul. Industriel
Chambly, QC J3L 4V2
450-572-6250
Jean Brunet, Branch Manager

Chelmsford
4633 Regional Rd. #15
Chelmsford, ON P0M 1L0
705-855-4519
Fax: 705-855-2032
Terry Wheatley, Branch Manager

Delta
7803 Progress Way
Delta, BC V4G 1A3
604-952-4700
Fax: 604-952-4701
Glenn Lundrigan, Branch Manager

Duncan
3014 Boys Rd., RR#6
Duncan, BC V9L 6W4
250-746-6246
Fax: 250-746-1997
Jim Brunet, Manager

London
1020 Hargrieve Rd., Unit 16
London, ON N6E 1P5
519-685-3040
Fax: 519-685-1655
Kevin Vine, Branch Manager

Nepean
89 Bentley Ave.
Nepean, ON K2E 6T7
613-226-1379
Fax: 613-226-4362
Matt Muzzi, Branch Manager

Nisku
500 - 13 Ave.
Nisku, AB T9E 7P6
780-955-2788
Fax: 780-955-2799
Jeff Huston, Branch Manager

Oshawa
1220 Skae Dr.
Oshawa, ON L1J 7A1
905-579-3221
Fax: 905-579-6063
Derek Poole, Branch Manager

Saint-Augustin-de-Desmaures
85, rue de Hambourg
St-Augustin-de-Desmaures, QC G3A 1S6
418-878-4570
Fax: 418-787-3533
Denis Chenier, Branch Manager

SAIC Canada
A wholly owned subsidiary of Science Applications International Corp.

#1516, 60 Queen St.
Ottawa, ON K1P 5Y7
613-563-7242
www.saiccanada.com
Firm Type: Management Consulting
Founded: 1986
Products/Services/Areas of Expertise: With offices in Ottawa, Calgary, Regina & Halifax, SAIC Canada provides technical services & solutions to both government & private business. Expertise is offered in the areas of energy services (energy efficiency & demand reduction, design-build services, services to the oil & gas industry, renewable energy & climate change services), environmental services (compliance, spill response, site decontamination/remediation, testing, training, etc.) health care technologies, information technology, & security & emergency management
Financial Information:
Type of Ownership: Foreign-owned
Domestic Markets:
National

Canadian Branches:
Halifax
#300, 1791 Barrington St.
Halifax, NS B3J 3K9
902-422-4255
Jim Bruce

Mississauga
6108 Edwards Blvd.
Mississauga, ON L5T 2V7
905-696-6701
David Broadley, Manager

Ottawa
335 River Rd.
Ottawa, ON K1A 1C7
613-991-2737

Regina
#240, 10 Research Dr.
Regina, SK S4S 7J7
306-791-3695
Products/Services/Areas of Expertise: In Western Canada, an office is also located at 240 - 4th Ave. SW, Calgary, AB
Al Clarke

St. Catharines Hydro Generation Inc.
P.O. Box 3083
340 Vansikle Rd.
St Catharines, ON L2R 6R8
905-323-3448
Fax: 905-684-3921
customerservice@schydro.com
www.schydro.com
Products/Services/Areas of Expertise: Electricity producer
Ecological Note: Renewable low-impact water-powered electricity
Contact(s):
John Kerklaan, President & CEO

St. George Power LP
J.D. Irving, Limited
P.O. Box 5666
300 Onion St.
Saint John, NB E2L 5B6
506-632-7777
Fax: 506-648-2205
Products/Services/Areas of Expertise: Renewable low-impact water powered electricity
Ecological Note: Hydro Facility, St. George, NB
Contact(s):
Mary Keith, 506-632-5122

St. Marys Cement Inc.
A wholly-owned subsidiary of Votorantim Cimentos
55 Industrial St., 4th Fl.
Toronto, ON M4G 3W9
416-696-4411
Fax: 416-696-4435
800-268-6148
customerservice@vcsmc.com
www.stmaryscement.com
Firm Type: Distributing, Manufacturing
Staff: 1500
Member of: Hutton Transport Ltd.
Products/Services/Areas of Expertise: Non-shrinking cement for waste containment applications; the firm is currently engaged in obtaining permits to initiate an Alternative Fuel Demonstration Project in 2011
Financial Information:
Type of Ownership: Private
Revenue: $1.5 Million - $3 Million
Domestic Markets:
National, Ontario
Foreign Activity:
USA
Contact(s):
Bram Vermeulen, President/CEO
Felipe Lima, CFO
John Vanderpas, Vice-President/General Manager
Dave Lumsden, President, Cement Division
Contact(s):
Fabio Cesconetto
Contact(s):
Marc Vermeire, Operations Manager

Canadian Branches:
Bowmanville
400 Waverley Rd. South
Bowmanville, ON L1C 3K3
905-623-3341
Fax: 905-623-4695

St. Marys
P.O. Box 1000
St. Marys, ON N4X 1B6
519-284-1020
Fax: 519-284-4045
Products/Services/Areas of Expertise: Located at 585 Water St. S., St. Mary's

SAL Engineering Ltd.
2220 Ave. C North
Saskatoon, SK S7L 6C3
306-653-4511
Fax: 306-664-1933
salengineering@shaw.ca
Firm Type: Engineering
Founded: 1980
Staff: 7
Member of: Association of Consulting Engineers of Canada.
Products/Services/Areas of Expertise: Water supply & treatment; sewage treatment & disposal; drainage & storm water management; solid waste management; cleanup
Financial Information:
Type of Ownership: Private
Revenue Sources: 80% nationwide; 10% Provincial; 10% Municipals
Domestic Markets:
Saskatchewan
Contact(s):
Don C.K. Poon, Managing Director

Sambrabec Inc.
5756, av Déom
Montréal, QC H3S 2N4
514-738-7241
Fax: 514-738-7324
sambrabec@videotron.ca
pages.videotron.com/sambrab
Firm Type: Manufacturing
Founded: 1984
Staff: 6
Products/Services/Areas of Expertise: Energy systems; energy produced using turbines which work on all fluids (water, gas, steam, wind, etc.); developed a wind application which does not experience overspeeding & produces twice as much energy as windmills
Financial Information:
Type of Ownership: Private
Revenue Sources: 10% Provincial; 5% Municipals; 85% Private Contracts
Domestic Markets:
Ontario, Québec
Foreign Activity:
Central America, South America
Contact(s):
Louis Beaulieu, President/CEO

Samco Resources & By-Products
360 Acadia Dr.
Hamilton, ON L8W 2R6
905-388-7620
Fax: 905-388-0671
info@samcoresources.ca
www.samcoresources.ca
Products/Services/Areas of Expertise: Recycling of scrap metal, hazardous & non-hazardous materials

Sanbec
Formerly: Solutions de Déversement Sanbec
58, rue Sauriol
Laval, QC H7N 3A8
450-688-3791
Fax: 450-688-0418
800-363-4280
info@sanbec.ca
www.sanbec.ca
Firm Type: Distributing, Manufacturing
Founded: 1977
Products/Services/Areas of Expertise: Liquid absorbents & adsorbents; cleaners & chemicals; cleaning services; safety & protective equipment; spill equipment
Domestic Markets:
New Brunswick, Newfoundland & Labrador, Nova Scotia, Nunavut, Ontario, Prince Edward Island, Québec
Foreign Activity:
Worldwide

Sanders Resource Manage Inc. / RMI
Formerly: Resource Management Inc.
Also Known As: Applied Microbe Consultants, Inc
P.O. Box 25149
Halifax, NS B3M 4H4
902-443-6796
Fax: 902-431-7282
resourcemanage@eastlink.ca
Firm Type: Management Consulting
Founded: 1989
Staff: 1
Products/Services/Areas of Expertise: Natural resource management
Recently Completed / Ongoing Projects: Development of NS 1 soybean innoculant for the atlantic region, establishment of a centre for compost study, study documenting ice in the Bay of Fundy
Domestic Markets:
New Brunswick, Nova Scotia, Ontario, Prince Edward Island, Québec
Foreign Activity:
Western Europe, USA
Contact(s):
Richard Sanders, Ph.D., President

Sandhill Disposal & Recycling Inc.
Formerly: Sandhill Disposal
5728 Old School Rd., RR#5
Caledon East, ON L0N 1E0
905-843-2552
Fax: 905-843-3495
sandhill@lincsat.com
www.sandhilldisposal.com
Firm Type: Waste Management
Founded: 1968
Staff: 55
Products/Services/Areas of Expertise: Waste transport & recycling
Contact(s):
John Devins, President

Sandwell Engineering Inc.
A member company of the Ausenco group
Park Place
#1580, 666 Burrard St.
Vancouver, BC V6C 2X8
604-684-0055
Fax: 604-684-7533
info@sandwell.com
www.sandwell.com
Firm Type: Management Consulting, Engineering
Founded: 1948
Staff: 495
Quality Environmental Management System(s): 14001:2004
Products/Services/Areas of Expertise: Engineering contractor in transportation, power, petroleum, industrial process, manufacturing & general industry; the firm is committed to delivering innovative solutions that enable clients to build & maintain competitive advantage, while reducing their environmental footprint & protecting the environment through conservation of resources & management of waste; the focus is

on a proactive approach to sustainable development policies & practices. Offices & projects around the world, including Belo Horizonte, & Rio de Janeiro, Brazil; Brisbane, & Perth, Australia; Chengdu, China; Johannesburg, South Africa; & Lima, Peru
Recently Completed / Ongoing Projects: EPC for landfill gas compression & conditioning equipment; preliminary & detailed desing engineering for replacement of biogas fuel engine-driven pumps; leaw 1,015 mw gas-fired electricity generating facility; wind power feasibility studies; waste management
Financial Information:
Revenue: $250,000 - $500,000
Domestic Markets:
National
Foreign Activity:
Worldwide
Contact(s):
Charles Birt, President
cbirt@sandwell.com
Richard A. Fraser, Vice President, Corporate & Project Development
rfraser@sandwell.com
Alf A. Price, Corporate Controller
aprice@sandwell.com
Graham K. Egli, Corporate Director, Health, Safety, Environment & Community
gegli@sandwell.com
Richard Ritchie, Manager, Management Information Systems
rritchie@sandwell.com

Canadian Branches:
Burlington - Sandwell Engineers Ltd.
#100, 1016B Sutton Dr.
Burlington, ON L7L 6B8
905-319-1698
Fax: 905-319-1801
Adrian VanSchouwen, Vice President/General Manager
avanschouwen@sandwell.com

Calgary
#805, 900 - 6th Ave. SW
Calgary, AB T2P 3K2
403-237-8035
Fax: 403-215-6350
Nick R. Krpan, Vice President, Oil Sands, Petrochemical & Mining Sectors
nkrpan@sandwell.com

Montréal
#200, 555, boul René-Lévesque ouest
Montréal, QC H2Z 1B1
514-866-1221
Fax: 514-866-0804
Serge Venne, Vice President/General Manager
svenne@sandwell.com

Vancouver
#600, 885 Dunsmuir St.
Vancouver, BC V6C 1N5
604-684-9311
Fax: 604-688-5913
Joel Cawker, Vice President/General Manager, Mining & Bulk Handling Div.
jcawker@sandwell.com

International Branch(es):
Atlanta - Sandwell Engineers Corp.
#390, 5300 Oakbrook Pkwy.
Norcross, GA USA
770-255-1640
Fax: 770-255-1649
Tom Marshall, Vice President, Operations
tmarshall@sandwell.com

Jakarta - Sandwell Inc.
Ariobimo Central Bldg. Lt.4
JL HR Rasuna Said Blok X-2 No.5
Jakarta Indonesi
-62-21-529-09125
Fax: -62-21-794-0728
Products/Services/Areas of Expertise: The Jakarta office is responsible for operations in Indonesia, Malaysia, Thailand, Singapore & Vietnam
Jim Chandra, Country Manager
jchandra@sandwell.com

Mumbai - Sandwell India Consulting Engineers Pvt. Ltd.
602/603 - Powai Plaza
Central Ave., Hiranandani Gardens
Mumbai India

91 22 6772 6666
Fax: 91 22 6772 6677
Peter Leekha, Managing Director, Sandwell India
pleekha@sandwell.com

Sanexen Environmental Services Inc.
Division of Logistec Corporation
#32, 1471, boul Lionel-Boulet
Varennes, QC J3X 1P7
450-652-9990
Fax: 450-652-2290
800-263-7870
info@sanexen.com
www.sanexen.com
Firm Type: Management Consulting, Engineering, Scientific/Technical Services, Waste Management
Founded: 1985
Member of: Association of Professional Engineers; National Solid Waste Management Association; American Water Works Association
Products/Services/Areas of Expertise: Site remediation service; PCB management; oil, water, soils clean-up; PCB destruction (chemical) & PCB transformer waste minimization; PCB building cleaning; water treatment; arctic soil remediation; biotreatment; building clean-up & equipment decommissioning; industrial waste management; underground tank removal; risk assessment
Domestic Markets:
National
Foreign Activity:
Central America, The Pacific Rim, South America, Mexico
Contact(s):
Alain Sauriol, President
asauriol@sanexen.com
Jean Paquin, Vice-President, Technology
jpaquin@sanexen.com
Joseph Loiacono, Manager, Business Development
jloiacono@sanexen.com

Canadian Branches:
Toronto
Bldg. 52, Marine Terminal
8 Unwin Ave.
Toronto, ON M5A 1A1
416-622-5011

Sani Gestion ONYX
Formerly: Groupe Sani Gestion Inc.
3383, boul de la Chaudière
Sainte-Foy, QC G1X 4B8
418-871-7089
Fax: 418-871-4415
Firm Type: Distributing, Waste Management
Founded: 1962
Products/Services/Areas of Expertise: Waste collection & transport; operation of solid waste disposal sites; distribution of waste containers & compactors, waste collection trucks; recycling centre
Contact(s):
Gaétan Blouin, President

Sanitherm Engineering Limited
#4, 431 Mountain Hwy.
North Vancouver, BC V7J 2L1
604-986-9168
Fax: 604-986-5377
saneng@sanitherm.com
www.sanitherm.com
Firm Type: Distributing, Manufacturing
Founded: 1946
Staff: 25
Products/Services/Areas of Expertise: Design & supply of water & sewage treatment plants; extended aeration wastewater treatment plants; water & wastewater treatment equipment
Domestic Markets:
Alberta, British Columbia, Manitoba, Northwest Territories, Saskatchewan
Foreign Activity:
Worldwide
Contact(s):
Richard Smyth, Partner
Dave Botwright, Partner
Joan Smyth

Canadian Branches:
Calgary
288 Woodside Circle SW
Calgary, AB T2W 3K5

403-251-0075
Fax: 403-251-0041
sanitherm.alberta@shaw.ca
Dan O'Brien

Sanix Incorporated
Formerly: Aqua-Plant Construction Co. Ltd
#329, 1508 Broadway West
Vancouver, BC V6J 1W8
604-734-3514
800-275-2082
sanix@telus.net
www.sanix.ca
Firm Type: Engineering
Founded: 1983
Staff: 10
Member of: Water Environment Federation; British Columbia Water & Wastes Association
Products/Services/Areas of Expertise: Designs & builds water recycling systems, groundwater arsenic treatment systems, industrial & municipal wastewater treatment
Recently Completed / Ongoing Projects: Physical/chemical treatment plant for food processing company; oil/water separation projects; arsenic treatment system for hotspring resort; small community sewage treatment plant
Financial Information:
Type of Ownership: Publicly Traded
Revenue Sources: 100% Private Contracts
Domestic Markets:
British Columbia
Foreign Activity:
Asia, The Pacific Rim, USA
Contact(s):
Robert Wyckham, Marketing & Sales
Seamus Frain, P.Eng., Manager, Engineering & Construction

International Branch(es):
Japan
Tobu Sendai Dai-ichi Building, 6F
4-6-1 Tsutsujioka, Miyagino-ku
Sendai Japan
-81-22-742-3026
Fax: -81-22-742-3027
w319202@sanix.co.jp
Toshiko Kumagai, Branch Manager

Santinel Inc.
1061, boul Ste-Foy
Longueuil, QC J4K 1W5
450-679-7801
Fax: 450-670-4504
sanitel@sanitel.com
www.santinel.com
Firm Type: Management Consulting, Scientific/Technical Services
Staff: 16
Products/Services/Areas of Expertise: Laboratory analysis; occupational health & safety consulting; project management; emergency measures; fire safety
Domestic Markets:
Québec
Contact(s):
Michel Dubeau, President/CEO

SAR Engineering
Formerly: Solar Applications & Research Ltd.
8884 - 15 Ave.
Burnaby, BC V3N 1Y3
604-525-2239
kacooper@sarengineering.com
Firm Type: Engineering, Scientific/Technical Services
Founded: 1974
Staff: 2
Products/Services/Areas of Expertise: Environmental & energy monitoring (short & long term); design, monitoring & simulation of residential buildings
Recently Completed / Ongoing Projects: Wall retrofit study for the Canada Mortgage & Housing Corporation (CMHC) includes residential energy simulation, database management, programming & management; advanced house testing & long-term monitoring for NRCan
Financial Information:
Revenue Sources: 50% nationwide; 20% Provincial; 10% Municipals; 20% Private Contracts
Domestic Markets:
National
Contact(s):

Products & Services Buyer's Guide

Ken Cooper, President

Sarafinchin Associates Ltd.
Also Known As: Sarafinchin Consulting Engineers
238 Galaxy Blvd.
Toronto, ON M9W 5R8
416-674-1770
Fax: 416-674-1997
geoeng@sarafinchin.com
www.sarafinchin.com
Firm Type: Engineering, Scientific/Technical Services
Founded: 1984
Staff: 10
Member of: Tunnelling Association of Canada
Member of: Professional Engineers of Ontario; Consulting Engineers of Ontario; Ordre des Ingenieurs du Québec; National Ground Water Association; Canadian Commission of Independent Laboratories; International Association of Hydrogeologists; Canadian EcoTechnical Societ
Products/Services/Areas of Expertise: Geotechnical, Geoenvironmental, Geotechnical & Hydrogeology engineering, inspection & testing; building sciences
Recently Completed / Ongoing Projects: Environmental site assessment, contaminate migration, site remediation, groundwater supply, watershed studies, wellhead protection, landfills, slopes, tunnels, foundations, escavations, erosion, mining
Financial Information:
Type of Ownership: Private
Domestic Markets:
Alberta, British Columbia, New Brunswick, Newfoundland & Labrador, Nova Scotia, Nunavut, Ontario, Prince Edward Island, Québec, Saskatchewan
Foreign Activity:
Africa, Asia, Caribbean, South America, Mexico, USA
Markets Sought:
Asia
Contact(s):
Murray G. Sarafinchin, P.Eng., M.A.Sc., President
geoeng@sarafinchin.com

SARCAN Recycling
Division of Saskatchewan Association of Rehabilitation Centres
111 Cardinal Cres.
Saskatoon, SK S7L 6H5
306-933-0616
Fax: 306-653-3932
www.sarcsarcan.ca
Firm Type: Waste Management
Founded: 1968
Staff: 365
Member of: Saskatchewan Waste Reduction Council; Recycling Council of Alberta; Recycling Council of BC
Products/Services/Areas of Expertise: Collects, processes & markets aluminum, plastic, glass & metal used beverage containers; recycle non-deposit milk cartons & plastic milk jugs
Recently Completed / Ongoing Projects: Operates over 70 recycling centres & 2 processing centres in over 60 Saskatchewan communities
Financial Information:
Type of Ownership: Non Profit
Revenue: Greater than $5 Million
Revenue Sources: 66% Provincial; 34% Private Contracts
Domestic Markets:
Saskatchewan
Contact(s):
Bob LeGoffe, Executive Director
Ken Homenick, Director, Operations
Kevin Acton, Manager, Special Projects
Bob Hnetka, Director, Finance

Saskferco Products Inc.
#215, 1874 Scarth St.
Regina, SK S4P 4B3
306-525-7600
Fax: 306-525-2942
www.saskferco.com
Firm Type: Manufacturing
Founded: 1990
Products/Services/Areas of Expertise: Manufacturers of nitrogen fertilizers, granular urea & anhydrous ammonia
Financial Information:
Type of Ownership: Private
Domestic Markets:
Alberta, British Columbia, Manitoba, Ontario, Québec, Saskatchewan

Foreign Activity:
USA
Canadian Branches:
Manitoba Warehouse
P.O. Box 670
Carman, MB R0G 0J0
204-745-6159
Fax: 204-745-6224
Belle Plaine Plant
P.O. Box 39
Belle Plaine, SK S0G 0G0
306-345-4200
Fax: 306-345-2353

SaskPower
Bulk Power Management
2025 Victoria Ave.
Regina, SK S4P 0S1
306-566-2095
888-757-6937
Ecological Note: Renewable low-impact electricity
Contact(s):
R. Stedwill, Manager, Environmental Programs, 306/566-3587
rstedwill@saskpower.com

Sass Manufacturing Ltd.
114 Sass Rd.
Chatham, ON N7M 5J4
514-352-0600
Fax: 514-352-6730
Canadian Branches:
Sass Manufacturing Ltd.
114 Sass Rd.
Chatham, ON N7M 5J4
514-352-0600
Fax: 514-352-6730

SatCon Power Systems (Canada)
Formerly: Inverpower Controls Ltd.
835 Harrington Ct.
Burlington, ON L7N 3P3
905-639-4692
Fax: 905-639-0961
Products/Services/Areas of Expertise: Electronic power systems for conversion of electrical energy; heating systems; motor drives

Satlantic
Richmond Terminal, Pier 9
3481 North Marginal Rd.
Halifax, NS B3K 5X8
902-492-4780
Fax: 902-492-4781
info@satlantic.com
www.satlantic.com
Firm Type: Manufacturing
Founded: 1990
Member of: Canadian Remote Sensing Society; Alliance of Marine Remote Sensing Association; Metro Halifax Chamber of Commerce
Member of: Canadian Manufacturers & Exporters Association
Products/Services/Areas of Expertise: Designs & manufactures a variety of precision sensors & systems for the study of aquatic environments; manufactures radiometers & standard light sensors for primary research, satellite calibration & validation & environmental prediction & assessment
Recently Completed / Ongoing Projects: Long-term ecosystem observatory at 15 meters, LFO-15, enables operators to monitor & control the underwater observatory securely & remotely while providing real time data to users worldwide via the internet
Financial Information:
Type of Ownership: Private
Revenue Sources: 80% nationwide; 20% Private Contracts
Domestic Markets:
National
Foreign Activity:
Worldwide
Contact(s):
Bill Ricketts, President/COO
Norman Countway, Vice-President, Sales
Scott MacLean, Vice-President, Engineering
Jennie King, Manager, Sales & Marketing
jking@satlantic.com

Scales Bioresource Consulting Ltd.
20 Keefe Rd.
Halifax, NS B3P 2J1
902-479-2600
Fax: 902-479-2601
Contact(s):
Pete Scales, President

SCC Environmental
137 LeMarchant Rd.
St. John's, NL A1C 2H3
709-726-0506
Fax: 709-726-7905
Firm Type: Waste Management
Founded: 1988
Member of: Newfoundland Environmental Industry Association; Nova Scotia Environmental Industry Association
Products/Services/Areas of Expertise:
Treatment/decontamination of hydrocarbon contaminated soils, sludges & sediments; treatment of contaminated drill muds & cuttings & recovery of drilling fluids; treatment of industrial wastewater; management of hazardous wastes & PCBs
Financial Information:
Type of Ownership: Private
Revenue Sources: 20% nationwide; 10% Provincial; 70% Private Contracts
Domestic Markets:
New Brunswick, Newfoundland & Labrador, Nova Scotia, Ontario, Québec
Foreign Activity:
Australia/New Zealand, The Middle East, South America, Mexico, USA
Canadian Branches:
Maritime Office
#550, 33 Alderney Dr.
Dartmouth, NS B2Y 2N4
902-461-9131
Fax: 902-461-0070
mkapila@ibm.net
Mukesh Kapila, Vice-President

Scepter Manufacturing Co. Ltd.
170 Midwest Rd.
Toronto, ON M1P 3A9
416-751-9445
Fax: 416-751-4451
800-387-6018
www.scepter.com
Firm Type: Manufacturing
Founded: 1948
Quality Environmental Management System(s): 9002
Products/Services/Areas of Expertise: Scepter makes a range of products for people who are environmentally conscious. They include garden gourmet - a backyard composter; rainsaver - a modern version of the rain barrel, curbside recycling containers, & recycling containers for offices
Financial Information:
Type of Ownership: Private
Domestic Markets:
National
Foreign Activity:
Asia, Australia/New Zealand, Western Europe, The Middle East, South America, Mexico, USA,

SCG Industries Ltd.
Spruce Lake Industrial Park
250 King William Rd.
Saint John, NB E2M 5Y5
506-674-1081
Fax: 506-674-1082
888-736-3348
remedi8@scgindustries.com
scgindustries.com
Firm Type: Manufacturing, Scientific/Technical Services
Founded: 1993
Staff: 7
Member of: New Brunswick Environmental Industry Association
Products/Services/Areas of Expertise: Remediation equipment provider; conducts testing & design for the appropriate application of remedial technologies
Recently Completed / Ongoing Projects: Fort Drum, NY, USAFB; Maryland, Andrews AFB; Argentia NL; Hamilton, Bermuda
Financial Information:
Type of Ownership: Private

Revenue Sources: 15% nationwide; 5% Provincial; 88% Private Contracts
Domestic Markets:
National
Markets Sought:
Caribbean, USA
Contact(s):
Michael C. Campbell, President
Dale Chambers, General Manager

Schlegel Canada Inc.
514 South Service Rd. East
Oakville, ON L6J 2X6
905-844-5039
800-268-5039
sales@schlegel.ca
Firm Type: Manufacturing
Founded: 1931
Member of: Canadian Window & Door Manufacturers Association
Quality Environmental Management System(s): 9001
Products/Services/Areas of Expertise: Weatherseals (pile, foam, compression) for window/door manufacturers & building/construction industries
Financial Information:
Type of Ownership: Foreign-owned
Domestic Markets:
National
Markets Sought:
USA
Contact(s):
Ralph Burlingham, General Manager

Schlumberger Oilfield Services
Canada GeoMarket
525 - 3 Ave. SW
Calgary, AB T2P 0G4
403-509-4100
Fax: 403-509-4120
www.slb.com
Products/Services/Areas of Expertise: Geological & hydrogeological engineering; resource management services
Contact(s):
Sarah Wilson, Manager, Marketing
Claude Durocher, General Manager

Schlumberger Water Services / SWS
Formerly: Waterloo Hydrogeologic Inc.
#101, 460 Phillip St.
Waterloo, ON N2L 5J2
519-746-1798
Fax: 519-885-5262
sws-info@slb.com; sws-sales@slb.com; sws-support@slb.com
www.swstechnology.com
Firm Type: Distributing, Engineering, Scientific/Technical Services
Founded: 1993
Products/Services/Areas of Expertise: Supplier of groundwater & environmental monitoring & modeling technologies; Clients include the mining, oil & gas, & power sectors
Activities: Developing, managing, & protecting water resources; Providing technical support for SWS software
Financial Information:
Type of Ownership: Foreign-owned
Domestic Markets:
National
Foreign Activity:
Australia/New Zealand, Central Europe, The Middle East, South America, USA
Contact(s):
Martin Draeger, Manager, Marketing

Canadian Branches:
Vancouver
#110, 3480 Gilmore Way
Burnaby, BC V5G 4Y1
604-430-4272
Fax: 604-430-3538
sws-westbay@slb.com

Schneider Electric Canada Inc.
5985 McLaughlin Rd.
Mississauga, ON L5R 1B8
905-366-3999
Fax: 859-334-9915
800-565-6699
canadian.pss@schneider-electric.com
www.schneider-electric.ca
Firm Type: Management Consulting, Distributing, Manufacturing
Products/Services/Areas of Expertise: Specializes in energy management solutions & products, with a focus on automation & control systems, energy efficient electrical distribution, building solutions, renewable energies, power & cooling services, RoHS compliance, & training; 21 sales & service offices, & 4 plants across Canada
Financial Information:
Type of Ownership: Foreign-owned
Domestic Markets:
National
Foreign Activity:
Worldwide
Contact(s):
Gary Abrams, President

Canadian Branches:
Calgary
2880 - 45th Ave. SE, Bay 288
Calgary, AB T2B 3M1
403-214-3130
Fax: 859-334-9902

Cambridge
#6, 150 Pinebush Rd.
Cambridge, ON N1R 8J8
519-621-5756
Fax: 859-334-9904

Sudbury
#15, 868 Falconbridge Rd.
Sudbury, ON P3A 5K7
705-560-9516
Fax: 859-344-9940

Winnipeg
21 Omands Creek Blvd.
Winnipeg, MB R2R 2V2
204-488-2305
Fax: 859-334-9957

Brossard
4200, Place de Java
Brossard, QC J4Y 0C4
450-444-0143
Fax: 859-334-9938

Edmonton
Bonaventure Industrial Park
12825 - 144th St.
Edmonton, AB T5L 4N7
780-453-3561
Fax: 859-334-9909

La Prairie
#200, 1400, rue Industrielle
La Prairie, QC J5R 2E5
450-724-6343
Fax: 450-659-8900

Richmond
22171 Fraserwood Way
Richmond, BC V6W 1J5
604-273-3711

Schwank Group
5205 Bradco Blvd.
Mississauga, ON L4W 2A6
905-712-4766
Fax: 905-712-8336
866-361-0417
csr@schwankgroup.com
www.schwankgroup.com
Firm Type: Manufacturing
Founded: 1972
Staff: 50
Quality Environmental Management System(s): 9001
Products/Services/Areas of Expertise: Energy-efficient heaters; infra-red & radiant heaters
Financial Information:
Type of Ownership: Private
Domestic Markets:
National
Foreign Activity:
Eastern Europe, Western Europe, The Middle East, The Pacific Rim, South America
Contact(s):
Bob Alcott, Manager, Products

International Branch(es):
Waynesboro Office
Two Shwank Way, Hwy 56N
Waynesboro, GA USA
706-554-6191
Fax: 706-554-9390
usacs@shwankgroup.com
Tim Weaver

Scicorp Systems Inc.
#15, 220 Bayview Dr.
Barrie, ON L4N 4Y8
705-733-2626
Fax: 705-733-2618
800-897-2053
sales@globalliquidscorp.com
www.scicorp.net
Firm Type: Distributing, Scientific/Technical Services
Founded: 1989
Staff: 17
Products/Services/Areas of Expertise: Products for biological treatment of wastewater, waste, odour control
Activities: Biological wastewater treatment research, manufacturing, marketing & sales
Recently Completed / Ongoing Projects: South Africa, Malaysia, Korea
Financial Information:
Type of Ownership: Private
Revenue: Greater than $5 Million
Revenue Sources: 100% Private Contracts
Domestic Markets:
British Columbia, Manitoba, New Brunswick, Ontario, Prince Edward Island, Québec
Foreign Activity:
Africa, Asia, Central America, China, Central Europe, The Middle East, The Pacific Rim, South Africa, Mexico, USA, United Kingdom, Vietnam
Markets Sought:
The Pacific Rim, South Africa, United Kingdom

International Branch(es):
Scicorp Biologic Inc. - North Tonawanda
908 Niagara Falls Blvd.
North Tonawanda, NY USA
1-800-897-2053
Rob Denis

Sciencetech Inc.
45 Meg Dr.
London, ON N6E 2V2
519-668-0131
Fax: 519-668-0132
sales@sciencetech-inc.com
www.sciencetech-inc.com
Firm Type: Scientific/Technical Services
Founded: 1985
Staff: 30
Products/Services/Areas of Expertise: Manufacturer of instrumentation for optical spectroscopy & new product developments
Recently Completed / Ongoing Projects: Calibration system for European Space Agency; Steady state fluorometer system, Univ. of North Carolina; far infrared spectrometer, Univ. of North California; high power xenon illumination system, Environment Canada
Financial Information:
Type of Ownership: Private
Revenue: $1.5 Million - $3 Million
Revenue Sources: 10% nationwide; 10% Provincial; 5% Municipals; 75% Private Contracts
Domestic Markets:
Ontario
Foreign Activity:
Asia, Central Europe, Mexico, USA, Worldwide
Contact(s):
Alexander Quaglia, President
alex@sciencetech-inc.com
Douglas Peng, Vice-President, Sales & Marketing
doug@sciencetech-inc.com
Mick Beattie, Plant Manager

Canadian Branches:
Concord
Sales & Marketing
96 Bradwick Dr.
Concord, ON L4K 1K8

519-964-3315
Fax: 519-668-0121
Douglas Peng, Vice-President

Scientific Instrumentation Ltd. / SIL
2233 Hanselman Ave.
Saskatoon, SK S7L 6A7
306-244-0881
Fax: 306-665-6263
s.i.l@sil.sk.ca
www.sil.sk.ca
Firm Type: Engineering, Manufacturing
Founded: 1980
Staff: 20
Quality Environmental Management System(s): 9001
Products/Services/Areas of Expertise: Advanced technology solutions to air, water & atmospheric monitoring; Ground based & airborne measurements; Expertise includes research & development, instrument design, manufacturing, systems engineering, data acquisition/analysis, data logging & telemetry systems (stack emission, ambient air, flue gas, flamescanning, field installations, others); multigas analyzer
Recently Completed / Ongoing Projects: CIBAOS - Chemical & Biological Detection & Identification System
Financial Information:
Type of Ownership: Private
Revenue: $1.5 Million - $3 Million
Revenue Sources: 10% nationwide; 90% Private Contracts
Domestic Markets:
Alberta, Ontario, Saskatchewan
Foreign Activity:
Africa, Asia, Australia/New Zealand, China, Central Europe, Western Europe, South America, USA, Vietnam
Contact(s):
Dale Sommerfeldt, Vice-President

Scimus Inc.
18 Aneta Circle
Toronto, ON M2M 3J2
416-225-1697
buchnea@sympatico.ca
Firm Type: Scientific/Technical Services
Founded: 1983
Staff: 2
Member of: Canadian Nuclear Society; Canadian Radiological Protection Association
Member of: Air & Waste Management Association
Products/Services/Areas of Expertise: Environmental consulting company specializing in solid wastes, environmental impact analysis, radiation & health physics
Activities: Site remediation
Recently Completed / Ongoing Projects: Decommissioning of phosphate fertilizer plant in Port Maitland, ON for Global Inc.; decommissioning of a former gold smelting site in Deloro, ON for the Ontario MOEE; site remediation of an automobile parts manufacturing plant in Oshawa, ON for A.G. Simpson; decommissioning of a gold mine in northern Ontario for Talisman Energy Co.
Financial Information:
Type of Ownership: Private
Revenue Sources: 20% Provincial; 80% Private Contracts
Domestic Markets:
Ontario, Saskatchewan
Markets Sought:
Eastern Europe, USA
Contact(s):
Alex Buchnea, President/CEO

Scintrex Ltd.
222 Snidercroft Rd.
Concord, ON L4K 1B5
905-669-2280
Fax: 905-669-6403
scintrex@scintrexltd.com
www.scintrexltd.com
Firm Type: Manufacturing
Founded: 1960
Quality Environmental Management System(s): 9001
Products/Services/Areas of Expertise: Developer & manufacturer of measuring & monitoring equipment, laboratory equipment, vapour detectors & odour detection, narcotics detectors, explosive detectors, radiation monitors
Financial Information:
Type of Ownership: Publicly Traded
Domestic Markets:
National

Foreign Activity:
Worldwide
Contact(s):
Abe Rolnick, President & CEO

Scitax Advisory Partners LLP
Formerly: David Hearn & Associates
#1000, 36 Toronto St.
Toronto, ON M5C 2C5
416-350-1214
Fax: 416-350-1215
info@scitax.com
www.scitax.com
Firm Type: Management Consulting
Founded: 1993
Staff: 41
Products/Services/Areas of Expertise: Tax services specializing in research & development technical tax services
Contact(s):
David Hearn, Managing Director
dhearn@scitax.com

Scotia Plastics
P.O. Box 69
Shubenacadie, NS B0N 2H0
902-758-2660
Fax: 902-758-2636
a.bezanson@scotiaplastics.ns.ca
www.scotiaplastics.ns.ca
Products/Services/Areas of Expertise: Supplies plastic bottles & plastic tubing; specializes in blowmolding HDPE plastic beverage bottles & blowmolding HDPE plastic industrial bottles & extruding HDPE plastic corrugated tubing or HDPE plastic corrugated pipe
Contact(s):
K. Reed, Contact

Scotia Recycling Ltd.
5 Brown Ave.
Dartmouth, NS B3B 1Z7
902-468-5650
Fax: 902-468-9769
scotiarecycling@scotiarecycling.com
www.scotiarecycling.com
Products/Services/Areas of Expertise: Collection and processing of paper products
Contact(s):
Darren Welner, Coordinator, Sales & Marketing

Scott & Stewart Forestry Consultants
2267 Antigonish Guysborough Rd., RR#1
St Andrews, NS B0H 1X0
902-863-5508
Fax: 902-863-5581
mainoffice@scottandstewart.com
www.scottandstewart.com/home.htm
Firm Type: Engineering, Scientific/Technical Services
Founded: 1986
Staff: 25
Member of: Nova Scotia Forest Products; Nova Scotia Silviculture Contractors Association
Products/Services/Areas of Expertise: Woodlot management plan preparation; reforestation; photo interpretation
Financial Information:
Type of Ownership: Private
Revenue: $1.5 Million - $3 Million
Revenue Sources: 60% Provincial; 5% Municipals; 35% Private Contracts
Domestic Markets:
Nova Scotia
Contact(s):
Ralph Stewart, President
Shaun Scott, Principal
Charles Bowers, Principal

Scott Resource Services Inc.
31856 Silverdale Ave.
Mission, BC V2V 2K9
604-820-1415
Fax: 604-820-1621
scottres@telus.net
Firm Type: Scientific/Technical Services
Founded: 1985
Staff: 8
Member of: American Fisheries Society; Canadian Society of Environmental Biologists

Products/Services/Areas of Expertise: Project administration & management; environmental counsel & monitoring; agency & municipal permits/approvals expedition; habitat impact mitigation (planning, construction procedures & sequencing, sediment control plans); compensation plans & mediation in relation to aquatic habitat altered or lost through land use developments; creek relocation design & construction; studies; surveys of sport fisheries; commercial & subsistence fishery survey; sport fishery development planning
Recently Completed / Ongoing Projects: Cedar Valley Connection, Mission BC, Coldwater Canyon, BC
Financial Information:
Type of Ownership: Private
Domestic Markets:
British Columbia
Contact(s):
Jim Scott, President
scottres@telus.net

Scott Tank Cleaning Co. Ltd.
#4, 34 Queen St. West
Mississauga, ON L5H 1L4
905-278-0231
Fax: 905-278-3225
800-289-8529
Firm Type: Engineering, Scientific/Technical Services
Founded: 1957
Staff: 10
Products/Services/Areas of Expertise: Hazardous waste transportation; spill cleanup; site rehabilitation; tank maintenance & removal
Contact(s):
John D. Thordarson, President/CEO
David Orr, Marketing

SDS Drilling Ltd.
A Division of Boart Longyear Inc.
4025 - 96 Ave. SE
Calgary, AB T2C 4T7
403-287-1460
Fax: 403-243-0580
info@boartlongyear.com
www.boartlongyear.com
Firm Type: Engineering, Scientific/Technical Services
Founded: 1978
Staff: 25
Products/Services/Areas of Expertise: Environmental & geotechnical drilling services
Financial Information:
Type of Ownership: Publicly Traded
Domestic Markets:
Alberta, British Columbia
Foreign Activity:
Africa

SEA Engineering Company Inc.
P.O. Box 23111
Dartmouth, NS B3A 4S9
902-469-1230
Fax: 902-463-5603
seaeas@fox.nstn.ca
www.designeng.com
Firm Type: Engineering
Founded: 1981
Staff: 2
Quality Environmental Management System(s): 9003
Products/Services/Areas of Expertise: Custom machine design, product development & product engineering; project management
Recently Completed / Ongoing Projects: Water vapour diffusion apparatus for testing breathable fabrics, Sweating Thermally Instrumented Manikin (TIM) for testing environmental protective garments; sweating hot plate for research, development & evaluation of components of environmental protective garments; iodine-based automated water treatment system; sub-sea heavy oil cargo extraction system for salvaging dangerous cargoes from sunken wrecks; commercial diving chamber environmental control system; plastics thermo forming machine
Financial Information:
Type of Ownership: Private
Domestic Markets:
National
Foreign Activity:
Worldwide
Markets Sought:
Central America

Contact(s):
Ed A. Smallhorn, President

Sea Scan International Inc. / SSII
16065 Humber Station Rd.
Caledon East, ON L7E 3A4
905-880-0528
Fax: 905-880-0528
seascan@ca.inter.net
Firm Type: Engineering, Scientific/Technical Services
Founded: 1984
Staff: 2
Member of: Remote Sensing Society; American Geophysical Union; Canadian Meteorological & Oceanographic Society; Alliance for Marine Remote Sensing
Products/Services/Areas of Expertise: Environmental satellite ground stations, data analysis & product development
Recently Completed / Ongoing Projects: Satellite ground station & processing for forest fire detection, Borneo; satellite data processing for limnology, Canada; satellite data processing for rice crop monitoring, Malaysia; satellite monitoring of smoke, Korea, Indonesia
Domestic Markets:
National
Foreign Activity:
Western Europe, The Pacific Rim, USA
Contact(s):
Brian Wannamaker, President

Seaboard Industrial Supply Co. Ltd.
15 School St.
Sydney, NS B1S 3G1
902-564-0400
Fax: 902-539-1090
sis@ns.sympatico.ca
Contact(s):
Bill Morrison, General Manager

Seacom International Inc.
19 Dunfield St.
St. John's, NL A1A 1W2
709-754-3255
Fax: 709-754-3215
seacom@seacomcanada.com
www.seacomcanada.com
Firm Type: Management Consulting, Scientific/Technical Services
Founded: 1995
Products/Services/Areas of Expertise: Provides consulting to petroleum & other industries in Canada & abroad; provides environmental services, emergency preparedness planning, training & exercise programs
Contact(s):
Paul R. Clay, President

Seaforth Engineering Group Inc.
#200, Inc. 300 Prince Albert Rd.
Dartmouth, NS B2Y 4J2
902-468-3579
Fax: 902-468-6865
info@seaforthengineering.com
www.seaforthengineering.com
Firm Type: Engineering, Manufacturing, Scientific/Technical Services
Founded: 1994
Staff: 10
Member of: Association of Professsional Engineers of Nova Scotia
Products/Services/Areas of Expertise: Emission control technologies; renewable/alternate energy systems; marine geomatics services; project management
Recently Completed / Ongoing Projects: Fiber optic cable marine route survey, Bahamas; law of the sea - extended continental shelf boundary claim, Nigeria; wind turbine sale, installation & commissioning
Financial Information:
Type of Ownership: Private
Revenue: $1.5 Million - $3 Million
Revenue Sources: 100% Private Contracts
Domestic Markets:
National
Foreign Activity:
Africa, Asia, Caribbean, The Middle East, USA
Markets Sought:
Central America, China, South America, Mexico, Vietnam
Contact(s):
David Lombardi, President

S. Mason, Vice-President

SEAL-OGIC Innovations Corp.
P.O. Box 23089
43-C Putman Industrial Rd.
Belleville, ON K8P 5J3
613-966-4567
Fax: 613-966-9854
info@seal-ogic.com
www.seal-ogic.com
Firm Type: Manufacturing
Founded: 1991
Products/Services/Areas of Expertise: Industry sealing products & solutions
Financial Information:
Type of Ownership: Private
Domestic Markets:
National

Sealcon Liner Systems Inc.
26020 - 31B Ave.
Aldergrove, BC V4W 2Z6
604-607-7755
Fax: 604-607-7756
sealcon@gu-international.com
Firm Type: Manufacturing
Products/Services/Areas of Expertise: Manhole liner products for sanitary & storm sewers
Financial Information:
Type of Ownership: Private
Revenue Sources: 100% Municipals
Domestic Markets:
Alberta, British Columbia, Manitoba
Foreign Activity:
Central Europe, Mexico, USA
Markets Sought:
USA
Contact(s):
John Chappell, President
Brian Lingnau, Manager, Sales & Technical Support

Sealtech Restorations Inc.
6224D - 2 St. SE
Calgary, AB T2H 1J4
403-253-5002
Fax: 403-253-2636
sealtech@shaw.ca

Sears Canada Inc.
222 Jarvis St.
Toronto, ON M5B 2B8
416-941-3982
Fax: 416-941-4856
Products/Services/Areas of Expertise: Consumer, office & industry products; Ecologo certified paints & surface coatings
Ecological Note: Complete line of interior & exterior paints & stains including: Easy Living & Weatherbeater
Contact(s):
Greig Carson, Contact

Secter Environmental Resource Consulting / SERC
A Division of Secter Pacific Services Inc.
1396 Hillside Ave.
Victoria, BC V8T 2B5
250-477-6912
Fax: 250-477-7573
info@sercbc.com
www.sercbc.com
Firm Type: Management Consulting
Founded: 1989
Products/Services/Areas of Expertise: Secter Environmental Resource Consulting is a natural resources consulting firm which is engaged in professional environmental resource consulting services, natural resource planning, & environmental assessment.
Recently Completed / Ongoing Projects: Victoria Shipyards Co. Ltd.; Kwantlen First Nation; British Columbia Ministry of Transportation & the Snuneymuxw First Nation; Canada Zinc Metals Ltd.
Domestic Markets:
Alberta, British Columbia
Foreign Activity:
USA
Contact(s):
Jonathan Secter, B.S.A., M.S., R.P.Bio., Principal & Ecologist, Natural Resources

Jordan Secter, B.A., B.Sc., B.L.A., M.L., Landscape Architect & Environmental Planner
William Hubbard, M.Sc., P.Ag., Plant Ecologist & Manager, Land Resources
Darryl Anderson, MBA, Specialist, Transportation & Port Development
Jack Farrell, P.Eng., Water Resource Engineer & Regulatory Specialist

Secural Inc.
Also Known As: Secural WaterCare; Secural Datashred Inc.; Secural Site Solutions
#4, 150 Rivermede Rd.
Vaughan, ON L4K 3M8
905-763-7428
Fax: 905-763-7429
info@secural.com
www.secural.com
Firm Type: Distributing
Founded: 1988
Staff: 8
Products/Services/Areas of Expertise: Secural provides water treatment products, data shredding services, & site solutions. WaterCare solutions are provided without the use of chemicals, & include industrial water treatment & the treatment of ponds & pools for municipalities, golf courses, & private owners. Secural Datashred services feature the recycling of recycling of shredded paper, binders, hanging files, & clips. Secural Environmental Products include waste & recycling containers, benches made from recycled plastic wood, barriers, & smoking shelters.
Domestic Markets:
National
Contact(s):
Wendy Banting, President/CEO

Sedac Inc.
1740, rue Mitis, 2e étage
Chicoutimi, QC G7K 1H5
418-696-2259
Fax: 418-696-4669
Firm Type: Engineering, Scientific/Technical Services
Founded: 1986
Quality Environmental Management System(s): 9001
Products/Services/Areas of Expertise: Environmental consulting
Domestic Markets:
Québec
Contact(s):
Eric Lamontagne, President/CEO
Martin Peron, General Manager

Sedore Stoves Canada
Also Known As: Sedore Multi-Fuel Stoves
9060 Hwy. 542
Spring Bay, ON P0P 2B0
705-377-6071
888-282-8145
sedorestoves@xplornet.com; manitoulin.on@sedorestoves.com
www.sedorestoves.com
Firm Type: Distributing, Manufacturing
Founded: 1979
Products/Services/Areas of Expertise: Sedore Stove Company produces & distributes high efficiency multi-fuel biomass stoves.
Financial Information:
Type of Ownership: Private
Domestic Markets:
National
Foreign Activity:
USA
Contact(s):
Scott Willis, Contact

Seeker Green Products Ltd.
Formerly: Seeker Enterprises
Also Known As: Green Earth
28 Donhaven Rd.
Markham, ON L6E 1S6
905-209-0526
Fax: 905-209-0527
greenearth@seeker.com.hk
www.seeker.com.hk
Firm Type: Distributing
Founded: 2001

Member of: Ontario Environmental Industry Association (ONEIA)
Products/Services/Areas of Expertise: Seeker Green Products Ltd. provides alternative food packaging products, which are safe & biodegradable. Products include bowls, boxes, cups, plates, & trays. No wood or petroleum is used in the composition of these products. The company has obtained the Environmental Choice Program certificate.
Financial Information:
Type of Ownership: Private
Domestic Markets:
National
Foreign Activity:
Asia, China, The Pacific Rim, USA,

SEG Engineering Inc.
200 Tache Ave.
Winnipeg, MB R2H 1A7
204-233-2113
Fax: 204-233-2080
888-233-2113
seg@mts.net
www.mts.net/seg/
Firm Type: Engineering
Founded: 1980
Products/Services/Areas of Expertise: Municipal services; water treatment; sewage treatment; landfill sites; feasibility studies; design & contract administration
Financial Information:
Type of Ownership: Private
Revenue Sources: 50% nationwide; 10% Provincial; 20% Municipals; 20% Private Contracts
Domestic Markets:
Manitoba, Ontario
Foreign Activity:
USA

Seguro Projects Inc.
Formerly: Seguro Consulting Inc.
330 East 23rd St.
North Vancouver, BC V7L 3E5
604-986-5275
Fax: 425-984-9440
contact@seguroprojects.com
www.seguroprojects.com
Firm Type: Management Consulting, Scientific/Technical Services
Founded: 1989
Products/Services/Areas of Expertise: Seguro Projects Inc. is engaged in project financing & development.
Activities: Assisting junior exploration companies look for properties in North & South America
Financial Information:
Type of Ownership: Private
Domestic Markets:
National
Foreign Activity:
South America, Mexico, USA
Contact(s):
Donald (Tony) Simon, President & Chief Executive Officer

SEI Industries Ltd.
7400 Wilson Ave.
Delta, BC V4G 1E5
604-946-3131
Fax: 604-940-9566
seisales@sei-ind.com
www.sei-ind.com
Firm Type: Manufacturing
Founded: 1978
Staff: 100
Products/Services/Areas of Expertise: Emergency spill response storage tanks for land or water, collapsible fabric tanks (fuels/waters); secondary containment systems, spill trays & liners; ISO 9001:2000 certified; spill prevention protection; hazmat response, arctic condition
Recently Completed / Ongoing Projects: Bema Gold; Department of National Defense
Financial Information:
Type of Ownership: Private
Domestic Markets:
National
Foreign Activity:
Worldwide
Contact(s):
Mark McCooey, President
Greg Emry, Marketing Manager

Rob Fergusen, Sales

Semco Systems Limited
Also Known As: SEMCO
8485 Parkhill Dr.
Milton, ON L9T 5E9
905-670-9301
Fax: 905-693-9432
800-730-5859
info@semcotbs.com
www.semcotbs.com
Firm Type: Engineering, Manufacturing
Founded: 1969
Products/Services/Areas of Expertise: Semco Systems Limited is involved in designing, engineering, manufacturing, & installing bulk chemical handling equipment systems. Products include a continuous railcar unloading system, a bulk storage & slaker feed system, & a hydrated lime slurry makedown system. The company serves municipal & industrial environmental clients, such as water & wastewater treatment facilites.
Recently Completed / Ongoing Projects: Supplemental cementaeous materials for an existing cement facility; Starch makedown for a paper facility; Dry sorbent injection for flue gas desulphurization of industrial stack emissions
Domestic Markets:
National
Contact(s):
Terry Frank, Vice-President
terry@semcotbs.com
Paul Skirrow, Vice-President, Operations
Anil Chopra, Manager, Engineering
Patric Morris, Manager, Regional Sales
Dean Salloch, Manager, Applications

Sendex Environmental Corp.
417 Exeter Rd.
London, ON N6E 2Z3
519-680-3868
Fax: 519-680-3870
inquiries@sendex.com
www.sendex.com
Firm Type: Management Consulting, Engineering, Scientific/Technical Services
Founded: 1987
Products/Services/Areas of Expertise: Sendex is a company of environmental consulting engineers & scientists, including environmental scientists, hydrogeologists, & technologists. Services include environmental site assessments, remediation & contracting, auditing, & regulatory compliance.
Financial Information:
Type of Ownership: Private
Domestic Markets:
National

SENES Consultants Limited
Also Known As: Specialists in Energy, Nuclear and Environmental Sciences
#12, 121 Granton Dr.
Richmond Hill, ON L4B 3N4
905-764-9380
Fax: 905-764-9386
senes@senes.ca
www.senes.ca
Firm Type: Engineering, Scientific/Technical Services
Founded: 1980
Staff: 100
Member of: EPAS (Trinidad & Tobago); Pulles Howard & DeLang (South Africa); Brenk Systemplanung (Germany); G&A (Chile)
Quality Environmental Management System(s): 14001
Products/Services/Areas of Expertise: A Canadian, employee-owned group of companies with offices in Canada, the U.S. & India. Environmental & risk assessments; EMS services & environmental audits; site investigations; air quality assessment, air emission control & noise assessments; assessment of industrial & municipal water & waste treatment technologies; preparation of solid waste management master plans; development of waste management strategies, including low-level radioactive waste management; design & supervision of remedial action projects; pathways analysis of contaminant migration; data management; strategic planning; services to the mining & energy industries. In Canada, other offices are located in Vancouver, Ottawa & Yellowknife. The Richmond Hill head office also houses Decommissioning Consulting Services Limited, part of the SENES group
Recently Completed / Ongoing Projects: Organization of Eastern Caribbean States Solid & Ship-generated Waste Management Project (design of solid waste landfill, St. Kitts & Nevis)
Financial Information:
Type of Ownership: Private
Revenue: Greater than $5 Million
Revenue Sources: 30% nationwide; 20% Provincial; 10% Municipals; 40% Private Contracts
Domestic Markets:
National
Foreign Activity:
Worldwide
Contact(s):
Donald M. Gorber, Ph.D., P.Eng., President & CEO
Murali Ganapathy, P.Eng, M.A.Sc., M.F.M., Manager, Marketing
Douglas B. Chambers, Ph.D., Executive Vice-President

International Branch(es):
Delhi - SENES Consultants India Pvt. Ltd.
1st Fl., Tower B, Logix Techno Park
Plot #5, Sect. 127, Noida (UP)
Delhi India
91-120-4368400
senes@senesindia.com
www.senesindia.com

Kolkata - SENES Consultants India Pvt. Ltd.
MBL House, 5th Fl.
DD 18/8, Sect. 1, Salt Lake
Kolkata India
91-33-23598070
seneskilkata@senesindia.com
www.senesindia.com
Debanjan Bandyopadhyay

Mumbai - SENES Consultants India Pvt. Ltd.
711 Mayuresh Cosmos, Plot 37, Sect. 11, CBD Belapur
Mumbai India
91 22 32986995
senesmumbai@senesindia.com
www.senesindia.com
Founded: 2001
Products/Services/Areas of Expertise: This is the regional office; other offices located in Kolkata, Hyderabad & Delhi. Specializes in environmental management services, with potential to offer GIS-based urban planning, design & development of information systems & related services

Oak Ridge - SENES Oak Ridge Inc., Center for Risk Analysis
102 Donner Dr.
Oak Ridge, TN USA
615-483-6111
Fax: 615-481-0060
senesor@senes.com
www.senes.com
Staff: 10
Products/Services/Areas of Expertise: Specializes in human health & ecological risk estimation, assessment & communication; site characterization, exposure & toxicity assessment, risk; research
F. Owen Hoffman, Ph.D., President/Director

Sensible Life Products
Also Known As: Benefect
A Division of LBD Ltd.
#34, 7 Innovation Dr.
Flamborough, ON L9H 7H9
905-690-7474
Fax: 905-690-7575
800-909-2813
customerservice@benefect.com
www.benefect.com
Firm Type: Manufacturing
Founded: 1999
Products/Services/Areas of Expertise: Sensible Life Products offers sustainable cleaning & disinfection products, without using chemicals. Products include Benefect Disinfectant, Atomic Degreaser, Impact Cleaner, & Multi-Purpose Cleaner. Benefect's botanical technology kills over 99.99% of bacteria.
Financial Information:
Type of Ownership: Private
Domestic Markets:
National
Foreign Activity:
USA
Contact(s):
S. Samuel DeAth, Founder & Chief Executive Officer

Seprotech Systems Inc.
2378 Holly Lane
Ottawa, ON K1V 7P1
613-523-1641
Fax: 613-731-0851
contact@seprotech.com
www.seprotech.com
Firm Type: Engineering, Manufacturing, Scientific/Technical Services
Founded: 1984
Products/Services/Areas of Expertise: Crossflow membrane filtration technology; water production systems; wastewater treatment & purification systems; RotoDisk
Financial Information:
Type of Ownership: Publicly Traded
Revenue Sources: 100% Private Contracts
Domestic Markets:
National
Foreign Activity:
Africa, The Middle East, South America, USA
Markets Sought:
The Pacific Rim

Canadian Branches:
Toronto
3100 Steeles Ave. West
Toronto, ON L4K 3R1
905-660-7580
Fax: 905-660-0243

Septo-Clean Co. Ltd.
#1, 700 Finley Ave.
Ajax, ON L1S 3Z2
905-683-0111
Fax: 905-683-4030
800-558-4845
www.septoclean.ca
Firm Type: Manufacturing
Founded: 1963
Products/Services/Areas of Expertise: Septo-Clean Co. Ltd. manufactures natural source nutrient products, such as Septo Clean, an activator for septic & holding tanks, Revive, for the start-up of seasonal pumped systems, Revive Ultimate, for older tanks, & Manuguest, for backyard composting & animal waste treatment. All products include healthy waste digesting bacteria. Material safety data sheets are available for each product.
Financial Information:
Type of Ownership: Private
Domestic Markets:
National
Foreign Activity:
Worldwide

Servco Environmental Solutions Inc.
P.O. Box 13501 A
21 Cashin Ave.
St. John's, NL A1B 4B8
709-722-4475
Fax: 709-722-2219
sesi@nf.sympatico.ca; jdaniels@servco.nf.net
www.servco.nf.net
Firm Type: Engineering, Scientific/Technical Services
Founded: 1989
Member of: Canadian Emergency Response Services Association (CERSA)
Products/Services/Areas of Expertise: Servco Environmental Solutions Inc. provides emergency response to hazardous materials incidents in Newfoundland & Labrador, such as oil & chemical spills & oiled bird response. Related services include environmental consulting & auditing, environmental & occupational health & safety training, asbestos & lead abatement, site remediation, & site decommissioning.
Recently Completed / Ongoing Projects: Aircraft accident; Freshwater cleanup; Land cleanup; PCB spill
Financial Information:
Type of Ownership: Private
Domestic Markets:
Newfoundland & Labrador
Contact(s):
J. Daniels, General Manager

Service de rebuts Soulanges inc.
3756, ch des Sables
Hudson, QC J0P 1H0
450-458-7016
Fax: 450-458-3235
info@rebutssoulanges.ca
www.rebutssoulanges.ca
Firm Type: Waste Management
Founded: 1981
Staff: 15
Products/Services/Areas of Expertise: Waste management
Financial Information:
Revenue: $500,000 - $1.5 Million
Revenue Sources: 15% Municipals; 85% Private Contracts
Contact(s):
Jean St. Pierre, President
jean@rebutssoulanges.ca

ServiceMaster of Canada
5462 Timberlea Blvd.
Mississauga, ON L4W 2T7
800-263-5928
www.servicemaster.ca
Firm Type: Waste Management
Founded: 1953
Products/Services/Areas of Expertise: ServiceMaster of Canada restores buildings & personal properties affected by fire, water, or smoke damage. ServiceMaster Clean in Canada also provides commercial maintenance, janitorial services, & residential carpet & upholstery cleaning.
Financial Information:
Type of Ownership: Foreign-owned
Domestic Markets:
Alberta, British Columbia, New Brunswick, Newfoundland & Labrador, Nova Scotia, Ontario, Prince Edward Island, Québec, Saskatchewan
Foreign Activity:
USA

Services d'Évaluation Santé/Toxicologie Inc. / SESTE
4933, av Isabella
Montréal, QC H3W 1S8
514-733-9481
800-661-3303
Firm Type: Scientific/Technical Services
Founded: 1988
Staff: 4
Member of: Environmental Assessment Association of Arizona; Ordre des chimistes du Québec; Associated Sites Assessors of Canada; Canadian Audit Association; Association québecoise de la verification environnementale
Products/Services/Areas of Expertise: Environmental health & environmental toxicology; ecotoxicology studies; environmental impact assessments; environmental audits & monitoring; environmental baseline evaluation; real estate environmental inspection
Domestic Markets:
Ontario
Foreign Activity:
USA
Markets Sought:
Central America, USA
Contact(s):
S. Savary, Chemist/Toxicologist
Reada Tucker, Accountant
Edith Pierre-Louis, Public Relations

Services industriels Newalta
111, rue des Routiers
Chicoutimi, QC G7H 5K3
418-543-3811
Fax: 418-543-3661
www.newalta.com
Firm Type: Waste Management

Products/Services/Areas of Expertise: This facility is a safe & secure transfer centre for hazardous wastes; materials are consolidated here for authorized treatment facilities. The head office for Newalta in Québec is located in Brossard - contact 866-546-1150. Newalta has locations across Canada & is engaged in comprehensive & innovative industrial waste management & environmental services
Financial Information:
Type of Ownership: Publicly Traded
Domestic Markets:
Québec
Contact(s):
Michel Dufour, Branch Manager
Eric Gagnon, Operations Supervisor
Danny Gauthier, Sales Representative

Services Matrec inc.
Also Known As: Matrec, A TransForce company
Une société de TransForce
4, ch du Tremblay
Boucherville, QC J4B 6Z5
450-641-3070
Fax: 450-641-4458
www.matrec.ca
Firm Type: Waste Management
Founded: 1993
Staff: 800
Products/Services/Areas of Expertise: Regroupe des entreprises spécialisées dans la gestion intégrée des résidus domestiques et commerciaux, des matières recyclables, des résidus verts, & des matériaux secs
Financial Information:
Type of Ownership: Private
Revenue: Greater than $5 Million
Revenue Sources: 25% Municipals; 75% Private Contracts
Domestic Markets:
Québec

Canadian Branches:
Brossard
8005, boul Grande-Allée
Brossard, QC J4Z 3H8
450-462-0503
Fax: 450-462-4887

Chicoutimi
3199, boul. Talbot
Chicoutimi, QC G7H 5B1
418-549-8074
Fax: 418-549-7973

Québec
#100, 2850, boul. Wilfrid-Hamel
Québec, QC G1P 2J1
418-628-8666
Fax: 418-628-2025
877-906-8666

Saint-Hubert
5300, Albert-Millchamp
Saint-Hubert, QC J3Y 8X7
450-656-2171
Fax: 450-656-0554

Saint-Joachim-de-Shefford
278, ch. Grande Ligne
Saint-Joachim-de-Shefford, QC J0E 2G0
450-539-3217
Fax: 450-539-2855

Saint-Marc-des-Carrières
139, rue du Parc Industriel
St-Marc-des-Carrières, QC G0A 4B0
418-268-4816
Fax: 418-268-4818
877-210-2911

Trois-Rivières
2920, rue Bellefeuille
Trois-Rivières, QC G9A 5R5
819-378-4881
Fax: 819-378-1243

Servicestat Ltd.
2675 Rena Rd.
Mississauga, ON L4T 1G6
905-678-1394
Fax: 905-678-1416
servstat@aol.com
www.servicestat.ca
Firm Type: Distributing
Founded: 1978
Member of: Ontario Petroleum Contractor's Association; Petroleum Equipment Institute; Technical Standards & Safety Authority
Products/Services/Areas of Expertise: Representing over thirty manufacturers, Servicestat Ltd. supplies petroleum & industrial equipment in the Greater Toronto Area. The company has a service department, which provides equipment start-up, training, maintenance, repair, & emergency service. Servicestat also provides the WOTEC system, which refines & purifies used oil on-site & blends it into diesel or heating fuel. Organizations served include municipalities, oil companies, transit & trucking companies, marinas, & automobile dealerships.

Products & Services Buyer's Guide

Financial Information:
Type of Ownership: Private
Domestic Markets:
Ontario
Contact(s):
Bill Robertson, Partner
Ray Blanchette, Partner

Settlement Surveys Ltd.
17 Wellington St.
New Liskeard, ON P0J 1P0
705-647-8833
Firm Type: Management Consulting, Scientific/Technical Services
Founded: 1979
Products/Services/Areas of Expertise: The environmental consultants conduct environment assessments.
Recently Completed / Ongoing Projects: Cultural resources overview study of provincial parks in the Temagami Planning Area, Ontario; An archaeological impact assessment of the Red Squirrel Road Extension, Ontario; Native background information report & values map for portions of the Cochrane Crown Timber Management Unit, the Driftwood Forest Management Unit, & the Smooth Rock Falls Management Unit
Contact(s):
John Pollock, Contact

SEW Eurodrive Co. of Canada Ltd.
210 Walker Dr.
Brampton, ON L6T 3W1
905-791-1553
Fax: 905-791-2999
800-567-8039
marketing@sew-eurodrive.ca
www.sew-eurodrive.ca
Firm Type: Manufacturing
Founded: 1974
Staff: 163
Quality Environmental Management System(s): 9002
Products/Services/Areas of Expertise: Drive systems for wastewater treatment applications; clarifiers, sludge collectors, travelling bridges, pumps, screw pumps; conveyor applications; gearmotors, frequency controls; gear reducers
Domestic Markets:
National

Canadian Branches:
Bramalea
905-791-1553
Fax: 905-791-2999
1-800-567-8039

British Columbia Branch
Tilbury Industrial Park
7188 Honeyman St.
Delta, BC V4G 1E2
604-946-5535
Fax: 604-946-2513
W.S. Wake, Western Operations Manager

Québec Branch
2555, rue Leger
Lasalle, QC H8N 2V9
514-367-1124
Fax: 514-367-3677
Anthony Peluso, Eastern Canada Operations Manager

SGE Hatch Ltd.
Formerly: SGE Acres Ltd.
Also Known As: Hatch Ltd; Hatch Mott McDonald
Bally Rou Place
#E200, 280 Torbay Rd.
St. John's, NL A1A 3W8
709-576-7376
Fax: 709-754-2717
stjohns@sgeacres.com
www.sgeacres.com
Products/Services/Areas of Expertise: Project management; cold climate engineering; environmental engineering: site decommissioning & remediation, solid waste management, wastewater treatment, water resources engineering; Hydro power; structural engineering; transportation engineering; & municipal planning
Contact(s):
Allan C. Green, P.Eng., Managing Director, Industrial/Regional Projects

Canadian Branches:
Corner Brook
355 O'Connell Dr.
Corner Brook, NL A2H 7E4
709-634-6973
Fax: 709-634-1739
cornerbrook@hatch.ca
Jack Carlson, P.Eng, Manager

Fredericton
#302, 231 Regent St.
Fredericton, NB E3B 3W8
506-450-4170
Fax: 506-450-4175
fredericton@sgeacres.com

Halifax
CIBC Bldg.
#1009, 1809 Barrington St.
Halifax, NS B3J 3K8
902-421-1065
Fax: 902-429-3525
halifax@hatch.ca
Frank LeBlanc, P.Eng., Manager

Moncton
50 Cameron Dr.
Moncton, NB E1C 9A9
506-857-8708
Fax: 506-857-8989
moncton@hatch.ca
Paul Stockton, P.Eng., Manager

Sydney
325 Vulcan Ave.
Sydney, NS B1P 5X1
902-564-5583
Fax: 902-564-9158
sydney@hatch.ca
Floyd Butts, P.Eng., Manager

SGS Canada Inc.
6490 Vipond Dr.
Mississauga, ON L5T 1W8
905-364-3757
Fax: 905-364-0344
www.ca.sgs.com
Firm Type: Scientific/Technical Services
Founded: 1948
Staff: 1200
Quality Environmental Management System(s): 14000; 900
Products/Services/Areas of Expertise: Provides auditing, monitoring, inspection, sampling & laboratory testing for raw materials, bulk, containerized & finished products; ISO 14001/9000 certification & training services; accredited by the Standards Council of Canada as an ISO 14000/9000 registrar. This location also provides services to the automotive sector, & laboratory services to the life sciences sector
Financial Information:
Type of Ownership: Private
Domestic Markets:
National
Foreign Activity:
Worldwide
Contact(s):
Gerard O'Dell, Managing Director
Chris Bates, Operations Manager

Canadian Branches:
Arnold's Cove - Laboratory Services
P.O. Box 439
Whiffen Head Rd.
Arnold's Cove, NL A0B 1A0
709-463-2540
Fax: 709-463-2542
Products/Services/Areas of Expertise: Laboratory services to the oil, gas & chemicals sector

Calgary
1120 - 44th Ave. SE, Bay E
Calgary, AB T2J 4W9
403-290-0903
Fax: 403-287-3715
Products/Services/Areas of Expertise: Services to the agriculture sector

Delta - Laboratory Services
7500 - 76th St.
Delta, BC V4G 1E6
604-946-2249
Fax: 604-946-2257
Products/Services/Areas of Expertise: Laboratory services to the minerals sector

Delta - Western Operations Office
1005 Derwent Way
Delta, BC V3M 5R4
604-525-5212
Fax: 604-525-5779
Products/Services/Areas of Expertise: Regional office for Western Canada; services to the automotive sector

Fort McMurray - Alberta Regional Office
235 MacDonald Cres.
Fort McMurray, ON T9H 4B5
780-791-6454
Fax: 780-791-1018

Garson - Laboratory Services
1209 O'Neil Dr. West
Garson, ON P3L 1L5
705-693-4555
Fax: 705-693-1678
Products/Services/Areas of Expertise: Laboratory services to the minerals sector

Ingersoll - Eastern Region Office
274180 Wallace Line
Ingersoll, ON N5C 3J7
519-485-7082
Fax: 519-485-6840
Products/Services/Areas of Expertise: Services to the automotive sector

Lakefield
P.O. Box 4300
185 Concession St.
Lakefield, ON K0L 2H0
705-652-2000
Fax: 705-652-6365
Products/Services/Areas of Expertise: Liaison office with services to the environmental & minerals sectors; laboratory services for geochemistry

London - Laboratory Services
657 Consortium Crt.
London, ON N6E 2S8
519-672-4500
Fax: 519-672-0361
Products/Services/Areas of Expertise: Laboratory services to the environmental sector

Montréal
3420, boul St-Joseph est
Montréal, QC H1X 1W6
514-255-1679
Fax: 514-252-0071
Products/Services/Areas of Expertise: Head Office for QC; services to the industrial sector; systems & services certification

Montréal - Laboratory Services
11 000A, rue Sherbrooke est
Montréal, QC H1B 5W1
514-645-8754
Fax: 514-640-3039
Products/Services/Areas of Expertise: Laboratory services to the oil, gas & chemicals sector

Point Tupper - Laboratory Services
4092 Port Malcolm Rd.
Point Tupper, NS B9A 1A5
902-625-3233
Fax: 902-625-5147
Products/Services/Areas of Expertise: Laboratory services to the oil, gas & chemicals sector

Red Lake - Laboratory Services
P.O. Box 1349
16A Young St.
Red Lake, ON P0V 2M0
807-727-2939
Fax: 807-727-3183
Products/Services/Areas of Expertise: Laboratory services to the minerals sector

Saint John
156 Johnston Rd.
Saint John, NB E2N 1M6
506-633-1788
Fax: 506-633-1788

Products/Services/Areas of Expertise: Services to the environmental sector

Sarnia - Laboratory Services
Building 1010
1086 Modeland Rd.
Sarnia, ON N7S 6L2
519-333-6871
Fax: 519-333-6873

Saskatoon
3815 Thatcher Ave., Bays 13 & 14
Saskatoon, SK S7R 1A3
306-934-3559
Fax: 306-934-6024
Products/Services/Areas of Expertise: Services to the agriculture sector

St. John's
Icon Building
#207, 187 Kenmount Rd.
St. John's, NL A1B 3P9
709-739-7797
Fax: 709-739-7798
Products/Services/Areas of Expertise: Services to the oil, gas & chemicals sector

Vancouver - Laboratory Services
Kent Corporate Centre
#50, 655 West Kent Ave. N.
Vancouver, BC V6P 6T7
604-324-1166
Fax: 604-324-1177
Products/Services/Areas of Expertise: Laboratory services to the minerals, agriculture, environmental, & industrial sectors; consumer testing services

Winnipeg - Laboratory Services
#103, 138 Portage Ave. E.
Winnipeg, MB R3C 0A1
204-942-8557
Fax: 204-942-8599
Products/Services/Areas of Expertise: Laboratory services to the agriculture sector

SHAL Consulting Engineers Ltd.
#202, 20 Packham Circle
Brampton, ON L7Z 2N6
905-495-7272
Fax: 905-846-0957
shal@shal.ca
Firm Type: Engineering
Founded: 1966
Staff: 10
Products/Services/Areas of Expertise: Consulting engineering services
Domestic Markets:
Ontario
Foreign Activity:
Africa, The Middle East
Contact(s):
T.H. Hluchan, P.Eng., President
T. Mahabir, P.Eng., SHAL International President

Sharp Electronics of Canada Ltd.
335 Britannia Rd. East
Mississauga, ON L4Z 1W9
905-890-2100
Fax: 905-890-7198
www.sharp.ca
Firm Type: Manufacturing
Founded: 1912
Products/Services/Areas of Expertise: A wholly owned subsidiary of Sharp Corporation of Osaka, Japan, Sharp Electronics of Canada Ltd. develops technologies in the following areas: home entertainment, digital office equipment systems, the appliance market, & air purification.
Activities: Developing Plasmacluster Ion technology for improved air purification
Financial Information:
Type of Ownership: Foreign-owned
Domestic Markets:
National
Contact(s):
Mikio Katayama, President & Chief Operating Officer, Sharp Corporation
Bill Friend, Vice-President, Consumer Products Division, Sharp Canada

Shaver Industries Inc.
Formerly: Copri Canada Inc.
#8, 20 Steckle Pl.
Kitchener, ON N2E 2C3
519-894-4800
Fax: 519-894-4726
888-766-8328
sales@shaverinc.com
www.shaverinc.com
Firm Type: Management Consulting, Distributing, Engineering, Manufacturing
Founded: 1986
Products/Services/Areas of Expertise: Shaver Industries Inc. is engaged in designing, manufacturing, installing, & providing after sales support for environmental & machine protection systems. Products include power roll-up doors & curtains, noise abatement solutions, chip disk filtration systems, & chip conveyors.
Financial Information:
Type of Ownership: Private
Domestic Markets:
National
Foreign Activity:
USA
Contact(s):
Bob Courtney, Contact, Machine Protection Product Sales
Dianne Finn, Contact, Environmental Protection Product Sales
Ken Knechtel, Contact, Engineering
Bob Penner, Contact, Machine & Environmental Installations
Mark Shaver, Contact, International Sales

Shaw Precast Solutions
P.O. Box 2130
1101 Hwy. 2
Lantz, NS B2S 3G4
902-883-2201
Fax: 902-883-1273
1-888-777-7429
sales@shawprecastsolutions.com
www.shawpipe.com
Firm Type: Engineering, Manufacturing
Founded: 1945
Quality Environmental Management System(s): 9001:2000
Products/Services/Areas of Expertise: Shaw Precast Solutions designs, engineers, & manufactures concrete pipe, manholes & catchbasins, & retaining wall systems. Specialty products are also developed for transportation & industrial purposes. The company serves the construction industry. It is both CSA & ISO 9001 certified.
Recently Completed / Ongoing Projects: Shaw Peat Sewage Treatment; CDS Stormwater Treatment System
Domestic Markets:
Nova Scotia
Contact(s):
John Greer, General Manager
greer@shawprecastsolutions.com

Sheldons Engineering Inc.
A Division of Earlscourt Metal Industries Ltd.
6660 Ordan Dr.
Mississauga, ON L5T 1J7
905-564-5072
Fax: 905-564-9004
800-265-3572
sales@sheldonsengineering.com
www.sheldonsengineering.com
Firm Type: Engineering, Manufacturing
Founded: 1896
Products/Services/Areas of Expertise: Sheldons Engineering Inc. builds commercial & industrial blowers. Products include standard centrifugal fan & axial fan designs. The company is also engaged in custom manufacturing to meet customers' needs.
Financial Information:
Type of Ownership: Private
Domestic Markets:
National
Foreign Activity:
USA,

Shell Canada Limited
P.O. Box 100 M
Calgary, AB T2P 2H5
403-691-3111
800-661-1600
questions@shell.com; publicaffairs-canada@shell.com
www.shell.ca
Firm Type: Engineering, Information Technology
Founded: 1911
Staff: 8200
Products/Services/Areas of Expertise: Shell Canada is an intergrated oil & gas company. In Canada, the company has the following operating facilities: more than 1,600 retail stations; natural gas plants in Alberta; heavy oil production facilities in Alberta; the oil sands mine & extraction plant in northern Alberta; an oil sands upgrader as part of the Athabasca Oil Sands Project; a chemical plant in Alberta; lubricant facilities in Alberta & Ontario; refineries in Alberta, Ontario, & Québec; & offshore natural gas production facilities in Nova Scotia.
Activities: Conducting research into engineering & technical services, materials testing & engineering, oil sands technology, & unconventional oil research, at the Calgary Research Centre; Seeking ways to reduce environmental impact
Recently Completed / Ongoing Projects: Establishing the Shell Environmental Fund (admin-sef@shell.com)
Contact(s):
Marvin Odum, Chair
Lorraine Mitchelmore, President
John Abbott, Executive Vice-President
David Brinley, General Counsel & Vice-President
Dwight van Kampen, Controller & Vice-President
Shannon Cosmescu, Secretary
Rob Dargewitcz, Treasurer

SHER-PAC Container Systems Ltd.
#204, 146 Laird St.
Toronto, ON M4G 3V7
416-481-0605
Fax: 416-481-8107
800-766-8494
alan@sherpac.com
Firm Type: Distributing
Founded: 1992
Staff: 3
Products/Services/Areas of Expertise: Returnable, reusable plastic containers used primarily in the food industry to replace cardboard boxes; designs & manufactures to client specifications
Financial Information:
Type of Ownership: Private
Revenue Sources: 100% Private Contracts
Domestic Markets:
Alberta, British Columbia, Manitoba, New Brunswick, Newfoundland & Labrador, Nova Scotia, Ontario, Québec, Saskatchewan
Foreign Activity:
South America, USA
Markets Sought:
Asia
Contact(s):
Alan Prussky, President

Sherwin-Williams Canada Inc.
A Division of Sherwin-Williams
P.O. Box 217
Fort Erie, ON L2A 5M9
905-871-2724
Fax: 905871-5455
800-263-8108
www.sherwin-williams.com
Firm Type: Distributing, Manufacturing
Quality Environmental Management System(s): 9001
Products/Services/Areas of Expertise: Sherwin-Williams Canada specializes in manufacturing wood finishes.
Financial Information:
Type of Ownership: Foreign-owned
Domestic Markets:
National
Foreign Activity:
USA
Contact(s):
Paul Sivilotti, Manager, Plant
paul.e.sivilotti@sherwin.com
Dave Macdonald, Manager, Production
dave.r.macdonald@sherwin.com

Shigawake Organics Ltd.
252, rte 132
Shigawake, QC G0C 3E0
418-752-2549
Fax: 418-752-7242

contact@shigawakeorganics.com
www.seagro.com
Products/Services/Areas of Expertise: Shigawake Organics produces natural, chemical free, & odourless compost mix, grower mix, & potting mix for indoor & outdoor gardening. For example, Seagro Professional Organic Grower Mix contains the following ingredients: Canadian sphagnum peat moss, composted ocean fish, composted cattle manure, perlite, & lime.
Domestic Markets:
National
Foreign Activity:
Worldwide

Showa-Best Glove, Inc.
Formerly: Best Glove Manufacturing Ltd.
253, rue Michaud
Coaticook, QC J1A 1A9
819-849-6381
Fax: 819-849-6120
800-565-2378
info@bestglove.ca
ShowaBestGlove.com
Products/Services/Areas of Expertise: Hand protection products for industrial applications
Domestic Markets:
National
Foreign Activity:
Africa, Asia, Central America, Western Europe, The Pacific Rim, South America, USA
Contact(s):
Bill Alico, President/COO
Tom Eggleston, Director, Sales and Marketing

International Branch(es):
Australia
32 Sargents Rd.
Minchinbury, NSW Australi
australia@bestglove.com

Belgium
Draaiboomstraat 6, bus 12
Wommelgem Belgium
europe@bestglove.com

Guatemala
Avenida Petapa 55-00
Zona 12 Guatemal
rcahueque@bestglove.com

USA, Alabama
931 Second Ave. SE
Fayette, AL USA
jlocke@bestglove.com

USA, Georgia
#200, 50 Old Ivy Rd.
Atlanta, GA USA
ggonzales@bestglove.com

USA, Georgia - Menlo
P.O. Box 8
579 Edison St.
Menlo, GA USA
800-241-0323
Fax: 888-393-2666
usa@bestglove.com

USA, Georgia - Rome
29 Yarbrough Bend Rd.
Rome, GA USA
usa@bestglove.com

Shred-It
2794 South Sheridan Way
Oakville, ON L6J 7T4
905-829-2794
Fax: 905-829-1999
877-607-4733
info@shredit.com
www.shredit.com
Firm Type: Manufacturing, Waste Management
Founded: 1988
Products/Services/Areas of Expertise: With over 140 branches on five continents, Shred-It provides secure document destruction services & recycles tons of paper each year. The information security company also manufactures industrial shredding equipment & secure consoles. To reduce its environmental impact, Shred-It trucks use recyclable, biodegradable hydraulic fluids, & meet or exceed emissions standards.

Financial Information:
Type of Ownership: Private
Domestic Markets:
National
Foreign Activity:
Asia, Central Europe, Western Europe, South Africa, South America, Mexico, USA, United Kingdom
Contact(s):
Vincent R. De Palma, President & Chief Executive Officer
Pat Capparelli, Executive Vice-President, Sales & Marketing
Brenda Frank, Executive Vice-President & General Counsel
Robert Guice, Executive Vice-President, Europe, Middle East, & Africa
Colette Raymond, Executive Vice-President Operations, North America
Jim Rudyk, Executive Vice-President & Chief Financial Officer

Sick Building Solutions / SBS
200 Brown's Line
Toronto, ON M8W 3T4
416-259-8833
877-742-5253
info@sickbuildingsolutions.com
www.sickbuildingsolutions.com
Firm Type: Management Consulting, Engineering, Scientific/Technical Services, Waste Management
Founded: 1995
Products/Services/Areas of Expertise: Sick Building Solutions offers the following services: indoor air quality; mould inspection & control; & growhouse inspection & remediation.
Financial Information:
Type of Ownership: Private
Domestic Markets:
Ontario
Foreign Activity:
Caribbean
Contact(s):
Art Robinson, President
Brett Robison, Vice-Presient

Sico
2505, rue de la Métropole
Longueuil, QC J4G 1E5
514-495-5712
Fax: 514-277-4457
800-463-7426
info@sico.ca
www.sico.ca
Firm Type: Distributing, Manufacturing
Founded: 1937
Products/Services/Areas of Expertise: Sico is a paint manufacturer, which has worked through the years to reduce the use of Volatile Organic Compounds in its paints. Products are identified with the following logos: "Meets Canadian VOC Standards" & "Zero VOC".
Domestic Markets:
National

Siemens Building Technologies, Ltd. / SBT
A Division of Siemens Canada Limited
Formerly: Landis & Staefa; Cerberus Pyrotronics; Security Technologies Group2185 Derry Rd. West
Mississauga, ON L5N 7A6
905-819-8000
corporate.communications.ca@siemens.com
www.siemens.ca
Firm Type: Manufacturing
Founded: 1998
Staff: 700
Products/Services/Areas of Expertise: Siemens Building Technologies provides fire safety, electronic security, & energy efficiency in buildings & public places. Customized building solutions are also offered.
Domestic Markets:
National

Canadian Branches:
Brampton
2 Kenview Blvd.
Brampton, ON L6T 5E4
905-799-9937
Fax: 905-799-9858

Calgary
#24, 1930 Maynard Rd. SE
Calgary, AB T2E 6J8
403-259-3404
Fax: 403-252-8578

Dartmouth
#100, 120 Troop Ave.
Dartmouth, NS B3B 1Z1
902-835-8316
Fax: 902-835-6682

Edmonton
6652 - 50th St. NW
Edmonton, AB T6B 2N7
780-486-1234
Fax: 780-486-1817

Hamilton
#2, 735 South Service Rd.
Stoney Creek, ON L8E 5Z2
905-643-2200
Fax: 905-643-6775

London
514 Newbold St.
London, ON N6E 1K6
519-680-2380
Fax: 519-680-2410
www.siemens.ca

Montréal
8455 - 19e av
Montréal, QC H1Z 4J2
514-374-0044
Fax: 514-374-0045

Ottawa
2435 Holly Lane
Ottawa, ON K1V 7P2
613-733-9781
Fax: 613-737-4985

Québec
#190, 2800, rue St. Jean Baptiste
Québec, QC G2E 6J5
418-622-2991
Fax: 418-622-3685

Sudbury
#4, 1899 Lasalle Blvd.
Sudbury, ON P3A 2A3
705-521-1959
Fax: 705-521-1960

Vancouver
#150, 4011 Viking Way
Richmond, BC V6V 2K9
604-273-7733
Fax: 604-273-1373

Winnipeg
1572 Dublin Ave.
Winnipeg, MB R3E 0L4
204-774-3411
Fax: 204-786-0033

Siemens Milltronics Process Instruments Inc.
A Division of Siemens Canada Limited
Formerly: Milltronics Ltd.P.O. Box 4225
1954 Technology Dr.
Peterborough, ON K9J 7B1
705-745-2431
www.automation.siemens.com/w1/smpi-peterborough-home-118 34.htm
Firm Type: Engineering, Manufacturing
Founded: 1954
Staff: 365
Quality Environmental Management System(s): 9001:2000
Products/Services/Areas of Expertise: Siemens Milltronics is a designer & manufacturer of sophisticated measurement instruments for the process industries. Examples of product use include waste water treatment, water distribution, & chemical processing. The company's products control the runtimes of pumps in water treatment plants & are also used as alarms on chemical tanks to prevent chemical spills.
Activities: Engaging in research & development activities
Domestic Markets:
National
Foreign Activity:
Worldwide
Contact(s):
Dave Bignell, President & Chief Executive Officer

Siemens Water Technologies
A Division of Siemens Canada Limited
215 Konrad Cres.
Markham, ON L3R 8T9
905-944-2800
866-926-8420
information.water@siemens.com
www.water.siemens.com
Firm Type: Manufacturing, Scientific/Technical Services
Founded: 1990
Products/Services/Areas of Expertise: Siemens Water Technologies provides water & wastewater treatment equipment & services. Examples of the company's products & services are as follows: activated carbon pellets & powder for air & water filtration; aeration products; biological treatment; chemical feed & disinfection; controls, instrumentation, & analyzers; conventional filtration; ion exchange; laboratory water products; liquid & vapour phase odour control; membrane filtration & separation products; chemical treatment products; separation & clarification products; sludge & biosolids processing; & specialty products, such as flow meters, hemodialysis water systems, & surge & storage tanks. Siemens Water Technologies serves municipal, institutional, industrial, & aquatics clients.
Activities: Engaging in research & development activities
Recently Completed / Ongoing Projects: Water reuse & recycling systems for automotive assembly plants in Mexico
Financial Information:
Type of Ownership: Foreign-owned
Domestic Markets:
National
Foreign Activity:
Worldwide
Contact(s):
Charles Gordon, President & Chief Executive Officer
Brent Hillier, Executive Vice-President, Services Segment
Lutz Kranz, Executive Vice President, Municipal Segment
Bill Mertes, Executive Vice President, Chemical Feed & Disinfection Segment
Dave Spyker, Executive Vice President, Industrial Segment

Canadian Branches:
Burnaby
3999 Phillips Ave.
Burnaby, BC V5A 3K4
604-639-1212

Calgary
4120 - 23rd St. NE
Calgary, AB T2E 6W9
403250-2650

Lachine
2126 - 32nd Ave.
Lachine, QC H8T 3H7
514-631-1111
Fax: 514-422-1111

London
317 Adelaide St. South
London, ON N5Z 3L3

Milton
555 Industrial Dr.
Milton, ON L9T 5E1
905-693-0339

Mississauga
5889 Coopers Ave.
Mississauga, ON L4Z 1P6

Repentigny
243, boul Brien
Repentigny, QC J6A 6M4

Sigma Engineering Ltd.
#400, 1444 Alberni St.
Vancouver, BC V6G 2Z4
604-688-8271, ext. 379
gmcdonnell@synex.com
www.sigmaengineering.com
Firm Type: Engineering, Scientific/Technical Services
Founded: 1973
Products/Services/Areas of Expertise: A wholly owned subsidiary of Synex International Inc., Sigma Engineering provides solutions for the control & use of water. The firm serves both public & private corporations, as well as government agencies.
Activities: Conducting research; Providing feasibility studies; Offering technical design services
Recently Completed / Ongoing Projects: Hydology; Fisheries & environmental assessment; River engineering; Flood control; Stormwater management; Site development services; Water supply & quality; Wastewater treatment & disposal
Contact(s):
Glenn S. McDonnell, Contact

Sika Canada Inc.
601, rue Delmar
Pointe-Claire, QC H9R 4A9
514-697-2610
Fax: 514-697-3087
866-697-2829
marketing.construction@ca.sika.com;marketing.industry@ca.sika.com
www.sika.ca
Firm Type: Distributing, Manufacturing
Founded: 1957
Staff: 150
Quality Environmental Management System(s): 9001; ISO
Products/Services/Areas of Expertise: Sika Canada is a manufacturer & distributor of products for the industrial & construction markets. Examples of products used by industry include auto glass, appliances, components, & sealing, bonding, & protecting products. Products used in the construction market include grouts, adhesives, sealants, moisture protection products, speciality mortars, structural strengthening systems, industrial flooring, & surface hardeners. Sika Canada meets or exceeds municipal, provincial, & federal environmental standards & legislation for it operations & processes.
Activities: Providing sales & marketing services across Canada; Engaging in research & development activities
Domestic Markets:
National

Canadian Branches:
Edmonton
18131 - 114th Ave. NW
Edmonton, AB T5S 1T8
780-486-6111
Fax: 780-483-1580
866-697-2829
marketing.construction@ca.sika.com;marketing.industry@ca.sika.com
www.sika.ca

Mississauga
6915 Davand Dr.
Mississauga, ON L5T 1L5
905-795-3177
Fax: 905-795-3192
866-697-2829
marketing.construction@ca.sika.com;marketing.industry@ca.sika.com
www.sika.ca

Silex Innovations Inc.
6659 Ordan Dr.
Mississauga, ON L5T 1K6
905-612-4000
Fax: 905-612-8999
800-387-7818
info@silex.com
www.silex.com
Firm Type: Distributing, Engineering, Manufacturing
Founded: 1985
Products/Services/Areas of Expertise: Silex is engaged in the design, manufacture, & supply of products for industrial applications, which contribute to a quieter environment. Examples of products include industrial silencers, insulation blankets, emission control products, expansion bellows, connectors, & exhaust accessories. Silex environmental products are used in the following industries: power generation, gas compression, marine, pneumatic conveying, building, locomotion, & the military.
Domestic Markets:
National
Foreign Activity:
USA
Contact(s):
Stephen Halkett, Vice-President, Sales & Marketing
stephenh@silex.com
Ovidiu Turlea, Territory Manager, Western Canada
ovit@silex.com

Silliker Canada Co.
A part of Mérieux NutriSciences Corp.
#4, 90 Gough Rd.
Markham, ON L3R 5V5
905-479-5255
Fax: 905-479-4645
customercare@canada.silliker.com
canada.silliker.com
Firm Type: Management Consulting, Scientific/Technical Services
Member of: Ocean Nutrition Canada
Quality Environmental Management System(s): 9001:2000;
Products/Services/Areas of Expertise: Comprehensive testing & consulting services for safety, nutritional value & quality of products from the food & consumer goods industries
Activities: Silliker JR Laboratories, ULC, a division in Vancouver, BC
Recently Completed / Ongoing Projects: Analysis of omega fatty acids in fish oil products to verify nutrient levels
Financial Information:
Type of Ownership: Foreign-owned
Domestic Markets:
British Columbia, Ontario
Contact(s):
Jim Ondyak, President, Silliker North America
Jocelyn Alfieri, Laboratory Director
jocelyn.alfieri@sillikercanada.com

Silliker JR Laboratories, ULC
A division of Silliker Canada Co.
Formerly: JR Laboratories Inc.#12, 3871 North Fraser Way
Burnaby, BC V5J 5G6
604-432-9311
Fax: 604-432-7768
info@jrlabs.ca
canada.silliker.com
Firm Type: Management Consulting, Scientific/Technical Services
Founded: 2007
Member of: Canadian Association of Environmental Analytical Laboratories
Quality Environmental Management System(s): 9001:2000;
Products/Services/Areas of Expertise: Food testing & technical consulting; laboratory analysis for monitoring, surveillance, compliance & regulatory enforcement of pesticide residues, wastewater discharge, soil contaminants & industrial pollutants, using high performance liquid chromatographic & mass spectrometric techniques
Recently Completed / Ongoing Projects: Pesticides & chlorinated pollutants, Agriculture Canada; microbiology & chemical analysis, Ministry of Environment; wastewater testing BC Fish Processing Association
Financial Information:
Type of Ownership: Foreign-owned
Domestic Markets:
Alberta, British Columbia, Manitoba, Nova Scotia, Ontario
Foreign Activity:
China, USA
Contact(s):
Ray Cheung, Division President
Jimmy Chang, Divison Vice-President

Canadian Branches:
Atlantic Division
#14, 4 Westwood Blvd.
Upper Tantallon, NS B3Z 1H3
902-483-2759
Fax: 902-826-1768

Silo Clean International
Also Known As: Anteby Enterprises Inc.
#174, 1136-3 Centre St.
Thornhill, ON L4J 3M8
905-660-7022
Fax: 905-660-1755
866-660-7456
info@siloclean.com
www.siloclean.com
Firm Type: Distributing, Engineering, Scientific/Technical Services
Founded: 1980
Products/Services/Areas of Expertise: Silo Clean invented a system for cleaning the interior of dry storage silos, without manual entry. The Silo Clean method utilizes compressed air as a power source to clean out silos, as well as hoppers, tanks, bins, & reactors. The dry process cleaning does not damage the environment, & meets or exceeds all government health & safety

regulations throughout the world. Silo Clean workers are WHMIS & MSHA trained.
Domestic Markets:
National
Foreign Activity:
Worldwide

Silva Forest Foundation
Formerly: Silva Ecosystem Consultants Ltd
P.O. Box 9
Slocan Park, BC V0G 2E0
250-226-7222
Fax: 250-226-7446
silvafor@netidea.com
www.silvafor.org
Firm Type: Scientific/Technical Services
Founded: 1977
Staff: 10
Member of: Association of BC Professional Foresters
Products/Services/Areas of Expertise: Forestry; water resources; GIS, mapping, remote sensing & image analysis; environmental impact assessment; site assessment; land use planning; project management; environmental data acquisition; planning & operations for ecosytem-based forest management
Financial Information:
Type of Ownership: Private
Revenue: $500,000 - $1.5 Million
Revenue Sources: 100% Private Contracts
Domestic Markets:
British Columbia, Newfoundland & Labrador
Foreign Activity:
USA
Contact(s):
Rami Rothkop, Chair
Susan Hammond, Executive Director

Silvana Import Trading Inc.
Also Known As: Commerce d'importation Silvana inc
#304, 4269, rue Ste-Catherine ouest
Montréal, QC H3Z 1P7
514-939-3523
Fax: 514-939-3863
info@silvanatrading.com
www.silvanatrading.com
Firm Type: Distributing
Founded: 1984
Products/Services/Areas of Expertise: Reforestation equipment; biodegradable lubricants; mapping; satellite images & remote sensing capabilities
Domestic Markets:
National
Foreign Activity:
Worldwide

Silvicon Services Inc.
P.O. Box 490
3560 Victoria Dr.
Smithers, BC V0J 2N0
250-847-3680
Fax: 250-847-2530
www.silvicon.com
Firm Type: Scientific/Technical Services
Staff: 40
Products/Services/Areas of Expertise: Mapping/surveying; fisheries consulting; wildlife consulting
Contact(s):
Bill Golding, Partner & Operations Manager

Simark Controls Ltd.
7725 - 46 St. SE
Calgary, AB T2C 2Y5
403-236-0580
Fax: 403-279-6553
800-565-7431
www.simark.com
Firm Type: Distributing
Founded: 1971
Staff: 45
Quality Environmental Management System(s): 9001
Products/Services/Areas of Expertise: SCADA systems for remote site monitoring & control; flow meters & totalizers; GAS detection, portable & fixed
Recently Completed / Ongoing Projects: City of Calgary storm water monitoring
Financial Information:
Type of Ownership: Private
Revenue: Greater than $5 Million
Revenue Sources: 2% Municipals; 98% Private Contracts
Domestic Markets:
Alberta, British Columbia, Manitoba, Northwest Territories, Saskatchewan, Yukon Territory
Contact(s):
Mark Wheeler, General Manager
mark.wheeler@simark.com
Perry Jamart, Sales Manager
perry.jamart@simark.com

Simcoe Engineering Group Limited
#10, 1815 Ironstone Manor
Pickering, ON L1W 3W9
905-831-1715
Fax: 905-831-0531
800-678-6578
simcoe@segl.com
www.segl.com
Firm Type: Engineering
Founded: 1974
Staff: 35
Member of: American Water Works Association; Water Environment Federation; Water Environment Association of Ontario; Canadian Society for Civil Engineers; Association of Professional Engineers (Ontario); Consulting Engineers of Ontario
Products/Services/Areas of Expertise: Water supply; wastewater treatment; stormwater management; civil, mechanical, electrical engineering; SCADA; instrumentation & controls
Recently Completed / Ongoing Projects: Region of Durham, Cortice Water Pollution Control Plant (on-going); Water Treatment Plants for Blind River, Vermilion Bay, Georgina & Township of Smith-Ennismore-Lakefield; sewage treatment plant upgrades for City of Toronto, Highland Creek PCP; various WTP upgrades; process control strategy report for City of Toronto
Financial Information:
Type of Ownership: Private
Revenue Sources: 5% Provincial; 85% Municipals; 10% Private Contracts
Domestic Markets:
Alberta, New Brunswick, Nova Scotia, Ontario, Québec
Foreign Activity:
Caribbean, Central America, USA
Markets Sought:
The Middle East, The Pacific Rim, Mexico
Contact(s):
D.D.B. Cane, P.Eng, President
G.R. Baker, Director
R.M. Zucchetti, C.E.T., Director
L.J. Manley, P.Eng., Director

Canadian Branches:
Kingston Branch
#200, 1020 Bayridge Dr.
Kingston, ON K7P 2S2
613-389-1661
Fax: 613-389-2442
simcoe@kos.net
Cameron Smith, P.Eng.

Simcoe Plastics Ltd.
#204, 7089 Yonge St.
Thornhill, ON L3T 2A7
905-881-1501
Fax: 905-881-9389
Firm Type: Distributing
Founded: 1980
Staff: 4
Member of: Society of Plastics Engineers
Products/Services/Areas of Expertise: Buyers of clean & segregated industrially generated plastic scrap; reprocessing & regrinding
Financial Information:
Type of Ownership: Private
Revenue: $1.5 Million - $3 Million
Revenue Sources: 100% Private Contracts
Domestic Markets:
British Columbia, New Brunswick, Nova Scotia, Ontario, Québec
Foreign Activity:
USA
Contact(s):
William L. Wheeler, President

Simon Fraser University
Centre for Tourism Policy & Research
c/o Simon Fraser University.
8888 University Dr.
Burnaby, BC V5A 1S6
604-291-3074
Fax: 604-291-4968
www.sfu.ca/~dossa/index.htm
Firm Type: Management Consulting, Information Technology, Scientific/Technical Services
Founded: 1987
Staff: 4
Member of: Travel & Tourism Research Association
Products/Services/Areas of Expertise: Basic & applied research relevant to issues in the tourism industry; research issues include management concerns such as market identification, social impact evaluation, community planning, carrying capacity management, coastal & alpine resource development, ecotourism & ski industry demand assessment
Recently Completed / Ongoing Projects: Environmental management systems, ski areas; growth management monitoring systems, resort communities & national parks; environmental best practice programs for tourism operations
Financial Information:
Type of Ownership: Non Profit
Revenue Sources: 25% nationwide; 35% Provincial; 40% Private Contracts
Domestic Markets:
Alberta, British Columbia, Yukon Territory
Foreign Activity:
Asia, Australia/New Zealand, Central America, The Pacific Rim, South America, USA
Markets Sought:
Western Europe,
Contact(s):
Peter Williams, Director
peter_williams@sfu.ca

SimplexGrinnell
A Tyco International Company
Formerly: Grinnell Fire Protectionc/o Tyco International of Canada
2400 Skymark Ave.
Mississauga, ON L4W 5K5
905-212-4600
Fax: 905-212-4601
www.simplexgrinnell.com
Firm Type: Engineering, Manufacturing, Scientific/Technical Services

Products/Services/Areas of Expertise: Fire detection & alarm systems; sprinklers, fire extinguishers & fire suppression equipment; integrated security systems; emergency communication solutions; healthcare communication systems; training & education. The company is committed to energy conservation, waste reduction & recycling, & a high standard of health & safety in the workplace
Financial Information:
Type of Ownership: Foreign-owned

Canadian Branches:
Calgary
431 Manitou Rd. SE
Calgary, AB T2G 4C2
403-287-3202
Fax: 403-243-6966
Bruce Ellis, Manager

Dartmouth
#G, 600 Windmill Rd.
Dartmouth, NS B3B 1B5
902-468-9100
Fax: 902-468-3253

Edmonton
17402 - 116 Ave.
Edmonton, AB T5S 2X2
780-452-5280
Fax: 780-451-3583
Barry Popoff, Manager

Fort McMurray
985 Memorial Dr.
Fort McMurray, AB T9H 2X3
780-790-1525
Fax: 780-743-9193
Fred Wilson, Manager

Hamilton
#1, 40 Hempstead Dr.
Hamilton, ON L8W 2E7
905-577-4077
Fax: 905-577-0091
John Wrycraft, Manager

Kingston
595 McKay St.
Kingston, ON K7M 5V8
613-634-8486
Fax: 613-634-8487
Greg Golding, Manager

London
#44-46, 150 Exeter Rd.
London, ON N2L 1A2
519-680-2001
Fax: 519-680-2008
John Wrycraft, Manager

Moncton
105 Engelhart St.
Dieppe, NB E1A 8K2
506-859-4206
Fax: 506-859-4477

Montréal
5800, boul. Henri-Bourassa ouest
Montréal, QC H4R 3A6
514-737-5505
Fax: 514-737-1602
Nicholas Zigayer, Manager

Mount Pearl
153 Glencoe Dr.
Mount Pearl, NL A1N 4P4
709-745-6666
Fax: 709-634-6966

Ottawa
1257 Algoma Rd., Unit 4
Ottawa, ON K1B 3W7
613-526-0435
Fax: 613-526-0379
Greg Golding, Manager

Québec
765, rue Godin
Vanier, QC G1M 2W8
418-681-4242
Fax: 418-681-7112
Nicholas Zigayer, Manager

Regina
496 Henderson Dr.
Regina, SK S4N 6E3
306-543-1314
Fax: 306-543-5535

Saskatoon
#1, 3006 Cleveland Ave.
Saskatoon, SK S7K 8B5
306-934-8184
Fax: 306-242-3930

Toronto
2400 Skymark Ave.
Mississauga, ON L4W 5K5
905-212-4600
Fax: 905-212-4601
John Wrycraft, Manager

Vancouver
Vancouver Delta
1485 Lindsey Pl.
Vancour, BC V3M 6V1
604-515-8872
Fax: 604-519-1477
Brian Gowing, Manager

Windsor
#700, 4525 Rhodes Dr.
Windsor, ON N8W 5R8
519-966-1910
Fax: 519-966-5857
John Wrycraft, Manager

Winnipeg
989 Century St.
Winnipeg, MB R3H 0W4
204-694-0140
Fax: 204-694-1590
Jesse Standing, Manager

Sinanni Inc.
#580, 3333, Queen Mary
Montréal, QC H3V 1AZ
514-940-3332
Fax: 514-940-3435
info@sinanni.com
www.sinanni.com
Firm Type: Engineering, Scientific/Technical Services, Waste Management
Founded: 1999
Staff: 5
Member of: Ordre de Ingenieur du Québec
Products/Services/Areas of Expertise: Air quality; remediation; site assessment; audit; project management; research & development
Recently Completed / Ongoing Projects: Remediation of a former radar station in Arctic; development & implementation of a waste water treatment system for fluoride at a glass etching plant
Financial Information:
Type of Ownership: Private
Revenue: $250,000 - $500,000
Revenue Sources: 10% Municipals; 90% Private Contracts
Domestic Markets:
Nunavut, Québec
Contact(s):
Philippe Simon, President
Karl Côté, Vice-President

Sinclair Technologies
616 Chester
Delta, BC V3M 5V8
604-525-5344
800-663-4670
Products/Services/Areas of Expertise: Laboratory measuring & monitoring equipment
Contact(s):
Sid Smith, Technologist

Sinnott Farm Services Ltd.
P.O. Box 426
Pincher Creek, AB T0K 1W0
403-627-2001
Fax: 403-627-5096
cgs128@telusplanet.net
Firm Type: Manufacturing
Staff: 6
Products/Services/Areas of Expertise: Owner/operator of a single grid connected 65 kw windmatic wind turbine; Also has one parcel of property leased to Canadian Hydro Developers who currently operate five Nordex 1300 kw machines
Contact(s):
Curtis Sinnott

Sintra Inc.
911, rue St-Mathieu
Bon-Conseil, QC J0C 1A0
819-336-2666
Fax: 819-336-2953
Products/Services/Areas of Expertise: Water & wastewater management equipment
Contact(s):
Robert Boudreau

Sittler Environmental
Formerly: SEL Recycling
P.O. Box 36
2660 Arthur St. North
Elmira, ON N3B 2Z5
519-669-2456
info@sittler.ca
www.selrecycling.com
Firm Type: Waste Management
Founded: 1949
Staff: 15
Products/Services/Areas of Expertise: On-site wood grinding; resource recovery; waste transfer; composting
Recently Completed / Ongoing Projects: Operates transfer/recovery facility in Kitchener, ON
Financial Information:
Type of Ownership: Private
Domestic Markets:
Ontario
Foreign Activity:
USA
Contact(s):
Steven Sittler, General Manager
Richard Sittler, Operations

Sittler Excavating Ltd.
2600 Arthur St. North
Elmira, ON N3B 2Z5
519-669-2456
Fax: 519-669-5710
Products/Services/Areas of Expertise: Engineering consulting services; construction & excavation services
Contact(s):
Steven Sittler, President

Sittler's Manufacturing
Global Repair Ltd.
33 Bellefair Ave.
Toronto, ON M4L 3T7
416-686-3690
Fax: 416-686-1744
866-271-0719
sales@globalrepair.ca
www.globalrepair.ca/compost.htm
Firm Type: Manufacturing
Founded: 1965
Staff: 2
Products/Services/Areas of Expertise: Composting equipment
Financial Information:
Type of Ownership: Private
Domestic Markets:
Ontario

Skelton Brumwell & Associates Inc.
#107, 93 Bell Farm Rd.
Barrie, ON L4M 5G1
705-726-1141
Fax: 705-726-0331
mail@skeltonbrumwell.ca
www.skeltonbrumwell.ca
Firm Type: Management Consulting, Engineering
Founded: 1970
Staff: 17
Member of: Ontario Sand, Stone & Gravel Association
Products/Services/Areas of Expertise: Municipal planning & engineering; land development; environmental management; aggregate resources; recreation & tourism; institutional
Recently Completed / Ongoing Projects: Lakeshore Dr. drainage, City of Barrie; planning, environmental management & engineering 1.8 km shoreline subdivision, Lake Simcoe; off-site sludge storage facilities, City of Barrie; environmental impact assessment, Tay Township; comprehensive ESR, The Blue Mountains; elevated water storage tank, Barrie
Financial Information:
Type of Ownership: Private
Revenue Sources: 10% Provincial; 40% Municipals; 50% Private Contracts
Domestic Markets:
Ontario
Contact(s):
Gary K. Bell, M.C.I.P., President
Scott W. Brumwell, P.Eng., Vice-President

Sky Generation
P.O. Box 1064
191 Isthmus Bay Rd.
Lions Head, ON N0H 1W0
519-793-6212
Fax: 519-793-6214
glen@skygeneration.ca
www.skygeneration.com
Firm Type: Distributing, Manufacturing
Founded: 2000
EcoLogo Certified Products & Services: Renewable low-impact wind-power
Products/Services/Areas of Expertise: The power is sold into the Ontario power pool. The project will be supported through the sale of green tags through greentagsontario.com, a renewable energy co-operative.
Recently Completed / Ongoing Projects: Sky Generation's first wind turbine has been installed south of Ferndale, on the Bruce Peninsula. First power was produced on November 27, 2002. The turbine is a Vestas 1.8 MW V80 & will generate enough power to supply 500 homes.
Ecological Note: Renewable low-impact wind-power

Domestic Markets:
Ontario
Contact(s):
Glen Estill, President/CEO
glen@skygeneration.com

Skylark Controls
1160 Ellesmere Rd.
Toronto, ON M1P 2X4
416-444-6614
Fax: 416-444-0353
888-297-6649
www.skylarkcontrols.com
Firm Type: Distributing, Manufacturing
Founded: 1990
Products/Services/Areas of Expertise: Manufacturer of melt pressure gauges, melt pressure transmitters, melt pressure transducers, melt temperature sensors, & controllers, such as the Skylark low voltage electronic dimmer; Clients include plastics processors & extrusion machinery builders
Domestic Markets:
National

SL Ross Environmental Research Ltd.
#200, 717 Belfast Rd.
Ottawa, ON K1G 0Z4
613-232-1564
Fax: 613-232-6660
info@slross.com
www.slross.com
Firm Type: Management Consulting, Scientific/Technical Services
Founded: 1980
Staff: 7
Products/Services/Areas of Expertise: A consulting firm specializing in oil spill research, & spill control. Expertise in evaluation & design of spill countermeasures, equipment, & techniques, in situ burning, dispersants, development of contingency plans & training programs, environmental impact assessments, computer modeling of oil & chemical spill behaviour, GIS, consultation for litigation & expert testimony. Clients have come from industry, government or other organizations. For a list of reports & other publications produced by the firm, please consult the website
Financial Information:
Type of Ownership: Private
Revenue Sources: 50% nationwide; 50% Private Contracts
Domestic Markets:
British Columbia, New Brunswick, Newfoundland & Labrador, Nova Scotia, Northwest Territories, Ontario
Foreign Activity:
Asia, Caribbean, Central America, The Middle East, Mexico, USA
Contact(s):
Stephen Potter, B.A.Sc., Managing Director

Sleegers Engineering Inc.
649 - 3 St.
London, ON N5V 2C1
519-451-5480
Fax: 519-451-9922
dperry@sleegers.on.ca
www.sleegers.on.ca
Firm Type: Engineering, Manufacturing
Founded: 1963
Products/Services/Areas of Expertise: Design & manufacture of special purpose equipment: de-watering presses, material handling, test & assembly equipment
Financial Information:
Type of Ownership: Private
Domestic Markets:
National
Foreign Activity:
USA
Contact(s):
Joseph L. Adams, Vice-President/Manager
j.adams@sleegers.on.ca

Canadian Branches:
First St. Branch
406 First St.
London, ON N5W 4N1
519-451-5400
Fax: 519-451-7487
dperry@sleegers.on.ca
Don Perry, Plant Manager

Green Valley Rd. Branch
980 Green Valley Rd.
London, ON N6N 1E3
519-685-7444
Fax: 519-685-2882
wlileikis@sleegers.on.ca
Walt Lileikis, Plant Manager

Slope Indicator Canada
#120, 6091 Dyke Rd.
Richmond, BC V7E 3R3
604-271-2585
Fax: 604-271-2580
800-663-2374
www.slopeindicator.com
Products/Services/Areas of Expertise: Manufacturer of geotechnical engineering equipment for various applications
Contact(s):
Simon Cornwallace, Contact

SLR Consulting Ltd. (Canada)
Formerly: SEACOR Environmental Inc.
#200, 1620 - West 8th Ave.
Vancouver, BC V6J 1V4
604-738-2500
Fax: 604-738-2508
www.slrconsulting.com
Firm Type: Management Consulting, Engineering

Products/Services/Areas of Expertise: Multidisciplinary environmental consulting in the areas of sustainability, greenhouse gas emissions, climate change, & site specific issues regarding energy, waste management, infrastructure, planning & development
Financial Information:
Type of Ownership: Foreign-owned
Domestic Markets:
National
Foreign Activity:
Worldwide
Contact(s):
James Malick, B.Sc., M.Sc., Ph.D., Exec. Vice-President/Director, Canada

Canadian Branches:
Calgary
#134, 12143 40th St. SE
Calgary, AB T2Z 4E6
403-266-2030
Fax: 403-263-7906

Dartmouth
115 Joseph Zatzman Dr.
Dartmouth, NS B3B 1N3
902-420-0040
Fax: 902-420-9703

Edmonton
6940 Roper Rd.
Edmonton, AB T6B 3H9
780-490-7893
Fax: 780-490-7819

Fort St. John
9943 - 100 Ave.
Fort St John, BC V1J 1Y4
250-785-0969
Fax: 250-785-0928

Grande Prairie
10015 - 102nd St.
Grande Prairie, AB T8V 2V5
780-513-6819
Fax: 780-513-6821

Kamloops
#A, 8 West St. Paul St.
Kamloops, BC V2C 1G1
250-374-8749
Fax: 250-374-8656

Kelowna
#200, 1475 Ellis St.
Kelowna, BC V1Y 2A3
250-762-7202
Fax: 250-763-7303

Markham
#101, 260 Town Centre Blvd.
Markham, ON L3R 8H8

905-415-7248
Fax: 905-415-1019

Mississauga
Plaza 4
#310, 2000 Argentia Rd.
Mississauga, ON L5N 1W1
905-670-5521
Fax: 905-670-5159

Nanaimo
#9, 6421 Applecross Rd.
Nanaimo, BC V9V 1N1
250-390-5050
Fax: 250-390-5042

Prince George
1586 Ogilvie St.
Prince George, BC V2N 1W9
250-562-4452
Fax: 250-562-4458

Regina
1054 Winnipeg St.
Regina, SK S4R 8P8
306-525-4690
Fax: 306-525-4691

Saskatoon
1141 8th St. E.
Saskatoon, SK S7H 5H9
306-374-6800
Fax: 306-374-6077

Sydney
P.O. Box 791 A
Sydney, NS B1P 6J1
902-564-7911
Fax: 901-564-7910
Products/Services/Areas of Expertise: Office location: 107B, 45 Wabana Court, Sydney

Victoria
#6, 40 Cadillac Ave.
Victoria, BC V8Z 1T2
250-475-9595
Fax: 250-475-9596

Winnipeg
1420 Clarence Ave., Unit D
Winnipeg, MB R3T 1T6
204-477-1848
Fax: 204-475-1649

Smart Turner Pumps
P.O. Box 28066
392 Hardy Rd.
Brantford, ON N3R 7X5
519-727-1746
Fax: 519-757-1747
contact@smartturner.ca
www.smartturner.ca
Products/Services/Areas of Expertise: Centrifugal & positive displacement pumps & mixers for municipal & industrial water/wastewater treatment
Domestic Markets:
National

Smith & Andersen Consulting Engineering
#500, 4211 Yonge St.
Toronto, ON M4P 2A9
416-487-8151
Fax: 416-487-9104
toronto@smithandersen.com
www.smithandersen.com
Firm Type: Engineering, Scientific/Technical Services
Founded: 1965
Staff: 70
Products/Services/Areas of Expertise: Feasibility studies; reports; computer control systems; thermal storage systems; energy conservation; computer-aided design & preparation of contract documents for complete mechanical systems incorporating plumbing, drainage, fire protection & energy-efficient heating, ventilation & air conditioning systems
Recently Completed / Ongoing Projects: Terminal 1, Lester B. Pearson Airport
Domestic Markets:
National
Contact(s):
D.I. Smith, P.Eng., B.A.Sc., Corporate Partner

Canadian Branches:
Calgary
#201, 1000 - 9 Ave. SW
Calgary, AB T2P 2Y6
403-261-8897
Fax: 403-233-0285
general@emanssmithandersen.com

Ottawa
738A Bank St.
Ottawa, ON K1S 3V4
613-230-1186
Fax: 613-230-2598
ottawa@smithandandersen.com

Smith-Way Ltd.
75 Freshway Dr.
Concord, ON L4K 1R9
905-669-4340
Fax: 905-669-9945
sales@ecowood-products.com
www.ecowood-products.com
Products/Services/Areas of Expertise: Rear-packer trucks for loose, non-recyclable garbage; recycling bins; containers for mixed fine paper, computer printout paper, cardboard
Contact(s):
Don Smith, Sales

SmithBrook Waste Management Services Inc.
P.O. Box 686
Brooks, AB T1R 1B3
403-362-4071
Fax: 403-362-3671
dispatch@smithtrucking.com
www.smithtrucking.com/sbwm.htm
Contact(s):
Richard Smith, President

Smiths Detection / BRL
Formerly: Barringer Technologies Canada
7030 Century Ave.
Mississauga, ON L5N 2V8
905-817-5990
Fax: 905-817-5992
info@smithsdetection.com
www.smithsdetection.com
Firm Type: Manufacturing, Scientific/Technical Services
Quality Environmental Management System(s): 9001
Products/Services/Areas of Expertise: Air pollution control products & systems; remote sensing & image analysis; research & development; air measuring & monitoring systems
Financial Information:
Type of Ownership: Foreign-owned
Contact(s):
David Martinak, Vice-President, Project Development
david.martinak@smithsdetection.com
Mark Elliott, Vice-President, Product Management
mark.elliott@smithsdetection.com

SMS Engineering Ltd.
Formerly: Scouten, Mitchell, Sigurdson
770 Bradford St.
Winnipeg, MB R3H 0N3
204-775-0291
Fax: 204-772-2153
888-775-0291
SMS@SMSeng.com
www.smseng.com
Firm Type: Engineering
Founded: 1965
Products/Services/Areas of Expertise: Provides engineering services to all building sectors such as commercial buildings, health care facilities, laboratory & pharmaceutical manufacturing facilities, schools, universities, correctional facilities, recreational centres, gaming facilities, air terminal buildings, vehicle maintenance garages, aircraft maintenance hangers
Financial Information:
Revenue Sources: 20% Provincial; 80% Private Contracts
Domestic Markets:
Manitoba, Northwest Territories, Ontario, Saskatchewan
Contact(s):
Ian D. Kelly, Principal
Garry Brown, Principal
Andy Lohse, Principal
Helmut Waedt, Principal

SNC-Lavalin Environment Inc.
2271, boul Fernand-Lafontaine
Longueuil, QC J4G 2R7
450-442-8809
Fax: 450-651-0885
www.snc-lavalin.com
Firm Type: Engineering, Waste Management

Products/Services/Areas of Expertise: Works with government & industry clients to ensure compliance with regulations & standards, & provides consultation & technical assistance. Expertise includes: site assessment & remediation, impact assessment & permitting, waste management, marine studies & coastal zone management, air quality monitoring, acoustics, climate change, auditing & EMS, water management & sanitation, engineering for geotechnical, environmental & agro-environment, LEED certifications. Offices across Canada, please consult website for details
Recently Completed / Ongoing Projects: Dockside Green planned community (LEED Platinum certification) - BC; Southeast False Creek, Vancouver, BC - soil & groundwater investigation; 45 MW Apaqui Hydroelectric Project, Ecuador
Financial Information:
Type of Ownership: Publicly Traded
Domestic Markets:
New Brunswick, Newfoundland & Labrador, Nova Scotia, Prince Edward Island
Foreign Activity:
South America
Markets Sought:
South America, Mexico
Contact(s):
Jean-Luc Allard, Vice President, Environment
Jacques Benoit, Sr. Vice President/General Manager, Montréal Office, 514-393-1000
Grant Byers, Sr. Vice President/General Manager, Calgary Office, 403-253-4333

Canadian Branches:
New Brunswick Branch
P.O. Box 1238
500 Beaverbrook Ct.
Fredericton, NB E3B 5C8
506-459-2645
Fax: 506-459-4175

SNC-Lavalin Group Inc.
455, boul René-Lévesque ouest
Montréal, QC H2Z 1Z3
514-393-1000
Fax: 514-866-0795
www.snc-lavalin.com
Firm Type: Engineering
Founded: 1911
Quality Environmental Management System(s): 9001; ISO
Products/Services/Areas of Expertise: With some 21,000 employees worldwide, SNC-Lavalin & its subsidiaries are a global leader in engineering & construction, providing expertise & client-centred services in agriculture & agrifood, chemicals & petroleum, environmental engineering, infrastructure, mass transit, mining & metallurgy, pharmaceuticals & biotechnology, power, procurement, & project management. Policies & practices which enhance sustainable development, & protect the environment are a focus. In the environment sector, expertise includes impact assessment, solid & industrial waste management, site assessment & remediation, marine studies & coastal zone management, air quality, acoustics, climate change, water infrastructure management & sanitation. SNC-Lavalin maintains a Training & Sustainable Development department which offers training to government & private sector clients. Office locations & projects around the world
Recently Completed / Ongoing Projects: Union Station-Pearson Airport rail link, Toronto - due to be completed in 2014; Goreway Power Plant, ON; Canada Line extension of the SkyTrain RT in Vancouver, BC - due for completion in 2009; James Bay Project, completed 1979
Financial Information:
Type of Ownership: Publicly Traded
Revenue Sources: 20% nationwide; 20% Provincial; 30% Municipals; 30% Private Contracts
Domestic Markets:
National
Foreign Activity:
Africa, Asia, Australia/New Zealand, Central Europe, Eastern Europe, Western Europe, The Middle East, The Pacific Rim, South Africa, South America, Mexico, USA, United Kingdom, Vietnam
Contact(s):
Pierre Duhaime, President/CEO
Gilles Laramée, Exec. Vice President/CFO
Parveen Khan, Vice President, External Training & Sustainable Development

Canadian Branches:
Toronto
2200 Lake Shore Blvd. West
Toronto, ON M8V 1A4
416-252-5311
Fax: 416-231-5356
Products/Services/Areas of Expertise: A 2nd Toronto office is located at 789 Don Mills Rd., Suite 1000 - contact 416-422-4056

Snowcap Waters Ltd.
A subsidiary of Norzan Enterprises Ltd.
7375 Island Hwy.
Fanny Bay, BC V0R 3B0
250-335-0999
Fax: 250-335-1055
Firm Type: Manufacturing
Founded: 1989
Products/Services/Areas of Expertise: Processes, packages & distributes pure, uncarbonated, glacier water
Financial Information:
Type of Ownership: Publicly Traded
Revenue Sources: 100% Private Contracts
Contact(s):
Joseph Yelder, President

Société d'énergie de la rivière Ste-Anne/AXOR
c/o AXOR
1950, rue Sherbrooke ouest
Montréal, QC H3H 1E7
514-846-4000
Fax: 514-846-4020
axor@axor.com
www.axor.com
Products/Services/Areas of Expertise: Electricity producer
Ecological Note: Renewable low impact water-powered electriciy
Contact(s):
Frédéric Debieuvre, Contact

Société Laurentide inc.
Also Known As: Laurentide Paint Cafe
4660, av 12
Shawinigan, QC G9N 6T5
819-537-6636
Fax: 819-537-5293
800-567-9481
www.paintcafe.com
Firm Type: Manufacturing
Founded: 1950
Staff: 150
Quality Environmental Management System(s): 9002
EcoLogo Certified Products & Services: 1
Products/Services/Areas of Expertise: Paint manufactuter, wood coatings, automobile fluids, bottled water
Ecological Note: 1
Financial Information:
Revenue Sources: 25% nationwide; 25% Provincial; 50% Private Contracts
Domestic Markets:
New Brunswick, Newfoundland & Labrador, Ontario, Prince Edward Island, Québec
Foreign Activity:
USA
Contact(s):
Andre Buisson, President
Catherine Courtois, Marketing
Denis Hogue, Sales

Socodec Inc.
Subsidiary of SNC Lavalin Inc.
Place Félix-Martin
455, boul René-Lévesque ouest
Montréal, QC H2Z 1Z3
514-393-1000
Fax: 514-861-5349
Firm Type: Engineering, Scientific/Technical Services
Founded: 1985
Staff: 100

Products & Services Buyer's Guide

Products/Services/Areas of Expertise: Project & construction management; turnkey projects; procurement services
Recently Completed / Ongoing Projects: Project management, PCB treatment, Québec; construction management, tunnel, Venezuela; turnkey project, deep water well drilling, Africa; management, energy efficiency, Québec
Financial Information:
Revenue Sources: 100% Provincial
Domestic Markets:
National
Foreign Activity:
Africa, Asia, Central America, Eastern Europe, The Pacific Rim, South America, Mexico, USA
Markets Sought:
Asia, The Pacific Rim, Mexico
Contact(s):
François Dionne, President

Softrisk Technologies Ltd.
#2060, 130 Adelaide St. West
Toronto, ON M5H 3P5
416-865-9300
Fax: 416-865-1153
www.softrisk.com
Products/Services/Areas of Expertise: Developing emergency/critical incident management software since 1989, SoftRisk Technologies has spent over a decade designing and refining the most robust and complete Emergency Management Software program

Solaction Inc.
5000, rue Jean-Arnaud
Québec, QC G2C 2C1
418-842-0122
Fax: 418-842-7888
solaction@qbc.clic.net; solaction@megaquebec.ne
Firm Type: Management Consulting
Founded: 1994
Staff: 5
Products/Services/Areas of Expertise: Soil decontamination, soil treatment plant, management of soil decontamination projects, civil work & excavation
Recently Completed / Ongoing Projects: Soil decontamination of commercial & industrial sites
Financial Information:
Type of Ownership: Private
Revenue: $500,000 - $1.5 Million
Revenue Sources: 15% Municipals; 85% Private Contracts
Domestic Markets:
Québec
Markets Sought:
Eastern Europe
Contact(s):
Pierre Thibault, President
Yves Talbot, Finance Director

Canadian Branches:
Soil Treatment Centre
16001, boul de la Colline
Québec, QC G2C 2C1
418-841-4535

Solar Solutions Inc.
#6, 130 Midland St.
Winnipeg, MB R3E 3R3
204-632-5554
Fax: 204-632-5577
800-285-7652
solar@solarengineers.com
www.solarsolutions.ca
Firm Type: Distributing, Engineering, Manufacturing
Founded: 1990
Staff: 12
Products/Services/Areas of Expertise: Assembly, manufacturing & distribution of photovoltaic (solar electric) systems & wind generation power systems for remote/independent living, telecommunications, cathodic protection traffic lighting; water pumping, etc.
Financial Information:
Type of Ownership: Private
Revenue: Greater than $5 Million
Domestic Markets:
National
Foreign Activity:
Africa, Caribbean, Central America, South America
Contact(s):
Tim Yusishen, President

Jake Fehr, Manager, Sales

Solarmart
2084 Vickery Dr.
Oakville, ON L6L 2J3
905-827-2579
Firm Type: Distributing, Manufacturing
Founded: 1979
Staff: 2
Member of: Solar Energy Society of Canada Inc.
Products/Services/Areas of Expertise: Solar heating equipment manufacture; installation; service & sales
Financial Information:
Type of Ownership: Private
Revenue Sources: 100% Private Contracts
Domestic Markets:
Ontario
Contact(s):
Dick Potma, Owner

Solcan Ltd.
126 Wychwood Park
London, ON N6G 1R7
519-473-0501
Fax: 519-474-1539
866-765-2263
solarheating@rogers.com
www.solcan.com
Firm Type: Manufacturing
Founded: 1975
Staff: 3
Member of: Canadian Solar Industries Association
Products/Services/Areas of Expertise: Canada's oldest solar company, manufactures solar collectors & solar water heaters, & sells other solar-related products which conserve energy & use renewable energy, such as PV equipment & wind turbines; specializes in turnkey solar heating projects for commercial & industrial applications & has developed solar water heaters for residential customers; provides full technical support to a network of dealer-installers
Recently Completed / Ongoing Projects: Fifteen Solcan flat-plate solar collectors in a system for preheating the domestic hot water, Parkway Apartments, Owen Sound, ON; residential systems which combine solar heating with radiant floor heating & potable hot water; ongoing project of combining solar heating potable hot water with air heating through a heat recovery ventilator
Financial Information:
Type of Ownership: Private
Revenue: $250,000 - $500,000
Revenue Sources: 10% Municipals; 90% Private Contracts
Domestic Markets:
National
Foreign Activity:
USA
Contact(s):
R.K. Swartman, President

Solenco Environnement inc.
5395, ch St-Jean
La Prairie, QC J5R 3X8
514-845-1344
Contact(s):
Patrick Cloutier

Soleno Inc.
CP 837
1160, rte 133
Saint-Jean-sur-Richelieu, QC J2X 4J5
450-347-7855
Fax: 450-359-4150
877-633-7473
service.quebec@soleno.com
www.soleno.com
Firm Type: Manufacturing
Staff: 300
EcoLogo Certified Products & Services: Corrugated polyethylene drainage & storm sewer pipe
Products/Services/Areas of Expertise: Manufactures corrugated polyethylene pipe & accessories
Ecological Note: Corrugated polyethylene drainage & storm sewer pipe

Canadian Branches:
Iberville
P.O. Box 147
1160, rte 133
Iberville, QC J2X 4J5

1-877-633-7473

New Brunswick Branch
64 Northlane
McAdam, NB E6J 1K6
1-877-633-7473
service.maritimes@soleno.com

Ontario Branch
RR#5, Bldg. 7, 304 Conc. 11
Hagersville, ON N0A 1H0
1-877-633-7473
service.ontario@soleno.com

Saint-Nicolas Branch
1185, ch Industriel
Saint-Nicolas, QC G7A 1B2
1-877-633-7473
service.quebec@soleno.com

Sainte-Madeleine Branch
2676, ch Plamondon
Sainte-Madeleine, QC J0H 1S0
1-877-633-7473
service.quebec@soleno.com

Solid Waste Reclamation Inc.
Also Known As: SWR
P.O. Box 200 A
1 James St. South, 16th Fl.
Hamilton, ON L8N 3A2
905-523-0036
Fax: 905-523-6036
800-893-1582
Firm Type: Waste Management
Founded: 1982
Staff: 3
Products/Services/Areas of Expertise: Locates recycling applications for wastes through main line resources as well as research of new markets for wastes that are presently being land filled; disposal & transportation options for construction & demolition rubble, municipal solid waste, sewage sludge, asbestos, non-hazardous wastes, hazardous wastes & contaminated solids; technical waste characterization, laboratory analysis & densification of landfill items
Domestic Markets:
Ontario, Québec
Foreign Activity:
USA
Contact(s):
Michael S. Waxman, President
Morris J. Waxman, Chair
Douglas A. Waxman, Vice-President

Solignum
UCP Group
Formerly: Peintures UCP Inc19500, rte Trans-Canada
Baie-d'Urfé, QC H9X 3S8
514-457-1512
Fax: 514-457-0883
800-361-9465
solignum@total.net
www.solignum.ca/main.htm
Firm Type: Manufacturing
Founded: 1960
Products/Services/Areas of Expertise: Paints & coatings

Canadian Branches:
Toronto
200 Norelco Dr.
Toronto, ON M9L 1S4
416-749-5542
Fax: 416-792-2985

Solignum Inc.
200 Norelco Dr.
Weston, ON M9L 1S4
416-749-5542
Fax: 416-742-2985
www.solignum.ca
Products/Services/Areas of Expertise: Manufacturer of egologo paints and surface coverings
Ecological Note: Paints & surface coatings
Domestic Markets:
National
Contact(s):
Sheldon Smaye, Contact

Solinov Inc.
#240, 100, rue Richelieu
Saint-Jean-sur-Richelieu, QC J3B 6X3
450-348-5693
Fax: 450-348-3607
fforcier@solinov.com
Firm Type: Management Consulting, Scientific/Technical Services

Products/Services/Areas of Expertise: Agriculture & agronomy management; engineering consulting services; environmental consulting & contracting; integrated special waste management/treatment facilities; solid waste management consulting
Financial Information:
Type of Ownership: Private
Domestic Markets:
New Brunswick, Nova Scotia, Ontario, Québec
Contact(s):
Françoise Forcier, ing.agr., M.Ing.

Solinst Canada Ltd.
35 Todd Rd.
Georgetown, ON L7G 4R8
905-873-2255
Fax: 905-873-1992
800-661-2023
instruments@solinst.com
www.solinst.com
Firm Type: Manufacturing
Founded: 1975
Staff: 42
Member of: National Ground Water Association; Canadian Water Well Association; Canadian Geotechnical Society
Products/Services/Areas of Expertise: Groundwater monitoring instrumentation; sampling & monitoring systems; water level indicators & loggers; hydrogeological instrumentation for site characterizations, spill investigations & long-term water monitoring; drive-point piezometers & profilers, oil/water interface meters
Financial Information:
Type of Ownership: Private
Domestic Markets:
National
Foreign Activity:
Worldwide
Contact(s):
Jim Pianosi, Sales Manager

Solmax International Inc.
Formerly: Côté inc., Matériaux techniques
Also Known As: Solmax Geosynthetics
2801, boul Marie-Victorin
Varennes, QC J3X 1P7
450-929-1234
Fax: 450-929-1227
international@solmax.com
www.solmax.com
Firm Type: Manufacturing
Founded: 1981
Member of: Canadian Plastics Industry Association; Industrial Fabrics Association International; International Geosynthetics Society; Geosynthetic Institute
Products/Services/Areas of Expertise: Manufacturing geomembrane (HDPE, VFPE, LLDPE, VLDPE, PVC); installation & supply of geosynthetics including geomembranes for waterproofing containment structures; geotextiles for separation, filtration, drainage
Financial Information:
Type of Ownership: Private

Solmax-Texel Geosynthetics Inc.
#790, 2954, boul Laurier
Sainte-Foy, QC G1V 4T2
418-658-0200
Fax: 418-658-0477
800-463-0088
info@sol-tex.qc.ca
www.sol-tex.qc.ca
Firm Type: Engineering, Scientific/Technical Services
Founded: 1993
Member of: International Association of Geosynthetics Installers
Products/Services/Areas of Expertise: Products serve to reduce hydraulic conductivity in earthwork structures; are designed principally to meet needs in civil engineering, geotechnology & environmental engineering fields; teams work all over the world performing on-site assembly of geomembranes & related geosynthetic products; installers are required to respect demanding quality control programs; are IAGI-certified & comply with GRI industry standards; has assembled & installed millions of square metres of geomembranes around the world.
Financial Information:
Revenue: Greater than $5 Million
Domestic Markets:
Newfoundland & Labrador, Québec
Contact(s):
André Noiseux, General Manager
andre.noiseux@sol-tex.qc.ca
Stéphane Leblanc, Project Manager
stephane.leblanc@sol-tex.qc.ca

Solmers Internationale Experts-Conseils Inc.
#22, 1471, boul Lionel Boulet
Varennes, QC J3X 1P7
450-929-0303
Fax: 450-929-4334
info@solmers.ca
www.solmers.ca
Firm Type: Engineering
Founded: 1986
Products/Services/Areas of Expertise: Covers all key aspects of environmental analyses and audits: site evaluations & characterizations, environmental audits, environmental studies, & environmental management systems; erosion control services, geosynthetic/geomembrane liners; storage tanks & equipment; solid waste collection services & equipment
Domestic Markets:
National
Foreign Activity:
Africa, Asia, Western Europe, The Middle East, USA

Canadian Branches:
Québec
3, rue Bégin
Québec, QC G6V 4B6
418-833-3885
Fax: 418-833-4969

Sols Consultants Ltée
133, av King
Pointe-Claire, QC H9R 4H5
514-697-1690
Fax: 514-697-0285
Firm Type: Engineering, Scientific/Technical Services
Founded: 1987
Staff: 10
Products/Services/Areas of Expertise: Engineering services for air pollution control; soil waste management; mine closure consulting & equipment design; coolingtowers; chimneys; filter design; recycling research & development
Domestic Markets:
Ontario, Québec
Contact(s):
Adalbert W. Goraczko, President
Stan Mileuski, Marketing Director

Solution 3R
3780, rue Panet
Jonquière, QC G7X 0E5
418-695-5556
Fax: 418-695-3340
Products/Services/Areas of Expertise: Accredited lab

Sonepar Canada
A member company of le groupe Sonepar
#303, 989 Derry Rd. E.
Mississauga, ON L5T 2J8
905-696-2838
soneparcanada.com
Firm Type: Distributing
Staff: 1500
Member of: CenturyVallen; Gescan; Lumen; Osso Electric; Texcan; Hagemeyer
Products/Services/Areas of Expertise: B2B technical distribution of electrical materials & related products & services; safety equipment & products; wire & cable products; renewable energy solutions; turnkey solar energy systems; innovating to find green, sustainable energy solutions; 90 offices across Canada
Financial Information:
Type of Ownership: Private; Foreign-owned
Contact(s):
Keith Moss, President/CEO
Contact(s):
Jeff Derkuch, President
Contact(s):
Ivan Romanow, Director, Sales & Marketing
ivan.romanow@sonepardis.ca

Canadian Branches:
CenturyVallen
4810 - 92nd Ave.
Edmonton, AB T6B 2X4
780-468-3366

Gescan - B.C. & Prairies Head Office
5005 - 12A St. SE
Calgary, AB T2G 5L5
403-253-7171
Fax: 403-255-7141
www.gescan.com

Gescan Ontario
8160 Parkhill Dr.
Milton, ON L9T 5V7
905-693-6311
Fax: 905-693-6315

Lumen
117, boul. Hymus
Pointe-Claire, QC H9R 1E5
514-426-9249
Fax: 514-697-4293
800-599-9249

Osso Electric Supplies
209 Bloor St. E.
Oshawa, ON L1H 3M3
905-576-4166
Fax: 905-576-7577

TEXCAN
1420 Derwent Way
Delta, BC V3M 6H9
604-528-3600
Fax: 604-528-3790
800-665-1025

Sonic Environmental Solutions Inc.
#7, 8765 Ash St.
Vancouver, BC V6P 6T3
604-736-2552
Fax: 604-736-2558
877-736-2552
info@sonicenvironmental.com
www.sesi.ca
Firm Type: Scientific/Technical Services
Founded: 1993
Quality Environmental Management System(s): 14001
Products/Services/Areas of Expertise: Environmental site remediation using proprietary sustainable technologies; works with owners of Brownfield sites to reduce harmful pollutants
Recently Completed / Ongoing Projects: Soil remediation at sites in: Cape Canaveral, Florida; Greater Toronto Area; Vancouver Lower Mainland; Sparrevohn Long Range Radar System, Alaska; Fernald Uranium Feed Plant, Ohio
Financial Information:
Type of Ownership: Publicly Traded
Domestic Markets:
National
Foreign Activity:
Asia, Australia/New Zealand, USA
Contact(s):
Adam Sumel, President/CEO
asumel@sesi.ca
Larry Rodricks, Vice President, Remediation Services
lrodricks@sesi.ca

Canadian Branches:
Eastern Canada
326 Edenwood Place
Waterloo, ON N2T 2S2
877-736-2552

International Branch(es):
USA
11494 Sorrento Valley Rd.
San Diego, CA USA
877-736-2552

Products & Services Buyer's Guide

Sonic Soil Sampling Inc.
Formerly: C.W. Archibald Limited
Also Known As: Sonic
#15, 668 Millway Ave.
Concord, ON L4K 3V2
905-660-0501
Fax: 905-660-7143
877-897-6642
sonic@sonicsoil.com
www.sonicsoil.com
Firm Type: Scientific/Technical Services
Founded: 1981
Staff: 12
Member of: Ontario Groundwater Association
Products/Services/Areas of Expertise: Environmental sampling & geotechnical testing for the engineering, industrial & commercial sectors; also offers geological & mining sampling services, world-wide
Recently Completed / Ongoing Projects: Public Works Canada soil sampling, Northern Ontario; Metro Toronto Works Department soil site assessments; Ontario Ministry of Northern Development & Mines abandoned mines projects & mine inspection & consulting; Chemical Valley monitoring & assessments, Sarnia
Financial Information:
Type of Ownership: Private
Revenue Sources: 20% nationwide; 80% Private Contracts
Domestic Markets:
National
Foreign Activity:
Worldwide
Markets Sought:
Asia, South America, USA
Contact(s):
John Archibald, President
Alan Archibald, Vice-President
Ted Nedelkopoulos, Director, Operations

Sonic Technology Solutions Inc.
Corporate Office
#7, 8765 Ash St.
Vancouver, BC V6P 6T3
604-736-2552
Fax: 604-736-2558
info@sesi.ca
www.sonictsi.com
Firm Type: Engineering, Scientific/Technical Services

Products/Services/Areas of Expertise: Developer of advanced processes using proprietary sonic energy technology, used for the remediation of soils contaminated with organic pollutants, & for applications in the oil industry
Financial Information:
Type of Ownership: Publicly Traded
Contact(s):
David Coe, Chair
Adam R. Sumel, President/CEO
Lisa Sharp, CGA, Chief Financial Officer
James Hill, B.Sc., M.B.A., Ph.D., P., Executive Vice-President

Sonitec Inc.
4020, ch Bois-Franc
Montréal, QC H4S 1A7
514-335-2200
Fax: 514-335-2295
sonitec@vortisand.com
Firm Type: Manufacturing
Founded: 1984
Staff: 25
Member of: Association québécoise des techniques de l'eau
Quality Environmental Management System(s): 9002
Products/Services/Areas of Expertise: Multi-media sand filtration system for removal of suspended solids down to .45 microns; for cooling water & potable wastewater applications
Recently Completed / Ongoing Projects: Filtration of process water for paper production for Rolland Inc. (Cascades Inc.); pre-filtration before reverse osmosis for reuse of sewage water, Florida Power; filtration with ozone system for potable water application, Bexar Metropolitan, San Antonio, TX
Financial Information:
Type of Ownership: Private
Revenue Sources: 30% Municipals; 70% Private Contracts
Domestic Markets:
Alberta, British Columbia, New Brunswick, Nova Scotia, Ontario, Québec

Foreign Activity:
Australia/New Zealand, Central America, Mexico, USA
Markets Sought:
Asia, Western Europe,
Contact(s):
Alain Blais, President

sonnevera international corp.
P.O. Box 23
Bluffton, AB T0C 0M0
403-843-6563
Fax: 403-843-4156
cseidel@telusplanet.net
Firm Type: Management Consulting
Founded: 1989
Staff: 1
Member of: Recycling Council of Alberta
Products/Services/Areas of Expertise: Specializes in waste minimization programs; recycling program design & evaluation; development of waste reduction plans; education/promotion design
Financial Information:
Type of Ownership: Private
Revenue Sources: 10% Municipals; 90% Private Contracts
Domestic Markets:
Alberta, British Columbia, Manitoba, Northwest Territories, Saskatchewan, Yukon Territory
Foreign Activity:
Caribbean
Contact(s):
Christina Seidel, President

Sonoco Recycling Ltd.
242 Cherry St.
Toronto, ON M5A 3L2
613-407-8272
Firm Type: Waste Management
Staff: 22
Products/Services/Areas of Expertise: Recycles waste paper, telephone books, old newspapers, magazines & corrugated boxes, for repulp by mills

Soper's
P.O. Box 277
Hamilton, ON L8N 3E8
905-528-7636
Fax: 905-528-8128
800-263-8334
inquiry@sopers.com
www.sopers.com
Firm Type: Manufacturing
Founded: 1875
Staff: 30
Products/Services/Areas of Expertise: Softwall enclosure systems, grinding booths, cleanrooms, retractable enclosures, partitions, flow control baffles for water/wastewater treatment, portable water tanks for rural firefighting
Financial Information:
Type of Ownership: Private
Revenue: $1.5 Million - $3 Million
Domestic Markets:
National
Foreign Activity:
USA
Contact(s):
Lincoln Gallagher, President
Ted Portz, Vice-President, Sales
Bob Finch, Marketing
Alex Gaal, Manager, General Sales

Soren Construction Ltd.
3304 Mainsail Cres.
Mississauga, ON L5L 1I12
905-820-8243
Firm Type: Scientific/Technical Services
Founded: 1986
Products/Services/Areas of Expertise: Erosion & soil-erosion control
Financial Information:
Type of Ownership: Private
Domestic Markets:
National
Foreign Activity:
USA
Contact(s):
Soren Broman, President

SOTAR Inc.
Also Known As: Société technique d'aménagement régional
P.O. Box 1601 St-Martin
Laval, QC H7V 3P8
514-335-4001
Fax: 514-733-5225
sotar@bellnet.cat
Firm Type: Engineering, Scientific/Technical Services
Founded: 1962
Staff: 5
Products/Services/Areas of Expertise: Environmental consulting & engineering services; GIS applications; resource & land mapping; field sampling & monitoring; erosion control; agriculture, soil & water conservation
Domestic Markets:
Québec
Contact(s):
Richard Bienvenu

Souris Valley Industries Ltd.
P.O. Box 121
8 - 16, 13 West of 2nd.
Weyburn, SK S4H 2J9
306-842-5854
Fax: 306-842-1011
Firm Type: Manufacturing
Founded: 1977
Staff: 4
Products/Services/Areas of Expertise: Concrete storage tanks for raw sewage
Contact(s):
Barry Allen, President

Southern Ontario Waste Inc.
Formerly: R.J. Ferrier Disposal Inc.
1 Thompson Cr.
Erin, ON N0B 1T0
519-833-1269
800-834-3446
Firm Type: Waste Management

Products/Services/Areas of Expertise: The firm is engaged in scrap metal removal & recycling for clients in the industrial, commercial & construction sectors
Financial Information:
Type of Ownership: Private
Domestic Markets:
Ontario
Contact(s):
Les Sanderson, Principal

Southwell Controls Ltd.
857 - 3 St. West
North Vancouver, BC V7P 1E3
604-980-3688
Fax: 604-980-6578
sales@southwellcontrols.com
www.southwellcontrols.com
Firm Type: Manufacturing
Founded: 1964
Staff: 10
Member of: Water Environment Federation; Instrument Society of America
Products/Services/Areas of Expertise: Manufacturer of high quality water & wastewater samplers, & seller of instrumentation products
Financial Information:
Type of Ownership: Private
Domestic Markets:
National
Foreign Activity:
Australia/New Zealand, South America, USA
Contact(s):
Rick van Rikxoort, Owner

Canadian Branches:
London
6 Trellis Cres.
London, ON N6K 4H2
519-641-2258
Fax: 519-641-2496

Southwestern Flowtech & Environmental Ltd.
Also Known As: SFE Global
#201, 26641 Fraser Hwy.
Aldergrove, BC V4W 3L1

604-856-2220
Fax: 604-856-3003
888-567-9994
vancouver@sfeonline.com
www.sfeonline.com
Firm Type: Engineering
Founded: 1990
Products/Services/Areas of Expertise: Field services engineering company
Domestic Markets:
National
Foreign Activity:
Asia, Eastern Europe, Western Europe, South America, USA
Canadian Branches:
Calgary
Calgary, AB T2E 6V2
403-293-0181
Fax: 403-293-0180
1-877-293-0173
calgary@sfeonline.com

Edmonton
10743 - 178 St.
Edmonton, AB T5S 1J6
780-461-0171
Fax: 780-443-4613
edmonton@sfeonline.com

Spanach Construction Ltd.
12015 - 154 St.
Edmonton, AB T5V 1N5
780-452-9121
Fax: 780-452-9129
spanach@telusplanet.net

SPD Sales Ltd.
6467 Northam Dr.
Mississauga, ON L4V 1J2
905-678-2882
Fax: 905-293-9774
800-811-2811
info@spdsales.com
www.spdsales.com
Products/Services/Areas of Expertise: Distributor for process products & instrumentation: chemical feed systems, control solutions, data & alarm management, fibreglass enclosures, flow measurement, gas detection, level measurement, liquid samplers, process calibrators, water quality analyzers

Specialty Technical Publishers
#10, 1225 East Keith Rd.
North Vancouver, BC V7J 1J3
604-983-3434
Fax: 604-983-3445
800-251-0381
info@stpub.com
www.stpub.com
Firm Type: Information Technology
Staff: 70
Products/Services/Areas of Expertise: Publishers of resource guides dealing with environmental health & safety, law, transportation regulations for USA, Canada & Mexico; division of Glacier Ventrues International Corp.
Financial Information:
Type of Ownership: Publicly Traded
Revenue: Greater than $5 Million
Revenue Sources: 70% nationwide; 30% Provincial; 20% Municipals; 80% Private Contracts
Domestic Markets:
National
Foreign Activity:
Africa, Asia, Australia/New Zealand, Caribbean, Central America, China, Central Europe, Western Europe, South Africa, South America, Mexico, USA, United Kingdom, Vietnam, Worldwide
Contact(s):
Steve Britten, Director, Publishing
steveb@stpub.com
Lee Grindley-Ferris, Corporate Sales
leegf@stpub.com
Deon Kopke, Vice-President, Sales
dkeon@stpub.com

Spectrum Resource Group Inc.
Formerly: Bugbusters Pest Management Inc.
3810 - 18th Ave.
Prince George, BC V2N 4V5
250-564-0383
Fax: 250-562-4885
srg@spectrumresourcegroup.com
www.spectrumresourcegroup.com
Firm Type: Management Consulting, Scientific/Technical Services
Founded: 1985
Staff: 300
Member of: Western Silviculture Contractors Association
Products/Services/Areas of Expertise: Silviculture contracting & consulting; specializes in vegetation & pest management; reforestation consulting
Financial Information:
Type of Ownership: Private
Domestic Markets:
Alberta, British Columbia, Yukon Territory
Contact(s):
Duane Maki, General Manager
dmaki@spectrumresourcegroup.com
Crawford Young, President
cyoung@spectrumresourcegroup.com

Canadian Branches:
Chetwynd Branch
P.O. Box 685
#207, 5016 - 50th Ave.
Chetwynd, BC V0C 2J0
250-788-3662
Fax: 250-788-3666

Spencer-Lemaire Industries Ltd.
Also Known As: Rootrainers Corp.
11406 - 119 St.
Edmonton, AB T5G 2X3
780-451-4318
Fax: 780-452-0920
800-668-8530
info@Spencer-Lemaire.com
www.spencer-lemaire.com
Firm Type: Manufacturing
Founded: 1961
Staff: 7
Products/Services/Areas of Expertise: Range of spill containers for refineries, chemical plants, field installations for preventing ground pollution; Flagship product is Rootrainers, openable containers for starting plants, growing forest seedlings, etc.
Domestic Markets:
National
Foreign Activity:
Worldwide
Contact(s):
Henry A. Spencer, P.Eng., President & General Manager
info@roctrainers.com
Lorraine Austin, Marketing

SPG Hydro International Inc.
Formerly: Subdev Canada Inc.
#101, 2151, Léonard de Vinci
Sainte-Julie, QC J3E 1Z3
450-922-3515
Fax: 450-922-3510
info@spghydro.com
www.spghydro.com
Firm Type: Management Consulting, Engineering, Scientific/Technical Services
Founded: 1983
Staff: 15
Member of: Association québécoise des techniques de l'eau; Association canadienne-française pour l'avancement des sciences
Products/Services/Areas of Expertise: Aquatic & underwater structure & site investigations; expertise in environmental biology & engineering consulting; pest monitoring & control (zebra mussels); impact assessments related to projects/processes affecting the aquatic milieu; waterway management studies; damage & remediation analysis for hydropower intakes, docks, bridges, dams, locks, ships & sewers
Recently Completed / Ongoing Projects: Zebra mussel monitoring & control programs in industry; zebra mussel population dynamics synthesis in the St. Lawrence River, & modelling for future evaluation; underwater structure investigation & engineering expertise offered
Financial Information:
Type of Ownership: Private
Revenue Sources: 15% Provincial; 5% Municipals; 80% Private Contracts
Domestic Markets:
Alberta, Manitoba, Newfoundland & Labrador, Northwest Territories, Prince Edward Island, Québec, Saskatchewan, Yukon Territory
Foreign Activity:
Central America, Western Europe, USA
Markets Sought:
Asia, South America
Contact(s):
Yves Richer, Président
Patrick Guillot, P.E., Director, Engineering
Jérôme Dion, Director, Quality SST & Environment

Sphag Sorb (Canada) Inc.
Subsidiary of Lakeland Peat Moss Ltd.
7430 - 52nd St.
Edmonton, AB T6B 2G3
780-468-5444
Fax: 780-447-1810
1-866-468-5411
ecp@earthcareproducts.com
www.sphagsorb.com
Products/Services/Areas of Expertise: Bioremediation & spill clean-up services; hydrocarbon absorbents; spill containment booms; microbe nutrients
Domestic Markets:
National
Foreign Activity:
Mexico, USA
Contact(s):
Jim Clark, President

Sphere Research Corp.
3394 Sunnyside Rd.
Kelowna, BC V1Z 2V4
250-769-1834
Fax: 250-769-4106
walter2@sphere.bc.ca
www.sphere.bc.ca
Firm Type: Scientific/Technical Services
Founded: 1992
Products/Services/Areas of Expertise: Used electronic test equipment; slide rules
Contact(s):
Walter Shawlee, President

SPI Industries Inc.
Formerly: Superior Precast
P.O. Box 10
RR#2
Shallow Lake, ON N0H 2K0
519-935-2211
Fax: 519-935-2174
800-269-6533
spi@spiplastics.com
www.spiplastics.com
Firm Type: Distributing, Manufacturing
Founded: 1930
Products/Services/Areas of Expertise: Precast concrete septic tanks; cable concrete erosion control mats for riverbank & shoreline use
Domestic Markets:
Ontario
Foreign Activity:
Worldwide
Contact(s):
S. Eric Robinson, President/CEO
Bob Saunders, Sales Manager

SpilKleen
Division of AgraMax Inc.
#1, 2395 Drew Rd.
Mississauga, ON L5S 1A1
905-293-9995
Fax: 905-293-9996
877-455-5336
sales@spilkleen.com
www.spilkleen.com
Firm Type: Distributing, Manufacturing
Founded: 1990
Staff: 15
Products/Services/Areas of Expertise: Industrial absorbents, non-controlled, non-toxic, non-hazardous, loose fill, socks, pads, booms, spill kits; designed for hydrocarbon & oil absorption
Domestic Markets:
National

Foreign Activity:
USA

Contact(s):
Stephen Laakso, President
Ian Tingey, Vice-President, Sales

Canadian Branches:
Calgary
#30, 4216 - 54th Ave. SE
Calgary, AB T2C 2E3
403-236-0015
Fax: 403-236-0016
Jamie Lacount, Manager

Spill Management Inc.
45 Upper Mount Albion Rd.
Hamilton, ON L8J 2R9
905-578-9666
Fax: 905-578-6644
contact@spillmanagement.ca
www.spillmanagement.ca
Firm Type: Management Consulting, Scientific/Technical Services
Founded: 1989
Staff: 2
Member of: Chemical Institute of Canada
Products/Services/Areas of Expertise: Site assessments, training & development of emergency planning; product-specific training for chemical spill response
Recently Completed / Ongoing Projects: Training for: Ontario Power, Ministry of Environment, Dept. of National Defence, Hydro One, Manitoba Hydro, Dofasco Tube, Accuride, Manitoba Conseration, Environment Canada, Alberta Environment
Financial Information:
Type of Ownership: Private
Domestic Markets:
National
Contact(s):
Clifford L. Holland, President
Ruth A. Holland, General Manager

Sprayaway Marine Services Ltd.
5735 Dorset St.
Burnaby, BC V5J 1L8
604-433-4413
Fax: 604-437-5546
sprayaway@axionnet.com
Firm Type: Management Consulting, Scientific/Technical Services, Waste Management
Founded: 1977
Staff: 10
Member of: Canadian Environment Industry Association - BC
Products/Services/Areas of Expertise: Recycling of oil; oil spills cleanup, emergency response; oil/water separation from bilge & ballast; truck & barge services available; heavy metals removal from water
Contact(s):
James L. Gwin, President
Contact(s):
James L. Gwin

Canadian Branches:
Sprayaway Enterprises Ltd.
5735 Dorset St.
Burnaby, BC V5J 1L8
604-437-4413
Fax: 604-437-5546

Sprecher + Schuh Inc.
#10, 3610 Nashua Dr.
Mississauga, ON L4V 1L2
905-677-7514
Fax: 905-677-7663
corporate@sprecherschuh.com
www.sprecherschuh.com
Firm Type: Manufacturing
Staff: 12
Products/Services/Areas of Expertise: Low voltage electrical controls
Domestic Markets:
Ontario

Spriet Associates London Ltd.
155 York St.
London, ON N6A 1A8
519-672-4100
Fax: 519-433-9351

mail@spriet.on.ca
www.spriet.on.ca
Firm Type: Engineering, Scientific/Technical Services
Founded: 1961
Staff: 22
Products/Services/Areas of Expertise: Consulting engineering & architects; municipal, water, sewage, landfill
Domestic Markets:
National,

Spring Air Silver Services Ltd.
2921 - 58 Ave. SE
Calgary, AB T2C 0B4
403-720-2828
Fax: 403-236-9811
Firm Type: Waste Management
Founded: 1987
Staff: 3
Products/Services/Areas of Expertise: Application of Silver Recovery Systems; photo, X-Ray chemical processing; film disposal
Financial Information:
Type of Ownership: Private
Revenue: $250,000 - $500,000
Revenue Sources: 5% nationwide; 20% Provincial; 10% Municipals; 65% Private Contracts
Domestic Markets:
Alberta, British Columbia
Foreign Activity:
USA
Contact(s):
Wayne Kettleson, President
Bill Mourie, General Manager
Barry Wilson, Production Manager

Canadian Branches:
Edmonton Office
780-486-2735
Barry Wilson

Sprung Instant Structures Ltd.
1001 - 10 Ave. SW
Calgary, AB T2R 0B7
403-245-3371
Fax: 403-229-1980
800-528-9899
info@sprung.com
www.sprung.com
Firm Type: Manufacturing
Founded: 1887
Staff: 500
Products/Services/Areas of Expertise: Manufacturers of stressed membrane structures for waste treatment & storage, hazardous waste, soil remediation, asbestos abatement; sludge pond covers, recycling, composting

Canadian Branches:
Oakville
#302, 2904 South Sheridan Way
Oakville, ON L6J 7L7
905-829-1600
Fax: 905-829-1555

SRB Controls Inc.
#135, 50 McIntosh Dr.
Markham, ON L3R 9T3
905-477-9333
Fax: 905-477-8129
sales@srbcontrols.com
www.srbcontrols.com
Firm Type: Distributing, Manufacturing
Founded: 1985
Staff: 5
Member of: Instrument Society of America; Professional Engineers of Ontario
Products/Services/Areas of Expertise: Manufacturers distributor of measuring & monitoring instrumentation
Financial Information:
Type of Ownership: Private
Contact(s):
Blair R. Finlayson, P.Eng., General Manager & President

SRI Petro Chemical Inc.
Also Known As: SRI Inc.
11020 Neff Rd.
Port Colborne, ON L3K 5V4
905-834-5228
Fax: 905-834-0065

sri@itcanada.com
www.oilsponge.com
Firm Type: Manufacturing
Founded: 1984
EcoLogo Certified Products & Services: Oil Sponge is supplied in powder form. Zorbolite is supplied in boom, pad & snake form. These products will dramatically improve the speed, efficiency, cost & capacity of oil/fuel spill absorption
Products/Services/Areas of Expertise: Provides the latest generation of petroleum spill absorbents, bulk powder bioremediates toxic oils, booms, pads & snakes absorb oil & fuel 400% more propylene or cellulose-based products, vertical axis wind turbines
Recently Completed / Ongoing Projects: Completeion of 3 vertical axis wind turbines
Ecological Note: Oil Sponge is supplied in powder form. Zorbolite is supplied in boom, pad & snake form. These products will dramatically improve the speed, efficiency, cost & capacity of oil/fuel spill absorption
Financial Information:
Type of Ownership: Private
Revenue: $3 Million - $5 Million
Revenue Sources: 5% nationwide; 5% Municipals; 90% Private Contracts
Domestic Markets:
National
Foreign Activity:
Eastern Europe, Western Europe, The Middle East
Contact(s):
George Scott, Trading Manager, Sales
Ken Thompson, Technical Sales Representative

SRK Consulting (Canada) Inc. / SRK
Formerly: Steffen Robertson & Kirsten (North America) Inc.
Oceanic Plaza
1066 West Hastings St., 22nd Fl.
Vancouver, BC V6E 3X2
604-681-4196
Fax: 604-687-5532
info@srk.com
www.srk.com
Firm Type: Management Consulting, Engineering
Founded: 1974
Staff: 1000
Products/Services/Areas of Expertise: With 40 offices worldwide, offers consulting services & expertise in geotechnical, civil, hydrotechnical, mining & geological engineering, geology & hydrogeology, hydrology, geochemistry, waste management & permitting; due diligence, feasibility studies, & confidential internal reviews; client sectors include earth & water resources, mining & metals, exploration, construction, & government
Financial Information:
Type of Ownership: Private
Domestic Markets:
National
Foreign Activity:
Africa, Australia/New Zealand, Central America, South Africa, South America, Mexico, USA, United Kingdom
Contact(s):
Andy Barrett, Group CEO, 604-601-8402
abarrett@srk.com

Canadian Branches:
Saskatoon
#205, 2100 Airport Dr.
Saskatoon, SK S7L 6M6
306-955-4778
Fax: 306-955-4750
saskatoon@srk.com
www.na.srk.com
Mark Liskowich, Principal Consultant
mliskowich@srk.com

Sudbury
#101, 1984 Regent St. S.
Sudbury, ON P3E 5S1
705-682-3270
sudbury@srk.com
www.na.srk.com

Toronto
#2100, 25 Adelaide St. E.
Toronto, ON M5C 3A1
416-601-1445
Fax: 416-601-9046

toronto@srk.com
www.na.srk.com
Glen Cole, M.Sc., M.Eng., B.Comm., Principal Resource Geologist
gcole@srk.com
Brian Connolly, Principal Mining Engineer
bconnolly@srk.com

Yellowknife
#202, 5204 - 50th Ave.
Yellowknife, NT X1A 1E2
867-873-8670
Fax: 866-380-3458
yellowknife@srk.com
www.na.srk.com
Daniel Hewitt, B.Eng., P.Eng., Principal Consultant
dhewitt@srk.com

SRP Control Systems Ltd.
#19, 5155 Spectrum Way
Mississauga, ON L4W 5A1
905-238-2880
Fax: 905-238-9590
800-268-2605
sales@srpcontrol.com
www.srpcontrol.com
Firm Type: Distributing
Founded: 1980
Staff: 13
Products/Services/Areas of Expertise: Metering & monitoring devices; sampling equipment; flowmeters; depth/level transmitters

SRT Soil Remediation Technologies
P.O. Box 2129
Dartmouth, NS B2W 3Y2
902-434-5040
Fax: 902-434-1737
800-434-1737
conradgroup@conrads.ns.ca
www.conrads.ns.ca
Firm Type: Waste Management
Founded: 1995
Products/Services/Areas of Expertise: Treats hydrocarbon contaminated soil using environmentally friendly method enhanced bioremediation
Contact(s):
Brent Conrad, Vice-President

SSI Schaefer Systems International Ltd.
140 Nugget Ct.
Brampton, ON L6T 5H4
905-458-5399
Fax: 905-458-7951
www.ssi-schaefer.ca
Firm Type: Distributing, Manufacturing
Staff: 25
Products/Services/Areas of Expertise: Waste container systems
Domestic Markets:
National
Contact(s):
Otto F. Fasthuber, Vice-President, General Manager
Maureen Von Ameln, Sales Coordinator

Canadian Branches:
Delta
#120, 10050 River Way
Delta, BC V4G 1M9
604-953-5440
Fax: 604-953-5444

St-Laurent Branch
#205, 100, boul Alexis-Nihon
Saint-Laurent, QC H4M 2N7
514-748-9395
Fax: 514-748-8311

Stabilis Environment Inc.
#580, ch Queen Mary
Montréal, QC H3V 1A2
514-940-1230
Fax: 514-940-3435
info@stabilis.ca
www.stabilis.ca
Products/Services/Areas of Expertise: Site assessment and remediation, hazardous materials, environmental risk management, air quality, and training.

Stablex Canada Inc.
760, boul Industriel
Blainville, QC J7C 3V4
450-430-9230
Fax: 450-430-9934
www.stablex.com
Firm Type: Waste Management
Founded: 1983
Staff: 150
Quality Environmental Management System(s): 9001; ISO
Products/Services/Areas of Expertise: Inorganic hazardous waste management; waste & contaminated soil treatment & stabilization; final disposal facility
Financial Information:
Type of Ownership: Private
Revenue Sources: 5% nationwide; 5% Provincial; 90% Private Contracts
Domestic Markets:
New Brunswick, Newfoundland & Labrador, Nova Scotia, Ontario, Prince Edward Island, Québec
Foreign Activity:
USA
Markets Sought:
Central America, Eastern Europe
Contact(s):
Roger S. Gibb, Vice-President/General Manager
roger.gibb@stablex.com
Richard Dufresne, Canadian Sales Vice-President
Guy Grondin, Marketing Manager
Serge St-Laurent, Quality/Compliance

Canadian Branches:
Stablex - Ontario
460 Sugarloaf St.
Port Colborne, ON L3K 2P3
905-834-1426
Fax: 905-834-1418
jpboisvenue@qc.aibn.com
John Paul Boisvenue

International Branch(es):
Stablex
Sales
9172 Rosemary Lena Way
Alexandria, VA USA
703-799-7805
Fax: 703-799-7806
sbruni@cox.rr.com
Steven Bruni, Vice-President

Stantec Inc.
10160 - 112 St.
Edmonton, AB T5K 2L6
780-917-7000
Fax: 780-917-7330
www.stantec.com
Firm Type: Management Consulting, Engineering, Scientific/Technical Services, Waste Management
Founded: 1954
Quality Environmental Management System(s): 9001:2000
Products/Services/Areas of Expertise: Professional design & consulting services, planning, engineering, architecture, surveying/geomatics, project management, electrical engineering, environmental management, facilities planning & operations, geotechnical engineering, industrial infrastructure engineering, infrastructure managementment, land development engineering, land planning, traffic engineering, water supply & treatment, wastewater treatment & conveyance, waste management; support public & private sector clients at every stage, from initial concept & financial feasibility to project completion & beyond
Recently Completed / Ongoing Projects: Niagara Falls International Airport; Kamloops Centre for Water Quality; Nogales International Wastewater Treatment Plant; Gold Bar Wastewater Treatment Plant; Fort Hills Oil Sands Project
Financial Information:
Type of Ownership: Publicly Traded
Revenue: Greater than $5 Million
Revenue Sources: 15% nationwide; 20% Provincial; 20% Municipals; 45% Private Contracts
Domestic Markets:
National
Foreign Activity:
Africa, Asia, Caribbean, Central America, China, Mexico, USA, Vietnam
Contact(s):
Robert J. (Bob) Gomes, President & CEO
bgomes@stantec.com
Ronald P. Triffo, Chairman
Anthony P. Franceschini, Director

Canadian Branches:
Abbotsford
#500, 34077 Gladys Ave.
Abbotsford, BC V2S 2E8
604-855-7890
Fax: 604-855-7891
rcorra@stantec.com
, Richard Corra

Antigonish
2847 Highway 104
Antigonish, NS B2G 2K7
902-863-5805
Fax: 902-863-5806

Barrie
#18, 15 Cedar Pointe Dr.
Barrie, ON L4N 5R7
705-719-1813
Fax: 705-719-1814

Burlington
#203, 3430 South Service Rd.
Burlington, ON L7N 3T9
905-631-8684
Fax: 905-631-8960

Burnaby
4370 Dominion St., 5th Fl.
Burnaby, BC V5G 4L7
604-436-3014
Fax: 604-436-3752

Calgary - 10th SW
#200, 1719 - 10 Ave. SW
Calgary, AB T3C 0K1
403-245-5661
Fax: 403-244-4701

Calgary - 25th SE
Main Branch
#200, 325 - 25 St. SE
Calgary, AB T2A 7H8
403-716-8000
Fax: 403-716-8109
RMackenzie@stantec.com
Russ Mackenzie, Vice-President

Calgary - 8th SW
#300, 805 - 8th Ave. SW
Calgary, AB T2P 1H7
403-263-7113
Fax: 403-269-5245

Charlottetown
165 Maple Hills Ave.
Charlottetown, PE C1C 1N9
902-566-2866
Fax: 902-566-2004

Corner Brook
P.O. Box 772
19 Union St.
Corner Brook, NL A2H 6G7
709-639-9712
Fax: 709-639-3001

Dartmouth - Highfield Park
#102, 40 Highfield Park Dr.
Dartmouth, NS B3A 0A3
902-468-7777
Fax: 902-468-9009

Dartmouth - Wyse
#1300, 99 Wyse Rd.
Dartmouth, NS B3A 4S5
902-461-8500
Fax: 902-461-1502

Edmonton
10160 - 112 St.
Edmonton, AB T5K 2L6
780-917-7000
Fax: 780-917-7330

Fort McMurray
#212, 300 B MacKenzie Blvd.
Fort McMurray, AB T9H 4C4

Products & Services Buyer's Guide

780-791-7117
Fax: 780-743-6191

Fredericton
845 Prospect St.
Fredericton, NB E3B 2T7
506-452-7000
Fax: 506-452-0112

Guelph
#1, 70 Southgate Dr.
Guelph, ON N1G 4P5
519-836-6050
Fax: 519-836-2493
dcharlton@stantec.com
David Charlton, Principal

Hamilton
1400 Rymal Rd. East
Hamilton, ON L8W 3N9
905-385-3234
Fax: 905-385-3534
demery@stantec.com
Dave Emery, Principal

Happy Valley-Goose Bay
P.O. Box 482 C
#19, 21 Burnwood Dr.
Happy Valley - Goose Bay, NL A0P 1C0
709-896-5860
Fax: 709-896-5863

Kamloops
#300, 175 - 2nd St.
Kamloops, BC V2C 5W1
250-374-0311
Fax: 250-828-1196
bchristianson@stantec.com
Brian Christianson, Senior Associate

Kelowna
#400, 1620 Dickson Ave.
Kelowna, BC V1Y 9Y2
250-860-3225
Fax: 250-860-3367
swoodmass@stantec.com
Steve Woodmass, Principal

Kitchener
49 Frederick St.
Kitchener, ON N2H 6M7
519-579-4410
Fax: 519-579-6733
pallen@stantec.com
Paul Allen, Vice-President

Lethbridge
#290, 220 - 4 St. South
Lethbridge, AB T1J 4J7
403-329-3344
Fax: 403-328-0664
mbellamy@stantec.com
Mark Bellamy, Principal

London
171 Queens Ave., 8th Fl.
London, ON N6A 5J7
519-645-2007
Fax: 519-645-6575
rhughes@stantec.com
Rob Hughes, Senior Project Manager

Markham
West Tower
#300, 675 Cochrane Dr.
Markham, ON L3R 0B8
905-944-7777
Fax: 905-474-9889
bfrizzell@stantec.com
Brad Frizzell, Principal

Medicine Hat
641 - 4th St. South
Medicine Hat, AB T1A 0L1
403-527-7545
Fax: 403-527-5218

Mississauga
#160, 7070 Mississauga Rd.
Mississauga, ON L5N 7G2

905-858-4424
Fax: 905-858-4426
rrobinson@stantec.com
Rob Robinson, Principal

Moncton
115 Harrisville Blvd.
Moncton, NB E1H 3T3
506-857-8607
Fax: 506-858-8698

North Bay
#200, 147 McIntyre St. West
North Bay, ON P1B 2Y5
705-494-8255
Fax: 705-474-2652

Ottawa - Lancaster
#200, 2781 Lancaster Rd.
Ottawa, ON K1B 1A7
613-738-0708
Fax: 613-738-0721

Ottawa - Lapierre
1505 Lapierre Ave.
Ottawa, ON K1Z 7T1
613-722-4420
Fax: 613-722-2799
mleger@stantec.com
Maurice Leger, Vice-President

Red Deer
#600, 4808 Ross St.
Red Deer, AB T4N 1X5
403-341-3320
Fax: 403-342-0969
rwlad@stantec.com
Russell Wlad, Principal

Regina - 11th
#701, 2010 - 11th Ave.
Regina, SK S4P 0J3
306-781-6550
Fax: 305-790-3100

Regina - Rose
#300, 1919 Rose St.
Regina, SK S4P 3P1
306-781-6400
Fax: 306-781-6500
bellard@stantec.com
Bob Ellard, Vice-President

Saint John
130 Somerset St.
Saint John, NB E2K 2X4
506-634-2185
Fax: 506-634-8104

Saint-Laurent
#110, 100 boul Alexis-Nihon
Saint-Laurent, QC H4M 2N6
514-739-0708
Fax: 514-739-8499

Sidney
#11, 2042 Mills Rd.
Sidney, BC V8L 5X4
250-656-7966
Fax: 205-656-4789

St. John's - Torbay
607 Torbay Rd.
St. John's, NL A1A 4Y6
709-576-1458
Fax: 709-576-2126

St. John's - Water
#230, 434 Water St.
St. John's, NL A1C 1E2
709-738-0122
Fax: 709-738-0566

Sudbury
1760 Regent St.
Sudbury, ON P3E 3Z8
705-566-6891
Fax: 705-566-5589

Surrey
13401 - 108th Ave.
Surrey, BC V3T 5T3

604-587-8400
Fax: 604-587-8489

Sydney
#207, 201 Churchill Dr.
Membertou, NS B1S 0H1
902-564-1855
Fax: 902-564-8756

Toronto - Queen's Quay West
#420, 207 Queen's Quay West
Toronto, ON M5J 1A7
416-203-1010
Fax: 416-203-1755

Toronto - Wellington
#100, 401 Welligton St. West
Toronto, ON M5V 1E7
416-596-6686
Fax: 416-596-6680

Vancouver
#1100, 111 Dunsmuir St.
Vancouver, BC V6B 6A3
604-696-8000
Fax: 604-696-8100
mkennedy@stantec.com
Michael Kennedy, P.Eng., Principal

Victoria
#400, 655 Tyee Rd.
Victoria, BC V9A 6X5
250-388-9161
Fax: 250-388-9161

Windsor
#100, 140 Ouellette Pl.
Windsor, ON N8X 1L9
519-966-2250
Fax: 519-966-5523
stsui@stantec.com
Stephen Tsui, Principal

Winnipeg - Broadway
#603, 386 Broadway Ave.
Winnipeg, MB R3C 3R6
204-942-2505
Fax: 204-942-2548

Winnipeg - Taylor
#100, 1355 Taylor Ave.
Winnipeg, MB R3M 3Y9
204-928-8840
Fax: 204-453-9012

Winnipeg - Waverley
905 Waverley St.
Winnipeg, MB R3T 5P4
204-489-5900
Fax: 204-453-9012
ewiens@stantec.com
Eric Wiens, Principal

Yellowknife
P.O. Box 1680
5021 - 49 St.
Yellowknife, NT X1A 2N4
867-920-2216
Fax: 867-920-2278

Startco Engineering Ltd.
406 Jessop Ave.
Saskatoon, SK S7N 2S5
306-373-5505
Fax: 306-374-2245
info@startco.ca
www.startco.ca
Firm Type: Manufacturing
Founded: 1975
Products/Services/Areas of Expertise: Measuring & monitoring equipment; protective relays; electrical monitoring equipment; power distribution systems
Financial Information:
Type of Ownership: Private
Revenue Sources: 100% Private Contracts
Domestic Markets:
National
Foreign Activity:
Australia/New Zealand, Western Europe, South Africa, South America, USA, United Kingdom
Contact(s):

Garry Paulson, President

Statiflo Inc.
#203, 2175 Sheppard Ave. East
Toronto, ON M2J 1W8
416-756-2406
Fax: 416-490-6937
sales@statiflo.com
www.statiflo.net
Products/Services/Areas of Expertise: Motionless mixers used for effluent treatment
Contact(s):
Don Ewing, President

Statutory Publications
#20, 200 Vaughan St.
Winnipeg, MB R3C 1T5
204-945-3101
Fax: 204-945-7172
800-321-1203
statpub@gov.mb.ca
www.gov.mb.ca/chc/statpub
Products/Services/Areas of Expertise: Today's Statutory Publications continues a tradition which began in 1870, by providing government and the public with information on the proceedings and laws of the government of the day. As the population of Manitoba has grown, so has the government and the laws enacted by the elected officials. Correspondingly, Statutory Publications has enlarged its operations to keep pace with this growing body of material and the increased demand for information. Statutory Publications makes information available through the publication and distribution of statutes, regulations and other Legislative material, the Manitoba Gazette, the CCSM (Continuing Consolidation of the Statutes of Manitoba), Special Sets and Re-enacted Regulations

Staveley Services Canada Inc. / SSCI
Formerly: CONAM Quantum Inspection & Testing; Quantum Inspection & Testing Ltd.
916 Gateway
Burlington, ON L7L 5K7
905-632-5869
Fax: 905-632-3741
800-897-0067
www.staveleycan.com
Firm Type: Scientific/Technical Services
Founded: 1968
Staff: 45
Quality Environmental Management System(s): 17025; ISO
Products/Services/Areas of Expertise: Non-destructive testing (above-ground tank inspections, aircraft maintenance inspections, compliance inspections for airworthiness, inspections for bridges & cranes, eddy current, field & lab radiography, Level 3 services, liquid penetrant testing, magnetic particle testing, NDT improvement audits, plant maintenance safety inspections, quality control, shutdown support, ultrasonic & visual inspections); test & measurement equipment calibration (mechanical, electrical, pressure, torque, optics & RF); & coordinate measuring machine (CMM) dimensional inspection services. NDT lab located at 5305 John Lucas Dr., Burlington, ON - contact Vince Vincelli, 905-331-8810 Ext. 16
Domestic Markets:
National
Contact(s):
Blair Croswell, Manager, Metrology Services Canada
blair.croswell@staveleycan.com
Russell Davis, Manager, Key Accounts & Sales
russell.davis@staveleycan.com

Stedtnitz Maritime Technology Ltd.
P.O. Box 374
141 Duquette Rd.
Eganville, ON K0J 1T0
613-628-2064
Fax: 613-628-2265
www.affra.com
Firm Type: Manufacturing
Founded: 1984
Staff: 5
Products/Services/Areas of Expertise: Continual measuring acoustic flowmeters for rivers & open canals
Financial Information:
Type of Ownership: Private
Revenue Sources: 80% nationwide; 20% Provincial
Domestic Markets:
Alberta, Ontario
Foreign Activity:
China, Western Europe, USA, Vietnam
Markets Sought:
China, Vietnam
Contact(s):
Wolfgang Stedtnitz, President
Sigrun Stedtnitz, Vice-President

Stemmer Steel Craft Industries Limited
Formerly: SteelCraft Industries Limite; FCF-Bowers Inc.
P.O. Box 339
904 Downie Rd.
Stratford, ON N5A 6T3
519-271-4750
Fax: 519-271-1092
800-567-3223
mail@steelcraft.ca
www.clemmersteelcraft.com
Firm Type: Manufacturing
Founded: 1972
Staff: 200
Quality Environmental Management System(s): 9001
Products/Services/Areas of Expertise: Manufacturer of custom designed pressure & process vessels, industrial mixers, mix tanks & storage tanks
Financial Information:
Type of Ownership: Private
Revenue: Greater than $5 Million
Domestic Markets:
National
Foreign Activity:
USA
Markets Sought:
Central America, South America, Mexico
Contact(s):
Keith Zehr, President
J. Ken Halwachs, Vice Chair & Chief Engineer
Graham Barraclough, CFO

Sterling Power Systems
Division of Sterling Electric Motors Inc.
P.O. Box 3313 C
799 Rennie St.
Hamilton, ON L8H 7L4
905-547-2345
Fax: 905-547-2381
800-809-0330
sterpwr@iprimus.ca
www.sterlingpowersystems.com
Firm Type: Distributing, Manufacturing

Products/Services/Areas of Expertise: Variable speed drives; motors & gear reducers
Financial Information:
Type of Ownership: Private
Domestic Markets:
National

Sterling Press
458 Logy Bay Rd.
St. John's, NL A1C 5R7
709-726-7060
Fax: 709-726-8227
sundayherald@nf.sympatico.ca
Firm Type: Manufacturing
Founded: 1989
Staff: 25
Quality Environmental Management System(s): 9001
Products/Services/Areas of Expertise: Custom designed paperboard folding cartons including confectionery, food, chocolate, hardware, etc.
Domestic Markets:
National
Foreign Activity:
USA
Contact(s):
Jim Hickson, Owner
jim@sterlingpackaginginc.com

Stewart Group
EcoTech Laboratory Ltd.
10041 Dallas Dr.
Kamloops, BC V2C 5J3
250-573-5700
Fax: 250-573-4557
lynne.bruce@stewartgroupglobal.com
www.stewartgroupglobal.com
Firm Type: Scientific/Technical Services
Founded: 1976
Member of: BC Water & Wastewater Association; Canadian Association for Environmental Analytical Laboratories
Products/Services/Areas of Expertise: Water & wastewater analyses: air, soils, sludges, industrial & municipal effluents; microbiological analyses; acid/base accounting; pulp & paper industry environmental services
Financial Information:
Type of Ownership: Private
Revenue: $1.5 Million - $3 Million
Revenue Sources: 1% nationwide; 30% Municipals; 69% Private Contracts
Domestic Markets:
British Columbia
Contact(s):
Jutta Jealouse, President/CEO
John Andrew, Environmental Lab Manager
Lynne Bruce, Manager, Quality Control

STOBEC Inc.
Formerly: Canadian Chemical Exchange
900, Blondin
Sainte-Adèle, QC J8B 2R1
450-436-2525
Fax: 450-436-2332
800-561-6511
stobec@stobec.com
www.stobec.com
Firm Type: Distributing
Founded: 1977
Staff: 5
Products/Services/Areas of Expertise: Consulting services to industries in waste management; match waste users with waste generators; brokerage of surplus chemicals & raw materials; buy & resell surplus chemicals, obsolete & off-spec raw materials, out-dated chemicals, slow-moving inventories
Domestic Markets:
National
Foreign Activity:
USA
Contact(s):
Philippe LaRoche, President/CEO
laroche@stobec.com
Gabrielle Lambert, Director of Operations

StonCor Canada
95 Sunray St.
Whitby, ON L1N 9C9
905-430-3333
Fax: 905-430-3056
canada@stoncor.com
www.stoncor.com
Firm Type: Distributing, Manufacturing
Founded: 1931
Quality Environmental Management System(s): 9002
Products/Services/Areas of Expertise: Coatings & linings systems for corrosion control; fibregrate & fibreglass reinforced grating systems; seamless epoxy flooring; intumescent fireproofing
Financial Information:
Type of Ownership: Publicly Traded
Revenue Sources: 15% nationwide; 20% Provincial; 20% Municipals; 45% Private Contracts
Domestic Markets:
National,
Contact(s):
Tim Stover, Manager
Michael Ford, Engineer

Stora Enso North America
Port Hawkesbury Mill
P.O. Box 9500
Port Hawkesbury, NS B9A 1A1
902-625-2460
Fax: 902-625-1105
www.storaenso.com
Products/Services/Areas of Expertise: Produces newsprint & supercalendered papers
Domestic Markets:
National

Canadian Branches:
Montréal
1351, rue Gay-Lussac
Montréal, QC J4B 7L4

Products & Services Buyer's Guide

450-449-2304
Fax: 450-449-3213
Toronto
#101A, 2100 Ellesmere Rd.
Toronto, ON M1H 3B7
416-226-5500
Fax: 416-226-4300

Stork Bronswerk Inc.
Formerly: Stork Canada, Inc.
3755C, boul Matte
Brossard, QC J4Y 2P4
450-659-6571
Fax: 450-659-1035
800-465-7749
info.sbi@stork.com
www.storkmarine.com
Firm Type: Engineering, Manufacturing, Scientific/Technical Services
Founded: 1960
Staff: 23
Quality Environmental Management System(s): 9001; ISO
Products/Services/Areas of Expertise: Manufacturers & suppliers of heating, ventilation, air conditioning & refrigeration equipment & systems for marine & offshore applications
Financial Information:
Revenue: Greater than $5 Million
Revenue Sources: 5% nationwide; 95% Private Contracts
Domestic Markets:
National
Foreign Activity:
Central America, China, Central Europe, Western Europe, The Pacific Rim, South Africa, South America, Mexico, USA, United Kingdom, Vietnam

Stormceptor Canada Inc.
Formerly: Fibresep Limited
#2100, 2 St. Clair Ave. West
Toronto, ON M4V 1L5
416-960-9900
Fax: 416-960-5637
800-565-4801
info@stormceptor.com; info@imbriumsystems.com
www.stormceptor.com
Firm Type: Manufacturing
Founded: 1993
Staff: 15
Products/Services/Areas of Expertise: North American leader of engineered stormwater oil & sediment treatment systems, removes pollutants & ensures compliance; Stormceptor Systems treat all rainfall events & prevent scouring
Recently Completed / Ongoing Projects: Installed over 9,000 Stormceptor & 5,000 Proceptor interceptors worldwide
Financial Information:
Type of Ownership: Private
Domestic Markets:
National
Foreign Activity:
Australia/New Zealand, Western Europe, USA
Contact(s):
Scott Monteith, President
Tim Patriquin, Group Manager
Cynthia Arsenault, Marketing Communicatons Specialist

Canadian Branches:
Filamat Composites Inc. - Mississauga
880 Rangeview Rd.
Mississauga, ON L5E 1G9
905-891-3993
Fax: 905-891-3514
info@filamat.com

International Branch(es):
Stormceptor Corp.- Hydro Conduit Division
Bldg. #3
6560 Longfield Rd.
Houston, TX USA
1-832-590-5399

Strait Engineering Ltd.
#9, 298 Reeves St.
Port Hawkesbury, NS B9A 2B4
902-625-3631
Fax: 902-625-3634
strait@straiteng.com
www.straiteng.com
Firm Type: Engineering
Founded: 1983
Staff: 8
Member of: Nova Scotia Consulting Engineers Association; Nova Scotia Environmental Industry Association
Products/Services/Areas of Expertise: Wastewater management; site assessment & remediation plans; erosion control; conceptual planning; feasibility, design & construction; land development
Recently Completed / Ongoing Projects: Sewage treatment plant replacement, St. Peters; Water & sewer extension & water tower, Port Hasting; Residential Sub-division, sidewalks & I&I investigation, Eskasons
Financial Information:
Type of Ownership: Private
Revenue: $500,000 - $1.5 Million
Revenue Sources: 22% nationwide; 8% Provincial; 55% Municipals; 15% Private Contracts
Domestic Markets:
Nova Scotia
Contact(s):
H. Basil Mattie, President & Owner
Sr. Project Engineer, P.Eng., Tim, Gilfoy

Strasser Alloy Steels Ltd.
4375 Corporate Dr.
Burlington, ON L7L 5P7
905-335-6337
Fax: 905-335-9687
Products/Services/Areas of Expertise: Recycling of stainless steel & nickel
Contact(s):
Ian Deakin

Strata Environmental Ltd.
5807 - 51 Ave.
Vermilion, AB T9X 1V8
780-853-3396
Fax: 780-853-2817
darcy@strataenv.ca
www.strataenv.ca
Products/Services/Areas of Expertise: Site assessment studies; soil remediation services
Domestic Markets:
Alberta, Saskatchewan
Contact(s):
D'Arcy White, President

Strata Soil Sampling Inc.
#2, 147 West Beaver Creek Rd.
Richmond Hill, ON L4B 1C6
905-764-9304
Fax: 905-764-1124
886-778-7282
jandean@stratasoil.com
www.stratasoil.com
Firm Type: Management Consulting
Staff: 20
Products/Services/Areas of Expertise: Canada's leader in environmental & geotechnical drilling services; innovative technology from Geoprobe systems; computerized drilling applications in the field
Financial Information:
Type of Ownership: Private
Revenue: $500,000 - $1.5 Million
Revenue Sources: 10% nationwide; 5% Provincial; 5% Municipals; 80% Private Contracts
Domestic Markets:
National
Foreign Activity:
Africa, Asia, Caribbean, Central America, Central Europe, Eastern Europe, Mexico
Markets Sought:
Asia, China, Mexico, Vietnam
Contact(s):
Ron Reid, President
Jan Dean, Manager, Marketing
Johan Fenelius, Manager, Operations

Strategies for the Environment
#411, 1 Yorkdale Place
Toronto, ON M6A 3A1
416-789-3713
Fax: 416-789-7668
info@strategies4enviro.com
www.strategies4enviro.com
Products/Services/Areas of Expertise: Environmental management services; Occupational health & safety
Contact(s):
Ivana Strgacic, President

Stratem Inc.
#2810, 1155, boul René-Lévesque ouest
Montréal, QC H3B 4N4
514-393-9088
Fax: 514-393-3579
stratem@stratem.ca
www.stratem.ca
Firm Type: Management Consulting
Founded: 1988
Staff: 5
Products/Services/Areas of Expertise: Feasibility studies for recycled products, sorting centre; landfill site economic projections; small-waste water treatment facilitator; taxation information systems; business plans
Recently Completed / Ongoing Projects: Feasibility study of waste treatment plant & waste residuals plant
Financial Information:
Type of Ownership: Private
Revenue Sources: 20% nationwide; 20% Provincial; 10% Municipals; 50% Private Contracts
Domestic Markets:
Québec
Foreign Activity:
Africa, Asia, China, Western Europe, The Middle East, USA, Vietnam
Contact(s):
E. Prefontaine, President

Stratos Inc.
Formerly: Resources Futures International
#1404, One Nicholas St.
Ottawa, ON K1N 7B7
613-241-1001
Fax: 613-241-4758
mail@stratos-sts.com
www.stratos-sts.com
Firm Type: Management Consulting
Founded: 2000
Staff: 18
Member of: Canadian Environment Industry Association
Products/Services/Areas of Expertise: Corporate responsibility & sustainability; performance, measurement & assurance; corporate sustainability reporting; environmental management; stakeholder engagement; public policy to promote sustainability
Recently Completed / Ongoing Projects: Benchmark survey Stepping Forward, Corporate Sustainability Reporting in Canada; North American comparison of voluntary compliance approaches; analysis of certification programs for environmental products; advice to parliamentary review of the Canadian Environmental Protection Act; Benchmark Survey Building Confidence, Corporate Sustainability Reporting
Financial Information:
Type of Ownership: Private
Revenue: $500,000 - $1.5 Million
Domestic Markets:
National
Foreign Activity:
Western Europe
Markets Sought:
Central America, Eastern Europe
Contact(s):
Michael van Aanhout, President
Dave Fairbaird, Managing Partner

Straub Tadco Inc.
Formerly: TADCO Manufacturing Inc.
Also Known As: Straub
1239 Aerowood Dr.
Mississauga, ON L4W 1B9
905-629-9114
Fax: 905-629-9116
info@straub.ca
www.straubcouplings.com
Firm Type: Distributing, Manufacturing
Founded: 1983
Staff: 10
Products/Services/Areas of Expertise: Pipe couplings; pipe repair clamps

Financial Information:
Type of Ownership: Private
Revenue Sources: 50% Municipals; 50% Private Contracts
Domestic Markets:
National,
Contact(s):
Peter Vermes

Strum Environmental
Formerly: Strum Environmental Services Ltd.
1355 Bedford Hwy.
Bedford, NS B4A 1C5
902-835-5560
Fax: 902-835-5574
mail@strumenvironmental.com
www.strumenvironmental.com
Firm Type: Management Consulting, Scientific/Technical Services
Founded: 1995
Staff: 20
Products/Services/Areas of Expertise: Site assessment services; site remedial planning & coordination; air & water quality
Domestic Markets:
New Brunswick, Newfoundland & Labrador, Nova Scotia, Prince Edward Island
Foreign Activity:
Western Europe
Contact(s):
Bruce Strum, President

Stuart Energy USA
USA
626-440-1962
Fax: 626-744-5610
pscott@stuartenergy.com
Contact(s):
Paul Scott, Dr., Director of Projects

Canadian Branches:
Systèmes Energetiques Stuart
4162, rue Burril
Shawinigan, QC G9N 6T6

Stuart Energy USA
USA
626-440-1962
Fax: 626-744-5610
pscott@stuartenergy.com

The Electrolyser Corporation
1800, One M&T Plaza
Buffalo, NY USA

Stuart Hunt & Associates
373 Munster Ave.
Toronto, ON M8Z 3C8
780-458-0291
Fax: 780-459-0746
800-661-4591
stuarth@stuarthunt.com
www.stuarthunt.com
Firm Type: Scientific/Technical Services
Founded: 1983
Staff: 7
Member of: Canadian Radiation Protection Association
Products/Services/Areas of Expertise: Provides consulting & technical support services for users of radioactive materials
Domestic Markets:
National
Contact(s):
Stuart Hunt, Principal Consultant

SUBBOR
Also Known As: Super Blue Box Recycling Corp.
#100, 304 The East Mall
Toronto, ON M9B 8E2
416-234-1301
Fax: 416-234-8336
estrnpwr@interlog.com
home.interlog.com/~estrnpwr/index.htm
Products/Services/Areas of Expertise: The SUBBOR process is a patented Canadian biotechnology which processes unsorted Municipal Solid Wastes and produces sustainable electricity & re-usable products without the use of landfilling or incineration. 100% is recycled & 0% goes to landfill or incineration
Contact(s):
Matt Larmour, Contact

Suimon Engineering Canada Ltd.
#618, 475 Howe St.
Vancouver, BC V6E 2B3
604-669-2021
Fax: 604-669-2022
info@suimon.com
www.suimon.com
Firm Type: Management Consulting, Engineering
Founded: 1992
Staff: 4
Member of: BC Water & Wastewater Association; Water Environment Federation
Products/Services/Areas of Expertise: Strive to harmonize the link between Environmental & Construction Engineering companies in Japan & North America
Recently Completed / Ongoing Projects: BioGreen Demonstration Project, Newfoundland; engineering technology investigation, Tokyo, Japan; medium size BioGreen design & install
Financial Information:
Type of Ownership: Private
Domestic Markets:
British Columbia, Newfoundland & Labrador
Foreign Activity:
Asia

Sultech Consulting Ltd.
PO Box 14, Site 6, RR#3
Rocky Mountain House, AB T4T 2A3
403-722-3032
Firm Type: Engineering, Scientific/Technical Services
Founded: 1985
Staff: 2
Products/Services/Areas of Expertise: Feasibility & pre-feasibility studies; process evaluation & selection services; tires recycling; product development services
Financial Information:
Type of Ownership: Private
Revenue Sources: 100% Private Contracts
Domestic Markets:
Alberta, British Columbia, Saskatchewan
Foreign Activity:
Central America, Eastern Europe, Western Europe, USA
Contact(s):
Allan Soderberg, President

Sumas Environmental Services Inc.
4623 Byrne Rd.
Burnaby, BC V5J 3H6
604-682-6678
Fax: 604-687-8108
866-887-8627
www.sumas.net
Firm Type: Scientific/Technical Services, Waste Management
Founded: 1995
Staff: 12
Member of: Sumas Remediation Services Inc.
Products/Services/Areas of Expertise: A full service waste management & environmental services company; site remediation; industrial & hazardous waste management; pollution prevention; offsite treatment & disposal of contaminated soil & hazardous wastes & sludges; excavating; transportation; vacuum truck services; storage tank decommissioning; water treatment services; equipment rental; emergency response service. Corporate office & Burnaby Facility at this location
Recently Completed / Ongoing Projects: Imperial Oil & Coast Guard, Victoria BC; Imperial Oil, Agassiz, BC
Financial Information:
Type of Ownership: Private
Revenue: $1.5 Million - $3 Million
Revenue Sources: 5% nationwide; 5% Municipals; 90% Private Contracts
Domestic Markets:
Alberta, British Columbia
Contact(s):
Saeed H.S. Javadi, Ph.D., P.Eng., President
saeed@sumas.net
Alan E. Avery, Manager, BC Operations
aavery@sumas.net
Contact(s):
Dale O'Krane, Manager, Remediation Services
dale@sumas.net

Canadian Branches:
Big Valley Facility
P.O. Box 312
Big Valley, AB T0J 0G0
403-876-2220
Fax: 403-876-2332
Products/Services/Areas of Expertise: Located 4 km north of Big Valley, AB
Rick Bourgon, Customer Service Manager
rbourgon@telusplanet.net

Calgary
#303, 6707 Elbow Dr. SW
Calgary, AB T2V 0E5
403-212-0250
Fax: 403-216-1404

Kamloops Facility
1347 Kootenay Way
Kamloops, BC V2C 5L7
250-374-4151
Fax: 250-374-4128
Geoff Barker, Manager
geoff@sumas.net

Nisku Facility
1402 - 8th St.
Nisku, AB T9E 7M1
780-955-2390
Fax: 780-955-2070
Perry Surdhar, Manager, Alberta Operations
perrys@sumas.net

Vancouver - Sumas Remediation Services Inc.
#705, 1489 Marine Dr.
West Vancouver, BC V7T 1B8
604-990-8229
Fax: 604-990-8289

Summa Engineering Ltd.
6423 Northam Dr.
Mississauga, ON L4V 1J2
905-678-3388
Fax: 905-678-0444
800-811-2811
postmaster@summaeng.com
www.summaeng.com
Firm Type: Engineering, Manufacturing
Founded: 1980
Staff: 32
Member of: Ontario Pollution Control Equipment Association; Water Environment Association of Ontario; Instrument Society of America
Products/Services/Areas of Expertise: Manufacturer of custom-built control panels; supplier of SCADA system; automation maintenance services; calibration services
Recently Completed / Ongoing Projects: Ashbridges Bay WPCP; GTAA de-icing facility; City of London
Financial Information:
Type of Ownership: Private
Domestic Markets:
National
Contact(s):
Fernando Chua, Director, Engineering
Frank Cosentino, Director, Sales & Marketing

Summerhill Group
Formerly: Lourie & Love Environmental Management Consulting Inc.
#201, 1216 Yonge St.
Toronto, ON M4T 1W1
416-922-9038
Fax: 416-922-1028
info@summerhillgroup.ca
www.summerhillgroup.ca
Firm Type: Management Consulting
Founded: 1990
Staff: 30
Products/Services/Areas of Expertise: Develops & executes strategies that move the market toward better choices for consumers & the environment
Recently Completed / Ongoing Projects: Manages the operations of the Clean Air Foundation, promote consumer adoption of energy efficient, low emissions products, services & practices
Domestic Markets:
National
Contact(s):
Ian Morton, Partner

Products & Services Buyer's Guide

Summit Structures
3815 Wanuskewin Rd.
Saskatoon, SK S7P 1A4
800-615-4777
info@summitstructures.com
www.summitstructures.com
Products/Services/Areas of Expertise: Supply & installation of steel framed fabric membrane buildings in widths of up to 260' & to any length; manufacturing, design/build & turn key management services
Recently Completed / Ongoing Projects: Hatch Project, Halifax, NS; Brownville Remediation, Bond Brook, NS; Lac de Gras, NWT; Pine River Remediation, St. Louis, MI
Domestic Markets:
National
Foreign Activity:
Australia/New Zealand, Central Europe, Eastern Europe, Western Europe, Mexico, USA, Former USSR,
Contact(s):
Jim Kumpula, Sr. Vice-President
Lance Cory, Inside Sales
Sterling Mumaw, Industrial Sales

Sun Prairie Organic
Formerly: SunTerra Environmental
P.O. Box 1063
Nanton, AB T0L 1R0
403-646-5752
Fax: 403-646-5992
info@sunprairie-organic.com
Contact(s):
Neall Coulson

Sun Ross Energy Systems Ltd.
P.O. Box 9
393 Grantville Rd.
Cleveland, NS B0E 1J0
902-625-1539
Fax: 902-625-3444
info@sunrossenergy.ca
Firm Type: Engineering
Member of: Canadian Solar Industries Association
Products/Services/Areas of Expertise: Sales, service & installation - solar assist in-floor heating, domestic/commercial hotwater, R.E.D.I./Retscreen capable, complete off-grid power systems for homes & cottages.
Contact(s):
John Ross, President

Sunarc of Canada Inc.
1597 Cunard St.
Laval, QC H7S 2B4
450-686-2960
Fax: 450-686-7741
866-688-2960
www.sunarc.ca
Firm Type: Management Consulting
Products/Services/Areas of Expertise: Producers of patented liquid insulation and shade-mimicing liquid foam; Enables commerical greenhouse growers to gain better control of their environment using on-demand systems
Financial Information:
Type of Ownership: Private
Domestic Markets:
National
Foreign Activity:
USA
Contact(s):
Dror Amar, Manager, Operations
damar@sunarc.ca
International Branch(es):
USA
245 First St., 18th Fl.
Cambridge, MA USA
617-444-8772
Fax: 617-444-8405
rfield@sunarc.ca
Richard K. Field, Director, International Business Development

SunBridge Wind Power
c/o Enbridge Income Fund
3000 Fifth Ave. Place - 425 - 1st St. SW
Calgary, AB T2P 3L8
403-231-3900
Fax: 403-231-3920
www.enbridgeincomefund.com
Products/Services/Areas of Expertise: Electricity generator
Ecological Note: Renewable low-impact wind-powered electricity

Suncor Energy Products
36 York Mills Rd.
Toronto, ON M2P 2C5
416-733-7089
Fax: 416-733-2113
888-858-7242
www.suncor.com; www.suncor.ca
Products/Services/Areas of Expertise: Sunoco Ethanol-Blended gasolines are blended to control volatility & octane; computer controlled precision in-line blending is utilized to ensure a consistent quality product; environmentally-friendly Ecowash car washes; Sunoco Biodiesel fuel blends are microblended for quality & are available for commercial customers
Ecological Note: Sunoco Ethanol-Blended gasolines four octane grades: Regular 87, Plus 89.5, Supreme 92, Ultra 94.; Sunoco Ecowash car washes
Contact(s):
Elizabeth Lazarou, Manager, Brand Marketing
elazarou@suncor.com
Neil Levine, Contact
nlevine@suncor.com
Patricia Anderson, Director, Marketing
panderson@suncor.com

Suncurrent Industries Inc.
P.O. Box 6044 A
Calgary, AB T2H 2L3
403-264-2880
Fax: 403-264-2881
pliddy@suncurrent.ab.ca
www.suncurrent.ab.ca
Firm Type: Management Consulting, Financial
Staff: 4
Products/Services/Areas of Expertise: Project development, management in renewable energy technologies
Recently Completed / Ongoing Projects: Cedar Road LFG, Landfill gas to electricity; Eco efficiency community initiative, rural development, developing water distribution, MNDP programming
Financial Information:
Type of Ownership: Private
Revenue: $500,000 - $1.5 Million
Revenue Sources: 20% nationwide; 50% Municipals; 30% Private Contracts
Domestic Markets:
Alberta, British Columbia
Foreign Activity:
Caribbean
Markets Sought:
Central America
Contact(s):
Paul Liddy, President/CEO
pliddy@suncurrent.ab.ca
Geraldine Byrne, Vice-President
gbyrne@suncurrent.ab.ca

Sundog Energy Management
387 Constance Ave.
Victoria, BC V9A 6N2
250-361-9333
Fax: 250-361-9339
Firm Type: Distributing, Engineering
Founded: 1985
Products/Services/Areas of Expertise: Energy control products; window film, light reflectors, window & curtain wall systems; conducts energy management studies & general renovations; high performance window & curtain wall systems
Domestic Markets:
British Columbia
Contact(s):
William Ross, President & CEO

Sunergy Systems Ltd.
P.O. Box 70
Cremona, AB T0M 0R0
403-637-3973
Fax: 403-637-3973
sunergy@compostingtoilet.com
www.compostingtoilet.com
Firm Type: Distributing, Engineering, Scientific/Technical Services
Founded: 1977
Products/Services/Areas of Expertise: Solar energy-efficient design; building, supply & installation of Phoenix composting (waterless) toilets; mainly serves the public facility sector; solar electrical design
Domestic Markets:
National
Contact(s):
Michael Kerfoot

Sunmotor International Ltd.
5037 - 50 St.
Olds, AB T4H 1R8
403-556-8755
Fax: 403-556-7799
office@sunpump.com
www.sunpump.com
Firm Type: Distributing, Manufacturing
Staff: 2
Products/Services/Areas of Expertise: Manufactures top quality d.c. submersible pumps for operation at remote locations, battery, solar or wind powered 12 volt & 24 volt pumps. Custom design larger 90 volt systems; Sunmotor pumps can supply water at remote locations anywhere in the world, including developing countries, with no fuel or emissions; also manufactures a line of specialty air blowers which are powered directly by solar modules to provide specified volumes & pressures for aeration, soil vapor extraction & sparging
Contact(s):
Eric Jensen, M.Sc., P.Eng.

Sunoco Inc.
c/o Suncor Energy Products Inc.
36 York Mills Rd.
Toronto, ON M2P 2C5
416-733-7000
Fax: 416-733-0774
Products/Services/Areas of Expertise: Wholly owned subsidiary of Suncor Energy Inc Suncor is investing in clean, renewable energy sources; it operates two wind power projects, a third is under construction; a site near Ripley, Ontario has been confirmed as the location of a fourth wind power project.; operates an ethanol production facility in the Sarnia-Lambton region of Ontario
Contact(s):
Ian Stewart, Contact
Canadian Branches:
Sarnia refinery
P.O. Box 307
1900 River Rd.
Sarnia, ON N7T 7J3
519-337-2301
Fax: 519-332-3309

SunOpta
2838 Bovair Dr. West
Brampton, ON L7A 0H2
905-455-2528, ext 103
Fax: 905-455-5744
susan.wikenkamp@sunopta.com
www.sunopta.com
Firm Type: Engineering, Scientific/Technical Services
Founded: 1973
Products/Services/Areas of Expertise: Steam explosion for pulping
Financial Information:
Type of Ownership: Publicly Traded
Domestic Markets:
National
Foreign Activity:
Worldwide
Contact(s):
Steven R. Bromley, Chair/CEO

Sunset Solar Systems Ltd. / LRPM
Also Known As: Little River Pond Mills Division
P.O. Box 1327
301 Hwy. #2 North
Assiniboia, SK S0H 0B0
306-642-4240
Fax: 306-642-4420
888-766-3645
info@pondmill.com
www.pondmill.com

Firm Type: Distributing, Manufacturing
Founded: 1986
Staff: 5
Member of: Saskatchewan Chamber of Commerce; Saskatoon Business Association; Assiniboia Chamber of Commerce; Federation of Independent Business; Prairie Implement Manufacturers Association
Products/Services/Areas of Expertise: Manufactures Little River Pond Mills, a bio-remediation facilitator (which functions as a rotating inverse biological contractor) for remediation of open air water supplies & human & livestock wastewater facilities; manufactures Row Hoe Tree Weeder, rotary cultivator for row cropping of trees
Recently Completed / Ongoing Projects: Treatment of lakes for control of milfoil & algae growth; decrease/eliminating E-Coli & coliform bacteria to safe levels in water & wastewater
Financial Information:
Type of Ownership: Private
Revenue: $250,000 - $500,000
Revenue Sources: 2% nationwide; 2% Provincial; 40% Municipals; 56% Private Contracts
Domestic Markets:
Alberta, British Columbia, Manitoba, New Brunswick, Newfoundland & Labrador, Nova Scotia, Ontario, Prince Edward Island, Saskatchewan
Foreign Activity:
Central America, Western Europe, South America, Mexico, USA
Markets Sought:
South Africa, United Kingdom
Contact(s):
Kathleen Cameron, Manager, Environmental Management

Canadian Branches:
Saskatoon
#2, 350 - 103 St. East
Saskatoon, SK S7N 1Z1
306-373-5040
Fax: 306-373-4547
1-866-247-5277

Supervac 2000
1043, rue Renault
Saint-Jean-Chrysostome, QC G6Z 1B6
418-839-5702
Fax: 418-839-1816
info@supervac2000.com
www.supervac2000.com
Products/Services/Areas of Expertise: Vacuum trucks

Supremex Inc.
7213, rue Cordner
LaSalle, QC H8N 2J7
514-595-0555
Fax: 514-595-1112
vente@supremex.com
www.supremex.com
Firm Type: Distributing, Manufacturing
EcoLogo Certified Products & Services: Globe Green envelopes
Products/Services/Areas of Expertise: Manufacturer & distributor of envelopes, including environmentally friendly envelopes with degradable window film
Ecological Note: Globe Green envelopes
Financial Information:
Type of Ownership: Publicly Traded
Domestic Markets:
National
Foreign Activity:
USA
Contact(s):
Gilles Cyr, President/CEO

Canadian Branches:
Calgary
#213, 7710 - 5th St. SE
Calgary, AB T2H 2L9
403-258-4466
Fax: 403-252-5699
info.calgary@supremex.com

Etobicoke
400 Humberline Dr.
Etobicoke, ON M9W 5T3
416-675-9370
Fax: 416-848-8388
sales.central@supremex.com

Mississauga
5300 Tomken Rd.
Mississauga, ON L4W 1P2
905-624-4973
Fax: 905-624-1539
sales.central@supremex.com

Moncton
300 Baig Blvd.
Moncton, NB E1E 1C8
506-857-8147
Fax: 506-853-6994
vente@supremex.com

Montréal
7355, rue Notre-Dame est
Montréal, QC H1N 3S7
514-251-7355
Fax: 514-251-0610
vente@supremex.com

Edmonton
16424 - 117th Ave.
Edmonton, AB T5M 3W2
780-453-5912
Fax: 780-455-3775
info.edmonton@supremex.com

Regina
2361 2nd Ave.
Regina, SK S4R 1A5
306-359-3000
Fax: 306-525-8244
info.regina@supremex.com

Vancouver
8189 River Way
Delta, BC V4G 1G9
604-940-4488
Fax: 604-940-6511
reception.bc@supremex.com

Winnipeg
33 Plymouth St.
Winnipeg, MB R2X 2V5
204-633-2416
Fax: 204-632-7954
info.winnipeg@supremex.com

Surpac Minex (Canada) Ltd. / SSI
Formerly: Surpac Software International (Canada) Ltd.
#330, 1122 Mainland St.
Vancouver, BC V6B 5L1
604-602-1200
Fax: 604-602-1201
can@surpac.com
www.surpac.com
Firm Type: Engineering, Scientific/Technical Services
Founded: 1982
Products/Services/Areas of Expertise: Sales & support software for mining, engineering & environmental; groundwater modelling; site assessment & remediation; database; geostatic; geological modelling; engineering design; air dispersion modelling; contouring; volumes; landfill design
Financial Information:
Type of Ownership: Private
Revenue Sources: 1% nationwide; 99% Private Contracts
Domestic Markets:
National
Foreign Activity:
Worldwide
Contact(s):
Rob Ferguson, Divisional Manager, North america
robf@surpac.com

Survalent Technology Corporation
Formerly: Quindar Products Ltd.
2600 Argentia Rd.
Mississauga, ON L5N 5V4
905-826-5000
Fax: 905-826-7144
info@survalent.com
www.survalent.com
Firm Type: Manufacturing
Founded: 1964
Products/Services/Areas of Expertise: Providing advanced process automation solutions to the oil, water, power & mass transportation industries; supervisory control & data acquisition systems; computer-based master stations

Domestic Markets:
National
Foreign Activity:
USA
Contact(s):
Steve Mueller, President
Benjamin Perez, Vice-President, International Sales
Paul A. Stirpe, Sales Manager, Canada

Sustainable EDGE Ltd.
Formerly: Allen Kani Associates
#305, 250 Merton St.
Toronto, ON M4S 1B1
416-481-0400
Fax: 416-849-0148
info@s-edge.com
www.s-edge.com
Firm Type: Engineering
Founded: 1986
Staff: 8
Member of: Solar Energy Society of Canada; American Society of Heating, Refrigerating, & Air Conditioning Engineers; Windshare; Energy Action Council of Toronto
Products/Services/Areas of Expertise: Comprehensive energy & environmental engineering consulting for minimum environmental impact of buildings
Recently Completed / Ongoing Projects: Southdown Retreat Centre, Aurora; sustainable energy plan, Toronto; YMCA, Kitchener/Waterloo; Regent Park, Toronto
Financial Information:
Type of Ownership: Private
Revenue Sources: 10% nationwide; 20% Municipals; 70% Private Contracts
Domestic Markets:
Ontario
Foreign Activity:
USA
Contact(s):
Greg Allen, P.Eng., Senior Associate
greg.allen@s-edge.com
Mario Kani, P.Eng., President
mario.kani@s-edge.com
Kerry Philpott, Office Manager

Sustainable Energy Technologies Ltd. / SET
Campana Place
#500, 609 - 14th St. NW
Calgary, AB T2N 2A1
403-508-7177
Fax: 403-205-2509
info@sustainableenergy.com
www.sustainableenergy.com
Firm Type: Engineering, Manufacturing, Scientific/Technical Services
Founded: 1999
Products/Services/Areas of Expertise: Develops, manufactures & markets advanced power electronics products for the emerging alternative & renewable energy markets
Financial Information:
Type of Ownership: Publicly Traded
Contact(s):
Michael Carten, President

Sustainable Resources Management Group
6 Morning Glory Way
Toronto, ON M2H 3M2
416-493-9232
Fax: 416-493-5366
dkatz@sustainable.on.ca
www.sustainable.on.ca
Products/Services/Areas of Expertise: Professional consulting services in the areas of energy efficiency, environmental economics, and renewable energy.
Domestic Markets:
National
Contact(s):
David Katz, CEO
dkatz@sustainable.on.ca

SustaiNet Software Solutions Inc.
#900, 1111 Melville St.
Vancouver, BC V6E 3V6
604-717-4327
Fax: 604-736-9531
800-763-1686
www.sustainet.com

Firm Type: Management Consulting
Founded: 2004
Staff: 3
Products/Services/Areas of Expertise: SustaiNet is the North American distributor of environmental & stakeholder engagement information management software systems
Contact(s):
Howard Adam, President
Donna Flynn, Executive Assistant
donnaf@sustainet.com

Sutherland Excavating Ltd.
5224 Route 108 Millerton
Miramichi, NB E1V 5H7
506-622-6437
Fax: 506-627-1217
blake@nb.aibn.com
www.sutherlandexcavating.com
Contact(s):
Blake Sutherland, President

Sutherland-Schultz Inc.
P.O. Box 5006
401 Fountain St. North
Cambridge, ON N3H 5P3
519-653-4123
Fax: 519-653-3232
admin@sutherland-schultz.com
www.sutherland-schultz.com
Firm Type: Engineering, Waste Management
Founded: 1922
Member of: Mechanical Contractors Association
Quality Environmental Management System(s): 9002
Products/Services/Areas of Expertise: Control systems for water & waste treatment plants & material recovery
Financial Information:
Type of Ownership: Private
Domestic Markets:
Ontario,

Swan Hills Treatment Centre
Also Known As: SHTC
P.O. Box 1500
Swan Hills, AB T0G 2C0
780-333-4197
Fax: 780-333-4196
jom.shostak@earthtech.ca
www.shtc.ca
Firm Type: Waste Management
Founded: 1987
Staff: 110
Products/Services/Areas of Expertise: SHTC is a fully integrated hazardous waste treatment facility, the only one of its kind in Canada; principle role is in treating hazardous wastes from across Canada including PCB's, dioxins, furans & other hazardous waste compounds; is capable of achieving complete treatment of all wastes with the exception of pathological, explosive & radioactive wastes; is operated by Earth Tech Canada
Contact(s):
Jim Shostak, Plant Manager
Ken Fossey, Director, Sales & Marketing

Swish Maintenance Ltd.
P.O. Box 3000
2060 Fisher Dr.
Peterborough, ON K9J 8N4
705-745-5763
Fax: 705-745-0220
800-461-7695
peterborough@swish.ca
www.swish.ca
Firm Type: Distributing
Founded: 1956
Quality Environmental Management System(s): 9002
Products/Services/Areas of Expertise: Environmental cleaning chemicals
Financial Information:
Type of Ownership: Private
Contact(s):
Anthony Ambler, President
Canadian Branches:
Barrie Branch
526 Byrne Dr., #A
Barrie, ON L4M 6E7
705-721-4780
Fax: 705-721-9951
1-800-461-5478
barrie@swish.ca

Dartmouth Branch
#H, 81 Wright Ave.
Dartmouth, NS B3B 1B4
902-468-3756
Fax: 902-468-3721
1-800-717-9474

Kingston Branch
760 Development Dr.
Kingston, ON K7M 4W8
613-384-2410
Fax: 613-384-8908
1-800-267-2232
kingston@swish.ca

London Branch
540 Admiral Dr.
London, ON N5V 4L5
519-659-2101
Fax: 519-659-7702
1-800-265-4116
london@swish.ca

Oakville Branch
2512 Bristol Circle
Oakville, ON L6H 5S1
905-829-9366
Fax: 905-829-9375
1-800-509-3563
oakville@swish.ca

Ottawa Branch
2410 Don Reid Dr.
Ottawa, ON K1H 8P5
613-247-9550
Fax: 613-247-9553
1-800-267-5210
ottawa@swish.ca

Sudbury
705-745-5763
Fax: 705-745-0220
1-800-461-7695

Thunder Bay
581 Red River Rd.
Thunder Bay, ON P7B 1H4
807-344-6666
Fax: 807-345-4446

Timmins Branch
2031 Riverside Dr.
Timmins, ON P4N 7C3
705-360-4355
Fax: 705-360-5155
1-800-461-9823
usupply@ntl.sympatico.ca

Timmins Branch (Hollinger Ct.)
100 Waterloo Rd.
Timmins, ON P4N 4X5
705-360-5744
Fax: 705-360-5755

Wawa Branch
4 McKinley Ave.
Wawa, ON P0S 1K0
705-856-2333
Fax: 705-856-1679

Whitby Branch
500 Hopkins St.
Whitby, ON L1N 2B9
905-666-1224
Fax: 905-686-7616
1-800-263-2703
whitby@swish.ca

Winnipeg Branch
#9, 1680 Notre Dame Ave.
Winnipeg, MB R3H 1H6
204-786-8894
Fax: 204-786-4714
1-800-262-8833
winnipeg@swish.ca

International Branch(es):
Burlington
703 Pine St.
Burlington, VT USA
802-864-0585
Fax: 802-864-0365
1-800-649-4149
swishusa@swish.ca

Marcy, NY Branch
P.O. Box 275
9559 Rte. 49
Marcy, NY USA
315-735-8354
Fax: 315-735-6531
1-800-649-4149

Swiss Environment & Safety Inc. / SES
145 Evergreen Way SW
Calgary, AB T2Y 3K8
403-233-2291
Fax: 403-253-1625
jjswiss@aol.com
www.swissenvironment.com
Firm Type: Management Consulting, Scientific/Technical Services
Founded: 1995
Products/Services/Areas of Expertise: Environmental & safety consulting firm
Contact(s):
James J. Swiss, President

Sydney Environmental Resources Ltd.
P.O. Box 1028
1 Inglist St.
Sydney, NS B1P 6J7
902-567-1133
Fax: 902-564-0027
serl@serl-ns.com
Contact(s):
Brenda Tattrie, Manager

Sylvain Léger
CP 659
Sainte-Julie, QC J3E 1X9
450-649-8311
Fax: 450-649-1095
sylvainleger@sympatico.ca
Firm Type: Management Consulting

Financial Information:
Type of Ownership: Private
Revenue: Less than $50,000
Revenue Sources: 100% Private Contracts
Domestic Markets:
Ontario, Québec
Contact(s):
Sylvain Léger

Sylvametrics Consulting
4672 Cordova Bay Rd.
Victoria, BC V8X 3V7
250-658-8349
Fax: 250-658-8460
pdc@sylva.com
www.edinet.ca
Firm Type: Engineering, Scientific/Technical Services
Founded: 1985
Staff: 3
Products/Services/Areas of Expertise: Consulting services in forest resources measurement, management, information systems
Domestic Markets:
British Columbia
Foreign Activity:
The Pacific Rim
Contact(s):
David W. Ormerod, RPF, President

Symbion Consultants
#415, 70 Arthur St.
Winnipeg, MB R3B 1G7
204-982-2940
Fax: 204-982-2949
gen.symbion@shawbiz.ca
Firm Type: Management Consulting
Founded: 1986
Staff: 3

Products/Services/Areas of Expertise: Consulting services - natural resources management; environmental & social impact assessment; Environmental Assessment Review Process hearings; aboriginal land claims; commercial & domestic wildlife/fishing development planning; land/resource use evaluation
Recently Completed / Ongoing Projects: Valuation of natural resources in Tribal Council; Innu Nation review of Voisey's Bay environmental impact assessment; treaty land entitlement land selection
Financial Information:
Type of Ownership: Private
Revenue Sources: 10% nationwide; 10% Provincial; 80% Private Contracts
Domestic Markets:
National
Foreign Activity:
USA
Contact(s):
P. Larcombe, Partner
W. Wysocki, Partner

Symbiose Consultants inc
#100, 1764, boul Wilfred-Hamel ouest
Québec, QC G1N 3Y8
418-686-1955
Fax: 418-686-1963
888-686-1955
info@symbiose.ca
www.symbiose.ca
Firm Type: Scientific/Technical Services
Founded: 1995
Quality Environmental Management System(s): 9001:2008
Products/Services/Areas of Expertise: Environmental assessment & impact studies; characterization & decontamination of soil, water & air; sector studies; restoration of wildlife habitat; forest inventory, management
Financial Information:
Type of Ownership: Private
Domestic Markets:
Québec
Contact(s):
Claude Champagne, Directeur

Symplastics Ltd.
21 Tideman Dr.
Orangeville, ON L9W 3K3
519-941-5300
Fax: 519-941-4489
800-661-2387
info@symplastics.com
www.symplastics.com
Firm Type: Manufacturing
Founded: 1973
Products/Services/Areas of Expertise: Consumer, office & industry products; plastic products

Syndel International Inc.
Formerly: Syndel Laboratories Ltd.
9211 Shaughnessy St.
Vancouver, BC V6P 6R5
604-321-7131
Fax: 604-321-3900
800-663-2232
info@syndel.com
www.syndel.com
Firm Type: Manufacturing, Scientific/Technical Services
Founded: 1977
Products/Services/Areas of Expertise: Aquaculture chemicals & pharmaceutical products
Domestic Markets:
National
Contact(s):
Steven Becker, CEO

Canadian Branches:
New Brunswick Office
#2, 4 Magaguadavic Dr.
St George, NB E0G 2Y0
506-755-8982
Fax: 506-755-3599
1-800-830-4885

International Branch(es):
Syndel Asia
Subang New Village
62 Jalan ID, 40000 Shah Alam
Selangor Darul Ehsan Malaysia

603-746-8541
Fax: 603-746-8542
Gopinath Nagaraj

Synex International Inc.
Formerly: Synex Systems Corp.
1444 Alberni St., 4th Fl.
Vancouver, BC V6G 2Z4
604-688-8271
Fax: 604-688-1286
sigma@synex.com
www.synex.com
Products/Services/Areas of Expertise: Water & hydraulic modelling software; software development with client/sewer technology
Contact(s):
Alan Stephens, Chair
Greg Sunell, President

System Ecotechnologies Inc.
#222, 111 Research Dr.
Saskatoon, SK S7N 3R2
306-955-0872
Fax: 306-975-7011
lakshmang@innovationplace.com
Firm Type: Scientific/Technical Services
Founded: 1987
Staff: 4
Products/Services/Areas of Expertise: Provides expertise in design, implementation & monitoring engineered wetland treatment systems for municipal, agricultural, industrial & mining effluents; in-house laboratory facilities to conduct client-driven R&D work, development of innovative treatment processes, production of value-added products from agricultural & forest wastes; R&D for environmental solutions; technology development
Recently Completed / Ongoing Projects: Treatment systems for distilleries, tanneries & textile mills in India; presently searching for partnering alliances; team leader for United Nations projects
Financial Information:
Revenue Sources: 30% Municipals; 70% Private Contracts
Domestic Markets:
Alberta, British Columbia, New Brunswick, Saskatchewan
Foreign Activity:
Asia, Central America, The Pacific Rim, South America, USA
Markets Sought:
The Middle East
Contact(s):
G. Lakshman, President

Systems Plus
1457 Gingerich Rd.
Baden, ON N3A 3J7
519-634-5708
Fax: 519-634-5779
800-604-3645
sales@splus.ca
www.splus.ca
Firm Type: Distributing, Manufacturing
Founded: 1984
Staff: 24
Products/Services/Areas of Expertise: Laboratory equipment & supplies; sampling containers & accessories; precleaned containers
Financial Information:
Type of Ownership: Private
Domestic Markets:
National
Foreign Activity:
USA
Markets Sought:
Mexico
Contact(s):
Garry Ruttan, President/CEO
Chris Morton, General Manager

T-G Burgmann
3225 Mainway Dr.
Burlington, ON L7M 1A6
905-335-1440
Fax: 905-335-4033
800-863-4001
info@tgburgmann.com
www.tgburgmann.com
Firm Type: Distributing, Manufacturing
Founded: 1916

Staff: 100
Quality Environmental Management System(s): 9001
Products/Services/Areas of Expertise: Products & application advice for sealing technology, fluids & gases; mechanical seals; expansion joints; hydraulic & pneumatic seals; packing; magnetic couplings; dry gas seals
Financial Information:
Type of Ownership: Private
Domestic Markets:
National,
Contact(s):
Al Marques, Division Manager

Canadian Branches:
Edmonton Branch
3456 - 78 Ave. NW
Edmonton, AB T6B 2X9
780-434-4928
Fax: 780-438-0658
info@tgburgmann.com

T. Harris Environmental Management Inc. / THEM Gestion environnementale T. Harris inc.
Formerly: T. Harris Partnership Inc./Fisher Lovegrove Environmental
#101, 93 Skyway Ave.
Toronto, ON M9W 6N6
416-679-8914
Fax: 416-679-8915
888-275-8436
info@tharris.ca
www.tharris.ca
Firm Type: Management Consulting, Scientific/Technical Services
Founded: 1979
Staff: 35
Products/Services/Areas of Expertise: Detailed facility surveys for hazardous materials; toxic mould assessments; site inspection & air monitoring programs; asbestos & lead laboratory testing services; worker exposure & health risk assessments; heat stress & noise level assessments; indoor air quality & ventilation system assessments; project management programs; training seminars; plant audits & decommissioning; environmental & regulatory audits; Phase I, II & III environmental site assessments; underground storage tank evaluations & environmental risk management programs; indoor air quality assessment; toxic mould assessments
Recently Completed / Ongoing Projects: Toxic mould assessments of various educational, hospital & commercial facilities; Numerous ESA projects (I, II, III) for ICI facilities
Financial Information:
Type of Ownership: Private
Domestic Markets:
National
Contact(s):
Trevor J. Harris, Chair & CEO
John C. Fisher, Chief Operating Officer
Richard Quenneville, Director, Occupational Hygiene

Canadian Branches:
London
#100, 931 Commissioners Rd. East
London, ON N5Z 3H9
519-685-9048
Fax: 519-685-1042
dpenny@tharris.ca
Dave Penny

Montréal
#100, 5, place du Commerce
Brossard, QC J4W 3E7
450-465-9990
Fax: 450-465-4494
ygagnon@tharris.ca
Yrieix Gagnon

Ottawa
#305, 19 Fairmont Ave.
Ottawa, ON K1Y 1X4
613-725-1554
Fax: 613-725-5147
rnelligan@tharris.ca
Richard Nelligan

T.D. Rooke Associates Ltd.
#201, 20 Floral Pkwy.
Concord, ON L4K 4R1

Products & Services Buyer's Guide

905-326-5666
Fax: 905-326-5667
pgreen@tdrooke.com
www.tdrooke.com
Firm Type: Distributing, Engineering, Manufacturing
Founded: 1979
Products/Services/Areas of Expertise: Liquids-solids separation equipment; gravity screens, filter presses, fluids mixing, solids suspension; mixers & agitators, aeration equipment, metering pumps; heat exchangers; demineralization; fiberglass storage tanks; blowers; complete treatment systems; centrifugal pumps
Financial Information:
Type of Ownership: Private
Revenue Sources: 35% Municipals; 65% Private Contracts

T.D. ThermoDesign / TDV
Formerly: T.D. Enviro Inc.
P.O. Box 5557 L
Edmonton, AB T6C 4E9
780-440-6064
Fax: 780-440-1657
www.thermodesign.com
Firm Type: Engineering, Scientific/Technical Services
Founded: 1993
Staff: 10
Products/Services/Areas of Expertise: Designing & supplying equipment for some of the worlds harshest climatic conditions & most demanding environments; design & manufacture of production modules for installation on fixed offshore production platforms & floating production, storage & off loading (FPSO) vessels; equipment for air, railroad, boat & barge as well as truck transportation
Financial Information:
Type of Ownership: Private
Domestic Markets:
Alberta, British Columbia, Saskatchewan
Foreign Activity:
Central America, The Pacific Rim, South America
Contact(s):
Tony Rojek, President
Les Ignasiak, Director, Technology
Jim Kramer, Manager

Taco Canada Ltd.
6180 Ordan Dr.
Mississauga, ON L5T 2B3
905-564-9422
Fax: 905-564-9436
www.taco-hvac.com
Firm Type: Manufacturing
Founded: 1930
Staff: 13
Quality Environmental Management System(s): 9001
Products/Services/Areas of Expertise: Centrifugal pumps; pressure storage tanks; shell & tube exchangers; heating/cooling system controls
Financial Information:
Type of Ownership: Private
Revenue: Greater than $5 Million
Revenue Sources: 15% nationwide; 5% Provincial; 5% Municipals; 75% Private Contracts
Domestic Markets:
National
Contact(s):
John White, President

Talkie Tooter Canada Ltd.
#101, 7188 Progress Way
Delta, BC V4G 1M6
604-946-8276
Fax: 604-946-8241
info@talkietooter.ca
www.talkietooter.ca
Firm Type: Manufacturing
Founded: 1973
Products/Services/Areas of Expertise: Design of custom portable radio systems; industrial, waterproof portable radios, radio control systems, radio remote detonators
Financial Information:
Type of Ownership: Private
Revenue Sources: 1% Municipals; 99% Private Contracts
Domestic Markets:
National
Foreign Activity:
Australia/New Zealand, South America, USA

Markets Sought:
Former USSR
Contact(s):
Pete Ruese, General Manager
Wally Weir, Contact, Sales/Marketing

Talon Projects Inc.
Formerly: Talon Geotechnical Engineering Inc
P.O. Box C10
RR#1, Group 20
Dufresne, MB R0A 0J0
866-667-3905
info@talongeotech.com
www.talongeotech.com
Products/Services/Areas of Expertise: Geotechnical investigations & characterizations for landfills, lagoons, buildings; geotechnical design, mitigation & remedial action; environmental audits; environmental impact assessments
Contact(s):
Wayne Pitura, President, 204/261-4488 Fax: 204/275-2428

Tang G. Lee Architect
Environmental Design, University of Calg
2500 University Dr. NW
Calgary, AB T2N 1N4
403-220-6608
lee@ucalgary.ca
Firm Type: Engineering, Scientific/Technical Services
Founded: 1979
Staff: 5
Member of: Royal Architectural Institute of Canada; Alberta Society of Environmental Housing & Health; Canadian Commission on Construction Material Evaluation; Alberta Building Envelope Council
Products/Services/Areas of Expertise: Designs environmentally clean facilities, houses, apartments & medical clinics; indoor air quality investigations, environmental health, courses & seminars on indoor contaminants; design & manufacturing of high efficiency air filtration & make-up air units
Domestic Markets:
Alberta, British Columbia, Manitoba, Ontario, Prince Edward Island, Saskatchewan
Contact(s):
Tang G. Lee, Professor of Architecture, Environmental Design

Tank-Craft Ltd.
Also Known As: Can-Jet Ltd.
2063 Oxford St. East
London, ON N5V 2Z7
519-451-4210
Fax: 519-451-8120
Firm Type: Manufacturing
Founded: 1954
Staff: 6
Products/Services/Areas of Expertise: Sewage treatment equipment; hose & cable reels; access covers
Contact(s):
Evan March, General Manager

Tankless Water Heater Company
#2, 1335 Dalhousie Dr.
Kamloops, BC V2C 5P6
250-374-2690
Fax: 250-374-2692
866-376-2690
info@gotankless.com
www.gotankless.com
Firm Type: Manufacturing
Founded: 1998
EcoLogo Certified Products & Services: Domestic water heaters
Products/Services/Areas of Expertise: Domestic & industrial tankless hot water heaters
Ecological Note: Domestic water heaters
Domestic Markets:
National
Foreign Activity:
USA
Contact(s):
Mark J. Morabito, President

Tankman
Division of ETT Chemicals Inc.
108 Parkview Way SE
Calgary, AB T2J 4M8
403-271-4525
Fax: 403-271-5623

Products/Services/Areas of Expertise: Storage equipment
Contact(s):
John S. Jochmann, CEO

Tanknology Canada Inc.
#8, 3455 Fairview St.
Burlington, ON L7N 2R4
905-681-5542
Fax: 905-681-6473
800-465-1577
info@tanknology.ca
www.tanknology.ca
Firm Type: Scientific/Technical Services
Founded: 1988
Staff: 25
Member of: Canadian Environment Industry Association
Products/Services/Areas of Expertise: Leak testing & management of storage tank systems, using precision leak test technologies & statistical inventory reconciliation
Financial Information:
Type of Ownership: Publicly Traded
Revenue Sources: 10% nationwide; 5% Provincial; 5% Municipals; 80% Private Contracts
Domestic Markets:
National
Foreign Activity:
Asia, Australia/New Zealand, Western Europe, South America, Mexico, USA,
Contact(s):
Peter Sutherland, President
Delaina Legere, Sales
Canadian Branches:
Montréal
#301, 560, boul Henri Bourassa ouest
Montréal, QC H3L 1P4
Frank Hattat

Calgary
#19, 2000 Pegasus Rd. NE
Calgary, AB T2E 8K7
403-262-2241
Fax: 403-269-5509
1-800-668-7885

Tanks-A-Lot Ltd.
1810 Yellowhead Trail NE
Edmonton, AB T6S 1B4
780-472-8265
Fax: 780-478-5699
800-661-5667
info@tanks-a-lot.com
www.tanks-a-lot.com
Firm Type: Distributing, Engineering, Manufacturing, Waste Management
Founded: 1982
Products/Services/Areas of Expertise: Sewage treatment equipment; composting odorless outdoor toilet tanks; oil/water separators; septic tanks; aquatic plants for sewage treatment; wastewater treatment plants; water cisterns; holding tanks & sumps
Financial Information:
Type of Ownership: Private
Contact(s):
Tom Welch, General Manager

International Branch(es):
Mucho Tanque S.A.
Apdo Postal 1736-7050
Cartago Costa Ri
506-573-8181
Fax: 506-573-8484
tanques@sol.racsa.co.cr

TankTek Environmental Services Ltd.
16 Knox St.
Acton, ON L7J 1C7
519-853-1819
Fax: 519-853-0064
877-789-6224
inquiries@tanktek.com
www.tanktek.com
Firm Type: Engineering
Founded: 1999
Member of: Professional Engineers Ontario, Ontario Petroleum Contractors Association, Canadian Federation of Independent Business

Products/Services/Areas of Expertise: Precision leak detection testing of storage tanks & lines, tank removals, impact assessments & remediation
Financial Information:
Type of Ownership: Private
Revenue: $250,000 - $500,000
Domestic Markets:
Ontario
Contact(s):
Thomas Burt, General Manager
tom.burt@tanktek.com

Tansley Associates Environmental Services
#3, 1470 - 28th St. NE
Calgary, AB T2A 7W6
403-569-8566
Fax: 403-207-5110
888-213-5838
info@tansleyaes.com
www.tansleyaes.com
Firm Type: Scientific/Technical Services
Staff: 36
Products/Services/Areas of Expertise: Oil field environmental service company; drillings fluid disposal; oil field waste disposal; reclamation & remediation; chloride soil washing; biological services; geo-services
Financial Information:
Type of Ownership: Private
Revenue Sources: 100% Private Contracts
Domestic Markets:
Alberta, British Columbia, Saskatchewan
Contact(s):
Mark G. Tansley, President
Kris Mikkelborg, Vice President
Jason Sikora, Manager, Sales
Norman Oliver, Manager, Operations, T-Line Division
Renee Heshka, Senior Manager, Operations, Biological and Soil Sciences Division

Tarandus Associates Limited
#24, 18 Regan Rd.
Brampton, ON L7A 1C2
905-840-6563
Fax: 905-840-6128
info@tarandus.ca
www.tarandus.ca
Firm Type: Scientific/Technical Services
Founded: 1982
Staff: 5
Products/Services/Areas of Expertise: Provides comprehensive environmental consulting services to industry, governments, special-interest groups & the public sector; services include impact assessments, environmental planning, fisheries/habitat studies & biological surveys, waterfront studies, wetland studies, contaminant studies, statistical analyses, baseline surveys, waste-site assessments & project management
Recently Completed / Ongoing Projects: Environmental monitoring, Darlington Nuclear Generating Station; design, construction, monitoring & assessment of wetland/fish habitat, Jordan Harbour; fisheries studies for the upgrading of the Queen Elizabeth Way (QEW), near St. Catharines, Ont.; Interim Waste Authority site search for a proposed landfill site in Peel Region, Ont.
Domestic Markets:
National
Foreign Activity:
Africa, Central America, The Pacific Rim, South America

Target Recycling Inc.
3312 Smiley Rd., RR#1
Chemainus, BC V0R 1K4
250-246-9886
Fax: 250-246-4403
office@targetrecycling.bc.ca
www.targetrecycling.bc.ca
Firm Type: Manufacturing, Scientific/Technical Services, Waste Management
Founded: 1991
Staff: 15
Member of: Explosives Engineers Society; North American Recycled Rubber Association; Scrap Rubber Recycling Association
Products/Services/Areas of Expertise: Tire derived products; product development, market development, manufacturers systems; collection systems; energy recovery systems

Foreign Activity:
USA,
Contact(s):
Anthony P. Stock, President
Lee Chapman, Research & Development
Kerri Keller, Administration

Taylor Mazier Associates
RR#3
St Andrews, NS B0H 1X0
902-783-2129
btaylor@auracom.com
Firm Type: Scientific/Technical Services
Founded: 1996
Staff: 1
Member of: Nova Scotia Environmental Industry Association; Alberta Society of Professional Biologists; B.C. College of Applied Biology
Products/Services/Areas of Expertise: Analysis & interpretation of biological, chemical & environmental data, covering water quality, aquatic biology, ecotoxicology, soil biology, environmental chemistry & conservation
Recently Completed / Ongoing Projects: Site assessment of forests, rural lakes in NS; literature review on effects of multiple stressors on aquatic ecosystems; vegetation/rare plant survey at road crossing
Financial Information:
Type of Ownership: Private
Revenue: Less than $50,000
Revenue Sources: 100% Private Contracts
Domestic Markets:
National
Contact(s):
Barry Taylor, President

Taylor Munro Energy Systems Inc.
#11, 7157 Honeyman St.
Delta, BC V4G 1E2
604-946-4433
Fax: 604-946-3804
info@taylormunro.com
www.taylormunro.com
Firm Type: Distributing, Manufacturing, Scientific/Technical Services
Founded: 1995
Staff: 10
Member of: Canadian Solar Industries Association; Solar Energy Society of Canada; Better Business Bureau
Products/Services/Areas of Expertise: Solar water heating, design, distribution, installation, consulting, repair, renewable energy education, research
Recently Completed / Ongoing Projects: YVR; Hyde Creek
Financial Information:
Type of Ownership: Private
Revenue: $500,000 - $1.5 Million
Domestic Markets:
Alberta, British Columbia, Manitoba, Ontario, Saskatchewan, Yukon Territory
Foreign Activity:
USA
Contact(s):
Joe Thwaites, President
Morgan McDonald, Environmental Contact

TEAM-1 Environmental Services Inc.
Also Known As: TEAM-1 Emergency Services
1650 Upper Ottawa St.
Hamilton, ON L8W 3P2
905-383-5550
Fax: 905-574-0492
800-327-7455
www.team-1.com
Firm Type: Engineering, Waste Management
Founded: 1995
Staff: 50
Quality Environmental Management System(s): 14001
Products/Services/Areas of Expertise: Provides 24/7 emergency response to any spill or dangerous goods occurrence; confined space entry/rescue; mobile lab services for E/R & recovery work; contracted by police & fire departments for highend specialized services
Recently Completed / Ongoing Projects: Mobile analytical lab services & state of the art decontamination units
Financial Information:
Type of Ownership: Private
Revenue: Greater than $5 Million

Revenue Sources: 5% nationwide; 5% Provincial; 10% Municipals; 80% Private Contracts
Domestic Markets:
National
Foreign Activity:
USA
Contact(s):
Scott Connor, Manager, Training Services
scott@team-1.com
Bill Abbott, Manager, Sales
bill@team-1.com
Mitchell Gibbs, Manager, Emergency Services
mitch@team-1.com

Tech Sales Co.
#220, 10520 Yonge St., Unit 35B
Richmond Hill, ON L4C 3C7
416-410-1313
www.tech-sales.com
Firm Type: Distributing
Founded: 1983
Staff: 5
Products/Services/Areas of Expertise: Compressed air saving systems; oil skimmers; non-hazardous chemicals; oil recycling
Financial Information:
Type of Ownership: Private
Revenue: $3 Million - $5 Million
Revenue Sources: 100% Private Contracts
Domestic Markets:
National
Foreign Activity:
Asia, Central Europe, Eastern Europe, Western Europe, Mexico, USA
Contact(s):
Les Rapchak, President
lesr@tech-sales.com
Robert Borja, Inside Marketing

Canadian Branches:
British Columbia, Alberta & Saskatchewan
2959 Pasture Circle
Coquitlam, BC V3C 2C3
604-552-3131
Fax: 604-552-6996
lylef@tech-sales.com
Lyle Faulks

Techint Goodfellow Technologies Inc. / TGTI
Formerly: Stantec Global Technologies Ltd.; Goodfellow Consultants Inc.
#170, 7070 Mississauga Rd.
Mississauga, ON L5N 7G2
905-567-3030
Fax: 905-567-3899
800-567-3030
info@tgti.ca
www.techint-technologies.com
Firm Type: Engineering, Information Technology
Founded: 2004
Staff: 24
Member of: Asssociation for Iron & Steel Technology; American Iron & Steel Institute; South East Asia Iron & Steel Institute; Steel Manufacturers Association
Products/Services/Areas of Expertise: Products: Goodfellow EFSOP Process Control System, installation & commissioning; EAF steelmaking; high combustion furnace processes
Financial Information:
Type of Ownership: Private
Revenue: $1.5 Million - $3 Million
Revenue Sources: 100% Private Contracts
Domestic Markets:
National
Foreign Activity:
Western Europe, The Pacific Rim, Mexico, USA
Markets Sought:
Eastern Europe, Western Europe, South America,
Contact(s):
Howard D. Goodfellow, Ph.D., P.Eng., President
Eduardo Cordsva, Vice-President, Sales & Marketing
Evan Evenson, Principal

Technel Engineering Inc.
#2, 60 Marycroft Ave.
Woodbridge, ON L4L 5Y5
905-851-4244
Fax: 905-851-5743
888-882-1172

Products & Services Buyer's Guide

info@technel.com
www.technel.com
Firm Type: Distributing
Founded: 1986
Products/Services/Areas of Expertise: Calibration standards; pressure & position transducers; instrumentation; data acquisition
Contact(s):
Carlo Rea, Owner

Technisol Environnement
325, rue de L'Espinay
Québec, QC G1L 2J2
418-647-1402
Fax: 418-648-9288
800-265-1402
plefrancois@groupetechnisol.com
www.groupetechnisol.com
Firm Type: Engineering, Scientific/Technical Services
Founded: 1982
Staff: 50
Member of: Réseau Environnement; Association pour la prévention de la contamination de l'air et du sol (APCAS); Association québécoise de vérification environnementale (AQVE); Centre patronal de l'environnement du Québec (CPEQ)
Products/Services/Areas of Expertise: Services as: consultants, project managers or contractors; environmental site assessment, site remediation, environmental management systems & various other environmental expertise
Activities: Environmental consulting services; Phase I, II, III environmental site assessments (ESA's); environmental impact studies; environmental audits; environmental rehabilitation of contaminated sites; contaminated groundwater mobile unit treatment facility
Recently Completed / Ongoing Projects: Environmental ESA's of 225 navigational aid sites; introduction of an EMS & confirmation of the system with ISO 14001 standards at a landing gear manufacture plant; site remediation of bulk plans; various sites assessment & characterization; industrial remediation strategies; market centres remedial work supervision; legal/technical expertises
Financial Information:
Type of Ownership: Private
Revenue: Greater than $5 Million
Revenue Sources: 10% nationwide; 5% Provincial; 5% Municipals; 80% Private Contracts
Domestic Markets:
New Brunswick, Ontario, Québec
Foreign Activity:
USA
Markets Sought:
USA
Contact(s):
Paul Lefrançois, President
Andre Renfer, Asst. Manager
Pierre Lupien, Asst. Manager
plupien@groupetechnisol.com
Christian Leblanc, Asst. Manager
cleblanc@groupetechnisol.com

Canadian Branches:
Longueuil
#120, 825, boul Guimond
Longueuil, QC J4G 1M1
450-646-2535
Fax: 450-646-1774
longueuil@groupetechnisol.com
Pierre Lupien

Montréal
11450 rue Hamon
Montréal, QC H3M 3A3
514-331-1134
Fax: 514-331-9091
montreal@groupetechnisol.com
Marc Desaulniers

New Brunswick
23 Boom Rd., #F
Atholville, NB E3N 4E8
506-759-9678
Fax: 506-753-4188
nb@groupetechnisol.com
Sylvain Comeau

Rimouski
561, rue Lausanne
Rimouski, QC G5L 4A7
418-723-1144
Fax: 418-722-4691
rimouski@groupetechnisol.com
Alexandre Coulombe

Techstar Plastics Inc.
15400 Old Simcoe Rd.
Port Perry, ON L9L 1L8
905-985-8479
Fax: 905-985-0265
800-263-7943
sales@techstarplastics.com
www.techstarplastics.com
Firm Type: Distributing, Manufacturing
Founded: 1978
Quality Environmental Management System(s): 9001
Products/Services/Areas of Expertise: Plastic carts for waste paper & recyclable materials; recycling bins, composters, source separation containers

Teckn-O-Laser
2101N, rue Nobel
Sainte-Julie, QC J3E 1Z8
450-922-0555
Fax: 450-922-0707
800-361-1539
marketing@teckn-o-laser.com
www.teckn-o-laser.com
Firm Type: Manufacturing
Founded: 1988
Staff: 220
Member of: Canadian Imaging Products Remanufacturers Association; International Imaging Technology Council
Quality Environmental Management System(s): 9002
Products/Services/Areas of Expertise: Remanufactured toner cartridges for laser printers, fax machines & copiers; collect & recondition used toner cartridges. Sales offices in Toronto, Quebec City & Sainte-Julie; distribution centres in Memphis, TN
Financial Information:
Type of Ownership: Private
Revenue: Greater than $5 Million
Revenue Sources: 90% Private Contracts
Domestic Markets:
National
Foreign Activity:
Western Europe, The Middle East, South America, USA,
Contact(s):
Yvon Leveillé, President
Alain Lachambre, Executive Vice-President, Sales

Canadian Branches:
Ontario Branch
850 Magnetic Dr.
North York, ON M3J 2C4
416-663-8494
Fax: 416-663-2289

Québec Branch
1841B, boul Hamel est
Québec, QC G1N 3Y9
418-688-1523
Fax: 418-688-4281

Tecsult Inc.
Also Known As: Tecsult International Inc.
85, rue Ste-Catherine ouest
Montréal, QC H2X 3P4
514-287-8500
Fax: 514-287-8643
tecsult@tecsult.com
www.tecsult.com
Firm Type: Engineering
Founded: 1961
Staff: 1100
Member of: Water Environment Federation; American Water Works Association
Quality Environmental Management System(s): 9001
Products/Services/Areas of Expertise: Services offered include expertise, market analyses, risk analyses, technico-economic studies, arbitration, preliminary studies, feasibility studies, engineering, procurement, supervision of construction, project management & personnel training; branch offices in 20 countries. Tecsult Environnement Inc. is a wholly-owned subsidiary
Recently Completed / Ongoing Projects: Provided technical assistance to fight desertification, Niger; flood control, irrigation & agricultural studies in the Baral River basin, Bangladesh; contaminated site characterization & decontamination, Ile aux Chats; study of fauna & habitat in wetlands, James Bay
Domestic Markets:
Newfoundland & Labrador, Nova Scotia, Northwest Territories, Ontario, Québec
Foreign Activity:
Worldwide
Contact(s):
Pierre Asselin, Eng., Vice-President, Infrastructures, Transportation and Urban Engineering
Luc Benoît, P.Eng., President & CEO

Canadian Branches:
Baie-Comeau Branch
857, rue Puyjalon
Baie-Comeau, QC G5C 1N3
418-589-2345
Fax: 418-589-2322

Châteauguay
301, boul Industriel
Châteauguay, QC J6J 4Z2
450-699-9974
Fax: 450-691-7929

Gatineau Branch
#204, boul Saint-Joseph
Gatineau, QC J8Y 4A1
819-777-1630
Fax: 819-777-2047

Halifax-Dartmouth Branch
#1100, 99 Wyse Rd.
Dartmouth, NS B3A 4S5
902-461-6600
Fax: 902-461-6601

Laval Branch
#200, 1, Place Laval
Montréal, QC H7N 1A1
450-967-1260
Fax: 450-629-8737

Lévis Branch
415, av 3
Lévis, QC G6W 5M6
418-834-7878
Fax: 418-834-7997

Montréal Branch
#1200, 2001, rue University
Montréal, QC H3A 2A6
514-287-8500
Fax: 514-282-2808

Notre-Dame-du-Lac
#10, 3, rue de l'Église
Notre-Dame-du-Lac, QC G0L 1X0
418-899-0110
Fax: 418-899-0210

Ottawa Branch
#1111, 151 Slater St.
Ottawa, ON K1P 5H3
613-232-1563
Fax: 613-232-3424

Québec Branch
4700, boul Wilfrid-Hamel
Québec, QC G1P 2J9
418-871-2444
Fax: 418-871-5868

Rivière-du-Loup Branch
2, rue de la Cour
Rivière-du-Loup, QC G5R 1J2
418-863-6457
Fax: 418-871-9898

Saint-Bruno Branch
#102, 63, ch de la Rabastalière Ouest
St-Bruno-de-Montarville, QC J3V 1Y7
450-461-1616
Fax: 450-461-3297

St-Jérôme Branch
480, rue St-Georges
Saint-Jérôme, QC J7Z 5B3
450-431-1261
Fax: 450-431-1225

Tekmar Control Systems Ltd.
5100 Silver Star Rd.
Vernon, BC V1B 3K4
250-545-7749
Fax: 250-545-0650
www.tekmarcontrols.com
Firm Type: Manufacturing
Founded: 1984
Products/Services/Areas of Expertise: Heating, ventilating & air conditioning equipment
Financial Information:
Type of Ownership: Private
Revenue Sources: 100% Private Contracts
Domestic Markets:
National
Foreign Activity:
Australia/New Zealand, China, Western Europe, USA, Vietnam
Contact(s):
Don Gibbs, President
Steffen Knuever, Vice-President & Sales & Marketing Manager

Teknion Corporation
Also Known As: Teknion Furniture Systems
1150 Flint Rd.
Toronto, ON M3J 2J5
416-661-3370
Fax: 416-661-4586
info.can@teknion.com
www.teknion.com
Firm Type: Distributing, Manufacturing
Founded: 1983
Staff: 1000
EcoLogo Certified Products & Services: Office furniture
Products/Services/Areas of Expertise: Design for Environment (DfE) guidelines into product development processes. DfE principles enable evaluation based upon reducing a product's impact on the environment by considering its entire life cycle; locations across Canada, check url
Ecological Note: Office furniture
Contact(s):
Sholem Prason, Contact

Tekran Canada
R&D Facility
330 Nantucket Blvd.
Toronto, ON M1P 2P4
416-449-3084
fhs@tekran.com
tekran.com
Firm Type: Manufacturing
Founded: 1989
Staff: 5
Products/Services/Areas of Expertise: Mercury ultra-trace monitoring equipment
Domestic Markets:
National
Foreign Activity:
Asia, South America
Contact(s):
Frank Schaedlich, President
Dan Schneeberger, Sec.-Treas.

Telamode
P.O. Box 280
15036 Colonial Dr.
Ingleside, ON K0C 1M0
613-537-2424
Fax: 613-537-8444
800-263-2951
telamode@telamode.com
www.telamode.on.ca
Products/Services/Areas of Expertise: Canadian made septic tank additives composed of 100% naturally occurring, non-pathogenic microorganisms, selected for their abilities to digest detergents, paper, oil, grease & hydrocarbons as well as a wide range of organic drain line deposits & blockages, designed for residential & commercial septic systems, grease traps, drain lines & sewage pits
Ecological Note: Manufacturer & formulator of biological septic tank additives SEPTI-ZONE, septic tank cleaner; RC-4, septic tank & drain field cleaner; tela-CHEM, drain line, grease digester; tel-ax MSB, all purpose odour controller & waste degrader
Domestic Markets:
National
Markets Sought:
USA
Contact(s):
Al Millward, Contact

Teleflex Canada Ltd.
Also Known As: Teleflex Energy Systems; Proheat wholly owned division of Teleflex Ltd.
3851 - 6th Rd.
Richmond, BC V6V 1P6
604-270-6899
Fax: 604-270-7172
www.teleflexcanada.com
Firm Type: Manufacturing
Founded: 1939
Staff: 175
Products/Services/Areas of Expertise: Fluid control products for emission reduction & fuel efficiency; marine & thermal divisions of US parent
Financial Information:
Type of Ownership: Publicly Traded
Revenue Sources: 100% Private Contracts
Domestic Markets:
National
Foreign Activity:
Worldwide

Temprite Industries Ltd.
Div. of Mestek Canada
5211 Creekbank Rd.
Mississauga, ON L4W 1R3
905-625-2991
Fax: 905-629-9886
Firm Type: Manufacturing
Founded: 1963
Staff: 80
Products/Services/Areas of Expertise: Heat exchangers; catalytic incinerators
Financial Information:
Type of Ownership: Publicly Traded
Revenue Sources: 100% Private Contracts
Domestic Markets:
Ontario
Foreign Activity:
USA
Contact(s):
Eric Watson, Sales & Marketing
Diana Miller, Customer Service/Inside Sales

Tera Environmental Consultants (Alta) Ltd.
#1100, 815 - 8th Ave. SW
Calgary, AB T2P 3P2
403-265-2885
Fax: 403-266-6471
tera@teraenv.com
www.teraenv.com
Firm Type: Scientific/Technical Services
Founded: 1983
Staff: 26
Products/Services/Areas of Expertise: Environmental studies relating to pipelines & oilfield facilities; oil spill contingency plans; route selection; regulatory applications; environmental impact assessment; expert testimony; environmental protection planning; environmental inspection/monitoring of pipeline construction; environmental manuals for construction & operations/maintenance; facilities siting; environmental training programs; terrain analysis, soil erosion control; environmental audits, land use planning, wildlife management; reclamation planning & inspection; fisheries & water quality studies
Financial Information:
Type of Ownership: Private
Revenue Sources: 100% Private Contracts
Domestic Markets:
Alberta, British Columbia, Manitoba, Northwest Territories, Saskatchewan
Foreign Activity:
USA
Markets Sought:
Asia, Central America, Mexico
Contact(s):
Dean F. Mutrie, President
Karl Gilmore, Senior. Vice-President
Piers Fothergill, Vice-President
Randal Glaholt, Sr. Wildlife Biologist/Partner

Terasen Waterworks
Subsidiary of Terasen Inc.
Formerly: BCG Services 9716 - 40 St. SE
Calgary, AB T2C 2P3
403-203-4100
Fax: 403-221-0213
info.waterworks@terasen.com
www.terasen.com/Waterworks/Default.htm
Firm Type: Distributing, Scientific/Technical Services

Products/Services/Areas of Expertise: Waterworks & related services for municipalities & institutions; energy services; water utility & supply services; measurement services
Financial Information:
Type of Ownership: Private
Revenue: Greater than $5 Million
Revenue Sources: 30% Municipals; 70% Private Contracts

TeraWind Ltd.
887 Knowlesville Rd.
Knowlesville, NB E7L 4R1
506-375-9816
Fax: 506-375-9816
fwbrown@nbnet.nb.ca
Contact(s):
Fred Brown, Contact

Terex Ltd.
Formerly: Bartell Industries Inc.
31 Sunpac Blvd.
Brampton, ON L6S 5P6
905-458-5455
Fax: 905-458-5484
sales@terexbartell.com
www.terex.com
Firm Type: Manufacturing
Founded: 1959
Staff: 40
Products/Services/Areas of Expertise: Light construction equipment; power trowel; vibratory plate compactors; replacement power trowel blades; surface preparation equipment & dust control units
Financial Information:
Type of Ownership: Private
Domestic Markets:
National
Foreign Activity:
Worldwide
Contact(s):
Tom Foskett, General Manager
tfoskett@terexbartell.com

Terinex International Ltd.
5338, Rte. Harwood
Hudson, QC J0P 1H0
450-458-5591
Fax: 450-458-0195
plastic@terinex.com
www.terinex.com
Firm Type: Distributing
Founded: 1976
Staff: 6
Member of: Society of Plastics Engineers; Canadian Plastics Industry Association; Plasttics Academy
Products/Services/Areas of Expertise: Distribution of plastic raw materials, virgin & recycled; technical service; color concentrates
Financial Information:
Type of Ownership: Private
Domestic Markets:
National
Foreign Activity:
USA
Contact(s):
Terry Browitt, President

Terminal City Iron Works Ltd.
#2, 9494 - 198th St.
Surrey, BC V1M 3C8
604-513-8313
Fax: 604-513-8347
info@tciw-bc.com
www.tciw-bc.com
Firm Type: Manufacturing
Founded: 1910
Staff: 80
Member of: BC Water & Waste Association; American

Products & Services Buyer's Guide

Waterworks Association
Quality Environmental Management System(s): 9002
Products/Services/Areas of Expertise: Municipal waterworks fittings; fire hydrants; gate valves; specialty castings
Financial Information:
Type of Ownership: Private
Domestic Markets:
Alberta, British Columbia, Manitoba, Ontario, Québec, Yukon Territory
Foreign Activity:
USA
Contact(s):
Dale Baldry, General Manager
dbaldry@tciw-bc.com

Canadian Branches:
Northlands Water & Sewer Supplies Ltd.
1733 South Lyon St.
Prince George, BC V2N 1T3
250-561-1884
Fax: 250-561-1830
Phil Ehnes

Central Water Sewer & Services Ltd.
Reid's Corner
194 Adams Rd.
Kelowna, BC V1V 1K1
250-765-5186
Fax: 250-765-5187
Ernie Naka

Terra Experts Conseils Inc.
#3, 2006, ch Saint-Louis
Sillery, QC G1T 1P1
418-681-6336
Contact(s):
Robert Marquis

TerraChoice Environmental Marketing
#801, 1280 Old Innes
Ottawa, ON K1B 5M7
613-247-1900
Fax: 613-247-2228
800-478-0399
Enquiries@terrachoice.com
www.terrachoice.com
Firm Type: Scientific/Technical Services
Founded: 1995
Staff: 14
Products/Services/Areas of Expertise: Environmental service; performance reporting, rating & recognition strategies; product lifecycle management; program development & delivery
Financial Information:
Type of Ownership: Private
Domestic Markets:
National
Foreign Activity:
Worldwide
Contact(s):
John C. Polak, President
Kevin Gallagher, Vice-President
David Bugden, Director, Corporate Sales

Terracon Geotechnique Ltd.
#140, 2723 - 37th Ave. NE
Calgary, AB T1Y 5R8
403-266-1150
Fax: 403-233-0841
terracon@terracon.ca
www.terracon.ca
Firm Type: Engineering
Founded: 1978
Staff: 85
Products/Services/Areas of Expertise: Geotechnical engineering consulting services; geological & hydrogeological engineering
Contact(s):
Lee Nichols, Principal

Canadian Branches:
Fort MacMurray
10208 Centennial Dr.
Fort McMurray, AB T9H 1Y5
780-743-9343
Fax: 780-743-2420
terracon.fm@terracon.ca

Mission
33047 - 5th Ave.
Mission, BC V2V 1V6
604-820-7835
terracon@terracon.ca

Terrafix Geosynthetics Inc.
Formerly: Terrafix Environmental Tech Inc.
178 Bethridge Rd.
Toronto, ON M9W 1N3
416-674-0363
Fax: 416-674-1159
terrafix@terrafixgeo.com
www.terrafixgeo.com
Firm Type: Engineering, Scientific/Technical Services
Founded: 1974
Staff: 30
Products/Services/Areas of Expertise: Clay containment liners; erosion control products; design & specifications; turnkey services; geomembrane installation; full range of geosynthetics
Domestic Markets:
National
Contact(s):
Dennis Hewitt, President

TerraLink Horticulture Inc.
Formerly: AGRO Pacific Industries Ltd. - Coast Agri Crop Products
464 Riverside Rd.
Abbotsford, BC V2S 7M1
604-864-9044
Fax: 604-864-8418
800-661-4559
info@terralink-horticulture.com
www.terralink-horticulture.com
Firm Type: Distributing, Manufacturing
Founded: 1973
Products/Services/Areas of Expertise: Crop products: fertilizer & chemicals; farm services: spreading, spraying & fumigation; pest management & consulting
Financial Information:
Type of Ownership: Private
Revenue Sources: 100% Private Contracts
Contact(s):
Stan Loewen, Manager

Terralog Technologies Inc.
#300, 1131 Kensington Rd. NW
Calgary, AB T2N 3P4
403-216-4730
Fax: 403-216-4739
tticalgary@terralog.com
www.terralog.com
Firm Type: Scientific/Technical Services, Waste Management
Founded: 1990
Products/Services/Areas of Expertise: Deep well injection using slurry fracture injection (SFI) for disposal of waste materials
Financial Information:
Type of Ownership: Private
Domestic Markets:
Alberta, British Columbia, Saskatchewan
Foreign Activity:
USA,
Contact(s):
Susanne Adamson

International Branch(es):
USA Office
332 E. Foothill Blvd., Suite B
Arcadia, CA USA
626-305-8460
Fax: 626-305-8462
msbruno@terralog.com
Mike Bruno, USA Operations

Terrapex Environmental Ltd.
#108, 557 Dixon Rd.
Toronto, ON M9W 6K1
416-245-0011
Fax: 416-245-0012
888-330-8739
toronto@terrapex.com
www.terrapex.com
Firm Type: Management Consulting, Engineering, Scientific/Technical Services
Founded: 1995
Staff: 40
Member of: Association of Professional Engineers of Ontario; Association of Groundwater Scientists & Engineers
Products/Services/Areas of Expertise: Soil & groundwater evaluation; environmental site assessments & audits; soil & groundwater remediation; underground storage tank removal & replacement; industrial site decommissioning; environmental sampling & monitoring; environmental engineering
Financial Information:
Type of Ownership: Private
Revenue: Greater than $5 Million
Revenue Sources: 5% nationwide; 5% Provincial; 10% Municipals; 80% Private Contracts
Domestic Markets:
Ontario, Québec
Foreign Activity:
Western Europe
Contact(s):
Michael Osborne, P.Eng., President
Jennifer O'Grady, P.Eng., Vice-President

Canadian Branches:
Boucherville Branch
#200, 1470, rue De Coulombe
Boucherville, QC J4B 7K2
450-449-3260
Fax: 450-449-1654
montreal@terrapex.com
Tony Hawke

Burlington
#8, 920 Brant St.
Burlington, ON L7R 4J1
905-632-5939
Fax: 905-632-6793
burlington@terrapex.com
George Kosztyo, P.Geo.

Montréal
3653, ch Chambly
Longueuil, QC J4L 1N9
450-928-3260
Fax: 450-928-0663
1-888-448-3899
montreal@terrapex.com
Tony Hawke

Québec City
#202, 917, rue Monseigneur-Grandin
Sainte-Foy, QC G1V 3X8
418-657-3260
Fax: 418-657-3085
quebec@terrapex.com
Sheila Pitre, ing

Sioux Lookout
P.O. Box 2047
Sioux Lookout, ON P8T 1J7
807-737-7132
Fax: 807-737-1091
Randy Edwards

Terratec Environmental Ltd.
200 Eastport Blvd.
Hamilton, ON L8H 7S4
905-544-0444
Fax: 905-544-0266
877-544-4070
rscholtens@amwater.com
Firm Type: Scientific/Technical Services, Waste Management
Founded: 1974
Staff: 150
Products/Services/Areas of Expertise: Vacuum clean-out services for sewage & water treatment plants, pumping stations, digesters, lagoons & incinerators; consulting & contracting services for sludge utilization on agricultural lands, including tanker haulage, flotation & injecting; hazardous waste transportation & spills response service
Financial Information:
Type of Ownership: Private
Domestic Markets:
National
Contact(s):
Phil Sidhwa, Vice-President
Reuben Scholtens, Manager, Sales

Terratech
275, rue Benjamin-Hudon
Montréal, QC H4N 1J1

514-331-6910
henri.madjar@snclavalin.com
Firm Type: Engineering, Scientific/Technical Services
Founded: 1960
Staff: 25
Products/Services/Areas of Expertise: Geotechnical & geohydrological engineering for civil, mining, pulp & paper projects; tailings dams & industrial waste disposal; soils, concrete, asphalt testing services
Domestic Markets:
New Brunswick, Newfoundland & Labrador, Nova Scotia, Ontario, Prince Edward Island, Québec
Contact(s):
Henri Madjar, President
Gilbert Haddad, Chief Operating Officer

Terratechnik Environmental Limited
#12, 2355 Royal Windsor Dr.
Mississauga, ON L5J 4S8
905-855-4943
Fax: 905-855-4936
admin@terratechnik.ca
www.terratechnik.ca
Firm Type: Distributing, Engineering
Founded: 1996
Staff: 20
Member of: Technical Standards & Safety Association; Ontario Petroleum Contractors Association
Products/Services/Areas of Expertise: Incapsulation of hazardous metal contaminated soils; on-site waste reduction & disposal; chemical oxidation & biological remediation of hydrocarbon contaminated soil & groundwater; brownfield site remediation; underground tank removals; insitu chemical & bio remediation of soil & groundwater
Recently Completed / Ongoing Projects: Remediation of former landfill; continuing remediation of former gun club
Financial Information:
Type of Ownership: Private
Revenue: $3 Million - $5 Million
Revenue Sources: 10% Municipals; 90% Private Contracts
Domestic Markets:
Alberta, Ontario, Saskatchewan
Markets Sought:
Caribbean, The Middle East, South America, USA
Contact(s):
J.P. Francois, Operations

Terratlantic Engineering Ltd.
#203, 880 Hanwell Rd.
Fredericton, NB E3B 6A3
506-460-8660
Fax: 506-460-8679
888-968-8011
info@terratlantic.nb.ca
www.terratlantic.nb.ca
Firm Type: Engineering
Founded: 1999
Products/Services/Areas of Expertise: Environmental, geotechnical & hydrogeological engineering
Contact(s):
Geoff Dickinson, Contact

Tertec Enterprises Inc.
#1, 450 Esna Park Dr.
Markham, ON L3R 1H5
905-477-5727
Fax: 905-470-2236
info@tertec.com
www.tertec.com
Firm Type: Scientific/Technical Services
Founded: 1978
Products/Services/Areas of Expertise: Measuring & monitoring equipment; laboratory equipment
Domestic Markets:
Ontario, Québec
Foreign Activity:
Asia, Australia/New Zealand, China, Central Europe, USA, Vietnam

Testwell Instruments
165 Rexway Dr.
Georgetown, ON L7G 1S2
905-873-8370
Fax: 905-873-1915
800-567-0004
info@testwell.ca
www.testwell.ca

Firm Type: Manufacturing
Founded: 1989
Products/Services/Areas of Expertise: Water level meters & interface meters
Financial Information:
Type of Ownership: Private
Revenue Sources: 10% nationwide; 15% Provincial; 15% Municipals; 60% Private Contracts
Domestic Markets:
National
Foreign Activity:
Worldwide
Contact(s):
Peter Kuryllowicz, President & CEO
Lisa Green, Marketing

TetrES Consultants Inc. / TCI
#603, 386 Broadway
Winnipeg, MB R3C 3R6
204-942-2505
Fax: 204-942-2548
info@tetres.ca
www.tetres.ca
Firm Type: Management Consulting, Engineering, Scientific/Technical Services
Founded: 1990
Staff: 28
Products/Services/Areas of Expertise: Environmental impact assessment; air quality; hydrological analysis; biology/ecology; expert testimony; environmental approvals/licensing; environmental audits, site reclamation; corporate environmental risk assessment; water quality studies; water resource development; solid & hazardous waste management; pollution assessment & control; environmental monitoring & program design; management of interdisciplinary study teams; toxic real estate assessment; ground & surface water hydrology
Recently Completed / Ongoing Projects: Red River Floodway Expansion; Manitoba Hydro Generating Stations; wind energy turbine farms; City of Winnipeg Drinking Water Treatment Plant; mining remediation
Financial Information:
Type of Ownership: Private
Revenue Sources: 30% Provincial; 40% Municipals; 30% Private Contracts
Domestic Markets:
Alberta, Manitoba, Ontario, Saskatchewan
Contact(s):
George Rempel, P.Eng, President/CEO
J. Michael McKernan, Vice-President
David Morgan, Vice-President
Roger Rempel, Associate
rrempel@tetres.ca

Texel Géomembrane Inc.
Formerly: Texel Inc.
485, des Érables
Saint-Elzéar, QC G0S 2J0
418-387-5910
Fax: 418-387-4326
Products/Services/Areas of Expertise: Synthetic liner materials

The Battery Broker Environmental Services Inc.
Also Known As: Battery Broker
11 Tupper Ave.
Toronto, ON M8Z 5H5
416-255-3321
Fax: 416-255-7707
administration@batterybroker.on.ca
www.batterybroker.on.ca
Firm Type: Management Consulting, Scientific/Technical Services, Waste Management
Founded: 1980
Staff: 6
Member of: Canadian Association of Recycling Industries; Ontario Waste Mangement Association
Products/Services/Areas of Expertise: Specialists in waste battery recycling; site audits; handling, shipping, storage & disposal of hazardous waste
Financial Information:
Type of Ownership: Private
Revenue: $250,000 - $500,000
Revenue Sources: 1% nationwide; 7% Provincial; 10% Municipals; 82% Private Contracts
Domestic Markets:
Ontario

Contact(s):
Ron Bebee, President/Site Manager
rbebee@netrover.com
William Love, Manager, Environmental Operations
administration@batterybroker.on.ca

The Beer Store
590 Explorer Dr.
Mississauga, ON L4W 5L2
905-361-1005
Fax: 905-361-4170
888-948-2337
customerservice@thebeerstore.ca
www.thebeerstore.ca
Products/Services/Areas of Expertise: Highly efficient & successful packaging management system; waste handling procedures meet the stringent guidelines & criteria set out by the Environmental Choice Program. Province-wide, return, reuse & recycle program takes back all of its packaging for reuse or recycling, committed to reaching a 100% return rate & are continually working with our customers towards achieving this goal.
Ecological Note: Packaging management system
Domestic Markets:
Ontario
Contact(s):
Lucio DiClemente, President
T-Jay Upper, Contact
t-jay.upper@thebeerstore.ca

The Brofield Group
P.O. Box 42015
Stoney Creek, ON L8E 1J9
905-643-8996
Fax: 905-643-6698
800-361-0453
brofield32@aol.com
Firm Type: Management Consulting, Distributing, Engineering
Founded: 1985
Staff: 3
Products/Services/Areas of Expertise: Design & engineering of recycling, transfer & waste material handling facilities; baling twine & wire
Domestic Markets:
National
Foreign Activity:
USA
Contact(s):
James H. Dutfield, Owner/Manager

The Cadmus Group
#204, 411 Roosevelt Ave.
Ottawa, ON K2A 3X9
613-761-1464
Fax: 613-761-7653
Contact(s):
Dwayne Moore, Principal

The Cintec Group
#309, 7475, boul Newman
Lasalle, QC H8N 1X3
514-368-4861
Fax: 514-368-4669
cintec@arobas.net
www.cintec.ca
Firm Type: Waste Management
Founded: 1987
Member of: Cintec Environnement Inc.; Cindesol Inc.
Products/Services/Areas of Expertise: Provider of transportation, treatment, recycling, & disposal services for municipal solid & hazardous wastes & contaminated soils
Financial Information:
Type of Ownership: Private
Domestic Markets:
Québec
Foreign Activity:
Asia, Central America, South America

The Conserver Group Inc.
356 Hargrave St.
Winnipeg, MB R3B 2J9
204-956-2129
Fax: 204-949-0627
info@conservergroup.com
Firm Type: Engineering
Founded: 1977
Staff: 4

Products & Services Buyer's Guide

Products/Services/Areas of Expertise: Energy management & retrofit; indoor air quality investigations & correction; design of industrial ventilation systems; mechanical & electrical engineering design services for new buildings & renovations; R&D in related fields
Financial Information:
Type of Ownership: Private
Domestic Markets:
Manitoba, Ontario, Saskatchewan
Contact(s):
Dave Waldman, P.Eng., President
david@conservergroup.com

The Cord Group Ltd.
50A Mount Hope Ave.
Dartmouth, NS B2Y 4K9
902-465-5544
Fax: 902-465-2717
ppotter@cordgroup.ca
www.cordgroup.ca
Firm Type: Scientific/Technical Services
Founded: 1983
Products/Services/Areas of Expertise: Testing & evaluation of marine-related safety equipment; contract research & development
Domestic Markets:
British Columbia, Newfoundland & Labrador, Ontario
Foreign Activity:
Australia/New Zealand, Western Europe, USA,
Contact(s):
Paul Potter, President, 902-465-5535

The DATA Group of Companies
Formules d'affaires Data
Formerly: Data Business Forms
9195 Torbram Rd.
Brampton, ON L6S 6H2
905-791-3151
Fax: 905-791-3277
800-268-0128
info@datagroup.ca
www.datagroup.ca
Firm Type: Distributing, Manufacturing
Founded: 1959
Staff: 1200
Quality Environmental Management System(s): 9001
EcoLogo Certified Products & Services: Customized business forms & labels
Products/Services/Areas of Expertise: EcoLogo-certified printing, business forms
Ecological Note: Customized business forms & labels
Financial Information:
Type of Ownership: Publicly Traded
Revenue: $100,000 - $250,000
Revenue Sources: 20% nationwide; 15% Provincial; 10% Municipals; 55% Private Contracts
Domestic Markets:
Alberta, British Columbia, Manitoba, New Brunswick, Newfoundland & Labrador, Nova Scotia, Northwest Territories, Ontario, Québec, Saskatchewan
Contact(s):
David Odell, President/CEO
Bradley Hains, Vice-President, Ontario Sales
Andrew MacGregor, Manager, Communications
Douglas Groff, Director, Environment, Health & Safety

The Delphi Group
428 Gilmour St.
Ottawa, ON K1S 0L2
613-562-2005
Fax: 613-562-2008
866-335-7443
info@delphi.ca
www.delphi.ca
Firm Type: Management Consulting
Founded: 1988
Staff: 12
Member of: Ontario Environmental Industry Association, Ottawa Centre for Research & Innovation
Products/Services/Areas of Expertise: Environmental business consulting; market entry strategies for environmental technologies; climate change strategic planning, analysis, capacity building; market creation plans for energy efficient, clean energy & climate change technologies; strategic environmental management; health & environment strategic development; business risk analysis & management related to environmental issues; policy for environment, climate change & clean energy sectors; GHG verification
Recently Completed / Ongoing Projects: Designed & implemented a capacity building project in Argentina; designed & developed an institutional foundation & tools to attract, design, assss, support & process CDM projects; defined & designed climate change capacity building & research project in China; assisted CIDA's China Program staff & project proponents operationalize cimate change technology transfer projects funded under CCCDF in China
Financial Information:
Type of Ownership: Private
Revenue: $500,000 - $1.5 Million
Domestic Markets:
National
Foreign Activity:
Worldwide
Markets Sought:
South America
Contact(s):
Christopher Henderson, Chairman
Michael Gerbis, President/CEO
Bruce Dudley, Sr. Vice-President, Health & Environment

The Enviro-Connect
142 Guest Dr.
Truro, NS B2N 6N9
902-895-5447
enviro-connect@iname.com
Products/Services/Areas of Expertise: A quarterly newspaper, to educate & promote environmental improvement & awareness among government, business & residential districts
Contact(s):
Margaret Traverse, Manager

The Greer Galloway Group Inc., Engineers & Planners
973 Crawford Dr.
Peterborough, ON K9J 3X1
705-743-5780
Fax: 705-743-9592
general@greergalloway.com
www.greergalloway.com
Firm Type: Engineering
Founded: 1965
Staff: 70
Products/Services/Areas of Expertise: Environmental engineering, including landfill, hydrogeological & water quality studies, water distribution design, sewage plant design & noise & air permits; environmental planning services
Recently Completed / Ongoing Projects: London St. Dam, Highway 7, Sherbrooke St., Peterborough; Emily Creek Bridge replacement; Highway 115, Clarington
Financial Information:
Type of Ownership: Private
Contact(s):
Steve Blakey, Contact
Canadian Branches:
Belleville
1620 Wallbridge Loyalist Rd., RR#5
Belleville, ON K8N 4Z5
613-966-3068
Fax: 613-966-3087
belleville@greergalloway.com
D. Blakey, P.Eng.

The Impact Group
78 Sullivan St.
Toronto, ON M5T 1C1
416-481-7070
Fax: 416-481-7120
info@impactg.com
www.impactg.com
Firm Type: Management Consulting
Founded: 1987
Staff: 10
Products/Services/Areas of Expertise: Provides policy, communications & marketing activities to environmental companies & organizations concerned with science & technology
Financial Information:
Type of Ownership: Private
Domestic Markets:
National
Contact(s):
Jeffrey Crelinston, President
Ron Freedman, Vice-President

The Lowe-Martin Group
P.O. Box 9702
400 Hunt Club Rd.
Ottawa, ON K1G 4E9
613-741-0962
Fax: 613-741-2144
866-521-9871
info@lmgroup.com
www.lmgroup.com
Firm Type: Scientific/Technical Services
Member of: Canadian Printers Industry Association
Quality Environmental Management System(s): 9001
EcoLogo Certified Products & Services: Commercial offset printing services; EcoLogo certified paper products & printeing services; Forest Stewardship Council (ESC) Certification
Products/Services/Areas of Expertise: Commercial offset printing electronic publishing, including design full prepress & post-press production warehousing & distribution services
Ecological Note: Commercial offset printing services; EcoLogo certified paper products & printeing services; Forest Stewardship Council (ESC) Certification
Financial Information:
Type of Ownership: Private
Revenue: Greater than $5 Million
Revenue Sources: 30% nationwide; 70% Private Contracts
Domestic Markets:
Prince Edward Island, Québec
Foreign Activity:
USA
Contact(s):
Ward Griffin, CEO
ward.griffin@lmgroup.com
Michael Renaud, Vice-President, Sales & Marketing
michael.renaud@lmgroup.com
Steve Grieveson, Vice-President, Corporate Services, 613/741-0962
steve.grieveson@lmgroup.com
Hakan Agyar, Senior Quality Assurance Advisor, 613/741-0962
hakan.agyar@lmgroup.com
Canadian Branches:
Kanata
555 Legget Dr.
Kanata, ON K2K 1X3
613-271-8755
Fax: 613-271-8756

Toronto Production
6006 Kestrel Rd.
Mississauga, ON L5T 1S8
905-670-7100
Fax: 905-670-7108

Toronto Warehouse
7330 Pacific Circle
Mississauga, ON L5T 1V1
905-696-9493
Fax: 905-696-9499

International Branch(es):
Ireland Office
Parkmore Industrial Estate
Galway Ireland
-(353) 91-756825

The MEP Environmental Products Ltd.
68 Paramount Rd.
Winnipeg, MB R2X 2W3
204-632-4118
Fax: 204-632-5809
mep@mts.net
www.mepenvironmental.com
Firm Type: Distributing
Founded: 1982
Staff: 1
Member of: Manitoba Environmental Industries Association; Manitoba Heavy Construction Association
Products/Services/Areas of Expertise: Adsorbents, absorbents for chemical spills on land or in water; secondary containment products; bioremediation products; safety products; 24-hour emergency availability
Financial Information:
Type of Ownership: Private
Revenue: $3 Million - $5 Million
Revenue Sources: 10% nationwide; 10% Provincial; 30% Municipals; 50% Private Contracts
Domestic Markets:
National

Markets Sought:
Australia/New Zealand, The Pacific Rim
Contact(s):
Paul Bauer, President
Dave Gural, Vice-President

The National Testing Laboratories Ltd.
199 Henlow Bay
Winnipeg, MB R3Y 1G4
204-488-6999
Fax: 204-488-6947
ntl@mb.sympatico.ca
www.nationaltestlabs.com
Firm Type: Scientific/Technical Services
Founded: 1923
Staff: 20
Member of: Canadian Association of Environmental Analytical Laboratories; Association of Official Analytical Chemists; Manitoba Environmental Industry Association
Products/Services/Areas of Expertise: Testing services; field sampling of contaminated soil, groundwater & air; laboratory analysis
Activities: Site assessment; project management; environmental audits; noise assessment; field services & sampling, monitoring & measuring services
Financial Information:
Type of Ownership: Private
Revenue Sources: 50% Provincial; 50% Private Contracts
Domestic Markets:
Manitoba, Ontario, Saskatchewan
Contact(s):
Don Flatt, President/CEO
Peter Giesbrecht, Manager, Environmental Services
Maria Santos, Supervisor, Laboratory

The Paint Recycling Company
Also Known As: Preferred Environment Inc.
9322 Main St.
Richibucto, NB E4W 4C7
506-523-4469
Fax: 506-523-7301
ohoh@nbnet.nb.ca
Firm Type: Waste Management
Founded: 1994
Staff: 12
Member of: Nova Scotia Environmental Industry Association; New Brunswick Environmental Industry Association
Products/Services/Areas of Expertise: Collecting & recycling waste paint; selling paints made from post-consumer paint; recycling metal paint containers
Financial Information:
Type of Ownership: Private
Revenue Sources: 75% Provincial; 25% Private Contracts
Domestic Markets:
New Brunswick, Newfoundland & Labrador, Nova Scotia, Prince Edward Island,
Contact(s):
Pierre Landry, Contact
Contact(s):
Leigh St. Peter

Canadian Branches:
Springhill Plant
100 Main St.
Springhill, NS B0M 1X0
902-597-8000
Fax: 902-597-8399
leigh_st.peter@hotmail.com

The PEI Energy Corp.
Jones Bldg.
P.O. Box 2000
11 Kent St., 4th Fl.
Charlottetown, PE C1A 7N8
902-894-0288
Fax: 902-368-4242
Products/Services/Areas of Expertise: Renewable low-impact wind-power electricity from the Atlantic Wind Test Site
Ecological Note: Wind-powered electricity
Contact(s):
Wayne MacQuarrie, CEO
dwmacquarrie@gov.pe.ca

The Recycle Systems Company Inc.
1508 - 10th St.
Nisku, AB T9E 7S4
780-955-2508
Fax: 780-955-2509
800-387-4459
recycle@recyclesystems.com
www.recyclesystems.com
Firm Type: Waste Management
Founded: 1992
Staff: 8
Products/Services/Areas of Expertise: Recycling services & facilities; fuel & aerosol recycling; compressed gas cylinder recycling; solvent sales; specialty by-product management; consulting services; technology demonstration; site remediation
Financial Information:
Type of Ownership: Private
Revenue Sources: 10% nationwide; 25% Provincial; 25% Municipals; 40% Private Contracts
Domestic Markets:
Alberta, British Columbia, Manitoba, Northwest Territories, Ontario, Saskatchewan
Foreign Activity:
USA
Contact(s):
Tim Underwood, President
Ryan McDermid, Operations Manager

The St. George Co. Ltd.
P.O. Box 430
20 Consolidated Dr.
Paris, ON N3L 3T5
519-442-2046
Fax: 519-442-7191
800-461-4299
sales@thestgeorgeco.com
www.thestgeorgeco.com
Firm Type: Distributing, Manufacturing
Founded: 1982
Staff: 8
Member of: Ontario Wholesale Farm Equipment Association
Products/Services/Areas of Expertise: Industrial/agricultural helmet respirators
Financial Information:
Type of Ownership: Private
Domestic Markets:
National
Foreign Activity:
Central America, South America, USA
Contact(s):
Peter Quail, President
Nick Quail, Technical Manager

Canadian Branches:
Alberta
P.O. Box 10
Foremost, AB T0K 0X0
403-867-2226
Fax: 403-867-2553
western@thestgeorgeco.com

The Sernas Group Inc.
#41, 110 Scotia Ct.
Whitby, ON L1N 8Y7
905-686-6402
info@sernas.com
www.sernasgroup.com
Firm Type: Engineering
Founded: 1962
Staff: 60
Member of: Professional Engineers of Ontario; Consulting Engineers of Ontario; Association of Consulting Engineers of Canada
Products/Services/Areas of Expertise: Transportation & transit planning services; municipal engineering services; utilities infrastructure design services; land development planning & engineering; water resources engineering
Recently Completed / Ongoing Projects: Phase I & II environmental site assessments for a marina, broadcasting facilities, a commercial plaza, agricultural properties, a metal fabricating company, a proposed pumping station; noise & impact studies
Financial Information:
Type of Ownership: Private
Revenue Sources: 25% Municipals; 75% Private Contracts
Domestic Markets:
Ontario
Contact(s):
Reg D. Webster, P.Eng., President
Gord Patterson, Chief Operating Officer

Canadian Branches:
Mississauga Branch
141 Brunel Rd.
Mississauga, ON L4Z 1X3
416-213-7121

Richmond Hill Branch
#306, 45 Vogell Rd.
Richmond Hill, ON L4B 3P6
416-508-3371
Fax: 416-508-2599

Toronto Branch
#300, 49 Ontario St.
Toronto, ON M5A 2V1
416-703-2612
Fax: 416-703-5804

The Water Shed
782 Main St.
Dartmouth, NS B2W 5G2
902-462-5566
Fax: 902-462-3399
800-667-5566
general@thewatershedonline.ca
www.thewatershedonline.ca
Firm Type: Engineering
Founded: 1980
Staff: 12
Products/Services/Areas of Expertise: Water treatment equipment
Contact(s):
Steve Burke, President

The Westford Group Inc.
#202, 2120 Queen St. East
Toronto, ON M4E 1E2
416-694-7587
Fax: 416-694-1793
800-579-5307
westford@idirect.com
Ecological Note: Maximatch Warming/Cooking Gel
Contact(s):
Don Haldenby, Contact

Theodor D. Sterling & Associates Ltd.
Also Known As: TDSA Ltd.
#310, 1122 Mainland St.
Vancouver, BC V6B 5L1
604-681-2701
Fax: 604-681-2702
877-993-9933
mglassco@sterlingiaq.com
www.sterlingiaq.com
Firm Type: Scientific/Technical Services
Founded: 1971
Staff: 6
Member of: Air & Waste Management Association; American Society of Heating, Refrigerating & Air Conditioning Engineers; Canadian Environment Industry Association
Products/Services/Areas of Expertise: Indoor air quality, mould, hazardous materials & health & safety consulting services
Financial Information:
Revenue: $500,000 - $1.5 Million
Revenue Sources: 5% Provincial; 5% Municipals; 90% Private Contracts
Domestic Markets:
National
Foreign Activity:
USA
Contact(s):
Elia Sterling, President
Michael Glassco, Operations Manager

Therm-O-Comfort Co. Ltd.
75 South Edgeware Rd.
St Thomas, ON N5P 2H7
519-631-3400
Fax: 519-631-9533
877-684-3766
Firm Type: Manufacturing
Founded: 1977
Staff: 32
Member of: Canadian Cellulose Insulation Manufacturing Association

Products & Services Buyer's Guide

Products/Services/Areas of Expertise: Cellulose insulation; insulation consulting for commercial & residential properties; hydroseeding mulch, recycling
Domestic Markets:
Ontario
Markets Sought:
USA
Contact(s):
Linda Smith, Manager
Paul Reehill, Sales & Marketing Manager

Thermal Energy International Inc. / TEI
364 Bentley Ave., 2nd Fl.
Nepean, ON K2E 6T8
613-723-6776
Fax: 613-723-7368
general@thermalenergy.com
www.thermalenergy.com
Firm Type: Management Consulting, Engineering
Founded: 1985
Products/Services/Areas of Expertise: Engineering & design-build services, specializing in heat recovery & air pollution control; environmental compliance & energy conservation
Financial Information:
Type of Ownership: Publicly Traded
Contact(s):
Tim Angus, President
Oliver Toffoli, CFO
Stuart McCarthy, Investor Relations & Communications

Thermal Hydronics Supply Ltd.
101 Sharer Rd.
Woodbridge, ON L4L 8Z3
905-760-1527
Fax: 905-760-1528
877-836-7772
info@thermalhydronics.com
www.thermalhydronics.com
Products/Services/Areas of Expertise: Over 30 years of combined experience in the hydronic industry have allowed us to become one of the industry's preferred service oriented part suppliers and manufacturers; wide spectrum of products & replacement parts for all types of heating & hydronic equipment
Contact(s):
Robert Ruscio, President

Thermal Technics Corporation
6665 Tomken Rd., #9
Mississauga, ON L5T 1Y8
905-795-9500
Fax: 905-795-9506
800-265-9500
Firm Type: Distributing, Engineering, Manufacturing
Founded: 1982
Staff: 3
Products/Services/Areas of Expertise: Heat reclaim systems; closed circuit water source heat pumps; geo-thermal heat pumps; compax chillers; fan coils; commercial & industrial supply & exhaust fans; corrosive resistant fans; electric humidifers; steam injection humidifiers
Domestic Markets:
National
Foreign Activity:
Asia, Central America, Eastern Europe, Western Europe, The Pacific Rim, USA,
Contact(s):
Tony Monk, President
Craig Monk, Marketing

Thermo Design Engineering Ltd.
Mapleridge Industrial Park
1624 - 70 Ave.
Edmonton, AB T6P 1P5
780-440-6064
Fax: 780-440-1657
sales@thermodesign.com
www.thermodesign.com
Firm Type: Engineering, Manufacturing
Founded: 1979
Member of: Canadian Manufacturers Association; Canadian Gas Processor Suppliers' Association; Alberta Pressure Vessel Manufacturers' Association
Products/Services/Areas of Expertise: Design & manufacturing of natural gas & oil clean-up & processing equipment; contaminated soil remediation; specializes in the removal of contaminants (including heavy oils, light oils, tars, VOC's, cyanides & heavy metals) from refinery & heavy oil processing wastes & sites. Has 12 offices worldwide, check website for locations
Financial Information:
Type of Ownership: Private
Domestic Markets:
Alberta, Saskatchewan
Foreign Activity:
Africa, Asia, Eastern Europe, The Middle East, USA, Former USSR

Thermo Dynamics Ltd.
101 Frazee Ave.
Dartmouth, NS B3B 1Z4
902-468-1001
Fax: 902-468-1002
solarinfo@thermo-dynamics.com
www.thermo-dynamics.com
Firm Type: Manufacturing
Founded: 1981
Staff: 10
Products/Services/Areas of Expertise: Research, development & manufacture of solar thermal heating products: solar collectors, heat exchangers & solar domestic hot water systems
Financial Information:
Type of Ownership: Private
Revenue Sources: 10% nationwide; 90% Private Contracts
Domestic Markets:
National
Foreign Activity:
Asia, Central Europe, South America
Markets Sought:
Asia, Eastern Europe
Contact(s):
Peter L. Allen, P.Eng., President/CEO
Paul R. Sajko, P.Eng., General Manager

Thermo Electric (Canada) Ltd.
12 Rutherford Rd. South
Brampton, ON L6W 3J2
905-451-0813
Fax: 905-451-0938
800-663-3278
sales@thermoelectric.ca
www.thermo-electric-direct.com
Firm Type: Manufacturing
Founded: 1954
Staff: 10
Products/Services/Areas of Expertise: Temperature sensors controllers & precision calibrator; wire & cable products
Financial Information:
Type of Ownership: Private
Domestic Markets:
National
Foreign Activity:
Worldwide
Contact(s):
Sydney Patel

Thermo Electron Corp.
Formerly: Ramsey REC
#4, 14 Gormley Industrial Ave.
Gormley, ON L0H 1G0
905-888-8808
Fax: 905-888-8828
www.thermo.com
Firm Type: Manufacturing
Founded: 1961
Products/Services/Areas of Expertise: Liquid samplers; open channel flow; portable analyzers
Domestic Markets:
National
Contact(s):
John Simpson, Marketing & Sales Manager

Thermo-Cell Industries Ltd.
2015 Lanthier Dr.
Orleans, ON K4A 3V2
613-837-9797
Fax: 613-837-5537
800-267-1433
www.thermocell.com
Firm Type: Manufacturing
Founded: 1977
Staff: 35
Quality Environmental Management System(s): 9002
EcoLogo Certified Products & Services: Weathershield thermal insulation
Products/Services/Areas of Expertise: Manufacture of cellulose loose-fill insulation, mulch hydroseeding, specialty fibres; type-2 cellulose wall spray insulation
Ecological Note: Weathershield thermal insulation
Domestic Markets:
New Brunswick, Newfoundland & Labrador, Nova Scotia, Ontario, Prince Edward Island, Québec
Contact(s):
Leigh Vradenburg
Contact(s):
John Surette

Canadian Branches:
Nova Scotia
1822 Plains Rd.
Debert, NS B0M 1G0
902-662-3600
Fax: 902-662-2882

Thermon Heat Tracing Services
Chippewa Industrial Park
255 Henry Dr.
Sarnia, ON N7T 7H5
519-337-2773
Fax: 519-337-1522
800-626-8874
www.thermon.com
Products/Services/Areas of Expertise: Heat tracing systems for temperature maintenance of pipes, tanks & vessels
Contact(s):
Gary Craig, Regional Manager
gcraig@thermon.com
Kandis Trachu, Customer Service, Inside Sales
ktrachy@thermon.com
Sam Palmer, Vice-President, Sales & Marketing
spalmer@thermon.com

Canadian Branches:
Calgary
333 - 28th St. NE
Calgary, AB T2A 7P4
403-273-5558
Fax: 403-273-5695
bbrown@thermon.com
Bob Brown, Managing Director

Edmonton
10436 - 14 Ave.
Edmonton, AB T6J 5S9
780-437-6326
Fax: 780-437-0372

London
151 Meg Dr.
London, ON
519-680-1232
Fax: 519-680-0213
gcraig@thermon.com

New Brunswick
3237 Main St.
Salisbury, NB 32J 4K8
506-372-5600
Fax: 506-372-5599
karl.steeves@thermon.com
Karl Steeves

Newfoundland - Vigilant
285 Symonds Ave.
St. John's, NL A1E 5B1
709-753-6685
Fax: 709-753-7759
info@vigilanttechnicalsales.ca

Québec
2535, rue Halpern
Saint-Laurent, QC H4S 1S3
514-335-2108
Fax: 514-335-2811
michel.jolicoeur@thermon.com
Michel Jolicoeur

Thermotech Windows Ltd.
Formerly: Peter Eder Ltd.
#101, 42 Antares Dr.
Nepean, ON K2E 7Y4
613-839-6158
Fax: 613-839-9066

888-930-9445
info@thermotechwindows.com
www.thermotechwindows.com
Firm Type: Distributing
Staff: 3
Products/Services/Areas of Expertise: Energy-efficient windows; window air tightness testing
Financial Information:
Type of Ownership: Private
Revenue: $1.5 Million - $3 Million
Revenue Sources: 100% Private Contracts
Domestic Markets:
National
Foreign Activity:
Western Europe, USA
Contact(s):
Peter Eder, President/CEO
Stephen Thwaites, Marketing

Thimm Engineering Inc.
#214, 3916 - 64th Ave. SE
Calgary, AB T2C 2B4
403-265-0792
Fax: 403-265-0793
hft@hfthimm.com
www.hfthimm.com/te/
Firm Type: Management Consulting, Engineering
Founded: 1986
Staff: 1
Products/Services/Areas of Expertise: Consulting services on water pollution, greenhouse gases, petroleum spill or pollution
Financial Information:
Type of Ownership: Private
Domestic Markets:
National
Foreign Activity:
Worldwide
Contact(s):
Harold Thimm, P.Eng, President

Thompson Engineering Consultants Ltd.
Formerly: McCabe (H. Bruce) & Associates Engineering Ltd.
P.O. Box 1083
186 Arthur St.
Truro, NS B2N 5G9
902-893-8455
Fax: 902-893-3670
tec@thompsoneng.ca
www.thompsoneng.ca
Firm Type: Engineering
Founded: 1972
Staff: 7
Products/Services/Areas of Expertise: Energy conservation
Contact(s):
Bruce L. Thompson, P.Eng., President

Thompson Rosemount Group / TRG
1345 Rosemount Ave.
Cornwall, ON K6J 3E5
613-933-5602
Fax: 613-936-0335
mail@trg.ca
www.trg.ca
Firm Type: Management Consulting, Engineering
Founded: 1956
Products/Services/Areas of Expertise: TRG offers a multi-disciplinary approach to healthcare, municipal service,s schools, colleges, water resources, security/detection, postal, environmental, transportation or energy management; architects & engineers provide cost effective & functional investigations, designs, construction review & project management solutions
Financial Information:
Type of Ownership: Private
Domestic Markets:
Ontario

Canadian Branches:
Fergus
#1 - 367 Woodlawn Rd. W
Guelph, ON N1H 7K9
519-827-1453
Fax: 519-827-1483

Kingston
#201, 780 Midpark Dr.
Kingston, ON K7M 7P6
613-634-7373
Fax: 613-634-3523

Ottawa
#300, 2197 Riverside Dr.
Ottawa, ON K1H 7X3
613-749-9685
Fax: 613-749-7918

Thomson & Howe Energy Systems Inc. / THES
8107 Hwy. 95A
Kimberley, BC V1A 3L6
250-427-4326
Fax: 250-427-3577
thes@cymberlink.bc.ca
Firm Type: Manufacturing, Scientific/Technical Services
Founded: 1982
Staff: 5
Member of: Kimberley Chamber of Commerce
Products/Services/Areas of Expertise: Design & manufacture of electronic governors, micro-hydro electric systems & controls for micro-hydro systems
Recently Completed / Ongoing Projects: Governor & controls for Lopez De Micay Project, Columbia; generator controls for city of Buffalo, Wyoming, USA; complete hydro system, Island Lake Lodge, BC
Financial Information:
Type of Ownership: Private
Revenue Sources: 5% Provincial; 95% Private Contracts
Domestic Markets:
British Columbia, Newfoundland & Labrador, Nova Scotia, Northwest Territories, Ontario, Québec, Yukon Territory
Foreign Activity:
Africa, Asia, Central America, China, South Africa, South America, Mexico, USA, United Kingdom, Vietnam
Markets Sought:
Caribbean, Former USSR
Contact(s):
Fred Howe, President

Thomson Technology Inc.
9087A - 198 St.
Langley, BC V1M 3B1
604-888-0110
Fax: 604-888-3381
info@thomsontechnology.com
www.thomsontechnology.com
Firm Type: Manufacturing
Founded: 1973
Staff: 50
Quality Environmental Management System(s): 9001
Products/Services/Areas of Expertise: Emergency standby power equipment for use in hospitals, etc.
Domestic Markets:
National
Foreign Activity:
Asia, China, South America, USA, Former USSR, Vietnam
Contact(s):
Bob Thomson, President
Rick Martin, Vice-President, Sales & Marketing

Canadian Branches:
Eastern Canada
Mississauga, ON
905-670-2233
Fax: 905-670-7833
toronto@thomsontechnology.com

Western Canada
Edmonton, AB
780-413-1800
Fax: 780-413-1887
edmonton@thomsontechnology.com

International Branch(es):
China - Beijing
-8610 6870 0433
Fax: -8610 8404 7075
beijing@thomsontechnology.com

China - Shanghai
8621 6334 5588
Fax: 8621 3358 0585
shanghai@thomsontechnology.com

US Regional
1-888-888-0110

Thor Global Enterprises Ltd.
Formerly: Thor Steel & Welding Ltd.
Also Known As: Thor Aggregate Equipment
839 Westport Cres.
Mississauga, ON L5T 1E7
905-564-0440
Fax: 905-564-9602
888-801-8467
bmacdougall@thor-global.com
www.thor-global.com
Firm Type: Manufacturing
Founded: 1969
Staff: 20
Member of: Aggregate Producers of Ontario
Products/Services/Areas of Expertise: Aggregated manufacturing equipment, trommel screens, portable stackers, portable radial conveyors
Domestic Markets:
National
Foreign Activity:
Australia/New Zealand, USA,
Contact(s):
Thor Jorhannsen, President

3M Canada Company
Compagnie 3M Canada
300 Tartan Dr.
London, ON N5V 4M9
Fax: 800-479-4453
888-364-3577
www.3m.com
Firm Type: Manufacturing
Founded: 1951
Staff: 2000
EcoLogo Certified Products & Services: Consumer Products
Products/Services/Areas of Expertise: Sorbents; respirators; spill control kits; air filters; safety & protective equipment; cleaners & chemicals; office industrial products; pharmaceuticals
Ecological Note: Consumer Products
Financial Information:
Type of Ownership: Foreign-owned
Domestic Markets:
National
Contact(s):
David Marsh, Manager, Operations
dwmarsh@mmm.com

360 Energy Inc.
#5, 920 Brant St.
Burlington, ON L7R 4J1
905-634-8877
Fax: 905-634-0999
877-431-0332
info@360energy.net
www.360energy.net
Products/Services/Areas of Expertise: Energy consulting; customized energy solutions

Thurber Engineering Ltd. / TEL
Formerly: Thurber Environmental Consultants Ltd.
#200, 1445 West Georgia St.
Vancouver, BC V6G 2T3
604-684-4384
Fax: 604-684-5124
www.thurber.ca
Firm Type: Engineering, Scientific/Technical Services
Founded: 1957
Staff: 20
Products/Services/Areas of Expertise: Environmental impact assessment; hazardous waste management; environmental audits; effluent & leachate monitoring; air & water quality
Domestic Markets:
Alberta, British Columbia, Northwest Territories, Ontario, Saskatchewan, Yukon Territory
Contact(s):
Dave Hill, P.Eng., Managing Director

Canadian Branches:
Calgary
#190, 550 - 71 Ave. SE
Calgary, AB T2H 0S6
403-253-9217
Fax: 403-252-8159
hheinz@thurber.ca
Heinrich Heinz

Products & Services Buyer's Guide

Edmonton
#200, 9636 - 51 Ave.
Edmonton, AB T6E 6A5
780-438-1684
Fax: 780-437-7125
cchow@thurber.ca
Campbell Chow

Fort McMurray
#B4, 380 MacKenzie Blvd.
Fort McMurray, AB T9H 4C4
780-743-1566
Fax: 780-743-1955
Robert Mills

Kamloops
#104, 1383 McGill Rd.
Kamloops, BC V2C 6K1
250-372-1058
Tim Bryan

Squamish
#40, 38922 Queens Way
Squamish, BC V0N 3G0
604-892-5112
Fax: 604-892-5118
squamish@thurber.ca
Dave Regehr

Toronto
#103, 2010 Winston Park Dr.
Oakville, ON L6H 5R7
905-829-8666
Fax: 905-829-1166
toronto-manager@thurber.ca
Steven M. Sather

Victoria
#100, 4396 West Saanich Rd.
Victoria, BC V8Z 3E9
250-727-2201
Fax: 250-727-3710
victoria-manager@thurber.ca
Stephen Bean

Thuro Inc.
4650 - 50th Ave. SE
Calgary, AB T2G 3R4
403-243-0276
Fax: 403-243-3371
thuro@cadvision.com
www.thuro.ab.ca
Firm Type: Engineering
Founded: 1969
Staff: 20
Member of: Environmental Services Association of Alberta; American Water Works Association; Association of Professional Engineers
Products/Services/Areas of Expertise: High pressure cleaning & flushing of sanitary & storm drain lines; TV inspection of underground lines; oilfield pump & valve sales; repair/rehabilitation of infrastructure (sewer, water)
Recently Completed / Ongoing Projects: TV inspection project, Lethbridge, Calgary, Edmonton, Coaldale, Mile River
Financial Information:
Type of Ownership: Private
Revenue: $1.5 Million - $3 Million
Revenue Sources: 2% nationwide; 10% Provincial; 50% Municipals; 38% Private Contracts
Domestic Markets:
Alberta, British Columbia, Saskatchewan,
Contact(s):
Alex Varro, President

Tiger-Vac International Inc.
2020, boul Dagenais
Laval, QC H7L 5W2
450-625-0099
Fax: 450-625-3388
800-668-4437
support@tiger-vac.com
www.tiger-vac.com
Firm Type: Manufacturing
Founded: 1985
Member of: National Asbestos Council
Quality Environmental Management System(s): 9002
Products/Services/Areas of Expertise: Vacuum cleaners for contamination-controlled environments; critical filter vacuums; explosion-proof vacuum systems; cleanroom vacuums

Financial Information:
Type of Ownership: Private
Domestic Markets:
National

Tinari Energy Management Services Inc. / TEMS
Also Known As: Pacific Institute for Advanced Study
936 Thermal Dr.
Coquitlam, BC V3J 6R8
604-469-7946
Fax: 604-469-3552
pacific@imag.net
www.pacificinstitute.com
Firm Type: Engineering, Scientific/Technical Services
Founded: 1982
Staff: 5
Member of: Ontario Association of Professional Engineers; British Columbia Waste Water Association; Simon Fraser University; Canadian Executive Service Organization; National Energy Institute of Ecuador; Von Karman Institute for Fluid Dynamics; Pacific Institute for Advanced Study Network
Products/Services/Areas of Expertise: Energy & environmental audits; environmental engineering; energy-efficient design; solar engineering; environmental management & engineering; bioremediation; earthquake-proof buildings; corporate research & development; third world development
Activities: Bioremediation studies; solar energy & energy efficient design research & development; toxic waste studies; fluid dynamics; solar engineering
Recently Completed / Ongoing Projects: 30000 CFM Biofilter for composting plant; contaminated site remediation; lower back pain treatment studies
Financial Information:
Type of Ownership: Private
Revenue Sources: 10% nationwide; 30% Provincial; 10% Municipals; 50% Private Contracts
Domestic Markets:
National
Foreign Activity:
Asia, Australia/New Zealand, China, Western Europe, The Pacific Rim, South America, Mexico, USA, Vietnam, Worldwide
Markets Sought:
Central Europe, Eastern Europe, The Middle East
Contact(s):
Paul D. Tinari, Director
Nancy Tinari, Vice-President, Marketing & Sales

TIR Systems Ltd.
Also Known As: Total International Reflection
7700 Riverfront Gate
Burnaby, BC V5J 5M4
604-294-8477
Fax: 604-294-3733
800-663-2036
info@tirsys.com
www.tirsys.com
Firm Type: Scientific/Technical Services
Founded: 1982
Staff: 140
Member of: Lighting Industry Resource Council (LIRC); American Institute of Architects (AIA)
Products/Services/Areas of Expertise: Provides energy efficient, longlife solid state lighting technology which replaces conventional lighting; through environmentally friendly energy conservation, provides lighting solutions to the commercial & industrial & corporate identity markets
Recently Completed / Ongoing Projects: Madrid City Square, Spain; Yorkdale Shopping Centre, Toronto; Cedar Point Amusement Park, OH
Financial Information:
Type of Ownership: Publicly Traded
Revenue: $1.5 Million - $3 Million
Revenue Sources: 100% Private Contracts
Domestic Markets:
National
Foreign Activity:
Asia, Australia/New Zealand, China, Western Europe, USA, Vietnam
Contact(s):
Neil McDonnell, COO
Gary Brown, CFO
Ken Piaggio, Vice-President, Operations, Manufacturing & Quality

Tiru Canada Inc.
900, av Industrielle
Québec, QC G1L 3V9
418-648-8818
Fax: 418-648-8801

Titan Logix Corp.
Formerly: Titan Pacific Resources Ltd.
4130 - 93 St.
Edmonton, AB T6E 5P5
780-462-4085
Fax: 780-450-8369
877-462-4085
www.titanlogix.com
Firm Type: Manufacturing
Founded: 1991
Products/Services/Areas of Expertise: Fluid measurement equipment
Financial Information:
Type of Ownership: Publicly Traded
Domestic Markets:
Alberta, British Columbia, Saskatchewan
Foreign Activity:
USA
Markets Sought:
Asia
Contact(s):
Les Evans, President/CEO

Canadian Branches:
Saskatchewan
P.O. Box 460
106 Cenaiko St.
Lampman, SK S0C 1N0
306-487-2883
Fax: 306-487-2889

TJ Consulting Ltd.
P.O. Box 659
Macklin, SK S0L 2C0
306-753-2897
Fax: 306-753-2971
Firm Type: Scientific/Technical Services
Founded: 1988
Staff: 2
Member of: Saskatchewan Institute of Agrologists; Canadian Consulting Agrologists Association; Saskatchewan Consulting Agrologists Association; Agricultural Institute of Canada; Saskatchewan Soil & Water Conservation Association; Soil & Water Conservation Society
Products/Services/Areas of Expertise: Soils classification & mapping; land inventory & information database systems; land use evaluation & planning; soil conservation & reclamation; irrigation/drainage feasibility rating, salinity investigation; environmental impact assessment & audit; education/public relations/communications; siting of intensive livestock operations & effluent irrigation
Domestic Markets:
Alberta, Saskatchewan
Contact(s):
Therell W. Johnston, P.Ag., President

TLT Co-Vent
Formerly: Co-Vent Engineering Inc.
1381, rue Hocquart
Montréal, QC J3V 6B5
450-441-3233
Fax: 450-441-2189
888-244-7644
info@tltcovent.com
www.tltcovent.com
Firm Type: Manufacturing
Quality Environmental Management System(s): 9001
Products/Services/Areas of Expertise: Design & manufacture custom centrifugal fans & blowers; carbon steel, aluminum, specialty alloys
Recently Completed / Ongoing Projects: Aluminum smelter fume control system fans for project in Iceland; baghouse fans at Sidbec-Dosco, Québec
Financial Information:
Type of Ownership: Private
Revenue Sources: 100% Private Contracts
Domestic Markets:
National
Foreign Activity:
Asia, Central Europe, Western Europe, The Middle East, The Pacific Rim, South America, Mexico, USA

Contact(s):
J. Cohen, P.Eng., President
D. McKinnon, P.Eng., Vice-President, Sales
Canadian Branches:
North American Sales Office
#302, 684 Belmont Ave. W
Kitchener, ON N2M 1N6
519-884-7788
Fax: 519-884-7588

International Branch(es):
TLT CO-VENT South America
Av. Ibirapuero, 2.120 - cj.193
Sao Paulo Brazil
(55) 11 5052-9501
Fax: (55) 1150529513
tltcovent_southamerica@tltcovent.com

TMK IPSCO Inc.
A division of OAO TMK
#3000, 150 - 6th Ave.
Calgary, AB T2P 3Y7
403-538-2182
800-667-1616
www.tmk-group.com/ipsco.php
Firm Type: Manufacturing
Quality Environmental Management System(s): 9002:1994
Products/Services/Areas of Expertise: Steelmaking; seamless, tubular goods, drill pipe, coupling stock & line pipe used in the exploration, production, transmission of oil & natural gas
Financial Information:
Type of Ownership: Foreign-owned
Contact(s):
Dmitry Butorin, Manager & Director, Sales - Canada
John Kearsey, Sales Manager

Tomark Compliance Centre
Also Known As: Tormark Industries Ltd.
#58, 5329 - 72 Ave. SE
Calgary, AB T2C 4X6
403-272-5505
Fax: 403-272-4397
800-661-8344
www.tomark.ca
Firm Type: Management Consulting, Information Technology, Manufacturing
Founded: 1987
Staff: 8
Products/Services/Areas of Expertise: Training seminars relating to transportation of dangerous goods & WHMIS; packaging of dangerous goods for air shipment, sea shipment & ground; books, placards, labels, all supplies for meeting the IATA regulations
Domestic Markets:
National
Foreign Activity:
USA, Worldwide
Contact(s):
Peter Pilling, President
peter.pilling@tomark.ca

Tomlinson Environmental Services
Formerly: Amazing Waste Disposal
970 Moodie Dr.
Ottawa, ON K2R 1H3
613-820-2332
Fax: 613-820-4334
tes@tomlinsongroup.com
www.tomlinsongroup.com
Products/Services/Areas of Expertise: Industrial, commercial waste hauling; recycling services; solid waste disposal
Contact(s):
Kevin Cinq-Mars, Vice-President
John Foley, General Manager, 613-820-2332
jfoley@tomlinsongroup.com

Canadian Branches:
Cornwall
120 Boundary Rd.
Cornwall, ON K6H 6M1
613-933-4410

TOR Geoscience Corp.
#6, 2280 - 39th Ave. NE
Calgary, AB T2E 6P7
403-291-4445
star@torgeo.ab.ca
www.torgeo.ab.ca
Firm Type: Distributing
Founded: 1986
Products/Services/Areas of Expertise: Sale & rental of air sampling equipment, laser particle counters, magnetometers, gravity meters, spectrometers, & other geophysical equipment; supplies expertise in areas of geophysical equipment application for environmental studies
Domestic Markets:
National

Tornatech
Formerly: Cusco Industries, Pump Control Division
2891, rue Halpern
Saint-Laurent, QC H4S 1P8
514-334-0523
Fax: 514-334-5448
1-800-363-8448
info@tornatech.com
www.tornatech.com
Firm Type: Distributing, Manufacturing
Founded: 1985
Products/Services/Areas of Expertise: Manufacturer of fire pump controllers & industrial pump controllers
Domestic Markets:
National
Foreign Activity:
Central America, The Middle East, The Pacific Rim, Mexico, USA
Contact(s):
Bruno Goupil, President/CEO & Manager, General Sales
brunog@tornatech.com
Ana Alves, Vice-President, Finance & Manager, Human Resources
anaa@tornatech.com
Daniel Gendebien, Director, Engineering & Research & Development
danielg@tornatech.com
Michael Pietrangelo, Manager, Sales & Marketing
mikep@tornatech.com

Toromont Caterpillar
Division of Toromont Industries Limited
Formerly: Crothers Limited 313 Hwy. 7 West
Concord, ON L4K 1B7
416-667-5511
Fax: 416-667-5687
800-268-1965
www.toromont.com
Firm Type: Distributing
Founded: 1945
Member of: Ontario Waste Management Association; Solid Waste Association of North America
Products/Services/Areas of Expertise: Power generation using bio gases, natural gas, & diesel fuel; distribution of power generation equipment; caterpillar products; landfill & earthmoving equipment
Financial Information:
Type of Ownership: Publicly Traded
Domestic Markets:
Manitoba, Newfoundland & Labrador, Nunavut, Ontario
Contact(s):
Hugo Sorenson, President

Canadian Branches:
Barrie
2344 Bowman St.
Innisfil, ON L9S 3V7
705-436-7770
Fax: 705-436-7820
Ed Balko, Manager

Brandon
Machine Sales.
1825 - 18th St. North
Brandon, MB R7C 1A6
204-571-2460
Fax: 204-727-4603
Bob Gladden, Manager

Cambridge
P.O. Box 3010
290 Industrial Rd.
Cambridge, ON N3H 4S1
519-650-1211
Fax: 519-650-1372
Dave NcClure, Manager

Cambridge Bay
Operations
P.O. Box 1082
Cambridge Bay, NU X0E 0C0
867-983-2041
Fax: 867-983-2141
Barry Walsh, Manager

Concord - REMAN Branch
P.O. Box 5480
548 Edgeley Blvd.
Concord, ON L4K 1B6
905-667-5900
Fax: 905-667-5919
Peter Born, Manager

Concord Branch - Power Division
Bldg. A
P.O. Box 5511
3131 Hwy. 7
Concord, ON L4K 1B7
416-667-5758
Fax: 416-667-5514
Glenn Keenan, General Manager

Concord Branch - Truck Shop
Bldg. A
P.O. Box 5511
3131 Hwy. 7
Concord, ON L4K 1B7
416-667-5754
Fax: 416-667-5682
Larry Moffat, General Manager

Corner Brook
P.O. Box 430
22 Confederation Dr.
Corner Brook, NL A2H 6E3
709-634-8258
Fax: 709-634-5370
Rick Casaletto, Manager

Dryden
P.O. Box 129
319 Kennedy Rd.
Dryden, ON P2N 2Y2
807-223-4505
Fax: 807-223-4440
Mike Schlereth, Manager

Elie
P.O. Box 272
Hwy. 1 West
Elie, MB R0H 0H0
204-353-3850
Fax: 204-353-4000
Gil St. Hilaire, General Manager

Grand Falls-Windsor
Product Support.
P.O. Box 100
56 Hardy Ave.
Grand Falls-Windsor, NL A2A 2J3
709-489-2131
Fax: 709-489-7807
Carl Hamlyn, Manager

Hamilton
460 South Service Rd.
Stoney Creek, ON L8E 2P8
905-561-5901
Fax: 905-664-6306
Tim Hurt, Vice-President & General Manager

Happy Valley-Goose Bay
P.O. Box 510
20 Halifax St.
Happy Valley-Goose Bay, NL A0P 1C0
709-896-5864
Fax: 709-896-9222
Ed Gillingham, Parts Manager

Iqaluit
P.O. Box 1149
Iqaluit, NU X0A 0H0
867-979-4178
Fax: 867-979-4179
Barry Walsh, Manager

London
50 Enterprise Dr.
London, ON N6N 1A7
519-681-1900
Fax: 519-668-3321
Mike Rugeroni, Manager

Orillia
Forest Home Ind. Park
8 Forest View Dr.
Orillia, ON L3V 6H1
705-327-1801
Fax: 705-327-5058
Ron Konig, Product Support Manager

Ottawa
5 Edgewater St.
Kanata, ON K2L 1V7
613-836-5171
Fax: 613-836-7354
Miles Gregg, Manager

Peterborough
3 Consumers Place
Peterborough, ON K9J 6X9
705-742-2436
Fax: 705-742-2445
Larry McLean, Branch Coordinator

Rankin Inlet
Operations
P.O. Box 530
Rankin Inlet, NU X0C 0G0
867-645-3422
Fax: 867-645-3423
Barry Walsh, Manager

Sault Ste Marie
1207 Great Northern Rd.
Sault Ste Marie, ON P6A 5K7
705-759-2444
Fax: 705-759-6148
Peter beard, Manager

St Catharines
5 Neilson St.
St Catharines, ON L2M 5V9
905-688-6224
Fax: 905-688-2923
Glenn Forbes, Product Support Manager

St. John's
NFLD & Labrador
P.O. Box 8940
82 Kenmount Rd.
St. John's, NL A1B 3S2
709-722-5660
Fax: 709-722-2290
Vic Casaletto, VP

Sudbury
Walden Industrial Park
25 Mumford Dr.
Lively, ON P3Y 1K9
705-692-4764
Fax: 705-692-5277
Dana Matson, Manager

Thompson
Parts Operations
108 Hayes Rd.
Thompson, MB R8N 1M4
204-677-1975
Fax: 204-677-9832
Mel Wickens, Manager

Thunder Bay
P.O. Box 1500
620 Beaverhall Pl.
Thunder Bay, ON P7C 5E5
807-475-7535
Fax: 807-475-3717
Jeff McKnight, Manager

Timmins
P.O. Box 1002
99 Jaguar Dr.
Timmins, ON P4N 7H6
705-268-9900
Fax: 705-268-9909
Horace Webb, Manager

Windsor
3740 Webster Dr., RR#3
Maidstone, ON N0R 1K0
519-737-7386
Fax: 519-650-7351
Tim Hurt, VP Southwest Region

Winnipeg
Western Region
140 Inksbrook Dr.
Winnipeg, MB R2R 2W3
204-453-4343
Fax: 204-475-7964
Mike Schlereth, Vice-President

Toromont Energy Ltd.
Subsidiary of Toromont Industries Ltd.
A
P.O. Box 5511
3131 Hwy.#7 West.
Concord, ON L4K 1B7
416-667-5758
Fax: 416-667-5694
energyinquirites@toromont.com
www.toromontenergy.com
Products/Services/Areas of Expertise: The company designs, constructs, owns, operates & markets green energy from powerplants fuelled by landfill gas, digester/sewage gas & biogas produced from large scale composting processes.
Ecological Note: Alternative source energy
Contact(s):
Peter Ronson, Contact

Torrie Smith Associates Inc. / TSA
125 Perry St.
Cobourg, ON K9A 1N8
905-372-0216
info@torriesmith.com
www.torriesmith.com
Firm Type: Information Technology, Scientific/Technical Services
Founded: 1979
Staff: 4
Member of: Association of Energy Economists; Environmental Assessment Association; Economic Development Corporation
Products/Services/Areas of Expertise: Greenhouse gas emission reduction strategies & software; energy conservation potential; economic analysis; resource management; policy analysis; technical studies & forecasts; cumulative environmental assessment; policy analysis on energy conservation; cumulative environmental impact assessments; science & technology management strategies
Activities: Energy conservation; climate change; environmental assessment; urban energy & transportation studies
Recently Completed / Ongoing Projects: Software tools for greenhouse gas reduction strategies for municipalities & private sector
Financial Information:
Type of Ownership: Private
Revenue Sources: 50% Municipals; 50% Private Contracts
Domestic Markets:
National
Foreign Activity:
Australia/New Zealand, Eastern Europe, The Pacific Rim, South Africa, Mexico, USA, United Kingdom
Markets Sought:
Caribbean, Western Europe
Contact(s):
Judy Smith, CAO
Ralph Torrie, President
Michael Bein, B.M., Software Architect

Toshiba of Canada Ltd.
191 McNabh St
Markham, ON L3R 8H2
905-470-3500
Fax: 905-470-3509
gkokot@toshiba.ca
www.toshiba.ca
Products/Services/Areas of Expertise: Manufacturer & distributor of mobile computer systems, home entertainment products, office products & medical diagnostic imaging equipment; incorporates features to reduce power consumption, noise levels & ozone emissions in copier systems, all electrical circuit boards maintain minimal usage of toxic halogen & lead substances & almost all screws & sheet metal parts are chromium free
Ecological Note: Photocopiers

Contact(s):
Glenn Kokot, Manager, Marketing
Canadian Branches:
Calgary Office
349 - 25th St. SE
Calgary, AB T2A 7H8
403-248-3883
Fax: 403-248-3926
Edmonton Office
11810 Kingsway Ave.
Edmonton, AB T5G 1X5
780-455-5685
Fax: 780-455-5102
Halifax Office
#S, 61 Raddall Ave.
Dartmouth, NS B3B 1T4
902-468-2671
Fax: 902-268-6861
Montréal Office
18050 Trans Canada Hwy.
Kirkland, QC H9A 4A1
514-390-7766
Fax: 514-390-7770
Ottawa Office
#218, 440 Laurier Ave. West
Ottawa, ON K1R 7X6
613-782-2360
Fax: 613-782-2219
Québec Office
3107, av des Hôtels
Québec, QC G1W 4W5
418-626-2080
Fax: 418-626-5044
Richmond
13551 Commerce Pkwy.
Richmond, BC V6W 1J5
604-303-2500
Fax: 604-303-2501

Total Combustion Inc.
#1510, 734 - 7 Ave. SW
Calgary, AB T2P 3P2
403-309-7731
Fax: 403-263-6352
Firm Type: Manufacturing
Founded: 1998
Staff: 18
Member of: Petroleum Technology Alliance; Environmental Services Association of Alberta
Products/Services/Areas of Expertise: Incineration
Financial Information:
Type of Ownership: Private
Domestic Markets:
National
Contact(s):
Tom Wiseman, CFO

Total Comfort Solution Inc. / TCS
P.O. Box 2730
83 - 4th Ave. West
Cardston, AB T0K 0K0
403-653-3547
Fax: 403-653-3458
877-653-3455
www.totalcomfortsolution.com
Firm Type: Distributing
Founded: 1998
Staff: 6
EcoLogo Certified Products & Services: Energy efficient heating & cooling for multi-residential, single residential & hospitality facilities
Products/Services/Areas of Expertise: 30% to 50% energy savings using the Total Comfort Solution Innovative Integrated Piping HVAC System. Installation costs for this hydronic system are lowered through the integration of a building existing infrastructure. The energy savings come from innovative design practices including the dual function of the buildings domestic hot water plant to also provide space heating. Air conditioning is provided from a central hydronic plant, lowering the operating costs. Conditioned air is delivered by thermostatically controlled non-central fan coil units, offering increased comfort for the occupant & increased efficiency through zone control

Ecological Note: Energy efficient heating & cooling for multi-residential, single residential & hospitality facilities
Contact(s):
Rod Shaw, President/CEO
Shellee Shaw, Vice-President/COO
shellee@totalcomfortsolution.com

Total Safety Canada Inc.
6541A Mississauga Rd. North
Mississauga, ON L5N 1A6
Fax: 905-858-3192
800-361-3201
www.totalsafety.com

Totten Sims Hubicki Associates Ltd. / TSH
300 Water St.
Whitby, ON L1N 9J2
905-668-9363
800-668-1983
tsh@tsh.ca
www.tsh.ca
Firm Type: Engineering
Founded: 1962
Staff: 375
Member of: Municipal Waste Integration Network; The Compost Council of Canada
Products/Services/Areas of Expertise: Design & construction of municipal & industrial water & wastewater systems & solid waste disposal facilities; site remediation, assessment & decommissioning
Recently Completed / Ongoing Projects: Detailed design of Cells 1 & 2 Lindsay/Ops Landfill; Co-Composting study, City of Sault Ste. Marie; Waste Diversion System Analysis, District Municipality of Muskoka
Financial Information:
Type of Ownership: Private
Revenue Sources: 90% Municipals; 10% Private Contracts
Domestic Markets:
Ontario
Foreign Activity:
Asia
Contact(s):
Doug Allingham, P.Eng., President
Robert B. Baker, M.A.Sc., P.Eng., Sr. Vice-President, Environmental Engineering
Ray Tufgar, P.Eng., Vice-President, Water Resources
Michael Cant, Manager, Solid Waste
Michael Gundry, P.Eng., Manager, Water & Wastewater Treatment

Canadian Branches:
Barrie
10 High St.
Barrie, ON L4N 1W1
705-721-9222
Fax: 705-734-0764
Ron Robinson, Branch Manager

Bracebridge
49 Manitoba St.
Bracebridge, ON P1L 2A9
705-645-5992
Fax: 705-645-1841
bracebridge@tsh.ca
Fred Clayton, Branch Manager

Cobourg
513 Division St.
Cobourg, ON K9A 5G6
905-372-2121
Fax: 905-372-3621
cobourg@tsh.ca
Bill Wilcox, Branch Manager

Kingston
654 Norris Ct.
Kingston, ON K7P 2R9
613-389-3703
Fax: 613-389-6729
kingston@tsh.ca
Guy Laporte, Branch Manager

Kitchener-Waterloo
#202, 72 Victoria St. South
Kitchener, ON N2G 4Y9
519-886-2160
Fax: 519-886-1697
waterloo@tsh.ca
R. Tufgar, Branch Manager

Ottawa
240 Terence Matthews Cres.
Ottawa, ON K2M 2C4
613-592-7070
Fax: 613-592-7702
ottawa@tsh.ca
Gary Craig, Branch Manager

Sault Ste Marie
523 Wellington St. East
Sault Ste Marie, ON P6A 2M4
705-942-2612
Fax: 705-942-3642
ssmarie@tsh.ca
Rick Talvitie, Branch Manager

St Catharines
#200, 36 Hiscott St.
St Catharines, ON L2R 1C8
905-682-0212
Fax: 905-682-4495
niagara@tsh.ca
Tim Stuart, Branch Manager

Touchie Engineering / TE
Division of R.V. Anderson Associates Limited
#801, 860 Main St.
Moncton, NB E1C 1G2
506-857-8525
Fax: 506-858-5972
moncton@touchieengineering.nb.ca
www.touchieengineering.nb.ca
Firm Type: Engineering
Staff: 8
Products/Services/Areas of Expertise: Engineering consulting services, municipal, environmental
Financial Information:
Type of Ownership: Private
Domestic Markets:
New Brunswick, Nova Scotia, Prince Edward Island
Contact(s):
Rodney Hopper
Contact(s):
Hans Arisq, P.Eng., Manager

Canadian Branches:
Fredericton Branch
P.O. Box 1057
Fredericton, NB E3B 5C2
506-450-2820
Fax: 506-450-3282
Dave Silliphant

Hydro-Com Technologies, Div. of R.V. Anderson Assoc. Ltd
445 Urquhart Cres.
Fredericton, NB E3B 8K4
506-455-2888

Townsend Engineering
151 Ontario Ave.
Elliot Lake, ON P5A 2T2
705-461-1781
Fax: 705-848-0370
Contact(s):
N. McMillan, Manager

Canadian Branches:
Townsend Engineering
151 Ontario Ave.
Elliot Lake, ON P5A 2T2
705-461-1781
Fax: 705-848-0370

ToxCo Waste Management Ltd.
Division of ToxCo Inc.
P.O. Box 232
9384 Highway 22A
Trail, BC V1R 4L5
250-367-9882
Fax: 250-367-9875
877-367-9875
toxcokat@xplornet.com
www.toxco.com
Firm Type: Waste Management
Founded: 1992
Staff: 10
Products/Services/Areas of Expertise: Recycling lithium & magnesium batteries & metals
Recently Completed / Ongoing Projects: Received $10.5 million (U.S.) contract from the U.S. Navy to recycle 570 lbs. MESP lithium batteries
Financial Information:
Type of Ownership: Private
Revenue Sources: 100% Private Contracts
Domestic Markets:
National
Foreign Activity:
Western Europe, The Pacific Rim, USA,
Contact(s):
Kathy Bruce, Plant Manager
toxcokat@xplornet.com

International Branch(es):
Toxco Inc. Head Office
A, 125 East Commercial St.
Anaheim, CA USA
714-879-2067
Fax: 714-441-0857
David Miller, President

Toxicology Centre
University of Saskatchewan
44 Campus Dr.
Saskatoon, SK S7N 5B3
306-966-7441
Fax: 306-931-1664
tox.centre@usask.ca
www.usask.ca/toxicology
Firm Type: Scientific/Technical Services
Founded: 1982
Products/Services/Areas of Expertise: Contract research; environmental consulting; analytical toxicology & chemical analyses; field studies; acute & chronic tests in plant & animal species
Recently Completed / Ongoing Projects: Bioavailability of uranium series radionuclides in food chains; sediment toxicity
Financial Information:
Revenue Sources: 40% nationwide; 10% Provincial; 50% Private Contracts
Domestic Markets:
National
Foreign Activity:
Asia, Western Europe, USA
Contact(s):
K. Liber, Director
karsten.liber@usask.ca

Toxprobe Inc.
#1801, 215 Wynford Dr.
Toronto, ON M3C 3P5
416-467-5106
Fax: 416-423-8276
mullerpavel@toxprobe.com
www.toxprobe.com
Firm Type: Management Consulting
Founded: 1998
Staff: 2
Products/Services/Areas of Expertise: Consultation services in risk assessment, risk management, contaminated site assessment, management option analysis, scientific peer review, expert witness services, risk communication, complex mixtures assessment, & custom scientific services
Contact(s):
Pavel Muller, Ph.D., President

TPE Technologies Inc.
Formerly: Aquarius Services & Technologies Inc.
Also Known As: UVTECH
12260 Green Lane
Montréal, QC H4K 2C3
514-745-6665
Fax: 514-745-8652
sales@uvtech.ca
www.uvtech.ca
Firm Type: Engineering, Manufacturing
Founded: 1995
Staff: 12
Products/Services/Areas of Expertise: Products & services for treatment of industrial process water/wastewater
Financial Information:
Type of Ownership: Private
Revenue Sources: 100% Private Contracts
Domestic Markets:
National
Foreign Activity:
Africa, Caribbean, South America, USA

Contact(s):
P. Van de Voorde, President

TRACC (NB)
Also Known As: Tire Recycling Atlantic Canada Corporation
Minto Industrial Park
Minto, NB E0E 1J0
506-327-4355
Fax: 506-327-3757
traccsales@nb.aibn.com
www.traccnb.ca/home.html
Firm Type: Waste Management
Member of: Crumb Rubber Universal Marketing Bureau
Contact(s):
John Leonard, President/CEO
Stephen Richardson, General Manager

Tract Consulting Inc.
P.O. Box 504
St. John's, NL A1C 5K4
709-738-2500
Fax: 709-738-2499
tract@nfld.com
Contact(s):
Neil Dave, President

Traders Metal Company Ltd.
Poscor Mill Services
P.O. Box 459
131 Yates St.
Sault Ste Marie, ON P6A 5M1
705-759-1090
Fax: 705-759-1209
Firm Type: Manufacturing
Founded: 1901
Staff: 15
Member of: Canadian Association of Recycling Industries
Products/Services/Areas of Expertise: Recycling of all ferrous & non-ferrous metals
Financial Information:
Type of Ownership: Private
Revenue Sources: 100% Municipals
Domestic Markets:
Ontario, Québec
Foreign Activity:
USA
Contact(s):
Robert L. Cohen, President
Peter Immonen, General Manager

Training & Development Services
AMEC TransTech Ltd.
Formerly: Interactive Training & Development Corporation#400,
111 Dunsmuir St.
Vancouver, BC V6B 5W3
604-664-4367
Fax: 604-664-4903
atd.na.amec.com
Firm Type: Management Consulting
Founded: 1986
Staff: 40
Quality Environmental Management System(s): 9001
Products/Services/Areas of Expertise: Design, development & delivery of specific training programs
Domestic Markets:
National
Foreign Activity:
The Pacific Rim, South America, USA
Contact(s):
Reilly Montgomery, General Manager

Transalta Utilities
P.O. Box 1900 M
110 - 12th Ave. SW
Calgary, AB T2P 2M1
403-267-7110
www.transalta.com
Products/Services/Areas of Expertise: Provides electricity directly & indirectly to about 1.7 million Albertans across its 212,000 square kilometer service area; supplies the municipal utilities of the cities of Calgary, Lethbridge & Red Deer; owns & operates 3 coal fired plants, 50% of another coal plant & 13 hydro plants with a net generating capacity of 4,476 megawatts. Also has other power plants throughout North America and Australia

Domestic Markets:
Alberta, New Brunswick, Ontario, Saskatchewan
Foreign Activity:
Australia/New Zealand, Mexico, USA
Contact(s):
Stephen G. Snyder, President & CEO

Transchem Inc.
155 Werlich Dr.
Cambridge, ON N1T 1Y2
519-740-0150
Fax: 519-740-2008
800-265-9100
info@transchem.com
www.transchem.com
Firm Type: Manufacturing
Founded: 1976
Staff: 10
EcoLogo Certified Products & Services: Car wash chemical supplies including: Touchless Presoaks, Foaming Detergents, Sealer Waxes & Foamy Waxes
Products/Services/Areas of Expertise: Manufacture & develop specialized products for vehicle cleaning; touchless car & truck washing
Ecological Note: Car wash chemical supplies including: Touchless Presoaks, Foaming Detergents, Sealer Waxes & Foamy Waxes
Financial Information:
Type of Ownership: Private
Revenue Sources: 100% Private Contracts
Domestic Markets:
National
Foreign Activity:
USA

Transco Plastic Industries
9405, Esplanade
Montréal, QC H2N 1V8
514-733-9951
Fax: 514-733-5481
800-724-5978
info@transco.net
www.transco.net
Ecological Note: Transco Ecolene 3: poly bags of rolls, monolayer & tri-extruded plain & printed
Contact(s):
Marvin Shaffer, Contact

International Branch(es):
US Office
#900, 2330 Tipton Dr.
Charlotte, NC USA

Transcontinental Energy Saving Products Inc.
Also Known As: TESP Inc.
#7, 4179 Harvester Rd.
Burlington, ON L7L 5M4
905-639-0937
Fax: 905-639-8731
800-669-6513
Firm Type: Distributing, Manufacturing
Founded: 1980
Staff: 7
Products/Services/Areas of Expertise: Low volume, high pressure, brass shower heads
Contact(s):
Art Fretz, President

Transcontinental Printing Inc.
725 Hampstead Close
Delta, BC V3M 6R6
604-540-2333
Fax: 604-527-9244
877-540-2333
www.transcontinental.com
Firm Type: Information Technology, Manufacturing
Staff: 180
EcoLogo Certified Products & Services: Lithographic printing services
Products/Services/Areas of Expertise: Transcontinental Printing plant uses recycled papers, re-using over 90% of all inks & solvents & using vegetable-based oils & inks in printing process
Ecological Note: Lithographic printing services
Financial Information:
Type of Ownership: Publicly Traded

Revenue Sources: 5% Provincial; 5% Municipals; 90% Private Contracts
Domestic Markets:
Alberta, British Columbia
Foreign Activity:
USA
Contact(s):
Jim Nicholson, General Manager
Gerry Maginn, Sales Manager
maginng@transcontinental.ca
James Grady, Sales Coordinator
jamesgrady@transcontinental.ca

Transform Compost Systems Ltd.
#211, 33119 South Fraser Way
Abbotsford, BC V2S 2B1
604-504-5660
Fax: 604-504-5666
info@transformcompost.com
www.transformcompost.com
Firm Type: Manufacturing
Founded: 1998
Member of: Composting Council of Canada; Agricultural Institute of Canada; US Composting Council
Products/Services/Areas of Expertise: Provides composting expertise, design & equipment for aerated or agited bed composting facilities
Recently Completed / Ongoing Projects: Design & equipment for: 200 tonnes/day organic waste in China; 40 tonnes/day organic waste in New York; 100 tonnes/day in California
Financial Information:
Type of Ownership: Private
Revenue: $500,000 - $1.5 Million
Revenue Sources: 100% Private Contracts
Domestic Markets:
National
Foreign Activity:
Worldwide
Contact(s):
John Paul, President
Dieter Geesing, Project Manager
dieter@transformcompost.com

TransGas Limited
#500, 1777 Victoria Ave.
Regina, SK S4P 4K5
306-777-9900
Fax: 306-525-3422
www.transgas.com
Firm Type: Distributing
Founded: 1988
Staff: 220
Products/Services/Areas of Expertise: Transports, stores, compresses & gathers natural gas in Saskatchewan
Contact(s):
Daryl Posehn, Sr. Vice-President, TransGas Limited

Transway Systems Inc.
314 Lake Ave. North
Hamilton, ON L8E 3A2
905-578-1000
Fax: 905-561-9176
800-263-4508
toby@transway.on.ca
www.transway.on.ca
Firm Type: Manufacturing
Founded: 1983
Staff: 25
Products/Services/Areas of Expertise: Manufacturer of mobile equipment used for removal, transportation & disposal of liquid & semi-solid wastes, hazardous & non-hazardous; vacuum, pressure pumps
Financial Information:
Type of Ownership: Private
Domestic Markets:
National
Foreign Activity:
Asia, China, The Middle East, South America, USA, Vietnam
Markets Sought:
Eastern Europe, Former USSR
Contact(s):
Mike Dziuba, Sales Manager

Trecan Combustion Ltd.
4049 St. Margaret's Bay Rd.
Hubley, NS B3Z 1C2

902-876-0457
Fax: 902-876-8275
sales@trecan.com
www.trecan.com
Firm Type: Manufacturing
Founded: 1969
Staff: 25
Products/Services/Areas of Expertise: Industrial combustion systems; incinerators for solid, liquid & gaseous wastes; snow melters
Financial Information:
Type of Ownership: Private
Revenue Sources: 10% Provincial; 90% Private Contracts
Domestic Markets:
National
Foreign Activity:
Worldwide
Contact(s):
David Burnett, President
Steve Meredith, Engineering

Canadian Branches:
Calgary Office
#6, 4620 Manilla Rd. SE
Calgary, AB T2G 4B7
403-243-5570
Fax: 403-287-0550
Peter Richardson, Sales Manager

Treeline Well Abandonment & Reclamation Ltd.
#750, 333 - 11 Ave. SW
Calgary, AB T2R 1L9
403-264-6900
Fax: 403-237-8271
www.treelinewell.com
Contact(s):
Dan Bryson, Vice-President
dan.bryson@treelinewell.com
Les Yakemchuk, Vice-president, Operations & Sales
les@treelinewell.com

Trellcan Rubber Ltd.
6150 Kennedy St.
Mississauga, ON L5T 2J4
905-671-3641
Fax: 905-671-3648
lydia@trellcan.com
www.trellcan.com
Firm Type: Distributing
Founded: 1979
Products/Services/Areas of Expertise: Industrial rubber protective products; military tents' anti-vibration mounts
Contact(s):
Elvind Hoff, President
Bibi Hallgren, Office Manager

Tremcar inc.
790, av Montrichard
Saint-Jean-sur-Richelieu, QC J2X 5G4
450-347-7822
Fax: 450-347-8372
800-363-2158
cburton@tremcarusa.com
www.tremcar.com/index.htm
Firm Type: Manufacturing
Founded: 1962
Staff: 85
Member of: Association québécoise des techniques de l'eau
Products/Services/Areas of Expertise: Stainless steel tank fabrication; custom built stainless steel products; pressure vessels; processor tank mixers; silos; water treatment filters; water softener shells; subcontracting
Domestic Markets:
National
Foreign Activity:
USA
Markets Sought:
Mexico
Contact(s):
Jacques Tremblay, President
Daniel Tremblay, Vice-President, Operations

Tremco Ltd.
220 Wicksteed Ave.
Toronto, ON M4H 1G7
416-421-3300
Products/Services/Areas of Expertise: Sealants, coatings, concrete protection systems; roofing systems; insulating glass products; energy conserving products
Contact(s):
Bart Francis, President
Geoff Hearns, Manager, OHS&E
Les Greenwood, Director, Manufacturing

International Branch(es):
Tremco Inc.
3735 Green Rd.
Beachwood, OH USA

Trent Metals Ltd.
P.O. Box 4088
2040 Fisher Dr.
Peterborough, ON K9J 6X6
705-745-4736
Fax: 705-745-7240
www.trentmetals.com
Firm Type: Manufacturing
Founded: 1953
Staff: 40
Products/Services/Areas of Expertise: Heat recovery ventilators; electrostatic air filters
Financial Information:
Type of Ownership: Private
Revenue Sources: 100% Private Contracts
Domestic Markets:
Alberta, British Columbia, Manitoba, New Brunswick, Newfoundland & Labrador, Nova Scotia, Ontario, Prince Edward Island, Saskatchewan
Foreign Activity:
USA
Contact(s):
Bill Edmanson, President

Tri-Arrow Industrial Recovery Inc.
13364 Comber Way
Surrey, BC V3W 7H5
604-597-7334
Fax: 604-594-1240
877-579-9988
sales@tri-arrow.com
www.tri-arrow.com
Firm Type: Waste Management
Founded: 1994
Staff: 11
Products/Services/Areas of Expertise: Liquid hazardous waste management & integrated special waste management/treatment services & facilities; designs & builds waste treatment operations
Financial Information:
Type of Ownership: Private
Domestic Markets:
Alberta, British Columbia
Foreign Activity:
USA
Contact(s):
Herb Locke, General Manager

Triangle Fluid Controls Ltd.
Formerly: Durabla Canada Ltd.
P.O. Box 186
269 University Ave.
Belleville, ON K8N 5A2
613-968-1100
Fax: 613-968-1099
866-537-1133
info@trianglefluid.com
www.trianglefluid.com
Firm Type: Manufacturing
Founded: 1922
Staff: 30
Quality Environmental Management System(s): 9001
Products/Services/Areas of Expertise: Valves/gasket material used in sewage treatment systems & other water treatment equipment
Domestic Markets:
National
Foreign Activity:
Australia/New Zealand, Western Europe, The Middle East, South America, Mexico, USA
Contact(s):
D.W. Moser, President
Dick Deegan, Vice-President
Mike Shorts, General Manager

Canadian Branches:
Red Deer Branch
403-343-1969
Fax: 403-342-1959
John Anderson

Trihedral Engineering Limited
#400, 1160 Bedford Hwy.
Bedford, NS B4A 1C1
902-835-1575
Fax: 902-835-0369
800-463-2783
vts@trihedral.com
www.trihedral.com
Firm Type: Engineering, Information Technology
Founded: 1986
Staff: 30
Products/Services/Areas of Expertise: Process control; process monitoring software development, HMI, Scada software; telemetry
Activities: Waste management research & development; waste research analysis
Domestic Markets:
National
Contact(s):
Glenn Wadden, President
Robert D. Spencer, Vice-President
Barry A. Baker, Vice-President, Business Development
Patrick M. Cooke, Director, Marketing

Trimax Residuals Management Inc.
9402 - 31 Ave.
Edmonton, AB T6N 1C4
780-433-7373
Fax: 780-433-5577
800-465-2115
bobn@paceds.com
www.trimaxenv.com
Firm Type: Waste Management
Founded: 1990
Staff: 44
Products/Services/Areas of Expertise: Mobile sludge dewatering services; complete residuals management programs
Recently Completed / Ongoing Projects: San Diego, CA; Tembec Mill, BC; New York City, NY
Financial Information:
Type of Ownership: Publicly Traded
Revenue: Greater than $5 Million
Revenue Sources: 70% Municipals; 30% Private Contracts
Domestic Markets:
National
Foreign Activity:
USA
Contact(s):
Blake Dermott, General Manager
Scott Urquhart, Manager, Finance
John Mazereeuw, Manager, Field Operations

Triple M Fiberglass Mfg. Ltd.
ZCL Composites Inc.
3608 - 69 Ave.
Edmonton, AB T6B 2V2
780-465-0726
Fax: 780-466-9801
877-874-7536
triplem@compusmart.ab.ca
Firm Type: Manufacturing
Founded: 1982
Staff: 50
Products/Services/Areas of Expertise: Waste storage containers; air pollution control equipment; scrubbers; fiberglass chemical storage tanks & piping systems; underground fuel storage tanks
Recently Completed / Ongoing Projects: Sectional tank, INCO, Thompson, MB; scrubber, Sterline Pulp Chemicals, Saskatoon, SK
Financial Information:
Type of Ownership: Publicly Traded
Revenue Sources: 100% Private Contracts
Domestic Markets:
Alberta, British Columbia, Manitoba, Ontario, Saskatchewan
Foreign Activity:
USA
Contact(s):
Glenn Maber, President
R.A. (Bob) Schaefer, Sales Manager
Larry Grant, Sales

Triple M Metal
471 Intermodal Dr.
Brampton, ON L6T 5G4
905-793-7083
Fax: 905-793-7285
bfarley@triplemmetal.com
www.triplemmetal.com
Firm Type: Waste Management
Founded: 1975
Products/Services/Areas of Expertise: Canada's leading metal recycling company with operations in Great Britain & the US; under construction is an aluminum remelt plant
Domestic Markets:
National
Contact(s):
Michael Giampaolo, President
Bryan Farley, Director, EHS

Canadian Branches:
Brantford
144 Mohawk Rd.
Brantford, ON N3T 5L9
519-752-4351
Fax: 519-752-5455

Hamilton
1640 Brampton St.
Hamilton, ON L8H 3S1
905-545-7083
Fax: 905-545-0232

Kitchener
61 Balzer Rd.
Kitchener, ON N2C 1X5
519-894-1360
Fax: 519-894-0970

Montréal
Montréal, QC
514-798-8600

Scarborough
80 Sinnott Rd.
Toronto, ON M1L 4M7
416-759-4167
Fax: 416-759-3898

St. Thomas
245 Edward St.
St. Thomas, ON N5P 1Z5
519-637-5934
Fax: 519-637-1148

Triton Consultants Ltd.
3530 - 43rd Ave. West
Vancouver, BC V6N 3J9
604-263-3500
Fax: 604-676-2252
info@triton.ca
www.triton.ca
Firm Type: Engineering, Scientific/Technical Services
Founded: 1986
Staff: 4
Products/Services/Areas of Expertise: Coastal, ocean, dredging; river & port engineers & physical oceanographers
Financial Information:
Type of Ownership: Private
Revenue Sources: 15% nationwide; 15% Provincial; 15% Municipals; 55% Private Contracts
Domestic Markets:
National
Foreign Activity:
Worldwide
Contact(s):
Michael R. Tarbotton, President

Canadian Branches:
Port Moody Office
618 Thurston Terrace
Port Moody, BC V3H 4E4
604-469-3563
Fax: 604-676-2252
mrlarson@triton.ca
Max R. Larson

Victoria Office
4935 Cordova Bay Rd.
Victoria, BC V8Y 2K1
250-658-4803
rfhenry@triton.ca

R. Falconer Henry

Triton Engineering Services Ltd.
#8, 18 Robb Blvd.
Orangeville, ON L9W 3L2
519-941-0330
Fax: 519-941-1830
info@tritoneng.on.ca
Firm Type: Engineering
Founded: 1964
Staff: 26
Products/Services/Areas of Expertise: Feasibility studies; technical assistance & advisory services; preliminary & final design; construction administration & inspection; water resources management; roads; bridges; water & wastewater systems
Contact(s):
Dale B. Murray, P.Eng., President/Principal
Gary W. Ezard, Sec.-Treas./Principal

Canadian Branches:
Fergus Branch
175 Provost Lane
Fergus, ON N1M 3N3
519-843-3920
Fax: 519-843-1943
dmurray@tritoneng.on.ca
Dale B. Murray, P.Eng, Principal

Gravenhurst Branch
P.O. Box 971
820 Muskoka Rd. South
Gravenhurst, ON P1P 1V3
705-687-4475
Fax: 705-687-7933
triton@muskoka.net
Bruce E. Vardon, Principal

Triton Environmental Consultants Ltd.
8971 Beckwith Rd.
Richmond, BC V6X 1V4
604-279-2093
Fax: 604-279-2047
info@triton-env.com
www.triton-env.com
Firm Type: Engineering, Scientific/Technical Services
Founded: 1989
Staff: 42
Member of: Canadian Environmental Industry Association; Independent Power Association of BC; Canadian Water Resources Association
Products/Services/Areas of Expertise: Environmental management; environmental performance assessment; water resources engineering; fisheries science & resource assessment; fish & wildlife forestry interactions; GIS-Geographical Information Systems
Recently Completed / Ongoing Projects: Nechako Fisheries Conservation Program (NFCP) for Alcan Inc.; environmental impact assessment for Tahtsa Narrows Project on the Nechako Reservoir for Alcan Inc., environmental assessment & habitat compensation for Riverwalk on the Coquitlam Project for Aplin Martin consultants; environmental management systems auditing & training; stream lake inventory for Canfor
Financial Information:
Type of Ownership: Private
Revenue: $3 Million - $5 Million
Revenue Sources: 10% nationwide; 20% Provincial; 10% Municipals; 60% Private Contracts
Domestic Markets:
British Columbia
Contact(s):
A.C. Mitchell, President & Senior Partner
Tom Watson, Vice-President/Senior Biologist
Dave Warburton, Manager, Prince George Office/GIS Manager, 250/562-9155
J Harris, Manager, Terrace Office, 250/635-1494

Canadian Branches:
Prince George Office
#201, 1157 - 5th Ave.
Prince George, BC V2L 3L1
250-562-9155
Fax: 250-562-9135
dwarburton@triton-env.com
D. Warburton

Terrace Office
Harris
#300, 4546 Park Ave.
Terrace, BC V8G 1V4
250-635-1494
Fax: 250-635-1495
jharris@triton-env.com
, J.

Trivalent Data Systems Ltd.
2813 Cartwright Cres.
Mississauga, ON L5M 5C4
905-826-2487
Fax: 905-826-1714
866-616-8527
sales@trivalent.com
www.trivalent.com
Firm Type: Scientific/Technical Services
Founded: 1970
Staff: 10
Products/Services/Areas of Expertise: Computer program enables companies to produce accurate MSDSs (Material Safety Data Sheets) & WHMIS (Workplace Hazardous Materials Information System) labels in both official languages
Domestic Markets:
British Columbia, Newfoundland & Labrador, Ontario, Québec
Foreign Activity:
USA
Markets Sought:
Mexico
Contact(s):
Richard Aldred, Manager

Trivar Inc.
#9, 188 Wilkinson Rd.
Brampton, ON L6T 4W9
905-595-1744
Fax: 905-595-1747
info@trivar.com
www.trivar.com
Firm Type: Manufacturing
Founded: 1980
Products/Services/Areas of Expertise: Electronic ballasts for fluorescent lighting; electronic ballasts for wastewater treatment systems; fluorescent power reducers; motor speed controls for fans & air purification systems; lamp touch controls, dimmers
Activities: Electronic ballasts for flouresent lighting & wastewater treatment systems
Financial Information:
Type of Ownership: Private
Domestic Markets:
National

TriWaste Services Inc.
1 Connie St.
Toronto, ON M6L 2H8
416-243-7000
Fax: 416-243-2000
Firm Type: Waste Management

Products/Services/Areas of Expertise: Commercial, industrial hazardous/non-hazardous waste hauling; site remediation; asbestos removal; site assessment; decommissioning services
Financial Information:
Type of Ownership: Private
Domestic Markets:
Ontario

Trojan Technologies Inc.
Also Known As: Trojan UV
3020 Gore Rd.
London, ON N5V 4T7
519-457-3400
Fax: 519-457-3030
888-220-6118
www.trojanuv.com
Firm Type: Manufacturing
Founded: 1976
Staff: 400
Member of: Aquafine Corporation; Viqua - A Trojan Technologies Company; US Peroxide, LLC; Trojan Marinex
Member of: Water Environment Federation; Water Quality Association; American Water Works Association; Canadian Association on Water Quality
Quality Environmental Management System(s): 9001:2000
Products/Services/Areas of Expertise: Ultra-violet disinfection equipment & systems for water & wastewater treatment;

technical & engineering support in design, installation & servicing; Environmental Contaminant Treatment, such as NDMA, 1, 4 Dioxane, using UV & H2D2 (hydrogenperoxide)
Activities: Environmental analysis & treatment; domestic water sterilization equipment; commercial water treatment systems; water & wastewater treatment & disinfection for domestic, industrial & municipal systems
Financial Information:
Type of Ownership: Publicly Traded
Revenue: Greater than $5 Million
Domestic Markets:
National
Foreign Activity:
Worldwide
Contact(s):
Marvin R. DeVries, M.Eng., P.Eng., President/CEO
Wesley D. From, M.A.Sc., P.Eng., Vice-President, Engineering
Trevor J.L. Noye, C.A., Vice-President, Manufacturing Operations
Ted Mao, Ph.D., P.Eng., Vice-President, Research

Canadian Branches:
European
Hampton Lovert Droitwich
5 De Salis Court
Worcestershire UK
-31-70-391-3020
Fax: -31-70-391-3330

Noka AS
Storgaten 52
P.O. Box 165
N-3251
Larvik Norway
-47-3319-0530
Fax: -47-3318-0531
noka@noka.com

Pureflow Ultraviolet
1750 Spectrum Dr.
Lawrenceville, GA USA
770-277-6330
Fax: 770-277-6344
info@pureflow.com
www.pureflow.com

Trojan Technologies Deutschland
Postfach 12 48
Aschaffenburger Strasse, 72, 63825
Schöllkrippen Germany
-49 (0) 6024 6347583
Fax: -49 (0) 6024 63
ballen@trojanuv.com; info-de@trojanuv.com

US Peroxide
23 Morningwood Dr.
Laguna Niguel, CA USA
404-589-9381
Fax: 404-589-9778
www.h2o2.com

Ueberall GmbH
Otto-Hahn Str. 9A
D-25337
Elmshorn Germany
-49 4121 57 80 690
Fax: -49 0 700 83 23
mueberall@trojanuv.com; info-de@trojanuv.com

United Kingdom
5 De Salis Court
Hampton Lovett, Droitwich
Worcestershire UK
-44 (0) 1905 771117
Fax: -44 (0) 1905 77
bsmith@trojanuv.com

Water Processing Sweden AB
Hammarbyvagen 37A
SE - 120 32
Stockholm Sweden
-46-8-702-3484
Fax: -46-8-702-3486
water@water.se

International Branch(es):
Benelux
Laan van Vredestein
160, 2552 DZ
The Hague Netherla

-011 317 0391 3020
Fax: -011 317 0391 3
jbourseul@trojanuv.com; hschuurman@trojanuv.com

Trow Consulting Engineers Ltd.
#301, 56 Queen St. East
Brampton, ON L6V 4M8
905-796-3200
Fax: 905-793-5533
brampton@trow.com
www.trow.com
Firm Type: Engineering
Founded: 1957
Member of: Air & Waste Management Association; Association of Professional Engineers; Association of Consulting Engineers of Canada; Geologists & Geophysicists of the Northwest Territories
Products/Services/Areas of Expertise: Engineering services in areas of environmental assessments, spill response, site cleanup, decommissioning waste management, & occupational & environmental health
Domestic Markets:
National
Foreign Activity:
Caribbean, The Middle East, South America, USA
Contact(s):
Colin Parsons, FCA, Chair
Vlad Stritesky, P.Eng., President
Khurshid Mirza, Sr. Vice-President
Joe Mangione, Vice-President, Business Development
Anthony Gussin, Corporate Marketing Manager

Canadian Branches:
Barrie
561 Bryne Dr., #D
Barrie, ON L4N 9Y3
705-734-6222
Fax: 705-734-6224
barrie@trow.com
Roger Tudhope, P.Eng, Office Manager

Brampton
1595 Clark Blvd.
Brampton, ON L6T 4V1
905-793-9800
Fax: 905-793-0641
brampton@trow.com
John McKee, P.Eng, Office Manager

Cornwall
1100 Marleau Ave.
Cornwall, ON K2H 2W8
613-936-9973
Fax: 613-938-4988
cornwall@trow.com
Dan McNicoll, P.Geo., Office Manager

Hamilton
428 Millen Rd.
Stoney Creek, ON L8E 3N9
905-664-3300
Fax: 905-662-4144
hamilton@trow.com
Klaus Stolch, MBA, P.Eng, Office Manager

Iqaluit
Bldg. 1342
P.O. Box 6
Iqaluit, NU X0A 0H0
867-979-5914
Fax: 867-979-0347
nunavut@trow.com
Dan McNicoll, P.Geo, Office Manager

Kingston
The Woolen Mill
#210, 4 Cataraqui St.
Kingston, ON K2K 1Z7
613-542-1253
Fax: 613-547-3767
kingston@trow.com
Paula Formanek, P.Geo., Office Manager

London
Operations
15 Cuddy Blvd.
London, ON N5V 3Y3
519-453-1480
Fax: 519-453-1551
london@trow.com

Bo Chiu, P.Eng., Vice-President

Markham
#12, 70 Gibson Dr.
Markham, ON L3R 4C2
905-470-0073
Fax: 905-470-9848
markham@trow.com
Peter Chan, P.Eng, Office Manager

North Bay (Northland)
1850 Bond St.
North Bay, ON P1B 8G5
705-474-2720
Fax: 705-474-8515
northbay@trow.ca
Dave Richards, P.Eng., Office Manager

Oshawa
#6, 1200 Philip Murray Ave.
Oshawa, ON L1J 6Z8
905-928-4974
Fax: 905-728-7581
oshawa@trow.com
Edward P. Wong, P.Eng, Office Manager

Ottawa
154 Colonnade Rd. South
Nepean, ON K2E 7J5
613-225-9940
Fax: 613-225-7337
ottawa@trow.com
Dan McNicoll, P.Geo, Office Manager

Sarnia
265 North Front St., 4th Fl.
Sarnia, ON N9A 4K9
519-332-1550
Fax: 519-332-5662
sarnia@trow.com
Bo Chiu, P.Eng., Office Manager

Sudbury
1074 Webbwood Dr.
Sudbury, ON P3C 3B7
705-674-9681
Fax: 705-674-8271
sudbury@trow.com
Tom Crilly, Office Manager

Sudbury - Durham St.
121 Durham St.
Sudbury, ON P3E 3M9
705-674-4401
Fax: 705-674-5583
sudbury-durham@trow.com
Ray Spangler, P.Eng, Office Manager

Thunder Bay
1142 Roland St..
Thunder Bay, ON P7B 5M4
807-623-9495
Fax: 807-623-8070
thunderbay@trow.com
Demetri Georgiou, P.Eng, Office Manager

Toronto (C&W)
#600, 970 Lawrence Ave. West
Toronto, ON M6A 3B6
416-789-2600
Fax: 416-789-3600
clw@cw-eng.com
Chris Andrews, P.Eng, Office Manager

Valleyfield (LBCD)
40, rue Sainte-Cécile
Salaberry-de-Valleyfield, QC J6T 1L7
450-371-5722
Fax: 450-371-6955
valleyfield@trow.com
Jean Noël, P.Eng, Office Manager

Vaudreuil-Dorion (LBCD)
#1008, 1000, ave St. Charles, 10e étage
Vaudreuil-Dorion, QC J7V 8P5
405-455-6119
Fax: 405-455-6388
vaudreuil@trow.com
Michel Lalande, Office Manager

Products & Services Buyer's Guide

Victoria
761 Enterprise Cres., #E
Victoria, BC V8Z 6P7
250-658-8114
Fax: 250-658-8115
victoria@trow.com
Jim West, P.Eng, Office Manager

Windsor
430 Pelissier St.
Windsor, ON N9A 4K9
519-988-0145
Fax: 519-988-0158
windsor@trow.com
Bo Chiu, P.Eng, Office Manager

International Branch(es):
Trow Engineering Consultants Inc.
#200, 1300 Metropolitan Blvd.
Tallahasse, FL USA
850-385-5441
Fax: 850-385-5523
tallahasse@trow.com
Mike Koski, Vice-President

Troy-Ontor Inc.
#1A, 230 Bayview Dr.
Barrie, ON L4N 5E9
705-721-8246
Fax: 705-721-5851
troy-ontor@troy-ontor.ca
Products/Services/Areas of Expertise: Specialists in supply & application of electric valve actuators for both new & existing installations with related controls & hardware, including 2-wire digital communication
Contact(s):
Martin Doyle, Sales

Trux Route Management Systems Inc.
P.O. Box 21175
260 Holiday Inn Dr.
Cambridge, ON N3C 4E8
519-658-4322
Fax: 519-658-9762
infor@trux.com
www.trux.com
Products/Services/Areas of Expertise: Software, hardware & consulting services for the waste management industry
Contact(s):
Allen Ische, President

Try Recycling Inc.
#230, 341 Talbot St.
London, ON N6A 2R5
519-457-1566
Fax: 519-457-1570
csr@tryrecycling.com
www.tryrecycling.com
Firm Type: Waste Management
Founded: 1991
Products/Services/Areas of Expertise: Recycling of concrete, sod, tar & chips, drywall, roofing material, wood; all construction & demolition material except insulation ceiling tile
Contact(s):
Jim Graham, President
jim.graham@tryrecycling.com

TTA Technology Training Associates Ltd.
#760, 555 Seymour St.
Vancouver, BC V6B 3H6
604-412-7706
Fax: 604-688-7037
tta@techtraining.org
www.techtraining.org
Firm Type: Management Consulting, Information Technology
Founded: 1989
Products/Services/Areas of Expertise: Training & seminar management; EMS 14000 training
Domestic Markets:
National
Foreign Activity:
Worldwide
Contact(s):
Jeanne Kurz, President

TurboSonic Inc.
#A14, 550 Parkside Dr.
Waterloo, ON N2L 5V4
519-885-5513
Fax: 519-885-6992
800-269-0298
info@turbosonic.com
www.turbosonic.com
Firm Type: Engineering
Founded: 1961
Staff: 30
Products/Services/Areas of Expertise: Air pollution control, gas conditioning & evaporative cooling applications for industries including: pulp & paper, wood products, mining, metallurgical - non-ferrous, iron & steel; chemical, food & beverage, waste processing - biomedical, municipal & hazardous waste incineration; power generation, mineral processing & general manufacturing; particulate & acid gas emission control
Financial Information:
Type of Ownership: Publicly Traded
Domestic Markets:
National
Foreign Activity:
Worldwide
Contact(s):
Ed Spink, CEO
Robert Berube, Vice-President, Marketing & Sales
Ron Allan, Vice-President, Engineering

Turcal
Division of Kruger Inc.
5770, rue Notre-Dame ouest
Montréal, QC H4C 1V2
514-937-4255
Fax: 514-937-2275
Firm Type: Waste Management
Founded: 1979
Staff: 12
Products/Services/Areas of Expertise: Recycling of paper
Domestic Markets:
Ontario, Québec
Contact(s):
Normand Manfield, Vice-President, Recycling Division

Turtle Island Recycling Co.
Formerly: Turtle Island Paper Co.
P.O. Box 6762 A
Toronto, ON M5W 1X5
416-406-2040
Fax: 416-406-2044
800-224-5325
www.turtleislandrecycling.com
Products/Services/Areas of Expertise: Multi-material recycling programs; recycled office paper products
Domestic Markets:
Ontario, Québec
Foreign Activity:
Asia, Eastern Europe, Western Europe, South America, Mexico, USA
Markets Sought:
Australia/New Zealand
Contact(s):
Louis Anagnostakos, President

Twin Falls Limited Partnership
P.O. Box 1747
Cambridge, ON N1R 7G8
519-632-7674
Products/Services/Areas of Expertise: Owns and operates a 5 MW hydroelectric generating station on the Kagiano River, west of Manitowadge, ON.
Ecological Note: Renewable low-impact water-powered electricity
Contact(s):
David Buehlow, Contact

2cg Inc.
451 Ferndale Ave.
London, ON N6C 2Z2
519-645-7733
Fax: 519-645-0337
www.2cg.ca
Firm Type: Management Consulting, Waste Management
Member of: Ontario Waste Management Association; Municipal Waste Association; Recycling Council of Ontario; Recycling Council of Alberta; Composting Council of Canada; Composting Association of Ireland; London Chamber of Commerce; London Composts; Habitat for Humanity; Goodwill Industries; TD Friends of the Environment; London Community Foundation
Products/Services/Areas of Expertise: Specialists in waste prevention & diversion; developing economically & environmentally sound strategies for public & private sectors; developing solutions to maximize waste diversion & minimize cost; expertise in composting of organic wastes, recycling, waste diversion programs, waste auditing, training, communications; brokering of wastes
Financial Information:
Type of Ownership: Private
Contact(s):
Paul van der Werf, B.Sc. (Agr.), M.Sc., MCIW, President

2R Services Inc.
Formerly: Wel-Chem Environmental Services Inc.
60 Churchill Dr.
Barrie, ON L4N 8Z5
705-733-2573
Fax: 705-733-2772
800-668-8475
Paul@2R.ca
www.2r.ca
Firm Type: Scientific/Technical Services, Waste Management
Founded: 1990
Staff: 14
Products/Services/Areas of Expertise: Waste handling, disposal & recycling services; hazardous & non-hazardous liquid, sludge, & solid waste; transportation service; small quantity/lab-pack services; dry cleaning services; solvent recycling & supply; certified testing services, profiling, MSDS preparation; industrial site services, including vacuum truck service, pumping, tank clean-out, pit clean-out, facility decontamination & dismantling; on-site waste management & technical service; emergency response service
Financial Information:
Type of Ownership: Private
Revenue Sources: 5% Provincial; 5% Municipals; 90% Private Contracts
Domestic Markets:
Ontario, Québec
Markets Sought:
USA
Contact(s):
Paul Weinwurm, President

Tyler Research Instruments Corp.
10328 - 73 Ave.
Edmonton, AB T6E 6N5
780-448-1249
Fax: 780-433-0479
tyler@tylerresearch.com
www.tylerresearch.com
Firm Type: Engineering, Manufacturing
Founded: 1987
Staff: 9
Products/Services/Areas of Expertise: Provides solutions to scientists & clinicians, applying engineering principles; creates proof-of-principle & research prototypes, investigates production methodologies through commercial prototype development & performs limited run manufacturing of advanced technology instrumentation; designs & develops the following products & services: Molecular separation technologies based on electrophoresis & chromatography; DNA sequencing systems; ultrafiltration, micro- & macrodialysis; solid state fluorimeters, hybridization incubators, peptide synthesizers; biofilm technologies, cell & tissue culture systems for growth & analysis of mammalian nerves; contract mechanical, electronic & biomedical engineering
Recently Completed / Ongoing Projects: Ultraviolet irradiation systems; ultraviolet dosmeters; diofilm manifolds & biofilm analysis systems
Financial Information:
Type of Ownership: Private
Revenue: $500,000 - $1.5 Million
Domestic Markets:
Alberta, British Columbia, Manitoba, Newfoundland & Labrador, Nova Scotia, Ontario, Prince Edward Island, Québec, Saskatchewan
Foreign Activity:
Asia, Australia/New Zealand, Central America, Central Europe, Eastern Europe, Western Europe, The Pacific Rim, South America, Mexico, USA
Contact(s):
Jonathan Tyler, President & CEO

U-pak Disposal Ltd.
Also Known As: U-Pak Recycling
15 Tidemore Ave.
Toronto, ON M9W 7E9
416-675-3700
Fax: 416-747-8878
Firm Type: Waste Management
Founded: 1972
Products/Services/Areas of Expertise: Waste management
Financial Information:
Type of Ownership: Publicly Traded
Domestic Markets:
Ontario
Contact(s):
Tim O'Connor, President

U.S. Filter/Asdor Ltd.
250 Royal Crest Ct.
Markham, ON L3R 3S1
905-944-2828
Fax: 905-474-1334
www.usfilter.com
Firm Type: Distributing
Staff: 20
Member of: Water Environment Federation; American Water Works Association; Water Environment Association of Ontario
Products/Services/Areas of Expertise: Equipment for transport, dewatering & storage of sewer sludge, including screw conveyors with live bottoms & storage hoppers, sludge cake pumps, screw pumps, plate & frame filter presses
Financial Information:
Revenue: Greater than $5 Million
Domestic Markets:
National
Foreign Activity:
The Middle East, USA

Ultra-Chem Industries Ltd.
#1, 7107 Venture St.
Delta, BC V4G 1H7
604-946-8357
Fax: 604-946-8457
888-858-7224
info@ultrachemlabs.com; smsmarshall@spring.ca
www.ultrachemlabs.com
Firm Type: Manufacturing
Quality Environmental Management System(s): 9001
EcoLogo Certified Products & Services: Industrial & commercial cleaners, strippers, disinfectants
Products/Services/Areas of Expertise: Manufactures janitorial cleaning chemicals including: floor finish, stripper, carpet cleaners, general cleaners & disinfectants; floor & carpet care, general cleaning & disinfecting
Ecological Note: Industrial & commercial cleaners, strippers, disinfectants
Financial Information:
Type of Ownership: Private
Domestic Markets:
National
Foreign Activity:
Asia, China, USA, Vietnam
Markets Sought:
Australia/New Zealand, Caribbean, Central Europe, Eastern Europe, The Pacific Rim, Mexico,
Contact(s):
Ian Marshall
dmmsmarshall@sprint.ca
Ian Marshall, Marketing
smsmarshall@sprint.ca

UMA Group Ltd.
Formerly: UMA Environmental
#275, 3001 Wayburne Dr.
Vancouver, BC V5G 4W3
604-689-3431
Fax: 604-685-1035
www.umagroup.com
Firm Type: Management Consulting, Engineering, Scientific/Technical Services, Waste Management
Founded: 1911
Staff: 1000
Products/Services/Areas of Expertise: Environmental engineering for municipalities & industries: water supply, treatment & distribution; pollution control planning; pollution prevention; wastewater collection, treatment & disposal; solid waste management; hazardous waste management; site assessment & remediation; storm water management; value engineering; environmental science: environmental inventory & monitoring; environmental impact assessment; hydrogeology & geotechnique; risk assessment; workplace health & safety; environmental planning & administration: environmental assessment (process); environmental management systems; approvals management; institutional capacity building; policy development & delivery; sustainability planning; watershed planning & management; dispute resolution
Domestic Markets:
National
Foreign Activity:
Asia, Australia/New Zealand, Central America, Eastern Europe, South America, Mexico, USA
Contact(s):
Jim Stewart, P.Eng., President/CEO
Sheila Jordan, Director
Bruce Richet, Sr. Vice-President, Community Infrastructure
Tom Wingrove, Sr. Vice-President, Earth & Water
Tom Knight, Sr. Vice-President, Transportation

Canadian Branches:
Burnaby
3030 Gilmore Diversion
Burnaby, BC V5G 3B4
604-438-5311
Fax: 604-438-5587

Calgary
2540 Kensington Rd. NW
Calgary, AB T2N 3S3
403-270-9200
Fax: 403-270-0399

Edmonton
17007 - 107 Ave.
Edmonton, AB T5S 1G3
780-486-7000
Fax: 780-486-7070

Hinton
217 Pembina Ave.
Hinton, AB T7V 2B3
780-865-4363
Fax: 780-865-5812

Lethbridge
514 Stafford Dr. North
Lethbridge, AB T1H 2B2
403-329-4822
Fax: 403-329-1678

Medicine Hat
#101, 552 - 18 St. SW
Medicine Hat, AB T1A 8A7
403-527-3183
Fax: 403-526-0403

Montréal
#6400, 1060, rue University
Montréal, QC H3B 4V3
514-940-6862
Fax: 514-940-6868

North Battleford
P.O. Box 548
962 - 102 St.
North Battleford, SK S9A 2Y7
306-446-4266
Fax: 306-446-4268

Red Deer
4920 - 54 St.
Red Deer, AB T4N 2G8
403-342-1141
Fax: 403-342-6863

Regina
1125 Pettigrew Ave. East
Regina, SK S4N 5W1
306-789-9900
Fax: 306-789-7422

Saskatoon
P.O. Box 539
#200, 2100 - 8th St. East
Saskatoon, SK S7H 0V1
306-955-3300
Fax: 306-955-0044

Sparwood
P.O. Box 580
#3, 115 Elk Valley
Sparwood, BC V0B 2G0
250-425-2167
Fax: 250-425-2577

Toronto
5080 Commerce Blvd.
Mississauga, ON L4W 4P2
905-238-0007
Fax: 905-238-0038

Victoria
#200, 415 Gorge Rd. East
Victoria, BC V0B 2G0
250-475-6355
Fax: 250-475-6388

Winnipeg
1479 Buffalo Pl.
Winnipeg, MB R3T 1L7
204-284-0580
Fax: 204-475-3646

Underwriters' Laboratories of Canada
7 Underwriters Rd.
Toronto, ON M1R 3B4
416-757-3611
Fax: 416-757-8727
sales@ulc.ca
www.ulc.ca
Products/Services/Areas of Expertise: ISO 9000 accredited quality systems registrar
Contact(s):
Martin J. Oughton, Regional Operations Leader

Canadian Branches:
Montreal
6505, rte Transcanadiene
Saint-Laurent, QC H4T 1S3
514-363-5941
Fax: 514-363-7014
1-866-937-3852

Ottawa
Ottawa Standards and Government Relation
#20, 440 Laurier Ave. West
Ottawa, ON K1R 7X6
613-755-2729
Fax: 613-231-5977

Vancouver
#130, 13775 Commerce Pkwy.
Richmond, BC V6V 2V4
604-214-9555
Fax: 604-214-9550

Unies Limited
#101, 1555 St. Kames St.
Winnipeg, MB A3H 1B5
204-633-6363
Fax: 204-632-1442
www.unies.mb.ca
Firm Type: Engineering
Founded: 1970
Products/Services/Areas of Expertise: Engineering consulting services
Contact(s):
Bert Phillips, Principal
Campbell MacInnes, Principal
Brian Bradley, Principal
Gordon Spafford, Principal

UniFold Shelters Ltd.
19 Fairleigh Cres.
Hamilton, ON L8M 2L1
905-528-4448
Fax: 905-528-4439
Products/Services/Areas of Expertise: Shelters; plastics fabricated materials; safety and rescue equipment
Contact(s):
Steve Ostrowski, Vice-President
Steve Richards, President

Unisearch Associates Inc.
96 Bradwick Dr.
Concord, ON L4K 1K8
905-669-3547
Fax: 905-669-8652

Products & Services Buyer's Guide

info@unisearch-associates.com
www.unisearch-associates.com
Firm Type: Manufacturing, Scientific/Technical Services
Founded: 1980
Staff: 26
Member of: Air & Waste Management Association
Products/Services/Areas of Expertise: Manufactures instrument systems for environmental monitoring & gas emissions & process control using spectroscopic methods; offers measurement services
Recently Completed / Ongoing Projects: Installation of systems into aluminum smelters in Québec, Australia & England; semi-conductor industry, auto exhaust emissions, paint facilities
Financial Information:
Type of Ownership: Private
Revenue Sources: 10% nationwide; 10% Provincial; 80% Private Contracts
Domestic Markets:
Alberta, British Columbia, Ontario, Québec
Foreign Activity:
Central Europe, South America, Mexico, USA, Former USSR, Worldwide
Contact(s):
Douglas Beynon, President/CEO
Stephen Dwight, Vice-President, Sales

United Oil Services
Also Known As: Lloyd Ward Enterprises Ltd.
13181 - 116 Ave.
Surrey, BC V3R 2S8
604-580-2132
Fax: 604-580-1500
Firm Type: Waste Management
Founded: 1960
Products/Services/Areas of Expertise: Removal & disposal of underground tanks & metals; removal & disposal of water, fuel, etc. from tanks, barrels above & below ground
Financial Information:
Type of Ownership: Private
Revenue: $100,000 - $250,000
Revenue Sources: 10% Provincial; 30% Municipals; 60% Private Contracts
Domestic Markets:
British Columbia
Contact(s):
Lloyd Ward, Owner
Al Greaves, Manager

United Safety Ltd.
Formerly: United Resource Safety Ltd.
104 East Lake Rd.
Airdrie, AB T4A 2J8
403-912-3690
Fax: 403-912-3696
800-432-1809
info@unitedcalgary.com
www.unitedsafetyworld.com
Firm Type: Scientific/Technical Services
Founded: 1987
Member of: Canadian Society of Safety Engineering, Inc.
Quality Environmental Management System(s): 14001
Products/Services/Areas of Expertise: Safety management services; safety equipment rentals; safety/loss prevention consulting & supervision; emergency response planning & training
Activities: Emergency response development; safety/loss prevention consulting & research
Financial Information:
Type of Ownership: Private
Revenue Sources: 100% Private Contracts
Domestic Markets:
Alberta, British Columbia, Nova Scotia, Saskatchewan
Foreign Activity:
Africa, Australia/New Zealand, Western Europe, The Middle East, The Pacific Rim

Universal Drum Reconditioning Company
2460 Royal Windsor Dr.
Mississauga, ON L5J 1K7
905-822-3280
Fax: 905-822-1248
Firm Type: Waste Management
Founded: 1940
Staff: 150
Products/Services/Areas of Expertise: Plant audits; recycling of steel & plastic drums; wastewater processing; steel shredding, bailing & decontamination; plastic recycling
Recently Completed / Ongoing Projects: Plastic recycling/decontamination facility; ISO 9000
Domestic Markets:
Newfoundland & Labrador, Nova Scotia, Ontario, Québec
Foreign Activity:
USA

Universal Filter Media
Also Known As: UFM
#23, 4 Vata Ct.
Aurora, ON L4G 4B6
905-841-1800
Fax: 905-841-8782
800-544-3386
afisher@nfm-filter.com
Firm Type: Distributing, Manufacturing
Founded: 1906
Products/Services/Areas of Expertise: Environmental filtration technologies, including filter medias, cloth & synthetic, replacement parts
Financial Information:
Type of Ownership: Foreign-owned
Revenue Sources: 10% Municipals; 90% Private Contracts
Domestic Markets:
National
Contact(s):
Anita Fisher, Manager, Customer Service

Universal Handling Equipment Company Limited / UHE
P.O. Box 3488 C
100 Burland Cres.
Hamilton, ON L8H 7L5
905-547-0161; 905-549-6922
Fax: 905-547-3364
888-843-4232
www.universalhandling.com
Firm Type: Engineering, Manufacturing
Founded: 1975
Products/Services/Areas of Expertise: Manufacturer of waste & recycling containers
Contact(s):
Erik Breivik, Manager, Engineering
ebreivik@uhecl.com
Bill Leslie, Manager, Parts & Services
service@uhecl.com
Andrea Tziatis, Manager, Client Support
atziatis@uhecl.com
Pierre St. Amand, Director, Sales
sales@uhecl.com
Rachel Baker, Coordinator, Inside Sales
rbaker@uhecl.com

Canadian Branches:
Red Deer
Blindman Industrial Park
4024 - 39139 Hwy. 2A
Red Deer County, AB T4S 2A8
403-346-1233
Fax: 403-340-8720
Carson Dyson, Vice-President, Western Canadian Operations
cdyson@uhecl.com
Denis Flageol, General Manager
dflageol@uhecl.com
Matt Kidd, Manager, Area Sales, 403-350-5439
mkidd@uhecl.com
Marie Drechsler, Manager, Office
mdrechsler@uhecl.com

International Branch(es):
Owosso, Michigan, USA
1650 Industrial Dr.
Owosso, MI USA
989-725-1640
Fax: 989-725-1322
Len Montague, General Manager
lmontague@uhecl.com
Earl Alexander, Manager, Area Sales
lmontague@uhecl.com
Susan Huska, Manager, Office
shuska@uhecl.com

Universal Industries
Head Office & Manufacturing Facility
5014 - 65th St.
Lloydminster, AB T9V 2K2
780-875-6161
Fax: 780-875-6169
www.uic.ca
Firm Type: Distributing, Engineering, Manufacturing
Founded: 1949
Member of: Alberta Manufacturers Health & Safety Association
Products/Services/Areas of Expertise: Manufacturer of pressure vessels; Fabricator of oil & gas processing equipment & tanks for all industries; Product lines include field storage tanks, process tanks, UIC/COLT flash treaters, HDT horizontal treaters, steam generation, & SKUD inclined FWKO
Activities: Project management; Crane service; Field construction; Troubleshooting & maintenance

Canadian Branches:
Calgary
Foremost Universal LP
#990, 630 - 6th Ave. SW
Calgary, AB T2P 0S8
Fax: 403-269-9445
888.966.4556
sales@uic.ca

Université du Québec / INRS-ETE
National Institute of Science Research - Water, Earth & E
Institut national de la recherche scientifique - Eau, Terre & Environne
490, de la Couronne
Québec, QC G1K 9A9
418-654-2524
Fax: 418-654-2600
info@ete.inrs.ca
www.ete.inrs.ca
Firm Type: Scientific/Technical Services
Founded: 1970
Staff: 150
Products/Services/Areas of Expertise: Experts in hydrology & integrated watershed management, biogrochemistry & contamination issues, natural resources & environmental geodynamics, sanitation & environmental decontamination
Financial Information:
Revenue: Greater than $5 Million
Revenue Sources: 20% nationwide; 10% Provincial; 10% Municipals; 60% Private Contracts
Domestic Markets:
National
Foreign Activity:
Africa, Eastern Europe, South America
Contact(s):
Jean-Pierre Villeneuve, Directeur

University of Saskatchewan
Toxicology Research Centre
44 Campus Dr.
Saskatoon, SK S7N 5B3
306-966-7441
Fax: 306-931-1664
tox.centre@usask.ca
www.usask.ca/toxicology
Firm Type: Scientific/Technical Services
Founded: 1982
Products/Services/Areas of Expertise: Contract research; analytical services; consultation in general toxicology, veterinary toxicology, environmental toxicology; education & training
Activities: Terrestrial & aquatic ecotoxicology research design & execution, including collaborative field assessment; toxicity research
Domestic Markets:
National
Foreign Activity:
Western Europe, USA
Contact(s):
Karsten Liber, Director
karsten.liber@usask.ca

University Technologies International / UTI
#130, 3553 - 31st St. NW
Calgary, AB T2L 2K7
403-270-7027
Fax: 403-270-2384
info@uti.ca
www.uti.ca
Firm Type: Management Consulting, Scientific/Technical Services
Founded: 1989

Products/Services/Areas of Expertise: The University of Calgary's Technology Transfer & Commericalization Centre to link the university's fundamental & applied research engine with commercialization partners
Activities: Invention assessments; Intellectual property protection; Licensing & business development; Creating new technology companies
Financial Information:
Type of Ownership: Private
Contact(s):
Kevin Casement, Vice-President, Licensing & Business Development
Sabina Bruehlmann, Project Manager, Medical & Life Sciences
Christopher Chow, Manager, Agreements
Marinela Ionita, Manager, Intellectual Property Administration
Leah McCartney, Project Manager, Engineering & Physical Sciences
David Reese, Project Manager, Engineering & Physical Sciences
Janet Scholz, Manager, Southern Alberta Intellectual Property

UNOTEC
Also Known As: Unique Oilfield Technologies Services
#100, 525 - 11 Ave. SW
Calgary, AB T2R 0C9
403-205-3443
Fax: 403-262-9182
888-205-3760
francisco@unotec.com
www.unotec.com/home.html
Firm Type: Waste Management
Founded: 1998
Staff: 100
Products/Services/Areas of Expertise: Drilling waste: handling, fluid recovery/recycling, management & disposal; creative consulting
Financial Information:
Type of Ownership: Private
Revenue: Greater than $5 Million
Revenue Sources: 100% Private Contracts
Domestic Markets:
Alberta, British Columbia, Yukon Territory
Markets Sought:
South America, Mexico, USA
Contact(s):
Paul Sicotte, President
Ari Laurell, Sales & Marketing
Bill McDougall, Operations
Francisco Fernandez, Technical

Unterman McPhail Associates
540 Runnymede Rd.
Toronto, ON M6S 2Z7
416-766-7333
Fax: 416-763-4082
Firm Type: Management Consulting
Founded: 1989
Staff: 3
Member of: Canadian Association of Professional Heritage Consultants; International Centre on Monuments & Sites Canada
Products/Services/Areas of Expertise: Heritage conservation & planning consultants; environmental assessment; heritage conservation district studies; heritage policy planning; heritage property inventories; historical research; architectural evaluation; expert witness testimony; land use planning; cultural heritage resource management; building documentation & heritage impact studies
Recently Completed / Ongoing Projects: Long-term water supply project, York; North Pickering Land Development Corporation, structure plan review; Highway 407 cultural heritage documentation
Financial Information:
Type of Ownership: Private
Revenue Sources: 20% nationwide; 30% Provincial; 30% Municipals; 20% Private Contracts
Domestic Markets:
Ontario
Markets Sought:
Caribbean,
Contact(s):
Richard M. Unterman, Principal
Barbara E. McPhail, Principal

UPI Inc.
#200, 105 Silvercreek Pkwy. North
Guelph, ON N1H 8M1
519-821-2667
Fax: 519-821-4919
800-396-2667
info@upi.on.ca
www.upienergylp.com
Products/Services/Areas of Expertise: Marketer of petroleum & propane products
Ecological Note: Ethanol-Blended Gasoline: UPI, FS & Co-op
Ethanol Blends, Regular, Midgrade & Premium
Contact(s):
Barbara Skipper, Manager, Corporate Programs
bskipper@upi.on.ca
Robert P. Sicard, President & CEO

Canadian Branches:
Cornwall
11201 Brookdale Ave.
Cornwall, ON K6J 4P7
613-932-8974
Fax: 613-932-7367

Elmira
30 Church St. West
Elmira, ON N3B 1M5
519-669-2645
Fax: 519-669-0578

Fenelon Falls
798 County Rd., #121
Fenelon Falls, ON K0M 1N0
705-887-3796
Fax: 705-887-1562

Guelph
P.O. Box 246
#124, 7060 Wellington Rd.
Guelph, ON N1H 6J9
519-824-7370
Fax: 519-824-1780

Hanover
P.O. Box 7
585 First St.
Hanover, ON N4N 3C3
519-364-4953
Fax: 519-364-5069

Lindsay - Sunderland
P.O. Box 186
36 Harvest St.
Lindsay, ON K9V 4S1
705-324-2242
Fax: 705-324-1839

Lion's Head
P.O. Box 375
2875 Hwy. 6
Lions Head, ON N0H 1W0
519-793-4499
Fax: 519-793-4723

London
3462 White Oak Rd.
London, ON N6E 2Z9
519-681-3772
Fax: 519-681-4680

St-Isidore
4593-A, rue St. Catherine
St-Isidore, ON K0C 2B0
613-524-3113
Fax: 613-524-2733

Thamesville
98 London Rd.
Thamesville, ON N0P 2K0
519-692-5788
Fax: 519-692-5955

Val Gagné
579, rue Principale
Val Gagné, ON P0K 1W0
705-232-6996
Fax: 705-232-2490

Waterdown
P.O. Box 1290
609 Hamilton St. North
Waterdown, ON L0R 2H0
905-689-7295
Fax: 905-689-3354

Waterford
P.O. Box 430
Waterford, ON N0E 1Y0
519-443-8681
Fax: 519-443-8621

Urban Ecology Centre of Montréal
Centre d'écologie urbaine de Montréal
3516, av du Parc
Montréal, QC H2X 2H7
514-282-8378
info@ecologieurbaine.net
www.urbanecology.net; www.ecologieurbaine.net
Firm Type: Management Consulting

Products/Services/Areas of Expertise: Provider of awareness services related to urban sustainability
Activities: Administering a green roof program; Operating a database about greening cities; Organizing conferences, workshops, roundtables, & displays about the impact of urban development upon the environment & health; Contributing to changes in sustainable urban development policy in Montréal
Recently Completed / Ongoing Projects: Green neighbourhoods, active & healthy / Quartiers verts, actifs et en santé, to promote urban planning to encourage walking & cycling
Financial Information:
Type of Ownership: Non Profit
Domestic Markets:
Québec,

Urban Impact Recycling Ltd.
10071 River Dr.
Richmond, BC V6X 2L2
604-273-0089
Fax: 604-273-0499
nicole@urbanimpact.com
www.urbanimpact.com
Firm Type: Waste Management
Founded: 1990
Staff: 20
Products/Services/Areas of Expertise: Recycling services
Domestic Markets:
British Columbia
Contact(s):
Nicole Stefenelli, General Manager

Urban Systems Ltd. / USL
#200, 286 St. Paul St.
Kamloops, BC V2C 6G4
250-374-8311
Fax: 250-374-5334
kamloops@urban-systems.com
www.urban-systems.com
Firm Type: Management Consulting, Engineering
Founded: 1975
Products/Services/Areas of Expertise: Consulting firm, with expertise in the areas of transportation planning & engineering, stormwater engineering, civil engineering, water & wastewater services, community planning, landscape architecture, & local government & First Nations consulting; Clients include provincial & crown agencies, public institutions, resort & urban land developers, First Nations, & local & regional governments
Domestic Markets:
Alberta, British Columbia
Contact(s):
Steve Frith, Branch Leader
Anthony Comazzetto, P.Eng., Professional Engineer
Glen Shkurhan, P.Eng., Professional Engineer
Samantha Ward, P.Eng., Professional Engineer
Christine Mighton, Senior Technologist, Planning
Theresa Foley, Advisor, Human Resources
careers@urban-systems.com
Gordon Petersen, Contact, Urban Systems Foundation

Canadian Branches:
Calgary
#101, 2716 Sunridge Way NE
Calgary, AB T1Y 0A5
403-291-1193
Fax: 403-291-1374
calgary@urban-systems.com
Roberto Binda, Branch Leader

Edmonton
#200, 10345 - 105th St.
Edmonton, AB T5J 1E8

Products & Services Buyer's Guide

780-430-4041
Fax: 780-435-3538
edmonton@urban-systems.com
Matt Brassard, Branch Leader

Fort St. John
10808 - 100th St.
Fort St John, BC V1J 3Z6
250-785-9697
Fax: 250-785-9691
fsj@urban-systems.com
Rob Close, Branch Leader

Kelowna
#500, 1708 Dolphin Ave.
Kelowna, BC V1Y 9S4
250-762-2517
Fax: 250-763-5266
kelowna@urban-systems.com
Ken Gauthier, Branch Leader

Nelson
515E Vernon St.
Nelson, BC V1L 4E9
250-352-9774
Fax: 250-352-5322
nelson@urban-systems.com
Ken Gauthier, Branch Leader

Richmond
#2353, 13353 Commerce Pkwy.
Richmond, BC V6V 3A1
604-273-8700
Fax: 604-273-8752
vancouver@urban-systems.com
John Steiner, Branch Leader

Urecon Ltée
1800, boul Bédard
Saint-Lazare, QC J7T 2G4
450-455-0961
Fax: 450-455-0350
urecon@urecon.com
www.urecon.com
Products/Services/Areas of Expertise: Water & wastewater management equipment

Canadian Branches:
Urecon Insulation Ltd.
5010 - 43 Ave.
Calmar, AB T0C 0V0
780-985-3636
Fax: 780-985-2466
sales.west@urecon.com

Urecon Ltd.- Newfoundland
3 Bluebell Bend
Portugal Cove/St. Philips, NL A1M 2G5
709-895-8100
Fax: 709-895-8101
sales.east@urecon.com

Urecon Ltd.- Ontario
#625, 268 Lakeshore Rd. East
Oakville, ON L6J 7S4
905-257-3797
Fax: 905-257-9723
sales.east@urecon.com

International Branch(es):
Urecon Systems Inc.
#102, 4185 South US Hwy #1
Rockledge, FL USA
321-638-2364
Fax: 321-638-2371
sales.usa@urecon.com

Urgel Delisle & Associés inc.
CP 60
426, ch des Patriotes
St-Charles-sur-Richelieu, QC J0H 2G0
450-584-2207
Fax: 450-584-2523
uda@udainc.com
www.udainc.com/eindex.html
Firm Type: Engineering, Scientific/Technical Services
Founded: 1978
Staff: 25
Quality Environmental Management System(s): 9001

Products/Services/Areas of Expertise: Energy reclamation; feasibility studies; agriculture; biomass
Activities: Manure management; municipal waste disposal; drainage research
Domestic Markets:
Québec
Foreign Activity:
Africa, South America
Contact(s):
Urgel Delisle, President/CEO

URS Canada Inc.
Formerly: Norecol, Dames & Moore Inc.
P.O. Box 11507
#1900, 650 Georgia St. West
Vancouver, BC V6B 4NT
604-681-1672
Fax: 604-687-3446
urs_vancouver@urscorp.com
www.urscorp.com
Firm Type: Engineering
Founded: 1993
Staff: 37
Member of: Environmental Managers Association of BC; Alberta Construction Safety Association; The Association of Professional Engineers; Geologists & Geophysicists of Alberta
Quality Environmental Management System(s): 14001
Products/Services/Areas of Expertise: Environmental planning & environmental sciences; property assessment/hazardous materials management services; site investigation/remediation & hydrology; risk assessment & risk management; mine development & closure, acid rock drainage; geotechnical engineering
Recently Completed / Ongoing Projects: Manulife remediation project; Public Works, Tundra Mine remediation design project; Hudson Bay Mining; Chevron oil & gas projects
Financial Information:
Type of Ownership: Publicly Traded
Revenue: $1.5 Million - $3 Million
Revenue Sources: 50% nationwide; 30% Provincial; 15% Municipals; 5% Private Contracts
Domestic Markets:
Alberta, British Columbia, Manitoba, Northwest Territories, Yukon Territory
Foreign Activity:
Africa, Asia, The Pacific Rim, South America, Mexico, USA
Contact(s):
Stephen Pellerin, Vice-President
stephen_pellerin@urscorp.com
Lynda Smithard, Coordinator, Marketing
lynda_smithard@urscorp.ca
Eva Gerencher, Senior Environmental Scientist
eva_gerencher@urscorp.ca

Utility Risk Management Ltd. / URM
Also Known As: URM Consulting
171 Charles St.
Arnprior, ON K7S 3V5
613-623-6601
Fax: 613-623-5218
mjustus@urmconsulting.com
www.urmconsulting.com
Firm Type: Management Consulting
Founded: 1993
Products/Services/Areas of Expertise: Consulting firm, with expertise in the implementation of a safe work management system, in order to eliminate serious accidents
Activities: Providing workshops on topics such as accident investigation, job safety planning, performance leadership, safety program management, safety strategy, & work observation; Offering safety auditing certification; Providing safety management audits & safety perception surveys
Recently Completed / Ongoing Projects: Accident investigation workshop, SaskPower; Job safety planning, Manitoba Hydro; Safety perception survey, Great Lakes Power Ltd.; Safety strategy workshop, Waterloo North Hydro; Work observation workshop, Newfoundland Power
Domestic Markets:
National
Contact(s):
Yvan Desrochers, P.Eng., Managing Partner
Jim Fawcett, Managing Partner
Don Watson, Managing Partner

UV Pure Technologies
#19, 60 Venture Dr.
Toronto, ON M1B 3S4
416-208-9884
Fax: 416-208-5808
888-407-9997
info@uvpure.com
www.uvpure.com
Firm Type: Distributing, Manufacturing, Scientific/Technical Services
Founded: 1998
Products/Services/Areas of Expertise: UV Pure's Hallett water systems for residential, municipal & commercial water applications, for up to 5,000 households; systems are NSF/ANSI 55 Class A Certified, the global gold standard accepted by environmental regulatory agents worldwide
Contact(s):
Ron Hallett, Founder

V. Fournier & Associates
#305, 1009, rte de l'Église
Sainte-Foy, QC G1V 3V8
418-656-1233
Fax: 418-656-9988
Firm Type: Engineering, Scientific/Technical Services, Waste Management
Founded: 1985
Staff: 12
Quality Environmental Management System(s): 9001
Products/Services/Areas of Expertise: Landfill design; site assessment; groundwater monitoring; soil & groundwater remediation; environmental audits
Contact(s):
Vincent Fournier, President

V.J. Rice Concrete Ltd.
P.O. Box 399
Bridgetown, NS B0S 1C0
902-665-4444
Fax: 902-665-4017
800-465-7500
info@riceconcrete.ca
www.riceconcrete.ca
Firm Type: Manufacturing
Founded: 1960
Staff: 30
Products/Services/Areas of Expertise: Ready-mixed concrete, manholes, pipes, septic tanks
Financial Information:
Type of Ownership: Private
Domestic Markets:
Nova Scotia,
Contact(s):
V.J. Rice, President
T.J. Rice, Manager

Vacuum Products Canada Inc.
Formerly: Leybold Canada Inc.
#5, 7050 Telford Way
Mississauga, ON L5S 1V7
905-672-7704
Fax: 905-672-2249
800-269-6030
reachus@vpcinc.ca
www.vpcinc.ca
Products/Services/Areas of Expertise: Distributor of vacuum equipment, vacuum instrumentation & tools; Products include vacuum pumps, cryogenic pumps, turbopumps, diffusion pumps, leak detectors, lubricants, fittings, gauges, thin film instrumentation, & gas analysis instrumentation; Vacuum brands include Sogevac, INFICON, Seiler, Oerlikon Leybold, & Pfeiffer
Activities: Providing maintenance & technical support
Domestic Markets:
National
Contact(s):
Christina Carere, Contact, Key Accounts, Ontario
c.carere@vpcinc.ca
Rick Lang, Contact, Technical Sales - Thin Film & Coating, Western Canada
r.lang@vpcinc.ca
Linda McCrea, Contact, Customer Support
l.mccrea@vpcinc.ca
Adil Merchant, Contact, Technical Sales, Eastern Canada & Québec
a.merchant@vpcinc.ca

Kayvan Separi, Contact, Technical Sales, Ontario & Applications Support
k.separi@vpcinc.ca
Arlene Thorne, Contact, Finance & Quality Management
finance@vpcinc.ca

Val Temp Sales Ltd. / VTS
601 Manitou Rd. SE
Calgary, AB T2G 4C2
403-221-8181
general@valtempsales.com
www.valtempsales.com
Firm Type: Distributing
Founded: 1971
Products/Services/Areas of Expertise: Distributor of engineered products; Clients include the industrial, institutional, commercial & design build markets
Domestic Markets:
National
Contact(s):
James E. (Jim) McNeil, Principal
jmcneil@valtempsales.com

Valerie Falls Limited Partnership / VFLP
c/o Brookfield Renewable Power, Wawa
P.O. Box 320
Wawa, ON P0S 1K0
705-856-2632, ext. 436
Fax: 705-856-1338
Products/Services/Areas of Expertise: Owner of the Valerie Falls Generating Station, which produces power solde to the Ontario Electrical Finance Corporation
Domestic Markets:
Ontario
Contact(s):
Bruce Welbourne, Water Resource Manager, VFLP, Brookfield Renewable Power, Wawa Hydro Operation
bruce.welbourne@brookfieldpower.com

Valley Associates Inc.
#3, 860 Taylor Creek Dr.
Orleans, ON K1C 1T1
613-830-1880
Fax: 613-830-3008
877-226-2219
sales@valleyassociates.com
www.valleyassociates.com
Products/Services/Areas of Expertise: Providers of tactical equipment, protective gear & technical support to response authorities; equipment to manage & control ballistic, bomb, fire rescue & bio-chemical threats.
Domestic Markets:
National
Foreign Activity:
Asia
Contact(s):
Michael Martin, President
mmartin@valleyassociates.com
Marc Lavigne, Manager, Business Development
mlavigne@valleyassociates.com

Valley Comfort Systems Inc.
Also Known As: Blaze King
1290 Commercial Way
Penticton, BC V2A 3H5
250-493-7444
Fax: 250-493-5833
vsales@vip.net
www.blazeking.com
Firm Type: Manufacturing
Founded: 1953
Staff: 36
Member of: Canadian Wood Energy Institute
Products/Services/Areas of Expertise: High-efficiency woodburning furnaces, heaters, stoves
Financial Information:
Type of Ownership: Private
Domestic Markets:
National
Markets Sought:
The Pacific Rim, USA
Contact(s):
Patrick Turner, President
Garth Bates, Manager

Valley Waste Resource Management
P.O. Box 895
11 Calkin Dr.
Kentville, NS B4N 4H8
902-679-1325
Fax: 902-679-1327
877-927-8300
info@vwrm.com
www.vwrm.com
Products/Services/Areas of Expertise: Waste management; outsourcing of recycling & organics processing
Domestic Markets:
Nova Scotia
Contact(s):
Ross Maybee, General Manager

Vanbots Construction Corp.
A Division of Carillion Construction Inc.
#200, 50 Acadia Ave.
Markham, ON L3R 0B3
905-477-7718
Fax: 905-477-8689
info@vanbots.com
www.vanbots.com
Firm Type: Engineering
Founded: 1959
Products/Services/Areas of Expertise: A construction contracting company, which has completed LEED projects such as the Cambridge City Hall, McMaster University's Les Prince Hall & the David Braley Athletic Centre, The Royal Inland Hospital, Hillside Centre in Kamloops BC, & the University of Toronto's Hazel McCallion Academic Learning Centre
Recently Completed / Ongoing Projects: The Royal Ontario Museum's Michael Lee-Chin Crystal, Toronto, ON; Expansion of the Vancouver International Airport, Vancouver, BC; Honda manufacturing facilities, Canada, USA, & UK
Domestic Markets:
National
Foreign Activity:
USA, United Kingdom
Contact(s):
Joel Parke, Vice-President, Client Services
jparke@vanbots.com

Canadian Branches:
Kanata
#202, 300 March Rd.
Kanata, ON K2K 2E2
613-592-5274
Fax: 613-592-4121
info@vanbots.com
Erin Matthews, P.Eng., Vice President & General Manager, Eastern Ontario
em@vanbots.com

Vancouver Fraser Port Authority
Formerly: Vancouver Pt Authority; Fraser River Pt Authority; N. Fraser Pt Authority
Also Known As: Port Metro Vancouver
999 Canada Place
100 The Pointe
Vancouver, BC V6C 3T4
604-665-9000
866-284-4271
info@portmetrovancouver.com
www.portmetrovancouver.com
Firm Type: Management Consulting
Founded: 1983
Products/Services/Areas of Expertise: Canada's largest port, responsible for the development & operation of the assets & jurisdictions of the combined Vancouver Port Authority, Fraser River Port Authority, & the North Fraser Port Authority
Activities: Environmental management of all port operations; Integration of environmental, social, & economic sustainability initiatives into all areas of port operations; Mitigation of environmental impacts related to development & expansion
Contact(s):
Robin Silvester, President/CEO
Chris Badger, Chief Operating Officer
Allan Baydala, Chief Financial Officer
Tom Winkler, Chief Strategic Development Officer
Lori Lindahl, Vice-President, Human Resources & Sustainability

Vancouver Gear Works Ltd.
14451 Burrows Rd.
Richmond, BC V6V 1K9

604-278-3111
Fax: 604-270-1433
877-888-3111
info@vangear.com
www.vangear.com
Products/Services/Areas of Expertise: Precision gears for oil, natural gas, mining, forestry, marine, steel, cement, pulp & paper & manufacturing industries
Contact(s):
Jim Mantei, General Manager
John Belton, Manager, Manufacturing
Vittorio Dente, Manager, Forest Products

Vanport Sterilizers Inc.
Formerly: R.G. Tennant & Associates Ltd.
Also Known As: VPS
1032 Delestre Ave.
Coquitlam, BC V3K 2H2
604-936-3705
Fax: 604-936-4194
sterilizers@excite.com
Firm Type: Engineering, Manufacturing
Founded: 1978
Member of: British Columbia Environment Industry Association
Products/Services/Areas of Expertise: Developer & manufacturer of steam process technologies for sterilizing wastes & soils
Activities: Developing Soils-from-Wastes systems for the forestry industry
Recently Completed / Ongoing Projects: Introduction of the CFIA-licensed & federally licensed Agriculture Quarantine Control plant, known as the "Shred and Steam" plant to handle wastes & soils
Domestic Markets:
National
Foreign Activity:
Worldwide
Contact(s):
Richard G. Tennant, President

Vansco Electronics Ltd.
1305 Clarence Ave.
Winnipeg, MB R3T 1T4
204-452-6776
Fax: 204-452-1749
info@vansco.ca
www.vansco.ca
Products/Services/Areas of Expertise: Agricultural measuring & monitoring equipment
Contact(s):
André Granger, Vice President, Sales and Marketing
John Lion, Sales Manager

Varcon Inc.
Formerly: Varcon Environmental
#100, 56 Avonlea Ct.
Fredericton, NB E3C 1N8
506-454-3233
Fax: 506-454-4647
info@varcon.ca
www.varcon.ca
Firm Type: Management Consulting, Engineering
Founded: 1987
Products/Services/Areas of Expertise: Consulting firm, with expertise in professional engineering & project management services related to communication site development & communication structures
Recently Completed / Ongoing Projects: Aliant Telecom inspections & routine maintenance supervision, NL, NB, NS, & PEI; CBC tower inspections & routine maintenance, SK, MB, ON, & NL; Canadian Coast Guard engineering inspections of Loran C towers, NL & BC; NorthwesTel Inc. maintenance inspections of towers, YK, NWT, BC; MTS Allstream Inc. corrosion assessments on towers, MB
Domestic Markets:
National
Contact(s):
T.M. (Tom) Vardy, P.Eng., President, 506-454-3233
Elizabeth Vardy, B.A., M.Ed., Vice-President
Matt Vardy, B.Com., M.B.A., Manager, Business Development
Steven Godbout, P.Eng., Regional Manager, Maritimes & Québec

Canadian Branches:
Barrie
#1, 237 Mapleview Dr. East
Barrie, ON L4N 0W5

Products & Services Buyer's Guide

705-734-3668
Fax: 705-734-1933
Trevor Bolt, P.Eng., Regional Manager

Burnaby
#262, 4664 Lougheed Hwy.
Burnaby, BC V5C 5T5
604-297-0551
Fax: 604-297-0747

Varian Canada Inc.
#5, 6705 Millcreek Dr.
Mississauga, ON L5N 5M4
905-819-8181
Fax: 800-394-6482
800-387-2216
www.varianinc.com
Firm Type: Distributing

Products/Services/Areas of Expertise: Distributor of chromatography systems, chromatography consumables & supplies, optical spectroscopy instruments, dissolution products, nuclear magnetic resonance spectrometers, & vacuum products
Activities: Providing preventive, corrective, or qualification service; Offering training courses on topics such as gas chromatography, high performance liquid chromatography, galaxie chromatography data systems, & gas chromatography troubleshooting & maintenance
Financial Information:
Type of Ownership: Foreign-owned

Vegewax Candleworx Ltd.
#1B, 1300 Alness St.
Vaughan, ON L4K 2W6
905-760-7942
Fax: 905-760-7944
866-835-3929
info@vegewax.com
www.vegewax.com
Products/Services/Areas of Expertise: Ecologo-certified consumer products
Ecological Note: Vegewax & Naturlite candles made of plant source
Contact(s):
Laura Sinclair

Velan Inc.
7007, Côte de Liesse
Montréal, QC H4T 1G2
514-748-7743
Fax: 514-748-8635
sales@velan.com; service@velan.com
www.velan.com
Firm Type: Manufacturing
Founded: 1950
Staff: 1800
Quality Environmental Management System(s): 9001
Products/Services/Areas of Expertise: Manufacturer of cast & forged globe, triple-offset, steel gate, knife gate, ball, check, & engineered service valves; Clients include the water & wastewater, mining, pulp & paper, refining & petrochemical, oil & gas, chemical & pharmaceutical, marine, nuclear power, & HVAC industries
Domestic Markets:
National
Foreign Activity:
China, Central Europe, Eastern Europe, Western Europe, The Pacific Rim, USA, United Kingdom
Contact(s):
John Ball, Chief Financial Officer
Sabine Bruckert, General Cousel & Vice-President, Human Resources
Tracy Fairchild, Manager, Marketing Communications
Michael Mogianesi, Regional Manager, Sales

Canadian Branches:
Calgary
17 Simcrest Manor SW
Calgary, AB T3H 3L2
403-232-6482
Fax: 403-686-6485
leo.shewchuk@velan.com
Leo Shewchuk, Regional Manager, Sales

Edmonton
7127 - 56 Ave.
Edmonton, AB T6B 3L2

780-490-3793
Fax: 780-465-0403
bill.patrick@velan.com
Bill Patrick, Regional Manager, Sales

Mississauga
871 Kowal Dr.
Mississauga, ON L5H 3T3
905-278-7522
Fax: 905-278-8155
george.lysakowski@velan.com
George Lysakowski, Regional Manager, Sales

Granby
1010, rue Cowie
Granby, QC J2J 1E7
450-378-2305

Montréal - McArthur
550, rue McArthur
Montréal, QC H4T 1X8
514-748-7743

Montréal - Ward
2125 rue Ward
Montréal, QC H4M 1T6
514-748-7743

Vemco Ltd.
A Division of AMIRIX Systems Inc.
211 Horseshoe Lake Dr.
Halifax, NS B3S 0B9
902-450-1700
Fax: 902-450-1704
www.vemco.com
Firm Type: Distributing, Engineering, Manufacturing
Founded: 1979
Products/Services/Areas of Expertise: Designer, manufacturer, & distributor of underwater acoustic telemetry transmitters & receivers, such as depth data storage recorders & hydrophones; Clients include aquatic research specialists, fisheries, & biologists
Activities: Providing after sale support for all products
Domestic Markets:
National
Foreign Activity:
The Pacific Rim, United Kingdom, Worldwide
Contact(s):
Doug Pincock, Founder & Chair, AMIRIX
Sandra Greer, President/CEO
Nancy Edwards, Manager, Marketing Communications
nancy.edwards@amirix.com

Venables Machine Works Ltd.
502 - 50th St. East
Saskatoon, SK S7K 6L9
306-931-7100
Fax: 306-933-4004
877-634-4968
info@venables.ca
www.venables.ca
Firm Type: Distributing, Manufacturing
Founded: 1931
Products/Services/Areas of Expertise: Provider of custom steel manufacturing services; Products include oilfield storage tanks, custom-built hydraulic cylinders, & tangential abrasive dehulling devices (TADD); Clients include the agricultural, construction, electronics, mining, oilfield, & food processing markets
Activities: Welding & pressure vessel repair; Heat exchanger retubing; Multi-stage pump rebuilds
Domestic Markets:
Alberta, Manitoba, Saskatchewan
Contact(s):
Devin Klotz, Contact, Saskatchewan Sales

Canadian Branches:
Edmonton
4124 - 97th St.
Edmonton, AB T6E 5Y6
780-487-9966
Fax: 780-487-9983
Adam Vaxvick, Contact, Alberta Sales

Venerus International Purification Inc.
Also Known As: VIP
P.O. Box 4508 Main
RR#6
Guelph, ON N1H 6J3

519-823-1252
Fax: 519-823-2046
vipinc@on.aibn.com
Firm Type: Management Consulting, Engineering
Founded: 1990
Quality Environmental Management System(s): 14001
Products/Services/Areas of Expertise: Provider of water & wastewater management services, air pollution assessment, & soil monitoring, analysis, & research; Clients include governments & industries such as resource & manufacturing
Contact(s):
Angelo Venerus, President

Venmar CES, Inc. / CES
2525 Wentz Ave.
Saskatoon, SK S7K 2K9
306-242-3663
Fax: 306-242-3484
866-483-6627
info@venmarces.com
www.venmarces.com
Firm Type: Engineering, Manufacturing
Founded: 1952
Member of: Canada Green Building Council; U.S. Green Building Council (USGBC)
Products/Services/Areas of Expertise: Designer & manufacturer of a variety of energy recovery equipment; Products include Energy recovery ventilators with enthalpy wheels, heat recovery ventilators with plate heat exchangers, classroom ventilators with or without energy recovery, & preconditioners with enthalpy wheels
Activities: Engaging in research & development activities; Offering technical support services
Recently Completed / Ongoing Projects: Development of a "carbon ticker" to demonstrate the amount of CO_2 emissions saved when energy recovery equipment is used
Financial Information:
Type of Ownership: Private
Domestic Markets:
National
Foreign Activity:
Worldwide

Canadian Branches:
St-Léonard-d'Aston
200, rue Carter
St-Léonard-d'Aston, QC J0C 1M0
819-399-2175
Fax: 819-399-2612
info@venmarces.com

Venmar Ventilation Inc.
550, boul Lemire
Drummondville, QC J2C 7W9
819-477-6226
Fax: 819-475-2660
800-567-3855
www.venmar.ca
Firm Type: Manufacturing
Founded: 1976
Products/Services/Areas of Expertise: Manufacturer of indoor air pollution control equipment & ventilation systems
Domestic Markets:
National
Foreign Activity:
USA
Contact(s):
Pascal Ialenti, President

Ventax Robot Inc.
P.O. Box 1180
53 Northumberland St.
Ayr, ON N0B 1E0
519-632-7834
Fax: 519-632-7702
800-440-2771
salesinfo@ventax.com
www.ventax.com
Firm Type: Manufacturing
Founded: 1984
Staff: 16
Products/Services/Areas of Expertise: Plastics automation equipment; robots, stackers, cutting routers
Domestic Markets:
Alberta, British Columbia, Ontario, Québec
Foreign Activity:
Central America, Western Europe, USA

Contact(s):
Hans-Armin Ohlmann, President
hans@ventax.com
Rick Delogu, CEO/CFO
rdelogu@ventax.com

Ventes Techniques Nimatec inc.
Nimatec Technical Sales Inc.
9, rue des Écureuils
Mercier, QC J6R 1Y5
450-691-9427
Fax: 450-691-4949
mstonely@nimatec.com
Firm Type: Distributing
Founded: 1983
Staff: 7
Products/Services/Areas of Expertise: SGL Acotec Inc. - Ceilcote corrosion control products, coatings, linings & floor protection; F.E. Myers Company - pumps for potable & waste water; corrosion protection
Recently Completed / Ongoing Projects: Interquisa Montréal
Financial Information:
Type of Ownership: Private
Domestic Markets:
Québec
Contact(s):
Martin Stonely, President
Stéphane Stonely, Vice-President
Marco Di Cesare, Representative

Venture Foam Products Inc. / VFP Inc.
A division of Industrial Thermo Polymers Ltd.
153 Van Kirk Dr.
Brampton, ON L7A 1A4
905-846-5704
866-855-3626
info@ecosleeve.com
www.ecosleeve.com
Firm Type: Manufacturing
Member of: MasterNet Ltd.; TDL Group Corp. (Tim Hortons)
EcoLogo Certified Products & Services: EcoSleeve, a degradable & recyclable beverage sleeve
Products/Services/Areas of Expertise: Extruded polyethylene foam products
Ecological Note: EcoSleeve, a degradable & recyclable beverage sleeve
Domestic Markets:
National
Foreign Activity:
USA
Contact(s):
Dave VanCasteren, Manager

Veolia ES Canada Industrial Services Inc.
Also Known As: Veolia Environmental Services
A division of Veolia Environnement, (VE-NYSE)
Formerly: Onyx Industries Inc.; Groupe Sani Mobile inc.141 Prosperity Way, RR #6
Chatham, ON N7M 5J6
519-352-7773
Fax: 519-352-7212
866-873-0086
veoliase.com/home
Firm Type: Scientific/Technical Services, Waste Management

Products/Services/Areas of Expertise: Industrial cleaning; hazardous waste handling; collection, disposal & recycling of trash & industrial waste; environmental emergency response
Financial Information:
Type of Ownership: Foreign-owned
Revenue: Greater than $5 Million
Domestic Markets:
New Brunswick, Ontario, Québec
Contact(s):
Richard Burke, President & CEO, Veolia Environmental Services North America Corp.

Canadian Branches:
Alma
575, rue Claire-Fontaine
Alma, QC G8B 5W1
418-662-9710
Fax: 418-662-3986
André Doucet, Gestionnaire
andre.doucet@veoliase.com

Baie-Comeau
51, boul Comeau
Baie-Comeau, QC G4Z 3A7
418-296-3967
Fax: 418-296-0504
Théo Poirier, Gestionnaire
theo.poirier@veoliase.com

Beauceville
139, 181e rue
Beauceville, QC G5X 2S9
418-774-5275
Denis Bénard, Gestionnaire
denis.bedard@veoliase.com

Blainville
750, boul Industriel
Blainville, QC J7C 3V4
450-434-2499
Alain Fontaine, Gestionnaire
alain.fontaine@veoliase.com

Burlington
2250 Industrial St.
Burlington, ON L7P 1A1
905-319-2262
Fax: 905-319-2265
Patricia McLaughlin, Manager
patricia.mclaughlin@veoliaes.com

Chambly
#100, 2630, boul Industriel
Chambly, QC J3L 4V2
450-447-3022
Fax: 450-447-1311
François Gordon, Gestionnaire
francois.gordon@veoliase.com

Contrecoeur
Division Regional Office
4050, rue Industrielle
Contrecoeur, QC J0L 1C0
450-746-0006
Fax: 450-746-2581
Eric Isabelle, Manager

Coquitlam
Division Regional Office
10 King Edward St.
Coquitlam, BC V3K 4S9
604-525-5261
Fax: 604-525-5699
Tom Peterson, Manager
tom.peterson@veoliaes.com

Edmonton
Divison Regional Office
7805 - 34 St.
Edmonton, AB T6B 2V5
780-466-9934
Fax: 780-466-7759
Joe Richards, Manager
joe.richards@veoliaes.com

Hamilton
Divison Regional Office
80 Birmingham St.
Hamilton, ON L8L 6W5
905-547-5661
Fax: 905-547-0511
Graham Wathen, Manager
graham.wathen@veoliaes.com

Jonquière
CP 1128
1995, rue Fay
Jonquière, QC G7S 4K7
418-548-8247
Fax: 418-548-9831
André Doucet, Gestionnaire
andre.doucet@veoliase.com

Kamloops
2305 Rosewood Ave.
Kamloops, BC V2B 4Y9
604-525-5261
Fax: 604-525-5699
Tom Peterson, Manager
tom.peterson@veoliaes.com

L'Ancienne-Lorette
1701, rte de l'Aéroport
L'Ancienne-Lorette, QC G2G 2P4
418-877-4077
Dany Blanchette, Gestionnaire
dany.blanchette@veoliase.com

La Tuque
509, rue Joffre
La Tuque, QC G9X 3P3
819-523-4763
Fax: 819-523-6046
André Doucet, Gestionnaire
andre.doucet@veoliase.com

London
459 Exeter Rd.
London, ON N6E 3Z3
519-668-3149
Tyrone Heiman, Manager
tyrone.heiman@veoliaes.com

Lévis
2800, rue de l'Etchemin
Lévis, QC G6W 7X6
418-835-3750
Fax: 418-835-6679
André Lamy, Gestionnaire
andre.lamy@veoliase.com

Matane
CP 398
88, rue Durette
Matane, QC G4W 3N3
418-562-6085
Fax: 418-562-3981
Pierre Savard, Gestionnaire
pierre.savard@veoliase.com

Montréal - Ontario est
11455, rue Ontario est
Montréal, QC H1B 5J3
514-645-4242
Fax: 514-645-1033
Céline Pearson, Gestionnaire
celine.pearson@veoliase.com

Montréal - Siège social
1705, 3e avenue
Montréal, QC H1B 5M9
514-645-1621
Fax: 514-645-5133
800-361-8920

Ottawa
4140 Belgreen Dr.
Ottawa, ON K1G 3N2
613-739-1449
Fax: 613-739-1955
Jocelyn Chouinard, Manager
jocelyn.chouinard@veoliase.com

Pickering
820 McKay Rd.
Pickering, ON L1W 2Y4
905-683-8111
Fax: 905-683-4668
Ser DaSilva, Manager
ser.dasilva@veoliaes.com

Powell River
5558 Manson Ave.
Powell River, BC V8A 3R5
604-525-5261
Fax: 604-525-5699
Tom Peterson, Manager
tom.peterson@veoliaes.com

Québec
2244, rue Lavoisier
Québec, QC G1N 4H2
418-872-6439
Daniel Labrie, Gestionnaire
daniel.labrie@veoliase.com

Rouyn-Noranda
137, av Marcel-Baril
Rouyn-Noranda, QC J9X 7B9
819-762-6577
Fax: 819-797-0400

Products & Services Buyer's Guide

André Poulin, Gestionnaire
andre.poulin@veoliase.com

Saint-Hyacinthe
7950, av Pion
Saint-Hyacinthe, QC J2R 1R9
450-796-6060
Fax: 450-796-4525
Réal Maihot, Gestionnaire
real.mailhot@veoliase.com

Saint-Romuald
857, rue de l'Église
Saint-Romuald, QC G6W 5M6
418-839-5500
Fax: 418-839-0109
Stéphane Marcotte, Gestionnaire
stephane.marcotte@veoliase.com

Saint-Rémi
77, boul St-Rémi
Saint-Rémi, QC J0L 2L0
450-454-7531
Fax: 450-454-7663
Eric Isabelle, Gestionnaire
eric.isabelle@veolase.com

Sarnia
Division Regional Office
605 Scott Rd.
Sarnia, ON N7T 2H2
519-336-3330
Todd Jardine, Manager
todd.jardine@veoliaes.com

Sept-Iles
CP 100
268, rue des Pionniers
Sept-Iles, QC G4R 4K3
418-962-0233
Fax: 418-962-6776
Théo Poirier, Gestionnaire
theo.poirier@veoliase.com

Timmins
#2, 374 Crawford St.
South Porcupine, ON P0N 1H0
705-235-3955
Fax: 705-235-2877
Kirk Dicks, Manager
kirk.dicks@veoliase.com

Trois-Rivières
2895, boul Jules-Vachon nord
Trois-Rivières, QC G9A 5E1
819-372-0803
Fax: 819-372-1357
André Doucet, Gestionnaire
andre.doucet@veoliase.com

Témiscaming
CP 54
#4, 200, rue de la Carriére
Témiscaming, QC J0Z 3R0
819-762-6577
Fax: 819-797-0400
André Poulin, Gestionnaire
andre.poulin@veoliase.com

Windsor
316, rue du Parc Industriel
Windsor, QC J1S 3A8
819-822-1820
Fax: 819-845-9132
Michel Gagnon, Gestionnaire
michel.gagnon@veoliase.com

Veolia Water Canada
#2, 150 Pony Dr.
Newmarket, ON L3Y 7B6
905-868-9683
www.veoliawaterna.com
Firm Type: Waste Management

Products/Services/Areas of Expertise: Veolia Water North America & Veolia Water Canada are components of Veolia Eau, based in Paris, France. The company provides water services for local & federal governments, as well as industry, & is engaged in water & wastewater treatment & reclamation, water distribution, wastewater collection systems, groundwater remediation, residuals & composting programs, & sewer overflow facilities. Veolia Water Solutions & Technologies is the design/build arm & provides expertise & service in the areas of testing, design, project management, construction & execution of water & wastewater solutions (see entry for John Meunier Inc.)
Financial Information:
Type of Ownership: Foreign-owned
Revenue Sources: 20% Municipals; 80% Private Contracts
Domestic Markets:
Ontario, Québec
Contact(s):
Laurent Auguste, President/CEO, Veolia Water North America
John M. Wood, President, Veolia Water North America - Central, LLC

Verdyol Mulch of Canada Ltd.
5009 Concession #13
RR#4
Cookstown, ON L0L 1L0
705-458-9601
Fax: 705-458-1047
866-250-5592
info@verdyol.ca
www.verdyol.ca
Firm Type: Manufacturing
Founded: 1976
Staff: 10
Products/Services/Areas of Expertise: Manufacturing of hydroseeding mulch from old newspapers, raw cotton, straw specially designed to prevent erosion
Domestic Markets:
New Brunswick, Newfoundland & Labrador, Nova Scotia, Ontario, Québec
Foreign Activity:
USA
Contact(s):
Rob Soczka, General Manager
Peter Davy, Manager, Production & Sales

Versatech Industries Inc.
612 Welham Rd.
Barrie, ON L4N 8Z8
705-726-3000
Fax: 705-726-9990
www.versatechindustriesltd.com
Products/Services/Areas of Expertise: Recycling systems & equipment
Contact(s):
Robert Lee, President

Versatech Products Inc.
4623 Byrne Rd.
Burnaby, BC V5J 3H6
604-271-7500
Fax: 604-271-7501
info@versatech.com; support@versatech.com; accounts@versatech.com
www.versatech.com
Firm Type: Distributing, Engineering, Manufacturing
Founded: 1968
Products/Services/Areas of Expertise: Designer & manufacturer of oil spill containment & recovery products; Products include oil recovery skimmers, oil spill containment booms, boom storage reels, plus the HeliPak & DeckPak Deployment Systems for response to oil spill emergencies; Supplier of Versatank storage tanks & sorbents for oil spill & chemical cleanup
Activities: Offering training & contingency planning courses
Financial Information:
Type of Ownership: Private
Domestic Markets:
National
Foreign Activity:
Worldwide
Contact(s):
Leo Rimanic, Vice-President, Marketing & Sales
Jeff Randall, Manager, Technical Sales

Canadian Branches:
Vancouver
60 Riverside Dr.
North Vancouver, BC V7H 1T4

Versatile Measuring Instruments Inc. / VMI
A subsidiary of The Amidyne Group
Formerly: Sigma Instruments (Canada) Ltd.#7, 1245 Maple Hill Ct.
Newmarket, ON L3Y 9E8
905-954-0582
Fax: 905-954-0415
800-742-1413
info@amidyne.com
www.amidyne.com
Firm Type: Distributing, Manufacturing
Founded: 1983
Staff: 14
Products/Services/Areas of Expertise: Manufacturer & distributor of panel meters & other nuclear instrumentation for use in nuclear power plants. Under new management since 2005, the company is focused on expanding its quality assurance scope to meet the needs of both the Canadian & American markets. The design process includes specification, prototyping, & qualification testing. Registered with QMI to CSA CAN3-Z299.2-1985, with scope to include design, manufacture, commercial grade dedication, & distribution of electronic instruments, panel meters, controlling panel meters, sensor & electronic components for the power generation industries
Recently Completed / Ongoing Projects: Provided instrumentation of nuclear power plants in United States, China & Korea
Financial Information:
Type of Ownership: Private
Revenue: $1.5 Million - $3 Million
Revenue Sources: 40% Provincial; 60% Private Contracts
Domestic Markets:
National
Foreign Activity:
USA
Contact(s):
Edmund Corrente, President
edcorrente@versatile.com
Sydney Platel, Vice-President, Sales/Marketing
sydplatel@versatile.com
William Aumon, Vice-President, Engineering
billaumon@versatile.com

Vestar
#301, 10451 - 170 St.
Edmonton, AB T5P 4T2
780-444-1630
Fax: 780-489-4999
lawrence.bazin@keen.ca
Contact(s):
Lawrence Bazin

Canadian Branches:
Calgary
Calgary
#200, 602 - 12 Ave. SW
Calgary, AB T2R 1J3
403-233-9044
Fax: 403-266-4549
jim.sawers@keen.ca
Jim Sawers, P.Eng., Regional Manager

Edmonton
Edmonton
#301, 10451 - 170 St.
Edmonton, AB T5P 4T2
780-444-1630
Fax: 780-489-4999
chris.jepson@keen.ca
Christopher Jepson, P.Eng., Regional Manager

Fraser Valley
Fraser Valley
#102, 33119 South Fraser Way
Abbotsford, BC V2S 2B1
604-855-7890
Fax: 604-855-7891
richard.corra@keen.ca
Richard Corra, P.Eng., Regional Manager

Kamloops
Kamloops
#201, 1425 Pearson Pl.
Kamloops, BC V1S 1J9
250-828-6766
Fax: 250-372-2241
art.mcdonald@keen.ca
Art McDonald, P.Eng., Regional Manager

Ottawa
#402, 1111 Prince of Wales Dr.
Ottawa, ON K2C 3T2

613-225-8414
Fax: 613-225-9421
kevin.courneya@keen.ca
Kevin Courneya

Toronto
Toronto
372 Bay St., 18th Fl.
Toronto, ON M5H 2W9
416-366-0220
Fax: 416-366-1808
mark.mitchell@keen.ca
Mark Mitchell, P.Eng., Regional Manager

Victoria
Victoria
1010 Langley St.
Victoria, BC V8W 1V8
250-382-2177
Fax: 250-382-4614
tom.wilson@keen.ca
Tom Wilson, P.Eng., Regional Manager

Vestar
#301, 10451 - 170 St.
Edmonton, AB T5P 4T2
780-444-1630
Fax: 780-489-4999
lawrence.bazin@keen.ca

International Branch(es):
San Francisco
2742 - 17th St
San Francisco, CA USA
415-626-6864
Fax: 415-626-1268
don.nurisso@keeneng.com
Don Murisso, Office Manager

Seattle
Seattle
#308, 1932 First Ave.
Seattle, WA USA
206-770-7779
Fax: 206-770-5941
paul.anseeuw@keeneng.com
Paul Anseeuw, P.Eng., Regional Manager

Vestas Canada
Formerly: Port Albert Wind Farms Ltd.
1475 Concession 5, RR#5
Kincardine, ON N2Z 2X6
519-396-6922
Fax: 519-396-6158
www.vestas.com
Products/Services/Areas of Expertise: Renewable low-impact wind-powered electricity
Ecological Note: Wind energy

Via Disposal Services Ltd.
145 Fenmar Dr.
Toronto, ON M9L 1M7
416-665-0505
Fax: 416-665-3785
Firm Type: Waste Management
Founded: 1971
Staff: 12
Member of: Ontario Waste Management Association
Products/Services/Areas of Expertise: Waste management; recycling services: industrial, commercial, construction, institutional; mini-bins for small projects, home renovations, minor clean-ups, etc.
Financial Information:
Type of Ownership: Private
Domestic Markets:
Ontario
Contact(s):
Domenic Baldasserra, President

Via-Sat Data Systems
124 Garden Ave.
North Vancouver, BC V7P 3H2
604-980-6062
Fax: 604-980-9262
pcr@via-sat.com; info@via-sat.com
www.via-sat.com
Firm Type: Scientific/Technical Services
Founded: 1988
Member of: Canadian Environment Industry Association, Air & Waste Management Assoc., Canadian Water Resources Assoc., Canadian Institute for Climate Studies, Alliance for Marine Remote Sensing, Canadian Hydropower Assoc., Independent Power Assoc. of BC, Western Snow Conference, North Shore Economic Development Commission
Products/Services/Areas of Expertise: Environmental data collection; installation & servicing of climate station networks with primary mode of transmission using satellite telemetry; installation & servicing of hydrometric & sedimentation networks; air quality monitoring
Domestic Markets:
Northwest Territories, Yukon Territory
Foreign Activity:
Asia
Markets Sought:
Central America, South America, Mexico
Contact(s):
Paul Rocchetti, President
Dennis Morgan, Vice-President & Project Engineer

Vibec International Inc.
161, rue Laurier est
Victoriaville, QC G6P 6P8
819-758-7212
Fax: 819-758-7290
vibec@ivic.qc.ca
Firm Type: Engineering
Founded: 1958
Staff: 150
Products/Services/Areas of Expertise: Construction of roads, bridges, dykes, dams, industrial, commercial & institutional buildings; completion of civil engineering projects, airports, sewage projects, soil decontamination, mining projects, works related to the production & distribution of electricity, building of hospitals & any type of BOOT projects
Financial Information:
Revenue Sources: 100% Private Contracts
Domestic Markets:
Québec
Foreign Activity:
Africa, Central America, South America
Contact(s):
Denis Roy, P.Eng., President
Gaetan Ducharme, P.Eng., Vice-President, Contract Administration
Edward Kteily, P.Eng., Vice-President, Operations
Michel Roy, Engineer

Victaulic Co. of Canada Ltd.
123 Newkirk Rd.
Richmond Hill, ON L4K 3G5
905-884-7444
Fax: 905-884-7446
viccanada@victaulic.com
www.victaulic.com
Firm Type: Manufacturing
Founded: 1931
Quality Environmental Management System(s): 9001
Products/Services/Areas of Expertise: Pipe fittings & valves for water & wastewater treatment
Domestic Markets:
National
Contact(s):
Gary Moore, President

Canadian Branches:
Edmonton Branch
11659 - 180 St. NW
Edmonton, AB T5S 2H6
780-452-0680
Fax: 780-452-2430

Montréal Branch
975, rue Selkirk
Pointe-Claire, QC H9R 4S4
514-426-3500
Fax: 514-426-2818

Sudbury Branch
1070 Elisabella St.
Sudbury, ON P3A 5K2
705-560-9595
Fax: 705-560-9490

Vancouver Branch
8129 River Way
Delta, BC V4G 1L2
604-940-3301
Fax: 604-940-3360

Viessmann Manufacturing Company Inc.
750 McMurray Rd.
Waterloo, ON N2V 2G5
519-885-6300
Fax: 519-885-5342
mail@viessmann.com
www.viessmann.ca
Firm Type: Manufacturing
Member of: Professional Engineers of Ontario, Certified Engineering Technicians Ontario
EcoLogo Certified Products & Services: Gas-fired hot water heating boilers
Products/Services/Areas of Expertise: Vertomat & Vitodens series of gas-fired hot water heating boilers, condensing boilers available, constructed of corrosion resistant stainless steel, can achieve seasonal efficiencies in excess of 95%, low NOX emissions meet or exceed all international guidelines including CCME initiatives
Ecological Note: Gas-fired hot water heating boilers
Financial Information:
Type of Ownership: Private
Domestic Markets:
National
Contact(s):
Kenneth Webster, Director, Sales & Marketing
Katharina Schmidt, Supervisor, Marketing
skth@viessmann.com

VIQUA - A Trojan Technologies Company
Formerly: R-Can Environmental Inc.; AMF Cuno/Sterilight
425 Clair Rd. West
Guelph, ON N1L 1R1
519-763-1032
Fax: 519-763-5069
800-265-7246
info@viqua.com
www.viqua.com
Firm Type: Distributing, Manufacturing
Founded: 1986
Member of: Canadian Water Quality Association, Water Quality Association; Ontario Bottled Water Association; Canadian Automatic Merchandising Association; Canadian Restaurant & Food Services Association; Canadian Institute of Plumbing & Heating
Quality Environmental Management System(s): 9001:2008
Products/Services/Areas of Expertise: Consumer, commercial & industrial water treatment products, such as filters, ultra-violet sterilizers & ozonators
Contact(s):
Ronald K. Braun, Managing Director

Viridis Environmental Inc. / VEI
777 Kingfisher Cres.
Orleans, ON K1E 2L5
613-845-9819
Fax: 613-482-4879
viridis@cyberus.ca
www.viridisenvironmental.com
Firm Type: Management Consulting
Founded: 1994
Staff: 8
Member of: Recycling Council of Ontario; Green Building Information Council
Products/Services/Areas of Expertise: Development & implementation of environmental management systems & sustainable development strategies; waste audits; environmental audits; water management
Financial Information:
Type of Ownership: Private
Revenue Sources: 70% nationwide; 30% Municipals
Domestic Markets:
Ontario
Markets Sought:
Asia, South America, Mexico
Contact(s):
Peter Landry, Director

Vision Quest - TransAlta's Wind Business
Formerly: Vision Quest Windelectric
Also Known As: TransAlta Wind
110 - 12th Ave. SW
Calgary, AB T2P 2M1

403-267-2000
Fax: 403-267-2005
877-547-3365
wind@transalta.com
www.visionquestwind.com
Products/Services/Areas of Expertise: Renewable energy project marketing, management, development & financing
Contact(s):
Fred Gallagher

Vision Quest Windelectric Inc.
Formerly: Chinook Project Inc.
#255, 3553 - 31st NW
Calgary, AB T2L 2K7
403-532-4250
Fax: 403-284-6415
877-547-3365
info@visionquestwind.com
www.visionquestwind.com
Firm Type: Manufacturing
Founded: 1996
Staff: 11
Member of: Canadian Wind Energy Association; Independent Power Producers Society of Alberta
EcoLogo Certified Products & Services: Green energy from emissions-free wind energy
Products/Services/Areas of Expertise: Renewable energy project management & development; ownership & operation selling energy & emissions offsets
Ecological Note: Green energy from emissions-free wind energy
Foreign Activity:
USA
Contact(s):
Paula Ohreen
Joe Miller, Director, Financial Operations

Visionwall Corporation
Formerly: Visionwall Technologies Inc.
17915 - 118 Ave.
Edmonton, AB T5S 1L6
780-451-4000
Fax: 780-451-4745
800-400-8633
marketing@visionwall.com
www.visionwall.com
Firm Type: Engineering, Manufacturing
Founded: 1986
Products/Services/Areas of Expertise: Custom-engineered & precision-manufactured energy-efficient windows & curtain wall systems for use in commercial, institutional & industrial buildings
Domestic Markets:
National
Foreign Activity:
USA
Contact(s):
Gregory L. Clarahan, President
Randy L. Pederson, B.Comm, MBA,CGA, Vice-Presdent, Finance & CFO

Vitafoam Products Canada Ltd.
150 Toro Rd.
Toronto, ON M3J 2A9
416-630-6633
Fax: 416-630-9921
800-268-1247
vitaca@vitacanada.ca
www.vitausa.com
Firm Type: Waste Management
Founded: 1958
Staff: 200
Products/Services/Areas of Expertise: Recycling of polyurethane foam; fabric & fibre; Supplier of filling & cushionings to home furnishing & flooring industries; recycled & new foam to automotive industry
Domestic Markets:
Alberta, British Columbia, Manitoba, Ontario, Québec
Contact(s):
Gerry Hannan, Manager

Viterra Inc.
Formerly: United Grain Growers Ltd., Saskatchewan Wheat Board, Agricore United
2625 Victoria Ave.
Regina, SK S4T 7T9
306-569-4411
Fax: 306-569-4708
866-569-4411
www.viterra.ca
Firm Type: Distributing, Information Technology
Founded: 2007
Staff: 5000
Member of: Crop Protection Institute
Quality Environmental Management System(s): 9001
Products/Services/Areas of Expertise: Operates businesses in grain handling and marketing, agri-products, food and feed processing, and financial services
Financial Information:
Type of Ownership: Publicly Traded
Domestic Markets:
Alberta, British Columbia, Manitoba, Ontario, Saskatchewan
Foreign Activity:
Australia/New Zealand, China, Western Europe, The Pacific Rim, USA,
Contact(s):
Mayo Schmidt, President & Chief Executive Officer
Rex Mclennan, Chief Financial Officer
Fran Malecha, Chief Operating Officer, Operations
Karl Gerrand, Sr. Vice-President, Food Processing
Colleen Vancha, Sr. Vice-President, Investor Relations and Corporate Affairs

Canadian Branches:
Calgary
Bow Valley Square 2
3400 - 205 5th Avenue SW
Calgary, AB T2P 2V7
403-440-1119
Firm Type: Distributing, Information Technology

Financial Information:
Type of Ownership: Publicly Traded

Winnipeg
CanWest Global Pl.
P.O. Box 6600
201 Portage Ave.
Winnipeg, MB R3C 3A7
204-944-5411
Firm Type: Distributing, Information Technology

Financial Information:
Type of Ownership: Publicly Traded

Vizon SciTec Inc. / BCRI
Formerly: BC Research Inc.
BC Research Complex
3650 Westbrook Mall
Vancouver, BC V6S 2L2
604-224-4331
Fax: 604-224-0540
info@vizonscitec.com
www.vizonscitec.com
Firm Type: Scientific/Technical Services
Founded: 1993
Staff: 80
Products/Services/Areas of Expertise: Privately operated multidisciplinary research & technology firm; develops international markets in leading edge technologies & sustainable development; provides laboratory services, contract research & development in areas of natural resource extraction & processing, biological treatment for wastes & effluents, pulp mill effluents & domestic sewage, methanation of hydrocarbons; predictive testing & remediation of acid mine drainage, biological toxicity studies, research on treatment of stormwater runoff, municipal wastewater, pulp mill effluent & other liquid wastes
Financial Information:
Type of Ownership: Private
Domestic Markets:
National
Foreign Activity:
Worldwide
Contact(s):
Brian Nixon, President/CEO

Voghel Inc.
1681, rue de l'Industrie
Beloeil, QC J3G 4S5
514-990-6636
voghel@videotron.ca
Contact(s):
Jean-Yves Voghel

Voice Construction Ltd.
5015 - 76 Ave.
Edmonton, AB T6B 2G2
780-469-1351
Fax: 780-466-9378
voice@voiceconst.com
www.voiceconst.com
Firm Type: Engineering
Member of: International Union of Operating Engineers 955
Products/Services/Areas of Expertise: Construction firm specializing in industrial site preparation and heavy construction projects
Contact(s):
Scott Shea, President

VQUIP Inc.
4430 Mainway Dr.
Burlington, ON L7L 5Y5
905-336-1611
Fax: 905-336-3035
info@vquip.com
www.vquip.com
Firm Type: Distributing, Manufacturing, Waste Management
Founded: 1986
Staff: 25
Products/Services/Areas of Expertise: Sweepers; scrubbers; spill control response units; recycling & waste collection systems; transfer systems
Domestic Markets:
National
Foreign Activity:
USA
Contact(s):
Doug Vanderlinden, President

VWR International, LLC / VWR
Formerly: VWR Scientific of Canada Ltd.
2360 Argentia Rd.
Mississauga, ON L5N 5Z7
800-932-5000
www.vwr.com
Firm Type: Distributing
Founded: 1852
Products/Services/Areas of Expertise: A laboratory supply & distribution company, with expertise in chemicals, lab supplies, instruments, equipment, apparel, & furniture; Clients include pharmaceutical & biotech companies, industries, governments, & educational organizations
Financial Information:
Type of Ownership: Foreign-owned
Domestic Markets:
National
Foreign Activity:
Worldwide

W. Ralston (Canada) Inc.
455, Côte Vertu
Montréal, QC H4N 1E8
800-334-1567
info@cttgroup.com
www.cttgroup.com
Products/Services/Areas of Expertise: Ecologo certified plastic products
Ecological Note: Retail & industrial garbage bags, construction films

W. Sodin (Gravity) Ltd.
#18, 95 West Beaver Creek Rd.
Richmond Hill, ON L4B 1H2
905-886-8632
Fax: 905-886-4477
Firm Type: Manufacturing, Scientific/Technical Services
Founded: 1970
Staff: 4
Products/Services/Areas of Expertise: Measuring & monitoring equipment; laboratory equipment; gravity meter used for mineral & oil exploration or scientific investigation
Contact(s):
W. Sodin, President

W.B. Beatty & Associates
Formerly: Beatty Franz & Associates
18 King St. East
Bolton, ON L7E 1E8
905-857-9919
Fax: 905-857-9082

info@bbeatty.com
www.bbeatty.com
Firm Type: Engineering
Founded: 1994
Staff: 20
Member of: Professional Engineers of Ontario; Canadian Groundwater Association; National Groundwater Association; Ontario Groundwater Association; International Association of Hydrogeologists; Canadian Geotechnical Society; Ontario Waste Management Association
Products/Services/Areas of Expertise: Environmental assessment & remediation services; risk assessment; GIS
Financial Information:
Type of Ownership: Private
Domestic Markets:
Alberta, New Brunswick, Newfoundland & Labrador, Nova Scotia, Ontario, Québec
Foreign Activity:
Eastern Europe, USA
Contact(s):
Brian Beatty, P.Eng., President
Joanne Thompson, MSc., P.Eng, Vice-President
Nancy Rennie, P.Geo., Hydrogeologist

W.D. Cookson Ltd.
RR#3
Simcoe, ON N3Y 4K2
519-426-1351
Products/Services/Areas of Expertise: Waste management
Contact(s):
Vera E. Cookson, President
James D. Cookson, Vice-President

W.F. Baird & Associates Coastal Engineers Ltd.
Also Known As: Baird & Associates
#500, 1145 Hunt Club Rd.
Ottawa, ON K1V 0Y3
613-731-8900
Fax: 613-731-9778
info@baird.com
www.baird.com/
Firm Type: Engineering
Founded: 1981
Products/Services/Areas of Expertise: Specialized services for practical, cost-effective & innovative solutions for water-related projects; studies of the force of waves & currents; defines natural processes of oceans, lakes & rivers; evaluation & analyses of coastal & shoreline processes; hydraulics & hydrodynamics; design of coastal & waterfront structures; planning; coastal zone management; numerical & physical modelling; research & development; field investigations; surveys & mapping; construction services
Domestic Markets:
National
Foreign Activity:
Caribbean, Central America, South America, USA
Contact(s):
Bill Baird, President

Canadian Branches:
Oakville Branch
#200, 627 Lyons Lane
Oakville, ON L6J 5Z7
905-845-5385
Fax: 905-845-0698

International Branch(es):
Atria Baird Consultores S.A.
Fidel Oteiza 1953, Oficina 602
Santiago Chile
562-341-4833
Fax: 562-204-6094

W.F. Baird & Associates - Madison
2981 Yarmouth Greenway Dr.
Madison, WI USA
608-273-0592
Fax: 608-273-2010

W.F. Baird & Associates - Barbados
#4 Evergreen House
3rd Avenue, Belleville
St. Michael Barbados
246-430-0845

W.G. Shaw & Associates
Highland Professional Centre
65 Beech Hill Rd.
Antigonish, NS B2G 2P9
902-863-1903
Firm Type: Management Consulting, Engineering, Scientific/Technical Services
Staff: 3
Products/Services/Areas of Expertise: Consulting geoscientists; ground & surface water studies; site assessments; mine development & reclamation
Contact(s):
W.G. Shaw, President

W.J. Sheldrick Sanitation Ltd.
Also Known As: Sheldrick Sanitation
West Lincoln, ON L0R 2A0
905-957-3165
800-263-8513
Firm Type: Waste Management
Founded: 1971
Staff: 19
Member of: Ontario Waste Management Association; National Solid Waste Management Association
Products/Services/Areas of Expertise: Waste management; municipal, industrial, commercial & institutional non-hazardous waste collection; recycling collections for Blue Box items, cardboard & tires; yard waste collection & composting; container service - rear loaders, luggers & roll-offs; front-end bins
Contact(s):
Steve Washuta, President
Stanley J. Sheldrake, General Manager
Mark Sheldrake, Operations Manager

W.L. Whelan Environmental Consultants Ltd.
46 Academy Park Rd.
Regina, SK S4S 4T7
306-584-0056
wwhelan@accesscomm.ca
Firm Type: Management Consulting
Staff: 2
Products/Services/Areas of Expertise: Site Assessments
Financial Information:
Type of Ownership: Private
Revenue Sources: 100% Private Contracts
Domestic Markets:
Saskatchewan
Contact(s):
W.L. Whelan, General Manager

W.R. Graham Services Ltd.
P.O. Box 375
New Glasgow, NS B2H 5E5
902-752-8936
Fax: 902-755-9932
888-935-3745
bill.graham@ns.sympatico.ca
www3.ns.sympatico.ca/bill.graham
Firm Type: Engineering, Manufacturing
Founded: 1986
Staff: 5
Products/Services/Areas of Expertise: Geothermal heat pumps
Contact(s):
Bill Graham, Owner

W.T. McGinn & Associates Ltd.
1457 Albert St.
Regina, SK S4R 2R8
306-565-0411
Fax: 306-757-9471
mcginn@sasktel.net
Firm Type: Engineering
Founded: 1964
Staff: 18
Member of: Association of Professional Engineers, Geologists & Geoscientists of Saskatchewan
Products/Services/Areas of Expertise: Engineering consulting services; building engineering; industrial plant engineering; processing engineering
Recently Completed / Ongoing Projects: Processing engineering, Agrevo, Regina; wastewater management/treatment study, Ipsco-Steel; numerous phase I, II & III audits
Financial Information:
Type of Ownership: Private
Revenue Sources: 15% nationwide; 15% Provincial; 70% Private Contracts
Domestic Markets:
Alberta, British Columbia, Manitoba, Ontario, Saskatchewan
Contact(s):
Michael McGinn, P.Eng., President
Patrick McGinn, P.Eng., Vice-President
Guy Sander, P.Eng., Vice-President, Mechanical
K. Parmar, Vice-President, Electrical

Wainbee Limited
5789 Coopers Ave.
Mississauga, ON L4Z 3S6
905-568-1700
Fax: 905-568-0083
888-924-6233
marketing@wainbee.com
www.wainbee.com
Firm Type: Distributing
Founded: 1957
Staff: 190
Quality Environmental Management System(s): 9002
Products/Services/Areas of Expertise: Air handling equipment used for soil remediation, air & water sampling & monitoring; aerobic sewage treatment; wastewater handling products
Domestic Markets:
National
Contact(s):
R.J. Rodger, President/CEO
John Bachmann, Manager, Sales & Marketing

Canadian Branches:
Calgary
3518 - 62 St. SE, Bay B
Calgary, AB T2C 1Z8
403-236-1133
Fax: 403-279-9367
calgary@wainbee.com

Chicoutimi
135, rue des Routiers
Chicoutimi, QC G7H 5B1
418-698-4884
Fax: 418-698-4909
chicoutimi@wainbee.com

Edmonton
10336 - 59 Ave.
Edmonton, AB T6H 1E6
780-434-9528
Fax: 780-437-7931
edmonton@wainbee.com

Halifax
#5, 10 Thornhill Dr.
Dartmouth, NS B3B 1S1
902-468-1787
Fax: 902-468-3225
dartmouth@wainbee.com

Kitchener
#14, 65 Trillium Park Pl.
Kitchener, ON N2E 1X1
519-748-5391
Fax: 519-748-4893
kitchener@wainbee.ca

London
#45, 1909 Oxford St.
London, ON N5V 4L9
519-451-6266
Fax: 519-451-5566

Montréal
215, boul Brunswick
Pointe-Claire, QC H9R 4R7
514-697-8810
Fax: 514-697-3070
montreal@wainbee.com

North Bay
#8, 191 Booth Rd.
North Bay, ON P1A 4K3
705-472-4244
Fax: 705-472-3864
1-800-461-9534
northbay@wainbee.ca

Ottawa
2212 Gladwin Cr., #B6
Ottawa, ON K1B 5N1
613-744-1720
Fax: 613-744-8472

Products & Services Buyer's Guide

Québec
950, av St-Jean-Baptiste
Québec, QC G2E 5E9
418-683-1956
Fax: 418-688-9885
quebec@wainbee.com

Saskatoon
1031 Main St.
Saskatoon, SK S7H 0K6
306-652-1433
Fax: 306-652-1436
saskatoon@wainbee.com

Vancouver
2231 Vauxhall Pl.
Richmond, BC V6V 1Z5
604-278-4288
Fax: 604-278-3490
vancouver@wainbee.com

Winnipeg
#4, 1393 Border St.
Winnipeg, MB R3H 0N1
204-632-4558
Fax: 204-694-5494
1-800-663-1393
winnpeg@wainbee.com

Wakefield Acoustics Ltd.
301 - 2250 Oak Bay Ave.
Victoria, BC V8R 1G5
250-370-9302
Fax: 250-370-9309
clair@wakefieldacoustics.com
www.wakefieldacoustics.com
Firm Type: Engineering
Founded: 1988
Staff: 12
Member of: National Council of Acoustical Consultants
Products/Services/Areas of Expertise: Consulting engineering services; environmental/community noise impact assessment & control; vibration control; architectural acoustics & building/HVAC noise control; industrial noise exposure assessment & control; noise by-law development & application; training services & expert testimony
Recently Completed / Ongoing Projects: Preliminary environmental noise studies, Lions Gate Crossing; theatre/drama facility acoustics & noise control, Edward Milne Community School; chipper noise control, Timberwest Sawmill, Quesnel, BC
Financial Information:
Type of Ownership: Private
Revenue Sources: 10% nationwide; 50% Provincial; 10% Municipals; 30% Private Contracts
Domestic Markets:
British Columbia
Markets Sought:
The Pacific Rim, USA
Contact(s):
Clair W. Wakefield, President

Walinga Inc.
Hwy. 6, RR#5
Guelph, ON N1H 6J2
519-824-8520
Fax: 519-824-5651
888-925-4642
www.walinga.com
Firm Type: Manufacturing
Founded: 1954
Staff: 190
Member of: Municipal Equipment Operation Association; National Solid Waste Management Association; Solid Waste Association of North America; Ontario Solid Waste Management; Association of Municipal Recycling Coordinators
Products/Services/Areas of Expertise: Curbside recycling collection truck bodies & loading mechanism; organic & rendering collection top load truck bodies for the recycling industry; walking floor transfer trailers
Financial Information:
Type of Ownership: Private
Revenue Sources: 60% Municipals; 40% Private Contracts
Domestic Markets:
National
Foreign Activity:
Asia, Australia/New Zealand, The Middle East, USA
Contact(s):
Butch Medemblik, Engineering & Plant Operations
chm@walinga.com
Terry Medemblik, Transportation Equipment Sales
tjm@walinga.com
Paul Broekema, P.Eng., Export Sales
pamb@walinga.com

Walker Industries Holdings Ltd.
P.O. Box 100
Thorold, ON L2V 3Y8
905-227-4142
Fax: 905-227-1034
800-263-2526
info@walkerind.com
www.walkerind.com
Firm Type: Waste Management
Founded: 1887
Staff: 200
Member of: Ontario Waste Management Association; Ontario Trucking Association; Recycling Council of Ontario; National Solid Wastes Management Association; Chemical Waste Transporters Institute; Association of Municipal Recycling Coordinators; Waste Reduction Council
Products/Services/Areas of Expertise: Waste disposal, transfer & transport; composting; recycling design, building & operation for municipal waste
Recently Completed / Ongoing Projects: Landfill licensing in Ontario; Landfill gas collection/utilization; Recycling centre construction; Biosolids processing facility
Financial Information:
Type of Ownership: Private
Revenue: Greater than $5 Million
Revenue Sources: 1% nationwide; 25% Municipals; 74% Private Contracts
Domestic Markets:
Ontario
Contact(s):
Bill Costello, President
Joseph Lyne, Manager, Sales & Marketing, 905/680-3702
jlyne@walkerind.com
Shawn Jordan, Environmental Coordinator, 905/680-1900
Alison Braithwaite, Director, Environmental Performance, 905/680-1900

Walker Technologies Corporation
Formerly: Walker Systems Corp.
3001B Moray Ave.
Courtenay, BC V9N 7S7
250-334-0447
Fax: 250-334-0467
sales@walkersys.com
www.walkertechnologies.com
Products/Services/Areas of Expertise: Microprocessor based control systems for major OEMs; environmental analysis & treatment; thermal measuring & controlling instruments; process & multi-function control machinery & apparatus; computer equipment & software
Contact(s):
Al Walker, President

Wallace, Van Egmond Spankle Inc. / WAVES
27 Hall Rd.
Georgetown, ON L7G 5Y7
905-877-6496
Fax: 905-877-6821
800-267-4797
john_van_egmond@egmondassociates.com
www.egmondassociates.com
Firm Type: Distributing, Engineering
Founded: 1994
Staff: 1
Member of: Professional Engineers of Ontario, Minnesota Architect Engineer
Products/Services/Areas of Expertise: Soil environmental testing; storm & groundwater management & consulting; distribution of storm water products; stormwater infiltration products
Recently Completed / Ongoing Projects: Stormwater control; aquifer replenishment; NPDES control
Financial Information:
Type of Ownership: Private
Revenue Sources: 100% Private Contracts
Domestic Markets:
Ontario
Foreign Activity:
USA
Contact(s):
John Van Egmond, President

Walter Dow Associates Ltd.
4180 Dundas St. West
Toronto, ON M8X 1X8
416-236-8880
Fax: 416-236-9160
walterdow@bellnet.ca
www.walterdow.com
Firm Type: Engineering
Founded: 1947
Staff: 20
Products/Services/Areas of Expertise: Complete engineering services
Recently Completed / Ongoing Projects: Mining, cement, water & sewage projects
Financial Information:
Type of Ownership: Private
Revenue: $500,000 - $1.5 Million
Revenue Sources: 50% Provincial; 50% Private Contracts
Domestic Markets:
National
Foreign Activity:
Worldwide
Markets Sought:
Asia, Australia/New Zealand, Caribbean, Central America, China, Vietnam
Contact(s):
Bill Marshall, President

Warco Process Technologies
Formerly: Warco Equipment Ltd.
1904, boul. St-Regis
Montréal, QC H9P 1H6
514-685-7878
Fax: 514-685-8871
warco@warco.ca
www.warco.ca
Firm Type: Distributing
Founded: 1950
Staff: 12
Member of: Canadian Pulp & Paper Association
Products/Services/Areas of Expertise: Air pollution treatment equipment; water treatment systems & equipment; liquid filtration; mist elimination; magnetic separation; metal detection; precision porous metals; gravity separation; power transmission equipment; automatic strainers
Financial Information:
Revenue: $3 Million - $5 Million
Domestic Markets:
New Brunswick, Newfoundland & Labrador, Nova Scotia, Ontario, Prince Edward Island, Québec
Contact(s):
Jeff Steinberg, Sales
Dan Levine, Sales Contact

Canadian Branches:
Central Ontario
#102, 1050 Simcoe St. North
Oshawa, ON L1G 4W5
905-725-8431
Fax: 905-725-4626
jsteinberg@warco.ca
Jeff Steinberg

Ward Chemical
6015 - 103A St. NW
Edmonton, AB T6H 2J7
780-436-4832
Fax: 780-431-0288

Wardrop Engineering Inc.
Formerly: W.L. Wardrop & Associates
6725 Airport Rd., 6th Fl.
Mississauga, ON L4V 1V2
905-673-3788
Fax: 905-673-8007
877-987-3211
toronto@wardrop.com
www.wardrop.com
Firm Type: Management Consulting, Engineering
Founded: 1955
Staff: 400
Member of: Consulting Engineers of Ontario, Manitoba, Saskatchewan, Alberta & British Columbia
Quality Environmental Management System(s): 9001

Products/Services/Areas of Expertise: Multi-disciplined engineering & environmental consulting firm, providing services to the oil & gas, power, nuclear, manufacturing, forest products & infrastructure centres; ecological field studies; environmental impact assessment & permitting (mining/oil & gas/hydroelectric/transportation/industrial/land development); fish habitat compensation planning; mine site reclamation
Recently Completed / Ongoing Projects: Metal mining EEM studies; Environment license applications for base/precious metal mintes; NI 43-101 base metal/precious metal mine feasibility studies; Large scale remediation of petroleum hydrocarbon & other chemical impacted soil & groundwater; Industrial wastewater process design; Environmental impact assessments & environmental approvals for mining, oil & gas, forestry, industrial, infrastructure & power generation developments; particular expertise in aquatic biology as it relates to the Department of Fisheries & Oceans matters
Financial Information:
Type of Ownership: Private
Revenue: Greater than $5 Million
Revenue Sources: 5% nationwide; 5% Provincial; 10% Municipals; 80% Private Contracts
Domestic Markets:
National
Foreign Activity:
Worldwide
Contact(s):
Brent Thompson, P.Eng., President
Dave Kelly, Vice-President, Oil & Gas & Industrial, 204/956-0980
dave.kelly@wardrop.com
Greg Turchyn, Vice-President, Business Development, 705/673-3788
gregory.turchyn@wardrop.com
Jim Mucklow, P.Eng., Manager, Environmental Sciences, 807/345-5453
jim.mucklow@wardrop.com
Doug Ramsey, Manager, Environmental Services, 204/956-0980
doug.ramsey@wardrop.com

Canadian Branches:
Calgary
815 - 8th Ave. SW
Calgary, AB T2P 3P2
403-514-6908
Fax: 403-514-8086
calgary@wardrop.com

Edmonton
#11, 900 - 10665 Jasper Ave.
Edmonton, AB T5J 3S9
780-429-5656
Fax: 780-429-5686
edmonton@wardrop.com

Markham
#206, 8901 Woodbine Ave.
Markham, ON L3R 0Y4
905-475-3477
Fax: 905-4753506

Pickering
#2, 975 Dillingham Rd.
Pickering, ON L1W 1Z7
905-837-5053
Fax: 905-837-9953
pickering@wardrop.com

Regina
#212, 2505 - 11th Ave.
Regina, SK S4P 0K6
306-352-1686
Fax: 306-352-1687
regina@wardrop.com

Saskatoon
#1400, 410 - 22 St. East
Saskatoon, SK S7K 5T6
306-244-4888
Fax: 306-664-7074
saskatoon@wardrop.com

Sudbury
#102, 957 Cambrian Heights Dr.
Sudbury, ON P3C 5M6
705-671-9518
Fax: 705-671-6139
sudbury@wardrop.com

Thunder Bay
725 Hewitson St.
Thunder Bay, ON P7B 6B5
807-345-5453
Fax: 807-345-8708
thunderbay@wardrop.com

Toronto
#604, 330 Bay St.
Toronto, ON M5H 2S8
416-368-9080
Fax: 416-368-1963
tim.maunula@wardrop.com
Ian Pritchard

Vancouver
#905, 1130 West Pender St.
Vancouver, BC V6E 4A4
604-408-3788
Fax: 604-408-3722
vancouver@wardrop.com

Winnipeg
#400, 386 Broadway Ave.
Winnipeg, MB R3C 4M8
204-956-0980
Fax: 204-988-0546
winnipeg@wardrop.com

International Branch(es):
Minneapolis, USA
#405, 6465 Wayzata Blvd.
Minneapolis, MN USA
952-546-1028
Fax: 952-546-1035
minneapolis@wardrop.com

Nigeria
18 Hassan Estate
Dakarta, Kano Nigeria
-011-234-64-947-150
paulmaycher@wardropnigeria.com

Uganda - MBW Consulting Engineers
P.O. Box 8493
Plot 4, Kanjokya St.
Kampala Uganda
-011-256-41-540140
Fax: -011-256-41-540
wardrop@imul.com

Warren's Imaging & Dryography Inc.
711 Clayson Rd.
Toronto, ON M9M 2H2
416-745-8200
Fax: 416-747-7199
800-820-7702
info@warrenswateless.com
www.warrenswaterless.com
Firm Type: Scientific/Technical Services
Founded: 1972
Staff: 30
Member of: Waterless Print Association; Forest Stewardship Council; Terrachoice
Quality Environmental Management System(s): 14001
EcoLogo Certified Products & Services: Pre-press & commercial sheetfed waterless printing (dryography)
Products/Services/Areas of Expertise: Eco-Logo certified printing services, environmentally friendly waterless printing of all types
Ecological Note: Pre-press & commercial sheetfed waterless printing (dryography)
Financial Information:
Type of Ownership: Private
Revenue: $3 Million - $5 Million
Revenue Sources: 5% nationwide; 5% Provincial; 5% Municipals; 85% Private Contracts
Domestic Markets:
Ontario
Foreign Activity:
USA
Contact(s):
Glen Warren, Manager
gwarren@warrenwaterless.com
Glen Laycock, Sales
glaycock@warrenwaterless.com
Dave Dixon, Environmental Manager
ddixon@warrenwaterless.com

Wascana Recycling & Resource Recovery Corp.
Formerly: Barker & Associates
1121 Scarth St.
Regina, SK S4R 2E3
306-586-6044
Fax: 306-352-0655
888-927-2262
Firm Type: Waste Management
Founded: 1999
Staff: 6
Products/Services/Areas of Expertise: Processing of recyclable materials
Financial Information:
Type of Ownership: Private
Revenue: $1.5 Million - $3 Million
Domestic Markets:
Alberta, British Columbia, Saskatchewan
Contact(s):
John Barker, 306/352-0346

Waste Alternatives Inc. / WAI
60 Wingold Ave.
Toronto, ON M6B 1P5
416-256-2010
Fax: 416-256-2022
Firm Type: Management Consulting
Founded: 1991
Staff: 6
Member of: Trash Research Corporation; Quick Service Restaurant Council; Canadian Restaurant & Foodservices Association
Products/Services/Areas of Expertise: Solid waste audits; hands-on development & implementation of solid waste diversion programs; process & equipment evaluation; market development; system design; sewage & wastewater compliance issues; composting; environmental management systems
Domestic Markets:
National
Foreign Activity:
USA
Contact(s):
Ray Leach, President
Karl Brown, Vice-President

Waste Logic Inc.
#202, 17704 - 103 Ave.
Edmonton, AB T5S 1J9
780-496-7697
Fax: 780-489-8481
logicedm@telusplanet.net
www.wastelogic.com
Firm Type: Management Consulting
Founded: 1992
Staff: 4
Products/Services/Areas of Expertise: Solid waste, recycling audits
Recently Completed / Ongoing Projects: Primary waste/recycling consultation, Canada Safeway Limited & Lucerne Foods, Western Canada
Financial Information:
Type of Ownership: Private
Domestic Markets:
British Columbia, Manitoba, Ontario
Contact(s):
Blair Penner, Director

Waste Management of Canada
Technical Service Center
117 Wentworth Ct.
Brampton, ON L6T 5L4
866-221-5556
Fax: 866-221-5557
800-963-4776
TSCECanada@wm.com
www.wmcanada.com
Firm Type: Waste Management
Staff: 3400
Products/Services/Areas of Expertise: Owner & operator of residential, commercial & industrial collection services, recycling recovery facilities, & landfills
Financial Information:
Type of Ownership: Private
Contact(s):
David P. Steiner, Chief Executive Officer, Waste Management, Inc.

Products & Services Buyer's Guide

Dan Grosshauser, General Manager, Western Canada Market Area, 877-784-7336
Rick Growden, General Manager, Greater Toronto Market Area, 905-595-3360
Brad Muter, General Manager, Southwest Ontario Market Area, 519-883-3000
Dave Richmond, General Manager, Eastern Canada Market Area, 800-475-4725

Canadian Branches:
Blenheim - Base Rd.
Blenheim Landfill
20277 Base Rd.
Blenheim, ON N0P 1A0
800-963-4776

Blenheim - County Rd.
Gore Landfill
County Rd. 19
Blenheim, ON N0P 1A0
800-665-1898
Fax: 519-676-0211
swo@wm.com

Brampton
Wentworth Hauling & Transfer Station
117 Wentworth Ct.
Brampton, ON L6T 5L4
905-791-5505
Fax: 905-791-5505
800-963-4776
GTACS@wm.com
Products/Services/Areas of Expertise: Residential hauling & transfer

Brandon
Brandon Hauling
934 Douglas Ave., #D
Brandon, MB R7A 7B2
204-725-2570
Fax: 204-727-4044
800-463-0958
wccs@wm.com; ibcwcana@wm.com

Brockville
Hauling/Transfer Stn/Material Recycling
1380 California Ave.
Brockville, ON K6V 6K8
800-267-7874
Fax: 613-549-3520
800-963-4776
gtacs@wm.com

Calgary
Calgary Hauling
4668 - 25th St. SE
Calgary, AB T2B 3M2
403-720-7201
Fax: 403-279-0962
877-784-7336
ibcwcana@wm.com

Campbell River
Waste Management - Campbell River
1622 Coulter Rd.
Campbell River, BC V9W 7M1
250-286-6311
Fax: 250-286-0499
877-784-7336
ibcwcana@wm.com

Camrose
3830 - 47 Ave.
Camrose, AB T4V 3W8
877-784-7336
Fax: 780-672-0393
866-418-4065
ibcwcana@wm.com

Carp
West Carleton Landfill
2301 Carp Rd., RR#2
Carp, ON K0A 1L0
800-267-7874
Fax: 613-831-2461
800-963-4776
gtacs@wm.com

Castlegar
Waste Management - Castlegar
1844 Co-op Lane
Castlegar, BC V1N 3H5
877-784-7336
Fax: 866-242-9285
ibcwcana@wm.com

Chicoutimi
Chicoutimi Hauling
4214, boul Talbot
Chicoutimi, QC G7H 5B1
800-267-7874
Fax: 418-543-4850
800-267-7874
swo@wm.com

Concord
Bowes Hauling
550 Bowes Rd.
Concord, ON L4K 1K2
905-669-7166
Fax: 905-660-1567
800-463-9691
gtacs@wm.com

Coquitlam
Waste Management - Vancouver
2330 United Blvd.
Coquitlam, BC V3K 6S1
604-520-7800
Fax: 604-520-7878
877-784-7336
ibcwcana@wm.com

Courtice
Courtice Hauling & Transfer Station
1 McKnight Rd.
Courtice, ON L1E 2T3
905-433-5077
Fax: 905-433-3896
800-963-4776
gtacs@wm.com

Cranbrook
Cdn Waste Svs - Cranbrook/East Kootenay
2000 - 17th St. North
Cranbrook, BC V1C 6H3
877-784-7336
Fax: 250-489-1480
ibcwcana@wm.com

Dartmouth
Halifax Hauling
20 Simmonds Dr.
Dartmouth, NS B3B 1R3
800-267-7874
Fax: 902-468-2543
swo@wm.com

Drayton Valley
Drayton Valley Hauling
5450 - 55 St.
Drayton Valley, AB T7A 1R3
780-542-6764
Fax: 780-542-6453
888-513-3179
ibcwcana@wm.com

Dundas
Dundas Transfer Station
Olympic Dr.
Dundas, ON L8E 3X8
800-665-1898
Fax: 905-578-2332
swo@wm.com

Edmonton - 170 St.
West Edmonton Landfill & MRF
12707 - 170 St.
Edmonton, AB T5V 1L9
780-447-2141
Fax: 780-447-1083
800-963-4776
ibcwcana@wm.com

Edmonton - 25th St.
Edmonton Hauling
P.O. Box 12006
7940 - 25th St.
Edmonton, AB T6P 1M9
780-440-1700
Fax: 780-440-4776
877-784-7336
ibcwcana@wm.com

Edmonton - Meridian St.
Edmonton Material Recycling Facility
1311 Meridian St.
Edmonton, AB T6S 1A3
800-963-4776

Fort McMurray
Fort McMurray Hauling
230G MacKay Cres.
Fort McMurray, AB T9H 5C6
877-784-7336
Fax: 780-791-0400
877-784-7336
ibcwcana@wm.com

Fort St. John
9412 Sikanni Rd.
Fort St John, BC V1J 4V1
877-784-7336
Fax: 250-787-0194
ibcwcana@wm.com

Grande Prairie
Grande Prairie Hauling
10964 - 97th Ave.
Grande Prairie, AB T8V 3J8
780-532-3476
Fax: 780-539-1219
877-784-7336
ibcwcana@wm.com

Hamilton - Kenora Ave. North
Kenora Transfer Station
460 Kenora Ave. North
Hamilton, ON L8E 3X8
800-665-1898
Fax: 905-578-4243
swo@wm.com

Hamilton - Kilbride Rd.
Mountain Transfer Station
37 Kilbride Rd.
Hamilton, ON L8E 3X8
800-665-1898
Fax: 905-578-4243
swo@wm.com

Kamloops
734 Sarcee St. East
Kamloops, BC V2H 1E7
250-374-0095
Fax: 250-766-9111
877-784-7336
ibcwcana@wm.com

Kelowna
Waste Management - Kelowna
350 Beaver Lake Rd.
Kelowna, BC V4V 1S6
250-861-8788
Fax: 250-766-9111
877-784-7336
ibcwcana@wm.com

Kenora
Redditt Rd., RR#1
Kenora, ON P9N 3W7
800-463-0958
wccs@wm.com; ibcwcana@wm.com

Kingston - St. Remy Pl.
Kingston Transfer Station
62 St. Remy Pl.
Kingston, ON K7K 6C4
800-963-4776

Kingston - West St.
Kingston Hauling
270 West St.
Kingston, ON K7L 4V5
800-267-7874
Fax: 613-549-3520
800-963-4776
gtacs@wm.com

Lethbridge
Lethbridge Hauling
2230 - 39th St. North
Lethbridge, AB T1H 5J2
403-328-4449
Fax: 403-328-4443
800-463-0958
ibcwcana@wm.com

Lloydminster
Lakeland / Lloydminster Hauling
P.O. Box 1349
5104 - 42 Ave.
Lloydminster, SK S9V 1K4
306-825-0256
Fax: 306-825-9897
800-463-0958
ibcwcana@wm.com

London
London Hauling & Transfer Station
290 Exeter Rd.
London, ON N6L 1A3
800-665-1898
Fax: 519-652-1812
800-963-4776
swo@wm.com

Magog - Ayer's Cliff
WM Québec Inc. Landfill 082
P.O. Box 718
1992, ch d'Ayer's Cliff
Magog, QC J1X 5A8
800-267-7874
Fax: 819-847-3597
800-963-4776
swo@wm.com

Magog - Ayers Cliff
District Magog Hauling 086
P.O. Box 718
1994, ch d'Ayers Cliff
Magog, QC J1X 5A8
800-267-7874
Fax: 819-868-1912
800-267-7874
csupstateny@wm.com (Customer Service); swo@wm.com (Sales)

Maidstone
Windsor District Hauling
5000 - 8th Conc., RR#3
Maidstone, ON N0R 1K0
519-737-2900
Fax: 519-974-4146
800-665-1898
swo@wm.com

Miramichi
Miramichi Landfill
1092 Beaverbrook Rd.
Miramichi, NB E1V 4R5
800-963-4776

Mississauga
Mavis Transfer Station
3525 Mavis Rd.
Mississauga, ON L5C 1T7
905-615-1116
Fax: 905-615-1116
800-463-9691
GTACS@wm.com; gta@wm.com

Moncton
Moncton Landfill
Melvin Rd.
Indian Mountain, NB E1G 2Y9
800-963-4776

Mount Forest
Mount Forest Hauling
200 Sligo Rd. West
Mount Forest, ON N0G 2L2
519-323-3682
Fax: 519-323-2677
800-665-1898
swo@wm.com

Nanaimo
Waste Managment - Nanaimo
241 Southside Dr.
Nanaimo, BC V9R 5K1
250-753-3533
Fax: 250-753-0466
877-784-7336

Napanee
Napanee Hauling & Richmond Landfill
1271 Beechwood Rd., RR#6
Napanee, ON K7R 3L1
800-267-7874
Fax: 613-549-3520
800-963-4776
gtacs@wm.com

New Glasgow
New Glasgow Solid Waste
P.O. Box 44
108 Acheron Ct.
New Glasgow, NS B2H 5E1
800-267-7874
Fax: 902-752-2301
swo@wm.com

Ottawa
Ottawa Hauling
254 Westbrook Rd.
Ottawa, ON K0A 1L0
800-267-7874
Fax: 613-831-7450
gtacs@wm.com; gta@wm.com

Peterborough
Bensfort Road Landfill Site
Lot 14, Conc. 14
Peterborough, ON K9J 1C5
800-267-7874
GTACS@wm.com

Petrolia - Oil Heritage Rd.
Petrolia Landfill
4052 Oil Heritage Rd.
Petrolia, ON N0N 1R0
519-882-3044
Fax: 519-882-4879
800-963-4776
swo@wm.com

Prince George
Prince George Hauling
4760 Banzar Dr.
Prince George, BC V2K 4H2
250-962-8898
Fax: 250-962-8335
877-784-7336
ibcwcana@wm.com

Red Deer
Red Deer Hauling
6207 - 47A Ave.
Red Deer, AB T4N 6V8
403-343-8844
Fax: 403-346-6477
800-463-0958
ibcwcana@wm.com

Regina
Regina Hauling / Moose Jaw Hauling
60 Kress St.
Regina, SK S4N 5Y3
306-721-5600
Fax: 306-721-5600
877-784-7336
wccs@wm.com; ibcwcana@wm.com

Rouyn-Noranda
Rouyn Hauling
505, boul Temiscaminque
Rouyn-Noranda, QC J9X 7C8
800-267-7874
swo@wm.com

Saanichton
Waste Management - Victoria
6808 Kirkpatrick Cres.
Saanichton, BC V8M 1Z9
250-544-2330
Fax: 250-544-2305

866-418-7065
ibcwcana@wm.com

Saint-Nicéphore
WM Québec Inc. Landfill
25, rue Gagnon
Saint-Nicéphore, QC J2A 3H3
800-267-7874
800-963-4776
swo@wm.com

Saint-Étienne-des-Grès
#200, 1, boul de la Gabelle
Saint-Étienne-des-Grès, QC G0X 2P0
800-267-7874
Fax: 819-376-5649
800-267-7874
swo@wm.com

Sainte-Sophie
WM Québec Inc. Landfill & Hauling
2535, Premiere rue
Sainte-Sophie, QC J5J 2R7
800-267-7874
Fax: 450-438-4342
800-963-4776
swo@wm.com
Products/Services/Areas of Expertise: Landfill & Montréal North Shore Hauling (Lachute)

Salaberry-de-Valleyfield
WM Québec Inc., Transfer & Transit II
978, boul Cadieux
Salaberry-de-Valleyfield, QC J6T 4L6
800-267-7874
Fax: 450-377-4230
800-963-4776
swo@wm.com

Saskatoon
Saskatoon/Prince Albert/Melfort Hauling
805 - 50th St. East
Saskatoon, SK S7K 3Y5
877-784-7336
Fax: 306-934-3939
wccs@wm.com; ibcwcana@wm.com

Sault Ste. Marie
Sault Ste. Marie Hauling
120 Industrial Ct. A
Sault Ste Marie, ON P6B 5W6
800-267-7874
Fax: 705-949-1377
800-267-7874
swo@wm.com

Scoth Village
West Hants Landfill
1569 Walton Woods Rd.
Scoth Village, NS B0N 2G0
800-963-4776

St Catharines
124 Cushman Rd.
St Catharines, ON L2M 6T6
905-687-9605
Fax: 905-687-8919
800-665-1898
swo@wm.com

St. John's
P.O. Box 21014
43 Sugarloaf Rd.
St. John's, NL A1A 5B2
709-753-3030
Fax: 709-753-3624
800-267-7874
swo@wm.com

Stoney Creek
407 McNeilly Rd.
Stoney Creek, ON L8E 5E3
800-665-1898
Fax: 905-643-1204
swo@wm.com

Sudbury
Sudbury Hauling
P.O. Box 2051 A
1865 Lasalle Blvd.
Sudbury, ON P3A 4R8

800-267-7874
Fax: 705-566-2333
800-267-7874
swo@wm.com

Swift Current
Swift Current Hauling
P.O. Box 994
1951 North Railway St. West
Swift Current, SK S9H 3X1
306-773-7596
Fax: 306-773-0623
800-463-0958
wccs@wm.com; ibcwcana@wm.com

Timmins
Timmins Hauling
P.O. Box 1301
Feldman Rd.
Timmins, ON P4N 7J8
800-267-7874
Fax: 705-264-8923
swo@wm.com

Toronto - Brydon Dr.
Brydon Transfer Station
5 Brydon Dr.
Toronto, ON M9W 4M7
416-744-9535
Fax: 416-744-9535
800-463-9691
GTACS@wm.com; gta@wm.com

Toronto - Esandar Dr.
Esandar Drive Hauling & Transfer Station
20 Esandar Dr.
Toronto, ON M4G 1Y2
416-423-6396
800-963-4776
GTACS@wm.com

Toronto - Unwin Ave.
Unwin Transfer Station
100 Unwin Ave.
Toronto, ON M5A 1A1
416-469-3840
Fax: 416-469-3840
800-463-9691
GTACS@wm.com; gta@wm.com

Trenton
Trenton Hauling & Transfer Station
26 Chester Rd.
Trenton, ON K8V 6X4
800-267-7874
800-963-4776
GTACS@wm.com; gta@wm.com

Val d'Or
Val D'Or Hauling
1061, rues des Manufacturiers
Val-d'Or, QC J9P 4N9
800-267-7874
swo@wm.com

Waterloo
Waterloo Hauling/Transfer Stn/Recycling
645 Conrad Pl.
Waterloo, ON N2V 1C4
800-665-1898
Fax: 519-886-1693
800-963-4776
swo@wm.com
Products/Services/Areas of Expertise: Waterloo Hauling; Transfer Station; Material Recycling Facility

Watford
Warwick Landfill
8039 Zion Line, RR#4
Watford, ON N0M 2S0
519-849-5810
Fax: 519-849-5811
800-963-4776
swo@wm.com

Windsor
Windsor Transfer Station
5000 - 8th Conc.
Windsor, ON N0R 1K0
800-963-4776

Winnipeg - Paramount Rd.
99 Paramount Rd.
Winnipeg, MB R2X 2W6
800-463-0958
wccs@wm.com; ibcwcana@wm.com

Winnipeg - Paramount Rd.
Winnipeg Hauling
70 Paramount Rd.
Winnipeg, MB R2X 2W3
877-784-7336
Fax: 204-694-7007
877-784-7336
wccs@wm.com; ibcwcana@wm.com

Waste Opportunities Inc.
#406, 1 Eva Rd.
Toronto, ON M9C 4Z5
416-621-1779
Fax: 416-622-4130

Waste Resource Containers
75 Akerley Blvd.
Dartmouth, NS B3B 1R7
902-468-9495
Fax: 902-468-2589
mike@caster-rack.com
Contact(s):
Michael Mathews, President

Waste Services (CA) Inc.
Formerly: Huneault Waste Management
601, 122 International Blvd.
Burlington, ON L7L 6Z8
905-319-1237
Fax: 905-319-9050
866-974-2255
info@wsii.ca
www.wsii.ca
Products/Services/Areas of Expertise: Contaminated soil centre; industrial waste hauling; landfill
Contact(s):
Robert Ross, Vice-President

Canadian Branches:
Abbotsford
P.O. Box 8000
34321 Industrial Way
Abbotsford, BC V2S 6H1
604-864-9177
Fax: 604-855-0565

Barrie
176A Saunders Rd.
Barrie, ON L4N 9A4
705-733-1200
Fax: 705-733-9998
1-877-733-1300

Barrie Northern
10 Hooper Rd.
Barrie, ON L4N 8Z9
705-792-0944
Fax: 705-792-0941

Bracebridge
P.O. Box 1779
580 Ecclestone Dr.
Bracebridge, ON P1L 1V7
705-645-4453
Fax: 705-645-9485
1-800-461-4448

Brantford
779 Powerline Rd.
Brantford, ON N3T 5V7
519-759-4370
Fax: 519-759-7204
1-800-265-9918

Brockville
Brockville Transfer Station
P.O. Box 386
4800 Development Dr.
Brockville, ON K6V 5V6
613-345-2442
Fax: 613-345-8023

Calgary
#117, 5025 - 90th Ave. SE
Calgary, AB T2C 2S9

403-236-8074

Comox
4624 Cumberland Rd.
Courtenay, BC V9N 5N5
250-336-2172
Fax: 250-336-2176

Coronation
P.O. Box 848
Coronation, AB T0C 1C0
403-578-3299
Fax: 403-578-3313

Edmonton
185 Strathmoor Way
Sherwood Park, AB T8H 1Z7
780-464-9401
Fax: 780-464-9402

Hamilton
306 Lake Ave. North
Hamilton, ON L8E 3A2
905-573-0774
Fax: 905-578-5805

Kamloops
8465 Dallas Dr.
Kamloops, BC V2C 6X5
250-573-5517
Fax: 250-573-5534

Keswick
23082 McCowan Rd.
Sutton West, ON L0E R10
905-478-1940
Fax: 905-478-1572
1-888-726-3131

Kingston
1266 McAdoo Lane, RR#1
Glenburnie, ON K7L 5C7
613-548-4428
Fax: 613-542-5612

Kitchener
147 Ardelt Ave.
Kitchener, ON N2C 2E1
519-745-8080
Fax: 519-519-4934

Lindsay
P.O. Box 236
2829 Hwy. 35 South
Lindsay, ON K9V 4S1
705-324-2889
Fax: 705-324-0198

Orillia
P.O. Box 814
180 James St. West
Orillia, ON L3V 6K8
705-326-9671
Fax: 705-325-8756
1-800-930-3535

Ottawa
1152 Kenaston St., 2nd. Fl.
Ottawa, ON K1B 3P5
613-749-1077
Fax: 613-749-0008
1-866-974-2255

Ottawa Navan
3354 Navan Rd.
Navan, ON K4B 1H9
613-824-7289
Fax: 613-824-7139
1-866-974-2255

Parksville
1151 Herring Gull Way
Parksville, BC V9P 1R2
250-248-8109
Fax: 250-248-2109

Penticton

Peterborough
P.O. Box 174
688 Harper Rd.
Peterborough, ON K9J 6Y8

705-742-4268
Fax: 705-742-2619

Ram-Pak
117 Advance Blvd.
Brampton, ON L6T 4H9
905-791-0392
Fax: 905-791-4671
1-800-461-5971

Red Deer
8028 Edgar Industrial Green
Red Deer, AB T4P 3S2
403-343-1691
Fax: 403-340-0894

Sarnia
1223 Confederation St.
Sarnia, ON N7S 4M7
519-337-3218
Fax: 519-332-1463

Saskatchewan
P.O. Box 10
Gladmor, SK S0C 1A0
306-969-4427

Toronto
117 Advance Blvd.
Brampton, ON L6T 4H9
905-791-5250
Fax: 905-791-2441

Vernon
1200 Carmi Ave.
Penticton, BC V2A 3H2
250-545-3191
Fax: 250-545-8041

Wasteco
Division of Southern Sanitation Inc.
161 Bridgeland Ave.
Toronto, ON M6A 1Z1
416-787-5000
Fax: 416-787-6210
toronto@wastecogroup.com
www.wastecogroup.com
Firm Type: Waste Management
Founded: 1978
Staff: 250
Member of: Ontario Waste Management Association; Recycling Council of Toronto; Building Owners & Managers Association; Toronto Building Superintendents Association
Products/Services/Areas of Expertise: Waste removal & recycling
Financial Information:
Type of Ownership: Private
Revenue Sources: 5% Provincial; 2% Municipals; 93% Private Contracts
Domestic Markets:
Ontario
Contact(s):
Stephen G. Caudwell, President & Owner
Carl J. Lorusso, Vice-President & General Manager
Peter Starr, Vice-President, Sales & Marketing
Linda Easwaran, Controller
Paul Weisman, Sales Manager
Anita Strano, Director, Customer Service

Canadian Branches:
Columbus Recycling Centre
6710 Columbus Rd.
Mississauga, ON L5T 2G1
905-564-5210
Fax: 905-564-9175

Imperial Recycling Centre
235 Curtis Dr.
Guelph, ON N1K 1Y3
519-836-1610
Fax: 519-836-4531

Orenda Recycling Centre
150 Orenda Rd.
Brampton, ON L6W 1W2
905-459-2716
Fax: 905-452-2606

Wastequip Cusco
305 Enford Rd.
Richmond Hill, ON L4C 3E9
905-883-1214
Fax: 905-883-1778
800-490-3541
www.wastequip-cusco.com
Firm Type: Manufacturing
Founded: 1969
Products/Services/Areas of Expertise: Manufacturer of custom fabricated mobile vacuum equipment, such as pressure vessels & tanks; Clients include the environmental, industrial, & commercial markets
Domestic Markets:
National
Foreign Activity:
USA
Contact(s):
Steve Guidoin, President
steveg@wastequipcusco.com
Stan Jones, Vice-President, Sales & Marketing & Regional Sales Mgr., Western Canada & USA
stanj@wastequipcusco.com
Glenn Eichler, Regional Sales Manager, USA Eastern Seaboard, 813-374-4094Fax: 813-374-4094
geichler@wastequip.com
Adam Franklin, Regional Sales Manager, South Central & South Western USA, 609-207-8542Fax: 205-991-2053
afranklin@wastequip.com
Doug Hinde, Regional Sales Manager, Central Canada & USA, 905-841-7438Fax: 905-841-7438
wastequipcusco@sympatico.ca
Sarathi Chilukuri, Manager, Quality Control
sarathi@wastequipcusco.com
Rob Huber, Manager, Production
robh@wastequipcusco.com
Scott Rae, Manager, Service
scottr@wastequipcusco.com
Tim Walter, Manager, Purchasing
timw@wastequipcusco.com
Joey Sooknanan, Supervisor, Engineering
joeys@wastequipcusco.com

Water & Earth Science Associates Ltd. / WESA
Envir-Eau
P.O. Box 430
3108 Carp Rd.
Carp, ON K0A 1L0
613-839-3053
Fax: 613-839-5376
wesacarp@wesa.ca
www.wesa.ca
Firm Type: Engineering, Scientific/Technical Services
Founded: 1976
Staff: 8
Products/Services/Areas of Expertise: Consulting organization with expertise in health, safety, environmental sciences, & engineering; Clients include government, industry, business, & professionals
Activities: Providing environmental & occupational health & safety training courses; Offering air quality, noise, vibration, & environmental field monitoring services; Providing solutions for the remediation & rehabilitation of water, soil, air, & facilities
Recently Completed / Ongoing Projects: Assisting the Recycling Council of Ontario in the development of waste reduction initiatives; Environmental assessment & engineering design for the development of a waterpower project, South River, Ontario; Assisting with the design & construction of a surface flow treatment system at an explosives plant, Missouri, USA
Financial Information:
Type of Ownership: Private
Domestic Markets:
National
Foreign Activity:
Mexico, USA, Worldwide
Contact(s):
Harry J. Marshall, President
hmarshall@wesa.ca

Canadian Branches:
Burlington
3380 South Service Rd., Garden Level
Burlington, ON L7N 3J5
905-639-5789
Fax: 905-639-9460
wesaburlington@wesa.ca

Gatineau
Envir-Eau
#204, 160, boul de l'Hôpital
Gatineau, QC J8T 8J1
819-243-7555
Fax: 819-243-0167
envireau@envireau.ca

Kingston
The Tower, The Woolen Mill
4 Cataraqui St.
Kingston, ON K7K 1Z7
613-531-2725
Fax: 613-531-1852
wesaking@wesa.ca

Kitchener
171 Victoria St. North
Kitchener, ON N2H 5C5
519-742-6685
Fax: 519-742-9810
wesakw@wesa.ca

Montréal
Envir-Eau
#350, 440, boul René-Lévesque ouest
Montréal, QC H2Z 1V7
514-844-7199
Fax: 514-841-9111
montreal@envireau.ca

Sudbury
273 Elm St.
Sudbury, ON P3C 1V5
705-525-6075
Fax: 705-525-6077
wesasud@wesa.ca

Yellowknife
3533B McDonald Dr.
Yellowknife, NT X1A 2H2
867-873-3500
Fax: 867-873-3500
yellowknife@wesa.ca

Toronto
WESA Technologies
#1, 4 Kern Rd.
Toronto, ON M3B 1T1
416-383-0957
Fax: 416-383-0956
wesatoronto@wesa.ca

Water Conservation Company Ltd. / WCC Ltd.
Formerly: Water Conservation Technologies Inc.
9E, 1912-A Avenue Rd.
Toronto, ON M5M 4A1
416-785-7185
Fax: 416-785-7403
www.water-conservation-company.com
Firm Type: Distributing
Founded: 1989
Products/Services/Areas of Expertise: Supplier of water & energy saving fixtures; Products include water saving toilets & shower head; Clients include multi-unit residential, institutional, commercial, & industrial buildings
Activities: Preparing water saving reports & recommendations; Installing water saving fixtures
Domestic Markets:
Ontario

Canadian Branches:
Ottawa
1411 Carling Ave.
Ottawa, ON K1Z 1A7
613-725-3700
Fax: 613-715-9064

Water Matrix
#3, 331 Trowers Rd.
Woodbridge, ON L4L 6A2
905-850-8080
Fax: 905-850-9100
800-668-4420
sales@watermatrix.com
www.watermatrix.com
Firm Type: Management Consulting, Distributing
Founded: 1989
Products/Services/Areas of Expertise: Provider of water efficiency services, such as analysis, auditing, implementation, &

monitoring; Distributor of the Niagara Flapperless Toilet, the Zero Flush Urinal, & other water-saving products; Clients include individual homeowners & multi-unit residential, institutional, & commercial buildings
Activities: Offering training programs; Providing technical support
Financial Information:
Type of Ownership: Private
Domestic Markets:
National
Contact(s):
Sean Kimmons, President
seank@watermatrix.com

Canadian Branches:
Water Matrix West
2038 - 70th Ave.
Edmonton, AB T6P 1N6
780-414-9965
Fax: 780-465-0680
daryl@watermatrix.com

Water Pik Canada
Formerly: Teledyne Water Pik Canada
#2B, 4961 Hwy. 7 East, 2nd Fl.
Markham, ON L3R 1N1
905-947-1393
888-226-3042
www.waterpik.com
Firm Type: Distributing, Manufacturing
Founded: 1962
Products/Services/Areas of Expertise: Distributor of water & energy conserving personal & oral health care products; Products include dental water jets & massaging showerheads
Financial Information:
Type of Ownership: Foreign-owned
Domestic Markets:
National

Water Resource Consultants Ltd.
3216 Winchester Rd.
Regina, SK S4V 2S8
306-751-0655
Fax: 306-751-0655
Firm Type: Management Consulting, Engineering, Scientific/Technical Services
Member of: Saskatchewan Environmental Industry & Managers' Association (SEIMA); Consulting Engineers of Saskatchewan (CES)
Products/Services/Areas of Expertise: A consulting firm, with expertise in areas such as water resource engineering, irrigation, hydraulics, & flood control
Recently Completed / Ongoing Projects: The Lake Diefenbaker Irrigation Projects, Saskatchewan
Domestic Markets:
Saskatchewan
Contact(s):
R.S. (Ray) Pentland, P. Eng., President
rpentland@accesscomm.ca

Waterford Group
70 Ewart Ave., RR#8
Brantford, ON N3T 5M1
519-752-1300
Fax: 519-752-1395
www.waterfordgroup.ca
Products/Services/Areas of Expertise: A diverse company serving the construction industry; supplies premium natural stone & sands, recycled asphalt & concrete products, ready-mix concrete, & washed & unwashed limestone products; services include screening, crushing, washing, & recovering waste streams from various industrial processes, dewatering & decontaminating material to client specifications, materials loading & transport. Quarries & other properties located in Dunnville, Vinemount, Waterford, Hamilton, & Wainfleet Twp.
Contact(s):
Bob Neate, Manager, Aggregate Sales
bneate@waterfordgroup.ca

Waterline Environmental Inc.
#4, 4151 Morris Dr.
Burlington, ON L7L 5L5
905-333-6604
Fax: 905-333-0368
info@waterlineenvironmental.com
www.waterlineenvironmental.ca

Firm Type: Management Consulting, Waste Management
Founded: 1991
Products/Services/Areas of Expertise: Licensed by the T.S.S.A., the Ministry of the Environment, & the Canadian Safety Association, the firm is engaged in the assessment, installation, removal, & disposal of all types & sizes of storage tanks; Clients include governments, institutions, industries, residents, & the commercial & retail sectors
Activities: Presenting seminars; Sending removed tanks to a registered recycler; Sending removed oils & sludges to a company that re-processes the fuel; Employing a company that naturally treats the earth, if soils are found to be contaminated
Financial Information:
Type of Ownership: Private
Domestic Markets:
Ontario,

Waterloo Barrier Inc.
P.O. Box 385
Rockwood, ON N0B 2K0
519-856-1352
Fax: 519-856-0759
www.waterloo-barrier.com
Firm Type: Distributing, Scientific/Technical Services
Founded: 1994
Products/Services/Areas of Expertise: A firm involved in the commercialization of the Waterloo Barrier, a groundwater containment wall, which is installed at contaminated sites; Clients include chemical companies, manufacturers, & public utilites
Recently Completed / Ongoing Projects: Containment of methane gas at the Ottawa Street Landfill, Kitchener, Ontario; Site remediation at former Shell site, Toronto, Ontario
Financial Information:
Type of Ownership: Private
Domestic Markets:
National
Foreign Activity:
Mexico, USA
Contact(s):
Robin Jowett, Contact
robin@waterloo-barrier.com

Waterloo Biofilter Systems Inc.
P.O. Box 400
143 Dennis St.
Rockwood, ON N0B 2K0
519-856-0757
Fax: 519-856-0759
wbs@waterloo-biofilter.com
www.waterloo-biofilter.com
Firm Type: Distributing, Manufacturing
Founded: 1991
Products/Services/Areas of Expertise: Manufacturer & marketer of sewage treatment systems
Activities: Offering training courses
Financial Information:
Type of Ownership: Private
Domestic Markets:
National
Foreign Activity:
The Pacific Rim, USA, United Kingdom
Contact(s):
Craig Jowett, President & Inventor
Robin Jowett, Manager, Business
robin@waterloo-biofilter.com

Canadian Branches:
Ridgetown
13448 Klondyke Line, RR#1
Ridgetown, ON N0P 2C0
519-674-2271
Fax: 519-674-5883
Marianne Wilson, Contact
mwillson@mnsi.net

Waterloo Concrete Products
RR#2
Cambridge, ON N1R 5S3
519-622-7574
Fax: 519-621-8233
Products/Services/Areas of Expertise: Liquid/hazardous waste management; storage tanks

Waterloo Evaporateurs Inc.
Also Known As: Waterloo Environmental Inc.
201, rue Western
Waterloo, QC J0E 2N0
450-539-3663
Fax: 450-539-2660
Firm Type: Engineering, Manufacturing, Scientific/Technical Services
Founded: 1919
Staff: 50
Member of: Water Environment Federation, Ordre des ingénieurs du Québec
Products/Services/Areas of Expertise: Process recovery; wastewater recovery; primary water treatment
Domestic Markets:
New Brunswick, Ontario, Québec
Foreign Activity:
USA
Contact(s):
Ernest Bieri, CEO
Claire Mercure, Marketing Director
Jacques Bieri, Vice-President

Waterous Power Systems
10025 - 51st Ave.
Edmonton, AB T6E 0A8
780-437-8200
www.waterouspower.com
Firm Type: Distributing
Founded: 1905
Products/Services/Areas of Expertise: Waterous Power Systems is a distributor of big engine & transmission brands. The company distributes the following product lines: GE Energy, Detroit Diesel, MTU, MTU Onsite Energy, Mercedes-Benz, & Allison Transmission. In addition to supplying parts, the compnay also provides service & aftermarket support. The following industries are served by Waterous Power Systems: power generation, oilfield, construction, industrial, transportation, agriculture, mining, & forestry.
Domestic Markets:
Alberta, British Columbia, Manitoba, Ontario, Saskatchewan
Contact(s):
Tim W. Zawislak, President
tzawislak@waterouspower.com
Richard Plain, Vice-President, Sales & Marketing
rplain@waterouspower.com
Steve Di Loreto, Director, Supply Chain
sdiloreto@waterouspower.com
Terry Keefe, General Manager, Aftermarket
tkeefe@waterouspower.com
Harvey Wood, Manager, Parts
hwood@waterouspower.com
Dave Janzen, Manager, Service, Off-Highway
djanzen@waterouspower.com

Canadian Branches:
Calgary
4343 - 114th Ave. SE
Calgary, AB T2Z 3M5
403-253-7601
Fax: 403-252-7532
Lyall Megaw, Vice-President, Operations
lmegaw@waterouspower.com
Tim G. Lindsay, Manager, Branch
tlindsay@waterouspower.com
Stafford Bezak, Manager, Service
sbezak@waterouspower.com
Craig Evans, Manager, Parts
cevans@waterouspower.com

Fort McMurray
430 MacAlpine Cres.
Fort McMurray, AB T9H 4B1
780-743-6252
Fax: 780-743-4953
Alfred Hamer, Manager, Branch
ahamer@waterouspower.com
Ben Brignall, Manager, Service
bbrignall@waterouspower.com

Fort St. John
P.O. Box 6658
Mile 48.5 Alaska Hwy.
Fort St. John, BC V1J 4J1
250-785-4191
Ken Mitchell, Manager, Branch
kmitchell@waterouspower.com

Rhonda McNee, Manager, Service
rmcnee@waterouspower.com
Murray Gall, Territory Manager, Allison Transmission

Grande Prairie
10906 - 97th Ave.
Grande Prairie, AB T8V 3J8
780-532-2396
Dave Miller, Manager, Branch
dmiller@waterouspower.com
Gary Atkinson, Manager, Service
gatkinson@waterouspower.com

Medicine Hat
1750 Broadway Ave. East
Redcliff, AB T0J 2P0
403-529-9557
Fax: 403-527-8901
Tim Lindsay, Manager, Branch
tlindsay@waterouspower.com
Jeff Nicholson, Manager, Service
jnicholson@waterouspower.com

Red Deer
7980 Edgar Industrial Dr.
Red Deer, AB T4P 3R2
403-346-8981
Fax: 403-347-3711
Wilf Ruskowksy, Manager, Branch
wruskowsky@waterouspower.com
Tony Rombouts, Manager, Service
trombouts@waterouspower.com
Albert Wandler, Manager, Parts
awandler@waterouspower.com

Regina
133 - 4th Ave.
Regina, SK S4N 6T2
306-522-2652
Fax: 306-565-0633
Joe Rudnicki, Manager, Branch
jrudnicki@waterouspower.com
Bruce Kumitch, Territory Manager, Sales
bkumitch@waterouspower.com
Steve Tidy, Manager, Service
stidy@waterouspower.com

Saskatoon
3210 Idylwyld Dr. North
Saskatoon, SK S7L 5Y7
306-242-3113
Fax: 306-242-2965
Joe Rudnicki, Manager, Branch
jrudnicki@waterouspower.com
Eldon Funk, Territory Manager, Allison Transmission
efunk@waterouspower.com
Terry Lishchynsky, Manager, Service
tlishchynsky@waterouspower.com

Thunder Bay
1100 Walsh St.
Thunder Bay, ON P7E 4X4
807-577-1101
Fax: 807-475-8330
Bob Johnston, Branch, Manager
Bill Stokaluk, Manager, Parts
bstokaluk@waterouspower.com

Winnipeg
2529 Inkster Blvd.
Winnipeg, MB R3C 2E6
204-452-8244
Fax: 204-452-2153
877-456-4010
Chris Cortvriendt, Manager, Parts
ccortvriendt@waterouspower.com
Randy Zyzniewski, Manager, Service
rzyzniewski@waterouspower.com

Waterra Pumps Limited
#44, 5200 Dixie Rd.
Mississauga, ON L4W 1E4
905-238-5242
Fax: 905-238-5704
sales@waterra.com
www.waterra.com
Products/Services/Areas of Expertise: Waterra Pumps Limited provides groundwater monitoring equipment & supplies. Applications for Waterra products include bailing, capping wells, conventional sampling, drivepoint sampling, hydrocarbon detection, metals sampling, purging, surging, VOC sampling, water level detection, well development, & well sediment removal.
Domestic Markets:
National
Foreign Activity:
USA, United Kingdom,

Waters Limited
6427 Northam Dr.
Mississauga, ON L4V 1J2
Fax: 905-678-9237
800-252-4752
canada@waters.com
www.waters.com
Firm Type: Scientific/Technical Services

Products/Services/Areas of Expertise: Developer of analytical science solutions to support client operations & regulatory compliance; Clients include laboratory-dependent organizations
Financial Information:
Type of Ownership: Foreign-owned
Domestic Markets:
National
Contact(s):
Aaron Wolkoff, President
Richard Blais, Vice-President & Manager, National Sales
Nancy Mosteko, Administrator, Marketing
nancy_mosteko@waters.com
Debbie Oliver, Coordinator, Service
Jane Hartson, Specialist, Chemistry Inside Sales

Canadian Branches:
Montréal
1850 - 55e av
Montréal, QC H8T 3J5
Fax: 514-636-1555

Watson & Associates Economists Ltd.
Formerly: C.N. Watson & Associates Ltd.
4304 Village Centre Ct.
Mississauga, ON L4Z 1S2
905-272-3600
Fax: 905-272-3602
info@watson-econ.ca
www.watson-econ.ca
Firm Type: Management Consulting
Founded: 1982
Staff: 26
Products/Services/Areas of Expertise: Economic impact assessment; land economics; landfill valuation; financial analysis of waste management systems
Financial Information:
Type of Ownership: Private
Domestic Markets:
Alberta, Ontario
Foreign Activity:
The Pacific Rim
Contact(s):
Cam Watson, President
watson@watson-econ.ca
Gary Scandlan, Associate Director
scandlan@watson-econ.ca
Cynthia Clarke, Associate Director
clarke@watson-econ.ca

Watson Petroleum Services Ltd.
P.O. Box 84
Mount Pearl, NL A1N 2C1
709-745-5600
Fax: 709-745-5606
Firm Type: Engineering
Member of: Newfoundland & Labrador Environmental Industry Association
Products/Services/Areas of Expertise: Installer of underground piping & petroleum tanks; Inspector of precision tanks & piping
Contact(s):
Ed Watson, President
ewatson@nl.rogers.com

Watson Process Systems
#202, 5511 Tomken Rd.
Mississauga, ON L4W 4B8
905-475-2511
Fax: 905-475-7638
contact@watsonprocess.com
www.watsonprocess.com
Firm Type: Distributing, Manufacturing
Founded: 1983
Member of: Air & Waste Management Association
Member of: Professional Engineers of Ontario; Ontario Society of Professional Engineers
Products/Services/Areas of Expertise: Mist elimination equipment; wet scrubbers; gas processing equipment; particulate monitors
Contact(s):
David Cui, Technical Director
dcui@watsonprocess.com

Wavefront Technology Solutions Inc.
#100, 17608 - 103 Ave.
Edmonton, AB T5S 1J9
780-486-2222
Fax: 780-484-7177
www.onthewavefront.com
Firm Type: Engineering

Products/Services/Areas of Expertise: Developer & designer of tools & techniques for environmental groundwater remediation, oil well stimulation, & secondary oil recovery
Financial Information:
Type of Ownership: Private
Contact(s):
Steven W. Percy, Chair
Brett Davidson, President/CEO
D. Brad Paterson, Chief Financial Officer

Canadian Branches:
Cambridge
26 Cranston Ave.
Cambridge, ON N1T 1J8
519-624-1312
Fax: 519-623-9103

Calgary
Wavefront Reservoir Technologies Ltd.
Bow Valley Square II, #700, 202 - 5th Ave. SW
Calgary, AB T2P 2V7
403-510-1522

Lloydminster
Wavefront Sand Pumps & Rentals Ltd.
6606 - 50th Ave.
Lloydminster, AB T9V 2W8
780-875-7883
Fax: 780-875-8443

International Branch(es):
Houston, Texas, USA
Wavefront Technology Solutions USA Inc.
9774 Whithom Dr.
Houston, TX USA
832-220-1400
Fax: 832-220-1405

Raleigh
Wavefront Technology Solutions USA Inc.
8004 Looking Glass Ct.
Raleigh, NC USA
919-424-7563

WDA Consultants Inc.
4827 Vienna Dr. NW
Calgary, AB T3A 0W7
403-233-9222
Fax: 403-233-9166
wda@wda-consultants.com
www.wda-consultants.com
Products/Services/Areas of Expertise: Hydrogeology; contaminant hydrogeology; environmental studies, remediation & decommissioning; hydrology; geology & engineering geology
Contact(s):
Udo Weyer, President

Web Engineering Ltd.
4173 Dawson St.
Burnaby, BC V5C 4B3
604-294-8588
Fax: 604-294-8580
postmaster@webengineering.ca
www.webengineering.ca
Products/Services/Areas of Expertise: The consulting civil engineers at Web Engineering provide services related to public

& private infrastructure, such as transportation, stormwater management, & land development.
Domestic Markets:
British Columbia

Weir Power & Industrial
A Division of The Weir Group PLC
2360 Millrace Ct.
Mississauga, ON L5N 1WR
905-812-7100
Fax: 905-812-8170
info@weirgroup.com; valveservices@weirgroup.com
www.weirpowerindustrial.com
Firm Type: Distributing, Manufacturing
Founded: 1897
Quality Environmental Management System(s): 9001; ISO
Products/Services/Areas of Expertise: Weir Power & Industrial serves renewable energy, fossil fuel, nuclear power, & industrial activities. Products include accredited pump equipment & safety critical valves.
Financial Information:
Type of Ownership: Foreign-owned
Domestic Markets:
National
Foreign Activity:
USA
Contact(s):
Phil Clifton, Divisional Managing Director
David Frost, Contact, Centrifuges
dfrost@weiramericas.com
Colin Harrison, Contact, Steam Turbines
charrison@weiramericas.com
Josh Jensen, Contact, Weir Specialty Pumps (Wemco-Hidrostal, Roto-Jet)
Kevin Lemieux, Contact, Hydro
klemieux@weiramericas.com
Rajan Muthukrishnan, Contact, Condition Monitoring
rmuthukrishnan@weiramericas.com

Canadian Branches:
Calgary
2715 - 18th St. NE
Calgary, AB T2E 7E6
403-250-7000
Fax: 403-250-2032
sonny.baytaluke@weirgroup.com
www.weirpowerindustrial.com
Products/Services/Areas of Expertise: The Calgary office conducts valve maintenance. It serves the oil & gas industry.

Fort St. John
10508 - 89th Ave.
Fort St. John, BC V1J 5P9
250-785-6627
Fax: 250-785-4501
david.austin@weirgroup.com
www.weirpowerindustrial.com
Products/Services/Areas of Expertise: The Fort St. John branch offers valve maintenance services. It serves the oil & gas industry.

Mississauga
1180 Aerowood Dr.
Mississauga, ON L4W 1Y5
905-625-7202
Fax: 905-624-0097
david.driesman@weirgroup.com
www.weirpowerindustrial.com
Products/Services/Areas of Expertise: The Mississauga service centre conducts crusher repair & valve maintenance tasks. It serves the oil & gas industry.

International Branch(es):
Boston
29 Old Right Rd.
Ipswich, MA 01938 USA
978-744-5690
Fax: 978-741-3626
sales@weirvalveusa.com
www.weirpowerindustrial.com
Products/Services/Areas of Expertise: The Boston branch is a sales & manufacturing facility.

Salt Lake City
440 West 800 South
Salt Lake City, UT 84101 USA
801-359-8171
Fax: 801-355-9203

info@weirsp.com
www.weirpowerindustrial.com
Products/Services/Areas of Expertise: The Salt Lake City location is a manufacturing & sales facility for Weir Specialty Pumps.

Washington
339 Old Bath Hwy.
Washington, NC 27889R2 USA
252-946-7763
Fax: 252-975-6334
sales@weirvalveusa.com
www.weirpowerindustrial.com
Products/Services/Areas of Expertise: The Washington branch is engaged in both manufacturing & sales.

Well To Wire Emissions Control Inc. / WWEC
#17, 1700 Varsity Estates Dr. NW
Calgary, AB T3B 2W9
403-288-3647
Fax: 403-286-3696
877-988-3647
wwe@welltowire.com
www.emissionscontrol.ca
Firm Type: Engineering
Founded: 2000
Products/Services/Areas of Expertise: Well To Wire Emissions Control Inc. uses portable Emission Defense Units to remove undesirable gases from gas streams. With its parent company, Well to Wire Energy Corporation, the company converts oil & gas industry waste gases into energy & safe chemical by-products. Well To Wire Emissions Control is also engaged in odour control at sewer processing plants.
Financial Information:
Type of Ownership: Private

Wellmaster Pipe & Supply
Formerly: TPS Industries Inc.
P.O. Box 456
1494 Bell Mill Rd.
Tillsonburg, ON N4G 4J1
519-688-0500
Fax: 519-688-0563
800-387-9355
carts@wellmaster.ca
www.wellmaster.ca
Firm Type: Distributing, Manufacturing
Founded: 1987
Products/Services/Areas of Expertise: Water products include water treatment devices, various pumps, hydrants, fittings to hook up water systems, switches & gauges, adapters, & pressure tanks
Domestic Markets:
National
Contact(s):
Doug White, President
dwhite@wellmaster.ca

Wellons Canada
Formerly: Salton Fabrication Ltd.
19087 - 96 Ave.
Surrey, BC V4N 3P2
604-888-0122
Fax: 604-888-2959
sales@wellons.ca
www.wellons.ca
Firm Type: Engineering, Manufacturing
Products/Services/Areas of Expertise: Designer & manufacturer of lumber drying kilns & biomass & gas fired thermal energy systems
Activities: Providing technical service
Recently Completed / Ongoing Projects: Primary crude oil heating system, Enbridge Midstream, Hardisty, Alberta; Two double track thermal oil kilns, Lakeland Mills, Prince George, British Columbia; Gas fired thermal oil heater, Murphy Plywood, Sutherlin, Oregon; Wood fired thermal oil energy system, Coastland Wood Industries, Nanaimo, British Columbia
Financial Information:
Type of Ownership: Private
Domestic Markets:
National
Foreign Activity:
USA

Canadian Branches:
Montréal
153, Henriette-Caron
Châteauguay, QC J6J 2J9
450-633-6767
Fax: 450-669-7003
1-888-234-4480
drykilns@on.aibn.com
Marie-Josee Dumont

Wenvor Technologies Inc.
P.O. Box 1482
Guelph, ON N1H 6N9
519-767-5227
Fax: 519-767-5228
info@wenvortechnologies.com
www.wenvortechnologies.com
Firm Type: Manufacturing
Founded: 1992
Products/Services/Areas of Expertise: Manufacturer of 30 kW wind turbines
Financial Information:
Type of Ownership: Private
Contact(s):
Al Paulissen, President
apaulissen@wenvortechnologies.com
Randy Seager, Manager, Business
rseager@wenvortechnologies.com

Canadian Branches:
Aberfoyle
#3, 43 Winer Rd.
Aberfoyle, ON N1H 6H9

West Coast Spill Supplies Ltd.
Formerly: Kleen Island Environmental Products
Also Known As: Kleen Island Spill Supplies
1570 Kersey Rd.
Brentwood Bay, BC V8M 1J5
250-652-4549
Fax: 250-652-5052
888-548-3800
info@spillsupply.com
www.spillsupply.com
Firm Type: Distributing
Founded: 1995
Products/Services/Areas of Expertise: Distributor of spill control products, spill response absorbent products, custom spill response kits, & secondary containment products to prevent hazardous materials spills
Financial Information:
Type of Ownership: Private
Domestic Markets:
National
Foreign Activity:
Worldwide

West Penetone Inc.
Formerly: West Chemical Products of Canada Ltd.
10900, rue Secant
Montréal, QC H1J 1S5
514-355-4660
Fax: 514-355-2319
800-361-8927
www.westpenetoneinc.com
Firm Type: Distributing, Manufacturing
Founded: 1907
Products/Services/Areas of Expertise: Manufacturer & distributor of environmentally friendly cleaning products; Clients include the aerospace, mining, petrochemical, pulp & paper, & transportation industries, in addition to supermarkets & the military
Financial Information:
Type of Ownership: Private
Domestic Markets:
National

Canadian Branches:
Edmonton
11411 - 160 St.
Edmonton, AB T5M 3T7
780-455-9161
Fax: 780-451-0761
800-661-8805

West Point Products Canada
210 James A. Brennan Rd.
Gananoque, ON K7G 1N7

613-382-1115
Fax: 866-338-6767
800-338-2274
orders@westpointproducts.com
www.multilaser.com
Firm Type: Distributing, Manufacturing
Founded: 1988
Products/Services/Areas of Expertise: West Point Products remanufactures toner cartridges, in an effort to redirect waste from landfills. The company supplies replacement toner cartridges & related services.
Financial Information:
Type of Ownership: Foreign-owned
Domestic Markets:
National
Foreign Activity:
USA
Contact(s):
Tom Day, Chief Executive Officer
Joe Lucot, President & Chief Operating Officer
Charlie Fitzgerald, Vice-President, Business Development
Brent Sallee, Vice-President, Finance & Information
Aldo Spensieri, Vice-President, Sales (Canada)

Wesman Salvage
855 - 49th St. East
Brandon, MB R7A 6S3
204-726-8080
Fax: 204-726-8654
877-284-7278
www.wesmansalvage.com
Firm Type: Waste Management
Member of: Automobile Recyclers of Manitoba
Products/Services/Areas of Expertise: Wesman Salvage specializes in recycling scrap metal. It is a supplier of both new & used steel products, such as auto parts, beams, flats, sheets, plates, & channels.
Activities: Utilizing the Eden Network & the Allied Network to connect with auto recyclers worldwide
Domestic Markets:
Manitoba

West-Lock Fastener Corp.
4303 - 50th Ave.
Athabasca, AB T9S 1M4
Fax: 780-675-3113
888-326-2547
mail@ecoclip.com
www.ecoclip.com
Firm Type: Distributing, Manufacturing
Founded: 1987
EcoLogo Certified Products & Services: Company is licensed by the federal government to use the "Environmental Choice" Eco-logo on all its products & literature
Products/Services/Areas of Expertise: Developer, manufacturer, & marketer of reusable plastic bag closures, called Ecoclips
Activities: Manufacturing Ecoclips from recycled beverage bottle flake material
Ecological Note: Company is licensed by the federal government to use the "Environmental Choice" Eco-logo on all its products & literature
Foreign Activity:
Eastern Europe, The Pacific Rim, USA, United Kingdom
Contact(s):
Lou W. Koppe, Contact, Sales Division

Westburne Canada
A Division of Rexel Canada Electrical Inc.
Formerly: Northern Electric CompanyRexel Canada Corporate Office
5600 Keaton Cres.
Mississauga, ON L5R 3G3
905-712-4004
Fax: 905-568-2987
866-853-0775
www.westburne.ca
Firm Type: Distributing
Founded: 1911
Products/Services/Areas of Expertise: Westburne is an electrical & telecommunication distributor. Products include wire & cable, lighting, controls, & other electrical applications. Westburne serves the institutional, commercial, & residential sectors across Canada.
Financial Information:
Type of Ownership: Foreign-owned
Domestic Markets:
National
Contact(s):
Larry Weber, Manager, Branch
larry.weber@westburne.ca
Canadian Branches:
Abbotsford
#1, 2080 Carpenter St.
Abbotsford, BC V2T 6B3
604-864-9444
Fax: 604-864-0808
www.westburne.ca
Roy Hannah, Manager, Customer Service
roy.hannah@westburne.ca

Ajax
#2, 539 Westney Rd. South
Ajax, ON L1S 4N7
905-426-7682
Fax: 905-426-7703
www.westburne.ca
Norm Crosbie, Manager, Branch
norm.crosbie@westburne.ca

Anjou
10330, boul Louis-H. Lafontaine
Anjou, QC H1J 2T3
514-788-5333
Fax: 514-788-1894
anjou@westburne.ca
www.westburne.ca
Pierre Poulin, Directeur

Barrie
80 Morrow Rd.
Barrie, ON L4N 3V8
705-726-2331
Fax: 705-726-0575
www.westburne.ca
John Forsey, Manager, Branch
john.forsey@westburne.ca

Belleville
291 Coleman St.
Belleville, ON K8P 3H9
613-968-5746
Fax: 613-968-4268
www.westburne.ca
Mike Kelly, Manager, Branch
mike.kelly@westburne.ca

Bracebridge
#2, 440 Ecclestone Dr.
Bracebridge, ON P1L 1Z6
705-645-8288
Fax: 705-645-6074
www.westburne.ca
Dennis Barkley, Manager, Branch
dennis.barkley@westburne.ca

Brampton
#2, 19 Melanie Dr.
Brampton, ON L6T 4K8
905-796-6138
Fax: 905-796-8073
www.westburne.ca
Colin Beisel, Manager, Branch
colin.beisel@westburne.ca

Brandon
346 Park Ave. East
Brandon, MB R7A 7A7
204-571-2333
Fax: 204-725-4479
www.westburne.ca
Darin Swallow, Manager, Customer Service
darin.swallow@westburne.ca

Brantford
71 Craig St.
Brantford, ON N3R 7H9
519-759-7300
Fax: 519-759-2433
www.westburne.ca
Lynn Cooper, Manager, Branch
lynn.cooper@westburne.ca

Whitecourt
4224 - 42nd Ave.
Whitecourt, AB T7S 1P1
780-778-3605
Fax: 780-778-3526
www.westburne.ca

Yellowknife
P.O. Box 968
135 Enterprise Dr.
Yellowknife, NT X1A 2N7
867-669-9690
Fax: 867-669-9695
www.westburne.ca

Victoria
872 Cloverdale Ave.
Victoria, BC V8X 2S8
250-475-1900
Fax: 250-475-1905
www.westburne.ca

Winnipeg - Turenne St.
400A Turenne St.
Winnipeg, MB R2J 3W8
204-954-9901
Fax: 204-954-9899
www.westburne.ca

Winnipeg - Notre Dame Ave.
#1, 1650 Notre Dame Ave.
Winnipeg, MB R3H 0Y7
204-954-9900
Fax: 204-954-9898
www.westburne.ca

Waterloo
75 Northland Rd.
Waterloo, ON N2V 1Y8
519-746-0330
Fax: 519-746-3412
www.westburne.ca

Woodstock
80 Clarke St. South
Woodstock, ON N4S 8Y7
519-539-8588
Fax: 519-539-0515
www.westburne.ca

Brockville
P.O. Box 1618
#6, 1415 California Ave.
Brockville K6V 6E6 ON
613-345-1857
Fax: 613-345-7664
www.westburne.ca
Ron Kleinlagel, Manager, Branch
ron.kleinlagel@westburne.ca

Vaughan
676 Westburne Way
Vaughan, ON L4K 4R8
905-879-2642
Fax: 905-879-0063
www.westburne.ca

Vanier
#150, 220, rue Fortin
Vanier, QC G1M 3S5
418-627-7201
Fax: 418-627-5660
quebec@westburne.ca
www.westburne.ca

Valleyfield
564, rue Ellen
Valleyfield, QC J6S 0B1
450-373-8573
Fax: 450-373-0472
valleyfield@westburne.ca
www.westburne.ca

Guelph
362 Silvercreek Pkwy.
Guelph, ON N1H 1E7
519-821-4020
Fax: 519-821-9075
www.westburne.ca

Burlington
#19-#20, 975 Fraser Dr.
Burlington, ON L7L 4X8

905-681-7110
Fax: 905-681-7221
www.westburne.ca
Andrew Hannon, Manager, Branch
andrew.hannon@westburne.ca

Burnaby
5700 Kingsland Dr.
Burnaby, BC V5B 4W6
604-205-2700
Fax: 604-294-3617
www.westburne.ca
Barry Anderson, Supervisor, Branch
barry.anderson@westburne.ca

Calgary - 32nd Ave. NE
1659 - 32nd Ave. NE
Calgary, AB T2E 7Z5
403-250-9497
Fax: 403-250-2206
www.westburne.ca
Mike Witmer, Manager, Branch Operations
mike.witmer@westburne.ca

Calgary - 40th St. SE
#10, 11133 - 40th St. SE
Calgary, AB T2C 2Z4
403-279-5100
Fax: 403-279-3222
www.westburne.ca
Dan Putz, Manager, Branch
Dan.Putz@westburne.ca

Calgary - 8th St.
3724 - 8th St. SE
Calgary, AB T2G 3A7
403-243-4214
Fax: 403-214-6238
www.westburne.ca
Martin Curtis, Manager, Branch
martin.curtis@westburne.ca
Martin Emery, Manager, Branch Operations
martin.emery@westburne.ca

Cambridge
543 Conestoga Blvd.
Cambridge, ON N1R 6T4
519-623-6710
Fax: 519-623-6291
www.westburne.ca
Dave Atwood, Manager, Branch
Dave.atwood@westburne.ca

Cobourg
#1, 20 Strathy Rd.
Cobourg, ON K9A 5J7
905-373-1717
Fax: 905-373-1733
www.westburne.ca
Tracet Chiodi, Manager, Branch
tracey.chiodi@westburne.ca

Collingwood
#1, 100 High St.
Collingwood, ON L9Y 4K2
705-445-2582
Fax: 705-445-4849
www.westburne.ca
Ian Ross, Manager, Branch
ian.ross@westburne.ca

Cornwall
2900 Marleau St.
Cornwall, ON K6H 6G5
613-933-1075
Fax: 613-933-5027
www.westburne.ca
Denis Paquette, Manager, Branch
denis.paquette@westburne.ca

Courtenay
2920B Moray Ave.
Courtenay, BC V9N 7S7
250-334-3148
Fax: 250-334-2461
www.westburne.ca
James Rose, Supervisor, Branch
james.rose@westburne.ca

Cranbrook
421A Slater Rd.
Cranbrook, BC V1C 4Y5
250-426-6263
Fax: 250-426-5855
www.westburne.ca
Tony Simmonds, Manager, Branch
tony.simmonds@westburne.ca
Carol Sloan, Manager, Branch Operations
carol.sloan@westburne.ca

Dauphin
P.O. Box 688
423 - 1st Ave. SE
Dauphin, MB R7N 3B3
204-638-5328
Fax: 204-638-5617
www.westburne.ca
Randy Parker, Supervisor, Branch
randy.parker@westburne.ca

Drummondville
Produtech
654, rue Farrell
Drummondville, QC J2C 7Y7
819-477-6112
Fax: 819-477-0332
drummondville@westburne.ca
www.westburne.ca
Sylvain Laliberté, Directeur

Edmonton - 149th St.
Westburne Major Projects
13155 - 149th St.
Edmonton, AB T5L 4L6
780-733-2249
Fax: 780-733-2251
www.westburne.ca
Lisa Somerton, Manager, Branch
lisa.somerton@westburne.ca

Edmonton - 184th St.
10640 - 184th St.
Edmonton, AB T5S 0B2
780-452-3131
Fax: 780-452-3492
www.westburne.ca
Mark Hill, Manager, Branch
mark.hill@westburne.ca
David Gibb, Manager, Branch Operations
david.gibb@westburne.ca

Edmonton - McIntyre Rd.
8330 McIntyre Rd.
Edmonton, AB T6E 6R6
780-469-0475
Fax: 780-469-0479
www.westburne.ca
Brian Mann, Manager, Branch
brian.mann@westburne.ca

Edmundston
P.O. Box 608 Main
Edmundston, NB E3V 3L2
506-737-8849
Fax: 506-737-8829
edmundston@westburne.ca
www.westburne.ca
Jacques Desjardins, Directeur

Estevan
P.O. Box 1428
300 Kensington Ave.
Estevan, SK S4A 2K9
306-634-7225
Fax: 306-634-7287
www.westburne.ca
Kevin Krantz, Supervisor, Branch
kevin.krantz@westburne.ca

Fort McMurray
205 Mackay Cres.
Fort McMurray, AB T9H 4T5
780-743-0378
Fax: 780-743-4675
www.westburne.ca
Kelly Smith-Morken, Manager, Branch
kelly.smith@westburne.ca
Laura Oele, Manager, Branch Operations
laura.oele@westburne.ca

Fort St. John
9419 Alaska Rd.
Fort St. John, BC V1J 1A3
250-785-8905
Fax: 250-785-0961
www.westburne.ca
Dianne Barnes, Manager, Branch Operations
dianne.barnes@westburne.ca

Goderich
121 Huckins St.
Goderich, ON N7A 3X8
519-524-9801
Fax: 519-524-2402
www.westburne.ca
Rob Pedlar, Manager, Branch
rob.pedlar@westburne.ca

Granby
236, rue Saint-Urbain
Granby, QC J2G 7T4
450-375-7370
Fax: 450-375-6827
granby@westburne.ca
www.westburne.ca
Michel Daudelin, Directeur

Grande Prairie
#101, 10850 - 97th Ave.
Grande Prairie, AB T8V 3J7
780-532-9021
Fax: 780-539-5153
www.westburne.ca
Steve Schollaardt, Manager, Branch
steve.schollaardt@westburne.ca
Ed Nellis, Manager, Branch Operations
ed.nellis@westburne.ca

Hamilton
120 Nebo Rd.
Hamilton, ON L8W 2E4
905-574-8688
Fax: 905-574-4797
www.westburne.ca
Galliano Campagna, Manager, Branch
galliano.campagna@westburne.ca

Joliette
1368, rue Raoul Charrette
Joliette, QC J6E 8S7
450-759-4313
Fax: 450-759-5205
joliette@westburne.ca
www.westburne.ca
Pierre Lafond, Directeur

Jonquière
2424, rue Cantin, #B
Jonquière, QC G7X 8S6
418-547-2130
Fax: 418-547-9327
jonquiere@westburne.ca
www.westburne.ca
Johanne Ainsley, Directeur

Kamloops
980 Camosun Cres.
Kamloops, BC V2C 6G2
250-374-1331
Fax: 250-374-1477
www.westburne.ca
Caroline Ralston, Manager, Customer Service
caroline.ralston@westburne.ca

Kelowna
#102, 2270 Hunter Rd.
Kelowna, BC V1X 7J8
250-860-4988
Fax: 250-860-1466
www.westburne.ca
Mike Klassen, Manager, Customer Service
mike.klassen@westburne.ca

Kenora
P.O. Box 5020
#4, 1 Dennis Pl.
Kenora, ON P9N 3X9
807-548-4266
Fax: 807-548-5445
www.westburne.ca

Bruce Loranger, Manager, Customer Service
bruce.loranger@westburne.ca

Kingston
#190-200, 1407 John Counter Blvd.
Kingston, ON K7K 6A9
613-546-5400
Fax: 613-546-5330
www.westburne.ca
Dennis Galpin, Manager, Branch
dennis.galpin@westburne.ca

Kitchener
101 Webster Rd.
Kichener, ON N2G 3Y4
519-893-1711
Fax: 519-893-8363
www.westburne.ca
Bunting Doug, Manager, Branch
doug.Bunting@westburne.ca

Kitimat
716 Enterprise Ave.
Kitimat, BC V8C 2E6
250-632-2148
Fax: 250-632-4452
www.westburne.ca
Jason Turyk, Manager, Branch Sales
jason.turyk@westburne.ca

Laval
3410, boul Industriel
Laval, QC H7L 4R9
450-663-5333
Fax: 450-663-3357
laval@westburne.ca
www.westburne.ca
Pierre Dinel, Directeur

Lethbridge
3115 - 16th Ave. North
Lethbridge, AB T1H 5E8
403-327-8561
Fax: 403-328-0354
www.westburne.ca
Joe Rougeau, Manager, Branch
joe.rougeau@westburne.ca
Jim Richardson, Manager, Branch Operations
jim.richardson@westburne.ca

Lindsay
46 Colborne St. East
Lindsay, ON K9V 1K5
705-324-6301
Fax: 705-324-3934
www.westburne.ca
Chris Elliot, Manager, Branch
chris.elliot@westburne.ca

Lloydminster
5113B - 63rd St.
Lloydminster, AB T9V 2E7
780-875-6236
Fax: 780-875-7931
www.westburne.ca
Todd Lamoureux, Manager, Branch
todd.lamoureux@westburne.ca
Shelly Callahan, Manager, Branch Operations
shelly.callahan@westburne.ca

London
600 Little Simcoe St.
London, ON N5Z 1P4
519-434-5755
Fax: 519-673-5188
www.westburne.ca
Bryan Melville, Manager, Branch
bryan.melville@westburne.ca

Longueuil
990, place Trans-Canada
Longueuil, QC J4G 2M1
450-651-9200
Fax: 450-651-8704
longueuil@westburne.ca
www.westburne.ca
Michel Pronovost, Directeur

Medicine Hat
814 - 23rd St. SW
Medicine Hat, AB T1A 8R6

403-526-2866
Fax: 403-580-1838
www.westburne.ca
Don Scott, Manager, Branch
don.scott@westburne.ca
Rudy Schlaht, Manager, Branch Operations
rudy.schlaht@westburne.ca

Midland
P.O. Box 395
405 Cranston Cres.
Midland, ON L4R 4L1
705-526-3710
Fax: 705-526-8316
www.westburne.ca
Felix Ladouceur, Manager, Branch
felix.ladouceur@westburne.ca

Mississauga - Ambassador Dr.
260 Ambassador Dr.
Mississauga, ON L5T 2J2
905-670-2800
Fax: 905-670-4023
www.westburne.ca
Mark Livingston, Manager, Branch
mark.livingston@westburne.ca

Mississauga - Laird Dr.
3495 Laird Dr.
Mississauga, ON L5L 5S5
905-608-1010
Fax: 905-608-0606
www.westburne.ca
Peter Ansell, Manager, Branch
peter.ansell@westburne.ca

Montréal
10045, boul. Henri Bourassa ouest
St-Laurent, QC H4S 1A1
514-337-5331
Fax: 514-332-9177
montreal@westburne.ca
www.westburne.ca
Robert Gauthier, Directeur

Nanaimo
1950 Boxwood Rd.
Nanaimo, BC V9S 5Y2
250-716-1333
Fax: 250-716-1337
www.westburne.ca
Christine Foy, Manager, Branch Sales
christine.foy@westburne.ca

New Richmond
115, boul Perron est
New Richmond, QC G0C 2B0
418-392-4401
Fax: 418-392-6608
newrichmond@westburne.ca
www.westburne.ca
Richard Rivière, Directeur

Newmarket
110 Harry Walker Pkwy.
Newmarket, ON L3Y 7B2
905-895-8625
Fax: 905-895-8143
www.westburne.ca
Rob Crooks, Manager, Branch
rob.crooks@westburne.ca

North Bay
825 Wallace Rd.
North Bay, ON P1B 8G4
705-472-0590
Fax: 705-472-7359
www.westburne.ca
Greg Walker, Manager, Branch
greg.walker@westburne.ca

North Vancouver
170 Donaghy Ave.
North Vancouver, BC V7P 2L5
604-985-9531
Fax: 604-985-4083
www.westburne.ca
Kasia Cobb, Supervisor, Branch
kasia.cobb@westburne.ca

Orangeville
#11 & #12, 48 Centennial Rd.
Orangeville, ON L9W 3T4
519-941-2006
Fax: 519-941-4631
www.westburne.ca
Rob Smith, Manager, Branch
rob.smith@westburne.ca

Oshawa
600 Thornton Rd. South
Oshawa, ON
905-576-7100
Fax: 905-728-5939
www.westburne.ca
Mike Krieger, Manager, Branch
mike.krieger@westburne.ca

Ottawa - Merivale Rd.
1867 Merivale Rd.
Nepean, ON K2G 1E3
613-225-9910
Fax: 613-225-9973
www.westburne.ca
Marc Desforges, Manager, Branch
marc.desforges@westburne.ca

Ottawa - Newmarket St.
1173-1175 Newmarket St.
Ottawa, ON K1B 3V1
613-747-9573
Fax: 613-747-1961
www.westburne.ca
Travis Humphreys, Manager, Branch

Owen Sound
1170 Second Ave.
Owen Sound, ON N4K 2H9
519-376-4310
Fax: 519-376-3892
www.westburne.ca
Keith Spry, Manager, Branch
keith.spry@westburne.ca

Parry Sound
32 Joseph St.
Parry Sound, ON P2A 2G3
705-746-1140
Fax: 705-746-7850
www.westburne.ca
Jason Phillips, Manager, Branch
Jason.phillips@westburne.ca

Pembroke
935 MacKay St.
Pembroke, ON K8B 1A2
613-735-1015
Fax: 613-735-1394
www.westburne.ca
Wayne Humphreys, Manager, Branch
wayne.humphreys@westburne.ca

Peterborough
700 Neal Dr.
Peterborough, ON K9J 6X7
705-743-1313
Fax: 705-743-6891
www.westburne.ca
Craig Schroter, Manager, Branch
craig.schroter@westburne.ca

Port Alberni
4737 Tebo Ave.
Port Alberni, BC V9Y 8A9
250-723-2451
Fax: 250-723-1211
www.westburne.ca
Trent Martin, Manager, Customer Service
trent.martin@westburne.ca

Prince Albert
380 - 16th St. West
Prince Albert, SK S6V 3V7
306-922-4545
Fax: 306-763-1144
www.westburne.ca
Jason Budd, Manager, Customer Service
jason.budd@westburne.ca

Products & Services Buyer's Guide

Prince George
2251 Nicholson St.
Prince George, BC V2N 1V9
250-562-3111
Fax: 250-562-0284
www.westburne.ca
Terri Langton, Manager, Branch
terri.langton@westburne.ca

Red Deer
6857 - 52nd Ave.
Red Deer, AB T4N 4L2
403-343-2155
Fax: 403-347-9955
www.westburne.ca
Darcy Robinson, Manager, Branch
darcy.robinson@westburne.ca
Caroline Ouellet, Manager, Branch Operations
caroline.ouellet@westburne.ca

Richmond
#110, 4320 Viking Way
Richmond, BC V6V 2L4
604-270-0450
Fax: 604-273-3871
www.westburne.ca
Angie Schwan, Supervisor, Branch
angie.schwan@westburne.ca

Rosemont
2961, rue Bélanger est
Rosemont, QC H1Y 3G4
514-729-5331
Fax: 514-729-5095
rosemont@westburne.ca
www.westburne.ca
Michel Clermont, Directeur

Rouyn
233, boul Industriel
Rouyn, QC J9X 6P2
819-764-6771
Fax: 819-764-5315
rouyn@westburne.ca
www.westburne.ca
Gilles Théberge, Directeur

Saint-Georges-de-Beauce
635, 94e rue
Saint-Georges-de-Beauce, QC G5Y 3K3
418-228-6421
Fax: 418-228-5616
stgeorges@westburne.ca
www.westburne.ca
Roger Doyon, Directeur

Saint-Jérôme
861, rue Alfred-Viau
Saint-Jérôme, QC J7Y 4N7
450-436-5553
Fax: 450-436-7021
stjerome@westburne.ca
www.westburne.ca
Pierre Dinel, Directeur

Sarnia
1231 Confederation St.
Sarnia, ON N7S 4M7
519-336-0015
Fax: 519-336-0016
www.westburne.ca
Steve Pepper, Manager, Branch
steve.pepper@westburne.ca

Saskatoon
2727 First Ave. North
Saskatoon, SK S7K 6Z6
306-933-2992
Fax: 306-242-2585
www.westburne.ca
Yvonne Yourkowski, Manager, Customer Service
yvonne.yourkowski@westburne.ca

Sault Ste Marie
#4, 64 White Oak Dr. East
Sault Ste Marie, ON P6B 4J8
705-949-5994
Fax: 705-949-6418
www.westburne.ca

Sheilagh Muncaster, Manager, Branch
sheilagh.muncaster@westburne.ca

Sherbrooke
4055, boul. Industriel
Sherbrooke, QC J1L 2S7
819-562-2660
Fax: 819-562-5187
sherbrooke@westburne.ca
www.westburne.ca
Denis Grenier, Directeur

Simcoe
47 Park Rd.
Simcoe, ON N3Y 4N5
519-428-0650
Fax: 519-428-2081
www.westburne.ca
Steve Long, Manager, Branch
steve.long@westburne.ca

Smiths Falls
94 Cornelia St. West
Smiths Falls, ON K7A 4W7
613-283-2270
Fax: 613-283-9581
www.westburne.ca
Len Cardiff, Manager, Branch
len.cardiff@westburne.ca

Squamish
#122, 39002 Discovery Way
Squamish, BC V8B 0E5
604-892-9330
Fax: 604-892-9392
www.westburne.ca
Phil Urch, Supervisor, Branch
phil.urch@westburne.ca

St Catharines
485 Eastchester Ave. East, #B
St Catharines, ON L2M 6S2
905-988-3881
Fax: 905-988-1194
www.westburne.ca
April Campbell, Manager, Branch
april.campbell@westburne.ca

St-Laurent
Westburne Centre de Câble
10045, boul. Henri Bourassa ouest
St-Laurent, QC H4S 1A1
514-337-6090
Fax: 514-337-6030
ccwq@westburne.ca
www.westburne.ca
Christian Loranger, Directeur

St. Thomas
6 Duckworth Ave.
St. Thomas, ON N5P 2A8
519-633-6613
Fax: 519-663-3367
www.westburne.ca
Scott Marr, Manager, Branch
scott.marr@westburne.ca

Stoney Creek
337 Barton St.
Stoney Creek, ON L8E 2L2
905-662-6468
Fax: 905-662-6807
www.westburne.ca
Jeff Pearce, Manager, Branch
jeff.pearce@westburne.ca

Strathroy
309 High St. East
Strathroy, ON N7G 3Z4
519-245-2300
Fax: 519-245-5341
www.westburne.ca
Steve Joos, Manager, Branch
steve.joos@westburne.ca

Sudbury
878 Falconbridge Rd.
Sudbury, ON P3A 4S4
705-560-2111
Fax: 705-560-5287
www.westburne.ca

Randy Hodgson, Manager, Branch
randy.hodgson@westburne.ca

Surrey
#101 & #102, 5521 - 192nd St.
Surrey, BC V3S 8E5
604-574-7882
Fax: 604-574-7858
www.westburne.ca
Terry Rhodes, Supervisor, Branch
terry.rhodes@westburne.ca
Mike Medway, Manager, Customer Service
mike.medway@westburne.ca

Thompson
200 Hayes Rd.
Thompson, MB R8N 1M4
204-778-7041
Fax: 204-778-8007
www.westburne.ca
Peter Ouellette, Manager, Customer Service
peter.ouellette@westburne.ca

Thunder Bay
1231 Amber Dr.
Thunder Bay, ON P7B 6M4
807-344-3100
Fax: 807-344-3255
www.westburne.ca
Tammy Mastalerz, Manager, Customer Service
tammy.mastalerz@westburne.ca

Tillsonburg
#3 & #4, 25 Spruce St.
Tillsonburg, ON N4G 4W6
519-842-3651
Fax: 519-842-2398
www.westburne.ca
Roger Ross, Manager, Branch
roger.ross@westburne.ca

Timmins
800 Birch St. South
Timmins, ON P4N 7H1
705-267-1436
Fax: 705-264-1925
www.westburne.ca
Rory MacKenzie, Manager, Branch
rory.mackenzie@westburne.ca

Toronto - Keele St.
3645 Keele St.
Toronto, ON M3J 1M6
416-635-2999
Fax: 416-633-6143
www.westburne.ca
John Carter, Manager, Branch
john.carter@westburne.ca

Toronto - Markham Rd.
1210 Markham Rd.
Toronto, ON M1H 3B3
416-751-4310
Fax: 416-751-8984
www.westburne.ca
Robert Farraway, Manager, Branch
robert.farraway@westburne.ca

Toronto - Queens Quay East
200 Queens Quay East
Toronto, ON M5A 4K9
416-863-1444
Fax: 416-863-4979
www.westburne.ca
Anthony Huber, Manager, Branch
anthony.huber@westburne.ca

Toronto - The East Mall
24 The East Mall
Toronto, ON M8W 4W5
416-503-4778
Fax: 416-503-2233
www.westburne.ca
Maurizio Pio, Manager, Branch
maurizio.pio@westburne.ca

Trois-Rivières
5230, rue Saint-Joseph
Trois-Rivières, QC G8Z 4L8
819-378-4071
Fax: 819-376-7492

troisrivieres@westburne.ca
www.westburne.ca
Richard Turgeon, Directeur

Val d'Or
1149, rue des Foreurs
Val d'Or, QC J9P 4P8
819-825-7272
Fax: 819-825-7779
valdor@westburne.ca
www.westburne.ca
Gilles Théberge, Directeur
Hugues Sauvé, Directeur
Germain Bourque, Directeur
Tony Rocca, Manager, Branch
tony.rocca@westburne.ca
Shawn Turner, Manager, Branch
shawn.turner@westburne.ca
Rob Hesch, Manager, Branch
Rob.Hesch@westburne.ca
Shane Stevens, Supervisor, Branch
shane.stevens@westburne.ca
Dave Arbour, Manager, Customer Service
dave.arbour@westburne.ca
Dan Glowacki, Supervisor, Branch
dan.glowacki@westburne.ca
Brent Hunniford, Manager, Branch
brent.hunniford@westburne.ca
Kelly Gabruck, Manager, Branch
kelly.gabruck@westburne.ca
Kim Smale, Manager, Branch Operations
kim.smale@westburne.ca

Westchem Mfg. Ltd.
#16, 31550 South Fraser Way
Abbotsford, BC V2T 4C6
604-857-1335
Fax: 604-852-4895
carl@westchem.com
www.westchem.com
Firm Type: Manufacturing
Founded: 1983
EcoLogo Certified Products & Services: RV products received certification from Environment Canada for environmental safety & performance.
Products/Services/Areas of Expertise: Westchem Mfg. Ltd. produces high performance terpolymer technologies for use in industrial water treatment. Specialty products are also manufactured to meet the specific needs of customers. The company serves cooling tower, boiler, food production, & wastewater facilities.
Ecological Note: RV products received certification from Environment Canada for environmental safety & performance.
Domestic Markets:
British Columbia
Contact(s):
Carl Cooke, Contact
carl@westchem.com

Westech Industrial Ltd.
5636 Burbank Cres. SE
Calgary, AB T2H 1Z6
403-252-8803
Fax: 403-253-6803
sales-export@westech-ind.com
www.westech-ind.com
Firm Type: Distributing, Manufacturing
Founded: 1966
Staff: 60
Member of: Ontario Pollution Control Equipment Association
Products/Services/Areas of Expertise: Analytical & control instrumentation; waste gas burners & control equipment for sewage treatment & landfill plants; on-line effluent & emission monitors; flare ignition systems; on-line wastewater analyzers, emission monitors, process analyzers; area monitors, trace pollutants monitors
Financial Information:
Type of Ownership: Private
Domestic Markets:
National
Foreign Activity:
Worldwide
Contact(s):
Ken Lapp, President/CEO
Etienne Patenaude, International Sales

Canadian Branches:
Edmonton
P.O. Box 4242
Edmonton, AB T6E 4T3
780-464-4740
Fax: 780-467-1605
sales-west@westech-ind.com
Alex Frei

Halifax
16 Lanshaw Close
Halifax, NS B3S 1E7
902-457-1171
Fax: 902-457-1731
sales-east@westech-ind.com
Fabian Beaton

Mississauga
240 Matheson Blvd. East
Mississauga, ON L4Z 1X1
905-890-5265
Fax: 905-890-6213
sales-east@westech-ind.com
Norm Williams

Montréal
#124, 10500, Côte de Liesse
Lachine, QC H8T 3E3
514-636-8761
Fax: 514-631-0857
sales-montreal@westech-ind.com
Jean-Paul Jean

Vancouver
#300, 1275 West 6th Ave/
Vancouver, BC V6H 4E4
604-737-8358
Fax: 604-737-8315
sales-west@westech-ind.com
Linda Ross

Westeel
A division of Vicwest Operating Limited Partnership
P.O. Box 792
450 Desautels St.
Winnipeg, MB R3C 2N5
204-233-7133
Fax: 204-235-0796
800-465-0463
info@westeel.com
www.westeel.com
Firm Type: Manufacturing
Founded: 1905
Member of: Steel Tank Institute; American Society of Mechanical Engineers; Canadian Standards Association; Society of Automotive Engineers
Quality Environmental Management System(s): 9001
Products/Services/Areas of Expertise: Design, engineering & manufacture of storage units for bulk commodities, including grain, fertilizer & petroleum products
Financial Information:
Type of Ownership: Publicly Traded
Domestic Markets:
National
Foreign Activity:
Asia, Australia/New Zealand, Central Europe, Eastern Europe, The Middle East, USA
Contact(s):
J.R. Skull, President
Jim Weeda, Sales & Marketing Manager

Western Bio Resources Consulting Ltd. / WBR
2248 Columbia Ave.
Castlegar, BC V1N 2X1
250-365-2028
Fax: 250-365-3607
info@westernbioresources.com
www.westernbioresources.com
Firm Type: Engineering
Founded: 1997
Staff: 4
Member of: Association of Professional Engineers & Geoscientists
Products/Services/Areas of Expertise: Contaminated sites; waste management & beneficial use; small-seal sewage; composting
Recently Completed / Ongoing Projects: Power pole management; smelter site remediation; transfer site design; large diesel spill bioremediation; pulp biosolid composting
Financial Information:
Type of Ownership: Private
Revenue: $250,000 - $500,000
Revenue Sources: 5% nationwide; 15% Municipals; 80% Private Contracts
Domestic Markets:
British Columbia
Markets Sought:
USA
Contact(s):
Chris Bullock, P.Eng., President

Western Canadian Spill Services Ltd. / WCSS
P.O. Box 503
3545 - 32nd Ave. NE
Calgary, AB T1Y 6M6
403-250-9606
Fax: 403-291-9408
www.wcss.ab.ca
Firm Type: Management Consulting, Scientific/Technical Services
Founded: 1972
Products/Services/Areas of Expertise: Cooperative of petroleum companies that work together to attain a state of spill response readiness
Activities: Maintaining spill contingency plans; Conducting training exercises; Providing educational funding for members; Participating in research & development activities
Financial Information:
Type of Ownership: Non Profit
Contact(s):
Alan B. McFadyen, Managing Director, 403-250-0882Fax: 403-291-9408
amcfadyen@enform.ca
Michael Locke, Coordinator, Oil Spills, 780-955-6008Fax: 780-955-2454
mlocke@enform.ca
Shannon Jarrell, Advisor, Environmental Training, 403-250-0887Fax: 403-291-9408
sjarrell@enform.ca
Sheila Wooldridge, Advisor, Accounting, 403-250-6277Fax: 403-291-9408
swooldridge@enform.ca

Western Industrial Services Ltd.
300 Dawson Rd.
Winnipeg, MB R2J 0S7
204-956-9475
Fax: 204-956-9470
western@wisl.ca
www.wisl.ca
Firm Type: Engineering, Scientific/Technical Services
Founded: 1964
Member of: National Association of Corrosion Engineers; Manitoba Building Contractors Safety Program; Steel Structures Painting Council; International Concrete Repair Institute; American Concrete Institute; Asbestos Abatement Association of Canada; Winnipeg Construction Association
Quality Environmental Management System(s): 9001
Products/Services/Areas of Expertise: Industrial & specialty painting & coating; blast & industrial cleaning; asbestos & lead abatement; hazardous waste removal; mould removal; concrete rehabilitation; shot blasting; fireproofing & fire stopping
Domestic Markets:
National
Foreign Activity:
USA
Contact(s):
George Rajotte, President
Kent Johnston, P.Eng., Estimator/Project Coordinator
Marcel Vincent, Estimator/Project Coordinator
L. Turenne, Project Coordinator

Western Scrap Metals
Also Known As: Western Recycling Services Ltd.
18 Sutherland Ave.
Winnipeg, MB R2W 3C2
204-947-0251
Fax: 204-947-5697
Firm Type: Waste Management
Founded: 1956
Staff: 10
Products/Services/Areas of Expertise: Recycling of all scrap metal, clean glass (bottles & jars only), PET plastic bottles, tin & aluminum cans, HDPE plastic

Products & Services Buyer's Guide

Contact(s):
Al Linder, President

Western Site Technologies Inc. / WSTI
Bay 6
2280 - 39th Ave. NE
Calgary, AB T2E 6P7
403-520-0101
Fax: 403-520-0105
1-877-520-0101
mudloc.westernsite.com
Firm Type: Management Consulting, Waste Management
Founded: 1996
Products/Services/Areas of Expertise: Provider of solutions for invert & hydrocarbon based disposal problems; Products include MUD-loc, AGROW-loc, THERM-tec, & BIO-dex; Services include envionmental consulting, environmental impact assessment, eco system surveys, landfill design & construction, hazardous waste management & project management; Clients include drilling groups using Invert Mud Systems
Recently Completed / Ongoing Projects: Treatment of invert drilling waste, northern Canada
Financial Information:
Type of Ownership: Private
Domestic Markets:
National
Foreign Activity:
China, The Middle East, The Pacific Rim, USA
Contact(s):
Gary Barnes, President
gbarnes@westernsite.com
Darryl Hartley, Director, Internation Operations
Edward Johnson, Associate & Professional Engineer

Canadian Branches:
Edmonton
7722 - 9th St.
Edmonton, AB T2P 1L6
780-940-7440
Mike Dansereau, Contact
mdansereau@westernsite.com

Vancouver
3350 Bridgeway
Vancouver, BC V5K 1H9
604-294-9378
Fax: 604-687-8697
kbarnes@westernsite.com
Bill Barnes, Contact
bbarnes@westernsite.com

Western Solutions 2000 Ltd.
P.O. Box 6897 Main
Drayton Valley, AB T7A 1S2
780-542-3364
Fax: 780-621-0018
arnold@westernsolutions2000.com
www.westernsolutions2000.com
Products/Services/Areas of Expertise: Provider of coating & environmental solutions; Clients include the forestry, mining, oil & gas, agricultural, & automotive industries
Activities: Providing line-x polyurethane, endura, epoxy, & powder coatings; Offering erosion control products, precidium spray in liners, portable berm systems, "Zero Ground Disturbance" corrugated steel containment berms, LDPE containment sheet liners, & ESSI spill absorbant materials
Domestic Markets:
Alberta, British Columbia, Saskatchewan
Contact(s):
Mark Baker, Contact
mark@westernsolutions2000.com

Western Subsea Technology Ltd.
Pacific Marine Technology Centre
#1, 203 Harbour Rd.
Victoria, BC V9A 3S2
250-380-2830
wst@islandnet.com
www.islandnet.com/subsea
Firm Type: Engineering, Scientific/Technical Services
Founded: 1984
Products/Services/Areas of Expertise: Services include research & development, environmental surveys, diving services, fish stock assessments, & habitat classifications
Financial Information:
Type of Ownership: Private
Contact(s):
Mike Muirhead, P.Eng., President

Westest
Also Known As: Western Canada Testing Inc.
P.O. Box 1060
390 River Rd.
Portage la Prairie, MB R1N 3C5
204-857-4811
Fax: 204-239-7124
800-561-8378
info@westest.ca
www.westest.ca
Firm Type: Engineering, Scientific/Technical Services
Founded: 1992
Quality Environmental Management System(s): 9001-2000
Products/Services/Areas of Expertise: Provider of physical testing & product performance evaluation services
Activities: Mower, tow dynamometer, RPC simulation, standards, package, & multi-axial simulation testing
Contact(s):
David Gullacher, B.E., General Manager
dgullacher@westest.ca
Troy Lucyshyn, P.Eng., Leader, Mower Testing Service
Steve Swiddle, P.Eng., Leader
Portage Division
Terry Carr, Test Technician, Package Testing Division

Canadian Branches:
Humboldt
P.O. Box 1150
Hwy. 5 West
Humboldt, SK S0K 2A0
306-682-2442
Fax: 306-682-5080
info@westest.ca
Philip Leduc, B.E., Leader, Humboldt Division

Westhoff Engineering Resources Inc.
#601, 1040 - 7 Ave. SW
Calgary, AB T2P 3C9
403-264-9366
Fax: 403-264-8796
dennis@westhoff.ab.ca
Firm Type: Management Consulting
Founded: 1996
Products/Services/Areas of Expertise: Water resources management consultants
Contact(s):
Dennis R Westoff, M.Eng., P.Eng., President/Chief Engineer

Westland Plastics Ltd.
12 Rothwell Rd.
Winnipeg, MB R3P 2H7
204-488-6075
Fax: 204-488-2376
sales@westland.ca
Firm Type: Distributing, Manufacturing
Founded: 1982
Member of: Canadian Marine Manufacturers Association; National Marine Manufacturers Association; American Boat & Yachting Council
Products/Services/Areas of Expertise: ISO certified manufacturer & distributor of rotationally molded plastic products; Products include water & sewage tanks, sump & sewage basins, components for the RV & van conversion industry, boat seat shells & dock floats, & polyland refuse lids; Clients include the marine, water, sewer, agricultural, industrial, recreational vehicle, & van conversion sectors

Westland Resource Group Inc.
#203, 830 Shamrock St.
Victoria, BC V8X 2V1
250-592-8500
Fax: 250-592-1633
info@westland.com
www.westland.com
Firm Type: Management Consulting, Scientific/Technical Services
Founded: 1986
Products/Services/Areas of Expertise: Consulting firm offering environmental & planning services; Clients include the private & public sectors & the First Nations
Activities: Preparing environmental assessments, research studies, & environmental management strategies
Recently Completed / Ongoing Projects: Land use, resource, & environmental studies, First Nations
Domestic Markets:
National
Contact(s):

Wayne G. Biggs, M.Sc., P.Ag., R.P.Bio, Biologist, Habitat & Land Use
Carmen I. Holschuh, B.Sc., M.Sc., R.P.Bio., Wildlife Biologist & Environmental Planner
Steve Young, B.Sc., PgDip, M.En.S., Specialist, Geographic Information Systems
David E. Harper, Ph.D., P.Ag., CPESC, MCIP, Planner, Environmental & Land Use
Rahul E. Ray, B.Sc., DEIA, M.R.M., Planner, Environmental & Land Use

Westport Innovations Inc.
#101, 1700 - 75 West Ave.
Vancouver, BC V6P 6G2
604-718-2000
Fax: 604-718-2001
info@westport.com
www.westport.com
Firm Type: Scientific/Technical Services
Staff: 140
Products/Services/Areas of Expertise: Technologies to allow diesel engines to operate on alternative fuels
Contact(s):
David Demers, CEO

Westra & Associates Inc.
P.O. Box 303
Rochester, AB T0G 1Z0
780-698-2142
Fax: 780-698-2293
Firm Type: Information Technology, Manufacturing, Scientific/Technical Services
Founded: 1983
Staff: 1
Products/Services/Areas of Expertise: Expert in nutrition physiology of plants & animals; toxicity of minerals & compounds to animals; water, feeds & product analysis & interpretation; forage & grain management; soil management; wildlife nutrition & management; biology of wild plants & animals; seminar preparation & teaching; scientific research studies
Recently Completed / Ongoing Projects: Development of export markets for local businesses in Germany, Italy, Mexico & Argentina for the storage of farm forages & grains for animal use; ongoing consultations with dairy farmers in Western Canada; research projects include growth of grass pastures & barley grain in eroded soils; arbitration of conflict crisis for two-farm families
Domestic Markets:
Alberta, British Columbia, Manitoba, Saskatchewan
Foreign Activity:
Australia/New Zealand, Central America, Eastern Europe, Western Europe, The Middle East, Mexico, USA
Contact(s):
Robert Westra, President

Westworth Associates Environmental Ltd.
#203, 4208 - 97 St.
Edmonton, AB T6E 5Z9
780-466-9992
Fax: 780-466-9979
lbrusnyk@wael.ca
www.wael.ca
Products/Services/Areas of Expertise: Consulting firm with expertise in environmental impact assessment & natural resource management
Activities: Researching wildlife & fisheries; Identifying regulatory requirements; Preparing mitigation plans
Recently Completed / Ongoing Projects: Northern River Basins Study
Domestic Markets:
National
Foreign Activity:
Worldwide

Weyerhaeuser Company Ltd.
P.O. Box 800
1850 Mission Flats Rd.
Kamloops, BC V2C 5M7
250-372-2217
Fax: 250-828-7585
www.weyerhaeuser.com
Ecological Note: Pulp
Contact(s):
David Lloyd, Customer Service Director
david.lloyd@weyerhaeuser.com

whatIf? Technologies Inc.
Formerly: Robbert Associates
338 Somerset St. West, 3rd Fl.
Ottawa, ON K2P 0J9
613-232-5613
Fax: 613-232-5997
info@whatiftechnologies.com
www.whatiftechnologies.com
Firm Type: Information Technology
Founded: 1994
Staff: 6
Products/Services/Areas of Expertise: Provider of software technology, consulting & services for systems models & simulation; models are used for strategic planning, scenario analysis, risk analysis, policy analysis & education; designs & implements simulation models, based on WhatIf? Technology platform; custom modelling work includes urban & regional planning; energy & emissions analysis; natural resource management; demography; sustainable development; farm-scale nutrient management; & industrial process modelling
Recently Completed / Ongoing Projects: Canadian Transportation energy & emissions model; population/land use models for Waterloo & Peel; process model for Taiwan textile industry; farm scale nutrient management model; energy end-use models; Canadian electric power generation & capacity planning; Melbourne Region stocks & flows model; Australian stocks & flows model
Financial Information:
Type of Ownership: Private
Revenue: $250,000 - $500,000
Revenue Sources: 75% nationwide; 25% Municipals
Domestic Markets:
National
Foreign Activity:
Australia/New Zealand
Markets Sought:
China, Central Europe, Western Europe, USA, Vietnam,
Contact(s):
Robert Hoffman, President, 613/232-5613
robert.hoffman@whatiftechnologies.com
Bert McInnis, 613/232-5613
bert.mcinnis@whatiftechnologies.com
Joe Collins, Director, Business Development, 613/232-5613
joe.collins@whatiftechnologies.com
Lloyd Switzer, Partner

Wheatland Regional Centre Inc. & SARCAN Recycling / WRC
A Division of The Saskatchewan Association of Rehabilitation Centres
P.O. Box 1540
802 - 6th St. East
Rosetown, SK S0L 2V0
306-882-4257
Fax: 306-882-2652
wrcf@sasktel.net
Firm Type: Manufacturing, Waste Management
Staff: 26
Member of: Saskatchewan Waste Reduction Council
Products/Services/Areas of Expertise: Recycler of beverage cans, bottles, milk jugs, glass containers, cardboard, & paper; Operator of a composting site for Rosetown
Activities: Recycling computers & electronics with Rosetown Recycling
Contact(s):
S. Lidsler, Chief Executive Officer

Wheelabrator Canada Co.
P.O. Box 100
401 Wheelabrator Way
Milton, ON L9T 4B7
905-875-1662
Fax: 905-875-1675
800-327-8727
info@wapc.com
www.wapc.com
Firm Type: Manufacturing
Founded: 1959
Staff: 22
Products/Services/Areas of Expertise: Air pollution control equipment; dry dust collectors
Domestic Markets:
National
Foreign Activity:
USA
Contact(s):
Edwin Formanek, President
Larry Martyniuk, Manager, Sales
Harry Cheng, Operations Manager
International Branch(es):
Wheelabrator Air Pollution Control
441 Smithfield St.
Pittsburgh, PA USA
412-562-7300
Fax: 412-562-7254
info@wapc.com
John Foster, International Sales

Whisco Ltd.
158 Clark St.
Fredericton, NB E3A 5G8
506-458-9490
Fax: 506-459-8698
whisco@nbnet.nb.ca
Firm Type: Distributing
Founded: 1970
Staff: 14
Products/Services/Areas of Expertise: Sanitation supplies; chemicals; recycling of paper products & plastics
Domestic Markets:
New Brunswick, Nova Scotia
Contact(s):
Bruce W. Wishart, President
David Milbury General Manager, Sales
Paul Cronkite, Office Manager

Whitecourt Power Limited Partnership
67 Yonge St., 16th Fl.
Toronto, ON M5E 1J8
416-777-2800
Fax: 416-777-9745
group@probyngroup.com
Firm Type: Manufacturing
Staff: 34
EcoLogo Certified Products & Services: Biomass power generation
Products/Services/Areas of Expertise: Alternative power generation in Whitecourt, AB
Ecological Note: Biomass power generation
Domestic Markets:
Alberta
Contact(s):
Peter Keskinen, Contact

Whitman Benn Group
1874 Brunswick St., 4th Fl.
Halifax, NS B3J 2G7
902-420-8900
Fax: 902-420-8949
whitbenn@fox.nstn.ca
Firm Type: Management Consulting, Engineering, Scientific/Technical Services
Staff: 7
Member of: NS Consulting Engineers Association; Association of Consulting Engineers of Canada
Products/Services/Areas of Expertise: Broad scope engineering, architectural & project management consulting services; erosion & sediment control; sewage collection & treatment; water treatment & distribution; municipal engineering & land development services, surveing; marine engineering; industrial pollution control; support services to the oil & gas industry onshore & offshore
Recently Completed / Ongoing Projects: Project management & environmental support to the Sable Energy Project
Financial Information:
Type of Ownership: Private
Revenue Sources: 30% nationwide; 10% Provincial; 10% Municipals; 50% Private Contracts
Domestic Markets:
New Brunswick, Newfoundland & Labrador, Nova Scotia, Prince Edward Island
Contact(s):
Aubrey Palmeter, President/CEO
Ian Tillard, Marketing
Tom Swanson, P.Eng., Vice-President, Municipal Services
Leo Brooks, Senior Municipal Engineering
Canadian Branches:
NB Office
80 Driscoll Cres.
Moncton, NB E1E 3R8
506-855-5542
Fax: 506-857-9974

WHMIS Inc.
11412 - 102 Ave. NW
Edmonton, AB T5K 0P9
780-488-7359
whmis@telusplanet.net
Firm Type: Engineering
Founded: 1990
Staff: 5
Member of: Alberta Professional Engineers Geologist Association; Association of the Professional Engineers of the Province of Ontario
Products/Services/Areas of Expertise: Safety training; waste management training; environmental consulting; design of refineries; patents on soil cleaning equipment
Financial Information:
Type of Ownership: Private
Revenue: $50,000 - $100,000
Revenue Sources: 100% Private Contracts
Domestic Markets:
Alberta
Foreign Activity:
Asia, Australia/New Zealand
Contact(s):
Norman Arrison, President/CEO

Wiebe Environmental Services Inc.
1212 - 58th Ave. SE
Calgary, AB T2H 2C9
403-271-4442
Fax: 403-271-4489
kelly@wesinc.ca
www.wesinc.ca
Products/Services/Areas of Expertise: Environmental Consulting services
Contact(s):
Craig Robertson, Manager
Canadian Branches:
Edmonton
9120 - 37 Ave. NW
Edmonton, AB T6E 5L4
780-435-4477
Fax: 780-435-4471

Grande Prairie
#205, 9914 - 109th Ave.
Grande Prairie, AB T8V 1R6
780-538-1757
Fax: 780-538-1417

Wilcorp Manufacturing
117 Tycos Dr.
Toronto, ON M6B 1W3
416-789-1164
Fax: 416-785-3626
800-465-3267
www.wilcorp.com
Firm Type: Distributing
Founded: 1965
Staff: 22
Quality Environmental Management System(s): 9002
Products/Services/Areas of Expertise: Residential & industrial ceiling fans; portable fans & pedestal fans
Financial Information:
Type of Ownership: Private
Domestic Markets:
National
Contact(s):
John Maraj, Sales Manager

Wilkinson Heavy Precast Ltd.
588 Hwy. 5 West, RR#2
Dundas, ON L9H 5E2
905-628-5611
Fax: 905-628-9292
800-263-8503
wilk@on.aibn.com
www.wilkinsonheavyprecast.com
Firm Type: Manufacturing
Founded: 1957
Staff: 15
Products/Services/Areas of Expertise: Sewage treatment systems & equipment; water treatment systems & equipment; industrial solid waste treatment equipment; precast concrete boxes & vessels for containment/treatment of potable water, wastewater, fire water storage, oil/water separators
Domestic Markets:
Ontario

Products & Services Buyer's Guide

Contact(s):
Jim Wilkinson, President
jim@wilkinsonheavyprecast.com

William Alexander & Associates Ltd.
#300, 5171 George St.
Halifax, NS B3J 1M6
902-492-0008
Fax: 902-492-0128
www.williamalexander.ca
Firm Type: Management Consulting, Information Technology
Founded: 1991
Staff: 14
Products/Services/Areas of Expertise: Provides community consultation services including documentation & strategic recommendations; environmental permitting, programming & management of multi-disciplinary projects directed at federal &/or provincial permitting requirements
Financial Information:
Type of Ownership: Private
Revenue Sources: 100% Private Contracts
Domestic Markets:
New Brunswick, Newfoundland & Labrador, Nova Scotia, Prince Edward Island
Contact(s):
James O'Hagan, Senior Partner
Peter Dwyer, Senior Partner

William Dam Seeds Ltd.
279 Hwy 8, RR#1
Dundas, ON L9H 5E1
905-628-6641
Fax: 905-627-1729
info@damseeds.com
www.damseeds.com
Firm Type: Distributing
Founded: 1949
Products/Services/Areas of Expertise: Chemically untreated & organically grown flower & vegetable seeds; gardening accessories
Domestic Markets:
National
Foreign Activity:
USA
Contact(s):
René Dam, President/CEO

Williams Engineering Inc.
Formerly: A.D. Williams Engineeering Inc.
Scotia Tower 2, Scotia Place
#1661, 10060 Jasper Avenue
Edmonton, AB T5J 3R8
780-409-5300
Fax: 780-409-5309
800-263-2393
info@williamsengineering.com
www.williamsengineering.com
Firm Type: Engineering
Founded: 1978
Staff: 200
Products/Services/Areas of Expertise: Civil/structural, mechanical, electrical, geotechnical, environmental, building science & forensic science
Financial Information:
Type of Ownership: Private
Domestic Markets:
Alberta, British Columbia, Manitoba, Northwest Territories, Nunavut
Foreign Activity:
The Pacific Rim, USA, Former USSR
Contact(s):
Naseem Bashir, P.Eng., President
nbashir@williamsengineering.com

Canadian Branches:
Calgary
#195, 3015-5 Avenue NE
Calgary, AB T2A 6T8
403-263-2393
Fax: 403-262-9075
800-263-2393
jmckay@williamsengineering.com
John McKay, P.Eng, Regional Director, Southern Alberta
jmckay@williamsengineering.com

Edmonton
10010 - 100 St.
Edmonton, AB T5J 0N3
780-424-2393
Fax: 780-425-1520
grajewski@williamsengineering.com
Gord Rajewski, Regional Director, Northern Alberta
grajewski@williamsengineering.com

Red Deer
#210, 7240 Johnstone Dr.
Red Deer, AB T4P 3Y6
403-755-2395
Fax: 403-755-4049
wgustafson@williamsengineering.com
Wayne Gustafson, P.Eng, Regional Director, Central Alberta
wgustafson@williamsengineering.com

Winnipeg
#500, 321 McDermot Ave.
Winnipeg, MB R3A 0A3
204-943-2393
Fax: 204-943-2251
tz@williamsengineering.coming.com
Henry Hunter, Regional Director, Manitoba
hhunter@williamsengineering.com

Yellowknife
P.O. Box 1529
4903 - 47 St.
Yellowknife, NT X1A 2P2
867-873-2395
Fax: 867-873-2547
800-263-2393
Brian F. George, P.Eng, Regional Director, Arctic
bgeorge@williamsengineering.com

Williams Milton Roy
Formerly: Williams Instrument Company Inc.
9357 - 45th Ave.
Edmonton, AB T6E 5Z7
780-434-9471
Fax: 780-435-6560
800-331-2674
hubert@williamspumps.com
www.williamspumps.com
Firm Type: Distributing
Staff: 5
Products/Services/Areas of Expertise: Measuring & monitoring equipment

Willis Energy Services Ltd.
#500, 885 Dunsmuir St.
Vancouver, BC V6C 1N5
604-685-2206
Fax: 604-685-1713
info7willisenergy.com
www.willisenergy.com
Firm Type: Scientific/Technical Services
Founded: 1988
Products/Services/Areas of Expertise: Energy use auditing & anaylsis; energy management planning; conservation & cogeneration studies; training; workshops
Contact(s):
Paul Willis, Contact

Willms Construction Ltd.
P.O. Box 267
Pincher Creek, AB T0K 1W0
403-627-2052
Fax: 403-627-3047
willmsd@telusplanet.net
Firm Type: Engineering
Staff: 2
Products/Services/Areas of Expertise: Construction firm with experience in the installation of bases of all ports; has done civil work for several wind projects.
Contact(s):
David Willms

Willowglen Systems Inc.
8522 Davies Rd.
Edmonton, AB T6E 4Y5
780-465-1530
Fax: 780-465-0130
marketing@willowglen.ca; info@willowglen.ca
www.willowglen.ca
Firm Type: Manufacturing
Founded: 1971
Staff: 35
Products/Services/Areas of Expertise: Measuring & monitoring equipment
Recently Completed / Ongoing Projects: Water systems, Manila; powergas system, Singapore
Financial Information:
Type of Ownership: Private
Domestic Markets:
National
Foreign Activity:
Eastern Europe, Western Europe, The Middle East, The Pacific Rim, USA
Markets Sought:
South America, Mexico
Contact(s):
Vic Thomas, Senior Vice-President
Dallas Hauge, Vice-President

Winchurch Environmental Inc.
P.O. Box 71612
Aurora, ON L4G 6S9
905-841-5074
Fax: 905-841-5494
winchurch@sympatico.ca
Firm Type: Engineering
Founded: 1995
Staff: 8
Products/Services/Areas of Expertise: Environmental site assessments phase I & II; site remediation programs; underground tank compliance programs
Financial Information:
Type of Ownership: Private
Revenue Sources: 100% Private Contracts
Domestic Markets:
Manitoba, New Brunswick, Newfoundland & Labrador, Nova Scotia, Ontario, Québec

Wind Energy Institute of Canada / WEICan
Formerly: Atlantic Wind Test Site Inc.
21741 Route 12
North Cape, PE C0B 2B0
902-882-2746
Fax: 902-882-3823
info@weican.ca
www.weican.ca
Firm Type: Management Consulting, Scientific/Technical Services
Founded: 1981
Staff: 5
Member of: PEI Energy Corporation; Canadian Wind Energy Association
Products/Services/Areas of Expertise: Working collaboratively with private & public sector partners, the Institute is engaged in wind energy research & development, with a focus on distributed generation, small wind turbines, wind-diesel systems, & wind-hydrogen applications. Services include testing & demonstration, data acquisition & analysis, technical consultation & assistance, training & outreach, & public education. The University of New Brunswick's Renewable Energy Technology Research Facility is located on-site, & the provincially-owned North Cape Wind Farm is located adjacent
Financial Information:
Type of Ownership: Non Profit
Revenue: $250,000 - $500,000
Revenue Sources: 70% nationwide; 30% Provincial
Domestic Markets:
New Brunswick, Nova Scotia, Prince Edward Island, Québec
Contact(s):
Scott Harper, CEO
scott.harper@weican.ca

Wind Energy Solutions Canada
Also Known As: WES Canada
P.O. Box 552
2952 Thompson Rd.
Smithville, ON L0R 2A0
905-957-8791
Fax: 905-957-8789
info@windenergysolutions.ca
www.windenergysolutions.com
Firm Type: Manufacturing
Member of: Wind Energy Solutions BV (Netherlands); Greely Construction
Products/Services/Areas of Expertise: Delivers turnkey wind energy projects, service, and maintenance; Wind turbine manufacturing up to 500 kW

Financial Information:
Type of Ownership: Private
Domestic Markets:
National
Contact(s):
Johan De Leeuw, Director

Wind Power Inc. / WPI
P.O. Box 609
#222, 696 Kettles St.
Pincher Creek, AB T0K 1W0
403-627-2923
Fax: 403-627-3239
wpi@windpower.ca
www.windpower.ca
Firm Type: Management Consulting, Engineering, Manufacturing
Founded: 1983
Products/Services/Areas of Expertise: Manufacturer of motors & generators
Activities: Wind assessment; Project management; Maintenance services
Contact(s):
Dale Johnson, President

Winds & Voices Environmental Services Inc.
245 McDermot Ave., 3rd Fl.
Winnipeg, MB R3B 0S6
204-946-5780
Fax: 204-956-1895
waves@cier.ca
Firm Type: Management Consulting
Founded: 1999
Staff: 3
Products/Services/Areas of Expertise: Communications; consultations; traditional knowledge
Financial Information:
Type of Ownership: Private
Revenue: $250,000 - $500,000
Revenue Sources: 80% nationwide; 20% Private Contracts
Domestic Markets:
National
Markets Sought:
South America
Contact(s):
Merrell Ann Phare, President

Windsor Barrel & Drum Ltd.
2215 Janette Ave.
Windsor, ON N8X 1Z9
519-253-4887
Fax: 519-253-9568
Firm Type: Scientific/Technical Services, Waste Management
Member of: Association of Container Reconditioners
Products/Services/Areas of Expertise: Reconditioning & recycling of steel & plastic drums
Foreign Activity:
USA
Contact(s):
Larry Polsky
Ron Polsky

Windsor Pump Co. Ltd.
3057 Marentette Ave.
Windsor, ON N8X 4G1
519-969-2190
Fax: 519-969-2047
888-296-7867
peter@winsorpump.com
www.windsorpump.com
Firm Type: Distributing, Engineering, Manufacturing
Founded: 1982
Products/Services/Areas of Expertise: Engineer & manufacturer of pump-based systems; Products include air operated diaphragm pumps, sanitary, marine, & industrial centrifugal pumps, self priming, turbine, & submersible pumps, solids & slurry handling centrifugal pumps, & magnetic drive alloy gear & centrifugal pumps
Activities: Providing installation, parts, maintenance, & repair
Canadian Branches:
Oakville
Oakville, ON 847-2334
905-847-2334
Fax: 905-847-2425

Wittmann Canada, Inc.
Formerly: Nucon Wittmann; Nucon Systems
35 Leek Cres.
Richmond Hill, ON L4B 4C2
905-887-5355
Fax: 905-887-1162
888-466-8266
info@wittmann-canada.com
www.wittmann-canada.com
Firm Type: Manufacturing
Founded: 1985
Staff: 35
Member of: Canadian Plastics Industry Association; Society of Plastics Industry; Society of Plastics Engineers
Products/Services/Areas of Expertise: Total plant engineering of pneumatic raw material handling systems; plastic grinders, dryers & blenders
Financial Information:
Type of Ownership: Foreign-owned
Domestic Markets:
National
Foreign Activity:
The Middle East, Mexico, USA, Former USSR, Worldwide
Contact(s):
Rob Miller, President

WJF Instrumentation (1990) Ltd.
#5, 3610 - 29th St. NE
Calgary, AB T1Y 5Z7
403-291-5570
Fax: 403-291-3714
877-291-5572
info@wjf.ca
www.wjf.ca
Firm Type: Distributing
Founded: 1984
Staff: 6
Products/Services/Areas of Expertise: Provides air quality monitoring; water quality monitoring; hazardous locations monitoring, environmental & laboratory measuring instrumentation
Recently Completed / Ongoing Projects: On-line monitoring (water, wastewater); gas detection installations; chlorination station/pump station monitoring; automatic sampling; environmental monitoring (air, water)
Financial Information:
Type of Ownership: Private
Revenue Sources: 5% nationwide; 5% Provincial; 40% Municipals; 50% Private Contracts
Domestic Markets:
Alberta, British Columbia, Manitoba, Northwest Territories, Saskatchewan
Contact(s):
Jim Algeo, President
Sheldon Wrubleski, Sales Manager
Roger Mazereeuw, Service Manager

Wood Laboratory Ltd.
#13, 3871 North Fraser Way
Burnaby, BC V5J 5G6
604-684-8732
Fax: 604-684-3917
Firm Type: Scientific/Technical Services
Founded: 1984
Products/Services/Areas of Expertise: Analyzing & sampling agency
Contact(s):
I. Zalyvadna, Supervisor, Laboratory

Woodington Systems Inc.
P.O. Box 100
Thorold, ON L2V 3Y8
905-680-1900
Fax: 905-680-1916
customerservice@woodingtonsystems.com
www.walkerind.com/Woodington_Sytems_Inc
Firm Type: Scientific/Technical Services, Waste Management
Member of: Ontario Waste Management Association; Ontario Trucking Association; Recycling Council of Ontario; National Solid Wastes Management Association; Chemical Waste Transporters Institute; Association of Municipal Recycling Coordinators
Products/Services/Areas of Expertise: Waste management services; waste transport; transfer station; non-hazardous landfill; wood & corrugated recycling; emergency response; remedial cleanup programs; tank removals

Domestic Markets:
National
Foreign Activity:
USA,

WorkLab Inc.
#507, 1280 Finch Ave. West
Toronto, ON M3J 3K6
416-663-8242
Fax: 416-663-9485
877-967-5522
worklab@interlog.com
Firm Type: Management Consulting
Founded: 1996
Member of: Occupational & Environmental Medical Association of Canada
Products/Services/Areas of Expertise: Medical assessments in keeping with guidelines of Bill 99; independent medical & functional abilities evaluation; post-offer pre-placement screening; physical demands analysis; post-rehab testing; modified job safety testing
Financial Information:
Type of Ownership: Private
Revenue: $500,000 - $1.5 Million
Revenue Sources: 100% Private Contracts
Domestic Markets:
National
Markets Sought:
Central Europe, Eastern Europe, Western Europe, USA
Contact(s):
Paul Fuso

World Ecology Enviro Store Ltd.
9845 - 99 Ave.
Grande Prairie, AB T8V 4B2
780-539-6547
Fax: 780-814-7133
Contact(s):
Leon Pendleton

Canadian Branches:
World Ecology Enviro Store Ltd.
9845 - 99 Ave.
Grande Prairie, AB T8V 4B2
780-539-6547
Fax: 780-814-7133

Worldware Enterprises Ltd.
30 Rosslinn Rd.
Cambridge, ON N1S 3K1
519-621-8244
Fax: 519-622-5281
866-621-8244
info@eatoils.com; sales@eatoils.com
www.eatoils.ca
Firm Type: Distributing, Manufacturing
Founded: 1987
Member of: Cleaning Equipment Trade Assoication (CETA); International Sanitary Supply Association (ISSA)
Quality Environmental Management System(s): 9002
EcoLogo Certified Products & Services: Eatoils Ecologo certified green cleaning products
Products/Services/Areas of Expertise: Supplier of green cleaning products; Products include Eatoils, which are solvent free & septic friendly cleaners, Eatscales, which are an acid free alternative to harsh chemicals, & Multizorb, which is a landfill friendly granular absorbent,; Clients include commercial, industrial, & home users
Ecological Note: Eatoils Ecologo certified green cleaning products
Domestic Markets:
National
Foreign Activity:
USA
Contact(s):
Charles Robinson, Manager, National Sales
crobinson@eatoils.ca

WorleyParsons Canada Ltd.
Formerly: Colt Engineering Corporation
#400, 10201 Southport Rd. SW
Calgary, AB T2W 4X9
403-258-8000
Fax: 403-258-5875
800-668-6772
www.worleyparsons.com

Firm Type: Management Consulting, Engineering, Waste Management
Founded: 1973
Staff: 5800
Member of: Cord WorleyParsons Ltd.; CoSyn Technology
Products/Services/Areas of Expertise: Provider of consulting engineering services to the resources & energy sectors, & industry; service areas include hydrocarbons (heavy oil production, mineable oil sands, pipelines); power & nuclear; minerals & metals; infrastructure; & environment. Offices across Canada
Activities: Designing & constructing the following: pipeline & related facilities; oil sands upgrading & extraction projects; conventional heavy oil & thermal in situ heavy oil production, processing, & transportation facilities; petroleum, refining, & upgrading projects; conventional oil & natural gas production systems; & natural gas production & processing projects
Recently Completed / Ongoing Projects: Shell Albian Project; EPCM services for EPCOR, TransAlta; engineering services for OPG Nuclear, Bruce Power; Run of River Project for Plutonic Power; OPG Coal-to-Biomass Conversion Project; Vale Inco Long Harbour Project
Financial Information:
Type of Ownership: Publicly Traded
Domestic Markets:
National
Foreign Activity:
Caribbean, The Pacific Rim, South America, Worldwide
Contact(s):
Larry M. Benke, P.Eng., Managing Director
Michael W. King, Sr. Vice-President, Business Development
michael.w.king@worleyparsons.com
Contact(s):
Ewart Cameron, General Manager
Contact(s):
Bob Bowhay, P.Eng., General Manager

Canadian Branches:
Calgary - Heavy Oil Business Unit
520 - 12 Ave. SW
Calgary, AB T2R 0H4
403-508-5300
Fax: 403-508-5301
Founded: 2002

Edmonton - 86th St.
#120, 5008 - 86th St.
Edmonton, AB T6E 5S2
780-440-5300
Fax: 780-440-5555
877-566-3933
Jacob Kellerman, General Manager

Markham
8133 Warden Ave.
Markham, ON L6G 1B3
905-940-4774
Fax: 905-940-4778
Founded: 1988
Products/Services/Areas of Expertise: Services focused on the nuclear energy sector
Brian Faulkner, P.Eng., General Manager

Sarnia
Bldg. 1040
1086 Modeland Rd.
Sarnia, ON N7S 6L2
519-332-0160
Fax: 519-344-1186
Founded: 1992
Marty Gaulin, P.Emg., General Manager

Calgary - Cord WorleyParsons Ltd.
#1000, 10201 Southport Rd. SW
Calgary, AB T2W 4X9
403-258-8660
Fax: 403-258-8661
Founded: 1978
Products/Services/Areas of Expertise: An open-shop merit contractor, with expertise in engineering, procurement, & construction; client sectors include oil & gas, gas processing, petrochemical, power generation, & heavy oil

Edmonton - CoSyn Technology
#101, 9405 - 50th St.
Edmonton, AB T9M 1P1
780-440-7000
Fax: 780-462-3897
Founded: 1991

Products/Services/Areas of Expertise: Provider of engineering & procurement services

Edmonton - Cord WorleyParsons Ltd.
Cord Projects Ltd., Operations Office
#130, 5008 - 86th St.
Edmonton, AB T6E 5S2
780-465-5516
Fax: 780-468-2905

WORX Environmental Products Inc.
#10, 2305 52nd Ave. SE
Calgary, AB T2C 4X7
403-273-7600
Fax: 403-248-1428
800-424-9679
info@worx.ca
www.worxtm.com
Products/Services/Areas of Expertise: Develops, manufactures, markets & distributes 100% biodegradable, 100% organic & natural cleaning products
Ecological Note: Biodegradable hand cleaner WORX Clean 'n Gentle, removes printer's ink, grease, oil, fresh paint, soot, carbon, big game & fish odour & other common industrial & household soil from skin
Domestic Markets:
National
Foreign Activity:
USA
Contact(s):
Brent Keeley, Vice-President, Marketing & Sales
Jack Neufeld

Wotherspoon Environmental Inc.
Formerly: Paul Wotherspoon & Associates Inc.
#104, 429 - 14th St. NW
Calgary, AB T2N 2A3
403-269-4351
Fax: 403-263-6999
infoenv@wenv.com
www.wenv.com
Firm Type: Management Consulting, Engineering, Scientific/Technical Services
Founded: 1988
Products/Services/Areas of Expertise: Provider of environmental management consulting services; Clients include the industrial insurance sector & the petroleum industry
Activities: Environmental site assessments; Operational audits; Waste management plans; Site reclamations; Oil spill equipment research; Spill contingency & emergency response plans
Domestic Markets:
Alberta, Newfoundland & Labrador, Northwest Territories, Nunavut, Yukon Territory
Foreign Activity:
Caribbean, Central America, The Middle East, South America, USA, Former USSR
Contact(s):
Paul Wotherspoon, BSc, ME, P.Eng., CEAS, CC, President

Woznuk Brothers Ltd.
P.O. Box 1704 Galt
1050 Main St.
Cambridge, ON N1R 7G8
519-621-9840
Fax: 519-621-9312
Firm Type: Waste Management
Founded: 1950
Staff: 10
Products/Services/Areas of Expertise: Recycling of scrap metal
Financial Information:
Type of Ownership: Private
Domestic Markets:
Ontario
Contact(s):
George Wosnuk, President

WPI Safety & Environmental Consultants
355 Union St., RR#4
Meaford, ON N4L 1W7
519-379-2530
Fax: 519-538-5611
800-265-7455
wpi@wpisafety.com
www.wpisafety.com
Firm Type: Management Consulting, Scientific/Technical Services

Founded: 1986
Staff: 4
Member of: Environmental Management Association; Canadian Society of Safety Engineering; World Safety Organization; Canada Safety Council; Canadian Federation of Independent Business
Products/Services/Areas of Expertise: Emergency management & planning; risk assessment; hazardous waste assessment; field sampling & monitoring; occupational health & safety; risk management; training & education; noise assessment; project management; design & specifications; site reclamation & remedial action; mould assessment; asbestos management services
Recently Completed / Ongoing Projects: Workplace mould assessments (3), specifications & supervision of remediation; Well water management for public facility; Asbestos assessments for jail & factory
Domestic Markets:
National
Contact(s):
Wolfgang Pantelmann, President & Senior Project Consultant
Wayne Boyd, Project Consultant
Raymond E.A. Harris, Project Consultant

WRS Environmental
Formerly: WRS Waste & Recycling
940 Redonda St.
Winnipeg, MB R2C 2Z2
204-661-3683
Fax: 204-222-0804
info@wrs.mb.ca
www.wrs.mb.ca
Firm Type: Waste Management
Founded: 1998
Staff: 12
Products/Services/Areas of Expertise: Removal of used oil, oil filters & containers, anti-freeze, waste fuel; absorbents; parts cleaner, service & rental; specializing in transporting industry wastes
Contact(s):
Ric Henkel

WSH Laboratories Ltd.
Also Known As: Clearwater Treatment Systems
3851B - 21 St. NE
Calgary, AB T2E 6T5
403-250-9164
Fax: 403-291-4597
800-449-6544
support@wshlabs.com
www.wshlabs.com
Firm Type: Distributing, Engineering, Manufacturing, Scientific/Technical Services
Founded: 1978
Staff: 8
Member of: American Water Works Association; Alberta Water Well Drilling Association; National Association of Corrosion Engineers
Products/Services/Areas of Expertise: Water treatment products including filtration & reverse osmosis; removal of hydrocarbons from water; water/wastewater & soil environmental testing & consulting
Domestic Markets:
Alberta, British Columbia
Foreign Activity:
Asia, The Middle East, USA
Markets Sought:
South America
Contact(s):
Bill Wong, President

Wyckomar Inc.
111 Malcolm Rd.
Guelph, ON N1K 1A8
519-822-1886
Fax: 519-763-6580
sales@wyckomaruv.com
www.wyckomaruv.com
Firm Type: Distributing, Manufacturing
Founded: 1978
Products/Services/Areas of Expertise: Manufacturer & distributor of residential & commercial chemical-free UV water disinfection equipment; Water system integratorl; Products include the solar powered UV-250, UV-200 fail-safe, Multi-step hazardous environment U, & Custom skid-mounted water purification systems

Financial Information:
Type of Ownership: Private
Domestic Markets:
National
Foreign Activity:
Worldwide
Contact(s):
Gerry Ottema, President
Walt Boduch, General Manager
Greg McLean, Sales

Wynn's Canada Ltd.
a subsidiary of Illinois Tool Works
7090 Edwards Blvd.
Mississauga, ON L5S 1Z1
905-670-3881
Fax: 905-670-3829
800-668-5626
info@wynns-canada.com
www.wynns.ca
Firm Type: Distributing
Founded: 1951
Staff: 13
Member of: Automotive Industries Association of Canada
Products/Services/Areas of Expertise: Automotive specialty chemical additives & flushing equipment
Financial Information:
Type of Ownership: Foreign-owned
Revenue: Greater than $5 Million
Revenue Sources: 100% Private Contracts
Domestic Markets:
National
Contact(s):
Ross Ayrhart, National Account Sales Manager
rayrhart@wynns-canada.com
Walter Lubberts, Technical Support Manager
wlubberts@wynss-canada.com
Nelson Verissimo, Customer Service Manager
nverissimo@wynns-canada.com

XCG Consultants Ltd.
Formerly: H2O Inc.
#300, 2620 Bristol Circle
Oakville, ON L6H 6Z7
905-829-8880
Fax: 905-829-8890
gta@xcg.com
www.xcg.com
Firm Type: Management Consulting, Engineering, Scientific/Technical Services
Founded: 1990
Staff: 70
Products/Services/Areas of Expertise: A full-service environmental consulting firm; Clients include government, industries, & legal, insurance, real estate, & financial organizations
Activities: Cleaning up & redeveloping Brownfield Sites; Site assessment & remediation; Wastewater & water treatment; Air quality related services; Solid waste management services; Training; Infrastructure management
Domestic Markets:
National
Foreign Activity:
USA, Worldwide
Canadian Branches:
Edmonton
#108, 10410 - 81st Ave.
Edmonton, AB T6E 1X5
780-432-5770
Fax: 780-437-0122
edmonton@xcg.com
Kingston
West Wing, Woolen Mill
#105, 6 Cataraqui St.
Kingston, ON K7K 1Z7
613-542-5888
Fax: 613-542-0844
kingston@xcg.com
Kitchener
820 Trillium Dr.
Kitchener, ON N2R 1K4
519-741-5774
Fax: 519-741-5627
kitchener@xcg.com

International Branch(es):
Cincinnati, Ohio, USA
#260, 4350 Glendale-Milford Rd.
Cincinnati, OH USA
513-841-9246
Fax: 513-841-9257
cinci@xcq.com

Xeneca Power Development Inc.
#520, 5160 Yonge St.
Toronto, ON M2N 6L9
416-590-9362
Fax: 416-590-9955
info@xeneca.com
www.xeneca.com
Firm Type: Management Consulting, Engineering

Products/Services/Areas of Expertise: Privately financed by the Firelight Limited Partnership, Xeneca identifies, develops, and constructs waterpower electricity generating facilities in Ontario. The focus is on ethical and sustainable practices in the creation of green, renewable energy. Xeneca partners with all levels of government, other private sector businesses, and First Nations communities, and consults with similar firms in the conduct of its business.
Financial Information:
Type of Ownership: Private
Domestic Markets:
Ontario
Contact(s):
Patrick Gillette, MES, M.P.A., President/COO

Xerox Canada Ltd.
#900, 5650 Yonge St.
Toronto, ON M2M 4G7
416-299-3769
Fax: 416-733-6811
800-275-9376
can.ask.xerox@can.xerox.com
www.xerox.ca
Firm Type: Distributing, Manufacturing
Founded: 1953
Staff: 5000
EcoLogo Certified Products & Services: FaxCentre & Document WorkCentre facsimile machines; Xerox photocopiers; Xerox printers
Products/Services/Areas of Expertise: Offers the broadest array of document products, services & solutions: printers, multifunction machines, copiers, fax machines, production printers & copiers, scanners & software
Ecological Note: FaxCentre & Document WorkCentre facsimile machines; Xerox photocopiers; Xerox printers
Financial Information:
Type of Ownership: Publicly Traded
Revenue: Greater than $5 Million
Domestic Markets:
National
Foreign Activity:
Worldwide
Contact(s):
Doug Lord, President/CEO & Chair

Xylon Biotechnologies Ltd.
The Fortinek Building (UBC)
2665 East Mall
Vancouver, BC V6T 1W5
604-224-7701
Fax: 604-224-7703
info@xylon.ca
www.xylon.ca
Products/Services/Areas of Expertise: Development, manufacture, and supply of chemicals found in the Western Red Cedar; also the premier manufacturer and supplier of tropolones
Contact(s):
David Jones, Ph.D., President/Director

YES Environment Technologies Inc.
Formerly: Young Environmental Systems
Also Known As: YES
#145, 7391 Vantage Way
Delta, BC V4G 1M3
604-940-8741
Fax: 604-940-8745
877-940-8741
www.yestek.com
Firm Type: Distributing, Engineering, Manufacturing
Founded: 1987

Products/Services/Areas of Expertise: Developer & manufacturer of indoor air quality instruments & related products; Products include miniature electronic recording IAQ monitors, the YESAIR IAQ monitor & datalogger, the YES Plus 12 sensor IAQ monitor, & the Falcon-II economical air quality monitor
Financial Information:
Type of Ownership: Private
Domestic Markets:
National
Foreign Activity:
Worldwide
Contact(s):
Frank Britton, General Manager, International Sales
fbritton@cetci.com
Shirley Britton, Manager, Customer Service
shirley@cetci.com
Bob Davidson, Manager, Sales & Marketing, Western Canada & USA
bdavidson@cetci.com
Ron Sweet, Manager, Eastern Regional Sales, Eastern Canada & USA
rsweet@@cetci.com
Kevin Batdorf, Development Engineer
kevin@@cetci.com
Mirza Baig, Specialist, Portables Products
mirza@@cetci.com
Rene Flores, Contact, Inside Sales
rene@cetci.com
Jeff Hung, Contact, Portables Service Department

York Disposal Service Ltd.
131 Freshway Dr.
Concord, ON L4K 1S2
905-669-1900
Fax: 905-669-9525
Products/Services/Areas of Expertise: Waste management; recycling services; waste disposal systems
Contact(s):
Rob Gill, General Manager

York Fluid Controls Ltd.
2 Westwyn Ct.
Brampton, ON L6T 4T5
905-454-4013
Fax: 905-454-8423
877-454-6066
www.yorkfluid.com
Firm Type: Distributing, Manufacturing
Founded: 1960
Products/Services/Areas of Expertise: Liquid & compressed air filtration, pumping systems; chemical transfers & spills; emergency response pumps
Domestic Markets:
National
Contact(s):
D. Knapman, President/CEO
Simba Mohamed, Technical

Yugo-Tech
1050 Britannia Rd. East, Units 11, 12
Mississauga, ON L4W 4N9
905-670-0860
Fax: 905-670-7586
joco@yugo-tech.com
www.yugo-tech.com
Products/Services/Areas of Expertise: Natural gas vehicle conversion kits, systems
Contact(s):
Joco Djurdevic, President

Z-Tech/Geogard Inc.
#3, 4025, rue Lavoisier
Boisbriand, QC J7N 1N1
450-430-5333
Fax: 450-430-9352
800-361-3510
acq-laur@acq.org
Firm Type: Distributing, Engineering, Manufacturing
Member of: Association de la construction du Québec
Products/Services/Areas of Expertise: Designer & manufacturer of bearings & expansion joints for bridges & other structures; Distributor & installer of geotechnical engineering materials; Products include geomembrane linings used for environmental protection applications
Activities: Installing geomembrane linings at landfill sites & wastewater treatment lagoons

Products & Services Buyer's Guide

Financial Information:
Type of Ownership: Private

Zazula Process Equipment Ltd.
1526 - 10 Ave. SW
Calgary, AB T3C 0J5
403-244-0751
Fax: 403-245-5808
zazula@zazula.com; sales@zazula.com; parts@zazula.com
www.zazula.com
Firm Type: Distributing, Engineering
Founded: 1963
Products/Services/Areas of Expertise: Designer, assembler, & distributor of integrated custom package systems; Products include industrial controls, pumps, tanks, mixers, heat exchangers, valves, & fittings; Clients include the chemical industry, food & beverage producers & processors, oil refiners & natural gas plants, printed circuit board manufacturers, & the domestic & industrial water & wastewater sector
Activities: Customed engineered projects include water & wastewater treatment plants
Domestic Markets:
National
Foreign Activity:
Worldwide

Zbeetnoff Agro-Environmental Consulting
15787 Buena Vista Ave.
White Rock, BC V4B 1Z9
604-535-7721
Fax: 604-535-4421
zbeetnoff@telus.net
www.zbeetnoffagro-environmental.com
Firm Type: Management Consulting
Founded: 1989
Products/Services/Areas of Expertise: A consulting firm with expertise in the food & agricultural industry; Clients include governments, agencies, associations, institutions, & private organizations
Activities: Agro-environmental analysis & planning; Policy, program, & project evaluation
Recently Completed / Ongoing Projects: Preparation of a farm plan for organic vegetable production, Chilliwack, BC; Update of the North American greenhouse vegetable industry, Regina, SK; Spallumcheen agricultural area plan, Township of Spallumcheen, BC; Marketing strategy for greenhouse vegetables, ON; Development of the Surrey agricultural plan. Surrey, BC; Vancouver food security study, Vancouver, BC; Agricultural profile of the BC egg sector, BC; Development of a grain farm business plan, Peace River Region, BC; Development of on-farm microbial food safety check lists, BC; Assessment of the Biodiversity Guide for BC farmers & ranchers; Durrell Creek watershed management plan, District of Saanich, BC; Preparation of environmental guidelines for the BC Greenhouse Growers
Financial Information:
Type of Ownership: Private
Domestic Markets:
National
Contact(s):
Darrell M. Zbeetnoff, MSc, MNRM, MA, PAg, CAC, Principal
Bruce McTavish, M.Sc, MBA, P.Ag., RPBio,, Associate
Hubert J. Timmenga, Ph.D., P.Ag., CAC, Associate

ZCL Composites Inc.
Formerly: ZCL Mfg. Canada Inc.
6907 - 36 St.
Edmonton, AB T6B 2Z6
Fax: 780-466-6126
800-661-8265
ir@zcl.com
www.zcl.com
Firm Type: Distributing, Engineering, Manufacturing
Founded: 1987
Products/Services/Areas of Expertise: Designer, manufacturer, & supplier of fiberglass tank systems; Clients include the petroleum industry, as well as other industrial & retail sectors
Financial Information:
Type of Ownership: Publicly Traded
Domestic Markets:
National
Foreign Activity:
Central Europe, USA
Contact(s):
James S. Edwards, Chair
Venence (Ven) Coté, President/CEO

Canadian Branches:
Edmonton - 69th Ave. NW
ZCL Everlast
3912 - 69 Ave. NW
Edmonton, AB T6B 2V2
780-465-9834
Fax: 780-469-0586
Products/Services/Areas of Expertise: Provider of secondary containment oilfield tanks; Clients include the oil & gas industry, as well as other industrial & retail sectors

Edmonton - 69th Ave. NW
Triple M Fiberglass Mfg. Ltd.
3608 - 69 Ave.
Edmonton, AB T6B 2V2
780-465-0726
Fax: 780-466-9801
877-874-7536
mail@triplemfiberglass.com
www.triplemfiberglass.com
Founded: 1982
Products/Services/Areas of Expertise: Manufacturer of fiberglass above ground tanks & fiberglass piping; Clients include the oil & gas, pulp & paper, & chemical industries

Helmond, The Netherlands
Parabeam BV
P.O. Box 134
5700 AC
Helmond, The Netherlands
+31 (0)492 591 222
Fax: +31(0)492591220
sales@parabeam.nl
www.parabeam.nl
Products/Services/Areas of Expertise: Manufacturer of a glass fabric for the corrosion, marine, transport, & construction industries

Minneapolis, MN, USA
Xerxes Corporation
7901 Xerxes Ave. South
Minneapolis, MN USA
952-887-1890
Fax: 952-887-1882
info@xerxescorp.com
www.xerxescorp.com
Products/Services/Areas of Expertise: Designer & manufacturer of fiberglass products; Products include single-wall & double-wall tanks, multicompartment tanks, triple-wall tanks, oil / water separators, & water & wastewater tanks; Clients include the petroleum, chemical, water, & wastewater markets

Zell Oilfield Service Ltd.
P.O. Box 3712
Spruce Grove, AB T7X 3A9
780-675-8875
Fax: 780-675-8874
zell@connect.ab.ca
Firm Type: Scientific/Technical Services
Founded: 1982
Staff: 30
Products/Services/Areas of Expertise: Drilling waste sampling, analysis, disposal; reclamation assessments; phase I & II assessments; fluid detoxification & irrigation; on-site lab testing
Financial Information:
Type of Ownership: Private
Domestic Markets:
Alberta, British Columbia, Saskatchewan
Markets Sought:
USA
Contact(s):
Les Zeller, President
Jeff Robbins, Environmental Manager
Tony Greenwood, Northern Area Manager

Zep Manufacturing Company of Canada
A Unit of Acuity Specialty Products Group, Inc.
11627 - 178th St. NW
Edmonton, AB T5S 1N6
780-453-5800
Fax: 780-453-6861
800-661-7408
www.zepcan.com
Firm Type: Distributing, Manufacturing
Founded: 1937
Quality Environmental Management System(s): 9001; ISO

Products/Services/Areas of Expertise: Manufacturer & distributor of industrial & institutional maintenance & sanitation products; Products include hand cleaners, deodorants, detergents, lubricants, degreasers, disinfectants, & floor finishes
Domestic Markets:
National
Foreign Activity:
Worldwide
Contact(s):
John K. Morgan, President/CEO, Acuity Specialty Products Group
Ralph Puertas, President, Zep Canada
Mark Bachmann, Chief Financial Officer
Bill Holl, Chief Commercial Officer

Canadian Branches:
Brandon
440 Richmond Ave. East
Brandon, MB R7A 7G7
204-728-1215
Fax: 204-727-4439

Calgary
Bay C
7004 - 5 St. SE
Calgary, AB T2H 2G3
403-253-3160
Fax: 403-258-2425

Camrose
5011 - 46 St.
Camrose, AB T4V 3G3
780-672-1780

Dartmouth
Burnside Industrial Park
#23, 10 Morris Dr.
Dartmouth, NS B3B 1K8
902-468-8209
Fax: 902-468-8213
877-428-9937
Chuck Boyd, Branch Manager
chuck.boyd@zepmfg.com

Delta
1210 Cliveden Ave.
Delta, BC V3M 6G4
604-520-1148

Grande Prairie
#102, 12627 - 100th St.
Grande Prairie, AB T8V 4H2
780-532-7133
Fax: 780-532-7166
800-532-7166

Kamloops
921B Laval Cres.
Kamloops, BC V2C 5P4
250-372-5242
Fax: 250-372-2272

Kelowna
#225, 1891 Springfield Rd.
Kelowna, BC V1Y 5V5
250-860-5116
Fax: 250-860-5533

Lethbridge
234F - 12B St. North
Lethbridge, AB T1H 2K7
403-329-4800
Fax: 403-380-4755
877-428-9937

Mississauga
#10, 1795 Meyerside Dr.
Mississauga, ON L5T 1E3
905-670-5050
Fax: 905-670-1717
877-425-9937

Montréal
660, av Lepine
Montréal, QC H9P 1G2
514-631-9041
Fax: 514-631-8049
877-428-9937

Prince George
2133 Ogilvie St. South
Prince George, BC V2N 1X2

250-564-4382
Fax: 250-563-2186

Red Deer
#8, 7419 - 50th Ave.
Red Deer, AB T4P 1M5
403-346-6631
Fax: 403-346-6330

Regina
603 Henderson Dr.
Regina, SK S4N 6A8
306-721-1919
Fax: 306-721-6065

Winnipeg
450 Provencher Blvd.
Winnipeg, MB R2J 0B9
204-233-3342
Fax: 204-233-2083

Zephyr Alternative Power
80 East Humber Dr.
King City, ON L7B 1B6
416-636-9001
Fax: 905-833-4401
info@zephyrpower.com
www.zephyrpower.com
Firm Type: Engineering
Founded: 2002
Products/Services/Areas of Expertise: Develops, promotes, and markets various alternative energy and energy efficient technologies.
Contact(s):
Edward Tsang, President
etsang@zephyrpower.com

Zephyr North
#20, 850 Legion Rd.
Burlington, ON L7S 1T5
905-335-9670
Fax: 905-335-0119
info@zephyrnorth.com
www.zephyrnorth.com
Firm Type: Engineering, Scientific/Technical Services
Founded: 1981
Staff: 5
Member of: Canadian Meteorological & Oceanographic Society; Canadian Wind Energy Association
Products/Services/Areas of Expertise: Meteorological measurement; automated weather stations; wind energy measurement, siting analysis; wind farm analysis; numerical modelling of wind flow
Domestic Markets:
National
Foreign Activity:
Worldwide
Contact(s):
Jim Salmon, Consultant

Zeton Inc.
740 Oval Ct.
Burlington, ON L7L 6A9
905-632-3123
Fax: 905-632-0301
pilotplants@zeton.com
www.zeton.com
Firm Type: Engineering
Founded: 1986
Staff: 100
Quality Environmental Management System(s): 9001
Products/Services/Areas of Expertise: Pilot plants for research & verification of processes for drinking water/wastewater treatment, hydrocarbons, polymers, chemicals, waste biomass conversion technologies, small skid-mounted processing plants for waste treatment processes
Financial Information:
Type of Ownership: Private
Revenue Sources: 100% Private Contracts
Domestic Markets:
National
Foreign Activity:
Asia, China, Western Europe, The Middle East, The Pacific Rim, South America, Mexico, USA, Vietnam
Contact(s):
David Beckman, President
Peter W. Smith, P.Eng., Vice-President, Marketing & Sales

International Branch(es):
Zeton B.V.
P.O. Box 9
Enschede Netherla
-31 (0)53 428 41 00
Fax: -31 (0)53 428 4
info@zeton.nl
Johan Ter Harmsel

Zimmark Inc.
4380 South Service Rd.
Burlington, ON L7L 5Y6
905-632-5410
Fax: 905-632-5171
zimmark@zimmark.com
www.zimmark.com
Firm Type: Waste Management
Founded: 1985
Products/Services/Areas of Expertise: On-site recycling systems & equipment; oil recycling system
Domestic Markets:
National
Foreign Activity:
Asia, Mexico, USA
Contact(s):
L.A. Wilson, President

Zodiac Fabrics Inc.
Formerly: Big O Inc.
688 Sovereign Rd.
London, ON N5V 4K7
519-457-7166
Fax: 519-457-3277
866-457-7166
www.zodiacfabrics.com
Firm Type: Manufacturing
Founded: 1996
Staff: 30
Quality Environmental Management System(s): 9001
Products/Services/Areas of Expertise: Circular knitted fabric for use in filtering drainage systems & tube material for absorbent socks & pillows, well mepoint filters
Financial Information:
Type of Ownership: Private
Domestic Markets:
National
Foreign Activity:
USA
Contact(s):
Paul Mutter, Sales Manager
Kathy Musch, Customer Service

Zorbit Technologies Inc.
#241, 2155 Leanne Blvd.
Mississauga, ON L5K 2K8
905-855-8500
Fax: 905-855-8502
800-461-0300
mbond@peatsorb.ca
www.peatsorb.ca
Firm Type: Distributing
Founded: 1990
Staff: 10
Member of: Canadian Environment Industry Association
Products/Services/Areas of Expertise: Distributors of environmentally friendly, non-leaching, non-biodegradeable industrial oil absorbent to absorb hydrocarbons on contact on land & water; made from 100% Canadian peat moss; floor absorbents to absorb hydrocarbons & aqueous solutions
Recently Completed / Ongoing Projects: Opened distributors in South America, South Africa, Australia, Mexico, Middle East, Eastern & Western Europe
Financial Information:
Type of Ownership: Private
Domestic Markets:
National
Foreign Activity:
Worldwide
Contact(s):
Meredith Bond, President
Allen Shully, Director, International Sales
Patricia Jimenez, Manager, Accounting
pjimenez@peatsorb.ca

International Branch(es):
Michigan
#112, 3605 - 32nd St.
Port Huron, MI USA
810-364-0228
Lou Marini

Zurn Industries Limited
3544 Nashua Dr.
Mississauga, ON L4V 1L2
905-405-8272
Fax: 905-671-9078
zurn.mail@zurncanada.com
www.zurn.com
Firm Type: Distributing
Founded: 1991
Staff: 30
Products/Services/Areas of Expertise: Water & wastewater management & equipment
Contact(s):
Khaled Zaied, General Manager
Andy Russell, Director, Sales & Marketing
andy.russell@zurncanada.com

SECTION 3

Environmental Government Listings

Included in this section:
- Government Quick Reference Guide 441
- Government Acts & Regulations 489
- Federal/Provincial Government 507
- Municipal Governments 669
- Waste & Water Commissions 757
- Intergovernmental Offices & Councils 763
- Environmental Trade Representatives Abroad 767

Government Quick Reference Guide

ABORIGINAL AFFAIRS

Alberta
Alberta Aboriginal Relations, Commerce Place, 19th Fl., 10155 - 102 St., Edmonton, T5K 2B6 AB
780-422-4144, Fax: 780-644-8389
Canadian Heritage, 15 Eddy St., Gatineau, K1A 0M5 QC
819-997-0055, 866-811-0055
Indian & Northern Affairs Canada, 10 Wellington St., North Tower, Gatineau, K1A 0H4 QC
819-997-0380, Fax: 819-953-3017, 866-817-3977, infopubs@ainc-inac.gc.ca

Alberta
Métis Settlements Appeal Tribunal, #1100, 10055 - 106 St., Edmonton, AB T5J 2Y2
780-422-1541, Fax: 780-422-0019, 800-661-8864

Manitoba
Manitoba Aboriginal & Northern Affairs, 59 Elizabeth Dr., PO Box 37, Thompson, R8N 1X4 MB
204-677-6607, Fax: 204-677-6753, amartin@gov.mb.ca
Aboriginal Affairs Secretariat, #200, 500 Portage Ave., Winnipeg, R3C 3X1 MB
204-945-2510, Fax: 204-945-3689

Newfoundland & Labrador
Department of Labrador & Aboriginal Affairs, Confederation Bldg., East Block, 6th Fl., PO Box 8700, St. John's, A1B 4J6 NL
709-729-4776, Fax: 709-729-4900, 877-788-8822, laa@gov.nl.ca

Northwest Territories
Department of Aboriginal Affairs & Intergovernmental Relations, 4910 - 52nd St., PO Box 1320, Yellowknife, X1A 2L9 NT
867-873-7143, Fax: 867-873-0233, 877-838-8194, nancy_gardiner@gov.nt.ca

Nunavut
Department of Culture, Language, Elders & Youth, PO Box 1000 800, Iqaluit, X0A 0H0 NU
867-975-5500, Fax: 867-975-5504, 866-934-2035

Saskatchewan
Saskatchewan First Nations & Métis Relations, #210, 1855 Victoria Ave., Regina, S4P 3T2 SK
306-787-6250, Fax: 306-787-5832

ACTS & REGULATIONS

New Brunswick
Legislative Services, Centennial Bldg., #418, 670 King St., PO Box 6000, Fredericton, E3B 5H1 NB
506-453-2855, Fax: 506-457-7342

Newfoundland & Labrador
Department of Transportation & Works, Confederation Bldg., West Block, 6th Fl., PO Box 8700, St. John's, A1B 4J6 NL
709-729-3679, Fax: 709-729-4285, twminister@gov.nl.ca

Nova Scotia
Department of Service Nova Scotia & Municipal Relations, 1505 Barrington St., PO Box 216, Halifax, B3J 2M4 NS
902-424-4141, Fax: 902-424-0581, public-enquiries@gov.ns.ca

Prince Edward Island
Office of the Attorney General, Shaw Building, North, 105 Rochford St., 4th Fl., PO Box 2000, Charlottetown, C1A 7N8 PE
902-368-5152, Fax: 902-368-4910

AGRICULTURE
See Also: Land Resources
Agriculture & Agri-Food Canada, Sir John Carling Bldg., 930 Carling Ave., Ottawa, K1A 0C5 ON
613-759-1000, Fax: 613-759-6726, info@agr.gc.ca
Plant Biotechnology Institute, 110 Gymnasium Pl., Saskatoon, S7N 0W9 SK
306-975-5248, Fax: 306-975-4839, pbi-info@nrc-cnrc.gc.ca
Prairie Farm Rehabilitation Administration, CIBC Tower, #408, 1800 Hamilton St., Regina, S4P 4L2 SK
306-780-5070, Fax: 306-780-5018

Alberta
Alberta Agriculture & Food, J.G. O'Donoghue Bldg., 7000 - 113 St., 1st Fl., Edmonton, T6H 5T6 AB
780-427-2727, Fax: 780-427-2861, 866-882-7677
Agriculture Financial Services Corporation, 5718 - 56 Ave., Lacombe, AB T4L 1B1
403-782-8200, Fax: 403-782-4226, 800-396-0215

British Columbia
Ministry of Agriculture & Lands, PO Box 9120 Prov Govt, Victoria, V8W 9E2 BC
250-387-5121, Fax: 250-387-1522, agf.webmaster@gems2.gov.bc.ca

Manitoba
Agricultural Societies, 1129 Queens Ave., Brandon, MB R7A 1L9
204-726-6195, Fax: 204-726-6260
Manitoba Agriculture, Food & Rural Initiatives, Norquay Bldg., 401 York Ave., Winnipeg, R3C 0P8 MB
Food Development Centre, 810 Phillips St., PO Box 1240, Portage la Prairie, MB R1N 3J9
204-239-3150, Fax: 204-239-3180, 800-870-1044

New Brunswick
Department of Agriculture & Aquaculture, PO Box 6000, Fredericton, E3B 5H1 NB
506-453-2666, Fax: 506-453-7170, DAA-MAA@gnb.ca

Newfoundland & Labrador
Agrifoods Branch, Provincial Agriculture Bldg., Brookfield Rd., PO Box 8700, St. John's, A1B 4J6 NL
709-729-6588, Fax: 709-729-2674

Northwest Territories
Department of Environment & Natural Resources, PO Box 1320, Yellowknife, X1A 2L9 NT

Nova Scotia
Department of Agriculture, 1741 Brunswick St., 3rd Fl., PO Box 2223, Halifax, B3J 3C4 NS
902-424-4560, Fax: 902-424-4671

Ontario
Ministry of Agriculture, Food & Rural Affairs, 1 Stone Rd. West, Guelph, N1G 4Y2 ON
519-826-3100, 888-466-2372

Prince Edward Island
Department of Agriculture, Jones Bldg., 11 Kent St., PO Box 2000, Charlottetown, C1A 7N8 PE
902-368-4880, Fax: 902-368-4857

Quebec
Ministère de l'Agriculture, des Pêcheries et de l'Alimentation, 200, ch Sainte-Foy, Québec, G1R 4X6 QC
418-380-2110, 888-222-6272,

Saskatchewan
Saskatchewan Agriculture, Walter Scott Bldg., 3085 Albert St., Regina, S4S 0B1 SK
306-787-5140, 866-457-2377, aginfo@gov.sk.ca

AGRICULTURE & FOOD
Agriculture & Agri-Food Canada, Sir John Carling Bldg., 930 Carling Ave., Ottawa, K1A 0C5 ON
613-759-1000, Fax: 613-759-6726, info@agr.gc.ca
Plant Biotechnology Institute, 110 Gymnasium Pl., Saskatoon, S7N 0W9 SK
306-975-5248, Fax: 306-975-4839, pbi-info@nrc-cnrc.gc.ca
Soil, Plant & Feed Laboratory, Brookfield Rd., PO Box 8700, St. John's, A1B 4J6 NL
709-729-6738, Fax: 709-729-6734

Alberta
Alberta Agriculture & Food, J.G. O'Donoghue Bldg., 7000 - 113 St., 1st Fl., Edmonton, T6H 5T6 AB
780-427-2727, Fax: 780-427-2861, 866-882-7677
Agriculture Financial Services Corporation, 5718 - 56 Ave., Lacombe, AB T4L 1B1
403-782-8200, Fax: 403-782-4226, 800-396-0215
Farmers' Advocate of Alberta, 7000 - 113 St., 3rd Fl., Edmonton, AB T6H 5T6
780-427-2433, Fax: 780-427-3913, farmers.advocate@gov.ab.ca

Irrigation Council, Provincial Bldg., 200 - 5 Ave. South, 3rd Fl., PO Bag 3014, Lethbridge, AB T1J 4L1
403-381-5176, Fax: 403-382-4406

British Columbia
Agricultural Land Commission, #133, 4940 Canada Way, Burnaby, BC V5G 4K6
604-660-7000, Fax: 604-660-7033
Ministry of Agriculture & Lands, PO Box 9120 Prov Govt, Victoria, V8W 9E2 BC
250-387-5121, Fax: 250-387-1522, agf.webmaster@gems2.gov.bc.ca

Manitoba
Agricultural Societies, 1129 Queens Ave., Brandon, MB R7A 1L9
204-726-6195, Fax: 204-726-6260
Manitoba Agriculture, Food & Rural Initiatives, Norquay Bldg., 401 York Ave., Winnipeg, R3C 0P8 MB
Farm Lands Ownership Board, #812, Norquay Bldg., 401 York Ave., Winnipeg, MB R3C 0P8
204-945-3149, Fax: 204-945-1489, 800-282-8069, robert.mckenzie@gov.mb.ca
Farm Machinery Board, Norquay Bldg., #812, 401 York Ave., Winnipeg, MB R3C 0P8
204-945-3856, Fax: 204-948-2844, randy.ozunko@gov.mb.ca
Manitoba Agricultural Services Corporation, #100, 1525 First St. South, Brandon, MB R7A 7A1
204-726-6850, Fax: 204-726-6849, mailbox@masc.mb.ca

New Brunswick
New Brunswick Crop Insurance Commission, PO Box 6000, Fredericton, NB E3B 5H1
506-453-2185, Fax: 506-453-7406
New Brunswick Farm Products Commission, c/o Department of Agriculture & Aquaculture, PO Box 6000, Fredericton, NB E3B 5H1
506-453-3647, Fax: 506-444-5969

Newfoundland & Labrador
Agrifoods Branch, Provincial Agriculture Bldg., Brookfield Rd., PO Box 8700, St. John's, A1B 4J6 NL
709-729-6588, Fax: 709-729-2674
Department of Natural Resources, Natural Resources Bldg., 50 Elizabeth Ave., 7th Fl., PO Box 8700, St. John's, A1B 4J6 NL
709-729-2920, Fax: 709-729-0059

Nova Scotia
Department of Agriculture, 1741 Brunswick St., 3rd Fl., PO Box 2223, Halifax, B3J 3C4 NS
902-424-4560, Fax: 902-424-4671

Ontario
AGRICORP, 1 Stone Rd. West, PO Box 3660 Central, Guelph, ON N1H 8M4
Fax: 519-826-4118, 888-247-4999, cac@agricorp.com
Agricultural Research Institute of Ontario, 1 Stone Rd. West, 2nd Fl. NW, Guelph, ON N1G 4Y2
519-826-4199, Fax: 519-826-4211
Agriculture, Food & Rural Affairs Tribunal, 1 Stone Rd. West, 1st Fl., Guelph, ON N1G 4Y2
519-826-3433, Fax: 519-826-4232, appeals.tribunal@omafra.gov.on.ca
Ministry of Agriculture, Food & Rural Affairs, 1 Stone Rd. West, Guelph, N1G 4Y2 ON
519-826-3100, 888-466-2372

Prince Edward Island
Agricultural Insurance Corporation, 29 Indigo Cres., PO Box 1600, Charlottetown, PE C1A 7N3
902-368-4842, Fax: 902-368-6677, peiaic@gov.pe.ca
Department of Agriculture, Jones Bldg., 11 Kent St., PO Box 2000, Charlottetown, C1A 7N8 PE
902-368-4880, Fax: 902-368-4857
Food Technology Centre, 101 Belvedere Ave., PO Box 2000, Charlottetown, PE C1A 7N8
902-368-5548, Fax: 902-368-5549, 877-368-5548, ftcweb@gov.pe.ca

Quebec
Ministère de l'Agriculture, des Pêcheries et de l'Alimentation, 200, ch Sainte-Foy, Québec, G1R 4X6 QC
418-380-2110, 888-222-6272

Government Quick Reference Guide / Air

Commission de protection du territoire agricole du Québec, 200, ch Ste-Foy, 2e étage, Québec, QC G1R 4X6
418-643-3314, Fax: 418-643-2261, 800-667-5294, info@cptaq.gouv.qc.ca

Régie des marchés agricoles et alimentaires du Québec, 201, boul Crémazie est, 5e étage, Montréal, QC H2M 1L3
514-873-4024, Fax: 514-873-3984, rmaaqc@rmaaq.gouv.qc.ca

Saskatchewan
Saskatchewan Agriculture, Walter Scott Bldg., 3085 Albert St., Regina, S4S 0B1 SK
306-787-5140, 866-457-2377, aginfo@gov.sk.ca

Saskatchewan Crop Insurance Corporation, 484 Prince William Dr., PO Box 3000, Melville, SK S0A 2P0
306-728-7200, Fax: 306-728-7268, 888-935-0000, customer.service@scic.gov.sk.ca

Yukon Territory
Yukon Environment, PO Box 2703, Whitehorse, Y1A 2C6 YT
867-667-5652, Fax: 867-393-6213, 800-661-0408, environmentyukon@gov.yk.ca

AIR
Atmospheric Science & Technology, 2121, rte Transcanadienne, Dorval, H9P 1J3 QC
514-421-4771, Fax: 514-421-2106

AIR POLLUTION
See Also: Environment
Atmospheric Science & Technology, 2121, rte Transcanadienne, Dorval, H9P 1J3 QC
514-421-4771, Fax: 514-421-2106

Environmental Stewardship Branch, 351 boul St-Joseph, Gatineau, K1A 0H3 QC
819-997-1575, Fax: 819-953-9452

International Joint Commission, 234 Laurier Ave. West, 22nd Fl., Ottawa, K1P 6K6 ON
613-947-1420, Fax: 613-993-5583

Meteorological Service of Canada, 4905 Dufferin St., Toronto, M3H 5T4 ON
416-739-4770, Fax: 416-739-4232

Alberta
Alberta Environment, South Tower, Petroleum Plaza, 9915 - 108 St., Main Fl., Edmonton, T5K 2G8 AB
780-427-2700, Fax: 780-422-4086,-310-0000, env.infocent@gov.ab.ca

British Columbia
Ministry of Environment, PO Box 9339 Prov Govt,Victoria, V8W 9M1 BC
250-387-1161, Fax: 250-387-5669, www.envmail@gov.bc.ca

Manitoba
Manitoba Conservation, 200 Saulteaux Cres., Winnipeg, R3J 3W3 MB
204-945-6784, 800-214-6497, mincon@leg.gov.mb.ca

New Brunswick
Department of the Environment, Marysville Place, 20 McGloin St., PO Box 6000, Fredericton, E3B 5H1 NB
506-453-2690, Fax: 506-457-4991

Environmental Management, Marysville Place, 20 McGloin St., PO Box 6000, Fredericton, E3B 5H1 NB
506-444-5119, Fax: 506-457-7333

Department of Natural Resources, PO Box 6000, Fredericton, E3B 5H1 NB
506-453-2510, Fax: 506-444-5839, dnrweb@gnb.ca

Sciences & Planning, Marysville Place, 20 McGloin St., 2nd Fl., PO Box 6000, Fredericton, E3B 5H1 NB
506-453-2862, Fax: 506-453-2265

Newfoundland & Labrador
Department of Environment & Conservation, Confederation Bldg., West Block, 4th Fl., PO Box 8700, St. John's, A1B 4J6 NL
709-729-2664, Fax: 709-729-6639, 800-563-6181, info@gov.nl.ca

Northwest Territories
Department of Environment & Natural Resources, PO Box 1320, Yellowknife, X1A 2L9 NT

Nova Scotia
Department of Environment, 5151 Terminal Rd., 5th Fl., PO Box 442, Halifax, B3J 2T8 NS
902-424-3600, Fax: 902-424-0503, 877-936-8476

Nunavut
Department of Environment, PO Box 1000 1300,Iqaluit, X0A 0H0 NU
867-975-7700, Fax: 867-975-7742, 866-222-9063, environment@gov.nu.ca

Ontario
Ministry of Environment, 135 St. Clair Ave. West, Toronto, M4V 1P5 ON
416-325-4000, Fax: 416-325-3159, 800-565-4923

Prince Edward Island
Department of Environment, Energy & Forestry, Jones Bldg., 11 Kent St., 4th & 5th Fl., PO Box 2000, Charlottetown, C1A 7N8 PE
902-368-5000, Fax: 902-368-5830

Quebec
Ministère du Développement durable, de l'Environnement et des Parcs, Édifice Marie-Guyart, 675, boul René-Lévesque est, 29e étage, Québec, G1R 5V7 QC
418-521-3830, Fax: 418-646-5974, 800-561-1616, info@mddep.gouv.qc.ca

Saskatchewan
Saskatchewan Environment, 3211 Albert St., 2nd Fl., Regina, S4S 5W6 SK
306-953-3750, Fax: 306-787-9544, 800-567-4224, inquiry@serm.gov.sk.ca

Yukon Territory
Yukon Environment, PO Box 2703, Whitehorse, Y1A 2C6 YT
867-667-5652, Fax: 867-393-6213, 800-661-0408, environmentyukon@gov.yk.ca

AIRPORTS & AVIATION
See Also: Transportation
Canadian Air Transport Security Authority, 99 Bank St., 13th Fl., Ottawa, ON K1P 6B9
Fax: 613-991-6726, 888-294-2202

Institute for Aerospace Research, 1200 Montreal Rd., Ottawa, K1A 0R6 ON
613-991-5738, Fax: 613-952-7214

Transport Canada, Place de Ville, 330 Sparks St., Tower C, Ottawa, K1A 0N5 ON
613-990-2309, Fax: 613-954-4731, minTC@tc.gc.ca

Transportation Appeal Tribunal of Canada, 333 Laurier Ave. West, 12th Fl., Ottawa, ON K1A 0N5
613-990-6906, Fax: 613-990-9153, info@tatc.gc.ca

Newfoundland & Labrador
Department of Transportation & Works, Confederation Bldg., West Block, 6th Fl., PO Box 8700, St. John's, A1B 4J6 NL
709-729-3679, Fax: 709-729-4285, twminister@gov.nl.ca

Northwest Territories
Airports, YK Centre, 4922 - 28th St., 4th fl., PO Box 1320, Yellowknife, X1A 2L9 NT
867-873-7725, Fax: 867-873-0297

Department of Transportation, Lahm Ridge Bldg., 4501 50 Ave., PO Box 1320, Yellowknife, X1A 2L9 NT
867-920-3460, Fax: 867-873-0363

Nunavut
Department of Community & Government Services, J.G. Brown Bldg., PO Box 1000 700,Iqaluit, X0A 0H0 NU
867-975-5400, Fax: 867-975-5305

Ontario
Ministry of Transportation, Ferguson Block, 77 Wellesley St. West, 3rd Fl., Toronto, M7A 1Z8 ON
416-235-4686, Fax: 416-327-9185, 800-268-4686

Saskatchewan
Saskatchewan Highways & Infrastructure, 1855 Victoria Ave., Regina, S4P 3T2 SK
306-787-4800

Yukon Territory
Yukon Highways & Public Works, PO Box 2703, Whitehorse, Y1A 2C6 YT
867-393-7193, Fax: 867-393-6218, 800-661-0408, hpw-info@gov.yk.ca

APPRENTICESHIP PROGRAMS
Canadian Council of Directors of Apprenticeship, Red Seal Secretariat, Place du Portage, Phase IV, 5th F, Gatineau, QC K1A 0J9
819-953-7442, Fax: 819-994-0202

Alberta
Alberta Advanced Education & Technology, Legislature Bldg., #324, 10800 - 97 Ave., Edmonton, T5K 2B6 AB
780-422-5400, Fax: 780-422-0821,-310-0000, aet.info@gov.ab.ca

Apprenticeship & Industry Training Division, Phipps-McKinnon Bldg., 5th Fl., 10020 - 101A Ave., Edmonton, T5J 3G2 AB
780-427-8517

New Brunswick
Apprenticeship & Occupational Certification Board, PO Box 6000, Fredericton, NB E3B 5H1
506-453-2260, Fax: 506-453-5317

Department of Post-Secondary Education, Training & Labour, 470 York St., PO Box 6000, Fredericton, E3B 5H1 NB
506-453-2597, Fax: 506-453-3618, dpetlinfo@gnb.ca

Northwest Territories
Northwest Territories Apprenticeship, Trade & Occupations Certification Board, PO Box 1320, Yellowknife, NT X1A 2L9
867-873-7357, Fax: 867-873-0200

Prince Edward Island
Community & Labour Development, Shaw Bldg., 105 Rochford St., 5th Fl., PO Box 2000, Charlottetown, C1A 7N8 PE
902-368-4244, Fax: 902-368-4242,

Quebec
Conseil consultatif du travail et de la main d'oeuvre, #9.400, 500, boul René-Lévesque ouest, Montréal, QC H2Z 1W7
514-873-2880, Fax: 514-873-1129, cctm@cctm.gouv.qc.ca

ARCTIC & NORTHERN AFFAIRS
Canadian Polar Commission, Constitution Square, #1710, 360 Albert St., Ottawa, K1R 7X7 ON
613-943-8605, Fax: 613-943-8607, 888-765-2701, mail@polarcom.gc.ca

Indian & Northern Affairs Canada, 10 Wellington St., North Tower, Gatineau, K1A 0H4 QC
819-997-0380, Fax: 819-953-3017, 866-817-3977, infopubs@ainc-inac.gc.ca

Polar Continental Shelf Project, #487, 615 Booth St., Ottawa, K1A 0E4 ON
613-947-1650, Fax: 613-947-1611, pcsp@NRCan.gc.ca

Alberta
Northern Alberta Development Council, Provincial Bldg., #206, 9621 - 96 Ave., PO Box 900-14, Peace River, T8S 1T4 AB
780-624-6274, Fax: 780-624-6184, nadc.council@gov.ab.ca

British Columbia
Northern Development Initiative Trust, #301, 1268 Fifth Ave., Prince George, BC V2L 3L2
250-561-2525, Fax: 250-561-2563, admin@nditrust.ca

Manitoba
Manitoba Aboriginal & Northern Affairs, 59 Elizabeth Dr., PO Box 37, Thompson, R8N 1X4 MB
204-677-6607, Fax: 204-677-6753, amartin@gov.mb.ca

Newfoundland & Labrador
Department of Labrador & Aboriginal Affairs, Confederation Bldg., East Block, 6th Fl., PO Box 8700, St. John's, A1B 4J6 NL
709-729-4776, Fax: 709-729-4900, 877-788-8822, laa@gov.nl.ca

Northwest Territories
Department of Environment & Natural Resources, PO Box 1320, Yellowknife, X1A 2L9 NT

Northwest Territories Business Development & Investment Corporation, #701, 5201 - 50 Ave., Yellowknife, NT X1A 3S9
867-920-6455, Fax: 867-765-0652, bdicinfo@gov.nt.ca

Nunavut
Department of Executive & Intergovernmental Affairs, 1084 Aeroplex bldg., PO Box 1000 200,Iqaluit, X0A 0H0 NU
867-975-6000, Fax: 867-975-6090

Ontario
Ministry of Northern Development & Mines, 159 Cedar St., Sudbury, P3E 6A5 ON
705-564-0032, Fax: 705-564-7357

Northern Development Division, Roberta Bondar Place, #200, 70 Foster Dr., Sault Ste Marie, P6A 6V8 ON
705-945-5900, Fax: 705-945-5931, 800-461-2287

Saskatchewan
Saskatchewan Northern Affairs, Mistasinihk Place, 1328 La Ronge Ave., PO Box 5000, La Ronge, S0J 1L0 SK

306-425-4207, Fax: 306-425-4349, 866-663-4065, admin@sna.gov.sk.ca

Yukon Territory
Yukon Economic Development, PO Box 2703, Whitehorse, Y1A 2C6 YT
867-393-7191, Fax: 867-395-7199, 800-661-0408

ARTS & CULTURE

Canada Science & Technology Museum Corporation, PO Box 9724 T,Ottawa, K1G 5A3 ON
613-991-6090, Fax: 613-990-3636, info@technomuses.ca
Canadian Heritage, 15 Eddy St., Gatineau, K1A 0M5 QC
819-997-0055, 866-811-0055
Parks Canada, 25 Eddy St., Gatineau, K1A 0M5 QC
888-773-8888, information@pc.gc.ca

Alberta
Alberta Foundation for the Arts, Standard Life Centre, #901, 10405 Jasper Ave., Edmonton, AB T5J 4R7
780-427-9968, Fax: 780-422-1162

British Columbia
Islands Trust, #200, 1627 Fort St., Victoria, BC V8R 1H8
250-405-5151, Fax: 250-405-5155, information@islandstrust.bc.ca

Manitoba
Communications Services Manitoba, 155 Carlton St., 10th Fl., Winnipeg, R3C 3H8 MB
204-945-3765, Fax: 204-948-2147
Manitoba Culture, Heritage, Tourism & Sport, Legislative Building, #118, 450 Broadway Ave., Winnipeg, R3C 0V8 MB
204-945-3729, Fax: 204-945-5223, mincht@leg.gov.mb.ca
Heritage Grants Advisory Council, 213 Notre Dame Ave., 3rd Fl., Winnipeg, MB R3B 1N3
204-945-2213, Fax: 204-948-2086
Le Centre Culturel franco-manitobain/Franco-Manitoban Cultural Centre, 340, boul Provencher, St Boniface, MB R2H 0G7
204-233-8972, Fax: 204-233-3324, ccfm@ccfm.mb.ca
Manitoba Arts Council, #525, 93 Lombard Ave., Winnipeg, MB R3B 3B1
204-945-2237, Fax: 204-945-5925, 866-994-2787, info@artscouncil.mb.ca
Manitoba Centennial Centre Corporation, 555 Main St., Winnipeg, MB R3B 1C3
204-956-1360, Fax: 204-944-1390
Manitoba Film Classification Board, #216, 301 Weston St., Winnipeg, MB R3E 3H4
204-945-8962, Fax: 204-945-0890, 866-612-2399, mfcb@gov.mb.ca
Manitoba Heritage Council, 213 Notre Dame Ave., Main Fl., Winnipeg, MB R3B 1N3
204-945-2118, Fax: 204-948-2384, hrb@gov.mb.ca
Manitoba Museum, 190 Rupert Ave., Winnipeg, MB R3B 0N2
204-956-2830, Fax: 204-942-3679, info@manitobamuseum.mb.ca
Multiculturalism Secretariat, 213 Notre Dame Ave., 4th Fl., Winnipeg, MB R3B 1N3
204-945-1156, Fax: 204-948-2323

New Brunswick
Ministerial Advisory Committee on Multiculturalism, PO Box 6000, Fredericton, NB E3B 5H1
New Brunswick Arts Board, #300, 634 Queen St., Fredericton, NB E3B 1C2
506-444-4444, Fax: 506-444-5543, 1-866-460-2787
New Brunswick Film, Assumption Pl., 770 Main St., 16th Fl., PO Box 5001, Moncton, NB E1C 8R3
506-869-6868, Fax: 506-869-6840, nbfilm@gnb.ca
Department of Wellness, Culture & Sport, Place 2000, 250 King St., 4th Fl., PO Box 6000, Fredericton, E3B 5H1 NB
506-453-2909, Fax: 506-453-6548

Newfoundland & Labrador
Department of Tourism, Culture & Recreation, Confederation Bldg., West Block, 2nd Fl., PO Box 8700, St. John's, A1B 4J6 NL
709-729-0862, Fax: 709-729-0870, tcrinfo@gov.nl.ca

Northwest Territories
Department of Education, Culture & Employment, PO Box 1320, Yellowknife, X1A 2L9 NT
867-669-2399, Fax: 867-873-0431, 866-606-5627
NWT Arts Council, PO Box 1320 Main, Yellowknife, NT X1A 2L9
867-920-6370, Fax: 867-873-0205

Nova Scotia
Culture Division, #601, 1800 Argyle St., PO Box 456, Halifax, B3J 2R5 NS
Fax: 902-424-0710
Film Nova Scotia, Collins Bank Bldg., 1869 Upper Water St., 3rd Fl., Halifax, NS B3J 1S9
902-424-7177, Fax: 902-424-0617, 888-360-2111, connorkm@gov.ns.ca
Nova Scotia Tourism Partnership Council, World Trade & Convention Centre, #603, 1800 Argyle St., Halifax, NS B3J 3N8
902-424-0048, Fax: 902-424-0723, pashermc@gov.ns.ca

Nunavut
Department of Culture, Language, Elders & Youth, PO Box 1000 800,Iqaluit, X0A 0H0 NU
867-975-5500, Fax: 867-975-5504, 866-934-2035

Ontario
Art Gallery of Ontario, 317 Dundas St. West, Toronto, ON M5T 1G4
416-977-0414, Fax: 416-979-6646
Culture Policy, Programs & Services Division, 400 University Ave., 5th Fl., Toronto, M7A 2R9 ON
416-314-7265, Fax: 416-314-7461
Ministry of Culture, Mowat Block, 900 Bay St., 5th Fl., Toronto, M7A 1L2 ON
416-325-1660, Fax: 416-325-1726, 866-454-0049
McMichael Canadian Art Collection, 10365 Islington Ave., Kleinburg, ON L0J 1C0
905-893-1121, Fax: 905-893-0692, 888-213-1121, info@mcmichael.com
Minister's Advisory Council for Arts & Culture, 400 University Ave., 5th Fl., Toronto, ON M7A 2R9
416-314-8321, Fax: 416-314-7091, 866-888-5829
Ontario Arts Council, 151 Bloor St. West, 5th Fl., Toronto, ON M5S 1T6
416-961-1660, Fax: 416-961-7796
Ontario Heritage Trust, 10 Adelaide St. East, Toronto, ON M5C 1J3
416-325-5000, Fax: 416-325-5071, marketing@heritagefdn.on.ca
Ontario Library Service - North, 334 Regent St., Sudbury, ON P3C 4E2
705-675-6467, Fax: 705-675-2285, 800-461-6348
Ontario Media Development Corporation, South Tower, #501, 175 Bloor St. East, Toronto, ON M4W 3R8
416-314-6858, Fax: 416-314-6876, mail@omdc.on.ca
Ontario Northland, 555 Oak St. East, North Bay, ON P1B 8L3
705-472-4500, Fax: 705-476-5598, 800-363-7512, info@ontc.on.ca
Ontario Place Corporation, 955 Lake Shore Blvd. West, Toronto, ON M6K 3B9
416-314-9900, Fax: 416-314-9992
Ontario Tourism Marketing Partnership Corporation, Hearst Block, 900 Bay St., 10th Fl., Toronto, ON M7A 2E1
416-212-0757, Fax: 416-325-6004, 800-668-2746
Ontario Trillium Foundation, 45 Charles St. East, 5th Fl., Toronto, ON M4Y 1S2
416-963-4927, Fax: 416-963-8781, 800-263-2887, trillium@trilliumfoundation.org
Ottawa Congress Centre, 55 Colonel By Dr., Ottawa, ON K1N 9J2
613-563-1984, Fax: 613-563-7646
Royal Ontario Museum, 100 Queen's Park Cres., Toronto, ON M5S 2C6
416-586-5549, Fax: 416-586-5685, info@rom.on.ca
Southern Ontario Library Service, #902, 111 Peter St., Toronto, ON M5V 2H1
416-961-1669, Fax: 416-961-5122, 800-387-5765
Ministry of Tourism, Hearst Block, 900 Bay St., 9th Fl., Toronto, M7A 2E1 ON
416-326-9326, Fax: 416-314-7854, 800-668-2746

Prince Edward Island
Department of Communities, Cultural Affairs & Labour, Shaw Bldg., 95 Rochford St., 4th Fl., PO Box 2000, Charlottetown, C1A 7N8 PE
902-368-5250, Fax: 902-368-4121
PEI Museum & Heritage Foundation, 2 Kent St., PO Box 2000, Charlottetown, PE C1A 1M6
902-368-6600, Fax: 902-368-6608, mhpei@gov.pe.ca

Quebec
Bibliothèque et Archives nationales du Québec (BAnQ), 475, boul De Maisonneuve est, Montréal, H2L 5C4 QC
514-873-1100, Fax: 514-873-9312, 800-363-9028

Commission de reconnaissance des associations d'artistes et des associations de producteurs, #14.60, 500, boul René-Lévesque ouest, Montréal, H2Z 1W7 QC
514-873-6012, Fax: 514-873-6267, tribunal@craaap.gouv.qc.ca
Commission des biens culturels du Québec, Bloc A-RC, 225, Grande Allée est, Québec, G1R 5G5 QC
418-643-8378, Fax: 418-643-8591, info@cbcq.gouv.qc.ca
Conseil des arts et des lettres du Québec, #320, 79, boul René-Lévesque est, Québec, G1R 5N5 QC
418-643-1707, Fax: 418-643-4558, 800-897-1707, info@calq.gouv.qc.ca
Ministère de la Culture, des Communications & de la Condition féminine, 225, Grande Allée est, Québec, G1R 5G5 QC
Fax: 418-380-2364, 888-380-8882, infos@mcccf.gouv.qc.ca
Musée d'art contemporain de Montréal, 185, rue Ste-Catherine ouest, Montréal, H2X 3X5 QC
514-847-6226, Fax: 514-847-6290
Musée de la civilisation, 85, rue Dalhousie, CP 155 B,Québec, G1K 7A6 QC
418-643-2158, Fax: 418-646-9705, 866-710-8031, mcqweb@mcq.org
Musée national des beaux-arts du Québec, Parc des Champs-de-Bataille, 1, av Wolfe-Montcalm, Québec, G1R 5H3 QC
418-643-2150, Fax: 418-646-3330, 866-220-2150, webmestre@mnba.qc.ca
Régie du cinéma, #100, 390, rue Notre-Dame ouest, Montréal, H2Y 1T9 QC
514-873-2371, Fax: 514-873-2142, 800-463-2463, regieducinema@rcq.gouv.qc.ca
Secrétariat à la politique linguistique, 225 Grande-Allée est, 4e étage, Québec, G1R 5G5 QC
418-643-4248, Fax: 418-646-7832, info@spl.gouv.qc.ca
Société de développement des entreprises culturelles, #800, 215, rue Saint-Jacques, Montréal, H2Y 1M6 QC
514-841-2200, Fax: 514-841-8606, 800-363-0401, info@sodec.gouv.qc.ca
Société de la Place des Arts de Montréal, 260, boul de Maisonneuve ouest, Montréal, H2X 1Y9 QC
514-285-4200, Fax: 514-285-1968, info@pda.qc.ca
Société de télédiffusion du Québec (Télé-Québec), 1000, rue Fullum, Montréal, H2K 3L7 QC
514-521-2424, Fax: 514-873-7739, 800-361-4301, info@telequebec.tv
Société du Grand Théâtre de Québec, 269, boul René-Lévesque est, Québec, G1R 2B3 QC
418-644-8921, Fax: 418-646-7670

Saskatchewan
Royal Saskatchewan Museum, 2445 Albert St., Regina, SK S4P 4W7
306-787-2815, Fax: 306-787-2820, info@royalsaskmuseum.ca
Sask Film, 1831 College Ave., Regina, SK S4P 3V7
306-798-3456, Fax: 306-798-7768, 800-561-9933
Saskatchewan Archives Board, University of Regina, 3303 Hillsdale St., Regina, SK S4S 0A2
306-787-4068, Fax: 306-787-1197, info.regina@archives.gov.sk.ca
Saskatchewan Arts Board, 2135 Broad St., Regina, SK S4P 3V7
306-787-4056, Fax: 306-787-4199, 800-667-7526, sab@artsboard.sk.ca
Saskatchewan Communications Network, #313E, 2440 Broad St., Regina, SK S4P 0A5
306-787-0490, Fax: 306-787-0496, 800-667-5055, inquiries@scn.ca
Saskatchewan Tourism, Parks, Culture, & Sport, 1919 Saskatchewan Dr., 4th Fl., Regina, S4P 4H2 SK
306-787-5729, Fax: 306-787-8560
Wanuskewin Heritage Park, RR#4, Saskatoon, SK S7K 3J7
306-931-6767, Fax: 306-931-4522, wanuskewin@wanuskewin.com

Yukon Territory
Yukon Tourism & Culture, PO Box 2703, Whitehorse, Y1A 2C6 YT
867-667-5036, Fax: 867-667-3546

AUDITORS-GENERAL

Auditor General of Canada, 240 Sparks St., Ottawa, K1A 0G6 ON
613-995-3708, Fax: 613-957-0474, communications@oag-bvg.gc.ca

AUTOMOBILE INSURANCE
See Also: Insurance (Life, Fire Property)

Nova Scotia
Nova Scotia Utility and Review Board, Summit Place, 1601 Lower Water St., 3rd Fl., Halifax, NS B3J 3P6
902-424-4448, uarb.board@gov.ns.ca

Quebec
Société de l'assurance automobile du Québec, 333, boul Jean-Lesage, CP 19600 Terminus, Québec, QC G1K 8J6
418-643-7620, Fax: 418-644-0339, 800-361-7620, courrier@saaq.gouv.qc.ca

BANKING & FINANCIAL INSTITUTIONS
Business Development Bank of Canada, #400, 5, Place Ville-Marie, Montréal, H3B 5E7 QC
514-283-5904, Fax: 514-283-2872, 877-232-2269
Finance Canada, L'esplanade Laurier, 140 O'Connor St., Ottawa, K1A 0G5 ON
613-992-1573, Fax: 613-996-2690, finpub@fin.gc.ca

Newfoundland & Labrador
Credit Union Deposit Guarantee Corporation, PO Box 340, Marystown, NL A0E 2M0
709-279-0170, Fax: 709-279-0177, 877-279-0170

Nunavut
Nunavut Business Credit Corporation, PO Box 224, Cape Dorset, NU X0A 0C0
867-897-3647, 800-758-0038

BILINGUALISM
Canadian Heritage, 15 Eddy St., Gatineau, K1A 0M5 QC
819-997-0055, 866-811-0055

Manitoba
Le Centre Culturel franco-manitobain/Franco-Manitoban Cultural Centre, 340, boul Provencher, St Boniface, MB R2H 0G7
204-233-8972, Fax: 204-233-3324, ccfm@ccfm.mb.ca

Nunavut
Department of Culture, Language, Elders & Youth, PO Box 1000 800, Iqaluit, X0A 0H0 NU
867-975-5500, Fax: 867-975-5504, 866-934-2035

Quebec
Secrétariat à la politique linguistique, 225 Grande-Allée est, 4e étage, Québec, G1R 5G5 QC
418-643-4248, Fax: 418-646-7832, info@spl.gouv.qc.ca

BIOTECHNOLOGY
Biotechnology Research Institute, 6100, av Royalmount, Montréal, H4P 2R2 QC
514-496-6100, Fax: 514-496-1928, bri-info@cnrc-nrc.gc.ca
Plant Biotechnology Institute, 110 Gymnasium Pl., Saskatoon, S7N 0W9 SK
306-975-5248, Fax: 306-975-4839, pbi-info@nrc-cnrc.gc.ca

BOARDS OF REVIEW
Canadian Nuclear Safety Commission, 280 Slater St., PO Box 1046 B, Ottawa, K1P 5S9 ON
613-995-5894, Fax: 613-995-5086, 800-668-5284, info@cnsc-ccsn.gc.ca
Commission for Public Complaints Against the Royal Canadian Mounted Police, PO Box 3423 D, Ottawa, ON K1P 6L4
613-952-1471, Fax: 613-952-8045, 800-267-6637, org@cpc-cpp.gc.ca
Committee on the Status of Endangered Wildlife in Canada, c/o Canadian Wildlife Service, Ottawa, ON K1A 0H3
819-997-4991, Fax: 819-994-3684, cosewic@ec.gc.ca
Mackenzie Valley Environmental Impact Review Board, 200 Scotia Centre, 5102 - 50th Ave., PO Box 938, Yellowknife, NT X1A 2N7
867-766-7050, Fax: 867-766-7074, 866-912-3472
Merchant Seamen Compensation Board, Secretary, Merchant Seamen Compensation Board, Phase II, Place du Portage, 10th Fl., Gatineau, QC K1A 0J2
819-953-8001, Fax: 819-994-5368
National Energy Board, 444 - 7 Ave. SW, Calgary, T2P 0X8 AB
403-292-4800, Fax: 403-292-5503, 800-899-1265, info@neb-one.gc.ca
National Secretariat on Homelessness, 165, rue Hôtel-de-Ville, Gatineau, K1A 0J2 QC
Nunavut Impact Review Board, PO Box 2379, Cambridge Bay, NU X0B 0C0
867-983-4600, Fax: 867-983-2594, info@nirb.nunavut.ca
Nunavut Water Board, PO Box 119, Gjoa Haven, NU X0B 1J0
867-360-6338, Fax: 867-360-6369
Porcupine Caribou Management Board, PO Box 31723, Whitehorse, YT Y1A 6L3
867-633-4780, Fax: 867-393-3904, pcmb@taiga.net
Royal Canadian Mounted Police External Review Committee, PO Box 1159 B, Ottawa, ON K1P 5R2
613-998-2134, Fax: 613-990-8969, org@erc-cee.gc.ca

Northwest Territories
Territorial Board of Revision, PO Box 1320, Yellowknife, NT X1A 2L9
867-873-7125, Fax: 867-873-0609

Ontario
Animal Care Review Board, 77 Grenville St., 8th Fl., Toronto, ON M5S 1B3
416-314-3509, Fax: 416-314-3518
Medical Eligibility Committee, 370 Select Dr., PO Box 168, Kingston, ON K7M 8T4
613-548-6405
Ontario Film Review Board, 1075 Millwood Rd., Toronto, ON M4G 1X6
416-314-3626, Fax: 416-314-3632
Ontario Review Board, 151 Bloor St. West, 10th Fl., Toronto, ON M5S 2T5
416-327-8866, Fax: 416-327-8867

Quebec
Bureau d'audiences publiques sur l'environnement, Édifice Lomer-Gouin, #2.10, 575, rue Saint-Amable, 2e étage, Québec, QC G1R 6A6
418-643-7447, Fax: 418-643-9474, 800-463-4732, communication@bape.gouv.qc.ca

BROADCASTING

Alberta
Alberta Public Affairs Bureau, Park Plaza, 10611 - 98 Ave., 6th Fl., Edmonton, T5K 2P7 AB
403-427-2754, Fax: 403-422-4168

Quebec
Société de télédiffusion du Québec (Télé-Québec), 1000, rue Fullum, Montréal, H2K 3L7 QC
514-521-2424, Fax: 514-873-7739, 800-361-4301, info@telequebec.tv

BUDGET PLANNING

Prince Edward Island
Department of the Provincial Treasury, Shaw Bldg., 95 Rochford St., 2nd Fl. South, PO Box 2000, Charlottetown, C1A 7N8 PE
902-368-4050, Fax: 902-368-6575

BUSINESS & FINANCE
Atlantic Canada Opportunities Agency, Blue Cross Centre, 644 Main St., 3rd Fl., PO Box 6051, Moncton, E1C 9J8 NB
506-851-2271, Fax: 506-851-7403, 800-561-7862,
Auditor General of Canada, 240 Sparks St., Ottawa, K1A 0G6 ON
613-995-3708, Fax: 613-957-0474, communications@oag-bvg.gc.ca
Business Development Bank of Canada, #400, 5, Place Ville-Marie, Montréal, H3B 5E7 QC
514-283-5904, Fax: 514-283-2872, 877-232-2269
Calgary, Home Oil Tower, #606, 3240 - 8 Ave. SW, Calgary, T2P 2Z2 AB
403-537-9800, Fax: 403-537-9811
Canada Business, 235 Queen St., Ottawa, K1A 0H5 ON
Fax: 888-417-0442, 888-576-4444
Canada Economic Development for Québec Regions, Édifice Dominion Square, #900, 1255, rue Peel, Montréal, H3B 2T9 QC
514-283-6412, Fax: 514-203-3302, 800-385-0412
Canada Investment & Savings, #900, 110 Yonge St., Toronto, ON M5C 1T4
416-952-1252, Fax: 416-952-1270, 800-575-5151, csb@csb.gc.ca
Canada Mortgage & Housing Corporation, 700 Montreal Rd., Ottawa, K1A 0P7 ON
613-748-2000, Fax: 613-748-2098, 800-668-2642, chic@cmhc-schl.gc.ca
Canada Revenue Agency, 875 Heron Rd., Ottawa, K1A 0L5 ON
613-952-0384, 800-267-6999
Canadian Commercial Corporation, 50 O'Connor St., 11th Fl., Ottawa, K1A 0S6 ON
613-996-0034, Fax: 613-995-2121, 800-748-8191
Canadian International Development Agency, 200, Promenade du Portage, Gatineau, K1A 0G4 QC
819-997-5006, Fax: 819-953-6088, 800-230-6349, info@acdi-cida.gc.ca
Cape Breton Development Fund Corporation, Silicon Island, 70 Crescent St., PO Box 1264, Sydney, NS B1P 6T7
902-564-3600, Fax: 902-564-3825, 800-705-3926
Competition Bureau, Place du Portage, Phase I, 50, rue Victoria, 21e étage, Ottawa, K1A 0C9 ON
613-997-4282, Fax: 613-997-0324, 800-348-5358, compbureau@ic.gc.ca
Competition Tribunal, Thomas D'Arcy McGee Bldg., #600, 90 Sparks St., Ottawa, ON K1P 5B4
613-957-3172, Fax: 613-957-3170, tribunal@ct-tc.gc.ca
Electronic Commerce Branch, 300 Slater St., Ottawa, ON K1A 0C8
613-990-4268, Fax: 613-941-0178, 800-328-6189
Enterprise Cape Breton Corporation, Silicon Island, 70 Crescent St., Sydney, NS B1S 2Z7
902-564-3600, Fax: 902-564-3825, 800-705-3926, ecbcinfo@ecbc.ca
Export Development Canada, 151 O'Connor St., Ottawa, K1A 1K3 ON
613-598-2500, Fax: 613-598-3811, 888-332-3320
Finance Canada, L'esplanade Laurier, 140 O'Connor St., Ottawa, K1A 0G5 ON
613-992-1573, Fax: 613-996-2690, finpub@fin.gc.ca
Financial Transactions & Reports Analysis Centre of Canada, 234 Laurier Ave. West, 24th Fl., Ottawa, ON K1P 1H7
Fax: 613-943-7931, 866-346-8722, guidelines-lignesdirectrices@fintrac-canafe.gc.ca
Foreign Affairs & International Trade Canada, 125 Sussex Dr., Ottawa, K1A 0G2 ON
613-944-4000, Fax: 613-996-9709, 800-267-8376, enqserv@international.gc.ca
Global Operations & Chief Trade Commissioner, 125 Sussex Dr., Ottawa, K1A 0G2 ON
613-944-2697, Fax: 613-996-1667
Industry Canada, 235 Queen St., Ottawa, K1A 0H5 ON
Fax: 613-954-6436, 800-328-6189, info@ic.gc.ca
National Round Table on the Environment & Economy, #200, 344 Slater St., Ottawa, K1R 7Y3 ON
613-992-7189, Fax: 613-992-7385, admin@nrtee-trnee.ca
Public Sector Pension Investment Board, #200, 440 Laurier Ave. West, Ottawa, ON K1R 7X6
613-782-3095, Fax: 613-782-6864, info@investpsp.ca
Purchasing Branch, 1920 Rose St., Regina, S4P 0A9 SK
306-787-6871, Fax: 306-787-3023
Statistics Canada, R.H. Coats Bldg., Tunney's Pasture, 100 Tunney's Pasture Driveway, Ottawa, K1A 0T6 ON
Fax: 877-287-4369, 800-263-1136, infostats@statcan.ca
Treasury Board of Canada, 300 Laurier Ave. West, 10th Fl., Ottawa, K1A 0R5 ON
613-957-2400, Fax: 613-941-4000, 877-636-0656, info@tbs-sct.gc.ca
Western Economic Diversification Canada, Canada Place, #1500, 9700 Jasper Ave. NW, Edmonton, T5J 4H7 AB
780-495-4164, Fax: 780-495-4557, 888-338-9378

Alberta
Agriculture Financial Services Corporation, 5718 - 56 Ave., Lacombe, AB T4L 1B1
403-782-8200, Fax: 403-782-4226, 800-396-0215
Alberta Economic Development, Commerce Place, 4th Fl., 10155 - 102 St., Edmonton, T5J 4L6 AB
780-427-4323, Fax: 780-415-1759
Industry & Regional Development Division, Commerce Place, 10155 - 102 St., 6th Fl., Edmonton, T5J 4L6 AB
Fax: 780-422-0626
International Offices & Trade, Commerce Place, 10155 - 102 St., 4th Fl., Edmonton, T5J 4L6 AB
780-427-3325, Fax: 780-427-0392
Northern Alberta Development Council, Provincial Bldg., #206, 9621 - 96 Ave., PO Box 900-14, Peace River, T8S 1T4 AB
780-624-6274, Fax: 780-624-6184, nadc.council@gov.ab.ca

British Columbia
Asia Pacific Foundation of Canada, #666, 999 Canada Pl., Vancouver, BC V6C 3E1
604-684-5986, info@asiapacific.ca; researchgrants@asiapacific.ca
British Columbia Innovation Council, 1188 West Georgia St., 9th Fl., Vancouver, BC V6E 4A2
604-683-2724, Fax: 604-683-6567, 800-665-7222, info@bcic.ca

Government Quick Reference Guide / Business Development

British Columbia Pension Corporation, 2995 Jutland Rd., PO Box 9460, Victoria, BC V8W 9V8
250-387-1002, Fax: 250-953-0429, 800-663-8823, PensionCorp@pensionsbc.ca; Retired.Members@pensionsbc.ca
International Financial Centre British Columbia, Park Place, #1170, 666 Burrard St., Vancouver, BC V6C 2X8
604-683-6626, Fax: 604-683-6646, info@ifcvancouver.com
Office of the Superintendent of Motor Vehicles, 940 Blanshard St., PO Box 9254 Prov Govt,Victoria, V8W 9J2 BC
250-387-7747, Fax: 250-387-4891, OSMV.Mailbox@gov.bc.ca
Timber Export Advisory Committee, 1520 Blanshard St., 2nd Fl., PO Box 9514 Prov Govt, Victoria, BC V8W 9C2
250-387-8916, Fax: 250-387-5050

Manitoba
Communities Economic Development Fund, #100, 23 Station Rd., Thompson, MB R8N 0N6
204-778-4138, Fax: 204-778-4313, 800-561-4315
Manitoba Competitiveness, Training & Trade, International Business Centre, The Paris Building, 259 Portage Ave., Winnipeg, R3B 3P4 MB
204-945-2475, Fax: 204-945-3977, minctt@leg.gov.mb.ca
Heritage Grants Advisory Council, 213 Notre Dame Ave., 3rd Fl., Winnipeg, MB R3B 1N3
204-945-2213, Fax: 204-948-2086
Manitoba Intergovernmental Affairs, #301, 450 Broadway Ave., Winnipeg, R3C 0V8 MB
Fax: 204-945-1383, mnia@leg.gov.mb.ca
Manitoba Agricultural Services Corporation, #100, 1525 First St. South, Brandon, MB R7A 7A1
204-726-6850, Fax: 204-726-6849, mailbox@masc.mb.ca
Manitoba Bureau of Statistics, #824, 155 Carlton St., Winnipeg, R3C 3H9 MB
204-945-2406, Fax: 204-945-0695
Manitoba Round Table for Sustainable Development, #160, 123 Main St., Winnipeg, R3C 1A5 MB
204-945-1671, Fax: 204-948-2357, mrtsd@gov.mb.ca
Mineral Resources Division, #360, 1395 Ellice Ave., Winnipeg, R3G 3P2 MB
Fax: 204-945-8427
Pension Commission of Manitoba, #1004, 401 York Ave., Winnipeg, MB R3C 0P8
204-945-2740, Fax: 204-948-2375, pensions@gov.mb.ca

New Brunswick
Department of Business New Brunswick, Centennial Bldg., 670 King St., PO Box 6000, Fredericton, E3B 5H1 NB
506-444-5228, Fax: 506-453-5428
Corporate Services, Centennial Bldg., 670 King St., 5th Fl., PO Box 6000, Fredericton, E3B 5H1 NB
506-453-3707, Fax: 506-453-3993
New Brunswick Crop Insurance Commission, PO Box 6000, Fredericton, NB E3B 5H1
506-453-2185, Fax: 506-453-7406
New Brunswick Farm Products Commission, c/o Department of Agriculture & Aquaculture, PO Box 6000, Fredericton, NB E3B 5H1
506-453-3647, Fax: 506-444-5969
New Brunswick Round Table on Environment & Economy, 20 McGloin St., PO Box 6000, Fredericton, NB E3B 5H1
506-453-3703, Fax: 506-453-3876
Regional Development Corporation, RDC Bldg., 836 Churchill Row, PO Box 428, Fredericton, E3B 5R4 NB
506-453-2277, Fax: 506-453-7988
Department of Supply & Services, PO Box 6000, Fredericton, E3B 5H1 NB
506-453-3742, Fax: 506-444-4400, Reception.Marysville@gnb.ca

Newfoundland & Labrador
Credit Union Deposit Guarantee Corporation, PO Box 340, Marystown, NL A0E 2M0
709-279-0170, Fax: 709-279-0177, 877-279-0170
Department of Innovation, Trade & Rural Development, West Block, Confederation Bldg., PO Box 8700, St. John's, A1B 4J6 NL
709-729-7000, Fax: 709-729-0654, 800-563-2299, itrd@gov.nl.ca
Ireland Business Partnership, PO Box 8700, St. John's, NL A1B 4J6
709-729-1684, Fax: 709-729-2236,
Department of Labrador & Aboriginal Affairs, Confederation Bldg., East Block, 6th Fl., PO Box 8700, St. John's, A1B 4J6 NL
709-729-4776, Fax: 709-729-4900, 877-788-8822, laa@gov.nl.ca
Nearshore Atlantic, 84 Elizabeth Ave., 1st Fl., St. John's, NL A1A 1W7
709-772-8324, Fax: 709-757-6284, info@nearshoreatlantic.com

Northwest Territories
Northwest Territories Business Development & Investment Corporation, #701, 5201 - 50 Ave., Yellowknife, NT X1A 3S9
867-920-6455, Fax: 867-765-0652, bdicinfo@gov.nt.ca
Department of Public Works & Services, PO Box 1320, Yellowknife, X1A 2L9 NT
867-873-7114, Fax: 867-873-0226

Nova Scotia
Department of Economic & Rural Development, Centennial Building, #600, 1660 Hollis St., PO Box 2311, Halifax, B3J 1V7 NS
902-424-0377, Fax: 902-424-7008, comm@gov.ns.ca
Nova Scotia Business Inc., World Trade & Convention Centre, #701, 1800 Argyle St., PO Box 2374, Halifax, NS B3J 3E4
902-424-6650, Fax: 902-424-5739, 800-260-6682, info@nsbi.ca
Nova Scotia Securities Commission, Joseph Howe Bldg., 1690 Hollis St., 2nd Fl., PO Box 458, Halifax, NS B3J 2P8
902-424-7768, Fax: 902-424-4625
Pension Regulation Division, PO Box 2531, Halifax, B3J 3N5 NS
902-424-8915, Fax: 902-424-0662

Ontario
Advertising Review Board, Macdonald Block, #M2-56, 900 Bay St., 2nd Fl., Toronto, ON M7A 1N3
416-327-2183, Fax: 416-327-2179
Agriculture, Food & Rural Affairs Tribunal, 1 Stone Rd. West, 1st Fl., Guelph, ON N1G 4Y2
519-826-3433, Fax: 519-826-4232, appeals.tribunal@omafra.gov.on.ca
Ministry of Economic Development, Hearst Block, 900 Bay St., 8th Fl., Toronto, M7A 2E1 ON
416-325-6666, Fax: 416-325-6688, 866-668-4249, info@edt.gov.on.ca
Ministry of Government Services & Consumer Services, Whitney Block, #4320, 99 Wellesley St. West, 4th Fl., Toronto, M7A 1W3 ON
416-326-1234, Fax: 416-327-3790, 800-268-1142
Grain Financial Protection Board, 1 Stone Rd. West, PO Box 3660, Guelph, ON N1H 8M4
519-826-3949, Fax: 519-826-3367
Infrasutucture Ontario, 777 Bay St., 9th Fl., Toronto, M5G 2C8 ON
416-212-7289, Fax: 416-325-4646, info@infrastructureontario.ca
Licence Appeal Tribunal (LAT), 1 St. Clair Ave. West, 12th Fl., Toronto, ON M4V 1K6
416-314-4260, Fax: 416-314-4270, 800-255-2214
Liquor Control Board of Ontario, 55 Lake Shore Blvd. East, Toronto, ON M5E 1A4
416-365-5900, Fax: 416-864-2476, 800-668-5226, infoline@lcbo.com
Livestock Financial Protection Board, 1 Stone Rd. West, 5th Fl. NW, Guelph, ON N1G 4Y2
519-826-3886, Fax: 519-826-4375, jim.wideman@omaf.gov.on.ca
Metro Toronto Convention Centre Corporation, 255 Front St. West, Toronto, ON M5V 2W6
416-585-8000, Fax: 416-585-8270, info@mtcc.com
Normal Farm Practices Protection Board, 1 Stone Rd. West, 3rd Fl., Northeast, Guelph, ON N1G 4Y2
519-826-3549, Fax: 519-826-6611
Ontario Farm Products Marketing Commission, 1 Stone Rd. West, 5th Fl., Guelph, ON N1G 4Y2
519-826-4220, Fax: 519-826-3400
Ontario Food Terminal Board, 165 The Queensway, Toronto, ON M8Y 1H8
416-259-5479, Fax: 416-259-4303
Ontario Place Corporation, 955 Lake Shore Blvd. West, Toronto, ON M6K 3B9
416-314-9900, Fax: 416-314-9992
Ottawa Congress Centre, 55 Colonel By Dr., Ottawa, ON K1N 9J2
613-563-1984, Fax: 613-563-7646
Pay Equity Commission, 400 University Ave., 11th Fl., Toronto, ON M7A 1T7
416-314-1896, Fax: 416-314-8741, 800-387-8813

Prince Edward Island
Agricultural Insurance Corporation, 29 Indigo Cres., PO Box 1600, Charlottetown, PE C1A 7N3
902-368-4842, Fax: 902-368-6677, peiaic@gov.pe.ca
Department of Innovation & Advanced Learning, Shaw Bldg., 105 Rochford St., 5th Fl., PO Box 2000, Charlottetown, C1A 7N8 PE
902-368-4240, Fax: 902-368-4242
Island Investment Development Inc., 94 Euston St., 2nd Fl., Charlottetown, PE C1A 1W4
902-894-0351, Fax: 902-368-5886
Prince Edward Island Business Development Inc., 94 Euston St., 1st & 2nd Fl., PO Box 910, Charlottetown, PE C1A 7L9
902-368-6300, Fax: 902-368-6301, 800-563-3734, business@gov.pe.ca
Prince Edward Island Lending Agency, Confederation Court Office Tower, #201, 134 Kent St., PO Box 1420, Charlottetown, PE C1A 7N1
902-368-6200, Fax: 902-368-6201
Prince Edward Island Lotteries Commission, Office of the Deputy Provincial Treasurer, 95 Rochford St., PO Box 2000, Charlottetown, PE C1A 7N8
902-368-4053, Fax: 902-368-6575
Department of the Provincial Treasury, Shaw Bldg., 95 Rochford St., 2nd Fl. South, PO Box 2000, Charlottetown, C1A 7N8 PE
902-368-4050, Fax: 902-368-6575

Quebec
Fonds de la recherche en santé du Québec, 500, rue Sherbrooke ouest, 8e étage, Montréal, QC H3A 3C6
514-873-2114, Fax: 514-873-8768
Société du Centre des congrès de Québec, 900, boul René-Lévesque est, 2e étage, Québec, QC G1R 2B5
418-644-4000, Fax: 418-644-6455, 888-679-4000
Société Innovatech du sud du Québec, #20, 2100, rue King ouest, Sherbrooke, QC J1J 2E8
819-820-3305, Fax: 819-820-3320, isq@isq.qc.ca
Société Innovatech Québec, 10, rue Pierre Olivier Chauveau, Québec, QC G1R 4J3
418-528-9770, Fax: 418-528-9783, info@innovatechquebec.com
Société Innovatech Régions ressources, #500, 1200, rte de l'Église, Sainte-Foy, QC G1V 5A3
866-870-0437, info@innovatech-regions.qc.ca

Saskatchewan
Saskatchewan Energy & Resources, #300, 2103 - 11th Ave., Regina, S4P 3Z8 SK
306-787-2528, Fax: 306-787-8447, 866-727-5427
Saskatchewan Crop Insurance Corporation, 484 Prince William Dr., PO Box 3000, Melville, SK S0A 2P0
306-728-7200, Fax: 306-728-7268, 888-935-0000, customer.service@scic.gov.sk.ca
Saskatchewan Trade & Export Partnership, #320, 1801 Hamilton St., PO Box 1787, Regina, SK S4P 3C6
306-787-9210, Fax: 306-787-6666, 877-313-7244, inquire@sasktrade.sk.ca

Yukon Territory
Yukon Lottery Commission, 312 Wood St., Whitehorse, YT Y1A 2E6
867-633-7890, Fax: 867-668-7561, lotteriesyukon@gov.yk.ca

BUSINESS DEVELOPMENT
See Also: Industry; Science & Technology
Atlantic Canada Opportunities Agency, Blue Cross Centre, 644 Main St., 3rd Fl., PO Box 6051, Moncton, E1C 9J8 NB
506-851-2271, Fax: 506-851-7403, 800-561-7862
Business Development Bank of Canada, #400, 5, Place Ville-Marie, Montréal, H3B 5E7 QC
514-283-5904, Fax: 514-283-2872, 877-232-2269
Canada Business, 235 Queen St., Ottawa, K1A 0H5 ON
Fax: 888-417-0442, 888-576-4444
Canada Economic Development for Québec Regions, Édifice Dominion Square, #900, 1255, rue Peel, Montréal, H3B 2T9 QC
514-283-6412, Fax: 514-283-3302, 866-385-6412
Cape Breton Development Fund Corporation, Silicon Island, 70 Crescent St., PO Box 1264, Sydney, NS B1P 6T7
902-564-3600, Fax: 902-564-3825, 800-705-3926
Enterprise Cape Breton Corporation, Silicon Island, 70 Crescent St., Sydney, NS B1S 2Z7
902-564-3600, Fax: 902-564-3825, 800-705-3926, ecbcinfo@ecbc.ca

Government Quick Reference Guide / Business Regulations

Export Development Canada, 151 O'Connor St., Ottawa, K1A 1K3 ON
 613-598-2500, Fax: 613-598-3811, 888-332-3320
Global Operations & Chief Trade Commissioner, 125 Sussex Dr,, Ottawa, K1A 0G2 ON
 613-944-2697, Fax: 613-996-1667
Industry Canada, 235 Queen St., Ottawa, K1A 0H5 ON
 Fax: 613-954-6436, 800-328-6189, info@ic.gc.ca
Western Economic Diversification Canada, Canada Place, #1500, 9700 Jasper Ave. NW, Edmonton, T5J 4H7 AB
 780-495-4164, Fax: 780-495-4557, 888-338-9378

Alberta

Alberta Economic Development Authority, McDougall Centre, 455 - 6 St. SW, Calgary, AB T2P 4E8
 403-297-3022, Fax: 403-297-6435,
Alberta Economic Development, Commerce Place, 4th Fl., 10155 - 102 St., Edmonton, T5J 4L6 AB
 780-427-4323, Fax: 780-415-1759
Northern Alberta Development Council, Provincial Bldg., #206, 9621 - 96 Ave., PO Box 900-14, Peace River, T8S 1T4 AB
 780-624-6274, Fax: 780-624-6184, nadc.council@gov.ab.ca

British Columbia

Asia Pacific Foundation of Canada, #666, 999 Canada Pl., Vancouver, BC V6C 3E1
 604-684-5986, info@asiapacific.ca; researchgrants@asiapacific.ca
British Columbia Innovation Council, 1188 West Georgia St., 9th Fl., Vancouver, BC V6E 4A2
 604-683-2724, Fax: 604-683-6567, 800-665-7222, info@bcic.ca
British Columbia Progress Board, #730, 999 Canada Pl., Vancouver, BC V6C 3E1
 604-775-1664, Fax: 604-775-2129, ideas@bcprogressboard.com
Columbia Basin Trust, Southwest Basin, 5400, 445 - 13 Ave., Castlegar, BC V1N 1G1
 250-365-6633, Fax: 250-365-6670, 800-505-8998, cbt@cbt.org
Economic Competitiveness Division, 1810 Blanshard St., 7th Fl., PO Box 9327 Prov Govt,Victoria, V8W 9N3 BC
 250-952-0367, Fax: 250-952-0137
International Financial Centre British Columbia, Park Place, #1170, 666 Burrard St., Vancouver, BC V6C 2X8
 604-683-6626, Fax: 604-683-6646, info@ifcvancouver.com
Northern Development Initiative Trust, #301, 1268 Fifth Ave., Prince George, BC V2L 3L2
 250-561-2525, Fax: 250-561-2563, admin@nditrust.ca
Small Business BC, #82, 601 West Cordova St., Vancouver, BC V6B 1G1
 800-775-5525, Fax: 604-775-5520, 800-667-2272, askus@smallbusinessbc.ca
Ministry of Technology, Trade, & Economic Development, 1810 Blanshard St., PO Box 9324 Prov Govt,Victoria, V8W 9N3 BC
 250-356-7411, Fax: 250-356-6376, Feedback.CSE@gov.bc.ca

Manitoba

Manitoba Competitiveness, Training & Trade, International Business Centre, The Paris Building, 259 Portage Ave., Winnipeg, R3B 3P4 MB
 204-945-2475, Fax: 204-945-3977, minctt@leg.gov.mb.ca

New Brunswick

Department of Business New Brunswick, Centennial Bldg., 670 King St., PO Box 6000, Fredericton, E3B 5H1 NB
 506-444-5228, Fax: 506-453-5428
Regional Development Corporation, RDC Bldg., 836 Churchill Row, PO Box 428, Fredericton, E3B 5R4 NB
 506-453-2277, Fax: 506-453-7988

Newfoundland & Labrador

Department of Innovation, Trade & Rural Development, West Block, Confederation Bldg., PO Box 8700, St. John's, A1B 4J6 NL
 709-729-7000, Fax: 709-729-0654, 800-563-2299, itrd@gov.nl.ca
Ireland Business Partnership, PO Box 8700, St. John's, NL A1B 4J6
 709-729-1684, Fax: 709-729-2236
Department of Labrador & Aboriginal Affairs, Confederation Bldg., East Block, 6th Fl., PO Box 8700, St. John's, A1B 4J6 NL
 709-729-4776, Fax: 709-729-4900, 877-788-8822, laa@gov.nl.ca

Northwest Territories

Department of Industry, Tourism & Investment, PO Box 1320, Yellowknife, X1A 2L9 NT
 Fax: 867-873-0306, info@iti.ca
Northwest Territories Business Development & Investment Corporation, #701, 5201 - 50 Ave., Yellowknife, NT X1A 3S9
 867-920-6455, Fax: 867-765-0652, bdicinfo@gov.nt.ca

Nova Scotia

Department of Economic & Rural Development, Centennial Building, #600, 1660 Hollis St., PO Box 2311, Halifax, B3J 1V7 NS
 902-424-0377, Fax: 902-424-7008, comm@gov.ns.ca
InNOVACorp, #1400, 1801 Hollis St., Halifax, NS B3J 3N4
 902-424-8670, Fax: 902-424-4679, 800-565-7051, communications@innovacorp.ca
Nova Scotia Business Inc., World Trade & Convention Centre, #701, 1800 Argyle St., PO Box 2374, Halifax, NS B3J 3E4
 902-424-6650, Fax: 902-424-5739, 800-260-6682, info@nsbi.ca
Trade Centre Limited, 1800 Argyle St., PO Box 955, Halifax, NS B3J 2V9
 902-421-8686, Fax: 902-422-2922

Nunavut

Department of Economic Development & Transportation, #1104 Inuksugait Plaza, PO Box 1000 1500,Iqaluit, X0A 0H0 NU
 867-975-7800, Fax: 867-975-7870, 888-975-5999, edt@gov.nu.ca

Ontario

Ministry of Economic Development, Hearst Block, 900 Bay St., 8th Fl., Toronto, M7A 2E1 ON
 416-325-6666, Fax: 416-325-6688, 866-668-4249, info@edt.gov.on.ca
Northern Development Division, Roberta Bondar Place, #200, 70 Foster Dr., Sault Ste Marie, P6A 6V8 ON
 705-945-5900, Fax: 705-945-5931, 800-461-2287
Ministry of Research & Innovation, 56 Wellesley St. West, 7th Fl., Toronto, M7A 2E7 ON
 416-325-5181, Fax: 416-325-3877

Prince Edward Island

Department of Innovation & Advanced Learning, Shaw Bldg., 105 Rochford St., 5th Fl., PO Box 2000, Charlottetown, C1A 7N8 PE
 902-368-4240, Fax: 902-368-4242
Prince Edward Island Business Development Inc., 94 Euston St., 1st & 2nd Fl., PO Box 910, Charlottetown, PE C1A 7L9
 902-368-6300, Fax: 902-368-6301, 800-563-3734, business@gov.pe.ca

Quebec

Ministère du Développement économique, de l'Innovation et de l'Exportation, 710, place D'Youville, 3e étage, Québec, G1R 4Y4 QC
 418-691-5950, Fax: 418-644-0118, 866-680-1884

Saskatchewan

Saskatchewan Energy & Resources, #300, 2103 - 11th Ave., Regina, S4P 3Z8 SK
 306-787-2528, Fax: 306-787-8447, 866-727-5427
Saskatchewan Enterprise & Innovation, #200, 3085 Albert St., Regina, S4S 0B1 SK
 Fax: 306-798-0629, 800-265-2001, RECDWebmaster@gov.sk.ca

Yukon Territory

Yukon Development Corporation, PO Box 2703 D-1,Whitehorse, Y1A 2C6 YT
 867-393-5337, Fax: 867-393-5401
Yukon Economic Development, PO Box 2703, Whitehorse, Y1A 2C6 YT
 867-393-7191, Fax: 867-395-7199, 800-661-0408

BUSINESS REGULATIONS

Canada Revenue Agency, 875 Heron Rd., Ottawa, K1A 0L5 ON
 613-952-0384, 800-267-6999
Industry Canada, 235 Queen St., Ottawa, K1A 0H5 ON
 Fax: 613-954-6436, 800-328-6189, info@ic.gc.ca

Alberta

Technology Services, John E. Brownlee Bldg., 10365 - 97 St., 8th Fl., Edmonton, T5J 3W7 AB
 780-422-8545

Northwest Territories

Northwest Territories Business Development & Investment Corporation, #701, 5201 - 50 Ave., Yellowknife, NT X1A 3S9
 867-920-6455, Fax: 867-765-0652, bdicinfo@gov.nt.ca

Nova Scotia

Nova Scotia Business Inc., World Trade & Convention Centre, #701, 1800 Argyle St., PO Box 2374, Halifax, NS B3J 3E4
 902-424-6650, Fax: 902-424-5739, 800-260-6682, info@nsbi.ca

Ontario

ServiceOntario, College Park, 777 Bay St., 15th fl., Toronto, M7A 2J3 ON
 416-326-6205, Fax: 416-326-5106

CANADIANS & SOCIETY

Beverly & Qamanirjuaq Caribou Management Board, Secretariat, PO Box 629, Stonewall, MB R0C 2Z0
 204-467-2438, rossthompson@mts.net
British Columbia Treaty Commission, #203, 1155 West Pender St., Vancouver, BC V6E 2P4
 604-482-9200, Fax: 604-482-9222, 800-665-8330, info@bctreaty.net
Canadian Heritage, 15 Eddy St., Gatineau, K1A 0M5 QC
 819-997-0055, 866-811-0055
Foreign Affairs & International Trade Canada, 125 Sussex Dr., Ottawa, K1A 0G2 ON
 613-944-4000, Fax: 613-996-9709, 800-267-8376, enqserv@international.gc.ca
Government of Canada, 111 Wellington St., PO Box 1103, Ottawa, K1A 0A6 ON
Historic Sites & Monuments Board of Canada, Terrasses de la Chaudière, 25 Eddy St., Gatineau, QC K1A 0M5
 819-997-4059, Fax: 819-934-1115, hsmbc-clmhc@pc.gc.ca
Human Resources & Skills Development Canada, 140 Promenade du Portage, Ottawa, K1A 0J9 ON
Indian & Northern Affairs Canada, 10 Wellington St., North Tower, Gatineau, K1A 0H4 QC
 819-997-0380, Fax: 819-953-3017, 866-817-3977, infopubs@ainc-inac.gc.ca
Indian Taxation Advisory Board, 90 Elgin St., 2nd Fl., Ottawa, ON K1A 0H4
 613-954-9972, Fax: 613-954-2073
National Capital Commission, #202, 40 Elgin St., Ottawa, K1P 1C7 ON
 613-239-5555, Fax: 613-239-5063, 800-704-8227, info@ncc-ccn.ca
National Round Table on the Environment & Economy, #200, 344 Slater St., Ottawa, K1R 7Y3 ON
 613-992-7189, Fax: 613-992-7385, admin@nrtee-trnee.ca
National Secretariat on Homelessness, 165, rue Hôtel-de-Ville, Gatineau, K1A 0J2 QC
Nunavut Impact Review Board, PO Box 2379, Cambridge Bay, NU X0B 0C0
 867-983-4600, Fax: 867-983-2594, info@nirb.nunavut.ca
Nunavut Planning Commission, PO Box 2101, Cambridge Bay, NU X0B 0C0
 867-983-2730, Fax: 867-983-2732
Nunavut Water Board, PO Box 119, Gjoa Haven, NU X0B 1J0
 867-360-6338, Fax: 867-360-6369
Passport Canada, Le 70 Crémazie, 70 Crémazie St., Gatineau, K1A 0G3 QC
 Fax: 819-953-5856, 800-567-6868
Porcupine Caribou Management Board, PO Box 31723, Whitehorse, YT Y1A 6L3
 867-633-4780, Fax: 867-393-3904, pcmb@taiga.net
Secteur du Québec de la Force terrestre, Montréal,QC
 514-252-2777

Alberta

Alberta Human Rights & Citizenship Commission, Northern Regional Office, Standard Life Centre, #800, 10405 Jasper Ave., Edmonton, AB T5J 4R7
 780-427-7661, Fax: 780-427-6013,-310-0000, humanrights@gov.ab.ca.
Alberta Sport, Recreation, Parks & Wildlife Foundation, Standard Life Centre, 10405 Jasper Ave., 9th Fl., Edmonton, AB T5J 4R7
 780-415-1167, Fax: 780-415-0308
Government House Foundation, 12845 - 102 Ave., Edmonton, AB T5N 0M6
 780-427-2281, Fax: 780-422-6508
Alberta Health & Wellness, TELUS Plaza North Tower, 10025 Jasper Ave., 22nd Fl., PO Box 1360 Main,Edmonton, T5J

2N3 AB
780-427-7164, health.ahinform@gov.ab.ca
Labour Relations Board, #503, 10808 - 99 Ave., Edmonton, AB T5K 0G5
780-427-5926, Fax: 780-422-0970, 800-463-2572, alrbinfo@lab.gov.ab.ca
Alberta Tourism, Parks, Recreation & Culture, Communications Branch, Standard Life Centre, 10405 Jasper Ave., 7th Fl., Edmonton, T5J 4R7 AB
780-427-6530, Fax: 780-427-1496, Comdev.Communications@gov.ab.ca

British Columbia
Ministry of Community Development, 800 Johnson St., 6th Fl., PO Box 9490 Prov Govt,Victoria, V8W 9N7 BC
250-387-2283, Fax: 250-387-4312, Feedback@gov.bc.ca
Local Government Department, 800 Johnson St., 6th Fl., PO Box 9490 Prov Govt,Victoria, V8W 9N7 BC
lgd_feedback@gov.bc.ca

Manitoba
Manitoba Aboriginal & Northern Affairs, 59 Elizabeth Dr., PO Box 37, Thompson, R8N 1X4 MB
204-677-6607, Fax: 204-677-6753, amartin@gov.mb.ca
Aboriginal Affairs Secretariat, #200, 500 Portage Ave., Winnipeg, R3C 3X1 MB
204-945-2510, Fax: 204-945-3689
Communications Services Manitoba, 155 Carlton St., 10th Fl., Winnipeg, R3C 3H8 MB
204-945-3765, Fax: 204-948-2147
Communities Economic Development Fund, #100, 23 Station Rd., Thompson, MB R8N 0N6
204-778-4138, Fax: 204-778-4313, 800-561-4315
Manitoba Culture, Heritage, Tourism & Sport, Legislative Building, #118, 450 Broadway Ave., Winnipeg, R3C 0V8 MB
204-945-3729, Fax: 204-945-5223, mincht@leg.gov.mb.ca
Heritage Grants Advisory Council, 213 Notre Dame Ave., 3rd Fl., Winnipeg, MB R3B 1N3
204-945-2213, Fax: 204-948-2086
Le Centre Culturel franco-manitobain/Franco-Manitoban Cultural Centre, 340, boul Provencher, St Boniface, MB R2H 0G7
204-233-8972, Fax: 204-233-3324, ccfm@ccfm.mb.ca
Manitoba Centennial Centre Corporation, 555 Main St., Winnipeg, MB R3B 1C3
204-956-1360, Fax: 204-944-1390
Manitoba Film Classification Board, #216, 301 Weston St., Winnipeg, MB R3E 3H4
204-945-8962, Fax: 204-945-0890, 866-612-2399, mfcb@gov.mb.ca
Manitoba Heritage Council, 213 Notre Dame Ave., Main Fl., Winnipeg, MB R3B 1N3
204-945-2118, Fax: 204-948-2384, hrb@gov.mb.ca
Multiculturalism Secretariat, 213 Notre Dame Ave., 4th Fl., Winnipeg, MB R3B 1N3
204-945-1156, Fax: 204-948-2323
Primary Care & Healthy Living, 300 Carlton St., 2nd Floor, Winnipeg, R3B 3M9 MB

New Brunswick
Department of Health, PO Box 5100, Fredericton, E3B 5G8 NB
506-457-4800, Fax: 506-453-5243, dh-ms@dh-ms.ca
Ministerial Advisory Committee on Multiculturalism, PO Box 6000, Fredericton, NB E3B 5H1
Regional Development Corporation, RDC Bldg., 836 Churchill Row, PO Box 428, Fredericton, E3B 5R4 NB
506-453-2277, Fax: 506-453-7988

Newfoundland & Labrador
Department of Labrador & Aboriginal Affairs, Confederation Bldg., East Block, 6th Fl., PO Box 8700, St. John's, A1B 4J6 NL
709-729-4776, Fax: 709-729-4900, 877-788-8822, laa@gov.nl.ca
Department of Tourism, Culture & Recreation, Confederation Bldg., West Block, 2nd Fl., PO Box 8700, St. John's, A1B 4J6 NL
709-729-0862, Fax: 709-729-0870, tcrinfo@gov.nl.ca

Northwest Territories
Department of Aboriginal Affairs & Intergovernmental Relations, 4910 - 52nd St., PO Box 1320, Yellowknife, X1A 2L9 NT
867-873-7143, Fax: 867-873-0233, 877-838-8194, nancy_gardiner@gov.nt.ca
Department of Municipal & Community Affairs, PO Box 1320, Yellowknife, X1A 2L9 NT
867-873-7118, Fax: 867-873-0309

Nova Scotia
Nova Scotia Advisory Commission on AIDS, Dennis Bldg., 1740 Granville St., 6th Fl., Halifax, NS B3J 1X5
902-424-5730, Fax: 902-424-4727
Pay Equity Commission, 5151 Terminal Rd., 7th Fl., PO Box 697, Halifax, NS B3J 2T8
902-424-2385, Fax: 902-424-0575
Seniors' Secretariat, Dennis Bldg., 1740 Granville St., 4th Fl., PO Box 2065, Halifax, NS B3J 2Z1
902-424-0065, Fax: 902-424-0561, 800-670-0065, scs@gov.ns.ca
Department of Service Nova Scotia & Municipal Relations, 1505 Barrington St., PO Box 216, Halifax, B3J 2M4 NS
902-424-4141, Fax: 902-424-0581, public-enquiries@gov.ns.ca

Ontario
Ministry of Government Services & Consumer Services, Whitney Block, #4320, 99 Wellesley St. West, 4th Fl., Toronto, M7A 1W3 ON
416-326-1234, Fax: 416-327-3790, 800-268-1142
McMichael Canadian Art Collection, 10365 Islington Ave., Kleinburg, ON L0J 1C0
905-893-1121, Fax: 905-893-0692, 888-213-1121, info@mcmichael.com
Ontario Arts Council, 151 Bloor St. West, 5th Fl., Toronto, ON M5S 1T6
416-961-1660, Fax: 416-961-7796
Ontario Heritage Trust, 10 Adelaide St. East, Toronto, ON M5C 1J3
416-325-5000, Fax: 416-325-5071, marketing@heritagefdn.on.ca
Ontario Northland, 555 Oak St. East, North Bay, ON P1B 8L3
705-472-4500, Fax: 705-476-5598, 800-363-7512, info@ontc.on.ca
Royal Ontario Museum, 100 Queen's Park Cres., Toronto, ON M5S 2C6
416-586-5549, Fax: 416-586-5685, info@rom.on.ca

Prince Edward Island
Advisory Council on the Status of Women, Sherwood Business Centre, 161 St. Peter's Rd., PO Box 2000, Charlottetown, PE C1A 7N8
902-368-4510, Fax: 902-368-4516, peistatusofwomen@eastlink.ca
Department of Communities, Cultural Affairs & Labour, Shaw Bldg., 95 Rochford St., 4th Fl., PO Box 2000, Charlottetown, C1A 7N8 PE
902-368-5250, Fax: 902-368-4121

Quebec
Commission des biens culturels du Québec, Bloc A-RC, 225, Grande Allée est, Québec, G1R 5G5 QC
418-643-8378, Fax: 418-643-8591, info@cbcq.gouv.qc.ca
Conseil des arts et des lettres du Québec, #320, 79, boul René-Lévesque est, Québec, G1R 5N5 QC
418-643-1707, Fax: 418-643-4558, 800-897-1707, info@calq.gouv.qc.ca
Ministère de la Culture, des Communications & de la Condition féminine, 225, Grande Allée est, Québec, G1R 5G5 QC
Fax: 418-380-2364, 888-380-8882, infos@mcccf.gouv.qc.ca
Fonds québécois de la recherche sur la société et la culture, #470, 140, Grande-Allée est, Québec, QC G1R 5M8
418-643-7582, Fax: 418-644-5248, fqrsc@fqrsc.gouv.qc.ca
Office des personnes handicapées du Québec, 309, rue Brock, Drummondville, QC J2B 1C5
819-475-8585, Fax: 819-475-8753, 800-567-1477, communications@ophq.gouv.qc.ca
Ministère de la Santé et des Services sociaux, Direction des communications et Renseignements généraux, 1075, ch Sainte-Foy, Québec, G1S 2M1 QC
418-266-8900, 800-707-3380, regisseur.web@msss.gouv.qc.ca
Secrétariat à la politique linguistique, 225 Grande-Allée est, 4e étage, Québec, G1R 5G5 QC
418-643-4248, Fax: 418-646-7832, info@spl.gouv.qc.ca
Société de développement des entreprises culturelles, #800, 215, rue Saint-Jacques, Montréal, H2Y 1M6 QC
514-841-2200, Fax: 514-841-8606, 800-363-0401, info@sodec.gouv.qc.ca

Saskatchewan
Saskatchewan First Nations & Métis Relations, #210, 1855 Victoria Ave., Regina, S4P 3T2 SK
306-787-6250, Fax: 306-787-5832

Saskatchewan Government Relations, 1855 Victoria Ave., Regina, S4P 3T2 SK
306-787-2635
Sask Heritage Foundation, 1919 Saskatchewan Dr., 9th Fl., Regina, SK S4P 3V7
306-787-4188, Fax: 306-787-0069
Saskatchewan Tourism, Parks, Culture, & Sport, 1919 Saskatchewan Dr., 4th Fl., Regina, S4P 4H2 SK
306-787-5729, Fax: 306-787-8560

Yukon Territory
Yukon Community Services, PO Box 2703, Whitehorse, Y1A 2C6 YT
867-667-5811, Fax: 867-393-6295, 800-661-0408, inquiry@gov.yk.ca
Yukon Health & Social Services, PO Box 2703, Whitehorse, Y1A 2C6 YT
867-667-3673, Fax: 867-667-3096, 800-661-0408, hss@gov.yk.ca

CENSORSHIP (MEDIA)

Manitoba
Manitoba Film Classification Board, #216, 301 Weston St., Winnipeg, MB R3E 3H4
204-945-8962, Fax: 204-945-0890, 866-612-2399, mfcb@gov.mb.ca

Nunavut
Department of Community & Government Services, J.G. Brown Bldg., PO Box 1000 700,Iqaluit, X0A 0H0 NU
867-975-5400, Fax: 867-975-5305

Ontario
Ontario Film Review Board, 1075 Millwood Rd., Toronto, ON M4G 1X6
416-314-3626, Fax: 416-314-3632

Quebec
Régie du cinéma, #100, 390, rue Notre-Dame ouest, Montréal, H2Y 1T9 QC
514-873-2371, Fax: 514-873-2142, 800-463-2463, regieducinema@rcq.gouv.qc.ca

CHEMICALS
Institute for Chemical Process & Environmental Technology, Bldg. M-12, 1200 Montreal Rd., Ottawa, K1A 0R6 ON
613-993-4041, Fax: 613-957-8231

CHILD WELFARE
See Also: Day Care Services

Northwest Territories
Department of Health & Social Services, Centre Square Tower, PO Box 1320, Yellowknife, X1A 2L9 NT
Fax: 867-873-0266

Nunavut
Department of Health & Social Services, Sivummut bldg., PO Box 1007 1000,Iqaluit, X0A 0H0 NU
867-975-5700, Fax: 867-975-5705, health@gov.nu.ca

CITIZENSHIP

Alberta
Libraries, Community & Voluntary Services, Standard Life Centre, 10405 Jasper Ave., 8th Fl., Edmonton, T5J 4R7 AB

CLIMATE & WEATHER
Atmospheric Science & Technology, 2121, rte Transcanadienne, Dorval, H9P 1J3 QC
514-421-4771, Fax: 514-421-2106
Canadian Hurricane Centre, 45 Alderney Dr., 16th Fl., Dartmouth, B2Y 2N6 NS
902-426-7231, Fax: 902-426-6348, 15th.reception@ec.gc.ca
Canadian Space Agency, 6767, rte de l'Aéroport, Longueuil, J3Y 8Y9 QC
450-926-4800, Fax: 450-926-4352, webmaster@space.gc.ca
Meteorological Service of Canada, 4905 Dufferin St., Toronto, M3H 5T4 ON
416-739-4770, Fax: 416-739-4232
Weather & Environmental Monitoring, 4905 Dufferin St., Toronto, M3H 5T4 ON
416-739-4965, Fax: 416-739-4261

Government Quick Reference Guide / Climate Change

CLIMATE CHANGE

Manitoba
Energy Climate Change & Green Strategy Initiatives Branch, #1202 - 155 Carlton St., Winnipeg, R3C 3H8 MB
204-945-7382, Fax: 204-948-3739, ccinfo@gov.mb.ca

Quebec
Ministère du Développement durable, de l'Environnement et des Parcs, Édifice Marie-Guyart, 675, boul René-Lévesque est, 29e étage, Québec, G1R 5V7 QC
418-521-3830, Fax: 418-646-5974, 800-561-1616, info@mddep.gouv.qc.ca

COAL
See Also: Energy

Alberta
Alberta Energy & Utilities Board, 640 - 5 Ave. SW, Calgary, AB T2P 3G4
403-297-8311, Fax: 403-297-7336
Alberta Energy Research Institute, AMEC Place, #2540, 801 - 6 Ave. SW, Calgary, AB T2P 3W2
403-297-8650, Fax: 403-297-3638, aeri@gov.ab.ca

New Brunswick
New Brunswick Power Group of Companies, 515 King St., PO Box 2000, Fredericton, E3B 4X1 NB
506-458-4444, Fax: 506-458-4000, questions@nbpower.com

Ontario
Ontario Power Generation, 700 University Ave., Toronto, M5G 1X6 ON
416-592-2555, 877-592-2555

Saskatchewan
Saskatchewan Power Corporation (SaskPower), 2025 Victoria Ave., Regina, S4P 0S1 SK
306-566-2121, Fax: 306-566-2330, 800-667-4749

COMMUNICATIONS
See: Telecommunications
Chief Informatics Office, 235 Queen St., Ottawa, ON K1A 0H5
613-954-3570, Fax: 613-941-1938
Communications Research Centre Canada, 3701 Carling Ave., PO Box 11490 H, Ottawa, ON K2H 8S2
613-991-3313, Fax: 613-998-5355, info@crc.ca
Global Operations & Chief Trade Commissioner, 125 Sussex Dr,, Ottawa, K1A 0G2 ON
613-944-2697, Fax: 613-996-1667
Institute for Information Technology, Bldg. M-50, 1200 Montreal Rd., Ottawa, K1A 0R6 ON
613-993-9101, Fax: 613-952-0074, 877-672-2672
Spectrum, Information Technologies & Telecommunications, Journal Tower North, 300 Slater St., 20th Fl., Ottawa, K1A 0C8 ON

Alberta
Alberta Public Affairs Bureau, Park Plaza, 10611 - 98 Ave., 6th Fl., Edmonton, T5K 2P7 AB
403-427-2754, Fax: 403-422-4168

Manitoba
Communications Services Manitoba, 155 Carlton St., 10th Fl., Winnipeg, R3C 3H8 MB
204-945-3765, Fax: 204-948-2147

New Brunswick
Business Development, Centennial Bldg., 670 King St., 5th Fl., PO Box 6000, Fredericton, E3B 5H1 NB
506-453-2111, Fax: 506-444-4182
Legislative Services, Centennial Bldg., #418, 670 King St., PO Box 6000, Fredericton, E3B 5H1 NB
506-453-2855, Fax: 506-457-7342

Ontario
Ontario Library Service - North, 334 Regent St., Sudbury, ON P3C 4E2
705-675-6467, Fax: 705-675-2285, 800-461-6348

Quebec
Ministère de la Culture, des Communications & de la Condition féminine, 225, Grande Allée est, Québec, G1R 5G5 QC
Fax: 418-380-2364, 888-380-8882, infos@mcccf.gouv.qc.ca

COMMUNITY & MUNICIPAL DEVELOPMENT
Atlantic Canada Opportunities Agency, Blue Cross Centre, 644 Main St., 3rd Fl., PO Box 6051, Moncton, E1C 9J8 NB
506-851-2271, Fax: 506-851-7403, 800-561-7862

Canada Economic Development for Québec Regions, Édifice Dominion Square, #900, 1255, rue Peel, Montréal, H3B 2T9 QC
514-283-6412, Fax: 514-283-3302, 866-385-6412
Western Economic Diversification Canada, Canada Place, #1500, 9700 Jasper Ave. NW, Edmonton, T5J 4H7 AB
780-495-4164, Fax: 780-495-4557, 888-338-9378

Alberta
Northern Alberta Development Council, Provincial Bldg., #206, 9621 - 96 Ave., PO Box 900-14, Peace River, T8S 1T4 AB
780-624-6274, Fax: 780-624-6184, nadc.council@gov.ab.ca
Alberta Tourism, Parks, Recreation & Culture, Communications Branch, Standard Life Centre, 10405 Jasper Ave., 7th Fl., Edmonton, T5J 4R7 AB
780-427-6530, Fax: 780-427-1496, Comdev.Communications@gov.ab.ca

British Columbia
Local Government Department, 800 Johnson St., 6th Fl., PO Box 9490 Prov Govt,Victoria, V8W 9N7 BC
lgd_feedback@gov.bc.ca

Manitoba
Manitoba Aboriginal & Northern Affairs, 59 Elizabeth Dr., PO Box 37, Thompson, R8N 1X4 MB
204-677-6607, Fax: 204-677-6753, amartin@gov.mb.ca
Community Land Use Planning Services, #604, 800 Portage Ave., Winnipeg, R3G 0N4 MB
Provincial-Municipal Support Services, #508, 800 Portage Ave., Winnipeg, R3G 0N4 MB

New Brunswick
Regional Development Corporation, RDC Bldg., 836 Churchill Row, PO Box 428, Fredericton, E3B 5R4 NB
506-453-2277, Fax: 506-453-7988

Newfoundland & Labrador
Department of Health & Community Services, West Block, Confederation Bldg., PO Box 8700, St. John's, A1B 4J6 NL
709-729-5021, Fax: 709-729-5824

Northwest Territories
Department of Municipal & Community Affairs, PO Box 1320, Yellowknife, X1A 2L9 NT
867-873-7118, Fax: 867-873-0309

Nova Scotia
Department of Service Nova Scotia & Municipal Relations, 1505 Barrington St., PO Box 216, Halifax, B3J 2M4 NS
902-424-4141, Fax: 902-424-0581, public-enquiries@gov.ns.ca

Nunavut
Department of Community & Government Services, J.G. Brown Bldg., PO Box 1000 700,Iqaluit, X0A 0H0 NU
867-975-5400, Fax: 867-975-5305

Ontario
Ministry of Municipal Affairs & Housing, 777 Bay St., 17th Fl., Toronto, M5G 2E5 ON
416-585-7041, Fax: 416-585-6227, 866-220-2290, mininfo.mah@ontario.ca

Prince Edward Island
Community & Labour Development, Shaw Bldg., 105 Rochford St., 5th Fl., PO Box 2000, Charlottetown, C1A 7N8 PE
902-368-4244, Fax: 902-368-4242

Quebec
Ministère des Affaires municipales et des Régions, Aile Chaveau, 10, rue Pierre-Olivier-Chauveau, 3e étage, Québec, G1R 4J3 QC
418-691-2019, Fax: 418-643-7385, communications@mamr.gouv.qc.ca
Ministère du Développement économique, de l'Innovation et de l'Exportation, 710, place D'Youville, 3e étage, Québec, G1R 4Y4 QC
418-691-5950, Fax: 418-644-0118, 866-680-1884

Saskatchewan
Saskatchewan Enterprise & Innovation, #200, 3085 Albert St., Regina, S4S 0B1 SK
Fax: 306-798-0629, 800-265-2001, RECDWebmaster@gov.sk.ca

COMMUNITY FINANCING
Atlantic Canada Opportunities Agency, Blue Cross Centre, 644 Main St., 3rd Fl., PO Box 6051, Moncton, E1C 9J8 NB
506-851-2271, Fax: 506-851-7403, 800-561-7862

Business Development Bank of Canada, #400, 5, Place Ville-Marie, Montréal, H3B 5E7 QC
514-283-5904, Fax: 514-283-2872, 877-232-2269
Canada Economic Development for Québec Regions, Édifice Dominion Square, #900, 1255, rue Peel, Montréal, H3B 2T9 QC
514-283-6412, Fax: 514-283-3302, 866-385-6412
Canada Investment & Savings, #900, 110 Yonge St., Toronto, ON M5C 1T4
416-952-1252, Fax: 416-952-1270, 800-575-5151, csb@csb.gc.ca
Finance Canada, L'esplanade Laurier, 140 O'Connor St., Ottawa, K1A 0G5 ON
613-992-1573, Fax: 613-996-2690, finpub@fin.gc.ca
Western Economic Diversification Canada, Canada Place, #1500, 9700 Jasper Ave. NW, Edmonton, T5J 4H7 AB
780-495-4164, Fax: 780-495-4557, 888-338-9378

Manitoba
Communities Economic Development Fund, #100, 23 Station Rd., Thompson, MB R8N 0N6
204-778-4138, Fax: 204-778-4313, 800-561-4315
Provincial-Municipal Support Services, #508, 800 Portage Ave., Winnipeg, R3G 0N4 MB

Nova Scotia
Nova Scotia Municipal Finance Corporation, Maritime Centre, 1505 Barrington St., 10th Fl. South, PO Box 850 M, Halifax, NS B3J 2V2
902-424-4590, Fax: 902-424-0525

Prince Edward Island
Community & Labour Development, Shaw Bldg., 105 Rochford St., 5th Fl., PO Box 2000, Charlottetown, C1A 7N8 PE
902-368-4244, Fax: 902-368-4242

Quebec
Ministère des Affaires municipales et des Régions, Aile Chaveau, 10, rue Pierre-Olivier-Chauveau, 3e étage, Québec, G1R 4J3 QC
418-691-2019, Fax: 418-643-7385, communications@mamr.gouv.qc.ca

Yukon Territory
Yukon Economic Development, PO Box 2703, Whitehorse, Y1A 2C6 YT
867-393-7191, Fax: 867-395-7199, 800-661-0408

COMMUNITY SERVICES

Alberta
Northern Alberta Development Council, Provincial Bldg., #206, 9621 - 96 Ave., PO Box 900-14, Peace River, T8S 1T4 AB
780-624-6274, Fax: 780-624-6184, nadc.council@gov.ab.ca
Alberta Tourism, Parks, Recreation & Culture, Communications Branch, Standard Life Centre, 10405 Jasper Ave., 7th Fl., Edmonton, T5J 4R7 AB
780-427-6530, Fax: 780-427-1496, Comdev.Communications@gov.ab.ca

British Columbia
Ministry of Community Development, 800 Johnson St., 6th Fl., PO Box 9490 Prov Govt,Victoria, V8W 9N7 BC
250-387-2283, Fax: 250-387-4312, Feedback@gov.bc.ca

Manitoba
Local Government Development Division, 59 Elizabeth Dr., PO Box 33, Thompson, R8N 1X4 MB
204-677-6794, Fax: 204-677-6525

Newfoundland & Labrador
Department of Health & Community Services, West Block, Confederation Bldg., PO Box 8700, St. John's, A1B 4J6 NL
709-729-5021, Fax: 709-729-5824

Northwest Territories
Department of Municipal & Community Affairs, PO Box 1320, Yellowknife, X1A 2L9 NT
867-873-7118, Fax: 867-873-0309

Nunavut
Department of Community & Government Services, J.G. Brown Bldg., PO Box 1000 700,Iqaluit, X0A 0H0 NU
867-975-5400, Fax: 867-975-5305

Prince Edward Island
Department of Communities, Cultural Affairs & Labour, Shaw Bldg., 95 Rochford St., 4th Fl., PO Box 2000, Charlottetown, C1A 7N8 PE
902-368-5250, Fax: 902-368-4121

Yukon Territory
Yukon Community Services, PO Box 2703, Whitehorse, Y1A 2C6 YT
  867-667-5811, Fax: 867-393-6295, 800-661-0408, inquiry@gov.yk.ca

CONSERVATION & ECOLOGY
See Also: Heritage Resources; Natural Resources

Arctic Goose, c/o Prairie & Northern Region, CWS, #200, 4999 - 98 Ave., Edmonton, T6B 2X3 AB
  780-951-8652, Fax: 780-495-2615, deanna.dixon@ec.gc.ca
Black Duck, c/o Ontario Region, CWS, 49 Camelot Dr., Nepean, K1A 0H3 ON
  613-952-2408, Fax: 613-952-9027
Canadian Heritage, 15 Eddy St., Gatineau, K1A 0M5 QC
  819-997-0055, 866-811-0055
Canadian Museum of Nature, PO Box 3343 D, Ottawa, K1P 6P4 ON
  613-566-4700, Fax: 613-364-4021
Canadian Polar Commission, Constitution Square, #1710, 360 Albert St., Ottawa, K1R 7X7 ON
  613-943-8605, Fax: 613-943-8607, 888-765-2701, mail@polarcom.gc.ca
Eastern Habitat, c/o Environment Canada, PO Box 1590, Sackville, E0A 3C0 NB
  506-364-5036, Fax: 506-364-5062
Environment Canada, 10 Wellington St., Gatineau, K1A 0H3 QC
  819-997-2800, Fax: 819-994-1412, 800-668-6767, enviroinfo@ec.gc.ca
Commission for Environmental Cooperation, Secretariat, #200, 393, rue St-Jacques ouest, Montréal, H2Y 1N9 QC
  514-350-4300, Fax: 514-350-4314, info@cec.org
Environmental Management, 2975 Jutland Rd., 3rd Fl., Victoria, V8T 5J9 BC
  250-387-9971, Fax: 250-387-8897
Fisheries Resource Conservation Council, PO Box 2001 D, Ottawa, ON K1P 5W3
  613-998-0433, Fax: 613-998-1146, info@frcc-ccrh.ca
Natural Resources Canada, 580 Booth St., Ottawa, K1A 0E4 ON
  613-995-0947, Fax: 613-992-7211
North American Bird Conservation Initiative, Canadian Wildlife Service, 351, boul St-Joseph, 3e étage, Gatineau, QC K1A 0H3
  819-994-0512, Fax: 819-994-4445, s.neve@ec.gc.ca
North American Waterfowl Management Plan, c/o Canadian Wildlife Service, Place Vincent-Massey, 351 St-Joseph Blvd., 16th Fl., Gatineau, ON K1A 0H3
  819-934-6034, Fax: 819-934-6017, nabci@ec.gc.ca
Pacific Coast, c/o Pacific & Yukon Region, CWS, #201, 401 Burrard St., Vancouver, V6C 3S5 BC
  604-666-2342, Fax: 604-664-4068
Parks Canada, 25 Eddy St., Gatineau, K1A 0M5 QC
  888-773-8888, information@pc.gc.ca
Prairie Habitat, c/o Prairie & Northern Region, CWS, #200, 4999 - 98 Ave., Edmonton, T6B 2X3 AB
  780-951-8652, Fax: 780-495-2615,

Alberta
Alberta Environmental Appeal Board, Peace Hills Trust Tower, #306, 10011 - 109 St. NW, Edmonton, AB T5J 3S8
  780-427-6207, Fax: 780-427-4693
Alberta Special Areas Board, 212 - 2nd Ave. West, PO Box 820, Hanna, AB T0J 1P0
  403-854-5600, Fax: 403-854-5527, specarea@telusplanet.net
Alberta Used Oil Management Association, Scotia One, Scotia Place, #1050, 10060 Jasper Ave., Edmonton, AB T5J 3R8
  780-414-1510, Fax: 780-414-1519, reception@usedoilrecycling.ca
Beverage Container Management Board, #1010, 10707 - 100 Ave., Edmonton, AB T5J 3M1
  780-424-3193, Fax: 780-428-4620, 888-424-7671, info@bcmb.ab.ca
Clean Air Strategic Alliance, Centre West Bldg, 10035 - 108 St., 10th Fl., Edmonton, AB T5J 3E1
  780-427-9793, Fax: 780-422-3127, casa@casahome.org
Alberta Environment, South Tower, Petroleum Plaza, 9915 - 108 St., Main Fl., Edmonton, T5K 2G8 AB
  780-427-2700, Fax: 780-422-4086,-310-0000, env.infocent@gov.ab.ca
Natural Resources Conservation Board, Sterling Place, 9940 - 106 St., 4th Fl., Edmonton, AB T5K 2N2
  780-422-1977, Fax: 780-427-0607, 866-383-6722

British Columbia
British Columbia Assessment Authority, 1537 Hillside Ave., Victoria, BC V8T 4Y2
  250-595-6211, Fax: 250-595-6222, info@bcassessment.ca
Ministry of Environment, PO Box 9339 Prov Govt, Victoria, V8W 9M1 BC
  250-387-1161, Fax: 250-387-5669, www.envmail@gov.bc.ca
Environmental Appeal Board, 747 Fort St., 4th Fl., PO Box 9425 Prov Govt, Victoria, BC V8W 9V1
  250-387-3464, Fax: 250-356-9923, eabinfo@gov.bc.ca
Environmental Stewardship Division, 2975 Jutland Rd., 5th Fl., PO Box 9339 Prov Govt, Victoria, V8T 5J9 BC
  250-356-0121, Fax: 250-953-3414
Forest Practices Board, 1675 Douglas St., 3rd Fl., PO Box 9905 Prov Govt, Victoria, BC V8W 9R1
  250-387-7964, Fax: 250-387-7009, 800-994-5899, fpboard@gov.bc.ca
Fraser Basin Council, Central Office, 470 Granville St., 1st Fl., Vancouver, BC V6C 1V5
  604-488-5350, Fax: 604-488-5351, info@fraserbasin.bc.ca
Mediation & Arbitration Board, #310, 9900 - 100 Ave., Fort St John, BC V1J 5S7
  250-787-3403, Fax: 250-787-3228, mab.office@gov.bc.ca
Northern Interior, 1011 - 4 Ave., 5th Fl., Prince George, V2L 3H9 BC
  250-565-6100, Fax: 250-565-6671, www.for.gov.bc.ca/rni

Manitoba
Clean Environment Commission, #305, 155 Carlton St., Winnipeg, MB R3C 3H8
  204-945-0594, Fax: 204-945-0090
Manitoba Conservation, 200 Saulteaux Cres., Winnipeg, R3J 3W3 MB
  204-945-6784, 800-214-6497, mincon@leg.gov.mb.ca
Ecological Reserves Advisory Committee, c/o Manitoba Conservation, Parks & Natural Areas Branch, 200 Saulteaux Cres., Winnipeg, MB R3J 3W3
  204-945-4148, Fax: 204-945-0012, hhernandez@gov.mb.ca
Manitoba Conservation Districts Commission, Secretariat c/o Planning & Coordination Branch, 123 Main St., PO Box 20000, Neepawa, MB R0J 1H0
  204-476-7033, Fax: 204-476-7539, whildebran@gov.mb.ca

New Brunswick
Assessment & Planning Appeal Board, #201, 435 King St., PO Box 6000, Fredericton, NB E3B 5H1
  506-453-2126, Fax: 506-444-4881
Department of the Environment, Marysville Place, 20 McGloin St., PO Box 6000, Fredericton, E3B 5H1 NB
  506-453-2690, Fax: 506-457-4991

Newfoundland & Labrador
Department of Environment & Conservation, Confederation Bldg., West Block, 4th Fl., PO Box 8700, St. John's, A1B 4J6 NL
  709-729-2664, Fax: 709-729-6639, 800-563-6181, info@gov.nl.ca

Northwest Territories
Department of Environment & Natural Resources, PO Box 1320, Yellowknife, X1A 2L9 NT

Nova Scotia
Environmental & Natural Areas Management, PO Box 697, Halifax, B3J 3T8 NS
  902-424-3571
Department of Natural Resources, Founder's Square, 1701 Hollis St., 3rd Fl., PO Box 698, Halifax, B3J 2T9 NS
  902-424-5935, Fax: 902-424-0594, 800-565-2224

Ontario
Ministry of Environment, 135 St. Clair Ave. West, Toronto, M4V 1P5 ON
  416-325-4000, Fax: 416-325-3159, 800-565-4923
Ministry of Natural Resources, Whitney Block, #6630, 99 Wellesley St. West, 6th Fl., Toronto, M7A 1W3 ON
  800-667-1940
Niagara Escarpment Commission, 232 Guelph St., Georgetown, L7G 4B1 ON
  905-877-5191, Fax: 905-873-7452

Prince Edward Island
Department of Environment, Energy & Forestry, Jones Bldg., 11 Kent St., 4th & 5th Fl., PO Box 2000, Charlottetown, C1A 7N8 PE
  902-368-5000, Fax: 902-368-5830
Environmental Advisory Council, 11 Kent St., PO Box 2000, Charlottetown, PE C1A 7N8

Department of Tourism, PO Box 2000, Charlottetown, C1A 7N8 PE
  800-463-4734

Quebec
Comité consultatif de l'environnement Kativik, CP 930, Kuujjuaq, QC J0M 1C0
  819-964-2961, Fax: 819-964-0694, ndea@krg.ca
Ministère du Développement durable, de l'Environnement et des Parcs, Édifice Marie-Guyart, 675, boul René-Lévesque est, 29e étage, Québec, G1R 5V7 QC
  418-521-3830, Fax: 418-646-5974, 800-561-1616, info@mddep.gouv.qc.ca
Fondation de la faune du Québec, Place Iberville II, #420, 1175, av Lavigerie, Québec, QC G1V 4P1
  418-644-7926, Fax: 418-643-7655, 877-639-0742, ffq@riq.qc.ca
Société de développement de la Baie James, 110, boul Matagami, CP 970, Matagami, QC J0Y 2A0
  819-739-4717, Fax: 819-739-4329
Société québécoise de récupération et de recyclage, Siège social, #200, 420, boul Charest est, Québec, QC G1K 8M4
  418-643-0394, Fax: 418-643-6507, 866-523-8290, info@recyc-quebec.gouv.qc.ca

Saskatchewan
Saskatchewan Assessment Management Agency, #200, 2201 - 11 Ave., Regina, S4P 0J8 SK
  306-924-8000, Fax: 306-924-8070, 800-667-7262, info.request@sama.sk.ca
Saskatchewan Environment, 3211 Albert St., 2nd Fl., Regina, S4S 5W6 SK
  306-953-3750, Fax: 306-787-9544, 800-567-4224, inquiry@serm.gov.sk.ca
Saskatchewan Conservation Data Centre, 3211 Albert St., Regina, SK S4S 5W6
  306-787-9038, Fax: 306-787-9544
Saskatchewan Watershed Authority, 111 Fairford St. East, Moose Jaw, SK S6H 7X9
  306-694-3900, Fax: 306-694-3465, comm@swa.ca

Yukon Territory
Alsek Renewable Resource Council, PO Box 2077, Haines Junction, YT Y0B 1L0
  867-634-2524, Fax: 867-634-2527
Carmacks Renewable Resource Council, PO Box 122, Carmacks, YT Y0B 1C0
  867-863-6838, Fax: 867-863-6429, carmacksrrc@lscfn.ca
Dawson District Renewable Resource Council, PO Box 1380, Dawson City, YT Y0B 1G0
  867-993-6976, Fax: 867-993-6093, dawsonrrc@yknet.yk.ca
Yukon Environment, PO Box 2703, Whitehorse, Y1A 2C6 YT
  867-667-5652, Fax: 867-393-6213, 800-661-0408, environmentyukon@gov.yk.ca
Mayo District Renewable Resources Council, PO Box 249, Mayo, YT Y0B 1M0
  867-996-2942, Fax: 867-996-2948, mayorrc@yknet.yk.ca
North Yukon Renewable Resources Council, PO Box 80, Old Crow, YT Y0B 1N0
  vgrrc@yknet.yk.ca
Selkirk Renewable Resources Council, PO Box 32, Pelly Crossing, YT Y0B 1P0
  867-537-3937, Fax: 867-537-3939, selkirkrre@yknet.yk.ca
Teslin Renewable Resource Council, PO Box 186, Teslin, YT Y0A 1B0
  867-390-2323, Fax: 867-390-2919, teslinrrc@yknet.yk.ca
Yukon Land Use Planning Council, #201, 307 Jarvis St., Whitehorse, YT Y1A 2H3
  867-667-7397, Fax: 867-667-4624, ylupc@planyukon.ca

CONSTRUCTION
Canada Mortgage & Housing Corporation, 700 Montreal Rd., Ottawa, K1A 0P7 ON
  613-748-2000, Fax: 613-748-2098, 800-668-2642, chic@cmhc-schl.gc.ca
Defence Construction Canada, Constitution Square, 350 Albert St., 19th Fl., Ottawa, K1A 0K3 ON
  613-998-9548, Fax: 613-998-1061, 800-514-3555, info@dcc-cdc.gc.ca
Infrastructure Canada, 90 Sparks St., 6th Fl., Ottawa, K1P 5B4 ON
  613-948-1148, Fax: 613-946-9888, 800-622-6232, info@infc.gc.ca
Institute for Research in Construction, Bldg. M-24, 1500 Montreal Rd., Ottawa, K1A 0R6 ON
  613-993-6189, Fax: 613-952-0268, ccmc@nrc-cnrc.gc.ca

Government Quick Reference Guide / Consumer Protection

Alberta
Alberta Infrastructure & Transportation, Twin Atria Bldg., 4999 - 98 Ave., Edmonton, T6B 2X3 AB
780-427-2731, Fax: 780-466-3166,-310-0000

Manitoba
Construction & Maintenance Branch, #1610, 215 Garry St., Winnipeg, R3C 3Z1 MB
Fax: 204-945-3841

Newfoundland & Labrador
Department of Transportation & Works, Confederation Bldg., West Block, 6th Fl., PO Box 8700, St. John's, A1B 4J6 NL
709-729-3679, Fax: 709-729-4285, twminister@gov.nl.ca

Nova Scotia
Labour Relations Board & Construction Industry Panel, 5151 Terminal Rd.,7th Fl., PO Box 697, Halifax, NS B3J 2T8
902-424-6730, Fax: 902-424-1744

Nunavut
Department of Community & Government Services, J.G. Brown Bldg., PO Box 1000 700,Iqaluit, X0A 0H0 NU
867-975-5400, Fax: 867-975-5305

Ontario
Building Code Commission, 777 Bay St., 2nd Fl., Toronto, ON M5G 2E5
416-585-6503, Fax: 416-585-7531
Building Materials Evaluation Commission, 777 Bay St., 2nd Fl., Toronto, ON M5G 2E5
416-585-4234, Fax: 416-585-7531

Quebec
Commissaire de l'industrie de la construction, 150, boul René-Lévesque est, 18e étage,, Québec, QC G1R 5B1
418-646-7200, Fax: 418-644-9977
Commission de la construction du Québec, 3530, rue Jean-Talon ouest, Montréal, QC H3R 2G3
514-341-7740, Fax: 514-341-6354, 888-842-8222
Régie du bâtiment du Québec, 545, boul Crémazie est, 4e étage, Montréal, QC H2M 2V2
514-873-0976, Fax: 514-864-2903, 800-361-0761, crc@rbq.gouv.qc.ca

CONSUMER PROTECTION
See Also: Public Safety

Nova Scotia
Department of Service Nova Scotia & Municipal Relations, 1505 Barrington St., PO Box 216, Halifax, B3J 2M4 NS
902-424-4141, Fax: 902-424-0581, public-enquiries@gov.ns.ca

Nunavut
Department of Community & Government Services, J.G. Brown Bldg., PO Box 1000 700,Iqaluit, X0A 0H0 NU
867-975-5400, Fax: 867-975-5305

CORONERS

British Columbia
Coroners Service of British Columbia, Metrotower II, #800, 4720 Kingsway, Burnaby, BC V5H 4N2
604-660-7745, Fax: 604-660-7766, BC.CorSer@gov.bc.ca

Quebec
Bureau du coroner, #390, 2875, boul Laurier, Sainte-Foy, QC G1V 5B1
418-643-1845, Fax: 418-643-6174, clientele.coroner@msp.gouv.qc.ca

CORRECTIONAL SERVICES

British Columbia
Corrections Branch, 1001 Douglas St., 7th Fl., PO Box 9278 Prov Govt,Victoria, V8W 9J7 BC
250-387-5059, Fax: 250-307-5698

Saskatchewan
Saskatchewan Corrections, Public Safety & Policing, 1874 Scarth St., Regina, S4P 4B3 SK
306-787-7872, Fax: 306-787-8747

CULTURE & HERITAGE
See: Arts & Culture
Canadian Heritage, 15 Eddy St., Gatineau, K1A 0M5 QC
819-997-0055, 866-811-0055
Culture & Heritage, PO Box 310, Igloolik, X0A 0L0 NU
867-975-2046, Fax: 867-934-2047, cleypermits@gov.nu.ca

Historic Sites & Monuments Board of Canada, Terrasses de la Chaudière, 25 Eddy St., Gatineau, QC K1A 0M5
819-997-4059, Fax: 819-934-1115, hsmbc-clmhc@pc.gc.ca
Indian & Northern Affairs Canada, 10 Wellington St., North Tower, Gatineau, K1A 0H4 QC
819-997-0380, Fax: 819-953-3017, 866-817-3977, infopubs@ainc-inac.gc.ca
Saskatchewan Lotteries Trust for Sport, Culture & Recreation, 1870 Lorne St., Regina, S4P 2L7 SK
306-780-9300, sasksport@sasksport.sk.ca

Alberta
Alberta Sport, Recreation, Parks & Wildlife Foundation, Standard Life Centre, 10405 Jasper Ave., 9th Fl., Edmonton, AB T5J 4R7
780-415-1167, Fax: 780-415-0308
Alberta International & Intergovernmental Relations, Commerce Place, 10155 - 102 St., 12th Fl., Edmonton, T5J 4G8 AB
780-422-1510, Fax: 780-427-0699

British Columbia
Ministry of Community Development, 800 Johnson St., 6th Fl., PO Box 9490 Prov Govt,Victoria, V8W 9N7 BC
250-387-2283, Fax: 250-387-4312, Feedback@gov.bc.ca

Manitoba
Manitoba Culture, Heritage, Tourism & Sport, Legislative Building, #118, 450 Broadway Ave., Winnipeg, R3C 0V8 MB
204-945-3729, Fax: 204-945-5223, mincht@leg.gov.mb.ca
Manitoba Heritage Council, 213 Notre Dame Ave., Main Fl., Winnipeg, MB R3B 1N3
204-945-2118, Fax: 204-948-2384, hrb@gov.mb.ca

New Brunswick
Department of Wellness, Culture & Sport, Place 2000, 250 King St., 4th Fl., PO Box 6000, Fredericton, E3B 5H1 NB
506-453-2909, Fax: 506-453-6548

Newfoundland & Labrador
Department of Tourism, Culture & Recreation, Confederation Bldg., West Block, 2nd Fl., PO Box 8700, St. John's, A1B 4J6 NL
709-729-0862, Fax: 709-729-0870, tcrinfo@gov.nl.ca

Northwest Territories
Department of Aboriginal Affairs & Intergovernmental Relations, 4910 - 52nd St., PO Box 1320, Yellowknife, X1A 2L9 NT
867-873-7143, Fax: 867-873-0233, 877-838-8194, nancy_gardiner@gov.nt.ca
Department of Education, Culture & Employment, PO Box 1320, Yellowknife, X1A 2L9 NT
867-669-2399, Fax: 867-873-0431, 866-606-5627

Nova Scotia
Culture Division, #601, 1800 Argyle St., PO Box 456, Halifax, B3J 2R5 NS
Fax: 902-424-0710

Ontario
Ontario Trillium Foundation, 45 Charles St. East, 5th Fl., Toronto, ON M4Y 1S2
416-963-4927, Fax: 416-963-8781, 800-263-2887, trillium@trilliumfoundation.org

Saskatchewan
Saskatchewan First Nations & Métis Relations, #210, 1855 Victoria Ave., Regina, S4P 3T2 SK
306-787-6250, Fax: 306-787-5832
Saskatchewan Government Relations, 1855 Victoria Ave., Regina, S4P 3T2 SK
306-787-2635

CUSTOMS
Canada Border Services Agency, Ottawa, K1A 0L8 ON
613-952-3200, CBSA-ASFC@canada.gc.ca

DAIRY INDUSTRY

Manitoba
Manitoba Milk Prices Review Commission, c/o Boards, Commissions & Legislation Branch, #812, 401 York Ave., Winnipeg, MB R3C 0P2
204-945-3854, Fax: 204-948-2844, randy.ozunko@gov.mb.ca

Prince Edward Island
Department of Agriculture, Jones Bldg., 11 Kent St., PO Box 2000, Charlottetown, C1A 7N8 PE
902-368-4880, Fax: 902-368-4857

DANGEROUS GOODS & HAZARDOUS MATERIALS
See Also: Occupational Safety; Waste Management

Manitoba
Environmental Approvals Branch, #160, 123 Main St., Winnipeg, R3C 1A5 MB
204-945-8321, Fax: 204-945-5229
Environmental Management, 2975 Jutland Rd., 3rd Fl., Victoria, V8T 5J9 BC
250-387-9971, Fax: 250-387-8897
Hazardous Materials Information Review Commission, 427 Laurier Ave. West, 7th Fl., Ottawa, ON K1A 1M3
613-993-4331, Fax: 613-993-4686, hmirc-ccrmd@hc-sc.gc.ca

British Columbia
Ministry of Transportation & Infrastructure, 940 Blanshard St., PO Box 9850 Prov Govt,Victoria, V8W 9T5 BC
250-387-3198, Fax: 250-356-7706, tran.webmaster@gov.bc.ca

Northwest Territories
Department of Transportation, Lahm Ridge Bldg., 4501 50 Ave., PO Box 1320, Yellowknife, X1A 2L9 NT
867-920-3460, Fax: 867-873-0363

Nova Scotia
Department of Transportation & Infrastructure Renewal, Johnston Bldg., 1672 Granville St., 2nd Fl., PO Box 186, Halifax, B3J 2N2 NS
902-424-2297, Fax: 902-424-0171, 888-432-3233, tpwpaff@gov.ns.ca

Ontario
Ministry of Transportation, Ferguson Block, 77 Wellesley St. West, 3rd Fl., Toronto, M7A 1Z8 ON
416-235-4686, Fax: 416-327-9185, 800-268-4686

Prince Edward Island
Department of Transportation & Public Works, Jones Bldg., 11 Kent St., PO Box 2000, Charlottetown, C1A 7N8 PE
902-368-5100, Fax: 902-368-5395

Quebec
Ministère du Développement durable, de l'Environnement et des Parcs, Édifice Marie-Guyart, 675, boul René-Lévesque est, 29e étage, Québec, G1R 5V7 QC
418-521-3830, Fax: 418-646-5974, 800-561-1616, info@mddep.gouv.qc.ca

Saskatchewan
Saskatchewan Highways & Infrastructure, 1855 Victoria Ave., Regina, S4P 3T2 SK
306-787-4800

Yukon Territory
Yukon Highways & Public Works, PO Box 2703, Whitehorse, Y1A 2C6 YT
867-393-7193, Fax: 867-393-6218, 800-661-0408, hpw-info@gov.yk.ca

DEBT MANAGEMENT
Finance Canada, L'esplanade Laurier, 140 O'Connor St., Ottawa, K1A 0G5 ON
613-992-1573, Fax: 613-996-2690, finpub@fin.gc.ca

DEFENCE
See Also: Emergency Response; Public Safety
Defence Construction Canada, Constitution Square, 350 Albert St., 19th Fl., Ottawa, K1A 0K3 ON
613-998-9548, Fax: 613-998-1061, 800-514-3555, info@dcc-cdc.gc.ca
Military Police Complaints Commission, 270 Albert St., 10th Fl., Ottawa, ON K1P 5G8
613-947-5625, Fax: 613-947-5713, 800-632-0566, commission@mpcc-cppm.gc.ca
National Defence Canada, Major-General George R. Pearkes Bldg., 101 Colonel By Dr., Ottawa, K1A 0K2 ON
613-995-2534, Fax: 613-992-4739, 800-856-8488

DISABLED PERSONS SERVICES
Transportation Development Centre, Tour Ouest, Complexe Guy-Favreau, 800, boul René-Lévesque ouest, 6e étage, Montréal, H3B 1X9 QC
514-283-0000, Fax: 514-283-7158, tdccdt@tc.gc.ca

Nunavut
Department of Culture, Language, Elders & Youth, PO Box 1000 800,Iqaluit, X0A 0H0 NU
867-975-5500, Fax: 867-975-5504, 866-934-2035

Quebec
Office des personnes handicapées du Québec, 309, rue Brock, Drummondville, QC J2B 1C5
819-475-8585, Fax: 819-475-8753, 800-567-1477, communications@ophq.gouv.qc.ca

DISCRIMINATION & EMPLOYMENT EQUITY

Alberta
Labour Relations Board, #503, 10808 - 99 Ave., Edmonton, AB T5K 0G5
780-427-5926, Fax: 780-422-0970, 800-463-2572, alrbinfo@lab.gov.ab.ca

Quebec
Commission de l'équité salariale, 200, ch Ste-Foy, 4e étage, Québec, QC G1R 6A1
418-528-8765, Fax: 418-528-6999, 888-528-8765, equite.salariale@ces.gouv.qc.ca

DRIVERS' LICENCES

Alberta
Technology Services, John E. Brownlee Bldg., 10365 - 97 St., 8th Fl., Edmonton, T5J 3W7 AB
780-422-8545

British Columbia
Ministry of Transportation & Infrastructure, 940 Blanshard St., PO Box 9850 Prov Govt,Victoria, V8W 9T5 BC
250-387-3198, Fax: 250-356-7706, tran.webmaster@gov.bc.ca

Manitoba
Manitoba Infrastructure & Transportation, Legislative Building, #203, 450 Broadway Ave., Winnipeg, R3C 0V8 MB
204-945-3723, Fax: 204-945-7610

Northwest Territories
Road Licensing & Safety, 4510 - 50 Ave., 1st fl., PO Box 1320, Yellowknife, X1A 2L9 NT
867-873-7972, Fax: 867-873-0120

Ontario
Licence Appeal Tribunal (LAT), 1 St. Clair Ave. West, 12th Fl., Toronto, ON M4V 1K6
416-314-4260, Fax: 416-314-4270, 800-255-2214
Ministry of Transportation, Ferguson Block, 77 Wellesley St. West, 3rd Fl., Toronto, M7A 1Z8 ON
416-235-4686, Fax: 416-327-9185, 800-268-4686

Prince Edward Island
Department of Transportation & Public Works, Jones Bldg., 11 Kent St., PO Box 2000, Charlottetown, C1A 7N8 PE
902-368-5100, Fax: 902-368-5395

Quebec
Société de l'assurance automobile du Québec, 333, boul Jean-Lesage, CP 19600 Terminus, Québec, QC G1K 8J6
418-643-7620, Fax: 418-644-0339, 800-361-7620, courrier@saaq.gouv.qc.ca

Yukon Territory
Driver Control Board, 308 Steele St., PO Box 2703, Whitehorse, YT Y1A 2C6
867-667-3774, Fax: 867-393-6483, dcb@gov.yk.ca

DRUGS & ALCOHOL
See Also: Liquor Control

Alberta
Alberta Alcohol & Drug Abuse Commission, Associated Engineering Plaza, 10909 Jasper Ave., 6th Fl., Edmonton, AB T5J 3M9
780-415-0370, Fax: 780-423-1419

British Columbia
Ministry of Health Services, 1515 Blanshard St., Victoria, V8W 3C8 BC
250-952-1742, Fax: 250-356-9587, 800-465-4911, hlth.health@gems1.gov.bc.ca

Quebec
Centre québécois de lutte aux dépendances, 105, rue Normand, Montréal, QC H2Y 2K6
514-389-6336, Fax: 514-389-1830, info@cqld.ca
Ministère de la Santé et des Services sociaux, Direction des communications et Renseignements généraux, 1075, ch Sainte-Foy, Québec, G1S 2M1 QC
418-266-8900, 800-707-3380, regisseur.web@msss.gouv.qc.ca

EDUCATION
Canadian Council of Directors of Apprenticeship, Red Seal Secretariat, Place du Portage, Phase IV, 5th F, Gatineau, QC K1A 0J9
819-953-7442, Fax: 819-994-0202
Canadian Forces College, Toronto,ON
416-482-6800
Royal Military College, Kingston,ON
613-541-6000

Alberta
Alberta Advanced Education & Technology, Legislature Bldg., #324, 10800 - 97 Ave., Edmonton, T5K 2B6 AB
780-422-5400, Fax: 780-422-0821,-310-0000, aet.info@gov.ab.ca
Alberta Apprenticeship & Industry Training Board, 10155 - 102 St., 10th Fl., Edmonton, AB T5J 4L5
780-427-8765, Fax: 780-422-7376
Alberta Council on Admissions & Transfer, 10155 - 102 St., 11th Fl., Edmonton, AB T5J 4L5
780-422-9021, Fax: 780-427-0423, acat@gov.ab.ca
Alberta Learning Information Service, South Tower, Capital Health Centre, 10030 - 107 St., 12th Fl., Edmonton, AB T5J 3E4
780-427-3722,-310-0000, info@alis.gov.ab.ca
Apprenticeship & Industry Training Division, Phipps-McKinnon Bldg., 5th Fl., 10020 - 101A Ave., Edmonton, T5J 3G2 AB
780-427-8517
Campus Alberta Quality Council, Commerce Place, 10155 - 102 St., 11th Fl., Edmonton, AB T5J 4L5
780-427-8921, Fax: 780-427-0423, caqc@gov.ab.ca
Private Vocational Schools Advisory Council, Commerce Place, 10155 - 102 St., 10th Fl., Edmonton, AB T5J 4L5
780-427-5609, Fax: 780-427-5920

British Columbia
Premier's Technology Council, #730, 999 Canada Pl., Vancouver, BC V6C 3E1
604-775-2122, Fax: 604-775-2129, premiers.technologycouncil@gov.bc.ca

Manitoba
Manitoba Education, Research & Learning Information Networks, #100 - 135 Innovation Dr., University of Manitoba, Winnipeg, MB R3T 6A8
204-474-7800, Fax: 204-474-7830, 800-430-6404

New Brunswick
Apprenticeship & Occupational Certification Board, PO Box 6000, Fredericton, NB E3B 5H1
506-453-2260, Fax: 506-453-5317
Department of Post-Secondary Education, Training & Labour, 470 York St., PO Box 6000, Fredericton, E3B 5H1 NB
506-453-2597, Fax: 506-453-3618, dpetlinfo@gnb.ca

Northwest Territories
Aurora Research Institute, 191 MacKenzie Rd., PO Box 1450, Inuvik, X0E 0T0 NT
867-777-3298, Fax: 867-777-4264, webmaster@nwtresearch.com
Department of Education, Culture & Employment, PO Box 1320, Yellowknife, X1A 2L9 NT
867-669-2399, Fax: 867-873-0431, 866-606-5627

Nova Scotia
Council of Ministers of Education & Training, PO Box 2044, Halifax, NS B3J 2Z1
902-424-5352, Fax: 902-424-8976, camet_camef@cap-cpma.ca

Ontario
Academic & Experience Requirements Committee of the Association of Ontario Land Surveyors, 1043 McNicoll Ave., Toronto, ON M1W 3W6
416-491-9020, Fax: 416-491-2576, 800-268-0718, admin@aols.org
College of Veterinarians of Ontario, 2106 Gordon St., Guelph, ON N1L 1G6
519-824-5600, Fax: 519-824-6497, 800-424-2856

Saskatchewan
Saskatchewan Research Council, #125, 15 Innovation Blvd., Saskatoon, S7N 2X8 SK
306-933-5400, Fax: 306-933-7446, info@src.sk.ca

EDUCATION & TRAINING
Human Resources & Skills Development Canada, 140 Promenade du Portage, Ottawa, K1A 0J9 ON

Department of Labour & Workforce Development, 5151 Terminal Rd., 6th Fl., PO Box 697, Halifax, B3J 2T8 NS
902-424-5301, Fax: 902-424-0575

Alberta
Alberta Employment, Immigration & Industry, Minister's Office, Legislature Bldg., #208, 10800 - 97 Ave., Edmonton, T5K 2B6 AB
780-415-4800, Fax: 780-422-9556, 866-644-5135, eii.communications@gov.ab.ca

British Columbia
Ministry of Labour & Citizens' Services, PO Box 9052 Prov Govt,Victoria, V8W 9E2 BC
250-356-6348, Fax: 250-356-6595, LCS.Minister@gov.bc.ca

New Brunswick
Department of Post-Secondary Education, Training & Labour, 470 York St., PO Box 6000, Fredericton, E3B 5H1 NB
506-453-2597, Fax: 506-453-3618, dpetlinfo@gnb.ca

Northwest Territories
Department of Education, Culture & Employment, PO Box 1320, Yellowknife, X1A 2L9 NT
867-669-2399, Fax: 867-873-0431, 866-606-5627

Ontario
Ministry of Labour, 400 University Ave., 14th Fl., Toronto, M7A 1T7 ON
416-326-7770, 800-268-8013

EMERGENCY MEASURES
Environment Canada, 10 Wellington St., Gatineau, K1A 0H3 QC
819-997-2800, Fax: 819-994-1412, 800-668-6767, enviroinfo@ec.gc.ca
National Search & Rescue Secretariat, 275 Slater St., 4th Fl., Ottawa, K1A 0K2 ON
613-992-0054, Fax: 613-996-3746, 800-727-9414, inquiry@nss.gc.ca
Public Safety Canada, 269 Laurier Ave. West, Ottawa, K1A 0P8 ON
613-991-3301, Fax: 613-954-5186, 866-222-3006, communications@ps.gc.ca
Spills Action Centre, 5775 Yonge St., 5th Fl., Toronto, M2M 4J1 ON
416-325-3000, Fax: 416-325-3011, 800-268-6060

Alberta
Emergency Management Alberta, 14515 - 122 Ave., Edmonton, T5L 2W4 AB
Fax: 780-422-1549
Alberta Environment, South Tower, Petroleum Plaza, 9915 - 108 St., Main Fl., Edmonton, T5K 2G8 AB
780-427-2700, Fax: 780-422-4086,-310-0000, env.infocent@gov.ab.ca

British Columbia
British Columbia Provincial Emergency Program, PO Box 9201 Prov Govt,Victoria, V8W 9J1 BC
250-952-4913, Fax: 250-952-4888, 888-257-4777

Manitoba
Emergency Measures Organization, 405 Broadway Ave., 15th Floor, Winnipeg, R3C 3L6 MB
204-945-4772, Fax: 204-945-4929, 888-267-8298, emo@gov.mb.ca

New Brunswick
New Brunswick Emergency Measures Organization, Victoria Health Centre, 65 Brunswick Ave., Fredericton, NB E3B 1G5
506-453-2133, Fax: 506-453-5513, 800-561-4034, emo@gnb.ca

Newfoundland & Labrador
Newfoundland & Labrador Emergency Measures Organization, PO Box 8700, St. John's, A1B 4J6 NL
709-729-3703, Fax: 709-729-3857

Nova Scotia
Nova Scotia Emergency Management Office, PO Box 2581, Halifax, B3J 3N5 NS
902-424-5620, Fax: 902-424-5376, 866-424-5620, emo@gov.ns.ca

Nunavut
Nunavut Emergency Management, PO Box 1000 700,Iqaluit, X0A 0H0 NU
867-975-5403, Fax: 867-979-4221, 800-693-1666

Government Quick Reference Guide / Employment

Ontario
Emergency Management Ontario, 77 Wellesley St. W, PO Box 222, Toronto, M7A 1N3 ON
416-314-3723, Fax: 416-314-3758

Prince Edward Island
Prince Edward Island Emergency Measures Organization, National Bank Tower, #600, 134 Kent St., PO Box 2000, Charlottetown, C1A 7N8 PE
902-894-0385, Fax: 902-368-6362

Saskatchewan
Saskatchewan Emergency Management Organization, #100, 1855 Victoria Ave., Regina, S4P 3V7 SK
306-787-9563, Fax: 306-787-1694, infosafety@cps.gov.sk.ca

Yukon Territory
Emergency Measures Organization, PO Box 2703, Whitehorse, Y1A 2C6 YT
867-667-5220, Fax: 867-393-6266, 800-661-0408, emo.yukon@gov.yk.ca

EMPLOYMENT

Alberta
Alberta Employment, Immigration & Industry, Minister's Office, Legislature Bldg., #208, 10800 - 97 Ave., Edmonton, T5K 2B6 AB
780-415-4800, Fax: 780-422-9556, 866-644-5135, eii.communications@gov.ab.ca

Manitoba
Manitoba Labour & Immigration, Legislative Building, 317, 450 Broadway Ave., Winnipeg, R3C 0V8 MB
204-945-4079, Fax: 204-945-8312, minlab@leg.gov.mb.ca

Quebec
Ministère du Travail, 200, ch Ste-Foy, 6e étage, Québec, G1R 5S1 QC
418-643-4817, Fax: 418-528-0559, 800-643-4817, service_clientele@travail.gouv.qc.ca

EMPLOYMENT INSURANCE
Canada Employment Insurance Commission, 140, Promenade du Portage, Phase IV, Gatineau, QC K1A 0J9
800-206-7218

Saskatchewan
Saskatchewan Advanced Education, Employment & Labour, 1945 Hamilton St., Regina, S4P 2C8 SK
306-787-9478, Fax: 306-787-2315

ENERGY
See Also: Natural Resources
Atomic Energy of Canada Limited, Head Office, 2251 Speakman Dr., Mississauga, L5K 1B2 ON
905-823-9040, webmaster@aecl.ca
Canadian Nuclear Safety Commission, 280 Slater St., PO Box 1046 B,Ottawa, K1P 5S9 ON
613-995-5894, Fax: 613-995-5086, 800-668-5284, info@cnsc-ccsn.gc.ca
CANMET Energy Technology Centre-Varennes, 1615, Montée Ste-Julie, CP 4800, Varennes, J3X 1S6 QC
450-652-6639, Fax: 450-652-0999
Chalk River Laboratories, Chalk River, K0J 1J0 ON
613-584-3311
Energy Solutions Centre, 206A Lowe St., 1st Fl., Whitehorse, Y1A 1WG YT
867-393-7063, Fax: 867-393-7061, info@nrgsc.yk.ca
Indian Oil & Gas Canada, #100, 9911 Chula Blvd., Tsuu T'ina (Sarcee), AB T2W 6H6
Fax: 403-292-5618
National Energy Board, 444 - 7 Ave. SW, Calgary, T2P 0X8 AB
403-292-4800, Fax: 403-292-5503, 800-899-1265, info@neb-one.gc.ca
Yukon Energy Corporation, 2 Miles Canyon Rd., PO Box 5920, Whitehorse, Y1A 6S7 YT
867-393-5300, 866-926-3749, communications@yukonenergy.ca

Alberta
Alberta Energy & Utilities Board, 640 - 5 Ave. SW, Calgary, AB T2P 3G4
403-297-8311, Fax: 403-297-7336
Alberta Energy Research Institute, AMEC Place, #2540, 801 - 6 Ave. SW, Calgary, AB T2P 3W2
403-297-8650, Fax: 403-297-3638, aeri@gov.ab.ca

Alberta Energy, North Petroleum Plaza, 9945 - 108 St., 7th Fl., Edmonton, T5K 2G6 AB
780-427-7425, Fax: 780-422-0698, 780-310-0000

British Columbia
Ministry of Energy, Mines & Petroleum Resources, PO Box 9318 Prov Govt,Victoria, V8W 9N3 BC
250-952-0241
British Columbia Hydro, 333 Dunsmuir St., 18th Fl., Vancouver, V6B 5R3 BC
604-224-9376, Fax: 604-623-4467, 800-224-9376
Oil & Gas Commission, #100, 10003 - 110 Ave., Fort St John, BC V1J 6M7
250-261-5700, 800-663-7867
Powerex Corp., #1400, 666 Burrard St., Vancouver, BC V6C 2X8
604-891-5000, Fax: 604-891-6060, 800-220-4907, customer.service@bchydro.com
Powertech Labs Inc., 12388 - 88 Ave., Surrey, BC V8W 7R7
604-590-7500, Fax: 604-590-5347, info@powertechlans.com
British Columbia Utilities Commission, 900 Howe St., 6th Fl., PO Box 250, Vancouver, V6Z 2N3 BC
604-660-4700, Fax: 604-660-1102, 800-663-1385, commission.secretary@bcuc.com

Manitoba
Manitoba Hydro, PO Box 815 Main,Winnipeg, R3C 2P4 MB
204-474-3311, Fax: 204-475-0069, publicaffairs@hydro.mb.ca
Petroleum, #360, 1395 Ellice Ave., Winnipeg, R3G 3P2 MB
204-945-6577, Fax: 204-945-0586
Manitoba Science, Technology, Energy & Mines, #333, 450 Broadway, Winnipeg, R3C 0V8 MB

New Brunswick
Efficiency NB, #101, 33 Charlotte St., Saint John, NB E2L 2H3
506-643-7826, Fax: 506-643-7835, 866-643-8833
Department of Energy, Brunswick Square, #100M, 1 Germain St., PO Box 5001, Saint John, E2L 4Y9 NB
506-658-3180, Fax: 506-658-3191
Department of Natural Resources, PO Box 6000, Fredericton, E3B 5H1 NB
506-453-2510, Fax: 506-444-5839, dnrweb@gnb.ca
New Brunswick Power Group of Companies, 515 King St., PO Box 2000, Fredericton, E3B 4X1 NB
506-458-4444, Fax: 506-458-4000, questions@nbpower.com

Newfoundland & Labrador
Canada-Newfoundland Offshore Petroleum Board, TD Place, 140 Water St., 5th Fl., St. John's, NL A1C 6H6
709-778-1400, Fax: 709-778-1473, postmaster@cnlopb.nl.ca
Churchill Falls (Labrador) Corporation Limited, Hydro Place, 500 Columbus Dr., PO Box 12500, St. John's, A1B 4K7 NL
709-737-1859, Fax: 709-737-1816
Newfoundland & Labrador Hydro, Hydro Place, Columbus Dr., PO Box 12400, St. John's, A1B 4K7 NL
709-737-1400, Fax: 709-737-1800
Newfoundland & Labrador Board of Commissioners of Public Utilities, PO Box 21040, St. John's, A1A 5B2 NL
709-726-8600, Fax: 709-726-9604, 866-782-0006, ito@pub.nf.ca
Twin Falls Power Corporation, PO Box 12500, St. John's, A1B 3T5 NL

Northwest Territories
Department of Environment & Natural Resources, PO Box 1320, Yellowknife, X1A 2L9 NT
Northwest Territories Power Corporation, 4 Capital Dr., Hay River, X0E 1G2 NT
867-874-5200, Fax: 867-874-5229, info@ntpc.com

Nova Scotia
Canada-Nova Scotia Offshore Petroleum Board, TD Centre, 1791 Barrington St., 6th Fl., Halifax, NS B3J 3K9
902-422-5588, Fax: 902-422-1799, postmaster@cnsopb.ns.ca
Department of Energy, Bank of Montreal Bldg., #400, 5151 George St., PO Box 2664, Halifax, B3J 3P7 NS
902-424-4575, Fax: 902-424-0528, energyinfo@gov.ns.ca
Nova Scotia Utility & Review Board, 1601 Lower Water St., 3rd Fl., PO Box 1692 M,Halifax, B3J 3S3 NS
902-424-4448, Fax: 902-424-3919, uarb.board@gov.ns.ca

Ontario
Ministry of Energy and Infrastructure, Hearst Block, 900 Bay St., 4th Fl., Toronto, M7A 2E1 ON
416-327-6758, Fax: 416-327-0033, 888-668-4939

Ministry of Environment, 135 St. Clair Ave. West, Toronto, M4V 1P5 ON
416-325-4000, Fax: 416-325-3159, 800-565-4923
Hydro One Inc., North Tower, 483 Bay St., Toronto, M5G 2P5 ON
416-345-5000, 877-955-1155, webmaster@HydroOne.com
Independent Electricity System Operator, PO Box 4474 A,Toronto, M5W 4E5 ON
905-403-6900, Fax: 905-403-6921, 888-448-7777, customer.relations@ieso.ca
Ontario Energy Board, #2700, 2300 Yonge St., Toronto, ON M4P 1E4
416-481-1967, Fax: 416-440-7656, 888-632-6273
Ontario Power Authority, #1600, 120 Adelaide St. West, Toronto, ON M5H 1T1
416-967-7474, Fax: 416-967-1947, info@powerauthority.on.ca
Ontario Power Generation, 700 University Ave., Toronto, M5G 1X6 ON
416-592-2555, 877-592-2555

Prince Edward Island
Department of Environment, Energy & Forestry, Jones Bldg., 11 Kent St., 4th & 5th Fl., PO Box 2000, Charlottetown, C1A 7N8 PE
902-368-5000, Fax: 902-368-5830,
PEI Energy Corporation, Jones Bldg., 11 Kent St., 4th Fl., PO Box 2000, Charlottetown, PE C1A 7N8
902-894-0288, Fax: 902-368-0290

Quebec
Agence de l'efficacité énergétique, #B-405, 5700, 4e av ouest, Québec, QC G1H 6R1
418-627-6379, Fax: 418-643-5828, 877-727-6655, aee@aee.gouv.qc.ca
Hydro-Québec, 75, boul René-Lévesque ouest, 20e étage, Montréal, H2Z 1A4 QC
514-289-2211
Régie de l'énergie, Tour de la Bourse, #255, 800, Place Victoria, CP 1, Montréal, QC H4Z 1A2
514-873-2452, Fax: 514-873-2070, 888-873-2452, secretariat@regie-energie.qc.ca
Société d'énergie de la Baie-James, 888, de Maisonneuve est, 2e étage, Montréal, H2L 5B2 QC
514-286-2020

Saskatchewan
Saskatchewan Energy & Resources, #300, 2103 - 11th Ave., Regina, S4P 3Z8 SK
306-787-2528, Fax: 306-787-8447, 866-727-5427
Saskatchewan Power Corporation (SaskPower), 2025 Victoria Ave., Regina, S4P 0S1 SK
306-566-2121, Fax: 306-566-2330, 800-667-4749
SaskEnergy Incorporated, 1777 Victoria Ave., Regina, S4P 4K5 SK
306-777-9225, Fax: 306-777-9200, 800-567-8899

Yukon Territory
Yukon Energy, Mines & Resources, PO Box 2703, Whitehorse, Y1A 2C6 YT
867-667-5466, Fax: 867-667-8601, 800-661-0408, emr@gov.yk.ca

ENGINEERING & CONSULTING
Canadian Environmental Assessment Agency, Place Bell Canada, 160 Elgin St., 22nd Fl., Ottawa, K1A 0H3 ON
613-957-0700, Fax: 613-957-0946, info@ceaa-acee.gc.ca
Defence Construction Canada, Constitution Square, 350 Albert St., 19th Fl., Ottawa, K1A 0K3 ON
613-998-9548, Fax: 613-998-1061, 800-514-3555, info@dcc-cdc.gc.ca
Natural Sciences & Engineering Research Council of Canada, Constitution Square, Tower II, 350 Albert St., Ottawa, K1A 1H5 ON
613-995-4273, Fax: 613-992-5337

British Columbia
Transportation Planning & Policy Department, #5C, 940 Blanshard St., PO Box 9850 Prov Govt,Victoria, V8W 9T5 BC
250-387-5062, Fax: 250-387-6431

Manitoba
Manitoba Infrastructure & Transportation, Legislative Building, #203, 450 Broadway Ave., Winnipeg, R3C 0V8 MB
204-945-3723, Fax: 204-945-7610

Northwest Territories
Highways, 4510 - 50 Ave., 2nd fl., PO Box 1320, Yellowknife, X1A 2L9 NT
867-920-8771, Fax: 867-873-0288

Saskatchewan
Saskatchewan Highways & Infrastructure, 1855 Victoria Ave., Regina, S4P 3T2 SK
306-787-4800

ENVIRONMENT
Commissioner of the Environment & Sustainable Development, 240 Sparks St., Ottawa, K1A 0G6 ON
613-995-3708, Fax: 613-957-0474
Environment Canada, 10 Wellington St., Gatineau, K1A 0H3 QC
819-997-2800, Fax: 819-994-1412, 800-668-6767, enviroinfo@ec.gc.ca
National Round Table on the Environment & Economy, #200, 344 Slater St., Ottawa, K1R 7Y3 ON
613-992-7189, Fax: 613-992-7385, admin@nrtee-trnee.ca

Alberta
Alberta Environment, South Tower, Petroleum Plaza, 9915 - 108 St., Main Fl., Edmonton, T5K 2G8 AB
780-427-2700, Fax: 780-422-4086,-310-0000, env.infocent@gov.ab.ca
Alberta Sustainable Resource Development, Information Centre, 9920 - 108 St., Main Fl., Edmonton, T5K 2M4 AB
780-944-0313, Fax: 780-427-4407, 877-944-0313, srd.infocent@gov.ab.ca

British Columbia
Ministry of Environment, PO Box 9339 Prov Govt,Victoria, V8W 9M1 BC
250-387-1161, Fax: 250-387-5669, www.envmail@gov.bc.ca

Manitoba
Manitoba Conservation, 200 Saulteaux Cres., Winnipeg, R3J 3W3 MB
204-945-6784, 800-214-6497, mincon@leg.gov.mb.ca
Manitoba Water Stewardship, 200 Saulteaux Cres., PO Box 11, Winnipeg, R3J 3W3 MB
204-945-6398, 800-282-8069, wsd@gov.mb.ca

New Brunswick
Department of the Environment, Marysville Place, 20 McGloin St., PO Box 6000, Fredericton, E3B 5H1 NB
506-453-2690, Fax: 506-457-4991

Newfoundland & Labrador
Department of Environment & Conservation, Confederation Bldg., West Block, 4th Fl., PO Box 8700, St. John's, A1B 4J6 NL
709-729-2664, Fax: 709-729-6639, 800-563-6181, info@gov.nl.ca

Northwest Territories
Department of Environment & Natural Resources, PO Box 1320, Yellowknife, X1A 2L9 NT

Nova Scotia
Department of Environment, 5151 Terminal Rd., 5th Fl., PO Box 442, Halifax, B3J 2T8 NS
902-424-3600, Fax: 902-424-0503, 877-936-8476

Nunavut
Department of Environment, PO Box 1000 1300,Iqaluit, X0A 0H0 NU
867-975-7700, Fax: 867-975-7742, 866-222-9063, environment@gov.nu.ca

Ontario
Ministry of Environment, 135 St. Clair Ave. West, Toronto, M4V 1P5 ON
416-325-4000, Fax: 416-325-3159, 800-565-4923
Environmental Commissioner of Ontario, #605, 1075 Bay St., Toronto, M5S 2B1 ON
416-325-3377, Fax: 416-325-3370, 800-701-6454, commissioner@eco.on.ca

Prince Edward Island
Department of Environment, Energy & Forestry, Jones Bldg., 11 Kent St., 4th & 5th Fl., PO Box 2000, Charlottetown, C1A 7N8 PE
902-368-5000, Fax: 902-368-5830

Quebec
Bureau d'audiences publiques sur l'environnement, Édifice Lomer-Gouin, #2.10, 575, rue Saint-Amable, 2e étage, Québec, QC G1R 6A6
418-643-7447, Fax: 418-643-9474, 800-463-4732, communication@bape.gouv.qc.ca
Ministère du Développement durable, de l'Environnement et des Parcs, Édifice Marie-Guyart, 675, boul René-Lévesque est, 29e étage, Québec, G1R 5V7 QC
418-521-3830, Fax: 418-646-5974, 800-561-1616, info@mddep.gouv.qc.ca

Saskatchewan
Saskatchewan Environment, 3211 Albert St., 2nd Fl., Regina, S4S 5W6 SK
306-953-3750, Fax: 306-787-9544, 800-567-4224, inquiry@serm.gov.sk.ca

ENVIRONMENT DEPARTMENTS/MINISTRIES
Environment Canada, 10 Wellington St., Gatineau, K1A 0H3 QC
819-997-2800, Fax: 819-994-1412, 800-668-6767, enviroinfo@ec.gc.ca

Alberta
Alberta Environment, South Tower, Petroleum Plaza, 9915 - 108 St., Main Fl., Edmonton, T5K 2G8 AB
780-427-2700, Fax: 780-422-4086,-310-0000, env.infocent@gov.ab.ca

British Columbia
Ministry of Environment, PO Box 9339 Prov Govt,Victoria, V8W 9M1 BC
250-387-1161, Fax: 250-387-5669, www.envmail@gov.bc.ca

Manitoba
Manitoba Conservation, 200 Saulteaux Cres., Winnipeg, R3J 3W3 MB
204-945-6784, 800-214-6497, mincon@leg.gov.mb.ca

New Brunswick
Department of the Environment, Marysville Place, 20 McGloin St., PO Box 6000, Fredericton, E3B 5H1 NB
506-453-2690, Fax: 506-457-4991

Newfoundland & Labrador
Department of Environment & Conservation, Confederation Bldg., West Block, 4th Fl., PO Box 8700, St. John's, A1B 4J6 NL
709-729-2664, Fax: 709-729-6639, 800-563-6181, info@gov.nl.ca

Northwest Territories
Department of Environment & Natural Resources, PO Box 1320, Yellowknife, X1A 2L9 NT

Nova Scotia
Department of Environment, 5151 Terminal Rd., 5th Fl., PO Box 442, Halifax, B3J 2T8 NS
902-424-3600, Fax: 902-424-0503, 877-936-8476

Nunavut
Department of Environment, PO Box 1000 1300,Iqaluit, X0A 0H0 NU
867-975-7700, Fax: 867-975-7742, 866-222-9063, environment@gov.nu.ca

Ontario
Ministry of Environment, 135 St. Clair Ave. West, Toronto, M4V 1P5 ON
416-325-4000, Fax: 416-325-3159, 800-565-4923

Prince Edward Island
Department of Environment, Energy & Forestry, Jones Bldg., 11 Kent St., 4th & 5th Fl., PO Box 2000, Charlottetown, C1A 7N8 PE
902-368-5000, Fax: 902-368-5830

Quebec
Ministère du Développement durable, de l'Environnement et des Parcs, Édifice Marie-Guyart, 675, boul René-Lévesque est, 29e étage, Québec, G1R 5V7 QC
418-521-3830, Fax: 418-646-5974, 800-561-1616, info@mddep.gouv.qc.ca

Saskatchewan
Saskatchewan Environment, 3211 Albert St., 2nd Fl., Regina, S4S 5W6 SK
306-953-3750, Fax: 306-787-9544, 800-567-4224, inquiry@serm.gov.sk.ca

Yukon Territory
Yukon Environment, PO Box 2703, Whitehorse, Y1A 2C6 YT
867-667-5652, Fax: 867-393-6213, 800-661-0408, environmentyukon@gov.yk.ca

ENVIRONMENTAL ASSESSMENT
Canadian Environmental Assessment Agency, Place Bell Canada, 160 Elgin St., 22nd Fl., Ottawa, K1A 0H3 ON
613-957-0700, Fax: 613-957-0946, info@ceaa-acee.gc.ca
Environmental Assessment & Approvals Branch, 2 St. Clair Ave. West, 12th Fl., Toronto, M4V 1L5 ON
416-314-8001, Fax: 416-314-8452, 800-461-6290
Environmental Assessment Branch, #486, 3211 Albert St., Regina, S4S 5W6 SK
306-787-6132, Fax: 306-787-0930

British Columbia
British Columbia Environmental Assessment Office, 836 Yates St., 1st Fl., PO Box 9426 Prov Govt,Victoria, V8W 9V1 BC
250-356-7441, Fax: 250-356-7440, eaoinfo@gov.bc.ca

New Brunswick
Environmental Management, Marysville Place, 20 McGloin St., PO Box 6000, Fredericton, E3B 5H1 NB
506-444-5119, Fax: 506-457-7333

EROSION CONTROL
Quebec
Commission de protection du territoire agricole du Québec, 200, ch Ste-Foy, 2e étage, Québec, QC G1R 4X6
418-643-3314, Fax: 418-643-2261, 800-667-5294, info@cptaq.gouv.qc.ca

Saskatchewan
Saskatchewan Agriculture, Walter Scott Bldg., 3085 Albert St., Regina, S4S 0B1 SK
306-787-5140, 866-457-2377, aginfo@gov.sk.ca

EXPORT DEVELOPMENT
Business Development Bank of Canada, #400, 5, Place Ville-Marie, Montréal, H3B 5E7 QC
514-283-5904, Fax: 514-283-2872, 877-232-2269
Export Development Canada, 151 O'Connor St., Ottawa, K1A 1K3 ON
613-598-2500, Fax: 613-598-3811, 888-332-3320
Global Operations & Chief Trade Commissioner, 125 Sussex Dr,, Ottawa, K1A 0G2 ON
613-944-2697, Fax: 613-996-1667
Industry Canada, 235 Queen St., Ottawa, K1A 0H5 ON
Fax: 613-954-6436, 800-328-6189, info@ic.gc.ca
Western Economic Diversification Canada, Canada Place, #1500, 9700 Jasper Ave. NW, Edmonton, T5J 4H7 AB
780-495-4164, Fax: 780-495-4557, 888-338-9378

Alberta
Alberta Economic Development, Commerce Place, 4th Fl., 10155 - 102 St., Edmonton, T5J 4L6 AB
780-427-4323, Fax: 780-415-1759

New Brunswick
Business Development, Centennial Bldg., 670 King St., 5th Fl., PO Box 6000, Fredericton, E3B 5H1 NB
506-453-2111, Fax: 506-444-4182

Northwest Territories
Northwest Territories Business Development & Investment Corporation, #701, 5201 - 50 Ave., Yellowknife, NT X1A 3S9
867-920-6455, Fax: 867-765-0652, bdicinfo@gov.nt.ca

Ontario
Ministry of Economic Development, Hearst Block, 900 Bay St., 8th Fl., Toronto, M7A 2E1 ON
416-325-6666, Fax: 416-325-6688, 866-668-4249, info@edt.gov.on.ca

Saskatchewan
Saskatchewan Energy & Resources, #300, 2103 - 11th Ave., Regina, S4P 3Z8 SK
306-787-2528, Fax: 306-787-8447, 866-727-5427
Saskatchewan Trade & Export Partnership, #320, 1801 Hamilton St., PO Box 1787, Regina, SK S4P 3C6
306-787-9210, Fax: 306-787-6666, 877-313-7244, inquire@sasktrade.sk.ca

EXPROPRIATION
National Defence Canada, Major-General George R. Pearkes Bldg., 101 Colonel By Dr., Ottawa, K1A 0K2 ON
613-995-2534, Fax: 613-992-4739, 800-856-8488

Alberta
Land Compensation/Surface Rights Board, Phipps-McKinnon Bldg., 10020 - 101A Ave., 18th Fl., Edmonton, AB T5J 3G2
780-427-2444, Fax: 780-427-5798

Manitoba
Manitoba Land Value Appraisal Commission, 800 Portage Ave., Winnipeg, MB R3G 0N4
204-945-2941, Fax: 204-948-2235

Quebec
Ministère des Transports, 700, boul René-Lévesque est, 27e étage, Québec, G1R 5H1 QC
Fax: 514-643-1269, 888-355-0511, communications@mtq.gouv.qc.ca

Saskatchewan
Saskatchewan Government Services, Century Plaza, 1920 Rose St., Regina, S4P 0A9 SK
306-787-6911, Fax: 306-787-1061

FAMILY BENEFITS
See Also: Income Security; Social Services
Social Development, L'esplanade Laurier, Level 2, 300 Laurier Ave. West, Ottawa, K1A 0J6 ON
613-990-5100, Fax: 613-990-5091

Northwest Territories
Department of Education, Culture & Employment, PO Box 1320, Yellowknife, X1A 2L9 NT
867-669-2399, Fax: 867-873-0431, 866-606-5627

FEDERAL-PROVINCIAL AFFAIRS

Alberta
Alberta International & Intergovernmental Relations, Commerce Place, 10155 - 102 St., 12th Fl., Edmonton, T5J 4G8 AB
780-422-1510, Fax: 780-427-0699

Northwest Territories
Department of Aboriginal Affairs & Intergovernmental Relations, 4910 - 52nd St., PO Box 1320, Yellowknife, X1A 2L9 NT
867-873-7143, Fax: 867-873-0233, 877-838-8194, nancy_gardiner@gov.nt.ca

Nova Scotia
Department of Intergovernmental Affairs, Joseph Howe Bldg., 1690 Hollis St., 7th Fl., PO Box 1617, Halifax, B3J 2Y3 NS
902-424-5153, Fax: 902-424-0728, iga@gov.ns.ca

Nunavut
Department of Executive & Intergovernmental Affairs, 1084 Aeroplex bldg., PO Box 1000 200, Iqaluit, X0A 0H0 NU
867-975-6000, Fax: 867-975-6090

Saskatchewan
Canadian Intergovernmental Relations, #800, 1919 Saskatchewan Dr., Regina, S4P 4H2 SK
Fax: 306-787-7317

FILM PRODUCTION & COLLECTIONS

Alberta
Alberta Film Commission, 10155 - 102 St., 5th Fl., Edmonton, AB T5J 4L6
780-422-8584, Fax: 780-422-8582, 888-813-1738

Manitoba
Manitoba Film & Sound Recording Development Corporation, #410, 93 Lombard Ave., Winnipeg, MB R3B 3B1
204-947-2040, Fax: 204-956-5261, carole@mbfilmsound.mb.ca

New Brunswick
New Brunswick Film, Assumption Pl., 770 Main St., 16th Fl., PO Box 5001, Moncton, NB E1C 8R3
506-869-6868, Fax: 506-869-6840, nbfilm@gnb.ca

Newfoundland & Labrador
Newfoundland & Labrador Film Development Corporation, 12 King's Bridge Rd., St. John's, NL A1C 3K3
709-738-3456, Fax: 709-739-1680, 877-738-3456, info@nlfdc.ca

Nova Scotia
Film Nova Scotia, Collins Bank Bldg., 1869 Upper Water St., 3rd Fl., Halifax, NS B3J 1S9
902-424-7177, Fax: 902-424-0617, 888-360-2111, connorkm@gov.ns.ca

Ontario
Ontario Media Development Corporation, South Tower, #501, 175 Bloor St. East, Toronto, ON M4W 3R8
416-314-6858, Fax: 416-314-6876, mail@omdc.on.ca

Saskatchewan
Sask Film, 1831 College Ave., Regina, SK S4P 3V7
306-798-3456, Fax: 306-798-7768, 800-561-9933

FINANCE
See Also: Banking & Financial Institutions
Finance Canada, L'esplanade Laurier, 140 O'Connor St., Ottawa, K1A 0G5 ON
613-992-1573, Fax: 613-996-2690, finpub@fin.gc.ca

Prince Edward Island
Department of the Provincial Treasury, Shaw Bldg., 95 Rochford St., 2nd Fl. South, PO Box 2000, Charlottetown, C1A 7N8 PE
902-368-4050, Fax: 902-368-6575

FINANCING & LOANS
See Also: Investment
Business Development Bank of Canada, #400, 5, Place Ville-Marie, Montréal, H3B 5E7 QC
514-283-5904, Fax: 514-283-2872, 877-232-2269,
Canada Mortgage & Housing Corporation, 700 Montreal Rd., Ottawa, K1A 0P7 ON
613-748-2000, Fax: 613-748-2098, 800-668-2642, chic@cmhc-schl.gc.ca

British Columbia
International Financial Centre British Columbia, Park Place, #1170, 666 Burrard St., Vancouver, BC V6C 2X8
604-683-6626, Fax: 604-683-6646, info@ifcvancouver.com

Manitoba
Manitoba Agricultural Services Corporation, #100, 1525 First St. South, Brandon, MB R7A 7A1
204-726-6850, Fax: 204-726-6849, mailbox@masc.mb.ca

Northwest Territories
Department of Industry, Tourism & Investment, PO Box 1320, Yellowknife, X1A 2L9 NT
Fax: 867-873-0306, info@iti.ca

Nova Scotia
Nova Scotia Farm Loan Board, PO Box 550, Truro, NS B2N 5E3
902-893-6506, Fax: 902-895-7693, flb@gov.ns.ca

Nunavut
Nunavut Business Credit Corporation, PO Box 224, Cape Dorset, NU X0A 0C0
867-897-3647, 800-758-0038

Prince Edward Island
Prince Edward Island Lending Agency, Confederation Court Office Tower, #201, 134 Kent St., PO Box 1420, Charlottetown, PE C1A 7N1
902-368-6200, Fax: 902-368-6201

Quebec
La financière agricole de Québec, 1400, boul de la Rive-Sud, Saint-Romuald, QC G6W 8K7
418-838-5602, Fax: 418-833-3871, 800-749-3646, dir.comm@fadq.qc.ca
Société Innovatech du sud du Québec, #20, 2100, rue King ouest, Sherbrooke, QC J1J 2E8
819-820-3305, Fax: 819-820-3320, isq@isq.qc.ca
Société Innovatech Québec, 10, rue Pierre Olivier Chauveau, Québec, QC G1R 4J3
418-528-9770, Fax: 418-528-9783, info@innovatechquebec.com

Saskatchewan
Saskatchewan Trade & Export Partnership, #320, 1801 Hamilton St., PO Box 1787, Regina, SK S4P 3C6
306-787-9210, Fax: 306-787-6666, 877-313-7244, inquire@sasktrade.sk.ca

Yukon Territory
Yukon Economic Development, PO Box 2703, Whitehorse, Y1A 2C6 YT
867-393-7191, Fax: 867-395-7199, 800-661-0408

FIRE PREVENTION

Ontario
Aviation & Forest Fire Management Branch, #400, 70 Foster Dr., Sault Ste Marie, P6A 6V5 ON
Office of the Fire Marshal, Victoria Health Centre, PO Box 6000, Fredericton, E3B 5H1 NB
506-453-2004, Fax: 506-457-4889, fire.marshal@gnb.ca

British Columbia
Emergency Management BC, 525 Fort St., 2nd Fl., PO Box 9223 Prov Govt, Victoria, V8W 9J1 BC
250-953-4002, Fax: 250-953-4081, BC.CorSer@gov.bc.ca (Coroner); OFC@gov.bc.ca (Fire Commissioner)

Manitoba
Office of the Fire Commissioner, #508, 401 York Ave., Winnipeg, MB R3C 0P8
204-945-3322, Fax: 204-948-2089, 800-282-8069, firecomm@gov.mb.ca

Newfoundland & Labrador
Office of the Fire Commissioner, 2 Wellon Dr., Deer Lake, NL A8A 2G5
709-635-4153, Fax: 709-635-4163

Northwest Territories
Department of Municipal & Community Affairs, PO Box 1320, Yellowknife, X1A 2L9 NT
867-873-7118, Fax: 867-873-0309

Nunavut
Nunavut Emergency Management, PO Box 1000 700, Iqaluit, X0A 0H0 NU
867-975-5403, Fax: 867-979-4221, 800-693-1666

Ontario
Fire Safety Commission, Place Nouveau Bldg., 5775 Yonge St., 7th Fl., Toronto, ON M2M 4J1
416-325-3100, Fax: 416-314-1217

Quebec
Commissariat des incendies, 455, rue Dupont, Québec, QC G1K 6N2
418-529-5706, Fax: 418-529-9922

Saskatchewan
Lands & Forests Division, 3211 Albert St., 5th fl., Regina, S4S 5W6 SK
306-787-5407, Fax: 306-787-2947

Yukon Territory
Fire Marshal's Office, PO Box 2703, Whitehorse, Y1A 2C6 YT
867-667-5811, Fax: 867-393-6295, inquiry@gov.yk.ca

FIREARMS
Canada Firearms Centre, Ottawa, ON K1A 1M6
Fax: 613-957-7325, 800-731-4000, cfc-cafc@cfc-cafc.gc.ca

FISHERIES

British Columbia
Fish & Wildlife Branch, 2975 Jutland Rd., 4th Fl., Victoria, V8T 5J9 BC
250-387-9717, Fax: 250-387-9568
Fisheries & Oceans Canada, 200 Kent St., Ottawa, K1A 0E6 ON
613-993-0999, Fax: 613-996-1866, info@dfo-mpo.gc.ca
Fisheries Resource Conservation Council, PO Box 2001 D, Ottawa, ON K1P 5W3
613-998-0433, Fax: 613-998-1146, info@frcc-ccrh.ca
Gulf Fisheries Centre, 343, av Université, 5th Fl., Moncton, E1C 9B6 NB
506-851-3886, Fax: 506-851-7732

British Columbia
Ministry of Agriculture & Lands, PO Box 9120 Prov Govt, Victoria, V8W 9E2 BC
250-387-5121, Fax: 250-387-1522, agf.webmaster@gems2.gov.bc.ca
Oceans & Marine Fisheries Division, 2975 Jutland Rd., 3rd Fl., PO Box 9309, Victoria, V8W 9N1 BC
250-387-0389, Fax: 250-953-3401, fishstats@gov.bc.ca; fishinfo@gov.bc.ca

New Brunswick
Department of Agriculture & Aquaculture, PO Box 6000, Fredericton, E3B 5H1 NB
506-453-2666, Fax: 506-453-7170, DAA-MAA@gnb.ca
Department of Business New Brunswick, Centennial Bldg., 670 King St., PO Box 6000, Fredericton, E3B 5H1 NB
506-444-5228, Fax: 506-453-5428

Newfoundland & Labrador
Department of Fisheries & Aquaculture, Petten Bldg., 30 Strawberry Marsh Rd., PO Box 8700, St. John's, A1B 4J6 NL
709-729-3723, Fax: 709-729-6082, fishaqwebmaster@gov.nl.ca

Northwest Territories
Department of Environment & Natural Resources, PO Box 1320, Yellowknife, X1A 2L9 NT

Nova Scotia
Fisheries & Aquaculture Loan Board, PO Box 2223, Halifax, NS B3J 3C4
902-424-4560, Fax: 902-424-1766
Department of Fisheries & Aquaculture, 1741 Brunswick St., 3rd Fl., PO Box 2223, Halifax, B3J 3C4 NS
902-424-4560, Fax: 902-424-4671

Ontario
Fish & Wildlife Heritage Commission, Robinson Pl., 300 Water St., PO Box 7000, Peterborough, ON K9J 8M5
Fax: 705-755-5093
Natural Resources Management Division, Whitney Block, #6540, 99 Wellesley St. West, Toronto, M7A 1W3 ON
416-314-2000, Fax: 416-314-1994

Prince Edward Island
Department of Agriculture, Jones Bldg., 11 Kent St., PO Box 2000, Charlottetown, C1A 7N8 PE
902-368-4880, Fax: 902-368-4857

FISHERIES & WILDLIFE

Arctic Goose, c/o Prairie & Northern Region, CWS, #200, 4999 - 98 Ave., Edmonton, T6B 2X3 AB
780-951-8652, Fax: 780-495-2615, deanna.dixon@ec.gc.ca
Beverly & Qamanirjuaq Caribou Management Board, Secretariat, PO Box 629, Stonewall, MB R0C 2Z0
204-467-2438, rossthompson@mts.net
Black Duck, c/o Ontario Region, CWS, 49 Camelot Dr., Nepean, K1A 0H3 ON
613-952-2408, Fax: 613-952-9027
Committee on the Status of Endangered Wildlife in Canada, c/o Canadian Wildlife Service, Ottawa, ON K1A 0H3
819-997-4991, Fax: 819-994-3684, cosewic@ec.gc.ca
Eastern Habitat, c/o Environment Canada, PO Box 1590, Sackville, E0A 3C0 NB
506-364-5036, Fax: 506-364-5062
Fish & Wildlife Branch, 300 Water St., PO Box 7000, Peterborough, K9J 8M5 ON
705-755-5954, Fax: 705-755-1900
Fisheries & Oceans Canada, 200 Kent St., Ottawa, K1A 0E6 ON
613-993-0999, Fax: 613-996-1866, info@dfo-mpo.gc.ca
Natural Resources Canada, 580 Booth St., Ottawa, K1A 0E4 ON
613-995-0947, Fax: 613-992-7211
North American Bird Conservation Initiative, Canadian Wildlife Service, 351, boul St-Joseph, 3e étage, Gatineau, QC K1A 0H3
819-994-0512, Fax: 819-994-4445, s.neve@ec.gc.ca
North American Waterfowl Management Plan, c/o Canadian Wildlife Service, Place Vincent-Massey, 351 St-Joseph Blvd., 16th Fl., Gatineau, ON K1A 0H3
819-934-6034, Fax: 819-934-6017, nabci@ec.gc.ca
Pacific Coast, c/o Pacific & Yukon Region, CWS, #201, 401 Burrard St., Vancouver, V6C 3S5 BC
604-666-2342, Fax: 604-664-4068
Porcupine Caribou Management Board, PO Box 31723, Whitehorse, YT Y1A 6L3
867-633-4780, Fax: 867-393-3904, pcmb@taiga.net
Prairie Habitat, c/o Prairie & Northern Region, CWS, #200, 4999 - 98 Ave., Edmonton, T6B 2X3 AB
780-951-8652, Fax: 780-495-2615

Alberta
Alberta Environment, South Tower, Petroleum Plaza, 9915 - 108 St., Main Fl., Edmonton, T5K 2G8 AB
780-427-2700, Fax: 780-422-4086,-310-0000, env.infocent@gov.ab.ca

British Columbia
Ministry of Environment, PO Box 9339 Prov Govt,Victoria, V8W 9M1 BC
250-387-1161, Fax: 250-387-5669, www.envmail@gov.bc.ca
Strategic Industry Development, 808 Douglas St., 5th Fl., PO Box 9120 Prov Govt,Victoria, V8W 9B4 BC
250-356-1821, Fax: 250-356-7279

Manitoba
Endangered Species Advisory Committee, 200 Saulteaux Cres., PO Box 24, Winnipeg, MB R3J 3W3
204-945-7465, Fax: 204-945-3077
Manitoba Habitat Heritage Corporation, #200, 1555 St. James St., Winnipeg, MB R3H 1B5
204-784-4350, Fax: 204-784-7359, mhhc@mhhc.mb.ca

New Brunswick
Department of Agriculture & Aquaculture, PO Box 6000, Fredericton, E3B 5H1 NB
506-453-2666, Fax: 506-453-7170, DAA-MAA@gnb.ca

Newfoundland & Labrador
Department of Fisheries & Aquaculture, Petten Bldg., 30 Strawberry Marsh Rd., PO Box 8700, St. John's, A1B 4J6 NL
709-729-3723, Fax: 709-729-6082, fishaqwebmaster@gov.nl.ca
Forest Resources, Fortis Bldg., PO Box 2006, Corner Brook, A2H 6J8 NL
709-637-2284, Fax: 709-634-4378

Northwest Territories
Department of Environment & Natural Resources, PO Box 1320, Yellowknife, X1A 2L9 NT

Nova Scotia
Department of Natural Resources, Founder's Square, 1701 Hollis St., 3rd Fl., PO Box 698, Halifax, B3J 2T9 NS
902-424-5935, Fax: 902-424-0594, 800-565-2224

Ontario
Ministry of Natural Resources, Whitney Block, #6630, 99 Wellesley St. West, 6th Fl., Toronto, M7A 1W3 ON
800-667-1940

Prince Edward Island
Department of Environment, Energy & Forestry, Jones Bldg., 11 Kent St., 4th & 5th Fl., PO Box 2000, Charlottetown, C1A 7N8 PE
902-368-5000, Fax: 902-368-5830
Department of Tourism, PO Box 2000, Charlottetown, C1A 7N8 PE
800-463-4734

Quebec
Ministère de l'Agriculture, des Pêcheries et de l'Alimentation, 200, ch Sainte-Foy, Québec, G1R 4X6 QC
418-380-2110, 888-222-6272

Yukon Territory
Yukon Environment, PO Box 2703, Whitehorse, Y1A 2C6 YT
867-667-5652, Fax: 867-393-6213, 800-661-0408, environmentyukon@gov.yk.ca
Yukon Fish & Wildlife Management Board, 106 Main St., Whitehorse, YT Y1A 5P7
867-667-3754, Fax: 867-393-6947, yfwmbadmin@yknet.yk.ca

FOREST RESOURCES

Northwest Territories
Forest Management Division, PO Box 7, Fort Smith, X0E 0P0 NT
Fax: 867-874-2077, forestmanagement.enr.gov.nt/

Alberta
Alberta Forestry Research Institute, 10365 - 97 St., Edmonton, AB T5J 3W7
780-427-1488, Fax: 780-427-0979
Alberta Research Council, 250 Karl Clark Rd., Edmonton, T6N 1E4 AB
780-450-5111, Fax: 780-450-5333

British Columbia
Ministry of Forests & Range, PO Box 9529 Prov Govt,Victoria, V8W 9C3 BC
250-387-4809, Fax: 250-953-3687

New Brunswick
Forest Protection Limited, 2502 Hwy. 102, Lincoln, NB E3B 7E6
506-446-6930, Fax: 506-446-6934, info@forestprotectionlimited.com
New Brunswick Forest Products Commission, PO Box 6000, Fredericton, NB E3B 5H1
506-453-2196, Fax: 506-457-4966

Newfoundland & Labrador
Forest Resources, Fortis Bldg., PO Box 2006, Corner Brook, A2H 6J8 NL
709-637-2284, Fax: 709-634-4378

Nova Scotia
NS Primary Forest Products Marketing Board, #804, 45 Alderney Dr., Dartmouth, NS B2Y 2N6
902-424-7598, Fax: 902-424-6965

Nunavut
Department of Environment, PO Box 1000 1300,Iqaluit, X0A 0H0 NU
867-975-7700, Fax: 867-975-7742, 866-222-9063, environment@gov.nu.ca

Ontario
Algonquin Forestry Authority - Huntsville, 222 Main St. West, Huntsville, ON P1H 1Y1
705-789-9647, Fax: 705-789-3353
Algonquin Forestry Authority - Pembroke, Victoria Centre, 84 Isabella St., 2nd Fl., Pembroke, ON K8A 5S5
613-735-0173, Fax: 613-735-4192
Forests Division, Roberta Bondar Place, #400, 70 Foster Dr., Sault Ste Marie, P6A 6V5 ON
Fax: 705-945-5977, 800-667-1940

Quebec
Forêt Québec, 880, ch Ste-Foy, 10e étage, Québec, G1S 4X4 QC
418-627-8652, Fax: 418-528-1278, foretquebec@mrnf.gouv.qc.ca

Saskatchewan
Lands & Forests Division, 3211 Albert St., 5th fl., Regina, S4S 5W6 SK
306-787-5407, Fax: 306-787-2947

Yukon Territory
Yukon Energy, Mines & Resources, PO Box 2703, Whitehorse, Y1A 2C6 YT
867-667-5466, Fax: 867-667-8601, 800-661-0408, emr@gov.yk.ca
Yukon Environment, PO Box 2703, Whitehorse, Y1A 2C6 YT
867-667-5652, Fax: 867-393-6213, 800-661-0408, environmentyukon@gov.yk.ca

FORESTRY & PAPER

Ontario
Forest Management Branch, #400, 70 Foster Dr., Sault Ste Marie, P6A 6V5 ON
705-945-6661, Fax: 705-945-6667
Natural Resources Canada, 580 Booth St., Ottawa, K1A 0E4 ON
613-995-0947, Fax: 613-992-7211
Policy Coordination Division, Herald Bldg., PO Box 2006, Corner Brook, A2H 6J8 NL
709-729-3752, Fax: 709-729-3374
Research Branch, 712 Yates St., Victoria, V8W 3E7 BC

Alberta
Alberta Forestry Research Institute, 10365 - 97 St., Edmonton, AB T5J 3W7
780-427-1488, Fax: 780-427-0979

British Columbia
Forest Practices Board, 1675 Douglas St., 3rd Fl., PO Box 9905 Prov Govt, Victoria, BC V8W 9R1
250-387-7964, Fax: 250-387-7009, 800-994-5899, fpboard@gov.bc.ca
Ministry of Forests & Range, PO Box 9529 Prov Govt,Victoria, V8W 9C3 BC
250-387-4809, Fax: 250-953-3687
Timber Export Advisory Committee, 1520 Blanshard St., 2nd Fl., PO Box 9514 Prov Govt, Victoria, BC V8W 9C2
250-387-8916, Fax: 250-387-5050

New Brunswick
Forest Protection Limited, 2502 Hwy. 102, Lincoln, NB E3B 7E6
506-446-6930, Fax: 506-446-6934, info@forestprotectionlimited.com
New Brunswick Forest Products Commission, PO Box 6000, Fredericton, NB E3B 5H1
506-453-2196, Fax: 506-457-4966

Newfoundland & Labrador
Forest Resources, Fortis Bldg., PO Box 2006, Corner Brook, A2H 6J8 NL
709-637-2284, Fax: 709-634-4378
Department of Natural Resources, Natural Resources Bldg., 50 Elizabeth Ave., 7th Fl., PO Box 8700, St. John's, A1B 4J6 NL
709-729-2920, Fax: 709-729-0059

Nova Scotia
Department of Natural Resources, Founder's Square, 1701 Hollis St., 3rd Fl., PO Box 698, Halifax, B3J 2T9 NS
902-424-5935, Fax: 902-424-0594, 800-565-2224

Ontario
Algonquin Forestry Authority - Huntsville, 222 Main St. West, Huntsville, ON P1H 1Y1
705-789-9647, Fax: 705-789-3353
Algonquin Forestry Authority - Pembroke, Victoria Centre, 84 Isabella St., 2nd Fl., Pembroke, ON K8A 5S5
613-735-0173, Fax: 613-735-4192

Government Quick Reference Guide / Geological Services

Ministry of Natural Resources, Whitney Block, #6630, 99 Wellesley St. West, 6th Fl., Toronto, M7A 1W3 ON
800-667-1940

Quebec
Ministère du Développement durable, de l'Environnement et des Parcs, Édifice Marie-Guyart, 675, boul René-Lévesque est, 29e étage, Québec, G1R 5V7 QC
418-521-3830, Fax: 418-646-5974, 800-561-1616, info@mddep.gouv.qc.ca

Saskatchewan
Saskatchewan Environment, 3211 Albert St., 2nd Fl., Regina, S4S 5W6 SK
306-953-3750, Fax: 306-787-9544, 800-567-4224, inquiry@serm.gov.sk.ca

Yukon Territory
Yukon Environment, PO Box 2703, Whitehorse, Y1A 2C6 YT
867-667-5652, Fax: 867-393-6213, 800-661-0408, environmentyukon@gov.yk.ca

GEOLOGICAL SERVICES

Geological Survey of Canada, 601 Booth St., Ottawa, K1A 0E8 ON
613-996-3919, Fax: 613-943-8742, info-ottawa@gsc.nrcan.gc.ca
Mapping Services Branch - Geomatics Canada, 615 Booth St., Ottawa, K1A 0E9 ON
613-995-4945, Fax: 613-995-8737,
Northwest Territories Geoscience Office, 4601 B - 52 Ave., PO Box 1500, Yellowknife, X1A 2R3 NT
867-669-2636, Fax: 867-669-2725, NTGO@gov.nt.ca
Ontario Geological Survey, Willet Green Miller Centre, 933 Ramsey Lake Rd.,Level B6, Sudbury, P3E 6B5 ON
705-670-5758, Fax: 705-670-5754

Alberta
Alberta Energy & Utilities Board, 640 - 5 Ave. SW, Calgary, AB T2P 3G4
403-297-8311, Fax: 403-297-7336

British Columbia
Ministry of Energy, Mines & Petroleum Resources, PO Box 9318 Prov Govt,Victoria, V8W 9N3 BC
250-952-0241

Manitoba
Manitoba Geological Survey, #360, 1394 Ellice Ave., Winnipeg, R3G 3P2 MB
Fax: 204-945-1406, 800-223-5215, minesinfo@gov.mb.ca

Nova Scotia
Nova Scotia Geomatics Centre, 160 Willow St., Amherst, B4H 3W3 NS
902-667-7231, Fax: 902-667-6008, 800-798-0706, info@nsgc.gov.ns.ca

GOVERNMENT

Auditor General of Canada, 240 Sparks St., Ottawa, K1A 0G6 ON
613-995-3708, Fax: 613-957-0474, communications@oag-bvg.gc.ca
British Columbia Treaty Commission, #203, 1155 West Pender St., Vancouver, BC V6E 2P4
604-482-9200, Fax: 604-482-9222, 800-665-8330, info@bctreaty.net
Business Development Bank of Canada, #400, 5, Place Ville-Marie, Montréal, H3B 5E7 QC
514-283-5904, Fax: 514-283-2872, 877-232-2269
Canada Economic Development for Québec Regions, Édifice Dominion Square, #900, 1255, rue Peel, Montréal, H3B 2T9 QC
514-283-6412, Fax: 514-283-3302, 866-385-6412
Canada Revenue Agency, 875 Heron Rd., Ottawa, K1A 0L5 ON
613-952-0384, 800-267-6999
Canadian Nuclear Safety Commission, 280 Slater St., PO Box 1046 B,Ottawa, K1P 5S9 ON
613-995-5894, Fax: 613-995-5086, 800-668-5284, info@cnsc-ccsn.gc.ca
Defence Construction Canada, Constitution Square, 350 Albert St., 19th Fl., Ottawa, K1A 0K3 ON
613-998-9548, Fax: 613-998-1061, 800-514-3555, info@dcc-cdc.gc.ca
Finance Canada, L'esplanade Laurier, 140 O'Connor St., Ottawa, K1A 0G5 ON
613-992-1573, Fax: 613-996-2690, finpub@fin.gc.ca

Foreign Affairs & International Trade Canada, 125 Sussex Dr., Ottawa, K1A 0G2 ON
613-944-4000, Fax: 613-996-9709, 800-267-8376, enqserv@international.gc.ca
Government of Canada, 111 Wellington St., PO Box 1103, Ottawa, K1A 0A6 ON
Indian & Northern Affairs Canada, 10 Wellington St., North Tower, Gatineau, K1A 0H4 QC
819-997-0380, Fax: 819-953-3017, 866-817-3977, infopubs@ainc-inac.gc.ca
Indian Taxation Advisory Board, 90 Elgin St., 2nd Fl., Ottawa, ON K1A 0H4
613-954-9972, Fax: 613-954-2073
Industry Canada, 235 Queen St., Ottawa, K1A 0H5 ON
Fax: 613-954-6436, 800-328-6189, info@ic.gc.ca
International Development Research Centre, 150 Kent St., PO Box 8500, Ottawa, K1P 0B2 ON
613-236-6163, Fax: 613-238-7230, info@idrc.ca
National Defence Canada, Major-General George R. Pearkes Bldg., 101 Colonel By Dr., Ottawa, K1A 0K2 ON
613-995-2534, Fax: 613-992-4739, 800-856-8488
Nunavut Impact Review Board, PO Box 2379, Cambridge Bay, NU X0B 0C0
867-983-4600, Fax: 867-983-2594, info@nirb.nunavut.ca
Nunavut Planning Commission, PO Box 2101, Cambridge Bay, NU X0B 0C0
867-983-2730, Fax: 867-983-2732
Public Works & Government Services Canada, Place du Portage, Phase III, 11, rue Laurier, Ottawa, K1A 0S5 ON
819-997-6363, Fax: 819-956-9062, 800-622-6232
Statistics Canada, R.H. Coats Bldg., Tunney's Pasture, 100 Tunney's Pasture Driveway, Ottawa, K1A 0T6 ON
Fax: 877-287-4369, 800-263-1136, infostats@statcan.ca
Treasury Board of Canada, 300 Laurier Ave. West, 10th Fl., Ottawa, K1A 0R5 ON
613-957-2400, Fax: 613-941-4000, 877-636-0656, info@tbs-sct.gc.ca

Alberta
Alberta Apprenticeship & Industry Training Board, 10155 - 102 St., 10th Fl., Edmonton, AB T5J 4L5
780-427-8765, Fax: 780-422-7376
Alberta Special Areas Board, 212 - 2nd Ave. West, PO Box 820, Hanna, AB T0J 1P0
403-854-5600, Fax: 403-854-5527, specarea@telusplanet.net
Government of Alberta, 9718 - 107 St., Edmonton, T5K 1E4 AB
Alberta Infrastructure & Transportation, Twin Atria Bldg., 4999 - 98 Ave., Edmonton, T6B 2X3 AB
780-427-2731, Fax: 780-466-3166,-310-0000
Alberta International & Intergovernmental Relations, Commerce Place, 10155 - 102 St., 12th Fl., Edmonton, T5J 4G8 AB
780-422-1510, Fax: 780-427-0699
Alberta Municipal Affairs & Housing, Communications Branch, Commerce Place, 10155 - 102 St., 18th Fl., Edmonton, T5J 4L4 AB
780-427-2732, Fax: 780-422-1419, comments@gov.ab.ca
Alberta Public Affairs Bureau, Park Plaza, 10611 - 98 Ave., 6th Fl., Edmonton, T5K 2P7 AB
403-427-2754, Fax: 403-422-4168

British Columbia
Agricultural Land Commission, #133, 4940 Canada Way, Burnaby, BC V5G 4K6
604-660-7000, Fax: 604-660-7033
British Columbia Assessment Authority, 1537 Hillside Ave., Victoria, BC V8T 4Y2
250-595-6211, Fax: 250-595-6222, info@bcassessment.ca
Client Services, 525 Superior St., 2nd Fl., PO Box 9472 Prov Govt,Victoria, V8W 9W6 BC
250-952-6861, Fax: 250-952-6803
Government of British Columbia, Parliament Bldgs., Victoria, V8V 1X4 BC
EnquiryBC@gov.bc.ca
British Columbia Utilities Commission, 900 Howe St., 6th Fl., PO Box 250, Vancouver, V6Z 2N3 BC
604-660-4700, Fax: 604-660-1102, 800-663-1385, commission.secretary@bcuc.com

Manitoba
Aboriginal Affairs Secretariat, #200, 500 Portage Ave., Winnipeg, R3C 3X1 MB
204-945-2510, Fax: 204-945-3689
Government of Manitoba, Legislative Building, Rm. 237, Winnipeg, R3C 0V8 MB
204-945-3636, Fax: 204-948-2507, clerkla@leg.gov.mb.ca

Manitoba Intergovernmental Affairs, #301, 450 Broadway Ave., Winnipeg, R3C 0V8 MB
Fax: 204-945-1383, mnia@leg.gov.mb.ca
Local Government Development Division, 59 Elizabeth Dr., PO Box 33, Thompson, R8N 1X4 MB
204-677-6794, Fax: 204-677-6525
Manitoba Civil Service Commission, #935, 155 Carlton St., Winnipeg, MB R3C 3H8
204-945-2332, Fax: 204-945-1486, cschrp@gov.mb.ca
Manitoba Land Value Appraisal Commission, 800 Portage Ave., Winnipeg, MB R3G 0N4
204-945-2941, Fax: 204-948-2235
Manitoba Municipal Board, #1144, 363 Broadway, Winnipeg, MB R3C 3N9
204-945-2941, Fax: 204-948-2235
Mineral Resources Division, #360, 1395 Ellice Ave., Winnipeg, R3G 3P2 MB
Fax: 204-945-8427
Provincial-Municipal Support Services, #508, 800 Portage Ave., Winnipeg, R3G 0N4 MB

New Brunswick
Corporate Services, Centennial Bldg., 670 King St., 5th Fl., PO Box 6000, Fredericton, E3B 5H1 NB
506-453-3707, Fax: 506-453-3993
Government of New Brunswick, PO Box 6000, Fredericton, E3B 5H1 NB
Department of Supply & Services, PO Box 6000, Fredericton, E3B 5H1 NB
506-453-3742, Fax: 506-444-4400, Reception.Marysville@gnb.ca

Newfoundland & Labrador
Government of Newfoundland & Labrador, Confederation Bldg., St. John's, A1B 4J6 NL
info@gov.nl.ca
Department of Government Services, PO Box 8700, St. John's, A1B 4J6 NL
709-729-4860
Department of Municipal Affairs, West Block, Main Fl., Confederation Bldg., PO Box 8700, St. John's, A1B 4J6 NL
709-729-3053

Northwest Territories
Department of Aboriginal Affairs & Intergovernmental Relations, 4910 - 52nd St., PO Box 1320, Yellowknife, X1A 2L9 NT
867-873-7143, Fax: 867-873-0233, 877-838-8194, nancy_gardiner @gov.nt.ca
Government of the Northwest Territories, PO Box 1320, Yellowknife, X1A 2L9 NT
Department of Public Works & Services, PO Box 1320, Yellowknife, X1A 2L9 NT
867-873-7114, Fax: 867-873-0226

Nova Scotia
Council of Atlantic Premiers, Council Secretariat, #1006, 5161 George St., PO Box 2044, Halifax, B3J 2Z1 NS
902-424-7590, Fax: 902-424-8976, info@cap-cpma.ca
Crown Lands Record Centre, Founders Square, #501, 1701 Hollis St., PO Box 698, Halifax, NS B3J 2T9
902-424-8681
Government of Nova Scotia, Province House, Halifax, B3J 2T3 NS
Department of Service Nova Scotia & Municipal Relations, 1505 Barrington St., PO Box 216, Halifax, B3J 2M4 NS
902-424-4141, Fax: 902-424-0581, public-enquiries@gov.ns.ca
Nova Scotia Utility & Review Board, 1601 Lower Water St., 3rd Fl., PO Box 1692 M,Halifax, B3J 3S3 NS
902-424-4448, Fax: 902-424-3919, uarb.board@gov.ns.ca

Nunavut
Department of Community & Government Services, J.G. Brown Bldg., PO Box 1000 700,Iqaluit, X0A 0H0 NU
867-975-5400, Fax: 867-975-5305
Department of Culture, Language, Elders & Youth, PO Box 1000 800,Iqaluit, X0A 0H0 NU
867-975-5500, Fax: 867-975-5504, 866-934-2035
Nunavut Emergency Management, PO Box 1000 700,Iqaluit, X0A 0H0 NU
867-975-5403, Fax: 867-979-4221, 800-693-1666
Department of Environment, PO Box 1000 1300,Iqaluit, X0A 0H0 NU
867-975-7700, Fax: 867-975-7742, 866-222-9063, environment@gov.nu.ca
Department of Executive & Intergovernmental Affairs, 1084 Aeroplex bldg., PO Box 1000 200,Iqaluit, X0A 0H0 NU
867-975-6000, Fax: 867-975-6090

Government of the Nunavut Territory, PO Box 1200, Iqaluit, X0A 0H0 NU
888-252-9869
Department of Health & Social Services, Sivummut bldg., PO Box 1007 1000,Iqaluit, X0A 0H0 NU
867-975-5700, Fax: 867-975-5705, health@gov.nu.ca

Ontario
Cancer Care Ontario, 620 University Ave., 15th Fl., Toronto, ON M5G 2L7
416-971-9800, Fax: 416-971-6888
Government of Ontario, Queen's Park, Toronto, M7A 1A2 ON
Healing Arts Radiation Protection Commission, 5700 Yonge St., 3rd Fl., Toronto, ON M2M 4K5
416-327-7952, Fax: 416-327-8805
Ministry of Municipal Affairs & Housing, 777 Bay St., 17th Fl., Toronto, M5G 2E5 ON
416-585-7041, Fax: 416-585-6227, 866-220-2290, mininfo.mah@ontario.ca
Ontario Housing Corporation, 777 Bay St., 2nd Fl., Toronto, ON M5G 2E5
Ontario Mental Health Foundation, #508, 489 College St., Toronto, ON M6G 1A5
416-920-7721, Fax: 416-920-0026, grants@omhf.on.ca
Ontario Northland, 555 Oak St. East, North Bay, ON P1B 8L3
705-472-4500, Fax: 705-476-5598, 800-363-7512, info@ontc.ca
Ontario Pension Board, #1100, 1 Adelaide St. East, Toronto, ON M5C 2X6
416-364-8558, Fax: 416-364-7578, 800-668-6203, office.services@opb.on.ca

Prince Edward Island
Government of Prince Edward Island, PO Box 2000, Charlottetown, C1A 7N8 PE
902-368-4000, Fax: 902-368-5544, island@gov.pe.ca
Department of the Provincial Treasury, Shaw Bldg., 95 Rochford St., 2nd Fl. South, PO Box 2000, Charlottetown, C1A 7N8 PE
902-368-4050, Fax: 902-368-6575

Quebec
Ministère des Affaires municipales et des Régions, Aile Chaveau, 10, rue Pierre-Olivier-Chauveau, 3e étage, Québec, G1R 4J3 QC
418-691-2019, Fax: 418-643-7385, communications@mamr.gouv.qc.ca
Bureau du coroner, #390, 2875, boul Laurier, Sainte-Foy, QC G1V 5B1
418-643-1845, Fax: 418-643-6174, clientele.coroner@msp.gouv.qc.ca
Centre de recherche industrielle du Québec, 333, rue Franquet, Sainte-Foy, QC G1P 4C7
418-659-1550, Fax: 418-652-2251, 800-667-2386, infocriq@criq.qc.ca
Comité de déontologie policière, Tour du Saint-Laurent, #A-200, 2525, boul Laurier, 2e étage, Québec, QC G1V 4Z6
418-646-1936, Fax: 418-528-0987, comite.deontologie@msp.gouv.qc.ca
Commissaire à la déontologie policière, 1200, rte de l'Église, R-C20, Sainte-Foy, QC G1V 4Y9
418-643-7897, Fax: 418-528-9473, 877-237-7897
Commissariat des incendies, 455, rue Dupont, Québec, QC G1K 6N2
418-529-5706, Fax: 418-529-9922
Commission québécoise des libérations conditionnelles, #1.32A, 300, boul Jean-Lesage, Québec, QC G1K 8K6
418-646-8300, Fax: 418-643-7217, liberation.conditionnel@msp.gouv.
Direction générale de la Sûreté du Québec, 1701, rue Parthenais, Montréal, QC H2K 3S7
514-598-4488, Fax: 514-598-4957, info@surete.qc.ca
Ministère du Développement économique, de l'Innovation et de l'Exportation, 710, place D'Youville, 3e étage, Québec, G1R 4Y4 QC
418-691-5950, Fax: 418-644-0118, 866-680-1884
Gouvernement du Québec, Hôtel du Parlement, 1045, rue des Parlementaires, Québec, G1A 1A4 QC
418-643-7239, Fax: 418-646-4271, 866-337-8837
Ministère des Ressources naturelles et de la Faune, #A303, 5700, 4e av ouest, Québec, G1H 6R1 QC
418-627-8600, Fax: 418-643-0720, 866-248-6936, service.citoyens@mrnf.gouv.qc.ca
Régie des alcools, des courses et des jeux, 560, boul Charest est, Québec, QC G1K 3J3
418-643-7667, Fax: 418-643-5971, 800-363-0320, racj.quebec@racj.gouv.qc.ca

École nationale de police du Québec, 350, rue Marguerite-d'Youville, Nicolet, QC J3T 1X4
819-293-8631, Fax: 819-293-4018, courriel@enpq.qc.ca

Saskatchewan
Government of Saskatchewan, Regina, S4S 0B3 SK
Saskatchewan Government Relations, 1855 Victoria Ave., Regina, S4P 3T2 SK
306-787-2635
Saskatchewan Government Services, Century Plaza, 1920 Rose St., Regina, S4P 0A9 SK
306-787-6911, Fax: 306-787-1061
Saskatchewan Tourism, Parks, Culture, & Sport, 1919 Saskatchewan Dr., 4th Fl., Regina, S4P 4H2 SK
306-787-5729, Fax: 306-787-8560

Yukon Territory
Government of the Yukon Territory, PO Box 2703, Whitehorse, Y1A 2C6 YT
867-667-5811, 800-661-0408

GOVERNMENT (GENERAL INFORMATION)
Auditor General of Canada, 240 Sparks St., Ottawa, K1A 0G6 ON
613-995-3708, Fax: 613-957-0474, communications@oag-bvg.gc.ca
Canada Business, 235 Queen St., Ottawa, K1A 0H5 ON
Fax: 888-417-0442, 888-576-4444
Communications & Consultations Branch, 930 Carling Ave., Ottawa, K1A 0C7 ON
613-759-1000, Fax: 613-759-7976
Consultations & Communications Branch, East Tower, 140 O'Connor St., 19th Fl., Ottawa, K1A 0G5 ON
613-992-1573, consltcomm@fin.gc.ca
Environment Canada, 10 Wellington St., Gatineau, K1A 0H3 QC
819-997-2800, Fax: 819-994-1412, 800-668-6767, enviroinfo@ec.gc.ca
Fisheries & Oceans Canada, 200 Kent St., Ottawa, K1A 0E6 ON
613-993-0999, Fax: 613-996-1866, info@dfo-mpo.gc.ca
Foreign Affairs & International Trade Canada, 125 Sussex Dr., Ottawa, K1A 0G2 ON
613-944-4000, Fax: 613-996-9709, 800-267-8376, enqserv@international.gc.ca
Health Canada, Tunney's Pasture, Ottawa, K1A 0K9 ON
613-957-2991, Fax: 613-941-5366, Info@hc-sc.gc.ca
Human Resources & Skills Development Canada, 140 Promenade du Portage, Ottawa, K1A 0J9 ON
Indian & Northern Affairs Canada, 10 Wellington St., North Tower, Gatineau, K1A 0H4 QC
819-997-0380, Fax: 819-953-3017, 866-817-3977, infopubs@ainc-inac.gc.ca
Industry Canada, 235 Queen St., Ottawa, K1A 0H5 ON
Fax: 613-954-6436, 800-328-6189, info@ic.gc.ca
National Defence Canada, Major-General George R. Pearkes Bldg., 101 Colonel By Dr., Ottawa, K1A 0K2 ON
613-995-2534, Fax: 613-992-4739, 800-856-8488
Service Canada, 140, Promenade du Portage, Gatineau, K1A 0J9 QC
800-622-6232
Statistics Canada, R.H. Coats Bldg., Tunney's Pasture, 100 Tunney's Pasture Driveway, Ottawa, K1A 0T6 ON
Fax: 877-287-4369, 800-263-1136, infostats@statcan.ca
Transport Canada, Place de Ville, 330 Sparks St., Tower C, Ottawa, K1A 0N5 ON
613-990-2309, Fax: 613-954-4731, minTC@tc.gc.ca
Treasury Board of Canada, 300 Laurier Ave. West, 10th Fl., Ottawa, K1A 0R5 ON
613-957-2400, Fax: 613-941-4000, 877-636-0656, info@tbs-sct.gc.ca

Alberta
Alberta Public Affairs Bureau, Park Plaza, 10611 - 98 Ave., 6th Fl., Edmonton, T5K 2P7 AB
403-427-2754, Fax: 403-422-4168
Alberta Service Alberta, John E. Brownlee Bldg., 10365 - 97 St., Mezzanine Fl., Edmonton, T5J 3W7 AB
780-427-2711, 877-427-4088, government.services@gov.ab.ca

British Columbia
Chief Information Office, 4000 Seymour Pl., PO Box 9412 Prov Govt,Victoria, V8W 9V1 BC
250-356-7970, Fax: 250-387-1940

Newfoundland & Labrador
Department of Government Services, PO Box 8700, St. John's, A1B 4J6 NL
709-729-4860

Nova Scotia
Department of Service Nova Scotia & Municipal Relations, 1505 Barrington St., PO Box 216, Halifax, B3J 2M4 NS
902-424-4141, Fax: 902-424-0581, public-enquiries@gov.ns.ca

Nunavut
Department of Executive & Intergovernmental Affairs, 1084 Aeroplex bldg., PO Box 1000 200,Iqaluit, X0A 0H0 NU
867-975-6000, Fax: 867-975-6090

Ontario
ServiceOntario, College Park, 777 Bay St., 15th fl., Toronto, M7A 2J3 ON
416-326-6205, Fax: 416-326-5106

Quebec
Services Québec, Bureau de la qualité, 800, place D'Youville, 20e étage, Québec, G1R 3P4 QC
418-646-4011

GRANTS & SUBSIDIES
See Also: Student Aid
Atlantic Canada Opportunities Agency, Blue Cross Centre, 644 Main St., 3rd Fl., PO Box 6051, Moncton, E1C 9J8 NB
506-851-2271, Fax: 506-851-7403, 800-561-7862
Business Development Bank of Canada, #400, 5, Place Ville-Marie, Montréal, H3B 5E7 QC
514-283-5904, Fax: 514-283-2872, 877-232-2269
Canada Economic Development for Québec Regions, Édifice Dominion Square, #900, 1255, rue Peel, Montréal, H3B 2T9 QC
514-283-6412, Fax: 514-283-3302, 866-385-6412
Canada Mortgage & Housing Corporation, 700 Montreal Rd., Ottawa, K1A 0P7 ON
613-748-2000, Fax: 613-748-2098, 800-668-2642, chic@cmhc-schl.gc.ca
Canadian Institutes of Health Research, 160 Elgin St., 9th Fl., Ottawa, K1A 0W9 ON
613-941-2672, Fax: 613-954-1800, info@cihr-irsc.gc.ca
International Development Research Centre, 150 Kent St., PO Box 8500, Ottawa, K1P 0B2 ON
613-236-6163, Fax: 613-238-7230, info@idrc.ca
Natural Sciences & Engineering Research Council of Canada, Constitution Square, Tower II, 350 Albert St., Ottawa, K1A 1H5 ON
613-995-4273, Fax: 613-992-5337
Western Economic Diversification Canada, Canada Place, #1500, 9700 Jasper Ave. NW, Edmonton, T5J 4H7 AB
780-495-4164, Fax: 780-495-4557, 888-338-9378

Alberta
Local Government Services, Commerce Place, 10155 - 102 St., 17th Fl., Edmonton, T5J 4L4 AB
Fax: 780-427-0453

Ontario
Culture Policy, Programs & Services Division, 400 University Ave., 5th Fl., Toronto, M7A 2R9 ON
416-314-7265, Fax: 416-314-7461

Prince Edward Island
Department of the Provincial Treasury, Shaw Bldg., 95 Rochford St., 2nd Fl. South, PO Box 2000, Charlottetown, C1A 7N8 PE
902-368-4050, Fax: 902-368-6575

Saskatchewan
Saskatchewan Energy & Resources, #300, 2103 - 11th Ave., Regina, S4P 3Z8 SK
306-787-2528, Fax: 306-787-8447, 866-727-5427

HAZARDOUS MATERIALS
Hazardous Materials Information Review Commission, 427 Laurier Ave. West, 7th Fl., Ottawa, ON K1A 1M3
613-993-4331, Fax: 613-993-4686, hmirc-ccrmd@hc-sc.gc.ca
Institute for Chemical Process & Environmental Technology, Bldg. M-12, 1200 Montreal Rd., Ottawa, K1A 0R6 ON
613-993-4041, Fax: 613-957-8231
Low-Level Radioactive Waste Management Office, #200, 1900 City Park Dr., Ottawa, K1J 1A3 ON
613-998-9442, Fax: 613-952-0760
Spills Action Centre, 5775 Yonge St., 5th Fl., Toronto, M2M 4J1 ON
416-325-3000, Fax: 416-325-3011, 800-268-6060

Government Quick Reference Guide / Health

Standards Development Branch, 40 St. Clair Ave. West, 7th Fl., Toronto, M4V 1M2 ON
416-327-5519

British Columbia
British Columbia Provincial Emergency Program, PO Box 9201 Prov Govt,Victoria, V8W 9J1 BC
250-952-4913, Fax: 250-952-4888, 888-257-4777

Manitoba
Emergency Measures Organization, 405 Broadway Ave., 15th Floor, Winnipeg, R3C 3L6 MB
204-945-4772, Fax: 204-945-4929, 888-267-8298, emo@gov.mb.ca

Ontario
Ministry of Environment, 135 St. Clair Ave. West, Toronto, M4V 1P5 ON
416-325-4000, Fax: 416-325-3159, 800-565-4923
Pesticides Advisory Committee, #1203, 2300 Yonge St., 12th Fl., Toronto, ON M4P 1E4
416-314-9230, Fax: 416-314-9237,

HEALTH

Canadian Centre for Occupational Health & Safety, 135 Hunter St. East, Hamilton, L8N 1M5 ON
905-572-2981, Fax: 905-572-2206, 800-668-4284, clientservices@ccohs.ca
Canadian Food Inspection Agency, 59 Camelot Dr., Ottawa, K1A 0Y9 ON
613-225-2342, Fax: 613-228-6629, 800-442-2342
Food Value Chain Bureau, 930 Carling Ave., 5th Fl., Ottawa, K1A 0C5 ON
Fax: 613-759-7480
Hazardous Materials Information Review Commission, 427 Laurier Ave. West, 7th Fl., Ottawa, ON K1A 1M3
613-993-4331, Fax: 613-993-4686, hmirc-ccrmd@hc-sc.gc.ca
Health Canada, Tunney's Pasture, Ottawa, K1A 0K9 ON
613-957-2991, Fax: 613-941-5366, Info@hc-sc.gc.ca
Public Health Agency of Canada, 130 Colonnade Rd., Ottawa, ON K1A 0K9

Alberta
Alberta Alcohol & Drug Abuse Commission, Associated Engineering Plaza, 10909 Jasper Ave., 6th Fl., Edmonton, AB T5J 3M9
780-415-0370, Fax: 780-423-1419
Alberta Cancer Board, Standard Life Centre, #1220, 10405 Jasper Ave., Edmonton, AB T5J 3N4
780-412-6328, Fax: 780-412-6326, info@cancerboard.ab.ca
Alberta Mental Health Board, 10025 Jasper Ave., 19th Fl., PO Box 1360, Edmonton, AB T5J 2N3
780-422-2233, Fax: 780-422-2472, 877-303-2642, info@amhb.ab.ca
Alberta Mental Health Patient Advocate Office, #1202, 10035 - 108 St., Edmonton, AB T5J 3E1
780-422-1812, Fax: 780-422-0695
Alberta Health & Wellness, TELUS Plaza North Tower, 10025 Jasper Ave., 22nd Fl., PO Box 1360 Main,Edmonton, T5J 2N3 AB
780-427-7164, health.ahinform@gov.ab.ca
Health Disciplines Board, North Tower, 17th Fl., Telus Plaza, Health Professions Bran, 10025 Jasper Ave., Edmonton, AB T5J 2N3
780-415-0486, Fax: 780-422-2880
Health Facilities Review Committee, Garneau Professional Centre, #250, 11044 - 82 Ave., Edmonton, AB T6G 0T2
780-427-4924, Fax: 780-427-0806
Occupational Health & Safety Council, Labour Bldg, 10808 - 99 Ave., 10th Fl., Edmonton, AB T5K 0G5
780-427-6452, Fax: 780-427-7548

British Columbia
Ministry of Health Services, 1515 Blanshard St., Victoria, V8W 3C8 BC
250-952-1742, Fax: 250-356-9587, 800-465-4911, hlth.health@gems1.gov.bc.ca

Manitoba
Addictions Foundation of Manitoba, 1031 Portage Ave., Winnipeg, MB R3G 0R8
204-944-6200, Fax: 204-786-7768, library@afm.mb.ca
Manitoba Health & Healthy Living, #100, 300 Carlton St., Winnipeg, R3B 3M9 MB
204-786-7191, minhlt@leg.gov.mb.ca
Manitoba Drug Standards & Therapeutics Committee, #1014, 300 Carlton St., Winnipeg, MB R3B 3M9
204-786-7317, Fax: 204-942-2030

Primary Care & Healthy Living, 300 Carlton St., 2nd Floor, Winnipeg, R3B 3M9 MB

New Brunswick
Department of Health, PO Box 5100, Fredericton, E3B 5G8 NB
506-457-4800, Fax: 506-453-5243, dh-ms@dh-ms.ca
Workplace Health, Safety & Compensation Commission of New Brunswick, 1 Portland St., PO Box 160, Saint John, E2L 3X9 NB
506-632-2200, 800-222-9775, communications@ws-ts.nb.ca

Newfoundland & Labrador
Department of Health & Community Services, West Block, Confederation Bldg., PO Box 8700, St. John's, A1B 4J6 NL
709-729-5021, Fax: 709-729-5824
Newfoundland & Labrador Health Boards Associations, Board of Trade Bldg., #202, 66 Kenmount Rd., St. John's, NL A1B 3V7
709-364-7701, Fax: 709-364-6460, nlhba@nlhba.nf.ca

Northwest Territories
Department of Health & Social Services, Centre Square Tower, PO Box 1320, Yellowknife, X1A 2L9 NT
Fax: 867-873-0266

Nova Scotia
Department of Health, Joseph Howe Bldg., 1690 Hollis St., 4th Fl., PO Box 488, Halifax, B3J 2R8 NS
902-424-5818, Fax: 902-424-0730, 800-387-6665, DoHweb@gov.ns.ca
Nova Scotia Advisory Commission on AIDS, Dennis Bldg., 1740 Granville St., 6th Fl., Halifax, NS B3J 1X5
902-424-5730, Fax: 902-424-4727
Occupational Health & Safety Advisory Council, PO Box 697, Halifax, NS B3J 2T8
902-424-2484, Fax: 902-424-5640
Occupational Health & Safety Appeal Panel, 5151 Terminal Rd., 7th Fl., PO Box 697, Halifax, NS B3J 2T8
902-424-6730

Nunavut
Department of Culture, Language, Elders & Youth, PO Box 1000 800,Iqaluit, X0A 0H0 NU
867-975-5500, Fax: 867-975-5504, 866-934-2035
Department of Health & Social Services, Sivummut bldg., PO Box 1007 1000,Iqaluit, X0A 0H0 NU
867-975-5700, Fax: 867-975-5705, health@gov.nu.ca

Ontario
Cancer Care Ontario, 620 University Ave., 15th Fl., Toronto, ON M5G 2L7
416-971-9800, Fax: 416-971-6888
Consent & Capacity Board, 151 Bloor St. West, 10th Fl., Toronto, ON M5S 2T5
416-327-4142, Fax: 416-327-4207
Healing Arts Radiation Protection Commission, 5700 Yonge St., 3rd Fl., Toronto, ON M2M 4K5
416-327-7952, Fax: 416-327-8805
Ministry of Health & Long-Term Care, Hepburn Block, 80 Grosvenor St., 10th Fl, Toronto, M7A 2C4 ON
416-327-4327, 800-268-1153
Health Boards Secretariat, 151 Bloor St. West, 9th Fl., Toronto, ON M5S 2T5
416-327-8512, Fax: 416-327-8524
Medical Eligibility Committee, 370 Select Dr., PO Box 168, Kingston, ON K7M 8T4
613-548-6405
Ontario Mental Health Foundation, #508, 489 College St., Toronto, ON M6G 1A5
416-920-7721, Fax: 416-920-0026, grants@omhf.on.ca
Ontario Review Board, 151 Bloor St. West, 10th Fl., Toronto, ON M5S 2T5
416-327-8866, Fax: 416-327-8867
Pesticides Advisory Committee, #1203, 2300 Yonge St., 12th Fl., Toronto, ON M4P 1E4
416-314-9230, Fax: 416-314-9237
Smart Systems for Health, #1900, 415 Yonge St., Toronto, ON M5B 2E7
416-586-6500, Fax: 416-586-4363
Trillium Gift of Life Network, #1440, 155 University Ave., Toronto, ON M5H 3B7
416-363-4001, Fax: 416-363-4002

Prince Edward Island
Food Technology Centre, 101 Belvedere Ave., PO Box 2000, Charlottetown, PE C1A 7N8
902-368-5548, Fax: 902-368-5549, 877-368-5548, ftcweb@gov.pe.ca

Department of Health, Jones Bldg., 11 Kent St., 2nd Fl., PO Box 2000, Charlottetown, C1A 7N8 PE
902-368-4900, Fax: 902-368-4974

Quebec
Agence d'évaluation des technologies et des modes d'intervention en santé, #1040, 2021, av Union, Montréal, QC H3A 2S9
514-873-2563, Fax: 514-873-1369
Bureau du coroner, #390, 2875, boul Laurier, Sainte-Foy, QC G1V 5B1
418-643-1845, Fax: 418-643-6174, clientele.coroner@msp.gouv.qc.ca
Centre québécois de lutte aux dépendances, 105, rue Normand, Montréal, QC H2Y 2K6
514-389-6336, Fax: 514-389-1830, info@cqld.ca
Commission de la santé et de la sécurité du travail, 425, rue du Pont, CP 4900 Terminus, Québec, QC G1K 7S6
418-266-4000, Fax: 418-266-4015, 800-668-6811
Conseil de la santé et du bien-être, #700, 1020, rte de l'Église, Sainte-Foy, QC G1V 3V9
418-643-3040, Fax: 418-644-0654, csbe@csbe.gouv.qc.ca
Conseil du médicament, #100, 1195, av Lavigerie, Sainte-Foy, QC G1V 4N3
418-644-8103, Fax: 418-644-8120, cdm@cdm.gouv.qc.ca
Conseil médical du Québec, 1020, rte de l'Église, 7e étage, Sainte-Foy, QC G1V 3V9
418-646-4379, Fax: 418-646-9895, cmed@cmed.gouv.qc.ca
Conseil québécois de lutte contre le cancer, 1075, ch Sainte-Foy, 6e étage, Québec, QC G1S 2M1
418-266-6944, Fax: 418-266-6938, cqlc@msss.gouv.qc.ca
Corporation d'hébergement du Québec, 2535, boul Laurier, 5e étage, Sainte-Foy, QC G1V 4M3
418-644-3600, Fax: 418-644-3609, danielle.dussault@chq.gouv.qc.ca
Fonds de la recherche en santé du Québec, 500, rue Sherbrooke ouest, 8e étage, Montréal, QC H3A 3C6
514-873-2114, Fax: 514-873-8768
Institut national de santé publique du Québec, 945, av Wolfe, Sainte-Foy, QC G1V 5B3
418-650-5115, Fax: 418-646-9328
Protecteur des usagers en matière de santé et de services sociaux, #6.400, 500, boul René-Lévesque ouest, Montréal, QC H2Z 1W7
514-873-3205, Fax: 514-873-5665, 877-658-2625, protecteur@msss.gouv.qc.ca
Régie de l'assurance maladie du Québec, 1125, ch Saint-Louis, Québec, QC G1S 1E7
418-646-4636
Commission de la santé et de la sécurité au travail, 524, rue Bourdages, CP 1200 Terminus postal,Québec, G1K 7E2 QC
418-266-4850, Fax: 418-266-4389, 866-302-2778
Ministère de la Santé et des Services sociaux, Direction des communications et Renseignements généraux, 1075, ch Sainte-Foy, Québec, G1S 2M1 QC
418-266-8900, 800-707-3380, regisseur.web@msss.gouv.qc.ca

Saskatchewan
Health Quality Council, 241, 111 Research Dr., Saskatoon, SK S7N 3R2
306-668-8810, Fax: 306-668-8820
Saskatchewan Health, T.C. Douglas Bldg., 3475 Albert St., Regina, S4S 6X6 SK
306-787-0146, 800-667-7766, info@health.gov.sk.ca

Yukon Territory
Yukon Health & Social Services, PO Box 2703, Whitehorse, Y1A 2C6 YT
867-667-3673, Fax: 867-667-3096, 800-661-0408, hss@gov.yk.ca

HEALTH & SAFETY

Ontario
Aviation & Forest Fire Management Branch, #400, 70 Foster Dr., Sault Ste Marie, P6A 6V5 ON
Canadian Centre for Occupational Health & Safety, 135 Hunter St. East, Hamilton, L8N 1M5 ON
905-572-2981, Fax: 905-572-2206, 800-668-4284, clientservices@ccohs.ca
Canadian Coast Guard, Centennial Towers, #6S018, 200 Kent St., Ottawa, K1A 0E6 ON
613-998-1573, Fax: 613-990-2780
Canadian Environmental Assessment Agency, Place Bell Canada, 160 Elgin St., 22nd Fl., Ottawa, K1A 0H3 ON
613-957-0700, Fax: 613-957-0946, info@ceaa-acee.gc.ca

Canadian Food Inspection Agency, 59 Camelot Dr., Ottawa, K1A 0Y9 ON
  613-225-2342, Fax: 613-228-6629, 800-442-2342
Canadian Food Inspection Agency, 59 Camelot Dr., Ottawa, ON K1A 0Y9
  613-225-2342, 800-442-2342
Finance & Administration Division, 910 Government St., 5th Fl., PO Box 9256 Prov Govt,Victoria, V8W 9J4 BC
  250-387-6856, Fax: 250-356-9185
Hazardous Materials Information Review Commission, 427 Laurier Ave. West, 7th Fl., Ottawa, ON K1A 1M3
  613-993-4331, Fax: 613-993-4686, hmirc-ccrmd@hc-sc.gc.ca
Health Canada, Tunney's Pasture, Ottawa, K1A 0K9 ON
  613-957-2991, Fax: 613-941-5366, Info@hc-sc.gc.ca
Human Resources & Skills Development Canada, 140 Promenade du Portage, Ottawa, K1A 0J9 ON
Department of Labour & Workforce Development, 5151 Terminal Rd., 6th Fl., PO Box 697, Halifax, B3J 2T8 NS
  902-424-5301, Fax: 902-424-0575
National Defence Canada, Major-General George R. Pearkes Bldg., 101 Colonel By Dr., Ottawa, K1A 0K2 ON
  613-995-2534, Fax: 613-992-4739, 800-856-8488
Occupational Health & Safety Branch, 655 Bay St., 14th Fl., Toronto, M7A 1T7 ON
  416-326-7770, Fax: 416-326-7242
Public Safety Canada, 269 Laurier Ave. West, Ottawa, K1A 0P8 ON
  613-991-3301, Fax: 613-954-5186, 866-222-3006, communications@ps.gc.ca
Transportation Safety Board of Canada, 200 Promenade du Portage, 4th Fl., Ottawa, K1A 1K8 ON
  819-994-3741, Fax: 819-997-2239, 800-387-3557

Alberta
Alberta Employment, Immigration & Industry, Minister's Office, Legislature Bldg., #208, 10800 - 97 Ave., Edmonton, T5K 2B6 AB
  780-415-4800, Fax: 780-422-9556, 866-644-5135, eii.communications@gov.ab.ca
Alberta Health & Wellness, TELUS Plaza North Tower, 10025 Jasper Ave., 22nd Fl., PO Box 1360 Main,Edmonton, T5J 2N3 AB
  780-427-7164, health.ahinform@gov.ab.ca
Occupational Health & Safety Council, Labour Bldg, 10808 - 99 Ave., 10th Fl., Edmonton, AB T5K 0G5
  780-427-6452, Fax: 780-427-7548
Transportation Safety Board, Twin Atria Bldg., 4999 - 98 Ave., Edmonton, AB T6B 2X3
  780-427-7178, Fax: 780-422-9739

British Columbia
Ministry of Health Services, 1515 Blanshard St., Victoria, V8W 3C8 BC
  250-952-1742, Fax: 250-356-9587, 800-465-4911, hlth.health@gems1.gov.bc.ca
Ministry of Labour & Citizens' Services, PO Box 9052 Prov Govt,Victoria, V8W 9E2 BC
  250-356-6348, Fax: 250-356-6595, LCS.Minister@gov.bc.ca
British Columbia Provincial Emergency Program, PO Box 9201 Prov Govt,Victoria, V8W 9J1 BC
  250-952-4913, Fax: 250-952-4888, 888-257-4777
Workers' Compensation Board of British Columbia, PO Box 5350 Terminal,Vancouver, V6B 5L5 BC
  604-276-3100, Fax: 604-244-6490, 888-621-7233

Manitoba
Advisory Council on Workplace Safety & Health, #200, 401 York Ave., Winnipeg, MB R3C 0P8
  204-945-3446, Fax: 204-945-4556
Emergency Measures Organization, 405 Broadway Ave., 15th Floor, Winnipeg, R3C 3L6 MB
  204-945-4772, Fax: 204-945-4929, 888-267-8298, emo@gov.mb.ca
Manitoba Health & Healthy Living, #100, 300 Carlton St., Winnipeg, R3B 3M9 MB
  204-786-7191, minhlt@leg.gov.mb.ca
Manitoba Labour & Immigration, Legislative Building, 317, 450 Broadway Ave., Winnipeg, R3C 0V8 MB
  204-945-4079, Fax: 204-945-8312, minlab@leg.gov.mb.ca
Workplace Safety & Health Division, #200, 401 York Ave., Winnipeg, R3C 0P8 MB
  204-945-3446, Fax: 204-948-2209, wshcompl@gov.mb.ca

New Brunswick
Department of Health, PO Box 5100, Fredericton, E3B 5G8 NB
  506-457-4800, Fax: 506-453-5243, dh-ms@dh-ms.ca

Department of Post-Secondary Education, Training & Labour, 470 York St., PO Box 6000, Fredericton, E3B 5H1 NB
  506-453-2597, Fax: 506-453-3618, dpetlinfo@gnb.ca
Workplace Health, Safety & Compensation Commission of New Brunswick, 1 Portland St., PO Box 160, Saint John, E2L 3X9 NB
  506-632-2200, 800-222-9775, communications@ws-ts.nb.ca

Newfoundland & Labrador
Newfoundland & Labrador Emergency Measures Organization, PO Box 8700, St. John's, A1B 4J6 NL
  709-729-3703, Fax: 709-729-3857
Department of Environment & Conservation, Confederation Bldg., West Block, 4th Fl., PO Box 8700, St. John's, A1B 4J6 NL
  709-729-2664, Fax: 709-729-6639, 800-563-6181, info@gov.nl.ca
Department of Health & Community Services, West Block, Confederation Bldg., PO Box 8700, St. John's, A1B 4J6 NL
  709-729-5021, Fax: 709-729-5824
Newfoundland & Labrador Workplace Health, Safety & Compensation Commission, 146 - 148 Forest Rd., PO Box 9000, St. John's, A1A 3B8 NL
  709-778-1000, Fax: 709-738-1714, 800-563-9000, general.inquiries@whscc.nl.ca

Northwest Territories
Department of Health & Social Services, Centre Square Tower, PO Box 1320, Yellowknife, X1A 2L9 NT
  Fax: 867-873-0266
Northwest Territories & Nunavut Workers' Compensation Board, Centre Square Tower, 5022 - 49th St., 5th Fl., PO Box 8888, Yellowknife, X1A 2R3 NT
  867-920-3888, Fax: 867-873-4596, 800-661-0792, wcb@wcb.nt.ca

Nova Scotia
Nova Scotia Emergency Management Office, PO Box 2581, Halifax, B3J 3N5 NS
  902-424-5620, Fax: 902-424-5376, 866-424-5620, emo@gov.ns.ca
Department of Health, Joseph Howe Bldg., 1690 Hollis St., 4th Fl., PO Box 488, Halifax, B3J 2R8 NS
  902-424-5818, Fax: 902-424-0730, 800-387-6665, DoHweb@gov.ns.ca
Occupational Health & Safety Advisory Council, PO Box 697, Halifax, NS B3J 2T8
  902-424-2484, Fax: 902-424-5640
Occupational Health & Safety Appeal Panel, 5151 Terminal Rd., 7th Fl., PO Box 697, Halifax, NS B3J 2T8
  902-424-6730

Ontario
Ministry of Government Services & Consumer Services, Whitney Block, #4320, 99 Wellesley St. West, 4th Fl., Toronto, M7A 1W3 ON
  416-326-1234, Fax: 416-327-3790, 800-268-1142
Ministry of Health & Long-Term Care, Hepburn Block, 80 Grosvenor St., 10th Fl, Toronto, M7A 2C4 ON
  416-327-4327, 800-268-1153
Ministry of Labour, 400 University Ave., 14th Fl., Toronto, M7A 1T7 ON
  416-326-7770, 800-268-8013
Road User Safety Division, #191, Bldg A, 1201 Wilson Ave., Toronto, M3M 1J8 ON
  416-235-2999, Fax: 416-235-4153

Prince Edward Island
Prince Edward Island Emergency Measures Organization, National Bank Tower, #600, 134 Kent St., PO Box 2000, Charlottetown, C1A 7N8 PE
  902-894-0385, Fax: 902-368-6362
Department of Health, Jones Bldg., 11 Kent St., 2nd Fl., PO Box 2000, Charlottetown, C1A 7N8 PE
  902-368-4900, Fax: 902-368-4974
Prince Edward Island Workers Compensation Board, 14 Weymouth St., PO Box 757, Charlottetown, C1A 7L7 PE
  902-368-5680, Fax: 902-368-5705, 800-237-5049

Quebec
Commission de la santé et de la sécurité au travail, 524, rue Bourdages, CP 1200 Terminus postal,Québec, G1K 7E2 QC
  418-266-4850, Fax: 418-266-4389, 866-302-2778
Ministère de la Santé et des Services sociaux, Direction des communications et Renseignements généraux, 1075, ch Sainte-Foy, Québec, G1S 2M1 QC
  418-266-8900, 800-707-3380, regisseur.web@msss.gouv.qc.ca

Ministère de la Sécurité publique, Tour des Laurentides, 2525, boul Laurier, 5e étage, Québec, G1V 2L2 QC
  Fax: 418-643-0275, 866-644-6826
Ministère du Travail, 200, ch Ste-Foy, 6e étage, Québec, G1R 5S1 QC
  418-643-4817, Fax: 418-528-0559, 800-643-4817, service_clientele@travail.gouv.qc.ca

Saskatchewan
Saskatchewan Advanced Education, Employment & Labour, 1945 Hamilton St., Regina, S4P 2C8 SK
  306-787-9478, Fax: 306-787-2315
Saskatchewan Health, T.C. Douglas Bldg., 3475 Albert St., Regina, S4S 6X6 SK
  306-787-0146, 800-667-7766, info@health.gov.sk.ca

Yukon Territory
Emergency Measures Organization, PO Box 2703, Whitehorse, Y1A 2C6 YT
  867-667-5220, Fax: 867-393-6266, 800-661-0408, emo.yukon@gov.yk.ca
Yukon Health & Social Services, PO Box 2703, Whitehorse, Y1A 2C6 YT
  867-667-3673, Fax: 867-667-3096, 800-661-0408, hss@gov.yk.ca
Yukon Workers' Compensation Health & Safety Board, 401 Strickland St., Whitehorse, Y1A 5N8 YT
  867-667-5645, Fax: 867-393-6279, 800-661-0443, worksafe@gov.yk.ca

HEALTH CARE INSURANCE
Health Canada, Tunney's Pasture, Ottawa, K1A 0K9 ON
  613-957-2991, Fax: 613-941-5366, Info@hc-sc.gc.ca

British Columbia
Medical Services Commission, 1515 Blanshard St., 3rd Fl., Victoria, BC V8W 3C8
  250-952-3073, Fax: 250-952-3131

Newfoundland & Labrador
Department of Health & Community Services, West Block, Confederation Bldg., PO Box 8700, St. John's, A1B 4J6 NL
  709-729-5021, Fax: 709-729-5824

Northwest Territories
Department of Health & Social Services, Centre Square Tower, PO Box 1320, Yellowknife, X1A 2L9 NT
  Fax: 867-873-0266

Nunavut
Department of Health & Social Services, Sivummut bldg., PO Box 1007 1000,Iqaluit, X0A 0H0 NU
  867-975-5700, Fax: 867-975-5705, health@gov.nu.ca

Prince Edward Island
Department of Health, Jones Bldg., 11 Kent St., 2nd Fl., PO Box 2000, Charlottetown, C1A 7N8 PE
  902-368-4900, Fax: 902-368-4974

Quebec
Régie de l'assurance maladie du Québec, 1125, ch Saint-Louis, Québec, QC G1S 1E7
  418-646-4636

HEALTH SERVICES
See Also: Health Care Insurance; Occupational Safety
Canadian Centre for Occupational Health & Safety, 135 Hunter St. East, Hamilton, L8N 1M5 ON
  905-572-2981, Fax: 905-572-2206, 800-668-4284, clientservices@ccohs.ca
Canadian Institutes of Health Research, 160 Elgin St., 9th Fl., Ottawa, K1A 0W9 ON
  613-941-2672, Fax: 613-954-1800, info@cihr-irsc.gc.ca
Health Canada, Tunney's Pasture, Ottawa, K1A 0K9 ON
  613-957-2991, Fax: 613-941-5366, Info@hc-sc.gc.ca

Alberta
Alberta Health & Wellness, TELUS Plaza North Tower, 10025 Jasper Ave., 22nd Fl., PO Box 1360 Main,Edmonton, T5J 2N3 AB
  780-427-7164, health.ahinform@gov.ab.ca

British Columbia
Ministry of Health Services, 1515 Blanshard St., Victoria, V8W 3C8 BC
  250-952-1742, Fax: 250-356-9587, 800-465-4911, hlth.health@gems1.gov.bc.ca
Medical Services Commission, 1515 Blanshard St., 3rd Fl., Victoria, BC V8W 3C8
  250-952-3073, Fax: 250-952-3131

Government Quick Reference Guide / Heritage Resources

Manitoba
Manitoba Health & Healthy Living, #100, 300 Carlton St., Winnipeg, R3B 3M9 MB
204-786-7191, minhlt@leg.gov.mb.ca
Manitoba Healthy Child Office, #219, 114 Garry St., Winnipeg, R3C 1G1 MB
204-945-2266, 888-848-0140, healthychild@gov.mb.ca
Manitoba Health Appeal Board, #4011, 300 Carlton St., Winnipeg, MB R3B 3M9
204-788-6704, Fax: 204-948-2024, 866-744-3257

New Brunswick
Department of Health, PO Box 5100, Fredericton, E3B 5G8 NB
506-457-4800, Fax: 506-453-5243, dh-ms@dh-ms.ca

Newfoundland & Labrador
Department of Health & Community Services, West Block, Confederation Bldg., PO Box 8700, St. John's, A1B 4J6 NL
709-729-5021, Fax: 709-729-5824,

Northwest Territories
Department of Health & Social Services, Centre Square Tower, PO Box 1320, Yellowknife, X1A 2L9 NT
Fax: 867-873-0266

Nova Scotia
Department of Health Promotion & Protection, Summit Place, 1601 Lower Water St., 5th Fl., PO Box 487, Halifax, B3J 2R7 NS
902-424-4807, Fax: 902-424-4716, 866-231-3882, healthpromotion@gov.ns.ca
Department of Health, Joseph Howe Bldg., 1690 Hollis St., 4th Fl., PO Box 488, Halifax, B3J 2R8 NS
902-424-5818, Fax: 902-424-0730, 800-387-6665, DoHweb@gov.ns.ca

Nunavut
Department of Health & Social Services, Sivummut bldg., PO Box 1007 1000,Iqaluit, X0A 0H0 NU
867-975-5700, Fax: 867-975-5705, health@gov.nu.ca

Prince Edward Island
Department of Health, Jones Bldg., 11 Kent St., 2nd Fl., PO Box 2000, Charlottetown, C1A 7N8 PE
902-368-4900, Fax: 902-368-4974

Quebec
Institut national de santé publique du Québec, 945, av Wolfe, Sainte-Foy, QC G1V 5B3
418-650-5115, Fax: 418-646-9328
Ministère de la Santé et des Services sociaux, Direction des communications et Renseignements généraux, 1075, ch Sainte-Foy, Québec, G1S 2M1 QC
418-266-8900, 800-707-3380, regisseur.web@msss.gouv.qc.ca

Saskatchewan
Saskatchewan Health, T.C. Douglas Bldg., 3475 Albert St., Regina, S4S 6X6 SK
306-787-0146, 800-667-7766, info@health.gov.sk.ca

HERITAGE RESOURCES
See Also: Land Resources; Parks
Canadian Heritage, 15 Eddy St., Gatineau, K1A 0M5 QC
819-997-0055, 866-811-0055
Culture & Heritage, PO Box 310, Igloolik, X0A 0L0 NU
867-975-2046, Fax: 867-934-2047, cleypermits@gov.nu.ca
Parks Canada, 25 Eddy St., Gatineau, K1A 0M5 QC
888-773-8888, information@pc.gc.ca

Alberta
Alberta Historical Resources Foundation, Old St. Stephen's College, 8820 - 112 St., Edmonton, AB T6G 2P8
780-431-2300

Manitoba
Manitoba Culture, Heritage, Tourism & Sport, Legislative Building, #118, 450 Broadway Ave., Winnipeg, R3C 0V8 MB
204-945-3729, Fax: 204-945-5223, mincht@leg.gov.mb.ca
Heritage Grants Advisory Council, 213 Notre Dame Ave., 3rd Fl., Winnipeg, MB R3B 1N3
204-945-2213, Fax: 204-948-2086
Manitoba Heritage Council, 213 Notre Dame Ave., Main Fl., Winnipeg, MB R3B 1N3
204-945-2118, Fax: 204-948-2384, hrb@gov.mb.ca

Nova Scotia
Heritage Division, 1747 Summer St., Halifax, B3H 3A6 NS
902-424-7344, Fax: 902-424-0560, 800-632-1114, heritage@gov.ns.ca

Nunavut
Department of Culture, Language, Elders & Youth, PO Box 1000 800,Iqaluit, X0A 0H0 NU
867-975-5500, Fax: 867-975-5504, 866-934-2035

Ontario
Conservation Review Board, 400 University Ave. 4th Fl., Toronto, ON M7A 2R9
416-314-7137, Fax: 416-314-7175
Ontario Heritage Trust, 10 Adelaide St. East, Toronto, ON M5C 1J3
416-325-5000, Fax: 416-325-5071, marketing@heritagefdn.on.ca

Quebec
Commission des biens culturels du Québec, Bloc A-RC, 225, Grande Allée est, Québec, G1R 5G5 QC
418-643-8378, Fax: 418-643-8591, info@cbcq.gouv.qc.ca

Saskatchewan
Sask Heritage Foundation, 1919 Saskatchewan Dr., 9th Fl., Regina, SK S4P 3V7
306-787-4188, Fax: 306-787-0069
Saskatchewan Tourism, Parks, Culture, & Sport, 1919 Saskatchewan Dr., 4th Fl., Regina, S4P 4H2 SK
306-787-5729, Fax: 306-787-8560

Yukon Territory
Yukon Tourism & Culture, PO Box 2703, Whitehorse, Y1A 2C6 YT
867-667-5036, Fax: 867-667-3546

HISTORY & ARCHIVES
Alberta
Culture & Community Development Division, Standard Life Centre, 10405 Jasper Ave., 9th Fl., Edmonton, T5J 4R7 AB
780-415-1167, Fax: 780-422-2891

Nova Scotia
Culture Division, #601, 1800 Argyle St., PO Box 456, Halifax, B3J 2R5 NS
Fax: 902-424-0710

Ontario
Archives of Ontario, 77 Grenville St., 3rd Fl., Toronto, M5S 1B3 ON
416-327-1600, Fax: 416-327-1999, 800-668-9933

Quebec
Bibliothèque et Archives nationales du Québec (BAnQ), 475, boul De Maisonneuve est, Montréal, H2L 5C4 QC
514-873-1100, Fax: 514-873-9312, 800-363-9028

HOSPITALS
See Also: Health Care Insurance

Alberta
Alberta Health & Wellness, TELUS Plaza North Tower, 10025 Jasper Ave., 22nd Fl., PO Box 1360 Main,Edmonton, T5J 2N3 AB
780-427-7164, health.ahinform@gov.ab.ca

British Columbia
Ministry of Health Services, 1515 Blanshard St., Victoria, V8W 3C8 BC
250-952-1742, Fax: 250-356-9587, 800-465-4911, hlth.health@gems1.gov.bc.ca
Hospital Appeal Board, 747 Fort St., 4th Fl., PO Box 9425 Prov Govt, Victoria, BC V8W 9V1
250-387-3464, Fax: 250-356-9923, 800-663-7867, hab@gov.bc.ca

Northwest Territories
Department of Health & Social Services, Centre Square Tower, PO Box 1320, Yellowknife, X1A 2L9 NT
Fax: 867-873-0266,

Nunavut
Department of Health & Social Services, Sivummut bldg., PO Box 1007 1000,Iqaluit, X0A 0H0 NU
867-975-5700, Fax: 867-975-5705, health@gov.nu.ca

Prince Edward Island
Department of Health, Jones Bldg., 11 Kent St., 2nd Fl., PO Box 2000, Charlottetown, C1A 7N8 PE
902-368-4900, Fax: 902-368-4974

Quebec
Ministère de la Santé et des Services sociaux, Direction des communications et Renseignements généraux, 1075, ch Sainte-Foy, Québec, G1S 2M1 QC
418-266-8900, 800-707-3380, regisseur.web@msss.gouv.qc.ca

HOUSING
Canada Mortgage & Housing Corporation, 700 Montreal Rd., Ottawa, K1A 0P7 ON
613-748-2000, Fax: 613-748-2098, 800-668-2642, chic@cmhc-schl.gc.ca

British Columbia
Local Government Department, 800 Johnson St., 6th Fl., PO Box 9490 Prov Govt,Victoria, V8W 9N7 BC
lgd_feedback@gov.bc.ca

New Brunswick
Department of Local Government, Marysville Place, 20 McGloin St., PO Box 6000, Fredericton, E3B 5H1 NB
506-453-2807, Fax: 506-453-3988

Nova Scotia
Department of Service Nova Scotia & Municipal Relations, 1505 Barrington St., PO Box 216, Halifax, B3J 2M4 NS
902-424-4141, Fax: 902-424-0581, public-enquiries@gov.ns.ca

Nunavut
Department of Community & Government Services, J.G. Brown Bldg., PO Box 1000 700,Iqaluit, X0A 0H0 NU
867-975-5400, Fax: 867-975-5305

Quebec
Société d'habitation du Québec, Aile St-Amable, 1054, rue Louis-Alexandre-Taschereau, 3e étage, Québec, QC G1R 5E7
Fax: 418-643-5560, 800-463-4315

HYDRO, ELECTRIC POWER
National Energy Board, 444 - 7 Ave. SW, Calgary, T2P 0X8 AB
403-292-4800, Fax: 403-292-5503, 800-899-1265, info@neb-one.gc.ca
Yukon Energy Corporation, 2 Miles Canyon Rd., PO Box 5920, Whitehorse, Y1A 6S7 YT
867-393-5300, 866-926-3749, communications@yukonenergy.ca

Alberta
Alberta Energy & Utilities Board, 640 - 5 Ave. SW, Calgary, AB T2P 3G4
403-297-8311, Fax: 403-297-7336
Alberta Utilities Consumer Advocate, TD Tower, 10088 - 102 Ave., Edmonton, T5J 2Z1 AB
780-644-5130, Fax: 780-644-5129, 866-714-4455, UtilitiesConsumerAdvocate@gov.ab.

British Columbia
British Columbia Hydro, 333 Dunsmuir St., 18th Fl., Vancouver, V6B 5R3 BC
604-224-9376, Fax: 604-623-4467, 800-224-9376
Powertech Labs Inc., 12388 - 88 Ave., Surrey, BC V8W 7R7
604-590-7500, Fax: 604-590-5347, info@powertechlans.com

Manitoba
Manitoba Hydro, PO Box 815 Main,Winnipeg, R3C 2P4 MB
204-474-3311, Fax: 204-475-0069, publicaffairs@hydro.mb.ca

New Brunswick
New Brunswick Power Group of Companies, 515 King St., PO Box 2000, Fredericton, E3B 4X1 NB
506-458-4444, Fax: 506-458-4000, questions@nbpower.com

Newfoundland & Labrador
Churchill Falls (Labrador) Corporation Limited, Hydro Place, 500 Columbus Dr., PO Box 12500, St. John's, A1B 4K7 NL
709-737-1859, Fax: 709-737-1816
Newfoundland & Labrador Hydro, Hydro Place, Columbus Dr., PO Box 12400, St. John's, A1B 4K7 NL
709-737-1400, Fax: 709-737-1800
Twin Falls Power Corporation, PO Box 12500, St. John's, A1B 3T5 NL

Northwest Territories
Northwest Territories Power Corporation, 4 Capital Dr., Hay River, X0E 1G2 NT
867-874-5200, Fax: 867-874-5229, info@ntpc.com

Nova Scotia
Nova Scotia Utility & Review Board, 1601 Lower Water St., 3rd Fl., PO Box 1692 M,Halifax, B3J 3S3 NS
902-424-4448, Fax: 902-424-3919, uarb.board@gov.ns.ca

Ontario
Hydro One Inc., North Tower, 483 Bay St., Toronto, M5G 2P5 ON
 416-345-5000, 877-955-1155, webmaster@HydroOne.com
Independent Electricity System Operator, PO Box 4474 A,Toronto, M5W 4E5 ON
 905-403-6900, Fax: 905-403-6921, 888-448-7777, customer.relations@ieso.ca
Ontario Power Authority, #1600, 120 Adelaide St. West, Toronto, ON M5H 1T1
 416-967-7474, Fax: 416-967-1947, info@powerauthority.on.ca
Ontario Power Generation, 700 University Ave., Toronto, M5G 1X6 ON
 416-592-2555, 877-592-2555

Quebec
Hydro-Québec, 75, boul René-Lévesque ouest, 20e étage, Montréal, H2Z 1A4 QC
 514-289-2211
Société d'énergie de la Baie-James, 888, de Maisonneuve est, 2e étage, Montréal, H2L 5B2 QC
 514-286-2020

Saskatchewan
Saskatchewan Power Corporation (SaskPower), 2025 Victoria Ave., Regina, S4P 0S1 SK
 306-566-2121, Fax: 306-566-2330, 800-667-4749

IMMIGRATION
See Also: Citizenship
Passport Canada, Le 70 Crémazie, 70 Crémazie St., Gatineau, K1A 0G3 QC
 Fax: 819-953-5856, 800-567-6868

Manitoba
Immigration & Multiculturalism Division, 213 Notre Dame Ave., 5th Floor, Winnipeg, R3B 1N3 MB
 204-945-6300, Fax: 204-948-2148, immigratemanitoba@gov.mb.ca

IMPORTS
See Also: Trade
Canada Border Services Agency, Ottawa, K1A 0L8 ON
 613-952-3200, CBSA-ASFC@canada.gc.ca

New Brunswick
Investment & Export Development, Centennial Bldg., 670 King St., 5th F., PO Box 6000, Fredericton, E3B 5H1 NB
 506-453-2875, Fax: 506-444-4277

INCOME SECURITY
See Also: Social Services

Yukon Territory
Yukon Health & Social Services, PO Box 2703, Whitehorse, Y1A 2C6 YT
 867-667-3673, Fax: 867-667-3096, 800-661-0408, hss@gov.yk.ca

INCORPORATION OF COMPANIES & ASSOCIATIONS

Alberta
Technology Services, John E. Brownlee Bldg., 10365 - 97 St., 8th Fl., Edmonton, T5J 3W7 AB
 780-422-8545

New Brunswick
Service New Brunswick, Westmorland Place, #200, 82 Westmorland St., PO Box 1998, Fredericton, E3B 5G4 NB
 506-457-3581, Fax: 506-457-7520, 888-762-8600, snb@snb.ca

Nova Scotia
Department of Economic & Rural Development, Centennial Building, #600, 1660 Hollis St., PO Box 2311, Halifax, B3J 1V7 NS
 902-424-0377, Fax: 902-424-7008, comm@gov.ns.ca
Registry of Joint Stock Companies, Martime Centre, 1505 Barrington St., 9th Fl., Halifax, B3J 3K5 NS
 902-424-7770, Fax: 902-424-4633, 800-225-8227, joint-stock@gov.ns.ca

Ontario
ServiceOntario, College Park, 777 Bay St., 15th fl., Toronto, M7A 2J3 ON
 416-326-6205, Fax: 416-326-5106

Yukon Territory
Yukon Community Services, PO Box 2703, Whitehorse, Y1A 2C6 YT
 867-667-5811, Fax: 867-393-6295, 800-661-0408, inquiry@gov.yk.ca

INDUSTRY
See Also: Business Development
Agriculture & Agri-Food Canada, Sir John Carling Bldg., 930 Carling Ave., Ottawa, K1A 0C5 ON
 613-759-1000, Fax: 613-759-6726, info@agr.gc.ca
Atlantic Canada Opportunities Agency, Blue Cross Centre, 644 Main St., 3rd Fl., PO Box 6051, Moncton, E1C 9J8 NB
 506-851-2271, Fax: 506-851-7403, 800-561-7862
Atomic Energy of Canada Limited, Head Office, 2251 Speakman Dr., Mississauga, L5K 1B2 ON
 905-823-9040, webmaster@aecl.ca
Canada Mortgage & Housing Corporation, 700 Montreal Rd., Ottawa, K1A 0P7 ON
 613-748-2000, Fax: 613-748-2098, 800-668-2642, chic@cmhc-schl.gc.ca
Canadian Food Inspection Agency, 59 Camelot Dr., Ottawa, K1A 0Y9 ON
 613-225-2342, Fax: 613-228-6629, 800-442-2342
Canadian International Development Agency, 200, Promenade du Portage, Gatineau, K1A 0G4 QC
 819-997-5006, Fax: 819-953-6088, 800-230-6349, info@acdi-cida.gc.ca
Canadian Nuclear Safety Commission, 280 Slater St., PO Box 1046 B,Ottawa, K1P 5S9 ON
 613-995-5894, Fax: 613-995-5086, 800-668-5284, info@cnsc-ccsn.gc.ca
Canadian Space Agency, 6767, rte de l'Aéroport, Longueuil, J3Y 8Y9 QC
 450-926-4800, Fax: 450-926-4352, webmaster@space.gc.ca
Canadian Tourism Commission, #1400, 1055 Dunsmuir St., PO Box 49230, Vancouver, BC V7X 1L2
 604-638-8300, Fax: 604-638-8425, ctc_feedback@businteractive.com
Cape Breton Development Fund Corporation, Silicon Island, 70 Crescent St., PO Box 1264, Sydney, NS B1P 6T7
 902-564-3600, Fax: 902-564-3825, 800-705-3926
Centre for Surface Transportation Technology, 2320 Lester Rd., Ottawa, K1V 1S2 ON
 613-998-9639, Fax: 613-957-0831, inquiries.cstt@nrc-cnrc.gc.ca
Chief Informatics Office, 235 Queen St., Ottawa, ON K1A 0H5
 613-954-3570, Fax: 613-941-1938
Communications Research Centre Canada, 3701 Carling Ave., PO Box 11490 H, Ottawa, ON K2H 8S2
 613-991-3313, Fax: 613-998-5355, info@crc.ca
Competition Bureau, Place du Portage, Phase I, 50, rue Victoria, 21e étage, Ottawa, K1A 0C9 ON
 613-997-4282, Fax: 613-997-0324, 800-348-5358, compbureau@ic.gc.ca
Competition Tribunal, Thomas D'Arcy McGee Bldg., #600, 90 Sparks St., Ottawa, ON K1P 5B4
 613-957-3172, Fax: 613-957-3170, tribunal@ct-tc.gc.ca
Defence Construction Canada, Constitution Square, 350 Albert St., 19th Fl., Ottawa, K1A 0K3 ON
 613-998-9548, Fax: 613-998-1061, 800-514-3555, info@dcc-cdc.gc.ca
Enterprise Cape Breton Corporation, Silicon Island, 70 Crescent St., Sydney, NS B1S 2Z7
 902-564-3600, Fax: 902-564-3825, 800-705-3926, ecbcinfo@ecbc.ca
Export Development Canada, 151 O'Connor St., Ottawa, K1A 1K3 ON
 613-598-2500, Fax: 613-598-3811, 888-332-3320
Fisheries & Oceans Canada, 200 Kent St., Ottawa, K1A 0E6 ON
 613-993-0999, Fax: 613-996-1866, info@dfo-mpo.gc.ca
Food Value Chain Bureau, 930 Carling Ave., 5th Fl., Ottawa, K1A 0C5 ON
 Fax: 613-759-7480
Foreign Affairs & International Trade Canada, 125 Sussex Dr., Ottawa, K1A 0G2 ON
 613-944-4000, Fax: 613-996-9709, 800-267-8376, enqserv@international.gc.ca
Hazardous Materials Information Review Commission, 427 Laurier Ave. West, 7th Fl., Ottawa, ON K1A 1M3
 613-993-4331, Fax: 613-993-4686, hmirc-ccrmd@hc-sc.gc.ca
Indian Oil & Gas Canada, #100, 9911 Chula Blvd., Tsuu T'ina (Sarcee), AB T2W 6H6
 Fax: 403-292-5618

Industry Canada, 235 Queen St., Ottawa, K1A 0H5 ON
 Fax: 613-954-6436, 800-328-6189, info@ic.gc.ca
Institute for Aerospace Research, 1200 Montreal Rd., Ottawa, K1A 0R6 ON
 613-991-5738, Fax: 613-952-7214
Institute for Information Technology, Bldg. M-50, 1200 Montreal Rd., Ottawa, K1A 0R6 ON
 613-993-9101, Fax: 613-952-0074, 877-672-2672
National Energy Board, 444 - 7 Ave. SW, Calgary, T2P 0X8 AB
 403-292-4800, Fax: 403-292-5503, 800-899-1265, info@neb-one.gc.ca
National Research Council Canada, Bldg. M-58, 1200 Montreal Rd., Ottawa, K1A 0R6 ON
 613-993-9101, Fax: 613-952-7928, 877-672-2672, info@nrc-cnrc.ca
National Round Table on the Environment & Economy, #200, 344 Slater St., Ottawa, K1R 7Y3 ON
 613-992-7189, Fax: 613-992-7385, admin@nrtee-trnee.ca
Natural Resources Canada, 580 Booth St., Ottawa, K1A 0E4 ON
 613-995-0947, Fax: 613-992-7211
Natural Sciences & Engineering Research Council of Canada, Constitution Square, Tower II, 350 Albert St., Ottawa, K1A 1H5 ON
 613-995-4273, Fax: 613-992-5337
Prairie Farm Rehabilitation Administration, CIBC Tower, #408, 1800 Hamilton St., Regina, S4P 4L2 SK
 306-780-5070, Fax: 306-780-5018
Prime Minister's Advisory Council on Science & Technology, 235 Queen St., 9th Fl., Ottawa, K1A 0H5 ON
 613-998-5646, Fax: 613-990-2007, acst-ccst@ic.gc.ca
Spectrum, Information Technologies & Telecommunications, Journal Tower North, 300 Slater St., 20th Fl., Ottawa, K1A 0C8 ON
Standards Council of Canada, #200, 270 Albert St., Ottawa, K1P 6N7 ON
 613-238-3222, Fax: 613-569-7808, info@scc.ca
Western Economic Diversification Canada, Canada Place, #1500, 9700 Jasper Ave. NW, Edmonton, T5J 4H7 AB
 780-495-4164, Fax: 780-495-4557, 888-338-9378

Alberta
Agricultural Products Marketing Council, 7000 - 113 St., 3rd Fl., Edmonton, AB T6H 5T6
 780-427-2164, Fax: 780-422-9690,
Alberta Agriculture & Food, J.G. O'Donoghue Bldg., 7000 - 113 St., 1st Fl., Edmonton, T6H 5T6 AB
 780-427-2727, Fax: 780-427-2861, 866-882-7677
Alberta Economic Development Authority, McDougall Centre, 455 - 6 St. SW, Calgary, AB T2P 4E8
 403-297-3022, Fax: 403-297-6435
Alberta Energy & Utilities Board, 640 - 5 Ave. SW, Calgary, AB T2P 3G4
 403-297-8311, Fax: 403-297-7336
Alberta Energy Research Institute, AMEC Place, #2540, 801 - 6 Ave. SW, Calgary, AB T2P 3W2
 403-297-8650, Fax: 403-297-3638, aeri@gov.ab.ca
Alberta Grain Commission, 7000 - 113 St., 3rd Fl., Edmonton, AB T6H 5T6
 780-427-7329, Fax: 780-422-9690
Alberta Science & Research Authority, Phipps-McKinnon Bldg., #500, 10020 - 101A Ave., Edmonton, AB T5J 3G2
 780-427-1488, Fax: 780-427-0979, asra@gov.ab.ca
Apprenticeship & Industry Training Division, Phipps-McKinnon Bldg., 5th Fl., 10020 - 101A Ave., Edmonton, T5J 3G2 AB
 780-427-8517
Alberta Economic Development, Commerce Place, 4th Fl., 10155 - 102 St., Edmonton, T5J 4L6 AB
 780-427-4323, Fax: 780-415-1759
Alberta Energy, North Petroleum Plaza, 9945 - 108 St., 7th Fl., Edmonton, T5K 2G6 AB
 780-427-7425, Fax: 780-422-0698, 780-310-0000
Alberta Environment, South Tower, Petroleum Plaza, 9915 - 108 St., Main Fl., Edmonton, T5K 2G8 AB
 780-427-2700, Fax: 780-422-4086,-310-0000, env.infocent@gov.ab.ca
Farmers' Advocate of Alberta, 7000 - 113 St., 3rd Fl., Edmonton, AB T6H 5T6
 780-427-2433, Fax: 780-427-3913, farmers.advocate@gov.ab.ca
Industry & Regional Development Division, Commerce Place, 10155 - 102 St., 6th Fl., Edmonton, T5J 4L6 AB
 Fax: 780-422-0626
International Offices & Trade, Commerce Place, 10155 - 102 St., 4th Fl., Edmonton, T5J 4L6 AB
 780-427-3325, Fax: 780-427-0392

Land Compensation/Surface Rights Board, Phipps-McKinnon Bldg., 10020 - 101A Ave., 18th Fl., Edmonton, AB T5J 3G2
780-427-2444, Fax: 780-427-5798

British Columbia
Agricultural Land Commission, #133, 4940 Canada Way, Burnaby, BC V5G 4K6
604-660-7000, Fax: 604-660-7033
Ministry of Agriculture & Lands, PO Box 9120 Prov Govt,Victoria, V8W 9E2 BC
250-387-5121, Fax: 250-387-1522, agf.webmaster@gems2.gov.bc.ca
British Columbia Farm Industry Review Board, 1007 Fort St., 3rd Fl., PO Box 9129 Prov Govt, Victoria, BC V8W 9B5
250-356-8945, Fax: 250-356-5131, firb@gov.bc.ca
Ministry of Energy, Mines & Petroleum Resources, PO Box 9318 Prov Govt,Victoria, V8W 9N3 BC
250-952-0241
Forest Practices Board, 1675 Douglas St., 3rd Fl., PO Box 9905 Prov Govt, Victoria, BC V8W 9R1
250-387-7964, Fax: 250-387-7009, 800-994-5899, fpboard@gov.bc.ca
Ministry of Forests & Range, PO Box 9529 Prov Govt,Victoria, V8W 9C3 BC
250-387-4809, Fax: 250-953-3687
British Columbia Hydro, 333 Dunsmuir St., 18th Fl., Vancouver, V6B 5R3 BC
604-224-9376, Fax: 604-623-4467, 800-224-9376
Industry Training Authority, #1223, 13351 Commerce Pkwy., Richmond, BC V6V 2X7
604-214-8700, Fax: 604-214-8701, 866-660-6011, info@itabc.ca; customerservice@itabc.ca
Ministry of Labour & Citizens' Services, PO Box 9052 Prov Govt,Victoria, V8W 9E2 BC
250-356-6348, Fax: 250-356-6595, LCS.Minister@gov.bc.ca
Oil & Gas Commission, #100, 10003 - 110 Ave., Fort St John, BC V1J 6M7
250-261-5700, 800-663-7867
Strategic Industry Development, 808 Douglas St., 5th Fl., PO Box 9120 Prov Govt,Victoria, V8W 9B4 BC
250-356-1821, Fax: 250-356-7279
Ministry of Technology, Trade, & Economic Development, 1810 Blanshard St., PO Box 9324 Prov Govt,Victoria, V8W 9N3 BC
250-356-7411, Fax: 250-356-6376, Feedback.CSE@gov.bc.ca
British Columbia Utilities Commission, 900 Howe St., 6th Fl., PO Box 250, Vancouver, V6Z 2N3 BC
604-660-4700, Fax: 604-660-1102, 800-663-1385, commission.secretary@bcuc.com

Manitoba
Manitoba Aboriginal & Northern Affairs, 59 Elizabeth Dr., PO Box 37, Thompson, R8N 1X4 MB
204-677-6607, Fax: 204-677-6753, amartin@gov.mb.ca
Advisory Council on Workplace Safety & Health, #200, 401 York Ave., Winnipeg, MB R3C 0P8
204-945-3446, Fax: 204-945-4556
Agricultural Societies, 1129 Queens Ave., Brandon, MB R7A 1L9
204-726-6195, Fax: 204-726-6260
Manitoba Agriculture, Food & Rural Initiatives, Norquay Bldg., 401 York Ave., Winnipeg, R3C 0P8 MB
Community & Economic Development Committee of Cabinet Secretariat, #648, 155 Carlton St., Winnipeg, R3C 3H8 MB
204-945-8221, Fax: 204-945-8229
Manitoba Competitiveness, Training & Trade, International Business Centre, The Paris Building, 259 Portage Ave., Winnipeg, R3B 3P4 MB
204-945-2475, Fax: 204-945-3977, minctt@leg.gov.mb.ca
Farm Lands Ownership Board, #812, Norquay Bldg., 401 York Ave., Winnipeg, MB R3C 0P8
204-945-3149, Fax: 204-945-1489, 800-282-8069, robert.mckenzie@gov.mb.ca
Farm Machinery Board, Norquay Bldg., #812, 401 York Ave., Winnipeg, MB R3C 0P8
204-945-3856, Fax: 204-948-2844, randy.ozunko@gov.mb.ca
Manitoba Hydro, PO Box 815 Main,Winnipeg, R3C 2P4 MB
204-474-3311, Fax: 204-475-0069, publicaffairs@hydro.mb.ca
Manitoba Labour & Immigration, Legislative Building, 317, 450 Broadway Ave., Winnipeg, R3C 0V8 MB
204-945-4079, Fax: 204-945-8312, minlab@leg.gov.mb.ca
Manitoba Agricultural Services Corporation, #100, 1525 First St. South, Brandon, MB R7A 7A1
204-726-6850, Fax: 204-726-6849, mailbox@masc.mb.ca
Manitoba Bureau of Statistics, #824, 155 Carlton St., Winnipeg, R3C 3H9 MB
204-945-2406, Fax: 204-945-0695
Manitoba Habitat Heritage Corporation, #200, 1555 St. James St., Winnipeg, MB R3H 1B5
204-784-4350, Fax: 204-784-7359, mhhc@mhhc.mb.ca
Manitoba Labour Board, A.A. Heaps Bldg., #402, 258 Portage Ave., Winnipeg, MB R3C 0B6
204-945-3783, Fax: 204-945-1296, mlb@gov.mb.ca
Manitoba Minimum Wage Board, 614 - 401 York Ave., Winnipeg, MB R3C 0P8
204-945-4889, Fax: 204-948-2085, mw@gov.mb.ca
Taxicab Board, #200, 301 Weston St., Winnipeg, MB R3E 3H4
Fax: 204-948-2315
Tourism Secretariat & Travel Manitoba, 155 Carlton St., 7th Fl., Winnipeg, R3C 3H8 MB
800-665-0040
Manitoba Workers' Compensation Board, 333 Broadway Ave., Winnipeg, R3C 4W3 MB
204-954-4321, Fax: 204-954-4999, 800-362-3340, wcb@wcb.mb.ca
Workplace Safety & Health Division, #200, 401 York Ave., Winnipeg, R3C 0P8 MB
204-945-3446, Fax: 204-948-2209, wshcompl@gov.mb.ca

New Brunswick
Department of Agriculture & Aquaculture, PO Box 6000, Fredericton, E3B 5H1 NB
506-453-2666, Fax: 506-453-7170, DAA-MAA@gnb.ca
Board of Examiners under the Scaler's Act, 1350 Regent St. South, PO Box 6000, Fredericton, NB E3B 5H1
506-453-2441, Fax: 506-453-6689
Department of Business New Brunswick, Centennial Bldg., 670 King St., PO Box 6000, Fredericton, E3B 5H1 NB
506-444-5228, Fax: 506-453-5428
Corporate Services, Centennial Bldg., 670 King St., 5th Fl., PO Box 6000, Fredericton, E3B 5H1 NB
506-453-3707, Fax: 506-453-3993
Department of the Environment, Marysville Place, 20 McGloin St., PO Box 6000, Fredericton, E3B 5H1 NB
506-453-2690, Fax: 506-457-4991
Forest Protection Limited, 2502 Hwy. 102, Lincoln, NB E3B 7E6
506-446-6930, Fax: 506-446-6934, info@forestprotectionlimited.com
Investment & Export Development, Centennial Bldg., 670 King St., 5th F., PO Box 6000, Fredericton, E3B 5H1 NB
506-453-2875, Fax: 506-444-4277
Department of Natural Resources, PO Box 6000, Fredericton, E3B 5H1 NB
506-453-2510, Fax: 506-444-5839, dnrweb@gnb.ca
New Brunswick Crop Insurance Commission, PO Box 6000, Fredericton, NB E3B 5H1
506-453-2185, Fax: 506-453-7406
New Brunswick Farm Products Commission, c/o Department of Agriculture & Aquaculture, PO Box 6000, Fredericton, NB E3B 5H1
506-453-3647, Fax: 506-444-5969
New Brunswick Film, Assumption Pl., 770 Main St., 16th Fl., PO Box 5001, Moncton, NB E1C 8R3
506-869-6868, Fax: 506-869-6840, nbfilm@gnb.ca
New Brunswick Industrial Development Board, Business New Brunswick, Centennial Bldg., 670 King St., PO Box 6000, Fredericton, NB E3B 5H1
506-453-4200, Fax: 506-444-4182
New Brunswick Round Table on Environment & Economy, 20 McGloin St., PO Box 6000, Fredericton, NB E3B 5H1
506-453-3703, Fax: 506-453-3876,
New Brunswick Power Group of Companies, 515 King St., PO Box 2000, Fredericton, E3B 4X1 NB
506-458-4444, Fax: 506-458-4000, questions@nbpower.com
Regional Development Corporation, RDC Bldg., 836 Churchill Row, PO Box 428, Fredericton, E3B 5R4 NB
506-453-2277, Fax: 506-453-7988
New Brunswick Research & Productivity Council, 921 College Hill Rd., Fredericton, E3B 6Z9 NB
506-452-1212, Fax: 506-452-1395, info@rpc.ca
Workplace Health, Safety & Compensation Commission of New Brunswick, 1 Portland St., PO Box 160, Saint John, E2L 3X9 NB
506-632-2200, 800-222-9775, communications@ws-ts.nb.ca

Newfoundland & Labrador
Canada-Newfoundland Offshore Petroleum Board, TD Place, 140 Water St., 5th Fl., St. John's, NL A1C 6H6
709-778-1400, Fax: 709-778-1473, postmaster@cnlopb.nl.ca
Department of Fisheries & Aquaculture, Petten Bldg., 30 Strawberry Marsh Rd., PO Box 8700, St. John's, A1B 4J6 NL
709-729-3723, Fax: 709-729-6082, fishaqwebmaster@gov.nl.ca
Newfoundland & Labrador Hydro, Hydro Place, Columbus Dr., PO Box 12400, St. John's, A1B 4K7 NL
709-737-1400, Fax: 709-737-1800
Department of Innovation, Trade & Rural Development, West Block, Confederation Bldg., PO Box 8700, St. John's, A1B 4J6 NL
709-729-7000, Fax: 709-729-0654, 800-563-2299, itrd@gov.nl.ca
Department of Labrador & Aboriginal Affairs, Confederation Bldg., East Block, 6th Fl., PO Box 8700, St. John's, A1B 4J6 NL
709-729-4776, Fax: 709-729-4900, 877-788-8822, laa@gov.nl.ca
Department of Natural Resources, Natural Resources Bldg., 50 Elizabeth Ave., 7th Fl., PO Box 8700, St. John's, A1B 4J6 NL
709-729-2920, Fax: 709-729-0059
Professional Fish Harvesters Certification Board, 15 Hallett Cres., PO Box 8541, St. John's, NL A1B 3P2
709-722-8170, Fax: 709-722-8201, pfh@pfhcb.com
Newfoundland & Labrador Board of Commissioners of Public Utilities, PO Box 21040, St. John's, A1A 5B2 NL
709-726-8600, Fax: 709-726-9604, 866-782-0006, ito@pub.nf.ca

Northwest Territories
Department of Environment & Natural Resources, PO Box 1320, Yellowknife, X1A 2L9 NT
Highways, 4510 - 50 Ave., 2nd fl., PO Box 1320, Yellowknife, X1A 2L9 NT
867-920-8771, Fax: 867-873-0288
Department of Industry, Tourism & Investment, PO Box 1320, Yellowknife, X1A 2L9 NT
Fax: 867-873-0306, info@iti.ca
Northwest Territories Business Development & Investment Corporation, #701, 5201 - 50 Ave., Yellowknife, NT X1A 3S9
867-920-6455, Fax: 867-765-0652, bdicinfo@gov.nt.ca
Northwest Territories Power Corporation, 4 Capital Dr., Hay River, X0E 1G2 NT
867-874-5200, Fax: 867-874-5229, info@ntpc.com

Nova Scotia
Department of Agriculture, 1741 Brunswick St., 3rd Fl., PO Box 2223, Halifax, B3J 3C4 NS
902-424-4560, Fax: 902-424-4671
Canada-Nova Scotia Offshore Petroleum Board, TD Centre, 1791 Barrington St., 6th Fl., Halifax, NS B3J 3K9
902-422-5588, Fax: 902-422-1799, postmaster@cnsopb.ns.ca
Crane Operators Appeal Board, 5151 Terminal Rd., 7th Fl., PO Box 697, Halifax, NS B3J 2T8
902-424-8595, Fax: 902-424-0217, fraserej@gov.ns.ca
Department of Economic & Rural Development, Centennial Building, #600, 1660 Hollis St., PO Box 2311, Halifax, B3J 1V7 NS
902-424-0377, Fax: 902-424-7008, comm@gov.ns.ca
Film Nova Scotia, Collins Bank Bldg., 1869 Upper Water St., 3rd Fl., Halifax, NS B3J 1S9
902-424-7177, Fax: 902-424-0617, 888-360-2111, connorkm@gov.ns.ca
InNOVACorp, #1400, 1801 Hollis St., Halifax, NS B3J 3N4
902-424-8670, Fax: 902-424-4679, 800-565-7051, communications@innovacorp.ca
Department of Natural Resources, Founder's Square, 1701 Hollis St., 3rd Fl., PO Box 698, Halifax, B3J 2T9 NS
902-424-5935, Fax: 902-424-0594, 800-565-2224
Nova Scotia Crop & Livestock Insurance Commission, MacRae Library Bldg., #2, 137 College Rd., PO Box 1092, Truro, NS B2N 5G9
902-893-7755, Fax: 902-895-4622, 800-565-6371, nsclic@gov.ns.ca
Nova Scotia Farm Loan Board, PO Box 550, Truro, NS B2N 5E3
902-893-6506, Fax: 902-895-7693, flb@gov.ns.ca
Trade Centre Limited, 1800 Argyle St., PO Box 955, Halifax, NS B3J 2V9
902-421-8686, Fax: 902-422-2922
Nova Scotia Utility & Review Board, 1601 Lower Water St., 3rd Fl., PO Box 1692 M,Halifax, B3J 3S3 NS
902-424-4448, Fax: 902-424-3919, uarb.board@gov.ns.ca
Waterfront Development Corporation Ltd., 1751 Lower Water St., 2nd Fl., Halifax, NS B3J 1S5
902-422-6591, Fax: 902-422-7582, info@wdcl.ca

Nunavut

Department of Economic Development & Transportation, #1104 Inuksugait Plaza, PO Box 1000 1500,Iqaluit, X0A 0H0 NU
867-975-7800, Fax: 867-975-7870, 888-975-5999, edt@gov.nu.ca

Ontario

AGRICORP, 1 Stone Rd. West, PO Box 3660 Central, Guelph, ON N1H 8M4
Fax: 519-826-4118, 888-247-4999, cac@agricorp.com

Agricultural Research Institute of Ontario, 1 Stone Rd. West, 2nd Fl. NW, Guelph, ON N1G 4Y2
519-826-4199, Fax: 519-826-4211

Ministry of Agriculture, Food & Rural Affairs, 1 Stone Rd. West, Guelph, N1G 4Y2 ON
519-826-3100, 888-466-2372

Building Code Commission, 777 Bay St., 2nd Fl., Toronto, ON M5G 2E5
416-585-6503, Fax: 416-585-7531

Building Materials Evaluation Commission, 777 Bay St., 2nd Fl., Toronto, ON M5G 2E5
416-585-4234, Fax: 416-585-7531

Ministry of Economic Development, Hearst Block, 900 Bay St., 8th Fl., Toronto, M7A 2E1 ON
416-325-6666, Fax: 416-325-6688, 866-668-4249, info@edt.gov.on.ca

Ministry of Environment, 135 St. Clair Ave. West, Toronto, M4V 1P5 ON
416-325-4000, Fax: 416-325-3159, 800-565-4923

Environmental Commissioner of Ontario, #605, 1075 Bay St., Toronto, M5S 2B1 ON
416-325-3377, Fax: 416-325-3370, 800-701-6454, commissioner@eco.on.ca

Ministry of Government Services & Consumer Services, Whitney Block, #4320, 99 Wellesley St. West, 4th Fl., Toronto, M7A 1W3 ON
416-326-1234, Fax: 416-327-3790, 800-268-1142

Hydro One Inc., North Tower, 483 Bay St., Toronto, M5G 2P5 ON
416-345-5000, 877-955-1155, webmaster@HydroOne.com

Independent Electricity System Operator, PO Box 4474 A,Toronto, M5W 4E5 ON
905-403-6900, Fax: 905-403-6921, 888-448-7777, customer.relations@ieso.ca

Industry Division, Hearst Block, 900 Bay St., 7th fl., Toronto, M7A 2E1 ON
416-325-6964, Fax: 416-325-2102

Ministry of Labour, 400 University Ave., 14th Fl., Toronto, M7A 1T7 ON
416-326-7770, 800-268-8013

Ministry of Municipal Affairs & Housing, 777 Bay St., 17th Fl., Toronto, M5G 2E5 ON
416-585-7041, Fax: 416-585-6227, 866-220-2290, mininfo.mah@ontario.ca

Ministry of Natural Resources, Whitney Block, #6630, 99 Wellesley St. West, 6th Fl., Toronto, M7A 1W3 ON
800-667-1940

Ministry of Northern Development & Mines, 159 Cedar St., Sudbury, P3E 6A5 ON
705-564-0032, Fax: 705-564-7357

Office of the Employer Advisor, #704, 151 Bloor St. West., Toronto, ON M5S 1S4
416-327-0020, Fax: 416-327-0726, 800-387-0774

Ontario Media Development Corporation, South Tower, #501, 175 Bloor St. East, Toronto, ON M4W 3R8
416-314-6858, Fax: 416-314-6876, mail@omdc.on.ca

Ontario Power Generation, 700 University Ave., Toronto, M5G 1X6 ON
416-592-2555, 877-592-2555

ServiceOntario, College Park, 777 Bay St., 15th fl., Toronto, M7A 2J3 ON
416-326-6205, Fax: 416-326-5106

Ministry of Tourism, Hearst Block, 900 Bay St., 9th Fl., Toronto, M7A 2E1 ON
416-326-9326, Fax: 416-314-7854, 800-668-2746

Workplace Safety & Insurance Board, 200 Front St. West, Ground Fl., Toronto, M5V 3J1 ON
416-344-1000, Fax: 416-344-4684, 800-387-0750

Prince Edward Island

Agricultural Insurance Corporation, 29 Indigo Cres., PO Box 1600, Charlottetown, PE C1A 7N3
902-368-4842, Fax: 902-368-6677, peiaic@gov.pe.ca

Department of Agriculture, Jones Bldg., 11 Kent St., PO Box 2000, Charlottetown, C1A 7N8 PE
902-368-4880, Fax: 902-368-4857

Community & Labour Development, Shaw Bldg., 105 Rochford St., 5th Fl., PO Box 2000, Charlottetown, C1A 7N8 PE
902-368-4244, Fax: 902-368-4242

Employment Development Agency, Sullivan Bldg., 1st Fl., PO Box 2000, Charlottetown, PE C1A 7N8
902-368-5805, Fax: 902-368-5909,

Employment Standards Board, 161 St. Peters Rd., PO Box 2000, Charlottetown, PE C1A 7N8
902-368-5550, Fax: 902-368-5476

Food Technology Centre, 101 Belvedere Ave., PO Box 2000, Charlottetown, PE C1A 7N8
902-368-5548, Fax: 902-368-5549, 877-368-5548, ftcweb@gov.pe.ca

Grain Elevators Corporation, PO Box 250, Kensington, PE C0B 1M0
902-836-8929

Department of Innovation & Advanced Learning, Shaw Bldg., 105 Rochford St., 5th Fl., PO Box 2000, Charlottetown, C1A 7N8 PE
902-368-4240, Fax: 902-368-4242

Island Investment Development Inc., 94 Euston St., 2nd Fl., Charlottetown, PE C1A 1W4
902-894-0351, Fax: 902-368-5886

Prince Edward Island Business Development Inc., 94 Euston St., 1st & 2nd Fl., PO Box 910, Charlottetown, PE C1A 7L9
902-368-6300, Fax: 902-368-6301, 800-563-3734, business@gov.pe.ca

Technology PEI Inc., 94 Euston St., 2nd Fl., PO Box 340, Charlottetown, PE C1A 7K7
902-368-6300, Fax: 902-368-6301, techpei@gov.pe.ca

Department of Tourism, PO Box 2000, Charlottetown, C1A 7N8 PE
800-463-4734

Department of Transportation & Public Works, Jones Bldg., 11 Kent St., PO Box 2000, Charlottetown, C1A 7N8 PE
902-368-5100, Fax: 902-368-5395

Prince Edward Island Workers Compensation Board, 14 Weymouth St., PO Box 757, Charlottetown, C1A 7L7 PE
902-368-5680, Fax: 902-368-5705, 800-237-5049

Quebec

Agence de l'efficacité énergétique, #B-405, 5700, 4e av ouest, Québec, QC G1H 6R1
418-627-6379, Fax: 418-643-5828, 877-727-6655, aee@aee.gouv.qc.ca

Ministère de l'Agriculture, des Pêcheries et de l'Alimentation, 200, ch Sainte-Foy, Québec, G1R 4X6 QC
418-380-2110, 888-222-6272

Centre de recherche industrielle du Québec, 333, rue Franquet, Sainte-Foy, QC G1P 4C7
418-659-1550, Fax: 418-652-2251, 800-667-2386, infocriq@criq.qc.ca

Comité conjoint de chasse, de pêche et de piégeage, #C220, 383 rue Saint-Jacques, Montréal, QC H2Y 1N9
514-284-2151, Fax: 514-284-0039, hftcc@bellnet.ca

Commissaire de l'industrie de la construction, 150, boul René-Lévesque est, 18e étage,, Québec, QC G1R 5B1
418-646-7200, Fax: 418-644-9977

Commission de protection du territoire agricole du Québec, 200, ch Ste-Foy, 2e étage, Québec, QC G1R 4X6
418-643-3314, Fax: 418-643-2261, 800-667-5294, info@cptaq.gouv.qc.ca

Conseil consultatif du travail et de la main d'oeuvre, #9.400, 500, boul René-Lévesque ouest, Montréal, QC H2Z 1W7
514-873-2880, Fax: 514-873-1129, cctm@cctm.gouv.qc.ca

Ministère de la Culture, des Communications & de la Condition féminine, 225, Grande Allée est, Québec, G1R 5G5 QC
Fax: 418-380-2364, 888-380-8882, infos@mcccf.gouv.qc.ca

Ministère du Développement durable, de l'Environnement et des Parcs, Édifice Marie-Guyart, 675, boul René-Lévesque est, 29e étage, Québec, G1R 5V7 QC
418-521-3830, Fax: 418-646-5974, 800-561-1616, info@mddep.gouv.qc.ca

Ministère du Développement économique, de l'Innovation et de l'Exportation, 710, place D'Youville, 3e étage, Québec, G1R 4Y4 QC
418-691-5950, Fax: 418-644-0118, 866-680-1884

Hydro-Québec, 75, boul René-Lévesque ouest, 20e étage, Montréal, H2Z 1A4 QC
514-289-2211

La financière agricole de Québec, 1400, boul de la Rive-Sud, Saint-Romuald, QC G6W 8K7
418-838-5602, Fax: 418-833-3871, 800-749-3646, dir.comm@fadq.qc.ca

Régie des marchés agricoles et alimentaires du Québec, 201, boul Crémazie, 5e étage, Montréal, QC H2M 1L3

514-873-4024, Fax: 514-873-3984, rmaaqc@rmaaq.gouv.qc.ca

Régie du bâtiment du Québec, 545, boul Crémazie est, 4e étage, Montréal, QC H2M 2V2
514-873-0976, Fax: 514-864-2903, 800-361-0761, crc@rbq.gouv.qc.ca

Société d'habitation du Québec, Aile St-Amable, 1054, rue Louis-Alexandre-Taschereau, 3e étage, Québec, QC G1R 5E7
Fax: 418-643-5560, 800-463-4315

Société de développement des entreprises culturelles, #800, 215, rue Saint-Jacques, Montréal, H2Y 1M6 QC
514-841-2200, Fax: 514-841-8606, 800-363-0401, info@sodec.gouv.qc.ca

Société Innovatech du sud du Québec, #20, 2100, rue King ouest, Sherbrooke, QC J1J 2E8
819-820-3305, Fax: 819-820-3320, isq@isq.qc.ca

Société Innovatech Québec, 10, rue Pierre Olivier Chauveau, Québec, QC G1R 4J3
418-528-9770, Fax: 418-528-9783, info@innovatechquebec.com

Société Innovatech Régions ressources, #500, 1200, rte de l'Église, Sainte-Foy, QC G1V 5A3
866-870-0437, info@innovatech-regions.qc.ca

Société québécoise de récupération et de recyclage, Siège social, #200, 420, boul Charest est, Québec, QC G1K 8M4
418-643-0394, Fax: 418-643-6507, 866-523-8290, info@recyc-quebec.gouv.qc.ca

Ministère du Tourisme, Direction des Communications, 900, boul René-Lévesque est, Québec, G1R 2B5 QC
418-643-5959, Fax: 418-646-8723, 800-482-2433

Saskatchewan

Agri-Food Council, #302, 3085 Albert St., Regina, SK S4S 0B1
306-787-5139, Fax: 306-787-5134, james.kettel@gov.sk.ca

Saskatchewan Agriculture, Walter Scott Bldg., 3085 Albert St., Regina, S4S 0B1 SK
306-787-5140, 866-457-2377, aginfo@gov.sk.ca

Saskatchewan Energy & Resources, #300, 2103 - 11th Ave., Regina, S4P 3Z8 SK
306-787-2528, Fax: 306-787-8447, 866-727-5427

Saskatchewan Environment, 3211 Albert St., 2nd Fl., Regina, S4S 5W6 SK
306-953-3750, Fax: 306-787-9544, 800-567-4224, inquiry@serm.gov.sk.ca

Farm Stress Unit, #329, 3085 Albert St., Regina, SK S4S 0B1
306-787-5196, Fax: 306-798-3042, 800-667-4442, ken.imhoff@gov.sk.ca

Labour Relations Board, #1600, 1920 Broad St., Regina, SK S4P 3V2
306-787-2406, Fax: 306-787-2664, mbaldwin@lrb.gov.sk.ca

Saskatchewan Power Corporation (SaskPower), 2025 Victoria Ave., Regina, S4P 0S1 SK
306-566-2121, Fax: 306-566-2330, 800-667-4749

Prairie Agricultural Machinery Institute, Hwy#5 West, PO Box 1900, Humboldt, SK S0K 2A0
306-682-2555, Fax: 306-682-5080, 800-567-7264, humboldt@pami.ca

Saskatchewan Crop Insurance Corporation, 484 Prince William Dr., PO Box 3000, Melville, SK S0A 2P0
306-728-7200, Fax: 306-728-7268, 888-935-0000, customer.service@scic.gov.sk.ca

Saskatchewan Lands Appeal Board, #202, 3085 Albert St., Regina, SK S4S 0B1
306-787-4693, Fax: 306-787-1315, dbrooks@agr.gov.sk.ca

Saskatchewan Trade & Export Partnership, #320, 1801 Hamilton St., PO Box 1787, Regina, SK S4P 3C6
306-787-9210, Fax: 306-787-6666, 877-313-7244, inquire@sasktrade.sk.ca

Saskatchewan Water Corporation (SaskWater), #200, 111 Fairford St. East, Moose Jaw, S6H 1C8 SK
306-694-3098, Fax: 306-694-3207, 888-230-1111, comm@saskwater.com

Saskatchewan Workers' Compensation Board, #200, 1881 Scarth St., Regina, SK S4P 4L1
306-787-4370, Fax: 306-787-7582, 800-667-7590, internet_clientsvc@wcbsask.com

SaskEnergy Incorporated, 1777 Victoria Ave., Regina, S4P 4K5 SK
306-777-9225, Fax: 306-777-9200, 800-567-8899

Saskatchewan Workers' Compensation Board, #200, 1881 Scarth St., Regina, S4P 4L1 SK
306-787-4370, Fax: 306-787-7582, 800-667-7590, internet_clientsvc@wcbsask.com

Government Quick Reference Guide / Industry & Trade

Yukon Territory

Yukon Development Corporation, PO Box 2703 D-1,Whitehorse, Y1A 2C6 YT
867-393-5337, Fax: 867-393-5401

Yukon Economic Development, PO Box 2703, Whitehorse, Y1A 2C6 YT
867-393-7191, Fax: 867-395-7199, 800-661-0408

Yukon Environment, PO Box 2703, Whitehorse, Y1A 2C6 YT
867-667-5652, Fax: 867-393-6213, 800-661-0408, environmentyukon@gov.yk.ca

Yukon Tourism & Culture, PO Box 2703, Whitehorse, Y1A 2C6 YT
867-667-5036, Fax: 867-667-3546

INDUSTRY & TRADE

Atlantic Canada Opportunities Agency, Blue Cross Centre, 644 Main St., 3rd Fl., PO Box 6051, Moncton, E1C 9J8 NB
506-851-2271, Fax: 506-851-7403, 800-561-7862

Business Development Bank of Canada, #400, 5, Place Ville-Marie, Montréal, H3B 5E7 QC
514-283-5904, Fax: 514-283-2872, 877-232-2269

Defence Construction Canada, Constitution Square, 350 Albert St., 19th Fl., Ottawa, K1A 0K3 ON
613-998-9548, Fax: 613-998-1061, 800-514-3555, info@dcc-cdc.gc.ca

Export Development Canada, 151 O'Connor St., Ottawa, K1A 1K3 ON
613-598-2500, Fax: 613-598-3811, 888-332-3320

Foreign Affairs & International Trade Canada, 125 Sussex Dr., Ottawa, K1A 0G2 ON
613-944-4000, Fax: 613-996-9709, 800-267-8376, enqserv@international.gc.ca

Industrial Materials Institute, 75, boul de Montagne, Boucherville, J4B 6Y4 QC
450-641-5100, Fax: 450-641-5101, imi-info@nrc.ca

Industry Canada, 235 Queen St., Ottawa, K1A 0H5 ON
Fax: 613-954-6436, 800-328-6189, info@ic.gc.ca

Institute for Research in Construction, Bldg. M-24, 1500 Montreal Rd., Ottawa, K1A 0R6 ON
613-993-6189, Fax: 613-952-0268, ccmc@nrc-cnrc.gc.ca

Integrated Manufacturing Technologies Institute, 800 Collip Circle, London, N6G 4X8 ON
519-430-7000, Fax: 519-430-7032

Standards Council of Canada, #200, 270 Albert St., Ottawa, K1P 6N7 ON
613-238-3222, Fax: 613-569-7808, info@scc.ca

Western Economic Diversification Canada, Canada Place, #1500, 9700 Jasper Ave. NW, Edmonton, T5J 4H7 AB
780-495-4164, Fax: 780-495-4557, 888-338-9378

Alberta

Alberta Economic Development Authority, McDougall Centre, 455 - 6 St. SW, Calgary, AB T2P 4E8
403-297-3022, Fax: 403-297-6435

Alberta Economic Development, Commerce Place, 4th Fl., 10155 - 102 St., Edmonton, T5J 4L6 AB
780-427-4323, Fax: 780-415-1759

Workers' Compensation Board of Alberta, 9925 - 107 St., PO Box 2415, Edmonton, T5J 2S5 AB
780-498-3999, Fax: 780-498-7999, 800-661-9608

British Columbia

Timber Export Advisory Committee, 1520 Blanshard St., 2nd Fl., PO Box 9514 Prov Govt, Victoria, BC V8W 9C2
250-387-8916, Fax: 250-387-5050

Manitoba

Manitoba Competitiveness, Training & Trade, International Business Centre, The Paris Building, 259 Portage Ave., Winnipeg, R3B 3P4 MB
204-945-2475, Fax: 204-945-3977, minctt@leg.gov.mb.ca

New Brunswick

Board of Examiners under the Scaler's Act, 1350 Regent St. South, PO Box 6000, Fredericton, NB E3B 5H1
506-453-2441, Fax: 506-453-6689

Department of Business New Brunswick, Centennial Bldg., 670 King St., PO Box 6000, Fredericton, E3B 5H1 NB
506-444-5228, Fax: 506-453-5428

New Brunswick Industrial Development Board, Business New Brunswick, Centennial Bldg., 670 King St., PO Box 6000, Fredericton, NB E3B 5H1
506-453-4200, Fax: 506-444-4182

Regional Development Corporation, RDC Bldg., 836 Churchill Row, PO Box 428, Fredericton, E3B 5R4 NB
506-453-2277, Fax: 506-453-7988

Newfoundland & Labrador

Department of Innovation, Trade & Rural Development, West Block, Confederation Bldg., PO Box 8700, St. John's, A1B 4J6 NL
709-729-7000, Fax: 709-729-0654, 800-563-2299, itrd@gov.nl.ca

Department of Labrador & Aboriginal Affairs, Confederation Bldg., East Block, 6th Fl., PO Box 8700, St. John's, A1B 4J6 NL
709-729-4776, Fax: 709-729-4900, 877-788-8822, laa@gov.nl.ca

Northwest Territories

Department of Environment & Natural Resources, PO Box 1320, Yellowknife, X1A 2L9 NT

Northwest Territories Business Development & Investment Corporation, #701, 5201 - 50 Ave., Yellowknife, NT X1A 3S9
867-920-6455, Fax: 867-765-0652, bdicinfo@gov.nt.ca

Nova Scotia

Department of Agriculture, 1741 Brunswick St., 3rd Fl., PO Box 2223, Halifax, B3J 3C4 NS
902-424-4560, Fax: 902-424-4671

Department of Economic & Rural Development, Centennial Building, #600, 1660 Hollis St., PO Box 2311, Halifax, B3J 1V7 NS
902-424-0377, Fax: 902-424-7008, comm@gov.ns.ca

Labour Relations Board & Construction Industry Panel, 5151 Terminal Rd.,7th Fl., PO Box 697, Halifax, NS B3J 2T8
902-424-6730, Fax: 902-424-1744

Labour Standards Tribunal, 5151 Terminal Rd., 7th Fl., PO Box 697, Halifax, NS B3J 2T8
902-424-6730, Fax: 902-424-1744, noeljl@gov.ns.ca

Pay Equity Commission, 5151 Terminal Rd., 7th Fl., PO Box 697, Halifax, NS B3J 2T8
902-424-2385, Fax: 902-424-0575

Workers' Compensation Board of Nova Scotia, 5668 South St., PO Box 1150, Halifax, B3J 2Y2 NS
902-491-8999, Fax: 902-491-8002, 800-870-3331, info@wcb.gov.ns.ca

Ontario

Ministry of Economic Development, Hearst Block, 900 Bay St., 8th Fl., Toronto, M7A 2E1 ON
416-325-6666, Fax: 416-325-6688, 866-668-4249, info@edt.gov.on.ca

Ministry of Northern Development & Mines, 159 Cedar St., Sudbury, P3E 6A5 ON
705-564-0032, Fax: 705-564-7357

Prince Edward Island

Department of Innovation & Advanced Learning, Shaw Bldg., 105 Rochford St., 5th Fl., PO Box 2000, Charlottetown, C1A 7N8 PE
902-368-4240, Fax: 902-368-4242

Quebec

Commission des lésions professionnelles, #700, 900, Place d'Youville, Québec, QC G1R 3P7
418-644-7777, Fax: 418-644-6443, 800-463-1591

Société Innovatech du sud du Québec, #20, 2100, rue King ouest, Sherbrooke, QC J1J 2E8
819-820-3305, Fax: 819-820-3320, isq@isq.qc.ca

Société Innovatech Québec, 10, rue Pierre Olivier Chauveau, Québec, QC G1R 4J3
418-528-9770, Fax: 418-528-9783, info@innovatechquebec.com

Société Innovatech Régions ressources, #500, 1200, rte de l'Église, Sainte-Foy, QC G1V 5A3
866-870-0437, info@innovatech-regions.qc.ca

Saskatchewan

Saskatchewan Energy & Resources, #300, 2103 - 11th Ave., Regina, S4P 3Z8 SK
306-787-2528, Fax: 306-787-8447, 866-727-5427

Saskatchewan Trade & Export Partnership, #320, 1801 Hamilton St., PO Box 1787, Regina, SK S4P 3C6
306-787-9210, Fax: 306-787-6666, 877-313-7244, inquire@sasktrade.sk.ca

Tourism Saskatchewan, 1922 Park St., Regina, SK S4N 7M4
306-787-9600, 877-237-2273

Yukon Territory

Yukon Development Corporation, PO Box 2703 D-1,Whitehorse, Y1A 2C6 YT
867-393-5337, Fax: 867-393-5401

INFORMATION RESOURCES

Industry Canada, 235 Queen St., Ottawa, K1A 0H5 ON
Fax: 613-954-6436, 800-328-6189, info@ic.gc.ca

Mapping Services Branch - Geomatics Canada, 615 Booth St., Ottawa, K1A 0E9 ON
613-995-4945, Fax: 613-995-8737

Public Works & Government Services Canada, Place du Portage, Phase III, 11, rue Laurier, Ottawa, K1A 0S5 ON
819-997-6363, Fax: 819-956-9062, 800-622-6232

Statistics Canada, R.H. Coats Bldg., Tunney's Pasture, 100 Tunney's Pasture Driveway, Ottawa, K1A 0T6 ON
Fax: 877-287-4369, 800-263-1136, infostats@statcan.ca

New Brunswick

Service New Brunswick, Westmorland Place, #200, 82 Westmorland St., PO Box 1998, Fredericton, E3B 5G4 NB
506-457-3581, Fax: 506-457-7520, 888-762-8600, snb@snb.ca

Nova Scotia

Nova Scotia Geomatics Centre, 160 Willow St., Amherst, B4H 3W3 NS
902-667-7231, Fax: 902-667-6008, 800-798-0706, info@nsgc.gov.ns.ca

Ontario

Ontario Geographic Names Board, Robinson Place, 300 Water St., 2nd Fl., PO Box 7000, Peterborough, ON K9J 8M5
705-755-2134, Fax: 705-755-2131

Science & Information Resources Division, Robinson Place, North Tower, 300 Water St., 2nd Fl., Peterborough, K9J 8M5 ON
705-755-2000, Fax: 705-755-2802, 800-667-1940,

Saskatchewan

Saskatchewan Conservation Data Centre, 3211 Albert St., Regina, SK S4S 5W6
306-787-9038, Fax: 306-787-9544

INSURANCE (LIFE, FIRE, PROPERTY)

See Also: Automobile Insurance; Health Care Insurance

Manitoba

Manitoba Agricultural Services Corporation, #100, 1525 First St. South, Brandon, MB R7A 7A1
204-726-6850, Fax: 204-726-6849, mailbox@masc.mb.ca

New Brunswick

New Brunswick Crop Insurance Commission, PO Box 6000, Fredericton, NB E3B 5H1
506-453-2185, Fax: 506-453-7406

Nova Scotia

Nova Scotia Utility and Review Board, Summit Place, 1601 Lower Water St., 3rd Fl., Halifax, NS B3J 3P6
902-424-4448, uarb.board@gov.ns.ca

Prince Edward Island

Agricultural Insurance Corporation, 29 Indigo Cres., PO Box 1600, Charlottetown, PE C1A 7N3
902-368-4842, Fax: 902-368-6677, peiaic@gov.pe.ca

Saskatchewan

Saskatchewan Crop Insurance Corporation, 484 Prince William Dr., PO Box 3000, Melville, SK S0A 2P0
306-728-7200, Fax: 306-728-7268, 888-935-0000, customer.service@scic.gov.sk.ca

INTELLECTUAL PROPERTY

Canadian Intellectual Property Office, Place du Portage I, 50, rue Victoria, Gatineau, K1A 0C9 QC
819-997-1936, Fax: 819-953-7620, 866-997-1936

Integrated Manufacturing Technologies Institute, 800 Collip Circle, London, N6G 4X8 ON
519-430-7000, Fax: 519-430-7032

INTERNATIONAL AFFAIRS

See Also: Trade

Canadian International Development Agency, 200, Promenade du Portage, Gatineau, K1A 0G4 QC
819-997-5006, Fax: 819-953-6088, 800-230-6349, info@acdi-cida.gc.ca

Foreign Affairs & International Trade Canada, 125 Sussex Dr., Ottawa, K1A 0G2 ON
613-944-4000, Fax: 613-996-9709, 800-267-8376, enqserv@international.gc.ca

International Development Research Centre, 150 Kent St., PO Box 8500, Ottawa, K1P 0B2 ON
613-236-6163, Fax: 613-238-7230, info@idrc.ca

National Defence Canada, Major-General George R. Pearkes
  Bldg., 101 Colonel By Dr., Ottawa, K1A 0K2 ON
  613-995-2534, Fax: 613-992-4739, 800-856-8488

Alberta
Alberta International & Intergovernmental Relations, Commerce
  Place, 10155 - 102 St., 12th Fl., Edmonton, T5J 4G8 AB
  780-422-1510, Fax: 780-427-0699

Manitoba
Manitoba Intergovernmental Affairs, #301, 450 Broadway Ave.,
  Winnipeg, R3C 0V8 MB
  Fax: 204-945-1383, mnia@leg.gov.mb.ca

Saskatchewan
Trade & International Relations, #800, 1919 Saskatchewan Dr.,
  Regina, S4P 4H2 SK
  306-787-6445, Fax: 306-787-7317

INTERNATIONAL AID
Canadian International Development Agency, 200, Promenade
  du Portage, Gatineau, K1A 0G4 QC
  819-997-5006, Fax: 819-953-6088, 800-230-6349,
  info@acdi-cida.gc.ca
International Development Research Centre, 150 Kent St., PO
  Box 8500, Ottawa, K1P 0B2 ON
  613-236-6163, Fax: 613-238-7230, info@idrc.ca

INVESTMENT
See Also: Business Development; Industry
Canada Economic Development for Québec Regions, Édifice
  Dominion Square, #900, 1255, rue Peel, Montréal, H3B 2T9
  QC
  514-283-6412, Fax: 514-283-3302, 866-385-6412
Canada Investment & Savings, #900, 110 Yonge St., Toronto,
  ON M5C 1T4
  416-952-1252, Fax: 416-952-1270, 800-575-5151,
  csb@csb.gc.ca
Finance Canada, L'esplanade Laurier, 140 O'Connor St.,
  Ottawa, K1A 0G5 ON
  613-992-1573, Fax: 613-996-2690, finpub@fin.gc.ca
Global Operations & Chief Trade Commissioner, 125 Sussex
  Dr,, Ottawa, K1A 0G2 ON
  613-944-2697, Fax: 613-996-1667
Industry Canada, 235 Queen St., Ottawa, K1A 0H5 ON
  Fax: 613-954-6436, 800-328-6189, info@ic.gc.ca
Public Sector Pension Investment Board, #200, 440 Laurier Ave.
  West, Ottawa, ON K1R 7X6
  613-782-3095, Fax: 613-782-6864, info@investpsp.ca

Alberta
International Offices & Trade, Commerce Place, 10155 - 102 St.,
  4th Fl., Edmonton, T5J 4L6 AB
  780-427-3325, Fax: 780-427-0392

British Columbia
Forestry Innovation Investments, #1200, 1130 West Pender St.,
  Vancouver, BC V6E 4A4
  604-685-7507, Fax: 604-685-5373, info@bcfii.ca
Technology, Research & Innovation Division, #730, 999 Canada
  Place, Vancouver, V6C 3E1 BC
  Fax: 604-775-2070

New Brunswick
Investment & Export Development, Centennial Bldg., 670 King
  St., 5th F., PO Box 6000, Fredericton, E3B 5H1 NB
  506-453-2875, Fax: 506-444-4277

Northwest Territories
Department of Industry, Tourism & Investment, PO Box 1320,
  Yellowknife, X1A 2L9 NT
  Fax: 867-873-0306, info@iti.ca
Northwest Territories Business Development & Investment
  Corporation, #701, 5201 - 50 Ave., Yellowknife, NT X1A 3S9
  867-920-6455, Fax: 867-765-0652, bdicinfo@gov.nt.ca

Nova Scotia
InNOVACorp, #1400, 1801 Hollis St., Halifax, NS B3J 3N4
  902-424-8670, Fax: 902-424-4679, 800-565-7051,
  communications@innovacorp.ca

Ontario
Investment & Trade Division, Hearst Block, 900 Bay St., 5th fl.,
  Toronto, M7A 2E1 ON
  416-325-9802, Fax: 416-325-5617,

Prince Edward Island
Island Investment Development Inc., 94 Euston St., 2nd Fl.,
  Charlottetown, PE C1A 1W4
  902-894-0351, Fax: 902-368-5886

Prince Edward Island Business Development Inc., 94 Euston St.,
  1st & 2nd Fl., PO Box 910, Charlottetown, PE C1A 7L9
  902-368-6300, Fax: 902-368-6301, 800-563-3734,
  business@gov.pe.ca

Quebec
Investissement Québec, #500, 1200, rte de l'Église, Sainte-Foy,
  QC G1V 5A3
  866-870-0437

JUSTICE DEPARTMENTS
Prince Edward Island
Office of the Attorney General, Shaw Building, North, 105
  Rochford St., 4th Fl., PO Box 2000, Charlottetown, C1A 7N8
  PE
  902-368-5152, Fax: 902-368-4910

LABOUR
Canadian Council of Directors of Apprenticeship, Red Seal
  Secretariat, Place du Portage, Phase IV, 5th F, Gatineau, QC
  K1A 0J9
  819-953-7442, Fax: 819-994-0202
Human Resources & Skills Development Canada, 140
  Promenade du Portage, Gatineau, Ottawa, K1A 0J9 ON
Department of Labour & Workforce Development, 5151 Terminal
  Rd., 6th Fl., PO Box 697, Halifax, B3J 2T8 NS
  902-424-5301, Fax: 902-424-0575
Merchant Seamen Compensation Board, Secretary, Merchant
  Seamen Compensation Board, Phase II, Place du Portage,
  10th Fl., Gatineau, QC K1A 0J2
  819-953-8001, Fax: 819-994-5368
Public Service Labour Relations Board, CD Howe Building, 240
  Sparks St., 6th Fl., PO Box 1525 B, Ottawa, ON K1P 5V2
  613-990-1800, Fax: 613-990-1849, 866-931-3454,
  mail.courrier@pslrb-crtfp.gc.ca

Alberta
Alberta Apprenticeship & Industry Training Board, 10155 - 102
  St., 10th Fl., Edmonton, AB T5J 4L5
  780-427-8765, Fax: 780-422-7376
Apprenticeship & Industry Training Division, Phipps-McKinnon
  Bldg., 5th Fl., 10020 - 101A Ave., Edmonton, T5J 3G2 AB
  780-427-8517
Alberta Employment, Immigration & Industry, Minister's Office,
  Legislature Bldg., #208, 10800 - 97 Ave., Edmonton, T5K 2B6
  AB
  780-415-4800, Fax: 780-422-9556, 866-644-5135,
  eii.communications@gov.ab.ca
Health Disciplines Board, North Tower, 17th Fl., Telus Plaza,
  Health Professions Bran, 10025 Jasper Ave., Edmonton, AB
  T5J 2N3
  780-415-0486, Fax: 780-422-2880
Labour Relations Board, #503, 10808 - 99 Ave., Edmonton, AB
  T5K 0G5
  780-427-5926, Fax: 780-422-0970, 800-463-2572,
  alrbinfo@lab.gov.ab.ca
Occupational Health & Safety Council, Labour Bldg, 10808 - 99
  Ave., 10th Fl., Edmonton, AB T5K 0G5
  780-427-6452, Fax: 780-427-7548
Workers' Compensation Board of Alberta, 9925 - 107 St., PO
  Box 2415, Edmonton, T5J 2S5 AB
  780-498-3999, Fax: 780-498-7999, 800-661-9608

British Columbia
British Columbia Labour Relations Board, Oceanic Plaza, #600,
  1066 West Hastings St., Vancouver, BC V6E 3X1
  604-660-1300, Fax: 604-660-1892, information@lrb.bc.ca
Employment Standards Tribunal, Oceanic Plaza, #650, 1066
  West Hastings St., Vancouver, BC V6E 3X1
  604-775-3512, Fax: 604-775-3372, registrar.est@bcest.bc.ca
Ministry of Labour & Citizens' Services, PO Box 9052 Prov
  Govt,Victoria, V8W 9E2 BC
  250-356-6348, Fax: 250-356-6595, LCS.Minister@gov.bc.ca
Workers' Compensation Appeal Tribunal, #150, 4600 Jacombs
  Rd., Richmond, BC V6V 3B1
  604-664-7800, Fax: 604-664-7898, 800-663-2782
Workers' Compensation Board of British Columbia, PO Box
  5350 Terminal,Vancouver, V6B 5L5 BC
  604-276-3100, Fax: 604-244-6490, 888-621-7233

Manitoba
Advisory Council on Workplace Safety & Health, #200, 401 York
  Ave., Winnipeg, MB R3C 0P8
  204-945-3446, Fax: 204-945-4556

Manitoba Labour & Immigration, Legislative Building, 317, 450
  Broadway Ave., Winnipeg, R3C 0V8 MB
  204-945-4079, Fax: 204-945-8312, minlab@leg.gov.mb.ca
Manitoba Civil Service Commission, #935, 155 Carlton St.,
  Winnipeg, MB R3C 3H8
  204-945-2332, Fax: 204-945-1486, cschrp@gov.mb.ca
Manitoba Labour Board, A.A. Heaps Bldg., #402, 258 Portage
  Ave., Winnipeg, MB R3C 0B6
  204-945-3783, Fax: 204-945-1296, mlb@gov.mb.ca
Manitoba Minimum Wage Board, 614 - 401 York Ave., Winnipeg,
  MB R3C 0P8
  204-945-4889, Fax: 204-948-2085, mw@gov.mb.ca
Pension Commission of Manitoba, #1004, 401 York Ave.,
  Winnipeg, MB R3C 0P8
  204-945-2740, Fax: 204-948-2375, pensions@gov.mb.ca
Manitoba Workers' Compensation Board, 333 Broadway Ave.,
  Winnipeg, R3C 4W3 MB
  204-954-4321, Fax: 204-954-4999, 800-362-3340,
  wcb@wcb.mb.ca
Workplace Safety & Health Division, #200, 401 York Ave.,
  Winnipeg, R3C 0P8 MB
  204-945-3446, Fax: 204-948-2209, wshcompl@gov.mb.ca

New Brunswick
Apprenticeship & Occupational Certification Board, PO Box
  6000, Fredericton, NB E3B 5H1
  506-453-2260, Fax: 506-453-5317
Department of Post-Secondary Education, Training & Labour,
  470 York St., PO Box 6000, Fredericton, E3B 5H1 NB
  506-453-2597, Fax: 506-453-3618, dpetlinfo@gnb.ca
Workplace Health, Safety & Compensation Commission of New
  Brunswick, 1 Portland St., PO Box 160, Saint John, E2L 3X9
  NB
  506-632-2200, 800-222-9775, communications@ws-ts.nb.ca

Newfoundland & Labrador
Newfoundland & Labrador Workplace Health, Safety &
  Compensation Commission, 146 - 148 Forest Rd., PO Box
  9000, St. John's, A1A 3B8 NL
  709-778-1000, Fax: 709-738-1714, 800-563-9000,
  general.inquiries@whscc.nl.ca

Northwest Territories
Department of Education, Culture & Employment, PO Box 1320,
  Yellowknife, X1A 2L9 NT
  867-669-2399, Fax: 867-873-0431, 866-606-5627
Northwest Territories Apprenticeship, Trade & Occupations
  Certification Board, PO Box 1320, Yellowknife, NT X1A 2L9
  867-873-7357, Fax: 867-873-0200
Northwest Territories & Nunavut Workers' Compensation Board,
  Centre Square Tower, 5022 - 49th St., 5th Fl., PO Box 8888,
  Yellowknife, X1A 2R3 NT
  867-920-3888, Fax: 867-873-4596, 800-661-0792,
  wcb@wcb.nt.ca

Nova Scotia
Labour Relations Board & Construction Industry Panel, 5151
  Terminal Rd.,7th Fl., PO Box 697, Halifax, NS B3J 2T8
  902-424-6730, Fax: 902-424-1744
Labour Standards Tribunal, 5151 Terminal Rd., 7th Fl., PO Box
  697, Halifax, NS B3J 2T8
  902-424-6730, Fax: 902-424-1744, noeljl@gov.ns.ca
Occupational Health & Safety Advisory Council, PO Box 697,
  Halifax, NS B3J 2T8
  902-424-2484, Fax: 902-424-5640
Pay Equity Commission, 5151 Terminal Rd., 7th Fl., PO Box
  697, Halifax, NS B3J 2T8
  902-424-2385, Fax: 902-424-0575
Workers' Advisers Program, #502, 5670 Spring Garden Rd., PO
  Box 1063, Halifax, NS B3J 2X1
  902-424-5050, Fax: 902-424-0530, 800-774-4712
Workers' Compensation Board of Nova Scotia, 5668 South St.,
  PO Box 1150, Halifax, B3J 2Y2 NS
  902-491-8999, Fax: 902-491-8002, 800-870-3331,
  info@wcb.gov.ns.ca

Ontario
Ministry of Labour, 400 University Ave., 14th Fl., Toronto, M7A
  1T7 ON
  416-326-7770, 800-268-8013
Office of the Employer Advisor, #704, 151 Bloor St. West.,
  Toronto, ON M5S 1S4
  416-327-0020, Fax: 416-327-0726, 800-387-0774
Office of the Worker Advisor, #1300, 123 Edward St., Toronto,
  ON M5G 1E2
  416-325-8570, Fax: 416-325-4830, 800-435-8980,

Ontario Labour Relations Board, 505 University Ave., 2nd Fl., Toronto, ON M5G 2P1
416-326-7500, Fax: 416-326-7531, 877-339-3335
Pay Equity Commission, 400 University Ave., 11th Fl., Toronto, ON M7A 1T7
416-314-1896, Fax: 416-314-8741, 800-387-8813
Workplace Safety & Insurance Board, 200 Front St. West, Ground Fl., Toronto, M5V 3J1 ON
416-344-1000, Fax: 416-344-4684, 800-387-0750

Prince Edward Island
Employment Development Agency, Sullivan Bldg., 1st Fl., PO Box 2000, Charlottetown, PE C1A 7N8
902-368-5805, Fax: 902-368-5909
Employment Standards Board, 161 St. Peters Rd., PO Box 2000, Charlottetown, PE C1A 7N8
902-368-5550, Fax: 902-368-5476
Labour Relations Board, PO Box 2000, Charlottetown, PE C1A 7N8
902-368-5550, Fax: 902-368-5476
Prince Edward Island Workers Compensation Board, 14 Weymouth St., PO Box 757, Charlottetown, C1A 7L7 PE
902-368-5680, Fax: 902-368-5705, 800-237-5049

Quebec
Commission de l'équité salariale, 200, ch Ste-Foy, 4e étage, Québec, QC G1R 6A1
418-528-8765, Fax: 418-528-6999, 888-528-8765, equite.salariale@ces.gouv.qc.ca
Commission de la construction du Québec, 3530, rue Jean-Talon ouest, Montréal, QC H3R 2G3
514-341-7740, Fax: 514-341-6354, 888-842-8222
Commission des lésions professionnelles, #700, 900, Place d'Youville, Québec, QC G1R 3P7
418-644-7777, Fax: 418-644-6443, 800-463-1591
Commission des normes du travail, Hall Est, 400, boul Jean-Lesage, 7e étage, Québec, QC G1K 8W1
418-644-0817, Fax: 418-643-5132, 800-563-9058
Conseil consultatif du travail et de la main d'oeuvre, #9.400, 500, boul René-Lévesque ouest, Montréal, QC H2Z 1W7
514-873-2880, Fax: 514-873-1129, cctm@cctm.gouv.qc.ca
Conseil des services essentiels du Québec, 800, tour de la place-Victoria, 25e étage, CP 365, Montréal, QC H4Z 1H9
514-873-7246, Fax: 514-873-3839, 800-337-7246, info@cses.gouv.qc.ca
Régie du bâtiment du Québec, 545, boul Crémazie est, 4e étage, Montréal, QC H2M 2V2
514-873-0976, Fax: 514-864-2903, 800-361-0761, crc@rbq.gouv.qc.ca
Commission de la santé et de la sécurité au travail, 524, rue Bourdages, CP 1200 Terminus postal, Québec, G1K 7E2 QC
418-266-4850, Fax: 418-266-4389, 866-302-2778
Ministère du Travail, 200, ch Ste-Foy, 6e étage, Québec, G1R 5S1 QC
418-643-4817, Fax: 418-528-0559, 800-643-4817, service_clientele@travail.gouv.qc.ca

Saskatchewan
Saskatchewan Advanced Education, Employment & Labour, 1945 Hamilton St., Regina, S4P 2C8 SK
306-787-9478, Fax: 306-787-2315
Labour Relations Board, #1600, 1920 Broad St., Regina, SK S4P 3V2
306-787-2406, Fax: 306-787-2664, mbaldwin@lrb.gov.sk.ca
Minimum Wage Board, #400, 1870 Albert St., Regina, SK S4P 4W1
306-787-2391, Fax: 306-787-7229, webmaster@lab.gov.sk.ca
Office of the Worker's Advocate, #400, 1870 Albert St., Regina, SK S4P 4W1
306-787-2456, Fax: 306-787-0249, 877-787-2456
Saskatchewan Workers' Compensation Board, #200, 1881 Scarth St., Regina, SK S4P 4L1
306-787-4370, Fax: 306-787-7582, 800-667-7590, internet_clientsvc@wcbsask.com
Saskatchewan Workers' Compensation Board, #200, 1881 Scarth St., Regina, S4P 4L1 SK
306-787-4370, Fax: 306-787-7582, 800-667-7590, internet_clientsvc@wcbsask.com

Yukon Territory
Yukon Workers' Compensation Health & Safety Board, 401 Strickland St., Whitehorse, Y1A 5N8 YT
867-667-5645, Fax: 867-393-6279, 800-661-0443, worksafe@gov.yk.ca

LAND RESOURCES
See Also: Agriculture; Forest Resources; Parks
Natural Resources Canada, 580 Booth St., Ottawa, K1A 0E4 ON
613-995-0947, Fax: 613-992-7211
Parks Canada, 25 Eddy St., Gatineau, K1A 0M5 QC
888-773-8888, information@pc.gc.ca

Alberta
Alberta Special Areas Board, 212 - 2nd Ave. West, PO Box 820, Hanna, AB T0J 1P0
403-854-5600, Fax: 403-854-5527, specarea@telusplanet.net

British Columbia
Crown Land Administration, 808 Douglas St., 5th Fl., PO Box 9120 Prov Govt, Victoria, V8W 9B4 BC
250-356-3076, Fax: 250-356-7279

Manitoba
Farm Lands Ownership Board, #812, Norquay Bldg., 401 York Ave., Winnipeg, MB R3C 0P8
204-945-3149, Fax: 204-945-1489, 800-282-8069, robert.mckenzie@gov.mb.ca
Manitoba Conservation Districts Commission, Secretariat c/o Planning & Coordination Branch, 123 Main St., PO Box 20000, Neepawa, MB R0J 1H0
204-476-7033, Fax: 204-476-7539, whildebran@gov.mb.ca
Manitoba Land Value Appraisal Commission, 800 Portage Ave., Winnipeg, MB R3G 0N4
204-945-2941, Fax: 204-948-2235

New Brunswick
Service New Brunswick, Westmorland Place, #200, 82 Westmorland St., PO Box 1998, Fredericton, E3B 5G4 NB
506-457-3581, Fax: 506-457-7520, 888-762-8600, snb@snb.ca

Northwest Territories
Department of Environment & Natural Resources, PO Box 1320, Yellowknife, X1A 2L9 NT
Department of Municipal & Community Affairs, PO Box 1320, Yellowknife, X1A 2L9 NT
867-873-7118, Fax: 867-873-0309

Nunavut
Department of Environment, PO Box 1000 1300, Iqaluit, X0A 0H0 NU
867-975-7700, Fax: 867-975-7742, 866-222-9063, environment@gov.nu.ca

Ontario
Natural Resources Management Division, Whitney Block, #6540, 99 Wellesley St. West, Toronto, M7A 1W3 ON
416-314-2000, Fax: 416-314-1994

Prince Edward Island
Department of Environment, Energy & Forestry, Jones Bldg., 11 Kent St., 4th & 5th Fl., PO Box 2000, Charlottetown, C1A 7N8 PE
902-368-5000, Fax: 902-368-5830

Quebec
Commission de protection du territoire agricole du Québec, 200, ch Ste-Foy, 2e étage, Québec, QC G1R 4X6
418-643-3314, Fax: 418-643-2261, 800-667-5294, info@cptaq.gouv.qc.ca
Foncier Québec, #E306, 5700, 4e av ouest, Québec, G1H 6R1 QC
418-643-3582, Fax: 418-528-8721, 866-226-0977, assistance.clientele@mrnf.registrefoncier.gouv.qc.ca
Territoire, #A300, 5700, 4e av ouest, Québec, G1H 6R1 QC
418-627-8638, Fax: 418-646-0042, territoire@mrnf.gouv.qc.ca

Saskatchewan
Saskatchewan Government Services, Century Plaza, 1920 Rose St., Regina, S4P 0A9 SK
306-787-6911, Fax: 306-787-1061
Saskatchewan Lands Appeal Board, #202, 3085 Albert St., Regina, SK S4S 0B1
306-787-4693, Fax: 306-787-1315, dbrooks@agr.gov.sk.ca

Yukon Territory
Yukon Land Use Planning Council, #201, 307 Jarvis St., Whitehorse, YT Y1A 2H3
867-667-7397, Fax: 867-667-4624, ylupc@planyukon.ca

LAND TITLES
See Also: Real Estate

British Columbia
British Columbia Assessment Authority, 1537 Hillside Ave., Victoria, BC V8T 4Y2
250-595-6211, Fax: 250-595-6222, info@bcassessment.ca

New Brunswick
Service New Brunswick, Westmorland Place, #200, 82 Westmorland St., PO Box 1998, Fredericton, E3B 5G4 NB
506-457-3581, Fax: 506-457-7520, 888-762-8600, snb@snb.ca

Nova Scotia
Registry of Deeds, PO Box 2205, Halifax, B3J 3C4 NS
Fax: 902-424-5872

LANDLORD & TENANT REGULATIONS

Ontario
Ontario Rental Housing Tribunal, 777 Bay St., 12th Fl., Toronto, ON M5G 2E5
416-585-7295, Fax: 416-585-6363, 888-332-3234

Prince Edward Island
Island Regulatory & Appeals Commission, National Bank Tower, #501, 134 Kent St., PO Box 577, Charlottetown, C1A 7L1 PE
902-892-3501, Fax: 902-566-4076, 800-501-6268, irac@irac.pe.ca

Quebec
Régie du logement du Québec, Pyramide Ouest, #2360, 5199, rue Sherbrooke est, Montréal, QC H1T 3X1
514-873-6575, Fax: 514-873-6805, 800-683-2245

LANDS & SOILS
Agriculture & Agri-Food Canada, Sir John Carling Bldg., 930 Carling Ave., Ottawa, K1A 0C5 ON
613-759-1000, Fax: 613-759-6726, info@agr.gc.ca
Canada Centre for Remote Sensing - Geomatics Canada, 588 Booth St., Ottawa, K1A 0Y7 ON
613-947-1216, Fax: 613-947-1382
Indian & Northern Affairs Canada, 10 Wellington St., North Tower, Gatineau, K1A 0H4 QC
819-997-0380, Fax: 819-953-3017, 866-817-3977, infopubs@ainc-inac.gc.ca
Natural Resources Canada, 580 Booth St., Ottawa, K1A 0E4 ON
613-995-0947, Fax: 613-992-7211
Soil, Plant & Feed Laboratory, Brookfield Rd., PO Box 8700, St. John's, A1B 4J6 NL
709-729-6738, Fax: 709-729-6734

Alberta
Irrigation Council, Provincial Bldg., 200 - 5 Ave. South, 3rd Fl., PO Bag 3014, Lethbridge, AB T1J 4L1
403-381-5176, Fax: 403-382-4406
Land Compensation/Surface Rights Board, Phipps-McKinnon Bldg., 10020 - 101A Ave., 18th Fl., Edmonton, AB T5J 3G2
780-427-2444, Fax: 780-427-5798

British Columbia
Ministry of Environment, PO Box 9339 Prov Govt, Victoria, V8W 9M1 BC
250-387-1161, Fax: 250-387-5669, www.envmail@gov.bc.ca
Forest Practices Board, 1675 Douglas St., 3rd Fl., PO Box 9905 Prov Govt, Victoria, BC V8W 9R1
250-387-7964, Fax: 250-387-7009, 800-994-5899, fpboard@gov.bc.ca
Timber Export Advisory Committee, 1520 Blanshard St., 2nd Fl., PO Box 9514 Prov Govt, Victoria, BC V8W 9C2
250-387-8916, Fax: 250-387-5050

Manitoba
Manitoba Geological Survey, #360, 1394 Ellice Ave., Winnipeg, R3G 3P2 MB
Fax: 204-945-1406, 800-223-5215, minesinfo@gov.mb.ca

New Brunswick
Assessment & Planning Appeal Board, #201, 435 King St., PO Box 6000, Fredericton, NB E3B 5H1
506-453-2126, Fax: 506-444-4881
Department of the Environment, Marysville Place, 20 McGloin St., PO Box 6000, Fredericton, E3B 5H1 NB
506-453-2690, Fax: 506-457-4991
Department of Natural Resources, PO Box 6000, Fredericton, E3B 5H1 NB
506-453-2510, Fax: 506-444-5839, dnrweb@gnb.ca

Newfoundland & Labrador
Department of Government Services, PO Box 8700, St. John's, A1B 4J6 NL
709-729-4860

Northwest Territories
Department of Environment & Natural Resources, PO Box 1320, Yellowknife, X1A 2L9 NT

Nova Scotia
Department of Natural Resources, Founder's Square, 1701 Hollis St., 3rd Fl., PO Box 698, Halifax, B3J 2T9 NS
902-424-5935, Fax: 902-424-0594, 800-565-2224

Prince Edward Island
Department of Environment, Energy & Forestry, Jones Bldg., 11 Kent St., 4th & 5th Fl., PO Box 2000, Charlottetown, C1A 7N8 PE
902-368-5000, Fax: 902-368-5830
Department of Tourism, PO Box 2000, Charlottetown, C1A 7N8 PE
800-463-4734

Quebec
Ministère du Développement durable, de l'Environnement et des Parcs, Édifice Marie-Guyart, 675, boul René-Lévesque est, 29e étage, Québec, G1R 5V7 QC
418-521-3830, Fax: 418-646-5974, 800-561-1616, info@mddep.gouv.qc.ca
Territoire, #A300, 5700, 4e av ouest, Québec, G1H 6R1 QC
418-627-8638, Fax: 418-646-0042, territoire@mrnf.gouv.qc.ca

Saskatchewan
Saskatchewan Assessment Management Agency, #200, 2201 - 11 Ave., Regina, S4P 0J8 SK
306-924-8000, Fax: 306-924-8070, 800-667-7262, info.request@sama.sk.ca
Saskatchewan Government Services, Century Plaza, 1920 Rose St., Regina, S4P 0A9 SK
306-787-6911, Fax: 306-787-1061

Yukon Territory
Carmacks Renewable Resource Council, PO Box 122, Carmacks, YT Y0B 1C0
867-863-6838, Fax: 867-863-6429, carmacksrrc@lscfn.ca
Yukon Environment, PO Box 2703, Whitehorse, Y1A 2C6 YT
867-667-5652, Fax: 867-393-6213, 800-661-0408, environmentyukon@gov.yk.ca
Selkirk Renewable Resources Council, PO Box 32, Pelly Crossing, YT Y0B 1P0
867-537-3937, Fax: 867-537-3939, selkirkrre@yknet.yk.ca
Yukon Land Use Planning Council, #201, 307 Jarvis St., Whitehorse, YT Y1A 2H3
867-667-7397, Fax: 867-667-4624, ylupc@planyukon.ca

LAW & JUSTICE
Auditor General of Canada, 240 Sparks St., Ottawa, K1A 0G6 ON
613-995-3708, Fax: 613-957-0474, communications@oag-bvg.gc.ca
Commission for Public Complaints Against the Royal Canadian Mounted Police, PO Box 3423 D, Ottawa, ON K1P 6L4
613-952-1471, Fax: 613-952-8045, 800-267-6637, org@cpc-cpp.gc.ca
Financial Transactions & Reports Analysis Centre of Canada, 234 Laurier Ave. West, 24th Fl., Ottawa, ON K1P 1H7
Fax: 613-943-7931, 866-346-8722, guidelines-lignesdirectrices@fintrac-canafe.gc.ca
International Joint Commission, 234 Laurier Ave. West, 22nd Fl., Ottawa, K1P 6K6 ON
613-947-1420, Fax: 613-993-5583
Military Police Complaints Commission, 270 Albert St., 10th Fl., Ottawa, ON K1P 5G8
613-947-5625, Fax: 613-947-5713, 800-632-0566, commission@mpcc-cppm.gc.ca
Passport Canada, Le 70 Crémazie, 70 Crémazie St., Gatineau, K1A 0G3 QC
Fax: 819-953-5856, 800-567-6868
Royal Canadian Mounted Police External Review Committee, PO Box 1159 B, Ottawa, ON K1P 5R2
613-998-2134, Fax: 613-990-8969, org@erc-cee.gc.ca
Transportation Appeal Tribunal of Canada, 333 Laurier Ave. West, 12th Fl., Ottawa, ON K1A 0N5
613-990-6906, Fax: 613-990-9153, info@tatc.gc.ca
Transportation Safety Board of Canada, 200 Promenade du Portage, 4th Fl., Ottawa, K1A 1K8 ON
819-994-3741, Fax: 819-997-2239, 800-387-3557

Alberta
Alberta Human Rights & Citizenship Commission, Northern Regional Office, Standard Life Centre, #800, 10405 Jasper Ave., Edmonton, AB T5J 4R7
780-427-7661, Fax: 780-427-6013,-310-0000, humanrights@gov.ab.ca.
Alberta Mental Health Patient Advocate Office, #1202, 10035 - 108 St., Edmonton, AB T5J 3E1
780-422-1812, Fax: 780-422-0695
Land Compensation/Surface Rights Board, Phipps-McKinnon Bldg., 10020 - 101A Ave., 18th Fl., Edmonton, AB T5J 3G2
780-427-2444, Fax: 780-427-5798
Workers' Compensation Board of Alberta, 9925 - 107 St., PO Box 2415, Edmonton, T5J 2S5 AB
780-498-3999, Fax: 780-498-7999, 800-661-9608

British Columbia
British Columbia Office of the Police Complaint Commissioner, 756 Fort St., 3rd Fl., PO Box 9895 Prov Govt, Victoria, BC V8W 9T8
250-356-7458, Fax: 250-356-6503, 800-663-7867, info@opcc.bc.ca
British Columbia Environmental Assessment Office, 836 Yates St., 1st Fl., PO Box 9426 Prov Govt, Victoria, V8W 9V1 BC
250-356-7441, Fax: 250-356-7440, eaoinfo@gov.bc.ca
Management Services Branch, 910 Government St., 5th Fl., PO Box 9256 Prov Govt, Victoria, V8W 9J4 BC
250-387-5258, Fax: 250-387-0081
Mediation & Arbitration Board, #310, 9900 - 100 Ave., Fort St John, BC V1J 5S7
250-787-3403, Fax: 250-787-3228, mab.office@gov.bc.ca

Manitoba
Advisory Council on Workplace Safety & Health, #200, 401 York Ave., Winnipeg, MB R3C 0P8
204-945-3446, Fax: 204-945-4556
Highway Traffic Board/Motor Transport Board, #200, 301 Weston St., Winnipeg, MB R3E 3H4
204-945-8912, Fax: 204-783-6529
License Suspension Appeal Board/Medical Review Committee, #200, 301 Weston St., Winnipeg, MB R3E 3H4
204-945-7350, Fax: 204-948-2682
Manitoba Film Classification Board, #216, 301 Weston St., Winnipeg, MB R3E 3H4
204-945-8962, Fax: 204-945-0890, 866-612-2399, mfcb@gov.mb.ca
Manitoba Labour Board, A.A. Heaps Bldg., #402, 258 Portage Ave., Winnipeg, MB R3C 0B6
204-945-3783, Fax: 204-945-1296, mlb@gov.mb.ca
Manitoba Land Value Appraisal Commission, 800 Portage Ave., Winnipeg, MB R3G 0N4
204-945-2941, Fax: 204-948-2235
Manitoba Liquor Control Commission, 1555 Buffalo Pl., PO Box 1023, Winnipeg, MB R3C 2X1
204-284-2501, Fax: 204-475-7666, info@mlcc.mb.ca
Manitoba Minimum Wage Board, 614 - 401 York Ave., Winnipeg, MB R3C 0P8
204-945-4889, Fax: 204-948-2085, mw@gov.mb.ca
Office of the Fire Commissioner, #508, 401 York Ave., Winnipeg, MB R3C 0P8
204-945-3322, Fax: 204-948-2089, 800-282-8069, firecomm@gov.mb.ca
Manitoba Workers' Compensation Board, 333 Broadway Ave., Winnipeg, R3C 4W3 MB
204-954-4321, Fax: 204-954-4999, 800-362-3340, wcb@wcb.mb.ca
Workplace Safety & Health Division, #200, 401 York Ave., Winnipeg, R3C 0P8 MB
204-945-3446, Fax: 204-948-2209, wshcompl@gov.mb.ca

New Brunswick
Assessment & Planning Appeal Board, #201, 435 King St., PO Box 6000, Fredericton, NB E3B 5H1
506-453-2126, Fax: 506-444-4881
Board of Examiners under the Scaler's Act, 1350 Regent St. South, PO Box 6000, Fredericton, NB E3B 5H1
506-453-2441, Fax: 506-453-6689
Department of Public Safety, 364 Argyle St., PO Box 6000, Fredericton, E3B 5H1 NB
506-453-3992, Fax: 506-453-3870, DPS-MSP.Information@gnb.ca
Workplace Health, Safety & Compensation Commission of New Brunswick, 1 Portland St., PO Box 160, Saint John, E2L 3X9 NB
506-632-2200, 800-222-9775, communications@ws-ts.nb.ca

Northwest Territories
Assessment Appeal Tribunal of the Northwest Territories, #500, 5201 - 50th Ave., PO Box 1320, Yellowknife, NT X1A 2L9
867-873-7125, Fax: 867-873-0609
Territorial Board of Revision, PO Box 1320, Yellowknife, NT X1A 2L9
867-873-7125, Fax: 867-873-0609
Northwest Territories & Nunavut Workers' Compensation Board, Centre Square Tower, 5022 - 49th St., 5th Fl., PO Box 8888, Yellowknife, X1A 2R3 NT
867-920-3888, Fax: 867-873-4596, 800-661-0792, wcb@wcb.nt.ca

Nova Scotia
Labour Relations Board & Construction Industry Panel, 5151 Terminal Rd.,7th Fl., PO Box 697, Halifax, NS B3J 2T8
902-424-6730, Fax: 902-424-1744
Labour Standards Tribunal, 5151 Terminal Rd., 7th Fl., PO Box 697, Halifax, NS B3J 2T8
902-424-6730, Fax: 902-424-1744, noeljl@gov.ns.ca
Pay Equity Commission, 5151 Terminal Rd., 7th Fl., PO Box 697, Halifax, NS B3J 2T8
902-424-2385, Fax: 902-424-0575
Workers' Compensation Board of Nova Scotia, 5668 South St., PO Box 1150, Halifax, B3J 2Y2 NS
902-491-8999, Fax: 902-491-8002, 800-870-3331, info@wcb.gov.ns.ca

Ontario
Alcohol & Gaming Commission of Ontario, 20 Dundas St. West, Toronto, ON M5G 2N6
416-326-8700, Fax: 416-326-5555, 800-522-2876
Association of Ontario Land Surveyors, 1043 McNicoll Ave., Toronto, ON M1W 3W6
416-491-9020, Fax: 416-491-2576, admin@aols.org
Ministry of Community Safety & Correctional Services, George Drew Bldg., 25 Grosvenor St., 18th Fl., Toronto, M7A 1Y6 ON
416-326-5000, Fax: 416-325-6067, 866-517-0571, jus.g.sgcs.webmaster@jus.gov.on.ca
Licence Appeal Tribunal (LAT), 1 St. Clair Ave. West, 12th Fl., Toronto, ON M4V 1K6
416-314-4260, Fax: 416-314-4270, 800-255-2214
Liquor Control Board of Ontario, 55 Lake Shore Blvd. East, Toronto, ON M5E 1A4
416-365-5900, Fax: 416-864-2476, 800-668-5226, infoline@lcbo.com
Ontario Civilian Commission on Police Services, 25 Grosvenor St., 1st Fl., Toronto, ON M7A 1Y6
416-326-1189, Fax: 416-314-2036, 888-515-5005
Ontario Film Review Board, 1075 Millwood Rd., Toronto, ON M4G 1X6
416-314-3626, Fax: 416-314-3632
Ontario Labour Relations Board, 505 University Ave., 2nd Fl., Toronto, ON M5G 2P1
416-326-7500, Fax: 416-326-7531, 877-339-3335
Ontario Parole & Earned Release Board, 415 Yonge St., Toronto, ON M5B 2E7
416-325-4480, Fax: 416-325-4485
Ontario Police Arbitration Commission, George Drew Bldg., 25 Grosvenor St., 1st Fl., Toronto, ON M7A 1Y6
416-314-3520, Fax: 416-314-3522
Ontario Racing Commission, 20 Dundas St. West, 9th Fl., Toronto, ON M5G 2C2
416-327-0520, Fax: 416-325-3478, orcinqry@cbs.gov.on.ca
Ontario Review Board, 151 Bloor St. West, 10th Fl., Toronto, ON M5S 2T5
416-327-8866, Fax: 416-327-8867
OPSEU Pension Trust, #1200, 1 Adelaide St. East, Toronto, ON M5C 3A7
416-681-6161, Fax: 416-681-6175
Road User Safety Division, #191, Bldg A, 1201 Wilson Ave., Toronto, M3M 1J8 ON
416-235-2999, Fax: 416-235-4153
ServiceOntario, College Park, 777 Bay St., 15th fl., Toronto, M7A 2J3 ON
416-326-6205, Fax: 416-326-5106
Workplace Safety & Insurance Board, 200 Front St. West, Ground Fl., Toronto, M5V 3J1 ON
416-344-1000, Fax: 416-344-4684, 800-387-0750,

Prince Edward Island
Office of the Attorney General, Shaw Building, North, 105 Rochford St., 4th Fl., PO Box 2000, Charlottetown, C1A 7N8 PE
902-368-5152, Fax: 902-368-4910
Employment Standards Board, 161 St. Peters Rd., PO Box 2000, Charlottetown, PE C1A 7N8
902-368-5550, Fax: 902-368-5476
Labour Relations Board, PO Box 2000, Charlottetown, PE C1A 7N8
902-368-5550, Fax: 902-368-5476

Government Quick Reference Guide / Legal & Regulatory

Island Regulatory & Appeals Commission, National Bank Tower, #501, 134 Kent St., PO Box 577, Charlottetown, C1A 7L1 PE
902-892-3501, Fax: 902-566-4076, 800-501-6268, irac@irac.pe.ca
Prince Edward Island Workers Compensation Board, 14 Weymouth St., PO Box 757, Charlottetown, C1A 7L7 PE
902-368-5680, Fax: 902-368-5705, 800-237-5049

Quebec
Bureau du coroner, #390, 2875, boul Laurier, Sainte-Foy, QC G1V 5B1
418-643-1845, Fax: 418-643-6174, clientele.coroner@msp.gouv.qc.ca
Comité de déontologie policière, Tour du Saint-Laurent, #A-200, 2525, boul Laurier, 2e étage, Québec, QC G1V 4Z6
418-646-1936, Fax: 418-528-0987, comite.deontologie@msp.gouv.qc.ca
Commissaire à la déontologie policière, 1200, rte de l'Église, R-C20, Sainte-Foy, QC G1V 4Y9
418-643-7897, Fax: 418-528-9473, 877-237-7897
Commissariat des incendies, 455, rue Dupont, Québec, QC G1K 6N2
418-529-5706, Fax: 418-529-9922
Commission des lésions professionnelles, #700, 900, Place d'Youville, Québec, QC G1R 3P7
418-644-7777, Fax: 418-644-6443, 800-463-1591
Commission québécoise des libérations conditionnelles, #1.32A, 300, boul Jean-Lesage, Québec, QC G1K 8K6
418-646-8300, Fax: 418-643-7217, liberation.conditionnel@msp.gouv.
Direction générale de la Sûreté du Québec, 1701, rue Parthenais, Montréal, QC H2K 3S7
514-598-4488, Fax: 514-598-4957, info@surete.qc.ca
Régie des alcools, des courses et des jeux, 560, boul Charest est, Québec, QC G1K 3J3
418-643-7667, Fax: 418-643-5971, 800-363-0320, racj.quebec@racj.gouv.qc.ca
Ministère de la Sécurité publique, Tour des Laurentides, 2525, boul Laurier, 5e étage, Québec, QC G1V 2L2 QC
Fax: 418-643-0275, 866-644-6826
École nationale de police du Québec, 350, rue Marguerite-d'Youville, Nicolet, QC J3T 1X4
819-293-8631, Fax: 819-293-4018, courriel@enpq.qc.ca

Saskatchewan
Agricultural Implements Board, #202, 3085 Albert St., Regina, SK S4S 0B1
306-787-4693, Fax: 306-787-1315
Saskatchewan Workers' Compensation Board, #200, 1881 Scarth St., Regina, S4P 4L1 SK
306-787-4370, Fax: 306-787-7582, 800-667-7590, internet_clientsvc@wcbsask.com

Yukon Territory
Driver Control Board, 308 Steele St., PO Box 2703, Whitehorse, YT Y1A 2C6
867-667-3774, Fax: 867-393-6483, dcb@gov.yk.ca
Yukon Workers' Compensation Health & Safety Board, 401 Strickland St., Whitehorse, Y1A 5N8 YT
867-667-5645, Fax: 867-393-6279, 800-661-0443, worksafe@gov.yk.ca
Yukon Motor Transport Board, PO Box 2703, Whitehorse, YT Y1A 2C6
867-667-5782, Fax: 867-393-6408, Laurie.Hrynuik@gov.yk.ca

LEGAL & REGULATORY
Canadian Coast Guard, Centennial Towers, #6S018, 200 Kent St., Ottawa, K1A 0E6 ON
613-998-1573, Fax: 613-990-2780
Commission for Environmental Cooperation, Secretariat, #200, 393, rue St-Jacques ouest, Montréal, H2Y 1N9 QC
514-350-4300, Fax: 514-350-4314, info@cec.org
Institute for National Measurement Standards, Bldg. M-36, 1500 Montreal Rd., Ottawa, K1A 0R6 ON
613-998-7018, Fax: 613-952-1394, alexandra.shaw@nrc-cnrc.gc.ca
Investigations & Enforcement Branch, 5775 Yonge St., 8th Fl., Toronto, M2M 4J1 ON
416-326-6700, Fax: 416-326-5276
Standards Council of Canada, #200, 270 Albert St., Ottawa, K1P 6N7 ON
613-238-3222, Fax: 613-569-7808, info@scc.ca
Standards Development Branch, 40 St. Clair Ave. West, 7th Fl., Toronto, M4V 1M2 ON
416-327-5519

Alberta
Workers' Compensation Board of Alberta, 9925 - 107 St., PO Box 2415, Edmonton, T5J 2S5 AB
780-498-3999, Fax: 780-498-7999, 800-661-9608

British Columbia
British Columbia Environmental Assessment Office, 836 Yates St., 1st Fl., PO Box 9426 Prov Govt,Victoria, V8W 9V1 BC
250-356-7441, Fax: 250-356-7440, eaoinfo@gov.bc.ca
Mediation & Arbitration Board, #310, 9900 - 100 Ave., Fort St John, BC V1J 5S7
250-787-3403, Fax: 250-787-3228, mab.office@gov.bc.ca

New Brunswick
Board of Examiners under the Scaler's Act, 1350 Regent St. South, PO Box 6000, Fredericton, NB E3B 5H1
506-453-2441, Fax: 506-453-6689
Environmental Management, Marysville Place, 20 McGloin St., PO Box 6000, Fredericton, E3B 5H1 NB
506-444-5119, Fax: 506-457-7333

Northwest Territories
Assessment Appeal Tribunal of the Northwest Territories, #500, 5201 - 50th Ave., PO Box 1320, Yellowknife, NT X1A 2L9
867-873-7125, Fax: 867-873-0609

Nova Scotia
Crane Operators Appeal Board, 5151 Terminal Rd., 7th Fl., PO Box 697, Halifax, NS B3J 2T8
902-424-8595, Fax: 902-424-0217, fraserej@gov.ns.ca
Labour Relations Board & Construction Industry Panel, 5151 Terminal Rd.,7th Fl., PO Box 697, Halifax, NS B3J 2T8
902-424-6730, Fax: 902-424-1744
Labour Standards Tribunal, 5151 Terminal Rd., 7th Fl., PO Box 697, Halifax, NS B3J 2T8
902-424-6730, Fax: 902-424-1744, noelj@gov.ns.ca
Occupational Health & Safety Advisory Council, PO Box 697, Halifax, NS B3J 2T8
902-424-2484, Fax: 902-424-5640
Pay Equity Commission, 5151 Terminal Rd., 7th Fl., PO Box 697, Halifax, NS B3J 2T8
902-424-2385, Fax: 902-424-0575
Workers' Advisers Program, #502, 5670 Spring Garden Rd., PO Box 1063, Halifax, NS B3J 2X1
902-424-5050, Fax: 902-424-0530, 800-774-4712
Workers' Compensation Board of Nova Scotia, 5668 South St., PO Box 1150, Halifax, B3J 2Y2 NS
902-491-8999, Fax: 902-491-8002, 800-870-3331, info@wcb.gov.ns.ca

Ontario
Ministry of Community Safety & Correctional Services, George Drew Bldg., 25 Grosvenor St., 18th Fl., Toronto, M7A 1Y6 ON
416-326-5000, Fax: 416-325-6067, 866-517-0571, jus.g.sgcs.webmaster@jus.gov.on.ca
Environmental Commissioner of Ontario, #605, 1075 Bay St., Toronto, M5S 2B1 ON
416-325-3377, Fax: 416-325-3370, 800-701-6454, commissioner@eco.on.ca
Environmental Review Tribunal, #1700, 2300 Yonge St., PO Box 2382, Toronto, ON M4P 1E4
416-314-4600, Fax: 416-314-4506
Road User Safety Division, #191, Bldg A, 1201 Wilson Ave., Toronto, M3M 1J8 ON
416-235-2999, Fax: 416-235-4153

Prince Edward Island
Island Regulatory & Appeals Commission, National Bank Tower, #501, 134 Kent St., PO Box 577, Charlottetown, C1A 7L1 PE
902-892-3501, Fax: 902-566-4076, 800-501-6268, irac@irac.pe.ca

LEISURE CRAFT & VEHICLE REGULATIONS

Alberta
Technology Services, John E. Brownlee Bldg., 10365 - 97 St., 8th Fl., Edmonton, T5J 3W7 AB
780-422-8545,

Northwest Territories
Road Licensing & Safety, 4510 - 50 Ave., 1st fl., PO Box 1320, Yellowknife, X1A 2L9 NT
867-873-7972, Fax: 867-873-0120

Nova Scotia
Department of Transportation & Infrastructure Renewal, Johnston Bldg., 1672 Granville St., 2nd Fl., PO Box 186, Halifax, B3J 2N2 NS
902-424-2297, Fax: 902-424-0171, 888-432-3233, tpwpaff@gov.ns.ca

Ontario
Ministry of Transportation, Ferguson Block, 77 Wellesley St. West, 3rd Fl., Toronto, M7A 1Z8 ON
416-235-4686, Fax: 416-327-9185, 800-268-4686

Quebec
Ministère des Transports, 700, boul René-Lévesque est, 27e étage, Québec, G1R 5H1 QC
Fax: 514-643-1269, 888-355-0511, communications@mtq.gouv.qc.ca

LIBRARIES

Nunavut
Department of Culture, Language, Elders & Youth, PO Box 1000 800,Iqaluit, X0A 0H0 NU
867-975-5500, Fax: 867-975-5504, 866-934-2035

Ontario
Ontario Library Service - North, 334 Regent St., Sudbury, ON P3C 4E2
705-675-6467, Fax: 705-675-2285, 800-461-6348
Southern Ontario Library Service, #902, 111 Peter St., Toronto, ON M5V 2H1
416-961-1669, Fax: 416-961-5122, 800-387-5765

Quebec
Bibliothèque et Archives nationales du Québec (BAnQ), 475, boul De Maisonneuve est, Montréal, H2L 5C4 QC
514-873-1100, Fax: 514-873-9312, 800-363-9028

Saskatchewan
Saskatchewan Tourism, Parks, Culture, & Sport, 1919 Saskatchewan Dr., 4th Fl., Regina, S4P 4H2 SK
306-787-5729, Fax: 306-787-8560

LIQUOR CONTROL
See Also: Drugs & Alcohol

British Columbia
Liquor Distribution Branch, 2625 Rupert St., Vancouver, V5M 3T5 BC
604-252-3000, Fax: 604-252-3026

Manitoba
Manitoba Liquor Control Commission, 1555 Buffalo Pl., PO Box 1023, Winnipeg, MB R3C 2X1
204-284-2501, Fax: 204-475-7666, info@mlcc.mb.ca

Nova Scotia
Alcohol & Gaming Division, Alderney Gate, 40 Alderney Dr., 5th Fl., PO Box 545, Dartmouth, B2Y 3Y8 NS
902-424-6160, Fax: 902-424-6313, 877-565-0556

Ontario
Alcohol & Gaming Commission of Ontario, 20 Dundas St. West, Toronto, ON M5G 2N6
416-326-8700, Fax: 416-326-5555, 800-522-2876
Liquor Control Board of Ontario, 55 Lake Shore Blvd. East, Toronto, ON M5E 1A4
416-365-5900, Fax: 416-864-2476, 800-668-5226, infoline@lcbo.com

Quebec
Régie des alcools, des courses et des jeux, 560, boul Charest est, Québec, QC G1K 3J3
418-643-7667, Fax: 418-643-5971, 800-363-0320, racj.quebec@racj.gouv.qc.ca

LOTTERIES & GAMING

British Columbia
British Columbia Lottery Corporation, 74 West Seymour St., Kamloops, BC V2C 1E2
250-828-5500, Fax: 250-828-5631, 866-815-0222

Newfoundland & Labrador
Department of Government Services, PO Box 8700, St. John's, A1B 4J6 NL
709-729-4860

Nova Scotia
Alcohol & Gaming Division, Alderney Gate, 40 Alderney Dr., 5th Fl., PO Box 545, Dartmouth, B2Y 3Y8 NS
902-424-6160, Fax: 902-424-6313, 877-565-0556

Nunavut
Department of Community & Government Services, J.G. Brown Bldg., PO Box 1000 700, Iqaluit, X0A 0H0 NU
867-975-5400, Fax: 867-975-5305

Ontario
Alcohol & Gaming Commission of Ontario, 20 Dundas St. West, Toronto, ON M5G 2N6
416-326-8700, Fax: 416-326-5555, 800-522-2876
Ontario Lottery & Gaming Corporation, Roberta Bondar Pl., #800, 70 Foster Dr., Sault Ste Marie, ON P6A 6V2
705-946-6464
Ontario Racing Commission, 20 Dundas St. West, 9th Fl., Toronto, ON M5G 2C2
416-327-0520, Fax: 416-325-3478, orcinqry@cbs.gov.on.ca

Prince Edward Island
Prince Edward Island Lotteries Commission, Office of the Deputy Provincial Treasurer, 95 Rochford St., PO Box 2000, Charlottetown, PE C1A 7N8
902-368-4053, Fax: 902-368-6575

Quebec
Régie des alcools, des courses et des jeux, 560, boul Charest est, Québec, QC G1K 3J3
418-643-7667, Fax: 418-643-5971, 800-363-0320, racj.quebec@racj.gouv.qc.ca

Yukon Territory
Yukon Lottery Commission, 312 Wood St., Whitehorse, YT Y1A 2E6
867-633-7890, Fax: 867-668-7561, lotteriesyukon@gov.yk.ca

MAPS, CHARTS & AERIAL PHOTOGRAPHS
Canada Centre for Remote Sensing - Geomatics Canada, 588 Booth St., Ottawa, K1A 0Y7 ON
613-947-1216, Fax: 613-947-1382
Mapping Services Branch - Geomatics Canada, 615 Booth St., Ottawa, K1A 0E9 ON
613-995-4945, Fax: 613-995-8737

Nova Scotia
Nova Scotia Geomatics Centre, 160 Willow St., Amherst, B4H 3W3 NS
902-667-7231, Fax: 902-667-6008, 800-798-0706, info@nsgc.gov.ns.ca

Ontario
Association of Ontario Land Surveyors, 1043 McNicoll Ave., Toronto, ON M1W 3W6
416-491-9020, Fax: 416-491-2576, admin@aols.org

MINERALS & MINING

British Columbia
Mining & Minerals, 1675 Douglas St., 7th Fl., PO Box 9320 Prov Govt, Victoria, V8W 9N3 BC
250-952-0596, Fax: 250-952-0491

Manitoba
Mines Branch, #360, 1395 Ellice Ave., Winnipeg, R3G 3P2 MB
Fax: 204-948-2578
Mining Board, #360, 1395 Ellice Ave., Winnipeg, MB R3G 3P2
204-489-0018

Northwest Territories
Department of Industry, Tourism & Investment, PO Box 1320, Yellowknife, X1A 2L9 NT
Fax: 867-873-0306, info@iti.ca

Nova Scotia
Department of Energy, Bank of Montreal Bldg., #400, 5151 George St., PO Box 2664, Halifax, B3J 3P7 NS
902-424-4575, Fax: 902-424-0528, energyinfo@gov.ns.ca

Nunavut
Department of Environment, PO Box 1000 1300, Iqaluit, X0A 0H0 NU
867-975-7700, Fax: 867-975-7742, 866-222-9063, environment@gov.nu.ca

Ontario
Mines & Minerals Division, Willet Green Miller Centre, 933 Ramsey Lake Rd., 6th Fl., Sudbury, P3E 6B5 ON
705-670-5755, Fax: 705-670-5818

Quebec
Mines, RC, 880, ch Ste-Foy, Québec, G1S 4X4 QC
418-627-6278, Fax: 418-418-6432, 800-363-7233, service.mines@mrnf.gouv.qc.ca

Énergie, #A405, 5700, 4e av ouest, Québec, G1H 6R1 QC
418-627-6377, Fax: 418-643-0701

Saskatchewan
Saskatchewan Energy & Resources, #300, 2103 - 11th Ave., Regina, S4P 3Z8 SK
306-787-2528, Fax: 306-787-8447, 866-727-5427

Yukon Territory
Yukon Energy, Mines & Resources, PO Box 2703, Whitehorse, Y1A 2C6 YT
867-667-5466, Fax: 867-667-8601, 800-661-0408, emr@gov.yk.ca

MINES & MINERALS

Alberta
Alberta Sport, Recreation, Parks & Wildlife Foundation, Standard Life Centre, 10405 Jasper Ave., 9th Fl., Edmonton, AB T5J 4R7
780-415-1167, Fax: 780-415-0308

British Columbia
Ministry of Energy, Mines & Petroleum Resources, PO Box 9318 Prov Govt, Victoria, V8W 9N3 BC
250-952-0241

Manitoba
Manitoba Geological Survey, #360, 1394 Ellice Ave., Winnipeg, R3G 3P2 MB
Fax: 204-945-1406, 800-223-5215, minesinfo@gov.mb.ca
Mining Board, #360, 1395 Ellice Ave., Winnipeg, MB R3G 3P2
204-489-0018

Northwest Territories
Department of Environment & Natural Resources, PO Box 1320, Yellowknife, X1A 2L9 NT

Ontario
Mines & Minerals Division, Willet Green Miller Centre, 933 Ramsey Lake Rd., 6th Fl., Sudbury, P3E 6B5 ON
705-670-5755, Fax: 705-670-5818
Ministry of Northern Development & Mines, 159 Cedar St., Sudbury, P3E 6A5 ON
705-564-0032, Fax: 705-564-7357

Quebec
Mines, RC, 880, ch Ste-Foy, Québec, G1S 4X4 QC
418-627-6278, Fax: 418-418-6432, 800-363-7233, service.mines@mrnf.gouv.qc.ca

MINIMUM WAGES
See Also: Labour

British Columbia
Ministry of Labour & Citizens' Services, PO Box 9052 Prov Govt, Victoria, V8W 9E2 BC
250-356-6348, Fax: 250-356-6595, LCS.Minister@gov.bc.ca

Quebec
Commission des normes du travail, Hall Est, 400, boul Jean-Lesage, 7e étage, Québec, QC G1K 8W1
418-644-0817, Fax: 418-643-5132, 800-563-9058

Saskatchewan
Minimum Wage Board, #400, 1870 Albert St., Regina, SK S4P 4W1
306-787-2391, Fax: 306-787-7229, webmaster@lab.gov.sk.ca

MULTICULTURALISM

Manitoba
Manitoba Ethnocultural Advisory & Advocacy Council, 215 Notre Dame Ave. 4th Fl., Winnipeg, MB R3B 1N3
204-945-2339, Fax: 204-948-2323, 800-665-8332, meaac@gov.mb.ca
Multiculturalism Secretariat, 213 Notre Dame Ave., 4th Fl., Winnipeg, MB R3B 1N3
204-945-1156, Fax: 204-948-2323

New Brunswick
Ministerial Advisory Committee on Multiculturalism, PO Box 6000, Fredericton, NB E3B 5H1

Northwest Territories
Department of Education, Culture & Employment, PO Box 1320, Yellowknife, X1A 2L9 NT
867-669-2399, Fax: 867-873-0431, 866-606-5627,

Nova Scotia
Department of Tourism, Culture & Heritage, World Trade & Convention Centre, 1800 Argyle St., 6th Fl., PO Box 456, Halifax, B3J 2R5 NS
902-424-5000, Fax: 902-424-4872, 800-565-0000, tns@gov.ns.ca

Ontario
Culture Policy, Programs & Services Division, 400 University Ave., 5th Fl., Toronto, M7A 2R9 ON
416-314-7265, Fax: 416-314-7461

Quebec
Ministère de la Culture, des Communications & de la Condition féminine, 225, Grande Allée est, Québec, G1R 5G5 QC
Fax: 418-380-2364, 888-380-8882, infos@mcccf.gouv.qc.ca

MUNICIPAL & RURAL AFFAIRS
Canada Economic Development for Québec Regions, Édifice Dominion Square, #900, 1255, rue Peel, Montréal, H3B 2T9 QC
514-283-6412, Fax: 514-283-3302, 866-385-6412
Canada Mortgage & Housing Corporation, 700 Montreal Rd., Ottawa, K1A 0P7 ON
613-748-2000, Fax: 613-748-2098, 800-668-2642, chic@cmhc-schl.gc.ca
Indian & Northern Affairs Canada, 10 Wellington St., North Tower, Gatineau, K1A 0H4 QC
819-997-0380, Fax: 819-953-3017, 866-817-3977, infopubs@ainc-inac.gc.ca
Mackenzie Valley Environmental Impact Review Board, 200 Scotia Centre, 5102 - 50th Ave., PO Box 938, Yellowknife, NT X1A 2N7
867-766-7050, Fax: 867-766-7074, 866-912-3472
Nunavut Impact Review Board, PO Box 2379, Cambridge Bay, NU X0B 0C0
867-983-4600, Fax: 867-983-2594, info@nirb.nunavut.ca
Nunavut Planning Commission, PO Box 2101, Cambridge Bay, NU X0B 0C0
867-983-2730, Fax: 867-983-2732

Alberta
Alberta Agriculture & Food, J.G. O'Donoghue Bldg., 7000 - 113 St., 1st Fl., Edmonton, T6H 5T6 AB
780-427-2727, Fax: 780-427-2861, 866-882-7677
Alberta Municipal Government Board, Commerce Place, 10155 - 102 St., 15th Fl., Edmonton, AB T5J 4L4
780-427-4864, Fax: 780-427-0986, mbgmail@gov.ab.ca
Alberta Municipal Affairs & Housing, Communications Branch, Commerce Place, 10155 - 102 St., 18th Fl., Edmonton, T5J 4L4 AB
780-427-2732, Fax: 780-422-1419, comments@gov.ab.ca
Northern Alberta Development Council, Provincial Bldg., #206, 9621 - 96 Ave., PO Box 900-14, Peace River, T8S 1T4 AB
780-624-6274, Fax: 780-624-6184, nadc.council@gov.ab.ca
Alberta Tourism, Parks, Recreation & Culture, Communications Branch, Standard Life Centre, 10405 Jasper Ave., 7th Fl., Edmonton, T5J 4R7 AB
780-427-6530, Fax: 780-427-1496, Comdev.Communications@gov.ab.ca

British Columbia
Local Government Department, 800 Johnson St., 6th Fl., PO Box 9490 Prov Govt, Victoria, V8W 9N7 BC
lgd_feedback@gov.bc.ca

Manitoba
Manitoba Aboriginal & Northern Affairs, 59 Elizabeth Dr., PO Box 37, Thompson, R8N 1X4 MB
204-677-6607, Fax: 204-677-6753, amartin@gov.mb.ca
Community Land Use Planning Services, #604, 800 Portage Ave., Winnipeg, R3G 0N4 MB
Manitoba Intergovernmental Affairs, #301, 450 Broadway Ave., Winnipeg, R3C 0V8 MB
Fax: 204-945-1383, mnia@leg.gov.mb.ca
Manitoba Municipal Board, #1144, 363 Broadway, Winnipeg, MB R3C 3N9
204-945-2941, Fax: 204-948-2235

New Brunswick
Assessment & Planning Appeal Board, #201, 435 King St., PO Box 6000, Fredericton, NB E3B 5H1
506-453-2126, Fax: 506-444-4881
Department of Health, PO Box 5100, Fredericton, E3B 5G8 NB
506-457-4800, Fax: 506-453-5243, dh-ms@dh-ms.ca
Regional Development Corporation, RDC Bldg., 836 Churchill Row, PO Box 428, Fredericton, E3B 5R4 NB
506-453-2277, Fax: 506-453-7988

Government Quick Reference Guide / Municipal Affairs

Newfoundland & Labrador
Department of Health & Community Services, West Block, Confederation Bldg., PO Box 8700, St. John's, A1B 4J6 NL
709-729-5021, Fax: 709-729-5824
Department of Labrador & Aboriginal Affairs, Confederation Bldg., East Block, 6th Fl., PO Box 8700, St. John's, A1B 4J6 NL
709-729-4776, Fax: 709-729-4900, 877-788-8822, laa@gov.nl.ca
Department of Municipal Affairs, West Block, Main Fl., Confederation Bldg., PO Box 8700, St. John's, A1B 4J6 NL
709-729-3053

Northwest Territories
Department of Municipal & Community Affairs, PO Box 1320, Yellowknife, X1A 2L9 NT
867-873-7118, Fax: 867-873-0309

Nova Scotia
Department of Service Nova Scotia & Municipal Relations, 1505 Barrington St., PO Box 216, Halifax, B3J 2M4 NS
902-424-4141, Fax: 902-424-0581, public-enquiries@gov.ns.ca
Department of Transportation & Infrastructure Renewal, Johnston Bldg., 1672 Granville St., 2nd Fl., PO Box 186, Halifax, B3J 2N2 NS
902-424-2297, Fax: 902-424-0171, 888-432-3233, tpwpaff@gov.ns.ca

Ontario
Ministry of Agriculture, Food & Rural Affairs, 1 Stone Rd. West, Guelph, N1G 4Y2 ON
519-826-3100, 888-466-2372
Ministry of Municipal Affairs & Housing, 777 Bay St., 17th Fl., Toronto, M5G 2E5 ON
416-585-7041, Fax: 416-585-6227, 866-220-2290, mininfo.mah@ontario.ca
Ministry of Northern Development & Mines, 159 Cedar St., Sudbury, P3E 6A5 ON
705-564-0032, Fax: 705-564-7357
Northern Development Division, Roberta Bondar Place, #200, 70 Foster Dr., Sault Ste Marie, P6A 6V8 ON
705-945-5900, Fax: 705-945-5931, 800-461-2287

Prince Edward Island
Department of Transportation & Public Works, Jones Bldg., 11 Kent St., PO Box 2000, Charlottetown, C1A 7N8 PE
902-368-5100, Fax: 902-368-5395

Quebec
Ministère des Affaires municipales et des Régions, Aile Chaveau, 10, rue Pierre-Olivier-Chauveau, 3e étage, Québec, G1R 4J3 QC
418-691-2019, Fax: 418-643-7385, communications@mamr.gouv.qc.ca
Comité consultatif de l'environnement Kativik, CP 930, Kuujjuaq, QC J0M 1C0
819-964-2961, Fax: 819-964-0694, ndea@krg.ca
Commission municipale du Québec, Mezzanine, aile Chaveau, 10, rue Pierre-Olivier-Chauveau, Tour 5e étage, Québec, QC G1R 4J3
418-691-2014, Fax: 418-644-4676, cmq@mamr.gouv.qc.ca
Ministère du Développement économique, de l'Innovation et de l'Exportation, 710, place D'Youville, 3e étage, Québec, G1R 4Y4 QC
418-691-5950, Fax: 418-644-0118, 866-680-1884

Saskatchewan
Saskatchewan Northern Affairs, Mistasinihk Place, 1328 La Ronge Ave., PO Box 5000, La Ronge, S0J 1L0 SK
306-425-4207, Fax: 306-425-4349, 866-663-4065, admin@sna.gov.sk.ca

Yukon Territory
Yukon Community Services, PO Box 2703, Whitehorse, Y1A 2C6 YT
867-667-5811, Fax: 867-393-6295, 800-661-0408, inquiry@gov.yk.ca

MUNICIPAL AFFAIRS

Alberta
Alberta Municipal Affairs & Housing, Communications Branch, Commerce Place, 10155 - 102 St., 18th Fl., Edmonton, T5J 4L4 AB
780-427-2732, Fax: 780-422-1419, comments@gov.ab.ca

British Columbia
Local Government Department, 800 Johnson St., 6th Fl., PO Box 9490 Prov Govt,Victoria, V8W 9N7 BC
lgd_feedback@gov.bc.ca

Manitoba
Manitoba Aboriginal & Northern Affairs, 59 Elizabeth Dr., PO Box 37, Thompson, R8N 1X4 MB
204-677-6607, Fax: 204-677-6753, amartin@gov.mb.ca
Manitoba Intergovernmental Affairs, #301, 450 Broadway Ave., Winnipeg, R3C 0V8 MB
Fax: 204-945-1383, mnia@leg.gov.mb.ca
Local Government Development Division, 59 Elizabeth Dr., PO Box 33, Thompson, R8N 1X4 MB
204-677-6794, Fax: 204-677-6525
Manitoba Municipal Board, #1144, 363 Broadway, Winnipeg, MB R3C 3N9
204-945-2941, Fax: 204-948-2235
Provincial-Municipal Support Services, #508, 800 Portage Ave., Winnipeg, R3G 0N4 MB

New Brunswick
Department of Local Government, Marysville Place, 20 McGloin St., PO Box 6000, Fredericton, E3B 5H1 NB
506-453-2807, Fax: 506-453-3988
Regional Development Corporation, RDC Bldg., 836 Churchill Row, PO Box 428, Fredericton, E3B 5R4 NB
506-453-2277, Fax: 506-453-7988

Newfoundland & Labrador
Department of Municipal Affairs, West Block, Main Fl., Confederation Bldg., PO Box 8700, St. John's, A1B 4J6 NL
709-729-3053

Northwest Territories
Department of Municipal & Community Affairs, PO Box 1320, Yellowknife, X1A 2L9 NT
867-873-7118, Fax: 867-873-0309

Nova Scotia
Nova Scotia Municipal Finance Corporation, Maritime Centre, 1505 Barrington St., 10th Fl. South, PO Box 850 M, Halifax, NS B3J 2V2
902-424-4590, Fax: 902-424-0525
Department of Service Nova Scotia & Municipal Relations, 1505 Barrington St., PO Box 216, Halifax, B3J 2M4 NS
902-424-4141, Fax: 902-424-0581, public-enquiries@gov.ns.ca

Nunavut
Department of Community & Government Services, J.G. Brown Bldg., PO Box 1000 700,Iqaluit, X0A 0H0 NU
867-975-5400, Fax: 867-975-5305

Ontario
Economic Development Division, 1 Stone Road W., 2nd Fl., Guelph, N1G 4Y2 ON
519-826-6636, Fax: 519-826-4328
Ministry of Municipal Affairs & Housing, 777 Bay St., 17th Fl., Toronto, M5G 2E5 ON
416-585-7041, Fax: 416-585-6227, 866-220-2290, mininfo.mah@ontario.ca

Prince Edward Island
Department of Communities, Cultural Affairs & Labour, Shaw Bldg., 95 Rochford St., 4th Fl., PO Box 2000, Charlottetown, C1A 7N8 PE
902-368-5250, Fax: 902-368-4121

Quebec
Ministère des Affaires municipales et des Régions, Aile Chaveau, 10, rue Pierre-Olivier-Chauveau, 3e étage, Québec, G1R 4J3 QC
418-691-2019, Fax: 418-643-7385, communications@mamr.gouv.qc.ca

MUSEUMS

Canada Science & Technology Museum Corporation, PO Box 9724 T,Ottawa, K1G 5A3 ON
613-991-6090, Fax: 613-990-3636, info@technomuses.ca
Canadian Heritage, 15 Eddy St., Gatineau, K1A 0M5 QC
819-997-0055, 866-811-0055

Alberta
Culture & Community Development Division, Standard Life Centre, 10405 Jasper Ave., 9th Fl., Edmonton, T5J 4R7 AB
780-415-1167, Fax: 780-422-2891

British Columbia
Ministry of Healthy Living & Sport, PO Box 9067 Prov Govt,Victoria, V8W 9E2 BC
250-387-3504, Fax: 250-387-3420, Feedback@gov.bc.ca

Manitoba
Manitoba Museum, 190 Rupert Ave., Winnipeg, MB R3B 0N2
204-956-2830, Fax: 204-942-3679, info@manitobamuseum.mb.ca

Newfoundland & Labrador
Department of Fisheries & Aquaculture, Petten Bldg., 30 Strawberry Marsh Rd., PO Box 8700, St. John's, A1B 4J6 NL
709-729-3723, Fax: 709-729-6082, fishaqwebmaster@gov.nl.ca

Nova Scotia
Culture Division, #601, 1800 Argyle St., PO Box 456, Halifax, B3J 2R5 NS
Fax: 902-424-0710

Ontario
Ministry of Culture, Mowat Block, 900 Bay St., 5th Fl., Toronto, M7A 1L2 ON
416-325-1660, Fax: 416-325-1726, 866-454-0049
Royal Ontario Museum, 100 Queen's Park Cres., Toronto, ON M5S 2C6
416-586-5549, Fax: 416-586-5685, info@rom.on.ca

Prince Edward Island
PEI Museum & Heritage Foundation, 2 Kent St., PO Box 2000, Charlottetown, PE C1A 1M6
902-368-6600, Fax: 902-368-6608, mhpei@gov.pe.ca

Quebec
Ministère de la Culture, des Communications & de la Condition féminine, 225, Grande Allée est, Québec, G1R 5G5 QC
Fax: 418-380-2364, 888-380-8882, infos@mcccf.gouv.qc.ca
Musée d'art contemporain de Montréal, 185, rue Ste-Catherine ouest, Montréal, H2X 3X5 QC
514-847-6226, Fax: 514-847-6290
Musée de la civilisation, 85, rue Dalhousie, CP 155 B,Québec, G1K 7A6 QC
418-643-2158, Fax: 418-646-9705, 866-710-8031, mcqweb@mcq.org
Musée national des beaux-arts du Québec, Parc des Champs-de-Bataille, 1, av Wolfe-Montcalm, Québec, G1R 5H3 QC
418-643-2150, Fax: 418-646-3330, 866-220-2150, webmestre@mnba.qc.ca

Saskatchewan
Royal Saskatchewan Museum, 2445 Albert St., Regina, SK S4P 4W7
306-787-2815, Fax: 306-787-2820, info@royalsaskmuseum.ca
Western Development Museum, 2935 Melville St., Saskatoon, SK S7J 5A6
306-934-1400, Fax: 306-934-4467, 800-363-6345, info@wdm.ca

Yukon Territory
Yukon Tourism & Culture, PO Box 2703, Whitehorse, Y1A 2C6 YT
867-667-5036, Fax: 867-667-3546

NATIVE PEOPLES & NORTHERN AFFAIRS

British Columbia
Northern Interior, 1011 - 4 Ave., 5th Fl., Prince George, V2L 3H9 BC
250-565-6100, Fax: 250-565-6671, www.for.gov.bc.ca/rni

Yukon Territory
Yukon Development Corporation, PO Box 2703 D-1,Whitehorse, Y1A 2C6 YT
867-393-5337, Fax: 867-393-5401
Yukon Land Use Planning Council, #201, 307 Jarvis St., Whitehorse, YT Y1A 2H3
867-667-7397, Fax: 867-667-4624, ylupc@planyukon.ca

NATURAL RESOURCES

Natural Resources Canada, 580 Booth St., Ottawa, K1A 0E4 ON
613-995-0947, Fax: 613-992-7211

Alberta
Natural Resources Conservation Board, Sterling Place, 9940 - 106 St., 4th Fl., Edmonton, AB T5K 2N2
780-422-1977, Fax: 780-427-0607, 866-383-6722

Alberta Sustainable Resource Development, Information Centre, 9920 - 108 St., Main Fl., Edmonton, T5K 2M4 AB
780-944-0313, Fax: 780-427-4407, 877-944-0313, srd.infocent@gov.ab.ca

British Columbia
Ministry of Energy, Mines & Petroleum Resources, PO Box 9318 Prov Govt,Victoria, V8W 9N3 BC
250-952-0241
Ministry of Environment, PO Box 9339 Prov Govt,Victoria, V8W 9M1 BC
250-387-1161, Fax: 250-387-5669, www.envmail@gov.bc.ca
Ministry of Forests & Range, PO Box 9529 Prov Govt,Victoria, V8W 9C3 BC
250-387-4809, Fax: 250-953-3687

Manitoba
Manitoba Conservation, 200 Saulteaux Cres., Winnipeg, R3J 3W3 MB
204-945-6784, 800-214-6497, mincon@leg.gov.mb.ca
Manitoba Conservation Districts Commission, Secretariat c/o Planning & Coordination Branch, 123 Main St., PO Box 20000, Neepawa, MB R0J 1H0
204-476-7033, Fax: 204-476-7539, whildebran@gov.mb.ca

New Brunswick
Department of Natural Resources, PO Box 6000, Fredericton, E3B 5H1 NB
506-453-2510, Fax: 506-444-5839, dnrweb@gnb.ca

Newfoundland & Labrador
Department of Natural Resources, Natural Resources Bldg., 50 Elizabeth Ave., 7th Fl., PO Box 8700, St. John's, A1B 4J6 NL
709-729-2920, Fax: 709-729-0059

Northwest Territories
Department of Environment & Natural Resources, PO Box 1320, Yellowknife, X1A 2L9 NT

Nova Scotia
Department of Natural Resources, Founder's Square, 1701 Hollis St., 3rd Fl., PO Box 698, Halifax, B3J 2T9 NS
902-424-5935, Fax: 902-424-0594, 800-565-2224

Nunavut
Department of Environment, PO Box 1000 1300,Iqaluit, X0A 0H0 NU
867-975-7700, Fax: 867-975-7742, 866-222-9063, environment@gov.nu.ca

Ontario
Ministry of Natural Resources, Whitney Block, #6630, 99 Wellesley St. West, 6th Fl., Toronto, M7A 1W3 ON
800-667-1940
Ministry of Northern Development & Mines, 159 Cedar St., Sudbury, P3E 6A5 ON
705-564-0032, Fax: 705-564-7357

Prince Edward Island
Department of Agriculture, Jones Bldg., 11 Kent St., PO Box 2000, Charlottetown, C1A 7N8 PE
902-368-4880, Fax: 902-368-4857
Department of Environment, Energy & Forestry, Jones Bldg., 11 Kent St., 4th & 5th Fl., PO Box 2000, Charlottetown, C1A 7N8 PE
902-368-5000, Fax: 902-368-5830

Quebec
Ministère du Développement durable, de l'Environnement et des Parcs, Édifice Marie-Guyart, 675, boul René-Lévesque est, 29e étage, Québec, G1R 5V7 QC
418-521-3830, Fax: 418-646-5974, 800-561-1616, info@mddep.gouv.qc.ca
Ministère des Ressources naturelles et de la Faune, #A303, 5700, 4e av ouest, Québec, G1H 6R1 QC
418-627-8600, Fax: 418-643-0720, 866-248-6936, service.citoyens@mrnf.gouv.qc.ca

Saskatchewan
Saskatchewan Energy & Resources, #300, 2103 - 11th Ave., Regina, S4P 3Z8 SK
306-787-2528, Fax: 306-787-8447, 866-727-5427
Saskatchewan Environment, 3211 Albert St., 2nd Fl., Regina, S4S 5W6 SK
306-953-3750, Fax: 306-787-9544, 800-567-4224, inquiry@serm.gov.sk.ca

Yukon Territory
Yukon Energy, Mines & Resources, PO Box 2703, Whitehorse, Y1A 2C6 YT
867-667-5466, Fax: 867-667-8601, 800-661-0408, emr@gov.yk.ca
Yukon Environment, PO Box 2703, Whitehorse, Y1A 2C6 YT
867-667-5652, Fax: 867-393-6213, 800-661-0408, environmentyukon@gov.yk.ca

NUCLEAR ENERGY
Atomic Energy of Canada Limited, Head Office, 2251 Speakman Dr., Mississauga, L5K 1B2 ON
905-823-9040, webmaster@aecl.ca
Canadian Nuclear Safety Commission, 280 Slater St., PO Box 1046 B,Ottawa, K1P 5S9 ON
613-995-5894, Fax: 613-995-5086, 800-668-5284, info@cnsc-ccsn.gc.ca

Alberta
Alberta Energy, North Petroleum Plaza, 9945 - 108 St., 7th Fl., Edmonton, T5K 2G6 AB
780-427-7425, Fax: 780-422-0698, 780-310-0000

Ontario
Ontario Power Generation, 700 University Ave., Toronto, M5G 1X6 ON
416-592-2555, 877-592-2555

Quebec
Hydro-Québec, 75, boul René-Lévesque ouest, 20e étage, Montréal, H2Z 1A4 QC
514-289-2211

NUTRITION
Food Value Chain Bureau, 930 Carling Ave., 5th Fl., Ottawa, K1A 0C5 ON
Fax: 613-759-7480

Manitoba
Manitoba Healthy Child Office, #219, 114 Garry St., Winnipeg, R3C 1G1 MB
204-945-2266, 888-848-0140, healthychild@gov.mb.ca
Primary Care & Healthy Living, 300 Carlton St., 2nd Floor, Winnipeg, R3B 3M9 MB

Newfoundland & Labrador
Department of Health & Community Services, West Block, Confederation Bldg., PO Box 8700, St. John's, A1B 4J6 NL
709-729-5021, Fax: 709-729-5824,

Northwest Territories
Department of Health & Social Services, Centre Square Tower, PO Box 1320, Yellowknife, X1A 2L9 NT
Fax: 867-873-0266

Nunavut
Department of Health & Social Services, Sivummut bldg., PO Box 1007 1000,Iqaluit, X0A 0H0 NU
867-975-5700, Fax: 867-975-5705, health@gov.nu.ca

Ontario
Ministry of Health & Long-Term Care, Hepburn Block, 80 Grosvenor St., 10th Fl, Toronto, M7A 2C4 ON
416-327-4327, 800-268-1153

Prince Edward Island
Department of Health, Jones Bldg., 11 Kent St., 2nd Fl., PO Box 2000, Charlottetown, C1A 7N8 PE
902-368-4900, Fax: 902-368-4974

Quebec
Ministère de la Santé et des Services sociaux, Direction des communications et Renseignements généraux, 1075, ch Sainte-Foy, Québec, G1S 2M1 QC
418-266-8900, 800-707-3380, regisseur.web@msss.gouv.qc.ca

Saskatchewan
Saskatchewan Health, T.C. Douglas Bldg., 3475 Albert St., Regina, S4S 6X6 SK
306-787-0146, 800-667-7766, info@health.gov.sk.ca

OCCUPATIONAL SAFETY
See Also: Dangerous Goods & Hazardous Materials
Canadian Centre for Occupational Health & Safety, 135 Hunter St. East, Hamilton, L8N 1M5 ON
905-572-2981, Fax: 905-572-2206, 800-668-4284, clientservices@ccohs.ca
Occupational Health & Safety Branch, 655 Bay St., 14th Fl., Toronto, M7A 1T7 ON
416-326-7770, Fax: 416-326-7242

Alberta
Labour Standards & Workplace Safety Division, Labour Bldg., 10808 - 99 Ave., 8th Fl., Edmonton, T5K 0G5 AB
780-415-9057, Fax: 780-644-2100
Occupational Health & Safety Council, Labour Bldg, 10808 - 99 Ave., 10th Fl., Edmonton, AB T5K 0G5
780-427-6452, Fax: 780-427-7548
Workers' Compensation Board of Alberta, 9925 - 107 St., PO Box 2415, Edmonton, T5J 2S5 AB
780-498-3999, Fax: 780-498-7999, 800-661-9608

British Columbia
Ministry of Labour & Citizens' Services, PO Box 9052 Prov Govt,Victoria, V8W 9E2 BC
250-356-6348, Fax: 250-356-6595, LCS.Minister@gov.bc.ca
Workers' Compensation Board of British Columbia, PO Box 5350 Terminal,Vancouver, V6B 5L5 BC
604-276-3100, Fax: 604-244-6490, 888-621-7233

Manitoba
Advisory Council on Workplace Safety & Health, #200, 401 York Ave., Winnipeg, MB R3C 0P8
204-945-3446, Fax: 204-945-4556
Workplace Safety & Health Division, #200, 401 York Ave., Winnipeg, R3C 0P8 MB
204-945-3446, Fax: 204-948-2209, wshcompl@gov.mb.ca

New Brunswick
Workplace Health, Safety & Compensation Commission of New Brunswick, 1 Portland St., PO Box 160, Saint John, E2L 3X9 NB
506-632-2200, 800-222-9775, communications@ws-ts.nb.ca

Newfoundland & Labrador
Newfoundland & Labrador Workplace Health, Safety & Compensation Commission, 146 - 148 Forest Rd., PO Box 9000, St. John's, A1A 3B8 NL
709-778-1000, Fax: 709-738-1714, 800-563-9000, general.inquiries@whscc.nl.ca

Northwest Territories
Northwest Territories & Nunavut Workers' Compensation Board, Centre Square Tower, 5022 - 49th St., 5th Fl., PO Box 8888, Yellowknife, X1A 2R3 NT
867-920-3888, Fax: 867-873-4596, 800-661-0792, wcb@wcb.nt.ca

Nova Scotia
Occupational Health & Safety Advisory Council, PO Box 697, Halifax, NS B3J 2T8
902-424-2484, Fax: 902-424-5640
Workers' Compensation Board of Nova Scotia, 5668 South St., PO Box 1150, Halifax, B3J 2Y2 NS
902-491-8999, Fax: 902-491-8002, 800-870-3331, info@wcb.gov.ns.ca

Ontario
Workplace Safety & Insurance Board, 200 Front St. West, Ground Fl., Toronto, M5V 3J1 ON
416-344-1000, Fax: 416-344-4684, 800-387-0750

Prince Edward Island
Prince Edward Island Workers Compensation Board, 14 Weymouth St., PO Box 757, Charlottetown, C1A 7L7 PE
902-368-5680, Fax: 902-368-5705, 800-237-5049

Quebec
Commission des lésions professionnelles, #700, 900, Place d'Youville, Québec, QC G1R 3P7
418-644-7777, Fax: 418-644-6443, 800-463-1591
Commission de la santé et de la sécurité au travail, 524, rue Bourdages, CP 1200 Terminus postal,Québec, G1K 7E2 QC
418-266-4850, Fax: 418-266-4389, 866-302-2778

Saskatchewan
Office of the Worker's Advocate, #400, 1870 Albert St., Regina, SK S4P 4W1
306-787-2456, Fax: 306-787-0249, 877-787-2456
Saskatchewan Workers' Compensation Board, #200, 1881 Scarth St., Regina, S4P 4L1 SK
306-787-4370, Fax: 306-787-7582, 800-667-7590, internet_clientsvc@wcbsask.com

Yukon Territory
Yukon Workers' Compensation Health & Safety Board, 401 Strickland St., Whitehorse, Y1A 5N8 YT
867-667-5645, Fax: 867-393-6279, 800-661-0443, worksafe@gov.yk.ca

OCCUPATIONAL TRAINING

Alberta
Apprenticeship & Industry Training Division, Phipps-McKinnon Bldg., 5th Fl., 10020 - 101A Ave., Edmonton, T5J 3G2 AB
780-427-8517

British Columbia
Ministry of Labour & Citizens' Services, PO Box 9052 Prov Govt,Victoria, V8W 9E2 BC
250-356-6348, Fax: 250-356-6595, LCS.Minister@gov.bc.ca

New Brunswick
Department of Post-Secondary Education, Training & Labour, 470 York St., PO Box 6000, Fredericton, E3B 5H1 NB
506-453-2597, Fax: 506-453-3618, dpetlinfo@gnb.ca

Quebec
École nationale de police du Québec, 350, rue Marguerite-d'Youville, Nicolet, QC J3T 1X4
819-293-8631, Fax: 819-293-4018, courriel@enpq.qc.ca
École nationale des pompiers du Québec, #3.08, 2800, boul Saint-Martin ouest, Laval, QC H7T 2S9
450-680-6800, Fax: 450-680-6818, 866-680-3677, enpq@enpq.gouv.qc.ca

OCEANOGRAPHY

Bayfield Institute, 867 Lakeshore Rd., PO Box 5050, Burlington, L7R 4A6 ON
905-336-6240
Bedford Institute of Oceanography, 1 Challenger Dr., PO Box 1006, Dartmouth, B2Y 4A2 NS
902-426-3492, Fax: 902-426-8484
Fisheries & Oceans Canada, 200 Kent St., Ottawa, K1A 0E6 ON
613-993-0999, Fax: 613-996-1866, info@dfo-mpo.gc.ca
Institut Maurice-Lamontagne, 850, rte de le Mer, CP 1000, Mont-Joli, G5H 3Z4 QC
418-775-0555, Fax: 418-775-0730
Institute for Marine Biosciences, 1411 Oxford St., Halifax, B3H 3Z1 NS
902-426-8332, Fax: 902-426-9413, communications.imb@nrc-cnrc.gc.ca
Institute for Ocean Technology, Kerwin Pl. & Arctic Ave., PO Box 12093, St. John's, A1B 3T5 NL
709-772-4939, Fax: 709-772-2462, noel.murphy@nrc.ca
Institute of Ocean Sciences, 9860 West Saanich Rd., PO Box 6000, Sidney, V8L 4B2 BC
250-363-6517, Fax: 250-363-6390

OIL & NATURAL GAS RESOURCES

See Also: Energy; Natural Resources
Indian Oil & Gas Canada, #100, 9911 Chula Blvd., Tsuu T'ina (Sarcee), AB T2W 6H6
Fax: 403-292-5618
National Energy Board, 444 - 7 Ave. SW, Calgary, T2P 0X8 AB
403-292-4800, Fax: 403-292-5503, 800-899-1265, info@neb-one.gc.ca

Alberta
Alberta Energy & Utilities Board, 640 - 5 Ave. SW, Calgary, AB T2P 3G4
403-297-8311, Fax: 403-297-7336
Alberta Energy, North Petroleum Plaza, 9945 - 108 St., 7th Fl., Edmonton, T5K 2G6 AB
780-427-7425, Fax: 780-422-0698, 780-310-0000

British Columbia
Ministry of Energy, Mines & Petroleum Resources, PO Box 9318 Prov Govt,Victoria, V8W 9N3 BC
250-952-0241
Oil & Gas Commission, #100, 10003 - 110 Ave., Fort St John, BC V1J 6M7
250-261-5700, 800-663-7867
British Columbia Utilities Commission, 900 Howe St., 6th Fl., PO Box 250, Vancouver, V6Z 2N3 BC
604-660-4700, Fax: 604-660-1102, 800-663-1385, commission.secretary@bcuc.com

Manitoba
Petroleum, #360, 1395 Ellice Ave., Winnipeg, R3G 3P2 MB
204-945-6577, Fax: 204-945-0586
Surface Rights Board, #360, 1395 Ellice Ave., Winnipeg, MB R3G 3P2
204-945-0731, Fax: 204-948-2578, 800-282-8069, bmiskimmin@gov.mb.ca

Newfoundland & Labrador
Canada-Newfoundland Offshore Petroleum Board, TD Place, 140 Water St., 5th Fl., St. John's, NL A1C 6H6
709-778-1400, Fax: 709-778-1473, postmaster@cnlopb.nl.ca

Nova Scotia
Canada-Nova Scotia Offshore Petroleum Board, TD Centre, 1791 Barrington St., 6th Fl., Halifax, NS B3J 3K9
902-422-5588, Fax: 902-422-1799, postmaster@cnsopb.ns.ca
Nova Scotia Utility & Review Board, 1601 Lower Water St., 3rd Fl., PO Box 1692 M,Halifax, B3J 3S3 NS
902-424-4448, Fax: 902-424-3919, uarb.board@gov.ns.ca

Nunavut
Department of Environment, PO Box 1000 1300,Iqaluit, X0A 0H0 NU
867-975-7700, Fax: 867-975-7742, 866-222-9063, environment@gov.nu.ca

Ontario
Ministry of Natural Resources, Whitney Block, #6630, 99 Wellesley St. West, 6th Fl., Toronto, M7A 1W3 ON
800-667-1940

Saskatchewan
SaskEnergy Incorporated, 1777 Victoria Ave., Regina, S4P 4K5 SK
306-777-9225, Fax: 306-777-9200, 800-567-8899

OIL SPILLS

Canadian Coast Guard, Centennial Towers, #6S018, 200 Kent St., Ottawa, K1A 0E6 ON
613-998-1573, Fax: 613-990-2780
Spills Action Centre, 5775 Yonge St., 5th Fl., Toronto, M2M 4J1 ON
416-325-3000, Fax: 416-325-3011, 800-268-6060

Newfoundland & Labrador
Canada-Newfoundland Offshore Petroleum Board, TD Place, 140 Water St., 5th Fl., St. John's, NL A1C 6H6
709-778-1400, Fax: 709-778-1473, postmaster@cnlopb.nl.ca

PARKS & RECREATION

Canadian Heritage, 15 Eddy St., Gatineau, K1A 0M5 QC
819-997-0055, 866-811-0055
Historic Sites & Monuments Board of Canada, Terrasses de la Chaudière, 25 Eddy St., Gatineau, QC K1A 0M5
819-997-4059, Fax: 819-934-1115, hsmbc-clmhc@pc.gc.ca
Parks & Protected Areas, 2975 Jutland Rd., 4th Fl., Victoria, V8T 5J9 BC
Fax: 250-387-5757
Parks & Recreation Division, RR#1, Belmont, B0M 1C0 NS
902-662-3030
Parks Branch, 3211 Albert St., 2nd Fl., Regina, S4S 5W6 SK
306-787-3105, Fax: 306-787-7000
Parks Canada, 25 Eddy St., Gatineau, K1A 0M5 QC
888-773-8888, information@pc.gc.ca
Saskatchewan Lotteries Trust for Sport, Culture & Recreation, 1870 Lorne St., Regina, S4P 2L7 SK
306-780-9300, sasksport@sasksport.sk.ca

Alberta
Alberta Special Areas Board, 212 - 2nd Ave. West, PO Box 820, Hanna, AB T0J 1P0
403-854-5600, Fax: 403-854-5527, specarea@telusplanet.net
Alberta Sport, Recreation, Parks & Wildlife Foundation, Standard Life Centre, 10405 Jasper Ave., 9th Fl., Edmonton, AB T5J 4R7
780-415-1167, Fax: 780-415-0308
Parks, Conservation, Recreation & Sport Division, Oxbridge Place, 9820 - 106 St., 2nd Fl., Edmonton, T5K 2J6 AB
780-427-3582, Fax: 780-427-5980, 866-427-3582

British Columbia
Ministry of Environment, PO Box 9339 Prov Govt,Victoria, V8W 9M1 BC
250-387-1161, Fax: 250-387-5669, www.envmail@gov.bc.ca

Manitoba
Manitoba Competitiveness, Training & Trade, International Business Centre, The Paris Building, 259 Portage Ave., Winnipeg, R3B 3P4 MB
204-945-2475, Fax: 204-945-3977, minctt@leg.gov.mb.ca
Ecological Reserves Advisory Committee, c/o Manitoba Conservation, Parks & Natural Areas Branch, 200 Saulteaux Cres., Winnipeg, MB R3J 3W3
204-945-4148, Fax: 204-945-0012, hhernandez@gov.mb.ca

New Brunswick
Department of Business New Brunswick, Centennial Bldg., 670 King St., PO Box 6000, Fredericton, E3B 5H1 NB
506-444-5228, Fax: 506-453-5428
Department of Tourism & Parks, Centennial Bldg., 670 King St., Fredericton, E3B 1G1 NB
506-444-5205, Fax: 506-457-4984, taponlinedirectory@gnb.ca

Newfoundland & Labrador
Department of Tourism, Culture & Recreation, Confederation Bldg., West Block, 2nd Fl., PO Box 8700, St. John's, A1B 4J6 NL
709-729-0862, Fax: 709-729-0870, tcrinfo@gov.nl.ca

Northwest Territories
Department of Environment & Natural Resources, PO Box 1320, Yellowknife, X1A 2L9 NT

Nova Scotia
Department of Economic & Rural Development, Centennial Building, #600, 1660 Hollis St., PO Box 2311, Halifax, B3J 1V7 NS
902-424-0377, Fax: 902-424-7008, comm@gov.ns.ca

Nunavut
Department of Environment, PO Box 1000 1300,Iqaluit, X0A 0H0 NU
867-975-7700, Fax: 867-975-7742, 866-222-9063, environment@gov.nu.ca

Ontario
Ministry of Economic Development, Hearst Block, 900 Bay St., 8th Fl., Toronto, M7A 2E1 ON
416-325-6666, Fax: 416-325-6688, 866-668-4249, info@edt.gov.on.ca

Prince Edward Island
Department of Innovation & Advanced Learning, Shaw Bldg., 105 Rochford St., 5th Fl., PO Box 2000, Charlottetown, C1A 7N8 PE
902-368-4240, Fax: 902-368-4242
Department of Tourism, PO Box 2000, Charlottetown, C1A 7N8 PE
800-463-4734

Quebec
Ministère du Développement durable, de l'Environnement et des Parcs, Édifice Marie-Guyart, 675, boul René-Lévesque est, 29e étage, Québec, G1R 5V7 QC
418-521-3830, Fax: 418-646-5974, 800-561-1616, info@mddep.gouv.qc.ca
Société des établissements en plein air du Québec, Place de la Cité, #250, 2640, boul Laurier, Sainte-Foy, QC G1V 5C2
418-890-6527, Fax: 418-528-6025, 800-665-6527, inforeservation@sepaq.com

Saskatchewan
Tourism Saskatchewan, 1922 Park St., Regina, SK S4N 7M4
306-787-9600, 877-237-2273

Yukon Territory
Yukon Tourism & Culture, PO Box 2703, Whitehorse, Y1A 2C6 YT
867-667-5036, Fax: 867-667-3546

PAROLE BOARDS

See Also: Correctional Services

New Brunswick
Department of Public Safety, 364 Argyle St., PO Box 6000, Fredericton, E3B 5H1 NB
506-453-3992, Fax: 506-453-3870, DPS-MSP.Information@gnb.ca

Ontario
Ontario Parole & Earned Release Board, 415 Yonge St., Toronto, ON M5B 2E7
416-325-4480, Fax: 416-325-4485

Quebec
Commission québecoise des libérations conditionnelles, #1.32A, 300, boul Jean-Lesage, Québec, QC G1K 8K6
418-646-8300, Fax: 418-643-7217, liberation.conditionnel@msp.gouv.

PASSPORT INFORMATION

See Also: Citizenship; Immigration
Passport Canada, Le 70 Crémazie, 70 Crémazie St., Gatineau, K1A 0G3 QC
Fax: 819-953-5856, 800-567-6868

PAY EQUITY
Human Resources & Skills Development Canada, 140 Promenade du Portage, Ottawa, K1A 0J9 ON

British Columbia
Employment Standards Tribunal, Oceanic Plaza, #650, 1066 West Hastings St., Vancouver, BC V6E 3X1
604-775-3512, Fax: 604-775-3372, registrar.est@bcest.bc.ca
Ministry of Labour & Citizens' Services, PO Box 9052 Prov Govt,Victoria, V8W 9E2 BC
250-356-6348, Fax: 250-356-6595, LCS.Minister@gov.bc.ca

Nova Scotia
Pay Equity Commission, 5151 Terminal Rd., 7th Fl., PO Box 697, Halifax, NS B3J 2T8
902-424-2385, Fax: 902-424-0575

Ontario
Pay Equity Commission, 400 University Ave., 11th Fl., Toronto, ON M7A 1T7
416-314-1896, Fax: 416-314-8741, 800-387-8813

Prince Edward Island
Labour Relations Board, PO Box 2000, Charlottetown, PE C1A 7N8
902-368-5550, Fax: 902-368-5476

Quebec
Commission de l'équité salariale, 200, ch Ste-Foy, 4e étage, Québec, QC G1R 6A1
418-528-8765, Fax: 418-528-6999, 888-528-8765, equite.salariale@ces.gouv.qc.ca

PENSIONS
Finance Canada, L'esplanade Laurier, 140 O'Connor St., Ottawa, K1A 0G5 ON
613-992-1573, Fax: 613-996-2690, finpub@fin.gc.ca
Office of the Commissioner of Review Tribunals, PO Box 8250 T, Ottawa, ON K1G 5S5
Fax: 613-941-3348, 800-363-0076, info@ocrt-bctr.gc.ca
Pension Appeals Board, PO Box 8567 T, Ottawa, ON K1G 3H9
613-995-0612, Fax: 613-995-6834, 888-640-8001, info@pab-cap.gc.ca
Public Sector Pension Investment Board, #200, 440 Laurier Ave. West, Ottawa, ON K1R 7X6
613-782-3095, Fax: 613-782-6864, info@investpsp.ca

British Columbia
British Columbia Pension Corporation, 2995 Jutland Rd., PO Box 9460, Victoria, BC V8W 9V8
250-387-1002, Fax: 250-953-0429, 800-663-8323, PensionCorp@pensionsbc.ca; Retired.Members@pensionsbc.ca

Manitoba
Pension Commission of Manitoba, #1004, 401 York Ave., Winnipeg, MB R3C 0P8
204-945-2740, Fax: 204-948-2375, pensions@gov.mb.ca

Nova Scotia
Pension Regulation Division, PO Box 2531, Halifax, B3J 3N5 NS
902-424-8915, Fax: 902-424-0662

Ontario
Ontario Pension Board, #1100, 1 Adelaide St. East, Toronto, ON M5C 2X6
416-364-8558, Fax: 416-364-7578, 800-668-6203, office.services@opb.on.ca
OPSEU Pension Trust, #1200, 1 Adelaide St. East, Toronto, ON M5C 3A7
416-681-6161, Fax: 416-681-6175

Prince Edward Island
Office of the Attorney General, Shaw Building, North, 105 Rochford St., 4th Fl., PO Box 2000, Charlottetown, C1A 7N8 PE
902-368-5152, Fax: 902-368-4910

PESTICIDES, HERBICIDES
Manitoba
Environmental Approvals Branch, #160, 123 Main St., Winnipeg, R3C 1A5 MB
204-945-8321, Fax: 204-945-5229
Environmental Assessment & Approvals Branch, 2 St. Clair Ave. West, 12th Fl., Toronto, M4V 1L5 ON
416-314-8001, Fax: 416-314-8452, 800-461-6290
Environmental Management, 2975 Jutland Rd., 3rd Fl., Victoria, V8T 5J9 BC
250-387-9971, Fax: 250-387-8897

Pest Management Regulatory Agency, 2720 Riverside Dr., Ottawa, ON K1A 0K9
613-736-3401, Fax: 613-736-3798
Standards Development Branch, 40 St. Clair Ave. West, 7th Fl., Toronto, M4V 1M2 ON
416-327-5519

Alberta
Alberta Research Council, 250 Karl Clark Rd., Edmonton, T6N 1E4 AB
780-450-5111, Fax: 780-450-5333

New Brunswick
Environmental Management, Marysville Place, 20 McGloin St., PO Box 6000, Fredericton, E3B 5H1 NB
506-444-5119, Fax: 506-457-7333

Ontario
Pesticides Advisory Committee, #1203, 2300 Yonge St., 12th Fl., Toronto, ON M4P 1E4
416-314-9230, Fax: 416-314-9237

PIPELINES
National Energy Board, 444 - 7 Ave. SW, Calgary, T2P 0X8 AB
403-292-4800, Fax: 403-292-5503, 800-899-1265, info@neb-one.gc.ca

Alberta
Alberta Energy & Utilities Board, 640 - 5 Ave. SW, Calgary, AB T2P 3G4
403-297-8311, Fax: 403-297-7336
Alberta Energy, North Petroleum Plaza, 9945 - 108 St., 7th Fl., Edmonton, T5K 2G6 AB
780-427-7425, Fax: 780-422-0698, 780-310-0000

British Columbia
British Columbia Hydro, 333 Dunsmuir St., 18th Fl., Vancouver, V6B 5R3 BC
604-224-9376, Fax: 604-623-4467, 800-224-9376

Northwest Territories
Department of Environment & Natural Resources, PO Box 1320, Yellowknife, X1A 2L9 NT

Nova Scotia
Department of Energy, Bank of Montreal Bldg., #400, 5151 George St., PO Box 2664, Halifax, B3J 3P7 NS
902-424-4575, Fax: 902-424-0528, energyinfo@gov.ns.ca
Nova Scotia Utility & Review Board, 1601 Lower Water St., 3rd Fl., PO Box 1692 M,Halifax, B3J 3S3 NS
902-424-4448, Fax: 902-424-3919, uarb.board@gov.ns.ca

Saskatchewan
SaskEnergy Incorporated, 1777 Victoria Ave., Regina, S4P 4K5 SK
306-777-9225, Fax: 306-777-9200, 800-567-8899
TransGas Limited, 1777 Victoria Ave, Regina, S4P 4K5 SK
Fax: 306-352-8892

POLICING SERVICES
British Columbia
Management Services Branch, 910 Government St., 5th Fl., PO Box 9256 Prov Govt,Victoria, V8W 9J4 BC
250-387-5258, Fax: 250-387-0081

Ontario
Ontario Provincial Police, Lincoln M. Alexander Bldg., 777 Memorial Ave., Orillia, L3V 7V3 ON
705-329-6111, 888-310-1122

Prince Edward Island
Office of the Attorney General, Shaw Building, North, 105 Rochford St., 4th Fl., PO Box 2000, Charlottetown, C1A 7N8 PE
902-368-5152, Fax: 902-368-4910

Quebec
Direction générale de la Sûreté du Québec, 1701, rue Parthenais, Montréal, QC H2K 3S7
514-598-4488, Fax: 514-598-4957, info@surete.qc.ca

POLITICS & SOCIETY
Auditor General of Canada, 240 Sparks St., Ottawa, K1A 0G6 ON
613-995-3708, Fax: 613-957-0474, communications@oag-bvg.gc.ca
Canadian International Development Agency, 200, Promenade du Portage, Gatineau, K1A 0G4 QC
819-997-5006, Fax: 819-953-6088, 800-230-6349, info@acdi-cida.gc.ca

Commission for Environmental Cooperation, Secretariat, #200, 393, rue St-Jacques ouest, Montréal, H2Y 1N9 QC
514-350-4300, Fax: 514-350-4314, info@cec.org
Finance Canada, L'esplanade Laurier, 140 O'Connor St., Ottawa, K1A 0G5 ON
613-992-1573, Fax: 613-996-2690, finpub@fin.gc.ca
Foreign Affairs & International Trade Canada, 125 Sussex Dr., Ottawa, K1A 0G2 ON
613-944-4000, Fax: 613-996-9709, 800-267-8376, enqserv@international.gc.ca
International Development Research Centre, 150 Kent St., PO Box 8500, Ottawa, K1P 0B2 ON
613-236-6163, Fax: 613-238-7230, info@idrc.ca
International Joint Commission, 234 Laurier Ave. West, 22nd Fl., Ottawa, K1P 6K6 ON
613-947-1420, Fax: 613-993-5583
National Capital Commission, #202, 40 Elgin St., Ottawa, K1P 1C7 ON
613-239-5555, Fax: 613-239-5063, 800-704-8227, info@ncc-ccn.ca
National Defence Canada, Major-General George R. Pearkes Bldg., 101 Colonel By Dr., Ottawa, K1A 0K2 ON
613-995-2534, Fax: 613-992-4739, 800-856-8488,
National Round Table on the Environment & Economy, #200, 344 Slater St., Ottawa, K1R 7Y3 ON
613-992-7189, Fax: 613-992-7385, admin@nrtee-trnee.ca
Public Safety Canada, 269 Laurier Ave. West, Ottawa, K1A 0P8 ON
613-991-3301, Fax: 613-954-5186, 866-222-3006, communications@ps.gc.ca
Public Works & Government Services Canada, Place du Portage, Phase III, 11, rue Laurier, Ottawa, K1A 0S5 ON
819-997-6363, Fax: 819-956-9062, 800-622-6232
Purchasing Branch, 1920 Rose St., Regina, S4P 0A9 SK
306-787-6871, Fax: 306-787-3023

Alberta
Alberta International & Intergovernmental Relations, Commerce Place, 10155 - 102 St., 12th Fl., Edmonton, T5J 4G8 AB
780-422-1510, Fax: 780-427-0699
Alberta Public Affairs Bureau, Park Plaza, 10611 - 98 Ave., 6th Fl., Edmonton, T5K 2P7 AB
403-427-2754, Fax: 403-422-4168

British Columbia
Ministry of Community Development, 800 Johnson St., 6th Fl., PO Box 9490 Prov Govt,Victoria, V8W 9N7 BC
250-387-2283, Fax: 250-387-4312, Feedback@gov.bc.ca

Manitoba
Manitoba Round Table for Sustainable Development, #160, 123 Main St., Winnipeg, R3C 1A5 MB
204-945-1671, Fax: 204-948-2357, mrtsd@gov.mb.ca

New Brunswick
New Brunswick Round Table on Environment & Economy, 20 McGloin St., PO Box 6000, Fredericton, NB E3B 5H1
506-453-3703, Fax: 506-453-3876
Department of Supply & Services, PO Box 6000, Fredericton, E3B 5H1 NB
506-453-3742, Fax: 506-444-4400, Reception.Marysville@gnb.ca

Newfoundland & Labrador
Department of Government Services, PO Box 8700, St. John's, A1B 4J6 NL
709-729-4860
Department of Transportation & Works, Confederation Bldg., West Block, 6th Fl., PO Box 8700, St. John's, A1B 4J6 NL
709-729-3679, Fax: 709-729-4285, twminister@gov.nl.ca

Northwest Territories
Department of Aboriginal Affairs & Intergovernmental Relations, 4910 - 52nd St., PO Box 1320, Yellowknife, X1A 2L9 NT
867-873-7143, Fax: 867-873-0233, 877-838-8194, nancy_gardiner@gov.nt.ca
Department of Public Works & Services, PO Box 1320, Yellowknife, X1A 2L9 NT
867-873-7114, Fax: 867-873-0226

Nova Scotia
Nova Scotia Emergency Management Office, PO Box 2581, Halifax, B3J 3N5 NS
902-424-5620, Fax: 902-424-5376, 866-424-5620, emo@gov.ns.ca

Ontario
Environmental Commissioner of Ontario, #605, 1075 Bay St., Toronto, M5S 2B1 ON

416-325-3377, Fax: 416-325-3370, 800-701-6454, commissioner@eco.on.ca
Environmental Review Tribunal, #1700, 2300 Yonge St., PO Box 2382, Toronto, ON M4P 1E4
416-314-4600, Fax: 416-314-4506

Prince Edward Island
Prince Edward Island Emergency Measures Organization, National Bank Tower, #600, 134 Kent St., PO Box 2000, Charlottetown, C1A 7N8 PE
902-894-0385, Fax: 902-368-6362
Department of Health, Jones Bldg., 11 Kent St., 2nd Fl., PO Box 2000, Charlottetown, C1A 7N8 PE
902-368-4900, Fax: 902-368-4974
Department of the Provincial Treasury, Shaw Bldg., 95 Rochford St., 2nd Fl. South, PO Box 2000, Charlottetown, C1A 7N8 PE
902-368-4050, Fax: 902-368-6575

Saskatchewan
Saskatchewan First Nations & Métis Relations, #210, 1855 Victoria Ave., Regina, S4P 3T2 SK
306-787-6250, Fax: 306-787-5832
Saskatchewan Government Relations, 1855 Victoria Ave., Regina, S4P 3T2 SK
306-787-2635

Yukon Territory
Emergency Measures Organization, PO Box 2703, Whitehorse, Y1A 2C6 YT
867-667-5220, Fax: 867-393-6266, 800-661-0408, emo.yukon@gov.yk.ca

POPULATION
See Also: Statistics
Statistics Canada, R.H. Coats Bldg., Tunney's Pasture, 100 Tunney's Pasture Driveway, Ottawa, K1A 0T6 ON
Fax: 877-287-4369, 800-263-1136, infostats@statcan.ca

Manitoba
Manitoba Bureau of Statistics, #824, 155 Carlton St., Winnipeg, R3C 3H9 MB
204-945-2406, Fax: 204-945-0695

Nunavut
Department of Executive & Intergovernmental Affairs, 1084 Aeroplex bldg., PO Box 1000 200,Iqaluit, X0A 0H0 NU
867-975-6000, Fax: 867-975-6090

PROPERTY ASSESSMENT
British Columbia
British Columbia Assessment Authority, 1537 Hillside Ave., Victoria, BC V8T 4Y2
250-595-6211, Fax: 250-595-6222, info@bcassessment.ca

New Brunswick
Assessment & Planning Appeal Board, #201, 435 King St., PO Box 6000, Fredericton, NB E3B 5H1
506-453-2126, Fax: 506-444-4881

Newfoundland & Labrador
Department of Municipal Affairs, West Block, Main Fl., Confederation Bldg., PO Box 8700, St. John's, A1B 4J6 NL
709-729-3053

Northwest Territories
Assessment Appeal Tribunal of the Northwest Territories, #500, 5201 - 50th Ave., PO Box 1320, Yellowknife, NT X1A 2L9
867-873-7125, Fax: 867-873-0609

Prince Edward Island
Island Regulatory & Appeals Commission, National Bank Tower, #501, 134 Kent St., PO Box 577, Charlottetown, C1A 7L1 PE
902-892-3501, Fax: 902-566-4076, 800-501-6268, irac@irac.pe.ca

Saskatchewan
Saskatchewan Assessment Management Agency, #200, 2201 - 11 Ave., Regina, S4P 0J8 SK
306-924-8000, Fax: 306-924-8070, 800-667-7262, info.request@sama.sk.ca

PUBLIC SAFETY
See Also: Occupational Safety
Canadian Coast Guard, Centennial Towers, #6S018, 200 Kent St., Ottawa, K1A 0E6 ON
613-998-1573, Fax: 613-990-2780
Canadian Transportation Agency, Les Terrasses de la Chaudière, 15, rue Eddy, Gatineau, K1A 0N9 QC
819-997-0344, Fax: 819-997-6727, 888-222-2592, info@otc-cta.gc.ca
Communications Security Establishment, PO Box 9703 Terminal, Ottawa, ON K1G 3Z4
613-991-7600
National Defence Canada, Major-General George R. Pearkes Bldg., 101 Colonel By Dr., Ottawa, K1A 0K2 ON
613-995-2534, Fax: 613-992-4739, 800-856-8488
Office of the Communications Security Establishment Commissioner, PO Box 1984 B, Ottawa, ON K1P 5R5
613-992-3044
Public Safety Canada, 269 Laurier Ave. West, Ottawa, K1A 0P8 ON
613-991-3301, Fax: 613-954-5186, 866-222-3006, communications@ps.gc.ca

British Columbia
Ministry of Public Safety & Solicitor General, PO Box 9282 Prov Govt,Victoria, V8W 9J7 BC
250-387-6121, 800-663-7867, pssgwebfeedback@gov.bc.ca

New Brunswick
Department of Public Safety, 364 Argyle St., PO Box 6000, Fredericton, E3B 5H1 NB
506-453-3992, Fax: 506-453-3870, DPS-MSP.Information@gnb.ca

Prince Edward Island
Prince Edward Island Emergency Measures Organization, National Bank Tower, #600, 134 Kent St., PO Box 2000, Charlottetown, C1A 7N8 PE
902-894-0385, Fax: 902-368-6362

Quebec
Ministère de la Sécurité publique, Tour des Laurentides, 2525, boul Laurier, 5e étage, Québec, G1V 2L2 QC
Fax: 418-643-0275, 866-644-6826

Saskatchewan
Saskatchewan Corrections, Public Safety & Policing, 1874 Scarth St., Regina, S4P 4B3 SK
306-787-7872, Fax: 306-787-8747

PUBLIC SERVICES
Canadian Centre for Occupational Health & Safety, 135 Hunter St. East, Hamilton, L8N 1M5 ON
905-572-2981, Fax: 905-572-2206, 800-668-4284, clientservices@ccohs.ca
Canadian Coast Guard, Centennial Towers, #6S018, 200 Kent St., Ottawa, K1A 0E6 ON
613-998-1573, Fax: 613-990-2780
Commission for Public Complaints Against the Royal Canadian Mounted Police, PO Box 3423 D, Ottawa, ON K1P 6L4
613-952-1471, Fax: 613-952-8045, 800-267-6637, org@cpc-cpp.gc.ca
Human Resources & Skills Development Canada, 140 Promenade du Portage, Ottawa, K1A 0J9 ON
Military Police Complaints Commission, 270 Albert St., 10th Fl., Ottawa, ON K1P 5G8
613-947-5625, Fax: 613-947-5713, 800-632-0566, commission@mpcc-cppm.gc.ca
National Capital Commission, #202, 40 Elgin St., Ottawa, K1P 1C7 ON
613-239-5555, Fax: 613-239-5063, 800-704-8227, info@ncc-ccn.ca
National Defence Canada, Major-General George R. Pearkes Bldg., 101 Colonel By Dr., Ottawa, K1A 0K2 ON
613-995-2534, Fax: 613-992-4739, 800-856-8488
National Search & Rescue Secretariat, 275 Slater St., 4th Fl., Ottawa, K1A 0K2 ON
613-992-0054, Fax: 613-996-3746, 800-727-9414, inquiry@nss.gc.ca
Prairie Farm Rehabilitation Administration, CIBC Tower, #408, 1800 Hamilton St., Regina, S4P 4L2 SK
306-780-5070, Fax: 306-780-5018
Public Works & Government Services Canada, Place du Portage, Phase III, 11, rue Laurier, Ottawa, K1A 0S5 ON
819-997-6363, Fax: 819-956-9062, 800-622-6232
Royal Canadian Mounted Police External Review Committee, PO Box 1159 B, Ottawa, ON K1P 5R2
613-998-2134, Fax: 613-990-8969, org@erc-cee.gc.ca

Alberta
Alberta Alcohol & Drug Abuse Commission, Associated Engineering Plaza, 10909 Jasper Ave., 6th Fl., Edmonton, AB T5J 3M9
780-415-0370, Fax: 780-423-1419
Alberta Energy & Utilities Board, 640 - 5 Ave. SW, Calgary, AB T2P 3G4
403-297-8311, Fax: 403-297-7336
Alberta Municipal Government Board, Commerce Place, 10155 - 102 St., 15th Fl., Edmonton, AB T5J 4L4
780-427-4864, Fax: 780-427-0986, mbgmail@gov.ab.ca
Alberta Infrastructure & Transportation, Twin Atria Bldg., 4999 - 98 Ave., Edmonton, T6B 2X3 AB
780-427-2731, Fax: 780-466-3166,-310-0000
Labour Relations Board, #503, 10808 - 99 Ave., Edmonton, AB T5K 0G5
780-427-5926, Fax: 780-422-0970, 800-463-2572, alrbinfo@lab.gov.ab.ca
Alberta Municipal Affairs & Housing, Communications Branch, Commerce Place, 10155 - 102 St., 18th Fl., Edmonton, T5J 4L4 AB
780-427-2732, Fax: 780-422-1419, comments@gov.ab.ca
Northern Alberta Development Council, Provincial Bldg., #206, 9621 - 96 Ave., PO Box 900-14, Peace River, T8S 1T4 AB
780-624-6274, Fax: 780-624-6184, nadc.council@gov.ab.ca
Alberta Tourism, Parks, Recreation & Culture, Communications Branch, Standard Life Centre, 10405 Jasper Ave., 7th Fl., Edmonton, T5J 4R7 AB
780-427-6530, Fax: 780-427-1496, Comdev.Communications@gov.ab.ca

British Columbia
British Columbia Assessment Authority, 1537 Hillside Ave., Victoria, BC V8T 4Y2
250-595-6211, Fax: 250-595-6222, info@bcassessment.ca
British Columbia Transit, 520 Gorge Rd. East, PO Box 610, Victoria, BC V8W 2P3
250-385-2551, Fax: 250-995-5639
Client Services, 525 Superior St., 2nd Fl., PO Box 9472 Prov Govt,Victoria, V8W 9W6 BC
250-952-6861, Fax: 250-952-6803
Local Government Department, 800 Johnson St., 6th Fl., PO Box 9490 Prov Govt,Victoria, V8W 9N7 BC
lgd_feedback@gov.bc.ca
Management Services Branch, 910 Government St., 5th Fl., PO Box 9256 Prov Govt,Victoria, V8W 9J4 BC
250-387-5258, Fax: 250-387-0081
British Columbia Provincial Emergency Program, PO Box 9201 Prov Govt,Victoria, V8W 9J1 BC
250-952-4913, Fax: 250-952-4888, 888-257-4777

Manitoba
Advisory Council on Workplace Safety & Health, #200, 401 York Ave., Winnipeg, MB R3C 0P8
204-945-3446, Fax: 204-945-4556
Manitoba Culture, Heritage, Tourism & Sport, Legislative Building, #118, 450 Broadway Ave., Winnipeg, R3C 0V8 MB
204-945-3729, Fax: 204-945-5223, mincht@leg.gov.mb.ca
Emergency Measures Organization, 405 Broadway Ave., 15th Floor, Winnipeg, R3C 3L6 MB
204-945-4772, Fax: 204-945-4929, 888-267-8298, emo@gov.mb.ca
Manitoba Health & Healthy Living, #100, 300 Carlton St., Winnipeg, R3B 3M9 MB
204-786-7191, minhlt@leg.gov.mb.ca
Manitoba Hydro, PO Box 815 Main,Winnipeg, R3C 2P4 MB
204-474-3311, Fax: 204-475-0069, publicaffairs@hydro.mb.ca
Manitoba Infrastructure & Transportation, Legislative Building, #203, 450 Broadway Ave., Winnipeg, R3C 0V8 MB
204-945-3723, Fax: 204-945-7610
Manitoba Labour & Immigration, Legislative Building, 317, 450 Broadway Ave., Winnipeg, R3C 0V8 MB
204-945-4079, Fax: 204-945-8312, minlab@leg.gov.mb.ca
Local Government Development Division, 59 Elizabeth Dr., PO Box 33, Thompson, R8N 1X4 MB
204-677-6794, Fax: 204-677-6525
Manitoba Bureau of Statistics, #824, 155 Carlton St., Winnipeg, R3C 3H9 MB
204-945-2406, Fax: 204-945-0695
Manitoba Film Classification Board, #216, 301 Weston St., Winnipeg, MB R3E 3H4
204-945-8962, Fax: 204-945-0890, 866-612-2399, mfcb@gov.mb.ca
Manitoba Labour Board, A.A. Heaps Bldg., #402, 258 Portage Ave., Winnipeg, MB R3C 0B6
204-945-3783, Fax: 204-945-1296, mlb@gov.mb.ca
Manitoba Land Value Appraisal Commission, 800 Portage Ave., Winnipeg, MB R3G 0N4
204-945-2941, Fax: 204-948-2235

Government Quick Reference Guide / Public Services

Manitoba Minimum Wage Board, 614 - 401 York Ave., Winnipeg, MB R3C 0P8
 204-945-4889, Fax: 204-948-2085, mw@gov.mb.ca
Office of the Fire Commissioner, #508, 401 York Ave., Winnipeg, MB R3C 0P8
 204-945-3322, Fax: 204-948-2089, 800-282-8069, firecomm@gov.mb.ca
Primary Care & Healthy Living, 300 Carlton St., 2nd Floor, Winnipeg, R3B 3M9 MB
Provincial-Municipal Support Services, #508, 800 Portage Ave., Winnipeg, R3G 0N4 MB
Manitoba Workers' Compensation Board, 333 Broadway Ave., Winnipeg, R3C 4W3 MB
 204-954-4321, Fax: 204-954-4999, 800-362-3340, wcb@wcb.mb.ca
Workplace Safety & Health Division, #200, 401 York Ave., Winnipeg, R3C 0P8 MB
 204-945-3446, Fax: 204-948-2209, wshcompl@gov.mb.ca

New Brunswick
Department of Health, PO Box 5100, Fredericton, E3B 5G8 NB
 506-457-4800, Fax: 506-453-5243, dh-ms@dh-ms.ca
Legislative Services, Centennial Bldg., #418, 670 King St., PO Box 6000, Fredericton, E3B 5H1 NB
 506-453-2855, Fax: 506-457-7342
Department of Post-Secondary Education, Training & Labour, 470 York St., PO Box 6000, Fredericton, E3B 5H1 NB
 506-453-2597, Fax: 506-453-3618, dpetlinfo@gnb.ca
New Brunswick Power Group of Companies, 515 King St., PO Box 2000, Fredericton, E3B 4X1 NB
 506-458-4444, Fax: 506-458-4000, questions@nbpower.com

Newfoundland & Labrador
Newfoundland & Labrador Emergency Measures Organization, PO Box 8700, St. John's, A1B 4J6 NL
 709-729-3703, Fax: 709-729-3857
Department of Government Services, PO Box 8700, St. John's, A1B 4J6 NL
 709-729-4860
Department of Municipal Affairs, West Block, Main Fl., Confederation Bldg., PO Box 8700, St. John's, A1B 4J6 NL
 709-729-3053
Office of the Fire Commissioner, 2 Wellon Dr., Deer Lake, NL A8A 2G5
 709-635-4153, Fax: 709-635-4163
Department of Transportation & Works, Confederation Bldg., West Block, 6th Fl., PO Box 8700, St. John's, A1B 4J6 NL
 709-729-3679, Fax: 709-729-4285, twminister@gov.nl.ca

Northwest Territories
Department of Health & Social Services, Centre Square Tower, PO Box 1320, Yellowknife, X1A 2L9 NT
 Fax: 867-873-0266
Department of Municipal & Community Affairs, PO Box 1320, Yellowknife, X1A 2L9 NT
 867-873-7118, Fax: 867-873-0309
Northwest Territories Power Corporation, 4 Capital Dr., Hay River, X0E 1G2 NT
 867-874-5200, Fax: 867-874-5229, info@ntpc.com
Department of Public Works & Services, PO Box 1320, Yellowknife, X1A 2L9 NT
 867-873-7114, Fax: 867-873-0226
Northwest Territories Water Board, 5114 - 49th St., PO Box 1326, Yellowknife, X1A 1N9 NT
 867-765-0106, Fax: 867-765-0114, info@nwtwb.com

Nova Scotia
Alcohol & Gaming Division, Alderney Gate, 40 Alderney Dr., 5th Fl., PO Box 545, Dartmouth, B2Y 3Y8 NS
 902-424-6160, Fax: 902-424-6313, 877-565-0556
Nova Scotia Emergency Management Office, PO Box 2581, Halifax, B3J 3N5 NS
 902-424-5620, Fax: 902-424-5376, 866-424-5620, emo@gov.ns.ca
Department of Health, Joseph Howe Bldg., 1690 Hollis St., 4th Fl., PO Box 488, Halifax, B3J 2R8 NS
 902-424-5818, Fax: 902-424-0730, 800-387-6665, DoHweb@gov.ns.ca
Department of Transportation & Infrastructure Renewal, Johnston Bldg., 1672 Granville St., 2nd Fl., PO Box 186, Halifax, B3J 2N2 NS
 902-424-2297, Fax: 902-424-0171, 888-432-3233, tpwpaff@gov.ns.ca
Workers' Advisers Program, #502, 5670 Spring Garden Rd., PO Box 1063, Halifax, NS B3J 2X1
 902-424-5050, Fax: 902-424-0530, 800-774-4712

Nunavut
Department of Community & Government Services, J.G. Brown Bldg., PO Box 1000 700, Iqaluit, X0A 0H0 NU
 867-975-5400, Fax: 867-975-5305
Nunavut Emergency Management, PO Box 1000 700, Iqaluit, X0A 0H0 NU
 867-975-5403, Fax: 867-979-4221, 800-693-1666
Department of Health & Social Services, Sivummut bldg., PO Box 1007 1000, Iqaluit, X0A 0H0 NU
 867-975-5700, Fax: 867-975-5705, health@gov.nu.ca

Ontario
Advertising Review Board, Macdonald Block, #M2-56, 900 Bay St., 2nd Fl., Toronto, ON M7A 1N3
 416-327-2183, Fax: 416-327-2179
Ministry of Community Safety & Correctional Services, George Drew Bldg., 25 Grosvenor St., 18th Fl., Toronto, M7A 1Y6 ON
 416-326-5000, Fax: 416-325-6067, 866-517-0571, jus.g.sgcs.webmaster@jus.gov.on.ca
Fire Safety Commission, Place Nouveau Bldg., 5775 Yonge St., 7th Fl., Toronto, ON M2M 4J1
 416-325-3100, Fax: 416-314-1217
Hydro One Inc., North Tower, 483 Bay St., Toronto, M5G 2P5 ON
 416-345-5000, 877-955-1155, webmaster@HydroOne.com
Independent Electricity System Operator, PO Box 4474 A, Toronto, M5W 4E5 ON
 905-403-6900, Fax: 905-403-6921, 888-448-7777, customer.relations@ieso.ca
Ministry of Municipal Affairs & Housing, 777 Bay St., 17th Fl., Toronto, M5G 2E5 ON
 416-585-7041, Fax: 416-585-6227, 866-220-2290, mininfo.mah@ontario.ca
Office of the Employer Advisor, #704, 151 Bloor St. West., Toronto, ON M5S 1S4
 416-327-0020, Fax: 416-327-0726, 800-387-0774
Office of the Worker Advisor, #1300, 123 Edward St., Toronto, ON M5G 1E2
 416-325-8570, Fax: 416-325-4830, 800-435-8980
Ontario Housing Corporation, 777 Bay St., 2nd Fl., Toronto, ON M5G 2E5
Ontario Pension Board, #1100, 1 Adelaide St. East, Toronto, ON M5C 2X6
 416-364-8558, Fax: 416-364-7578, 800-668-6203, office.services@opb.on.ca
Ontario Rental Housing Tribunal, 777 Bay St., 12th Fl., Toronto, ON M5G 2E5
 416-585-7295, Fax: 416-585-6363, 888-332-3234
Ontario Power Generation, 700 University Ave., Toronto, M5G 1X6 ON
 416-592-2555, 877-592-2555
Public Safety Division, George Drew bldg, 25 Grosvenor St., 12th fl., Toronto, M7A 2H3 ON
 416-314-3000, Fax: 416-314-4037
Southern Ontario Library Service, #902, 111 Peter St., Toronto, ON M5V 2H1
 416-961-1669, Fax: 416-961-5122, 800-387-5765
Ministry of Transportation, Ferguson Block, 77 Wellesley St. West, 3rd Fl., Toronto, M7A 1Z8 ON
 416-235-4686, Fax: 416-327-9185, 800-268-4686

Prince Edward Island
Office of the Attorney General, Shaw Building, North, 105 Rochford St., 4th Fl., PO Box 2000, Charlottetown, C1A 7N8 PE
 902-368-5152, Fax: 902-368-4910
Department of Communities, Cultural Affairs & Labour, Shaw Bldg., 95 Rochford St., 4th Fl., PO Box 2000, Charlottetown, C1A 7N8 PE
 902-368-5250, Fax: 902-368-4121
Community & Labour Development, Shaw Bldg., 105 Rochford St., 5th Fl., PO Box 2000, Charlottetown, C1A 7N8 PE
 902-368-4244, Fax: 902-368-4242
Prince Edward Island Emergency Measures Organization, National Bank Tower, #600, 134 Kent St., PO Box 2000, Charlottetown, C1A 7N8 PE
 902-894-0385, Fax: 902-368-6362
Department of Health, Jones Bldg., 11 Kent St., 2nd Fl., PO Box 2000, Charlottetown, C1A 7N8 PE
 902-368-4900, Fax: 902-368-4974
Island Waste Management Corporation, 110 Watts Ave., Charlottetown, PE C1E 2C1
 902-894-0330, Fax: 902-894-0331, 888-280-8111, reception@iwmc.pe.ca; info@iwmc.pe.ca

Quebec
Ministère des Affaires municipales et des Régions, Aile Chaveau, 10, rue Pierre-Olivier-Chauveau, 3e étage, Québec, G1R 4J3 QC
 418-691-2019, Fax: 418-643-7385, communications@mamr.gouv.qc.ca
Centre québécois de lutte aux dépendances, 105, rue Normand, Montréal, QC H2Y 2K6
 514-389-6336, Fax: 514-389-1830, info@cqld.ca
Commissariat des incendies, 455, rue Dupont, Québec, QC G1K 6N2
 418-529-5706, Fax: 418-529-9922
Commission municipale du Québec, Mezzanine, aile Chauveau, 10, rue Pierre-Olivier-Chauveau, Tour 5e étage, Québec, QC G1R 4J3
 418-691-2014, Fax: 418-644-4676, cmq@mamr.gouv.qc.ca
Conseil des services essentiels du Québec, 800, tour de la place-Victoria, 25e étage, CP 365, Montréal, QC H4Z 1H9
 514-873-7246, Fax: 514-873-3839, 800-337-7246, info@cses.gouv.qc.ca
Hydro-Québec, 75, boul René-Lévesque ouest, 20e étage, Montréal, H2Z 1A4 QC
 514-289-2211
Office des personnes handicapées du Québec, 309, rue Brock, Drummondville, QC J2B 1C5
 819-475-8585, Fax: 819-475-8753, 800-567-1477, communications@ophq.gouv.qc.ca
Palais des congrès de Montréal, 159, rue Saint-Antoine ouest, 9é étage, Montréal, QC H2Z 1H2
 514-871-8122, Fax: 514-871-3188, 800-268-8122, pcmcomm@congresmtl.com
Protecteur des usagers en matière de santé et de services sociaux, #6.400, 500, boul René-Lévesque ouest, Montréal, QC H2Z 1W7
 514-873-3205, Fax: 514-873-5665, 877-658-2625, protecteur@msss.gouv.qc.ca
Régie de l'assurance maladie du Québec, 1125, ch Saint-Louis, Québec, QC G1S 1E7
 418-646-4636,
Régie du logement du Québec, Pyramide Ouest, #2360, 5199, rue Sherbrooke est, Montréal, QC H1T 3X1
 514-873-6575, Fax: 514-873-6805, 800-683-2245
Ministère de la Santé et des Services sociaux, Direction des communications et Renseignements généraux, 1075, ch Sainte-Foy, Québec, G1S 2M1 QC
 418-266-8900, 800-707-3380, regisseur.web@msss.gouv.qc.ca
Société d'habitation du Québec, Aile St-Amable, 1054, rue Louis-Alexandre-Taschereau, 3e étage, Québec, QC G1R 5E7
 Fax: 418-643-5560, 800-463-4315
Société de l'assurance automobile du Québec, 333, boul Jean-Lesage, CP 19600 Terminus, Québec, QC G1K 8J6
 418-643-7620, Fax: 418-644-0339, 800-361-7620, courrier@saaq.gouv.qc.ca
Société immobilière du Québec, 1075, rue de l'Amérique-Française, Québec, QC G1R 5P8
 418-646-1766, Fax: 418-646-6911, 877-747-9911, courrier@siq.gouv.qc.ca
Ministère de la Sécurité publique, Tour des Laurentides, 2525, boul Laurier, 5e étage, Québec, G1V 2L2 QC
 Fax: 418-643-0275, 866-644-6826
École nationale des pompiers du Québec, #3.08, 2800, boul Saint-Martin ouest, Laval, QC H7T 2S9
 450-680-6800, Fax: 450-680-6818, 866-680-3677, enpq@enpq.gouv.qc.ca

Saskatchewan
Saskatchewan Assessment Management Agency, #200, 2201 - 11 Ave., Regina, S4P 0J8 SK
 306-924-8000, Fax: 306-924-8070, 800-667-7262, info.request@sama.sk.ca
Saskatchewan Power Corporation (SaskPower), 2025 Victoria Ave., Regina, S4P 0S1 SK
 306-566-2121, Fax: 306-566-2330, 800-667-4749
Saskatchewan Water Corporation (SaskWater), #200, 111 Fairford St. East, Moose Jaw, S6H 1C8 SK
 306-694-3098, Fax: 306-694-3207, 888-230-1111, comm@saskwater.com
SaskEnergy Incorporated, 1777 Victoria Ave., Regina, S4P 4K5 SK
 306-777-9225, Fax: 306-777-9200, 800-567-8899

Yukon Territory
Yukon Community Services, PO Box 2703, Whitehorse, Y1A 2C6 YT

867-667-5811, Fax: 867-393-6295, 800-661-0408, inquiry@gov.yk.ca
Emergency Measures Organization, PO Box 2703, Whitehorse, Y1A 2C6 YT
867-667-5220, Fax: 867-393-6266, 800-661-0408, emo.yukon@gov.yk.ca
Yukon Health & Social Services, PO Box 2703, Whitehorse, Y1A 2C6 YT
867-667-3673, Fax: 867-667-3096, 800-661-0408, hss@gov.yk.ca

PUBLIC UTILITIES

Yukon Territory
Yukon Energy Corporation, 2 Miles Canyon Rd., PO Box 5920, Whitehorse, Y1A 6S7 YT
867-393-5300, 866-926-3749, communications@yukonenergy.ca

Alberta
Alberta Energy & Utilities Board, 640 - 5 Ave. SW, Calgary, AB T2P 3G4
403-297-8311, Fax: 403-297-7336
Alberta Utilities Consumer Advocate, TD Tower, 10088 - 102 Ave., Edmonton, T5J 2Z1 AB
780-644-5130, Fax: 780-644-5129, 866-714-4455, UtilitiesConsumerAdvocate@gov.ab.

British Columbia
British Columbia Hydro, 333 Dunsmuir St., 18th Fl., Vancouver, V6B 5R3 BC
604-224-9376, Fax: 604-623-4467, 800-224-9376
British Columbia Transmission Corporation, Four Bentall Centre, #1100, 1055 Dunsmuir St., PO Box 49260, Vancouver, V7X 1V5 BC
604-699-7300, Fax: 604-699-7333, 866-647-3334, contact.us@bctc.com
British Columbia Utilities Commission, 900 Howe St., 6th Fl., PO Box 250, Vancouver, V6Z 2N3 BC
604-660-4700, Fax: 604-660-1102, 800-663-1385, commission.secretary@bcuc.com

Manitoba
Manitoba Hydro, PO Box 815 Main,Winnipeg, R3C 2P4 MB
204-474-3311, Fax: 204-475-0069, publicaffairs@hydro.mb.ca

New Brunswick
NB Board of Commissioners of Public Utilities, #1400, 15 Market Sq., PO Box 5001, Saint John, NB E2L 4Y9
506-658-2504, Fax: 506-643-7300, 866-766-2782, general@pub.nb.ca
New Brunswick Power Group of Companies, 515 King St., PO Box 2000, Fredericton, E3B 4X1 NB
506-458-4444, Fax: 506-458-4000, questions@nbpower.com

Newfoundland & Labrador
Churchill Falls (Labrador) Corporation Limited, Hydro Place, 500 Columbus Dr., PO Box 12500, St. John's, A1B 4K7 NL
709-737-1859, Fax: 709-737-1816
Newfoundland & Labrador Hydro, Hydro Place, Columbus Dr., PO Box 12400, St. John's, A1B 4K7 NL
709-737-1400, Fax: 709-737-1800
Newfoundland & Labrador Board of Commissioners of Public Utilities, PO Box 21040, St. John's, A1A 5B2 NL
709-726-8600, Fax: 709-726-9604, 866-782-0006, ito@pub.nf.ca

Northwest Territories
Northwest Territories Power Corporation, 4 Capital Dr., Hay River, X0E 1G2 NT
867-874-5200, Fax: 867-874-5229, info@ntpc.com
Northwest Territories Water Board, 5114 - 49th St., PO Box 1326, Yellowknife, X1A 1N9 NT
867-765-0106, Fax: 867-765-0114, info@nwtwb.com

Nova Scotia
Nova Scotia Utility & Review Board, 1601 Lower Water St., 3rd Fl., PO Box 1692 M,Halifax, B3J 3S3 NS
902-424-4448, Fax: 902-424-3919, uarb.board@gov.ns.ca

Ontario
Hydro One Inc., North Tower, 483 Bay St., Toronto, M5G 2P5 ON
416-345-5000, 877-955-1155, webmaster@HydroOne.com
Independent Electricity System Operator, PO Box 4474 A,Toronto, M5W 4E5 ON
905-403-6900, Fax: 905-403-6921, 888-448-7777, customer.relations@ieso.ca

Ontario Power Generation, 700 University Ave., Toronto, M5G 1X6 ON
416-592-2555, 877-592-2555

Prince Edward Island
Island Regulatory & Appeals Commission, National Bank Tower, #501, 134 Kent St., PO Box 577, Charlottetown, C1A 7L1 PE
902-892-3501, Fax: 902-566-4076, 800-501-6268, irac@irac.pe.ca

Quebec
Hydro-Québec, 75, boul René-Lévesque ouest, 20e étage, Montréal, H2Z 1A4 QC
514-289-2211
Régie de l'énergie, Tour de la Bourse, #255, 800, Place Victoria, CP 1, Montréal, QC H4Z 1A2
514-873-2452, Fax: 514-873-2070, 888-873-2452, secretariat@regie-energie.qc.ca

Saskatchewan
Saskatchewan Power Corporation (SaskPower), 2025 Victoria Ave., Regina, S4P 0S1 SK
306-566-2121, Fax: 306-566-2330, 800-667-4749
Saskatchewan Water Corporation (SaskWater), #200, 111 Fairford St. East, Moose Jaw, S6H 1C8 SK
306-694-3098, Fax: 306-694-3207, 888-230-1111, comm@saskwater.com
SaskEnergy Incorporated, 1777 Victoria Ave., Regina, S4P 4K5 SK
306-777-9225, Fax: 306-777-9200, 800-567-8899

PUBLIC WORKS
Public Works & Government Services Canada, Place du Portage, Phase III, 11, rue Laurier, Ottawa, K1A 0S5 ON
819-997-6363, Fax: 819-956-9062, 800-622-6232

Alberta
Alberta Infrastructure & Transportation, Twin Atria Bldg., 4999 - 98 Ave., Edmonton, T6B 2X3 AB
780-427-2731, Fax: 780-466-3166,-310-0000,

British Columbia
Ministry of Labour & Citizens' Services, PO Box 9052 Prov Govt,Victoria, V8W 9E2 BC
250-356-6348, Fax: 250-356-6595, LCS.Minister@gov.bc.ca

Manitoba
Manitoba Infrastructure & Transportation, Legislative Building, #203, 450 Broadway Ave., Winnipeg, R3C 0V8 MB
204-945-3723, Fax: 204-945-7610

Newfoundland & Labrador
Department of Transportation & Works, Confederation Bldg., West Block, 6th Fl., PO Box 8700, St. John's, A1B 4J6 NL
709-729-3679, Fax: 709-729-4285, twminister@gov.nl.ca

Northwest Territories
Department of Public Works & Services, PO Box 1320, Yellowknife, X1A 2L9 NT
867-873-7114, Fax: 867-873-0226

Nova Scotia
Department of Transportation & Infrastructure Renewal, Johnston Bldg., 1672 Granville St., 2nd Fl., PO Box 186, Halifax, B3J 2N2 NS
902-424-2297, Fax: 902-424-0171, 888-432-3233, tpwpaff@gov.ns.ca

Nunavut
Department of Community & Government Services, J.G. Brown Bldg., PO Box 1000 700,Iqaluit, X0A 0H0 NU
867-975-5400, Fax: 867-975-5305

Ontario
Ministry of Public Infrastructure Renewal, Mowat Block, 900 Bay St., 6th Fl., Toronto, M7A 1L2 ON
416-325-0424, Fax: 416-325-8851

Prince Edward Island
Department of Transportation & Public Works, Jones Bldg., 11 Kent St., PO Box 2000, Charlottetown, C1A 7N8 PE
902-368-5100, Fax: 902-368-5395

Quebec
Ministère des Services gouvernementaux, Édifice H, 875, Grande Allée est, Québec, G1R 5R8 QC
418-643-8383, Fax: 418-528-6153, communication@msg.gouv.qc.ca

Saskatchewan
Saskatchewan Government Services, Century Plaza, 1920 Rose St., Regina, S4P 0A9 SK
306-787-6911, Fax: 306-787-1061

Yukon Territory
Yukon Highways & Public Works, PO Box 2703, Whitehorse, Y1A 2C6 YT
867-393-7193, Fax: 867-393-6218, 800-661-0408, hpw-info@gov.yk.ca

PUBLICATIONS
Public Works & Government Services Canada, Place du Portage, Phase III, 11, rue Laurier, Ottawa, K1A 0S5 ON
819-997-6363, Fax: 819-956-9062, 800-622-6232

New Brunswick
Legislative Services, Centennial Bldg., #418, 670 King St., PO Box 6000, Fredericton, E3B 5H1 NB
506-453-2855, Fax: 506-457-7342

Newfoundland & Labrador
Office of the Queen's Printer, Queen's Printer-Earl Tucker, Ground Fl., Confederation Blg., PO Box 8700, St. John's, A1B 4J6 NL
709-729-3649, Fax: 709-729-1900, queensprinter@gov.nl.ca

Nova Scotia
Department of Service Nova Scotia & Municipal Relations, 1505 Barrington St., PO Box 216, Halifax, B3J 2M4 NS
902-424-4141, Fax: 902-424-0581, public-enquiries@gov.ns.ca

Quebec
Ministère de la Culture, des Communications & de la Condition féminine, 225, Grande Allée est, Québec, G1R 5G5 QC
Fax: 418-380-2364, 888-380-8882, infos@mcccf.gouv.qc.ca

Yukon Territory
Yukon Highways & Public Works, PO Box 2703, Whitehorse, Y1A 2C6 YT
867-393-7193, Fax: 867-393-6218, 800-661-0408, hpw-info@gov.yk.ca

PURCHASING

Saskatchewan
Purchasing Branch, 1920 Rose St., Regina, S4P 0A9 SK
306-787-6871, Fax: 306-787-3023

Alberta
Alberta Infrastructure & Transportation, Twin Atria Bldg., 4999 - 98 Ave., Edmonton, T6B 2X3 AB
780-427-2731, Fax: 780-466-3166,-310-0000

British Columbia
Ministry of Labour & Citizens' Services, PO Box 9052 Prov Govt,Victoria, V8W 9E2 BC
250-356-6348, Fax: 250-356-6595, LCS.Minister@gov.bc.ca

Manitoba
Government Services, Legislative Bldg., #332, 450 Broadway, Winnipeg, R3C 0V8 MB

Newfoundland & Labrador
Department of Government Services, PO Box 8700, St. John's, A1B 4J6 NL
709-729-4860

Northwest Territories
Department of Public Works & Services, PO Box 1320, Yellowknife, X1A 2L9 NT
867-873-7114, Fax: 867-873-0226

Nunavut
Department of Community & Government Services, J.G. Brown Bldg., PO Box 1000 700,Iqaluit, X0A 0H0 NU
867-975-5400, Fax: 867-975-5305

Ontario
Ministry of Public Infrastructure Renewal, Mowat Block, 900 Bay St., 6th Fl., Toronto, M7A 1L2 ON
416-325-0424, Fax: 416-325-8851

Prince Edward Island
Department of Transportation & Public Works, Jones Bldg., 11 Kent St., PO Box 2000, Charlottetown, C1A 7N8 PE
902-368-5100, Fax: 902-368-5395

Saskatchewan
Saskatchewan Government Services, Century Plaza, 1920 Rose St., Regina, S4P 0A9 SK
306-787-6911, Fax: 306-787-1061

RAIL TRANSPORTATION
See Also: Transportation
Transportation Safety Board of Canada, 200 Promenade du Portage, 4th Fl., Ottawa, K1A 1K8 ON
819-994-3741, Fax: 819-997-2239, 800-387-3557,

Manitoba
Manitoba Infrastructure & Transportation, Legislative Building, #203, 450 Broadway Ave., Winnipeg, R3C 0V8 MB
204-945-3723, Fax: 204-945-7610

New Brunswick
Department of Transportation, Kings Pl., 440 KingSt., PO Box 6000, Fredericton, E3B 5H8 NB
506-453-3939, Fax: 506-453-2900, Transportation.Web@gnb.ca

Newfoundland & Labrador
Department of Transportation & Works, Confederation Bldg., West Block, 6th Fl., PO Box 8700, St. John's, A1B 4J6 NL
709-729-3679, Fax: 709-729-4285, twminister@gov.nl.ca

Nova Scotia
Department of Transportation & Infrastructure Renewal, Johnston Bldg., 1672 Granville St., 2nd Fl., PO Box 186, Halifax, B3J 2N2 NS
902-424-2297, Fax: 902-424-0171, 888-432-3233, tpwpaff@gov.ns.ca

Ontario
GO Transit, #600, 20 Bay St., Toronto, ON M5J 2W3
416-869-3600, Fax: 416-869-1755, 888-438-6646

Quebec
Société du port ferroviaire Baie-Comeau-Hauterive, 18, rte Maritime, Baie-Comeau, QC G4Z 2L6
418-296-6785, Fax: 418-296-2377, soport@globetrotter.qc.ca
Ministère des Transports, 700, boul René-Lévesque est, 27e étage, Québec, G1R 5H1 QC
Fax: 514-643-1269, 888-355-0511, communications@mtq.gouv.qc.ca

Saskatchewan
Saskatchewan Highways & Infrastructure, 1855 Victoria Ave., Regina, S4P 3T2 SK
306-787-4800

REAL ESTATE
See Also: Land Titles
Canada Mortgage & Housing Corporation, 700 Montreal Rd., Ottawa, K1A 0P7 ON
613-748-2000, Fax: 613-748-2098, 800-668-2642, chic@cmhc-schl.gc.ca

Alberta
Technology Services, John E. Brownlee Bldg., 10365 - 97 St., 8th Fl., Edmonton, T5J 3W7 AB
780-422-8545

Nova Scotia
Department of Service Nova Scotia & Municipal Relations, 1505 Barrington St., PO Box 216, Halifax, B3J 2M4 NS
902-424-4141, Fax: 902-424-0581, public-enquiries@gov.ns.ca

Ontario
Ontario Realty Corporation, #2000, 1 Dundas St. West, Toronto, ON M5G 2L5
416-327-3937, Fax: 416-327-1906, 877-863-9672, feedback@ontariorealty.ca

Quebec
Société immobilière du Québec, 1075, rue de l'Amérique-Française, Québec, QC G1R 5P8
418-646-1766, Fax: 418-646-6911, 877-747-9911, courrier@siq.gouv.qc.ca

REAL ESTATE

Ontario
Ontario Realty Corporation, #2000, 1 Dundas St. West, Toronto, ON M5G 2L5
416-327-3937, Fax: 416-327-1906, 877-863-9672, feedback@ontariorealty.ca

RECREATION
See Also: Tourism & Tourist Information
Canadian Heritage, 15 Eddy St., Gatineau, K1A 0M5 QC
819-997-0055, 866-811-0055
Canadian Tourism Commission, #1400, 1055 Dunsmuir St., PO Box 49230, Vancouver, BC V7X 1L2
604-638-8300, Fax: 604-638-8425, ctc_feedback@businteractive.com
Parks Canada, 25 Eddy St., Gatineau, K1A 0M5 QC
888-773-8888, information@pc.gc.ca

Alberta
Alberta Sport, Recreation, Parks & Wildlife Foundation, Standard Life Centre, 10405 Jasper Ave., 9th Fl., Edmonton, AB T5J 4R7
780-415-1167, Fax: 780-415-0308
Alberta Economic Development, Commerce Place, 4th Fl., 10155 - 102 St., Edmonton, T5J 4L6 AB
780-427-4323, Fax: 780-415-1759

British Columbia
British Columbia 2010 Olympic & Paralympic Games Secretariat, 3585 Graveley St., 7th Fl., Vancouver, BC V5K 5J5
604-660-2010, Fax: 604-660-3437, 877-604-2010, bcsecretariat@gov.bc.ca
British Columbia Lottery Corporation, 74 West Seymour St., Kamloops, BC V2C 1E2
250-828-5500, Fax: 250-828-5631, 866-815-0222
Office of the Superintendent of Motor Vehicles, 940 Blanshard St., PO Box 9254 Prov Govt, Victoria, V8W 9J2 BC
250-387-7747, Fax: 250-387-4891, OSMV.Mailbox@gov.bc.ca

Manitoba
Manitoba Competitiveness, Training & Trade, International Business Centre, The Paris Building, 259 Portage Ave., Winnipeg, R3B 3P4 MB
204-945-2475, Fax: 204-945-3977, minctt@leg.gov.mb.ca
Manitoba Horse Racing Commission, c/o Boards, Commissions & Legislation Branch, #812, 401 York Ave., Winnipeg, MB R3C 0P8
204-945-4495, Fax: 204-948-2844, gordon.mackenzie@gov.mb.ca
Tourism Secretariat & Travel Manitoba, 155 Carlton St., 7th Fl., Winnipeg, R3C 3H8 MB
800-665-0040

New Brunswick
Department of Business New Brunswick, Centennial Bldg., 670 King St., PO Box 6000, Fredericton, E3B 5H1 NB
506-444-5228, Fax: 506-453-5428
Investment & Export Development, Centennial Bldg., 670 King St., 5th F., PO Box 6000, Fredericton, E3B 5H1 NB
506-453-2875, Fax: 506-444-4277
Department of Wellness, Culture & Sport, Place 2000, 250 King St., 4th Fl., PO Box 6000, Fredericton, E3B 5H1 NB
506-453-2909, Fax: 506-453-6548

Newfoundland & Labrador
Department of Tourism, Culture & Recreation, Confederation Bldg., West Block, 2nd Fl., PO Box 8700, St. John's, A1B 4J6 NL
709-729-0862, Fax: 709-729-0870, tcrinfo@gov.nl.ca

Nova Scotia
Alcohol & Gaming Division, Alderney Gate, 40 Alderney Dr., 5th Fl., PO Box 545, Dartmouth, B2Y 3Y8 NS
902-424-6160, Fax: 902-424-6313, 877-565-0556

Ontario
Alcohol & Gaming Commission of Ontario, 20 Dundas St. West, Toronto, ON M5G 2N6
416-326-8700, Fax: 416-326-5555, 800-522-2876
Ministry of Economic Development, Hearst Block, 900 Bay St., 8th Fl., Toronto, M7A 2E1 ON
416-325-6666, Fax: 416-325-6688, 866-668-4249, info@edt.gov.on.ca
Metro Toronto Convention Centre Corporation, 255 Front St. West, Toronto, ON M5V 2W6
416-585-8000, Fax: 416-585-8270, info@mtcc.com
Niagara Parks Commission, 7400 Portage Rd. South, PO Box 150, Niagara Falls, ON L2E 6T2
905-356-2241, Fax: 905-354-6041, 877-642-7275,
Ontario Film Review Board, 1075 Millwood Rd., Toronto, ON M4G 1X6
416-314-3626, Fax: 416-314-3632
Ontario Lottery & Gaming Corporation, Roberta Bondar Pl., #800, 70 Foster Dr., Sault Ste Marie, ON P6A 6V2
705-946-6464
Ontario Place Corporation, 955 Lake Shore Blvd. West, Toronto, ON M6K 3B9
416-314-9900, Fax: 416-314-9992
Ontario Racing Commission, 20 Dundas St. West, 9th Fl., Toronto, ON M5G 2C2
416-327-0520, Fax: 416-325-3478, orcinqry@cbs.gov.on.ca
Ottawa Congress Centre, 55 Colonel By Dr., Ottawa, ON K1N 9J2
613-563-1984, Fax: 613-563-7646
St. Lawrence Parks Commission, RR#1, Morrisburg, ON K0C 1X0
613-543-3704, Fax: 613-543-2847, 800-437-2233
Ministry of Tourism, Hearst Block, 900 Bay St., 9th Fl., Toronto, M7A 2E1 ON
416-326-9326, Fax: 416-314-7854, 800-668-2746

Prince Edward Island
Department of Communities, Cultural Affairs & Labour, Shaw Bldg., 95 Rochford St., 4th Fl., PO Box 2000, Charlottetown, C1A 7N8 PE
902-368-5250, Fax: 902-368-4121
Department of Innovation & Advanced Learning, Shaw Bldg., 105 Rochford St., 5th Fl., PO Box 2000, Charlottetown, C1A 7N8 PE
902-368-4240, Fax: 902-368-4242
Maritime Provinces Harness Racing Commission, 5 Gerald McCarville Dr., PO Box 128, Kensington, PE C0B 1M0
902-836-5500, Fax: 902-836-5390, dwalsh@mphrc.ca
Prince Edward Island Lotteries Commission, Office of the Deputy Provincial Treasurer, 95 Rochford St., PO Box 2000, Charlottetown, PE C1A 7N8
902-368-4053, Fax: 902-368-6575
Department of Tourism, PO Box 2000, Charlottetown, C1A 7N8 PE
800-463-4734

Quebec
Comité conjoint de chasse, de pêche et de piégeage, #C220, 383 rue Saint-Jacques, Montréal, QC H2Y 1N9
514-284-2151, Fax: 514-284-0039, hftcc@bellnet.ca
Régie des alcools, des courses et des jeux, 560, boul Charest est, Québec, QC G1K 3J3
418-643-7667, Fax: 418-643-5971, 800-363-0320, racj.quebec@racj.gouv.qc.ca
Société des établissements en plein air du Québec, Place de la Cité, #250, 2640, boul Laurier, Sainte-Foy, QC G1V 5C2
418-890-6527, Fax: 418-528-6025, 800-665-6527, inforeservation@sepaq.com

Saskatchewan
Saskatchewan Science Centre, 2903 Powerhouse Dr., Regina, SK S4N 0A1
306-522-4629, Fax: 306-525-0194, 800-667-6300, info@sasksciencecentre.com
Saskatchewan Tourism, Parks, Culture, & Sport, 1919 Saskatchewan Dr., 4th Fl., Regina, S4P 4H2 SK
306-787-5729, Fax: 306-787-8560
Western Development Museum, 2935 Melville St., Saskatoon, SK S7J 5A6
306-934-1400, Fax: 306-934-4467, 800-363-6345, info@wdm.ca

Yukon Territory
Yukon Tourism & Culture, PO Box 2703, Whitehorse, Y1A 2C6 YT
867-667-5036, Fax: 867-667-3546
Yukon Lottery Commission, 312 Wood St., Whitehorse, YT Y1A 2E6
867-633-7890, Fax: 867-668-7561, lotteriesyukon@gov.yk.ca

RECYCLING

Alberta
Alberta Recycling Management Authority, PO Box 189, Edmonton, AB T5J 2J1
780-990-1111, Fax: 780-990-1122, 888-999-8762, info@albertarecycling.ca

Newfoundland & Labrador
Multi-Materials Stewardship Board, PO Box 8131 A, St. John's, NL A1B 3M9
709-753-0948, Fax: 709-753-0974

RESEARCH & DEVELOPMENT
Atmospheric Science & Technology, 2121, rte Transcanadienne, Dorval, H9P 1J3 QC
514-421-4771, Fax: 514-421-2106
Bayfield Institute, 867 Lakeshore Rd., PO Box 5050, Burlington, L7R 4A6 ON
905-336-6240

Bedford Institute of Oceanography, 1 Challenger Dr., PO Box 1006, Dartmouth, B2Y 4A2 NS
902-426-3492, Fax: 902-426-8484
Biotechnology Research Institute, 6100, av Royalmount, Montréal, H4P 2R2 QC
514-496-6100, Fax: 514-496-1928, bri-info@cnrc-nrc.gc.ca
Canada Centre for Remote Sensing - Geomatics Canada, 588 Booth St., Ottawa, K1A 0Y7 ON
613-947-1216, Fax: 613-947-1382
Canadian Hydraulics Centre, M-32, 1200 Montreal Rd., Ottawa, K1A 0R6 ON
613-993-9381, Fax: 613-952-7679, info.chc@nrc-cnrc.gc.ca
Canadian Hydrographic Service, 615 Booth St., Ottawa, K1A 0E6 ON
613-998-4931, Fax: 613-998-1217, chsinfo@dfo-mpo.gc.ca
Canadian Ice Service, 373 Sussex Dr., Block E, 3rd Fl., Ottawa, K1A 0H3 ON
613-996-1550, Fax: 613-947-9160, 800-767-2885, cis-scg.cient@ec.gc.ca
Canadian Museum of Nature, PO Box 3343 D, Ottawa, K1P 6P4 ON
613-566-4700, Fax: 613-364-4021
Canadian Space Agency, 6767, rte de l'Aéroport, Longueuil, J3Y 8Y9 QC
450-926-4800, Fax: 450-926-4352, webmaster@space.gc.ca
CANMET Energy Technology Centre-Varennes, 1615, Montée Ste-Julie, CP 4800, Varennes, J3X 1S6 QC
450-652-6639, Fax: 450-652-0999
Centre for Surface Transportation Technology, 2320 Lester Rd., Ottawa, K1V 1S2 ON
613-998-9639, Fax: 613-957-0831, inquiries.cstt@nrc-cnrc.gc.ca
Chalk River Laboratories, Chalk River, K0J 1J0 ON
613-584-3311
Fisheries Resource Conservation Council, PO Box 2001 D, Ottawa, ON K1P 5W3
613-998-0433, Fax: 613-998-1146, info@frcc-ccrh.ca
Freshwater Institute, 501 University Cres., Winnipeg, R3T 2N6 MB
204-983-5000, Fax: 204-983-6285
Herzberg Institute of Astrophysics, 5071 West Saanich Rd., Victoria, V9E 2E7 BC
250-363-0001, Fax: 250-363-0045, hia-www@nrc-cnrc.gc.ca
Industrial Materials Institute, 75, boul de Montagne, Boucherville, J4B 6Y4 QC
450-641-5100, Fax: 450-641-5101, imi-info@nrc.ca
Institut Maurice-Lamontagne, 850, rte de le Mer, CP 1000, Mont-Joli, G5H 3Z4 QC
418-775-0555, Fax: 418-775-0730
Institute for Aerospace Research, 1200 Montreal Rd., Ottawa, K1A 0R6 ON
613-991-5738, Fax: 613-952-7214
Institute for Biological Sciences, Bldg. M-54, 1200 Montreal Rd., Ottawa, K1A 0R6 ON
613-993-5812, Fax: 613-957-7867
Institute for Chemical Process & Environmental Technology, Bldg. M-12, 1200 Montreal Rd., Ottawa, K1A 0R6 ON
613-993-4041, Fax: 613-957-8231
Institute for Marine Biosciences, 1411 Oxford St., Halifax, B3H 3Z1 NS
902-426-8332, Fax: 902-426-9413, communications.imb@nrc-cnrc.gc.ca
Institute for National Measurement Standards, Bldg. M-36, 1500 Montreal Rd., Ottawa, K1A 0R6 ON
613-998-7018, Fax: 613-952-1394, alexandra.shaw@nrc-cnrc.gc.ca
Institute for Ocean Technology, Kerwin Pl. & Arctic Ave., PO Box 12093, St. John's, A1B 3T5 NL
709-772-4939, Fax: 709-772-2462, noel.murphy@nrc.ca
Institute for Research in Construction, Bldg. M-24, 1500 Montreal Rd., Ottawa, K1A 0R6 ON
613-993-6189, Fax: 613-952-0268, ccmc@nrc-cnrc.gc.ca
Institute of Ocean Sciences, 9860 West Saanich Rd., PO Box 6000, Sidney, V8L 4B2 BC
250-363-6517, Fax: 250-363-6390
Integrated Manufacturing Technologies Institute, 800 Collip Circle, London, N6G 4X8 ON
519-430-7000, Fax: 519-430-7032
Laboratory Services Branch, 125 Resources Rd., Toronto, M9P 3V6 ON
416-235-5743, Fax: 416-235-5744
National Institute of Nanotechnology, Bldg. NINT, University of Alberta, 11421 Saskatchewan Dr., Edmonton, T6G 2M9 AB
780-641-1600, Fax: 780-641-1601, nintinfo@nrc.gc.ca

National Research Council Canada, Bldg. M-58, 1200 Montreal Rd., Ottawa, K1A 0R6 ON
613-993-9101, Fax: 613-952-7928, 877-672-2672, info@nrc-cnrc.ca
Natural Sciences & Engineering Research Council of Canada, Constitution Square, Tower II, 350 Albert St., Ottawa, K1A 1H5 ON
613-995-4273, Fax: 613-992-5337
Pacific Biological Station, 3190 Hammond Bay Rd., Nanaimo, V9T 6N7 BC
250-756-7000, Fax: 250-756-7053
Plant Biotechnology Institute, 110 Gymnasium Pl., Saskatoon, S7N 0W9 SK
306-975-5248, Fax: 306-975-4839, pbi-info@nrc-cnrc.gc.ca
Polar Continental Shelf Project, #487, 615 Booth St., Ottawa, K1A 0E4 ON
613-947-1650, Fax: 613-947-1611, pcsp@NRCan.gc.ca
Research Branch, 712 Yates St., Victoria, V8W 3E7 BC
Safe Environments Programme, Environmental Health Centre, Bldg. 8, 120 Parkdale Ave., Ottawa, K1A 0K9 ON
613-954-0291, Fax: 613-952-2206
St. Andrews Biological Station, 531 Brandy Cove Rd., St Andrews, E5B 2L9 NB
506-529-8854, Fax: 506-529-5862, XMARSABS@mar.dfo-mpo.gc.ca
Transportation Development Centre, Tour Ouest, Complexe Guy-Favreau, 800, boul René-Lévesque ouest, 6e étage, Montréal, H3B 1X9 QC
514-283-0000, Fax: 514-283-7158, tdccdt@tc.gc.ca

Alberta
Alberta Science & Research Authority, Phipps-McKinnon Bldg., #500, 10020 - 101A Ave., Edmonton, AB T5J 3G2
780-427-1488, Fax: 780-427-0979, asra@gov.ab.ca
Alberta Research Council, 250 Karl Clark Rd., Edmonton, T6N 1E4 AB
780-450-5111, Fax: 780-450-5333

British Columbia
Powertech Labs Inc., 12388 - 88 Ave., Surrey, BC V8W 7R7
604-590-7500, Fax: 604-590-5347, info@powertechlans.com

New Brunswick
New Brunswick Research & Productivity Council, 921 College Hill Rd., Fredericton, E3B 6Z9 NB
506-452-1212, Fax: 506-452-1395, info@rpc.ca
Service New Brunswick, Westmorland Place, #200, 82 Westmorland St., PO Box 1998, Fredericton, E3B 5G4 NB
506-457-3581, Fax: 506-457-7520, 888-762-8600, snb@snb.ca

Newfoundland & Labrador
Department of Innovation, Trade & Rural Development, West Block, Confederation Bldg., PO Box 8700, St. John's, A1B 4J6 NL
709-729-7000, Fax: 709-729-0654, 800-563-2299, itrd@gov.nl.ca

Northwest Territories
Aurora Research Institute, 191 MacKenzie Rd., PO Box 1450, Inuvik, X0E 0T0 NT
867-777-3298, Fax: 867-777-4264, webmaster@nwtresearch.com

Ontario
Ministry of Research & Innovation, 56 Wellesley St. West, 7th Fl., Toronto, M7A 2E7 ON
416-325-5181, Fax: 416-325-3877
Science & Information Resources Division, Robinson Place, North Tower, 300 Water St., 2nd Fl., Peterborough, K9J 8M5 ON
705-755-2000, Fax: 705-755-2802, 800-667-1940

Prince Edward Island
Agricultural Insurance Corporation, 29 Indigo Cres., PO Box 1600, Charlottetown, PE C1A 7N3
902-368-4842, Fax: 902-368-6677, peiaic@gov.pe.ca
Food Technology Centre, 101 Belvedere Ave., PO Box 2000, Charlottetown, PE C1A 7N8
902-368-5548, Fax: 902-368-5549, 877-368-5548, ftcweb@gov.pe.ca

Quebec
Centre de recherche industrielle du Québec, 333, rue Franquet, Sainte-Foy, QC G1P 4C7
418-659-1550, Fax: 418-652-2251, 800-667-2386, infocriq@criq.qc.ca

Fonds de la recherche en santé du Québec, 500, rue Sherbrooke ouest, 8e étage, Montréal, QC H3A 3C6
514-873-2114, Fax: 514-873-8768
Fonds québécois de la recherche sur la nature et les technologies, #450, 140, Grande-Allée est, Québec, QC G1R 5M8
418-643-8560, Fax: 418-643-1451, info@fqrnt.gouv.qc.ca
Société Innovatech du sud du Québec, #20, 2100, rue King ouest, Sherbrooke, QC J1J 2E8
819-820-3305, Fax: 819-820-3320, isq@isq.qc.ca
Société Innovatech Québec, 10, rue Pierre Olivier Chauveau, Québec, QC G1R 4J3
418-528-9770, Fax: 418-528-9783, info@innovatechquebec.com
Société Innovatech Régions ressources, #500, 1200, rte de l'Église, Sainte-Foy, QC G1V 5A3
866-870-0437, info@innovatech-regions.qc.ca

Saskatchewan
Saskatchewan Power Corporation (SaskPower), 2025 Victoria Ave., Regina, S4P 0S1 SK
306-566-2121, Fax: 306-566-2330, 800-667-4749
Saskatchewan Research Council, #125, 15 Innovation Blvd., Saskatoon, S7N 2X8 SK
306-933-5400, Fax: 306-933-7446, info@src.sk.ca

ROUND TABLES
National Round Table on the Environment & Economy, #200, 344 Slater St., Ottawa, K1R 7Y3 ON
613-992-7189, Fax: 613-992-7385, admin@nrtee-trnee.ca

Manitoba
Manitoba Round Table for Sustainable Development, #160, 123 Main St., Winnipeg, R3C 1A5 MB
204-945-1671, Fax: 204-948-2357, mrtsd@gov.mb.ca

New Brunswick
New Brunswick Round Table on Environment & Economy, 20 McGloin St., PO Box 6000, Fredericton, NB E3B 5H1
506-453-3703, Fax: 506-453-3876

SALES TAX
Nova Scotia
Tax Commission, Maritime Centre, 1505 Barrington St., Halifax, B3J 3K5 NS
902-424-5200, Fax: 902-424-0720, 800-670-4357

Prince Edward Island
Department of the Provincial Treasury, Shaw Bldg., 95 Rochford St., 2nd Fl. South, PO Box 2000, Charlottetown, C1A 7N8 PE
902-368-4050, Fax: 902-368-6575

SCIENCE & NATURE
Agriculture & Agri-Food Canada, Sir John Carling Bldg., 930 Carling Ave., Ottawa, K1A 0C5 ON
613-759-1000, Fax: 613-759-6726, info@agr.gc.ca
Atomic Energy of Canada Limited, Head Office, 2251 Speakman Dr., Mississauga, L5K 1B2 ON
905-823-9040, webmaster@aecl.ca
Beverly & Qamanirjuaq Caribou Management Board, Secretariat, PO Box 629, Stonewall, MB R0C 2Z0
204-467-2438, rossthompson@mts.net
Canada Centre for Remote Sensing - Geomatics Canada, 588 Booth St., Ottawa, K1A 0Y7 ON
613-947-1216, Fax: 613-947-1382
Canadian Institutes of Health Research, 160 Elgin St., 9th Fl., Ottawa, K1A 0W9 ON
613-941-2672, Fax: 613-954-1800, info@cihr-irsc.gc.ca
Canadian Nuclear Safety Commission, 280 Slater St., PO Box 1046 B, Ottawa, K1P 5S9 ON
613-995-5894, Fax: 613-995-5086, 800-668-5284, info@cnsc-ccsn.gc.ca
Canadian Polar Commission, Constitution Square, #1710, 360 Albert St., Ottawa, K1R 7X7 ON
613-943-8605, Fax: 613-943-8607, 888-765-2701, mail@polarcom.gc.ca
Canadian Space Agency, 6767, rte de l'Aéroport, Longueuil, J3Y 8Y9 QC
450-926-4800, Fax: 450-926-4352, webmaster@space.gc.ca
Centre for Surface Transportation Technology, 2320 Lester Rd., Ottawa, K1V 1S2 ON
613-998-9639, Fax: 613-957-0831, inquiries.cstt@nrc-cnrc.gc.ca
Committee on the Status of Endangered Wildlife in Canada, c/o Canadian Wildlife Service, Ottawa, ON K1A 0H3
819-997-4991, Fax: 819-994-3684, cosewic@ec.gc.ca

Electronic Commerce Branch, 300 Slater St., Ottawa, ON K1A 0C8
613-990-4268, Fax: 613-941-0178, 800-328-6189
Environment Canada, 10 Wellington St., Gatineau, K1A 0H3 QC
819-997-2800, Fax: 819-994-1412, 800-668-6767, enviroinfo@ec.gc.ca
Commission for Environmental Cooperation, Secretariat, #200, 393, rue St-Jacques ouest, Montréal, H2Y 1N9 QC
514-350-4300, Fax: 514-350-4314, info@cec.org
Fisheries & Aquaculture Management, 200 Kent St., Ottawa, K1A 0E6 ON
Fisheries & Oceans Canada, 200 Kent St., Ottawa, K1A 0E6 ON
613-993-0999, Fax: 613-996-1866, info@dfo-mpo.gc.ca
Fisheries Resource Conservation Council, PO Box 2001 D, Ottawa, ON K1P 5W3
613-998-0433, Fax: 613-998-1146, info@frcc-ccrh.ca
Geological Survey of Canada, 601 Booth St., Ottawa, K1A 0E8 ON
613-996-3919, Fax: 613-943-8742, info-ottawa@gsc.nrcan.gc.ca
Hazardous Materials Information Review Commission, 427 Laurier Ave. West, 7th Fl., Ottawa, ON K1A 1M3
613-993-4331, Fax: 613-993-4686, hmirc-ccrmd@hc-sc.gc.ca
Indian & Northern Affairs Canada, 10 Wellington St., North Tower, Gatineau, K1A 0H4 QC
819-997-0380, Fax: 819-953-3017, 866-817-3977, infopubs@ainc-inac.gc.ca
Indian Oil & Gas Canada, #100, 9911 Chula Blvd., Tsuu T'ina (Sarcee), AB T2W 6H6
Fax: 403-292-5618
Institute for Aerospace Research, 1200 Montreal Rd., Ottawa, K1A 0R6 ON
613-991-5738, Fax: 613-952-7214
Institute for Information Technology, Bldg. M-50, 1200 Montreal Rd., Ottawa, K1A 0R6 ON
613-993-9101, Fax: 613-952-0074, 877-672-2672
International Development Research Centre, 150 Kent St., PO Box 8500, Ottawa, K1P 0B2 ON
613-236-6163, Fax: 613-238-7230, info@idrc.ca
Mackenzie Valley Environmental Impact Review Board, 200 Scotia Centre, 5102 - 50th Ave., PO Box 938, Yellowknife, NT X1A 2N7
867-766-7050, Fax: 867-766-7074, 866-912-3472
National Energy Board, 444 - 7 Ave. SW, Calgary, T2P 0X8 AB
403-292-4800, Fax: 403-292-5503, 800-899-1265, info@neb-one.gc.ca
National Research Council Canada, Bldg. M-58, 1200 Montreal Rd., Ottawa, K1A 0R6 ON
613-993-9101, Fax: 613-952-7928, 877-672-2672, info@nrc-cnrc.ca
National Round Table on the Environment & Economy, #200, 344 Slater St., Ottawa, K1R 7Y3 ON
613-992-7189, Fax: 613-992-7385, admin@nrtee-trnee.ca
Natural Resources Canada, 580 Booth St., Ottawa, K1A 0E4 ON
613-995-0947, Fax: 613-992-7211
Natural Sciences & Engineering Research Council of Canada, Constitution Square, Tower II, 350 Albert St., Ottawa, K1A 1H5 ON
613-995-4273, Fax: 613-992-5337
North American Bird Conservation Initiative, Canadian Wildlife Service, 351, boul St-Joseph, 3e étage, Gatineau, QC K1A 0H3
819-994-0512, Fax: 819-994-4445, s.neve@ec.gc.ca
North American Waterfowl Management Plan, c/o Canadian Wildlife Service, Place Vincent-Massey, 351 St-Joseph Blvd., 16th Fl., Gatineau, ON K1A 0H3
819-934-6034, Fax: 819-934-6017, nabci@ec.gc.ca
Nunavut Impact Review Board, PO Box 2379, Cambridge Bay, NU X0B 0C0
867-983-4600, Fax: 867-983-2594, info@nirb.nunavut.ca
Nunavut Water Board, PO Box 119, Gjoa Haven, NU X0B 1J0
867-360-6338, Fax: 867-360-6369
Pest Management Regulatory Agency, 2720 Riverside Dr., Ottawa, ON K1A 0K9
613-736-3401, Fax: 613-736-3798
Polar Continental Shelf Project, #487, 615 Booth St., Ottawa, K1A 0E4 ON
613-947-1650, Fax: 613-947-1611, pcsp@NRCan.gc.ca
Porcupine Caribou Management Board, PO Box 31723, Whitehorse, YT Y1A 6L3
867-633-4780, Fax: 867-393-3904, pcmb@taiga.net
Prairie Farm Rehabilitation Administration, CIBC Tower, #408, 1800 Hamilton St., Regina, S4P 4L2 SK
306-780-5070, Fax: 306-780-5018

Prime Minister's Advisory Council on Science & Technology, 235 Queen St., 9th Fl., Ottawa, K1A 0H5 ON
613-998-5646, Fax: 613-990-2007, acst-ccst@ic.gc.ca
Science Sector, 200 Kent St., Ottawa, K1A 0E6 ON

Alberta

Agricultural Products Marketing Council, 7000 - 113 St., 3rd Fl., Edmonton, AB T6H 5T6
780-427-2164, Fax: 780-422-9690
Alberta Agriculture & Food, J.G. O'Donoghue Bldg., 7000 - 113 St., 1st Fl., Edmonton, T6H 5T6 AB
780-427-2727, Fax: 780-427-2861, 866-882-7677
Alberta Agricultural Research Institute, John E. Brownlee Bldg., 10365 - 97 St. North, 9th Fl., Edmonton, AB T5J 3W7
780-427-1956, Fax: 780-427-3252, AARIMAIL@gov.ab.ca
Alberta Cancer Board, Standard Life Centre, #1220, 10405 Jasper Ave., Edmonton, AB T5J 3N4
780-412-6328, Fax: 780-412-6326, info@cancerboard.ab.ca
Alberta Energy Research Institute, AMEC Place, #2540, 801 - 6 Ave. SW, Calgary, AB T2P 3W2
403-297-8650, Fax: 403-297-3638, aeri@gov.ab.ca
Alberta Environmental Appeal Board, Peace Hills Trust Tower, #306, 10011 - 109 St. NW, Edmonton, AB T5J 3S8
780-427-6207, Fax: 780-427-4693
Alberta Heritage Foundation for Medical Research, #1500, 10104 - 103 Ave, Edmonton, AB T5J 4A7
780-423-5727, Fax: 780-429-3509, postmaster@ahfmr.ab.ca
Alberta Ingenuity Fund, Manulife Place, #2410, 10180 - 101 St., Edmonton, AB T5J 3S4
780-423-5735, Fax: 780-420-0018, info@albertaingenuity.ca
Alberta Recycling Management Authority, PO Box 189, Edmonton, AB T5J 2J1
780-990-1111, Fax: 780-990-1122, 888-999-8762, info@albertarecycling.ca
Alberta Science & Research Authority, Phipps-McKinnon Bldg., #500, 10020 - 101A Ave., Edmonton, AB T5J 3G2
780-427-1488, Fax: 780-427-0979, asra@gov.ab.ca
Alberta Special Areas Board, 212 - 2nd Ave. West, PO Box 820, Hanna, AB T0J 1P0
403-854-5600, Fax: 403-854-5527, specarea@telusplanet.net
Alberta Sport, Recreation, Parks & Wildlife Foundation, Standard Life Centre, 10405 Jasper Ave., 9th Fl., Edmonton, AB T5J 4R7
780-415-1167, Fax: 780-415-0308
Alberta Used Oil Management Association, Scotia One, Scotia Place, #1050, 10060 Jasper Ave., Edmonton, AB T5J 3R8
780-414-1510, Fax: 780-414-1519, reception@usedoilrecycling.ca
Beverage Container Management Board, #1010, 10707 - 100 Ave., Edmonton, AB T5J 3M1
780-424-3193, Fax: 780-428-4620, 888-424-7671, info@bcmb.ab.ca
Clean Air Strategic Alliance, Centre West Bldg, 10035 - 108 St., 10th Fl., Edmonton, AB T5J 3E1
780-427-9793, Fax: 780-422-3127, casa@casahome.org
Alberta Energy, North Petroleum Plaza, 9945 - 108 St., 7th Fl., Edmonton, T5K 2G6 AB
780-427-7425, Fax: 780-422-0698, 780-310-0000
Alberta Environment, South Tower, Petroleum Plaza, 9915 - 108 St., Main Fl., Edmonton, T5K 2G8 AB
780-427-2700, Fax: 780-422-4086, -310-0000, env.infocent@gov.ab.ca
Farmers' Advocate of Alberta, 7000 - 113 St., 3rd Fl., Edmonton, AB T6H 5T6
780-427-2433, Fax: 780-427-3913, farmers.advocate@gov.ab.ca
Informatics Circle of Research Excellence, 3608 - 33 St. NW, Calgary, AB T2L 2A6
403-210-5335, Fax: 403-210-5337, info@icore.ca
Irrigation Council, Provincial Bldg., 200 - 5 Ave. South, 3rd Fl., PO Bag 3014, Lethbridge, AB T1J 4L1
403-381-5176, Fax: 403-382-4406
Land Compensation/Surface Rights Board, Phipps-McKinnon Bldg., 10020 - 101A Ave., 18th Fl., Edmonton, AB T5J 3G2
780-427-2444, Fax: 780-427-5798
Natural Resources Conservation Board, Sterling Place, 9940 - 106 St., 4th Fl., Edmonton, AB T5K 2N2
780-422-1977, Fax: 780-427-0607, 866-383-6722
Alberta Research Council, 250 Karl Clark Rd., Edmonton, T6N 1E4 AB
780-450-5111, Fax: 780-450-5333
Alberta Sustainable Resource Development, Information Centre, 9920 - 108 St., Main Fl., Edmonton, T5K 2M4 AB
780-944-0313, Fax: 780-427-4407, 877-944-0313, srd.infocent@gov.ab.ca

British Columbia

Agricultural Land Commission, #133, 4940 Canada Way, Burnaby, BC V5G 4K6
604-660-7000, Fax: 604-660-7033
Ministry of Agriculture & Lands, PO Box 9120 Prov Govt, Victoria, V8W 9E2 BC
250-387-5121, Fax: 250-387-1522, agf.webmaster@gems2.gov.bc.ca
British Columbia Farm Industry Review Board, 1007 Fort St., 3rd Fl., PO Box 9129 Prov Govt, Victoria, V8W 9B5
250-356-8945, Fax: 250-356-5131, firb@gov.bc.ca
Emergency Management BC, 525 Fort St., 2nd Fl., PO Box 9223 Prov Govt, Victoria, V8W 9J1 BC
250-953-4002, Fax: 250-953-4081, BC.CorSer@gov.bc.ca (Coroner); OFC@gov.bc.ca (Fire Commissioner)
Ministry of Energy, Mines & Petroleum Resources, PO Box 9318 Prov Govt, Victoria, V8W 9N3 BC
250-952-0241
Ministry of Environment, PO Box 9339 Prov Govt, Victoria, V8W 9M1 BC
250-387-1161, Fax: 250-387-5669, www.envmail@gov.bc.ca
Environmental Appeal Board, 747 Fort St., 4th Fl., PO Box 9425 Prov Govt, Victoria, BC V8W 9V1
250-387-3464, Fax: 250-356-9923, eabinfo@gov.bc.ca
British Columbia Environmental Assessment Office, 836 Yates St., 1st Fl., PO Box 9426 Prov Govt, Victoria, V8W 9V1 BC
250-356-7441, Fax: 250-356-7440, eaoinfo@gov.bc.ca
Environmental Protection Division, 2975 Jutland Rd., 5th Fl., PO Box 9339, Victoria, V8W 9M1 BC
250-387-1288, Fax: 250-387-5669
Environmental Stewardship Division, 2975 Jutland Rd., 5th Fl., PO Box 9339 Prov Govt, Victoria, V8T 5J9 BC
250-356-0121, Fax: 250-953-3414
Forest Appeals Commission, 747 Fort St., 4th Fl., PO Box 9425 Prov Govt, Victoria, BC V8W 9V1
250-387-3464, Fax: 250-356-9923, facinfo@gov.bc.ca
Forest Practices Board, 1675 Douglas St., 3rd Fl., PO Box 9905 Prov Govt, Victoria, BC V8W 9R1
250-387-7964, Fax: 250-387-7009, 800-994-5899, fpboard@gov.bc.ca
Forestry Innovation Investments, #1200, 1130 West Pender St., Vancouver, BC V6E 4A4
604-685-7507, Fax: 604-685-5373, info@bcfii.ca
Ministry of Forests & Range, PO Box 9529 Prov Govt, Victoria, V8W 9C3 BC
250-387-4809, Fax: 250-953-3687
Fraser Basin Council, Central Office, 470 Granville St., 1st Fl., Vancouver, BC V6C 1V5
604-488-5350, Fax: 604-488-5351, info@fraserbasin.bc.ca
Islands Trust, #200, 1627 Fort St., Victoria, BC V8R 1H8
250-405-5151, Fax: 250-405-5155, information@islandstrust.bc.ca
Oil & Gas Commission, #100, 10003 - 110 Ave., Fort St John, BC V1J 6M7
250-261-5700, 800-663-7867
Operations, 1520 Blanshard St., 3rd Fl., PO Box 9525 Prov Govt, Victoria, V8W 9C3 BC
250-387-1236, Fax: 250-953-3687, Forests.OperationsDivisionExecutiveOffice@gov.bc.ca
Timber Export Advisory Committee, 1520 Blanshard St., 2nd Fl., PO Box 9514 Prov Govt, Victoria, BC V8W 9C2
250-387-8916, Fax: 250-387-5050

Manitoba

Manitoba Aboriginal & Northern Affairs, 59 Elizabeth Dr., PO Box 37, Thompson, R8N 1X4 MB
204-677-6607, Fax: 204-677-6753, amartin@gov.mb.ca
Aboriginal Affairs Secretariat, #200, 500 Portage Ave., Winnipeg, R3C 3X1 MB
204-945-2510, Fax: 204-945-3689
Agricultural Societies, 1129 Queens Ave., Brandon, MB R7A 1L9
204-726-6195, Fax: 204-726-6260
Manitoba Agriculture, Food & Rural Initiatives, Norquay Bldg., 401 York Ave., Winnipeg, R3C 0P8 MB
Clean Environment Commission, #305, 155 Carlton St., Winnipeg, MB R3C 3H8
204-945-0594, Fax: 204-945-0090
Manitoba Conservation, 200 Saulteaux Cres., Winnipeg, R3J 3W3 MB
204-945-6784, 800-214-6497, mincon@leg.gov.mb.ca
Ecological Reserves Advisory Committee, c/o Manitoba Conservation, Parks & Natural Areas Branch, 200 Saulteaux Cres., Winnipeg, MB R3J 3W3
204-945-4148, Fax: 204-945-0012, hhernandez@gov.mb.ca

Government Quick Reference Guide / Science & Nature

Endangered Species Advisory Committee, 200 Saulteaux Cres., PO Box 24, Winnipeg, MB R3J 3W3
204-945-7465, Fax: 204-945-3077
Farm Lands Ownership Board, #812, Norquay Bldg., 401 York Ave., Winnipeg, MB R3C 0P8
204-945-3149, Fax: 204-945-1489, 800-282-8069, robert.mckenzie@gov.mb.ca
Farm Machinery Board, Norquay Bldg., #812, 401 York Ave., Winnipeg, MB R3C 0P8
204-945-3856, Fax: 204-948-2844, randy.ozunko@gov.mb.ca
Manitoba Hydro, PO Box 815 Main,Winnipeg, R3C 2P4 MB
204-474-3311, Fax: 204-475-0069, publicaffairs@hydro.mb.ca
Local Government Development Division, 59 Elizabeth Dr., PO Box 33, Thompson, R8N 1X4 MB
204-677-6794, Fax: 204-677-6525
Manitoba Habitat Heritage Corporation, #200, 1555 St. James St., Winnipeg, MB R3H 1B5
204-784-4350, Fax: 204-784-7359, mhhc@mhhc.mb.ca

New Brunswick
Department of Agriculture & Aquaculture, PO Box 6000, Fredericton, E3B 5H1 NB
506-453-2666, Fax: 506-453-7170, DAA-MAA@gnb.ca
Board of Examiners under the Scaler's Act, 1350 Regent St. South, PO Box 6000, Fredericton, NB E3B 5H1
506-453-2441, Fax: 506-453-6689
Business Development, Centennial Bldg., 670 King St., 5th Fl., PO Box 6000, Fredericton, E3B 5H1 NB
506-453-2111, Fax: 506-444-4182
Department of the Environment, Marysville Place, 20 McGloin St., PO Box 6000, Fredericton, E3B 5H1 NB
506-453-2690, Fax: 506-457-4991
Forest Protection Limited, 2502 Hwy. 102, Lincoln, NB E3B 7E6
506-446-6930, Fax: 506-446-6934, info@forestprotectionlimited.com
Department of Natural Resources, PO Box 6000, Fredericton, E3B 5H1 NB
506-453-2510, Fax: 506-444-5839, dnrweb@gnb.ca
New Brunswick Crop Insurance Commission, PO Box 6000, Fredericton, NB E3B 5H1
506-453-2185, Fax: 506-453-7406
New Brunswick Farm Products Commission, c/o Department of Agriculture & Aquaculture, PO Box 6000, Fredericton, NB E3B 5H1
506-453-3647, Fax: 506-444-5969
New Brunswick Round Table on Environment & Economy, 20 McGloin St., PO Box 6000, Fredericton, NB E3B 5H1
506-453-3703, Fax: 506-453-3876
New Brunswick Research & Productivity Council, 921 College Hill Rd., Fredericton, E3B 6Z9 NB
506-452-1212, Fax: 506-452-1395, info@rpc.ca
Service New Brunswick, Westmorland Place, #200, 82 Westmorland St., PO Box 1998, Fredericton, E3B 5G4 NB
506-457-3581, Fax: 506-457-7520, 888-762-8600, snb@snb.ca

Newfoundland & Labrador
Canada-Newfoundland Offshore Petroleum Board, TD Place, 140 Water St., 5th Fl., St. John's, NL A1C 6H6
709-778-1400, Fax: 709-778-1473, postmaster@cnlopb.nl.ca
Department of Environment & Conservation, Confederation Bldg., West Block, 4th Fl., PO Box 8700, St. John's, A1B 4J6 NL
709-729-2664, Fax: 709-729-6639, 800-563-6181, info@gov.nl.ca
Department of Fisheries & Aquaculture, Petten Bldg., 30 Strawberry Marsh Rd., PO Box 8700, St. John's, A1B 4J6 NL
709-729-3723, Fax: 709-729-6082, fishaqwebmaster@gov.nl.ca
Department of Innovation, Trade & Rural Development, West Block, Confederation Bldg., PO Box 8700, St. John's, A1B 4J6 NL
709-729-7000, Fax: 709-729-0654, 800-563-2299, itrd@gov.nl.ca
Department of Natural Resources, Natural Resources Bldg., 50 Elizabeth Ave., 7th Fl., PO Box 8700, St. John's, A1B 4J6 NL
709-729-2920, Fax: 709-729-0059
Professional Fish Harvesters Certification Board, 15 Hallett Cres., PO Box 8541, St. John's, NL A1B 3P2
709-722-8170, Fax: 709-722-8201, pfh@pfhcb.com

Northwest Territories
Aurora Research Institute, 191 MacKenzie Rd., PO Box 1450, Inuvik, X0E 0T0 NT
867-777-3298, Fax: 867-777-4264, webmaster@nwtresearch.com

Department of Environment & Natural Resources, PO Box 1320, Yellowknife, X1A 2L9 NT

Nova Scotia
Department of Agriculture, 1741 Brunswick St., 3rd Fl., PO Box 2223, Halifax, B3J 3C4 NS
902-424-4560, Fax: 902-424-4671
Canada-Nova Scotia Offshore Petroleum Board, TD Centre, 1791 Barrington St., 6th Fl., Halifax, NS B3J 3K9
902-422-5588, Fax: 902-422-1799, postmaster@cnsopb.ns.ca
Crown Lands Record Centre, Founders Square, #501, 1701 Hollis St., PO Box 698, Halifax, NS B3J 2T9
902-424-8681
Department of Natural Resources, Founder's Square, 1701 Hollis St., 3rd Fl., PO Box 698, Halifax, B3J 2T9 NS
902-424-5935, Fax: 902-424-0594, 800-565-2224
Nova Scotia Crop & Livestock Insurance Commission, MacRae Library Bldg., #2, 137 College Rd., PO Box 1092, Truro, NS B2N 5G9
902-893-7755, Fax: 902-895-4622, 800-565-6371, nsclic@gov.ns.ca
Nova Scotia Farm Loan Board, PO Box 550, Truro, NS B2N 5E3
902-893-6506, Fax: 902-895-7693, flb@gov.ns.ca
Nova Scotia Geomatics Centre, 160 Willow St., Amherst, B4H 3W3 NS
902-667-7231, Fax: 902-667-6008, 800-798-0706, info@nsgc.gov.ns.ca

Nunavut
Department of Environment, PO Box 1000 1300,Iqaluit, X0A 0H0 NU
867-975-7700, Fax: 867-975-7742, 866-222-9063, environment@gov.nu.ca

Ontario
Advisory Council on Drinking Water Quality & Testing Standards, 40 St. Clair Ave. West, 3rd Fl., Toronto, ON M4V 1M2
416-212-7779, Fax: 416-212-7595
Ministry of Agriculture, Food & Rural Affairs, 1 Stone Rd. West, Guelph, N1G 4Y2 ON
519-826-3100, 888-466-2372
Algonquin Forestry Authority - Huntsville, 222 Main St. West, Huntsville, ON P1H 1Y1
705-789-9647, Fax: 705-789-3353
Algonquin Forestry Authority - Pembroke, Victoria Centre, 84 Isabella St., 2nd Fl., Pembroke, ON K8A 5S5
613-735-0173, Fax: 613-735-4192
Animal Care Review Board, 77 Grenville St., 8th Fl., Toronto, ON M5S 1B3
416-314-3509, Fax: 416-314-3518
Association of Ontario Land Surveyors, 1043 McNicoll Ave., Toronto, ON M1W 3W6
416-491-9020, Fax: 416-491-2576, admin@aols.org
Cancer Care Ontario, 620 University Ave., 15th Fl., Toronto, ON M5G 2L7
416-971-9800, Fax: 416-971-6888
Conservation Review Board, 400 University Ave. 4th Fl., Toronto, ON M7A 2R9
416-314-7137, Fax: 416-314-7175
Crown Timber Board of Examiners, Roberta Bondar Place, #400, 70 Foster Dr., Sault Ste Marie, ON P6A 6V5
705-945-6643
Ministry of Environment, 135 St. Clair Ave. West, Toronto, M4V 1P5 ON
416-325-4000, Fax: 416-325-3159, 800-565-4923
Environmental Commissioner of Ontario, #605, 1075 Bay St., Toronto, M5S 2B1 ON
416-325-3377, Fax: 416-325-3370, 800-701-6454, commissioner@eco.on.ca
Environmental Review Tribunal, #1700, 2300 Yonge St., PO Box 2382, Toronto, ON M4P 1E4
416-314-4600, Fax: 416-314-4506
Fish & Wildlife Heritage Commission, Robinson Pl., 300 Water St., PO Box 7000, Peterborough, ON K9J 8M5
Fax: 705-755-5093
Lake of the Woods Control Board, c/o Executive Engineer, Ottawa, ON K1A 0H3
Fax: 819-953-4666, 800-661-5922, secretariat@lwcb.ca
Livestock Medicines Advisory Committee, 1 Stone Rd. West, 3rd Fl. NE, Guelph, ON N1G 4Y2
519-826-4110, Fax: 519-826-3254
Mines & Minerals Division, Willet Green Miller Centre, 933 Ramsey Lake Rd., 6th Fl., Sudbury, P3E 6B5 ON
705-670-5755, Fax: 705-670-5818

Ministry of Natural Resources, Whitney Block, #6630, 99 Wellesley St. West, 6th Fl., Toronto, M7A 1W3 ON
800-667-1940
Niagara Parks Commission, 7400 Portage Rd. South, PO Box 150, Niagara Falls, ON L2E 6T2
905-356-2241, Fax: 905-354-6041, 877-642-7275
Ministry of Northern Development & Mines, 159 Cedar St., Sudbury, P3E 6A5 ON
705-564-0032, Fax: 705-564-7357
Ontario Clean Water Agency, 1 Yonge St., 17th Fl., Toronto, ON M5E 1E5
416-314-5600, Fax: 416-314-8300, 800-667-6292
Ontario Geographic Names Board, Robinson Place, 300 Water St., 2nd Fl., PO Box 7000, Peterborough, ON K9J 8M5
705-755-2134, Fax: 705-755-2131
Ontario Moose & Bear Allocation Advisory Committee, PO Box 964, Sioux Lookout, ON P8T 1B3
807-737-2615, Fax: 807-737-4173
Ontario Science Centre, 770 Don Mills Rd., Toronto, ON M3C 1T3
416-696-1000, Fax: 416-696-3124
Pesticides Advisory Committee, #1203, 2300 Yonge St., 12th Fl., Toronto, ON M4P 1E4
416-314-9230, Fax: 416-314-9237
Rabies Advisory Committee, Trent University Science Complex, PO Box 4840, Peterborough, ON K9J 8N8
705-755-2270
Royal Botanical Gardens, 680 Plains Rd. West, Burlington, ON L7T 4H4
905-527-1158, Fax: 905-577-0375, 800-694-4769
Science & Information Resources Division, Robinson Place, North Tower, 300 Water St., 2nd Fl., Peterborough, K9J 8M5 ON
705-755-2000, Fax: 705-755-2802, 800-667-1940
Science North, 100 Ramsey Lake Rd., Sudbury, ON P3E 5S9
705-522-3701, Fax: 705-522-4954, 800-461-4898
Shibogama Interim Planning Board, PO Box 105, Wunnumin, ON P0V 2Z0
807-442-2559, Fax: 807-442-2627
St. Lawrence Parks Commission, RR#1, Morrisburg, ON K0C 1X0
613-543-3704, Fax: 613-543-2847, 800-437-2233
Windigo Interim Planning Board, PO Box 299, Sioux Lookout, ON P8T 1A3
807-737-1585, Fax: 807-737-3133

Prince Edward Island
Agricultural Insurance Corporation, 29 Indigo Cres., PO Box 1600, Charlottetown, PE C1A 7N3
902-368-4842, Fax: 902-368-6677, peiaic@gov.pe.ca
Department of Agriculture, Jones Bldg., 11 Kent St., PO Box 2000, Charlottetown, C1A 7N8 PE
902-368-4880, Fax: 902-368-4857
Grain Elevators Corporation, PO Box 250, Kensington, PE C0B 1M0
902-836-8929
PEI Energy Corporation, Jones Bldg., 11 Kent St., 4th Fl., PO Box 2000, Charlottetown, PE C1A 7N8
902-890-0288, Fax: 902-368-0290

Quebec
Ministère de l'Agriculture, des Pêcheries et de l'Alimentation, 200, ch Sainte-Foy, Québec, G1R 4X6 QC
418-380-2110, 888-222-6272
Bureau d'audiences publiques sur l'environnement, Édifice Lomer-Gouin, #2.10, 575, rue Saint-Amable, 2e étage, Québec, QC G1R 6A6
418-643-7447, Fax: 418-643-9474, 800-463-4732, communication@bape.gouv.qc.ca
Comité consultatif de l'environnement Kativik, CP 930, Kuujjuaq, QC J0M 1C0
819-964-2961, Fax: 819-964-0694, ndea@krg.ca
Conseil de la science et de la technologie, #3.45, 1200, rue de l'Église, Sainte-Foy, QC G1V 4Z2
418-644-1165, Fax: 418-646-0920, cst@cst.gouv.qc.ca
Fondation de la faune du Québec, Place Iberville II, #420, 1175, av Lavigerie, Québec, QC G1V 4P1
418-644-7926, Fax: 418-643-7655, 877-639-0742, ffq@riq.qc.ca
Fonds québécois de la recherche sur la nature et les technologies, #450, 140, Grande-Allée est, Québec, QC G1R 5M8
418-643-8560, Fax: 418-643-1451, info@fqrnt.gouv.qc.ca
Ottawa River Regulation Planning Board, 351 St Joseph Blvd., Gatineau, QC J8Y 3Z5
613-997-1735, 800-778-1246, secretariat@ottawariver.ca

Ministère des Ressources naturelles et de la Faune, #A303, 5700, 4e av ouest, Québec, G1H 6R1 QC
418-627-8600, Fax: 418-643-0720, 866-248-6936, service.citoyens@mrnf.gouv.qc.ca
Régie de l'énergie, Tour de la Bourse, #255, 800, Place Victoria, CP 1, Montréal, QC H4Z 1A2
514-873-2452, Fax: 514-873-2070, 888-873-2452, secretariat@regie-energie.qc.ca
Société de développement de la Baie James, 110, boul Matagami, CP 970, Matagami, QC J0Y 2A0
819-739-4717, Fax: 819-739-4329

Saskatchewan
Agri-Food Council, #302, 3085 Albert St., Regina, SK S4S 0B1
306-787-5139, Fax: 306-787-5134, james.kettel@gov.sk.ca
Agricultural Implements Board, #202, 3085 Albert St., Regina, SK S4S 0B1
306-787-4693, Fax: 306-787-1315
Saskatchewan Agriculture, Walter Scott Bldg., 3085 Albert St., Regina, S4S 0B1 SK
306-787-5140, 866-457-2377, aginfo@gov.sk.ca
Saskatchewan Enterprise & Innovation, #200, 3085 Albert St., Regina, S4S 0B1 SK
Fax: 306-798-0629, 800-265-2001, RECDWebmaster@gov.sk.ca
Saskatchewan Environment, 3211 Albert St., 2nd Fl., Regina, S4S 5W6 SK
306-953-3750, Fax: 306-787-9544, 800-567-4224, inquiry@serm.gov.sk.ca
Farm Stress Unit, #329, 3085 Albert St., Regina, SK S4S 0B1
306-787-5196, Fax: 306-798-3042, 800-667-4442, ken.imhoff@gov.sk.ca
Health Quality Council, 241, 111 Research Dr., Saskatoon, SK S7N 3R2
306-668-8810, Fax: 306-668-8820
Saskatchewan Northern Affairs, Mistasinihk Place, 1328 La Ronge Ave., PO Box 5000, La Ronge, S0J 1L0 SK
306-425-4207, Fax: 306-425-4349, 866-663-4065, admin@sna.gov.sk.ca
Prairie Agricultural Machinery Institute, Hwy#5 West, PO Box 1900, Humboldt, SK S0K 2A0
306-682-2555, Fax: 306-682-5080, 800-567-7264, humboldt@pami.ca
Saskatchewan Research Council, #125, 15 Innovation Blvd., Saskatoon, S7N 2X8 SK
306-933-5400, Fax: 306-933-7446, info@src.sk.ca
Saskatchewan Conservation Data Centre, 3211 Albert St., Regina, SK S4S 5W6
306-787-9038, Fax: 306-787-9544
Saskatchewan Crop Insurance Corporation, 484 Prince William Dr., PO Box 3000, Melville, SK S0A 2P0
306-728-7200, Fax: 306-728-7268, 888-935-0000, customer.service@scic.gov.sk.ca
Saskatchewan Lands Appeal Board, #202, 3085 Albert St., Regina, SK S4S 0B1
306-787-4693, Fax: 306-787-1315, dbrooks@agr.gov.sk.ca
Saskatchewan Watershed Authority, 111 Fairford St. East, Moose Jaw, SK S6H 7X9
306-694-3900, Fax: 306-694-3465, comm@swa.ca

Yukon Territory
Alsek Renewable Resource Council, PO Box 2077, Haines Junction, YT Y0B 1L0
867-634-2524, Fax: 867-634-2527
Carmacks Renewable Resource Council, PO Box 122, Carmacks, YT Y0B 1C0
867-863-6838, Fax: 867-863-6429, carmacksrrc@lscfn.ca
Dawson District Renewable Resource Council, PO Box 1380, Dawson City, YT Y0B 1G0
867-993-6976, Fax: 867-993-6093, dawsonrrc@yknet.yk.ca
Yukon Development Corporation, PO Box 2703 D-1,Whitehorse, Y1A 2C6 YT
867-393-5337, Fax: 867-393-5401
Yukon Environment, PO Box 2703, Whitehorse, Y1A 2C6 YT
867-667-5652, Fax: 867-393-6213, 800-661-0408, environmentyukon@gov.yk.ca
Mayo District Renewable Resources Council, PO Box 249, Mayo, YT Y0B 1M0
867-996-2942, Fax: 867-996-2948, mayorrc@yknet.yk.ca
North Yukon Renewable Resources Council, PO Box 80, Old Crow, YT Y0B 1N0
vgrrc@yknet.yk.ca
Selkirk Renewable Resources Council, PO Box 32, Pelly Crossing, YT Y0B 1P0
867-537-3937, Fax: 867-537-3939, selkirkrre@yknet.yk.ca

Teslin Renewable Resource Council, PO Box 186, Teslin, YT Y0A 1B0
867-390-2323, Fax: 867-390-2919, teslinrrc@yknet.yk.ca
Yukon Fish & Wildlife Management Board, 106 Main St., Whitehorse, YT Y1A 5P7
867-667-3754, Fax: 867-393-6947, yfwmbadmin@yknet.yk.ca
Yukon Land Use Planning Council, #201, 307 Jarvis St., Whitehorse, YT Y1A 2H3
867-667-7397, Fax: 867-667-4624, ylupc@planyukon.ca

SCIENCE & TECHNOLOGY
See Also: Business Development
Atmospheric Science & Technology, 2121, rte Transcanadienne, Dorval, H9P 1J3 QC
514-421-4771, Fax: 514-421-2106
Bedford Institute of Oceanography, 1 Challenger Dr., PO Box 1006, Dartmouth, B2Y 4A2 NS
902-426-3492, Fax: 902-426-8484
Biotechnology Research Institute, 6100, av Royalmount, Montréal, H4P 2R2 QC
514-496-6100, Fax: 514-496-1928, bri-info@cnrc-nrc.ca
Canada Centre for Remote Sensing - Geomatics Canada, 588 Booth St., Ottawa, K1A 0Y7 ON
613-947-1216, Fax: 613-947-1382
Canada Science & Technology Museum Corporation, PO Box 9724 T,Ottawa, K1G 5A3 ON
613-991-6090, Fax: 613-990-3636, info@technomuses.ca
Canadian Food Inspection Agency, 59 Camelot Dr., Ottawa, K1A 0Y9 ON
613-225-2342, Fax: 613-228-6629, 800-442-2342
Canadian Hydraulics Centre, M-32, 1200 Montreal Rd., Ottawa, K1A 0R6 ON
613-993-9381, Fax: 613-952-7679, info.chc@nrc-cnrc.gc.ca
Canadian Institutes of Health Research, 160 Elgin St., 9th Fl., Ottawa, K1A 0W9 ON
613-941-2672, Fax: 613-954-1800, info@cihr-irsc.gc.ca
Canadian Space Agency, 6767, rte de l'Aéroport, Longueuil, J3Y 8Y9 QC
450-926-4800, Fax: 450-926-4352, webmaster@space.gc.ca
CANMET Energy Technology Centre-Devon, 1 Oil Patch Dr., PO Box 1280, Devon, T0C 1E0 AB
780-987-8214, Fax: 780-987-8690
Chalk River Laboratories, Chalk River, K0J 1J0 ON
613-584-3311
Environmental Trade & Innovation, 5151 Terminal Rd., PO Box 697, Halifax, B3J 2T8 NS
Freshwater Institute, 501 University Cres., Winnipeg, R3T 2N6 MB
204-983-5000, Fax: 204-983-6285
Herzberg Institute of Astrophysics, 5071 West Saanich Rd., Victoria, V9E 2E7 BC
250-363-0001, Fax: 250-363-0045, hia-www@nrc-cnrc.gc.ca
Industrial Materials Institute, 75, boul de Montagne, Boucherville, J4B 6Y4 QC
450-641-5100, Fax: 450-641-5101, imi-info@nrc.ca
Institut Maurice-Lamontagne, 850, rte de le Mer, CP 1000, Mont-Joli, G5H 3Z4 QC
418-775-0555, Fax: 418-775-0730
Institute for Biological Sciences, Bldg. M-54, 1200 Montreal Rd., Ottawa, K1A 0R6 ON
613-993-5812, Fax: 613-957-7867
Institute for Chemical Process & Environmental Technology, Bldg. M-12, 1200 Montreal Rd., Ottawa, K1A 0R6 ON
613-993-4041, Fax: 613-957-8231
Institute for Marine Biosciences, 1411 Oxford St., Halifax, B3H 3Z1 NS
902-426-8332, Fax: 902-426-9413, communications.imb@nrc-cnrc.gc.ca
Institute for National Measurement Standards, Bldg. M-36, 1500 Montreal Rd., Ottawa, K1A 0R6 ON
613-998-7018, Fax: 613-952-1394, alexandra.shaw@nrc-cnrc.gc.ca
Institute for Ocean Technology, Kerwin Pl. & Arctic Ave., PO Box 12093, St. John's, A1B 3T5 NL
709-772-4939, Fax: 709-772-2462, noel.murphy@nrc.ca
Institute for Research in Construction, Bldg. M-24, 1500 Montreal Rd., Ottawa, K1A 0R6 ON
613-993-6189, Fax: 613-952-0268, ccmc@nrc-cnrc.gc.ca
Institute of Ocean Sciences, 9860 West Saanich Rd., PO Box 6000, Sidney, V8L 4B2 BC
250-363-6517, Fax: 250-363-6390
International Development Research Centre, 150 Kent St., PO Box 8500, Ottawa, K1P 0B2 ON
613-236-6163, Fax: 613-238-7230, info@idrc.ca

Laboratory Services Branch, 125 Resources Rd., Toronto, M9P 3V6 ON
416-235-5743, Fax: 416-235-5744
National Research Council Canada, Bldg. M-58, 1200 Montreal Rd., Ottawa, K1A 0R6 ON
613-993-9101, Fax: 613-952-7928, 877-672-2672, info@nrc-cnrc.ca
Natural Sciences & Engineering Research Council of Canada, Constitution Square, Tower II, 350 Albert St., Ottawa, K1A 1H5 ON
613-995-4273, Fax: 613-992-5337
Pacific Biological Station, 3190 Hammond Bay Rd., Nanaimo, V9T 6N7 BC
250-756-7000, Fax: 250-756-7053
Plant Biotechnology Institute, 110 Gymnasium Pl., Saskatoon, S7N 0W9 SK
306-975-5248, Fax: 306-975-4839, pbi-info@nrc-cnrc.gc.ca
Polar Continental Shelf Project, #487, 615 Booth St., Ottawa, K1A 0E4 ON
613-947-1650, Fax: 613-947-1611, pcsp@NRCan.gc.ca
Research Branch, 712 Yates St., Victoria, V8W 3E7 BC
Safe Environments Programme, Environmental Health Centre, Bldg. 8, 120 Parkdale Ave., Ottawa, K1A 0K9 ON
613-954-0291, Fax: 613-952-2206
Prime Minister's Advisory Council on Science & Technology, 235 Queen St., 9th Fl., Ottawa, K1A 0H5 ON
613-998-5646, Fax: 613-990-2007, acst-ccst@ic.gc.ca
Science Sector, 200 Kent St., Ottawa, K1A 0E6 ON
Soil, Plant & Feed Laboratory, Brookfield Rd., PO Box 8700, St. John's, A1B 4J6 NL
709-729-6738, Fax: 709-729-6734
Spectrum, Information Technologies & Telecommunications, Journal Tower North, 300 Slater St., 20th Fl., Ottawa, K1A 0C8 ON
St. Andrews Biological Station, 531 Brandy Cove Rd., St Andrews, E5B 2L9 NB
506-529-8854, Fax: 506-529-5862, XMARSABS@mar.dfo-mpo.gc.ca
Transportation Development Centre, Tour Ouest, Complexe Guy-Favreau, 800, boul René-Lévesque ouest, 6e étage, Montréal, H3B 1X9 QC
514-283-0000, Fax: 514-283-7158, tdccdt@tc.gc.ca

Alberta
Alberta Science & Research Authority, Phipps-McKinnon Bldg., #500, 10020 - 101A Ave., Edmonton, AB T5J 3G2
780-427-1488, Fax: 780-427-0979, asra@gov.ab.ca
Alberta Innovation & Science, 10365 - 97 St., 9th Fl., Edmonton, T5J 3W7 AB
780-427-0285, Fax: 780-415-9824, is.inq@gov.ab.ca
Alberta Research Council, 250 Karl Clark Rd., Edmonton, T6N 1E4 AB
780-450-5111, Fax: 780-450-5333

British Columbia
Powertech Labs Inc., 12388 - 88 Ave., Surrey, BC V8W 7R7
604-590-7500, Fax: 604-590-5347, info@powertechlans.com
Premier's Technology Council, #730, 999 Canada Pl., Vancouver, BC V6C 3E1
604-775-2122, Fax: 604-775-2129, premiers.technologycouncil@gov.bc.ca

Manitoba
Industrial Technology Centre, #200, 78 Innovation Dr., Winnipeg, MB R3T 6C2
Manitoba Education, Research & Learning Information Networks, #100 - 135 Innovation Dr., University of Manitoba, Winnipeg, MB R3T 6A8
204-474-7800, Fax: 204-474-7830, 800-430-6404
Manitoba Science, Technology, Energy & Mines, #333, 450 Broadway, Winnipeg, R3C 0V8 MB

New Brunswick
Business Development, Centennial Bldg., 670 King St., 5th Fl., PO Box 6000, Fredericton, E3B 5H1 NB
506-453-2111, Fax: 506-444-4182
New Brunswick Research & Productivity Council, 921 College Hill Rd., Fredericton, E3B 6Z9 NB
506-452-1212, Fax: 506-452-1395, info@rpc.ca
Sciences & Planning, Marysville Place, 20 McGloin St., 2nd Fl., PO Box 6000, Fredericton, E3B 5H1 NB
506-453-2862, Fax: 506-453-2265

Northwest Territories
Aurora Research Institute, 191 MacKenzie Rd., PO Box 1450, Inuvik, X0E 0T0 NT
867-777-3298, Fax: 867-777-4264, webmaster@nwtresearch.com

Nova Scotia
InNOVACorp, #1400, 1801 Hollis St., Halifax, NS B3J 3N4
902-424-8670, Fax: 902-424-4679, 800-565-7051, communications@innovacorp.ca

Ontario
Ontario Science Centre, 770 Don Mills Rd., Toronto, ON M3C 1T3
416-696-1000, Fax: 416-696-3124
Ministry of Research & Innovation, 56 Wellesley St. West, 7th Fl., Toronto, M7A 2E7 ON
416-325-5181, Fax: 416-325-3877
Science North, 100 Ramsey Lake Rd., Sudbury, ON P3E 5S9
705-522-3701, Fax: 705-522-4954, 800-461-4898

Prince Edward Island
Department of Environment, Energy & Forestry, Jones Bldg., 11 Kent St., 4th & 5th Fl., PO Box 2000, Charlottetown, C1A 7N8 PE
902-368-5000, Fax: 902-368-5830

Quebec
Centre de recherche industrielle du Québec, 333, rue Franquet, Sainte-Foy, QC G1P 4C7
418-659-1550, Fax: 418-652-2251, 800-667-2386, infocriq@criq.qc.ca
Conseil de la science et de la technologie, #3.45, 1200, rte de l'Église, Sainte-Foy, QC G1V 4Z2
418-644-1165, Fax: 418-646-0920, cst@cst.gouv.qc.ca
Fonds québécois de la recherche sur la nature et les technologies, #450, 140, Grande-Allée est, Québec, QC G1R 5M8
418-643-8560, Fax: 418-643-1451, info@fqrnt.gouv.qc.ca
Société Innovatech Québec, 10, rue Pierre Olivier Chauveau, Québec, QC G1R 4J3
418-528-9770, Fax: 418-528-9783, info@innovatechquebec.com

Saskatchewan
Saskatchewan Research Council, #125, 15 Innovation Blvd., Saskatoon, S7N 2X8 SK
306-933-5400, Fax: 306-933-7446, info@src.sk.ca

Yukon Territory
Yukon Energy, Mines & Resources, PO Box 2703, Whitehorse, Y1A 2C6 YT
867-667-5466, Fax: 867-667-8601, 800-661-0408, emr@gov.yk.ca

SECURITIES ADMINISTRATION
See Also: Finance

Nova Scotia
Nova Scotia Securities Commission, Joseph Howe Bldg., 1690 Hollis St., 2nd Fl., PO Box 458, Halifax, NS B3J 2P8
902-424-7768, Fax: 902-424-4625

SENIOR CITIZENS SERVICES
Office of the Commissioner of Review Tribunals, PO Box 8250 T, Ottawa, ON K1G 5S5
Fax: 613-941-3348, 800-363-0076, info@ocrt-bctr.gc.ca

British Columbia
Rural Development, 800 Johnson St., 6th Fl., PO Box 9824 Prov Govt, Victoria, V8W 9W4 BC
250-953-3005, Fax: 250-387-7935

Nova Scotia
Seniors' Secretariat, Dennis Bldg., 1740 Granville St., 4th Fl., PO Box 2065, Halifax, NS B3J 2Z1
902-424-0065, Fax: 902-424-0561, 800-670-0065, scs@gov.ns.ca

Nunavut
Department of Culture, Language, Elders & Youth, PO Box 1000 800, Iqaluit, X0A 0H0 NU
867-975-5500, Fax: 867-975-5504, 866-934-2035

Quebec
Ministère de la Santé et des Services sociaux, Direction des communications et Renseignements généraux, 1075, ch Sainte-Foy, Québec, G1S 2M1 QC
418-266-8900, 800-707-3380, regisseur.web@msss.gouv.qc.ca

Yukon Territory
Yukon Health & Social Services, PO Box 2703, Whitehorse, Y1A 2C6 YT
867-667-3673, Fax: 867-667-3096, 800-661-0408, hss@gov.yk.ca

SEXUALLY TRANSMITTED DISEASE CONTROL
See Also: AIDS

Prince Edward Island
Department of Health, Jones Bldg., 11 Kent St., 2nd Fl., PO Box 2000, Charlottetown, C1A 7N8 PE
902-368-4900, Fax: 902-368-4974

SOCIAL AFFAIRS

Ontario
Ontario Trillium Foundation, 45 Charles St. East, 5th Fl., Toronto, ON M4Y 1S2
416-963-4927, Fax: 416-963-8781, 800-263-2887, trillium@trilliumfoundation.org

SOCIAL SERVICES
See Also: Community Services
National Secretariat on Homelessness, 165, rue Hôtel-de-Ville, Gatineau, K1A 0J2 QC
Social Development, L'esplanade Laurier, Level 2, 300 Laurier Ave. West, Ottawa, K1A 0J6 ON
613-990-5100, Fax: 613-990-5091,

British Columbia
Ministry of Community Development, 800 Johnson St., 6th Fl., PO Box 9490 Prov Govt, Victoria, V8W 9N7 BC
250-387-2283, Fax: 250-387-4312, Feedback@gov.bc.ca

Northwest Territories
Department of Health & Social Services, Centre Square Tower, PO Box 1320, Yellowknife, X1A 2L9 NT
Fax: 867-873-0266

Nunavut
Department of Health & Social Services, Sivummut bldg., PO Box 1007 1000, Iqaluit, X0A 0H0 NU
867-975-5700, Fax: 867-975-5705, health@gov.nu.ca

Quebec
Ministère de la Santé et des Services sociaux, Direction des communications et Renseignements généraux, 1075, ch Sainte-Foy, Québec, G1S 2M1 QC
418-266-8900, 800-707-3380, regisseur.web@msss.gouv.qc.ca

SOIL RESOURCES
Prairie Farm Rehabilitation Administration, CIBC Tower, #408, 1800 Hamilton St., Regina, S4P 4L2 SK
306-780-5070, Fax: 306-780-5018
Soil, Plant & Feed Laboratory, Brookfield Rd., PO Box 8700, St. John's, A1B 4J6 NL
709-729-6738, Fax: 709-729-6734
Soils & Crops Research & Development Centre, 2560, boul Hochelaga, Québec, G1V 2J3 QC
418-657-7980, Fax: 418-648-2402

Quebec
Commission de protection du territoire agricole du Québec, 200, ch Ste-Foy, 2e étage, Québec, QC G1R 4X6
418-643-3314, Fax: 418-643-2261, 800-667-5294, info@cptaq.gouv.qc.ca

SOLICITORS GENERAL

British Columbia
Ministry of Public Safety & Solicitor General, PO Box 9282 Prov Govt, Victoria, V8W 9J7 BC
250-387-6121, 800-663-7867, pssgwebfeedback@gov.bc.ca

Ontario
Ministry of Community Safety & Correctional Services, George Drew Bldg., 25 Grosvenor St., 18th Fl., Toronto, M7A 1Y6 ON
416-326-5000, Fax: 416-325-6067, 866-517-0571, jus.g.sgcs.webmaster@jus.gov.on.ca

Quebec
Ministère de la Sécurité publique, Tour des Laurentides, 2525, boul Laurier, 5e étage, Québec, G1V 2L2 QC
Fax: 418-643-0275, 866-644-6826

SPACE & ASTRONOMY
Canada Science & Technology Museum Corporation, PO Box 9724 T, Ottawa, K1G 5A3 ON
613-991-6090, Fax: 613-990-3636, info@technomuses.ca
Canadian Space Agency, 6767, rte de l'Aéroport, Longueuil, J3Y 8Y9 QC
450-926-4800, Fax: 450-926-4252, webmaster@space.gc.ca

Herzberg Institute of Astrophysics, 5071 West Saanich Rd., Victoria, V9E 2E7 BC
250-363-0001, Fax: 250-363-0045, hia-www@nrc-cnrc.gc.ca
Institute for Aerospace Research, 1200 Montreal Rd., Ottawa, K1A 0R6 ON
613-991-5738, Fax: 613-952-7214

STANDARDS
Institute for National Measurement Standards, Bldg. M-36, 1500 Montreal Rd., Ottawa, K1A 0R6 ON
613-998-7018, Fax: 613-952-1394, alexandra.shaw@nrc-cnrc.gc.ca
Standards Council of Canada, #200, 270 Albert St., Ottawa, K1P 6N7 ON
613-238-3222, Fax: 613-569-7808, info@scc.ca

STATISTICS
See Also: Vital Statistics
Statistics Canada, R.H. Coats Bldg., Tunney's Pasture, 100 Tunney's Pasture Driveway, Ottawa, K1A 0T6 ON
Fax: 877-287-4369, 800-263-1136, infostats@statcan.ca

British Columbia
Client Services, 525 Superior St., 2nd Fl., PO Box 9472 Prov Govt, Victoria, V8W 9W6 BC
250-952-6861, Fax: 250-952-6803

Manitoba
Manitoba Bureau of Statistics, #824, 155 Carlton St., Winnipeg, R3C 3H9 MB
204-945-2406, Fax: 204-945-0695

Nunavut
Department of Executive & Intergovernmental Affairs, 1084 Aeroplex bldg., PO Box 1000 200, Iqaluit, X0A 0H0 NU
867-975-6000, Fax: 867-975-6090

Ontario
Registrar General Branch, 189 Red River Rd., PO Box 4600, Thunder Bay, P7B 6L8 ON
807-343-7414, Fax: 807-343-7411, 800-461-2156

Prince Edward Island
Department of Health, Jones Bldg., 11 Kent St., 2nd Fl., PO Box 2000, Charlottetown, C1A 7N8 PE
902-368-4900, Fax: 902-368-4974

STATISTICS (ENVIRONMENTAL)
Statistics Canada, R.H. Coats Bldg., Tunney's Pasture, 100 Tunney's Pasture Driveway, Ottawa, K1A 0T6 ON
Fax: 877-287-4369, 800-263-1136, infostats@statcan.ca

SUSTAINABLE DEVELOPMENT
Commissioner of the Environment & Sustainable Development, 240 Sparks St., Ottawa, K1A 0G6 ON
613-995-3708, Fax: 613-957-0474

Manitoba
Manitoba Round Table for Sustainable Development, #160, 123 Main St., Winnipeg, R3C 1A5 MB
204-945-1671, Fax: 204-948-2357, mrtsd@gov.mb.ca

Quebec
Ministère du Développement durable, de l'Environnement et des Parcs, Édifice Marie-Guyart, 675, boul René-Lévesque est, 29e étage, Québec, G1R 5V7 QC
418-521-3830, Fax: 418-646-5974, 800-561-1616, info@mddep.gouv.qc.ca

TAXATION
See Also: Sales Tax
Canada Revenue Agency, 875 Heron Rd., Ottawa, K1A 0L5 ON
613-952-0384, 800-267-6999
Indian Taxation Advisory Board, 90 Elgin St., 2nd Fl., Ottawa, ON K1A 0H4
613-954-9972, Fax: 613-954-2073

Nova Scotia
Tax Commission, Maritime Centre, 1505 Barrington St., Halifax, B3J 3K5 NS
902-424-5200, Fax: 902-424-0720, 800-670-4357

TELECOMMUNICATIONS
See Also: Broadcasting
Communications Research Centre Canada, 3701 Carling Ave., PO Box 11490 H, Ottawa, ON K2H 8S2
613-991-3313, Fax: 613-998-5355, info@crc.ca

Spectrum, Information Technologies & Telecommunications, Journal Tower North, 300 Slater St., 20th Fl., Ottawa, K1A 0C8 ON

Prince Edward Island
Department of Innovation & Advanced Learning, Shaw Bldg., 105 Rochford St., 5th Fl., PO Box 2000, Charlottetown, C1A 7N8 PE
902-368-4240, Fax: 902-368-4242

Quebec
Ministère de la Culture, des Communications & de la Condition féminine, 225, Grande Allée est, Québec, G1R 5G5 QC
Fax: 418-380-2364, 888-380-8882, infos@mcccf.gouv.qc.ca
Société de télédiffusion du Québec (Télé-Québec), 1000, rue Fullum, Montréal, H2K 3L7 QC
514-521-2424, Fax: 514-873-7739, 800-361-4301, info@telequebec.tv

TOURISM & TOURIST INFORMATION
Canadian Tourism Commission, #1400, 1055 Dunsmuir St., PO Box 49230, Vancouver, BC V7X 1L2
604-638-8300, Fax: 604-638-8425, ctc_feedback@businteractive.com
Parks Canada, 25 Eddy St., Gatineau, K1A 0M5 QC
888-773-8888, information@pc.gc.ca

British Columbia
British Columbia 2010 Olympic & Paralympic Games Secretariat, 3585 Graveley St., 7th Fl., Vancouver, BC V5K 5J5
604-660-2010, Fax: 604-660-3437, 877-604-2010, bcsecretariat@gov.bc.ca
Ministry of Healthy Living & Sport, PO Box 9067 Prov Govt,Victoria, V8W 9E2 BC
250-387-3504, Fax: 250-387-3420, Feedback@gov.bc.ca

Manitoba
Tourism Secretariat & Travel Manitoba, 155 Carlton St., 7th Fl., Winnipeg, R3C 3H8 MB
800-665-0040

New Brunswick
Department of Tourism & Parks, Centennial Bldg., 670 King St., Fredericton, E3B 1G1 NB
506-444-5205, Fax: 506-457-4984, taponlinedirectory@gnb.ca

Newfoundland & Labrador
Department of Tourism, Culture & Recreation, Confederation Bldg., West Block, 2nd Fl., PO Box 8700, St. John's, A1B 4J6 NL
709-729-0862, Fax: 709-729-0870, tcrinfo@gov.nl.ca

Northwest Territories
Department of Industry, Tourism & Investment, PO Box 1320, Yellowknife, X1A 2L9 NT
Fax: 867-873-0306, info@iti.ca

Ontario
Ministry of Tourism, Hearst Block, 900 Bay St., 9th Fl., Toronto, M7A 2E1 ON
416-326-9326, Fax: 416-314-7854, 800-668-2746

Prince Edward Island
Department of Tourism, PO Box 2000, Charlottetown, C1A 7N8 PE
800-463-4734

Quebec
Société des établissements en plein air du Québec, Place de la Cité, #250, 2640, boul Laurier, Sainte-Foy, QC G1V 5C2
418-890-6527, Fax: 418-528-6025, 800-665-6527, inforeservation@sepaq.com
Ministère du Tourisme, Direction des Communications, 900, boul René-Lévesque est, Québec, G1R 2B5 QC
418-643-5959, Fax: 418-646-8723, 800-482-2433

Saskatchewan
Tourism Saskatchewan, 1922 Park St., Regina, SK S4N 7M4
306-787-9600, 877-237-2273

Yukon Territory
Yukon Tourism & Culture, PO Box 2703, Whitehorse, Y1A 2C6 YT
867-667-5036, Fax: 867-667-3546

TRADE
See Also: Business Development; Imports

Business Development Bank of Canada, #400, 5, Place Ville-Marie, Montréal, H3B 5E7 QC
514-283-5904, Fax: 514-283-2872, 877-232-2269
Canadian Commercial Corporation, 50 O'Connor St., 11th Fl., Ottawa, K1A 0S6 ON
613-996-0034, Fax: 613-995-2121, 800-748-8191
Commission for Environmental Cooperation, Secretariat, #200, 393, rue St-Jacques ouest, Montréal, H2Y 1N9 QC
514-350-4300, Fax: 514-350-4314, info@cec.org
Export Development Canada, 151 O'Connor St., Ottawa, K1A 1K3 ON
613-598-2500, Fax: 613-598-3811, 888-332-3320
Global Operations & Chief Trade Commissioner, 125 Sussex Dr., Ottawa, K1A 0G2 ON
613-944-2697, Fax: 613-996-1667
Inter-American Development Bank, 1300 New York Ave. NW, Washington,DC
202-623-1000, Fax: 202-623-3096
International Trade Canada, 125 Sussex Dr., Ottawa, K1A 0G2 ON
613-995-2901, Fax: 613-996-8924
Northstar Trade Finance Inc., #833, 595 Burrard St., PO Box 49058, Vancouver, V7X 1C4 BC
604-664-5828, Fax: 604-664-5838, 800-663-9288, vancouver@northstar.ca
The World Bank Group, 1818 H St. NW, Washington,DC
202-473-1000, Fax: 202-477-6391

Alberta
International Offices & Trade, Commerce Place, 10155 - 102 St., 4th Fl., Edmonton, T5J 4L6 AB
780-427-3325, Fax: 780-427-0392

British Columbia
Asia Pacific Trade Council, #730, 999 Canada Pl., Vancouver, BC V6C 3E1
604-775-2100, Fax: 604-775-2070
Economic Competitiveness Division, 1810 Blanshard St., 7th Fl., PO Box 9327 Prov Govt,Victoria, V8W 9N3 BC
250-952-0367, Fax: 250-952-0137
Technology, Research & Innovation Division, #730, 999 Canada Place, Vancouver, V6C 3E1 BC
Fax: 604-775-2070

Manitoba
Manitoba Competitiveness, Training & Trade, International Business Centre, The Paris Building, 259 Portage Ave., Winnipeg, R3B 3P4 MB
204-945-2475, Fax: 204-945-3977, minctt@leg.gov.mb.ca

New Brunswick
Department of Business New Brunswick, Centennial Bldg., 670 King St., PO Box 6000, Fredericton, E3B 5H1 NB
506-444-5228, Fax: 506-453-5428

Newfoundland & Labrador
Department of Innovation, Trade & Rural Development, West Block, Confederation Bldg., PO Box 8700, St. John's, A1B 4J6 NL
709-729-7000, Fax: 709-729-0654, 800-563-2299, itrd@gov.nl.ca

Nova Scotia
Department of Economic & Rural Development, Centennial Building, #600, 1660 Hollis St., PO Box 2311, Halifax, B3J 1V7 NS
902-424-0377, Fax: 902-424-7008, comm@gov.ns.ca

Ontario
Investment & Trade Division, Hearst Block, 900 Bay St., 5th fl., Toronto, M7A 2E1 ON
416-325-9802, Fax: 416-325-5617

Prince Edward Island
Department of Innovation & Advanced Learning, Shaw Bldg., 105 Rochford St., 5th Fl., PO Box 2000, Charlottetown, C1A 7N8 PE
902-368-4240, Fax: 902-368-4242

Quebec
Ministère du Développement économique, de l'Innovation et de l'Exportation, 710, place D'Youville, 3e étage, Québec, G1R 4Y4 QC
418-691-5950, Fax: 418-644-0118, 866-680-1884

Saskatchewan
Saskatchewan Trade & Export Partnership, #320, 1801 Hamilton St., PO Box 1787, Regina, SK S4P 3C6
306-787-9210, Fax: 306-787-6666, 877-313-7244, inquire@sasktrade.sk.ca

Trade & International Relations, #800, 1919 Saskatchewan Dr., Regina, S4P 4H2 SK
306-787-6445, Fax: 306-787-7317

Yukon Territory
Yukon Economic Development, PO Box 2703, Whitehorse, Y1A 2C6 YT
867-393-7191, Fax: 867-395-7199, 800-661-0408

TRADE - MEXICAN
Canadian Chamber of Commerce in Mexico, Zaragoza 1300 ur, Edificio Kalos, Piso A2, Oficina 201,, Monterrey,NL
info@cancham.org.mx
Embassy of Mexico in Canada, #1000, 45 O'Connor St., Ottawa, K1P 1A4 ON
613-233-8988, Fax: 613-235-9123, info@embamexcan.com
NAFTA Office of Mexico in Canada, #1030, 45 O'Connor St., Ottawa, K1P 1A4 ON
613-235-7782, Fax: 613-235-1129, info@nafta-mexico.org
North American Development Bank, #300, 203 St. Mary's, San Antonio,TX
210-231-8000, Fax: 210-231-6232

TRADE - UNITED STATES
American National Standards Institute, 25 West 43rd St., New York,NY
212-642-4900, Fax: 212-398-0023
Environmental Protection Agency: Office of Acquisition Management, 1200 Pennsylvania Ave. NW, Washington,DC
202-564-4310, oam-web@epa.gov
General Services Administration, 1800 F St. NW, Washington,DC
202-501-0112, 877-495-4849, vendor.support@gsa.gov
Government Printing Office, 732 North Capitol St., Washington,DC
202-512-0526, Fax: 202-512-1782, gpoaccess@gpo.gov
National Electronic Procurement Assistance Center, #304, 55 Maple Ave., Rockville Center,NY
516-255-0500, Fax: 516-255-0509, 800-932-7761, online@cbdweb.com
National Technical Information Service, c/o Department of Commerce, 5285 Port Royal Rd., Springfield,VA
703-605-6000, Fax: 703-321-8547, info@ntis.gov
North American Development Bank, #300, 203 St. Mary's, San Antonio,TX
210-231-8000, Fax: 210-231-6232
United States Embassy in Canada, 490 Sussex Dr., Ottawa, K1N 1G8 ON
613-238-5335, Fax: 613-688-3082, ottawareference@state.gov
US Commercial Service in Canada, c/o Department of Commerce, 14th & Constitution Ave. NW, Washington,DC
202-482-5777, Fax: 202-482-5013

TRAINING, ENVIRONMENTAL
Alberta
Apprenticeship & Industry Training Division, Phipps-McKinnon Bldg., 5th Fl., 10020 - 101A Ave., Edmonton, T5J 3G2 AB
780-427-8517

TRANSPORTATION
Ontario
Aviation & Forest Fire Management Branch, #400, 70 Foster Dr., Sault Ste Marie, P6A 6V5 ON
Canadian Air Transport Security Authority, 99 Bank St., 13th Fl., Ottawa, ON K1P 6B9
Fax: 613-991-6726, 888-294-2202
Canadian Coast Guard, Centennial Towers, #6S018, 200 Kent St., Ottawa, K1A 0E6 ON
613-998-1573, Fax: 613-990-2780
Canadian Transportation Agency, Les Terrasses de la Chaudière, 15, rue Eddy, Gatineau, K1A 0N9 QC
819-997-0344, Fax: 819-997-6727, 888-222-2592, info@otc-cta.gc.ca
Centre for Surface Transportation Technology, 2320 Lester Rd., Ottawa, K1V 1S2 ON
613-998-9639, Fax: 613-957-0831, inquiries.cstt@nrc-cnrc.gc.ca
Federal Bridge Corporation Limited, #1210, 55 Metcalfe St., Ottawa, ON K1P 6L5
613-993-6880, Fax: 613-993-6945, info@federalbridge.ca
Institute for Aerospace Research, 1200 Montreal Rd., Ottawa, K1A 0R6 ON
613-991-5738, Fax: 613-952-7214

Government Quick Reference Guide / Transportation of Dangerous Goods

Transport Canada, Place de Ville, 330 Sparks St., Tower C, Ottawa, K1A 0N5 ON
613-990-2309, Fax: 613-954-4731, minTC@tc.gc.ca
Transportation Appeal Tribunal of Canada, 333 Laurier Ave. West, 12th Fl., Ottawa, ON K1A 0N5
613-990-6906, Fax: 613-990-9153, info@tatc.gc.ca
Transportation Development Centre, Tour Ouest, Complexe Guy-Favreau, 800, boul René-Lévesque ouest, 6e étage, Montréal, H3B 1X9 QC
514-283-0000, Fax: 514-283-7158, tdccdt@tc.gc.ca
Transportation Safety Board of Canada, 200 Promenade du Portage, 4th Fl., Ottawa, K1A 1K8 ON
819-994-3741, Fax: 819-997-2239, 800-387-3557

Alberta
Alberta Infrastructure & Transportation, Twin Atria Bldg., 4999 - 98 Ave., Edmonton, T6B 2X3 AB
780-427-2731, Fax: 780-466-3166,-310-0000,
Transportation Safety Board, Twin Atria Bldg., 4999 - 98 Ave., Edmonton, AB T6B 2X3
780-427-7178, Fax: 780-422-9739

British Columbia
British Columbia Transit, 520 Gorge Rd. East, PO Box 610, Victoria, BC V8W 2P3
250-385-2551, Fax: 250-995-5639
Passenger Transportation Board, #202, 940 Blanshard St., PO Box 9850 Prov Govt, Victoria, BC V8W 9T5
250-953-3777, Fax: 250-953-3788, ptboard@gov.bc.ca
Ministry of Transportation & Infrastructure, 940 Blanshard St., PO Box 9850 Prov Govt,Victoria, V8W 9T5 BC
250-387-3198, Fax: 250-356-7706, tran.webmaster@gov.bc.ca
Transportation Planning & Policy Department, #5C, 940 Blanshard St., PO Box 9850 Prov Govt,Victoria, V8W 9T5 BC
250-387-5062, Fax: 250-387-6431

Manitoba
Highway Traffic Board/Motor Transport Board, #200, 301 Weston St., Winnipeg, MB R3E 3H4
204-945-8912, Fax: 204-783-6529
Manitoba Infrastructure & Transportation, Legislative Building, #203, 450 Broadway Ave., Winnipeg, R3C 0V8 MB
204-945-3723, Fax: 204-945-7610
License Suspension Appeal Board/Medical Review Committee, #200, 301 Weston St., Winnipeg, MB R3E 3H4
204-945-7350, Fax: 204-948-2682
Taxicab Board, #200, 301 Weston St., Winnipeg, MB R3E 3H4
Fax: 204-948-2315

New Brunswick
New Brunswick Transportation Authority, Kings Place, 440 King St., PO Box 6000, Fredericton, NB E3B 5H1
506-453-3939, Fax: 506-453-2900
Department of Transportation, Kings Pl., 440 KingSt., PO Box 6000, Fredericton, E3B 5H8 NB
506-453-3939, Fax: 506-453-2900, Transportation.Web@gnb.ca

Newfoundland & Labrador
Department of Transportation & Works, Confederation Bldg., West Block, 6th Fl., PO Box 8700, St. John's, A1B 4J6 NL
709-729-3679, Fax: 709-729-4285, twminister@gov.nl.ca

Northwest Territories
Highways, 4510 - 50 Ave., 2nd fl., PO Box 1320, Yellowknife, X1A 2L9 NT
867-920-8771, Fax: 867-873-0288
Department of Transportation, Lahm Ridge Bldg., 4501 50 Ave., PO Box 1320, Yellowknife, X1A 2L9 NT
867-920-3460, Fax: 867-873-0363

Nova Scotia
Department of Transportation & Infrastructure Renewal, Johnston Bldg., 1672 Granville St., 2nd Fl., PO Box 186, Halifax, B3J 2N2 NS
902-424-2297, Fax: 902-424-0171, 888-432-3233, tpwpaff@gov.ns.ca

Nunavut
Department of Community & Government Services, J.G. Brown Bldg., PO Box 1000 700,Iqaluit, X0A 0H0 NU
867-975-5400, Fax: 867-975-5305
Department of Economic Development & Transportation, #1104 Inuksugait Plaza, PO Box 1000 1500,Iqaluit, X0A 0H0 NU
867-975-7800, Fax: 867-975-7870, 888-975-5999, edt@gov.nu.ca

Ontario
GO Transit, #600, 20 Bay St., Toronto, ON M5J 2W3
416-869-3600, Fax: 416-869-1755, 888-438-6646
Licence Appeal Tribunal (LAT), 1 St. Clair Ave. West, 12th Fl., Toronto, ON M4V 1K6
416-314-4260, Fax: 416-314-4270, 800-255-2214
Ontario Highway Transport Board, 151 Bloor St. West, 10th Fl., Toronto, ON M5S 2T5
416-326-6732, Fax: 416-326-6738, ohtb@mto.gov.on.ca
Owen Sound Transportation Company Ltd., RR#5, Hwy 6 & 21, Owen Sound, ON N4K 5N7
519-376-8740
Road User Safety Division, #191, Bldg A, 1201 Wilson Ave., Toronto, M3M 1J8 ON
416-235-2999, Fax: 416-235-4153
Ministry of Transportation, Ferguson Block, 77 Wellesley St. West, 3rd Fl., Toronto, M7A 1Z8 ON
416-235-4686, Fax: 416-327-9185, 800-268-4686

Prince Edward Island
Department of Transportation & Public Works, Jones Bldg., 11 Kent St., PO Box 2000, Charlottetown, C1A 7N8 PE
902-368-5100, Fax: 902-368-5395

Quebec
Abitibi-Témiscamingue-Nord-du-Québec, 80, av Québec, Rouyn-Noranda, J9X 6R1 QC
819-763-3271, Fax: 819-763-3493, datnq@mtq.gouv.qc.ca
Bas-Saint-Laurent-Gaspésie-Iles-de-la-Madeleine, #101, 92, 2e rue ouest, Rimouski, G5L 8E6 QC
418-727-3674, Fax: 418-727-3673, dtbgi@mtq.gouv.qc.ca
Capitale-Nationale, 475, boul de l'Atrium, 2e étage, Québec, G1H 7H9 QC
418-643-1911, Fax: 418-646-0003, dcnat@mtq.gouv.qc.ca
Chaudière-Appalaches, 1156, boul de la Rive-Sud, Saint-Romuald, G6W 5M6 QC
418-839-5581, Fax: 418-834-7338, dtca@mtq.gouv.qc.ca
Commission des transports du Québec, 200, ch Sainte-Foy, 7e étage, Québec, QC G1R 5V5
Fax: 418-644-8034, 888-461-2433, courrier@ctq.gouv.qc.ca
Côte-Nord, #110, 625, boul Laflèche, Baie-Comeau, G5C 1C5 QC
418-295-4765, Fax: 418-295-4766, dtcn@mtq.gouv.qc.ca
Est-de-la-Montérégie, 201, place Charles-Lemoyne, 5e étage, Longueuil, J4K 2T5 QC
450-677-3413, Fax: 450-442-1317, dtem@mtq.gouv.qc.ca
Estrie, #2.02, 200, rue Belvédère nord, Sherbrooke, J1H 4A9 QC
819-820-3280, Fax: 819-820-3118, dte@mtq.gouv.qc.ca
Ile-de-Montréal, 440, boul René-Lévesque ouest, 10e étage, Montréal, H2Z 2A6 QC
514-873-7781, Fax: 514-864-3867, dtim@mtq.gouv.qc.ca
Laurentides-Lanaudière, 222, rue Saint-Georges, 2e étage, Saint-Jérôme, J7Z 4Z9 QC
450-569-3057, Fax: 450-569-3072, dll@mtq.gouv.qc.ca
Laval-Mille-Iles, 1725, boul Le Corbusier, Laval, H7S 2K7 QC
450-680-6330, Fax: 450-973-4959, dtlmi@mtq.gouv.qc.ca
Mauricie-Centre-du-Québec, 100, rue Laviolette, 4e étage, Trois-Rivières, G9A 5S9 QC
819-371-6896, Fax: 819-371-6136, dmcq@mtq.gouv.qc.ca
Ouest-de-la-Montérégie, #200, 180, boulevard d'Anjou, Châteauguay, J6K 1C4 QC
450-698-3400, Fax: 450-698-3452, dtom@mtq.gouv.qc.ca
Outaouais, #5.110, 170, rue de l'Hôtel-de-Ville, Gatineau, J8X 4C2 QC
819-772-3849, Fax: 819-772-3338, dto@mtq.gouv.qc.ca
Saguenay-Lac-Saint-Jean-Chibougamau, 3950, boul Harvey, Jonquière, G7X 8L6 QC
418-695-7916, Fax: 418-695-7926, dt.slsjc@mtq.gouv.qc.ca
Société de l'assurance automobile du Québec, 333, boul Jean-Lesage, CP 19600 Terminus, Québec, QC G1K 8J6
418-643-7620, Fax: 418-644-0339, 800-361-7620, courrier@saaq.gouv.qc.ca
Société des traversiers du Québec, 250, rue Saint-Paul, Québec, QC G1K 9K9
418-643-2019, Fax: 418-643-7308, stq@traversiers.gouv.qc.ca
Société du port ferroviaire Baie-Comeau-Hauterive, 18, rte Maritime, Baie-Comeau, QC G4Z 2L6
418-296-6785, Fax: 418-296-2377, soport@globetrotter.qc.ca
Ministère des Transports, 700, boul René-Lévesque est, 27e étage, Québec, G1R 5H1 QC
Fax: 514-643-1269, 888-355-0511, communications@mtq.gouv.qc.ca

Saskatchewan
Saskatchewan Highways & Infrastructure, 1855 Victoria Ave., Regina, S4P 3T2 SK
306-787-4800
Saskatchewan Highway Traffic Board, 1550 Saskatchewan Dr., Regina, SK S4P 0E4
306-775-6674

Yukon Territory
Yukon Community Services, PO Box 2703, Whitehorse, Y1A 2C6 YT
867-667-5811, Fax: 867-393-6295, 800-661-0408, inquiry@gov.yk.ca
Driver Control Board, 308 Steele St., PO Box 2703, Whitehorse, YT Y1A 2C6
867-667-3774, Fax: 867-393-6483, dcb@gov.yk.ca
Yukon Highways & Public Works, PO Box 2703, Whitehorse, Y1A 2C6 YT
867-393-7193, Fax: 867-393-6218, 800-661-0408, hpw-info@gov.yk.ca
Yukon Motor Transport Board, PO Box 2703, Whitehorse, YT Y1A 2C6
867-667-5782, Fax: 867-393-6408, Laurie.Hrynuik@gov.yk.ca

TRANSPORTATION OF DANGEROUS GOODS

Alberta
Dangerous Goods Control & Rail Safety, Twin Atria Bldg., 4999 - 98 Ave., Edmonton, T6B 2X3 AB
780-422-9600, Fax: 780-427-1044, 800-272-9600

Nova Scotia
Department of Transportation & Infrastructure Renewal, Johnston Bldg., 1672 Granville St., 2nd Fl., PO Box 186, Halifax, B3J 2N2 NS
902-424-2297, Fax: 902-424-0171, 888-432-3233, tpwpaff@gov.ns.ca

Ontario
Road User Safety Division, #191, Bldg A, 1201 Wilson Ave., Toronto, M3M 1J8 ON
416-235-2999, Fax: 416-235-4153

Prince Edward Island
Department of Transportation & Public Works, Jones Bldg., 11 Kent St., PO Box 2000, Charlottetown, C1A 7N8 PE
902-368-5100, Fax: 902-368-5395

Saskatchewan
Saskatchewan Highways & Infrastructure, 1855 Victoria Ave., Regina, S4P 3T2 SK
306-787-4800

TRAPPING & FUR INDUSTRY

Ontario
Ontario Moose & Bear Allocation Advisory Committee, PO Box 964, Sioux Lookout, ON P8T 1B3
807-737-2615, Fax: 807-737-4173

Quebec
Comité conjoint de chasse, de pêche et de piégeage, #C220, 383 rue Saint-Jacques, Montréal, QC H2Y 1N9
514-284-2151, Fax: 514-284-0039, hftcc@bellnet.ca

Saskatchewan
Saskatchewan Environment, 3211 Albert St., 2nd Fl., Regina, S4S 5W6 SK
306-953-3750, Fax: 306-787-9544, 800-567-4224, inquiry@serm.gov.sk.ca

TREASURY SERVICES
See Also: Finance
Treasury Board of Canada, 300 Laurier Ave. West, 10th Fl., Ottawa, K1A 0R5 ON
613-957-2400, Fax: 613-941-4000, 877-636-0656, info@tbs-sct.gc.ca

Prince Edward Island
Department of the Provincial Treasury, Shaw Bldg., 95 Rochford St., 2nd Fl. South, PO Box 2000, Charlottetown, C1A 7N8 PE
902-368-4050, Fax: 902-368-6575

URBAN RENEWAL & DESIGN
See Also: Municipal Affairs

Alberta
Local Government Services, Commerce Place, 10155 - 102 St., 17th Fl., Edmonton, T5J 4L4 AB
Fax: 780-427-0453

Northwest Territories
Department of Municipal & Community Affairs, PO Box 1320, Yellowknife, X1A 2L9 NT
867-873-7118, Fax: 867-873-0309

Ontario
Ministry of Municipal Affairs & Housing, 777 Bay St., 17th Fl., Toronto, M5G 2E5 ON
416-585-7041, Fax: 416-585-6227, 866-220-2290, mininfo.mah@ontario.ca

Prince Edward Island
Community & Labour Development, Shaw Bldg., 105 Rochford St., 5th Fl., PO Box 2000, Charlottetown, C1A 7N8 PE
902-368-4244, Fax: 902-368-4242

Quebec
Société d'habitation du Québec, Aile St-Amable, 1054, rue Louis-Alexandre-Taschereau, 3e étage, Québec, QC G1R 5E7
Fax: 418-643-5560, 800-463-4315

VITAL STATISTICS

British Columbia
Vital Statistics, 818 Fort St., Victoria, V8W 1H8 BC
250-952-2681, Fax: 250-952-2587

Northwest Territories
Vital Statistics, Bag #9, Inuvik, X0E 0T0 NT
867-777-7400, Fax: 867-777-3197, 800-661-0830, hsa@gov.nt.ca

Nova Scotia
Vital Statistics, Joseph Howe Bldg., 1690 Hollis St., Ground Floor, PO Box 157, Halifax, B3J 2M9 NS
902-424-4071, Fax: 902-424-0678, 877-848-2578, vstat@gov.ns.ca

Ontario
Registrar General Branch, 189 Red River Rd., PO Box 4600, Thunder Bay, P7B 6L8 ON
807-343-7414, Fax: 807-343-7411, 800-461-2156

Prince Edward Island
Department of Health, Jones Bldg., 11 Kent St., 2nd Fl., PO Box 2000, Charlottetown, C1A 7N8 PE
902-368-4900, Fax: 902-368-4974

WASTE & GARBAGE

Low-Level Radioactive Waste Management Office, #200, 1900 City Park Dr., Ottawa, K1J 1A3 ON
613-998-9442, Fax: 613-952-0760

Newfoundland & Labrador
Department of Government Services, PO Box 8700, St. John's, A1B 4J6 NL
709-729-4860
Department of Municipal Affairs, West Block, Main Fl., Confederation Bldg., PO Box 8700, St. John's, A1B 4J6 NL
709-729-3053,

Ontario
Ministry of Environment, 135 St. Clair Ave. West, Toronto, M4V 1P5 ON
416-325-4000, Fax: 416-325-3159, 800-565-4923

Quebec
Bureau d'audiences publiques sur l'environnement, Édifice Lomer-Gouin, #2.10, 575, rue Saint-Amable, 2e étage, Québec, QC G1R 6A6
418-643-7447, Fax: 418-643-9474, 800-463-4732, communication@bape.gouv.qc.ca
Société québécoise de récupération et de recyclage, Siège social, #200, 420, boul Charest est, Québec, QC G1K 8M4
418-643-0394, Fax: 418-643-6507, 866-523-8290, info@recyc-quebec.gouv.qc.ca

WASTE MANAGEMENT

See Also: Dangerous Goods & Hazardous Materials

British Columbia
Environmental Quality, 2978 Jutland Rd., 3rd Fl., Victoria, V8T 5J9 BC
250-387-9933, Fax: 250-356-7197

Alberta
Alberta Recycling Management Authority, PO Box 189, Edmonton, AB T5J 2J1
780-990-1111, Fax: 780-990-1122, 888-999-8762, info@albertarecycling.ca
Alberta Used Oil Management Association, Scotia One, Scotia Place, #1050, 10060 Jasper Ave., Edmonton, AB T5J 3R8
780-414-1510, Fax: 780-414-1519, reception@usedoilrecycling.ca
Beverage Container Management Board, #1010, 10707 - 100 Ave., Edmonton, AB T5J 3M1
780-424-3193, Fax: 780-428-4620, 888-424-7671, info@bcmb.ab.ca
Alberta Environment, South Tower, Petroleum Plaza, 9915 - 108 St., Main Fl., Edmonton, T5K 2G8 AB
780-427-2700, Fax: 780-422-4086,-310-0000, env.infocent@gov.ab.ca

New Brunswick
Department of Local Government, Marysville Place, 20 McGloin St., PO Box 6000, Fredericton, E3B 5H1 NB
506-453-2807, Fax: 506-453-3988

Newfoundland & Labrador
Multi-Materials Stewardship Board, PO Box 8131 A, St. John's, NL A1B 3M9
709-753-0948, Fax: 709-753-0974

Northwest Territories
Department of Municipal & Community Affairs, PO Box 1320, Yellowknife, X1A 2L9 NT
867-873-7118, Fax: 867-873-0309

Prince Edward Island
Island Waste Management Corporation, 110 Watts Ave., Charlottetown, PE C1E 2C1
902-894-0330, Fax: 902-894-0331, 888-280-8111, reception@iwmc.pe.ca; info@iwmc.pe.ca

Quebec
Société québécoise de récupération et de recyclage, Siège social, #200, 420, boul Charest est, Québec, QC G1K 8M4
418-643-0394, Fax: 418-643-6507, 866-523-8290, info@recyc-quebec.gouv.qc.ca

Saskatchewan
Saskatchewan Environment, 3211 Albert St., 2nd Fl., Regina, S4S 5W6 SK
306-953-3750, Fax: 306-787-9544, 800-567-4224, inquiry@serm.gov.sk.ca

Yukon Territory
Yukon Environment, PO Box 2703, Whitehorse, Y1A 2C6 YT
867-667-5652, Fax: 867-393-6213, 800-661-0408, environmentyukon@gov.yk.ca

WATER & WASTEWATER

Bedford Institute of Oceanography, 1 Challenger Dr., PO Box 1006, Dartmouth, B2Y 4A2 NS
902-426-3492, Fax: 902-426-8484
Canadian Hydraulics Centre, M-32, 1200 Montreal Rd., Ottawa, K1A 0R6 ON
613-993-9381, Fax: 613-952-7679, info.chc@nrc-cnrc.gc.ca
Canadian Hydrographic Service, 615 Booth St., Ottawa, K1A 0E6 ON
613-998-4931, Fax: 613-998-1217, chsinfo@dfo-mpo.gc.ca
Environment Canada, 10 Wellington St., Gatineau, K1A 0H3 QC
819-997-2800, Fax: 819-994-1412, 800-668-6767, enviroinfo@ec.gc.ca
Fisheries & Oceans Canada, 200 Kent St., Ottawa, K1A 0E6 ON
613-993-0999, Fax: 613-996-1866, info@dfo-mpo.gc.ca
Freshwater Institute, 501 University Cres., Winnipeg, R3T 2N6 MB
204-983-5000, Fax: 204-983-6285
Institut Maurice-Lamontagne, 850, rte de le Mer, CP 1000, Mont-Joli, G5H 3Z4 QC
418-775-0555, Fax: 418-775-0730
Institute for Marine Biosciences, 1411 Oxford St., Halifax, B3H 3Z1 NS
902-426-8332, Fax: 902-426-9413, communications.imb@nrc-cnrc.gc.ca
Institute for Ocean Technology, Kerwin Pl. & Arctic Ave., PO Box 12093, St. John's, A1B 3T5 NL
709-772-4939, Fax: 709-772-2462, noel.murphy@nrc.ca
Institute of Ocean Sciences, 9860 West Saanich Rd., PO Box 6000, Sidney, V8L 4B2 BC
250-363-6517, Fax: 250-363-6390
Nunavut Water Board, PO Box 119, Gjoa Haven, NU X0B 1J0
867-360-6338, Fax: 867-360-6369

Alberta
Alberta Environment, South Tower, Petroleum Plaza, 9915 - 108 St., Main Fl., Edmonton, T5K 2G8 AB
780-427-2700, Fax: 780-422-4086,-310-0000, env.infocent@gov.ab.ca
Irrigation Council, Provincial Bldg., 200 - 5 Ave. South, 3rd Fl., PO Bag 3014, Lethbridge, AB T1J 4L1
403-381-5176, Fax: 403-382-4406

British Columbia
Ministry of Environment, PO Box 9339 Prov Govt,Victoria, V8W 9M1 BC
250-387-1161, Fax: 250-387-5669, www.envmail@gov.bc.ca
British Columbia Utilities Commission, 900 Howe St., 6th Fl., PO Box 250, Vancouver, V6Z 2N3 BC
604-660-4700, Fax: 604-660-1102, 800-663-1385, commission.secretary@bcuc.com

Manitoba
Manitoba Conservation, 200 Saulteaux Cres., Winnipeg, R3J 3W3 MB
204-945-6784, 800-214-6497, mincon@leg.gov.mb.ca
Manitoba Water Services Board, PO Box 22080, Brandon, MB R7A 6Y9
204-726-6076, Fax: 204-726-6290

New Brunswick
Department of the Environment, Marysville Place, 20 McGloin St., PO Box 6000, Fredericton, E3B 5H1 NB
506-453-2690, Fax: 506-457-4991
Department of Natural Resources, PO Box 6000, Fredericton, E3B 5H1 NB
506-453-2510, Fax: 506-444-5839, dnrweb@gnb.ca

Newfoundland & Labrador
Department of Environment & Conservation, Confederation Bldg., West Block, 4th Fl., PO Box 8700, St. John's, A1B 4J6 NL
709-729-2664, Fax: 709-729-6639, 800-563-6181, info@gov.nl.ca
Newfoundland & Labrador Board of Commissioners of Public Utilities, PO Box 21040, St. John's, A1A 5B2 NL
709-726-8600, Fax: 709-726-9604, 866-782-0006, ito@pub.nf.ca

Northwest Territories
Department of Environment & Natural Resources, PO Box 1320, Yellowknife, X1A 2L9 NT
Northwest Territories Water Board, 5114 - 49th St., PO Box 1326, Yellowknife, X1A 1N9 NT
867-765-0106, Fax: 867-765-0114, info@nwtwb.com

Nova Scotia
Department of Natural Resources, Founder's Square, 1701 Hollis St., 3rd Fl., PO Box 698, Halifax, B3J 2T9 NS
902-424-5935, Fax: 902-424-0594, 800-565-2224
Nova Scotia Utility & Review Board, 1601 Lower Water St., 3rd Fl., PO Box 1692 M,Halifax, B3J 3S3 NS
902-424-4448, Fax: 902-424-3919, uarb.board@gov.ns.ca
Waterfront Development Corporation Ltd., 1751 Lower Water St., 2nd Fl., Halifax, NS B3J 1S5
902-422-6591, Fax: 902-422-7582, info@wdcl.ca

Ontario
Ministry of Environment, 135 St. Clair Ave. West, Toronto, M4V 1P5 ON
416-325-4000, Fax: 416-325-3159, 800-565-4923
Lake of the Woods Control Board, c/o Executive Engineer, Ottawa, ON K1A 0H3
Fax: 819-953-4666, 800-661-5922, secretariat@lwcb.ca
Ministry of Natural Resources, Whitney Block, #6630, 99 Wellesley St. West, 6th Fl., Toronto, M7A 1W3 ON
800-667-1940
Ontario Clean Water Agency, 1 Yonge St., 17th Fl., Toronto, ON M5E 1E5
416-314-5600, Fax: 416-314-8300, 800-667-6292
Walkerton Clean Water Centre, PO Box 160, Walkerton, ON N0G 2V0
519-881-2003, Fax: 519-881-4947, inquiry@wcwc.ca

Prince Edward Island
Department of Environment, Energy & Forestry, Jones Bldg., 11 Kent St., 4th & 5th Fl., PO Box 2000, Charlottetown, C1A 7N8 PE
902-368-5000, Fax: 902-368-5830
Department of Tourism, PO Box 2000, Charlottetown, C1A 7N8 PE
800-463-4734

Quebec
Ministère du Développement durable, de l'Environnement et des Parcs, Édifice Marie-Guyart, 675, boul René-Lévesque est, 29e étage, Québec, G1R 5V7 QC

418-521-3830, Fax: 418-646-5974, 800-561-1616, info@mddep.gouv.qc.ca

Saskatchewan
Saskatchewan Environment, 3211 Albert St., 2nd Fl., Regina, S4S 5W6 SK
 306-953-3750, Fax: 306-787-9544, 800-567-4224, inquiry@serm.gov.sk.ca
Saskatchewan Water Corporation (SaskWater), #200, 111 Fairford St. East, Moose Jaw, S6H 1C8 SK
 306-694-3098, Fax: 306-694-3207, 888-230-1111, comm@saskwater.com
Saskatchewan Watershed Authority, 111 Fairford St. East, Moose Jaw, SK S6H 7X9
 306-694-3900, Fax: 306-694-3465, comm@swa.ca

Yukon Territory
Yukon Environment, PO Box 2703, Whitehorse, Y1A 2C6 YT
 867-667-5652, Fax: 867-393-6213, 800-661-0408, environmentyukon@gov.yk.ca

WATER RESOURCES
See Also: Oceanography

Ontario
Environmental Innovations & Emerging Sciences Branch, 40 St. Clair Ave. West, 14th Fl., Toronto, M4V 1M2 ON
 416-314-0713, Fax: 416-314-0251
Environmental Protection Branch, #B21, 3085 Albert St., Regina, S4S 0B1 SK
 306-787-6169, Fax: 306-787-0197
Environmental Stewardship Branch, 351 boul St-Joseph, Gatineau, K1A 0H3 QC
 819-997-1575, Fax: 819-953-9452
Freshwater Institute, 501 University Cres., Winnipeg, R3T 2N6 MB
 204-983-5000, Fax: 204-983-6285
International Joint Commission, 234 Laurier Ave. West, 22nd Fl., Ottawa, K1P 6K6 ON
 613-947-1420, Fax: 613-993-5583
National Water Research Institute, 867 Lakeshore Rd., PO Box 5050, Burlington, L7R 4A6 ON
 905-336-4625, Fax: 905-336-6444, nwriscience.liaison@ec.gc.ca
Nunavut Water Board, PO Box 119, Gjoa Haven, NU X0B 1J0
 867-360-6338, Fax: 867-360-6369

Alberta
Alberta Environment, South Tower, Petroleum Plaza, 9915 - 108 St., Main Fl., Edmonton, T5K 2G8 AB
 780-427-2700, Fax: 780-422-4086,-310-0000, env.infocent@gov.ab.ca

British Columbia
Environmental Protection Division, 2975 Jutland Rd., 5th Fl., PO Box 9339, Victoria, V8W 9M1 BC
 250-387-1288, Fax: 250-387-5669
Water Stewardship Division, 2975 Jutland Rd., 5th Fl., PO Box 9339 Prov Govt,Victoria, V8W 9M1 BC
 250-356-9443, Fax: 250-953-3414

Manitoba
Manitoba Water Services Board, PO Box 22080, Brandon, MB R7A 6Y9
 204-726-6076, Fax: 204-726-6290
Office of Drinking Water, 1007 Century St., Winnipeg, R3H 0W4 MB
 204-945-5762, Fax: 204-945-1365
Manitoba Water Stewardship, 200 Saulteaux Cres., PO Box 11, Winnipeg, R3J 3W3 MB
 204-945-6398, 800-282-8069, wsd@gov.mb.ca

New Brunswick
Department of the Environment, Marysville Place, 20 McGloin St., PO Box 6000, Fredericton, E3B 5H1 NB
 506-453-2690, Fax: 506-457-4991
Environmental Management, Marysville Place, 20 McGloin St., PO Box 6000, Fredericton, E3B 5H1 NB
 506-444-5119, Fax: 506-457-7333
Department of Local Government, Marysville Place, 20 McGloin St., PO Box 6000, Fredericton, E3B 5H1 NB
 506-453-2807, Fax: 506-453-3988
Sciences & Planning, Marysville Place, 20 McGloin St., 2nd Fl., PO Box 6000, Fredericton, E3B 5H1 NB
 506-453-2862, Fax: 506-453-2265

Northwest Territories
Northwest Territories Water Board, 5114 - 49th St., PO Box 1326, Yellowknife, X1A 1N9 NT
 867-765-0106, Fax: 867-765-0114, info@nwtwb.com

Nova Scotia
Department of Agriculture, 1741 Brunswick St., 3rd Fl., PO Box 2223, Halifax, B3J 3C4 NS
 902-424-4560, Fax: 902-424-4671

Nunavut
Department of Health & Social Services, Sivummut bldg., PO Box 1007 1000,Iqaluit, X0A 0H0 NU
 867-975-5700, Fax: 867-975-5705, health@gov.nu.ca

Ontario
Advisory Council on Drinking Water Quality & Testing Standards, 40 St. Clair Ave. West, 3rd Fl., Toronto, ON M4V 1M2
 416-212-7779, Fax: 416-212-7595
Ontario Clean Water Agency, 1 Yonge St., 17th Fl., Toronto, ON M5E 1E5
 416-314-5600, Fax: 416-314-8300, 800-667-6292
Walkerton Clean Water Centre, PO Box 160, Walkerton, ON N0G 2V0
 519-881-2003, Fax: 519-881-4947, inquiry@wcwc.ca

Quebec
Ministère du Développement durable, de l'Environnement et des Parcs, Édifice Marie-Guyart, 675, boul René-Lévesque est, 29e étage, Québec, G1R 5V7 QC
 418-521-3830, Fax: 418-646-5974, 800-561-1616, info@mddep.gouv.qc.ca

Saskatchewan
Saskatchewan Environment, 3211 Albert St., 2nd Fl., Regina, S4S 5W6 SK
 306-953-3750, Fax: 306-787-9544, 800-567-4224, inquiry@serm.gov.sk.ca
Saskatchewan Water Corporation (SaskWater), #200, 111 Fairford St. East, Moose Jaw, S6H 1C8 SK
 306-694-3098, Fax: 306-694-3207, 888-230-1111, comm@saskwater.com
Saskatchewan Watershed Authority, 111 Fairford St. East, Moose Jaw, SK S6H 7X9
 306-694-3900, Fax: 306-694-3465, comm@swa.ca

Yukon Territory
Yukon Environment, PO Box 2703, Whitehorse, Y1A 2C6 YT
 867-667-5652, Fax: 867-393-6213, 800-661-0408, environmentyukon@gov.yk.ca

WEIGHTS & MEASURES
Standards Council of Canada, #200, 270 Albert St., Ottawa, K1P 6N7 ON
 613-238-3222, Fax: 613-569-7808, info@scc.ca

WILDLIFE RESOURCES
Committee on the Status of Endangered Wildlife in Canada, c/o Canadian Wildlife Service, Ottawa, ON K1A 0H3
 819-997-4991, Fax: 819-994-3684, cosewic@ec.gc.ca
Fish & Wildlife Branch, 300 Water St., PO Box 7000, Peterborough, K9J 8M5 ON
 705-755-5954, Fax: 705-755-1900
North American Bird Conservation Initiative, Canadian Wildlife Service, 351, boul St-Joseph, 3e étage, Gatineau, QC K1A 0H3
 819-994-0512, Fax: 819-994-4445, s.neve@ec.gc.ca
North American Waterfowl Management Plan, c/o Canadian Wildlife Service, Place Vincent-Massey, 351 St-Joseph Blvd., 16th Fl., Gatineau, ON K1A 0H3
 819-934-6034, Fax: 819-934-6017, nabci@ec.gc.ca
Resource Stewardship Branch, #436, 3211 Albert Street, Regina, S4S 5W6 SK
 306-787-2314, Fax: 306-787-9544
Wildlife Division, Provincial Building, 136 Exhibition St., Kentville, B4N 4E5 NS
 902-678-6091

Alberta
Alberta Sport, Recreation, Parks & Wildlife Foundation, Standard Life Centre, 10405 Jasper Ave., 9th Fl., Edmonton, AB T5J 4R7
 780-415-1167, Fax: 780-415-0308

British Columbia
Environmental Stewardship Division, 2975 Jutland Rd., 5th Fl., PO Box 9339 Prov Govt,Victoria, V8T 5J9 BC
 250-356-0121, Fax: 250-953-3414

Manitoba
Endangered Species Advisory Committee, 200 Saulteaux Cres., PO Box 24, Winnipeg, MB R3J 3W3
 204-945-7465, Fax: 204-945-3077

Newfoundland & Labrador
Forest Resources, Fortis Bldg., PO Box 2006, Corner Brook, A2H 6J8 NL
 709-637-2284, Fax: 709-634-4378

Nunavut
Department of Environment, PO Box 1000 1300,Iqaluit, X0A 0H0 NU
 867-975-7700, Fax: 867-975-7742, 866-222-9063, environment@gov.nu.ca

Ontario
Ministry of Environment, 135 St. Clair Ave. West, Toronto, M4V 1P5 ON
 416-325-4000, Fax: 416-325-3159, 800-565-4923
Fish & Wildlife Heritage Commission, Robinson Pl., 300 Water St., PO Box 7000, Peterborough, ON K9J 8M5
 Fax: 705-755-5093

Quebec
Fondation de la faune du Québec, Place Iberville II, #420, 1175, av Lavigerie, Québec, QC G1V 4P1
 418-644-7926, Fax: 418-643-7655, 877-639-0742, ffq@riq.qc.ca
Ministère des Ressources naturelles et de la Faune, #A303, 5700, 4e av ouest, Québec, G1H 6R1 QC
 418-627-8600, Fax: 418-643-0720, 866-248-6936, service.citoyens@mrnf.gouv.qc.ca

WOMEN'S ISSUES
See Also: Pay Equity

Alberta
Alberta Tourism, Parks, Recreation & Culture, Communications Branch, Standard Life Centre, 10405 Jasper Ave., 7th Fl., Edmonton, T5J 4R7 AB
 780-427-6530, Fax: 780-427-1496, Comdev.Communications@gov.ab.ca

British Columbia
Rural Development, 800 Johnson St., 6th Fl., PO Box 9824 Prov Govt,Victoria, V8W 9W4 BC
 250-953-3005, Fax: 250-387-7935

Manitoba
Manitoba Women's Advisory Council, #301, 155 Carlton St., Winnipeg, MB R3C 3H8
 204-945-6281, Fax: 204-945-6511, 800-282-8069, 001women@gov.mb.ca
Status of Women, #409, 401 York Ave., Winnipeg, R3C 0P8 MB
 204-945-3476, Fax: 204-945-0013, 800-263-0234, mwd@gov.mb.ca

Nunavut
Department of Culture, Language, Elders & Youth, PO Box 1000 800,Iqaluit, X0A 0H0 NU
 867-975-5500, Fax: 867-975-5504, 866-934-2035

Prince Edward Island
Advisory Council on the Status of Women, Sherwood Business Centre, 161 St. Peter's Rd., PO Box 2000, Charlottetown, PE C1A 7N8
 902-368-4510, Fax: 902-368-4516, peistatusofwomen@eastlink.ca

Saskatchewan
Status of Women, #400, 1870 Albert St., Regina, SK S4P 4W1
 306-787-7401, Fax: 306-787-2058

WORKERS' COMPENSATION
Merchant Seamen Compensation Board, Secretary, Merchant Seamen Compensation Board, Phase II, Place du Portage, 10th Fl., Gatineau, QC K1A 0J2
 819-953-8001, Fax: 819-994-5368

Alberta
Appeals Commission for Alberta Workers' Compensation, #206, 1701 Centre St. North, Calgary, AB T2E 6Y2
 403-508-8800, Fax: 403-508-8822
Workers' Compensation Board of Alberta, 9925 - 107 St., PO Box 2415, Edmonton, T5J 2S5 AB
 780-498-3999, Fax: 780-498-7999, 800-661-9608

British Columbia
Workers' Compensation Appeal Tribunal, #150, 4600 Jacombs Rd., Richmond, BC V6V 3B1
604-664-7800, Fax: 604-664-7898, 800-663-2782

Workers' Compensation Board of British Columbia, PO Box 5350 Terminal,Vancouver, V6B 5L5 BC
604-276-3100, Fax: 604-244-6490, 888-621-7233

Manitoba
Manitoba Workers' Compensation Board, 333 Broadway Ave., Winnipeg, R3C 4W3 MB
204-954-4321, Fax: 204-954-4999, 800-362-3340, wcb@wcb.mb.ca

New Brunswick
Workplace Health, Safety & Compensation Commission of New Brunswick, 1 Portland St., PO Box 160, Saint John, E2L 3X9 NB
506-632-2200, 800-222-9775, communications@ws-ts.nb.ca

Newfoundland & Labrador
Newfoundland & Labrador Workplace Health, Safety & Compensation Commission, 146 - 148 Forest Rd., PO Box 9000, St. John's, A1A 3B8 NL
709-778-1000, Fax: 709-738-1714, 800-563-9000, general.inquiries@whscc.nl.ca

Northwest Territories
Northwest Territories & Nunavut Workers' Compensation Board, Centre Square Tower, 5022 - 49th St., 5th Fl., PO Box 8888, Yellowknife, X1A 2R3 NT
867-920-3888, Fax: 867-873-4596, 800-661-0792, wcb@wcb.nt.ca

Nova Scotia
Workers' Compensation Board of Nova Scotia, 5668 South St., PO Box 1150, Halifax, B3J 2Y2 NS
902-491-8999, Fax: 902-491-8002, 800-870-3331, info@wcb.gov.ns.ca

Ontario
Workplace Safety & Insurance Board, 200 Front St. West, Ground Fl., Toronto, M5V 3J1 ON
416-344-1000, Fax: 416-344-4684, 800-387-0750

Prince Edward Island
Prince Edward Island Workers Compensation Board, 14 Weymouth St., PO Box 757, Charlottetown, C1A 7L7 PE
902-368-5680, Fax: 902-368-5705, 800-237-5049

Quebec
Commission des lésions professionnelles, #700, 900, Place d'Youville, Québec, QC G1R 3P7
418-644-7777, Fax: 418-644-6443, 800-463-1591

Commission de la santé et de la sécurité au travail, 524, rue Bourdages, CP 1200 Terminus postal,Québec, G1K 7E2 QC
418-266-4850, Fax: 418-266-4389, 866-302-2778

Saskatchewan
Saskatchewan Workers' Compensation Board, #200, 1881 Scarth St., Regina, S4P 4L1 SK
306-787-4370, Fax: 306-787-7582, 800-667-7590, internet_clientsvc@wcbsask.com

Yukon Territory
Yukon Workers' Compensation Health & Safety Board, 401 Strickland St., Whitehorse, Y1A 5N8 YT
867-667-5645, Fax: 867-393-6279, 800-661-0443, worksafe@gov.yk.ca

YOUNG OFFENDERS

Prince Edward Island
Office of the Attorney General, Shaw Building, North, 105 Rochford St., 4th Fl., PO Box 2000, Charlottetown, C1A 7N8 PE
902-368-5152, Fax: 902-368-4910

YOUTH SERVICES

Nunavut
Department of Culture, Language, Elders & Youth, PO Box 1000 800,Iqaluit, X0A 0H0 NU
867-975-5500, Fax: 867-975-5504, 866-934-2035

Quebec
Ministère de la Santé et des Services sociaux, Direction des communications et Renseignements généraux, 1075, ch Sainte-Foy, Québec, G1S 2M1 QC
418-266-8900, 800-707-3380, regisseur.web@msss.gouv.qc.ca

ZONING

Alberta
Local Government Services, Commerce Place, 10155 - 102 St., 17th Fl., Edmonton, T5J 4L4 AB
Fax: 780-427-0453

British Columbia
Ministry of Community Development, 800 Johnson St., 6th Fl., PO Box 9490 Prov Govt,Victoria, V8W 9N7 BC
250-387-2283, Fax: 250-387-4312, Feedback@gov.bc.ca

Manitoba
Manitoba Municipal Board, #1144, 363 Broadway, Winnipeg, MB R3C 3N9
204-945-2941, Fax: 204-948-2235

New Brunswick
Department of Local Government, Marysville Place, 20 McGloin St., PO Box 6000, Fredericton, E3B 5H1 NB
506-453-2807, Fax: 506-453-3988

Quebec
Commission municipale du Québec, Mezzanine, aile Chauveau, 10, rue Pierre-Olivier-Chauveau, Tour 5e étage, Québec, QC G1R 4J3
418-691-2014, Fax: 418-644-4676, cmq@mamr.gouv.qc.ca

Government Acts & Regulations

Federal Legislation

Environment Canada/Environnement Canada
Antarctic Environmental Protection Act
Canada Emission Reduction Incentives Agency Act
Canada Water Act
Canada Wildlife Act
    Administration, Management & Control of Certain Public Lands
    Wildlife Area Regulations
Canadian Environment Week Act
Canadian Environmental Assessment Act
    Canada Port Authority Environmental Assessment Regulations
    Comprehensive Study List Regulation
    Exclusion List Regulation
    Federal Authorities Regulations
    Inclusion List Regulation
    Law List Regulation
    Projects Outside Canada Environmental Assessment Regulations
Canadian Environmental Protection Act
    Alberta Equivalency Order
    Asbestos Mines & Mills Release Regulations
    Benzene in Gasoline Regulations
    Chlor-Alkali, Mercury Release Regulations
    Chlorobiphenyls Regulations
    Contaminated Fuel Regulations
    Disposal at Sea Regulations
    Environmental Emergency Regulations
    Export Control List of Notification Regulations
    Export & Import of Hazardous Wastes Regulations
    Export of Substances under the Rotterdam Convention Regulations
    Federal Halocarbon Regulations
    Federal Mobile PCB Treatment & Destruction Regulations
    Federal Registration of Storage Tank Systems for Petroleum Products & Allied Petroleum Products on Federal Lands or Aboriginal Lands Regulations
    Fuels Information Regulations, No. 1
    Gasoline & Gasoline Blend Dispensing Flow Rate Regulations
    Gasoline Regulations
    Interprovincial Movement of Hazardous Waste Regulations
    List of Hazardous Waste Authorities
    List of Toxic Substances Authorities
    Masked Name Regulations
    New Substances Fees Regulations
    New Substances Notification Regulations
    Off-Road Small Spark-Ignition Engine Emission Regulations
    On-Road Vehicle & Engine Emission Regulations
    Ozone Depleting Substances Regulations
    PCB Waste Export Regulations
    Persistence & Bioaccumulation Regulations
    Phosphorus Concentration Regulations
    Prohibition of Certain Toxic Substances
    Pulp & Paper Mill Defoamer & Wood Chip Regulations
    Pulp & Paper Mill Effluent Chlorinated Dioxins & Furans Regulations
    Regulations respecting Applications for Permits for Disposal at Sea
    Rules for Procedures for Boards of Review
    Secondary Lead Smelter Release Regulations
    Solvent Degreasing Regulations
    Sulphur in Diesel Fuel Regulations
    Sulphur in Gasoline Regulations
    Storage of PCB Material Regulations
    Tetrachloroethylene (Use in Dry Cleaning & Reporting Requirements) Regulations
    Tributyltetradeclyphosphonium Chloride Regulations
    Vinyl Chloride Release Regulations
Convention on International Trade in Endangered Species of Wild Fauna & Flora
Department of the Environment Act
    Kemano Completion Project Guidelines Order
International River Improvements Act
Lac Seul Conservation Act, 1928
Lake of the Woods Control Board Act
Manganese-Based Fuel Additives Act
Migratory Birds Convention Act, 1994
    Migratory Bird Regulations
    Migratory Bird Sanctuary Regulations
National Wildlife Week Act
Species at Risk Act
Weather Modification Information Act
Wild Animal & Plant Protection & Regulation of International & Interprovincial Trade Act

Acts Administered in Part by Environment Canada
James Bay & Northern Québec Native Claims Settlement Act
Resources & Technical Surveys Act (jointly with Natural Resources/Fisheries & Oceans)

Environment Canada Related Acts & Regulations
Agricultural & Rural Development Act (jointly with Industry)
Alternative Fuels Act & Regulations (jointly with Treasury Board)
Canada Marine Act (jointly with Transport)
Canada Oil & Gas Operations Act (jointly with Indian & Northern Affairs/Natural Resources)
    Canada Oil & Gas Certificate of Fitness Regulations
    Canada Oil & Gas Drilling Regulations
    Canada Oil & Gas Geophysical Operations Regulations
    Canada Oil & Gas Operations Regulations
    Canada Oil & Gas Production & Conservation Regulations
Canada Petroleum Resources Act (jointly with Indian Affairs & Northern Development/Natural Resouces)
    Environmental Studies Research Fund Regions Regulations
Canadian Transportation Accident Investigation & Safety Board Act (jointly with Privy Council)
Transportation Safety Board Regulations
Food & Drugs Act (jointly with Agriculture & Agri-Foods/Industry)
Mackenzie Valley Resource Management Act (jointly with Indian & Northern Affairs)
National Energy Board Act (jointly with Natural Resources/Transport Canada)
    Electricity Regulations
    Oil & Gas Regulations
    Onshore Pipeline Regulations
    Rules of Practice & Procedure
National Round Table on the Environment & the Economy Act (jointly with Environment)
Northern Pipeline Act (jointly with Natural Resources)
    Northern Pipeline Socio-Economic & Environmental Terms & Conditions (jointly with Northern BC, Southern BC, AB, SK & Swift River Portion in BC)
Oceans Act (jointly with Fisheries & Oceans)

Agriculture & Agri-Food Canada/Agriculture et Agro-alimentaire Canada
Agricultural Marketing Programs Act
Agricultural Products Marketing Act
Canada Agricultural Products Act
Canada Grain Act
Canadian Food Inspection Agency Act (CFIA)
Consumer Packaging & Labelling Act (jointly with Industry)
Department of Agriculture & Agri-Food Act
Experimental Farm Stations Act
Prairie Farm Rehabilitation Act

Canada Revenue Agency/Agence du revenu du Canada
Customs & Excise Offshore Application Act

Canadian Food Inspection Agency/Agence canadienne d'inspection des aliments
Canada Agricultural Products Act
Canadian Food Inspection Agency Act
Feeds Act
Fertilizers Act
Fish Inspection Act
Health of Animals Act
Meat Inspection Act
Plant Breeders' Rights Act
Plant Protection Act
Seeds Act

Acts Administered in Part by the Canadian Food Inspection Agency
Consumer Packaging & Labelling Act
Food & Drugs Act

Canadian Heritage/Patrimoine canadien
Cultural Property Export & Import Act
Department of Canadian Heritage Act
Fitness & Amateur Sport Act (jointly with Health)
Historic Sites & Monuments Act
Library & Archives of Canada Act
Museums Act
National Sports of Canada Act
Physical Activity & Sport Act (jointly with Health)

Government Acts & Regulations

Citizenship & Immigration Canada/Citoyenneté et Immigration Canada
Canadian Multiculturalism Act

Fisheries & Oceans Canada/Pêches et Océans Canada
Canada Shipping Act, 2001 (jointly with Transport)
   Air Pollution Regulations
   Dangerous Chemicals & Noxious Liquid Substances Regulations
   Garbage Pollution Prevention Regulations
   Great Lakes Sewage Pollution Prevention Regulations
   Non-Pleasure Craft Sewage Pollution Prevention Regulations
   Oil Pollution Prevention Regulations
   Pleasure Craft Sewage Pollution Prevention Regulations
   Pollutant Discharge Reporting Regulations
   Pollutant Substances Regulations
   Ship-Source Oil Pollution Fund Regulations
Coastal Fisheries Protection Act
Department of Fisheries & Oceans Act
Fisheries Act
   Aboriginal Communal Fishing Licences Regulations
   Alberta Fishery Regulations, 1998
   Alice Arm Tailings Deposit Regulations
   Atlantic Fishery Regulations
   British Columbia Gravel Removal Order
   British Columbia Logging Order
   British Columbia Sport Fishing Regulations
   Fish Health Protection Regulations
   Fish Toxicant Regulations
   Fishery (General) Regulations
   Foreign Vessel Fishing Regulations
   Management of Contaminated Fisheries Regulations
   Manitoba Fishery Regulations
   Marine Mammal Regulations
   Maritime Provinces Fishery Regulations
   Newfoundland & Labrador Fishery Regulations
   Northwest Territories Fishery Regulations
   Ontario Fishery Regulations
   Pacific Fishery Management Area Regulations
   Pacific Fishery Regulations
   Potato Processing Plant Liquid Effluent Regulations
   Provincial Regulations
   Pulp & Paper Effluent Regulations
   Quebec Fishery Regulations
   Saskatchewan Fishery Regulations
   Yukon Territory Fishery Regulations
Fisheries Development Act
Fisheries Improvement Loans Act
   Fisheries & Oceans Canada Orders
Fishing & Recreational Harbours Act
Freshwater Fish Marketing Act
Oceans Act
   Basic Head Marine Protected Area Regulations
   Confederation Bridge Area Provincial (PEI) Laws Application Regulations
   Eastport Marine Protected Area Regulations
   Endeavour Hydrothermal Vents Marine Protected Areas Regulations
   Fishing Zones of Canada (Zones 1, 2 & 3) Order
   Fishing Zones of Canada (Zones 4 & 5) Order
   Fishing Zones of Canada (Zone 6) Order
   Gilbert Bay Marine Protected Area Regulations
   Gully Marine Protected Area Regulations
   Territorial Sea Geographical Coordinates (Area 7) Order
   Territorial Sea Geographical Coordinated Order

Foreign Affairs & International Trade Canada/Affaires étrangères et Commerce international Canada
Canada-Chile Free Trade Agreement
   Implementation Act
Comprehensive Nuclear Test-Ban Treaty Implementation Act
Department of Foreign Affairs & International Trade Act
Export Development Act
Export & Import Permits Act
Food & Agriculture Organization of the United Nations Act
International Boundary Waters Treaty Act
North American Free Trade Agreement Implementation Act
Rainy Lake Watershed Emergency Control Act
Roosevelt-Campobello International Park Commission Act
Skagit River Valley Treaty Implementation Act
United Nations Act

Health Canada/Santé Canada
Canada Health Act
Department of Health Act
Fitness & Amateur Sport Act (jointly with Heritage)
Food & Drugs Act (jointly with Agriculture)
Hazardous Materials Information Review Act (jointly with Human Resources & Skills Development)
   Appeal Board Procedures Regulations
   Hazardous Material Information Review Regulations
Hazardous Products Act
   Carbonated Beverage Glass Containers Regulations
   Consumer Chemicals & Containers Regulations
   Controlled Products Regulations
   Hazardous Products Regulations (Cellulose Insulation, Charcoal, Crocidolite Asbestos, Liquid Coating Materials, etc.)
   Ingredient Disclosure List
Pest Control Products Act, 2002 & Regulations
Pesticide Residue Compensation Act
Physical Activity & Sport Act (jointly with Heritage)
Quarantine Act, 2005
Radiation Emitting Devices Act
Tobacco Act

Human Resources & Social Development Canada/Ressources humaines et développement social Canada
Canada Labour Code
   Aviation Occupational Safety & Health Regulations
   Canada Occupational Health & Safety Regulations
   Coal Mines (CBDC) Occupational Safety & Health Regulations
   Coal Mining Safety Commission Regulations
   Marine Occupational Safety & Health Regulations
   Oil & Gas Occupational Safety & Health Regulations
   On Board Trains Occupational Safety & Health Regulations
Canadian Centre for Occupational Health & Safety Act
Non-smokers' Health Act (Transport Canada)

Indian & Northern Affairs Canada/Affaires indiennes et du Nord Canada
Arctic Waters Pollution Prevention Act (jointly with Transport/Natural Resources)
Department of Indian & Northern Affairs Development Act
Canada Lands Surveys Act (jointly with Natural Resources)
Canada Oil & Gas Operations Act (jointly with Natural Resources)
Canada Petroleum Resources Act (jointly with Natural Resources)
Canada - Yukon Oil & Gas Accord Implementation Act
Canadian Polar Commission Act
Claims Settlement (Alberta & Saskatchewan) Implementation Act
Fort Nelson Indian Reserve Minerals Revenue Sharing Act
Indian Act (jointly with Health)
Indian Lands Agreement Act
Indian Lands Settlement of Differences Act
   Indian Reserve Waste Disposal Regulations
   Territorial Land Titles Offices Regulations
Indian Oil & Gas Act
Land Titles Repeal Act
Mackenzie Valley Resource Management Act
Nelson House First Nation Flooded Land Act
Northern Canada Power Commission (Share Issuance & Sale Authorization) Act
Northern Canada Power Commission Yukon Assets Disposal Authorization Act
Northwest Territories Act
Northwest Territories Waters Act
Nunavut Act
Nunavut Waters & Nunavut Surface Rights Tribunal Act, 2002
Railway Belt Act
Railway Belt Water Act
Saskatchewan Natural Resources Act
Split Lake Cree First Nation Flooded Land Act
Territorial Lands Act
   Canada Mining Regulations
   Canada Oil & Gas Drilling & Production Regulations
   Canada Oil & Gas Land Regulations
   Crown Waiver Orders
   Government Employees Land Acquisition Orders
   Northwest Territories Mining Districts Order & Nunavut Mining District
   Oil & Gas Land Orders
   Orders Authorizing Acquisition of Interest in Certain Lands
   Orders Respecting Withdrawal from Disposal of Certain Lands
   Polar Bear Pass Withdrawal Order
   Reservations to Crown Waiver Orders
   Territorial Coal Regulations
   Territorial Dredging Regulations
   Territorial Land Use Regulations
   Territorial Lands Act Exclusion Orders
   Territorial Lands Regulations

Territorial Quarrying Regulations
Withdrawal of Certain Lands from Disposal Orders
Withdrawals of Disposal Orders
York Factory First Nation Flooded Land Act
Yukon Act
Yukon Environmental & Socio-Economic Assessment Act, 2003
Yukon Placer Mining Act
Yukon Quartz Mining Act
Yukon Waters Act

Industry Canada/Industrie Canada
Agricultural & Rural Development Act
Canadian Space Agency Act
Canadian Tourism Commission Act
Consumer Packaging & Labelling Act (jointly with Agriculture)
Corporations Returns Act
Department of Industry Act
Electricity & Gas Inspection Act
Industrial Design Act
National Research Council Act
Natural Sciences & Engineering Research Council Act
Standards Council of Canada Act
Timber Marking Act

Minister for the purposes of the Atlantic Canada Opportunities Agency Act
Cape Breton Development Corporation Act

National Defence (Canada)/Défense nationale
Emergencies Act

Natural Resources Canada/Ressources naturelles Canada
Canada Foundation for Sustainable Development Technology Act
Canada-Newfoundland Atlantic Accord Implementation Act
   Canada-Newfoundland Oil & Gas Spills & Debris Liability Regulations
   Newfoundland Offshore Area Oil & Gas Operations Regulations
   Newfoundland Offshore Area Petroleum Diving Regulations
   Newfoundland Offshore Area Petroleum Geophysical Operations Regulations
   Newfoundland Offshore Area Petroleum Production & Conservation Regulations
   Newfoundland Offshore Area Registration Regulations
   Newfoundland Offshore Certificate of Fitness Regulations
   Newfoundland Offshore Petroleum Drilling Regulations
   Newfoundland Offshore Petroleum Installations Regulations
Canada-Nova Scotia Offshore Petroleum Resources Accord Implementation Act
   Canada-Nova Scotia Oil & Gas Spills & Debris Liability Regulations
   Nova Scotia Offshore Area Certificate of Fitness Regulations
   Nova Scotia Offshore Area Petroleum Diving Regulations
   Nova Scotia Offshore Area Petroleum Drilling Regulations
   Nova Scotia Offshore Area Petroleum Geophysical Operations Regulations
   Nova Scotia Offshore Area Petroleum Installations Regulations
   Nova Scotia Offshore Area Petroleum Production & Conservation Regulations
   Nova Scotia Resources (Ventures) Ltd. Drilling Assistance Regulations
Canada Oil & Gas Operations Act (Indian Affairs & Northern Development)
   Canada Oil & Gas Certificate of Fitness Regulations
   Canada Oil & Gas Diving Regulations
   Canada Oil & Gas Drilling Regulations
   Canada Oil & Gas Geophysical Operations Regulations
   Canada Oil & Gas Installations Regulations
   Canada Oil & Gas Operations Regulations
   Canada Oil & Gas Production & Conservation Regulations
   Nova Scotia Offshore Area Production & Conservation Regulations
   Oil & Gas Spills & Debris Liability Regulations
Canadian Ownership & Control Determination Act
Co-operative Energy Act
Department of Natural Resources Act
   Report on the State of Canada's Forests Regulations
Energy Administration Act
Energy Efficiency Act
Energy Monitoring Act
Energy Supplies Emergency Act
Explosives Act
Forestry Act
   Gros Morne Forestry Timber Regulations
   Timber Regulations
Hibernia Development Project Act
International Boundary Commission Act
National Energy Board Act (jointly with Transport)
   National Energy Board Coast Recovery Regulations
   National Energy Board Electricity Regulations
   National Energy Board Export & Import Reporting Regulations
   National Energy Board Pipeline Crossing Regulations, I & II
   National Energy Board Processing Plant Regulations
   National Energy Board Rules of Practice & Procedure
   National Energy Board Substituted Service Regulations
   Onshore Pipeline Regulations
   Pipeline Arbitration Committee Procedure Rules
   Power Line Crossing Regulations
Northern Pipeline Act
   Uranium Mines (Ontario) Occupational Health & Safety Regulations
Nuclear Energy Act
   Transport Packaging of Radioactive Materials Regulations
   Uranium & Thorium Mining Regulations
Nuclear Energy Act
Nuclear Fuel Waste Act, 2002
Nuclear Liability Act
Nuclear Safety & Control Act
   Canadian Nuclear Safety Commission Rules of Procedure
   Class I Nuclear Facilities Regulations
   Class II Nuclear Facilities & Prescribed Equipment Regulations
   General Nuclear Safety & Control Regulations
   Nuclear Non-Proliferation Import & Export Control Regulations
   Nuclear Security Regulations
   Nuclear Substances & Radiation Devices Regulations
   Packaging & Transport of Nuclear Substances Regulations
   Radiation Protection Regulations
   Uranium Mines & Mills Regulations
   Uranium Mines (Ontario) Occupational Health & Safety Regulations
Oil Substitution & Conservation Act

Administration of Acts with respect to Changes in Provincial Boundaries
Alberta Act
Alberta/BC Boundary Act, 1974
Alberta/NWT Boundary Act, 1958
British Columbia 1857, 1866
BC-Yukon-NWT Boundary Act, 1967
Keewatin Act
Manitoba Boundaries Extension Act, 1912
Manitoba-NWT Boundary Act, 1966
Manitoba/Saskatchewan Boundary Act, 1966
New Brunswick, 1851
Newfoundland, 1949
Northwest Territories, 1905
Nova Scotia, 1851
Nunavut, 1993
Ontario, 1889
Ontario Boundaries Extension Act, 1912
Ontario-Manitoba Boundary Act
Prince Edward Island, 1873
Energy Supplies Emergency Act
Québec Boundaries Extension Act, 1912
Saskatchewan, 1905
Saskatchewan/NWT Boundary Act, 1966
Yukon, 1898

Acts Administered in Part by Natural Resources Canada
Arctic Waters Pollution Prevention Act (jointly with Transport Canada/Indian & Northern Affairs)
   Arctic Shipping Pollution Prevention Regulations
   Arctic Waters Experimental Pollution Regulations
   Arctic Waters Pollution Prevention Regulations
   Order Exempting the United States Coast Guard Icebreaker "Healy" from the Application of the Arctic Shipping Pollution Prevention Regulations
Canada Lands Survey Act (jointly with Indian & Northern Affairs)
   Canada Lands Surveys Examination Regulation
   Canada-Newfoundland Oil & Gas Spills & Debris Liability Regulations
   Land Survey Tariff Regulations
   Newfoundland & Labrador Offshore Area Line Regulations
   Newfoundland Offshore Area Oil & Gas Operations Regulations
   Newfoundland Offshore Area Petroleum Diving Regulations
   Newfoundland Offshore Area Petroleum Geophysical Operations Regulations
   Newfoundland Offshore Area Petroleum Production & Conservation Regulations
   Newfoundland Offshore Area Registration Regulations
   Newfoundland Offshore Petroleum Drilling Regulations
   Newfoundland Offshore Petroleum Installations Regulations
   Newfoundland Offshore Petroleum Resource Revenue Fund Regulations
   Nova Scotia Resources (Ventures) Limited Drilling Assistance Regulations
   Shipping Safety Control Zones Order
Canada Petroleum Resources Act (jointly with Indian & Northern Affairs)
   Environmental Studies Research Fund Regions Regulations
   Frontier Lands Petroleum Royalty Regulations
   Frontier Lands Registration Regulations

Government Acts & Regulations

Lancaster Sound Designated Area Regulations
Orders Prohibiting the Issuance of Interests at Lapierre House Historic Site (Yukon) & Rampart House (Yukon)
National Energy Board Act (jointly with Transport Canada)
Resources & Technical Surveys Act (jointly with Fisheries & Oceans/Environment)

Privy Council Office/Bureau du Conseil privé
Anti-Personnel Mines Convention Implementation Act

Public Safety/Sécurité publique Canada
Emergency Preparedness Act

Public Works & Government Services Canada/Travaux publics et services gouvernementaux
Bridges Act
Expropriation Act
Federal District Commission to have acquired certain lands, An Act to Confirm the Authority of
Government Property Traffic Act (jointly with Transport)
Ottawa River, Act Respecting Certain Works
Public Works & Government Services Act

Transport Canada/Transports Canada
Aeronautics Act
Arctic Waters Pollution Prevention Act (jointly with Natural Resources/Indian Affairs & Northern Development)
Canada Marine Act
Canada Shipping Act, 2001 (jointly with Fisheries & Oceans)
Canada Transportation Act
Canadian Air Transport Security Authority Act
Department of Transport Act
Government Property Traffic Act (jointly with Public Works)
Marine Transportation Security Act
Motor Vehicle Fuel Consumption Standards Act
Motor Vehicle Safety Act
Motor Vehicle Transport Act, 1987
National Energy Board Act (jointly with Natural Resources)
Navigable Waters Protection Act
Pilotage Act
Railway Safety Act
Safe Containers Convention Act
Transportation Appeal Tribunal of Canada Act
Transportation of Dangerous Goods Act, 1992

Treasury Board of Canada/Conseil du Trésor du Canada
Alternative Fuels Act
Auditor General Act
Federal Real Property & Federal Immovables Act
Motor Vehicle Safety Act, 1993

Alberta Legislation

Alberta Environment
Climate Change & Emissions Management Act, 2003
    Specified Gas Reporting Regulation
Drainage District Act, 2000
Energy Statutes Amendment Act
Environmental Protection & Enhancement (Clean-Up) Instructions Amendment Act, 2002, (Unproclaimed)
Environmental Protection & Enhancement Act (Community Development & Sustainable Resource Development)
    Activities Designation Amendment Regulation
    Activities Designation Regulation
    Approvals & Registration Procedures Regulation
    Beverage Container Recycling Regulation
    Codes of Practice (Waterworks System Consisting Solely of a Water Distribution System; Asphalt Paving Plants; Compost Facilities; Landfills; Pesticides, etc.)
    Conservation Easement Registration Regulation
    Conservation & Reclamation Regulation
    Designated Material Recycling & Management Regulation
    Disclosure of Information Regulation
    Electronics Designation Regulation
    Emissions Trading Regulation
    Environmental Appeal Board Regulation
    Environmental Assessment Regulation
    Environmental Assessment (Mandatory & Exempted Activities) Regulation
    Environmental Protection & Enhancement (Miscellaneous) Regulation
    Forest Resources Improvement Regulation
    Lubricating Oil Material Environmental Handling Charge By-Law
    Lubricating Oil Material Recycling & Management By-Law
    Lubricating Oil Material Recycling Management Regulation
    Mercury Emissions from Coal-fired Power Plants Regulation
    Ozone-depleting Substances & Halocarbons Regulation
    Pesticide (Ministerial) Regulation
    Pesticide Sales, Handling, Use & Application Regulation
    Potable Water Regulation
    Release Reporting Regulation
    Substance Release Regulation
    Tire Designation Regulation
    Waste Control Regulation
    Wastewater & Storm Drainage Regulation
    Wastewater & Storm Drainage (Ministerial) Regulation
Mines & Minerals Act (jointly with Energy/Sustainable Resource Development)
Natural Resources Conservation Board Act (jointly with Sustainable Resource Development)
    Rules of Practice of the Natural Resources Conservation Board
North Red Deer Water Authorization Act
Stettler Regional Water Authorization Act
Water Act
    Codes of Practice (Various) Regulations
    Water Allocation Orders (Various) Regulation
    Water (Ministerial) Regulation
    Water (Offences & Penalities) Regulation
Wilderness Areas, Ecological Reserves & Natural Areas Amendment Act
Wilderness Areas, Ecological Reserves, Natural Areas & Heritage Rangelands Act

Alberta Agriculture, Food & Rural Development
Agricultural Operations Practices Act
Agricultural Pest Act
    Pest & Nuisance Control Regulation
Agricultural Services Board Act
Alberta Wheats & Barley Test Market Act
Animal Keepers Act
Animal Protection Act
Federal-Provincial Farm Assistance Act
Fuel Tax Act
Fur Farms Act & Regulation
Gas Distribution Act
Irrigation Districts Act
    Irrigation Forms Regulation
    Irrigation Plebiscite Regulation
    Irrigation Seepage Claims Exemption Regulation
Livestock Diseases Act
    Destruction & Disposal of Dead Animals Regulation
    Designated Communicable Diseases Regulation
    Livestock Disease Control Regulation
    Livestock Market & Assembly Station Regulation
    Production Animal Medicine Regulation
Marketing of Agricultural Products Act
Rural Utilities Act
Soil Conservation Act
Weed Control Act
    Seed Cleaning Plant Regulations
    Weed Designation Regulations

Alberta Community Development
Alberta Sport, Recreation, Parks & Wildlife Foundation Act
Black Creek Heritage Rangeland Trails Act
Environmental Protection & Enhancement Act 35(d) to (f.4)
Historical Resources Act
    Archaeological & Palaeontological Research Permit Regulation
    Fort Mcleod Provincial Historic Area Establishment Regulation
Provincial Parks Act
Recreation Development Act
Wilderness Areas, Ecological Reserves & Natural Areas Act (amendment 2000-not yet proclaimed)
Willmore Wilderness Park Act

Alberta Energy
Alberta Energy & Utilities Board Act Security Management Regulation
Coal Conservation Act
Coal Sales Act
Electric Utilities Act
    Flare Gas Generation Regulation
    Independent Power & Small Power Regulation
Energy Resources Conservation Act
Freehold Mineral Rights Tax Act
Gas Resources Preservation Act
Gas Utilities Act
Hydro & Electric Energy Act
The Mineral Titles Redemption Act

Government Acts & Regulations

Mines & Minerals Act
   Ammonite Shell Regulations
   CO2 Projects Royalty Credit Regulation
   Exploration Regulation
   Gas Processing Efficiency Assistance Regulation
   Innovative Energy Technologies Regulation
   Metallic & Industrial Minerals Exploration Regulation
   Metallic & Industrial Minerals Regulation
   Mineral Rights Compensation Regulation
   Oil Sands Tenure Regulation
Natural Gas Marketing Act
Oil & Gas Conservation Act
Oil Sands Conservation Act
Petroleum Marketing Act
Pipeline Act
Small Power Research & Development Act
Turner Valley Unit Operations Act
Water, Gas & Electric Companies Act

Alberta Government Services
Land Titles Act
Surveys Act, Section 5(1)(d) & (2)(b) (jointly with Alberta Sustainable Development)

Alberta Health & Wellness
Public Health Act
   Communicable Disease Regulation
   Nuisance & General Sanitation Regulations
   Regulated Matter Regulations
Smoke-free Places Act

Alberta Human Resources & Employment
Agrologists Act
Land Surveyors Act
Occupational Health & Safety Act
   Occupational Health & Safety Code
   Occupational Health & Safety Regulation
Radiation Protection Act & Regulations
Regulated Forestry Profession Act
Workers' Compensation Act

Alberta Infrastructure & Transportation
City Transportation Act
Dangerous Goods Transportation & Handling Act
Highways Development & Protection Act
Public Highways Development Act
Railway (Alberta) Act
Regional Airports Authorities Act
Water Act (jointly with Environment)
Water, Gas & Electric Companies Act (jointly with Energy)

Alberta Innovation & Science
Alberta Heritage Foundation for Medical Research Act
Alberta Science, Research & Technology Authority Act

Alberta Justice & Attorney General
Expropriation Act (jointly with Sustainable Resource Development)

Alberta Municipal Affairs
Disaster Services Act
   Disaster Recovery Regulation
   Government Emergency Planning Regulation
Municipal Government Act
   Waste Management Services, Water Services & Wastewater Commissions Regulations
Safety Codes Act

Alberta Sustainable Resource Development
Boundary Surveys Act
Environmental Protection & Enhancement Act (jointly with Environment)
Expropriation Act (sections 25 to 28 & 72)
Fisheries (Alberta) Act
Forest & Prairie Protection Act
Forest Reserves Act
Forests Act
Government Organization Act (jointly with Environment/Infrastructure)
Natural Resources Conservation Board Act (jointly with Environment)
Public Lands Act
Surface Rights Act
Surveys Act (jointly with Service Alberta)
Wildlife Act

British Columbia Legislation

Ministry of Environment
Ecological Reserve Act
   Application of Park Legislation to Ecological Reserves Regulation
   Ecological Reserve Regulations
Environmental Assessment Act
   Concurrent Approval Regulation
   Public Consultation Policy Regulation
   Regional District Definition Regulation
   Transition Regulation
Environmental Management Act (jointly with Attourney General/Forests, Lands & Natural Resource Operations)
   Agricultural Waste Control Regulation
   Antisapstain Chemical Waste Control Regulation
   Asphalt Plant Regulation
   Cleaner Gasoline Regulation
   Code of Practice for the Discharge of Produced Water from Coalbed Gas Operations
   Conservation Office Service Authority Regulation
   Contaminated Sites Regulation
   Environmental Appeal Board Procedure Regulation
   Environmental Data Quality Assurance Regulation
   Environmental Impact Assessment Regulation
   Finfish Aquaculture Waste Control Regulation
   Gasoline Vapour Control Regulation
   Hazardous Waste Regulation
   Land-based Fin Fish Waste Control Regulation
   Motor Vehicle Emissions Control Warranty Regulation
   Municipal Sewage Regulations
   Mushroom Composting Pollution Prevention Regulation
   Oil & Gas Waste Regulation
   Ootsa Lake Beehive Burner Regulation
   Open Burning Smoke Control Regulation
   Organic Matter Recycling Regulation
   Ozone Depleting Substances & Other Halocarbons Regulation
   Permit Fees Regulation
   Petroleum Storage & Distribution Facilities Storm Water Regulation
   Placer Mining Waste Control Regulation
   Post-Consumer Residual Stewardship Program Regulation
   Public Notification Regulation
   Pulp Mill & Pulp & Paper Mill Liquid Effluent Control Regulation
   Rebate of Waste Management Fee Regulation
   Recycling Regulation
   Solid Fuel Burning Domestic Appliance Regulation
   Spill Cost Recovery Regulation
   Spill Reporting Regulation
   Storage of Recyclable Material Regulation
   Sulphur Content of Fuel Regulation
   Waste Discharge Regulation
   Wood Residue Burner & Incinerator Regulation
Forest Land Reserve Act
Integrated Pest Management Act, 2003
Ministry of Environment Act
Okanagan River Boundaries Settlement Act
Park Act
Parks & Protected Areas Statutes Amendment Act, 2004
   Park & Recreation Area Regulation
Protected Areas of British Columbia Act
Sustainable Environment Fund Act
Wildlife Act (jointly with Forests, Lands & Natural Resource Operations)
   Angling & Scientific Collection Regulation
   Closed Areas Regulation
   Designation & Exemption Regulation
   Designation of Officers Regulation
   Freshwater Fish Regulation
   Habitat Conservation Trust Fund Regulation
   Hunter Safety Training Regulation
   Hunting Licensing Regulation
   Hunting Regulation
   Limited Entry Hunting Regulation
   Management Unit Regulation
   Motor Vehicle Prohibition Regulation
   Permit Regulation
   Public Access Prohibition Regulation
   Tofino Mudflats Wildlife Management Area Regulation
   Wildlife Act Commercial Activities Regulation
   Wildlife Act General Regulation
   Wildlife Management Areas Regulations

Government Acts & Regulations

Wildlife Amendment Act
Ministry of Aboriginal Relations & Reconciliation
Indian Cut-off Lands Dispute
Treaty Commission Act

Ministry of Agriculture
Agri-Food Choice & Quality Act
    Organic Agricultural Products Certification Regulation
Agricultural Land Commission Act
Animal Disease Control Act
Columbia Basin Trust Act
Farm Practices Protection (Right to Farm) Act
Farming & Fishing Industries Development Act
Fisheries Act (jointly with Forests, Lands & Natural Resource Operations)
Food Products Standards Act
Fur Farm Act
Game Farm Act
Livestock Act
Livestock Protection Act
Ministry of Agriculture & Food Act
Natural Products Marketing (BC) Act
Pesticide Control Act
Plant Protection Act
Prevention of Cruelty to Animals Act
Range Act (jointly with Finance/Forests)
Veterinarians Act

Ministry of the Attorney General
Coastal Ferry Act (jointly with Transportation)
Expropriation Act
Forest & Range Practices Act (jointly with Finance/Forests)
Forest Practices Code of British Columbia Act (jointly with Finance/Forests)
Utilities Commission Act

Ministry of Community, Sport & Cultural Development
Arts Council Act
Assessment Act
Assessment Authority Act
Capital Commission Act
Capital Region Water Supply & Sooke Hills Protection
Community Charter Act
Islands Trust Act
Local Government Act (jointly with Agriculture/Energy & Mines)
Local Services Act
Museum Act
Recreational Facility Act

Ministry of Energy & Mines
BC Hydro Public Power Legacy & Heritage Contract Act
Clean Energy Act (jointly with Aboriginal Relations & Reconciliation)
Coal Act
Coalbed Gas Act, 2003
Columbia Basin Trust Act
Energy Efficiency Act
    Energy Efficiency Standards Regulation
Gas Utility Act
Geothermal Resources Act
Hydro & Power Authority Act
Hydro Power Measures Act
Mineral Land Tax Act (jointly with Finance)
Mineral Tax Act (jointly with Finance)
Mineral Tenure Act
Mines Act
    Mine Reclamation Fund Regulation
    Mines Regulation
    Workplace Hazardous Materials Information
        System Regulation (Mines)
Mining Right of Way Act
Mining Tax Act
Ministry of Energy & Mines Act
Oil & Gas Activities Act (jointly with Attorney General)
Petroleum & Natural Gas Act
Petroleum & Natural Gas (Vancouver Island Railway Lands) Act
Safety Authority Act
Safety Standards Act
Vancouver Island Natural Gas Pipeline Act
West Kootenay Power & Light Company, Ltd. Act

Ministry of Finance
Budget Measures Implementation Act
Financial Administration Act

Forest Act
Forest & Range Practices Act (jointly with Attorney General/Forests)
Forest Practices Code of British Columbia Act (jointly with Attorney General/Forests)
Forest Stand Management Fund Act (jointly with Forests)
Range Act (jointly with Agriculture/Forests)
Wildfire Act, 2004 (jointly with Forests)

Ministry of Forests, Lands & Natural Resource Operations
Boundary Act
Creston Valley Wildlife Act
    Discharge of Firearms Regulation
    Summit Creek Campground & Recreation Area
Dike Maintenance Act
Drainage, Ditch & Dike Act
Drinking Water Protection Act
    Ground Water Protection Regulations
Environment & Land Use Act
Fisheries Act
Fish Protection Act
    Riparian Areas Regulation
    Sensitive Streams Designation & Licensing Regulation
    Streamside Protection Regulation
Flood Hazard Statutes Amendment Act, 2003
Forest Act (jointly with Finance)
    Advertising, Deposits & Disposition Regulation
    Allowable Annual Cut Proportionate Reduction Regulation
    Annual Rent Regulation
    BC Timber Sales Business Areas Regulation
    BC Timber Sales Business Regulation
    Christmas Tree Regulation
    Community Forest Agreement Regulation
    Credit to Stumpage Regulation
    Cut Control Regulation
    Effective Director Regulation
    Forest Accounts Receivable Interest Regulation
    Forest Regions Regulation
    Free Use Permit Regulation
    Innovative Forestry Practices Regulation
    Interest Rate Under Various Statutes Regulation
    Log Salvage Regulation (Vancouver District)
    Manufactured Forest Products Regulation
    Minimum Stumpage Rate Regulation
    Performance Based Harvesting Regulation
    Scaling Regulation
    Special Forest Products Regulation
    Timber Definition Regulation
    Timber Harvesting Contract & Subcontract Regulation
    Timber Marketing & Transportation Regulation
    Woodlot Licence Regulation
Forest & Range Practices Act (jointly with Attorney General/Finance)
Forest Practices Code of British Columbia Act (jointly with Finance/Attorney General)
    Government Actions Regulation
    Provincial Forest Use Regulation
    Stillwater Pilot Project Regulation
Forest & Range Practises Act (jointly with Finance/Attorney General)
    Administrative Remedies Regulation
    Administrative Review & Appeal Procedure (Forest Practices) Regulation
    Forest Planning & Practices Regulation
    Forest Practices Board Regulation
    Forest Recreation Regulation
    Forest Service Road Use Regulation
    Fort St. John Pilot Project Regulation
    Invasive Plants Regulation
    Range Planning & Practices Regulation
    Security for Forest Practice Liabilities Regulation
    TFL 49 Pilot Project Regulation
    Woodlot Licence Planning & Practices Regulation
Forest Stand Management Fund Act (jointly with Finance)
    Forest Stand Management Fund Regulation
Foresters Act
Forestry Revitalization Act, 2003
Greenbelt Act
Heritage Conservation Act
Hunting & Fishing Heritage Act
Industrial Operation Compensation Act
Land Act
Land Survey Act
Land Surveyors Act
Land Title & Survey Authority Act

Libby Dam Reservoir Act
Manufactured Forest Products Regulation
Ministry of Forests Act
Motor Vehicle (All Terrain) Act
Muskwa-Kechika Management Area Act
Private Managed Forest Land Act
Protected Areas Forests Compensation Act
Railway Act (jointly with Transportation)
Range Act (jointly with Agriculture/Finance)
Skagit Environmental Enhancement Act
Water, Land & Air Protection Statutes Amendment Act, 2003
Water Act
Water Protection Act
   Groundwater Protection Regulations
Water Utility Act
Weed Control Act
Wildfire Act, 2004 (jointly with Finance)

Ministry of Health
Drinking Water Protection Act
Food Safety Act
Health Act
   Health Hazard Regulation
   Industrial Camps Health Regulations
   Sanitary Regulations
   Sewage Disposal Regulations
   Sewage System Regulation
   West Nile Virus Control Regulations
Health Emergency Act
   Health Emergency Regulation
Ministry of Health Act
Tobacco Damages & Health Care Costs Recovery Act
Tobacco Control Act

Ministry of Jobs, Tourism & Innovation
BC-Alcan Northern Development Fund Act
British Columbia Enterprise Corporation Act (jointly with Community)
Economic Development Act
Ministry of International Business & Immigration Act
Northern Development Initiative Trust Act
Tourism Act

Ministry of Labour, Citizens' Services & Open Government
Coastal Forest Industry Dispute Settlement Act
Employment Standards Act
Labour Relations Code
Ministry of Labour Act (except in relation to gas, electrical, elevating devices, boiler & pressure vessel safety)
Workers' Compensation Act

Ministry of Public Safety & Solicitor General
Commercial Transport Act (jointly with Transportation)
Emergency Communications Corporations Act
Emergency Program Act
   Compensation & Disaster Financial Assistance Regulation
   Emergency Program Management Regulation
   Local Authority Emergency Management Regulation
   Environment & Land Use Act (Sustainable Resource Management)
Fire Services Act
Flood Relief Act
Motor Vehicle Act (jointly with Transportation)

Ministry of Transportation & Infrastructure
Commercial Transport Act (jointly with Public Safety)
Coastal Ferry Act (jointly with Attorney General)
South Coast British Columbia Transportation Authority Act
Industrial Roads Act
Motor Vehicle Act (jointly with Public Safety)
   Emission Inspection Exemption Regulation
   Heavy Vehicle Diesel Emission Standards Regulation
   Inspection Standards (Safety & Repair) Regulation
Passenger Transportation Act
Railway Act (jointly with Forests)
Transport of Dangerous Goods Act
   Tunnel Transportation of Dangerous Commodities Regulation
Transportation Act

Manitoba Legislation

Manitoba Conservation
Contaminated Sites Remediation Act
Crown Lands Act

Dangerous Goods Handling & Transportation Act
   Anhydrous Ammonia Handling & Transport Regulations
   Classification for Products, Substances & Organisms Regulation
   Dangerous Goods Handling & Transportation Fees Regulation
   Dangerous Goods Handling & Transportation Regulation
   Environmental Accident Reporting Regulation
   Generator Registration & Carrier Licensing Regulation
   Manifest Regulation
   PCB Storage Site Regulation
   Special Waste (Shredder Residue) Regulation
   Storage & Handling of Petroleum Products & Allied Products Regulation
Ecological Reserves Act
   Ecological Reserves Designation Regulation
Endangered Species Act
Environment Act
   Burning of Crop Residue & Non-Crop Herbage Regulation
   Campgrounds Regulation
   Classes of Development Regulation
   Disposal of Whey Regulation
   Environment Act Fees Regulation
   Environmental Assessment Hearing Costs Recovery Regulation
   Incinerators Regulation
   Inco Ltd. & Hudson Bay Mining & Smelting Co., Ltd. Smelting Complex Regulation
   Joint Environmental Assessment Regulation
   Litter Regulation
   Livestock Manure & Mortalities Management Regulation
   Onsite Wastewater Management Systems Regulation
   Participant Assistance Regulation
   Peat Smoke Control Regulation
   Pesticides Regulation
   Rockwood Sensitive Area Regulation
   Waste Disposal Grounds Regulation
   Wastewater Management Systems Regulations
   Water & Wastewater Facility Operators Regulation
Forest Act
Forest Health & Protection Act & Regulations
High-Level Radioactive Waste Act
International Peace Garden Act
Manitoba Hazardous Waste Management Corporation Act
Manitoba Natural Resources Transfer Act
Manitoba Natural Resources Transfer Act, Amendment Act
Manitoba Natural Resources Transfer Act, Amendment Act, 1963
Ozone Depleting Substances Act
Provincial Parks Act
Plant Pests & Diseases Act
Polar Bear Protection Act, 2003
   Protection of Water Resources Regulation
   Sanitary Areas Regulation
   Water Supplies Regulation
   Water Works, Sewage & Sewage Disposal Regulations
Resource Tourism Operators Act
Surveys Act (Part II)
Sustainable Development Act
Waste Reduction & Prevention Act
   Multi-Material Stewardship (Interim Measures) Regulation
   Tire Stewardship Regulation
   Used Oil, Oil Filters & Containers Stewardship Regulation
Wildlife Act
   Designation of Wild Animals Regulation
   Designation of Wildlife Lands Regulation
   Threatened, Endangered & Extirpated Species Regulation
Wild Rice Act

Manitoba Aboriginal & Northern Affairs
Northern Affairs Act
Planning Act

Manitoba Agriculture, Food & Rural Initiatives
Animal Diseases Act
Crown Lands Act, (in part) Sections 6, 7, 10, 12(1), 14, 16, 17, 18, 21, 23, 24 to 28 both inclusive
Department of Agriculture, Food & Rural Initiatives Act
Farm Lands Ownership Act
Farm Practices Protection Act
Farm Products Marketing Act
Land Rehabilitation Act
Livestock Industry Diversification Act
Livestock & Livestock Products Act
Noxious Weeds Act
Pesticides & Fertilizers Control Act

Government Acts & Regulations

Prescribed Spraying Equipment & Controlled Products
Plant Pests & Diseases Act
Wildlife Act, (in part) Section 89(e)

Manitoba Conservation
Sustainable Development Act

Manitoba Culture, Heritage & Tourism
Heritage Manitoba Act
Heritage Resources Act
Travel Manitoba Act

Manitoba Finance
Manitoba Hydro Act (responsibility of Hon. Rosann Wowchuk)

Manitoba Health
Public Health Act
   Atmospheric Pollution Regulation
   Collection & Disposal of Wastes Regulation
   Fumigation & Pest Control Regulation
   Protection of Water Sources Regulation
   Sanitation Regulation
   Water Supplies Regulation
   Water Works, Sewerage & Sewage Disposal Regulation
   X-Ray Safety Regulation

Manitoba Infrastructure & Transportation
Crown Lands Act
Drivers & Vehicles Act
Emergency Measures Act (responsibility of Hon. Steve Ashton)
Emergency 911 Public Safety Answering Point Act (responsibility of Hon. Steve Ashton)
Highway Traffic Act
Highways Protection Act
Highways & Transportation Act
Land Acquisition Act
Manitoba Floodway and East Side Road Authority Act
Manitoba Water Services Board Act
Off-Road Vehicles Act
Provincial Parks Act
Provincial Railways Act
Trans-Canada Highway Act
Wild Rice Act

Manitoba Innovation, Energy & Mines
Biofuels Act
Economic Innovation & Technology Council Act
Energy Act
Gas Allocation Act
Gas Pipe Line Act
Greater Winnipeg Gas Distribution Act (S.M. 1988-89, C.40)
Mines & Minerals Act
Mining & Metallurgy Compensation Act
Oil & Gas Act
   Drilling & Production Regulation
Oil & Gas Production Tax Act

Manitoba Justice
Expropriation Act
Gaming Control Act (responsibility of Hon. David Walter)
Transboundary Pollution Reciprocal Act

Manitoba Labour & Immigration
Employment Standards Code
Fires Prevention & Emergency Response Act
Gas & Oil Burner Act
Steam & Pressure Plants Act
Workplace Safety & Health Act
   Construction Industry Safety Regulation
   Fibrosis & Silicosis Regulation
   Forestry, Logging & Log Hauling Regulation
   Hearing Conservation & Noise Control Regulation
   Operation of Mines Regulation
   Sanitary & Hygienic Welfare Regulation
   Workplace Hazardous Materials Information System Regulation
   Workplace Health Hazard Regulation
   Workplace Safety & Health Committee Regulation
   Workplace Safety Regulation
   Minimum Wage & Working Conditions Regulation

Manitoba Local Government
Municipal Act
Municipal Assessment Act
Planning Act (in part)

Northern Manitoba Planning & Bylaws Regulation
Provincial Land Use Policies Regulation
Subdivision Regulation
Regional Waste Management Authorities Act

Manitoba Water Stewardship
Conservation Agreements Act
   Conservation Agreement Forms Regulation
   Eligible Conservation Agencies Regulation
Conservation Districts Act
Drinking Water Safety Act, 2004
Dyking Authority Act
Fisheries Act
Fishermen's Assistance & Polluter's Liability Act
Ground Water & Water Well Act
   Well Drilling Regulation
Lake of the Woods Control Board Act
Manitoba Habitat Heritage Act
Manitoba Natural Resources Transfer Act
Natural Resources Agreement Act
Red River Floodway Act
Water Power Act
Water Protection Act
Water Resources Administration Act
Water Resources Conservation & Protection Act
Water Rights Act
Water Supply Commissions Act

New Brunswick Legislation

Department of the Environment/Environnement
Agricultural Land Protection & Development Act (in part)
Assessment & Planning Appeal Board Act (jointly with Local Government)
Beverage Containers Act
Clean Air Act
   Administrative Penalties Regulation
   Air Quality Regulation
   Appeal Regulation
   Ozone Depleting Substances Regulation
Clean Environment Act
   Appeal Regulation
   Environmental Impact Assessment Regulation
   Petroleum Product Storage & Handling Regulation
   New Brunswick Tire Stewardship Regulation
   Public Participation Regulation
   Regional Solid Waste Commissions Regulation
   Used Oil Regulation
   Water Quality Regulation
Clean Water Act
   Appeal Regulation
   Fees for Industrial Approvals
   Potable Water Regulation
   Protected Area Exemption Regulation
   Protected Areas Order
   Water Classification Regulation
   Water Well Regulation
   Watercourse & Wetland Alteration Regulation
   Watershed Protected Area Designation Order
   Wellfield Protected Area Designation Order
Community Planning Act
Environmental Trust Fund Act
Gas Distribution Act (in part)
Highway Act (Sections 58 to 62.1)
Mining Act (Subsection 68(2))
Pesticides Control Act
Pipeline Act (in part)
Topsoil Preservation Act

Department of Attorney General/Procureur général
Municipalities Act
Protected Natural Areas Act
   Establishment of Protected Natural Areas Regulation
   General Regulation, Protected Natural Areas Act

Department of Agriculture, Fisheries & Aquaculture/Agriculture, Pêches et Aquaculture
Agricultural Land Protection & Development Act
Agricultural Operation Practices Act
Aquaculture Act
Diseases of Animals Act

Government Acts & Regulations

Fisheries & Aquaculture Development Act
Fish Processing Act
Fish & Wildlife Act (in part)
Inshore Fisheries Representation Act
Livestock Operations Act
Livestock Incentives Act
Marshland Reclamation Act
Natural Products Act
Plant Health Act
Potato Disease Eradication Act

Department of Business New Brunswick/Entreprises Nouveau-Brunswick
Economic Development Act

Department of Energy/Énergie
Electricity Act
Energy Efficiency Act
Energy Efficiency and Conservation Agency of New Brunswick Act
Gas Distribution Act, 1999
Petroleum Products Pricing Act
Pipeline Act, 2005

Department of Health/Santé
Clean Air (Paragraph 8(2a) & Subsection 4)
Clean Water Act (in part)
Motor Vehicle Act (in part)
Pesticides Control Act (in part)
Public Health Act
Smoke-Free Places Act, 2004

Department of Local Government/Gouvernements locaux
Assessment & Planning Appeal Board Act (jointly with Environment)
Control of Municipalities Act
Unsightly Premises Act

Department of Natural Resources/Ressources naturelles
An Act respecting Angling Lease Number 7
Bituminous Shale Act
Conservation Easements Act
Crown Grant Restrictions Act
Crown Lands & Forests Act
    Leasing Regulation
Endangered Species Act
Fish & Wildlife Act
Forest Fires Act
Forest Products Act
Grants Act
Kouchibougac National Park Act
Maritime Forestry Complex Coporation Act
Metallic Minerals Tax Act
Mining Act (in part)
National Parks Act
Natural Products Act (in part)
Off-Road Vehicle Act
Oil & Natural Gas Act
Ownership of Minerals Act
Parks Act
Protected Natural Areas Act, 2003
Quarriable Substances Act
Scalers Act
Territorial Divisions Act
Transportation of Primary Forest Products Act
Underground Storage Act

Department of Post-Secondary Education & Training/Éducation postsecondaire et Formation
Occupational Health & Safety Act
    Code of Practice for Working with Material Containing Asbestos
    Underground Mine Regulation
    Workplace Hazardous Materials Information System (WHMIS) Regulation
Silicosis Compensation Act
Workplace Health, Safety & Compensation Commission Act

New Brunswick Power Group of Companies/Énergie NB
Electric Power Act

Department of Public Safety/Sécurité publique
Boiler & Pressure Vessel Act
Elevators & Lifts Act
Emergency 911 Act
Emergency Measures Act
Fire Prevention Act

Motor Vehicle Act
Salvage Dealers Licensing Act
Transportation of Dangerous Goods Act

Service New Brunswick/Services Nouveau-Brunswick
Boundaries Confirmation Act
Land Titles Act
Surveys Act

Department of Supply & Services/Approvisionnement et services
Public Purchasing Act
Public Works Act

Department of Tourism & Parks/Tourisme et Parcs
Parks Act
Tourism Development Act, 2008 (unproclaimed)

Department of Transportation/Transports
Highway Act
Motor Carrier Act
New Brunswick Highway Corporation Act
New Brunswick Transportation Authority Act
Public Landings Act
Shortline Railways Act

Newfoundland & Labrador Legislation

Department of Environment & Conservation
Endangered Species Act
    Endangered Species Regulation
    Species Status Advisory Committee Regulations
Environmental Protection Act
    Air Pollution Control Regulations, 2004
    Environmental Assessment Regulations, 2003
    Gasoline Volatility Control Regulations, 2003
    Halocarbon Regulations
    Heating Oil Storage Tank System Regulations
    Ozone Depleting Substances Regulations, 2003
    Pesticides Control Regulations, 2003
    Storage & Handling of Gasoline & Associated Products Regulations, 2003
    Storage of PCB Waste Regulations, 2003
    Used Oil Control Regulations
    Waste Management Regulations, 2003
    Waste Material Disposal Areas Regulations
Geographical Name Act
Land Surveyors Act
Lands Act
National Parks Lands Act
Provincial Parks Act
Water Resources Act
    Environmental Control Water & Sewage Regulations
    Notices of Protected Water Supplies, Watershed Areas, Wellhead Protected Water Supplies
    Water Power Rental Regulations, 2003
    Well Drilling Regulations, 2003
Wild Life Act
    Wild Life Park Order
    Wild Life Park Regulations
    Wild Life Regulations
    Wild Life Reserve Regulations
Wilderness & Ecological Reserves Act

Department of Fisheries & Aquaculture
Aquaculture Act
Fish Inspection Act
Fish Processing Licensing Board Act
Fisheries Act
Fisheries Restructuring Act
Fishing Industry Collective Bargaining Act
Professional Fish Harvesters Act

Department of Government Services
Architects Act
Occupational Health & Safety Act
    Asbestos Abatement Regulations
    Asbestos Exposure Code Regulations
    Mines Safety of Workers Regulations
    Occupational Health & Safety Electrical & Fisheries Advisory Committees Regulations
    Occupational Health & Safety Regulations
    Workplace Hazardous Materials Information System (WHMIS) Regulations
Petroleum Products Act

Government Acts & Regulations

Radiation Health & Safety Act

Acts Shared in Part with Other Ministries
Building Standards Act (Municipal Affairs)
Dangerous Goods Transportation Act (Justice)
Environmental Protection Act (Environment & Conservation)
Fire Prevention Act, 1991 (Municipal Affairs)
Health & Community Services Act (Health & Community Services)
Highway Traffic Act (Transportation & Works)
Motor Carrier Act (Transportation & Works)
Motorized Snow Vehicles & All-Terrain Vehicles Act (Natural Resources)
Tobacco Act (Federal) (Health & Community Services)
Urban & Rural Planning Act (Municipal Affairs)
Water Resources Act (Environment & Conservation)

Department of Health & Community Services
Food & Drug Act
Health & Community Services Act
   Public Health (Sanitation) Regulation
Smoke-Free Environment Act, 2005

Department of Innovation, Trade & Rural Development
Economic Diversification & Growth Enterprises (EDGE) Act
Research Council Act

Department of Municipal Affairs
Assessment Act, 2006
Building Standards Act
Emergency Services Act
Evacuated Communities Act
Fire Prevention Act, 1991
Municipalities Act, 1999
Regional Service Boards Act
St. John's Municipal Council Parks Act
Urban & Rural Planning Act, 2000

Department of Natural Resources
Animal Health & Protection Act
Canada-Newfoundland Atlantic Accord Implementation Act, 1986
   Canada-Newfoundland & Labrador Oil & Gas Spills & Debris Liability Newfoundland & Labrador Regulations
   Certificate of Fitness Newfoundland & Labrador Regulations
   Offshore Area Oil & Gas Operations Regulations
   Offshore Area Petroleum Geophysical
   Operations Newfoundland & Labrador Regulations
   Offshore Area Petroleum Production & Conservation Newfoundland & Labrador Regulations
   Offshore Petroleum Drilling Newfoundland & Labrador Regulations
   Offshore Petroleum Installations Newfoundland & Labrador Regulations
Electrical Power Control Act, 1994
Forest Protection Act
   Cutting of Timber Regulations
   Forest Fire Regulations
   Forest Management Districts Proclamation
Forestry Act
   Cutting of Timber Regulations
   Forest Fire Offence & Penalty Regulation
   Forest Fire Regulations
   Forest Fires Liability & Compensation Regulations
   Forest Land Management & Taxation Regulations
   Forest Management Districts Proclamation Regulations
   Mill Regulations
   Timber Royalty Regulations
   Timber Scaling Regulations
Heritage Animals Act
Hydro Corporation Act, 2007
Lower Churchill Development Act
Mineral Act
Mineral Holdings Impost Act
Mining Act
Motorized Snow Vehicles & All-Terrain Vehicles Act (jointly with Government Services)
Natural Products Marketing Act
Petroleum & Natural Gas Act
Plant Protection Act
   Seed Potato Regulations
Quarry Materials Act, 1998
Undeveloped Minerals Areas Act

Department of Tourism, Culture & Recreation
Colonial Buildings Act
Historic Resources Act
Tourist Establishments Act

Department of Transportation & Works
Expropriation Act
Local Road Boards Act
Motor Carrier Act
Pippy Park Commission Act
Rail Services Act
Transportation & Works Act

Northwest Territories Legislation

Department of Environment & Natural Resources
Environmental Protection Act
   Asphalt Paving Industry Emission Regulations
   Spill Contingency Planning & Reporting Regulations
   Used Oil & Waste Fuel Management Regulations
Environmental Rights Act
Forest Management Act
Forest Protection Act
Natural Resources Conservation Trust Act
Pesticide Act
Species at Risk (NWT) Act
Waste Reduction & Recovery Act
   Beverage Container Regulations
   Single-Use Retail Bag Regulations
Water Resources Agreement Act
Wildlife Act
   Big Game Hunting Regulations
   Birds of Prey Regulations
   Certification and Disposal of Wildlife Regulations
   Critical Wildlife Areas Regulations
   Dempster Highway Special Management Area Regulations
   Inuvialuit Settlement Region Hunters and Trappers Committees Regulations
   Nuisance Bison Control Regulations
   Sale of Wildlife Regulations
   Small Game Hunting Regulations
   Trapping Regulations
   Wildlife Business Regulations
   Wildlife Export Regulations
   Wildlife General Regulations
   Wildlife Licences and Permits Regulations
   Wildlife Management Barren-Ground Caribou Areas Regulations
   Wildlife Management Areas Regulations
   Wildlife Preserves Regulations
   Wildlife Regions Regulations
   Wildlife Sanctuaries Regulations

Department of Health & Social Services
Public Health Act
   Disease Surveillance Regulations
   Food Establishment Safety Regulations General Sanitation Exemption Regulations
   General Sanitation Regulations
   Public Pool Regulations
   Public Sewerage Systems Regulations
   Reportable Disease Control Regulations
   Tourist Accommodation Health Regulations
   Water Supply System Regulations

Department of Industry, Tourism & Investment
Agricultural Products Marketing Act
Co-operative Associations Act
Freshwater Fish Marketing Act
Herd and Fencing Act
Northwest Territories Business Development and Investment Corporation Act
Territorial Parks Act
Tourism Act

Department of Municipal & Community Affairs
Area Development Act
Cities, Towns & Villages Act
Civil Emergency Measures Act
Commissioner's Land Act
Fire Prevention Act
Hamlets Act
Planning Act
Property Assessment & Taxation Act
Settlements Act
Tåîchô Community Government Act

Department of Public Works & Services
Boilers & Pressure Vessels Act
Electrical Protection Act

Government Acts & Regulations

Gas Protection Act
Public Utilities Act

Department of Transportation
All-Terrain Vehicles Act
Motor Vehicles Act
Public Airports Act
Public Highways Act
Transportation of Dangerous Goods Act
    Transportation of Dangerous Goods Regulations

Northwest Territories & Nunavut Workers' Compensation Board
Explosives Use Act
Mine Health & Safety Act
    Environmental Tobacco Smoke Worksite Regulations
Safety Act
    Asbestos Safety Regulations
    Work Site Hazardous Materials Information System Regulations
Workers' Compensation Act

Nova Scotia Legislation

Nova Scotia Environment
Anti-idling Act
Environment Act
    Activities Designation Regulations
    Air Quality Regulations
    Approvals Procedure Regulations
    Asbestos Waste Management Regulations
    Dangerous Goods Management Regulations
    Emergency Spill Regulations
    Environmental Assessment Regulations
    Environment Act & Regulations Fees Regulations
    Greenhouse Gas Emissions Regulations
    Motive Fuel & Fuel Oil Approval Regulations
    NS Environmental Assessment Boards Regulations
    NS Environmental Trust Regulations
    On-Site Services Advisory Board Regulations
    On-Site Sewage Disposal Systems Regulations
    Ozone Layer Protection Regulations
    PCB Management Regulations
    Pesticides Regulations
    Petroleum Management Regulations
    Solid Waste-Resource Management Regulations
    Sulphide Bearing Material Disposal Regulations
    Used Oil Regulations
    Water and Wastewater Facilities and Public Drinking Water Supplies Regulations
    Well Construction Regulations
Environmental Goals and Sustainable Prosperity Act
Non-essential Pesticides Control Act
Off Highway Vehicles Act
Water Resources Protection Act
Voluntary Carbon Emissions Offset Fund Act
Wilderness Area Protection Act

Department of Agriculture
Agriculture & Marketing Act
Agriculture Marshland Conservation Act
    Marsh Land Use Regulations: Bishop-Beckwith, Dentiballis, Dugau/ Ryerson, Grand Pré, Lower Truro, Masstown, St. Croix, Victoria Diamond Jubilee, Wellington
    Non-Agricultural Use Land Exemption Regulations
Animal Health & Protection Act
    Animal Health & Protection Regulations
Bee Industry Act
Dairy Industry Act
Farm Practices Act
Livestock Health Services Act
    Livestock Health Services Regulations
Meat Inspection Act
Natural Products Act
Potato Industry Act
Weed Control Act
Wildlife Act
    Game Farming Regulations (jointly with Natural Resources)

Department of Communities, Culture and Heritage
Heritage Property Act
Sherbrooke Restoration Commission Act

Department of Economic and Rural Development and Tourism
Cooperative Associations Act
Tourist Accommodations Act

Nova Scotia Emergency Management Office
Emergency 911 Act
Emergency Management Act

Department of Energy
Canada-Nova Scotia Offshore Petroleum Resources Accord Implementation (Nova Scotia) Act
    Nova Scotia Offshore Area Certificate of Fitness Regulations
    Nova Scotia Offshore Area Oil & Gas Spills & Debris Liability Regulations
    Nova Scotia Offshore Area Petroleum Diving Regulations
    Nova Scotia Offshore Area Petroleum Drilling & Production Regulations
    Nova Scotia Offshore Area Petroleum Geophysical Operations Regulations
    Nova Scotia Offshore Area Petroleum Installations Regulations
Electricity Act
Energy-Efficient Appliances Act
Energy Resources Conservation Act
    Gas Plant Facility Regulations
    Onshore Petroleum Geophysical Exploration Regulations
    Sable Offshore Energy Project Regulations
Gas Distribution Act
Petroleum Resources Act
    Onshore Petroleum Drilling Regulations
    Onshore Petroleum Geophysical Exploration Regulations
    Petroleum Resources Regulations
    Withdrawal of Petroleum Products from the Act Regulations
Petroleum Resources Removal Permit Act
Pipeline Act
    Gas Plant Facility Regulations
    Land Acquisition Regulations
    Pipeline Benefits Plan Regulations
    Pipeline Regulations
Underground Hydrocarbons Storage Act

Nova Scotia Fisheries & Aquaculture
Fisheries & Coastal Resources Act
Fisheries Organizations Support Act
Wildlife Act
    Fishing Regulations (jointly with Natural Resources)

Department of Health & Wellness
Health Act
Health Protection Act (jointly with Department of Agriculture)
Health Research Foundation Act
Medical Laboratory Technology Act
Safer Needles in Healthcare Workplaces Act
Smoke Free Places Act
Tobacco Access Act

Department of Labour & Advanced Education
Amusement Devices Safety Act
Apprenticeship and Trades Qualifications Act
Building Code Act
Electrical Installation and Inspection Act
Elevators and Lifts Act
Fire Safety Act
Labour Standards Code
Occupational Health and Safety Act
    Occupational Health & Safety Appeal Panel Regulations
    Occupational Safety General Regulations
    Underground Mining Regulations
    Workplace Hazardous Materials Information System Regulations
Technical Safety Act
Workers' Compensation Act

Department of Natural Resources
Beaches Act
Conservation Easements Act
Endangered Species Act
    Species At Risk List Regulations
Forests Act
    Christmas Tree Grading Regulations
    Christmas Tree Levy Regulations
    Dutch Elm Disease Regulations
    Forest Fire Protection Regulations
    Forest Sustainability Regulations
    Registration & Statistical Returns Regulations
    Timber Loan Board Regulations
    Wildlife Habitat & Watercourses Protection Regulations
Land Surveyors Act

Government Acts & Regulations

Mineral Resources Act
Mines Act
Nova Scotia Federation of Anglers & Hunters Act
Off Highway Vehicles Act (jointly with Environment/Service Nova Scotia & Municipal Relations/Transportation & Infrastructure Renewal)
Primary Forest Products Marketing Act
Provincial Parks Act
Scalers Act
Trails Act
Wildlife Act
   Bear Harvesting Regulations
   Deer Farming and Marketing of Deer Products Regulations
   Deer Hunting Regulations
   Fishing Regulations (jointly with Fisheries & Aquaculture)
   Forfeiture of Seized Property Regulations
   Fur Buyers, Hide Dealers and Taxidermists Regulations
   Fur Harvesting Regulations
   Game Farming Regulations (jointly with Agriculture)
   General Wildlife Regulations
   Guide Regulations
   Hunter Education, Safety, and Training Regulations
   Licence and Permit Suspension Regulations
   Moose Hunting Regulations
   Pheasant Shooting Preserve Regulations
   Small Game Hunting Regulations

Department of Service Nova Scotia & Municipal Relations
Assessment Act
Land Registration Act
Motor Vehicle Act
Municipal Government Act
Off-Highway Vehicles Act (jointly with Environment/Natural Resources/Transportation & Infrastructure Renewal)
   Off-Highway Vehicles Designated Trails
   Off-Highway Vehicle Infrastructure Fund Regulations
   Off-Highway Vehicles Closed Courses Regulations
   Off-Highway Vehicles Designated Trails and Trail Permits Regulations
   Off-Highway Vehicles Fees Regulations
   Off-Highway Vehicles General Regulations
   Off-Highway Vehicles Safety and Training Regulations
   Off-Highway Vehicles Vulnerable Areas Licensing Regulations

Department of Economic & Rural Development & Tourism
Peggy's Cove Commission Act

Department of Communities, Culture & Heritage
Heritage Property Act
Schooner Bluenose Foundation Act Special Places Protection Act (Ecological Site Designations: Abraham Lake, Bornish Hill,
   Duncans Cove, Great Barren & Quinan Lakes, Indian Man Lake, MacFarlane Woods, Panuke Lake, Ponhook Lake,
   Quinns Meadow, River Inhabitants, Roman Valley, Spinneys Health, Sporting Lake, Tusket River, Washabuck River;
   Protected Site Designations: Certain lands at Debert, Colchester County, Fletcher Lake, Joggins Fossil Cliff, Parrsboro
   Fossil Site, Port Morien French Mine Site)

Department of Transportation & Infrastructure Renewal
Dangerous Goods Transportation Act
   Dangerous Goods Transportation Regulations
Ferries Act
Highway 104 Western Alignment Act
Motor Carrier Act
Motor Vehicle Act
Off-Highway Vehicles Act (jointly with Environment/Natural Resources/Service Nova Scotia & Municipal Relations)
Public Highways Act
Railways Act
Surplus Crown Property Disposal Act

Nova Scotia Utility & Review Board
Petroleum Products Pricing Act
Public Utilities Act
Utility & Review Board Act

Nunavut Territory Legislation

Department of Environment
Environmental Protection Act
   Asphalt Paving Industry Emission Regulations
   Spill Contingency Planning & Reporting

Environmental Rights Act
Flood Damage Reduction Agreements Act
Forest Management Act
   Forest Management Regulations
Forest Protection Act
Freshwater Fish Marketing Act
   Establishing Freshwater Fish Marketing Corporation Regulations
Herd & Fencing Act
Natural Resource Conservation Trust Act
Pesticides Act
Territorial Park Act
   Community Parks Order
   Historical Parks Order
   Territorial Parks Regulations
Travel & Tourism Act
   Outfitter Regulations
   Tourist Establishment Regulations
Water Resources Agreements Act
Wildlife Act
   Big Game Hunting Regulations
   Birds of Prey Regulations
   Certification & Disposal of Wildlife Regulations
   Critical Wildlife Areas Regulations
   Dempster Highway Special Management Area Regulations
   Nuisance Bison Control Regulations
   Polar Bear Defence Kill Regulations
   Sale of Wildlife Regulations
   Small Game Hunting Regulations
   Trapping Regulations
   Wildlife Business Regulations
   Wildlife Export Regulations
   Wildlife General Regulations
   Wildlife Licenses & Permits Regulations
   Wildlife Management Barren Ground Caribou Area Regulation
   Wildlife Management Grizzly Bear Area Regulations
   Wildlife Management Muskox Areas Regulations
   Wildlife Management Outfitter Area Regulations
   Wildlife Management Polar Bear Areas Regulations
   Wildlife Management Units Regulations
   Wildlife Management Wood Bison Area Regulations
   Wildlife Management Zones Regulations
   Wildlife Preserves Regulations
   Wildlife Regions Regulations
   Wildlife Sanctuaries Regulations

Department of Community & Government Services
Area Development Act
   Resolute Bay Development Area Regulations
   Strathcona Sound Development Area Regulations
Cities, Towns & Villages Act
   Iqaluit By-Law Exemption Order
   Town of Iqaluit Continuation Order
Commissioner's Land Act
   Commissioner's Airport Lands Regulations
   Commissioner's Land Regulations
Consumer Protection Act
Dog Act
Emergency Measures Act
Fire Prevention Act
   Fire Prevention Regulations
   Fireworks Regulations
   Propane Cylinder Storage
Gas Protection Act
Hamlets Act
Planning Act
Settlements Act
Safety Act

Department of Economic Development & Transportation
All-Terrain Vehicles Act
   All-Terrain Vehicles Regulations
   Special All-Terrain Vehicles Fees Regulations
   Special All-Terrain Vehicles Helmet Regulations
Economic Development Agreements Act
Motor Vehicles Act
   Carrier Fitness Regulations
   Exemption of Motor Vehicles Act Regulations
   Hours of Service Regulations
   Large Vehicle Control Regulations
   Motor Vehicle Equipment Regulations

School Bus Regulations
Seasonal Highway Regulations
Nunavut Development Corporation
Public Highways Act
Highway Designation & Classification Regulations
Highway Signs Regulations
Transportation of Dangerous Goods Act
Transportation of Dangerous Goods Regulations
Travel & Tourism Act
Guide Exemption Regulations
Outfitter Regulations
Tourist Establishment Regulations
Travel Development Area Regulations

Department of Executive & Intergovernmental Affairs
Nunavut Power Corporation Assets Transfer Confirmation Act
Public Utilities Act
Public Utilities Regulations

Department of Finance
Consolodation of Workers' Compensation Act
Explosives Use Act
Explosives Regulations
Mine Health & Safety Act
Mine Health & Safety Regulations
Safety Act
Asbestos Safety Regulations
Environmental Tobacco Smoke Work Site Regulations
General Safety Regulations
Safety Forms Regulations
Silica Sand Blasting Safety Regulations
Work Site Hazardous Materials Information System Regulations

Department of Health & Social Services
Boards of Management Dissolution Act
Disease Registries Act
Reportable Diseases Order
Public Health Act
Camp Sanitation Regulations
Communicable Diseases Regulations
General Sanitation Exemption Regulations
General Sanitation Regulations
Meat Inspection Regulations
Public Sewerage Systems Regulations
Public Water Supply Regulations
Tourist Accomodation Health Regulations
Tobacco Control Act

Ontario Legislation

Ministry of Environment
Environmental Assessment Act
Designations & Exemptions
Electricity Projects Regulation
Environmental Assessment General Regulations
Environmental Protection Act
Air Pollution - Local Air Quality Regulations
Airborne Contaminant Discharge Monitoring & Reporting Regulations
Boilers Regulation
Certificates of Approval Exemptions Air Regulation
Cessation of Coal Use - Atikokan, Lambton, Nanticoke and Thunder Bay Generating Stations Regulations
Classes of Contaminants Exemption Regulations
Classification & Exemption of Spills & Reporting of Discharges Regulations
Containers Regulation
Deep Well Disposal Regulation
Designation of Waste Regulation
Discharge of Sewage from Pleasure Boats Regulation
Disposable Containers for Milk Regulations
Disposable Paper Containers for Milk Regulations
Dry Cleaners Regulations
Effluent Monitoring & Effluent Limits Regulations (organic chemicals, inorganic chemicals, iron & steel manufacturers, electric power generation, petroleum sector, metal mining sector, industrial minerals sector, metal casting sector, pulp & paper sector)
Emissions Trading Regulation
Environmental Penalities Regulation
Ethanol in Gasoline
Exemption Regulations
Gasoline Volatility Regulation
General Waste Management Regulation
Greenhouse Gas Emissions Reporting Regulations
Ground Source Heat Pumps Regulation
Halon Fire Extinguishing Equipment Regulation
Hot Mix Asphalt Facilities Regulation
Industrial, Commercial & Institutional Source Separation Programs Regulation
Industry Emissions - Nitrogen Oxides & Sulphur Dioxide
Lakeview Generating Station Regulations
Lambton Industry Meteorological Alert Regulation
Landfilling Sites Regulation
Marinas Regulation
Mobile PCB Destruction Facilities Regulation
Motor Vehicles Regulation
Municipal Sewage & Water & Roads Class Environmental Assessment Project Regulation
Municipalities, Secured Creditors, Receivers, Trustees in Bankruptcy & Fiduciaries, Pt.XV.2 of the Act Regulations, 2002
Ontario Power Generation Regulations
Ozone Depleting Substances & Other Halocarbons Regulation
Packaging Audits & Packaging Reduction Work Plans Regulation
Plasco Demonstration Project Regulation
Records of Site Condition, Pt.XV.1 of the Act Regulations, 2004
Recovery of Gasoline Vapour in Bulk Transfers Regulation
Recycling & Composting of Municipal Waste Regulation
Refillable Containers for Carbonated Soft Drink Regulation
Refrigerants Regulation
Renewable Energy Approvals Under Part V.0.1. of the Act Regulation
Solvents Regulation
Spill Prevention & Contingency Plans Regulation
Spills Regulation
Sulphur Content of Fuels Regulation
Transitional Provisions Relating to the Repeal of Pt.VIII of the Act Regulations
Waste Audits & Waste Reduction Workplans Regulation
Waste Disposal Sites & Waste Management Systems Subject to Approval Under or Exempt from the Environmental Assessment Act Regulations
Waste Management (PCBs) Regulation
Environmental Review Tribunal
Ministry of the Environment Act
Ontario Water Resources Act
Additional Charges Regulation
Charges for Industrial & Commercial Water Users Regulation
Environmental Penalties Regulation
Exemption - City of Detroit Regulation
Lake Simcoe Protection Regulation
Licensing of Sewage Works Operators Regulations
Municipal Sewage & Water & Roads Class Environmental Assessment Projects Regulation
Secured Creditors, Receivers, Trustees in Bankruptcy Regulations, 2002
Sewage Works Subject to Approval under the Environmental Assessment Act Regulations
Transitional Provisions Relating to the Repeal of Pt.VIII of the Environmental Protection Act Regulations
Water Taking Regulation
Wells Regulation
Pesticides Act
Safe Drinking Water Act, 2002
Certification of Drinking-Water System Operators & Water Quality Analysts
Compliance & Enforcement
Definitions of "Deficiency" & "Municipal Drinking-Water System" Regulations, 2003
Definitions of Words & Expressions Used the Act Regulations, 2003
Drinking-Water Systems Regulations, 2003
Drinking-Water Testing Services Regulations, 2003
Licensing of Municipal Drinking Water Systems Regulation
Ontario Drinking-Water Quality Standards Regulations, 2003
Schools, Private Schools & Day Nurseries Regulations, 2003
Sustainable Water & Sewage Systems Act, 2002 (not in Force)
Toxics Reduction Act
Waste Diversion Act, 2002
Blue Box Waste Regulations, 2002
Municipal Hazardous or Special Waste Regulation
Stewardship Ontario Regulation
Used Oil Material Regulations, 2003
Used Tires Regulations, 2003
Waste Electrical & Electronic Equipment

Ministry of Agriculture, Food & Rural Affairs
Agricorp Act
Agricultural Employees Protection Act 2002
Agricultural & Horticultural Organizations Act

Government Acts & Regulations

Agricultural Research Institute of Ontario Act
    Agricultural Lands Regulations
Agricultural Tile Drainage Installation Act
Animals for Research Act
Dead Animal Disposal Act
Drainage Act
Farm Products Container Act
Farm Products Marketing Act
Farming & Food Production Protection Act
Food Safety & Quality Act, 2001
Livestock & Livestock Products Act
Meat Inspection Act (Ontario)
Ministry of Agriculture, Food & Rural Affairs Act
Nutrient Management Act, 2002
Plant Diseases Act
Tile Drainage Act
Weed Control Act

Ministry of Community Safety & Correctional Services
Emergency Management and Civil Protection Act
Fire Protection & Prevention Act, 1997

Ministry of Culture
AGO Act
Arts Council Act
George R. Gardiner Museum of Ceramic Art Act
Historical Parks Act
Hummingbird Performing Arts Centre Corporation Act
McMichael Canadian Art Collection Act
Metropolitan Toronto Convention Centre Act
Ontario Heritage Act
Ontario Place Corporation Act
Public Libraries Act
Royal Ontario Museum Act
St. Lawrence Parks Commission Act
Science North Act

Ministry of Economic Development & Trade
Ministry of Economic Development & Trade Act
Research Foundation Act

Ministry of Energy
Electricity Restructuring Act, 2004
Energy Efficiency Act
Green Energy Act
Ministry of Energy Act
Ontario Energy Board Act
Ontario Energy Board Amendment Act (Electricity Pricing), 2003
Toronto District Heating Corporation Act

Ministry of Government Services
Archives & Recordkeeping Act
Boundaries Act
Electricity Act
Land Registration Reform Act
Land Titles Act
Safety & Consumer Statutes Administration Act
Technical Standards & Safety Act, 2000

Ministry of Health & Long-Term Care
Excellent Care for All Act, 2010
Health Protection & Promotion Act
Health System Improvements Act, 2007
Ministry of Health & Long-Term Care Act
Tobacco Control Act, 1994

Ministry of Infrastructure
Places to Grow Act, 2005
    Growth Plan Areas Regulation

Ministry of Labour
Occupational Health & Safety Act
    Control of Exposure to Biological or Chemical Agents Regulations
    Designated Substance Regulations (Various)
    Farming Operations Regulation
    Oil & Gas - Offshore Regulation
    Workplace Hazardous Materials Information System (WHMIS) Regulations
Rights of Labour Act
Workplace Safety & Insurance Act

Ministry of Municipal Affairs & Housing
Greenbelt Act
Housing Development Act
Ministry of Municipal Affairs & Housing Act
Municipal Act
Municipal Water & Sewage Transfer Act
Oak Ridges Moraine Conservation Act
Oak Ridges Moraine Protection Act, 2001
    Oak Ridges Moraine Conservation Plan
Ontario Planning & Development Act
Planning Act
Public Utilities Act
Road Access Act
Shoreline Property Assistance Act
Snow Roads & Fences Act
Toronto Islands Residential Community Stewardship Act

Ministry of Natural Resources
Aggregate Resources Act
Algonquin Forestry Authority Act
Beds of Navigable Waters Act
Conservation Authorities Act
Conservation Land Act
    Conservation Bodies Land Regulation
Crown Forest Sustainability Act
Endangered Species Act
    Endangered Species Regulation
Fish Inspection Act
Fish & Wildlife Conservation Act
    Possession, Buying & Selling of Wildlife
    Wildlife in Captivity
    Wildlife Management Units
    Wildlife Schedules
Forest Fires Prevention Act
Forestry Act
Gas & Oil Leases Act
Heritage Hunting & Fishing Act, 2002
Indian Lands Act
Indian Lands Agreement Confirmation Act
Industrial & Mining Lands Compensation Act
Kawartha Highlands Signature Park Act
Lac Seul Conservation Act
Lake of the Woods Control Board Act
Lakes & Rivers Improvement Act
Manitoba-Ontario Lake St. Joseph Diversion Agreement Authorization Act
Migratory Birds Convention Act (Canada)
    Ontario Regulations
Mining Act
Ministry of Natural Resources Act
Niagara Escarpment Planning & Development Act
North Georgian Bay Recreational Reserve Act
Northern Ontario Heritage Fund Act
Northern Services Boards Act
Oil, Gas & Salt Resources Act
Ontario Geographic Names Board Act
Ontario Harbours Agreement Act
Ottawa River Water Powers Act
Professional Foresters Act
Provincial Parks & Conservation Reserves Act
    Conservation Reserves: General Provisions Regulation
    Designation & Classification of Provincial Parks Regulation
    Designation of Conservation Reserves Regulation
    Mechanized Travel in Wilderness Parks Regulation
    Provincial Parks: General Provisions Regulation
Public Lands Act
Surveys Act
Wild Rice Harvesting Act
Wilderness Areas Act

Ministry of Northern Development, Mines & Forestry
Mining Act
Ministry of Northern Development, Mines & Forestry Act
Ontario Northland Transportation Commission Act

Ministry of Transportation
Airports Act
Dangerous Goods Transportation Act
Highway Traffic Act
Ministry of Transportation Act
Motorized Snow Vehicles Act
Off-Road Vehicles Act
Ontario Highway Transport Board Act

Government Acts & Regulations

Public Service Works on Highways Act
Public Transportation & Highway Improvement Act
Public Vehicles Act
Shortline Railways Act

Prince Edward Island Legislation

Department of Environment, Energy & Forestry
Agicultural Crop Rotation Act
Automobile Junk Yards Act
Beverage Containers Act
   General Regulations
   Recyclable Beverage Container Deposit Regulations
Boilers & Pressure Vessels Act
Electrical Inspection Act
Elevators & Lifts Act
Energy Corporation Act
Environmental Protection Act
   Air Quality Regulations
   Code for Plumbing Services Regulations
   Environmental Assessment Fees Regulation
   Environmental Records Review Regulations
   Drinking Water & Wastewater Facility Operating Regulations
   Excavation Pits Regulations
   Litter Control Regulation
   Materials Recycling Regulation
   Ozone Layer Protection Regulations
   Petroleum Hydrocarbon Remediation Regulations
   Petroleum Storage Tank Regulations
   Sewage Disposal Regulations
   Waste Resource Management Regulations
   Watercourse & Wetland Protection Regulations
   Water Well Regulations
Fisheries Act (related)
Forest Management Act
   Forest Renewal Program Regulations
   Provincial Forests Regulations
Mineral Resources Act
Natural Areas Protection Act
Oil & Natural Gas Act
   Oil & Gas Conservation Regulations
Pesticides Control Act
Power Engineers Act
Provincial Building Code Act
Public Forest Council Act
Renewable Energy Act
Unsightly Property Act
Wildlife Conservation Act
   Angling Regulations
   Fur Harvesting Regulations
   Ground Hemlock Regulations
   Hunting & Trapping Seasons Regulation
   Hunting Guide Regulations
   Snowshoe Hare Snaring Regulations
   Wildlife Conservation Fund Regulations
   Wildlife Management Areas Regulations

Department of Agriculture, Fisheries & Aquaculture
Agricultural Products Standards Act
Animal Health & Protection Act
Dairy Industry Act
Environmental Protection Act (in part)
Farm Machinery Dealers & Vendors Act
Farm Practices Act
Fire Prevention Act
Occupational Health & Safety Act
Plant Health Act
Weed Control Act

Department of Community & Cultural Affairs DELETE
Archaeological Sites Protection Act
Electrical Inspection Act
Elevators & Lifts Act
Emergency 911 Act
Emergency Measures Act
Employment Standards Act
Fathers of Confederation Buildings Act
Fire Prevention Act
Heritage Places Protection Act
Lucy Maud Montgomery Foundation Act
Museum Act
Power Engineers Act
Rural Community Fire Companies Act

Department of Community Services, Seniors & Labour
Employment Standards Act

Department of Finance & Municipal Affairs
Environment Tax Act
Gasoline Tax Act

Department of Health
Health Services Act
Public Health Act
Smoke-Free Places Act

Department of Innovation & Advanced Learning
Area Industrial Commission Act

Department of Justice & Public Safety
Emergency 911 Act
Emergency Measures Act
Fire Prevention Act
Rural Community Fire Companies Act

Island Regulatory & Appeals Commission
Electric Power Act
Petroleum Products Act
Water & Sewerage Act

Department of Tourism & Culture
Fathers of Confederation Buildings Act
Heritage Places Protection Act
Lucy Maud Montgomery Foundation Act
Museum Act
National Park Act
Recreation Development Act
   Provincial Parks Regulations
Tourism Industry Act
Tourism PEI Act
Trails Act

Department of Transportation & Infrastructure Renewal
Dangerous Goods (Transportation) Act
Expropriation Act
Highway Traffic Act
Land Survey Act
Off Highway Vehicle Act
Public Works Act
Roads Act
   Closing of Roads Regulations
   Highway Access Regulations
   Public Utility Easement (Fees) Regulations
   Vehicle Weights & Dimensions Regulations

Prince Edward Island Workers Compensation Board
Occupational Health & Safety Act
Workers Compensation Act

Québec Legislation

Ministère du Développement durable, de l'Environnement et des Parcs/Sustainable Development, Environment & Parks
Loi portant restrictions à l'élevage de porcs/Act to Impose Restrictions on Pig Farming, 2002
Loi portant sur la délimitation de la ligne des hautes eaux du Fleuve Saint-Laurent sur le territoire de la municipalité régionale
   de comté de la Côte-de-Beaupré/An Act to delimit the high water mark of the St. Lawrence River in the territory of
   Municipalité régionale de comté de La Côte-de-Beaupré
Loi sur la conservation du patrimoine naturel/Natural Heritage Conservation Act
Loi sur la conservation et la mise en valeur de la faune/Act respecting the Conservation & Development of Wildlife (in part)
Loi sur la protection des arbres/Tree Protection Act
Loi sur la provocation artificielle de la pluie/Act respecting the artificial inducement of rain
Loi sur la qualité de l'environnement/Environment Quality Act
   Agricultural Operations Regulation, 2002
   Groundwater Catchment Regulation, 2002
   Land Protection & Rehabilitation Regulation, 2003
   Regulation respecting certain bodies for the protection of the environment and social milieu of the territory of James Bay and

Government Acts & Regulations

Northern Québec
Regulation respecting Compensation for Municipal Services Provided to Recover & Reclaim Residual Materials
Regulation respecting Environmental Impact Assessments in Northeastern Québec
Regulation respecting Halocarbons
Regulation respecting Hazardous Materials
Regulation respecting Hot Mix Asphalt Plants
Regulation respecting Industrial Depollution Attestations
Regulation respecting Motor Vehicle Traffic in Certain Fragile Environments
Regulation respecting Ozone-Depleting Substances
Regulation respecting Permits & Certificates for the Sale & Use of Pesticides
Regulation respecting Pits & Quarries
Regulation respecting Prevention of Water
Pollution in Livestock Operations
Regulation respecting Public Swimming & Wading Pools
Regulation respecting Pulp & Paper Mills
Regulation respecting Sanitary Conditions in Industrial or other Camps
Regulation respecting Snow Elimination Sites
Regulation respecting Solid Waste
Regulation respecting the Application of the Environment Quality Act
Regulation respecting the Artificial Inducement of Rain
Regulation respecting the Burial of Contaminated Soils
Regulation respecting the environmental and social impact assessment and review procedure applicable to the territory of James Bay and Northern Québec
Regulation respecting the environmental impact assessment and review applicable to a part of the northeastern Québec region
Regulation respecting the Liquid Effluents of Petroleum Refineries
Regulation respecting the Quality of Drinking Water
Regulation respecting the Quality of the Atmosphere
Regulation respecting the Recovery & Reclamation of Discarded Paint Containers & Paints
Regulation respecting the Recovery & Reclamation of Used Oils, Oil or Fluid Containers & Used Filters
Regulation respecting threatened or vulnerable plant species and their habitats
Regulation respecting Used Tire Storage
Regulation Respecting Waste Water Disposal Systems for Isolated Dwellings
Regulation respecting the Water Property in the Domain of the State, 2003
Regulation respecting Waterworks & Sewer Services
Rules of internal management of the James Bay Advisory Committee on the Environment
Rules of internal management of the Kativik Environmental Advisory Committee
Loi sur la sécurité des barrages/Dam Safety Act
Loi sur la Société des établissements de plein air du Québec
Loi sur la Société québécoise de récupération et de recyclage
Loi sur la vente et la distribution de bière et de boissons gazeuses dans des contenants à remplissage unique/Act respecting the Sale & Distribution of Beer & Soft Drinks in Non-returnable Containers
Loi sur le développement durable
Loi sur le ministère du Développement durable, de l'Environnement et des Parcs
Loi sur le parc de la Mauricie et ses environs
Loi sur le Parc Forillon et des environs
Loi sur le parc marin du Saguenay-Saint-Laurent
Loi sur le régime des eaux/Watercourses Act
Loi sur les espèces menacées ou vulnérables/Act respecting Threatened or Vulnerable Species
Loi sur les pesticides/Pesticides Act
Pesticides Management Code, 2003
Loi sur les parcs
Loi visant la préservation des ressources en eau/Water Resources Preservation Act

Ministère des Affaires municipales et des Régions/Municipal Affairs
Code municipal du Québec
Loi concernant la réglementation municipale des édifices publics
Loi sur l'aménagement et l'urbanisme
Loi sur la Régie du logement
Loi sur la Société québécoise d'assainissement des eaux
Loi sur les abus préjudiciables à l'agriculture
Loi sur les cités et villes
Loi sur les conseils intermunicipaux de transport dans la région de Montréal
Loi sur les immeubles industriels municipaux
Loi sur les travaux municipaux

Ministère de l'Agriculture, des Pêcheries et de l'Alimentation/Agriculture, Fisheries & Food
Loi sur l'acquisition de terres agricoles par des non-résidants/An Act governing the acquisition of farm land by non-residents
Loi sur l'aquaculture commerciale/ An Act respecting commercial aquaculture
Loi sur l'assurance-récolte/Crop Insurance Act
Loi sur la commercialisation des produits marins/An Act respecting the marketing of marine products
Loi sur la conservation et la mise en valeur de la faune/An Act respecting the conservation & development of wildlife
Loi sur la prévention des maladies de la pomme de terre/An Act respecting prevention of disease in potatoes
Loi sur la protection sanitaire des animaux/Animal Health Protection Act
Loi sur le ministère de l'Agriculture, des Pêcheries et de l'Alimentation/An Act respecting the Ministère de l'Agriculture, des Pêcheries et de l'Alimentation
Loi sur les abus préjudiciables à l'agriculture/Agricultural Abuses Act
Loi sur les cités et villes/Cities & Towns Act (certaines sections)
Loi sur les terres agricoles du domaine de l'État/An Act respecting agricultural lands in the domain of the state

Ministère de la Culture et des Communications/Culture & Communications
Loi sur les musées nationaux

Ministère des Ressources naturelles et de la Faune/Natural Resources & Wildlife
Loi approuvant la convention de la Baie-James et du nord québécois/An Act approving the Agreement concerning James Bay and Northern Québec
Loi approuvant la convention du nord-est québécois/An Act approving the Northeastern Québec Agreement
Loi assurant la mise en oeuvre de l'entente concernant une nouvelle relation entre le gouvernement du Québec et les Cris du Québec/An Act to ensure the implementation of the Agreement Concerning a New Relationship Between the Government of Québec and the Crees of Québec
Loi concernant la construction par Hydro-Québec d'infrastructures et d'équipements par suite de la tempête de verglas survenue du 5 au 9 janvier 1998
Loi concernant les droits sur les mines/Mining Duties Act
Loi de 1994 sur la convention concernant les oiseaux migrateurs
Loi favorisant la réforme du cadastre québécois/An Act to promote the reform of the cadastre in Québec
Loi sur les forêts/Forest Act
Loi régissant les activités d'aménagement forestier de bénéficiaires de contrats d'approvisionnement et d'aménagement forestier pour les années 2000-2001 et 2001-2002
Loi sur Hydro-Québec/Hydro-Québec Act
Loi sur l'agence de l'efficacité énergétique/An Act respecting the Agence de l'efficacité énergétique
Loi sur l'efficacité énergétique d'appareils fonctionnant à l'électricité ou aux hydrocarbures/An Act respecting the energy efficiency of electrical or hydrocarbon-fuelled appliances
Loi sur la conservation et la mise en valeur de la faune/Act respecting the conservation and development of wildlife
Regulation respecting aquaculture and the sale of fish
Lands in the Domain of the State Designated for Development of Wildlife Resources Regulation
Regulation respecting hunting and fishing controlled
Regulation respecting the enforcement of certain legislative and regulatory provisions respecting the protection of the environment by wildlife protection officers
Regulation respecting wildlife habitats
Regulation respecting wildlife sanctuaries
Loi sur la division territoriale/Territorial Division Act
Loi sur la Régie de l'énergie/An Act respecting the Régie de l'énergie
Loi sur la société de développement autochtone de la Baie James/An Act respecting the James Bay Native Development Corporation
Loi sur la société Eeyou de la Baie-James/An Act respecting the James Bay Eeyou Corporation
Loi sur la société nationale de l'amiante/An Act respecting the Société nationale de l'amiante
Loi sur le cadastre/Cadastre Act
Loi sur le développement et l'organisation municipale de la région de la Baie-James/James Bay Region Development and Municipal Organization Act
Loi sur le ministère des ressources naturelles, de la faune et des parcs/An Act respecting the Ministère des Ressources naturelles, de la Faune et des Parcs
Loi sur le programme d'aide aux Inuits bénéficiaires de la convention de la Baie-James et du nord québécois pour leurs activités de chasse, de pêche et de piégeage/An Act respecting the support program for Inuit beneficiaries of the James Bay and Northern Québec agreement for their hunting, fishing and trapping activities
Loi sur le régime des eaux/Watercourses Act
Regulation respecting the water property in the domain of the State
Loi sur le régime des terres dans les territoires de la Baie-James et du Nouveau-Québec/An Act respecting the land regime in the James Bay and New Québec territories

Loi sur les arpentages/An Act respecting land survey
Loi sur les bureaux de la publicité des droits/An Act respecting registry offices
Loi sur les clubs de chasse et de pêche/Fish and Game Clubs Act
Loi sur les compagnies de flottage/ Timber-Driving Companies Act
Loi sur les droits de chasse et de pêche dans les territoires de la Baie James et du Nouveau-Québec/An Act respecting hunting and fishing rights in the James Bay and New Québec territories
Loi sur les espèces menacées ou vulnérables/An Act respecting threatened or vulnerable species
Loi sur les mines/Mining Act
Loi sur les Pêches
Loi sur les produits et les équipements pétroliers/An Act respecting petroleum products and equipment
Loi sur les systèmes municipaux et les systèmes privés d'électricité/An Act respecting municipal and private electric power systems
Loi sur les terres du domaine de l'état/An Act respecting the lands in the domain of the State
Loi sur les titres de propriété dans certains districts électoraux/An Act respecting land titles in certain electoral districts
Loi sur l'exportation de l'électricité/An Act respecting the exportation of electric power

Ministère de la Santé et des Services sociaux/Health & Social Services
Loi sur la protection de la santé publique/Public Health Protection Act
Loi sur la santé publique/Public Health Act
Loi sur le tabac/Tobacco Act

Ministère de la Sécurité publique/Public Security
Loi sur la sécurité civile/Civil Protection Act
Loi sur la sécurité incendie/Fire Safety Act
Loi sur le ministère de la Sécurité publique/An Act respecting the Ministère de la Sécurité publique
Loi sur les bombes lacrymogènes/Act respecting tear bombs
Loi sur les explosifs/An Act respecting explosives

Ministère des Transports/Transportation
Code de la sécurité routière/Highway Safety Code
Loi concernant les partenariats en matière d'infrastructures de transport/Act respecting transport infrastructure partnerships
Loi concernant les propriétaires et exploitants de véhicules lourds/Act respecting owners and operators of heavy vehicles
Loi modifiant la Loi sur les transports en matière de camionnage en vrac/Act to amend the Transport Act as regards bulk trucking
Loi sur l'expropriation/Expropriation Act
Loi sur la sécurité du transport terrestre guidé/Act to ensure safety in guided land transportation
Loi sur les chemins de fer/Railway Act
Loi sur les sociétés de transport en commun/Act respecting public transit authorities
Loi sur les véhicules hors route/Act respecting off-highway vehicles

Ministère du Travail/Labour
Loi sur les accidents du travail et les maladies professionnelles/Act respecting accidents at work & professional illness or sickness
Loi sur la santé et la sécurité du travail/Occupational Health & Safety Act

Saskatchewan Legislation

Saskatchewan Environment
Clean Air Act
    Clean Air Regulation
Conservation Easements Act
    Potash Refining Air Emissions Regulations
Ecological Reserves Act
    Assiniboine Slopes Provincial Ecological Reserves Regulations
    Buffalograss Ecological Reserve Regulations
    Provincial Ecological Reserves Regulation
    Qu'Appelle Coulee Provincial Ecological Reserves Regulations
    Representative Area Ecological Reserve Regulations
Environmental Assessment Act
Environmental Management & Protection Act, 2002
    Environmental Spill Control Regulations
    Halocarbon Control Regulations
    Hazardous Substances & Dangerous Goods Regulations
    Mineral Industry Environmental Protection Regulations
    Municipal Refuse Management Regulations
    Ozone-Depleting Substances Control Regulations
    PCB Waste Storage Regulations
    Reservoir Development Area Regulations
    Scrap Tire Management Regulations
    Used Oil Collection Regulations
    Waste Electronic Equipment Regulations
    Waste Paint Management Regulations
    Water Regulations
Fisheries Act
    Fisheries Regulations
Forest Resources Management Act
    Dutch Elm Disease Regulations
    Forest Resources Management Regulations
    Indian Treaty Obligations Regulations
    Surface Lease Agreement Regulations: Beaverlodge, Cigar Lake, Cluff Lake, Jolu Project, Key Lake, Konuto Project, McArthur River Operation, McClean Lake, Midwest Joint, Rabbit Lake
    Wild Rice Regulations
    Withdrawal of Land from Forests; Historical Interest Regulations
Grasslands National Park Act
Litter Control Act
Natural Resources Act
    Commercial Activities Regulations
    Commercial Fishing Production Incentive Regulations
    Outfitter & Guide Regulations, 1996
    Resource Protection & Development Services Regulations
    Park Land Reserve Regulations
    Parks Regulations
    Recreation Site Regulations, 1991
Parks Act
    Government Land Reserves Regulation
    Historic Sites Regulations
    Park Land Reserves Regulations
Prairie & Forest Fires Act, 1982
Provincial Lands Act
    Crown Resource Lands Regulations, 1989
    Provincial Lands Regulations
    Surface Rights Regulations (Grasslands Park, Komis Project, Parks Lake Uranium Mining, Seabee)
Regional Parks Act, 1979
Sale or Lease of Certain Lands Act
State of the Environment Report Act
Water Appeal Board Act
Water Regulations Act, 2002
Wildlife Act, 1998
    Captive Wildlife Regulations
    Dog Training Regulations
    Open Seasons Game Regulations
    Wild Species at Risk Regulations
    Wildlife Landowner Assistance Regulations, 1991
    Wildlife Management Zones & Special Areas Boundaries Regulations, 1990
    Wildlife Regulations, 1981
Wildlife Habitat Protection Act
    Treaty Land Entitlement Withdrawal Regulations
    Wildlife Habitat Lands Designation Regulations
    Wildlife Habitat Lands Disposition & Alteration Regulations

Saskatchewan Agriculture & Food
Agri-Food Act, 2004
Agri-Food Innovation Act
Animal Products Act
Department of Agriculture, Food & Rural Revitalization Act
Disease of Animal Act
Expropriation (Rehabilitation Projects) Act
Farming Communities Land Act
Irrigation Act
Line Fence Act
Pastures Act
Pest Control Act
    Bacterial Ring Rot Control Regulations
    Dutch Elm Disease Control Regulations
Pest Control Products (Saskatchewan) Act
Provincial Lands Act
Sale or Lease of Certain Lands Act
    Saskatchewan Wetland Conservation Corporation Land Regulation
Soil Drifting Control Act

Saskatchewan Health
Department of Health Act
Public Health Act, 1994
Tobacco Control Act

Saskatchewan Highways & Infrastructure
Dangerous Goods Transportation Act
Highways & Transportation Act, 1997
Railway Act

Government Acts & Regulations

Saskatchewan Industry & Resources
Crown Minerals Act
Department of Energy & Mines Act
Ethanol Fuel Act, 2002
    Ethanol Fuel (General) Regulations
    Ethanol Fuel (Grant) Regulations
Mineral Resources Act
    Seismic Exploration Regulations
Oil & Gas Conservation Act
    Oil & Gas Conservation Regulations
Pipelines Act

Saskatchewan Labour Relations & Workplace Safety
Occupational Health & Safety Act, 1993 (Mines Regulation)
Occupational Health & Safety Regulations, 1996
Radiation Health & Safety Act, 1985
    Radiation Health & Safety Regulations
Worker's Compensation Act
    Worker's Compensation Act Exclusion Regulations
Worker's Compensation General Regulations, 1985

Saskatchewan Municipal Affairs
Border Areas Act
Cities Act
Department of Rural Development Act
Municipal Expropriation Act
Municipalities Act
Northern Municipalities Act, 2010
Planning & Development Act, 2007
Rural Development Act

Saskatchewan Watershed Authority
Conservation & Development Act
Saskatchewan Watershed Authority Act 2005
    Drainage Control Regulations
    Groundwater Regulations
    Reservoir Development Area Regulations
Water Power Act
Watershed Associations Act

SaskEnergy Incorporated
SaskEnergy Act

SaskWater
Saskatchewan Water Corporation Act, 2002

Yukon Territory Legislation

Yukon Environment
Animal Health Act, (jointly with Energy, Mines & Resources)
Environment Act
    Administrative Regulation
    Air Emissions Regulations
    Beverage Container Regulation
    Contaminated Sites Regulations
    Designated Materials
    Ozone Depleting Substances & Other
    Halocarbons Regulation
    Pesticides Regulations
    Recycling Fund Regulation
    Solid Waste Regulations
    Special Waste Regulations
    Spills Regulations
    Storage Tank Regulations
    Yukon Council on the Economy & the Environment Regulation
Environmental Assessment Act
    Activities Requiring Environmental Assessment (Inclusion List) Regulations
    Comprehensive Study List Regulation
    Coordination of Environmental Assessment Procedures & Requirement Regulations
    Exclusion List Regulation
    Law List Regulation
Mackenzie River Basin Agreement Act
Parks & Land Certainty Act
    Campground Regulations
    Coal River Springs Ecological Reserve
    Establish Ni'iinlii Njik (Fishing Branch) Ecological Reserve
    Establish Ni'iinlii Njik (Fishing Branch) Wilderness Preserve
    Herschel Island Nature Preserve
    Herschel Island Park Regulations
    Tombstone Territorial Park Regulations
    Waters Act, (jointly with Energy, Mines & Resources & the Executive Council Office)
        Waters Regulation
Wilderness Tourism Licensing Act
Wildlife Act
    Concession & Compensation Review Board Regulations
    Conservation Fund Regulations
    Game Farm Regulations
    Game Management Sub-zone Regulations
    Outfitting Concession Area Boundary Regulations
    Trapping Concession Area Boundary Regulations
    Trapping Regulations
    Wildlife Sanctuary Regulation
Yukon River Basin & Alsek River Basin Agreements Act

Yukon Community Services
Animal Protection Act (jointly with Energy, Mines & Resources)
Assessment & Taxation Act
Building Standards Act
Civil Emergency Measures Act
Fire Prevention Act
Forest Protection Act (jointly with Department of Energy, Mines & Resources
Gasoline Handling Act
Miner's Lien Act
Motor Vehicles Act (jointly with Highways & Public Works)
Municipal Act
Recreation Act

Yukon Energy, Mines & Resources
Agriculture Development Act
Animal Health Act, (jointly with Environment)
Area Development Act
Forest Protection Act, (jointly with Community Services)
Lands Act
Oil & Gas Act
    Oil & Gas Disposition Regulations
    Oil & Gas Drilling & Production Regulations
    Oil & Gas Geoscience & Exploration Regulations
    Oil & Gas Licence Administration Regulations
Placer Mining Act
Quartz Mining Act
Territorial Lands (Yukon) Act
Waters Act, (jointly with Environment & the Executive Council Office)

Yukon Health & Social Services
Public Health & Safety Act
    Regulations to Establish Butylnitrite as Regulated Matter
    Rubbish Disposal
    Sewage Disposal Systems Regulations

Yukon Highways & Public Works
Dangerous Goods Transportation Act
Highways Act
Motor Transport Act
Motor Vehicles Act (jointly with Community Services)

Yukon Tourism & Culture
Archives Act
Arts Act
Historical Resources Act
Scientists & Explorers Act

Yukon Workers' Compensation Health & Safety Board
Occupational Health & Safety Act
Worker's Compensation Act
    Workplace Hazardous Materials Information System (WHMIS) Regulations

Federal/Provincial Government

Government of Canada
c/o Canada Enquiry Centre, Service Canada
Ottawa, ON K1A 0J9
613-941-1827
800-622-6232
TDD: 800-926-9105
sitecanadasite@canada.gc.ca
www.canada.gc.ca
All political authority in Canada is divided between the federal & provincial governments, according to the provisions of the Constitution Act, 1867. Local municipalities are a concern of the provinces, & derive their authority from Acts of provincial legislation. The Parliament of Canada consists of Her Majesty Queen Elizabeth II (represented in Canada by the Governor General, His Excellency the Right Honourable David Johnston), an Upper House called the Senate, & an elected House of Commons.
Acts Administered:
National Round Table on the Environment & the Economy Act

Agriculture & Agri-Food Canada / Agriculture et Agro-alimentaire Canada
1341 Baseline Rd.
Ottawa, ON K1A 0C5
613-773-1000
Fax: 613-773-2772
866-345-7972
TDD: 613-773-2600
info@agr.ca
www.agr.ca
Other Communication: AgriInvest & AgriStability, Toll-Free Phone: 1-866-367-8506; Developing Innovative Agri-Products: 1-866-857-2287; Community Development Program: 1-877-295-7160
Agriculture & Agri-Food Canada is responsible for all matters related to agriculture. Examples of services provided by Agriculture & Agri-Food Canada include the following: research, development, & technology; policies & programs; the inspection & regulation of animals & plant-life forms; the coordination of rural development; the support of agricultural productivity & trade; the stabilization of farm incomes; & the provision of information. The goals of Agriculture & Agri-Food Canada are as follows: to achieve security of the food system; to ensure health of the environment; & to provide innovation for growth. Agriculture & Agri-Food Canada reports to Parliament & Canadians through the Minister of Agriculture & Agri-Food & the Minister for the Canadian Wheat Board.
Acts Administered:
Agricultural Marketing Programs Act
Agricultural Products Marketing Act
Animal Pedigree Act
Canada Grain Act
Canadian Agricultural Loans Act
Canadian Dairy Commission Act
Canadian Wheat Board Act
Department of Agriculture & Agri-Food Act
Experimental Farm Stations Act
Farm Debt Mediation Act
Farm Credit Canada Act
Farm Income Protection Act
Farm Products Agencies Act
Prairie Farm Rehabilitation Act
Minister, Agriculture & Agri-Food; Minister, Canadian Wheat Board, Hon. Gerry Ritz
613-773-1059, Fax: 613-773-1060
Ritz.G@parl.gc.ca
Minister, Veterans Affairs; Minister of State (Agriculture), Hon. Jean-Pierre Blackburn
613-947-9472, Fax: 613-773-1081
BlackJ@parl.gc.ca
• Canadian Dairy Commission(CDC) / Commission canadienne du lait
Building 55, NCC Driveway, Central Experimental Farm
960 Carling Ave.
Ottawa, ON K1A 0Z2
613-792-2000
Fax: 613-792-2009
866-366-0676
TDD: 613-792-2082cdc-ccl@cdc-ccl.gc.ca;
carole.cyr@cdc-ccl.gc.ca
www.cdc-ccl.gc.ca
Other Communication: Special Milk Class Permits, Phone: 613-792-2057; Dairy Imports & Exports, Phone: 613-792-2010
• Canadian Food Inspection Agency(CFIA) / Agence canadienne d'inspection des aliments
1400 Merivale Rd.
Ottawa, ON K1A 0Y9
613-225-2342
Fax: 613-228-6601
800-442-2342
TDD: 800-465-7735www.inspection.gc.ca
Other Communication: Atlantic Area, Phone: 506-851-7400; Ontario Area: 519-837-9400; Québec Area: 514-283-8888; Western Area: 403-292-4301
• Canadian Grain Commission(CGC) / Commission canadienne des grains
#603, 303 Main St.
Winnipeg
Winnipeg, MB R3C 3G8
204-983-2770
Fax: 204-983-2751
800-853-6705
TDD: 866-317-4289contact@grainscanada.gc.ca
www.grainscanada.gc.ca
Other Communication: Grain Sanitation & Infestation Control Industry Services, Fax: 204-984-7550; Licensing & Security Unit, Fax: 204-983-4654; Statistics Unit, Phone: 204-983-2739
• Farm Credit Canada(FCC) / Financement agricole Canada
1800 Hamilton St.
PO Box 4320
Regina, SK S4P 4L3
306-780-8100
Fax: 306-780-8919
888-332-3301
TDD: 306-780-6974csc@fcc-fac.ca
www.fcc-fac.ca
Other Communication: Careers, E-mail: hr-rh@fcc-fac.ca; Media & Publications: Communications@fcc-fac.ca; Legal Services: legal_services@fcc-fac.ca; FCC Learning: fcclearning@fcc-fac.ca
• Canadian Wheat Board(CWB)
423 Main St.
PO Box 816 Main
Winnipeg, MB R3C 2P5
204-983-0239
Fax: 204-983-3841
800-275-4292
questions@cwb.ca; farmers@cwb.ca
www.cwb.ca
Other Communication: Media relations, Phone: 204-983-3101; Government relations, Phone: 204-984-8167
• Canadian Pari-Mutuel Agency(CPMA)
800-268-8835
cpmawebacpm@agr.gc.ca
www4.agr.gc.ca/AAFC-AAC/display-afficher.do?id=1204043533186&lang
Other Communication: Toll-Free Phone, French: 1-800-326-3344; Equine Drug Control Program, Phone: 613-949-0745

Agri-Environment Services Branch (AESB)
Tower 4
1341 Baseline Rd.
Ottawa, ON K1A 0C5
613-759-1000
Fax: 613-773-1211
www4.agr.gc.ca/AAFC-AAC/display-afficher.do?id=1187362338955&lang
Other Communication: Agroforestry Development Centre, Phone: 1-866-766-2284, Fax: 306-695-2568; Canada-Manitoba Crop Diversification Centre, Phone: 204-834-6000, Fax: 204-834-3777
The Agri-Environment Services Branch integrates the following components: Prairie Farm Rehabilitation Administration; National Land & Water Information Service; & Agri-Environmental Policy Bureau. The mission of the branch is to deliver innovative environmental solutions to the agriculture & agri-food sector. Applied Technology Development Centres of the Agri-Environment Services Branch include the following: Agroforestry Development Centre (formerly known as the Prairie Farm Rehabilitation Administration); Canada-Saskatchewan Irrigation Diversification Centre; & the Canada-Manitoba Crop Diversification Centre.

Communications & Consultations Branch
Tower 7
1341 Baseline Rd.
Ottawa, ON K1A 0C7
613-759-1000
Fax: 613-773-2772

Corporate Management
Tower 4
1341 Baseline Rd.
Ottawa, ON K1A 0C5
613-759-1000
Fax: 613-773-0911

Deputy Minister's Office / Bureau du sous-ministre
Tower 7
1341 Baseline Rd.
Ottawa, ON K1A 0C5
613-759-1011
Fax: 613-759-1040
The Deputy Minister's Office oversees the following organizations: Corporate Secretariat; Food Safety Review Secretariat; & Portfolio Coordination Secretariat.
Manager, Governance Committees Secretariat, Corporate Secretariat, Monique Deguire
613-773-1096, Fax: 613-773-1061
monique.deguire@agr.gc.ca

Farm Financial Programs Branch / Direction générale des programmes de financement agricoles
Tower 7
1341 Baseline Rd.
Ottawa, ON K1A 0C5
613-759-1000
Fax: 613-773-2121
The Farm Financial Programs Branch of Agriculture & Agri-Food Canada oversees the following organizations: Agriculture Transformation Programs Directorate; Business Risk Management Program Development; Centre of Program Excellence (COPE); Farm Income Programs Directorate; Finance & Renewal Programs Directorate; & Service Policy & Transformation Directorate.
Assistant Deputy Minister, Farm Financial Programs Branch, Rita Moritz
613-773-2815, Fax: 613-773-2121
rita.moritz@agr.gc.ca
Director General, Finance & Renewal Programs Directorate, Jody Aylard
613-773-2005, Fax: 613-773-2099
jody.aylard@agr.gc.ca

Human Resources Branch / Direction générale des ressources humaines
Tower 1
560 Rochester St.
Ottawa, ON K1A 0C5
613-759-1000
Fax: 613-759-7105

Information Systems Branch
Tower 4
1341 Baseline Rd.
Ottawa, ON K1A 0C5
613-759-1000
Fax: 613-773-0676
The Information Systems Branch of Agriculture & Agri-Food Canada is reponsible for the following organizations: Applications Development Directorate; Information Management Services; IT Operations; & the Strategic Management Directorate.

Legal Services
Tower 7
1341 Baseline Rd.
Ottawa, ON K1A 0C5
613-759-1000
Fax: 613-773-2929

Federal/Provincial Government / Government of Canada

Market & Industry Services Branch (MISB) / Direction générale des services à l'industrie et aux marchés
Tower 5
1341 Baseline Rd.
Ottawa, ON K1A 0C5
613-759-1000
Fax: 613-773-1755
Other Communication: Government of Canada Export Services Information, Toll-Free Phone: 1-888-576-4444
The Market & Industry Services Branch of Agriculture & Agri-Food Canada oversees the following organizations: Bilateral Relations & Technical Trade Policy Directorate; Food Value Chain Bureau; International Markets Bureau; Market Access Secretariat; Negotiations & Multilateral Trade Policy Directorate; & the Operations Directorate. The Operations Directorate operates regional offices throughout Canada, which provide access to market & trade programs & services. Marketing & trade officers offer the following information: statistics by country & product; market access advice; investment opportunities; regulatory issues; export counselling; & news about promotional events.
Assistant Deputy Minister, Steve Tierney
613-773-1790, Fax: 613-773-1755
steve.tierney@agr.gc.ca
Director General, Bilateral Relations & Technical Trade Policy Directorate, Blair Coomber
613-773-1600, Fax: 613-773-1616
blair.coomber@agr.gc.ca
Director General & Chief Agriculture Negotiator, Negotiations & Multilateral Trade Policy Directorate, Gilles Gauthier
613-773-0985, Fax: 613-773-1755
gilles.gauthier@agr.gc.ca
Director General, Market Access Secretariat, Fred Gorrell
613-773-1512, Fax: 613-773-0199
fred.gorrell@agr.gc.ca
Director General, Operations Directorate, Dr. Jaspinder Komal
613-773-1501, Fax: 613-773-1500
jaspinder.komal@agr.gc.ca
Director General, Food Value Chain Bureau, Susie Miller
613-773-1750, Fax: 613-773-0300
susie.miller@agr.gc.ca
Director General, International Markets Bureau, Paul Murphy
613-773-1517, Fax: 613-773-1500
paul.murphy@agr.gc.ca

Market & Industry Services Branch Regional Offices:

Alberta & Territories Regional Office
#720, 9700 Jasper Ave.
Edmonton, AB T5J 4G5
780-495-4141
Fax: 780-495-3324
Regional Director, Alberta & Territories Regional Office, Rodney Dlugos
780-495-5525, Fax: 780-495-3324
rodney.dlugos@agr.gc.ca
Deputy Director, Janet Dorey
780-495-5526, Fax: 780-495-3324
janet.dorey@agr.gc.ca

Atlantic Regional Office
#405, 1791 Barrington St.
PO Box 248
Halifax, NS B3J 2N7
902-426-3198
Fax: 902-426-3439
The Atlantic Regional Office in Halifax, Nova Scotia, is the headquarters for the following operations: New Brunswick Operations (Phone: 506-452-3706, Fax: 506-452-3509); Newfoundland & Labrador Operations (Phone: 709-772-4063, Fax: 709-772-4803); Nova Scotia Operations (Phone: 902-896-0332, Fax: 902-896-0100); & Prince Edward Island Operations (Phone: 902-566-7300, Fax: 902-566-7316).
Regional Director, Atlantic Regional Office, Janet Steele
902-426-7171, Fax: 902-426-3439
janet.steele@agr.gc.ca
Deputy Director, Prince Edward Island Operations, Heath Coles
902-566-7305, Fax: 902-566-7316
heath.coles@agr.gc.ca
Deputy Director, Newfoundland & Labrador Operations, Brian Goldsworthy
709-772-4055, Fax: 709-772-4803
brian.goldsworthy@agr.gc.ca
Deputy Director, New Brunswick Operations, Bernard P. Mallet
506-452-3732, Fax: 506-452-3509
bernard.mallet@agr.gc.ca
Deputy Director, Nova Scotia Operations, Shelley Manning
902-896-0098, Fax: 902-896-0100
shelley.manning@agr.gc.ca

British Columbia Regional Office
#420, 4321 Stillcreek Dr.
Burnaby, BC V5C 6S7
604-666-6344
Fax: 604-666-7235
Regional Director, British Columbia Regional Office, John Berry
604-666-6344, Fax: 604-666-7235
john.berry@agr.gc.ca
Deputy Director, Michelle Soucie
604-666-3054, Fax: 604-666-7235
michelle.soucie@agr.gc.ca

Manitoba Regional Office
303 Main St.
Winnipeg, MB R3C 3G7
204-983-3032
Fax: 204-983-4583
Regional Director, Manitoba Regional Office, Brian Lemon
204-983-8622, Fax: 204-983-4583
brian.lemon@agr.gc.ca
Deputy Director, Bob Nawolsky
204-983-3891, Fax: 204-983-4583
bob.nawolsky@agr.gc.ca

Ontario Regional Office
174 Stone Rd. West
Guelph, ON N1G 4S9
519-837-9400
Fax: 519-837-9782
Regional Director, Ontario Regional Office, Ezio Di Emanuele
519-837-5825, Fax: 519-837-9782
ezio.diemanuele@agr.gc.ca
Deputy Director, Ezio Di Emanuele
519-837-5821, Fax: 519-837-9782
marg.bancroft@agr.gc.ca
Deputy Director, Bill Robinson
519-837-5822, Fax: 519-837-9782
bill.robinson@agr.gc.ca

Québec Regional Office
2001, rue Université, 7e étage
Montréal, QC H3A 3N2
514-283-8888
Fax: 514-496-3966
Regional Director, Québec Regional Office, Sandra Gagné
514-315-6170, Fax: 514-496-3966
sandra.gagne@agr.gc.ca
Regional Deputy Director, Scott Patterson
514-315-6171, Fax: 514-496-3966
scott.patterson2@agr.gc.ca

Saskatchewan Regional Office
1800 Hamilton St.
Regina, SK S4P 4K7
306-780-5545
Fax: 306-780-7360
Regional Director, Saskatchewan Regional Office, Dean L. Vey
306-780-7065, Fax: 306-780-7360
dean.vey@agr.gc.ca
Deputy Director, Saskatchewan Regional Office, Wendy Collinge
306-780-5452, Fax: 306-780-7360
wendy.collinge@agr.gc.ca
Deputy Director, Markets & Trade, Gavin M. Conacher
306-780-5216, Fax: 306-780-7360
gavin.conacher@agr.gc.ca

Office of Audit & Evaluation
Tower 4
1341 Baseline Rd.
Ottawa, ON K1A 0C5
613-759-1000
Fax: 613-773-0660
Agriculture & Agri-Food Canada's Office of Audit & Evaluation is responsible for the following services: evaluation; governance & review; & internal audit & assurance.

Canada-Saskatchewan Irrigation Diversification Centre
901 McKenzie St. South
PO Box 700
Outlook, SK S0L 2N0
306-867-5400
Fax: 306-867-9656
csidc@agr.gc.ca

Manitoba
#200, 303 Main St.
Winnipeg, MB R3C 3G7
204-984-3695
Fax: 204-983-2178

Manitoba Crop Diversification Centre
PO Box 309
Carberry, MB R0K 0H0
204-834-6005
Fax: 204-834-3777

Northern Alberta & BC
Canada Place
#945, 9700 Jasper Ave. NW
Edmonton, AB T5J 4C3
780-495-3307
Fax: 780-495-4504

Northern Saskatchewan
#1101, 11 Innovation Blvd.
Saskatoon, SK S7N 3H5
306-975-4693
Fax: 306-975-4594

Shelterbelt Centre
PO Box 940
Indian Head, SK S0G 2K0
306-695-2284
Fax: 306-695-2568
pfratree@agr.gc.ca

Southern Alberta
Harry Hays Bldg.
#600, 138 - 4 Ave. SE
Calgary, AB T2G 4Z2
403-292-5638
Fax: 403-292-5659

Southern Saskatchewan
#603, 1800 Hamilton St.
Regina, SK S4P 4L2
306-780-5150
Fax: 306-780-6778

Research Branch / Direction générale de la recherche
Tower 5
1341 Baseline Rd.
Ottawa, ON K1A 0C5
613-759-1000
Fax: 613-773-1866
Agriculture & Agri-Food Canada's Research Branch consists of the following organizations: Innovation Directorate; International Scientific Cooperation Bureau; Land Resources; Science Centres Directorate, Science Partnerships Directorate; & Science Policy & Planning. Scientists from Agriculture & Agri-Food Canada work on projects to benefit the agricultural & agri-food sector at research centres located across Canada.
Assistant Deputy Minister, Dr. Marc Fortin, PhD
613-773-1860, Fax: 613-773-1866
marc.fortin@agr.gc.ca
Director General, Science Policy & Planning, Dr. Christiane Deslauriers, PhD
613-773-1870, Fax: 613-773-1877
christiane.deslauriers@agr.gc.ca
Director General, Science Partnerships Directorate, Dr. Stephen D. Morgan Jones, PhD
403-317-2200, Fax: 403-317-2197
steve.morganjones@agr.gc.ca
Director General, Science Centres Directorate, Dr. Gilles Saindon, PhD
613-773-1843, Fax: 613-773-1844
gilles.saindon@agr.gc.ca
Director General, Innovation Directorate, Michael J. Whittaker
613-773-2308, Fax: 613-773-1822
michael.j.whittaker@agr.gc.ca
Director, Multilateral Science Relations, International Scientific Cooperation Bureau, Brad Fraleigh
613-773-1838, Fax: 613-773-1822
brad.fraleigh@agr.gc.ca
Chief Scientist, International Scientific Cooperation Bureau, Dr. Yvon Martel, PhD
613-773-1830, Fax: 613-773-1833
yvon.martel@agr.gc.ca
Chief Officer for Scientific Relations, China, International Scientific Cooperation Bureau, Jianqiang (Joe) Zhou, PhD
613-759-1744, Fax: 613-773-1833
joe.zhou@agr.gc.ca

Federal/Provincial Government / Government of Canada

Senior Officer, Land Resources, Warren D. Eilers
306-975-4062, Fax: 306-966-4226
warren.eilers@agr.gc.ca

Research Centres:

Atlantic Food & Horticulture Research Centre
32 Main St.
Kentville, NS B4N 1J5
902-679-5333
Fax: 902-679-2311
Manager, Research, Dr. D. Mark Hodges, PhD
902-679-5544, Fax: 902-679-5784
mark.hodges@agr.gc.ca
Manager, Facilities, Brian Wagner
902-679-5583, Fax: 902-679-2311
brian.wagner@agr.gc.ca
Manager, Farm, Innovation & Renewal, David L. Bowlby
902-679-5589, Fax: 902-670-0004
david.bowlby@agr.gc.ca
Science Director, Crop Production Systems, Peter Hickleton
902-679-5760, Fax: 902-679-5344
peter.hickleton@agr.gc.ca

Brandon Research Centre
RR#3
PO Box 1000A
Brandon, MB R7A 5Y3
204-726-7650
Fax: 204-728-3858
Manager, Research, Dr. Fernando Selles, PhD
204-578-3539, Fax: 204-578-3528
fernando.selles@agr.gc.ca
Manager, Building, Frank Thompson
204-578-3525, Fax: 204-728-3858
frank.thompson@agr.gc.ca
Manager, Farm, Clay Jackson
204-578-3610, Fax: 204-578-3522
clayton.jackson@agr.gc.ca

Cereal Research Centre
195 Dafoe Rd.
Winnipeg, MB R3T 2M9
204-983-5533
Fax: 204-983-4604
Manager, Research, Dr. David Wall
204-983-0099, Fax: 204-984-6333
david.wall@agr.gc.ca
Manager, Integrated Services, Bill Atkinson
204-983-0293, Fax: 204-984-8053
william.atkinson@agr.gc.ca
Science Director, Water & Soil Resources, Dr. Johanne B. Boisvert, PhD
204-983-0466, Fax: 204-983-4604
johanne.boisvert@agr.gc.ca

Crops & Livestock Research Centre
440 University Ave.
Charlottetown, PE C1A 4N6
902-566-6800
Fax: 902-566-6821
The Crops and Livestock Research Centre (CLRC) in Charlottetown, Prince Edward Island is one of Agriculture and Agri-Food Canada's network of 19 research centres. The Centre's mandate is to develop scientific knowledge and new technologies in agriculture with the prime focus on Prince Edward Island and Atlantic Canada.
Manager, Research, Dr. Maria Rodriguez
902-566-6817, Fax: 902-566-6821
maria.rodriguez@agr.gc.ca
Manager, Research Operations, Roddy C. Pratt
902-672-6426, Fax: 902-566-6821
roddy.pratt@agr.gc.ca
Manager, Facilities, Kenny J. MacInnis
902-566-7353, Fax: 902-566-6821
kenneth.macinnis@agr.gc.ca
Manager, Integrated Services, Jamie Coffin
902-566-6811, Fax: 902-566-6821
jamie.coffin@agr.gc.ca

Dairy & Swine Research & Development Centre
2000, rue College
CP 90 Lennoxville
Sherbrooke, QC J1M 1Z3
819-565-9171
Fax: 819-564-5507
The Dairy & Swine Research & Development Centre oversees the operations of the Beef Research Farm in Kapuskasing, Ontario, as well as the Office of Intellectual Property & Commercialization in Sherbrooke, Québec.
Manager, Research, Dr. Alain Giguère
819-565-9174, Fax: 819-564-5407
alain.guiere@agr.gc.cagc.ca
Science Director, Livestock Production Systems, Dr. Jacques Surprenant, PhD, MPA
819-565-9174, Fax: 819-564-4974
jacques.surprenant@agr.gc.ca
Commercialization Officer, Office of Intellectual Property & Commercialization, Denise Call
613-759-1708, Fax: 613-759-1765
calld@agr.gc.ca
Head Herdsman, Kapuskasing Beef Research Farm, Maurice Portelance
705-335-6148, Fax: 705-337-6000
maurice.portelance@agr.gc.ca

Eastern Cereal & Oilseed Research Centre
960 Carling Ave.
Ottawa, ON K1A 0C6
613-759-1858
Fax: 613-759-1970
Manager, Research, Dr. Marc Savard
613-759-1683, Fax: 613-759-1970
marc.savard@agr.gc.ca
Manager, Research Support, Ron Wheeler
613-759-1544, Fax: 613-952-6438
ron.wheeler@agr.gc.ca
Science Director, Food & Health, Dr. Michèle Marcotte, PhD, Eng
613-759-1525, Fax: 613-759-1970
michele.marcotte@agr.gc.ca
Director, System Architecture, National Science Programs, Peter Schut, PhD, Eng
613-759-1874, Fax: 613-759-1937
peter.schut@agr.gc.ca

Food Research & Development Centre
3600, boul Casavant ouest
Saint-Hyacinthe, QC J2S 8E3
450-773-1105
Fax: 450-773-8461
Manager, Research, Dr. Christian J. Toupin, PhD
450-768-3331, Fax: 450-773-2888
christian.toupin@agr.gc.ca
Manager, Integrated Services & Industry, Jean C. Gagnon
450-768-3260, Fax: 450-773-8461
jean.gagnon@agr.gc.ca
Science Director, Food Production, Safety, & Quality, Gabriel Piette
450-768-3304, Fax: 450-773-2888
gabriel.piette@agr.gc.ca

Greenhouse & Processing Crops Research Centre
2585 Country Rd. 20
Harrow, ON N0R 1G0
519-738-2251
Fax: 519-738-2929
Manager, Research, Ranjana Sharma
519-738-1208, Fax: 519-738-2929
ranjana.sharma@agr.gc.ca
Manager, Integrated Services, Adrian Lancop
519-738-1210, Fax: 519-738-2929
adrian.lancop@agr.gc.ca
Science Director, Integrated Pest Management, Environmental Health, Dr. Gary Whitfield
519-738-1218, Fax: 519-738-3756
gary.whitfield@agr.gc.ca

Guelph Food Research Centre
93 Stone Rd. West
Guelph, ON N1G 5C9
519-829-2400
Fax: 519-829-2600
Manager, Research, Dr. Punidadas Piyasena
519-780-8063, Fax: 519-829-2602
puni.piyasena@agr.gc.ca
Manager, Facility, Michael Kerr
519-780-8084, Fax: 519-829-2600
mike.kerr@agr.gc.ca
Manager, Integrated Services, Joan Leatherdale
519-780-8039, Fax: 519-829-2601
joan.leatherdale@agr.gc.ca

Horticulture Research & Development Centre
430, boul Gouin
Saint-Jean-sur-Richelieu, QC J3B 3E6
450-346-4494
Fax: 450-346-7740
Manager, Research, Roger Chagnon
450-515-2001, Fax: 450-346-7908
roger.chagnon@agr.gc.ca
Manager, Integrated Services, Sylvie Joncas
450-515-2111, Fax: 450-346-7740
sylvie.joncas@agr.gc.ca
Manager, Facilities, Guy Lahaie
450-515-2090, Fax: 450-346-7740
guy.lahaie@agr.gc.ca
Manager, Greenhouse, Guy Boulet
450-515-2016, Fax: 450-346-7740
guy.boulet@agr.gc.ca

Lacombe Research Centre
6000 C & E Trail
Lacombe, AB T4L 1W1
403-782-8100
Fax: 403-782-6120
The Lacombe Research Centre is responsible for the operations of research farms in Beaverlodge & Fort Vermilion in Alberta.
Manager, Research, Rick Lawrence
403-782-8110, Fax: 403-782-4308
rick.lawrence@agr.gc.ca
Manager, Integrated Services, Danielle Girard
403-782-8105, Fax: 403-782-6120
danielle.girard@agr.gc.ca
Manager, Farm, Ken B. Grimson
403-782-8139, Fax: 403-782-8186
ken.grimson@agr.gc.ca
Facilities Management Officer, Beaverlodge Research Farm, Mervin R. Hegland
780-354-5120, Fax: 780-354-5150
merv.hegland@agr.gc.ca
Foreman, Fort Vermilion Research Farm, Mervin R. Hegland
780-927-3253, Fax: 780-927-3330
joe.unruh@agr.gc.ca

Lethbridge Research Centre
5403 - 1st Ave. South
PO Box 3000
Lethbridge, AB T1J 4B1
403-327-4561
Fax: 403-382-3156
The Lethbridge Research Centre oversees the operations of the Onefour Research Substation, the Stavely Research Substation, & the Vauxhall Research Substation in Alberta.
Manager, Research, Dr. Brian Freeze, PhD
403-317-3445, Fax: 403-317-2211
brian.freeze@agr.gc.ca
Manager, Facility, Donavan T. Casson
403-317-2233, Fax: 403-317-3491
donavan.casson@agr.gc.ca
Manager, Feed Mill, Dave Dancoisne
403-317-3383, Fax: 403-382-3156
dave.dancoisne@agr.gc.ca
Manager, Stavely Research Substation Site, Albert J. Middleton
403-549-2152, Fax: 403-549-3744
albert.middleton@agr.gc.ca
Manager, Vauxhall Research Substation Site, Jim Sukeroff
403-654-2255, Fax: 403-654-4243
jim.sukeroff@agr.gc.ca
Manager, Onefour Research Substation Site, Ian Walker
403-868-2364, Fax: 403-868-2489
ian.walker@agr.gc.ca
Science Director, Crop Genetic Enhancement, Dr. Jeff Stewart
403-317-2208, Fax: 403-317-2197
jeff.stewart@agr.gc.ca

Pacific Agri-Food Research Centre (PARC)
4200 Hwy. 97
PO Box 5000
Summerland, BC V0H 1Z0
250-494-7711
Fax: 250-494-0755
The Pacific Agri-Food Research Centre oversees the following organizations: the Agassiz Site, the Kamloops Range Research Unit, & the Summerland Site.
Research Manager, Summerland Site, Kenna MacKenzie
250-494-6358, Fax: 250-494-6415
kenna.mackenzie@agr.gc.ca
Facility Manager, Agassiz Site, Lorne Primeau
604-796-1719, Fax: 604-796-0359
lorne.primeau@agr.gc.ca

Federal/Provincial Government / Government of Canada

Facility Manager, Kamloops Range Research Unit, Larry Maio
250-554-5227, Fax: 250-554-5229
larry.maio@agr.gc.ca
Integrated Services Manager, Summerland Site, Bruce Jensen
250-494-6357, Fax: 250-494-0755
bruce.jensen@agr.gc.ca
Field Services Manager, Summerland Site, Mark Neufield
250-494-6427, Fax: 250-494-0755
mark.neufield@agr.gc.ca
Grounds & Greenhouse Manager, Summerland Site, David Weir
250-494-6387, Fax: 250-494-0755
david.weir@agr.gc.ca

Potato Research Centre
850 Lincoln Rd.
PO Box 20280
Fredericton, NB E3B 4Z7
506-452-3260
Fax: 506-452-3316
The Potato Research Centre is also responsible for the Senator Hervé J. Michaud Research Farm, located in Bouctouche, New Brunswick.
Manager, Research, Jacques Millette, PhD
506-452-4845, Fax: 506-452-3212
jacques.millette@agr.gc.ca
Manager, Facilities, Sean Brown
506-452-4839, Fax: 506-452-3316
sean.brown@agr.gc.ca
Manager, Integrated Services, Senator Hervé J Michaud Research Farm, Louise Boucher
506-743-1140, Fax: 506-743-8316
louise.boucher@agr.gc.ca
Manager, Integrated Services, Potato Research Centre, Jeanne Caissie
506-452-4951, Fax: 506-452-3316
jeanne.caissie@agr.gc.ca
Manager, Farm, Larry McMillan
506-452-4838, Fax: 506-452-3316
larry.mcmillan@agr.gc.ca

Saskatoon Research Centre
107 Science Pl.
Saskatoon, SK S7N 0X2
306-956-7200
Fax: 306-956-7247
Manager, Research, Dr. Felicitas Katepa-Mupondwa
306-956-2489, Fax: 306-956-7248
felicitas.katepa-mupondwa@agr.gc.ca
Science Director, Bioproducts Platforms & Genomics, Dr. Paul McCaughey
306-956-7211, Fax: 306-956-7248
paul.mccaughey@agr.gc.ca

Semiarid Prairie Agricultural Research Centre
PO Box 1030
Swift Current, SK S9H 3X2
306-778-7200
Fax: 306-778-3188
The Semiarid Prairie Agricultural Research Centre is responsible for the operations of research farms in Indian Head & Regina, Saskatchewan.
Manager, Research, Dr. Campbell G. Davidson
306-778-7270, Fax: 306-778-3186
campbell.davidson@agr.gc.ca
Manager, Integrated Services, Debbie Biese
306-778-7223, Fax: 306-778-3188
debbie.biese@agr.gc.ca
Manager, Regina Research Farm, Myron Knelsen
306-780-7426, Fax: 306-780-5501
myron.knelsen@agr.gc.ca
Head, Facilities Management, Brad Olfert
306-778-7219, Fax: 306-778-3188
brad.olfert@agr.gc.ca
Supervisor, Indian Head Research Farm, Darren Pollock
306-695-5264, Fax: 306-695-3445
darren.pollock@agr.gc.ca

Soils & Crops Research & Development Centre
2560, boul Hochelaga
Québec, QC G1V 2J3
418-657-7980
Fax: 418-648-2402
The Soils & Crops Research & Development Centre is also responsible for a research farm in Normandin, Québec.
Manager, Research, Claude Lapierre, MSc
418-210-5002, Fax: 418-648-2402
claude.lapierre@agr.gc.ca
Manager, Facilities, Rémi Lafrenière
418-210-5029, Fax: 418-648-2402
remi.lafreniere@agr.gc.ca
Manager, Integrated Services, Normandin Research Farm, Mario Fortin
418-274-5881, Fax: 418-274-3386
mario.fortin@agr.gc.ca
Chief, Greenhouse, Normand Charest
418-210-5014, Fax: 418-648-2402
normand.charest@agr.gc.ca

Southern Crop Protection & Food Research Centre
1391 Sandford St.
London, ON N5V 4T3
519-457-1470
Fax: 519-457-3997
The Southern Crop Protection & Food Research Centre oversees the operations of research farms in Delhi & Vineland, Ontario, as well as an Office of Intellectual Property & Commercialization in London, Ontario.
Manager, Research, Southern Crop Protection & Food Research Centre, Dr. Karl Volkmar
519-457-1470, Fax: 519-457-3503
karl.volkmar@agr.gc.ca
Manager, Research, Vineland Research Farm, Antonet Svircev
604-796-1709, Fax: 604-796-0359
antonet.svircev@agr.gc.ca
Manager, Facility, Joe Pratt
519-457-1470, Fax: 519-457-3997
joe.pratt@agr.gc.ca
Supervisor, Farm Services, Delhi Research Farm, Albert Asztalos
519-582-1950, Fax: 519-582-4223
albert.asztalos@agr.gc.ca

Rural & Co-operatives Secretariat
Tower 7
1341 Baseline Rd.
Ottawa, ON K1A 0C5
613-759-1000
Fax: 613-773-2727
Executive Director, Rural & Co-operatives Secretariat, Donna Mitchell
613-773-2946, Fax: 613-773-2727
donna.mitchell@agr.gc.ca
Associate Executive Director, Rural & Co-operatives Secretariat, Christine Burton
613-773-2955, Fax: 613-773-2727
christine.burton@agr.gc.ca
Director, Partnerships & Programs, Louise Boudreau
613-773-2988, Fax: 613-773-2198
louise.boudreau@agr.gc.ca
Manager, Program Development & Implementation, Rural Programs, Lawrence Euteneier
613-773-2943, Fax: 613-773-2198
lawrence.euteneier@agr.gc.ca
Manager, Financial Services, Theresa Hedquist
613-773-2947, Fax: 613-773-2727
theresa.hedquist@agr.gc.ca
Manager, Co-op Policy & Research Unit, Co-operatives Secretariat, Anne Marie McInnis
613-773-2971, Fax: 613-773-2199
anne-marie.mcinnis@agr.gc.ca

Strategic Policy Branch / Direction générale des politiques stratégiques
Tower 7
1341 Baseline Rd.
Ottawa, ON K1A 0C5
613-759-1000
Fax: 613-773-2111
The Strategic Policy Branch of Agriculture & Agri-Food Canada includes the following organizations: Policy Development & Analysis Directorate; Policy, Planning, & Integration Directorate; & the Research & Analysis Directorate.
Assistant Deputy Minister, Greg Meredith
613-773-2930, Fax: 613-773-2121
greg.meredith@agr.gc.ca
Director General, Policy Development & Analysis Directorate, Paul Martin
613-773-2700, Fax: 613-773-2111
paul.martin@agr.gc.ca
Director General, Research & Analysis Directorate, Thomas Shenstone
613-773-2400, Fax: 613-773-2499
tom.shenstone@agr.gc.ca

Agri-Environment Policy Bureau / Bureau des politiques agro-environnementales
Provides a focal point for environmental analysis & policy development activities within the Department as well as information & advice in the area of environmental sustainability for the agricultural sector. Participates on interdepartmental committees dealing with federal environmental policy & program issues.
Director, Greg Strain
613-759-7323
Senior Environmental Analyst, Alexandre Lefebvre
613-759-7278

National Land & Water Information Service / Service national d'information sur les terres et les eaux
www.agr.gc.ca/nlwis/main_e.htm
National Land & Water Information Service (NLWIS) is an internet-based initiative that will provide land use decision makers with one-stop access to current, local & relevant land & water data. NLWIS will be the key analytical & planning source for agricultural producers, & for municipal, provincial & federal land planners in every region of Canada. Preliminary capabilities will be available, with final delivery planned for 2009.
Asst. Deputy Minister & Project Leader, Susan Till
613-759-1712

Atlantic Canada Opportunities Agency (ACOA) / Agence de promotion économique du Canada atlantique (APECA)

Blue Cross Centre
644 Main St., 3rd Fl.
PO Box 6051
Moncton, NB E1C 9J8
506-851-2271
Fax: 506-851-7403
800-561-7862
TDD: 877-456-6500
information@acoa-apeca.gc.ca
www.acoa-apeca.gc.ca
The role of the Atlantic Canada Opportunities Agency is the development of opportunities for economic growth in Atlantic Canada. The agency achieves its mission in the following ways: assisting businesses to become more innovative, productive, & competitive; promoting the strengths of Atlantic Canada; & helping communities to develop more diversified local economies.
Minister, National Revenue; Minister, Atlantic Canada Opportunities Agency; Minister, Atlantic Gateway, Hon. Keith Ashfield
613-992-1067, Fax: 613-996-9955
Ashfield.K@parl.gc.ca
Other Communications: National Revenue, Phone: 613-995-2960
President, Monique Collette
506-851-6128, Fax: 506-851-7403
President-presidente@acoa-apeca.gc.ca
Executive Vice-President, Paul J. LeBlanc
506-851-7075, Fax: 506-851-7403
Senior Vice-President, David Slade
506-851-6141
Vice-President, Finance & Corporate Services, Denise Frenette
506-851-6438
Director General, Human Resources, Charlene Sullivan
506-851-2141
Director General, Communications, Susan Wisking
506-851-7731, Fax: 613-952-6393
Director, Energy, Environment Policy, & Coordination, Daniel McCarthy
613-952-8216
Director, Regional Affairs, Raymond Vogan
506-444-6120

New Brunswick Regional Office
570 Queen St.
PO Box 578
Fredericton, NB E3B 5A6
506-452-3285
Fax: 506-452-3296
800-561-4030
TDD: 877-456-6500
The New Brunswick Regional Office oversees operations at the following offices: Campbellton (Phone: 506-789-4735); Edmundston (Phone: 506-735-4236); Fundy Region (Phone: 506-636-4485); Miramichi (506-778-1909); Northeast (Phone: 506-548-7420); Northwest (Phone: 506-473-5556); Southeast (Phone: 506-851-6432); Southwest (506-452-3135); & Tracadie-Sheila (506-395-1025).

Director General, New Brunswick Regional Operations, Janet Gagnon
506-452-3342
Executive Director, New Brunswick Federal Council, Raymond Gallant
506-452-4986
Director, Business Programs, André Charron
506-452-2413
Director, Communications, Patricia Field
506-452-4287
Director, Financial Management Services, David Hubbard
506-452-2423
Director, Policy, Advocacy, & Coordination, Gail Moser
506-452-3155

Newfoundland & Labrador Regional Office
John Cabot Building
10 Barter's Hill, 11th Fl.
PO Box 1060 C
St. John's, NL A1C 5M5
709-772-2751
Fax: 709-772-2712
800-668-1010
TDD: 877-456-6500
The Atlantic Canada Opportunities Agency's Newfoundland & Labrador Regional Office oversees the following offices throughout the province: Clarenville (Phone: 709-466-5980); Corner Brook (Phone: 709-637-4477); Gander (Phone: 709-651-4457); Grand Bank (Phone: 709-832-2517); Grand Falls-Windsor (Phone: 709-489-6600); & Labrador (Phone: 709-896-2648).

Nova Scotia Regional Office
#600, 1801 Hollis St.
PO Box 2284 M
Halifax, NS B3J 3C8
902-426-6743
Fax: 902-426-2054
800-565-1228
TDD: 877-456-6500
The Nova Scotia Regional Office of the Atlantic Canada Opportunities Agency oversees the following offices throughout Nova Scotia: Antigonish (Phone: 902-867-6075); Bridgewater (Phone: 902-541-5543); Digby (Phone: 902-245-7308); Kentville (902-679-5356); Pictou (Phone: 902-755-3746); Truro (902-895-2743), & Yarmouth (Phone: 902-742-0809).
Vice-President, Deborah Windsor
902-426-8364
Director General, Regional Operations, Peter Hogan
902-426-1288
Director, Finance & Management Services, Nancy Ives
902-426-5968
Director, Intergovernmental Affairs & Coordination, Lisa Muton
902-426-4820
Director, Communications, Alexander Smith
902-426-9417, Fax: 902-426-5843

Prince Edward Island Regional Office
Royal Bank Building
100 Sydney St., 3rd Floor
PO Box 40
Charlottetown, PE C1A 7K2
902-566-7492
Fax: 902-566-7098
800-871-2596
TDD: 877-456-6500
The Prince Edward Island Regional Office oversees the Summerside District Office (Phone: 902-888-4145).
Vice-President, Prince Edward Island & Tourism, Patrick Dorsey
902-368-0760
Director General, Enterprise Development & Policy, Wayne Hooper
902-626-2877, Fax: 902-566-7098
Director General, Atlantic Tourism, Robert McCloskey
902-626-2479, Fax: 902-566-7098
Executive Director, Prince Edward Island Federal Council, Catherine MacInnis
902-368-0889, Fax: 902-566-7489
Director, Corporate Programs & Services, Lynne Beairsto
902-566-7499
Director, Infrastructure Programs, Pat McAulay
902-626-2794
Director, Communicatons, Cindy Roy
902-566-7569, Fax: 902-566-7098
Director, Business Programs & Strategic Infrastructure, Brian Schmeisser
902-566-7422

Director, Trade & Business Programs, Douglas Smith
902-368-0890

Atomic Energy of Canada Limited (AECL) / Énergie atomique du Canada Ltée (EACL)

Head Office, Sheridan Science & Technology Park
2251 Speakman Dr.
Mississauga, ON L5K 1B2
905-823-9040
866-886-2325
librarycr@aecl.ca (Library); speakers@aecl.ca (Community speakers)
www.aecl.ca
Other Communication: Community inquiries, Toll-Free: 1-800-364-6989
Established in 1952, Atomic Energy of Canada Limited is a nuclear technology & services company, which employs 4,300 employees. It provides services to utilities in Canada & throughout the world. Atomic Energy of Canada Limited's head office in Mississauga employs more than 1,500 people. The head office provides the following services: nuclear service initiatives; the development, manufacturing, & testing of commercial products; engineering; the management & support of nuclear projects; commercial operations; & international sales & marketing. Atomic Energy of Canada Limited is also responsible for the management & operation of laboratories. Laboratories include the Chalk River Laboratories (Phone: 613-584-3311), northwest of Ottawa, Ontario, the Whiteshell Laboratories (Phone: 204-753-2311), situated northeast of Winnipeg, Manitoba, & the Underground Research Laboratory, located northeast of Winnipeg, Manitoba. At the Chalk River Laboratories, many of the organization's major research & development efforts are conducted. Atomic Energy of Canada Limited is widely known as the designer & builder of CANDU technology, including the CANDU 6.
President & Chief Executive Officer, Hugh MacDiarmid
Senior Vice-President, External Relations & Communications, George Bothwell
Senior Vice-President & Chief Technology Officer, Dr. Anthony (Tony) De Vuono
Senior Vice-President, Operations, Ramzi Fawaz
Senior Vice-President & Chief Financial Officer, Kent Harris
Senior Vice-President, Strategic Contracting, Allan A. Hawryluk
Senior Vice-President, General Counsel & Corporate Secretary, Jonathan Lundy
Senior Vice-President, Human Resources, Beth Medhurst
Senior Vice-President & Chief Nuclear Officer, Bill Pilkington
Senior Vice-President, Restructuring, Michael Robins
Vice-President, Marketing & Business Development, Ala Alizadeh
Vice-President, Contracts, Bruce Ambeault
Vice-President, Commercial, Richard V. Coté
Vice-President & General Manager, Operations, Earnest (Hank) Drumhiller
Vice-President, Supply Chain, Tracy Greig
Vice-President, Product Development, Jerry Hopwood
Vice-President, Finance, Georgina Kossivas
Vice-President & General Manager, Research & Development, William Kupferschmidt
Vice-President, Engineering & Technical Delivery, Joseph Lau
Vice-President & General Manager, Waste Management & Decommissioning, Joan Miller
Vice-President, Life Extension Projects & Project Management, Ian Trotman

Chalk River Laboratories
Chalk River, ON K0J 1J0
613-584-3311
Programs cover a wide range of topics associated with atomic power. Supports all aspects of nuclear technology & serves as a national laboratory in nuclear sciences. Developmental work is performed to demonstrate that low & intermediate level radioactive wastes arising from reactor operation can be immobilized in a stable form before disposal in a repository. The Fuel Packaging & Storage Project is underway to replace aging waste fuel storage containers, with 2010 as a completion date for the project.

Low-Level Radioactive Waste Management Office (LLRWMO) / Bureau de gestion des déchets radioactifs de faible activité
#200, 1900 City Park Dr.
Ottawa, ON K1J 1A3

613-998-9442
Fax: 613-952-0760
Carries out the responsibilities of the federal government for low-level radioactive waste (LLRW) management in Canada.
Director, Robert L. Zelmer

Auditor General of Canada / Vérificateur général du Canada

240 Sparks St.
Ottawa, ON K1A 0G6
613-995-3708
Fax: 613-957-0474
888-761-5953
TDD: 613-954-8042
communications@oag-bvg.gc.ca; infomedia@oag-bvg.gc.ca
www.oag-bvg.gc.ca
Other Communication: Media Relations, Phone: 613-952-0213, ext. 6292; Publications, Toll-Free Phone: 1-888-761-5953; Work Opportunities, E-mail: emplo@oag-bvg.gc.ca
The Office of the Auditor General of Canada was established in 1878. Today, the head office in Ottawa & regional offices in Halifax, Montréal, Edmonton, & Vancouver employ approximately 650 employees. The Office of the Auditor General of Canada provides objective, fact-based information required by Parliament to hold the federal government accountable for its stewardship of public funds. An Officer of Parliament, the Auditor General of Canada is responsible for auditing the following organizations: federal government departments; federal government agencies; most Crown corporations; many federal organizations; the government of the Yukon; the government of the Northwest Territories; & the government of Nunavut. The Auditor General, Sheila Fraser, reports publicly to the House of Commons about matters she believes should be brought to the attention of the House of Commons.stainable development matters that she believes should be brought to the attention of the House of Commons. The report can include chapters on audits & studies, sustainable development strategies, & environmental petitions.
Auditor General, Sheila Fraser
613-992-2512

Commissioner of the Environment & Sustainable Development / Commissaire à l'environnement et au développement durable
240 Sparks St.
Ottawa, ON K1A 0G6
613-995-3708
Fax: 613-957-0474
petitions@oag-bvg.gc.ca
www.oag-bvg.gc.ca
Commissioner, Environment & Sustainable Development, Scott Vaughan
613-952-0213
Principal, Sustainable Development Strategies, Audits, & Studies, Richard Arseneault
613-952-0213
Principal, Sustainable Development Strategies, Audits, & Studies, Andrew Ferguson
613-952-0213
Principal, Sustainable Development Strategies, Audits, & Studies, James McKenzie
613-952-0213

Regional Offices:

Edmonton
Manulife Place
#2460, 10180 - 101st St.
Edmonton, AB T5J 3S4
780-495-2028
Fax: 780-495-2031

Halifax
Centennial Building
#414, 1660 Hollis St.
Halifax, NS B3J 1V7
902-426-7721
Fax: 902-426-8591
Principal, Kevin Potter
902-426-9371
Director, Glenn Doucette
902-426-2097
Director, Heather McManaman
902-426-7728

Montréal
#545, 1255, rue Peel
Montréal, QC H3B 2T9

Federal/Provincial Government / Government of Canada

514-283-6086
Fax: 514-283-1715
Principal, René Béliveau
514-283-8324
Director, Jean-Pierre Morin
514-283-8136
Director, Tina Swiderski
514-283-7793
Vancouver
#250, 351 Abbott St.
Vancouver, BC V6B 0G6
604-666-3596
Fax: 604-666-6162
Principal, Eric Hellsten
604-666-7600

Business Development Bank of Canada (BDC) / Banque de développement du Canada (BDC)

#400, 5, Place Ville-Marie
Montréal, QC H3B 5E7
514-283-5904
Fax: 514-283-2872
877-232-2269
www.bdc.ca
Other Communication: Toll-Free Fax 1-877-329-9232; Corporate Financing (Québec & Atlantic Regions), Fax: 514-283-8410
The Business Development Bank of Canada is a financial institution which is wholly owned by the Goverment of Canada. It was created by an Act of Parliament in 1944. The Bank is governed by an independent Board of Directors, & reports to the Minister of Industry. The mission of the Business Development Bank of Canada is to assist in the establishment & development of Canadian businesses in all industries. The Bank focuses its efforts on small & medium-sized enterprises. The following services are carried out by the Business Development Bank of Canada: consulting services; flexible financing, such as long term business financing & subordinate financing; & venture capital. Branches of the Business Development Bank of Canada are located throughout Canada. Smaller communities are served by satellite branches, consultants, & travelling account managers.
Chair, John A. MacNaughton
President & Chief Executive Officer, Jean-René Halde
Executive Vice-President & Chief Financial Officer, Paul Buron
Executive Vice-President, Financing & Consulting, Edmée Métivier
Executive Vice President, Investments, Jacques Simoneau
Senior Vice President, Human Resources, Mary Karamanos

Alberta Branches:

Calgary Area Branch
Barclay Centre
#110, 444 - 7 Ave. SW
Calgary, AB T2P 0X8
403-292-5600
Fax: 403-292-6616

Calgary North Branch
#100, 1935 - 32 Ave. NE
Calgary, AB T2E 7C8
403-292-5333
Fax: 403-292-6651

Calgary South Branch
#200, 6700 MacLeod Trail SE
Calgary, AB T2H 0L3
403-292-8882
Fax: 403-292-4345

Edmonton Branch
#200, 10665 Jasper Ave.
Edmonton, AB T5J 3S9
780-495-2277
Fax: 780-495-6616

Edmonton South Branch
#201, 4628 Calgary Trail NW
Edmonton, AB T6H 6A1
780-495-7200
Fax: 780-495-7198

Grande Prairie Branch
#203, 10625 West Side Dr.
Grande Prairie, AB T8V 8E6
780-532-8875
Fax: 780-539-5130

Lethbridge Branch
520 - 5th Ave. South
Lethbridge, AB T1J 0T8
403-382-3000
Fax: 403-382-3162

Medicine Hat Branch
#101, 2248 - 13th Ave. SE
Medicine Hat, AB T1A 8G6
403-527-2601
Fax: 403-528-6899

Red Deer Branch
#107, 4815 - 50th Ave.
Red Deer, AB T4N 4A5
403-340-4203
Fax: 403-340-4243

British Columbia Branches:

Cranbrook Branch
205B Cranbrook St. North
Cranbrook, BC V1C 3R1
250-417-2200
Fax: 250-417-2213

Fort St. John Branch
#7, 10230 - 100 St.
Fort St. John, BC V1J 3Y9
250-787-0622
Fax: 250-787-9423

Kamloops Branch
205 Victoria St.
Kamloops, BC V2C 2A1
250-851-4900
Fax: 250-851-4925

Kelowna Branch
313 Bernard Ave.
Kelowna, BC V1Y 6N6
250-470-4802
Fax: 250-470-4832

Langley Branch
#101B, 6424 - 200th St.
Langley, BC V2Y 2T3
250-532-5150
Fax: 250-532-5166

Nanaimo Branch
#500, 6581 Aulds Rd.
Nanaimo, BC V9T 6J6
250-390-5757
Fax: 250-390-5753

North Vancouver Branch
#6, 221 West Esplanade
North Vancouver, BC V7M 3J3
604-666-7703
Fax: 604-666-1957
Branch Manager, Chris Boissevain
604-666-6007

Prince George Branch
#150, 177 Victoria St.
Prince George, BC V2L 5R8
250-561-5323
Fax: 250-561-5512

Surrey Branch
#160, 10362 King George Blvd.
Surrey, BC V3T 2W5
604-586-2400
Fax: 604-586-2430

Terrace Branch
3233 Emerson St.
Terrace, BC V8G 5L2
250-615-5300
Fax: 250-615-5320

Vancouver Branch
One Bentall Centre
#2100, 505 Burrard St.
PO Box 6
Vancouver, BC V7X 1M6
604-666-7850
Fax: 604-666-1068
Other Communication: Subordinate Financing (British Columbia & Yukon), Phone: 604-666-7875

Victoria Branch
990 Fort St.
Victoria, BC V8V 3K2
250-363-0161
Fax: 250-363-8029

Manitoba Branches:

Brandon Branch
#10, 940 Princess Ave.
Brandon, MB R7A 0P6
204-726-7570
Fax: 204-726-7555

Winnipeg Branch
#1100, 155 Carlton St.
Winnipeg, MB R3C 3H8
204-983-7900
Fax: 204-983-0870

Winnipeg West Branch
#200, 1655 Kenaston Blvd.
Winnipeg, MB R3P 2M4
204-983-6530
Fax: 204-983-6531

New Brunswick Branches:

Bathurst Branch
#205, 275 Main St.
Bathurst, NB E2A 1A9
506-548-7360
Fax: 506-548-7381

Edmundston Branch
#407, 121, rue de l'Église
Edmundston, NB E3V 1J9
506-739-8311
Fax: 506-735-0019

Fredericton Branch
#504, 570 Queen St.
PO Box 754
Fredericton, NB E3B 5B4
506-452-3030
Fax: 506-452-2416

Moncton Branch
766 Main St.
Moncton, NB E1C 1E7
506-851-6120
Fax: 506-851-6033

Saint John Branch
53 King St.
Saint John, NB E2L 1G5
506-636-4751
Fax: 506-636-3892

Newfoundland & Labrador Branches:

Corner Brook Branch
4 Herald Ave., 1st Fl.
Corner Brook, NL A2H 4B4
709-637-4515
Fax: 709-637-4522

Grand Falls-Windsor Branch
42 High St.
PO Box 744
Grand Falls-Windsor, NL A2A 2M4
709-489-2181
Fax: 709-489-6569

St. John's Branch
215 Water St.
PO Box 520
St. John's, NL A1C 5K4
709-722-5505
Fax: 709-772-2516

Northwest Territories Branches:

Yellowknife Branch
4912 - 49th St.
Yellowknife, NT X1A 1P3
867-873-3565
Fax: 867-873-3501

Nova Scotia Branches:

Halifax Branch
#1400, 2000 Barrington St.
Halifax, NS B3J 2Z7
902-426-7850
Fax: 902-426-6783
Vice-President & Area Manager, Craig Levangie
902-426-7865,
craig.levangie@bdc.ca

Sydney Branch
#117, 275 Charlotte St.
Sydney, NS B1P 1C6
902-564-7700
Fax: 902-564-3975

Truro Branch
622 Prince St.
PO Box 1378
Truro, NS B2N 5N2
902-895-6377
Fax: 902-893-7957
Senior Manager Business Development, Matthew Fraser
902-895-6378,
matthew.fraser@bdc.ca

Yarmouth Branch
103 Water St.
PO Box 98
Yarmouth, NS B5A 4B1
902-742-7119
Fax: 902-742-8180

Ontario Branches:

Barrie Branch
#301, 151 Ferris Lane
PO Box 876
Barrie, ON L4M 4Y6
705-725-2533
Fax: 705-739-0467

Brampton Branch
#100, 24 Queen St. East
Brampton, ON L6V 1A3
905-450-9845
Fax: 905-450-7514

Burlington / Halton Branch
#401, 4145 North Service Rd.
Burlington, ON L7L 6A3
905-315-9230
Fax: 905-315-9243

Durham (Whitby) Branch
400 Dundas St. West
Whitby, ON L1N 2M7
905-666-6694
Fax: 905-666-1059

Hamilton Branch
#1900, 25 Main St. West
Hamilton, ON L8P 1H1
905-572-2954
Fax: 905-572-4282

Kenora Branch
227 - 2nd St. South
Kenora, ON P9N 1G1
807-467-3535
Fax: 807-467-3533

Kingston Branch
#201, 1000 Gardiners Rd.
Kingston, ON K7L 3C4
613-389-0999
Fax: 613-389-2543

Kitchener-Waterloo Branch
#110, 50 Queen St. North
Kitchener, ON N2H 6P4
519-571-6676
Fax: 519-571-6685

London Branch
380 Wellington St.
London, ON N6A 5B5
519-645-4229
Fax: 519-645-5450
Other Communication: Subordinate Financing (Southwestern Ontario), Phone: 519-675-3114, Fax: 519-645-5989

Markham Branch
3130 Hwy. 7 East
Markham, ON L3R 5A1
905-305-6867
Fax: 905-305-1969

Mississauga Branch
#100, 4310 Sherwoodtowne Blvd.
Mississauga, ON L4Z 4C4
905-566-6417
Fax: 905-566-6425
Other Communication: Corporate Financing (Ontario), Fax: 905-566-5425

North Bay Branch
222 McIntyre St. West
North Bay, ON P1B 2Y8
705-495-5700
Fax: 705-495-5707

Ottawa Branch
55 Metcalfe St., Ground Fl.
Ottawa, ON K1P 6L5
613-995-0234
Fax: 613-995-9045
Other Communication: Subordinate Financing (Ottawa & Atlantic Regions), Phone: 613-995-4084, Fax: 613-943-9866

Peterborough Branch
340 George St. North, 4th Fl.
PO Box 1419
Peterborough, ON K9J 7H6
705-750-4800
Fax: 705-750-4808

Sault Ste Marie Branch
153 Great Northern Rd.
Sault Ste Marie, ON P6B 4Y9
705-941-3030
Fax: 705-941-3040

St Catharines Branch
#100, 39 Queen St.
PO Box 1193
St Catharines, ON L2R 7A7
905-988-2874
Fax: 905-988-2890

Stratford Branch
516 Huron St.
Stratford, ON N5A 5T7
519-271-5650
Fax: 519-271-8472

Sudbury Branch
#10, 233 Brady St.
Sudbury, ON P3B 4H5
705-670-6482
Fax: 705-670-6387

Thunder Bay Branch
#102, 1136 Alloy Dr.
Thunder Bay, ON P7B 6M9
807-346-1780
Fax: 807-346-1790

Timmins Branch
#214, 119 Pine St. South
Timmins, ON P4N 2K3
705-267-6416
Fax: 705-268-5437

Toronto (Finch Ave. West) Branch
#502, 1120 Finch Ave. West
Toronto, ON M3J 3H7
416-736-3420
Fax: 416-736-3425

Toronto (King St.) Branch
#1200, 121 King St. West
Toronto, ON M5H 3T9
416-973-0341
Fax: 416-954-5009
Other Communication: Subordinate Financing (Greater Toronto Area), Phone: 416-952-9673, Fax: 416-954-2630
The King Street West branch offers corporate financing for the Greater Toronto Area.

Toronto (Milner Ave.) Branch
#112, 305 Milner Ave.
Toronto, ON M1B 3V4

416-954-0709
Fax: 416-954-0716

Vaughan Branch
#600, 3901 Hwy. 7 West
Vaughan, ON L4L 8L5
905-264-2100
Fax: 905-264-2122

Windsor Branch
#200, 2485 Ouellette Ave.
Windsor, ON N8X 1L5
519-257-6808
Fax: 519-257-6811

Prince Edward Island Branches

Charlottetown Branch
#230, 119 Kent St.
PO Box 488
Charlottetown, PE C1A 7L1
902-566-7454
Fax: 902-566-7459

Québec Branches:

Brossard Branch
#200, 4255, boul Lapinière
Brossard, QC J4Z 0C7
450-926-7220
Fax: 450-926-7221

Chaudière - Appalaches (Saint-Romuald) Regional Branch
#100, 1175, boul de la Rive sud
Saint-Romuald, QC G6W 5M6
418-834-5144
Fax: 418-834-1855

Des Moulins - Lanaudière (Terrebonne) Regional Branch
2785, boul des Plateaux
Terrebonne, QC J6X 4J9
450-964-8778
Fax: 450-964-8773

Drummondville Branch
1010, boul René-Lévesque
Drummondville, QC J2C 5W4
819-478-4951
Fax: 819-478-5864

Gatineau Branch
#104, 259, boul St-Joseph
Gatineau, QC J8Y 6T1
819-997-4434
Fax: 819-997-4435

Granby Branch
#302, 155, rue St-Jacques
Granby, QC J2G 9A7
450-372-5202
Fax: 450-372-2423

Laval Branch
#100, 2525, Daniel-Johnson
Laval, QC H7T 1S9
450-973-6868
Fax: 450-973-6860

Longueuil Branch
#100, 550, ch de Chambly
Longueuil, QC J4H 3L8
450-928-4120
Fax: 450-928-4127

Montréal Branch
#12525, 5, Place Ville-Marie
Montréal, QC H3B 2G2
514-496-7966
Fax: 514-496-7974
Other Communication: Subordinate Financing (Montréal), Phone: 514-496-0626, Fax: 514-496-1020; Subordinate Financing (North-Shore & South-Shore), Phone: 514-283-8265, Fax: 514-496-1020

Pointe-Claire Branch
#110, 755, boul St-Jean
Pointe-Claire, QC H9R 5M9
514-697-8014
Fax: 514-697-3160

Québec (Grande Allée ouest) Branch
1134, Grande-Allée ouest
Québec, QC G1S 1E5

Federal/Provincial Government / Government of Canada

418-648-3972
Fax: 418-648-5525
Other Communication: Subordinate Financing (Eastern Quebec), Phone: 418-648-5517, Fax: 418-649-6301

Québec (Lebourgneuf) Branch
#310, 1165, boul Lebourgneuf
Québec, QC G2K 2C9
418-648-4740
Fax: 418-648-4745

Rimouski Branch
391, boul Jessop
Rimouski, QC G5L 1M9
418-722-3304
Fax: 418-722-3362

Rouyn-Noranda Branch
#301, 139, boul Québec
Rouyn-Noranda, QC J9X 6M8
819-764-6701
Fax: 819-764-5472

Saint-Jérôme Branch
#102, 55, rue Castonguay
Saint-Jérôme, QC J7Y 2H9
450-432-7111
Fax: 450-432-8366

Saint-Laurent Branch
#160, 3100, boul de la Côte-Vertu
Saint-Laurent, QC H4R 2J8
514-496-7500
Fax: 514-496-7510

Saint-Léonard Branch
6347, rue Jean-Talon est
Saint-Léonard, QC H1S 3E7
514-251-2818
Fax: 514-251-2758

Sherbrooke Branch
2532, rue King ouest
Sherbrooke, QC J1J 2E8
819-564-5700
Fax: 819-564-4276

Thérèse-de-Blainville (Boisbriand) Regional Branch
3000, rue Cours le Corbusier
Boisbriand, QC J7G 3E8
450-420-4900
Fax: 450-420-4904

Trois-Rivières Branch
#150, 1500, rue Royale
Trois-Rivières, QC G9A 6E6
819-371-5215
Fax: 819-371-5220

Saskatchewan Branches:

Regina
#320, 2220 - 12th Ave.
Regina, SK S4P 0M8
306-780-6478
Fax: 306-780-7516

Saskatoon
135 - 21st St. East, Main Fl.
Saskatoon, SK S7K 0B4
306-975-4822
Fax: 306-975-5955

Yukon Branches:

Whitehorse
204 Lambert St.
Whitehorse, YT Y1A 1Z4
867-633-7510
Fax: 867-667-4058

Canada Border Services Agency (CBSA) / Agence des services frontaliers du Canada (ASFC)

Headquarters
191 Laurier Ave. West
Ottawa, ON K1A 0L8
800-461-9999
TDD: 866-335-3237
CBSA-ASFC@canada.gc.ca; communications@ps.gc.ca (Public Safety)
www.cbsa-asfc.gc.ca
Other Communication: Border Information Service, Service in French, Toll-Free Phone: 1-800-959-2036; Public Safety Canada, Phone: 613-944-4875, Toll-Free: 1-800-830-3118
Established in 2003, as a response to the need for increased border services, the Canada Border Services Agency ensures the security & prosperity of Canada. The agency is responsible for managing the access of people & goods to & from Canada. To carry out its mission, Canada Border Services Agency administers more than ninety pieces of legislation. Some of the agencies duties include the following: managing over 100 border crossings; offering services at points throughout Canada & internationally; operating detention centres across the nation; conducting marine operations at the ports of Prince Rupert, Vancouver, Montréal, & Halifax; managing postal services at major mail centres in Montréal, Toronto, & Vancouver; & forming part of more than twenty Integrated Border Enforcement Teams across Canada.

Acts Administered:
Access to Information Act
Act to Establish the Canada Border Services Agency
Aeronautics Act
Anti-Personnel Mines Convention Implementation Act (through EIPA)
Blue Water Bridge Authority Act
Bretton Woods & Related Agreements Act
Canada Agricultural Products Act
Canada Customs & Revenue Agency Act
Canada Grain Act
Canada Post Corporation Act
Canada Shipping Act
Canada-Chile Free Trade Agreement Implementation Act
Canada-Costa Rica Free Trade Agreement Implementation Act
Canada-Israel Free Trade Agreement Implementation Act
Canada-United States Free Trade Agreement Implementation Act
Canadian Dairy Commission Act
Canadian Environmental Protection Act, 1999
Canadian Food Inspection Agency Act
Canadian International Trade Tribunal Act
Canadian Wheat Board Act
Carriage by Air Act
Chemical Weapons Convention Implementation Act (through EIPA)
Civil International Space Station Agreement Implementation Act
Coastal Fisheries Protection Act
Coasting Trade Act
Consumer Packaging & Labelling Act
Controlled Drug & Substances Act
Convention on International Trade in Endangered Species of Wild Fauna & Flora
Copyright Act
Criminal Code
Cultural Property Export & Import Act
Customs Act
Customs & Excise Offshore Application Act
Customs Tariff Act
Defence Production Act
Department of Health Act
Department of Industry Act
Energy Administration Act
Energy Efficiency Act
Excise Act
Excise Act, 2001
Excise Tax Act
Explosives Act
Export Act
Export & Import of Rough Diamonds Act
Export & Import Permits Act
Federal-Provincial Fiscal Arrangements Act
Feeds Act
Fertilizers Act
Financial Administration Act
Firearms Act
Fish Inspection Act
Fisheries Act
Foods & Drugs Act
Foreign Missions & International Organizations Act
Freshwater Fish Marketing Act
Hazardous Products Act
Health of Animals Act
Immigration & Refugee Protection Act
Importation of Intoxicating Liquors Act
Integrated Circuit Topography Act
International Boundary Commission Act
Manganese-based Fuel Additives Act
Meat Inspection Act
Motor Vehicle Fuel Consumption Standards Act (not in force)
Motor Vehicle Safety Act
National Energy Board Act
Navigable Waters Protection Act
North American Free Trade Agreement Implementation Act
Nuclear Energy Act
Nuclear Safety & Control Act
Pest Control Products Act
Pilotage Act
Plant Breeders' Rights Act
Plant Protection Act
Precious Metals Marking Act
Preclearance Act
Privacy Act
Privileges & Immunities (North Atlantic Organization Act)
Proceeds of Crime (Money Laundering) & Terrorist Financing Act
Quarantine Act
Quebec Harbour, Port Warden Act
Radiation Emitting Devices Act
Radiocommunication Act
Seeds Act
Special Economic Measures Act
Special Import Measures Act
Statistics Act
Telecommunications Act
Textile Labelling Act
Trade-Marks Act
Transportation of Dangerous Goods Act, 1992
United Nations Act
United States Wreckers Act
Visiting Forces Act
Wild Animals & Plant Protection & Regulation of International & Interprovincial Trade Act

Minister, Public Safety, Hon. Vic Toews
613-992-3128, Fax: 613-995-1049
Toews.V@parl.gc.ca
Other Communications: Public Safety & Emergency Preparedness: 613-991-2924
President, Stephen Rigby
Executive Vice-President, Luc Portelance
Regional Director General, Québec Region, Martin Bolduc
514-283-8700, Fax: 514-496-5181
Regional Director General, Greater Toronto Area Region, Rick Comerford
905-803-5595
Regional Director General, Pacific Region, Blake Delgaty
604-666-0760,
Other Communications: Executive Assistant, Phone: 604-666-3305
Regional Director General, Windsor - St. Clair Region, Pete Diponio
519-967-4010
Regional Director General, Niagara - Fort Erie Region, Tony Geoghegan
905-994-6011,
Other Communications: Administrative Assistant, Phone: 905-994-6002

Canada Business (CBSC) / Entreprises Canada (CSEC)

235 Queen St.
Ottawa, ON K1A 0H5
Fax: 888-417-0442
888-576-4444
TDD: 800-457-8466
www.canadabusiness.ca
Canada Business provides a wide range of information on government services, programs & regulations to Canadian business people. The base framework is an organized network of centres across Canada, one in each province & territory. The network of Canada Business is expanding to include regional access partners in many other communities across Canada. The centres offer various products and services aimed at helping clients obtain quick, accurate & comprehensive business information. Each centre exists as a result of cooperative arrangements between federal & provincial governments, & the private sector in some cases. Administration & management of the CBSC varies depending on location between the following federal agencies: Western Economic Diversification (WD), Industry Canada, the Canada Economic Development for Quebec Regions (CEDQR) & the Atlantic Canada Opportunities Agency (ACOA). The Federal Business Information System (BIS) is a collection of information on business-related programs, services & selected regulations which are accessible through the CBSC & on the

CBSC web site (www.cbsc.org). The Federal BIS acts as a single window for individuals or businesses to access relevant information from all federal departments
Executive Director, Marcie Girouard
613-954-3576, Fax: 613-954-5463

Regional Offices:

The Business Link Business Service Centre
#100, 10237 - 104 St. NW
Edmonton, AB T5J 1B1
780-422-7722
Fax: 780-422-0055
800-272-9675
TDD: 800-457-8466
buslink@cbsc.ic.gc.ca
www.cbsc.org/alberta
Other Communication: Info-Fax: 780/422-0055

Small Business BC
82 - 601 West Cordova St.
Vancouver, BC V6B 1G1
604-775-5525
Fax: 604-775-5520
800-667-2272
TDD: 800-457-8466
askus@smallbusinessbc.ca
www.smallbusinessbc.ca

Canada/Manitoba Business Service Centre
#250, 240 Graham Ave.
PO Box 2609
Winnipeg, MB R3C 4B3
204-984-2272
Fax: 204-983-3852
800-665-2019
TDD: 800-457-8466
manitoba@canadabusiness.ca
www.cbsc.org/manitoba

Canada/New Brunswick Business Service Centre
570 Queen St.
Fredericton, NB E3B 6Z6
506-444-6140
Fax: 506-444-6172
888-576-4444
TDD: 800-457-8466
infonb@canadabusiness.ca
www.cbsc.org/nb

Canada/Newfoundland & Labrador Business Service Centre
90 O'Leary Ave.
PO Box 8687 A
St. John's, NL A1B 3T1
709-772-6022
Fax: 709-772-6090
800-668-1010
TDD: 800-457-8466
info@cbsc.ic.gc.ca
www.cbsc.org/nf

Canada/NWT Business Service Centre
#701, 5201 - 50 Ave.
PO Box 1320
Yellowknife, NT X1A 3S9
867-873-7958
Fax: 867-873-0573
888-576-4444
TDD: 800-457-8466
yel@cbsc.ic.gc.ca
www.cbsc.org/nwt

Canada/Nova Scotia Business Service Centre (CNSBSC)
1575 Brunswick St.
Halifax, NS B3J 2G1
902-426-8604
Fax: 902-426-6530
888-576-4444
TDD: 800-457-8466
halifax@cbsc.ic.gc.ca
www.cbsc.org/ns

Canada/Nunavut Business Service Centre
Inuksugait Plaza
PO Box 1000 1198
Iqaluit, NU X0A 0H0
867-975-7860
Fax: 867-975-7885
877-499-5199
cnbsc@gov.nu.ca

www.cbsc.org/nunavut
Other Communication: Toll Free Fax: 1-877-499-5299

Canada/Ontario Business Service Centre (COBSC)
151 Yonge St., 3rd Fl.
Toronto, ON M5C 2W7
416-775-3456
Fax: 416-954-8597
888-576-4444
TDD: 800-457-8466
ontario@cbsc.ic.gc.ca
www.cbsc.org/ontario

Canada/Prince Edward Island Business Service Centre (CPEIBSC)
Jean Canfield Building
191 University Ave., 1st Fl.
Charlottetown, PE C1A 4L2
902-368-0771
Fax: 902-566-7377
888-576-4444
Info.cb.pei@acoa-apeca.gc.ca
www.cbsc.org/pe

Canada/Saskatchewan Business Service Centre (CSBSC)
#2, 345 Third Ave. South
Saskatoon, SK S7K 1M6
306-956-2323
Fax: 306-956-2328
800-667-4374
TDD: 800-457-8466
saskatchewan@canadabusiness.ca
www.cbsc.org/sask/index.cfm

Canada/Yukon Business Service Centre
#101, 307 Jarvis St.
Whitehorse, YT Y1A 2H3
867-633-6257
Fax: 867-667-2001
888-576-4444
TDD: 800-457-8466
yukon@cbsc.ic.gc.ca
www.cbsc.org/yukon

Info entrepreneurs
380, rue St-Antoine ouest, local 6000
Montréal, QC H2Y 3X7
514-496-4636
Fax: 514-496-5934
888-576-4444
TDD: 800-457-8466
infoentrepreneurs@cbsc.ic.gc.ca
http://infoentrepreneurs.org
Other Communication: Toll Free Fax: 1-888-417-0442

Canada Economic Development for Québec Regions / Développement économique Canada pour les régions du Québec

Édifice Dominion Square
#900, 1255, rue Peel
Montréal, QC H3B 2T9
514-283-6412
Fax: 514-283-3302
866-385-6412
www.dec-ced.gc.ca
Defines federal objectives relating to development opportunities & delivers business assistance programs for small- & medium-sized businesses in Qu‚bec for innovation, entrepreneurial & market development purposes. Supports a series of programs for appropriate environmental initiatives in various regions of Québec. The agency fosters alliances among the various environmental industry stakeholders including small- & medium-sized enterprises & industrial associations. Goals include a strengthening of existing & new partnerships, & an improvement of access to government programs. The agency also provides a significant amount of support for research & development in areas of environmental technology, demonstration, marketing & transfer projects. Supports initiatives that contribute to making Montréal an industrial centre of excellence in the environment. Aids small- & medium-sized firms in gaining access to federal procurement process, & encourages training & education focusing on business management. Helps business develop export markets through cooperative efforts with Industry Canada & Foreign Affairs & International Trade Canada
Minister responsible, Hon. Christian Paradis
613-995-1377, Fax: 613-943-1562
Paradis.C@parl.gc.ca

Minister of State, Economic Development Agency of Canada for the Regions of Québec, Hon. Denis Lebel
613-996-6236, Fax: 613-996-6252
Lebel.D@parl.gc.ca; denis.lebel@dec-ced.gc.ca
Other Communications: Economic Development Agency (QC):514-496-1282
President, Suzanne Vinet
514-283-4843, Fax: 514-283-7778

Operations

Abitibi-Témiscamingue
906, 5e av
Val-d'Or, QC J9P 1B9
819-825-5260
Fax: 819-825-3245
800-567-6451

Bas St-Laurent
Édifice Trust général du Canada
#310, 2, rue Saint-Germain Est
Rimouski, QC G5L 8T7
418-722-3282
Fax: 418-722-3285
800-463-9073
Director, Pierre Roberge

Centre-du-Québec
Place du Centre
#502, 150, rue Marchand
Drummondville, QC J2C 4N1
819-478-4664
Fax: 819-478-4666
800-567-1418
Acting Director, Mariette Larochelle

Estrie
Place Andrew Paton
#240, 65, rue Belvédère nord
Sherbrooke, QC J1H 4A7
819-564-5904
Fax: 819-564-5912
800-567-6084

Gaspésie-Îles-de-la-Madeleine
Place Jacques-Cartier
120, rue de la Reine, 3e étage
Gaspé, QC G4X 2S1
418-368-5870
Fax: 418-368-6256
866-368-0044
Director, France Simard

Ile-de-Montréal
3340, boul de l'Assomption
Montréal, QC H1N 3S4
514-283-2500
Fax: 514-496-8310
800-322-4636

Laval - Laurentides - Lanaudière
#410, 2990, av Pierre-Péladeau
Laval, QC H7T 3B3
450-973-6844
Fax: 450-973-6851
800-430-6844

Mauricie
Immeuble Bourg du Fleuve
#413, 25, rue des Forges
Trois-Rivières, QC G9A 2G4
819-371-5182
Fax: 819-371-5186
800-567-8637

Montérégie
Place Agropur
#400, 101, boul Roland-Therrien
Longueuil, QC J4H 4B9
450-928-4088
Fax: 450-928-4097
800-284-0335
Director, Stéphane Dufour

Nord-du-Québec
Édifice Dominion Square
#900, 1255 rue Peel
Montréal, QC H3B 2T9

Federal/Provincial Government / Government of Canada

514-283-8131
Fax: 514-283-3637
800-561-0633
Director, Daniel Ricard

Outaouais
#202, 259 boul Saint-Joseph
Gatineau, QC J8Y 6T1
819-994-7442
Fax: 819-994-7846
800-561-4353
Director, Marc Boily

Québec - Chaudière - Appalaches
Place Iberville IV
#030, 2954, boul Laurier
Québec, QC G1V 4T2
418-648-4826
Fax: 418-648-7291
800-463-5204

Policy & Planning / Politiques et planification

Saguenay - Lac-Saint-Jean
#203, 170, rue Saint-Joseph sud
Alma, QC G8B 3E8
418-668-3084
Fax: 418-668-7584
800-463-9808

Inter-regional Intervention & Partnership / Intervention et partenariat entre régions

Responsible for the Agency's Sustainable Development Strategy, both within & outside the department. Promotes SD practices internally & emphasizes adoption of new business practices aimed at increasing productivity through pollution prevention & eco-efficiency; development & commercialization of innovations associated with sustainable development; partnerships with Government of Canada departments & agencies & environment industry representatives for the evaluation of projects & delivery of services with respect to sustainable development.
Director, François Yassa
514-283-8224, Fax: 514-283-4131

Canada Science & Technology Museum Corporation (CSTM) / Musée des sciences et de la technologie du Canada (MSTC)

PO Box 9724 T
Ottawa, ON K1G 5A3
613-991-6090
Fax: 613-990-3636
info@technomuses.ca
www.technomuses.ca
The Corporation is the only comprehensive science & technology collecting institution in Canada, & focuses on the following major subject areas: aviation, communications, manufacturing, natural resources, renewable resources including agriculture, scientific instrumentation, & transportation. The Corporation operates three Museums: the Canada Agriculture Museum, the Canada Aviation Museum & the Canada Science & Technology Museum.
President/CEO CSTM Corporation, Denise Amyot
613-993-0775
Director General Canada Science & Technology Museum,
Claude Faubert
613-991-0372
Curator Agriculture, Franz Klingender
613-996-7822
Curator Transportation, Garth Wilson
613-991-3087

Canada Mortgage & Housing Corporation (CMHC) / Société canadienne d'hypothèques et de logement (SCHL)

700 Montreal Rd.
Ottawa, ON K1A 0P7
613-748-2000
Fax: 613-748-2098
800-668-2642
TDD: 613-748-2447
chic@cmhc-schl.gc.ca
www.cmhc.ca; www.schl.ca
Other Communication: Canadian Housing Information Centre:
613/748-2367
CMHC works closely with a network of professional associations, groups & institutions concerned with regional planning & the residential sector. It prepares various research projects for the examination of relationships between urban areas, housing & sustainable development issues. Involved in numerous technical research projects addressing interrelationships between housing, energy & resource use. Through its research & information transfer function, CMHC will undertake initiatives such as identifying approaches & solutions that lead to more sustainable & healthy communities, examining barriers to potential development of brownfield sites.CMHC will focus on ways to reduce residential energy consumption in multiple-unit housing, educate consumers on energy-saving changes to homes. The Net Zero Healthy Healthy Housing Initiative combines passive solar, energy-efficient design, construction & appliances, integrated with renewable energy systems, to achieve net zero energy consumption on an annual basis, significantly reducing environmental impacts & GHG emissions. Twenty demonstration projects across Canada are underway
Acts Administered:
CMHC Act
National Housing Act (NHA)
Chair, Dino Chiesa

Atlantic Region
Barrington Tower, 9th Fl.
1894 Barrington St.
Halifax, NS B3J 2A8
902-426-3530
Fax: 902-426-9991

British Columbia
#200, 1111 West Georgia St.
Vancouver, BC V6E 4S4
604-731-5733
Fax: 604-737-4139

Ontario
#300, 100 Sheppard Ave. East
Toronto, ON M2N 6Z1
416-221-2642
Fax: 416-218-3310

Prairie & Territories Region
#200, 1000 - 7 Ave. SW
Calgary, AB T2P 5L5
403-515-3000
Fax: 403-515-2930

Québec
1100, boul René-Levesque ouest, 1er étage
Montréal, QC H3B 5J7
514-283-2222
888-772-0772

Canada Revenue Agency (CRA) / Agence du revenu du Canada

875 Heron Rd.
Ottawa, ON K1A 0L5
613-952-0384
800-267-6999
TDD: 800-665-0354
www.cra-arc.gc.ca
Other Communication: Individual Income Tax Enquiries:
1-800-959-8281; Telerefund: 1-800-959-1956; Business & Self-Employed Individuals: 1-800-959-5525; GST/HST Credit: 1-800-959-1953
The Canada Revenue Agency administers tax laws for the Canadian federal government & for most provincial & territorial governments. The Agency is also responsible for various social & economic benefit & incentive programs, which are delivered through the tax system.
Acts Administered:
Canada Pension Plan Act, Part I
Customs Act
Customs & Excise Offshore Application Act
Customs Tariff Act
Department of National Revenue Act
Excise Act
Excise Tax Act
Special Import Measures Act
Unemployment Insurance Act, Part III & VII
Minister, National Revenue; Minister, Atlantic Canada Opportunities Agency; Minister, Atlantic Gateway, Hon. Keith Ashfield
613-992-1067, Fax: 613-996-9955
Ashfield.K@parl.gc.ca
Other Communications: National Revenue, Phone:
613-995-2960
Commissioner & CEO, Linda Lizotte-MacPherson
613-957-3688

Tax Services Offices

Atlantic Region

Bathurst
201 George St.
PO Box 8888
Bathurst, NB E2A 4L8
Fax: 506-548-9905

Charlottetown
161 St. Peters Rd.
PO Box 8500
Charlottetown, PE C1A 8L3
Fax: 902-566-7197

Halifax
1557 Hollis St.
PO Box 638
Halifax, NS B3J 2T5
Fax: 902-426-7170

Moncton
50 King St.
PO Box 1070
Moncton, NB E1C 4M2
Fax: 506-851-7018

Newfoundland & Labrador
Sir Humphrey Gilbert Building
165 Duckworth St.
PO Box 12075
St. John's, NL A1B 4R5
709-754-5928

Saint John
126 Prince William St.
Saint John, NB E2L 4H9
Fax: 506-636-5200

St. John's Tax Centre
290 Empire Ave.
St. John's, NL A1B 3Z1
Fax: 709-754-3416

Summerside Tax Centre
275 Pope Rd.
Summerside, PE C1N 6A2
Fax: 902-432-6287

Sydney
47 Dorchester St.
PO Box 1300
Sydney, NS B1P 6K3
Fax: 902-564-3095

Northern Ontario Region

Barrie
81 Mulcaster St.
Barrie, ON L4M 6T7
Fax: 705-721-0056

Belleville
11 Station St.
Belleville, ON K8N 2S3
Fax: 613-969-7845

Kingston
31 Hyperion Ct.
PO Box 2600
Kingston, ON K7L 5P3
Fax: 613-545-3272

Ottawa & Nunavut
333 Laurier Ave. West
Ottawa, ON K1A 0L9
Fax: 613-238-7125

Peterborough
185 King St. West, 5th Fl.
Peterborough, ON K9J 8M3
Fax: 705-876-6422

Sudbury Tax Centre
1050 Notre Dame Ave.
Sudbury, ON P3A 5C1
Fax: 705-671-3994

Thunder Bay
130 South Syndicate Ave.
Thunder Bay, ON P7E 1C7
Fax: 807-622-8512

Federal/Provincial Government / Government of Canada

Pacific Region

Burnaby-Fraser
9737 King George Hwy.
Surrey, BC V3T 5W6
Fax: 604-587-2010

Northern BC & Yukon
280 Victoria St.
Prince George, BC V2L 5N8
Fax: 250-561-7869

Southern Interior
277 Winnipeg St.
Penticton, BC V2A 1N6
Fax: 250-492-8346

Surrey Tax Centre
9755 King George Hwy.
Surrey, BC V3T 5E1
Fax: 604-585-5769

Vancouver
1166 West Pender St.
Vancouver, BC V6E 3H8
Fax: 604-689-7536

Vancouver Island
1415 Vancouver St.
Victoria, BC V8V 3W4
Fax: 250-363-8188

Prairie Region

Edmonton & NWT
#10, 9700 Jasper Ave.
Edmonton, AB T5J 4C8
Fax: 780-495-3533

Lethbridge
#200, 419 - 7 St. South
Lethbridge, AB T1J 4A9
Fax: 403-382-4765

Red Deer
4996 - 49 Ave.
Red Deer, AB T4N 6X2
Fax: 403-341-7053

Regina
#260, 1783 Hamilton St.
Regina, SK S4P 2B6
Fax: 306-757-1412

Saskatoon
340 - 3rd Ave. North
Saskatoon, SK S7K 0A8
Fax: 306-652-3211

Calgary
220 - 4 Ave. SE
Calgary, AB T2G 0L1
Fax: 403-264-5843

Winnipeg
325 Broadway
Winnipeg, MB R3C 4T4
Fax: 204-984-5164

Winnipeg Tax Centre
66 Stapon Rd.
Winnipeg, MB R3C 3M2
Fax: 204-984-5164

Southern Ontario Region

Hamilton
55 Bay St.
PO Box 2220
Hamilton, ON L8N 3E1
Fax: 905-546-1615

Kitchener-Waterloo
166 Frederick St.
Kitchener, ON N2G 4N1
Fax: 519-579-4532

London
451 Talbot St.
London, ON N6A 5E5
Fax: 519-645-4029

St Catharines
32 Church St.
PO Box 3038
St Catharines, ON L2R 3B9
Fax: 905-688-5996

Toronto Centre
1 Front St. West
Toronto, ON M5J 2X6
Fax: 416-360-8908

Toronto East
Rm 427, 200 Town Centre Court
Toronto, ON M1P 4Y3
Fax: 416-973-5126

Toronto North
#1000, 5001 Yonge St.
Toronto, ON M2N 6R9
Fax: 416-512-2558

Toronto West
5800 Hurontario St.
PO Box 6000
Mississauga, ON L5R 4B4
Fax: 905-566-6182

Windsor
185 Ouellette Ave.
Windsor, ON N9A 5S8
Fax: 519-257-6558

Québec Region

Chicoutimi
#123, 100, rue Lafontaine
Chicoutimi, QC G7H 6X2
Fax: 418-698-6387

Jonquière Tax Centre
2251, boul René-Lévesque
Jonquière, QC G7S 5J1
Fax: 418-548-0846

Laval
3400, av Jean-Béraud
Laval, QC H7T 2Z2
Fax: 514-956-7071

Montérégie-Rive-Sud
3250, boul Lapinière
Brossard, QC J4Z 3T8
Fax: 450-926-7100

Montréal
305, boul René-Lévesque ouest
Montréal, QC H2Z 1A6
Fax: 514-496-1309

Outaouais
1100, boul Maloney ouest
Gatineau, ON K1A 1L4
Fax: 819-994-1103

Québec
165, rue de la Pointe-aux-Lièvres sud
Québec, QC G1K 7L3
Fax: 418-649-6478

Rimouski
#101, 180, av de la Cathédrale
Rimouski, QC G5L 5H9
Fax: 418-722-3027

Rouyn-Noranda
44, av du Lac
Rouyn-Noranda, QC J9X 6Z9
Fax: 819-797-8366

Shawinigan-Sud Tax Centre
4695, 12e av
Shawinigan-Sud, QC G9P 5H9
Fax: 819-536-7078

Sherbrooke
50, Place de la Cité
CP 1300
Sherbrooke, QC J1H 5L8
Fax: 819-821-8582

Trois-Rivières
#111, 25, rue des Forges
Trois-Rivières, QC G9A 2G4
Fax: 819-371-2744

Canadian Centre for Occupational Health & Safety (CCOHS) / Centre canadien d'hygiène et de sécurité au travail (CCHST)

135 Hunter St. East
Hamilton, ON L8N 1M5
905-572-2981
Fax: 905-572-2206
800-668-4284
clientservices@ccohs.ca
www.ccohs.ca
Provides occupational health & safety & environmental information in the form of publications, responses to inquiries & a computerized information service available in various formats. Topics include: environmental acts & regulations; occupational & environmental health data; toxic effects of chemical substances; transport of dangerous goods; chemical evaluation; hazardous substances; & domestic substances listed under the Canadian Environmental Protection Act; biological hazards; ergonomics
President/CEO, S. Len Hong
905-572-2981
Vice-President, Dr. Patabendi K. Abeytunga
905-572-2981
Controller, Bonnie Easterbrook
905-572-2981
Manager Communications, Eleanor Westwood
905-572-2981
Manager Computer Systems & Services, David Brophy
905-572-2981
Manager General Health & Safety Services, Norma Gibson-MacDonald
905-572-2981
Manager Inquiries & Client Services, Renzo Bertolini
905-572-2981

Canadian Commercial Corporation (CCC) / Corporation commerciale canadienne

50 O'Connor St., 11th Fl.
Ottawa, ON K1A 0S6
613-996-0034
Fax: 613-995-2121
800-748-8191
www.ccc.ca
A Crown Corporation mandated to facilitate international trade, particularly in government markets.CCC specializes in international procurement markets for Canadian companies & provides services to help them win, negotiate & manage export contracts. As prime contractor, CCC offers a government-to-government agreement that simplifies customer access to Canadian technology & expertise. CCC contracts have a government guarantee for performance.
Chair, Robert C. Kay
President, Marc Whittingham
613-996-0042, Fax: 613-992-2134
Vice-President Strategy & Organizational Development, Mariette Fyfe-Fortin
613-943-4360
Vice-President Defence Procurement, Jacques Greffe
613-996-0161
Vice-President Business Development & Sales, Pierre Alarie
613-943-0953
Vice-President/CFO Risk & Finance, Martin Zablocki
613-992-9638
Vice-President/Legal General Counsel & Corporate Secretary Legal Services, Tamara Parschin-Rybkin, Q.C.
613-992-4419, Fax: 613-947-3903

Canadian Environmental Assessment Agency (CEAA) / Agence canadienne d'évaluation environnementale (ACEE)

Place Bell Canada
160 Elgin St., 22nd Fl.
Ottawa, ON K1A 0H3
613-957-0700
Fax: 613-957-0862
866-582-1884
info@ceaa-acee.gc.ca
www.ceaa-acee.gc.ca
The Canadian Environmental Assessment Agency (CEAA) was established to administer the Canadian Environmental Assessment Act (the Act). The environmental assessment process identifies the environmental effects of proposed projects & measures to address those effects, in support of sustainable development. CEAA promotes environmental assessment as a tool to protect & sustain a healthy environment in harmony with a growing economy. The CEAA advocates high-quality environmental

Federal/Provincial Government / Government of Canada

assessments by assisting federal departments & agencies with training & guidance & by investing in the research & development of best practices. CEAA provides administrative support to mediators & review panels & ensures that the public has opportunities to participate effectively in the environmental assessment process. Public participation strengthens the quality & credibility of environmental assessments by providing local & traditional knowledge, & insight into possible environmental effects. A publicly accessible master index of environmental assessments carried out by federal departments is available in the Canadian Environmental Assessment Registry (projects beginning before November 2003 are available in the Federal Environmental Assessment Index) located on the CEAA web site. In addition, CEAA's participant funding program provides limited funds to ensure that interested individuals & groups have the opportunity to participate in mediations & panel reviews. Accountable to the Minister of the Environment.
President, Peter Sylvester
613-948-2671,
peter.sylvester@ceaa-acee.gc.ca
Vice-President Operations, Thao Pham
613-948-2665,
thao.pham@ceaa-acee.gc.ca
Vice-President Policy Development, Yves Leboeuf
613-948-2662,
yves.leboeuf@ceaa-acee.gc.ca
Executive Director Project Reviews, Steve Burgess
613-948-2663,
steve.burgess@ceaa-acee.gc.ca
Director General Corporate Services, Richard Gagné
613-957-0467,
richard.gagne@ceaa-acee.gc.ca
Director Operational Support, Andrée Chevrier
613-957-0641,
andree.chevrier@ceaa-acee.gc.ca
Director Communications, Charlene Gaudet
613-957-0712,
charlene.gaudet@ceaa-acee.gc.ca
Director Finance & Administration, Daniel Nadeau
613-948-2677,
daniel.nadeau@ceaa-acee.gc.ca
Director Human Resources, Brigitte Schryer
613-954-2201,
brigitte.schryer@ceaa-acee.gc.ca
Director Legislative & Regulatory Affairs, John D. Smith
613-948-1942,
john.smith@ceaa-acee.gc.ca
Director Policy Analysis, Margaret Bailey
613-957-0065,
Margaret.bailey@ceaa-acee.gc.ca
General Counsel Legal Services, Irene V. Gendron
613-957-0735,
irene.gendron@ceaa-acee.gc.ca

Alberta & Northwest Territories
61 Airport Rd. NW
Edmonton, AB T5G 0W6
780-495-2037
Fax: 780-495-2876
ceaa.alberta@ceaa-acee.gc.ca
Director, Lanny Coulson
780-495-2388

Atlantic Region
#200, 1801 Hollis St.
Halifax, NS B3J 3N4
902-426-0564
Fax: 902-426-6550
ceaa.atlantic@ceaa.gc.ca
Director, William Coulter
902-426-0564

Ontario
#907, 55 St. Clair Ave. East
Toronto, ON M4T 1M2
416-952-1576
Fax: 416-952-1573
ceaa.ontario@ceaa-acee.gc.ca
Director, Louise Knox
416-952-1575

Nunavut
c/o Place Bell Canada, 22nd Floor
160 Elgin St.
Ottawa, ON K1A 0H3
613-957-0748
Fax: 613-948-1354
clare.cattrysse@ceaa-acee.gc.ca
Acting Director Policy Analysis, Claire Cattrysse

Pacific & Yukon
#320, 757 West Hastings St.
Vancouver, BC V6C 1A1
604-666-2434
Fax: 604-666-6990
ceaa.pacific@ceaa-acee.gc.ca
Director, Jason Quigley
604-666-6989

Prairie Region
#445, 123 Main St.
Winnipeg, MB R3C 4W2
204-983-5127
Fax: 204-983-7174
ceaa.prairies@ceaa-acee.gc.ca
Director, Dan McNaughton
204-984-2457

Québec
1141, rte de l'Église, 2e étage
CP 9514 Ste-Foy
Québec, QC G1V 4B8
418-649-6444
Fax: 418-649-6443
ceaa.quebec@ceaa-acee.gc.ca
Director, François Boulanger
418-649-6438

Canadian Food Inspection Agency (CFIA) / Agence canadienne d'inspection des aliments (ACIA)
1400 Merivale Rd.
Ottawa, ON K1A 0Y9
613-225-2342
Fax: 613-228-6629
800-442-2342
TDD: 800-465-7735
www.inspection.gc.ca
The agency is responsible for all inspection services related to food safety, economic fraud, trade-related requirements, & animal & plant health programs.
Acts Administered:
Agriculture & Agri-Food Administration Monetary Penalties Act
Canada Agricultural Products Act
Canadian Food Inspection Agency Act
Feeds Act
Fertilizers Act
Fish Inspection Act
Health of Animals Act
Meat Inspection Act
Plant Breeders' Rights Act
Plant Protection Act
Seeds Act
Acts Administered in Part by the Canadian Food Inspection Agency
Consumer Packaging & Labelling Act
Food & Drugs Act
President, Carole Swan
613-773-6000, Fax: 613-773-6060
carole.swan@inspection.gc.ca
Executive Vice-President Office of the President, Dr. Brian Evans
613-773-5763,
brian.evans@inspection.gc.ca
Vice-President Finance, Administration & Information Technology, Stephen Baker
613-773-5700, Fax: 613-773-5792
Stephen.Baker@inspection.gc.ca
Vice-President Human Resources, Omer Boudreau
613-773-5725, Fax: 613-773-5795
Omer.Boudreau@inspection.gc.ca
Vice-President Operations, Cameron Prince
613-773-5717, Fax: 613-773-5671
Cameron.Prince@inspection.gc.ca
Vice-President Policy & Programs, Sandra Wing
613-773-5734, Fax: 613-773-5791
Sandra.Wing@inspection.gc.ca
Vice-President Science, Martine Dubuc
613-773-5722, Fax: 613-773-5797
Martine.Dubuc@inspection.gc.ca
Assoc. Vice-President Integration & Management Services, Jim Butcher
613-773-6298, Fax: 613-773-5791
Jim.Butcher@inspection.gc.ca
Executive Director Audit, Evaluation & Risk Oversight, Peter Everson
613-773-5759, Fax: 613-773-5696
Peter.Everson@inspection.gc.ca
Executive Director Corporate Secretariat, Veronica McGuire
613-773-5751, Fax: 613-773-5791
Veronica.McGuire@inspection.gc.ca
Executive Director Programs Communications, Laurel Herwig
613-773-5501, Fax: 613-773-5618
Laurel.Herwig@inspection.gc.ca
Director Executive Support & Coordination, Cynthia Richardson
613-773-5542, Fax: 613-773-5606
Cynthia.Richardson@inspection.gc.ca
Director Corporate Planning & Reporting, Dr. Raman Srivastava
613-773-5528, Fax: 613-773-5605
Raman.Srivastava@inspection.gc.ca

Atlantic
1081 Main St., 5th Fl.
Moncton, NB E1C 8R2
506-851-7400
Fax: 506-851-2689
Executive Director, Doug Steadman
506-851-7670,
steadmanb@inspection.gc.ca

Ontario
174 Stone Rd. West
Guelph, ON N1G 4S9
519-837-9400
Fax: 519-837-9766
Executive Director, Bill Teeter
519-837-5802,
bteeter@inspection.gc.ca

Québec
2001, av Université, 7e étage
Montréal, QC H3A 3N2
514-283-8888
Fax: 514-283-3143
Executive Director, Yvon Bertrand

Western
#654, 220 - 4 Ave. SE
Calgary, AB T2G 4X3
403-292-4301
Fax: 403-292-5707
Executive Director, Philip H. Amundson
403-292-4364,
pamundson@inspection.gc.ca

Canadian Museum of Nature (CMN) / Musée Canadien de la Nature (MCN)
PO Box 3343 D
Ottawa, ON K1P 6P4
613-566-4700
Fax: 613-364-4021
www.nature.ca
A diverse natural history collection encompassing some 10 million specimens, & thousands of species. Provides access to specimens & data for research & access to knowledge on biodiversity, biosystematics & the environment. Carries out research on management & care of collections & employs a staff of researchers working on national & international projects. Through public programs, CMN communicates knowledge & promotes understanding of science & nature to diverse audiences. It includes permanent, special & travelling exhibits, curriculum-based & interpretive programs, & print, electronic, audiovisual & multimedia publications.
President/CEO, Joanne DiCosimo
613-566-4733, Fax: 613-364-4020
jdicosimo@mus-nature.ca
Director Collection Services, Roger Baird
613-364-4138, Fax: 613-364-4022
rbaird@mus-nature.ca
Director Research Services, Dr. Mark S. Graham
613-566-4743, Fax: 613-364-4022
mgraham@mus-nature.ca

Canadian Centre for Biodiversity (CCB) / Centre canadien de la biodiversité
A repository for the understanding, interpretation & dissemination of knowledge on biodiversity & conservation issues. The Centre supports & participates in the activities of COSEWIC (Committee of the Status of Endangered Wildlife in Canada) & the Ecological Monitoring & Assessment Network (EMAN), the Working Group on Museums & Sustainable Communities. It is home to the Secretariat for the Canadian Committee for IUCN - the World Conservation Union. The Biological Survey acts as a clearing house & source of information on insects & related animals of general concern to biologists.
Chief, Anne Breau
613-566-4795, Fax: 613-364-4022
abreau@mus-nature.ca
Environmental Specialist, Jean Lauriault
613-566-4217, Fax: 613-364-4022
jlauriault@mus-nature.ca

Canadian Heritage / Patrimoine canadien

15 Eddy St.
Gatineau, QC K1A 0M5
819-997-0055
866-811-0055
TDD: 888-997-3123
info@pch.gc.ca
www.pch.gc.ca
Canadian Heritage works to achieve a more cohesive & creative nation. Goals of the department are for Canadians to express & share their cultural experiences with others in their own country & globally & for Canadians to live in an inclusive society with intercultural understanding & citizen participation. Responsibilities are carried out by the following sectors: Citizenship & Heritage; Cultural Affairs; International & Intergovernmental Affairs & Sport; Planning & Corporate Affairs; & Public & Regional Affairs.
Acts Administered:
An Act to Incorporate the Jules & Paul-Émile Léger Foundation
Broadcasting Act
Canada Council Act
Canadian Film Development Corporation Act
Canadian Heritage Languages Institute Act
Canadian Multiculturalism Act
Canadian Race Relations Foundation Act
Canadian Radio-television & Telecommunications Commission
Cultural Property Export & Import Act
Department of Canadian Heritage Act
Fitness & Amateur Sport Act
Historic Sites & Monuments Act
Holidays Act
Library & Archives of Canada Act
Lieutenant Governors Superannuation Act
Museums Act
National Anthem Act
National Arts Centre Act
National Battlefields at Québec Act
National Capital Act
National Film Act
National Flag of Canada Manufacturing Standards Act
National Library Act
National Sports of Canada Act
National Symbol of Canada Act
Official Languages Act
Physical Activity & Sport Act
Public Service Employment Act
Salaries Act
Status of the Artist Act
Trademarks Act
Minister, Canadian Heritage & Official Languages, Hon. James Moore
819-997-7788, Fax: 613-992-9868
Moore.J@parl.gc.ca
Deputy Minister, Judith A. LaRocque
819-994-1132, Fax: 819-997-0979
Judith.A.LaRocque@pch.gc.ca
Associate Deputy Minister, Stephen Wallace
819-997-1356, Fax: 819-997-2978
Stephen.Wallace@pch.gc.ca
Parliamentary Secretary to the Minister of Canadian Heritage, Dean Del Mastro
613-995-6411, Fax: 613-996-9800
DelMastro.D@parl.gc.ca
Parliamentary Secretary for Official Languages, Greg Rickford
613-996-1161, Fax: 613-996-1759
Rickford.G@parl.gc.ca

- Canada Council for the Arts
350 Albert St.
PO Box 1047
Ottawa, ON K1P 5V8
613-566-4414
Fax: 613-566-4390
800-263-5588
TDD: 613-565-5194www.canadacouncil.ca
- Canada Science & Technology Museum Corporation
- Canadian Broadcasting Corporation(CBC) / Société Radio-Canada (SRC)
- Canadian Museum of Civilization
- Canadian Museum of Nature
- Canadian Museum of Civilization(CMC) / Musée canadien des civilisations
- Canadian Museum of Nature
- Canadian Radio-television & Telecommunications Commission(CRTC) / Conseil de la radiodiffusion et des télécommunications canadiennes
- Library & Archives Canada
- National Arts Centre(NAC) / Centre national des Arts (CNA)
- National Battlefields Commission
- National Film Board of Canada
- National Gallery of Canada
- National Gallery of Canada
- Public Service Commission of Canada
- Status of Women Canada
- Telefilm Canada

Citizenship & Heritage Sector / Citoyenneté et patrimoine
Asst. Deputy Minister, Diane Fulford
819-997-2832, Fax: 819-994-5032
Executive Director Heritage Group, Lyn Elliot Sherwood
819-997-7774, Fax: 819-997-8392
Director General Canadian Conservation Institute & Chief Operating Officer, Jeanne E. Inch
819-998-3721, Fax: 819-998-4721
Director General Canadian Heritage Information Network (CHIN), Gabrielle Blais
819-997-0091, Fax: 819-994-9555

Atlantic
#106, 1045 Main St.
Moncton, NB E1C 1H1
506-851-7069
Fax: 506-851-7079

Ontario
#400, 150 John St.
Toronto, ON M5V 3T6
416-954-0396
Fax: 416-954-2909

Prairies & Northern Region
275 Portage Ave., 2nd Fl.
PO Box 2160
Winnipeg, MB R3C 3R5
204-983-2630
Fax: 204-984-6996

Québec
Complexe Guy-Favreau, Tour Ouest
200, boul René-Lévesque ouest, 6e étage
Montréal, QC H2Z 1X4
514-283-5797
Fax: 514-283-8762

Western
300 West Georgia St., 4th Fl.
Vancouver, BC V6B 6C6
604-666-1893
Fax: 604-666-6040

Canadian Institutes of Health Research (CIHR) / Instituts de recherche en santé du Canada (IRSC)

160 Elgin St., 9th Fl.
Ottawa, ON K1A 0W9
613-941-2672
Fax: 613-954-1800
888-603-4178
info@cihr-irsc.gc.ca
www.cihr-irsc.gc.ca
Promotes health research excellence in Canada through training & funding programs in basic, clinical, health systems & services, & population health research. Research is carried out in universities, in the health sciences faculties, affiliated hospitals & institutions & other faculties where research projects are highly relevant to human health. University-Industry programs create the opportunity for collaboration between Canadian companies & researchers conducting research in Canadian universities or affiliated institutions. Also manages the health-related Networks of Centres of Excellence.
President, Alain Beaudet
613-954-1974
Executive Vice-President, Christine Fitzgerald
613-957-6134
Vice-President Research, Dr. Pierre Chartrand
613-954-1805
Director Human Resources, Sandra Cooper
613-957-8762
Executive Director Secretariat on Research Ethics, Susan Zimmerman
613-947-7148
Director Communications & Marketing, Karen Spierkel
613-954-1812
Director Ethics Office, Geneviève Dubois-Flynn
613-954-1801

Institute of Population & Public Health
#207-L, Banting Bldg., University of Toronto
100 College St.
Toronto, ON M5G 1L5
ipph@cihr-irsc.gc.ca
One of 13 CIHR Institutes, IPPH focuses on the interactions (biological, social, cultural, environmental) that determines the health of individuals, communities & global populations. Research includes environment & health issues, such as radiation, contaminants, ecosystems, air quality.
Scientific Director, Dr. John Frank
416-946-7986, Fax: 416-946-7984

Canadian International Development Agency (CIDA) / Agence canadienne de développement international (ACDI)

200, Promenade du Portage
Gatineau, QC K1A 0G4
819-997-5006
Fax: 819-953-6088
800-230-6349
TDD: 819-953-5023
info@acdi-cida.gc.ca
www.acdi-cida.gc.ca
Other Communication: Toll Free TDD: 1-800-331-5018; Public Inquiries: 819-997-5006
Major agency responsible for delivering most of Canada's foreign aid.CIDA is committed to supporting sustainable development in developing countries to meet the needs of current & future generations. The mission statement demands that criteria of sustainability be integrated into each project undertaken by the Agency in order to improve the economic, social, cultural, ecological & political condition of the world's developing nations. Many of the projects CIDA supports are aimed directly at the environment. Projects include reforestation & watershed rehabilitation, small scale fishing development (to increase output & food), water projects (to improve health), increased food production, improved rural quality, & supply & generation of electricity. Various other projects help nations develop the legal & administrative framework needed to promote environmentally sustainable development.In February, 2004, the Agency released its Sustainable Development Strategy 2004-2006: Enabling Change." This strategy sets out a number of key directions for the Agency to advance sustainable development. The $100-million five-year Canada Climate Change Development Fund was extended to 2005-2006
Minister, International Cooperation, Hon. Beverley J. (Bev) Oda
613-992-2792, Fax: 613-992-2794
Oda.B@parl.gc.ca; minister@acdi-cida.gc.ca
Parliamentary Secretary to the Minister of International Cooperation, Hon. Jim Abbott
613-995-7246, Fax: 613-996-9923
Abbott.J@parl.gc.ca
Chief of Staff, Amy Baker
819-997-0843
Administration & Information Officer, Claudine Taillefer
819-997-6912, Fax: 819-997-0866
Senior Vice-President Geographic Programs Branch, Hau Sing Tse
819-997-1665,

Federal/Provincial Government / Government of Canada

Acting Vice-President Afghanistan & Pakistan Task Force, Francoise Ducros
819-997-1408
Acting Vice-President Canadian Partnership Branch, Naresh Singh
819-956-8266, Fax: 819-934-3587
Vice-President Multilateral & Global Programs Branch, Diane Jacovella
819-997-7537, Fax: 819-953-5348
Vice-President Pan Geographic Programs, Allan Culham
819-997-1643, Fax: 819-994-6174
Vice-President Strategic Policy & Performance Branch, Christine Hogan
819-997-6133, Fax: 819-953-6356
Acting Director General Communications Branch, Bernard Etzinger
819-953-9574
Acting Director General Human Resources Branch, Sheila Tenasco-Banerjee
819-994-4418
Director General Strategic Policy Directorate, Paul Samson
819-953-3139, Fax: 819-953-5229
Acting Chief Information Officer, Jacques Mailloux
819-994-3855

Canadian Nuclear Safety Commission (CNSC) / Commission canadienne de sûreté nucléaire (CCSN)

280 Slater St.
PO Box 1046 B
Ottawa, ON K1P 5S9
613-995-5894
Fax: 613-995-5086
800-668-5284
info@cnsc-ccsn.gc.ca
www.nuclearsafety.gc.ca

Federal agency which regulates activities involving nuclear energy & prescribed substances in the interests of health & safety for workers & the public. Areas covered under the AECB's licensing process include the nuclear fuel cycle (from mining to waste disposal), heavy water plants, research reactors & accelerators, & radioisotopes. Operations ensure that the use of nuclear energy in Canada does not pose undue risk to health, safety, security & the environment. The Research & Support Program (RSP) augments & extends the AECB's regulatory program beyond the capability of in-house resources. It produces pertinent & independent information that will assist the Board & its staff in making sound, timely & credible decisions on regulating nuclear facilities & materials. The nine sectors of the program include: safety of nuclear facilities; radioactive waste management; health physics; physical security; development of regulatory processes; & social services
President, Michael Binder
613-992-8828, Fax: 613-995-5086
Executive Vice-President/Chief Regulatory Operations Officer, Ramzi Jammal
613-947-8899, Fax: 613-995-5086
Vice-President Corporate Services & CFO, Gordon White
Vice-President Regulatory Affairs, Patricia McDowell
613-943-7662, Fax: 613-995-5086
Director General Environmental & Radiation Protection & Assessment, Patsy Thompson
613-947-3352, Fax: 613-995-5086
Director General Nuclear Cycle & Facilities Regulation, Peter H. Elder
613-943-8948, Fax: 613-995-5086
Director Systems Engineering Division, Robert Lojk
613-947-3992, Fax: 613-995-5086

Canadian Polar Commission (CPC) / Commission canadienne des affaires polaires (CCAP)

Constitution Square
#1710, 360 Albert St.
Ottawa, ON K1R 7X7
613-943-8605
Fax: 613-943-8607
888-765-2701
mail@polarcom.gc.ca
www.polarcom.gc.ca

Mandated to enhance the public's awareness of polar regions & to foster both international & domestic liaison & cooperation in circumpolar research & technology development. One of the Commission's main objectives in the short term is focus on climate change & energy. Maintains the Canadian Polar Information System (CPIS) which, in addition to polar data & information, includes services such as the Polar Science Forum, Researcher's Directory, Researcher's Toolbox, & links to International Partners. In September 2005, the federal government announced it will provide $150 million in new funding over six years for International Polar Year 2007-2008, an international research program.
Chair, Peter Johnson
613-943-8605, Fax: 613-943-8607
Executive Director, Steven Bigras
613-943-8606,
bigrass@polarcom.gc.ca
Financial Officer, Bill Ryan
613-943-0718, Fax: 613-943-8607
Manager Communications & Information, John Bennett
613-943-0716, Fax: 613-943-8607
bennettj@polarcom.gc.ca
Manager Polar Science, Jean-Marie Beaulieu
613-947-9108, Fax: 613-943-8607
beaulieuj@polarcom.gc.ca
Executive Secretary, Sandy Bianchini
613-943-8605
Research Assistant, Elaine Anderson
613-947-9107,
andersone@polarcom.gc.ca

Canadian Space Agency (CSA) / Agence spatiale canadienne (ASC)

6767, rte de l'Aéroport
Saint-Hubert, QC J3Y 8Y9
450-926-4800
Fax: 450-926-4352
webmaster@space.gc.ca
www.space.gc.ca

Established in 1989, & responsible for coordinating all civil, space-related policies & programs on behalf of the Government of Canada. Scientific research & industrial development in earth observation, space science & exploration, satellite communications, & space awareness & learning. RADARSAT International (RSI) develops products & services demanded by world markets. RADARSAT-1, the first Canadian commercial Earth Observation (EO) satellite, is uniquely capable of responding to disasters around the world. The system can support the operational mapping & monitoring of natural disasters in four critical ways: prevention, preparedness, emergency response & recovery. Moreover, the development of the high performance RADARSAT-2 to be launched in 2007, will further enhance Canada's competitive position. RADARSAT-2 will offer improved quality of data images to meet the growing world demand of Earth observation information. The SCISAT satellite is used in ozone depletion research.
Acts Administered:
Canadian Space Agency Act
Minister, Industry; Minister Responsible, Canadian Space Agency, Hon. Tony Clement
613-944-7740, Fax: 613-992-5092
ClemeT@parl.gc.ca; ministre.industrie@ic.gc.ca
President & Chief Astronaut, Steven MacLean
450-926-4301, Fax: 450-926-4315
Vice-President, Jean Paquette
450-926-4760, Fax: 450-926-4332
CFO, Jacques Côté
450-926-4407, Fax: 450-926-4424
Director Operations Engineering/Program Manager CSSP, Pierre Jean
450-926-4515, Fax: 450-926-4722
Director Satellite Operations, Surendra Parashar
450-926-4412, Fax: 450-926-4888
Director Communications & Public Affairs, Paul Engel
450-926-4342, Fax: 450-926-4377
paul.engel@space.gc.ca
Director Government Liaison, Manon Larocque
613-993-3771, Fax: 613-990-4994

Canadian Transportation Agency (CTA) / Office des transports du Canada (OTC)

Les Terrasses de la Chaudière
15, rue Eddy
Gatineau, QC K1A 0N9
819-997-0344
Fax: 819-997-6727
888-222-2592
TDD: 819-953-9705
info@otc-cta.gc.ca
www.cta-otc.gc.ca

Responsible for the economic regulation of transportation in Canada. The agency requires that all applications for new railway lines, modifications to existing railway lines, disputed railway crossings at grade, grade separation, utility crossings & private crossings be accompanied by an environment impact assessment
Chair/CEO, Geoffrey C. Hare
819-997-9233, Fax: 819-953-9979
Vice-Chair, John Scott
819-953-8915, Fax: 819-953-9979
Director General Corporate Management Branch, Arun Thangaraj
819-997-6764, Fax: 819-953-9842
Director General Industry Regulation & Determinations Branch, Ghislain Blanchard
819-953-4657, Fax: 819-994-8807
Director General Dispute Resolution Branch, Joan MacDonald
819-953-5074, Fax: 819-953-5562
Director Communications Directorate, Jacqueline Bannister
819-953-7666, Fax: 819-953-8353
Director Rail, Air & Marine Disputes Directorate, Joseph Dion
819-953-0327, Fax: 819-953-8353
Investigation Officer Regulatory Approvals & Compliance Directorate, Darryl Salmaso
819-953-9924, Fax: 819-934-0631

Atlantic
#109, 1045 Main St.
Moncton, NB E1C 1H1
506-851-6950
Fax: 506-851-2518

Central
#702, 269 Main St.
PO Box 27007 Winnipeg Square
Winnipeg, MB R3C 4T3
204-984-6092
Fax: 204-984-6093

Ontario
#300, 4900 Yonge St.
Toronto, ON M2N 6A5
416-952-7895
Fax: 416-952-7897

Pacific
#560, 800 Burrard St.
Vancouver, BC V6Z 2V8
604-666-0620
Fax: 604-666-1267

Québec
#510, 101, boul Roland-Therrien
Longueuil, QC J4H 4B9
450-928-4173
Fax: 450-928-4174

Western
#1100, 9700 Jasper Ave. NW
Edmonton, AB T5J 4C3
780-495-6618
Fax: 780-495-5639
Minister, Citizenship, Immigration, & Multiculturalism, Hon. Jason Kenney
613-992-2235, Fax: 613-992-1920
kenneJ@parl.gc.ca; Minister@cic.gc.ca

Defence Construction Canada (DCC) / Construction de Défense Canada (CDC)

Constitution Square
350 Albert St., 19th Fl.
Ottawa, ON K1A 0K3
613-998-9548
Fax: 613-998-1061
800-514-3555
info@dcc-cdc.gc.ca
www.dcc-cdc.gc.ca

Federal government crown corporation responsible for the contracting & supervising of major military construction & maintenance projects required by National Defence. Services include construction, project management, environmental services & operational support services. DCC provides environmental science & environmental engineering services to help fulfill the Department of National Defence's sustainable development strategy, including: environmental impact & site assessment; environmental site remediation; environmental support for project & program

management; sustainable development strategy support services; policy, compliance & advisory services; site decommissioning services; facility deconstruction & demolition; firing range decommissioning; waste management auditing & planning; waste reduction planning; landfill inventories & investigations; hazardous waste management; UST removals; training & education; ISO 14000 environmental management systems; environmental CIS applications; environmental checklists for property transactions & decommissioning; environmental monitoring & compliance auditing; designated substances inventories; environmental disclosures reporting; treatment & disposal facilities conceptual designs; environmental contracting & contract management; energy conservation. Projects include: the DEW (Distant Early Warning) Line cleanup, a dismantling of the DEW sites, scheduled for completion in 2012, & a major environmental project in the Canadian Arctic; green demolition at CFB Comox; biodiesel pilot program at 4 Wing Cold Lake, launched in 2005.
President/CEO, James S. Paul
613-998-9541, Fax: 613-998-1218
Senior Vice-President Operations, Ron de Vries, P.Eng
613-998-9543, Fax: 613-998-1218
Vice-President Operations, Steve Irwin, P.Eng
613-949-7721, Fax: 613-998-1218
Vice-President Operations, Randy McGee, P.Eng., GSC
613-949-0052, Fax: 613-998-1218
Vice-President Corporate Services & CFO, Angelo Ottoni, C.A.
613-998-1001
Manager Business Operations - Atlantic Region, George Theoharopoulos
902-426-4040, Fax: 902-426-9655
Manager Environmental Services - Ontario, Dennis Katic
613-384-1256, Fax: 613-384-7747
Manager Environmental Services - Québec, Alain Dufresne
514-283-8165, Fax: 514-496-6934
Manager Environmental Services - Western Region, Sabrina Rock
780-495-3979, Fax: 780-495-5959
Executive Administrative Assistant, Claire Péladeau
613-991-3475, Fax: 613-998-1218

Environmental Protection Review Canada / Révision de la protection de l'environnement Canada

240 Sparks St., 1st Fl. West
Ottawa, ON K1A 1A1
613-995-7599
Fax: 613-992-4918
eprc-rpec@eprc-rpec.gc.ca
www.eprc-rpec.gc.ca
Environmental Protection Review Canada is a group of expert adjudicators, entirely separate from Environment Canada, that conducts reviews of Environmental Protection Compliance Orders (EPCOs). Under the Canadian Environmental Protection Act, 1999 (CEPA, 1999), enforcement officers have the power to issue EPCOs to prevent a violation, to stop an on-going violation or to require that violations be corrected. Any person who has been issued an EPCO may ask for an independent review conducted by a Review Officer. Review Officers have the authority to confirm or cancel an EPCO. They may also amend, suspend, add or delete a term or condition of the Order. The decisions of Review Officers may be appealed to the Federal Court, Trial Division.
Chief Review Officer, Margot Priest
613-947-4060, Fax: 613-992-4918
Review Officer, Louis LaPierre
506-858-4152, Fax: 506-863-2000

Environment Canada (EC) / Environnement Canada

10 Wellington St.
Gatineau, QC K1A 0H3
819-997-2800
Fax: 819-994-1412
800-668-6767
TDD: 819-994-0736
enviroinfo@ec.gc.ca
www.ec.gc.ca
Other Communication: Environmental Emergencies (24-hour):|819/997-3742; TTY: 819/994-0736
Fosters a national capacity for sustainable development in cooperation with other governments, departments of government & the private sector that will result in a safe & healthy environment & a sound & prosperous economy by:undertaking & promoting programs to augment understanding of the environment; supporting environmentally responsible public & private decision-making; warning Canadians of risks to & from the environment; engaging Canadians as partners in measurably beneficial action to conserve, protect & restore the integrity of Canada's environment for the benefit of present & future generations.
Acts Administered:
Antarctic Environmental Protection Act
Canada Emission Reduction Incentives Agency Act
Canada Water Act
Canada Wildlife Act
Administration, Management & Control of Certain Public Lands
Wildlife Area Regulations
Canadian Environment Week Act
Canadian Environmental Assessment Act
Canada Port Authority Environmental Assessment Regulations
Comprehensive Study List Regulation
Exclusion List Regulation
Federal Authorities Regulations
Inclusion List Regulation
Law List Regulation
Projects Outside Canada Environmental Assessment Regulations
Canadian Environmental Protection Act
Alberta Equivalency Order
Asbestos Mines & Mills Release Regulations
Benzene in Gasoline Regulations
Chlor-Alkali, Mercury Release Regulations
Chlorobiphenyls Regulations
Clean Air Act
Contaminated Fuel Regulations
Disposal at Sea Regulations
Environmental Emergency Regulations
Export Control List of Notification Regulations
Export & Import of Hazardous Wastes Regulations
Export of Substances under the Rotterdam Convention Regulations
Federal Halocarbon Regulations
Federal Mobile PCB Treatment & Destruction Regulations
Federal Registration of Storage Tank Systems for Petroleum Products & Allied Petroleum Products on Federal Lands or Aboriginal Lands Regulations
Fuels Information Regulations, No. 1
Gasoline & Gasoline Blend Dispensing Flow Rate Regulations
Gasoline Regulations
Interprovincial Movement of Hazardous Waste Regulations
List of Hazardous Waste Authorities
List of Toxic Substances Authorities
Masked Name Regulations
New Substances Fees Regulations
New Substances Notification Regulations
Off-Road Small Spark-Ignition Engine Emission Regulations
On-Road Vehicle & Engine Emission Regulations
Ozone Depleting Substances Regulations
PCB Waste Export Regulations
Persistence & Bioaccumulation Regulations
Phosphorus Concentration Regulations
Prohibition of Certain Toxic Substances
Pulp & Paper Mill Defoamer & Wood Chip Regulations
Pulp & Paper Mill Effluent Chlorinated Dioxins & Furans Regulations
Regulations respecting Applications for Permits for Disposal at Sea
Rules for Procedures for Boards of Review
Secondary Lead Smelter Release Regulations
Solvent Degreasing Regulations
Sulphur in Diesel Fuel Regulations
Sulphur in Gasoline Regulations
Storage of PCB Material Regulations
Tetrachloroethylene (Use in Dry Cleaning & Reporting Requirements) Regulations
Tributyltetradeclyphosphonium Chloride Regulations
Vinyl Chloride Release Regulations
Department of the Environment Act
Kemano Completion Project Guidelines Order
Greenhouse Gas Technology Investment Fund Act
International River Improvements Act
Lac Seul Conservation Act
Lake of the Woods Control Board Act
Manganese-Based Fuel Additives Act
Migratory Birds Convention Act
Migratory Bird Regulations
Migratory Bird Sanctuary Regulations
National Wildlife Week Act
Species at Risk Act, 2002
Weather Modification Information Act
Wild Animal & Plant Protection & Regulation of International & Interprovincial Trade Act
Acts Administered in Part by Environment Canada
Auditor General Act (Treasury Board)
Energy Supplies Emergency Act (National Research)
Fisheries Act (Fisheries & Oceans)
Chlor-alkali Mercury Liquid Effluent Regulations
Meat & Poultry Products Plant Liquid Effluent Regulations
Metal Mining Effluent Regulations
Petroleum Refinery Liquid Effluent Regulations
Port Alberni Pulp & Paper Effluent Regulations
Potato Processing Plant Liquid Effluent Regulations
Pulp & Paper Effluent Regulations
James Bay & Northern Québec Native Claims Settlement Act
Motor Vehicle Safety Act (Transport)
Resources & Technical Surveys Act (Natural Resources/Fisheries & Oceans)
Acts in which Environment Canada Provides Assistance
Arctic Waters Pollution Prevention Act
Arctic Shipping Pollution Prevention Regulations
Arctic Waters Pollution Prevention Regulations
Atomic Energy Control Act
Transport Packaging of Radioactive Materials Regulations
Uranium & Thorium Mining Regulations
Canada Agricultural Products Act
Canada Shipping Act
Air Pollution Regulations
Dangerous Chemicals & Noxious Liquid Substances Regulations
Garbage Pollution Prevention Regulations
Great Lakes Sewage Pollution Prevention Regulations
Non-Pleasure Craft Sewage Pollution Prevention Regulations
Oil Pollution Prevention Regulations
Pleasure Craft Sewage Pollution Prevention Regulations
Pollutant Discharge Reporting Regulations
Pollutant Substances Regulations
Ship-Source Oil Pollution Fund Regulations
Canada-Chile Free Trade Agreement Implementation Act (International Trade)
Canada-Newfoundland Atlantic Accord Implementation Act
Newfoundland Offshore Area Oil & Gas Operations Regulations
Newfoundland Offshore Area Petroleum Geophysical Operations Regulations
Newfoundland Offshore Area Petroleum Production & Conservation Regulations
Newfoundland Offshore Certificate of Fitness Regulations
Newfoundland Offshore Petroleum Drilling Regulations
Newfoundland Offshore Petroleum Installations Regulations
Canada-Nova Scotia Offshore Petroleum Resources Accord Implementation Act
Nova Scotia Offshore Petroleum Drilling Regulations
Emergency Preparedness Act (National Defence)
Hazardous Products Act (Health Canada)
Controlled Products Regulations
International Boundary Waters Treaty Act (Foreign Affairs)
North American Free Trade Agreement Implementation Act
Nuclear Energy Act (Natural Resources)
Pest Control Products Act & Regulations (Health Canada)
Transportation of Dangerous Goods Act & Regulations (Transport Canada)
Environment Canada Related Acts & Regulations
Agricultural & Rural Development Act (Agriculture & Agri-Foods)
Alternative Fuels Act & Regulations (Treasury Board)
Canada Marine Act (Transport Canada)
Canada Oil & Gas Operations Act (Indian & Northern Affairs/Natural Resources)
Canada Oil & Gas Certificate of Fitness Regulations
Canada Oil & Gas Drilling Regulations
Canada Oil & Gas Geophysical Operations Regulations
Canada Oil & Gas Operations Regulations
Canada Oil & Gas Production & Conservation Regulations
Canada Petroleum Resources Act (Indian Affairs & Northern Development/Natural Resouces)
Environmental Studies Research Fund Regions Regulations
Canadian Transportation Accident Investigation & Safety Board Act (Privy Council)
Transportation Safety Board Regulations
Food & Drugs Act (Agriculture & Agri-Foods/Health Canada)
Mackenzie Valley Resource Management Act (Indian & Northern Affairs)
National Energy Board Act (Natural Resources/Transport Canada)
Electricity Regulations
Oil & Gas Regulations
Onshore Pipeline Regulations
Rules of Practice & Procedure

Federal/Provincial Government / Government of Canada

National Round Table on the Environment & the Economy Act (Prime Minister)
Northern Pipeline Act (Natural Resources)
Northern Pipeline Socio-Economic & Environmental Terms & Conditions (Northern BC, Southern BC, AB, SK & Swift River Portion in BC)
Oceans Act (Fisheries & Oceans)
Minister, Environment, Hon. Peter Kent
819-997-1441, Fax: 819-953-0279
Kent.P@parl.gc.ca
Director, Parliamentary Affairs, Lori Dawe
819-997-1441
Deputy Minister, Paul Boothe
819-997-4203, Fax: 819-953-6897
Associate Deputy Minister, Vacant
819-953-2832
Assistant Deputy Minister Human Resources, Lynette Cox
819-997-1847, Fax: 819-953-2757
Director General Corporate Secretariat, Pierre Bernier
819-953-2743, Fax: 819-953-0749
Chief Enforcement Officer, Gordon T. Owen
819-997-2019, Fax: 819-997-0086
Assistant Deputy Minister & Chief Information Officer, Chuck Shawcross
819-994-3634, Fax: 819-934-7975

Environmental Stewardship Branch / Direction générale de l'intendance environnementale
351 boul St-Joseph
Gatineau, QC K1A 0H3
819-997-1575
Fax: 819-953-9452
Assessment & management of risk associated with domestic & international sources of pollution. The range of activity is broad, assessment of substances & practices that pose a risk to the environment, development & implementation of environmental protection measures including pollution prevention, regulations, permits & technology advancement & ensuring compliance with federal pollution & wildlife laws. These activities lead to improvements in environmental quality which helps to support the health of Canadians & their economic security.
Acting Asst. Deputy Minister, Cynthia Wright
819-953-1711, Fax: 819-953-9452
Acting Assoc. Asst. Deputy Minister, Mike Beale
819-956-9500
Director General Canadian Wildlife Service, Virginia Poter
819-994-1360, Fax: 819-953-7177
Director General Climate Change International, John Moffet
819-953-6830, Fax: 819-953-9333
Director General Energy & Transportation, Steve McCauley
819-997-1298, Fax: 819-953-9547
Director General Environmental Protection Operations, Sue Milburn-Hopwood
819-934-5666, Fax: 819-934-6531
Chief GHG Reporting Section, Lo Chiang Cheng
819-994-6143, Fax: 819-953-3006
Director Greenhouse Gas Division, Art Jaques
819-994-3098, Fax: 819-953-3006
Executive Director Habitat & Ecosystem Conservation, Robert McLean
819-997-1303, Fax: 819-994-4445
Executive Director Outreach, Pat Dolan
819-953-4950, Fax: 819-953-9748
Director General Public and Resources Sectors, Randa Meades
819-934-4205

Human Resources Branch / Direction générale des ressources humaines
819-997-1847
Fax: 819-953-2757
Asst. Deputy Minister, Lynette Cox
819-997-1847, Fax: 819-953-2757
Director General National HR Services, Donna Richard
819-934-7215, Fax: 819-953-2675
Acting Director General Performance Measurement & Monitoring Business Systems, Donald Bilodeau
819-994-0201
Director General Strategic Planning & Corporate Programs, Deirdre Keane
819-953-0432, Fax: 819-953-6963

Chief Information Officer / Direction générale du dirigeant principal de l'information
819-934-4151
Fax: 819-934-7975

Asst. Deputy Minister & Chief Information Officer, Chuck Shawcross
819-994-3634, Fax: 819-934-7975
Director General Business Applications & Solutions Directorate, Denis Benoit
819-934-1523
Director General Infrastructure Operations Directorate, Connie MacDonald
819-953-1162, Fax: 819-994-4224
Director General Major Projects & Supercomputing Directorate, Mike Minuk
514-421-4765, Fax: 514-421-4703
Acting Director MSC Regional Operations, Lina Assad
819-997-8810, Fax: 819-953-4509

Finance & Corporate Branch / Finances et services corporatifs
819-953-7026
Fax: 819-953-4064
Asst. Deputy Minister & Chief Financial Officer, Basia Ruta
Director General Assets, Contracting & Environmental Management, Karen Anderson
819-997-2991, Fax: 819-997-1781
Director General Corporate Management, David Henley
819-953-4171, Fax: 819-953-3388
Director General Finance Directorate, Robert D'Aoust
819-953-5471, Fax: 819-953-2459
Director General Integrated Enterprise Services, Randy Larkin
819-953-9569, Fax: 819-953-4064

International Affairs / Direction générale des affaires internationales
819-997-4882
Fax: 819-953-5981
Asst. Deputy Minister, David McGovern
819-934-6020
Director General Americas, Dean Knudson
819-994-1670, Fax: 819-997-0199
Director General Climate Change International, John Moffet
819-953-6830, Fax: 819-953-9333
Director General Multilateral & Bilateral Affairs, France Jacovella
819-956-5263, Fax: 819-994-6227
Executive Director Strategic Engagement, Darren Goetze
819-953-9525, Fax: 819-953-9333

Meteorological Service of Canada (MSC) / Le service météorologique du Canada
4905 Dufferin St.
Toronto, ON M3H 5T4
416-739-4770
Fax: 416-739-4232
www.msc-smc.ec.gc.ca/index_e.cfm
Other Communication: Weather Office:
weatheroffice.ec.gc.ca/canada_e.html
The Meteorological Service of Canada monitors water quantities, provides information & conducts research on climate, atmospheric science, air quality, ice & other environmental issues.
Asst. Deputy Minister, David Grimes
613-943-5585, Fax: 613-943-5737
Director General Business Policy, Danielle Lacasse
613-943-5532, Fax: 613-995-0389
Director General Weather & Environmental Operations, Angèle Simard
514-421-4601
Director General Weather & Environmental Monitoring, Jim Abraham
416-739-4965, Fax: 416-739-4261
Director General Weather & Environmental Prediction & Services, Diane E. Campbell
613-947-9200, Fax: 613-943-6440
Coordinator GEOSS Interdepartmental Secretariat, Kenneth D. Korporal
613-995-2466, Fax: 613-947-1261

Science & Technology Branch / Direction générale des sciences et de la technologie
819-994-4751
Fax: 819-997-1541
Asst. Deputy Minister, Brian Gray
819-934-6851
Director General Atmospheric Science & Technology, Charles A. Lin
416-739-4995, Fax: 416-739-4265

Acting Director General Science & Risk Assessment, George Enei
819-997-4977, Fax: 819-953-5371
Director General Science & Technology Strategies, Dr. Javier A. Gracia-Garza
819-953-3090, Fax: 819-953-9029
Director General Water Science & Technology, Dr. John H. Carey
905-336-4625
Director General Wildlife & Landscape Science, Dan Wicklum
613-998-0329

Strategic Policy / Direction générale de la politique stratégique
819-953-4818
Fax: 819-953-5981
Asst. Deputy Minister, Michael Keenan
819-953-4818
Director General Economic Analysis Directorate, Tony Young
819-953-7624, Fax: 819-953-5916
Director General Strategic Information & Integration, Brenda McKelvey
819-934-6028, Fax: 819-994-8864
Director General Strategic Policy Directorate, Lawrence Hanson
819-934-4149, Fax: 819-953-4679

Environment Canada Regional Directors General:

Atlantic
Queen Sq.
45 Alderney Dr.
Dartmouth, NS B2Y 2N6
902-426-7231
Fax: 902-426-6348
TDD: 819-994-0736
15th.reception@ec.gc.ca
Regional Director General, Daniel Lebel
902-426-6700, Fax: 902-426-5168

Pacific & Yukon
401 Burrard St.
Vancouver, BC V6C 3S5
604-664-9100
Fax: 604-713-9517
greenlane.pyr@ec.gc.ca
Regional Director General, Paul Kluckner
604-664-9145, Fax: 604-664-9190

Ontario
4905 Dufferin St.
Toronto, ON M3H 5T4
416-739-4826
Fax: 416-739-4776
EnviroInfo.Ontario@ec.gc.ca
Regional Director General, Jim Vollmershausen
416-739-4666, Fax: 416-739-4691

Pacific & Yukon: Yukon Office
Canadian Wildlife Service
91782 Alaska Hwy.
Yellowknife, YT Y1A 5B7
867-393-6700
Fax: 867-393-7970
greenlane.pyr@ec.gc.ca

Prairie & Northern
#200, 4999 - 98 Ave.
Edmonton, AB T6B 2X3
780-951-8600
Fax: 780-495-2615
Regional Director General, Randal Cripps
780-951-8869, Fax: 780-495-3086

Prairie & Northern: Manitoba Office
#150, 123 Main St.
Winnipeg, MB R3C 4W2
204-984-6203
Fax: 204-983-0964
800-263-0595

Québec
1141, rte de l'Église, 6e étage
CP 10100
Québec, QC G1V 4H5

Fax: 418-648-4613
800-463-4311
quebec.lavoieverte@ec.gc.ca
Regional Director General, Philippe Morel
418-648-4077, Fax: 418-649-6213
• Committee on the Status of Endangered Wildlife in Canada(COSEWIC) / Comité sur la situation des espèces en péril au Canada
c/o Canadian Wildlife Service
Ottawa, ON K1A 0H3
819-997-4991
Fax: 819-994-3684
cosewic@ec.gc.ca
www.cosewic.gc.ca
Other Communication: Species at Risk Act Public Registry:
www.sararegistry.gc.ca
Chair, Dr. Jeffrey Hutchings
Committee of experts that assesses & designates which wild species are in some danger of disappearing from Canada. COSEWIC determines the national status of wild Canadian species, subspecies & separate populations suspected of being at risk. COSEWIC bases its decisions on the best up-to-date scientific information & Aboriginal traditional knowledge available. All native mammals, birds, reptiles, amphibians, fish, mollusks, lepidopterans (butterflies & moths), vascular plants, mosses & lichens are included in its current mandate. As of April 2006, COSEWIC's assessment results indicate there are 516 species in the risk category (extirpated, endangered, threatened or of special concern) & 13 species found to be extinct.
• National Round Table on the Environment & Economy
• North American Waterfowl Management Plan(NAWMP) / Le plan nord-américain de gestion de la sauvagine
c/o Canadian Wildlife Service, Place Vincent-Massey
351 St-Joseph Blvd., 16th Fl.
Gatineau, ON K1A 0H3
819-934-6034
Fax: 819-934-6017
nabci@ec.gc.ca
www.nawmp.ca
• North American Bird Conservation Initiative(NAWCC)
Canadian Wildlife Service
351, boul St-Joseph, 3e étage
Gatineau, QC K1A 0H3
819-994-0512
Fax: 819-994-4445
s.neve@ec.gc.ca
www.cws-scf.ec.gc.ca/mbc-com/
Canadian Coordinator, Martin Damus
The NABCI is a coordinated effort among Canada, the United States & Mexico to maintain the diversity & abundance of all North American birds. National coordination of this effort in Canada occurs through the NABCI Canada Council, chaired by the Asst. Deputy Minister of Environment Canada's Environmental Conservation Service. Council members include representatives from provincial governments, non-government organizations, four bird plans (waterfowl, landbirds, shorebirds, waterbirds), & habitat joint ventures. In Canada, the joint venture conservation projects has three habitat joint ventures (Pacific Coast, Prairie Habitat, Eastern Habitat) & three species (Arctic Goose, Black Duck, Sea Duck.)

Enforcement Branch / Direction de l'application de la loi
819-997-2019
Fax: 819-997-0086
ele-ale@ec.gc.ca
www.ec.gc.ca/ele-ale
From the Environmental Protection perspective, Environment Canada administers two acts. The Canadian Environmental Protection Act 1999 (CEPA, 1999) which was passed by Parliament to replace the Canadian Environmental Protection Act of 1988, & the pollution prevention provisions of the Fisheries Act (FA). Enforcement officers, designated under CEPA, 1999, & inspectors/fishery officers, designated under the Fisheries Act, ensure compliance with the two acts & corresponding regulations. An enforcement & compliance policy to guide enforcement officers in the performance of their duties has been adopted.
Chief Enforcement Officer, Albin Tremblay
819-997-2019
National Director Environmental Enforcement, Renzo A. Benocci
819-953-1523, Fax: 819-953-3459
National Director Enforcement Services, Kim Hibbeln
819-997-4712, Fax: 819-994-0724
National Director Wildlife Enforcement, Richard Charette
819-953-4811, Fax: 819-994-5836

Canadian Wildlife Service (CWS) / Service canadien de la faune
National Wildlife Research Centre
Carleton University
Ottawa, ON K1S 5B6
819-997-1095
Fax: 819-997-2751
cws-scf@ec.gc.ca
www.cws-scf.ec.gc.ca/nwrc-cnrf/default.asp?lang=En&n=79FF6764-1
Other Communication: Ecological Gifts Program:
www.cws-scf.ec.gc.ca/ecogifts/intro_e.cfm
The Canadian Wildlife Service (CWS) handles wildlife matters that are the responsibility of the federal government. This includes protection & management of migratory birds, nationally significant habitat & endangered species, & work on other wildlife issues of national & international importance. CWS conducts research on wildlife topics, particularly migratory birds. Its research provides the science base for conservation actions. The most ambitious migratory birds conservation program to date is the North American Waterfowl Management Plan (NAWMP). It is a $1.5 billion joint Canada/U.S. program designed to protect & enhance wetland habitat throughout North America. The objective of NAWMP is to restore the populations of ducks, swans, & geese to the levels of the 1970s. CWS sits on an international management board that has been established to ensure the well-being of caribou & other herds by providing expertise in research & conservation. CWS is a leading player in the efforts to protect endangered species & is a founding member of the Committee on the Status of Endangered Wildlife in Canada (COSEWIC), which produces the official list of Canadian endangered species. CWS developed & promoted the adoption of the Species at Risk Act (SARA). This act, which came into effect in 2003, protects species from extinction & their critical habitat from disappearance, & it ensures their recovery. CWS is involved in numerous international activities. The Convention on International Trade in Endangered Species of Wild Fauna & Flora (CITES) is an effort to protect endangered species by regulating trade in over 15,000 species of wild plants & animals & their parts or derivatives. Canada is a party to CITES & CSW is responsible for implementing CITES in Canada. CWS works with other agencies & groups to minimize the impact on critical wildlife habitat. CWS's most direct role is in the establishment & management of National Wildlife Areas & Migratory Bird Sanctuaries. There are more than 140 of these refuges across the country. Environmental impact studies are conducted by CWS to determine the effects of large-scale development projects on wildlife habitat. Many of these studies are in the north, a region that has just begun to feel the effects of resource development. CWS provides advice on projects such as planning the location of highways & pipelines to avoid sensitive habitats. Other industrial activities, such as hydro developments in the James Bay region & a tidal power proposal in the Bay of Fundy, have shown the need for studies of vital shorebird feeding & resting areas.
Director General, Virginia Poter
819-994-1360, Fax: 819-953-7177
Executive Director Habitat & Ecosystem Conservation, Robert McLean
819-997-1303, Fax: 819-994-4445
Director Conservation Service Delivery & Permitting, Mary Taylor
819-953-9097, Fax: 819-953-6283
Director Population Conservation & Management, Basile van Havre
819-997-2957, Fax: 819-964-3684

Partners in Flight / Partenaires d'envol
c/o Canadian Wildlife Service
Ottawa, ON K1A 0H3
819-953-4390
Fax: 819-994-4445
martin.damus@ec.gc.ca
www.cws-scf.ec.gc.ca/birds/lb_ot_e.cfm
The goal of Partners in Flight - Canada (PIF) is to ensure the long-term viability of populations of native Canadian landbirds across their range of habitats. The Canadian Wildlife Service, with its mandate for migratory bird conservation, is working with partners to build a national landbird conservation program. Implementation of this goal will occur at national, regional & local levels. Work is overseen by the National Working Group & includes representatives from government & non-government conservation agencies & regional PIF programs & welcomes participation from industry, academia, & other interested stakeholders. Activities & products of the National Working Group support landbird conservation at international, national, regional & local levels. To date, these include the Framework for Landbird Conservation in Canada (provides context for a Canadian landbird conservation program) the Canadian Landbird Monitoring Strategy (highlights existing surveys & discusses how to fill gaps in our knowledge of landbird populations), the National Action Needs for Canadian Landbird Conservation (outlines priority research & monitoring needs for specific landbird species.) Regional & provincial/territorial landbird conservation efforts are undertaken independently through conservation plans developed by partnerships. PIF encourages regional efforts to use Bird Conservation Regions as the geographic framework for conservation plans.
Contact, Martin Damus

Clean Air Directorate / Direction générale de l'air pur
Fax: 819-953-9547
Other Communication: National Pollutant Release Inventory:
www.ec.gc.ca/pdb/npri/npri_home_e.cfm
Manages & coordinates pollution prevention activities for global air issues (climate change & ozone depletion), transboundary air issues (smog, acid rain, particulates, & hazardous air pollutants), pollution data (National Pollution Release Inventory, greenhouse gases & conventional pollutants), transportation systems & related industries, & oil, gas & energy industries.
Director General, Gord Owen
819-998-1298, Fax: 819-953-9029
Director Domestic Clean Air Program Operations, Vincenza Galatone
819-934-4533
Director Electricity & Industrial Combustion, Shannon Glenn
819-956-5560
Director Oil, Gas & Energy, Helen Ryan
819-997-1221
Director Transboundary Air Issues, Peggy Farnsworth
819-994-9535
Director Transportation, Steve McCauley
819-994-3706

Environmental Protection Operations Directorate / Direction générale des activités de protection de l'environnement
Acting Director General, Peter Blackall
780-951-8862,
Acting Director Compliance Promotion & Operations, René Drolet
819-994-0738
Director Environmental Assessment Program, Diane Campbell
819-953-1690
Director Environmental Emergencies, Tom Foote
819-953-0607

GHG Reductions Directorate / Direction générale de réduction des émissions de gaz à l'effet de serre
Acting Director General, Mike Beale
819-996-1521, Fax: 819-995-3663
Director GHG Operations, Louise Métivier
613-947-6602
Acting Director Mining & Manufacturing, Carmelita Olivotto
613-995-4643
Manager Energy, Geoff Browning
613-943-1695

Integrated Ecosystem Management Directorate / Direction générale de gestion intégrée des écosystèmes
Acting Director General, Robert McLean
819-997-1303
Director Biodiversity Convention Office, John Karau
819-953-9669
Director Sustainable Water Management, Kate Moir
819-953-1101

EcoAction
Queen's Square
45 Alderley Dr.
Dartmouth, NS B2Y 2N6
902-426-8521
Fax: 902-426-0262
ecoaction@ec.gc.ca
www.ec.gc.ca/ecoaction/index_e.htm
The EcoAction Community Funding Program provides financial support to community groups for projects that have measurable, positive impacts on the environment. Non-profit groups & organizations are eligible to apply to the Funding Program. EcoAction encourages projects that deal with climate change, clean water, nature & clean air.
Manager Community & Outreach, Ted Jennex
902-426-7696

Federal/Provincial Government / Government of Canada

Offset Systems Directorate / Direction générale de mécanisme de compensation pour le gaz à l'effet de serre au Canada
Director General, Suzanne Matheson
913-993-6730
Director Offset Credit System Management, Dominic Demers
613-949-5530
Director Quantification Methodologies & Protocol, Jane Owen
613-949-1290
Director Regional Operations & Coordination, Judith Hull
613-949-1294

Pollution Prevention Directorate / Direction générale de la prévention de la pollution
819-953-8060
Fax: 819-953-8098
Areas of responsibility include CEPA Registry, contaminated sites, intellectual property, municipal wastewater effluent, technology outreach.
Director General, Anne O'Toole
819-934-4205
Director Natural Resources, Caroline Ladanowski
819-994-4705
Director Public Sector, Sheila Gariepy
819-994-3503
Director Waste Management, France Jacovella
819-953-5263
Director National Office of Pollution Prevention, James Riordan
819-953-3353, Fax: 819-953-7970
james.riordan@ec.gc.ca

Canadian Ice Service / Service canadien des glaces
373 Sussex Dr., Block E, 3rd Fl.
Ottawa, ON K1A 0H3
613-996-1550
Fax: 613-947-9160
800-767-2885
cis-scg.cient@ec.gc.ca
ice-glaces.ec.gc.ca
The Canadian Ice Service (CIS) is the leading authority for information about ice in Canada's navigable waters. CIS provides daily ice hazard bulletins & charts describing ice conditions in active navigable waters; an ice warning service for extreme ice events within ice-encumbered waters; daily iceberg bulletins & charts for Canadian waters south of 60 ree N; weekly ice analyses of active ice areas for strategic planning purposes; conducts ice reconnaissance with a specially instrumented Dash-7 aircraft, as well as by helicopter; maintains the Canadian Ice Service Archive for climatological purposes; contributes Canadian ice data to the World Data Center for Glaciology.
Director, Lina Assad
613-996-4489

Weather & Environmental Monitoring
4905 Dufferin St.
Toronto, ON M3H 5T4
416-739-4965
Fax: 416-739-4261
AMWSD provides national leadership for MSC activities in atmospheric & water monitoring, archiving & data management & includes responsibility for establishing national standards for observing systems & the national archives. AMWSD provides national leadership on network design, the evaluation & implementation of new technologies & the development of planning strategies to meet current & future requirements for data.MSC manages a number of national monitoring networks, upper air (radiosonde, Doppler Radar, lightning, surface weather, climate, hydrometric & marine (Buoy & Volunteer Observing Ship).
Director General, Jim Abraham
Director Atmospheric Monitoring, Dave Wartman
416-739-4121
Acting Director Data Analysis & Archives, Diane C. Johnston
416-739-4128
Acting Director Hydrometric Monitoring, Al Pietroniro
306-975-4394

Weather & Environmental Prediction & Services (SCPD)
10, rue Wellington
Gatineau, QC K1A 0H3
819-997-0142
Fax: 819-994-8864
Services, Clients & Partners Directorate (SCPD) ensures the provision of equitable & response-oriented weather, marine & ice services to Canadians. The SCPD's mandate is to strengthen meteorological & hydrological services to Canadians as well as interactions with clients & relationships with partners. Through the development & implementation of departmental policies, strategies & standards frameworks, the Directorate also ensures cohesive national meteorological (atmospheric & climatic) & hydrological services to Canadians & specialized clients groups.
Director General, Diane E. Campbell
613-947-9200, Fax: 613-943-6440
Director National Service Operations, Bill Appleby
613-943-5788, Fax: 613-943-6440
Director National Prediction Operations, Richard Hogue
514-421-4622, Fax: 514-421-4679
Acting Director Aviation & Defence Services, Abdoulaye Harou
613-992-3917, Fax: 613-992-4288

Canadian Hurricane Centre / Centre canadien de prévision d'ouragan
45 Alderney Dr., 16th Fl.
Dartmouth, NS B2Y 2N6
902-426-7231
Fax: 902-426-6348
15th.reception@ec.gc.ca
www.atl.ec.gc.ca/weather/hurricane/index_e.html
The CHC exists to advise Canadians on the threat of hurricanes & tropical storms. The Centre serves to provide guidance to weather centres in all regions potentially affected by one of these storms.The CHC gathers information on tropical & post-tropical cyclones, predicts their evolution, & assesses their potential impact on Canadian territory. The CHC's Area of Forecast Responsibility lies along the Canada-United States border & extends into Canadian waters to 200 nautical miles. The CHC makes presentations about hurricanes to schools, businesses, the media, & other governmental agencies & receives calls from the public for more information about hurricanes in Canada.

National Climate Data & Information Archive / Archives nationales d'information et de données climatologiques
Fax: 416-739-4446
climate.services@ec.gc.ca
www.climate.weatheroffice.ec.gc.ca/Welcome_e.html
The National Climate Data & Information Archive, operated & maintained by Environment Canada, contains official climate & weather observations for Canada. Climate elements, such as temperature, precipitation, relative humidity, atmospheric pressure, wind speed, wind direction, visibility, cloud types, cloud heights & amounts, soil temperature, evaporation, solar radiation & sunshine as well as occurrences of thunderstorms, hail, fog or other weather phenomena are warehoused in a digital database. Access to selected portions of this data, as well as related products such as CD-ROMS & climate normals & averages are available on their website. Information regarding obtaining extremes, monthly summaries, microfilm, microfiche, paper documents & technical documents, is also available.

Atmospheric Science & Technology
2121, rte Transcanadienne
Dorval, QC H9P 1J3
514-421-4771
Fax: 514-421-2106
Conducts research in climate, meteorology, air quality, & environmental impacts & adaptation.It produces science assessments on pressing environmental issues, such as climate change, acid rain, & the depletion of the ozone layer, etc., for Canadians & government policy makers.
Director General, Michel Béland
514-421-4771
Director Adaptation & Impacts Research, Don McIver
416-739-4271
Director Air Quality Research, Keith Puckett
416-739-4836
Director Climate Research, Dr. Doug Whelpdale
416-739-4869
Acting Director Prediction Development, Louis Lefaivre
514-421-4654

Science Horizons: Environment Canada's Youth Internship Program
351, boul St-Joseph
Gatineau, QC K1A 0H3
Fax: 819-956-5602
800-668-6767
science.horiz@ec.gc.ca
www.ec.gc.ca/sci_hor
Environment Canada's Science Horizons Program is a collaborative effort with Canadian universities, the private sector & NGOs which offers promising young scientists & post-secondary graduates hands-on experience working on environmental projects under the mentorship & coaching of experienced scientists & program managers. Approximately one hundred youth placements, lasting from 6 months to 1 year, are awarded annually across Canada.

Science & Risk Assessment Directorate / Direction générale de Science et évaluation des risques
Director General, John Arseneau
819-953-1114, Fax: 819-953-5371
Director Existing Substances, George Enei
819-997-4977
Director Greenhouse Gas Division, Art Jaques
819-994-3098
Acting Director New Substances, Bernard Madé
819-997-4336
Director Pollution Data, Alain Chung
819-994-3127

Environmental Effects Monitoring Office (EEM) / Bureau national des études de suivi des effets sur l'environnement (ESEE)
819-953-1553
Fax: 819-953-0641
EEM-ESEE@ec.gc.ca
www.ec.gc.ca/eem
EEM provides national leadership for the regulated environmental effects monitoring (EEM) programs for the pulp & paper & metal mining sectors.
Manager, Kathleen Hedley
Head Metal Mining, Lise Trudel
819-953-1527

National Guidelines & Standards Office (NGSO) / Bureau national des recommandations et des normes (BNRN)
819-953-1550
Fax: 819-956-5602
cegg-rcqe@ec.gc.ca
www.ec.gc.ca/ceqg-rcqe/
The National Guidelines & Standards Office (NGSO)provides nationally approved, science-based measures of environmental quality including guidelines, standards, & objectives. The primary focus of the group is developing national guidelines for water, sediment, & soil quality & aquatic tissue residues. Guidelines are recommended numerical or narrative limits for a variety of substances & environmental quality characteristics (such as dissolved oxygen or pH), which, if exceeded, may impair the health of Canadian ecosystems. Guidelines are mandated federally under the Canadian Environmental Protection Act (CEPA) & nationally under various federal-provincial agreements (Canadian Council of Ministers of the Environment, Great Lakes Water Quality Agreement). In addition, the NGSO leads & supports various ecosystem management initiatives (with a focus on consultative, community-based, right-to-know approaches) cooperatively with the CCME, Environment Canada Regions & other federal departments. The NGSO's thrust is to develop & promote effective implementation of science-based guidelines, objectives & indicators to achieve ecosystem health & sustainable development
Acting Manager, Doug Spry
819-953-3206

Science & Technology Strategies / Science et technologies, statégies
Acting Director General, Alex Bielak
905-336-4503
Director Science Policy & Priorities, Phillip Enros
819-994-5434
Acting Director Science & Technology Liaison, Karl Schaefer
905-336-4884
Director Technology Strategies, Shirley Anne Scharf
819-953-9364, Fax: 819-997-8427

Water Science & Technology / Science et technologie de l'eau
Director General, Dr. J.H. Carey
905-336-4625
Director Aquatic Ecosystem Impacts Research, Fred J. Wrona
250-472-5134
Director Aquatic Ecosystem Management Research, John Lawrence
905-336-4913
Director Aquatic Ecosystem Protection Research, Jim Maguire
905-336-4927
Director Water Quality Monitoring & Surveillance, Jacinthe Leclerc
514-283-5869, Fax: 514-283-1719

National Hydrology Research Centre (NHRC) / Centre national de recherche en hydrologie (CNRH)
www.nwri.ca/nhrcdesc-e.html

NHRC houses five groups: the western centre of the National Water Research Institute, the Water Quality Laboratory of the Environmental Protection Service, Prairie & Northern Region, which provides analytical services to support government & university research & monitoring programs in western Canada, the Climate Processes & Earth Observation Division, the Prairie & Northern Region, & the Saskatchewan Inspection Office of the Meteorological Service of Canada(MSC).These MSC groups monitor the state of Canada's climate, install, maintain & regularly inspect weather stations in Saskatchewan, & disseminates weather information & warnings of extreme weather events.

National Laboratory of Environmental Testing (NLET) / Laboratoire national des essais environnementaux
867 Lakeshore Rd.
PO Box 5050
Burlington, ON L7R 4A6
905-336-4563
Fax: 905-336-6404
NLET delivers a range of specialized & accredited analytical laboratory services, including sample characterization, technical consulting, quality mangement & laboratory information management systems development, in support of Environment Canada monitoring, assessment & research programs across the country.This isaccomplished at facilities located in Burlington, Ontario & at the Regional Water Quality Laboratory in Saskatoon, Saskatchewan.The mission is to support the laboratory science needs of Environment Canada research & monitoring programs & to deliver quality management products & services through responsive, cost-effective laboratory services that meet international standards of quality. The role of NLET within Environment Canada is a national analytical support laboratory capable of providing Environment Canada program managers with standarized & fully accredited environmental analysis capability for a wide range of organic & inorganic chemicals, unique analytical capabilities used to deliver collaborative projects outside the normal boundaries of the QA framework & usually delivered through MOUs, & partnership-based applied research projects such as developing/adapting new methods. NLET consists of two operational laboratories, the associated enabling infrastructure & a quality assurance/management group.
Director, Dave Warry
dave.warry@cciw.ca

National Water Research Institute (NWRI) / Centre canadien des eaux intérieures (CCIW)
867 Lakeshore Rd.
PO Box 5050
Burlington, ON L7R 4A6
905-336-4625
Fax: 905-336-6444
nwriscience.liaison@ec.gc.ca
www.nwri.ca
The National Water Research Institute (NWRI) is Canada's largest freshwater research facility, with centres in Burlington, Ontario & Saskatoon, Saskatchewan. As part of the Environmental Conservation Service of Environment Canada, NWRI conducts research & development in the aquatic sciences, often in collaboration with Canadian & international science communities. NWRI generates scientific knowledge through ecosystem-based research to support the development of sound government policies & programs, public decision making, & early identification of environmental problems.

St. Lawrence Centre (SLC) / Centre Saint-Laurent
105, rue McGill, 7e étage
Montréal, QC H2Y 2E7
514-283-7000
Fax: 514-283-1719
quebec.csl@ec.gc.ca
www.qc.ec.gc.ca/csl/
SLC is the only federal research & development centre devoted entirely to the river ecosystem. SLC experts study the ecosystems of the St. Lawrence River & conduct research programs with the aim of better understanding how these ecosystems function & maintaining knowledge of the St. Lawrence River up to date. SLC is divided into four sections Environmental Chemistry, Environmental Biology, State of the St. Lawrence Environment & Information Management.

Wildlife & Landscape Science
Acting Director General, Kevin Cash
306-975-4676
Acting Director Wildlife Research, Robert Clark
613-306-9754
Acting Director Wildlife Toxicology, Keith Marshall
613-998-0450

North American Waterfowl Management Plan (NAWMP) / Plan nord-américain de gestion de la sauvagine
Place Vincent Massey
351 St. Joseph Blvd.
Gatineau, QC K1A 0H3
819-934-6034
Fax: 819-934-6017
nawmp@ec.gc.ca
www.nawmp.ca
The North American Waterfowl Management Plan is an international action plan to conserve migratory birds throughout the continent. The Plan's goal is to return waterfowl populations to their 1970s levels by conserving wetland and upland habitat.

Joint Venture Coordinators:

Arctic Goose
c/o Prairie & Northern Region, CWS
#200, 4999 - 98 Ave.
Edmonton, AB T6B 2X3
780-951-8652
Fax: 780-495-2615
deanna.dixon@ec.gc.ca
Coordinator, Deanna Dixon

Black Duck
c/o Ontario Region, CWS
49 Camelot Dr.
Nepean, ON K1A 0H3
613-952-2408
Fax: 613-952-9027
Coordinator, Brigitte Collins

Eastern Habitat
c/o Environment Canada
PO Box 1590
Sackville, NB E0A 3C0
506-364-5036
Fax: 506-364-5062

Pacific Coast
c/o Pacific & Yukon Region, CWS
#201, 401 Burrard St.
Vancouver, BC V6C 3S5
604-666-2342
Fax: 604-664-4068
Coordinator, Saul Schneider
saul.schneider@ec.gc.ca

Prairie Habitat
c/o Prairie & Northern Region
CWS, #200, 4999 - 98 Ave.
Edmonton, AB T6B 2X3
780-951-8652
Fax: 780-495-2615
Coordinator, Deanna Dixon
deanna.dixon@ec.gc.ca

Commission for Environmental Cooperation (CEC) / Commission coopération environnementale
Secretariat
#200, 393, rue St-Jacques ouest
Montréal, QC H2Y 1N9
514-350-4300
Fax: 514-350-4314
info@cec.org
www.cec.org
The Commission for Environmental Cooperation (CEC) is an international organization created by Canada, Mexico & the United States under the North American Agreement on Environmental Cooperation (NAAEC). The CEC was established to address regional environmental concerns, help prevent potential trade & environmental conflicts & to promote the effective enforcement of environmental law. The Agreement complements the environmental provisions of the North American Free Trade Agreement (NAFTA).
Executive Director, Evan Lloyd
514-350-4318,
mvulpescu@cec.org
Legal Officer Submission on Enforcement Matters Unit, Marcelle Marion
514-350-4337,
mmarion@cec.org
Legal Officer Submission on Enforcement Matters Unit, Paolo Solano
514-350-4321,
psolano@cec.org

Program Manager Air Quality, Orlando Cabrera-Rivera
514-350-4323,
ocabrera@cec.org
Program Manager Biodiversity, Thomas Hammond
514-350-4336,
thammond@cec.org
Program Manager Environmental Information, Karen Richardson
514-350-4326,
krichardson@cec.org
Program Manager Environmental Law, Marco Antonio Heredia Fragoso
514-350-4302,
maheredia@cec.org
Council Secretary, Nathalie Daoust
514-350-4310,
ndaoust@cec.org

Export Development Canada (EDC) / Exportation et développement Canada (SEE)
151 O'Connor St.
Ottawa, ON K1A 1K3
613-598-2500
Fax: 613-598-3811
800-267-8510
TDD: 866-574-0451
www.edc.ca
A financial services corporation assisting Canadian business to succeed in foreign markets. EDC provides a wide range of financial solutions to exporters across Canada & their customers around the world. The corporation's risk management services include: export-credit insurance protecting exporters against losses due to non-payment relating to commercial & political risks; & flexible medium- or long-term financing & guarantees. As a financially self-sustaining Crown corporation, EDC operates on commercial principles, charging fees & premiums for its products & interest on its loans. EDC is governed by a board of directors composed of representatives from both the private & public sectors, & reports to Parliament through the minister for international trade. An Environmental Review Directive is used to assess the environmental impacts of projects EDC is asked to support. EDC pursues an international multilateral consensus on environmental review practices so that all exporters are subject to the same rules. EDC has adopted & implemented the OECD Recommendation on Common Approaches on Environment & Officially Supported Export Credits. EDC has signed the UNEP Statement of Financial Institutions. Through the EnviroExport initiative, EDC helps Canadian environmental exporters succeed internationally through financing products. Where EDC is considering providing financing support, political risk insurance or equity to the sponsor of a Category A project under the Environmental Review Directive, EDC will seek consent to inform the public on its website that it is considering support to such a project. The Chief Environmental Advisor's annual report for 2005 reported that 20 project-related transactions were assessed as meeting the ERD's criteria, & EDC facilitated $1.24 billion in exports of environmental goods & services with 283 Canadian companies.
President/CEO, Eric D. Siegel
Senior Vice-President Insurance, Pierre Gignac

EDC Regional Offices:

Calgary
Home Oil Tower
#606, 3240 - 8 Ave. SW
Calgary, AB T2P 2Z2
403-537-9800
Fax: 403-537-9811

Edmonton
#1000, 10810 - 101 St.
Edmonton, AB T5J 3S4
780-702-5233
Fax: 780-702-5235

Halifax
Purdy's Wharf Tower II
#1605, 1969 Upper Water St.
Halifax, NS B3J 3R7
902-442-5205
Fax: 902-442-5204

London
#1512, 148 Fullarton St.
London, ON N6A 5P3
519-963-5400
Fax: 519-963-5407

Federal/Provincial Government / Government of Canada

Moncton
#400, 735 Main St.
Moncton, NB E1C 1E5
506-851-6066
Fax: 506-851-6406

Montréal
Tour de la Bourse
#4520, 800, Victoria Square
CP 124
Montréal, QC H4Z 1C3
514-908-9200
Fax: 514-878-9891

Québec
#1340, 2875, boul Laurier
Québec, QC G1V 2M2
418-266-6130
Fax: 418-266-6131

St. John's
90 O'Leary Ave.
St. John's, NL A1B 2C7
709-772-8808
Fax: 709-772-8693

Toronto
#810, 150 York St.
PO Box 810
Toronto, ON M5H 3S5
416-640-7600
Fax: 416-862-1267

Vancouver
#1030, 505 Burrard St.
PO Box 58
Vancouver, BC V7X 1M5
604-638-6950
Fax: 604-638-6955

Winnipeg
Commodity Exchange Tower
#2075, 360 Main St.
Winnipeg, MB R3C 3Z3
204-975-5090
Fax: 204-975-5094

Finance Canada / Finances Canada

L'esplanade Laurier
140 O'Connor St.
Ottawa, ON K1A 0G5
613-992-1573
Fax: 613-943-0938
TDD: 613-995-1455
finpub@fin.gc.ca
www.fin.gc.ca
Other Communication: Library Services: 613-995-5877; Human Resources: 613-992-1105
The Department of Finance Canada is responsible for providing the federal government with analysis & advice on financial & economic issues. It also monitors & researches the performance of the Canadian economy's major factors (output, growth, employment, income, price stability, monetary policy, & long-term change). Interacting with various other federal departments & agencies, the Department encourages coordination in all federal initiatives with an impact on the economy. Emphasis is placed on consulting with the public regarding policy directions & options.
Acts Administered:
Bank Act
Bank of Canada Act
Banks & Banking Law Revision Act
Bills of Exchange Act
Bretton Woods & Related Agreements Act
Canada Deposit Insurance Corporation Act
Canada Development Corporation Reorganization Act
Canada Mortgage & Housing Corporation Act
Canada-Newfoundland Atlantic Accord Implementation Act
Canada Pension Plan Act
Canadian International Trade Tribunal Act
Canadian National Railways Capital Revision Act
Canadian National Railways Refunding Act
Canadian National Steamship (West Indies Service) Act
Co-operative Credit Association Act
Currency Act
Customs & Excise Offshore Application Act
Customs Tariff, Debt Servicing & Reduction Account Act
Diplomatic Service (Special) Superannuation Act
Excise Tax Act
Export Credit Insurance Act
Federal Provincial Fiscal Arrangements & Federal Post-Secondary Education & Health Contributions Act
Financial Administration Act
Garnishment Attachment & Pension Diversion Act
Governor General's Retiring Annuity Act
Halifax Relief Commission Pension Continuation Act
Income Tax Act
Income Tax Conventions Interpretation Act
Insurance Companies Canadian & British Act
Insurance Companies Foreign Act
Interest Act
International Development (Financial Institutions) Assistance Act
Investment Companies Act
Loan Companies Act
Members of Parliament Retiring Allowances Act
Newfoundland Additional Finance Assistance Act
Nova Scotia Offshore Retail Sales Tax Act
Office of the Superintendent of Financial Institutions Act
Pension Benefits Standards Act
Prince Edward Island Subsidy Act
Provincial Subsidies Act
Public Service Superannuation Act
Québec Savings Bank Act
Residential Mortgage Financing Act
Small Business Loans Act
Special Import Measures Act
Tax Rental Agreements Act
Trust & Loans Companies Act
Winding Up Act
Minister, Finance, Hon. James Michael (Jim) Flaherty, B.A., LL.B.
613-992-6344, Fax: 513-992-8320
FlaheJ@parl.gc.ca; jflaherty@fin.gc.ca
Deputy Minister, Michael Horgan
613-992-4925, Fax: 613-952-9569
Associate Deputy Minister & G-7 Deputy for Canada, Tiff Macklem
613-943-2314, Fax: 613-952-9569
Associate Deputy Minister, Stephen Richardson
613-996-1963
Assistant Deputy Minister, Denis Gauthier
613-992-1527, Fax: 613-992-0387
• Auditor General of Canada
• Bank of Canada
• Canada Deposit Insurance Corporation
• Canada Investment & Savings(CI&S) / Placements Épargne Canada (PEC)
#900, 110 Yonge St.
Toronto, ON M5C 1T4
416-952-1252
Fax: 416-952-1270
800-575-5151
csb@csb.gc.ca
www.csb.gc.ca
• Canada Revenue Agency
• Financial Consumer Agency of Canada
• Financial Transactions & Reports Analysis Centre of Canada(FINTRAC) / Centre d'analyse des opérations et déclarations financières du Canada (CANAFE)
234 Laurier Ave. West, 24th Fl.
Ottawa, ON K1P 1H7
Fax: 613-943-7931
866-346-8722
guidelines-lignesdirectrices@fintrac-canafe.gc.ca
www.fintrac.gc.ca
• Office of the Superintendent of Financial Institutions

Sectoral Policy Analysis / Analyse des politiques sectorielles
Fax: 613-992-0387
As part of the Economic Development & Corporate Finance Branch, Sectoral Policy Analysis advises the Minister on issues related to environment, resources, energy, transport, privatization, Crown corporations.
Chief Agriculture & Fisheries, Martine Bérubé
613-995-9118, Fax: 613-957-7874
Chief Resources, Energy & Environment, Leah Anderson
613-992-6516, Fax: 613-995-7090

Consultations & Communications Branch / Direction des consultations et des communications
East Tower
140 O'Connor St., 19th Fl.
Ottawa, ON K1A 0G5
613-992-1573
consltcomm@fin.gc.ca

Corporate Services Branch / Direction des services ministériels
Provides joint services for the federal Treasury Board Secretariat & Finance Canada.

Tax Policy Branch / Direction de la politique de l'impôt
Asst. Deputy Minister, Clément Gignac
613-996-9903, Fax: 613-952-9569
Chief Resource & Environmental Taxation, James Greene
613-992-0960, Fax: 613-943-2486

Fisheries & Oceans Canada (DFO) / Pêches et Océans Canada (MPO)

200 Kent St.
Ottawa, ON K1A 0E6
613-993-0999
Fax: 613-996-1866
TDD: 800-465-7735
info@dfo-mpo.gc.ca
www.dfo-mpo.gc.ca
The Department of Fisheries & Oceans (DFO), on behalf of the Government of Canada, is responsible for policies & programs in support of Canada's economic, ecological & scientific interests in the oceans & freshwater fish habitat; for the conservation & sustainable utilization of Canada's fisheries resources in marine & inland waters; & for safe, effective & environmentally soundmarine services responsive to the needs of Canadians in a global economy. The Department's mandate is extremely broad & covers management & protection of the marine & fisheries resources inside the 200-mile exclusive economic zone; management & protection of freshwater fisheries resources; marine safety along the world's longest coastline; facilitation of marine transportation; protection of the marine environment; support to other federal government institutions & objectives, as the government's civilian marine service; & research to support government priorities such as climate change & biodiversity. Because of its broad mandate, DFO does not operate alone. Federal & provincial governments share jurisdiction in a number of areas related to the Department's mandate. A $28-million investment over two years for the first phase of the Oceans Action Plan was announced in February, 2005. The Plan is designed to develop ocean resources while protecting marine ecosystems, through sustainable development, integrated management plans, & marine protected areas.
Acts Administered:
Atlantic Fisheries Restructuring Act
Canada Shipping Act
Pleasure Craft Sewage Pollution Prevention Regulations
Coastal Fisheries Protection Act
Department of Fisheries & Oceans Act
Fisheries Act
Aboriginal Communal Fishing Licences Regulations
Alberta Fishery Regulations, 1998
Alice Arm Tailings Deposit Regulations
Atlantic Fishery Regulations
British Columbia Gravel Removal Order
British Columbia Logging Order
British Columbia Sport Fishing Regulations
Fish Health Protection Regulations
Fish Toxicant Regulations
Fishery (General) Regulations
Foreign Vessel Fishing Regulations
Management of Contaminated Fisheries Regulations
Manitoba Fishery Regulations
Marine Mammal Regulations
Maritime Provinces Fishery Regulations
Newfoundland & Labrador Fishery Regulations
Northwest Territories Fishery Regulations
Ontario Fishery Regulations
Pacific Fishery Management Area Regulations
Pacific Fishery Regulations
Potato Processing Plant Liquid Effluent Regulations
Provincial Regulations
Pulp & Paper Effluent Regulations
Quebec Fishery Regulations
Saskatchewan Fishery Regulations
Yukon Territory Fishery Regulations
Fisheries Development Act
Fisheries Improvement Loans Act
Fisheries & Oceans Canada Orders
Fishing & Recreational Harbours Act
Freshwater Fish Marketing Act

Great Lakes Fisheries Convention Act
Navigable Waters Protection Act
Oceans Act
Basic Head Marine Protected Area Regulations
Confederation Bridge Area Provincial (PEI) Laws Application Regulations
Eastport Marine Protected Area Regulations
Endeavour Hydrothermal Vents Marine Protected Areas Regulations
Fishing Zones of Canada (Zones 1, 2 & 3) Order
Fishing Zones of Canada (Zones 4 & 5) Order
Fishing Zones of Canada (Zone 6) Order
Gilbert Bay Marine Protected Area Regulations
Gully Marine Protected Area Regulations
Territorial Sea Geographical Coordinates (Area 7) Order
Territorial Sea Geographical Coordinated Order
Species at Risk Act
Minister, Fisheries & Oceans, Hon. Gail Shea
613-992-9223, Fax: 613-992-1974
Shea.G@parl.gc.ca; Min@dfo-mpo.gc.ca
Other Communications: Fisheries & Oceans, Phone: 613-992-3474
Deputy Minister, Claire Dansereau
613-993-2200, Fax: 613-993-2194
Executive Advisor to the Deputy Minister, Christine Lavergne
613-993-9226, Fax: 613-993-2194
Assistant Deputy Minister Special Envoy for Asia-Pacific, Donna Petrachenko
604-666-8922, Fax: 604-666-8959
Director General Communications, Susan Gardner-Barclay
613-990-0219, Fax: 613-993-8277
Acting Senior General Counsel, Lynn Lovett
613-993-0966,
Parliamentary Secretary to the Minister of Fisheries and Oceans, Randy Kamp
613-947-4613, Fax: 613-947-4615
Kamp.R@parl.gc.ca
• Fisheries Resource Conservation Council(FRCC) / Le Conseil pour la conservation desressources halieutiques (CCRH)
PO Box 2001 D
Ottawa, ON K1P 5W3
613-998-0433
Fax: 613-998-1146
info@frcc-ccrh.ca
www.frcc.ca
Executive Director, Arthur Willett
Created in 1993 to form a partnership between scientific & academic expertise, & all sectors of the fishing industry.Council members make public recommendations to the Minister of Fisheries & Oceans on conservation measures for the Atlantic fishery.
• Freshwater Fish Marketing Corporation

Canadian Coast Guard (CCG) / Garde côtière canadienne
Centennial Towers
#6S018, 200 Kent St.
Ottawa, ON K1A 0E6
613-998-1573
Fax: 613-990-2780
www.ccg-gcc.gc.ca
The Canadian Coast Guard provides the following maritime programs & services: search & rescue; marine communications & traffic services, including radio communications & radio navigational aids services; marine navigation services, a program which establishes & maintains navigational aids to assist vessels in safe navigation; enrvironmental response program, which works to minimize impacts of marine pollution incidents & to provide humanitarian aid in disasters; aids to navigation, such as the Differential Global Positioning System (DGPS) & Notices to Mariners (NOTMAR); icebreaking services; & client relations & international affairs.
Commissioner, George DaPont
613-998-1571, Fax: 613-990-2780
Acting Deputy Commissioner, Charles Gadula
613-998-1570, Fax: 613-990-2780
Director General Fleet, Gary B. Sidock
613-990-9172
Director General Integrated Business Management Directorate, Claudine Gagnon
613-998-1440
Director General Integrated Technical Services, David G. Faulkner
613-998-1638, Fax: 613-993-5333
Director General Maritime Services, Michel Vermette
613-990-5608

Director Safety & Environmental Response Systems, Stevn Troy
613-990-3115, Fax: 613-996-8902

Human Resources & Corporate Services / Services généraux
200 Kent St.
Ottawa, ON K1A 0E6

Fisheries & Aquaculture Management / Gestion des pêches et de l'aquaculture
200 Kent St.
Ottawa, ON K1A 0E6
Responsible for the management & development of all federal fisheries & habitat in Canada. The division conserves, protects, develops & enhances fishery resources & habitats, encompassing the Atlantic & Pacific sectors, adjacent provinces, & the 200-mile offshore zone. Also manages Canadian parts of trans-boundary rivers.
Assistant Deputy Minister, David Bevan
613-990-9864, Fax: 613-990-9557
Director General Aboriginal Policy & Governance, David Balfour
613-993-2574
Director General Conservation & Protection, Paul Steele
613-998-9537
Director General International Affairs Directorate, Guy Beaupré
613-993-1873, Fax: 613-993-5995
Director General Resource Management, Kevin Stringer
613-990-6794

Oceans & Habitats / Océans et habitats
200 Kent St.
Ottawa, ON K1A 0E6
Services include: oceans sciences (ocean's physical properties, behaviour of organic & inorganic materials & their impact on fish & ecosystems, pollutants); regulation, enforcement & management of fisheries resources & habitat that are exploited for aboriginal, commercial & recreational purposes. The Marine Protected Areas Policy & the National Framework for Establishing & Managing Marine Protected Areas represents DFO's approach to establishing & maintaining MPOs in Canada.
Assistant Deputy Minister, Mimi Breton
613-993-9850
Director General Habitat Management Directorate, David McBain
613-991-1280
Director General Oceans Directorate, Wayne Moore
613-990-0001

Policy / Politiques
200 Kent St.
Ottawa, ON K1A 0E6
Provides leadership in recommending, developing & monitoring policy frameworks that advance DFO's initiatives, support DFO programs, & are responsive to the changing needs of DFO clients.Provides strategic advice on departmental programs, develops long-term planning priorities for the department & coordinates cross-sectoral activities in support of government goals & departmental objectives.
Assistant Deputy Minister, Michaela Huard
613-993-1808
Director General International Policy & Integration, Lori Ridgeway
613-993-1914
Director General Economic Analysis & Statistics, Bill Doubleday
613-991-6867

Science Sector / Secteur des sciences
200 Kent St.
Ottawa, ON K1A 0E6
Services provided by the science sector include the following: research & data gathering; provision of information & advice in the fields of fisheries sciences (fish, invertebrates, marine mammals & plants, & ecosystems), oceans sciences (ocean's physical properties, behaviour of organic & inorganic materials & their impact on fish & ecosystems, pollutants), & hydrography (bathymetric, tide & current systems); regulation, enforcement & management of fisheries resources & habitat that are exploited for aboriginal, commercial & recreational purposes. The sector assesses major stocks of exploited species of anadromous & marine fish, invertebrates, mammals & plants in Canada's Atlantic, Pacific, Arctic & marine waters, as well as freshwater fish in the Yukon & Northwest Territories. Research is conducted in the following areas: the biology & population of fish stocks, in order to provide scientific information & advice to fishery managers; the effects of changes in the ocean environment on the recruitment & distribution of fish populations; & studies to improve the productivity of aquaculture.
Assistant Deputy Minister, Wendy M. Watson-Wright
613-990-5123, Fax: 613-990-5113
Senior Director General Science Renewal, Serge Labonté
613-990-9082
Director General Canadian Hydrography Service, Savithri Narayanan
613-995-4413
Director General Ecosystem Science, Sylvain Paradis
613-990-0271
Director General Integrated Business Management, Jacqueline Gonçalves
613-991-0475
Director General Species at Risk Secretariat, Pardeep Ahluwalia
613-990-0417
Associate Director Ocean Sciences - Canadian Hydrographic Service, Howard Freeland
613-991-6850
Executive Director Strategic Directions & Science Outreach, Barbara Adams
613-993-1884

Central & Arctic
#703, 201 Front St.
Sarnia, ON N7T 8B1
519-383-1810
Fax: 519-464-5128
Regional Director, Bob Lambe

Gulf
PO Box 5030
Moncton, NB E1C 9B6
506-851-7747
Fax: 506-851-2435
Regional Director General, Jim Jones
506-851-7750

Maritimes
176 Portland St.
Halifax, NS B2Y 4T3
902-426-2581
Fax: 902-426-2479
Acting Regional Director, Faith Scattolon
902-426-2581

Newfoundland & Labrador
PO Box 5667 Whitehills
St. John's, NL A1C 5X1
709-772-4423
Fax: 709-772-4880
Regional Director General, Wayne Follett
709-772-4417, Fax: 709-772-6306

Pacific
#200, 401 Burrard St.
Vancouver, BC V6C 3S4
604-666-0384
Fax: 604-666-8956
Regional Director General, Paul Sprout
604-666-6098, Fax: 604-666-8756

Québec
104, rue Dalhousie
Québec, QC G1K 7Y7
418-648-7747
Fax: 418-648-4758
Regional Director General, Marc Demonceaux

Bayfield Institute
867 Lakeshore Rd.
PO Box 5050
Burlington, ON L7R 4A6
905-336-6240
Comprises fisheries research, habitat management, hydrographic surveys & chart production & ships support. Together with the Freshwater Institute in Winnipeg, it provides the federal Fisheries & Oceans science programs for the Central & Arctic Region. Multiple partnerships with a variety of external stakeholders allow the Institute to be recognized internationally as a site of leading research in freshwater science.
District Manager, Ron DesJardine
705-750-4017

Bedford Institute of Oceanography (BIO) / L'institut océanographique de Bedford

Federal/Provincial Government / Government of Canada

1 Challenger Dr.
PO Box 1006
Dartmouth, NS B2Y 4A2
902-426-3492
Fax: 902-426-8484
www.bio.gc.ca
Administered by Fisheries & Oceans, Bedford Institute of Oceanography (BIO) is Canada's largest centre for ocean research. Scientists, engineers & technicians primarily from Fisheries & Oceans, & Natural Resources Canada, (smaller components are from National Defense & Environment Canada) perform targeted research & provide advice on Atlantic marine environments. Programs include: fisheries research, ocean sciences & management, habitat ecology, marine chemistry, Canadian Hydrographic Service (producing navigation charts for the Atlantic & Arctic areas), marine environmental regional & resources geoscience, & seabird research & management. BIO based staff also conduct joint projects, such as sea floor mapping & exploration, & provide scientific response to marine environmental emergencies. Also located at Bedford is the Canadian Shark Research Laboratory & the Otolith Research Laboratory.
Regional Science Director, Dr. Michael Sinclair
sinclairm@mar.dfo-mpo.gc.ca

Freshwater Institute / Institut des eaux douces
501 University Cres.
Winnipeg, MB R3T 2N6
204-983-5000
Fax: 204-983-6285
Main areas of research are: fish habitats; limnology emphasizing mechanisms & processes of biological production & decomposition in lakes; studies related to energy development use, acidification, radionuclide & heavy metal pollution. Arctic research emphasizes commercially important fish & marine mammals & associated ecosystems, & the effects of hydroelectric developments & toxic chemical pollution on aquatic ecosystems. The Institute supports a major field camp at the Experimental Lakes Area. Activities include freshwater & arctic science, science oceans initiative, fish habitat management, fisheries management, small craft harbours, corporate services, communications & regional senior management. The federal fish inspection program, recently transferred to the new Canadian Food Inspection Agency (CFIA), continues to operate out of the FWI.
Administrative Assistant, Judy Fredette
204-983-5118

Gulf Fisheries Centre / Centre de poissonerie du gulfe
343, av Université, 5th Fl.
Moncton, NB E1C 9B6
506-851-3886
Fax: 506-851-7732
Regional Director General, James B. Jones
506-851-7750, Fax: 506-851-2224

Institut Maurice-Lamontagne / Maurice Lamontagne Institute
850, rte de le Mer
CP 1000
Mont-Joli, QC G5H 3Z4
418-775-0555
Fax: 418-775-0730
www.qc.dfo.ca/iml/en/intro.htm
Provides extensive research on: fisheries, fish habitat, oceanography, hydrography; development of marine renewable resources in the fields of fisheries, ocean industry development, commercial shipping & recreational boating. Main area of focus centres on the Gulf of St. Lawrence & estuary, Saguenay Fjord, Canadian Arctic, & the James, Hudson & Ungava Bays. Also performs the following research: environmental chemistry research on the distribution, transport & fate of contaminants in sediments, water & the food chain; ecotoxicology research & field assessments for biomarkers, fish pathology & embryotoxicity; molecular toxicology research for biomarkers, fish reproduction & steroid hormones; bioremediation study on the microbial degradation of petroleum oil hydrocarbons & microbial bioassays. Projects include the temporal & spatial monitoring of organic & inorganic contaminants in fish, shellfish & sediments of the St. Lawrence gulf & estuary. Also studying the effects of pulp & paper effluents & mercury & municipal effluents on the reproduction of fish.
Regional Director Regional Science Branch, Ariane Plourde

Centre for Aquaculture & Environmental Research
4160 Marine Dr.
West Vancouver, BC V7V 1N6
604-666-7453
Fax: 604-666-3497
The Center for Aquaculture & Environmental Research (CAER) is a specialized centre for aquaculture and coastal research co-founded by Fisheries and Oceans Canada and the University of British Columbia.
Regional Director Science Branch, Laura Richards
250-729-8369, Fax: 250-756-7053

Institute of Ocean Sciences (IOS) / Institut des sciences de la mer (ISM)
9860 West Saanich Rd.
PO Box 6000
Sidney, BC V8L 4B2
250-363-6517
Fax: 250-363-6390
Science divisions at IOS include: Canadian Hydrographic Service, Marine Environment & Habitat Science, Ocean Science & Productivity. Other departments & organizations at the IOS facility include: GSC Pacific - Sidney Pacific Geoscience Centre, Canadian Wildlife Service, Canadian Coast Guard, North Pacific Marine Science Organization (PICES). Science Division also includes Pacific Biological Station, West Vancouver Laboratory, Cultus Lake Laboratory.
Director, Denis D'Amours
250-363-6347

Pacific Biological Station (PBS) / La station de biologie du Pacifique
3190 Hammond Bay Rd.
Nanaimo, BC V9T 6N7
250-756-7000
Fax: 250-756-7053
Research at PBS responds to stock assessment, aquaculture, marine environment & habitat science, & ocean science & productivity priorities.
Regional Director Science Branch, Laura Richards
250-729-8369

St. Andrews Biological Station / La Station biologique de St. Andrews
531 Brandy Cove Rd.
St Andrews, NB E5B 2L9
506-529-8854
Fax: 506-529-5862
XMARSABS@mar.dfo-mpo.gc.ca
www.mar.dfo-mpo.gc.ca/sabs
Chemical & ecological studies on the interaction between oceanography & fisheries/aquaculture & the aquatic environment. Stock assessments & associated research on commercially important groundfish, pelagic finfish, invertebrate species in the Bay of Fundy & other areas of Atlantic Canada. Research in support of the existing salmon aquaculture industry & research on other species with potential for aquaculture in Atlantic Canada. Major environmental research projects include: risk assessment of organic chemicals to fisheries; biochemical indicators of health of aquatic animals; aquatic toxicity of marine phytotoxins; molluscan toxins, techniques & improvements; phytotoxin research; aquaculture ecology research; effectiveness of acid rain control programs; effects of aquaculture in the coastal environment.
Head Environmental Sciences & Research Scientist, Dr. Kats Haya
506-529-5916

Fleet / Flotte
Fax: 613-995-4700

Integrated Business Management (IBM) / Gestion des affaires intégré
Fax: 613-990-3480

Integrated Technical Support / Support technique intégré
Fax: 613-993-5333

Marine Programs
Fax: 613-991-4982
Director Safety & Environmental Response Systems, Steve Troy
613-990-3115, Fax: 613-996-8902

Aboriginal Policy & Governance
Fax: 613-993-7651

Conservation & Protection Directorate / Direction de la préservation et protection
Fax: 613-941-2718

Resource Management Directorate

Finance & Administration
Fax: 613-990-1932

Human Resources, Strategies & Programs
Fax: 613-990-3009

Information Management & Technology Services / Gestion de l'information et de la technologie
Fax: 613-990-3264

Habitat Management / Gestion de l'habitat
Fax: 613-993-7493
Activities include regulatory, freshwater & oceans planning, habitat enhancement, community outreach & stewardship, scientific support.
Director General, Richard Wex
613-991-1280
Chief Environmental Assessments & Major Projects, Bruce Hood
613-993-4922
Director Habitat Program Services Branch, Brian Torrie
613-993-7354
Director Habitat Protection & Sustainable Development, Patrice Leblanc
613-990-5252

Oceans Directorate / Direction générale des océans
Fax: 613-990-4810
Develops & implements the national Oceans Action Plan.
Director General, Céline Gaulin
613-990-0001
Oceans Policy Advisor Oceans Action Plan Secretariat, Pamela J. Rizzo
613-990-0253
Director Oceans Policy & Planning, Camille Mageau
613-991-1285
Director Regional Oceans Operations, Michael Murphy
613-991-2283

Economic & Policy Analysis / Analyse économique et politique
Fax: 613-990-9574

Policy, Coordination & Liaison / Politique, coordination et liaison
Fax: 613-990-2811

Strategic Priorities & Planning / Planification et priorités stratégiques
Fax: 613-993-5085

Canadian Hydrographic Service (CHS) / Service hydrographique du Canada
615 Booth St.
Ottawa, ON K1A 0E6
613-998-4931
Fax: 613-998-1217
chsinfo@dfo-mpo.gc.ca
www.chs-shc.gc.ca/pub
Federal program which offers the following: conducts field studies & gathers hydrographic information on tides, water levels & currents; compiles & publishes navigational charts & manuals for Canadian & adjacent international waters; works with Natural Resources Canada to cooperatively map boundary waters.
Director General, Savithri Narayanan
613-995-4413, Fax: 613-947-4369
Acting Director Hydrography, Steve Forbes
613-996-9163

Canadian Hydrographic Service / Service hydrographique du Canada
Fax: 613-998-1217

Fisheries, Environment & Biodiversity Science / Sciences halieutiques et biodiversité

Ecosystem Science
Director General, Sylvain Paradis
613-990-0271
Assoc. Director General, Denis Rivard
613-990-0281
Senior Advisor Aquaculture, Edward Black
613-990-0272
Acting Director Environment & Biodiversity Science, Paul Keizer
613-990-0314

Program Planning & Coordination
Fax: 613-990-0313

Ocean Sciences
Research Scientist & Senior Advisor, Jim Helbig
613-990-0314
Assoc. Director, Howard Freeland
613-991-6850
Senior Policy Advisor Oceanography & Climate, Leah Braithwaite
613-991-1313

Marine Environmental Data Service
613-990-6065
Fax: 613-993-4658
service@meds-sdmm.dfo-mpo.gc.ca
www.meds-sdmm.dfo-mpo.gc.ca
Manages & archives ocean data collected by DFO or acquired through national or international programmes conducted in ocean areas adjacent to Canada; disseminates data, data products & services to the marine community. MEDS is a member of the International Oceanographic Data & Information Exchange, whose mission is to enhance marine research, exploitation & development by facilitating the exchange of oceanographic information between participating member countries.
Chief Data Management & Client Services Division, Jean J. Gagnon
Senior Technical & Policy Advisor, J. Robert Keeley

Foreign Affairs & International Trade Canada (FAIT) / Affaires étrangères et Commerce international Canada (AECT)

125 Sussex Dr.
Ottawa, ON K1A 0G2
613-944-4000
Fax: 613-996-9709
800-267-8376
enqserv@international.gc.ca
www.international.gc.ca
Other Communication: Media Relations: 613/995-1874
FAIT works to ensure that its policies, programmes & operations reflect sustainable development criteria & to make a difference in sustainable development terms in the international arena. The Department defines its intent in a 3-year SD strategy which is tabled in Parliament. Annual progress reports are also tabled in Parliament. The current strategy, Agenda 2006, covers the 2004-2006 period. FAIT strives to defend & advance Canada's international interests in environmental protection & sustainable development in bilateral, multilateral & regional fora including issues relating to climate change, trade & environment, sustainable forest management, hazardous & toxic substances, desertification, human settlements, biological diversity, biosafety, genetic resources for food & agriculture, air & marine pollution, whaling, & non-Canada-USA freshwater. To achieve progress in this area of responsibility, FAIT's Environmental & Sustainable Development Bureau works with the major international environmental & sustainable development organizations. It also recommends & oversees funding where appropriate. Domestically, the Bureau works toward agreement & productive partnerships with other government departments, agencies & non-governmental environmental, non-nuclear energy, developmental & business organizations. It prepares & monitors implementation of the Department's Sustainable Development Strategy & provides advice & assistance in the areas of environmental assessment & the greening of departmental operations both in Canada & at the 157 missions abroad. FAIT established an environmental management system (EMS), based on the International Organization for Standardization's (ISO) 14000 series, in a commitment to incorporate best environmental management practices into its operations. A database of international environmental agreements & arrangements to which Canada is a party may be searched at pubx.dfait-maeci.gc.ca/A_Branch/AES/Env_commitments.nsf/VE Welcome/Homepage

Acts Administered:
Asia-Pacific Foundation of Canada Act
Bretton Woods Agreements Act
Canadian Commercial Corporation Act
Canadian Institute for International Peace & Security Act
Comprehensive Nuclear Test-Ban Treaty Implementation Act
Cultural Property Export & Import Act
Department of Foreign Affairs & International Trade Act
Diplomatic & Consular Privileges & Immunities Act
Export Development Act
Export & Import Permits Act
Food & Agriculture Organization of the United Nations Act
Forgiveness of Certain Official Development Assistance Debts Act
Fort-Falls Bridge Authority Act
Geneva Conventions Act
High Commissioner of the United Kingdom Act
International Boundary Waters Treaty Act
International Development (Financial Institutions) Continuing Assistance Act
International Development Research Centre Act
Meat Import Act
North American Free Trade Agreement Implementation Act
Northern Pipeline Act
Privileges & Immunities (International Organizations) Act
Privileges & Immunities (North Atlantic Treaty Organization) Act
Prohibition of International Air Services Act
Rainy Lake Watershed Emergency Control Act
Roosevelt-Campobello International Park Commission Act
Skagit River Valley Treaty Implementation Act
State Immunity Act
United Nations Act

Minister, Foreign Affairs, Hon. Lawrence Cannon
613-992-5516, Fax: 613-992-6802
CannoL@parl.gc.ca; L.Cannon@international.gc.ca
Deputy Minister Foreign Affairs, Morris Rosenberg
613-944-4911
Deputy Minister International Trade, Louis Lévesque
613-944-5000, Fax: 613-944-8493
Parliamentary Secretary to the Minister of Foreign Affairs, Deepak Obhrai
613-947-4566, Fax: 613-947-4569
Obhrai.D@parl.gc.ca

Foreign Affairs / Affaires étrangères
Deputy Minister, Leonard Edwards
613-944-4911

Global Issues / Enjeux mondiaux
Assistant Deputy Minister, Keith Christie
613-944-2273

International Security Branch & Political Director / Sécurité international et directeur politique
Assistant Deputy Minister, Colleen Swords
613-944-4228, Fax: 613-944-1180
Director General Secretariat for the Stabilization & Reconstruction Task Force, Robert Derouin
613-995-6689
Director Global Partnership Program, Troy Lulashnyk
613-944-3311, Fax: 613-944-1130
Director Nuclear & Chemical Disarmament Implementation Agency, James A. Junke
613-996-6901, Fax: 613-944-3105
Senior Coordinator Mine Action & Small Arms Team, Earl Turcotte
613-995-9282, Fax: 613-944-2501

Office of Protocol / Bureau du Protocole
613-996-8683
Fax: 613-943-1075

Strategic Policy & Planning
Assistant Deputy Minister, Drew Fagan
613-944-3022, Fax: 613-944-0285
Director General Intergovernmental Affairs & Domestic Outreach, Don Costello
613-944-7162
Director General Policy Planning Bureau, Robert McRae
613-944-3179
Director General Public Policy Bureau, James Lambert
613-996-0232
- Canadian International Development Agency
- Canadian International Grains Institute
- International Joint Commission (Canadian Section)

Passport Canada
Le 70 Crémazie
70 Crémazie St.
Gatineau, QC K1A 0G3
Fax: 819-953-5856
800-567-6868
www.pptc.gc.ca
Other Communication: TTY: 1-866-255-7655

Brampton
#401, 40 Gillingham Dr.
Brampton, ON

Calgary
Harry Hays Bldg.
#254, 220 - 4th Ave. SE
Calgary, AB

Calgary South
14331 Macleod Trail SW
Calgary, AB

Edmonton
Canada Place Building
#126, 9700 Jasper Ave.
Edmonton, AB

Fredericton
Frederick Square
#430, 77 Westmorland St.
Fredericton, NB

Gatineau
Place du Centre, Commercial Level 2
200 Promenade du Portage
Gatineau, QC

Halifax
Maritime Centre
#1508, 1505 Barrington St.
Halifax, NS

Hamilton
Standard Life Bldg.
#330, 120 King St. West
Hamilton, ON

Kitchener
The Galleria
#630, 101 Frederick St.
Kitchener, ON

Laval
#500, 3, place Laval
Laval, QC

London
#201, 400 York St., 2nd Fl.
London, ON

Mississauga
Central Parkway Mall
#116, 377 Burnhamthorpe Rd. East, 2nd Fl.
Mississauga, ON

Montréal
Complexe Guy Favreau, Tour Ouest
#803, 200, boul René-Lévesque ouest
Montréal, QC

North York
Joseph Shepard Bldg.
#380, 4900 Yonge St.
North York, ON

Ottawa
Level C, East Tower, C.D. Howe Bldg.
240 Sparks St.
Ottawa, ON

Pointe Claire
Centre commercial Fairview
6818, rte Transcanadienne
Pointe-Claire, QC

Québec
Tour Cominar, Place de la Cité
#200, 2640, boul Laurier, 2e étage
Québec, QC

Regina
#500, 1870 Albert St.
Regina, SK

Richmond
#135, 8011 Saba Rd.
Richmond, BC

Saguenay
Immeuble St-Michel
#408, 3885, boul Harvey
Saguenay, QC

St. Catharines
Landmark Bldg.
#600, 43 Church St.
St Catharines, ON

Federal/Provincial Government / Government of Canada

St. John's
TD Place
#802, 140 Water St.
St. John's, NL

Saint-Laurent
#112, 3300, boul Côte Vertu
Saint-Laurent, QC

Saskatoon
Federal Bldg.
#405, 101 - 22 St. East
Saskatoon, SK

Scarborough
#210, 200 Town Centre Crt.
Scarborough, ON

Surrey
#900, 13401 - 108 Ave.
Surrey, BC

Thunder Bay
979 Alloy Dr., 2nd Fl.
Thunder Bay, ON

Toronto
#300, 74 Victoria St.
Toronto, ON

Vancouver
Sinclair Centre
#200, 757 West Hastings St.
Vancouver, BC

Victoria
747 Fort St., 5th Fl.
Victoria, BC

Whitby
Whitby Mall
1615 Dundas St. East
Whitby, ON

Windsor
CIBC Building
#503, 100 Ouellette Ave.
Windsor, ON

Winnipeg
#400, 433 Main St.
Winnipeg, MB

Baie Comeau
235, boul Lasalle, 2e étage
Baie-Comeau, QC

Bridgewater
77 Dufferin St.
Bridgewater, NS

Brandon
#100, 1039 Princess Ave.
Brandon, MB

Cambridge Bay
PO Box 2010
Cambridge Bay, NU

Campbellton
157 Water St.
Campbellton, NB

Chibougamau
623, 3e rue
Chibougamau, QC

Collingwood
44 Hurontario St.
Collingwood, ON

Comox Valley
130 - 19th St.
Comox Valley, BC

Corner Brook
1 Regent Sq.
Corner Brook, NL

Drummondville
1525 Saint-Joseph Blvd.
Drummondville, QC

Flin Flon
111 Main St.
Flin Flon, MB

Fort McMurray
Provincial Bldg., Main Fl.
9915 Franklin Ave.
Fort McMurray, AB

Fort Simpson
9606 - 100 St.
Fort Simpson, NT

Fort Smith
136 McDougal Rd.
Fort Smith, NT

Gander
1 Markham Pl.
Gander, NL

Hay River
#204, 41 Capital Dr.
Hay River, NT

Inuvik
170 McKenzie Rd.
Inuvik, NT

Iqaluit
#300, Iqaluit House
Iqaluit, NU

Kamloops
235 Lansdowne St.
Kamloops, BC

Kenora
308 Second St.
Kenora, ON

La Tuque
290, rue St-Joseph
La Tuque, QC

Miramichi
150 Pleasant St.
Miramichi, NB

Montague
541 Main St.
Montague, PE

New Glasgow
340 East River Rd.
New Glasgow, NS

North Battleford
9800 Territorial Dr.
North Battleford, SK

Pembroke
141 Lake St.
Pembroke, ON

Rankin Inlet
PO Box 97
Rankin Inlet, NU

Terrace
4630 Lazelle Ave.
Terrace, BC

Thompson
#118, 3 Station Rd.
Thompson, MB

Timmins
#300, 273 - 3 Ave.
Timmins, ON

Val d'Or
400 Central Ave.
Val-d'Or, QC

Whitehorse
#125, 300 Main St.
Whitehorse, YT

Yellowknife
5020 - 48th St.
Yellowknife, NT

Yorkton
214 Smith St. East
Yorkton, SK

International Trade Canada (ITCan) / Commerce international Canada

125 Sussex Dr.
Ottawa, ON K1A 0G2
613-995-2901
Fax: 613-996-8924
International Trade Canada works to position Canada as a business leader for the 21st century. ITCan helps large & small Canadian companies expand & succeed internationally, promotes Canada as a dynamic place to do business, & negotiates & administers trade agreements.
Deputy Minister, Louis Lévesque
613-944-5000, Fax: 613-944-8493
Executive Director, Peter McGovern
613-944-0979, Fax: 613-947-8117
Director Briefing & Correspondence Services, Noelle Grosse
613-944-6288
Director Resource Management, Jean Guertin
613-996-2326, Fax: 613-943-2058

Global Operations & Chief Trade Commissioner

125 Sussex Dr,
Ottawa, ON K1A 0G2
613-944-2697
Fax: 613-996-1667
Assistant Deputy Minister & Chief Trade Commissioner, Ken Sunquist
613-944-2695, Fax: 613-944-3473
Director General Bilateral Commercial Relations: Asia & Americas, Peter McGovern
613-944-0979, Fax: 613-947-8117
Director General Bilateral Commercial Relations: Europe, Africa & Middle East, James K. Hill
613-944-0506, Fax: 613-944-0556
Director General Trade Commissioner Service - Initiatives, Grant Manuge
613-944-1678, Fax: 613-947-8390
Director General Trade Commissioner Service - Operations, Louise Leger
613-992-8785, Fax: 613-995-5773

International Business Development, Investment & Innovation

111 Sussex Dr.
Ottawa, ON K1N 1J1
Fax: 613-944-3178
Assistant Deputy Minister, Stewart Beck
613-944-3122
Principal Advisor Pacific Gateway International Marketing Group, Michael Fine
613-944-3146, Fax: 613-995-7832
Director General Global Business Opportunities, Paul Thoppil
613-996-1745
Director General Invest in Canada, Mario Ste-Marie
613-944-3125, Fax: 613-944-3178
Director General Economic Policy Analysis & Consultations, Robert Clark
613-992-7979, Fax: 613-992-8727

Communications Bureau

125 Sussex Dr.
Ottawa, ON K1A 0G2
613-944-0404
Fax: 613-944-0811

Canadian Trade Commissioner Service / Service des délégués commerciaux du Canada

Fax: 613-944-1078
www.infoexport.gc.ca/
Other Communication: Toll Free Fax: 1-800-667-3802
The Virtual Trade Commissioner (VTC) is a federal service that provides Canadian businesses with export assistance to increase overseas sales. VTC provides access to free services of the Canadian Trade Commissioner Service, with over 500 trade officers in 140 cities worldwide, information & services available through a personalized web page & access to International business leads from the International Business Opportunities Centre.

International Business Opportunities Centre / Centre des occasions d'affaires internationales

Fax: 613-996-2635
support@e-leads.ca
www.iboc.gc.ca/
Operates an electronic trade leads system that is made available to companies registered through the Virtual Trade Commissioner. The service is free of charge & exclusive to Canadian companies.
Acting Director, Anne Argyris
613-944-2010

Federal/Provincial Government / Government of Canada

Trade Law Bureau
125 Sussex Dr.
Ottawa, ON K1A 0G2
613-943-2804
Fax: 613-944-0027
Senior General Counsel & Director General, Meg Kinnear
613-943-2803
Acting General Counsel Trade Law Bureau, Matthew Kronby
613-944-3046
Director, Cynthia A. Westaway
613-944-3046

Trade Policy & Negotiations / Politique commercial et négociations
111 Sussex Dr.
Ottawa, ON K1N 1J1
613-996-5677
Fax: 613-996-1667
Assistant Deputy Minister, Don Stephenson
613-992-0293, Fax: 613-996-1667
Director General Bilateral & Regional Trade Policy, David Plunkett
613-944-9171
Director General Export & Import Controls, Suzanne McKellips
613-995-2947
Director General Multilateral Trade Policy, Gilles Gauthier
613-944-2002, Fax: 613-944-0757
Director General North America Trade Policy, Paul Robertson
613-944-0462, Fax: 613-944-0231
Chief Trade Negotiator Bilateral & Regional, Ian Burney
613-992-3386

Americas Strategy
125 Sussex Dr.
Ottawa, ON K1A 0G2
613-944-1903
Fax: 613-944-1910
Assistant Deputy Minister, Alex Bugailiskis
613-944-1909
Special Advisor, Randolph Harwood
613-944-1907

BC & Yukon
#2000, 300 West Georgia St.
Vancouver, BC V6B 6E1
604-666-0434
Fax: 604-666-0954
itc-vancouver@ic.gc.ca
www.bctradeevents.com
Director & Senior Trade Commissioner, Bill Johnston
johnston.william@ic.gc.ca

Calgary
#400, 639 - 5 Ave. SW
Calgary, AB T2P 0M9
403-292-4575
Fax: 403-292-4578
itc-calgary@ic.gc.ca
www.alberta-canada.com/tta/about/index.cfm
Trade Commissioner, Barry Schlinker
403-292-4509

Charlottetown
75 Fitzroy St.
PO Box 1115
Charlottetown, PE C1A 7K2
902-566-7382
Fax: 902-566-7450
itc-charlottetown@ic.gc.ca
www.tradeteampei.com
Acting Provincial Director & Sr. Trade Commissioner, Bernard Postma
902-566-7426

Edmonton
Canada Place
#725, 9700 Jasper Ave.
Edmonton, AB T5J 4C3
780-495-2944
Fax: 780-495-4507
Acting Sr. Trade Commissioner, Dee Pannu
780-495-3329

Halifax
1800 Argyle St., 5th Fl.
PO Box 940 M
Halifax, NS B3J 2V9
902-426-7540
Fax: 902-426-5218
itc-halifax@ic.gc.ca
Acting Senior Trade Commissioner, Ron Rose
902-426-6660

Manitoba (NWT & Nunavut)
400 St. Mary Ave., 4th Fl.
Winnipeg, MB R3C 4K5
204-983-5851
Fax: 204-983-3182
itc-winnipeg@ic.gc.ca
www.gov.mb.ca/trade/index.html
Senior Trade Commissioner, Suzanne Cormie
cormie.suzanne@ic.gc.ca

New Brunswick
#103, 1045 Main St.
Moncton, NB E1C 1H1
506-851-6452
Fax: 506-851-6429
800-332-3801
itc-moncton@ic.gc.ca
www.ttnb.ca
Senior Trade Commissioner & Provincial Director, Michelyne Paulin
506-851-6440

Newfoundland & Labrador
John Cabot Bldg.
Phase II, 10 Barter's Hill, 10th Fl.
PO Box 8950
St. John's, NL A1B 3R9
709-772-5511
Fax: 709-772-5093
itc-stjohns@ic.gc.ca
www.cbsc.org/nf/search/display.cfm?CODE=2438&coll=FE_FEDSBIS_E
Sr. Trade Commissioner, Anthony McLevey
709-772-4910

Québec
#800, 5, Place Ville Marie
Montréal, QC H3B 2G2
514-283-6328
Fax: 514-283-8794
itc.montreal@ic.gc.ca
www.eciq.net/public/
Director, Michel Charland
charland.michel@ic.gc.ca

Regina
#320, 1801 Hamilton St.
Regina, SK S4P 3N8
306-780-6124
Fax: 306-780-8797
itc-regina@ic.gc.ca
www.cbsc.org/sask/trade_export.cfm

Saskatoon
Princeton Tower
123 - 2nd Ave. South, 7th Fl.
Saskatoon, SK S7K 7E6
306-975-5315
Fax: 306-975-5334
itc-saskatoon@ic.gc.ca
www.cbsc.org/trade_export.cfm

Senior Trade Commissioner, Rod Johnson
johnson.rod@ic.gc.ca

Toronto
Yonge-Richmond Centre
151 Yonge St., 4th Fl.
Toronto, ON M5C 2W7
416-973-5053
Fax: 416-973-8161
itc-toronto@ic.gc.ca
napoleon.ic.gc.ca/ontario_region/tcontario.nsf
Director International Business & Senior Trade Commissioner, Randy Harwood
416-954-6326

Bancomext
#1540, 1501, McGill College
Montréal, QC H3A 3M8
514-287-1669
Fax: 514-287-1844
cc-montreal@bancomext.gob.mx
www.bancomext.com
Main business development bank in Mexico which promotes international competitiveness within Mexican companies, & develops Mexico's foreign trade. It also encourages the inflow of foreign investment & the establishment of cooperative investments with companies & agencies from other countries.
Trade Commissioner, Ana Elvia Mejia Moysen

Toronto
#2110, 1 Dundas St. West
PO Box 11
Toronto, ON M5G 1Z3
416-867-9292
Fax: 416-867-1847
cc-toronto@bancomext.gob.mx
Trade Commissioner, Rafael Jose Cortes Gomez

Vancouver
#1365, 200 Granville St.
Vancouver, BC V6C 1S4
604-682-3648
Fax: 604-682-1355
bancomext@trademexnc.com
Trade Commissioner, Sergio Rios Martinez

Canada Trade Mission to Mexico / Mission commerciale du Canada au Mexique
www.tcm-mec.gc.ca/mexico/links-en.asp
Website contains links to useful webpages such as embassies, trade fairs, government departments & industry sectors, including environmental technologies.

Canadian Chamber of Commerce in Mexico / Chambre de commerce du Canada au Mexique
Zaragoza 1300 ur, Edificio Kalos, Piso A2, Oficina 201,
Monterrey, NL
info@cancham.org.mx
Other Communication: 81-8343-1899

Embassy of Mexico in Canada / Ambassade du Mexique au Canada
#1000, 45 O'Connor St.
Ottawa, ON K1P 1A4
613-233-8988
Fax: 613-235-9123
info@embamexcan.com
www.embamexcan.com
Ambassador, Teresa Garcia Segocia de Madero
First Secretary Economic Section, Carlos Obrador-Garrido
ext-226-5

NAFTA Office of Mexico in Canada / Bureau de l'ALENA du Mexique au Canada
#1030, 45 O'Connor St.
Ottawa, ON K1P 1A4
613-235-7782
Fax: 613-235-1129
info@nafta-mexico.org
www.nafta-mexico.org
Participates in NAFTA committees & working groups, including those on environment & labour issues. Analyzes & provides information on Mexico-Canada trade, develops trade relations, information on government export programs, Mexican manufacturing contacts, import regulations & trade statistics.
Chief Representative, Carlos Piñera
Trade Policy & Legal Affairs, Alejandro Trujillo
Trade & Investment Promotion, Leonor Yañez

North American Development Bank
#300, 203 St. Mary's
San Antonio, TX 78205 USA
210-231-8000
Fax: 210-231-6232
www.nadbank.org
NADB is a bilaterally funded, international organization, funded & governed by the United States & Mexico for the purpose of financing environmental infrastructure projects along their joint border.
Managing Director, Jorge Garces

Secretariat of Environment & Natural Resources (SEMARNAT)
Jardines en la Montana, Tlalpan
4209 Blvd. Adolfo Ruiz Cortines
México DF, 14210 Mexico
525-286-7766
Fax: 525-286-6872

Federal/Provincial Government / Government of Canada

contactodgeia@semernat.gob.mx
www.semarnat.gob.mx/
Government agency whose main purpose is to developenvironmental protection policy.

American National Standards Institute
25 West 43rd St.
New York, NY 10036 USA
212-642-4900
Fax: 212-398-0023
www.ansi.org
Provides services as the administrator & coordinator of the US private sector voluntary standardization system. This is a private, not-for-profit membership organization supported by a diverse constituency of private & public sector organizations. The goal of the Institute is to enhance the global compeitiveness of US business & the American quality of life by promoting & facilitating voluntary consensus standards & conformity assessment systems.
President/CEO, Joe Bhatia

Environmental Protection Agency: Office of Acquisition Management (EPA)
1200 Pennsylvania Ave. NW
Washington, DC 20460 USA
202-564-4310
oam-web@epa.gov
www.epa.gov/oam/
Responsible for the policies, procedures, operations & support of the Environmental Protection Agency's procurement & contracts management program.Also responsible for serving as the Procurement Executive for the Agency & performing special projects. Oversees four service centres within the Superfund/RCRA Procurement Operations Division which coordinates contract services in areas covered under the Comprehensive Environmental Response, Compensation & Liability Act CERCLA), commonly known as "Superfund", & the Resources Conservation & Recovery Act (RCRA). This includes supervision of the emergency response, remedial action, enforcement, & federal facility oversight contracting programs
Administrator, Stephen L. Johnson
Acting Director Office of Acquisition Management, John Gherardini
Contact Headquarters Program Operations Division, Robert Krumhansl
krumhansl.robert@epa.gov
Contact Superfund/RCRA Procurement Operations Division, Maria Ondrish

General Services Administration
1800 F St. NW
Washington, DC 20405 USA
202-501-0112
877-495-4849
vendor.support@gsa.gov
www.gsa.gov/
Other Communication: FedBizOpps (Federal Contracting Opportunities): 1-877-472-3779; Email: fbo.support@gsa.gov.ca; www.fedbizopps.gov
Secures buildings, products, services, technology & other workplace essentials for over 1 million federal government workers located in 8,000 government-owned & leased buildings in the US & overseas. The new Federal Acquisition Service is a major reorganization of the Federal Technology Service & the Federal Supply Service.
Administrator, Lurita A. Doan
Commissioner Federal Acquisition Service, James A. Williams
703-605-5400
Chief Acquisition Officer, Emily W. Murphy
202-501-1043

Government Printing Office (GPO)
732 North Capitol St.
Washington, DC 20401 USA
202-512-0526
Fax: 202-512-1782
gpoaccess@gpo.gov
www.gpo.gov/
Other Communication: Contractor Connection URL: contractorconnect.gpo.gov/
The GPO produces & distributes Federal Government information products for public access to Government information online or in print. Acquisition Services provides products & services for the GPO & provides support for other federal agencies for warehouse & office space leasing, surplus & scrap item disposal.
Chief Acquisition Services, Herbert H. Jackson
202-512-0937

National Technical Information Service (NTIS)
c/o Department of Commerce
5285 Port Royal Rd.
Springfield, VA 22161 USA
703-605-6000
Fax: 703-321-8547
info@ntis.gov
www.ntis.gov
NTIS is the official source for government-sponsored US & worldwide scientific, technical, engineering &business related information.It is a non-appropriated agency of the US Department of Commerce's Technology Administration, & does not rely on taxpayer funds to operate.All NTIS operating costs are paid for by the sale of its products & services.

United States Embassy in Canada
490 Sussex Dr.
Ottawa, ON K1N 1G8
613-238-5335
Fax: 613-688-3082
ottawareference@state.gov
ottawa.usembassy.gov
Charge d'affaires, Terry Breese

US Commercial Service in Canada
c/o Department of Commerce
14th & Constitution Ave. NW
Washington, DC 20230 USA
202-482-5777
Fax: 202-482-5013
www.export.gov; www.buyusa.gov/canada
Other Communication: Trade Information Center:
1-800-USA-TRADE Commercial News USA: 1-800-581-8533
Assists US firms in developing their export potential by providing expert counseling, advice, foreign market information, international contacts, & advocacy services.Operates Export Assistance Centers throughout the US & in more than 70 countries internationally.Domestic & international offices are linked through an international communications & information network, to provide liaison services between companies & multilateral development banks.Prints & distributes Commercial News USA to subscribers outside the US. The publication lists new products & services which US companies wish to export, & identifies whether they seek agents, distributors or representatives in foreign markets. The US Commercial Service sponsors "Environmental Technology Matchmakers" providing opportunities for American firms to partner with Canadian firms, & offer products or services in Canada. International Buyer Program brings international buyers to major trade shows in the U.S., promoting business opportunities, & strategic partnerships, including environmental products & services. International Partner Search has networks in 80 countries to research strategic partners.

Regional Offices
Provides assistance for Canadian firms attempting to locate a particular product or service in the US.CS Canada advertises such requests through the US Department of Commerce's Electronic Bulletin Board & the Journal of Commerce. Maintains six Business Information Centres in Canada, located in the six regional Canadian CS offices.The Centres provide Canadian companies with useful information about US products & companies.

Halifax
#904, 1969 Upper WAter St.
Halifax, NS B3J 3R7
902-429-2482
Fax: 902-429-7690
Halifax.Office.Box@mail.doc.gov
Commercial Specialist CS Halifax, Richard Vinson

Calgary
615 Macleod Trail, 10th Fl.
Calgary, AB T2G 4T8
403-265-2116
Fax: 403-403-2664
calgary.office.box@mail.doc.gov
Commercial Specialist, Charon Atkins

Montréal
1155, rue St-Alexandre
Montréal, QC H3B 3Z1
514-398-9695
Fax: 514-398-0711
Montreal.Office.Box@mail.doc.gov
Senior Commercial Specialist CS Montréal, Pierre Richer
514-398-0673, Fax: 514-398-0711

Ottawa
Commercial Service Ottawa
490 Sussex Dr.
Ottawa, ON K1N 1G8
613-688-5217
Fax: 613-238-5999
ottawa.office.box@mail.doc.gov
Commercial Officer, Thomas Boam
613-688-5388, Fax: 613-238-5999

Toronto
#602, 480 University Ave.
Toronto, ON M5G 1V2
416-595-5412
Fax: 416-595-5419
toronto.office.box@mail.doc.gov
Principal Commercial Officer, Michael Keaveny
ext- 22-2
Sr. Commercial Specialist, Madellon C. Lopes
ext- 22-7

Vancouver
#1950, 1095 West Pender St.
Vancouver, BC V6E 2M6
604-685-3382
Fax: 604-687-6095
vancouver.office.box@mail.doc.gov
Commercial Specialist, Cheryl Schell
604-642-6679

Inter-American Development Bank (IADB)
1300 New York Ave. NW
Washington, DC 20577 USA
202-623-1000
Fax: 202-623-3096
www.iadb.org
The oldest & largest regional multilateral development institution, established to foster sustainable economic & social development in Latin America & the Caribbean. The IDB is owned by 47 member states, including Canada.
President, Luis Alberto Moreno

Northstar Trade Finance Inc.
#833, 595 Burrard St.
PO Box 49058
Vancouver, BC V7X 1C4
604-664-5828
Fax: 604-664-5838
800-663-9288
vancouver@northstar.ca
www.northstar.ca
A cooperative agency which coordinates the export strengths of Bank of Montr,al, Royal Bank, HSBC Bank Canada, National Bank of Canada, Caisse de D,pt et Placement du Québec, Export Development Canada & Western Economic Diversification Canada & the government of British Columbia. Branches: Toronto: #501, 1 University Ave., Toronto ON M5J 2P1, 416/861-8222; Fax: 416/861-8233 Email: toronto@northstar.ca Montréal: #1630, 630, boul René-Lévesque ouest, Montréal QC H3B 1S6, 514/874-3366; Fax: 514/874-8428; Email: montreal@northstar.ca Calgary:407 - 8 Ave. SW, 8th Fl., Calgary AB T2P 1E5 403/693-8557; Fax: 403/693-8626; Email: calgary@northstar.ca

The World Bank Group
1818 H St. NW
Washington, DC 20433 USA
202-473-1000
Fax: 202-477-6391
www.worldbank.org
Other Communication: Global Environment Facility:
202/473-1816; Fax: 202/522-3256; Email:
eadvisor@worldbank.org
The World Bank Group is made up of five organizations: the International Bank for Reconstruction & Development (IBRD), the International Development Association (IDA), the International Finance Corporation (IFC), the Multilateral Investment Guarantee Agency (MIGA) & the International Centre for Settlement of Investment Disputes (ICSID).The organization offers partnership services, procurement opportunities, information services & advisory services to assist foreign governments in building the foundations for growth. The Global Environment Facility Coordination Team includes global environmental specialists who work closely with World Bank clients & partners to identify & prepare projects that conform to the Conference to the Parties for the UN Conventions on Biodiversity, Climate Change & Persistent Organic

Pollutants, & meet the financing criteria of the GEF & Montreal Protocol.
GEF Executive Coordinator, Steve Gorman

National Electronic Procurement Assistance Center (NEPAC)
#304, 55 Maple Ave.
Rockville Center, NY 11570 USA
516-255-0500
Fax: 516-255-0509
800-932-7761
online@cbdweb.com
www.cbd-net.com/
One of the largest sources of government bid & award information both online & offline. Formerly the Commerce Business Daily (CBD), it has been replaced by FedBizOpps (FBO). Email service is also available.

Health Canada / Santé Canada

Tunney's Pasture
Ottawa, ON K1A 0K9
613-957-2991
Fax: 613-941-5366
Info@hc-sc.gc.ca
www.hc-sc.gc.ca
Other Communication: Media Relations: 613-957-2983; Office of the Access to Information: 613-954-8744; Public Services Health Medical Centre: 613-954-6582; Emergency Svs: 613-957-7711
In partnership with provincial & territorial governments, Health Canada (HC) develops health policy, enforces health regulations, promotes disease prevention, & enhances healthy living for all Canadians. HC ensures that health services are available & accessible to First Nations & Inuit communities. It works closely with other federal departments, agencies & health stakeholders to reduce health & safety risks to Canadians. Through its Health Intelligence Network, HC works with other levels of government & the health care system in the surveillance, prevention, control & research of disease outbreaks across Canada & around the world. It also monitors health & safety risks related to the sale & use of drugs, food, chemicals, pesticides, medical devices & certain consumer products. HC negotiates agreements regarding hazardous materials in the workplace, performs medical assessments for pilots & air traffic controllers, & conducts environmental health assessments.

Acts Administered:
Canada Health Act
Canada Medical Act
Canadian Centre on Substance Abuse Act
Canadian Institutes of Health Research Act
Controlled Drug Substances Act
Department of Health Act
Financial Administration Act
Fitness & Amateur Sport Act
Food & Drugs Act (Agriculture & Agri-Food Canada)
Hazardous Materials Information Review Act (Human Resources & Skills Development)
Appeal Board Procedures Regulations
Hazardous Material Information Review Regulations
Hazardous Products Act
Carbonated Beverage Glass Containers Regulations
Consumer Chemicals & Containers Regulations
Controlled Products Regulations
Hazardous Products Regulations (Cellulose Insulation, Charcoal, Crocidolite Asbestos, Liquid Coating Materials, etc.)
Ingredient Disclosure List
Health Resources Fund Act
Medical Research Council Act
Narcotic Control Act
Patent Act
Pest Control Products Act, 2002
Pesticide Residue Compensation Act
Quarantine Act
Queen Elizabeth II Canadian Research Fund Act
Radiation Emitting Devices Act
Tobacco Act
Minister, Health, Hon. Leona Aglukkaq
613-992-2848, Fax: 613-996-9764
Aglukkaq.L@parl.gc.ca; Minister_Ministre@hc-sc.gc.ca
Other Communications: Health Canada, Phone: 613-957-0200
Deputy Minister, Glenda Yeates
613-957-0212, Fax: 613-952-8422
glenda.yeates@hc-sc.gc.ca
Assistant Deputy Minister, Meena Ballantyne
613-957-1804, Fax: 613-957-3954
meena.ballantyne@hc-sc.gc.ca

Director General, Jane Hazel
613-957-0215, Fax: 613-948-8092
jane.hazel@hc-sc.gc.ca
Director General, Michelle Kovacevic
613-957-3402, Fax: 613-952-5770
michelle_kovacevic@hc-sc.gc.ca
Chief Scientist, Wendy Sexsmith
613-941-3003, Fax: 613-941-3007
wendy.sexsmith@hc-sc.gc.ca
• Canadian Institutes of Health Research
• Hazardous Materials Information Review Commission(HMIRC) / Conseil de contrôle des renseignements relatifs aux matières dangereuses
427 Laurier Ave. West, 7th Fl.
Ottawa, ON K1A 1M3
613-993-4331
Fax: 613-993-4686
hmirc-ccrmd@hc-sc.gc.ca
www.hmirc-ccrmd.gc.ca
President/CEO, Sharon Watts
Independent agency that examines applications from suppliers & employers seeking exemptions from WHMIS disclosure requirements. Reviews the product labels & material safety data sheets related to claims &, if satisfied, keeps the actual ingredients on file & issues confidential numbers to safeguard the formulas. Fees are charged for the screening process & for administering appeals against the Commission's decisions.
• Pest Management Regulatory Agency(PMRA) / Agence de réglementation de la lutte antiparasitaire (ARLA)
2720 Riverside Dr.
Ottawa, ON K1A 0K9
613-736-3401
Fax: 613-736-3798
www.pmra-arla.gc.ca
Other Communication: Pesticides Information: 1-800-267-6315
Executive Director, Karen Dodds
The PMRA is responsible for protecting human health & the environment by minimizing the risks associated with pest control products. The Agency carries out its responsibility by evaluating pesticides to ensure they meet the latest human health & environmental safety standards before being registered for use in Canada; re-evaluating older pesticides to ensure they remain acceptable for use based on the latest standards; & setting the safe residue levels for pesticides in food. The Agency collaborates with Environment Canada, Agriculture & Agri-Food Canada, the Canadian Food Inspection Agency& other organizations in environmental pesticide research & monitoring, including sustainable pest management.
• Public Health Agency of Canada
130 Colonnade Rd.
Ottawa, ON K1A 0K9
www.phac-aspc.gc.ca/new_e.html
Chief Public Health Officer, Dr. David Butler-Jones
Promotes & protects the health & safety of all Canadians. Its activities focus on preventing chronic diseases, including cancer & heart disease, preventing injuries, & responding to public health emergencies & infectious disease outbreaks.

Corporate Services Branch / Direction générale aux services de gestion
Fax: 613-952-7580

First Nations & Inuit Health Branch / Direction générale de la santé des Premières nations et des Inuits
Fax: 613-957-1118
Assists First Nations & Inuit communities & people to address health inequalities & diseases threats through health surveillance & population health interventions. Ensures the availability of, or access to, health services for First Nations & Inuit people. Devolves control & management of community-based health services to First Nations & Inuit communities & organizations. The Environmental Health Division addresses conditions in the environment that could affect the health of community members, such as drinking water quality, mould, food safety, facilities inspections, transportation of dangerous goods. The Environmental Research Division conducts, coordinates & funds contaminants-related research, coordinates the replacement or upgrading of diesel-fuel tanks & remediation of fuel oil-contaminated sites, lab services for testing of PCBs & mercury, drinking water-related research & testing.
Acting Asst. Deputy Minister, Michelle Kovacevic
613-957-7700,
michelle.kovacevic@hc-sc.gc.ca
Director General Primary Health Care & Public Health, Shelagh Jane Woods

613-941-1956, Fax: 613-941-8904
shelagh.jane.woods@hc-sc.gc.ca
Director Environmental Health, Ivy Chan
613-948-7773, Fax: 613-952-8639
ivy.chan@hc-sc.gc.ca
Director Environmental Health Research, Roy Kwiatkowski
613-952-2828, Fax: 613-954-0692
roy.kwiatkowski@hc-sc.gc.ca
Manager Drinking Water Program, Dominique Poulin
613-954-6655, Fax: 613-952-8639
dominique.poulin@hc-sc.gc.ca

Fort Qu'Appelle Indian Hospital
Fort Qu'appelle, SK S0G 1S0
306-332-5611

Mayo General Hospital
Mayo, YT Y0B 1M0
867-996-2345

Moose Factory General Hospital
Moose Factory, ON P0L 1W0
705-658-4544

Percy E. Moore Hospital
Hodgson, MB R0C 1N0
204-372-8444

Sioux Lookout Zone Hospital
Sioux Lookout, ON P0V 2T0
807-737-3030

Whitehorse General Hospital
5 Hospital Rd.
Whitehorse, YT Y1A 3H8
867-668-9444

Health Policy / Direction générale de la politique de la santé
Fax: 613-954-0336

Health Products & Food Branch / Produits de santé et des aliments
HPFB's mandate is to take an integrated apporach to the management of risks & benefits related to health products & food by minimizing health factors to Canadians while maximizing the safety provided by the regulatory system for health products & food; & to promote conditions that enable Canadians to make healthy choices & provide information so that they can make informed decisions about their health. The Environmental Impact Initiative develops strategy & policy in response to the Canadian Environmental Protection Act requirement that all new substances for use in Canada must be assessed f or direct & indirect impact on human health & the environment.
Asst. Deputy Minister, Meena Ballantyne
613-957-1804, Fax: 613-957-3954
meena.ballantyne@hc-sc.gc.ca
Director Environmental Impact Initiative, Gordon Stringer
613-957-6682, Fax: 613-954-1556
gordon.stringer@hc-sc.gc.ca

Healthy Environments & Consumer Safety Branch / Santé environnementale et sécurité des consommateurs
613-946-6700
Fax: 613-946-6666
www.hc-sc.gc.ca/ahc-asc/branch-dirgen/hecs-dgsesc/index-eng.php
The Healthy Environments & Consumer Safety Branch promotes healthy & safe living, working & recreational environments with emphasis on health in the work environment & occupational health & safety. It assesses & reduces health risks posed by environmental factors & it regulates the safety of industrial & consumer goods. The branch also regulates tobacco & controlled substances, coordinates Canada's Drug Strategy, promotes initiatives that reduce or prevent the harm associated with tobacco, alcohol & other substances, & provides expert advice & drug analysis services to law enforcement agencies across the country. Finally, it is responsible for coordinating & monitoring Health Canada's Sustainable Development Strategy
Asst. Deputy Minister, Paul Glover
613-946-6701,
paul.glover@hc-sc.gc.ca
Director General Policy, Planning & Integration Directorate, Hilary Geller
613-946-6706, Fax: 613-954-5268
hilary.geller@hc-sc.gc.ca
Director Environmental Health Science & Research, David Blakey

Federal/Provincial Government / Government of Canada

613-957-3966, Fax: 613-957-3952
david.blakey@hc-sc.gc.ca
Director Office of Controlled Substances, Diane Allan
613-952-2177, Fax: 613-946-4224
diane.allan@hc-sc.gc.ca
Director Office of Workforce Initiatives, Debbie Holbrook
613-952-8773, Fax: 613-946-5692
debbie.holbrook@hc-sc.gc.ca
Director Water, Air & Climate Change Bureau, John Cooper
613-948-2568, Fax: 613-952-2574
john.cooper@hc-sc.gc.ca

Alberta
9700 Jasper Ave.
Edmonton, AB T5J 4C3
780-495-5147
Fax: 780-495-5551

Atlantic
1505 Barrington St.
Halifax, NS B3J 3Y6
902-426-6861
Fax: 902-426-3768

British Columbia
757 Hastings St. West
Vancouver, BC V6C 3E6
604-666-2396
Fax: 604-775-8716

Manitoba/Saskatchewan Region
391 York Ave.
Winnipeg, MB R3C 4W1
204-983-4764
Fax: 204-983-5325

Northern Region
60 Queen St.
Ottawa, ON K1A 0K9
613-954-2038
Fax: 613-948-2428

Ontario
180 Queen St. West
Toronto, ON M5V 3L7
416-954-3593
Fax: 416-954-3599

Québec
Guy-Favreau Complexe, Tour Est
200, boul René-Lévesque ouest, 2e étage
Montréal, QC H2Z 1X4
514-283-2569
Fax: 514-283-1364

Assets Management Directorate / Gestion des biens
Fax: 613-954-0737

Departmental Planning & Financial Administration Directorate / Planification ministérielle et administration financière
Fax: 613-957-4020

Community Programs Directorate
613-954-5810

Non-Insured Health Benefits Directorate / Direction des Services de santé non assurés
Fax: 613-941-6249

Intergovernmental Affairs Directorate / Direction des affaires entre gouvernement
Fax: 613-957-2726

Food Directorate / Direction des aliments
613-957-0365
Fax: 613-941-5070
Research, analysis of risk & benefit & policy development regarding chemical & microbiological contaminants of food, food processes, genetically modified foods.
Director General, Janet Beauvais
613-957-1821
Acting Director Bureau of Food Safety Assessment, Ashwani Wadhera
613-954-2996
Director Bureau of Chemical Safety, Samuel Benrejeb
613-957-0973

Healthcare Policy
Fax: 613-954-0336

International Affairs Directorate / Direction des affaires internationaux

Policy, Planning & Priorities Directorate / Politiques, planifications et priorités
Fax: 613-957-2738

Safe Environments Programme
Environmental Health Centre, Bldg. 8
120 Parkdale Ave.
Ottawa, ON K1A 0K9
613-954-0291
Fax: 613-952-2206
Investigates, monitors & assesses health risks in the work, home & natural environments. Areas investigated & regulated include: medical devices, chemicals & biotechnology products in the environment, drinking water, air quality, tobacco, hazardous products & toxic waste, as well as anything that emits radiation from natural & human sources. Aims to protect Canadians from health hazards associated with natural & man-made environments through assessment & investigation of the health effects of environmental pollutants & health hazards associated with radiation sources & hazardous products.
Director General, Paul Glover
613-954-0291, Fax: 613-952-2206
Director Environmental Health Science Bureau, David Blakey
613-957-3966, Fax: 613-957-3952
Director Radiation Protection Bureau, Jack Cornett
613-954-6647, Fax: 613-952-9071
Director Water, Air & Climate Change Bureau, John Cooper
613-948-2568, Fax: 613-952-2574
Director Bureau of Risk & Impact Assessment, Steve Clarkson
613-957-3133

Workplace Hazardous Materials Information System (WHMIS)
Fax: 613-952-1994
www.hc-sc.gc.ca/ewh-semt/occup-travail/whmis-simdut/index_e.html
A nationwide hazard communication system providing information on hazardous materials used in the workplace. Key elements of the system are cautionary labelling on containers of hazardous materials, material safety data sheets (MSDSs) that contain more detailed information, & worker training. Suppliers must ensure that products are appropriately labelled & that MSDSs are provided to purchasers. Employers are required to make MSDSs available to their employees & provide workers with training on WHMIS & the safe use of hazardous materials. WHMIS supports the workers' right to know the hazards of the materials they use. WHMIS requirements are administered through federal & provincial coordinators.

Workplace Health & Public Safety
Vanguard Bldg.
171 Slater St., 9th Fl.
Ottawa, ON K1A 0K9
corporate_whpsp@hc-sc.gc.ca
Workplace Health & Public Safety Programme (WHPSP) is responsible for helping Canadian private & public sector employers maintain & improve the health of their workers. WHPSP provides national leadership to develop health policy, best practices in the workplace, & enhance healthy living for all working Canadians.
Director General, Stéphane Hardy
613-957-7669, Fax: 613-954-5822
stephane_hardy@hc-sc.gc.ca

Drug Strategy & Controlled Substances Programme / Stratégie antidrogue et substances controlés

Office of Tobacco Control Program / Bureau pour le contrôle du tabac

Product Safety Programme / Programme de la sécurité des produits

Alberta Region
Harry Hayes Bldg.
#654, 220 - 4 Ave. SE
Calgary, AB T2G 4X3
Fax: 403-292-6629

Atlantic Region
1081 Main St., 5th Fl.
PO Box 6088
Moncton, NB E1C 8R2
Fax: 506-851-2689

British Columbia Region
#101, 620 Royal Ave.
Westminister, BC V3M 1J2
Fax: 604-666-6130

Manitoba Region
#613, 269 Main St.
Winnipeg, MB R3C 1B2
Fax: 204-983-8022

Ontario Region
174 Stone Rd. West
Guelph, ON N1G 4S9
Fax: 519-837-9773

Québec Region
746-E, 2001, Université
Montréal, QC H3A 3N2
Fax: 514-283-1919

Saskatchewan Region
Walter Scott Bldg.
#300, 3085 Albert St.
PO Box 8060
Regina, SK S4P 4E3
Fax: 306-780-5177

Human Resources & Skills Development Canada (HRSDC) / Ressources humaines et Développement des compétences Canada (RHDCC)
140 Promenade du Portage
Ottawa, ON K1A 0J9
www.hrsdc.gc.ca
Other Communication: Employment Insurance: 1-800-206-7218; Income Security Programs: 1-800-277-9914
HRSDC works to build a competitive country & to support Canadians in making choices to live productively. The following are key responsibilities of the federal department: developing policies to assist Canadaians to use their talents, skills & resources to participate in learning, work, & their community; creating programs to support initiative to help citizens in life transitions; improving outcomes for people through services offered by Service Canada & other partners; & establishing a healthy work environment.

Acts Administered:
Canada Labour Code
Aviation Occupational Safety & Health Regulations
Canada Occupational Health & Safety Regulations
Coal Mines (CBDC) Occupational Safety & Health Regulations
Coal Mining Safety Commission Regulations
Marine Occupational Safety & Health Regulations
Oil & Gas Occupational Safety & Health Regulations
On Board Trains Occupational Safety & Health Regulations
Canada Pension Plan
Canada Student Financial Assistance Act
Canada Student Loans Act
Canadian Centre for Occupational Health & Safety Act
Corporations & Labour Unions Returns Act
Department of Human Resources Development Act
Employment Equity Act
Employment Insurance Act
Fair Wages & Hours of Labour Act
Family Orders & Agreements Enforcement Assistance Act
Federal-Provincial Fiscal Arrangements Act
Government Annuities Act
Government Employees Compensation Act
Labour Adjustment Benefits Act
Merchant Seamen Compensation Act
Non-smokers' Health Act (Transport Canada)
Old Age Security Act
Status of the Artist Act
Unemployment Assistance Act
Vocational Rehabilitation of Disabled Persons Act
Wages Liability Act
Minister, Human Resources & Skills Development, Hon. Diane Finley, B.A., M.B.A.
613-996-4974, Fax: 613-996-9749
Finley.D@parl.gc.ca; diane.finley@hrsdc-rhdsc.gc.ca
Minister, Labour, Hon. Lisa Raitt
613-996-7046, Fax: 613-992-0851
Raitt.L@parl.gc.ca
Other Communications: Labour, Phone: 819-953-5646, Fax: 819-994-5168
Deputy Minister of Human Resources & Skills Development Canada, Ian Shugart

819-994-4514, Fax: 819-953-5603
ian.shugart@hrsdc-rhdcc.gc.ca
• Canada Employment Insurance Commission(CEIC) /
Commission de l'assurance-emploi du Canada (CAEC)
140, Promenade du Portage, Phase IV
Gatineau, QC K1A 0J9
800-206-7218
www.ei-ae.gc.ca
• Canada Industrial Relations Board
• Canadian Centre for Occupational Health & Safety
• Canadian Council of Directors of Apprenticeship
140 Promenade du Portage, 5th Fl, Phase IV
Gatineau, QC K1A 0J9
819-953-7443
Fax: 819-994-0202
redseal-sceaurouge@hrsdc-rhdcc.gc.ca
www.red-seal.ca
• Merchant Seamen Compensation Board
Secretary, Merchant Seamen Compensation Board
Phase II, Place du Portage, 10th Fl.
Gatineau, QC K1A 0J2
819-953-8001
Fax: 819-994-5368
• Office of the Commissioner of Review Tribunals
PO Box 8250 T
Ottawa, ON K1G 5S5
613-954-1313
Fax: 613-946-1588
800-363-0076
info@ocrt-bctr.gc.ca
www.ocrt-bctr.gc.ca
• Pension Appeals Board
PO Box 8567 T
Ottawa, ON K1G 3H9
613-995-0612
Fax: 613-995-6834
888-640-8001
info@pab-cap.gc.ca
www.pab-cap.gc.ca

Citizen Service Branch / Direction générale de service aux citoyens

Corporate Stakeholder Relations / Relations avec les intervenants
Part II of the Canada Labour Code - Occupational Health & Safety - promotes & enforces federal occupational safety & health legislation & regulations. The Labour Program also uses its technical expertise in specialized fields such as industrial hygiene & industrial safety engineering to administer the legislation.

Homelessness Partnering Secretariat / Secrétariat des partenariats de lutte contre l'itinérance
165, rue Hôtel-de-Ville
Gatineau, QC K1A 0J2

Labour / Travail
Deputy Minister, Hélène Gosselin
819-934-3320, Fax: 819-934-7066
gosselin.helene@labour-travail.gc.ca
Asst. Deputy Minister, Marie-Geneviève Mounier
819-997-1493, Fax: 819-953-5685
mg.mounier@labour-travail.gc.ca
Senior Director Labour Standards & Workplace Equity, Jan Michaels
819-934-5745, Fax: 819-997-3701
jan.michaels@labour-travail.gc.ca
Director Occupational Health & Safety Tribunal Canada, Pierre Rousseau
613-957-6344, Fax: 613-954-6404
pierre.rousseau@ohstc-tsstc.gc.ca
Laboratory Manager, Ian Fraser
613-990-8423, Fax: 613-990-7709
ian.fraser@labour-travail.gc.ca

Learning Branch / Apprentissage

Service Canada
140, Promenade du Portage
Gatineau, QC K1A 0J9
800-622-6232
TDD: 800-926-9105
www.servicecanada.gc.ca

Service Canada was created in 2005 to improve the delivery of government programs and services to Canadians, by making access to them faster, easier, and more convenient. Service Canada offers single-window access to a wide range of Government of Canada programs and services for citizens through more than 600 points of service located across the country, call centres, and the Internet.
Senior Assist. Deputy Minister, Carolina Giliberti
819-934-1504, Fax: 819-934-1505
carolina.giliberti@servicecanada.gc.ca
Head Service Delivery, Robin Flaherty
613-991-8061, Fax: 613-941-1827
robin.flaherty@servicecanada.gc.ca

Service Canada Centres:

Calgary Centre
#270, 220 - 4 Ave. SE
Calgary, AB T2G 4X3
Fax: 403-292-6561
800-622-6232

Calgary East
#1502, 515 Marlborough Way NE
Calgary, AB T2A 7E7
Fax: 403-292-6845
800-622-6232

Calgary North
1816 Crowchild Trail NW
PO Box 65037 North Hill
Calgary, AB T2N 4T6
Fax: 403-292-4076
800-622-6232

Calgary South
Fisher Park Place II
#100, 6712 Fisher St. SE
Calgary, AB T2H 1X3
Fax: 403-292-5763
800-622-6232

Cambridge Bay
15 Amogok
PO Box 2010
Cambridge Bay, NU X0C 0E0
867-983-4025
800-622-6232

Camrose
4901 - 50 Ave.
Camrose, AB T2H 1X3
780-672-1440
800-622-6232

Canmore
Bldg. C
#113, 802 Bow Valley Trail
Canmore, AB T1W 1N6
403-609-6456
800-622-6232

Edmonton Canada Place
Canada Place
#1440, 9700 Jasper Ave.
Edmonton, AB T5J 4C1
800-829-6891
Other Communication: Toll Free Fax: 1-800-622-6232

Edmonton Meadowlark
#120, 15710 - 87 Ave. NW
Edmonton, AB T5R 5W9
Fax: 780-495-7717
800-622-6232

Edmonton North
#2000, 9499 - 137 Ave. NW
Edmonton, AB T5E 5R8
780-495-3904
800-622-6232

Edmonton South
6325 Gateway Blvd.
Edmonton, AB T6H 5H6
Fax: 780-495-3902
800-622-6232

Edson
#102, 111 - 54 St.
Edson, AB T7E 1T2

780-723-3634
800-622-6232

Fort McMurray
9915 Franklin Ave.
Fort McMurray, AB T9H 2K4
800-622-6232

Fort Simpson
9606 - 100 St.
PO Box 380
Fort Simpson, NT X0E 0P0
867-695-2238
Fax: 867-695-2229

Fort Smith
136 McDougal Rd.
PO Box 1018
Fort Smith, NT X0E 0P0
867-872-2747
Fax: 867-872-2616

Hay River
#204, 41 Capital Dr.
PO Box 204
Hay River, NT X0E 1G2
867-874-6739
Fax: 867-874-6100

Red Deer
4911 - 51 St., 2nd Fl.
PO Box 5050
Lethbridge, AB T4N 6A1
Fax: 403-341-7105
800-622-6232

Grande Prairie
#100, 9845 - 99 Ave.
Grande Prairie, AB T8V 0R3
Fax: 780-532-3488
800-622-6232

Inuvik
170 McKenzie Rd.
PO Box 1678
Inuvik, NT X0E 0T0
867-777-2122
Fax: 867-777-4369

Iqaluit
#300, Iqaluit House
PO Box 639
Iqaluit, NU X0A 0H0
867-975-4700
Fax: 867-975-4711

Lethbridge
200 - 5 Ave. South
Lethbridge, AB T1J 4L1
Fax: 403-381-5668
800-622-6232

Lloydminster
5016 - 48 St.
Lloydminster, AB T9V 0H8
780-871-7065
800-622-6232

Medicine Hat
#4, 346 - 3 St. SE
Medicine Hat, AB T1A 0G7
403-529-1755
800-622-6232

Rankin Inlet
PO Box 97
Rankin Inlet, NU X0C 0G0
867-645-4092
800-260-0877

St Paul
5126 - 50 Ave.
St Paul, AB T0A 3A0
780-645-777
800-622-6232

Slave Lake
101 Main St. South, 2nd Fl.
Slave Lake, AB T0G 2A0
780-849-3377
800-622-6232

Federal/Provincial Government / Government of Canada

Yellowknife
5101 - 50 Ave.
PO Box 1170
Yellowknife, NT X1A 3Z4
867-766-8300
Fax: 867-873-3621

BC/Yukon Regional Headquarters
#1400, 300 Georgia St. West
Vancouver, BC V6B 6G3
604-666-2282
Fax: 604-666-8222
Other Communication: BC/Yukon Email:
bcytprograminquiry@servicecanada.gc.ca

Abbotsford
32525 Simon Ave.
Abbotsford, BC V2T 6T6
604-854-5852
Fax: 604-870-2765

Burnaby
4729 Canada Way
Burnaby, BC V5G 4Y2
604-437-3761
Fax: 604-666-1015

Central & Northern Vancouver Island
#201, 60 Front St.
Nanaimo, BC V9R 5H7
250-754-0222
Fax: 250-754-0319

Coquitlam
#100, 2963 Glen Dr.
Coquitlam, BC V3B 2P7
604-464-7144
Fax: 604-945-1600

CPP/OAS BC/Yukon Processing Centre
PO Box 1177
Victoria, BC V8W 2V2
800-277-9914
bcytispinquiry@servicecanada.gc.c
Other Communication: Ligne sans frais: 1-800-277-9915

Kamloops
235 Lansdowne St.
Kamloops, BC V2C 1X8
250-372-2515
Fax: 250-372-0761

Kelowna
471 Queensway Ave.
Kelowna, BC V1Y 6S5
250-762-3018
Fax: 250-762-0357

Nelson
333 Victoria St.
Nelson, BC V1L 4K3
250-352-3155
Fax: 250-352-5170

North Shore
#100, 221 West Esplanade
North Vancouver, BC V7M 3N7
604-988-1151
Fax: 604-666-6494

Prince George
1363 - 4 Ave.
Prince George, BC V2L 3J6
250-561-5200
Fax: 250-561-5504

Southern Vancouver Island
595 Pandora Ave.
Victoria, BC V8W 1N5
250-220-3200
Fax: 250-363-0553

Surrey
7404 King George Hwy.
Surrey, BC V3W 0L4
604-590-3346
Fax: 604-590-5351

Terrace
4630 Lazelle Ave.
Terrace, BC V8G 1S6

250-635-7134
Fax: 250-635-4073

Vancouver
125 - 10 Ave. East
Vancouver, BC V5T 1Z3
604-872-7431
Fax: 604-666-1205

Whitehorse
#125, 300 Main St.
Whitehorse, YT Y1A 2B5
867-667-5083
Fax: 867-668-6801

Brandon
1039 Princess Ave.
Brandon, MB R7A 6E2
204-726-7700
Fax: 204-726-7744

Dauphin
135 - 2 Ave. NE
Dauphin, MB R7N 0Z6
Fax: 204-622-4045
800-622-6232

Flin Flon
111 Main St.
Flin Flon, MB R8A 1J9
Fax: 204-687-4607
TDD: 800-622-6232

La Verendrye
#100, 614 Des Meurons St.
Winnipeg, MB R2H 2P9
204-984-3438
Fax: 204-983-3719

Morden
158 Stephen St.
Morden, MB R6M 1T3
204-822-7370
Fax: 204-822-7384

Notre-Dame-des-Lourdes
51 Rodgers St.
PO Box 82
Notre Dame de Lourdes, QC R0G 1M0
204-248-7201
Fax: 204-248-7207

Portage la Prairie
1016 Saskatchewan Ave. East
Portage la Prairie, MB R1N 3V2
Fax: 204-239-8432
800-622-6232

Saint-Pierre-Jolys
427 Sabourin St.
PO Box 98
Saint-Pierre-Jolys, MB R0A 1V0
204-433-7373
Fax: 204-433-7356

Selkirk
237 Manitoba Ave.
PO Box 7000
Selkirk, MB R1A 2M8
204-785-6200
Fax: 204-785-6222

Steinbach
321 Main St.
Steinbach, MB R5G 1Z2
204-326-1371
Fax: 204-326-1275

Swan River
201 - 4 Ave. South
Swan River, MB R0L 1Z0
Fax: 204-734-5151
800-206-7218

The Pas
305 - 4 Ave. SW
PO Box 660
The Pas, MB
Fax: 204-623-7205
800-623-2

Thompson
#118, 3 Station Rd.
Thompson, MB R8N 0N3
Fax: 204-677-7147
800-622-6232

Winnipeg Centre
#201, 391 York Ave.
PO Box 8850
Winnipeg, MB R3C 3E6
Fax: 204-984-8029
800-206-7218

Winnipeg Northeast
1122 Henderson Hwy.
Winnipeg, MB R2G 1L1
Fax: 204-983-4404
800-622-6232

Winnipeg Southwest
3338 Portage Ave.
Winnipeg, MB R3K 0Z1
Fax: 204-983-0319
800-206-7218

Winnipeg St. Boniface
1031 Autumnwood Dr.
Winnipeg, MB R2J 1C6
Fax: 204-983-0535
800-206-7218

Bathurst
120 Harbourview Blvd.
PO Box 4000
Bathurst, NB E2A 1R6
506-548-7998
Fax: 506-548-7186

Campbellton
157 Water St.
PO Box 5002
Campbellton, NB E3N 3L3
Fax: 506-789-4547
800-206-7218

Edmundston
22 Emmerson St.
Edmundston, NB E3V 1R7
506-739-0222
Fax: 506-739-0228
nb.inquiries@hrdc-drhc.gc.ca

Fredericton
633 Queen St.
PO Box 12000
Fredericton, NB E3B 5G4
506-452-3823
Fax: 506-452-3303

Miramichi
150 Pleasant St.
PO Box 1030
Miramichi, NB E1V 1Y1
506-627-2033
Fax: 506-627-2049
nb.inquiries@hrdc-dhrc.gc.ca

Moncton
#310, 95 Foundry St.
PO Box 5003
Moncton, NB E1C 8R5
506-851-6718
Fax: 506-851-6941

Saint John
1 Agar Place
PO Box 7000
Saint John, NB E2L 4V4
Fax: 506-636-3808
800-206-7218

Clarenville
50 Manitoba Dr.
Clarenville, NL A5A 1K5
709-466-8200
Fax: 709-466-8210

Corner Brook
1 Regent Sq.
PO Box 2004
Corner Brook, NL A2H 49I

Federal/Provincial Government / Government of Canada

709-637-4243
Fax: 709-637-4224

Gander
1 Markham Place
PO Box 347
Gander, NL A1V 1W7
709-256-6519
Fax: 709-256-6506

Happy Valley-Goose Bay
23 Broomfield St.
PO Box 3010 B
Happy Valley-Goose Bay, NL A0P 1E0
709-896-6270
Fax: 709-896-6268

Labrador West
500 Vanier Ave.
Labrador City, NL A2V 2W7
709-944-3655
Fax: 709-944-3381

Placentia
61 Blockhouse Rd.
PO Box 339
Placentia, NL A0B 2Y0
709-227-4001
Fax: 709-227-5588

Port Aux Basques
#4, 10 High St.
PO Box 849
Port aux Basques, NL A0M 1C0
709-695-5002
Fax: 709-695-9671

St. John's
223 Churchill Ave.
PO Box 8548
St. John's, NL A1B 3P3
709-772-2982
Fax: 709-772-0354

Amherst
#202, 26-28 Prince Arthur St.
Amherst, NS B4H 1V6
902-661-6619
Fax: 902-661-6637

Antigonish
325 Main St., 2nd Fl.
Antigonish, NS B2G 2C3
902-863-7069
Fax: 902-863-7053

Bedford
1597 Bedford Hwy.
PO Box 44176
Bedford, NS B4A 1E7
902-426-7698
Fax: 902-426-5552

Bridgewater
77 Dufferin St.
PO Box 3100
Bridgewater, NS B4V 3J1
902-527-5524
Fax: 902-527-5570

Dartmouth
46 Portland St.
PO Box 2400
Dartmouth, NS B2Y 1H3
902-426-5512
Fax: 902-426-7301

Digby
84 Warwick St.
PO Box 1540
Digby, NS B0V 1A0
902-245-4784
Fax: 902-245-6226

Glace Bay
#201, 633 Main St.
Glace Bay, NS B1A 6J3
902-842-2414
Fax: 902-842-2655

Halifax
7001 Mumford Rd.
PO Box 1800
Halifax, NS B3J 3V1
902-426-9617
Fax: 902-426-7690

Kentville
495 Main St., 2nd Fl.
Kentville, NS B4N 3W5
902-679-5772
Fax: 902-679-5786

New Glasgow
340 East River Rd.
New Glasgow, NS B2H 3P7
902-755-7826
Fax: 902-755-7869

North Sydney
105 King St.
North Sydney, NS B2A 3S1
902-794-5715
Fax: 902-794-5724

Port Hawkesbury
#8, 811 Reeves St.
Port Hawkesbury, NS B9A 2S4
902-625-4115
Fax: 902-625-4137

Shelburne
218 Water St.
PO Box 819
Shelburne, NS B0T 1W0
902-875-3940
Fax: 902-875-3505

Sydney
15 Dorchester St.
PO Box 850
Sydney, NS B1P 6J3
902-564-7249
Fax: 902-564-7104

Truro
#8, 60 Lorne St.
Truro, NS B2N 3K3
902-893-0016
Fax: 902-893-0075

Windsor
90 Water St.
PO Box 2760
Windsor, NS B0N 2T0
902-798-6518
Fax: 902-798-5816

Yarmouth
13 Willow St.
PO Box 249
Yarmouth, NS B5A 4B2
902-742-6178
Fax: 902-742-0815

Ajax
320 Harwood Ave.
Ajax, ON L1S 2J1
905-725-2001
Fax: 905-428-8410
ontario.inquiry@hrsdc-rhdcc.gc.ca

Arnprior
#1 & 2, 75 Elgin St. West
Arnprior, ON K7S 3T9
613-623-3173
Fax: 613-623-2104
ontario.inquiry@hrsdc-rhdcc.gc.ca

Bancroft
5 Fairway Blvd.
Bancroft, ON K0L 1C0
Fax: 613-332-5517
800-206-7218
ontario.inquiry@hrsdc-rhdcc.gc.ca

Barrie
#301, 48 Owen St.
Barrie, ON L4M 3H1
705-728-2468
Fax: 705-725-2501
ontario.inquiry@hrsdc-rhdcc.gc.ca

Belleville
1 North Front St., 2nd Fl.
PO Box 4800
Belleville, ON K8N 5E2
613-969-3350
Fax: 613-969-3347
ontario.inquiry@hrsdc-rhdcc.gc.ca

Bracebridge
98 Manitoba St., 2nd Fl.
Bracebridge, ON P1L 1S1
705-645-2204
Fax: 705-645-7313
ontario.inquiry@hrsdc-rhdcc.gc.ca

Brampton
18 Corporation Dr.
Brampton, ON L6S 6B2
905-790-2525
Fax: 905-789-3885
ontario.inquiry@hrsdc-rhdcc.gc.ca

Brantford
58 Dalhousie St., 2nd Fl.
Brantford, ON N3T 2J2
519-751-6500
Fax: 519-751-6529
ontario.inquiry@hrsdc-rhdcc.gc.ca

Brockville
153 King St. West
Brockville, ON K6V 3R4
613-342-4487
Fax: 613-342-7580
ontario.inquiry@hrsdc-rhdcc.gc.ca

Burlington
440 Elizaebth St.
Burlington, ON L7R 2M1
905-637-4525
Fax: 905-637-9585
ontario.inquiry@hrsdc-rhdcc.gc.ca

Cambridge
73 Water St. North
Cambridge, ON N1R 7L6
519-579-1550
Fax: 519-571-5508
ontario.inquiry@hrsdc-rhdcc.gc.ca

Carleton Place
46 Lansdowne Ave.
Carleton Place, ON K7C 3S9
613-257-3344
Fax: 613-257-2505
ontario.inquiry@hrsdc-rhdcc.gc.ca

Chatham-Kent
120 Wellington St. West
Chatham, ON N7M 4V9
519-380-6800
Fax: 519-380-6846
ontario.inquiry@hrsdc-rhdcc.gc.ca

Cobourg
#103, 1005 Elgin St. West
Cobourg, ON K9A 5J4
905-372-3326
Fax: 905-372-1277
ontario.inquiry@hrsdc-rhdcc.gc.ca

Collingwood
44 Hurontonario St.
Collingwood, ON L9Y 2L6
705-445-1010
Fax: 705-445-8643

Cornwall
111 Water St. East
Cornwall, ON K6H 6S4
613-938-5731
Fax: 613-938-9876
ontario.inquiry@hrsdc-rhdcc.gc.ca

Dryden
41C Duke St.
Dryden, ON P8N 1E6

Federal/Provincial Government / Government of Canada

807-223-2331
Fax: 807-223-6615
ontario.inquiry@hrsdc-rhdcc.gc.ca

Elliot Lake
151 Ontario Ave.
Elliot Lake, ON P5A 2T2
705-848-2231
Fax: 705-848-0971
ontario.inquiry@hrsdc-rhdcc.gc.ca

Espanola
#200, 800 Centre St.
Espanola, ON P5E 1J3
705-869-7030
Fax: 705-869-7035
ontario.inquiry@hrsdc0rhdcc.gc.ca

Fort Frances
301 Scott St.
Fort Frances, ON P9A 1H1
807-274-5307
Fax: 807-274-7858
ontario.inquiry@hrsdc-rhdcc.gc.ca

Gananoque
5 Charles St. South
Gananoque, ON K7G 1V9
613-382-2124
Fax: 613-382-8942
ontario.inquiry@hrsdc-rhdcc.gc.ca

Georgetown
232 Guelph St.
Georgetown, ON L7G 4B1
905-877-6915
Fax: 905-877-4370
ontario.inquiry@hrsdc-hrdcc.gc.ca

Geraldton
208 Beamish St.
PO Box 640
Geraldton, ON P0T 1M0
807-854-0635
Fax: 807-854-0335
ontario.inquiry@hrsdc-rhdcc.gc.ca

Goderich
52 East St.
Goderich, ON N7A 1N3
519-524-8342
Fax: 519-524-6809
ontario.inquiry@hrsdc-rhdcc.gc.ca

Guelph
259 Woodlawn Rd. West, Unit C
Guelph, ON N1H 8J1
Fax: 519-826-2257
800-265-3595
ontario.inquiry@hrsdc-rhdcc.gc.ca

Hamilton Central/East
2255 Barton St. East
Hamilton, ON L8H 7T4
905-572-2211
Fax: 905-573-4117
ontario.inquiry@hrsdc-rhdcc.gc.ca

Hamilton Mountain
1550 Upper James St.
PO Box 2066 A
Hamilton, ON L9B 1K3
905-572-2211
Fax: 905-572-2563
ontario.inquiry@hrsdc-rhdcc.gc.ca

Hawkesbury
134 Main St. East
Hawkesbury, ON K6A 1A3
613-632-2759
Fax: 613-632-6976

Kapuskasing
8 Queen St.
Kapuskasing, ON P5N 1G7
705-335-2337
Fax: 705-337-1197
ontario.inquiry@hrsdc-rhdcc.gc.ca

Kenora
308 Second St. South, 2nd Fl.
PO Box 5170
Kenora, ON P9N 3X9
807-467-5700
Fax: 807-468-6209
ontairo.inquiry@hrsdc-rhdcc.gc.ca

Kingston
299 Concession St.
Kingston, ON K7L 5H5
613-545-8559
Fax: 613-545-8808

Kirkland Lake
10 Government Rd. East
PO Box 576
Kirkland Lake, ON P2N 1A2
705-567-9205
Fax: 705-568-8086
ontario.inquiry@hrsdc-rhdcc.gc.ca

Kitchener
409 Weber St. West
PO Box 9011
Kitchener, ON N2G 4L6
519-579-1550
Fax: 519-571-5508
ontario.inquiry@hrsdc-rhdcc.gc.ca

Leamington
215 Talbot St. East
Leamington, ON N8H 3X5
519-326-8695
Fax: 519-326-9203
ontario.inquiry@hrsdc-rhdcc.gc.ca

Lindsay
65 Kent St. West
Lindsay, ON K9V 2Y3
705-324-3562
Fax: 705-328-1202
ontario.inquiry@hrsdc-rhdcc.gc.ca

Listowel
210 Main St. East
Listowel, ON N4W 2B7
519-291-2920
Fax: 519-291-5848
ontario.inquiry@hrsdc-rhdcc.gc.ca

London
120 Queen's Ave.
PO Box 5711
London, ON N6A 4S7
519-645-5944
Fax: 519-645-4613
ontario.inquiry@hrsdc-rhdcc.gc.ca

Malton
#5, 6877 Goreway Dr.
Mississauga, ON L4V 1L9
905-608-7000
Fax: 905-677-3025
ontario.inquiry@hrsdc-rhdcc.gc.ca

Marathon
#105, 52 Peninsula Rd.
PO Box 958
Marathon, ON P0T 2E0
807-229-0959
Fax: 807-229-1592

Midland
9225 Hwy. 93
Midland, ON L4R 4K4
705-526-2224
Fax: 705-526-0316

Milton
310 Main St. East
Milton, ON L9T 1P4
905-878-8418
Fax: 905-878-6861
ontario.inquiry@hrsdc-rhdcc.gc.ca

Mississauga East
2525 Dixie Rd.
Mississauga, ON L4Y 2A1

905-608-7000
Fax: 905-803-7449
ontario.inquiry@hrsdc-rhdcc.gc.ca

Mississauga West
3085 Glen Erin Dr.
Mississauga, ON L5L 1J3
905-608-7000
Fax: 905-608-7108
ontario.inquiry@hrsdc-rhdcc.gc.ca

Napanee
2 Dairy Ave.
Napanee, ON K7R 3T1
Fax: 613-354-3728
800-206-7218
ontario.inquiry@hrsdc-rhdcc.gc.ca

New Liskeard
290 Armstrong St. North
PO Box 6001
New Liskeard, ON P0J 1P0
705-647-6741
Fax: 705-647-3078
ontario.inquiry@hrsdc-rhdcc.gc.ca

Newmarket
#100, 465 David Dr.
Newmarket, ON L3Y 7T9
905-953-4052
Fax: 905-895-5069
ontario.inquiry@hrsdc-rhdcc.gc.ca

Niagara Falls
5853 Peer St.
Niagara Falls, ON L2G 1X4
905-988-2700
Fax: 905-354-2591
ontario.inquiry@hrsdc-rhdcc.gc.ca

North Bay
#102, 107 Shirreff Ave.
North Bay, ON P1B 7K8
705-472-3700
Fax: 705-472-0870
ontario.inquiry@jrsdc-rhdcc.gc.ca

Oakville
1090 Speers Rd.
Oakville, ON L6L 2X4
Fax: 905-845-4055
800-959-9522

Orangeville
#102, 210 Broadway
Orangeville, ON L9W 5G4
519-941-4898
Fax: 519-941-2504
ontario.inquiry@hrsdc-rhdcc.gc.ca

Orillia
50 Andrew St. South
Orillia, ON L3V 7T5
705-326-7336
Fax: 705-326-6375

Oshawa
78 Richmond St. West
Oshawa, ON L1G 1E1
905-725-2001
Fax: 905-725-7001

Ottawa Centre
300 Laurier Ave. West, Level 2
Ottawa, ON K2P 1W5
613-990-5100
Fax: 613-990-5091

Ottawa East
2339 Ogilvie Rd.
Gloucester, ON K1A 0J6
613-900-5100
Fax: 613-954-0676

Ottawa Government Services Centre
110 Laurier Ave. West
Ottawa, ON K1P 1J1
613-990-5100
Fax: 613-990-5091

Ottawa West
2525 Carling Ave.
Ottawa, ON K2B 7Z2
613-990-5100
Fax: 613-991-1447
ontario.inquiry@hrsdc-rhdcc.gc.ca

Owen Sound
#1, 1450 - 1 Ave. West
Owen Sound, ON N4K 6X7
519-376-4280
Fax: 519-376-4715

Parry Sound
74 James St.
Parry Sound, ON P2A 1T8
705-746-9374
Fax: 705-746-5331

Pembroke
141 Lake St.
Pembroke, ON K8A 5L8
613-735-0681
Fax: 613-735-0047
ontario.inquiry@hrsdc-rhdcc.gc.ca

Perth
13 Herriott St.
PO Box 336
Perth, ON K7H 3E4
613-267-1921
Fax: 613-267-3947

Peterborough
185 King St.
Peterborough, ON K9J 2R8
705-750-4500
Fax: 705-750-4520
ontario.inquiry@hrsdc-rhdcc.gc.ca

Picton
229 Main St.
PO Box 970
Picton, ON K0K 2T0
Fax: 613-476-8569
800-206-7218
ontario.inquiry@hrsdc-rhdcc.gc.ca

Prescott
292 Centre St.
PO Box 1780
Prescott, ON K0E 1T0
613-925-2808
Fax: 613-925-3846
ontario.inquiry@hrsdc-rhdcc.gc.ca

Renfrew
39 Renfrew Ave. West
Renfrew, ON K7V 2Y2
613-432-4878
Fax: 613-432-4087
ontario.inquiry@hrsdc-rhdcc.gc.ca

Richmond Hill
35 Beresford Dr.
Richmond Hill, ON L4B 4M3
905-886-7662
Fax: 905-707-6924
ontario.inquiry@hrsdc-rhdcc.gc.ca

St Catherines
43 Church St.
PO Box 21
St Catharines, ON L2R 5C7
905-988-2700
Fax: 905-988-2722
ontario.inquiry@hrsdc-rhdcc.gc.ca

St Thomas
#400, 408 Talbot St.
PO Box 515
St Thomas, ON N2P 3V6
519-631-5470
Fax: 519-631-3565
ontario.inquiry@hrsdc-rhdcc.gc.ca

Sarnia
150 Christina St. North
Sarnia, ON N7T 7W5

519-464-5025
Fax: 519-464-5040
ontario.inquiry@hrsdc-rhdcc.gc.ca

Sault Ste Marie
22 Bay St.
PO Box 2400
Sault Ste Marie, ON P6A 5S2
705-941-4500
Fax: 705-941-4545
ontario.inquiry@hrsdc-rhdcc.gc.ca

Simcoe
5 Queensway Dr. East
Simcoe, ON N3Y 5K2
519-426-5270
Fax: 519-428-4096
ontario.inquiry@hrsdc-rhdcc.gc.ca

Smiths Falls
#115, 91 Cornelia St. West
Smiths Falls, ON K7A 5L3
613-283-4790
Fax: 613-283-9002

Stratford
100 Albert St.
Stratford, ON N5A 3K4
519-271-4122
Fax: 519-271-7096
ontario.inquiry@hrsdc-rhdcc.gc.ca

Sudbury
19 Lisgar St.
Sudbury, ON P3E 6L1
705-670-6600
Fax: 705-670-6669

Thunder Bay
975 Alloy Dr.
Thunder Bay, ON P7B 6N5
807-346-2000
Fax: 807-346-2132
ontario.inquiry@hrsdc-rhdcc.gc.ca

Tillsonburg
96 Tillson Ave.
Tillsonburg, ON N4G 3A1
519-842-9008
Fax: 519-688-3671
ontario.inquiry@hrsdc-rhdcc.gc.ca

Timmins
#300, 273 Third Ave.
Timmins, ON P4N 1E2
705-267-6271
Fax: 705-267-7099
ontario.inquiry@hrsdc-rhdcc.gc.ca

Toronto Canada Quay
235 Queens Quay West
Toronto, ON M5J 2G8
416-954-6059
Fax: 416-954-6064
ontario.inquiry@hrsdc-rhdcc.gc.ca

Toronto Centre
25 St. Clair Ave. East
Toronto, ON M4T 3A4
416-973-6915
Fax: 416-973-6040
ontario.inquiry@hrsdc-rhdcc.gc.ca

Toronto East
811 Danforth Ave.
Toronto, ON M4J 1L2
416-461-3511
Fax: 416-462-7373
ontario.inquiry@hrsdc-rhdcc.gc.ca

Toronto Etobicoke
Dundas-Kipling Centre, Phase II
#105, 5343 Dundas St. West
Toronto, ON M9B 6K6
416-954-1500
Fax: 416-954-1520
ontario.inquiry@hrsdc-rhdcc.gc.ca

Toronto Lakeside
Dufferin Mall
900 Dufferin St.
Toronto, ON M6H 4B1

416-583-4700
Fax: 416-583-4779
ontario.inquiry@hrsdc-rhdcc.gc.ca

Toronto Lawrence Square
Lawrence Square Mall
700 Lawrence Ave. West
Toronto, ON M6B 4L4
416-780-4100
Fax: 416-954-8814
ontario.inquiry@hrsdc-rhdcc.gc.ca

Toronto North
373 Chesswood Dr.
Toronto, ON M3J 2P6
416-954-8700
Fax: 416-954-8702
ontario.inquiry@hrsdc-rhdcc.gc.ca

Toronto Scarborough
200 Town Centre Ct.
Toronto, ON M1P 4X9
416-973-4400
Fax: 416-973-3434
ontario.inquiry@hrsdc-rhdcc.gc.ca

Toronto Willowdale
4900 Yonge St.
Toronto, ON M2N 6B1
Fax: 416-954-2097
800-277-9914
ontario.inquiry@hrsdc-rhdcc.gc.ca

Trenton
50 Dundas St. West
Trenton, ON K8V 6R5
Fax: 613-392-6148
800-206-7218
ontario.inquiry@hrsdc-rhdcc.gc.ca

Walkerton
200 McNab St.
PO Box 1139
Walkerton, ON N0G 2V0
519-881-2010
Fax: 519-881-0377
ontario.inquiry@hrsdc-rhdcc.gc.ca

Wallaceburg
786 Dufferin Ave., 2nd Fl.
Wallaceburg, ON N8A 2V3
519-627-3348
Fax: 519-627-8885
ontario.inquiry@hrsdc-rhdcc.gc.ca

Welland
250 Thorold Rd. West
Welland, ON L3C 3W3
905-988-2700
Fax: 905-735-7036

Windsor
400 City Hall Sq.
Windsor, ON N9A 7K6
519-560-2500
Fax: 519-560-2545
ontario.inquiry@hrsdc-rhdcc.gc.ca

Woodstock
#101, 959 Dundas St.
Woodstock, ON N4S 1H2
519-421-7225
Fax: 519-421-1916
ontario.inquiry@hrsdc-rhdcc.gc.ca

Charlottetown
161 St. Peters Rd.
PO Box 20105
Charlottetown, PE C1A 9E3
902-566-7723
Fax: 902-368-0178

Montague
541 Main St.
Montague, PE C0A 1R0
902-838-5562
Fax: 902-838-3439

Federal/Provincial Government / Government of Canada

O'Leary
371 Main St.
PO Box 700
O'Leary, PE C0B 1V0
902-859-1918
Fax: 902-859-1286

Souris
173 Main St., 2nd Fl.
PO Box 40
Souris, PE C0A 2B0
902-687-7202
Fax: 902-687-3722

Summerside
120 Harbour Dr.
PO Box 2000
Summerside, PE C1N 5P5
902-432-6804
Fax: 902-432-6808

Wellington
48 Mill Rd.
Wellington, PE C0B 2E0
902-854-2083
Fax: 902-854-2516

Abitibi-Témiscamingue
#300, 151, av du Lac
Rouyn-Noranda, QC J9X 6C3
819-764-6711
Fax: 819-762-4605

Bas-Saint-Laurent
140, av Belzile
Rimouski, QC G5L 8Y1
418-722-3200
Fax: 418-722-3369

Brossard
2501, boul Lapinière
Brossard, QC J4Z 3P1
450-445-0411
Fax: 450-445-3792

Centre-du-Québec
1525, boul St-Joseph
Drummondville, QC J2C 2E9
819-477-4150
Fax: 819-478-8137

Côte-Nord
701, boul Laure, 3e étage
Sept-Iles, QC G4R 1X8
418-962-5501
Fax: 418-962-8301

Est-de-Montréal
7141, rue Jean-Talon est
Anjou, QC H1M 3A4
514-355-3330
Fax: 514-514-3558

Gaspésie-Iles-de-la-Madeleine
98, rue de la Reine, 2e étage
Gaspé, QC G4X 2V4
418-368-3331
Fax: 418-368-2785

Laval
1575, boul Chomedey
Laval, QC H7V 2X2
450-682-8950
Fax: 450-682-3856

Longueuil
#114, 365, rue St-Jean
Longueuil, QC J4H 2X8
450-677-9471
Fax: 450-442-0708

Mauricie
#200, 444 - 5e rue
Shawinigan, QC G9N 1E6
819-536-5633
Fax: 819-536-7063

Montréal Centre-Ville/Sud-ouest-de-Montréal
1001, boul de Maisonneuve est, 2e étage
Montréal, QC H2L 5A1
514-522-4444
Fax: 514-283-6085

Nord-de-Montréal
#300, 1415, rue Jarry est
Montréal, QC H2E 3B2
514-723-7273
Fax: 514-723-6249

Ouest-de-Montréal
#3015, 6900, boul Decarie
Montréal, QC H3X 2T8
514-731-0060
Fax: 514-496-1335

Outaouais
920, boul St-Joseph
Gatineau, QC J8Z 1S9
819-953-2830
Fax: 819-953-0267

Québec
CP 10800 Ste-Foy
Québec, QC G1V 5B4
418-681-2599
Fax: 418-681-4810

Repentigny
#54, 155, rue Notre-Dame
Repentigny, QC J6A 7G5
450-585-2044
Fax: 450-585-2180

Richelieu-Yamaska
1225, rue Gauvin, 2e étage
Saint-Hyacinthe, QC J2S 8T8
450-773-7481
Fax: 450-773-8276

Rive-Sud-de-Québec
940, rte du Sault
Saint-Romuald, QC G6W 5M6
418-834-7697
Fax: 418-834-2551

Saguenay-Lac-Saint-Jean
3223, rue Ste-Émilie
Jonquière, QC G7S 5L1
418-699-5700
Fax: 418-699-5760

Saint-Jérôme
#1520, 500, boul Des Laurentides
Saint-Jérôme, QC J7Z 4M2
450-436-4230
Fax: 450-436-7886

Sainte-Thérèse
100, boul Ducharme
Sainte-Thérèse, QC J7E 1X2
450-430-2800
Fax: 450-430-5885

Sherbrooke
124 Wellington St. North
PO Box 340
Sherbrooke, QC J1H 5X8
819-564-5864
Fax: 819-564-5769

Thetford Mines
#200, 222, boul Frontenac ouest
Thetford Mines, QC G6G 6N7
418-335-2972
Fax: 418-335-3715

Vaudreuil-Dorion
2555, av Dutrisac, local GR 23
Vaudreuil-Dorion, QC J7V 7E6
450-424-5717
Fax: 450-424-0506

Assiniboia
110 - 4 Ave. West
Assiniboia, SK S0H 0B0
Fax: 306-642-3768
800-622-6232

Carlyle
100 Main St.
Carlyle, SK S0C 0R0
Fax: 306-453-2796
800-622-6232

Estevan
1314 - 3 St.
Estevan, SK S7K 0E2
Fax: 306-975-6426
800-622-6232

La Ronge
1016 La Ronge Ave.
La Ronge, SK S0J 1L0
Fax: 306-425-6515
800-622-6232

Meadow Lake
106 - 1 St. East
Meadow Lake, SK S9X 1Y1
Fax: 306-236-7866
800-622-6232

Melfort
104 McKendry Plaza
Melfort, SK S0E 1A0
Fax: 306-752-6640
800-622-6232

Moose Jaw
111 Fairford St. East
Moose Jaw, SK S6H 7X5
Fax: 306-691-0048
800-622-6232

Nipawin
435 Centre St.
Nipawin, SK S0E 1E0
Fax: 306-862-1755
800-622-6232

North Battleford
9800 Territorial Dr.
North Battleford, SK S9A 3N6
Fax: 306-446-1812
800-622-6232

Prince Albert
1288 Central Ave.
Prince Albert, SK S6V 4V8
Fax: 306-953-8404
800-622-6232

Regina
2045 Broad St.
Regina, SK S4P 2N6
Fax: 306-780-5370
800-622-6232

Regina North Central
2901 - 5 Ave.
Regina, SK S4T 0L3
Fax: 306-780-6571
800-622-6232

Saskatoon
101 - 22 St. East
Saskatoon, SK S7K 0E2
306-975-6426
800-622-6232

Shaunavon
410 Centre St.
Shaunavon, SK S0M 2M0
Fax: 306-297-3738
800-622-6232

Swift Current
250 Central Ave. North
Swift Current, SK S9H 4G3
Fax: 306-778-4388
800-622-6232

Weyburn
110 Souris Ave.
Weyburn, SK S4H 2Z8
Fax: 306-848-4458
800-622-6232

Wynyard
435 Bosworth St.
Wynyard, SK S0A 4T0
800-622-6232

Yorkton
214 Smith St. East
Yorkton, SK S3N 3S6

Federal/Provincial Government / Government of Canada

Fax: 306-786-5249
800-622-6232

Social Development / Développement social
L'esplanade Laurier, Level 2
300 Laurier Ave. West
Ottawa, ON K1A 0J6
613-990-5100
Fax: 613-990-5091
www.sdc.gc.ca

Helps to secure & strengthen Canada's social foundation. Does this by helping families with children, supporting people with disabilities & ensuring that seniors can fully participate in their communities. Also provides the policies, services & programs for Canadians who need assistance in overcoming challenges they encounter in their lives & their communities. This includes income security programs, such as the Canada Pension Plan.

Strategic Policy & Planning / Politique stratégique
Fax: 819-997-7329

Workplace Skills / Compétences en milieu de travail

Alberta-NWT-Nunavut
Canada Place
#1440, 9700 Jasper Ave. Northwest
Edmonton, AB T5J 4C1

British Columbia & Yukon
Library Sq. Tower
300 West Georgia St., 15th Fl.
Vancouver, BC V6B 6G3
604-666-2282

Manitoba
Canada Post Office Bldg.
#750, 266 Graham Ave.
Winnipeg, MB R3C 0K3
204-983-3781
Fax: 204-984-2113
TDD: 866-886-6166

New Brunswick
1081 Main St.
PO Box 6044
Moncton, NB E1C 9G8

Newfoundland & Labrador
689 Topsail Rd.
PO Box 12051
St. John's, NL A1B 3Z4
709-772-6204
Fax: 709-772-0815

Nova Scotia
Metropolitan Place
99 Wyse Rd.
PO Box 1350
Dartmouth, NS B2Y 4B9
902-426-5383
Fax: 902-426-1840

Ontario
#900, 4900 Yonge St.
Toronto, ON M2N 6A8
416-954-7700
Fax: 416-954-7707

Prince Edward Island
85 Fitzroy St.
PO Box 8000
Charlottetown, PE C1A 8K1

Québec
Complexe Guy-Favreau, Tour Ouest
200, boul René-Levesque ouest, 5e étage
Montréal, QC H2Z 1X4
514-982-2384
Fax: 514-283-5549

Saskatchewan
2045 Broad St., 4th Fl.
Regina, SK S4P 2N6

Indian & Northern Affairs Canada (INAC) / Affaires indiennes et du Nord Canada (AINC)
10 Wellington St., North Tower
Gatineau, QC K1A 0H4

819-997-0380
Fax: 819-953-3017
866-817-3977
TDD: 866-553-0554
infopubs@ainc-inac.gc.ca
www.ainc-inac.gc.ca
Other Communication: Toll Free Fax: 1-800-567-9604

INAC is responsible for two separate mandates, Indian & Inuit Affairs, & Northern Affairs. This mandate is derived largely from the Department of Indian & Northern Development Act, the Indian Act, territorial acts & legal obligations arising from section 91(24) of the Constitution Act, 1867. The department administers over 50 statutes. INAC has responsibility to meet the government's responsibilities to First Nations, Inuit & Northerners & must work collaboratively with First Nations, Inuit, Northerners, departments, agencies, provinces & territories. The primary role is to support First Nations & Inuit in developing healthy, sustainable communities & assist in achieving their economic & social aspirations.

Acts Administered:
(An Act to confirm an) Agreement between the Governments of Canada & the province of New Brunswick respecting the Indian Reserves
(An Act to confirm an) Agreement between the Governments of Canada & the province of Nova Scotia respecting the Indian Reserves
Alberta Natural Resources Act
Arctic Waters Pollution Prevention Act (Transport Canada & Natural Resources)
Department of Indian & Northern Affairs Development Act
British Columbia Indian Cut-off Lands Settlement Act
British Columbia Indian Lands Settlement Act
British Columbia Treaty Commission Act
Canada Lands Surveys Act (Natural Resources)
Canada Oil & Gas Operations Act (Natural Resources)
Canada Petroleum Resources Act (Natural Resources)
Canada - Yukon Oil & Gas Accord Implementation Act
Canadian Polar Commission Act
Caughnawaga Indian Reserve Act
Claims Settlement (Alberta & Saskatchewan) Implementation Act
Condominium Ordinance Validation Act
Cree-Naskapi (of Québec) Act
Dominion Water Power Act
Fort Nelson Indian Reserve Minerals Revenue Sharing Act
Grassy Narrows & Islington Indian Band Mercury Pollution Claims Settlement Act
Gwich'in Land Claim Settlement Act
Indian Act (Health Canada)
Indian Lands Agreement Act
Indian Lands Settlement of Differences Act
Indian Reserve Waste Disposal Regulations
Territorial Land Titles Offices Regulations
Indian Oil & Gas Act
Indian (Soldier Settlement) Act
James Bay & Northern Quebec Native Claims Settlement Act
Land Titles Repeal Act
Mackenzie Valley Resource Management Act
Manitoba Natural Resources Act
Manitoba Supplementary Provisions Act
Natural Resources Transfer (School Lands) Amendments, Alberta, Manitoba & Saskatchewan
Nelson House First Nation Flooded Land Act
Northern Canada Power Commission (Share Issuance & Sale Authorization) Act
Northern Canada Power Commission Yukon Assets Disposal Authorization Act
Northwest Territories Act
Northwest Territories Waters Act
Nunavut Act
Nunavut Land Claims Agreement Act
Nunavut Waters & Nunavut Surface Rights Tribunal Act, 2002
Pictou Landing Indian Band Agreement Act
Railway Belt Act
Railway Belt & Peace River Block Act
Railway Belt Water Act
St. Peters Indian Reserve Act
St. Regis Islands Act
Sahtu Dene & Metis Land Claim Settlement Act
Saskatchewan Natural Resources Act
Saskatchewan Treaty Land Entitlement Act
Sechelt Indian Band Self-Government Act
(An Act for the) Settlement of Certain Questions Between the Governments of Canada & Ontario Respecting the Indian Reserve Lands Act
(An Act Respecting) Songhees Indian Reserve Act
Split Lake Cree First Nation Flooded Land Act
Territorial Lands Act
Canada Mining Regulations
Canada Oil & Gas Drilling & Production Regulations
Canada Oil & Gas Land Regulations
Crown Waiver Orders
Government Employees Land Acquisition Orders
Northwest Territories Mining Districts Order & Nunavut Mining District
Oil & Gas Land Orders
Orders Authorizing Acquisition of Interest in Certain Lands
Orders Respecting Withdrawal from Disposal of Certain Lands
Polar Bear Pass Withdrawal Order
Reservations to Crown Waiver Orders
Territorial Coal Regulations
Territorial Dredging Regulations
Territorial Land Use Regulations
Territorial Lands Act Exclusion Orders
Territorial Lands Regulations
Territorial Quarrying Regulations
Withdrawal of Certain Lands from Disposal Orders
Withdrawals of Disposal Orders
Western Arctic (Inuvialuit) Claims Settlement Act
York Factory First Nation Flooded Land Act
Yukon Act
Yukon Environmental & Socio-Economic Assessment Act, 2003
Yukon First Nations Land Claims Settlement Act
Yukon First Nations Self-Government Act
Yukon Placer Mining Act
Yukon Quartz Mining Act
Yukon Waters Act

Minister, Indian Affairs & Northern Development; Minister of the Canadian Northern Economic Development Agency; Federal Interlocutor for Métis & Non-Status Indians, Hon. John Duncan, B.Sc.F.
613-992-2503, Fax: 613-996-3306
Duncan.J@parl.gc.ca; Minister@ainc-inac.gc.ca
Other Communications: Indian Affairs & Northern Development: 819-997-0002

Deputy Minister, Michael Wernick
819-997-0133, Fax: 819-953-2251

Associate Deputy Minister, Colleen Swords
819-934-0583, Fax: 819-953-2251

• Beverly & Qamanirjuaq Caribou Management Board
Secretariat
PO Box 629
Stonewall, MB R0C 2Z0
204-467-2438
rossthompson@mymts.net
www.arctic-caribou.com
Chair, Albert Thorassie
Group of hunters, biologists & wildlife managers working together to conserve Canada's vast Beverly & Qamanirjuaq caribou herds for the welfare of traditional caribou-using communities in northern Manitoba, Saskatchewan, Northwest Territories & Nunavut.

• First Nations Tax Commission(FNTC) / Commission de la fiscalité des premières nations (CFPN)
#200, 160 Grorge St.
Ottawa, ON K1N 9M2
613-789-5000
Fax: 613-789-5008
mail@fntc.ca
www.fntc.ca

• Indian Oil & Gas Canada(IOGC) / Pétrole et gaz des Indiens du Canada
#100, 9911 Chula Blvd.
Tsuu T'ina (Sarcee), AB T2W 6H6
403-292-5625
Fax: 403-292-5618
ContactIOGC@inac-ainc.gc.ca
www.iogc-pgic.gc.ca
CEO & Executive Director, Strater Crowfoot
Indian Oil and Gas Canada (IOGC) is an organization committed to managing and regulating oil and gas resources on First Nation reserve lands. It is a special operating agency within Indian and Northern Affairs Canada.

• Mackenzie Valley Environmental Impact Review Board
200 Scotia Centre
5102 - 50th Ave.
PO Box 938
Yellowknife, NT X1A 2N7
867-766-7050
Fax: 867-766-7074

Federal/Provincial Government / Government of Canada

866-912-3472
tcharlo@reviewboard.ca
www.mveirb.nt.ca
Chair, Richard Edjericon
In 1998, the Mackenzie Valley Environmental Impact Review Board was established, under the Mackenzie Valley Resources Management Act. The co-management Review Board is made up of members nominated by First Nations & federal & territorial governments. Board members represent the interests of all residents of the Mackenzie Valley.

• Nunavut Impact Review Board
PO Box 1360
Cambridge Bay, NU X0B 0C0
867-983-4600
Fax: 867-983-2594
866-233-3033
info@nirb.ca
www.nirb.ca
Executive Director, Stephanie Autut
An institution of the government established under the Nunavut Land Claims Agreement to conduct environmental & socio-economic assessments. The NIRB process involves participation by members of the community, Inuit organizations, the Government of Nunavut & the Government of Canada through the entire environmental assessment. Under the Canadian Environmental Assessment Act, the federal departments with specific responsibilities for the project must ensure that the requirements of the Act are met throughout the assessment process. This open process facilitates sound environmental stewardship & promotes economic & sustainable development.

• Nunavut Planning Commission
PO Box 2101
Cambridge Bay, NU X0B 0C0
867-983-4625
Fax: 867-983-4626
staptuna@nunavut.ca
www.nunavut.ca
Executive Director, Sharon Ehaloak
Responsible for land use planning & environmental reporting & management in Nunavut.

• Nunavut Water Board
PO Box 119
Gjoa Haven, NU X0B 1J0
867-360-6338
Fax: 867-360-6369
www.nunavutwaterboard.org
Executive Director, Dionne Filiatrault
Responsible for the regulation, use & management of water in the Nunavut Settlement Area.

• Porcupine Caribou Management Board
PO Box 31723
Whitehorse, YT Y1A 6L3
867-633-4780
Fax: 867-393-3904
pcmb@taiga.net
http://taiga.net/pcmb
Chair, Joe Tetlichi
Works to manage the Porcupine Caribou herd, one of the largest herds of migratory caribou in North America, & to protect & maintain its habitat.

Chief Financial Officer Sector / Secteur du dirigeant principal des finances
819-953-1201
Fax: 819-953-4094

Lands & Trusts Services / Services fonciers et fiduciaires
Manages land-related statutory duties under the Indian Act & duties related to transferring land management services to First Nations. The Environment Directorate maintains an Inventory of Contaminated Sites on reserve land & coordinates remediation planning; responsible for the design & implementation of the Indian & Inuit Affairs Program Environmental Stewardship Strategy Action Plan; development of First Nations capacity, tools & enabling legislation inorder that first Nations undertake their own environmental protection initiatives; administers Indian Environmental Assistance Fund (IEAF). Environment Capacity Development Initiative (ECDI) supports First Nation, Innu & Inuit communities in efforts to promote environmental stewardship in a manner that is consistent with the principles of sustainable development.
Director General Governance, Brenda Kustra
819-997-8154, Fax: 819-997-9541
Director Strategic Policy & Integration Directorate, John Kozij
819-934-7018, Fax: 819-997-0552

Northern Affairs / Affaires du Nord
819-994-0044
Fax: 819-953-6121
Supports northern political & economic development through the management of federal interests; promotes sustainable development of the North's natural resources & northern communities. Works toward the devolution of all province-like responsibilities to northern governments of NWT, Nunavut & the Yukon. Develops & coordinates policies & programs related to northern environment & conservation, like the federal Northern Affairs Program Sustainable Development Strategy, the cleanup of northern hazardous waste sites, climate change & interdepartmental liaison with key policy departments like Environment Canada. Northern Contaminants Program is managed by INAC in partnership with the federal departments of Health, Environment & Fisheries & Oceans, the territorial governments, Aboriginal organizations & university researchers, & its aim is to work toward reducing & eliminating, where possible, contaminants in traditionally harvested foods. The Northern Information Network is designed to link users to information about the Yukon, the Northwest Territories & Nunavut for more effective decision making in the areas such as resource management & economic development. NIN supports various research initiatives about the North, including project impact assessments sustainable development strategies, wildlife management planning, land use planning & emergency preparedness. NIN has a directory of geo-referenced databases, provides a forum for discussion & has information & research documents pertaining to the North.
Asst. Deputy Minister, Patrick Borbey
819-953-3760
Director Circumpolar Liaison Directorate, Harald Finkler
819-997-8318, Fax: 819-953-0546

Vancouver
Comprehensive Claims Branch
#600, 1168 Melville St.
Vancouver, BC V6E 4S3
604-775-7114
Fax: 604-666-2546

Victoria
#309, 1230 Government St.
Victoria, BC V8W 2Z4
250-363-6910
Fax: 250-363-6911

Policy & Strategic Direction Sector / Politique et direction stratégique
Fax: 819-953-5082

Socio Policy & Programs Branch
Fax: 819-953-1974

Treaties & Aboriginal Government / Traités et gouvernement autochtone
Director General Financial Management & Strategic Services, Tony Richard
819-997-9757, Fax: 819-994-0273

Alberta
#630, Canada Place
9700 Jasper Ave.
Edmonton, AB T5J 4G2
780-495-2834
Fax: 780-495-4354

Acting Regional Director General, Jim Sisson
780-495-2839

Atlantic
40 Havelock St.
PO Box 160
Amherst, NS B4H 3Z3
902-661-6201
Fax: 902-661-6237
Regional Director General, Ian Gray
902-661-6262

British Columbia
#600, 1138 Melville St.
Vancouver, BC V6E 4S3
604-666-5201
Fax: 604-666-2546
Regional Director General, George Arcand
Fax: 604-775-7149

Manitoba
#200, 365 Hargrave St.
Winnipeg, MB R3B 3A3
204-983-7849
Fax: 204-983-2936
Regional Director General, Anna Fontaine
204-983-2474

Northwest Territories
PO Box 1500
Yellowknife, NT X1A 2R3
867-669-2507
Fax: 867-669-2709
Regional Director General, Trish Merrithew-Mercredi
867-669-2501, Fax: 867-669-2703
Director Renewable Resources & Environment, Teresa Joudrie
867-669-2647, Fax: 867-669-2707
Acting Director Contaminants & Remediation, Bill Mitchell
867-669-2434, Fax: 867-669-2439

Nunavut
PO Box 2200
Iqaluit, NU X0A 0H0
867-975-4500
Fax: 867-975-4560
Acting Regional Director General, Bernie MacIsaac
867-975-4501
Director Contaminated Sites, Natalie Plato
867-975-4730

Ontario
25 St. Clair Ave. East, 8th Fl.
Toronto, ON M4T 1M2
416-973-6599
Fax: 416-954-4326
Acting Regional Director General, Leigh Jessen
416-973-6201
Acting Director Executive & Communications, Natalie Pennefather
416-973-6110, Fax: 416-973-3421

Québec
#400, 320, rue St-Joseph est
Québec, QC G1K 9J2
418-648-7551
Fax: 418-648-2266
800-567-9604
TDD: 866-553-0554
Regional Director General, Pierre Nepton
418-648-3270
Director Education & Social Development Programs, Céline Laverdière
418-648-4104, Fax: 418-648-7685
Director Lands & Economic Development, Stéphane Greffard
418-648-7743, Fax: 418-648-3930

Saskatchewan
#200, 1 First Nations Way
Regina, SK S4S 7K5
306-780-6486
Fax: 306-780-5733
Regional Director General, Riel Bellegarde
306-780-6486, Fax: 306-780-7305
Director Lands & Economic Development, Dwayne Johns
306-780-6420, Fax: 306-780-6128
Director Strategic Initiatives & Innovations, Cherie Moreau
306-780-6442, Fax: 306-780-6897

Yukon
#415C, 300 Main St.
Whitehorse, YT Y1A 2B5
867-667-3888
Fax: 867-667-6038
Regional Director General, Joanne Wilkinson
306-667-3300, Fax: 867-667-3801
Director Environment, Michelle Edwards
867-393-7934, Fax: 867-667-3861
Director Strategic Investments, Shari Borgford
867-667-3310, Fax: 867-667-3801

Implementation Branch / Direction générale de la mise en oeuvre
Fax: 819-953-6430

Self-Government Branch / Autonomie gouvernementale
Fax: 819-994-1831

Natural Resources & Environment Branch / Direction générale des ressources naturelles et de l'environnement
Director General, Steven Joudry
819-997-9381
Director Environment & Renewable Resources Directorate, Leslie Whitby
819-997-2728
Director Lands & Waters, Chris Cuddy
819-994-7483
Director Mineral Resources, Rick Meyers
819-997-9828
Acting Director Northern Science & Contaminants Research, Russel Shearer
819-994-7484
Director Resource Policy & Programs, Stephen Van Dine
819-953-8613
Manager Aboriginal & Northern Climate Change Program, Jesse George
819-994-7425
Manager Contaminated Sites Program, Joanna Ankersmit
819-997-7247
Acting Manager Sustainable Development Division, Martha Johnson
819-953-6773, Fax: 819-953-9066

Natural Resources & Environment Branch / Ressources naturelles et Environnement
Fax: 819-953-8766

Northern Oil & Gas Branch / Direction générale du pétrole et du gaz du nord
Director Northern Oil & Gas, Mimi Fortier
819-997-0878
Senior Environmental Advisor, George McCormick
819-953-8491

Industry Canada / Industrie Canada

235 Queen St.
Ottawa, ON K1A 0H5
Fax: 613-954-6436
800-328-6189
TDD: 866-694-8389
info@ic.gc.ca
www.ic.gc.ca
The mission of Industry Canada is to help make Canadians more productive & competitive in a global, knowledge-based economy. The department's policies, programs & services assists in the creation of an economy that offers the following: provides more & better-paying jobs for Canadians; supports stronger business growth through sustained improvements in productivity; & gives consumers, businesses & investors confidence that the marketplace is fair, efficient & competitive. To reach its clients, Industry Canada collaborates extensively with partners at all levels of government & the private sector.

Acts Administered:
Agreement on Internal Trade Implementation Act
Bankruptcy & Insolvency Act
Boards of Trade Act
Canada Business Corporations Act
Canada Co-operative Associations Act
Canada Corporations Act
Canada Small Business Financing Act
Canadian Space Agency Act
Canadian Tourism Commission Act
Companies' Creditors Arrangement Act
Department of Industry Act
Departmental Legislation
Electricity & Gas Inspection Act
Radiocommunication Act
Telecommunications Act
Teleglobe Canada Reorganization & Divestiture Act
Telesat Canada Reorganization & Divestiture Act
Marketplace & Trade Regulation
Competition Act
Consumer Packaging & Labelling Act
Government Corporations Operations Act
Telecommunications Legislation
Investment Canada Act
Lobbyists Registration Act
Small Business Loans Act
Winding-up & Restructuring Act
Canadian Intellectual Property Office (CIPO) Legislation
Copyright Act
Industrial Design Act
Integrated Circuit Topography Act
Patent Act
Public Servants Inventions Act
Trade-marks Act
Consumer Legislation
Bills of Exchange Act
Electricity & Gas Inspection Act
Precious Metals Marking Act
Textile Labelling Act
Timber Marking Act
Weights & Measures Act
Registrar General Functions
Public Documents Act
Public Officers Act
Seals Act
Trade Unions Act
Portfolio & Agency Legislation
Business Development Bank of Canada Act
Canada Foundation for Innovation Act (Part I & XI)
Competition Tribunal Act
Copyright Board: Sections 66ff of the Copyright Act
National Research Council Act
Natural Sciences & Engineering Research Council Act
Social Sciences & Humanities Research Council Act
Standards Council of Canada Act
Statistics Act
Largely Inactive or Minimal Involvement
Atlantic Fisheries Restructuring Act
Agricultural & Rural Development Act
Bell Canada Act
Corporations & Labour Unions Returns Act
Pension Fund Societies Act
Regional Development Incentives Act
Special Areas Act
Minister, Industry, Hon. Tony Clement
613-944-7740, Fax: 613-992-5092
ClemeT@parl.gc.ca; ministre.industrie@ic.gc.ca
Deputy Minister, Richard Dicerni
613-992-4292, Fax: 613-954-3272
richard.dicerni@ic.gc.ca
Director General Information & Communications Technologies Branch, Alain Beaudoin
613-954-5598, Fax: 613-957-4076
alain.beaudoin@ic.gc.ca
• Canadian Tourism Commission(CTC) / Commission canadienne du Tourisme (CCT)
#1400, 1055 Dunsmuir St.
PO Box 49230
Vancouver, BC V7X 1L2
604-638-8300
Fax: 604-638-8425
ctc_feedback@businteractive.com
www.canadatourism.com
• Cape Breton Development Fund Corporation
Silicon Island
70 Crescent St.
PO Box 1264
Sydney, NS B1P 6T7
902-564-3600
Fax: 902-564-3825
800-705-3926
www.cbgf.ca
• Chief Informatics Office
235 Queen St.
Ottawa, ON K1A 0H5
613-954-3570
Fax: 613-941-1938
• Communications Research Centre Canada(CRC) / Centre de recherches sur les communications
3701 Carling Ave.
PO Box 11490 H
Ottawa, ON K2H 8S2
613-991-3313
Fax: 613-998-5355
info@crc.ca
www.crc.ca
• Competition Tribunal
Thomas D'Arcy McGee Bldg.
#600, 90 Sparks St.
Ottawa, ON K1P 5B4
613-957-3172
Fax: 613-957-3170
tribunal@ct-tc.gc.ca
www.ct-tc.gc.ca
• Electronic Commerce Branch
300 Slater St.
Ottawa, ON K1A 0C8
613-990-4268
Fax: 613-941-0178
800-328-6189
www.ic.gc.ca/eic/site/ecic-ceac.nsf/eng/home
• Enterprise Cape Breton Corporation(ECBC) / Société d'expansion du Cap-Breton
Silicon Island
70 Crescent St.
Sydney, NS B1S 2Z7
902-564-3600
Fax: 902-564-3825
800-705-3926
information@ecbc-secb.gc.ca
www.ecbc-secb.gc.ca
• Standards Council of Canada

Competition Bureau / Bureau de la concurrence
Place du Portage, Phase I
50, rue Victoria, 21e étage
Ottawa, ON K1A 0C9
613-997-4282
Fax: 613-997-0324
800-348-5358
TDD: 800-642-3844
compbureau@ic.gc.ca
www.competitionbureau.gc.ca
The Competition Bureau is the organization responsible for the enforcement of the Competition Act, the Consumer Packaging & Labelling Act except as it relates to food, the Precious Metals Marking Act & the Textile Labelling Act. The Competition Bureau ensures compliance by the business community with legislation administered by the Bureau, & oversees the development of policy & dissemination of information aimed at ensuring optimal compliance levels.
Commissioner of Competition, Melanie Aitken
819-997-3304, Fax: 819-953-5013

Industry Sector / Secteur de l'industrie
Industry Sector (IS) assists Canadian industry & businesses compete, expand & create jobs in the knowledge-based economy. IS contributes to Industry Canada's strategic objectives, trade, investment, innovation, connectedness & marketplace. It facilitates delivery of industrial, related policy analyses & strategies to promote global competitiveness of Canadian industry. IS provides a broad range of services, information resources, sector policies & strategies to support business growth. IS provides Canadian businesses with timely information products, business tools, research, strategic analyses, data & information resources. For more information about Industry Sector's products, visit the Business Information by Sector area on Strategis, Industry Canada's on-line business information source at
http://www.ic.gc.ca/eic/site/ic1.nsf/eng/h_00066.html
Senior Asst. Deputy Minister, Ron Parker
613-954-3798, Fax: 613-941-1134
Director General Aerospace, Defence and Marine Branch, Brian Gear
613-941-8123, Fax: 613-998-6703
Director General Policy and Sector Services Branch, Colette Jubinville
613-954-9633, Fax: 613-948-1230

Aerospace, Defence & Marine Branch / Aérospatiale, defense et la marine
Fax: 613-941-2379
Director General, Brian Gear
613-941-8123, Fax: 613-998-6703
Director Aerospace, Sharon Harrison
613-954-3166, Fax: 613-998-6703
Acting Director Defence & Marine Directorate, André Bernier
613-954-3774, Fax: 613-998-6703
Director Industrial & Regional Benefit Directorate, Daniel Duguay
613-957-2651, Fax: 613-998-6703

Automotive & Industrial Materials Branch / Automobile et matériaux industriels
613-952-0441
Fax: 613-952-8088

Energy & Environment Industries Branch / Énergie et industries environnementales
Director General, Bruce Bowie
613-946-7317

Federal/Provincial Government / Government of Canada

Director Energy Directorate, Glenn MacDonell
613-954-2703

Life Sciences Industries Branch / Sciences de la vie
Fax: 613-946-3144
Director General, Leah Clark
613-954-5258, Fax: 613-952-5822

Resource Processing Industries Branch / Industries de transformation des ressources naturelles
Director General, Tim Elliot
613-954-3394, Fax: 613-941-8048
Director Energy Industries Directorate, Tim Karlsson
613-954-2991, Fax: 613-941-2463
Director Forest Industries Directorate, Jyotsna Dalvi
613-941-2274, Fax: 613-952-8988
Director Resource Manufacturing & Value-added Products Directorate, Simon Tuck
613-954-5609, Fax: 613-952-8988

Services Industries Branch / Industries de services
Deputy Director, Philippe Richer
613-941-3361, Fax: 613-952-9054
Director, Patrick Hurens
613-952-1710, Fax: 613-952-9054

Operations Sector / Secteur des opérations
Asst. Deputy Minister, Matthew King
613-957-4392, Fax: 613-995-2233
Assoc. Asst. Deputy Minister, Iain Stewart
613-960-1850
President Measurement Canada, Alan E. Johnston
613-952-0655, Fax: 613-957-1265
Director General Corporations Canada, Richard G. Shaw
613-941-2837, Fax: 613-941-5783
Director General Sectorial Strategies & Services, Jeff Moore
613-941-2479, Fax: 613-952-9026
Director General Small Business Financing Directorate, Nathalie Poirier-Mizon
613-946-3391, Fax: 613-952-0290

Office of the Superintendent of Bankruptcy / Bureau du surintendant des faillites
613-941-1000
Fax: 613-941-2862

Canadian Intellectual Property Office / Office de la propriété intellectuelle du Canada
Place du Portage I
50, rue Victoria
Gatineau, QC K1A 0C9
819-997-1936
Fax: 819-953-7620
866-997-1936
TDD: 866-442-2476
www.cipo.ic.gc.ca
The Canadian Intellectual Property Office (CIPO), a Special Operating Agency (SOA) associated with Industry Canada, is responsible for the administration and processing of the greater part of intellectual property in Canada.

Spectrum, Information Technologies & Telecommunications / Spectre, technologies de l'information et télécommunications
Journal Tower North
300 Slater St., 20th Fl.
Ottawa, ON K1A 0C8
613-998-0368
Fax: 613-952-1203
Contributes to the Industry Canada mandate by fostering the early development & use of information & communications technologies, infrastructures & services. The sector uses its policy & regulatory rule-making powers, & marketplace & industry sectoral development services to: ensure Canada has a world-class telecommunications & information infrastructure; promote the international competitiveness of Canadian information technologies by all sectors of the Canadian economy; & ensure effective & efficient use of the radio frequency spectrum.

Infrastructure Canada / L'infrastructure Canada
90 Sparks St., 6th Fl.
Ottawa, ON K1P 5B4
613-948-1148
Fax: 613-946-9888
800-622-6232
TDD: 800-465-7735
info@infc.gc.ca
www.infrastructure.gc.ca
Infrastructure Canada consists of the following branches: Policy & Communications; Corporate Services, & Program Operations. The Program Operations sector undertakes the following functions: implentation of programs; management of infrastructure funding agreements; provision of risk management & analysis; promotion of environmental stewardship; management of the federal Gas Tax transfer to Canadian municipalities to support environmentally sustainable infrastructure; & program evaluation. In 2007, a team was established to develop a National Transit Strategy.
Minister, Transport, Infrastructure, & Communities, Hon. Charles (Chuck) Strahl
613-992-2940, Fax: 613-944-9376
Strahl.C@parl.gc.ca
Parliamentary Secretary, Brian Jean
613-992-1154, Fax: 613-992-4603
Jean.B@parl.gc.ca
Deputy Minister, Yaprak Baltacioglu
613-990-4507, Fax: 613-991-0851
yaprak.baltacioglu@infc.gc.ca
Assistant Deputy Minister, John Forster
613-948-8157, Fax: 613-948-6062
john.forster@infc.gc.ca
Assistant Deputy Minister Corporate Services, David Miller
613-948-9161, Fax: 613-960-6348
david.miller@infc.gc.ca
Senior Counsel Legal Services, Jean-Philippe Dallaire
613-952-2310, Fax: 613-954-5356
ouellet.richard@ic.gc.ca

Policy & Communications Branch
#605, 90 Sparks St.
Ottawa, ON K1P 5B4
The branch conducts research, both independently & with partners, on infrastructure issues for potential federal action. Policy & Communications also shares knowledge to further understanding of infrastructure issues affecting cities & communities. Policy advice is also offered to the Minister.
Assistant Deputy Minister, John Forster
613-948-8157
Director General Communications Directorate, Gerry Maffre
613-948-2940
Director General Policy & Priorities Directorate, Taki Sarantakis
613-946-5188
Director General Policy & Strategic Initiatives Directorate, Adam Ostry
613-952-9940

Program Operations Branch / Direction générale des opérations du programme
#605, 90 Sparks St.
Ottawa, ON K1P 5B4
Assistant Deputy Minister, Carol Beal
613-948-6050
Director General Intergovernmental Operations Directorate, Jocelyne St. Jean
613-948-8003
Director General Issues Management Directorate, Shirley Anne Scharf
613-948-3996
Director General Partnerships & Operations Directorate, Claude Blanchette
613-948-9392

International Development Research Centre (IDRC) / Centre de recherches pour le développement international (CRDI)
150 Kent St.
PO Box 8500
Ottawa, ON K1P 0B2
613-236-6163
Fax: 613-238-7230
info@idrc.ca
www.idrc.ca
Helps scientists in developing countries identify long-term, practical solutions to pressing development problems. Support is given directly to scientists working in universities, private enterprise, government & non-profit-making organizations. Priority is given to research aimed at achieving equitable & sustainable development. One of the three program areas of focus is Environmental & Natural Resource Management. Initiatives in this area include a rural poverty & environment program initiative, an urban poverty & environment program, ecosystem approaches to human health, an international model forest network, biodiversity & regional water demand initiative
Chair, Barbara McDougall
613-236-6163, Fax: 613-565-8212
bmcdougall@idrc.ca
President, David M. Malone
613-236-6163, Fax: 613-235-6391
dmalone@idrc.ca
Vice-President Resources & CFO, Denys Vermette
613-236-6163, Fax: 613-236-7293
dvermette@idrc.ca
Vice-President Programs & Partnership Branch, Rohinton Medhora
613-236-6163, Fax: 613-567-7748
rmedhora@idrc.ca
Director Communications Division, Angela Prokopiak
613-236-6163, Fax: 613-563-2476
aprokopiak@idrc.ca
Director Environmental & Natural Resource Management, Jean Lebel
613-236-6163, Fax: 613-567-7748
jlebel@idrc.ca
Chief Public Affairs & Parliamentary Relations, Jennifer Pepall
613-236-6163, Fax: 613-238-7230
jpepall@idrc.ca

Eastern & Southern Africa
IDRC, Liasion House
State House Avenue
PO Box 62084
Nairobi
vngugi@idrc.or.ke
www.idrc.ca/esaro
Other Communication: 254-20-2713160; Fax: 254-20-2711063

Latin America & the Caribbean
Avenida Brasil 2655
Montevideo, 11300 Uruguay
lacroinf@idrc.org.uy
www.idrc.ca/lacro
Other Communication: 598-2-709-0042; Fax: 598-2-708-6776

Middle East & North Africa
8 Ahmed Niseem St., 8th fl.
PO Box 14
Cairo
skamel@idrc.org.eg
www.idrc.ca/cairo
Other Communication: 20-2-336-7051; Fax: 20-2-336-7056

South Asia
IDRC, 208 Jor Bagh
New Delhi, 110 003 India
saro@idrc.org.in
www.idrc.ca/saro
Other Communication: 91-11-461-9411; Fax: 91-11-462-2707

Southeast and East Asia
IDRC, Tanglin
#02-55 - 22 Cross St.
Singapore, 048421 Singapore
asro@idrc.org.sg
www.idrc.org.sg
Other Communication: 65-6438-7877; Fax: 65-6438-4844

West & Central Africa
CRDI
CD Annexe, BP 11007, Peytavin
Dakar
waro@idrc.ca
www.idrc.ca/waro
Other Communication: 221-33-864-0000; Fax: 221-33-825-3255

International Joint Commission (IJC) / Commission mixte internationale (CMI)
234 Laurier Ave. West, 22nd Fl.
Ottawa, ON K1P 6K6
613-947-1420
Fax: 613-993-5583
beckhoffb@ottawa.ijc.org
www.ijc.org
Other Communication: Great Lakes Water Quality Information: 519/257-6700
Established by the Boundary Waters Treaty of 1909 & is responsible for approving (by Order of Approval) certain works in boundary waters which affect levels & flows on both sides of the Canada-US border. The commission provides recommendations

on matters along the common boundary which have been referred to the Commission by the governments. Also monitors & assesses theGreat Lakes Water Quality Agreement (GLWQA) & is responsible for reviewing & commenting on Remedial Action Plans (RAPs) in coordination with eight US States & the province of Ontario.
Chair & Commissioner, Rt. Hon. Herb Gray, P.C., C.C., Q.C.
613-992-2417, Fax: 613-947-9386
Secretary, Dr. Murray Clamen
613-995-0113
Administrative Assistant, Marie Lalonde
613-947-2527, Fax: 613-993-5583

Great Lakes Regional Office
100 Ouellette Ave., 8th fl.
Windsor, ON N9A 6T3
Fax: 519-257-6740
Other Communication: Information: 519/257-6700
Director Great Lakes Regional Office, Karen E. Vigmostad
519-257-6715

United States Section / Section des États-Unis
#100, 1250 - 23 St. Northwest
Washington, DC 20440 USA
202-736-9000
Fax: 202-736-9015
Communications Officer, Joanne Laurin
418-649-6251, Fax: 418-648-3809
Executive Secretary, Nathalie Marcotte

National Capital Commission (NCC) / Commission de la capitale nationale (CCN)

#202, 40 Elgin St.
Ottawa, ON K1P 1C7
613-239-5555
Fax: 613-239-5063
800-704-8227
TDD: 866-661-3530
info@ncc-ccn.ca
www.canadascapital.gc.ca
Responsible for the planning, development & preservation of the National Capital Region. Maintains a "greenbelt" which includes historical bogs & swamps & a 40-hectare farm circa 1875. Responsible for the operation of Gatineau Park.
CEO, Marie Lemay
613-239-5194, Fax: 613-239-5039
Director Communications, Kathryn Keyes
613-239-5636, Fax: 613-239-5180

National Defence Canada / Défense nationale

Major-General George R. Pearkes Bldg.
101 Colonel By Dr.
Ottawa, ON K1A 0K2
613-995-2534
Fax: 613-992-4739
800-856-8488
TDD: 800-467-9877
www.forces.gc.ca
Other Communication: Access to Information: 613-992-0996; Media Inquiries: 613-996-2353
The Minister of National Defence is responsible for the Department of National Defence (DND), the Canadian Forces (CF), & related organizations. Canadian Forces members protect Canada, defend North America, & contribute to international peace & security. The work of DND & CF includes the following: assisting civil authorities to protect national interests, to handle national emergencies & to maintain an adequate level of emergency preparedness throughout Canada; protecting Canadian approaches to the continent; promoting Arctic security; pursuing opportunities for Canada-U.S.A. defence co-operation; participating in multilateral operations through international organizations, such as the United Nations (UN) & the North Atlantic Treaty Organization (NATO); supporting humanitarian relief efforts; assisting in the restoration of conflict-devastated places; & participating in confidence-building measures, like arms-control programs.
Acts Administered:
Aeronautics Act, with respect to any matter relating to defence
Army Benevolent Act
Canadian Forces Superannuation Act
Defence Services Pension Continuation Act
Emergencies Act
Emergency Preparedness Act
Garnishment, Attachment & Pension Diversion Act, with respect to members & former members of the Canadian Forces
National Defence Act
Pension Benefits Division Act, with respect to members & former members of the Canadian Forces
Visiting Forces Act
In addition, the DND administers, under the general direction of the Chief Electoral Officer, the Special Voting Rules (Schedule II to the Canada Elections Act) as they relate to Canadian Forces elect
Minister, National Defence, Hon. Peter Gordon MacKay
613-992-6022, Fax: 613-992-2337
MacKay.P@parl.gc.ca; Mackay.P@forces.gc.ca
Parliamentary Secretary to the Minister of National Defence, Laurie Hawn
613-992-4524, Fax: 613-943-0044
Hawn.L@parl.gc.ca
Deputy Minister, Robert Fonberg
613-992-4258, Fax: 613-995-2028
Chief of the Defence Staff, Gen. Walt Natynczyk
613-992-5054, Fax: 613-995-8578
Vice-Chief of Defence Staff, V.-Adm. Denis Rouleau
613-992-6052, Fax: 613-992-3945
Assistant Deputy Minister Finance & Corporate Services, Bryn Weadon
613-992-5669, Fax: 613-992-9693
Assistant Deputy Minister Information Management, John Turner
613-995-2017, Fax: 613-995-2189
Assistant Deputy Minister Infrastructure & Environment, J. Scott Stevenson
613-945-7545, Fax: 613-995-6653
Assistant Deputy Minister Human Resources - Civilian, Cynthia Binnington
613-992-7447, Fax: 613-995-8938
Assistant Deputy Minister Materiel, Dan Ross
613-992-6622, Fax: 613-945-0949
Assistant Deputy Minister Policy, Jill Sinclair
613-992-3458, Fax: 613-995-2876
Assistant Deputy Minister Public Affairs, Josée Touchette
613-995-0383, Fax: 613-995-2610
Assistant Deputy Minister Science & Technology; CEO, Defence R&D Canada, Dr. Robert S. Walker
613-996-2020, Fax: 613-995-3402
Associate Deputy Minister National Defence, William F. Pentney
613-992-0275, Fax: 613-945-7011
Director General Environment, Ginger Stones
613-995-0923, Fax: 613-992-9422
Director General General Military Engineering, Robert Testa
613-995-2415, Fax: 613-995-8261
Director General Nuclear Safety, Keith Dewar
613-995-6729, Fax: 613-995-5537
Director General Realty Policy & Plans, Marie McDonald
613-995-5586, Fax: 613-995-1031
Director Infrastructure & Environment Corporate Services, Don Edgecombe
613-995-7243, Fax: 613-996-9527
Director Infrastructure & Environment Issues Management, Kathryn Brown
613-995-1064, Fax: 613-995-1031
Comptroller Infrastructure & Environment, Jim Carter
613-992-7980, Fax: 613-995-6653
Chief Review Services, Greg Jarvis
613-992-7975, Fax: 613-992-0528
Associate Chief Communications Security Establishment, Penny Reedie
613-991-7501, Fax: 613-991-8514
Judge Advocate General, B.Gen. Ken Watkin
613-992-3019, Fax: 613-992-5078
Ombudsman, Pierre Daigle
613-992-0787, Fax: 613-992-3167
• Communications Security Establishment
PO Box 9703 Terminal
Ottawa, ON K1G 3Z4
613-991-7600
www.cse-cst.gc.ca
• Office of the Communications Security Establishment Commissioner
PO Box 1984 B
Ottawa, ON K1P 5R5
613-992-3044
csec-ccst.gc.ca
• Military Police Complaints Commission
270 Albert St., 10th Fl.
Ottawa, ON K1P 5G8
613-947-5625
Fax: 613-947-5713
800-632-0566
commission@mpcc-cppm.gc.ca
Other Communication: Toll Free Fax: 1-877-947-5713

Commands / Commandes

Operational Commands

Land Force Atlantic Area (Headquarters)
Halifax, NS
902-427-7580

Land Force Central Area (Headquarters)
Toronto, ON
416-633-6200

Land Force Western Area (Headquarters)
Edmonton, AB
780-973-4011

Maritime Forces Atlantic (Headquarters)
Halifax, NS
902-427-6355

Maritime Forces Pacific (Headquarters)
Victoria, BC
250-363-2800

Secteur du Québec de la Force terrestre
Montréal, QC
514-252-2777

BFC Bagotville
Alouette, QC G0C 1A0

CFB Borden
Borden, ON L0M 1C0

CFB Cold Lake
Cold Lake, AB T9M 2C6

CFB Comox
Lazo, BC V0R 2K0

CFB Edmonton
PO Box 10500
Edmonton, AB T5J 4J5

CFB Esquimalt
FMO
Victoria, BC V9A 7N2

CFB Gagetown
Oromocto, NB E2V 4J5

CFB Gander
PO Box 6000
Gander, NL A1V 1X1

CFB Goose Bay
Goose Airport
Happy Valley-Goose Bay, NL A0P 1S0

CFB Greenwood
Greenwood, NS B0P 1N0

CFB Halifax
Halifax, NS B3K 5X5

CFB Kingston
Vimy Post Office
Kingston, ON K7K 7B4

BFC Montréal
Richelain, QC J0J 1R0

CFB Moose Jaw
PO Box 5000
Moose Jaw, SK S6H 7Z8

CFB North Bay
Hornell Heights, ON P0H 1P0

CFB Petawawa
Petawawa, ON K8H 2X3

CFB Shilo

Shilo, MB R0K 2A0

CFB Suffield
PO Box 6000
Medicine Hat, AB T1A 8K8

CFB Trenton
Astra, ON K0K 3W0

BFC Valcartier
Courcelette, QC G0A 4Z0

CFB Winnipeg
Westwin, MB R3J 3Y5

CFS Alert
Belleville, ON K8N 5W6

CFS Leitrim
Ottawa, ON K1A 0K5

CFS Masset
PO Box 2000
Masset, BC V0T 1M0

CFS St. John's
PO Box 2028
St. John's, NL A1C 6B5

Canadian Forces College
Toronto, ON
416-482-6800

Canadian Land Forces Command & Staff College
Kingston, ON
613-451-5818

Royal Military College
Kingston, ON
613-541-6000

Calgary
#418, 100 - 4th Ave. SW
Calgary, AB T2P 3N2
403-974-2822

Moncton
#102, 95 Foundry St.
Moncton, NB E1C 5H7
506-851-0556

Québec
Tour Ouest, Guy-Favreau Complex
#911, 200, boul René-Lévesque
Montréal, QC H2Z 1X4
514-283-5286

Toronto
4900 Yonge St., 6th Fl.
Toronto, ON M2N 6B7
416-635-4406
888-564-8625

Vancouver
#201, 1090 West Pender
Vancouver, BC V6E 2N7
604-666-0199

National Energy Board (NEB) / Office national de l'énergie (ONE)

444 - 7 Ave. SW
Calgary, AB T2P 0X8
403-292-4800
Fax: 403-292-5503
800-899-1265
TDD: 800-632-1663
info@neb-one.gc.ca
www.neb-one.gc.ca
Other Communication: Toll free fax: 877-288-8803
Federal regulatory tribunal whose powers include: authorizing oil, natural gas & electricity exploration; certifying interprovincial & international pipelines & designated power lines; & setting tolls & tariffs for oil & gas pipelines under federal jurisdiction. The NEB reviews Canadian supply of all major commodities, with emphasis on electricity, oil, natural gas, & oil & natural gas by-products. It also reviews the demand for Canadian energy in Canada & in export markets. In addition to its regulatory role, the NEB is responsible for advising the government on the development & use of energy resources. Its responsibilities include regulating exploration, development & production of oil & gas on frontier lands in a manner that promotes worker safety, environmental protection & resource conservation. The NEB is responsible for environmental matters relating to the construction & operation of facilities & programs within its jurisdiction. Its environmental activities are carried out in three phases: The first phase involves evaluating the potential environmental effects of proposed projects. In the second phase, the environment is protected through monitoring & enforcement of terms & conditions attached to project approval. The third phase includes ongoing monitoring of operations to ensure that cleanup, restoration & maintenance of sites & rights of way are conducted to acceptable standards. The Board also verifies that emergency response plans are in place & that it or the operator can respond immediately to any incidents.
Acts Administered:
Canada Oil & Gas Operations Act
Canada Petroleum Resources Act
Canada Transportation Act
Canadian Environmental Assessment Act
Energy Administration Act
National Energy Board Act
Northern Pipeline Act
Chair/CEO, Gaétan Caron
403-299-2724, Fax: 403-299-5503
gaetan.caron@neb-one.gc.ca
Professional Leader Environment, Robert Steedman
403-299-3178,
rsteedman@neb-one.gc.ca
Government Film Commissioner & Chair, Tom Perlmutter
514-283-9245

National Research Council Canada (NRC) / Conseil national de recherches Canada (CNRC)

Bldg. M-58
1200 Montreal Rd.
Ottawa, ON K1A 0R6
613-993-9101
Fax: 613-952-7928
877-672-2672
TDD: 613-952-9907
info@nrc-cnrc.ca
www.nrc-cnrc.ca
Other Communication: IRAP Information: 613/993-1790; CISTI Information: 613/993-1600
NRC is Canada's principal public science & technology agency. It performs, supports & promotes scientific & industrial research for economic & social benefits, research & development in the national interest. Contributions are made to the national science & technology infrastructure & the development of a highly skilled workforce is fostered. Activities focus on strengthening industrial partnerships to bolster competitiveness in key information & telecommunications technologies. The Canada Institute for Scientific & Technical Information (CISTI), a component of NRC, provides access to hundreds of national/international databases, more than 50,000 journals, millions of books, technical reports & conference proceedings. Provides: customized literature searches; current awareness services; access to scientific, technical & medical databases; & referrals to experts. CISTI has an integrated online catalog accessible via the Internet. It publishes 14 international research journals including "Environmental Reviews". The NRC Industrial Research Assistance Program (IRAP) is Canada's national technology transfer & diffusion network helping Canadian firms develop world-class technology they cannot generate on their own. Advisory services involve assisting firms to: define technical needs; identify technical opportunities; obtain technical information & assistance; solve process & production problems; access or acquire technology & expertise from Canadian or foreign firms; & access financial assistance where appropriate. Technical & financial assistance is provided for R&D projects & for adapting existing technologies, with emphasis on advancing unproven technologies to the point of performance testing.
President, Dr. John R. McDougall
613-993-2024, Fax: 613-957-8850
Vice-President Research, Life Sciences, Dr. Roman Szumski
613-993-9244, Fax: 613-954-2066
Vice-President Research, Physical Sciences, Dr. Danial D. Wayner
613-998-5404, Fax: 613-949-1314
Vice-President Technology & Industry Support, Patricia Mortimer
613-998-3664, Fax: 613-998-3839
Acting Vice-President Engineering, John M. Coleman
613-949-5955, Fax: 613-949-5987
Acting Vice-President Corporate Management & CFO, Shane Brunas
613-991-3773, Fax: 613-991-3774
Acting Secretary General, Robert G. James
613-998-4579, Fax: 613-991-0398
Director General Canada Institute for Scientific & Technical Information, Pam Bjornson
613-993-2341, Fax: 613-952-9112
Director General Industrial Research Assistance Program (IRAP), Dr. Tony Rahilly
613-993-0695, Fax: 613-954-0501

Alberta & Northwest Territories
250 Karl Clark Rd.
Edmonton, AB T6N 1E4
780-495-6509
Fax: 780-495-6510

Atlantic/Nunavut Region
1411 Oxford St.
Halifax, NS B3H 3Z1
902-426-3138
Fax: 902-426-1624
Executive Director, Bradley C. Goodyear
902-426-1055, Fax: 902-426-1624

Pacific Region
#650 - 1185 West Georgia St.
Vancouver, BC V6E 4E6
604-221-3100
Fax: 604-221-3101
Executive Director, Christopher Ryan
604-221-3163, Fax: 604-221-3101
christopher.ryan@nrc-cnrc.gc.ca

Newfoundland & Labrador
Kerwin Place & Arctic Ave., Memorial University
PO Box 12093
St. John's, NL A1B 3T5
709-772-5228
Fax: 709-772-5067
Director, David W. Rideout
709-772-2838, Fax: 709-772-5067
dave.rideout@nrc-cnrc.gc.ca

New Brunswick
PO Box 5678 W
Fredericton, NB E3B 5G4
506-452-3831
Fax: 506-452-3827
877-994-4727

Ontario
#903 55 St. Clair Ave. E
Toronto, ON M4T 1M2
416-973-4484
Fax: 416-973-4303

Québec
#P-101, 75, boul de Montagne
Boucherville, QC J4B 6Y4
450-641-5300
Fax: 450-641-5301
Executive Director, Bogdan Ciobanu
450-641-5305, Fax: 450-641-5301
bogdan.ciobanu@cnrc-nrc.gc.ca

Saskatchewan & Manitoba
435 Ellice Ave.
Winnipeg, MB R3B 1X6
204-983-0092
Fax: 204-983-8835

Biotechnology Research Institute (BRI) / Institut de recherche en biotechnologie (IRB)
6100, av Royalmount
Montréal, QC H4P 2R2
514-496-6100
Fax: 514-496-1928
bri-info@cnrc-nrc.gc.ca
www.nrc-cnrc.gc.ca/eng/ibp/bri.html

Prevention & pollution control, including technology & process development, identification & behaviour of pollutants, monitoirng & ecotoxicological risk evaluation; green technologies & sustainable development. BRI scientists have unique expertise in the biotreatment of contaminated soils, groundwater, sediments, air, & industrial wastewater. The Sector works closely with industry on the R&D of innovative environmental technologies. BRI is also a founding member of the Montreal Centre of Excellence in Brownfields Rehabilitation (MCEBR), a joint initiative between government & industry to carry out research, development, & demonstration projects associated with soil decontamination & site rehabilitation.
Director General, Dr. Michel Desrochers
514-496-6101, Fax: 514-496-6388
Director Bioprocess Centre, Bernard Massie
514-496-6131, Fax: 514-496-7251
Bernard.Massie@cnrc-nrc.gc.ca
Director Environment Sector, Adrien Pilon
514-496-6180, Fax: 514-496-1575
Acting Director Health Sector, Eugene Lepekhin
514-496-7065, Fax: 514-496-5143
Eugene.Lepekhin@cnrc-nrc.gc.ca
Director Industrial Affairs, Eileen Raymond
514-496-6349, Fax: 514-496-5007
Eileen.Raymond@cnrc-nrc.gc.ca
Group Leader Applied Ecotoxicology, Dr. Geoffrey Sunahara
514-496-8030, Fax: 514-496-6265
Geoffrey.Sunahara@cnrc-nrc.gc.ca
Group Leader Bioconversion & Sustainable Development, Dr. Peter Lau
514-496-6325, Fax: 514-496-6265
Peter.Lau@cnrc-nrc.gc.ca
Group Leader Environmental & Analytical Chemistry, Dr. Jalal Al-Hawari
514-496-6267, Fax: 514-496-6265
Jalal.Hawari@cnrc-nrc.gc.ca
Group Leader Environmental Bio-Engineering, Dr. Serge Guiot
514-496-6181, Fax: 514-496-6265
Serge.Guiot@cnrc-nrc.gc.ca
Group Leader Environmental Microbiology, Dr. Charles Greer
514-496-6182, Fax: 514-496-6265
Charles.Greer@cnrc-nrc.gc.ca
Group Leader Genetics, Dr. Malcolm Whiteway
514-496-6146, Fax: 514-496-6213
Malcolm.Whiteway@cnrc-nrc.gc.ca
Group Leader Nanobiotechnology, Dr. John Luong
416-496-6175, Fax: 514-496-6265
John.Luong@cnrc-nrc.gc.ca

Herzberg Institute of Astrophysics (HIA) / Institut Herzberg d'astrophysique (IHA)
5071 West Saanich Rd.
Victoria, BC V9E 2E7
250-363-0001
Fax: 250-363-0045
hia-www@nrc-cnrc.gc.ca
www.nrc-cnrc.gc.ca/eng/ibp/hia.html
Operation & maintenance of astronomical observatories as national facilities available to all interested scientists. Conducts research programs in the fields of astronomy, space science & studies solar activity measurements of trace elements in the atmosphere.
Director General, Dr. Greg Fahlman
250-363-0040, Fax: 250-363-8483
Gregory.Fahlman@nrc-cnrc.gc.ca
Director Dominion Astrophysical Observatory, James E. Hesser
250-363-0007, Fax: 250-363-6970
James.Hesser@nrc-cnrc.gc.ca
Director Operations, Susanna Gibson
250-363-0567, Fax: 250-363-0063
Susanna.Gibson@nrc-cnrc.gc.ca

Industrial Materials Institute (IMI) / Institut des matériaux industriels
75, boul de Mortagne
Boucherville, QC J4B 6Y4
450-641-5000
Fax: 450-641-5101
Imi-Info@cnrc-nrc.gc.ca
www.nrc-cnrc.gc.ca/imi-imi
Materials processing technologies for the metal, polymer, aerospace & automotive sectors; virtual fabrication; advanced instrumentation & materials; envionmental technologies.
Director General, Dr. Blaise Champagne, Eng., Ph.D.
450-641-5050, Fax: 450-641-5101
Blaise.Champagne@cnrc-nrc.gc.ca
Acting Director Aluminium Technology Centre, Bernard Arsenault
418-545-5546, Fax: 418-545-5543
Bernard.Arsenault@cnrc-nrc.gc.ca
Director Modelling and Diagnostics, Jean F. Bussière
450-641-5252, Fax: 450-641-5106
Jean.Bussiere@cnrc-nrc.gc.ca
Director London - Center for Automotive Materials & Manufacturing (CAMM), Sylvain Pelletier
450-641-5239, Fax: 450-641-5105
Sylvain.Pelletier@imi.cnrc-nrc.gc.ca

Institute for Aerospace Research (NRC) / Institut de recherche aérospatiale (IAR)
1200 Montreal Rd.
Ottawa, ON K1A 0R6
613-990-0765
Fax: 613-952-7214
www.nrc-cnrc.gc.ca/iar-ira
Development & use of national aeronautical facilities; advanced design & manufacture; transportation & safety; aerospace & the environment; international programs & strategic intelligence.
Director General, Jerzy P. Komorowski
613-993-0141,
jerzy.komorowski@nrc-cnrc.gc.ca
Director Aerodynamics Laboratory, Dr. Steven J. Zan
613-993-2423, Fax: 613-957-4309
Director Aerospace Manufacturing Technology Centre, Pierre Dicaire
514-283-9139, Fax: 514-283-9484
Director Flight Research Laboratory, Stewart W. Baillie
613-998-3071, Fax: 613-952-1704
Director Gas Turbine Laboratory, Dr. Ibrahim A. Yimer
613-991-1139
Director Operations, Andrew B. Sullivan
613-993-9447
Director Structures, Materials and Performance Laboratory, Dr. Prakash Patnaik
613-991-6915, Fax: 613-990-7444

Institute for Biodiagnostics / Institut du biodiagnostic
435 Ellice Ave.
Winnipeg, MB R3B 1Y6
204-983-7692
Fax: 204-984-7217
Neela.Mitra@nrc-cnrc.gc.ca
www.nrc-cnrc.gc.ca/ibd-ibd

Institute for Biological Sciences (IBS) / Institut des sciences biologiques
Bldg. M-54
1200 Montreal Rd.
Ottawa, ON K1A 0R6
613-993-5812
Fax: 613-957-7867
www.nrc-cnrc.gc.ca/ibs-isb
Research in molecular genetics, immunochemistry, microbiology, biochemistry, neurobiology including cell signaling, transduction, in vivo & in vitro models for therapeutics evaluation.
Director General, Dr. James Richards
613-993-7506, Fax: 613-957-7867
James.Richards@nrc-cnrc.gc.ca
Director Business Development & Research Services, Scott Ferguson
613-990-5948, Fax: 613-952-5136
Scott.Ferguson@nrc-cnrc.gc.ca
Director Immunobiology Program, Jean-Robert Brisson
613-990-3244, Fax: 613-941-1327
Jean-Robert.Brisson@nrc-cnrc.gc.ca

Institute for Chemical Process & Environmental Technology (ICPET) / Institut de technologie des procédés chimiques et de l'environnement
Bldg. M-12
1200 Montreal Rd.
Ottawa, ON K1A 0R6
613-993-4041
Fax: 613-957-8231
www.nrc-cnrc.gc.ca/icpet-itpce
Focuses expertise in the areas of process & materials chemistry, process technology & related environmental technology. Supports environmentally responsible manufacturing in the fuel cell, oil sands & bioproducts sectors. Aids manufacturing & industrial clients in optimizing their process operations & reducing the impact of their operations on the environment. Promotes business opportunities in collaborative research, technology licensing & fee-for-service arrangements.
Director General, Dr. Janusz Lusztyk
Janusz.Lusztyk@nrc-cnrc.gc.ca
Director Commericalization, Kanu Sikka
613-990-4624, Fax: 613-991-2384
Kanu.Sikka@nrc-cnrc.gc.ca

Institute for Fuel Cell Innovation (IFCI) / Institut d'innovation en piles à combustible
4250 Wesbrook Mall
Vancouver, BC V6T 1W5
604-221-3000
Fax: 604-221-3001
info.itci-iipac@nrc-cnrc.gc.ca
www.nrc-cnrc.gc.ca/ifci-iipc
Strategic research aimed at advancing fuel cell science & technology & facilitating the commercialization of hydrogen & fuel cell systems.
Director General, Maja Veljkovic
604-221-3024, Fax: 604-221-3002
Maja.Veljkovic@nrc-cnrc.gc.ca
Director Operations, David Semczyszyn
604-221-3013,
David.Semczyszyn@nrc-cnrc.gc.ca
Director Science & Technology, Dr. Dave Ghosh
604-221-3040,
Dave.Ghosh@nrc-cnrc.gc.ca

Institute for Information Technology (IIT) / Institut de technologie de l'information
Bldg. M-50
1200 Montreal Rd.
Ottawa, ON K1A 0R6
613-991-3373
Fax: 613-952-0074
877-672-2672
www.nrc-cnrc.gc.ca/iit-iti
Director General, Christian Couturier
506-444-0555, Fax: 506-444-6187
christian.couturier@nrc-cnrc.gc.ca
Director Business Development & Research Support, Marc-Alain Mallet
506-444-0375, Fax: 506-452-3859
Marc-Alain.Mallet@nrc-cnrc.gc.ca
Acting Director Research Programs, NCR, Charles-Antoine Gauthier
613-993-8551, Fax: 613-952-7998
Charles-Antoine.Gauthier@nrc-cnrc.gc.ca
Director Research Programs, New Brunswick, Andrew Reddick
506-444-0540, Fax: 506-452-3814
Andrew.Reddick@nrc-cnrc.gc.ca

Institute for Marine Biosciences (IMB) / Institut des biosciences marines (IBM)
1411 Oxford St.
Halifax, NS B3H 3Z1
902-426-8332
Fax: 902-426-9413
communications.imb@nrc-cnrc.gc.ca
www.nrc-cnrc.gc.ca/imb-ibm
Aquatic animal health & nutrition; natural toxins; mass spectrometry & proteomics; cell & molecular biology.
Director General, Dr. Joan C. Kean-Howie
902-426-8278, Fax: 902-426-8514
Joan.Kean-Howie@nrc-cnrc.gc.ca

Institute for Microstructural Sciences (IMS) / Institut des sciences des microstructures
Bldg. M-50
1200 Montreal Rd.
Ottawa, ON K1A 0R6
613-949-9660
Fax: 613-957-8734
ims.info@nrc-cnrc.gc.ca
www.nrc-cnrc.gc.ca/ims-ism
Director General, Marie D'lorio
613-993-4597, Fax: 613-957-8734
Marie.D'iorio@nrc-cnrc.gc.ca
Director Applications Technologies, Sylvain Charbonneau
613-998-9414,
Sylvain.Charbonneau@nrc-cnrc.gc.ca

Federal/Provincial Government / Government of Canada

Director Materials Technologies, Thomas E. Jackman
613-993-6711,
Thomas.Jackman@nrc-cnrc.gc.ca
Director Research Support Operations, Cheryl Lambert
613-991-4650,
Cheryl.Lambert@nrc-cnrc.gc.ca

Institute for National Measurement Standards / Institut des étalons nationaux de mesure
Bldg. M-36
1500 Montreal Rd.
Ottawa, ON K1A 0R6
613-998-7018
Fax: 613-954-1473
alexandra.shaw@nrc-cnrc.gc.ca
www.nrc-cnrc.gc.ca/inms-ienm
Canada's national metrology institute (NMI), charged with the responsibility to investigate & determine standards & methods of measurement.
Director General, Dr. James W. McLaren
613-993-7319, Fax: 613-952-5113
James.McLaren@nrc-cnrc.gc.ca
Director Business & Research Support, Katalin Deczky
613-991-6942, Fax: 613-952-8154
Katalin.Deczky@nrc-cnrc.gc.ca
Director Metrology, Dr. Alan G. Steele
613-993-9384, Fax: 613-990-6439
Alan.Steele@nrc-cnrc.gc.ca

Institute for Nutrisciences & Health / Institut des sciences nutritionelles et de la santé
550 University Ave.
Charlottetown, PE C1A 4P3
902-566-7000
Fax: 902-569-4289
inh@nrc-cnrc.gc.ca
www.nrc-cnrc.gc.ca/inh-isns

Institute for Ocean Technology (IOT) / Institut des technologies océaniques (ITO)
Kerwin Pl. & Arctic Ave.
PO Box 12093
St. John's, NL A1B 3T5
709-772-4939
Fax: 709-772-2462
Noel.Murphy@nrc-cnrc.gc.ca
www.nrc-cnrc.gc.ca/iot-ito
Ocean technology research in the areas of offshore engineering, marine vessel design, underwater vehicles, propulsion, electronic navigation, ice-vessel & ice structure interaction. Provides assistance to Canadian ocean technology companies & Canadian government departments. Research services performed in the following areas: tanker offloading & stationkeeping, offshore platform efficiency, navigation safety, all aspects of ocean technology. The Ocean Technology Enterprise Centre assists in the growth & development of new ventures in ocean technology. The centre helps new & established enterprises to develop their concepts & technologies in a supportive environment, with access to IOT facilities & expertise.
Director General, Dr. F. Mary Williams
709-772-2469, Fax: 709-772-3101
f.williams@nrc-cnrc.gc.ca
Director Facilities, Carl J. Harris
709-772-2326, Fax: 709-772-2462
Carl.Harris@nrc-cnrc.gc.ca
Director Research, Dr. Bruce Parsons
709-772-2326, Fax: 709-772-2462
bruce.parsons@nrc-cnrc.gc.ca

Institute for Research in Construction (IRC) / Institut de recherche en construction
Bldg. M-24
1500 Montreal Rd.
Ottawa, ON K1A 0R6
613-993-2607
Fax: 613-952-7673
Irc.Client-Services@nrc-cnrc.gc.ca
www.nrc-cnrc.gc.ca/irc-irc
Research areas include building envelope & structure, indoor environment, urban infrastructure, fire research, sustainable built environment & climate change. A special initiative is the National Guide to Sustainable Municipal Infrastructure, in partnership with the Federation of Canadian Municipalities, Infrastructure Canada & the Canadian Public Works Association, a collection of best practices for core infrastructure.
Director General, Morad R. Atif
613-993-2443, Fax: 613-941-0822
Morad.Atif@nrc-cnrc.gc.ca
Director Building Envelope & Structure, Dr. Ralph M. Paroli
613-993-9714, Fax: 613-954-5984
ralph.paroli@nrc-cnrc.gc.ca
Director Business Services, Daniel B. Roy
613-993-3772, Fax: 613-941-0822
Daniel.Roy@nrc-cnrc.gc.ca
Director Codes & Evaluation, Denis Bergeron
613-993-5659, Fax: 613-952-0268
Denis.Bergeron@nrc-cnrc.gc.ca
Director Fire Research, J.R. Thomas
613-993-0817, Fax: 613-954-0483
J.Thomas@nrc-cnrc.gc.ca
Director Urban Infrastructure, Zoubir Lounis
613-993-5412, Fax: 613-952-8102
Zoubir.Lounis@nrc-cnrc.gc.ca
Manager Centre for Sustainable Infrastructure Research, Dr. David W. Hubble
306-780-3332, Fax: 306-780-3421
david.hubble@nrc-cnrc.gc.ca

London - Centre for Automotive Materials and Manufacturing (CAMM) / Centre des matériaux et fabrication pour l'automobile
800 Collip Circle
London, ON N6G 4X8
519-430-7166
Fax: 519-430-7064
John.Lyons@nrc-cnrc.gc.ca
www.nrc-cnrc.gc.ca/eng/facilities/imi/camm.html
The Centre for Automotive Materials and Manufacturing serves as the national headquarters for the National Research Council's automotive-related capabilities and facilities across Canada. Their purpose is to lead in the development of scalable, sustainable manufacturing technologies for green vehicles. CAMM research is focused on laser materials processing, electrolytic, physical and chemical vapor deposition technologies and composites in manufacturing.
Director, Dr. Sylvain Pelletier
450-641-5239, Fax: 450-641-5105
Sylvain.Pelletier@imi.cnrc-nrc.gc.ca

National Institute of Nanotechnology / Institut national de nanotechnologie
Bldg. NINT, University of Alberta
11421 Saskatchewan Dr.
Edmonton, AB T6G 2M9
780-641-1600
Fax: 780-641-1601
nintinfo@nrc.gc.ca
www.nrc-cnrc.gc.ca/nint-innt
Multi-disciplined research in physics, chemistry, engineering, biology, informatics, pharmacy & medicine, with applications in medicine & biotechnology, energy & environment, computing & telecommunications.
Director General, Dr. Nils O. Petersen
780-641-1610,
Nils.Petersen@nrc-cnrc.gc.ca
Director Business Development & External Relations, Richard Brommeland
780-641-1620,
Richard.Brommeland@nrc-cnrc.gc.ca
Director Research Programs, Dr. Christopher J. Haugen
780-641-1615,
Chris.Haugen@nrc-cnrc.gc.ca
Research Officer Nano Ethical, Environmental, Economic, Legal & Societal Issues (NEEELS), Michael D. Lounsbury
780-492-1684, Fax: 780-492-3325
ml37@ualberta.ca

Plant Biotechnology Institute (PBI) / Institut de biotechnologie des plantes (IBP)
110 Gymnasium Pl.
Saskatoon, SK S7N 0W9
306-975-5248
Fax: 306-975-4839
pbi-info@nrc-cnrc.gc.ca
www.nrc-cnrc.gc.ca/pbi-ibp
Canada's national laboratory for advanced research in new exploitable methods for genetic alteration of plants & for biochemical control of plant development in agriculture. Engineering projects include cell & molecular biology of higher plants. Technical services include: DNA synthesis & sequencing, bio-nuclear magnetic resonance spectroscopy, mass spectroscopy, advanced training services, & expert consultancy.
Director General, Jerome Konecsni
306-975-5575, Fax: 306-975-4191
Jerome.Konecsni@nrc-cnrc.gc.ca
Director Business & Corporate Services, Jeffrey P. Parker
306-975-5568, Fax: 306-975-4839
Jeff.Parker@nrc-cnrc.gc.ca
Director Research, Suzanne R. Abrams
306-975-5569, Fax: 306-975-4191
Sue.Abrams@nrc-cnrc.gc.ca

Steacie Institute for Molecular Sciences / Institut Steacie des sciences moléculaires
100 Sussex Dr.
Ottawa, ON K1A 0R6
613-993-1212
Fax: 613-954-5242
Huguette.Morin-Dumais@nrc-cnrc.gc.ca
www.nrc-cnrc.gc.ca/sims-issm
NRC-SIMS conducts cutting-edge interdisciplinary research in selected areas of molecular sciences that have the potential to stimulate entirely new or emerging sectors of the Canadian economy. Strategic molecular sciences research fields for NRC-SIMS include: nanoscience, chemical biology, diagnostics, laser science, molecular interfaces, advanced materials, and their related technologies.

Canadian Hydraulics Centre (CHC) / Centre canadien d'hydraulique (CCH)
1200 Montreal Rd.
Ottawa, ON K1A 0R6
613-993-9381
Fax: 613-952-7679
info.chc@nrc-cnrc.gc.ca
www.nrc-cnrc.gc.ca/chc-chc
One of North America's largest hydraulic engineering laboratories, with expertise & experience in physical & numerical modeling, analysis & field studies to solve a wide range of hydraulic engineering problems. Specializations include: coastal engineering; marine structures; cold regions; environmental hydraulics; laboratory technologies; numerical models. Environmental hydraulics services include: coastal ecosystem management; river & watershed management; flood management & dam break; chemical & oil spill migration; water quality & pollutant transport; sediment transport, including shoreline erosion & dredged spoil disposal; aquaculture management; environmental information & simulation systems.
Acting General Manager, Dr. Garry W. Timco
613-993-6673,
Garry.Timco@nrc-cnrc.gc.ca
Group Leader Coastal Engineering, Andrew M. Cornett
613-993-6690,
Andrew.Cornett@nrc-cnrc.gc.ca

Centre for Surface Transportation Technology (CSTT) / Centre de technologie des transports de surface (CTTS)
2320 Lester Rd.
Ottawa, ON K1V 1S2
613-998-9639
Fax: 613-957-0831
inquiries.cstt@nrc-cnrc.gc.ca
www.nrc-cnrc.gc.ca/cstt-ctts
Road & rail vehicle performance technology, studies & rail tribology; climatic engineering.
Director General, Paul Treboutat
613-998-9635,
Paul.Treboutat@nrc-cnrc.gc.ca
Director Rail Division, Harold M. Kohn
613-991-5522,
Harold.Kohn@nrc-cnrc.gc.ca
Director Road Vehicles & Military Systems Division, Michael S. Halasz
613-998-8015,
Michael.Halasz@nrc-cnrc.gc.ca

National Round Table on the Environment & Economy (NRTEE) / Table ronde nationale sur l'environnement et l'économie (TRNEE)
#200, 344 Slater St.
Ottawa, ON K1R 7Y3
613-992-7189
Fax: 613-992-7385
admin@nrtee-trnee.ca
www.nrtee-trnee.ca

Federal/Provincial Government / Government of Canada

The National Round Table on the Environment & the Economy is an independent agency of the federal government committed to providing decision makers & opinion leaders with reliable information &objective views on the current state of the debate on the environment & the economy. Working with stakeholders across Canada, the NRTEE carries out its mandate by identifying key issues with both environmental &economic implications, fully exploring these implications, & suggesting action designed to balance economic prosperity with environmental preservation. A multistakeholder approach, combined with impartiality & neutrality, are the hallmarks of the NRTEE's activities. By creating an atmosphere in which all points of view can be expressed freely & debated openly, the NRTEE has established a process whereby stakeholders themselves define the environment/economy interface within issues, determine areas of consensus & identify the reasons for disagreement in other areas. The NRTEE's programs focus on the following areas: energy & climate change; capital markets & sustainability; climate change adaptation
President & CEO, David McLaughlin
613-943-0399,
mclaughlind@nrtee-trnee.ca
Director Communications & Public Affairs, Brian Laghi
613-943-2054,
laghib@nrtee-trnee.ca
Director Corporate Services, Jim McLachlan
613-947-4507,
mclachlanj@nrtee-trnee.ca
Director Policy & Research, René Drolet
613-996-4501,
droletr@nrtee-trnee.ca

National Search & Rescue Secretariat / Secrétariat national de recherches et sauvetage

#400, 275 Slater St.
Ottawa, ON K1A 0K2
613-992-0054
Fax: 613-996-3746
800-727-9414
inquiry@nss.gc.ca
www.nss.gc.ca
Provides a central managerial role in the overall coordination of search & rescue. It addresses program & policy issues related to the National Search & Rescue Program, & advises the Lead Minister for search & rescue.
Executive Director, Géraldine Underdown
613-992-0054, Fax: 613-996-3746
Communications Officer, Kim Fauteux
613-992-3472, Fax: 613-996-3746

Natural Resources Canada (NRCan) / Ressources naturelles Canada (RNCan)

580 Booth St.
Ottawa, ON K1A 0E4
613-995-0947
Fax: 613-992-7211
TDD: 613-996-4397
www.nrcan-rncan.gc.ca/com/
Other Communication: Emergency Operations Centre:
613/995-5555, 943-0000
Advances development of Canada's economy by contributing to the development & use of Canada's mineral & energy resources in a manner consistent with federal environmental & social objectives; advances knowledge of the Canadian landmass through scientific & science-related activities.
Acts Administered:
Arctic Waters Pollution Prevention Act
Arctic Waters Experimental Pollution Regulations
Order Exempting the United States Coast Guard Icebreaker \Healy\" from the Application of the Arctic Shipping Pollution Prevention Regulations"
Canada Foundation for Sustainable Development Technology Act
Canada-Newfoundland Atlantic Accord Implementation Act
Canada-Newfoundland Oil & Gas Spills & Debris Liability Regulations
Newfoundland Offshore Area Oil & Gas Operations Regulations
Newfoundland Offshore Area Petroleum Diving Regulations
Newfoundland Offshore Area Petroleum Geophysical Operations Regulations
Newfoundland Offshore Area Petroleum Production & Conservation Regulations
Newfoundland Offshore Area Registration Regulations
Newfoundland Offshore Certificate of Fitness Regulations
Newfoundland Offshore Petroleum Drilling Regulations
Newfoundland Offshore Petroleum Installations Regulations
Canada-Nova Scotia Offshore Petroleum Resources Accord Implementation Act
Canada-Nova Scotia Oil & Gas Spills & Debris Liability Regulations
Nova Scotia Offshore Area Certificate of Fitness Regulations
Nova Scotia Offshore Area Petroleum Diving Regulations
Nova Scotia Offshore Area Petroleum Drilling Regulations
Nova Scotia Offshore Area Petroleum Geophysical Operations Regulations
Nova Scotia Offshore Area Petroleum Installations Regulations
Nova Scotia Offshore Area Petroleum Production & Conservation Regulations
Nova Scotia Resources (Ventures) Ltd. Drilling Assistance Regulations
Canada Oil & Gas Operations Act (Indian Affairs & Northern Development)
Canada Oil & Gas Certificate of Fitness Regulations
Canada Oil & Gas Diving Regulations
Canada Oil & Gas Drilling Regulations
Canada Oil & Gas Geophysical Operations Regulations
Canada Oil & Gas Installations Regulations
Canada Oil & Gas Operations Regulations
Canada Oil & Gas Production & Conservation Regulations
Nova Scotia Offshore Area Production & Conservation Regulations
Oil & Gas Spills & Debris Liability Regulations
Canada Petroleum Resources Act
Canadian Ownership & Control Determination Act
Co-operative Energy Act
Department of Natural Resources Act
Report on the State of Canada's Forests Regulations
Energy Administration Act
Energy Efficiency Act
Energy Monitoring Act
Energy Supplies Emergency Act
Explosives Act
Forestry Act
Gros Morne Forestry Timber Regulations
Timber Regulations
Hibernia Development Project Act
International Boundary Commission Act
Lands Surveys Act
Lands Surveyors Act
Motor Vehicle Fuel Consumption Standards Act
National Energy Board Act
National Energy Board Coast Recovery Regulations
National Energy Board Electricity Regulations
National Energy Board Export & Import Reporting Regulations
National Energy Board Pipeline Crossing Regulations, I & II
National Energy Board Processing Plant Regulations
National Energy Board Rules of Practice & Procedure
National Energy Board Substituted Service Regulations
Onshore Pipeline Regulations
Pipeline Arbitration Committee Procedure Rules
Power Line Crossing Regulations
Northern Pipeline Act
Uranium Mines (Ontario) Occupational Health & Safety Regulations
Nuclear Energy Control Act
Nuclear Fuel Waste Act, 2002
Nuclear Liability Act
Nuclear Safety & Control Act
Canadian Nuclear Safety Commission Rules of Procedure
Class I Nuclear Facilities Regulations
Class II Nuclear Facilities & Prescribed Equipment Regulations
General Nuclear Safety & Control Regulations
Nuclear Non-Proliferation Import & Export Control Regulations
Nuclear Security Regulations
Nuclear Substances & Radiation Devices Regulations
Packaging & Transport of Nuclear Substances Regulations
Radiation Protection Regulations
Uranium Mines & Mills Regulations
Uranium Mines (Ontario) Occupational Health & Safety Regulations
Oil Substitution & Conservation Act
Administration of Acts with respect to Changes in Provincial Boundaries
Alberta Act
Alberta/BC Boundary Act, 1974
Alberta/NWT Boundary Act, 1958
British Columbia 1857, 1866
BC-Yukon-NWT Boundary Act, 1967
Keewatin Act
Manitoba Boundaries Extension Act, 1912
Manitoba-NWT Boundary Act, 1966
Manitoba/Saskatchewan Boundary Act, 1966
New Brunswick, 1851
Newfoundland, 1949
Northwest Territories, 1905
Nova Scotia, 1851
Nunavut, 1993
Ontario, 1889
Ontario Boundaries Extension Act, 1912
Ontario-Manitoba Boundary Act
Prince Edward Island, 1873
Québec Boundaries Extension Act, 1912
Saskatchewan, 1905
Saskatchewan/NWT Boundary Act, 1966
Yukon, 1898
Acts Administered in Part by Natural Resources Canada
Arctic Waters Pollution Prevention Act (Transport Canada/Indian & Northern Affairs)
Arctic Shipping Pollution Prevention Regulations
Arctic Waters Pollution Prevention Regulations
Canada Lands Survey Act (Indian & Northern Affairs)
Canada Lands Surveys Examination Regulation
Canada-Newfoundland Oil & Gas Spills & Debris Liability Regulations
Land Survey Tariff Regulations
Newfoundland & Labrador Offshore Area Line Regulations
Newfoundland Offshore Area Oil & Gas Operations Regulations
Newfoundland Offshore Area Petroleum Diving Regulations
Newfoundland Offshore Area Petroleum Geophysical Operations Regulations
Newfoundland Offshore Area Petroleum Production & Conservation Regulations
Newfoundland Offshore Area Registration Regulations
Newfoundland Offshore Petroleum Drilling Regulations
Newfoundland Offshore Petroleum Installations Regulations
Newfoundland Offshore Petroleum Resource Revenue Fund Regulations
Nova Scotia Resources (Ventures) Limited Drilling Assistance Regulations
Shipping Safety Control Zones Order
Canada Petroleum Resources Act (Indian & Northern Affairs)
Environmental Studies Research Fund Regions Regulations
Frontier Lands Petroleum Royalty Regulations
Frontier Lands Registration Regulations
Lancaster Sound Designated Area Regulations
Orders Prohibiting the Issuance of Interests at Lapierre House Historic Site (Yukon) & Rampart House (Yukon)
Cape Breton Development Corporation Act
National Energy Board Act (Transport Canada)
Resources & Technical Surveys Act (Fisheries & Oceans/Environment)
Minister, Natural Resources, Hon. Christian Paradis
613-996-2007, Fax: 613-943-1562
ParadC@parl.gc.ca
Deputy Minister, Cassie J. Doyle
613-992-3280, Fax: 613-992-3828
CassieJ.Doyle@NRCan-RNCan.gc.ca
Associate Deputy Minister, Malcolm Brown
613-996-9753, Fax: 613-992-3828
Malcolm.Brown@NRCan-RNCan.gc.ca
Assistant Deputy Minister Energy Sector, Christine Donoghue
613-947-2751, Fax: 613-992-1405
Christine.Donoghue@NRCan-RNCan.gc.ca
Chief Scientist, Marian Chiu
613-947-9094, Fax: 613-944-4747
Marian.Chiu@NRCan-RNCan.gc.ca
Director General External Relations, Mark Pearson
613-996-6055, Fax: 613-996-0478
Mark.Pearson@NRCan-RNCan.gc.ca
Chief Audit Executive, Joe Freamo
613-996-4940, Fax: 613-992-8799
Joe.Freamo@NRCan-RNCan.gc.ca
Director General Corporate Renewal Office, Sylvie Letellier
613-947-7403, Fax: 613-992-8922
Sylvie.Letellier@NRCan-RNCan.gc.ca
• Atomic Energy of Canada Ltd.
• National Energy Board

Canadian Forest Service (CFS) / Service canadien des forêts

613-995-0947
Fax: 613-947-1208
TDD: 613-996-4397

Federal/Provincial Government / Government of Canada

cfs-scf@nrcan.gc.ca
http://cfs.nrcan.gc.ca
Promotes the sustainable development of Canada's forests & competitiveness of the Canadian forest sector for the well-being of present & future generations of Canadians. It focuses on forest science & technology, & related national policy coordination. The CFS maintains five research centres across the country that share responsibility for research in the areas of biodiversity; biotechnology; climate change; ecology & ecosystems; entomology; forest conditions, monitoring & reporting; forest fires; forest & landscape management; pathology; silviculture & regeneration; & socioeconomics.
Asst. Deputy Minister, Jim Farrell
613-990-5555,
Jim.Farrell@NRCan-RNCan.gc.ca
Jr. Program Officer, Amanda Chickite
250-363-8975,
Amanda.Chickite@NRCan-RNCan.gc.ca

Atlantic Forestry Centre / Centre de foresterie de l'Atlantique
1350 Regent St. South
PO Box 4000
Fredericton, NB E3B 5P7
506-452-3500
Fax: 506-452-3525
http://cfs.nrcan.gc.ca/regions/afc
Responsible for the overall Canadian Forest Service operations & programs in the Atlantic region. Liaises & negotiates with provincial government, industry officials, & other sector-related senior management on behalf of the CFS in the region.
Regional Director General, John E. Richards
506-452-3508,
JohnE.Richards@NRCan-RNCan.gc.ca
Director Forest Production and Protection, Derek MacFarlane
506-452-3680,
Derek.MacFarlane@NRCan-RNCan.gc.ca
Director Science, Bruce Pendrel
506-452-3505,
Bruce.Pendrel@NRCan-RNCan.gc.ca

Canadian Wood Fibre Centre (CWFC) / Centre canadien sur la fibre de bois (CCFB)
580 Booth Street, 8th Floor
Ottawa, ON K1A 0E4
613-947-9001
Fax: 613-947-8863
http://cfs.nrcan.gc.ca/subsite/cwfc
The Canadian Wood Fibre Centre (CWFC) brings together forest sector researchers to develop solutions for the Canadian forest sector's wood fibre related industries in an environmentally responsible manner. Its mission is to create innovative knowledge to expand the economic opportunities for the forest sector to benefit from Canadian wood fibre.

Great Lakes Forestry Centre / Centre de foresterie des Grands Lacs
1219 Queen St. East
PO Box 490
Sault Ste Marie, ON P6A 2E5
705-949-9461
Fax: 705-541-5700
http://cfs.nrcan.gc.ca/regions/glfc
Responsibilities include: forest research & regional forestry activities in Ontario; provides the primary federal focus for forestry in Ontario; emphasis on boreal mixed wood forest management & environmental impacts of pollutants & forestry practices; efforts also directed at the reduction of losses from insects, disease & fire; ecosystem dynamics & classification; nutrient problems & impacts from forestry practices; acid rain impacts (carbon dioxide/nitrogen oxide interactions).
Director General, Theodore Van Lunen
705-541-5555,
Theodore.VanLunen@NRCan-RNCan.gc.ca
Director Forest Ecology & Productivity, David Nanang
705-541-5558,
David.Nanang@NRCan-RNCan.gc.ca
Director Integrated Pest Management, Anthony Hopkin
705-541-5568,
Anthony.Hopkin@NRCan-RNCan.gc.ca
Director Policy, Planning & Liaison, Rod Smith
705-541-5561,
Rod.CFS.Smith@NRCan-RNCan.gc.ca

Laurentian Forestry Centre / Centre de foresterie des Laurentides
1055, rue du PEPS
CP 10380 Sainte-Foy
Québec, QC G1V 4C7
418-648-3335
Fax: 418-648-5849
lucie.labrecque@RNCan-NRCan-gc.ca
http://scf.rncan.gc.ca/regions/cfl
Responsibilities include: increasing scientific & technical knowledge in the area of forest biology which includes biodiversity, tree biotechnology & advanced genetics, pest management methods, & in the area of forest ecosystem which cover forest ecosystem processes, effects of forestry practices, landscape management & climate change.
Director General, Jacinthe Leclerc
418-648-3957,
Jacinthe.Leclerc@RNCan-NRCan.gc.ca
Director Forest Biology Program, Lise Caron
418-648-7616, Fax: 418-649-6956
Lise.Caron@RNCan-NRCan.gc.ca
Research Director Forest Ecosystems, Vincent Roy
418-648-3770, Fax: 418-649-6956
Vincent.Roy@RNCan-NRCan.gc.ca
Director Planning & Development, Normand Laflamme
418-648-2528, Fax: 418-648-2529
Normand.Laflamme@RNCan-NRCan.gc.ca

Northern Forestry Centre / Centre de foresterie du Nord
5320 - 122 St.
Edmonton, AB T6H 3S5
780-435-7210
Fax: 780-435-7359
http://cfs.nrcan.gc.ca/regions/nofc
Responsibilities include: socio-economics & forest sociology; fire ecology, environment, & advanced fire management & prediction systems; climate change & forest interactions; carbon budget modeling; forest health, insect, & disease monitoring & management systems; remote sensing applications & landscape level classification systems; ecosystems productivity; biodiversity. Regional coordination of national programs relating to Model Forests & First Nation Forestry. Responsible for the direction of forestry programs in the provinces of Alberta, Saskatchewan, Manitoba & the NWT, including R&D, & four federal-provincial partnership agreements in forestry.
Director General, Timothy Sheldan
780-435-7202, Fax: 780-435-7396
Timothy.Sheldan@NRCan-RNCan.gc.ca
Director Climate Change & Forests Research Program, Kelvin Hirsch
780-435-7319,
Kelvin.Hirsch@NRCan-RNCan.gc.ca
Director Ecosystems Health Science Program, Maria Teresa Fernandez de Castro
780-430-3848,
MariaTeresa.FernandezdeCastro@NRCan-RNCan.gc.ca
Director Strategic Policy & Planning Branch, Ken Mallett
780-435-7201,
Ken.Mallett@NRCan-RNCan.gc.ca

Pacific Forestry Centre / Centre de foresterie du Pacifique
506 West Burnside Rd.
Victoria, BC V8Z 1M5
250-363-0600
Fax: 250-363-0775
http://cfs.nrcan.gc.ca/regions/pfc
Responsibilities include: forest management of federal lands; first nations programs; first nations land claims resource analysis; economic analysis of the regional forest sector (value-added, labour costs, & industrial sustainability); national strategic planning for the forestry practices & landscape management networks; science & technology programs in both forest biology (ecosystems processes, climate change, pest management, & tree biotechnology). Advises the CFS ADM on all forestry matters relating to the Pacific & Yukon region. The Mountain Pine Beetle Action Plan 2005-2010 set out strategies for confronting the infestation.
Director General, Kami Ramcharan
250-363-0608, Fax: 250-363-6088
Kami.Ramcharan@NRCan-RNCan.gc.ca
Director Forest Information, Jeff Dechka
250-363-0627,
Jeff.Dechka@NRCan-RNCan.gc.ca
Director Forest Resources Division, Jim Wood
250-363-6008, Fax: 250-363-6004
Jim.Wood@NRCan-RNCan.gc.ca

Director Forest Science, Judi Beck
250-363-0705,
Judi.BECK@NRCan-RNCan.gc.ca
Director MPB Policy & Research, Bill Wilson
250-363-0721, Fax: 250-363-6004
Bill.Wilson@NRCan-RNCan.gc.ca

Corporate Management & Services Sector / Secteur de la gestion et des services intégrés
613-995-4243
Fax: 613-922-8922

Earth Sciences Sector / Secteur des sciences de la Terre
http://ess.nrcan.gc.ca/index_e.php
Provides Canadians with timely & reliable geomatics & geoscience knowledge, products & services of the highest standards & in the most cost-effective manner possible. The Earth Sciences Sector is a predominantly science- and technology-based sector & includes the Geological Survey of Canada, Geomatics Canada, & the Polar Continental Shelf Project. These groups are major contributors to the comprehensive geoscience knowledge base of Canada & provide surveying, mapping, remote sensing, & digital information services describing the Canadian landmass.
Asst. Deputy Minister, Dr. David Boerner
613-992-9983, Fax: 613-995-1509
David.Boerner@NRCan-RNCan.gc.ca
Chief Geologist, Donald James
867-975-4412, Fax: 867-979-0708
Donald.James@NRCan-RNCan.gc.ca
Director General Coordination & Strategic Issues Branch, Marian Campbell Jarvis
613-992-5032,
Marian.CampbellJarvis@NRCan-RNCan.gc.ca

Geological Survey of Canada (GSC) / Commission géologique du Canada
601 Booth St.
Ottawa, ON K1A 0E8
613-996-3919
Fax: 613-943-8742
esic@nrcan.gc.ca
http://gsc.nrcan.gc.ca
Other Communication: Bookstore: 613-995-4342
Geoscientific information & research, geoscience surveys, sustainable development of Canada's resources, environmental protection, technology innovation.
Executive Manager Atlantic & Western Branch, Laurie Lee McGuire
613-996-6574, Fax: 613-996-6575
LaurieLee.McGuire@NRCan-RNCan.gc.ca
Director General Central & Northern Canada Branch, Dr. David Boerner
613-995-4314, Fax: 613-996-6575
David.Boerner@NRCan-RNCan.gc.ca
Director GSC Atlantic, Dr. Jacob Verhoef
902-426-3448, Fax: 902-426-1466
Jacob.Verhoef@NRCan-RNCan.gc.ca
Director GSC Calgary, Bill Reynen
403-292-7156, Fax: 403-292-5377
Bill.Reynen@NRCan-RNCan.gc.ca
Director GSC Central Canada, Dr. Alan Galley
613-992-7867, Fax: 613-992-5694
Alan.Galley@NRCan-RNCan.gc.ca
Director GSC Northern Canada, Dr. David J. Scott
613-992-3218,
DavidJ.Scott@NRCan-RNCan.gc.ca
Director GSC Pacific, Dr. Carmel Lowe
250-363-6763, Fax: 250-363-6739
Carmel.Lowe@NRCan-RNCan.gc.ca
Director GSC Québec, Donna Kirkwood
418-654-2675, Fax: 418-654-2615
Donna.Kirkwood@RNCan-NRCan.gc.ca

Energy Policy Sector / Secteur de la politique énergétique
613-996-7432
Fax: 613-992-1405
www.nrcan-rncan.gc.ca/eneene/polpol/index-eng.php
Develops & promotes economic, regulatory & voluntary approaches to encourage sustainable development of energy resources to meet domestic needs & export markets. Advises the government on federal energy policies, strategies, emergency plans & activities; promotes efficient energy use.
Asst. Deputy Minister, Mark Corey
613-947-2751,
Mark.Corey@NRCan-RNCan.gc.ca

Senior Director International Environment Policy Division, Margaret E. Martin
613-996-6474, Fax: 613-947-6799
Margaret.Martin@nrcan-rncan.gc.ca

Innovation and Energy Technology Sector / Secteur de l'innovation et de la technologie énergétique
Asst. Deputy Minister, Geoff Munro
613-947-1435, Fax: 613-944-4747
Geoff.Munro@NRCan-RNCan.gc.ca

CANMET Energy Technology Centre / Direction de la technologie de l'énergie
613-996-6220
Fax: 613-947-1016
www.nrcan.gc.ca/es/etb/
CETC develops & delivers knowledge & technology-based programs for the sustainable production & use of Canada's energy supply. Key areas include advanced combustion, greener buildings, sustainable hydrocarbons, energy-efficient industrial technologies, sustainable communities, renewable energy, distributed power. Programs & services are delivered through three regional centres
Acting Director General, Richard Davies
613-996-8115
Director TEAM Operations Office, Wayne Richardson
613-996-5419

CANMET Energy Technology Centre-Devon
1 Oil Patch Dr.
PO Box 1280
Devon, AB T0C 1E0
780-987-8214
Fax: 780-987-8690
The federal government's primary research group for the development of hydrocarbon supply technologies & related environmental technologies, with an emphasis on oil sands & heavy oil. CWRC comprises of two S&T groups: Advanced Separation Technologies (AST) & the National Centre for Upgrading Technology (NCUT). CWRC conducts fee-for-service, cost-shared & task-shared S&T activities, & performs exploratory, public-good research in strategic areas such as environmental technologies. By developing hydrocarbon technologies that use less energy & have fewer environmental impacts, CWRC is helping to ensure that the oil industry is a sustainable, environmentally responsible contributor to Canada's energy supply.
Director General, Hassan Hamza
780-780-8617

CANMET Energy Technology Centre-Ottawa (CETC)
1 Haanel Dr.
Nepean, ON K1A 1M1
613-996-8201
Fax: 613-995-9584
www.nrcan.gc.ca/es/etb/cetc/cetchome.htm
One of Canada's premier organizations in the field of energy science & technology. Fosters the research, development & deployment of innovative, environmentally responsible solutions for conventional, alternative & renewable energy technologies. Research carried out in renewable energy, energy-efficient technologies for industry, communities & buildings, alternative transportation fuels, district heating & cooling & integrated energy systems, advanced low-emission combustion technologies, processing & environmental catalysis for fuels production & hydrocarbon conversion, & energy-efficient metallurgical fuel products & technologies. Offers an Interlaboratory Sample Exchange Program (CANSPECS) for the characterization of standards, R&D testing services, technology & market assessments, & energy-related workshops.
Director General, John Marrone
613-996-8201

CANMET Energy Technology Centre-Varennes (CEDRL)
1615, Montée Ste-Julie
CP 4800
Varennes, QC J3X 1S6
450-652-6639
Fax: 450-652-0999
R&D & related technology transfer in efficiency technologies in the industrial & buildings sector; vehicle & engine efficiencies; alternative transportation fuels; renewable energy technology.
Director General, Gilles Jean
450-652-6639, Fax: 450-652-5177

Minerals & Metals Sector (MMS) / Secteur des minéraux et des métaux
613-947-6580
TDD: 613-996-4397
info-mms@nrcan-rncan.gc.ca
www.nrcan-rncan.gc.ca/mms-smm
MMS is the federal government's primary source of scientific & technological knowledge, & policy advice, on Canada's mineral & metal resources & on explosives regulation & technology. In addition to housing three scientific research institutions, MMS has the government lead in promoting sustainable development & responsible use of Canada's mineral & metal resources. The Sector is a leader in the generation & dissemination of knowledge on the Canadian minerals & metals industry, & collaborates with & provides research services to governmental, institutional & industrial clients for the development of new technology with economic, environmental & social benefits to Canadians.
Asst. Deputy Minister, Anil Arora
613-992-2490, Fax: 613-996-7425
Anil.Arora@NRCan-RNCan.gc.ca

Minerals & Metals Sector / Secteur des minéraux et des métaux
Other Communication: Canadian Metals & Minerals Recycling Database: www.recycle.nrcan.gc.ca/recyclingdb.asp
MMS is the federal government's primary source of scientific & technological knowledge, & policy advice, on Canada's mineral & metal resources & on explosives regulation & technology. In addition to housing three scientific research institutions, MMS has the government lead in promoting sustainable development & responsible use of Canada's mineral & metal resources. The Sector is a leader in the generation & dissemination of knowledge on the Canadian minerals & metals industry, & collaborates with & provides research services to governmental, institutional & industrial clients for the development of new technology with economic, environmental & social benefits to Canadians
Asst. Deputy Minister, Gary Nash
613-992-2490, Fax: 613-996-7425
Director General Industry Analysis & Business Development, Leonard Surges
613-995-2662
Director General Policy & Planning, Chrystia Chudczak
613-995-8851
Director General Programs Branch, Denis Lagacé
613-995-7029

Climate Change Impacts & Adaptation Directorate / Direction des impacts et de l'adaptation liés aux changements climatiques
613-947-4848
Fax: 613-947-0126
adaptation@nrcan.gc.ca
adaptation.nrcan.gc.ca
Provides funding for research & activities to improve knowledge of Canada's vulnerability to climate change. Acts as facilitator between stakeholders & researchers through support of C-CIARN (Canadian Climate Impacts & Adaptation Research Network).
Executive Director, Paul Egginton
613-947-4880

Canada Centre for Remote Sensing - Geomatics Canada (CCRSO) / Centre canadien de télédétection (CCT)
588 Booth St.
Ottawa, ON K1A 0Y7
613-995-0947
Fax: 613-947-1382
TDD: 613-996-4397
http://ccrs.nrcan.gc.ca
Remote sensing data for Canada; development of remote sensing technology & applications in conjunction with the private sector, & in support of environmental monitoring; development of the Canadian geospatial data infrastructure for distribution of remote sensing & other geographical databases, in partnership with other departments; development of GIS applications.
Director General, Douglas Bancroft
613-947-1358, Fax: 613-947-1382
Douglas.Bancroft@NRCan-RNCan.gc.ca
Director Business, Policy & Planning, Gordon Deecker
613-947-1280, Fax: 613-947-1408
Gordon.Deecker@NRCan-RNCan.gc.ca
Director Data Acquisition Division, Caroline Cloutier
613-995-0802, Fax: 613-947-1408
Caroline.Cloutier@NRCan-RNCan.gc.ca
Director Earth Observation & GeoSolutions Divison, E. Paola de Rose
613-947-1350, Fax: 613-947-1385
E.Paola.deRose@NRCan-RNCan.gc.ca

Director Geodetic Survey Division, Denis Hains
613-995-4282, Fax: 613-995-3215
Denis.Hains@NRCan-RNCan.gc.ca

Mapping Services Branch - Geomatics Canada
615 Booth St.
Ottawa, ON K1A 0E9
613-995-4945
Fax: 613-995-8737
Surveys Canadian lands & waters; prepares & distributes topographic, geographic, electoral & aeronautical maps & digital products, surveys federal-provincial boundaries; manages a national program for acquiring & using remote sensing data. Mapping Branch is responsible for the Canada Map Office, Geogrpahical Names Board of Canada & National Air Photo Library.
Director General, Jean Cooper
613-947-0793

Mapping Information Branch / Direction de l'information cartographique
615 Booth St.
Ottawa, ON K1A 0E9
613-995-4945
Fax: 613-995-8737
Other Communication: Canada Map Office: 1-800-465-6277 or 613/952-7009; Help Desk: 613/996-5916

Programs Branch / Direction des programmes
Acting Director General, David Boerner
613-995-4314
Acting Director Sustainable Resources, Joan Tod
613-992-6438
Acting Director Environment, Safety & Security, Dr. Geneviève Béchard
613-943-4119

Polar Continental Shelf Project (PCSP) / Étude du plateau continental polaire (EPCP)
#487, 615 Booth St.
Ottawa, ON K1A 0E4
613-947-1650
Fax: 613-947-1611
TDD: 613-996-4397
pcsp@NRCan.gc.ca
http://polar.nrcan.gc.ca
Other Communication: Resolute NWT Base: 867/252-3872; Fax: 867/252-3605
A logistics network that allows scientists to conduct research in the Arctic each year by providing ground & air transportation support, accommodations & communications. Maintains a comprehensive field logistical network, & promotes & coordinates scientific activities in the Canadian Arctic, including protecting the environment.
Director, Martin Bergmann
613-947-1601,
Martin.Bergmann@NRCan-RNCan.gc.ca

Legal Services / Services juridiques
613-992-7837
Fax: 613-995-2598

Electricity Resources Branch / Direction des ressources en électricité
Legislative, policy & regulatory responsibilities for renewable energies, electricity, oil & gas, frontier lands activities. Provides leadership on policy on nuclear energy, uranium, radioactive waste & related environmental issues.
Director General, Tom Wallace
613-996-3027
Director Nuclear Energy, Sylvana Guindon
613-995-2870
Director Renewable & Electrical Energy, Christopher Padfield
613-947-5101
Director Uranium & Radioactive Waste, P.A. Brown
613-996-2395
Director, David Burpee
613-995-7460

Office of Energy Research & Development (OERD) / Bureau de recherche et développement énergétique (BRDE)
Coordinates the federal indepartmental program of Energy Research & Development (PERD) for research & development in energy efficiency & climate change, transportation, renewable energy, & coordinates & represents Canada in international collaboration energy R&D through international mechanisms such

Federal/Provincial Government / Government of Canada

as the International Energy Agency & the MOU with US DOE International Energy Agency.
Director, Graham R. Campbell
613-995-8860,
Director Energy Technology Policy, Milena Sejnoha
613-947-1021
Director PERD Program Operations, Mary Preville
613-995-3590

Petroleum Resources Branch / Direction des ressources pétrolières
Legislative, policy & regulatory responsibilities for all sources of energy supplies, such as renewable energies, electricity, oil & gas, frontier lands activities.
Director General, Phillipp Jennings
613-944-6171
Director Energy Infrastructure Protection Division, Felix Kwamena
613-995-3190
Director Frontier Lands Management, Eric Landry
613-992-3794
Director Oil Division, Kevin Cliffe
613-995-1525
Director Natural Gas Division, J.S. Booth
613-992-9780

Office of Energy Efficiency / Office de l'éfficacité énergétique
Policy & programs in support of efficient use of energy, use of alternative energy & transportation fuels.
Acting Director General, Carol Buckley
613-944-7501
Director Buildings Division, Anne Auger
613-996-4079
Director Demand Policy & Analysis Division, Tim McIntosh
613-943-2396
Director Housing & Equipment, Louis Marmen
613-996-7512
Director Industrial Programs, Michael Burke
613-996-6872
Director Outreach & Information, Colleen Paton
613-996-0765
Director Transportation Energy Use Division, Vacant
613-995-7300

CANMET Mineral Technology Branch (MTB) / Direction de la technologie minérale
Includes the Mining & Mineral Sciences Laboratories, the Materials Technology Laboratory & the Canadian Explosives Research Laboratory. R&D, technological solutions to to reduce environmental liabilities.
Director CANMET Materials Technology Laboratory, Dr. Jennifer Jackman
613-995-8248
Manager Climate Change, Linda Wilson
613-995-4133

Natural Sciences & Engineering Research Council of Canada (NSERC) / Conseil des recherches en sciences naturelles et en génie du Canada (CRSNG)
Constitution Square, Tower II
350 Albert St.
Ottawa, ON K1A 1H5
613-995-4273
Fax: 613-943-1624
marie-josee.duval@nserc-crsng.gc.ca
www.nserc.gc.ca
Science & Engineering Research Canada (NSERC) is a federal agency whose role is to make investments in people, discovery & innovation for the benefit of all Canadians. With an annual budget of more than $860 million, it supports more than 20,000 university students & postdoctoral fellows in their advanced studies. NSERC promotes discovery by funding more than 10,000 university professors every year & helps make innovation happen by encouraging more than 500 Canadian companies to participate & invest in university research projects.
President, Dr. Suzanne Fortier
613-995-5840,
suzanne.fortier@nserc-crsng.gc.ca
Vice-President Research Grants & Scholarships Directorate, Isabelle Blain
613-995-5833,
isabelle.blain@nserc-crsng.gc.ca
Vice-President Research Partnerships Programs Directorate, Janet Walden

616-139-9215, Fax: 613-947-6371
janet.walden@nserc-crsng.gc.ca
Director Communications Division, Jacqueline Couture
613-995-5993,
Jacqueline.Couture@nserc-crsng.gc.ca
Commissioner, Cassie J. Doyle
613-992-3280, Fax: 613-995-1913
Acting Assistant Commissioner & Comptroller, Jim Booth
613-992-9780, Fax: 613-995-1913

Parks Canada / Parcs Canada
25 Eddy St.
Gatineau, QC K1A 0M5
613-860-1251
888-773-8888
TDD: 866-787-6221
information@pc.gc.ca
www.pc.gc.ca
Responsible for the protection, management, operation & maintenance of national parks, historic sites, canals & other significant examples of Canada's natural & cultural heritage, for the benefit, understanding & enjoyment of Canadians. Administers one of the largest park systems in the world. Working towards establishing parks in each of 39 distinct natural regions. In addition to the national parks, national historic sites & national marine conservation areas, Parks Canada coordinates other heritage programs, including federal heritage buildings, heritage railway stations, grave sites of Canadian Prime Ministers, heritage rivers, archaeology programs, international programs.
CEO, Alan Latourelle
819-997-9525, Fax: 819-953-9745
Director General National Parks, Ron Hallman
819-994-2657, Fax: 819-994-5140
Director General National Historic Sites, Larry S. Ostola
819-994-1808, Fax: 819-934-1526
Chief Administrative Officer, Céline Gaulin
819-953-4013, Fax: 819-953-5632
Communications Advisor, Joanne Huppé
819-953-8699, Fax: 819-953-5523
joanne.huppe@pc.gc.ca
Other Communications: Alt. Phone: 613/799-6269
• Historic Sites & Monuments Board of Canada
Terrasses de la Chaudière
25 Eddy St.
Gatineau, QC K1A 0M5
819-997-4059
Fax: 819-934-1115
hsmbc-clmhc@pc.gc.ca
www.pc.gc.ca/clmhc-hsmbc/
Chair, Dr. Richard M. Alway
A seventeen-member advisory board which reports to the Minister of Environment & recommends whether persons, places or events are of national historic &/or architectural significance, & therefore warrant commemoration. The board also makes recommendations concerning the designation of heritage railway stations.

National Parks Directorate / Direction générale des parcs nationaux
Director General, Doug C. Stewart
819-994-2657, Fax: 819-994-5140
Executive Director Ecological Integrity, Mike P. Wong
819-994-2639, Fax: 819-997-3380
Director Parks Establishment, Kevin McNamee
819-997-4908

Carillon
230, rue du Barrage
Carillon, QC J0V 1C0
450-447-4888
Fax: 450-658-2428
888-773-8888
www.pc.gc.ca/canalcarillon

Chambly
1899, boul Périgny
Chambly, QC J3L 4C3
450-447-4888
Fax: 450-658-2428
888-773-8888
www.pc.gc.ca/canalchambly

Lachine
200, boul René-Lévesque ouest, tour Ouest, 6e étage
Montréal, QC H2Z 1X4

514-283-6054
Fax: 514-496-1263
888-773-8888
www.pc.gc.ca/canallachine

Rideau
34A Beckwith St. South
Smiths Falls, ON K7A 2A8
613-283-5170
Fax: 613-283-0677
TDD: 866-787-6221
www.pc.gc.ca/lhn-nhs/on/rideau

Sainte-Anne-de-Bellevue
170, rue Sainte-Anne
Sainte-Anne-de-Bellevue, QC H9X 1N1
450-447-4888
Fax: 450-658-2428
www.pc.gc.ca/canalsteanne

Saint-Ours
2930, ch des Patriotes
Saint-Ours, QC G1K 7R3
450-785-2212
Fax: 450-658-2428
www.pc.gc.ca/canalstours

St. Peters
PO Box 8
St Peters, NS B0E 3B0
902-733-2280
Fax: 902-733-2362
www.pc.gc.ca/stpeterscanal

Sault
1 Canal Dr.
Sault Ste Marie, ON P6A 6W4
705-941-6262
Fax: 705-941-6206
www.pc.gc.ca/lhn-nhs/on/ssmarie

Trent-Severn Waterway
PO Box 567
Peterborough, ON K9J 6Z6
705-750-4900
Fax: 705-742-9644
TDD: 705-750-4949
www.pc.gc.ca/trentsevern

Alexander Graham Bell Historic Site of Canada
PO Box 159
Baddeck, NS B0E 1B0
902-295-2069
Fax: 902-295-3496
information@pc.gc.ca
www.pc.gc.ca/lhn-nhs/ns/grahambell/

Ardgowan National Historic Site of Canada
2 Palmer's Lane
Charlottetown, PE C1A 5V6
902-566-7050
Fax: 902-566-7226
pc.gc.ca/lhn-nhs/pe/ardgowan/

Bank Fishery National Heritage Exhibit
PO Box 9080 A
Halifax, NS B3K 5M7
902-426-5080
Fax: 902-426-4228
information@pc.gc.ca
www.pc.gc.ca/lhn-nhs/ns/bank/

Boishébert & Beaubears Shipbuilding National Historic Sites of Canada
186, route 117
Kouchibouguac National Park, NB E4X 2P1
506-876-2443
Fax: 506-876-4802
TDD: 506-876-4205
kouch.info@pc.gc.ca
www.pc.gc.ca/lhn-nhs/nb/boishebert

Canso Islands National Historic Site of Canada
PO Box 159
Baddeck, NS B0E 1E0

902-295-2069
Fax: 902-295-3496
pc.gc.ca/lhn-nhs/ns/canso/

Cape Breton Highlands National Park of Canada
Ingonish Beach, NS B0C 1L0
902-224-2306
Fax: 902-285-2866
TDD: 902-224-2306
pc.gc.ca/pn-np/ns/cbreton/

Cape Spear National Historic Site of Canada
PO Box 1268
St. John's, NL A1C 5M9
709-772-5367
Fax: 709-772-6302
cape.spear@pc.gc.ca
pc.gc.ca/lhn-nhs/nl/spear/

Carleton Martello Tower National Historic Site of Canada
454 Whipple St.
Saint John, NB E2M 2R3
506-636-4011
Fax: 506-636-4574
TDD: 506-887-6015
fundy.info@pc.gc.ca
pc.gc.ca/lhn-nhs/nb/carleton/

Castle Hill National Historic Site of Canada
PO Box 10, Jerseyside
Placentia Bay, NL A0B 2G0
709-227-2401
Fax: 709-227-2452
castle.hill@pc.gc.ca
pc.gc.ca/lhn-nhs/nl/castlehill/
Other Communication: Off-season: 709/772-5367, Fax: 709/772-6302

Fort Amherst/Port-La-Joye National Historic Site of Canada
2 Palmer's Lane
Charlottetown, PE C1A 5V6
902-566-7626
Fax: 902-566-8295
pc.gc.ca/lhn-nhs/pe/amherst/

Fort Anne National Historic Site of Canada
PO Box 9
Annapolis Royal, NS B0S 1A0
902-532-2397
Fax: 902-532-2232
www.pc.gc.ca/lhn-nhs/ns/fortanne/
Other Communication: Off-season: 902/532-2321

Fort Beauséjour National Historic Site of Canada
111 Fort Beauséjour Rd.
Aulac, NB E4L 2W5
506-364-5080
Fax: 506-536-4399
fort.beausejour@pc.gc.ca
pc.gc.ca/lhn-nhs/nb/beausejour/

Fort Edward National Historic Site of Canada
PO Box 9
Annapolis Royal, NS B0S 1A0
902-532-2321
Fax: 902-532-2232
pc.gc.ca/lhn-nhs/ns/edward/
Other Communication: July & August: 902/798-4706

Fort McNab National Historic Site of Canada
PO Box 9080 A
Halifax, NS B3K 5M7
902-426-5080
Fax: 902-426-4228
halifax.citadel@pc.gc.ca
pc.gc.ca/lhn-nhs/ns/mcnab/

Fortress of Louisbourg National Historic Site
259 Park Service Rd.
Louisbourg, NS B1C 2L2
902-733-2280
Fax: 902-733-2362
TDD: 902-733-3607
pc.gc.ca/lhn-nhs/ns/louisbourg/

Fundy National Park of Canada
PO Box 1001
Alma, NB E4H 1B4
506-887-6000
Fax: 506-887-6008
TDD: 506-887-6015
fundy.info@pc.gc.ca
pc.gc.ca/pn-np/nb/fundy/

Grand Pré National Historic Site of Canada
PO Box 150
Grand Pré, NS B0P 1M0
902-542-3631
Fax: 902-542-1691
866-542-3631
TDD: 902-532-7472
grandpre.info@pc.gc.ca; contact@grand-pre.com
pc.gc.ca/lhn-nhs/ns/grandpre/; www.grand-pre.com

Georges Island National Historic Site of Canada
PO Box 9080 A
Halifax, NS B3K 5M7
902-426-5080
Fax: 902-426-4228
halifax.citadel@pc.gc.ca
pc.gc.ca/lhn-nhs/ns/georges/

Green Gables Heritage Place
2 Palmer's Lane
Charlottetown, PE C1A 5V6
902-963-7874
peinp-pnipe@pc.gc.ca
pc.gc.ca/lhn-nhs/pe/greengables/

Gros Morne National Park of Canada
PO Box 130
Rocky Harbour, NL A0K 4N0
709-458-2417
Fax: 709-458-2059
grosmorne.info@pc.gc.ca
pc.gc.ca/pn-np/nl/grosmorne/

Halifax Citadel National Historic Site of Canada
PO Box 9080 A
Halifax, NS B3K 5M7
902-426-5080
Fax: 902-426-4228
halifax.citadel@pc.gc.ca
pc.gc.ca/lhn-nhs/ns/halifax/

Hawthorne Cottage National Historic Site of Canada
PO Box 5542
St. John's, NL A1C 5W4
709-753-9262
Fax: 709-772-0879
pc.gc.ca/lhn-nhs/nl/hawthorne/
Other Communication: Off-season: 709/528-4004

Kejimkujik National Park of Canada
PO Box 236
Maitland Bridge, NS B0T 1B0
902-682-2772
Fax: 902-682-3367
kejimkujik.info@pc.gc.ca
pc.gc.ca/pn-np/ns/kejimkujik/index_e.asp

Kouchibouguac National Park of Canada
186, Route 117
Kouchibouguac National Park, NB E4X 2P1
506-876-2443
Fax: 506-876-4802
TDD: 506-876-4205
kouch.info@pc.gc.ca
pc.gc.ca/pn-np/nb/kouchibouguac/

L'Anse aux Meadows National Historic Site of Canada
PO Box 70
St-Lunaire-Criquet, NL A0K 2X0
709-623-2608
Fax: 709-623-2028
viking.lam@pc.gc.ca
www.pc.gc.ca/lhn-nhs/nl/meadows/

Marconi National Historic Site of Canada
PO Box 159
Baddeck, NS B0E 1B0
902-295-2069
Fax: 902-295-3496
www.pc.gc.ca/lhn-nhs/ns/marconi/

Monument Lefebvre National Historic Site of Canada
480 rue Centrale
Memramcook, NB E4K 3S6
506-536-0720
Fax: 506-758-9813
monument@nbnet.nb.ca
www.pc.gc.ca/lhn-nhs/nb/lefebvre/
Other Communication: Summer: 506/758-9808

Port-au-Choix National Historic Site of Canada
PO Box 140
Port au Choix, NL A0K 4C0
709-458-2417
Fax: 709-861-3827
pc.gc.ca/lhn-nhs/nl/portauchoix/
Other Communication: Seasonal: 709/861-3522

Port Royal National Historic Site of Canada
PO Box 9
Annapolis Royal, NS B0S 1A0
902-532-2898
Fax: 902-532-2232
www.pc.gc.ca/lhn-nhs/ns/portroyal/
Other Communication: Off-season: 902/532-2232

Prince Edward Island National Park of Canada
2 Palmers Lane
Charlottetown, PE C1A 5V6
902-672-6350
Fax: 902-672-6370
TDD: 902-566-7061
pnipe.peinp@pc.gc.ca
http://pc.gc.ca/pn-np/pe/pei-ipe

Prince of Wales Tower National Historic Site
PO Box 9080 A
Halifax, NS B3K 5M7
902-426-5080
Fax: 902-426-4228
halifax.citadel@pc.gc.ca
www.pc.gc.ca/lhn-nhs/ns/prince/

Province House National Historic Site of Canada
2 Palmer's Lane
Charlottetown, PE C1A 5V6
902-566-7626
Fax: 902-566-8295
pc.gc.ca/lhn-nhs/pe/provincehouse/

Red Bay National Historic Site of Canada
PO Box 103
Red Bay, NL A0K 4K0
709-920-2142
Fax: 709-920-2144
redbay.info@pc.gc.ca
pc.gc.ca/lhn-nhs/nl/redbay/

Ryan Premises National Historic Site
PO Box 1451
Bonavista, NL A0C 1B0
709-468-1600
Fax: 709-468-1604
ryan.premises@pc.gc.ca
pc.gc.ca/lhn-nhs/nl/ryan/

St. Andrews Blockhouse National Historic Site of Canada
454 Whipple St.
Saint John, NB E2M 2R3
506-636-4011
Fax: 506-636-4574
TDD: 506-887-6015
fundy.info@pc.gc.ca
pc.gc.ca/lhn-nhs/nb/standrews/
Other Communication: Summer: 506/529-4270

St. Peters Canada National Historic Site of Canada
PO Box 8
St Peters, NS B0A 1M0
902-733-2280
Fax: 902-733-2362
www.pc.gc.ca/lhn-nhs/ns/stpeters/

Federal/Provincial Government / Government of Canada

Signal Hill National Historic Site of Canada
PO Box 1268
St. John's, NL A1C 5M9
709-772-5367
Fax: 709-772-6302
signal.hill@pc.gc.ca
pc.gc.ca/lhn-nhs/nl/signalhill/

Terra Nova National Park of Canada
General Delivery
Glovertown, NL A0G 2L0
709-533-2801
Fax: 709-533-2706
info.tnnp@pc.gc.ca
pc.gc.ca/pn-np/nl/terranova/

York Redoubt National Historic Site of Canada
PO Box 9080 A
Halifax, NS B3K 5M7
902-426-5080
Fax: 902-426-4228
halifax.citadel@pc.gc.ca
www.pc.gc.ca/lhn-nhs/ns/york/

Battle of the Windmill National Historic Site of Canada
370 Vankoughnet St.
PO Box 479
Prescott, ON K0E 1T0
613-925-2896
Fax: 613-925-1536
ont.wellington@pc.gc.ca
www.pc.gc.ca/lhn-nhs/on/windmill/

Bellevue House National Historic Site of Canada
35 Centre St.
Kingston, ON K7L 4E5
613-545-8666
Fax: 613-545-8721
TDD: 613-545-8668
bellevue.house@pc.gc.ca
www.pc.gc.ca/lhn-nhs/on/bellevue/

Bethune Memorial House National Historic Site of Canada
235 John St. North
Gravenhurst, ON P1P 1G4
705-687-4261
Fax: 705-687-4935
TDD: 705-687-7969
ont-bethune@pc.gc.ca
pc.gc.ca/lhn-nhs/on/bethune/

Bois Blanc Island Lighthouse National Historic Site of Canada
c/o Fort Malden N.H.S.
100 Laird Ave.
PO Box 38
Amherstburg, ON N9V 2Z2
519-736-5416
Fax: 519-736-6603
ont.fort-malden@pc.gc.ca
pc.gc.ca/lhn-nhs/on/boisblanc/

Bruce Peninsula National Park
PO Box 189
Tobermory, ON N0H 2R0
519-596-2233
Fax: 519-596-2298
bruce-fathomfive@pc.gc.ca
pc.gc.ca/pn-np/on/bruce/

Butler's Barracks c/o Fort George National Historic Site
26 Queen St.
PO Box 787
Niagara on the Lake, ON L0S 1J0
905-468-4257
Fax: 905-468-4638
www.pc.gc.ca/lhn-nhs/on/fortgeorge/

Fort George National Historic Site of Canada
26 Queen St.
PO Box 787
Niagara on the Lake, ON L0S 1J0
905-468-4257
Fax: 905-468-4638

ont-niagara@pc.gc.ca
pc.gc.ca/lhn-nhs/on/fortgeorge/

Fathom Five National Marine Park of Canada
PO Box 189
Tobermory, ON N0H 2R0
519-596-2233
Fax: 519-596-2298
bruce-fathomfive@pc.gc.ca
www.pc.gc.ca/lhn-nhs/on/fathomfive

Fort Malden National Historic Site
100 Laird Ave.
PO Box 38
Amherstburg, ON N9V 2Z2
519-736-5416
Fax: 519-736-6603
ont.fort-malden@pc.gc.ca
www.pc.gc.ca/lhn-nhs/on/fortmalden/

Fort Mississauga National Historic Site of Canada
26 Queen St.
PO Box 787
Niagara on the Lake, ON L0S 1J0
905-468-4257
Fax: 905-468-4638

Fort St. Joseph National Historic Site of Canada
PO Box 220
Richards Landing, ON P0R 1J0
705-246-2664
Fax: 705-246-1796
fortstjoseph-info@pc.gc.ca
www.pc.gc.ca/lhn-nhs/on/fortstjoseph

Fort Wellington National Historic Site of Canada
PO Box 479
Prescott, ON K0E 1T0
613-925-2896
Fax: 613-925-1536
TDD: 613-925-2896
ont-wellington@pc.gc.ca
www.pc.gc.ca/lhn-nhs/on/fortwellington/

Georgian Bay Islands National Park of Canada
901 Wye Valley Rd.
PO Box 9
Midland, ON L4R 4K6
705-526-9804
Fax: 705-526-5939
info.gbi@pc.gc.ca
www.pc.gc.ca/lhn-nhs/on/gbi/

Inverarden House National Historic Site of Canada
370 Vankoughnet St.
PO Box 479
Prescott, ON K0E 1T0
613-925-2896
Fax: 613-925-1536
www.pc.gc.ca/lhn-nhs/on/inverarden/

Kingston Martello Towers
35 Centre St.
Kingston, ON K7L 4E5
613-545-8666
Fax: 613-545-8721
TDD: 613-545-8668
www.pc.gc.ca/lhn-nhs/on/bellevue

Laurier House National Historic Site of Canada
335 Laurier Ave. East
Ottawa, ON K1A 6R4
613-992-8142
Fax: 613-947-4851
laurier.house@pc.gc.ca
www.pc.gc.ca/lhn-nhs/on/laurierhouse/

Point Clark Lighthouse National Historic Site of Canada
c/o Woodside National Historic Site
528 Wellington St. North
Kitchener, ON N2H 5L5
519-571-5684
Fax: 519-571-5286
ont-woodside@pc.gc.ca
www.pc.gc.ca/lhn-nhs/on/pointclark/

Point Pelee National Park of Canada
407 Monarch Lane, RR#1
Leamington, ON N8H 3V4
519-322-2365
Fax: 519-322-1277
TDD: 866-787-6221
pelee.info@pc.gc.ca
www.pc.gc.ca/lhn-nhs/on/pointpelee/

Pukaskwa National Park of Canada
Hwy. 627, Hattie Cove
PO Box 212
Heron Bay, ON P0T 1R0
807-229-0801
Fax: 807-229-2097
ont-pukaskwa@pc.gc.ca
www.pc.gc.ca/lhn-nhs/on/pukaskwa/

Queenston Heights & Brock's Monument
Niagara Court House
26 Queen St.
PO Box 787
Niagara on the Lake, ON L0S 1J0
905-468-4257
Fax: 905-468-4638
www.pc.gc.ca/lhn-nhs/on/queenston/

St. Lawrence Islands National Park of Canada
2 County Rd. 5, RR#3
Mallorytown Landing, ON K0E 1R0
613-923-5261
Fax: 613-923-1021
ont-sli@pc.gc.ca
www.pc.gc.ca/pn-np/on/lawren/

Sir John Johnson National Historic Site of Canada
c/o Fort Wellington National Historic Site
370 Vanhoughnet St.
PO Box 479
Prescott, ON K0E 1T0
613-925-2896
Fax: 613-925-1536
ont.wellington@pc.gc.ca
www.pc.gc.ca/lhn-nhs/on/johnjohnson/

Woodside National Historic Site of Canada
528 Wellington St. North
Kitchener, ON N2H 5L5
519-571-5684
Fax: 519-571-5686
ont.woodside@pc.gc.ca
www.pc.gc.ca/lhn-nhs/on/woodside/
Rob Watt

Artillery Park National Historic Site of Canada
2, rue d'Auteuil
CP 10 B
Québec, QC G1K 7A1
418-648-4205
Fax: 418-648-4825
TDD: 866-787-6221
www.pc.gc.ca/lhn-nhs/qc/artillery/

Carillon Barracks National Historic Site of Canada
1899, boul. Périgny
Chambly, QC J3L 4C3
450-537-3861
Fax: 450-537-0975
TDD: 866-787-6221
www.pc.gc.ca/lhn-nhs/qc/carillon/

Cartier-Brébeuf National Historic Site of Canada
175, rue de l'Espinay
CP 10 B
Québec, QC G1K 7R3
418-648-4038
Fax: 418-648-4367
888-773-8888
www.pc.gc.ca/lhn-nhs/qc/brebeuf/

Battle of the Châteauguay National Historic Site of Canada
2371, ch de la Rivière Châteauguay nord
CP 250
Howick, QC J0S 1G0

Federal/Provincial Government / Government of Canada

450-829-2003
Fax: 450-829-3325
www.pc.gc.ca/lhn-nhs/qc/chateauguay/

Battle of the Restigouche National Historic Site of Canada
Route 132
CP 359
Pointe-à-la-Croix, QC G0C 1L0
418-788-5676
Fax: 418-788-5895
www.pc.gc.ca/lhn-nhs/qc/restigouche

Forges du Saint-Maurice National Historic Site of Canada
10000, boul des Forges
Trois-Rivières, QC G9C 1B1
819-378-5116
Fax: 819-378-0887
www.pc.gc.ca/lhn-nhs/qc/forges/

Coteau-du-Lac National Historic Site of Canada
308 A, ch du Fleuve
Coteau-du-Lac, QC J0P 1B0
450-763-5631
Fax: 450-763-1654
www.pc.gc.ca/lhn-nhs/qc/coteau/

Forillon National Park of Canada
122, boul Gaspé
Gaspé, QC G4X 1A9
418-368-5505
Fax: 418-368-6837
www.pc.gc.ca/lhn-nhs/qc/forillon/

Fort Chambly National Historic Site of Canada
2, rue de Richelieu
Chambly, QC J3L 2B9
450-658-1585
Fax: 450-658-7216
www.pc.gc.ca/lhn-nhs/qc/fortchambly/

Fort Lennox National Historic Site of Canada
1 - 61e av
St-Paul-de-l'Ile-aux-Noix, QC J0J 1G0
450-291-5700
Fax: 450-291-4389
www.pc.gc.ca/lhn-nhs/qc/fortlennox/

Fort Témiscamingue National Historic Site of Canada
830, ch du Vieux-Fort
Duhamel ouest, QC J9V 1N7
819-629-3222
Fax: 819-629-2977
fort.temiscaminque@pc.gc.ca
www.pc.gc.ca/lhn-nhs/qc/forttemiscamingue/

Fortifications of Québec National Historic Site of Canada
100, rue St-Louis
PO Box 10 B
Québec, QC G1K 7R3
418-648-7016
Fax: 418-648-9068
www.pc.gc.ca/lhn-nhs/qc/fortifications/

Grosse Ile & the Irish Memorial National Historic Site of Canada
2 rue D'Auteuil
CP 10 B
Québec, QC G1K 7R3
418-248-8841
Fax: 866-790-8991
www.pc.gc.ca/lhn-nhs/qc/grosseile/

La Mauricie National Park of Canada
702, 5e rue
CP 160 Bureau-Chef
Shawinigan, QC G9N 6T9
819-538-3232
Fax: 819-536-3661
parkscanada-que @pc.gc.ca
www.pc.gc.ca/lhn-nhs/qc/mauricie

Lévis Forts National Historic Site of Canada
41, ch du Gouvernement
CP 10 B
Québec, QC G1K 7R3

418-835-5182
Fax: 418-948-9119
www.pc.gc.ca/lhn-nhs/qc/levis/

Louis S. St-Laurent National Historic Site of Canada
6790, rte Louis-St-Laurent
Compton, QC J0B 1L0
819-835-5448
Fax: 819-835-9101
www.pc.gc.ca/lhn-nhs/qc/st-laurent/

Manoir Papineau National Historic Site of Canada
500, rue Notre-Dame
Montebello, QC J0V 1L0
819-423-6965
Fax: 819-423-6455
www.pc.gc.ca/lhn-nhs/qc/papineau/

Mingan Archipelago National Park Reserve of Canada
1340, rue de la Digue
CP 1180
Ha@vre-Saint-Pierre, QC G0G 1P0
418-538-3331
Fax: 418-538-3595
www.pc.gc.ca/lhn-nhs/qc/mingan/

Old Port of Québec Interpretation Centre
100, rue Saint-André
CP 2474 Terminus postal
Québec, QC G1K 7R3
418-648-3300
Fax: 418-648-3678
www.pc.gc.ca/lhn-nhs/qc/vieuxport/

Pointe-au-Père Lighthouse National Historic Site of Canada
1034, rue du Phare
Pointe-au-Père, QC G5M 1L8
418-724-6214
Fax: 418-721-0815
888-773-8888
TDD: 866-787-6221
parkscanada-que@pc.gc.ca
www.pc.gc.ca/lhn-nhs/qc/pointaupere

Saguenay St. Lawrence Marine Park of Canada
182, rte de l'Église
CP 220
Tadoussac, QC G0T 2A0
418-235-4703
Fax: 418-235-4686
parkscanada-que @pc.gc.ca
www.pc.gc.ca/lhn-nhs/qc/saguenay-saint-laurent

Sir George-Étienne Cartier National Historic Site of Canada
458, rue Notre-Dame est
Montréal, QC H2Y 1C8
514-283-2282
Fax: 514-283-5560
888-773-8888
TDD: 866-558-2950
parkscanada-que @pc.gc.ca
www.pc.gc.ca/lhn-nhs/qc/cartier

Sir Wilfrid Laurier National Historic Site of Canada
#945, 12e av
St-Lin-Laurentides, QC J5M 2W4
450-439-3702
Fax: 450-439-5721
888-773-8888
TDD: 866-787-6221
parkscanada-que @pc.gc.ca
www.pc.gc.ca/lhn-nhs/qc/laurier

The Fur Trade at Lachine National Historic Site of Canada
1255, boul Saint-Joseph
Lachine, QC H8S 2M2
514-637-7433
Fax: 514-637-5325
888-773-8888
TDD: 866-787-6221
parkscanada-que@pc.gc.ca
www.pc.gc.ca/lhn-nhs/qc/lachine

Aulavik National Park of Canada
PO Box 29
Sachs Harbour, NT X0E 0Z0

867-690-3904
Fax: 867-690-4808
inuvik.info@pc.gc.ca
http://pc.gc.ca/pn-np/nt/aulavik/index_e.asp

Auyuittuq National Park of Canada
PO Box 353
Pangnirtung, NU X0A 0R0
867-473-2500
Fax: 867-473-8612
nunavut.info@pc.gc.ca
http://pc.gc.ca/pn-np/nu/auyuittuq/index_e.asp

Banff National Park of Canada
PO Box 900
Banff, AB T1L 1K2
403-762-1550
Fax: 403-762-3380
banff.vrc@pc.gc.ca
www.pc.gc.ca/pn-np/ab/banff/index_e.asp

Banff Park Museum National Historic Site of Canada
PO Box 900
Banff, AB T1L 1K2
403-762-1558
Fax: 403-762-1565
banff.vrc@pch.gc.ca
www.pc.gc.ca/lhn-nhs/ab/banff/index_E.asp

Bar U Ranch National Historic Site of Canada
PO Box 168
Longview, AB T0L 1H0
403-395-2212
Fax: 403-395-2331
888-773-8888
TDD: 866-787-6221
BarU.Info@pc.gc.ca
http://pc.gc.ca/lhn-nhs/ab/baru/index_e.asp
Ian Church

Batoche National Historic Site of Canada
RR#1 Box 1040
Wakaw, SK S0K 4P0
306-423-6227
Fax: 306-423-5400
TDD: 306-423-5540
batoche@pc.gc.ca
pc.gc.ca/lhn-nhs/sk/batoche/imdex_e.asp

Cave & Basin National Historic Site of Canada
PO Box 900
Banff, AB T1L 1K2
403-762-1566
Fax: 403-762-1565
banff.vrc@pc.gc.ca
http://pc.gc.ca/lhn-nhs/ab/caveandbasin/index_e.asp

Chilkoot Trail National Historic Site of Canada
#205, 300 Main St.
Whitehorse, YT Y1A 2B5
867-667-3910
Fax: 867-393-6701
800-661-0486
whitehorse.info@pc.gc.ca
http://pc.gc.ca/lhn-nhs/yt/chilkoot/index_e.asp

Dawson Historical Complex National Historic Site of Canada
PO Box 390
Dawson City, YT Y0B 1G0
867-993-7200
Fax: 867-993-7203
dawson.info@pc.gc.ca
http://pc.gc.ca/lhn-nhs/yt/dawson/index_E.asp

Dredge No. 4 National Historic Site of Canada
PO Box 390
Dawson City, YT Y0B 1G0
867-993-7200
Fax: 867-993-7203
dawson.info@pc.gc.ca
http://pc.gc.ca/lhn-nhs/yt/dn4/index_E.asp

Elk Island National Park of Canada
RR#1, Site 4
Fort Saskatchewan, AB T8L 2N7

Federal/Provincial Government / Government of Canada

780-992-5790
Fax: 780-992-2951
elk.island@pc.gc.ca
http://pc.gc.ca/pn-np/ab/elkisland/index_e.asp

Fisgard Lighthouse National Historic Site of Canada
603 Fort Rodd Hill Rd.
Victoria, BC V9C 2W8
250-478-5849
Fax: 250-478-2816
fort.rodd@pc.gc.ca
http://pc.gc.ca/lhn-nhs/bc/fisgard/index_e.asp

Fort Battleford National Historic Site of Canada
PO Box 70
Battleford, SK S0M 0E0
306-937-2621
Fax: 306-937-3370
TDD: 306-937-3199
battleford-info@pc.gc.ca
http://pc.gc.ca/lhn-nhs/sk/battleford/index_e.asp

Fort Langley National Historic Site of Canada
23433 Mavis Ave.
PO Box 129
Fort Langley, BC V1M 2R5
604-513-4777
Fax: 604-513-4798
fort.langley@pc.gc.ca
http://pc.gc.ca/lhn-nhs/bc/langley/index_e.asp

Fort Rodd Hill National Historic Site of Canada
603 Fort Rodd Hill Rd.
Victoria, BC V9C 2W8
250-478-5849
Fax: 250-478-2816
fort.rodd@pc.gc.ca
http://pc.gc.ca/lhn-nhs/bc/fortroddhill/index_e.asp

Fort St. James National Historic Site of Canada
PO Box 1148
Fort St James, BC V0J 1P0
250-996-7191
Fax: 250-996-8566
http://pc.gc.ca/lhn-nhs/bc/stjames/index_e.asp

Fort Walsh National Historic Site of Canada
PO Box 278
Maple Creek, SK S0N 1N0
306-662-3590
Fax: 306-662-2711
TDD: 306-662-3124
fort.walsh@pc.gc.ca
http://pc.gc.ca/lhn-nhs/sk/walsh/index_e.asp

Gitwangak Battle Hill National Historic Site of Canada
PO Box 37
Queen Charlotte, BC V0T 1S0
250-559-8818
Fax: 250-559-8366
TDD: 250-559-8139
gwaii.haanas@pc.gc.ca
www.pc.gc.ca/lhn-nhs/bc/kitwanga/index_E.asp

Glacier National Park of Canada
PO Box 350
Revelstoke, BC V0E 2S0
250-837-7500
Fax: 250-837-7536
revglacier.reception@pc.gc.ca
http://pc.gc.ca/pn-np/bc/glacier/index_e.asp

Grasslands National Park of Canada
PO Box 150
Val Marie, SK S0N 2T0
306-298-2257
Fax: 306-298-2042
grasslands.info@pc.gc.ca
http://pc.gc.ca/pn-np/sk/grasslands/index_e.asp

Gulf Islands National Park Reserve of Canada
2220 Harbour Rd.
Sidney, BC V8L 2P6
250-654-4000
Fax: 250-654-4014
866-944-1744
gulf.islands@pc.gc.ca
http://pc.gc.ca/pn-np/bc/gulf/index_E.asp

Gulf of Georgia Cannery National Historic Site of Canada
12138 Fourth Ave.
Richmond, BC V7E 3J1
604-664-9009
Fax: 604-664-9008
gog.info@pc.gc.ca
http://pc.gc.ca/lhn-nhs/bc/georgia/index_e.asp

Gwaii Haanas National Park Reserve & Haida Heritage Site of Canada
60 Second Beach Rd.
PO Box 37
Queen Charlotte, BC V0T 1S0
250-559-8818
Fax: 250-559-8366
877-559-8818
gwaii.haanas@pc.gc.ca
http://pc.gc.ca/pn-np/bc/gwaiihaanas/index_e.asp

Ivvavik National Park of Canada
PO Box 1840
Inuvik, NT X0E 0T0
867-777-8800
Fax: 867-777-8820
inuvik.info@pc.gc.ca
http://pc.gc.ca/pn-np/yt/ivvavik/index_e.asp

Jasper National Park of Canada
PO Box 10
Jasper, AB T0E 1E0
780-852-6176
Fax: 780-852-6152
jnp_info@pc.gc.ca
http://pc.gc.ca/pn-np/ab/jasper/index_e.asp

Kluane National Park & Reserve of Canada
PO Box 5495
Haines Junction, YT Y0B 1L0
867-634-7250
Fax: 867-634-7208
kluane.info@pc.gc.ca
http://pc.gc.ca/pn-np/yt/kluane/index_e.asp

Kootenay National Park of Canada
PO Box 220
Radium Hot Springs, BC V0A 1M0
250-347-9505
Fax: 250-347-9980
TDD: 866-787-6221
kootenay.info@pc.gc.ca
http://pc.gc.ca/pn-np/bc/kootenay/index_e.asp

Lower Fort Garry National Historic Site of Canada
5925 Highway 9
St. Andrews, MB R1A 4A8
204-785-6050
Fax: 204-482-5887
888-773-8888
LFGNHS_Info@pc.gc.ca
http://pc.gc.ca/lhn-nhs/mb/fortgarry/index_e.asp

Motherwell Homestead National Historic Site of Canada
PO Box 70
Abernethy, SK S0A 0A0
306-333-2116
Fax: 306-333-2210
Motherwell-Homestead@pc.gc.ca
http://pc.gc.ca/lhn-nhs/sk/motherwell/index_e.asp

Mount Revelstoke National Park of Canada
PO Box 350
Revelstoke, BC V0E 2S0
250-837-7500
Fax: 250-837-7536
TDD: 866-787-6221
revglacier.reception@pc.gc.ca
http://pc.gc.ca/pn-np/bc/revelstoke/index_e.asp

Nahanni National Park Reserve of Canada
10002 - 100 Street
PO Box 348
Fort Simpson, NT X0E 0N0
867-695-3151
Fax: 867-695-2446
nahanni.info@pc.gc.ca
http://pc.gc.ca/pn-np/nt/nahanni/index_e.asp

Pacific Rim National Park Reserve of Canada
2185 Ocean Terrace Rd.
PO Box 280
Ucluelet, BC V0R 3A0
250-726-3500
Fax: 250-726-3520
pacrim.info@pc.gc.ca
http://pc.gc.ca/pn-np/bc/pacificrim/index_e.asp

Prince Albert National Park of Canada
PO Box 100
Waskesiu Lake, SK S0J 2Y0
306-663-4522
panp.info@pc.gc.ca
http://pc.gc.ca/pn-np/sk/princealbert/index_e.asp

Prince of Wales Fort National Historic Site of Canada
PO Box 127
Churchill, MB R0B 0E0
204-675-8863
Fax: 204-675-2026
TDD: 866-787-6221
mannorth.nhs@pc.gc.ca
http://pc.gc.ca/lhn-nhs/mb/prince/index_e.asp

Quttinirpaaq National Park of Canada
PO Box 278
Iqaluit, NU X0A 0H0
867-975-4673
Fax: 867-975-4674
nunavut.info@pc.gc.ca
http://pc.gc.ca/pn-np/nu/quttinirpaaq/index_e.asp

Riding Mountain National Park of Canada
Wasagaming, MB R0J 2H0
204-848-7275
Fax: 204-848-2596
TDD: 866-787-6221
rmnp.info@pc.gc.ca
http://pc.gc.ca/pn-np/mb/riding/index_e.asp

Riel House National Historic Site of Canada
330 River Rd. (St. Vidal)
PO Box 73
Winnipeg, MB R2N 3X9
204-257-1783
Fax: 204-983-2221
TDD: 866-787-6221
FORKSNHS.Info@pc.gc.ca
http://pc.gc.ca/lhn-nhs/mb/riel/index_E.asp

Rocky Mountain House National Historic Site of Canada
Site 127, Comp 6, RR#4
Rocky Mountain House, AB T4T 2A4
403-845-2412
Fax: 403-845-5320
rocky.info@pc.gc.ca
www.pc.gc.ca/lhn-nhs/ab/rockymountain/index_E.asp

Sirmilik National Park of Canada
PO Box 300
Pond Inlet, NU X0A 0S0
867-899-8092
Fax: 867-899-8104
sirmilik.info@pc.gc.ca
http://pc.gc.ca/pn-np/nu/sirmilik/index_E.asp

SS Keno National Historic Site of Canada
PO Box 390
Dawson City, YT Y0B 1G0
867-993-7200
Fax: 867-993-7203
dawson.info@pc.gc.ca
http://pc.gc.ca/lhn-nhs/yt/sskeno/index_e.asp

SS Klondike National Historic Site of Canada
#205, 300 Main St.
Whitehorse, YT Y1A 2B5
Fax: 867-393-6701
800-661-0486

Federal/Provincial Government / Government of Canada

whitehorse.info@pc.gc.ca
http://pc.gc.ca/lhn-nhs/yt/ssklondike/index_E.asp

St. Andrews Rectory National Historic Site of Canada
374, chemin River
St. Andrews, MB R1A 2Y1
204-334-6405
Fax: 204-338-3790
888-773-8888
TDD: 866-787-6221
LFGNHS_Info@pc.gc.ca
http://pc.gc.ca/lhn-nhs/mb/standrews/contact_e.asp

The Forks National Historic Site of Canada
401-25 Forks Market Rd.
Winnipeg, MB R3C 4S8
204-983-6757
Fax: 204-983-2221
888-773-8888
TDD: 866-787-6221
FORKSNHS.Info@pc.gc.ca
http://pc.gc.ca/lhn-nhs/mb/forks/index_e.asp

Tuktut Nogait National Park of Canada
PO Box 91
Paulatuk, NT X0E 1N0
867-580-3233
Fax: 867-580-3234
inuvik.info@pc.gc.ca
http://pc.gc.ca/pn-np/nt/tuktutnogait/index_e.asp

Ukkusiksalik National Park of Canada
PO Box 220
Repulse Bay, NU X0C 0H0
867-462-4500
Fax: 867-462-4095
ukkusiksalik.info@ pc.gc.ca
www.pc.gc.ca/pn-np/nu/ukkusiksalik/index_E.asp

Wapusk National Park of Canada
Churchill Office
PO Box 127
Churchill, MB R0B 0E0
204-675-8863
Fax: 204-675-2026
888-773-8888
TDD: 866-787-6221
wapusk.np@pc.gc.ca
pc.gc.ca/pn-np/mb/wapusk/index_e.asp

Vuntut National Park of Canada
c/o Yukon Field Unit - Parks Canada
#205, 300 Main St.
Whitehorse, YT Y1A 2B5
867-667-3910
Fax: 867-393-6701
whitehorse.info@pc.gc.ca
http://pc.gc.ca/pn-np/yt/vuntut/index_E.asp

Waterton Lakes National Park of Canada
PO Box 200
Waterton Park, AB T0K 2M0
403-859-2224
Fax: 403-859-5152
waterton.info@pc.gc.ca
http://pc.gc.ca/pn-np/ab/waterton/index_E.asp

York Factory National Historic Site of Canada
PO Box 127
Churchill, MB R0B 0E0
204-675-8863
Fax: 204-675-2026
888-773-8888
TDD: 866-787-6221
mannorth.nhs@pc.gc.ca
http://pc.gc.ca/lhn-nhs/mb/yorkfactory/index_E.asp

Wood Buffalo National Park of Canada
PO Box 750
Fort Smith, NT X0E 0P0
867-872-7900
Fax: 867-872-3910
TDD: 867-872-7961
wbnp.info@pc.gc.ca
http://pc.gc.ca/pn-np/nt/woodbuffalo/index_e.asp

Yoho National Park of Canada
PO Box 99
Field, BC V0A 1G0
250-343-6783
Fax: 250-343-6012
TDD: 866-787-6221
yoho.info@pc.gc.ca
http://pc.gc.ca/pn-np/bc/yoho/index_E.asp

Public Safety Canada / Sécurité publique Canada

269 Laurier Ave. West
Ottawa, ON K1A 0P8
613-944-4875
Fax: 613-954-5186
866-222-3006
TDD: 866-865-5667
communications@ps.gc.ca
www.publicsafety.gc.ca; www.securitepublique.gc.ca
Other Communication: National Crime Prevention Centre Toll Free: 1-877-302-6272; E-mail: prevention@ps.gc.ca; National Office for Victims Toll-Free: 866-525-0554; Media: 613-991-0657
Public Safety Canada works to keep Canadians safe in cases of natural disasters, crime, & terrorism. Policies are developed, & programs & services are delivered in the following areas: emergency management, including information about emergency preparedness; national security, which features the administration of the Government Operations Centre to monitor potential threats to the national interest; law enforcement, including the contribution of funds for policing services in First Nations & Inuit communities; federal corrections effectiveness, efficiency & accountability, with the development of federal policy & legislation; & crime prevention, such as work with other governments, businesses, & volunteer groups to support projects to reduce offences.
Acts Administered:
Canadian Security Intelligence Act
Corrections & Conditional Release Act
Criminal Records Act
Customs Act
Department of the Solicitor General Act
DNA Identification Act
Emergency Preparedness Act
Firearms Act
Prisons & Reformatories Act
Royal Canadian Mounted Police Act
Royal Canadian Mounted Police Pension Continuation Act
Transfer of Offenders Act
Witness Protection Program Act
Minister, Public Safety, Hon. Vic Toews
613-992-3128, Fax: 613-995-1049
ToewsV@parl.gc.ca
Other Communications: Public Safety & Emergency Preparedness: 613-991-2924
Deputy Minister, William V. Baker
613-991-2895
Assistant Deputy Minister Corporate Management, Elisabeth Nadeau
613-990-2615
Assistant Deputy Minister Emergency Management, Lynda Clairmont
613-990-4976
Associate Assistant Deputy Minister Emergency Management & National Security, Daniel Lavoie
613-990-2743
Inspector General Canadian Security Intelligence Service (CSIS), Eva Plunkett
613-949-0675
Senior Counsel / Strategic Policy Advisor, Mary-Anne Kirvan
613-954-1067
Counsel Legal Services, Caroline Fobes
613-949-9724
Parliamentary Secretary to the Minister of Public Safety, Dave MacKenzie
613-995-4432, Fax: 613-995-4433
MacKenzie.D@parl.gc.ca
• Canada Firearms Centre(CAFC) / Centre des armes à feu Canada
Ottawa, ON K1A 1M6
Fax: 613-825-0297
800-731-4000
cfp-pcaf@rcmp-grc.gc.ca
www.rcmp.gc.ca/cfp

• Canadian Security Intelligence Service(CSIS) / Service canadien du renseignement de sécurité (SCRS)
• Commission for Public Complaints Against the Royal Canadian Mounted Police
#102, 7337 137 St.
Surrey, BC V3W 1A4
Fax: 613-952-8045
800-665-6878
TDD: 866-432-5837org@cpc-cpp.gc.ca
www.cpc-cpp.gc.ca
• Correctional Service of Canada
• National Parole Board
• Royal Canadian Mounted Police
• Royal Canadian Mounted Police External Review Committee
PO Box 1159 B
Ottawa, ON K1P 5R2
613-998-2134
Fax: 613-990-8969
org@erc-cee.gc.ca
www.erc-cee.gc.ca

Community Safety & Partnerships Branch / Sécurité de la population et des partenariats
340 Laurier Ave. West
Ottawa, ON K1A 0P8
The Community Safety & Partnerships Branch consist of the Aboriginal Policing Directorate, the Corrections & Criminal Justice Directorate, & the National Crime Prevention Centre.

Emergency Management & National Security Branch / Secteur de la gestion des urgences et de la sécurité nationale
340 Laurier Ave. West
Ottawa, ON K1A 0P8
The Emergency Management & National Security Branch consists of the following directorates & secretariat: Coordination Directorate; Emergency Management Policy Directorate; National Security Policy Directorate; Operations Directorate; Preparedness & Recovery Directorate; & the Cyber Security Strategy Secretariat.
Assistant Deputy Minister, Lynda Clairmont
613-990-4976
Associate Assistant Deputy Minister, Daniel Lavoie
613-990-2743
Director General National Cyber Security, Robert Dick
613-990-2661
Director General National Security Operations, Michael MacDonald
613-993-4595
Director General National Security Policy, Paul MacKinnon
613-991-1970
Director General Preparedness & Recovery, Serge C. Beaudoin
613-991-2944
Director General Preparedness & Recovery, Robert Lesser
613-944-4853
Director General Regional Operations Directorate, Jamie Deacon
613-991-1699
Senior Director Public Service Renewal, Kevin Phillips
613-947-6492
Executive Director Canadian Emergency Management College, Susan Daly
613-949-5000
Acting Associate Director General Operations, Craig Oldham
613-991-7728
Senior Analyst National Cyber Security, Tom Campbell
613-990-3577

Law Enforcement & Policing Branch / Secteur de la Police, et de l'application de la loi
340 Laurier Ave. West
Ottawa, ON K1A 0P8
The Policing, Law Enforcement & Interoperability Branch includes the following directorates: Law Enforcement & Border Strategies; Policing Policy; & Public Safety Interoperability.

Strategic Policy Branch
340 Laurier Ave. West
Ottawa, ON K1A 0P8

Federal/Provincial Government / Government of Canada

Public Works & Government Services Canada (PWGSC) / Travaux publics et services gouvernementaux

Place du Portage, Phase III
11, rue Laurier
Ottawa, ON K1A 0S5
819-997-6363
Fax: 819-956-9062
800-622-6232
TDD: 800-926-9105
questions@tpsgc-pwgsc.gc.ca
www.tpsgc-pwgsc.gc.ca

Primary department responsible for purchasing goods & services for the Government of Canada. Purchases a variety of goods & services, construction, architectural, engineering & maintenance services & provides leasing services related to federal government works & facilities. Also maintains source lists of potential suppliers for some products. Ensures that the government's operational requirements are met in a cost-effective & timely manner, while taking into account the government's objectives including environmental considerations. As builders & caretakers of buildings, the department protects the environment by reducing solid waste, greening the construction & operation of buildings, conserving energy & water, improving fleet management, minimizing the effects of operations on climate change, & increasing environmental protection & conservation.

Acts Administered:
Anti-Personnel Mines Convention Implementation Act
Bridges Act
Canadian Arsenals Limited Divestiture Authorization Act
Defence Production Act
Dry Docks Subsidies Act
Expropriation Act
Federal District Commission to have acquired certain lands, An Act to Confirm the Authority of
Garnishment, Attachment & Pension Diversion Act
Government Property Traffic Act
Ottawa River, Act Respecting Certain Works
Pension Benefits Division Act
Public Works & Government Services Act
Seized Property Management Act
Statutes Act
Surplus Crown Assets Act
Translation Bureau Act

Minister, Public Works & Government Services; Minister for Status of Women, Hon. Rona Ambrose
613-996-9778, Fax: 613-996-0785
Ambrose.R@parl.gc.ca; ministre@tpsgc-pwgsc.gc.ca
Parliamentary Secretary, Jacques Gourde
613-992-2639, Fax: 613-992-1018
Gourdj@parl.gc.ca
Deputy Minister, François Guimont
819-956-1706, Fax: 819-956-8280
francois.guimont@tpsgc-pwgsc.gc.ca
Assoc. Deputy Minister, Andrew Treusch
819-956-4472, Fax: 819-956-8280
Andrew.Treusch@tpsgc-pwgsc.gc.ca
Asst. Deputy Minister Human Resources, Diane Lorenzato
819-956-7548, Fax: 819-934-2523
diane.lorenzato@tpsgc-pwgsc.gc.ca
Senior General Counsel, Sarah Paquet
819-956-0993, Fax: 819-953-3974
sarah.paquet@tpsgc-pwgsc.gc.ca
• Canadian Wheat Board
• Defence Construction Canada

Acquisitions Branch / Direction générale des approvisionnements

Provides departments & agencies with expert assistance at each stage of the supply cycle & offers tools that simplify & accelerate the acquisition of goods & services. It ensures that the government exercises due diligence & maintains the integrity of the procurement process. It is a primary service provider offering client departments a broad base of procurement solutions aimed at securing best value for their procurement dollar.
Asst. Deputy Minister, Liliane Saint-Pierre
819-956-1711, Fax: 819-953-1058
liliane.saintpierre@tpsgc-pwgsc.gc.ca

Consulting & Audit Canada / Conseils et vérification Canada
Tower B, Place de Ville
112 Kent St.
Ottawa, ON K1A 0S5
613-996-0188

Finance, Accounting, Banking & Compensation Branch / Finances, comptabilité, gestion bancaire et rémunération

Responsible for managing the operations of the federal treasury, including issuing Receiver General payments for major government programs as well as maintaining the Accounts of Canada & producing the Government's financial statements. Responsible for providing government-wide accounting & reporting services. Directs the management & delivery of the administration of the public service pension & group insurance plans & maintains accounts for the various pension funds. Focuses in the financial management & control framework for the Department.

Government Purchasing Information

www.pwgsc.gc.ca/acquisitions/text/sm/chapter04-e.html
Most federal government purchasing is centralized in the department of Public Works & Government Services Canada (PWGSC), which purchases all goods, certain services, & most construction. Individual departments work through PWGSC to obtain the supplies & some of the services they need. Contracting for the majority of services is done by individual departments. Federal departments & agencies are establishing purchasing practices to make government procurement more environmentally responsible, using online resources to identify products, services & companies that supply them: Agreements & Opportunities: Agreement on Internal Trade (AIT), which came into effect July 1, 1995, is designed to reduce barriers to trade within Canada. This agreement, between the federal government, the provinces & territories, opens up public procurement to all Canadian companies. Procurement for goods for $25,000, or more or service & construction contracts for $100,000 or more are covered by the AIT. These opportunities are advertised on MERX. World Trade Organization Agreement on Government Procurement (referred to as WTO-AGP) that expands on the General Agreement on Tariffs & Trade (GATT), also covers services. Service contracts of federal departments worth $245,000 or more & construction contracts worth $9.4 million or more are covered by WTO-AGP. These opportunities are also publicized through MERX. The North American Free Trade Agreement was the first international trade agreement signed by Canada to cover services, including construction-related services. In opening up the Mexican, U.S. & Canadian government service markets to each other's suppliers, NAFTA ensures equal treatment to all North American businesses. Service contracts worth $84,000 or more & construction contracts estimated at $10.9 million or more are covered by NAFTA when the purchases are made for government departments. For Crown corporations, NAFTA kicks in when service contracts are worth $420,000 or more & the estimated value of construction contracts is $13.4 million, or greater. Canadian opportunities affected by NAFTA are publicized through MERX. Mexican opportunities are advertised in that country's major daily newspapers & in the Diario Oficial de la Federación, as well as on MERX. U.S. purchases are published in the Commerce Business Daily (CBD). Extracts of the CBD appear on MERX.

Information Technology Services Branch / Services d'infotechnologie

Provides common telecommunications & informatics services to government departments, agencies & organizations, to facilitate universal access to information throughout the federal government. Focussing on network & computer services, telecommunications, & application development, ITS is a key player in government-wide initiatives such as the Secure Channel, IM/IT community renewal, & Government-On-Line (GoL).

MERX
Fax: 888-235-5800
www.merx.com
Other Communication: Suppliers Support: 1-800-964-MERX (6379); Buyers Support: 1-888-738-3005 (Ottawa: 613/737-3796)
The federal government's Government Electronic Tendering Service (GETS) contracts MERX to advertise government procurement opportunities online. Architectural & engineering consulting services, or services related to real property above $84,000 are advertised on MERX; below $84,000, they are handled through SELECT. Construction opportunities above $100,000 are advertised through MERX; below are handled through SELECT. MERX is used for printing services valued at $10,000 or above, & most goods & services valued at $25,000 or above. Below this level PWGSC uses a variety of bid solicitation methods: T-buys (purchasing by telephone when the product or service is required quickly and can easily be identified over the phone); RFQ (Request for Quotation); an Invitation to Tender (ITT) is used for straightforward requirements above $25,000 & where the lowest price will determine the awarding of the contract; RFP (Request for Proposal) for more complex requirements above $25,000; RFSO (Request for Standing Offer); RFSA (Request for Supply Arrangement); Sole-sourcing, subject to trade agreements & government contracting regulations. For products, individual departments have authority to buy up to $5,000 directly from suppliers; above $5,000, the department must go to PWGSC. Departments have authority to purchase nearly all their services; for program delivery services, departments may buy directly from suppliers up to $400,000 competitively or up to $100,000 without competition; they may also buy competitively up to $2 million when they advertise their requirements through MERX. Subscribers to MERX have access to an opportunity matching service, may view historical opportunities, review contract awards & international opportunities.

Real Property Branch / Biens immobiliers
Fax: 613-736-2789
Manages office space & other general-purpose property; acts as custodian for $7.6 billion of real property holdings; administers 2,000 lease contracts; provides working space for 241,000 public servants in 1,810 locations across Canada; provides professional & technical services to government departments & agencies. Government buildings are 34 per cent more energy efficient & 24 per cent more greenhouse gas efficient than in 1990. Green Leases address key environmental standards such as proper management of wastewater, indoor air quality, recycling, energy efficient lighting fixtures, greenhouse gas reduction. Works with other departments on the remediation of contaminated sites & is the federal lead in the cleanup of the Sydney Tar Ponds in Nova Scotia.
Asst. Deputy Minister, John McBain
819-956-3189, Fax: 819-956-7130
john.mcbain@tpsgc-pwgsc.gc.ca
Director General Accelerated Infrastructure Program, Jean Vézina
819-956-7426, Fax: 819-934-0980
jean.vezina@tpsgc-pwgsc.gc.ca
Acting Director General Major Crown Projects, Pierre Vaillancourt
819-956-4935, Fax: 819-956-7384
pierre.vaillancourt@tpsgc-pwgsc.gc.ca

Translation Bureau / Bureau de traduction
Richelieu Bldg.
975 St-Joseph Blvd., 5th Fl.
Gatineau, QC K1A 0S5
819-934-0496
Fax: 819-997-9227

Commercial Acquisition & Supply Management Sector / Secteur des achats commerciaux et de la gestion de l'approvisionnement
Director General, Bruce Fletcher
819-956-6040
Director General Land, Aerospace & Marine Systems & Major Projects Sector, Terry Williston
819-956-0010

Commercial & Consumer Products Directorate (CCPD) / Direction des produits commerciaux et de consommation
819-956-1663
Responsible for acquiring scientific items, medical supplies, clothing & textiles, food, furniture & office supplies.
Senior Director, Céline Bédard
819-956-6098

Crown Assets Distribution Centre (CADC) / Direction de la distribution des biens de la couronne
613-952-0272
Fax: 613-941-0155
crownassets.pwgsc.gc.ca/text/home-e.htm
Director, Dave Keys
819-956-9857

Logistics, Electrical, Fuel & Transportation Directorate (LEFTD) / Direction du transport et des produits logistiques, électriques et pétroliers
Responsible for procuring clothing & textiles; electrical & electronics products; fuel & construction products; industrial vehicles; machinery products & logistics; light & medium vehicles; vehicles & industrial products.
Acting Director, Gary Reny
819-956-3529

Federal/Provincial Government / Government of Canada

Real Property Contracting Directorate / Direction de l'attribution des marchés immobiliers
Responsible for procuring various services related to real property on behalf of PWGSC & other federal departments.
Senior Director, Jacques Leclerc
819-956-0148
Acting Manager Construction Service, Tom Von Schoenberg
819-956-3918
Manager Consultant Services Division, Stephanie Duggan
819-956-5978
Acting Manager Facility Maintenance Service, Louise Sullivan
819-956-3924

Services & Specialized Acquisitions Management Sector / Secteur de la gestion des services et des approvisionnements spéciaux
Director General, George Butts
819-956-0867
Senior Director Major Projects Services, Monty Mukerji
819-934-0960

Canadian General Standards Board (CGSB) / Office des normes générales du Canada
www.pwgsc.gc.ca/cgsb
In support of environmental initiatives, CGSB develops national standards & specifications for products & services. The Board maintains extensive certified & qualified product lists, which are used widely by governments & business for procurement, including environmental management systems (ISO 14001), quality management systems (ISO 9000 series), & occupational health & safety management system BSI-OHSAS 18001:1999. The office also distributes & sells CGSB standards. CGSB delivers the HACCP Advantage Program, a new standard in the field of food safety.
Actying Director, Chantal Marin-Comeau
819-956-0383

Services & Technology Acquisition Management Sector / Secteur de la gestion de l'approvisionnement en services et en technologies
Director General, Pierre Benoît
819-956-1649
Acting Senior Director Special Procurement Initiatives Directorate, Scott Leslie
819-956-1326

Science Procurement Directorate / Direction de l'approvisionnement en travaux scientifiques
Senior Director, Michel J. Rancourt
819-956-1788
Manager Defence Sciences Division, Suzanne Lorrain
819-956-1328
Manager Earth Sciences Division, Patricia Mortimer
819-956-1688
Manager Human, Life & Environmental Sciences, Linda Latray
819-956-1384

Small & Medium Enterprises Sector / Seceur des petites et moyennes entreprises
Launched September 2005.
Director General, Marshall Moffatt
819-956-8416
Acting Director Policy, Samuel Millar
819-956-7850
Manager Client Services & Communications, Julie Desroches
819-956-0920

Office of Greening Government Operations / Direction du bureau de l'écologisation des opérations gouvernementales
Greening@pwgsc.gc.ca
www.pwgsc.gc.ca/greening/
Consolidates the department's environmental expertise. Provides advice & functional guidance for federal departments regarding green procurement, green construction, green property management, recycling & waste management, remediation of contaminated sites. Policy on Green Procurement took effect on April 1, 2006, integrating environmental considerations into all procurement decisions.
Acting Director General, Margaret Kenny
819-956-1613

Environmental & Sustainable Development Services Directorate
Director Environmental Services, Peggy Farnsworth
613-993-4408
National Manager Environmental Engineering, Craig Legare
613-993-5501

Senior Asbestos Control Officer, William Drysdale
613-993-5318
Manager Contaminated Sites, Michael Billowits
819-956-4042,

Professional & Technical Programs / Programmes professionnels et techniques
Acting Director General, Garnet Strong
819-956-2039
Acting Director Asset & Facilities Management, Ralph Collins
613-736-2073
Acting Director Geomatics Services, Dan Brown
613-244-3002
Director Heritage Conservation Service, Jack Vandenberg
819-997-6792
Manager Energy Task Group, Alan Ham
819-956-7338

Business Access Canada / Accès entreprises Canada
6C1, Portage III
11, rue Laurier
Gatineau, QC K1A 0S5
819-956-3440
Fax: 819-956-6123
ncr.contractscanada@pwgsc.gc.ca
Other Communication: Infoline: 1-800-811-1148
Formerly known as Contracts Canada. Interdepartmental initiative to improve supplier & buyer awareness & simplify federal government purchasing information. There are 31 participating departments. Refer to contractscanada.gc.ca/en/partn-e.htm where links to most individual departments provide information on how the department buys goods & services. A list of departmental materiel managers is found at contractscanada.gc.ca/en/materi-e.html.
Chief, Fred Albert
819-956-3449

Procurement Allocation Directory (PAD) / Répertoire des attributions des approvisionnements (RAA)
pad.contractscanada.gc.ca/
List of key purchasing contacts in PWGSC offices, & what products & services they buy.

Supplier Registration Information (SRI) / Données d'inscription des fournisseurs
contractscanada.gc.ca/en/regist-e.htm
Other Communication: Suppliers Registration Points of Contact: contractscanada.gc.ca/en/natcon-e.htm; SELECT: select.pwgsc-tpsgc.gc.ca
Companies register as potential suppliers to the government; used by federal government buyers to identify potential suppliers for purchases not subject to any trade agreements. Procurement Business Number (PBN) identifies a branch, division or office of a company & is used by PWGSC as a supplier identification code. Architectural & engineering consulting services, including environmental services, valued between $25,000 & $84,000 (construction up to $100,000) are handled through the online SELECT system, which contains a list of pre-qualified real property firms (architects, engineers, construction contractors) identified by their expertise or the service they provide. To get on the list, companies need to register in the SRI service. Supplier Registration Officers are located in regional offices across Canada.

Standards Council of Canada (SCC) / Conseil canadien des normes (CCN)
#200, 270 Albert St.
Ottawa, ON K1P 6N7
613-238-3222
Fax: 613-569-7808
info@scc.ca
www.scc.ca
Federal Crown corporation with the mandate to promote efficient & effective standardization. The organization reports to Parliament through the Minister of Industry & oversees Canada's National Standards System. The National Standards System comprises organizations & individuals involved in voluntary standards development, promotion & implementation. In addition, more than 400 organizations have been accredited by the Standards Council, including environmental management systems (EMS) registration organizations that perform registrations to ISO 14000 series standards. The Council offers accreditation to registration bodies for specialized environmental management systems in industry-specific areas, including sustainable forestry management (CAN/CSZ809-02). Manages the Program for the Accreditation of Laboratories - Canada (PALCAN) which seeks to identify & accredit competent testing laboratories. Initial assessment is made & regular follow-up audits are performed; accredited organizations are included in the Standards Council directory of accredited testing organizations. Users of testing services can eliminate or reduce their need to establish the competence of a prospective lab. In cooperation with the Canadian Association of Environmental Analytical Laboratories (CAEAL), SCC operates an accreditation program for environmental analytical laboratories. SCC's website provides free access to a wide variety of standards information, including searchable databases containing information on Canadian, foreign & international standards, regulations & SCC-accredited organizations. More speacialized information is available through SCC's information & Research Service. Other accreditation programs include ones for registrars of ISO 14000 environmental management systems; environmental auditor certifiers & auditor training course providers.
Chair, Hugh Krentz
613-238-3222, Fax: 613-569-7808
Executive Director, John Walter
613-238-3222, Fax: 613-569-7808
gclarke@scc.ca
Manager Communications, Pilar Castro
613-238-3222, Fax: 613-569-7808
pcastro@scc.ca

Statistics Canada / Statistique Canada
R.H. Coats Bldg., Tunney's Pasture
100 Tunney's Pasture Driveway
Ottawa, ON K1A 0T6
613-951-8116
Fax: 877-287-4369
800-263-1136
TDD: 800-363-7629
infostats@statcan.ca
www.statcan.ca
Agency of the federal government, headed by the Chief Statistician of Canada which reports to Parliament through the Minister of Industry. As Canada's central statistical agency, it has a mandate to collect, compile, analyse, abstract & publish statistical information relating to the commercial, industrial, financial, social, economic & general activities & condition of the people of Canada; coordinates activities with its federal & provincial partners in the national statistical system to avoid duplication of effort & to ensure the consistency & usefulness of statistics. The agency profiles & measures both social & economic changes in Canada. It presents a comprehensive picture of the national economy through statistics on manufacturing, agriculture, retail sales, services, prices, productivity changes, trade, transportation, employment & unemployment, & aggregate measures such as gross domestic product. It also presents a comprehensive picture of social conditions through statistics on demography, health, areas.
Acts Administered:
Corporations Returns Act
Statistics Act
Chief Statistician of Canada, Wayne Smith
613-951-9757, Fax: 613-951-3880
Wayne.Smith@statcan.gc.ca
Director Communications & Information Services, Lynn Barr-Telford
613-951-1518,
Lynn.Barr-Telford@statcan.gc.ca

Business & Trade Statistics / Statistique du commerce et des entreprises
Includes: distributive trades; enterprise statistics; manufacturing, construction & energy; service industries
Director General Economy-Wide Statistics, Louis Marc Ducharme
613-951-0688, Fax: 613-951-0411
LouisMarc.Ducharme@statcan.gc.ca
Director General Industry Statistics, Peter Lys
613-951-4071, Fax: 613-951-0411
Peter.Lys@statcan.gc.ca

Environment Accounts & Statistics Division / Division des comptes et de la statistique de l'environnement
Fax: 613-951-0634
Statistical information on forests, air, water, animal & plant life, environment industry, environmental practices & pollution control. Learning resources for students. Publishes Human Activity & the Environment (annual overview of data on population, economic activities & the environment).

Federal/Provincial Government / Government of Canada

Acting Director, Rowena Orok
613-951-4341, Fax: 613-951-0634
Rowena.Orok@statcan.gc.ca
Acting Chief, Joan Forbes
613-951-1801
Chief/Advisor, John Marshall
613-951-0347,
John.Marshall@statcan.gc.ca
Section Chief, Bruce Mitchell
613-951-5347,
Bruce.Mitchell@statcan.gc.ca
Section Chief, François Soulard
613-951-1777,
Francois.Soulard@statcan.gc.ca
Section Chief, Joe St Lawrence
613-951-7709,
Joe.St.Lawrence@statcan.gc.ca
Section Chief, Doug Trant
613-951-3829,
Doug.Trant@statcan.gc.ca

Edmonton
Pacific Plaza
#900, 10909 Jasper Ave. NW
Edmonton, AB T5J 4J3
780-495-3027
Fax: 780-495-5318

Halifax
1888 Brunswick St., 1st Fl.
Halifax, NS B3J 2G7

Montréal
Tour Est, Complexe Guy-Favreau
200, boul René-Lévesque ouest, 4e étage
Montréal, QC H2Z 1X4

Ottawa
R.H. Coats Bldg., Lobby, West Wing
100 Tunney's Pasture Driveway
Ottawa, ON K1A 0T6

Regina
Park Plaza
#440, 2365 Albert St.
Regina, SK S4P 4K1

Toronto
Arthur Meighen Bldg.
25 St. Clair Ave. East, 10th Fl.
Toronto, ON M4T 1M4

Vancouver
Library Square Tower
#600, 300 West Georgia St.
Vancouver, BC V6B 6C7

Winnipeg
Via Rail Bldg.
#200, 123 Main St.
Winnipeg, MB R3C 4V9
Minister, Public Works & Government Services; Minister for Status of Women, Hon. Rona Ambrose
613-996-9778, Fax: 613-996-0785
Ambrose.R@parl.gc.ca
Parliamentary Secretary for Status of Women, Sylvie Boucher
613-992-4406, Fax: 613-992-4544
Boucher.S@parl.gc.ca

Transport Canada (TC) / Transports Canada

Place de Ville
330 Sparks St., Tower C
Ottawa, ON K1A 0N5
613-990-2309
Fax: 613-954-4731
minTC@tc.gc.ca
www.tc.gc.ca
Other Communication: TTY: 1-888-675-6863
Using EMS 14000 standards, Transport Canada incorporates environmental considerations in all decision-making to fulfill the department's sustainable development strategy. Working with airports & airlines to minimize environmental effects of de-icing fluids; working with Environment Canada & industry to more effectively manage road salt; participating with ICAO's Committee on Aviation Environmental Protection (CAEP) concerning aircraft emissions, noise & land use planning. Ongoing contaminated sites management program. The Moving on Sustainable Transportation (MOST) Program supports projects that educate, raise awareness & provide tools to understand, promote & encourage sustainable transportation, such as neighbourhood transit passes, idle-free workplaces, school walking routes. Development of strategies to reduce greenhouse gas emissions from freight transportation; information on fuel consumption. Urban Transportation Showcase Program aims to reduce greenhouse gas emissions through showcasing demonstrations in communities across Canada (www.tc.gc.ca/programs/environment/utsp/menu.htm).

Acts Administered:
Aeronautics Act
(Act respecting regulations made pursuant to section 5 of the) Aeronautics Act
Air Canada Public Participation Act
Airport Transfer (Miscellaneous Matters) Act
Arctic Waters Pollution Prevention Act (Indian & Northern Affairs)
Bills of Landing Act
Blue Water Bridge Authority Act
Buffalo & Fort Erie Public Bridge Company Act
Canada Marine Act
Canada Post Corporation Act
Canada Shipping Act
Canada Shipping Act, 2001 (Fisheries & Oceans)
Canada Strategic Infrastructure Fund Act
Canada Transportation Act
Canadian Air Transport Security Authority Act
Canadian National Montréal Terminals Act
Canadian National Toronto Terminals Act
Carriage by Air Act
Civil Air Navigation Services Commercialization Act
CN Commercialization Act
Coasting Trade Act
Department of Transport Act
Government Property Traffic Act
Harbour Commissions Act
Harbour of Québec Act, The Corporation of Pilots for & below the
Intercolonial & PEI Railways Employees' Provident Fund Act
International Interests in Mobile Equipment (aircraft equipment) Act
International Rapids Power Development Act
Marine & Aviation War Risks Act
Marine Atlantic Inc. Acquisition Authorization Act
Marine Insurance Act
Marine Liability Act
Marine Transportation Security Act
Maritime Code Act
Meaford Harbour Act
Montréal Port Wardens Act
Motor Vehicle Fuel Consumption Standards Act
Motor Vehicle Safety Act
Motor Vehicle Transport Act, 1987
National Capital Act
National Transcontinental Railway Act
Navigable Waters Projection Act
Northern Transportation Company Ltd. Disposal Authorization Act
Northumberland Strait Crossing Act
Ontario Harbours Agreement Act
Pilotage Act
Pre-clearance Act
Québec Port Wardens Act
Railway Relocation & Crossing Act
Railway Safety Act
Royal Canadian Mint Act
Safe Containers Convention Act
Transportation Appeal Tribunal of Canada Act
Transportation of Dangerous Goods Act, 1992
Shipping Conferences Exemption Act, 1987
United States Wreckers Act
Winnipeg Terminals Act
Minister, Transport, Infrastructure, & Communities, Hon. Charles (Chuck) Strahl
613-992-2940, Fax: 613-944-9376
Strahl.C@parl.gc.ca
Deputy Minister, Yaprak Baltacioglu
613-990-4507, Fax: 613-991-0851
yaprak.baltacioglu@tc.gc.ca
Director General Communications & Marketing, Jean Valin
613-990-6138, Fax: 613-991-6719
jean.valin@tc.gc.ca

Senior General Counsel & Head, Legal Services, Henry K. Schultz
613-990-5768, Fax: 613-990-5777
henry.schultz@tc.gc.ca
- Atlantic Pilotage Authority Canada
- Canada Lands Company
- Canada Mortgage & Housing Corporation
- Canada Post Corporation
- Canadian Air Transport Security Authority(CATSA) / Administration canadienne de la sûreté du transport aérien (ACSTA)
99 Bank St., 13th Fl.
Ottawa, ON K1P 6B9
Fax: 613-991-6726
888-294-2202
www.catsa-acsta.gc.ca
- Canadian Transportation Agency
- Federal Bridge Corporation Limited
#1210, 55 Metcalfe St.
Ottawa, ON K1P 6L5
613-993-6880
Fax: 613-993-6945
info@federalbridge.ca
www.federalbridge.ca
- Great Lakes Pilotage Authority
- Laurentian Pilotage Authority
- Marine Atlantic Inc.
- Pacific Pilotage Authority
- Royal Canadian Mint
- Transportation Appeal Tribunal of Canada
333 Laurier Ave. West, 12th Fl.
Ottawa, ON K1A 0N5
613-990-6906
Fax: 613-990-9153
info@tatc.gc.ca
- Transportation Safety Board of Canada
- VIA Rail Canada Inc.

Corporate Services Group / Services généraux
Corporate Services is part of the Department's administration business line & is responsible for providing services & functional expertise in the areas of finance & administration, technology & information management, human resources & access to information, Crown corporation portfolio coordination, internal audit & evaluation services.

Transportation Development Centre (TDC) / Centre de développement des transports
Tour Ouest, Complexe Guy-Favreau
800, boul René-Lévesque ouest, 6e étage
Montréal, QC H3B 1X9
514-283-0000
Fax: 514-283-7158
tdccdt@tc.gc.ca
www.tc.gc.ca/tdc/menu.htm
Conducts research & development on new technologies in transportation to support Transport Canada's objectives of safety, security & economic competitiveness, as well as broader national concerns, such as accessibility, energy efficiency & the environment.
Director General Transportation Technology & Innovations, Marc Fortin
613-998-8242, Fax: 613-998-3987
marc.fortin@tc.gc.ca
Chief Advanced Technology, Howard Posluns
613-993-6254,
howard.posluns@tc.gc.ca
Chief Technology Applications, Sesto Vespa
514-283-0059,
sesto.vespa@tc.gc.ca
Chief Strategic Policy, Bill Benoit
613-990-9141, Fax: 613-990-1719
bill.benoit@tc.gc.ca

Policy Group / Groupe de politiques
Responsible for setting policies relating to rail, marine, highways & borders, motor carrier, air, airports & accessible transportation, as well as setting departmental strategic policy & coordinating intergovernmental relations; assessing the performance of the overall transportation systems & its components, & developing supporting databases, forecasts & economic analysis; administering the management agreement with the St. Lawrence Seaway Management Corporation; & supporting rail passenger services through payments to VIA Rail & three regional railways, & ferry services through payments to Marine Atlantic & to

provincial & private operators & border infrastructure improvements.
Asst. Deputy Minister, Kristine Burr
613-998-1880, Fax: 613-991-1440
Senior Advisor to the Asst. Deputy Minister Policy, Valerie Dufour
613-991-6435, Fax: 613-991-1440
Director General Air Policy, Brigita Gravitis-Beck
613-993-0054
Director General International & Intergovernmental Relations, Arlene Turner
613-991-6500, Fax: 613-991-6422
Director General Economic Analysis, Roger Roy
613-998-0684, Fax: 613-957-3280
Director General Marine Policy, Emile Di Sanza
613-991-3536, Fax: 613-998-1845
Acting Director General Surface Transportation Policy, Helena Borges
613-998-2689, Fax: 613-998-2686

Programs Group / Groupe des programmes
www.tc.gc.ca/programs/menu.htm
Responsible for the transfer of ports, harbours & airports to communities & other interests; the oversight & lease management of divested facilities; the operation of facilities not yet divested; &real property management. Responsible for environmental programs & policies, including environmental management system, sustainable development strategies, environmental assessment & national environmental issues in transportation, such as climate change.
Asst. Deputy Minister, Ronald Sully
613-990-3001, Fax: 613-998-5008

Safety & Security Group / Groupe de sécurité et sûreté
The ADM, Safety & Security, directs the development of transportation safety & security legislation, regulations & national standards; is responsible for the uniform implementation of monitoring, testing, inspection, research & development, & subsidy programs in the aviation, marine, rail & road modes of transport; oversees the delivery of aircraft services to government & other transportation bodies; & is responsible for development & enforcement of regulations & standards under federal jurisdiction, to protect public safety in the transportation of dangerous goods, & to prevent unlawful interference in the aviation, marine & railways modes of transport, as well as ensuring that the department is prepared to respond to transportation & transportation-related emergencies.
Asst. Deputy Minister, Marc Grégoire
613-990-3838, Fax: 613-990-2947
Assoc. Asst. Deputy Minister, John Forster
613-949-2394
Director General Aircraft Services, Michel Gaudreau
613-998-3316, Fax: 613-991-0365
Director General Civil Aviation, Merlin Preuss
613-990-1322
Director General Marine Security, Laureen Kinney
613-991-4173
Executive Director Rail & Mass Transit Task Force, Tony Ritchie
613-990-3885
Acting Director General Strategies & Integration, Sheila K. Smith
613-990-1115

Environmental Affairs / Affaires environnementales
Director General, Robert Lyman
613-991-5995, Fax: 613-993-8674
Director Environmental Initiatives, Catherine Higgens
613-998-5693
Director Environmental Programs, Alec Simpson
613-990-0512
Director Sustainable Development, Phil Kurys
613-993-5065

Marine Safety Directorate / Sécurité maritime
www.tc.gc.ca/marine/menu.htm
Responsible for the administration of national & international laws designed to ensure the safe operation, navigation, design & maintenance of ships, protection of life & property, & prevention of ship-source pollution. Transport Canada has assumed responsibility for environmental response from Fisheries & Oceans Canada. Strictly enforces pollution prevention regulations through the inspection of ships for compliance with pollution prevention regulations & through investigation of pollution incidents.
Director General, William Nash
613-998-0610
Manager Environmental Protection, Tom Morris
613-991-3170

Rail Safety Directorate / Sécurité ferroviaire
www.tc.gc.ca/rail/menu.htm
Administers the Railway Safety Act & associated regulations; provides funding for improvements to railway grade crossings; administers Part II of the Canada Labour Code, relating to the safety & health of employees; & ensures, for specific railway works, that environmental impacts are assessed in compliance with the Canadian Environmental Assessment Act.
Director General, Luc Bourdon
613-998-2984, Fax: 613-990-2924
Director Engineering, T.M. Coghlan
613-990-7068
Environmental Engineer, Ryan Rickard
613-990-4517

Road Safety & Motor Vehicle Registration / Direction de la sécurité routière et de la réglementation automobile
613-998-8616
800-333-0371
www.tc.gc.ca/road/menu.htm
Administers the Motor Vehicle Safety Act by developing vehicle & motor vehicle equipment safety standards, emission standards & testing procedures; responds to public enquiries & complaints of alleged vehicle safety defects, emission defects & fuel consumption deficiencies; &, in conjunction with Natural Resources Canada, provides fuel consumption information through vehicle labels & the Fuel Consumption Guide. Also administers the Motor Vehicle Transport Act, which governs the safety fitness of extra-provincial trucks & buses. The enforcement of this act is largely delegated to the provinces.
Director General, Kash Ram
613-993-6735
Director Road Safety Programs, Brian Jonah
613-998-1968

Security & Emergency Preparedness Directorate / Sûreté et préparatifs d'urgence
Responsible for the development & enforcement of regulations & standards to prevent unlawful interference with air, rail & marine transportation; management of departmental security.
Director General, Debra Normoyle
613-990-3651, Fax: 613-996-6381

Transport Dangerous Goods Directorate / Transport des marchandises dangereuses
Regulatory development, information & guidance on dangerous goods transport for the public, industry & government. Represents Canada on international organizations responsible for establishing uniform international requirements, such as the United Nations Committee of Experts on the Transport of Dangerous Goods, Association of American Railroads (AAR) Tankcar Committee & International Civil Aviation Organization (ICAO) Dangerous Goods Panel. Branches are responsible for regulatory affairs, research, evaluation, compliance & response, review of remedial measures, development of training programs.
Director General, Dr. J.A. Read
613-990-1147, Fax: 613-993-5925
Director Regulatory Affairs, Jacques Savard
613-990-1154

Canada Transport Emergency Centre (CANUTEC) / Centre canadien d'urgence du Ministère des transports
613-992-4624
Fax: 613-954-5101
canutec@tc.gc.ca
www.tc.gc.ca/canutec/
Assists emergency response personnel in handling dangerous goods emergencies; established a scientific data bank on chemicals manufactured, stored & transported in Canada; staffed by professional chemists specialized in emergency response & experienced in interpreting technical information; provides advice & serves as a communication link during emergencies; primary contact point for the Transport of Dangerous Goods Directorate; & provides assistance with regulations administration. Developed an Emergency Response Guide with the US Dept. of Transportation & the secretariat of Communications & Transportation of Mexico. The Guide is a reference source on chemical hazards and recommended responses to accidents involving dangerous goods.
Director, Michel Cloutier

Atlantic
95 Foundry St., 6th Fl.
Moncton, NB E1C 5H7
800-387-4999

Regional Director General, Michel Doiron
506-851-7315, Fax: 506-851-3099
michel.doiron@tc.gc.ca

Ontario
#300, 4900 Yonge St.
Toronto, ON M2N 6A5
416-952-0230
Fax: 416-952-0159
888-231-2330
Regional Director General, Debra D. Taylor
416-952-2170, Fax: 416-952-2174
debra.taylor@tc.gc.ca

Pacific
#620, 800 Burrard St.
Vancouver, BC V6Z 2J8
604-666-3518
Fax: 604-666-7255
pacific-pacifique@tc.gc.ca
Regional Director General, Michael A. Henderson
604-666-5849,
michael.henderson@tc.gc.ca

Prairie & Northern
344 Edmonton St.
Winnipeg, MB R3C 0P6
204-983-3152
888-463-0521
pnrweb@tc.gc.ca
Regional Director General, Sylvain Giguère
204-984-8105,
sylvain.giguere@tc.gc.ca

Québec
700, Leigh Capreol, Zone 3A
Dorval, QC H4Y 1G7
514-633-2714
Fax: 514-633-2751
Regional Director General, André Lapointe
514-633-2717, Fax: 514-633-2720
andre.lapointe@tc.gc.ca

Transportation Safety Board of Canada / Bureau de la sécurité des transports du Canada
200 Promenade du Portage, 4th Fl.
Ottawa, ON K1A 1K8
819-994-3741
Fax: 819-997-2239
800-387-3557
TDD: 819-953-7287
www.tsb.gc.ca
The Board is an independent agency reporting to Parliament through the President of the Queen's Privy Council. The formal name for the Board is the Canadian Transportation Accident Investigation & Safety Board. Its sole aim is the advancement of transportation safety in the marine, rail, pipeline & air modes of transport. The TSB conducts independent investigations into selected transportation occurences in order to make findings as to their causes & contributing factors; identifies safety deficiencies, & makes recommendations designed to prevent further occurences. Because the Board is independent, its transportation accident investigations are completely separate from the regulatory agencies responsible for transportation. In making findings & recommendations it is not the function of the Board to assign fault or determine civil liability.
Chair, Wendy A. Tadros
819-994-8000, Fax: 819-994-9759
Wendy.Tadros@tsb.gc.ca
COO, Jean L. Laporte
819-994-8004, Fax: 819-994-9759
Jean.Laporte@bst-tsb.gc.ca
Director Communications, Aarin Masson
819-994-8051, Fax: 819-953-1733
aarin.bronson@bst-tsb.gc.ca

Treasury Board of Canada / Conseil du Trésor du Canada
300 Laurier Ave. West, 10th Fl.
Ottawa, ON K1A 0R5
613-957-2400
Fax: 613-941-4000
877-636-0656
TDD: 613-957-9090

Federal/Provincial Government / Government of Alberta

info@tbs-sct.gc.ca
www.tbs-sct.gc.ca
The Treasury Board is a Cabinet Committee of government headed by the President of the Treasury Board. The committee constituting the Treasury Board includes, in addition to the President, the Minister of Finance & four other ministers appointed by the Governor-in-Council. The main role of the Treasury Board is the management of the government's financial, personnel & administrative responsibilities. The Treasury Board derives its authority primarily from the Financial Administration Act & is supported by the Treasury Board Secretariat.

Acts Administered:
Alternative Fuels Act
Federal Real Property & Federal Immovables Act
Minister, Asia-Pacific Gateway; President, Treasury Board,
Hon. Stockwell Burt Day
613-995-1702, Fax: 613-995-1154
DayS@parl.gc.ca; president@tbs-sct.gc.ca
• Public Sector Pension Investment Board
#200, 440 Laurier Ave. West
Ottawa, ON K1R 7X6
613-782-3095
Fax: 613-782-6864
info@investpsp.ca
www.investpsp.ca
• Canada Public Service Agency(CPSA) / Agence de la fonction publique du Canada (AFPC)
269 Laurier Ave. West, 10th Fl.
Ottawa, ON K1A 0R3
613-946-5015
Fax: 613-948-4758
www.infosource.gc.ca/inst/hrh/fed00-eng.asp
• Public Service Labour Relations Board
CD Howe Building
240 Sparks St., 6th Fl.
PO Box 1525 B
Ottawa, ON K1P 5V2
613-990-1800
Fax: 613-990-1849
866-931-3454
mail.courrier@pslrb-crtfp.gc.ca
www.pslrb-crtfp.gc.ca

Federal Contaminated Sites & Solid Waste Landfills Inventory
www.tbs-sct.gc.ca/dfrp-rbif/cs-sc/home-accueil.asp?Language=EN
Includes all known federal contaminated sites for which federal departments & agencies (excluding Crown corporations) are accountable. Also includes some non-federal sites for which the government has accepted some or all responsibility. Sites are classified at the time of assessment for contaminants, in a system developed by the Canadian Council of Ministers of Environment.
Executive Director Real Property & Materiel Policy Directorate, Bob Hirst
613-957-0517, Fax: 613-957-2405
hirst.bob@tbs-sct.gc.ca

Office of the Registrar of Lobbyists
255 Albert St., 10th Fl.
Ottawa, ON K1A 0R5
613-957-2760
Fax: 613-957-3078
Minister, Veterans Affairs; Minister of State (Agriculture),
Hon. Jean-Pierre Blackburn
613-996-4649, Fax: 613-996-0287
Blackburn.J@parl.gc.ca

Western Economic Diversification Canada (WD) / Diversification de l'économie de l'Ouest Canada (DEO)

Canada Place
#1500, 9700 Jasper Ave. NW
Edmonton, AB T5J 4H7
780-495-4164
Fax: 780-495-4557
888-338-9378
www.wd-deo.gc.ca
Responsible for promoting economic growth & diversification in the West. By investing in innovation, fostering entrepreneurship & using partnerships to enhance community sustainability, WD is helping to create a more prosperous future for western Canadians. Invests in R&D & commercialization in environmental technologies as a focus area for innovation strategies.

Minister of State (Western Economic Diversification), Hon. Lynne Yelich
613-952-2768, Fax: 613-952-9384
Yelich.L@parl.gc.ca; lynne.yelich@wd.gc.ca
Deputy Minister, Daniel Watson
780-495-5772, Fax: 780-495-6222
Other Communications: Ottawa: 613/952-9382; Fax: 613/954-1044
Executive Director Finance & Corporate Management, Jim Saunderson
780-495-4301, Fax: 780-495-7618

Regional Offices:

Edmonton
Canada Place
#1500, 9700 Jasper Ave. Northwest
Edmonton, AB T5J 4H7
780-495-4164
Fax: 780-495-4557
888-338-9378
TDD: 877-303-3388

Vancouver
Price Waterhouse Bldg.
#700, 333 Seymour St.
Vancouver, BC V6B 5G9
604-666-6256
Fax: 604-666-2353
888-338-9378
TDD: 877-303-3388
Asst. Deputy Minister, Gerry Salembier
604-666-6366, Fax: 604-666-1510

Calgary
#400, 639 - 5 Ave. SW
Calgary, AB T2P 0M9
403-292-5458
Fax: 403-292-5487
888-338-9378
TDD: 877-303-3388

Winnipeg
The Cargill Bldg.
#620, 240 Graham Ave.
Winnipeg, MB R3C 0J7
204-983-4472
Fax: 204-983-3852
888-338-9378
TDD: 877-303-3388
Asst. Deputy Minister, Marilyn Kapitany
204-983-5715, Fax: 204-983-0966

Ottawa
#500, 141 Laurier Ave. West
Ottawa, ON K1P 5J3
613-952-2768
Fax: 613-952-9384
TDD: 877-303-3388
Asst. Deputy Minister, Janet King
613-952-7096, Fax: 613-954-1044

Saskatoon
S.J. Cohen Bldg.
#601, 119 - 4 Ave. South
PO Box 2025
Saskatoon, SK S7K 3S7
306-975-4373
Fax: 306-975-5484
888-338-9378
TDD: 877-303-3388
Asst. Deputy Minister, Sharon Lee Smith
306-975-5858, Fax: 306-975-5484

Government of Alberta

Seat of Government: 9718 - 107 St.
Edmonton, AB T5K 1E4
www.alberta.ca
The Province of Alberta entered Confederation September 1, 1905. It has an area of 640,044.57 km2, & the StatsCan census population in 2009 was 3,687,700.

Land & Resource Issues

Alberta Advanced Education & Technology

Legislature Bldg.
#324, 10800 - 97 Ave.
Edmonton, AB T5K 2B6

780-422-5400
Fax: 780-422-1263
aet.info@gov.ab.ca
www.advancededandtech.gov.ab.ca
In 2006-2007, the Ministry of Advanced Education & Technology was created to combine the responsibilities of the ministries of Advanced Education & Innovation & Science. The mission of the Ministry of Advanced Education & Technology is to assist Alberta to be a learning & innovative society. The goals of the ministry are to ensure that advanced learning is a lifelong pursuit that is accessible & affordable to Albertans. The province's advanced learning & innovation system continues work to respect a diversity of communities, learner aspirations & abilities. In order to ensure an adaptable learning system & to create value through innovation, partnerships, coalitions & networks are sought & built. Investments in Alberta's advanced learning system & innovation framework focus upon sustainability. The aim is for the province's advanced learning system's research, technology & knowledge transfer to be competitive & to achieve global excellence.

Acts Administered:
Access to the Future Act
Alberta Enterprise Corporation Act
Alberta Research & Innovation Act
Apprenticeship & Industry Training Act
Post-secondary Learning Act (PSLA)
Private Vocational Training Act
Student Support Legislation (various)
Advanced Education & Technology Grants Regulation
• Alberta Agricultural Research Institute(AARI)
Phipps-McKinnon Bldg.
#500, 10020 - 101A Ave.
Edmonton, AB T5J 3G2
780-427-1956
Fax: 780-427-3252
aarimail@gov.ab.ca
www.aari.ab.ca
• Alberta Prion Research Institute(APRI)
Scotia Place, Tower 2
#2001, 10060 Jasper Ave.
Edmonton, AB T5J 3R8
780-638-3790
Fax: 780-643-1432
www.prioninstitute.ca
Managing Director, Donald Harrison
APRI was established in response to the devastion that BSE brought to the province's beef industry in 2003. The institute is a research hub to challenge the economic and social threat posed by BSE and other prion-related diseases. In 2010, APRI became part of Alberta Innovates - Bio Solutions, an umbrella corporation that supports the growth and development of Alberta's agricultural, forestry and associated industries:
www.albertainnovates.ca/bio.
• Alberta Innovates - Health Solutions
#1500, 10104 - 103 Ave
Edmonton, AB T5J 4A7
780-423-5727
Fax: 780-429-3509
877-423-5727
health@albertainnovates.ca
www.albertainnovates.ca/health
• Alberta Science & Research Authority(ASRA)
Phipps-McKinnon Bldg.
#500, 10020 - 101A Ave.
Edmonton, AB T5J 3G2
780-427-1488
Fax: 780-427-0979
asra@gov.ab.ca
www.asra.gov.ab.ca
Chair, Dr. Marvin Fritzler
Created in 1994, the Alberta Science & Research Authority (ASRA) is an independent board of members from Alberta's academic, business & research communities, appointed by provincial Cabinet. ASRA functions as the senior science & research body of the Government. It works collaboratively with government departments & agencies & stakeholders to stimulate & develop research & related scientific activities, policies & priorities compatible with economic & social priorities of the government. ASRA conducts annual reviews & evaluations of government science & research policies, priorities & programs, promotes communication on matters related to science & research & encourages Alberta's science & research sector to attain international competitiveness & recognition. In Jan., 2010, ASRA was placed under the umbrella of Alberta Innovates - Alberta Research and Innovation Authority: www.albertainnovates.ca/research.

- Informatics Circle of Research Excellence(iCORE)
3608 - 33 St. NW
Calgary, AB T2L 2A6
780-450-5111
Fax: 403-210-5337
techfutures@albertainnovates.ca
www.icore.ca
President/CEO, Randy Goebel
iCORE operates grant programs to develop chairs at Alberta universities. It invests in research scientists who work on fundamental and applied problems in informatics, in areas such as computer science, electrical and computer engineering, physics, mathematics and other disciplines related to information and communications technology (ICT). iCORE has been placed under the umbrella of Alberta Innovates - Technology Futures, a research and innovation system that helps technical industries find solutions, develop products and move technologies to market, building on Alberta's platform technologies, like nanotechnology, information communications technologies, and genomics:
www.albertainnovates.ca/technology.
- Alberta Learning Information Service(ALIS)
City Centre
10242 - 105 St.
Edmonton, AB T5J 3L5
780-427-9674
info@alis.gov.ab.ca
www.alis.gov.ab.ca
Other Communication: Alberta Career Information Hotline:
780-422-4266; Toll Free: 1-800-661-3753
- Alberta Council on Admissions & Transfer(ACAT)
Commerce Place
10155 - 102 St., 11th Fl.
Edmonton, AB T5J 4L5
780-422-9021
Fax: 780-422-3688
800-232-7215
TDD: 780-427-9999
acat@gov.ab.ca
www.acat.gov.ab.ca
- Campus Alberta Quality Council
Commerce Place
10155 - 102 St., 11th Fl.
Edmonton, AB T5J 4L5
780-427-8921
Fax: 780-427-0423
caqc@gov.ab.ca
www.caqc.gov.ab.ca
- Alberta Apprenticeship & Industry Training Board
South Tower
10030 - 107 St., 7th Fl.
Edmonton, AB T5J 4X7
780-427-8517
Fax: 780-422-3734
800-232-7215
TDD: 780-427-9999
- Private Vocational Schools Advisory Council
Commerce Place
10155 - 102 St., 10th Fl.
Edmonton, AB T5J 4L5
780-427-5609
Fax: 780-427-5920

Research & Innovation Division
Phipps-McKinnon Bldg.
10020 - 101A Ave., 5th Fl.
Edmonton, AB T5J 3G2
780-427-1488
Fax: 780-427-0979
Some of the branches, units & services include: Cross Ministry Initiatives; Innovation Planning & Accountability (Reporting & Accountability, Research Capacity Planning, Strategic Integration); Alberta Research & Innovation Authority - ARIA; Innovation Policy; Alberta Innovates (Bio Solutions, Energy & Environment Solutions, Health Solutions, Technology Futures).
Executive Director Cross Ministry Initiatives, Daphne Cheel
780-422-0054, Fax: 780-427-3252
daphne.cheel@gov.ab.ca
Executive Director Innovation Planning & Accountability, Michele Kirchner
780-427-5634,
michele.kirchner@gov.ab.ca
Executive Director Alberta Research & Innovation Authority, Lee Kruszewski
780-638-3795, Fax: 780-427-0979
lee.kruszewski@gov.ab.ca

Director Innovation Policy, Sandra Duxbury
780-427-4498, Fax: 780-415-9823
sandra.duxbury@gov.ab.ca

Advanced Technology Industries Division
Phipps-McKinnon Bldg.
10020 - 101A Ave., 5th Fl.
Edmonton, AB T5J 3G2
Branches, units & services in this division include: Emerging Technology Industries; Information & Technology Management (Client Service Delivery, External Client Liaison, Information & Applicatin Services, Strategic Technology Planning); Innovation Client Services; Technology Industry Development (Business Development, ICT Industries, Strategic Iniatives, Life Sciences Industries).
Assistant Deputy Minister, Mel Wong
780-427-2084, Fax: 780-427-5924
mel.wong@gov.ab.ca
Executive Director & CIO Information and Technology Management Section, Leslie Sim-Kaiser
780-415-0813, Fax: 780-422-0880
leslie.sim-kaiser@gov.ab.ca
Executive Director Technology Industry Development Section, Robert Lai
780-427-7722, Fax: 780-427-5924
robert.lai@gov.ab.ca
Branch Head Emerging Technology Industries Branch, Ken Langhorn
780-415-8751, Fax: 780-427-5924
ken.langhorn@gov.ab.ca
Branch Head Life Sciences Industries Branch, Brad Guthrie
780-427-6618, Fax: 780-427-5924
brad.guthrie@gov.ab.ca

Post Secondary Excellence Division
Commerce Place, 7th Fl.
10155 - 102 St.
Edmonton, AB T5J 4L5
Some of the branches, units and services included in this division are: Campus Alberta Partnerships (Alberta Council on Admissions and Transfer - ACAT, Community Partnerships and Literacy, Inspiring Excellence, International Education); Investments and Quality (Campus Alberta Quality Council, Financial Planning, Post-Secondary Planning and Investment, Post-Secondary Programs, Private Vocational Training); System Capacity and Development (Business Integration & Consultation, Policy Development and Intergovernmental, Policy Research and Analysis, Business Operations & Reporting)

Community, Learner & Industry Connections Division
Phipps-McKinnon Bldg., 5th Fl.
10020 - 101A Ave.
Edmonton, AB T5J 3G2
780-427-8517
Some of the branches, units and services offered are: Apprenticeship & Industry Training (International & Provincial Assessment Services, Technical Solutions & Support, Apprenticeship Technical Training & Certification); Learner Funding (Loans Administration, Assessing & Processing); Financial Operations & Control Services (Program & Awards Support, Program Compliance & Investigations); Program, Policy & Systems Support (Policy & Planning, Business & Systems Support, Program Services & Delivery, Student Funding Contact Centre).
Assistant Deputy Minister, Shirley Dul
780-422-1185, Fax: 780-422-2420
shirley.dul@gov.ab.ca
Director Apprenticeship Policy & Legislation, Susan Johnston
780-422-1183, Fax: 780-422-2420
susan.johnston@gov.ab.ca
Director Apprenticeship Technical Training & Certification, James Tyler
780-638-3329, Fax: 780-422-7376
tyler.james@gov.ab.ca
Director Learner Assistance, Schubert Kwan
780-422-4498, Fax: 780-422-4517
schubert.kwan@gov.ab.ca

Alberta Aboriginal Relations
Commerce Place, 19th Fl.
10155 - 102 St.
Edmonton, AB T5J 4G8
780-422-4144
Fax: 780-644-8389
TDD: 800-232-7215
www.aboriginal.alberta.ca

Alberta Aboriginal Relations works with Aboriginal communities and other partners to enhance social and economic opportunities for Aboriginal people in Alberta.
Acts Administered:
Constitution of Alberta Amendment Act, 1990
Metis Settlements Accord Implementation Act
Metis Settlements Amendment Act, 2004
Metis Settlements Act
Metis Settlements Land Protection Act
Minister, Hon. Len Webber
780-422-4144, Fax: 780-644-8389
Deputy Minister, Maria David-Evans
780-415-0900, Fax: 780-415-6144
maria.david-evans@gov.ab.ca
Assistant Deputy Minister First Nations and Métis Relations, Donavon Young
780-422-5925, Fax: 780-427-4019
donavon.young@gov.ab.ca
Assistant Deputy Minister Consultation and Land Claims, Stan Rutwind
780-643-1731, Fax: 780-427-0401
stan.rutwind@gov.ab.ca
Assistant Deputy Minister Corporate Services, Lorne Harvey
780-422-2429, Fax: 780-427-0939
lorne.harvey@gov.ab.ca
Executive Director Policy and Planning, Cameron Henry
780-427-2008, Fax: 780-427-1760
cameron.henry@gov.ab.ca
- Métis Settlements Appeal Tribunal
14605 - 134 St.
Edmonton, AB T5L 4S9
780-422-1541
Fax: 780-422-0019
800-661-8864
www.msat.gov.ab.ca

First Nations & Métis Relations
Commerce Place
10155 - 102 St., 13th Fl.
Edmonton, AB T5J 4G8
780-422-9526
Fax: 780-427-4019
Assistant Deputy Minister, Donavon Young
780-422-5925, Fax: 780-427-4019
donavon.young@gov.ab.ca
Executive Director Métis Relations, Thomas Droege
780-427-9431, Fax: 780-427-1760
thomas.droege@gov.ab.ca
Director First Nations Relations, Cynthia Dunnigan
780-415-6141, Fax: 780-427-4019
cynthia.dunnigan@gov.ab.ca
Director, Aboriginal Justice Initiatives Aboriginal Community Initiatives, Bronwyn Shoush
780-427-3060, Fax: 780-227-1760
bronwyn.shoush@gov.ab.ca
Director Aboriginal Economic Partnerships, Lanny Der
780-644-1057, Fax: 780-427-1760
lanny.der@gov.ab.ca
Director First Nations Development Fund, Peter Crossen
780-415-6142, Fax: 780-427-0401
peter.crossen@gov.ab.ca
Director Land Claims, Steven Andres
780-427-6084, Fax: 780-427-0401
steven.andres@gov.ab.ca
Registrar Métis Settlements Land Registry, Lisa Chartrand
780-415-0168, Fax: 780-427-3656
lisa.chartrand@gov.ab.ca

Métis Settlements Ombudsman Office
#203, 10525 - 170 St.
Edmonton, AB T5P 4W2
a80-427-9828
Fax: 780-427-9962
866-427-6813
Ombudsman, Harley Johnson
780-427-9463, Fax: 780-427-9962
harley.johnson@gov.ab.ca

Alberta Agriculture & Rural Development
J.G. O'Donoghue Bldg.
7000 - 113 St., 1st Fl.
Edmonton, AB T6H 5T6
780-427-2727
Fax: 780-427-2861
866-882-7677

Federal/Provincial Government / Government of Alberta

www.agric.gov.ab.ca
Other Communication: Publications Office: 780/427-0391, Toll Free: 1-800-292-5697
The Ministry of Agriculture & Food provides a variety of services to Alberta's agricultural industry. Programs are aimed towards farmers & production, & to ag & food processing industries.

Acts Administered:
Agricultural Operations Practices Act
Agricultural Pests Act
Agricultural Service Board Act
Agricultural Societies Act
Agriculture Financial Services Act
Alberta Wheat and Barley Test Market Act
Animal Health Act
Animal Keepers Act
Animal Protection Act
Bee Act
Brand Act
Crop Liens Priorities Act
Crop Payments Act
Dairy Industry Act
Farm Implement Act
Farm Implement Dealerships Act
Federal-Provincial Farm Assistance Act
Feeder Associations Guarantee Act
Fuel Tax Act
Fur Farms Act
Gas Distribution Act
Government Accountability Act
Government Organization Act, Sched 2
Heating Oil & Propane Rebate Act
Irrigation Districts Act
Line Fence Act
Livestock Diseases Act
Livestock Identification and Brand Inspection Act
Livestock Identification and Commerce Act
Livestock Industry Diversification Act
Livestock and Livestock Products Act
Marketing of Agricultural Products Act
Meat Inspection Act
Rural Electrification Loan Act
Rural Electrification Long-term Financing Act
Rural Utilities Act
Soil Conservation Act
St. Mary and Milk Rivers Water Agreements (Termination) Act
Stray Animals Act
Weed Control Act
Wheat Board Money Trust Act
Women's Institute Act

Minister, Hon. Jack Hayden
780-427-2137, Fax: 780-422-6035
Deputy Minister, John Knapp
780-427-2145, Fax: 780-415-6002
john.knapp@gov.ab.ca
Executive Director Human Resource Services & Facilities Management Services, Heather K.M. Behman
780-427-2430, Fax: 780-427-3398
heather.behman@gov.ab.ca
Director Communications Branch, Cathy Housdorff
780-422-7683, Fax: 780-427-2861
cathy.housdorff@gov.ab.ca
Senior Financial Officer Financial & Business Planning Services Division, Jim Carter
780-427-2162, Fax: 780-422-6529
• Agriculture Financial Services Corporation(AFSC)
5718 - 56 Ave.
Lacombe, AB T4L 1B1
403-782-8200
Fax: 403-782-4226
800-396-0215
www.afsc.ca
Chair, Harry Haney
The provincial crown corporation provides farmers, agribusinesses, & other small businesses loans, crop insurance, & farm income disaster assistance.
• Alberta Grain Council
7000 - 113 St., 3rd Fl.
Edmonton, AB T6H 5T6
780-427-7329
Fax: 780-422-9690
www1.agric.gov.ab.ca/$department/deptdocs.nsf/all/agc2620
Chair, Greg Porozni
Provincial government agency within the Ministry of Agriculture and Rural Development (ARD), comprised of ten Alberta Grains Council (AGC) members appointed by the Minister of ARD (eight farmers, and two government employees). A small staff supports the AGC members. This body advises and makes recommendations to the Minister of ARD on current and emerging issues and trends in the grain industry.
• Farmers' Advocate of Alberta
7000 - 113 St., 3rd Fl.
Edmonton, AB T6H 5T6
780-427-2433
Fax: 780-427-3913
farmers.advocate@gov.ab.ca
Farmers' Advocate, Jim Kiss
• Irrigation Council
Provincial Bldg.
200 - 5 Ave. South, 3rd Fl., PO Bag 3014
Lethbridge, AB T1J 4L1
403-381-5176
Fax: 403-382-4406
Chair, Vern Hoff
• Alberta Livestock & Meat Agency(ALMA)
Ellwood Office Park South
1003 Ellwood Rd. SW
Edmonton, AB T6X 0B3
780-638-1699
Fax: 780-638-6496
info@almaltd.ca
www.alma.alberta.ca
• Alberta Centre for Livestock Genomics
College Plaza
8215 - 112 St., 14th Fl.
Edmonton, AB T6G 2C8
780-427-2442
Fax: 780-428-1900

Industry Development & Food Safety Sector
JG O'Donoghue
7000 - 113 Street, 3rd fl.
Edmonton, AB T6H 5T6
Asst. Deputy Minister, Jason Krips
780-427-2439, Fax: 780-422-6317
jason.krips@gov.ab.ca
Director Bio-Industrial Technologies Division, Connie Phillips
780-644-8124, Fax: 780-638-3586
connie.phillips@gov.ab.ca
Branch Head Bio-Industrial Technology Branch, Hong Qi
780-644-8128, Fax: 780-638-3586
hong.qi@gov.ab.ca
Branch Head Bio-Industrial Development Branch, Kirsty Piquette
780-644-2410, Fax: 780-638-3586
kirsty.piquette.ab.ca
Director Rural Extension & Industry Development Division, Jo-Ann Hall
780-968-3512, Fax: 780-963-4709
jo-ann.hall@gov.ab.ca
Acting Branch Head Local/Domestic Market Expansion Branch, Shauna Johnston
780-968-3553, Fax: 780-968-3554
shauna.johnston@gov.ab.ca
Branch Head Alberta Ag-Info Centre, Ross Hutchison
403-742-7542, Fax: 403-742-7527
ross.hutchison@gov.ab.ca
Branch Head Processing Industry Business Development Branch, Lynn Stegman
403-340-7010, Fax: 403-340-4896
lynn.stegman@gov.ab.ca
Branch Head Agriculture Grant Programs Branch, Murray Greer
780-980-4722, Fax: 780-980-4737
murray.greer@gov.ab.ca
Branch Head Livestock Business Development Branch, Rod Carlyon
780-349-4466, Fax: 780-349-5240
rod.carlyon@gov.ab.ca
Branch Head Crop Business Development Branch, James Calpas
403-340-5329, Fax: 403-340-4896
james.calpas@gov.ab.ca
Branch Head Ag-Industry Extension Branch, Barb Shackel-Hardman
780-968-3550, Fax: 780-968-3554
barb.shackel.hardman@gov.ab.ca
Branch Head 4-H & Agriculture Education Branch, Marguerite Stark
403-948-8510, Fax: 403-948-2069
marguerite.stark@gov.ab.ca

Executive Director Traceability Division, Brent McEwan
780-427-2799, Fax: 780-422-3655
brent.mcewan@gov.ab.ca

Policy & Environment Sector
Same address as above sector.
Asst. Deputy Minister, Colin Jeffares
780-427-1957, Fax: 780-422-6317
colin.jeffares@gov.ab.ca
Director Irrigation & Farm Water Division, Brent Paterson
780-381-5143, Fax: 780-381-5903
brent.paterson@gov.ab.ca
Branch Head Rural Water Branch, Marshall Eliason
780-427-4615, Fax: 780-422-9745
marshall.eliason@gov.ab.ca
Branch Head Water Resources Branch,vacant
403-381-5140, Fax: 403-381-5903
arliss.boschee@gov.ab.ca
Branch Head Irrigation Secretariat, Roger Hohm
403-381-5176, Fax: 403-382-4406
roger.hohm@gov.ab.ca.ab.ca

Business Service & Rural Utilities Sector
Executive Director, Jamie curran
780-422-6166, Fax: 780-422-6317
jamie.curran@gov.ab.ca
Acting Director Information Technology Division, Rob Pungor
780-422-6660, Fax: 780-422-4004
rob.pungor@gov.ab.ca

Food Safety Division
Director, Greg Orriss
780-427-6159, Fax: 780-427-1437
Head Agri-Food Laboratories, Ken Manninen
780-422-0808, Fax: 780-415-4527
ken.manninen@gov.ab.ca
Head Agri-Food Systems, Dr. Sandra Honour
780-427-4054, Fax: 780-427-7535
sandra.honour@gov.ab.ca
Head Safe Food Systems Section, Kim Whitehead
780-415-4522, Fax: 780-427-7535
kim.whitehead@gov.ab.ca

Resource Management & Irrigation
Fax: 780-422-0474
Director, John Tackaberry
780-422-4596,
john.tackaberry@gov.ab.ca
Head Conservation & Development, John Hermans
780-427-3908, Fax: 780-422-0474
john.hermans@gov.ab.ca
Head Irrigation, Brent Paterson
403-381-5143, Fax: 403-381-5903
brent.paterson@gov.ab.ca

Technical Services Division
Director, Carol Bettac
780-427-0674, Fax: 780-422-9745
carol.bettac@gov.ab.ca
Head Agricultural Engineering, Rick Atkins
403-329-1212, Fax: 403-328-5562
rick.atkins@gov.ab.ca
Head Environmental Practices & Livestock Welfare, Barb Shackel-Hardman
780-427-9801, Fax: 780-422-9745
barb.shackel.hardman@gov.ab.ca
Unit Leader Environmental Practices, Sandi Jones
403-340-7609, Fax: 403-340-4896
sandi.jones@gov.ab.ca
Provincial Livestock Welfare Specialist, Dr. Derek Haley
403-340-5524, Fax: 403-340-4896
derek.haley@gov.ab.ca

Agriculture Research Division
780-427-5341
Director, Dr. Cornelia Kreplin
780-427-5341, Fax: 780-427-1057
cornelia.kreplin@gov.ab.ca
Branch Head Aquaculture,Vacant
403-381-5171, Fax: 403-381-5903
Branch Head Crop Development - Food, Henry Nadja
403-362-1346, Fax: 403-362-1306
henry.nadja@gov.ab.ca
Branch Head Crop Development - Non-Food, Dr. Christine Murray

Federal/Provincial Government / Government of Alberta

403-644-1986, Fax: 403-427-1057
christine.murray@gov.ab.ca
Branch Head Feeds & Feeding, Dave Dyson
403-782-8697, Fax: 403-782-5514
dave.dyson@gov.ab.ca
Branch Head Livestock Production & Meat Quality, Michelle Follensbee
780-415-0828, Fax: 780-427-1057
michelle.follensbee@gov.ab.ca
Team Leader Meat Quality Unit, Jake Kotowich
780-644-1741

Commercialization Division
Fax: 780-963-4709
Director, Jo-Ann Hall
780-968-3557,
jo-ann.hall@gov.ab.ca
Head Agri-preneur Feasability Team, Heather Loeppky
780-963-6101,
heather.loeppky@gov.ab.ca

Agri-Business Expansion Division
780-427-3166
Director Business Expansion and Commercialization Division, Marilynn Boehm
780-422-1851, Fax: 780-644-2400
marilyn.boehm@gov.ab.ca

Economics & Competitiveness Division
Fax: 780-427-5220

Strategy & Business Planning Division
780-422-9167
Director, Lloyd Andruchow
780-427-3338, Fax: 780-422-7755
lloyd.andruchow@gov.ab.ca
Head Program Policy Development & Coordination, Marcia Hewitt-Fisher
780-427-3315, Fax: 780-427-5921
marcia.hewitt.fisher@gov.ab.ca
Head Strategic Planning, Cam Swan
780-427-4463, Fax: 780-427-5921
cam.swan@gov.ab.ca

Culture & Community Development Division
Standard Life Centre
10405 Jasper Ave., 9th Fl.
Edmonton, AB T5J 4R7
780-415-1167
Fax: 780-422-2891
Other Communication: Board Development Information:
780-427-2001; Lottery Funding Programs Information:
780-447-8600
The Culture & Community Development Division oversees the following areas: Community Spirit Program; Arts; Human Rights & Citizenship; Alberta Foundation for the Arts; Alberta Sport, Recreation, Parks & Wildlife Foundation; Strategic Information; Board Development; Lottery Funding Programs; Voluntary Sector Services & Initiatives; Financial Services; & the Wild Rose Foundation.
Acting Assistant Deputy Minister, Sue Bohaichuk
780-415-4874, Fax: 780-422-2891
sue.bohaichuk@gov.ab.ca
Executive Director Arts, Jeffrey Anderson
780-415-0283,
jeffrey.anderson@gov.ab.ca
Director Human Rights & Citizenship, Marie Riddle
780-427-3116, Fax: 780-422-3563
marie.riddle@gov.ab.ca
Director Voluntary Sector Services, Pat Blakney
780-422-1724

Parks, Conservation, Recreation & Sport Division
Oxbridge Place
9820 - 106 St., 2nd Fl.
Edmonton, AB T5K 2J6
780-427-3582
Fax: 780-427-5980
866-427-3582
The Division is responsible for the following program & branches: Parks & Protected Areas Program; Sport & Recreation Branch; & Historic Resources Management Branch.
Assistant Deputy Minister, Bill Werry
780-427-7896,
bill.werry@gov.ab.ca b.ca

Executive Director Field Operations, Fred Moffatt
780-427-8441,
fred.moffatt@gov.ab.ca
Director Policy & Program Coordination, Brian Kelly
780-427-9382,
brian.kelly@gov.ab.ca
Director Heritage Protection & Recreation Management Branch, Archie Landals
780-427-9470,
archie.landals@gov.ab.ca
Director Visitor Services Branch, June Markwart
780-427-9383,
june.markwart@gov.ab.ca
Director Sport and Recreation Branch, Lloyd Bentz
780-415-0263, Fax: 780-415-0308
lloyd.bentz@gov.ab.ca
Director Historic Resources Management Branch, David Link
780-431-2313,
david.link@gov.ab.ca
Calgary
Standard Life Bldg.
639 - 5 Ave. SW, 3rd Fl.
Calgary, AB T2P 0M9
Fax: 403-297-6168
Director, Walter Valentini
403-297-8920,
walter.valentini@gov.ab.ca
Camrose
5005 - 49 St.
Camrose, AB T4V 1N5
780-679-1235
Fax: 780-679-1250
Director, Al Walkey
780-679-1235, Fax: 780-679-1250
al.walkey@gov.ab.ca
Edmonton
Commerce Place
10155 - 102 St., 5th Fl.
Edmonton, AB T5J 4L6
780-427-6656
Fax: 780-422-5804
Executive Director, Rick Siddle
780-427-6656, Fax: 780-422-5804
rick.siddle@gov.ab.ca
Senior Director Defence Industry Development, Bill Werny
780-427-5299
Director Regional Alliance Development, George Brosseau
780-427-0802, Fax: 780-422-5804
george.brosseau@gov.ab.ca
Director Aerospace Industry and Regional Development, Larry Pana
780-427-6764, Fax: 780-422-5804
Director North Central Region, Garry Krause
780-415-8745, Fax: 780-422-5804
garry.krause@gov.ab.ca
Director Transportation & Logistics, Gary Haynes
780-427-6643, Fax: 780-422-2091
gary.haynes@gov.ab.ca
Edmonton - Provincial Nominee Program
North Tower, Telus Plaza
10025 Jasper Ave., 9th Fl.
Edmonton, AB T5J 1S6
780-427-6496
Fax: 780-427-6560
Senior Director, Brad Trefan
brad.trefan@gov.ab.ca
Edson
Provincial Bldg.
111 - 54 St.
Edson, AB T7E 1T2
780-723-8229
Fax: 780-723-8240
Director, Tammy Powell
780-723-8229, Fax: 780-723-8240
tammy.powell@gov.ab.ca
Grande Prairie
Provincial Bldg.
10320 - 99 St., 3rd Fl.
PO Box 20
Grande Prairie, AB T8V 6J4
780-538-5636
Fax: 780-538-5332
Director, Bob Hall
780-538-5636, Fax: 780-538-5332
bob.hall@gov.ab.ca

Lethbridge
Provincial Bldg.
#105, 200 - 5 Ave. South
Lethbridge, AB T1J 4L1
403-381-5414
Fax: 403-381-5741
Director, Linda Erickson
403-381-5741, Fax: 403-381-5741
linda.erickson@gov.ab.ca
Medicine Hat
Provincial Bldg.
346 - 3 St. SE, 1st Fl.
Medicine Hat, AB T1A 0G7
403-529-3633
Fax: 403-529-3564
Senior Advisor Alberta Economic Development Authority, Elvira Smid
403-529-3633, Fax: 403-529-3564
elvira.smid@gov.ab.ca
Pincher Creek
Provincial Bldg.
782 Main St., 2nd Fl.
PO Box 2813
Pincher Creek, AB T0K 1W0
403-627-1165
Fax: 403-627-1169
Director, Beverley Thornton
403-627-1165, Fax: 403-627-1169
bev.thornton@gov.ab.ca
Red Deer
Provincial Bldg.
4920 - 51 St., 2nd Fl.
Red Deer, AB T4N 6K8
403-340-5302
Fax: 403-340-5231
Regional Manager, Dawna Allard
403-340-5302, Fax: 403-340-5231
dawna.allard@gov.ab.ca
St. Paul
Provincial Bldg.
5025 - 49 Ave., 3rd Fl.
St Paul, AB T0A 3A4
780-645-6358
Fax: 780-645-6241
Regional Manager, Cathy Goulet
780-645-6358, Fax: 780-645-6241
cathy.goulet@gov.ab.ca

Beijing
c/o Canadian Embassy
19 Dongzhimenwai Dajie, Chaoyang District
Beijing, 100600 China
Other Communication: International Number: 86-10-5139-4272;
International Fax: 86-10-5139-4465
Managing Director Alberta China Office (Beijing), David Wong
david.wong@international.gc.ca

Hong Kong
Alberta Government Office, Admiralty Centre, Tower Two
#1004, 18 Harcourt Rd.
Hong Kong
www.alberta.org.hk
Other Communication: International Number:
011-852-2528-4729; International Fax: 011-852-2529-8115
Trade Director, Christopher Liu
chris.liu@alberta.org.hk
Other Communications: International Number:
011-852-2528-4729

Mexico
Calle Schiller No. 529
Colonia Palanco, Del. Miguel Hidalgo
Mexico, 11560 Mexico
www.alberta-canada.com/mexico
Other Communication: International Number:
011-52-555-387-9302; International Fax: 011-52-555-724-7913
Managing Director, David Nygaard
david.nygaard@international.gc.ca

Munich
Canadian Consulate
Tal 29
Munich, 80331 Germany
Other Communication: International Number:
011-49-(0)89-2199-5740; International Fax:
011-49-(0)89-2199-5745

Federal/Provincial Government / Government of Alberta

Consul - Alberta Alberta Germany Office, Wes Sawatzky
wes.sawatzky@international.gc.ca

London
Canadian High Commission, Macdonald House
1 Grosvenor Sq.
London, W1K 4AB United Kingdom
Other Communication: International Number:
011-44-20-7258-6472; International Fax: 011-44-20-7258-6309
Business Development Officer Alberta United Kingdom Office, Lesley Cairns
lesley.cairns@international.gc.ca

Seoul
c/o Alberta Government Office, Canadian Embassy
16-1 Jeong-dong, Jung-gu
Seoul, 100-120 South Korea
www.albertakorea.com
Other Communication: International Number:
011-82-2-3783-6142; International Fax: 011-82-2-3783-6147
Commercial Director Alberta Korea Office, Won-il Chung
Director Trade & Investment, Ha-Kyun Yoon
ha-kyun.yoon@dfait-maeci.gc.ca
Other Communications: International Number:
011-82-2-3783-6142

Taipei
Canadian Trade Office
365 Fu Hsing North Rd., 13th Fl.
Taipei 105
Other Communication: International Number:
011-866-2-2715-3637; International Fax: 011-886-22-715-1717
Trade Representative Alberta Taiwan Office, Li-an Chen
lian.chen@dfait-maeci.gc.ca

Tokyo
Alberta Government Office, Place Canada
3-37 Akasaka 7-chome, 3rd Fl., Minato-Ku
Tokyo, 107-0052 Japan
www.altanet.or.jp
Other Communication: International Number:
011-81-3-3475-1298; International Fax: 011-81-3-3470-3939
Managing Director Alberta Japan Office, Sean Crockett
sean.crockett@altanet.or.jp

Tourism Marketing & Heritage Division
Commerce Place
10155 - 102 St., 6th Fl.
Edmonton, AB T5J 4L6
Fax: 780-427-6454
The Tourism Marketing & Heritage Division oversees the following areas: Divisional Services; Historic Sites & Museums; Royal Alberta Museum; Royal Tyrrell Museum of Palaeontology; Provincial Archives of Alberta; & the Tourism Development & Services Branch.
Minister, Hon. Dave Hancock
780-427-5010, Fax: 780-427-5018
education.minister@gov.ab.ca
Deputy Minister, Keray Henke
780-427-3659, Fax: 780-427-7733
keray.henke@gov.ab.ca

Alberta Employment & Immigration
Minister's Office, Legislature Bldg.
#208, 10800 - 97 Ave.
Edmonton, AB T5K 2B6
780-644-5135
Fax: 780-422-9556
866-644-5135
eii.communications@gov.ab.ca
www.employment.alberta.ca
The Ministry's major responsibilities are: developing and delivering policies, programs and services to promote labour force development; helping Albertans train for, find and keep employment; providing financial and health benefits, child support services and employment training support to Albertans in need; ensuring Alberta's workplaces are safe, healthy, fair, and productive for employees and employers; providing leadership for immigration and interprovincial labour mobility policy for the Government of Alberta; coordinating resources to support the settlement and integration of new Albertans.
Acts Administered:
Agrology Profession Act
Architects Act
Blind Workers' Compensation Act
Consulting Engineers of Alberta Act
Employment Standards Code
Engineering, Geological & Geophysical Professions Act
Government Organization Act, Sched 3, 8, 10
Income & Employment Supports Act
Labour Relations Code
Land Agents Licensing Act
Land Surveyors Act
Managerial Exclusion Act
M.L.A. Compensation Act
Occupational Health and Safety Act
Police Officers Collective Bargaining Act
Professional and Occupational Associations Registration Act
Public Service Employee Relations Act
Radiation Protection Act
Regulated Accounting Profession Act
Regulated Forestry Profession Act
Special Payment Act
Office of Statistics & Information Act
Veterinary Profession Act
Widows' Pension Act
Workers' Compensation Act
Minister, Hon. Thomas A. Lukaszuk
780-415-4800, Fax: 780-422-9556
Deputy Minister, Shirley Howe
780-427-8305, Fax: 780-422-9205
shirley.howe@gov.ab.ca
Director Communications, Janice Schroeder
780-427-5649, Fax: 780-427-5988
janice.schroeder@gov.ab.ca
• Alberta Economic Development Authority(AEDA)
McDougall Centre
455 - 6 St. SW
Calgary, AB T2P 4E8
403-297-3022
Fax: 403-297-6435
aeda.alberta.ca

• Alberta Workers' Compensation Board
9912 - 107 St.
PO Box 2415
Edmonton, AB T5J 2S5
780-498-3999
866-922-9221
TDD: 780-498-7895
www.wcb.ab.ca
Other Communication: Calgary: 403-517-6000; Toll free outside Alberta: 1-800-661-9608 (in Canada)
• Appeals Commission for Alberta Workers' Compensation
Energy Square Bldg.
#901, 10109 - 106th St.
Edmonton, AB T5J 3L7
780-412-8700
Fax: 780-412-8701
www.appealscommission.ab.ca
• Labour Relations Board
#503, 10808 - 99 Ave.
Edmonton, AB T5K 0G5
780-422-5926
Fax: 780-422-0970
800-463-2572
alrboard@lab.gov.ab.ca
www3.gov.ab.ca/alrb
• Northern Alberta Development Council(NADC)
Provincial Bldg
#206, 9621 - 96 Ave.
PO Box 900-14
Peace River, AB T8S 1T4
780-624-6274
Fax: 780-624-6184
nadc.council@gov.ab.ca
www.nadc.gov.ab.ca
Executive Director, Dan Dibbelt
The Northern Alberta Development Council's (NADC) mandate is outlined in the Alberta Act of legislature. NADC objectives are to identify & implement measures that will advance northern development & advise government on opportunities & issues. Focus is on advancing development of the northern economy. Northern Alberta includes 60% of Alberta's landmass & has 10% of the province's population. It is resource rich, with 90% of alberta's forests, all of Canada's oil sands development, nearly 40% of Alberta's conventional oil & gas activity & 20% of Alberta's agricultural land. The NADC is involved with projects and initiatives in transportation, value-added agriculture, tourism, educational initiatives and inter-jurisdictional projects.

• Occupational Health & Safety Council
Labour Bldg
10808 - 99 Ave., 9th Fl.
Edmonton, AB T5K 0G5
780-415-0599
Fax: 780-422-8944
employment.alberta.ca/SFW/6446.html
Chair, Patty Whiting
The Occupational Health & Safety Council (the Council) is a group appointed by the Minister of Alberta Human Resources & Employment to hear appeals. The Council deals with matters that come under the Occupational Health & Safety Act & associated legislation. The issues that can be appealed before the Council are orders issued by Occupational Health & Safety Officers.

Immigration Division
Labour Bldg.
10808 - 99 Ave., 9th Fl.
Edmonton, AB T5K 0G5
780-638-3531
Assistant Deputy Minister, Maryann Everett
780-422-9493, Fax: 780-422-2889
maryann.everett@gov.ab.ca
Executive Director Immigration Policy & Programs, Percy Cummings
780-415-8945, Fax: 780-643-0905
percy.cummings@gov.ab.ca
Director Alberta Immigrant Nominee Program, Brad Trefan
780-427-6496, Fax: 780-427-6560
brad.trefan@gov.ab.ca
Executive Director Labour Attraction, Wendy Blackwell
780-427-1637, Fax: 780-644-3329
wendy.blackwell@gov.ab.ca
Director Strategic Marketing, Danielle Comeau
780-427-0528, Fax: 780-422-2889
danielle.comeau@gov.ab.ca

Delivery Services Division
Labour Bldg.
10808 - 99 Ave., 10th Fl.
Edmonton, AB T5K 0G5

Workplace Standards Division
Labour Bldg.
10808 - 99 Ave., 8th Fl.
Edmonton, AB T5K 0G5
780-415-9057
Fax: 780-644-2100
The Division includes Mediation Services, Professions & Occupations & Land Agent Licensing, Workplace Innovation & Continuous Improvement, Workplace Partnerships Director's Office, Workplace Policy & Standards Development, & Workplace Health & Safety & Employment Standards Compliance.
Assistant Deputy Minister, Dan Kennedy
780-415-0458, Fax: 780-644-2100
dan.kennedy@gov.ab.ca
Director Mediation Services (Labour Mediation), Bertha Greenstein
780-415-0530, Fax: 780-427-6327
bertha.greenstein@gov.ab.ca
Executive Director Workplace Policy & Legislation, Tim Thompson
780-415-0527, Fax: 780-422-0014
tim.thompson@gov.ab.ca
Executive Director Occupational Health & Safety, Vacant
780-415-0603, Fax: 780-644-1508
Executive Director Employment Standards, Eric Reitsma
780-422-5932, Fax: 780-644-5424
eric.reitsma@gov.ab.ca

Strategic Corporate Services Division
Labour Building
10808 - 99 Ave.
Edmonton, AB T5K 0G5
780-427-6765
The Strategic Services & Information Division consists of Data Development & Evaluation, Intergovernmental Relations, Legislative Services, Organizational Planning & Effectiveness, & People, Skills & Workplace Resources.

Workforce Supports Division
Labour Building
10808 - 99 Ave., 10th Fl.
Edmonton, AB T5K 0G5

780-722-0010
The Workforce Supports Division features the following components: Income & Child Support; Strategic Policy & Supports; Business Innovations; Employment & Training Services; & Labour Force Development.
Assistant Deputy Minister, Shannon Marchand
780-422-0194, Fax: 780-422-1651
shannon.marchand@gov.ab.ca

Alberta Energy

North Petroleum Plaza
9945 - 108 St., 10th Fl.
Edmonton, AB T5K 2G6
780-427-8050
Fax: 780-422-0698
780-310-0000
TDD: 780-427-9999
www.energy.gov.ab.ca
Other Communication: Calgary: 403-297-8955; Public Information Centre: 780-427-0265; TTY Toll Free: 1-800-232-7215
The Alberta Department of Energy's mission is to guide the development of the province's non-renewable resources. The sustained development of these resources is managed by the Department, with the goal of maximizing long-term benefits to Alberta. Alberta Energy is organzied around ten business units: aboriginal relations; bioenergy; coal, electricty; environment and resource services; minerals; natural gas; oil; oil sands; and tenure. Tenure is the process of leasing and administering petroleum and natural gas (P&NG) rights owned by the Province of Alberta.
Acts Administered:
Alberta Corporate Tax Act
Alberta Utilities Commission Act
Security Management Regulation
Coal Conservation Act
Coal Sales Act
Electric Utilities Act
Flare Gas Generation Regulation
Independent Power & Small Power Regulation
Energy Resources Conservation Act
Energy Statutes Amendment Act, 2009
Freehold Mineral Rights Tax Act
Gas Resources Preservation Act
Gas Utilities Act
Hydro & Electric Energy Act
The Mineral Titles Redemption Act
Mines & Minerals Act
Ammonite Shell Regulations
CO2 Projects Royalty Credit Regulation
Exploration Regulation
Gas Processing Efficiency Assistance Regulation
Innovative Energy Technologies Regulation
Metallic & Industrial Minerals Exploration Regulation
Metallic & Industrial Minerals Regulation
Mineral Rights Compensation Regulation
Oil Sands Tenure Regulation
Natural Gas Marketing Act
Natural Gas Price Protection Act
Oil & Gas Conservation Act
Oil Sands Conservation Act
Petroleum Marketing Act
Pipeline Act
Public Utilities Act
Small Power Research & Development Act
Turner Valley Unit Operations Act
Water, Gas & Electric Companies Act
Minister, Hon. Ron Liepert
780-427-3740, Fax: 780-422-0195
minister.energy@gov.ab.ca
Deputy Minister, Peter Watson
780-415-8434, Fax: 780-644-3103
peter.watson@gov.ab.ca
• Energy Resources Conservation Board(ERCB)
#1000, 250 - 5 Ave. SW
Calgary, AB T2P 0R4
403-297-8311
Fax: 403-297-7336
inquiries@ercb.ca
www.ercb.ca
Chair, Neil McCrank, Q.C., P.Eng
The ERCB is an independent, quasi-judicial agency of the Government of Alberta that regulates the safe, responsible, and efficient development of Alberta's energy resources: oil, natural gas, oil sands, coal, and pipelines.

• Alberta Utilities Commission(AUC)
Fifth Avenue Place
425 - 1 St. SW
Calgary, AB T2P 3L8
403-592-8845
Fax: 403-592-4406
www.auc.ab.ca

Energy Future Division
Petroleum Plaza NT
9945 - 108 St., 10th Fl.
Edmonton, AB T5K 2G6
Executive Lead, Jeff Kucharski
780-638-3136, Fax: 780-427-7737
jeff.kucharski@gov.ab.ca
Project Coordinator Manager Regulatory Enhancement Project, Anoushka Fernandes
780-427-2364, Fax: 780-427-7737
anoushka.m.fernandes@gov.ab.ca
Director Business Planning & Performance, Sandra Stemmer
780-643-1438, Fax: 780-422-0800
sandra.stemmer@gov.ab.ca
Director Strategic Energy Secretariat, Katherine Braun
780-427-7738, Fax: 780-427-7737
katherine.braun@gov.ab.ca

Resource Development Policy Division
Petroleum Plaza NT
9945 - 108 St.
Edmonton, AB T5K 2G6
Asst. Deputy Minister, Jennifer Steber
780-427-6370, Fax: 780-427-7737
jennifer.steber@gov.ab.ca
Executive Director Resource Development, Sharla Rauschning
780-427-6230, Fax: 780-644-3604
sharla.rauschning@gov.ab.ca

Strategic Initiatives Division
Petroleum Plaza NT
9945 - 108 St., 10th Fl.
Edmonton, AB T5K 2G6
Asst. Deputy Minister, Mike Ekelund
780-422-0813, Fax: 780-427-7737
mike.ekelund@gov.ab.ca

Electricity, Alternative Energy, & Carbon Capture & Storage Division
Petroleum Plaza NT
9945 - 108 St., 10th Fl.
Edmonton, AB T5K 2G6
Asst. Deputy Minister, Tim Grant
780-644-2384, Fax: 780-427-7737
tim.grant@gov.ab.ca
Executive Director Electricity Markets Branch, Kathryn Wood
780-644-1232, Fax: 780-427-8065
kathryn.wood@gov.ab.ca
Director Infrastructure & Alternative Energy Branch, Ian McKay
780-422-8726, Fax: 780-427-8065
ian.mckay@gov.ab.ca
Executive Director Carbon Capture & Storage (CCS) Development / Energy Efficiency & Conservation Branch, Sandra Locke
780-644-7126, Fax: 780-638-3031
sandra.locke@gov.ab.ca

Resource Revenue & Operations Division
Petroleum Plaza NT
9945 - 108 St., 10th Fl.
Edmonton, AB T5K 2G6
Asst. Deputy Minister, Rhonda Wehrhahn
780-422-9430, Fax: 780-422-1123
rhonda.wehrhahn@gov.ab.ca
Acting Branch Head Coal & Mineral Development, Gary V. White
780-415-0349, Fax: 780-422-5447
gary.v.white@gov.ab.ca
Branch Head Tenure, Brenda Allbright
780-422-9393, Fax: 780-422-1123
brenda.allbright@gov.ab.ca
Branch Head Compliance & Assurance, Larry McGuinness
403-297-6742, Fax: 403-297-5199
larry.mcguinness@gov.ab.ca
Executive Director Petroleum Registry of Alberta (PRA), Wally Goeres
780-415-2079, Fax: 780-422-0229
wally.goeres@gov.ab.ca

Branch Head Royalty Operations, Salim Merali
780-422-9124, Fax: 780-427-0865
salim.merali@gov.ab.ca
Branch Head Petroleum Marketing & Valuation, & Site Services, Gale Robins
403-297-5460,
gale.robins@gov.ab.ca

Oil Sands Strategy & Operations
Petroleum Plaza NT
9945 - 108 St., 14th Fl.
Edmonton, AB T5K 2G6
Asst. Deputy Minister, Matthew Machielse
780-644-8030, Fax: 780-427-7737
matthew.machielse@gov.ab.ca
Executive Director Strategic Integration & Development, Anne Denman
780-422-9212, Fax: 780-427-8065
anne.denman@gov.ab.ca
Branch Head Operations, Steve Tkalcic
780-422-9121, Fax: 780-422-0692
steve.tkalcic@gov.ab.ca
Branch Head Business Design & Evaluation, Larry Ziegenhagel
780-427-6384, Fax: 780-422-0692
larry.ziegenhagel@gov.ab.ca
Branch Head External Relations & Advocacy, Charlotte Moran
780-415-6187, Fax: 780-422-0800
charlotte.moran@gov.ab.ca
Branch Head Value Added Development, Matthew Machielse
780-644-8030, Fax: 780-427-8065
matthew.machielse@gov.ab.ca
• Alberta Environmental Appeals Board
Peace Hills Trust Tower
#306, 10011 - 109 St. NW
Edmonton, AB T5J 3S8
780-427-6207
Fax: 780-427-4693
www.eab.gov.ab.ca
Chair, Justice Delmar Perras
• Alberta Recycling Management Authority(ARMA)
Scotia Tower 1
#1310, 10060 Jasper Ave.
PO Box 189
Edmonton, AB T5J 2J1
780-990-1111
Fax: 780-990-1122
888-999-8762
info@albertarecycling.ca
www.albertarecycling.ca
Other Communication: Toll Free Fax: 1-866-990-1122; Electronics Recycling: electronics@albertarecycling.ca; Tire Recycling: tires@albertarecycling.ca
• Alberta Used Oil Management Association(AUMA)
Scotia One, Scotia Place
#1050, 10060 Jasper Ave.
Edmonton, AB T5J 3R8
780-414-1510
Fax: 780-414-1519
reception@usedoilrecycling.ca
www.usedoilrecycling.com
Other Communication: Info Line: 1-888-922-2298
Executive Director, Roger Jackson
With the approval by the provincial government of the LubricatingOil Material Recycling & Management in 1997, AUOMA was established as the Delegated Administrative Organization. AUOMA manages programs to facilitate the collection & recycling of used oil materials in Alberta.
• Beverage Container Management Board(BCMB)
#750, 10707 - 100 Ave.
Edmonton, AB T5J 3M1
780-424-3193
Fax: 780-428-4620
888-424-7671
info@bcmb.ab.ca
www.bcmb.ab.ca
Managing Director, John Bachinski
The non-profit management board was established under Alberta's Environmental Protection & Enhancement Act. BCMB regulates the recycling system of beverage containers in Alberta.
• Clean Air Strategic Alliance(CASA)
Centre West Bldg
10035 - 108 St., 10th Fl.
Edmonton, AB T5J 3E1
780-427-9793
Fax: 780-422-3127

Federal/Provincial Government / Government of Alberta

casa@casahome.org
www.casahome.org
Executive Director, Kerra Chomlak
• Environmental Response Centre
Twin Atria Bldg.
4999 - 98 Ave., 1st Fl.
Edmonton, AB T6B 2X3
780-422-4505
Fax: 780-427-3178
800-222-6514

Alberta Environment (AE)

South Tower, Petroleum Plaza
9915 - 108 St., 10th Fl.
Edmonton, AB T5K 2G8
780-427-2700
Fax: 780-422-4086
TDD: 800-232-7215
env.infocent@gov.ab.ca
environment.alberta.ca
Other Communication: 24-hour Environment Hotline (to report an environmental emergency or file a complaint):
1-800-222-6514
To assure the effective stewardship of Alberta's environmental systems to sustain a high quality of life is the mission of Alberta Environment. In order to accomplish this mission, the department has staff in over 120 communities in Alberta. Alberta Environment consists of the following four business divisions: Environmental Stewardship, Environmental Assurance, Environmental Management, & Strategic Support and Integration.

Acts Administered:
Climate Change & Emissions Management Act, 2003
Drainage District Act, 2000
Environmental Protection & Enhancement Act (Community Development & Sustainable Resource Development)
Activities Designation Amendment Regulation
Activities Designation Regulation
Approvals & Registration Procedures Regulation
Beverage Container Recycling Regulation
Codes of Practice (Waterworks System Consisting Solely of a Water Distribution System; Asphalt Paving Plants; Compost Facilities; Landfills; Pesticides, etc.)
Conservation Easement Registration Regulation
Conservation & Reclamation Regulation
Designated Material Recycling & Management Regulation
Disclosure of Information Regulation
Electronics Designation Regulation
Emissions Trading Regulation
Environmental Appeal Board Regulation
Environmental Assessment Regulation
Environmental Assessment (Mandatory & Exempted Activities) Regulation
Environmental Protection & Enhancement (Miscellaneous) Regulation
Forest Resources Improvement Regulation
Lubricating Oil Material Environmental Handling Charge By-Law
Lubricating Oil Material Recycling & Management By-Law
Lubricating Oil Material Recycling Management Regulation
Mercury Emissions from Coal-fired Power Plants Regulation
Ozone-depleting Substances & Halocarbons Regulation
Pesticide (Ministerial) Regulation
Pesticide Sales, Handling, Use & Application Regulation
Potable Water Regulation
Release Reporting Regulation
Substance Release Regulation
Tire Designation Regulation
Waste Control Regulation
Wastewater & Storm Drainage Regulation
Wastewater & Storm Drainage (Ministerial) Regulation
Specified Gas Reporting Regulation
Environmental Protection & Enhancement (Clean-Up) Instructions Amendment Act, 2002, (Unproclaimed)
Mines & Minerals Act (Energy & Sustainable Resource Development)
Natural Resources Conservation Board Act (Sustainable Resource Development)
Rules of Practice of the Natural Resources Conservation Board
North Red Deer Water Authorization Act
Stettler Regional Water Authorization Act
Water Act
Codes of Practice (Various) Regulations
Water Allocation Orders (Various) Regulation
Water (Ministerial) Regulation
Water (Offences & Penalities) Regulation

Minister, Hon. Rob Renner
780-427-2391, Fax: 780-422-6259
Deputy Minister, Jim Ellis
780-427-6236, Fax: 780-427-0923
jim.ellis@gov.ab.ca
Executive Director Finance & Administration, Mike Dalrymple
780-427-9148, Fax: 780-427-0923
mike.dalrymple@gov.ab.ca
Director CEMS Transformation Secretariat, Tom Davis
780-644-3205, Fax: 780-427-2278
tom.davis@gov.ab.ca
Director Communications, Mark Cooper
780-427-2848, Fax: 780-427-1874
mark.cooper@gov.ab.ca
Director Environmental Law Section, Darin Stepaniuk
780-427-6121, Fax: 780-427-4343
darin.stepaniuk@gov.ab.ca
Leader People Services, Mary Jefferies
780-422-7699, Fax: 780-644-7832
mary.jefferies@gov.ab.ca

Corporate Services
Petroleum Plaza NT
9945 - 108 St., 10th Fl.
Edmonton, AB T5K 2G6
Asst. Deputy Minister, John Buie
780-427-2159, Fax: 780-427-7737
john.buie@gov.ab.ca
Branch Head Business & Facility Services, Mike G. Boyd
780-427-6382, Fax: 780-422-0800
mike.g.boyd@gov.ab.ca
Branch Head Finance, Douglas Borland
780-427-6223, Fax: 780-422-4281
douglas.borland@gov.ab.ca
Branch Head FOIP & Records Management Branch, Marlene Bruyere
780-644-3778, Fax: 780-644-3786
marlene.bruyere@gov.ab.ca
Branch Head Information Technology, Carolanne Pasutto
780-415-2083, Fax: 780-427-5696
carolanne.pasutto@gov.ab.ca

Legal Services
Petroleum Plaza NT
9945 - 108 St., 11th Fl.
Edmonton, AB T5K 2G6
Branch Head, Bruce Laycock
780-422-8085, Fax: 780-427-1871
bruce.laycock@gov.ab.ca

Environmental Assurance Division
Petroleum Plaza ST
9915 - 108 St., 10th Fl.
Edmonton, AB T5K 2G8
Asst. Deputy Minister, Ernie Hui
780-415-8183, Fax: 780-415-6492
ernie.hui@gov.ab.ca
Director Climate Change Secretariat, Andy Ridge
780-644-7970, Fax: 780-415-1718
andy.ridge@gov.ab.ca
Director Monitoring Reporting & Innovation Branch, Bob Stone
780-415-9356, Fax: 780-422-8606
bob.stone@gov.ab.ca
Director Integrated Monitoring, Evaluation & Reporting Framework (IMERF) Project, Albert Poulette
780-644-3771, Fax: 780-427-6334
albert.poulette@gov.ab.ca
Director Water Policy Branch, Bob Barraclough
780-427-0029, Fax: 780-422-4192
bob.barraclough@gov.ab.ca
Director Air, Land & Strategic Policy Branch, Keith Leggat
780-427-2234, Fax: 780-422-4192
keith.leggat@gov.ab.ca
Project Director NE Plan, Chris Hunt
780-644-1259, Fax: 780-415-1718
chris.hunt@gov.ab.ca
Director Oil Sands & Clean Energy Policy Branch, Roger Ramcharita
780-644-5290, Fax: 780-415-1718
roger.ramcharita@gov.ab.ca

Environmental Stewardship Division
Petroleum Plaza ST
9915 - 108 St., 10th Fl.
Edmonton, AB T5K 2G8

Environmental Management Division
Petroleum Plaza ST
9915 - 108 St., 10th Fl.
Edmonton, AB T5K 2G8
Asst. Deputy Minister, Rick Brown
780-427-1335, Fax: 780-422-4715
rick.brown@gov.ab.ca
Director Regional Integration, Luke Pantin
780-427-2010, Fax: 780-427-2278
luke.pantin@gov.ab.ca
Regional Director Central Region - Red Deer, Andy Lamb
403-340-4326, Fax: 403-340-5022
andy.lamb@gov.ab.ca
Regional Director Northern Region - Edmonton, Shannon Flint
780-422-8463, Fax: 780-427-7824
shannon.flint@gov.ab.ca
Regional Director Southern Region, Jay Litke
403-297-6070, Fax: 403-297-6069
Director Water Management Operations, Dave Ardell
403-297-5892, Fax: 403-297-6389
dave.ardell@gov.ab.ca

Strategic Support & Integration Division
Petroleum Plaza ST
9915 - 108 St., 10th Fl.
Edmonton, AB T5K 2G8
Asst. Deputy Minister, Al Sanderson
780-643-0890, Fax: 780-644-8469
al.sanderson@gov.ab.ca
Section Head Geographic Information Office, Lana Robinson
403-382-4106, Fax: 403-381-5969
lana.robinson@gov.ab.ca
Chief Information Officer Office of the CIO & Integrated Information Solutions, Roger Burns
780-644-5065,
roger.burns@gov.ab.ca
Director Performance Leadership Branch, Larry Williams
780-644-1094, Fax: 780-644-8946
larry.williams@gov.ab.ca
Minister, Hon. Lloyd Snelgrove
780-415-4855, Fax: 780-415-4853
min.finance@gov.ab.ca
• Alberta Ingenuity Fund
250 Karl Clark Rd.
Edmonton, AB T6N 1E4
780-450-5111
Fax: 780-450-5333
info@albertaingenuity.ca
www.albertaingenuity.ca
President, Dr. Gary Albach
The Alberta Ingenuity Fund was established to develop internationally competitive science and engineering expertise and build greater capacity for innovation, particularly in areas with lasting social and economic impact. Alberta Ingenuity has become part of Alberta Innovates - Technology Futures,
www.albertainnovates.ca/technology.

Alberta Health & Wellness

Telus Plaza NT
10025 Jasper Ave., 22nd Fl.
PO Box 1360 Main
Edmonton, AB T5J 2N3
780-427-7164
TDD: 800-232-7215
health.ahinform@gov.ab.ca
www.health.alberta.ca
The Government has endorsed broad health goals for Albertans which support Alberta's vision for health.These health goals reflect the range of factors which determine health, families, communities & environments, public policy, information, behaviour, coping skills, heredity & health services. The goals of Alberta Health & Wellness reflect the interrelationship of health, prosperity & the environment. It's mandate is to work to improve the health by providing leadership & encouraging actions to address health concerns, protect & promote good health, & prevent disease & injury. The government also works to ensure that Albertans are well informed & able to make decisions about their health & services.

Acts Administered:
ABC Benefits Corporation Act
Alberta Evidence Act (Section 9)
Alberta Health Care Insurance Act
Charitable Donation of Food Act
Emergency Health Services Act
Emergency Medical Aid Act

Government Organization Act, Schedule 7.1
Health Disciplines Act
Health Facilities Review Committee Act
Health Information Act
Health Insurance Premiums Act
Health Professions Act
Hospitals Act
Human Tissue & Organ Donation Act
Mandatory Testing & Disclosure Act
Mental Health Act
M.S.I. Foundation Act
Nursing Homes Act
Opticians Act
Pharmacy & Drug Act
Physical Therapy Profession Act
Podiatry Act
Prevention of Youth Tobacco Use Act
Protection of Children Abusing Drugs Act
Provincial Health Authorities of Alberta Act
Public Health Act
Regional Health Authorities Act
Tobacco Reduction Act
Alberta Cancer Prevention Legacy Act
Health Care Protection Act
Health Governance Transition Act
Minister, Hon. Gene Zwozdesky
780-427-3665, Fax: 780-415-0961
health.minister@gov.ab.ca
Deputy Minister, Jay Ramotar
780-422-0747, Fax: 780-427-1016
jay.ramotar@gov.ab.ca
Chief Medical Officer of Health, Dr. André Corriveau
780-415-2809, Fax: 780-427-7683
andre.corriveau@gov.ab.ca
Mental Health Patient Advocate, Fay Orr
780-422-1812, Fax: 780-422-0695
fay.orr@gov.ab.ca v.ab.ca
• Alberta Health Services(AHS)
Manulife Place
10180 - 101 St.
Edmonton, AB T5J 3S4
780-342-2000
Fax: 780-342-2060
888-342-2471
www.albertahealthservices.ca
• Health Disciplines Board
Telus Plaza NT, Health Professions Branch
10025 Jasper Ave., 17th Fl.
Edmonton, AB T5J 2N3
780-415-0486
Fax: 780-422-2880

• Health Facilities Review Committee(HFRC)
First Edmonton Place
#590, 10665 Jasper Ave.
Edmonton, AB T5J 3S9
780-427-2791
Fax: 780-427-0806

Corporate Support Division
Telus Plaza NT
10025 Jasper Ave., 19th Fl.
Edmonton, AB T5J 1S6

Health Workforce Division
Telus Plaza NT
10025 Jasper Ave., 10th Fl.
Edmonton, AB T5J 1S6
Asst. Deputy Minister, Glenn Monteith
780-415-2745, Fax: 780-415-8455
glenn.monteith@gov.ab.ca
Executive Director Innovative Compensation, Yolanda Lackie
780-427-0380, Fax: 780-422-5208
yolanda.lackie@gov.ab.ca

Community & Population Health Division
Telus Plaza NT
10025 Jasper Ave., 24th Fl.
Edmonton, AB T5J 1S6
Asst. Deputy Minister, Margaret King
780-415-2783, Fax: 780-422-3671
margaret.king@gov.ab.ca
Executive Director Community Health, Silvia Vajushi
780-422-1344, Fax: 780-422-6663
silvia.vajushi@gov.ab.ca

Executive Director Health Protection, Alex MacKenzie
780-422-4549, Fax: 780-427-1470
alex.mackenzie@gov.ab.ca
Acting Executive Director Surveillance & Assessment, Kathy Ness
780-422-2561, Fax: 780-427-1470
kathy.ness@gov.ab.ca
Executive Director Public Health Strategic Policy and Planning Branch, Neil MacDonald
780-415-2759, Fax: 780-422-5474
neil.macdonald@gov.ab.ca

Financial Accountability Division
Telus Plaza NT
10025 Jasper Ave., 16th Fl.
Edmonton, AB T5J 1S6

Financial Accountability Division
Telus Plaza NT
10025 Jasper Ave., 21st Fl.
Edmonton, AB T5J 1S6

Health Policy & Service Standards Division
Telus Plaza NT
10025 Jasper Ave., 18th Fl.
Edmonton, AB T5J 1S6

Alberta Housing & Urban Affairs
44 Capital Blvd.
10044 - 108 St., 3rd fl.
Edmonton, AB T5J 5E6
780-422-0122
Fax: 780-422-8462
housing@gov.ab.ca
www.housing.alberta.ca
The Ministry promotes the independence of lower-income Albertans through safe, sustainable and affordable housing, and assists urban communities with their unique needs.
Acts Administered:
Alberta Housing Act
Social Care Facilities Licensing Act
Government Organization Act
Minister, Hon. Jonathan Denis, Q.C.
780-644-8954, Fax: 780-644-8959
Deputy Minister, Marcia Nelson
780-644-5253, Fax: 780-644-5240
marcia.nelson@gov.ab.ca
Director Communications,Vacant
780-644-6838, Fax: 780-644-5796
Director Human Resource Services, Sandra Kraatz
780-422-8681, Fax: 780-422-0214
sandra.kraatz@gov.ab.ca
• Gunn Centre
PO Box 130
Gunn, AB T0E 1Ao
780-967-2221
Fax: 780-967-3494
Director, Lynn Bell
The Centre has provided services for disadvantaged men to a capacity of 115 since 1941. It offers temporary accommodation to men who are homeless, or at risk of homelessness. It aims to establish links to affordable housing and services within the community meeting the special needs of each individual.
Asst. Deputy Minister, Mike Leathwood
780-643-1020, Fax: 780-422-8462
mike.leathwood@gov.ab.ca
Executive Director Corporate Projects, Rai Batra
780-427-2925, Fax: 780-422-8462
rai.batra@gov.ab.ca
Executive Director Housing Development, Don Squire
780-427-5786, Fax: 780-422-5124
don.squire@gov.ab.ca
Executive Director Housing Operations, Clarence Bereska
780-427-5784, Fax: 780-422-8551
clarence.bereska@gov.ab.ca
Asst. Deputy Minister, Lana Lougheed
780-643-0766, Fax: 780-422-5124
lana.lougheed@gov.ab.ca
Executive Director & Senior Financial Officer Finance & Administrative Services, Bev Walkner
780-643-1324, Fax: 780-427-0418
bev.walkner@gov.ab.ca
Director & CIO Information Management & Technology, Dean Lussier

780-427-1751, Fax: 780-427-0418
dean.lussier@gov.ab.ca
Acting Executive Director Policy & Urban Affairs, Lora Pillipow
780-422-2816, Fax: 780-422-5124
lora.pillipow@gov.ab.ca
Calgary
Cantury Park Place
855 - 8 Ave. SWt, 11th Fl.
Calgary, AB T2P 3P1
403-297-4575
Fax: 403-297-5988
Central
Provincial Bldg.
4920 - 51 St., 5th Fl.
Red Deer, AB T4N 6K8
403-340-7022
Fax: 403-340-7057
Edmonton
South Tower
10030 - 107 St., 8th Fl.
Edmonton, AB T5J 4X7
780-427-0003
Fax: 780-422-5125
Northeast
Lakeview Bldg.
15 Nipewan Rd.
PO Box 1410
Lac La Biche, AB T0A 2C0
780-623-5283
Fax: 780-623-5355
Northwest
205 - 1 St. East
McLennan, AB T0H 2L0
780-324-3200
Fax: 780-324-3235

South
2105 - 20 Ave.
Coaldale, AB T1M 1M2
403-345-2277
Fax: 403-345-4915

Alberta Infrastructure
Infrastructure Building
6950 - 101 St., 3rd Fl.
Edmonton, AB T6H 5V7
780-415-0507
Fax: 780-427-2187
www.infrastructure.alberta.ca
The Ministry anticipates the growth of the province, and takes the necessary actions to build essential roads and highways, schools and hospitals, utilities and facilities to accommodate the changing Alberta.
Acts Administered:
Government Organization Act, Sched 1, 5, 11, 14
Highways Development and Protection Act
Hospitals Act
Mental Health Act
Nursing Homes Act
Post-secondary Learning Act
School Act
Water, Gas and Electric Companies Act
Minister, Hon. Ray Danyluk
780-427-5041, Fax: 780-422-2002
Deputy Minister, Barry Day
780-427-3835, Fax: 780-422-6565
barry.day@gov.ab.ca
• Alberta Research Council(ARC)
250 Karl Clark Rd.
Edmonton, AB T6N 1E4
780-450-5111
Fax: 780-450-5333
www.arc.ab.ca
Chair, Ron Triffo
ARC is an R&D corporation with a mandate to develop and commercialize technology. It aims to convert early stage ideas into marketable products and services. It is a not-for-profit corporation, wholly-owned by the province of Alberta and now operates under the umbrella of Alberta Innovates — Technology Futures:
www.albertainnovates.ca/technology.

Capital Projects Division
Infrastructure Building
6950 - 113 St., 2nd Fl.
Edmonton, AB T6H 5V7

Federal/Provincial Government / Government of Alberta

Asst. Deputy Minister, Diane Dagleish
780-422-7436, Fax: 780-422-7599
diane.dalgleish@gov.ab.ca
Executive Director Project Delivery Branch, Kent Phillips
780-422-0770, Fax: 780-422-9749
kent.phillips@gov.ab.ca
Director Divisional Coordination Branch, Roberta Killips
780-415-0678, Fax: 780-422-7599
roberta.killips@gov.ab.ca
Executive Director Capital Programs Branch, Mike Irving
780-422-7224, Fax: 780-427-5816
mike.irving@gov.ab.ca
Executive Director Program Management Branch, Brian Soutar
780-422-7461, Fax: 780-422-9594
brian.soutar@gov.ab.ca
Executive Director Technical Services Branch, Tom O'Neill
780-422-7447, Fax: 780-422-7479
tom.o'neill@gov.ab.ca

Policy & Corporate Services Division
Twin Atria Building
4999 - 98 Ave., 3rd Fl.
Edmonton, AB T6B 2X3

Properties Division
Infrastructure Building
6950 - 113 St., 3rd Fl.
Edmonton, AB T6H 5V7
Asst. Deputy Minister, Bob Smith
780-427-3875, Fax: 780-422-1389
bob.smith@gov.ab.ca
Executive Director Property Development Branch, Rod Dushnicky
780-422-3597, Fax: 780-422-5832
rod.dushnicky@gov.ab.ca
Acting Executive Director Property Management Branch - North Region, Dave Bentley
780-427-9225, Fax: 780-422-0284
dave.bentley@gov.ab.ca
Executive Director Property Management Branch - South Region, John Enns
780-427-2710, Fax: 780-422-0284
john.enns@gov.ab.ca
Executive Director Realty Services Branch, Larry James
780-427-7489, Fax: 780-415-1641
larry.james@gov.ab.ca
Director Divisional Coordination Branch, Dennis Mitchell
780-427-3900, Fax: 780-427-6905
dennis.mitchell@gov.ab.ca

Southern
Administration Bldg.
909 - 3 Ave. North
Lethbridge, AB T1H 0H5
Fax: 403-382-4412

Dangerous Goods Control & Rail Safety
Twin Atria Bldg.
4999 - 98 Ave.
Edmonton, AB T6B 2X3
780-422-9600
Fax: 780-427-1044
800-272-9600
Director, Terry Wallace
780-427-7508,
terry.wallace@gov.ab.ca
Manager Rail Safety, Bob Clyne
780-415-6147, Fax: 780-422-9193
bob.clyne@gov.ab.ca

Drive Safety, Research & Traffic Safety Initiative
Fax: 780-422-3682

Vehicle Safety & Carrier Services
Provincial Bldg.
#401, 4920 - 51 St.
Red Deer, AB T4N 6K8
Fax: 403-340-4811

Alberta International & Intergovernmental Relations
Commerce Place
10155 - 102 St., 12th Fl.
Edmonton, AB T5J 4G8
780-422-1510
Fax: 780-427-0699
www.international.aberta.ca

Alberta's International & Intergovernmental Relations (IIR) Ministry coordinates the province's relationships with different levels of government both nationally & internationally. The IIR works in areas such as export, trade & govermental relations to enhance & develop Alberta's presence.
Acts Administered:
Constitutional Referendum Act
Government Organization Act
International Interests in Mobile Aircraft Equipment Act (unproclaimed)
International Trade and Investment Agreements Implementation Act
Senatorial Selection Act
Minister, Hon. Iris Evans
780-427-2585, Fax: 780-422-9023
Deputy Minister, Paul Whittaker
780-427-6644, Fax: 780-423-6654
paul.whittaker@gov.ab.ca
Director Communications, Mike Deising
780-422-2524, Fax: 780-422-2635
mike.deising@gov.ab.ca

Corporate Services
Commerce Place
10155 - 102 St., 12th Fl.
Edmonton, AB T5J 4L8
Intergovernmental Relations works with other Alberta government ministries & the federal government to ensure that Alberta's interests are represented in the Canadian federation by reviewing policies, programs & legislation; participating in the negotiation of intergovernmental agreements; providing stragic advice & making recommendations on the intergovernmental implications of issues & policy initiatives advanced by the Alberta government, & coordinating & providing logistical support for intergovernmental meetings, including meetings of the Council of the Federation & Western Premiers' Conferences.
Asst. Deputy Minister, Lorne Harvey
780-422-2429, Fax: 780-422-0939
lorne.harvey@gov.ab.ca
Executive Director Human Resource Services, Georgina Riddell
780-422-1341, Fax: 780-427-1272
georgina.riddell@gov.ab.ca
Executive Director Finance & Administration, Howard Wong
780-427-0793, Fax: 780-422-0939
howard.wong@gov.ab.ca
Director Corporate Planning, Carol Mayers
780-644-1160, Fax: 780-644-4939
carol.mayers@gov.ab.ca
Director IMIT, Carol Lawrence
780-427-0269, Fax: 780-427-4625
carol.lawrence@gov.ab.ca
Director FOIP, Gerry Kushlyk
780-427-9658, Fax: 780-644-4939
gerry.kushlyk@gov.ab.ca

Intergovernmental Relations
Commerce Place
10155 - 102 St., 12th Fl.
Edmonton, AB T5J 4L8
Intergovernmental Relations works with other Alberta government ministries & the federal government to ensure that Alberta's interests are represented in the Canadian federation by reviewing policies, programs & legislation; participating in the negotiation of intergovernmental agreements; providing stragic advice & making recommendations on the intergovernmental implications of issues & policy initiatives advanced by the Alberta government, & coordinating & providing logistical support for intergovernmental meetings, including meetings of the Council of the Federation & Western Premiers' Conferences.
Assistant Deputy Minister Intergovernmental Relations, Garry Pocock
780-422-0453, Fax: 780-427-0939
garry.pocock@gov.ab.ca
Intergovernmental Officer Intergovernmental Coordination, David Liles
780-422-0098, Fax: 780-427-0939
david.liles@gov.ab.ca
Executive Director Federal/Provincial Relations, Bruce Tait
780-422-1127, Fax: 780-427-0939
bruce.tait@gov.ab.ca
Executive Director Social and Economic Policy, Gordon Vincent
780-415-6548, Fax: 780-427-0939
gordon.vincent@gov.ab.ca

International Relations
Commerce Place
10155 - 102 St., 12th Fl.
Edmonton, AB T5J 4G8
780-427-6543
Assistant Deputy Minister, John Cotton
780-422-2789, Fax: 780-427-0392
john.cotton@gov.ab.ca
Executive Director Advocacy, US Relations & Mission Planning, Marvin Schneider
780-422-2332, Fax: 780-422-5486
marvin.schneider@gov.ab.ca
Executive Director Europe & US Branch, Chris Heseltine
403-297-6377, Fax: 403-297-6168
chris.heseltine@gov.ab.ca
Minister & Attorney General, Hon. Alison Redford
780-427-2339, Fax: 780-422-6621
Acts Administered:
Expropriation Act (Sustainable Resource Development)
Deputy Minister & Deputy Attorney General, Ray Bodnarek, Q.C.
780-427-5032, Fax: 780-422-9639
ray.bodnarek@gov.ab.ca
Asst. Deputy Minister, Grant Sprague, Q.C.
780-415-2388, Fax: 780-422-9639
grant.sprague@gov.ab.ca
Chief Medical Examiner, Dr. Graeme P. Dowling
780-427-4987, Fax: 780-422-1265
graeme.dowling@gov.ab.ca
Executive Director, Legal Aid & Corporate Legal Services Civil Law Branch, R. Neil Dunne, Q.C.
780-422-8787, Fax: 780-425-0307
r.neil.dunne@gov.ab.ca

Alberta Municipal Affairs
Communications Branch, Commerce Place
10155 - 102 St., 18th Fl.
Edmonton, AB T5J 4L4
780-427-2732
Fax: 780-422-1419
comments@gov.ab.ca
www.municipalaffairs.alberta.ca
The Ministry works to provide well-managed, accountable local governments. It aims to ensure safety standards in construction and maintenance of buildings & equipment and it manages the municipal & library system boards.
Acts Administered:
City of Lloydminster Act
Emergency Management Act
Government Organization Act, Sched 10, 13
Libraries Act
Local Authorities Election Admendment Act, 2009
Municipal Government Amendment Act
Parks Towns Act
Public Highways Development Act
Safety Codes Act
Special Areas Act
Minister, Hon. Hector Goudreau
780-427-3744, Fax: 780-422-9550
Deputy Minister, Ray Gilmour
780-427-4826, Fax: 780-422-9561
ray.gilmour@gov.ab.ca
Director Communications, Donna Babchishin
780-415-4758, Fax: 780-422-1419
donna.babchishin@gov.ab.ca
Director Human Resource Services, Sandra Kraatz
780-422-8681, Fax: 780-422-0214
sandra.kraatz@gov.ab.ca .ca
Director & Solicitor Legal Services, Bill Nugent
780-422-8795, Fax: 780-427-0996
bill.nugent@gov.ab.ca
• Alberta Municipal Government Board
Commerce Place
10155 - 102 St., 15th Fl.
Edmonton, AB T5J 4L4
780-427-4864
Fax: 780-427-0986
Chair, Ken Lesniak
The Municipal Government Board is an independent & impartial body set up to make decisions on certain appeals & disputes stemming from the Municipal Government Act, including appeals on property assessment, equalized assessment, linear property assessment & subdivisions involving provincial interest, intermunicipal disputes, conflicts between municipalities & housing authorities, annexation matters & any other matters referred by the Minister or Lieutenant Governor.

- Alberta Special Areas Board
212 - 2nd Ave. West
PO Box 820
Hanna, AB T0J 1P0
403-854-5600
Fax: 403-854-5527
specarea@telusplanet.net
www.specialareas.ab.ca
Chair, Jay J. Slemp
The Special Areas Board reports directly to the Assistant Deputy Minister of the Local Government Services Division. The Special Areas Board was set up under the Special Areas Act (1938) to administer this area where municipal services could not be provided due to financial hardship resulting from the Depression & drought of the 1930s. The board provides cost-effective, responsive municipal services & effective, long-term land resource management for the Special Areas. Special Areas is made up of a unique rural municipal area covering approximately 2.1 million hectares in southeastern Alberta. The Special Areas Board is made up of three members appointed by the Lieutenant Governor in Council, who also designates one member as Chairman.

- Alberta Emergency Management Agency (AEMA)
c/o Alberta Municipal Affairs, Communications Br.
10155 - 102 St., 18th Fl.
Edmonton, AB T5J 4L4
780-422-9000
Fax: 780-644-1044
866-618-2362
aema@gov.ab.ca
www.aema.alberta.ca

- Safety Codes Council (SCC)
#1000, 10665 Jasper Ave. NW
Edmonton, AB T5J 3S9
780-413-0099
Fax: 780-424-5134
888-413-0099
sccinfo@safetycodes.ab.ca
www.safetycodes.ab.ca
Chair, Robert Blakely
The Council recommends codes and standards to the Ministry under the authority of the Safety Codes Act. It administers a system to accredit municipalities, corporations and agencies to pursue activities under the Act. It aims to promote uniform standards and barrier-free designs & access on behalf of the Ministry.

Corporate Strategic Services Division
Commerce Place
10155 - 102 St., 18th Fl.
Edmonton, AB T5J 4L4
Asst. Deputy Minister, Anthony Lemphers
780-427-8099, Fax: 780-422-4923
anthony.lemphers@gov.ab.ca
Executive Director Corporate Planning & Policy, Indira Breitkreuz
780-422-7317, Fax: 780-422-4923
indira.breitkreuz@gov.ab.ca
Director Information Management, Legislative & Administrative Services, Wilma Sisk
780-422-8834, Fax: 780-643-1090
wilma.sisk@gov.ab.ca
Executive Director & Senior Financial Officer Financial Services, Dan Balderston
780-644-8098, Fax: 780-422-5840
dan.balderston@gov.ab.ca

Local Government Services Division
Commerce Place
10155 - 102 St., 17th Fl.
Edmonton, AB T5J 4L4
The Local Government Services Division provides support services & advice to municipalities to assist them in developing sustainable & effective local government. Services focus on innovation & cooperation, municipal viability, & assessment & tax policy. The division is divided into three branches, Municipal Services, Assessment Services & the Special Areas Board. Municipal Services provides policy, planning, & analytical support for municipal legislation, property taxation, land-use planning, intermunicipal & regional cooperation & municipal status changes. The branch also provides advisory & financial support to assist municipalities to operate efficiently. Assessment Services creates & develops the assessment standards & guidelines & audits municipal assessments to ensure standards are met. The Special Areas Board falls under this Division.

Asst. Deputy Minister, Michael Merritt
780-427-9660, Fax: 780-427-0453
michael.merritt@gov.ab.ca
Executive Director Municipal Services Branch, Gary Sandberg
780-422-8034, Fax: 780-420-1016
gary.sandberg@gov.ab.ca
Executive Director Assessment Services Branch, Steve White
780-422-1377, Fax: 780-422-3110
steve.white@gov.ab.ca
Director Legislative Projects, Ronald Cust
780-422-8322, Fax: 780-644-4941
ron.cust@gov.ab.ca

Public Safety Division
Commerce Place
10155 - 102 St., 16th Fl.
Edmonton, AB T5J 4L4
866-421-6929
The Public Safety Division consists of three branches designed to help ensure safe buildings, equipment & facilities, & effective emergency response, Emergency Management Alberta, Safety Services & the Fire Commissioner's Office. The division works in partnership with Alberta's municipalities, other government departments, local authorities & various local organizations.
Asst. Deputy Minister, Ivan Moore
780-638-3245, Fax: 780-427-2538
ivan.moore@gov.ab.ca
Director Legislation & Strategic Projects, Joan Armstrong
780-427-2279, Fax: 780-427-2538
joan.armstrong@gov.ab.ca
Executive Director Safety Services, Chris Tye
780-644-5691, Fax: 780-427-8686
safety.services@gov.ab.ca
Manager Operational Support Services, Don Rebus
780-644-1010, Fax: 780-427-8686
safety.services@gov.ab.ca
Director Codes and Standards, James Orr
780-644-1010, Fax: 780-427-8686
safety.services@gov.ab.ca
Director Field Technical Services, Randy Paulson
780-644-1010, Fax: 780-427-8686
safety.services@gov.ab.ca
Director Safety Assurance Services, Alex Morrison
780-644-1010, Fax: 780-297-4174
safety.services@gov.ab.ca
Director Risk Management & Finance, Diane McLean
780-427-6133, Fax: 780-427-2538
diane.mclean@gov.ab.ca
Program Coordinator Tank Site Remediation Program, Stephen Hoare
780-415-8665, Fax: 780-415-8664
stephen.hoare@gov.ab.ca

Alberta Public Affairs Bureau
Park Plaza
10611 - 98 Ave., 6th Fl.
Edmonton, AB T5K 2P7
403-427-9261
Fax: 403-422-4168
www.pab.gov.ab.ca
The PAB gives communication support to government ministries and coordinates cross-gervernmental initiatives. It is also a means by which the public can ask questions about the government's programs & services.
Managing Director, Lee Funke
780-644-5655, Fax: 780-427-1010
lee.funke@gov.ab.ca
Executive Director Corporate Services, Elaine Dougan
780-422-4097, Fax: 780-422-4168
elaine.dougan@gov.ab.ca

Alberta Service Alberta
103 Legislature Bldg.
10800 - 97 Ave.
Edmonton, AB T5K 2B6
780-427-2711
877-427-4088
government.services@gov.ab.ca
www.servicealberta.gov.ab.ca
Service Alberta is engaged in the following major areas: providing licensing & registry services for consumers & businesses; regulating & enforcing standards of consumer protection & business practices; providing secure & accessible services to Albertans; leveraging Alberta SuperNet, a high-speed network to connect Albertans with government; administering the Freedom of Information & Protection of Privacy legislation; delivering shared services to ministries; promoting a streamlined regulatory environment; working with ministries to achieve cost savings in information technology & business processes; ensuring computer systems operate in the same way across government; & managing government vehicles & air transportation.
Acts Administered:
Agricultural & Recreational Land Ownership Act
Business Corporations Act
Cemeteries Act
Cemetery Companies Act
Change of Name Act
Charitable Fund-Raising Act
Companies Act
Condominium Property Act
Cooperatives Act
Debtors' Assistance Act
Dower Act
Electronic Transactions Act
Fair Trading Act
Franchises Act
Freedom of Information & Protection of Privacy Act
Funeral Services Act
Garage Keepers' Lien Act
Government Organization Act, Sched 11, 12, 13
Land Titles Act
Law of Property Act
Marriage Act
Mobile Home Sites Tenancies Act
Motor Vehicle Accident Claims Act
Partnership Act
Personal Information Protection Act
Personal Property Security Act
Possessory Liens Act
Public Service Act
Queen's Printer Act
Real Estate Act
Religious Societies' Land Act
Residential Tenancies Act
Surveys Act
Traffic Safety Act
Vital Statistics Act
Warehousemen's Lien Act
Woodmen's Lien Act
Builders' Lien Act
Minister, Hon. Heather Klimchuk
780-422-6880, Fax: 780-422-2496
Deputy Minister, Paul Pellis
780-427-1990, Fax: 780-427-4999
paul.pellis@gov.ab.ca
Executive Director Human Resource Services, Gerry Jacubo
780-427-8352, Fax: 780-644-1015
gerry.jacubo@gov.ab.ca
Director Communications, Sharon Lopatka
780-422-8049, Fax: 780-422-9816
cameron.traynor@gov.ab.ca

Technology Services
John E. Brownlee Bldg.
10365 - 97 St., 8th Fl.
Edmonton, AB T5J 3W7
780-422-8545
Assistant Deputy Minister, Dennis Mudryk
780-427-6005, Fax: 780-422-0956
dennis.mudryk@gov.ab.ca
Director Operations - Planning & Support, Ian Phimester
780-427-6326,
ian.phimester@gov.ab.ca
Asst. Deputy Minister, Reegan McCullough
780-638-2808, Fax: 780-638-2813
reegan.mccullough@gov.ab.ca
Committee Secretariat & Project Coordinator, Barbara Reid
780-638-2807, Fax: 780-638-2821
barbara.reid@gov.ab.ca
Deputy Minister & Deputy Solicitor General, Brad Pickering
780-427-3841, Fax: 780-427-0727
brad.pickering@gov.ab.ca

Alberta Sustainable Resource Development
Information Centre
9920 - 108 St., Main Fl.
Edmonton, AB T5K 2M4
780-944-0313
Fax: 780-427-4407
877-944-0313

Federal/Provincial Government / Government of Alberta

srd.infocent@gov.ab.ca
www.srd.alberta.ca
Sustainable Resource Development works with Albertans to manage fish & wildlife, to oversee the development of the province's forests, to fight forest fires, & to manage the use of public lands. Programs & services are provided in the following areas: hunting & fishing, including species, news, licenses, regulations & management programs; wildlife, including diseases, species at risk, status reports, & watchable wildlife; Alberta species, such as bears & bighorn sheep; forests & wildfires, including forest health, meanagement & fire reports; public lands, featuring information about management, access & use, & photographs; & information about Alberta, such as areas & maps.

Acts Administered:
Boundary Surveys Act
Environmental Protection & Enhancement Act (jointly with Environment & Community Development)
Expropriation Act (sections 25 to 28 & 72)
Fisheries (Alberta) Act
Forest & Prairie Protection Act
Forest Reserves Act
Forests Act
Government Organization Act (jointly with Alberta Environment & Infrastructure)
Mines & Minerals Act (jointly with Alberta Energy)
Natural Resources Conservation Board Act (jointly with Alberta Environment)
Public Lands Act
Surface Rights Act
Surveys Act (jointly with Alberta Government Services)
Wildlife Act
Minister, Hon. Ted Morton
780-415-4815, Fax: 780-415-4818
Deputy Minister, Eric McGhan
780-427-1799, Fax: 780-415-9669
eric.mcghan@gov.ab.ca
Executive Director Corporate Business Support, Joyce Ingram
780-415-2634, Fax: 780-415-9669
joyce.ingram@gov.ab.ca
Director Communications, Carol Chawrun
780-427-8122, Fax: 780-422-6339
carol.chawrun@gov.ab.ca
Manager Issues Management, Denine Westman
780-415-0845, Fax: 780-422-8762
denine.westman@gov.ab.ca
Director Strategic Projects, Mike Poscente
780-427-6350, Fax: 780-427-7434
mike.poscente@gov.ab.ca
• Land Compensation/Surface Rights Board
Phipps-McKinnon Bldg.
10020 - 101A Ave., 18th Fl.
Edmonton, AB T5J 3G2
780-427-2444
Fax: 780-427-5798
Chair, Brian Gifford
• Natural Resources Conservation Board(NRCB)
Sterling Place
9940 - 106 St., 4th Fl.
Edmonton, AB T5K 2N2
780-422-1977
Fax: 780-427-0607
866-383-6722
www.nrcb.gov.ab.ca
Chair, Vern Hartwell

Fish & Wildlife Division
Fish & Wildlife Management ensures Albertans benefit economically, environmentally & socially from the province's fish & wildlife resources.Goals are to provide a balanced approach to fish & wildlife management through a fish & wildlife policy, legislative & regulatory framework that maximizes the benefits received from these resources, sustains the recreational enjoyment of fish & wildlife resources with appropriate allocation & licensing decisions, mitigates & reduces negative interactions between wildlife & humans & partner with Aboriginal communities to sustain traditional uses of fish & wildlife resources.Management plans are up-to-date for all game species & species at risk.Sustainable fishing has improved the viability of the commercial fishing industry, along with habitat maintenance, restoration, the system of stocking fish & appropriate management information.
Asst. Deputy Minister, Ken Ambrock
780-427-6749, Fax: 780-427-8884
ken.ambrock@gov.ab.ca

Executive Director Fisheries Management, Ken Crutchfield
780-427-7763, Fax: 780-422-9559
ken.crutchfield@gov.ab.ca
Executive Director Wildlife Management, Ron Bjorge
780-427-9503, Fax: 780-422-9557
ron.bjorge@gov.ab.ca
Director Enforcement Field Services, Deryl Empson
780-422-0044, Fax: 780-422-9560
deryl.empson@gov.ab.ca

Forestry Division
Forest Protection protects the multiple values received from forests within the Forest Protection Area of the province by working co-operatively with municipalities, industry & other stakeholders to prevent & suppress wildfires.
Asst. Deputy Minister, Don Harrison
780-427-3542, Fax: 780-422-6068
don.harrison@gov.ab.ca
Director Wildfire Prevention, Hugh Boyd
780-427-7811, Fax: 780-427-0292
hugh.boyd@gov.ab.ca
Director Wildfire Operations, John Brewer
780-427-7925, Fax: 780-422-7230
john.brewer@gov.ab.ca
Section Head Business Planning & Information, Deanna McCullough
780-427-4293, Fax: 780-415-1831
deanna.mccullough@gov.ab.ca
Director Wildfire Service,Vacant
780-427-2545

Public Lands & Forests Division
Approximately 60 per cent of the province's land base is public land. It is managed under an integrated resource management philosophy that supports forest production, watershed protection, wildlife habitat, recreation, oil & gas well sites, agricultural production & industrial development, to mention only a few of the uses. Public land management focuses on establishing & sustaining an optimum balance of use, conservation & development of resources, in harmony with the values & needs of Albertans. Historically, public land management was directed at homesteading & agricultural development in the White (settled) area of the province, & timber management in the Green (forested) area. Today, land management practices & policies addressesa greater variety of competing demands including recreation, watershed management, agricultural uses, industrial uses, commercial uses & conservation.
Asst. Deputy Minister, Craig Quintillo
780-422-4415, Fax: 780-422-6068
craig.quintillo@gov.ab.ca
Executive Director Forest Management Branch, Doug Sklar
780-422-4590, Fax: 780-427-0085
doug.sklar@gov.ab.ca
Acting Executive Director Forest Operations Branch, Ken McCrae
780-644-5497, Fax: 780-427-0085
ken.mccrae@gov.ab.ca
Executive Director Land Management Branch, Glenn Selland
780-427-3570, Fax: 780-724-1185
glenn.selland@gov.ab.ca
Executive Director Rangeland Management Branch, Keith Lyseng
780-427-3595, Fax: 780-422-0454
keith.lyseng@gov.ab.ca

Strategic Forestry Initiative Division
Senior Manager Economics & Trade,Ron, Dunnigan
780-422-4799, Fax: 780-644-5728
ron.dunnigan@gov.ab.ca
Executive Director Forest Business and Bio-economy Initiatives, Pat Guidera
780-427-4351, Fax: 780-644-5728
pat.guidera@gov.ab.ca
Senior Manager Value Added Section, Paul Short
780-427-6571, Fax: 780-644-5728
paul.short@gov.ab.ca

Sustainable Resource & Environmental Management
Asst. Deputy Minister, Morris Seiferling
780-644-7978, Fax: 780-644-1034
morris.seiferling@gov.ab.ca

Alberta Tourism, Parks, Recreation & Culture
Communications Branch, Standard Life Centre
10405 Jasper Ave., 7th Fl.
Edmonton, AB T5J 4R7
780-427-6530
Fax: 780-427-1496
TDD: 780-427-9999
Comdev.Communications@gov.ab.ca
www.tprc.alberta.ca
Committed to the development & preservation of Alberta's tourism, culture & heritage, the Ministry of Tourism, Parks, Recreation & Culture provides programs & services to support active & inclusive communities. Tourist destinations are developed & marketed. Community enhancement is provided through financial support. Support is also given to the non-profit sector, including the arts, film, sport & recreation. The province's natural heritage is preserved, through a network of parks & protected areas. Preservation of Alberta's historical resources is realized, through Provincial Archives of Alberta, as well as museums & historic sites. The natural heritage & historical resources of the province are promoted to tourists.

Acts Administered:
Alberta Centennial Medal Act
Alberta Foundation for the Arts Act
Alberta Sport, Recreation, Parks and Wildlife Foundation Act
Amusements Act
Emblems of Alberta Act
First Nations Sacred Ceremonial Objects Repatriation Act
Foreign Cultural Property Immunity Act
Glenbow-Alberta Institute Act
Government House Act
Historical Resources Act
Holocaust Memorial Day & Genocide Remembrance Act
Human Rights, Citizenship & Multiculturalism Act
Provincial Parks Act
Queen Elizabeth II Golden Jubilee Recognition Act
Recreation Development Act
Wild Rose Foundation Act
Wilderness Areas, Ecological Reserves, Natural Areas and Heritage Rangelands Act
Willmore Wilderness Park Act
Minister, Hon. Hector Goudreau
780-427-4928, Fax: 780-427-0188
TPRC.minister@gov.ab.ca
Associate Minister Tourism Promotion, Hon. Cindy Ady
Fax: 780-644-8960
Deputy Minister, Fay Orr
780-427-2921
Director Communications, Anne Douglas
780-427-2395
• Alberta Film Commission
10155 - 102 St., 5th Fl.
Edmonton, AB T5J 4L6
780-422-8584
Fax: 780-422-8582
888-813-1738
• Alberta Foundation for the Arts
Standard Life Centre
#901, 10405 Jasper Ave.
Edmonton, AB T5J 4R7
780-427-9968
Fax: 780-422-1162
www.affta.ca
• Alberta Historical Resources Foundation
Old St. Stephen's College
8820 - 112 St.
Edmonton, AB T6G 2P8
780-431-2300
• Alberta Human Rights & Citizenship Commission
Northern Regional Office, Standard Life Centre
#800, 10405 Jasper Ave.
Edmonton, AB T5J 4R7
780-427-7661
Fax: 780-427-6013
TDD: 780-297-5639
humanrights@gov.ab.ca
www.albertahumanrights.ab.ca
Other Communication: Southern Regional Office (Calgary): 403-297-6571; Fax: 403-297-6567; TTY: 403-297-5639; Toll Free TTY: 1-800-232-7215
• Alberta Sport, Recreation, Parks & Wildlife Foundation
Standard Life Centre
10405 Jasper Ave., 9th Fl.
Edmonton, AB T5J 4R7

780-415-1167
Fax: 780-415-0308
www.cd.gov.ab.ca/asrpwf
Chair, Orest Korbutt
To enhance the quality of life in Alberta, the Alberta Sport, Recreation, Parks & Wildlife Foundation provides financial support to eligible sport & recreation organizations.The Development Initiatives Program provides support to those working in the areas of sport, recreation, parks & wildlife for project & program related endeavors.The Hosting Program encourages the development of youth in sport, recreation, parks & wildlife & promotes economic growth.
• Government House Foundation
12845 - 102 Ave.
Edmonton, AB T5N 0M6
780-427-2281
Fax: 780-422-6508
www.cd.gov.ab.ca/all_about_us/commissions/government_house/index.
• Wild Rose Foundation
#901, 10405 Jasper Ave.
Edmonton, AB T5J 4R7
780-422-9305

Alberta Transportation

Twin Atria Building
4999 - 98 Jasper Ave., 2nd Fl.
Edmonton, AB T6B 2X3
780-427-2731
Acts Administered:
City Transportation Act
Dangerous Goods Transportation & Handling Act
Highways Development & Protection Act
Public Highways Development Act
Railway (Alberta) Act
Regional Airports Authorities Act
Traffic Safety Act
Government Organization Act
Provincial Parks Act
Water Act
Water, Gas and Electric Companies Act
Minister, Hon. Luke Ouellette
780-427-2080, Fax: 780-422-2722
Deputy Minister, Gary Boddez
780-427-6912, Fax: 780-422-6515
gary.boddez@gov.ab.ca
Director Communications, Tammy Forbes
780-415-1841, Fax: 780-466-3166
tammy.forbes@gov.ab.ca
Executive Director Human Resources Branch, Lynn Cook
780-415-1811, Fax: 780-422-5138
lynn.cook@gov.ab.ca
• Transportation Safety Board
Twin Atria Bldg.
4999 - 98 Ave., Main Fl.
Edmonton, AB T6B 2X3
780-427-7178
Fax: 780-422-9739
Chair, Ron Smitten
The Board was established under the Traffic Safety Act. It functions as the final administrative authority charged with making operator licence determinations, and it holds hearings in relation to driver conduct, reinstatement of licences for suspended drivers through the Alberta Administrative Licence Suspension Program & the Alberta Zero Tolerance Program, impaired driving convictions through the Ignition Interlock Program, & early release of vehicles under the Vehicle Seizure Program. In addition, the Board functions as the appeal body for decisions of the Registrar, relating to driver training schools, driver instructors, driver examiners, vehicle inspection stations & technicians, operating authority certificates, safety fitness certificates, carrier safety ratings, exemption permits, & assessed administrative penalties. It is responsible for appeals surrounding decisions & actions taken under the Railway (Alberta) Act.
• Transportation Safety Board - Calgary
Willowglen Business Park
803 Manning Rd. NE, Main Fl.
Calgary, AB T2E 7M8

Francophone Secretariat
HSBC Bldg.
10055 - 106 St., 5th Fl.
Edmonton, AB T5J 1G3
Fax: 780-422-7533

Executive Director, Denis Tardif
780-415-3348,
denis.tardif@gov.ab.ca

Policy & Corporate Services Division
Twin Atria Building
4999 - 98 Ave., 3rd Fl.
Edmonton, AB T6B 2X3

Strategic Transportation Initiatives
Twin Atria Building
4999 - 98 Ave., 3rd Fl.
Edmonton, AB T6B 2X3

Transportation Safety Services
Twin Atria Building
4999 - 98 Ave., Main Fl.
Edmonton, AB T6B 2X3
Transportation Safety Services is responsible for vehicle/driver safety, driver licensing & drivers license enforcement, impaired driving intervention programs, road safety programs, dangerous goods control, & monitoring the motor carrier industry & provincial railways.
Asst. Deputy Minister, Shaun Hammond
780-415-1146, Fax: 780-415-0782
shaun.hammond@gov.ab.ca
Executive Director Vehicle Safety & Carrier Services, Roger Clarke
403-340-5033, Fax: 403-340-4811
roger.clarke@gov.ab.ca
Director Transport Engineering, Kim Durdle
403-340-5189, Fax: 403-340-5092
kim.durdle@gov.ab.ca

Transportation & Civil Engineering
Twin Atria Building
4999 - 98 Ave., 2nd Fl.
Edmonton, AB T6B 2X3
Asst. Deputy Minister, Bruno Zutautas
780-422-2184, Fax: 780-415-1268
bruno.zutautas@gov.ab.ca
Executive Director Program Management Branch, John Engleder
780-644-4004, Fax: 780-427-0783
john.engleder@gov.ab.ca
Executive Director Technical Standards Branch, Moh Lali
780-415-1083, Fax: 780-422-2027
moh.lali@gov.ab.ca
Executive Director Planning Branch, Jim Der
780-415-1300, Fax: 780-422-2027
jim.der@gov.ab.ca
Regional Director Southern Region, Darrell Camplin
403-382-4060, Fax: 403-382-4412
darrell.camplin@gov.ab.ca
Regional Director Central Region, Stu Becker
403-340-4325, Fax: 403-340-4810
stu.becker@gov.ab.ca
Regional Director North Central Region,Vacant
780-674-8221, Fax: 780-674-8383
Regional Director Peace Region, Wayne Franklin
780-674-6280, Fax: 780-674-2440
wayne.franklin@gov.ab.ca
Regional Director Northeast Alberta Transportation Corridor (NATC) - Fort McMurray, Ranjit Tharmalingam
780-422-7672, Fax: 780-427-0369
ranjit.tharmalingam@gov.ab.ca

Strategic Corporate Services Division
Standard Life Centre
10405 Jasper Ave., 7th Fl.
Edmonton, AB T5J 4R7
780-415-0257
Other Communication: Information Management & Technology Services Help Desk: 780-427-2450
Acting Assistant Deputy Minister, Wilma Haas
780-415-6092, Fax: 780-422-3142
wilma.haas@gov.ab.ca
Executive Director Policy, Planning & Legislative Services Branch, Susan Cribbs
780-422-1290,
susan.cribbs@gov.ab.ca
Executive Director Financial Services Branch, Pam Arnston
780-427-0120,
pam.arnston@gov.ab.ca

Executive Director & Chief Information Officer, Marsha Capell
780-427-1075, Fax: 780-644-1286
marsha.capell@gov.ab.ca

Travel Alberta
PO Box 2500
Edmonton, AB T5J 2Z4
780-427-4321
Fax: 780-427-0867
800-252-3782
travelinfo@TravelAlberta.com
www.travelalberta.com
Managing Director Travel Alberta, Derek Coke-Kerr
403-297-2849, Fax: 403-297-5068
derek.coke-kerr@travelalberta.com
Director Communications, Don Boynton
403-297-8753,
don.boynton@travelalberta.com

Alberta Utilities Consumer Advocate
TD Tower
10088 - 102 Ave.
Edmonton, AB T5J 2Z1
780-644-5130
Fax: 780-644-5129
866-714-4455
UtilitiesConsumerAdvocate@gov.ab.
www.utilitiesconsumeradvocate.gov.ab.ca
The Office of the Utilities Consumer Advocate was created in October 2003 to provide a voice for electricity & natural gas consumers in Alberta's restructured utilities market. The Office of the Utilities Consumer Advocate works closely with other consumer advocacy agencies to ensure that retail utility consumers in Alberta; homeowners & tenants, farmers & small businesses, are represented fairly in their dealings with electricity & natural gas companies, regulatory agencies such as the Alberta Energy & Utilities Board (EUB) & the provincial government.
Acting Utilities Consumer Advocate, Cathryn Landreth
780-415-8761, Fax: 780-422-8191
cathryn.landreth@gov.ab.ca

Northern Development Branch
780-624-6274
Fax: 780-624-6184
Director Projects & Research, Allen Geary
780-624-6337, Fax: 780-624-6184
allen.geary@gov.ab.ca
Senior Northern Development Officer, Audrey DeWit
780-624-6342,
audrey.dewit@gov.ab.ca
Senior Northern Development Officer, Kim Pinnock
780-624-6432,
kim.pinnock@gov.ab.ca
Senior Northern Development Officer, Kris Rollheiser
780-624-6336,
kris.rollheiser@gov.ab.ca
Research Officer, Natalie Butler
780-624-6350,
natalie.butler@gov.ab.ca
Research Officer, Sam Warrior
780-624-6433,
sam.warrior@gov.ab.ca

Government of British Columbia
Seat of Government: Parliament Bldgs.
Victoria, BC V8V 1X4
EnquiryBC@gov.bc.ca
www.gov.bc.ca
The Province of British Columbia entered Confederation on July 20, 1871. It has an area of 924,815.43 km2. According to Statistics Canada, the population of the province in 2010 was 4,551,853.
Director Operations & Management Services, Jerymy Brownridge
250-387-2087
Premier, Hon. Christy Clark
• British Columbia Treaty Commission(BCTC)
#203, 1155 West Pender St.
Vancouver, BC V6E 2P4
604-482-9200
Fax: 604-482-9222
800-665-8330
info@bctreaty.net
www.bctreaty.net
Acts Administered:

Ministry of International Business & Immigration Act
• British Columbia Pension Corporation
2995 Jutland Rd.
PO Box 9460
Victoria, BC V8W 9V8
250-387-1002
Fax: 250-953-0429
800-663-8823
PensionCorp@pensionsbc.ca;
Retired.Members@pensionsbc.ca
www.pensionsbc.ca
Other Communication: College Pension Plan: 250-953-4324; Municipal Pension Plan: 250-953-3000; Public Service Pension Plan: 250-953-3033; Teachers' Pension Plan: 250-953-3022
• Industry Training Authority(ITA)
#1223, 13351 Commerce Pkwy.
Richmond, BC V6V 2X7
604-214-8700
Fax: 604-214-8701
866-660-6011
info@itabc.ca; customerservice@itabc.ca
www.itabc.ca
Other Communication: Customer Service: 778-328-8700
Executive Lead, Lisa Dooling
British Columbia's Industry Training Authority is a provincial government agency which oversees the province's training & apprenticeship system. The ITA works with industry, employers, training providers, trainees, & apprentices.

Ministry of Agriculture

PO Box 9120 Prov Govt
Victoria, BC V8W 9E2
250-387-5121
Fax: 250-387-1522
www.gov.bc.ca/agri
The mission of the Ministry is to provide a business climate for a competitive & profitable industry that supplies safe, high quality food for consumers & the export market.
Acts Administered:
Agri-Food Choice & Quality Act
Organic Agricultural Products Certification Regulation
Agricultural Lands Commission
Agricultural Produce Grading Act
Animal Disease Control Act
Bee Act
Boundary Act
British Columbia Wine Act
Cattle (Horned) Act
Environment & Land Use Act
Farm Income Insurance Act
Farm Practices Protection (Right to Farm) Act
Farmers & Womens Institutes Act
Farming & Fishing Industries Development Act
Fisheries Act
Food Products Standards Act
Fur Farm Act
Game Farm Act
Greenbelt Act
Insurance for Crops Act
Land Act
Land Survey Act
Land Surveyors Act
Land Title & Survey Authority
Libby Dam Reservoir Act
Livestock Act
Livestock Identification Act
Livestock Lien Act
Livestock Protection Act
Livestock Public Sale Act
Local Government Act (in part)
Ministry of Agriculture & Food Act
Muskwa-Kechika Management Area Act
Natural Products Marketing (BC) Act
Pharmacists, Pharmacy Operations & Drug Scheduling Act (in part)
Plant Protection Act
Prevention of Cruelty to Animals Act
Private Managed Forest Land Act
Veterinarians Act
Weed Control Act
Wine Act
Minister Agriculture, Hon. Don McRae
250-387-1023, Fax: 250-387-1522
AGR.Minister@gov.bc.ca

Deputy Minister, Wes Shoemaker
250-356-1800, Fax: 250-356-8392
• Agricultural Land Commission(ALC)
#133, 4940 Canada Way
Burnaby, BC V5G 4K6
604-660-7000
Fax: 604-660-7033
www.alc.gov.bc.ca
Director, Brian Underhill
The independent Crown agency strives to preserve agricultural land in British Columbia. The Provincial Agricultural Land Commission also works to encourage & enable farm businesses throughout the province. The Commission's chief responsibility is the administration of the Agricultural Land Commission Act.
• British Columbia Farm Industry Review Board(BCFIRB)
1007 Fort St., 3rd Fl.
PO Box 9129 Prov Govt
Victoria, BC V8W 9B5
250-356-8945
Fax: 250-356-5131
firb@gov.bc.ca
www.firb.gov.bc.ca
Chair, Richard Bullock
The British Columbia Farm Industry Review Board is a statutory appeal body. It is engaged in the general supervision of marketing boards & commodity boards which operate in the agricultural & aquaculture sectors.

Agriculture Operations
808 Douglas St., 5th Fl
PO Box 9120 Prov Govt
Victoria, BC V8W 9B4
250-356-7279
Assistant Deputy Minister, Lindsay Kislock
250-356-1815
Director Food Safety & Plant Health, Marney K. James
604-556-3058, Fax: 604-556-3117
Acting Director Regional Operations, Wray McDonnell
250-861-7201
Director Animal Health, Dr. Ron Lewis
604-556-3038, Fax: 604-556-3010
Director Sustainable Agriculture Management, Ken Nickel
604-556-3103, Fax: 604-556-3099

Corporate Services
2975 Jutland Rd., 5th Fl.
PO Box 9339 Prov Govt
Victoria, BC V8W 9M1
250-387-9878
Fax: 250-953-3414
Assistant Deputy Minister, Denise Bragg
250-387-9878
Acting Chief Information Officer & Executive Director Information Management, Doug Say
250-387-1348, Fax: 250-387-1085
Executive Director People Strategies, Duff McCaghey
250-356-6243, Fax: 250-387-3522
Executive Director Finance & Administration, Anne Minnings
250-356-9220
Director Corporate Services Delivery, Trish Dohan
250-356-9221

Crown Land Administration
808 Douglas St., 5th Fl.
PO Box 9120 Prov Govt
Victoria, BC V8W 9B4
250-356-3076
Fax: 250-356-7279
Assistant Deputy Minister, Grant Parnell
Director Crown Land Opportunities, Randy Wenger
604-586-2889, Fax: 604-586-2900
Director Crown Contaminated Sites, Brian D. Clarke
250-387-9659, Fax: 250-356-6791
Director Land Program Services, Ward Trotter
250-356-2166, Fax: 250-356-5450
Director Strategic Initiatives, Jane Spackman
250-356-0911, Fax: 250-356-7830
Acting Director Strategic Land Policy & Legislation, Allan Lidstone
250-356-1659, Fax: 250-356-7830

Strategic Industry Development
808 Douglas St., 5th Fl.
PO Box 9120 Prov Govt
Victoria, BC V8W 9B4

250-356-1821
Fax: 250-356-7279
Assistant Deputy Minister, Harvey Sasaki
250-356-1122
Director Governance & Legislation, Mark Parsons
250-387-3195
Director Strategic Policy & Planning, Daphne Sidaway-Wolf
250-356-2945, Fax: 250-387-0357
Director Business Risk Management, Gary Falk
250-861-7232
Director Investment & Innovation, Grant Thompson
250-356-8299, Fax: 250-356-2949
Director Aquaculture Policy, Al Castledine
250-387-9574, Fax: 250-356-0358
Acting Director Aquaculture Operations, Jim Russell
250-897-7561, Fax: 250-334-1410
Attorney General, Hon. Barry Penner
250-387-1866, Fax: 250-387-6411
barry.penner.mla@leg.bc.ca
Acts Administered:
Commissioner on Resources & Environment Act
Expropriation Act
Indian Cut-off Lands Dispute
Treaty Commission Act
Deputy Attorney General, David Loukidelis
250-356-0149, Fax: 250-387-6224
Executive Director Court Administration, William Grandage
604-660-9823, Fax: 604-660-9580

Columbia Power Corporation (CPC)

#200, 445 - 13th Ave.
Castlegar, BC V1N 1G1
250-365-8585
Fax: 250-365-8537
cpc.info@columbiapower.org
www.columbiapower.org
Columbia Power Corporation was established under the Company Act in 1994. A Crown corporation, it is wholly owned & controlled by the Province of British Columbia. On a joint venture basis with the Columbia Basin Trust, Columbia Power Corporation undertakes power project investments as the agent of the Province of British Columbia. Some power projects include the following: Arrow Lakes Generating Station, Brilliant Expansion Project, & Waneta Expansion Project.
President/CEO, Barry Chuddy
250-365-8529
Vice-President Human Resources & Corporate Services, Debbie Martin
250-365-8595
Vice-President Sales & Development, Victor Jmaeff
250-304-6023,
Vice-President Project Implementation, Giulio Ambrosone
250-365-9930
Vice-President Operations & Environment, Health & Safety Affairs, Amy Stevenson
250-359-6738
Chief Financial Officer & Vice-President Finance & Stakeholder Relations, Robert Krysac
250-365-9331
General Counsel & Corporate Secretary, Don Rose
604-267-1945,
don.rose@columbiapower.org

Ministry of Community, Sport & Cultural Development

800 Johnson St., 6th Fl.
PO Box 9490 Prov Govt
Victoria, BC V8W 9N7
250-387-2283
Fax: 250-387-4312
www.gov.bc.ca/cscd
The Ministry of Community, Sport and Cultural Development supports healthier, greener, & more inclusive communities in British Columbia.
Acts Administered:
Capital Region Water Supply & Sooke Hills Protection
Community Charter Act
Community Charter Council Act
Islands Trust Act
Land Title Act (in part)
Local Government Act
Local Government Grants Act
Local Services Act
Manufactured Home Tax Act
Ministry of Municipal Affairs Act

Mountain Resort Associations act
Municipal Aid Act
Municipal Finance Authority Act
Nanaimo & Southwest Water Supply Act
Ports Property Tax Act
Resort Municipality of Whistler Act
Sechelt Indian Government District Enabling Act
University Endowment Land Act
Vancouver Charter Act
Minister, Hon. Ida Chong
250-356-2771, Fax: 250-356-3000
ida.chong.mla@leg.bc.ca
Deputy Minister, Don Fast
250-387-4104, Fax: 250-387-7973
Don.Fast@gov.bc.ca
• Columbia Basin Trust(CBT)
Southwest Basin
5400, 445 - 13 Ave.
Castlegar, BC V1N 1G1
250-365-6633
Fax: 250-365-6670
800-505-8998
cbt@cbt.org
www.cbt.org
Other Communication: Northwest Basin: 250-265-9936; Southeast Basin: 250-426-8810; Northeast Basin: 250-344-7065
Chair, Garry Merkel
The Columbia Basin Trust manages its assets to benefit the economy, environment, & social well-being of the region. The Trust works to establish collaborative partnerships to achieve improved self-sufficiency.
• Islands Trust
#200, 1627 Fort St.
Victoria, BC V8R 1H8
250-405-5151
Fax: 250-405-5155
information@islandstrust.bc.ca
www.islandstrust.bc.ca
Other Communication: Northern Office: 250-247-2063; Salt Spring Office: 250-537-9144
Chair, Kim Benson
The Islands Trust area covers the following islands & waters between the British Columbia mainland & southern Vancouver Island: Bowen, Denman, Gabriola, Galiano, Gambier, Hornby, Lasqueti, Mayne, North Pender, Salt Spring, Saturna, South Pender, & Thetis. The Trust is a federation of independent local governments. The federation plans land use & regulates development to preserve & protect the area and its environment.
• Northern Development Initiative Trust
#301, 1268 Fifth Ave.
Prince George, BC V2L 3L2
250-561-2525
Fax: 250-561-2563
admin@nditrust.ca
www.nditrust.ca
Chair, Bruce Sutherland
The Northern Trust consists of a Board of Directors which makes funding decisions for programs of the Trust. According to provincial legislation, investments can be made in the following areas: agriculture, economic development, energy, forestry, mining, Olympic opportunities; pine beetle recovery, small business, tourism, & transportation.
Southern Interior Development Initiative Trust
103, 2903 - 35th Ave.
Vernon, BC V1T 2S7
250-545-6829
Fax: 250-545-6896
min@sidit-bc.ca
www.sidit-bc.ca
Chair, Jim Thomson
The government of British Columbia enacted legislation in 2006 to establish the Southern Interior Development Initiative Trust. The mission of the Trust is to grow & diversify the economy of the Southern Interior of British Columbia through investments in economic development projects that will benefit the area.

Community Development Trust
634 Humboldt St., 2nd Fl.
PO Box 9595 Prov Govt
Victoria, BC V8W 9K4
877-238-8882
Fax: 250-387-4425
Executive Director Community Development Trust, Tracey Thompson
250-387-3130

Program Manager, Donna Brand
250-387-4491

Local Government Department
800 Johnson St., 6th Fl.
PO Box 9490 Prov Govt
Victoria, BC V8W 9N7
lgd_feedback@gov.bc.ca
www.cd.gov.bc.ca/lgd
Working with a great range of partners, the Local Government Department develops communities that can manage change & offer affordable services to residents of British Columbia. The Department's programs include the following: developing local government legislation; facilitating partnerships with local governments & First Nations; fostering positive inter-governmental relations to facilitate community & regional planning; offering financial support; & providing information & advice.
Assistant Deputy Minister, Mike Furey
250-356-6575, Fax: 250-387-7973
Executive Director Intergovernmental Relations & Planning, Alan Osborne
250-387-0089, Fax: 250-387-6212
Director Local Government Infrastructure & Finance, Julia Duff
250-387-4069, Fax: 250-356-1873
lgsi@gov.bc.ca

Management Services
800 Johnson St., 6th Fl.
PO Box 9842 Prov Govt
Victoria, BC V8W 9T2
250-387-8705
Fax: 250-387-7973

Rural Development
800 Johnson St., 6th Fl.
PO Box 9824 Prov Govt
Victoria, BC V8W 9W4
250-953-3005
Fax: 250-387-7935

Pine Beetle Epidemic Response
#390, 546 St. Paul St.
Kamloops, BC V2C 5T1
250-371-3725
Fax: 250-371-3735
Assistant Deputy Minister Pine Beetle Epidemic Response, Ray Schultz
250-371-3725, Fax: 250-371-3735
Ray.Schultz@gov.bc.ca

Ministry of Jobs, Tourism, & Innovation
PO Box 9071 Prov Govt
Victoria, BC V8W 9E9
250-356-2771
Fax: 250-356-3000
JTI.Minister@gov.bc.ca
www.gov.bc.ca/tti
The ministry combines the power of tourism, investment attraction and export market development to market British Columbia as never before and to fully realize this province's potential as Canada's Pacific Gateway. By bringing together synergistic elements from the former Ministry of Tourism, Culture and the Arts and the former Ministry of Small Business, Technology and Economic Development, the ministry is attracting new visitors, more investment and new customers for B.C. products in all of the province's traditional markets, as well as opening up new tourism, trade and investment opportunities in Asia, particularly in Japan, China, Korea and India.
Acts Administered:
British Columbia Enterprise Corporation Act
British Columbia Innovation Council Act
Builders Lien Act
Business Paper Reduction Act
Employee Investment Act
International Financial Activity Act (except Parts 3, 4, & 5, & Part 6, as it pertains to Parts 3, 4, & 5)
Ministry of International Business & Immigration Act (except as the act relates to immigrant recruitment & labour market development, & programs respecting immigrant & refugee settlement)
Small Business Venture Capital Act
Special Accounts Appropriation & Control Act (s. 9.5)
Trade, Investment, & Labour Mobility Agreement Implementation Act

Minister, Hon. Pat Bell
250-387-6240, Fax: 250-387-1040
pat.bell.mla@leg.bc.ca
Deputy Minister, Dana Hayden
250-356-6981, Fax: 250-356-1195
Dana.Hayden@gov.bc.ca
• Asia Pacific Foundation of Canada
#666, 999 Canada Pl.
Vancouver, BC V6C 3E1
604-684-5986
info@asiapacific.ca; researchgrants@asiapacific.ca
www.asiapacific.ca
Other Communication: Research Grants Program, Address: #220, 890 West Pender St., Vancouver, BC V6C 1J9
• Asia Pacific Trade Council
#730, 999 Canada Pl.
Vancouver, BC V6C 3E1
604-775-2100
Fax: 604-775-2070
www.asiapacifictradecouncil.ca
Chair, Arthur Hara, O.C., LLD
The Asia Pacific Trade Council advises the Premier of British Columbia on investment & trade opportunities with the Asia Pacific Region.
• British Columbia Innovation Council(BCIC)
1188 West Georgia St., 9th Fl.
Vancouver, BC V6E 4A2
604-683-2724
Fax: 604-683-6567
800-665-7222
info@bcic.ca
www.bcic.ca
Chair, Hector Mackay-Dunn, Q.C.
The British Columbia Innovation Council strives to advance innovation & commercialization by focusing on the following strategies: developing, recruiting & retaining science & technology professionals; fostering innovation & entrepreneurship; & bringing innovation to commercial success by establishing partnerships.
• British Columbia Progress Board
#730, 999 Canada Pl.
Vancouver, BC V6C 3E1
604-775-1664
Fax: 604-775-2129
ideas@bcprogressboard.com
www.bcprogressboard.com
Executive Director, Athana Mentzelopoulos
The BC Progress Board has the following responsibilities: Determining if the province is improving its competitiveness & quality of life; & Making recommendations to the Premier to enhance the province's economy & social well-being.
• International Financial Centre British Columbia(IFC BC)
Park Place
#1170, 666 Burrard St.
Vancouver, BC V6C 2X8
604-683-6626
Fax: 604-683-6646
info@ifcvancouver.com
www.ifcbc.com
• Premier's Technology Council
#730, 999 Canada Pl.
Vancouver, BC V6C 3E1
604-775-2122
Fax: 604-775-2129
premiers.technologycouncil@gov.bc.ca
www.gov.bc.ca/premier/technology_council

Asia Pacific, Trade, & Investment Division
#730, 999 Canada Pl.
Vancouver, BC V6E 3C1
604-775-2251
Fax: 604-775-2070

Economic Competitiveness Division
1810 Blanshard St., 7th Fl.
PO Box 9327 Prov Govt
Victoria, BC V8W 9N3
250-952-0367
Fax: 250-952-0137

Assistant Deputy Minister, Shannon Baskerville
Director Labour Market Development, Mark Gillis
250-952-0678, Fax: 250-952-0705

Management Services Division

Federal/Provincial Government / Government of British Columbia

1810 Blanshard St., 8th Fl.
PO Box 9324 Prov Govt
Victoria, BC V8W 9N3
250-952-0126
Fax: 250-952-0101

Technology, Research & Innovation Division
#730, 999 Canada Place
Vancouver, BC V6C 3E1
Fax: 604-775-2070
Minister, Hon. Shirley Bond
Minister.Educ@gov.bc.ca; shirley.bond.mla@leg.bc.ca
Deputy Minister, James Gorman
250-387-2026, Fax: 250-356-2011
dm.Education@gov.bc.ca

Resource Management Division
620 Superior St., 4th Fl
PO Box 9151 Prov Govt
Victoria, BC V8W 9H1
250-356-2588
Fax: 250-356-8003
www.bced.gov.bc.ca/departments/resource_man
• British Columbia Lottery Corporation
74 West Seymour St.
Kamloops, BC V2C 1E2
250-828-5500
Fax: 250-828-5631
866-815-0222
www.bclc.com
Other Communication: Lottery Player Complaint Centre Toll-Free Phone: 1-866-601-1818; BCLC Marketing & Sales Phone: 604-270-0649

Ministry of Energy, Mines & Petroleum Resources

PO Box 9318 Prov Govt
Victoria, BC V8W 9N3
250-952-0241
www.gov.bc.ca/empr
The development of sustainable & competitive energy & mineral resource sectors in British Columbia is the focus of the Ministry.
Acts Administered:
BC Hydro Public Power Legacy & Heritage Contract
Coal Act
Coalbed Gas Act, 2003
Columbia Basin Trust Act
Energy Efficiency Act
Energy Efficiency Standards Regulation
Gas Utility Act
Geothermal Resources Act
Hydro & Power Authority Act
Hydro Power Measures Act
Mineral Land Tax Act
Mineral Tax Act
Mineral Tenure Act
Mines Act
Mine Reclamation Fund Regulation
Mines Regulation
Workplace Hazardous Materials Information System Regulation (Mines)
Mining Right of Way Act
Mining Tax Act
Ministry of Energy & Mines Act
Natural Gas Price Act
Oil & Gas Commission Act
Petroleum & Natural Gas Act
Petroleum & Natural Gas (Vancouver Island Railway Lands) Act
Pipeline Act
Sour Pipeline Regulation
Transmission Corporation Act
Utilities Commission Act
Vancouver Island Natural Gas Pipeline Act
West Kootenay Power & Light Company, Ltd. Act
Minister, Hon. Richard Neufeld
250-387-5896, Fax: 250-356-2965
empr.minister@gov.bc.ca; richard.neufeld.mla@leg.bc.ca
Minister of State Mining, Hon. Gordon Hogg
250-953-4100, Fax: 250-387-1803
gordon.hogg.mla@leg.bc.ca
Deputy Minister, Greg Reimer
250-952-0504, Fax: 250-952-0269
Officer Public Affairs, Jake Jacobs
250-952-0628, Fax: 250-952-0627
Jake.Jacobs@gov.bc.ca

• Mediation & Arbitration Board
#310, 9900 - 100 Ave.
Fort St John, BC V1J 5S7
250-787-3403
Fax: 250-787-3228
mab.office@gov.bc.ca
www.empr.gov.bc.ca/OG/mab
Chair, Cheryl Vickers
The Mediation & Arbitration Board is an independent, quasi-judicial organization which was established under the authority of the Petroleum & Natural Gas Act. The Board functions under the following acts: the Geothermal Resources Act, the Mineral Tenure Act, the Mining Right of Way Act, & the Coal Act. It assists in resolving disputes between companies & landowners concerning petroleum or natural gas resources.
• Oil & Gas Commission(OGC)
#100, 10003 - 110 Ave.
Fort St John, BC V1J 6M7
250-261-5700
800-663-7867
www.ogc.gov.bc.ca
Other Communication: Incident Reporting: 1-800-663-3456
Commissioner & Chief Executive Officer, Alex Ferguson
The Oil & Gas Commission was enacted under the Oil & Gas Commission Act, The Commission regulates British Columbia's oil & gas activities & pipelines.

Electricity & Alternative Energy
1810 Blanshard St., 4th Fl.
PO Box 9314 Prov Govt
Victoria, BC V8W 9N1
250-952-0204
Fax: 250-952-0258
Assistant Deputy Minister, Les MacLaren
Fax: 250-952-0926
Acting Executive Director Alternative Energy Policy, Dan Green
250-952-0279
Director Bioenergy & Renewable, Janice Larson
250-952-0706
Director Electricity Policy, Shelley Murphy
250-952-0264
Director Independent Power Producers, Neil Banera
250-952-0655

Management Services
1810 Blanshard St., 8th Fl.
PO Box 9324 Prov Govt
Victoria, BC V8W 9N3
250-952-0606
Fax: 250-952-0101
Assistant Deputy Minister, Doug Callbeck
250-952-0126
Chief Information Officer & Director Information Management, Stewart Symmers
250-952-0229, Fax: 250-952-0739
Director Strategic Human Resources, Brenda Vachon
250-952-0601
Acting Director Finance & Administration, Terry Gelinas
250-952-0174

Marketing, Aboriginal & Community Relations
1810 Blanshard St., 4th Fl.
PO Box 9396 Prov Govt
Victoria, BC V8W 9M3
250-356-9569
Fax: 250-356-5092
Assistant Deputy Minister, Jody Shimkus
Executive Director Marketing & Community Relations, Ellen Frisch
250-952-0651, Fax: 250-356-5092
Acting Executive Director Aboriginal Relations, Giovanni Puggioni
250-952-0530, Fax: 250-952-0111
Executive Director Corporate Policy, Planning & Legislation, Karen Koncohrada
250-952-0274, Fax: 250-952-0637

Mining & Minerals
1675 Douglas St., 7th Fl.
PO Box 9320 Prov Govt
Victoria, BC V8W 9N3
250-952-0596
Fax: 250-952-0491
Assistant Deputy Minister, John Cavanagh

Chief Inspector Mines, Douglas Sweeney
250-952-0793
Chief Geologist & Director British Columbia Geological Survey, Dave Lefebvre
250-952-0374, Fax: 250-952-0381
Executive Director Policy & Sustainability, Karina Brino
250-952-0868

Oil & Gas
1810 Blanshard St., 5th Fl.
PO Box 9323 Prov Govt
Victoria, BC V8W 9N3
250-952-0115
Fax: 250-952-0926
Executive Director Innovation & Investment, Alex McMillan
250-952-6277
Acting Executive Director Business Development, Ines Piccinino
250-356-9825
Executive Director Major Initiatives, Linda Beltrano
250-356-1183, Fax: 250-952-0255
Acting Executive Director Oil & Gas Policy, Paula Barrett
250-953-3766, Fax: 250-953-3770
Executive Director Resource Development & Geoscience, Vic Levson
250-952-0391, Fax: 250-952-0922

Titles & Offshore
1675 Douglas St., 2nd Fl.
PO Box 9312 Prov Govt
Victoria, BC V8W 9N2
250-356-0510
Fax: 250-356-0582
Assistant Deputy Minister, Bill Phelan
250-356-0552
Acting Executive Director Offshore Oil & Gas, Susan Kelly
250-356-7512, Fax: 250-952-0541
Director Land Use Coordination, Norman Marcy
250-387-1780
Director Compliance & Administration, Debbie Fischer
250-952-0336, Fax: 250-952-0331
Director Oil & Gas Titles, Laurel Nash
250-952-0335, Fax: 250-952-0331
Director Mineral Titles, Rick Conte
604-660-2814, Fax: 604-660-2653
Mineral.Titles@gov.bc.ca

Ministry of Environment

PO Box 9339 Prov Govt
Victoria, BC V8W 9M1
250-387-1161
Fax: 250-387-5669
www.envmail@gov.bc.ca
www.gov.bc.ca/env
Other Communication: Environmental Emergencies:
1-800-663-3456; Conservation Officer Svs.: 1-877-952-7277;
Recycling Hotline: 1-800-667-4321; Dangerous Wildlife Conflicts:
1-800-663-9453
The Ministry provides sustainable environmental management to work towards a healthy, clean, & naturally diverse environment.
Acts Administered:
Agriculture Land Commission Act
Assessment Act
Assessment Authority Act
Boundary Act
Budget Measures Implementation Act
Commercial Rafting Safety Act
Creston Valley Wildlife Act
Discharge of Firearms Regulation
Summit Creek Campground & Recreation Area
Dike Maintenance Act
Drainage, Ditch & Dike Act
Ground Water Protection Regulations
Ecological Reserve Act
Application of Park Legislation to Ecological Reserves Regulation
Ecological Reserve Regulations
Emergency Program Act
Compensation & Disaster Financial Assistance Regulation
Emergency Program Management Regulation
Local Authority Emergency Management Regulation
Environment & Land Use Act (Sustainable Resource Management)
Environmental Assessment Act
Concurrent Approval Regulation
Public Consultation Policy Regulation

Regional District Definition Regulation
Transition Regulation
Environmental Management Act
Agricultural Waste Control Regulation
Antisapstain Chemical Waste Control Regulation
Asphalt Plant Regulation
Cleaner Gasoline Regulation
Code of Practice for the Discharge of Produced Water from Coalbed Gas Operations
Conservation Office Service Authority Regulation
Contaminated Sites Regulation
Environmental Appeal Board Procedure Regulation
Environmental Data Quality Assurance Regulation
Environmental Impact Assessment Regulation
Finfish Aquaculture Waste Control Regulation
Gasoline Vapour Control Regulation
Hazardous Waste Regulation
Land-based Fin Fish Waste Control Regulation
Motor Vehicle Emissions Control Warranty Regulation
Municipal Sewage Regulations
Mushroom Composting Pollution Prevention Regulation
Oil & Gas Waste Regulation
Ootsa Lake Beehive Burner Regulation
Open Burning Smoke Control Regulation
Organic Matter Recycling Regulation
Ozone Depleting Substances & Other Halocarbons Regulation
Permit Fees Regulation
Petroleum Storage & Distribution Facilities Storm Water Regulation
Placer Mining Waste Control Regulation
Post-Consumer Residual Stewardship Program Regulation
Public Notification Regulation
Pulp Mill & Pulp & Paper Mill Liquid Effluent Control Regulation
Rebate of Waste Management Fee Regulation
Recycling Regulation
Solid Fuel Burning Domestic Appliance Regulation
Spill Cost Recovery Regulation
Spill Reporting Regulation
Storage of Recyclable Material Regulation
Sulphur Content of Fuel Regulation
Waste Discharge Regulation
Wood Residue Burner & Incinerator Regulation
Environmental Protection Act
Fish Protection Act
Riparian Areas Regulation
Sensitive Streams Designation & Licensing Regulation
Streamside Protection Regulation
Financial Administration Act
Flood Hazard Statutes Amendment Act, 2003
Forest & Range Practices Act
Forest Land Reserve Act
Hunting & Fishing Heritage Act
Industrial Operation Compensation Act
Integrated Pest Management Act, 2003
Land Act
Ministry of Environment Act
Okanagan River Boundaries Settlement
Park Act
Parks & Protected Areas Statutes Amendment Act, 2004
Park & Recreation Area Regulation
Pesticide Control Act
Protected Areas of British Columbia Act
Skagit Environmental Enhancement Act
Sustainable Environment Fund Act
Waste Management Act
Water, Land & Air Protection Statutes Amendment Act, 2003
Water Act
Water Protection Act
Groundwater Protection Regulations
Water Utility Act
Wildlife Act
Angling & Scientific Collection Regulation
Closed Areas Regulation
Designation & Exemption Regulation
Designation of Officers Regulation
Freshwater Fish Regulation
Habitat Conservation Trust Fund Regulation
Hunter Safety Training Regulation
Hunting Licensing Regulation
Hunting Regulation
Limited Entry Hunting Regulation
Management Unit Regulation
Motor Vehicle Prohibition Regulation
Permit Regulation
Public Access Prohibition Regulation

Tofino Mudflats Wildlife Management Area Regulation
Wildlife Act Commercial Activities Regulation
Wildlife Act General Regulation
Wildlife Management Areas Regulations
Wildlife Amendment Act
Minister, Hon. Barry Penner
250-387-1187, Fax: 250-387-1356
env.minister@gov.bc.ca; barry.penner.mla@leg.bc.ca
Deputy Minister, Doug Konkin
250-387-5429
• British Columbia Environmental Assessment Office
• Environmental Appeal Board
747 Fort St., 4th Fl.
PO Box 9425 Prov Govt
Victoria, BC V8W 9V1
250-387-3464
Fax: 250-356-9923
eabinfo@gov.bc.ca
www.eab.gov.bc.ca
Chair, Alan Andison
The Environmental Appeal Board is an independent agency which was created under the Environment Management Act. The Board hears appeals from administrative decisions under the following acts: the Environmental Management Act, the Health Act, the Integrated Pest Management Act, the Water Act, & the Wildlife Act. Notices of appeal are reviewed & evaluated to determine if an alternative dispute resolution is possible.
• Fraser Basin Council(FBC)
Central Office
470 Granville St., 1st Fl.
Vancouver, BC V6C 1V5
604-488-5350
Fax: 604-488-5351
info@fraserbasin.bc.ca
www.fraserbasin.bc.ca
Other Communication: Thompson: 250-314-9660; Upper Fraser: 250-612-0252; Fraser Valley: 604-826-1661; Cariboo-Chilcotin: 250-392-1400; Greater Vancouver Sea to Sky: 604-488-5365
Chair, Dr. Charles Jago
The Fraser Basin Council is a not-for-profit, non-partisan organization. The Council works to advance sustainability throughout the Fraser River Basin.

Compliance Division
2975 Jutland Rd., 5th Fl.
PO Box 9339 Prov Govt
Victoria, BC V8W 9M1
250-387-9997
Fax: 250-387-5669
Director Compliance Policy & Planning, Gwenda Laughland
250-387-9641, Fax: 250-387-8433

Corporate Services Division
2975 Jutland Rd., 5th Fl.
PO Box 9339 Prov Govt
Victoria, BC V8W 9M1
250-387-9878
Fax: 250-953-3414
Assistant Deputy Minister, Denise Bragg
Chief Information Officer & Executive Director Information Management, Doug Say
250-387-1348, Fax: 250-387-1085
Executive Director Finance & Administration, Anne Minnings
250-356-9220, Fax: 250-356-9239
Executive Director People Strategies, Duff McCaghey
250-356-6243, Fax: 250-356-7286
Director Corporate Services Delivery, Trish Dohan
250-356-9221, Fax: 250-356-9836

Environmental Protection Division
2975 Jutland Rd., 5th Fl.
PO Box 9339
Victoria, BC V8W 9M1
250-387-1288
Fax: 250-387-5669
Assistant Deputy Minister, Lynn Bailey
Acting Director Environmental Quality, Glen Okrainetz
250-387-9933, Fax: 250-356-7197
Director Environmental Management, Jim Hofweber
250-387-9971, Fax: 250-387-8897
Director Regional Operations, Jim Standen
250-397-9990, Fax: 250-356-5496
Regional Manager Kootenay & Okanagan Regional Office, Robyn Roome
250-354-6362, Fax: 250-354-6332

Regional Manager Lower Mainland Regional Office, Steffanie Warriner
604-582-5284, Fax: 604-584-9791
Regional Manager Omineca Regional Office, Sean Sharpe
250-565-6443, Fax: 250-565-6629
Regional Manager Skeena Regional Office, Ian Sharpe
250-847-7251, Fax: 250-847-7591
Regional Manager Thompson Regional Office, Rick Adams
250-371-6225, Fax: 250-371-6234
Regional Manager Vancouver Island Regional Office, Randy Alexander
250-751-3176, Fax: 250-751-3103
Section Head Cariboo Regional Office, Douglas Hill
250-398-4542, Fax: 250-398-4214

Environmental Stewardship Division
2975 Jutland Rd., 5th Fl.
PO Box 9339 Prov Govt
Victoria, BC V8T 5J9
250-356-0121
Fax: 250-953-3414
Assistant Deputy Minister, Ralph Archibald
Executive Director Protected Areas, Scott Benton
250-387-3637, Fax: 250-387-5757
Director Protected Areas Visitor Services, Christine Houghton
250-356-9241, Fax: 250-387-5757
Director Parks Planning & Management, Brian Bawtinheimer
250-387-4355, Fax: 250-387-5757
Director Ecosystems, Kaaren Lewis
250-387-9731, Fax: 250-356-9145
Director Fish & Wildlife, Tom Ethier
250-387-5657, Fax: 250-387-9568
Director Regional Operations, Brian J. Clark
250-356-0874, Fax: 250-356-9299
Regional Manager Cariboo Regional Office, Rodger Stewart
250-398-4214, Fax: 250-398-4214
Regional Manager Kootenay Regional Office, Wayne Stetski
250-489-8523, Fax: 250-489-8506
Regional Manager Lower Mainland Regional Office, Jennifer McGuire
604-582-5370, Fax: 604-930-7119
Regional Manager Okanagan Regional Office, Drew Carmichael
250-490-8262, Fax: 250-490-2231
Regional Manager Omineca Regional Office, Don Cadden
250-614-9915, Fax: 250-565-6940
Regional Manager Peace Regional Office, Maurice Lirette
250-787-3426, Fax: 250-787-3490
Regional Manager Thompson Regional Office, John Metcalfe
250-371-6304, Fax: 250-828-4000
Regional Manager Vancouver Island Regional Office, Dick Heath
250-751-3211, Fax: 250-751-3208
Section Head Skeena Regional Office, Peter Levy
250-847-7303, Fax: 250-847-7728

Oceans & Marine Fisheries Division (OMFD)
2975 Jutland Rd., 3rd Fl.
PO Box 9309
Victoria, BC V8W 9N1
250-387-0389
Fax: 250-953-3401
fishstats@gov.bc.ca; fishinfo@gov.bc.ca
Director, Jamie Alley
250-953-3417
Manager Operations, Barron Carswell
Manager Seafood Development, Lorraine Saunders
Manager Sustainablility, Bob Williams
Manager Marine Fisheries, Martin Paish

Strategic Policy Division
2975 Jutland Rd., 5th Fl.
PO Box 9335 Prov Govt
Victoria, BC V8W 9M1
250-387-9666
Fax: 250-387-8894
Executive Director, Anthony J. Danks
250-387-8483
Director Intergovernmental & External Relations, Lisa Paquin
250-387-9661, Fax: 250-387-8894
Director Policy & Legislation, Peter Trotzki
250-953-5147, Fax: 250-387-8894
Manager Planning & Performance Management, Rozlynne Mitchell
250-387-7980, Fax: 250-387-8894
Manager Science Policy & Economics, Jennifer A. Maxwell
250-387-9642, Fax: 250-387-8894

Federal/Provincial Government / Government of British Columbia

Water Stewardship Division
2975 Jutland Rd., 5th Fl.
PO Box 9339 Prov Govt
Victoria, BC V8W 9M1
250-356-9443
Fax: 250-953-3414
Assistant Deputy Minister, Jim Mattison
Director Innovation & Planning, Lynn Kriwoken
250-387-9481, Fax: 250-356-1202
Director Management & Standards, Glen Davidson
250-387-6949, Fax: 250-356-0605
Director Science & Information, Fern Schultz
250-387-6722, Fax: 250-356-1202
Director Regional Operations, Brian Symonds
250-490-8255
Regional Manager Thompson Regional Office, Valerie Cameron
250-371-6270, Fax: 250-828-4000
Regional Manager Vancouver Island Regional Office, Larry Barr
250-751-7105, Fax: 250-751-7079
Regional Manager Lower Mainland Regional Office, Julia Berardinucci
604-582-5353, Fax: 604-582-5235
Regional Manager Okanagan / Kootenay Regional Offices, Ken Cunningham
250-490-8232, Fax: 250-490-2231
Regional Manager Omineca, Peace, & Skeena Regional Offices, Norm Bilodeau
250-565-6424,

Enforcement Program/Conservation Officer Service
250-387-6041
Fax: 250-356-5240
The ministry's Enforcement Program supports other ministry programs in the development of new legislative initiatives or amendments to existing regimes to ensure the enforceability of new environmental protection laws. The program manages the Conservation Officer Service by establishing its strategic objectives, allocating the budget & auditing the effectiveness of the Chief Conservation Officer. The Conservation Officer Service (COS) is the delivery arm of the Enforcement program in the Ministry. It works with other professional staff in the ministry to achieve compliance with provincial & federal environmental legislation. The Special Investigation Unit, undercover, investigates many large-scale & organized-crime style cases related to environmental resources. Its objective is to focus on illegal activities that have the greatest impact on the environment
Director & Chief Conservation Officer, Mark Hayden
250-387-6479
Manager Conservation Officer Service, Northern Region, Doug Gillett
250-565-6135
Manager Conservation Officer Service, South Coast Region, Lance Sundquist
250-751-3119
Manager Interior Region, Rick Hildebrand
250-371-6208

Environmental Quality
2978 Jutland Rd., 3rd Fl.
Victoria, BC V8T 5J9
250-387-9933
Fax: 250-356-7197
The Environmental Quality Branch develops legislation & policies to protect air & water quality, & the land. It sets standards for, & does monitoring & reporting for, ambient air & water quality. The branch is a co-leader within the BC government in developing & implementing measures to address global climate change. These key climate change actions, in conjunction with federal initiatives, involve policies & programs to reduce greenhouse gas emissions, as well as the development of adaptation measures.
Director, Hu Wallis
250-356-0345
Manager Air Protection, Glen Okrainetz
250-953-3080
Manager Climate Change, Lee Thiessen
250-387-6338
Manager Community Waste Management, Kris Ord
250-953-3866
Manager Water & Air Monitoring & Reporting, Chris Jenkins
250-387-9944

Environmental Management
2975 Jutland Rd., 3rd Fl.
Victoria, BC V8T 5J9
250-387-9971
Fax: 250-387-8897
Develops legislation & policies to manage & reduce discharges of potential contaminants & to remediate contaminated sites. Along with the Regional Operations Branch, it directs the remediation of complex, high-risk contaminated sites, & manages remediation of low-to moderate-risk sites. The Branch sets regulations, standards & guidelines for a wide range of industrial & municipal operations, both urban & rural. These deal with discharges, & the handling of toxics, special (hazardous) waste, pesticides & other potential contaminants. It also leads pollution-prevention, product-stewardship & flood-hazard-management programs in BC.
Director, Jim Hofweber
250-387-9971
Acting Deputy Director IPM & Industry, Christine Houghton
250-387-9952
Acting Manager Environmental Emergencies, Graham Knox
250-356-8383
Acting Manager Hazard Management, Duncan Ferguson
250-387-9950
Acting Manager Land Remediation, Mike MacFarlane
250-356-0557
Hazardous Waste Specialist, Dr. Kuldip Bindra
250-387-3648

Ecosystems Branch
Fax: 250-356-9145
Director, Rod Davis
250-356-7725
Acting Manager Conservation Planning, Stewart Guy
250-387-0060
Manager Fisheries Science, Ted Down
250-387-9715
Acting Manager Habitat Management, Bob Cox
250-356-6831
Acting Manager Wildlife Science, Sean Sharpe
250-387-1577

Fish & Wildlife Branch
2975 Jutland Rd., 4th Fl.
Victoria, BC V8T 5J9
250-387-9717
Fax: 250-387-9568
Director, Al Martin
250-387-9599
Manager Data & Licensing, John Thornton
250-387-9776
Manager Permit & Authorization Bureau, Yvonne Foxall
Manager Wildlife Act, Bob Williams
250-356-0830
Acting Manager Wildlife Management, Tom Ethier
250-387-5657

Parks & Protected Areas
2975 Jutland Rd., 4th Fl.
Victoria, BC V8T 5J9
Fax: 250-387-5757
Director, Lynn Kennedy
250-387-3974
Manager Land Acquisition & Management Section, Ken Morrison
250-356-5298
Manager Protected Areas Recreation & Conservation, Brian Bawtinheimer
250-387-4355
Manager Visitor Information & Planning Services, David Ranson
250-387-5036

British Columbia Environmental Assessment Office
836 Yates St., 1st Fl.
PO Box 9426 Prov Govt
Victoria, BC V8W 9V1
250-350-7441
Fax: 250-356-7440
eaoinfo@gov.bc.ca
www.eao.gov.bc.ca
Operating independently, the Environmental Assessment Office (EAO) coordinates the assessment of proposed projects in British Columbia. The Office acts under the requirements of the Environmental Assessment Act. Working with the public, government agencies, & First Nations, the Environmental Assessment Office ensures that projects are developed in a sustainable manner.
Associate Deputy Minister & Executive Director, Robin Junger
250-356-7475

Director Strategic Policy & Planning, Alan Moyes
250-387-2307, Fax: 250-356-6448
Director Communications, Sarah Harrison
250-387-9973, Fax: 250-387-4966
Project Assessment Director Shoreline Modification Projects, Garry Alexander
Acting Project Assessment Director Mining, Joe Truscott
Project Assessment Director Climate Change, Kathy Eichenberger
Project Assessment Director Industrial & Waste Disposal Projects, Derek Griffin
Project Assessment Director Oil & Gas (Pipeline), & Food Processing Projects, Graeme McLaren
Project Assessment Director Energy (Power) & General Water Projects (Dams), Brian Murphy
Project Assessment Director Destination Resorts, & Groundwater Projects, Archie Riddell
Minister Finance & Deputy Premier, Hon. Kevin Falcon
250-387-3751, Fax: 250-387-5594
Fin.Minister@gov.bc.ca; kevin.falcon.mla@leg.bc.ca
Deputy Minister, Graham Whitmarsh
250-387-3184, Fax: 250-387-1655
• British Columbia 2010 Olympic & Paralympic Games Secretariat
3585 Graveley St., 7th Fl.
Vancouver, BC V5K 5J5
604-660-2010
Fax: 604-660-3437
877-604-2010
bcsecretariat@gov.bc.ca
www.2010bcsecretariat.ca

Ministry of Forests, Lands & Natural Resource Operations
PO Box 9529 Prov Govt
Victoria, BC V8W 9C3
250-387-4809
Fax: 250-953-3687
www.gov.bc.ca/for
Other Communication: Report Wildfires Toll Free:
1-800-663-5555
The Ministry of Forests, Mines and Lands supports the sustainable development of forest, mineral and land resources. The Ministry is committed to a globally competitive resource sector that can provide enormous benefits for workers, communities and future generations.
Acts Administered:
Forest Act
Advertising, Deposits & Disposition Regulation
Allowable Annual Cut Proportionate Reduction Regulation
Annual Rent Regulation
BC Timber Sales Business Areas Regulation
BC Timber Sales Business Regulation
Christmas Tree Regulation
Community Forest Agreement Regulation
Credit to Stumpage Regulation
Cut Control Regulation
Effective Director Regulation
Forest Accounts Receivable Interest Regulation
Forest Regions Regulation
Free Use Permit Regulation
Innovative Forestry Practices Regulation
Interest Rate Under Various Statutes Regulation
Log Salvage Regulation (Vancouver District)
Manufactured Forest Products Regulation
Minimum Stumpage Rate Regulation
Performance Based Harvesting Regulation
Scaling Regulation
Special Forest Products Regulation
Timber Definition Regulation
Timber Harvesting Contract & Subcontract Regulation
Timber Marketing & Transportation Regulation
Woodlot Licence Regulation
Forest Practices Code of British Columbia Act
Government Actions Regulation
Provincial Forest Use Regulation
Stillwater Pilot Project Regulation
Forest & Range Practices Act
Administrative Remedies Regulation
Administrative Review & Appeal Procedure (Forest Practices) Regulation
Forest Planning & Practices Regulation
Forest Practices Board Regulation
Forest Recreation Regulation
Forest Service Road Use Regulation

Fort St. John Pilot Project Regulation
Invasive Plants Regulation
Range Planning & Practices Regulation
Security for Forest Practice Liabilities Regulation
TFL 49 Pilot Project Regulation
Woodlot Licence Planning & Practices Regulation
Forest Stand Management Fund Act
Forest Stand Management Fund Regulation
Foresters Act
Forestry Revitalization Act, 2003
Manufactured Forest Products Regulation
Ministry of Forests Act
Protected Areas Forests Compensation Act
Range Act
Safety Authority Act
Safety Standards Act
South Moresby Implementation Account Act
Timber Licences Settlement Act
Timber Sale Licence Replacement (Sliammon First Nation) Act
Wildfire Act, 2004
Minister, Hon. Steve Thomson
250-356-6611, Fax: 250-952-0223
steve.thomson.mla@leg.bc.ca
Deputy Minister, Dana Hayden
250-356-5012, Fax: 250-953-3687
Forests.DeputyMinistersOffice@gov.bc.ca
• Forest Appeals Commission
747 Fort St., 4th Fl.
PO Box 9425 Prov Govt
Victoria, BC V8W 9V1
250-387-3464
Fax: 250-356-9923
facinfo@gov.bc.ca
www.fac.gov.bc.ca
Chair, Alan Andison
Established in 1996 under the Forest Practices Code of British Columbia Act, the Forest Appeals Commission is an independent agency which now continues under the Forest & Range Practices Act. The Commission hears appeals from administrative decisions made under the following statutes: Forest Act, Forest & Range Practices Act, Forest Practices Code of British Columbia Act, Private Managed Forest Land Act, Range Act, & the Wildfire Act.
• Forest Practices Board
1675 Douglas St., 3rd Fl.
PO Box 9905 Prov Govt
Victoria, BC V8W 9R1
250-387-7964
Fax: 250-387-7009
800-994-5899
fpboard@gov.bc.ca
www.fpb.gov.bc.ca
Chair, Bruce Fraser
British Columbia's Forest Practices Board is responsible for reporting to the government & public about compliance with the Forest & Range Practices Act. The Board engages in the following activities: Investigation of public complaints; Undertaking special investigations; Auditing forest practices of government, government enforcement of the Forest & Range Practices Act, & licence holders on public lands; Participation in appeals; & Provision of reports & recommendations.
• Forestry Innovation Investments(FII)
#1200, 1130 West Pender St.
Vancouver, BC V6E 4A4
604-685-7507
Fax: 604-685-5373
info@bcfii.ca
www.bcfii.ca
Chief Executive Officer, Ken Baker
British Columbia's Forestry Innovation Investment strives to support a prosperous & environmentally sustainable forest economy in the province. The role of the organization includes the following activities: Promotion of British Columbia's forest practices & wood products to international markets; Working in partnership with the forestry sector, the Government of British Columbia, & the Government of Canada; & Assisting the forestry sector with issues such as Mountain Pine Beetle outbreak.
• Timber Export Advisory Committee
1520 Blanshard St., 2nd Fl.
PO Box 9514 Prov Govt
Victoria, BC V8W 9C2
250-387-8916
Fax: 250-387-5050
Secretary, John R. Cook

British Columbia Timber Sales
727 Fisgard St., 3rd Fl.
PO Box 9510 Prov Govt
Victoria, BC V8W 9C2
250-387-1261
Fax: 250-356-6209
Forests.BCTimberSalesHQOffice@gov.bc.ca
www.for.gov.bc.ca/bcts/
Assistant Deputy Minister BC Timber Sales, Dave Peterson
Director Operations, Mike Falkiner
250-387-8309
Acting Director Business Operations, Jerry Kennah
250-387-8643
Director Forestry, Jim Sutherland
250-356-1473

Corporate Services
1520 Blanshard St., 3rd Fl.
PO Box 9525 Prov Govt
Victoria, BC V8W 9C3
250-387-1300
Fax: 250-953-3687
Forests.CorporateServicesExecutiveOffice@gov.bc.ca
Assistant Deputy Minister, Joan Elangovan
Chief Information Officer Information Management, Guy Gondor
250-387-8400, Fax: 250-387-5132
Forests.InformationManagementGroup@gov.bc.ca
Executive Director Organizational Development, Shelagh Ryan-McNee
250-387-9016, Fax: 250-387-9086
Acting Director Finance & Management Services, Mary Myers
250-356-6624, Fax: 250-387-8818
Forests.FinanceandManagementServicesBranch@gov.bc.ca
Acting Director Strategic Policy & Planning, Rick Brand
250-356-6675, Fax: 250-356-7903
Forests.StrategicPolicyAndPlanningBranchOffice@gov.bc.ca
Director Strategic Corporate Initiatives, Sue Stephen
250-387-2248, Fax: 250-356-7903

Forest Stewardship
1520 Blanshard St., 3rd Fl.
PO Box 9525 Prov Govt
Victoria, BC V8W 9C3
250-387-1296
Fax: 250-953-3687
Forests.ForestStewardshipExecutiveOffice@gov.bc.ca
Chief Forester, Jim Snetsinger
Deputy Chief Forester, Craig Sutherland
Acting Director Climate Change & Forest Carbon, Dale Draper
250-217-7735, Fax: 250-356-8124
Forests.ClimateChangeandForestCarbon@gov.bc.ca
Director Forest Analysis & Inventory, Melanie Boyce
250-356-5958, Fax: 250-387-5999
Forests.ForestAnalysisBranchOffice@gov.bc.ca
Acting Director Forest Practices, Lorne Bedford
250-387-8901, Fax: 250-387-1467
Forests.ForestPracticesBranchOffice@gov.bc.ca
Director Research, Gerry Still
250-387-6579, Fax: 250-387-0046
Forests.ResearchBranchOffice@gov.bc.ca
Director Tree Improvement, Brian Barber
250-356-0888, Fax: 250-356-8124
Forests.TreeImprovementBranchOffice@gov.bc.ca
Ministry Librarian BC Ministry of Forests & Range Library, Pamela Wilkins
250-387-2169, Fax: 250-953-3079
Forests.Library@gov.bc.ca
Coordinator Provincial Bark Beetle, Rod DeBoice
250-371-3734

Operations
1520 Blanshard St., 3rd Fl.
PO Box 9525 Prov Govt
Victoria, BC V8W 9C3
250-387-1236
Fax: 250-953-3687
Forests.OperationsDivisionExecutiveOffice@gov.bc.ca
Assistant Deputy Minister, Tim R. Sheldan
Executive Director Operations, Peter Fuglem
250-387-1236
Director Forest Worker Safety, Mark Vieweg
250-356-9287
Director Protection Program, Brian Simpson
250-356-1068, Fax: 250-387-5685
Forests.ProtectionBranchOffice@gov.bc.ca

Director Range, David Borth
250-371-3827, Fax: 250-828-4987

Coast
2100 Labieux Rd.
Nanaimo, BC V9T 6E9
250-751-7001
Fax: 250-751-7190
Forests.CoastRegionOffice@gov.bc.ca
www.for.gov.bc.ca/rco
Regional Executive Director, Jim Gowriluk
250-751-7163

Northern Interior
1011 - 4 Ave., 5th Fl.
Prince George, BC V2L 3H9
250-565-6100
Fax: 250-565-6671
www.for.gov.bc.ca/rni
Forests.NorthernInteriorRegionOffice@gov.bc.ca
Regional Executive Director, Bill I. Warner
250-565-6102

Southern Interior
515 Columbia St.
Kamloops, BC V2C 2T7
250-828-4131
Fax: 250-828-4154
Forests.SouthernInteriorRegionOffice@gov.bc.ca
www.for.gov.bc.ca/rsi
Regional Executive Director, T.P. (Phil) Zacharatos
250-828-4120

Tenure & Revenue
1520 Blanshard St., 3rd Fl.
PO Box 9525 Prov Govt
Victoria, BC V8W 9C3
250-387-3656
Fax: 250-953-3687
Forests.TenureRevenueExecutiveOffice@gov.bc.ca
Assistant Deputy Minister, Bob S. Friesen
Director Aboriginal Affairs, Darrell A. Robb
250-387-6719, Fax: 250-356-6076
Forests.AboriginalAffairsBranchOffice@gov.bc.ca
Director Resource Tenures & Engineering, Jim Langridge
250-387-8300, Fax: 250-387-6445
Forests.ResourceTenuresAndEngineeringBranchOffice@gov.bc.ca

Forest Analysis & Inventory Branch
1520 Blanshard St, 1st Fl.
Victoria, BC V8W 3J9
250-365-5947
Fax: 250-953-3838
Director, Melanie Boyce

Forest Practices Branch
727 Fisgard St., 9th Fl.
Victoria, BC V8W 3E7
Policy & procedures for forest planning, timber supply, resource management, & public involvement; collects grazing & hay-cutting fees; maintains inventory; administers weed control & soil conservation services; monitors resource use; audits the forest wilderness & recreation resources & plans for various uses.
Director, Ralph Archibald
250-387-3541, Fax: 250-387-2136

Research Branch
712 Yates St.
Victoria, BC V8W 3E7
The Research Branch is part of the Forest Sciences Program & provides scientific basis for forest practices & policy decisions in BC. The branch has provided forest research for nearly 75 years in varied disciplines such as forest productivity, ecology, soil science, wildlife biology, hydrology, tree genetics, fisheries, & growth & yield. Over 55 scientists & technicians from the Research Branch work in Victoria, regional & district offices, & research stations. 40 scientists & technicians in Regional Forest Sciences Groups comprise the remainder of the Forest Sciences Program. The focus of the Branch is on program leadership, conducting research with province-wide application, & supporting the mandate of the Chief Forester & Forestry Division. Each Forest Region also shares part of the Forest Sciences Program & maintains a Regional Forest Sciences Group, which conducts locally relevant research & provides specialized technical advice to operational decision-makers.
Acting Director, Barrie Philips
250-387-6642, Fax: 250-387-0046

Federal/Provincial Government / Government of British Columbia

Research Scientist, Dr. W. Binder

Tree Improvement Branch
722 Johnson St.
Victoria, BC V8W 1N1
250-387-8939
Fax: 250-356-8124
Tree Improvement Branch core business functions undertake to protect, manage & improve public land genetic assets & to set the required standards for forest practices influencing these genetic assets.
Director, Dale Draper
250-387-3179

Compliance & Enforcement
1520 Blanshard St., 1st Fl.
Victoria, BC V8W 3C8
250-356-9841
Fax: 250-350-2539
Ensures that forestry laws are being followed in BC's public forests, & takes action where there is non-compliance. C&E staff enforce forest management laws & combat forest crimes such as theft, arson & mischief. Officials conduct more than 16,000 inspections a year to assess compliance with forest laws. Where there is evidence of a contravention, an investigation is conducted, which may lead to the issuance of a violation ticket, penalty or other enforcement action. The most serious forest crimes are prosecuted through the court system.
Director, Dan Graham

Aboriginal Affairs
Coordinates & develops policies, initiatives & support to First Nations' issues as they pertain to forest management. Ensures that existing aboriginal & treaty rights are acknowledged & respected in Ministry legislation, policies & programs & that current case law is reflected in the Ministry's business.
Director, Darrell Robb
250-387-6719

Economics & Trade
Responsible for changes to methods of pricing of timber; log export policy; analyses regarding the forest industry; provides advice to individuals & forest companies considering investing in the province.
Acting Director, Jim Gowriluk
250-356-8610

Resource Tenure & Engineering
1675 Douglas St., 2nd Fl.
Victoria, BC V8W 2G5
Fax: 250-387-6445
Primary business is timber tenure administration & road access management.
Director, Jim Langridge
250-387-8300

Ministry of Health Services

1515 Blanshard St.
Victoria, BC V8W 3C8
250-952-1742
Fax: 250-356-9587
800-465-4911
hlth.health@gems1.gov.bc.ca
www.gov.bc.ca/healthservices
Other Communication: Media Relations Phone: 250-952-1887; Fax: 250-952-1883
The Ministry of Health Services is responsible for guiding & enhancing British Columbia's health system. The goal of the Ministry is to improve health care & ensure that citizens of the province have access to the care they require, when they need it.

Acts Administered:
Access to Abortion Services Act
Anatomy Act
BC Benefits (Income Assistance) Act
Community Care Facility Act
Continuing Care Act
Drinking Water Protection Act
Forensic Psychiatry Act
Health Act
Health Hazard Regulation
Industrial Camps Health Regulations
Sanitary Regulations
Sewage Disposal Regulations
Sewage System Regulation
West Nile Virus Control Regulations
Health Authorities Act
Health Care (Consent) & Care Facility (Admission) Act (not in force)
Health Emergency Act
Health Emergency Regulation
Health Special Account Act
Hearing Aid Act
Hospital Act
Hospital District Act
Hospital Insurance Act
Human Tissue Gift Act
Marriage Act
Meat Inspection Act
Mental Health Act
Milk Industry Act
Ministry of Health Act
Name Act
Tobacco Sales Act
Vital Statistics Act
Wills Act (Part II)
Minister, Hon. George Abbott
250-953-3547, Fax: 250-356-9587
hlth.health@gov.bc.ca; george.abbott.mla@leg.bc.ca
Deputy Minister, Gordon Macatee
250-952-1911, Fax: 250-952-1909
hlth.dmoffice@gov.bc.ca
Executive Director Program Integration, Jan Wheeler
250-952-1410
• Hospital Appeal Board(HAB)
747 Fort St., 4th Fl.
PO Box 9425 Prov Govt
Victoria, BC V8W 9V1
250-387-3464
Fax: 250-356-9923
800-663-7867
hab@gov.bc.ca
www.hab.gov.bc.ca
Chair, Derek A. Brindle
The Hospital Appeal Board of British Columbia is an independent, quasi-judicial administrative appeal tribunal, which was created by the Hospital Act. The Board provides an appeal process for medical practitioners. The role of the Board is to review hospital board of management decisions concerning hospital privileges. Board members are appointed by British Columbia's Minister of Health.
• Medical Services Commission(MSC)
1515 Blanshard St., 3rd Fl.
Victoria, BC V8W 3C8
250-952-3073
Fax: 250-952-3131
www.health.gov.bc.ca/msp/legislation/msc.html

Corporate Policy, Legislation, & Intergovernmental Relations
1515 Blanshard St., 5th Fl.
Victoria, BC V8W 3C8
250-952-2165
Fax: 250-952-2109

Financial & Corporate Services
1515 Blanshard St., 4th Fl.
Victoria, BC V8W 3C8
250-952-2067
Fax: 250-952-1573

Health Authorities
1515 Blanshard St., 6th Fl.
Victoria, BC V8W 3C8
250-952-1049
Fax: 250-952-1052

Vital Statistics
818 Fort St.
Victoria, BC V8W 1H8
250-952-2681
Fax: 250-952-2587
www.vs.gov.bc.ca
For a certificate of a registration or record: $25 per copy. For each search for one registration or record for each three-year period or fraction thereof over which the search is conducted: $25.

Health Sector Information Management / Information Technology
1515 Blanshard St., 7th Fl.
Victoria, BC V8W 3C8
250-952-2563
Fax: 250-952-1827

Health System Planning
1515 Blanshard St., 3rd Fl.
Victoria, BC V8W 3C8
250-952-3465
Fax: 250-952-3131

Medical Services
1515 Blanshard St., 3rd Fl.
Victoria, BC V8W 3C8
250-952-3465
Fax: 250-952-3131

Pharmaceutical Services
1515 Blanshard St., 3rd Fl.
Victoria, BC V8W 3C8
250-952-1859
Fax: 250-952-1584

Social Development Policy Office
1515 Blanshard St., 2nd Fl.
Victoria, BC V8W 3C8
250-952-1112
Fax: 250-952-1186
Executive Director, John Phillips
250-952-1432, Fax: 250-952-1186

System Evaluation & Accountability Office
1483 Douglas St., 5th Fl.
Victoria, BC V8W 3K4
250-952-1109
Fax: 250-356-6221

Health Protection
250-952-1433
Fax: 250-952-1713
Provides advocacy & leadership in the development & management of appropriate strategies to minimize environmental health risks to the public. Services include: food safety & monitoring; drinking water & recreational pool safety & monitoring; environmental contaminants & waste disposal concerns; institutional monitoring; public health bylaw approval coordination.
Executive Director, Kersteen Johnston
250-952-1110

British Columbia Hydro

333 Dunsmuir St., 18th Fl.
Vancouver, BC V6B 5R3
604-224-9376
Fax: 604-623-4467
800-224-9376
www.bchydro.com
BC Hydro is a provincial Crown corporation. It reports to the Minister of Energy & Mines, & is regulated by the British Columbia Utilities Commission. BC Hydro is engaged in the generation & distribution of electricity throughout British Columbia. It strives to provide these services in an environmentally & socially responsible manner. On behalf of BC Hydro, BC Transmission Corporation facilitates the transmission of electricity.
Chair, Mossadiq S. Umedaly
President/CEO, Robert G. Elton
Senior Vice-President Engineering, Aboriginal Relations & Generation, Chris O'Riley
Chief Officer Safety, Health, & Environment, Ray Stewart
Chief Officer Human Resources, Debbie Nagle
• Powerex Corp.
#1400, 666 Burrard St.
Vancouver, BC V6C 2X8
604-891-5000
Fax: 604-801-6060
800-220-4907
customer.service@bchydro.com
www.powerex.com
Other Communication: Toronto Location, Phone: 416-345-8854
President/CEO, Teresa Conway
A wholly-owned subsidiary of BC Hydro, Powerex Corp. markets wholesale energy products & services to utilities, power pools, industrials, & power marketers in North America, particularly western Canada, the western United States.
• Powertech Labs Inc.
12388 - 88 Ave.
Surrey, BC V8W 7R7
604-590-7500
Fax: 604-590-5347

info@powertechlans.com
www.powertechlabs.com
President/COO, Eamonn Percy
A wholly owned subsidiary of BC Hydro, Powertech Labs offers environmental, mechanical, electrical, metallurgical, civil, chemical, gas technologies, & structural engineering to deal with technical problems with power equipment & systems.

Ministry of Labour, Citizens' Services & Open Government
PO Box 9052 Prov Govt
Victoria, BC V8W 9E2
250-356-6348
Fax: 250-356-6595
LCS.Minister@gov.bc.ca
www.gov.bc.ca/citz
Other Communication: Employment Standards Inquiries: 1-800-663-3316, 250-612-4100 (Prince George area)
Responsibilities of the Ministry of Labour include the following: Labour relations; Employment standards; Workers' Compensation Act; Occupational health & safety; Chief Information Officer; Information & privacy; Alternative Service Delivery Secretariat; Queen's Printer; Solutions BC; BC Stats; BC Internet Services; BC Online; Enquiry BC; BC Bid; Enquiry BC; & Canada-BC Business Service Centre.
Acts Administered:
BC Online Act
Business Number Act (s. 10.1)
Coastal Forest Industry Dispute Settlement Act
Community Services Labour Relations Act
Document Disposal Act
Education Services Collective Agreement Act
Electronic Transactions Act
Employment Standards Act
Fire & Police Services Collective Bargaining Act
Fire Department Act
Fishing Collective Bargaining Act
Freedom of Information and Protection of Privacy Act
Labour Relations Code
Legislative Assembly Management Committee Act
Legislative Assembly Privilege Act
Legislative Library Act
Legislative Procedure Review Act
Members' Remuneration & Pensions Act
Ministry of Labour Act (except in relation to gas safety, electrical safety, elevating devices, boiler & pressure vessel safety)
Ministry of Provincial Secretary & Government Services Act (ss. 1, 2 (4) & 4)
Personal Information Protection Act
Procurement Services Act
Public Agency Accommodation Act
Queen's Printer Act
Statistics Act
Workers' Compensation Act
Minister, Hon. Stephanie Cadieux
250-387-2283, Fax: 250-387-4312
stephanie.cadieux.mla@leg.bc.ca
Deputy Minister, Robert Lapper
250-387-3914, Fax: 250-356-5186
SDL.DeputyMinister@gems3.gov.bc.ca
• British Columbia Labour Relations Board
Oceanic Plaza
#600, 1066 West Hastings St.
Vancouver, BC V6E 3X1
604-660-1300
Fax: 604-660-1892
information@lrb.bc.ca
www.lrb.bc.ca
Chair, Brent Mullin
The British Columbia Labour Relations Board is an independent, administrative tribunal. The Board is responsible for mediating & adjudicating employment & labour relations matters related to unionized workplaces.
• Employment Standards Tribunal
Oceanic Plaza
#650, 1066 West Hastings St.
Vancouver, BC V6E 3X1
604-775-3512
Fax: 604-775-3372
registrar.est@bcest.bc.ca
www.bcest.bc.ca
Chair, Brent Mullin
Established under the Employment Standards Act, the Employment Standards Tribunal operates as an administrative tribunal. The responsibility of the Tribunal is to provide an independent appeal of Determinations made by the Director of Employment Standards.
• Workers' Compensation Appeal Tribunal(WCAT)
#150, 4600 Jacombs Rd.
Richmond, BC V6V 3B1
604-664-7800
Fax: 604-664-7898
800-663-2782
www.wcat.bc.ca
Chair, Jill Callan
The Workers' Compensation Appeal Tribunal of British Columbia is an independent appeal tribunal, which was established by the Workers Compensation Amendment Act (No. 2), 2002. The Tribunal decides appeals from workers & employers from decisions of the Workers' Compensation Board (WorkSafeBC).
• Workers' Compensation Board

Alternative Service Delivery Secretariat
548 Michigan St.
PO Box 9438 Prov Govt
Victoria, BC V8W 9V3
250-387-1911
Fax: 250-356-2805
Assistant Deputy Minister, John Bethel
250-387-4503, Fax: 250-952-8299
Executive Director New Business Development & Acting Executive Director, Alliance Support, Wayne Powell
250-387-1911
Executive Director Solutions Development, Dave Bacharach
250-217-4788

Chief Information Office
4000 Seymour Pl.
PO Box 9412 Prov Govt
Victoria, BC V8W 9V1
250-356-7970
Fax: 250-387-1940
www.cio.gov.bc.ca
Chief Information Officer, Dave Nikolejsin
250-387-8509
Executive Director Advanced Communication & Collaboration Services, Gary Cooney
250-387-5975
Executive Director Architecture & Standards, Bob Duggan
250-387-8583
Executive Director Community & External Initiatives, Wilf R. Bangert
250-387-9637
Executive Director Cross Government Information Management / Information Technology Initiatives, Peter Watkins
250-387-2184
Executive Director Cross Government Research, Policy & Practice, Wendy Taylor
250-952-6161, Fax: 250-356-1182
Executive Director Finance, Matt Mannix
250-356-8321
Executive Director Information Management / Information Governance, Bruce Cuthbert
250-387-2194, Fax: 250-952-6250
Acting Executive Director Information Security, Rob Todd
250-387-8823
Executive Director Intergration Infrastructure Program, Don Henkelman
604-660-6442

Client Services
525 Superior St., 2nd Fl.
PO Box 9472 Prov Govt
Victoria, BC V8W 9W6
250-952-6861
Fax: 250-952-6803
Assistant Deputy Minister, Trish Shwart
Executive Director Coordinated Client Relationship Management Program, Bobbi Plecas
250-952-6952, Fax: 250-387-0380
Executive Director Strategic Planning, Operations, & Development, Gary Swift
250-952-6841
Lead Client Services Integration, Ron Colquhoun
250-387-3890, Fax: 250-387-4722
WTS.ClientServices@gov.bc.ca; Ron.Colquhoun@gov.bc.ca

Common Business Services
548 Michigan St, 2nd Fl.
PO Box 9451 Prov Govt
Victoria, BC V8W 9V7
250-356-5846
Fax: 250-387-1399
Assistant Deputy Minister, Richard Poutney
Executive Director Strategic Acquisitions & Intellectual Property, Frank Hudson
250-356-0843, Fax: 250-356-0846
SATP@gov.bc.ca; Frank.Hudson@gov.bc.ca
Executive Director Corporate Accounting Services, Nashater Sanghera
250-356-9116, Fax: 250-953-3352
Queen's Printer for British Columbia & Executive Director Procurement & Supply Services (P&SS), Vern Burkhardt
250-356-9969, Fax: 250-387-0388
Vern.Burkhardt@gov.bc.ca
Other Communications: URL:www.pss.gov.bc.ca; Customer Service: 250-387-3309

Service BC
548 Michigan St., 2nd Fl.
PO Box 9804 Prov Govt
Victoria, BC V8W 9W1
604-660-2421
Fax: 250-387-5633
800-663-7867
TDD: 800-661-8773
EnquiryBC@gov.bc.ca
www.servicebc.gov.bc.ca
Other Communication: Service BC Contact Centre - Enquiry BC, Victoria Phone: 387-6121; Outside B.C. Phone: 604-660-2421; Metro Vancouver TTY: 604-775-0303
Service BC provides frontline government services & information. Citizens in British Columbia are assisted in accessing services they need. These programs & services are available in person, by phone, & online. Service BC Centres are located in 59 places throughout British Columbia. The following are examples of services offered by Service BC: Doing business in B.C.; Education; Employment & labour standards; Exploring B.C.; Fees & payments; Health; Land & property; Legal services; License & registration; Life events; Living in B.C.; Reports & publications; & Taxation.
Assistant Deputy Minister Service BC, Lois Fraser
250-387-4823
Executive Director Online Channel Office, Laurie Barker
250-953-3679, Fax: 250-387-2144
Executive Director Service Solutions & Planning, Deborah Ainsworth
250-387-8574, Fax: 250-387-9843
Executive Director BC Stats, Don McRae
250-356-2119, Fax: 250-387-0380
BC.Stats@gov.bc.ca; Don.McRae@gov.bc.ca
Other Communications: URL: www.bcstats.gov.bc.ca
Executive Director Service Delivery Operations, Bette-Jo Hughes
250-356-2031, Fax: 250-387-5633
Other Communications: URL: www.governmentagents.gov.bc.ca
Regional Director Service Delivery Operations, Northwest Service BC Centre, Perry Slump
250-565-6001, Fax: 250-992-4314
Customer Service Representative Service Delivery Operations, Vancouver Island / South Coast Service BC Centre, Jason Bell
250-741-3636, Fax: 250-741-3663

Strategic Infrastructure
548 Michigan St, 2nd Fl.
PO Box 9438 Prov Govt
Victoria, BC V8W 9V3
250-387-4632
Fax: 250-356-2805
Assistant Deputy Minister Strategic Infrastructure, Wayne Jensen
250-387-4524, Fax: 250-387-9332
Executive Director Business Planning & Development Services, Gary Lakusta
250-387-7849, Fax: 250-387-9332
Executive Director Strategic Telecommunications Services, Roman Mateyko
250-387-7915, Fax: 250-387-3623

Workplace Technology Services
4000 Seymour Pl.
PO Box 9412 Prov Govt
Victoria, BC V8W 9V1

Federal/Provincial Government / Government of British Columbia

250-387-0672
Fax: 250-387-5693
Assistant Deputy Minister Workplace Technology Services, Jill Kot
Jill.Kot@gov.bc.ca
Executive Director Business Strategy & Planning Services, Brian Bowman
250-387-9533, Fax: 250-387-5693
Executive Director Client Services, Sue Goldsmith
250-387-4821, Fax: 250-387-5693
Executive Director Workplace Application Services, Randy Fehr
250-387-8083
Acting Executive Director Workplace Communication Services, Workstations, Steve Banks
250-953-3637, Fax: 250-387-8419
Acting Executive Director Workplace Communication Services, Communications,
250-387-9322, Fax: 250-387-8419
Executive Director Workplace Hosting Services, Nelson Lah
250-356-5600

British Columbia Provincial Emergency Program (PEP)

PO Box 9201 Prov Govt
Victoria, BC V8W 9J1
250-952-4913
Fax: 250-952-4888
888-257-4777
www.pep.gov.bc.ca
Other Communication: Emergency Coordination Centre: 1-800-663-3456; Recovery & Funding Programs Phone: 250-952-5505
The Provincial Emergency Program (PEP) is a division of the Ministry of Public Safety & Solicitor General, Emergency Management BC. PEP works with local governments to provide the following training & support services for emergencies: Awareness & education to lessen the effects of emergencies; Promotion of preparedness for disasters, through planning & exercises; Coordination & assistance in response to emergencies; & Development & implementation of recovery measures.
Executive Director, Cam Filmer
Cam.Filmer@gov.bc.ca
Director Management Services & Programs, Steve Bachop
250-952-4892
Director Operations, Chris Duffy
250-952-4544

Ministry of Public Safety & Solicitor General

PO Box 9290 Prov Govt
Victoria, BC V8W 9J7
250-387-6121
800-663-7867
pssgwebfeedback@gov.bc.ca
www.gov.bc.ca/pssg
Other Communication: Public Affairs Bureau Phone: 250-356-6961, Fax: 250-387-1753; B.C. Coroners Service: 604-660-7745; Provincial Emergency Program: 250-952-4846
The goal of the Ministry of Public Safety & Solicitor General is the maintenance & enhancement of public safety in communities across British Columbia. The following are the key responsibilities of the Ministry: Crime prevention programs; Police & correctional services; Criminal record check & protection order registry; Victim assistance; Provincial emergency management; Emergency social services; Consumer services; & Gaming enforcement.
Acts Administered:
Attorney General Act (ss. 2(e), 5 & 6, as they relate to the powers, duties, & functions of the Minister of Public Safety & the Solicitor General)
BC Neurotrauma Fund Contribution Act
Business Practices & Consumer Protection Act
Business Practices & Consumer Protection Authority Act
Civil Forfeiture Act
Commercial Transport Act (ss. 2, 6, 7, 10, 13; & ss. 1, 4, 5, 8, 9, 11, 12 & 14, as they relate to affairs of the Insurance Corporation of British Columbia)
Coroners Act
Correction Act
Cremation, Interment & Funeral Services Act
Crime Victim Assistance Act
Criminal Injury Compensation Act
Criminal Records Review Act
Emergency Communications Corporations Act
Emergency Program Act
Fire Services Act (as it relates to the portfolio of the minister)
Firearm Act
Fireworks Act
Flood Relief Act
Food Donor Encouragement Act
Guide Animal Act
Insurance Corporation Act (Part 1)
Insurance (Vehicle) Act
Ministry of Consumer & Corporate Affairs Act (ss. 3 & 4(a), in relation to consumer affairs; s. 4(b)-(d))
Motion Picture Act
Motor Dealer Act
Motor Vehicle Act
Parental Responsibility Act
Police Act
Sale of Goods Act
Senior Citizen Automobile Insurance Grant Act
Sex Offender Registry Act
Special Accounts Appropriation & Control Act (ss. 7 & 10 (2) (a) & (b))
Victims of Crime Act
Minister, Hon. Shirley Bond
250-387-1978, Fax: 250-356-2290
shirley.bond.mla@leg.bc.ca
• British Columbia Office of the Police Complaint Commissioner
756 Fort St., 3rd Fl.
PO Box 9895 Prov Govt
Victoria, BC V8W 9T8
250-356-7458
Fax: 250-356-6503
800-663-7867
info@opcc.bc.ca
www.opcc.bc.ca
Other Communication: Vancouver Phone: 604-660-2385
Police Complaint Commissioner, Dirk Ryneveld, Q.C.
Established under the Police Act, the British Columbia Office of the Police Complaint Commissioner is an independent agency. The responsibility of the agency is overseeing complaints against municipal police & ensuring that these complaints are dealt with in a fair & impartial manner. The Office reports directly to the Legislature.
• Coroners Service of British Columbia
Metrotower II
#800, 4720 Kingsway
Burnaby, BC V5H 4N2
604-660-7745
Fax: 604-660-7766
BC.CorSer@gov.bc.ca
www.pssg.gov.bc.ca/coroners
Chief Coroner, Terry Smith
Governed by the Coroners Act, the Coroners Service of British Columbia investigates all unnatural, unexplained, unattended, or sudden & unexpected deaths. Based on its fact-finding, the agency recommends public safety improvements in order to prevent similar deaths.

Corrections Branch

1001 Douglas St., 7th Fl.
PO Box 9278 Prov Govt
Victoria, BC V8W 9J7
250-387-5059
Fax: 250-387-5698
www.pssg.gov.bc.ca/corrections
Other Communication: Adult Custody Phone: 250-387-5098; Community Corrections & Corporate Programs Phone: 250-356-7930
The Corrections Branch consists of the Adult Custody Division & the Community Corrections & Corporate Programs Division. The Adult Custody Division operates correctional centres for persons awaiting trial or serving a provincial custody sentence. The Community Corrections & Corporate Programs Division operates over fifty community corrections offices throughout British Columbia.

Emergency Management BC

525 Fort St., 2nd Fl.
PO Box 9223 Prov Govt
Victoria, BC V8W 9J1
250-953-4002
Fax: 250-953-4081
BC.CorSer@gov.bc.ca (Coroner); OFC@gov.bc.ca (Fire Commissioner)
www.pssg.gov.bc.ca/coroners; www.pssg.gov.bc.ca/firecom
Other Communication: Office of the Chief Coroner: 604-660-7745; Office of the Fire Commissioner Phone: 250-356-9000, Toll Free: 1-888-988-9488; Provincial Emergency Program: 250-952-4913
Emergency Management BC oversees the Coroners Service of British Columbia, the Office of the Fire Commissioner, & the Provincial Emergency Program (www.pep.bc.ca). B.C. Coroners Service investigates all unexpected, unnatural, unexplained, & unattended deaths in the province. Improvements to public safety & recommendations to prevent similar deaths are made by the Coroners Service. The Office of the Fire Commissioner administers & enforces fire safety legislation, trains local assistants to the fire commissioner, certifies fire fighters, provides public fire safety education, advises local governments, responds to major fires, & investigates fires. The Provincial Emergency Program provides training & support to local governments.
Associate Deputy Minister Emergency Management BC, Wes Shoemaker
250-953-4083

Finance & Administration Division

910 Government St., 5th Fl.
PO Box 9256 Prov Govt
Victoria, BC V8W 9J4
250-387-6856
Fax: 250-356-9185

Information Technology Services Division

910 Government St., 4th Fl.
PO Box 9262 Prov Govt
Victoria, BC V8W 9J4
250-356-8787
Fax: 250-356-7699

Liquor Distribution Branch

2625 Rupert St.
Vancouver, BC V5M 3T5
604-252-3000
Fax: 604-252-3026

Management Services Branch

910 Government St., 5th Fl.
PO Box 9256 Prov Govt
Victoria, BC V8W 9J4
250-387-5258
Fax: 250-387-0081

Office of the Superintendent of Motor Vehicles (OSMV)

940 Blanshard St.
PO Box 9254 Prov Govt
Victoria, BC V8W 9J2
250-387-7747
Fax: 250-387-4891
OSMV.Mailbox@gov.bc.ca
www.pssg.gov.bc.ca/osmv
The Office of the Superintendent of Motor Vehicles is responsible for regulating drivers in British Columbia. The following services are provided: Establishment & maintenance of standards for driving behaviour & medical fitness; Provision of an independent method of appeal of certain Insurance Corporation of British Columbia decisions; Scheduling & hearing evidence related to proposals by the Insurance Corporation of British Columbia concerning licences, driving training schools, & AirCare Certified repair facilities; & Reviewing driving prohibitions & vehicle impoundments imposed by police.

Policing & Community Safety Branch

1001 Douglas St., 10th Fl.
PO Box 9285
Victoria, BC V8W 9J7
250-387-1100
Fax: 250-356-7747
sgpcsb@gov.bc.ca; vsdvistimservices@gov.bc.ca
www.pssg.gov.bc.ca/victim_services
Other Communication: Victim Services Phone: 604-660-5199; VictimLINK: 1-800-563-0808
• British Columbia Assessment Authority(BCAA)
1537 Hillside Ave.
Victoria, BC V8T 4Y2
250-595-6211
Fax: 250-595-6222
info@bcassessment.ca
www.bcassessment.bc.ca
Executive Director, Laurie McAmmond
The British Columbia Assessment Authority is an independent, provincial Crown corporation. Governed by a Board of Directors,

the role of BC Assessment is the production of annual property assessments for each property owner in British Columbia. Area offices are located across the province.
• Small Business BC
#82, 601 West Cordova St.
Vancouver, BC V6B 1G1
800-775-5525
Fax: 604-775-5520
800-667-2272
TDD: 800-457-8466
askus@smallbusinessbc.ca
www.smallbusinessbc.ca

Ministry of Healthy Living & Sport
PO Box 9067 Prov Govt
Victoria, BC V8W 9E2
250-387-3504
Fax: 250-387-3420
Feedback@gov.bc.ca
www.gov.bc.ca/hls
Other Communication: Public Affairs Bureau Phone: 250-812-4012
The main responsibilities of the Ministry of Healthy Living & Sport are as follows: Aboriginal health promotion; ActNow BC; Addictions services promotion; Chronic disease prevention; Communicable diseases prevention; Dial-a-Dietician; Health promotion & protection; Healthy living; Provincial Health Officer; Provincial Nutritionist; Public health planning; Sports & recreation; Water & air monitoring & reporting; & Women & seniors.
Acts Administered:
Drinking Water Protection Act
Food Safety Act
Milk Industry Act (s. 12, except in respect of tank milk receiver licences)
Public Toilet Act
Special Accounts Appropriation & Control Act
Tobacco Control Act
Tobacco Damages & Health Care Costs Recovery Act
Venereal Disease Act
Minister Healthy Living & Sport, Hon. Mary Polak
mary.polak.mla@leg.bc.ca
Deputy Minister, Grant Main
250-952-1164, Fax: 250-952-1390
Executive Director Strategic Financial Services & Operations, Wes Boyd
• BC Games Society
990 Fort St.
Victoria, BC V8V 3K2
250-387-1375
Fax: 250-387-4489
info@bcgames.org
www.bcgames.org
Co-Chair, Wendy Ladner-Beaudry
The BC Games Society is incorporated under the Societies Act. With responsibility to British Columbia's Minister of Healthy Living & Sport, the Crown Agency works with its partners to provide event management leadership. The Society strives to create development opportunities for athletes, coaches, & officials, sport organizations, & host communities.

Office of the Provincial Health Officer
1515 Blanshard St., 4th Fl.
Victoria, BC V8W 3C8
250-952-1330
Fax: 250-952-1362
Provincial Health Officer, Dr. Perry Kendall
Perry.Kendall@gov.bc.ca
Deputy Provincial Health Officer, Dr. Eric Young
250-952-1329

Population & Public Health
1515 Blanshard St., 4th Fl.
Victoria, BC V8W 3C8
Assistant Deputy Minister, Andrew G. Hazlewood
Director, Margo, Ross
250-356-7168
Assistant Director, Graham McKay
250-356-0364

British Columbia Transmission Corporation
Four Bentall Centre
#1100, 1055 Dunsmuir St.
PO Box 49260
Vancouver, BC V7X 1V5
604-699-7300
Fax: 604-699-7333
866-647-3334
contact.us@bctc.com
www.bctc.com
Other Communication: Media inquiries: 604-699-7445; Customer Services: 604-699-7391; Settlements & Billing: 604-699-7383; Emergencies: 1-888-769-3766; Before Digging: 1-800-474-6886
The British Columbia Transmission Corporation is a provincial Crown corporation. In accordance with the Transmission Corporation Act, the Minister for the Crown holds 100 percent of the shares of the Corporation. Its main activities include the planning, operation, & maintenance of British Columbia's publicly-owned electrical transmission system.
President/CEO, Jane Peverett
Chief Financial Officer & Vice-President Corporate Services, Janet P. Woodruff
Vice-President System Operations, Martin Huang
Vice-President & General Counsel, John Irving
Vice-President Customer & Strategy Development, Doug Little
Vice-President Major Projects, Bruce Barrett
Vice-President System Planning & Asset Management, Julius Pataky
Director Human Resources, Scott oogemans

Ministry of Transportation & Infrastructure
940 Blanshard St.
PO Box 9850 Prov Govt
Victoria, BC V8W 9T5
250-387-3198
Fax: 250-356-7706
tran.webmaster@gov.bc.ca
www.gov.bc.ca/tran
In carrying out its mission to move people & goods safely in British Columbia, the Ministry of Transportation & Infrastructure is responsible for the following: Transportation planning & policy; Highway construction & maintenance; Commercial vehicle safety & inspections; Infrastructure grants; & Port & airport development.
Acts Administered:
British Columbia Rail Benefits (First Nations) Trust Act
British Columbia Railway Act
British Columbia Transit Act
Coastal Ferry Act (Parts 1-3; & ss. 71, & 74-77)
Commercial Transport Act (s. 3; ss. 1, 4, 5, 8, 9, 11, & 12, as they relate to highway infrastructure & weigh scales; & ss. 1, 4, 5, 8, 9, 11, 12, & 14, as they relate to Commercial Vehicle Safety & E
Industrial Roads Act
Land Title Act (s. 77.2)
Motor Vehicle Act (ss. 116.1, 118.94-118.992, 119-125.1, 126-135.1, 136-148.1, 149-169.1, 170-182, 185-209, 212-212.2, 213, 214, 216-218, 219, 223, 237, 239-240; ss. 1, 75-76, 78, 83, 83.1, 183 & 210;
Passenger Transportation Act
Public Works Agreement Act
Railway Act (ss. 1-5, 14-27, 30, 32, 34-63, 135, 136, 138, 161, 180, 183, 185 (1), (2) & (5)-(10), 186, 187, 197 (1)-(6), 198, 204-207, 225, 229-232, 253, 255-257, & 282)
Railway Safety Act
Significant Projects Streamlining Act
South Coast British Columbia Transportation Authority Act
Transport of Dangerous Goods Act
Transportation Act
Transportation Investment Act
Minister, Hon. Kevin Falcon
250-387-1978, Fax: 250-356-2290
Minister.Transportation@gov.bc.ca; kevin.falcon.mla@leg.bc.ca
Deputy Minister, John Dyble
250-387-3280, Fax: 250-387-6431
DeputyMinister.Transportation.gov.bc.ca
• British Columbia Ferry Services Inc.
• British Columbia Transit
520 Gorge Rd. East
PO Box 610
Victoria, BC V8W 2P3
250-385-2551
Fax: 250-995-5639
www.bctransit.com
Chair, Kevin Mahoney
A provincial crown agency, BC Transit coordinates the delivery of public transportation in British Columbia, outside the Greater Vancouver Regional District. The corporation's specific role, in accordance with the BC Transit Act, is the planning, acquisition, construction, operation, & maintenance of public passenger transportation systems & rail systems.
• Passenger Transportation Board
#202, 940 Blanshard St.
PO Box 9850 Prov Govt
Victoria, BC V8W 9T5
250-953-3777
Fax: 250-953-3788
ptboard@gov.bc.ca
www.ptboard.bc.ca
Chair, Dennis Day
The Passenger Transportation Board carries out its responsibilities in accordance with the Passenger Transportation Act. The independent tribunal makes decisions regarding the operation of passenger directed vehicles and inter-city buses in British Columbia.

Finance & Management Services Department
#5B, 940 Blanshard St.
PO Box 9850
Victoria, BC V8W 9T5
250-387-3100
Fax: 250-387-5012
Assistant Deputy Minister Finance & Management Services, Sheila A. Taylor
Director Transit, Jim Hester
250-387-6024, Fax: 250-387-3059
Chief Information Officer & Director Information Management, Bob Buckingham
250-953-3111, Fax: 250-356-7184

Highways Department
940 Blanshard St.
PO Box 9850
Victoria, BC V8W 9T5
250-387-3260
Fax: 250-387-6431
Assistant Deputy Minister, Mike Proudfoot
Executive Director Properties & Business Management, John Dowler
250-387-7767, Fax: 250-356-8767
Director Commercial Vehicle Safety & Enforcement, Greg Gilks
250-953-4024, Fax: 250-952-0578
Regional Director South Coast Regional Office, Tracy Cooper
604-660-8205, 877-660-8218, Fax: 604-660-0350
Tracy.Cooper@gov.bc.ca
Regional Director Southern Interior Regional Office, Kevin Richter
250-828-4220, Fax: 250-828-4204
Kevin.Richter@gov.bc.ca
Regional Director Northern Regional Office, Shanna Mason
250-565-6479, Fax: 250-565-6065
Deputy Director Commercial Vehicle Safety & Enforcement, Dawn Major
250-953-4024, Fax: 250-952-0578
Chief Engineer, Dirk Nyland
250-387-2310, Fax: 250-387-7735

Partnerships Department
#5A, 940 Blanshard St.
PO Box 9850 Prov Govt
Victoria, BC V8W 9T5
250-356-0517
Fax: 250-387-6431
Assistant Deputy Minister, Frank Blasetti
250-356-1403,
Frank.Blasetti@gov.bc.ca
Executive Director Gateway Program, Geoff Freer
604-775-0489, Fax: 604-775-0348
Executive Project Director Sea to Sky Highway Improvement Project, Peter Milburn
604-775-1152, Fax: 604-775-1144
Acting Director Partnership & Project Development, Bob Steele
250-356-2051, Fax: 250-356-2112
Director Operations Transitions & Procurement, Bruce McAllister
250-356-7108, Fax: 250-356-2112

Transportation Planning & Policy Department
#5C, 940 Blanshard St.
PO Box 9850 Prov Govt
Victoria, BC V8W 9T5
250-387-5062
Fax: 250-387-6431
Assistant Deputy Minister, Sandra Carroll
Sandra.Carroll@gov.bc.ca

Executive Director Infrastructure Development, Kirk Handrahan
250-952-0678, Fax: 250-952-0688
Executive Director Pacific Gateway, Lisa Gow
250-387-2672, Fax: 250-387-5812
Executive Director Planning & Programming, David Marr
250-356-2100, Fax: 250-953-4974
Director Highway Planning, Jim Hester
250-387-6024
Director Project Management Support Services, Svein Haugen
250-356-0515, Fax: 250-953-4974
Director Transportation Policy, Kirsten Pedersen
250-387-0882, Fax: 250-356-0897
Director Project Delivery, Border Infrastructure Program, John Bodnarchuk
250-751-3287, Fax: 250-953-4975
Director & Registrar Passenger Transportation, Tom Greene
604-453-4278, 888-453-4280,Fax: 604-453-4253
passengertransportationbr@gov.bc.ca; Tom.Greene@gov.bc.ca
Other Communications: URL: www.th.gov.bc.ca/rpt
Deputy Registrar & Manager Business Standards & Planning, Passenger Transportation, Doris Sundquist
604-453-4235, 888-453-4280,Fax: 604-453-4253
passengertransportationbr@gov.bc.ca

British Columbia Utilities Commission
900 Howe St., 6th Fl.
PO Box 250
Vancouver, BC V6Z 2N3
604-660-4700
Fax: 604-660-1102
800-663-1385
commission.secretary@bcuc.com
www.bcuc.com
The British Columbia Utilities Commission is an independent regulatory agency of the Provincial Government of British Columbia. The Commission's regulates the province's natural gas & electricity utilities. Other activities of the Utilities Commission include the regulation of universal compulsory automobile insurance & intra-provincial pipelines.
Acts Administered:
Utilities Commission Act
Chair/CEO, Len Kelsey
604-660-4757
Commission Secretary, Erica Hamilton
604-660-4727,
commission.secretary@bcuc.com; Erica.Hamilton@bcuc.com
Director Strategic Services, James W. Fraser
604-660-4740
Director Rates & Finance, Philip W. Nakoneshny
604-660-4736
Director Engineering & Energy Markets, J. Brian Williston
604-660-4773

Workers' Compensation Board of British Columbia
PO Box 5350 Terminal
Vancouver, BC V6B 5L5
604-276-3100
Fax: 604-244-6490
888-621-7233
www.worksafebc.com
Other Communication: Head Office Physical Address: 6951 Westminster Hwy., Richmond; Health care benefits: 604-276-3085; Employer Service Centre: 604-244-6181; Compensation: 604-231-8888
The Workers' Compensation Board of British Columbia, or WorkSafeBC, assists workers & employers in British Columbia by promoting health & safety in workplaces. WorkSafeBC's key repsonsiblities are as follows: Consultation with & education of employers & workers; Monitoring compliance with the Occupational Health & Safety Regulation; & Provision of return-to-work compensation, rehabilitation, health care benefits, & other services for parties affected by work-related injuries or diseases.
Chair, Roslyn Kunin
President/CEO, David Anderson
Chief Financial Officer Finance Division, Steve Barnett
Vice-President Human Resources & Facilities, Pamela Cohen
Vice-President Policy, Investigations & Review, Roberta Ellis
Vice-President Worker & Employer Services, Diana Miles
General Counsel & Secretary, Ed Bates

Government of Manitoba
Seat of Government: Legislative Building, Rm. 237
Winnipeg, MB R3C 0V8
204-945-3636
Fax: 204-948-2507
clerkla@leg.gov.mb.ca
www.gov.mb.ca
The Province of Manitoba entered Confederation July 15, 1870. It has an area of 647,797 km2, & the StatsCan census population in 2008 was 1,196,291.

Manitoba Aboriginal & Northern Affairs
59 Elizabeth Dr.
PO Box 37
Thompson, MB R8N 1X4
204-677-6607
Fax: 204-677-6753
amartin@gov.mb.ca
www.gov.mb.ca/ana/
To improve the quality of life & opportunities for Aboriginal & Northern people. To facilitate better services, opportunities & results for Manitoba's Aboriginal & northern people. Goals are: to support the mental, emotional, physical & spiritual health of northern communities & Aboriginal people; to resolve outstanding provincial obligations to Aboriginal/northern communities; to foster self-determination, accountability & sustainable growth; to strengthen the participation of Aboriginal & northern people in Manitoba's economy
Acts Administered:
Northern Affairs Act
Planning Act
Minister, Hon. Oscar Lathlin
204-945-3719, Fax: 204-954-8374
minna@leg.gov.mb.ca
Deputy Minister, Harvey Bostrom
204-945-0565, Fax: 204-945-1256
dmna@leg.gov.mb.ca
Executive Director Aboriginal Affairs Secretariat, Joe Morrisseau
204-945-3689
• Communities Economic Development Fund
#100, 23 Station Rd.
Thompson, MB R8N 0N6
204-778-4138
Fax: 204-778-4313
800-561-4315
www.cedf.mb.ca

Aboriginal Affairs Secretariat
#200, 500 Portage Ave.
Winnipeg, MB R3C 3X1
204-945-2510
Fax: 204-945-3689

Agreements Management
#200, 500 Portage Ave.
Winnipeg, MB R3C 3X1
204-945-8337
Fax: 204-945-3689

Local Government Development Division
59 Elizabeth Dr.
PO Box 33
Thompson, MB R8N 1X4
204-677-6794
Fax: 204-677-6525
Provides support to 50 northern & remote communities, including public works, environmental services, infrastructure development. Promotes cooperative, community-driven sustainable development
Executive Director, Freda Albert
204-677-6795,
falbert@gov.mb.ca
Director Program Planning & Development, Jeff Gordon
204-945-1713,
jgordon@gov.mb.ca

Dauphin
Provincial Bldg.
27 Second Ave. SW
PO Box 15
Dauphin, MB R7N 3E5
204-622-2152
Fax: 204-622-2305

Thompson
59 Elizabeth Dr.
PO Box 27
Thompson, MB R8N 1X4
204-677-6786
Fax: 204-677-6525

Manitoba Agriculture, Food & Rural Initiatives
Norquay Bldg.
401 York Ave.
Winnipeg, MB R3C 0P8
www.gov.mb.ca/agriculture/
Acts Administered:
Agricultural Credit Corporation Act
Agricultural Productivity Council Act
Agricultural Producers' Organization Funding Act
Animal Care Act
Animal Diseases Act
Crop Insurance Act
Crown Lands Act, (in part) Sections 6, 7, 10, 12(1), 14, 16, 17, 18, 21, 23, 24 to 28 both inclusive
Dairy Act
Department of Agriculture, Food & Rural Initiatives Act
Family Farm Protection Act
Farm Income Assurance Plans Act
Farm Lands Ownership Act
Farm Machinery & Equipment Act
Farm Practices Protection Act
Fruit & Vegetable Sales Act
Horse Racing Regulation Act
Land Rehabilitation Act
Livestock Industry Diversification Act
Livestock & Livestock Products Act
Margarine Act
Milk Prices Review Act
Natural Products Marketing Act
Noxious Weeds Act
Pesticides & Fertilizers Control Act
Prescribed Spraying Equipment & Controlled Products
Plant Pests & Diseases Act
Seed & Fodder Relief Act
Veterinary Medical Act
Veterinary Science Scholarship Fund Act
Veterinary Services Act
Wildlife Act, (in part) Section 89(e)
Women's Institute Act
Minister, Hon. Rosann Wowchuk
204-945-3722, Fax: 204-945-3470
minagr@leg.gov.mb.ca
Deputy Minister, Barry Todd
204-945-3734, Fax: 204-948-2095
dmagr@leg.gov.mb.ca
Executive Director Strategic Planning, Maurice Bouvier
204-792-5406
• Agricultural Societies
1129 Queens Ave.
Brandon, MB R7A 1L9
204-726-6195
Fax: 204-726-6260
Superintendent, Liz Roberts
Promotes improvement in agriculture & development of Manitoba agricultural products. Provide organizational assistance to rural & urban people.
• Farm Lands Ownership Board
#812, Norquay Bldg.
401 York Ave.
Winnipeg, MB R3C 0P8
204-945-3149
Fax: 204-945-1489
800-282-8069
robert.mckenzie@gov.mb.ca
www.web2gov.mb.ca/agriculture/programs/
Program Specialist, Robert McKenzie
• Farm Machinery Board
Norquay Bldg.
#812, 401 York Ave.
Winnipeg, MB R3C 0P8
204-945-3856
Fax: 204-948-2844
randy.ozunko@gov.mb.ca
www.web2.gov.mb.ca/agriculture/programs/
Program Specialist, Randy Ozunko

- Food Development Centre
810 Phillips St.
PO Box 1240
Portage la Prairie, MB R1N 3J9
204-239-3150
Fax: 204-239-3180
800-870-1044
www.gov.mb.ca/agriculture/fdc
General Manager/COO, Lynda Lowry
The Food Development Centre (FDC) is a Special Operating Agency of Manitoba Agriculture, Food and Rural Initiatives (MAFRI). Its mandate is to assist the agri-food industry in the development and commercialization of conventional and functional foods and natural health products.
- Manitoba Agricultural Services Corporation(MASC)
#100, 1525 First St. South
Brandon, MB R7A 7A1
204-726-6850
Fax: 204-726-6849
mailbox@masc.mb.ca
www.masc.mb.ca
President/CEO, Neil Hamilton
Formerly the Manitoba Agricultural Credit Corporation & the Manitoba Crop Insurance Corporation. Manitoba Agricultural Services Corporation (MASC) fully supports the province's producers and rural communities, through innovative and targeted risk management and financial programs. MASC is represented across Manitoba by 19 insurance offices and 16 lending offices, with corporate offices located in Portage la Prairie and Brandon.
- Manitoba Farm Mediation Board
c/o Boards, Commissions & Legislation Branch
#812, 401 York Ave.
Winnipeg, MB R3C 0P8
204-945-0357
Fax: 204-945-1489
robert.mckenzie@gov.mb.ca
www.web2.gov.mb.ca/agriculture/programs/
- Farm Practices Protection Board
c/o Boards, Commissions & Legislation Branch
#812, 401 York Ave.
Winnipeg, MB R3C 0P8
204-945-0630
Fax: 204-948-2844
www.web2.gov.mb.ca/agriculture/programs/
- Farm Products Marketing Council
c/o Boards, Commissions & Legislation Branch
#812, 401 York Ave.
Winnipeg, MB R3C 0P8
204-945-4495
Fax: 204-948-2844
gordon.mackenzie@gov.mb.ca
www.web2.gov.mb.ca/agriculture/programs/
- Manitoba Horse Racing Commission
c/o Boards, Commissions & Legislation Branch
#812, 401 York Ave.
Winnipeg, MB R3C 0P8
204-945-4495
Fax: 204-948-2844
gordon.mackenzie@gov.mb.ca
www.web2.gov.mb.ca/agriculture/programs/
- Manitoba Milk Prices Review Commission
c/o Boards, Commissions & Legislation Branch
#812, 401 York Ave.
Winnipeg, MB R3C 0P8
204-945-3854
Fax: 204-948-2844
randy.ozunko@gov.mb.ca
www.web2.gov.mb.ca/agriculture/programs/

Agri-Food & Rural Development Division
Asst. Deputy Minister, Dori Gingera-Beauchemin
204-945-3735

North Interlake
317 River Rd.
PO Box 2000
Arborg, MB R0C 0A0
Fax: 204-376-3311
GO Team Manager, Susan Nicoll
204-641-1454

South Interlake
77 Main St.
PO Box 70
Teulon, MB R0C 3B0
Fax: 204-886-3657

GO Team Manager, Wray Whitmore

Red River
67 - 2 St. NE
PO Box 969
Altona, MB R0G 0B0
Fax: 204-324-2803
GO Team Leader, Jacquie Cherewayko

Central Plains
Morris Ave.
PO Box 532
Gladstone, MB R0J 0T0
204-871-4219
GO Team Leader, Dennis Beernaert

Pembina
279 Carlton St.
PO Box 189
Somerset, MB R0G 2L0
GO Team Leader, Shane Dobson

Southwest
247 Wellington St.
PO Box 850
Virden, MB R0M 2C0
Fax: 204-748-4775
GO Team Manager, John Corbey
204-851-2442

South Parkland
221 Elm St., Hwy 21 N
PO Box 50
Hamiota, MB R0M 0T0

Valleys North
120 - 6th Ave. North
PO Box 370
Swan River, MB R0L 1Z0
Fax: 204-734-5271
GO Team Manager, Allen Muggaberg

Eastman
20 First St. South
PO Box 50
Beausejour, MB R0E 0C0
204-268-6099
Fax: 204-268-6060
GO Team Manager, Shaunda Rossington

North Parkland
27 - Second Ave. SW
Dauphin, MB R7N 3E5
Fax: 204-734-5271
GO Team Manager, Debra Watson

Agri-Industry Development & Innovation Division
Asst. Deputy Minister, Allan Preston
204-945-3736
Director Food Safety & Chief Veterinary Office, Dr. John Taylor
204-945-7690, Fax: 204-945-4327
Acting Director Land Use Planning & Manager, Agricultural Crown Lands, Robert Fleming
204-867-6551
Director Livestock Knowledge Centre, Brent McCannell
204-945-7650

Regional Agricultural Services Division
Acting Asst. Deputy Minister, Dory Gingera-Beauchemin
204-945-3735
Director Agricultural Crown Lands Branch, Dennis Hodgson
204-867-3419, Fax: 204-867-5696

Agri-Environment
Enhances development, diversification & productive capabilities of livestock producers & processors by providing technical & specialized services addressing environmental issues. The Branch works with Manitoba Conservation, Manitoba Health, & related producer groups; updates the farm practices guidelines & legislation to assist producers in managing their operations in a sustainable manner; assists the Farm Practices Protection Board in determining normal farm practices; coordinates & implements programs in support of agricultural sustainability.
Acting Director, Leloni Scott
204-745-5658

Agri-Food Innovation & Adaptation
Develops & delivers the province's programs regarding scientific innovation in agri-food & rural development, crop & livestock diversification. The Branch strives to achieve the province's goals regarding renewable energy from agricultural sources. The Branch also establishes strategic partnerships among research providers including universities, colleges, NGOs, federal agencies & the private sector.
Acting Director, Daryl Domitruk
204-745-5636
Director Agri-Energy, Henry Nelson
204-945-5222

Crops Branch
Agricultural land-use planning, soil & water management, crop production information.
Director, Don Dixon
204-745-5653

Manitoba Competitiveness, Training & Trade
International Business Centre, The Paris Building
259 Portage Ave.
Winnipeg, MB R3B 3P4
204-945-2475
Fax: 204-945-3977
minctt@leg.gov.mb.ca
www.gov.mb.ca/ctt/
Mission is to support the growth of business in the province, meet provincial labour demands, increase training opportunities, and expand global trade relations
Acts Administered:
Biofuels Act
Crocus Investment Fund
Design Institute Act
Development Corporations Act
Economic Innovation & Technology Council Act
Electronic Commerce & Information Act (except part 5)
Energy Act
Gas Allocation Act
Gas Pipe Line Act
Greater Winnipeg Gas Distribution Act (S.M. 1988-89, C.40)
Income Tax Act (S. 7.5 & 7.10)
Labour-Sponsored Venture Capital Corporations Act
Manitoba Health Research Council Act
Mines & Minerals Act
Mining & Metallurgy Compensation Act
Oil & Gas Act
Drilling & Production Regulation
Oil & Gas Production Tax Act
Statistics Act
Surface Rights Act
Sustainable Development Act
Minister, Hon. Andrew Swan
204-945-0067, Fax: 204-945-4882
minctt@leg.gov.mb.ca
Deputy Minister, Hugh Eliasson
204-945-4076, Fax: 204-945-1561

Community & Economic Development Committee of Cabinet Secretariat
#648, 155 Carlton St.
Winnipeg, MB R3C 3H8
204-945-8221
Fax: 204-945-8229

Business Services Division - Financial Services
To encourage & facilitate entrepreneurial & employment opportunities within the Province through the establishment of new businesses or the expansion/retention of existing Manitoba businesses.The Branch promotes increased access to capital for industry by serving as a principal source of financial advice & assistance for businesses to expand or locate in Manitoba. The Branch develops & administers a number of third party delivered pools of risk capital

Manitoba Bureau of Statistics
#824, 155 Carlton St.
Winnipeg, MB R3C 3H9
204-945-2406
Fax: 204-945-0695

Premier's Economic Advisory Council
#648, 155 Carlton St.
Winnipeg, MB R3C 3N8
204-945-6133
Fax: 204-945-8229

Small Business Development

Federal/Provincial Government / Government of Manitoba

#250, 240 Graham Ave.
PO Box 2609
Winnipeg, MB R3C 4B3
204-984-2272
Fax: 204-983-3852
manitoba@cbsc.ic.gc.ca
www.cbsc.org/manitoba
Director, Tony Romeo
204-945-2019

Manitoba Conservation

200 Saulteaux Cres.
Winnipeg, MB R3J 3W3
204-945-6784
800-214-6497
mincon@leg.gov.mb.ca
www.gov.mb.ca/conservation
Manitoba Conservation protects, conserves, manages & sustains development of forest, fisheries, wildlife, water, energy & Crown & Park land resources, protects environmental integrity & ensures a high level of environmental quality. The department is the lead agency for providing outdoor recreational opportunities for Manitobans & visitors. The department is a contributor to the economic development & wellbeing of the province, through resource-based harvesting operations & in co-operation with other departments responsible for agriculture & tourism. Providing for domestic use & protecting people & property from floods, wildfires & adverse effects of other natural occurrences, are also major roles. The department administers legislation & regulations protecting the environment & public health, participates in approval, licensing & appeals for industrial development activities, administers waste reduction & pollution prevention activities & monitors environmental quality

Acts Administered:
Contaminated Sites Remediation Act
Crown Lands Act
Dangerous Goods Handling & Transportation Act
Anhydrous Ammonia Handling & Transport Regulations
Classification for Products, Substances & Organisms Regulation
Dangerous Goods Handling & Transportation Fees Regulation
Dangerous Goods Handling & Transportation Regulation
Environmental Accident Reporting Regulation
Generator Registration & Carrier Licensing Regulation
Manifest Regulation
PCB Storage Site Regulation
Special Waste (Shredder Residue) Regulation
Storage & Handling of Petroleum Products & Allied Products Regulation
Dutch Elm Disease Act
Ecological Reserves Act
Ecological Reserves Designation Regulation
Endangered Species Act
Environment Act
Burning of Crop Residue & Non-Crop Herbage Regulation
Campgrounds Regulation
Classes of Development Regulation
Disposal of Whey Regulation
Environment Act Fees Regulation
Environmental Assessment Hearing Costs Recovery Regulation
Incinerators Regulation
Inco Ltd. & Hudson Bay Mining & Smelting Co., Ltd. Smelting Complex Regulation
Joint Environmental Assessment Regulation
Litter Regulation
Livestock Manure & Mortalities Management Regulation
Onsite Wastewater Management Systems Regulation
Participant Assistance Regulation
Peat Smoke Control Regulation
Pesticides Regulation
Rockwood Sensitive Area Regulation
Waste Disposal Grounds Regulation
Wastewater Management Systems Regulations
Water & Wastewater Facility Operators Regulation
Forest Act
Ground Water & Water Well Act
Well Drilling Regulation
High Level Radioactive Waste Act
Homeowners Tax & Insulation Assistance Act
International Peace Garden Act
Manitoba Hazardous Waste Management Corporation Act
Manitoba Natural Resources Transfer Act
Manitoba Natural Resources Transfer Act, Amendment Act
Manitoba Natural Resources Transfer Act, Amendment Act, 1963
Ozone Depleting Substances Act
Provincial Parks Act
Plant Pests & Diseases Act
Polar Bear Protection Act, 2003
Public Health Act
Protection of Water Resources Regulation
Sanitary Areas Regulation
Water Supplies Regulation
Water Works, Sewage & Sewage Disposal Regulations
Resource Tourism Operators Act
Surveys Act (Part II)
Sustainable Development Act
Waste Reduction & Prevention Act
Multi-Material Stewardship (Interim Measures) Regulation
Tire Stewardship Regulation
Used Oil, Oil Filters & Containers Stewardship Regulation
Water Commission Act
Wildlife Act
Designation of Wild Animals Regulation
Designation of Wildlife Lands Regulation
Threatened, Endangered & Extirpated Species Regulation
Water Resources Conservation & Protection Act
Water Rights Act
Wild Rice Act
Minister, Hon. Bill Blaikie
204-945-3730, Fax: 204-945-3586
mincon@leg.gov.mb.ca
Deputy Minister, Fred Meier
204-945-3785, Fax: 204-948-2403
dmcon@leg.gov.mb.ca
• Clean Environment Commission
#305, 155 Carlton St.
Winnipeg, MB R3C 3H8
204-945-0594
Fax: 204-945-0090
www.cecmanitoba.ca/
Chair, Terry Sargeant
Arm's-length provincial agency that holds public hearings on the subject of the regulation of a broad range of private industry, municipal or provincial government operations. Investigates environmental matters or considers proposed abatement projects with public hearings. Reports to the Minister with advice & recommendations & acts as a mediator between two or more parties to an environmental dispute.
• Ecological Reserves Advisory Committee
c/o Manitoba Conservation, Parks & Natural Areas Branch
200 Saulteaux Cres.
Winnipeg, MB R3J 3W3
204-945-4148
Fax: 204-945-0012
hhernandez@gov.mb.ca
Secretary, Helios Hernandez
• Endangered Species Advisory Committee
200 Saulteaux Cres.
PO Box 24
Winnipeg, MB R3J 3W3
204-945-7465
Fax: 204-945-3077
Co-Chair, Jim Duncan
• Lake of the Woods Control Board
c/o Executive Engineer
Ottawa, ON K1A 0H3
Fax: 819-953-4666
800-661-5922
secretariat@lwcb.ca
www.lwcb.ca
Chair, Allan Chow

Conservation Programs Division
Manages Manitoba's natural resources, parks, lands, forests, fish, wildlife, & the environment. Implements the principles of sustainable development.
Asst. Deputy Minister, Fred Meier
204-945-7008, Fax: 204-945-3125
Director Forestry, John Dojack
204-945-7998
Director Lands & Geomatics, Harley Jonasson
204-945-8288
Director Parks & Natural Areas, Barry J. Bentham
204-945-4413

Environmental Stewardship Division
The Branch co-ordinates & integrates departmental policy, natural resource allocation & crown land-use planning, environmental impact assessment, legislative interpretation & co-management in accordance with principles of sustainable development. The Branch monitors cross-boundary water projects, administers licensing of resource-based tourism facilities, represents the department in issues related to internal & international trade agreements, co-ordinates settlements & litigation arising out of hydro-electric & water-control projects & Treaty Land Entitlement.
Asst. Deputy Minister, Serge Scrafield
204-945-7107, Fax: 204-945-5229
Director Environmental Assessment & Licensing, Tracey Braun
204-945-7071

Manitoba Round Table for Sustainable Development (MRTSD)
#160, 123 Main St.
Winnipeg, MB R3C 1A5
204-945-1671
Fax: 204-948-2357
mrtsd@gov.mb.ca
Advisory body to the provincial government that provides advice & support to decision makers toward making responsible resource, land use, environment, social & economic development decisions for the province
Chair, Hon. Stan Struthers

Regional Operations Division
Operates six regional offices in rural Manitoba & co-ordinated from Headquarters operations in Winnipeg. The Division co-ordinates the delivery of programs & services at the community level
Asst. Deputy Minister, Bruce Bremner
204-945-4842

Eastern
Provincial Hwy #502
CP 4000
Lac du Bonnet, MB R0E 1A0
204-345-1431
Fax: 204-345-1440
Regional Director, Bruce Bremner

Central (Gimli)
75 - 7th Ave.
PO Box 6000
Gimli, MB R0C 1B0
204-642-6070
Fax: 204-642-6108
Regional Director, Brian Gillespie

Northeastern
59 Elizabeth Dr.
PO Box 28
Thompson, MB R8N 1X4
204-677-6648
Fax: 204-677-6359
Regional Director, Steve Kearney

Northwestern
3rd St. & Ross Ave.
PO Box 2550
The Pas, MB R9A 1M4
204-627-8215
Fax: 204-623-1773

Central (Winnipeg)
#160, 123 Main St.
Winnipeg, MB R3C 1A5
204-945-7100
Fax: 204-948-2338

Western
1129 Queens Ave.
Brandon, MB R7A 1L9
204-726-6441
Fax: 204-726-6567
Regional Director, Bruce Wright

Air Quality Management Section
204-945-7100
The Air Quality Management section measures air quality & provides scientific & technical support. The section develops & reviews objectives & guidelines for pollutants, monitors air quality in urban areas & selected industrial sources, undertakes special project investigations, assists review & assessment of developments, participates in development & implementation of national strategies & assists in development of strategies to address global climate change.
Manager, David Bezak
204-945-7046

Pollution Prevention Branch
204-945-8443
Coordinates the Waste Reduction & Prevention Program; provides support to the Ozone Depleting Substances Program; develops technical support materials to promote the application of pollution prevention by generators of waste & pollution. Promotes wider pollution prevention applications in the Department; developing cost-effective options to command & control programs; provides support to the Sustainable Development Innovations Fund, the Environmental Youth Corps & other environmental funding programs.
Director, Laurie Streich
204-945-7482

Wildlife & Ecosystem Protection
204-945-7775
The mandate of the Wildlife & Ecosystem Protection Branch is to protect wildlife resources in a manner consistent with the conservation of species & ecosystems. This responsibility is carried out under the authority of The Wildlife Act, The Endangered Species Act & The Conservation Agreements Act of Manitoba & by applying the principles of sustainable development. The Branch develops programs, policies & legislation for hunting & trapping, biodiversity conservation, & habitat & land management on Crown & private land. The Branch also represents Manitoba in numerous provincial, national & international initiatives.
Director, Jack Dubois
204-945-7761

Aboriginal Relations Branch
200 Saulteaux Cres.
PO Box 26
Winnipeg, MB R3J 3W3
204-945-2821
Fax: 204-945-4552
The Branch sets the overall direction for the Department for programs, policies & legislation that impact Aboriginal & treaty rights; is accountable for the development & implementation of a departmental framework to address Aboriginal issues as they relate to the department; educates, & facilitates dialogue, & bridges opposing views & philosophies.
Director, Ron Missyabit
204-945-5229

Environmental Approvals Branch
#160, 123 Main St.
Winnipeg, MB R3C 1A5
204-945-8321
Fax: 204-945-5229
Administers & manages the approval process, considerations for approval made through the Environment Act, Dangerous Goods Handling Act, Transportation Act & Public Health Act. Branch activities are carried out by three sections, Municipal, Industrial & Hazardous Waste Approvals, Environmental Land Use Approvals & Pesticide Approvals. The branch controls municipal, industrial & hazardous waste sources of pollutants, ensures safe drinking water, minimizes the environmental impact of development proposals & adverse effects to the environment & public health from pesticide use.

Sustainable Resource Management Branch
Coordinates & integrates departmental policy, natural resource allocation & Crown land-use planning, environmental impact assessment, legislative interpretation, & co-management, in accordance with principles & guidelines of sustainable development. Planning & policy assistance to local planning authorities, licensing of resource-based tourism facilities, representing the Department in issues related to internal & international trade agreements, provides support on communications issues, coordination of departmental settlements & litigation arising out of Treaty Land Entitlement.
Senior Planner, William Barto
204-945-3957

Manitoba Culture, Heritage, Tourism & Sport
Legislative Building
#118, 450 Broadway Ave.
Winnipeg, MB R3C 0V8
204-945-3729
Fax: 204-945-5223
mincht@leg.gov.mb.ca
www.gov.mb.ca/chc
Committed to the development & implementation of programs & services which promote & enhance the well-being, identity & creativity of Manitobans & which contribute to Manitoba's continued economic growth & steadily rising quality of life. Working with its partners in the community & with government, the Department raises the national & international profile of the talents & abilities of our people, encourages healthy active living, promotes pride of place, creates jobs & attracts & maintains investment in our province

Acts Administered:
Amusements Act (except Part II)
Arts Council Act
Boxing Commission Act
Centennial Centre Corporation Act
Le Centre Culturel Franco-Manitobain Act
Coat of Arms, Emblems & The Manitoba Tartan Act
Convention Centre Corporation Act
Foreign Cultural Objects Immunity from Seizure Act
Freedom of Information & Protection of Privacy Act
Heritage Manitoba Act
Heritage Resources Act
Legislative Library Act
Manitoba Film & Sound Recording Development Corporation Act
Museums & Miscellaneous Grants Act
Public Libraries Act
Public Printing Act
Travel Manitoba Act
Minister, Hon. Eric Robinson
204-945-3729, Fax: 204-945-5223
mincht@leg.gov.mb.ca
Deputy Minister, Sandra Hardy
204-945-4136, Fax: 204-948-3102
dmcht@leg.gov.mb.ca
• Le Centre Culturel franco-manitobain/Franco-Manitoban Cultural Centre
340, boul Provencher
St Boniface, MB R2H 0G7
204-233-8972
Fax: 204-233-3324
ccfm@ccfm.mb.ca
www.ccfm.mb.ca
• Heritage Grants Advisory Council
213 Notre Dame Ave., 3rd Fl.
Winnipeg, MB R3B 1N3
204-945-2213
Fax: 204-948-2086
• Manitoba Arts Council
#525, 93 Lombard Ave.
Winnipeg, MB R3B 3B1
204-945-2237
Fax: 204-945-5925
866-994-2787
info@artscouncil.mb.ca
www.artscouncil.mb.ca
• Manitoba Centennial Centre Corporation
555 Main St.
Winnipeg, MB R3B 1C3
204-956-1360
Fax: 204-944-1390
• Manitoba Film Classification Board
#216, 301 Weston St.
Winnipeg, MB R3E 3H4
204-945-8962
Fax: 204-945-0890
866-612-2399
mfcb@gov.mb.ca
www.gov.mb.ca/filmclassification
• Manitoba Heritage Council
213 Notre Dame Ave., Main Fl.
Winnipeg, MB R3B 1N3
204-945-2118
Fax: 204-948-2384
hrb@gov.mb.ca
Secretary, Donna Dul
Protects, interprets & promotes the heritage resources of the province; offers advice & recommendations on places & events which should be protected by the department; protection of significant buildings & sites.
• Manitoba Museum
190 Rupert Ave.
Winnipeg, MB R3B 0N2
204-956-2830
Fax: 204-942-3679
info@manitobamuseum.mb.ca
www.manitobamuseum.mb.ca
Other Communication: Info Line:|204/943-3139
• Manitoba Film & Sound Recording Development Corporation
#410, 93 Lombard Ave.
Winnipeg, MB R3B 3B1
204-947-2040
Fax: 204-956-5261
carole@mbfilmsound.mb.ca
www.mbfilmsound.mb.ca

Administration & Finance Division
Fax: 204-945-5760

Communications Services Manitoba
155 Carlton St., 10th Fl.
Winnipeg, MB R3C 3H8
204-945-3765
Fax: 204-948-2147
Asst. Deputy Minister, Cindy Stevens
204-945-4271, Fax: 204-948-2219
Director Public Affairs, Debbie MacKenzie
204-945-4971, Fax: 204-948-2147
Supervisor Statutory Publications, Keith Holness
204-945-3101, Fax: 204-945-7172
statpub@gov.mb.ca

Culture, Heritage & Recreation Programs Division
Acting Asst. Deputy Minister, Ann Hultgren-Ryan
204-945-4078, Fax: 204-948-2739
Director Historic Resources, Donna Dul
204-945-4389, Fax: 204-948-2384

Provincial Services Division
#100, 200 Vaughan St.
Winnipeg, MB R3C 1T5

Tourism Secretariat & Travel Manitoba
155 Carlton St., 7th Fl.
Winnipeg, MB R3C 3H8
800-665-0040
www.travelmanitoba.com
Acting Executive Director Tourism Manitoba, Terry Welsh
204-945-2449,
Minister, Hon. Peter Bjornson
204-945-3720, Fax: 204-945-1291
minedu@leg.gov.mb.ca

Manitoba Health & Healthy Living
#100, 300 Carlton St.
Winnipeg, MB R3B 3M9
204-786-7191
minhlt@leg.gov.mb.ca
www.gov.mb.ca/health/index.html
Responsible for the overall quality of the health system in the province, for maintaining the health system, & for ensuring that the health needs of Manitobans are met. Services are provided through regional delivery systems, hospitals & other health care facilities. The Department also makes insured benefits claims payments for residents of Manitoba related to the cost of medical, hospital, personal care, pharmacare & other health services. To lead the way to quality health care, built with creativity, compassion, confidence, trust & respect; empower Manitobans through knowledge, choices & access to the best possible health resources; & build partnerships & alliances for healthy & supportive communities. To foster innovation in the health care system. This is accomplished through: developing mechanisms to assess & monitor quality of care, utilization & cost effectiveness; fostering behaviours & environments which promote health; & promoting responsiveness & flexibility of delivery systems, & alternative & less expensive services.

Acts Administered:
Ambulance Services Act
Anatomy Act
Cancer Care Manitoba Act
Dental Association Act
Dental Health Services Act
Dental Health Workers Act
Denturists Act
Department of Health Act
District Health & Social Services Act
Elderly & Infirm Persons' Housing Act (with respect to elderly persons housing units as defined in the Act)
(Manitoba) Health Research Council Act
Health Sciences Centre Act, 1988-89
Health Services Act
Health Services Insurance Act
Hearing Aid Act
Hospitals Act
Human Tissue Act
Licensed Practical Nurses Act

Federal/Provincial Government / Government of Manitoba

Medical Act
Manitoba Medical Association Dues Act
Mental Health Act (except parts 9 & 10 & clauses 125 (1)(i) & (j)
Midwifery Act
Occupational Therapists Act
Personal Health Information Act
Pharmaceutical Act
Physiotherapists Act
Podiatrists Act
Prescription Drugs Cost Assistance Act
Private Hospitals Act
Protection for Persons in Care Act
Public Health Act
Atmospheric Pollution Regulation
Collection & Disposal of Wastes Regulation
Fumigation & Pest Control Regulation
Protection of Water Sources Regulation
Sanitation Regulation
Water Supplies Regulation
Water Works, Sewerage & Sewage Disposal Regulation
X-Ray Safety Regulation
Regional Health Authorities Act
Registered Dieticians Act
Registered Nurses Act
Registered Psychiatric Nurses Act
Registered Respiratory Therapists Act
Sanitorium Board of Manitoba Act
Minister, Hon. Theresa Oswald
204-945-3731, Fax: 204-945-0441
minhlt@leg.gov.mb.ca
Deputy Minister, Arlene Wilgosh
204-945-3771, Fax: 204-945-4564
dmhlt@leg.gov.mb.ca
Chief Medical Officer of Health, Dr. Joel Kettner
204-788-6766, Fax: 204-948-2204
• Appeal Panel for Home Care
#4012, 300 Carlton St.
Winnipeg, MB R3B 3M9
204-788-6788
Fax: 204-948-2024
800-491-4993
appeals@gov.mb.ca
• Manitoba Drug Standards & Therapeutics Committee
#1014, 300 Carlton St.
Winnipeg, MB R3B 3M9
204-786-7317
Fax: 204-942-2030
• Manitoba Health Appeal Board
#4011, 300 Carlton St.
Winnipeg, MB R3B 3M9
204-788-6704
Fax: 204-948-2024
866-744-3257
• Addictions Foundation of Manitoba(AFM) / Fondation manitobaine de lutte contre les dépendances
1031 Portage Ave.
Winnipeg, MB R3G 0R8
204-944-6200
Fax: 204-786-7768
library@afm.mb.ca
www.afm.mb.ca
• Manitoba Seniors & Health Aging Secretariat

Corporate & Provincial Program Support
Fax: 204-775-3712

Finance

Primary Care & Healthy Living
300 Carlton St., 2nd Floor
Winnipeg, MB R3B 3M9
Mission is to encourage the prevention of illness & injury, coordinate access to health care, & strengthen existing primary health care services with new initiatives
Asst. Deputy Minister, Marie O'Neill
204-786-6656, Fax: 204-948-2366
Executive Director Primary Health Care, Barbara Wasilewski
204-786-7176

Public Health
300 Carlton St., 4th Fl.
Winnipeg, MB R3B 3M9
204-788-6701
Fax: 204-948-2040

Mission is to assure conditions in which people can be healthy, by applying scientific & medical knowledge to systematically identify & analyze the health of groups & populations, & by assisting communities to organize, implement & monitor efforts aimed at the prevention & control of disease & promotion of health.The Environmental Health Unit of the Public Health Branch responds to biological, chemical or social health threats to the public. The Unit manages several programs including Environmental Health, Food Protection, Tobacco Reduction & Dental/Oral Health
Chief Provincial Public Health Officer, Dr. Joel Kettner
204-788-6766

Manitoba Healthy Child Office
#219, 114 Garry St.
Winnipeg, MB R3C 1G1
204-945-2266
888-848-0140
healthychild@gov.mb.ca
Office provides leadership & encourages actions that address health concerns & reduces the need for medical care for children
Acts Administered:
The Addictions Foundation Act
The Non-Smokers Health Protection Act
Manitoba Prenatal Benefit Regulation
Minister, Hon. Kerri Irvin-Ross
204-945-1373, Fax: 204-948-2703
Director Programs, Susan Tessler
204-945-1275

Manitoba Hydro
PO Box 815 Main
Winnipeg, MB R3C 2P4
204-474-3311
Fax: 204-475-0069
publicaffairs@hydro.mb.ca
www.hydro.mb.ca
Manitoba Hydro (MH) is a major energy utility. One of the largest electricity & natural gas utilities in Canada, it serves 521,600 electric customers throughout Manitoba & 261,150 gas customers in various communities throughout southern Manitoba. Virtually all electricity generated by the provincial Crown Corporation is from self-renewing water power. MH is the major distributor of natural gas in the province. Developing & implementing an environmental management system consistent with ISO standards. Actively pursuing a vairety or projects & programs aimed at reducing GHG & vehicle emissions, recycling, conserving energy, digging out contaminated soils, partnering with NGOs
Minister responsible, Hon. Gregory F. Selinger
204-945-3952, Fax: 204-945-6057
minfin@leg.gov.mb.ca
President/CEO, Bob B. Brennan
204-474-3600
Vice-President Finance & Administration & CFO, Vince A. Warden
Vice-President Transmission & Distribution, Al M. Snyder

Manitoba Infrastructure & Transportation
Legislative Building
#203, 450 Broadway Ave.
Winnipeg, MB R3C 0V8
204-945-3723
Fax: 204-945-7610
www.gov.mb.ca/mit/
Acts Administered:
Crown Lands Act
Drivers & Vehicles Act
Government Air Services Act
Government House Act
Government Purchases Act
Highway Traffic Act
Highways Protection Act
Highways & Transportation Act
Highways & Transportation Construction Contracts
  Disbursement Act
Land Acquisition Act
Manitoba Floodway Authority Act
Manitoba Water Services Board Act
Off-Road Vehicles Act
Provincial Parks Act
Provincial Railways Act
Public Works Act
Taxicab Act
Trans-Canada Highway Act
Wild Rice Act

Minister, Hon. Ron Lemieux
204-945-3723, Fax: 204-945-7610
mininfratran@leg.gov.mb.ca
• Lake Winnipeg Stewardship Board
PO Box 305
Gimli, MB R0C 1B0
204-642-4899
www.lakewinnipeg.org
Chair, William Barlow
Established in 2003 to assist the government of Manitoba to achieve the main commitments in the Lake Winnipeg Action Plan of reducing phosphorus & nitrogen in the lake to pre-1970 levels. The Lake Winnipeg Stewardship Board's Interim Report (Jan. 2005), contained 32 sets of recommendations & was followed by public discussions.
• Highway Traffic Board/Motor Transport Board
#200, 301 Weston St.
Winnipeg, MB R3E 3H4
204-945-8912
Fax: 204-783-6529
Secretary, Iris Murrell
• Manitoba Floodway Authority(MFA)
#200, 155 Carlton St.
Winnipeg, MB R3C 3H8
204-945-4900
Fax: 204-948-2462
866-356-6355
floodway@gov.mb.ca
CEO, Ernie Gilroy
Separate, independent, publicly accountable provincial agency that will manage the expansion & maintenance of the Red River Floodway on behalf of Manitobans.
• Manitoba Habitat Heritage Corporation
#200, 1555 St. James St.
Winnipeg, MB R3H 1B5
204-784-4350
Fax: 204-784-7359
mhhc@mhhc.mb.ca
www.mhhc.mb.ca
COO, Lorne Colpitts
• License Suspension Appeal Board/Medical Review Committee
#200, 301 Weston St.
Winnipeg, MB R3E 3H4
204-945-7350
Fax: 204-948-2682
• Manitoba Water Services Board
PO Box 22080
Brandon, MB R7A 6Y9
204-726-6076
Fax: 204-726-6290
www.gov.mb.ca/waterstewardship/mwsb/
Chair, Gerry Berezuk
Assists rural residents outside Winnipeg in developing safe & sustainable water &/or sewerage facilities.
• Manitoba Land Value Appraisal Commission
800 Portage Ave.
Winnipeg, MB R3G 0N4
204-945-2941
Fax: 204-948-2235
• Taxicab Board
#200, 301 Weston St.
Winnipeg, MB R3E 3H4
Fax: 204-948-2315

Canada-Manitoba Infrastructure Secretariat
204-945-4074
Fax: 204-945-2035
800-268-4883
infra@gov.mb.ca

Government Services
Legislative Bldg.
#332, 450 Broadway
Winnipeg, MB R3C 0V8

Accommodation Services
1700 Portage Ave.
Winnipeg, MB R3J 0E1
Asst. Deputy Minister, Chris Hauch
204-945-7535, Fax: 204-945-2546
Director Corporate Accommodation Planning, Hilary Oakman
204-945-7965
Director Project Services, Pat Landry
204-945-6615

Director Operations, Rod Berscheid
204-945-7528
Director Security Branch, Gary Walker
204-945-7608

Supply & Services Division
270 Osborne St. North
Winnipeg, MB R3C 1V7
Asst. Deputy Minister, Tracey Danowski
204-945-6340, Fax: 204-948-2509
COO Materials Distribution Agency, David Bishop
204-945-6043, Fax: 204-948-3273

Transportation
Legislative Bldg.
#209, 450 Broadway
Winnipeg, MB R3C 0V8
Deputy Minister, Andrew Horosko
204-945-3768, Fax: 204-945-4766

Construction & Maintenance Branch
#1610, 215 Garry St.
Winnipeg, MB R3C 3Z1
Fax: 204-945-3841
Other Communication: Highway Condition Information:
204/945-3705, 1-877-627-6237
Executive Director, Ron Weatherburn
204-945-3775
Director Mechanical Equipment Services, Mike Knight
204-945-8567, Fax: 204-948-3274

Administrative Services Division
215 Garry St., 17th Fl.
Winnipeg, MB R3C 3Z1
Fax: 204-945-5115

Engineering & Operations Division
215 Garry St., 16th Fl.
Winnipeg, MB R3C 3Z1
Fax: 204-945-3841
Asst. Deputy Minister, Lance Vigfusson
204-945-3733

Highway Engineering Branch
Executive Director, Walter Burdz
204-945-3772
Director Highway Planning & Design, Eric Christiansen
204-945-0236
Director Materials Engineering, Said Kass
204-945-2279
Director Traffic Engineering, Glenn Cuthbertson
204-945-0329

Transportation Policy Division
215 Garry St., 15th Fl.
Winnipeg, MB R3C 3Z1
Fax: 204-945-5539

Manitoba Intergovernmental Affairs
#301, 450 Broadway Ave.
Winnipeg, MB R3C 0V8
Fax: 204-945-1383
mnia@leg.gov.mb.ca
www.gov.mb.ca/ia/
Mission is to improve the economic, social & environmental wellbeing of Manitoba communities & citizens. The Department serves individuals, local governments, community organizations & businesses; & establishes a legislative, financial, planning & policy framework that supports democratic, accountable, effective & financially efficient local government, & the sustainable development of our communities. Programs are aimed at meeting particular needs for training, on-going advice, technical analysis & funding related to community revitalization & development, infrastructure development, land management, business support & local governance. The Department functions as an advocate of community needs, a catalyst & co-ordinator of action, promotes & participates in partnerships with private sector & non-government organizations & intergovernmental alliances
Acts Administered:
Capital Region Partnership Act
City of Winnipeg Charter
Convention Centre Corporation Act
An Act respecting Debts Owing by Municipalities to School Districts
Emergency Measures Act
Emergency 911 Public Safety Answering Point Act
Liquor Control Act
Local Authorities Election Act
Local Government Districts Act
Manitoba Lotteries Corporation Act
Manitoba Trade & Investment Corporation Act
Municipal Act
Municipal Affairs Administration Act
Municipal Assessment Act
Municipal Board Act
Municipal Councils & School Boards Elections Act
Municipal Revenue (Grants & Taxation) (Part 2)
Official Time Act
Planning Act (in part)
Northern Manitoba Planning & Bylaws Regulation
Provincial Land Use Policies Regulation
Subdivision Regulation
Soldiers' Taxation Relief Act
Regional Waste Management Authorities Act
Unconditional Grants Act
Minister, Hon. Steve Ashton
204-945-3788, Fax: 204-945-1383
minia@leg.gov.mb.ca
Deputy Minister Intergovernmental Affairs, Linda McFadyen
204-945-4309, Fax: 204-945-5255
dmnia@leg.gov.mb.ca
• Manitoba Liquor Control Commission
1555 Buffalo Pl.
PO Box 1023
Winnipeg, MB R3C 2X1
204-284-2501
Fax: 204-475-7666
info@mlcc.mb.ca
www.mlcc.mb.ca
• Manitoba Municipal Board
#1144, 363 Broadway
Winnipeg, MB R3C 3N9
204-945-2941
Fax: 204-948-2235
Chair, Peter Diamant

Provincial-Municipal Support Services
#508, 800 Portage Ave.
Winnipeg, MB R3G 0N4
Provincial Municipal Assessor Assessment Branch, Mark Boreskie
204-945-2604, Fax: 204-945-1994

Community Land Use Planning Services
#604, 800 Portage Ave.
Winnipeg, MB R3G 0N4
Asst. Deputy Minister, Vacant
Director Community Planning Services, David Neufeld
204-945-2192, Fax: 204-945-5059
Director Provincial Planning Services, Michael Teillet
204-945-2592, Fax: 204-945-5059

Emergency Measures Organization (EMO)
405 Broadway Ave., 15th Floor
Winnipeg, MB R3C 3L6
204-945-4772
Fax: 204-945-4929
888-267-8298
emo@gov.mb.ca
www.manitobaemo.ca
Coordinates emergency response, municipal emergency planning & training, & disaster recovery programs
Executive Director, Chuck Sanderson
204-945-5228, Fax: 204-945-4929

Urban Strategic Initiatives
#607, 800 Portage Ave.
Winnipeg, MB R3G 0N4
Fax: 204-948-3512
Asst. Deputy Minister, Vacant
Director Programs & Policy, Jon Gunn
204-945-3864
Director Winnipeg Partnership Agreement, Vacant
204-984-1806, Fax: 204-983-3844
Coordinator Neighbourhoods Alive!, Bob Dilay
204-945-3379, Fax: 204-945-5059
Deputy Minister & Deputy Attorney General, Ron Perozzo, Q.C.
204-945-3739, Fax: 204-945-4133
dmjus@leg.gov.mb.ca
Acts Administered:
Expropriation Act
Transboundary Pollution Reciprocal Access Act

Manitoba Labour & Immigration
Legislative Building
317, 450 Broadway Ave.
Winnipeg, MB R3C 0V8
204-945-4079
Fax: 204-945-8312
minlab@leg.gov.mb.ca
www.gov.mb.ca/labour
Acts Administered:
Amusements Act (Part II)
Architects Act
Architects & Engineers Scope of Practice Dispute Settlement Act
Buildings & Mobile Homes Act
Construction Industry Wages Act
Department of Labour & Immigration Act
Electricians' Licence Act
Elevator Act
Employment Services Act
Employment Standards Code
Engineering & Geoscientific Professions Act
Firefighters & Paramedics Arbitration Act
Fires Prevention & Emergency Response Act
Gas & Oil Burner Act
Holocaust Memorial Day Act
Labour Relations Act
Manitoba Ethnocultural Advisory & Advocacy Council Act
Manitoba Immigration Council Act
Manitoba Multiculturalism Act
Manitoba Women's Advisory Council Act
Pay Equity Act
Pension Benefits Act
Power Engineers Act
Remembrance Day Act
Retail Business Holiday Closing Act
Steam & Pressure Plants Act
Workplace Safety & Health Act
Construction Industry Safety Regulation
Fibrosis & Silicosis Regulation
Forestry, Logging & Log Hauling Regulation
Hearing Conservation & Noise Control Regulation
Operation of Mines Regulation
Sanitary & Hygienic Welfare Regulation
Workplace Hazardous Materials Information System Regulation
Workplace Health Hazard Regulation
Workplace Safety & Health Committee Regulation
Workplace Safety Regulation
Minimum Wage & Working Conditions Regulation
Minister, Hon. Nancy Allan
204-945-4079, Fax: 204-945-8312
minlab@leg.gov.mb.ca
Deputy Minister, Jeff Parr
204-945-3782, Fax: 204-948-2203
dmlab@leg.gov.mb.ca
• Advisory Council on Workplace Safety & Health
#200, 401 York Ave.
Winnipeg, MB R3C 0P8
204-945-3446
Fax: 204-945-4556
www.gov.mb.ca/labour/safety/council.html
Acting Chairperson, Ilana Warner
The Advisory Council on Workplace Safety & Health was established in 1977 under the authority of the Workplace Safety & Health Act. The council reports directly to the Minister of Labour & Immigration. The council advises & makes recommendations to the Minister of Labour & Immigration concerning general workplace safety & health issues, protection of workers in specific situations & appointment of consultants & advisors.
• Manitoba Civil Service Commission
#935, 155 Carlton St.
Winnipeg, MB R3C 3H8
204-945-2332
Fax: 204-945-1486
cschrp@gov.mb.ca
www.gov.mb.ca/csc/
• Manitoba Ethnocultural Advisory & Advocacy Council
215 Notre Dame Ave. 4th Fl.
Winnipeg, MB R3B 1N3
204-945-2339
Fax: 204-948-2323
800-665-8332
meaac@gov.mb.ca
www.gov.mb.ca/labour/immigrate/multiculturalism/5.html

Federal/Provincial Government / Government of Manitoba

- Manitoba Labour Board
A.A. Heaps Bldg.
#402, 258 Portage Ave.
Winnipeg, MB R3C 0B6
204-945-3783
Fax: 204-945-1296
mlb@gov.mb.ca
www.gov.mb.ca/labour/labbrd
- Manitoba Minimum Wage Board
614 - 401 York Ave.
Winnipeg, MB R3C 0P8
204-945-4889
Fax: 204-948-2085
mw@gov.mb.ca
www.gov.mb.ca/labour/labmgt/resbr/wages/minwagbd.html
- Manitoba Women's Advisory Council
#301, 155 Carlton St.
Winnipeg, MB R3C 3H8
204-945-6281
Fax: 204-945-6511
800-282-8069
001women@gov.mb.ca
- Multiculturalism Secretariat
213 Notre Dame Ave., 4th Fl.
Winnipeg, MB R3B 1N3
204-945-1156
Fax: 204-948-2323
- Office of the Fire Commissioner
#508, 401 York Ave.
Winnipeg, MB R3C 0P8
204-945-3322
Fax: 204-948-2089
800-282-8069
firecomm@gov.mb.ca
www.firecomm.gov.mb.ca/
Fire Commissioner, Douglas M. Popowich
- Pension Commission of Manitoba
#1004, 401 York Ave.
Winnipeg, MB R3C 0P8
204-945-2740
Fax: 204-948-2375
pensions@gov.mb.ca
www.gov.mb.ca/labour/pension/index.html

Employment Standards Division
204-945-3352
Fax: 204-948-3046
800-821-4307
employmentstandards@gov.mb.ca

Immigration & Multiculturalism Division
213 Notre Dame Ave., 5th Floor
Winnipeg, MB R3B 1N3
204-945-6300
Fax: 204-948-2148
immigratemanitoba@gov.mb.ca
www.immigrationmanitoba.com

Status of Women
#409, 401 York Ave.
Winnipeg, MB R3C 0P8
204-945-3476
Fax: 204-945-0013
800-263-0234
mwd@gov.mb.ca

Workplace Safety & Health Division
#200, 401 York Ave.
Winnipeg, MB R3C 0P8
204-945-3446
Fax: 204-948-2209
wshcompl@gov.mb.ca
www.gov.mb.ca/labour/safety/index.html
Operates a 24-hour response service to accidents & complaints; monitors & evaluates workplace areas for chemical, physical, biological & ergonomic factors; participates in worker education & training programs for workers, employers & other interested parties on matters relating to maintaining a safe & healthy workplace
Asst. Deputy Minister, Don Hurst
204-945-3605
Director Inspection Services, Bryan Zirk
204-945-8429,
bzirk@gov.mb.ca

Acting Director Mining Safety Unit, Bill Comaskey
204-677-6821,
bcomaskey@gov.mb.ca
Chief Occupational Medical Officer, Dr. Ted Redekop
204-945-3608,
tredekop@gov.mb.ca
President/CEO, Winston Hodgins

Manitoba Science, Technology, Energy & Mines
#333, 450 Broadway
Winnipeg, MB R3C 0V8
www.gov.mb.ca/stem/index.html
Acts Administered:
Gaming Control Act
Manitoba Hydro Act
Minister, Jim Rondeau
204-945-5356, Fax: 204-948-2692
minstem@leg.gov.mb.ca
Deputy Minister, John Clarkson
204-945-2771, Fax: 204-948-2747
dmstem@leg.gov.mb.ca
- Industrial Technology Centre
#200, 78 Innovation Dr.
Winnipeg, MB R3T 6C2
www.itc.mb.ca
Chief Operating Officer, Trevor Cornell
- Mining Board
#360, 1395 Ellice Ave.
Winnipeg, MB R3G 3P2
204-489-0018
Presiding Member, Roy McPhail, P.Eng.
Arbitration of disputes between surface rights holders & mineral rights holders with respect to accessing of minerals other than oil & gas.
- Surface Rights Board
#360, 1395 Ellice Ave.
Winnipeg, MB R3G 3P2
204-945-0731
Fax: 204-948-2578
800-282-8069
bmiskimmin@gov.mb.ca
Presiding Member, Art Cowan
Arbitrates disputes relating to right of entry or compensation for surface rights used by holders of oil & gas rights.
- Manitoba Education, Research & Learning Information Networks(MERLIN)
#100 - 135 Innovation Dr., University of Manitoba
Winnipeg, MB R3T 6A8
204-474-7800
Fax: 204-474-7830
800-430-6404
www.merlin.mb.ca
- Manitoba Health Research Council
#P216, 770 Bannatyne Ave.
Winnipeg, MB R3E 0W3
204-775-1096
Fax: 204-786-5401
info@mhrc.mb.ca
mhrc.mb.ca

Energy Development Initiative
The Initiative's focus is on: Agri-Energy, Biofuels, Geothermal systems, Wind Energy, Green Building & Energy Efficiency, Hydrogen, as well as hybrid-electric vehicles, solar energy, ethanol fuels
Asst. Deputy Minister Energy Development Initiative, Garry Hastings
204-945-1454, Fax: 204-943-0031
Director Energy Economic Development, Jim Crone
204-945-1874, Fax: 204-943-0031
jcrone@gov.mb.ca
Director Energy Policy, Shaun Loney
204-945-5804, Fax: 204-943-0031
sloney@gov.mb.ca

Energy Climate Change & Green Strategy Initiatives Branch
#1202 - 155 Carlton St.
Winnipeg, MB R3C 3H8
204-945-7382
Fax: 204-948-3739
ccinfo@gov.mb.ca
www.manitoba.ca
The Branch promotes awareness, programs & funding for climate change initiatives, facilitates partnerships between government & community to develop green initiatives that result in environmental, economic & social benefits, advances climate change mitigation & adaptation research, & develops regional partnerships for climate change action
Acting Executive Director, Andrea Merredew
204-945-2245
Director Communications, Colin Lemoine
204-945-1494

Mineral Resources Division
#360, 1395 Ellice Ave.
Winnipeg, MB R3G 3P2
Fax: 204-945-8427
Promotes wise land management & environmentally sustainable economic development in the province based on Manitoba's mineral & petroleum resources; fosters & enhances business development opportunities in mineral & petroleum economic development through promotion & marketing activities; provides authoritative documentation of the province's mineral & petroleum endowment & development potential; administers the delivery of mineral & petroleum industry support programs; administers legislation governing the disposition of mineral rights, oil & gas rights, exploration, development & production of Manitoba's mineral & petroleum resources
Assistant Deputy Minister, John Fox
204-945-4317, Fax: 204-945-1406
jfox@gov.mb.ca

Manitoba Geological Survey
#360, 1394 Ellice Ave.
Winnipeg, MB R3G 3P2
Fax: 204-945-1406
800-223-5215
minesinfo@gov.mb.ca
Generates technical information on the geology of Manitoba in order to encourage & guide mineral exploration in the province & to provide a database for developing mineral policy & for determining effective land-use policies.
Director, Ric Syme
204-945-6556,
rsyme@gov.mb.ca

Mineral Policy & Business Development
Manager, Gary Ostry
204-945-6564, Fax: 204-945-8427
gostry@gov.mb.ca
MEAP Coordinator Minerals Policy & Business Development, Linda Rogoski
204-945-6586, Fax: 204-945-8427
lrogoski@gov.mb.ca

Flin Flon
Barrow Bldg.
143 Main St.
Flin Flon, MB R8K 1K2
Fax: 204-687-1634

Thompson
Provincial Bldg.
59 Elizabeth Dr.
Thompson, MB R8N 1X4
Fax: 204-677-6888

Mines Branch
#360, 1395 Ellice Ave.
Winnipeg, MB R3G 3P2
Fax: 204-948-2578
The Mines Branch administers legislation governing the disposition of mineral rights (permits, claims & leases), exploration, development, & production of the province's non-fuel mineral resources & the rehabilitation of mines & quarries.
Director, Ernie Armitt
204-945-6505,
earmitt@gov.mb.ca

Brandon Mining Engineering Office
Provincial Bldg.
340 - 9th St.
Brandon, MB R7A 6C2
Fax: 204-677-6888

Petroleum
#360, 1395 Ellice Ave.
Winnipeg, MB R3G 3P2
204-945-6577
Fax: 204-945-0586
Administers provisions under The Oil & Gas Act & The Oil & Gas Production Tax Act relating to exploration, development, production & transportation of oil & gas. The Branch develops, recom-

mends, implements & administers policies & legislation, to provide for the sustainable development of Manitoba's oil & gas resources. The Branch deals with matters relating to well spacing, production allowables, pool designations, salt water disposal, enhanced recovery projects & unitization. The Branch publishes several reports each year, providing the public, industry & government with information on the petroleum industry in Manitoba
Director, Keith Lowdon
klowdon@gov.mb.ca

Virden
Petroleum Inspection
227 King St.
Virden, MB R0M 2C0
204-748-4260
Fax: 204-748-2208

Waskada
Petroleum Inspection
23 Railway Ave.
Waskada, MB R0M 2E0
204-673-2472
Fax: 204-673-2767

ICT Services Manitoba
#300 - 259 Portage Ave.
Winnipeg, MB R3B 2A9
800-665-0204
www.gov.mb.ca/est/KnowledgeEnterprises

Knowledge Enterprises Branch
259 Portage Ave.
Winnipeg, MB R3B 3P4
204-945-6298
Fax: 204-945-3977

Manitoba Water Stewardship
200 Saulteaux Cres.
PO Box 11
Winnipeg, MB R3J 3W3
204-945-6398
800-282-8069
wsd@gov.mb.ca
www.gov.mb.ca/waterstewardship/index.html
Provides leadership in environmental stewardship for the benefit of current & future generations of Manitobans, so that the social, economic & inherent environmental value of water is protected & realized, Manitoba's water & fish resources are managed sustainably, & people are safe from water hazards. Comprised of the former Water Branch, Fisheries Branch, & Office of Drinking Water from Manitoba Conservation, the Manitoba Water Services Board, & the Conservation Districts Program from the Department of Intergovernmental Affairs
Acts Administered:
Conservation Agreements Act
Conservation Agreement Forms Regulation
Eligible Conservation Agencies Regulation
Conservation Districts Act
Drinking Water Safety Act, 2004
Dyking Authority Act
Fisheries Act
Fishermen's Assistance & Polluter's Liability Act
Ground Water & Water Well Act
Lake of the Woods Control Board Act
Manitoba Habitat Heritage Act
Manitoba Natural Resources Transfer Act
Natural Resources Agreement Act
Red River Floodway Act
Water Power Act
Water Protection Act
Water Resources Administration Act
Water Resources Conservation Act
Water Rights Act
Water Supply Commissions Act
Minister, Hon. Christine Melnick
204-945-1133, Fax: 204-948-2684
minwsd@leg.gov.mb.ca
Deputy Minister, Don Norquay
204-945-0982, Fax: 204-948-2519
dmwsd@leg.gov.mb.ca
• Manitoba Conservation Districts Commission
Secretariat c/o Planning & Coordination Branch
123 Main St.
PO Box 20000
Neepawa, MB R0J 1H0
204-476-7033
Fax: 204-476-7539
whildebran@gov.mb.ca

Ecological Services Division
Asst. Deputy Minister, Dwight Williamson
204-945-7030
Director Fisheries Branch, Joe O'Connor
204-945-7814, Fax: 204-945-2308
Director Planning & Coordination, Rhonda McDougal
204-945-8271
Director Water Science & Management Branch, Nicole Armstrong
204-945-3991

Office of Drinking Water
1007 Century St.
Winnipeg, MB R3H 0W4
204-945-5762
Fax: 204-945-1365
Coordinates the activities of the province's drinking water program; provides guidance, technical expertise, information & education materials; ensures water suppliers provide safe, adequate & aesthetically pleasing water
Manager, P.Eng. Don Rocan
204-945-7010

Regulatory & Operational Services
Executive Director, Steven Topping
204-945-7488
Manager Water Control Systems Management, Eugene Kozera
204-945-7474
Manager Water Use Licensing Section, Rob Matthews
204-945-6118
Manager Flood Forecasting Coordination, Alfred Warkentin
204-945-6698
Acting Manager Water Control Works & Drainage Licensing, Perry Stonehouse
204-726-6764

Manitoba Workers' Compensation Board
333 Broadway Ave.
Winnipeg, MB R3C 4W3
204-954-4321
Fax: 204-954-4999
800-362-3340
wcb@wcb.mb.ca
www.wcb.mb.ca
President/CEO, Doug Sexsmith
Vice President Prevention, Assessments & Customer Service, Alice Sayant
Vice President Rehabilitation & Compensation Services, Dave Scott
Director Communications/SAFE Work, Warren Preece

Government of New Brunswick
Seat of Government: PO Box 6000
Fredericton, NB E3B 5H1
www.gnb.ca
The Province of New Brunswick entered Confederation July 1, 1867. It has an area of 71,355.12 km2. The Statistics Canada census population in 2006 was 730,000.

Population Growth Secretariat
Centennial Bldg.
670 King St.
PO Box 6000
Fredericton, NB E3B 5H1
506-453-3981
Fax: 506-444-6729
immigration@gnb.ca
www.gnb.ca/3100/index-e.asp
The Population Growth Secretariat consists of the Immigration Division & the Population Support Division. Issues such as settlement & multiculturalism, retention, & repatriation are handled by the Secretariat.
Minister, Business New Brunswick; Minister Responsible, Service New Brunswick; Minister Responsible Population Growth Secretariat; Minister Responsible, Communications New Brunswick, Minister Responsible, Red Tape Reduction, Hon. Greg Byrne
506-453-5898, Fax: 506-453-5893
greg.byrne@gnb.ca

Chief Executive Officer, Humprhey Sheehan
506-457-7640, Fax: 506-453-3899
humphrey.sheehan@gnb.ca
Executive Director Immigration, Tony Lampart
506-453-3455, Fax: 506-444-6729
tony.lampart@gnb.ca
Executive Director Population Support, Monique Drapeau-Miles
506-453-8786, Fax: 506-453-3899
Monique.Drapeau-Miles@gnb.ca
Officer Marketing & Communications, Karen Vessey
506-444-2483, Fax: 506-453-5329
karen.vessey@gnb.ca

Department of Agriculture, Aquaculture & Fisheries / Agriculture, Aquaculture et Pêches
PO Box 6000
Fredericton, NB E3B 5H1
506-453-2666
Fax: 506-453-7170
DAAF-MAAP@gnb.ca
www.gnb.ca/aquaculture
Acts Administered:
Agricultural Commodity Price Stabilization Act
Agricultural Land Protection & Development Act
Agricultural Operation Practices Act
Apiary Inspection Act
Aquaculture Act
Crop Insurance Act
Diseases of Animals Act
Farm Income Assurance Act
Fish Processing Act
Fish & Wildlife Act (in part)
Injurious Insect & Pest Act
Inshore Fisheries Representation Act
Livestock Operations Act
Livestock Yard Sales Act
Marshland Reclamation Act
Natural Products Act
New Brunswick Grain Act
Pipeline Act
Plant Health Act
Potato Disease Eradication Act
Poultry Health Protection Act
Sheep Protection Act
Weed Control Act
Women's Institute & Institut féminin Act
Minister Agriculture, Aquaculture & Fisheries, Hon. Michael Olscamp
506-453-2662, Fax: 506-453-3402
Mike.Olscamp@gnb.ca
Deputy Minister, Jean-Marc Dupuis
506-453-2450, Fax: 506-444-5022
jean-marc.dupuis@gnb.ca
Director Communications, Gisèle Regimbal
506-444-4218, Fax: 506-444-5022
Gisele.Regimbal@gnb.ca
• New Brunswick Agricultural Insurance Commission
PO Box 6000
Fredericton, NB E3B 5H1
506-453-2185
Fax: 506-453-7406
Manager, Margaret Mann
To provide farmers with insurance protection against production losses caused by natural hazards beyond their control through the Canada / Agricultural Insurance Program.
• New Brunswick Farm Products Commission
c/o Department of Agriculture, Aquaculture & Fisheries
PO Box 6000
Fredericton, NB E3B 5H1
506-453-3647
Fax: 506-444-5969
Chair, Bob Shannon
Products Act. ment/administrative support to the Commission in the monitoring of commodity boards under the provisions of the Natural Products Act.

Agriculture & Bio-Economy Division / Agriculture et Bioéconomie
To encourage the development of a prosperous, globally competitive & sustainable agriculture & agri-food business using the latest technologies to produce & market innovative & safe food as well as other bio-products.

Federal/Provincial Government / Government of New Brunswick

Asst. Deputy Minister, Kevin McKendy
506-453-2366, Fax: 506-444-5022
kevin.mckendy@gnb.ca
Executive Director Livestock Development, Michael Maloney
506-453-5443
Director Crop Development, Kevin McCully
506-453-3481
Director Business Risk Management, Cathy Larochelle
506-444-2728
Director Land & Environment, Lynn Moore
506-453-2109
Director Regional Agri-Business Development, Gerry Chevrier
506-453-2172

Central
Miramichi, NB
506-778-6030
Fax: 506-778-6679

East
Bathurst, NB
506-547-2088
Fax: 506-547-2064

Northwest
Grand Falls, NB
506-473-7755
Fax: 506-473-6641

South
Sussex, NB
506-432-2000
Fax: 506-432-2044

Southeast
Moncton, NB
506-856-2277
Fax: 506-856-2092

West
Wicklow, NB

Fisheries Division / Pêches
To foster the continued development of & innovation within the commercial fisheries & aquaculture sectors & to provide policy & planning support for all departmental programs.
Asst. Deputy Minister, Roland Cormier
506-457-6964, Fax: 506-444-5022
roland.cormier@gnb.ca
Executive Director Resource Management & Operations, Yvon Chiasson
506-453-8432, Fax: 506-462-5929
yvon.chiasson@gnb.ca
Director Business Development, Louis Arsenault
506-444-4218, Fax: 506-444-5022
louis.rsenault@gnb.ca
Director Licensing & Technical Services, Ghislain Chiasson
506-453-5229, Fax: 506-453-5210
ghislain.chiasson@gnb.ca

St. George
506-755-4000
Fax: 506-755-4001
Regional Director, Marc Johnston

Bouctouche
506-743-7222
Fax: 506-743-7229
Regional Director, Louis Arsenault

Caraquet
506-726-2400
Fax: 506-726-2419
Regional Director, Mario Gaudet

Legislative Services
Centennial Bldg.
#418, 670 King St.
PO Box 6000
Fredericton, NB E3B 5H1
506-453-2855
Fax: 506-457-7342

Department of Business New Brunswick / Entreprises Nouveau-Brunswick

Centennial Bldg.
670 King St.
PO Box 6000
Fredericton, NB E3B 5H1
506-453-3707
Fax: 506-453-3993
investnb@gnb.ca
www.gnb.ca/0398/index-e.asp
The Department of Business New Brunswick provides the following serices: Business expansion & innovation; Export development; Investment, for the establishment of new business in the province; & Services & support to the film & television industry in New Brunswick.
Acts Administered:
Agricultural Associations Act
Economic Development Act
Farm Credit Corporation Assistance Act
Farm Improvement Assistance Loans Act
Farm Machinary Loans Act
Fisheries Development Act
Industrial Relations Act
Livestock Incentives Act
Youth Assistance Act
Minister Responsible, Business New Brunswick, Hon. Paul Robichaud
506-453-5898, Fax: 506-453-6389
paul.robichaud@gnb.ca
Deputy Minister, Bill Levesque
506-453-5897, Fax: 506-453-6389
bill.levesque@gnb.ca
Director Human Resource Services, Karen Tucker
506-457-6710, Fax: 506-444-5440
karen.tucker@gnb.ca
Director Communications, Marie-Josée Groulx
506-444-3465, Fax: 506-453-3993
marie-josee.groulx@gnb.ca
• New Brunswick Industrial Development Board
Business New Brunswick, Centennial Bldg.
670 King St.
PO Box 6000
Fredericton, NB E3B 5H1
506-453-4200
Fax: 506-444-4182

Business Financial Support & Corporate Services
Centennial Bldg.
#571, 670 King St.
PO Box 6000
Fredericton, NB E3B 5H1
506-453-2794
Fax: 506-444-4277
Helps companies be more successful by offering financial assistance and capital investment to new and existing entrepreneurs that want to grow and create sustainable employment in New Brunswick.
Assistant Deputy Minister, Sadie Perron
506-453-7499,
sadie.perron@gnb.ca
Executive Director Business Financial Support, John Rosengren
506-453-3929,
john.rosengren@gnb.ca
Executive Director Financial Administration, Barbara Yerxa
506-444-5197, Fax: 506-453-5428
Barbara.YERXA@gnb.ca
Executive Director Policy & Planning, Shannon Sanford
506-444-5854,
shannon.sanford@gnb.ca
Manager Financial Programs, Kevin Kearns
506-444-5888, Fax: 506-453-7904
Kevin.kearns@gnb.ca

Communications
Centennial Bldg.
670 King St., 5th Fl.
PO Box 6000
Fredericton, NB E3B 5H1
506-453-3707
Fax: 506-453-3993
Spreads the word about Business New Brunswick's efforts to help attract investment, retain and expand businesses and develop key economic clusters.
Director, Marie-Josée Groulx
506-444-3465,
marie-josee.groulx@gnb.ca

Investment, Export & Business Development
Centennial Bldg.
670 King St., 5th Fl.
PO Box 6000
Fredericton, NB E3B 5H1
506-453-2875
Fax: 506-444-4277
They get the word out among international corporate leaders that New Brunswick is the place to be in business, attracting new investment and jobs with specific focus on knowledge-based industries, value-added natural resources, bio-technologies and advanced manufacturing. Their export and trade staff members help companies be more profitable by exporting their products to new and existing markets, providing counseling, trade assistance and specialized services to export-ready businesses and existing exporters.
Assistant Deputy Minister, Jeff Trail
506-444-5775,
jeff.trail@gnb.ca
Executive Director Industry Services, Roger Y. Cyr
506-453-2402, Fax: 506-457-7282
roger.cyr@gnb.ca
Executive Director Knowledge Industries and Innovation, Joanne Walker
506-457-4921, Fax: 506-444-4182
joanne.walker@gnb.ca
Director Export Development, Michel Albert
506-444-5053, Fax: 506-453-3783
michel.albert@gnb.ca
Director Investment, Joel Richardson
506-457-7545,
joel.richardson@gnb.ca
Manager Marketing, Monique Arsenault
506-444-2135, Fax: 506-444-4586
monique.arsenault@gnb.ca

Northern Development / Développement des entreprises
Harbourview Place
275 Main St.
Bathurst, NB E2A 1A9
506-547-2227
Fax: 506-547-2269
Assistant Deputy Minister, Roger Robichaud
roger.robichaud@gnb.ca
Director, Rick Lloyd
rick.lloyd@gnb.ca
Director, Denis Roy
denis.roy2@gnb.ca

Special Initiatives / Initiatives spéciales
Centennial Building
PO Box 6000
Fredericton, NB E3B 5H1
506-453-3707
Fax: 506-453-5428
Executive Director, Gary Jochelman
506-444-4238,
gary.jochelman@gnb.ca
Director Office of Red Tape Reduction, Wendy L. Betts
506-444-4167,
Wendy.Betts@gnb.ca

Department of Energy / Énergie

Brunswick Square
#100M, 1 Germain St.
PO Box 5001
Saint John, NB E2L 4Y9
506-658-3180
Fax: 506-658-3191
www.gnb.ca/0085/index-e.asp
The New Brunswick Department of Energy is responsible for the following: Ensuring a reliable & cost effective energy supply; Promoting economic efficiency in energy systems; Encouraging economic development opportunities; Protecting & improving the environment; & Ensuring an effective regulatory regime.
Acts Administered:
Electricity Act
Energy Efficiency Act
Energy Efficiency & Conservation Agency of New Brunswick Act
Gas Distribution, 1999 Act
Petroleum Products Pricing Act
Pipeline, 2005 Act
Minister, Energy; Minister, Supply & Services; Minister Responsible, Efficiency NB, Hon. Jack Keir
506-658-3177, Fax: 506-658-3191
Jack.Keir2@gnb.ca

Federal/Provincial Government / Government of New Brunswick

Deputy Minster, Claire Lepage
506-658-3179,
Claire.Lepage@gnb.ca
• Efficiency NB
#101, 33 Charlotte St.
Saint John, NB E2L 2H3
506-643-7826
Fax: 506-643-7835
866-643-8833
www.efficiencynb.ca
Minister, Energy; Minister, Supply & Services; Minister Responsib, Hon. Jack Keir
Efficiency NB is engaged in the following activities: Promoting energy efficiency measures throughout New Brunswick; Encouraging the development of an energy efficiency services industry; Implementing & offering programs related to energy efficiency; & Increasing awareness of the relation between energy efficiency measures & a reliable energy supply for the province.

Alternative Energy & Market Development
Brunswick Square
#M100, 1 Germain St.
Saint John, NB E2L 4V1
506-658-3180
Fax: 506-658-3191
Assistant Deputy Minister Alternative Energy & Market Development, Neil Jacobsen
506-658-3132, Fax: 506-658-3191
Director Science & Technology, Bill Breckenridge
506-658-3144,
bill.breckenridge@gnb.ca
Director Pipeline, Petroleum, & Natural Gas, Patrick Ervin
506-658-3124,
patrick.ervin@gnb.ca
Director Electricity, Stephen Waycott
506-658-3126,
Stephen.Waycott@gnb.ca
Coordinator Corporate Services, Education & Awareness, Bonnie Doyle
506-658-2410,
bonnie.doyle@gnb.ca
Senior Consultant Corporate Services, Education & Awareness, David Duplisea
506-658-3158,
David.Duplisea@gnb.ca

Policy Development & Planning
Brunswick Square
#100M, 1 Germain St.
Saint John, NB E2L 4V1
506-658-3180
Fax: 506-658-3191
Executive Director Policy Development & Planning, Shelley Rinehart
506-658-3180,
shelley.rinehart@gnb.ca
Policy Advisor, Laura Delong
506-658-3184
• New Brunswick Round Table on Environment & Economy
20 McGloin St.
PO Box 6000
Fredericton, NB E3B 5H1
506-453-3703
Fax: 506-453-3876
Executive Secretary, Dean Mundee
Mandate is to monitor/report on New Brunswick's progress towards implementing the elements of its Plan for Action & to act as a catalyst for change towards sustainable development within the Province.

Department of the Environment / Environnement
Marysville Place
20 McGloin St.
PO Box 6000
Fredericton, NB E3B 5H1
506-453-2690
Fax: 506-457-4991
env-info@gnb.ca
www.gnb.ca/0009/index-e.asp
Other Communication: To report oil, pesticide, chemical spills, & other environmental emergencies, Toll-Free: 1-800-565-1633.
The Department of the Environment carries out the following responsibilities: Provision of integrated stewardship; Ensuring enforcement of environmental legislation & regulations; & Consultation with municipal governments & Local Service Districts.
Acts Administered:
Beverage Containers Act
Clean Air Act
Clean Environment Act
Clean Water Act
Community Planning Act
Environmental Trust Fund Act (except administration of fund)
Gas Distribution, 1999 Act (subsection 18(2), paragraph 32(1)(a), & subsection 39(1))
Mining Act (subsection 68(2))
Pesticides Control Act
Topsoil Preservation Act
Minister, Hon. Richard Miles
506-444-5136, Fax: 506-453-3377
rick.miles@gnb.ca
Deputy Minister, Bonny Hoyt-Hallett
506-453-3256, Fax: 506-453-3377
Bonny.Hoyt-Hallett@gnb.ca
Executive Director Corporate Initiatives, K. Bradford Marshall
506-453-3700, Fax: 506-453-3676
Brad.Marshall@gnb.ca
Director Strategic Planning & Policy Development, Kim Hughes
506-453-3700,
Kim.HUGHES@gnb.ca
Director Public Affairs, Vicky Deschênes
506-453-3700, Fax: 506-453-3843
Vicky.Deschenes@gnb.ca

Environmental Management / Gestion de l'environnement
Marysville Place
20 McGloin St.
PO Box 6000
Fredericton, NB E3B 5H1
506-444-5119
Fax: 506-457-7333
The main responsibility of the Environmental Management Division is initiatives to control pollutants, promote pollution prevention, & protect the environment. The Division acts as a major regulatory arm of the Department.
Assistant Deputy Minister, Perry Haines
Perry.Haines@gnb.ca
Executive Director Regional Services, Kirk M. Gordon
Kirk.Gordon@gnb.ca
Director Environmental Technologies & Innovation, Michael R. Sprague
506-444-5416,
mike.sprague@gnb.ca
Director Stewardship, Gregory Shanks
506-453-7945, Fax: 506-453-2390
greg.shanks@gnb.ca
Director Project Assessment & Approvals, Paul Vanderlaan
506-444-4599, Fax: 506-457-7805
Paul.Vanderlaan@gnb.ca

Approvals Branch
Provides authorization to control or limit the discharge of contaminants into the environment, regulates issuing of approvals & permits & monitors compliance with the conditions of approvals, permits, & established standards. Making the public aware of issues related to the release of contaminants, soliciting public input to decisions on approvals, responding in a timely fashion to public & media inquiries to promote a better understanding of environmental issues are all activities focused within this Branch.
Director, Perry Haines
506-444-4599

Climate Change & Environmental Services
Executive Director, David Schellenberg
506-453-3925, Fax: 506-453-2265
Director Climate Change Secretariat, Dean Mundee
506-453-3925, Fax: 506-453-2265

Remediation Branch
506-453-2690
Remediation Branch focuses on all aspects of identification & remediation, redevelopment & management of contaminated sites including: dump closures, petroleum storage & soil remediation, tank decommissioning & thermal absorption.
Director, Michael Sprague
506-444-5955

Stewardship Branch
Encompasses those areas focusing on the management of environmental issues, which are not specifically related to pollution control such as pesticides, dredge disposal, used oil, municipal water & wastewater approvals, landfills, composting & C&D site approvals as well as aquaculture approvals.
Director, Greg Shanks
506-453-7945,
greg.shanks@gnb.ca
Manager Bioscience & Resource Recovery, Mark Boldon
Manager Waste Management, Timothy Leblanc

Regional Environmental Services

Bathurst Regional Office
#202, 159 Main St.
Bathurst, NB E2A 1A6
506-547-2092
Fax: 506-547-7655
elg.egl-region1@gnb.ca
Regional Director, Paul Fournier
Paul.Fournier@gnb.ca

Fredericton Regional Office
Priestman Centre
565 Priestman St.
PO Box 6000
Fredericton, NB E3B 5H1
506-444-5149
Fax: 506-453-2893
elg.egl-region5@gnb.ca
Regional Director, Serge Gagnon
Serge.Gagnon@gnb.ca

Grand Falls Regional Office
#200, 65 Broadway Blvd.
PO Box 5001
Grand Falls, NB E3Z 1G1
506-473-7744
Fax: 506-475-2510
elg.egl-region6@gnb.ca
Regional Director, Richard Keeley
Richard.Keeley@gnb.ca

Miramichi Regional Office
Industrial Park
316 Dalton Ave.
Miramichi, NB E1V 3N9
506-778-6032
Fax: 506-778-6796
elg.egl-region2@gnb.ca
Regional Director, Denis Daigle
Denis.Daigle@gnb.ca

Moncton Regional Office
Provincial Bldg.
428 Collishaw St.
PO Box 5001
Moncton, NB E1C 8R3
506-856-2374
Fax: 506-856-2370
elg.egl-region3@gnb.ca

Regional Director, Laurie Collette
Laurie.Collette@gnb.ca

Saint John Regional Office
8 Castle St.
PO Box 5001
Saint John, NB E2L 4Y9
506-658-2558
Fax: 506-658-3046
elg.egl-region4@gnb.ca
Regional Director, Susan M. Atkinson

Sciences & Planning / Science et planification
Marysville Place
20 McGloin St., 2nd Fl.
PO Box 6000
Fredericton, NB E3B 5H1
506-453-2862
Fax: 506-453-2265
Scientific assessment, monitoring functions, & planning for sustainability are the major activities of the Sciences & Planning Division.
Assistant Deputy Minister Sciences & Planning, Diane Kent Gillis
diane.kentgillis@gnb.ca

Federal/Provincial Government / Government of New Brunswick

Executive Director Environmental Services, David Schellenberg
506-444-2654, Fax: 506-444-2734
dave.schellenberg@gnb.ca
Director Science & Reporting, Daryl Pupek
506-457-4844,
Darryl.Pupek@gnb.ca
Director Climate Change Secretariat, Dean Mundee
506-457-4844,
Dean.Mundee@gnb.ca

Analytical Services Branch
Provides scientific testing resources to the department for the determination of selected environmental contaminates in water, soil, sediment, air & food. Laboratory analysis of environmental samples is performed in support of government legislation & programs. The laboratory also serves other government departments & agencies, municipalities, & the general public on a fee for service basis.
Director, Peter McLaughlin
506-453-2477

Project Assessment Branch
Responsible for ensuring that new developments & expansions are designed & planned in a manner that minimizes or eliminates impacts on the environment. The Branch coordinates the review of project-related information by provincial & federal agencies to avoid costly remedial measures.
Director, Paul Vanderlaan
506-444-5382

Sciences & Reporting Branch
Provides broad environmental monitoring & scientific assessment to the Department, & also provides information to the public sector, private sector & other government agencies. Focus is given to four main component areas: air quality science; general hydrology; surface water quality & hydrogeological resource assessments.
Director, Daryl Pupek
506-457-4844

Sustainable Planning Branch
Contributes to the maintenance of the ecosystem through integrated land, water, & air planning, focusing on all aspects of comprehensive environmental planning with due consideration to economic, social & governance issues. Some of the areas of responsibility are; contributing to the maintenance of water quality in sources of public drinking water, promoting watershed management & appropriate use of lands, addressing water quality & quantity associated with private wells, coordinating Land Use Planning approvals & overseeing the Community Planning Act, as well as working with community groups to enhance sustainable planning activities, such as watershed groups.
Director, Kim Hughes
506-453-2862

Acts Administered:
Environmental Trust Fund (administration of fund)
Fishermen's Disaster Fund Act (functions vested in Provincial Secretary-Treasurer)
Gasoline & Motive Fuel Tax Act

Department of Health / Santé

PO Box 5100
Fredericton, NB E3B 5G8
506-457-4800
Fax: 506-453-5243
dh-ms@dh-ms.ca
www.gnb.ca/0051/index-e.asp
To work with New Brunswickers in achieving well-being by promoting self-sufficiency & personal responsibility, & providing approved services as required. The development & delivery of health programs & services to New Brunswick residents is supported by a range of internal department functions such as administration, planning & evaluation, & program support. Provides the continuum of services to prevent illness & disability. The department's education & awareness raising initiatives promote the health & well-being of New Brunswickers of all ages so that they can achieve their best potential while enjoying an independent & healthy lifestyle for as long as possible.

Acts Administered:
Ambulance Services Act
Anatomy Act
Cemetery Companies Act
Change of Name Act
Clean Air (Paragraph 8(2a) & Subsection 4)
Clean Water Act (in part)
Fish Inspection Act
Health Act
Hospital Act
Hospital Services Act
Human Tissues Act
Human Tissues Gift Act
Insurance Act
Liquor Control Act
Marriage Act
Medical Consent of Minors Act
Medical Services Payment Act
Mental Health Act
Mental Health Services Act
Motor Vehicle Act (in part)
Municipalities Act
Pesticides Control Act (in part)
Prescription Drug Payment Act
Public Health
Radiological Health Protection Act
Regional Health Authorities Act
Smoke-Free Places Act, 2004
Tobacco Sales Act
Venereal Disease Act
Vital Statistics Act
Minister, Hon. Michael B. Murphy
MichaelB.Murphy@gnb.ca
Deputy Minister, Donald Ferguson
don.j.ferguson@gnb.ca
Director Communications, Tracey Burkhardt
506-453-2536,
tracey.burkhardt@gnb.ca
Administrative Support, Kathy Densmore
506-453-2536, Fax: 506-444-4697
kathy.densmore@gnb.ca

Addiction & Mental Health Services Division / Services de traitement des dépendances et de santé mentale
506-444-4442

Public Health & Medical Services / Santé publique et services médicaux
Public Health services are delivered through the province's seven health regions, under the management of Regional Directors. A Chief Medical Officer of Health & a Deputy Chief Medical Officer of Health oversee the development of policy & regulations, & provide medical operational support to the regional Medical Officers of Health. Public Health Services support healthy growth & development, foster healthy lifestyles, control communicable diseases, & protect the public from adverse health consequences of exposure to chemical, physical & biological agents.
Chief Medical Officer, Dr. Wayne MacDonald
506-453-2323
Provincial Epidemiologist, Dr. B. Christofer Balram
506-453-3092
Director Medicare Services, Linda M. Lingley
506-453-6851
Manager Medical Services, Cheryl Saunders
Acts Administered:
Easements Act
Expropriation Act

Department of Local Government / Gouvernementaux locales

Marysville Place
20 McGloin St.
PO Box 6000
Fredericton, NB E3B 5H1
506-453-2807
Fax: 506-453-3988
www.gnb.ca/0370/index-e.asp
The Department of Local Government oversees the following areas: Assessment & planning appeals; Local governance & regional collaboration for New Brunswick; Local Service Districts; Municipalities (cities, towns, & villages) & rural communities, including municipal capital borrowing, orientation, & restructuring; Registration of dogs & dog kennels in unincorporated areas; Resource manuals for local government in New Brunswick; & grants.

Acts Administered:
Agricultural Land Protection & Development Act (subsection 10(2) & section 11)
Assessment & Planning Appeal Board Act
Business Improvement Areas Act
Cemetery Companies Act (paragraph 5(1)(c))
Control of Municipalities Act
Days of Rest Act
Edmundston, 1998 Act
Evidence Act (sections 88, 89, & 90)
Highway Act (sections 58 - 62.1)
Metric Conversion Act
Municipal Assistance Act
Municipal Capital Borrowing Act
Municipal Debentures Act
Municipalities Act (except subsection 19(8), 125(1), & 188(3))
Municipal Thoroughfare Easements Act
New Brunswick Municipal Finance Corporation Act (section 14 & subsection 16(4))
Police Act (paragraph 17.05(2)(b), subsections 17.06(3), & (4), paragraph 17.2(3)(b), & subsections 17.4(3) & (4))
Real Property Tax (section 4 & subsection 5(10))
Service New Brunswick Act (paragraph 15.1(3)(b))
Society for the Prevention of Cruelty to Animals Act
Unsightly Premises Act
Minister Local Government, Hon. Carmel Robichaud
carmel.robichaud@gnb.ca
Deputy Minister, Bonny Hoyt-Hallett
506-453-3256, Fax: 506-453-3988
Bonny.Hoyt-Hallett@gnb.ca
• Assessment & Planning Appeal Board
#201, 435 King St.
PO Box 6000
Fredericton, NB E3B 5H1
506-453-2126
Fax: 506-444-4881
Chair, Scott R. MacGregor

Corporate & Community Finance
Marysville Place
20 McGloin St.
PO Box 6000
Fredericton, NB E3B 5H1
506-453-2154
Fax: 506-457-4933
Executive Director Community Finance, Dan Rae
506-453-2154, Fax: 506-453-7128
Dan.Rae@gnb.ca
Director Community Finance, Sandra Jessop-Roach
506-453-2154, Fax: 506-453-7128
Sandra.Roach@gnb.ca
Director Corporate Finance, Yvonne Samson
Yvonne.Samson@gnb.ca

Corporate Services / Services généraux
Marysville Place
20 McGloin St.
PO Box 6000
Fredericton, NB E3B 5H1
506-453-2020
Fax: 506-457-7800
Executive Director Corporate Services, Alan J. Roy
506-453-2020, Fax: 506-457-7800
alan.roy@gnb.ca
Director Information & Technology Management, Laurie Robichaud
506-453-2020, Fax: 506-453-7128
Laurie.Robichaud@gnb.ca

Local Governance & Community Infrastructure
Marysville Place
20 McGloin St., 2nd Fl.
PO Box 6000
Fredericton, NB E3B 5H1
506-444-4423
Fax: 506-457-4933
Executive Director Community Infrastructure, Stephen Battah
506-444-4423, Fax: 506-457-4933
stephen.battah@gnb.ca
Director Community Restructuring, Johnny St. Onge
506-444-4423, Fax: 506-457-4933
Johnny.St-Onge@gnb.ca
Director Capacity Building, Thierry Arseneau
506-444-4423, Fax: 506-457-4933
Thierry.arseneau@gnb.ca

Local Service District
Marysville Place
20 McGloin St., 2nd Fl.
PO Box 6000
Fredericton, NB E3B 5H1
506-453-2434
Fax: 506-457-4933

Offices of the Local Service District Division are located in the following places: Bathurst, Edmundston, Richibucto, Tracadie-Sheila, Miramichi, St, Stephen, & Woodstock.
Director Local Service District, Colleen Mullin
506-453-2434, Fax: 506-457-4933
Colleen.Mullin@gnb.ca

Policy, Planning & Public Affairs
Marysville Place
20 McGloin St., 2nd Fl.
PO Box 6000
Fredericton, NB E3B 5H1
506-453-2434
Fax: 506-457-4933
Executive Director Policy, Planning & Public Affairs, Elizabeth Hayward
506-453-2434, Fax: 506-457-4933
bebo.hayward@gnb.ca
Director Policy & Legislative Affairs, Christy Shaw
506-453-2434, Fax: 506-453-7128
Christy.Shaw@gnb.ca
Manager Strategic Initiatives Development, Martin Corbett
506-453-2434, Fax: 506-457-4933
martin.corbett@gnb.ca

Department of Natural Resources / Ressources naturelles

PO Box 6000
Fredericton, NB E3B 5H1
506-453-2510
Fax: 506-444-5839
dnrweb@gnb.ca
www.gnb.ca/0078/index-e.asp
Manages all natural resources within the province including fish & wildlife, timber, minerals, Crown lands & water resources. Responsible for the development, protection, allocation & utilization of resources in a way that is considered economically, environmentally & socially acceptable.
Acts Administered:
Act Respecting Angling Lease Number 7
Bituminous Shale Act
Conservation Easements Act
Crown Grant Restrictions Act
Crown Lands & Forests Act
Leasing Regulation
Endangered Species Act
Fish & Wildlife Act
Forest Fires Act
Grants Act
Kouchibouguac National Park, An Act to Implement Recommendation 16 of the Report of the Special Inquiry on Mining Act (in part)
National Parks Act
Natural Products Act (in part)
Off-Road Vehicle Act
Oil & Natural Gas Act
Ownership of Minerals Act
Parks Act
Pipe Line Act
Protected Natural Areas Act, 2003
Quarriable Substances Act
Scalers Act
Territorial Divisions Act
Transportation of Primary Forest Products Act
Underground Storage Act
Acts administered by an Associated Agency, Board, Commission or Corporation
Forest Products Act
Maritime Forestry Complex Coporation Act
Roosevelt Campobello International Park Act
St. Croix International Waterway Commission Act
Minister, Hon. Wally Stiles
wally.stiles@gnb.ca
Deputy Minister, Tom Reid
506-453-2501, Fax: 506-453-2930
Tom.REID@gnb.ca
Director Communications, Steven Benteau
506-453-2614, Fax: 506-457-4881
Steve.Benteau@gnb.ca
Office Manager, Geoff Payne
506-453-2614, Fax: 506-457-4881
Geoff. Payne@gnb.ca

• Board of Examiners under the Scaler's Act
1350 Regent St. South
PO Box 6000
Fredericton, NB E3B 5H1
506-453-2441
Fax: 506-453-6689
Secretary, Chris Bringloe
• Forest Protection Limited
2502 Hwy. 102
Lincoln, NB E3B 7E6
506-446-6930
Fax: 506-446-6934
info@forestprotectionlimited.com
www.forestprotectionlimited.com
General Manager, David C. Davies
Forest Protection Limited (FPL) is a non-profit aerial forest protection company whose mandate is to protect forests through assistance to the Forest Management Branch, for fire protection, fire fighting assistance & aerial surveys.
• New Brunswick Forest Products Commission
PO Box 6000
Fredericton, NB E3B 5H1
506-453-2196
Fax: 506-457-4966
www.gnb.ca/0078/fpc/index.asp
Executive Director, Linda D. Gould
The New Brunswick Forest Products Commission is an independent Commission overseeing the marketing relationships involving forest industries (pulp mills & sawmills), forest products marketing boards (private woodlot owners & producers) & the provincial government.

Minerals, Policy & Planning Division / Ressources minières, politique et planification
506-453-2206
Fax: 506-457-6762
Asst. Deputy Minister, Ellen Barry
506-453-2684
Director Mineral & Petroleum Development Branch, Samuel K. McEwan
506-444-5005, Fax: 506-453-3671
Director Geological Surveys Branch, Les Fyffe
506-453-2206, Fax: 506-453-3671

Renewable Resources / Ressources renouvelables
Asst. Deputy Minister, Tom Reid
506-453-3063, Fax: 506-453-2930
Executive Director Regional Operations, Julius Tarjan
506-453-3063, Fax: 506-453-2930

Fish & Wildlife Branch
Manages the province's fisheries & wildlife.By managing fish populations & habitats the Branch develops sport fisheries.Over 160 species of birds, mammals, reptiles & amphibians live in New Brunswick's forests.A Branch goal is to conserve the habitat to support these species.The staff develops environmental protection plans to ensure these resources are protected & maintained.
Director, Mike Sullivan
506-453-2440, Fax: 506-453-6699
Manager Big Game/Furbearer, Kevin Craig
506-453-2440
Manager Fisheries, Peter Cronin
Manager Species at Risk, Pascal Giasson

Forest Management Branch
506-453-2516
Fax: 506-453-6689
To manage Crown timber resource in accordance with Government Policy.
Director, Daniel Murphy
506-453-2432, Fax: 506-453-6689
Manager, Robert Dick
506-453-2516, Fax: 506-453-6689
robert.dick@gnb.ca
Manager Forest Pest Management, Nelson Carter
506-453-2516, Fax: 506-453-6689
nelson.carter@gnb.ca

Department of Post-Secondary Education, Training & Labour / Éducation postsecondaire, Formation et Travail

470 York St.
PO Box 6000
Fredericton, NB E3B 5H1

506-453-2597
Fax: 506-453-3618
dpetlinfo@gnb.ca
www.gnb.ca/0105/index.htm
Formerly the Department of Training & Employment.
Acts Administered:
Adult Education & Training Act
Apprenticeship & Occupational Certification Act
Blind Workmen's Compensation Act
Degree Granting Act
Employment Development Act
Employment Standards Act
Fisheries Bargaining Act
Higher Education Foundation Act
Human Rights Act
Industrial Relations Act
Labour & Employment Board Act
Labour Market Research Act
Maritime Provinces Higher Education Commission Act
New Brunswick Public Libraries Act
New Brunswick Public Libraries Foundation Act
Occupational Health & Safety Act
Code of Practice for Working with Material Containing Asbestos
Underground Mine Regulation
Workplace Hazardous Materials Information System (WHMIS) Regulation
Pension Benefits Act
Private Occupational Training Act
Public Service Labour Relations Act
Silicosis Compensation Act
Special Payment to Certain Dependent Spouses of Deceased Workers Act
Workers' Compensation Act (administered by Workplace Health, Safety & Compensation Commission)
Workplace Health, Safety & Compensation Commission Act
Youth Assistance Act
Minister, Hon. Donald Arseneault
506-453-2342, Fax: 506-453-3038
donald.arseneault@gnb.ca
Deputy Minister, Byron James
506-453-2343, Fax: 506-453-3038
Byron.James@gnb.ca
Director Communications, Marie-Josée Groulx
506-444-3465, Fax: 506-444-4314
marie-josee.groulx@gnb.ca
Media Relations Coordinator, Sheri Strickland
506-453-8617, Fax: 506-444-4314
sheri.strickland@gnb.ca
• Apprenticeship & Occupational Certification Board
PO Box 6000
Fredericton, NB E3B 5H1
506-453-2260
Fax: 506-453-5317
• Ministerial Advisory Committee on Multiculturalism
PO Box 6000
Fredericton, NB E3B 5H1
• New Brunswick Human Rights Commission
• Workplace Health, Safety & Compensation Commission(WHSCC) / Commission de la santé, de la sécurité et de l'indemnisation des accidents au travail
• Workplace Health, Safety & Compensation Commission of New Brunswick(WHSC) / Commission de la santé, de la sécurité et de l'indemnisation des accidents au travail

Labour & Legislative Development / Travail et Élaboration des législations
Asst. Deputy Minister, Paul G. Blackmore
506-453-8202, Fax: 506-444-4314
Director Industrial Relations, David Moore
506-453-2261, Fax: 506-453-2678

NBCC / CCNB

New Brunswick Community Colleges
800-376-5353
www.nbcc.nb.ca

New Brunswick Power Group of Companies (NBPC) / Énergie NB

515 King St.
PO Box 2000
Fredericton, NB E3B 4X1
506-458-4444
Fax: 506-458-4000
questions@nbpower.com
www.nbpower.com

Federal/Provincial Government / Government of New Brunswick

NB Power will be restructured to form a holding company with four subsidiary companies, NB Power Generation, NB Power Nuclear, NB Power Transmission & NB Power Distribution & Customer Service. NB Power is legislated to provide electric power to the province of NB. It is the largest electric utility in Atlantic Canada. Economic generation is from hydro, oil, nuclear, coal & Orimulsion powered facilities. NB Power is developing a comprehensive station environmental management system & is moving towards ISO 14001 certification. The Corporate Environmental Policy applies to all aspects of NB Power's activities. These include the generation of electricity from various energy sources, including nuclear, oil, coal, Orimulsion(193), & hydro, the transmission & distribution of electricity to customers. It also includes those activities that support the generation, transmission & distribution of electricity, including management of land, raw materials, & by-products.
Acts Administered:
Electric Power Act
Chair, Derek Burney
President/CEO, David Hay
Director Environmental Affairs, Glen Wilson
Manager Environmental Assessment & Assurance, Charles Hickman

Department of Public Safety / Sécurité publique
364 Argyle St.
PO Box 6000
Fredericton, NB E3B 5H1
506-453-3992
Fax: 506-453-3870
DPS-MSP.Information@gnb.ca
www.gnb.ca/0276/index-e.asp
Provides leadership in the areas of public order & community safety. Provides fair, accessible, community-focused, & coordinated public safety programs & services. Ensures effective inspection & enforcement of designated public safety programs & services. Acts in partnership with communities to prevent crime, assist victims, & create opportunities for offenders to change. Coordinates & cooperates with the federal government in the administration of correctional services & law enforcement in New Brunswick.
Acts Administered:
All Terrain Vehicle Act
Boiler & Pressure Vessel Act
Coroners Act
Corrections Act
Custody & Detention of Young Persons Act
Electrical Installation & Inspection Act
Elevators & Lifts Act
Emergency 911 Act
Emergency Measures Act
Film & Video Act
Fire Prevention Act
Intoxicated Persons Detention Act
Liquor Control Act
Lotteries Act
Motor Vehicle Act
Plumbing Installation & Inspection Act
Police Act
Private Investigators & Security Services Act
Restricted Beverage Act
Salvage Dealers Licensing Act
Sheriffs Act
Transportation of Dangerous Goods Act
Victim Services Act
Minister, Hon. John W. Foran
506-453-7414,
John.Foran@gnb.ca
Deputy Minister, Marc Leger
506-453-7412,
Marc.Leger@gnb.ca
Director Communications & Public Awareness, Lisa Harrity
506-444-3425,
Lisa.Harrity@gnb.ca
Director Financial Services, Brian Wilkins
506-453-5446, Fax: 506-444-4743
Brian.Wilkins@gnb.ca
Director Human Resources, John Smith
506-453-3903, Fax: 506-453-7481
Director Information Technology, Virender Ambwani
506-444-4433, Fax: 506-453-3321
vic.ambwani@gnb.ca
Executive Assistant, Penné Buckley
506-453-7414,
Penne.Buckley@gnb.ca

• New Brunswick Emergency Measures Organization(EMO) / Organisation des mesures d'urgence (OMU)
Victoria Health Centre
65 Brunswick Ave.
Fredericton, NB E3B 1G5
506-453-2133
Fax: 506-453-5513
800-561-4034
emo@gnb.ca
www.gnb.ca/cnb/emo-omu/index-e.asp
Director, Ernest MacGillivray
Coordinates preparedness for emergencies by provincial government departments & municipal governments. NB EMO works at both provincial & municipal levels to ensure that communities are protcted by emergency plans. Coordinates provincial response operations during emergencies & administers disaster financial assistance programs.

Safety Services / Direction des services de sécurité
Provides leadership in the areas of law enforcement & community safety in order to preserve & enhance the quality of life in New Brunswick.
Asst. Deputy Minister, Marc Léger
506-453-7142, Fax: 506-453-3870
Executive Director Police, Fire & Emergency Services, Dick Isabelle
506-453-3603

Office of the Fire Marshal / Bureau du prévôt des incendies
Victoria Health Centre
PO Box 6000
Fredericton, NB E3B 5H1
506-453-2004
Fax: 506-457-4889
fire.marshal@gnb.ca
The Office of the Fire Marshal provides leadership for 221 permanent, volunteer & industrial fire departments. The Office is accountable for carrying out the provisions of the Fire Prevention Act.
Deputy Fire Marshal, Benoit Laroche

Regional Development Corporation (RDC) / Société d'aménagement régional (SAR)
RDC Bldg.
836 Churchill Row
PO Box 428
Fredericton, NB E3B 5R4
506-453-2277
Fax: 506-453-7988
www2.gnb.ca/content/gnb/en/departments/regional_development.html
The Regional Development Corporation is a Crown corporation which carries out its mandate in accordance with the Regional Development Corporation Act. The following are responsibilities of the Corporation; Administration & management of development agreements between the Province of New Brunswick & the federal government; Assistance in the establishment & development of enterprises & institutions; Assistance to municipalities in the planning & development of projects to benefit the public; Assistance in the development of tourism & recreational facilities; Planning, coordinating, & guiding regional development; & Performing duties assigned by the Lieutenant-Governor-in-Council.
Minister Responsible, Hon. Paul Robichaud
506-453-5898, Fax: 506-453-6389
paul.robichaud@gnb.ca
President, Denis Caron
506-453-8542,
denis.caron@gnb.ca
Corporate Secretary, Bruce Macfarlane
506-444-4606,
bruce.macfarlane@gnb.ca

New Brunswick Research & Productivity Council (RPC) / Conseil de la recherche et de la productivité du Nouveau-Brunswick (RPC)
921 College Hill Rd.
Fredericton, NB E3B 6Z9
506-452-1212
Fax: 506-452-1395
info@rpc.ca
www.rpc.ca
RPC's vision is to excel in technological innovation, enabling its partners in business & industry to create wealth & high quality employment opportunities in New Brunswick;to steadily improve its capacity to develop & apply new technology in partnership with firms in the private sector, & to provide an expanding range of high quality technical services to clients in the global marketplace. RPC is registered to the ISO 9001:2000 International Standard.
Executive Director, Eric Cook, P.Eng.
506-452-0585,
eric.cook@rpc.ca
CFO, Stephen A. Fox
506-452-1380,
stephen.fox@rpc.ca
Head Physical Metallurgy, John Aikens
506-460-5766,
john.aikens@rpc.ca
Head Food, Fisheries & Aquaculture, Dr. Rachael Ritchie
506-452-1365,
rachael.ritchie@rpc.ca
Head Inorganic Analytical Services, Ross Kean
506-452-1399,
ross.kean@rpc.ca
Head Mechanical Systems & Diagnostics, John Aikens
506-460-5766,
john.aikens@rpc.ca
Manager Organic Analytical Services, Bruce Phillips
506-452-1369,
bruce.phillips@rpc.ca
Manager High Res Section, Dr. John Macaulay
506-452-1369,
john.macaulay@rpc.ca
Manager Process Technology, Ross Gilders
506-460-5672,
ross.gilders@rpc.ca
Manager Air Quality Services, Thelma Green
506-452-0586,
thelma.green@rpc.ca
Coordinator, Susi Chamberlain
506-452-1244,
susi.chamberlain@rpc.ca
Executive Assistant, Linda Horsman
506-452-1363, Fax: 506-452-1386
linda.horsman@rpc.ca

Service New Brunswick (SNB) / Services Nouveau-Brunswick (SNB)
Westmorland Place
#200, 82 Westmorland St.
PO Box 1998
Fredericton, NB E3B 5G4
506-457-3581
Fax: 506-457-7520
888-762-8600
snb@snb.ca
www.snb.ca
Other Communication: Technical Assistance: 1-888-832-2762; SNB TeleServices outside the province: 506-684-7901
Service New Brunswick provides authoritative information to the public about federal, provincial, & municipal government services. The Crown corporation, which is owned by the Province of New Brunswick, operates the following services: New Brunswick's Land Registry; New Brunswick's Personal Property Registry; New Brunswick's Corporate Affairs Registry; & New Brunswick's Property Assessment & Taxation System.
Acts Administered:
Air Space Act
Assessment Act
Boundaries Confirmation Act
Business Corporation Act
Common Business Identifier Act
Companies Act
Condominium Property Act
Corporations Act
Foreign Resident Corporations Act
Land Titles Act
Limited Partnership Act
Partnership Act
Partnerships & Business Names Registration Act
Personal Property Security Act
Registry Act
Residential Property Tax Relief Act
Service New Brunswick Act
Special Corporate Continuance Act
Standard Forms of Conveyances Act
Surveys Act
Winding-Up Act

Minister Responsible, Hon. Bruce Fitch
506-453-2807, Fax: 506-453-3988
bruce.fitch@gnb.ca
Chair, Derek Pleadwell
506-444-2897, Fax: 506-457-7520
derek.pleadwell@snb.ca
President, Sylvie Levesque-Finn
506-444-2897,
sylvie.levesque-finn@snb.ca
Corporate Legal Counsel Corporate Counsel Directorate,
Claude Poirier
506-869-6389, Fax: 506-869-6523
claude.poirier@snb.ca
Vice-President Technology & Business Development, Carol MacDonald
506-444-2322, Fax: 506-453-5384
carol.macdonald@snb.ca
Vice-President Corporate Services, Dan Rae
506-457-4805, Fax: 506-444-5239
dan.rae@snb.ca
Vice-President Operations, Bernard Arseneau
506-457-3582, Fax: 506-457-7520
bernard.arseneau@snb.ca
Executive Director Strategy, Policy & Innovation, Judy Ross, C.A.
506-444-4103, Fax: 506-453-5384
judy.ross@snb.ca
Director Communications, Brand & Customer Experience,
Brent Staeben
506-453-6775, Fax: 506-453-5384
brent.staeben@snb.ca
Director Human Resources, Donat Theriault
506-453-3912, Fax: 506-453-3043
donat.theriault@snb.ca
Director Central Office Program Delivery, Luc J. Sirois
506-453-7450, Fax: 506-462-5150
Luc.Sirois@gnb.ca

Department of Supply & Services / Approvisionnement et services

PO Box 6000
Fredericton, NB E3B 5H1
506-453-3742
Fax: 506-444-4400
Reception.Marysville@gnb.ca
www.gnb.ca/0099/index-e.asp
Provides effective & efficient services within government. Among the varied & diverse services the department provides are: the procurement of goods & services; printing & postal services; translation services; records management; the construction & operation of government-owned buildings; & information technology management.
Acts Administered:
Archives Act
Public Purchasing Act
Public Works Act
Minister, Hon. Edward Doherty
506-453-6100, Fax: 506-462-5049
ed.doherty@gnb.ca
Deputy Minister, Louise Lemon
506-453-2504,
Louise.LEMON@gnb.ca
Executive Director Corporate Services, Byard A. Smith
506-444-2808,
byard.smith@gnb.ca
Director Technology Support, Christine Colborne
506-457-7279,
Christine.Colborne@gnb.ca
Director Human Resources & Administration, Ray Butler
506-453-3742,
ray.butler@gnb.ca
Chief Information Officer Corporate Information Management Services, Danny Keizer
506-453-3742, Fax: 506-462-2006
Danny.KEIZER@gnb.ca

Buildings Group / Direction générale des bâtiments
Asst. Deputy Minister, Ashley Cummings
506-453-2228
Executive Director Design & Construction, Barb Nicholson
506-453-2228
Executive Director Facilities Management, Greg Cook
506-444-4527
Director Property Management, Gary Lenehan
506-453-2221

Services / Direction générale des services
www.gov.nb.ca/supply/sgs/index.htm (Purchasing)
Asst. Deputy Minister, Dick Burgess
506-453-2245
Director Central Purchasing, Joanne Lynch
506-453-2245

Department of Tourism & Parks / Tourisme et Parcs

Centennial Bldg.
670 King St.
Fredericton, NB E3B 1G1
506-444-5205
Fax: 506-457-4984
taponlinedirectory@gnb.ca
www.gnb.ca/0397/index-e.asp
To increase the profile and performance of the tourism industry in New Brunswick and to ensure that provincial parks are an integral part of this effort.
Acts Administered:
Kings Landing Corporation Act
Municipalities Act (subsection 188 (3))
Parks Act
Tourism Development Act
Minister, Hon. Stuart Jamieson
506-453-3009,
Stuart.jamieson@gnb.ca
Deputy Minister, Ellen Barry
506-453-3261,
Ellen.Barry@gnb.ca
Asst. Deputy Minister, Clarence Lebreton
506-726-2600, Fax: 506-726-2601
clarence.lebreton@gnb.ca
Director Communications, Alison Aiton
506-444-4454,
alison.aiton@gnb.ca
Coordinator Human Resources Services, Maryse McFarlane
506-444-2757, Fax: 506-462-2202
maryse.mcfarlane@gnb.ca

Planning & Product Branch / Planification et production
506-453-2170
Fax: 506-453-2854
Executive Director, Jane Garbutt
Executive Director Kings Landing, Robert Moreau
506-363-4957, Fax: 506-363-4989
office.kingsland@gnb.ca
Director Planning & Research, Janet Cameron
506-444-4521, Fax: 506-453-2854
Janet.Cameron@gnb.ca

The Anchorage
506-453-4283
Fax: 506-662-7035

La République

Herring Cove
506-752-7012

Parlee Beach
506-533-3363
Fax: 506-533-3312

Sugarloaf
506-759-2365
Fax: 506-789-2099

Department of Transportation / Transports

Kings Pl.
440 KingSt.
PO Box 6000
Fredericton, NB E3B 5H8
506-453-3939
Fax: 506-453-2900
Transportation.Web@gnb.ca
www.gnb.ca/0113/index-e.asp
To ensure the effective development & implementation of an integrated transportation approach for New Brunswick (roads, airports, ports & other infrastructure), to support New Brunswick's economic & social goals; develop & maintain safe & efficient network of highways & roads; & maintain the long-term integrity of our transportation infrastructure including roads, ports & airports through effective planning, maintenance & oversight.
Acts Administered:
Highway Act
Motor Carrier Act
New Brunswick Highway Corporation Act
New Brunswick Transportation Authority Act
Public Landings Act
Shortline Railways Act
Minister, Hon. Denis Landry
506-457-7345, Fax: 506-453-7987
Denis.Landry2@gnb.ca
Deputy Minister, David J. Johnstone
506-453-2549, Fax: 506-453-7987
David.JOHNSTONE@gnb.ca
Director Communications, Andrew Holland
506-453-5634, Fax: 506-457-4968
andrew.holland@gnb.ca
• NB Board of Commissioners of Public Utilities
#1400, 15 Market Sq.
PO Box 5001
Saint John, NB E2L 4Y9
506-658-2504
Fax: 506-643-7300
866-766-2782
general@pub.nb.ca
www.pub.nb.ca
• New Brunswick Transportation Authority
Kings Place
440 King St.
PO Box 6000
Fredericton, NB E3B 5H1
506-453-3939
Fax: 506-453-2900
Deputy Minister, David J. Johnstone
Crown corporation responsible for the promotion, operation & development of transportation terminals in New Brunswick. Encourages the development of transport terminal-related services.

Assistant Deputy Minister & Chief Engineer Office / Sous-ministre adjoint et ingénieur en chef
Asst. Deputy Minister, Michael Trites
506-453-2351
Executive Director Operations, Henri Allain
506-453-2849
Executive Director Engineering Services, Neil Gilbert
506-453-2849
Director Trans Canada Highway Project, Denis LaChapelle
506-444-2007
Director Planning & Land Management, Brian McEwing
506-453-2754

Corporate Services & Fleet Management / Services généraux et gestion de flotte
Asst. Deputy Minister, Dale Wilson
506-453-2552,
dale.wilson@gnb.ca
Director Vehicle Management Agency, Andrew Aiton
506-453-2601,
Andy.AITON@gnb.ca

Policy, Strategic Development & Intergovernmental Relations / Politiques, développement et relations intergouvernementales
Asst. Deputy Minister, Doug L. Johnson
506-453-5818
Director Strategic Development, Margaret Grant-McGivney
506-453-5818

Department of Wellness, Culture & Sport / Mieux-être, Culture et Sport

Place 2000
250 King St., 4th Fl.
PO Box 6000
Fredericton, NB E3B 5H1
506-453-2909
Fax: 506-453-6548
www.gnb.ca/0131/index-e.asp
The Department of Wellness, Culture, & Sport is repsonsible for arts development, heritage, wellness, & sport, recreation, & active living.
Acts Administered:
Arts Development Trust Fund Act (except administration of fund)
Assessment Act (s. 15.3)
Historic Sites Protection Act
Municipal Heritage Preservation Act
Sport Development Trust Fund Act (except administration of fund)
Youth Assistance Act (section 11)

Federal/Provincial Government / Government of Newfoundland & Labrador

Minister, Wellness, Culture, & Sport; Minister Responsible, Francophonie, Hon. Hédard Albert
506-444-2517, Fax: 506-453-6668
Hedard.Albert2@gnb.ca
Deputy Minister, Ellen Barry
506-453-2909, Fax: 506-453-6668
ellen.barry@gnb.ca
• New Brunswick Arts Board
61 Carleton St.
Fredericton, NB E3B 3T2
506-444-4444
Fax: 506-444-5543
1-866-460-2787
www.artsnb.ca
• New Brunswick Film
Place 2000
250 King St., 4th Fl.
PO Box 6000
Fredericton, NB E1B 5H1
506-453-2555
Fax: 506-453-2416
nbfilm@gnb.ca
www.nbfilm.ca
Director, Nathalie Dubois
Responsible for fostering New Brunswick's film, television & new media industry.

Arts Development
Place 2000
250 King St.
Fredericton, NB E3B 9M9
506-453-2555
Fax: 506-453-2416
Director Arts Development, Nathalie Dubois
506-453-2729, Fax: 506-453-2416
nathalie.dubois@gnb.ca
Coordinator Art Bank Services, Caroline Walker
506-444-5303, Fax: 506-453-2416
Caroline.Walker@gnb.ca
Manager Programs, Alain Boisvert
506-453-2166, Fax: 506-453-2416
alain.boisvert@gnb.ca

Heritage
Place 2000
250 King St., 4th Fl.
PO Box 6000
Fredericton, NB E3B 5H1
506-453-2324
Fax: 506-453-2416
Director Heritage, Wayne Burley
506-453-8774, Fax: 506-453-2416
Wayne.Burley@gnb.ca
Manager Archaeological Services, Albert M. Ferguson
506-453-2756, Fax: 506-457-4880
albert.ferguson@gnb.ca
Manager Historic Places, William Hicks
506-444-5320, Fax: 506-453-2416
Bill.Hicks@gnb.ca
Manager Museum Services, Guy Tremblay
506-444-5892, Fax: 506-453-2416
Guy.Tremblay@gnb.ca
Manager Toponymy, Gilles Bourque
506-453-8125, Fax: 506-453-2416
Gilles.Bourque@gnb.ca
Project Manager Heritage Education, Cynthia Wallace-Casey
506-453-2915, Fax: 506-453-2416
Cynthia.Wallace-Casey@gnb.ca

New Brunswick Museum
277 Douglas Ave.
Saint John, NB E2K 1E5
506-643-2300
Fax: 506-643-2360
nbmuseum@nbm-mnb.ca
www.nbm-mnb.ca
Manager Natural Science, Randall Miller
506-643-2361, Fax: 506-643-2360
Randall.Miller@nbm-mnb.ca
Manager Library & Archives, Felicity Osepchook
506-643-2324, Fax: 506-643-2360
Felicity.Osepchook@nbm-mnb.ca
Manager Interpretation Services, Wendy Martindale
506-643-2338, Fax: 506-643-6081
wmrdale@nb.aibn.com

Manager Temporary Exhibitions, Regina Mantin
506-643-2330, Fax: 506-643-6081
rmantin@nb.aibn.com
Controller, Judith Brown
506-643-2356, Fax: 506-643-6081
jbrown@nb.aibn.com

Wellness, Sport, & Community Development
Place 2000
250 King St., 4th Fl.
PO Box 6000
Fredericton, NB E3B 5H1
506-444-2451
Fax: 506-453-6548
Assistant Deputy Minister Wellness, Sport, & Community Development, Jane Garbutt
506-444-2451, Fax: 506-453-6548
jane.garbutt@gnb.ca
Acting Director Sport & Recreation, Roger H. Duval
506-457-4950, Fax: 506-453-6548
roger.duval@gnb.ca
Acting Director Regional Operations & Community Development, Allen Bard
506-453-3193, Fax: 506-453-6548
Allen.Bard@gnb.ca
Director Wellness, Michelle Bourgoin
506-453-4217, Fax: 506-444-5722
michelle.bourgoin@gnb.ca

Workplace Health, Safety & Compensation Commission of New Brunswick (WHSCC) / La commission de la santé, de la sécurité et de l'indemnisation des accidents au travail du Nouveau-Brunswick

1 Portland St.
PO Box 160
Saint John, NB E2L 3X9
506-632-2200
800-222-9775
communications@ws-ts.nb.ca
www.whscc.nb.ca
The Workplace Health, Safety & Compensation Commission (WHSCC) of New Brunswick is a crown corporation charged with overseeing the implementation & application of the New Brunswick Occupational Health & Safety Act, the Workers' Compensation Act of New Brunswick, & the Workplace Health, Safety & Compensation Commission Act of New Brunswick on behalf of the workers & employers of this province. The Commission administers no-fault workplace accident & disability insurance & comprehensive accident prevention health & safety initiatives for employers & their workers, funded solely through premiums paid by employers.
Acts Administered:
Occupational Health & Safety Act
Workers' Compensation Act
Workplace Health, Safety & Compensation Commission Act
Chair, Roberta Dugas
President/CEO, Douglas C. Stanley
Chair Appeals Tribunal, Paul M. LeBreton
Corporate Secretary & General Counsel, Richard Tingley
506-632-2837
Vice-President Corporate Services, Peter Murphy
506-632-2204
Vice-President Worksafe Services, David Greason
506-632-2816
Manager Communications, Mary Tucker
506-632-2828

Government of Newfoundland & Labrador
Seat of Government: Confederation Bldg.
St. John's, NL A1B 4J6
info@gov.nl.ca
www.gov.nl.ca
The Province of Newfoundland & Labrador entered Confederation March 31, 1949.It has an area of 370,494.89 km2, & the StatsCan census population in 2006 was 505,469.
Minister, Hon. Joan Burke
709-729-5040, 866-838-5620,Fax: 709-729-0414
Joanburke@gov.nl.ca
Deputy Minister, Rebecca Roome
709-729-5086,
rebeccaroome@gov.nl.ca

Newfoundland & Labrador Emergency Measures Organization

PO Box 8700
St. John's, NL A1B 4J6
709-729-3703
Fax: 709-729-3857
www.ma.gov.nl.ca/ma/fes/emo
Other Communication: 24 hr. Emergencies: 709/729-3703
The Provincial Emergency Measures Program is responsible for the development & maintenance of provincial emergency preparedness, response & recovery measures with a view to mitigating the human suffering & loss of property caused by actual or imminent emergencies & disasters.Using its legislative support, The Emergency Measures Act, it has the responsibility to co-ordinate &/or manage an emergency situation. It is the only agency that is authorized to control & coordinate the activities of all Police, Fire, Health, Social Services, & other services in the area, either municipal or provincial, & to engage civilian personnel to assist in these services.Programs & Services provided include Emergency Response, Planning & Operations, Training & Education, Joint Emergency Preparedness, Disaster Financial Assistance Arrangements, Emergency Air Services & Emergency Response.
Director, Fred Hollett
709-729-3703
Clerk Typist, Ryan Hurley
709-729-3703, Fax: 709-729-3857
rhurley@gov.nl.ca

Department of Environment & Conservation
Confederation Bldg.
West Block, 4th Fl.
PO Box 8700
St. John's, NL A1B 4J6
709-729-2664
Fax: 709-729-6639
800-563-6181
info@gov.nl.ca
www.env.gov.nl.ca
To protect, conserve & enhance the Province's environment through the management of water resources, the environmental assessment of undertakings & the control & management of substances & activities that may pollute the environment. The Department is actively working towards reducing the number of landfill sites & implementing the Provincial Waste Management Strategy.The strategy will divert 50 percent of materials from landfill sites,phase out municipal solid waste incinerators by 2008 & prohibit such facilities from being built in the future.
Acts Administered:
Endangered Species Act
Endangered Species Regulation
Species Status Advisory Committee Regulations
Environmental Protection Act
Air Pollution Control Regulations, 2004
Environmental Assessment Regulations, 2003
Gasoline Volatility Control Regulations, 2003
Halocarbon Regulations
Heating Oil Storage Tank System Regulations
Ozone Depleting Substances Regulations, 2003
Pesticides Control Regulations, 2003
Storage & Handling of Gasoline & Associated Products Regulations, 2003
Storage of PCB Waste Regulations, 2003
Used Oil Control Regulations
Waste Management Regulations, 2003
Waste Material Disposal Areas Regulations
Geographical Name Act
Land Surveyors Act
Lands Act
National Parks Lands Act
Provincial Parks Act
Smoke-Free Environment Act
Water Resources Act
Environmental Control Water & Sewage Regulations
Notices of Protected Water Supplies, Watershed Areas, Wellhead Protected Water Supplies
Water Power Rental Regulations, 2003
Well Drilling Regulations, 2003
Wild Life Act
Wild Life Park Order
Wild Life Park Regulations
Wild Life Regulations
Wild Life Reserve Regulations
Wilderness & Ecological Reserves Act

Minister, Hon. Charlene Johnson
709-729-2577, Fax: 709-729-0112
charlenejohnson@gov.nl.ca
Deputy Minister, William Parrott
709-729-2572
Director Communications, Melony O'Neil
709-729-2575
Director Environmental Assessment, Bas Cleary
709-729-2562
Director Policy & Planning, John Drover
709-729-0027,
jdrover@gov.nl.ca
Director Pollution Prevention, Derrick Maddocks
709-729-2556
Acting Director Water Resources, Haseen Khan
709-729-2563
• Multi-Materials Stewardship Board(MMSB)
PO Box 8131 A
St. John's, NL A1B 3M9
709-753-0948
Fax: 709-753-0974
www.mmsb.nf.ca
Chair & CEO, John Scott

Environment Branch
Other Communication: Spill Reporting (24 hours): 709/772-2083;
Environmental Assessment: 1-800-563-6181
Director, Bas Cleary
709-729-0673, Fax: 709-729-5518
clearyb@gov.nl.ca
Director Policy & Planning, John Drover, P. Eng
709-729-1090,
jdrover@gov.nl.ca

Natural Heritage
Asst. Deputy Minister, Robert Warren
709-637-2135, Fax: 709-637-2180
rwarren@gov.nl.ca

Environmental Assessment Division
800-563-6181
The Environmental Assessment Division administers the environmental assessment process, including: consultation with interested government departments & the public, evaluation of submissions by proponents & reviewers, advising the Minister on potential environmental effects prior to decisions, & monitoring released projects to ensure compliance & effectiveness of mitigation
Acting Director, Michael Cahill
709-729-2562
Director, Phil Graham
709-729-5752
Manager Environmental Impact Management Section, John Eason
709-729-5706

Pollution Prevention
709-729-5782
Fax: 709-729-6969
Environmental science & monitoring; industrial compliance; pesticide control; waste management; petroleum storage & maintenance.
Director, Derrick Maddocks
709-729-2556
Manager Industrial Compliance, Dan Michielsen
709-729-6697
Manager Pesticides Control, Karen Linfield
709-729-3395
Manager Waste Management Section, Toby Matthews
709-729-5793

Water Resources
Administers various acts as they relate to the allocation of water, stream alterations, protection of water supply areas, licensing of well drillers & other aspects of water resource management.
Director, Martin Goebel
709-729-2563,
mgoebel@gov.nl.ca
Manager Groundwater Resources, Keith Guzzwell
709-729-2539,
kguzzwell@gov.nl.ca
Manager Hydrologic Modelling, Amir Ali Khan
709-729-2295,
akhan@gov.nl.ca

Manager Investigations, Clyde McLean
709-729-5713,
clydemclean@gov.nl.ca
Manager Surface Water, Haseen Khan
709-729-2535, Fax: 709-729-0320
hkhan@gov.nl.ca
Manager Water Rights, Dr. Abdel Razek
709-729-4795

Corner Brook
Sir Richard Squires Bldg.
Corner Brook, NL A2H 6J8
709-637-2431
Regional Water Quality Officer, Paul Barneable

Grand Falls
Provincial Bldg.
Grand Falls-Windsor, NL A2A 1W9
709-292-4298
Regional Water Quality Officer, Craig Cummings

Parks & Natural Areas Division
Responsible for planning, establishing, & managing Newfoundland & Labrador's Provincial Parks, Wilderness & Ecological Reserves, & Canadian Heritage Rivers. The Division is a member of the Canadian Parks Council & the Canadian Heritage Rivers Board & works with Parks Canada in planning new National Parks & National Marine Conservation Areas in the province. Newfoundland & Labrador's parks & reserves are created & maintained for five key reasons: biodiversity conservation, scientific research, recreation, education & ecotourism.
Acting Director, Calvin C. Yates
709-635-3849
Manager Natural Areas, Siân French
709-635-4533,
sianfrench@gov.nl.ca
Manager Parks Operations, Frank Turner
709-635-3851,
frankturner@gov.nl.ca
Director Special Projects, Michael Cahill
709-729-2222,
mikecahill@gov.nl.ca

Wildlife Division
Director, Jim Hancock
709-637-2008
Director Science, Rob Otto
709-637-2970
Manager Conservation Services, John Blake
709-637-2354
Chief Endangered Species & Biodiversity, Joe Brazil
709-637-2356
Minister & President, Treasury Board, Hon. Tom Marshall
709-729-3775, Fax: 709-729-2232
financeminister@gov.nl.ca

Department of Fisheries & Aquaculture
Petten Bldg.
30 Strawberry Marsh Rd.
PO Box 8700
St. John's, NL A1B 4J6
709-729-3723
Fax: 709-729-6082
fishaqwebmaster@gov.nl.ca
www.fishaq.gov.nl.ca
Contributes to economic & community growth in the province by encouraging sustainable growth & development of the harvesting, processing, & distribution sectors; includes providing support for the marketing of fish & aquaculture products produced in Newfoundland & Labrador for domestic & export markets. Responsible for: setting & enforcing standards for the processing & sale of fish products in the province; licensing fish processing establishments; undertaking developmental initiatives in the harvesting, processing, & marketing sectors of the fishing industry; developing, promoting & licensing of aquaculture facilities; developing & maintaining strategic fisheries infrastructure; articulating policies & providing advice for the management & development of fisheries & aquaculture; providing statistical information.
Acts Administered:
Aquaculture Act
Fish Inspection Act
Fish Processing Licensing Board Act
Fisheries Act
Fisheries Products International Limited Act
Fisheries Restructuring Act
Fishing Industry Collective Bargaining Act

Professional Fish Harvesters Act
Acting Minister, Hon. Trevor Taylor
trevortaylor@gov.nl.ca
Deputy Minister, Alastair O'Rielly
709-729-3707, Fax: 790-729-4219
aorielly@gov.nl.ca
• Professional Fish Harvesters Certification Board(PFHCB)
15 Hallett Cres.
PO Box 8541
St. John's, NL A1B 3P2
709-722-8170
Fax: 709-722-8201
pfh@pfhcb.com
www.pfhcb.com

Aquaculture Branch
Fax: 709-729-0360
The Branch is responsible for licensing & aquaculture development.
Asst. Deputy Minister, Brian Meaney
709-729-3710, Fax: 709-729-1882
bmeaney@gov.nl.ca
Director Aquaculture Development, Shawn Robinson
709-292-4111, Fax: 709-292-4113
srobinson@gov.nl.ca

Fisheries Branch
Fax: 709-729-6082
Asst. Deputy Minister, David Lewis
709-729-3713
Director, Ian Burford
709-729-3736
Director Processing & Marketing Development, Mike Handrigan
709-729-3749

Policy Development & Planning Branch
Provides policy & program planning services to the Department. Through the Sustainable Fisheries & Oceans Policy Division participates in oceans policy & governance issues, in addition to the resource assessment & management process of the federal Department of Fisheries & Oceans, including local, national, & international bodies responsible for fisheries conservation & management.
Executive Director, Mike Warren
709-729-3708, Fax: 709-729-6082
mikewarren@gov.nl.ca
Director Fishing Industry Renewal, Brian Delaney
709-729-3712, Fax: 709-729-6082
Director Sustainable Fisheries & Oceans Policy, Tom Dooley
709-729-0335

Gander
709-292-4102
Fax: 709-292-4113
Regional Director, Nelson Higdon
709-292-4109, Fax: 709-292-4113
nhigdon@gov.nl.ca

Avalon & Eastern
709-832-2860
Fax: 709-832-1669
Regional Director, Rex Matthews
709-832-2860

Labrador
709-896-3412
Fax: 709-896-3483
Regional Director, Craig Taylor
709-896-3412, Fax: 709-896-3483
craigtaylor@gov.nl.ca

Western
709-861-3537
Fax: 709-861-3556
Clerk, Vivian Hynes
709-861-3537,
vivianhynes@gov.nl.ca

Department of Government Services
PO Box 8700
St. John's, NL A1B 4J6
709-729-4834
gsinfo@gov.nl.ca
www.gs.gov.nl.ca
Departmental responsibilities include: motor vehicle registration, government service centres, consumer protection, trade prac-

Federal/Provincial Government / Government of Newfoundland & Labrador

tices, vital statistics, lotteries, registries, building accessibility, residential tenancies services, regulation of financial institutions, occupational health & safety, Office of the Queen's Printer, Government Purchasing Agency, permits, licences, approvals & inspections for public health & safety.

Acts Administered:
Accident & Sickness Insurance Act
Architects Act
Automobile Insurance Act
Bank of Nova Scotia Trust Company Act, 1997
Buildings Accessibility Act
Bulk Sales Act
Business Electronic Filing Act
Certified General Accountants Act
Certified Public Accountants Act
Change of Name Act
Chartered Accountants Act
Chartered Accountants & Certified Public Accountants Merger Act
Collections Act
Consumer Protection Act
Condominium Act
Consumer Reporting Agencies Act
Co-operatives Act
Conveyancing Act
Corporations Act
Corporations Guarantee Act
Credit Union Act
Criminal Code
Direct Sellers Act
Electronic Commerce Act
Embalmers & Funeral Director Act
Engineers & Geoscientists Act
Fire Insurance Act
Income Tax Savings Plan Act
Insurance Adjusters, Agents & Brokers Act
Insurance Companies Act
Insurance Contracts Act
Intergovernmental Joint Purchasing Act
Investment Contracts Act
Judgement Recovery (Nfld) Ltd. Act
Life Insurance Act
Limited Partnership Act
Lodgers' Goods Protection Act
Management Accountants Act
Maritime Hospital Service Association Re-Incorporation Act
Mechanics Lien Act
Mortgage Brokers Act
Occupational Health & Safety Act
 Asbestos Abatement Regulations
 Asbestos Exposure Code Regulations
 Mines Safety of Workers Regulations
 Occupational Health & Safety Electrical & Fisheries Advisory Committees Regulations
 Occupational Health & Safety Regulations
 Workplace Hazardous Materials Information System (WHMIS) Regulations
Pension Benefits Act, 1997
Pension Plans Designation of Beneficiaries Act
Perpetuities & Accumulations Act
Personal Property Security Act
Petroleum Products Act
Prepaid Funeral Services Act
Printing Services Act
Private Investigation & Security Services Act
Public Accountancy Act
Public Safety Act
Public Tender Act
Radiation Health & Safety Act
Real Estate Trading Act
Registration of Deeds Act
Residential Tenancies Act, 2000
Sale of Goods Act
Securities Act
Security Interest Registration Act
Solemnization of Marriage Act
Trade Practices Act
Trust & Loan Corporations Licensing Act
Trustee Act
Unconscionable Transactions Relief Act
Unsolicited Goods & Credit Cards Act
Vital Statistics Act
Warehouse Receipts Act
Warehouse's Lien Act
Workplace Health, Safety & Compensation Act

Acts Shared in Part with Other Ministries
Adoptions Act (Health & Community Services)
Building Standards Act (Municipal Affairs)
Child Care Services Act (Health & Community Services)
Child, Youth & Family Services Act (Health & Community Services)
Children's Law Act (Justice)
Communicable Diseases Act (Health & Community Services)
Dangerous Goods Transportation Act (Justice)
Employers' Liability Act (Justice)
Environmental Protection Act (Environment & Conservation)
Fire Prevention Act, 1991 (Municipal Affairs)
Food & Drug Act (Health & Community Services)
Fraudulent Conveyance Act (Justice)
Health & Community Services Act (Health & Community Services)
Highway Traffic Act (Transportation & Works)
Meat Inspection Act (Natural Resources)
Motor Carrier Act (Transportation & Works)
Motorized Snow Vehicles & All-Terrain Vehicles Act (Natural Resources)
Tobacco Act (Federal) (Health & Community Services)
Urban & Rural Planning Act (Municipal Affairs)
Water Resources Act (Environment & Conservation)

Minister, Hon. Harry Harding
709-729-4712, Fax: 709-729-4754
harryharding@gov.nl.ca
Deputy Minister, David Norman
709-729-4752, Fax: 709-729-4754
davidnorman@gov.nl.ca
Director Audit, Information & Training, Joseph Day
709-729-5429,
dayj@gov.nl.ca
Director Communications, Vanessa Colman-Sadd
709-729-4860, Fax: 709-729-4754
vanessacolmansadd@gov.nl.ca
Director Financial Services Regulation, Douglas Connolly
709-729-4909, Fax: 709-729-3205
connolly@gov.nl.ca
Director Government Purchasing, Policy & Administration, Wayne Hendry
709-729-3347, Fax: 709-729-5817
hendryw@gov.nl.ca
Director Policy & Planning, Elizabeth Day
709-729-6470, Fax: 709-729-4754
ElizabethDay@gov.nl.ca
Director Procurement & Development, Patricia Hearn
709-729-3344,
hearnp@gov.nl.ca
Manager Organizational Development, Leona O'Neill
709-729-0683, Fax: 709-729-6661
leonaoneill@gov.nl.ca

• Credit Union Deposit Guarantee Corporation
PO Box 340
Marystown, NL A0E 2M0
709-279-0170
Fax: 709-279-0177
877-279-0170
www.cudgcnl.com
Executive Director, William Langthorne
The Credit Union Deposit Guarantee Corporation guarantees deposits up to $250,000 per account type: demand accounts, registered retirement savings plans, registered retirement income fund, trust accounts, and joint accounts. Established in 1991 under the Co-operative Societies Act, replacing the Newfoundland and Labrador Stabilization fund, which was enacted in 1983.

Consumer & Commercial Affairs Branch
Promotes economic development by assisting businesses & protecting consumers. The branch is responsible for regulating the insurance industry, the securities industries, the trust & loan industry, the credit union industry, the real estate industry, collection agencies, mortgage brokers, automobile dealers, charitable gaming, private investigation agencies, & landlord-tenant relations.

Government Services Branch
Provides a one-stop service to the public & business community for a wide range of government regulatory & information functions. The Branch processes various permits, licences, & approvals, carries out inspections & investigations on behalf of various departments & conducts highway enforcement of the motor carrier industry. Also administers the Highway Traffic Act & registers vital events such as births, marriages, deaths & name changes. Through the Office of the Queen's Printer publishes, distributes & sells the Newfoundland & Labrador Consolidated Statutes, Regulations, the Newfoundland & Labrador Gazette & selected publications. Operates printing & micrographic services for all government departments.

Clarenville
2 Masonic Terrace
Clarenville, NL A5A 1N2
709-466-4060
Fax: 709-466-4070
Director, Guy Perry

Office of the Queen's Printer
Queen's Printer-Earl Tucker, Ground Fl., Confederation Blg.
PO Box 8700
St. John's, NL A1B 4J6
709-729-3649
Fax: 709-729-1900
queensprinter@gov.nl.ca
Provides a retail outlet for purchase of government legislation & various government reports. Publishes Hansard, Bills, Statutes & Regulations for the House of Assembly. Publishes weekly The Newfoundland & Labrador Gazette which contains government & public legal notices as well as subordinate legislation. Provides subscription & mail-out services for some of these publications. Provides ISBN numbers for government publications.

Vital Statistics Division
5 Mews Pl.
PO Box 8700
St. John's, NL A1B 4J6
709-729-3308
Fax: 709-729-0946
vstats@gov.nl.ca
Registers births, marriages & deaths in the province. In addition, the division registers adoptions & legal name changes & certifies clergy who are authorized to solemnize marriages. From this division, the public may obtain a birth, marriage, death, or change of name certificate, or a marriage licence. Vital Statistics services are also available from GSC offices.
Registrar, Brenda Andrews
709-729-3311

Eastern Office
15 Dundee Ave.
Mount Pearl, NL A1N 4R6
709-729-2706
Fax: 709-729-3445

Corner Brook
Noton Bldg.
133 Riverside Dr.
PO Box 2006
Corner Brook, NL A2H 6J8
709-637-2204
Fax: 709-637-2681

Gander
McCurdy Complex
PO Box 2222
Gander, NL A1V 2N9
709-256-1420
Fax: 709-256-1438
Director, Roger LeDrew

Grand Falls-Windsor
9 Queensway
Grand Falls-Windsor, NL A2A 1W9
709-292-4206
Fax: 709-292-4528
Manager, Rick Conway

Happy Valley-Goose Bay
13 Churchill St.
Happy Valley-Goose Bay, NL A0P 1E0
709-896-5428
Fax: 709-896-4340

Harbour Grace
Conception Bay Highway
Harbour Grace, NL
709-945-3014
Fax: 709-945-3114

St. John's
5 Mews Pl.
PO Box 8710
St. John's, NL A1B 4J5

709-729-3699
Fax: 709-729-2071

Stephenville
35 Alabama Dr.
Stephenville, NL A2N 3K9
709-643-8650

Occupational Health & Safety Branch
Other Communication: Accident Reporting Line: 709/729-4444 (24 hours); Toll Free for Occupational Health & Safety: 1-800-563-5471 (in Nfld. & Lab.)
Maintains & improves health & safety standards in the workplace through the administration of the Occupational Health & Safety Act & Regulations, The Mines Safety of Workers Regulations, the Radiation Health & Safety Act & Regulations &, other associated regulations, codes of practice & specified standards. The Division is supported by inspections officers, industrial hygienists, engineers & radiation specialists to per form various multi-disciplinary activities such as: investigating workplace accidents & statistics; conducting compliance inspections & detailed audits of workplaces; hygiene assessments of various physical, chemical, biological & ergonomic agents in the workplace in order to protect worker health; evaluating & inspecting radiation control measures in workplaces & enforcing occupational health & safety Legislation.
Asst. Deputy Minister, Kim Dunphy
709-729-5548, Fax: 709-729-4151
Director, Reg Bennett
709-729-7454, Fax: 709-729-3445
regbennett@gov.nl.ca

Corner Brook
Fortis Towers
4 Herald Ave., 2nd fl.
Corner Brook, NL
709-637-2946
Fax: 709-637-2928

Grand Falls-Windsor
7 High St.
Grand Falls-Windsor, NL
709-292-4400
Fax: 709-292-4430

Labrador City
Provincial Court Bldg.
Wabush, NL
709-282-2680
Fax: 709-282-2688

Department of Health & Community Services (HCS)
West Block, Confederation Bldg.
PO Box 8700
St. John's, NL A1B 4J6
709-729-5021
Fax: 709-729-5824
www.health.gov.nl.ca/
Provides a leadership role in health & community service programs & policy development for the Province. This involves working in partnership with a number of key stakeholders including regional boards, community organizations, professional associations, post-secondary educational institutions, unions, consumer & other government departments.
Acts Administered:
Adoption Act
Cancer Treatment & Research Foundation Act
Centre for Health Information Act
Child Care Services Act
Child, Youth & Family Services Act
Chiropractors Act
Communicable Diseases Act
Dental Act
Denturists Act
Dieticians Act
Dispensing Opticians Act
Emergency Medical Aid Act
Food & Drug Act
Health & Community Services Act
Health Care Association Act
Homes for Special Care Act
Public Health (Sanitation) Regulation
Hearing Aid Dealers Act
Hospital Insurance Agreement Act
Hospitals Act
Human Tissue Act
Licensed Practical Nurses Act
Massage Therapy Act
Medical Act
Medical Care Insurance Act, 1999
Mental Health Act
Midwifery Act
Neglected Adults Welfare Act
Occupational Therapists Act
Optometry Act
Pharmacy Act
Physiotherapy Act
Private Homes for Special Care Allowances Act
Psychologists Act
Registered Nurses Act
Self-managed Home Support Services Act
Smoke-free Environment Act
Social Workers Association Act
Tobacco Control Act
Venereal Disease Prevention Act
Young Persons Offences Act
Youth Criminal Justice Act (Canada)
Minister, Hon. Ross Wiseman
709-729-3124, 800-514-9073,Fax: 709-729-0121
rosswiseman@gov.nl.ca
Deputy Minister, Don Keats
709-729-3125, Fax: 709-729-0121
Director Communications, Glenda Power
709-729-1377, Fax: 709-729-0121
• Newfoundland & Labrador Health Boards Associations
Board of Trade Bldg.
#202, 66 Kenmount Rd.
St. John's, NL A1B 3V7
709-364-7701
Fax: 709-364-6460
nlhba@nlhba.nf.ca
www.nlhba.nf.ca

Public Health, Wellness, & Children & Youth Services
Asst. Deputy Minister, Jennifer Jeans
709-729-5864
Chief Medical Officer of Health Public Health Division, Dr. Faith Stratton
709-729-3430
Director Health Emergency Management,Vacant
Director Environmental Public Health, Darryl Johnson
709-729-3422, Fax: 709-729-0730
djohnson@gov.nl.ca
Director Public Health Labs, Dr. Sam Ratnam
709-777-7235
Director Health Promotion & Wellness, Eleanor Swanson
709-729-5023
Minister, Hon. Shawn Skinner
709-729-3580, Fax: 709-729-6996
ShawnSkinner@gov.nl.ca

Newfoundland & Labrador Hydro
Hydro Place
Columbus Dr.
PO Box 12400
St. John's, NL A1B 4K7
709-737-1400
Fax: 709-737-1800
Crown corporation, owned by the Province of Newfoundland & Labrador. Hydro generates, transmits & distributes electrical power & energy to utility, residential & industrial customers throughout the province. Hydro is the parent company of the Hydro Group of Companies (Hydro Group), comprising Newfoundland & Labrador Hydro, Churchill Falls (Labrador) Corporation Limited (CF(L)Co), Lower Churchill Development Corporation Limited (LCDC), Gull Island Power Company Limited (GIPCo), & Twin Falls Power Corporation Limited (TwinCo).The Hydro Group's installed generating capacity is the fourth largest of all utility companies in Canada, consisting of ten hydroelectric plants, including the Churchill Falls hydraulic plant, which is the largest underground powerhouse in the world with a rated capacity of 5,428 megawatts (MW) of power, one oil-fired plant, four gas turbines & 26 diesel plants.
President/CEO, Ed Martin
Vice-President Business Development, Jim Keating
Vice-President Engineering, John Mallam
Vice-President Finance & CFO, Derrick Sturge
Vice-President Human Resources, Gerard McDonald
Vice-President Regulated Operations, Jim Haynes

Churchill Falls (Labrador) Corporation Limited
Hydro Place
500 Columbus Dr.
PO Box 12500
St. John's, NL A1B 4K7
709-737-1859
Fax: 709-737-1816
Churchill Falls (Labrador) Corporation operates a hydroelectric generating plant & transmission facilities.
President/CEO, Ed Martin
General Manager, Andrew MacNeill
709-925-8227

Gull Island Power Co. Ltd.
President/CEO, Ed Martin
Vice-President Regulated Operations, Jim Haynes
CFO & Vice-President Finance, Derrick Sturge

Lower Churchill Development Corporation Ltd.
Vice-President, Gilbert Bennett

Twin Falls Power Corporation
PO Box 12500
St. John's, NL A1B 3T5
Twin Falls Power Corporation has developed a hydroelectric generating plant on the Unknown River in Labrador.The plant has been inoperative since 1974.
President, Jim Haynes
709-737-1400
General Manager, Andrew MacNeill

Department of Innovation, Trade & Rural Development
West Block, Confederation Bldg.
PO Box 8700
St. John's, NL A1B 4J6
709-729-7000
Fax: 709-729-0654
intrd@gov.nl.ca
www.intrd.gov.nl.ca
The department has a number of initiatives to assist businesses in the province or to open in the province.
Acts Administered:
Business Investment Corporation Act
Economic Diversification & Growth Enterprises (EDGE) Act
Industries Act
Research Council Act
Minister, Hon. Susan Sullivan
709-729-4728, Fax: 709-729-0654
SusanSullivan@gov.nl.ca
Deputy Minister, Meade Brent
709-729-4731, Fax: 709-729-0654
bmeade@gov.nl.ca
• Ireland Business Partnership
PO Box 8700
St. John's, NL A1B 4J6
709-729-1684
Fax: 709-729-2236
• Nearshore Atlantic
84 Elizabeth Ave., 1st Fl.
St. John's, NL A1A 1W7
709-772-8324
Fax: 709-757-6284
info@nearshoreatlantic.com
www.nearshoreatlantic.com

Innovation, Research & Advanced Technologies Branch
Asst. Deputy Minister, Dennis Hogan
709-729-7101, Fax: 709-729-7234
dhoghan@gov.nl.ca
Director, Diane Hooper

Regional Development
Asst. Deputy Minister, Rita Malone
709-637-2977, Fax: 709-639-7713
rmalone@gov.nl.ca
Director Regional Development & Planning, John Wickham
709-729-7260, Fax: 709-729-5124
jwickham@gov.nl.ca

Avalon
28 Pippy Place
St. John's, NL A1B 3X4
Fax: 709-729-7135

Federal/Provincial Government / Government of Newfoundland & Labrador

Central
McCurdy Complex, Markham Place
PO Box 2222
Gander, NL A1V 2N9
Fax: 709-256-1490

Eastern
211B Memorial Drive
Clarenville, NL A5A 1R3
Fax: 709-466-1306

Labrador
2 Hillcrest Rd.
PO Box 3014 B
Happy Valley-Goose Bay, NL A0P 1E0
709-896-2400
Fax: 709-896-0234

Western
PO Box 2006
Corner Brook, NL A2H 6J8
Fax: 709-639-7713

Strategic Industries & Business Development Branch
Asst. Deputy Minister, Peter Au
709-729-4711, Fax: 709-729-4858
PeterAu@gov.nl.ca
Director Business Analysis, Don Kavanagh
709-729-5622, Fax: 709-729-5124
dkavanagh@gov.nl.ca

Trade & Export Development Branch
Specializes in assisting provincial businesses develop an export plan to enter new markets, find export business partners & research national & international market opportunities.
Director, Linda Spurrell
709-729-7483, Fax: 709-729-5124
lspurrel@gov.nl.ca
Director Strategic Partnership, Derek Staubitzer
709-729-7043, Fax: 709-729-5124
derekstaubitzer@gov.nl.ca

Strategic Industries
This business line focuses on development of opportunities in three broad categories: further development of the province's manufacturing sector beyond traditional resource industries; emerging opportunities in new economy sectors such as biotechnology, marine communications, information technology & environmental industries; & value-added opportunities in traditional resource-based industries such as agrifoods & wood products.
Director, Kirk Tilley
709-729-7080, Fax: 709-729-6853
Minister, Hon. Felix Collins
709-729-2869, Fax: 709-729-0469
felixcollins@gov.nl.ca
Acts Administered:
Public Utilities Acquisition of Lands Act
Public Utilities Act
Deputy Minister, Donald Burrage, Q.C.
709-729-2872, Fax: 709-729-0469
donburrage@gov.nl.ca
Assistant Deputy Minister, Donna Ballard, Q.C.
709-729-0288, Fax: 709-729-2129
dballard@gov.nl.ca
Executive Director Human Rights Commission, Carey Majid
709-729-2709,
CareyMajid@gov.nl.ca
Director Fines Administration, Susan Roberts
709-729-0250, Fax: 709-729-0595
Director Legal Information Services, Sean Dawe
709-729-2861, Fax: 709-729-1370
seand@gov.nl.ca
Director Quality Management & Support Services, Dan Chafe
709-729-1078, Fax: 709-729-5100
Director Policy & Strategic Planning, Jackie Lake-Kavanagh
709-729-0543, Fax: 709-729-3949
jackiekavanagh@gov.nl.ca
Director Communications, Jennifer Tulk
709-729-6985, Fax: 709-729-0469
JenniferTulk@gov.nl.ca
Director Court Services, Pamela Ryder-Lahey
709-729-2081, Fax: 709-729-2161

Department of Labrador & Aboriginal Affairs

Confederation Bldg.
East Block, 6th Fl.
PO Box 8700
St. John's, NL A1B 4J6
709-729-4776
Fax: 709-729-4900
877-788-8822
laa@gov.nl.ca
www.laa.gov.nl.ca
Responsible for coordinating government's activities related to Labrador Affairs & Aboriginal Affairs, including developing policy & programs, managing federal-provincial agreements, negotiating land claims, public information & all matters of significant public interest in Labrador.The principal tasks of the Department in the field of Aboriginal Affairs are policy development for Aboriginal issues, negotiating land claims treaties & self-government agreements, implementing & managing land claims agreements once achieved & providing public information & education in matters related to land claims.The principal tasks of the Department in the field of Labrador Affairs are developing policies & programs related to significant issues of Government interest in Labrador, managing Federal-Provincial Agreements related to the development of Labrador & managing Federal-Provincial Agreements for the Innu & Inuit communities of Labrador.
Minister Responsible Labrador Affairs, Hon. John Hickey
709-896-3099, Fax: 709-896-4285
JHickey@gov.nl.ca
Minister Responsible Aboriginal Affairs, Hon. Patty Pottle
709-729-1069, 877-788-8822,Fax: 709-729-4900
pattypottle@gov.nl.ca
Deputy Minister, Robert Coombs
709-896-1711, Fax: 709-896-4648
Senior Negotiator Innu Land Claims, Robert Pelley
709-729-0166, Fax: 709-729-4900
bpelley@gov.nl.ca
Senior Negotiator Inuit Land Claims, Ruby Carter
709-729-0137, Fax: 709-729-4900
rcarter@gov.nl.ca

Department of Municipal Affairs

West Block, Main Fl., Confederation Bldg.
PO Box 8700
St. John's, NL A1B 4J6
709-729-3053
www.ma.gov.nl.ca
Works with municipalities to ensure communities are properly managed & planned to ensure residents have a high standard of living in a clean, healthy & safe environment.The department is responsible for community-related activities such as the Office of the Fire Commissioner, the Emergency Measures Organization, Engineering & Land Use Planning.
Acts Administered:
Assessment Act
Avian Emblem Act
Building Standards Act
City of Corner Brook Act
City of Mount Pearl Act
City of St. John's Act
Coat of Arms Act
Commemoration Day Act
Crown Corporations Local Taxation Act
Emergency Measures Act
Evacuated Communities Act
Family Homes Expropriation Act
Fire Prevention Act
Floral Emblem Act
Housing Act
Labrador Act
Mineral Emblem Act
Municipal Affairs Act
Municipal Elections Act
Municipalities Act
Provincial Anthem Act
Provincial Flag Act
Remembrance Day Act
Regional Service Boards Act
St. John's Assessment Act
St. John's Centennial Foundation Act
St. John's Municipal Council Parks Act
St. John's Municipal Elections Act
Standard Time Act
Taxation of Utilities & Cable Television Companies Act
Urban & Rural Planning Act, 2000
Minister, Hon. Dave Denine
709-729-3048, Fax: 709-729-0943
davedenine@gov.nl.ca
Deputy Minister, Rose Baxter
709-729-3052, Fax: 709-729-0943
brose@gov.nl.ca
Assistant Deputy Minister Municipal Support & Policy, Lori Anne Companion
709-729-3066, Fax: 709-729-4475
loriannecompanion@gov.nl.ca
Director Communications, Jennifer Collingwood
709-729-1983, Fax: 709-729-0943
jennifercollingwood@gov.nl.ca
• Office of the Fire Commissioner
2 Wellon Dr.
Deer Lake, NL A8A 2G5
709-635-4153
Fax: 709-635-4163
Fire Commissioner, Fred Hollett

Engineering & Land Use Planning
Provides professional engineering, administrative & technical support services to facilitate the provision of sustainable, suitable & affordable municipal infrastructure in a manner that will result in greater autonomy for communities; assists & advises departments of government & any public authority in planning for the orderly & economic development of land.
Asst. Deputy Minister, Wayne Churchill
709-729-5328
Director, Randy Dillon
709-729-5328,
wchurchill@mail.gov.nl.ca

Department of Natural Resources

Natural Resources Bldg.
50 Elizabeth Ave., 7th Fl.
PO Box 8700
St. John's, NL A1B 4J6
709-729-2920
Fax: 709-729-0059
www.nr.gov.nl.ca
Responsible for the management of the province's mineral, energy, land, forest & wildlife resources in a manner that will ensure optimum benefits for the people of the province.
Acts Administered:
Animal Protection Act
Canada-Newfoundland Atlantic Accord Implementation (Newfoundland) Act, 1986
Canada-Newfoundland & Labrador Oil & Gas Spills & Debris Liability Newfoundland & Labrador Regulations
Certificate of Fitness Newfoundland & Labrador Regulations
Offshore Area Oil & Gas Operations Regulations
Offshore Area Petroleum Geophysical Operations Newfoundland & Labrador Regulations
Offshore Area Petroleum Production & Conservation Newfoundland & Labrador Regulations
Offshore Petroleum Drilling Newfoundland & Labrador Regulations
Offshore Petroleum Installations Newfoundland & Labrador Regulations
Dog Act
Electrical Power Control Act
Food & Drug Act
Forest Protection Act
Cutting of Timber Regulations
Forest Fire Regulations
Forest Management Districts Proclamation
Forestry Act
Cutting of Timber Regulations
Forest Fire Offence & Penalty Regulation
Forest Fire Regulations
Forest Fires Liability & Compensation Regulations
Forest Land Management & Taxation Regulations
Forest Management Districts Proclamation Regulations
Mill Regulations
Timber Royalty Regulations
Timber Scaling Regulations
Heritage Animals Act
Hydro Corporation Act
Livestock Act
Livestock Health Act
Livestock Insurance Act
Lower Churchill Development Act
Meat Inspection Act
Mineral Act
Mineral Holdings Impost Act
Mining Act

Motorized Snow Vehicles & All-Terrain Vehicles Act (Shared with Government Services)
Natural Products Marketing Act
Petroleum & Natural Gas Act
Plant Protection Act
Poultry & Poultry Products Act
Seed Potato Regulations
Quarry Materials Act
Undeveloped Minerals Areas Act
Vegetable Grading Act
Veterinary Medical Act
Wildlife Act
Minister, Hon. Kathy Dunderdale
709-729-2920, Fax: 709-729-0059
KathyDunderdale@gov.nl.ca
Deputy Minister, Chris Kieley
709-729-2766, Fax: 709-729-0059
chriskieley@gov.nl.ca
Assistant Deputy Minister, Keith Deering
709-729-2269, Fax: 709-637-2461
keithdeering@gov.nl.ca
Director Communications, Tracy Barron
709-729-5282, Fax: 709-729-0059
tracybarron@gov.nl.ca
Director Animal Health & Provincial Veterinarian, Dr. Hugh Whitney
709-729-6879, Fax: 709-729-0055
hughwhitney@gov.nl.ca
• Canada-Newfoundland Offshore Petroleum Board
TD Place
140 Water St., 5th Fl.
St. John's, NL A1C 6H6
709-778-1400
Fax: 709-778-1473
postmaster@cnlopb.nl.ca
www.cnlopb.nl.ca
Chair/CEO, Max Ruelokke
The Canada-Newfoundland Offshore Petroleum Board manages the petroleum resources in the Newfoundland offshore area on behalf of the Government of Canada & the Government of Newfoundland & Labrador. The Board's authority is derived from the legislation implementing the 1985 Atlantic Accord between the two governments. The Environmental Affairs department ensures that offshore oil & gas industrial activities proceed in an environmentally acceptable manner & evaluates the effect of the offshore environment upon the safety of offshore activities & by ensuring protection of the environment during the conduct of these activities. Working in close consultation with the Operations & Safety department, Environmental Affairs assesses the effects of environmental conditions, such as winds, waves & ice conditions, in the Newfoundland offshore area upon the safety of operations. Environmental Affairs reviews operators' plans for collecting the weather, oceanographic & ice data that they are required to measure at offshore

Agrifoods Branch
Provincial Agriculture Bldg.
Brookfield Rd.
PO Box 8700
St. John's, NL A1B 4J6
709-729-6588
Fax: 709-729-2674
To contribute to economic & rural development throughout the province by promoting the continued development, expansion & diversification of competitive & sustainable primary & value-added agrifood businesses.
Asst. Deputy Minister, Jeffrey Whalen
709-729-3787, Fax: 709-729-0973
jeffwhalen@gov.nl.ca
Director Animal Health Division & Provincial Veterinarian, Dr. Hugh Whitney
709-729-6879, Fax: 709-729-0055
hughwhitney@gov.nl.ca
Director Land Resource Stewardship, Jeff Whalen
709-637-2081, Fax: 709-637-2586

Energy Branch
Acting Deputy Minister, Pierre Tobin
709-729-2349, Fax: 709-729-2871
ptobin@gov.nl.ca
Director Electricity Industry Development, David Bazeley
709-729-6760, Fax: 709-729-2508
dbazeley@gov.nl.ca
Assistant Deputy Minister Petroleum Resources Development, Wes Foote
709-729-2206, Fax: 709-729-2508
wesfoote@gov.nl.ca
Director Regulatory Affairs/Energy Policy, Fred Allen
709-729-2778, Fax: 709-729-2508
fredallen@gov.nl.ca

Forest Resources
Fortis Bldg.
PO Box 2006
Corner Brook, NL A2H 6J8
709-637-2284
Fax: 709-634-4378
Manages & conserves the Province's ecosystems, under the principles of sustainable development, using an ecologically based management philosophy, & sound environmental practices. This is achieved through the implementation of forest management programs, such as silviculture, access road construction, forest fire suppression, insect control, management planning, tree nursery operations, inventory, dealing with wildlife in residential areas, collisions or similar situations, & public relations. In addition the Department is responsible for issuing permits under various legislation as well as the enforcement of forestry & wildlife regulations in such areas as hunting & timber harvesting.

Forestry Branch (Newfoundland Forest Service) (NFS)
Fortis Bldg.
PO Box 2006
Corner Brook, NL A2H 6J8
709-637-2349
Fax: 709-637-2403
CEO, Len Moores
709-637-2339, Fax: 709-637-2461
Director Forest Ecosystem Management, Ivan Downton
709-634-2284,
idownton@gov.nl.ca
Director Legislation & Compliance, Tony Porter
709-535-0102, Fax: 709-535-0102
tonyporter@gov.nl.ca

Mines Branch
Promotes & facilitates the sustainable development of the province's mineral & energy resources through its resource assessment, management & development activities for the overall benefit of the citizens of Newfoundland & Labrador.
Asst. Deputy Minister, Richard Wardle
709-729-2768, Fax: 709-729-2871
richardwardle@gov.nl.ca
Director Mineral Lands Division, Kenneth Andrews
709-729-6425, Fax: 709-729-6782
kenandrews@gov.nl.ca
Acting Director Mineral Development, John D. Davis
709-729-6449, Fax: 709-729-3493
johnddavis@gov.nl.ca
Asst. Deputy Minister Industrial Benefits, Brian Condon
709-729-1644, Fax: 709-729-0868
bcondon@gov.nl.ca

Geological Survey
709-729-4014
Fax: 709-729-4270
Director, Dave Liverman
709-729-4014, Fax: 709-729-4270
dliverman@gov.nl.ca

Soil, Plant & Feed Laboratory
Brookfield Rd.
PO Box 8700
St. John's, NL A1B 4J6
709-729-6738
Fax: 709-729-6734
Research is focused on: animal waste & soil conservation; environmental sustainability issues (ESI);soil, plant & feed testing.
Supervisor Soil, Plant & Feed Laboratory, Dr. Jaswant Tomar
Specialist Soils, Jeff Whalen

Forest Engineering & Industry Services Division
709-637-2349
Fax: 709-637-2403
Services include mensuration, environmental & land use planning, inventory & cartography.
Director, G.J. Fleming
709-637-2349, Fax: 709-637-2403
Supervisor Industry Services, Barry Garland
709-637-2247
Supervisor Insect & Disease, Hubert Crummey
709-637-2424
Coordinator Fire Tracking & Consumption, Bruce Nicholl

Forest Ecosystem Management Division
709-637-2284
Senior Management Planner, Basil English
709-637-2343

Policy Coordination Division
Herald Bldg.
PO Box 2006
Corner Brook, NL A2H 6J8
709-729-3752
Fax: 709-729-3374
Responsible for forest fire control, reforestation, insect & pest control, prescribed burn, & forest products utilization & development.
Coordinator Cost Shared Agreement, Gary Small
709-729-3374

Eastern
PO Box 2222
Gander, NL A1V 5T4
709-256-1450
Fax: 709-256-1459

Labrador
PO Box 3014 B
Happy Valley-Goose Bay, NL A0P 1E0
709-896-3405
Other Communication: Fax: 709-896-3747 (Forestry); 896-0188 (Wildlife)
Regional Manager, Mildred Johnson
709-896-2732, Fax: 709-896-3747
mildredjohnson@gov.nl.ca

Western
Massey Drive Bldg.
PO Box 2006
Corner Brook, NL A2H 6J8
709-637-2409
Fax: 709-639-1377
Regional Ecosystem Director, Perry Benoit
709-637-2692

Bay D'Espoir
PO Box 179
Milltown, NL A0H 1W0
709-882-2200

Bishop Falls
PO Box 640
Bishop Falls, NL A0H 1C0
709-258-5334

Cartwright
PO Box 159
Cartwright, NL A0K 1V0
709-938-7362
Fax: 709-938-7399

Clarenville
#206, 97 Manitoba Dr.
Clarenville, NL A5A 1K3
709-466-7439
Fax: 709-466-3802
District Manager, Ed Stewart

Gambo
PO Box 25
Gambo, NL A0G 2E0
709-674-4625

Gander
PO Box 2222
Gander, NL A1V 2N9
709-256-1450

Lewisporte
PO Box 217
Lewisporte, NL A0G 1A0
709-535-2706

Massey Drive
PO Box 2006
Corner Brook, NL A2H 6J8
709-637-2370

Northwest River
PO Box 1200
Northwest River, NL A0P 1B0

Federal/Provincial Government / Government of the Northwest Territories

709-497-8479
Fax: 709-497-8482

Paddy's Pond
PO Box 13036
St. John's, NL A1B 3V8
709-729-4180
District Manager, William Clarke

Pasadena
PO Box 340
Pasadena, NL A0L 1K0
709-686-2071

Port Saunders
PO Box 69
Port Saunders, NL A0K 4H0
709-861-3502

Roddickton
PO Box 250
Roddickton, NL A0K 4P0
709-457-2300
District Manager, George Gibbons

St. George's
PO Box 279
St Georges, NL A0N 1Z0
709-647-3761
District Manager, Hubert Smith

Springdale
PO Box 220
Springdale, NL A0J 1T0
709-673-3821
Fax: 709-673-4525

Wabush
PO Box 419
Wabush, NL A0R 1D0
709-282-6881

Newfoundland & Labrador Board of Commissioners of Public Utilities

PO Box 21040
St. John's, NL A1A 5B2
709-726-8600
Fax: 709-726-9604
866-782-0006
ito@pub.nf.ca
www.pub.nf.ca
Regulates electrical utilities in Newfoundland & Labrador.
Acts Administered:
Act to Amend the Electric Power Control Act
Automobile Insurance Act
Electric Power Control Act
Expropriation Act
Motor Carrier Act
Motor Vehicle Act
Petroleum Products Act
Public Utilities Act
Public Utilities Acquisition of Lands Act
Chair & CEO, Andy Wells
709-726-1133,
awells@pub.nl.ca
Vice-Chair, Darlene Whalen
709-726-0955,
dwhalen@pub.nl.ca

Department of Tourism, Culture & Recreation

Confederation Bldg.
West Block, 2nd Fl.
PO Box 8700
St. John's, NL A1B 4J6
709 729 0862
Fax: 709-729-0870
tcrinfo@gov.nl.ca
www.tcr.gov.nl.ca
Ensures the development of provincial vacation & business travel markets.The department conserves, preserves & protects natural & cultural resources & promotes the resources for economic benefit, sport & recreation in the province. It also protects, preserves & develops the historic resources of the province.Programs promote the development of travel & tourism & assist in transforming the province's natural & cultural attractions into opportunities for employment & revenue generation.
Acts Administered:
Arts Council Act
Books Preservation of Copies Act
Boxing Authority Act
Colonial Buildings Act
Cruiseship Authority Act
Grand Concourse Authority Act
Historic Resources Act
Newspapers & Books Act
Rooms Act
Tourist Establishments Act
Minister, Hon. Clyde Jackman
709-729-0659, 877-787-0707,Fax: 709-729-0662
clydejackman@gov.nl.ca
Deputy Minister, Brent Meade
709-729-3555, Fax: 709-729-0662
bmeade@gov.nl.ca
• Newfoundland & Labrador Film Development Corporation
12 King's Bridge Rd.
St. John's, NL A1C 3K3
709-738-3456
Fax: 709-739-1680
877-738-3456
info@nlfdc.ca
www.nlfdc.ca

Culture & Heritage
The department administers archeology permits, the Art Procurement Program, the Heritage Foundation of Newfoundland & Labrador, provides grants to artists, arts organizations, museums & archives through the Newfoundland & Labrador Arts Council, provides grants to assists the Newfoundland & Labrador Film Development Corporation & administers provincial historic sites.
Asst. Deputy Minister,Vacant
709-729-3609
Director Heritage, Jerry Dick
709-729-7393, Fax: 709-729-0870
jerrydick@gov.nl.ca

Tourism
Director Tourism Product Development, Juanita Keel-Ryan
709-729-1708, Fax: 709-729-0474
jkeelryan@gov.nl.ca
Director Tourism Marketing Division, Carmela Murphy
709-729-2831, Fax: 709-729-0057
Manager Labrador Regional Office, Rose Dyson
709-896-8480

Department of Transportation & Works

Confederation Bldg.
West Block, 6th Fl.
PO Box 8700
St. John's, NL A1B 4J6
709-729-3679
Fax: 709-729-4285
twminister@gov.nl.ca
www.tw.gov.nl.ca
To provide a safe, efficient & sustainable transportation system & to provide landlord services & support services such as leasing & mail services for all government departments. The department liaises with other agencies & the federal government to ensure the overall public works & transportation needs & interest of the province are fully provided & protected.
Acts Administered:
Expropriation Act
Local Road Boards Act
Motor Carrier Act
Pippy Park Commission Act
Rail Services Act
Transportation & Works Act
Minister, Hon. Dianne C. Whalen
709-729-3679, 866-996-5670,Fax: 709-729-4285
twminister@gov.nl.ca
Deputy Minister, Robert Smart
709-729-3676, Fax: 709-729-4285
Director Communications, David Salter
709-729-3015, Fax: 709-729-4285
davidsalter@gov.nl.ca

Transportation Services
Asst. Deputy Minister, Cluney Mercer
709-729-3796, Fax: 709-729-0283
mercerc@gov.nl.ca
Director Highway Design & Construction, Gary Gosse
709-729-5483, Fax: 709-729-0283
Senior Engineer Highway Design, Garry Spencer
709-729-7293, Fax: 709-729-0283
Chief Operating Officer Marine Services, Tom Prim
709-429-3278, Fax: 709-729-6934
Environmental Specialist Policy & Planning, Ken Hannaford
709-729-5540, Fax: 709-729-3418
Environmental Planner Policy & Planning, Charlie Horwood
709-729-2632, Fax: 709-729-0646
horwoodc@gov.nl.ca

Works Branch
709-729-3019
Fax: 709-729-4658
Asst. Deputy Minister, Weldon Moores
709-729-6882, Fax: 709-729-3418
wmoores@gov.nl.ca
Director Design & Construction, Gunar Leja
709-729-1969, Fax: 709-729-0646
lejag@gov.nl.ca
Director Engineering Support Services, Keith Noel
709-729-5786, Fax: 709-729-5934
noelka@gov.nl.ca

Newfoundland & Labrador Workplace Health, Safety & Compensation Commission

146 - 148 Forest Rd.
PO Box 9000
St. John's, NL A1A 3B8
709-778-1000
Fax: 709-738-1714
800-563-9000
general.inquiries@whscc.nl.ca
www.whscc.nf.ca
Other Communication: Grand Falls toll-free: 800/563-3448;
Corner Brook toll-free: 800/563-2772
Utilizing skilled, professional employees, in partnership with workplace parties, the commission facilitates safe & healthy workplaces by assisting employers & workers to prevent accidents, & manage workplace injuries/illnesses & return-to-work processes. Operating as the administrator of the workers' compensation insurance program, the commission provides a reasonable level of benefits to injured workers & their dependents based on reasonable assessment rates for employers, while maintaining or exceeding service level performance when compared to other jurisdictions in Canada.
Chair, Ralph Tucker
CEO, Leslie Galway

Government of the Northwest Territories

Seat of Government:PO Box 1320
Yellowknife, NT X1A 2L9
www.gov.nt.ca
The Northwest Territories was reconstituted September 1, 1905.It has an area of 1,140,834.90 km2, & the StatsCan population in 2006 was 41,464. On April 1, 1999, the Northwest Territories was divided into two new territories: Nunavut Territories and the as yet unnamed territory (known as the Northwest Territories). The Northwest Territories is governed by a fully elected Legislative Assembly of 19 members elected for a four-year term. Government is by consensus rather than party politics. The Legislature elects the Premier & a seven-member Executive Council, which is charged with the operation of government & the establishment of program & spending priorities. The Commissioner of the Northwest Territories is appointed by the Federal Government, & serves a role similar to that of a Lieutenant Governor in provincial jurisdictions.

Department of Aboriginal Affairs & Intergovernmental Relations

4910 - 52nd St.
PO Box 1320
Yellowknife, NT X1A 2L9
867-873-7143
Fax: 867-873-0233
877-838-8194
nancy_gardiner@gov.nt.ca
www.daair.gov.nt.ca
The Department of Aboriginal Affairs & Intergovernmental Relations is charged with the following responsibilities: to negotiate, implement, & monitor land, resource & self-government agreements; to manage governmental relationships with Aboriginal, federal, provincial, & territorial governments, & with circumpolar countries; to provide advice on federal-provincial-territorial-Aboriginal relations; & to contribute to the political & constitutional development of the Northwest Territories.

Federal/Provincial Government / Government of the Northwest Territories

Minister, Hon. Floyd Roland
867-669-2311, Fax: 867-873-0385
floyd_roland@gov.nt.ca
Deputy Minister, Gabriela Sparling
867-873-7143, Fax: 867-873-0233
gabriela_sparling@gov.nt.ca
Director Intergovernmental Relations, Andy Bevan
867-920-8701,
andy_bevan@gov.nt.ca
Director Implementation, Scott Alexander
867-873-7149, Fax: 867-873-0540
scott_alexander@gov.nt.ca
Director Negotiations, Fred Talen
867-873-7388, Fax: 867-873-0593
fred_talen@gov.nt.ca

Aurora Research Institute (ARI)

191 MacKenzie Rd.
PO Box 1450
Inuvik, NT X0E 0T0
867-777-3298
Fax: 867-777-4264
webmaster@nwtresearch.com
www.nwtresearch.com

A division of Aurora College that is dedicated to excellence, leadership & innovations in Northern education & research. Administers the research licencing provisions of the Northwest Territories Scientists Act & provides year round logistical assistance for researchers.
Director, Andrew Applejohn
867-777-3298,
director@nwtresearch.com
Manager Fort Smith, Ruthann Gal
867-872-4909,
rgal@auroracollege.nt.ca
Manager Research & Technology, Sharon Katz
867-777-3298,
skatz@auroracollege.nt.ca

Department of Education, Culture & Employment (ECE)

PO Box 1320
Yellowknife, NT X1A 2L9
867-669-2399
Fax: 867-873-0431
866-606-5627
www.ece.gov.nt.ca
Other Communication: Jobs North Phone: 867-873-7690; Fax: 867-873-0636; Email: jobsnorth@gov.nt.ca
The Ministry's responsibilities cover the following areas: Early Childhood; Kindergarten to Grade 12; Adult & Post-Secondary Education; Career Development & Employment; Apprenticeship & Occupational Certification; Culture, Heritage & Languages; Income Security; & Labour Services.
Acts Administered:
Apprenticeship, Trade & Occupations Certification Act
Archives Act
Child Day Care Act
Education Act
Library Act
Occupational Training Agreements Act
Official Languages Act
Public Colleges Act
Scientists Act
Senior Citizens Benefits Act
Social Assistance Act
Student Financial Assistance Act
Minister, Hon. Jackson Lafferty
867-669-2399, Fax: 867-873-0274
jackson_lafferty@gov.nt.ca
Deputy Minister, Dan Daniels
867-920-6240, Fax: 867-873-0338
dan_daniels@gov.nt.ca
• Northwest Territories Apprenticeship, Trade & Occupations Certification Board
PO Box 1320
Yellowknife, NT X1A 2L9
867-873-7357
Fax: 867-873-0200
• NWT Arts Council
PO Box 1320 Main
Yellowknife, NT X1A 2L9
867-920-6370
Fax: 867-873-0205
pwnhc.learnnet.nt.ca/artscouncil/

College & Careers Development Branch
867-873-7252
Fax: 867-873-0155

Education & Culture
867-920-8061
Fax: 867-873-0155
Asst. Deputy Minister, Roy Erasmus
867-920-8061, Fax: 867-873-0338
roy_erasmus@gov.nt.ca
Director Culture & Heritage, Charles Arnold
867-873-7551,
charles_arnold@gov.nt.ca
Territorial Archaeologist, Tom Andrews
867-873-7688,
tom_andrews@gov.nt.ca

Department of Environment & Natural Resources (ENR)

PO Box 1320
Yellowknife, NT X1A 2L9
www.enr.gov.nt.ca
Operations cover a broad spectrum of activities directed at promoting a healthy environment that supports traditional lifestyles within a modern economy. The wise use & protection of natural resources are encouraged. The Department's activities are carried out through the following divisions: Environmental Protection, Forest Management, Policy, Legislation & Communications, Protected Areas Strategy, Informatics, & Wildlife.
Acts Administered:
Environmental Protection Act
Asphalt Paving Industry Emission Regulations
Spill Contingency Planning & Reporting Regulations
Used Oil & Waste Fuel Management Regulations
Environmental Rights Act
Forest Management Act
Forest Protection Act
Natural Resources Conservation Trust Act
Pesticide Act
Waste Reduction & Recovery Act
Beverage Container Regulations
Water Resources Agreement Act
Wildlife Act
Certification & Disposal of Wildlife Regulations
Critical Wildlife Areas Regulations
Sale of Wildlife Regulations
Trapping Regulations
Wildlife Export Regulations
Wildlife General Regulations
Wildlife Management Areas & Zones Regulations
Wildlife Preserves Regulations
Wildlife Sanctuaries Regulations
Minister, Hon. J. Michael Miltenberger
867-669-2355, Fax: 867-873-0596
michael_miltenberger@gov.nt.ca
Deputy Minister, Gary Bohnet
867-873-7401,
gary_bohnet@gov.nt.ca
Director Policy & Strategic Planning, Doris Eggers
867-920-8046, Fax: 867-873-0114
doris_eggers@gov.nt.ca
Director Shared Services, Finance & Administration, Nancy Magrum
867-920-8649, Fax: 867-873-0551
NANCY_MAGRUM@gov.nt.ca
Director Shared Services & Informatics, Rick Wind
867-920-3327, Fax: 867-873-0293
rick_wind@gov.nt.ca
Director Environment, Ray Case
867-873-7654, Fax: 867-873-0221
ray_case@gov.nt.ca
Director Wildlife, Susan Fleck
867-920-8043, Fax: 867-873-0293
susan_fleck@gov.nt.ca
Director Forest Management, William Mawdsley
867-872-7725,
WILLIAM_MAWDSLEY@gov.nt.ca

Deh Cho
Milton Bldg., 2nd Fl.
PO Box 240
Fort Simpson, NT X0E 0N0
867-695-7451
Fax: 867-695-2381

Regional Superintendent, Stephen Charlie
867-695-7451

Inuvik
Semmler Bldg., 2nd Fl.
Bag Service #1
Inuvik, NT X0E 0T0
867-678-6651
Fax: 867-678-6659
Regional Superintendent, Ron Morrison
867-678-6651,
ron_morrison@gov.nt.ca

North Slave
PO Box 2668
Yellowknife, NT X1A 2P9
867-920-6134
Fax: 867-873-6230
Acting Regional Superintendent, Lance Schmidt
867-920-6134, Fax: 867-873-6230
lance_schmidt@gov.nt.ca

Sahtu
PO Box 130
Norman Wells, NT X0E 0V0
867-587-3508
Regional Superintendent, Keith Hickling
867-587-3508,
keith_hickling@gov.nt.ca

Fort Smith
Sweetgrass Bldg.
PO Box 390
Fort Smith, NT X0E 0P0
867-872-6401
Fax: 867-872-4250
Regional Superintendent, Jack Bird
867-872-6401,
jack_bird@gov.nt.ca

Northwest Territories Geoscience Office
4601 B - 52 Ave.
PO Box 1500
Yellowknife, NT X1A 2R3
867-669-2636
Fax: 867-669-2725
NTGO@gov.nt.ca
www.nwtgeoscience.ca/
The Northwest Territories Geoscience Office (NTGO) advances the geoscience knowledge of the Northwest Territories for the benefit of northerners through: delivery of geoscience research; analysis of mineral & petroleum resources; excellence in data management. In collaboration with its partners, NTGO provides analysis, information & advice to individuals, communities, governments, & the mining & petroleum industry
Chief Geologist, Carolyn Relf
867-669-2635,
carolyn_relf@gov.nt.ca

Environmental Protection Division
867-873-7654
Fax: 867-873-0221
To protect & enhance the environmental quality in the North. Departmental programs are designed to control the discharge of contaminants & reduce their impacts on the natural environment. This is a shared responsibility with federal, territorial, Aboriginal & municipal agencies, as well as every resident of the Northwest Territories. To promote energy conservation & the use of energy efficient technology in the Northwest Territories, identify & facilitate the development of alternative, local energy sources which strengthen community economies, & promote & facilitate energy planning.
Director, Emery Paquin
867-873-7654,
Manager Environmental Protection, Ken Hall
867-920-6476
Coordinator Climate Change, Jim Sparling
867-920-6396
Specialist Hazardous Substances, Harvey Gaukel
867-873-7645,
harvey_gaukel@gov.nt.ca
Specialist Hazardous Waste, Don Helfrick
867-920-8044,
don_helfrick@gov.nt.ca

Federal/Provincial Government / Government of the Northwest Territories

Specialist Industrial Oil & Gas, Todd Paget
867-873-7178
Specialist Industrial Mining, Colleen Roche
867-920-3118

Forest Management Division
PO Box 7
Fort Smith, NT X0E 0P0
Fax: 867-874-2077
forestmanagement.enr.gov.nt/
Provides the policy, planning & regulatory framework for the stewardship, protection & sustainable management of forest resources on 33 million hectares of land in the Northwest Territories, eight per cent of Canada's entire forested area. Working with First Nations governments, communities, other governments & non-governmental agencies on such a vast land mass presents unique & complex challenges for forest managers. The FMD coordinates & facilitates the implementation of forest management programs & services among the five administrative regions of ENR. The regional offices have the primary responsibility for delivery of programs. Regional staff implement forest resource & fire management programs for the Department. Regional personnel receive applications for approval to harvest, supervise harvesting activities, ensure compliance with standards, support community protection planning efforts & carry out fire management activities under the direction of the Forest Management Division.
Director, Susan Corey
867-872-7700, Fax: 867-872-2077
susan_corey@gov.nt.ca
Manager Forest Management Services, William Maudsley
867-872-7725
Manager Fire Operations, Frank Lepine
867-872-7713
Manager Forest Resources, Tom Lakusta
867-874-2009
Manager Forest Science, Vacant
867-872-7707
Coordinator Standards & Environmental Assessment, David Purchase
867-870-7743
Forest Ecologist, Bob Decker
867-874-2009

Policy, Legislation & Communications Division
Fax: 867-873-0114
Provides services in the area of policy, legislation, environmental assessment, land claims & self-government, resource management & public affairs & communications.
Director, Doris Eggers
867-920-8046
Policy Analyst, Kevin Brezinski
867-920-3197
Senior Advisor Aboriginal Relations, Luke Coady
867-920-3296
Manager Environmental Assessment, Gavin More
867-873-7244

Wildlife
Fax: 867-874-2347
www.nwtwildlife.com/
Activities are directed towards maintaining productive populations of all native wildlife in their natural habitats, encouraging the wise use of wildlife populations within the limits of sustainable yield & encouraging the active participation of northern residents in the management of wildlife resources. In addition to assistance programs that are designed to support the hunting & trapping economy, the division provides support to organizations of resource users to allow them to become more involved in wildlife management.
Director, Susan Fleck
867-920-8043
Manager Technical Support, Ray Case
867-920-8067,
ray_case@gov.nt.ca
Acting Manager Wildlife & Environment, Inuvik Region & Environmental Assessment Specialist, Marsha Branigan
867-920-6315
Manager Wildlife & Environment, South Slave Region, Troy Ellsworth
867-872-6423
Manager Wildlife, Sahtu Region, Keith Hickling
867-920-3179
Acting Manager Wildlife & Environment, North Slave Region, Lance Schmidt

867-873-7765,
ron_graf@gov.nt.ca
Supervisor Sahtu Wildlife Management & Regional Biologist, Alasdair Veitch
867-587-3517
Manager Biodiversity & Information, Lynda Yonge
867-920-8675,
lynda_yonge@gov.nt.ca
Secretary & Comptroller General, Margaret Melhorn
867-873-7117, Fax: 867-873-0414
margaret_melhorn@gov.nt.ca

Vital Statistics
Bag #9
Inuvik, NT X0E 0T0
867-777-7400
Fax: 867-777-3197
800-661-0830
hsa@gov.nt.ca
Birth certificates: $10

Deh Cho
PO Box 246
Fort Simpson, NT X0E 0N0
867-695-3815
Fax: 867-695-2920

Tlicho
Bag #5
Behchoko, NT X0E 0Y0
867-392-3000
Fax: 867-392-3001

Fort Smith
PO Box 1080
Fort Smith, NT X0E 0P0
867-872-6200
Fax: 867-872-6275

Hay River
3 Gaetz Dr.
Hay River, NT X0E 0R8
867-874-7100
Fax: 867-874-7118

Beaufort-Delta
Bag #2, 285 Mackenzie Rd.
Inuvik, NT X0E 0T0
867-777-8000
Fax: 867-777-8062

Sahtu
PO Box 340
Norman Wells, NT X0E 0V0
867-587-3652
Fax: 867-587-3436

Stanton
PO Box 10
Yellowknife, NT X1A 2N1
867-669-4224
Fax: 867-669-4128
www.srhb.org

Yellowknife
Jan Stirling Bldg.
4702 Franklin Ave.
PO Box 608
Yellowknife, NT X1A 2N5
867-873-7276
Fax: 867-920-7025
yhssa@gov.nt.ca
www.yhssa.org

Department of Health & Social Services
Centre Square Tower
PO Box 1320
Yellowknife, NT X1A 2L9
Fax: 867-873-0266
www.hlthss.gov.nt.ca
The Department of Health & Social Services is mandated to provide a broad range of health & social programs & services to the residents of the NWT. Seven regional Health & Social Services Authorities plan, manage & deliver a full spectrum of community & facility-based services for health care & social services. Community health programs include daily sick clinics, public health clinics, home care, school health programs & educational programs. Visiting physicians & specialists routinely visit the communities.
Acts Administered:
Aboriginal Custom Adoption Recognition Act
Adoption Act
Change of Name Act
Child & Family Services Act
Child Welfare Act
Dental Auxiliaries Act
Dental Mechanics Act
Dental Professions Act
Disease Registries Act
Emergency Medical Aid Act
Guardianship & Trusteeship Act (jointly with Dept. of Justice)
Hospital Insurance & Health & Social Services Administration Act
Human Tissue Act
Intercountry Adoption (Hague Convention) Act
Licensed Practical Nurses Act
Marriage Act (jointly with Dept. of Justice)
Medical Care Act
Medical Profession Act
Mental Health Act
Midwifery Profession Act
Nursing Profession Act
Ophthalmic Medical Assistants Act
Optometry Act
Personal Directives Act
Pharmacy Act
Psychologists Act
Public Health Act
Communicable Diseases Regulation
General Sanitation Regulations
Meat Inspection Regulations
Public Sewerage Systems Regulation
Public Water Supply Regulations
Veterinary Profession Act
Vital Statistics Act
Minister, Hon. Sandy Lee
867-669-2344, Fax: 867-873-0481
sandy_lee@gov.nt.ca
Deputy Minister, Greb Cummings
867-920-6173, Fax: 867-873-0266
greg_cummings@gov.nt.ca

Integrated Community Services
Fax: 867-873-7706

Population Health
Fax: 867-873-0122
Director & Chief Medical Officer of Health, Andre Corriveau

Stanton
PO Box 10
Yellowknife, NT X1A 2N1
867-669-4224
Fax: 867-669-4128

Financial & Management Services
Fax: 867-920-4969

Policy, Legislation & Communications
Fax: 867-873-0484

Population Health
Fax: 867-873-0442

Director, Andre Corriveau
867-920-3231,
andre_corriveau@gov.nt.ca

Department of Industry, Tourism & Investment (ITI)
PO Box 1320
Yellowknife, NT X1A 2L9
Fax: 867-873-0306
info@iti.ca
www.iti.gov.nt.ca
The Department of Industry, Tourism & Investment promotes & supports economic prosperity & community self-reliance in the Northwest Territories by providing programs & services. Programs & services are available through the following departmental divisions: Diamonds; Energy Planning; Industrial Initiatives; Informatics; Investment & Economic Analysis; Mackenzie Valley Pipeline Office; Minerals, Oil & Gas; Policy, Legislation & Communications; & Tourism & Parks.

Acts Administered:
Agricultural Products Marketing Act
Business Development & Investment Corporation Act
Co-operative Associations Act
Credit Union Act
Freshwater Fish Marketing Act
Herd & Fencing Act
Industry, Tourism & Investment Act
Territorial Parks Act
Minister, Hon. Bob McLeod
867-669-2388, Fax: 867-873-0306
bob_mcleod@gov.nt.ca
Deputy Minister, Peter Vician
867-920-8048, Fax: 867-873-0563
peter_vician@gov.nt.ca
Assistant Deputy Minister Programs & Operations, Doug Doan
867-873-7115,
doug_doan@gov.nt.ca
Director Minerals, Oil & Gas, Deborah Archibald
867-920-3222,
DEBORAH_ARCHIBALD@gov.nt.ca
Director Mackenzie Valley Pipeline Office, Tim Coleman
867-874-5405,
tim_coleman@gov.nt.ca
Director Shared Services, Finance & Administration, Nancy Magrum
867-920-8649, Fax: 867-920-2756
NANCY_MAGRUM@gov.nt.ca
Director Energy Planning, Dave Nightingale
867-920-3274,
dave_nightingale@gov.nt.ca
Director Policy, Legislation & Communications, Sonya Saunders
867-873-7005, Fax: 867-873-0645
SONYA_SAUNDERS@gov.nt.ca
Director Investment & Economic Analysis, Kevin Todd
867-873-7361, Fax: 867-873-0101
KEVIN_TODD@gov.nt.ca
Director Shared Services, Informatics, Rick Wind
867-920-3327, Fax: 867-920-2756
rick_wind@gov.nt.ca
Director Tourism & Parks, Richard Zieba
867-873-7903, Fax: 867-873-0163
richard_zieba@gov.nt.ca
Chief Geologist, Scott Cairns
867-669-2479,
scott_cairns@gov.nt.ca
• Northwest Territories Business Development & Investment Corporation(BDIC)
#701, 5201 - 50 Ave.
Yellowknife, NT X1A 3S9
867-920-6455
Fax: 867-765-0652
bdicinfo@gov.nt.ca
www.bdic.ca
CEO, Pawan Chugh
Formerly the Northwest Territories Development Corporation (DEVCORP). The BDIC is a recognized leader in the NWT's regional economic development and the growth of a dynamic small and mid-sized business sector.

Mackenzie Valley Pipeline Office
Coordinates the territorial government's planning & response related to the Mackenzie Gas Project, including the regulatory review & environmental assessment processes. Also handles the territorial government's communications with respect to the Mackenzie Gas Project, & will manage selective funding programs to help Aboriginal groups & communities to prepare for the project.
Director Planning & Coordination, Tim Coleman
867-874-5405
Special Advisor, Ian Butters
867-874-5404

Investment & Economic Analysis
Fax: 867-873-0101
With general responsibilities for strategies, plans & programs to develop the NWT business community, the division provides expert advice & support in the production & marketing of arts & crafts, & acts as a link to national & international businesses & organizations.
Acting Director, Garry Singer
867-873-7361,
garry_singer@gov.nt.ca

Trade Officer, Terry Lancaster
867-873-7360,
terry_lancaster@gov.nt.ca
Manager Canada/NWT Business Service Centre, Claudia Kelly
867-873-7960, Fax: 867-873-0101

Minerals, Oil & Gas Division
Fax: 867-873-0254
The Minerals, Oil & Gas Division develops & implements strategies to encourage & attract non-renewable resource investment in the Northwest Territories. It also provides advice on the geological potential, industrial activity & potential opportunities associated with mineral, oil & gas exploration in the Territory.
Director, Deb Archibald
867-920-3214

Northwest Territories Remote Sensing Centre
#600, 5102 - 50 Ave.
Yellowknife, NT X1A 3S8
Fax: 867-920-2756
Provides expertise in remote sensing & geographic information systems as well as data to resource managers, developers & users in the public & private sectors. Integrating a database of vegetation types in the Mackenzie Valley Corridor with other geographic information system data & developing vegetation mapping for the Slave Geological Province.
Manager, Helmut Epp
867-920-3329,
helmut_epp@gov.nt.ca
Geomatics Analyst, Cindy Squires Taylor
867-920-3325,
cindy_squires_taylor@gov.nt.ca
Specialist Systems, David Taylor
867-920-3328,
david_taylor@gov.nt.ca
Specialist GIS, Cathie Harper
867-920-3326,
cathie_harper@gov.nt.ca
Technician Image Analysis, Norm Mair
norm_mair@gov.nt.ca

Tourism & Parks
Fax: 867-873-0163
Develops, operates & maintains facilities that include parks, visitor centres & interpretive displays. The division is also responsible for implementing the Protected Areas Strategy for the Northwest Territories, in conjunction with Canada's Federal Government & other stakeholders. The division also provides support for tourism marketing, research & product development.
Director, Gerry LePrieur
867-873-7902
Manager Parks & Protected Areas, Larry Adamson
867-920-6206,
larry_adamson@gov.nt.ca
Minister, Hon. Jackson Lafferty
867-669-2399, Fax: 867-873-0274
jackson_lafferty@gov.nt.ca
Deputy Minister, Bronwyn Watters
867-920-6197, Fax: 867-873-0307
brownyn_watters@gov.nt.ca
Assistant Deputy Minister & Attorney General, Karan Shaner
867-920-6197,
karan_shaner@gov.nt.ca
Assistant Deputy Minister & Solicitor General, Sylvia Haener
SYLVIA_HAENER@gov.nt.ca
Administrator & Deputy Chief Coroner Coroner's Office, Cathy Menard
867-973-7448, Fax: 867-873-0426
cathy_menard@gov.nt.ca
Chief Information Officer, Norm Embleton
867-920-6100, Fax: 867-873-0197
norm_embleton@gov.nt.ca
Public Trustee Public Trustee's Office, Larry Pontus
867-873-7464, 866-535-0423,Fax: 867-873-0184
larry_pontus@gov.nt.ca
Executive Director Legal Services Board, Lucy Austin
867-873-7450, Fax: 867-873-5320
lucy_austin@gov.nt.ca
Director Legislation Division, Mark Aitken
867-873-7462, Fax: 867-873-0234
mark_aitken@gov.nt.ca
Director Corrections Services, Colin G. Gordon
867-920-8922, Fax: 867-873-0299
colin_g_gordon@gov.nt.ca

Director Court Services, Anne Mould
867-920-8852, Fax: 867-873-0307
anne_mould@gov.nt.ca
Director Community Justice & Community Policing, Shirley KemeysJones
867-873-7002, Fax: 867-873-0199
shirley_kemeysjones@gov.nt.ca
Director Legal Registries, Gary MacDougall
867-873-7490, Fax: 867-873-0243
gary.macdougall@gov.nt.ca
Director Finance, Kim Schofield
867-873-7641, Fax: 867-873-0173
kim_schofield@gov.nt.ca
Director Policy & Planning, Laura Seddon
867-920-3225, Fax: 867-873-0659
laura_seddon@gov.nt.ca
Director Legal Division, Clarence Hudson
867-873-7787, Fax: 867-873-0234
clarence_hudson@gov.nt.ca
Registrar Land Titles, Tom Hall
867-920-8986, Fax: 867-873-0243
tom_hall@gov.nt.ca
Deputy Superintendent Legal & Enforcement, Donald MacDougall
867-920-8984, Fax: 867-873-0243
donald_macdougall@gov.nt.ca
Administrator Commissioner for Oaths / Notary Public, Cindy Pettes
867-920-8985, Fax: 867-873-0243
CINDY_PETTES@gov.nt.ca
• Assessment Appeal Tribunal of the Northwest Territories
#500, 5201 - 50th Ave.
PO Box 1320
Yellowknife, NT X1A 2L9
867-873-7125
Fax: 867-873-0609
Secretary, Michael Gagnon
• Territorial Board of Revision
PO Box 1320
Yellowknife, NT X1A 2L9
867-873-7125
Fax: 867-873-0609
Secretary, Michael Gagnon

Department of Municipal & Community Affairs
PO Box 1320
Yellowknife, NT X1A 2L9
867-873-7118
Fax: 867-873-0309
www.maca.gov.nt.ca
Supports capable, accountable & self-directed community governments providing a safe, sustainable & healthy environment for community residents. Works with community governments & other partners in supporting community residents as they organize & manage democratic, responsible & accountable community governments. The Department assists municipalities with administrative services & infrastructure project management, provides expertise in engineering to communities & arranges for debentures on behalf of communities which are undertaking public works programs.Advisory services are supplied to community councils for the planning, development & administration of public lands within municipal boundaries.Technical expertise is provided for mapping, surveying & air photography & zoning by-law administration.
Acts Administered:
Area Development Act
Civil Emergency Measures Act
Commissioner's Land Act
Community Employees Benefits Act
Consumer Protection Act
Curfew Act
Dog Act
Film Classification Act
Fire Prevention Act
Flood Damage Reduction Agreements Act
Hamlets Act
Home Owner's Property Tax Rebate Act
Local Authorities Elections Act
Lotteries Act
Municipal Employees Benefits Act
Municipal Statutes Replacement Act
Pawnbrokers & Second-Hand Dealers Act
Planning Act
Property Assessment & Taxation Act
Real Estate Agent's Licensing Act

Federal/Provincial Government / Government of the Northwest Territories

Religious Societies Land Act
Senior Citizens' & Disabled Persons' Property Tax Relief Act
Settlements Act
Western Canada Lotteries Act
Minister, Hon. Sandy Lee
867-669-2344, Fax: 867-873-0431
sandy_lee@gov.nt.ca
Deputy Minister, Jeff Polakoff
867-873-7118, Fax: 867-873-0309
heff_polakoff@gov.nt.ca
Asst. Deputy Minister Regional Operations, Sheila Bassi Kellett
867-920-6146, Fax: 867-873-0309
sheila_bassi-kellett@gov.nt.ca

Lands Administration
867-873-7569
Fax: 867-920-6156
Responsible for the administration of Commissioner's lands in & around the communities of the Northwest Territories. Commissioner's lands make up about 2 percent of all land in the North. The Federal Government administers about 97 percent & municipal corporations administer the remaining 1 percent. Under the Lands Program, MACA is in the process of transferring certain lands from the Commissioner to municipalities. Land administration is being decentralized from MACA headquarters to regional offices or to the communities. As authority for land devolves, MACA will take on a training & advisory role, teaching & advising communities how to look after their own lands. The division supplies information & advice regarding land leases, surrenders, transfers, & mortgage registration for Commissioner's land & notifications.
Director, Andy Tereposky
867-873-7569,
andy_tereposky@gov.nt.ca
Manager Lands Policy, Beverly Chamberlin
867-920-6284,
beverly_chamberlin@gov.nt.ca

School of Community Government
#400, 5201 - 50th Ave.
Yellowknife, NT X1A 3S9
867-920-3159
Fax: 867-873-0584
877-531-9194

Emergency Measures Organization
867-873-7083
EMO_Coordinator@gov.nt.ca
The EMO handles several duties related to emergency or disaster situations including coordinating operations during an emergency situation. Assists communities with emergency preparedness, or emergencies such as search & rescue of missing persons or a community-threatening forest fire. EMO responsibilities include coordination of the GNWT involvement in emergency operations at headquarters, assisting with community & regional emergency plans, search & rescue coordination, implementation, plans & training exercises, administration of the disaster assistance program, planning & emergency response, emergency preparedness training & exercises.
Coordinator, Eric Bussey
867-920-6133, Fax: 867-873-8193
eric_bussey@gov.nt.ca

Office of the Fire Marshal
Other Communication: 24 Hour Emergency: 867/873-7554
Handles fire prevention duties & the administration of the Fire Prevention Act, such as fire investigations & fire loss reporting, fire safety inspections, fire service training, public education in fire prevention, reviewing building plans to ensure compliance with fire prevention standards, Enforcement of the Fire Prevention Act.
Fire Marshal, Bernie Van Tighem
867-873-7469

Surveys & Mapping
Provides technical support to the department & community governments by obtaining & supplying photography, mapping & legal surveys. Legal Surveys provide the basis for titling real property & are necessary for the devolution of land ownership to community governments. Mapping shows land disposition & provides a base for the orderly development of community lands.
Manager, Robert Marchiori
867-920-8919

Sport, Recreation & Youth

Fax: 867-920-6467

Northwest Territories Power Corporation
4 Capital Dr.
Hay River, NT X0E 1G2
867-874-5200
Fax: 867-874-5229
info@ntpc.com
www.ntpc.com
Other Communication: Fort Simpson: 800/288-4784; Fort Smith: 800/661-0855; Inuvik: 800/661-0856; Yellowknife: 800/661-0854
Made up of 28 separate power systems, the NWT Power Corporation serves approximately 42,000 people in communities across the Northwest Territories. Facilities include hydro-electric, diesel & natural gas generation plants, transmission systems, & several isolated electrical distribution systems. The Corporation works to provide environmentally sound, safe, reliable, cost-effective energy & related services in the territories.
Minister Responsible, Hon. Floyd K. Roland
867-669-2311, Fax: 867-873-0169
floyd_roland@gov.nt.ca
Director Engineering, Stephen Kerr
Director/CFO Finance, Judith Goucher

Public Utilities Board of the Northwest Territories (PUB)
#203, 62 Woodland Dr.
PO Box 4211
Hay River, NT X0E 1G1
867-874-3944
Fax: 867-874-3639
www.nwtpublicutilitiesboard.ca
The independent, quasi-judicial agency of the Government of the Northwest Territories is responsible for the regulation of public utilities in the territory. Its authority is from the Public Utilities Act. Issues are handled by an application & decision process.
Minister Responsible, Hon. Bob McLeod
867-669-2388, Fax: 867-873-0431
bob_mcleod@gov.nt.ca
Chair, Joe Acorn

Department of Public Works & Services
PO Box 1320
Yellowknife, NT X1A 2L9
867-873-7114
Fax: 867-873-0226
www.pws.gov.nt.ca
Designs, constructs, maintains & operates territorial buildings; implements energy efficiency projects; provides essential petroleum products to the public where they are not available from the private sector; provides data systems & communication services to government departments.
Acts Administered:
Boilers & Pressure Vessels Act
Electrical Protection Act
Gas Protection Act
Public Utilities Act
Minister, Hon. Michael McLeod
867-669-2377, Fax: 867-873-0169
michael_mclwod@gov.nt.ca
Deputy Minister, Mike Aumond
867-873-7114, Fax: 867-873-0226
mike_aumond@gov.nt.ca

Asset Management Division
Estimates the cost of building construction & renovation; consults in the plan of buildings so they meet program needs; reviews consultant designs of buildings & works; implements the Safe Drinking Water Initiatives.
Director, Paul Guy
867-920-6142

Petroleum Products Division
Fax: 867-645-3554
Provides essential petroleum products to the public where they are not available from the private sector.
Director, Mike Burns

Department of Transportation
Lahm Ridge Bldg.
4501 50 Ave.
PO Box 1320
Yellowknife, NT X1A 2L9
867-920-3460
Fax: 867-873-0363
www.dot.gov.nt.can

Acts Administered:
All-Terrain Vehicles Act
Motor Vehicles Act
Public Highways Act
Public Service Vehicles Act
Transportation of Dangerous Goods Act, 1990
Transportation of Dangerous Goods Regulations
Minister, Hon. Michael McLeod
867-669-2377, Fax: 867-873-0388
michael_mcleod@gov.nt.ca
Deputy Minister, Russell Neudorf
867-920-3460, Fax: 867-873-0363
russell_neudorf@gov.nt.ca
Asst. Deputy Minister, Daniel Auger
867-920-3461, Fax: 867-873-0363
daniel_auger@gov.nt.ca

Airports
YK Centre
4922 - 28th St., 4th fl.
PO Box 1320
Yellowknife, NT X1A 2L9
867-873-7725
Fax: 867-873-0297

Highways
4510 - 50 Ave., 2nd fl.
PO Box 1320
Yellowknife, NT X1A 2L9
867-920-8771
Fax: 867-873-0288
Director, Kevin McLeod
867-873-7800, Fax: 867-920-3085
kevin_mcleod@gov.nt.ca
Head Structures, Ann Lanteigne
867-920-8010,
ann_lanteigne@gov.nt.ca
Project Environmental Coordinator, Vacant
867-920-8011

Planning & Policy
Fax: 867-920-2565
Director, Jim Stevens
867-920-3366
Environmental Analyst, Rob Thom
867-920-8920,
rob_thom@gov.nt.ca

Road Licensing & Safety
4510 - 50 Ave., 1st fl.
PO Box 1320
Yellowknife, NT X1A 2L9
867-873-7972
Fax: 867-873-0120

Northwest Territories Water Board
5114 - 49th St.
PO Box 1326
Yellowknife, NT X1A 1N9
867-765-0106
Fax: 867-765-0114
info@nwtwb.com
www.nwtwb.com
Responsible for the development, maintenance & conservation of water resources; administers licences for utilizing water or disposing wastes into water under the Northwest Territories Waters Act; has federal/territorial jurisdiction.
Chair, Eddie Dillon
Board Member, Emery Paquin

Northwest Territories & Nunavut Workers' Compensation Board (WCB)
Centre Square Tower
5022 - 49th St., 5th Fl.
PO Box 8888
Yellowknife, NT X1A 2R3
867-920-3888
Fax: 867-873-4596
800-661-0792
wcb@wcb.nt.ca
www.wcb.nt.ca; www.wcbnunavut.ca
Other Communication: Toll Free Fax: 1-866-277-3677; Incident/Accident Line: 1-800-661-0792
The Workers' Compensation Board of the Northwest Territories & Nunavut is engaged in the following activities: ensuring com-

pensation & pensions are awarded to injured workers or their dependents; assessubg enokiters sufficiently & fairly to meet obligations; maintaining balance in providing benefits to injured workers, while keeping costs to employers as low as possible; & promoting safe workplaces through education & enforcement.
Acts Administered:
Explosives Use Act
Mine Health & Safety Act
Environmental Tobacco Smoke Worksite Regulations
Safety Act
Asbestos Safety Regulations
Mine Health & Safety Regulations
Work Site Hazardous Materials Information System Regulations
Workers' Compensation Act
Minister Responsible Northwest Territories, Hon. J. Michael Miltenberger
867-669-2355, Fax: 867-873-0596
michael_miltenberger@gov.nt.ca
Vice-President Prevention Services, Sylvester Wong
867-669-4408,
SylvesterW@wcb.nt.ca

Council of Atlantic Premiers (CAP)
Council Secretariat
#1006, 5161 George St.
PO Box 2044
Halifax, NS B3J 2Z1
902-424-7590
Fax: 902-424-8976
info@cap-cpma.ca
www.cap-cpma.ca
The Premiers of New Brunswick, Newfoundland & Labrador, Nova Scotia & Prince Edward Island constitute the Council. It was established by memorandum of understanding to: promote unity of purpose among their respective Governments; ensure maximum coordination of the activities of the Governments & their agencies &; establish a framework for joint action & undertakings.The Council meets up to four times annually to discuss matters of mutual interest or concern to the four Atlantic governments.A Secretariat acts as the focal point for coordinating the efforts of the four Governments in identifying potential benefits that could result from a regional approach to policy formulation & program development.
Acting Secretary to Council, Rhéal Poirier
902-424-7600
• Council of Ministers of Education & Training
PO Box 2044
Halifax, NS B3J 2Z1
902-424-5352
Fax: 902-424-8976
camet_camef@cap-cpma.ca
www.camet-camef.ca
• Maritime Provinces Harness Racing Commission
5 Gerald McCarville Dr.
PO Box 128
Kensington, PE C0B 1M0
902-836-5500
Fax: 902-836-5390
dwalsh@mphrc.ca
www.mphrc.ca
Chair, Frank Balcom
To govern & regulate harness racing in the Maritime provinces.

Government of Nova Scotia
Seat of Government: Province House
Halifax, NS B3J 2T3
www.gov.ns.ca
The Province of Nova Scotia entered Confederation July 1, 1867.It has an area of 52,917,46 km2, & the StatsCan census population in 2006 was 913,462.

Department of Agriculture
1741 Brunswick St., 3rd Fl.
PO Box 2223
Halifax, NS B3J 3C4
902-424-4560
Fax: 902-424-4671
www.gov.ns.ca/nsaf
The Department of Agriculture has a legislated mandate to support & develop the agriculture & food industries, recognizing that these sectors are economic engines of Nova Scotia's rural communities. Fosters prosperous & sustainable agriculture & food industries through the delivery of quality public services for the betterment of rural communities in Nova Scotia.
Acts Administered:
Agriculture & Marketing Act
Agriculture & Rural Credit Act
Agriculture Marshland Conservation Act
Marsh Land Use Regulations: Bishop-Beckwith, Dentiballis, Dugau/Ryerson, Grand Pré, Lower Truro, Masstown, Victoria Diamond Jubilee, Wellington
Non-Agricultural Use Land Exemption Regulations
Agrologists Act
Animal Cruelty Prevention Act
Animal Health & Protection Act
Animal Health & Protection Regulations
Baby Chick Protection Act
Bee Industry Act
Cattle Pest Control Act
Crop & Livestock Insurance Act
Dairy Industry Act
Farm Practices Act
Farm Registration Act
Federations & Agriculture Act
Fences & Detention of Stray Livestock Act
Health Act (Food Safety, Inspection & Regulations)
Imitation Dairy Products Act
Livestock Brands Act
Livestock Health Services Act
Livestock Health Services Regulations
Margarine Act
Maritime Provinces Harness Racing Commission Act
Meat Inspection Act
Natural Products Act
Potato Industry Act
Provincial Berry Act
Sheep Protection Act
Veterinary Medical Act
Weed Control Act
Wildlife Act
Women's Institute of Nova Scotia Act
Minister, Hon. Mark Parent
902-424-4388,
min_dag@gov.ns.ca
Deputy Minister, Paul LaFleche
902-424-0300,
laflecpt@gov.ns.ca
Executive Director Agriculture Services, Alan Grant
902-893-6591,
grantac@gov.ns.ca
Executive Director Industry Development & Business Services, Linda MacDonald
902-424-8870,
macdonald@gov.ns.ca
Executive Director Policy & Planning, Diane Kenny
902-424-0308,
kennyd@gov.ns.ca
Acting President Nova Scotia Agricultural College, Dr. Leslie MacLaren
902-893-2773,
lmaclaren@nsac.ca
Director Communications, Celeste Sulliman
902-424-0192, Fax: 902-424-3948
sullimcc@gov.ns.ca
Executive Secretary, Yvelle Poirier
902-424-4388,
ypoirier@gov.ns.ca
• Nova Scotia Crop & Livestock Insurance Commission
MacRae Library Bldg.
#2, 137 College Rd.
PO Box 1092
Truro, NS B2N 5G9
902-893-7755
Fax: 902-895-4622
800-565-6371
nsclic@gov.ns.ca
www.gov.ns.ca/nsaf/ci
• Nova Scotia Farm Loan Board
PO Box 550
Truro, NS B2N 5E3
902-893-6506
Fax: 902-895-7693
flb@gov.ns.ca
www.gov.ns.ca/nsaf/loanboards/farmlb/
CEO, Derrick Jamieson
• Nova Scotia Farm Practices Board
PO Box 550
Truro, NS B2N 5E3
902-893-7314
Administrator, Arthur Pick
• Nova Scotia Natural Products Marketing Council
550
Truro, NS B2N 5E3
902-893-6306
www.gov.ns.ca/nsaf/npmc
Project Coordinator, David Livingstone

Agriculture Services
Provides regional agriculture services; land protection; environmental management including integrated pest management; 4-H & rural organizations; agricultural awareness; industry development programs; business risk management; crop & livestock insurance; orderly production & supply of major farm products.

Agriculture Services
Executive Director, G. Brian Smith
902-893-6591,
smithgb@gov.ns.ca
Manager Programs & Risk Management, Michael Johnson
902-893-7534

Resource Stewardship Division
Encourages the best available management of agricultural resources to ensure sustainable & sound environmental farm practices. Environmental Management conducts research & technology adaptation initiatives that support a sustainable economic atmosphere for rural people. It also has a close working relationship with the Nova Scotia Federation of Agriculture & provides resources in support of the Environmental Farm Plan Program. Pest Management, Regulation & Environmental Coordination adapts & develops regulatory programs & related methods to prevent or minimize introduction & spread of designated diseases & pests of concern to agriculture; delivers enforcement of related regulations; conducts regular assessments to determine risk invasion of agricultural pests. Land Protection has the responsibilities to carry out maintenance work on system of tidal dykes in Nova Scotia. Staff of the Resource Stewardship Division also chair & provide administrative services to the Nova Scotia Soils Institute
Acting Director, George Burris
902-893-6557
Resource Management Specialist Environmental Management, Lorne Crozier
902-893-6548
Acting Manager 4-H & Rural Organizations, Arthur Pick
902-893-7314
Supervisor Land Protection, Hank Kolstee
902-893-6569,
kolstehw@gov.ns.ca
Chief Inspector (Weed Control Act) Pest Management Regulation & Environmental Coordination, Joe Calder
902-893-6549
Manager Regional Services, Andrew Cameron
902-893-7314,
cameroad@gov.ns.ca

Legislation & Compliance Services
Licenses meat processing, retail food outlets & restaurants, fur & game farms, oversees activities related to food & consumer safety, as well as on-farm quality evaluation. Responsible for monitoring & enforcing compliance with departmental regulations.
Executive Director, Leo Muise
902-424-0337,
muiselj@gov.ns.ca

Department of Fisheries & Aquaculture
1741 Brunswick St., 3rd Fl.
PO Box 2223
Halifax, NS B3J 3C4
902-424-4560
Fax: 902-424-4671
www.gov.ns.ca/fish
The Department of Fisheries & Aquaculture's mission is to foster prosperous and sustainable fisheries, aquaculture and food industries through the delivery of quality public services for the betterment of coastal communities and of all Nova Scotians.
Acts Administered:
Fisheries & Coastal Resources Act
Fisheries Organizations Support Act
Minister, Hon. Ronald Chisholm
902-424-8953, Fax: 902-428-3145
min_dfa@gov.ns.ca
Deputy Minister / CEO, Paul LaFleche
902-424-0300,
laflecpt@gov.ns.ca

Federal/Provincial Government / Government of Nova Scotia

Asst. Deputy Minister, Gregory Roach
902-424-0348,
roachg@gov.ns.ca
Director Aquaculture, Marshall Giles
902-424-3664,
gilesm@gov.ns.ca
Director Inland Fisheries, Murray Hill
902-485-7021,
hillm@gov.ns.ca
Manager Innovations in Fisheries & Aquaculture, Bruce Osborne
902-424-0352,
osbornbd@gov.ns.ca
Admin. Assistant, Jo-Anne Sutherland
902-424-3735
• Fisheries & Aquaculture Loan Board
PO Box 2223
Halifax, NS B3J 3C4
902-424-4560
Fax: 902-424-1766
www.gov.ns.ca/nsaf/loanboards/fishlb/

Eastern
295 Charlotte St.
Sydney, NS B1P 1C6
902-563-2093
Fax: 902-563-1648
Controller, Winston Musgrave

Central
664 Prince St., 2nd Fl.
Truro, NS B2N 1G6
902-893-5896
Fax: 902-893-1648
Controller, Dominic Fewer

Western
151 Exhibition St.
Kentville, NS B4N 4E5
902-679-6100
Fax: 902-679-6322
Controller, Vern Fraser

Department of Economic & Rural Development
Centennial Building
#600, 1660 Hollis St.
PO Box 2311
Halifax, NS B3J 1V7
902-424-0377
Fax: 902-424-7008
comm@gov.ns.ca
www.gov.ns.ca/econ/
The office assists with knowledge management, trade policy, special projects, government relations regarding economic development issues, labour advice, regarding the work force of the future, information on the business climate & assistance on strategic infrastructure.The Office provides assistance withstrategic management & rural development regarding the business climate, & services such as the Rural Development Branch, Rural Development Service Locations & Co-operatives Branch, dealing with trade policy negotiations & agreements.
Acts Administered:
Business Development Corporation Act
Cooperation Associations Act
Economic Renewal Agency Act
Industrial Development Act
Industrial Estates Limited Act
Industrial Loan Act
Industrial Property Act
Industry Closing Act
Innovation Corporation Act
Nova Scotia Business Incorporated Act
Nova Scotia Film Development Corporation Act
Regional Community Development Act
Research Foundation Corporation Act
Small Business Development Act
Sydney Steel Corporation Act
Trade Development Authority Act
Venture Corporation Act
Venture Corporation Act - Regulations
Voluntary Planning Act
Minister, Hon. Percy Paris
902-424-5790, Fax: 902-424-0514
econmin@gov.ns.ca

Deputy Minister, Ian Thompson
902-424-2901, Fax: 902-424-0619
thompsia@gov.ns.ca
Director Decision Support, Chris Bryant
902-424-3545,
cbryant@gov.ns.ca
Director Communications, Heather Spidell
902-424-4998, Fax: 902-424-7008
spidelhd@gov.ns.ca
Director Corporate Information Strategies, Holly Fancy
902-424-2863,
fancyh@gov.ns.ca
Director Economic Strategies and Initiatives, Bruce Hennebury
902-424-5757,
hennebub@gov.ns.ca
• Canada-Nova Scotia Offshore Petroleum Board
TD Centre
1791 Barrington St., 6th Fl.
Halifax, NS B3J 3K9
902-422-5588
Fax: 902-422-1799
postmaster@cnsopb.ns.ca
www.cnsopb.ns.ca
Chair, Diana Lee Dalton
The Canada-Nova Scotia Offshore Petroleum Board (CNSOPB) is responsible for protection of the environment during all phases of offshore petroleum activities, from initial exploration to abandonment.The Board is a Federal Authority under the Canadian Environmental Assessment Act. The environmental assessment process starts at the Call for Bids stage. At this stage, a strategic or broad environmental assessment is conducted which identifies environmental concerns or issues. All subsequent projects, including seismic programs & exploratory wells, must undergo an environmental assessment prior to approval by the CNSOPB.The Board also uses class screenings or generic assessments to streamline the regulatory process.These more in-depth environmental assessments, usually jointly funded by a number of petroleum companies, provide more detailed overviews of potential environmental effects, research priorities & mitigation measure than can be accomplished in a single project-specific environmental assessment.
• InNOVACorp
#1400, 1801 Hollis St.
Halifax, NS B3J 3N4
902-424-8670
Fax: 902-424-4679
800-565-7051
communications@innovacorp.ca
www.innovacorp.ns.ca
President & CEO, Dr. Dan MacDonald
A network of critical business resources for the early stage technology entrepreneur. Key services include research & development support, business advice, investment & partnership advice. Focuses on two main growth sectors: life sciences & information technology.
• Nova Scotia Business Inc.(NSBI)
World Trade & Convention Centre
#701, 1800 Argyle St.
PO Box 2374
Halifax, NS B3J 3E4
902-424-6650
Fax: 902-424-5739
800-260-6682
info@nsbi.ca
www.novascotiabusiness.com
President/CEO, Stephen Lund
NSBI is the first point of contact for local companies that want to grow in Nova Scotia, and for international companies that have heard about the province and want to know more.
• Film Nova Scotia
Collins Bank Bldg.
1869 Upper Water St., 3rd Fl.
Halifax, NS B3J 1S9
902-424-7177
Fax: 902-424-0617
888-360-2111
connorkm@gov.ns.ca
www.film.ns.ca
President/CEO, Ann MacKenzie
Created in 1990 under the Film Development Corporation Act, Film Nova Scotia is a Provincial Crown Corporation reporting to the Minister of Economic and Rural Development. A Board of Directors, appointed by the Governor in Council, directs the Corporation's activities.

• Trade Centre Limited
1800 Argyle St.
PO Box 955
Halifax, NS B3J 2V9
902-421-8686
Fax: 902-422-2922
www.tradecentrelimited.com
Interim President/CEO, Scott Ferguson
Trade Centre Limited creates economic benefits by bringing people together in Halifax and Nova Scotia.
• Waterfront Development Corporation Ltd.
1751 Lower Water St., 2nd Fl.
Halifax, NS B3J 1S5
902-422-6591
Fax: 902-422-7582
info@wdcl.ca
www.wdcl.ca
President, Colin MacLean
Coordinates the commercial & recreational development of the downtown waterfront of Halifax & Dartmouth.

Antigonish
#4, 149 Church St.
Antigonish, NS B2G 2E2
902-863-7539
Fax: 902-863-7477

Amherst
35 Church St.
Amherst, NS B4H 4A1
902-667-3233
Fax: 902-667-2270

Bridgewater
220 North St.
Bridgewater, NS B4V 2V6
902-530-3117
Fax: 902-543-1156

Cape Breton
#207, 275 Charlotte St.
Sydney, NS B1P 1C6
902-563-2070
Fax: 902-563-0500

Capital Region
Centennial Building
#600, 1660 Hollis St.
Halifax, NS B3J 1V7
902-424-4319
Fax: 902-424-1263
800-565-2009

Kentville
#103, 35 Webster St.
Kentville, NS B4N 1H4
902-679-6116
Fax: 902-679-6094

Northeastern Region
#101, 35 Commercial St.
Truro, NS B2N 3H9
902-893-6212
Fax: 902-893-6108

Southwestern Shore/Valley
Pier One Complex
103 Water St.
Yarmouth, NS B5A 4P4
902-742-8404
Fax: 902-742-0019
Coordinator Environmental Health & Safety, Gerald Muise
902-424-7669, Fax: 902-424-0732
muisege@gov.ns.ca

Nova Scotia Emergency Management Office (EMO)
PO Box 2581
Halifax, NS B3J 3N5
902-424-5620
Fax: 902-424-5376
866-424-5620
emo@gov.ns.ca
www.gov.ns.ca/emo
Coordinating agency of the Nova Scotia Government with the responsibility of assisting municipalities to plan & prepare for emergencies; responsible for the implementation of the province-wide 911 service. Coordinates emergency efforts of provincial & federal departments & agencies, as well as private health & social

services, to provide assistance to disaster areas; sponsors the Ground Search & Rescue Program; maintains a professional planner at all offices. Coordinates all emergency preparedness training for municipal staff at the Emergency Preparedness College (Arnprior, ON) & through the Joint Emergency Preparedness Program (JEPP) which provides a federal government cost-sharing formula for emergency equipment for first-response agencies.

Acts Administered:
Emergency Management Act
Emergency 911 Act
Minister Responsible, Hon. Ernest Fage
CEO/Deputy Head, Craig D. MacLaughlan
Director Emergency Programs, Andy S. Lathem
Director Emergency Services, Michael Myette
Director Training & Strategic Planning, Dennis P. Kelly
Exec. Assistant/Office Manager, Dianne Caswell

Department of Energy

Bank of Montreal Bldg.
#400, 5151 George St.
PO Box 2664
Halifax, NS B3J 3P7
902-424-4575
Fax: 902-424-0528
energyinfo@gov.ns.ca
www.gov.ns.ca/energy

To serve as the government's focal point in the development of the province's energy resources, as outlined in the Energy Strategy. Responsible for a wide range of initiatives in the following areas: energy Transportation & utilization policy & analysis; resource assessment & royalties; climate change; business & technology; communications & public education.

Acts Administered:
Canada-Nova Scotia Offshore Petroleum Resources Accord Implementation (Nova Scotia) Act
Canada-Newfoundland Labrador Offshore Area Regulations
Nova Scotia Offshore Area Certificate of Fitness Regulations
Nova Scotia Offshore Area Oil & Gas Spills & Debris Liability Regulations
Nova Scotia Offshore Area Petroleum Diving Regulations
Nova Scotia Offshore Area Petroleum Drilling Regulations
Nova Scotia Offshore Area Petroleum Geophysical Operations Regulations
Nova Scotia Offshore Area Petroleum Installations Regulations
Nova Scotia Offshore Petroleum Production & Conservation Regulations
Sable Offshore Energy Project Regulations
Electricity Act
Energy-Efficient Appliances Act
Energy Resources Conservation Act
Gas Plant Facility Regulations
Onshore Petroleum Geophysical Exploration Regulations
Gas Distribution Act
Natural Gas Transmission Pipeline Assessment Regulations
Offshore Petroleum Royalty Act
Petroleum Resources Act
Onshore Petroleum Drilling Regulations
Onshore Petroleum Geophysical Exploration Regulations
Petroleum Resources Removal Permit Act
Pipeline Act
Land Acquisition Regulations
Pipeline Benefits Plan Regulations
Pipeline Regulations
Sable Offshore Energy Project Regulations
Underground Hydrocarbons Storage Act
Minister, Hon. Barry Barnet
902-424-7793,
barnetbe@gov.ns.ca
Deputy Minister, Alison Scott
902-424-1710, Fax: 902-424-3265
scottal@gov.ns.ca
Director Communications, Ross McLaren
902-424-4536, Fax: 902-424-0528
mclarenr@gov.ns.ca
Director Policy & Analysis, Bruce Cameron
902-424-2288, Fax: 902-499-8849
Executive Secretary to the Minister, Diane Bernard
902-424-7793, Fax: 902-424-3265
bernardm@gov.ns.ca

Energy Management, Markets & Climate Change
Director, Allan Crandlemire
902-424-6829,
crandlal@gov.ns.ca

Natural Gas Engineering Specialist, Bill O'Halloran, P.Eng.
902-424-8184,
ohallowe@gov.ns.ca
Manager Energy Management & Markets, Scott McCoombs, P.Eng.
902-424-7305,
srmccoom@gov.ns.ca
Director Intergovernmental & Climate Change Initiatives, George Foote
902-424-8168,
gffoote@gov.ns.ca

Resource Assessment & Royalties
Responsible for the development of policy, legislation, & regulations for the exploration & development of the province's offshore & onshore petroleum resources, which includes the administration of the royalty regulations & agreements. In the onshore, this division administers the granting of petroleum rights & coordinates the regulation of exploration activity. The Canada-Nova Scotia Offshore Petroleum Board regulates day-to-day offshore petroleum activity, while it is its job to actively promote Nova Scotia's onshore & offshore petroleum potential.
Director, Sandy MacMullin, P.Eng.
902-424-8129,
macmulsa@gov.ns.ca
Manager Petroleum Resources, Jack MacDonald
902-424-8125,
macdondj@gov.ns.ca
Petroleum Geologist/Environmental Coordinator, Kim Doane
902-424-7146,
doaneka@gov.ns.ca
Petroleum Projects Analyst, Andre Corkum
902-424-6117,
corkumap@gov.ns.ca
Petroleum Geophysicist, Kris Kendall
902-424-3234,
kendelkl@gov.ns.ca

Department of Environment

5151 Terminal Rd., 5th Fl.
PO Box 442
Halifax, NS B3J 2T8
902-424-3600
Fax: 902-424-0503
877-936-8476
www.gov.ns.ca/nse

Major program responsibilities for Nova Scotia Environment are environmental and natural areas management, environmental monitoring and compliance, and climate change. Pollution prevention, the NS Youth Conservation Corps., solid waste reduction and recycling, and environmental trade and innovation are all part of the new Nova Scotia Environment.

Acts Administered:
Amusement Device Safety Act
Building Code Act (Shared with Service Nova Scotia)
Court & Administrative Reform Act
Crane Operators & Power Engineers Act
Credit Union Act
Electrical Installation & Inspection Act
Elevators & Lifts Act
Environment Act
Activities Designation Regulations
Air Quality Regulations
Approvals Procedure Regulations
Asbestos Waste Management Regulations
Dangerous Goods Management Regulations
Emergency Spill Regulations
Environmental Assessment Regulations
Environment Act & Regulations Fees Regulations
Motive Fuel & Fuel Oil Approval Regulations
NS Environmental Assessment Boards Regulation
NS Environmental Trust Regulations
On-Site Services Advisory Board Regulations
On-Site Sewage Disposal Systems Regulations
Ozone Layer Protection Regulations
PCB Management Regulations
Pesticide Regulations
Petroleum Management Regulations
Protected Areas, Water Areas, Designations & Regulations : Bennery Lake, Forbes Lake, French Mill Brook, Hebb, Milipsigate & Minamkeak Lake, James River, Lake Major, McGee Lake, Mill Lakes, North Tynd
Round Table Regulations
Solid Waste-Resource Management Regulations
Sulphide Bearing Material Disposal Regulations

Used Oil Regulations
Water and Wastewater Facility Regulations
Well Construction Regulations
Fire Safety Act
Fuel Safety Regulations
Gaming Control Act
Health Act (in part)
Insurance Act
Insurance Premiums Tax Act
Labour Standards Code
Liquor Control Act
Mutual Insurance Companies Act
Occupational Health & Safety Act
Occupational Health & Safety Appeal Panel Regulations
Occupational Safety General Regulations
Underground Mining Regulations
Workplace Hazardous Materials Information System Regulations
Remembrance Day Act
Securities Act
Smoke-free Places Act
Special Places Protection Act (Shared with Tourism, Culture & Heritage)
Steam Boiler & Pressure Vessel Act
Teachers' Collective Bargaining Act
Theaters & Amusements Act
Trade Union Act
Trust & Loan Companies Act
Water Resources Protection Act
Wilderness Areas Protection Act
Workers' Compensation Act
Minister, Hon. Sterling Belliveau
902-424-3736, Fax: 902-424-1599
min_env@gov.ns.ca
Deputy Minister, Nancy Vanstone
902-424-8150,
nvanston@gov.ns.ca
Director Communications, Penny McCormick
902-424-2575,
mccormpl@gov.ns.ca
Executive Secretary, Virginia Messervey
902-424-3736,
messerv@gov.ns.ca
• Crane Operators Appeal Board
5151 Terminal Rd., 7th Fl.
PO Box 697
Halifax, NS B3J 2T8
902-424-8595
Fax: 902-424-0217
fraserej@gov.ns.ca
www.gov.ns.ca/lwd/coab
Acting Executive Officer, Joseph Fraser
The Crane Operators Appeal Board is one of the newest tribunals in Nova Scotia Labour and Workforce Development, created pursuant to the Crane Operators and Power Engineers Act which came into force on September 1, 2001. It is an independent adjudicative tribunal charged with considering appeals filed under Part I of the Act.
• Labour Relations Board & Construction Industry Panel
5151 Terminal Rd.,7th Fl.
PO Box 697
Halifax, NS B3J 2T8
902-424-6730
Fax: 902-424-1744
www.gov.ns.ca/lwd/lrb
CEO, Mary-Lou Stewart
The Labour Relations Board and Construction Industry Panel help to resolve disputes between labour and management that relate to the Trade Union Act.
• Labour Standards Tribunal
5151 Terminal Rd., 7th Fl.
PO Box 697
Halifax, NS B3J 2T8
902-424-6730
Fax: 902-424-1744
noeljl@gov.ns.ca
www.gov.ns.ca/lwd/lst
Chair, E.A. Nelson Blackburn, Q.C.
The Labour Standards Tribunal is a body that hears complaints of failure to comply with the Labour Standards Code. This Code came into effect by proclamation on February 1, 1973.
• Nova Scotia Securities Commission
Joseph Howe Bldg.
1690 Hollis St., 2nd Fl.
PO Box 458
Halifax, NS B3J 2P8

Federal/Provincial Government / Government of Nova Scotia

902-424-7768
Fax: 902-424-4625
www.gov.ns.ca/nssc
Director, J. William Slattery, C.A.
Their mission is to protect investors in Nova Scotia from practices and activities that tend to undermine their confidence in the fairness and efficiency of securities markets and to foster the process of capital formation, where it would not be inconsistent with an adequate level of investor protection.
• Occupational Health & Safety Advisory Council
PO Box 697
Halifax, NS B3J 2T8
902-424-2484
Fax: 902-424-5640
www.gov.ns.ca/lwd/abct/ohsadvisory.asp
Executive Officer, Jim Gordon
The Occupational Health and Safety Advisory Council advises the Minister of Labour and Workforce Development on occupational health and safety matters.
• Occupational Health & Safety Appeal Panel
5151 Terminal Rd., 7th Fl.
PO Box 697
Halifax, NS B3J 2T8
902-424-6730
www.gov.ns.ca/lwd/ohsapo
Executive Officer, Diana Hartley
The Occupational Health & Safety Appeal Panel adjudicates disputes relating to both the technical aspects of health & safety & the protection of individual employees from union & employer reprisals when they have discharged their responsibilities under the Occupational Health & Safety Act. The OHS Appeal Panel Office administers & coordinates the process of appeals of orders or decisions made by the executive director of the OHS Division. The OHS Appeal Panel is separate from & independent from the OHS Division.
• Pay Equity Commission
5151 Terminal Rd., 7th Fl.
PO Box 697
Halifax, NS B3J 2T8
902-424-2385
Fax: 902-424-0575
www.gov.ns.ca/lwd/payequity
Executive Director, Barb Jones Gordon
The Pay Equity Commission is responsible for administrating the Pay Equity Act. In addition to monitoring the pay equity process, the Commission has the power to resolve disputes when employers and employees cannot agree, conducts research, maintains statistics, and advises the Minister of Labour on matters relating to pay equity.
• Workers' Advisers Program
#502, 5670 Spring Garden Rd.
PO Box 1063
Halifax, NS B3J 2X1
902-424-5050
Fax: 902-424-0530
800-774-4712
www.gov.ns.ca/lwd/wap
Chief Worker Adviser, Kenny LeBlanc
The Workers' Advisers Program is a legal clinic that is funded by the provincial government offering services to injured workers. Our purpose is to provide legal assistance when an injured worker has been denied Workers' Compensation Board benefits.
• Workers' Compensation Board of Nova Scotia

Alcohol & Gaming Division
Alderney Gate
40 Alderney Dr., 5th Fl.
PO Box 545
Dartmouth, NS B2Y 3Y8
902-424-6160
Fax: 902-424-6313
877-565-0556
www.gov.ns.ca/lwd/agd
Responsible for licensing & regulating gaming activity, liquor activity, & film classification in Nova Scotia.

Environmental & Natural Areas Management
PO Box 697
Halifax, NS B3J 3T8
902-424-3571
Promotes sustainable management & protection of the environment through both regulatory & non-regulatory means, including developing & implementing plans, standards, guidelines, & policies for the management & protection of Nova Scotia's air, water & terrestrial resources including protected areas, & by providing regionally-based regulatory approval, inspection, monitoring & enforcement.
Executive Director, Robert Langdon, P.Eng.
902-424-2386,
langdobe@gov.ns.ca

Environmental Monitoring & Compliance
Responsible for the majority of field operations relating to environmental protection. Activities in this Division include processing applications, inspection & monitoring of approvals, enforcement activities & response to public issues & complaints. Services of Environmental Monitoring & Compliance include the Regional & District Offices Network & Solid Waste Resource Management.
Executive Director Regional & District Offices, Gerard MacLellan
902-424-2547, Fax: 902-424-0569
maclelgj@gov.ns.ca
Manager Solid Waste Resource Management, Barry Friesen
902-424-2645

Central
Sunnyside Mall
#224, 1595 Bedford Hwy.
Bedford, NS B4A 3Y4
902-424-2382
Fax: 902-424-0597
Regional Manager, Darlene Fenton

Eastern
#125, 400 Reeves St.
Port Hawkesbury, NS B9A 2R5
902-625-0791
Fax: 902-625-3722
District Manager, Terry MacPherson

Northern
32 Church St.
Amherst, NS B2H 3A8
902-667-6205
Fax: 902-667-6214
District Manager, Brad Skinner

Western
60 Logan Rd.
Briwdewater, NS B4V 3J8
902-543-4685
Fax: 902-527-5480
Acting District Manager, Adrian Fuller

Financial Institutions
902-424-6331
Fax: 902-424-1298
The Financial Institutions Division regulates the operations of credit unions, trust & loan companies & insurance companies, agents, brokers & adjusters in the Province. The Division also provides a complaint & enquiry service to the public relating to financial institutions & the insurance industry & collects & verifies the insurance premiums tax.

Information & Business Services
5151 Terminal Rd., 5th Fl.
PO Box 697
Halifax, NS B3J 2T8
902-424-4313
Fax: 902-424-6925
Is responsible for providing a focus within the department for the development, use, and access to our information holdings, including operational records and published material; providing consistency in the department's business practices; and developing and implementing the department's Occupational Health and Safety program.

Air Quality Branch
Responsible for the management of outdoor air quality in Nova Scotia. It monitors air quality, ensures that citizens can obtain information about the quality of the air that they breathe, & develops policies to improve air quality.
Manager, Andrew Murphy
902-424-2177
Air Quality Specialist, Kamila Tomcik
902-424-2324
Inspector Specialist, John McPherson
902-424-2566

Environmental Assessment Branch
902-424-3571
Fax: 902-424-3571
EA@gov.ns.ca
Responsible for assessing major projects in order to identify, correct or prevent adverse environmental impacts & to maximize sustainable development. The Branch monitors, analyses & reports on the ambient air & water resources & develops regional & national air quality management plans. Environmental assessment in Nova Scotia is legislated by Part IV of the Environment Act (1995). The environmental assessment process is set out in the Environmental Assessment Regulations & the Environmental Assessment Board Regulations.
Manager, Chris Daly
902-424-4936
Environmental Assessment Officer, Helen MacPhail
902-424-3960

Environmental Education
Directed towards increasing the environmental awareness of Nova Scotians. It develops & coordinates the delivery of environmental education & training programs & provides environmental skills development to Nova Scotia's youth through the Youth Conservation Corps.
Manager, Paul Schwartz
902-424-5206

Environmental Trade & Innovation
5151 Terminal Rd.
PO Box 697
Halifax, NS B3J 2T8
Provides assistance to environmental industries by coordinating the delivery of business assistance, financial & management. The branch supports & promotes the environmental industry sector by assisting its entrance into the global marketplace. It also leads in the development & delivery of a sustainable development program.
Manager, Craig Morrison
902-424-2541, Fax: 902-424-3571
morriscp@gov.ns.ca

Pollution Prevention Branch
Assists to identify pollution prevention opportunities; to research options, & develop pollution prevention plans & programs; & to identify required resources & support the development of partnerships to achieve these goals.
Pollution Prevention Specialist, Solveig Madsen
902-424-2173

Protected Areas
902-424-2117
Fax: 902-424-0501
Responsible for planning & managing Nova Scotia's wilderness areas, nature reserves & Heritage Rivers & for encouraging private land stewardship. Branch programs support the establishment of a comprehensive system of parks & protected areas which incorporates examples of the province's natural landscapes, as well as sites & features of outstanding natural value & outdoor recreational resources that offer quality wilderness recreation. Responsibilities are carried out in partnership with the Nova Scotia Department of Natural Resources, & through agreements with community groups & other organizations.
Manager, John Leduc
leducjm@gov.ns.ca
Ecologist, Robert Cameron
camerorp@gov.ns.ca

Water & Wastewater Branch
Responsible for the development & implementation of the provincial water & wastewater management regulations, policies, strategies & programs designed to protect public health, safety & the environment. Develops management practices for drinking water supply protection, establishes water & wastewater effluent quality standards & objectives, allocates provincial water resources to a variety of users, collects & reports on ambient water monitoring data, & maintains several databases related to water resource & wastewater management.
Manager, David Briggins
902-424-2571

Labour Services
902-424-4156

Labour Standards Division
902-424-4311
Fax: 902-424-0648
labrstd@gov.ns.ca
Deals with enquiries & complaints from the public about how the provincial Labour Standards Code applies to specific employment situations. Labour Standards staff help to facilitate settlements of complaints through a self-help process. If this process

fails, staff investigate & work to achieve compliance in areas where the Labour Standards Code has not been adhered to. The Labour Standards Division also promotes an understanding of the Labour Standards Code & respective legislation, through continuing education.
Director, Mary Belliveau
902-424-5404,
bellivma@gov.ns.ca

Occupational Health & Safety Division
902-424-5400
Fax: 902-424-5640
800-952-2687
Executive Director, Jim LeBlanc
leblajim@gov.ns.ca
Provincial Manager Inspection & Compliance Services, Ray O'Neil
902-424-8478,
oneilrx@gov.ns.ca
Provincial Manager Professional Services, Stewart Sampson
902-424-8055,
sampsons@gov.ns.ca

Public Safety
The Office of the Fire Marshal, through the Fire Prevention Act, has the authority & responsibility for the provision of fire safety in buildings & for safe storage of flammable & combustible materials. The Office advises various levels of government on fire-related matters, including fire protection, & is also responsible for the safe installation of propane & electricity.
Director & Fire Marshall, Robert Cormier
902-424-4553,
cormierr@gov.ns.ca
Deputy Fire Marshall, Marty Dobbin
902-424-3931

Pension Regulation Division
PO Box 2531
Halifax, NS B3J 3N5
902-424-8915
Fax: 902-424-0662
The Pension Regulation Division administers & enforces the Pension Benefits Act to safeguard benefits promised under pension plans. The Division supervises over 470 registered pension plans to ensure the plans are well managed & adequately funded in order to meet their obligations to pension plan members.
• Nova Scotia Utility and Review Board(NSUARB)
Summit Place
1601 Lower Water St., 3rd Fl.
Halifax, NS B3J 3P6
902-424-4448
uarb.board@gov.ns.ca
www.nsuarb.ca

Department of Health
Joseph Howe Bldg.
1690 Hollis St., 4th Fl.
PO Box 488
Halifax, NS B3J 2R8
902-424-5818
Fax: 902-424-0730
800-387-6665
TDD: 800-670-8888
DoHweb@gov.ns.ca
www.gov.ns.ca/health
Other Communication: TeleHealth Network: 1-800-889-5949
Mission: Working together to empower individuals, families, partners, and communities to promote, improve, and maintain the health of Nova Scotians through a proactive and sustainable health care system.
Acts Administered:
Chiropractic Act
Cobequid Multi-Service Centre Act
Dental Act
Dental Technicians Act
Denturist Act
Department of Health Promotion & Protection Act
Disabled Persons' Commission Act
Dispensing Opticians Act
Drug Dependency Act
Health Act
Health Authorities Act
Health Research Foundation Act
Health Services & Insurance Act
Homemakers' Services Act
Homes for Special Care Act
Hospitals Act
Municipal Hospitals Loan Act
Nursing Assistants Act
Occupational Therapists Act
Optometry Act
Pharmacy Act
Physiotherapy Act
Psychologists Act
Registered Nurses Association Act
Smoke Free Places Act
Tobacco Access Act
Minister, Hon. Karen Casey
902-424-3377, Fax: 902-424-0559
caseykl@gov.ns.ca
Deputy Minister, Cheryl A. Doiron
902-424-7570, Fax: 902-424-4570
doironca@gov.ns.ca
CFO, Allan Horsborough
Director NS TeleHealth Network, Ron MacFarlane
902-424-2152, Fax: 902-424-0270
macfarr@gov.ns.ca
• Nova Scotia Advisory Commission on AIDS
Dennis Bldg.
1740 Granville St., 6th Fl.
Halifax, NS B3J 1X5
902-424-5730
Fax: 902-424-4727
• Seniors' Secretariat
Dennis Bldg.
1740 Granville St., 4th Fl.
PO Box 2065
Halifax, NS B3J 2Z1
902-424-0065
Fax: 902-424-0561
800-670-0065
scs@gov.ns.ca
www.gov.ns.ca/scs

Emergency Health Services
Fax: 902-424-0155
Emergency Health Services Nova Scotia (EHS) is a division of the Nova Scotia Department of Health. It is responsible for the development, implementation, monitoring & evaluation of pre-hospital emergency health services.
Senior Director, Marilyn Pike
902-424-8902

Mental Health & Addiction Services
Fax: 902-424-0647

Continuing Care
Fax: 902-424-0506

Western Region - South Shore Health, South West Health, Annapolis Valley Health
23 Earnscliffe Ave.
PO Box 1180
Wolfville, NS B0P 1X0
902-542-6310
Fax: 902-542-6333
Medical Officer, Dr. Richard Gould

Central Region - Capital Health, IWK Health Centre
#4, 201 Brownlow Ave.
Dartmouth, NS B3B 1W2
902-481-5888
Fax: 902-481-5803
Medical Officer, Dr. Robert Strang

Eastern Region - Guysborough Antigonish Strait, Cape Breton
235 Townsend, 2nd Fl.
Sydney, NS B1P 5E7
902-563-2403
Fax: 902-563-0508
Medical Officer, Dr. Charles Badenhorst

Northern Region - Colchester East Hants, Cumberland, Pictou
Colchester Regional Hospital Annex 3rd Floor
201 Willow St.
Truro, NS B2N 4Z9
902-893-5820
Fax: 902-893-5839
Medical Officer, Dr. Shelly Sarwal
902-893-5820, Fax: 902-893-5839

Department of Health Promotion & Protection
Summit Place
1601 Lower Water St., 5th Fl.
PO Box 487
Halifax, NS B3J 2R7
902-424-4807
Fax: 902-424-4716
866-231-3882
healthpromotion@gov.ns.ca
www.gov.ns.ca/hpp
Dedicated to helping Nova Scotians live healthier and safer lives.
Minister, Hon. Pat Dunn
902-424-5627, Fax: 902-424-7983
dunnpr@gov.ns.ca
Deputy Minister, Duff Montgomerie
902-424-3095,
montgodm@gov.ns.ca
Chief Public Health Officer, Dr. Robert Strang
902-424-2358, Fax: 902-424-4716
robert.strang@gov.ns.ca
Director Addiction Services, Carolyn Davison
902-424-7218,
davisocj@gov.ns.ca
Senior Director Sport & Recreation, Farida Gabanni
902-424-7554,
gabbanfg@gov.ns.ca
Director Communications, Sue McKeage
902-424-0913, Fax: 902-428-3148
mckeagsm@gov.ns.ca

Office of the Chief Medical Officer of Health
The Office of the Chief Medical Officer of Health is responsible for the Department of Health's legislated responsibility to protect & promote the public's health in the following areas: communicable disease control, environmental health, emergency preparedness & response. In addition, staff in the Office of the Chief Medical Officer of Health, in collaboration with academic expertise at Dalhousie University, function as an expert resource in community health science & an epidemiological resource for the department, the health districts, & other relevant government & community groups.
Chief Medical Officer of Health, Dr. Jeff Scott
902-424-8698, Fax: 902-424-0550
medicalofficerofhealth@gov.ns.ca
Deputy Chief Medical Officer of Health, Dr. Maureen Baikie
902-424-2358, Fax: 902-424-0550

Tobacco Strategy for Nova Scotia
Tobacco Control Unit, Joseph Howe Bldg.
1690 Hollis St.
PO Box 488
Halifax, NS B3J 2R8
902-424-5187
Fax: 902-424-0663
Nova Scotia has the highest smoking rate in the country. The province has developed a comprehensive tobacco strategy to reduce smoking rates & reduce the burden of tobacco related illness. Through consultations, research & best-practices reviews, the strategy involves a multi-year approach in the areas of pricing & taxation, smoke free legislation, policy, treatment & cessation, community-based programming, youth smoking prevention, media & public awareness & monitoring & evaluation.
Coordinator, Nancy Hoddinott
902-424-5962,
hoddinnl@gov.ns.ca

Department of Intergovernmental Affairs
Joseph Howe Bldg.
1690 Hollis St., 7th Fl.
PO Box 1617
Halifax, NS B3J 2Y3
902-424-5153
Fax: 902-424-0728
iga@gov.ns.ca
http://gov.ns.ca/iga
Provides leadership in the development of corporate strategies for Nova Scotia's relations with governments & organizations.
Minister, Hon. Rodney MacDonald
902-424-6600, Fax: 902-424-7648
premier@gov.ns.ca
Deputy Minister, Judith Sullivan-Corney
902-424-3219,
corneyjm@gov.ns.ca

Federal/Provincial Government / Government of Nova Scotia

General Counsel, Pat Clahane
902-424-4894,
clahanpg@gov.ns.ca
Director Strategic Policy, Norma MacIsaac
902-424-7662,
macisanj@gov.ns.ca
Sr. Trade Policy Analyst, John Hoar
902-424-7108,
hoarj@gov.ns.ca
Director Environmental & Social Affairs, Albert Walzak
902-424-7748,
walzakag@gov.ns.ca
Director Regional Relations, Darryl C. Eisan
902-424-4535,
dceisan@gov.ns.ca
Director Economic Policy & Analysis, André Moore
902-424-7728,
mooreac@gov.ns.ca
Research Assistant Federal-Provincial, Cathy Richard
902-424-1198,
richarcl@gov.ns.ca
Minister & Attorney General, Hon. Ross Landry
902-424-4044, Fax: 902-424-0510
justmin@gov.ns.ca
Deputy Minister, Marian F. Tyson, Q.C.
902-424-4223,
tysonmf@gov.ns.ca
Director Communications, Sherri Aikenhead
902-424-3313,
aikenhsl@gov.ns.ca
Director Public Safety, Fred Sanford
902-424-0069,
sanforfg@gov.ns.ca

Department of Labour & Workforce Development

5151 Terminal Rd., 6th Fl.
PO Box 697
Halifax, NS B3J 2T8
902-424-5301
Fax: 902-424-0575
www.gov.ns.ca/lwd
The Department of Labour and Workforce Development focuses on labour issues, employment rights and responsibilities, adult learning, apprenticeship training and trade qualification, skill development, public and workplace safety, industry regulation, licensing and pensions.
Minister, Hon. Mark Parent
902-424-6647,
min_lwd@gov.ns.ca
Deputy Minister, Margaret F. MacDonald
902-424-6632,
macdonmf@gov.ns.ca
Director Communications, Karen Stone
902-424-2107, Fax: 902-424-0644
stonekk@gov.ns.ca
Executive Secretary, Lorna Kennedy
902-424-6647,
kennedlj@gov.ns.ca
Executive Director, Bill Wilson
902-424-3236
Director Solicitor Services & Registrar, Regulations, Jonathan Davies
902-424-5476

Department of Natural Resources

Founder's Square
1701 Hollis St., 3rd Fl.
PO Box 698
Halifax, NS B3J 2T9
902-424-5935
Fax: 902-424-0594
800-565-2224
www.gov.ns.ca/natr
Responsible for the administration & management of provincial Crown lands, development of mineral & energy resources, protection & sustainable development of forest resources & operation & maintenance of parks system, & promoting the conservation & sustainable use of wildlife populations, habitat & ecosystems.Initiatives include: a State of the Forest report; working with other departments on State of the Environment report; leading the development of a provincial climate change strategy; implementing recovery plans for endangered & threatened wildlife species; & developing strategic land use plans for Crown lands using an integrated resource management planning process.

Acts Administered:
Act to Confer Certain Powers upon the Lieutenant Governor in Council & to amend the Mines Act
Angling Act
Beaches Act
Blueberry Association Act
Bowater Mersey Agreement Act
Conservation Easements Act
Endangered Species Act
Species At Risk List Legislation
Expropriation Act
Forests Act
Christmas Tree Grading Regulations
Christmas Tree Levy Regulations
Dutch Elm Disease Regulations
Forest Fire Protection Regulations
Forest Sustainability Regulations
Registration & Statistical Returns Regulations
Timber Loan Board Regulations
Wildlife Habitat & Watercourses Protection Regulations
Gypsum Mining Income Tax Act
Indian Lands Act
Halifax Power & Pulp Company Limited Agreement Act, 1962
Land Holdings Disclosure Act
Land Surveyors Act
Mineral Resources Act
Mines Act
Nova Scotia Federation of Anglers & Hunters Act
Off Highway Vehicles Act
Primary Forest Products Marketing Act
Provincial Parks Act
Private Ways Act
Scalers Act
Scott Maritimes Limited Agreement (1965) Act
Special Places Protection Act (Shared with Tourism, Culture & Heritage)
Stora Forest Industries Agreement Act
Trails Act
Treasure Trove Act
Wildlife Act
General Wildlife Regulations
Minister, Hon. Carolyn Bolivar-Getson
902-424-4037, Fax: 902-424-0594
bolivargetson@gov.ns.ca
Deputy Minister, Peter Underwood
902-424-4121, Fax: 902-424-0594
underwpc@gov.ns.ca
Secretary to the Deputy Minister, Nancy Parsons
902-424-4121,
parsonn@gov.ns.ca
• Crown Lands Record Centre
Founders Square
#501, 1701 Hollis St.
PO Box 698
Halifax, NS B3J 2T9
902-424-8681
• NS Primary Forest Products Marketing Board
#804, 45 Alderney Dr.
Dartmouth, NS B2Y 2N6
902-424-7598
Fax: 902-424-6965

Land Services Branch
The Land Services Branch management oversees, coordinates & approves all activities within the Branch relating to the administration of Crown land. The Branch provides advice on legislative revisions & advises & drafts policies relating to the administration of Crown land & provides on all matters respecting Crown land administration.
Executive Director, Jo-Anne Himmelman
902-424-4267,
himmelgj@gov.ns.ca

Minerals Resources Branch
Fax: 902-424-7735
www.gov.ns.ca/natr/meb/
Implements policies & programs dealing with the exploration, development, management & efficient use of energy & mineral resources, promotes scientific studies of the geology of the province for use by government, industry & the public, provides a mineral rights tenure system to establish legal rights to minerals for exploration & development. Promotes concepts of environmental responsibility & sustainable, stewardship or the mineral & energy resource sector & integrated resource planning.
Executive Director, Scott Swinden
902-424-7943,
hsswinde@gov.ns.ca

Minerals Management Division
Receives & evaluates applications for & issues mineral rights; assesses exploration work reports submitted by industry & registers activities; provides technical & financial assessment & evaluation of minerals & energy resources & promotes development of same; develops & administers regulations relative to the mining industries.
Director, Don Jones, Ph.D., P.Eng.
902-424-5618,
jonesds@gov.ns.ca
Acting Manager Mineral Development & Policy, Thomas Lamb
902-424-4911,
lambtg@gov.ns.ca

Planning Secretariat
Provides planning & policy coordination support to the Department, ensures that policies & plans developed in the Department are coordinated, support the integrated management of our natural resources & are compatible with & support the strategic direction of the government.Also provides a range of administrative, planning, research, information management, information distribution, graphics, cartographic, communication, & occupational health & safety-related services.
Executive Director, Patricia MacNeil
902-424-4988,
macneipb@gov.ns.ca

Regional Services Branch
Delivers departmental programs & services through a field office network, responsible for forest protection & planning, forest nurseries, research & development, enforcement, coordination of the hunter safety program, regional geological services, Crown land surveys, operation & maintenance of provincial parks, resource conservation, forest fire prevention & monitoring of forest insects & diseases.
Executive Director, Brian Gilbert
902-424-3949,
giberbs@gov.ns.ca

Central
626 College Rd.
Bible Hill, NS B2N 2R2
902-893-5620
Fax: 902-893-5613
Regional Director, Roger Aggas
aggasr@gov.ns.ca

Eastern
300 Mountain Rd.
Sydney, NS B1L 1A9
902-563-3370
Fax: 902-567-2535
Regional Director, Dave Harris
harrisdl@gov.ns.ca

Western
Provincial Bldg.
99 High St.
Bridgewater, NS B4V 1V8
902-543-8167
Fax: 902-543-6157
Regional Director, Gerald Joudrey
gtjoudre@gov.ns.ca

Renewable Resources Branch
The Renewable Resources Branch provides coordination & leadership on policy, planning & program development including industry development & resource promotion, marketing, resource inventories & research, & the preparation of strategies & plans for the integrated development, management & conservation of the province's forests, parks & wildlife resources.
Executive Director, Ed MacAulay
902-424-4103,
emmacaul@gov.ns.ca

Land Administration
Acquires, leases & disposes of Crown lands administered by the department; maintains & researches records, map & title files for interest in Crown lands; acquires lands for other departments & agencies on request; & administers proclamations & designations of parks, special places & protected beaches.

Director, Dave Steeves
902-424-3160,
steeveda@gov.ns.ca
Manager Acquisitions & Leases, Jane Latremouille
902-424-4006,
jilatrem@gov.ns.ca
Manager Crown Land Disposals & Coastal Permits, Harry Ashcroft
ashcroht@gov.ns.ca

Surveys Division
Maintains surveying equipment standards, establishes & maintains surveys standards, administers orders of surveys & Crown lands boundary line maintenance contracts, resolves claims against Crown lands & maintains a registry of Crown lands.
Acting Director, Sandy Cameron
902-424-3144

Geological Services
Gathers & analyzes & provides geoscientific information to industry & the public to promote exploration & development of mineral resources; develops & maintains mineral inventory information; provides advice to the coordinated Integrated Resource Management (IRM) effort.
Director Geology, Mike Cherry, Ph.D
902-424-8135, Fax: 902-424-7735
cherryme@gov.ns.ca

Enforcement Division
Develops & coordinates the Department's enforcement & compliance program, & operates a province-wide wildlife crime prevention program.
Director, John Mombourquette
902-424-5254,
jamombou@gov.ns.ca

Fleet Management Division
PO Box 130
Shubenacadie, NS B0N 2H0
902-758-7019
Providing centralized aviation services to government departments & agencies for forest fire detection & suppression, provincial emergency situations, ground search & rescue, medical evacuations, & resource development & management; managing & maintaining the department's motorized equipment.
Director, Ross Wickwire
902-758-7019, Fax: 902-758-3355
wickwira@gov.ns.ca

Operations Division
Involved in work planning & financial reporting for Regional Services Branch; technical training for staff of Regional Services Branch; OH&S implementation for Regional Services Branch, parks program operations; natural resources stewardship & outreach activities including youth & hunter education & technical transfer of forest management information for woodlot owners & Christmas tree growers.
Director, Bill Smith
902-424-4445

Resource Management Division
Coordinating the implementation of forest management programs designed to help ensure the long term viability of the forest industry in the Province. The forest management programs incorporate forest/wildlife guidelines & the principles of integrated resource management & sustainable development.
Director, Dan Eidt
902-424-7594

Forestry Division
PO Box 68
Truro, NS B2N 5B8
902-893-6350
Fax: 902-893-5613
Conducts research to improve forest management practices, maintains a provincial forest inventory, coordinates the provincial forest fire management & integrated pest management programs & manages the provincial forest nursery.
Director, Jorg Beyeler
902-893-5673, Fax: 902-893-6102

Parks & Recreation Division
RR#1
Belmont, NS B0M 1C0
902-662-3030
Undertakes site planning, development, project management & inspection-related activities for parks, trails & outdoor recreational activities & coordinates the preparation of parks development & operating standards for the provincial parks system.
Director Parks & Recreation Division, Harold Carroll
902-662-5062, Fax: 902-662-2190

Program Development Division
Coordinates policy & program development activities related to forestry, parks & wildlife, provides information & advice on markets & market opportunities for forest products, manages federal-provincial agreements for renewable resources & assists in the development & delivery of the branch's education & extension programs.
Director, G. Peter MacQuarrie
902-424-7708,
gpmacqua@gov.ns.ca

Wildlife Division
Provincial Building
136 Exhibition St.
Kentville, NS B4N 4E5
902-678-6091
Develops legislation, policies & guidelines to ensure conservation & the sustainable use of wildlife, inventories & monitors wildlife populations & wildlife habitat, conducts wildlife & habitat-related research, develops protection & recovery programs for threatened & endangered species & their habitats & operates the provincial wildlife park.
Director, Julie Towers
902-678-6091, Fax: 902-679-6176
towersjk@gov.ns.ca

Department of Service Nova Scotia & Municipal Relations
1505 Barrington St.
PO Box 216
Halifax, NS B3J 2M4
902-424-4141
Fax: 902-424-0581
public-enquiries@gov.ns.ca
www.gov.ns.ca/snsmr
Other Communication: Nova Scotia Business Registry:
1-800-670-4357
Provides leadership in the achievement of effective local government, assessment services, business licensing & registration, vehicle registration & driver licensing, taxation & revenue collection, vital statistics & an integrated land information management system to meet the needs of local & provincial agencies & residents of Nova Scotia.

Acts Administered:
Assessment Act
Building Access Act
Business Electronic Filing Act
Cemetery & Funeral Services Act
Change of Name Act
Collection Agencies Act
Communications & Information Act
Companies Act
Condominium Act
Consumer Creditors' Conduct Act
Consumer Protection Act
Consumer Reporting Act
Consumer Services Act
Corporations Registration Act
Direct Sellers' Regulation Act
Embalmers & Funeral Directors Act
Land Registration Act
Limited Partnerships Act
Marketable Titles Act
Mortgage Brokers' & Lenders' Registration Act
Motor Vehicle Act
Municipal Conflict of Interest Act
Municipal Elections Act
Municipal Finance Corporation Act
Municipal Fiscal Year Act
Municipal Government Act
Municipal Grants Act
Municipal Housing Corporations Act
Municipal Loan & Building Fund Act
Off-Highway Vehicles Act
Off-Highway Vehicles Regulations
Snow Vehicles Regulations
Part X of the Bankruptcy & Insolvency Act
Part IV of the Revenue Act for administrative purposes
Partnerships & Business Names Registration Act
Personal Property Security Act
Private Investment Holding Companies Act
Public Accountants Act
Real Estate Trading Act
Registry Act
Rental Property Conversion Act
Residential Tenancies Act
Rural Fire District Act
Sales Tax Act
Shopping Centre Development Act
Societies Act
Solemnization of Marriage Act
Unconscionable Transactions Relief Act
Vital Statistics Act
Minister, Hon. Richard Hurlburt
902-424-5550, Fax: 902-424-0581
snsmrmin@gov.ns.ca
Deputy Minister, Kevin Malloy
902-424-4100,
keefeg@gov.ns.ca
Asst. Deputy Minister, Kevin Malloy
902-424-4559
Director Communications, Donna Chislett
902-424-6336, Fax: 902-424-0581
chisledp@gov.ns.ca
• Nova Scotia Municipal Finance Corporation
Maritime Centre
1505 Barrington St., 10th Fl. South
PO Box 850 M
Halifax, NS B3J 2V2
902-424-4590
Fax: 902-424-0525
www.gov.ns.ca/nsmfc
Chair, Greg Keefe
NSMFC issues pooled debentures that provide low-cost, long-term capital financing for municipal capital projects. The NSMFC issues in capital markets twice a year, generally in the spring and fall. On occasion the NSMFC will do a single issue, provided the size is large enough.

Assessment Services
Fax: 902-424-0587

Program Management & Corporate Services

Co-operative Branch
902-893-6190
Fax: 902-893-6108

Tax Commission
Maritime Centre
1505 Barrington St.
Halifax, NS B3J 3K5
902-424-5200
Fax: 902-424-0720
800-670-4357
www.gov.ns.ca/snsmr/taxcomm/

Integrated Service Delivery
Fax: 902-424-5510

Nova Scotia Geomatics Centre
160 Willow St.
Amherst, NS B4H 3W3
902-667-7231
Fax: 902-667-6008
800-798-0706
info@nsgc.gov.ns.ca
www.gov.ns.ca/snsmr/land/

Registry of Deeds
PO Box 2205
Halifax, NS B3J 3C4
Fax: 902-424-5872

Registry of Joint Stock Companies
Maritime Centre
1505 Barrington St., 9th Fl.
Halifax, NS B3J 3K5
902-424-7770
Fax: 902-424-4633
800-225-8227
joint-stock@gov.ns.ca
www.gov.ns.ca/snsmr/rjsc

Registry of Motor Vehicles
902-424-7801
Fax: 902-424-0772

Federal/Provincial Government / Government of Nova Scotia

Vital Statistics
Joseph Howe Bldg.
1690 Hollis St., Ground Floor
PO Box 157
Halifax, NS B3J 2M9
902-424-4071
Fax: 902-424-0678
877-848-2578
vstat@gov.ns.ca

Service Delivery
Maritime Centre
1505 Barrington St., 8th Fl. North
PO Box 2734
Halifax, NS B3J 3P7

Antigonish
20 St. Andrew's St.
Antigonish, NS B2G 2L4

Bridgewater
80 Logan Rd.
Bridgewater, NS B4V 3J8

Dartmouth
Super Store Mall
650 Portland St.
Dartmouth, NS B2W 6A3

Halifax
West End Mall
6960 Mumford Rd.
Halifax, NS B3L 4P1

Kentville
28 Aberdeen St.
Kentville, NS B4N 2N1

Municipal Services Division
Fax: 902-424-0821

Sydney
Moxam Centre
380 King's Rd.
Sydney, NS B1S 1A8

Associated Agencies, Boards & Commissions
Executive Director, Nathan Gorall
902-424-2499

Truro
#3, 80 Walker St.
Truro, NS B2N 4A7

Yarmouth
Provincial Bldg.
#127, 10 Starrs Rd.
Yarmouth, NS B5A 2T1

Department of Tourism, Culture & Heritage

World Trade & Convention Centre
1800 Argyle St., 6th Fl.
PO Box 456
Halifax, NS B3J 2R5
902-424-5000
Fax: 902-424-4872
800-565-0000
tns@gov.ns.ca
www.gov.ns.ca/tch

Acts Administered:
Art Council Act
Art Gallery of Nova Scotia Act
Cemeteries Protection Act
Cultural Foundation Act
Government Records Act
Heritage Property Act
Multiculturalism Act
Nova Scotia Museum Act
Nova Scotia Tartan Act
Peggy's Cove Commission Act
Public Archives Act
Schooner Bluenose Foundation Act
Sherbrooke Restoration Commission Act
Special Places Protection Act (Ecological Site Designations:
　Abraham Lake, Bornish Hill, Duncans Cove, Great Barren &
　Quinan Lakes, Indian Man Lake, MacFarlane Woods, Panuke
　Lake, Ponhook Lake, Quinns
Tourist Accommodations Act

Minister, Hon. William Dooks
902-424-4889, Fax: 902-424-4872
dooksbf@gov.ns.ca
Deputy Minister, Kelliann Dean
902-424-4869,
deankm@gov.ns.ca
Secretary to the Deputy Minister, Renata Aube
902-424-4869, Fax: 902-424-4872
auberg@gov.ns.ca
• Nova Scotia Tourism Partnership Council
World Trade & Convention Centre
#603, 1800 Argyle St.
Halifax, NS B3J 3N8
902-424-0048
Fax: 902-424-0723
pashermc@gov.ns.ca
www.nstpc.com

NS Archives & Records Management
Fax: 902-424-0628

Culture Division
#601, 1800 Argyle St.
PO Box 456
Halifax, NS B3J 2R5
Fax: 902-424-0710
Responsible for Nova Scotia museums which administer the Special Places Protection Act; preserves ecological sites in the province.
Executive Director, Dianne Coish
902-424-6471, Fax: 902-424-0710
coishdm@gov.ns.ca

Heritage Division
1747 Summer St.
Halifax, NS B3H 3A6
902-424-7344
Fax: 902-424-0560
800-632-1114
heritage@gov.ns.ca
The mission of Heritage Division is to protect, enhance, & celebrate heritage for all Nova Scotians & for future generations.
Executive Director, Bill Greenlaw
902-424-7344,
greenlbe@gov.ns.ca

Tourism Division
Fax: 902-424-2668
Director Tourism Development, Robert Book
902-424-3141
Manager Enquiries & Research, Robert Boyd
902-424-2906

Department of Transportation & Infrastructure Renewal

Johnston Bldg.
1672 Granville St., 2nd Fl.
PO Box 186
Halifax, NS B3J 2N2
902-424-2297
Fax: 902-424-0171
888-432-3233
tpwpaff@gov.ns.ca
http://gov.ns.ca/tran
Provides a transportation network for the safe & efficient movement of people & goods; serves the building, property & accommodation needs of government departments & agencies; employs professional, dedicated people & offers a high level of customer service.

Acts Administered:
Dangerous Goods Transportation Act
Dangerous Goods Transportation Regulations
Ferries Act
Highway 104: Western Alignment Act
Highway Workers Collective Bargaining Act
Motor Vehicle Act
Off-Highway Vehicles Act
Public Highways Act
Railways Act
Surplus Crown Property Disposal Act
Unsightly Premises Act
Minister, Hon. Brooke D. Taylor
902-424-5875, Fax: 902-424-0171
tirmin@gov.ns.ca

Deputy Minister, David Darrow
902-424-4036, Fax: 902-424-2014
ddarrow@gov.ns.ca
Executive Director Maintenance & Operations, Kevin Caines
Director Public Affairs & Communications, Cathy MacIsaac
902-424-8978, Fax: 902-424-0532
macisacl@gov.ns.ca
• Sydney Tar Ponds Agency
1 Inglis St.
PO Box 1028 A
Sydney, NS B1P 6J7
902-567-1035
Fax: 902-567-1032
www.tarpondscleanup.ca
Acting CEO, Frank Potter, P.Eng.

Highway Operations
This division provides for provincial highway & bridge maintenance, as well as the operation of the Department's fleet management & a strategic planning section.District Services provides general services on primary & secondary roads & works with private sector contractors to provide the public with enhanced road systems.

Environmental Services Group
The Environmental Services Group of Transportation & Public Works acts on behalf of government with regard to the environmental assessment & cleanup of contaminated sites. Environmental site assessments, environmental impact assessments, vegetation management, development & promotion of environmentally sound construction & maintenance practices, quantitative hazardous building material surveys, site investigations, air monitoring, water supply development, sewage treatment, hazardous chemical management, PCB & asbestos removal & disposal, building demolition & waste disposal/recycling, & public relations are some examples of current environmental activities undertaken by the Environmental Services Group.
Manager, Chris Moir
902-424-4725

Public Works
This division provides technical expertise & services required by the Department's highway, building & property divisions. The Highway Engineering Services section provides delivery of highway planning, geometric & structural design, traffic engineering, capital program maintenance & asset management business functions.The Engineering & Design section provides engineering, architectural, environmental & technical services & project management services for projects that are related to maintaining & constructing highway & building infrastructure.The Building Services & Operations section oversees the management, operation, maintenance & renovation of government buildings, infrastructure & properties, as well as the provision of trade & contract services in both leased & owned premises.
Executive Director, Al MacRae
902-424-5687
Acting Director Building Services & Operations, Neil Whyte
902-424-2281
Director Engineering & Design, John O'Connor
902-424-2756
Director Highway Engineering Services, Ralph Hessian
902-424-4268,
hessiara@gov.ns.ca

Nova Scotia Utility & Review Board

1601 Lower Water St., 3rd Fl.
PO Box 1692 M
Halifax, NS B3J 3S3
902-424-4448
Fax: 902-424-3919
uarb.board@gov.ns.ca
The Board has a very broad mandate encompassing a number of acts.Operations fall into two categories, regulatory & adjudicative. The regulatory category includes the regulation of public utilities, licensing of public passenger carriers, monitoring of automobile insurance rates, the approval of Halifax-Dartmouth bridge fares, & the regulation of natural gas distribution & pipelines. The Board conducts hearings relating to gaming control, liquor control & film classification. The adjudicative category includes appeals or applications relating to property assessments, expropriation compensation claims, planning & subdivisions, heritage properties, criminal injury compensation claims, municipal boundaries, municipal & school board electoral boundaries, as well as gasoline, diesel oil & tobacco taxes.The Board receives its authority from the Public Inquiries Act & the Utility & Review Board Act.

Acts Administered:
Assessment Act
Electrical Installation & Inspection Act
Education Act
Energy & Mineral Resources Conservation Act
Expropriation Act
Fire Safety Act
Gaming Control Act (Part II)
Gas Distribution Act
Halifax-Dartmouth Bridge Commission Act
Liquor Control Act
Motor Carrier Act (public passenger only)
Motor Vehicle Transport Act of Canada, 1987 (Federal)
Municipal Government Act
Nova Scotia Power Finance Corporation Act
Nova Scotia Power Privatization Act
Petroleum Resources Removal Permit Act
Pipeline Act
Public Utilities Act
Railways Act
Revenue Act
Theatres & Amusement Act
Underground Hydrocarbons Storage Act
Utility & Review Board Act
Victims' Rights & Services Act
Minister Responsible, Hon. Michael Baker, Q.C.
Chair, Peter W. Gurnham, Q.C.
uarb.board@gov.ns.ca

Workers' Compensation Board of Nova Scotia
5668 South St.
PO Box 1150
Halifax, NS B3J 2Y2
902-491-8999
Fax: 902-491-8002
800-870-3331
info@wcb.gov.ns.ca
www.wcb.ns.ca
Coordinates the workers' compensation system to assist injured workers & their employers by providing timely medical & rehabilitative support to help injured workers return to work.Also, to provide appropriate compensation for work-related injuries & illnesses.
Acting Chair, Chris Power
902-491-8382
CEO, Nancy MacCready-Williams
902-491-8300
Director Communications, Mary Kingston
902-491-8101
Administrative Assistant, Dianne Barnes
902-491-8317,
dianne.barnes@wcb.gov.ns.ca

Government of the Nunavut Territory
Seat of Government: PO Box 1200
Iqaluit, NU X0A 0H0
888-252-9869
www.gov.nu.ca
On April 1, 1999, Nunavut Territory was created as part of the Nunavut Land Claims Agreement signed in 1993. It has area of 1,932,254.97 km2, & the StatsCan population in 2006 was 29,474. Nunavut Territory is governed by a fully elected Legislative Assembly of 19 members elected for a five-year term. Government is by consensus rather than party politics. The Legislature elects the Premier & a seven-member Executive Council, which is charged with the operation of government & the establishment of program & spending priorities. Nunavut Territory acts under the same conditions as other territories in Canada. For an explanation of the difference between provinces & territories please see the Yukon Territory listing. The Commissioner of Nunavut Territory is appointed by the Federal Government, & serves a role similar to that of the Lieutenant Governor in provincial jurisdictions.
Legislative Librarian, Yvonne Earle
867-975-5132, Fax: 867-975-5190

Department of Community & Government Services
J.G. Brown Bldg.
PO Box 1000 700
Iqaluit, NU X0A 0H0
867-975-5400
Fax: 867-975-5305
To support the development, provision & maintenance of programs & services which affect the communities in all areas of municipal responsibility & transportation.

Acts Administered:
Area Development Act
Resolute Bay Development Area Regulations
Strathcona Sound Development Area Regulations
Boilers & Pressure Vessels Act
Business Licenses Act
Cities, Towns & Villages Act
Iqaluit By-Law Exemption Order
Land Administration By-law Exemption Order
Town of Iqaluit Continuation Order
Civil Emergency Measures Act
Commissioner's Land Act
Commissioner's Airport Lands Regulations
Commissioner's Land Regulations
Community Employees' Benefits Program Transfer Act
Conflict of Interest Act
Consumer Protection Act
Dog Act
Electrical Protection Act
Film Classification Act
Fire Prevention Act
Fire Prevention Regulations
Fireworks Regulations
Propane Cylinder Storage
Gas Protection Act
Hamlets Act
Home Owners Property Tax Rebate Act
Local Authorities Elections Act
Lotteries Act
Pawnbrokers & Second-Hand Dealers Act
Planning Act
Property Assessment & Taxation Act
Real Estate Agents Licencing Act
Religious Societies Lands Act
Residential Tenancies Act
Senior Citizens & Disabled Persons Property Tax Relief Act
Settlements Act
Technical Standards & Safety Act
Minister, Hon. Levinia Brown
867-975-5075, Fax: 867-975-5095
Deputy Minister, David Akeeagok
867-975-5306, Fax: 867-975-5305
Asst. Deputy Minister, Shawn Maley
867-645-8101, Fax: 867-645-8141
smaley@gov.nu.ca
Asst. Deputy Minister, Brent Boddy
867-975-5409, Fax: 867-975-5457
Director Policy, Lucy Magee
867-975-5309, Fax: 867-975-5305
lmagee@gov.nu.ca
Director Protection Services, Ed Zebedee
867-975-5319, Fax: 867-975-5453
ezebedee@gov.nu.ca
Manager Procurement, Logistics & Contract Support, Mark McCulloch
867-975-5427, Fax: 867-975-5450

Regional Offices:

Cambridge
PO Box 200
Cambridge Bay, NU X0B 0C0
Fax: 867-983-4123

Cape Dorset
PO Box 330
Cape Dorset, NU X0A 0C0

Pond Inlet
PO Box 379
Pond Inlet, NU X0A 0S0

Rankin Inlet
PO Box 490
Rankin Inlet, NU X0C 0G0
Fax: 867-645-8197

Department of Culture, Language, Elders & Youth (CLEY)
PO Box 1000 800
Iqaluit, NU X0A 0H0
867-975-5500
Fax: 867-975-5504
866-934-2035
www.gov.nu.ca/cley

Responsible for the protection, preservation & promotion of Inuit languages. Cultural initiatives & departmental goals are reached in coordination with & in support of elder & youth groups.CLEY acts in respect to issues concerning women & people with disabilities. The government is dedicated to preserving & promoting elements that make up the Inuit identity.
Acts Administered:
Archives Act
Historical Resources Act
Official Languages Act
Minister, Hon. Louis Tapardjuk
867-975-5070, Fax: 867-975-5095
Deputy Minister, Phoebe Hainnu
867-975-5501, Fax: 867-975-5504
Asst. Deputy Minister, Naullaq Arnaquq
867-975-5532, Fax: 867-975-5504
narnaquq@gov.nu.ca

Culture & Heritage
PO Box 310
Igloolik, NU X0A 0L0
867-975-2046
Fax: 867-934-2047
cleypermits@gov.nu.ca
This Division provides direction & planning related to the conservation of Nunavut's heritage resources & lends expertise to establish policies & programs in the interest of conserving, protecting & promoting Nunavut's heritage & culture. The archive preserves the territory's documentary heritage & makes the information available to the public.Archaeology staff is preparing regulations for archaeology & palaeontology research in Nunavut. The territorial toponymist recognizes & grants authority for official names or titles.
Director, Douglas Stenton
867-975-5524,
dstenton1@gov.nu.ca

Department of Economic Development & Transportation
#1104 Inuksugait Plaza
PO Box 1000 1500
Iqaluit, NU X0A 0H0
867-975-7800
Fax: 867-975-7870
888-975-5999
edt@gov.nu.ca
www.edt.gov.nu.ca
Acts Administered:
Agricultural Products Marketing Act
All-Terrain Vehicles Act
All-Terrain Vehicles Regulations
Special All-Terrain Vehicles Fees Regulations
Special All-Terrain Vehicles Helmet Regulations
Economic Development Agreements Act
Motor Vehicles Act
Carrier Fitness Regulations
Exemption of Motor Vehicles Act Regulations
Hours of Service Regulations
Large Vehicle Control Regulations
Motor Vehicle Equipment Regulations
School Bus Regulations
Seasonal Highway Regulations
Nunavut Development Corporation
Public Highways Act
Highway Designation & Classification Regulations
Highway Signs Regulations
Transportation of Dangerous Goods Act
Transportation of Dangerous Goods Regulations
Travel & Tourism Act
Guide Exemption Regulations
Outfitter Regulations
Tourist Establishment Regulations
Travel Development Area Regulations
Minister, Hon. Patterk Netser
867-975-5024, Fax: 867-975-5095
Deputy Minister, Rosemary Keenainak
867-975-7829, Fax: 867-975-7880
• Nunavut Business Credit Corporation
PO Box 224
Cape Dorset, NU X0A 0C0
867-897-3647
800-758-0038
www.nbcc.nu.ca

Economic Development

Federal/Provincial Government / Government of the Nunavut Territory

Asst. Deputy Minister, Jane Cooper
867-975-7832, Fax: 867-975-7880
Director Community Economic Development, Steve Hannah
867-473-2661, Fax: 867-473-2663
Director Minerals & Petroleum, Gordon MacKay
867-975-7822, Fax: 867-975-7870

Fisheries & Sealing
Focuses on developing viable & sustainable sectors that will ensure that all revenues & opportunities derived from the territorial resources benefit Nunavummiut. Through the development & implementation of the Nunavut Sealing Strategy, the Nunavut Fishing Strategy & support to the fur sector, fisheries & sealing programs work towards maximizing economic opportunities for Nunavummiut within the principles of conservation & sustainability.
Director, Wayne Lynch
867-975-5968

Transportation
Asst. Deputy Minister, Methusalah Kunuk
867-975-7832, Fax: 867-975-7880
Director Iqaluit Airports, John Graham
867-979-5224, Fax: 867-979-6985
Director Motor Vehicles, Lorna Gee
867-360-4614, Fax: 867-360-4619
Director Nunavut Airports, Neal Carmichael
867-645-8203, Fax: 867-645-8246
Director Transportation Policy & Planning, John Hawkins
867-975-7826, Fax: 867-795-7870

Kitikmeot
PO Box 316
Kugluktuk, NU X0B 0E0
Director, Beatrice Bernhardt
867-982-7459, Fax: 867-982-3204

Kivalliq
PO Box 2
Rankin Inlet, NU X0C 0G0
Acting Director, Robert Connely
867-645-8458, Fax: 867-645-8455

Qikiqtaaluk
#1045
PO Box 389
Pond Inlet, NU X0A 0S0
Director, Rhoda Katsak
867-899-7339, Fax: 867-899-7348
Minister, Hon. Ed Picco
867-975-5020, Fax: 867-979-5095

Nunavut Emergency Management

PO Box 1000 700
Iqaluit, NU X0A 0H0
867-975-5403
Fax: 867-979-4221
800-693-1666
cgs.gov.nu.ca/en/nunavut-emergency-management
Other Communication: Emergency Services Response Centre:
867/979-6262
Manager Emergency Services, Glen Higgins
867-975-5403, Fax: 867-979-4221
ghiggins@gov.nu.ca
Acting Fire Marshall, Robert Prima
867-975-5310, Fax: 867-975-5315

Department of Environment

PO Box 1000 1300
Iqaluit, NU X0A 0H0
867-975-7700
Fax: 867-975-7742
866-222-9063
environment@gov.nu.ca
Acts Administered:
Environmental Protection Act
Asphalt Paving Industry Emission Regulations
Spill Contingency Planning & Reporting
Used Oil & Waste Fuel Management
Environmental Rights Act
Flood Damage Reduction Agreements Act
Forest Management Act
Forest Management Regulations
Forest Protection Act
Freshwater Fish Marketing Act
Establishing Freshwater Fish Marketing Corporation Regulations

Herd & Fencing Act
Natural Resource Conservation Trust Act
Pesticides Act
Territorial Park Act
Community Parks Order
Heritage Parks, Natural Environment Parks & Recreation Parks Regulations
Natural Environment Recreation Park Order
Historic Parks Order
Outdoor Recreation Parks Order
Territorial Parks Regulations
Wayside Parks Order
Travel & Tourism Act
Outfitter Regulations
Tourist Establishment Regulations
Waste Reduction & Recovery Act
Travel Development Area Regulation
Water Resources Agreements Act
Wildlife Act
Big Game Hunting Regulations
Birds of Prey Regulations
Certification & Disposal of Wildlife Regulations
Critical Wildlife Areas Regulations
Dempster Highway Special Management Area Regulations
Nuisance Bison Control Regulations
Polar Bear Defence Kill Regulations
Sale of Wildlife Regulations
Small Game Hunting Regulations
Trapping Regulations
Wildlife Business Regulations
Wildlife Export Regulations
Wildlife General Regulations
Wildlife Licenses & Permits Regulations
Wildlife Management Barren Ground Caribou Area Regulation
Wildlife Management Grizzly Bear Area Regulations
Wildlife Management Muskox Areas Regulations
Wildlife Management Outfitter Area Regulations
Wildlife Management Polar Bear Areas Regulations
Wildlife Management Units Regulations
Wildlife Management Wood Bison Area Regulations
Wildlife Management Zones Regulations
Wildlife Preserves Regulations
Wildlife Regions Regulations
Wildlife Sanctuaries Regulations
Minister, Hon. Olayuk Akesuk
867-975-5026, Fax: 867-975-0595
Deputy Minister, Alukie Rojas
867-975-7705, Fax: 867-975-7740
Asst. Deputy Minister, Vacant
867-975-7705, Fax: 867-975-7740
Director Policy, Planning & Legislation, Steve Pinksen
867-975-7718, Fax: 867-975-7740
spinksen@gov.nu.ca

Environmental Protection
867-975-5907
The government is working towards the development & implementation of a strategy to address climate change. Environmental protection ensures that all spills of hazardous substances are cleaned up properly by the party responsible. Major areas of the environment, such as persistent organic pollutants & other contaminants that threaten the traditional food chain will be monitored.
Director, Earle Baddaloo
867-975-7729, Fax: 867-975-7739
Manager Land Use & Environmental Assessment, Mike Atkinson
867-975-7732
Manager Pollution Control & Air Quality, Rob Eno
867-975-4478

Parks & Conservation Areas
www.nunavutparks.com
Responsible for the planning, establishment, operations & the promotion of a system of territorial parks & conservation areas throughout Nunavut. In cooperation with Nunavummiut, Parks & Conservation Areas showcases Nunavut's protected areas locally, regionally, nationally, & internationally to ensure protected areas continue to reflect the Nunavut Territory's unique heritage & the spirit, principles & special relationships established through the Nunavut Land Claims Agreement & the Inuit Impact Benefit Agreements (IIBAs) for Territorial Parks.
Director, David Monteith
867-975-5934,
dmonteith@gov.nu.ca

Wildlife Management
Responsible for the management of terrestrial wildlife species in Nunavut. In addition to the Nunavut Wildlife Act, Wildlife Management is responsible for fulfilling responsibilities under a wide range of federal legislation & both national & international agreements & conventions.
Director, Drikus Gissing
867-899-8034, Fax: 867-899-8017

Regional Offices:

Baffin
PO Box 569
Pond Inlet, NU X0A 0S0

Kitikmeot
PO Box 377
Kugluktuk, NU X0B 0E0
Regional Wildlife Manager, Dustin Fredlund
867-982-7441, Fax: 867-982-3701

Kivalliq
PO Box 120
Arviat, NU X0C 0E0
Fax: 867-857-2986
Regional Wildlife Manager, Dan Shewchuk
867-857-2828, Fax: 867-857-2986

Department of Executive & Intergovernmental Affairs

1084 Aeroplex bldg.
PO Box 1000 200
Iqaluit, NU X0A 0H0
867-975-6000
Fax: 867-975-6090
The department provides advice & administrative support to Cabinet & the government, works to ensure that the Nunavut Land Claims Agreement & Nunavut's relationships with other governments in Canada & the circumpolar world are used to support common goals. The department compiles & communicates information & evaluates government programs & data. The Intergovernmental Affairs Division is responsible for the management & development of government strategies, policies & initiatives relating to federal, provincial, territorial, circumpolar & aboriginal affairs. This office participates in preparations for Intergovernmental activities such as the Western & Annual Premiers Conferences, First Ministers meetings & the Social Union Framework Agreement, the Arctic Council, the Nunavut Implementation Panel & the Clyde River Protocol.
Acts Administered:
Nunavut Power Corporation Assets Transfer Confirmation Act
Public Utilities Act
Public Utilities Regulations
Minister, Hon. Paul Okalik
867-975-5050, Fax: 867-975-5051
Asst. Deputy Minister Policy, Planning & Evaluation, Paul Suvega
867-975-6009, Fax: 867-975-6089
Director Aboriginal & Circumpolar Affairs, Letia Obed
867-975-6036, Fax: 867-975-6091
Director Policy, Planning & Evaluation, Rachel Mark
867-975-6029, Fax: 867-975-6029
Acting Director Communications, Lena Kilabuk
867-975-6048, Fax: 867-975-6099
Director Statistics, Ron McMahon
867-473-2693, Fax: 867-473-2626
Acts Administered:
Explosives Use Act
Mine Health & Safety Act
Safety Act
Environmental Tobacco Smoke Work Site Regulations
Technical Standards & Safety Act
Worker's Compensation Act

Department of Health & Social Services

Sivummut bldg.
PO Box 1007 1000
Iqaluit, NU X0A 0H0
867-975-5700
Fax: 867-975-5705
health@gov.nu.ca
www.gov.nu.ca/hsssite/hssmain.shtml
The Environmental Health Specialist provides recommendations & direction, consultation, development of standards, monitoring,

maintenance & evaluation of all environmental health programs within Nunavut. Reviews the Public Health Act & Regulations & environmental health standards & policies & makes recommendations for revisions. Guides the regional environmental health officers in development & implementation of programs & policies in prevention of diseases caused by environmental factors, including food, water, waste disposal, housing & the sanitation of public places, including schools, day cares & other institutional facilities. Guides the Regional Environmental Health Officers in water & food-borne related illness investigations & food recalls. Guides the regions in the monitoring of drinking water supplies. Assists with development of health education & promotional materials & activities related to environmental health.

Acts Administered:
Boards of Management Dissolution Act
Disease Registries Act
Reportable Diseases Order
Public Health Act
Camp Sanitation Regulations
Communicable Diseases Regulations
General Sanitation Exemption Regulations
General Sanitation Regulations
Meat Inspection Regulations
Public Sewerage Systems Regulations
Public Water Supply Regulations
Tourist Accomodation Health Regulations
Tobacco Control Act
Minister, Hon. Olayuk Akesuk
867-975-5026, Fax: 867-975-5095
Deputy Minister, Alex Campbell
867-975-5702, Fax: 867-975-5705
Chief Medical Officer of Health, Dr. Isaac Sobol
867-975-5744, Fax: 867-975-5755
Acting Executive Director Population Health, Janet Brewster
867-975-5703, Fax: 867-975-8648
Manager Public Health, Kristine Hutchinson
867-975-4813, Fax: 867-975-4830
Environmental Health Consultant, Peter Workman
867-975-5764, Fax: 867-975-5755
Deputy Minister, Koovian Flanagan
867-975-6213, Fax: 867-975-6216
Minister, Hon. Paul Okalik
867-975-5050, Fax: 867-975-5051
Acts Administered:
Engineers, Geologists & Geophysicists Act
Expropriation Act
Land Titles Act
Deputy Minister, Markus Weber
867-975-6180, Fax: 867-975-6195

Northwest Territories & Nunavut Workers Compensation Board

Other Communication: For a detailed listing please see Northwest Territories

Government of Ontario

Seat of Government: Queen's Park
Toronto, ON M7A 1A2
416-326-1234
800-267-8097
TDD: 800-268-7095
www.gov.on.ca
The Province of Ontario entered Confederation July 1, 1867. It has an area of 907,573.82 km2, & the StatsCan census population in 2006 was 12,160,282.
Secretary to the Cabinet & Clerk of the Executive Council, Shelly Jamieson
416-325-7641, Fax: 416-314-8980
shelly.jamieson@ontario.ca
Deputy Minister Policy & Associate Secretary of Cabinet, Giles Gherson
416-325-3759, Fax: 416-325-7631
giles.gherson@ontario.ca
Director Corporate Planning & Services, Kevin Owens
416-212-0786, Fax: 416-325-2388
kevin.owens@ontario.ca
Minister, Hon. Brad Duguid
416-314-8693, Fax: 416-314-2701
bduguid.mpp.co@liberal.ola.org

Ministry of Agriculture, Food & Rural Affairs (OMAF)

1 Stone Rd. West
Guelph, ON N1G 4Y2
519-826-3100
888-466-2372
www.omafra.gov.on.ca
The ministry works in partnership with an industry that employs over 640,000 people & contributes over $25 billion annually to the provincial economy. The ministry plays a key role in bringing a strong agricultural & rural perspective to provincial policies. The ministry works with other ministries to resolve local economic issues & assists rural communities in retaining & attracting business. Staff at the ministry's Guelph headquarters & across the province provide a wide range of agri-food & rural economic development programs & services to clients.

Acts Administered:
Agricorp Act
Agricultural Employees Protection Act 2002
Agricultural & Horticultural Organizations Act
Agricultural Rehabilitation & Development Act (Ontario)
Agricultural Research Institute of Ontario Act
Agricultural Lands Regulations
Agricultural Tile Drainage Installation Act
Animals for Research Act
Beef Cattle Marketing Act
Bees Act
Crop Insurance Act
Dead Animal Disposal Act
Drainage Act
Edible Oil Products Act
Farm Products Container Act
Farm Products Marketing Act
Farm Implements Act
Farm Products Grades & Sales Act
Farm Products Payments Act
Farm Registration & Farm Organizations Funding Act
Farming & Food Production Protection Act
Food Safety & Quality Act, 2001
Grain Corn Marketing Act
Grains Act
Livestock & Livestock Products Act
Livestock Community Sales Act
Livestock Identification Act
Livestock Medicines Act
Livestock, Poultry & Honey Bee Protection Act
Meat Inspection Act (Ontario)
Milk Act
Ministry of Agriculture, Food & Rural Affairs Act
Nutrient Management Act, 2002
Ontario Agricultural Museum Act
Ontario Agricultural Week Act, 1998
Ontario Food Terminal Act
Plant Diseases Act
Pounds Act
Tile Drainage Act
Veterinarians Act
Weed Control Act
Minister, Hon. Leona Dombrowsky
416-326-3074, Fax: 416-326-3083
minister.omafra@ontario.ca
Deputy Minister, Bruce Archibald
416-326-3101,
bruce.archibald@ontario.ca
• **AGRICORP**
1 Stone Rd. West
PO Box 3660 Central
Guelph, ON N1H 8M4
Fax: 519-826-4118
888-247-4999
cac@agricorp.com
CEO, Randy Jackiw
Responsible for delivering government & non-government priority products & services that assist Ontario's agri-food industry in managing risks. Since its inception, AGRICORP has developed a reputation for innovation, excellent customer service & reliable, cost-effective delivery
• **Agricultural Research Institute of Ontario**
1 Stone Rd. West, 2nd Fl. NW
Guelph, ON N1G 4Y2
519-826-4199
Fax: 519-826-4211
Chair, Murray Porteus
The role of ARIO is to enquire into programs of research with respect to agriculture, veterinary medicine & consumer studies, select & recommend areas of research for the betterment of agriculture, veterinary medicine & consumer studies, & stimulate interest in research as a means of developing a high degree of efficiency in the production & marketing of agricultural products in Ontario.
• **Agriculture, Food & Rural Affairs Tribunal**
1 Stone Rd. West, 1st Fl.
Guelph, ON N1G 4Y2
519-826-3433
Fax: 519-826-4232
appeals.tribunal@omafra.gov.on.ca
www.omafra.gov.on.ca/english/index.html
Chair, Rod Stork
• **College of Veterinarians of Ontario**
2106 Gordon St.
Guelph, ON N1L 1G6
519-824-5600
Fax: 519-824-6497
800-424-2856
• **Grain Financial Protection Board**
1 Stone Rd. West
PO Box 3660
Guelph, ON N1H 8M4
519-826-3949
Fax: 519-826-3367
• **Livestock Financial Protection Board**
1 Stone Rd. West, 5th Fl. NW
Guelph, ON N1G 4Y2
519-826-3886
Fax: 519-826-4375
jim.wideman@omaf.gov.on.ca
Administrator/Secretary, Jim Wideman
• **Livestock Medicines Advisory Committee**
1 Stone Rd. West, 3rd Fl. NE
Guelph, ON N1G 4Y2
519-826-4110
Fax: 519-826-3254
Chair, Harold Kloeze
• **Normal Farm Practices Protection Board**
1 Stone Rd. West, 3rd Fl., Northeast
Guelph, ON N1G 4Y2
519-826-3549
Fax: 519-826-6611
www.gov.on.ca/OMAFRA/english/engineer/nfppb/nfppb.htm
Chair, Robert Stephens
• **Ontario Farm Products Marketing Commission**
1 Stone Rd. West, 5th Fl.
Guelph, ON N1G 4Y2
519-826-4220
Fax: 519-826-3400
Chair, Dave Hope
• **Ontario Food Terminal Board**
165 The Queensway
Toronto, ON M8Y 1H8
416-259-5479
Fax: 416-259-4303
www.oftb.com

Food Safety & Environment Division
519-826-4304
Fax: 519-826-4416

Asst. Deputy Minister, Dr. Deb Stark
519-826-4301, Fax: 519-826-4416
deb.stark@ontario.ca

Innovation & Competitiveness Division
Asst. Deputy Minister, Bonnie Winchester
519-826-3528, Fax: 519-826-3259
bonnie.winchester@ontario.ca

Policy & Programs Division
519-826-4020
Fax: 519-826-3492
Responsible for the ministry's policy processes, the administration & delivery of several farm business risk management programs & the management of the ministry's strategic partnership with AGRICORP.
Asst. Deputy Minister, Dave Antle
519-826-4151, Fax: 519-826-3492
dave.antle@ontario.ca
Director Strategic Policy, Phil Malcolmson
416-326-3207,
phil.malcolmson@ontario.ca

Research & Corporate Services Division

Federal/Provincial Government / Government of Ontario

NW
1 Stone Road W., 2nd fl.
Guelph, ON N1G 4Y2
519-826-4551
Fax: 519-826-3390
Asst. Deputy Minister, Karen D. Chan
519-826-6599, Fax: 519-826-3390
karen.chan@ontario.ca

Economic Development Division
1 Stone Road W., 2nd Fl.
Guelph, ON N1G 4Y2
519-826-6636
Fax: 519-826-4328

Environmental Policy & Programs Branch
Director, Charles Lalonde
519-826-3577
Manager Agriculture Land Use, David Cooper
519-826-3117
Acting Manager Engineering & Technology, Finbar Desir
519-826-3549
Acting Manager Environmental Management, Brent Kennedy
519-826-3559

Food Inspection Branch
519-826-4230
Fax: 519-826-4375
The Food Inspection Branch ensures compliance with legislated standards for dairy, dairy analogs, eggs, fruit & vegetables, meat & livestock products, by providing inspection services at processing plants & other points of distribution, & by placing accountability for product safety on licensed operators. It is responsible for establishing standards & coordinating policy development to ensure a coordinated approach with other ministries, to provide a strategic & dynamic food inspection environment in Ontario.
Director, Tom Baker
519-826-4366
Acting Manager Dairy Food Safety Program, Brenda Mitchell
519-826-4378

Food Safety Programs Branch
Director, Gwen McBride
519-826-3112
Manager Enforcement & Compliance, Jim Cushing
519-826-4391
Manager Food Safety Animal Programs, Dawn Pate
519-826-3102
Manager Food Safety Plant Programs, Patricia Johnson
519-826-3667

Deputy Minister's Office
416-326-3104
Fax: 416-326-3106
Other Communication: Guelph Fax: 519/826-4335

Communications Branch
Fax: 519-826-3262

Client Services:
Fax: 519-826-3259
The staff in Client Services co-ordinate the delivery of leading edge technical information & services to a wide variety of clients & stakeholders across the province. Information & services are provided through the Agricultural Information Contact Centre, OMAF website, Resource Centres located across southern Ontario & the Northern Regional Office in Verner, Regional Information Coordinators & Agriculture & Rural Representatives working through partnerships with local stakeholders, agri-business & rural municipalities & businesses & Government Information Centres located in communities across the province.
Director, Michael Toombs
519-826-3781

Fergus
Wellington Pl.
RR#1
Fergus, ON N1M 2W3
519-846-0941
Fax: 519-846-8178

Simcoe
Hwy. 3 & Blueline Rd.
PO Box 587
Simcoe, ON N3Y 4N5
519-426-7120
Fax: 519-428-1142

Vineland
Advisory Services Bldg.
4890 Victoria Ave. North
PO Box 8000
Vineland Station, ON L0R 2E0
905-562-4147
Fax: 905-562-5933

Alfred
Regional OMAFRA Office
31 St. Paul St.
PO Box 430
Alfred, ON K0B 1A0
613-679-4411
Fax: 613-679-0929

Brighton
95 Dundas St., RR#3
Brighton, ON K0K 1H0
613-475-1630
Fax: 613-475-3835

Kemptville
ORC Government Bldg.
PO Box 2004
Kemptville, ON K0G 1J0
613-258-8295
Fax: 613-258-8392

Lindsay
322 Kent St. West
Lindsay, ON K9V 4T7
705-324-6125
Fax: 705-324-1638

Gore Bay
PO Box 328
Gore Bay, ON P0P 1H0
705-282-2043
Fax: 705-282-2792

New Liskeard
280 Armstrong St.
PO Box 4070
New Liskeard, ON P0J 1P0
705-647-6701
Fax: 705-647-7993

Verner
Caldwell Twp. Hall
Hwy. 64
PO Box 521
Verner, ON P0H 2M0
705-594-2312
Fax: 705-594-9675

Clinton
100 Don St.
PO Box 159
Clinton, ON N0M 1L0
519-482-3428
Fax: 519-482-5031

London
667 Exeter Rd.
London, ON N6E 1L3
519-873-4070
Fax: 519-873-4062

Ridgetown
Main St. East
PO Box 400
Ridgetown, ON N0P 2C0
519-674-1690
Fax: 519-674-1564

Stratford
581 Huron St.
Stratford, ON N5A 5T8
519-271-0280
Fax: 519-273-5278

Woodstock
Hwy. 59 North
PO Box 666
Woodstock, ON N4S 7Z5
519-537-6621
Fax: 519-539-5351
800-265-7896

Economic Development
519-826-4080
Fax: 519-826-3259
Economic Development provides support for business initiatives in agriculture & rural business sectors, including general extension programs, marketing, business planning, economic analysis, succession planning & project management for businesses. In addition, this area works with rural communities to increase their capacity to undertake community-based economic development. Key clients include farmers & growers, lenders, accountants, lawyers, rural entrepreneurs, municipalities & economic development officers.
Director, Thom Hagerty
519-826-4533

Crop Technology
Fax: 519-826-3567
The branch assists crop sectors to respond to new & evolving opportunities in the marketplace such as value chains, functional foods, nutraceuticals, bioenergy, biohealth & bioremediation; assesses crop protection issues, supports minor use initiatives & develops programs in integrated pest management, plant health &reduced risk strategies, assists commodity sectors in dealing with regulatory related impacts. It also assesses new &/or evolving crop production & management technologies to improve competitiveness in the domestic & global marketplace; promotes sustainable production & postharvest systems & practices that will ensure safe, high-quality agricultural products for the marketplace as well as assessing & promoting environmentally responsible use of new technologies, nutrients, pesticides & water for crop production & assess impacts & opportunities of climate change.
Director, Bill Ingratta
519-826-3151
Acting Manager Field Crops, John Finlay
519-826-6941
Manager Greenhouse, Agroforestry & Specialty Crops, Annette Anderson
519-826-3286
Acting Manager Horticultural Crops, Kelly Ward
519-826-3257

Food Industry Competitiveness Branch
Fax: 519-826-4333
The Branch supports the food industry by providing a wide range of information services & advice to clients. The branch consists of a Client Account Unit & an Investment Development Unit. Services are provided through a system of client account management whereby individual officers have specific sectoral & client assignments. Specialists in finance, infrastructure, training & research support the client account officers for food industry, value added & rural business development.
Director, Doug Chapman
519-826-4452

Livestock Technology
Fax: 519-826-3254
Responsible for program issues relating to livestock & poultry management. The group promotes high quality livestock production through the use of on-farm quality assurance, production systems, genetics, nutrition & animal health improvement technology programs.
Director, Allen MacNeil
519-826-6588

Rural Secretariat
The Rural Secretariat administers economic development programs, which include the Healthy Futures for Ontario Agriculture program, the Ontario Small Town & Rural Development (OSTAR) Initiative, the Rural Job Strategy Fund & the Rural Youth Jobs Strategy. Healthy Futures for Ontario Agriculture is designed to promote & enhance responsible production processing & distribution systems in the agri-food industry. OSTAR is a program to improve the quality of infrastructure & encourage economic development in Ontario's agricultural & rural areas, small towns & small cities. It provides assistance to municipalities to upgrade water & sewage treatment systems & for other health & safety projects, & for rural economic development initiatives.
Director, Christine Dukelow
519-826-3419

Market Development Branch
519-829-4210
Fax: 519-826-3460
Responsible for the development & expansion of international markets for Ontario agri-food products & for the Foodland On-

tario program, which promotes domestic consumption of Ontario grown fruits & vegetables. The branch consists of two units, the Domestic Marketing Unit & the Export Marketing Unit.
Acting Director, Andy Rankine
519-826-3510

Policy Development
Director, Gwen Zellen
519-826-6800,
Coordinator Food Safety Science, Mike Cassidy
519-826-4106

Financial Management Branch
519-826-4150
Fax: 519-826-3264
Acts Administered:
Assessment Review Board Act
Expropriation Act
Transboundary Pollution Reciprocal Access Act
Deputy Minister, Joan C. Andrew
416-325-6220, Fax: 416-325-6196
joan.andrew@ontario.ca
Acts Administered:
Historical Parks Act
Director Communications, Diane Gumbs
416-314-7606, Fax: 416-314-4965
diane.gumbs@ontario.ca

Ministry of Community Safety & Correctional Services

George Drew Bldg.
25 Grosvenor St., 18th Fl.
Toronto, ON M7A 1Y6
416-326-5000
Fax: 416-325-6067
866-517-0571
TDD: 416-326-5511
jus.g.sgcs.webmaster@jus.gov.on.ca
www.mpss.jus.gov.on.ca
Other Communication: TTY Toll Free: 1-866-517-0572
The Ministry ensures that communities across the province are protected by safe, effective & accountable law enforcement and public safety systems. General responsibilities of the ministry are as follows: correctional services; public safety & security; & policing services.
Acts Administered:
Ammunition Regulation Act, 1994
Anatomy Act
Christopher's Law (Sex Offender Registry), 2000
Coroners Act
Emergency Management Act
Fire Protection & Prevention Act, 1997
Firefighters' Memorial Day Act
Imitation Firearms Regulation Act
Lightning Rod Act
Ministry of Correctional Services Act
Ministry of the Solicitor General Act
Ontario Society for the Prevention of Cruelty to Animals Act
Police Services Act
Private Investigators & Security Guards Act
Public Works Protection Act
Minister, Hon. Rick Bartolucci
416-325-0408, Fax: 416-325-6067
rbartolucci.mpp@liberal.ola.org
Deputy Minister Community Safety, Deborah Newman
416-326-5060, Fax: 416-327-0469
deborah.newman@ontario.ca
• Animal Care Review Board
77 Grenville St., 8th Fl.
Toronto, ON M5S 1B3
416-314-3509
Fax: 416-314-3518
• Fire Safety Commission
Place Nouveau Bldg.
5775 Yonge St., 7th Fl.
Toronto, ON M2M 4J1
416-325-3100
Fax: 416-314-1217
Manager, Krystyna Paterson
• Ontario Civilian Commission on Police Services(OCCPS)
25 Grosvenor St., 1st Fl.
Toronto, ON M7A 1Y6
416-326-1189
Fax: 416-314-2036
888-515-5005
Other Communication: Toll Free Fax: 1-888-311-7555

• Ontario Parole & Earned Release Board
415 Yonge St.
Toronto, ON M5B 2E7
416-325-4480
Fax: 416-325-4485
• Ontario Police Arbitration Commission
George Drew Bldg.
25 Grosvenor St., 1st Fl.
Toronto, ON M7A 1Y6
416-314-3520
Fax: 416-314-3522
www.policearbitration.on.ca

Community Safety
416-314-3000
Fax: 416-314-4037

Emergency Management Ontario
77 Wellesley St. W
PO Box 222
Toronto, ON M7A 1N3
416-314-3723
Fax: 416-314-3758
Chief, Dan Hefkey
416-314-6186, Fax: 416-314-3758
dan.hefkey@ontario.ca
Asst. Chief Provincial Prevention/Mitigation & Preparedness, Maureen Griffiths
416-212-3459,
maureen.griffiths@jus.gov.on.ca
Deputy Chief Program Support, Randy Reid
416-314-8608, Fax: 416-314-3758
randy.r.reid@ontario.ca

Ontario Provincial Police (OPP)
Lincoln M. Alexander Bldg.
777 Memorial Ave.
Orillia, ON L3V 7V3
705-329-6111
888-310-1122
TDD: 888-310-1133
www.opp.ca
Other Communication: Crime Stoppers: 1-800-222-8477

Public Safety Division
George Drew bldg
25 Grosvenor St., 12th fl.
Toronto, ON M7A 2H3
416-314-3000
Fax: 416-314-4037
Asst. Deputy Minister, Glen Murray
416-325-3454, Fax: 416-314-4037
glenn.murray@ontario.ca
Fire Marshal, Patrick R. Burke
416-325-3101, Fax: 416-325-3119
patr.burke@ontario.ca

Corporate Planning & Services Division
George Drew bldg.
25 Grosvenor St., 13th fl.
Toronto, ON M7A 1Y6
416-325-3445
Fax: 416-325-3465

Correctional Services

Justice Technology Services Division
#300, 21 College St
Toronto, ON M5G 2B3
416-326-6950
Fax: 416-326-1104

Adult Community Corrections

Communications Branch
Fax: 416-326-0498

Legal Services Branch

Eastern
4685 Donnelly Dr.
Merrickville, ON K0G 1N0
613-269-2390
Fax: 613-269-2393

Northern
#403, 199 Larch St.
Sudbury, ON P3E 5P9

705-564-4227
Fax: 705-671-2980

Southern
2195 Yonge St., 3rd Fl.
Toronto, ON M4S 2B1
416-325-4487
Fax: 416-325-4491

Western
785 York Rd.
PO Box 1716
Guelph, ON N1H 6Z9
519-837-6320
Fax: 519-837-6324

Ministry of Culture

Mowat Block
900 Bay St., 5th Fl.
Toronto, ON M7A 1L2
416-325-1660
Fax: 416-325-1726
866-454-0049
TDD: 416-325-5170
www.culture.gov.on.ca
The Ministry is responsible for the following: encouraging the arts & cultural industries; protecting the province's heritage; advancing the public library system; implementing strategies to promote cultural & heritage attractions; & working with communities & agencies to preserve Ontario's culture & heritage.
Acts Administered:
AGO Act
Arts Council Act
George R. Gardiner Museum of Ceramic Art Act
Hummingbird Performing Arts Centre Corporation Act
McMichael Canadian Art Collection Act
Metropolitan Toronto Convention Centre Act
Ontario Heritage Act
Public Libraries Act
Royal Ontario Museum Act
Science North Act
Minister, Hon. Aileen M. Carroll
416-325-1600, 866-454-0049, Fax: 416-325-1726
acarroll.mpp.co@liberal.ola.org
TDD: 416-325-5170
Deputy Minister, Marg Rappolt
416-212-0646, Fax: 416-212-0641
marg.rappolt@ontario.ca
Director Culture & Innovation Audit Service Team, Charles Meehan
416-325-5983, Fax: 416-314-3467
charles.meehan@ontario.ca
Parliamentary Assistant, Laura Albanese
416-325-1800, Fax: 416-325-1802
lalbanese.mpp.co@liberal.ola.org
• Art Gallery of Ontario
317 Dundas St. West
Toronto, ON M5T 1G4
416-977-0414
Fax: 416-979-6646
www.ago.net
• Conservation Review Board
400 University Ave. 4th Fl.
Toronto, ON M7A 2R9
416-314-7137
Fax: 416-314-7175
Chair, Peter Zakarow
• McMichael Canadian Art Collection
10365 Islington Ave.
Kleinburg, ON L0J 1C0
905-893-1121
Fax: 905-893-0692
888-213-1121
info@mcmichael.com
www.mcmichael.com/
• Minister's Advisory Council for Arts & Culture
400 University Ave., 5th Fl.
Toronto, ON M7A 2R9
416-314-8321
Fax: 416-314-7091
866-888-5829
www.culture.gov.on.ca./english/about/macac.htm
• Ontario Arts Council
151 Bloor St. West, 5th Fl.
Toronto, ON M5S 1T6

Federal/Provincial Government / Government of Ontario

416-961-1660
Fax: 416-961-7796
www.arts.on.ca
• Ontario Heritage Trust(OHT)
10 Adelaide St. East
Toronto, ON M5C 1J3
416-325-5000
Fax: 416-325-5071
marketing@heritagefdn.on.ca
www.heritagetrust.on.ca; www.doorsopenontario.on.ca
Chair, Hon. Lincoln Alexander
For more than three decades, the Ontario Heritage Trust has preserved, protected & promoted Ontario's rich & varied heritage. The Trust celebrates the people, places & events that have influenced & continue to shape our culture. As Ontario's lead heritage agency, the Trust's work extends to every corner of the province.
• Ontario Library Service - North
334 Regent St.
Sudbury, ON P3C 4E2
705-675-6467
Fax: 705-675-2285
800-461-6348
www.olsn.ca
• Ontario Media Development Corporation(OMDC)
South Tower
#501, 175 Bloor St. East
Toronto, ON M4W 3R8
416-314-6858
Fax: 416-314-6876
mail@omdc.on.ca
www.omdc.on.ca
• Ontario Science Centre
770 Don Mills Rd.
Toronto, ON M3C 1T3
416-696-1000
Fax: 416-696-3124
www.OntarioScienceCentre.ca
• Ontario Trillium Foundation
45 Charles St. East, 5th Fl.
Toronto, ON M4Y 1S2
416-963-4927
Fax: 416-963-8781
800-263-2887
trillium@trilliumfoundation.org
www.trilliumfoundation.org
CEO, Robin Cardozo
The Ontario Trillium Foundation is an agency of the Ministry of Culture. Grants are provided to eligible not-for-profit & charitable organizations in the areas of arts & culture, sports and recreation, human & social services, & the environment.
• Royal Botanical Gardens
680 Plains Rd. West
Burlington, ON L7T 4H4
905-527-1158
Fax: 905-577-0375
800-694-4769
www.rbg.ca
Chair, Terry Yates
• Royal Ontario Museum(ROM)
100 Queen's Park Cres.
Toronto, ON M5S 2C6
416-586-5549
Fax: 416-586-5685
info@rom.on.ca
www.rom.on.ca/
• Science North
100 Ramsey Lake Rd.
Sudbury, ON P3E 5S9
705-522-3701
Fax: 705-522-4954
800 461 4808
www.sciencenorth.ca
• Southern Ontario Library Service
#902, 111 Peter St.
Toronto, ON M5V 2H1
416-961-1669
Fax: 416-961-5122
800-387-5765

Culture Policy, Programs & Services Division
400 University Ave., 5th Fl.
Toronto, ON M7A 2R9
416-314-7265
Fax: 416-314-7461

Office of the Chief Information Officer & Community Services I&IT Cluster
Mowat Block
900 Bay St., 3rd Fl.
Toronto, ON M7A 1L2
Corporate Chief Information, Information Technology Officer & Chief Strategist, Service Delivery, Ron McKerlie
416-327-9696, Fax: 416-327-3264
ron.mckerlie@ontario.ca
Director Technology & Business Solutions, Tricia Ireland
416-314-4954, Fax: 416-325-6388
Tricia.Ireland@ontario.ca
Director IT Negotiations & Coordination, Rick Morasch
416-326-9571, Fax: 416-325-2262
Rick.Morasch@ontario.ca

Regional & Corporate Services Division
400 University Ave., 2nd Fl.
Toronto, ON M7A 2R9
416-314-7311
Fax: 416-314-7313

Regional Offices:

Central
180 Dundas St. West, 5th Fl.
Toronto, ON M7A 2R9
416-314-6044
Fax: 416-314-2024
877-395-4105

Northern
#334, 435 James St. South
Thunder Bay, ON P7E 6S7
807-475-1683
Fax: 807-475-1297
800-465-6861

Southeast
347 Preston St., 4th Fl.
Ottawa, ON K1S 3J4
613-742-3360
Fax: 613-742-5300
800-267-9340

Southwest
#405, 30 Duke St. West
Kitchener, ON N2H 3W5
Fax: 519-578-1632
800-265-2189

Ministry of Economic Development & Trade
Hearst Block
900 Bay St., 8th Fl.
Toronto, ON M7A 2E1
416-325-6666
Fax: 416-325-6688
866-668-4249
TDD: 416-325-4402
info@edt.gov.on.ca
www.ontariocanada.com
Promotes economic development & job creation in Ontario by creating a climate for business to prosper & eliminate red tape as well as stimulating trade. This Ministry markets the province as a desirable place to live, work, invest & raise a family. It works with its private sector partners to ensure that its core responsibilities of employment & business development, investment & trade continue to help Ontario businesses compete globally; contribute to a highly-skilled, well-educated workforce; & generate prosperity for all Ontarians. In Northern Ontario, the Ministry is represented by the Northern Development Division of the Ministry of Northern Development & Mines.
Acts Administered:
Development Corporations Act
Idea Corporation Act
Ministry of Industry, Trade & Technology Act
Research Foundation Act
Telephone Act
Minister, Hon. Sandra Pupatello
416-325-6900, Fax: 416-325-6918
spupatello.mpp@liberal.ola.org
Deputy Minister, Wendy Tilford
416-325-6927,
wendy.tilford@ontario.ca

Industry Division

Hearst Block
900 Bay St., 7th fl.
Toronto, ON M7A 2E1
416-325-6964
Fax: 416-325-2102
Director Automotive Strategy Branch, Ken Albright
416-314-2126, Fax: 416-325-2102
ken.albright@ontario.ca
Director Trade & International Policy, Katherine McGuire
416-325-6930, Fax: 416-325-6949
katherine.mcguire@ontario.ca

Investment & Trade Division
Hearst Block
900 Bay St., 5th fl.
Toronto, ON M7A 2E1
416-325-9802
Fax: 416-325-5617
Asst. Deputy Minister, William Forward
416-325-9801, Fax: 416-325-5617
william.forward@ontario.ca
Director Investment Branch, John Langley
416-325-6758, Fax: 416-325-6799
john.langley@ontario.ca

Ministry of Energy and Infrastructure
Hearst Block
900 Bay St., 4th Fl.
Toronto, ON M7A 2E1
416-327-6758
Fax: 416-327-6754
888-668-4636
TDD: 800-239-4224
www.mei.gov.on.ca
The Ministry of Energy's responsibility is to ensure that Ontario's electricity system functions at the highest level of reliability & productivity. The electricity system lies at the heart of the economy & way of life & by ensuring the system remains reliable, efficient & secure, the ministry is making sure Ontario remains one of the best places in the world in which to live, work, invest & raise a family. The Ministry of Energy is also focused on promoting ingenuity & innovation in the energy sector. By encouraging the development of new ideas & technologies it is helping to make Ontario a world leader in the global energy market. Protecting the environment is also a top priority for the Ministry. Developing renewable sources of energy, cleaner forms of fuel, as well as fostering a conservation culture, are all cornerstones of the Ministry's vision for Ontario's electricity future.
Acts Administered:
Energy Efficiency Act
Hydro One Directors & Officers Act, 2002
Ministry of Energy Act
Ontario Energy Board Act
Power Corporation Act
Toronto District Heating Corporation Act
Minister, Hon. Brad Duguid
416-327-6758, Fax: 416-327-6754
bduguid.mpp@liberal.ola.org
Deputy Minister, Fareed Amin
416-327-6734,
Fareed.Amin@ontario.ca
• Hydro One
• Independent Electricity System Operator
• Ontario Energy Board
#2700, 2300 Yonge St.
Toronto, ON M4P 1E4
416-481-1967
Fax: 416-440-7656
888-632-6273
www.oeb.gov.on.ca
Chair, Howard Wetston, Q.C.
• Ontario Power Authority
#1600, 120 Adelaide St. West
Toronto, ON M5H 1T1
416-967-7474
Fax: 416-967-1947
info@powerauthority.on.ca
www.powerauthority.on.ca
Chief Energy Conservation Officer, Peter Love
• Ontario Power Generation

Office of Conservation & Strategic Policy
416-314-6246
Fax: 416-325-3438

Provides strategic policy coordination & development for the ministry as well as policy analysis & advice related to energy conservation & efficiency, demand management, & conservation.
Asst. Deputy Minister, Tony Rockingham
416-327-8552, Fax: 416-325-3438
tony.rockingham@ontario.ca

Conservation Branch
The branch provides analysis, advice & policy development on issues relating to energy efficiency, demand management & conservation as well as administering the Energy Efficiency Act.
Manager, Robert Stasko
416-325-6540
Secretary, Maureen Holland
416-325-6552

Office of Consumer & Regulatory Affairs
416-325-6559
Fax: 416-325-7041
Asst. Deputy Minister, Rosalyn Lawrence
416-325-6544, Fax: 416-325-7041
rosalyn.lawrence@ontario.ca
Policy Analyst Transmission & Distribution, Dmitry Balashov
416-325-6728, Fax: 416-325-7041
dmitry.balashov@ontario.ca
Senior Policy Advisor, John Lang
416-325-6810, Fax: 416-325-7041
john.lang@ontario.ca
Senior Advisor Electricity Planning, John Savage
416-325-6763, Fax: 416-325-7041
john.savage@ontario.ca
Senior Advisor Gas Distribution, Helmuth Schumann
416-325-6887, Fax: 416-325-7041
helmuth.schumann@ontario.ca
Advisor Natural Gas, Sing-Gin Louie
416-325-6836, Fax: 416-325-7041
sing-gin.louie@ontario.ca

Office of Corporate Services
416-327-7106
Fax: 416-314-3354
Provides a structure to identify strategic issues, to coordinate policy & program development; & to coordinate & integrate action by the Ministry & other governments.
Asst. Deputy Minister, Jeanette Dias D'Souza
416-327-3682, Fax: 416-314-3354
jeanette.diasdsouza@ontario.ca

Office of Energy Supply
416-327-7353
Fax: 416-314-6224
Asst. Deputy Minister, Rick Jennings
416-314-6190, Fax: 416-314-6224
rick.jennings@ontario.ca
Director Energy Supply & Competition, Garry McKeever
416-325-8627, Fax: 416-325-7023
garry.mckeever@ontario.ca
Manager Energy Economics, Tom Chapman
416-325-6869, Fax: 416-325-7023
tom.c.chapman@ontario.ca

Ministry of Environment (MOE)
135 St. Clair Ave. West
Toronto, ON M4V 1P5
416-325-4000
Fax: 416-325-3159
800-565-4923
TDD: 800-515-2759
www.ene.gov.on.ca
Other Communication: Pollution Hotline: 1-866-MOE-TIPS(1-866-663-8477); Spills or Emergencies: 1-800-268-6060; Public Information: 1-800-565-4923
The ministry is responsible for protecting clean & safe air, land & water to ensure healthy communities, ecological protection & sustainable development for present & future generations of Ontarians. Using stringent regulations, targeted enforcement & a variety of innovative programs & initiatives, the ministry continues to address environmental issues that have local, regional &/or global effects. The ministry has built a strong foundation of clear laws, stringent regulations, tough standards & rigorous permits & approvals. The ministry monitors pollution & restoration trends in an effort to determine the effectiveness of its activities & to assess risks to human health & the environment. This information is used to develop & implement environmental legislation, regulations, standards, policies, guidelines & programs to enhance environmental protection.

Acts Administered:
Adams Mine Lake Act, 2004
Environmental Assessment Act
Designations & Exemptions
Electricity Projects Regulation
Environmental Assessment General Regulations
Environmental Bill of Rights Act
Environmental Protection Act
Air Contaminants from Ferrous Foundries Regulation
Air Pollution - Local Quality Regulations
Airborne Contaminant Discharge Monitoring & Reporting Regulations
Ambient Air Quality Criteria Regulations
Boilers Regulation
Certificates of Approval Exemptions Air Regulation
Classes of Contaminants Exemption Regulations
Classification & Exemption of Spills Regulations
Containers Regulation
Deep Well Disposal Regulation
Designation of Waste Regulation
Discharge of Sewage from Pleasure Boats Regulation
Disposable Containers for Milk Regulations
Disposable Paper Containers for Milk Regulations
Dry Cleaners Regulations
Effluent Monitoring & Effluent Limits Regulations (organic chemicals, inorganic chemicals, iron & steel manufacturers, electric power generation, petroleum sector, metal mining sector, industrial mine
Emissions Trading Regulation
Ethanol in Gasoline
Exemption Regulations
Gasoline Volatility Regulation
General Waste Management Regulation
Ground Source Heat Pumps Regulation
Halon Fire Extinguishing Equipment Regulation
Hot Mix Asphalt Facilities Regulation
Industrial, Commercial & Institutional Source Separation Programs Regulation
Industry Emissions - Nitrogen Oxides & Sulphur Dioxide
Lakeview Generating Station Regulations
Lambton Industry Meteorology Alert Regulation
Land Disposal Restrictions
Landfilling Sites Regulation
Marinas Regulation
Mobil PCB Destruction Facilities Regulation
Motor Vehicles Regulation
Municipal Sewage & Water & Roads Class Environmental Assessment Project Regulation
Municipalities, Secured Creditors, Receivers, Trustees in Bankruptcy & Fiduciaries, Pt.XV.2 of the Act Regulations, 2002
Ontario Power Generation Regulations
Ozone Depleting Substances Regulation
Packaging Audits & Packaging Reduction Work Plans Regulation
Records of Site Condition, Pt.XV.1 of the Act Regulations, 2004
Recovery of Gasoline Vapour in Bulk Transfers Regulation
Recycling & Composting of Municipal Waste Regulation
Refillable Containers for Carbonated Soft Drink Regulation
Refrigerants Regulation
Reporting Requirements, Sulphur Levels in Gasoline Regulations
Sewage System Regulations & Exemptions
Solvents Regulation
Spills Regulation
Sterilants Regulation
Sulphur Content of Fuels Regulation
Transitional Provisions Relating to the Repeal of Pt.VIII of the Act Regulations
Waste Audits & Waste Reduction Workplans Regulation
Waste Disposal Sites & Waste Management Systems Subject to Approval under the Environmental Assessment Act Regulations
Waste Management (PCBs) Regulation
Environmental Review Tribunal, 2000
Ministry of the Environment Act
Ontario Water Resources Act
Additional Charges Regulation
Licensing of Sewage Works Operators Regulations
Municipal Sewage & Water & Roads Class Environmental Assessment Projects Regulation
Secured Creditors, Receivers, Trustees in Bankruptcy Regulations, 2002
Sewage Works Subject to Approval under the Environmental Assessment Act Regulations
Transitional Provisions Relating to the Repeal of Pt.VIII of the Environmental Protection Act Regulations
Water Taking & Transfer Regulation
Wells Regulation
Pesticides Act
Safe Drinking Water Act, 2002
Certification of Drinking-Water System Operators & Water Quality Analysts
Compliance & Enforcement
Definitions of \Deficiency\" & \"Municipal Drinking-Water System\" Regulations
Definitions of Words & Expressions Used the Act Regulations, 2003
Drinking-Water Systems Regulations, 2003
Drinking-Water Testing Services Regulations, 2003
Non-Residential & Non-Municipal Seasonal Residential Systems that do not Service Designated Facilities
Ontario Drinking-Water Quality Standards Regulations, 2003
Schools, Private Schools & Day Nurseries Regulations, 2003
Sustainable Water & Sewage Systems Act, 2002
Waste Diversion Act, 2002
Blue Box Waste Regulations, 2002
Used Oil Material Regulations, 2003
Used Tires Regulations, 2003
Waste Electrical & Electronic Equipment
Waste Management Act
Minister, Hon. John Gerretsen
416-314-6790, Fax: 416-314-7337
jgerretsen.mpp.co@liberal.ola.org
Deputy Minister, Gail Beggs
416-314-6753, Fax: 416-314-6791
Director Communications Branch, Garth Cramer
416-314-6677, Fax: 416-314-6711
Garth.Cramer@ontario.ca
• Office of Consolidated Hearings
#1700, 2300 Yonge St.
Toronto, ON M4P 1E4
416-314-4600
Fax: 416-314-4506
• Advisory Council on Drinking Water Quality & Testing Standards
40 St. Clair Ave. West, 3rd Fl.
Toronto, ON M4V 1M2
416-212-7779
Fax: 416-212-7595
Chair, Jim Merritt
• Environmental Review Tribunal
#1700, 2300 Yonge St.
PO Box 2382
Toronto, ON M4P 1E4
416-314-4600
Fax: 416-314-4506
www.ert.gov.on.ca
Chair, Toby Vigod
The Environmental Review Tribunal's primary role is adjudicating applications & appeals under various environmental & planning statutes. The Tribunal hears applications & appeals under the Environmental Assessment Act, the Environmental Protection Act, the Ontario Water Resources Act, & the Pesticides Act, & leave to appeal applications under the Environmental Bill of Rights, 1993. The Environmental Review Tribunal also functions as the Office of Consolidated Hearings to hear applications made under the Consolidated Hearings Act & as the Niagara Escarpment Hearing Office to hear development permit appeals & Niagara Escarpment Plan amendment applications under the Niagara Escarpment Planning & Development Act.
• Ontario Clean Water Agency(OCWA)
1 Yonge St., 17th Fl.
Toronto, ON M5E 1E5
416-314-5600
Fax: 416-314-8300
800-667-6292
www.ocwa.com
President/CEO, Dante Pontone
The Ontario Clean Water Agency (OCWA) was established as a Provincial Crown Agency in November 1993 & is committed to providing safe & reliable clean water services. The Agency is an established leader in the operation, maintenance & management of water & wastewater treatment facilities & their associated distribution & collection systems. OCWA operates hundreds of water & wastewater facilities, ranging in size from small wells & pumping stations to large-scale urban water & wastewater systems.

Federal/Provincial Government / Government of Ontario

- Pesticides Advisory Committee
#1203, 2300 Yonge St., 12th Fl.
Toronto, ON M4P 1E4
416-314-9230
Fax: 416-314-9237
www.opac.gov.on.ca
Chair, Dr. C.M. Switzer
This committee advises the Minister of the Environment on matters pertaining to pesticides. It annually reviews the Pesticides Act & regulations, & government publications respecting pesticides & control of pests. The committee also recommends classifications for all new pesticide products prior to their marketing & use in Ontario, & publishes an annual report, which is available upon request. For other ministry publications on pests & pest control & information on pesticide licensing, contact the Standards Development Branch, Pesticides Section.

- Walkerton Clean Water Centre
PO Box 160
Walkerton, ON N0G 2V0
519-881-2003
Fax: 519-881-4947
inquiry@wcwc.ca
www.wcwc.ca
CEO, Dr. Saad Jasim
The vision of the Walkerton Clean Water Centre is to create a world-class intitute dedicated to safe & secure drinking water for the people of Ontario. Established by Ontario Regulation 304/04 as a crown agency of the Ministry of the Environment in October 2004, & governed by a 12-member board of directors, the Centre's work will complement & support that of the Ministry with a focus on ensuring that training, education & information is available & accessible to owners, operators & operating authorities of Ontario's drinking water systems, particularly in rural & remote communities.

Deputy Minister's Office
416-314-6753
Fax: 416-314-6791
Deputy Minister, Paavo Kivisto

Environmental Bill of Rights Office
40 St. Clair Ave. West, 14th Fl.
Toronto, ON M4V 1M2
416-314-0197
Fax: 416-314-6872
Ensures the Ministry's compliance with the legal requirements of the Environmental Bill of Rights & manages & operates, on behalf of government, the Environmental Registry, which ensures the public's right to participate in government decision making.

Legal Services Branch
416-314-6569
Fax: 416-314-6579
Counsels the ministry on the interpretation of statutes & regulations & the preparation & review of proposed legislation, regulations & other legal documents. Branch lawyers conduct prosecutions under provincial environmental legislation, act as counsel at environmental hearings, represent the ministry before the National Energy Board & other tribunals & provides solicitors' services, including drafting contracts & setting of claims. The branch is part of the Ministry of the Attorney General.
Director, Rand Roszell
416-212-0853

Deputy Minister's Office
Fax: 416-314-6791

Corporate Management Division
416-314-6426
Fax: 416-314-6425
Asst. Deputy Minister, Debra Sikora
416-314-6424, Fax: 416-314-6425
debra.sikora@ontario.ca
Director Business & Fiscal Planning, Rob W. Campbell
416-314-7370, Fax: 416-314-7858
rob.w.campbell@ontario.ca
Director Information Management & Access Branch, Jim Lewis
416-314-3856, Fax: 416-314-6872
jim.d.lewis@ontario.ca
Director Human Resources Branch, Jacques LeGris
416-314-9305, Fax: 416-314-9313
jacques.legris@ontario.ca

Business & Fiscal Planning Branch
40 St. Clair Ave. West, 8th Fl.
Toronto, ON M4V 1M2

416-314-7360
Fax: 416-314-7858

Human Resources Branch
416-314-9300
Fax: 416-314-9313

Drinking Water Management Division

Drive Clean Office
40 St. Clair Ave. West, 4th Fl.
Toronto, ON M4V 1M2
416-314-5856
Fax: 416-314-4160
800-758-2999
www.driveclean.com
The Drive Clean Office is responsible for the development, implementation & administration of Drive Clean, Ontario's motor vehicle emission inspection & maintenance program for passenger & heavy duty vehicles. The Drive Clean Office has implemented the program through a number of contracts with private sector companies & facilities to carry out emission tests &/or repairs. The office also works closely with the Sector Compliance Branch, Investigations & Enforcement Branch & the Ministry of Transportation.
Director, Michael Burger
416-314-3920,
michael.burger@ontario.ca

Environmental Monitoring & Reporting Branch
West Wing
125 Resources Rd.
Toronto, ON M9P 3V6
416-235-6300
Fax: 416-235-6235
The Environmental Monitoring and Reporting Branch delivers a comprehensive framework of programs to monitor, assess and report on the quality of the natural environment in support of the ministry's mandate to safeguard healthy ecosystems and human health.
Director, John Mayes
416-235-6160,
john.mayes@ontario.ca
Manager Air Monitoring, Gary DeBrou
416-235-6157, Fax: 416-235-6037
gary.debrou@ontario.ca
Manager Water Monitoring, Wolfgang Scheider
416-235-5701,
wolfgang.scheider@ontario.ca
Manager Biomonitoring & Dorset Environmental Science Centre Section, Wolfgang Scheider
705-766-2418,
wolfgang.scheider@ontario.ca
Manager Hazardous Waste Information Systems, Anna Gortva
416-235-6264, Fax: 416-235-5818
anna.gortva@ontario.ca
Manager Business Monitoring and Reporting, Cynthia Carr
416-235-6262,
cynthia.carr@ontario.ca
Issues Management Coordinator, Stephanie DeSousa
416-235-5768,
stephanie.desousa@ontario.ca

Environmental Innovations & Emerging Sciences Branch
40 St. Clair Ave. West, 14th Fl.
Toronto, ON M4V 1M2
416-314-0713
Fax: 416-314-0251
The Environmental Innovations and Emerging Sciences Branch (EIESB) promotes innovation within the Ministry by bringing together expertise in environmental management, best practices and environmental sciences.
Director, Anne Buntic
416-314-5888,
Anne.Buntic@ontario.ca
Management Support Coordinator, Fil Aguiar
416-327-1488,
Fil.Aguiar@ontario.ca
Administrative Assistant, Sue Yuen
416-314-0713,
Sue.Yuen@ontario.ca

Laboratory Services Branch
125 Resources Rd.
Toronto, ON M9P 3V6
416-235-5743
Fax: 416-235-5744

Provides analytical support for the ministry's environmental monitoring & regulatory programs. It provides analytical method development, supports standard setting & ensures the data quality of ministry compliance, enforcement & emergency analytical testing.
Director, Dr. P.K. Misra
416-235-5747,
pk.misra@ontario.ca

Standards Development Branch
40 St. Clair Ave. West, 7th Fl.
Toronto, ON M4V 1M2
416-327-5519
Responsible for developing & promulgating environmental standards to protect both human & ecosystem health & the quality of the natural environment; providing toxicological advice & diagnostic services on environmental contaminants & pesticides; assessing the performance of new & emerging environmental technologies & promoting technology transfer; administering the Pesticides Act & providing direction on the responsible use of pesticides in Ontario.
Director, Dale Henry
416-327-5543, Fax: 416-327-2936
dale.henry@ontario.ca

Workforce Planning Office
40 St. Clair Ave. West, 2nd Fl.
Toronto, ON M4V 1M2
Manager, Heather Duncan
416-314-1302

Drinking Water Management Division
416-314-4475
Fax: 416-314-6935
The Drinking Water Management Division, led by the Chief Drinking Water Inspector, has lead responsibility for program & operational activities related to the protection & provision of safe drinking water in Ontario.
Asst. Deputy Minister & Inspector, Keith West
416-314-4463, Fax: 416-314-6935
keith.west@ontario.ca

Drinking Water Program Management Branch
Conducts program analysis to support policy development & the division's compliance program.
Director, Ian Smith
416-212-6459, Fax: 416-212-2757

Education & Outreach Branch
The Education & Outreach Branch works with its partners across the ministry on a broad range of drinking water-related activities, including: the coordination of outreach activities, managing stakeholder relations, facilitating internal communications, staff training & client services & managing the Operator Certification & Training program. It also provides project management support & business services to the division.
Director, Mary Anne Covelli
416-314-1501

Safe Drinking Water Branch
Responsible for drinking water compliance & delivery of the drinking water approvals & licensing program. The branch is also responsible for responding to & resolving adverse water quality incidents through its 21 field offices.
Director, Ed Gill
416-314-1977

Environmental Sciences & Standards Division
416-314-6357
Fax: 416-314-6358
The Environmental Sciences & Standards Division (ESSD) provides the best available science & technology to support decisions about the natural environment, & implements those decisions by developing & managing programs & partnerships, setting scientifically credible standards, monitoring the environment & providing valuable analytical & scientific expertise. Programs such as Drive Clean, that improve the environment & increase public awareness, are central to the ministry's efforts to strengthen environmental protection.
Asst. Deputy Minister, Carl Griffith
416-314-6310, Fax: 416-314-6358
carl.griffith@ontario.ca

Air Policy & Climate Change Branch
416-314-4148
Fax: 416-314-4128

Federal/Provincial Government / Government of Ontario

Land Use Policy Branch
416-325-4440
Fax: 416-326-0461

Strategic Policy Branch
416-314-3372
Fax: 416-314-2976
The Strategic Policy Branch provides the central strategic policy function for the ministry, including central cabinet liaison responsibilities. The branch's role is to provide integrated strategic policy capacity by forecasting the longer range strategic direction for the ministry. The branch looks at long range ministry issues & concepts to inform the development of sound public policy, & effectively integrates ministry policy development from among the core functional areas (air, climate change, waste, water & land) to ensure consistency with the government's priorities.
Director, Adrienne Scott
416-325-8726

Waste Management Policy Branch
416-325-4440
Fax: 416-325-4437

Water Policy Branch
135 St. Clair Ave. West, 5th Fl.
Toronto, ON M4V 1P5
416-314-4140
Fax: 416-314-3918

Environmental Assessment & Approvals Branch
2 St. Clair Ave. West, 12th Fl.
Toronto, ON M4V 1L5
416-314-8001
Fax: 416-314-8452
800-461-6290
Provides one-window service for regulatory environmental approvals in Ontario. The branch administers Ontario's Environmental Assessment Act, which applies to the planning of public sector projects & certain types of private sector projects. The Minister of the Environment is required to make decisions on the following types of submissions: individual environmental assessments, class environmental assessments, requests for exemption & review of each of the above submissions to inform & advise decision-makers, proponents (those proposing an undertaking) & the public, as necessary. The branch also reviews & approves technical applications under the Ontario Water Resources Act & Environmental Protection Act for new or modified waste, wastewater & sewage facilities, or facilities which may emit a contaminant, including noise, to the air; monitors, through an audit & acknowledgement process, compliance with soil & groundwater remediation requirements under the Brownfields Act; & administers the Pesticides Act, inc
Director, James O'Mara
416-314-7288,
james.o'mara@ene.gov.on.ca

Sector Compliance
#1003, 305 Milner Ave.
Toronto, ON M1B 3V4
416-314-4278
Fax: 416-314-4464
The Sector Compliance Branch (formerly called the Environmental SWAT Team) conducts province-wide inspection sweeps of entire sectors. This branch is dedicated to getting tough on polluters & increasing the number of companies & individuals who comply.
Director, Agatha Garcia-Wright
416-314-4241

Investigations & Enforcement Branch
5775 Yonge St., 8th Fl.
Toronto, ON M2M 4J1
416-326-6700
Fax: 416-326-5276
Responsible for all aspects of environmental enforcement within the ministry. This includes enforcement of the Environmental Protection Act, Ontario Water Resources Act, Environmental Assessment Act, Niagara Escarpment Planning Act & Pesticides Act. The branch complements the abatement & control activities of the Regional Operations Division through effective investigation & enforcement activity.
Director, Greg Sones
416-326-3444

Cornwall Area
113 Amelia St., 2nd Fl.
Cornwall, ON K6H 3P1
613-933-7402
Fax: 613-933-6402

Spills Action Centre
5775 Yonge St., 5th Fl.
Toronto, ON M2M 4J1
416-325-3000
Fax: 416-325-3011
800-268-6060
www.ene.gov.on.ca/en/emergency/actioncenter.php
Receives & initiates response to notification of spills & other urgent environmental matters on a 24-hour basis.
Senior Manager, Janet Woelfle
416-314-6370,
jan.woelfle@ontario.ca

Halton-Peel
#300, 4145 North Service Rd.
Burlington, ON L7L 6A3
905-319-3847
Fax: 905-319-9902
800-335-5906
District Manager, J. Budz
905-319-1389

Toronto
5775 Yonge St., 8th Fl.
Toronto, ON M2M 4J1
416-326-6700
Fax: 416-325-6345
Area Supervisor, Dick Worthington
416-326-5603

York-Durham
230 Westney Rd. South, 5th Fl.
Ajax, ON L1S 7J5
905-427-5600
Fax: 905-427-5602
800-376-4547
District Manager, Dave Fumerton
905-427-5626

Belleville Area
Belleville Mall
470 Dundas St. East
Belleville, ON K8N 1G1
613-962-9208
Fax: 613-962-6809
800-860-2763

Cornwall Area
113 Amelia St., 1st Fl.
Cornwall, ON K6H 3P1
800-860-2760
Acting Supervisor, John Romard

Kingston
133 Dalton Ave.
PO Box 820
Kingston, ON K7L 4X6
800-267-0974
ActingDistrict Manager, John Allen

Ottawa
2435 Holly Lane
Ottawa, ON K1V 7P2
613-521-3450
Fax: 613-521-5437
800-558-0595

Peterborough
Robinson Place, South Tower
300 Water St., 2nd Fl.
Peterborough, ON K9J 8M5
705-755-4300
Fax: 705-755-4321

Sudbury
#1101, 199 Larch St.
Sudbury, ON P3E 5P9
705-564-3237
Fax: 705-564-4180
800-890-8516
Area Supervisor, Tom Brown
705-564-3214

Thunder Bay
#331, 435 James St. South
Thunder Bay, ON P7E 6S7
807-475-1315
Fax: 807-475-1754
800-875-7772
District Manager, Arnie Laine
807-475-1690

Timmins
Government Complex
Hwy. 101 East, PO Bag 3080
South Porcupine, ON P0N 1H0
705-235-1500
Fax: 705-235-1520
800-380-6615
District Manager, Dennis Durocher
705-235-1505

Barrie
#1203, 54 Cedar Pointe Dr.
Barrie, ON L4N 5R7
705-739-6441
Fax: 705-739-6440
800-890-8511
District Manager, Phil Bye
705-739-6436

London
733 Exeter Rd.
London, ON N6E 1L3
519-873-5000
Fax: 519-873-5020
800-265-7672

District Manager, Lee Orphan
519-873-5031

Owen Sound
1580 - 20 St. East
Owen Sound, ON N4K 6H6
519-371-2901
Fax: 519-371-2905
800-265-3783
Acting District Supervisor, Phil Bye
519-381-6022

Sarnia
1094 London Rd.
Sarnia, ON N7S 1P1
519-336-4030
Fax: 519-336-4280
800-387-7784
District Manager, Mike Moroney
519-383-3780

Windsor
#620, 4510 Rhodes Dr.
Windsor, ON N8W 5K5
519-948-1464
Fax: 519-948-2396
800-387-8826
Area Supervisor, Kim Ferguson
519-254-7098

Guelph
1 Stone Rd. West, 4th Fl.
Guelph, ON N1G 4Y2
519-826-4255
Fax: 519-826-4286
800-265-8658
District Manager, Dolly Goyette
519-826-4258

Hamilton
Ellen Fairclough Bldg.
119 King St. West, 9th Fl.
Hamilton, ON L8P 4Y7
905-521-7640
Fax: 905-521-7820
800-668-4557
Acting District Manager, Mark Dunn
905-521-7642

Niagara
#15, 301 St. Paul St., 9th Fl.
St Catharines, ON L2R 3M8
905-704-3910
Fax: 905-704-4015
800-263-1035
District Manager, Rich Vickers
905-704-3904

Federal/Provincial Government / Government of Ontario

Integrated Environmental Planning Division
416-314-6338
Fax: 416-314-6346
Integrated Environmental Planning Division is responsible for integrating the overall policy development & planning functions of the Ministry. This involves integrating & synthesizing all information, data & perspectives on the many aspects of the Ministry's mandate. The division consults extensively on developing policies, strategies & programs that support the Ministry's core business of conservation & environmental protection.
Asst. Deputy Minister, John Lieou
416-314-6352, Fax: 416-314-6346
john.lieou@ontario.ca
Director Land & Water Policy, Sharon Bailey
416-314-7020, Fax: 416-314-7200
sharon.bailey@ontario.ca
Director Transformation Office, Vacant
416-325-8785

Operations Division
416-314-6378
Fax: 416-314-6396
The Operations Division is the operations & program delivery arm of the ministry. It is responsible for delivering programs to protect air quality, to protect surface & ground water quality & quantity, to ensure appropriate management of wastes, to ensure an adequate quality of drinking water & to control the use of pesticides. In addition, the division is responsible for administering the ministry's approvals & licensing programs as well as an investigative & enforcement program to ensure compliance with environmental laws. The division has a province-wide network of regional, district & area offices.
Asst. Deputy Minister, Michael Williams
416-314-6366, Fax: 416-314-6396
michael.williams@ontario.ca

Environmental Commissioner of Ontario (ECO)
#605, 1075 Bay St.
Toronto, ON M5S 2B1
416-325-3377
Fax: 416-325-3370
800-701-6454
commissioner@eco.on.ca
www.eco.on.ca
An independent officer of the Legislative Assembly of Ontario, the Environmental Commissioner of Ontario promotes the values, goals & purposes of the Environmental Bill of Rights (EBR) to improve the quality of Ontario's natural environment. The ECO monitors & reports on the application of the EBR, provides public education to facilitate Ontario residents' participation in the EBR & reviews government accountability for environmental decision-making.
Commissioner, Gord Miller
416-325-3377, Fax: 416-325-3370
commissioner@eco.on.ca
In-House Counsel/Senior Policy Advisor, David McRobert
416-325-3376, Fax: 416-325-3370
david.mcrobert@eco.on.ca
Senior Policy Advisor, Ellen Schwartzel
416-325-0559, Fax: 416-325-3370
ellen.schwartzel@eco.on.ca
Senior Policy Advisor, Dennis Draper
416-325-0530, Fax: 416-325-3370
dennis.draper@eco.on.ca

Ministry of Government Services (MGS)
Whitney Block
#4320, 99 Wellesley St. West, 4th Fl.
Toronto, ON M7A 1W3
416-326-1234
Fax: 416-327-3790
800-268-1142
TDD: 416-326-8566
www.mgs.gov.on.ca
Other Communication: Consumer Protection, Phone:
416-326-8800; Toll Free: 1-800-889-9768
MGS is responsible for the delivery of government services, the government workforce, procurement & technology resources. The ministry is engaged in the following main activities: providing government information to individuals & businesses, including distribution through Publications Ontario; protecting consumers through information about frauds & scams & mediating complaints about businesses; & issuing birth, death & marriage certificates, & managing Land Registry Offices throughout the province.

Acts Administered:
Alcohol & Gaming Regulation & Public Protection Act
Apportionment Act
Archives Act
Assignments & Preferences Act
Bailiffs Act
Boundaries Act
Bread Sales Act
Business Corporations Act
Business Names Act
Business Practices Act
Business Regulation Reform Act
Cemeteries Act
Certification of Titles Act
Change of Name Act
Collection Agencies Act
Condominium Act
Consumer Protection Act
Consumer Protection Bureau Act
Consumer Reporting Act
Corporations Act
Corporations Information Act
Debt Collectors Act
Discriminatory Business Practices Act
Electricity Act
Electronic Registration Act
Extra-Provincial Corporations Act
Factors Act
Funeral Directors & Establishments Act
Gaming Control Act
Land Registration Reform Act
Land Titles Act
Limited Partnerships Act
Liquor Licence Act
Loan Brokers Act
Management Board of Cabinet Act
Marriage Act
Ministry of Consumer & Commercial Relations Act
Ministry of Consumer & Commercial Relations Red Tape Reduction Act
Motor Vehicle Dealers Act
Motor Vehicle Repair Act
Ontario New Home Warranties Plan Act
Paperback & Periodical Distributors Act
Partnerships Act
Partnerships Registration Act
Personal Property Security Act
Petroleum Products Price Freeze Act
Prearranged Funeral Services Act
Prepaid Services Act
Public Service Act
Racing Commission Act
Real Estate & Business Brokers Act
Repair & Storage Liens Act
Residential Complex Sales Representation Act
Retail Business Holidays Act
Safety & Consumer Statutes Administration Act
Technical Standards & Safety Act, 2000
Travel Industry Act
Vintners Quality Alliance Act
Vital Statistics Act
Wine Content Act
Criminal Code (Canada), s. 207 (administration dealing with lottery licences issued to charitable & religious organizations to raise money for charitable or religious purposes)
Minister, Hon. Harinder S. Takhar
416-327-2333, Fax: 416-327-3790
htakhar.mpp@liberal.ola.org
• Advertising Review Board
Macdonald Block
#M2-56, 900 Bay St., 2nd Fl.
Toronto, ON M7A 1N3
416-327-2183
Fax: 416-327-2179
• Alcohol & Gaming Commission of Ontario
20 Dundas St. West
Toronto, ON M5G 2N6
416-326-8700
Fax: 416-326-5555
800-522-2876
www.agco.on.ca
• Licence Appeal Tribunal (LAT)
1 St. Clair Ave. West, 12th Fl.
Toronto, ON M4V 1K6
416-314-4260
Fax: 416-314-4270
800-255-2214
www.lat.gov.on.ca
Other Communication: Toll Free Fax: 1-800-720-5292
• Ontario Film Review Board
1075 Millwood Rd.
Toronto, ON M4G 1X6
416-314-3626
Fax: 416-314-3632
• Ontario Pension Board
#1100, 1 Adelaide St. East
Toronto, ON M5C 2X6
416-364-8558
Fax: 416-364-7578
800-668-6203
office.services@opb.on.ca
www.opb.on.ca
• Ontario Racing Commission
20 Dundas St. West, 9th Fl.
Toronto, ON M5G 2C2
416-327-0520
Fax: 416-325-3478
orcinqry@cbs.gov.on.ca
• OPSEU Pension Trust
#1200, 1 Adelaide St. East
Toronto, ON M5C 3A7
416-681-6161
Fax: 416-681-6175
www.optrust.com

Deputy Minister, MGS, Associate Secretary of the Cabinet & Secretary of Mgmt Board of Cabinet
416-325-1630
Fax: 416-325-1612
www.mgs.gov.on.ca

Archives of Ontario
77 Grenville St., 3rd Fl.
Toronto, ON M5S 1B3
416-327-1600
Fax: 416-327-1999
800-668-9933

Office of the Corporate Chief Information Officer (OCCIO)
416-327-3442
Fax: 416-327-3264

Policy & Consumer Protection Services Division
416-326-8578
Fax: 416-325-6192
Asst. Deputy Minister, Frank Denton
416-326-2826, Fax: 416-325-6192
frank.denton@ontario.ca

ServiceOntario
College Park
777 Bay St., 15th fl.
Toronto, ON M7A 2J3
416-326-6205
Fax: 416-326-5106

Registrar General Branch
189 Red River Rd.
PO Box 4600
Thunder Bay, ON P7B 6L8
807-343-7414
Fax: 807-343-7411
800-461-2156
Other Communication: Toronto: 416/325-8305
Fees are: Birth Certificate, $11; Marriage Certificate, $11; Death Certificate, $11; Certified Copies, $22; Genealogical Extracts, $22.

Algoma
420 Queen St. E
Sault Ste Marie, ON P6A 1Z7
705-253-8887
Fax: 705-253-9245

Brant
Court House
80 Wellington St.
Brantford, ON N3T 2L9
519-752-8321
Fax: 519-752-8321

Bruce
203 Cayley St.
PO Box 1690
Walkerton, ON N0G 2V0
519-881-2259
Fax: 519-881-2322

Cochrane
143 4th Ave.
PO Box 580
Cochrane, ON P0L 1C0
705-272-5791
Fax: 705-272-2951

Dufferin
#7 - 41 Briadway Ave.
Orangeville, ON L9W 1J7
519-941-1481
Fax: 519-941-6444

Dundas
8 Fifth St.
PO Box 645
Morrisburg, ON K0C 1X0
613-543-2583
Fax: 613-543-4541

Durham
590 Rossland Rd. East
Whitby, ON L1N 9G5
416-665-4007
Fax: 416-666-9806

Elgin
Courthouse Block
4 Wellington St.
St Thomas, ON N5R 2P2
519-631-3015
Fax: 519-631-8182

Essex
#100 - 949 McDougall St.
Windsor, ON N9A 1L9
519-971-9980
Fax: 519-971-9937

Frontenac
1 Court St.
Kingston, ON K7L 2N4
613-548-6767
Fax: 613-548-6766

Glengarry
63 Kenyon St. W.
Alexandria, ON K0C 1A0
613-525-1315
Fax: 613-525-0509

Grenville
499 Centre St.
PO Box 1660
Prescott, ON K0E 1T0
613-925-3177
Fax: 613-925-0302

Grey
East Court Plaza
#1-2 - 1555 16th St. E.
Owen Sound, ON N4K 5N3
519-376-1637
Fax: 519-376-1639

Haldimand
10 Echo St. W.
PO Box 310
Cayuga, ON N0A 1E0
905-772-3531

Haliburton
12 Newcastle St.
PO Box 270
Minden, ON K0M 2K0
705-286-1391
Fax: 705-286-4324

Halton
491 Steeles Ave. East
Milton, ON L9T 1Y7

905-878-7287
Fax: 905-876-8806

Hastings
#109 - 199 Front St.
Belleville, ON K8N 5H5
613-968-4597
Fax: 613-968-3606

Huron
38 North St.
Goderich, ON N7A 2T4
519-524-9562
Fax: 519-524-2482

Kenora
220 Main St. South
Kenora, ON P9N 1T2
807-468-2794
Fax: 807-468-2796

Kent
40 William St. North
Chatham, ON N7M 5L8
519-352-5520
Fax: 519-352-3222

Lambton
#102 - 700 North Christina St.
Sarnia, ON N7Y 7N5
519-337-2393
Fax: 519-337-8371

Lanark
2 Industrial Dr.
PO Box 1180
Almonte, ON K0A 1A0
613-256-1456
Fax: 613-256-0940

Leeds
7 King St. West
Brockville, ON K6V 3P7
613-345-5751
Fax: 613-345-7390

Lennox
Unit 2
7 Snow Rd.
Napanee, ON K7R 0A2
613-354-3751
Fax: 613-354-1474

Manitoulin
Courthouse
27 Phipps St.
PO Box 619
Gore Bay, ON P0P 1H0
705-282-2442
Fax: 705-282-2131

Middlesex East
100 Dundas St.
London, ON N6A 5B6
519-675-7600
Fax: 519-675-7611

Muskoka
15 Dominion St. N.
Bracebridge, ON P1L 2E7
705-645-4415
Fax: 705-645-7826

Niagara North
59 Church St.
St Catharines, ON L2R 3C3
905-684-6351
Fax: 905-684-5874

Niagara South
59 Church St.
St. Catharines, ON L2R 3C3
905-684-6351
Fax: 905-684-5874

Nipissing
360 Plouffe St.
North Bay, ON P1B 9L5
705-474-2270
Fax: 705-495-8511

Norfolk
Court House
530 Queensway W., 2nd Fl.
Simcoe, ON N3Y 4K8
519-426-2216
Fax: 519-426-9627

Northumberland
Fleming Bldg.
#105, 1005 Elgin St. W.
Cobourg, ON K9A 5J4
705-372-3813
Fax: 905-372-4758

Ottawa-Carleton
Court House
161 Elgin St., 4th Fl.
Ottawa, ON K2P 2K1
613-239-1230
Fax: 613-239-1422

Oxford
75 Graham St.
Woodstock, ON N4S 6J8
519-537-6287
Fax: 519-537-3107

Parry Sound
28 Miller St.
Parry Sound, ON P2A 1T1
705-746-5816
Fax: 705-746-6517

Peel
7765 Hurontario St., 1st Fl.
Brampton, ON L6W 4S8
905-874-4008
Fax: 905-874-4012

Perth
5 Huron St.
Stratford, ON N5A 5S4
519-271-3343
Fax: 519-271-2550

Peterborough
Robinson Pl. South Tower
300 Water St., 2nd Fl.
Peterborough, ON K9J 8M5
705-755-1342
Fax: 705-755-1343

Prescott
499 Centre St.
PO Box 1660
Prescott, ON K0E 1T0
613-925-3177
Fax: 613-925-0302

Prince Edward
1 Pitt St.
PO Box 1310
Picton, ON K0K 2T0
613-476-3219
Fax: 613-476-7908

Rainy River
353 Church St.
Fort Frances, ON P9A 1C9
807-274-5451
Fax: 807-274-1704

Renfrew
400 Pembroke St. E.
Pembroke, ON K8A 3K8
613-732-8331
Fax: 613-732-0297

Russell
1122 Concession St.
PO Box 10
Russell, ON K4R 1C8
613-445-2138
Fax: 613-445-0614

Federal/Provincial Government / Government of Ontario

Simcoe
Court House
114 Worsley St.
Barrie, ON L4M 1M1
705-734-2722
Fax: 705-725-7246

Stormont
127 Sydney St.
Cornwall, ON K6H 3H1
613-932-4522
Fax: 613-932-4524

Sudbury
199 Larch St., 3rd Fl.
Sudbury, ON P3E 5P9
705-675-4300
Fax: 705-675-4148

Thunder Bay
189 Red River Rd., 2nd Fl.
Thunder Bay, ON P7B 1A2
807-343-7436
Fax: 807-343-7439

Timiskaming
375 Main St.
PO Box 159
Haileybury, ON P0J 1K0
705-672-3332
Fax: 705-672-3906

Toronto (Metropolitan Registry)
#420, 20 Dundas St. West
PO Box 117
Toronto, ON M5G 2C2
416-314-4400
Fax: 416-314-4453

Toronto (Metropolitan Land Titles)
#420, 20 Dundas St. West
PO Box 117
Toronto, ON M5G 2C2
416-314-4430
Fax: 416-314-4453

Victoria
440 Kent St. West
Lindsay, ON K9V 6G8
705-324-4912
Fax: 705-324-6290

Waterloo
30 Duke St., 2nd Fl.
Kitchener, ON N2H 3W5
519-571-6043
Fax: 519-571-6067

Wellington
1 Stone Rd. W.
Guelph, ON N1G 4Y2
519-826-3372
Fax: 519-826-3373

Wentworth
119 King St. West, 4th Fl.
Hamilton, ON L8P 4Y7
905-521-7561
Fax: 905-521-7505

York Region
50 Bloomington Rd. W., 2nd Fl.
Aurora, ON L4G 3G8
905-713-7798
Fax: 905-713-7799

Ontario Shared Services
416-326-9300
866-979-9300
Assoc. Deputy Minister, David Hallett
416-212-7550, Fax: 416-212-7551
david.hallett@ontario.ca

Supply Chain Management
413-212-0967
Fax: 416-327-3573
www.ppitpb.gov.on.ca/mbs/psb/psb.nsf/english/index.html

Develops & implements an integrated corporate procurement strategy to: leverage & optimize government procurement of goods & services; identify and implement procurement process improvements; enhance procurement controllership; provide strategic advice on large scale procurements; develop innovative policy frameworks to support service delivery through third party service providers.
Asst. Deputy Minister, Neil Sentance
416-327-3536, Fax: 416-327-3573
neil.sentance@ontario.ca
Director Corporate Procurement Policy & Planning Branch,
Marian Macdonald
416-327-7508, Fax: 416-327-3573
marian.macdonald@ontario.ca

Ministry of Health & Long-Term Care
Hepburn Block
80 Grosvenor St., 10th Fl
Toronto, ON M7A 2C4
416-327-4327
800-268-1153
www.health.gov.on.ca
Other Communication: TTY: 1-800-387-5559
The ministry is responsible for administering the health care system & providing services to the Ontario public through such programs as health insurance, drug benefits, assistive devices, care for the mentally ill, long-term care, home care, community & public health, & health promotion & disease prevention. It also regulates hospitals & nursing homes, operates psychiatric hospitals & medical laboratories, & co-ordinates emergency health services.

Acts Administered:
Alcoholism & Drug Addiction Research Foundation Act
Ambulance Act
Audiology & Speech Pathology Act
Cancer Act
Cancer Remedies Act
Charitable Institutions Act
Chiropody Act
Chiropractic Act
Community Psychiatric Hospitals Act
Dental Hygiene Act, 1991
Dental Technology Act, 1991
Dentistry Act, 1991
Denturism Act, 1991
Developmental Services Act (long-term care programs & services)
Dietetics Act, 1991
Drug & Pharmacies Regulation Act
Drug Interchangeability & Dispensing Fee Act
Drugless Practitioners Act
Elderly Persons Centres Act
General Welfare Assistance Act (long-term care programs & services only)
Health Cards & Numbers Control Act, 1991
Health Care Accessibility Act
Health Care Consent Act
Health Facilities Special Orders Act
Health Insurance Act
Health Protection & Promotion Act
Homemakers & Nurses Services Act
Homes for Retarded Persons Act (long-term care programs & services)
Homes for Special Care Act
Homes for the Aged & Rest Homes Act
Human Tissue Gift Act
Hypnosis Act
Immunization of School Pupils Act
Independent Health Facilities Act
Laboratory & Specimen Collection Centres Licensing Act
Long Term Care Act, 1994
Massage Therapy Act
Mental Health Act
Mental Hospitals Act
Midwifery Act, 1991
Ministry of Community & Social Services Act (sections 11.1 & 12 re: long-term care programs & services only)
Ministry of Health & Long-Term Care Act
Nursing Homes Act
Occupational Therapy Act
Ontario Drug Benefit Act
Ontario Medical Association Dues Act, 1991
Ontario Mental Health Foundation Act
Opticianry Act, 1991
Optometry Act, 1991
Pharmacy Act, 1991
Physician Services Delivery Management Act, 1995
Physiotherapy Act, 1991
Private Hospitals Act
Psychology Act, 1991
Public Hospitals Act
Regulated Health Professions Act, 1991
Respiratory Therapy Act, 1991
Tobacco Control Act, 1994
War Veterans Burial Act
Minister, Hon. David Caplan
416-327-4300, Fax: 416-326-1571
dcaplan.mpp@liberal.ola.org
Deputy Minister, Ron Sapsford
416-327-4496, Fax: 416-326-1570
ron.sapsford@ontario.ca
Parliamentary Assistant, Laurel C. Broten
416-326-3981, Fax: 416-326-1571
laurel.broten@ontario.ca;lbroten.mpp.co@liberal.ola.org
• Cancer Care Ontario
620 University Ave., 15th Fl.
Toronto, ON M5G 2L7
416-971-9800
Fax: 416-971-6888
www.cancercare.on.ca
• Consent & Capacity Board
151 Bloor St. West, 10th Fl.
Toronto, ON M5S 2T5
416-327-4142
Fax: 416-327-4207
• Healing Arts Radiation Protection Commission(HARP)
5700 Yonge St., 3rd Fl.
Toronto, ON M2M 4K5
416-327-7952
Fax: 416-327-8805
• Health Boards Secretariat
151 Bloor St. West, 9th Fl.
Toronto, ON M5S 2T5
416-327-8512
Fax: 416-327-8524
• Medical Eligibility Committee
370 Select Dr.
PO Box 168
Kingston, ON K7M 8T4
613-548-6405
• Ontario Mental Health Foundation
#508, 489 College St.
Toronto, ON M6G 1A5
416-920-7721
Fax: 416-920-0026
grants@omhf.on.ca
www.omhf.on.ca
• Ontario Review Board
151 Bloor St. West, 10th Fl.
Toronto, ON M5S 2T5
416-327-8866
Fax: 416-327-8867
• Smart Systems for Health
#1900, 415 Yonge St.
Toronto, ON M5B 2E7
416-586-6500
Fax: 416-586-4363
www.ssha.com
• Trillium Gift of Life Network
#1440, 155 University Ave.
Toronto, ON M5H 3B7
416-363-4001
Fax: 416-363-4002
www.giftoflife.on.ca

Corporate Services & Direct Services Division
416-327-4266
Fax: 416-314-5915

Health Human Resources Strategy Division
416-212-6115
Fax: 416-314-3751

Health Services
Acting Asst. Deputy Minister, Dawn Ogram
416-327-4266
Medical Director Public Health Laboratories Branch, Dr. Donald Low
416-235-5944, Fax: 416-235-6063
don.low@ontario.ca

Health System Strategy Division
416-327-8295
Fax: 416-327-5109

Public Health Division
416-325-8412
Acting Chief Medical Officer of Health, Dr. David C. Williams
416-314-5487, Fax: 416-325-8412
david.williams@ontario.ca
Acting Director Emergency Management, Tiffany Jay
416-212-5229, Fax: 416-212-4466
tiffany.jay@ontario.ca

Infectious Diseases
5700 Yonge St., 8th Fl.
Toronto, ON M2M 4K5
416-327-7392
Fax: 416-327-7438
Provides leadership & support to Ontario's public health system including 36 boards of health; programs & services include: the Disease Control Service (DCS), Environmental Health & Toxicology Unit (EHTU), Safe Water/Food Safety Unit, Surveillance & Outbreak Management Section (SOMS), & Tuberculosis/Vaccine Preventable Diseases. The Infectious Diseases Branch provides public health, epidemiological, expert consultation & technical support to local boards of health & other health agencies in respect of the programs of the Mandatory Health Programs & Services Guidelines (MHPSG). The Infectious Diseases Branch is also responsible for disease-related databases, communications & support for health units during outbreaks.
Assoc. Chief Medical Officer of Health & Director, Dr. David Williams
416-314-5487
Manager Food Safety & Safe Water Unit & Acting Manager, Environmental Health & Toxicology Unit, Fred Ruf
416-327-7624
Minister, Hon. Margarett R. Best
416-326-8500, Fax: 416-326-8520
mbest.mpp@liberal.ola.org
Deputy Minister, Cynthia Morton
416-326-8475, Fax: 416-326-8409
cynthia.morton@ontario.ca

Public Health Division
Hepburn Block
80 Grosvenor St., 11th Fl.
Toronto, ON M7A 1R3
416-212-3831
Fax: 416-325-8412
General Counsel, Vella Mijal
819-953-1380, Fax: 819-953-9110

Hydro One Inc.
North Tower
483 Bay St.
Toronto, ON M5G 2P5
416-345-5000
877-955-1155
webmaster@HydroOne.com
www.HydroOne.com
President/CEO, Laura Formusa
Vice-President Engineering & Construction Services, Nairn McQueen
Vice-President Health, Safety & Environment, Michelle Morrissey O'Ryan

Independent Electricity System Operator (IESO)
PO Box 4474 A
Toronto, ON M5W 4E5
905-403-6900
Fax: 905-403-6921
888-448-7777
customer.relations@ieso.ca
www.ieso.ca
President/CEO, Paul Murphy
paul.murphy@ieso.ca
Vice-President Corporate Relations & Market Development, Bruce Campbell
416-506-2829,
bruce.campbell@ieso.ca
Vice-President Corporate Services, Gary Sherkey
gary.sherkey@ieso.ca
Vice-President Information Technology & Infrastructure, Bill Limbrick
Vice-President Market & System Operations, Ken Kozlik
ken.kozlik@ieso.ca

Vice-President Market Services, Derek Cowbourne
905-855-6211, Fax: 905-855-6471
derek.cowbourne@ieso.ca
Director Human Resources, Norm Thomas
Director Market Assessment & Compliance, Harry Chandler
905-855-6170, Fax: 905-855-6408
harry.chandler@ieso.ca

Ministry of Labour
400 University Ave., 14th Fl.
Toronto, ON M7A 1T7
416-326-7770
800-268-8013
www.labour.gov.on.ca
Advances safe, fair & harmonious workplace practices that are essential to the social & economic well-being of the people of Ontario. Through the ministry's key areas of occupational health & safety, employment rights & responsibilities, labour relations & internal administration, the ministry's mandate is to set, communicate & enforce workplace standards while encouraging greater workplace self-reliance. A range of specialized agencies, boards & commissions assist the ministry in its work.
Acts Administered:
Ambulance Services Collective Bargaining Act
Crown Employees Collective Bargaining Act
Employment Standards Act
Fire Protection & Prevention Act
Hospital Labour Disputes Arbitration Act
Labour Relations Act
Ministry of Labour Act
Occupational Health & Safety Act
Control of Exposure to Biological or Chemical Agents Regulations
Designated Substance Regulations (Various)
Workplace Hazardous Materials Information System (WHMIS) Regulations
Pay Equity Act
Public Sector Dispute Resolution Act
Public Sector Labour Relations Transitions Act
Public Sector Transition Stability Act
Rights of Labour Act
Workplace Safety & Insurance Act
Minister, Hon. Peter Fonseca
416-326-7600, Fax: 416-726-1449
pfonseca.mpp@liberal.ola.org; pfonseca.mpp.co@liberal.ola.org
Deputy Minister, Virginia M. West
416-326-7576, Fax: 416-326-0507
virginia.west@ontario.ca
• Office of the Employer Advisor
#704, 151 Bloor St. West.
Toronto, ON M5S 1S4
416-327-0020
Fax: 416-327-0726
800-387-0774
• Office of the Worker Advisor
#1300, 123 Edward St.
Toronto, ON M5G 1E2
416-325-8570
Fax: 416-325-4830
800-435-8980
Other Communication: 1-800-661-6365 (French)
• Ontario Labour Relations Board
505 University Ave., 2nd Fl.
Toronto, ON M5G 2P1
416-326-7500
Fax: 416-326-7531
877-339-3335
www.gov.on.ca/lab/olrb/home.htm
• Pay Equity Commission
400 University Ave., 11th Fl.
Toronto, ON M7A 1T7
416-314-1896
Fax: 416-314-8741
800-387-8813
www.payequity.gov.on.ca

• Workplace Safety & Insurance Board

Internal Administrative Services Division
416-326-7586
Fax: 416-326-7599

Operations Division
416-326-7606
Fax: 416-212-4455

Asst. Deputy Minister, Sophie Dennis
416-326-7665, Fax: 416-212-4455
sophie.dennis@ontario.ca

Regional Offices:

Central
West Bldg.
1201 Wilson Ave., 2nd Fl.
Toronto, ON M3M 1J8
416-235-5330
Fax: 416-235-5355

Eastern
#200, 1111 Prince of Wales Dr.
Ottawa, ON K2C 3T2
613-228-8050
Fax: 613-727-2900

Northern
#301, 159 Cedar St.
Sudbury, ON P3E 6A5
705-564-7400
Fax: 705-670-7435
800-461-6325
TDD: 866-567-8893

Western
1 Jarvis St., Main Fl.
Hamilton, ON L8R 3J2
905-577-6221
Fax: 905-577-1200
800-263-6906

Policy, Program Development & Dispute Resolution Services
416-326-7558
Fax: 416-326-7599
The Division provides the Minister & senior officials with information, analysis & advice to assist in the development, adoption & implementation of policies, programs & legislation related to the workplace. The division includes policy & information co-ordination.
Asst. Deputy Minister, Susanna Zagar
416-326-7555, Fax: 416-326-7599
susanna.zagar@ontario.ca
Director Health & Safety Policy & Program Development Branch, John Vander Doelen
416-326-7628, Fax: 416-314-7650
john.vanderdoelen@ontario.ca

Finance & Administration
416-326-7200
Fax: 416-326-9069

Freedom of Information & Privacy

Human Resources Branch
Fax: 416-326-7241
TDD: 416-314-5811

Employment Practices Branch
416-326-2450
Fax: 416-326-7061
800-531-5551

Occupational Health & Safety
416-326-7770
Fax: 416-326-7761
800-268-8013

Occupational Health & Safety Branch (OHSB)
655 Bay St., 14th Fl.
Toronto, ON M7A 1T7
416-326-7770
Fax: 416-326-7242
The branch provides program services related to the Construction Health & Safety Program, the Industrial Health & Safety Program & Mining Health & Safety Program. These services are provided through Regional & District Offices across the province. The programs enforce the Occupational Health & Safety Act & regulations made under the Act. The branch assists with the co-ordination of the development of occupational health & safety regulations.
Director, Alec Farquhar
416-326-7866
Provincial Coordinator Construction Health & Safety Program, Michael Chappell
416-326-5220

Federal/Provincial Government / Government of Ontario

Acting Provincial Coordinator Industrial Health & Safety, Wayne De L'Orme
416-326-7904
Provincial Coordinator Mining Health & Safety Program, Bernie Deck
705-670-5714
Manager Radiation Protection Service, Ken Gilmer
416-235-5916

Professional & Specialized Services
The unit identifies & reduces the risk of worker injury in the Ontario workplace through professional knowledge on the anticipation, recognition, evaluation & control of occupational hazards. The service is composed of professionals who set, communicate & enforce standards, provide health & safety assessments of chemicals, notifiability of new chemical & biological agents, statistical analysis of occupational health data. Engineers provide engineering expertise to the Construction, Industrial & Mining Health & Safety Programs. Occupational health professionals including physicians, hygienists, ergonomists, scientists & radiation technologists provide consultations to help prevent occupational diseases.
Acting Provincial Coordinator, Gabriel Mansour
416-326-1404, Fax: 416-326-7761

Labour Management Services
416-326-7575
Fax: 416-314-8755

Ministry of Municipal Affairs & Housing
777 Bay St., 17th Fl.
Toronto, ON M5G 2E5
416-585-7041
Fax: 416-585-6227
866-220-2290
TDD: 866-220-2290
mininfo.mah@ontario.ca
www.mah.gov.on.ca
Other Communication: TDD/TTY: 416-585-6991
Responsible for providing provincial leadership in defining the framework for governance, finances & management for the local government systems; as well as leadership in the development & administration of the legislative & policy framework for land use planning. It is also responsible for providing the operational, policy & accountability framework for local government to fund & administer social housing; policy & program instruments to create a competitive marketplace for rental housing; & the regulatory framework for buildings.

Acts Administered:
Barrie Innisfil Annexation Act
Barrie-Vespra Annexation Act
Brantford-Brant Annexation Act
Building Code Act
City of Cornwall Annexation Act
City of Gloucester Act
City of Greater Sudbury Act
City of Hamilton Act
City of Hazeldean-March Act
City of Kawartha Lakes Act
City of London Act
City of Nepean Act
City of Ottawa Act
City of Ottawa Road Closing & Conveyance Validation Act
City of Port Colborne Act
City of Sudbury Hydro-Electric Service Act
City of Thunder Bay Act
City of Thorold Act
City of Timmins-Porcupine Act
City of Toronto Act
City of Toronto Act (No. 2)
Commercial Tenancies Act
Community Economic Development Act
County of Haliburton Act
County of Oxford Act
County of Simcoe Act
Development Charges Act
District Municipality of Muskoka Act
District of Parry Sound Local Government Act
Elderly Person's Housing Aid Act
Geographic Township of Hansen Act
Greater Toronto Services Board Act
Greenbelt Act
Housing Development Act
Local Government Disclosure of Interest Act
London-Middlesex Act
Ministry of Municipal Affairs & Housing Act
Municipal Act
Municipal Affairs Act
Municipal Arbitrations Act
Municipal Conflict of Interest Act
Municipal Corporations Quieting Orders Act
Municipal Elderly Residents' Assistance Act
Municipal Elections Act
Municipal Extra - Territorial Tax Act
Municipal Franchises Act
Municipal Interest & Discount Rates Act
Municipal Private Acts Repeal Act
Municipal & School Tax Credit Assistance Acts
Municipal Subsidies Adjustment Repeal Act
Municipal Tax Assistance Act
Municipal Tax Sales Act
Municipal Unemployment Relief Act
Municipal Water & Sewage Transfer Act
Municipal Works Assistance Act
Municipality of Metropolitan Toronto Act
Municipality of Shuniah Act
North Pickering Development Corporation Act
Oak Ridges Moraine Conservation Act
Oak Ridges Moraine Protection Act, 2001
Designation of the Oak Ridges Moraine Area
Municipalities that are Required to Prepare & Adopt Official Plan Amendments
Oak Ridges Moraine Conservation Plan
Ontario Housing Corporation Act
Ontario Municipal Employees Retirement System Act
Ontario Municipal Support Grants Act
Ontario Planning & Development Act
Ottawa-Carleton Amalgamations & Elections Act
Planning Act
Police Village of St. George Act
Public Utilities Act
Public Utilities Corporations Act
Regional Municipalities Act
Regional Municipality of Durham Act
Regional Municipality of Halton Act
Regional Municipality of Hamilton-Wentworth Act
Regional Municipality of Niagara Act
Regional Municipality of Ottawa-Carleton Act
Regional Municipality of Ottawa-Carleton Land Acquisition Act
Regional Municipality of Peel Act
Regional Municipality of Waterloo Act
Regional Municipality of York Act
Road Access Act
Rural Housing Assistance Act
Sarnia-Lambton Act
Shoreline Property Assistance Act
Snow Roads & Fences Act
Social Housing Reform Act
Statute Labour Act
Tax Sales Confirmation Act
Tenant Protection Act
Territorial Division Act
Tom Longboat Act
Toronto Islands Residential Community Stewardship Act
Town of Haldimand Act
Town of Moosonee Act
Town of Norfolk Act
Town of Wasaga Beach Act
Township of North Plantagenet Act
Township of South Dumfries Act
Wharfs & Harbours Act
Minister, Hon. James J. Bradley
416-585-7000, Fax: 416-585-6470
jbradley.mpp.co@liberal.ola.org
Interim Deputy Minister, Dana Richardson
416-585-7100, Fax: 416-585-7211
Dana.Richardson@ontario.ca
• Building Code Commission
777 Bay St., 2nd Fl.
Toronto, ON M5G 2E5
416-585-6503
Fax: 416-585-7531
www.obc.mah.gov.on.ca
Secretary, Sally England-Bizjak
Works with the municipal & building sectors & consumer groups to improve & streamline the building regulatory system. This leads to efficient development & more construction jobs, while protecting public safety. The Branch administers the Building Code Act (BCA) & the Ontario Building Code (OBC), which govern the construction of new buildings & the renovation & maintenance of existing buildings. It provides enforcement officials & other building code users with advice & information so that they can apply building code requirements more consistently.
• Building Materials Evaluation Commission
777 Bay St., 2nd Fl.
Toronto, ON M5G 2E5
416-585-4234
Fax: 416-585-7531
Secretary, Penelope Horsfall
• Ontario Housing Corporation
777 Bay St., 2nd Fl.
Toronto, ON M5G 2E5
• Ontario Rental Housing Tribunal
777 Bay St., 12th Fl.
Toronto, ON M5G 2E5
416-585-7295
Fax: 416-585-6363
888-332-3234
www.orht.gov.on.ca

Business Management Division
416-585-7209
Fax: 416-585-6191

Housing Division
416-585-6277
Fax: 416-585-6800

Local Government & Planning Policy Division
416-585-6320
Fax: 416-585-6463
Asst. Deputy Minister, Dana Richardson
416-585-6320, Fax: 416-585-6463
dana.richardson@ontario.ca

Municipal Services Division
Fax: 416-585-6445

Municipal Services Offices:

Central
777 Bay St., 2nd Fl.
Toronto, ON M5G 2E5
416-585-6226
Fax: 416-585-6882
800-668-0230

Eastern
Rockwood House
8 Estate Lane, Postal Bag 2500
Kingston, ON K7M 9A8
613-548-4304
Fax: 613-548-6822
800-267-9438

Northeastern
#401, 159 Cedar St.
Sudbury, ON P3E 6A5
705-564-0120
Fax: 705-564-6863
800-461-1193

Northwestern
#223, 435 James St. South
Thunder Bay, ON P7E 6S7
807-475-1651
Fax: 807-475-1196
800-465-5027

Western
659 Exeter Rd., 2nd Fl.
London, ON N6E 1L3
519-873-4020
Fax: 519-873-4018
800-265-4736

Planning & Development Division
Asst. Deputy Minister, Elizabeth McLaren
416-585-6427
Director Building & Development, David Brezer
416-585-6656, Fax: 416-585-7531
david.brezer@ontario.ca
Director Provincial Planning Policy, Audrey Bennett
416-585-6072, Fax: 416-585-4245
audrey.bennett@ontario.ca

Corporate Planning Branch
Fax: 416-585-7328

Technology & Business Solutions
Fax: 416-585-7394

Municipal Finance Branch
Fax: 416-585-6315

Ministry of Natural Resources (MNR)

Whitney Block
#6630, 99 Wellesley St. West, 6th Fl.
Toronto, ON M7A 1W3
800-667-1940
www.mnr.gov.on.ca

The MNR manages & protects natural resources in the province for wise use. Working with environmental organizations, private industries, fish & game associations, researchers, & other government agencies, the MNR is responsible for the following areas: science & information resources; forest management; fish & wildlife management; land & waters management; Ontario Parks; aviation & forest fire management; & geographic information.

Acts Administered:
Aggregate Resources Act
Algonquin Forestry Authority Act
An Act for the Settlement of certain Questions between the Governments of Canada & Ontario respecting Indian Reserve Lands
An Act to Confirm the title of the Government of Canada to certain Lands & Indian Lands
Arboreal Emblem Act
Beds of Navigable Waters Act
Conservation Authorities Act
Conservation Land Act
Conservation Bodies Land Regulation
Crown Forest Sustainability Act
Endangered Species Act
Endangered Species Regulation
Fish Inspection Act
Fish & Wildlife Conservation Act
Possession, Buying & Selling of Wildlife
Wildlife in Captivity
Wildlife Management Units
Wildlife Schedules
Forest Fires Prevention Act
Forestry Act
Forestry Workers Lien for Wages Act
Freshwater Fish Marketing Act (Ontario)
Gas & Oil Leases Act
Heritage Hunting & Fishing Act, 2002
Indian Lands Act
Indian Lands Agreement Confirmation Act
Industrial & Mining Lands Compensation Act
Kawartha Highlands Signature Park Act
Lac Seul Conservation Act
Lake of the Woods Control Board Act
Lakes & Rivers Improvement Act
Manitoba-Ontario Lake St. Joseph Diversion Agreement Authorization Act
Mineral Emblem Act
Mining Act
Ministry of Natural Resources Act
Niagara Escarpment Planning & Development Act
North Georgian Bay Recreational Reserve Act
Northern Ontario Heritage Fund Act
Northern Services Boards Act
Oil, Gas & Salt Resources Act
Ontario Geographic Names Board Act
Ottawa River Water Powers Act
Provincial Parks Act
Designation of Parks
Guides in Quetico Provincial Park
Mining in Provincial Parks
Public Lands Act
Surveys Act
Water Transfer Control Act
Wild Rice Harvesting Act
Wilderness Areas Act

Minister, Hon. Donna H. Cansfield
416-314-2301, Fax: 416-325-5316
dcansfield.mpp@liberal.ola.org
Deputy Minister, David L. Lindsay
416-314-2150, Fax: 416-314-2159
Commissioner Mining & Lands, Linda Kamerman
416-314-2322, Fax: 416-314-2327
linda.kamerman@ontario.ca

Director Legal Services, Anne Marie Gutierrez
416-314-2025, Fax: 416-314-2030
annemarie.gutierrez@ontario.ca
Director Communications, John Whytock
416-314-2119, Fax: 416-314-2102
john.whytock@ontario.ca
Director Resources & Labour Audit Service Team, Ray Masse
416-314-9208, Fax: 416-314-9220
ray.masse2@ontario.ca
Parliamentary Assistant, Bill Mauro
416-314-6467, Fax: 416-314-6470
bmauro.mpp.co@liberal.ola.org
• Academic & Experience Requirements Committee of the Association of Ontario Land Surveyors(AERC)
1043 McNicoll Ave.
Toronto, ON M1W 3W6
416-491-9020
Fax: 416-491-2576
800-268-0718
admin@aols.org
• Algonquin Forestry Authority - Huntsville
222 Main St. West
Huntsville, ON P1H 1Y1
705-789-9647
Fax: 705-789-3353
www.algonquinforestry.on.ca
Other Communication: Email: huntsville.office@algonquinforestry.on.ca
General Manager, C.M. Corbett
Ensures the viability of the local forest industry while preserving the soil & water resources, fish & wildlife habitat & recreational areas in the park.
• Algonquin Forestry Authority - Pembroke
Victoria Centre
84 Isabella St., 2nd Fl.
Pembroke, ON K8A 5S5
613-735-0173
Fax: 613-735-4192
www.algonquinforestry.on.ca
Other Communication: EMail: pembroke.office@algonquinforestry.on.ca
Manager, J.R. Janke
• Association of Ontario Land Surveyors
1043 McNicoll Ave.
Toronto, ON M1W 3W6
416-491-9020
Fax: 416-491-2576
admin@aols.org
• Crown Timber Board of Examiners
Roberta Bondar Place
#400, 70 Foster Dr.
Sault Ste Marie, ON P6A 6V5
705-945-6643
• Fish & Wildlife Heritage Commission
Robinson Pl.
300 Water St.
PO Box 7000
Peterborough, ON K9J 8M5
Fax: 705-755-5093
Executive Director, Patrick Kennedy
• Ontario Geographic Names Board
Robinson Place
300 Water St., 2nd Fl.
PO Box 7000
Peterborough, ON K9J 8M5
705-755-2134
Fax: 705-755-2131
• Ontario Moose & Bear Allocation Advisory Committee
PO Box 964
Sioux Lookout, ON P8T 1B3
807-737-2615
Fax: 807-737-4173
• Ottawa River Regulation Planning Board
351 St Joseph Blvd.
Gatineau, QC J8Y 3Z5
613-997-1735
800-778-1246
secretariat@ottawariver.ca
www.ottawariver.ca
• Rabies Advisory Committee
Trent University Science Complex
PO Box 4840
Peterborough, ON K9J 8N8
705-755-2270

• Shibogama Interim Planning Board
PO Box 105
Wunnumin, ON P0V 2Z0
807-442-2559
Fax: 807-442-2627
• Windigo Interim Planning Board
PO Box 299
Sioux Lookout, ON P8T 1A3
807-737-1585
Fax: 807-737-3133

Niagara Escarpment Commission (NEC)
232 Guelph St.
Georgetown, ON L7G 4B1
905-877-5191
Fax: 905-873-7452
Other Communication: Toronto: 905/453-2468
Responsible for implementing the Niagara Escarpment Planning & Development Act, which is designed to maintain the escarpment & surrounding area as a continuous natural environment & to ensure that all new development in the escarpment area is compatible with provincial goals of environmental protection & conservation. The commission is also the main source of information on the Niagara Escarpment & the Niagara Escarpment Plan.
Chair, Don Scott
905-877-5594, Fax: 905-873-7452
don.scott@ontario.ca
Director, Mark Frawley
905-877-4810, Fax: 905-873-7452
mark.frawley@ontario.ca

Corporate Management Division
416-314-1900
Fax: 416-314-1901
Asst. Deputy Minister, David Lynch
416-314-1939, Fax: 416-314-1901
david.lynch@ontario.ca
Director Finance & Business Services, Larry Davis
705-755-2532, Fax: 705-755-2508
larry.davis@ontario.ca

Field Services Division
Fax: 416-314-2629
800-667-1940
Field Services Division is the ministry's local presence in communities across the province, delivering integrated programs on resource management through 3 regions & 25 districts. The division delivers programs on provincial enforcement, native affairs, fisheries, forests & provincial lands, in addition to resources such as finance, facilities & engineering infrastructure, equipment & vehicles.
Asst. Deputy Minister, Charlie Lauer
416-314-2621,
charlie.lauer@ontario.ca
Director Natural Spaces, Lynne Peterson
705-755-1748, Fax: 705-755-3289

Human Resources Branch
300 Water St., 3rd Fl.
PO Box 7000
Peterborough, ON K9J 8M5
Fax: 705-755-3108

Communications Services Branch
416-314-2101
Fax: 416-314-2102

Mining & Lands Commissioner
700 Bay St., 24th Fl.
PO Box 330
Toronto, ON M5G 1Z6
416-314-2320
Fax: 416-314-2327
Commissioner, Linda Kamerman
416-314-2322

Finance & Business Services Branch
300 Water St., 3rd Fl.
PO Box 7000
Peterborough, ON K9J 8M5
705-755-1855
Fax: 705-755-2508

Federal/Provincial Government / Government of Ontario

Aboriginal Affairs Unit
705-755-1826
Fax: 705-455-1372
Acting Manager, Dan Marinigh
705-755-1540

Aviation & Forest Fire Management Branch
#400, 70 Foster Dr.
Sault Ste Marie, ON P6A 6V5
Other Communication: General Inquiry: 705/779-2149 (Aviation); 705/945-5792 (Fire)
Provides forest fire management services to protect lives, resources & private property from wildfire; uses fire for the attainment of forest management & other land use objectives; coordinates the MNR airfleet for the purposes of natural resource management, such as wildlife population surveys, forest mapping, forest fire suppression, personnel & cargo transport & enforcement; provides a flood warning system in Ontario to prevent loss of life & minimize property damage associated with flooding.
Director, Ralph Wheeler
705-945-5937
Manager Aviation Services, Barry O'Brien
705-779-4030
Acting Manager Forest Fire Management, Al Tithecott
705-945-5782
Manager East Fire Region, Ken Gibbons
705-564-6030
Fire Program Manager Northwest Region Fire Management Centre, Terry Popowich
807-937-7210

Enforcement
705-755-1777
Fax: 705-755-1757
Provides assistance, advice & direction to ministry staff at all levels, on a variety of compliance & law enforcement matters. The branch is responsible for the development, coordination & delivery of an Integrated Provincial Compliance Program which focuses on the promotion, monitoring & enforcement aspects of compliance.
Director, Serge Tenaglia
705-755-1750

Regional Offices:

Northeast Region
Ontario Government Complex
Hwy. 101 East
PO Box 3020
South Porcupine, ON P0N 1H0
705-235-1157
Fax: 705-235-1246
Regional Director, Eric Doidge
705-235-1153,
eric.doidge@ontario.ca

Chapleau (Fire Management & Area Office)
190 Cherry St.
Chapleau, ON P0M 1K0
705-864-1710
Fax: 705-864-0681
Acting District Manager, Paul Bernier
705-864-3122,
paul.bernier@ontario.ca
Fire Management Supervisor, Wes Woods
705-864-3126,
wesley.woods@ontario.ca

Cochrane (Fire Management Office)
2 - 3rd Ave.
PO Box 730
Cochrane, ON P0L 1C0
705-272-4365
Fax: 705-272-7183
District Manager, Marty Blake
705-272-7137,
marty.blake@ontario.ca
Supervisor, Fred Welch
705-272-7141,
Fred.Welch@ontario.ca

Hearst
613 Front St.
PO Box 670
Hearst, ON P0L 1N0
705-362-4346
Fax: 705-372-2245

District Manager, Martha Heidenheim
705-273-2204,
martha.heidenheim@ontario.ca

Kirkland Lake
10 Government Rd. East
PO Box 910
Kirkland Lake, ON P2N 3K4
705-568-3222
Fax: 705-568-3200
District Manager, Corrinne Nelson
705-568-3201,
corrinne.nelson@ontario.ca

North Bay
3301 Trout Lake Rd.
North Bay, ON P1A 4L7
705-475-5550
Fax: 705-475-5500
District Manager, Dave Payne
705-457-5599,
dave.payne@ontario.ca

Sault Ste. Marie
64 Church St.
Sault Ste Marie, ON P6A 3H3
705-949-1231
Fax: 705-949-6450
District Manager, Bob Johnston
705-941-5120,
bob.johnston1@ontario.ca
Fire Management Supervisor, Daryl Curran
705-946-7855,
daryl.curran@ontario.ca

Sudbury
#5, 3767 Hwy. 69 South
Sudbury, ON P3G 1E7
705-564-7823
Fax: 705-564-7879
District Manager, Ed Tear
705-564-7872,
ed.tear@ontario.ca
Fire Management Supervisor, Ted Shannon
705-564-6003,
ted.shannon@ontario.ca

Timmins
Ontario Government Complex
5520 Hwy. 101 East
PO Box 3090
South Porcupine, ON P0N 1H0
705-235-1300
Fax: 705-235-1377
Other Communication: Fire Fax: 705/755-1373
Acting District Manager, Jim Duncan
705-235-1325,
jim.duncan@ontario.ca
Fire Management Supervisor, Anne-Marie Larivee
705-235-1362,
marie.larivee@ontario.ca

Wawa
48 Mission Rd. Hwy 101
PO Box 1160
Wawa, ON P0S 1K0
705-856-2396
Fax: 705-856-7511
District Manager, John Peluch
705-856-2396,
john.peluch@ontario.ca
Fire Management Supervisor, Vacant

Northwest Region
Ontario Government Bldg.
#221A, 435 James St. South
Thunder Bay, ON P7E 6S8
807-475-1261
Fax: 807-473-3023

Dryden
479 Government Rd.
PO Box 730
Dryden, ON P8N 2Z4
807-223-3341
Fax: 807-223-2824
Acting District Manager, Matt Myers
807-223-7515,
matt.myers@ontario.ca

Fire Management Supervisor, Rod Kellar
807-937-7321,
rod.kellar@ontario.ca

Fort Frances
922 Scott St.
Fort Frances, ON P9A 1J4
807-274-5337
Fax: 807-274-5553
District Manager, Bill Darby
807-274-8633,
bill.darby@ontario.ca
Acting Fire Management Supervisor, Harrold Boven
807-274-8647,
harrold.boven@ontario.ca

Kenora
808 Robertson St.
PO Box 5080
Kenora, ON P9N 3X9
807-468-2501
Fax: 807-468-2736
District Manager, Fred Hall
807-468-2528,
fred.hall@ontario.ca
Fire Management Supervisor, Walt Lesenke
807-548-8416

Nipigon
5 Wadsworth Dr.
PO Box 970
Nipigon, ON P0T 2J0
807-887-5000
Fax: 807-887-2993
District Manager, Kim Groenendyk
807-887-5013,
kim.groenendyk@ontario.ca

Red Lake
227 Howey St.
PO Box 5003
Red Lake, ON P0V 2M0
807-727-2253
Fax: 807-727-2861
Other Communication: Fire Headquarters Fax: 807/727-3182
District Manager, Graeme Swanwick
807-727-1333,
graeme.swanwick@ontario.ca
Acting Fire Management Supervisor, Randy Crampton
807-727-2041

Sioux Lookout
49 Prince St.
PO Box 309
Sioux Lookout, ON P8T 1A6
807-737-1140
Fax: 807-737-1813
District Manager, Bob David
807-737-5026,
bob.david@ontario.ca
Fire Management Supervisor, Darren McLarty
807-737-5005,
darren.mclarty@ontario.ca

Thunder Bay
Ontario Government Bldg.
#B001, 435 James St. South
Thunder Bay, ON P7E 6S8
807-475-1471
Fax: 807-475-1527
District Manager, Bill Baker
807-475-1174,
bill.baker@ontario.ca
Fire Management Supervisor, Dave Manol
807-476-2230,
Dave.Manol@ontario.vc

Southern Region
Robinson Place, South Tower
300 Water St., 4th Fl. South
PO Box 7000
Peterborough, ON K9J 8M5
705-755-2000
Fax: 705-755-3233
Regional Director, Ray Bonenberg
705-753-3235,
ray.bonenberg@ontario.ca

Aurora
50 Bloomington Rd. West, RR#2
Aurora, ON L4G 3G8
905-713-7400
Fax: 905-713-7359
District Manager, Tracey Smith
905-713-7372,
tracy.c.smith@ontario.ca

Aylmer
615 John St.
Aylmer, ON N5H 2S8
519-773-9241
Fax: 519-773-9014
District Manager, Mitch Wilson
519-773-4710,
mitch.wilson@ontario.ca

Bancroft
106 Monck St.
PO Box 500
Bancroft, ON K0L 1C0
613-332-3940
Fax: 613-332-0608
District Manager, Vince Ewing
613-332-3940,
vince.ewing@ontario.ca

Guelph
1 Stone Rd. West
Guelph, ON N1G 4Y2
519-826-4955
Fax: 519-826-4929
District Manager, Ian Hagman
519-826-4931,
ian.hagman@ontario.ca

Kemptville
Provincial Government Bldg.
10 Campus Dr.
PO Box 2002
Kemptville, ON K0G 1J0
613-258-8204
Fax: 613-258-3920
District Manager, Alex Gardner
613-258-8201,
Alex.Gardner@ontario.ca

Midhurst
2284 Nursery Rd.
Midhurst, ON L0L 1X0
705-725-7500
Fax: 705-725-7584
District Manager, Mark Shoreman
705-725-7504,
mark.shoreman@ontario.ca

Parry Sound
7 Bay St.
Parry Sound, ON P2A 1S4
705-746-4201
Fax: 705-746-8828
District Manager, Andy Heerschap
705-773-4236,
andy.heerschap@ontario.ca

Pembroke
31 Riverside Dr.
Pembroke, ON K8A 8R6
613-732-3661
Fax: 613-732-2972
District Manager, Paul V. Moreau
613-732-5520,
paul.v.moreau@ontario.ca

Peterborough
South Tower
300 Water St., 1st Fl.
PO Box 7000
Peterborough, ON K9J 8M5
705-755-2001
Fax: 705-755-3125
District Manager, Jane Ireland
705-755-3363,
jane.ireland@ontario.ca

Policy & Planning Coordination Branch
Fax: 416-314-1948

Forests Division
Roberta Bondar Place
#400, 70 Foster Dr.
Sault Ste Marie, ON P6A 6V5
Fax: 705-945-5977
800-667-1940
Provides assistance, advice & direction to ministry staff at all levels, on a variety of compliance & law enforcement matters. The branch is responsible for the development, coordination & delivery of an Integrated Provincial Compliance Program which focuses on the promotion, monitoring & enforcement aspects of compliance.
Asst. Deputy Minister, Bill Thornton
705-945-6660, Fax: 705-945-5977
bill.thornton@ontario.ca

Aviation, Forest & Fire Management Branch
705-945-5949
Fax: 705-945-5959

Forest Management Branch
#400, 70 Foster Dr.
Sault Ste Marie, ON P6A 6V5
705-945-6661
Fax: 705-945-6667
The branch coordinates development & implementation of forest legislation, policies, programs, standards & related forest management planning mechanisms. The branch leads initiatives to establish & maintain mechanisms for evaluating forest management practices & enhancing competency to meet standards to ensure forest sustainability.
Director, Rich Greenwood
705-945-6653
Manager Forest Evaluations & Standards, Chris Walsh
705-945-5768,
Manager Forest Health & Silviculture, Albert King
705-945-6718
Manager Forest Management & Planning, Dan Pyke
705-945-6708
Manager Forest Policy, Brian Hillier
705-945-6601

Forest Management Branch
705-945-6661
Fax: 705-945-6667

Industry Relations Branch
Fax: 705-945-6667

Fish & Wildlife Branch
300 Water St.
PO Box 7000
Peterborough, ON K9J 8M5
705-755-5954
Fax: 705-755-1900
The branch coordinates development, implementation & improvement of fisheries & wildlife legislation, policies, programs, standards & related management mechanisms, marketing & client services. The branch influences the development & implementation of fisheries & wildlife partnership programs, represents the ministry in management decisions with provincial, national & international agencies & organizations. The branch leads & directs the management of the Great Lakes fisheries & is responsible for Ontario's fish culture operations. It manages the Outdoors Card, licensing programs, associated information systems related to allocation of wildlife resources.
Director, Cameron Mack
705-755-1909
Manager Biodiversity Section, Debbie Ramsay
705-755-5204
Manager Fisheries Section, Dave Maraldo
705-755-1906
Manager Wildlife Section, Deb Stetson
705-755-1925

Lands & Waters Branch
705-755-1204
Fax: 705-755-1201

Ontario Parks
Fax: 705-755-1701
800-667-1940
www.ontarioparks.com
Development & management of 261 provincial parks, covering 6,328,407 hectares (6% of the provincial land base); parks are classified into broad categories to suit specific requirements for planning & management; categories include nature reserve parks (84), recreation parks (76), natural environment parks (60), waterway parks (29), wilderness parks (8) & historical parks (4).

Great Lakes Branch
705-755-2900
Fax: 705-755-2091
Director, Alec Denys
705-755-2902
Manager Fish Culture Section, Quentin Day
705-755-1804
Manager Lake Erie Management Unit, Michael Morencie
519-873-4609
Lake Manager Lake Ontario Management Unit, Rob MacGregor
705-755-1798
Manager Upper Great Lakes Management Unit - Lake Superior, David McLeish
519-371-5924

Natural Resources Management Division
Whitney Block
#6540, 99 Wellesley St. West
Toronto, ON M7A 1W3
416-314-2000
Fax: 416-314-1994
The division provides leadership & direction for the ministry's resource management programs. The division leads programs for the province's fish, wildlife, parks, Crown lands & waters & is responsible for the delivery of natural resource management programs, including fish hatcheries, the provincial parks system & the management of the Great Lakes.
Asst. Deputy Minister, Kevin J. Wilson
416-314-6131, Fax: 416-314-1994
kevin.j.wilson@ontario.ca

Science & Information Resources Division
Robinson Place, North Tower
300 Water St., 2nd Fl.
Peterborough, ON K9J 8M5
705-755-2000
Fax: 705-755-2802
800-667-1940
The division leads the development & application of scientific knowledge, information management systems & information technologies in support of the Ministry mandate. The division is responsible for ensuring operational decision-making requirements of the Ministry are supported by sound science & reliable data, by providing accurate, relevant & timely information to manage resources in an ecologically sustainable manner.
Asst. Deputy Minister, David de Launay
705-755-2800, Fax: 705-755-2802
david.delaunay@ontario.ca

Applied Research & Development Branch
1235 Queen St. East
Sault Ste Marie, ON P6A 2E5
705-946-2981
Fax: 705-946-3849

Information Geographical Branch
705-755-2363
Fax: 705-755-1640

Geographic Information Branch
300 Water St.
Peterborough, ON K9J 8M5
705-755-2363
Fax: 705-755-1640
Ontario GIO is responsible for implementation of the Ontario Land Information Infrastructure through Land Information Ontario, administers the Surveys Act, Surveyors Act & Ontario Geographic Names Board Act; manages surveying services; coordinates policy, priorities & development or programs in geodetic services, geographic names & Crown land surveying activities. Provincial Georeferencing develops & publishes standards, guidelines & Geographic Information Ontario provides leadership & coordination for Geomatics activities in specifications & stores provincial information related to horizontal & vertical geodetic networks & Global Positioning System (GPS) in the COSINE database. It also administers changes to the names of geographic features & maintains the official geographic names database. Geomatic Services provides leadership in Geomatic Services for the OPS Base Data Infrastructure (BDI) maintains base data & sets standards & manages related fundamental base data projects.

Federal/Provincial Government / Government of Ontario

Surveyor General, Brian Maloney
705-755-2204

Science & Information Branch
Roberta Bondar Pl.
#400, 70 Foster Dr.
Sault Ste Marie, ON P6A 6V5
705-945-5826
Fax: 705-945-6527
Acting Director, Frank Kennedy
705-945-6703

Ministry of Northern Development, Mines & Forestry

99 Wellesley St. West
Toronto, ON M7A 1W3
416-327-0633
Fax: 416-327-0665
TDD: 866-349-1388
www.mndm.gov.on.ca

The Ministry of Northern Development & Mines is the only regional ministry within the government & plays a central role in northern affairs. MNDM supports the mineral industry by providing it with valuable information about the province's geology. It also delivers & administers Ontario's Mining Act to improve the investment climate for mineral development. The ministry has a two-fold mandate, to promote northern economic development & support mineral sector competitiveness. The ministry is developing an initiative to help Ontario's Far North communities attract environmentally sound development, work with First Nation communities, partner ministries, the federal government, the mineral sector & private sector stakeholders to create opportunities for residents to help First Nation communities become more self-reliant. The ministry works with the Northern Ontario Heritage Fund Corporation & with the Ontario Northland Transportation Commission to bring much-needed service improvements to the northeast.

Acts Administered:
Mining Act
Ministry of Northern Development & Mines Act
Northern Services Boards Act
Ontario Mineral Exploration Projects Act
Ontario Northland Transportation Commission Act
Tourism Act

Minister, Hon. Michael Gravelle
807-345-3647, Fax: 807-345-2922
mgravelle.mpp@liberal.ola.org
Deputy Minister, David Lindsay
416-212-2701,
david.lindsay@ontario.ca
• Ontario Northland
555 Oak St. East
North Bay, ON P1B 8L3
705-472-4500
Fax: 705-476-5598
800-363-7512
info@ontc.on.ca
www.ontc.on.ca
• Owen Sound Transportation Company Ltd.
RR#5, Hwy 6 & 21
Owen Sound, ON N4K 5N7
519-376-8740
www.chicheemaun.com

Corporate Management Division
#704, 159 Cedar St.
Sudbury, ON P3E 6A5
705-564-7443
Fax: 705-564-7447

Mines & Minerals Division
Willet Green Miller Centre
933 Ramsey Lake Rd., 6th Fl.
Sudbury, ON P3E 6B5
705-670-5755
Fax: 705-670-5818

The Mines & Minerals Division works to generate new wealth & benefits for the residents of Ontario by providing basic geological information gathering & interpretation in support of Ontario's exploration, mine development & mining sectors & the administration of Ontario's Mining Act in a fair & consistent fashion. Collects, analyzes & publishes valuable information about the state of the mining & mineral industries, as well as specific information about the location & quality of mineral deposits. The field staff throughout the province provide consultative services to the industry through all phases of the mining sequence, & include resident geologists, mining recorders & mineral development officers.
Asst. Deputy Minister, Christine Kaszycki
705-670-5877, Fax: 705-670-5818
christine.kaszycki@ontario.ca

Northern Development Division
Roberta Bondar Place
#200, 70 Foster Dr.
Sault Ste Marie, ON P6A 6V8
705-945-5900
Fax: 705-945-5931
800-461-2287
Other Communication: Delivery of Government Services:
705/945-5904

Responsible for promoting business, industrial, community & regional economic development & diversification; improving access to social & health services for northerners; planning & coordinating an integrated transportation system to meet private & commercial transportation needs at local, regional & provincial levels; coordinating the policies & programs of other ministries to ensure the special needs of northerners are addressed by government.
Asst. Deputy Minister, Cal McDonald
705-945-5901, Fax: 705-945-5932
cal.mcdonald@ontario.ca
Executive Director Northern Ontario Heritage Fund Corporation, Aime Dimatteo
705-945-6734,
aime.dimatteo@ontario.ca
Director Programs & Transportation Branch, Tom Marcolini
705-945-5836,
tom.marcolini@ontario.ca
Director Regional Economic Development, Hial Newsome
705-564-7134,
hial.newsome@ontario.ca

Kenora
#104, 810 Robertson St.
Kenora, ON P9N 4J2
807-468-2937
Fax: 807-468-2930
Manager, Christine Hansen
807-468-2938,
christine.hansen@ontario.ca

North Bay
#203, 447 McKeown Ave.
North Bay, ON P1B 9S9
705-494-4045
Fax: 705-494-4069
Manager, Louise Brinkmann
705-494-4176,
louise.brinkmann@ontario.ca

Sault Ste. Marie
Roberta Bondar Place
#200, 70 Foster Dr.
Sault Ste Marie, ON P6A 6V8
705-945-5914
Fax: 705-945-5931
Manager, Eileen Forestell
705-945-5839,
eileen.forestell@ontario.ca

Sudbury
#601, 159 Cedar St.
Sudbury, ON P3E 6A5
705-564-7517
Fax: 705-564-7583
Manager, Murray Morello
705-564-7519,
murray.morello@ontario.ca

Thunder Bay
#332, 435 James St. South
Thunder Bay, ON P7E 6L3
807-475-1648
Fax: 807-475-1589
Manager, Dave Laderoute
807-475-1573,
dave.laderoute@ontario.ca

Timmins
Hwy. 101 East, Bag 3060
South Porcupine, ON P0N 1H0
705-235-1664
Fax: 705-235-1660

Manager, Brian Pountney
705-235-1654,
brian.pountney@ontario.ca

Mineral Development & Lands Branch
Willet Green Miller Centre
933 Ramsey Lake Rd., Level B4
Sudbury, ON P3E 6B5
705-670-5787
Fax: 705-670-5803

Director, Cindy Blancher-Smith
705-670-5784
Manager Mine Rehabilitation Section, John Robertson
705-670-5798
Senior Manager Mining Lands Section, Ron Gashinski
705-670-5840

Ontario Geological Survey
Willet Green Miller Centre
933 Ramsey Lake Rd., Level B6
Sudbury, ON P3E 6B5
705-670-5758
Fax: 705-670-5754
Director, Andy Fyon
705-670-5924
Senior Manager Geoscience Laboratories, Ed Debicki
705-670-5643
Senior Manager Precambrian Geoscience, Jack Parker
705-670-5976
Senior Manager Resident Geologist Program, Hial Newsome
705-670-5955
Senior Manager Sedimentary Geoscience, Cameron Baker
705-670-5902

Ontario Power Generation

700 University Ave.
Toronto, ON M5G 1X6
416-592-2555
877-592-2555
www.opg.com

Mandate is to meet Ontario's requirements for electricity so as to result in the greatest overall benefit to the community & the lowest cost to the consumer, while operating in a safe & environmentally responsible manner. Assets include 3 nuclear generating stations, 5 fossil generating stations, 64 hydroelectric stations, 3 wind generating stations.
Chair, Hon. Jake Epp
416-592-2115, Fax: 416-971-3691
President/CEO, James F. Hankinson
Executive Vice-President Corporate Development, Jim Burpee
Executive Vice-President Hydro, John Murphy
Executive Vice-President Fossil, Jim Twomey
Senior Vice-President & CFO, Donn Hanbridge
Senior Vice-President Corporate Affairs, Bruce Boland
Senior Vice-President Law & General Counsel, David Brennan

Agencies Division

Ontario Growth Secretariat
#425 - 777 Bay St., 4th Fl.
Toronto, ON M5G 2E5
416-325-1210
Fax: 416-325-7405
866-479-9781

Provides leadership in the development of a growth management agenda. Smart Growth will result in integrated decision-making that brings together all levels of government & to their stakeholders on issues such as transportation, infrastructure, land-use, the environment, housing & public investment to create a higher quality of life.
Asst. Deputy Minister, Brad Graham
416-325-5803, Fax: 416-325-7405
brad.graham@ontario.ca

Infrastucture Ontario
777 Bay St., 9th Fl.
Toronto, ON M5G 2C8
416-212-7289
Fax: 416-325-4646
info@infrastructureontario.ca
www.infrastructureontario.ca

Federal/Provincial Government / Government of Ontario

Ministry of Research & Innovation
Ferguson Block
77 Wellesley St. West, 12th Fl.
Toronto, ON M7A 1N3
416-325-5181
Fax: 416-325-3877
866-446-5216
TDD: 416-325-9275
www.mri.gov.on.ca
The Ministry of Research & Innovation works collaboratively across all government ministries to ensure improved coordination & alignment of research, commercialization & innovation activities & to foster a culture of innovation. The Ministry of Research & Innovation is also committed to engaging all external partners, including the private sector, education & research communities in supporting & delivering on the research & innovation agenda.
Minister, Hon. John Milloy
416-326-1600, Fax: 416-326-1656
jmilloy.mpp@liberal.ola.org
Deputy Minister, George Ross
416-325-7517, Fax: 416-325-5927
george.ross@ontario.ca

Corporate Services Division
416-325-6486
Fax: 416-325-6392

Research & Commercialization Division
416-314-1163
Fax: 416-314-4344
Acting Asst. Deputy Minister, Robert Taylor
416-314-8219,
robert.taylor@ontario.ca
Director Commercialization Branch, Bill Mantel
416-314-0670, Fax: 416-314-0680
bill.mantel@ontario.ca
Director Infrastructure & Innovation Partnerships Branch, Ian Bromley
416-925-0544
Acting Director Research Branch, Allison Barr
416-212-6990, Fax: 416-314-8224
allison.barr@ontario.ca
Deputy Minister, Angela Longo
416-327-8342, Fax: 416-314-7167
angela.longo@ontario.ca

Small & Medium Enterprise Division
416-325-9585
Fax: 416-326-5154
Asst. Deputy Minister, Neil Smith
416-212-7793, Fax: 416-326-5154
neil.h.smith@ontario.ca
Director Entrepreunership, Ann Hoy
416-314-3809, Fax: 416-325-6538
ann.hoy@ontario.ca
Director Business & Advisory Services, Bob Marrs
416-325-6522, Fax: 416-325-6757
bob.marrs@ontario.ca
Director Small & Medium Enterprise Policy & Outreach, Rob Swaffield
416-325-4595, Fax: 416-325-3732
rob.swaffield@ontario.ca

Ministry of Tourism
Hearst Block
900 Bay St., 9th Fl.
Toronto, ON M7A 2E1
416-326-9326
Fax: 416-314-7854
800-668-2746
TDD: 416-325-5807
www.tourism.gov.on.ca
Other Communication: Ontario Travel Information:
1-800-668-2746
Acts Administered:
Historical Parks Act
Ontario Place Corporation Act
St. Clair Parks Commission Act
St. Lawrence Parks Commission Act
Tourism Act
Minister, Hon. Monique M. Smith
416-326-9326, Fax: 416-314-7854
msmith.mpp.co@liberal.ola.org

• St. Clair Parks Commission
ACPC Administrative Office
264 Paget St.
Corunna, ON N0N 4G0
519-862-2291
Fax: 519-862-2294
info@stclairparkway.com
www.stclairparkway.com
Chair, Todd Case
The St. Clair Parks Commission is committed to creating, maintaining & operating, in cooperation with other agencies, regional parks for people of the region & tourists; people-oriented outdoor recreation facilities; fiscal accountability; environmental accountability by action, example & education.
• Metro Toronto Convention Centre Corporation
255 Front St. West
Toronto, ON M5V 2W6
416-585-8000
Fax: 416-585-8270
info@mtcc.com
www.mtcc.com
• Niagara Parks Commission
7400 Portage Rd. South
PO Box 150
Niagara Falls, ON L2E 6T2
905-356-2241
Fax: 905-354-6041
877-642-7275
www.niagaraparks.com
Chair, James Williams
• Ontario Place Corporation
955 Lake Shore Blvd. West
Toronto, ON M6K 3B9
416-314-9900
Fax: 416-314-9992
www.ontarioplace.com
• Ontario Tourism Marketing Partnership Corporation
Hearst Block
900 Bay St., 10th Fl.
Toronto, ON M7A 2E1
416-212-0757
Fax: 416-325-6004
800-668-2746
www.ontariotravel.net
• Ottawa Congress Centre
55 Colonel By Dr.
Ottawa, ON K1N 9J2
613-563-1984
Fax: 613-563-7646
www.ottawacongresscentre.com
• St. Lawrence Parks Commission
RR#1
Morrisburg, ON K0C 1X0
613-543-3704
Fax: 613-543-2847
800-437-2233
TDD: 613-543-4181
Chair, Peter Watson
The St. Lawrence Parks Commission is an Ontario provincial agency established in 1955 to provide recreation, tourism, cultural & educational opportunities for residents of Ontario & visitors to the province through the presentation & interpretation of historical attractions & the development & operation of parks, campgrounds, scenic parkways & recreational areas.

Deputy Minister's Office
416-326-9326
Fax: 416-314-7854

Regional & Corporate Services Division
416-314-7311
Fax: 416-314-7313

Tourism Policy & Development Division
416-326-9326
Fax: 416-325-6985
Acting Asst. Deputy Minister, Michael Kurts
416-325-6961, Fax: 416-325-6985
michael.kurts@ontario.ca
Acting Director Sport & Recreation, Anita Comella
416-314-7696,
anita.comella@ontario.ca
Director Tourism Agencies Unit, Susan Patterson
416-326-9579, Fax: 416-314-7003
susan.patterson@ontario.ca

Director Tourism Policy & Research, Joan MacDonald
416-325-6055, Fax: 416-314-7341
joan.macdonald@ontario.ca

Ministry of Transportation (MTO)
Ferguson Block
77 Wellesley St. West, 3rd Fl.
Toronto, ON M7A 1Z8
416-235-4686
Fax: 416-327-9185
800-268-4686
TDD: 905-704-2426
www.mto.gov.on.ca
Other Communication: TTY Toll Free: 1-866-471-8929; Driver and Vehicle Licensing: 1-800-387-3445; Road Test Booking: 1-888-570-6110
The Ministry performs the following functions: planning, designing & building highways; performing environmental assessments; rehabilitating existing highways to increase their efficiency & safety; performing ongoing highway maintenance; developing standards, operational guidelines & policies relating to highways; & researching & introducing new technologies for more effective highway management. MTO commits to providing & promoting transportation services in a way that sustains a healthful environment through the Ministry's Statement of Environmental Values. The Ministry applies & integrates environmental concerns, along with prevailing social, economic, scientific & other considerations when conducting its business activities.
Acts Administered:
Airports Act
Bluewater Bridge Act
Bridges Act
Commuter Services Act
Dangerous Goods Transportation Act
Ferries Act
Freedom of Information Act
Go Transit Act
Highway Traffic Act
Local Roads Boards Act
Ministry of Transportation Act
Motorized Snow Vehicles Act
Northern Transportation Commission Act
Off-Road Vehicles Act
Ontario Highway Transport Board Act
Ontario Transportation Development Corporation Act
Public Service Works on Highways Act
Public Transportation & Highway Improvement Act
Public Vehicles Act
Railways Act
Rainbow Bridge Act
Statute Labour Act (part)
Toll Bridges Act
Toronto Area Transit Operating Authority Act
Township of Pelee Act
Truck Transportation Act
Urban Transportation Development Corporation Ltd. Act
Minister, Hon. James J. Bradley
416-327-9200, 800-268-4686, Fax: 416-327-9188
jbradley.mpp@liberal.ola.org
TDD: 866-471-8929
Deputy Minister, Bruce McCuaig
416-327-9162, Fax: 416-327-9185
bruce.mccuaig@ontario.ca
Parliamentary Assistant, Michael A. Brown
416-325-3601, Fax: 416-325-3713
mbrown.mpp.co@liberal.ola.org
• GO Transit
#600, 20 Bay St.
Toronto, ON M5J 2W3
416-869-3600
Fax: 416-869-1755
888-438-6646
www.gotransit.com
Chair, Peter Smith
• Ontario Highway Transport Board
151 Bloor St. West, 10th Fl.
Toronto, ON M5S 2T5
416-326-6732
Fax: 416-326-6738
ohtb@mto.gov.on.ca
www.ohtb.gov.on.ca
Chair, Gary Stanley

Corporate Services Division

Federal/Provincial Government / Government of Prince Edward Island

Garden City Tower
301 St. Paul St., 6th Fl.
St Catharines, ON L2R 7R4
905-704-2693
Fax: 905-704-2445
Asst. Deputy Minister, Rob Fleming
905-704-2701, Fax: 905-704-2445
rob.fleming@ontario.ca

Human Resources Branch
905-704-2692
Fax: 905-704-2747

Economics & Transportation I&IT Cluster
416-327-3754
Fax: 416-327-3755

Policy & Planning Division
Ferguson Block
77 Wellesley St. West, 3rd Fl.
Toronto, ON M7A 1Z8
416-327-8521
Fax: 416-327-8746

Provincial Highways Management
Ferguson Block
77 Wellesley St. West, 3rd Fl.
Toronto, ON M7A 1Z8
416-327-9044
Fax: 416-327-9226
Asst. Deputy Minister, Brian Gaston
416-327-9044, Fax: 416-327-9226
brian.gaston@ontario.ca

Central
Atrium Tower
1201 Wilson Ave., 2nd Fl.
Toronto, ON M3M 1J8
416-235-5412
Fax: 416-235-5266

Eastern
1355 John Counter Blvd.
PO Box 4000
Kingston, ON K7L 5A3
613-545-4711
Fax: 613-545-4786
800-267-0295

Northeastern
Ontario Government Bldg.
#301, 447 McKeown Ave.
North Bay, ON P1B 9S9
705-472-7900
Fax: 705-497-5422
800-461-9547

Northwestern
615 James St. South
Thunder Bay, ON P7E 6P6
807-473-2000
Fax: 807-473-2157
800-465-5034

Southwestern
659 Exeter Rd.
London, ON N6A 1L3
519-873-4335
Fax: 519-873-4236
800-265-6072

Engineering Standards Branch
Garden City Tower
301 St. Paul St., 2nd Fl.
St Catharines, ON L2R 7R4
905-704-2089
Fax: 905-704-2055
Director & Chief Engineer, Gerry Chaput
905-704-2940, Fax: 905-704-2055

Strategic Policy Branch
#206, Bldg E, 2nd Fl.
1201 Wilson Ave.
Toronto, ON M3M 1J8
416-235-4504
Fax: 416-235-5243

Transportation Policy Branch
416-235-3502
Fax: 416-235-4932

Construction & Operations Branch
Garden City Tower
301 St. Paul St., 2nd Fl.
St Catharines, ON L2R 7R4
905-704-2032
Fax: 905-704-2030

Program Management Branch
Garden City Tower
301 St. Paul St., 4th Fl.
St Catharines, ON L2R 7R4
905-704-2600
Fax: 905-704-2626

Road User Safety Division
#191, Bldg A
1201 Wilson Ave.
Toronto, ON M3M 1J8
416-235-2999
Fax: 416-235-4153
The division sets safety standards, develops policies, legislation & regulation, & educates road users about road user safety. Responsibilities include evaluating the effectiveness of safety measures, inspecting, monitoring & enforcing compliance with standards, testing, licenses & drivers, & registering vehicles. Through public education, legislation & enforcement, the government strives to ensure all motorists take responsibility for their driving behaviour. The Assistant Deputy Minister, Road User Safety, is responsible for the co-ordination of all Road User Safety activities for the province & acts as the Registrar of Motor Vehicles for Ontario.
Asst. Deputy Minister, Bohodar Rubashewsky
416-235-4454, Fax: 416-235-4153
bohodar.rubashewsky@ontario.ca
Acting Director Business Services, Shelley Unterlander
416-235-4769,
shelley.unterlander@ontario.ca
Director Projects & Change Management, Paul Harbottle
416-235-4199, Fax: 416-235-4111
paul.harbottle@ontario.ca
Director Safety Policy & Education, Susan Lo
416-235-4050, Fax: 416-235-5139
sue.lo@ontario.ca
Acting Executive Director Road User Safety, Brian Gaston
416-235-4827, Fax: 416-235-5672

Service Development & Implementation Office
416-235-4396
Fax: 416-235-4111

Workplace Safety & Insurance Board
200 Front St. West, Ground Fl.
Toronto, ON M5V 3J1
416-344-1000
Fax: 416-344-4684
800-387-0750
TDD: 800-387-0050
www.wsib.on.ca
Other Communication: Information Centre: 416/344-4078
Chair, Hon. Steven W. Mahoney, P.C.
416-344-4451
President & CEO, Jill Hutcheon
416-344-4009
Vice-President & Chief Actuary Actuarial Services, Rob Hinrichs
416-344-5300,
rob_hinrichs@wsib.on.ca
Vice-President Health Services, Jane McCarthy
416-344-4334,
jane_mccarthy@wsib.on.ca

Government of Prince Edward Island
Seat of Government: PO Box 2000
Charlottetown, PE C1A 7N8
902-368-4000
Fax: 902-368-5544
island@gov.pe.ca
www.gov.pe.ca
The Province of Prince Edward Island entered Confederation July 1, 1873. It has an area of 5,683.91 km2, & the StatsCan census population in 2006 was 135,851.

Department of Agriculture
Jones Bldg.
11 Kent St.
PO Box 2000
Charlottetown, PE C1A 7N8
902-368-4880
Fax: 902-368-4857
www.gov.pe.ca/af/agweb/index.php3
Other Communication: Pest Information Line:|902/368-5658
Promotes the sustainable growth & development of Prince Edward Island's primary industries & improvement of the quality of products, co-administering projects demonstrating practical, cost-effective soil conservation practices, operates a potato composting program, instituted a pest information hotline to provide information of environmental significance.Financial & technical assistance is being offered to farmers & owners of agricultural & wood land to implement practices to protect the quality of the Island's soil, water & forest resources & to reduce the risk & use of pesticides. Projects include manure storage, structural soil erosion control, strip cropping, fuel & pesticide storage, deadstock composting, milkhouse waste storage, developing nutrient management plans & planting trees.Details are also being finalized for a forestry component, which would provide financial & technical assistance to woodlot owners in preparing forest management plans & carry out work identified in the plans.
Acts Administered:
Agricultural Crop Rotation Act
Agricultural Insurance Act
Agricultural Products Standards Act
Agrologists Act
Animal Health & Protection Act
Artificial Insemination Act
Companion Animal Protection Act
Dairy Industry Act
Dairy Producers Act
Dog Act
Environmental Protection Act (in part)
Farm Machinery Dealers & Vendors Act
Farm Practices Act
Fences & Detention of Stray Livestock Act
Fire Prevention Act
Fish Inspection Act
Fisheries Act
Gasoline Tax Act
Grain Elevators Corporation Act
Livestock Community Auction Sales Act
Natural Products Marketing Act
Occupational Health & Safety Act
Planning Act
Plant Health Act
Poultry & Poultry Products Act
Real Property Assessment Act
Real Property Tax Act
Revenue Tax Axt
Veterinary Profession Act
Weed Control Act
Women's Institute Act
Minister, Hon. George T. Webster
902-368-4880, Fax: 902-368-4846
gtwebster@gov.pe.ca
Deputy Minister, Brian Douglas
902-368-4830, Fax: 902-368-4846
bwdouglas@gov.pe.ca
Director Corporate & Financial Services, Jerry Gavin
902-368-5741, Fax: 902-368-4857
jpgavin@gov.pe.ca
• Agricultural Insurance Corporation
29 Indigo Cres.
PO Box 1600
Charlottetown, PE C1A 7N3
902-300-4042
Fax: 902-368-6677
peiaic@gov.pe.ca
www.gov.pe.ca/af/agweb/index.php3?number=1000214
Manager, David Aiton
In Prince Edward Island, production insurance is administered by the Prince Edward Island Agricultural Insurance Corporation. The province delivers the Production Insurance Program by sharing costs with the federal government through the Canada-Prince Edward Island Agricultural Policy Framework Agreement on Agricultural Business Risk Management.
• Grain Elevators Corporation(PEIGEC)
PO Box 250
Kensington, PE C0B 1M0

902-836-8929
www.peigec.com
President, Emmerson McMillan
The Prince Edward Island Grain Elevators Corporation will, in accordance with its mandate continue to play a leadership role in the cereal and protein sector of Prince Edward Island.
• Aquaculture & Fisheries Research Initiative Inc.
902-368-5790
Fax: 902-368-5542
Program Officer, Kelly Cantelo
Established to provide industry associations, private businesses, public institutions &/or individual fishers & aquaculturists with increased access to applied & developmental research to address priorities & opportunities in the industry.

Agriculture Policy & Regulatory Division
Works in partnership with general agriculture & agrifood organizations, provincial commodity organizations & education institutions in the development & implementation of industry led strategies that address short & long term critical issues & create wealth for the agri-food sector.
Director, Robert Morrison
902-368-5087, Fax: 902-368-4857
wrmorrison@gov.pe.ca
Acting Manager Farm Practices Review Board, Michael Delaney
902-836-8929
Manager Legislative & Regulatory Section, Vacant

Agriculture Resource Division
Research Station
University Avenue
PO Box 1600
Charlottetown, PE C1A 7N3
902-368-5600
Fax: 902-368-5661
Director, Brian Douglas
902-368-5645
Manager Laboratory, Tracey Wood
902-368-4190
Lab Supervisor Soil & Feed Testing Laboratory, Lori C. Connolly
902-368-6294, Fax: 902-368-6299
hhcairns@gov.pe.ca

District Agricultural Offices:

Charlottetown
Research Station
440 University Ave.
Charlottetown, PE C1A 4N6
902-368-5600
Fax: 902-368-5661
800-236-5214
Agriculture Innovation Manager, Linda MacSwain
902-368-4815, Fax: 902-368-5729
lemacswain@gov.pe.ca

Montague/Souris
Access PEI Montague
PO Box 1500
Montague, PE C0A 1R0
902-838-0600
Fax: 902-838-0610
ACCESSPEIMONTAGUE@gov.pe.ca

Summerside
Access PEI Summerside
PO Box 2063
Summerside, PE C1N 5L2
902-888-8000
Fax: 902-888-8306
accesspeisummerside@gov.pe.ca

West Prince
Access PEI O'Leary
West Prince Regional Services Centre
PO Box 8
O'Leary, PE C0B 1V0
902-859-8800
Fax: 902-859-8709
accesspeioleary@gov.pe.ca

Plant Health Regulatory Program
The Section is responsible for monitoring, management & control of regulated diseases, for enforcement of minimum planting standards & for the supervision of the cull burial, disinfection & virus testing programs. The Section establishes eligibility for planting & prepares Planting Permits for all seed potatoes brought into PEI & monitors all plantings to insure compliance with the Plant Health Act.
Manager, Brian Craig
902-368-4044, Fax: 902-368-4857
bncraig@gov.pe.ca

Agriculture & Agri-Food Development
Agriculture information officers offer on-farm visitation in the areas of crop & livestock management, environmental sustainability, financial management & human resources. Development Officers are available to partner with industry on industry development projects, research trials & program delivery. Staff at the Agriculture Information Centre provide clients with a first point-of-contact for accurate & timely information on a wide variety of aspects of commercial agriculture.
Manager, Shane Murphy
902-368-5611, Fax: 902-314-0823
smurphy@gov.pe.ca

Sustainable Agriculture Resources
The Sustainable Agriculture Section provides technical assistance to soil conservation & integrated pest management, & encourages more sustainable farm operations. The Agriculture & Environmental Resource Conservation program provides technical & financial assistance for a wide range of on-farm conservation projects to help achieve compliance with environmental protection legislation.
Acting Manager, Ron DeHaan
902-368-5642

Office of the Attorney General
Shaw Building, North
105 Rochford St., 4th Fl.
PO Box 2000
Charlottetown, PE C1A 7N8
902-368-5152
Fax: 902-368-4910
www.gov.pe.ca/attorneygeneral
The Attorney General is also responsible for the Coroners Office.

Acts Administered:
Affidavits Act
Age of Majority Act
Ancient Burial Grounds Act
Appeals Act
Apportionment Act
Arbitration Act
Auctioneers Act
Bailable Proceedings Act
Business Practices Act
Canada-United Kingdom Judgements Recognition Act
Canadian Judgements (Enforcement) Act
Cemeteries Act
Charities Act
Child Status Act
Collection Agencies Act
Commorientes Act
Companies Act
Condominium Act
Consumer Protection Act
Consumer Reporting Act
Contributory Negligence Act
Controverted Elections (Provincial) Act
Cooperative Associations Act
Coroners Act
Correctional Services Act
Court Security Act
Credit Unions Act
Crown Proceedings Act
Custody Jurisdiction & Enforcement Act
Defamation Act
Dependents of a Deceased Person Relief Act
Designation of Beneficiaries under Benefit Plans Act
Direct Sellers Act
Electronic Commerce Act
Electronic Evidence Act
Escheats Act, (jointly with Dept. of Transportation & Public Works)
Evidence Act
Factors Act
Family Law Act
Fatal Accidents Act
Films Act
Foreign Resident Corporations Act
Frauds on Creditors Act
Freedom of Information & Protection of Privacy Act
Frustrated Contracts Act
Garage Keepers' Lien Act
Garnishee Act
Gulf Trust Corporations Act
Habeas Corpus Act
Human Rights Act
Insurance Act
Intercountry Adoption (Hague Convention) Act
Interjurisdictional Support Orders Act
International Commercial Arbitration Act
International Sale of Goods Act
International Trusts Act
Interpretation Act
Investigation of Titles Act
Judgement & Execution Act
Judicial Review Act
Jury Act
Landlord & Tenant Act
Legal Profession Act
Licencing Act
Limited Partnerships Act
Maintenance Enforcement Act
Mechanics' Lien Act
Occupiers' Liability Act
Partnership Act
Perpetuities Act
Personal Property Security Act
Police Act
Powers of Attorney Act
Prearranged Funeral Services Act
Premium Tax Act
Private Investigators & Security Guards Act
Probate Act
Probation Act
Provincial Administrator of Estates Act
Provincial Court Act
Public Accounting & Auditing Act
Public Trustee Act
Quieting Titles Act
Real Estate Trading Act
Real Property Act
Reciprocal Enforcement of Judgements Act
Reciprocal Enforcement of Maintenance Orders Act
Retail Business Holidays Act
Sale of Goods Act
Securities Act
Sheriffs Act
Statute of Frauds
Statute of Limitations
Store Hours Act
Summary Proceedings Act
Supreme Court Act
Supreme Court Reporters Act
Survival of Actions Act
Transboundary Pollution (Reciprocal Access) Act
Trespass to Property Act
Truck Operators' Remuneration Act
Trust & Fiduciary Companies Act
Trustee Act
Unclaimed Articles Act
Unconscionable Transactions Relief Act
Uniformity Commissioners Act
Variation of Trusts Act
Vendors & Purchasers Act
Victims of Crime Act
Victims of Family Violence Act
Volunteers Liability Act
Warehousemen's Liens Act
Winding Up Act
Youth Employment Act
Youth Justice Act
Attorney General, Hon. Gerard Greenan
902-368-5152, Fax: 902-368-4910
glgreenan@edu.pe.ca
Deputy Attorney General, Edison J. Shea
902-368-5152, Fax: 902-368-4910
ejshea@gov.pe.ca
Director Justice Policy, Ellie Reddin
902-368-6619, Fax: 902-368-5335
eereddin@gov.pe.ca
Director Policy & Administration, Kevin Barnes
902-368-4865, Fax: 902-368-4224
kcbarnes@gov.pe.ca
Director, Barrie L. Grandy, Q.C.
902-368-4554, Fax: 902-368-4563

Federal/Provincial Government / Government of Prince Edward Island

Department of Communities, Cultural Affairs & Labour
Shaw Bldg.
95 Rochford St., 4th Fl.
PO Box 2000
Charlottetown, PE C1A 7N8
902-368-5250
Fax: 902-368-4121
www.gov.pe.ca/cca

The role of this department is to strengthen the communities by preserving the foundations of social development and public safety while setting new directions that encourage Islanders to maintain and enhance the province's unique physical and cultural characteristics.

Acts Administered:
Amusement Devices Act
Archaeological Sites Protection Act
Archives & Records Act
Blind Workers' Compensation Act
Boilers & Pressure Vessels Act
Charlottetown Area Municipalities Act
City of Summerside Act
Electrical Inspection Act
Elevators & Lifts Act
Emergency 911 Act
Emergency Measures Act
Employment Standards Act
Fathers of Confederation Buildings Act
Fire Prevention Act
Heritage Places Protection Act
Labour Act
Lands Protection Act, PEI
Lightning Rod Act
Lucy Maud Montgomery Foundation Act
Municipal Boundaries Act
Municipal Debenture Guarantee Act
Municipalities Act
Museum Act
North American Labour Cooperation Agreement Implementation Act
Pay Equity Act
P.E.I. Firefighters Long Service Medal Act
Planning Act
Power Engineers Act
Provincial Building Code Act
Public Libraries Act
Rural Community Fire Companies Act

Minister, Hon. Carolyn Bertram
902-368-5250, Fax: 902-368-4121
cibertram@gov.pe.ca
Deputy Minister, Tracey Cutcliffe
902-368-5290, Fax: 902-368-4121
tdcutcliffe@gov.pe.ca
Admin. Assistant, Gayle Roberts
902-368-5250, Fax: 902-368-4121
gfroberts@gov.pe.ca

• Employment Standards Board
161 St. Peters Rd.
PO Box 2000
Charlottetown, PE C1A 7N8
902-368-5550
Fax: 902-368-5476
www.gov.pe.ca/commcul/lair-info/index.php3
Chair, Donald G. MacCormac
The primary role of the Employment Standards Board is to hear appeal presentations from employers who have a complaint filed against them for alleged violations of the Employment Standards Act and also to make recommendations to the Lieutenant Governor in Council with regard to changes in the Minimum Wage Order.

• Labour Relations Board
PO Box 2000
Charlottetown, PE C1A 7N8
902-368-5550
Fax: 902-368-5476
www.gov.pe.ca/commcul/lair-info/index.php3
CEO, Shawn Shea
The Labour Relations Board provides a quasi-judicial process to resolve applications that either management or labour may bring before it. The board attempts to provide a speedy resolution for all matters while at the same time trying to provide for and maintain harmonious labour relations in the province.

• PEI Museum & Heritage Foundation
2 Kent St.
PO Box 2000
Charlottetown, PE C1A 1M6
902-368-6600
Fax: 902-368-6608
mhpei@gov.pe.ca
www.peimuseum.com
Executive Director, Dr. David L. Keenlyside
The PEI Museum and Heritage Foundation is an integral part of the Island's community. Museum and Heritage Prince Edward Island operates the seven provincial museums and heritage sites in Prince Edward Island, providing Islanders and visitors alike with an opportunity to discover our Island heritage and culture. The PEI Museum and Heritage Foundation is a Schedule B Provincial Crown Corporation governed by the Museum Act. It is a registered charitable corporation whose purpose is "to study, collect, preserve, interpret, and protect the human and natural heritage of Prince Edward Island for the use, benefit and enjoyment of the people of the province."

• Prince Edward Island Emergency Measures Organization

Culture, Heritage & Libraries
Fax: 902-368-4663
Director, Harry Holman
902-368-4784,
htholman@gov.pe.ca

Municipal Affairs
Serves as a primary liason with municipalities & municipal interest groups on all municipal matters. Maintains the legislative framework that provides for the existence of municipal government & specifies their duties & powers. Responsible for providing timely advisory & consulting services on most aspects of administration, operations, governance & municipal land use planning.
Acting Manager, John Chisholm
902-368-4744

Planning & Inspection Services
902-368-5490
Fax: 902-368-5526
Provides an integrated delivery of various Acts & regulations pertinent to land use planning for sustainable provincial growth as well as building & development control standards & central delivery of programs in the areas of fire prevention.
Director, Albert MacDonald
902-368-5582,
afmacdonald@gov.pe.ca
Chief Officer Building & Development Services, Don Walters
902-368-4874,
dewalters@gov.pe.ca

Fire Marshal's Office
Responsible for promoting fire prevention measures & training volunteer fire fighters as well as institutional & municipal officials.
Fire Marshal, David Blacquiere
902-368-4869

Policy & Administration
902-368-4865
Fax: 902-368-5335

Inspection Services Branch
Administers & enforces standards for building & development, on-site sewage disposal & subdivision of land.
Manager, Gerry MacDonald
902-368-4884

Provincial Planning Branch
Receiving its mandate from the province's Planning Act, the branch serves as the designated policy centre within government for land use & development on Prince Edward Island. The branch assists public & private individuals & organizations in an effort to achieve sustainable development in the province. General responsibilities include the preperation of management plans for Special Planning Areas, & the approval of subdivisions containing more than five lots.
Manager, Jack Saunders
Minister Education & Early Childhood Development;
Attorney General, Hon. L. Gerard Greenan
902-368-4610, Fax: 902-368-4699
glgreenan@edu.pe.ca
Deputy Minister Education & Early Childhood Development,
Shauna Sullivan Curley, Q.C.

902-368-4662, Fax: 902-368-4699
sscurley@edu.pe.ca
Communications Officer, Jean Doherty
902-368-6449, Fax: 902-368-4663
jmdoherty@edu.pe.ca

Prince Edward Island Emergency Measures Organization
National Bank Tower
#600, 134 Kent St.
PO Box 2000
Charlottetown, PE C1A 7N8
902-894-0385
Fax: 902-368-6362
www.gov.pe.ca/cca/index.php3?number=1002518
Prepares, approves & implements plans, programs, or procedures that are intended to mitigate the effects of an emergency or disaster; provides for the safety, health or welfare of the civil population & the protection of property & the environment in the event of such an occurrence. Conducts public information programs relating to the prevention & mitigation of damage due to disasters, & conducts training exercises for the effective implementation of emergency plans; procures emergency equipment & goods; coordinates emergency preparedness with federal authorities.
Emergency Measures Officer, Cindy MacDougall
902-368-6325, Fax: 902-368-6362
cdmacdougall@gov.pe.ca
Emergency Measures Officer, Barry Folland
902-368-6629,
bffolland@gov.pe.ca

Department of Environment, Energy & Forestry
Jones Bldg.
11 Kent St., 4th & 5th Fl.
PO Box 2000
Charlottetown, PE C1A 7N8
902-368-5000
Fax: 902-368-5830
www.gov.pe.ca/enveng/index.php3
Ensures the quality of the Island's natural environment for the benefit of all residents; encourages Islanders to become stewards of natural resources in order to sustain the resources for the future. Operates & maintains the Bunbury/Stratford Pollution Control Commission, Charlottetown Area Pollution Control Commission, Summerside Area Water Commission & Natural Areas Advisory Committee. Joint enforcement of fish & wildlife regulations with Fisheries & Oceans Canada & the Canadian Wildlife Service.

Acts Administered:
Agriculture Crop Rotation Act
Automobile Junk Yards Act
Energy Corporation Act
Environmental Protection Act
Air Quality Regulations
Code for Plumbing Services Regulations
Environmental Assessment Fees Regulation
Environmental Records Review Regulations
Drinking Water & Wastewater Facility Operating Regulations
Excavation Pits Regulations
Lead Acid Battery Regulations
Litter Control Regulation
Ozone Depleting Substances & Replacement Regulations
Petroleum Storage Tank Regulations
Sand Removal from Beaches Regulations
Sewage Disposal Regulations
Summary Proceeding Act Ticket Regulations
Used Oil Handling Regulations
Waste Resource Management Regulations
Water Quality Certification Regulations
Water Well Regulations
Fish Inspection Act (related)
Fisheries Act (related)
Forest Management Act
Forest Renewal Program Regulations
Provincial Forests Regulations
Mineral Resources Act
Natural Areas Protection Act
Oil & Natural Gas Act
Oil & Gas Conservation Regulations
Pesticides Control Act
Public Forest Council Act
Renewable Energy Act
Unsightly Property Act
Wildlife Conservation Act

Angling Regulation
Fur Harvesting Regulations
Ground Hemlock Regulations
Hunting & Trapping Seasons Regulation
Hunting Guide Regulations
Snowshoe Hare Snaring Regulations
Wildlife Conservation Fund Regulations
Wildlife Management Areas Regulations
Minister, Hon. Richard Brown
902-368-6410, Fax: 902-368-6488
rebrown@gov.pe.ca
Deputy Minister, John MacQuarrie
902-368-5340, Fax: 902-368-6488
jamacquarrie@gov.pe.ca
Director Administrative Services, Mary Kinsman
902-368-5032, Fax: 902-368-5830
makinsman@gov.pe.ca
Director Energy & Minerals, Wayne MacQuarrie
902-894-0289, Fax: 902-894-0290
dwmacquarrie@gov.pe.ca
Head Investigation & Enforcement, John Clements
902-368-4808, Fax: 902-368-5830
jkclements@gov.pe.ca
Communications Officer, Kim Devine
902-368-5286, Fax: 902-368-5830
kmdevine@gov.pe.ca
• Public Forest Council
Forestry Division
PO Box 2000
Charlottetown, PE C1A 7N8
Fax: 902-368-4713
publicforest@gov.pe.ca
• PEI Energy Corporation
Jones Bldg.
11 Kent St., 4th Fl.
PO Box 2000
Charlottetown, PE C1A 7N8
902-894-0288
Fax: 902-894-0290
www.gov.pe.ca/enveng/pec-info/index.php3
CEO, Wayne MacQuarrie
Responsible for pursuing & promoting the development of energy systems & the generation, production, transmission & distribution of energy, in all its forms, on an economic & efficient basis.
• Environmental Advisory Council
11 Kent St.
PO Box 2000
Charlottetown, PE C1A 7N8
Chair, Sherra Profit
Advises the Minister of Environment on environmental issues of concern.

Energy & Minerals
902-894-0288
Fax: 902-894-0290
Responsible for the development, implementation & administration of energy policies & programs; administration of mineral resources development; also supports gas exploration initiatives undertaken on Prince Edward Island.
Director, Wayne MacQuarrie
902-894-0289, Fax: 902-894-0290
dwmacquarrie@gov.pe.ca
Energy Officer, Mike Proud
902-368-5019,
mpproud@gov.pe.ca

Wind Energy Institute of Canada
21741 Rte. 12
Tignish, PE C0B 2B0
902-882-2746
Fax: 902-882-3823
info@weican.org
www.weican.ca
The Wind Energy Institute of Canada (WEICan) has evolved from the Atlantic Wind Test Site (AWTS), which had been a cornerstone of Canada's wind energy R&D program for the last 25 years. Located at North Cape, the northernmost tip of Prince Edward Island, the site offers one of the harshest environments in the world for the testing of wind technology. Its mission is to support the development of safe, reliable, efficient, sustainable & affordable wind power generation in Canada & the development of wind energy-related products & services for Canadian & export markets.

CEO, Scott Harper
902-882-4125,
scott.harper@weican.ca

Private Forest
The Private Forest Program provides financial & technical assistance to woodlot owners for management of private owned woodlots. The section also provides a Forest Management Education program for woodlot owners.
Manager, Brian Brown
902-368-6431,
bmbrown@gov.pe.ca

Pollution Prevention Division
Administers a wide range of programs, legislation & activities which are designed to protect the environment in the province. These include: air quality, protection of the ozone layer, management of hazardous wastes, litter, beverage containers, petroleum storage tanks, used oil, tires, lead-acid batteries, derelict vehicles, excavation pits, unsightly properties, & special projects.
Director, Don Jardine
902-368-5035,
dejardine@gov.pe.ca
Section Head Air Quality & Hazardous Materials, Todd Fraser
902-368-5037, Fax: 902-368-5830
tfraser@gov.pe.ca
Climate Change Coordinator, Erin Swansburg
902-368-6111, Fax: 902-894-0290
Coordinator Environmental Assessment, Greg Wilson
902-368-5052, Fax: 902-368-5830

Production Development
Production Development works to improve the quality & growth of selected tree species through intensive selection & breeding programs. The J. Frank Gaudet Tree Nursery in West Royalty is the primary seedling production facility on Prince Edward Island. Tree seedlings are produced for reforestation programs on private &provincial forest lands as well as for special projects such as watershed enhancements.
Manager, Bill Butler
902-368-7411,
jfnursery@gov.pe.ca

Provincial Forest
The Provincial Forest Section is responsible for the sustainable management of 18,700 ha of publicly owned forest. This is done through monitoring of the growth & health of the Provincial Forest, modeling of forest management options, delivery of forest management treatments to achieve multiple benefits from the forest through tenders or Provincial Forest Section crews, building partnerships with community groups, & periodic public consultations. In addition, the Section provides leadership in forest fire management for all lands, manages the tree planting contracts, delivers forest education & technical information programs for youth & the general public, & provides public access to maps at the district offices.
Manager, Dan McAskill
902-368-6730,
jdmcaskill@gov.pe.ca

Resource Inventory & Modeling
Provides inventory & mapping support for the agriculture & forestry community. This involves the acquisition of aerial photography, the production of land use & land cover mapping products, & the establishment & measurement of forest management plots. Other activities included monitoring forest growth & conducting special forestry projects.
Section Manager, Vacant
902-368-4700,
wmglen@gov.pe.ca

Pesticides Regulatory Program
The Pesticides Regulatory Program is responsible for the administration & enforcement of the PEI Pesticides Control Act & Regulations. This includes the training & licensing of commercial pesticide applicators & vendors, training & certification of private pesticide applicators, inspection audits, & issue of restricted-use pesticide application permits.
Manager, Don Reeves
902-368-5053, Fax: 902-368-5830
dbreeves@gov.pe.ca

Water Management Division
902-368-5028
Fax: 902-368-5830
866-368-5044

Responsible for sustainable management, protection & enhancement of the Province's drinking water, groundwater, inland surface water & coastal estuaries; regulates water & sewer infrastructure & assists in the administration of funding that supports this infrastructure; division provides water testing services (microbiological & chemical) & engineering advisory services to the general public, other provincial departments & agencies, industry & municipalities; also responsible for conducting baseline monitoring & assessment of the Province's water resources.
Director, Jim Young, P.Eng.
902-368-5034,
jyyoung@gov.pe.ca
Manager Drinking Water Management Section, George Somers
902-368-5046,
ghsomers@gov.pe.ca
Manager Watershed Management Section, Bruce Raymond
902-368-5054,
bgraymond@gov.pe.ca

Department of Fisheries, Aquaculture & Rural Development
Jones Bldg.
11 Kent St., 5th Fl.
PO Box 2000
Charlottetown, PE C1A 7N8
902-368-6330
Fax: 902-368-5542
www.gov.pe.ca/fa/faweb
This Department provides an advocacy role in the area of marine fisheries management and supports development of the marine fishery and the aquaculture sector. It also provides support to the processing sector, professional and technical services and fish inspection services.

Aquaculture
Jones Bldg.
11 Kent St., 5th Fl.
Charlottetown, PE C1A 7N8
902-368-5524
Fax: 902-368-5542
The Aquaculture Division delivers the following services: Advice & information to the provinces's aquaculture industry; Financial programs to assist in aquaculture development; & Biological & technical services to the shellfish & finfish sectors on the Island.
Director Aquaculture, Neil MacNair
902-368-5615
Aquaculture Biologist, Kim Gill
902-368-5252

Community Development
PO Box 2000
Charlottetown, PE C1A 7N8
902-368-4467
www.gov.pe.ca/communitydevelopment/index.php3
Prince Edward Island has been divided into six regions. Each region is represented by a Community Development Officer. The Officer helps communities in each region identify their needs, & encourages residents to assist community growth & prosperity.
Chief Community Development Bureau, Bill Buell
902-368-6360
Community Development Officer West Prince Region, Brenda Profit
902-859-8839, Fax: 902-859-8709
bfprofit@gov.pe.ca
Community Development Officer Evangeline Region, Marcel Bernard
902-854-7250, Fax: 902-854-7255
mjbernard@gov.pe.ca
Community Development Officer East Prince Region, Kellie Mulligan
902-432-2705, Fax: 902-432-2634
kamulligan@gov.pe.ca
Community Development Officer Central Queens Region, Nancy Murphy
902-894-0347, Fax: 902-368-4224
nkmurphy@gov.pe.ca
Community Development Officer Eastern Kings Region, Chris Blaisdale
902-687-7083, Fax: 902-687-7091
cwblaisdell@gov.pe.ca
Community Development Officer Southern Kings & Queens, Stephen Lewis
902-838-0618, Fax: 902-838-0610
sjlewis@gov.pe.ca

Federal/Provincial Government / Government of Prince Edward Island

Marine Fisheries & Seafood Services
Jones Bldg.
11 Kent St. 5th Fl.
Charlottetown, PE C1A 7N8
902-368-5251
Fax: 902-368-5542
The Marine Fisheries & Seafood Services Division is engaged in the following activities: Advocating for Prince Edward Island's fishing industry; Offering programs to support new technology, & value-added processing of seafood; Supporting development of emerging species; & Undertaking biological research in support of major fish species.
Director Marine Fisheries & Seafood Services, Barry MacPhee
902-569-7710, Fax: 902-368-5542
jbmacphee@gov.pe.ca
Manager Seafood Services, Lloyd Murphy
902-368-5259,
lgmurphy@gov.pe.ca
Officer Program Statistics, Parnell Trainor
902-368-5248,
patrainor@gov.pe.ca
Manager Marine Fisheries, Dave MacEwen
902-368-5244,
dgmacewen@gov.pe.ca
Lobster Biologist, Robert MacMillan
902-368-5593,
rjmacmillan@gov.pe.ca

Single Window Service
105 Rochford St.
PO Box 2000
Charlottetown, PE C1A 7N8
902-368-4136
Fax: 902-368-4224
www.gov.pe.ca/accesspei/index.php3
Programs & services include government service centres, known as Access PEI. At the eight Access PEI centres across Prince Edward Island, citizens obtain information about the Provincial Government & its programs & services. The Access PEI Centres are situated in the following places: Tignish (902-882-7351); Alberton (902-853-8622); O'Leary (902-859-8800); Wellington (902-854-7250); Summerside (902-888-8000); Charlottetown (902-368-5200); Montague (902-838-0600); & Souris (902-687-7000). Bilingual services are available at all locations, except Montague & Souris.
Director Single Window Service, Carol A. Mayne
902-368-4264, Fax: 902-368-5542
Manager Access PEI Summerside & Access PEI Wellington, Amand Arsenault
902-888-8001, Fax: 902-888-8306
accesspeisummerside@gov.pe.ca;
accesspeiwellington@gov.pe.ca
Other Communications: Access PEI Wellington Address: 48 Mill Rd.
Manager Access PEI Souris & Access PEI Montague, Eleanor Avery
902-687-7050, Fax: 902-687-7091
accesspeisouris@gov.pe.ca; accesspeimontague@gov.pe.ca
Other Communications: Access PEI Montague Address: 41 Wood Islands Hill
Manager Access PEI O'Leary, Access PEI Tignish, & Access PEI Alberton, Martha Dawson
902-859-8801, Fax: 902-859-8709
accesspeioleary@gov.pe.ca; accesspeitignish@gov.pe.ca
Other Communications: Access PEI Alberton Email
accesspeialberton@gov.pe.ca
Manager Access PEI Charlottetown, Mary Lynn Arsenault
902-368-6847, Fax: 902-569-7560
accesspeicharlottetown@gov.pe.ca
Other Communications: Access PEI Charlottetown Phone: 902-368-5200

Department of Health
Jones Bldg.
11 Kent St., 2nd Fl.
PO Box 2000
Charlottetown, PE C1A 7N8
902-368-4900
Fax: 902-368-4974
www.gov.pe.ca/health/index.php3
Provides public health services, primary care, acute care, community hospital and continuing care services to Islanders to help ensure their optimal health.
Acts Administered:
Adoption Act
Adult Protection Act
Change of Name Act
Chiropractic Act
Community Care Facilities & Nursing Homes Act
Consent to Treatment & Health Care Directives Act
Dental Profession Act
Dental Technicians Association Act
Dietitians Act
Dispensing Opticians Act
Donation of Food Act
Drug Cost Assistance Act
Family & Child Services Act
Funeral Directors & Embalmers Association Act
Health & Community Services Act
Health Services Payment Act
Hospital & Diagnostic Services Insurance Act
Hospitals Act
Housing Corporation Act
Human Tissue Donation Act
Licensed Practical Nurses Act
Marriage Act
Medical Act
Mental Health Act
Nurses Act
Occupational Therapists Act
Optometry Act
Pharmacy Act
Physiotherapy Act
Premarital Health Examination Act
Provincial Health Number Act
Psychologists Act
Public Health Act
Rehabilitation of Disabled Persons Act
Smoke-Free Places Act
Social Work Act
Tobacco Sales to Minors Act
Vital Statistics Act
Welfare Assistance Act
White Cane Act
Minister, Hon. Doug W. Currie
902-368-4930, Fax: 902-368-4974
dwcurrie@gov.pe.ca
Deputy Minister, Keith Dewar
902-368-4935, Fax: 902-368-4974
kdewar@gov.pe.ca
Director Community Hospitals & Continuing Care, Cecil Villard
902-894-0337, Fax: 902-894-0363
cfvillard@gov.pe.ca
Acting Director Corporate Services, Glen Doyle
902-368-6142, Fax: 902-368-4969
grdoyle@gov.pe.ca
Director Finance, Terry Keefe
902-368-6125, Fax: 902-368-6136
tekeefe@gov.pe.ca
Director Medical Programs, Dr. Richard Wedge
902-368-6261, Fax: 902-620-3072
rhwedge@gov.pe.ca
Director Primary Care, Leanne Sayle
902-368-6157, Fax: 902-368-6136
ilsayle@gov.pe.ca
Chief Health Officer, Dr. Heather G. Morrison
902-368-4996, Fax: 902-620-3354
hgmorrison@gov.pe.ca

Department of Innovation & Advanced Learning
Shaw Bldg.
105 Rochford St., 5th Fl.
PO Box 2000
Charlottetown, PE C1A 7N8
902-368-4240
Fax: 902-368-4242
www.gov.pe.ca/ial/index.php3
Acts Administered:
Apprenticeship & Trades Qualification Act
Area Industrial Commission Act
Business Development Inc. Act, P.E.I.
Employment Development Agency Act
Hairdressers Act
Holland College Act
Island Investment Development Act
Lending Agency Act
Liquor Control Act
Maritime Economic Cooperation Act
Maritime Provinces Higher Education Commission Act
Prince Edward Island Science & Technology Corporation Act
Private Training Schools Act
University Act
Minister, Hon. Allan V. Campbell
902-368-4230, Fax: 902-368-4242
avcampbell@gov.pe.ca
Deputy Minister, Dr. Michael Mayne
902-368-4250, Fax: 902-368-4242
mbmayne@gov.pe.ca
• Employment Development Agency
Sullivan Bldg., 1st Fl.
PO Box 2000
Charlottetown, PE C1A 7N8
902-368-5805
Fax: 902-368-5909
Acting Director, Birt Mackinnon
In Prince Edward Island, the Employment Development Agency strives to provide employment opportunities & training incentives.
• Food Technology Centre (FTC)
101 Belvedere Ave.
PO Box 2000
Charlottetown, PE C1A 7N8
902-368-5548
Fax: 902-368-5549
877-368-5548
ftcweb@gov.pe.ca
www.gov.pe.ca/ftc
Executive Director, James (Jim) Smith, PhD, MBA, FIFST
The Food Technology Centre provides technical support to the food processing industry. It is an ISO 9001:2000 registered company.
• Island Investment Development Inc. (IIDI)
94 Euston St., 2nd Fl.
Charlottetown, PE C1A 1W4
902-894-0351
Fax: 902-368-5886
• Prince Edward Island Business Development Inc.
94 Euston St., 1st & 2nd Fl.
PO Box 910
Charlottetown, PE C1A 7L9
902-368-6300
Fax: 902-368-6301
800-563-3734
business@gov.pe.ca
www.peibusinessdevelopment.com
Interim Chief Executive Officer, Dr. Michael Mayne
Prince Edward Island Business Development leads business development efforts in the province. Information is provided about investment opportunities, business services, finances, trade & marketing, & government services.
• Prince Edward Island Lending Agency
Confederation Court Office Tower
#201, 134 Kent St.
PO Box 1420
Charlottetown, PE C1A 7N1
902-368-6200
Fax: 902-368-6201
Chief Executive Officer, Peter Wilson
Assistance is provided by the Lending Agency to new & growing businesses. Loans are available for organizations with export potential in the following industries: agriculture, fisheries & aquaculture, tourism, manufacturing & processing, information technology, & small business.
• Technology PEI Inc.
94 Euston St., 2nd Fl.
PO Box 340
Charlottetown, PE C1A 7K7
902-368-6300
Fax: 902-368-6301
techpei@gov.pe.ca
www.techpei.com

Environmental Health
902-368-4970
Fax: 902-368-6468
800-958-6400
The Office of Environmental Health is part of the Division of Regulatory Services. Environmental Health provides the delivery of various programs & services under the PEI Public Health Act & Regulations, the Federal Tobacco Act, & the PEI Tobacco Sales to Minors Act & Regulations. Our main focus includes the enforcement of regulations, education, & illness prevention.
Manager, Joe Bradley

Federal/Provincial Government / Government of Prince Edward Island

Community & Labour Development
Shaw Bldg.
105 Rochford St., 5th Fl.
PO Box 2000
Charlottetown, PE C1A 7N8
902-368-4244
Fax: 902-368-4242
Working with economic development partners, the Community & Labour Development Division facilitates development of the rural areas of the provincial economy.
Director Community & Labour Development, Birt MacKinnon
902-368-4244,
bwmackinnon@gov.pe.ca
Manager Federal Provincial Relations, Mary Hunter
902-620-3488,
mehunter@gov.pe.ca

Finance & Administration
105 Rochford St.
Charlottetown, PE C1A 7N8
902-368-5878
Fax: 902-368-7087
Responsibilities include financial management, administration, the Prince Edward Island Business Development Inc., & human resource management.
Manager Human Resources, Leah Eldershaw
902-368-5876

Higher Education
Sullivan Bldg.
16 Fitzroy St., 3rd Fl.
Charlottetown, PE C1A 7N8
902-368-4615
Fax: 902-368-6144
Acting Director Higher Education & Corporate Services, Susan A. MacKenzie
samackenzie@edu.pe.ca
Manager Student Financial Services, Susan Graham
902-368-4603,
Manager Literacy Initiatives Secretariat; GED Chief Examiner & Chief Administrator, Barbara MacNutt
902-368-6286
Manager Apprenticeship, Karen Redmond
902-368-4625

Population Secretariat
94 Euston St.
PO Box 910
Charlottetown, PE C1A 7L9
902-368-6300
Fax: 902-368-6255
Populationsecretariat@gov.pe.ca
www.gov.pe.ca/popsec
The Population Secretariat promotes Prince Edward Island as a welcoming place to live. The Secretariat works to attract immigrants & former Islanders, & to retain youth & immigrants.
Director, Jane Mallard
902-569-7556,
jmallard@gov.pe.ca
Settlement & Retention Officer, Kate Flanagan
902-368-5018,
kgflanagan@gov.pe.ca
Recruitment Officer, Carson Birch
902-368-4861,
cfbirch@gov.pe.ca
Policy & Repatriation Officer, Erin Docherty
902-368-5127,
ecdocherty@gov.pe.ca

Island Regulatory & Appeals Commission
National Bank Tower
#501, 134 Kent St.
PO Box 577
Charlottetown, PE C1A 7L1
902-892-3501
Fax: 902-566-4076
800-501-6268
irac@irac.pe.ca
www.irac.pe.ca
The Commission is an independent tribunal that hears appeals on issues relating to land use, property & revenue (sales) tax & unsightly premises. It administers land ownership legislation in Prince Edward Island & regulates the petroleum industry & automobile insurance rates. The Commission also regulates electric utilities & certain water & wastewater utilities in Prince Edward Island & hears & considers appeals from decisions or orders of the Director of Residential Rental Property (Rentalsman).
Acts Administered:
Insurance Act
Electric Power Act
Petroleum Products Act
Rental of Residential Property Act
Water & Sewerage Act
Chair & CEO, Maurice (Moe) Rodgerson
902-892-3501, Fax: 902-566-4076
mrodgerson@irac.pe.ca
Vice-Chair, Brian J. McKenna
bmckenna@irac.pe.ca
Director Rental Division, Cathy Flanagan
cflanagan@irac.pe.ca
Director Technical & Regulatory Services Division, Donald G. Sutherland
dgsutherland@irac.pe.ca
Director Corporate Services Division, Eileen Callaghan
mecallaghan@irac.pe.ca
Commission Administrator, Susan D. Jefferson
sdjefferson@irac.pe.ca

Land, Corporate & Appellate Services Division
Regulation of land use, land purchases by non-residents & corporations, zoning & by-law appeals.
Director, Eileen Callaghan
Senior Land Officer, Sandy For
sandyf@irac.pe.ca

Technical & Regulatory Services Division
Regulation of electric power, water & sewage utilities; processing of sales tax appeals.
Director, Donald Sutherland
dons@irac.pe.ca
Research Analyst, Heather Walker
heatherw@irac.pe.ca

Department of Tourism
PO Box 2000
Charlottetown, PE C1A 7N8
800-463-4734
www.tourismpei.com/index.php3
The Tourism PEI mandate is to promote continued growth in the tourism sector; aggressively market PEI as a premier destination; proactively facilitate product and plant development; aggressively promote special events; provide continued emphasis on customer service; manage provincial infrastructure projects (i.e. golf courses and parks); and facilitate community development through tourism.
Acts Administered:
Highway Signage Act
National Park Act
Recreation Development Act
Provincial Parks Regulations
Tourism Industry Act
Tourism PEI Act
Trails Act
Minister, Hon. Valerie E. Docherty
902-368-4801, Fax: 902-368-5277
vedocherty@gov.pe.ca
Deputy Minister, Melissa MacEachern
902-368-5956, Fax: 902-368-5277
mamaceachern@gov.pe.ca
Director Policy, Planning & Research, Chris K. Jones
902-368-6342, Fax: 902-368-6155
ckjones@gov.pe.ca
Administrative Assistant, Janice Walters
902-368-4801, Fax: 902-368-5277
jwalters@gov.pe.ca
• Advisory Council on the Status of Women
Sherwood Business Centre
161 St. Peter's Rd.
PO Box 2000
Charlottetown, PE C1A 7N8
902-368-4510
Fax: 902-368-4516
peistatusofwomen@eastlink.ca
www.gov.pe.ca/acsw
Executive Director, Lisa Murphy
The advisory agency consists of nine members who are appointed by government. Issues addressed by the Council include equality & support for women's participation in the social, cultural, economic, legal, & political spheres.

Tourism Development
The Tourism Development Branch is responsible for delivering programs to assist the Island's travel industry, including the development of new tourism products. The Branch co-ordinates the development of major events & infrastructure through the Province. It has both an operational & a developmental role. It manages provincial parks & through Golf Links PEI, provincial golf courses.
Director, Ron MacNeill
902-368-5505, Fax: 902-368-4438
rnmacnei@gov.pe.ca
Manager Provincial Parks, Shane Arbing
902-368-4404, Fax: 902-368-5922
sdarbing@gov.pe.ca
Supervisor Visitor Services, Heather Pollard
902-368-4441, Fax: 902-368-4438
hlpollard@gov.pe.ca

Tourism Marketing
Fax: 902-368-4438

Department of Transportation & Public Works
Jones Bldg.
11 Kent St.
PO Box 2000
Charlottetown, PE C1A 7N8
902-368-5100
Fax: 902-368-5395
www.gov.pe.ca/tpwpei
Responsible for provincial coordination of the transportation of dangerous goods; holding discussions with the Environmental Advisory Council aimed at introducing environmental protection guidelines during construction & maintenance activities.
Acts Administered:
Architects Act
Crown Building Corporation Act
Dangerous Goods (Transportation) Act
Engineering Profession Act
Expropriation Act
Highway Traffic Act
Judgement Recovery (PEI) Ltd., An Act to Incorporate
Land Survey Act
Off Highway Vehicle Act
Public Works Act
Roads Act
Closing of Roads Regulations
Highway Access Regulations
Public Utility Easement (Fees) Regulation
Vehicle Weights & Dimensions Regulations
Minister, Hon. Ron W. MacKinley
902-368-5120, Fax: 902-368-5385
rwmackinley@gov.pe.ca
Deputy Minister, Steve MacLean, P. Eng
902-368-5130, Fax: 902-368-5385
scmaclean@gov.pe.ca
Director Finance, Human Resources & Operations, Bob S. Clow
902-368-5126, Fax: 902-368-5395
bsclow@gov.pe.ca
Director Highway Maintenance, Alan Maynard, P.Eng
902-368-5103, Fax: 902-368-6244
aemaynard@gov.pe.ca
Director Highway Safety, John B. MacDonald
902-368-5225, Fax: 902-368-5236
jbmacdonald@gov.pe.ca
Communications Officer, Andrew Sprague
902-368-5112, Fax: 902-368-5385
asgsprague@gov.pe.ca
• Island Waste Management Corporation(IWMC)
110 Watts Ave.
Charlottetown, PE C1E 2C1
902-894-0330
Fax: 902-894-0331
888-280-8111
reception@iwmc.pe.ca; info@iwmc.pe.ca
www.iwmc.pe.ca
CEO, Gerry Moore
Management, administration, & provision of solid waste management services throughout Prince Edward Island is the role of the Island Waste Management Corporation. The Crown Agency operates or oversees the following facilities: the Central Compost Facility, the East Prince Waste Management Facility, the Energy from Waste Facility, & the Waste Watch Drop-Off Centers.

Capital Projects Division

Federal/Provincial Government / Gouvernement du Québec / Government of Québec

902-368-5180
The Capital Projects Division is responsible for the design & construction of Government's highway & building infrastructure. The Division consists of four sections: Highway Construction, Planning & Design, Engineering Services & Materials Lab.
Acting Chief Engineer & Director, Stephen J. Yeo, P.Eng.
902-368-5105, Fax: 902-368-5425
sjyeo@gov.pe.ca
Manager Materials Testing, Terry Kelly
902-696-7979

Highway Maintenance
The Highway Maintenance Division provides a full range of operations & maintenance services for the entire provincial highway system. The Division is organized by function & into sections & work units.
Director, Alan Maynard
902-368-5090, Fax: 902-368-6244

Land & Environment
The Land & Environment Division provides a wide range of environmental services for both public works & transportation related projects. The Division also oversees highway construction & maintenance activities to ensure compliance with Federal & Provincial environmental legislation & regulations. Division staff develop & provide training to staff & the construction industry on policies, programs & guidelines to be followed on highway construction & maintenance projects. This division is also responsible for provincial lands.
Director, Brian Thompson, P.Eng.
902-368-5185, Fax: 902-368-5395
bfthompson@gov.pe.ca

Public Works & Planning Division
The Public Works & Planning Division is responsible for assessment & analysis of long term transportation requirements within the Province, combined with the planning & implementation of major projects required to meet the initiatives of various government departments, agencies & corporations. In addition, the Division is responsible for the planning, design & construction associated with building construction projects, including major repair & renovation, for Department building facilities required by Department clients. This division is also responsible for building maintenance & accommodations.
Director, Foster P. Millar
902-368-5147,
jfmillar@gov.pe.ca

Department of the Provincial Treasury
Shaw Bldg.
95 Rochford St., 2nd Fl. South
PO Box 2000
Charlottetown, PE C1A 7N8
902-368-4050
Fax: 902-368-6575
www.gov.pe.ca/pt/index.php3
The Department of the Provincial Treasury facilitates the effective & efficient management of government's human & financial resources. The Office of the Comptroller administers the Corporate Procurement Service.
Acts Administered:
Appropriation Act
Civil Service Act
Civil Service Superannuation Act
Deposit Receipt (Winding up) Act
Environment Tax Act
Financial Administration Act
Financial Corporation Capital Tax Act
Gasoline Tax Act
Health Tax Act
Income Tax Act
Lending Agency Act
Loan Act
Lotteries Commission Act
Maritime Province Harness Racing Commission Act
Northumberland Strait Crossing Act
Public Purchasing Act
Public Sector Pay Reduction Act
Queen's Printer Act
Real Property Assessment Act
Real Property Tax Act
Registry Act
Revenue Administration Act
Revenue Tax Act
Supplementary Appropriation Act

Provincial Treasurer, Hon. Wesley J. Sheridan
902-368-4050, Fax: 902-368-6575
wjsheridan@gov.pe.ca
Deputy Provincial Treasurer, Paul R. Jelley
902-368-4053, Fax: 902-368-6575
prjelley@gov.pe.ca
Communications Officer, Jennifer MacDonald-Donovan
902-620-3679, Fax: 902-368-6575
jwmacdonald@gov.pe.ca
• Prince Edward Island Lotteries Commission
Office of the Deputy Provincial Treasurer
95 Rochford St.
PO Box 2000
Charlottetown, PE C1A 7N8
902-368-4053
Fax: 902-368-6575
• Prince Edward Island Public Service Commission

Office of the Comptroller
902-368-4020
Fax: 902-368-6661
Comptroller, Scott K. Stevens
902-368-4001, Fax: 902-368-6661
ksstevens@gov.pe.ca
Manager Procurement, Ian K. Burge
902-368-4041, Fax: 902-368-5171
ikburge@gov.pe.ca

Fiscal Management
902-368-5802
Fax: 902-368-4077
Other Communication: Investments: 902/368-4167; Fax: 902/368-4077

Information Technology Shared Services
902-368-4100
Fax: 902-368-5444

Program Evaluation & Fiscal Relations
902-368-4178
Fax: 902-569-7632

Prince Edward Island Workers Compensation Board
14 Weymouth St.
PO Box 757
Charlottetown, PE C1A 7L7
902-368-5680
Fax: 902-368-5705
800-237-5049
www.wcb.pe.ca
Other Communication: Customer Liaison Service: 866-460-3074
WCB exists to promote safe workplaces & to protect employers & injured workers through a sustainable accident insurance program.
Acts Administered:
Occupational Health & Safety Act
Workers Compensation Act
Chair, Nancy Guptill
902-368-5688, Fax: 902-368-6359
CEO, Carol Anne Duffy
902-368-5688,
caduffy@wcb.pe.ca
Director Client Services, Mary Hughes Power
902-368-5687, Fax: 902-368-5705
mhpower@wcb.pe.ca
Director Corporate Services, Tammy Turner
902-368-4102,
teturner@wcb.pe.ca
Director Occupational Health & Safety Council, George Stewart
902-368-5562, Fax: 902-368-5696
gwstewart@wcb.pe.ca
Officer Communications, Mark Barrett
902-894-0362, Fax: 902-620-3885
mabarretta@wcb.pe.ca
Manager Employer Services, Greg MacCallum
902-368-5679,
ggmaccallum@wcb.pe.ca
Finance Officer, Annette Johnson
902-368-5708,
aljohnson@wcb.pe.ca
Manager Information Technology Services, Darren MacDonald
902-368-5669, Fax: 902-368-5696
dpmacdonald@wcb.pe.ca

Gouvernement du Québec / Government of Québec
Siège du gouvernement: Hôtel du Parlement
1045, rue des Parlementaires
Québec, QC G1A 1A4
418-643-7239
Fax: 418-646-4271
866-337-8837
www.gouv.qc.ca; www.asnat.qc.ca
La Province de Québec est entrée dans la Confédération le 1ère juillet, 1867. Terre: 1,356,366.78 km2. Population: 7,866,108 (2010)
• Commission municipale du Québec
Mezzanine, aile Chauveau
10, rue Pierre-Olivier-Chauveau, Tour 5e étage
Québec, QC G1R 4J3
418-691-2014
Fax: 418-644-4676
866-353-6767
cmq@mamr.gouv.qc.ca
www.cmq.gouv.qc.ca
Président, Pierre Delisle
CMQ est un tribunal et un organisme administratif, d'enquête et de conseil, spécialisé en matière municipale.
• Régie du logement du Québec
Pyramide Ouest
#2360, 5199, rue Sherbrooke est
Montréal, QC H1T 3X1
514-873-6575
Fax: 514-873-6805
800-683-2245
www.rdl.gouv.qc.ca
• Société d'habitation du Québec
Aile St-Amable
1054, rue Louis-Alexandre-Taschereau, 3e étage
Québec, QC G1R 5E7
418-643-4035
Fax: 418-643-4560
800-463-4315
www.habitation.gouv.qc.ca

Ministère des Affaires municipales et Occupation du territoire / Municipal Affairs
Aile Chaveau
10, rue Pierre-Olivier-Chauveau, 3e étage
Québec, QC G1R 4J3
418-691-2019
Fax: 418-643-7385
communications@mamrot.gouv.qc.ca
www.mamrot.gouv.qc.ca
A la charge de conseiller le gouvernement & d'assurer la coordination interministérielle dans ces domaines; a pour mission de favoriser la mise en place & le maintien d'un cadre de vie & de services municipaux de qualité pour des citoyens/citoyennes; le développement des régions & des milieux ruraux; & le progrès & le rayonnement de la métropole; intervient auprès des municipalités locales, régionales de comté, des communautés métropolitaines de Montréal & de Québec, & de l'administration régionale Kativik
Acts Administered:
Code municipal du Québec
Loi concernant la consultation des citoyens sur la réorganisation territoriale
Loi concernant la négociation d'ententes relatives à la réduction des coûts de main-d'oeuvre dans le secteur municipal
Loi concernant la réglementation municipale des édifices publics
Loi concernant la Ville de Schefferville
Loi concernant les droits sur les mutations immobilières
Loi instituant le fonds spécial de financement des activités locales
Loi modifiant de nouveau diverses dispositions législatives concernant le domaine municipal
Loi portant réforme de l'organisation territoriale municipale des régions métropolitaines de Montréal, de Québec et de l'Outaouais
Loi sur Immobilière SHQ
Loi sur l'aide municipale à la protection du public aux traverses de chemin de fer
Loi sur l'aménagement et l'urbanisme
Loi sur l'exercice de certaines compétences municipales dan certaines agglomérations
Loi sur l'expropriation
Loi sur l'instruction publique

Loi sur l'instruction publique pour les autochtones cris, inuits et naskapis
Loi sur l'interdiction de subventions municipales
Loi sur l'organisation territoriale municipale
Loi sur la Commission municipale
Loi sur la Communauté métropolitaine de Montréal
Loi sur la Communauté métropolitaine de Québec
Loi sur la conservation du patrimoine naturel
Loi sur la conservation et la mise en valeur de la faune
Loi sur la fiscalité municipale
Loi sur la police
Loi sur la qualité de l'environnement
Loi sur la Régie du logement
Loi sur la Société d'habitation du Québec
Loi sur la Société du Parc industriel et portuaire de Bécancour
Loi sur la Société Innovatech du grand Montréal
Loi sur la Société québécoise d'assainissement des eaux
Loi sur la vente des services publics municipaux
Loi sur le développement de la région de la Baie-James
Loi sur le Ministère de l'Agriculture, des Pêcheries et de l'Alimentation
Loi sur le Ministère du Développement durable, de l'Environnement et des Parcs
Loi sur le régime de retraite des élus municipaux
Loi sur les abus préjudiciables à l'agriculture
Loi sur les compétences municipales
Loi sur les cités et villes
Loi sur les conseils intermunicipaux de transport dans la région de Montréal
Loi sur les cours municipales
Loi sur les dettes et les emprunts municipaux
Loi sur les élections et les référendums dans les municipalités
Loi sur les espèces menacées ou vulnérables
Loi sur les immeubles industriels municipaux
Loi sur les impôts
Loi sur les régimes de retraite des maires et des conseillers des municipalités
Loi sur les sociétés de transport en commun
Loi sur les sociétés d'économie mixte dans le secteur municipal
Loi sur le traitement des élus municipaux
Loi sur les travaux municipaux
Loi sur les villages cris et le village Naskapi
Loi sur les villages Nordiques et l'Administration régionale Kativik
Ministre, L'hon. Laurent Lessard
418-691-2050, Fax: 418-643-1795
ministre@mamrot.gouv.qc.ca
Sous-ministre, Marc Lacoix
418-691-2040, Fax: 418-643-7708
Sous-ministre adjointe (Territoires), Linda Morin
Sous-ministre adjoint (Politiques), Sylvain Boucher
Sous-ministre adjoint (Infrastructures & finances municipales), Jacques A. Tremblay
Sous-ministre adjoint (Métropole), Jean Séguin

Territoires / Regions
Sous-ministre adjointe, Linda Morin
418-691-2040
Directeur Bureau municipal de la géomatique & de la statistique, Gilles W. Boivin
418-691-2088
Directrice (par intérim) Développement rural, Danielle Leduc
418-691-2078
Directeur Affaires régionales/Direction de la Capitale-Nationale, Stéphane Bouchard
418-691-2016
Directeur du projet Occupation des territoires, Yannick Routhier
418-691-2038

Abitibi-Témiscamingue
#105, 170, av Principale, 1er étage
Rouyn-Noranda, QC J9X 4P7
819-763-3582
Fax: 819-763-3803
Dr.Abitibi-Temis@mamrot.gouv.qc.ca
Directeur, Denis Moffet

Bas-Saint-Laurent
337, rue Moreault, 2e étage
Rimouski, QC G5L 1P4
418-727-3629
Fax: 418-727-3537
Dr.Bas-St-Laur@mamrot.gouv.qc.ca
Directeur, Gilles Julien

Capitale-Nationale
8, rue Cook, 5e étage
Québec, QC G1R 5J8
418-643-1343
Fax: 418-643-4086
Dr.CapNat@mamrot.gouv.qc.a
Directeur, Paul Arsenault

Centre-du-Québec
#S-05, 62, rue Saint-Jean-Baptiste
Victoriaville, QC G6P 4E3
819-752-2453
Fax: 819-795-3673
Dr.Centre-Quebec@mamrot.gouv.qc.ca
Directeur, Gaétan Désilets

Chaudière-Appalaches
#102, 1100, boul Frontenac est
Thetford Mines, QC G6G 6H1
418-338-4624
Fax: 418-338-1908
Dr.Chaud-App@mamrot.gouv.qc.ca
Directrice, Danie Croteau

Côte-Nord
#RC-708, 625, boul Laflèche
Baie-Comeau, QC G5C 1C5
418-295-4241
Fax: 418-295-4955
Dr.CoteNord@mamrot.gouv.qc.ca
Directeur, Jacques Tremblay

Estrie
#4.04, 200, rue Belvédère nord
Sherbrooke, QC J1H 4A9
819-820-3244
Fax: 819-820-3979
Dr.Estrie@mamrot.gouv.qc.ca
Directeur, Pierre Poulin

Gaspésie-Iles-de-la-Madeleine
#10B, 500, av Daigneault
CP 310
Chandler, QC G0C 1K0
418-689-5024
Fax: 418-689-4823
Dr.Gaspe-IlesMad@mamrot.gouv.qc.ca
Directeur, Michel Gionest

Lanaudière
#3200, 40, rue Gauthier sud
Joliette, QC J6E 4J4
450-752-5040
Fax: 450-752-8064
Dr.Lanaudiere@mamrot.gouv.qc.ca
Directeur, Jean Ouellet

Laurentides
#210, 161, rue de la Gare
Saint-Jérôme, QC J7Z 2B9
450-569-7646
Fax: 450-569-3131
Dr.Laurentides@mamrot.gouv.qc.ca
Directeur (par intérim), Jean Ouellet

Mauricie
#321, 100, rue Laviolette
Trois-Rivières, QC G9A 5S9
819-371-6653
Fax: 819-371-6953
Dr.Mauricie@mamrot.gouv.qc.ca
Directeur, Pierre Robert

Montérégie
#403, 201, place Charles-Le Moyne
Longueuil, QC J4K 2T5
450-928-5670
Fax: 450-928-5673
Dr.Monteregie@mamrot.gouv.c

Directeur, Robert Sabourin

Métropole
Tour de la Bourse
#2.17, 800, rue du Square-Victoria
CP 83
Montréal, QC H4Z 1B7
514-873-8246
Fax: 514-864-5912
courrier.ddrm@mamrot.gouv.qc.ca
Directrice, Johanne Dumont

Nord-du-Québec
#1, 215, 3e Rue
Chibougamau, QC G8P 1N3
418-748-7737
Fax: 418-748-7841
Nord-du-Quebec@mamrot.gouv.qc.ca
Directeur, Richard Leclerc

Outaouais
#9.300, 170, rue de l'Hôtel-de-Ville
Gatineau, QC J8X 4C2
819-772-3006
Fax: 819-772-3989
Dr.Outaouais@mamrot.gouv.qc.ca
Directeur, Pierre Ricard

Saguenay-Lac-Saint-Jean
#RC-03, 227, rue Racine est
Chicoutimi, QC G7H 7B4
418-698-3523
Fax: 418-698-3526
Dr.Sag-Lac@mamrot.gouv.qc.ca
Directrice, Lison Rhéaume

Infrastructures et finances municipales / Infrastructures & Municipal Financing
Sous-ministre adjoint, Jacques A. Tremblay
418-691-2040
Directeur général Finances municipales, Jean Monfet
418-691-2007
Directeur général Infrastructures, Jean-Pierre Beaumont
418-691-2005

Métropole / Metropolitan Regions
Sous-ministre adjoint, Jean Séguin
514-873-8395
Directrice Développement régional & métropolitain, Johanne Dumont
514-873-6992
Directrice métropolitaine Aménagement et des affaires municipales, Lucie Tremblay
514-873-8246

Politiques / Policy
Sous-ministre adjoint, Sylvain Boucher
418-691-2040
Directrice générale Urbanisme/Aménagement du territoire, Marie-Lise Côté
418-691-2015
Directrice générale Politiques, Sylvie Desaulniers
418-691-2039

Services à la gestion / Administrative Services

Gaspésie—Iles-de-la-Madeleine
195, boul Perron est
Caplan, QC G0C 1H0
418-388-2125
Fax: 418-388-2444
gaspesie-iles-de-la-madeleine@mrnf.gouv.qc.ca

Nord-du-Québec
1121, boul Industriel
CP 159
Lebel-sur-Quévillon, QC J0Y 1X0
819-755-4838
Fax: 819-755-3541
nord-du-quebec@mrnf.gouv.qc.ca

Nord-du-Québec
1121, boul Industriel
CP 159
Lebel-sur-Quévillon, QC J0Y 1X0
819-755-4838
Fax: 819-755-3541
nord-du-quebec@mrnf.gouv.qc.ca
Directeur général, Guy Hétu

Planification, performance et qualité / Planning, Performance and Quality
Sous-ministre adjoint, Denis Lalumière
418-266-5990
Directrice Qualité, Danielle St-Louis
418-266-7505
Directrice Évaluation, Monique Savoie
418-266-7030

Federal/Provincial Government / Gouvernement du Québec / Government of Québec

Directrice Affaires intergouvernementales & coopération internationale/Études et analyses, Patricia Caris
418-266-8740
Directrice Planification et orientations stratégiques, Andrée Quenneville
418-266-7088
Directrice Recherche, innovation et transfert des connaissances, Manon St-Pierre
418-266-7056

Services de santé et médecine universitaire / Health Services & Academic Medicine
Directeur général Services de santé et médecine universitaire, Michel A. Bureau
418-266-6930
Directeur Main d'oeuvre médicale, Daniel Poirier
418-266-6975
Directrice Organisation des services médicaux et technologiques, Sylvie Bernier
418-266-6946
Directrice Services médicaux généraux et préhospitaliers et traumatologie, Jeannine Auger
418-266-5827
Directeur Affaires universitaires, Louis Dufresne
418-266-7500
Directeur Lutte contre le cancer, Antoine Loutfi
418-266-6940
Directrice Organisation des services de première ligne intégrés, Yolaine Galarneau
418-266-6976
Directeur Santé mentale, André Delorme
418-266-6835
Directeur nationale Urgences, Daniel Lefrançois
418-266-5811
Directeur Biovigilance, Yves Jalbert
418-266-6710
Sous-ministre adjoint, Sylvain Gagnon
418-266-6800
Directrice Secrétariat à l'adoption internationale, Luce de Bellefeuille
514-873-4747
Directeur Personnes âgées en perte d'autonomie, Christian Gagné
418-266-6818
Directrice Personnes handicapées/Programme dépendances, Rachel Ruest
418-266-6852
Directeur Services sociaux généraux/Activités communautaires, Mario Frechette
418-266-6936,
Directrice Projet pour la mise en oeuvre de la Loi sur la représentation des RI-RTF, Diane Lapointe
418-663-5226
Directrice Jeunes et des familles, Chantal Maltais
418-226-6840

Services administratifs / Administrative Services
Sous-ministre associée Services à la gestion, Liette Larrivée
418-643-3500, Fax: 418-643-0275
Directeur Gestion immobilière, Jean Leclerc
418-646-6777, Fax: 418-646-1869
Directeur Planification et politiques, Louis Métiver
418-646-6777, Fax: 418-643-1713
Directrice Ressources financières et matérielles, Lucie Picard
418-646-6777, Fax: 418-643-1713
Directeur Ressources humaines, René Boulanger
418-646-6777, Fax: 418-528-6878
Directeur Technologies de l'information, Abdelaziz Younsi
418-646-6777, Fax: 418-644-4593

Services à la gestion / Administrative Services
Directeur Ressources financières, Francis Mathieu
Directrice Ressources humaines, Nicole Lévesque
Directeur Ressources informationnelles, Guy Leclerc

Services à la gestion / Administrative Services
Directrice (par intérim), Josée Dupont
418-528-0808
Directrice Ressources humaines, Hélène Verret
418-646-4157
Directrice Ressources financières, Danièle Cantin
418-646-9934
Directeur Contrats et ressources matérielles, Marcel Carpentier
418-643-5473

Directrice Technologies de l'information, Odile Béland
418-643-4431

Politiques et recherche / Policy & Research
Sous-ministre adjoint, Normand Pelletier
Directeur Politiques du travail, Steeve Audet
Directeur Information sur le travail, Gilles Fleury
Directeur Recherche et innovation en milieu de travail, Dalil Maschino

Relations du travail / Labour Relations
Sous-ministre adjointe, Suzanne Thérien
Directeur générale, Daniel Cholette
Directeur Médiation-conciliation & prévention (Montréal), Julien Perron
Directeur Médiation-conciliation, prévention & arbitrage (Québec), Jean Poirier
Directeur Bureau d'évaluation médicale, Dr André Perron

Ministère de la Culture, des Communications & de la Condition féminine / Culture, Communications & the Status of Women
225, Grande Allée est
Québec, QC G1R 5G5
Fax: 418-380-2364
888-380-8882
infos@mcccf.gouv.qc.ca
www.mcccf.gouv.qc.ca

Acts Administered:
Charte de la langue française
Loi sur Bibliothèque et archives nationales du Québec
Loi sur la programmation éducative
Loi sur la Société de développement des entreprises culturelles
Loi sur la Société de la Place des Arts de Montréal
Loi sur la Société de télédiffusion du Québec
Loi sur la Société du Grand Théâtre de Québec
Loi sur le cinéma
Loi sur le Conseil des arts et des lettres du Québec
Loi sur le Conservatoire
Loi sur le Conservatoire de musique et d'art dramatique du Québec
Loi sur le développement des entreprises québécoises dans le domaine du livre
Loi sur le ministère de la Culture et des Communications
Loi sur le Musée des beaux-arts de Montréal
Loi sur le statut professionnel des artistes des arts visuels, des métiers d'art et de la littérature et sur leurs contrats avec les diffuseurs
Loi sur le statut professionnel et les conditions d'engagement des artistes de la scène, du disque et du cinéma
Loi sur les archives
Loi sur les biens culturels
Loi sur les concours artistiques, littéraires et scientifiques
Loi sur les musées nationaux
Ministre, L'hon. Christine St-Pierre
418-380-2310, Fax: 418-380-2311
Sous-ministre, Sylvie Barcelo
418-380-2330, Fax: 418-380-2391
Sous-ministre adjoint Politiques, patrimoine, muséologie et communications, Louis Vallée
418-380-2330, Fax: 418-380-2391
Directrice Information/Bibliothèque, Monique Lachance
418-380-2358, Fax: 418-380-2364

Abitibi-Témiscamingue et Nord-du-Québec
#450, 19, rue Perreault ouest
Rouyn-Noranda, QC J9X 6N5
819-763-3517
Fax: 819-763-3382
dratnq@mcccf.gouv.qc.ca

Bas-St-Laurent
337, rue Moreault
Rimouski, QC G5L 1P4
418-727-3650
Fax: 418-727-3824
drbsl@mcccf.gouv.qc.ca

Capitale-Nationale
Bloc C, RC
225, Grande-Allée est
Québec, QC G1R 5G5
418-380-2346
Fax: 418-380-2347
dcn@mcccf.gouv.qc.ca

Chaudière-Appalaches
6210, rue St-Laurent
Lévis, QC G6V 3P4
418-838-9886
Fax: 418-838-1485
drca@mcccf.gouv.qc.ca

Côte-Nord
#1.806, 625, boul Laflèche
Baie-Comeau, QC G5C 1C5
418-295-4979
Fax: 418-295-4070
drcn@mcccf.gouv.qc.ca

Estrie
#410, 225, rue Frontenac
Sherbrooke, QC J1H 1K1
819-820-3007
Fax: 819-820-3930
dre@mcccf.gouv.qc.ca

Gaspésie/Iles-de-la-Madeleine
146, av de Grand-Pré
CP 370
Bonaventure, QC G0C 1E0
418-534-4431
Fax: 418-534-4564
drgim@mcccf.gouv.qc.ca

Laval, Lanaudière et les Laurentides
#200, 300, rue Sicard
Sainte-Thérèse, QC J7E 3X5
450-430-3737
Fax: 450-430-2475
drlll@mcccf.gouv.qc.ca

Mauricie et Centre-du-Québec
#315, 100, rue Laviolette
Trois-Rivières, QC G9A 5S9
819-387-6001
Fax: 819-371-6984
drmcq@mcccf.gouv.qc.ca

Montérégie
#500, 2, boul Desaulniers
Saint-Lambert, QC J4P 1L2
450-671-1231
Fax: 450-671-3884
drmonter@mcccf.gouv.qc.ca

Montréal
#600, 480, boul St-Laurent
Montréal, QC H2Y 3Y7
514-873-2255
Fax: 514-864-2448
dm@mcccf.gouv.qc.ca

Outaouais
#4.140, 170, rue de l'Hôtel-de-Ville, 4e étage
Gatineau, QC J8X 4C2
819-772-3002
Fax: 819-772-3950
dro@mcccf.gouv.qc.ca

Saguenay—Lac-Saint-Jean
202, rue Jacques-Cartier est
Chicoutimi, QC G7H 6R8
418-698-3500
Fax: 418-698-3522
drslstj@mcccf.gouv.qc.ca

Directions régionales/Regional Offices:

Bas-Saint-Laurent - Gaspésie - Iles-de-la-Madeleine - Saguenay - Lac Saint Jean
#2, 1600, rue Bersimis
Chicoutimi, QC G7K 1H9
418-698-3530
Fax: 418-698-3533

Laurentides - Outaouais - Abitibi-Témiscamingue
Galeries de Buckingham
999, rue Dollard
Gatineau, QC J8L 3E6
819-986-8985
Fax: 819-986-9793

Mauricie - Centre-du-Québec - Estrie
#55, 5195, boul des Forges
Trois-Rivières, QC G8Y 4Z3

Federal/Provincial Government / Gouvernement du Québec / Government of Québec

819-475-8506
Fax: 819-371-4907

Montérégie - Secteur Est
#3300, 1355, rue Gauvin
Saint-Hyacinthe, QC J2S 8W7
450-778-6530
Fax: 450-778-6540

Montréal - Laval - Lanaudière
201, boul Crémazie est, 2e étage
Montréal, QC H2M 1L4
514-873-8101
Fax: 514-873-9994

Québec - Chaudière-Appalaches
#C RC.245, 2700, rue Einstein
Québec, QC G1P 3W8
418-643-6140
Fax: 418-644-6327

Pêches et aquaculture commerciales / Commercial Fishing & Aquaculture
Sous-ministre adjoint, Louis Vallée
418-380-2136, Fax: 418-380-2171
Directeur Analyses et politiques, Abdoul Aziz Niang
418-380-2100, Fax: 418-380-2182
Directeur Centre de coordination des projects spéciaux, Denis Lacerte
418-380-2100, Fax: 418-380-2182
Directeur Innovation et technologies, Lucien Poirier
418-368-7637, Fax: 418-360-8400

Directions régionales/Regional Offices:

Côte-Nord
466, av Arnaud
Sept-Îles, QC G4R 3B1
418-964-8521
Fax: 418-964-8744
drcn@mapaq.gouv.qc.ca
Directeur régional, Alain Côté

Estuaire et Eaux intérieures
460, boul Louis-Fréchette, RC
Nicolet, QC J3T 1Y2
819-293-5677
Fax: 819-293-8519
dreei@mapaq.gouv.qc.ca

Gaspésie
#206, 96, montée de Sandy Beach
Gaspé, QC G4X 2V6
418-368-7631
Fax: 418-360-8851
drg@mapaq.gouv.qc.ca
Directeur régional, Marcel Roussy

Îles-de-la-Madeleine
Édifice Réjean-Richard
101-125, ch du Parc
Cap-aux-Meules, QC G4T 1B3
418-986-2098
Fax: 418-986-4421
drim@mapaq.gouv.qc.ca
Directeur régional, Donald Arseneau

Transformation Alimentaire Québec
Sous-ministre associé, Jean-Yves Lavoie
418-380-2136, Fax: 418-380-2171
Directeur Institut de technologie agroalimentaire, André Simard
Directrice (par intérim) Développement régional, Lyne Fournier
514-873-4147, Fax: 514-873-2364

Bibliothèque et Archives nationales du Québec (BAnQ) / National Library & Archives of Québec
475, boul De Maisonneuve est
Montréal, QC H2L 5C4
514-873-1100
Fax: 514-873-9312
800-363-9028
www.banq.qc.ca

Commission de reconnaissance des associations d'artistes et des associations de producteurs / Commission for Recognition of Artists & Production Associations
#14.60, 500, boul René-Lévesque ouest
Montréal, QC H2Z 1W7
514-873-6012
Fax: 514-873-6267
tribunal@craaap.gouv.qc.ca
www.craaap.gouv.qc.ca

Commission des biens culturels du Québec / Québec Cultural Property Commission
Bloc A-RC
225, Grande Allée est
Québec, QC G1R 5G5
418-643-8378
Fax: 418-643-8591
info@cbcq.gouv.qc.ca
www.cbcq.gouv.qc.ca
Président, Mario Dufour
Vice-présidente, Suzel Brunel

Conseil des arts et des lettres du Québec
#320, 79, boul René-Lévesque est
Québec, QC G1R 5N5
418-643-1707
Fax: 418-643-4558
800-897-1707
info@calq.gouv.qc.ca
www.calq.gouv.qc.ca

Institution nationale & sociétés d'État / Crown Corporations

Musée d'art contemporain de Montréal (MACM) / Montréal Museum of Contemporary Art
185, rue Ste-Catherine ouest
Montréal, QC H2X 3X5
514-847-6226
Fax: 514-847-6290
www.macm.org

Musée de la civilisation / Museum of Civilisation
85, rue Dalhousie
CP 155 B
Québec, QC G1K 7A6
418-643-2158
Fax: 418-646-9705
866-710-8031
mcqweb@mcq.org
www.mcq.org

Musée national des beaux-arts du Québec
Parc des Champs-de-Bataille
1, av Wolfe-Montcalm
Québec, QC G1R 5H3
418-643-2150
Fax: 418-646-3330
866-220-2150
webmestre@mnba.qc.ca
www.mnba.qc.ca

Politiques, patrimoine, muséologie & communications / Policy, Heritage, Museology & Communication

Régie du cinéma / Film Board
#100, 390, rue Notre-Dame ouest
Montréal, QC H2Y 1T9
514-873-2371
Fax: 514-873-2142
800-463-2463
regieducinema@rcq.gouv.qc.ca
www.rcq.gouv.qc.ca

Directions régionales/Regional Offices:

Secrétariat à la politique linguistique / French Language Board
225 Grande-Allée est, 4e étage
Québec, QC G1R 5G5
418-643-4248
Fax: 418-646-7832
info@spl.gouv.qc.ca
www.spl.gouv.qc.ca

Société de développement des entreprises culturelles (SODEC) / Arts & Cultural Enterprise Development Commission
#800, 215, rue Saint-Jacques
Montréal, QC H2Y 1M6
514-841-2200
Fax: 514-841-8606
800-363-0401
info@sodec.gouv.qc.ca
www.sodec.gouv.qc.ca

Société de la Place des Arts de Montréal / Montréal Place des Arts Corporation
260, boul de Maisonneuve ouest
Montréal, QC H2X 1Y9
514-285-4200
Fax: 514-285-1968
info@pda.qc.ca
www.pda.qc.ca

Société de télédiffusion du Québec (Télé-Québec) / Radio-Québec
1000, rue Fullum
Montréal, QC H2K 3L7
514-521-2424
Fax: 514-873-7739
800-361-4301
info@telequebec.tv
www.telequebec.tv

Société du Grand Théâtre de Québec / Grand Theatre of Québec
269, boul René-Lévesque est
Québec, QC G1R 2B3
418-644-8921
Fax: 418-646-7670
www.grandtheatre.qc.ca

Ministère de l'Agriculture, des Pêcheries et de l'Alimentation (MAPAQ) / Agriculture, Fisheries & Food

200, ch Sainte-Foy
Québec, QC G1R 4X6
418-380-2110
888-222-6272
www.mapaq.gouv.qc.ca
Le Ministère influence et appuie l'essor de l'industrie bioalimentaire québécoise dans une perspective de développement durable; réalise des interventions en production, transformation, commercialisation & consommation des produits agricoles, marins & alimentaires; & joue un rôle important en matière de recherche & de développement, d'enseignement & de formation

Acts Administered:
Code municipal du Québec/Municipal Code of Québec (certain sections)
Loi assurant la reprise des activités de Madelipêche inc.
Loi sur l'acquisition de terres agricoles par des non-résidants/An Act governing the acquisition of farm land by non-residents
Loi sur les appellations réservées
Loi sur l'aquaculture commerciale/ An Act respecting commercial aquaculture
Loi sur l'assurance-prêts agricoles et forestiers/An Act respecting farm-loan insurance & forestry-loan insurance
Loi sur l'assurance-récolte/Crop Insurance Act
Loi sur l'assurance-stabilisation des revenus agricoles/An Act respecting farm income stabilization insurance
Loi sur l'école de laiterie et lesécoles moyennes d'agriculture/An Act respecting the École de laiterie & intermediate agricultural schools
Loi sur la commercialisation des produits marins/An Act respecting the marketing of marine products
Loi sur la conservation et la mise en valeur de la faune/An Act respecting the conservation & development of wildlife
Loi sur la prévention des maladies de la pomme de terre/An Act respecting prevention of disease in potatoes
Loi sur la protection des animaux pur sang/Thoroughbred Cattle Act
Loi sur la protection des plantes/Plant Protection Act
Loi sur la protection sanitaire des animaux/Animal Health Protection Act
Loi sur la transformation des produits marins/The Marine Products Processing Act
Loi sur le financement de la pêche commerciale/Maritime Fisheries Credit Act
Loi sur le mérite national de la pêche et de l'aquaculture/Fishermen's Merit Act
Loi sur le Mérite national de la restauration et de l'alimentation/Restaurant Merit Act
Loi sur le ministère de l'Agriculture, des Pêcheries et de l'Alimentation/An Act respecting the Ministère de l'Agriculture, des Pêcheries et de l'Alimentation

Federal/Provincial Government / Gouvernement du Québec / Government of Québec

Loi sur les abus préjudiciables à l'agriculture/Agricultural Abuses Act
Loi sur les cités et villes/Cities & Towns Act (certain sections)
Loi sur les pêcheries commerciales et la récolte commerciale de végétaux aquatiques
Loi sur les produits agricoles, les produits marins et les aliments/Farm, Food & Fishery Products Act
Loi sur les producteurs agricoles/Farm Producers Act
Loi sur les produits alimentaires/Food Products Act
Loi sur les races animales du Patrimoine agricole du Québec
Loi sur les sociétés agricoles et laitières/An Act respecting farmers' & dairymen's associations
Loi sur les sociétés d'horticulture/Horticultural Societies Act
Loi sur les terres agricoles du domaine de l'État/An Act respecting agricultural lands in the domain of the state
Ordre national du mérite agricole/Agricultural Merit Act
La Charte de la ville de Québec/The Charter of the City of Québec (certain sections)
La Charte de la Ville de Sherbrooke/The Charter of the City of Sherbrooke (certain sections)
La Charte de la Ville de Trois-Rivières/The Charter of the City of Trois-Rivières (certain sections)
Ministre, Pierre Corbeil
418-380-2525, Fax: 418-380-2184
ministre.mapaq@mapaq.gouv.qc.ca
Sous-ministre, Marc Dion
418-380-2136, Fax: 418-380-2171
Sous-ministre associée Transformation Alimentaire Québec, Dominique Fortin
418-380-2136, Fax: 418-380-2171
Sous-ministre adjoint & Directeur général Politiques agroalimentaires, Norman Johnston
418-380-2136, Fax: 418-380-2171
Sous-ministre adjointe & Directrice générale Alimentation, Madeleine Fortin
418-380-2136, Fax: 418-380-2171
• Commission de protection du territoire agricole du Québec
200, ch Ste-Foy, 2e étage
Québec, QC G1R 4X6
418-643-3314
Fax: 418-643-2261
800-667-5294
info@cptaq.gouv.qc.ca
www.cptaq.gouv.qc.ca
Président, Roger Lefebvre
• La financière agricole de Québec
1400, boul de la Rive-Sud
Saint-Romuald, QC G6W 8K7
418-838-5602
Fax: 418-833-3871
800-749-3646
dir.comm@fadq.qc.ca
www.financiereagricole.qc.ca
• Régie des marchés agricoles et alimentaires du Québec
201, boul Crémazie est, 5e étage
Montréal, QC H2M 1L3
514-873-4024
Fax: 514-873-3984
rmaaqc@rmaaq.gouv.qc.ca
www.rmaaq.gouv.qc.ca
Président, Marc-A. Gagnon

Directions régionales/Regional Offices:

Abitibi-Témiscamingue - Nord-du-Québec
#2.01, 180, boul Rideau
Rouyn-Noranda, QC J9X 1N9
819-763-3287
Fax: 819-763-3359
Directrice régionale, Line Charland

Québec
Édifice 2
#RC22, 1685, boul Hamel ouest
Québec, QC G1N 3Y7
418-643-0033
Fax: 418-644-8263
Directrice régionale, Suzanne Pilote

Saguenay - Lac-Saint-Jean - Côte-Nord
801, ch du Pont-Taché nord
Alma, QC G8B 5W2
418-662-6457
Fax: 418-668-8694
Directeur régional, Alain Dessureault

Développement régional et développement durable / Regional Development/Sustainable Development
Sous-ministre adjoint, Michel Bonneau

Alimentation / Food
dga@mapaq.gouv.qc.ca
Other Communication: Centre québécois d'inspection des aliments et de santé animale: 1-800-463-5023
Sous-ministre adjointe, Madeleine Fortin
418-380-2136, Fax: 418-380-2171
Directrice (par intérim) Institut national de santé animale, Martine Bouchard
418-380-2100, Fax: 418-380-2169
Directrice Coordination administrative et Services à la clientèle, Michèle Lavoie
418-380-2100, Fax: 418-380-2169
Directeur Laboratoire d'expertises et d'analyses alimentaires, Jacques Ménard
418-266-4440, Fax: 418-266-4438

Ministère du Développement durable, de l'Environnement et des Parcs / Sustainable Development, Environment & Parks

Édifice Marie-Guyart
675, boul René-Lévesque est, 29e étage
Québec, QC G1R 5V7
418-521-3830
Fax: 418-646-5974
800-561-1616
info@mddep.gouv.qc.ca
www.mddep.gouv.qc.ca
A pour mission d'assurer la protection de l'environnement & des écosystèmes naturels; de promouvoir le développement durable & d'assurer à la population un environnement sain en harmonie avec le développement économique & le progrès social du Québec

Acts Administered:
Loi instituant le Fonds national de l'eau
Loi portant restrictions à l'élevage de porcs/Act to Impose Restrictions on Pig Farming, 2002
Loi portant sur la délimitation de la ligne des hautes eaux du Fleuve Saint-Laurent sur le territoire de la municipalité régionale de comté de la Côte-de-Beaupré/An Act to delimit the high water mark
Loi sur la conservation du patrimoine naturel/Natural Heritage Conservation Act
Loi sur la conservation et la mise en valeur de la faune/Act respecting the Conservation & Development of Wildlife (in part)
Loi sur la protection des arbres/Tree Protection Act
Loi sur la provocation artificielle de la pluie/Act respecting the artificial inducement of rain
Loi sur la qualité de l'environnement/Environment Quality Act
Agricultural Operations Regulation, 2002
Groundwater Catchment Regulation, 2002
Land Protection & Rehabilitation Regulation, 2003
Regulation respecting certain bodies for the protection of the environment and social milieu of the territory of James Bay and Northern Québec
Regulation respecting Compensation for Municipal Services Provided to Recover & Reclaim Residual Materials
Regulation respecting Environmental Impact Assessments in Northeastern Québec
Regulation respecting Halocarbons
Regulation respecting Hazardous Materials
Regulation respecting Hot Mix Asphalt Plants
Regulation respecting Industrial Depollution Attestations
Regulation respecting Motor Vehicle Traffic in Certain Fragile Environments
Regulation respecting Ozone-Depleting Substances
Regulation respecting Permits & Certificates for the Sale & Use of Pesticides
Regulation respecting Pits & Quarries
Regulation respecting Prevention of Water Pollution in Livestock Operations
Regulation respecting Public Swimming & Wading Pools
Regulation respecting Pulp & Paper Mills
Regulation respecting Sanitary Conditions in Industrial or other Camps
Regulation respecting Snow Elimination Sites
Regulation respecting Solid Waste
Regulation respecting the Application of the Environment Quality Act
Regulation respecting the Artificial Inducement of Rain
Regulation respecting the Burial of Contaminated Soils

Regulation respecting the environmental and social impact assessment and review procedure applicable to the territory of James Bay and Northern Québec
Regulation respecting the environmental impact assessment and review applicable to a part of the northeastern Québec region
Regulation respecting the Liquid Effluents of Petroleum Refineries
Regulation respecting the Quality of Drinking Water
Regulation respecting the Quality of the Atmosphere
Regulation respecting the Recovery & Reclamation of Discarded Paint Containers & Paints
Regulation respecting the Recovery & Reclamation of Used Oils, Oil or Fluid Containers & Used Filters
Regulation respecting threatened or vulnerable plant species and their habitats
Regulation respecting Used Tire Storage
Regulation Respecting Waste Water Disposal Systems for Isolated Dwellings
Regulation respecting the Water Property in the Domain of the State, 2003
Regulation respecting Waterworks & Sewer Services
Rules of internal management of the James Bay Advisory Committee on the Environment
Rules of internal management of the Kativik Environmental Advisory Committee
Loi sur la sécurité des barrages/Dam Safety Act
Loi sur la Société des établissements de plein air du Québec
Loi sur la Société québécoise de récupération et de recyclage
Loi sur la vente et la distribution de bière et de boissons gazeuses dans des contenants à remplissage unique/Act respecting the Sale & Distribution of Beer & Soft Drinks in Non-returnable Containers
Loi sur le développement durable
Loi sur le ministère du Développement durable, de l'Environnement et des Parcs
Loi sur le parc de la Mauricie et ses environs
Loi sur le Parc Forillon et des environs
Loi sur le parc marin du Saguenay-Saint-Laurent
Loi sur le régime des eaux/Watercourses Act
Loi sur les espèces menacées ou vulnérables/Act respecting Threatened or Vulnerable Species
Loi sur les pesticides/Pesticides Act
Pesticides Management Code, 2003
Loi sur les parcs
Loi sur les villages cris et le village naskapi/The Cree Villages and the Naskapi Village Act
Loi visant la préservation des ressources en eau/Water Resources Preservation Act
Ministre, L'hon. Pierre Arcand
418-521-3911, Fax: 418-643-4143
Sous-ministre, Diane Jean
418-521-3860, Fax: 418-643-3619
Directeur (par intérim) Affaires juridiques, Pierre Normandin
418-521-3816, Fax: 418-646-0908
Secrétaire générale et Directrice Vérification interne, Caroline Drouin
418-521-3810, Fax: 418-646-4762
Directeur Communications, Jérôme Thibaudeau
418-521-3823, Fax: 418-646-4852
Directeur du Cabinet, François Émond
418-521-3911
Sous-ministre adjoint Services à la gestion & au milieu terrestre, Frédéric Guay
Sous-ministre adjoint Changements climatiques, à l'air & à l'eau, Charles Larochelle
Sous-ministre adjoint Développement durable, Léopold Gaudreau
Sous-ministre adjoint Expertise hydrique, analyse et évaluations environnementales, Jacques Dupoint
Sous-ministre adjoint Analyse & expertise régionales/Centre de contrôle environnemental du Québec, Michel Rousseau
• Bureau d'audiences publiques sur l'environnement (BAPE) / Environmental Public Hearing Board
Édifice Lomer-Gouin
#2.10, 575, rue Saint-Amable, 2e étage
Québec, QC G1R 6A6
418-643-7447
Fax: 418-643-9474
800-463-4732
communication@bape.gouv.qc.ca
www.bape.gouv.qc.ca
Président, William J. Cosgrove

Federal/Provincial Government / Gouvernement du Québec / Government of Québec

- Comité consultatif de l'environnement Kativik(CCEK) / Kativik Environmental Advisory Committee
CP 930
Kuujjuaq, QC J0M 1C0
819-964-2961
Fax: 819-964-0694
ndea@krg.ca
Président, Gilles H. Tremblay
- Société des établissements en plein air du Québec(SÉPAQ)
Place de la Cité
#250, 2640, boul Laurier
Sainte-Foy, QC G1V 5C2
418-890-6527
Fax: 418-528-6025
800-665-6527
inforeservation@sepaq.com
www.sepaq.com
Président-directeur général, Yvan Bilodeau
- Société québécoise de récupération et de recyclage(RECYC-QUÉBEC)
Siège social
#200, 420, boul Charest est
Québec, QC G1K 8M4
418-643-0394
Fax: 418-643-6507
866-523-8290
info@recyc-quebec.gouv.qc.ca
www.recyc-quebec.gouv.qc.ca
Other Communication: Infoline: 1-800-807-0678; Montréal: 514/351-7835
Président-directeur général, Robert Lemieux

Analyse et expertise régionales / Regional Analysis & Expertise
Édifice Marie-Guyart
675, boul René-Lévesque est, 30e étage
Québec, QC G1R 5V7
418-521-3861
Fax: 418-646-1800
La mission est d'assurer l'analyse & la délivrance d'autorisations environnementales & d'offrir une expertise professionnelle en matière d'environnement
Sous-ministre adjoint, Michel Rousseau
418-521-3861, Fax: 418-646-1800

Changements climatiques / Climate Change
Sous-ministre adjoint, Charles Larochelle
418-521-3813, Fax: 418-646-4920
Directeur Bureau des changements climatiques, Marcel Gaucher
Directrice Relations intergouvernementales, Danielle Pronovost
Directeur (par intérim) Politiques de l'eau, Normand Bouliane
Directeur Politiques de la qualité de l'atmosphère, Michel Goulet

Baie-Comeau
20, boul Comeau
Baie-Comeau, QC G4Z 3A8
418-294-8888
Fax: 418-294-8018
cote-nord@mddep.gouv.qc.ca
Directeur, Alain Gaudreault

Gatineau
98, rue Lois
Gatineau, QC J8Y 3R7
819-772-3434
Fax: 819-772-3952
outaouais@mddep.gouv.qc.ca
Directeur, Marc Dubreuil

Laval
850, boul Vanier
Laval, QC H7C 2M7
450-661-2008
Fax: 450-661-2217
laval@mddep.gouv.qc.ca

Directeur, Pierre Robert

Longueuil
201, Place Charles-Le Moyne, 2e étage
Longueuil, QC J4K 2T5
450-928-7607
Fax: 450-928-7625
monteregie@mddep.gouv.qc.ca
Directeur, Pierre Paquin

Montréal
#3860, 5199, rue Sherbrooke est
Montréal, QC H1T 3X9
514-873-3636
Fax: 514-873-5662
montreal@mddep.gouv.qc.ca
Directeur, Pierre Robert

Nicolet
1579, boul Louis-Fréchette
Nicolet, QC J3T 2A5
819-293-4122
Fax: 819-293-8322
centre-du-quebec@mddep.gouv.qc.ca
Directeur, Luc St-Martin

Québec
365, 55e, rue Ouest
Québec, QC G1H 7M7
418-644-8844
Fax: 418-646-1214
capitale-nationale@mddep.gouv.qc.ca
Directeur, Jean-Marc Lachance

Repentigny
100, boul Industriel
Repentigny, QC J6A 4X6
450-654-4355
Fax: 450-654-6131
lanaudiere@mddep.gouv.qc.ca
Directeur, Pierre Robert

Rimouski
212, rue Belzile
Rimouski, QC G5L 3C3
418-727-3511
Fax: 418-727-3849
bas-saint-laurent@mddep.gouv.qc.ca
Directeur, Jean-Marie Dionne

Rouyn-Noranda
180, boul Rideau, 1er étage
Rouyn-Noranda, QC J9X 1N9
819-763-3333
Fax: 819-763-3202
abitibi-temiscamingue@mddep.gouv.qc.ca
Directrice, Edith van de Walle

Saguenay
3950, boul Harvey, 4e étage
Saguenay, QC G7X 8L6
418-695-7883
Fax: 418-695-7897
saguenay-lac-saint-jean@mddep.gouv.qc.ca
Directrice, Édith Tremblay

Sainte-Anne-des-Monts
124, 1e av ouest
Sainte-Anne-des-Monts, QC G4V 1C5
418-763-3301
Fax: 418-763-7810
gaspesie-iles-de-la-madeleine@mddep.gouv.qc.ca
Directeur, Jean-Marie Dionne

Sainte-Marie
#200, 675, rte Cameron
Sainte-Marie, QC G6E 3V7
418-386-8000
Fax: 418-386-8080
chaudiere-appalaches@mddep.gouv.qc.ca
Directeur, Jean-Marc Lachance

Sainte-Thérèse
#80, 300, rue Sicard
Sainte-Thérèse, QC J7E 3X5
450-433-2220
Fax: 450-433-1315
laurentides@mddep.gouv.qc.ca
Directeur, Pierre Robert

Sept-Iles
818, boul Laure, RC
Sept-Iles, QC G4R 1Y8
418-964-8888
Fax: 418-964-8023
cote-nord@mddep.gouv.qc.ca
Directeur, Alain Gaudreault

Sherbrooke
770, rue Goretti
Sherbrooke, QC J1E 3H4
819-820-3882
Fax: 819-820-3958
estrie@mddep.gouv.qc.ca
Directeur, Pierre Paquin

Trois-Rivières
100, rue Laviolette, 1er étage
Trois-Rivières, QC G9A 5S9
819-371-6581
Fax: 819-371-6987
mauricie@mddep.gouv.qc.ca
Directeur, Luc St-Martin

Centre de contrôle environnemental du Québec
Édifice Marie-Guyart
675, boul René-Lévesque est, 30e étage
Québec, QC G1R 5V7
418-521-3860
Fax: 418-643-7812
Sous-ministre adjoint, Michel Rousseau

Expertise hydrique, analyse & évaluations environnementales / Water Systems, Analysis & Environmental Assessment
Sous-ministre adjoint, Jacques Dupont
418-521-3860, Fax: 418-643-7812
Directrice Évaluations environnementales, Marie-Josée Lizotte
Directeur général Centre d'expertise en analyse environnementale, Guy Chouinard
Directeur général Centre d'expertise hydrique du Québec, Yvon Gosselin
Directeur Accréditation et Relations externes, Julien Moreault

Baie-Comeau
20, boulevard Comeau
Baie-Comeau, QC G4Z 3A8
418-294-8888
Fax: 418-294-8018
cote-nord@mddep.gouv.qc.ca
Directrice, Nadine Bégin

Gatineau
98, rue Lois
Gatineau, QC J8Y 3R7
819-772-3434
Fax: 819-772-3952
outaouais@mddep.gouv.qc.ca
Directeur, Léon Martin

Nicolet
1579, boulevard Louis-Fréchette
Nicolet, QC J3T 2A5
819-293-4122
Fax: 819-293-8322
centre-du-quebec@mddep.gouv.qc.ca
Directrice, Isabelle Olivier

Rimouski
212, avenue Belzile
Rimouski, QC G5L 3C3
418-727-3511
Fax: 418-727-3849
bas-saint-laurent@mddep.gouv.qc.ca
Directeur, Jules Boulanger

Rouyn-Noranda
180, boul Rideau, 1er étage
Rouyn-Noranda, QC J9X 1N9
819-763-3333
Fax: 819-763-3202
abitibi-temiscamingue@mddep.gouv.qc.ca
Directrice (par intérim), Édith van de Walle

Saguenay
3950, boul Harvey, 4e étage
Saguenay, QC G7X 8L6
418-695-7883
Fax: 418-695-7897
saguenay-lac-saint-jean@mddep.gouv.qc.ca
Directeur, Daniel Labrecque

Sainte-Marie
#200, 675, rte Cameron
Sainte-Marie, QC G6E 3V7
418-386-8000
Fax: 418-386-8080
chaudiere-appalaches@mddep.gouv.qc.ca
Directeur,VACANTE

Federal/Provincial Government / Gouvernement du Québec / Government of Québec

Sherbrooke
770, rue Goretti
Sherbrooke, QC J1E 3H4
819-820-3882
Fax: 819-820-3958
estrie@mddep.gouv.qc.ca
Directeur, Émile Grieco

Montréal
#3860, 5199, rue Sherbrooke est
Montréal, QC H1T 3X9
514-873-3636
Fax: 514-873-5662
montreal@mddep.gouv.qc.ca
Directrice (par intérim), Hélène Proteau

Développement durable / Sustainable Development
418-521-3860
Fax: 418-646-5883
Sous-ministre adjoint, Léopold Gaudreau
418-521-3860, Fax: 418-646-5883
Directeur Suivi de l'état de l'environnement, Luc Berthiaume
418-521-3820, Fax: 418-646-8483
Directeur Bureau de Coordination du développement durable, Luc Vézina
418-521-3848
Directeur Patrimoine écologique et des parcs, Patrick Beauchesne
418-521-3907, Fax: 418-646-6169

Services à la gestion & au milieu terrestre / Administrative Services & Earth Environment
418-521-3860
Fax: 418-643-9990
Sous-ministre adjoint (par intérim), Frédéric Guay
418-521-3860, Fax: 418-643-9990
Directeur Matières résiduelles & lieux contaminés, Mario Bérubé
Directeur Secteur agricole & pesticides, Didier Bicchi
Directeur Ressources informationnelles & matérielles, Yvan Déry

Centre d'expertise en analyse environnementale du Québec (CEAEQ)
#E-2-220, 2700, rue Einstein
Québec, QC G1P 3W8
418-643-8225
Fax: 418-661-8512
www.ceaeq.gouv.qc.ca
La mission: garantir la disponibilité, la qualité & la continuité de l'expertise & de l'information analytique pour les besoins de protection de l'environnement, & de conservation des ressources
Directeur général, Marc Bisson

Centre d'expertise hydrique du Québec
418-521-3866
Fax: 418-643-6900
cehq@mddep.gouv.qc.ca
www.cehq.gouv.qc.ca
A pour mission de gérer le régime hydrique de Québec avec une préoccupation de sécurité, d'équité & de développement durable, & d'assurer la régularisation du régime des eaux
Directeur général, Yvon Gosselin
Directeur Expertise hydrique et gestion des barrages publics, Pierre Aubé
Directeur Sécurité des barrages, Michel Dolbec
Directeur Maintenance des barrages, Serge Goulet
Directeur Gestion du domaine hydrique de l'État, Peter Stevenson
Directrice Surveillance des barrages & l'Hydrométrie, Paula Bergeron

Ministère du Développement économique, de l'Innovation et de l'Exportation / Economic Development, Innovation & Export Trade
710, place D'Youville, 3e étage
Québec, QC G1R 4Y4
418-691-5950
Fax: 418-644-0118
866-680-1884
www.mdeie.gouv.qc.ca
A pour mission de soutenir le développement économique, l'innovation & l'exportation; d'offrir des services-conseils; de promouvoir l'image du Québec à l'étranger auprès des investisseurs
Acts Administered:

Loi favorisant l'augmentation du capital des petites et moyennes entreprises/An Act to promote the capitalization of small and medium-sized businesses
Loi sur Investissement Québec et sur la Financière du Québec/An Act respecting Investissement Québec and La Financière du Québec
Loi sur l'aide au développement des coopérative et des personnes morales sans but lucratif/An Act respecting assistance for the development of cooperatives and non-profit legal persons
Loi sur la Régie des installations olympiques
Loi sur la Société des alcools du Québec/An Act respecting the Société des alcools du Québec
Loi sur la Société du Centre des congrès de Québec
Loi sur la Société du Palais de Congrés de Montréal
Loi sur la Société du parc industriel et portuaire de Bécancour/An Act respecting the Société du parc industriel et portuaire de Bécancour
Loi sur la Société générale de financement du Québec/ An Act respecting the Société générale de financement du Québec
Loi sur la Société Innovatech du Grand Montréal/An Act respecting the Société Innovatech du Grand Montréal
Loi sur la Société Innovatech du sud du Québec/An Act respecting the Société Innovatech du sud du Québec
Loi sur la Société Innovatech Québec et Chaudière-Appalaches/An Act respecting Société Innovatech Québec et Chaudiére-Appalaches
Loi sur la Société Innovatech Régions ressources/An Act respecting Société Innovatech Régions ressources
Loi sur le Centre de recherche industriel du Québec/An Act respecting the Centre de recherche industrielle du Québec
Loi sur le ministère des Relations internationales/An Act respecting the Ministère des Relations internationales
Loi sur le ministère du Développement économique et régional et de la Recherche/An Act respecting the Ministère du Développement économique et régional et de la Recherche
Loi sur les concours artistiques, littéraires et scientifiques/An Act respecting artistic, literary and scientific competitions
Loi sur les coopératives/Cooperatives Act
Loi sur les heures et les jours d'admission dans les établissements commerciaux/An Act respecting hours and days of admission to commercial establishments
Loi sur les matériaux de rembourrage et les articles rembourrés/An Act respecting stuffing and upholstered and stuffed articles
Loi sur les sociétés de placement dans l'entreprise québécoise
Ministre, L'hon. Clément Gignac
418-691-5650
Sous-ministre, Christyne Tremblay
418-691-5656, Fax: 418-646-6497
Directeur général Communications et services à la clientèle, Pierre Tessier
418-691-5653
Directeur (par intérim) Services à la gestion, Jean-Marc Sauvé
418-691-5963
Secrétaire général (par intérim), Linda Landry
418-691-5656, Fax: 418-646-6497
• Centre de recherche industrielle du Québec(CRIQ) / Industrial Research Centre of Québec
333, rue Franquet
Québec, QC G1P 4C7
418-659-1550
Fax: 418-652-2251
800-667-2386
infocriq@criq.qc.ca
www.criq.qc.ca
Président-directeur général, Serge Guérin
Recherche industrielle appliquée; services de RD pour des entreprises
• Conseil de la science et de la technologie
1150, Grande Allée ouest, RC
Québec, QC G1S 4Y9
418-691-5986
cst@cst.gouv.qc.ca
www.cst.gouv.qc.ca
Présidente, Marie-France Germain
• Fonds québécois de la recherche sur la nature et les technologies
#450, 140, Grande Allée est
Québec, QC G1R 5M8
418-643-8560
Fax: 418-643-1451
info@fqrnt.gouv.qc.ca
www.fqrnt.gouv.qc.ca

Présidente-directrice générale, Sylvie Dillard
• Fonds québécois de la recherche sur la société et la culture
#470, 140, Grande Allée est
Québec, QC G1R 5M8
418-643-7582
Fax: 418-644-5248
fqrsc@fqrsc.gouv.qc.ca
www.fqrsc.gouv.qc.ca
• Fonds de la recherche en santé du Québec
#800, 500, rue Sherbrooke ouest
Montréal, QC H3A 3C6
514-873-2114
Fax: 514-873-8768
www.frsq.gouv.qc.ca
• Investissement Québec
#500, 1200, rte de l'Église
Québec, QC G1V 5A3
418-643-5172
866-870-0437
www.investquebec.com
• Société générale de financement du Québec
#1500, 600, rue de La Gauchetière ouest
Montréal, QC H3B 4L8
514-876-9290
Fax: 514-395-8055
info@sgfqc.com
www.sgfqc.com
Présidente & Directrice générale, Francine Laurent
• Innovatech Québec
#120, 925, Grande Allée ouest
Québec, QC G1S 1C1
418-528-9770
Fax: 418-528-9783
866-605-1676
info@innovatech-regions.qc.ca
www.innovatechquebec.com
Président, Pierre B. Lafrenière

Affaires économiques régionales / Regional Economic Affairs
Sous-ministre adjoint, Jean-Marc Sauvé
Directrice Coordination régionale, Michèle Robert
418-528-0930, Fax: 418-528-8428
Directeur Projet ACCORD, Xavier Fonteneau
Directrice Programmes et mesures, Lise Mathieu
418-643-0060, Fax: 418-646-3609

Affaires économiques internationales / International Economic Affairs
Sous-ministre adjoint, Jean Séguin
514-499-2188, Fax: 514-873-4230
Directeur de la coordination (par intérim), Herman Vyncke
Directeur (par intérim) Amérique latine et Antilles, Rafaël Sanchez
418-691-5698, Fax: 418-643-0825
Directrice Amérique du Nord, Chantal Castonguay
Directeur Asie-Pacifique, Afrique et Moyen-Orient, Daniel Gagné
Directeur Europe, Yves Lafortune
514-499-2185, Fax: 514-873-1540
Directeur Promotion des investissements, Alain Proulx

Secteurs stratégiques et des projets économiques / Strategic Sectors and Economic Projects
Directrice Biens de consommation, Marie-Annick Drouin
Directeur Chimie, plasturgie, métallurgie et équipements, Clément Drolet
418-691-5976, Fax: 418-644-0519
Directrice Coordination, Lisette Seyer
Directrice Développement des industries, Diane Hastie
418-691-5698
Directeur Environnement et services aux entreprises, Gaétan Poiré
418-691-5815, Fax: 418-644-1687
Directeur (par intérim) Équipements de transport, Bernard Strauss
514-499-6535, Fax: 514-864-3755
Directrice (par intérim) Santé et biotechnologies, Michèle Houpert
514-499-6534, Fax: 514-864-3755
Directrice Technologies de l'information et des communications, Guylaine Leblanc
418-691-5957, Fax: 418-643-6947
Directeur Commerce et construction, Pierre A. Forgues

Politiques et sociétés d'État / Policy & Crown Corporations

Sous-ministre adjoint, Brian Girard
418-691-5698, Fax: 418-644-3109
Directrice (par intérim) Politiques économiques, Sylvie Miguel
Directeur Politique commerciale pour les accords internationaux, Jocelyn Savoie
Directeur Sociétés d'État & entrepreneuriat, Richard Carbonneau
Directeur (par intérim) Politique commerciale/Politique commercial pour l'Amérique du Nord, Patrick Muzzi
418-643-4347, Fax: 418-691-5995
Directeur Développement des entreprises, Bertrand Verbruggen

Recherche, innovation, science et société / Research, Innovation, Science & Society
Sous-ministre adjointe, Geneviève Tanguay
418-528-2515, Fax: 418-528-0234
Directrice Collaborations internationales, Marie-Josée Blais
Directeur Recherche universitaire & collégiale, Luc Castonguay
418-646-1447, Fax: 418-646-6888
Directeur Financement des infrastructures de recherche, Gaston Beaudoin
Directrice (par intérim) Innovation & transfert, Frédérique-Myriam Villemure
Directrice Science & société, Monique La Rue
Directeur (par intérim) Politiques & analyses, Mawana Pongo
Directrice (par intérim) Coordination & concertation, Marie-Odile Koch

Abitibi-Témiscamingue
#202, 170, av Principale
Rouyn-Noranda, QC J9X 4P7
819-763-3561
Fax: 819-763-3462

Bas-St-Laurent
#RC 04, 337, rue Moreault
Rimouski, QC G5L 1P4
418-727-3577
Fax: 418-727-3640

Capitale-Nationale
900, Place d'Youville, 3e étage
Québec, QC G1R 3P7
418-691-5824
Fax: 418-643-4099
Directeur (par intérim), Jean-François Talbot

Centre-du-Québec
Édifice provincial
#1.03, 62, rue Saint-Jean-Baptiste
Victoriaville, QC G6P 4E3
819-752-9781
Fax: 819-758-4306

Chaudière-Appalaches
#1, 1055, boul Vachon nord
Sainte-Marie, QC G6E 1M4
418-386-8677
Fax: 418-386-8037
Directeur, Normand Giguère

Côte-Nord
#RC 711, 625, boul Laflèche
Baie-Comeau, QC G5C 1C5
418-589-4349
Fax: 418-295-4199

Estrie
#4.05, 200, rue Belvédère nord
Sherbrooke, QC J1H 4A9
819-820-3731
Fax: 819-820-3929

Gaspésie/Îles-de-la-Madeleine
#10A, 500, av Daigneault
CP 1360
Chandler, QC G0C 1K0
418-689-2019
Fax: 418-689-4108

Lanaudière
#3300, 40, rue Gauthier sud
Joliette, QC J6E 4J4
450-752-8050
Fax: 450-752-8064

Laurentides
#C3.35, 85, rue de Martigny
Saint-Jérôme, QC J7Y 3R8
450-569-3031
Fax: 450-569-3039

Laval
#RC-30, 705, ch de Trait-Carré
Laval, QC H7N 1B3
450-680-6175
Fax: 450-972-3090

Mauricie
Édifice Capitanal
#114, 100, rue Laviolette
Trois-Rivières, QC G9A 5S9
819-371-6617
Fax: 819-371-6960

Montérégie
#101, 201, Place Charles-Lemoyne
Longueuil, QC J4K 2T5
450-928-7645
Fax: 450-928-7465

Montréal
380, rue Saint-Antoine ouest, 5e étage
Montréal, QC H2Y 3X7
514-499-2550
Fax: 514-873-9913

Nord-du-Québec
333, 3e rue
Chibougamau, QC G8P 1N4
418-748-6681
Fax: 418-748-6698

Outaouais
#7.200, 170, rue de l'Hôtel-de-Ville
Gatineau, QC J8X 4C2
819-772-3038
Fax: 819-772-3968

Saguenay/Lac-Saint-Jean
3950, boul Harvey, 2e étage
Jonquière, QC G7X 8L6
418-695-7971
Fax: 418-695-7870
Ministre, L'hon. Line Beauchamp
418-644-0664, Fax: 418-646-7551
Directeur Planification, stratégies & information de gestion, Richard St-Pierre
Sous-ministre adjoint, Claude Blouin
418-646-2876, Fax: 418-643-6329
Directeur général adjoint (par intérim) Administration & projets corporatifs, Michel Lalande
Directeur Coordination du développement des systèmes d'information, Beniamino Colombo
Directrice Modernisation des modes de prestation de services, Claudine Bouchard
Directeur Soutien & qualité des applications informatiques, Mario Godin
Directeur Budget & services administratifs, Michel Lalande

Hydro-Québec
75, boul René-Lévesque ouest, 20e étage
Montréal, QC H2Z 1A4
514-289-2211
www.hydroquebec.com
Président Conseil d'administration, Michael Louis Turcotte
Président-directeur général, Thierry Vandal
Présidente Hydro-Québec TransÉnergie, Isabelle Courville
Président Hydro-Québec Distribution, André Boulanger
Président Hydro-Québec Production, Richard Cacchione
Protectrice de la personne, Justine Sentenne

Développement durable / Sustainable Development
www.hydroquebec.com/developpementdurable/
Président-directeur général, Thierry Vandal

Subsidiaries/Filiales:

Hydro-Québec CapiTech
#1600, 1000, rue Sherbrooke ouest
Montréal, QC H3A 3G4
hqcapitech@hydro.qc.ca
www.hydroquebec.com/technologie/capitech/index.html
Une société de capitale de risque corporatif dont la mission est de fournir une meilleure connaissance des produits & des services liés au domaine de l'énergie. Elle favorise les investissements dans des entreprises québécoises

Hydro-Québec International
75, boul René-Lévesque ouest, 20e étage
Montréal, QC H2Z 1A4
514-289-4020

Société d'énergie de la Baie-James (SEBJ) / James Bay Energy
888, de Maisonneuve est, 2e étage
Montréal, QC H2L 5B2
514-286-2020
www.hydroquebec.com/sebj
Président-directeur général, Réal Laporte

Innovation technologique / Technological Innovation
www.hydroquebec.com/technologie/index.html
Président, Élie Saheb

Laboratoire des technologies de l'énergie (LTE) de Shawinigan / Shawinigan Energy Technology Laboratory
600, av de la Montagne
Shawinigan, QC G9N 7N5
819-539-1400
Fax: 819-539-1409
Research focuses on new applications for the use of electricity & co-energy. Areas of expertise include mechanical, metallurgical & civil engineering, electrical equipment, automation & measurement systems, power system analysis, operation & control, chemistry & materials, & energy use.

Laboratoires de recherche et d'essais de Varennes / Varennes Research & Testing Laboratories.
1800, boul Lionel-Boulet
Varennes, QC J3X 1S1
450-652-8011
Fax: 450-652-8990
R&D on high-voltage lines & equipment; testing facilities for mechanical & thermomechanical behaviour of equipment; power system simulation; calibration laboratory & equipment.

Ministère des Ressources naturelles et de la Faune / Natural Resources & Wildlife
880, ch Sainte-Foy
Québec, QC G1S 4X4
418-627-8600
Fax: 418-644-6513
866-248-6936
services.clientele@mrnf.gouv.qc.ca
www.mrnf.gouv.qc.ca
Acts Administered:
Loi approuvant la convention de la Baie-James et du nord québécois/An Act approving the Agreement concerning James Bay and Northern Québec
Loi approuvant la convention du nord-est québécois/An Act approving the Northeastern Québec Agreement
Loi assurant la mise en oeuvre de l'entente concernant une nouvelle relation entre le gouvernement du Québec et les Cris du Québec/An Act to ensure the implementation of the Agreement Concerning a New
Loi concernant la construction par Hydro-Québec d'infrastructures et d'équipements par suite de la tempête de verglas survenue du 5 au 9 janvier 1998
Loi concernant les droits sur les mines/Mining Duties Act
Loi de 1994 sur la convention concernant les oiseaux migrateurs
Loi favorisant la réforme du cadastre québécois/An Act to promote the reform of the cadastre in Québec
Loi favorisant le crédit forestier par les institutions privées/An Act to promote forest credit by private institutions
Loi sur les forêts/Forest Act
Loi régissant les activités d'aménagement forestier de bénéficiaires de contrats d'approvisionnement et d'aménagement forestier pour les années 2000-2001 et 2001-2002
Loi sur Hydro-Québec/Hydro-Québec Act
Loi sur l'agence de l'efficacité énergétique
Loi sur l'efficacité énergétique d'appareils fonctionnant à l'électricité ou aux hydrocarbures/An Act respecting the energy efficiency of electrical or hydrocarbon-fuelled appliances

Federal/Provincial Government / Gouvernement du Québec / Government of Québec

Loi sur la conservation et la mise en valeur de la faune/Act respecting the conservation and development of wildlife
Regulation respecting aquaculture and the sale of fish
Lands in the Domain of the State Designated for Development of Wildlife Resources Regulation
Regulation respecting hunting and fishing controlled
Regulation respecting the enforcement of certain legislative and regulatory provisions respecting the protection of the environment by wildlife protection officers
Regulation respecting wildlife habitats
Regulation respecting wildlife sanctuaries
Loi sur la division territoriale/Territorial Division Act
Loi sur la Régie de l'énergie/An Act respecting the Régie de l'énergie
Loi sur la société de développement autochtone de la Baie James/An Act respecting the James Bay Native Development Corporation
Loi sur la société Eeyou de la Baie-James/An Act respecting the James Bay Eeyou Corporation
Loi sur la société nationale de l'amiante/An Act respecting the Société nationale de l'amiante
Loi sur le cadastre/Cadastre Act
Loi sur le crédit forestier/Forestry Credit Act
Loi sur le développement et l'organisation municipale de la région de la Baie-James/James Bay Region Development and Municipal Organization Act
Loi sur le ministère des ressources naturelles, de la faune et des parcs/An Act respecting the Ministère des Ressources naturelles, de la Faune et des Parcs
Loi sur le mode de paiement des services d'électricité et de gaz dans certains immeubles/An Act respecting the mode of payment for electric and gas service in certain buildings
Loi sur le programme d'aide aux Inuits bénéficiaires de la convention de la Baie-James et du nord québécois pour leurs activités de chasse, de pêche et de piégeage/An Act respecting the support progra
Loi sur le régime des eaux/Watercourses Act
Regulation respecting the water property in the domain of the State
Loi sur le régime des terres dans les territoires de la Baie-James et du Nouveau-Québec/An Act respecting the land regime in the James Bay and New Québec territories
Loi sur les arpentages/An Act respecting land survey
Loi sur les bureaux de la publicité des droits/An Act respecting registry offices
Loi sur les clubs de chasse et de pêche/Fish and Game Clubs Act
Loi sur les compagnies de flottage/Timber-Driving Companies Act
Loi sur les droits de chasse et de pêche dans les territoires de la Baie James et du Nouveau-Québec/An Act respecting hunting and fishing rights in the James Bay and New Québec territories
Loi sur les espèces menacées ou vulnérables/An Act respecting threatened or vulnerable species
Loi sur les mesureurs de bois/Cullers Act
Loi sur les mines/Mining Act
Loi sur les Pêches
Loi sur les produits et les équipements pétroliers/An Act respecting petroleum products and equipment
Loi sur les systèmes municipaux et les systèmes privés d'électricité/An Act respecting municipal and private electric power systems
Loi sur les terres du domaine de l'état/An Act respecting the lands in the domain of the State
Loi sur les titres de propriété dans certains districts électoraux/An Act respecting land titles in certain electoral districts
Loi sur l'exportation de l'électricité/An Act respecting the exportation of electric power
Ministre, L'hon. Serge Simard
418-643-7295, Fax: 418-643-4318
Sous-ministre, Robert Sauvé
418-627-6370, Fax: 418-643-1443
Directeur général Administration/Services partagés, Guy Mercier
418-627-6260, Fax: 418-646-2614
• Agence de l'efficacité énergétique
#B-405, 5700, 4e av ouest
Québec, QC G1H 6R1
418-627-6379
Fax: 418-643-5828
877-727-6655
aee@aee.gouv.qc.ca
www.aee.gouv.qc.ca

Directeur général, Réjean Carrier
Promotes the efficient use of all forms of energy, in all sectors of activity, for the benefit of the people of Québec. The Agency achieves this through demonstration projects, which highlight new technologies, new approaches or new applications that save energy; design, management & evaluation of energy efficient programs; information, training & educational materials; technical & organizational support for export of products & services; review, commentary on proposed amendments to applicable laws & regulations.
• Comité conjoint de chasse, de pêche et de piégeage
#C220, 383 rue Saint-Jacques
Montréal, QC H2Y 1N9
514-284-2151
Fax: 514-284-0039
hftcc@bellnet.ca
www.cccpp-hftcc.com
Secrétaire-trésorière, Nicole Gougeon
• Fondation de la faune du Québec
Place Iberville II
#420, 1175, av Lavigerie
Québec, QC G1V 4P1
418-644-7926
Fax: 418-643-7655
877-639-0742
ffq@riq.qc.ca
www.fondationdelafaune.qc.ca
Président-directeur général, André Martin
Non-profit organization whose mission is to enhance the value & promote the conservation of wildlife & its habitats.
• Hydro Québec
75, boul René-Lévesque ouest
Montréal, QC H2Z 1A4
514-385-7252
800-790-2424
www.hydroquebec.com
Other Communication: Residential Customer Service: 1-888-385-7252; TTY: 711; Persons with a visual impairment: 1-888-385-7252
• Régie de l'énergie
Tour de la Bourse
#255, 800, Place Victoria
CP 1
Montréal, QC H4Z 1A2
514-873-2452
Fax: 514-873-2070
888-873-2452
secretariat@regie-energie.qc.ca
www.regie-energie.qc.ca
Président, Jean-Paul Théorêt
An economic regulation agency, its mission is to reconcile the public interest, consumer protection, & fair treatment of the electricity carrier & distributors.
• Société de développement de la Baie James(SDBJ) / James Bay Development Society
110, boul Matagami
CP 970
Matagami, QC J0Y 2A0
819-739-4717
Fax: 819-739-4329
www.sdbj.gouv.qc.ca
Président-directeur général (par intérim), Raymond Thibault
Developed in 1971, this organization uses its resources & vast knowledge of the territory, contributors, & development projects to promote & maintain activities in the James Bay area, with a perspective of integrated economic development & harmonious cohabitation with territorial residents.

Énergie / Energy
#B401, 5700, 4e av ouest
Québec, QC G1H 6R1
418-627-6377
Fax: 418-643-0701
Le gouvernement québécois prévoit le lancement des projets hydoélectriques représentant 4,500 MW, qui susciteront des investissements de l'ordre de 25m de dollars, et la création d'environ 70,000 emplois sur six ans. Il mise sur le développement du potential existant d'énergie éolienne, avec l'objectif de 4,000 MW d'ici 2015, et prend plusieurs moyens afin de renforcer la sécurité des approvisionnements en pétrole et gaz naturel
Sous-ministre associé, Mario Gosselin
Directeur général Électricité, René Paquette
Directeur général Hydrocarbures et Bioarburants, Alain Lefebvre

Directrice générale (par intérim) Politiques, coordination et analyse économique, Julie Grignon

Faune Québec / Wildlife Québec
RC-80, 880, ch Sainte-Foy
Québec, QC G1S 4X4
418-627-8688
Fax: 418-646-4223

Foncier Québec
#E306, 5700, 4e av ouest
Québec, QC G1H 6R1
418-643-3582
Fax: 418-528-8721
866-226-0977
assistance.clientele@mrnf.registrefoncier.gouv.qc.ca
Sous-ministre associée, Louise Ouellet
418-627-6252, Fax: 418-643-3954
Directeur général Arpentage et cadastre, Julien Arsenault
418-627-6267, Fax: 418-646-7405
Directrice générale Registre Foncier, Marie-Claude Rioux
418-643-3155

Forêt Québec / Québec Forests
880, ch Ste-Foy, 10e étage
Québec, QC G1S 4X4
418-627-8652
Fax: 418-528-1278
foretquebec@mrnf.gouv.qc.ca
Sous-ministre associé, Richard Savard
Sous-ministre associé/Forestier en chef, Pierre Levac
Directeur général Connaissance et gestion de l'information forestière, Francis Forcier
Directeur général Gestion du milieu forestier/Développement, Mario Gibeault
Directeur général Attribution des bois et développement industriel, Pierre Marineau
Directrice Inventaires forestiers, Élisabeth Bossert
Directeur Aménagement des forêts publiques et privées, Ronald Brizard
Directeur Recherche forestière, Robert Jobidon
Directeur Gestion de l'information forestière, Denis Robitaille
Directeur Développement de l'industrie et des produits forestiers, André Denis
Directeur Environnement et Protection des forêts, Paul Lamirande
Directeur Gestion des stocks ligneux, Réal Paris
Directrice Développement et Coordination, Cécile Tremblay

Mines
RC, 880, ch Ste-Foy
Québec, QC G1S 4X4
418-627-6278
Fax: 418-418-6432
800-363-7233
service.mines@mrnf.gouv.qc.ca
Sous-ministre associé Mines, Jean-Sylvain Lebel
418-627-8652,
Directeur général Géologie Québec, Robert Marquis
Directeur général Développement de l'industrie minérale, Pierre Verpaelst
Directrice générale Gestion du milieu minier, Lucie Ste-Croix

Territoire / Lands
#A313, 5700, 4e av ouest
Québec, QC G1H 6R1
418-627-6256
Fax: 418-528-2075
territoire@mrnf.gouv.qc.ca
Le Ministère favorise une utilisation du territoire qui rejoint les préoccupations économiques, sociales & environnementales des Québécois
Sous-ministre associé Plan Nord et Territoire, Christian Dubois
418-627-6260
Directeur général Affaires stratégiques et territoire, André Auclair
Directrice Coordination du Plan Nord, Andrée Bélanger
Directeur Environnement et Coordination, Marcel Grenier
Directeur Affaires autochtones, François Dupuis
Directeur Politiques et Intégité du territoire, Mario Perron

Centre de service des Mines (Capitale-Nationale)
RC, 880, ch Sainte-Foy
Québec, QC G1S 4X4
418-627-6278
Fax: 418-643-2816

Federal/Provincial Government / Gouvernement du Québec / Government of Québec

800-363-7233
service.mines@mrnf.gouv.qc.ca

Bureaux de la protection de la faune/Regional Wildlife Protection Offices:

Abitibi-Témiscamingue
70, av Québec
Rouyn-Noranda, QC J9X 6R1
819-763-3388
Fax: 819-763-3186

Bas-Saint-Laurent
#207, 92, 2e Rue ouest
Rimouski, QC G5L 8B3
418-727-3710
Fax: 418-727-3735

Capitale-Nationale
#1.14, 1685, boul Hamel
Québec, QC G1N 3Y7
418-643-4680
Fax: 418-644-8960

Mauricie—Centre-du-Québec
#207, 100, rue Laviolette
Trois-Rivières, QC G9A 5S9
819-371-6151
Fax: 819-371-6978

Chaudière-Appalaches
8400, av Sous-le-Vent
Charny, QC G6X 3S9
418-832-7222
Fax: 418-832-1827

Côte-Nord
818, boul Laure
Sept-Iles, QC G4R 1Y8
418-964-8889
Fax: 418-964-8021

Estrie
770, rue Goretti
Sherbrooke, QC J1E 3H4
819-820-3883
Fax: 819-820-3747

Gaspésie—Iles-de-la-Madeleine
124, 1re av ouest
Sainte-Anne-des-Monts, QC G4V 1C5
418-763-3302
Fax: 418-764-2378

Laval—Lanaudière—Laurentides
#1.50B, 999, rue Nobel
Saint-Jérôme, QC J7Z 7A3
450-569-3113
Fax: 450-569-7568

Montérégie et Montréal
Bureau local de Granby
329, rue Racine
Granby, QC J2G 3B6
450-776-7131
Fax: 450-776-7133
Autres bureau dans la région: Saint-Jean-sur-Richelieu, Salaberry-de-Valleyfield, et Sorel-Tracy. S.O.S. Braconnage: 1-800-463-2191 ou courriel: centralesos@mrnf.gouv.qc.ca

Nord-du-Québec
951, boul Hamel
Chibougamau, QC G8P 2Z3
418-748-7701
Fax: 418-748-3338

Outaouais
#RC-100, 16, impasse de la Gare-Talon
Gatineau, QC J8T 0B1
819-246-4827
Fax: 819-246-5049

Saguenay—Lac-Saint-Jean
3950, boul Harvey, 4e étage
Jonquière, QC G7X 8L6
418-695-8125
Fax: 418-695-8436
saguenay-lac-saint-jean@mrnf.gouv.qc.ca

Sous-ministre associé & Forestier en chef / Chief Forester
845, boul Saint-Joseph
Roberval, QC G8H 2L4
418-275-7770
Fax: 418-275-8884
bureau@forestierenchef.gouv.qc.ca
www.forestierenchef.gouv.qc.ca
Forestier en chef, Pierre Levac

Abitibi-Témiscamingue
70, av Québec
Rouyn-Noranda, QC J9X 6R1
819-763-3388
Fax: 819-763-3216
abitibi-temiscamingue@mrnf.gouv.qc.ca
Directeur général, Martin Gingras

Bas-Saint-Laurent
#207, 92, 2e Rue ouest
Rimouski, QC G5L 8B3
418-727-3710
Fax: 418-727-3735
bas-saint-laurent@mrnf.gouv.qc.ca
Directeur général (par intérim), Alain Lachapelle

Capitale-Nationale—Chaudières-Appalaches
#1.14, 1665, boul Hamel
Québec, QC G1N 3Y7
418-643-4680
Fax: 418-644-8960
capitale-nationale@mrnf.gouv.qc.ca

Côte-Nord
#RC702, 625, boul Laflèche
Baie-Comeau, QC G5C 1C5
418-295-4676
Fax: 418-295-4682
cote-nord.@mrnf.gouv.qc.ca
Directeur général, Normand Laprise

Gaspésie—Iles-de-la-Madeleine
195, boul Perron est
Caplan, QC G0C 1H0
418-388-2125
Fax: 418-388-2444
gaspesie-iles-de-la-madeleine@mrnf.gouv.qc.ca
Directeur général, Bernard Landry

Mauricie—Centre-du-Québec
#207, 100, rue Laviolette
Trois-Rivières, QC G9A 5S9
418-371-6151
Fax: 418-371-6978
mauricie@mrnf.gouv.qc.ca
Directeur général, Alain Simard

Estrie—Montréal—Montérégie et Laval—Lanaudière—Laurentides
545, boul Crémazie est, 8e étage
Montréal, QC H2M 2V1
514-873-2140
Fax: 514-873-8983
montreal@mrnf.gouv.qc.ca; laval@mrnf.gouv.qc.ca
Directeur général, André B. Lemay

Outaouais
#RC-100, 16, impasse de la Gare-Talon
Gatineau, QC J8T 0B1
819-246-4827
Fax: 819-246-5049
outaouais@mrnf.gouv.qc.ca
Directeur général, Jean Benoît

Saguenay—Lac-Saint-Jean
3950, boul Harvey, 3e étage
Jonquière, QC G7X 8L6
418-695-8125
Fax: 418-695-8133
saguenay-lac-saint-jean@mrnf.gouv.qc.ca
Directeur général, Alain Thibeault

Abitibi-Témiscamingue
70, av Québec
Rouyn-Noranda, QC J9X 6R1
819-763-3388
Fax: 819-763-3216
abitibi-temiscamingue@mrnf.gouv.qc.ca

Bas-Saint-Laurent
#207, 92, 2e rue ouest
Rimouski, QC G5L 8B3
418-727-3710
Fax: 418-727-3735
bas-saint-laurent@mrnf.gouv.qc.ca

Capitale-Nationale et Chaudière-Appalaches
#1.14, 1685, boul. Hamel
Québec, QC G1N 3Y7
418-643-4680
Fax: 418-644-8960
capitale-nationale@mrnf.gouv.qc.ca

Côte-Nord
#RC702, 625, boul Laflèche
Baie-Comeau, G5C 1C5
418-295-4676
Fax: 418-295-4682
cote-nord@mrnf.gouv.qc.ca

Estrie—Montréal—Montérégie et Laval—Lanaudière—Laurentides
545, boul Crémazie est, 8e étage
Montréal, QC H2M 2V1
514-873-2140
Fax: 514-873-8983
estrie@mrnf.gouv.qc.ca; lanaudiere@mrnf.gouv.qc.ca

Mauricie—Centre-du-Québec
#207, 100, rue Laviolette
Trois-Rivières, QC G9A 5S9
819-371-6151
Fax: 819-371-6978
866-821-4625
mauricie@mrnf.gouv.qc.ca

Outaouais
#RC100, 16, impasse de la Gare-Talon
Gatineau, QC J8T 0B1
819-246-4827
Fax: 819-246-5049
outaouais@mrnf.gouv.qc.ca

Saguenay—Lac-Saint-Jean
3950, boul Harvey, 3e étage
Jonquière, QC G7X 8L6
418-695-8125
Fax: 418-695-8133
saguenay-lac-saint-jean@mrnf.gouv.qc.ca

Gaspé
124, rte 132
CP 128
Percé, QC G0C 2L0
418-782-2061
Fax: 418-782-5551

Montréal
#RC10, 2050, rue de Bleury
Montréal, QC H3A 2J5
514-399-2055
Fax: 514-873-1670

Québec
#32, 300, boul Jean-Lesage
Québec, QC G1K 8K6
418-528-2688
Fax: 418-528-2000

Trois-Rivières
#RC12, 878, rue de Tonnancourt
Trois-Rivières, QC G9A 4P8
819-371-6100
Fax: 819-371-6956

Sherbrooke
#120, 3425, rue King ouest
Sherbrooke
819-820-3287
Fax: 819-820-3219
Directrice Santé et mieux-être au travail, Danielle Rheault
418-652-6433, Fax: 418-646-9546

Ministère de la Santé et des Services sociaux / Health & Social Services

Direction des communications et Renseignements généraux
1075, ch Sainte-Foy
Québec, QC G1S 2M1

Federal/Provincial Government / Gouvernement du Québec / Government of Québec

418-266-8900
800-707-3380
regisseur.web@msss.gouv.qc.ca
www.msss.gouv.qc.ca

Acts Administered:
Loi assurant l'exercice des droits des personnes handicapées/An Act to secure the handicapped in the exercise of their rights
Loi assurant la mise en oeuvre de la Convention sur la protection des enfants et la coopération en matière d'adoption internationale et modifiant diverses dispositions législatives en matière d'adopti
Loi assurant le maintien des services essentiels dans le secteur de la santé et des services sociaux/An Act to ensure that essential services are maintained in the health and social services sector
Loi concernant les unités de négociation dans le secteur des affaires sociales/An Act respecting bargaining units in the social affairs sector
Loi sur Héma-Québec et sur le Comité d'hémovigilance/An Act respecting Héma-Québec and the haemovigilance committee
Loi sur l'administration publique/Public Administration Act
Loi sur l'assurance-hospitalisation/Hospital Insurance Act
Loi sur l'assurance-maladie/Health Insurance Act
Loi sur l'assurance-médicaments/An Act respecting prescription drug insurance
Loi sur l'équilibre budgétaire du réseau public de la santé et des services sociaux/An Act to provide for balanced budgets in the public health and social services network
Loi sur l'Institut national de Santé publique du Québec/An Act respecting the Institut national de Santé publique du Québec
Loi sur la Corporation d'hébergement du Québec/An Act respecting the Corporation d'hébergement du Québec
Loi sur la protection de la jeunesse/Youth Protection Act
Loi sur la protection de la santé publique/Public Health Protection Act
Loi sur la protection des personnes dont l'état mental présente un danger pour elles-mêmes ou pour autrui/An Act respecting the protection of persons whose mental state presents a danger to themselves
Loi sur la Régie de l'assurance-maladie du Québec/An Act respecting la Régie de l'assurance-maladie du Québec
Loi sur la santé publique/Public Health Act
Loi sur le Commissaire à la santé et au bien-être/An Act respecting the Health and Welfare Commissioner
Loi sur le Conseil de la santé et du bien-être/An Act respection g the Conseil de la santé et du bien-être
Loi sur le Conseil médical du Québec/An Act respecting the Conseil médical du Québec
Loi sur le ministère de la Santé et des Services Sociaux/An Act respecting the Ministède la Santé des Services sociaux
Loi sur le Protecteur des usagers en matière de santé et de services sociaux/An Act respecting the Health and Social Services Ombudsman
Loi sur le tabac/Tobacco Act
Loi sur les activités cliniques et de recherche en matière de procréation assistée et modifiant d'autres dispositions législatives
Loi sur les agences de développement de réseaux locaux de services de santé et de services sociaux/An Act respecting local health and social services network development agencies
Loi sur les cimetières non-Catholiques/Non-Catholic Cemeteries Act
Loi sur les inhumations et les exhumations/Burial Act
Loi sur les laboratoires médicaux, la conservation des organes, des tissus, des gamètes et des embryons, les services ambulanciers et la disposition des cadavres/An Act respecting medical laboratories
Loi sur les sages-femmes/Midwives Act
Loi sur les services de santé et les services sociaux/An Act respecting health services and social services
Loi sur les services de santé et les services sociaux pour les autochtones cris/An Act respecting health services and social services for Cree Native persons

Ministre, L'hon. Dr Yves Bolduc
418-266-7171
Ministre déléguée Services sociaux, L'hon. Dominique Vien
418-266-7181
Sous-ministre, Jacques Cotton
418-266-8989, Fax: 418-266-8990
Sous-ministre adjoint Planification, performance & qualité, Denis Lalumière
418-266-5990

• Agence d'évaluation des technologies et des modes d'intervention en santé(AETMIS) / Technology Assessment & Health Solutions Agency
#10.083, 2021, av Union
Montréal, QC H3A 2S9
514-873-2563
Fax: 514-873-1369
www.aetmis.gouv.qc.ca
• Bureau des projets Centres hospitaliers universitaires de Montréal, CHUM, CUSM et CHU Sainte-Justine
#10.049, 2021, rue Union
Montréal, QC H3A 2S9
514-864-9883
Fax: 514-873-7362
www.construction3chu.msss.gouv.qc.ca
• Secrétariat à l'accès aux services en langue anglaise et aux communautés ethnoculturelles
#840, 2021, av Union
Montréal, QC H3A 2S9
514-873-5130
Fax: 514-873-9876
www.msss.gouv.qc.ca/ministere/saslacc
• Conseil du médicament
#100, 1195, av Lavigerie
Sainte-Foy, QC G1V 4N3
418-644-8103
Fax: 418-644-8120
cdm@cdm.gouv.qc.ca
www.cdm.gouv.qc.ca
• Commissaire à la santé et du bien-être
#700, 1020, rte de l'Église
Québec, QC G1V 3V9
418-643-3040
Fax: 418-644-0654
csbe@csbe.gouv.qc.ca
www.csbe.gouv.qc.ca
• Corporation d'hébergement du Québec
2535, boul Laurier, 5e étage
Québec, QC G1V 4M3
418-644-3600
Fax: 418-644-3609
danielle.dussault@chq.gouv.qc.ca
www.chq.gouv.qc.ca
• Institut national de santé publique du Québec
945, av Wolfe
Québec, QC G1V 5B3
418-650-5115
Fax: 418-646-9328
info@inspq.qc.ca
www.inspq.qc.ca
Président-directeur général, Richard Massé
• Office des personnes handicapées du Québec
309, rue Brock
Drummondville, QC J2B 1C5
819-475-8585
Fax: 819-475-8767
800-567-1465
www.ophq.gouv.qc.ca
Other Communication: Téléscripteur: 1-800-567-1477
• Urgences-santé Québec
3232, rue Bélanger
Montréal, QC H1Y 3H5
514-723-5600
info@urgences-sante.qc.ca
www.urgences-sante.qc.ca
• Régie de l'assurance maladie du Québec
1125, Grande Allée ouest
Québec, QC G1S 1E7
418-646-4636
www.ramq.gouv.qc.ca

Santé publique / Public Health
Sous-ministre adjoint, Alain Poirier
418-266-6700, Fax: 418-266-6707
Directrice Planification, évaluation et développement en santé publique/Surveillance de l'état de santé, Lyne Jobin
418-266-6780
Directeur Développement des individus et de l'environnement, André Dontigny
418-266-6714
Directrice Prévention des maladies chroniques et des traumatismes, Marie Rochette
418-266-6750
Directeur Protection de la santé publique, Horacio Arruda
418-266-6720

Commission de la santé et de la sécurité du travail du Québec (CSST) / Québec Occupational Health & Safety Commission
524, rue Bourdages
CP 1200 Terminus postal
Québec, QC G1K 7E2
418-266-4850
Fax: 418-266-4398
866-302-2778
www.csst.qc.ca
A pour mission de soutenir aux travailleurs & aux employeurs dans leurs démarches pour éliminer les dangers présents dans leur milieu de travail, inspecter des lieux de travail, & promouvoir la santé & sécurité du travail
Président & Chef de la direction, Luc Meunier
Vice-président Opérations, Paul Marceau

Ministère de la Sécurité publique / Ministry of Public Security
Tour des Laurentides
2525, boul Laurier, 5e étage
Québec, QC G1V 2L2
418-643-2112
Fax: 418-646-6168
866-644-6826
www.securitepublique.gouv.qc.ca
A pour mission d'assurer la sécurité publique au Québec

Acts Administered:
Loi de tempérance/Temperance Act
Loi favorisant la libération conditionnelle des détenus/An Act to promote the parole of inmates
Loi sur la police/Police Act
Loi sur la propriété des bicyclettes/Bicycle Ownership Act
Loi sur la recherche des causes et des circonstances des décès/An Act respecting the determination of the causes & circumstances of death
Loi sur la sécurité civile/Civil Protection Act
Loi sur la sécurité dans les sports/An Act respecting safety in sports
Loi sur la sécurité incendie/Fire Safety Act
Loi sur la Société des alcools du Québec/An Act respecting the Société des alcools du Québec (partially administered by MSP)
Loi sur la Société des loteries du Québec/An Act respecting the Société des loteries du Québec (partially administered by the MSP)
Loi sur le ministère de la Sécurité publique/An Act respecting the Ministère de la Sécurité publique
Loi sur le régime syndical applicable à la Sûreté du Québec/An Act respecting the Syndical Plan of the Sûreté du Québec
Loi sur le système correctionnel du Québec/An Act respecting the Québec correctional system
Loi sur les agences d'investigation ou de sécurité/An Act respecting detectives or security agencies
Loi sur les bombes lacrymogènes/Act respecting tear bombs
Loi sur les coffrets de sûreté/Safe-Deposit Boxes Act
Loi sur les courses/An Act respecting racing
Loi sur les explosifs/An Act respecting explosives
Loi sur les infractions en matière de boissons alcooliques/An Act respecting offences relating to Alcoholic Beverages
Loi sur les loteries, les concours publicitaires et les appareils d'amusement/An Act respecting lotteries, publicity, contests & amusement machines
Loi sur les permis d'alcool/An Act respecting liquor permits
Loi sur les services correctionnels/An Act respecting correctional services
Loi sur les villages nordiques et l'Administration régionale Kativik/An Act respecting Northern Villages & the Kativik Regional Government (partially administered by the MSP)

Ministre, L'hon. Robert Dutil
418-643-2112, Fax: 418-646-6168
ministre@msp.gouv.qc.ca
Sous-ministre, Robert Lafrenière
418-643-3500, Fax: 418-643-0275
• Bureau du coroner
#390, 2875, boul Laurier
Sainte-Foy, QC G1V 5B1
418-643-1845
Fax: 418-643-6174
clientele.coroner@msp.gouv.qc.ca
• Comité de déontologie policière
Tour du Saint-Laurent
#A-200, 2525, boul Laurier, 2e étage
Québec, QC G1V 4Z6

Federal/Provincial Government / Gouvernement du Québec / Government of Québec

418-646-1936
Fax: 418-528-0987
comite.deontologie@msp.gouv.qc.ca
www.deontologie-policiere.gouv.qc.ca
• Commissaire à la déontologie policière
1200, rte de l'Église, R-C20
Sainte-Foy, QC G1V 4Y9
418-643-7897
Fax: 418-528-9473
877-237-7897
www.deontologie-policiere.gouv.qc.ca
Other Communication:
deontologie-policiere.quebec@msp.gouv.qc.ca
• Commissariat des incendies
455, rue Dupont
Québec, QC G1K 6N2
418-529-5706
Fax: 418-529-9922
Commissaire, Cyrille Delâge
• Commission québecoise des libérations conditionnelles
#1.32A, 300, boul Jean-Lesage
Québec, QC G1K 8K6
418-646-8300
Fax: 418-643-7217
liberation.conditionnel@msp.gouv.
www.msp.gouv.qc.ca
• Direction générale de la Sûreté du Québec
1701, rue Parthenais
Montréal, QC H2K 3S7
514-598-4488
Fax: 514-598-4957
info@surete.qc.ca
www.surete.qc.ca
• École nationale de police du Québec
350, rue Marguerite-d'Youville
Nicolet, QC J3T 1X4
819-293-8631
Fax: 819-293-4018
courriel@enpq.qc.ca
www.enpq.qc.ca
• École nationale des pompiers du Québec
#3.08, 2800, boul Saint-Martin ouest
Laval, QC H7T 2S9
450-680-6800
Fax: 450-680-6818
866-680-3677
enpq@enpq.gouv.qc.ca
www.enpq.gouv.qc.ca
Directeur général, Yves Desjardins
• Régie des alcools, des courses et des jeux
560, boul Charest est
Québec, QC G1K 3J3
418-643-7667
Fax: 418-643-5971
800-363-0320
racj.quebec@racj.gouv.qc.ca

Affaires policières / Police Services
418-643-3500
Fax: 418-643-0275

Sécurité civile et Sécurité incendie / Public Safety & Fire Services
Sous-ministre associé & directeur général, Michel C. Doré
418-643-3500, Fax: 418-643-0275
Directeur général adjoint/Directeur (par intérim) Opérations, Éric Houde
418-646-6777, Fax: 418-646-5426
Directrice Mobilisation, Hélène Chagnon
418-646-6777, Fax: 418-646-5427
Directeur Gestion des risques, Martin Simard
418-643-3821, Fax: 418-644-4547
Directeur Rétablissement, Denis Landry
418-646-6638, Fax: 418-646-6628

Bas-Saint-Laurent, Gaspésie et Îles-de-la-Madeleine
#110, 70, rue Saint-Germain est
Rimouski, QC G5L 7J9
418-727-3589
Fax: 418-727-3643
securite.civile01@msp.gouv.qc.ca
Directrice, France-Sylvie Loisel

Capitale-Nationale, Chaudière Appalaches et Nunavik
#200, 1122, Grande-Allée ouest
Québec, QC G1S 1E5
418-643-3244
Fax: 418-644-2080
securite.civile03@msp.gouv.qc.ca
Directrice, Hélène Chagnon

Estrie et Montérégie
165, rue Jacques-Cartier nord
Saint-Jean-sur-Richelieu, QC J3B 6S9
450-346-3200
Fax: 450-346-5856
securite.civile16@msp.gouv.qc.ca
Directrice, Diane Migneault

Mauricie et Centre-du-Québec
4000, rue Louis-Pinard
Trois-Rivières, QC G8Y 4L9
819-371-6703
Fax: 819-371-6983
securite.civile04@msp.gouv.qc.ca
Directeur, Jacques Raymond

Montréal, Laval, Lanaudière et Laurentides
RC #23, 5100, rue Sherbrooke est
Montréal, QC H1V 3R9
514-873-1300
Fax: 514-864-8654
securite.civile06@msp.gouv.qc.ca
Directeur (par intérim), Yvan Leroux

Outaouais, Abitibi-Témiscamingue et Nord-du-Québec
817, boul St-René ouest
Gatineau, QC J8T 8M3
819-772-3737
Fax: 819-772-3954
securite.civile07@msp.gouv.qc.ca
Directeur, Jacques Viger

Saguenay-Lac-Saint-Jean et Côte-Nord
RC-01, 3950, boul Harvey
Jonquière, QC G7X 8L6
418-695-7872
Fax: 418-695-7875
securite.civile02@msp.gouv.qc.ca
Directeur, Réal Delisle

Services correctionnels / Correctional Services

Abitibi-Témiscamingue, Nord-du-Québec
#203, 170, av Principale
Rouyn-Noranda, QC J9X 4P7
819-763-3790
Fax: 819-763-3882

Bas-Saint-Laurent
Place Saint-Laurent
#101, 70, rue Saint-Germain est
Rimouski, QC G5L 7J9
418-727-3687
Fax: 418-727-3531

Capitale-Nationale, Chaudière-Appalaches
#3.05, 1200, rte de l'Église, 3e étage
Québec, QC G1V 4K9
418-646-0570
Fax: 418-646-9254

Côte-Nord
1191, boul Laflèche, 2e étage
Baie-Comeau, QC G5C 1E1
418-295-1333
Fax: 418-295-4819
866-640-3026

Estrie, Centre-du-Québec
#1.10, 200, Belvédère nord
Sherbrooke, QC J1H 4A9
819-820-3017
Fax: 819-820-3074
hebert@msp.gouv.qc.ca

Gaspésie-Îles-de-la-Madeleine
#101, 484, rue Hôtel-de-Ville, 1er étage
Chandler, QC G0C 1K0
418-689-4947
Fax: 418-689-5549

Laval, Lanaudière, Laurentides
#3.02, 2800, boul Saint-Martin ouest
Laval, QC H7T 2S9
450-680-6040
Fax: 450-680-6035

Mauricie, Centre-du-Québec
#212, 100, rue Laviolette
Trois-Rivières, QC G9A 5S9
819-371-6124
Fax: 819-371-6176

Montérégie
#3300, 5245, boul Cousineau
Saint-Hubert, QC J3Y 6Y8
450-656-3822
Fax: 450-656-7633
866-337-0184

Montréal
#11.87, 10, rue Saint-Antoine est
Montréal, QC H2Y 1A2
514-864-1800
Fax: 514-873-9362

Outaouais
#2.230, 17, rue Laurier
Gatineau, QC J9A 1B4
819-772-3929
Fax: 819-772-3025
866-466-7603

Saguenay-Lac-Saint-Jean
#4.09, 227, rue Racine est
Chicoutimi, QC G7H 7B4
418-698-3779
Fax: 418-690-8560
alain.dastous@msp.gouv.qc.ca

Ministère des Services gouvernementaux / Government Services
4e étage, Secteur 500
875, Grande Allée est
Québec, QC G1R 5R8
418-643-8383
Fax: 418-528-6153
communication@msg.gouv.qc.ca
www.msg.gouv.qc.ca
A pour mission de faire progresser la modernisation de l'État, simplifier l'accès aux services gouvernementaux, regrouper des services pour l'Administration, et développer le gouvernement en ligne
Acts Administered:
Loi concernant le cadre juridique des technologies de l'information
Loi sur la Société immobilière du Québec
Loi sur le Centre de services partagés du Québec
Loi sur le ministère des Services gouvernementaux
Loi sur le Service des achats du gouvernement
Loi sur les services gouvernementaux aux ministères et organismes publics
Loi sur Services Québec
Ministre, L'hon. Michelle Courchesne
418-643-5926, Fax: 418-643-7824
cabinet@sct.gouv.qc.ca
Sous-ministre & dirigeante principale de l'information (par intérim), Denis Garon
Sous-ministre associé Bureau de la recherche et de l'innovation, Sylvie Grondin
Directeur général Service aérien gouvernemental, Lucien Tremblay
Directeur (par intérim) Affaires publiques et Communications, Jean Talbot
• Services Québec
800, place D'Youville, 20e étage
Québec, QC G1R 3P4
418-644-4545
Fax: 418-528-9341
877-644-4545
TDD: 800-361-9596
www.gouv.qc.ca/portail/quebec/pgs/commun
Other Communication: Montréal Citizens: 514-644-4545;
Address: Place Dupuis, RC#2, 800, boul Maisonneuve est, Montréal, QC H2L 4L8
Ministre, L'hon. Clément Gignac
Services Québec est un guichet multiservices chargé d'offrir des services intégrés aux citoyens et aux entreprises

Federal/Provincial Government / Gouvernement du Québec / Government of Québec

• Société immobilière du Québec(SIQ) / Québec Buildings Corp.
1075, rue de l'Amérique-Française
Québec, QC G1R 5P8
418-646-1766
Fax: 418-646-6911
877-747-9911
courrier@siq.gouv.qc.ca
www.siq.gouv.qc.ca
Président & Chef de la direction, Richard Verreault
La Société immobilière du Québec (SIQ) a pour mission de mettre à la disposition des ministères et organismes publics des immeubles et de leur fournir des services de construction, d'exploitation et de gestion immobilière

Centre de services partagés / Shared Services Centre

Société immobilière du Québec
1075, rue de l'Amérique-Française, 1er étage
Québec, QC G1R 5P8
418-646-1766
Fax: 418-646-6911
courrier@siq.gouv.qc.ca
A pour mission à loger les ministères & organismes publics au meilleur rapport qualité & prix. Créée en 1984, la SIQ a remplacé le Ministère des Travaux publics et de l'Approvisionnement

Services Québec
877-644-4545
www.gouv.qc.ca/portail/quebec/
Créé en 2004 pour améliorer la façon d'offrir des services publics aux citoyens et aux entreprises

Services Québec

Bureau de la qualité
800, place D'Youville, 20e étage
Québec, QC G1R 3P4
418-646-4011
Fax: 418-528-9341
www.gouv.qc.ca/portail/quebec/servicesquebec/
Président-Directeur général (par-intérim) & Vice-président Services à la clientèle, Jocelyn Girard
418-528-9328
Directrice Planification, recherche et coordination intergouvernementale, Réjeanne Lachance

Ministère du Tourisme / Tourism Québec

#400, 900, boul René-Lévesque est
Québec, QC G1R 2B5
418-643-5959
Fax: 418-646-8723
800-482-2433
www.tourisme.gouv.qc.ca
Acts Administered:
Loi sur l'aide au développement touristique
Loi sur le ministère du Tourisme
Loi sur l'Institut de tourisme et d'hôtellerie du Québec
Loi sur les établissements d'hébergement touristique
Ministre, L'hon. Nicole Ménard
418-528-8063, Fax: 418-528-8066
Sous-ministre, Suzanne Giguère
418-643-9141, Fax: 418-643-2268
Directrice (par intérim) Communications, Dominique Lavoie
Sous-ministre adjoint Accueil/Hébergement touristique, Raymond Lesage
• Palais des congrès de Montréal
159, rue Saint-Antoine ouest, 9é étage
Montréal, QC H2Z 1H2
514-871-8122
Fax: 514-871-3188
800-268-8122
pcmcomm@congresmtl.com
congresmtl.com
• Société du Centre des congrès de Québec
900, boul René-Lévesque est, 2e étage
Québec, QC G1R 2B5
418-644-4000
Fax: 418-644-6455
888-679-4000
www.convention.qc.ca
Sous-ministre adjoint, Georges Vacher
514-864-1016, Fax: 514-864-6152
Directrice générale Marketing, Sylvie Quenneville
Directeur général Services à la clientèle touristique, Sylvain Lacombe

Directrice Centre d'affaires électroniques, Michèle Morel
Directrice Renseignements par téléphone et Internet, Nicole Desrochers

Ministère des Transports (MTQ) / Transportation

700, boul René-Lévesque est, 27e étage
Québec, QC G1R 5H1
418-643-6980
Fax: 418-643-2011
888-355-0511
communications@mtq.gouv.qc.ca
www.mtq.gouv.qc.ca
Other Communication: Au Québec: 5-1-1
Acts Administered:
Code de la sécurité routière/Highway Safety Code
Loi concernant la Compagnie de gestion de Matane inc./Act respecting the Compagnie de gestion de Matane Inc.
Loi concernant les partenariats en matière d'infrastructures de transport/Act respecting transport infrastructure partnerships
Loi concernant les propriétaires et exploitants de véhicules lourds/Act respecting owners and operators of heavy vehicles
Loi concernant les services de transport par taxi/Act respecting transportation services by taxi
Loi interdisant l'affichage publicitaire le long de certaines voies de circulation/Act to prohibit commercial advertising along certain thoroughfares
Loi modifiant la Loi sur les transports en matière de camionnage en vrac/Act to amend the Transport Act as regards bulk trucking
Loi sur l'Agence métropolitaine de transport/Act respecting the Agence métropolitaine de transport
Loi sur l'assurance automobile/Automobile Insurance Act
Loi sur l'expropriation/Expropriation Act
Loi sur la publicité le long des routes/Roadside Advertising Act
Loi sur la sécurité du transport terrestre guidé/Act to ensure safety in guided land transportation
Loi sur la Société de l'assurance automobile du Québec/Act respecting the Société de l'assurance automobile du Québec
Loi sur la Société des traversiers du Québec/Act respecting the Société des Traversiers du Québec
Loi sur la Société du port ferroviaire de Baie-Comeau-Hauterive/Act respecting the Société du port ferroviaire de Baie-Comeau-Hauterive
Loi sur la voirie/Act respecting roads
Loi sur le Ministère des Transports/Act respecting the Ministère des Transports
Loi sur les chemins de fer/Railway Act
Loi sur les conseils intermunicipaux de transport dans la région de Montréal/Act respecting intermunicipal boards of transport in the area of Montréal
Loi sur les sociétés de transport en commun/Act respecting public transit authorities
Loi sur les transports/Transport Act
Loi sur les transports instituant la Commission des transports du Québec/Transport Act established by the Commission des transports du Québec
Loi sur les véhicules hors route/Act respecting off-highway vehicles
Ministre, L'hon. Sam Hamad
418-643-6980, Fax: 418-643-2033
Ministre délégué, Norman MacMillan
418-643-6980, Fax: 418-643-2033
Sous-ministre, Michel Boivin
418-643-6740, Fax: 418-643-9836
Directeur général de Montréal & de l'Ouest, VACANTE
Directeur général de Québec & de l'Est, André Caron, s.m.a.
418-528-0808
Directrice générale Infrastructures & Technologies, Anne-Marie Leclerc
418-528-0808
Directrice générale (par intérim) Services à la gestion, Josée Dupont
418-528-0808
Directeur Politiques & sécurité en transport, André Meloche, s.m.a.
418-528-0808,
• Commission des transports du Québec
200, ch Sainte-Foy, 7e étage
Québec, QC G1R 5V5
Fax: 418-644-8034
888-461-2433
courrier@ctq.gouv.qc.ca
www.ctq.gouv.qc.ca
Présidente, Lise Lambert

• Société de l'assurance automobile du Québec
333, boul Jean-Lesage
CP 19600 Terminus
Québec, QC G1K 8J6
418-643-7620
Fax: 418-644-0339
800-361-7620
courrier@saaq.gouv.qc.ca
www.saaq.gouv.qc.ca
• Société du port ferroviaire Baie-Comeau-Hauterive
18, rte Maritime
Baie-Comeau, QC G4Z 2L6
418-296-6785
Fax: 418-296-2377
soport@globetrotter.qc.ca
• Société des traversiers du Québec
250, rue Saint-Paul
Québec, QC G1K 9K9
418-643-2019
Fax: 418-643-7308
stq@traversiers.gouv.qc.ca
www.traversiers.gouv.qc.ca
Président et Directeur général, Georges Farrah

Infrastructures et technologies / Infrastructure & Technologies

Directrice générale, Anne-Marie Leclerc, s.m.a.
418-528-0808
Directeur Laboratoire des chaussées, Claude Tremblay
418-643-6618
Directeur Structures, Daniel Bouchard
418-643-6906
Directeur Soutien aux opérations, Éric Breton
418-643-9298
Directeur Environnement et recherche, Christian Therrien
418-643-8326

Montréal et de l'Ouest / Montreal & the West

Directeur (par intérim) Planification & coordination des ressources, Pierre Fernandez Galvan
514-864-1730

Abitibi-Témiscamingue-Nord-du-Québec
80, av Québec
Rouyn-Noranda, QC J9X 6R1
819-763-3271
Fax: 819-763-3493
datnq@mtq.gouv.qc.ca

Est-de-la-Montérégie
201, place Charles-Lemoyne, 5e étage
Longueuil, QC J4K 2T5
450-677-3413
Fax: 450-442-1317
dtem@mtq.gouv.qc.ca

Estrie
#2.02, 200, rue Belvédère nord
Sherbrooke, QC J1H 4A9
819-820-3280
Fax: 819-820-3118
dte@mtq.gouv.qc.ca

Ile-de-Montréal
440, boul René-Lévesque ouest, 10e étage
Montréal, QC H2Z 2A6
514-873-7781
Fax: 514-864-3867
dtim@mtq.gouv.qc.ca

Laurentides-Lanaudière
222, rue Saint-Georges, 2e étage
Saint-Jérôme, QC J7Z 4Z9
450-569-3057
Fax: 450-569-3072
dll@mtq.gouv.qc.ca

Laval-Mille-Iles
1725, boul Le Corbusier
Laval, QC H7S 2K7
450-680-6330
Fax: 450-973-4959
dtlmi@mtq.gouv.qc.ca

Ouest-de-la-Montérégie
#200, 180, boulevard d'Anjou
Châteauguay, QC J6K 1C4

450-698-3400
Fax: 450-698-3452
dtom@mtq.gouv.qc.ca

Outaouais
#5.110, 170, rue de l'Hôtel-de-Ville
Gatineau, QC J8X 4C2
819-772-3849
Fax: 819-772-3338
dto@mtq.gouv.qc.ca

Politiques et sécurité en transport / Transportation Policy & Security
Directeur général, André Meloche, s.m.a.
418-528-0808
Directeur Transport routier des marchandises, Claude Larose
418-528-0631
Directeur Sécurité en transport, Claude Morin
418-643-1564
Directrice Transport terrestre des personnes, France Dompierre
418-644-0324
Directeur (par intérim) Transport maritime, aérien et ferroviaire, André Meloche
418-643-1864

Québec et de l'Est / Québec & the East
Directeur Coordination, planification & ressources, Robert Beaulieu
418-643-7726

Bas-Saint-Laurent-Gaspésie-Iles-de-la-Madeleine
#101, 92, 2e rue ouest
Rimouski, QC G5L 8E6
418-727-3674
Fax: 418-727-3673
dtbgi@mtq.gouv.qc.ca

Chaudière-Appalaches
1156, boul de la Rive-Sud
Saint-Romuald, QC G6W 5M6
418-839-5581
Fax: 418-834-7338
dtca@mtq.gouv.qc.ca

Côte-Nord
#110, 625, boul Laflèche
Baie-Comeau, QC G5C 1C5
418-295-4765
Fax: 418-295-4766
dtcn@mtq.gouv.qc.ca

Mauricie-Centre-du-Québec
100, rue Laviolette, 4e étage
Trois-Rivières, QC G9A 5S9
819-371-6896
Fax: 819-371-6136
dmcq@mtq.gouv.qc.ca

Capitale-Nationale
475, boul de l'Atrium, 2e étage
Québec, QC G1H 7H9
418-643-1911
Fax: 418-646-0003
dcnat@mtq.gouv.qc.ca

Saguenay-Lac-Saint-Jean-Chibougamau
3950, boul Harvey
Jonquière, QC G7X 8L6
418-695-7916
Fax: 418-695-7926
dt.slsjc@mtq.gouv.qc.ca

Ministère du Travail / Labour
200, ch Sainte-Foy, 6e étage
Québec, QC G1R 5S1
418-643-4817
Fax: 418-528-0559
800-643-4817
service_clientele@travail.gouv.qc.ca
www.travail.gouv.qc.ca
Acts Administered:
Code du travail/Labour Code
Loi assurant l'exercice des droits des personnes handicapées/Act to secure the handicapped in the exercise of their rights
Loi sur le ministère du Travail/Act respecting le Ministère du travail
Loi sur le régime de négociation des conventions collectives dans les secteurs public et parapublic/Act respecting the process of negotiating of the collective agreements in the public & parapublic se
Loi sur les décrets de convention collective/Act respecting Collective Agreement Decrees
Loi sur les relations du travail, la formation professionnelle et la gestion de la main-d'ouvre dans l'industrie de la construction/Act Respecting Labour Relations, Vocational Training, and Manpower M
Loi sur les syndicats professionnels/Professional Syndicates Act
Acts administered by Labour Agencies
Commission de l'équité salariale
Loi sur l'équité salariale/Pay Equity Act
Commission de la construction du Québec
Loi sur les relations du travail, la formation professionnelle et la gestion de la main-d'ouvre dans l'industrie de la construction/Act respecting labour relations vocational training & manpower manag
Commission de la santé et de la sécurité du travail
Loi sur les accidents du travail et les maladies professionnelles/Act respecting accidents at work & professional illness or sickness
Loi sur l'indemnisation des victimes d'amiantose ou de silicose dans les mines et les carrières/Act respecting compensation - victims of asbestos or silicosis in mines & quarries
Loi sur la santé et la sécurité du travail/Occupational Health & Safety Act
Commission des lésions professionnelles
Commission des normes du travail
Loi sur la fête nationale/National Holiday Act
Loi sur les normes du travail/Act respecting Labour Standards
Conseil consultatif du travail et de la main-d'oeuvre
Loi sur le bâtiment /Building Act
Loi sur le Conseil consultatif du travail et de la main-d'ouvre/Act respecting the Conseil consultatif du travail et de la main d'oeuvre
Loi sur les appareils sous pression/Act respecting pressure vessels
Régie du bâtiment du Québec
Loi sur l'économie de l'énergie dans le bâtiment/Act respecting the conservation of energy in buildings
Loi sur la distribution du gaz/Gas distribution Act
Loi sur la sécurité dans les édifices publics/Public Buildings Safety Act
Loi sur les mécaniciens de machines fixes/Master Pipe Mechanics Act
Ministre, L'hon. Lise Thériault
418-643-5297, Fax: 418-644-0003
ministre@travail.gouv.qc.ca
Sous-ministre, Jocelin Dumas
418-643-2902, Fax: 418-643-0735
Directeur Communications, Gilles Beaulé
418-643-4508
• Commissaire de l'industrie de la construction
150, boul René-Lévesque est, 18e étage,
Québec, QC G1R 5B1
418-646-7200
Fax: 418-644-9977
www.cic.gouv.qc.ca
• Commission de la construction du Québec
3530, rue Jean-Talon ouest
Montréal, QC H3R 2G3
514-341-7740
Fax: 514-341-6354
888-842-8222
www.ccq.org
• Commission de l'équité salariale
200, ch Ste-Foy, 4e étage
Québec, QC G1R 6A1
418-528-8765
Fax: 418-528-6999
888-528-8765
equite.salariale@ces.gouv.qc.ca
www.ces.gouv.qc.ca
• Commission des lésions professionnelles
#700, 900, Place d'Youville
Québec, QC G1R 3P7
418-644-7777
Fax: 418-644-6443
800-463-1591
www.clp.gouv.qc.ca
Other Communication: Montréal: 1-800-361-9593
Présidente, Micheline Bélanger
Administrative tribunal that is the last recourse for employers or workers who contest a decision made by the Commission de la sant, et de la s,curit, du travail.
• Commission des normes du travail
Hall Est
400, boul Jean-Lesage, 7e étage
Québec, QC G1K 8W1
418-644-0817
Fax: 418-643-5132
800-563-9058
www.cnt.gouv.qc.ca
Président-directeur général, André Brochu
• Commission des relations du travail
35, rue de Port-Royal est, 2e étage
Montréal, H3L 3T1
514-864-3646
Fax: 514-873-3112
866-864-3646
crtm@crt.gouv.qc.ca
www.crt.gouv.qc.ca
Présidente, Andrée St-Georges
• Commission de la santé et de la sécurité du travail(CSST) / Occupational Health & Safety Commission
425, rue du Pont
CP 4900 Terminus
Québec, QC G1K 7S6
418-266-4000
Fax: 418-266-4015
800-668-6811
www.csst.qc.ca
Other Communication: Ile-de-Montréal: 514-906-3000; Address: Tour Sud, 1, complexe Desjardins, 31e étage, CP 3, Succursale Place-Desjardins, Montréal, QC, H5B 1H1
• Conseil consultatif du travail et de la main d'oeuvre
#9.400, 500, boul René-Lévesque ouest
Montréal, QC H2Z 1W7
514-873-2880
Fax: 514-873-1129
cctm@cctm.gouv.qc.ca
www.cctm.gouv.qc.ca
• Conseil des services essentiels du Québec
800, tour de la place-Victoria, 25e étage
CP 365
Montréal, QC H4Z 1H9
514-873-7246
Fax: 514-873-3839
800-337-7246
info@cses.gouv.qc.ca
www.cses.gouv.qc.ca
• Régie du bâtiment du Québec
545, boul Crémazie est, 4e étage
Montréal, QC H2M 2V2
514-873-0976
Fax: 514-864-2903
800-361-0761
crc@rbq.gouv.qc.ca
www.rbq.gouv.qc.ca
Ministre responsable de l'Administration gouvernementale & Présidente du Conseil du trésor, L'hon. Michelle Courchesne
418-643-5926, Fax: 418-643-7824
cabinet@sct.gouv.qc.ca
Secrétaire associé, Alain Parenteau
418-643-9383, Fax: 418-528-6877

Government of Saskatchewan
Seat of Government: Regina, SK S4S 0B3
www.gov.sk.ca
The Province of Saskatchewan entered Confederation on September 1, 1905. It has an area of 588,276.09 km2, & the StatsCan census population in 2006 was 968,157.
Assistant Deputy Minister, Rob Cunningham
306-787-0952, Fax: 306-798-0975

Saskatchewan Agriculture
Walter Scott Bldg.
3085 Albert St.
Regina, SK S4S 0B1
306-787-5140
866-457-2377
aginfo@gov.sk.ca
www.agriculture.gov.sk.ca
The Ministry's mandate is to foster, in partnership with individuals, communities, industry, & government, a commercially viable, self-sufficient, & sustainable agricultural sector in Saskatchewan.

Federal/Provincial Government / Government of Saskatchewan

The Ministry addresses needs of individual farmers & ranchers, encourages & develops higher value production & processing, & promotes sustainable economic development in rural areas of the province. Some responsibilities are as follows: agri-business development through provision of agriculture-based business experts & technical support; agricultural research to promote development & diversification; corporate services to support the Information Technology Office & the Rural Economic Co-operative Development; crop development; financial programs; inspection & administration of regulations for food & crop protection, animal disease surveillance, environmental reviews, licenses, registrations, & complaint resolution; irrigation development; promotion of sustainable use of Crown land; livestock development; provision of food safety, quality, policy, regulatory, market & business development programs; policy analysis, strategies, & agricultural information services; & delivery of Saskatchewan Crop Insurance Corporation programs & services.

Acts Administered:
Agri-Food Act, 2004
Agri-Food Innovation Act
Agricultural Credit Corporation of Saskatchewan Act
Agricultural Equipment Dealerships Act
Agricultural Implements Act
Agricultural Operations Act
Agricultural Safety Net Act
Agricultural Societies Act
Agrologists Act, 1994
Animal Identification Act
Animal Products Act
Animal Protection Act, 1999
Apiaries Act
Cattle Marketing Deductions Act, 1998
Crop Insurance Act
Crop Payments Act
Department of Agriculture, Food & Rural Revitilization Act
Disease of Animal Act
Expropriation (Rehabilitation Projects) Act
Farm Financial Stability Act
Farmers' Counselling & Assistance Act
Farming Communities Land Act
Government Organization Act
Grain Charges Limitation Act
Horned Cattle Purchases Act
Irrigation Act
Land Bank Repeal & Temporary Provisions Act
Leafcutting Beekeepers Registration Act
Line Fence Act
Milk Control Act, 1992
Noxious Weeds Act, 1984
On-farm Quality Assurance Programs Act
Pastures Act
Pest Control Act
Bacterial Ring Rot Control Regulations
Dutch Elm Disease Control Regulations
Pest Control Products (Saskatchewan) Act
Prairie Agricultural Machinery Institute Act, 1999
Provincial Lands Act
Sale or Lease of Certain Lands Act
Saskatchewan 4-H Foundation Act
Saskatchewan Farm Security Act
Saskatchewan Wetland Conservation Corporation Land Regulation
Soil Drifting Control Act
Stray Animals Act
Vegetable, Fruit & Honey Sales Act
Veterinarians Act, 1987
Veterinary Services Act
Minister, Hon. Bob Bjornerud
306-787-0338, Fax: 306-787-0630
minister.ag@gov.sk.ca
Deputy Minister, Alanna Koch
306-787-5170, Fax: 306-787-2393
alanna.koch@gov.sk.ca
Assistant Deputy Minister, Rick Burton
306-787-8077, Fax: 306-787-2393
rick.burton@gov.sk.ca
Director Regional Services, Lee Giroux
306-787-5018, Fax: 306-787-9623
lee.giroux@gov.sk.ca
Director Agriculture Research, Abdul Jalil
306-787-5960, Fax: 306-787-2654
abdul.jalil@gov.sk.ca
Director Crop Development, Doug Billett
306-787-8061, Fax: 306-787-0428
doug.billett@gov.sk.ca

Director Lands Administration, Gloria Parisien
306-787-5154, Fax: 306-787-5180
gloria.parisien@gov.sk.ca
Director Livestock Development, Paul Johnson
306-787-6423, Fax: 306-787-1315
paul.johnson@gov.sk.ca
Director Policy, Scott Brown
306-787-5961, Fax: 306-787-5134
scott.brown@gov.sk.ca
Director Irrigation Development, John Babcock
306-787-8711, Fax: 306-787-9623
john.babcock@gov.sk.ca
• Agri-Food Council
#302, 3085 Albert St.
Regina, SK S4S 0B1
306-787-5139
Fax: 306-787-5134
james.kettel@gov.sk.ca
www.agr.gov.sk.ca/agrifood
Chair, Robert Tyler
The Agri-Food Council is an independent board appointed by the provincial government. The Council is accountable to the Minister of Agriculture for the supervision of all agencies established under The Agri-Food Act, 2004.
• Agricultural Implements Board
#202, 3085 Albert St.
Regina, SK S4S 0B1
306-787-4693
Fax: 306-787-1315
Secretary, Donald Brooks
• Farm Stress Unit
#329, 3085 Albert St.
Regina, SK S4S 0B1
306-787-5196
Fax: 306-798-3042
800-667-4442
ken.imhoff@gov.sk.ca
Manager, Ken Imhoff
• Prairie Agricultural Machinery Institute(PAMI)
Hwy#5 West
PO Box 1900
Humboldt, SK S0K 2A0
306-682-2555
Fax: 306-682-5080
800-567-7264
humboldt@pami.ca
www.pami.ca
President/CEO, David Gullacher
PAMI works for the advancement of technology in agriculture through research and development.
• Saskatchewan Crop Insurance Corporation
484 Prince William Dr.
PO Box 3000
Melville, SK S0A 2P0
306-728-7200
Fax: 306-728-7268
888-935-0000
customer.service@scic.gov.sk.ca
www.saskcropinsurance.com
Minister Responsible, Hon. Bob Bjornerud
The provincial Crown Corporation provides responsive & flexible risk management tools. Crop insurance programs are as follows: Multi-Peril Insurance; Organic Insurance; Forage Insurance; & Weather Based Insurance.
• Saskatchewan Lands Appeal Board
#202, 3085 Albert St.
Regina, SK S4S 0B1
306-787-4693
Fax: 306-787-1315
dbrooks@agr.gov.sk.ca
Secretary, Donald Brooks

Saskatchewan Assessment Management Agency (SAMA)
#200, 2201 - 11th Ave.
Regina, SK S4P 0J8
306-924-8000
Fax: 306-924-8070
800-667-7262
info.request@sama.sk.ca
www.sama.sk.ca
SAMA is an independent agency with responsibility to develop & maintain the province's assessment policies, standards & procedures, audit assessments, & review & confirm municipal assessment rolls & provide property valuation services to local governments (municipalities & school boards).
Chair, Neal Hardy
CEO, Irwin Blank
306-924-8046, 800-667-7262,Fax: 306-924-8060
irwin.blank@sama.sk.ca
Managing Director Finance, George Dobni
306-924-8025, Fax: 306-928-8060
george.dobni@sama.sk.ca

Saskatchewan Corrections, Public Safety & Policing
1874 Scarth St.
Regina, SK S4P 4B3
306-787-7872
Fax: 306-787-8747
www.cpsp.gov.sk.ca
The Ministry of Corrections, Public Safety & Policing promotes safe communities in Saskatchewan. Adult correction & young offender programs & services are delivered that serve individuals in conflict with the law. Public safety is also addressed through the following programs & services: protection & emergency planning & communication; monitoring of building standards; fire prevention & disaster assistance programs; & licensing & inspections services.

Acts Administered:
Amusement Ride Safety Act
Boiler & Pressure Vessel Act
Correctional Services Act
Electrical Licensing Act
Emergency 911 System Act
Emergency Planning Act
Fire Prevention Act, 1992
Gas Licensing Act
Passenger & Freight Elevator Act
Uniform Building & Accessibility Standards Act
Youth Justice Administration Act
Minister, Hon. Darryl Hickie
306-787-4377, Fax: 306-787-5331
minister.cpsp@gov.sk.ca
Deputy Minister, Terry Coleman
306-787-8065, Fax: 306-798-0270
terry.coleman@gov.sk.ca
Executive Director Strategic Policy, Karen Lautsch
306-787-7344, Fax: 306-798-0270
karen.lautsch@gov.sk.ca
Executive Director Corporate Services, Mae Boa
306-787-8081, Fax: 306-798-0270
mae.boa@gov.sk.ca
Co-Director Communications, Judy Orthner
306-787-5883, Fax: 306-787-3874
judy.orthner@gov.sk.ca
Co-Director Communications, Laur'Lei Silzer
306-787-0775, Fax: 306-787-3874
laurlei.silzer@gov.sk.ca
Director Corporate Services, Gord Sisson
306-787-5472, Fax: 306-787-5830
gord.sisson@gov.sk.ca
Director Human Resources, Marlys Tafelmeyer
306-787-5475, Fax: 306-798-2084
marlys.tafelmeyer@gov.sk.ca
Director Information Management, Jim Bingaman
306-787-9512, Fax: 306-787-6979
jim.bingaman@gov.sk.ca
Legislative Secretary to the Minister of Corrections, Public Safety & Policing, Corrections Facilities Initiative, Serge LeClerc
306-934-2847, Fax: 306-934-2867
sleclerc@mla.legassembly.sk.ca

Licensing & Inspections
306-787-1443
Fax: 306-787-9273
866-530-8599
Administers a wide range of regulatory, enforcement, & advisory services which provide safety standards to industry & the general public in the areas of boiler, pressure vessel, elevators, amusement rides, gas & electrical equipment installations.
Acting Executive Director, Brian Krasiun
306-787-4509, Fax: 306-787-9273
brian.krasiun@gov.sk.ca

Protection & Emergency Services
306-787-8568
Fax: 306-787-1694
www.cpsp.gov.sk.ca/ProtectionandEmergencyServices

Delivers emergency planning & preparedness services, including Sask 911 emergency calling, the Provincial Disaster Assistance Program (PDAP), building standards & the Office of the Fire Commissioner.
Executive Director, Tom Young
306-787-3316, Fax: 306-787-1694
tom.young@gov.sk.ca

Building & Fire Safety
306-787-4113
Fax: 306-787-9273
buildingstandards@cps.gov.sk.ca
The National Building Code of Canada (NBC) is the basis for Saskatchewan's building construction standards. These standards address fire safety, health safety, structural adequacy, & barrier-fee accessibility requirements for all types of buildings. Building & Fire Safety works with municipalities & other local authorities, building & fire officials, building owners, designers & contractors to promote construction of safe buildings.
Chief Building Official, William Hawkins
306-787-4517

Office of the Fire Commissioner
The Office of the Fire Commissioner provides communities, fire departments & emergency service organizations with information, education & leadership to enhance their capabilities to protect people, property & the environment from the devastation of fire. The Office includes the Fire Commissioner, Fire Prevention Officer supervisors in charge of regional services, technical services, programs & standards & Fire Prevention Officers who deliver programs to regions.
Fire Commissioner, Duane McKay
306-787-4516, Fax: 306-787-9273
duane.mckay@gov.sk.ca

Provincial Disaster Assistance Program (PDAP)
306-787-7800
Fax: 306-787-1694
The Provincial Disaster Assistance Program (PDAP) provides financial assistance in certain circumstances where there has been a natural disaster, such as flooding, tornadoes, plow winds & severe weather. PDAP does not provide financial assistance for drought losses, fire losses or fire-related costs.
Program Advisor, Nadine Ring
306-787-7800

Saskatchewan Emergency Management Organization (SaskEMO)
#100, 1855 Victoria Ave.
Regina, SK S4P 3V7
306-787-9563
Fax: 306-787-1694
infosafety@cps.gov.sk.ca
www.cpsp.gov.sk.ca/saskemo
Saskatchewan Emergency Management Organization (SaskEMO) maintains the Provincial Emergency Plan & related contingencies as part of their provincial preparedness program to deal with events that may affect government operations. SaskEMO also offers training & education for emergency measures officials, volunteer organizations & public service groups &, to support community preparedness, has municipal emergency measures advisors available 24 hours per day to advise & assist municipalities during local emergencies.
Director, Kevin Roche
306-787-9567, Fax: 306-787-1694
kevin.roche@gov.sk.ca

Saskatchewan Tourism, Parks, Culture, & Sport
1919 Saskatchewan Dr., 4th Fl.
Regina, SK S4P 4H2
306-787-5729
Fax: 306-787-8560
www.tpcs.gov.sk.ca
The Ministry enhances the province's cultural, artistic, recreational & social life by working cooperatively with diverse groups & communities as it strives to promote leadership, recognize accomplishments, & sustain excellence in the arts, culture & sport. It is dedicated to ensuring that Saskatchewan people, especially the young people, reach their fullest potential in provincial, national, & international communities. In November 2007, a new provincial government resulted in the reorganization of provincial government ministries. The work of Saskatchewan Culture, Youth & Recreation was merged into an expanded ministry. Christine Tell was named the Minister of Tourism, Parks, Culture & Sport.

Minister Tourism, Parks, Culture & Sport, Hon. Christine Tell
306-787-0354, Fax: 306-798-0264
minister.tpcs@gov.sk.ca
Deputy Minister Tourism, Parks, Culture & Sport, Van Isman
306-787-5050, Fax: 306-798-0033
van.isman@gov.sk.ca
Executive Director Culture & Heritage, Susan Hetu
306-787-0730, Fax: 306-787-3177
susan.hetu@gov.sk.ca
• Saskatchewan Communications Network(SCN)
#313E, 2440 Broad St.
Regina, SK S4P 0A5
306-787-0490
Fax: 306-787-0496
800-667-5055
inquiries@scn.ca
www.scn.ca
• Royal Saskatchewan Museum
2445 Albert St.
Regina, SK S4P 4W7
306-787-2815
Fax: 306-787-2820
info@royalsaskmuseum.ca
www.royalsaskmuseum.ca
• Saskatchewan Archives Board
University of Regina
3303 Hillsdale St.
Regina, SK S4S 0A2
306-787-4068
Fax: 306-787-1197
info.regina@archives.gov.sk.ca
www.saskarchives.com
• Sask Film
1831 College Ave.
Regina, SK S4P 3V7
306-798-3456
Fax: 306-798-7768
800-561-9933
www.saskfilm.com
• Sask Heritage Foundation
1919 Saskatchewan Dr., 9th Fl.
Regina, SK S4P 3V7
306-787-4188
Fax: 306-787-0069
Manager, Garth Pugh
• Saskatchewan Arts Board
2135 Broad St.
Regina, SK S4P 3V7
306-787-4056
Fax: 306-787-4199
800-667-7526
sab@artsboard.sk.ca
www.artsboard.sk.ca
• Saskatchewan Science Centre
2903 Powerhouse Dr.
Regina, SK S4N 0A1
306-522-4629
Fax: 306-525-0194
800-667-6300
info@sasksciencecentre.com
www.sasksciencecentre.com
Executive Director, Scott Langen
• Wanuskewin Heritage Park
RR#4
Saskatoon, SK S7K 3J7
306-931-6767
Fax: 306-931-4522
wanuskewin@wanuskewin.com
www.wanuskewin.com
• Western Development Museum
2935 Melville St.
Saskatoon, SK S7J 5A6
306-934-1400
Fax: 306-934-4467
800-363-6345
info@wdm.ca
www.wdm.ca
Executive Director, David Klatt

Saskatchewan Lotteries Trust for Sport, Culture & Recreation
1870 Lorne St.
Regina, SK S4P 2L7
306-780-9300
sasksport@sasksport.sk.ca
www.sasklotteries.ca/sk/about_us/SLTF.html
Sask. Trust for Sport, Culture & Recreation is the organization that holds the net profits of the Saskatchewan Lotteries. The trust holds funds for three umbrella organizations Sask. Sport Inc., SaskCulture, & Saskatchewan Parks & Recreation Association.

Saskatchewan Environment
3211 Albert St., 2nd Fl.
Regina, SK S4S 5W6
306-953-3750
Fax: 306-787-9544
800-567-4224
inquiry@serm.gov.sk.ca
www.environment.gov.sk.ca
Other Communication: Provincial Parks Information Toll Free: 1-800-205-7070; Firewatch Line: 1-800-667-9660; Spill Control Centre: 1-800-667-7525; TIPS (Turn in Poachers): 1-800-667-7561
Saskatchewan Environment protects & mananges the province's environmental & natural resources by offering the following programs & services: compliance & enforcement to protect the public's interests in the management of air, land, water & natural resources; protection & management of forest ecosystems; wildfire management; Green Strategy; environmental assessment; legislation, & policies to ensure that Crown land is used in ways that respect environmental, economic & social values; fishing & fisheries management; hunting management; licensing & guiding the trapping industry; protection of wildlife; recycling; waste management; & water resource & treatment plant operations management.

Acts Administered:
Clean Air Act
Clean Air Regulation
Conservation Development Act
Conservation Easements Act
Potash Refining Air Emissions Regulations
Ecological Reserves Act
Assiniboine Slopes Provincial Ecological Reserves Regulations
Buffalograss Ecological Reserve Regulations
Provincial Ecological Reserves Regulation
Qu'Appelle Coulee Provincial Ecological Reserves Regulations
Representative Area Ecological Reserve Regulations
Environmental Assessment Act
Environmental Management & Protection Act, 2002
Environmental Spill Control Regulations
Halocarbon Control Regulations
Hazardous Substances & Dangerous Goods Regulations
Mineral Industry Environmental Protection Regulations
Municipal Refuse Management Regulations
Ozone-Depleting Substances Control Regulations
PCB Waste Storage Regulations
Reservoir Development Area Regulations
Scrap Tire Management Regulations
Used Oil Collection Regulations
Waste Electronic Equipment Regulations
Waste Paint Management Regulations
Water Regulations
Fisheries Act
Fisheries Regulations
Forest Resources Management Act
Dutch Elm Disease Regulations
Forest Resources Management Regulations
Indian Treaty Obligations Regulations
Surface Lease Agreement Regulations: Beaverlodge, Cigar Lake, Cluff Lake, Jolu Project, Key Lake, Konuto Project, McArthur River Operation, McClean Lake, Midwest Joint, Rabbit Lake
Wild Rice Regulations
Withdrawal of Land from Forests; Historical Interest Regulations
Grasslands National Park Act
Litter Control Act
Natural Resources Act
Commercial Activities Regulations
Commercial Fishing Production Incentive Regulations
Outfitter & Guide Regulations, 1996
Resource Protection & Development Services Regulations
Park Land Reserve Regulations
Parks Regulations
Recreation Site Regulations, 1991
Parks Act
Government Land Reserves Regulation
Historic Sites Regulations

Federal/Provincial Government / Government of Saskatchewan

Park Land Reserves Regulations
Prairie & Forest Fires Act, 1982
Provincial Lands Act
Crown Resource Lands Regulations, 1989
Provincial Lands Regulations
Surface Rights Regulations (Grasslands Park, Komis Project, Parks Lake Uranium Mining, Seabee)
Regional Parks Act, 1979
Sale or Lease of Certain Lands Act
Saskatchewan Watershed Authority Act 2005
Drainage Control Regulations
Groundwater Regulations
Reservoir Development Area Regulations
State of the Environment Report Act
Water Appeal Board Act
Water Regulations Act, 2002
Water Power Act
Watershed Associations Act
Wildlife Act, 1998
Captive Wildlife Regulations
Dog Training Regulations
Open Seasons Game Regulations
Wild Species at Risk Regulations
Wildlife Landowner Assistance Regulations, 1991
Wildlife Management Zones & Special Areas Boundaries Regulations, 1990
Wildlife Regulations, 1981
Wildlife Habitat Protection Act
Treaty Land Entitlement Withdrawal Regulations
Wildlife Habitat Lands Designation Regulations
Wildlife Habitat Lands Disposition & Alteration Regulations

Minister, Hon. Nancy Heppner
306-787-0393, Fax: 306-787-1669
minister.env@gov.sk.ca
Deputy Minister, Liz Quarshie
306-787-2930, Fax: 306-787-2947
liz.quarshie@gov.sk.ca
Associate Deputy Minister, Bob Ruggles
306-787-5122, Fax: 306-798-0599
bob.ruggles@gov.sk.ca
Acting Executive Director Finance & Administration,
Laurel Welsh
306-787-2484, Fax: 306-787-8441
laurel.welsh@gov.sk.ca
Director Communications, Greg Leake
306-787-5511, Fax: 306-787-3941
greg.leake@gov.sk.ca
• Saskatchewan Conservation Data Centre
3211 Albert St.
Regina, SK S4S 5W6
306-787-9038
Fax: 306-787-9544
www.biodiversity.sk.ca
Contact, Steve Porter
The SKCDC was formed as a co-operative venture between the province, The Nature Conservancy USA & The Nature Conservancy of Canada. The SKCDC gathers, interprets & distributes scientific information on the ecological status of provincial wild species & communities. The SKCDC is committed to conserving biological diversity; producing scientific reports & being the provincial clearinghouse for threatened & endangered species information.
• Saskatchewan Watershed Authority
111 Fairford St. East
Moose Jaw, SK S6H 7X9
306-694-3900
Fax: 306-694-3465
comm@swa.ca
www.swa.ca
Minister Responsible, Hon. Nancy Heppner
The Saskatchewan Watershed Authority administers the following legislation and regulations: Conservation & Development Act; Saskatchewan Watershed Authority Act, 2005; Water Power Act; Watershed Associations Act; Conservation & Development Regulations; Drainage Control Regulations; Ground Water Regulations; & Reservoir Development Area Regulations.

Lands & Forests Division
3211 Albert St., 5th fl.
Regina, SK S4S 5W6
306-787-5407
Fax: 306-787-2947
Provides delivery of integrated resource management & environmental protection programs.

Compliance & Field Services
112 Research Dr.
Saskatoon, SK S7K 2H6
306-933-7950
Fax: 306-933-8442
Community relations, compliance & enforcement.
Executive Director, Kevin Callele
306-787-3388

Fire Management & Forest Protection
800 Central Ave.
PO Box 3003
Prince Albert, SK S6V 6G1
306-953-3459
Fax: 306-953-3575
Manages forest fire activities.
Executive Director, Steve Roberts
306-953-2206
Strategic Performance Manager, Dave Tulloch
306-787-1095

Forest Service Branch
1061 Central Ave.
PO Box 3003
Prince Albert, SK S6V 6G1
306-953-2437
Fax: 306-953-2360
Sustainable mangement of Saskatchewan's forest ecosystems.
Executive Director, Al Willcocks
306-953-2437
Project Administrator, Sharon Kent
306-953-2221

Environmental Assessment Branch
3211 Albert St., 4th Fl.
Regina, SK S4S 5W6
306-787-6132
Fax: 306-787-0930
Determines impacts of developments.
Acting Director, Ron Zukowsky
306-787-6285, Fax: 306-787-0930
ron.zukowsky@gov.sk.ca

Green Policy Branch
#520, 3211 Albert St.
Regina, SK S4S 5W6
306-787-7774
Fax: 306-787-1349
Development of a government-wide green strategy.
Director, Lin Gallagher
306-787-2327

Planning & Evaluation Branch
#534, 3211 Albert St.,
Regina, SK S4S 5W6
306-787-5852
Fax: 306-787-0024
Strategic planning, policy, integrated monitoring, & Aboriginal affairs.
Executive Director, Dennis Sherratt
306-787-9904
Acting Director Aboriginal Affairs, Jack Kinnear
306-787-9643

Conservation Division
3211 Albert St., 5th fl.
Regina, SK S4S 5W6
306-787-9075
Fax: 306-787-2947
Assistant Deputy Minister, Dave Phillips
306-787-9079, Fax: 306-787-2947
dave.phillips@gov.sk.ca

Environmental Protection & Audit Division
3211 Albert St., 5th Fl.
Regina, SK S4S 5W6
306-787-5407
Fax: 306-787-2947
Protects human health & ecosystem integrity.
Assistant Deputy Minister, Mark Wittrup
306-787-5419, Fax: 306-787-2947
mark.wittrup@gov.sk.ca
Executive Director Municipal Branch, Sam Ferris
306-787-6193, Fax: 306-787-0197
sam.ferris@gov.sk.ca

Manager Environmental Information, Marlon Killaby
306-787-5021, Fax: 306-787-0197
marlon.killaby@gov.sk.ca
Acting Manager Standards, Thon Phommavong
306-787-9986,
thon.phommavong@gov.sk.ca

Parks Branch
3211 Albert St., 2nd Fl.
Regina, SK S4S 5W6
306-787-3105
Fax: 306-787-7000
Manages & operates the provincial park system.
Executive Director, Syd Barber
306-787-2846
Manager Park Business Services, Bob McEachern
306-787-2948
Manager Facilities Management, Bob Stenzil
Asst. Executive Director Park Program Development, Ken Lozinsky
306-787-2854

Resource Stewardship Branch
#436, 3211 Albert Street
Regina, SK S4S 5W6
306-787-2314
Fax: 306-787-9544
Executive Director, Hugh Hunt
Fax: 306-787-2309
Director Ecosystem Management Section, Nancy Cherney
306-787-2796
Manager Fisheries Management Unit, Chris Dunn
Manager Wildlife Management Unit, Shawn Burke

Northern Field Services
McIntosh Mall
800 Central Ave.
PO Box 3003
Prince Albert, SK S6V 6G1
306-953-2896
Fax: 306-953-2502

Swift Current Compliance Area
350 Chedle St. West
PO Box 5000
Swift Current, SK S9H 4G3
306-778-8205
Fax: 306-778-8212

Saskatoon Compliance Area
112 Research Dr.
Saskatoon, SK S7K 2H6
306-933-6240
Fax: 306-933-5773

La Ronge Compliance Area
#1100 - 1328 La Ronge Ave.
PO Box 5000
La Ronge, SK S0J 1L0
306-425-4234
Fax: 306-425-2580

Meadow Lake Compliance Area
#1, 101 - Railway Place
Meadow Lake, SK S9X 1X6
306-236-7557
Fax: 306-236-7677
Minister, Hon. Rod Gantefoer
306-787-6060, Fax: 306-787-6055
minister.fin@gov.sk.ca
Provincial Comptroller, Terry Paton
306-787-9254, Fax: 306-787-9720
terry.paton@gov.sk.ca

Saskatchewan First Nations & Métis Relations
#210, 1855 Victoria Ave.
Regina, SK S4P 3T2
306-787-6250
Fax: 306-787-5832
www.fnmr.gov.sk.ca
Working with First Nations and Métis people, the Ministry carries out the following responsibilities: providing overall direction to the government's approach to issues concerning First Nations & Métis people; coordinating programs in other government departments; ensuring that Saskatchewan's commitments regarding lands & resources are fulfilled; & working in partnership with First Nations & Métis people on issues of education & economic participation.

Acts Administered:
Indian & Native Affairs Act
Métis Act
Saskatchewan Gaming Corporation Act, Part III
Treaty Land Entitlement Implementation Act
Government Organization Act (Dept. of First Nations & Métis Relations Regulations)
Minister, Hon. June Draude
306-787-0605, Fax: 306-798-8050
minister.fnmr@gov.sk.ca
Acting Deputy Minister & Assistant Deputy Minister, Ron Crowe
306-787-6253, Fax: 306-787-5832
ron.crowe@gov.sk.ca
Executive Director, Seonaid MacPherson
306-787-8142, Fax: 306-798-0083
seonaid.macpherson@gov.sk.ca

Aboriginal Policy & Operations
306-787-9709
Fax: 306-787-5832

Lands & Resources Branch
306-787-5722
Fax: 306-787-6336
Manages & coordinates Saskatchewan's obligations under Treaty Land Entitlement. The Branch also performs a similar function with respect to Specific Claims.
Executive Director, Trisha Delormier-Hill
306-787-6681, Fax: 306-787-6336
trisha.delormier-hill@gov.sk.ca
Project Manager, Lornette Pelletier
306-787-0003, Fax: 306-787-6336
lonette.pelletier@gov.sk.ca

Saskatchewan Government Relations

1855 Victoria Ave.
Regina, SK S4P 3T2
306-787-2635
www.gr.gov.sk.ca
The Ministry has the following main duties: to create & maintain effective partnerships with governments in Saskatchewan, Canada, & abroad; to promote the province's interests with other governments; to support local governance to meet the needs of municipal governments; to coordinate & manage matters related to Government House, French language services, official protocol, & provincial honours; & to provide administrative services to the Office of the Lieutenant Governor. In November 2007, a new provincial government resulted in the reorganization of provincial government ministries. Saskatchewan Government Relations established separate roles for the Provincial Secretary, Municipal Affairs, & Intergovernmental Affairs. Bill Hutchinson was named Minister of Municipal Affairs.
Acts Administered:
Assessment Appraisers Act
Assessment Management Agency Act
Border Areas Act
Cities Act
City of Lloydminster Act
Community Planning Profession Act
Controverted Municipal Elections Act
Cut Knife Reference Act
Department of Rural Development Act
Department of Urban Affairs Act
Flin Flon Extension of Boundaries Act, 1952
Lloydminster Municipal Amalgamation Act, 1930
Local Government Election Act
Local Improvements Act, 1993
Municipal Board Act
Municipal Debentures Repayment Act
Municipal Development & Loan (Saskatchewan) Act
Municipal Expropriation Act
Municipal Industrial Development Corporations Act
Municipal Revenue Sharing Act
Municipal Tax Sharing (Potash) Act
Municipalities Act
Municipality Improvements Assistance (Saskatchewan) Act
Northern Municipalities Act
Planning & Development Act, 1983
Provincial Emblems & Honours Act
Provincial Secretary's Act
Rural Development Act
Rural Municipal Administrators Act
Rural Municipality Act, 1989
Subdivisions Act
Tax Enforcement Act
Time Act
Urban Municipal Administrators Act
Urban Municipality Act, 1984
Minister Municipal Affairs, Hon. Bill Hutchinson
306-787-6100, Fax: 306-787-0399
minister.ma@gov.sk.ca
Minister Responsible Intergovernmental Affairs, Hon. Bill Boyd
306-787-9124, Fax: 306-787-0395
minister.er@gov.sk.ca
Deputy Minister Intergovernmental Affairs, Al Hilton
306-787-4220, Fax: 306-787-7317
alan.hilton@gov.sk.ca
Provincial Secretary, Hon. Wayne Elhard
306-787-6447, Fax: 306-787-1736
minister.hi@gov.sk.ca
Deputy Provincial Secretary; Clerk of the Executive Council; Deputy Cabinet Secretary, Rick Mantey
306-787-9630, Fax: 306-787-8299
rick.mantey@gov.sk.ca
Chief of Protocol Office of Protocol & Honours, Deborah Johnson
306-787-3109, 877-427-5505,Fax: 306-787-1269
deborah.johnson7@gov.sk.ca
Executive Director Communications, Jeff Welke
306-787-6156, Fax: 306-787-4181
jeff.welke@gov.sk.ca
Executive Director Government House, Deborah Johnson
306-787-3109, Fax: 306-787-5714
deborah.johnson7@gov.sk.ca
Director Office of Francophone Affairs Branch/Direction des affaires francophones (DAF), René Boudreau
306-787-8035, Fax: 306-787-6352
rboudreau@gr.gov.sk.ca

Municipal Affairs
www.municipal.gov.sk.ca
The Municipal Relations Division strengthens Saskatchewan communities by providing the legal framework, organizational support, financial assistance & other services for the operation of municipalities. Working in partnership with municipal organizations & other communities, the Division encourages cooperation, understanding & self-reliance.
Asst. Deputy Minister, Maryellen Carlson
306-787-5765, Fax: 306-787-1987
maryellen.carlson@gov.sk.ca
Director Community Planning, Ralph Leibel
306-787-7672, Fax: 306-798-0194
ralph.leibel@gov.sk.ca
Director Northern Municipal Services Branch, Randy Braaten
306-425-4322, Fax: 306-425-2401
randy.braaten@gov.sk.ca

Canadian Intergovernmental Relations
#800, 1919 Saskatchewan Dr.
Regina, SK S4P 4H2
Fax: 306-787-7317

Central Management Services
#1410, 1855 Victoria Ave.
Regina, SK S4P 3T2
306-787-2136
Fax: 306-787-4161

Trade & International Relations
#800, 1919 Saskatchewan Dr.
Regina, SK S4P 4H2
306-787-6445
Fax: 306-787-7317

Saskatchewan Health

T.C. Douglas Bldg.
3475 Albert St.
Regina, SK S4S 6X6
306-787-0146
800-667-7766
info@health.gov.sk.ca
www.health.gov.sk.ca
Other Communication: Family Health Benefits: 1-800-266-0695; HealthLine: 1-877-800-0002; Health Registration / Health Card: 1-800-667-7551; Prescription Drug Plan: 1-800-667-7581
Saskatchewan Health offers the following programs & services: continuing care to help people live independently; e-health & information systems for access to medical information; emergency services; health benefits; recruitment & retention of healthcare providers; promotion of mental health & treatment for mental illness & addictions; personal health services; prescription drug coverage; public health programs; privacy of health information; services for people with long term disabilities or illnesses; surgery & diagnostics initiatives; & vital statistics.
Acts Administered:
Ambulance Act
Cancer Foundation Act
Change of Name Act
Chiropody Profession Act
Chiropractic Act, 1994
Dental Care Act
Dental Disciplines Act
Department of Health Act
Dietitians Act
Emergency Medical Aid Act
Health Districts Act
Health Facilities Licensing Act
Health Information Protection Act
Health Quality Control Act
Hearing Aid Act
Hearing Aid Sales & Services Act
Hospital Standards Act
Housing & Special-care Homes Act
Human Tissue Gift Act
Licensed Practical Nurses Act
Medical & Hospitalization Tax Repeal Act
Medical Laboratory Licensing Act
Medical Laboratory Technologists Act
Medical Profession Act, 1981
Medical Radiation Technologists Act
Medical Scholarships & Bursaries Act
Mental Health Services Act
Midwifery Act
Mutual Medical & Hospital Benefit Associations Act
Naturopathy Act
Occupational Therapists Act
Opthalmic Dispensers Act
Optometry Act, 1985
Personal Care Homes Act
Pharmacy Act
Physical Therapists Act, 1988
Prescription Drugs Act
Psychologists Act
Public Health Act
Regional Health Services Act
Registered Nurses Act, 1988
Registered Psychiatric Nurses Act
Saskatchewan Health Research Foundation Act
Saskatchewan Medical Care Insurance Act
Speech Language Pathologists & Audiologists Act
Tobacco Control Act
Vital Statistics Act
White Cane Act
Youth Detoxification & Stabilization Act
Minister, Hon. Don McMorris
306-787-7345, Fax: 306-787-0237
minister.he@gov.sk.ca
Deputy Minister, Dan Florizone
306-787-3041, Fax: 306-787-4533
dflorizone@health.gov.sk.ca
Associate Deputy Minister, Mike Shaw
306-787-3160, Fax: 306-787-4533
mshaw@health.gov.sk.ca
Legislative Secretary to the Minister of Health Nurse Recruitment & Retention, Laura Ross
306-545-6333, Fax: 306-545-6112
lross@mla.legassembly.sk.ca
Legislative Secretary to the Minister of Health Addictions, Joceline Schriemer
306-244-5623, Fax: 306-244-5626
jschriemer@mla.legassembly.sk.ca
• Health Quality Council
241, 111 Research Dr.
Saskatoon, SK S7N 3R2
306-668-8810
Fax: 306-668-8820
www.hqc.sk.ca

Acute & Emergency Services
Fax: 306-787-6113

Community Care Branch

Federal/Provincial Government / Government of Saskatchewan

306-787-7239
Fax: 306-787-7095

Drug Plan & Extended Benefits
306-787-3317

Health Registration & Vital Statistics
306-787-3251
Fax: 306-787-8951
800-667-7551
Vital Statistics Unit is responsible for the issuance of provincial birth, marriage & death certificates. Fee for each certificate is $20.00.

Medical Services
306-787-3475
Fax: 306-787-3761
800-667-7523

Policy & Planning Branch
Fax: 306-787-2974

Population Health Branch
Fax: 306-787-3112
Coordinates & encourages initiatives that promote & protect health & prevent disease & injury. The branch actively supports research & evaluation into health status, health trends & the risks to & determinants of health. Population Health Branch also supports food Ssfety programs which work at reducing the risk of the public contracting a food-borne illness. It is a leader in the development of food safety legislation, regulations & guidelines.
Executive Director, Rick Trimp
306-787-8847, Fax: 306-787-3237
rtrimp@health.gov.sk.ca

Disease Prevention & Health Protection Unit
3475 Albert St.
Regina, SK S4S 6X6
306-787-3237
The unit consists of program areas related to public health nursing, dental health, food safety & environmental health.The unit is responsible for leading development & implementation of legislation, regulations, policies & guidelines relating to The Public Health Act & providing support to health districts responsible for the delivery of disease prevention & environmental health programs.
Director, Jim Myres
306-787-1580, Fax: 306-787-3823
jim.myres@health.gov.sk.ca

Environmental Health
Through medical health officers & public health inspectors, Saskatchewan health districts investigate, monitor & address environmental health concerns. The purpose of these initiatives is to prevent injury & disease related to exposure to biological, physical & chemical hazards.Areas of concentration include private water supplies, sewage disposal, plumbing, public swimming pools, indoor air quality, public accommodations, institutional sanitation, personal service facilities & recreational facilities.
Manager Environmental Health, Tim Macaulay
306-787-7128, Fax: 306-787-3237
Tmacaulay@health.gov.sk.ca

Health Promotion
Fax: 306-787-3823
Health Promotion active in developing communication links between organizations, practitioners, researchers & policy makers, disseminates research findings & working through partnerships to offer training in health promotion practice & research.The department works with Prairie Region Health Promotion Research Centre, University of Saskatchewan, Health Canada & the World Health Organization.
Director, Mary Martin-Smith
306-787-7110,
mmartin-smith@health.gov.sk.ca

Workforce Planning Branch
Fax: 306-798-0023

Saskatchewan Highways & Infrastructure
1855 Victoria Ave.
Regina, SK S4P 3T2
306-787-4800
www.highways.gov.sk.ca
Other Communication: Hotline for Road Information:
306-933-8333 (North SK); 306-787-7623 (South SK); Toll Free: 888-335-7623; Website: roadinfo.telenium.ca/shwyw.html

The Ministry operates, preserves, & guides the development of the transportation system in Saskatchewan.
Acts Administered:
Dangerous Goods Transportation Act
Engineering & Geoscience Professions Act
Highway Traffic Act
Highways & Transportation Act
Railway Act
Sand & Gravel Act
Minister, Hon. Wayne Elhard
306-787-6447, Fax: 306-787-1736
minister.hi@gov.sk.ca
Deputy Minister, John Law
306-787-4949, Fax: 306-787-9777
john.law@gov.sk.ca
Director Communications, Doug Wakabayashi
306-787-4804, Fax: 306-798-0438
doug.wakabayashi@gov.sk.ca
• Saskatchewan Highway Traffic Board
1550 Saskatchewan Dr.
Regina, SK S4P 0E4
306-775-6674
Chair, Isabelle Impey
The Highway Traffic Board's mandate is to establish & to administer legislation relating to the safe & legal operations of private vehicles, the bus-truck industry & the short line rail industry in Saskatchewan, where specifically legislated to do so.

Corporate Services Division
306-787-4904

Operations Division
306-787-4901
Asst. Deputy Minister, Terry Schmidt
306-787-4859,
terry.schmidt@gov.sk.ca
Senior Environmental Engineer Materials & Testing, Neil Richardson
306-933-5213, Fax: 306-933-5221
neil.richardson@gov.sk.ca
Principal Technical Engineer Materials & Testing, Jorge Antunes
306-787-4640
Executive Director Engineering Standards, Ron Gerbrandt
306-787-4858, Fax: 306-787-4836
ron.gerbrandt@gov.sk.ca

Policy & Programs Division
306-787-4904
Asst. Deputy Minister, George Stamatinos
306-787-5028, Fax: 306-787-9777
george.stamatinos@gov.sk.ca
Executive Director Transportation Programs and Services, Les Bell
306-787-0825, Fax: 306-787-3963
les.bell@gov.sk.ca
Director Transport Compliance, Blair Wagar
306-787-4072, Fax: 306-787-6697
blair.wagar@gov.sk.ca
Director Land Branch, Jeff Grigg
306-787-4885, Fax: 306-787-4100
jeff.grigg@gov.sk.ca
Executive Director Transportation Policy, Harold Hugg
306-787-5311, Fax: 306-787-3963
harold.hugg@gov.sk.ca

Saskatchewan Energy & Resources (SIR)
#300, 2103 - 11th Ave.
Regina, SK S4P 3Z8
306-787-2528
Fax: 306-787-0395
866-727-5427
www.er.gov.sk.ca
The Ministry encourages the growth & development of the provincial resource sector. The Ministry's two main roles are as follows: offering programs & services to individuals & businesses; & coordinating economic development activities with other departments & agencies. In November 2007, a new provincial government resulted in the reorganization of provincial government ministries. The work of Saskatchewan Industry & Resources was merged into a newly named ministry. Bill Boyd was named the Minister of Energy & Resources.
Acts Administered:
Crown Minerals Act
Department of Economic Development Act, 1993
Department of Energy & Mines Act
Ethanol Fuel Act, 2002
Ethanol Fuel (General) Regulations
Ethanol Fuel (Grant) Regulations
Mineral Resources Act
Seismic Exploration Regulations
Oil & Gas Conservation Act
Oil & Gas Conservation Regulations
Pipelines Act
Minister Energy & Resources, Hon. Bill Boyd
306-787-9124, Fax: 306-787-0395
minister.er@gov.sk.ca
Deputy Minister Energy & Resources, Kent Campbell
306-787-9580, Fax: 306-787-2159
kent.campbell@gov.sk.ca
Director Public Affairs, Bob Ellis
306-787-8983, Fax: 306-787-2198
robert.ellis@gov.sk.ca
• Saskatchewan Trade & Export Partnership(STEP)
#320, 1801 Hamilton St.
PO Box 1787
Regina, SK S4P 3C6
306-787-9210
Fax: 306-787-6666
877-313-7244
inquire@sasktrade.sk.ca
www.sasktrade.sk.ca
President/CEO, Lionel LaBelle
Works in partnership with provincial export companies & emerging export companies to maximize commercial success in foreign ventures. STEP provides marketing services using a team of trade professionals, innovative approaches & world-wide networks. By promoting & developing sales, contracts, projects & referrals, STEP increases exports to existing foreign markets & taps into new markets.
• Tourism Saskatchewan
1922 Park St.
Regina, SK S4N 7M4
306-787-9600
877-237-2273
www.sasktourism.com

Corporate & Financial Services
306-787-2188
Fax: 306-787-3872

Exploration & Geological Services
306-787-2585
Fax: 306-787-1284
Executive Director, George Patterson
306-787-2560, Fax: 306-787-1284
george.patterson@gov.sk.ca
Director Mines, Mike Detharet
306-787-2139, Fax: 306-798-0047
mike.detharet@gov.sk.ca
Director Northern Geological Survey, Dr. Gary Delaney
306-787-1160, Fax: 306-787-1284
gary.delaney@gov.sk.ca
Director Sedimentary Geodata & Director, Petroleum Geology, Chris Gilboy
306-787-2573, Fax: 306-787-2488
chris.gilboy@gov.sk.ca

Petroleum & Natural Gas
306-787-2592
Fax: 306-787-2478
Asst. Deputy Minister, Trevor Dark
306-787-2591, Fax: 306-787-2478
trevor.dark@gov.sk.ca
Director Geology & Petroleum Lands, Ed Dancsok
306-787-2602, Fax: 306-787-0620
ed.dancsok@gov.sk.ca
Acting Director Petroleum Development, Todd Han
306-787-2221, Fax: 306-787-2478
todd.han@gov.sk.ca
Director Petroleum Royalties, Mike Ferguson
306-787-2605, Fax: 306-787-2478
mike.ferguson@gov.sk.ca
Director Petroleum Statistics, Darwin Roske
306-787-2607, Fax: 306-787-8236
darwin.roske@gov.sk.ca

Resource & Economic Policy
306-787-0900
Fax: 306-787-2198

Director Mineral Policy, Vacant
306-787-3377, Fax: 306-787-2198
Minister & Attorney General, Hon. Don Morgan, Q.C.
306-787-5353, Fax: 306-787-1232
minister.ju@gov.sk.ca
Acts Administered:
Alberta-Saskatchewan Boundary Act, 1939
Expropriation Act
Land Titles Act, 2000
Land Surveys Act, 2000
Manitoba-Saskatchewan Boundary Act, 1937
Manitoba-Saskatchewan Boundary Act, 1942
Manitoba-Saskatchewan Boundary Act, 1966
Manitoba-Saskatchewan Boundary Act, 1978
Saskatchewan Northwest Territories Boundary Act, 1966
Surface Rights Acquisition & Compensation Act
Deputy Minister & Deputy Attorney General, Gerald Tegart
306-787-5351, Fax: 306-787-3874
gerald.tegart@gov.sk.ca
Executive Director Policy, Planning & Evaluation, Betty Ann Pottruff, Q.C.
306-787-8954, Fax: 306-787-9008
bettyann.pottruff@gov.sk.ca
Director Corporate Services, Dave Tulloch
306-787-5472, Fax: 306-787-5830
dave.tulloch@gov.sk.ca
Director Communications, Laur'Lei Silzer
306-787-0775, Fax: 306-787-3874
laurlei.silzer@gov.sk.ca
Executive Director & Director, Legislative Services, Susan Amrud, Q.C.
306-787-8990,
susan.amrud@gov.sk.ca

Saskatchewan Advanced Education, Employment & Labour

1945 Hamilton St.
Regina, SK S4P 2C8
306-787-9478
Fax: 306-787-2315
TDD: 306-787-2429
www.aeel.gov.sk.ca
The Ministry is responsible for labour standards, labour support services, labour relations, mediation, occupational health & safety, workers' advocacy, & the Status of Women Office. In November 2007, a new provincial government resulted in the reorganization of provincial government ministries. An expanded Ministry of Advanced Education, Employment & Labour was formed. Rob Norris was named the Minister of Advanced Education, Employment & Labour.
Acts Administered:
Building Trades Protection Act
Construction Industry Labour Relations Act, 1992
Employment Agencies Act
Labour Standards Act
Occupational Health & Safety Act, 1993
Mines Regulation
Occupational Health & Safety Regulations, 1996
Radiation Health & Safety Act, 1985
Radiation Health & Safety Regulations
Trade Union Act
Worker's Compensation Act
Worker's Compensation Act Exclusion Regulations
Worker's Compensation General Regulations, 1985
Minister Advanced Education, Employment & Labour; Minister Responsible, Immigration; Minister Responsible for the Workers Compensation Board, Hon. Rob Norris
306-787-0341, Fax: 306-787-6946
minister.aeel@gov.sk.ca
Deputy Minister Advanced Education, Employment & Labour, Wynne Young
306-787-7071, Fax: 306-798-0975
wynne.young@gov.sk.ca
Executive Director Policy & Evaluation, Linda Smith
306-787-2984, Fax: 306-787-5870
linda.smith@gov.sk.ca
Executive Assistant Work & Family Unit, Gayl Basler
306-933-7983, Fax: 306-933-5444
Director Marketing & Communications, Herman Hulshof
306-787-9715, Fax: 306-798-5021
herman.hulshof@gov.sk.ca
Executive Director HR Services, Greg Tuer
306-787-3292, Fax: 306-787-7149
gtuer@psc.gov.sk.ca

• Labour Relations Board
#1600, 1920 Broad St.
Regina, SK S4P 3V2
306-787-2406
Fax: 306-787-2664
mbaldwin@lrb.gov.sk.ca
• Minimum Wage Board
#400, 1870 Albert St.
Regina, SK S4P 4W1
306-787-2391
Fax: 306-787-7229
webmaster@lab.gov.sk.ca
www.labour.gov.sk.ca
• Office of the Worker's Advocate
#400, 1870 Albert St.
Regina, SK S4P 4W1
306-787-2456
Fax: 306-787-0249
877-787-2456
www.labour.gov.sk.ca
Director, Margaret Halifax
The Office of the Worker's Advocate provides free assistance to workers who are experiencing difficulties with workers' compensation claims. The Office offers information about the following programs & services: wage loss, benefits, survivor's benefits, medical aid, rehabilitation, & retraining. Working with advocacy groups & unions, The Office of the Worker's Advocate strives to improve service to injured workers. Workers' Compensation Board (WCB) decisions about claims can be reviewed & appealed.
• Saskatchewan Workers' Compensation Board
#200, 1881 Scarth St.
Regina, SK S4P 4L1
306-787-4370
Fax: 306-787-7582
800-667-7590
TDD: 888-844-7773
internet_clientsvc@wcbsask.com
www.wcbsask.com
Other Communication: Injury Reports: 1-800-787-9288; Employer Inquiries: reainquiry@wcbsask.com; Health Care Provider Inquiries: internet_healthcare@wcbsask.com; Appeal Fax: 306-787-1116
Minister Responsible, Hon. Rob Norris
• Status of Women
#400, 1870 Albert St.
Regina, SK S4P 4W1
306-787-7401
Fax: 306-787-2058

Finance & Administration Branch
306-787-2413
Fax: 306-787-4038

Labour Relations & Mediation Division
306-787-0817
Fax: 306-787-1064
Executive Director, Doug Forseth
306-787-9106, Fax: 306-787-1064
doug.forseth@gov.sk.ca

Labour Standards
306-787-2438
Fax: 306-787-4780
800-667-1783
Acting Executive Director, Glen McRorie
306-933-5087, Fax: 306-787-4780
glen.mcrorie@gov.sk.ca
Other Communications: Alt. phone: 306/787-2432

Occupational Health & Safety Division
306-787-4496
Fax: 306-787-2208
800-567-7233
www.labour.gov.sk.ca/ohs
The division protects employee's health & safety at work. Its goal is to prevent & reduce the number of accidents, injuries, illnesses & deaths on the job. OH&S staff work with Occupational Health Committees or representatives to ensure the workplace fulfils health & safety responsibilities, creates & trains Occupational Health Committees, enforces workplace health & safety laws, inspects workplaces, investigates workplace accidents, hazards, concerns & complaints, provides health & safety training, information & advice, provides lab & technical services on chemical, biological & radiological hazards, ensures hazardous substances are properly managed & provides health & safety resources.
Executive Director, Glennis Bihun
306-787-4481, Fax: 306-787-2208
glennis.bihun@gov.sk.ca
Chief Mine Inspector Mines Safety Unit, Neil Crocker
306-933-5106, Fax: 306-933-7339
Manager Occupational Hygiene Unit, Herb Wooley
306-787-4506, Fax: 306-787-2208
herb.wooley@gov.sk.ca
Manager Workplace Safety Unit South, Bob Ross
306-787-4134, Fax: 306-787-2208
Manager Workplace Safety Unit North, Shelley Chirpilo
306-933-5050, Fax: 306-933-7339
shelley.chirpilo@gov.sk.ca

Saskatchewan Northern Affairs

Mistasinihk Place
1328 La Ronge Ave.
PO Box 5000
La Ronge, SK S0J 1L0
306-425-4207
Fax: 306-425-4349
866-663-4065
admin@sna.gov.sk.ca
www.northern.gov.sk.ca
Northern Affairs has the following responsibilities: to stimulate & support business & employment development in northern Saskatchewan; to promote benefits & opportunities for northerners from development; to provide leadership & support for regional economic planning & sector development in northern Saskatchewan by working with agencies & northerners; & to advance northern perspectives & interests within government.
Minister Responsible, Hon. June Draude
306-787-0605, Fax: 306-798-8050
minister.fnmr@gov.sk.ca
Executive Director Resource & Industry Development, Richard Turkheim
306-787-2143, Fax: 306-787-6014
richard.turkheim@gov.sk.ca
Executive Director Planning & Financial Management, Anita Jones
306-787-0174, Fax: 306-787-6014
anita.jones@gov.sk.ca

Saskatchewan Power Corporation (SaskPower)

2025 Victoria Ave.
Regina, SK S4P 0S1
306-566-2121
Fax: 306-566-2330
800-667-4749
www.saskpower.com
A Crown Corporation which provides services to over 439,000 customers over 652,000 square kilometres of diverse terrain in Saskatchewan; operates 15 generating facilities including, four base-load thermal stations, seven hydroelectric stations, three gas-fired peaking stations, & the Cypress Wind Power facility; capacity of 3,655 megawatts. The SaskPower Environmental policy maintains a commitment to environmental responsibility. The policy includes compliance with relevant environmental legislation, regulations & corporate environmental committees; continual improvement of environmental management systems & prevention of pollution. SaskPower's management system is ISO 14001 registered.
Minister Crown Corporations, Hon. Ken Cheveldayoff
306-787-7339, Fax: 306-798-3140
minister.cc@gov.sk.ca
President/CEO, Pat Youzwa
306-566-3103
Acting President & CEO SaskPower International, Garner Mitchell
306-566-2667
Vice-President Customer Services, Judy May
306-566-2161
Vice-President Power Production, Garner Mitchell
306-566-2067
Vice-President Transmission & Distribution, Mike Marsh
306-566-3271
Manager Communications & Public Affairs, Keith Moen
306-566-3421
Exec. Assistant, Cecile Matysio
306-566-3103

SaskPower Shand GreenHouse

Federal/Provincial Government / Government of Saskatchewan

PO Box 280
Estevan, SK S4A 2A3
306-634-9771
Fax: 306-634-6682
greenhouse@saskpower.com
Environmentally advanced power station, completed in July of 1992; burns high-quality lignite coal; flyash is removed by an electrostatic precipitator; a calcium-bearing sorbent injection system removes sulphur dioxide; burner temperature & air quality controls nitrogen oxide formations; Rafferty reservoir & Estevan sewage are the primary water sources for cooling. The Shand Power Station is a Zero discharge plant. Fully operational in 1996.

Saskatchewan Government Services (SPM)

Century Plaza
1920 Rose St.
Regina, SK S4P 0A9
306-787-6911
Fax: 306-787-1061
www.gs.gov.sk.ca
Responsibilities of the Ministry include the following: management, operation, & maintenance of accommodation; administration of commercial services such as relocation services, information services, & distribution; & coordination of corporate support services, including protective services, planning, & policy. In November 2007, a new provincial government resulted in the reorganization of provincial government ministries. The work of Saskatchewan Property Management was merged into a newly named ministry. Dan D'Autremont was named Minister of Government Services.
Acts Administered:
Architects Act
Interior Designers Act
Purchasing Act
Saskatchewan Property Management Corporation Act
Minister Government Services; Minister Responsible, Information Technology Office, Hon. Dan D'Autremont
306-787-0942, Fax: 306-787-8677
minister.gs@gov.sk.ca
Acting Deputy Minister, Phil Lambert
306-787-6520, Fax: 306-787-6547
phil.lambert@gov.sk.ca
Assistant Deputy Minister Accommodation Services, Donald Koop
306-787-9909, Fax: 306-798-0370
donald.koop@gov.sk.ca

Purchasing Branch
1920 Rose St.
Regina, SK S4P 0A9
306-787-6871
Fax: 306-787-3023
SPMC's Purchasing Branch coordinates the purchase of goods & some services for government departments, boards, agencies, & commissions, & some Crown corporations. Purchasing's current tender distribution methods are goods tenders valued at $5,000 or more & services tenders valued at $100,000 or more, are advertised & distributed through MERX, an electronic advertisement & tender system. Goods tenders valued between $5,000 & $25,000 are restricted where possible to firms located in the four western provinces.Source lists are normally used for goods tenders valued at less than $5,000 & services tenders valued at less than $100,000.
Director Purchasing, Rob Isbister
306-787-6005

Enterprise Saskatchewan

#200, 3085 Albert St.
Regina, SK S4S 0B1
Fax: 306-798-0629
800-265-2001
Webmaster@enterprisesask.ca
www.enterprisesaskatchewan.ca
Enterprise Saskatchewan (ES) is a bold and innovative approach to creating sustainable economic growth in Saskatchewan. It is a special agency for co-ordinating the province's growth agenda, led by key economic development and community stakeholders with one ultimate goal: to ensure Saskatchewan has a competitive environment that will attract investment at every level. Enterprise Saskatchewan provides leadership as the central co-ordinating agency of the Government of Saskatchewan for economic development. In partnership with key stakeholders, Enterprise Saskatchewan advances a transformative sustainable economic growth agenda and develops a culture of innovation and entrepreneurship that encourages investment and population growth, creating prosperity for all Saskatchewan residents.
Acts Administered:
Economic & Co-operative Development Act
Regional Economic & Co-operative Development Act
Minister Enterprise, Hon. Ken Cheveldayoff
306-787-0804, Fax: 306-798-2009
minister.ei@gov.sk.ca
Interim Chief Executive Officer, Chris Dekker
306-933-6744, Fax: 306-933-8244
chris.dekker@enterprisesask.ca
Chief Financial Officer, Denise Haas
306-787-2756, Fax: 306-798-0629
denise.haas@enterprisesask.ca
Vice President Regional Enterprise, Ernest Heapy
306-787-2561, Fax: 306-787-7559
ernest.heapy@enterprisesask.ca
Acting Director Investment Programs, Marv Weismiller
306-787-5014, Fax: 306-787-8702
marv.weismiller@enterprisesask.ca

Saskatchewan Research Council (SRC)

#125, 15 Innovation Blvd.
Saskatoon, SK S7N 2X8
306-933-5400
Fax: 306-933-7446
info@src.sk.ca
www.src.sk.ca
Research activities include: gas emissions testing; indoor environment testing; groundwater pesticides testing; indoor air quality & source testing for rayon & asbestos; spray drift research; vegetation studies for range, forestry, conservation; aquatic monitoring & assessment methods; climate impact assessment for environmental economic & urban stormwater management; development of plant bioassays for assessing the effects of hazardous materials in aquatic ecosystems; radiochemistry, chromatographic analysis, water analysis; parenting verification centre for the Canadian livestock industry; develops the optimum engine & fuel system for natural gas operation; bioprocessing technology; emulsions research; studies to support mineral exploration; analyses various sample material used in mineral exploration; geoenvironmental research. SRC's Biofuels Test Centre opened in September, 2006.
President/CEO, Dr. Laurier Schramm
306-933-5402, Fax: 306-933-7519
schramm@src.sk.ca
Vice-President Agriculture, Biotechnology & Food, Dale Kelly
306-933-8136, Fax: 306-933-7662
kelly@src.sk.ca
Vice-President Energy, Ernie S. Pappas
306-787-9351, Fax: 306-787-8811
pappas@src.sk.ca
Vice-President Alternative Energy & Manufacturing, Craig Murray
306-933-5482, Fax: 306-933-7446
murray@src.sk.ca
Acting Vice-President Mining & Minerals, Craig Murray
306-933-5482, Fax: 306-933-7446
murray@src.sk.ca
Director Business Intelligence, Dave Grier
306-933-8131, Fax: 306-933-7299
grier@src.sk.ca
Corporate Relations Officer, Judy Peters
306-933-5429, Fax: 306-933-7896
petersj@src.sk.ca

Environment & Forestry
Vice-President, Michael E. Weekes
306-933-5439, Fax: 306-933-7299
weekes@src.sk.ca
Business Unit Manager Air & Climate, Keith Wallace
306-933-8120,
wallace@src.sk.ca
Business Unit Manager Climatology, Elaine Wheaton
306-933-8179,
wheaton@src.sk.ca
Business Unit Manager Ecosystems, Mark Johnston
306-933-8175,
johnston@src.sk.ca
Business Unit Manager Hydrogeology, Harm Maathuis
306-993-5496,
maathuis@src.sk.ca

Office of Energy Conservation

Petroleum Research Technology Centre Bldg.
6 Research Dr.
Regina, SK S4S 7J7
306-933-6865
800-668-4636
oecinfo@src.sk.ca
www.oec.ca
Encourages action by the public & industry by facilitating the development and implementation of cost-effective energy conservation initiatives, including public information & application of energy conservation measures.
Director, Grant McIvor
306-787-6033,
mcvicar@src.sk.ca

SaskEnergy Incorporated

1777 Victoria Ave.
Regina, SK S4P 4K5
306-777-9225
Fax: 306-777-9200
800-567-8899
TDD: 800-792-6665
www.saskenergy.com
Other Communication: Natural Gas Emergency:
1-888-700-0427; Line Locates: 1-866-828-4888; Emergency & Safety Line: 1-888-700-0427
The provincial Crown corporation provides natural gas to residential, farm, commercial, & industrial customers in 92% of Saskatchewan's communities.
Acts Administered:
SaskEnergy Act
Minister Crown Corporations, Hon. Ken Cheveldayoff
306-787-7339, Fax: 306-798-3140
minister.cc@gov.sk.ca
President/CEO, Doug Kelln
306-777-9568, Fax: 306-777-9889
dkelln@saskenergy.com
Executive Vice-President, Dean Reeve
306-777-9402, Fax: 306-522-2217
dreeve@saskenergy.com
Executive Director Corporate Affairs, Ron Podbielski
306-777-9432, Fax: 306-352-4438
rpodbielski@saskenergy.com
Sr. Vice-President Gas Supply & Business Development, Daryl Posehn
306-777-9567, Fax: 306-569-3522
Vice-President TransGas, Phil Sandham
306-777-9603, Fax: 306-352-8892
Sr. Admin. Coordinator Legal Dept., Candace LeBlanc
306-777-9403, Fax: 306-565-3332

TransGas Limited
1777 Victoria Ave
Regina, SK S4P 4K5
306-777-9225
Fax: 306-352-8892
TransGas & its affiliates, Many Islands Pipelines Canada Limited, MIPCL, & Swan Valley Gas Corporation, SVGC, own & operate over 13,800 kilometres of gathering & transmission pipeline in Saskatchewan, operates storage facilities to ensure safe & reliable operationduring the winter.TransGas transports natural gas for over 280 customers, producers & industrial & commercial customers. The TransGas pipeline system is connected to TransCanada pipelines, ATCO pipelines, & Havre pipeline, providing the Saskatchewan market access to Alberta & Montana gas supplies. TransGas' & MIPCL'sinterconnections with other transmission systems, Foothills Pipelines Ltd., TransCanada Pipelines Ltd., Swan Valley Gas & Williston Basin Interstate, provide access to Manitoba, eastern Canadian & United States markets for Saskatchewan, Alberta & United States-sourced gas supplies
President/CEO, Doug Kelln
306-777-9568, Fax: 306-777-9889
dkelln@saskenergy.com
Sr. Vice-President, Daryl Posehn
306-777-9567, Fax: 306-569-3522
Vice-President, General Counsel & Corporate Secretar, Mark Guillet
306-777-9427, Fax: 306-565-3332

Saskatchewan Water Corporation (SaskWater)

#200, 111 Fairford St. East
Moose Jaw, SK S6H 1C8
306-694-3098
Fax: 306-694-3207

888-230-1111
comm@saskwater.com
www.saskwater.com
Other Communication: SaskWater Customer Emergencies:
1-800-667-5799
SaskWater, a provincial Crown corporation, is Saskatchewan's water utility service provider. Lines of business are as follows: supply of potable & non-potable water; treatment & management of wastewater; & certified operations & maintenance. SaskWater is responsible for designing, building, & operating transmission, regional, & stand-alone water supply & wastewater systems. All systems must meet regulatory requirements.
Acts Administered:
Saskatchewan Water Corporation Act, 2002
Minister Crown Corporations, Hon. Ken Cheveldayoff
306-787-7339, Fax: 306-787-3140
minister.cc@gov.sk.ca
President, Stuart Kramer
306-694-3903, Fax: 306-694-7722
stuart.kramer@saskwater.com
Acting Vice-President Engineering & Business Development, Eric Light
306-694-3920, Fax: 306-694-3207
eric.light@saskwater.com
Vice-President Operations, Mart Cram
306-694-3909, Fax: 306-694-3207
mart.cram@saskwater.com

Saskatchewan Workers' Compensation Board
#200, 1881 Scarth St.
Regina, SK S4P 4L1
306-787-4370
Fax: 306-787-7582
800-667-7590
TDD: 888-844-7773
internet_clientsvc@wcbsask.com
www.wcbsask.com
Other Communication: Injury Reports: 1-800-787-9288; Employer Inquiries: reainquiry@wcbsask.com; Health Care Provider Inquiries: internet_healthcare@wcbsask.com; Appeal Fax: 306-787-1116
The Saskatchewan's Workers' Compensation Board was created by the following provincial legislation in Saskatchewan: the Workers' Compensation Act 1979, General Regulations, & Exclusion Regulations. The Board is an independent body that administers a no-fault compensation system to protect employers and workers against the result of work injuries. The WCB provides financial protection, medical benefits. & rehabilitation services to injured workers & their dependents in cases of injury or death arising from, & in the course of, employment.
Minister Responsible, Hon. Rob Norris
306-787-0341, Fax: 306-787-6946
minister.aeel@gov.sk.ca
Chairman, David Eberle
306-787-4379, Fax: 306-787-0213
CEO, Peter Federko
306-787-7398, Fax: 306-787-0213
pfederko@wcbsask.com
Vice President Prevention, Finance & Information Technology, Gail Kruger
306-787-2475, Fax: 306-787-4311
gkruger@wcbsask.com
Vice President Human Resources & Team Support, Donna Kane
306-787-4440, Fax: 306-787-3915
dkane@wcbsask.com
Vice President Operations, Graham Topp
306-787-4371, Fax: 306-787-7582
gtopp@wcbsask.com

Government of the Yukon Territory
Seat of Government: PO Box 2703
Whitehorse, YT Y1A 2C6
867-667-5811
800-661-0408
TDD: 867-393-7460
www.gov.yk.ca
The Yukon was created as a separate territory June 13, 1898. It has an area of 474,711.02 km2, & StatsCan's population estimate in 2010 was 34,500. A federally appointed commissioner (similar to a provincial lieutenant-governor) oversees federal interests in the territory, but the day-to-day operation of the government rests with the wholly elected executive council (cabinet). The territorial legislature has power to make acts on generally all matters of a local nature in the territory, including the imposition of local taxes, property & civil rights & the administration of justice, education & health & social services. Legislative powers vested in the provinces but not available to the territory include control of unoccupied Crown land, renewable & non-renewable resources (except wildlife & sport fisheries) & the power to amend the Yukon Act, a federal statute.
Acts Administered:
Environmental Assessment Act, 2003
Raven Act
Waters Act, (shared with Environment & Energy, Mines & Resources)
Yukon Environmental & Socio-Economic Assessment Act
Yukon Land Claim Final Agreements, An Act Approving

Yukon Community Services
PO Box 2703
Whitehorse, YT Y1A 2C6
867-667-5811
Fax: 867-393-6295
800-661-0408
TDD: 867-393-7460
inquiry@gov.yk.ca
www.community.gov.yk.ca
The main purpose of the department is to serve Yukoners & their communities by providing access to services to strengthen communities. The department focuses on community affairs & municipal relations within government on behalf of Yukon communities & acts as a liaison between community groups & government departments.
Acts Administered:
Animal Protection Act (shared with Energy, Mines & Resources)
Area Development Act
Assessment & Taxation Act
Boiler & Pressure Vessels Act
Builder's Lien Act
Building Standards Act
Business Corporation Act
Cemeteries & Burial Sites Act
Certified General Accountants Act
Certified Management Accountants Act
Chartered Accountants Act
Chiropractors Act
Choses in Action Act shared with Department of Justice
Civil Emergency Measures Act
Consumer Protection Act
Cooperative Associations Act
Dental Professions Act
Denture Technicians Act
Dog Act
Electrical Protection Act
Elevator & Fixed Conveyances Act
Emergency Medical Aid Act
Employment Agencies Act
Employment Standards Act
Engineering Profession Act
Factors Act
Fire Prevention Act
First Nation Indemnification (Fire Management) Act
Forest Protection Act shared with Department of Energy, Mines & Resources
Funeral Directors Act
Garage Keepers Lien Act
Gas Burning Devices Act
Gasoline Handling Act
Health Professions Act
Home Owner's Grant Act
Insurance Act
International Commercial Arbitration Act
International Sale of Goods Act
Landlord & Tenant Act
Licensed Practical Nurses Act
Lottery Licensing Act
Medical Profession Act
Miner's Lien Act
Motor Vehicles Act (shared with Highways & Public Works)
Municipal Act
Municipal Finance & Community Grants Act
Municipal Loans Act
Noise Prevention Act
Optometrists Act
Partnership & Business Name Act
Pawnbrokers & Second-Hand Dealers Act
Personal Property Security Act
Pharmacists Act
Private Investigators & Security Guards Act
Public Libraries Act
Real Estate Agents Act
Recreation Act
Registered Nurses Profession Act
Sales of Goods Act
Securities Act
Seniors Property Tax Deferment Act
Societies Act
Subdivision Act
Trustee Act (shared with Economic Development)
Warehouse Keepers Lien Act
Warehouse Receipts Act
Whitehorse Streets & Lanes Ordinance
Yukon Foundation Act
Minister, Hon. Archie Lang
867-667-8643, Fax: 867-393-7400
archie.lang@gov.yk.ca
Deputy Minister, Jeff O'Farrell
867-456-6512, Fax: 867-633-7957
jeff.o'farrell@gov.yk.ca
Director Communications, Matt King
867-456-6580, Fax: 867-393-6404
matt.king@gov.yk.ca
Director Community Affairs, Christine Smith
867-667-8684, Fax: 867-393-6258
christine.smith@gov.yk.ca
Director Corporate Policy, Charlene Beauchemin
867-667-5865, Fax: 867-393-6404
charlene.beauchemin@gov.yk.ca
Director Finance, Systems & Administration, Christine Mahar
867-667-5311, Fax: 867-393-6264
christine.mahar@gov.yk.ca
Director Human Resources, Judy Tomlin
867-667-5667, Fax: 867-393-6933
judy.tomlin@gov.yk.ca
• Assessment Appeal Board
867-668-6598
Fax: 867-633-2640
• Driver Control Board
308 Steele St.
PO Box 2703
Whitehorse, YT Y1A 2C6
867-667-3774
Fax: 867-393-6483
dcb@gov.yk.ca
• Yukon Lottery Commission
312 Wood St.
Whitehorse, YT Y1A 2E6
867-633-7890
Fax: 867-668-7561
lotteriesyukon@gov.yk.ca

Community Development
The branch assists, advises & organizes municipal & unincorporated communities, provides funding by administering the comprehensive municipal grants & grants in lieu of taxes, assesses properties, collects property taxes & administers the Rural Electrification & Telecommunication program & the Home Owner Grant program. The branch collaborates with communities for the planning, design, & construction of land development projects & includes residential, rural residential, commercial, industrial, & cottage lots. The branch is responsible for regulatory approvals & design, managing construction capital works projects, such as upgrading roads, water & sewage treatment facilities & solid waste disposal sites & assists communities in developing land use plans, working closely with the Yukon Municipal Board & the Association of Yukon Communities. The branch is responsible for the operation of Yukon Government owned facilities for water supply & distribution, sewage treatment & solid waste disposal.
Acting Asst. Deputy Minister, Pat Molloy
867-667-5707, Fax: 867-393-6216
Acting Director Community Affairs, Matt King
867-667-5154, Fax: 867-393-6258
Acting Director Community Infrastructure, Kriss Sarson
867-667-5425, Fax: 867-393-6216
Director Community Land Planning, George Stetkiewicz
867-667-8945, Fax: 867-393-6258
Director Property Assessment & Taxation, Kelly Eby
867-667-5234, Fax: 867-667-8276

Consumer & Safety Services
Acting Director, Dale Kozmen
867-667-8290
Registrar Corporate Affairs, Rhonda Horte
867-667-5005, Fax: 867-393-6251

Federal/Provincial Government / Government of the Yukon Territory

Protective Services
Asst. Deputy Minister, Dan Boyd
867-667-5486, Fax: 867-393-6251
Director Wildland Fire Management, Ken Colbert
867-456-3904, Fax: 867-667-3165

Emergency Measures Organization (EMO)
PO Box 2703
Whitehorse, YT Y1A 2C6
867-667-5220
Fax: 867-393-6266
800-661-0408
emo.yukon@gov.yk.ca
www.community.gov.yk.ca/emo/index.html
Responsible for coordinating the Territory's preparedness for, response to, & recovery from, major emergencies & disasters. EMO provides authority to ensure that contingency plans are in place to deal with foreseeable risks & hazards. The Yukon EMO is divided into 13 geographical preparedness areas, mirroring the RCMP detachment boundaries. Eight of these areas have incorporated Municipalities that have appointed a Municipal EMO Coordinator to chair the local Emergency Planning Committee. In the remaining areas, the Emergency Measures Branch appoints a co-ordinator.
Manager, Michael Templeton
867-667-5220, Fax: 867-393-6266

Fire Marshal's Office
PO Box 2703
Whitehorse, YT Y1A 2C6
867-667-5811
Fax: 867-393-6295
inquiry@gov.yk.ca
www.community.gov.yk.ca/fireprotection/index.html
The Fire Marshal's Office works to reduce the loss of life & property due to fire &is responsible for public education & fire fighter training, as well as for funding & administering volunteer fire departments in Yukon unincorporated communities. Staff carry out fire & life safety inspections on hotels, motels, public assembly buildings, schools, day care centers, homes for special care, restaurants, etc. throughout Yukon. The Office inspects & permits underground fuel storage tank installations.

Yukon Development Corporation (YDC)
#2 Miles Canyon Rd.
PO Box 5920
Whitehorse, YT Y1A 6S7
867-393-5337
Fax: 867-393-5401
shelley.dixon@yec.yk.ca
www.ydc.yk.ca
The Yukon Development Corporation (YDC) assists with implementation of energy policies from the Department of Energy, Mines & Resources, by designing & delivering related energy programs. YDC facilitates the generation, production, transmission & distribution of energy in a manner consistent with sustainable development. YDC has investments in electricity & related energy infrastructure & acts as the primary vehicle for delivery of territorial energy programs & services. YDC owns two subsidiary corporations, Yukon Energy Corporation, YEC, & the Energy Solutions Centre Inc., ESC. YEC is the primary producer & transmitter of electrical energy in the territory & operates under the Yukon Utilities Board & the Public Utilities Act. ESC provides technical services, promotes efficiency & renewable energy technologies, co-ordinates & delivers federal & territorial energy programs to households, businesses, institutions, First Nation & public governments.
Acts Administered:
Yukon Development Corporation Act
Minister Responsible, Hon. Dennis Fentie
867-393-7053, Fax: 867-393-6252
dennis.fentie@gov.yk.ca
CEO, David Morrison
867-393-5400, Fax: 867-393-5401

Yukon Energy Corporation
2 Miles Canyon Rd.
PO Box 5920
Whitehorse, YT Y1A 6S7
867-393-5300
866-926-3749
communications@yukonenergy.ca
www.yukonenergy.ca
The YEC distributes electricity to wholesale & industrial customers. YEC acts in an environmentally responsible manner while developing & maintaining energy infrastructure & services consistent with the principles of sustainable development. Sources of energy include solar power, wind power, geo-thermal power, hydro power & diesel power. YEC is also involved in fish ladder & hatchery.
President/CEO, David Morrison
Vice-President Operations & Engineering, David MacDonald

Yukon Economic Development
PO Box 2703
Whitehorse, YT Y1A 2C6
867-667-5387
Fax: 867-393-6412
800-661-0408
ecdev@gov.yk.ca
www.economicdevelopment.gov.yk.ca
The Department works with the Yukon business community & with other governments to support business development, trade & investment opportunities, & partnerships for the development of the Yukon economy. It co-ordinates & facilitates the Yukon Government's economic development agenda. The Department is focused on creating a positive business climate in Yukon & is committed to First Nation business development in the territory. Economic Development markets Yukon as a great place to do business.
Minister, Hon. Jim Kenyon
867-667-8628, Fax: 867-393-7400
jim.kenyon@gov.yk.ca
Deputy Minister, Harvey Brooks
867-393-7191, Fax: 867-667-3159
harvey.brooks@gov.yk.ca
Asst. Deputy Minister Operations, Terry Hayden
867-456-3912,
terry.hayden@gov.yk.ca
Director Business & Industry Development, Denny Kobayashi
867-667-3430, Fax: 867-393-6944
denny.kobayashi@gov.yk.ca
Director Economic Research, Scott Milton
867-667-8011, Fax: 867-393-6412
scott.milton@gov.yk.ca
Director Finance & Information Services, Karen Mason
867-667-5933, Fax: 867-393-7199
karen.mason@gov.yk.ca
Director Policy, Planning & Research, Stephen Rose
867-667-8416, Fax: 867-393-6412
stephen.rose@gov.yk.ca
Director Regional Economic Development, Bert Perry
867-667-8853, Fax: 867-393-6228
bert.perry@gov.yk.ca
Executive Assistant to the Deputy Minister, Judith Voswinkel
867-393-7191, Fax: 867-667-3159
judith.voswinkel@gov.yk.ca

Film & Sound Commission
PO Box 2703
Whitehorse, YT Y1A 2C6
867-667-5400
Fax: 867-393-7040
info@reelyukon.com
www.reelyukon.com

Yukon Energy, Mines & Resources
PO Box 2703
Whitehorse, YT Y1A 2C6
867-667-5466
Fax: 867-667-8601
800-661-0408
TDD: 867-393-7460
emr@gov.yk.ca
www.emr.gov.yk.ca
The territory has extensive mineral deposits, oil & gas potential, with two producing gas wells, which rank among the top producing wells in Canada, forest reserves & local manufacturing of wood products, such as furniture, wood laminate stock & lumber. The territory has abundant & diverse energy resources due to the presence of fossil fuel reserves, numerous lakes & rivers, windy & mountainous terrain, broad forest cover & sunny conditions. The Yukon is one of the few places left in Canada where Crown land can be obtained for agricultural purposes.
Acts Administered:
Agricultural Products Acts
Agriculture Development Act
Animal Health Act, (shared with Environment)
Animal Protection Act, (shared with Community Services)
Brands Act
Economic Development Act, (shared with Economic Development)
Energy Conservation Assistance Act
Forest Protection Act, (shared with Community Services)
Lands Act
Oil & Gas Act
Oil & Gas Disposition Regulations
Oil & Gas Drilling & Production Regulations
Oil & Gas Geoscience & Exploration Regulations
Oil & Gas Licence Administration Regulations
Pounds Act
Placer Mining Act
Quartz Mining Act
Territorial Lands (Yukon) Act
Waters Act, (shared with Environment & the Executive Council Office)
Minister, Hon. Brad Cathers
867-667-5806, Fax: 867-393-6252
Deputy Minister, Angus Robertson
867-667-5417, Fax: 867-393-7167
angus.robertson@gov.yk.ca
Executive Director Yukon Placer Secretariat, Robert Thomson
867-667-5802, Fax: 867-667-3632
Director Communications, Mark Roberts
867-667-5307, Fax: 867-393-7421
Acting Director Corporate Services, Ross McLachlan
867-456-3960, Fax: 867-456-3965
Director Human Resources, Ingrid Fawcus
867-667-3549, Fax: 867-393-7422

Energy Corporate Policy
Fax: 867-667-8601
Asst. Deputy Minister, Shirley Abercrombie
867-667-5496, Fax: 867-393-7421
Director Corporate Policy & Planning, John Spicer
867-393-7126, Fax: 867-393-7421
Director Energy & Resource Policy, Vacant
867-667-5032, Fax: 867-667-8601

Energy Solutions Centre
206A Lowe St., 1st Fl.
Whitehorse, YT Y1A 1WG
867-393-7063
Fax: 867-393-7061
info@nrgsc.yk.ca
www.nrgsc.yk.ca/index.php
The ESC is a non-profit organization that works in partnership with Natural Resources Canada (NRCan) to promote renewable energy programs & assist Yukon businesses, institutions, & municipal governments implement renewable energy solutions.
Director, Colin McDowell

Oil & Gas Mineral Resources
Fax: 867-393-6262
Asst. Deputy Minister, Greg Komaromi
867-667-3011, Fax: 867-667-8601
Senior Manager Faro Project Management Team, Stephen Mead
867-393-6904
Executive Director Oil & Gas Resources, Brian Love
867-667-3566, Fax: 867-393-7046
brian.love@gov.yk.ca

Mineral Resources
867-456-3830
Fax: 867-456-3832
mining@gov.yk.ca
Responsibilities include issuing & maintaining mineral titles; reviewing work filed for assessment credit; selling claim maps & providing information on land status; developing, implementing regulations governing mining & exploration activities; screening, approving proposed developments.
Director, Bob Holmes
867-667-3126

Oil & Gas Management
867-667-7042
Fax: 867-393-3427
Responsible for managing & regulating Yukon's oil & gas resources, facilities & operations & the Oil & Gas Business Development/Pipeline branch which promotes & facilitates oil & gas & pipeline development in the Yukon, also manages Yukon's interest in Offshore Beaufort Sea oil & gas development.
Director, John Masterson
867-667-5026

Yukon Geological Survey
867-667-8508
Fax: 867-393-6232
geosales@gov.yk.ca
www.geology.gov.yk.ca
Director, Carolyn Relf
867-667-8892,
carolyn.relf@gov.yk.ca
Environmental Geologist, Karen Pelletier
867-456-3808,
karen.pelletier@gov.yk.ca

Sustainable Resources
Fax: 867-667-8601
Asst. Deputy Minister, Jeff O'Farrell
867-456-3827, Fax: 867-393-6340

Agriculture Branch
867-667-5838
Fax: 867-393-6222
agriculture@gov.yk.ca
The branch administers sales & leases of Crown land for agricultural purposes, accepts applications for grazing leases on Yukon land & manages grazing land agreements, provides advice to commercial producers in all aspects of agricultural management, production, marketing & development, conducts research on improving production & yields, secures veterinary services for animal husbandry, encourages wholesome food production for public health & safety, works with federal agencies to seek & evaluate agricultural technologies & techniques, promotes infrastructure support &maintains a database on cost, value of production & amount of land in agriculture.
Director, Tony Hill
867-667-5838,
Director, Dave Beckman
david.beckman@gov.yk.ca

Forest Management Branch
Mile 918 Alaska Highway
PO Box 2703
Whitehorse, YT Y1A 2C6
867-456-3999
Fax: 867-667-3138
800-661-0408
forestry@gov.yk.ca
Oversees the development & management of Yukon's forest resources. The services & responsibilities include: taking inventory of & managing Yukon forests, conduct environmental assessments of proposed timber harvesting projects, forest renewal, forest management planning, identifying & allocating timber harvesting areas, issuing permits to harvest timber, conducting environmental assessments of proposed forest activities, collecting stumpage revenues; auditing activities, consultation, forestry legislations,forest practices planning & liaison, & maintaining & improving forestry GIS & mapping capabilities.
Director, Diane Reed
867-456-3838

Lands Branch
867-667-5215
Fax: 867-667-3214
land.disposition@gov.yk.ca
The branch administers residential, recreational, commercial & industrial lot sales, assists with land applications for commercial, industrial & enlargement of existing properties, information on finalizing a land application & permitting for a variety of uses. Since April 1, 2003, the Yukon government has assumed land-related responsibilities previously administered by the federal department of Indian Affairs & Northern Development. The Yukon government now controls the majority of vacant lands in the territory, Yukon First Nations control their settlement lands, & municipalities administer lands, community plans & zoning by-laws within their jurisdictions. Whitehorse & Dawson City also controls subdivision within their boundaries.
Director, Lyle Henderson
867-667-5218
Manager, Bryony McIntyre
867-667-5882,
byrony.mcintyre@gov.yk.ca

Yukon Environment
PO Box 2703
Whitehorse, YT Y1A 2C6
867-667-5652
Fax: 867-393-7197
800-661-0408
environmentyukon@gov.yk.ca
www.environmentyukon.gov.yk.ca
The department is responsible for legislation, regulations licensing, management, policies, programs, services, education & information regarding the natural environment in three program areas: fish & wildlife, environmental protection & assessment & parks & protection areas.The department's branches educate resource users & the general public, develop & enforce policies, regulations, & legislation & assist other departments in the sustainable use & management of the territory's natural resources. The department supports land claims negotiations & assists in implementing land claims agreements.The department represents the Yukon government at national & global environmental forums on issues such as climate change & biodiversity conservation.Through the Environmental Awareness Fund the government provides funding to assist registered non-government organizations to promote environmental education or awareness, resource planning & sustainable development in the Yukon.
Acts Administered:
Animal Health Act, (shared with Energy, Mines & Resources)
Environment Act
Administrative Regulation
Air Emissions Regulations
Beverage Container Regulation
Contaminated Sites Regulations
Designated Materials
Ozone Depleting Substances & Other Halocarbons Regulation
Pesticides Regulations
Recycling Fund Regulation
Solid Waste Regulations
Special Waste Regulations
Spills Regulations
Storage Tank Regulations
Yukon Council on the Economy & the Environment Regulation
Environmental Assessment Act
Activities Requiring Environmental Assessment (Inclusion List) Regulations
Comprehensive Study List Regulation
Coordination of Environmental Assessment Procedures & Requirement Regulations
Exclusion List Regulation
Law List Regulation
Fresh Water Fisheries Agreement Act
Mackenzie River Basin Agreement Act
Parks & Land Certainty Act
Campground Regulations
Coal River Springs Ecological Reserve
Establish Ni'iinlii Njik (Fishing Branch) Ecological Reserve
Establish Ni'iinlii Njik (Fishing Branch) Wilderness Preserve
Herschel Island Nature Preserve
Herschel Island Park Regulations
Tombstone Territorial Park Regulations
Waters Act, (shared with Energy, Mines & Resources & the Executive Council Office)
Waters Regulation
Wilderness Tourism Licensing Act
Wildlife Act
Concession & Compensation Review Board Regulations
Conservation Fund Regulations
Game Farm Regulations
Game Management Sub-zone Regulations
Outfitting Concession Area Boundary Regulations
Trapping Concession Area Boundary Regulations
Trapping Regulations
Wildlife Sanctuary Regulation
Yukon River Basin & Alsek River Basin Agreements Act
Minister, Hon. John Edzerza
867-667-5806, Fax: 867-393-6252
john.edzerza@gov.yk.ca
Deputy Minister, Kelvin Leary
867-667-5460, Fax: 867-393-6213
kelvin.leary@gov.yk.ca
Director Human Resources, Mindy Crayford
867-667-8486, Fax: 867-393-7012
mindy.crayford@gov.yk.ca
Director Policy & Planning, Ed Van Randen
867-667-3028, Fax: 867-393-6213
ed.vanranden@gov.yk.ca
Manager Client Services, Dee Balsam
867-667-5797, Fax: 867-393-7197
dee.balsam@gov.yk.ca
• Alsek Renewable Resource Council
PO Box 2077
Haines Junction, YT Y0B 1L0
867-634-2524
Fax: 867-634-2527
• Carmacks Renewable Resource Council
PO Box 122
Carmacks, YT Y0B 1C0
867-863-6838
Fax: 867-863-6429
carmacksrrc@lscfn.ca
• Dawson District Renewable Resource Council
PO Box 1380
Dawson City, YT Y0B 1G0
867-993-6976
Fax: 867-993-6093
dawsonrrc@yknet.yk.ca
• Mayo District Renewable Resources Council
PO Box 249
Mayo, YT Y0B 1M0
867-996-2942
Fax: 867-996-2948
mayorrc@yknet.yk.ca
• North Yukon Renewable Resources Council
PO Box 80
Old Crow, YT Y0B 1N0
vgrrc@yknet.yk.ca
• Selkirk Renewable Resources Council
PO Box 32
Pelly Crossing, YT Y0B 1P0
867-537-3937
Fax: 867-537-3939
selkirkrre@yknet.yk.ca
• Teslin Renewable Resource Council
PO Box 186
Teslin, YT Y0A 1B0
867-390-2323
Fax: 867-390-2919
teslinrrc@yknet.yk.ca
• Yukon Fish & Wildlife Management Board
106 Main St.
Whitehorse, YT Y1A 5P7
867-667-3754
Fax: 867-393-6947
yfwmbadmin@yknet.yk.ca
www.yfwmb.yk.ca
Chair, Pat Van Bibber
The Board was established as an independent advisory body under the Umbrella Final Agreement to make recommendations on fish & wildlife management.
• Yukon Land Use Planning Council
#201, 307 Jarvis St.
Whitehorse, YT Y1A 2H3
867-667-7397
Fax: 867-667-4624
ylupc@planyukon.ca
www.planyukon.ca/
Executive Director, Ron Cruikshank
The Yukon Land Use Planning Council assists government & Yukon First Nationsto co-ordinate efforts to conduct community based regional land use planning. This planning is necessary to resolve land use & resource conflicts. The plans ensure that use of lands & resources is consistent with social, cultural, economic & environmental values. These plans build upon traditional knowledge & experience of the residents of each region.

Conservation Officer Services
867-667-8005
Fax: 867-393-6206
800-661-0408
Ronalane.Anderson@gov.yk.ca
The Branch provides environmental education, environmental youth camps & projects, provides hunting, fishing & trapping licences, provides hunter & trapper education, resource management support, wildlife safety for the public & provides enforcement & compliance.
Director, John Russell
867-667-5786, Fax: 867-393-6206
Manager Enforcement & Compliance, Tony Grabowski
867-667-5115, Fax: 867-393-6206
Manager Field Operations, Torrie Hunter
867-993-5492

Environmental Programs
867-667-5683
Fax: 867-393-6205
800-661-0408
envprot@gov.yk.ca

Federal/Provincial Government / Government of the Yukon Territory

Formed in 1994, the Branch is responsible for development of regulations & standards under the Environment Act & programs associated with everyday waste management, contaminated sites, air quality & pesticides. The Branch is also responsible for monitoring & inspection of permits, spill cleanup & environmental assessments of development project, recycling education & promotion, public education & awareness.
Director, Jon Bowen
867-667-8177, Fax: 867-393-6213
Chief Water Resources, Kevin McDonnell
867-667-3145, Fax: 867-667-3195
Manager Environmental Affairs, Randy Lamb
867-667-5409, Fax: 867-667-3641
Manager Hydrology, Richard Janowicz
867-667-3223
Manager Monitoring & Inspections, Bryan Levia
867-667-3436, Fax: 867-393-6205
bryan.levia@gov.yk.ca
Manager Standards & Approvals, Shannon Jensen
867-667-8787, Fax: 867-393-6205
Manager Water Inspections, Rob Savard
867-667-3227
Manager Water Quality, Bob Truelson
867-667-3217
Climate Change Coordinator, Johanna Martin
867-633-7971, Fax: 867-456-6124

Fish & Wildlife Branch
867-667-5715
Fax: 867-393-6405
fish.wildlife@gov.yk.ca
The Branch maintains the ecosystem based on sound management of fish, wildlife & their habitats, preserves the sustainability of fish & wildlife populations, works with First Nations & community relations to preserve & enhance the ecosystem, develops management plans, provides policy & planning, collects, assesses & disseminates natural resource data & provides public education for resource users.
Director, Harvey Jessup
867-667-5715, Fax: 867-393-6405
Biologist Fisheries Management, Nathan Millar
867-667-5117
Acting Manager Habitat Programs, Karen Clyde
867-667-5464, Fax: 867-393-6405
Manager Species Programs, Rob Florkiewicz
867-667-5177, Fax: 867-393-6263
Manager Habitat Protection, Bruce McLean
867-667-5803, Fax: 867-393-6405

Parks Yukon
867-667-5639
Fax: 867-393-7003
800-661-0408
yukonparks@gov.yk.ca
www.environmentyukon.gov.yk.ca/parks/parks.html
Director, Erik Val
867-667-5639, Fax: 867-393-6223
Regional Superintendent Klondike Region, Gordon MacRae
867-993-6850, Fax: 867-993-6548
Regional Superintendent Kluane Region, George Nassiopoulos
867-634-2026, Fax: 867-634-2435
george.nassiopoulos@gov.yk.ca
Regional Superintendent Liard Region, Gary Vantell
867-667-5282, Fax: 867-393-6223

Yukon Finance
PO Box 2703
Whitehorse, YT Y1A 2C6
867-667-5343
Fax: 867-393-6217
fininfo@gov.yk.ca
www.finance.gov.yk.ca
Acts Administered:
Appropriation Acts
Banking Agency Guarantee Act
Faro Mine Loan Act
Financial Administration Act
Fireweed Fund Act
Fuel Oil Tax Act
Income Tax Act
Insurance Premium Tax Act
Interim Supply Appropriation Acts
Liquor Tax Act
Taxpayer Protection Act
Tobacco Tax Act
Yukon Development Corporation Loan Guarantee Act
Minister, Hon. Dennis Fentie
867-393-7053, Fax: 867-393-6252
dennis.fentie@gov.yk.ca
Deputy Minister, David Hrycan
867-667-3571, Fax: 867-393-6217
david.hrycan@gov.yk.ca
Director Finance & Administration, Bill Curtis
867-667-5276, Fax: 867-393-6217
bill.curtis@gov.yk.ca
Director Fiscal Relations, Tim Shoniker
867-667-5303, Fax: 867-393-6355
tim.shoniker@gov.yk.ca
Director Investments & Debt Services, Elaine Carlyly
867-667-5346,
elaine.carlyle@gov.yk.ca
Director Management Board Secretariat, Mary Rae Cafferty
867-667-3542, Fax: 867-393-6355
mary.cafferty@gov.yk.ca
Director Taxation, Gerald Gagnon
867-667-3074, Fax: 867-456-6709
gerald.gagnon@gov.yk.ca

Yukon Health & Social Services
PO Box 2703
Whitehorse, YT Y1A 2C6
867-667-3673
Fax: 867-667-3096
800-661-0408
hss@gov.yk.ca
www.hss.gov.yk.ca/
Committed to quality health & social services for Yukoners. This is achieved by helping individuals acquire the skills to live responsible, healthy & independent lives; & providing a range of accessible, affordable services that assist individuals, families & communities to reach their full potential.
Acts Administered:
Canadian Blood Agency/Canadian Blood Services Indemnification Act
Canadian Council for Donation & Transplantation Indemnifiction Act
Change of Name Act
Child Care Act
Children's Act
Decision Making, Support & Protection to Adults Act
Health Act
Health Care Insurance Plan Act
Hospital Act
Hospital Insurance Services Act
Intercounty Adoption (Hague Convention) Act
Marriage Act
Mental Health Act
Pioneer Utility Grant Act
Public Health & Safety Act
Regulations to Establish Butylnitrite as Regulated Matter
Rubbish Disposal
Sewage Disposal Systems Regulations
Rehabilitation Services Act
Seniors' Income Supplement Act
Social Assistance Act
Travel for Medical Treatment Act
Vital Statistics Act
Young Persons Offences Act
Youth Criminal Justice Act (Canada), (shared with Justice)
Yukon Family Services Association Rent Guarantee Act
Minister, Hon. Glenn Hart
867-667-8629, Fax: 867-393-6252
Deputy Minister, Stuart Whitley
867-667-5770, Fax: 867-667-3096
Asst. Deputy Minister Health Services, Joanne Fairlie
867-667-5689, Fax: 867-667-3096
Director Policy & Program Development, Drian Kitchen
867-667-5688, Fax: 867-667-3096

Environmental Health Services
2 Hospital Rd.
PO Box 2703
Whitehorse, YT Y1A 2C6
867-667-8391
Fax: 867-667-8322
800-661-0408
environmental.health@gov.yk.ca
Promotes care for the environment in the interest of human health. Engages in consultation & provides information, advice, inspections & enforcement services on water quality, sewage & solid waste disposal, food quality, institutional hygiene, special events, recreational facilities, communicable disease control, & other related matters.
Manager/Health Officer, Eric Bergsma
867-667-8370, Fax: 867-667-8322

Yukon Highways & Public Works
PO Box 2703
Whitehorse, YT Y1A 2C6
867-393-7193
Fax: 867-393-6218
800-661-0408
TDD: 867-393-7460
hpw-info@gov.yk.ca
www.hpw.gov.yk.ca
The Department of Highways & Public Works is responsible for ensuring safe & efficient public highways, airstrips, buildings & information systems.
Acts Administered:
Access to Information & Protection Act
Dangerous Goods Transportation Act
Highways Act
Languages Act
Motor Transport Act
Motor Vehicles Act (shared with Community Services)
Public Printing Act
Minister, Hon. Archie Lang
867-667-8643, Fax: 867-393-7400
Deputy Minister, Mike Johnson
867-667-3732, Fax: 867-393-6218
Asst. Deputy Minister Corporate Services Branch, Leslie Anderson
867-667-5128, Fax: 867-393-6218
Director Policy & Communications, Tim Hierlihy
867-667-5436, Fax: 867-393-6218
• Yukon Motor Transport Board
PO Box 2703
Whitehorse, YT Y1A 2C6
867-667-5782
Fax: 867-393-6408
Laurie.Hrynuik@gov.yk.ca

Property Management Agency
Asst. Deputy Minister, Steven Gasser
867-667-8191, Fax: 867-667-5349
Director Space Planning & Development, Pat Hogan
867-667-3064, Fax: 867-667-5349

Supply Services
Director, Carl Rumscheidt
867-667-5289, Fax: 867-667-2958
Senior Purchasing Officer Procurement Services, David Knight
867-393-6387, Fax: 867-667-2958
Manager Fleet Vehicle Agency, Stefan Voswinkel
867-667-5793, Fax: 867-393-6463
Manager Materiel Management, Vacant
867-667-5459

Transportation
Asst. Deputy Minister, Robert Magnuson
867-667-5196, Fax: 867-393-6218
Director Aviation & Marine Branch, Bill Blahitka
867-634-2440, Fax: 867-634-2131
Acting Director Transportation Maintenance Branch, Catherine Harwood
867-667-5761, Fax: 867-667-3648
Director Transportation Engineering, Robin Walsh
867-633-7928, Fax: 867-393-6447
Director Transport Services Branch, Vern Janz
867-667-5833, Fax: 867-667-5799
Minister Responsible, Hon. Jim Kenyon
867-667-0028, Fax: 867-393-7400
President & Deputy Minister, Ron Macmillan
867-667-5155, Fax: 867-393-6274
Director Corporate Policy & Communications, Janet Lecamp
867-667-5865, Fax: 867-393-6404
Minister, Hon. Marian Horne
867-633-7973, Fax: 867-393-7400
marian.horne@gov.yk.ca
Acts Administered:
Expropriation Act
Land Titles Act
Public Utilities Act

Deputy Minister, Dennis Cooley
867-667-5959, Fax: 867-393-5790
jus.dm@gov.yk.ca
Director Finance, Systems & Administration, Luda Ayzenberg
867-667-5615, Fax: 867-667-5790
luda.ayzenberg@gov.yk.ca
Director Policy & Communications, Dan Cable
867-667-3508,
dan.cable@gov.yk.ca
Executive Assistant to the Deputy Minister, Charmaine Hall
867-667-5959, Fax: 867-667-5790
charmaine.hall@gov.yk.ca

Yukon Tourism & Culture

PO Box 2703
Whitehorse, YT Y1A 2C6
867-667-5036
Fax: 867-667-3546
www.tc.gov.yk.ca/
The department focuses on business, tourism, cultural industries & technology/telecommunications to develop & promote economic capacity & entrepreneurial skills to stimulate economy. The department works with the Yukon's diverse arts communities to foster creativity & quality of life & with heritage interests to preserve & interpret heritage resources.
Acts Administered:
Archives Act
Arts Act
Arts Centre Act
Historical Resources Act
Hotel & Tourist Establishments Act
Scientists & Explorers Act
Minister, Hon. Elaine Taylor
867-667-8641, Fax: 867-393-6252
Deputy Minister, Sally Sheppard
867-667-5430, Fax: 867-667-8844

Cultural Services Branch
100 Hanson St., 2nd Fl.
Whitehorse, YT Y1A 6C2
867-667-8589
Fax: 867-667-3546
The Branch implements & administers all aspects of heritage protection, preservation & information, manages & supports Yukon museums, provides technical & financial support to the development of arts including community arts, professional arts & cultural industries & maintains the Yukon Archives & government records.
Director, Rick Lemaire
867-667-8592
Manager Heritage Resources, Jeff Hunston
867-667-5363
Archaeologist, Ruth Gotthardt
867-667-5983
Yukon Paleontologist, Paul Matheus
867-667-8089

Tourism Branch
867-667-3053
Fax: 867-667-3546
The Tourism Branch directs the development, implementation, & evaluation of the Yukon's tourism marketing programs to promote the Yukon as a travel destination.

Director, Pierre Germain
867-667-3087

Yukon Workers' Compensation Health & Safety Board (YWCHSB)

401 Strickland St.
Whitehorse, YT Y1A 5N8
867-667-5645
Fax: 867-393-6279
800-661-0443
worksafe@gov.yk.ca
wcb.yk.ca/
The Yukon Workers' Compensation Health and Safety Board (YWCHSB) administers workers' compensation and occupational health and safety in the Yukon.
Acts Administered:
Day of Mourning for Victims of Workplace Injuries Act
Occupational Health & Safety Act
Spousal Compensation Act
Worker's Compensation Act
Workplace Hazardous Materials Information System (WHMIS) Regulations
Minister Responsible, Hon. Glenn Hart
867-667-8629, Fax: 867-393-6252
glenn.hart@gov.yk.ca
President/CEO, Valerie Royle
867-667-5975, Fax: 867-393-6419
valerie.royle@gov.yk.ca

Municipal Governments

Alberta

Alberta Environment carries out its work under the authority of the Environmental Protection & Enhancement Act (EPEA), the Climate Change & Emissions Management Act and the Water Act. The EPEA mandate is to maintain air, land and water quality so that ecosystems and public health are protected. The Climate Change & Emissions Management Act provides the legislative backing for Alberta's Climate Change Program. The Water Act supports the conservation and management of water in the province.

Alberta Environment is organized into four main business divisions: Environmental Stewardship, Environmental Assurance, Environmental Management and Oil Sands Environmental Management. Each division is supported by People Services, Communications, Legal Services, Finance and Administration and the Strategic Planning Secretariat.

Alberta's air quality is maintained through a management system comprising protection, enforcement, monitoring and modelling.

Municipal waterworks, wastewater, storm drainage and solid waste disposal facilities may be municipally or privately owned. Alberta Municipal Management Facility guidelines require most facilities to demonstrate the financial capability to reclaim the site after its closure. Waste collection is the responsibility of the municipality. Those who operate or propose developments are subject to requirements that detail their environmental responsibilities. Alberta's Municipal Waste Action Plan calls for the Waste Management Stakeholder Group, comprising non-profit waste management associations in the province, to communicate waste management initiatives to interested parties, and to prepare recommendations.

"Water for Life: Alberta's Strategy for Sustainability" is mandated to establish a water management policy to ensure safe drinking water, healthy aquatic ecosystems and a reliable water supply-municipalities are active partners in this initiative. The Alberta Water Council was formed in April, 2004 to guide the implementation of the Strategy.

EPEA establishes a legislated process for environmental assessments. This process will ensure that potential environmental impacts are identified early during planning. A company will submit one comprehensive application to Alberta Environment. A designated director coordinates the preparation of a single, integrated approval for the project.

The EPEA regulates the beverage container collection program, which diverts containers from landfill to recycling. Containers are collected through over 200 privately owned beverage container depots. The recovery rate from regulated containers is close to 85%. An electronics recycling program is dedicated to recovering televisions, computers and other electronics with fees ranging from $5 to $45 per item. This is being managed by Electronics Recycling Alberta, of the Alberta Recycling Management Authority (which also operates Tire Recycling Alberta).

The municipal energy efficiency program (ME! First) provides interest-free loans to municipalities to achieve energy savings. The $100 million program is designed to reduce greenhouse gas emissions, and nearly 50 projects funded by this program are in operation. The Municipal Sponsorship Program provides municipalities with populations of 20,000 or under with grants. The program provided funding for projects such as the provision of solar energy sources for existing municipal buildings and the construction of new facilities. The Alberta Municipal Infrastructure Program provides financial assistance for core capital municipal infrastructure projects through Alberta Infrastructure & Transportation. Under the federal government's New Deal for Cities, Alberta received $477 million in federal gas tax funding from 2005 to 2010 for municipal infrastructure projects. In addition, the Alberta Infrastructure Program provided $600 million annually for the same period.

Counties & Municipal Districts in Alberta

Clearwater County
P.O. Box 550
4340 - 47th Ave.
Rocky Mountain House, AB T4T 1A4
403-845-4444
Fax: 403-845-7330
admin@county.clearwater.ab.ca
www.county.clearwater.ab.ca
Municipal Type: Municipal District
Incorporated: April 1, 1945 *Area:* 18,691.65 sq km
Population in 2006: 11,826
Next Election: 2013 (3 year terms)
Note: Incorporated as a municipal district on Jan. 1, 1985.
Ron Leaf, County Manager
rleaf@county.clearwater.ab.ca
Pat Alexander, Reeve
Joe Baker, Manager, Planning / West Country
jbaker@county.clearwater.ab.ca
Kim Nielsen, Manager, Agricultural Services
knielsen@county.clearwater.ab.ca
Marshall Morton, Manager, Public Works
mmorton@county.clearwater.ab.ca

Foothills No. 31
P.O. Box 5605
309 Macleod Trail
High River, AB T1V 1M7
403-652-2341
Fax: 403-652-7880
Emergencies: 1-888-808-3722
mdfthlls@mdfoothills.com
www.mdfoothills.com
Municipal Type: Municipal District
Incorporated: Dec. 23, 1912 *Area:* 3,643.6 sq km
Population in 2006: 19,736
Next Election: 2013 (3 year terms)
Note: Incorporated as a municipal district on Jan. 1, 1944.
Harry Riva Cambrin, Municipal Manager
hrc@mdfoothills.com
Roy McLean, Reeve
council@mdfoothills.com
Graham Clark, Fire Chief, Protective Services
graham.clark@mdfoothills.com
Tom Gillis, Director, Public Works & Engineering
tom.gillis@mdfoothills.com
Nasir Sheikh, Municipal Engineer
nasir.sheikh@mdfoothills.com
Judy Gordon, Coordinator, Planning & Development
judy.gordon@mdfoothills.com
Marilyn Gordon-Cooper, Contact, Property Tax & Utilities Department
marilyn.gordon-cooper@mdfoothills.com
Heather Hemingway, Contact, Environment Committee
heather.hemingway@mdfoothills.com
Ken McKay, Contact, Building Safety Codes & Bylaw Enforcement
ken.mckay@mdfoothills.com

Grande Prairie No. 1
10001 - 84 Ave.
Clairmont, AB T0H 0W0
780-532-9722
Fax: 780-539-9880
info@countygp.ab.ca
www.countygp.ab.ca
Municipal Type: County
Incorporated: Dec. 9, 1912 *Area:* 5,883.92 sq km
Population in 2006: 17,970
Next Election: 2013 (3 year terms)
Note: Incorporated as a county on Jan. 1, 1951.
W.A. Rogan, County Administrator
brogan1@countygp.ab.ca
Everett McDonald, Reeve
John Simpson, Director, Planning
780-513-3950
plan@countygp.ab.ca
Everett Cooke, Fire Chief
780-567-5590
fire@countygp.ab.ca
Steve Madden, Manager, Environment
780-532-7393
Herb Pfau, Superintendent, Public Works
780-532-7393
pubwks@countygp.ab.ca

Lacombe County
RR#3
Lacombe, AB T4L 2N3
403-782-6601
Fax: 403-782-3820
info@lacombecounty.com
www.lacombecounty.com
Municipal Type: County
Incorporated: Jan. 1, 1944 *Area:* 2,777.26 sq km
County or District: Lacombe No. 14; *Population in 2008:* 10,507
Next Election: 2013 (3 year terms)
Note: Incorporated as a county on Jan. 1, 1961.
Terry Hager, County Commissioner
thager@lacombecounty.com
Terry Engen, Reeve
Keith Boras, Manager, Agriculture Services
kboras@lacombecounty.com
Dale Freitag, Manager, Planning Services
dfreitag@lacombecounty.com
Julian Veuger, County Constable, Disaster Services
jveuger@lacombecounty.com
Dale Freitaq, Planner & Development Officer
dfreitaq@lacombecounty.com
Dale Kary, Project Coordinator, Public Works
dkary@lacombecounty.com
Phil Lodermeier, Supervisor, Public Works
plodermeier@lacombecounty.com

Leduc County
#101, 1101 - 5 St.
Nisku, AB T9E 2X3
780-955-3555
Fax: 780-955-3444
Toll free: 1-800-379-9052
shaunaf@leduc-county.com
www.leduc-county.com
Municipal Type: County
Incorporated: Jan. 1, 1944 *Area:* 2,610.25 sq km
County or District: Leduc No. 25; *Population in 2006:* 12,730
Next Election: 2013 (3 year terms)
Note: Incorporated as a county on Jan. 1, 1964.
Doug Wright, County Manager
780-955-6400
dougw@leduc-county.com
John Whaley, Reeve
Michael MacLean, Director, Public Works & Engineering
780-955-6416
michael@leduc-county.com
Phil Newman, Director, Planning & Development
780-955-6413
phil@leduc-county.com
Dean Ohnysty, Director, Parks & Recreation
780-955-4535
dean@leduc-county.com
Garett Broadbent, Director, Agricultural Services
780-955-6404
garett@leduc-county.com
Bob Galloway, Chief, Fire
780-955-7099
bobg@leduc-county.com
Deryld Dublanko, Manager, Maintenance & Materials Supply
780-955-2469
deryld@leduc-county.com
Janis Fong, Manager, Public Works & Infrastructure
Des Myglod, Manager, Engineering
Dave McPhee, Officer, Utilities
780-955-4541
dave@leduc-county.com

Mountain View County
P.O. Box 100
1408 Twp Rd. 320
Didsbury, AB T0M 0W0
403-335-3311
Fax: 403-335-9207
Toll Free Phone: 1-877-264-9754
info@mountainviewcounty.com
www.mountainviewcounty.com
Municipal Type: County
Incorporated: Dec. 9, 1912 *Area:* 3,804.43 sq km

See blue tabs following this section for Municipal Waste Management and Water & Wastewater Treatment.

Municipal Governments / Alberta

Population in 2007: 12,570
Next Election: 2013 (3 year terms)
Note: Incorporated as a county on Jan. 1, 1961.
Doug Plamping, CAO
doug.plamping@mountainviewcounty.com
Albert Kemmere, Reeve
Steve McInnis, Director, Operational Services
steve.mcinnis@mountainviewcounty.com
Tony Martens, Director, Legislative & Community Services
tony.martens@mountainviewcounty.com
Jeff Holmes, Manager, Agriculture & Parks Services
jeff.holmes@mountainviewcounty.com

Parkland County
53109A Sec Hwy. 779
Parkland County, AB T7Z 1R1
780-968-8888
Fax: 780-968-8413
Toll Free: 1-888-880-0858
inquiries@parklandcounty.com
www.parklandcounty.com
Municipal Type: County
Incorporated: March 1, 1918 Area: 2,392.61 sq km
Population in 2009: 30,089
Next Election: 2013 (3 year terms)
Note: Incorporated as a county on Jan. 1, 1969.
Pat Vincent, CAO
780-968-8411
pvincent@parklandcounty.com
Rodney Shaigec, Mayor
rshaigec@parklandcounty.com
Mark Cardinal, Manager, Agricultural Services
mcardinal@parklandcounty.com
Andy Haden, Manager, Planning & Development Services
ahaden@parklandcounty.com
Rob McGowan, Manager, Engineering Services
rmcgowan@parklandcounty.com
Daryl Phillips, Manager, Public Works
dphillips@parklandcounty.com
Ken Saulit, Manager, Protective Services
ksaulit@parklandcounty.com
Ken Van Buul, Manager, Recreation & Parks Services
kvanbuul@parklandcounty.com
Janette Szucs, Coordinator, Purchasing
jszucs@parklandcounty.com
Trent Tompkins, Coordinator, Solid Waste
ttompkins@parklandcounty.com
Kevin Bryant, Supervisor, Utilities & Waste Services
kbryant@parklandcounty.com
Brian Rimmer, Supervisor, Environmental Services
brimmer@parklandcounty.com
Grace Horsfield, Officer, Development
ghorsfield@parklandcounty.com

Red Deer County
Red Deer County Centre
38106 Range Rd. 275
Red Deer County, AB T4S 2L9
403-350-2150
Fax: 403-346-9840
info@rdcounty.ca
http://rdcounty.ca
Municipal Type: County
Incorporated: Jan. 1, 1944 Area: 4,002.58 sq km
Population in 2006: 19,108
Next Election: 2013 (3 year terms)
Note: Incorporated as a county on Jan. 1, 1963.
Curtis Herzberg, County Manager
cherzberg@reddeercounty.ab.ca
Jim Wood, Mayor
403-350-2152
Harry Harker, Director, Planning & Development
hharker@reddeercounty.ab.ca
Ric Henderson, Director, Community & Protective Services
rhenderson@reddeercounty.ab.ca
Frank Peck, Director, Operations Services
fpeck@reddeercounty.ab.ca
Cliff Fuller, Fire Chief
cfuller@reddeercounty.ab.ca
Don Bardonnex, Manager, Fire Services
dbardonnex@reddeercounty.ab.ca
Joe D'Onofrio, Manager, Land
jd'onofrio@reddeercounty.ab.ca
Linda Henrickson, Manager, Rural Planning
lhenrickson@reddeercounty.ab.ca

Johan van der Bank, Manager, Urban Planning
jvanderbank@reddeercounty.ab.ca
Marty Campbell, Coordinator, Engineering
mcampbell@reddeercounty.ab.ca
Jo-Ann Symington, Coordinator, Community Services
jsymington@reddeercounty.ab.ca
Andrew Treu, Coordinator, Environmental Services
atreu@reddeercounty.ab.ca
Donna Trottier, Coordinator, Conservation
Dawna Barnes, Specialist, Community Development
dbarnes@reddeercounty.ab.ca
Art Preachuk, Fieldman, Agricultural Services
apreachuk@reddeercounty.ab.ca

Rocky View No. 44
911 - 32 Ave. NE
Calgary, AB T2E 6X6
403-230-1401
Fax: 403-277-5977
comments@rockyview.ca
www.rockyview.ca
Municipal Type: Municipal District
Incorporated: Feb. 1, 1943 Area: 4,014.89 sq km
Population in 2006: 34,171
Next Election: 2013 (3 year terms)
Robert Coon, CAO
rcoon@rockyview.ca
Lois Habberfield, Reeve
council@rockyview.ca
Brian Jobson, Director, Transportation Services
bjobson@gov.mdrockyview.ab.ca
Frank Misura, Manager, Development/Utility Services
Linda Ratzlaff, Coordinator, Policy Planning
403-520-8166
Tim Dietzler, Fieldman, Agriculture
403-520-1271

Strathcona County
2001 Sherwood Dr.
Sherwood Park, AB T8A 3W7
780-464-8111
Fax: 780-464-8050
info@strathcona.ab.ca
www.strathcona.ab.ca
Municipal Type: Regional Municipality
Incorporated: Jan. 1, 1962 Area: 1,179.43 sq km
Population in 2009: 87,998
Next Election: 2013 (3 year terms)
Note: Incorporated as a specialized municipality on Jan. 1, 1996.
Robyn W. Singleton, Q.C., Chief Commissioner
780-464-8100
singleton@strathcona.ab.ca
Linda Osinchuk, Mayor
Peter Vana, Associate Commissioner, Infrastructure & Planning Services
780-464-8188
vana@strathcona.ab.ca
Denise Exton, Associate Commissioner, Community Services
780-464-8291
exton@strathcona.ab.ca

Sturgeon County
9613 - 100 St.
Morinville, AB T8R 1L9
780-939-4321
Fax: 780-939-3003
Toll free: 1-866-939-9303
sturgeonmail@sturgeoncounty.ab.ca
www.sturgeoncounty.ab.ca
Municipal Type: Municipal District
Incorporated: Feb. 1, 1943 Area: 2,108.9 sq km
Population in 2008: 19,105
Next Election: 2013 (3 year terms)
Case Van Herk, County Commissioner
780-939-8345
cvanherk@sturgeoncounty.ab.ca
Donald Rigney, B.Sc., MBA, Mayor
780-921-3041, Fax: 780-921-3041
drigney@sturgeoncounty.ab.ca
Ian McKay, General Manager, Infrastructure Services
780-939-8337
imckay@sturgeoncounty.ab.ca
Peter Tarnawsky, General Manager, Public Services
780-939-8344
ptarnawsky@sturgeoncounty.ab.ca

Bart Clark, Manager, Protective Services
780-939-0600
bclark@sturgeoncounty.ab.ca
Collin Steffes, Manager, Planning & Development
780-939-8275
csteffes@sturgeoncounty.ab.ca
Roy Lidgren, Manager, Transportation Services
780-939-8250
rlidgern@sturgeoncounty.ab.ca
Quentin Bochar, Manager, Agriculture Services
780-939-8325
qbochar@sturgeoncounty.ab.ca
Mike Hittinger, Coordinator, Municipal Conservation
780-939-8339
nwaci@sturgeoncounty.ab.ca

Wetaskiwin County No. 10
P.O. Box 6960
Wetaskiwin, AB T9A 2G5
780-352-3321
Fax: 780-352-3486
Toll Free: 1-800-661-4125
fcoutney@county.wetaskiwin.ab.ca
www.county.wetaskiwin.ab.ca
Municipal Type: County
Incorporated: Dec. 13, 1915 Area: 3,130.9 sq km
County or District: Wetaskiwin No. 10; Population in 2006: 10,535
Next Election: 2013 (3 year terms)
Note: Incorporated as a county on Jan. 1, 1958.
Frank Coutney, County Administrator
fcoutney@county.wetaskiwin.ab.ca
Garry Dearing, Reeve
Ken Carlson, Director, Disaster Services
780-361-6340
kcarlson@county.wetaskiwin.ab.ca
Dave Dextraze, Director, Public Works
780-361-6230
ddextraze@county.wetaskiwin.ab.ca
Steve Majek, Director, Agricultural Services
780-361-6226
smajek@county.wetaskiwin.ab.ca

Wood Buffalo
9909 Franklin Ave.
Fort McMurray, AB T9H 2K4
780-743-7000
Fax: 780-743-7028
Toll Free: 1-800-973-9663
communications@woodbuffalo.ab.ca
www.woodbuffalo.ab.ca
Municipal Type: Regional Municipality
Incorporated: April 1, 1995 Area: 63,342.89 sq km
Population in 2006: 51,496
Next Election: 2013 (3 year terms)
Kelly Kloss, Acting CAO
780-743-7023
kelly.kloss@woodbuffalo.ab.ca
Melissa Blake, Mayor
Wes Holodniuk, Manager, Operations & Maintenance
780-743-7931, Fax: 780-799-5909
wes.holodniuk@woodbuffalo.ab.ca
Salem Abushawashi, Superintendent, Fort Chipewyan
780-697-3600
salem.abushawashi@woodbuffalo.ab.ca
Guy Jette, Acting Superintendent, Operations & Facilities Maintenance
780-799-7486
guy.jette@woodbuffalo.ab.ca
Darcy Elder, Superintendent, Infrastructure
780-799-7475
darcy.elder@woodbuffalo.ab.ca
Michel Savard, Superintendent, Environment
780-799-7490
michel.savard@woodbuffalo.ab.ca
Dwayne Harvie, Project Engineer
780-743-7855
dwayne.harvie@woodbuffalo.ab.ca

Major Municipalities in Alberta

Airdrie
400 Main St. SE
Airdrie, AB T4B 3C3

See blue tabs following this section for Municipal Waste Management and Water & Wastewater Treatment.

Municipal Governments / Alberta

403-948-8800
Fax: 403-948-6567
information.systems@airdrie.ca
www.airdrie.ca
Municipal Type: City
Incorporated: Sept. 10, 1909 *Area:* 33.10 sq km
Population in 2010: 39,822
Provincial Electoral District(s): Airdrie-Chestermere
Federal Electoral District(s): Wild Rose
Next Election: 2013 (3 year terms)
Note: Incorporated as a city on Jan. 1, 1985.
Council
Peter Brown, Mayor
mayor@airdrie.ca
Administration
George Keene, City Manager
george.keen@airdrie.ca
Mark Locking, Director, Engineering & Public Works
Jeff Greene, City Planner & Team Leader
403-948-8848
planning.development@airdrie.ca
Dave Rimes, Leader, Parks
403-948-8402
parks@airdrie.ca
Mary Grace Curtis, Coordinator, Recycling & Composting
780-948-0246
environmental.services@airdrie.ca
Darryl Wolski, Coordinator, Solid Waste
403-948-0246
pubwrks@airdrie.ca

Brooks
P.O. Box 880
201 - 1 Ave. West
Brooks, AB T1R 0Z6
403-362-3333
Fax: 403-362-4787
admin@brooks.ca
www.brooks.ca
Municipal Type: City
Incorporated: July 14, 1910 *Area:* 17.7 sq km
Population in 2007: 13,581
Provincial Electoral District(s): Strathmore-Brooks
Federal Electoral District(s): Medicine Hat
Next Election: 2013 (3 year terms)
Note: Incorporated as a city on Sept. 1, 2005.
Council
Martin Shields, Mayor
mshields@brooks.ca
Administration
Kevin Stephenson, City Manager
kstephenson@brooks.ca
Neil Hollands, Director, Engineering & Property Services
nhollands@brooks.ca
Kevin Swanson, Director, Protective Services
403-362-2331
Terry Walsh, Director, Parks & Recreation
twalsh@brooks.ca
Maurice Landry, Manager, Development Services
mlandry@brooks.ca
Bill Prentice, Manager, Public Works
403-362-3146
bprentice@brooks.ca
Gord Shaw, Manager, Planning Services
gshaw@brooks.ca

Calgary
P.O. Box 2100 M
800 Macleod Trail SE
Calgary, AB T2P 2M5
403-268-2489
Fax: 403-538-6111
TTY: 403-268-4889
www.calgary.ca
Municipal Type: City
Incorporated: Nov. 7, 1884 *Area:* 726.5 sq km
Population in 2009: 1,230,248
Provincial Electoral District(s): Cal.-Bow; Cal.-Buffalo; Cal.-Cross; Cal.-Currie; Cal.-Egmont; Cal.-East; Cal.-Elbow; Cal.-Fish Creek; Cal.-Foothills; Cal.-Fort; Cal.-Glenmore; Cal.-Hays; Cal.-Lougheed; Cal.-McCall; Cal.-Mackay; Cal.-Montrose; Cal.-Mountain View; Cal.-North Hill; Cal.-Nose Hill; Cal.-Shaw; Cal.-Varsity; Cal.-West
Federal Electoral District(s): Calgary Centre; Calgary Centre-North; Calgary East; Calgary Northeast; Calgary-Nose Hill; Calgary Southeast; Calgary Southwest; Calgary West; Macleod; Wild Rose
Next Election: 2013 (3 year terms)
Note: Incorporated as a city on Jan. 1, 1894.
Council
Naheed K. Nenshi, Mayor
403-268-5622, Fax: 403-268-8130
themayor@calgary.ca
Dale Hodges, Aldermen, Ward(s): 1
403-268-2445, Fax: 403-268-8091
Frederick Gordon Lowe, Aldermen, Ward(s): 2
403-268-2430, Fax: 403-268-3823
Jim Stevenson, Aldermen, Ward(s): 3
403-268-2430, Fax: 403-268-8091
Gael MacLeod, Aldermen, Ward(s): 4
403-268-2430, Fax: 403-268-8091
Ray Jones, Aldermen, Ward(s): 5
403-268-2430, Fax: 403-268-3823
Richard Pootmans, Aldermen, Ward(s): 6
403-268-2430, Fax: 403-268-8091
Druh Farrell, Aldermen, Ward(s): 7
403-268-2475, Fax: 403-268-3823
John Mar, Aldermen, Ward(s): 8
403-268-2430, Fax: 403-268-3823
Gian-Carlo Carra, Aldermen, Ward(s): 9
403-268-2430, Fax: 403-268-8091
Andre Chabot, Aldermen, Ward(s): 10
403-268-2430, Fax: 403-268-3823
Brian Pincott, Aldermen, Ward(s): 11
403-268-2430, Fax: 403-268-8091
Shane A. Keating, Aldermen, Ward(s): 12
403-268-2430, Fax: 403-268-4673
Diane Colley-Urquhart, Aldermen, Ward(s): 13
403-268-2430, Fax: 403-268-8091
Linda Fox-Mellway, Aldermen, Ward(s): 14
403-268-2430, Fax: 403-268-3823
Administration
Diana L. Garner, City Clerk
403-268-5861, Fax: 403-268-2362
cityclerk@calgary.ca
George McLauchlan, Director, Human Resources
403-268-2201, Fax: 403-268-4680
Stuart Dalgleish, Director & City Assessor
403-268-4609, Fax: 403-268-8278
J. Bernie Trahan, Director, Fleet Services
403-268-1122, Fax: 403-266-2496
btrahan@calgary.ca
Anne Charlton, Director, Parks
403-268-3888
John Hubbell, General Manager, Transportation
Mary Axworthy, Director, Land Use Planning & Policy
David L. Day, Director, Environmental & Safety Management
403-268-3668
Dave Griffiths, Director, Waste & Recycling Services
Allyn Humber, Director, Water Services
403-268-2702
waterworks@calgary.ca
Ian Norris, Director, Transportation Infrastructure
403-974-4876
Wolf Keller, Director, Water Resources
403-268-6752
Jack Beaton, Chief of Police
403-206-5900
W. Bruce Burrell, Fire Chief
403-287-4255, Fax: 403-243-1490
Tom Sampson, Deputy Chief, Calgary Emergency Management Agency
tom.sampson@calgary.ca
Owen Tobert, P.Eng., City Manager
owens.tobert@calgary.ca
David Watson, General Manager, Planning Development & Assessment
403-268-2601
david.watson@calgary.ca
Rob Pritchard, General Manager, Utilities & Environmental Protection
403-268-2042, Fax: 403-537-3023
Erika Hargesheimer, General Manager, Community & Protective Services
403-268-5636
Kathy Strong-Duffin, Manager, Environmental Policy & Strategic Initiatives
403-268-4699
kstrongd@calgary.ca

Kevan van Velzen, M.Sc., P.Biol., Manager, Environmental Assessment & Liabilities
403-250-6448
Richard Binder, Manager, Infrastructure & Program Development
richard.binder@calgary.ca

Camrose
City Hall
5204 - 50 Ave.
Camrose, AB T4V 0S8
780-672-4426
Fax: 780-672-2469
admin@camrose.ca
www.camrose.ca
Municipal Type: City
Incorporated: May 4, 1905 *Area:* 31.14 sq km
Population in 2008: 16,543
Provincial Electoral District(s): Wetaskiwin-Camrose
Federal Electoral District(s): Crowfoot
Next Election: 2013 (3 year terms)
Note: Incorporated as a city on Jan. 1, 1955.
Council
Marshall Chalmers, Mayor
admin@camrose.ca
Administration
Brian Hamblin, P.Eng., City Manager
bhamblin@camrose.ca
Damian Herle, Manager, Corporate & Protective Services
Diane Urkow, Manager, Financial Services
Jeremy Enarson, Acting City Engineer, Engineering Services
Chris Clarkson, Director, Parks
780-672-9195
Jim Kupka, Director, Public Works
780-672-5513
Darrell Kambeitz, Police Chief
Peter Krich, Fire Chief/Deputy Director, Emergency Management
Brenda Hisey, Director, Planning & Development
780-672-4428
Doug Delmage, Chief Building Inspector
780-672-4428

Canmore
902 - 7 Ave.
Canmore, AB T1W 3K1
403-678-1500
Fax: 403-678-1524
info@canmore.ca
www.canmore.ca
Municipal Type: City
Incorporated: Jan. 1, 1965 *Area:* 68.9 sq km
Population in 2006: 12,039
Provincial Electoral District(s): Banff-Cochrane
Federal Electoral District(s): Wild Rose
Next Election: 2013 (3 year terms)
Note: Incorporated as a town on June 1, 1966.
Council
Ron Casey, Mayor
mayor@canmore.ca
Administration
Don Kochan, CAO
donkochan@canmore.ca
Don Kochan, Director, Environmental Services
donkochan@canmore.ca
Doug Townsend, Manager, Facilities
403-678-1586
Kevin Van Vliet, Manager, Engineering
403-678-1545, Fax: 403-678-1534

Cochrane
P.O. Box 10
101 Ranche House Rd.
Cochrane, AB T4C 2K8
403-851-2505
Fax: 403-851-2581
cochrane@cochrane.ca
www.cochrane.ca
Municipal Type: City
Incorporated: June 17, 1903 *Area:* 30.03 sq km
Population in 2006: 13,760
Provincial Electoral District(s): Banff-Cochrane
Federal Electoral District(s): Wild Rose
Next Election: 2013 (3 year terms)
Note: Incorporated as a town on Feb. 15, 1971.

See blue tabs following this section for Municipal Waste Management and Water & Wastewater Treatment.

Municipal Governments / Alberta

Council
Truper McBride, Mayor
truper.mcbride@cochrane.ca
Administration
Julian deCocq, Clerk
julian.decocq@cochrane.ca
Jim Anderson, Director, Operational Services
403-851-2560
jim.anderson@cochrane.ca
Lori Leipnitz, Director, Corporate Services
403-851-2510
lori.leipnitz@cochrane.ca
Ian Smith, Director, Community & Protective Services
403-851-2530
ian.smith@cochrane.ca
Frank Wesseling, Director, Planning & Engineering
403-851-2570
frank.wesseling@cochrane.ca
Elise Harnick, Engineer, Subdivision & Development
403-851-2575
elise.harnick@cochrane.ca

Cold Lake
5513 - 48 Ave.
Cold Lake, AB T9M 1A1
780-594-4494
Fax: 780-594-3480
city@coldlake.com
www.coldlake.com
Municipal Type: City
Incorporated: Dec. 31, 1953 *Area:* 59.3 sq km
Population in 2009: 13,924
Provincial Electoral District(s): Bonnyville-Cold Lake
Federal Electoral District(s): Westlock-St. Paul
Next Election: 2013 (3 year terms)
Note: Incorporated as a city on Oct. 1, 2000.
Council
Craig Copeland, Mayor
Administration
Gordon Frank, CAO
gfrank@coldlake.com
Allan Weiss, Chief, Fire
780-594-4494
Carry Grant, Manager, Operations
780-594-3776
cgrant@coldlake.com
George McIntosh, Foreman, Utilities
780-639-3604
wtp@coldlake.com
John McLean, Foreman, Parks & Facilities
780-594-3776
parks@coldlake.com

Edmonton
City Hall
1 Sir Winston Churchill Sq., 3rd Fl.
Edmonton, AB T5J 2R7
Fax: 780-496-8210
Telephone: 311 in Edmonton; or 780-442-5311
311@edmonton.ca
www.edmonton.ca
Municipal Type: City
Incorporated: Jan. 9, 1892 *Area:* 684.37 sq km
Population in 2009: 782,439
Provincial Electoral District(s): Ed.-Beverly-Clareview;
Ed.-Calder; Ed.-Castle Downs; Ed.-Centre; Ed.-Decore;
Ed.-Ellerslie; Ed.-Glenora; Ed.-Gold Bar;
Ed.-Highlands-Norwood; Ed.-Manning; Ed.-McClung;
Ed.-Meadowlark; Ed.-Mill Creek; Ed.-Mill Woods; Ed.-Riverview;
Ed.-Rutherford; Ed.-Strathcona; Ed.-Whitemud
Federal Electoral District(s): Edmonton Centre; Edmonton East;
Edmonton-Leduc; Edmonton-Mill Woods-Beaumont;
Edmonton-Sherwood Park; Edmonton-Spruce Grove;
Edmonton-St. Albert; Edmonton-Strathcona
Next Election: 2013 (3 year terms)
Note: Incorporated as a city on Oct. 08, 1904.
Council
Stephen Mandel, Mayor
780-496-8100, Fax: 780-496-8292
Linda Sloan, Councillor, Ward(s): 1
780-496-8122, Fax: 780-496-8113
linda.sloan@edmonton.ca
Kim Krushell, Councillor, Ward(s): 2
780-496-8128, Fax: 780-496-8113
kim.krushell@edmonton.ca
Dave Loken, Councillor, Ward(s): 3
dave.loken@edmonton.ca
Ed Gibbons, Councillor, Ward(s): 4
ed.gibbons@edmonton.ca
Karen Leibovici, Councillor, Ward(s): 5
780-496-8120, Fax: 780-496-8113
karen.leibovici@edmonton.ca
Jane Batty, Councillor, Ward(s): 6, Fax: 780-496-8113
jane.batty@edmonton.ca
Tony Caterina, Councillor, Ward(s): 7
780-496-8333, Fax: 780-496-8113
tony.caterina@edmonton.ca
Ben Henderson, Councillor, Ward(s): 8
780-496-8146, Fax: 780-496-8113
ben.henderson@edmonton.ca
Bryan Anderson, Councillor, Ward(s): 9
780-496-8130, Fax: 780-496-8113
bryan.anderson@edmonton.ca
Don Iveson, Councillor, Ward(s): 10
780-496-8132, Fax: 780-496-8113
don.iveson@edmonton.ca
Kerry Diotte, Councillor, Ward(s): 11, Fax: 780-496-8113
kerry.diotte@edmonton.ca
Amarjeet Sohi, Councillor, Ward(s): 12
780-496-8148, Fax: 780-496-8113
amarjeet.sohi@edmonton.ca
Administration
Simon Farbrother, City Manager
780-496-8231, Fax: 780-496-8220
simon.farbrother@edmonton.ca
David Edey, General Manager, Corporate Services
780-496-7201, Fax: 780-496-8854
david.edey@edmonton.ca
David Wiun, City Auditor
780-496-8315, Fax: 780-496-8062
david.wiun@edmonton.ca
Mike Boyd, Police Chief
780-421-3333
Dave Galea, Director, Office of Emergency Preparedness
780-944-6420, Fax: 780-496-3062
david.galea@edmonton.ca
Doug Costigan, Director, Asset Management & Public Works, Parks Branch
780-496-4956, Fax: 780-496-4978
doug.costigan@edmonton.ca
John Hodgson, Manager, Drainage Services
780-496-5658, Fax: 780-496-3629
Gerald W. Goodall, Consultant, Corporate Services, Materials Management Branch
780-496-3729, Fax: 780-496-5015
gerry.goodall@edmonton.ca
Audra Jones, Director, Transportation Planning
780-496-1790, Fax: 780-496-4287
Gary Klassen, General Manager, Planning & Development
780-496-6050, Fax: 780-496-6916
gary.klassen@edmonton.ca
Bob Boutilier, General Manager, Transportation
780-496-2808, Fax: 780-496-2803
transportation@edmonton.ca
Linda Cochrane, General Manager, Community Services
780-496-5804, Fax: 780-577-3525
linda.cochrane@edmonton.ca
Joyce Tustian, General Manager, Deputy City Manager's Office
780-442-6356, Fax: 780-496-8220
joyce.tustian@edmonton.ca
Mary Pat Barry, Manager, Deputy City Manager's Office, Communications Branch
780-496-8191, Fax: 780-496-4877
marypat.barry@edmonton.ca
Peter Muller, EMT-P, ABCP, Emergency Management Officer (Planning), Office of Emergency Preparedness
780-496-1530, Fax: 780-496-3062
peter.muller@edmonton.ca
Grant Pearsell, Director, Asset Management & Public Works, Parks Branch
780-496-6080, Fax: 780-496-5636
grant.pearsell@edmonton.ca
Garth Clyburn, Planner II, Planning & Development, Planning & Policy Branch
780-496-6209, Fax: 780-496-6299
garth.clyburn@edmonton.ca
Roy Neehall, Manager, Waste Management
780-496-5405, Fax: 780-496-5657

Fort Saskatchewan
10005 - 102 St.
Fort Saskatchewan, AB T8L 2C5
780-992-6200
Fax: 780-998-4774
lrosen@fortsask.ca
www.fortsask.ca
Municipal Type: City
Incorporated: March 1, 1899 *Area:* 48.12 sq km
Population in 2009: 17,469
Provincial Electoral District(s): Fort Saskatchewan-Vegreville
Federal Electoral District(s): Edmonton-Sherwood Park
Next Election: 2013 (3 year terms)
Note: Incorporated as a city on July 1, 1985.
Council
Gale Katchur, Mayor
Administration
Lorna Rosen, City Manager
John Rop, Treasurer
Scott Mack, Director, Planning
780-992-6573
smack@fortsask.ca
Todd Burge, Manager, Corporate Services
780-992-6255
tburge@fortsask.ca
Richard Hobson, Manager, Community & Protective Services
780-992-6205, Fax: 780-992-0192
rhobson@fortsask.ca
Dave Worman, Manager, Planning & Public Works
780-992-6207
dworman@fortsask.ca
Ken Lura, Superintendent, Public Works
780-992-6247
klura@fortsask.ca
Gale Katchur, Contact, Environmental Awareness Committee
gkatchur@fortsask.ca

Grande Prairie
P.O. Box 4000
10205 - 98 St.
Grande Prairie, AB T8V 6V3
780-538-0300
Fax: 780-538-0746
www.cityofgp.com
Municipal Type: City
Incorporated: April 30, 1914 *Area:* 61.08 sq km
Population in 2006: 47,076
Provincial Electoral District(s): Grande Prairie-Smoky; Grande Prairie-Wapiti
Federal Electoral District(s): Peace River
Next Election: 2013 (3 year terms)
Note: Incorporated as a city on Jan. 1, 1958.
Council
Bill Given, Mayor
bgiven@cityofgp.com
Administration
Greg Scerbak, City Manager
780-538-0312, Fax: 780-814-7560
gscerbak@cityofgp.com
Janette Ferguson, City Clerk
780-538-0314, Fax: 780-539-1056
jferguson@cityofgp.com
Frank Daskewech, Director, Public Works
780-538-0350, Fax: 780-538-4667
fdaskewech@cityofgp.com
Ken Anderson, Director, Financial Services
780-538-0302, Fax: 780-539-1056
kanderson@cityofgp.com
Josy Burrough, Manager, Parks
780-538-0476, Fax: 780-532-7588
jburrough@cityofgp.com
Michael MacIntyre, Planning Manager, Development Services
780-538-0440, Fax: 780-538-0746
mmacintyre@cityofgp.com
Valerie Norris-Kirk, Development Coordinator, Development Services
780-513-5236, Fax: 780-538-0746
vnorrisk@cityofgp.com
Uli Wolf, Solid Waste Services Supervisor, Aquatera Utilities Inc.
780-538-0360, Fax: 780-830-7060
uwolf@aquatera.ca
Amy Horne, Recycling Coordinator, Aquatera Utilities Inc.
780-538-0452, Fax: 780-830-7060
ahorne@aquatera.ca

See blue tabs following this section for Municipal Waste Management and Water & Wastewater Treatment.

Mark Simpson, Operations Coordinator, Aquatera Utilities Inc.
780-538-0442, Fax: 780-830-7430
msimpson@aquatera.ca
Dan Lemieux, Sr. Deputy Fire Chief
780-538-0398, Fax: 780-538-0395
dlemieux@cityofgp.com

Leduc
1 Alexandra Park
Leduc, AB T9E 4C4
780-980-7177
Fax: 780-980-7127
info@leduc.ca
www.leduc.ca
Municipal Type: City
Incorporated: Dec. 15, 1899 *Area:* 36.97 sq km
Population in 2010: 23,293
Provincial Electoral District(s): Leduc-Beaumont-Devon
Federal Electoral District(s): Edmonton-Leduc
Next Election: 2013 (3 year terms)
Note: Incorporated as a city on Sept. 01, 1983.
Council
Greg Krischke, Mayor
mayor@leduc.ca
Administration
Laura Knoblock, City Clerk
lknoblock@leduc.ca
Linda Kyluik, Treasurer
Paul Benedetto, City Manager
pbenedetto@leduc.ca
Kevin Cole, Director, Public Services
Doug Parrish, Director, Planning & Development
780-980-7124
dparrish@leduc.ca
Rick Sereda, Fire Chief & Director, Protective Services
Allan Yamashita, City Engineer & General Manager, Operations

Lethbridge
City Hall
910 - 4 Ave. South
Lethbridge, AB T1J 0P6
403-329-7355
Fax: 403-320-7575
info@lethbridge.ca
www.lethbridge.ca
Municipal Type: City
Incorporated: Nov. 29, 1890 *Area:* 121.97 sq km
Population in 2010: 86,659
Provincial Electoral District(s): Lethbridge-East; Lethbridge-West
Federal Electoral District(s): Lethbridge
Next Election: 2013 (3 year terms)
Note: Incorporated as a city on May 9, 1906.
Council
Rajko Dodic, Mayor
403-320-3823, Fax: 403-320-7575
mayor@lethbridge.ca
Bob Babki, Aldermen, Fax: 403-320-7575
Jeff Carlson, Aldermen
403-360-7550, Fax: 403-320-7575
aldermancarlson@gmail.com
Faron Ellis, Aldermen, Fax: 403-320-7575
Liz Iwaskiw, Aldermen, Fax: 403-320-7575
Joe Mauro, Aldermen, Fax: 403-320-7575
Bridget Mearns, Aldermen, Fax: 403-320-7575
Ryan Parker, Aldermen
403-380-4848, Fax: 403-320-7575
aldermanryanparker@gmail.com
Tom Wickersham, Aldermen
403-381-1521, Fax: 403-381-1571
thwicker@gmail.com
Administration
Dianne Nemeth, City Clerk
403-320-3821, Fax: 403-320-7575
dnemeth@lethbridge.ca
Garth Sherwin, B.Comm., CA, City Manager
gsherwin@lethbridge.ca
Douglas Hudson, Q.C., City Solicitor
dhudson@lethbridge.ca
Brian Cornforth, Fire Chief
403-320-3800, Fax: 403-327-3503
astrandlund@lethbridge.ca
Tom McKenzie, Police Chief
403-327-2210, Fax: 403-328-6999

Byron Buzunis, M.Eng., PMP, P.Eng., Urban Construction Manager
403-320-3975
Kathy Hopkins, Director, Community Services
403-320-3015, Fax: 403-380-2512
khopkins@lethbridge.ca
Warren Andrews, Manager, Public Operations
wandrews@lethbridge.ca
Kevin Viergutz, Manager, Transportation Operations
kviergutz@lethbridge.ab.ca
Bary Beck, Director, Corporate Initiatives
Jody Meli, Manager, Corporate & Community Relations
jmeli@lethbridge.ca
John King, Manager, Transit
403-320-3884, Fax: 403-380-3876
jking@lethbridge.ca
Craig Milley, Manager, Purchasing
403-320-3961
cmilley@lethbridge.ca
Kevin Theodore, Manager, Waste & Recycling
403-320-3088
ktheodore@lethbridge.ab.ca
Don Bulpitt, Manager, Water & Wastewater Operations
dbulpitt@lethbridge.ca
Kevin Jensen, Coordinator, Parks
403-330-5108
kjensen@lethbridge.ab.ca
George Kuhl, Senior Planner, Development Services
403-327-3926, Fax: 403-327-6571
gkuhl@lethbridge.ca

Lloydminster
City Hall
4420 - 50 Ave.
Lloydminster, AB T9V 0W2
780-875-6184
Fax: 780-871-8345
jkeeley@lloydminster.ca
www.lloydminster.ca
Municipal Type: City
Incorporated: Nov. 25, 1903 *Area:* 24.19 sq km
Population in 2009: 26,502
Provincial Electoral District(s): Vermilion-Lloydminster
Federal Electoral District(s): Vegreville-Wainwright
Next Election: 2013 (3 year terms)
Note: Population figure represents both the Alberta & Saskatchewan populations. Incorporated as a city on Jan. 1, 1958.
Council
Jeff Mulligan, Mayor
mayor@lloydminster.ca
Administration
Beth Kembel, City Clerk
780-871-8328
bkembel@lloydminster.ca
Diane Beecroft, Treasurer
780-875-6184
dbeecroft@lloydminster.ca
Adam Homes, Director, Planning & Public Works
780-875-8332
ahomes@lloydminster.ca
Corwin McCullagh, Director, Parks & Recreation
780-871-8340
cmccullagh@lloydminster.ca
Richard Power, Chief Development Officer
780-871-8335
rpower@lloydminster.ca
Kirk Morrison, Engineer, Transportation & Works
kmorrison@lloydminster.ca
Lindsay Parnwell, Engineer, Utilities
lparnwell@lloydminster.ca
Trisha Le, Urban Planner
tle@lloydminster.ca

Medicine Hat
City Hall
580 - 1 St. SE
Medicine Hat, AB T1A 8E6
403-529-8115
Fax: 403-529-8182
clerk@medicinehat.ca
www.medicinehat.ca
Municipal Type: City
Incorporated: May 31, 1894 *Area:* 112.01 sq km
Population in 2009: 61,097

Provincial Electoral District(s): Cypress-Medicine Hat; Medicine Hat
Federal Electoral District(s): Medicine Hat
Next Election: 2013 (3 year terms)
Note: Incorporated as a city on May 9, 1906.
Council
Normand Boucher, Mayor
403-529-8181, Fax: 403-529-8182
mayor@medicinehat.ca; norbou@medicinehat.ca
Ted Clugston, Aldermen
403-526-8760
tedclu@medicinehat.ca
Wayne Craven, Aldermen, Fax: 403-529-8182
waycra@medicinehat.ca
Robert C. Dumanowski, Aldermen
John Hamill, Aldermen
403-526-7196, Fax: 403-529-8282
johham@medicinehat.ca
Graham Kelly, Aldermen
403-527-1891, Fax: 403-528-2453
gldarops@shaw.ca
Les Pearson, Aldermen
lespea@medicinehat.ca
Jeremy Thompson, Aldermen
403-504-5647, Fax: 403-526-1422
jertho@medicinehat.ca
Phil Turnbull, Aldermen
Administration
Dave Leflar, City Clerk
403-529-8234, Fax: 403-529-8182
davlef@medicinehat.ca
Gerry Labas, COO
403-529-8222
gerlab@medicinehat.ca
John Hughes, City Solicitor
403-529-8350
johhug@medicinehat.ca
Andy McGrogan, Police Chief
403-529-8410, Fax: 403-529-8444
Ron Robinson, Fire Chief
403-502-8006, Fax: 403-526-1352
Albert Bizio, Commissioner, Public Services
403-529-8229
albbiz@medicinehat.ca
Don Knutson, Acting Commissioner, Corporate Services
403-529-8231
onknu@medicinehat.ca
John Komanchuk, Commissioner, Development & Infrastructure
403-529-8354
johjo@medicinehat.ca
Dwight Brown, General Manager, Planning, Building & Development Services
Dale Descoteau, General Manager, Information & Computer Services
403-529-8108
daldes@medicinehat.ca
John Fedoruk, General Manager, Environmental Utilities
403-529-8176, Fax: 403-528-4955
eu@medicinehat.ca
Tony Klauwers, General Manager, Municipal Works
Grant MacKay, General Manager, Human Resources
403-529-8239
gramac@medicinehat.ca
Dave Panabaker, General Manager, Gas Utility
403-529-8288
davepan@medicinehat.ca
Ron Webb, General Manager, Community Development
403-529-8310
ronweb@medicinehat.ca
Les Wickenheiser, General Manager, Corporate Asset Management
403-529-8327
leswic@medicinehat.ca
Kendall Woodacre, General Manager, Electric Utility
403-502-8081
kenwoo@medicinehat.ca
R. Vizbar, General Manager, Parks & Outdoor Recreation
403-529-8312, Fax: 403-527-4798
parks@medicinehat.ca
Russ Smith, Manager, Environment Management
403-529-8188
russmi@medicinhat.ca
Frank Wetsch, Manager, Water & WasteWater Treatment
403-529-8227

See blue tabs following this section for Municipal Waste Management and Water & Wastewater Treatment.

Municipal Governments / Alberta

S. Schentag, Coordinator, Recycling Development
403-502-8593
Ron Davis, Officer, Health & Safety
403-529-8359
rondav@medicine-hat.ca

Okotoks
P.O. Box 20 Main
5 Elizabeth St.
Okotoks, AB T1S 1K1
403-938-4404
Fax: 403-938-7387
info@okotoks.ca
www.okotoks.ca
Municipal Type: City
Incorporated: Oct. 25, 1899 *Area:* 18.55 sq km
Population in 2010: 23,201
Provincial Electoral District(s): Highwood
Federal Electoral District(s): Macleod
Next Election: 2013 (3 year terms)
Note: Incorporated as a town on June 1, 1904.
Council
Bill Robertson, Mayor
mayor@okotoks.ca
Administration
Rick Quail, Municipal Manager
403-938-8900
municipalmanager@okotoks.ca
Marley Oness, Municipal Engineer
403-938-8930
municipalengineer@okotoks.ca
Dave Robertson, Manager, Operations
403-938-8952
operations@okotoks.ca
Ken Thevenot, Fire Chief
403-938-4066
fire@okotoks.ca

Red Deer
City Hall
P.O. Box 5008
4914 - 48th Ave.
Red Deer, AB T4N 3T4
403-342-8111
Fax: 403-346-6195
feedback@reddeer.ca
www.reddeer.ca
Municipal Type: City
Incorporated: May 31, 1894 *Area:* 69.23 sq km
Population in 2010: 90,084
Provincial Electoral District(s): Red Deer-North; Red Deer-South
Federal Electoral District(s): Red Deer
Next Election: 2013 (3 year terms)
Note: Incorporated as a city on March 25, 1913.
Council
Morris Flewwelling, Mayor
403-342-8154, Fax: 403-342-8365
mayor@reddeer.ca
Buck Buchanan, Councillor
403-343-6550, Fax: 403-346-6195
buck.buchanan@reddeer.ca
Paul Harris, Councillor
Cindy Jefferies, Councillor
403-302-3706, Fax: 403-346-6195
cindy.jefferies@reddeer.ca
Lynne Mulder, Councillor
403-341-6418, Fax: 403-346-6195
lynne.mulder@reddeer.ca
Chris Stephan, Councillor
Tara Veer, Councillor
403-358-3568, Fax: 403-340-7466
tara.veer@reddeer.ca
Frank Wong, Councillor
403-347-6514, Fax: 403-346-6195
frank.wong@reddeer.ca
Dianne Wyntjes, Councillor
Administration
Craig Curtis, City Manager
403-342-8156, Fax: 403-342-8365
craig.curtis@reddeer.ca
Lorraine Poth, Director, Corporate Services
lorraine.poth@reddeer.ca
Don Simpson, City Solicitor
Brian Simpson, Superintendent, RCMP
rcmp@reddeer.ca

Paul Goranson, Director, Development Services
403-342-8162, Fax: 403-342-8211
paul.goranson@reddeer.ca
Colleen Jensen, Director, Community Services
403-342-8323, Fax: 403-342-8222
communityservices@reddeer.ca
Scott Cameron, Manager, Social Planning
403-342-8100
communityservices@reddeer.ca
Frank Colosimo, Manager, Public Works
403-342-8238, Fax: 403-343-7074
publicworks@reddeer.ca
Kevin Joll, Manager, Transit
403-342-8225, Fax: 403-342-8116
transit@reddeer.ca
Paul Meyette, Director, Planning Division
Rod Risling, Manager, Assessment & Taxation
assessment@reddeer.ca
Greg Scott, Manager, Recreation, Parks & Culture
403-342-8159, Fax: 403-342-8222
Dave Matthews, Supervisor, Planning & Technical Services
Tom Marstaller, Superintendent, Environmental Services
403-342-8238, Fax: 403-343-7074
publicworks@reddeer.ca

St. Albert
5 St. Anne St.
St. Albert, AB T8N 3Z9
780-459-1500
Fax: 780-460-2394
stalbert@st-albert.net
www.stalbert.ca
Municipal Type: City
Incorporated: Dec. 7, 1899 *Area:* 35.04 sq km
Population in 2010: 60,138
Provincial Electoral District(s): Spruce Grove-Sturgeon-St. Albert; St. Albert
Federal Electoral District(s): Edmonton-St. Albert
Next Election: 2013 (3 year terms)
Note: Incorporated as a city on Jan. 1, 1977.
Council
Nolan Crouse, Mayor
780-459-1606, Fax: 780-459-1591
mayor@st-albert.net
Len Bracko, Councillor
780-458-6478, Fax: 780-418-2961
len@bracko.ca
Wes Broadhead, Councillor
Cathy Heron, Councillor
Roger Lemieux, Councillor
780-460-7223, Fax: 780-651-6147
jrcl@shaw.ca
Cam MacKay, Councillor
Malcolm Parker, Councillor
Administration
Bill Holtby, City Manager
780-459-1607, Fax: 780-459-1591
bholtby@st-albert.net
Gail Barrington-Moss, General Manager, Community & Protective Services
N. Jamieson, General Manager, Planning & Engineering Services
D. Screpnek, General Manager, Corporate Services
B. Treidler, General Manager, Business & Strategic Services
C. Cundy, Director, Planning & Development
D. Irving, Manager, Planning
S. Laarhuis, Chief Legislative Officer
Tracy Young, Administrative Resources Coordinator, Fire & Emergency Medical Services
780-458-2020, Fax: 780-459-7636

Spruce Grove
315 Jespersen Ave.
Spruce Grove, AB T7X 3E8
780-962-2611
Fax: 780-962-2526
info@sprucegrove.org
www.sprucegrove.org
Municipal Type: City
Incorporated: March 14, 1907 *Area:* 26.4 sq km
Population in 2010: 24,646
Provincial Electoral District(s): Spruce Grove-Sturgeon-St. Albert
Federal Electoral District(s): Edmonton-Spruce Grove
Next Election: 2013 (3 year terms)
Note: Incorporated as a city on March 1, 1986.

Council
Stuart Houston, Mayor
shouston@sprucegrove.org
Administration
Doug Lagore, City Manager
dlagore@sprucegrove.org
Kathy Chan, Treasurer
Ken Luck, Director, FCSS & Recreation
Jackie Araujo, General Manager, Community Services
780-962-7617
David Hales, General Manager, Planning & Infrastructure
780-962-7622
Robert Kosterman, Chief, Fire
780-962-4496
Jeff Mustard, Superintendent, Engineering
780-962-7624
Paul Hanlan, Supervisor, Planning & Development
Jane Holmes, Coordinator, Sustainable Development

Wetaskiwin
P.O. Box 6210
4705 - 50th Ave.
Wetaskiwin, AB T9A 2E9
780-361-4400
Fax: 780-352-0930
Toll Free Phone: 1-800-989-6899
reception@wetaskiwin.ca
www.wetaskiwin.ca
Municipal Type: City
Incorporated: Dec. 4, 1899 *Area:* 16.74 sq km
Population in 2009: 12,285
Provincial Electoral District(s): Wetaskiwin-Camrose
Federal Electoral District(s): Wetaskiwin
Next Election: 2013 (3 year terms)
Note: Incorporated as a city on May 9, 1906.
Council
Bill Elliot, Mayor
mayor@wetaskiwin.ca
Administration
Ted Gillespie, City Manager
Merlin Klassen, Fire Chief
780-361-4429, Fax: 780-352-6261
fireservices@wetaskiwin.ca

Other Municipalities in Alberta

Alberta Capital Region Wastewater Commission
23262 Township Rd. 540
Fort Saskatchewan, AB T8L 4A2
780-467-8655
Fax: 780-467-5398
Municipal Type: Water Commission
Gordon Thompson, General Manager
gthompson@acrwc.ab.ca

Athabasca Regional Waste Management Services Commission
P.O. Box 90
Athabasca, AB T9S 2A2
780-675-1117
Fax: 780-675-8881
arwmsc@telusplanet.net
Municipal Type: Water Commission
Robert Smith, Manager

Beaver Regional Waste Management Services Commission
P.O. Box 322
Ryley, AB T0B 4A0
780-663-2038
Fax: 780-663-2006
brwmsccc@telusplanet.net
www.brwmsc.com
Municipal Type: Waste Commission
Forrest Wright, CAO
Owen Ligard, Director, Operations
owen.ligard@brwmsc.com

Beaver River Regional Waste Management Commission
Bag 1010
Bonnyville, AB T9N 2J7
780-826-3951
Fax: 780-826-5064

See blue tabs following this section for Municipal Waste Management and Water & Wastewater Treatment.

Municipal Type: Water Commission
Marco Schroeninger, Manager
marco@md.bonnyville.ab.ca

Big Country Waste Management Commission
P.O. Box 1906
Hanna, AB T0J 1P0
403-854-5600
Fax: 403-854-5527
Municipal Type: Waste Commission
Greg R. Sheppard, Operations Manager

Bow Valley Waste Management Commission
Wild Earth Associates Inc.
185 Carey
Canmore, AB T1W 2R7
403-609-7229
Fax: 403-609-0320
bvwmc@wildearth.ab.ca
Municipal Type: Water Commission
John Stutz, Chair
jstutz@telusplanet.net

Capital Region Northeast Water Services Commission
10005 - 102 St.
Fort Saskatchewan, AB T8L 2C5
780-992-6207
Fax: 780-992-1375
Municipal Type: Water Commission
Dave Worman, Manager
dworman@fortsask.ca

Capital Region Parkland Water Services
c/o 315 Jesperson Ave.
Spruce Grove, AB T7X 3E8
780-962-2611
Municipal Type: Water Commission

Capital Region Southwest Water Services Commission
#101, 1101 - 5 St.
Nisku, AB T9E 2X3
780-955-3555
Fax: 780-955-3444
Municipal Type: Water Commission
Darryl Rubis, Manager
darryl@leduc-county.com

Capital Region Vegreville Corridor Water Services Commission
P.O. Box 176
Chipman, AB T0B 0W0
780-363-3982
Fax: 780-363-2386
chipmanab@primus.ca
Municipal Type: Waste Commission
Pat Tomkow, Manager

Central Peace Regional Waste Management Commission
c/o Saddle Hills County
P.O. Box 69
Spirit River, AB T0H 3G0
780-864-3760
Fax: 780-864-3904
Municipal Type: Water Commission
Cliff Travis, Chair

Cold Lake Regional Utility
5513 - 48 Ave.
Cold Lake, AB T9M 1A1
780-594-4494
Fax: 780-594-3480
Municipal Type: Water Commission

Evergreen Regional Waste Management Services Commission
5015 - 49 Ave.
St Paul, AB T0A 3A4
780-645-3301
Fax: 780-645-3104
Municipal Type: Water Commission
Dennis Bergheim, Manager

Foothills Regional Services
P.O. Box 5605
High River, AB T1V 1M7
403-652-2341
Fax: 403-652-7880
Municipal Type: Waste Commission
Bill Robinson, Sec.-Treas.
wrobins@mdfoothills.com
Irv Cherneski, Chair

Greenview Regional Waste Management Commission
P.O. Box 115
Valleyview, AB T0H 3N0
780-524-7601
Fax: 780-524-4432
Municipal Type: Water Commission
Gordon Frank, Acting Administrator

Henry Kroeger Regional Water Services Commission
P.O. Box 25
Youngstown, AB T0J 3P0
403-779-3904
Fax: 403-779-2279
Municipal Type: Waste Commission
Evelyn Manion, Manager

Highway 14 Regional Water Services
P.O. Box 322
Ryley, AB T0B 4A0
780-663-2039
Fax: 780-663-2006
brwmsccc@telusplanet.net
Municipal Type: Water Commission
Forrest Wright, CAO
brwmscfw@telusplanet.net

Highway 43 East Waste Commission Services
P.O. Box 219
Sangudo, AB T0E 2A0
780-785-3411
Fax: 780-785-2359
bweldon@vennercs.com
Municipal Type: Waste Commission
Ron Kidd, Chair
Mark Anker, Manager
780-454-9414

Kneehill Regional Water Services Commission
P.O. Box 592
Acme, AB T0M 2A0
403-546-3783
Fax: 403-546-3014
vacme@telus.net
Municipal Type: Water Commission
John Van Doesburg, Manager

Lakeland Regional Waste Management Services Commission
P.O. Box 387
Lac La Biche, AB T0A 2C0
780-623-4323
Fax: 780-623-3510
townlib@telusplanet.net
Municipal Type: Water Commission
Gordon Elliott, Chair

Lamont County Regional Solid Waste Commission
General Delivery
Lamont, AB T0B 2R0
780-895-2233
Fax: 780-895-7404
Municipal Type: Water Commission
John Stribling, Chair

Lesser Slave Lake Regional Waste Management Services Commission
P.O. Box 722
Slave Lake, AB T0G 2A0
780-369-2590
Fax: 780-369-2599
md124@md124.ca
www.md124.ca
Municipal Type: Water Commission
George Snider, Interim Manager

Lethbridge Regional Waste Management Services
P.O. Box 1594
Lethbridge, AB T1J 4K3
403-732-4722
Fax: 403-732-4328
rsnowdon@county.lethbridge.ab.ca
Municipal Type: Waste Commission
Eugene Wauters, Chair
Larry Thomson, Vice-Chair
Sandy Trocakstad, Sec.-Treas.

Lethbridge Regional Water Services Commission
c/o County of Lethbridge
#100, 905 - 4 Ave. South
Lethbridge, AB T1J 4E4
403-328-5525
Fax: 403-328-5602
rrobinson@county.lethbridge.ab.ca
Municipal Type: Water Commission
Rick Robinson, Commission Manager
Duncan Lloyd, Chair

Long Lake Regional Waste Management Commission
P.O. Box 178
Grimshaw, AB T0H 1W0
780-971-2200
Fax: 780-971-2200
llrwmsc@telusplanet.net
Municipal Type: Waste Commission
Elzina Vance, Acting Manager
May Rowe, Chair

Mackenzie Regional Waste Management Commission
9813 - 102 St.
High Level, AB T0H 1Z0
780-926-2201
Fax: 780-926-2899
landfill@highlevel.ca
Municipal Type: Water Commission
Ron Pelensky, Manager
Pat Kulscar, Chair

Mountain View Regional Waste Management Commission
1230
Didsbury, AB T0M 0W0
403-335-2005
Fax: 403-335-8132
nrkivell@telusplanet.net
Municipal Type: Water Commission
Dave Derksen, Chair

Mountain View Regional Water Services
Site 22, Box 1, RR#1
Innisfail, AB T4G 1T6
403-227-5828
Fax: 403-227-5831
mtnwater@telusplanet.net
Municipal Type: Water Commission
John Van Doesburg, Administrator

North 43 Lagoon Commission
14403 - 110 Ave.
Edmonton, AB T5N 1J7
780-454-9414
Fax: 780-452-2322
Municipal Type: Water Commission
Mark Anker, Manager

North Forty Mile Regional Waste Management Services Commission
P.O. Box 276
Bow Island, AB T0K 0G0
403-833-3805
Municipal Type: Waste Commission
Bill Ressler, Chair
Ron Lane, Vice-Chair
Roselyn Pahl, Sec.-Treas.

North Peace Regional Landfill Commission
P.O. Box 2654
Fairview, AB T0H 1L0
780-835-2576
Fax: 780-835-2579

See blue tabs following this section for Municipal Waste Management and Water & Wastewater Treatment.

Municipal Governments / British Columbia

info@nprlandfill.com
www.nprlandfill.com
Municipal Type: Water Commission
Darren Lubeck, Manager
Brent Dechant, Chair

North Red Deer River Water Services Commission
5432 - 56 Ave.
Lacombe, AB T4L 1E9
403-391-0270
Municipal Type: Water Commission
Judy Gordon, Chair

Northeast Pigeon Lake Regional Services Commission
P.O. Box 6960
Wetaskiwin, AB T9A 2G5
780-352-3321
Fax: 780-352-3486
fcoutney@telusplanet.net
Municipal Type: Water Commission
Frank Coutney, Manager
Ralph B. Johnston, Chair

Roseridge Waste Management Services Commission
P.O. Box 19
Site 1, RR#1
Morinville, AB T8R 1P4
780-939-5678
Fax: 780-939-4788
sbberry@sturgeoncounty.ab.ca
Municipal Type: Water Commission
Susan Berry, Manager
Vic Pasay, Chair

Smoky River Regional Waste Management Commission
P.O. Box 155
Falher, AB T0H 1M0
780-837-2247
Fax: 780-837-2647
tnfalher@telusplanet.net
Municipal Type: Water Commission
Carmen Ewing, Chair

Smoky River Regional Water Management Commission
P.O. Box 155
Falher, AB T0H 1M0
780-837-2247
Fax: 780-837-2647
Municipal Type: Water Commission
Margaret Tardif, Chair

South Forty Waste Services Commission
P.O. Box 307
Foremost, AB T0K 0X0
403-867-3530
Fax: 403-867-2242
Municipal Type: Water Commission
Lynden Hutchinson, Chair
lhutch@telusplanet.net

Thorhild Regional Waste Management Services Commission
P.O. Box 10
Thorhild, AB T0A 3J0
780-398-3741
Fax: 780-398-3748
Municipal Type: Water Commission
Debbie Hamilton, Acting Commission Manager
debbie@thorhild.com

Thorhild Regional Water Services Commission
P.O. Box 310
Thorhild, AB T0A 3J0
780-398-3688
Fax: 780-398-2100
dhamilton@telusplanet.net
Municipal Type: Water Commission
Debbie Hamilton, Manager

Tri Village Regional Sewage Services
Box 16, Site 1, RR#2
Carvel, AB T0E 0H0
780-963-4211
Fax: 780-963-4260
Municipal Type: Water Commission
Don Boudreaux, Chair

Two Hills Regional Waste Management Commission
P.O. Box 8
Two Hills, AB T0B 4K0
780-567-2016
Municipal Type: Water Commission
Darren Banack, Operations Manager

Vulcan District Waste Commission
P.O. Box 180
Vulcan, AB T0L 2B0
403-485-2241
Fax: 403-482-2920
countyadmin@vulcancounty.ab.ca
www.vulcancounty.ab.ca
Municipal Type: Water Commission
Merle Wyatt, Chair

Westend Regional Sewage Services
P.O. Box 330
Turner Valley, AB T0L 2A0
403-933-4744
Fax: 403-933-5377
Municipal Type: Water Commission
Sharlene Brown, Chair

Westlock Regional Waste Management Commission
10336 - 106 St.
Westlock, AB T7P 2G1
780-349-3346
Fax: 780-349-2012
Municipal Type: Water Commission
Vacant, Manager

Willow Creek Regional Waste Management Services Commission
P.O. Box 2820
Claresholm, AB T0L 0T0
403-687-2603
Fax: 403-287-2602
wcrwmsc@telusplanet.net
Municipal Type: Water Commission
Gerry McGueire, Chair

British Columbia

Sewage and wastewater is provincially regulated. This is split between the Ministry of Environment for regional districts and the Ministry of Health for individual septic tank systems. Under the Municipal Sewage Regulations, municipalities, commercial entities and industries are responsible for treating sewage, generating and using reclaimed water and disposing of wastewater. British Columbia enacted the Municipal Sewage Regulation that replaced a permit system and provides rules for treating sewage, generating and using reclaimed water, and disposing of effluent that cannot be reused. Grants of up to $10,000 are available to local governments through the Water & Sewer Infrastructure Planning Grant Program to study proposed sewer, water, groundwater or stormwater drainage facilities.

The Drinking Water Protection Act is administered by the Ministry of Health, as is the Sewerage System Regulation, replacing the Sewage Disposal Regulation, dealing with on-site wastewater management in rural and regional municipalities. Community Water Improvement Program has been allocated $80 million to improve drinking water and wastewater management, with local governments responsible for an additional $40 million.

Regional districts were set up to initiate programs and develop regulations to reduce the amount of solid waste being sent to the 125 landfills in the province. British Columbia has reduced the amount of solid waste being sent to landfills by nearly 40%. The Environmental Management Act (July, 2004) accelerates and simplifies the process of rehabilitating low-risk contaminated sites. The Liquid Waste Management Plan provides guidance to local government seeking an approved liquid waste plant. The Organic Matter Recycling Regulation governs the production, quality and application of certain types of organic matter.

Product stewardship programs exist for the following: beverage containers, based on deposit refunds; lead acid batteries, funded from a $5 levy on the sale of all new vehicle type lead acid batteries weighing more than 2 kg; medications; paints; scrap tires, funded through a $3 levy on new tires; solvents, flammable liquids or gases; pesticides; used lubricating oil; household hazardous waste.

The Greenhouse Gas Action Guide assists local governments carry out initiatives to decrease greenhouse gases.

Under the federal government's New Deal for Cities, British Columbia received $635.6 million in federal gas tax funding from 2005 to 2010 for municipal infrastructure projects such as transit, clean drinking water, improved wastewater infrastructure, improved air quality.

Counties & Municipal Districts in British Columbia

Alberni-Clayoquot
3008 - 5 Ave.
Port Alberni, BC V9Y 2E3
250-720-2700
Fax: 250-723-1327
mailbox@acrd.bc.ca
www.acrd.bc.ca
Municipal Type: Regional Districts
Incorporated: April 21, 1966 Area: 6,596.58 sq km
Population in 2006: 28,601
Next Election: Nov. 2011 (3 year terms)
Hira Chopra, Chair
250-723-2146, Fax: 250-723-1003
citypa@portalberni.ca
Wendy Thompson, Deputy Secretary
250-720-2706, Fax: 250-723-1327
wendy.thomson@acrd.bc.ca
Sean McGinn, Coordinator, Public Works
250-720-2714
smcginn@acrd.bc.ca
Riley Varns, West Coast Landfill
250-726-7176
Robert A. Harper, Administrator
rharper@acrd.bc.ca
Richard Zoet, Bamfield Water System
250-728-1237
Cyril Johnson, Millstream Water System
250-726-7088
Mike Irg, Manager, Planning & Development
250-720-2710, Fax: 250-723-1327
mirg@acrd.bc.ca

Bulkley-Nechako
P.O. Box 820
37, 3rd Ave.
Burns Lake, BC V0J 1E0
250-692-3195
Fax: 250-692-3305
Toll Free Phone: 1-800-320-3339
inquiries@rdbn.bc.ca
www.rdbn.bc.ca
Municipal Type: Regional Districts
Incorporated: Feb. 1, 1966 Area: 73,440.95 sq km
Population in 2006: 38,243
Next Election: Nov. 2011 (3 year terms)
Eileen Benedict, Chair
250-692-3195, Fax: 250-692-3305
Jason Llewellyn, Director, Planning
250-692-3195, Fax: 250-692-3305
jason.llewellyn@rdbn.bc.ca
Janine Dougall, Director, Environmental Services
250-692-3195
janine.dougall@rdbn.bc.ca
Rory McKenzie, Supervisor, Field Operations, Environmental Services
250-692-3195, Fax: 250-692-3305
rory.mckenzie@rdbn.bc.ca
Gail Chapman, CAO
250-692-3195, Fax: 250-692-3305
gail.chapman@rdbn.bc.ca

Capital Regional District
625 Fisgard St.
Victoria, BC V8W 1R7
250-360-3000
Fax: 250-360-3234
Mailing address: PO Box 1000, Victoria, BC V8W 2S6
corporatecommunications@crd.bc.ca
www.crd.bc.ca

See blue tabs following this section for Municipal Waste Management and Water & Wastewater Treatment.

Municipal Type: Regional Districts
Incorporated: Feb. 1, 1966 Area: 2,341.02 sq km
Population in 2006: 345,164
Provincial Electoral District(s): Juan de Fuca; Southern Gulf Islands; Salt Spring Island.
Next Election: Nov. 2011 (3 year terms)
Note: Member municipalities: Central Saanich; Colwood; Esquimalt; Highlands; Langford; Metchosin; North Saanich; Oak Bay; Saanich; Sidney; Sooke; Victoria; and View Royal.
Geoff Young, Board Chair
250-385-5711
Diana Lokken, General Manager, Corporate Services
250-360-3010
Larissa Hutcheson, General Manager, Environmental Sustainability
250-360-3000
Tracy Corbett, Senior Manager, Regional Planning Services
250-360-3244
Dan Telford, Senior Manager, Environmental Engineering
250-360-3064
Glenn Harris, Senior Manager, Environmental Protection
250-360-3090
Alan Summers, Senior Manager, Environmental Resource Management
250-260-3080
Tom Watkins, Manager, Solid Waste Operations
250-360-3030
Malcolm MacPhail, Senior Manager, Transportation Planning
250-360-3052
Jack Hull, General Manager, Integrated Water Services
250-474-9604
Ted Robbins, Senior Manager, Water Management
250-360-3061
Jan van Niekerk, Senior Manager, Integrated Water Services - Customer & Technical Services
250-474-9655
Tim Tanton, Senior Manager, Infrastructure Engineering
250-474-9611
Gordon Joyce, Senior Manager, Watershed Protection
250-474-9621
John Craveiro, Manager, Environmental Resource Management Policy & Planning
250-360-3164
Chris Neilson, Senior Manager, Human Resources
250-360-3282
Rita Estock, Senior Manager, Financial Services
250-360-3011

Cariboo
180 North 3rd Ave., #D
Williams Lake, BC V2G 2A4
250-392-3351
Fax: 250-392-2812
Toll Free Phone: 1-800-665-1636
mailbox@cariboord.bc.ca
www.cariboord.bc.ca
Municipal Type: Regional Districts
Incorporated: July 9, 1968 Area: 80,629.34 sq km
Population in 2006: 58,920
Next Election: Nov. 2011 (3 year terms)
Al Richmond, Chairperson
Janis Bell, CAO
Mitch Minchau, Supervisor, Environmental Services
mminchae@cariboord.bc.ca
Rick Brundrige, Manager, Planning Services
rbrundrige@cariboord.bc.ca
Gordon Gillette, Manager, 108 Greenbelt
ggillette@cariboord.bc.ca
Rowena Bastien, Supervisor, Protective Services
rbastien@cariboord.bc.ca

Central Kootenay
P.O. Box 590
202 Lakeside Dr.
Nelson, BC V1L 5R4
250-352-6665
Fax: 250-352-9300
Toll Free Phone: 1-800-268-7325
info@rdck.bc.ca
www.rdck.bc.ca
Municipal Type: Regional Districts
Incorporated: Nov. 30, 1965 Area: 22,130.72 sq km
Population in 2006: 55,883
Next Election: Nov. 2011 (3 year terms)
Gary Wright, Board Chair
office@newdenver.ca
Jim Gustafson, CAO
Grant Roeland, CFO
Marianne Crowe, Manager, Engineering & Environmental Services
wastedept@rdck.bc.ca
Dave Wahn, Sr. Planner

Central Okanagan
1450 KLO Rd.
Kelowna, BC V1W 3Z4
250-763-4918
Fax: 250-763-0606
info@cord.bc.ca
www.cord.bc.ca
Municipal Type: Regional Districts
Incorporated: Aug. 24, 1967 Area: 2,904.01 sq km
Population in 2006: 162,276
Next Election: Nov. 2011 (3 year terms)
Robert Hobson, Chair
Robert.Hobson@cord.bc.ca
Harold Reay, Administrator
Bill Vos, Director, Parks & Recreation
250-868-5232
parks@cord.bc.ca
Ken Arcuri, Director, Planning
250-868-5227
planning@cord.bc.ca
Carol Suhan, Coordinator, Waste Reduction
250-469-6259
csuhan@cord.bc.ca
Hilary Hettinga, Director, Engineering Services
250-868-5241
engineer@cord.bc.ca

Columbia-Shuswap
P.O. Box 978
781 Marine Park Dr. NE
Salmon Arm, BC V1E 4P1
250-832-8194
Fax: 250-832-3375
Toll Free Phone: 1-888-248-2773
enquiries@csrd.bc.ca
www.csrd.bc.ca
Municipal Type: Regional Districts
Incorporated: Nov. 30, 1965 Area: 29,003.97 sq km
Population in 2006: 50,141
Next Election: Nov. 2011 (3 year terms)
Marty Bootsma, Chair
mbootsma@salmonarm.ca
Charles Hamilton, Administrator
admin@csrd.bc.ca, chamilton@csrd.bc.ca
Doug Dymond, Manager, Works Services
ddymond@csrd.bc.ca
Geoff Power, Manager, Development Services
gpower@csrd.bc.ca
Rhona Martin, Chair, Shuswap Emergency Management Program
semp@csrd.bc.ca
Darcy Mooney, Coordinator, Waste Management
dmooney@csrd.bc.ca
Hamish Kassa, Coordinator, Environmental Services
hkassa@csrd.bc.ca

Comox Valley
600 Comox Rd.
Courtenay, BC V9N 3P6
250-334-6000
Fax: 250-334-4358
Toll Free Phone: 1-800-331-6007
administration@comoxvalleyrd.ca
www.comoxvalleyrd.ca
Municipal Type: Regional Districts
Incorporated: Aug. 19, 1965 Area: 20,013.48 sq km
Population in 2006: 101,595
Next Election: Nov. 2011 (3 year terms)
Fred Bates, Chair
fbates@cumberlandbc.net
Debra Oakman, CAO
W. Whyte, Manager, Water Utilities & Services
Graeme Faris, General Manager, Operational Services
operations@rdcs.bc.ca
Ian Smith, General Manager, Community Services
Marci Crossan, Manager, Operational Communications
T. Knight, Manager, Planning Operations
J. Elliott, Manager, Wastewater Operations
R. Boogaards, General Manager, Park Services
parks@rdcs.bc.ca
B. Rees, Manager, Parks

Cowichan Valley
175 Ingram St.
Duncan, BC V9L 1N8
250-746-2500
Fax: 250-746-2513
cvrd@cvrd.bc.ca
www.cvrd.bc.ca
Municipal Type: Regional Districts
Incorporated: Sept. 26, 1967 Area: 3,473.12 sq km
Population in 2006: 73,338
Next Election: Nov. 2011 (3 year terms)
Gerry Giles, Chair
chairperson@cvrd.bc.ca
Brian Dennison, Manager, Engineering
Frank Raimondo, Administrator
Bob McDonald, Program Coordinator, Solid Waste Reduction
Tom Anderson, Manager, Development Services
Brian Farquhar, Manager, Parks
Dave Leitch, Manager, Utilities
Warren Jones, CAO
wjones@cvrd.bc.ca

East Kootenay
19 - 24 Ave. South
Cranbrook, BC V1C 3H8
250-489-2791
Fax: 250-489-3498
Toll Free Phone: 1-888-478-7335
rdek@rdek.bc.ca
www.rdek.bc.ca
Municipal Type: Regional Districts
Incorporated: Nov. 30, 1965 Area: 27,560.49 sq km
Population in 2006: 54,932
Next Election: Nov. 2011 (3 year terms)
Norman Walter, Chair
norm.walter@gmail.com
Andrew McLeod, Manager, Planning & Development Services
amcleod@rdek.bc.ca
Eric Sharpe, Manager, Environmental Services
esharpe@rdek.bc.ca
Dan McNeill, Manager, Building & Protective Services
dmcneill@rdek.bc.ca
Loree Duczek, Public Education Coordinator, Engineering & Environmental Services
lduczek@rdek.bc.ca
Carol Lind, Coordinator, Emergency Services
clind@rdek.bc.ca
Brian Funke, Superintendent, Utilities
bfunke@rdek.bc.ca
Eric Sharpe, Superintendent, Solid Waste
esharpe@rdek.bc.ca
Lee-Ann Crane, CAO & Manager, Administration
lcrane@rdek.bc.ca

Fraser Valley
#1, 45950 Cheam Ave.
Chilliwack, BC V2P 1N6
604-702-5000
Fax: 604-792-9684
Toll Free Phone: 1-800-528-0061
info@fvrd.bc.ca
www.fvrd.com
Municipal Type: Regional Districts
Incorporated: Dec. 12, 1995 Area: 13,361.74 sq km
Population in 2006: 257,031
Next Election: Nov. 2011 (3 year terms)
Patricia Ross, Chair
pross@fvrd.bc.ca
Gerald H. Kingston, CAO
gkingston@fvrd.bc.ca
Gale McMahon, Assistant, Administration
Doug Wilson, Manager, Parks
dwilson@fvrd.bc.ca
Tareq Islam, Director, Engineering
tislam@fvrd.bc.ca
Siri Bertelsen, Planner, Regional Growth
Hugh Sloan, Director, Planning
hsloan@fvrd.bc.ca

Municipal Governments / British Columbia

Mike Hofer, Coordinator, Environmental Services & Operations
mhofer@fvrd.bc.ca
Lance Lilley, Planner, Watershed
llilley@fvrd.bc.ca
Mike Hofer, Manager, Environmental Services & Operations
mhofer@fvrd.bc.ca

Fraser-Fort George
155 George St.
Prince George, BC V2L 1P8
250-960-4400
Fax: 250-563-7520
Toll Free Phone: 1-800-667-1959
district@rdffg.bc.ca
www.rdffg.bc.ca
Municipal Type: Regional Districts
Incorporated: March 8, 1967 *Area:* 50,705.84 sq km
Population in 2006: 92,063
Next Election: Nov. 2011 (3 year terms)
Art Kaehn, Chair
akaehn@rdffg.bc.ca
Tom Yates, General Manager, Corporate Services
tyates@rdffg.bc.ca
Terry McEachen, General Manager, Development & Community Services
tmceachen@rdffg.bc.ca
Diane Hiscock, General Manager, Financial Services
dhiscock@rdffg.bc.ca
Jim Martin, General Manager, Environmental Services
jmartin@rdffg.bc.ca

Kitimat-Stikine
#300, 4545 Lazelle Ave.
Terrace, BC V8G 4E1
250-615-6100
Fax: 250-635-9222
Toll Free Phone: 1-800-663-3208
info@rdks.bc.ca
www.rdks.bc.ca
Municipal Type: Regional Districts
Incorporated: Sept. 14, 1967 *Area:* 91,917.88 sq km
Population in 2006: 30,307
Next Election: Nov. 2011 (3 year terms)
Harry Nyce, Board Chair
Robert Marcellin, Administrator
Roger Tooms, Manager, Works & Services
250-615-6100
rtooms@rdks.bc.ca
Andrew Webber, Manager, Planning & Economic Development
awebber@rdks.bc.ca
Ted Pellegrino, Planner
tpellegrino@rdks.bc.ca

Kootenay Boundary
#202, 843 Rossland Ave.
Trail, BC V1R 4S8
250-368-9148
Fax: 250-368-3990
Toll Free Phone: 1-800-355-7352 (BC only)
ekumar@rdkb.com
www.rdkb.com
Municipal Type: Regional Districts
Incorporated: Feb. 22, 1966 *Area:* 8,095.63 sq km
Population in 2006: 30,742
Next Election: Nov. 2011 (3 year terms)
Marguerite Rotvold, Chair
250-449-2222
John MacLean, CAO
jmaclean@rdkb.com
Raymond Gaudart, Coordinator, Resource Recovery
zerowaste@rdkb.com
Marten Kruysse, Officer, Economic Development
Mark Andison, Director, Planning

Metro Vancouver
4330 Kingsway
Burnaby, BC V5H 4G8
604-432-6200
Fax: 604-436-6901
icentre@metrovancouver.org
www.metrovancouver.org
Municipal Type: Regional Districts
Incorporated: June 29, 1967 *Area:* 2,877.36 sq km
Population in 2006: 2,109,031
Next Election: Nov. 2011 (3 year terms)

Lois Jackson, Chair
mayor@corp.delta.bc.ca
George Peary, Directors, Ward(s): Abbotsford
Moe Gill, Directors, Ward(s): Abbotsford
Hal Weinberg, Directors, Ward(s): Anmore
Ralph Drew, Directors, Ward(s): Belcarra
Peter Frinton, Directors, Ward(s): Bowen Island
Derek Corrigan, Directors, Ward(s): Burnaby
Sav Dhaliwal, Directors, Ward(s): Burnaby
Colleen Jordan, Directors, Ward(s): Burnaby
Mae Reid, Directors, Ward(s): Coquitlam
Richard Stewart, Directors, Ward(s): Coquitlam
Lois Jackson, Directors, Ward(s): Delta
Maria Harris, Directors, Ward(s): Electoral Area A
Gayle Martin, Directors, Ward(s): Langley City
Rick Green, Directors, Ward(s): Langley Township
Brenda Boughton, Directors, Ward(s): Lions Bay
Judy Dueck, Directors, Ward(s): Maple Ridge
Wayne Wright, Directors, Ward(s): New Westminster
Darrell Mussatto, Directors, Ward(s): North Vancouver City
Richard Walton, Directors, Ward(s): North Vancouver District
Don MacLean, Directors, Ward(s): Pitt Meadows
Greg Moore, Directors, Ward(s): Port Coquitlam
Joe Trasolini, Directors, Ward(s): Port Moody
Malcolm Brodie, Directors, Ward(s): Richmond
Harold Steves, Directors, Ward(s): Richmond
Linda Hepner, Directors, Ward(s): Surrey
Marvin Hunt, Directors, Ward(s): Surrey
Judy Villeneuve, Directors, Ward(s): Surrey
Dianne Watts, Directors, Ward(s): Surrey
George Chow, Directors, Ward(s): Vancouver
Heather Deal, Directors, Ward(s): Vancouver
Raymond Louie, Directors, Ward(s): Vancouver
Andrea Reimer, Directors, Ward(s): Vancouver
Gregor Robertson, Directors, Ward(s): Vancouver
Pamela Goldsmith-Jones, Directors, Ward(s): West Vancouver
Catherine Ferguson, Directors, Ward(s): White Rock
Johnny Carline, CAO
Jim Rusnak, CFO
Linda Shore, Manager, Human Resources
Hugh Kellas, Manager, Policy & Planning
Heather Shoemaker, Manager, Corporate Relations
Tracy Husoy, Manager, Purchasing & Risk
Tim Jervis, P.Eng., Manager, Engineering & Construction
Ed Andrusiak, Manager, Regional Parks
Toivo Allas, Manager, Policy & Planning
Malcolm Graham, Manager, Labour Relations
Doug Humphris, P.Eng., Manager, Operations & Maintenance
Delia Laglagaron, Deputy CAO

Mount Waddington
P.O. Box 729
Port McNeill, BC V0N 2R0
250-956-3161
Fax: 250-956-3232
info@rdmw.bc.ca
www.rdmw.bc.ca
Municipal Type: Regional Districts
Incorporated: June 13, 1966 *Area:* 20,288.19 sq km
Population in 2006: 11,651
Next Election: Nov. 2011 (3 year terms)
Al Huddlestan, Chair
Greg Fletcher, Administrator
gfletcher@rdmw.bc.ca
Neil Smith, Manager, Economic Development
Paddy Hinton, Coordinator, Parks
Karl Digby, Supervisor, Salvage
Madeline McDonald, Manager, Local Services
250-956-3301
mmcdonald@rdmw.bc.ca
Joe MacKenzie, Treasurer

Nanaimo
6300 Hammond Bay Rd.
Nanaimo, BC V9T 6N2
250-390-4111
Fax: 250-390-4163
Toll Free Phone: 1-877-607-4111
corpsrv@rdn.bc.ca
www.rdn.bc.ca
Municipal Type: Regional Districts
Incorporated: Aug. 24, 1967 *Area:* 2,034.93 sq km
Population in 2006: 138,631
Next Election: Nov. 2011 (3 year terms)

Joseph Stanhope, Chair
jstanhope@shaw.ca
Carol Mason, CAO
Neil Connelly, General Manager, Community Services
Wayne Moorman, P.Eng., Manager, Engineering Services
Dennis Trudeau, Manager, Transportation & Solid Waste
John Finnie, Manager, Water & Wastewater
250-390-6560, Fax: 250-390-1542
envsrv@rdn.bc.ca
Alan Stanley, Coordinator, Solid Waste Program
John Finnie, General Manager, Environmental Services
250-390-6560, Fax: 250-390-1542
envsrv@rdn.bc.ca
Pam Shaw, Deputy Manager, Community Planning
250-390-6510, Fax: 250-390-7511
planning@rdn.bc.ca
Tom Osborne, General Manager, Parks & Recreation
Mike Donnelly, Manager, Utilities

North Okanagan
9848 Aberdeen Rd.
Coldstream, BC V1B 2K9
250-550-3700
Fax: 250-550-3701
info@nord.ca
www.nord.ca
Municipal Type: Regional Districts
Incorporated: Nov. 9, 1965 *Area:* 7,511.94 sq km
Population in 2006: 77,301
Next Election: Nov. 2011 (3 year terms)
Herman Halvorson, Chair
Greg Betts, Administrator
250-550-3714
greg.betts@rdno.ca
Nicole Kohnert, Manager, Solid Waste
nicole.kohnert@rdno.ca
Al McNiven, Director, Greater Vernon Parks & Recreation District
250-550-3664
Rob Smailes, Manager, Development Services
rob.smailes@rdno.ca
Doug Buchholz, Officer, Protective Services
doug.buchholz@rdno.ca
John Slater, Chair, Okanagan Basin Water Board
Maggie Knox, Manager, Infrastructure Services
maggie.knox@rdno.ca
Steve Noakes, Planner
steve.noakes@rdno.ca
Joseph Kennedy, Coordinator, Solid Waste & Noxious Weeds
joseph.kennedy@rdno.ca
Greg Armour, Field Supervisor, Okanagan Basin Water Board
Nicole Marzinzik, Coordinator, Waste Reduction
nicole.marzinzik@rdno.ca

Okanagan-Similkameen
101 Martin St.
Penticton, BC V2A 5J9
250-492-0237
Fax: 250-492-0063
Toll Free Phone: 1-877-610-3737
info@rdos.bc.ca
www.rdos.bc.ca
Municipal Type: Regional Districts
Incorporated: March 4, 1966 *Area:* 10,412.64 sq km
Population in 2006: 79,475
Next Election: Nov. 2011 (3 year terms)
Dan Ashton, Chair
Bill Newell, CAO
D. Hamilton, Superintendent, Solid Waste Management
Susanne Theurer, Director, Planning & Building Inspection
stheurer@rdos.bc.ca
D. Vaykovich, Coordinator, Special Projects
Andrew Reeder, Manager, Engineering Services

Peace River
P.O. Box 810
1981 Alaska Ave.
Dawson Creek, BC V1G 4H8
250-784-3200
Fax: 250-784-3201
prrd.dc@prrd.bc.ca
www.peaceriverrd.bc.ca
Municipal Type: Regional Districts
Incorporated: Oct. 31, 1987 *Area:* 117,761.07 sq km

See blue tabs following this section for Municipal Waste Management and Water & Wastewater Treatment.

Municipal Governments / British Columbia

Population in 2006: 58,264
Next Election: Nov. 2011 (3 year terms)
Karen Goodings, Chair
Fred Banham, CAO
250-784-3208
George Kunz, Supervisor, Public Works
Jeff Rahn, Manager, Regional Solid Waste Management
Bruce General Manager, Director, Development Services
Shannon Anderson, General Manager, Environmental Services
Paul Solmes, Coordinator, Parks & Recreation

Powell River
5776 Marine Ave.
Powell River, BC V8A 2M4
604-483-3231
Fax: 604-483-2229
administration@powellriverrd.bc.ca
www.powellriverrd.bc.ca
Municipal Type: Regional Districts
Incorporated: Dec. 19, 1967 *Area:* 5,092.05 sq km
Population in 2006: 19,599
Next Election: Nov. 2011 (3 year terms)
Colin Palmer, Chair
Frances Ladret, CAO
Don Turner, Regional Planner
Mike Bolch, Manager, Community & Infrastructure Services

Skeena-Queen Charlotte
100 - 1st Ave. East
Prince Rupert, BC V8J 1A6
250-624-2002
Fax: 250-627-8493
Toll Free Phone: 1-888-301-2002
sqcrd@sqcrd.bc.ca
www.sqcrd.bc.ca
Municipal Type: Regional Districts
Incorporated: Aug. 17, 1967 *Area:* 19,871.85 sq km
Population in 2006: 19,664
Next Election: Nov. 2011 (3 year terms)
Barry Pages, Chair
John Farrell, Interim Administrator
Bob Thompson, Chair, Mainland Solid Waste Advisory Committee
Janet Brown, Chair, Islands Solid Waste Advisory Committee
iswac@islands.net
Tim DesChamp, Operations Supervisor, Regional Recycling
Janet Beil, Director, Planning
jbeil@sqcrd.ca
Thor Collison, Contact, Islands Landfill
Barry Pages, Chair, Skeena-Queen Charlotte Regional District Board of Directors

Squamish-Lillooet
P.O. Box 219
Pemberton, BC V0N 2L0
604-894-6371
Fax: 604-894-6526
Toll Free Phone: 1-800-298-7753
info@slrd.bc.ca
www.slrd.bc.ca
Municipal Type: Regional Districts
Incorporated: Oct. 3, 1968 *Area:* 16,353.66 sq km
Population in 2006: 35,225
Next Election: Nov. 2011 (3 year terms)
Russ Oakley, Chair
Paul Edgington, CAO
pedgington@slrd.bc.ca
Rudy D'Souza, Manager, Utilities & Environmental Services
rdsouza@slrd.bc.ca
Steven Olmstead, Manager, Planning & Development
Wendy Horan, Coordinator, Waste Reduction
zerowaste@slrd.bc.ca

Sunshine Coast
1975 Field Rd.
Sechelt, BC V0N 3A1
604-885-6800
Fax: 604-885-7909
info@scrd.bc.ca
www.scrd.bc.ca
Municipal Type: Regional Districts
Incorporated: Jan. 4, 1967 *Area:* 3,778.08 sq km
Population in 2006: 27,759
Next Election: Nov. 2011 (3 year terms)
Donna Shugar, Chair

John France, CAO
604-885-6800
Paul Fenwick, General Manager, Community Services
Bryan Shoji, General Manager, Infrastructure Services

Thompson-Nicola
#300, 465 Victoria St.
Kamloops, BC V2C 2A9
250-377-8673
Fax: 250-372-5048
admin@tnrd.bc.ca
www.tnrd.bc.ca
Municipal Type: Regional Districts
Incorporated: Nov. 24, 1967 *Area:* 44,475.73 sq km
Population in 2006: 122,286
Next Election: Nov. 2011 (3 year terms)
Peter Milobar, Chair
mayor@kamloops.ca
Greg Toma, CAO
Andy Swetlishoff, Director, Development Services
Don May, P.Eng., Manager, Environmental Health Services
dmay@tnrd.bc.ca

Major Municipalities in British Columbia

Abbotsford
32315 South Fraser Way
Abbotsford, BC V2T 1W7
604-853-2281
Fax: 604-853-1934
Toll Free Phone: 1-866-853-2281
info@abbotsford.ca
www.abbotsford.ca; twitter.com/City_Abbotsford
Municipal Type: City
Incorporated: Jan. 1, 1995 *Area:* 359.36 sq km
County or District: Fraser Valley; *Population in 2006:* 123,864
Provincial Electoral District(s): Abbotsford-Mission; Abbotsford South; Abbotsford West
Federal Electoral District(s): Abbotsford
Next Election: Nov. 2011 (3 year terms)
Council
George Peary, Mayor
Les Barkman, Councillor
Simon Gibson, Councillor
Mohindar (Moe) Gill, Councillor
Lynne Harris, Councillor
Dave Loewen, Councillor
Bill MacGregor, Councillor
Patricia Ross, Councillor
John Smith, Councillor
Administration
Bill Flitton, City Clerk
604-864-5603
bflitton@abbotsford.ca
Judy Lewis, General Manager, Finance & Corporate Services
604-864-5532, Fax: 604-853-1934
jlewis@abbotsford.ca
Jay Teichroeb, General Manager, Economic Development/Development Services
604-864-5525
jteichroeb@abbotsford.ca
Jim Gordon, P.Eng., General Manager, Engineering & Regional Utilities
604-864-5556
jgordon@abbotsford.ca
Mark Taylor, General Manager, Parks, Recreation & Culture
604-859-3134, Fax: 604-853-1934
mtaylor@abbotsford.ca
Don Beer, Fire Chief
604-853-2281
dbeer@abbotsford.ca
Bob Rich, Chief Constable, Abbotsford Police Department
604-864-4724, Fax: 604-864-4809
Karen Sinclair, Manager, Strategic & Community Planning
604-557-4416
ksinclair@abbotsford.ca
Mike Pastro, General Manager, Airport
604-864-5651
mpastro@abbotsford.ca
Frank Pizzuto, City Manager
604-864-5501
fpizzuto@abbotsford.ca

Burnaby
4949 Canada Way
Burnaby, BC V5G 1M2
604-294-7944
Fax: 604-294-7537
postmaster@burnaby.ca
www.city.burnaby.bc.ca
Municipal Type: City
Incorporated: Sept. 22, 1892 *Area:* 89.12 sq km
County or District: Greater Vancouver; *Population in 2006:* 202,799
Provincial Electoral District(s): Burnaby-Edmonds; Burnaby North; Burnaby-Willingdon
Federal Electoral District(s): Burnaby-Douglas; Burnaby-New Westminster
Next Election: Nov. 2011 (3 year terms)
Council
Derek Corrigan, Mayor
Pietro Calendino, Councillor
Richard Chang, Councillor
Sav Dhaliwal, Councillor
Dan Johnston, Councillor
Colleen Jordan, Councillor
Anne Kang, Councillor
Paul McDonell, Councillor
Nick Volkow, Councillor
Administration
Debbie R. Comis, City Clerk
604-294-7290, Fax: 604-294-7537
Rick Earle, Director, Finance
604-294-7360, Fax: 604-294-7544
rick.earle@burnaby.ca
Basil Luksun, Director, Planning & Building
604-294-7432
D. Ellenwood, Director, Parks, Recreation & Cultural Services
604-294-7450, Fax: 604-294-7201
Lambert Chu, Director, Engineering
604-294-7460, Fax: 604-294-7425
Vacant, Deputy Director, Engineering
604-294-7466, Fax: 604-294-7425
Robert H. Moncur, City Manager
604-294-7110, Fax: 604-294-7733
Chad Turpin, Deputy City Manager
604-294-7110, Fax: 604-294-7733
B.R. Rose, City Solicitor
604-294-7382, Fax: 604-294-7985
Patrick Shek, P.Eng, Chief Building Inspector
Bob Cook, Fire Chief
604-294-7195, Fax: 604-294-0490
K. Basi, Coordinator, Emergency Program, Fax: 604-294-7733
Dipak Dattani, Supervisor, Environmental Services
604-294-7771, Fax: 604-294-7425
Robyn Wark, Planner, Ecosystem
604-294-7297, Fax: 604-570-3680
Gisele Caron, Agent, Purchasing, Fax: 604-294-7529

Campbell River
301 St. Ann's Rd.
Campbell River, BC V9W 4C7
250-286-5700
Fax: 250-286-5760
info@campbellriver.ca
www.campbellriver.ca
Municipal Type: City
Incorporated: June 24, 1947 *Area:* 143.48 sq km
County or District: Comox-Strathcona; *Population in 2006:* 29,572
Provincial Electoral District(s): North Island
Federal Electoral District(s): Vancouver Island North
Next Election: Nov. 2011 (3 year terms)
Council
Charlie Cornfield, Mayor
mayor.cornfield@campbellriver.ca
Administration
Tom Stevens, City Manager
tom.stevens@campbellriver.ca
Rob Harley, By-law Enforcement Officer & Manager, Property Services
Larry Samson, Coordinator, Provincial Emergency
Paul Stanton, Manager, Planning Services
Dave Morris, Manager, Materials
William Halstead, GM, Corporate Services
Rob Neufeld, GM, Operations Services
Ross Milnthrop, GM, Parks, Recreation & Culture
Debra Law, Manager, Finance

See blue tabs following this section for Municipal Waste Management and Water & Wastewater Treatment.

Municipal Governments / British Columbia

Ron Neufeld, Manager, Engineering Services
Gordon Brown, Manager, Public Works
Mary Ellen Callaghan, Manager, Information Services
Pat Mulcahy, Manager, Human Resources
Tyler Massee, Manager, Airport
Larry Stright, RCMP Inspector
Rob Owens, Fire Chief

Chilliwack
8550 Young Rd
Chilliwack, BC V2P 8A4
604-792-9311
Fax: 604-795-8443
info@chilliwack.com
www.chilliwack.com
Municipal Type: City
Incorporated: Jan. 1, 1980 *Area:* 260.19 sq km
County or District: Fraser Valley; *Population in 2006:* 69,217
Provincial Electoral District(s): Chilliwack-Kent, Chilliwack-Sumas
Federal Electoral District(s): Chilliwack-Fraser Canyon
Next Election: Nov. 2011 (3 year terms)
Council
Sharon Gaetz, Mayor
Sue Attrill, Councillor
Pat Clark, Councillor
Ken Huttema, Councillor
Diane Janzen, Councillor
Stewart McLean, Councillor
Chuck Stam, Councillor
Administration
Robert Carnegie, Clerk & Director, Corporate Services
604-793-2910
rcarnegie@chilliwack.com
Kathleen Fraser, Director, Finance
604-792-9311, Fax: 604-795-8443
David Blain, Director, Engineering
604-793-2841, Fax: 604-795-8443
Ian Crane, Director, Municipal Development
604-793-2906, Fax: 604-793-8443
Glen MacPherson, Director, Public Works
604-792-9311, Fax: 604-795-8443
Gordon Pederson, Director, Parks, Recreation & Culture
604-792-9311, Fax: 604-795-8443
Peter Monteith, CAO
604-793-2903, Fax: 604-792-2561
pmonteith@chilliwack.com
Rick Ryall, Fire Chief
604-792-9311, Fax: 604-795-8443
Janet Demarcke, Manager, Environmental Services
604-792-9311, Fax: 604-795-8443
Paul Whitehouse, Manager, Purchasing
604-792-9311, Fax: 604-795-8443
whitehouse@chilliwack.com
Keith Robinson, Superintendent, RCMP
604-702-4086, Fax: 604-702-4045
keith.robinson@rcmp-grc.gc.ca
Tara Friesen, Sr. Specialist, Environmental Services
604-792-9311, Fax: 604-795-8443

Colwood
3300 Wishart Rd.
Victoria, BC V9C 1R1
250-478-5541
Fax: 250-478-7516
generalinquiry@colwood.ca
www.colwood.bc.ca
Municipal Type: City
Incorporated: June 24, 1985 *Area:* 17.76 sq km
County or District: Capital; *Population in 2006:* 14,687
Provincial Electoral District(s): Esquimalt-Metchosin
Federal Electoral District(s): Esquimalt-Juan de Fuca
Next Election: Nov. 2011 (3 year terms)
Council
David Saunders, Mayor
mayor@colwood.bc.ca
Administration
Chris Pease, CAO
cpease@colwood.ca
Adia Mavrikos, Director, Finance
amavrikos@colwood.ca
Simon Lawrence, Director, Planning
250-478-5541
slawrence@colwood.bc.ca

Dan Brazier, Manager, Public Works
250-474-4133
dbrazier@colwood.bc.ca
Russ Cameron, Fire Chief
rcameron@colwood.bc.ca

Comox
Town Hall
1809 Beaufort Ave.
Comox, BC V9M 1R9
250-339-2202
Fax: 250-339-7110
town@comox.ca
www.comox.ca
Municipal Type: City
Incorporated: Jan. 14, 1946 *Area:* 15.16 sq km
County or District: Comox-Strathcona; *Population in 2006:* 12,136
Provincial Electoral District(s): Comox Valley
Federal Electoral District(s): Vancouver Island North
Next Election: Nov. 2011 (3 year terms)
Council
Paul Ives, Mayor
town@comox.ca
Administration
Gord Schreiner, Fire Chief
250-339-2432, Fax: 250-339-1988
gschreiner@comox.ca
Allan Fraser, Superintendent, Parks
250-339-2421
afraser@comox.ca
Marvin Kamenz, Municipal Planner
250-339-1118
mkamenz@comox.ca
Glenn Westendorp, Superintendent, Public Works
250-339-2485, Fax: 250-890-0698
gwestendorp@comox.ca
Richard Kanigan, Administrator
rkanigan@comox.ca

Coquitlam
3000 Guildford Way
Coquitlam, BC V3B 7N2
604-927-3000
Fax: 604-927-3015
feedback@coquitlam.ca
www.coquitlam.ca
Municipal Type: City
Incorporated: July 25, 1891 *Area:* 121.69 sq km
County or District: Greater Vancouver; *Population in 2006:* 114,565
Provincial Electoral District(s): Coquitlam-Maillardville
Federal Electoral District(s): New Westminster-Coquitlam; Port Moody-Westwood-Port Coquitlam
Next Election: Nov. 2011 (3 year terms)
Council
Richard Stewart, Mayor
rstewart@coquitlam.ca
Brent Asmundson, Councillor
Fin Donnelly, Councillor
Barrie Lynch, Councillor
Doug Macdonell, Councillor
Mae Reid, Councillor
Linda Reimer, Councillor
Selina Robinson, Councillor
Lou Sekora, Councillor
Administration
Jay Gilbert, City Clerk
jgilbert@coquitlam.ca
Sheena Macleod, Treasurer & Manager, Financial Services
Peter Steblin, City Manager
managersoffice@coquitlam.ca
Lori MacKay, General Manager, Leisure & Parks Services
604-927-3000
leisureandparks@coquitlam.ca
Jim McIntyre, General Manager, Planning & Development
604-927-3000, Fax: 604-927-3405
jmcintyre@coquitlam.ca
Bill Susak, General Manager, Engineering & Public Works
604-927-3000, Fax: 604-927-3015
bsusak@coquitlam.ca
Trevor Wingrove, General Manager, Corporate Services
twingrove@coquitlam.ca
Ron Price, Manager, Human Resources
humanresources@coquitlam.ca

Tony Delmonico, Fire Chief
firerescue@coquitlam.ca
Peter A. Lepine, Superintendent, RCMP Coquitlam Detachment
604-945-1550

Courtenay
830 Cliffe Ave.
Courtenay, BC V9N 2J7
250-334-4441
Fax: 250-334-4241
info@courtenay.ca
www.courtenay.ca
Municipal Type: City
Incorporated: Jan. 1, 1915 *Area:* 26.68 sq km
County or District: Comox-Strathcona; *Population in 2006:* 21,940
Provincial Electoral District(s): Comox Valley
Federal Electoral District(s): Vancouver Island North
Next Election: Nov. 2011 (3 year terms)
Council
Greg Phelps, Mayor
gphelps@courtenay.ca
Administration
Sandy Gray, City Administrator
sgray@courtenay.ca
D. Slobodan, Director, Regulatory & Property Services
Peter Crawford, Director, Planning Services
pcrawford@courtenay.ca
Randy Wiwchar, Director, Community Services
Kevin Lagan, Director, Operational Services
250-703-4860
klagan@courtenay.ca

Cranbrook
40 - 10 Ave. South
Cranbrook, BC V1C 2M8
250-426-4211
Fax: 250-426-4026
Toll Free Phone: 1-800-728-2726
hales@cranbrook.ca
www.cranbrook.ca
Municipal Type: City
Incorporated: Nov. 1, 1905 *Area:* 25.14 sq km
County or District: East Kootenay; *Population in 2006:* 18,267
Provincial Electoral District(s): East Kootenay
Federal Electoral District(s): Kootenay-Columbia
Next Election: Nov. 2011 (3 year terms)
Council
Scott Manjak, Mayor
mayor@cranbrook.ca
Administration
Roy Hales, Director, Corporate Services
hales@cranbrook.ca
Jamie Hodge, City Engineer
Joe McGowan, Director, Public Works
250-489-0240, Fax: 250-489-1828
mcgowan@cranbrook.ca
Wayne Price, Coordinator, Emergency Program
price@cranbrook.ca
Will Pearce, CAO
pearce@cranbrook.ca
Marnie Dueck, Municipal Clerk
dueck@cranbrook.ca
Wayne Staudt, Director, Finance
staudt@crankbook.ca

Dawson Creek
P.O. Box 150
10105 - 12A St.
Dawson Creek, BC V1G 4G4
250-784-3600
Fax: 250-782-3203
admin@dawsoncreek.ca
www.dawsoncreek.ca
Municipal Type: City
Incorporated: May 26, 1936 *Area:* 22.32 sq km
County or District: Peace River; *Population in 2006:* 10,994
Provincial Electoral District(s): Peace River South
Federal Electoral District(s): Prince George-Peace River
Next Election: Nov. 2011 (3 year terms)
Council
Mike Bernier, Mayor
Administration
Jim Chute, CAO
jchute@dawsoncreek.ca

See blue tabs following this section for Municipal Waste Management and Water & Wastewater Treatment.

Municipal Governments / British Columbia

Greg Dobrowolski, Manager, Special Projects
250-784-3619
gdobrowolski@dawsoncreek.ca
Rod Harmon, Manager, Water Resource
250-782-3114
rharmon@dawsoncreek.ca
Gordon (Shorty) Smith, Fire Chief
250-784-3635
shorty@dawsoncreek.ca
Kevin Henderson, Director, Operations
250-784-3622
khenderson@dawsoncreek.ca
Barry Reynard, Director, Parks & Recreation
250-784-3605
breynard@dawsoncreek.ca

Fort St. John
10631 - 100 St.
Fort St John, BC V1J 3Z5
250-787-8150
Fax: 250-787-8181
info@fortstjohn.ca
www.fortstjohn.ca
Municipal Type: City
Incorporated: Dec. 31, 1947 *Area:* 22.74 sq km
County or District: Peace River; *Population in 2006:* 17,402
Provincial Electoral District(s): Peace River North
Federal Electoral District(s): Prince George-Peace River
Next Election: Nov. 2011 (3 year terms)
Council
Bruce Lantz, Mayor
Administration
Janet Prestley, Director, Corporate Administration
jprestley@fortstjohn.ca
Fred Burrows, Fire Chief
250-785-4333, Fax: 250-785-0080
fburrows@fortstjohn.ca
Don Demers, Director, Public Works & Utilities
ddemers@fortstjohn.ca
Sarah Cockerill, Director, Community Services
scockerill@fortstjohn.ca
Horacio Galanti, Director, Engineering Services
hgalanti@fortstjohn.ca
Jeremy Garner, Superintendent, Utilities
jgarner@fortstjohn.ca

Kamloops
City Hall
7 Victoria St. West
Kamloops, BC V2C 1A2
250-828-3311
Fax: 250-828-3578
info@kamloops.ca
www.kamloops.ca
Municipal Type: City
Incorporated: Oct. 17, 1967 *Area:* 297.3 sq km
County or District: Thompson-Nicola; *Population in 2006:* 80,376
Provincial Electoral District(s): Kamloops; Kamloops-North Thompson
Federal Electoral District(s): Kamloops-Thompson-Cariboo
Next Election: Nov. 2011 (3 year terms)
Council
Peter Milobar, Mayor
mayor@kamloops.ca
Nancy Bepple, Councillor
John De Cicco, Councillor
Jim Harker, Councillor
Tina Lange, Councillor
John O'Fee, Councillor
Marg Spina, Councillor
Patricia Wallace, Councillor
Denis Walsh, Councillor
Administration
Len Hrycan, Director, Community & Corporate Affairs
Sally Edwards, Director, Finance & Information Technology
250-828-3413, Fax: 250-828-0845
Solange Belleforte, Manager, Human Resources
David Duckworth, Director, Public Works & Utilities
Byron McCorkell, Director, Parks, Recreation & Culture Services
250-828-3850, Fax: 250-372-7529
David A. Trawin, Director, Development & Engineering Services
250-828-3473

Randy H. Diehl, CAO
250-828-3498
cao@kamloops.ca
Kundan Bubbar, Chief Building Inspector
Neill Moroz, Fire Chief, Fire & Rescue Services
250-372-3311, Fax: 250-372-3578
Maurice J. Gravelle, Manager, Asset Management & Capital Projects
250-828-3463, Fax: 250-828-0952
D.C. Hilton, Manager, Parks
Randy Lambright, Manager, Planning & Development
J.B. McNeely, Manager, Streets & Environmental Services
250-828-3463
Errol Wild, Agent, Purchasing
Mike Warren, Manager, Engineering
Sharon E. Frissell, Chair, Water Treatment Committee

Kelowna
City Hall
1435 Water St.
Kelowna, BC V1Y 1J4
250-469-8500
Fax: 250-862-3399
ask@kelowna.ca
www.kelowna.ca
Municipal Type: City
Incorporated: May 4, 1905 *Area:* 211.69 sq km
County or District: Central Okanagan; *Population in 2006:* 106,707
Provincial Electoral District(s): Kelowna-Mission; Kelowna-Lake Country; Westside-Kelowna
Federal Electoral District(s): Kelowna-Lake Country; Okanagan-Coquihalla
Next Election: Nov. 2011 (3 year terms)
Council
Sharon Shepherd, Mayor
mayorandcouncil@kelowna.ca
Andre F. Blanleil, Councillor
Kevin Craig, Councillor
Robert Douglas Hobson, Councillor
Charlie Hodge, Councillor
Graeme James, Councillor
Angela Reid, Councillor
Michele Rule, Councillor
Luke Stack, Councillor
Administration
Ronald Mattiussi, City Manager
Stephen Fleming, Clerk
250-469-8500
cityclerk@kelowna.ca
John Vos, General Manager, Community Services
Jim Paterson, General Manager, Community Sustainability
Paul Macklem, General Manager, Corporate Sustainability
David Graham, Director, Strategic Initiatives
Joe Creron, Director, Civic Operations
William J. Berry, Director, Design & Construction Services
Ron Dickinson, Director, Development Services
Doug Gilchrist, Director, Real Estate & Building Services
Randy Cleveland, Director, Infrastructure Planning
Shelley Gambacort, Director, Land Use Management
Signe Bagh, Director, Policy & Planning
Ron W. Westlake, Director, Regional Services
Carla Stephens, Director, Community & Media Relations
Charlene Covington, Director, Human Resources
Rob Mayne, Director, Corporate Services
Rene M. Blanleil, Fire Chief

Langford
877 Goldstream Ave., 2nd Fl.
Victoria, BC V9B 2X8
250-478-7882
Fax: 250-391-3437
adminassist@cityoflangford.ca
www.cityoflangford.ca
Municipal Type: City
Incorporated: Dec. 8, 1992 *Area:* 39.55 sq km
County or District: Capital; *Population in 2006:* 22,459
Provincial Electoral District(s): Malahat-Juan de Fuca
Federal Electoral District(s): Esquimalt-Juan de Fuca
Next Election: Nov. 2011 (3 year terms)
Council
Stewart Young, Mayor
council@cityoflangford.ca

Administration
Jim Bowden, Acting Clerk Administrator
jbowden@cityoflangford.ca
Steve Ternent, Treasurer
sternent@cityoflangford.ca
Bob Beckett, Fire Chief
250-478-9555
firechief@cityoflangford.ca
John Manson, City Engineer
engineering@cityoflangford.ca
Matthew Baldwin, City Planner
mbaldwin@cityoflangford.ca
Trevor Auger, Chief Engineering Technologist
tauger@cityoflangford.ca

Langley
20399 Douglas Cres.
Langley, BC V3A 4B3
604-514-2800
Fax: 604-530-4371
council@city.langley.bc.ca
www.city.langley.bc.ca
Municipal Type: City
Incorporated: March 15, 1955 *Area:* 10.22 sq km
County or District: Greater Vancouver; *Population in 2006:* 23,606
Provincial Electoral District(s): Langley
Federal Electoral District(s): Langley
Next Election: Nov. 2011 (3 year terms)
Council
Peter Fassbender, Mayor
mayor@langleycity.ca
Jack Arnold, Councillor
Dave Hall, Councillor
Teri James, Councillor
Gayle Martin, Councillor
Rudy Storteboom, Councillor
Rosemary Wallace, Councillor
Administration
Tracey Arthur, Acting City Clerk
604-514-2803
Darrin W. Leite, Director, Corporate Services
604-514-2806
dleite@langleycity.ca
Gerald Minchuk, Director, Development Services & Economic Development
604-514-2815
gminchuk@langleycity.ca
Gary Vlieg, Director, Engineering, Parks & Environment
gvlieg@langleycity.ca
F. Cheung, CAO
604-514-2805
fcheung@langleycity.ca
Bruce Dundas, Fire Chief
604-514-2881
Kim Hilton, Manager, Recreation, Culture & Community Services
Len Walters, Manager, Park Operations
604-514-2912

Nanaimo
455 Wallace St.
Nanaimo, BC V9R 5J6
250-754-4251
Fax: 250-755-4440
mayor&council@nanaimo.ca
www.nanaimo.ca
Municipal Type: City
Incorporated: Dec. 24, 1874 *Area:* 89.3 sq km
County or District: Nanaimo; *Population in 2006:* 78,692
Provincial Electoral District(s): Nanaimo-Parksville; Nanaimo
Federal Electoral District(s): Nanaimo-Cowichan; Nanaimo-Alberni
Next Election: Nov. 2011 (3 year terms)
Council
John Ruttan, Mayor
250-754-4251
john.ruttan@nanaimo.ca
William Leslie (Bill) Bestwick, Councillor
bill.bestwick@nanaimo.ca
Bill Holdom, Councillor
bill.holdom@nanaimo.ca
Diana Johnstone, Councillor
diana.johnstone@nanaimo.ca
Jim Kipp, Councillor
jim.kipp@nanaimo.ca

See blue tabs following this section for Municipal Waste Management and Water & Wastewater Treatment.

Municipal Governments / British Columbia

Larry McNabb, Councillor
larry.mcnabb@nanaimo.ca
Fred Pattje, Councillor
fred.pattje@nanaimo.ca
Loyd Sherry, Councillor
loyd.sherry@nanaimo.ca
Mervin Wayne (Merv) Unger, Councillor
merv.unger@nanaimo.ca
Administration
Doug Holmes, General Manager, Corporate Services
250-755-4488
Doug.Holmes@nanaimo.ca
Brian Clemens, Director, Finance
250-755-4431
brian.clemens@nanaimo.ca
Richard Harding, Director, Parks, Recreation & Culture
250-755-7516
Richard.Harding@nanaimo.ca
Tom Hickey, Director, Engineering & Public Works
Tom.Hickey@nanaimo.ca
Ian Howat, Director, Legislative Services
506-755-4405
Terry Hartley, Director, Human Resources
250-755-4427
terry.hartley@nanaimo.ca
Andrew Tucker, Director, Planning & Development
250-754-4251
Andrew.Tucker@nanaimo.ca
Gerald (Jerry) Berry, City Manager
250-755-4401
gerry.berry@nanaimo.ca
Ron Lambert, Fire Chief
250-755-7550
Ron.Lambert@nanaimo.ca
Andy Laidlaw, General Manager, Community Services
250-756-5346
andy.laidlaw@nanaimo.ca
Ted Swabey, General Manager, Development Services
250-755-4429
Ted.Swabey@nanaimo.ca
Jim Bowden, Manager, Occupational Health & Rehabilitation
Brian Denbigh, Manager, Roads & Traffic Services
Kurtis Felker, Manager, Purchasing & Stores
250-756-5317
gino.dimenna@nanaimo.ca
John Elliot, Manager, Utilities
Gary Franssen, Manager, Sanitation, Recycling & Cemeteries
Bob Prokopenko, Manager, Engineering Services
Jeff Ritchie, Senior Manager, Parks
Jeff.Ritchie@nanaimo.ca
Graham Savage, Manager, Engineering & Environment Services
Andrew Tucker, Director, Community Planning
250-754-4251
andrew.tucker@nanaimo.ca
Kevin Brydges, Environmental Coordinator
250-755-4460
kevin.brydges@nanaimo.ca
Jim Kipp, Coordinator, Emergency Management
250-753-4572
jim.kipp@nanaimo.ca
Jeff Lott, Superintendent & Officer-in-Charge, Nanaimo RCMP Detachment
250-754-2345
Jeff.Lott@nanaimo.ca
Marilyn Hutchinson, Officer, Economic Development
250-755-4465
Marilyn.Hutchinson@nanaimo.ca
Rob Lawrance, Environmental Planner
250-755-4483
rob.lawrance@nanaimo.ca

New Westminster
511 Royal Ave.
New Westminster, BC V3L 1H9
604-521-3711
Fax: 604-521-3895
postmaster@newwestcity.ca
www.city.new-westminster.bc.ca
Municipal Type: City
Incorporated: July 16, 1860 *Area:* 15.41 sq km
County or District: Greater Vancouver; *Population in 2006:* 58,549
Provincial Electoral District(s): New Westminster
Federal Electoral District(s): Burnaby-New Westminster; New Westminster-Coquitlam
Next Election: Nov. 2011 (3 year terms)
Council
Wayne Wright, Mayor
604-527-4522
wwright@newwestcity.ca
Jonathan Cote, Councillor
jcote@newwestcity.ca
Bill Harper, Councillor
Jamie McEvoy, Councillor
jmcevoy@newwestcity.ca
Betty McIntosh, Councillor
bmcintosh@newwestcity.ca
Bob Osterman, Councillor
bosterman@newwestcity.ca
Lorrie Williams, Councillor
lwilliams@newwestcity.ca
Administration
Rick Page, Director, Legislative Services
rpage@newwestcity.ca
Gary Holowatiuk, Director, Finance & Information Technology
gholowatiuk@newwestcity.ca
Paul Daminato, CAO
pdaminato@newwestcity.ca
Dean Gibson, Director, Parks, Recreation & Culture
dgibson@newwestcity.ca
Jim Lowrie, Director, Engineering Services
jlowrie@newwestcity.ca
Carl Nepstad, Fire Chief, Fire & Rescue Services
cnepstad@newwestcity.ca
Lisa Spitale, Director, Development Services
lspitale@newwestcity.ca
Joan Burgess, Director, Human Resources
jburgess@newwestcity.ca
Lorne Zapotichny, Police Chief, Police Services
lzapotichny@newwestcity.ca
Rod Carle, General Manager, Electric Utility
rcarle@newwestcity.ca
Jon McDonald, Manager, Engineering Operations
604-521-6594
jmcdonald@newwestcity.ca
Roger Emanuels, Coordinator, Transportation & Infrastructure
604-527-4540
Roy Moulder, Manager, Purchasing
604-527-4632
rmoulder@newwestcity.ca
Bob Jack, Supervisor, Waste Management
604-526-4691
bjack@newwestcity.ca
Sheldon Rigby, Supervisor, Sewer & Drainage Branch
604-517-5416
srigby@newwestcity.ca

North Vancouver
141 - 14 St. West
North Vancouver, BC V7M 1H9
604-985-7761
Fax: 604-985-9417
info@cnv.org
www.cnv.org
Municipal Type: City
Incorporated: May 13, 1907 *Area:* 11.85 sq km
County or District: Greater Vancouver; *Population in 2006:* 45,165
Provincial Electoral District(s): N. Vancouver-Lonsdale; N. Vancouver-Seymour; W. Vancouver-Capilano; W. Vancouver-Garibaldi
Federal Electoral District(s): North Vancouver
Next Election: Nov. 2011 (3 year terms)
Council
Darrell R. Mussatto, Mayor
dmussatto@cnv.org
Administration
Sandra Dowey, City Clerk
sdowey@cnv.org
Isabel Gordon, Director, Finance
Barrie Penman, Fire Chief
604-980-5201, Fax: 604-980-8544
bpenman@cnv.org
Steven Ono, City Engineer
sono@cnv.org
Fred A. Smith, Director, Community Development
604-990-4206
Heather Turner, Director, Recreation
604-983-6305, Fax: 604-984-4294
Wolfgang Beier, Manager, Purchasing
604-983-7392
Allen Lynch, Manager, North Shore Recycling Program
604-984-9730, Fax: 604-984-3563
Nikii Hoglund, Manager, Public Works & Operations
604-983-7388
Doug Pope, Manager, Environment & Parks
604-983-7337
Michael Hunter, Environmental Coordinator
604-990-4224
John Guenther, Building Inspector
604-985-7761, Fax: 604-985-0576

Parksville
P.O. Box 1390
100 Jensen Ave. East
Parksville, BC V9P 2H3
250-248-6144
Fax: 250-248-6650
citypark@parksville.ca
www.parksville.ca
Municipal Type: City
Incorporated: June 19, 1945 *Area:* 14.6 sq km
County or District: Nanaimo; *Population in 2006:* 10,993
Provincial Electoral District(s): Nanaimo-Parksville
Federal Electoral District(s): Nanaimo-Alberni
Next Election: Nov. 2011 (3 year terms)
Council
Ed Mayne, Mayor
Administration
Fred Manson, CAO
250-954-4666
fmanson@city.parksville.bc.ca
Doug Banks, Fire Chief
250-954-4671
dbanks@parksville.ca
Gayle Jackson, Director, Community Planning
250-954-4660
gjackson@city.parksville.bc.ca
Mike Squire, Manager, Engineering
250-954-4698
msquire@parksville.ca
Alan Metcalf, Manager, Operations
250-954-4667
ametcalf@parksville.ca
Lynn Kitchen, Deputy Corporate Administrator, Administrative Services
lkitchen@parksville.ca

Penticton
171 Main St.
Penticton, BC V2A 5A9
250-490-2400
Fax: 250-490-2402
ask@penticton.ca
www.penticton.ca
Municipal Type: City
Incorporated: Jan. 1, 1909 *Area:* 42.02 sq km
County or District: Okanagan-Similkameen; *Population in 2006:* 31,909
Provincial Electoral District(s): Penticton-Okanagan Valley
Federal Electoral District(s): Okanagan-Coquihalla
Next Election: Nov. 2011 (3 year terms)
Council
Dan Ashton, Mayor
mayor@penticton.ca
Administration
Cathy Ingram, Manager, Legislative Services
250-490-2412
cathy.ingram@penticton.ca
Michael Ummenhofer, Agent, Purchasing
250-490-2555, Fax: 250-490-2557
purch-agent@city.penticton.bc.ca
Berne Udala, Supervisor, Water Quality
250-490-2550, Fax: 250-490-2552
berne.udala@penticton.ca
Douglas Leahy, Treasurer
John Kirbyson, Director, Parks, Recreation & Culture
250-490-2426, Fax: 250-490-2427
john.kirbyson@penticton.ca
Wayne Williams, Fire Chief
250-492-4209, Fax: 250-490-4288
wayne.williams@penticton.ca
Mitch Moroziuk, Director, Development & Engineering Services
mitch.moroziuk@penticton.ca

See blue tabs following this section for Municipal Waste Management and Water & Wastewater Treatment .

Brent Edge, Supervisor, Water
brent.edge@penticton.ca
Carolyn Stewart, Coordinator, Water Conservation Program
carolyn.stewart@penticton.ca

Pitt Meadows
Municipal Hall
12007 Harris Rd.
Pitt Meadows, BC V3Y 2B5
604-465-5454
Fax: 604-465-2404
info@pittmeadows.bc.ca
www.pittmeadows.bc.ca
Municipal Type: City
Incorporated: April 25, 1914 *Area:* 85.38 sq km
County or District: Greater Vancouver; *Population in 2006:* 15,623
Provincial Electoral District(s): Maple Ridge-Pitt Meadows
Federal Electoral District(s): Pitt Meadows-Maple Ridge-Mission
Next Election: Nov. 2011 (3 year terms)
Note: Effective Jan. 1, 2007, Pitt Meadows' designation was changed from a district to a city.
Council
Don MacLean, Mayor
604-465-2416
dmaclean@pittmeadows.bc.ca
Administration
Dean Rear, Director, Corporate Services
604-465-2449
drear@pittmeadows.bc.ca
Jake Rudolph, CAO
604-465-2413
jrudolph@pittmeadows.bc.ca
Don Jolley, Fire Chief, Protective Services
djolley@pittmeadows.bc.ca
Kelly Swift, Director, Recreation
kswift@mapleridge.org
Kim Grout, Director, Operations & Development Services
604-465-2420
kgrout@pittmeadows.bc.ca
Adrian Kopystynski, General Manager, Development Services
604-467-2432
akopystynski@pittmeadows.bc.ca
Y. (Ike) de Boer, Coordinator, Engineering Services
604-465-2425
ideboer@pittmeadows.bc.ca
Randy Evans, Superintendent, Operations
604-465-2435
revans@pittmeadows.bc.ca
Dana Parr, Planner
604-465-2497
dparr@pittmeadows.bc.ca

Port Alberni
4850 Argyle St.
Port Alberni, BC V9Y 1V8
250-723-2146
Fax: 250-723-1003
citypa@portalberni.ca
www.portalberni.ca
Municipal Type: City
Incorporated: Oct. 28, 1967 *Area:* 19.92 sq km
County or District: Alberni-Clayoquot; *Population in 2006:* 17,548
Provincial Electoral District(s): Alberni-Qualicum
Federal Electoral District(s): Nanaimo-Alberni
Next Election: Nov. 2011 (3 year terms)
Council
Ken McRae, Mayor
ken_mcrae@portalberni.ca
Administration
Russell Dyson, City Clerk
russell_dyson@portalberni.ca
Ann Hopkins, Director, Finance
ann_hopkins@portalberni.ca
Guy Cicon, Director/City Engineer, Public Works
guy_cicon@port-alberni.ca
Ken Watson, City Manager
ken_watson@port-alberni.ca
Scott Smith, Planner
scott_smith@port-alberni.ca
Scott Kenny, Director, Parks & Recreation
scott_kenny@portalberni.ca
Brian Mousley, Superintendent, Utilities
brian_mousley@portalberni.ca

Tim Pley, Fire Chief
250-724-1351
tim_pley@portalberni.ca

Port Coquitlam
2580 Shaughnessy St.
Port Coquitlam, BC V3C 2A8
604-927-5411
Fax: 604-927-5360
info@portcoquitlam.ca
www.portcoquitlam.ca
Municipal Type: City
Incorporated: March 7, 1913 *Area:* 28.85 sq km
County or District: Greater Vancouver; *Population in 2006:* 52,687
Provincial Electoral District(s): Port Coquitlam-Burke Mountain
Federal Electoral District(s): Port Moody-Westwood-Port Coquitlam
Next Election: Nov. 2011 (3 year terms)
Council
Greg Moore, Mayor
604-927-5498
mooreg@portcoquitlam.ca
Sherry Carroll, Councillor
Mike Forrest, Councillor
Darrell Penner, Councillor
Glenn Pollock, Councillor
Brad West, Councillor
Michael Wright, Councillor
Administration
Tony Chong, P. Eng., CAO
chongt@portcoquitlam.ca
Susan Rauh, CMC, Corporate Officer
rauhs@portcoquitlam.ca
Jim Maitland, Officer, Finance
maitlandj@portcoquitlam.ca
S. Gamble, Fire Chief
Barry Becker, Director, Parks & Recreation
Laura Lee Richard, Director, Development Services
Mindy Smith, Director, Corporate Services
smithm@portcoquitlam.ca
I. Zahynacz, Director, Engineering & Operations
engineering@portcoquitlam.ca
A. Jensen, Manager, Evironmental Services
Karen Laustrup, Manager, Purchasing
604-927-5430, Fax: 604-927-5408
L. Richard, Manager, Planning
Gordon Voncina, Manager, Operations
Robin Wishart, Manager, Information Services

Port Moody
P.O. Box 36
100 Newport Dr.
Port Moody, BC V3H 3E1
604-469-4500
Fax: 604-469-4550
info@cityofportmoody.com
www.cityofportmoody.com
Municipal Type: City
Incorporated: March 11, 1913 *Area:* 25.62 sq km
County or District: Greater Vancouver; *Population in 2006:* 27,512
Provincial Electoral District(s): Port Moody-Westwood
Federal Electoral District(s): Port Moody-Westwood-Port Coquitlam; New Westminster-Coquitlam
Next Election: Nov. 2011 (3 year terms)
Council
Joe Trasolini, Mayor
604-469-4501
joe.trasolini@cityofportmoody.com
Administration
Colleen Rohde, City Clerk
604-469-4505
colleen.rohde@cityofportmoody.com
Paul Rockwood, Director, Corporate Services
paul.rockwood@cityofportmoody.com
Tim Savoie, Director, Planning & Development Services
604-469-4545
planning@cityofportmoody.com
Gaetan Royer, City Manager
gaetan.royer@cityofportmoody.com
Jeff Lambert, Fire Chief
pmfd.info@cityofportmoody.com
Ron Higo, Director, Community Services
604-469-4542

Bob Parsons, Acting Director, Engineering & Operations

Powell River
6910 Duncan St.
Powell River, BC V8A 1V4
604-485-6291
Fax: 604-485-2913
info@cdpr.bc.ca
www.powellriver.ca
Municipal Type: City
Incorporated: Oct. 15, 1955 *Area:* 29.77 sq km
County or District: Powell River; *Population in 2006:* 12,957
Provincial Electoral District(s): Powell River-Sunshine Coast
Federal Electoral District(s): West Vancouver-Sunshine Coast-Sea to Sky Country
Next Election: Nov. 2011 (3 year terms)
Council
Stewart Alsgard, Mayor
Administration
Stan Westby, CAO
swestby@cdpr.bc.ca
Dave Douglas, Director, Financial Services
ddouglas@cdpr.bc.ca
Richard Stogre, Manager, Engineering Services
Barry Jantz, Director, Public Works
Dan Ouellette, Director, Fire & Emergency Services
Regina Sadilkova, Manager, Development Services
rsadilkova@cdpr.bc.ca
 Vacant, City Engineer

Prince George
City Hall
1100 Patricia Blvd.
Prince George, BC V2L 3V9
250-561-7600
Fax: 250-561-0183
cityclerk@city.pg.bc.ca
www.city.pg.bc.ca
Municipal Type: City
Incorporated: March 6, 1915 *Area:* 316 sq km
County or District: Fraser-Fort George; *Population in 2006:* 70,981
Provincial Electoral District(s): Pr. George-Mt. Robson; Pr. George N.; Pr. George-Omineca
Federal Electoral District(s): Prince George-Peace River; Cariboo-Prince George
Next Election: Nov. 2011 (3 year terms)
Council
Dan Rogers, Mayor
Don Bassermann, Councillor
Garth Frizzell, Councillor
Shari Green, Councillor
Murry Krause, Councillor
Debora Munoz, Councillor
Brian Skakun, Councillor
Cameron Stolz, Councillor
Dave Wilbur, Councillor
Administration
Walter Babicz, Corporate Officer
250-561-7605
wbabicz@city.pg.bc.ca
Sandra Stibrany, Manager, Financial Services
250-561-7677, Fax: 250-561-7759
Derek Bates, City Manager
250-561-7607, Fax: 250-561-0183
Dave Dyer, Chief Engineer
250-561-7663
ddyer@city.pg.bc.ca
Jeff Rowland, Fire Chief
250-561-7670, Fax: 250-561-7670
Tom Madden, Director, Community Services
250-561-7644, Fax: 250-561-7718
Grant Bain, Director, Development Services
250-561-7616, Fax: 250-561-0183
Kathleen Soltis, Director, Corporate Services
Rob Whitwham, Director, Administrative Services
250-561-7608, Fax: 250-561-0183
Dan Milburn, Manager, Long Range Planning
250-561-7614, Fax: 250-561-7721
Scott Bone, Manager, Supply & Fleet Services
250-561-7511, Fax: 250-612-5603
Frank Blues, Manager, Transportation
250-561-7503
fblues@city.pg.bc.ca

See blue tabs following this section for Municipal Waste Management and Water & Wastewater Treatment.

Municipal Governments / British Columbia

Mark Fercho, Manager, Environment
250-561-7698
Marco Fornari, Manager, Utilities
250-561-7509
mfornari@city.pg.bc.ca
Bill Gaal, Manager, Parks & Solid Waste Services
250-561-7691, Fax: 250-564-5809
Dan Milburn, Manager, Current Planning
250-561-7614, Fax: 250-561-7721
Gina Layte-Liston, Environmental Coordinator
250-614-7824
glayte@city.pg.bc.ca
Ann Bailey, Supervisor, RCMP Support Services
Tom Kadla, Supervisor, Solid Waste
250-561-7575
Tony Pirillo, Supervisor, Utility Plant (Pump Stations)
250-614-7830, Fax: 250-561-7519
Alan Clark, Engineer, Development & Projects
250-561-7617
Glenn Stanker, Engineer, Transportation
250-561-7757
Norm Gobbi, Chief Operator, Wastewater Treatment Plant
250-562-4578
ngobbi@city.pg.bc.ca

Prince Rupert
424 - 3rd Ave. West
Prince Rupert, BC V8J 1L7
250-627-0934
Fax: 250-627-0999
cityhall@princerupert.ca
www.princerupert.ca
Municipal Type: City
Incorporated: March 10, 1910 *Area:* 54.9 sq km
County or District: Skeena-Queen Charlotte; *Population in 2006:* 12,815
Provincial Electoral District(s): North Coast
Federal Electoral District(s): Skeena-Bulkley Valley
Next Election: Nov. 2011 (3 year terms)
Council
Jack Mussallem, Mayor
jmussallem@princerupert.ca
Administration
Gord Howie, City Manager
gord.howie@princerupert.ca
Dan Rodin, Chief Financial Officer
dan.rodin@princerupert.ca
Robert M. Thompson, General Manager, Engineering & Public Works
250-627-0954
bob.thompson@princerupert.ca
Ron Miller, Fire Chief
250-624-5115, Fax: 250-624-3407
ron.miller@princerupert.ca
T.J. Ireland, City Administrator & Planner

Richmond
6911 No. 3 Rd.
Richmond, BC V6Y 2C1
604-276-4000
Fax: 604-278-5139
cityclerk@richmond.ca
www.richmond.ca
Municipal Type: City
Incorporated: Nov. 10, 1879 *Area:* 128.76 sq km
County or District: Greater Vancouver; *Population in 2006:* 174,461
Provincial Electoral District(s): Richmond-Centre; Richmond E.; Richmond-Steveston
Federal Electoral District(s): Richmond; Delta-Richmond East
Next Election: Nov. 2011 (3 year terms)
Council
Malcolm D. Brodie, Mayor
mayorandcouncillors@richmond.ca
Linda Barnes, Councillor
Derek Dang, Councillor
Evelina Halsey-Brandt, Councillor
Sue Halsey-Brandt, Councillor
Greg Halsey-Brandt, Councillor
Ken Johnston, Councillor
Bill McNulty, Councillor
Harold Steves, Councillor
Administration
David Weber, Director, City Clerk's Office
604-276-4007

Andrew Nazareth, General Manager, Business & Finance Services
604-276-4095
finance@richmond.ca
George Duncan, CAO
604-276-4336, Fax: 604-276-4222
administratorsoffice@richmond.ca
Jim Hancock, Fire Chief
604-303-2700
fire@richmond.ca
Ward Clapham, RCMP Officer-in-Charge
604-207-4741
Jerry Chong, Director, Finance
604-276-4064
Allan Cameron, Director, Information Technology
604-276-4096
Robert Gonzalez, P. Eng., General Manager, Engineering & Public Works
604-276-4000
robert.gonzalez@richmond.ca
Mike Pellant, Director, Human Resources
604-276-4092
humanresources@richmond.ca
Dave Semple, Director, Operations
604-244-1206
dave.semple@richmond.ca
Cathryn Carlile, General Manager, Parks, Recreation & Cultural Services
604-276-4068
ccarlile@richmond.ca
Phyllis Carlyle, General Manager, Law & Community Safety
604-276-4104
pcarlyle@richmond.ca
Joe Erceg, General Manager, Planning & Development
604-276-4083
planningdevelopment@richmond.ca
Mike Kirk, General Manager, Corporate Services
604-276-4142
corporateservices@richmond.ca
Suzanne Bycraft, Manager, Fleet & Environmental Programs
604-233-3338
sbycraft@richmond.ca
Terry Crowe, Manager, Policy Planning
604-276-4139
tcrowe@richmond.ca
Margot Daykin, Asst. Manager, Environmental Programs
604-276-4130
mdaykin@richmond.ca

Salmon Arm
P.O. Box 40
500 - 2nd Ave. NE
Salmon Arm, BC V1E 4N2
250-832-6021
Fax: 250-832-5584
cityhall@salmonarm.ca
www.salmonarm.ca
Municipal Type: City
Incorporated: May 15, 1905 *Area:* 155.36 sq km
County or District: Columbia-Shuswap; *Population in 2006:* 16,012
Provincial Electoral District(s): Shuswap
Federal Electoral District(s): Okanagan-Shuswap
Next Election: Nov. 2011 (3 year terms)
Council
Marty Bootsma, Mayor
mbootsma@salmonarm.ca
Administration
Carl Bannister, CAO
cbannistser@salmonarm.ca
Charles Ward, Director, Operations
cward@salmonarm.ca
Brad Shirley, Fire Chief
250-803-4064
bshirley@salmonarm.ca
Dale McTaggart, Municipal Engineer
dmctaggart@salmonarm.ca
Monica Dennis, Treasurer
Corey Paiement, Director, Development Services
cpaiement@salmonarm.ca
John Rosenberg, Manager, Public Works, Utilities & Parks
Monica Dalziel, Director, Corporate Services
mdalziel@salmonarm.ca

Sidney
Municipal Hall
2440 Sidney Ave.
Sidney, BC V8L 1Y7
250-656-1184
Fax: 250-655-4508
townhall@sidney.ca
www.sidney.ca
Municipal Type: City
Incorporated: Sept. 30, 1952 *Area:* 5.04 sq km
County or District: Capital; *Population in 2006:* 11,315
Provincial Electoral District(s): Saanich N. & the Islands
Federal Electoral District(s): Saanich-Gulf Islands
Next Election: Nov. 2011 (3 year terms)
Alison Myerscough, Municipal Planner
250-655-5419
amyerscough@sidney.ca
Council
Larry Cross, Mayor
Administration
Murray Clarke, CAO/Corporate Administrator
250-656-1139
mclarke@sidney.ca
Andrew Hicik, Manager, Finance
ahicik@sidney.ca
Rob Hall, P.Eng., Director, Engineering & Works
250-656-4502
rhall@sidney.ca
Dan Holder, Fire Chief
250-656-2121
dholder@sidney.ca
Randy Humble, Director, Development Services
250-655-5418
rhumble@sidney.ca
Mike van der Linden, Manager, Engineering
mvanderlinden@sidney.ca

Surrey
14245 - 56 Ave.
Surrey, BC V3X 3A2
604-591-4011
Fax: 604-591-8731
www.surrey.ca
Municipal Type: City
Incorporated: Nov. 10, 1879 *Area:* 317.19 sq km
County or District: Greater Vancouver; *Population in 2006:* 394,976
Provincial Electoral District(s): Surrey-Cloverdale; Surrey-Green Timbers; Surrey-Newton; Surrey-Panorama Ridge; Surrey-Tynehead; Surrey-Whalley; Surrey-White Rock
Federal Electoral District(s): Surrey North; South Surrey-White Rock-Cloverdale; Newton-North Delta; Fleetwood-Port Kells
Next Election: Nov. 2011 (3 year terms)
Council
Dianne L. Watts, Mayor
604-591-4126, Fax: 604-591-4481
Robert Bose, Councillor
604-591-4624
Tom Gill, Councillor
604-591-4634
Linda Hepner, Councillor
604-591-4626
Marvin Hunt, Councillor
604-591-4635
Mary Martin, Councillor
604-591-4622
Barinder Rasode, Councillor
604-591-4011
H. Barbara Steele, Councillor
604-591-4623
Judy Villeneuve, Councillor
604-591-4625
Administration
Jane Sowik, City Clerk
604-591-4113, Fax: 604-591-8731
Vivienne Wilke, General Manager, Finance & Technology
604-591-4011, Fax: 604-591-8731
Murray Dinwoodie, City Manager
604-591-4441
Craig MacFarlane, City Solicitor
Len Garis, Fire Chief
604-541-4011
Laurie Cavan, General Manager, Parks, Recreation & Culture
604-598-5765
parksrecculture@surrey.ca

See blue tabs following this section for Municipal Waste Management and Water & Wastewater Treatment.

Vincent Lalonde, General Manager, Engineering
604-591-4011, Fax: 604-591-8731
Jean Lamontagne, General Manager, Planning & Development
604-591-4441, Fax: 604-591-2507
Nicola Webb, General Manager, Human Resources
Vincent Lalonde, P. Eng., Manager, Utilities & Transportation
604-591-4146
Violet McGregor, CMA, C.P.P., Manager, Purchasing & Payments
604-591-4011
Gerry McKinnon, Manager, Operations
604-590-4011
Rob Wilson, P. Eng., Manager, Land Development
604-591-4276
Erin Desautels, Coordinator, Environmental Stewardship
604-501-5158

Terrace
3215 Eby St.
Terrace, BC V8G 2X8
250-635-6311
Fax: 250-638-4777
cityhall@terrace.ca
www.city.terrace.bc.ca
Municipal Type: City
Incorporated: Dec. 31, 1927 *Area:* 41.52 sq km
County or District: Kitimat-Stikine; *Population in 2006:* 11,320
Provincial Electoral District(s): Skeena
Federal Electoral District(s): Skeena-Bulkley Valley
Next Election: Nov. 2011 (3 year terms)
Council
David Pernarowski, Mayor
dpernarowski@terrace.ca
Administration
Denise Fisher, Corporate Administrator
250-638-4722
dfisher@terrace.ca
Ron Bowles, Director, Finance
205-638-4725
rbowles@terrace.ca
Ron Poole, CAO
rpoole@terrace.ca
Lisa Teggarty, Deputy Treasurer
rbowles@terrace.ca
Ross Bretherick, Agent, Purchasing
250-615-4036
rbretherick@terrace.ca
David Block, City Planner
250-615-4028
dblock@terrace.ca
Brad North, Contact, Solid Waste Management
250-615-4032
bnorth@terrace.ca
Peter Weeber, Fire Chief
Herb Dusdal, Director, Public Works
250-615-4030
hdusdal@terrace.ca
Marvin Kwiatkowski, Director, Development Services
250-615-4041
mkwiatkowski@terrace.ca
Lyle Marleau, Contact, Environmental Health
250-635-6871
lmarleau@terrace.ca

Vancouver
453 West 12th Ave.
Vancouver, BC V5Y 1V4
604-873-7000
Fax: 604-873-7419
Telephone locally: 311
info@vancouver.ca
www.vancouver.ca
Municipal Type: City
Incorporated: November 15, 2008 *Area:* 114.71 sq km
County or District: Greater Vancouver; *Population in 2006:* 578,041
Provincial Electoral District(s): Vancouver Burrard; Vanc.-Fraserview; Vanc.-Hastings; Vanc.-Kensington; Vanc.-Kingsway; Vanc.-Langara; Vanc.-Mt. Pleasant; Vanc.-Point Grey; Vanc.-Quilchena; Vanc.-Fairview
Federal Electoral District(s): Vancouver Centre; Vancouver East; Vancouver-Kingsway; Vancouver Quadra; Vancouver South
Next Election: Nov. 2011 (3 year terms)
Council
Gregor Robertson, Mayor
604-873-7621, Fax: 604-873-7685
info@vancouver.ca
Suzanne Anton, Councillor
604-873-7248, Fax: 604-873-7750
suzanne.anton@vancouver.ca
David Cadman, Councillor
604-873-7244, Fax: 604-873-7750
david.cadman@vancouver.ca
George Chow, Councillor
604-873-7245, Fax: 604-873-7750
george.chow@vancouver.ca
Heather Deal, Councillor
604-873-7242, Fax: 604-873-7750
heather.deal@vancouver.ca
Kerry Jang, Councillor
604-873-7621, Fax: 604-873-7685
kerry.jang@vancouver.ca
Raymond Louie, Councillor
604-873-7243, Fax: 604-873-7750
raymond.louie@vancouver.ca
Geoff Meggs, Councillor
604-873-7011, Fax: 604-873-7419
geoff.meggs@vancouver.ca
Andrea Reimer, Councillor
604-873-7011, Fax: 604-873-7419
andrea.reimer@vancouver.ca
Tim Stevenson, Councillor
604-873-7247, Fax: 604-873-7750
tim.stevenson@vancouver.ca
Ellen Woodsworth, Councillor
604-873-7245, Fax: 604-873-7750
ellen.woodsworth@vancouver.ca
Administration
Marg Coulson, City Clerk
604-873-7266, Fax: 604-873-7419
marg.coulson@vancouver.ca
Ken Bayne, General Manager, Business Planning & Services
ken.bayne@vancouver.ca
Penny Ballem, City Manager
604-873-7625, Fax: 604-873-7641
penny.ballem@vancouver.ca
Jim Chu, Chief Constable, Vancouver Police Department
604-717-3321, Fax: 604-873-7419
chief@vpd.ca
Garrick Bradshaw, Director, Facilities Design & Management
garrick.bradshaw@vancouver.ca
Sue Harvey, Managing Director, Cultural Services
604-871-6001
sue.harvey@vancouver.ca
Frances J. Connell, Director, Legal Services
604-873-7506, Fax: 604-873-7445
frances.connell@vancouver.ca
Trish Doge, Director, Risk & Emergency Management
604-873-7011, Fax: 604-873-7419
trish.doge@vancouver.ca
Peter Kuran, Acting General Manager, Board of Parks & Recreation
peter.kuran@vancouver.ca
Brent Toderian, Director, Planning Services
604-873-7011, Fax: 604-873-7419
brent.toderian@vancouver.ca
Shari Wallace, Director, Information Technology
shari.wallace@vancouver.ca
Chris Warren, Director, Development Services
604-873-7011, Fax: 604-873-7419
christine.warren@vancouver.ca
David McLellan, General Manager, Community Services
604-276-4083, Fax: 604-276-4222
david.mclellan@vancouver.ca
John McKearney, General Manager & Fire Chief, Vancouver Fire & Rescue Services
604-665-6051, Fax: 604-654-0623
john.mckearney@vancouver.ca
Patrice Impey, Chief Financial Officer & General Manager, Human Resources
604-873-7011, Fax: 604-873-7419
patrice.impey@vancouver.ca
Tom Timm, P.Eng., General Manager, Engineering Services
604-873-7300, Fax: 604-871-6119
tom.timm@vancouver.ca
Brian Davies, P.Eng., Assistant City Engineer, Solid Waste/Sanitation/Landfill Operations
604-873-7348
brian.davies@vancouver.ca
Sean Pander, Acting Manager, Sustainability Group
604-871-6619
Brian Crowe, P.Eng., Assistant City Engineer, Water & Sewers Utilities
604-873-7313
brian.crowe@vancouver.ca
Neal Carley, P.Eng., Assistant City Engineer, Streets Division
604-873-7360
neal.carley@vancouver.ca
Rowan Birch, P.Eng., Assistant City Engineer, Departmental Services Division
604-873-7280
rowan.birch@vancouver.ca
Chris Underwood, Manager, Solid Waste Management
604-873-7992

Vernon
3400 - 30 St.
Vernon, BC V1T 5E6
250-545-1361
Fax: 250-545-7876
admin@vernon.ca
www.vernon.ca
Municipal Type: City
Incorporated: Dec. 30, 1892 *Area:* 94.2 sq km
County or District: North Okanagan; *Population in 2006:* 35,944
Provincial Electoral District(s): Okanagan-Vernon
Federal Electoral District(s): Okanagan-Shuswap; Vancouver Island North
Next Election: Nov. 2011 (3 year terms)
Council
Wayne Lippert, Mayor
Administration
Patti Bridal, Manager, Corporate Services
James Rice, Manager, Public Works
jrice@vernon.ca
Tony Kopp, Manager, Utilities
250-545-1361
Kevin Bertles, Manager, Finance
Marg Bailey, General Manager, Corporate Services
Kim Flick, Manager, Planning, Development & Engineering Services

Victoria
1 Centennial Sq.
Victoria, BC V8W 1P6
250-385-5711
Fax: 250-361-0348
publicsrv@victoria.ca
www.victoria.ca
Municipal Type: City
Incorporated: Aug. 2, 1862 *Area:* 19.68 sq km
County or District: Capital Regional District; *Population in 2006:* 78,057
Provincial Electoral District(s): Victoria-Beacon Hill; Victoria-Hillside; Oak Bay-Gordon Head. In Greater Victoria: Esquimalt-Metchosin; Saanich South; Saanich North & the Islands; and Malahat-Juan de Fuca
Federal Electoral District(s): Victoria
Next Election: Nov. 2011 (3 year terms)
Council
Dean Fortin, B.A., LL.B., M.Ed., Mayor
250-361-0200
Sonya Chandler, R.N., Councillor
schandler@victoria.ca
Chris Coleman, B.A., M.B.A., LL.B., Councillor
ccoleman@victoria.ca
Lynn Hunter, Councillor
lhunter@victoria.ca
Phillipe Lucas, B.A., Councillor
plucas@victoria.ca
John Luton, B.A., Councillor
jluton@victoria.ca
Pamela Madoff, Councillor
pmadoff@victoria.ca
Charlayne Thornton-Joe, B.A., Councillor
cthornton-joe@victoria.ca
Geoff Young, B.A., Ph.D., Councillor
gyoung@victoria.ca
Administration
Robert Woodland, Director, Legislative & Regulatory Services
250-361-0203
Gail Stephens, City Manager
250-361-0202

See blue tabs following this section for Municipal Waste Management and Water & Wastewater Treatment.

Doug Angrove, Fire Chief
250-920-3353
Jamie Graham, Chief Constable
250-995-7217
John Basey, City Solicitor
250-361-0588, Fax: 250-361-0348
Deborah Day, Director, Planning & Development
250-361-0511
Trina Scott, Director, Human Resources
250-361-0229
Peter Sparanese, General Manager, Operations
250-361-0292
Jocelyn Jenkyns, General Manager, Victoria Conference Centre
250-361-1000
Ed Robertson, Assistant Director, Public Works
250-361-0457
Katie Josephson, Director, Communications
250-361-0210
Kate Friars, Director, Parks, Recreation & Community Development
250-361-0355
Scott Clark, Manager, Information Systems
250-361-0265
Glen Oberg, Manager, Supply Management Services
250-361-0271
Kim Fowler, Director, Sustainability
250-361-0290
Don Schaffer, Manager, Legislative Services
250-361-0549
Donald Reichert, Supervisor, Solid Waste & Recycling
250-361-0417, Fax: 250-361-0409

White Rock
15322 Buena Vista Ave.
White Rock, BC V4B 1Y6
604-541-2100
Fax: 604-541-9348
whiterockcouncil@city.whiterock.bc.ca
www.city.whiterock.bc.ca
Municipal Type: City
Incorporated: April 15, 1957 *Area:* 5.16 sq km
County or District: Greater Vancouver; *Population in 2006:* 18,755
Provincial Electoral District(s): Surrey-White Rock
Federal Electoral District(s): South Surrey-White Rock-Cloverdale
Next Election: Nov. 2011 (3 year terms)
Council
Catherine Ferguson, Mayor
cferguson@city.whiterock.bc.ca
Administration
Tracey Arthur, City Clerk
604-541-2212
tarthur@city.whiterock.bc.ca
Sandra Kurylo, Director
Financial Services
Peggy Clark, CAO
Peggy Clark, City Manager
pclark@city.whiterock.bc.ca
Phil Lemire, Fire Chief
604-541-2122
plemire@city.whiterock.bc.ca
David Pollock, Director, Municipal Operations
604-541-2181
dpollock@city.whiterock.bc.ca
Greg Scott, P.Eng., City Engineer
gscott@city.whiterock.bc.ca
Dale T. Kitsul, Manager, Parks
604-541-2181
dkitsul@city.whiterock.bc.ca
Paul Stanton, Director, Development Services
pstanton@city.whiterock.bc.ca

Williams Lake
450 Mart St.
Williams Lake, BC V2G 1N3
250-392-2311
Fax: 250-392-4408
corporateservices@williamslake.ca
www.williamslake.ca
Municipal Type: City
Incorporated: March 15, 1929 *Area:* 33.11 sq km
County or District: Cariboo; *Population in 2006:* 10,744
Provincial Electoral District(s): Cariboo North; Cariboo South
Federal Electoral District(s): Cariboo-Prince George
Next Election: Nov. 2011 (3 year terms)
Council
Kerry Cook, Mayor
mayor@williamslake.ca
Administration
Sue Moxey, Director, Corporate Services
250-392-1774
smoxey@williamslake.ca
Darcy Lazzarin, General Manager, Corporate Services
dlazzarin@williamslake.ca
Alberto De Feo, CAO
250-392-1775
adefeo@williamslake.ca
Randy Isfeld, Director, Protective Services
250-392-1778
risfeld@williamslake.ca
Geoff Goodall, Director, Development Services
250-392-1766
ggoodall@williamslake.ca
Brian Carruthers, General Manager, Community Services
250-392-1763
bcarruthers@williamslake.ca
Kevin Goldfuss, Director, Municipal Services
250-392-1783
kgoldfuss@williamslake.ca
Joe Engelberts, Manager, Water/Sewer Division

Other Municipalities in British Columbia

Central Saanich
1903 Mt. Newton Cross Rd.
Saanichton, BC V8M 2A9
250-652-4444
Fax: 250-652-0135
municipalhall@csaanich.ca
www.centralsaanich.ca
Municipal Type: District
Incorporated: Dec. 12, 1950 *Area:* 41.42 sq km
County or District: Capital; *Population in 2006:* 15,745
Provincial Electoral District(s): Saanich North & the Islands
Federal Electoral District(s): Saanich-Gulf Islands
Next Election: Nov. 2011 (3 year terms)
Jack Mar, Mayor
jack.mar@csaanich.ca
Sara C. Ribeiro, Corp. Administrator
sara.ribeiro@csaanich.ca
Nirmal Bhattacharya, P.Eng., Municipal Engineer, Public Works & Operationss
250-652-4444
nirmal@saanich.ca
Roy Thomassen, Chief Building Inspector
Ron French, Fire Chief
250-544-4227
ron.french@csaanich.ca
Hope V. Burns, Director, Planning & Building Services
hope.burns@csaanich.ca
Gary C. Nason, Administrator
gary.nason@csaanich.ca

Delta
4500 Clarence Taylor Cres.
Delta, BC V4K 3E2
604-946-4141
Fax: 604-946-3390
clerks@corp.delta.bc.ca
www.corp.delta.bc.ca
Municipal Type: District
Incorporated: Nov. 10, 1879 *Area:* 183.7 sq km
County or District: Greater Vancouver; *Population in 2006:* 96,723
Provincial Electoral District(s): Delta North; Delta South
Federal Electoral District(s): Delta-Richmond East; Newton-North Delta
Next Election: Nov. 2011 (3 year terms)
Lois E. Jackson, Mayor
604-946-3210, Fax: 604-946-6055
mayor@corp.delta.bc.ca
Robert Campbell, Councillor
604-948-0623
rpc@telus.net
Scott Hamilton, Councillor
604-599-9261
shamilton@corp.delta.bc.ca
George Hawksworth, Councillor
604-946-4740
ghawksworth@corp.delta.bc.ca
Heather King, Councillor
604-946-4141
Bruce McDonald, Councillor
604-946-4141
Anne Peterson, Councillor
604-946-4141
Karl Preuss, Director, Finance
604-946-3230, Fax: 604-946-3962
kpreuss@corp.delta.bc.ca
Ken Kuntz, Director, Parks, Recreation & Culture
604-952-3537, Fax: 604-946-4693
kkuntz@corp.delta.bc.ca
Sean McGill, Director, Human Resources & Corporate Planning
604-946-3218, Fax: 604-946-3706
smcgill@corp.delta.bc.ca
Thomas Leathem, Director, Community Planning & Development
604-946-3380
tleathem@corp.delta.bc.ca
Dan Copeland, Fire Chief
604-952-3119
dcopeland@corp.delta.bc.ca
Jim Cessford, Chief Constable
604-946-3729, Fax: 604-946-3729
deltapolice@police.delta.bc.ca
George Harvie, CAO
604-946-3212, Fax: 604-946-3864
cao@corp.delta.bc.ca
Greg Vanstone, Municipal Solicitor
604-946-3213, Fax: 604-952-3801
gvanstone@corp.delta.bc.ca
Hugh Fraser, Deputy Director, Engineering
Ian Radnidge, Director, Engineering
604-946-3279, Fax: 604-946-2659
iradnidge@corp.delta.bc.ca
Verna Kucy, Manager, Environmental Services
604-946-3281, Fax: 604-946-3240
vkucy@corp.delta.bc.ca
Don Claybo, Manager, Purchasing
604-952-3640, Fax: 604-946-5796
dclybo@corp.delta.bc.ca
Wally Semenoff, Manager, Development
604-946-3384, Fax: 604-946-4148
wsemenoff@corp.delta.bc.ca
Marcy Sangret, Planning Manager, Environment & Agriculture
604-946-3219, Fax: 604-946-4148
msangret@corp.delta.bc.ca
Claudia Jesson, Acting Municipal Clerk
604-946-4141, Fax: 604-946-3390
cjesson@corp.delta.bc.ca

Esquimalt
1229 Esquimalt Rd.
Victoria, BC V9A 3P1
250-414-7100
Fax: 250-414-7111
info@esquimalt.ca
www.esquimalt.ca
Municipal Type: Township
Incorporated: Sept. 1, 1912 *Area:* 7.04 sq km
County or District: Capital; *Population in 2006:* 16,840
Provincial Electoral District(s): Esquimalt-Metchosin
Federal Electoral District(s): Esquimalt-Juan de Fuca
Next Election: Nov. 2011 (3 year terms)
Barbara Desjardins, Mayor
barb.desjardins@esquimalt.ca
Carolynne Evans, Municipal Clerk
Andy Katschor, Acting Director, Parks & Recreation
akatschor@esquimalt.ca
Barbara Snyder, Director, Development Services
barbara.snyder@esquimalt.ca
Paul Nelson, Fire Chief
250-414-7126, Fax: 250-414-7115
Trevor Parkes, Senior Planner, Development Services
Gilbert Cote, Director, Engineering & Public Works
gcote@esquimalt.ca
Vacant, Superintendent, Public Works
Andy Katschor, Manager, Parks
Paul Nelson, Coordinator, Emergency Program
250-414-7125
Laurie Hurst, Acting CAO
lhurst@esquimalt.ca

See blue tabs following this section for Municipal Waste Management and Water & Wastewater Treatment .

Kitimat
270 City Centre
Kitimat, BC V8C 2H7
250-632-8900
Fax: 250-632-4995
districtofkitimat@kitimat.ca
www.city.kitimat.bc.ca
Municipal Type: District
Incorporated: March 31, 1953 *Area:* 242.63 sq km
County or District: Kitimat-Stikine; *Population in 2006:* 8,987
Provincial Electoral District(s): Skeena
Federal Electoral District(s): Skeena-Bulkley Valley
Next Election: Nov. 2011 (3 year terms)
Joanne Monaghan, Mayor
mayor@city.kitimat.bc.ca
Walter McLellan, Municipal Clerk
wmclellan@city.kitimat.bc.ca
Zoelita (Zo) Mulder, Treasurer
zmulder@kitimat.ca
John Klie, Fire Chief
jklie@city.kitimat.bc.ca
Steve Lawson, Manager, Information Systems & Procurement
slawson@city.kitimat.bc.ca
Tim Gleig, Director, Engineering Services
tgleig@city.kitimat.bc.ca
Diane Hewlett, Manager, Economic Promotion & Investor Services
dhewlett@kitimat.ca
Gwendolyn Sewell, Director, Planning and Development
gsewell@city.kitimat.bc.ca

Langley
20338 - 65 Ave.
Langley, BC V2Y 3J1
604-534-3211
Fax: 604-533-6052
info@tol.bc.ca
www.tol.bc.ca
Municipal Type: Township
Incorporated: April 26, 1873 *Area:* 306.93 sq km
County or District: Greater Vancouver; *Population in 2006:* 93,726
Provincial Electoral District(s): Fort Langely-Aldergrove
Federal Electoral District(s): Langley
Next Election: Nov. 2011 (3 year terms)
Rick Green, Mayor
Jordan Bateman, Councillor
Bev Dornan, Councillor
Steve Ferguson, Councillor
Charlie Fox, Councillor
Mel Kositsky, Councillor
Bob Long, Councillor
Kim Richter, Councillor
Grant Ward, Councillor
Mark Bakken, Administrator
604-533-6002
Hilary Tsikayi, Director, Finance
604-533-6156, Fax: 604-533-6130
htsikayi@tol.bc.ca
Ramin Sefi, Director, Community Development
604-533-6059, Fax: 604-533-6110
kholden@tol.bc.ca
Christine Corfe, Director, Corporate Administration
604-533-6015, Fax: 604-533-6010
ccorfe@tol.bc.ca
Doug Wade, Fire Chief
604-532-7509, Fax: 604-532-7530
dwade@tol.bc.ca
Paul Crawford, Manager, Long Range Planning
604-533-6056
pcrawford@tol.bc.ca
Dellarae Sawchuk, Manager, Purchasing
604-533-7327, Fax: 604-533-6130
dsawchuk@tol.bc.ca
Shannon Harvey-Renner, Manager, Human Resources
604-533-6121, Fax: 604-533-6129

Maple Ridge
11995 Haney Pl.
Maple Ridge, BC V2X 6A9
604-463-5221
Fax: 604-467-7329
enquiries@mapleridge.ca
www.mapleridge.ca
Municipal Type: District
Incorporated: Sept. 12, 1874 *Area:* 265.79 sq km
County or District: Fraser Valley; *Population in 2006:* 68,949
Provincial Electoral District(s): Maple Ridge-Pitt Meadows; Maple Ridge-Mission
Federal Electoral District(s): Pitt Meadows-Maple Ridge-Mission
Next Election: Nov. 2011 (3 year terms)
Ernie Daykin, Mayor
edaykin@mapleridge.ca
Cheryl Ashlie, Councillor
Judy Dueck, Councillor
Al Hogarth, Councillor
Linda King, Councillor
Mike Morden, Councillor
Craig Speirs, Councillor
James Rule, CAO
604-463-5221
jrule@mapleridge.ca
Mike Murray, General Manager, Community Development, Parks & Recreation Services
mmurray@mapleridge.ca
Frank Quinn, General Manager, Public Works & Development Services
fquinn@mapleridge.ca
Brock McDonald, Director, Licences, Permits & Bylaws
604-467-7370
bmcdonald@mapleridge.ca
Gary Manson, Manager, Communications
Paul Gill, General Manager, Corporate & Financial Services
pgill@mapleridge.ca
Jake Sorba, Director, Finance
604-467-7317
Jane Pickering, Director, Planning
604-467-7471
jpickering@mapleridge.ca
David Boag, Director, Parks & Facilities
604-467-7344
dboag@mapleridge.ca
Russ Carmichael, Director, Engineering Operations
604-467-7363
rcarmichael@mapleridge.ca
Andrew Wood, Municipal Engineer
604-467-7496, Fax: 604-467-7425
Jim Sheehan, Environmental Technician
604-467-7499
jsheehan@mapleridge.org
Rod Stott, Environmental Planner
604-467-7390
rstott@mapleridge.org
Chuck Goddard, Manager, Development & Environmental Services
604-467-7487
cgoddard@mapleridge.org
Terry Fryer, Manager, Corporate & Development Engineering
604-467-7450
Peter Grootendorst, Director, Fire Operations
604-463-5221
pgrootendorst@mapleridge.ca
John Bastaja, Chief Information Officer
604-467-7479
jbastaja@mapleridge.ca
Sue Wheeler, Director, Community Services
604-467-7308
swheeler@mapleridge.ca
Dave Walsh, Superintendent, Police Services
604-463-6251
Ceri Marlo, P.Eng., Manager, Legislative Services
604-467-7482, Fax: 604-467-7329
cmarlo@mapleridge.ca

Mission
P.O. Box 20
8645 Stave Lake St.
Mission, BC V2V 4L9
604-820-3700
Fax: 604-826-1363
info@mission.ca
www.mission.ca
Municipal Type: District
Incorporated: June 2, 1892 *Area:* 225.78 sq km
County or District: Fraser Valley; *Population in 2006:* 34,505
Provincial Electoral District(s): Maple Ridge-Mission
Federal Electoral District(s): Pitt Meadows-Maple Ridge-Mission
Next Election: Nov. 2011 (3 year terms)
James Atebe, Mayor
Ian Fitzpatrick, Coordinator, Emergency Program
604-820-5390
Robert Ross, Director, Community Development
604-820-3751
RRoss@mission.ca
Beverly Endersby, Manager, Inspection Services
604-820-3732
bendersby@mission.ca
Brian Storrier, Director, Parks & Recreation
604-820-5355
Brian_Storrier@mission.ca
Michael Giesbrecht, Manager, Purchasing
604-820-3756
mgiesbrecht@mission.ca
Mike Hofer, Environmental Technician
604-820-3736
Mike_Hofer@mission.ca
Ken Bjorgaard, Director, Finance
Glenn Robertson, CAO
604-820-3704
grobertson@mission.ca
Ian Fitzpatrick, Fire Chief
604-820-5390
ifitzpatrick@mission.ca
Kim Allan, Director, Forest Management
604-820-3764
Kim_Allan@mission.ca
Greg Giles, Superintendent, Utilities
604-820-3765
Greg_Giles@mission.ca
Sharon Fletcher, Director, Planning
604-820-3752
sfletcher@mission.ca
Dennis Clark, Director, Corporate Administration
dclark@mission.ca
Rick Bomhof, Director, Engineering & Public Works
604-820-3736
rbomhof@mission.ca

North Cowichan
P.O. Box 278
7030 Trans Canada Hwy.
Duncan, BC V9L 3X4
250-746-3100
Fax: 250-746-3133
info@northcowichan.bc.ca
www.northcowichan.bc.ca
Municipal Type: District
Incorporated: June 18, 1873 *Area:* 193.66 sq km
County or District: Cowichan Valley; *Population in 2006:* 27,557
Provincial Electoral District(s): Cowichan-Ladysmith
Federal Electoral District(s): Nanaimo-Cowichan
Next Election: Nov. 2011 (3 year terms)
Tom Walker, Mayor
walker@northcowichan.bc.ca
Mark O. Ruttan, Director, Administration
ruttan@northcowichan.bc.ca
Mark Frame, Director, Finance
frame@northcowichan.bc.ca
Chris Hall, Director, Planning
hall@northcowichan.bc.ca
John Mackay, Director, Engineering
250-746-3103
mackay@northcowichan.bc.ca
Ernie Mansueti, Director, Parks & Recreation
mansueti@northcowichan.bc.ca
Darrell Frank, Forester
250-746-3104
frank@northcowichan.bc.ca
F.S. Rockwell, Medical Health Officer

North Saanich
1620 Mills Rd.
North Saanich, BC V8L 5S9
250-656-0781
Fax: 250-656-3155
admin@northsaanich.ca
www.northsaanich.ca
Municipal Type: District
Incorporated: Aug. 19, 1965 *Area:* 37.14 sq km
County or District: Capital; *Population in 2006:* 10,823
Provincial Electoral District(s): Saanich North & the Islands
Federal Electoral District(s): Saanich-Gulf Islands
Next Election: Nov. 2011 (3 year terms)

See blue tabs following this section for Municipal Waste Management and Water & Wastewater Treatment.

Municipal Governments / British Columbia

Alice Finall, Mayor
mayor@northsaanich.ca
Tim Tanton, Engineer
Curt Kingsley, Manager, Corporate Services
ckingsley@northsaanich.ca
Ralph Gillis, Director, Financial Services
rgillis@northsaanich.ca

North Vancouver
355 West Queens Rd.
North Vancouver, BC V7N 4N5
604-990-2311
Fax: 604-984-9637
infoweb@dnv.org
www.dnv.org
Municipal Type: District Municipality
Incorporated: Aug. 10, 1891 *Area:* 160.67 sq km
County or District: Greater Vancouver; *Population in 2006:* 82,562
Provincial Electoral District(s): N. Vancouver-Lonsdale; N. Vancouver-Seymour; W. Vancouver-Capilano; W. Vancouver-Garibaldi
Federal Electoral District(s): North Vancouver; West Vancouver-Sunshine Coast-Sea to Sky Country
Next Election: Nov. 2011 (3 year terms)
Richard Walton, Mayor
604-990-2208
council@dnv.org
Roger Bassam, Councillor
Robin Hicks, Councillor
Mike Little, Councillor
Doug Mackay-Dunn, Councillor
Lisa Muri, Councillor
Alan Nixon, Councillor
Agnes S. Hilsen, Municipal Clerk
604-990-2207
agnes_hilsen@dnv.org
Nicole Deveaux, CFO
604-990-2234
David Stuart, CAO
604-990-2209
dstuart@dnv.org
Doug Trussler, Chief, Fire & Rescue Services
604-990-3653
Jozsef Dioszeghy, Director, Environment, Parks & Engineering
604-990-3828
Margaret Eckenfelder, Director, Sustainability, Planning & Building
604-990-2398
Gavin Joyce, Director, Corporate Services
604-990-2336
Ken Bennett, Manager, Environment & Sustainability
604-990-2445
Richard Boulton, Manager, Parks & Environmental Services
604-990-3804
Brett Dwyer, Manager, Development Services
604-990-2247
Robert Huffman, P.Eng., Manager, Utilities
604-990-3861
Len Jensen, Manager, Engineering Operations
604-990-3845
Rick Pratt, Manager, Information Technology Services
604-990-2312
Cindy Rogers, Manager, Human Resources
604-990-2217
rogersc@dnv.org
Donna Howes, Section Manager, Transportation Planning
604-990-2450
Paula Huber, Section Manager, Planning Development
604-990-2328
Allen Lynch, Section Manager, Waste Reduction
604-984-9730
Graham Knell, Coordinator, Trails & Habitat
604-990-3806
Mark Brown, District Arborist

Oak Bay
2167 Oak Bay Ave.
Victoria, BC V8R 1G2
250-598-3311
Fax: 250-598-9108
lhilton@oakbaybc.org
www.oakbaybc.org
Municipal Type: District
Incorporated: July 2, 1906 *Area:* 10.38 sq km

County or District: Capital; *Population in 2006:* 17,908
Provincial Electoral District(s): Oak Bay-Gordon Head
Federal Electoral District(s): Victoria
Next Election: Nov. 2011 (3 year terms)
Christopher M. Causton, Mayor
mayor@oakbay.ca
Dave Marshall, Director, Engineering Services
Patricia A. Walker, Treasurer
pawalker@oakbay.ca
William E. Cochrane, CAO
bcochrane@oakbay.ca
Roy Thomassen, Director, Building & Planning
rthomassen@oakbay.ca
Agnes Szilos, Director, Parks & Recreation
250-595-7946
Phil Barnett, Superintendent, Public Works
250-598-4501
Gerry Adam, Fire Chief
250-592-9121
Lorne Middleton, Manager, Parks Services
250-592-7275
lmiddleton@oakbay.ca

Quesnel
410 Kinchant St.
Quesnel, BC V2J 7J5
250-992-2111
Fax: 250-992-2206
cityhall@city.quesnel.bc.ca
www.city.quesnel.bc.ca
Municipal Type: Town
Incorporated: March 21, 1928 *Area:* 35.34 sq km
County or District: Cariboo; *Population in 2006:* 9,326
Provincial Electoral District(s): Cariboo North
Federal Electoral District(s): Cariboo-Prince George
Next Election: Nov. 2011 (3 year terms)
Mary Sjostrom, Mayor
mayorsjostrom@city.quesnel.bc.ca
Byron Johnson, CAO
bjohnson@city.quesnel.bc.ca
Kari Bolton, Director, Finance
kbolton@city.quesnel.bc.ca
Jack Marsh, Director, Public Works & Engineering
jmarsh@city.quesnel.bc.ca
Ric Raynor, Director, Emergency Services
rraynor@city.quesnel.bc.ca
Richard Bergey, Manager, Development Services
rbergey@city.quesnel.bc.ca
Tanya Turner, Planner
tturner@city.quesnel.bc.ca
Chris Coben, Superintendent, Utilities
ccoben@city.quesnel.bc.ca
Alec Darragh, Supervisor, Parks & Solid Waste
adarragh@city.quesnel.bc.ca
Coralee Oakes, Councillor & Member, Environmental Advisory Committee
Jeff Norburn, Director, Community Services
jnorburn@city.quesnel.bc.ca
Ken Coombs, Deputy Superintendent, Works
kcoombs@city.quesnel.bc.ca
Harlene Hunt, Manager, Quesnel Airport & Quesnel Transit
hhunt@city.quesnel.bc.ca

Saanich
770 Vernon Ave.
Victoria, BC V8X 2W7
250-475-1775
Fax: 250-475-5440
clerksec@saanich.ca
www.saanich.ca
Municipal Type: District Municipality
Incorporated: Dec. 12, 1950 *Area:* 103.44 sq km
County or District: Capital; *Population in 2006:* 108,265
Provincial Electoral District(s): Oak Bay-Gordon Head; Saanich N. & the Islands; Saanich S.
Federal Electoral District(s): Esquimalt-Juan de Fuca; Saanich-Gulf Islands; Victoria
Next Election: Nov. 2011 (3 year terms)
Frank Leonard, Mayor
250-475-5510
mayor@saanich.ca
Susan Brice, Councillor
Judy Brownoff, Councillor
Vic Derman, Councillor
Paul Gerrard, Councillor

Wayne Hunter, Councillor
Dean Murdock, Councillor
Vicki Sanders, Councillor
Leif Wergeland, Councillor
Carrie M. MacPhee, Manager, Legislative Services, Fax: 250-475-5440
macpheec@saanich.ca
Ken Kreiger, Director, Parks & Recreation
250-475-5422, Fax: 250-475-5411
kreigerk@saanich.ca
Russ Fuoco, Director, Planning
250-475-5472, Fax: 250-475-5430
fuocor@saanich.ca
Marie Van Dyk, Director, Purchasing, Fax: 250-475-5460
vandykm@saanich.ca
Tim Wood, Administrator
250-475-5555, Fax: 250-475-5440
woodt@saanich.ca
Colin Doyle, Director, Engineering
250-475-5447, Fax: 250-475-5450
colin.doyle@saanich.ca
Bonnie Cole, Manager, Human Resources, Fax: 250-475-5550
bonnie.cole@saanich.ca
Mike Chadwick, Chief Constable
250-475-4321, Fax: 250-475-6138
community@saanichpolice.ca
Chris Nation, Municipal Solicitor, Fax: 250-475-5444
chris.nation@saanich.ca
Dave Ward, Fire Chief
250-475-5423, Fax: 250-475-5588
dave.ward@saanich.ca
Dwayne Halldorson, Manager, Underground Services
250-475-5574, Fax: 250-475-5450
dwayne.halldorson@saanich.ca
Adriane Pollard, Manager, Environmental Services, Fax: 250-475-5430
Dave McAra, Manager, Solid Waste Services
250-475-5432, Fax: 250-475-5590
mcarad@saanich.ca
Mike Ippen, Manager, Public Works
250-475-1775, Fax: 250-475-5487
mike.ippen@saanich.ca
Al Keiser, Manager, Waterworks
250-475-1775, Fax: 250-475-5438
keisera@saanich.ca
Quenton Lehmann, Manager, Recreation
250-475-5441, Fax: 250-475-5411
quenton.lehmann@saanich.ca
Nathalie Dechaine, Officer, Environmental Education
250-475-5475
dechainn@saanich.ca
Anne Topp, Manager, Community Planning
250-475-1775, Fax: 250-457-5430
anne.topp@saanich.ca
Paul Murray, Director, Finance
250-475-5521, Fax: 250-475-5429
paul.murray@saanich.ca
Kristine Kelly, Manager, Forestry, Horticulture & Natural Areas
250-475-5539
kellyk@saanich.ca
Angela Evans, Officer, Environmental Planning
250-475-1775
evansa@saanich.ca
Donavon (Von) Bishop, Manager, Development & Municipal Facilities
Mike Lai, Manager, Transportation
250-475-5492, Fax: 250-475-5450

Squamish
P.O. Box 310
37955 Second Ave
Squamish, BC V0N 3G0
604-892-5217
Fax: 604-892-1083
admdept@squamish.ca
www.squamish.ca
Municipal Type: District
Incorporated: May 18, 1948 *Area:* 106.11 sq km
County or District: Squamish-Lillooet; *Population in 2006:* 14,949
Provincial Electoral District(s): West Vancouver-Garibaldi
Federal Electoral District(s): West Vancouver-Sunshine Coast-Sea to Sky Country
Next Election: Nov. 2011 (3 year terms)

See blue tabs following this section for Municipal Waste Management and Water & Wastewater Treatment.

Municipal Governments / Manitoba

Greg Gardner, Mayor
ggardner@squamish.ca
Ray Saurette, Fire Chief
rsaurette@squamish.ca
Cameron Chalmers, Director, Planning
604-815-5010
cchalmers@squamish.ca
Rick Boulier, Manager, Technical Services
604-815-5015
rboulier@squamish.ca
Francesca Langford, Coordinator, Environment
604-815-5021
environment@squamish.ca
Kim Anema, CAO
604-815-5004
Ralph M. Hughes, Director, Finance
rhughes@squamish.ca
Mick Gottardi, Director, Community Development
604-815-5011
mgottardi@squamish.ca
Cliff Doherty, Director, Protective Services
cdoherty@squamish.ca
Rod Pleasance, Project Engineer
604-815-5016
rpleasance@squamish.ca
Gordon Prescott, Manager, Operations
gprescott@squamish.ca
Maurice Wutzke, Assistant Manager, Operations - Roads, Drainage & Parks
mwutzke@squamish.ca
Fred Hendy, Assistant Manager, Operations - Fleet & Buildings
fhendy@squamish.ca
Dennis Bell, Foreman, Waterworks
dbell@squamish.ca
Roy Mihalick, Chief Operator, Wastewater Treatment Plant
rmihalick@squamish.ca
Jim Lang, Coordinator, Emergency Program
jlang@squamish.ca

Summerland
P.O. Box 159
11321 Henry Ave.
Summerland, BC V0H 1Z0
250-494-6451
Fax: 250-494-1415
info@summerland.ca
summerland@summerland.ca
Municipal Type: District
Incorporated: Dec. 21, 1906 *Area:* 73.88 sq km
County or District: Okanagan-Similkameen; *Population in 2006:* 10,828
Provincial Electoral District(s): Okanagan-Westside
Federal Electoral District(s): Okanagan-Coquihalla
Next Election: Nov. 2011 (3 year terms)
Janice Perrino, Mayor
mayor@summerland.ca
Ken Ostraat, Director, Finance
kostraat@summerland.ca
Gordon Morley, District Planner & Approving Officer
gmorley@summerland.ca
Dale McDonald, Director, Parks & Recreation
dmacdonald@summerland.ca
Lloyd Miskiman, Fire Chief
lmiskiman@summerland.ca
Dave Hill, Superintendent, Public Works
works@summerland.ca
Don De Gagne, CAO
ddegagne@summerland.ca
Don Darling, Director, Engineering & Public Works
ddarling@summerland.ca
Joe Fitzpatrick, Officer, Water Conservation
jfitzpatrick@summerland.ca
Greg Mealing, Superintendent, Water Operations
gmealing@summerland.ca

West Vancouver
750 - 17 St.
West Vancouver, BC V7V 3T3
604-925-7000
Fax: 604-925-7006
info@westvancouver.ca
www.westvancouver.ca
Municipal Type: District
Incorporated: March 15, 1912 *Area:* 87.13 sq km
County or District: Greater Vancouver; *Population in 2006:* 42,131
Provincial Electoral District(s): N. Vancouver-Lonsdale; W. Vancouver-Capilano; W. Vancouver-Garibaldi
Federal Electoral District(s): West Vancouver-Sunshine Coast-Sea to Sky Country
Next Election: Nov. 2011 (3 year terms)
Pamela Goldsmith-Jones, Mayor
pgoldsmith-jones@westvancouver.ca
Anne Mooi, Director, Parks & Community Services
604-925-7206
Bob Sokol, Director, Planning, Lands & Permits
604-925-7058
Gareth Rowlands, Acting Manager, Transit
604-985-3500
Grant McRadu, CAO
604-925-7002
gmcradu@westvancouver.ca
Richard Laing, Director, Finance
Brent Dozzi, Manager, Roads & Transportation
604-925-7157
Jim Cook, Fire Chief
604-925-7370
Allen Lynch, Manager, North Shore Recycling Program
604-984-9730, Fax: 604-984-3563
Ray Fung, Director, Engineering & Transportation

Manitoba

The Manitoba Conservation Department administers the Environment Act for the province. Each municipality in the province is individually licensed and responsible for sewage and wastewater management under the guidelines of the Act.

There are approximately 270 landfill sites in the province. Some transfer stations burn brush and plain wood. There are no incinerators or open pit burning.

Under the Waste Reduction & Prevention Act, Manitoba Product Stewardship Corporation is mandated to establish and administer a waste reduction and prevention program for designated materials for Manitoba. Recycling is supported by the province, with the municipalities paying 20% of the cost. Glass, bottles, cans and paper are recycled at transfer stations. More than 90% of the population of Manitoba recycles. Beverage container recycling is encouraged with consumers paying an extra 2 cents per bottle as part of a non-refundable recycling fee. There are over 200 community recycling programs in Manitoba. For fiscal 2007/2008 material recovery increased by 6.2%.

Manitoba Water Stewardship manages the province's water resources. The Drinking Water Safety Act created the Office of Drinking Water, established to provide a regulatory and advisory function. The Act also provides regulations regarding livestock, waste systems, and other measures to ensure the drinking water supply. The Water Protection Act (June, 2005) is designed to protect water at its source and includes standards regarding treatment of municipal waste, watershed management plans, water management zones, and the establishment of the Manitoba Water Council. The first standard to be introduced related to municipal waste. Municipal water conservation is promoted through the Water Efficiency Program.

Municipalities are eligible for the Sustainable Development Innovations Fund, which supports the development, implementation and promotion of environmental innovation and sustainable development projects.

Major Municipalities in Manitoba

Brandon
410 - 9th St.
Brandon, MB R7A 6A2
204-729-2186
Fax: 204-729-8244
cityclerk@brandon.ca
www.brandon.ca
Municipal Type: City
Incorporated: May 3, 1882 *Area:* 76.89 sq km
Population in 2006: 41,511
Provincial Electoral District(s): Brandon East; Brandon West
Federal Electoral District(s): Brandon-Souris
Next Election: Oct. 2014 (4 year terms)
Council
Shari Decter Hirst, Mayor
mayor@brandon.ca
Jeff Fawcett, Councillor, Ward(s): 1. Assiniboine
Corey Roberts, Councillor, Ward(s): 2. Rosser
Murray Blight, Councillor, Ward(s): 3. Victoria
Jeff Harwood, Councillor, Ward(s): 4. University
James McCrae, Councillor, Ward(s): 5. Meadows
Garth Rice, Councillor, Ward(s): 6. South Centre
Shawn Berry, Councillor, Ward(s): 7. Linden Lanes
Stephen Montague, Councillor, Ward(s): 8. Richmond
Len Isleifson, Councillor, Ward(s): 9. Riverview
Jan Chaboyer, Councillor, Ward(s): 10. Green Acres
Administration
Conrad R. Arvisais, City Clerk
204-729-2207, Fax: 204-729-0975
c.arvisais@brandon.ca
Grant McMillan, General Manager & City Treasurer, Corporate Services
204-729-2209
g.mcmillan@brandon.ca
Brian MacRae, City Manager
204-729-2204, Fax: 204-729-0975
b.macrae@brandon.ca
Brian Kayes, Director, Emergency Coordination
best@brandon.ca
Rick Bailey, Director, Public Works
r.bailey@brandon.ca
Jeff Roziere, Director, Sanitation
204-573-6480
j.roziere@brandon.ca
Cathy Snelgrove, General Manager, Operations
204-729-2145, Fax: 204-729-2191
c.snelgrove@brandon.ca
Ted Snure, General Manager & City Engineer, Development Services
204-729-2214, Fax: 204-725-3235
t.snure@brandon.ca
Ian Christiansen, Manager, Engineering Services & Water Resources
i.christiansen@brandon.ca
Sandy Trudel, Officer, Economic Development
s.trudel@brandon.ca
Vivienne Lockerby, CPP, Supervisor, Purchasing
v.lockerby@brandon.ca
Brent Dane, Fire Chief
204-729-2404, Fax: 204-729-2153
b.dane@brandon.ca

Portage La Prairie
97 Saskatchewan Ave. East
Portage la Prairie, MB R1N 0L8
204-239-8337
Fax: 204-239-1532
tkirchener@city-plap.com
www.city-plap.com
Municipal Type: City
Incorporated: Jan. 3, 1907 *Area:* 24.67 sq km
Population in 2006: 12,728
Provincial Electoral District(s): Portage la Prairie
Federal Electoral District(s): Portage-Lisgar
Next Election: Oct. 2014 (4 year terms)
Council
Earl Porter, Mayor
Administration
Dale Lyle, City Manager
Kelly Braden, Director, Operations
204-239-8350, Fax: 204-857-7257
kbraden@city-plap.com
Dean Yaremchuk, Director, Economic & Community Development
dyaremchuk@city-plap.com
Dennis Nodrick, Chief, Fire
204-239-8340, Fax: 204-239-5154
dcnpes@escape.ca
Doug Campbell, Manager, Water Treatment
204-239-8373
dcampbell@city-plap.com
Dave Green, Manager, Parks
204-239-8325
dgreen@city-plap.com
Ian Milne, Manager, Engineering
204-239-8349
imilne@city-plap.com
Brian Taylor, Manager, Public Works
204-239-8352
btaylor@city-plap.com

See blue tabs following this section for Municipal Waste Management and Water & Wastewater Treatment.

Municipal Governments / New Brunswick

Wayne Wall, Manager, Water Pollution Control Facility
204-239-8359
wwall@city-plap.com

Thompson
226 Mystery Lake Rd.
Thompson, MB R8N 1S6
204-677-7910
Fax: 204-677-7936
ltaylor@city.thompson.mb.ca
www.thompson.ca
Municipal Type: City
Incorporated: Jan. 5, 1970 *Area:* 17.18 sq km
Population in 2006: 13,446
Provincial Electoral District(s): Thompson
Federal Electoral District(s): Churchill
Next Election: Oct. 2014 (4 year terms)
Council
Tim Johnston, Mayor
johnston@city.thompson.mb.ca
Administration
Lynn Taylor, City Manager
Dennis Fenske, Director, Personnel & Community Development
dfenske@city.thompson.mb.ca
Ken Thevenot, Fire Chief
204-677-7915
fchief@city.thompson.mb.ca
Ken Allard, Superintendent, Public Works
204-677-7900
kallard@city.thompson.mb.ca
Ray Janzen, Engineering Technician, Water & Sewer
204-677-7905
rjanzen@city.thompson.mb.ca
Nathan Steuart, Engineering Technician, Roads & Buildings
nsteuart@city.thompson.mb.ca
Wayne Koversky, Agent, Purchasing
204-677-7973
koversky@city.thompson.mb.ca

Winnipeg
City Hall
510 Main St.
Winnipeg, MB R3B 1B9
204-986-6432
Fax: 204-947-3452
Phone or Fax: 311 for information on city services
www.winnipeg.ca
Municipal Type: City
Incorporated: Nov. 8, 1873 *Area:* 464.01 sq km
Population in 2006: 633,451
Provincial Electoral District(s): Assiboina; Burrows; Charleswood; Concordia; Elmwood; Ft. Garry-Riverview; Ft. Rouge; Ft. Whyte; Inkster; Kildonan; Kirkfield Park; Logan; Minto; Point Douglas; Radisson; Riel; River East; River Heights; Rossmere; Seine River; Southdale; St. Boniface; St. James; St. Johns; St. Norbert; St. Vital; The Maples; Transcona; Tuxedo; Tyndall Park; Wollseley
Federal Electoral District(s): Charleswood-St. James-Assiniboia; Elmwood-Transcona; Kildonan-St. Paul; Saint Boniface; Winnipeg Centre; Winnipeg North; Winnipeg South; Winnipeg South Centre
Next Election: Oct. 2014 (4 year terms)
Council
Sam Katz, Mayor
204-986-2171, Fax: 204-949-0566
feedback@winnipeg.ca
Paula Havixbeck, Councillor, Ward(s): Charleswood-Tuxedo
Harvey Smith, Councillor, Ward(s): Daniel McIntyre
204-986-5951, Fax: 204-986-7000
Thomas Steen, Councillor, Ward(s): Elmwood-East Kildonan
Jenny Gerbasi, Councillor, Ward(s): Fort Rouge-East Fort Garry
204-986-5878, Fax: 204-986-5636
Ross Eadie, Councillor, Ward(s): Mynarski
Jeff Browaty, Councillor, Ward(s): North Kildonan
204-986-5196, Fax: 204-986-3725
Devi Sharma, Councillor, Ward(s): Old Kildonan
Mike Pagtakhan, Councillor, Ward(s): Point Douglas
204-986-8401, Fax: 204-986-3531
John Orlikow, Councillor, Ward(s): River Heights-Fort Garry
204-986-5236, Fax: 204-986-3725
Daniel Vandal, Councillor, Ward(s): St. Boniface
204-986-5206, Fax: 204-986-3725
Grant Nordman, Councillor, Ward(s): St. Charles
204-986-5920, Fax: 204-986-7359

Scott Fielding, Councillor, Ward(s): St. James-Brooklands
204-986-5848, Fax: 204-986-4320
Justin Swandel, Councillor, Ward(s): St. Norbert
204-986-6824, Fax: 204-986-3725
Gord Steeves, Councillor, Ward(s): St. Vital
204-986-5088, Fax: 204-986-3725
Russ Wyatt, Councillor, Ward(s): Transcona
204-986-8087, Fax: 204-986-4530
Administration
Richard Kachur, City Clerk
204-986-2428, Fax: 204-947-3452
Jo-Anne Ferrier, City Treasurer
Michael P. Ruta, Deputy CAO/CFO
Glen Laubenstein, CAO
Jim Brennan, Chief, Winnipeg Fire Paramedic Service
Keith McCaskill, Chief of Police, Winnipeg Police Service
Linda Black, Director, Corporate Support Services
Nelson Karpa, Director, Assessment & Taxation
Bill Larkin, Director, Public Works
Barry MacBride, Director, Water & Waste
Deepak Joshi, Director, Planning, Property & Development
Dave Wardrop, Director, Winnipeg Transit
Clive Wightman, Director, Community Services
Kelly Kjartanson, Manager, Environmental Standards
Dave Domke, Manager, Parks & Open Space
Brad Sacher, Manager, Transportation

Rural Municipality

Hanover
P.O. Box 1720
28 Westland Dr.
Steinbach, MB R5G 1N4
204-326-4488
Fax: 204-326-4830
general@rmhanover.mb.ca
Municipal Type: Rural Municipality
Incorporated: Jan. 7, 1881 *Area:* 740.31 sq km
Population in 2006: 11,871
Provincial Electoral District(s): Steinbach
Federal Electoral District(s): Provencher
Next Election: Oct. 2014 (4 year terms)
Douglas E. Cavers, CAO
Stan Toews, Reeve

St. Andrews
P.O. Box 130
500 Railway Ave.
Clandeboye, MB R0C 0P0
204-738-2264
Fax: 204-738-2500
Toll Free Phone: 1-866-738-2264
info@rmofstandrews.com
www.rmofstandrews.com
Municipal Type: Rural Municipality
Incorporated: Jan. 5, 1880 *Area:* 752.7 sq km
Population in 2006: 11,359
Provincial Electoral District(s): Gimli
Federal Electoral District(s): Selkirk-Interlake
Next Election: Oct. 2014 (4 year terms)
Danny Jo Sigmundson, CAO
cao@rmofstandrews.com
Don Forfar, Reeve
don@rmofstandrews.com
Ralph Bach, Chair, Public Works
Lawrie Hunt, Chair, Environment
Brad Pawluk, Superintendent, Public Works
Jack Robertson, District Fire Chief (St. Andrews South)
204-757-4748
Ray Kelsch, District Fire Chief (St. Andrews Central)
204-738-2607
Ron Lucyshen, District Fire Chief (St. Andrews North)
204-389-2004

Springfield
P.O. Box 219
628 Main St.
Oakbank, MB R0E 1J0
204-444-3321
Fax: 204-444-2137
ltetrault@rmofspringfield.ca
www.rmofspringfield.ca
Municipal Type: Rural Municipality
Incorporated: Jan. 4, 1873 *Area:* 1,100.81 sq km
Population in 2006: 12,990

Provincial Electoral District(s): Springfield
Federal Electoral District(s): Provencher; Selkirk-Interlake
Next Election: Oct. 2014 (4 year terms)
Laurent Tetrault, CAO
Peter Skrupski, Reeve
204-444-2970
pskrupski@mts.net
Shawn Tosh, Manager, Operations
204-444-2241
Tony Keoycga, Manager, Recreation
204-444-4119
David Donaghy, CAO

New Brunswick

The goal of New Brunswick's Department of Environment & Local Government is to protect, maintain or improve the water quality of its lakes and rivers and the air quality, and to provide appropriate reduction and disposal of waste. The Department relies on the Clean Air Act, the Clean Environment Act and the Clean Water Act to achieve these goals. All three stipulate that anyone discharging a contaminant needs approval from the Minister.

Municipalities oversee solid waste collection for their municipality and its surrounding area. The Province contracts with local haulers for waste collection in rural areas. There are six sanitary landfill sites, with five transfer stations that complete the province-wide waste management network. The Provincial government provides legislation, regulations and guidelines to manage the environment appropriately. Solid waste commissions, their establishment and operation, and the conditions under which they may accept solid waste, are outlined in the Clean Environment Act and the Regional Solid Waste Commissions Regulation. Between 1988 & 2001, waste going to landfills decreased by 41%, thanks to diversion programs and consumer awareness.

Water and wastewater systems are owned and operated by municipalities, the province and private companies. Under the Municipal Drinking Water Program established in 2003, certificates of approval for municipal water treatment and water distribution facilities are required to safeguard drinking water systems. The certificates cover training, certification, monitoring and reporting requirements. The Wellfield Protection Program & the Watershed Protection Programs are designed to ensure safe drinking water for municipalities that rely on groundwater for drinking water by designating the area that needs to be protected from industries or activities operating in the area of a wellfield or watershed. The Canada/New Brunswick Infrastructure Program has allocated 70% of its funding to green initiatives for municipalities, especially in the area of water quality infrastructure.

The Beverage Containers Program was devised to reduce the amount of waste going into landfills, or littered along roadsides and waterways. Each beverage distributor is responsible for their containers by refilling or recycling them. Scrap tires and used oil programs exist as well.

Major Municipalities in New Brunswick

Bathurst
150 St. George St.
Bathurst, NB E2A 1B5
506-548-0400
Fax: 506-548-0581
city@bathurst.ca
www.bathurst.ca
Municipal Type: City
Area: 91.55 sq km
County or District: Gloucester; *Population in 2006:* 12,714
Provincial Electoral District(s): Bathurst
Federal Electoral District(s): Acadie-Bathurst
Next Election: May 2012 (4 year terms)
Council
Stephen J. Brunet, Mayor
506-548-2171
Bob Anderson, Councillor
506-548-3536
bobelva@nb.sympatico.ca
Hugh L. Comeau, Councillor
506-548-2255
2868@nb.sympatico.ca
Scott A. Ferguson, Councillor
506-547-8993
scott.ferguson@nbed.nb.ca

See blue tabs following this section for Municipal Waste Management and Water & Wastewater Treatment.

Anne-Marie Gammon, Councillor
506-545-6821
amgammon@nbnet.nb.ca
Daniel (Danny) Roy, Councillor
506-546-1588
Graham Wiseman, Councillor
506-548-3600
gwiseman3600@rogers.com
Hugh J. Young, Councillor
506-548-1815
HughJYoung@GMAIL.com
Administration
Lola Doucet, City Clerk
506-548-0417
André Doucet, City Manager
506-548-0733
Gerald Pettigrew, Manager, Operations, Parks, Recreation & Tourism Department
506-548-0410
kcregionalcenter@bathurst.ca
Vincent Wood, General Foreman, Utilities
506-548-0444
Vincent.Wood@bathurst.ca
Marc Losier, Director, Design & Construction
city.operationalservices@bathurst.ca
Paul Godin, General Engineer
Robert Langlais, Fire Chief
506-548-0439
city.fire@bathurst.ca
Danny White, Manager, Operation Planning
Barry Veniot, Supervisor, Purchasing
506-548-0700
Barry.Veniot@bathurst.ca
Lucien Cormier, Building Inspector
Lucien.Cormier@bathurst.ca
Donald McLaughlin, Technician, Planning
Dave Moran, General Foreman, Above Ground Operational Services

Dieppe
333, av Acadie
Dieppe, NB E1A 1G9
506-877-7900
Fax: 506-877-7910
info@dieppe.ca, communications@dieppe.ca
www.dieppe.ca
Municipal Type: City
Incorporated: Jan. 1, 1952 *Area:* 51.17 sq km
County or District: Westmorland; *Population in 2006:* 18,565
Provincial Electoral District(s): Dieppe Centre-Lewisville
Federal Electoral District(s): Moncton-Riverview-Dieppe; Beauséjour
Next Election: May 2012 (4 year terms)
Jody Dallaire, Councillor at Large
506-387-8738
jody.dallaire@dieppe.ca
Council
Jean G. LeBlanc, Mayor
jean.leblanc@dieppe.ca
Yvon Comeau, Councillor at Large
506-388-3245
yvon.comeau@dieppe.ca
Jean J. Gaudet, Councillor at Large
506-854-8409
jean.gaudet@dieppe.ca
Dave A. Maltais, Councillor, Ward(s): 1
506-855-4299
dave.maltais@dieppe.ca
Paul J.L. LeBlanc, Councillor, Ward(s): 2
506-853-3974
paul.leblanc@dieppe.ca
Paul N. Belliveau, Councillor, Ward(s): 3
506-855-2637
paul.belliveau@dieppe.ca
Hélène Boudreau, Councillor, Ward(s): 4
506-866-2739
helene.boudreau@dieppe.ca
Roger J. LeBlanc, Councillor, Ward(s): 5
506-850-1604
roger.leblanc@dieppe.ca
Administration
Marc Melanson, Chief Administrative Officer
Jacques LeBlanc, Director, Public Works
Marc Melanson, Director, Community Services
communityservices@dieppe.ca

Desimil Chalmessin, Superintendent, Public Works
David Knowles, Superintendent, Public Works

Edmundston
7, ch Canada
Edmundston, NB E3V 1T7
506-739-4636
Fax: 506-737-6902
communication@edmundston.ca
www.ville.edmundston.nb.ca
Municipal Type: City
Area: 106.92 sq km
County or District: Madawaska; *Population in 2006:* 16,643
Provincial Electoral District(s): Edmundston-Saint-Basile
Federal Electoral District(s): Madawaska-Restigouche
Next Election: May 2012 (4 year terms)
Council
Jacques P. Martin, Mayor
André Lang, Councillor, Ward(s): 1
Aldéo D. Nadeau, Councillor, Ward(s): 1
Ben Beaulieu, Councillor, Ward(s): 2
Denis M. Pelletier, Councillor, Ward(s): 2
Martin (Tin) Albert, Councillor, Ward(s): 3
Gérald G. Morneault, Councillor, Ward(s): 3
Michel Dubé, Councillor, Ward(s): 4
Jean Guy Marquis, Councillor, Ward(s): 4
Administration
Marc Michaud, Acting Chief Administrative Officer
Paul Dionne, Director, Public Works and Environment
506-739-2103

Fredericton
City Hall
P.O. Box 130
397 Queen St.
Fredericton, NB E3B 4Y7
506-460-2020
Fax: 506-460-2042
www.fredericton.ca
Municipal Type: City
Incorporated: 1848 *Area:* 130.68 sq km
County or District: York; *Population in 2006:* 50,535
Provincial Electoral District(s): Fredericton-Lincoln; Fredericton-Silverwood; Fredericton-Fort Nashwaak; Fredericton-Nashwaaksis
Federal Electoral District(s): Fredericton
Next Election: May 2012 (4 year terms)
Council
Brad S. Woodside, Mayor
506-460-2085, Fax: 506-460-2134
Daniel R. Keenan, Councillor, Ward(s): 1
Bruce N. Grandy, Deputy Mayor & Councillor, Ward(s): 2
Michael G. O'Brien, Councillor, Ward(s): 3
Eric Megarity, Councillor, Ward(s): 4
Steven Hicks, Councillor, Ward(s): 5
Marilyn K. Kerton, Councillor, Ward(s): 6
Scott McConaghy, Councillor, Ward(s): 7
Tony J. Whalen, Councillor, Ward(s): 8
Stephen A. Chase, Councillor, Ward(s): 9
Stephen T. Kelly, Councillor, Ward(s): 10
Jordan S. Graham, Councillor, Ward(s): 11
David A.J. Kelly, Councillor, Ward(s): 12
Administration
Pamela G. Hargrove, City Clerk
pam.hargrove@fredericton.ca
Marven Grant, City Treasurer & Director, Financial Services
marven.grant@fredericton.ca
Bruce A. Noble, City Solicitor
bruce.noble@fredericton.ca
Paul R. Stapleton, City Administrator
cityadmin@fredericton.ca
Barry MacKnight, Police Chief & Director, Emergency Measures Organization
506-460-2300
policechief@fredericton.ca
Philip E. Toole, Fire Chief & Deputy Director, Emergency Measures Organization
506-460-2500
fire@fredericton.ca
Jane Blakely, Director, Corporate Services
jane.blakely@fredericton.ca
W. Frank Flanagan, Director, Development Services
planning@fredericton.ca
Murray Jamer, P.Eng., Director, Engineering & Public Works
publicworks@fredericton.ca

Wayne Tallon, Director, Community Services
wayne.tallon@fredericton.ca
Ken Forrest, Manager, Policy & Planning
506-460-2110, Fax: 506-460-2894
Sandy MacNeill, Manager, Transit
506-460-2200
transit@fredericton.ca
Andy Holyoke, Superintendent, Water & Sewer
publicworks@fredericton.ca
Brian Cochrane, Superintendent, Parks & Trees Division
506-460-2230
recreation@fredericton.ca

Miramichi
141 Henry St.
Miramichi, NB E1V 2N5
506-623-2200
Fax: 506-623-2201
jim.lamkey@miramichi.org
www.miramichi.org
Municipal Type: City
Incorporated: Jan. 1, 1995 *Area:* 179.84 sq km
County or District: Northumberland; *Population in 2006:* 18,129
Provincial Electoral District(s): Miramichi-Bay du Vin; Miramichi-Centre; Miramichi Bay-Neguac; Southwest Miramichi
Federal Electoral District(s): Miramichi
Next Election: May 2012 (4 year terms)
Council
Gerry Cormier, Mayor
Rupert Bernard, Councillor
Derek Burchill, Councillor
Joan M. Cripps, Councillor
Jason H. Harris, Councillor
Brian J. King, Councillor
Nancy Lordon, Councillor
Michael J. (Tanker) Malley, Councillor
Michael J. McCoombs, Councillor
Bill Treadwell, Councillor
Robert B. Trevors, Councillor
Administration
James F. Lamkey, Clerk
Doug Chase, City Manager
doug.chase@miramichi.org
Kevin Kerr, P.Eng., Director, Engineering & Public Works
506-623-2020, Fax: 506-623-2025
kevin.kerr@miramichi.org
David Keating, Fire Chief
506-623-2225, Fax: 506-623-2226
david.keating@miramichi.org

Moncton / Ville de Moncton
655 Main St.
Moncton, NB E1C 1E8
506-853-3333
Fax: 506-389-5904
info@moncton.ca
www.moncton.ca
Municipal Type: City
Incorporated: 1890 *Area:* 141.17 sq km
County or District: Westmorland; *Population in 2006:* 64,128
Provincial Electoral District(s): Moncton East; Moncton North; Moncton West; Moncton Crescent
Federal Electoral District(s): Moncton-Riverview-Dieppe; Beauséjour
Next Election: May 2012 (4 year terms)
Council
George H. LeBlanc, Mayor
506-856-4343, Fax: 506-853-3553
info.mayor@moncton.ca
Kathryn M. Barnes, Councillor at Large
Pierre A. Boudreau, Councillor at Large
Steven Boyce, Councillor, Ward(s): 1
Paulette Thériault, Councillor, Ward(s): 1
Merrill A. Henderson, Councillor, Ward(s): 2
Nancy L. Hoar, Councillor, Ward(s): 2
Daniel Bourgeois, Councillor, Ward(s): 3
Brian A.Q. Hicks, Councillor, Ward(s): 3
René (Pepsi) Landry, Councillor, Ward(s): 4
Paul A. Pellerin, Councillor, Ward(s): 4
Administration
Barbara A. Quigley, City Clerk & Director, Legislative Support
info.clerk@moncton.ca
John Martin, City Treasurer & CFO
506-853-3566
john.martin@moncton.ca

See blue tabs following this section for Municipal Waste Management and Water & Wastewater Treatment.

Municipal Governments / New Brunswick

Jacques Dubé, City Manager
506-853-3498
info.manager@moncton.ca
Stephen Trueman, City Solicitor
stephen.trueman@moncton.ca
Eric Arsenault, Fire Chief
506-857-8800, Fax: 506-856-4353
info.fire@moncton.ca
B. Butler, Constable, Codiac Regional RCMP
Bill Budd, Director, District Planning
C. Despres, Director, Corporate Planning & Policy Development
506-859-2608
info.support@moncton.ca
D. Morehouse, Director, Engineering Operations
info.engineering@moncton.ca
A. Richard, Director, Design & Construction
S. Sparks, Director, Building Inspection
info.inspection@moncton.ca
Paul Thomson, Director, Corporate Communications
info.communications@moncton.ca
Ian Fowler, General Manager, Recreation, Parks, Tourism & Culture
ian.fowler@moncton.ca
J. MacDonald, General Manager, Engineering & Public Works
info.publicworks@moncton.ca
T. Carter, Manager, Purchasing
506-853-3535
info.purchasing@moncton.ca
Catherine Dallaire, Assistant City Manager, Corporate Services
catherine.dallaire@moncton.ca
Donald MacLellan, Assistant City Manager
don.maclellan@moncton.ca
Rod Higgins, Assistant General Manager, Recreation, Parks, Tourism & Culture
rod.higgins@moncton.ca

Quispamsis
P.O. Box 21085
12 Landing Ct.
Quispamsis, NB E2E 4Z4
506-849-5778
Fax: 506-849-5799
quispamsis@quispamsis.ca
www.quispamsis.ca
Municipal Type: City
Area: 57.06 sq km
County or District: Kings; *Population in 2006:* 15,239
Provincial Electoral District(s): Quispamsis
Federal Electoral District(s): Fundy Royal; Saint John
Next Election: May 2012 (4 year terms)
Gary Losier, Director, Engineering & Works
506-849-5749
glosier@quispamsis.ca
Chris Vriezen, Supervisor, Utility
506-849-5734
cvriezen@quispamsis.ca
Phil Shedd, Superintendent, Works
506-849-5742
pshedd@quispamsis.ca
Beth Thompson, Councillor
506-849-2852
Margie McGrath, Secretary, Planning Advisory Committee
506-849-5745
mmcgrath@quispamsis.ca
Larry Greer, Fire Chief, Rothesay Regional Fire Dept.
506-848-6604, Fax: 506-848-6608
rrfd@nb.aibn.com
Council
Murray Driscoll, Mayor
506-849-5992
mayor@quispamsis.ca
Administration
Catherine Snow, Clerk
506-849-5738

Riverview
30 Honour House Ct.
Riverview, NB E1B 3Y9
506-387-2020
Fax: 506-387-2033
www.town.riverview.nb.ca
Municipal Type: City
Area: 33.88 sq km
County or District: Albert; *Population in 2006:* 17,832
Provincial Electoral District(s): Riverview
Federal Electoral District(s): Moncton-Riverview-Dieppe; Fundy Royal
Next Election: May 2012 (4 year terms)
Council
Clarence O. Sweetland, Mayor
506-386-1703
csweetland@town.riverview.nb.ca
Claude Curwin, Councillor, Ward(s): 1
506-860-6873
ccurwin@town.riverview.nb.ca
Ian Macdonald, Councillor, Ward(s): 2
506-386-8756
imacdonald@town.riverview.nb.ca
Bob Hyslop, Councillor, Ward(s): 3
506-866-2273
rhyslop@town.riverview.nb.ca
Wayne Bennett, Councillor, Ward(s): 4
506-386-3295
Don Lenehan, Councillor at Large
506-386-4483
lenehandon@yahoo.ca
Sherry Wilson, Councillor at Large
506-386-1133
swilson@town.riverview.nb.ca
Ann Seamans, Councillor at Large
506-386-4558
aseamans@town.riverview.nb.ca
Administration
David Muir, Chief Administrative Officer
506-387-2021
Denyse Richard, Deputy Town Clerk
506-387-2043
Robert Higson, Director, Finance
506-387-2023
Jim Steeves, Superintendent, Works
506-387-2027
Bob Clive, Director, Parks, Recreation & Community Relations
506-387-2031
Doug Hamer, Chief, Fire & Ambulance
506-387-2201
rivefire@nbnet.nb.ca
Kenneth L. Sharpe, Director, Works & Engineering
506-387-2035

Rothesay
70 Hampton Rd.
Rothesay, NB E2E 5L5
506-848-6600
Fax: 506-848-6677
info@rothesay.ca
www.rothesay.ca
Municipal Type: City
Incorporated: Jan. 1, 1998 *Area:* 34.73 sq km
County or District: Kings; *Population in 2006:* 11,637
Provincial Electoral District(s): Rothesay
Federal Electoral District(s): Saint John; Fundy Royal
Next Election: May 2012 (4 year terms)
Council
William J. Bishop, Mayor
BillBishop@rothesay.ca
Scott Cochrane, Councillor
jassco@rogers.com
Pat Gallagher Jette, Councillor
patgall@nbnet.nb.ca
Terry Kilfoil, Councillor
kilfoilt@nbnet.nb.ca
Norma Mullett, Councillor
normamullett@hotmail.com
Don Shea, Councillor
sheadoj@nbnet.nb.ca
Tom Young, Councillor
tomyoung@rogers.com
Administration
Mary Jane Banks, Clerk
MaryJaneBanks@rothesay.ca
Scott Hatcher, P.Eng., Director, Operations
506-848-6668
scotthatcher@rothesay.ca
Larry Greer, Fire Chief
506-848-6604
Gay Drescher, Director, Development Services
gaydrescher@rothesay.ca
Jeff Humphrey, Technologist, Engineering

Saint John
City Hall
P.O. Box 1971
15 Market Sq.
Saint John, NB E2L 4L1
506-649-6000
inquiries@saintjohn.ca
www.saintjohn.ca
Municipal Type: City
Incorporated: May 18, 1785 *Area:* 315.49 sq km
County or District: Saint John; *Population in 2006:* 68,043
Provincial Electoral District(s): Saint John East; Saint John Harbour; Saint John Portland; Saint John Lancaster; Saint John-Fundy
Federal Electoral District(s): Saint John
Next Election: May 2012 (4 year terms)
Council
Ivan Court, Mayor
ivan.court@saintjohn.ca
Stephen Chase, Deputy Mayor & Councillor
stephen.chase@saintjohn.ca
Christopher Titus, Councillor at Large
christopher.titus@saintjohn.ca
Bill Farren, Councillor, Ward(s): 1
bill.farren@saintjohn.ca
Peter McGuire, Councillor, Ward(s): 1
peter.mcguire@saintjohn.ca
Patricia (Patty) Higgins, Councillor, Ward(s): 2
patty.higgins@saintjohn.ca
H. Gary Sullivan, Councillor, Ward(s): 2
gary.sullivan@saintjohn.ca
Carl Killen, Councillor, Ward(s): 3
carl.killen@saintjohn.ca
Donnie Snook, Councillor, Ward(s): 3
donnie.snook@saintjohn.ca
Bruce Court, Councillor, Ward(s): 4
bruce.court@saintjohn.ca
Joe Mott, Councillor, Ward(s): 4
joe.mott@saintjohn.ca
Administration
J. Patrick Woods, City Manager
506-658-2913, Fax: 506-658-2802
citymanager@saintjohn.ca
Greg Yeomans, Treasurer & Commissioner, Finance & Corporate Services
506-658-2951, Fax: 506-649-7901
finance@saintjohn.ca
James R. Baird, Commissioner, Planning & Development
506-658-2835, Fax: 506-658-2837
planning@saintjohn.ca
William Edwards, Commissioner, Buildings & Inspection Services
506-658-2911, Fax: 506-632-6199
buildinginspection@saintjohn.ca
Paul Groody, P.Eng., Commissioner, Municipal Operations
506-658-4455, Fax: 506-658-4740
municipaloperations@saintjohn.ca
Margaret Totten, Manager, Tourism Saint John
506-658-2990, Fax: 506-632-6118
visitsj@saintjohn.ca
John Nugent, City Solicitor
506-658-2860, Fax: 506-649-7939
legal@saintjohn.ca
Allen Bodechon, Police Chief
506-648-3200, Fax: 506-648-3304
police@saintjohn.ca
Rob Simonds, Fire Chief
506-658-2910, Fax: 506-658-2916
fire@saintjohn.ca
Shayne Galbraith, Director, Works
506-658-2852
works@saintjohn.ca
Peter J. Hanlon, P.Eng., Manager, Water & Sewerage Services
506-658-2811, Fax: 506-658-4740
waterandsewerage@cityofsaintjohn.com
David Logan, Purchasing Agent, Material & Fleet Management
506-658-2930, Fax: 506-658-4742
mat-man@saintjohn.ca

See blue tabs following this section for Municipal Waste Management and Water & Wastewater Treatment.

Other Municipalities in New Brunswick

Commission de gestion des déchets solides de la péninsule Acadienne (COGEDES)
#4, 149, boul St-Pierre ouest
Caraquet, NB E1W 1B6
506-726-2911
Fax: 506-726-2912
cogedes@nbnet.nb.ca
www.cogedes.com
Municipal Type: Waste Commission
Jean-Marie Gionet, Chair
Gary LeBlanc, General Manager

Commission de gestion enviro ressources du Nord-Ouest (COGERNO)
248, ch Clément Roy
Rivière-Verte, NB E7C 2W7
506-263-3470
Fax: 506-263-3476
jean@nbnet.nb.ca
www.cogerno.com
Municipal Type: Water Commission
Jean A. Bourque, General Manager
Pierre Michaud, Chair

Fredericton Region Solid Waste Commission
P.O. Box 21 A
Fredericton, NB E3B 4Y2
506-453-9930
Fax: 506-453-9933
swc99@nbnet.nb.ca
www.frswc.ca
Municipal Type: Water Commission
Gordon Wilson, General Manager
506-444-0960
gordon@frswc.ca
Pierre Theriault, Operations Manager
506-453-9932
John Bigger, Chair

Fundy Region Solid Waste Commission
P.O. Box 3032
Grand-Bay Westfield, NB E5K 4V3
506-738-1212
Fax: 506-738-1207
hotline@fundyrecycles.com
www.fundyrecycles.com
Municipal Type: Water Commission
Jack Keir, General Manager
Rob Dean, Site Operations Supervisor, Crane Mountain Landfill
Ron Nelson, Environmental Coordinator
Chris Harned, Supervisor, Waste Diversion
Catherine Doucette, Officer, Public Education
Brenda MacCallum, Public Education Officer

Kent County Solid Waste Commission
2249 Rte. 134
Lakeville-Westmorland, NB E1H 1P3
506-384-9195
Fax: 506-384-6029
Toll Free Phone: 1-877-588-1125
Municipal Type: Water Commission
Roland Fougère, Chair
Florence Babineau, General Manager
fbabineau@rogers.com

Kings County Region Solid Waste Commission
P.O. Box 4861
Sussex, NB E4E 5L9
506-433-6502
Fax: 506-432-6435
kcrswc@nbnet.nb.ca
Municipal Type: Waste Commission
Garth Long, Chair
506-433-1341
gplong@nbnet.nb.ca

Nepisiguit-Chaleur Solid Waste Commission
1300, rte 360
Allardville, NB E8L 1H5
506-725-2402
Fax: 506-725-2410
redpine@nb.sympatico.ca
Municipal Type: Waste Commission
Raymond Bryar, General Manager
Graham Wiseman, Chair

Northumberland Solid Waste Commission
505 Old King George Hwy.
Miramichi, NB E1V 1J8
506-778-6646
Fax: 506-778-6642
info@nswc-cdsn.ca
www.nswc-cdsn.ca
Municipal Type: Waste Commission
Marie LeBlanc, Manager, Administration
Scotty Bernard, Chair
April Conroy, Coordinator, Waste Reduction

Restigouche Solid Waste Corporation
P.O. Box 93
162B Water St.
Campbellton, NB E3N 3G1
506-789-2111
Fax: 506-789-2111
Municipal Type: Waste Commission
Ian Comeau, General Manager
comeai@nbnet.nb.ca
Jean Perron, Chair

South West Solid Waste Commission
P.O. Box 243
St Stephen, NB E3L 2X2
506-466-7830
Fax: 506-466-7833
crww@nbnet.nb.ca
www.swswc.com
Municipal Type: Waste Commission
Ken Landmaid, Chair, Managed Forest Committee
Glenn Greenlaw, Chair, Technical Committee
Peter Fenety, Chair, Environmental Monitoring Committee

Valley Solid Waste Commission
P.O. Box 880
Hartland, NB E7P 3K4
506-375-3040
Fax: 506-375-3043
Toll Free Phone: 1-866-312-8800
vswc@nb.sympatico.ca
www.valleysolidwaste.com
Municipal Type: Water Commission
Denise Brown, Office Administrator

Westmorland-Albert Solid Waste Corporation
P.O. Box 1397
Moncton, NB E1C 8T6
506-877-1050
Fax: 506-877-1060
www.westmorlandalbert.com
Municipal Type: Waste Commission
Bill Slater, General Manager
Norman H. Crossman, Chair
Christa Methot, Coordinator, Community Relations
Yvon Gautreau, Vice-Chair
Greg Martin, Corporate Secretary
Trina Davidson, Supervisor, Site Operations

Newfoundland & Labrador

The Environmental Protection Act prohibits the pollution of air, water and soil. There are provisions in the act for the management of sewage, wastewater, landfills, solid waste, recycling and water quality.

Community Water & Wastewater Section relates to the review and approval of the design of public water supply and wastewater systems and issuance of certificates of approval for public water supply and wastewater projects. The Department of the Environment & Conservation, with municipal governments, monitors source and tap water quality of public water supplies. Water quality has benefited from government spending on additional inspectors, increased frequency of water testing and on providing municipalities with 100% funding up to a maximum of $100,000 to install or upgrade chlorination equipment.

The Environment Branch is working with the Department of Municipal & Provincial Affairs and the Multi-Materials Stewardship Board to implement the Newfoundland & Labrador Waste Management Strategy. The Waste Management Section is responsible for the administration of the Waste Material Disposal Act, which includes the management of solid waste, hazardous and special waste, landfill licensing and recycling programs. There are 240 dumps in Newfoundland & Labrador. The Department plans to reduce the number of waste disposal sites. Incinerators were phased out in 2008, and unlined landfills were phased out in 2010. The Multi-Materials Stewardship Board is responsible for the provincial beverage recycling and household hazardous waste programs. Consumers pay a deposit of 8 cents per beverage container, except milk, receiving 5 cents back when they return the recyclable containers to a depot. There is little recycling activity outside of the deposit program for beverage containers. Rules are in place for disposal of tires, oil and paper products. More recycling initiatives are planned with the goal to reduce the amount of waste being sent for disposal. Eleven of 15 regional waste management zones have operating committees that have been formed to deal with collection, disposal and diversion of waste. MMSB administers the Newfoundland & Labrador Waste Management Trust Fund, which provides financial assistance to develop and implement waste management initiatives.

The provincial government committed $85 million under the 2005-08 Multi-Year Capital Works Program for municipal infrastructure, administered by the Department of Municipal & Provincial Affairs, with costs shared equally between provincial and larger municipal governments.

The Climate Change Action Plan 2005 outlined two initiatives relevant to municipalities specifically-assessing vulnerabilities of local communities to climate change and educating municipalities on the impacts of climate change and the development of adaptation strategies.

Major Municipalities in Newfoundland & Labrador

Conception Bay South
106 Conception Bay Hwy.
Conception Bay South, NL A1W 3A5
709-834-6500
Fax: 709-834-8337
jmiller@conceptionbaysouth.ca
www.conceptionbaysouth.ca
Municipal Type: City
Incorporated: Sept. 1, 1971 Area: 59.27 sq km
Population in 2006: 21,966
Provincial Electoral District(s): Conception Bay South; Topsail
Federal Electoral District(s): St. John's East; Avalon
Next Election: Sept. 2009 (4 year terms)
Council
Woodrow French, Mayor
WFrench@conceptionbaysouth.ca
Administration
Keith Arns, CAO
karns@conceptionbaysouth.ca
Elaine Mitchell, Director, Planning
Ron Franey, Director, Public Works
Dave Tibbo, Director, Recreation & Leisure Services

Corner Brook
City Hall
P.O. Box 1080
Corner Brook, NL A2H 6E1
709-637-1500
Fax: 709-637-1625
cityhall@cornerbrook.com
www.cornerbrook.com
Municipal Type: City
Incorporated: April 27, 1955 Area: 148.27 sq km
Population in 2006: 20,083
Provincial Electoral District(s): Humber East; Humber West
Federal Electoral District(s): Humber-St. Barbe-Baie Verte
Next Election: Sept. 2009 (4 year terms)
Note: City Hall is located on Mount Bernard Ave. at Main St.
Council
Neville Greeley, Mayor
709-637-1537, Fax: 709-637-1543
ngreeley@cornerbrook.com
Leo Bruce, Councillor
lbruce@cornerbrook.com
Priscilla Boutcher, Councillor
pboutcher@cornerbrook.com
Donna Francis, Councillor
dfrancis@cornerbrook.com
Charlie Renouf, Councillor
crenouf@cornerbrook.com

See blue tabs following this section for Municipal Waste Management and Water & Wastewater Treatment.

Municipal Governments / Newfoundland & Labrador

Linda Chaisson, Councillor
lchaisson@cornerbrook.com
Administration
Marina Redmond, City Clerk
709-637-1534
mredmond@cornerbrook.com
Michael Dolter, CAO
709-637-1532
mdolter@cornerbrook.com
Neville Wheaton, Fire Chief
709-637-1615
nmwheaton@cornerbrook.com
Paul Barnable, Director, Community Services
709-637-1548, Fax: 709-637-1514
pbarnable@cornerbrook.com
Gerry Cole, Supervisor, Recreational Services
709-637-1232
gcole@cornerbrook.com
Trina Burden, Business Resource Manager
709-637-1558
tburden@cornerbrook.com
Steve May, Director, Operational Services
709-637-1541, Fax: 709-637-1502
smay@cornerbrook.com
Todd Pickett, Land Management Officer
709-637-1544
tpickett@cornerbrook.com
Colleen Humphries, Supervisor, Planning
709-637-1553
chumphries@cornerbrook.com
James Warford, P.Eng., Coordinator, Engineering Services
709-637-1626
jwarford@cornerbrook.com
Keith Costello, Superintendent, Water & Sewer
709-637-1595
kcostello@cornerbrook.com
Barry Ellsworth, Manager, Public Works
709-637-1509
bellsworth@cornerbrook.com
Percy Joyce, Officer, Land Management
709-637-1544
pjoyce@cornerbrook.com
Deon Rumbolt, Supervisor, Development & Inspection
709-637-1552
drumbolt@cornerbrook.com
Rhea Hutchings, Sustainable Development Officer, Operational Services
709-637-1574
rhutchings@cornerbrook.com
Craig Kennedy, Superintendent, Public Works
709-637-1607
ckennedy@cornerbrook.com

Grand Falls-Windsor
P.O. Box 439
Grand Falls-Windsor, NL A2A 2J8
709-489-0412
Fax: 709-489-0465
jrowsell@grandfallswindsor.com
www.grandfallswindsor.com
Municipal Type: City
Incorporated: Jan. 1, 1991 *Area:* 54.48 sq km
Population in 2006: 13,558
Provincial Electoral District(s): Grand Falls-Buchans; Windsor-Springdale
Federal Electoral District(s): Bonavista-Gander-Grand Falls-Windsor
Next Election: Sept. 2009 (4 year terms)
Council
Rex Barnes, Mayor
mayor@grandfallswindsor.com
Administration
Michael Pinsent, Town Manager
709-487-0407, Fax: 709-292-0018
mpinsent@grandfallswindsor.com
Jeff Saunders, Director, Engineering Works
709-489-0427, Fax: 709-489-0465
jsaunders@grandfallswindsor.com
Vince J. McKenzie, Fire Chief
709-489-0431, Fax: 709-489-0885
firechief@grandfallswindsor.com
Dave Nichols, Director, Parks & Recreation
709-489-0450, Fax: 709-489-0454
dnichols@grandfallswindsor.com

Robert Thompson, Supervisor, Engineering & Works
709-489-0421, Fax: 709-489-0467
rthompson@grandfallswindsor.com
Mark Kelly, Clerk, Purchasing
709-489-0422, Fax: 709-489-0465
purchasing@grandfallswindsor.com

Mount Pearl
3 Centennial St.
Mount Pearl, NL A1N 1G4
709-748-1000
Fax: 709-748-1150
info@mtpearl.nf.ca
info@mountpearl.ca
Municipal Type: City
Incorporated: Jan. 11, 1955 *Area:* 15.75 sq km
Population in 2006: 24,671
Provincial Electoral District(s): Mount Pearl; Waterford Valley
Federal Electoral District(s): St. John's South-Mount Pearl
Next Election: Sept. 2009 (4 year terms)
Council
Randy Simms, Mayor
rsimms@mountpearl.ca
Paul Lane, Deputy Mayor & Councillor
plane@mountpearl.ca
Ed Grant, Councillor
egrant@mountpearl.ca
Jim Locke, Councillor
jlocke@mountpearl.ca
Lucy Stoyles, Councillor
lstoyles@mountpearl.ca
Paula Tessier, Councillor
ptessier@mountpearl.ca
John Walsh, Councillor
jwalsh@mountpearl.ca
Administration
Gerard Lewis, CAO
709-748-1025
glewis@mountpearl.ca
Michelle Peach, C.A., City Treasurer
mpeach@mountpearl.ca
Stephen Jewcyzk, Director, Planning & Development
709-748-1029
sjewczyk@mountpearl.ca
James Oxford, Director, Infrastructure & Public Works
709-748-1028
joxford@mountpearl.ca
Raymond Osmond, Director, Community Services
709-748-1027
rosmond@mountpearl.ca
Bronda Aylward, Director, Economic Development
709-748-1096
baylward@mountpearl.ca

St. John's
City Hall
P.O. Box 908
10 New Gower St.
St. John's, NL A1C 5M2
709-754-2489
Fax: 709-576-7688
311 for city services
council@stjohns.ca
www.stjohns.ca
Municipal Type: City
Incorporated: Aug. 7, 1921 *Area:* 446.04 sq km
Population in 2006: 100,646
Provincial Electoral District(s): Kilbride; Signal Hill-Quidi Vidi; St. J. Centre; St. J. East; St. J. North; St. J. South; St. J. West; Virginia Waters; Mount Pearl North; Cape St. Francis
Federal Electoral District(s): St. John's East; St. John's South-Mount Pearl
Next Election: Sept. 2009 (4 year terms)
Council
Dennis O'Keefe, Mayor
709-576-8477, Fax: 709-576-8250
dokeefe@stjohns.ca
Shannie Duff, Deputy Mayor & Councillor
709-576-8583, Fax: 709-576-8474
sduff@stjohns.ca
Gerry Colbert, Councillor at Large
709-576-7689, Fax: 709-576-8474
gcolbert@stjohns.ca

Sheilagh O'Leary, Councillor at Large
709-576-8567, Fax: 709-576-8474
soleary@stjohns.ca
Tom Hann, Councillor at Large
709-576-8219, Fax: 709-576-8474
thann@stjohns.ca
Sandy Hickman, Councillor at Large
709-576-8045, Fax: 709-576-8474
shickman@stjohns.ca
Danny Breen, Councillor, Ward(s): 1
709-576-2332, Fax: 709-576-8474
dbreen@stjohns.ca
Frank Galgay, Councillor, Ward(s): 2
709-576-8577, Fax: 709-576-8474
fgalgay@stjohns.ca
Bruce Tilley, Councillor, Ward(s): 3
709-576-8643, Fax: 709-576-8474
btilley@stjohns.ca
Debbie Hanlon, Councillor, Ward(s): 4
709-576-2383, Fax: 709-576-8474
dhanlon@stjohns.ca
Wally Collins, Councillor, Ward(s): 5
709-576-8584, Fax: 709-576-8474
wcollins@stjohns.ca
Administration
Neil Martin, City Clerk, Director & Associate Commissioner, Corporate Services
709-576-8446, Fax: 709-576-8474
Robert Bishop, C.A., Treasurer & Director, Finance
709-576-8696, Fax: 709-576-8564
Ronald Penney, City Solicitor & City Manager
709-576-8557, Fax: 709-576-8561
legal@stjohns.ca
Walt Mills, Director, Engineering
709-576-8658, Fax: 709-576-8625
David Blackmore, Director, Building & Property Management
709-576-8701, Fax: 709-576-8160
Kevin Breen, Director, Human Resources
709-576-8213, Fax: 709-576-8575
Jill Brewer, Director, Recreation
709-576-8405, Fax: 709-576-8469
Cliff Johnston, Director, Planning
709-576-8383, Fax: 709-576-8625
Elizabeth Lawrence, Director, Economic Development, Tourism & Culture
709-576-8203, Fax: 709-576-8246
Paul Mackey, Director, Public Works & Parks
709-576-8303, Fax: 709-576-8026
Jim Clarke, Manager, Streets & Parks
709-576-8541, Fax: 709-576-8026
P.J. (Jim) Ford, Manager, Regulatory Services
709-576-8294, Fax: 709-576-8160
Gareth Griffiths, C.E.T., Manager, Real Estate Services
709-576-8440, Fax: 709-576-8561
Kevin Gushue, Manager, Tourism Development
709-567-8545, Fax: 709-576-8246
Geraldine King, Manager, Environmental Initiatives
709-576-8613, Fax: 709-576-8625
Joe Sampson, Manager, Development
Bob Wilson, Manager, Energy Efficiency
709-576-8238, Fax: 709-576-8160
Robin King, Transportation Engineer
709-576-8232, Fax: 709-576-8625

Other Municipalities in Newfoundland & Labrador

Gander
P.O. Box 280
Gander, NL A1V 1W6
709-651-2930
Fax: 709-256-5809
info@gandercanada.com
www.gandercanada.com
Municipal Type: Town
Incorporated: Dec. 28, 1954 *Area:* 104.25 sq km
Population in 2006: 9,951
Provincial Electoral District(s): Gander
Federal Electoral District(s): Bonavista-Gander-Grand Falls-Windsor
Next Election: Sept. 2009 (4 year terms)
Garry Brown, Town Clerk & Director, Finance
Claude Elliott, Mayor

See blue tabs following this section for Municipal Waste Management and Water & Wastewater Treatment.

Dermot Chafe, Director, Development
709-651-5912
dchafe@gandercanada.com
Dave Brett, Fire Chief
709-651-5928
Cluny Matchim, Director, Municipal Works & Services
709-651-5914
cmatchim@gandercanada.com
Kevin Waterman, Director, Parks, Recreation & Tourism
709-651-5928
kwaterman@gandercanada.com

Northwest Territories

The Government of the Northwest Territories funds and manages the water and wastewater, and waste management programs for small non-tax based communities. Major tax-based municipalities are fully responsible for the management and partially responsible for the funding for their municipal programs. The Environmental Protection Division of the Department. of Environment & Natural Resources is responsible for programs that cover hazardous substances, waste management, air quality and environmental impact assessment. The Waste Reduction & Recovery Act allows for community recovery depots to be funded and established, and for fees and deposits to be collected. A ready-to-serve beverage container recovery program was the first initiative to be implemented (November 2005), with a refundable deposit and handling fee (ranging from 15 to 35 cents) added to the cost of the beverage. Recycling depots and regional processing centres will process the returns for reuse or recycling markets.

Major Municipalities in Northwest Territories

Yellowknife
P.O. Box 580
4807 - 52 St.
Yellowknife, NT X1A 2N4
867-920-5600
Fax: 867-920-5649
cityclerk@yellowknife.ca
www.yellowknife.ca
Municipal Type: City
Incorporated: Jan. 1, 1970 *Area:* 105.22 sq km
Population in 2009: 19,711
Provincial Electoral District(s): Yellowknife South; Yellowknife Centre; Frame Lake; Great Slave; Weledeh; Kam Lake, Range Lake
Federal Electoral District(s): Western Arctic
Next Election: Oct. 19, 2011
Council
Gordon Van Tighem, Mayor
gvantighem@yellowknife.ca
Lydia Bardak, City Councillor
lbardak@yellowknife.ca
Bob Brooks, City Councillor
bbrooks@yellowknife.ca
Paul Falvo, City Councillor
pfalvo@yellowknife.ca
Mark Heyck, City Councillor
mheyck@yellowknife.ca
Amanda Mallon, City Councillor
amallon@yellowknife.ca
Shelagh Montgomery, City Councillor
smontgomery@yellowknife.ca
Cory Vanthuyne, City Councillor
cvanthuyne@yellowknife.ca
David Wind, City Councillor
dwind@yellowknife.ca
Administration
Debbie Gillard, City Clerk
867-920-5646
debbie.gillard@yellowknife.ca
Max Hall, City Administrator
867-920-5624
mhall@yellowknife.ca
Darcy Hernblad, Fire Chief
867-766-5501
dhernblad@yellowknife.ca
Carl Bird, Director, Corporate Services
867-920-5666
cbird@yellowknife.ca

Jeffrey Humble, Director, Planning & Lands
867-920-5633
jhumble@yellowknife.ca
Dennis Kefalas, Director, Public Works
867-920-5639
dkefalas@yellowknife.ca
Dennis Marchiori, Director, Public Safety
867-920-5661
dmarchiori@yellowknife.ca
Peter Neugebauer, Director, Economic Development
867-920-5660
pneugebauer@yellowknife.ca
Grant White, Director, Community Services
867-920-5636
gwhite@yellowknife.ca
Kerry Penney, Manager, Legal Services
kpenney@yellowknife.ca
Nalini Naidoo, Manager, Planning & Lands
867-920-5675
nnaidoo@yellowknife.ca
Marie Couturier, Manager, Human Resources
mcouturier@yellowknife.ca
Clem Hand, Manager, Procurement Services
867-920-5617
chand@yellowknife.ca
Bruce Underhay, Manager, Solid Waste Management Facility
867-669-3404
bunderhay@yellowknife.ca
Sharolynn Woodward, Manager, Information Technology
867-920-5651
swoodward@yellowknife.ca
Dennis Althouse, Superintendent, Operations & Maintenance
867-766-5512
dalthouse@yellowknife.ca

Nova Scotia

Municipalities are responsible for waste management, water treatment and supply, and wastewater treatment. The province is divided into eight solid waste management regions. The provincial Department of Environment's Solid Waste Management Branch is responsible for a number of initiatives, including recycling, composting, disposal bans and the province's Solid Waste Strategy. The private, not-for-profit Resource Recovery Fund Board funds municipal and regional waste diversion programs. Nearly all of the 55 municipalities have centralized composting facilities for the business sector. Ninety-nine percent of residents have access to curbside recycling programs. Draft regulations have been drawn up to ban electronics from landfills. All landfills are required to have containment landfill systems (liners). The current number of landfills has been reduced to nine.

Under the Drinking Water Strategy (2002), the province is auditing all municipal water systems to assess that all comply with provincial standards. Clarification and simplification of regulations regarding operation of water and wastewater facilities are under review. Standards regarding the treatment and application of sewage sludge on lands were established in 2004.

Under the federal government's New Deal for Cities, Nova Scotia was allocated $145.2 million in federal gas tax funding from 2005 to 2010 for municipal infrastructure projects.

Counties & Municipal Districts in Nova Scotia

Cape Breton
Civic Centre
320 Esplanade
Sydney, NS B1P 7B9
902-563-5005
Fax: 902-564-0481
cbrm@cbrm.ns.ca
www.cbrm.ns.ca
Municipal Type: Regional Municipality
Incorporated: Aug. 1, 1995 *Area:* 2,433.33 sq km
County or District: Cape Breton; *Population in 2006:* 102,250
Provincial Electoral District(s): Cape Breton Centre; Cape Breton East; Cape Breton North; Cape Breton Nova; Cape Breton South; Cape Breton-The Lakes
Federal Electoral District(s): Cape Breton-Canso; Sydney-Victoria
Next Election: Oct. 2008 (4 year terms)
Gordon MacLeod, Councillor, Ward(s): District 14
gmacleod@cbrm.ns.ca

Council
John W. Morgan, Mayor
jwmorgan@cbrm.ns.ca
Brian Lahey, Councillor, Ward(s): District 1
blahey@cbrm.ns.ca
Kevin Saccary, Councillor, Ward(s): District 2
ksaccary@cbrm.ns.ca
Lee McNeil, Councillor, Ward(s): District 3
lmcneil@cbrm.ns.ca
George MacDonald, Councillor, Ward(s): District 4
gmmacdonald@cbrm.ns.ca
Darren Bruckschwaiger, Councillor, Ward(s): District 5
drbruckschwaiger@cbrm.ns.ca
Kim Desveaux, Councillor, Ward(s): District 6
kadesveaux@cbrm.ns.ca
Jim MacLeod, Councillor, Ward(s): District 7
jmacleod@cbrm.ns.ca
Ray Paruch, Councillor, Ward(s): District 8
frparuch@cbrm.ns.ca
Tom Wilson, Councillor, Ward(s): District 9
twilson@cbrm.ns.ca
Derek Mombourquette, Councillor, Ward(s): District 10
dcmombourquette@cbrm.ns.ca
Dave LeBlanc, Councillor, Ward(s): District 11
dfleblanc@cbrm.ns.ca
Claire Detheridge, Councillor, Ward(s): District 12
mcdetheridge@cbrm.ns.ca
Mae Rowe, Councillor, Ward(s): District 13
mjrowe@cbrm.ns.ca
Clarence Prince, Councillor, Ward(s): District 15
cprince@cbrm.ns.ca
Wesley Stubbert, Councillor, Ward(s): District 16
wstubbert@cbrm.ns.ca
Administration
Bernie White, Municipal Clerk
902-563-5010
bjwhite@cbrm.ns.ca
Marie Walsh, Director, Finance
902-563-5014
Jerry Ryan, CAO
Robin B. Campbell, Regional Solicitor
902-563-5045
rbcampbell@cbrm.ns.ca
Edgar MacLeod, Police Chief
902-563-5095
eamacleod@cbrmps.cape-breton.ns.ca
Angus Fleming, Director, Human Resources
902-563-5058
acfleming@cbrm.ns.ca
Doug Foster, Director, Planning
902-563-5070
Kevin MacDonald, Director, Engineering & Public Works
902-563-5051
Bernie MacKinnon, Director, Fire Services
902-563-5132
Bob McNeil, Director, Technology & Communications
902-563-5066
rjmcneil@cbrm.ns.ca
Fred Brooks, Sr. Manager, Recreation
902-563-5510
ftbrooks@cbrm.ns.ca
Malcolm Gillis, Manager, Planning & Development
Mike MacKeigan, Manager, Utilities
Roger Munroe, Manager, Solid Waste
902-563-5182

Halifax Regional Municipality
P.O. Box 1749
1841 Argyle St.
Halifax, NS B3J 3A5
902-490-4000
Fax: 902-490-4208
Toll Free Phone: 1-800-835-6428
www.halifax.ca
Municipal Type: Regional Municipality
Incorporated: April 1, 1996 *Area:* 5,490.18 sq km
Population in 2006: 372,679
Provincial Electoral District(s): Bedford-Birch Cove; Cole Harbour; Cole Harbour-Eastern Passage; Dartmouth E.; Dartmouth N.; Dartmouth S.-Portland Valley; Eastern Shore; Hlfx Atlantic; Hlfx Chebucto; Hlfx Citadel-Sable Island; Hlfx-Clayton Park; Hlfx Fairview; Hlfx Needham; Hammonds Plains-Upper Sackville; Preston; Sackville-Cobequid; Timberlea-Prospect; Waverly-Fall River-Beaver Bank
Federal Electoral District(s): Central Nova;

See blue tabs following this section for Municipal Waste Management and Water & Wastewater Treatment.

Municipal Governments / Nova Scotia

Cumberland-Colchester-Musquodoboit Valley; Dartmouth-Cole Harbour; Halifax; Halifax West; Sackville-Eastern Shore; South Shore-St. Margaret's
Next Election: Oct. 2008 (4 year terms)
Council
Peter J. Kelly, M.B.A., Mayor
902-490-4010
kellyp@halifax.ca
Steve Streatch, Councillor, Ward(s): District 1
streats@halifax.ca
Barry Dalrymple, Councillor, Ward(s): District 2
barry.dalrymple@halifax.ca
David Hendsbee, Councillor, Ward(s): District 3
david.hendsbee@halifax.ca
Lorelei Nicoll, Councillor, Ward(s): District 4
lorelei.nicoll@halifax.ca
Gloria McCluskey, Councillor, Ward(s): District 5
mcclusg@halifax.ca
Darren Fisher, Councillor, Ward(s): District 6
darren.fisher@halifax.ca
Bill Karsten, Councillor, Ward(s): District 7
karsteb@halifax.ca
Jackie Barkhouse, Councillor, Ward(s): District 8
barkhoj@halifax.ca
Jim Smith, Councillor, Ward(s): District 9
smithj@halifax.ca
Mary Wile, Councillor, Ward(s): District 10
wilema@halifax.ca
Jerry Blumenthal, Councillor, Ward(s): District 11
blumenj@halifax.ca
Dawn Marie Sloane, Councillor, Ward(s): District 12
sloaned@halifax.ca
Sue Uteck, Councillor, Ward(s): District 13
utecks@halifax.ca
Jennifer Watts, Councillor, Ward(s): District 14
jennifer.watts@halifax.ca
Russell Walker, Councillor, Ward(s): District 15
walkerr@halifax.ca
Debbie Hum, Councillor, Ward(s): District 16
humd@halifax.ca
Linda Mosher, Councillor, Ward(s): District 17
mosherl@halifax.ca
Stephen Adams, Councillor, Ward(s): District 18
adamss@halifax.ca
Brad Johns, Councillor, Ward(s): District 19
brad.johns@halifax.ca
Robert (Bob) P. Harvey, Councillor, Ward(s): District 20
harveyb@halifax.ca
Tim Outhit, Councillor, Ward(s): District 21
outhitt@halifax.ca
Reg Rankin, Councillor, Ward(s): District 22
rankinr@halifax.ca
Peter Lund, Councillor, Ward(s): District 23
peter.lund@halifax.ca
Administration
Cathy Mellett, Acting Municipal Clerk
902-490-4210
clerks@halifax.ca
Cathie O'Toole, C.G.A., Director, Finance
Dan English, M.P.A., CAO
902-490-6430
Wayne Anstey, Q.C., B.Sc., LL.B., Deputy CAO, Operations
902-490-4426
Mike Labrecque, Deputy CAO, Corporate Services & Strategy
902-490-1520
Frank Beazley, Chief, Halifax Regional Police
902-490-6500
Bill Mosher, Chief Director, Fire & Emergency Services
Phillip Townsend, Director, Infrastructure & Asset Management
Brad Anguish, Director, Business Planning & Information Management and Harbour Solutions Project
Mary Ellen Donovan, B.Sc., LL.B., Director, Legal Services
902-490-4226
Paul Dunphy, B.A., Director, Community Development
Ken Reashor, Acting Director, Transportation & Public Works
Catherine Mullally, Director, Human Resources
Carl D. Yates, M.A.Sc., P.Eng., General Manager, Halifax Water
902-490-4827, Fax: 902-490-4808
general.manager@hrwc.ca
Jim Bauld, Manager, Solid Waste Resources
902-490-6606
Alan Brady, Manager, Wastewater Treatment
302-835-9566
Jim Donovan, Project Manager, Economic Strategy
902-490-1742

Shaune MacKinlay, Manager, Public Affairs
Cathie Osborne, P.Eng., Manager, Business Systems & Control
902-490-4093
John P. Sheppard, P.Eng., Manager, Environmental Engineering Services
902-490-6958, Fax: 902-490-4858
sheppaj@halifax.ca
Brian Taylor, Manager, Transit Services
902-490-6388
John Sibbald, Coordinator, Pollution Prevention
902-490-5527
sibbalj@halifax.ca
Peter Lund, Chair, Solid Waste Resource Advisory Committee

Major Municipalities in Nova Scotia

Truro
P.O. Box 427
695 Prince St.
Truro, NS B2N 5C5
902-895-4484
Fax: 902-893-0501
town@truro.ca
www.truro.ca
Municipal Type: City
Incorporated: May 6, 1875 *Area:* 37.63 sq km
County or District: Colchester; *Population in 2006:* 11,765
Provincial Electoral District(s): Truro-Bible Hill
Federal Electoral District(s):
Cumberland-Colchester-Musquodoboit Valley
Next Election: Oct. 2008 (4 year terms)
W.R. (Bill) Mills, Mayor
Diane Bennett Cook, Councillor, Ward(s): 1
Raymond Tynes, Councillor, Ward(s): 1
Charles Cox, Councillor, Ward(s): 2
Brian Kinsman, Councillor, Ward(s): 2
Sharron Byers, Councillor, Ward(s): 3
Greg MacArthur, Councillor, Ward(s): 3
Jim Langille, CAO
jlangille@truro.ca
Andrew McKinnon, Director, Public Works & Traffic Authority
amackinnon@truro.ca
Audrey Buchanan, Senior Engineer
Doug MacKenzie, Director, Parks & Recreation Committee
dmackenzie@truro.ca
Tom Bremner, Chief, Fire
Juanita Bigelow, Administrator, Planning
jbigelow@truro.ca
Genevieve DeCoste, Superintendent, Water Treatment Plant
wpt@truro.ca

Other Municipalities in Nova Scotia

Kings County
P.O. Box 100
87 Cornwallis St.
Kentville, NS B4N 3W3
902-690-6133
Fax: 902-678-9279
inquiry@county.kings.ns.ca
www.county.kings.ns.ca
Municipal Type: Municipality
Incorporated: April 17, 1879 *Area:* 2,122.18 sq km
County or District: Kings; *Population in 2006:* 60,035
Provincial Electoral District(s): Kings North; Kings South; Kings West
Federal Electoral District(s): Kings-Hants; West Nova
Next Election: Oct. 2008 (4 year terms)
Council
Fred Whalen, Warden
902-690-6132
warden.whalen@county.kings.ns.ca
Jim Taylor, Councillor, Ward(s): District 1
councillor.taylor@county.kings.ns.ca
Janet Newton, Councillor, Ward(s): District 2
councillor.newton@county.kings.ns.ca
Dick Killam, Councillor, Ward(s): District 3
councillor.killam@county.kings.ns.ca
Fred Whalen, Councillor, Ward(s): District 4
Wayne Atwater, Councillor, Ward(s): District 5
councillor.atwater@county.kings.ns.ca
Diana Brothers, Councillor, Ward(s): District 6
councillor.brothers@county.kings.ns.ca

Dale Lloyd, Councillor, Ward(s): District 8
councillor.lloyd@county.kings.ns.ca
Basil Hall, Councillor, Ward(s): District 9
councillor.hall@county.kings.ns.ca
Chris Parker, Councillor, Ward(s): District 10
councillor.parker@county.kings.ns.ca
Eric Smith, Councillor, Ward(s): District 11
councillor.smith@county.kings.ns.ca
Mike Ennis, Councillor, Ward(s): District 12
902-542-5217
councillor.ennis@county.kings.ns.ca
Administration
Ann L. Longley, Municipal Clerk
alongley@county.kings.ns.ca
Brian Smith, CAO
902-690-6131, Fax: 902-678-9279
bsmith@county.kings.ns.ca
Bill Butler, Director, Community Development
902-690-6137
bbutler@county.kings.ns.ca
Richard Lloyd, Director, Engineering & Public Works
902-690-6111, Fax: 902-679-0911
rlloyd@county.kings.ns.ca
Bill McKennan, CMA, Director, Corporate Services
902-690-6130
bmckennan@county.kings.ns.ca
Kathleen Leslie, Manager, Information Technology
902-690-6155, Fax: 902-690-6165
kleslie@county.kings.ns.ca
Gary Smith, Manager, Protective & Emergency Services
902-690-6117
gsmith@county.kings.ns.ca
Bob Suffron, Coordinator, Parks & Open Spaces
902-690-6153
bsuffron@county.kings.ns.ca
Chrystal Fuller, Manager, Planning
902-690-6173
cfuller@county.kings.ns.ca
Scott Quinn, Project Engineer
902-690-6194, Fax: 902-679-0911
Zane Long, Manager, Properties
Brian Hazlett, Supervisor, Water & Wastewater
902-690-6198
bhazlett@county.kings.ns.ca

Rural Municipality

Annapolis County
P.O. Box 100
752 George St.
Annapolis Royal, NS B0S 1A0
902-532-2331
Fax: 902-532-2096
info@annapoliscounty.ns.ca
www.annapoliscounty.ns.ca
Municipal Type: Rural Municipality
Incorporated: April 17, 1879 *Area:* 3,184.97 sq km
County or District: Annapolis; *Population in 2006:* 21,438
Provincial Electoral District(s): Annapolis; Digby-Annapolis
Federal Electoral District(s): West Nova
Next Election: Oct. 2008 (4 year terms)
Peter A. Newton, Warden
warden@annapoliscounty.ns.ca
Tom Vitiello, Chair, Emergency Measures Advisory Committee
Reginald C. Ritchie, Chair, Municipal Services (Priorities & Planning) Committee
Brenda Orchard, Chief Administrative Officer
admin@annapoliscounty.ns.ca
Jacquie Farrow-Lawrence, Clerk
Gerald Hackenschmidt, Director, Finance
902-532-3135
ghackenschmidt@annapoliscounty.ns.ca
David McCoubrey, Coordinator, Regional Emergency Measures
remo@annapoliscounty.ns.ca
Laurie Emms, Director, Municipal Services
902-584-2188
lmemms@annapolisvalley.ns.ca
Nelson Porteous, Coordinator, Public Works
902-532-3141
pwork@annapoliscounty.ns.ca

Antigonish County
285 Beech Hill Rd.
Antigonish, NS B2G 0B4

See blue tabs following this section for Municipal Waste Management and Water & Wastewater Treatment.

Municipal Governments / Nova Scotia

902-863-1117
Fax: 902-863-5751
clerk@antigonishcounty.ns.ca
www.antigonishcounty.ns.ca
Municipal Type: Rural Municipality
Incorporated: April 17, 1879 *Area:* 1,457.82 sq km
County or District: Antigonish; *Population in 2006:* 18,836
Provincial Electoral District(s): Antigonish
Federal Electoral District(s): Central Nova
Next Election: Oct. 2008 (4 year terms)
Alan J. Bond, Clerk-Treas.
Herbert J. DeLorey, Warden
Michael O'Leary, Director, Public Works
publicworks@antigonishcounty.ns.ca
Kemp MacDonald, Municipal Planner
planning@antigonishcounty.ns.ca
Daryl Myers, Supervisor, Beech Hill Sanitary Landfill Site
902-863-4744
landfill@antigonishcounty.ns.ca

Chester District
P.O. Box 369
151 King St.
Chester, NS B0J 1J0
902-275-3554
Fax: 902-275-4771
administration@district.chester.ns.ca
www.district.chester.ns.ca
Municipal Type: Rural Municipality
Incorporated: April 17, 1879 *Area:* 1,120.75 sq km
County or District: Lunenburg; *Population in 2006:* 10,741
Provincial Electoral District(s): Chester-St. Margaret's
Federal Electoral District(s): South Shore-St. Margaret's
Next Election: Oct. 2008 (4 year terms)
Allen Webber, Warden
awebber@district.chester.ns.ca
Pamela Myra, Clerk
Darrell Hiltz, CAO
darrell.hiltz@district.chester.ns.ca
Bruce Forest, Director, Public Works
902-275-1312
Earl Woodworth, Building Inspector
ewoodworth@district.chester.ns.ca
Geoff MacDonald, Planning Director
geoff.macdonald@district.chester.ns.ca
Karen Newton, Development Officer
colleen.clare@district.chester.ns.ca
Jennifer Veinotte, Recycling Coordinator
Chad Haughn, Director, Recreation & Parks

Colchester County
P.O. Box 697
1 Church St.
Truro, NS B2N 5E7
902-897-3160
Fax: 902-895-9983
cao@colchester.ca
www.colchester.ca
Municipal Type: Rural Municipality
Incorporated: April 17, 1879 *Area:* 3,627.69 sq km
County or District: Colchester; *Population in 2006:* 50,023
Provincial Electoral District(s): Colchester-Musqudoboit Valley;
Colchester North; Truro-Bible Hill
Federal Electoral District(s):
Cumberland-Colchester-Musquodoboit Valley
Next Election: Oct. 2008 (4 year terms)
Bob Taylor, Mayor
mayor@colchester.ca
Christine Blair, Councillor, Ward(s): District 1
councillordistrict1@colchester.ca
Bill Masters, Councillor, Ward(s): District 2
councillordistrict2@colchester.ca
Gerry Buott, Councillor, Ward(s): District 3
councillordistrict3@colchester.ca
Mike Cooper, Councillor, Ward(s): District 4
councillordistrict4@colchester.ca
Glen Edwards, Councillor, Ward(s): District 5
councillordistrict5@colchester.ca
Karen MacKenzie, Councillor, Ward(s): District 6
kdmackenzie@tru.eastlink.ca
Le Fresne Jimmie, Councillor, Ward(s): District 7
councillordistrict7@colchester.ca
Ron Cavanaugh, Councillor, Ward(s): District 8
councillordistrict8@colchester.ca

Bob White, Councillor, Ward(s): District 9
councillordistrict9@colchester.ca
Tom Taggart, Councillor, Ward(s): District 10
councillordistrict10@colchester.ca
Earl D. McKenna, Councillor, Ward(s): District 11
councillordistrict11@colchester.ca
Dan McDougall, CAO
dmcdougall@colchester.ca
Bruce Purchase, Director, Corporate Services
bpurchase@colchester.ca
Crawford Macpherson, Director, Community Development
cmacpherson@colchester.ca
Donna Campbell, Manager, Finance
dcampbell@colchester.ca

Cumberland County
E.D. Fullerton Municipal Bldg.
P.O. Box 428
1395 Blair Lake Rd., RR#6
Amherst, NS B4H 3Y4
902-667-2313
Fax: 902-667-1352
Toll Free Phone: 1-888-756-6262
info@cumberlandcounty.ns.ca
www.cumberlandcounty.ns.ca
Municipal Type: Rural Municipality
Incorporated: April 17, 1879 *Area:* 4,271.14 sq km
County or District: Cumberland; *Population in 2006:* 32,046
Provincial Electoral District(s): Cumberland North; Cumberland South
Federal Electoral District(s):
Cumberland-Colchester-Musquodoboit Valley
Next Election: Oct. 2008 (4 year terms)
Keith Hunter, Warden
Rennie Bugley, CAO
Connie Speight, Executive Secretary
Robert Streatch, Director, Public Works
902-667-3029
Jim Hannon, Coordinator, Emergency Measures
902-667-2313
jhannon@cumberlandcounty.ns.ca

Hants East District
P.O. Box 190
2361 Hwy. 2, Milford
Shubenacadie, NS B0N 2H0
902-758-2299
Fax: 902-758-3497
info@easthants.ca
www.easthants.ca
Municipal Type: Rural Municipality
Incorporated: April 17, 1879 *Area:* 1,787.64 sq km
County or District: Hants; *Population in 2006:* 21,387
Provincial Electoral District(s): Hants East
Federal Electoral District(s): Kings-Hants
Next Election: Oct. 2008 (4 year terms)
John Patterson, Warden
Ian Glasgow, CAO
iglasgow@easthants.ca
Edward Gillis, P.Eng., Director, Engineering Services
Roger Freeman, P.Eng., Engineer, Transportation
Andrea Trask, Coordinator & Educator, Waste Reduction
Heidi Achenbach, Manager, Solid Waste
902-758-2299
Jim Ashley, Manager, Public Works
Edward McQuillan, Operator, Water Distribution
John Woodford, Director, Planning & Development
902-758-2715
jwoodford@easthants.ca
Mike Brown, Foreman, Georgefield Municipal Landfill Site
902-261-2178
Krista Dewey, Director, Corporate & Residential Services
Terry Matheson, Officer, Environmental Compliance

Hants West District
Windsor-West Hants Industrial Park
P.O. Box 3000
76 Morrison Dr.
Windsor, NS B0N 2T0
902-798-8391
Fax: 902-798-8553
west.hants@westhants.ca
www.westhants.ca
Municipal Type: Rural Municipality
Incorporated: April 17, 1879 *Area:* 1,238.12 sq km

County or District: Hants; *Population in 2006:* 13,881
Provincial Electoral District(s): Hants West
Federal Electoral District(s): Kings-Hants
Next Election: Oct. 2008 (4 year terms)
Richard B. Dauphinee, Warden
admin@westhants.ca
Dwight Bennett, CAO
cao@westhants.ca
Rick Sherrard, Director, Public Works
public.works@westhants.ca
Paul DeMont, Operator, Water Treatment
drc@westhants.ca
Lynn Davis, Director, Planning
902-798-6900
ldavis@windsorwesthantsplanning.ns.ca
Doug MacInnes, Development Officer
dmacinnis@windsorwesthants.planning.ns.ca
Christine McClare, Coordinator, Waste Reduction
waste@westhants.ca

Inverness County
Municipal Bldg.
P.O. Box 179
375 Main St.
Port Hood, NS B0E 2W0
902-787-2274
Fax: 902-787-3110
joe.oconnor@invernesscounty.ca
www.invernesscounty.ca
Municipal Type: Rural Municipality
Incorporated: April 17, 1879 *Area:* 3,830.4 sq km
County or District: Inverness; *Population in 2006:* 19,036
Provincial Electoral District(s): Guysborough-Sheet Harbour;
Inverness; Victoria-The Lakes
Federal Electoral District(s): Cape Breton-Canso;
Sydney-Victoria
Next Election: Oct. 2008 (4 year terms)
Duart MacAulay, Warden
duartmaca@ns.sympatico.ca
Joe O'Connor, CAO
Joe O'Connor, Director, Public Works
902-787-3502, Fax: 902-787-2339
invworks@ns.sympatico.ca
William Gillis, Officer, Bylaw Enforcement

Lunenburg District
P.O. Box 200
210 Aberdeen Rd.
Bridgewater, NS B4V 4G8
902-543-8181
Fax: 902-543-7123
finance@municipality.lunenburg.ca
www.modl.ca
Municipal Type: Rural Municipality
Incorporated: April 17, 1879 *Area:* 1,759.14 sq km
County or District: Lunenburg; *Population in 2006:* 25,164
Provincial Electoral District(s): Chester-St. Margaret's
Lunenburg; Lunenburg West
Federal Electoral District(s): South Shore-St. Margaret's
Next Election: Oct. 2008 (4 year terms)
Don Downe, Warden
Tammy Wilson, CAO
twilson@modl.ca
Pierre A. Breau, P.Eng., Municipal Engineer & Director,
Engineering & Public Works
902-541-1331
pierrebreau@modl.ca
Ed Curran, Director, Planning & Development Services
902-541-1336
ecurran@modl.ca
Jim Annand, Manager, Solid Waste Operations
902-541-1325
jannand@modl.ca
Kevin Wentzell, Supervisor, Compost Plant
902-543-2991
Sally Steele, Coordinator, Recycling
902-543-2913
Bob Palmer, Emergency Measures
902-543-8650
emo@modl.ca
April Whynot-Lohnes, Officer, Development
awlohnes@modl.ca
Laura Barkhouse, Coordinator, Trails

See blue tabs following this section for Municipal Waste Management and Water & Wastewater Treatment.

CANADIAN ENVIRONMENTAL RESOURCE GUIDE 2011-2012

Municipal Governments / Nunavut

Pictou County
P.O. Box 910
46 Municipal Dr.
Pictou, NS B0K 1H0
902-485-4311
Fax: 902-485-6475
cmacintosh@county.pictou.ns.ca
www.county.pictou.ns.ca
Municipal Type: Rural Municipality
Incorporated: April 17, 1879 *Area:* 2,845.26 sq km
County or District: Pictou; *Population in 2006:* 46,513
Provincial Electoral District(s): Pictou Centre; Pictou East; Pictou West
Federal Electoral District(s): Central Nova
Next Election: Oct. 2008 (4 year terms)
Ronald Baillie, Warden
Brian Cullen, CAO
Carol MacKenzie, Manager, Waste Reduction Program
902-396-1495
cmackenzie@pcwastemgmt.com
Lonnie Ferguson, General Manager, Mount William Landfill Site
902-396-5062, Fax: 902-396-4782
lferguson@pcwastemgmt.com

Richmond County
P.O. Box 120
2357 Hwy. 206
Arichat, NS B0E 1A0
902-226-2400
Fax: 902-226-1510
ldigout@richmondcounty.ca
www.richmondcounty.ca
Municipal Type: Rural Municipality
Incorporated: April 17, 1879 *Area:* 1,244.24 sq km
County or District: Richmond; *Population in 2006:* 9,740
Provincial Electoral District(s): Richmond
Federal Electoral District(s): Cape Breton-Canso
Next Election: Oct. 2008 (4 year terms)
Louis Digout, CAO
John Boudreau, Warden
Darrin McLean, Director, Public Works/Municipal Engineer
902-226-3988
dmclean@richmondcounty.ca
Jason MacMillan, Technologist, Engineering
902-226-3989
jmacmillan@richmondcounty.ca

Yarmouth District
P.O. Box 21
932, Hwy 1
Hebron, NS B0W 1X0
902-742-7159
Fax: 902-742-3164
admin@district.yarmouth.ns.ca
www.district.yarmouth.ns.ca
Municipal Type: Rural Municipality
Incorporated: April 17, 1879 *Area:* 585.27 sq km
County or District: Yarmouth; *Population in 2006:* 10,304
Provincial Electoral District(s): Yarmouth
Federal Electoral District(s): West Nova
Next Election: Oct. 2008 (4 year terms)
Leland Anthony, Warden
warden@district.yarmouth.ns.ca
Ken Moses, CAO
cao@district.yarmouth.ns.ca
Greg Shay, Director, Finance
greg@district.yarmouth.ns.ca

Nunavut

One of Nunavut's challenges is the lack of well-developed infrastructure. There currently are no roads linking communities. As the population grows there will be an increasing need to further develop infrastructure, particularly in such environmental areas as water quality and waste management.

There are 26 active landfill sites for solid waste, one for each community in Nunavut. Each landfill site allows open pit burning. In municipalities, there is residential diversion of plastics and metals from the landfill sites. The territory is in the process of devising a recycling and diversion program for all municipalities.

Drinking water, collection, treatment and distribution is a territorial function. Regulated by the territory through the Public Health Water Supply Regulations for public drinking water, this dictates distribution and quality. Nunavut is reviewing the regulations to bring them up to standard and to align them with the requirements of the territory.

Each municipality disposes of its own sewage and wastewater by deep ocean discharge, or primary treatment in a sewage lagoon followed by deep ocean discharge where the municipality can do so. Sewage and wastewater discharge requires a license supplied by the Nunavut Water Board.

Under the federal government's New Deal for Cities, Nunavut received $69.5 million in federal gas tax funding and the Municipal Rural Infrastructure Fund between 2005 and 2010 for municipal infrastructure projects.

Major Municipalities in Nunavut

Iqaluit
P.O. Box 460
Iqaluit, NU X0A 0H0
867-979-5600
Fax: 867-979-5922
info@city.iqaluit.nu.ca
www.city.iqaluit.nu.ca
Municipal Type: City
Incorporated: 2001 *Area:* 52.34 sq km
Population in 2006: 6,184
Provincial Electoral District(s): Iqaluit East; Iqaluit West; Iqaluit Centre
Federal Electoral District(s): Nunavut
Next Election: 2012 (3 year terms)
Note: Formerly known as Frobisher Bay.
Council
Elisapee Sheutiapik, Mayor
mayor@city.iqaluit.nu.ca
Mary Akpalialuk, Councillor
Jimmy Kilabuk, Councillor
Natsiq Kango, Councillor
Mat Knicklebein, Councillor
Simon Nattaq, Councillor
Mary Ekho Wilman, Councillor
David Ell, Councillor
Romeyn Stevenson, Councillor
Administration
John Hussey, Chief Administration Officer
867-979-5666
j.hussey@city.iqaluit.nu.ca
John Mabberi-Mudonyi, Director, Corporate Services
867-979-5675
j.mabberi-mudonyi@city.iqaluit.nu.ca
Doug Vincent, Chief Enforcement Officer
867-979-6363
d.vincent@city.iqaluit.nu.ca
Michèle Bertol, Director, Planning & Lands
867-979-6363
m.bertol@city.iqaluit.nu.ca
Amy Elgersma, Director, Recreation
867-979-5616
a.elgersma@city.iqaluit.nu.ca
Vacant, Director, Engineering & Public Works
Meagan Leach, Director, Engineering & Sustainability
867-979-6363
m.leach@city.iqaluit.nu.ca
Sean Tiessen, Coordinator, Materials
s.tiessen@city.iqaluit.nu.ca
Vacant, Superintendent, Operations
Geneva Chislett, Controller
867-979-5610
g.chislett@city.iqaluit.nu.ca
Walter Oliver, Fire Chief, Emergency Services
867-976-5657
w.oliver@city.iqaluit.nu.ca
Joamie Eegeesiak, Officer, Community Economic Development
867-979-6363
j.eegeesiak@city.iqaluit.nu.ca
Rob Hogan, Foreman, Utilidor Water Treatment Plant
867-975-8509

Ontario

Ontario's Environmental Protection Act (EPA) is the Act that governs water and waste management for the province.

Bill 90 Waste Diversion Act was passed June, 2002. The Act promotes reduction, reuse and recycling of waste by creating Waste Diversion Ontario (WDO), a permanent non-crown, multi-stakeholder corporation with industry, municipal, non-government and Ministry of the Environment representatives on its board of directors. WDO will develop, implement and fund waste diversion programs in the province. This legislation will lead to increased diversion of waste materials, such as organics, scrap tires, used oil, household special wastes, electronics, pharmaceutical products, fluorescent lighting tubes and batteries. The first phase of the Waste Electrical and Electronic Equipment Program Plan was approved by the Minister on July 10, 2008 and commenced on April 1, 2009. The Used Tires Program Plan was approved on April 9, 2009 and commenced on September 1, 2009.

Sewage and wastewater management has been transferred to municipalities by the province. Most municipal governments own and operate their own sewage and wastewater systems. Certificates of approval under the Ontario Water Resources Act (OWRA) are issued by the Ministry for the treatment and disposal of sewage by municipal and private systems. Certificates of approval are required for facilities that discharge contaminants to groundwater and/or surface water.

Municipal residential drinking water systems are required to be tested regularly and meet stringent provincial standards. More than 99.8% of over 700,000 recent tests conducted on these systems met the standards set out in the Safe Drinking Water Act, 2002. Orders for not meeting regulatory requirements issued by Ministry drinking water inspectors fell to 3% in 2006-07 from 11% in 2004-05 and 39% in 2003-04, reflecting an improvement in drinking water systems and operations.

The Greenbelt Act, 2005 protects about 1.8 million acres of environmentally sensitive land and agricultural land in the Golden Horseshoe from urban development and sprawl.

Under the federal government's New Deal for Cities, Ontario was allocated $1.865 billion in federal gas tax funding betweem 2005 and 2010 for municipal infrastructure projects.

Counties & Municipal Districts in Ontario

Brant
P.O. Box 160
26 Park Ave.
Burford, ON N0E 1A0
519-449-2451
Fax: 519-449-2454
Toll Free Phone: 1-888-250-2297
brant@county.brant.on.ca
www.brant.ca
Municipal Type: County
Incorporated: Jan. 1, 1999 *Area:* 843.1 sq km
Population in 2006: 34,415
Provincial Electoral District(s): Brant
Federal Electoral District(s): Brant
Next Election: Oct. 2014 (4 year terms)
Ron Eddy, Mayor
Steve Schmitt, Councillor, Ward(s): 1
John Wheat, Councillor, Ward(s): 1
Roy Haggart, Councillor, Ward(s): 2
Shirley Simons, Councillor, Ward(s): 2
Cliff Atfield, Councillor, Ward(s): 3
Murray Powell, Councillor, Ward(s): 3
Robert Chambers, Councillor, Ward(s): 4
Kevin Hodge, Councillor, Ward(s): 4
Brian Coleman, Councillor, Ward(s): 5
Joan Gatward, Councillor, Ward(s): 5
Jayne Carman, Clerk & Coordinator, Council Committee, Administration
Don Glassford, Chief Administrative Officer, Administration
Heather Mifflin, Treasurer, Administration
Fran Bell, Director, Corporate Services, Administration
Cynthia Compeau, Director, Public Works, Administration
David Johnston, Director, Development Services, Administration
Paul Boissonneault, Fire Chief, Administration
Kathy Ballantyne, Manager, Parks & Facilities, Administration
Alex Davidson, Manager, Water Division, Administration
Lee Robinson, Manager, Infrastructure Services, Administration
Ed Sharp, Manager, Environmental Services, Administration
Mike Tout, Manager, Roads Operations, Administration

Bruce
P.O. Box 70
30 Park St.
Walkerton, ON N0G 2V0

See blue tabs following this section for Municipal Waste Management and Water & Wastewater Treatment.

Municipal Governments / Ontario

519-881-1291
Fax: 519-881-1619
www.brucecounty.on.ca
Municipal Type: County
Area: 4,079.17 sq km
Population in 2006: 65,349
Next Election: Oct. 2014 (4 year terms)
Council
Mike Smith, Warden & Councillor
Charlie Bagnato, Councillor
Bill Goetz, Councillor
Milt McIver, Councillor
Gwen Gilbert, Councillor
Larry Kraemer, Councillor
Mitch Twolan, Councillor
Ron Oswald, Councillor
Administration
J. Wayne Jamieson, Chief Administrative Officer, Administration
wjamieson@brucecounty.on.ca
Bettyanne Cobean, C.M.O., Clerk-Treasurer, Administration
bcobean@brucecounty.on.ca
Doug Harris, Director, Human Resources, Administration
Chris LaForest, Director, Planning, Administration
Terry Sanderson, Director, Social Services & Social Housing, Administration
Doug Smith, Director, Emergency Services, Administration
Brian Knox, County Engineer, Administration

Dufferin
51 Zina St.
Orangeville, ON L9W 1E5
519-941-2816
Fax: 519-941-4565
Toll Free Phone: 1-877-941-6991
info@dufferincounty.on.ca; treasury@dufferincounty.on.ca
www.dufferincounty.on.ca
Municipal Type: County
Incorporated: Jan. 24, 1881 *Area:* 1,485.58 sq km
Population in 2006: 54,436
Next Election: Oct. 2014 (4 year terms)
Council
Allen Taylor, Warden & Councillor, Ward(s): East Garafraxa
warden@dufferincounty.on.ca
Don MacIver, Councillor, Ward(s): Amaranth
Walter Kolodziechuk, Councillor, Ward(s): Amaranth
John Oosterhof, Councillor, Ward(s): East Luther Grand Valley
Debbie Fawcett, Councillor, Ward(s): Melancthon
Bill Hill, Councillor, Ward(s): Melancthon
Lorie Haddock, Councillor, Ward(s): Mono
Ken McGhee, Councillor, Ward(s): Mono
Sue Snider, Councillor, Ward(s): Mulmur
Gordon D. Montgomery, Councillor, Ward(s): Mulmur
Rob Adams, Councillor, Ward(s): Orangeville
Warren Maycock, Councillor, Ward(s): Orangeville
Ken Bennington, Councillor, Ward(s): Shelburne
Ed Crewson, Councillor, Ward(s): Shelburne
Administration
Pam Hillock, Clerk, Administration
clerk@dufferincounty.on.ca
Linda J. Dean, Chief Administrative Officer, Administration
cao@dufferincounty.on.ca
Alan Selby, Treasurer, Administration
treasurer@dufferincounty.on.ca
Trevor Lewis, Director, Public Works, Administration
directorofpublicworks@dufferincounty.on.ca
Michael A. Giles, Chief Building Official, Administration
cbo@dufferincounty.on.ca
Mark Bialkowski, Manager, Human Resources, Administration
hr@dufferincounty.on.ca
Melissa Kovacs-Reid, Coordinator, Waste Management, Administration
wastemgmt@dufferincounty.on.ca
Shara Bagnell, Officer, Health & Safety, Administration
health&safety@dufferincounty.on.ca

Durham
P.O. Box 623
605 Rossland Rd. East
Whitby, ON L1N 6A3
905-668-7711
Fax: 905-668-9963
Toll Free Phone: 1-800-372-1102
info@durham.ca; cishelp@durham.ca (Corporate Information)
www.durham.ca

Municipal Type: Regional Municipality
Incorporated: Jan. 1, 1974 *Area:* 2,523.15 sq km
Population in 2006: 561,258
Next Election: Oct. 2014 (4 year terms)
Council
Roger Anderson, Regional Chair & Chief Executive Officer, Councillor, Fax: 905-668-1567
chair@durham.ca
Scott Crawford, Councillor, Ward(s): Ajax
Steve Parish, Councillor, Ward(s): Ajax
Colleen Jordan, Councillor, Ward(s): Ajax
Debbie Bath, Councillor, Ward(s): Brock
John Grant, Councillor, Ward(s): Brock
Mary Novak, Councillor, Ward(s): Clarington 1 & 2
Willie Woo, Councillor, Ward(s): Clarington 3 & 4
John R. Aker, Councillor, Ward(s): Oshawa
Bob Chapman, Councillor, Ward(s): Oshawa
Nancy Diamond, Councillor, Ward(s): Oshawa
Amy England, Councillor, Ward(s): Oshawa
Tito-Dante Marimpietri, Councillor, Ward(s): Oshawa
John Neal, Councillor, Ward(s): Oshawa
Nester Pidwerbecki, Councillor, Ward(s): Oshawa
Jennifer O'Connell, Councillor, Ward(s): Pickering 1
Bill McLean, Councillor, Ward(s): Pickering 2
Peter Rodrigues, Councillor, Ward(s): Pickering 3
Bobbie Drew, Councillor, Ward(s): Scugog
Jack Ballinger, Councillor, Ward(s): Uxbridge
Lorne Earle Coe, Councillor, Ward(s): Whitby
Joe Drumm, Councillor, Ward(s): Whitby
Don Mitchell, Councillor, Ward(s): Whitby
Administration
Patricia M. Madill, Regional Clerk, Administration, Fax: 905-668-9963
clerks@durham.ca
Garry H. Cubitt, M.S.W., Chief Administrative Officer, Administration
cao@durham.ca
R. Jim Clapp, Commissioner, Finance Department, Administration, Fax: 905-666-6256
Cliff Curtis, Commissioner, Works Department, Administration, Fax: 905-668-2051
works@durham.ca
Hugh A. Drouin, Commissioner, Social Services Department, Administration, Fax: 905-666-6219
socserv@durham.ca
Alex L. Georgieff, Commissioner, Planning Department, Administration, Fax: 905-666-6208
planning@durham.ca
Garth S. Johns, Commissioner, Human Resources, Administration, Fax: 905-666-3327
Robert J. Kyle, Commissioner, Health Department & Medical Officer of Health, Administration, Fax: 905-666-3327
health@durham.ca
Pat W. Olive, Commissioner, Economic Development & Tourism, Administration
800-413-0017, Fax: 905-666-6228
business@durham.ca; tourism@durham.ca
Ivan Ciuciura, Director, Durham Emergency Management Office, Administration
905-430-2792, Fax: 905-430-8635
demo@durham.ca
Sherri Munns-Audet, Director, Corporate Communications, Administration, Fax: 905-668-1468
corporatecommunications@durham.ca
Ted Galinis, General Manager, Durham Region Transit, Administration, Fax: 905-666-6193
transit@durham.ca

Elgin
450 Sunset Dr.
St Thomas, ON N5R 5V1
519-631-1460
Fax: 519-633-7661
www.elgin-county.on.ca
Municipal Type: County
Incorporated: 1852 *Area:* 1,880.84 sq km
Population in 2006: 85,351
Next Election: Oct. 2014 (4 year terms)
Note: Restructuring of the county occurred in 1998.
Council
Graham Warwick, Warden & Councillor
warden@elgin-county.on.ca
Lynn Acre, Councillor
Bob Habkirk, Councillor
Sylvia Hofhuis, Councillor

Tom Marks, Councillor
James McIntyre, Councillor
Dave Mennill, Councillor
Bonnie Vowel, Councillor
John R. Wilson, Councillor
Administration
Mark G. McDonald, Chief Administrative Officer, Administration
mmcdonald@elgin-county.on.ca
Jim Bundschuh, Director, Financial Services, Administration
Brian Masschaele, Director, Community & Cultural Services, Administration
Harley Underhill, Director, Human Resources, Administration
Clayton Watters, Director, Engineering Services, Administration

Essex
360 Fairview Ave. West
Essex, ON N8M 1Y6
519-776-6441
Fax: 519-776-4455
Fax, Planning Department: 519-776-1253
www.countyofessex.on.ca
Municipal Type: County
Incorporated: 1999 *Area:* 1,851.34 sq km
Population in 2006: 393,402
Next Election: Oct. 2014 (4 year terms)
Council
Nelson Santos, Warden & Councillor
519-733-9936
nsantos@kingsville.ca
John Adams, Deputy Warden, Councillor
519-326-7010
jadams@leamington.ca
Wayne Hurst, Councillor
519-736-7646
whurst@amherstburg.ca
Robert Bailey, Councillor
519-978-0974
rbailey@amherstburg.ca
Ron McDermott, Councillor
519-776-8150
rmcdermott@essex.ca
Richard Meloche, Councillor
519-776-5726
rmeloche@essex.ca
Katherine Gunning, Councillor, Fax: 519-839-6222
kayway@kelcom.net
Tom Bain, Councillor
519-728-2394
tbain@lakeshore.ca
Robert Sylvester, Councillor
519-727-3849
rsylvester@lakeshore.ca
Gary Baxter, Councillor
mayor@town.lasalle.on.ca
Bill Varga, Councillor
bvarga@town.lasalle.on.ca
Robert Schmidt, Councillor
519-326-7443
rschmidt@leamington.ca
Gary McNamara, Councillor
519-735-6654
gmcnamara@tecumseh.ca
Tom Burton, Councillor
519-979-2339
tburton@tecumseh.ca
Administration
Mary S. Brennan, Clerk & Director, Council Services, Administration
mbrennan@countyofessex.on.ca
Brian Gregg, Chief Administrative Officer, Administration
Robert Maisonville, Director, Corporate Services & Treasurer, Administration
Greg Schlosser, Director, Human Resources, Administration
Bill King, Manager, Planning Services, Administration
Tom Bateman, County Engineer, Administration
Phillip Berthiaume, Planner, Emergency Measures, Administration

Frontenac
2069 Battersea Rd., RR#1
Glenburnie, ON K0H 1S0
613-548-9400
Fax: 613-546-8460
info@frontenaccounty.ca; communications@frontenaccounty.ca
www.frontenaccounty.ca

See blue tabs following this section for Municipal Waste Management and Water & Wastewater Treatment.

Municipal Governments / Ontario

Municipal Type: County
Incorporated: Jan. 1, 1998 *Area:* 3,672.49 sq km
Population in 2006: 143,865
Next Election: Oct. 2014 (4 year terms)
Council
Janet Gutowski, Warden & Councillor
cfmayor@frontenaccounty.ca
Gary Davison, Councillor
Ron Maguire, Councillor
Jim Vanden Hoek, Councillor
Administration
Liz Savill, Chief Administrative Officer & Clerk, Administration
Marian Van Bruinessen, Treasurer, Administration
Paul Charbonneau, Director, Emergency & Transportation Services & Chief, Paramedics, Administration
Anne Marie Young, Manager, Economic Development, Administration

Grey
County Administration Bldg.
595 Ninth Ave. East
Owen Sound, ON N4K 3E3
519-376-2205
Fax: 519-376-7970
Toll Free Phone: 1-800-567-4739
clerks@greycounty.ca; socialservices@greycounty.ca
www.greycounty.ca
Municipal Type: County
Incorporated: Jan. 1, 1852 *Area:* 4,508.12 sq km
Population in 2006: 92,411
Next Election: Oct. 2014 (4 year terms)
Council
Arlene Wright, Warden & Councillor
warden@grey.ca
Howard Greig, Mayor, Councillor, Ward(s): Chatsworth
howard.greig@grey.ca
Bob Pringle, Deputy Mayor & Councillor, Ward(s): Chatsworth
bob.pringle@grey.ca
Alan Barfoot, Mayor, Councillor, Ward(s): Georgian Bluffs
alan.barfoot@grey.ca
Dwight Burley, Deputy Mayor & Councillor, Ward(s): Georgian Bluffs
dwight.burley@grey.ca
Brian Mullin, Mayor, Councillor, Ward(s): Grey Highlands
brian.mullin@grey.ca
David Fawcett, Deputy Mayor & Councillor, Ward(s): Grey Highlands
david.fawcett@grey.ca
Kathi Maskell, Mayor, Councillor, Ward(s): Hanover
kathi.maskell@grey.ca
Gerald Rogers, Deputy Mayor & Councillor, Ward(s): Hanover
gerald.rogers@grey.ca
Francis Richardson, Mayor, Councillor, Ward(s): Meaford
francis.richardson@grey.ca
Michael Traynor, Deputy Mayor & Councillor, Ward(s): Meaford
michael.traynor@grey.ca
Ruth Lovell-Stanners, Mayor, Councillor, Ward(s): Owen Sound
ruth.lovell@grey.ca
Arlene Wright, City/County Councillor, Councillor, Ward(s): Owen Sound
arlene.wright@grey.ca
Don Lewis, Mayor, Councillor, Ward(s): Southgate
don.lewis@grey.ca
Brian Milne, Deputy Mayor & Councillor, Ward(s): Southgate
brian.milne@grey.ca
Ellen Anderson, Mayor, Councillor, Ward(s): The Blue Mountains
ellen.anderson@grey.ca
Duncan McKinlay, Deputy Mayor & Councillor, Ward(s): The Blue Mountains
duncan.mckinlay@grey.ca
Kevin Eccles, Mayor, Councillor, Ward(s): West Grey
kevin.eccles@grey.ca
Dan Sullivan, Deputy Mayor & Councillor, Ward(s): West Grey
dan.sullivan@grey.ca
Administration
Sharon Vokes, C.M.O., County Clerk & Director, Council Services, Administration
svokes@greycounty.ca
Lance Thurston, Chief Administrative Officer, Administration
lance.thurston@grey.ca
Kevin Weppler, Director, Finance, Administration
kevin.weppler@grey.ca
Barb Fedy, BA, Director, Social Services, Administration
barb.fedy@grey.ca; socialservices@grey.ca

Geoff Hogan, BSc, Director, Information Technology, Administration
geoff.hogan@grey.ca
Randy Scherzer, BES, MCIP, RPP, Director, Planning & Development, Administration
randy.scherzer@grey.ca; planning@grey.ca
Grant McLevy, Director, Human Resources, Administration
grant.mclevy@grey.ca; employment@grey.ca
Gary Shaw, Director, Transportation & Public Safety, Administration
gary.shaw@grey.ca; transportation@grey.ca

Haldimand
Cayuga Administration Bldg.
P.O. Box 400
45 Munsee St. North
Cayuga, ON N0A 1E0
905-318-5932
Fax: 905-772-3542
E-mail, Ops.: operations@haldimandcounty.on.ca
info@haldimandcounty.on.ca; clerk@haldimandcounty.on.ca
www.haldimandcounty.on.ca
Municipal Type: County
Incorporated: Jan. 1, 2001 *Area:* 1,251.58 sq km
Population in 2006: 45,212
Provincial Electoral District(s): Haldimand-Norfolk
Federal Electoral District(s): Haldimand-Norfolk
Next Election: Oct. 2014 (4 year terms)
Marie Trainer, Mayor
mayor@haldimandcounty.on.ca
Leroy Bartlett, Councillor, Ward(s): 1
lbartlett@haldimandcounty.on.ca
Buck Sloat, Councillor, Ward(s): 2
bsloat@haldimandcounty.on.ca
Craig Grice, Councillor, Ward(s): 3
cgrice@haldimandcounty.on.ca
Tony Dalimonte, Deputy Mayor & Councillor, Ward(s): 4
tdalimonte@haldimandcounty.on.ca
Don Ricker, Councillor, Ward(s): 5
dricker@haldimandcounty.on.ca
Lorne Boyko, Councillor, Ward(s): 6
lpboyko@haldimandcounty.on.ca
Janis Lankester, Clerk, Administration
jlankester@haldimandcounty.on.ca
D. Boyle, Chief Administrative Officer, Administration
K. General, General Manager, Corporate Services, Administration
R. Lane, General Manager, Community Services, Administration
C. Manley, General Manager, Planning & Economic Development, Administration
G. Rae, General Manager, Public Works, Administration

Haliburton
P.O. Box 399
11 Newcastle St.
Minden, ON K0M 2K0
705-286-1333
Fax: 705-286-4829
Toll Free: 1-866-886-8815
aballe@county.haliburton.on.ca
www.haliburtoncounty.ca
Municipal Type: County
Incorporated: Jan. 1, 2001 *Area:* 4,025.27 sq km
Population in 2006: 16,147
Next Election: Oct. 2014 (4 year terms)
Council
Dave Burton, Warden & Councillor
705-448-9355
dburton@highlandseast.ca
Eleanor Harrison, Councillor, Ward(s): Algonquin Highlands
705-489-2128
eharrison@algonquinhighlands.ca
Tom Gardner, Councillor, Ward(s): Algonquin Highlands
705-489-3703
tomgardner01@hotmail.com
Murray Fearrey, Councillor, Ward(s): Dysart et al
705-457-2557
mfearrey@dysartetal.ca
Bill Davis, Councillor, Ward(s): Dysart et al
705-457-1196
bdavis@county.haliburton.on.ca
James Mackie, Councillor, Ward(s): Highlands East
613-339-1714
james.mackie@sympatico.ca

James McMahon, Councillor, Ward(s): Minden Hills
705-286-2801
jmcmahon@mindenhills.ca
Cheryl Murdoch, Councillor, Ward(s): Minden Hills
705-286-1701
Administration
Tamara Wilbee, County Clerk & Coordinator, Human Resources, Administration
twilbee@county.haliburton.on.ca
Jim Wilson, Chief Administrative Officer, Administration
jwilson@county.haliburton.on.ca
Laura Janke, Treasurer, Administration
ljanke@county.haliburton.on.ca
Pat Kennedy, Director, Emergency Services, Administration
pkennedy@county.haliburton.on.ca
Doug Ray, Director, Public Works, Administration
dray@county.haliburton.on.ca
Robert Smith, Director, Economic Development & Tourism Marketing, Administration
rsmith@county.haliburton.on.ca
Jane Tousaw, Director, Planning, Administration
jtousaw@county.haliburton.on.ca
Roy Haig, Manager, Engineering, Administration
rhaig@county.haliburton.on.ca
Jim Young, Manager, Operations, Administration
jyoung@county.haliburton.on.ca

Halton
1151 Bronte Rd.
Oakville, ON L6M 3L1
905-825-6000
Fax: 905-825-9010
Toll Free Phone: 1-866-442-5866; TTY: 905-827-9833
accesshalton@halton.ca
www.halton.ca
Municipal Type: Regional Municipality
Incorporated: Jan. 1, 1974 *Area:* 967.17 sq km
Population in 2006: 439,256
Next Election: Oct. 2014 (4 year terms)
Council
Gary Carr, Regional Chair, Councillor
905-825-6115, Fax: 905-825-8273
gary.carr@halton.ca
Rick Goldring, Councillor, Ward(s): Burlington Mayor
Rick Craven, Councillor, Ward(s): Burlington 1
Marianne Meed Ward, Councillor, Ward(s): Burlington 2
John Taylor, Councillor, Ward(s): Burlington 3
Jack Dennison, Councillor, Ward(s): Burlington 4
Paul Sharman, Councillor, Ward(s): Burlington 5
Blair Lancaster, Councillor, Ward(s): Burlington 6
Rick Bonnette, Councillor, Ward(s): Halton Hills Mayor
Clark Somerville, Councillor, Ward(s): Halton Hills 1 & 2
Jane Fogal, Councillor, Ward(s): Halton Hills 3 & 4
Gordon Krantz, Councillor, Ward(s): Milton Mayor
Tony Lambert, Councillor, Ward(s): Milton 1, 6, 7, 8
Colin Best, Councillor, Ward(s): Milton 2, 3, 4, 5
Rob Burton, Councillor, Ward(s): Oakville Mayor
Alan Johnston, Councillor, Ward(s): Oakville 1
Cathy Duddeck, Councillor, Ward(s): Oakville 2
F. Keith Bird, Councillor, Ward(s): Oakville 3
Allan Elgar, Councillor, Ward(s): Oakville 4
Jeff Knoll, Councillor, Ward(s): Oakville 5
Tom Adams, Councillor, Ward(s): Oakville 6
Administration
Susan Lathan, Regional Clerk & Director, Council Services, Administration
regionalclerk@halton.ca
Pat Moyle, Chief Administrative Officer, Administration
J.E. MacCaskill, Regional Treasurer & Commissioner, Corporate Services, Administration
Mark Meneray, Commissioner, Legislative & Planning Services & Corporate Counsel, Administration
Robert Nosal, Commissioner & Medical Officer of Health, Administration
Adelina Urbanski, Commissioner, Social & Community Services, Administration
M. Zamojc, Commissioner, Public Works, Administration

Hastings
County Administration Bldg.
P.O. Box 4400
235 Pinnacle St.
Belleville, ON K8N 3A9
613-966-1319
Fax: 613-966-2574

See blue tabs following this section for Municipal Waste Management and Water & Wastewater Treatment.

Toll Free Phone: 1-800-510-3306
www.hastingscounty.com
Municipal Type: County
Incorporated: 1850 *Area:* 5,977.64 sq km
Population in 2006: 130,474
Next Election: Oct. 2014 (4 year terms)
Council
Ron Emond, Warden & Councillor, Ward(s): Hastings Highlands
emondr@hastingscounty.com
Lloyd Churchill, Councillor, Ward(s): Bancroft
Dave Panabaker, Councillor, Ward(s): Carlow/Mayo
Tom Deline, Councillor, Ward(s): Centre Hastings
Norm Clark, Councillor, Ward(s): Deseronto
Carl Tinney, Councillor, Ward(s): Faraday
Dave Golem, Councillor, Ward(s): Limerick
Bob Sager, Councillor, Ward(s): Madoc
Terry Clemens, Councillor, Ward(s): Marmora & Lake
Peter Kooistra, Councillor, Ward(s): Stirling-Rawdon
Wanda Donaldson, Councillor, Ward(s): Tudor & Cashel
Jo-Anne Albert, Councillor, Ward(s): Tweed
Margaret Walsh, Councillor, Ward(s): Tyendinaga
Dan McCaw, Councillor, Ward(s): Wollaston
Administration
James Pine, Chief Administrative Officer & Clerk, Administration
pinej@hastingscounty.com
Sue Horwood, Treasurer, Director, Finance, Asset Management & Services, Administration
Shaune Lightfoot, Director, Human Resources, Administration
Brian McComb, Director, Planning, Administration

Huron
1 Court House Sq.
Goderich, ON N7A 1M2
519-524-8394
Fax: 519-524-2044
Toll Free Phone: 1-888-524-8394 (in 519 area)
huronadmin@huroncounty.ca
www.huroncounty.ca
Municipal Type: County
Area: 3,396.68 sq km
Population in 2006: 59,325
Next Election: Oct. 2014 (4 year terms)
Council
Ken Oke, Warden & Councillor, Ward(s): South Huron
Ben Van Diepenbeek, Councillor, Ward(s): Ashfield-Colborne-Wawanosh
Neil Rintoul, Councillor, Ward(s): Ashfield-Colborne-Wawanosh
Bill Dowson, Councillor, Ward(s): Bluewater
Jim Fergusson, Councillor, Ward(s): Bluewater
Dave Johnston, Councillor, Ward(s): Bluewater
Bert Dykstra, Councillor, Ward(s): Central Huron
John Bezaire, Councillor, Ward(s): Central Huron
Tim Collyer, Councillor, Ward(s): Central Huron
Deb Shewfelt, Councillor, Ward(s): Goderich
John Grace, Councillor, Ward(s): Goderich
Max Demaray, Councillor, Ward(s): Howick
Joe Seili, Councillor, Ward(s): Huron East
Bernie MacLellan, Councillor, Ward(s): Huron East
Bill Siemon, Councillor, Ward(s): Huron East
Dorothy Kelly, Councillor, Ward(s): Morris-Turnberry
Neil Vincent, Councillor, Ward(s): North Huron
Murray Scott, Councillor, Ward(s): North Huron
George Robertson, Councillor, Ward(s): South Huron
Jim Dietrich, Councillor, Ward(s): South Huron
Administration
Barbara Wilson, Clerk, Administration
Dave Laurie, Director, Public Works, Administration
Scott Tousaw, Director, Planning & Development, Administration
Nancy Cameron, Medical Officer of Health, Administration

Lambton
P.O. Box 3000
789 Broadway St.
Wyoming, ON N0N 1T0
519-845-0801
Fax: 519-845-3160
Toll Free Phone: 1-866-324-6912
administration@county-lambton.on.ca
www.lambtononline.com
Municipal Type: County
Incorporated: 1853 *Area:* 3,001.7 sq km
Population in 2006: 128,204
Next Election: Oct. 2014 (4 year terms)

Council
Jim Burns, Warden & Councillor
jim.burns@county-lambton.on.ca
Anne Marie Gillis, Deputy Warden, Councillor
annemariegillis@sarnia.ca
Don McGugan, Councillor, Ward(s): Brooke-Alvinston
jdmcgugan@hotmail.com
William (Bill) Bilton, Councillor, Ward(s): Dawn-Euphemia
mayor@dawneuphemia.ca
Gord Minielly, Councillor, Ward(s): Lambton Shores
minielly1@execulink.com
Carolyn Jamieson, Councillor, Ward(s): Lambton Shores
cjscookies@execulink.com
Gord Perry, Councillor, Ward(s): Oil Springs
gord.perry@county-lambton.on.ca
John McCharles, Councillor, Ward(s): Petrolia
johnnyremax@bellnet.ca
Lonny Napper, Councillor, Ward(s): Plympton-Wyoming
lnapper@xcelco.on.ca
Dick Kirkland, Councillor, Ward(s): Point Edward
dkirkland@villageofpointedward.com
Mike Bradley, Councillor, Ward(s): Sarnia
mayor@city.sarnia.on.ca
David Boushy, Councillor, Ward(s): Sarnia
d.boushy@cogeco.ca
Jim Foubister, Councillor, Ward(s): Sarnia
jfoubister1@cogeco.ca
Bev MacDougall, Councillor, Ward(s): Sarnia
bevmacdougall@ebtech.net
Steve Arnold, Councillor, Ward(s): St. Clair
sarnold1@rogers.blackberry.net
Peter Gilliland, Councillor, Ward(s): St. Clair
pgillila@rivernet.net
Todd Case, Councillor, Ward(s): Warwick
cases@execulink.com
Administration
Ronald G. Van Horne, Chief Administrative Officer, Administration
Kenneth C.R. Dick, MSW, General Manager, Social & Health Services, Administration
Jim Kutyba, P.Eng., General Manager, Infrastructure & Development Services, Administration
Cindy Thayer, General Manager, Community Services, Administration
Stephane Thiffeault, General Manager, Corporate Services, Administration
Andrew Taylor, MSW, Manager, Environmental Health & Prevention Services, Administration

Lanark
County Administration Bldg.
P.O. Box 37
99 Christie Lake Rd.
Perth, ON K7H 3E2
613-267-4200
Fax: 613-267-2964
Toll Free Phone: 1-888-952-6275
info@county.lanark.on.ca
www.county.lanark.on.ca
Municipal Type: County
Incorporated: Jan. 1st 1998 *Area:* 2,979.14 sq km
Population in 2006: 63,785
Next Election: Oct. 2014 (4 year terms)
John MacTavish, Councillor, Ward(s): Montague
johnmactavish@bellnet.ca
Council
Paul Dulmage, Warden & Councillor, Ward(s): Carleton Place
Richard Kidd, Councillor, Ward(s): Beckwith Township
rkidd@ripnet.com
Sharon Mousseau, Councillor, Ward(s): Beckwith Township
smousseau@ripnet.com
Ed Sonnenburg, Councillor, Ward(s): Carleton Place
e.sonnenburg@rogers.com
Aubrey Churchill, Councillor, Ward(s): Drummond / North Elmsley
achurchill@storm.ca
Gord McConnell, Councillor, Ward(s): Drummond / North Elmsley
gmcconnell@ripnet.com
Bob Fletcher, Councillor, Ward(s): Lanark Highlands
bob.fletcher@xplornet.com
Bruce Horlin, Councillor, Ward(s): Lanark Highlands
b.horlin@sympatico.ca
Al Lunney, Councillor, Ward(s): Mississippi Mills
al.lunney@sympatico.ca

Brenda Hurrle, Councillor, Ward(s): Mississippi Mills
unitedway@trytel.com
Bill Dobson, Councillor, Ward(s): Montague
bdobson@ripnet.com
John Fenik, Councillor, Ward(s): Perth
jfenik@cogeco.ca
John Gemmell, Councillor, Ward(s): Perth
jgemmell.lc@cogeco.ca
Keith Kerr, Councillor, Ward(s): Tay Valley Township
kmkk@ripnet.com
Susan Freeman, Councillor, Ward(s): Tay Valley Township
sfreeman@rideau.net
Administration
Cathie Ritchie, Clerk, Administration
clerk@county.lanark.on.ca
Peter Wagland, Chief Administrative Officer, Administration
cao@county.lanark.on.ca
Kurt Greaves, Treasurer & Director, Finance, Administration
Steve Allan, Director, Public Works, Administration
Lisa Crosbie-Larmon, Director, Human Resources, Administration
Nancy Green, Director, Social Services, Administration
Sam Law, Director, Information Technology, Administration

Lennox & Addington
P.O. Box 1000
97 Thomas St. East
Napanee, ON K7R 3S9
613-354-4883
Fax: 613-354-3112
www.lennox-addington.on.ca
Municipal Type: County
Area: 2,776.48 sq km
Population in 2006: 40,542
Next Election: Oct. 2014 (4 year terms)
Council
Gord Schermerhorn, Warden & Councillor
613-354-4883
Gary Hodson, Councillor
613-354-3664
Henry Hogg, Councillor
613-336-0227
Bill Lowry, Councillor
613-583-2412
Clayton McEwen, Councillor
613-354-4883
Todd Steele, Councillor
613-379-5664
Debbie Thompson, Councillor
613-378-1553
Helen Yanch, Councillor
613-336-8774
Administration
Larry Keech, Chief Administrative Officer & Clerk, Administration
lkeech@lennox-addington.on.ca
Stephen Fox, Director, Financial & Physical Services, Administration
sfox@lennox-addington.on.ca
Bill Bishop, Director, Human Resources, Administration
bbishop@lennox-addington.on.ca
Brian Elo-Sheperd, Director, Social Services, Administration
elo-shepherdb@pelass.org
Mary Anne Evans, Director, Information Services, Administration
mevans@lennox-addington.on.ca
Tom Bedford, Manager, Ambulance Services & Emergency Programs, Administration
tbedford@lennox-addington.on.ca
Linda Andoney, Coordinator, Environmental Services, Administration
landoney@lennox-addington.on.ca

Middlesex
399 Ridout St. North
London, ON N6A 2P1
519-434-7321
Fax: 519-434-0638
www.county.middlesex.on.ca
Municipal Type: County
Area: 3,317.15 sq km
Population in 2006: 422,333
Next Election: Oct. 2014 (4 year terms)
Council
Jim Maudsley, Warden & Councillor, Ward(s): Thames Centre
warden@county.middlesex.on.ca
David Bolton, Councillor, Ward(s): Adelaide Metcalfe

Municipal Governments / Ontario

Paul Hodgins, Councillor, Ward(s): Lucan Biddulph
Al Edmondson, Councillor, Ward(s): Middlesex Centre
Albert Bannister, Councillor, Ward(s): Middlesex Centre
Wesley Hodgson, Councillor, Ward(s): North Middlesex
Ian Brebner, Councillor, Ward(s): North Middlesex
Doug Reycraft, Councillor, Ward(s): Southwest Middlesex
Vance Blackmore, Councillor, Ward(s): Southwest Middlesex
Mel Veale, Councillor, Ward(s): Strathroy Caradoc
Joanne Vanderheyden, Councillor, Ward(s): Strathroy Caradoc
Delia Reiche, Councillor, Ward(s): Thames Centre
Administration
Kathy Bunting, Clerk, Administration
kbunting@county.middlesex.on.ca
Bill Rayburn, Chief Administrative Officer, Administration
brayburn@county.middlesex.on.ca
Jim Gates, Treasurer, Administration
jgates@county.middlesex.on.ca
Sally Bennett, Director, Social Services, Administration
Steve Evans, Director, Planning & Economic Development & Deputy CAO, Administration
Denis Merrall, Director, Emergency Services, Administration
Chris Traini, County Engineer, Administration
Doug Spettigue, Human Resource Officer, Administration
John Trott, Woodlands Conservation Officer & Weed Inspector, Administration

Muskoka
70 Pine St.
Bracebridge, ON P1L 1N3
705-645-2231
Fax: 705-645-5319
Toll Free Phone: 1-800-461-4210 (In 705 area code)
info@muskoka.on.ca
www.muskoka.on.ca
Municipal Type: Regional Municipality
Incorporated: Jan. 1, 1971 *Area:* 3,890.24 sq km
Population in 2006: 57,563
Next Election: Oct. 2014 (4 year terms)
Janet Peake, Councillor, Ward(s): Lake of Bays
Council
Gord Adams, District Chair, Councillor
gadams@muskoka.on.ca
Susan Pryke, Acting Chair, Councillor
Steven Clement, Councillor, Ward(s): Bracebridge
Don Coates, Councillor, Ward(s): Bracebridge
Graydon Smith, Councillor, Ward(s): Bracebridge
Scott Young, Councillor, Ward(s): Bracebridge
Larry Braid, Councillor, Ward(s): Georgian Bay
Greg Sutcliffe, Councillor, Ward(s): Georgian Bay
Jim Walden, Councillor, Ward(s): Georgian Bay
Mark Clairmont, Councillor, Ward(s): Gravenhurst
Bob Colhoun, Councillor, Ward(s): Gravenhurst
John Klinck, Councillor, Ward(s): Gravenhurst
Terry Pilger, Councillor, Ward(s): Gravenhurst
Fran Coleman, Councillor, Ward(s): Huntsville
Claude Doughty, Councillor, Ward(s): Huntsville
Brian Thompson, Councillor, Ward(s): Huntsville
George Young, Councillor, Ward(s): Huntsville
Ben Boivin, Councillor, Ward(s): Lake of Bays
Margaret Casey, Councillor, Ward(s): Lake of Bays
Mary Grady, Councillor, Ward(s): Muskoka Lakes
Stewart Martin, Councillor, Ward(s): Muskoka Lakes
Susan Pryke, Councillor, Ward(s): Muskoka Lakes
Nancy Thompson, Councillor, Ward(s): Muskoka Lakes
Administration
Christine Lees, District Clerk, Administration
clees@muskoka.on.ca
Jim Green, Chief Administrative Officer, Administration
jgreen@muskoka.on.ca
Stephen Cairns, Commissioner, Finance & Corporate Services, Administration
scairns@muskoka.on.ca
Tony White, Commissioner, Engineering & Public Works, Administration
705-645-6764
publicworks@muskoka.on.ca
Rick Williams, Commissioner, Community Services, Administration
705-645-2412
rwilliams@muskoka.on.ca; mcsinfo@muskoka.on.ca
Geoff Bache, Director, Environmental Services, Administration
Terri Burton, Director, Emergency Services, Administration
tburton@muskoka.on.ca
Herman Clemens, Director, Water & Sewer Operations, Administration

Anna Landry, Director, Human Resources, Administration, Fax: 705-645-4065
alandry@muskoka.on.ca
Noel Waters, Director, Roads & Waste Management, Administration

Niagara
P.O. Box 1042
2201 St. David's Rd.
Thorold, ON L2V 4T7
905-685-1571
Fax: 905-687-4977
Toll Free Phone: 1-800-263-7215; TTY: 905-984-3613
www.niagararegion.ca
Municipal Type: Regional Municipality
Incorporated: Jan. 1, 1970 *Area:* 1,854.17 sq km
Population in 2006: 427,421
Next Election: Oct. 2014 (4 year terms)
Council
Peter Partington, Regional Chair & Councillor
chairman@niagararegion.ca
Douglas Martin, Councillor, Ward(s): Fort Erie
mayor@town.forterie.ca
Shirley Cordiner, Councillor, Ward(s): Fort Erie
shirley.cordiner@niagararegion.ca
Bob Bentley, Councillor, Ward(s): Grimsby
bob.bentley@niagararegion.ca
Debbie M. Zimmerman, Councillor, Ward(s): Grimsby
debbie.zimmerman@niagararegion.ca
Bill Hodgson, Councillor, Ward(s): Lincoln
bhodgson@lincoln.ca
Mark Bylsma, Councillor, Ward(s): Lincoln
mark.bylsma@niagararegion.ca
R.T. (Ted) Salci, Councillor, Ward(s): Niagara Falls
tsalci@niagarafalls.ca
Barbara Greenwood, Councillor, Ward(s): Niagara Falls
barbara.greenwood@niagararegion.ca
Norm Puttick, Councillor, Ward(s): Niagara Falls
norm.puttick@niagararegion.ca; nputtick@cogeco.net
Willian (Bill) Smeaton, Councillor, Ward(s): Niagara Falls
william.smeaton@niagararegion.ca
Gary Burroughs, Councillor, Ward(s): Niagara on the Lake
gburroughs@notl.org
Dave Lepp, Councillor, Ward(s): Niagara on the Lake
dave.lepp@niagararegion.ca
Dave Augustyn, Councillor, Ward(s): Pelham
mayordave@pelham.ca
Brian Baty, Councillor, Ward(s): Pelham
brian.baty@niagararegion.ca; batyregion@cogeco.net
Vance Badawey, Councillor, Ward(s): Port Colborne
mayor@portcolborne.ca
Bob Saracino, Councillor, Ward(s): Port Colborne
bob.saracino@niagararegion.ca
Brian McMullan, Councillor, Ward(s): St Catharines
bmcmullan@stcatharines.ca
Judy Casselman, Councillor, Ward(s): St Catharines
judy.casselman@niagararegion.ca
Brian Heit, Councillor, Ward(s): St Catharines
brian.heit@niagararegion.ca
Ronna Katzman, Councillor, Ward(s): St Catharines
ronna.katzman@niagararegion.ca
Tim Rigby, Councillor, Ward(s): St Catharines
tim.rigby@niagararegion.ca
D. Bruce Timms, Councillor, Ward(s): St Catharines
bruce.timms@niagararegion.ca
Henry D'Angela, Councillor, Ward(s): Thorold
mayor@thorold.com
Robert Gabriel, Councillor, Ward(s): Thorold
robert.gabriel@niagararegion.ca
Barbara Henderson, Councillor, Ward(s): Wainfleet
bhenderson@township.wainfleet.on.ca
Damian Goulbourne, Councillor, Ward(s): Welland
mayor@welland.ca
Cindy Forster, Councillor, Ward(s): Welland
cindy.forster@niagararegion.ca
George Marshall, Councillor, Ward(s): Welland
george.marshall@niagararegion.ca
Katie Trombetta, Councillor, Ward(s): West Lincoln
jthrower@westlincoln.com
Administration
Kevin Bain, Regional Clerk, Administration
Michael Trojan, Chief Administrative Officer, Administration
Gord Lockyer, Treasurer & Director, Financial Management & Reporting, Administration

John Bergsma, Commissioner, Corporate Services, Administration
Brian Hutchings, Commissioner, Social Services, Administration
Patrick Robson, Commissioner, Integrated Community Planning, Administration
patrick.robson@niagararegion.ca
Robin C. Williams, Commissioner, Public Health & Medical Officer of Health, Administration
robin.williams@niagararegion.ca
Betty Matthews-Malone, Director, Water & Wastewater Services, Administration
Andrew Pollock, Director, Waste Management Services, Administration
Denise Papaiz, Senior Manager, Corporate Communications, Administration
denise.papaiz@niagararegion.ca

Norfolk
Main Administration Bldg.
P.O. Box 545
50 Colborne St. South
Simcoe, ON N3Y 4N5
519-426-5870
Fax: 519-426-8573
Delhi Customer Service Ctr., Phone: 519-582-2100
www.norfolkcounty.on.ca
Municipal Type: County
Incorporated: Jan. 1, 2001 *Area:* 1,606.91 sq km
Population in 2006: 62,563
Provincial Electoral District(s): Haldimand-Norfolk
Federal Electoral District(s): Haldimand-Norfolk
Next Election: Oct. 2014 (4 year terms)
Dennis Travale, Mayor
dennis.travale@norfolkcounty.ca
John Hunt, Councillor, Ward(s): 1
john.hunt@norfolkcounty.ca
Roger Geysens, Councillor, Ward(s): 2
roger.geysens@norfolkcounty.ca
Michael J. Columbus, Councillor, Ward(s): 3
michael.columbus@norfolkcounty.ca
Jim Oliver, Councillor, Ward(s): 4
jim.oliver@norfolkcounty.ca
Charlie Luke, Councillor, Ward(s): 5
charlie.luke@norfolkcounty.ca
Heidy Van Dyk, Councillor, Ward(s): 5
heidy.vandyk@norfolkcounty.ca
John Wells, Councillor, Ward(s): 6
john.wells@norfolkcounty.ca
Harold Sonnenberg, Councillor, Ward(s): 7
harold.sonnenberg@norfolkcounty.ca
Bev Wood, Clerk & Manager, Council Services, Administration
bev.wood@norfolkcounty.ca
William F. Allcock, County Manager, Administration
allcock@norfolkcounty.ca
John Ford, Treasurer & Manager, Financial Services, Administration
john.ford@norfolkcounty.ca
Christopher D. Baird, CET, CMMIII, Ec.D., General Manager, Planning & Economic Development, Administration
Eric R. D'Hondt, P.Eng., General Manager, Public Works & Environmental Services, Administration, Fax: 519-582-4571
eric.dhondt@norfolkcounty.ca
Frank Gelinas, General Manager, Corporate Services, Administration
frank.gelinas@norfolkcounty.ca
Kevin Lichach, General Manager, Community Services, Administration
Patti Moore, General Manager, Health & Social Services, Administration
E. Bernard Dawtre, Manager, Environmental Services, Administration
bernard.dawtrey@norfolkcounty.ca
John Hamilton, Manager, Engineering, Administration
john.hamilton@norfolkcounty.ca
Frank Sams, Manager, Parks & Facilities, Administration
Terry Dicks, Fire Chief, Administration
519-426-4115, Fax: 519-426-4140

Northumberland
555 Courthouse Rd.
Cobourg, ON K9A 5J6
905-372-3329
Fax: 905-372-1696
Toll Free Phone: 1-800-354-7050
www.northumberland.ca

Municipal Type: County
Area: 1,902.97 sq km
Population in 2006: 80,963
Next Election: Oct. 2014 (4 year terms)
Council
Linda Thompson, Warden & Councillor, Ward(s): Port Hope
mayor@porthope.ca
William Finley, Councillor, Ward(s): Alnwick / Haldimand
finleyw@northumberlandcounty.ca
Christine Herrington, Councillor, Ward(s): Brighton
herringtonc@northumberlandcounty.ca
Peter Delanty, Councillor, Ward(s): Cobourg
delantyp@northumberlandcounty.ca
Marc Coombs, Councillor, Ward(s): Cramahe
coombsm@northumberlandcounty.ca
Mark Lovshin, Councillor, Ward(s): Hamilton
lovshinm@northumberlandcounty.ca
Hector Macmillan, Councillor, Ward(s): Trent Hills
macmillanh@northumberlandcounty.ca
Administration
Diane Cane, CMO, County Clerk, Administration
Bill Pyatt, Chief Administrative Officer, Administration
Jennifer Moore, Treasurer & Director, Finance, Administration
James Rogers, By-Law Officer, Forest Conservation, Administration
705-799-2470, Fax: 705-879-7297
Ken Stubbings, Coordinator, Emergency Management, Administration

Peel
10 Peel Centre Dr.
Brampton, ON L6T 4B9
905-791-7800
Fax: 905-791-7871
Toll Free Phone: 1-888-919-7800
info@peelregion.ca
www.peelregion.ca
Municipal Type: Regional Municipality
Incorporated: Oct. 15, 1973 Area: 1,242.40 sq km
Population in 2006: 1,159,405
Next Election: Oct. 2014 (4 year terms)
Council
Emil Kolb, Regional Chair & Councillor, Fax: 905-791-2567
chair@peelregion.ca
Susan Fennell, Mayor & Councillor, Ward(s): Brampton
susan.fennell@brampton.ca
Elaine Moore, Councillor, Ward(s): Brampton 1 & 5
elaine.moore@brampton.ca
Paul Palleschi, Councillor, Ward(s): Brampton 2 & 6
paul.palleschi@brampton.ca
John Sanderson, Councillor, Ward(s): Brampton 3 & 4
john.sanderson@brampton.ca
Gael Miles, Councillor, Ward(s): Brampton 7 & 8
gael.miles@brampton.ca
John Sprovieri, Councillor, Ward(s): Brampton 9 & 10
john.sprovieri@brampton.ca
Marolyn Morrison, Mayor, Ward(s): Caledon
marolyn.morrison@caledon.ca
Richard Paterak, Councillor, Ward(s): Caledon 1
richard.paterak@caledon.ca
Allan Thompson, Councillor, Ward(s): Caledon 2
allan.thompson@caledon.ca
Richard Whitehead, Councillor, Ward(s): Caledon 3 & 4
r.whitehead@sympatico.ca
Patti Foley, Councillor, Ward(s): Caledon 5
patti.foley@caledon.ca
Hazel McCallion, Mayor & Councillor, Ward(s): Mississauga
mayor@mississauga.ca
Jim Tovey, Councillor, Ward(s): Mississauga 1
jim.tovey@mississauga.ca
Patricia Mullin, Councillor, Ward(s): Mississauga 2
pat.mullin@mississauga.ca
Chris Fonseca, Councillor, Ward(s): Mississauga 3
chris.fonseca@mississauga.ca
Frank Dale, Councillor, Ward(s): Mississauga 4
frank.dale@mississauga.ca
Eve Adams, Councillor, Ward(s): Mississauga 5
eve.adams@mississauga.ca
Ron Starr, Councillor, Ward(s): Mississauga 6
ron.starr@mississauga.ca
Nando Iannicca, Councillor, Ward(s): Mississauga 7
nando.iannicca@mississauga.ca
Katie Mahoney, Councillor, Ward(s): Mississauga 8
katie.mahoney@mississauga.ca
Pat Saito, Councillor, Ward(s): Mississauga 9
pat.saito@mississauga.ca
Sue McFadden, Councillor, Ward(s): Mississauga 10
sue.mcfadden@mississauga.ca
George Carlson, Councillor, Ward(s): Mississauga 11
george.carlson@mississauga.ca
Administration
David Szwarc, Chief Administrative Officer, Administration
N. Trim, Chief Financial Officer & Commissioner, Corporate Services, Administration
R.K. Gillespie, Commissioner, Employee & Business Services, Administration
Dan Labrecque, Commissioner, Environment, Transportation, & Planning Services, Administration
Janette Smith, Commissioner, Health Services, Administration
Keith Ward, Commissioner, Human Services, Administration
D. Mowat, Medical Officer of Health, Administration
P. O'Connor, Regional Solicitor & Director, Legal & Risk Management, Administration
Damian Albanese, Director, Transportation, Administration
Norman Lee, Director, Waste Management, Administration
norman.lee@peelregion.ca

Perth
Courthouse
1 Huron St.
Stratford, ON N5A 5S4
519-271-0531
Fax: 519-271-6265
info@perthcounty.ca
www.perthcounty.ca
Municipal Type: County
Incorporated: Jan. 1850 Area: 2,218.41 sq km
Population in 2006: 74,344
Next Election: Oct. 2014 (4 year terms)
Note: Restructuring occurred in Jan. 1998.
Council
Julie Behrns, Warden & Councillor, Ward(s): North Perth
warden@perthcounty.ca
Ed Hollinger, Councillor, Ward(s): North Perth
ehollinger@northperth.ca
Terry Seiler, Councillor, Ward(s): North Perth
tdseiler@wightman.ca
Ian Forrest, Councillor, Ward(s): Perth East
iforrest@pertheast.on.ca
Bob McMillan, Councillor, Ward(s): Perth East
mcmillan@cyg.net
Robert J. McTavish, Councillor, Ward(s): Perth East
rjmct@rogers.com
Ron McKay, Councillor, Ward(s): Perth South
rlmckay@rogers.com
Robert Wilhelm, Councillor, Ward(s): Perth South
ulchtran@quadro.net
John Van Bakel, Councillor, Ward(s): West Perth
mvb@omniglobe.ca
Gerry Kehl, Councillor, Ward(s): West Perth
gerry@riverroots.ca
Administration
Bill Arthur, Chief Administrative Officer & Clerk, Administration
cao@perthcounty.ca
Renato Pullia, Treasurer & Director, Corporate Services, Administration
treasurer@perthcounty.ca
Matt Ash, Director, Public Works, Administration
mash@perthcounty.ca
Dave Hanly, Director, Planning & Development, Administration
dhanly@perthcounty.ca
Linda Rockwood, Director, Emergency Medical Services, Administration
lrockwood@perthcounty.ca
Cliff Eggleton, Manager, Operations, Administration
ceggleton@perthcounty.ca
Ann McKnight Duralia, Manager, Human Resources, Administration
amcknight@perthcounty.ca

Peterborough
County Court House
470 Water St.
Peterborough, ON K9H 3M3
705-743-0380
Fax: 705-876-1730
Toll Free Phone: 1-800-710-9586
gking@county.peterborough.on.ca
www.county.peterborough.on.ca

Municipal Type: County
Area: 3,805.71 sq km
Population in 2006: 133,080
Next Election: Oct. 2014 (4 year terms)
Council
Ronald Gerow, Warden & Councillor, Ward(s): Havelock-Belmont-Methuen
ron.gerow@sympatico.ca
Douglas Pearcy, Councillor, Ward(s): Asphodel-Norwood
dpearcy@accel.net
Terry Low, Councillor, Ward(s): Asphodel-Norwood
terry.low@sympatico.ca
Neal Cathcart, Councillor, Ward(s): Cavan Monaghan
ncathcart@cavanmonaghan.net
Brian Fallis, Councillor, Ward(s): Cavan Monaghan
bfallis@nexicom.net
Brian Bartlett, Councillor, Ward(s): Cavan Monaghan
bbartlett@cavanmonaghan.net
James Jones, Councillor, Ward(s): Douro-Dummer
dumnews@nexicom.net
Karl Moher, Councillor, Ward(s): Douro-Dummer
kmoher@nexicom.net
Thomas Flynn, Councillor, Ward(s): Galway-Cavendish & Harvey
Madeline Pearson, Councillor, Ward(s): Galway-Cavendish & Harvey
madelinepearson@sympatico.ca
Andy Sharpe, Councillor, Ward(s): Havelock-Belmont-Methuen
2andysharpe@gmail.com
Jim Whelan, Councillor, Ward(s): North Kawartha
reeve@northkawartha.on.ca; mjdmwh@sympatico.ca
Barry Rand, Councillor, Ward(s): North Kawartha
sallyandbarry@aol.com.ca
David Nelson, Councillor, Ward(s): Otonabee- South Monaghan
Paul Heath, Councillor, Ward(s): Otonabee- South Monaghan
paul.heath@sympatico.ca
Ron Millen, Councillor, Ward(s): Smith-Ennismore-Lakefield
rmillen@nexicom.net
Mary Smith, Councillor, Ward(s): Smith-Ennismore-Lakefield
mjsmith@peterboro.net
Administration
Sally Saunders, Clerk, Administration
ssaunders@county.peterborough.on.ca
Gary King, Chief Administrative Officer & Deputy Clerk, Administration
gking@county.peterborough.on.ca
John Butler, Treasurer, Administration
jbutler@county.peterborough.on.ca
Chris Bradley, Director, Public Works, Administration
cbradley@county.peterborough.on.ca
Mary Percy, Director, Human Resources, Administration
mpercy@county.peterborough.on.ca
Bryan Weir, Director, Planning, Administration
bweir@county.peterborough.on.ca
Sheridan Graham, General Manager, Strategic Services & Corporate Projects, Administration
sgraham@county.peterborough.on.ca
Sherry Arcaro, Manager, Environmental Services, Administration
sarcaro@county.peterborough.on.ca
Bill Linnen, Manager, Operations, Administration
blinnen@county.peterborough.on.ca
Bob English, Chief, Emergency Medical Services (EMS), Administration
benglish@county.peterborough.on.ca
Mark Cross, Specialist, Waste Diversion Operations, Administration
mcross@county.peterborough.on.ca

Prince Edward
332 Main St.
Picton, ON K0K 2T0
613-476-2148
Fax: 613-476-8356
info@pecounty.on.ca; council@pecounty.on.ca
www.pecounty.on.ca
Municipal Type: County
Incorporated: Jan. 1, 1998 Area: 1,050.14 sq km
Population in 2006: 25,496
Provincial Electoral District(s): Prince Edward-Hastings
Federal Electoral District(s): Prince Edward-Hastings
Next Election: Oct. 2014 (4 year terms)
Leo P. Finnegan, Mayor
lfinnegan@pecounty.on.ca
Bev Campbell, Councillor, Ward(s): 1 - Picton
bcampbell@pecounty.on.ca

Municipal Governments / Ontario

Laverne Bailey, Councillor, Ward(s): 1 - Picton
lbailey@pecounty.on.ca
Barry Turpin, Councillor, Ward(s): 2 - Bloomfield
bturpin@pecounty.on.ca
Peter Mertens, Councillor, Ward(s): 3 - Wellington
pmertens@pecounty.on.ca
Sandy Latchford, Councillor, Ward(s): 4 - Ameliasburgh
slatchford@pecounty.on.ca
Dianne O'Brien, Councillor, Ward(s): 4 - Ameliasburgh
dobrien@pecounty.on.ca
Lori Slik, Councillor, Ward(s): 4 - Ameliasburgh
lslik@pecounty.on.ca
Brian Marisett, Councillor, Ward(s): 5 - Athol
bmarisett@pecounty.on.ca
Richard Parks, Councillor, Ward(s): 6 - Hallowell
rparks@pecounty.on.ca
Keith MacDonald, Councillor, Ward(s): 6 - Hallowell
kmacdonald@pecounty.on.ca
Peggy Burris, Councillor, Ward(s): 7 - Hillier
pburris@pecounty.on.ca
Ray Best, Councillor, Ward(s): 8 - North Marysburgh
rbest@pecounty.on.ca
Monica Alyea, Councillor, Ward(s): 9 - South Marysburgh
malyea@pecounty.on.ca
Kevin Gale, Councillor, Ward(s): 10 - Sophiasburgh
kgale@pecounty.on.ca
John Thompson, Councillor, Ward(s): 10 - Sophiasburgh
jthompson@pecounty.on.ca
Victoria Leskie, Clerk, Administration
vleskie@pecounty.on.ca
Richard Shannon, Chief Administrative Officer, Administration
rshannon@pecounty.on.ca
James Hepburn, Treasurer, Administration
jhepburn@pecounty.on.ca
Barry Braun, Commissioner, Recreation, Parks, & Culture Department, Administration
bbraun@pecounty.on.ca
Gerry Murphy, Commissioner, Planning Services Department, Administration
gmurphy@pecounty.on.ca
Susan Turnbull, Commissioner, Corporate Services & Finance, Administration
sturnbull@pecounty.on.ca
Joe Angelo, P.Eng., Manager, Public Works Department Projects, Administration
jangelo@pecounty.on.ca
Grant Currie, Manager, Human Resources, Administration
gcurrie@pecounty.on.ca
Scott Manlow, Fire Chief, Administration
smanlow@pecounty.on.ca

Renfrew
9 International Dr.
Pembroke, ON K8A 6W5
613-735-7288
Fax: 613-735-2081
Toll Free Phone: 1-800-273-0183
info@countyofrenfrew.on.ca
www.countyofrenfrew.on.ca
Municipal Type: County
Incorporated: June 8, 1861 *Area:* 7,403.46 sq km
Population in 2006: 97,545
Next Election: Oct. 2014 (4 year terms)
Council
Don Rathwell, Warden & Councillor, Ward(s): Whitewater
613-646-2282
Raye-Anne Briscoe, Councillor, Ward(s): Admaston / Bromley
613-432-2885
Walter Stack, Councillor, Ward(s): Arnprior
613-623-4231
Zig Mintha, Councillor, Ward(s): Bonnechere Valley
613-628-3101
Norm Lentz, Councillor, Ward(s): Brudenell, Lyndoch, & Raglan
613-758-2061
Ann Aikens, Councillor, Ward(s): Deep River
613-584-2000
Peter Emon, Councillor, Ward(s): Greater Madawaska
613-752-2222
Tammy Stewart, Councillor, Ward(s): Head, Clara & Maria
613-586-2526
Robert A. Johnston, Councillor, Ward(s): Horton
613-432-6271
Janice Visneskie, Councillor, Ward(s): Killaloe, Hagarty & Richards
613-757-2300

Vance Gutzman, Councillor, Ward(s): Laurentian Hills
613-584-3114
Jack Wilson, Councillor, Ward(s): Laurentian Valley
613-584-3114
John Hildebrandt, Councillor, Ward(s): Madawaska Valley
613-756-2747
Mary Campbell, Councillor, Ward(s): McNab / Braeside
613-623-5756
Harold Weckworth, Councillor, Ward(s): North Algona Wilberforce
613-628-2080
Bob Sweet, Councillor, Ward(s): Petawawa
613-687-5536
Audrey R. Green, Councillor, Ward(s): Renfrew
613-432-4848
Administration
Norm Lemke, Chief Administrative Officer & Clerk, Administration
James D. Kutschke, CA, Treasurer & Deputy Clerk, Administration
Bruce Beakley, Director, Human Resources, Administration
Dave Darch, Director, Public Works & Engineering, Administration
613-732-4353
Michael Nolan, Director, Emergency Services, Administration
Jeff Muzzi, Manager, Forestry Services, Administration
613-735-3204
jmuzzi@countyofrenfrew.on.ca

Simcoe
County of Simcoe Administration Centre
1110 Hwy. 26
Midhurst, ON L0L 1X0
705-726-9300
Fax: 705-726-3991
Toll Free Phone: 1-866-893-9300, 1-800-263-3199
info@simcoe.ca
www.simcoe.ca
Municipal Type: County
Incorporated: Jan. 1, 1850 *Area:* 4,840.56 sq km
Population in 2006: 422,204
Next Election: Oct. 2014 (4 year terms)
Council
Tony Guergis, Warden & Councillor
tony.guergis@simcoe.ca; Warden@simcoe.ca
Tom Walsh, Councillor, Ward(s): Adjala-Tosorontio
Doug Little, Councillor, Ward(s): Adjala-Tosorontio
Doug White, Councillor, Ward(s): Bradford West Gwillimbury
Dennis Roughley, Councillor, Ward(s): Bradford West Gwillimbury
Ken Ferguson, Councillor, Ward(s): Clearview
Alicia Savage, Councillor, Ward(s): Clearview
Chris Carrier, Councillor, Ward(s): Collingwood
Sandra Cooper, Councillor, Ward(s): Collingwood
David Guergis, Councillor, Ward(s): Essa
Terry Dowdall, Councillor, Ward(s): Essa
Brian Jackson, Councillor, Ward(s): Innisfil
Gord Wauchope, Councillor, Ward(s): Innisfil
James Downer, Councillor, Ward(s): Midland
Ruth Hackney, Councillor, Ward(s): Midland
Mike MacEachern, Councillor, Ward(s): New Tecumseth
Rick Milne, Councillor, Ward(s): New Tecumseth
Harry Huges, Councillor, Ward(s): Oro-Medonte
Ralph Hough, Councillor, Ward(s): Oro-Medonte
Anita Dubeau, Councillor, Ward(s): Penetanguishene
Doug Leroux, Councillor, Ward(s): Penetanguishene
Bill Duffy, Councillor, Ward(s): Ramara
Basil Clarke, Councillor, Ward(s): Ramara
Phil Sled, Councillor, Ward(s): Severn
Judith Cox, Councillor, Ward(s): Severn
Tony Guergis, Councillor, Ward(s): Springwater
Tony Hope, Councillor, Ward(s): Springwater
Scott Warnock, Councillor, Ward(s): Tay
Michael Ladouceur, Councillor, Ward(s): Tay
Peggy Breckenridge, Councillor, Ward(s): Tiny
George Lawrence, Councillor, Ward(s): Tiny
Cal Patterson, Councillor, Ward(s): Wasaga Beach
David Foster, Councillor, Ward(s): Wasaga Beach
Administration
Glen R. Knox, County Clerk, Administration
Glen.Knox@simcoe.ca
Mark Aitken, Chief Administrative Officer, Administration
CAO@simcoe.ca

Craig Elliott, General Manager, Finance & Administration, Administration
Craig.Elliott@simcoe.ca
Rick Newlove, General Manager, Corporate Services, Administration
Rick.Newlove@simcoe.ca
Jane Sinclair, General Manager, Health & Cultural Services, Administration
Jane.Sinclair@simcoe.ca
Terry Talon, General Manager, Social Services, Administration
Terry.Talon@simcoe.ca
Dawn Hipwell, Director, Purchasing, Fleet, & Property, Administration
Dawn.Hipwell@simcoe.ca
Jim Hunter, Director, Transportation Construction, Administration
Jim.Hunter@simcoe.ca
Bryan MacKell, Director, Planning & Development, Administration
Bryan.MacKell@simcoe.ca
Rob McCullough, Director, Environmental Services, Administration
Rob.McCullough@simcoe.ca
Michael Moffatt, Director, Human Resources, Administration
Michael.Moffatt@simcoe.ca

Waterloo
Regional Administration Bldg.
P.O. Box 9051 C
150 Frederick St.
Kitchener, ON N2G 4J3
519-575-4400
Fax: 519-575-4481
Phone, Regional Councillors: 519-575-4581
regionalinquiries@region.waterloo.on.ca
www.region.waterloo.on.ca
Municipal Type: Regional Municipality
Incorporated: Jan. 1, 1973 *Area:* 1,368.64 sq km
Population in 2006: 478,121
Next Election: Oct. 2014 (4 year terms)
Council
Ken Seiling, Regional Chair & Councillor
519-575-4585, Fax: 519-575-4440
sken@region.waterloo.on.ca
Jane Brewer, Councillor, Ward(s): Cambridge
bjane@region.waterloo.on.ca
Doug Craig, Councillor, Ward(s): Cambridge
cdoug@region.waterloo.on.ca
Claudette Millar, Councillor, Ward(s): Cambridge
mclaudette@region.waterloo.on.ca
Tom Galloway, Councillor, Ward(s): Kitchener
gtom@region.waterloo.on.ca
Jean Haalboom, Councillor, Ward(s): Kitchener
hjean@region.waterloo.on.ca
Jake Smola, Councillor, Ward(s): Kitchener
sjake@region.waterloo.on.ca
Jim Wideman, Councillor, Ward(s): Kitchener
wjim@region.waterloo.on.ca
Carl Zehr, Councillor, Ward(s): Kitchener
zcarl@region.waterloo.on.ca
Kim Denouden, Councillor, Ward(s): North Dumfries
dekim@region.waterloo.on.ca
Brenda Halloran, Councillor, Ward(s): Waterloo
hbrenda@region.waterloo.on.ca
Jane Mitchell, Councillor, Ward(s): Waterloo
mjane@region.waterloo.on.ca
Sean Strickland, Councillor, Ward(s): Waterloo
ssean@region.waterloo.on.ca
Ross Kelterborn, Councillor, Ward(s): Wellesley
kross@region.waterloo.on.ca
Wayne Roth, Councillor, Ward(s): Wilmot
rwayne@region.waterloo.on.ca
William Strauss, Councillor, Ward(s): Woolwich
sbill@region.waterloo.on.ca
Administration
Kris Fletcher, Regional Clerk & Director, Council & Administrative Services, Administration
fkris@region.waterloo.on.ca
Mike Murray, Chief Administrative Officer
mmike@region.waterloo.on.ca
Larry Ryan, Chief Financial Officer, Administration
rlarry@region.waterloo.on.ca
Rob Horne, Commissioner, Planning, Housing & Community Services, Administration
hrob@region.waterloo.on.ca

Municipal Governments / Ontario

Thomas Schmidt, Commissioner, Transportation & Environmental Services, Administration
sthomas@region.waterloo.on.ca
Michael Schuster, Commissioner, Social Services, Administration
scmike@region.waterloo.on.ca
Penny Smiley, Commissioner, Human Resources, Administration
spenny@region.waterloo.on.ca
Gary Sosnoski, Commissioner, Corporate Resources, Administration
sogary@region.waterloo.on.ca
James Archibald, Director, Waste Management, Administration
ajames@region.waterloo.on.ca
Debra Arnold, Director, Legal Services & Regional Solicitor, Administration
adebra@region.waterloo.on.ca
Lucille Bish, Director, Community Services, Administration
blucille@region.waterloo.on.ca
Kevin Eby, Director, Community Planning, Administration
ekevin@region.waterloo.on.ca
Eric Gillespie, Director, Transit Services, Administration
geric@region.waterloo.on.ca
Nancy Kodousek, Director, Water Services, Administration
konancy@region.waterloo.on.ca
Ken Noonan, Director, Facilities Management & Fleet Services, Administration
nken@region.waterloo.on.ca
Graham Vincent, Director, Transportation Planning, Administration
vgraham@region.waterloo.on.ca
Liana Nolan, Medical Officer of Health, Administration

Wellington
74 Woolwich St.
Guelph, ON N1H 3T9
519-837-2600
Fax: 519-837-1909
Toll Free Phone: 1-800-663-0750
finance@county.wellington.on.ca (Treasury)
www.wellington.ca
Municipal Type: County
Incorporated: Jan. 1, 1852 *Area:* 2,656.66 sq km
Population in 2006: 200,425
Next Election: Oct. 2014 (4 year terms)
Note: The council of the County of Wellington is comprised of the mayors of its seven municipalities, plus nine elected county ward councillors.
Council
Joanne Ross-Zuj, Warden & Councillor, Ward(s): Centre Wellington
519-846-0213, Fax: 519-846-8593
warden@wellington.ca; joanner@wellington.ca
Rod Finnie, Warden & Councillor, Ward(s): Erin
519-833-2380
rodf@wellington.ca
Chris White, Councillor, Ward(s): Guelph / Eramosa
519-856-0450
chrisw@wellington.ca
John Green, Councillor, Ward(s): Mapleton
519-638-2126
johngr@wellington.ca
David Anderson, Councillor, Ward(s): Minto
519-343-3883
davida@wellington.ca
Brad Whitcombe, Councillor, Ward(s): Puslinch
519-623-7970
bradw@wellington.ca
Mike Broomhead, Councillor, Ward(s): Wellington North
519-323-1981
mikeb@wellington.ca
Mark MacKenzie, Councillor, Ward(s): 1
519-338-2641
markm@wellington.ca
Carl Hall, Councillor, Ward(s): 2
519-846-5235
carlh@wellington.ca
Walter Trachsel, Councillor, Ward(s): 3
519-323-2794
waltert@wellington.ca
Lynda White, Councillor, Ward(s): 4
519-848-2806
lyndaw@wellington.ca

Jean Innes, Councillor, Ward(s): 5
519-846-8460
jeani@wellington.ca
Robert Wilson, Councillor, Ward(s): 6
519-843-3329
robertw@wellington.ca
Gordon Tosh, Councillor, Ward(s): 8
519-856-9056
gordt@wellington.ca
Lou Maieron, Councillor, Ward(s): 9
519-833-2559
loum@wellington.ca
Administration
Donna Van Wyck, Clerk, Administration
donnav@wellington.ca
Scott Wilson, Chief Administrative Officer, Administration
scottw@wellington.ca
Craig Dyer, Treasurer, Administration
craigd@county.wellington.on.ca
Andrea Lawson, Administrator, Human Resources, Administration, Fax: 519-837-8882
andreal@county.wellington.on.ca
Heather Burke, Director, Housing, Administration
heatherb@wellington.ca; wghsinfo@wellington.ca
Gary Cousins, Director, Planning, Administration, Fax: 519-823-1694
garyc@wellington.ca
Luisa Della Croce, Director, Child Care Services, Administration
luisad@wellington.ca
Bonnie Blackmore, Manager, Community Services, Administration
bonnieb@wellington.ca
Linda Dickson, Coordinator, Community Emergency Management, Administration
519-846-8058, Fax: 519-846-8482
lindad@wellington.ca
Rob Johnson, Coordinator, Forestry, Administration
robj@wellington.ca
Barb McKay, Councillor, Ward(s): 7
519-822-2984
barbm@wellington.ca

York
17250 Yonge St.
Newmarket, ON L3Y 6Z1
905-895-1231
Fax: 905-895-1238
Toll Free Phone: 1-877-464-9675
info@york.ca; twgeneral@york.ca (Transportation & Works)
www.york.ca
Municipal Type: Regional Municipality
Incorporated: Jan. 1, 1971 *Area:* 1,761.84 sq km
Population in 2006: 892,712
Next Election: Oct. 2014 (4 year terms)
Council
Bill Fisch, Regional Chair & Councillor
regional.chair@york.ca
Geoff Dawe, Councillor, Ward(s): Aurora Mayor
Virginia Hackson, Councillor, Ward(s): East Gwillimbury Mayor
Robert Grossi, Councillor, Ward(s): Georgina Mayor
Danny Wheeler, Councillor, Ward(s): Georgina
Steve Pellegrini, Councillor, Ward(s): King Mayor
Frank Scarpitti, Councillor, Ward(s): Markham Mayor
Jack Heath, Councillor, Ward(s): Markham
Jim Jones, Councillor, Ward(s): Markham
Gordon Landon, Councillor, Ward(s): Markham
Joe Li, Councillor, Ward(s): Markham
A.J. (Tony) Van Bynen, Councillor, Ward(s): Newmarket Mayor
John Taylor, Councillor, Ward(s): Newmarket
David Barrow, Councillor, Ward(s): Richmond Hill Mayor
Brenda Hogg, Councillor, Ward(s): Richmond Hill
Vito Spatafora, Councillor, Ward(s): Richmond Hill
Maurizio Bevilacqua, Councillor, Ward(s): Vaughan Mayor
Michael Di Biase, Councillor, Ward(s): Vaughan
Deb Schulte, Councillor, Ward(s): Vaughan
Gino Rosati, Councillor, Ward(s): Vaughan
Wayne Emmerson, Councillor, Ward(s): Whitchurch-Stouffville Mayor
Administration
Denis Kelly, Regional Clerk, Administration
regionalclerk@york.ca
Bruce Macgregor, Chief Administrative Officer, Administration
Lloyd Russell, Regional Treasurer & Commissioner, Finance, Administration

Jim Davidson, Commissioner, Corporate Services, Administration
Kathleen Llewellyn-Thomas, Commissioner, Transportation Services, Administration
Erin Mahoney, Commissioner, Environmental Services, Administration
Joann Simmons, Commissioner, Community & Health Services, Administration
Bryan Tuckey, Commissioner, Planning & Development Services, Administration
Patrick Casey, Director, Corporate Communications, Administration
patrick.casey@york.ca
Karen Close, Director, Human Resource Services, Administration
Karim Kurji, Medical Officer of Health & Director, Public Health Programs, Administration

Major Municipalities in Ontario

Ajax
65 Harwood Ave. South
Ajax, ON L1S 2H9
905-683-4550
Fax: 905-683-1061
Corporate Communications: 905-619-2529, ext. 3362
info@townofajax.com
www.townofajax.com
Municipal Type: City
Incorporated: 1955 *Area:* 67.09 sq km
County or District: Durham Regional Municipality; *Population in 2006:* 90,167
Provincial Electoral District(s): Ajax-Pickering
Federal Electoral District(s): Ajax-Pickering
Next Election: Oct. 2014 (4 year terms)
Council
Steve Parish, Mayor, Fax: 905-683-9450
Shaun Collier, Regional Councillor, Ward(s): 1 & 2
shaun.collier@townofajax.com
Colleen Jordan, Regional Councillor, Ward(s): 3 & 4
colleen.jordan@townofajax.com
Marilyn Crawford, Councillor, Ward(s): 1
Renrick Ashby, Councillor, Ward(s): 2
renrick.ashby@townofajax.com
Joanne Dies, Councillor, Ward(s): 3
joanne.dies@townofajax.com
Pat Brown, Councillor, Ward(s): 4
pat.brown@townofajax.com
Administration
Brian J. Skinner, Chief Administrative Officer
Rob Ford, Director, Finance & Treasurer
Finance@townofajax.com
John Fleck, Director, Human Resource Services
Dave Meredith, Director, Operations & Environmental Services
operations@townofajax.com

Amherstburg
271 Sandwich St. South
Amherstburg, ON N9V 2A5
519-736-0012
Fax: 519-736-5403
TTY: 519-736-9860
inquiry@amherstburg.ca
www.amherstburg.ca
Municipal Type: City
Incorporated: 1851 *Area:* 185.65 sq km
County or District: Essex; *Population in 2006:* 21,748
Provincial Electoral District(s): Essex
Federal Electoral District(s): Essex
Next Election: Oct. 2014 (4 year terms)
Note: Incorporated as a town in 1878.
Council
Wayne Hurst, Mayor
519-736-7646
whurst@amherstburg.ca
Carolyn Davies, Councillor
John Sutton, Councillor
jsutton@amherstburg.ca
Bart DiPasquale, Councillor
Diane Pouget, Councillor
Robert (Bob) Pillon, Councillor
rpillon@amherstburg.ca
Ron Sutherland, Councillor

See blue tabs following this section for Municipal Waste Management and Water & Wastewater Treatment.

Municipal Governments / Ontario

Administration
Pam Malott, Chief Administrative Officer
pmalott@amherstburg.ca
Lou Zarlenga, P.Eng, Manager, Public Services
Antonietta Giofu, P.Eng, Engineer, Environmental Services
Dwayne Grondin, Superintendent, Sewer & Watermain
Tony DeThomasis, Superintendent, Roads & Parks

Aurora
P.O. Box 1000
1 Municipal Dr.
Aurora, ON L4G 6J1
905-727-1375
Fax: 905-726-4738
Alternative Phone: 905-727-3123; TTY: 905-726-4766
info@e-aurora.ca
www.e-aurora.ca
Municipal Type: City
Area: 49.62 sq km
County or District: York Regional Municipality; *Population in 2006:* 47,629
Provincial Electoral District(s): Newmarket-Aurora
Federal Electoral District(s): Newmarket-Aurora
Next Election: Oct. 2014 (4 year terms)
Council
Geoff Dawe, Mayor
John Abel, Councillor
Chris Ballard, Councillor
Evelyn Buck, Councillor
ebuck@e-aurora.ca.ca
Wendy Gaertner, Councillor
wgaertner@e-aurora.ca
John Gallo, Councillor
jgallo@e-aurora.ca
Sandra Humphries, Councillor
Paul Pirri, Councillor
Michael Thompson, Councillor
Administration
Lucille King, Town Clerk
905-727-3123
Ilmar Simanovskis, Director, Public Works
Peter Horvath, Manager, Operations Services

Barrie
P.O. Box 400
70 Collier St.
Barrie, ON L4M 4T5
705-726-4242
Fax: 705-739-4243
TTY: 705-792-7910; Council Info: 705-739-4204
cityinfo@barrie.ca
www.barrie.ca; www.facebook.com/cityofbarrie
Municipal Type: City
Incorporated: 1853 *Area:* 76.99 sq km
County or District: Simcoe; *Population in 2006:* 128,430
Provincial Electoral District(s): Barrie
Federal Electoral District(s): Barrie
Next Election: Oct. 2014 (4 year terms)
Council
Jeff Lehman, Mayor
705-792-7900
officeofthemayor@barrie.ca
Bonnie J. Ainsworth, Councillor, Ward(s): 1
Lynn M. Strachan, Councillor, Ward(s): 2
lstrachan@barrie.ca
Doug Shipley, Councillor, Ward(s): 3
Barry J. Ward, Councillor, Ward(s): 4
bward@barrie.ca
Peter Silveira, Councillor, Ward(s): 5
Michael Prowse, Councillor, Ward(s): 6
mprowse@barrie.ca
John Brassard, Councillor, Ward(s): 7
jbrassard@barrie.ca
Alison Eadie, Councillor, Ward(s): 8
Brian H. Jackson, Councillor, Ward(s): 9
Alexander Nuttall, Councillor, Ward(s): 10
anuttall@barrie.ca
Administration
Dawn McAlpine, City Clerk, Administration
705-739-4204
Jon Babulic, Chief Administrative Officer, Administration
Ed Archer, CMA, General Manager, Corporate Services, Administration
Richard Forward, M.Sc., P.Eng., General Manager, Infrastructure, Development & Culture Division, Administration
J.W. (Jim) Sales, General Manager, Community Operations, Administration
G. Allison, Director, Building Services & Chief Building Official, Administration
Sandy Coulter, B.Sc., Acting Director, Operations - Water, Wastewater & Environmental, Administration
Dave Friary, Acting Director, Operations - Roads, Parks & Fleet Operations, Administration
Hany Kirolos, Director, Strategy & Economic Development, Administration
Wendell McArthur, Director, Engineering, Administration
Debbie McKinnon, Director, Finance, Administration
Barbara Roth, Director, Leisure, Transit & Facilities, Administration
J. Taylor, Director, Planning Services Department, Administration
John Lynn, Fire Chief, Administration
Bruce L. Griffin, Community Emergency Planner, Administration

Belleville
City Hall
169 Front St.
Belleville, ON K8N 2Y8
613-968-6481
Fax: 613-967-3206
www.city.belleville.on.ca
Municipal Type: City
Area: 246.76 sq km
County or District: Hastings; *Population in 2006:* 48,821
Provincial Electoral District(s): Prince Edward-Hastings
Federal Electoral District(s): Prince Edward-Hastings
Next Election: Oct. 2014 (4 year terms)
Council
Neil R. Ellis, Mayor
613-967-3267, Fax: 613-967-3209
mayor.ellis@city.belleville.on.ca
Egerton Boyce, Councillor, Ward(s): 1
councillor.boyce@city.belleville.on.ca
Pat Culhane, Councillor, Ward(s): 1
councillor.culhane@city.belleville.on.ca
Jodie Jenkins, Councillor, Ward(s): 1
councillor.jenkins@city.belleville.on.ca
Tom Lafferty, Councillor, Ward(s): 1
councillor.lafferty@city.belleville.on.ca
Jack Miller, Councillor, Ward(s): 1
councillor.miller@city.belleville.on.ca
Garnet Thompson, Councillor, Ward(s): 1
councillor.thompson@city.belleville.on.ca
Taso Christopher, Councillor, Ward(s): 2
councillor.christopher@city.belleville.on.ca
Jackie Denyes, Councillor, Ward(s): 2
councillor.denyes@city.belleville.on.ca
Administration
Julie C. Oram, City Clerk & Director, Corporate Services, Administration
613-967-3271
joram@city.belleville.on.ca
Stephen G. Hyndman, Ec.D.(F), MCIP RPP, Chief Administrative Officer, Administration
shyndman@city.belleville.on.ca
Brian Cousins, Director, Finance & Treasurer, Administration
bcousins@city.belleville.on.ca
Mark Fluhrer, Director, Recreation Culture & Community Services, Administration
mfluhrer@city.belleville.on.ca
Rick Kester, Director, Engineering & Development Services, Administration
rkester@city.belleville.on.ca
John Martin, Director, Human Resources, Administration
jmartin@city.belleville.on.ca
Brad Wilson, Environmental & Operational Services, Administration
bwilson@city.belleville.on.ca
Ted Marecak, Chief Building Official, Administration
tmarecak@city.belleville.on.ca
Rhéaume Chaput, Fire Chief, Administration
rchaput@city.belleville.on.ca
Elizabeth Garrison, Manager, Transit Operations, Administration
phodgson@city.belleville.on.ca
Art MacKay, Manager, Policy Planning, Administration
amackay@city.belleville.on.ca
Pat McNulty, Manager, Transportation, Administration
pmcnulty@city.belleville.on.ca
Richard Reinert, Manager, Environmental Services, Administration
rreinert@city.belleville.on.ca

Bracebridge
1000 Taylor Ct.
Bracebridge, ON P1L 1R6
705-645-5264
Fax: 705-645-1262
Fax, Public Works: 705-645-4209
www.town.bracebridge.on.ca
Municipal Type: City
Area: 617.42 sq km
County or District: Muskoka Dist. Mun.; *Population in 2006:* 15,652
Provincial Electoral District(s): Parry Sound-Muskoka
Federal Electoral District(s): Parry Sound-Muskoka
Next Election: Oct. 2014 (4 year terms)
Council
Graydon Smith, Mayor
Steve Clement, District Councillor
Liam Craig, Councillor
Lori-Lynn Giaschi-Pacini, District Councillor
lpacini@sympatico.ca
Rick Maloney, Councillor
Barb McMurray, Councillor
Mark Quemby, Councillor
Gerry Tryon, Councillor
gtryon@vianet.ca
Scott Young, District Councillor
dsy4@vianet.ca
Administration
Lori McDonald, Clerk, Administration
mcdonald@town.bracebridge.on.ca
John R. Sisson, Chief Administrative Officer, Administration
Carol Wakefield, Treasurer, Administration
Kim Horrigan, Director, Development Services, Administration
Cheryl Kelley, Director, Economic Development, Administration
Ron Walton, Director, Public Works & Municipal Engineer, Administration
Murray Medley, Fire Chief, Administration

Bradford West Gwillimbury
Administration Centre
P.O. Box 160
3541 Line 11
Bradford, ON L3Z 2A8
905-775-5366
Fax: 905-775-0153
www.town.bradfordwestgwillimbury.on.ca
Municipal Type: City
Incorporated: 1857 *Area:* 201.03 sq km
County or District: Simcoe; *Population in 2006:* 24,039
Provincial Electoral District(s): York-Simcoe
Federal Electoral District(s): York-Simcoe
Next Election: Oct. 2014 (4 year terms)
Note: Incorporated as a town in 1960.
Council
Doug White, Mayor
dwhite@townofbwg.com
Rob Keffer, Deputy Mayor & Councillor
Raj Sandhu, Councillor, Ward(s): 1
Del Crake, Councillor, Ward(s): 2
Gary R. Lamb, Councillor, Ward(s): 3
Carl Hordyk, Councillor, Ward(s): 4
Ron Simpson, Councillor, Ward(s): 5
James Leduc, Councillor, Ward(s): 6
Peter Dykie, Jr., Councillor, Ward(s): 7
Administration
Patricia Nash, Municipal Clerk, Administration
pnash@townofbwg.com
Jay Currier, Chief Administrative Officer & Town Manager, Administration
Ian Goodfellow, Director, Finance & Treasurer, Administration
Debbie Korolnek, Director, Engineering Services, Administration
Geoff McKnight, Director, Planning & Development, Administration
Paul Feehely, Superintendent, Public Works, Administration
Edward O'Donnell, Supervisor, Water, Administration
Brad Sullivan, Supervisor, Waste Water, Administration
Lorne Arscott, Fire Chief, Administration

Brampton
2 Wellington St. West
Brampton, ON L6Y 4R2

See blue tabs following this section for Municipal Waste Management and Water & Wastewater Treatment.

905-874-2000
Fax: 905-874-2119
E-mail, Economic Development: edo@brampton.ca
cityhall@brampton.ca; tourism@brampton.ca (Tourism)
www.brampton.ca
Municipal Type: City
Incorporated: Jan. 1, 1974 *Area:* 266.71 sq km
County or District: Peel Reg. Mun.; *Population in 2006:* 433,806
Provincial Electoral District(s): Bramalea-Gore-Malton; Brampton Springdale; Brampton West; Brampton South-Mississauga
Federal Electoral District(s): Bramalea-Gore-Malton; Brampton Springdale; Brampton West; Mississauga-Brampton South
Next Election: Oct. 2014 (4 year terms)
Council
Susan Fennell, Mayor
mayor@brampton.ca
Grant Gibson, City Councillor, Ward(s): 1 & 5
John Hutton, City Councillor, Ward(s): 2 & 6
Bob Callahan, City Councillor, Ward(s): 3 & 4
Sandra Hames, City Councillor, Ward(s): 7 & 8
Vicky Dhillon, City Councillor, Ward(s): 9 & 10
Elaine Moore, Regional Councillor, Ward(s): 1 & 5
Paul Palleschi, Regional Councillor, Ward(s): 2 & 6
John Sanderson, Regional Councillor, Ward(s): 3 & 4
Gael Miles, Regional Councillor, Ward(s): 7 & 8
John Sprovieri, Regional Councillor, Ward(s): 9 & 10
Administration
Peter Fay, City Clerk, Administration
905-874-2100, Fax: 905-874-2119
cityclerksoffice@brampton.ca
Deborah Dubenofsky, City Manager, Administration
Mo Lewis, Commissioner, Finance, Administration
John Corbett, Commissioner, Planning, Design & Development, Administration
Dennis Cutajar, Commissioner, Economic Development & Communications, Administration
Jamie Lowery, Commissioner, Community Services, Administration
Tom Mulligan, Commissioner, Works & Transportation, Administration
Julian Patteson, Commissioner, Buildings & Property Management, Administration
Kathy Zammit, Commissioner, Corporate Services, Administration

Brantford
City Hall
P.O. Box 818
100 Wellington Sq.
Brantford, ON N3T 2M3
519-759-4150
Fax: 519-759-7840
new_webmaster@brantford.ca
www.brantford.ca
Municipal Type: City
Incorporated: May 31, 1877 *Area:* 72.47 sq km
County or District: Brant; *Population in 2006:* 90,192
Provincial Electoral District(s): Brant
Federal Electoral District(s): Brant
Next Election: Oct. 2014 (4 year terms)
Council
Chris Friel, Mayor
519-756-2242, Fax: 519-751-7109
Larry M. Kings, Councillor, Ward(s): 1
Jan C. Vander Stelt, Councillor, Ward(s): 1
Vince Bucci, Councillor, Ward(s): 2
John K. Utley, Councillor, Ward(s): 2
Debi Dignan-Rumble, Councillor, Ward(s): 3
Dan McCreary, Councillor, Ward(s): 3
Richard Carpenter, Councillor, Ward(s): 4
Dave Wrobel, Councillor, Ward(s): 4
Marguerite Ceschi-Smith, Councillor, Ward(s): 5
David E. Neumann, Councillor, Ward(s): 5
Administration
Darryl Lee, City Clerk, Administration
John Brown, City Manager, Administration
Sandra Lawson, General Manager, Engineering & Operational Services, Administration
Ted Salisbury, General Manager, Community Development Services, Administration
Dan Temprile, General Manager, Public Health, Safety, & Social Services, Administration

Brockville
Victoria Bldg.
P.O. Box 5000
1 King St. West
Brockville, ON K6V 7A5
613-342-8772
Fax: 613-342-8780
info@brockville.com; tourism@brockvillechamber.com
www.brockville.com
Municipal Type: City
Area: 20.74 sq km
County or District: Leeds & Grenville; *Population in 2006:* 21,957
Provincial Electoral District(s): Leeds-Grenville
Federal Electoral District(s): Leeds-Grenville
Next Election: Oct. 2014 (4 year terms)
Council
David L. Henderson, Mayor
Jason Baker, Councillor
David E. Beatty, Councillor
Leigh Z. Bursey, Councillor
Jeffery Earle, Councillor
Jane Fullerton, Councillor
Larry F. Journal, Councillor
Mike Kalivas, Councillor
David D. Lesueur, Councillor
Mary Jane McFall, Councillor
Administration
Sandra M. Seale, City Clerk, Administration
smseale@brockville.com
Bob Casselman, City Manager, Administration
bcasselman@brockville.com
Donna Cyr, Director, Finance, Administration
dcyr@brockville.com
Jim Baker, Director, Human Resources, Administration
jbaker@brockville.com
Valerie Harvey, Director, Parks & Recreation, Administration
vharvey@brockville.com
David C. Paul, Director, Economic Development, Administration
dpaul@brockville.com
Maureen Pascoe Merkley, Director, Planning, Administration
mpmerkley@brockville.com
Harry Jones, Fire Chief, Administration
hjones@brockville.com

Burlington
City Hall
P.O. Box 5013
426 Brant St.
Burlington, ON L7R 3Z6
905-335-7777
Fax: 905-335-7881
Toll Free Phone: 1-877-213-3609
cob@burlington.ca
www.burlington.ca
Municipal Type: City
Incorporated: 1914 *Area:* 185.74 sq km
County or District: Halton Regional Municipality; *Population in 2006:* 164,415
Provincial Electoral District(s): Ancaster-Dundas-Flamborough-Westdale; Burlington; Halton
Federal Electoral District(s): Burlington; Halton; Ancaster-Dundas-Flamborough-Westdale
Next Election: Oct. 2014 (4 year terms)
Note: Incorporated as a city in 1974.
Council
Rick Goldring, Mayor
905-335-7607, Fax: 905-335-7708
Rick Craven, Councillor, Ward(s): 1
cravenr@burlington.ca
Peter Thoem, Councillor, Ward(s): 2
thoemp@burlington.ca
John Taylor, Councillor, Ward(s): 3
taylorj@burlington.ca
Jack Dennison, Councillor, Ward(s): 4
dennisonj@burlington.ca
Paul Sharman, Councillor, Ward(s): 5
Blair Lancaster, Councillor, Ward(s): 6
Administration
Kim Phillips, City Clerk, Administration
905-335-7698, Fax: 905-335-7881
cityclerks@burlington.ca; phillipsk@burlington.ca
Roman Martiuk, City Manager, Administration
martiukr@burlington.ca
Steve Zorbas, City Treasurer, Administration
zorbass@burlington.ca
Leo DeLoyde, General Manager, Development & Infrastructure, Administration
Scott Stewart, General Manager, Community Services, Administration
Tom Eichenbaum, Director, Engineering, Administration
eichenbaumt@burlington.ca
Bruce Krushelnicki, Director, Planning & Building, Administration
krushelnickib@burlington.ca
Lynn Robichaud, Senior Coorindator, Environmental Services, Administration
robichaudl@burlington.ca

Caledon
Town Hall
6311 Old Church Rd.
Caledon, ON L7C 1J6
905-584-2272
Fax: 905-584-4325
Toll Free Phone: 1-888-225-3366
info@caledon.ca
www.caledon.ca
Municipal Type: City
Incorporated: Jan. 1, 1974 *Area:* 687.17 sq km
County or District: Peel Regional Municipality; *Population in 2006:* 57,050
Provincial Electoral District(s): Dufferin-Caledon
Federal Electoral District(s): Dufferin-Caledon
Next Election: Oct. 2014 (4 year terms)
Council
Marolyn Morrison, Mayor
marolyn.morrison@caledon.ca
Richard Paterak, Regional Councillor, Ward(s): 1
Allan Thompson, Regional Councillor, Ward(s): 2
Richard Whitehead, Regional Councillor, Ward(s): 3 & 4
Patti Foley, Regional Councillor, Ward(s): 5
Doug Beffort, Area Councillor, Ward(s): 1
Gord McClure, Area Councillor, Ward(s): 2
Nick deBoer, Area Councillor, Ward(s): 3 & 4
Rob Mezzapelli, Area Councillor, Ward(s): 5
Administration
Karen Landry, Town Clerk & Director, Administration, Administration
D. Barnes, Chief Administrative Officer, Administration
R. Kaufman, Treasurer, Deputy CAO, & Director, Corporate Services, Administration
L. Koehle, Director, Public Works & Engineering, Administration
M. Hall, Director, Planning & Development, Administration
G. Middlebrook, Chief Building Official, Administration
J. Schembri, Officer, Environmental Progress, Administration

Cambridge
P.O. Box 669
73 Water St. North
Cambridge, ON N1R 5W8
519-623-1340
Fax: 519-740-3011
E-mail, Corporate Services: corpserv@cambridge.ca
questions@cambridge.ca; csd@cambridge.ca (Community Svs.)
www.cambridge.ca
Municipal Type: City
Incorporated: Jan. 1973 *Area:* 112.86 sq km
County or District: Waterloo Regional Municipality; *Population in 2006:* 120,371
Provincial Electoral District(s): Cambridge
Federal Electoral District(s): Cambridge
Next Election: Oct. 2014 (4 year terms)
Council
Doug Craig, Mayor
519-740-4517
mayor@cambridge.ca; craigd@cambridge.ca
Donna Reid, City Councillor, Ward(s): 1
Rick Cowsill, City Councillor, Ward(s): 2
cowsillr@cambridge.ca
Karl Kiefer, City Councillor, Ward(s): 3
kieferk@cambridge.ca
Ben Tucci, City Councillor, Ward(s): 4
tuccib@cambridge.ca
Pam Wolf, City Councillor, Ward(s): 5
wolfp@cambridge.ca
Gary Price, City Councillor, Ward(s): 6
priceg@cambridge.ca
Frank Monteiro, City Councillor, Ward(s): 7
Nicholas Ermeta, City Councillor, Ward(s): 8

Municipal Governments / Ontario

Jane Brewer, Regional Councillor
Claudette Millar, Regional Councillor
Administration
Alex Mitchell, City Clerk, Administration
519-740-4680
clerks@city.cambridge.ca
Jim King, Chief Administrative Officer, Administration
519-740-4683
cao@cambridge.ca
Terry Allen, Commisssioner, Fire Services, Administration
Janet Babcock, Commisssioner, Planning Services, Administration
Steven Fairweather, Commisssioner, Corporate Services, Administration
Ed Kovacs, Commisssioner, Transportation & Public Works, Administration
Reg Weber, Commisssioner, Community Services, Administration

Clarence-Rockland
1560 Laurier St.
Rockland, ON K4K 1P7
613-446-6022
Fax: 613-446-1497
www.clarence-rockland.com
Municipal Type: City
Incorporated: Jan. 1, 1998 *Area:* 296.53 sq km
County or District: Prescott & Russell; *Population in 2006:* 20,790
Provincial Electoral District(s): Glengarry-Prescott-Russell
Federal Electoral District(s): Glengarry-Prescott-Russell
Next Election: Oct. 2014 (4 year terms)
Note: Amalgamation of the Town of Rockland and the Township of Clarence.
Council
Marcel Guibord, Mayor
613-446-4856
Michel Thivierge, Councillor, Ward(s): 1
André Henrie, Councillor, Ward(s): 2
Francine Mault, Councillor, Ward(s): 3
Raymond Serrurier, Councillor, Ward(s): 4
Kyle Cyr, Councillor, Ward(s): 5
Guy Desjardins, Councillor, Ward(s): 6
Jean-Pierre Chartrand, Councillor, Ward(s): 7
Garry M. Edwards, Councillor, Ward(s): 8
Administration
Daniel Gatien, Chief Administrative Officer & Clerk, Administration
dgatien@clarence-rockland.com
Chantal McLean-Leroux, Treasurer, Administration
cmcleanleroux@clarence-rockland.com
Thérèse Lefaivre, Director, Community Services, Administration
tlefaivre@clarence-rockland.com
Michael Michaud, Director, Planning, Administration
mmichaud@clarence-rockland.com
Yves Rivard, Director, By-law Enforcement, Administration
yrivard@clarence-rockland.com
Yves Rousselle, Director, Physical Services, Administration
yrousselle@clarence-rockland.com
Pierre Sabourin, Fire Chief, Administration
psabourin@clarence-rockland.com
Denis Longpré, Manager, Environment, Administration
dlongpre@clarence-rockland.com

Cobourg
55 King St. West
Cobourg, ON K9A 2M2
905-372-4301
Fax: 905-372-7421
Toll Free Phone: 1-888-262-6874
webmaster@cobourg.ca
www.cobourg.ca
Municipal Type: City
Area: 22.37 sq km
County or District: Northumberland; *Population in 2006:* 18,210
Provincial Electoral District(s): Northumberland-Quinte West
Federal Electoral District(s): Northumberland-Quinte West
Next Election: Oct. 2014 (4 year terms)
Council
Gil Brocanier, Mayor, Fax: 905-372-2910
gbrocanier@cobourg.ca
Stan Frost, Deputy Mayor & Councillor
stan.frost@sympatico.ca
John Henderson, Councillor
Miriam Mutton, Councillor
miriam.mutton@cogeco.ca
Forrest Rowden, Councillor
Larry E. Sherwin, Councillor
Donna Todd, Councillor
Administration
D.S. Robinson, Chief Administrative Officer, Administration
srobinson@cobourg.ca
Ian Davey, Director, Corporate Services, Administration
idavey@cobourg.ca
Glenn J. McGlashon, Director, Planning & Development Services, Administration
gmcglashon@cobourg.ca
Steven Peacock, Director, Public Works, Administration
speacock@cobourg.ca

Collingwood
P.O. Box 157
97 Hurontario St.
Collingwood, ON L9Y 3Z5
705-445-1030
Fax: 705-445-2448
Toll Free Phone, Economic Dev.: 1-888-265-9663
ddraper@collingwood.ca (Reception)
www.collingwood.ca
Municipal Type: City
Incorporated: 1858 *Area:* 33.46 sq km
County or District: Simcoe; *Population in 2006:* 17,290
Provincial Electoral District(s): Simcoe-Grey
Federal Electoral District(s): Simcoe-Grey
Next Election: Oct. 2014 (4 year terms)
Council
Sandra Cooper, Mayor
705-446-4704
scooper@collingwood.ca
Rick Lloyd, Deputy Mayor & Councillor
Ian Chadwick, Councillor
ichadwick@collingwood.ca
Sandy Cunningham, Councillor
Mike Edwards, Councillor
medwards@collingwood.ca
Joe Gardhouse, Councillor
Keith Hull, Councillor
Kevin Lloyd, Councillor
Dale West, Councillor
Administration
Sara J. Almas, Clerk, Administration
salmas@collingwood.ca
Gord Norris, Chief Administrative Officer, Administration
gnorris@collingwood.ca
Marjory Leonard, Treasurer, Administration
mleonard@collingwood.ca
Ed Houghton, Executive Director, Public Works, Administration
ehoughton@collingwood.ca
Peter Dunbar, Director, Leisure Services, Administration
pdunbar@collingwood.ca
Larry Irwin, Director, Information Technology, Administration
lirwin@collingwood.ca
Bill Plewes, Director, Building Services, Administration
bplewes@collingwood.ca
Gord Russell, Director, Planning Services, Administration
grussell@collingwood.ca
Trent Elyea, Fire Chief, Administration
telyea@collingwood.ca
Donald Green, Manager, Environmental Services, Administration
dgreen@collingwood.ca
Wendy Martin, Manager, Green Space, Administration
wmartin@collingwood.ca

Cornwall
P.O. Box 877
360 Pitt St.
Cornwall, ON K6H 5T9
613-932-6252
Fax: 613-932-8145
E-mail, Municipal Works: engineering@cornwall.ca
cityhall@cornwall.ca; ecodev@cornwall.ca (Economic Dev.)
www.cornwall.ca
Municipal Type: City
Incorporated: 1834 *Area:* 61.52 sq km
County or District: Stormont, Dundas & Glengarry; *Population in 2006:* 45,965
Provincial Electoral District(s): Stormont-Dundas-South Glengarry
Federal Electoral District(s): Stormont-Dundas-South Glengarry
Next Election: Oct. 2014 (4 year terms)
Note: Incorporated as a city in 1945.
Council
Bob Kilger, Mayor
mayor@cornwall.ca
Denis Carr, Councillor
Bernadette Clement, Councillor
Maurice Dupelle, Councillor
Syd Gardiner, Councillor
Glen Grant, Councillor
Elaine MacDonald, Councillor
David Murphy, Councillor
Leslie O'Shaugnessy, Councillor
André Rivette, Councillor
Denis Thibault, Councillor
Administration
Denise Labelle-Gelinas, City Clerk, Administration
dgelinas@cornwall.ca
Paul Fitzpatrick, Chief Administrative Officer, Administration
Maureen Adams, General Manager, Financial Services, Administration
Stephen Alexander, General Manager, Planning, Parks & Recreation Services, Administration
Norm Levac, General Manager, Infrastructure & Municipal Works, Administration
Tom Gemmell, Division Manager, Municipal Works, Administration
Morris McCormick, Division Manager, Environment, Administration
Len Tapp, Division Manager, Transit, Administration
Mark Boileau, Manager, Economic Development, Administration
Myles Cassidy, Manager, Emergency Services & Chief, Fire, Administration
Patrick Carrière, Supervisor, Waste Water Treatment Facility, Administration
Neil Dixon, Supervisor, Waste Management, Administration
Owen O'Keefe, Supervisor, Water Purification Plant, Administration

East Gwillimbury
19000 Leslie St.
Sharon, ON L0G 1V0
905-478-4282
Fax: 905-478-2808
Alternate Fax: 905-478-8545
town@eastgwillimbury.ca; engineering@eastgwillimbury.ca
www.eastgwillimbury.ca
Municipal Type: City
Incorporated: 1850 *Area:* 245.06 sq km
County or District: York Regional Municipality; *Population in 2006:* 21,069
Provincial Electoral District(s): York-Simcoe
Federal Electoral District(s): York-Simcoe
Next Election: Oct. 2014 (4 year terms)
Council
Virginia Hackson, Mayor
John Eaton, Councillor
Marlene Johnston, Councillor
mjohnston@eastgwillimbury.ca
Cathy Morton, Councillor
cmorton@eastgwillimbury.ca
Tara Roy-Diclemente, Councillor
Administration
Anna Knowles, Acting Clerk, Administration
aknowles@eastgwillimbury.ca
Thomas R. Webster, Chief Administrative Officer, Administration
twebster@eastgwillimbury.ca
Mark Valcic, General Manager, Corporate & Financial Services & Treasurer, Administration
mvalcic@eastgwillimbury.ca
Wayne Hunt, General Manager, Community Programs & Infrastructure, Administration
whunt@eastgwillimbury.ca
Don Sinclair, General Manager, Development & Legal Services, Administration
Ken Beckett, Fire Chief, Administration
Don Allan, Manager, Engineering Branch, Administration
dallan@eastgwillimbury.ca
Carolyn Kellington, Manager, Community Planning & Development Branch, Administration
ckellington@eastgwillimbury.ca
Steve Krystal, Manager, Capital Programs & Traffic Engineering Branch, Administration
skrystal@eastgwillimbury.ca

See blue tabs following this section for Municipal Waste Management and Water & Wastewater Treatment.

Municipal Governments / Ontario

Gary Shropshire, Manager, Community Parks & Programs Branch, Administration
gshropshire@eastgwillimbury.ca
Tim Gibson, Director, Building Approvals & Inspections, Administration
tgibson@eastgwillimbury.ca
Christopher Kalimootoo, Director, Engineering & Environmental Services, Administration
ckalimootoo@eastgwillimbury.ca
Robin Skinner, Environmental Planner, Administration
rskinner@eastgwillimbury.ca

Elliot Lake
45 Hillside Dr. North
Elliot Lake, ON P5A 1X5
705-848-2287
Fax: 705-461-7244
www.cityofelliotlake.com
Municipal Type: City
Area: 698.12 sq km
County or District: Algoma District; *Population in 2006:* 11,549
Provincial Electoral District(s): Algoma-Manitoulin
Federal Electoral District(s): Algoma-Manitoulin-Kapuskasing
Next Election: Oct. 2014 (4 year terms)
Council
Rick Hamilton, Mayor
Al Collett, Councillor
Tom Farquhar, Councillor
Sandy Finamore, Councillor
Norman Mann, Councillor
Chris Patrie, Councillor
Ken Rastin, Councillor
Administration
Lesley Sprague, City Clerk, Administration
Fred Bauthus, Chief Administrative Officer, Administration
Dawn Halcrow, Director, Finance, Administration
R. deBortoli, Director, Operations, Administration
D. Gagnon, Director, Economic Development, Administration
Paul Officer, Fire Chief, Administration

Erin
5684 Wellington Rd., RR#2
Hillsburgh, ON N0B 1Z0
519-855-4407
Fax: 519-855-4821
Toll Free Phone: 1-877-818-2888
council@erin.ca; cao@erin.ca (Town Manager)
www.erin.ca
Municipal Type: City
Incorporated: 1997 *Area:* 296.98 sq km
County or District: Wellington; *Population in 2006:* 11,148
Provincial Electoral District(s): Wellington-Halton Hills
Federal Electoral District(s): Wellington-Halton Hills
Next Election: Oct. 2014 (4 year terms)
Council
Lou Maieron, Mayor, Fax: 519-833-0208
John Brennan, Councillor, Fax: 519-833-0891
hejo@ca.inter.net
Deb Callaghan, Councillor
Barb Tocher, Councillor
barb.tocher@sympatico.ca
Josie Wintersinger, Councillor, Fax: 519-855-6927
jwintersinger@yahoo.ca
Administration
Kathryn Ironmonger, Clerk, Administration
Lisa Hass, Town Manager, Administration
Sharon Marshall, Director, Finance, Administration
Rhonda Buck, Administrator, Building & Planning, Administration
Louise Warn, Administrator, Water Compliance, Administration
Steve Goode, Fire Chief, Administration
Andrew Hartholt, Chief Building Official, Administration
Larry Van Wyck, Superintendent, Roads, Administration

Essex
33 Talbot St. South
Essex, ON N8M 1A8
519-776-7336
Fax: 519-776-8811
www.essex.ca
Municipal Type: City
Incorporated: 1883 *Area:* 277.95 sq km
County or District: Essex; *Population in 2006:* 20,032
Provincial Electoral District(s): Essex
Federal Electoral District(s): Essex
Next Election: Oct. 2014 (4 year terms)

Note: Incorporated as a town in 1890. Restructuring occurred in 1999.
Council
Ron McDermott, Mayor
519-776-8150
rmcdermott@essex.ca
Morley Bowman, Councillor, Ward(s): 1
Randy Voakes, Councillor, Ward(s): 1
Richard Meloche, Councillor, Ward(s): 2
Bill Baker, Councillor, Ward(s): 3
John Scott, Councillor, Ward(s): 3
Sherry Bondy, Councillor, Ward(s): 4
Administration
Cheryl Bondy, Clerk & Deputy-Treasurer, Administration
cbondy@essex.ca
Wayne Miller, Chief Administrative Officer, Administration
Donna Hunter, Director, Finance & Administration & Treasurer, Administration
Richard Beausoleil, Director, Public Works, Administration
Harry Hakim, Director, Parks & Recreation, Administration
Chris Nepszy, Director, Infasructure & Development, Administration
Ed Pillon, Fire Chief, Administration
519-776-6476, Fax: 519-776-7171
Heather Jablonski, Town Planner, Administration
Dan Boudreau, Superintendent, Drainage, Administration
Andy Graf, Superintendent, Water, Administration

Fort Erie
1 Municipal Centre Dr.
Fort Erie, ON L2A 2S6
905-871-1600
Fax: 905-871-4022
Fax, Community Services: 905-871-9984
townhall@town.forterie.on.ca
www.forterie.on.ca
Municipal Type: City
Incorporated: 1857 *Area:* 166.35 sq km
County or District: Niagara Regional Municipality; *Population in 2006:* 29,925
Provincial Electoral District(s): Niagara Falls
Federal Electoral District(s): Niagara Falls
Next Election: Oct. 2014 (4 year terms)
Council
Douglas G. Martin, Mayor
douglas.martin@town.forterie.ca
Stephen Passero, Councillor, Ward(s): 1
Richard Shular, Councillor, Ward(s): 2
rshular@town.forterie.ca
Bob Steckley, Councillor, Ward(s): 3
bsteckley@town.forterie.ca
John Hill, Councillor, Ward(s): 4
Don Lubberts, Councillor, Ward(s): 5
Paul Collard, Councillor, Ward(s): 6
John Teal, Regional Councillor
Administration
Carolyn J. Kett, Town Clerk, Administration
ckett@town.forterie.ca
H. Schlange, Chief Administrative Officer, Administration
H. Chamberlain, Director, Financial Services, Administration
R. Mostacci, Director, Community & Development Services, Administration
H. Salter, Director, Legal & Legislative Services & Town Solicitor, Administration
R. Tripp, Director, Infrastructure Services, Administration
Larry Coplen, Fire Chief & Coordinator, Community Emergency Management, Administration
S. Hansen, Manager, Parks & Open Space Development, Administration

Georgina
Georgina Civic Centre
26557 Civic Centre Rd., RR#2
Keswick, ON L4P 3G1
905-476-4301
Fax: 905-476-8100
Alternative Phones: 905-722-6516; 705-437-2210
info@georgina.ca; events@georgina.ca
www.georgina.ca
Municipal Type: City
Area: 287.72 sq km
County or District: York Reg. Mun.; *Population in 2006:* 42,346
Provincial Electoral District(s): York-Simcoe
Federal Electoral District(s): York-Simcoe
Next Election: Oct. 2014 (4 year terms)

Note: Amalgamation of the Village of Keswick, the Township of Georgina & Village of Sutton.
Council
Robert Grossi, Mayor, Fax: 905-476-1475
rgrossi@georgina.ca
Danny Wheeler, Deputy Mayor & Regional Councillor
dwheeler@georgina.ca
Naomi Davison, Councillor, Ward(s): 1
Dan Fellini, Councillor, Ward(s): 2
Dave Szollosy, Councillor, Ward(s): 3
dszollosy@georgina.ca
Ken Hackenbrook, Councillor, Ward(s): 4
khackenbrook@georgina.ca
Brad Smockum, Councillor, Ward(s): 5
bsmockum@georgina.ca
Administration
Roland Chénier, A.M.C.T., Town Clerk, Administration
rchenier@georgina.ca
Susan Plamondon, Chief Administrative Officer, Administration
splamondon@georgina.ca
Rebecca Mathewson, C.G.A., Director, Administrative Services, Administration
rmathewson@georgina.ca
Harold Lenters, M.Sc.Pl., MCIP, RPP, Director, Planning & Building, Administration
hlenters@georgina.ca
Robert Magloughlen, P.Eng., Director, Engineering & Public Works, Administration
rmagloughlen@georgina.ca
Bill O'Neill, C.M.M. III, Director, Emergency Services & Fire Chief, Administration
boneill@georgina.ca
Faye Richardson, Director, Leisure Services, Administration
frichardson@georgina.ca
Claire Marsden, C.H.R.P., C.M.M. I, Manager, Human Resources, Administration
cmarsden@georgina.ca

Gravenhurst
190 Harvie St.
Gravenhurst, ON P1P 1S9
705-687-3412
Fax: 705-687-7016
reception@gravenhurst.ca
www.gravenhurst.ca
Municipal Type: City
Area: 517.99 sq km
County or District: Muskoka District Municipality; *Population in 2006:* 11,046
Provincial Electoral District(s): Parry Sound-Muskoka
Federal Electoral District(s): Parry Sound-Muskoka
Next Election: Oct. 2014 (4 year terms)
Council
Paisley Donaldson, Mayor
705-689-8334
Sandy Cairns, District Councillor
Bob Colhoun, District Councillor
colhoun@muskoka.com
Rosemary King, District Councillor
Heidi Lorenz, Councillor, Ward(s): 1
Lola Bratty, Councillor, Ward(s): 2
Joe Donoghue, Councillor, Ward(s): 3
Randy Jorgensen, Councillor, Ward(s): 4
Jeff Watson, Councillor, Ward(s): 5
Administration
Candace Thwaites, Clerk, Administration
Kenneth Watson, Treasurer, Administration
D. Broderick, Manager, Recreation, Community Services, & Centennial Ctr. Ops., Administration
N. Popovich, Manager, Development Services, Administration
B. Rundle, Manager, Arts & Culture, Administration
D. Saunders, Manager, Public Works & Operations, Administration
L. Sherk, Officer, Community Economic Development, Administration

Greater Napanee
P.O. Box 97
124 John St.
Napanee, ON K7R 3L4
613-354-3351
Fax: 613-354-6545
E-mail, Programs: recreation@greaternapanee.com
info@greaternapanee.com; roads@greaternapanee.com
www.greaternapanee.com

See blue tabs following this section for Municipal Waste Management and Water & Wastewater Treatment.

Municipal Governments / Ontario

Municipal Type: City
Area: 459.71 sq km
County or District: Lennox-Addington; *Population in 2006:* 15,400
Provincial Electoral District(s): Lanark-Frontenac-Lennox & Addington
Federal Electoral District(s): Lanark-Frontenac-Lennox & Addington
Next Election: Oct. 2014 (4 year terms)
Council
Gord Schermerhorn, Mayor
613-354-0429
Roger Cole, Deputy Mayor & Councillor
613-354-3664
Shane Grant, Councillor, Ward(s): 2
613-354-5529
Marg Isbester, Councillor, Ward(s): 3
Shaune Lucas, Councillor, Ward(s): 5
Administration
Rebecca Murphy, Clerk & Director, Corporate & Legal Services, Administration
rmurphy@greaternapanee.com
Raymond Callery, Chief Administrative Officer, Administration
rcallery@greaternapanee.com
Mark Day, Director, Finance & Treasurer, Administration
mday@greaternapanee.com
Vern Amey, Director, Public Works, Administration
vamey@greaternapanee.com
George Hanmore, Director, Fire & Emergency Services, Administration
ghanmore@greaternapanee.com
Kevin Hill, Director, Parks, Recreation & Culture, Administration
khill@greaternapanee.com
Charles McDonald, Director, Development Services, Administration
cmcdonald@greaternapanee.com
Ron Vankoughnet, Supervisor, Roads & Landfill, Administration

Greater Sudbury / Grand Sudbury
Tom Davies Square
P.O. Box 5000 A
200 Brady St.
Sudbury, ON P3A 5P3
705-671-2489
Fax: 705-671-8118
Phone, Local Calls: 3-1-1
www.greatersudbury.ca
Municipal Type: City
Incorporated: Jan. 1, 2001 *Area:* 3,200.56 sq km
Population in 2006: 157,857
Provincial Electoral District(s): Nickel Belt; Sudbury
Federal Electoral District(s): Nickel Belt; Sudbury
Next Election: Oct. 2014 (4 year terms)
Council
Marianne Matichuk, Mayor
705-674-4455, Fax: 705-673-3096
mayor@greatersudbury.ca
Joe Cimino, Councillor, Ward(s): 1
joe.cimino@greatersudbury.ca
Jacques Barbeau, Councillor, Ward(s): 2
jacques.barbeau@greatersudbury.ca
Claude Berthiaume, Councillor, Ward(s): 3
claude.berthiaume@greatersudbury.ca
Evelyn Dutrisac, Councillor, Ward(s): 4
claude.berthiaume@greatersudbury.ca
Ron Dupuis, Councillor, Ward(s): 5
ron.dupuis@greatersudbury.ca
André Rivest, Councillor, Ward(s): 6
andre.rivest@greatersudbury.ca
Dave Kilgour, Councillor, Ward(s): 7
Fabio Belli, Councillor, Ward(s): 8
Doug Craig, Councillor, Ward(s): 9
doug.craig@greatersudbury.ca
Frances Caldarelli, Councillor, Ward(s): 10
frances.caldarelli@greatersudbury.ca
Terry Kett, Councillor, Ward(s): 11
Joscelyne Landry-Altmann, Councillor, Ward(s): 12
joscelyne.landry-altmann@greatersudbury.ca
Administration
Angie Hache, City Clerk, Administration
705-674-4455, Fax: 705-671-8118
angie.hache@greatersudbury.ca
Doug Nadorozny, Chief Administrative Officer, Administration
doug.nadorozny@greatersudbury.ca

Lorella M. Hayes, B.Comm., CA, Chief Financial Officer & Treasurer, Administration
lorella.hayes@greatersudbury.ca
Greg Clausen, P. Eng, General Manager, Infrastructure Services, Administration
greg.clausen@greatersudbury.ca
Bill Lautenbach, General Manager, Growth & Development, Administration
bill.lautenbach@greatersudbury.ca
Catherine Matheson, General Manager, Community Development, Administration
catherine.matheson@greatersudbury.ca
Bruno Mangiardi, Chief Information Officer, Administration
bruno.mangiardi@greatersudbury.ca
Tim P. Beadman, Chief, Emergency Services, Administration
tim.beadman@greatersudbury.ca
Marc Leduc, Fire Chief, Administration
marc.leduc@greatersudbury.ca
Nick Benkovich, Director, Water & Wastewater, Administration
nick.benkovich@greatersudbury.ca
Robert Falcioni, Director, Roads & Transportation, Administration
robert.falcioni@greatersudbury.ca
Guido Mazza, Director, Building Services, Administration
guido.mazza@greatersudbury.caa
Roger Sauvé, Director, Greater Sudbury Transit, Administration
roger.sauve@greatersudbury.ca
Kevin Shaw, Director, Engineering Services, Administration
kevin.shaw@greatersudbury.ca

Grimsby
P.O. Box 159
160 Livingston Ave.
Grimsby, ON L3M 4G3
905-945-9634
Fax: 905-945-5010
E-mail: pw-general@town.grimsby.on.ca
administration-office-general@town.grimsby.on.ca
www.town.grimsby.on.ca
Municipal Type: City
Area: 68.94 sq km
County or District: Niagara Reg. Mun.; *Population in 2006:* 23,937
Provincial Electoral District(s): Niagara West-Glanbrook
Federal Electoral District(s): Niagara West-Glanbrook
Next Election: Oct. 2014 (4 year terms)
Council
Robert N. Bentley, Mayor
905-945-2710
bbentley@grimsby.ca
Steve Berry, Aldermen, Ward(s): 1
905-945-2578
sberry@grimsby.ca
Dave Wilson, Aldermen, Ward(s): 1
905-309-0905
dwilson@grimsby.ca
Dave Kadwell, Aldermen, Ward(s): 2
905-945-8259
dkadwell@grimsby.ca
Michelle Seaborn, Aldermen, Ward(s): 2
David Finch, Aldermen, Ward(s): 3
905-945-4545
Nick Andreychuk, Aldermen, Ward(s): 3
Nick DiFlavio, Aldermen, Ward(s): 4
905-309-4133
ndiflavio@grimsby.ca
Carolyn Mullins, Aldermen, Ward(s): 4
Administration
Kathryn J. Vout, Town Clerk, Administration
905-945-9634
Gary D. Shay, Town Manager, Administration
S. Gruninger, CGA, Town Treasurer & Director, Finance, Administration
B. Atkinson, CGA, Director, Recreation, Facilities, & Culture, Administration
R. LeRoux, P.Eng., Director, Public Works, Administration
J. Schonewille, Director, Building & Enforcement, Administration
K. Vogl, Director, Planning, Administration
C.H. Halliday, Fire Chief, Administration
Brandon Wartman, Manager, EHS Compliance, Administration
905-309-2016

Guelph
City Hall
1 Carden St.
Guelph, ON N1H 3A1
519-822-1260
Fax: 519-763-1269
TTY: 519-826-9771
info@guelph.ca; communications@guelph.ca
www.guelph.ca
Municipal Type: City
Incorporated: 1879 *Area:* 86.72 sq km
County or District: Wellington; *Population in 2006:* 114,943
Provincial Electoral District(s): Guelph; Wellington-Halton Hills
Federal Electoral District(s): Guelph; Wellington-Halton Hills
Next Election: Oct. 2014 (4 year terms)
Council
Karen Farbridge, Mayor
519-837-5643, Fax: 519-822-8277
mayor@guelph.ca
Jim J. Furfaro, Councillor, Ward(s): 1
Bob Bell, Councillor, Ward(s): 1
Ian Findlay, Councillor, Ward(s): 2
Andy Van Hellemond, Councillor, Ward(s): 2
Maggie Laidlaw, Councillor, Ward(s): 3
June Hofland, Councillor, Ward(s): 3
Gloria Kovach, Councillor, Ward(s): 4
Cam G. Guthrie, Councillor, Ward(s): 4
Leanne Piper, Councillor, Ward(s): 5
Lise Burcher, Councillor, Ward(s): 5
Karl Wettstein, Councillor, Ward(s): 6
Dinnis Todd, Councillor, Ward(s): 6
Administration
L.A. Giles, City Clerk & Director, Information Services, Administration
clerks@guelph.ca
Hans Loewig, Chief Administrative Officer, Administration
519-837-5602, Fax: 519-822-8277
administration@guelph.ca
M. Neubauer, Director, Finance, Administration
finance@guelph.ca
M. Amorosi, Director, Human Resources, Administration
hr@guelph.ca
S. Armstrong, Director, Emergency Services, Administration
J. Laird, Director, Environmental Services, Administration
D. McCaughan, Director, Operations, Administration
operations@guelph.ca
A. Pappert, Director, Community Services, Administration
L.E. Payne, Director, Corporate Services & City Solicitor, Administration
J. Riddell, Director, Community Design & Development Services, Administration

Halton Hills
1 Halton Hills Dr.
Georgetown, ON L7G 5G2
905-873-2601
Fax: 905-873-2347
Toll Free Phone: 1-877-712-2205
www.haltonhills.ca
Municipal Type: City
Area: 276.26 sq km
County or District: Halton Reg. Mun.; *Population in 2006:* 55,289
Provincial Electoral District(s): Wellington-Halton Hills
Federal Electoral District(s): Wellington-Halton Hills
Next Election: Oct. 2014 (4 year terms)
Council
Rick Bonnette, Mayor
Clark A. Somerville, Regional Councillor, Ward(s): 1 & 2
Jane Fogal, Regional Councillor, Ward(s): 3 & 4
Jon Hurst, Councillor, Ward(s): 1
Mike O'Leary, Councillor, Ward(s): 1
Joan Robson, Councillor, Ward(s): 2
Bryan Lewis, Councillor, Ward(s): 2
Moya Johnson, Councillor, Ward(s): 3
David Kentner, Councillor, Ward(s): 3
Bob Inglis, Councillor, Ward(s): 4
Ann Lawlor, Councillor, Ward(s): 4
Administration
Debbie Edmonds, Town Clerk, Administration
D. Perlin, Chief Administrative Officer, Administration
Ed DeSousa, Treasurer & Director, Corporate Services, Administration
Terry Alyman, Director, Recreation & Parks, Administration

Municipal Governments / Ontario

Bruce D. MacLean, Director, Planning, Development, & Sustainability, Administration
Chris Mills, Director, Infrastructure Services & Town Engineer, Administration
D. Szybalski, Coordinator, Sustainability, Administration

Hamilton
Hamilton City Centre
P.O. Box 2040 LCD1
#220, 77 James St. North
Hamilton, ON L8R 2K3
905-546-2489
Fax: 905-546-2095
E-mail, Dev.: economicdevelopment@hamilton.ca
askCITY@hamilton.ca; communications@hamilton.ca
www.hamilton.ca
Municipal Type: City
Incorporated: 1846 *Area:* 1,117.21 sq km
Population in 2006: 504,559
Provincial Electoral District(s):
Ancaster-Dundas-Flamborough-Westdale; Hamilton Centre; Hamilton East-Stoney Creek; Hamilton Mountain; Niagara West-Glanbrook
Federal Electoral District(s): Hamilton Centre; Hamilton East-Stoney Creek; Hamilton Mountain; Niagara West-Glanbrook; Ancaster-Dundas-Flamborough-Westdale
Next Election: Oct. 2014 (4 year terms)
Note: Incorporated as a city on Jan. 1, 2001.
Council
Bob Bratina, Mayor
Brian McHattie, Councillor, Ward(s): 1
bmchattie@hamilton.ca
Jason Farr, Councillor, Ward(s): 2
Bernie Morelli, Councillor, Ward(s): 3
bmorelli@hamilton.ca
Sam Merulla, Councillor, Ward(s): 4
smerulla@hamilton.ca
Chad Collins, Councillor, Ward(s): 5
ccollins@hamilton.ca
Tom Jackson, Councillor, Ward(s): 6
tjackson@hamilton.ca
Scott Duvall, Councillor, Ward(s): 7
sduvall@hamilton.ca
Terry Whitehead, Councillor, Ward(s): 8
twhitehead@hamilton.ca
Brad Clark, Councillor, Ward(s): 9
bclark@hamilton.ca
Maria Pearson, Councillor, Ward(s): 10
mpearson@hamilton.ca
Brenda Johnson, Councillor, Ward(s): 11
Lloyd Ferguson, Councillor, Ward(s): 12
lferguson@hamilton.ca
Russ Powers, Councillor, Ward(s): 13
rpowers@hamilton.ca
Robert Pasuta, Councillor, Ward(s): 14
rpasuta@hamilton.ca
Judi Partridge, Councillor, Ward(s): 15
Administration
Rose Caterini, City Clerk, Administration
clerk@hamilton.ca
Chris Murray, City Manager, Administration
905-540-5420
Roberto Rossini, General Manager, Finance & Corporate Services, Administration
Jim Kay, General Manager, Hamilton Emergency Services, Administration
Tim McCabe, General Manager, Planning & Economic Development, Administration
Joe-Anne Priel, General Manager, Community Services, Administration
Scott Stewart, C.E.T., General Manager, Public Works, Administration

Hawkesbury
600 Higginson St.
Hawkesbury, ON K6A 1H1
613-632-0106
Fax: 613-632-2463
www.hawkesbury.ca
Municipal Type: City
Area: 9.46 sq km
County or District: Prescott & Russell; *Population in 2006:* 10,869
Provincial Electoral District(s): Glengarry-Prescott-Russell

Federal Electoral District(s): Glengarry-Prescott-Russell
Next Election: Oct. 2014 (4 year terms)
Council
Rene Berthiaume, Mayor
Michel A. Beaulne, Councillor
mbeaulne@hawkesbury.ca
André Chamaillard, Councillor
Alain Fraser, Councillor
Johanne Portelance, Councillor
Michel Thibodeau, Councillor
Marc Tourangeau, Councillor
Administration
Christine Groulx, Clerk, Administration
Normand Beaulieu, Chief Administrative Officer & Treasurer, Administration
Liette Valade, Director, Recreation & Culture, Administration
Gérald Campbell, Superintendent, Public Works, Administration
Richard Guertin, Superintendent, Water Treatment Plant, Administration
Jean-Claude Miner, Chief Building Official, Administration
Ghislain Pigeon, Fire Chief, Administration
Danielle Fredette-Thériault, Officer, Human Resources, Administration
Manon Belle-Isle, Planner, Administration

Huntsville
37 Main St. East
Huntsville, ON P1H 1A1
705-789-1751
Fax: 705-789-6689
administration@huntsville.ca
www.huntsville.ca
Municipal Type: City
Area: 703.23 sq km
County or District: Muskoka Dist. Mun.; *Population in 2006:* 18,280
Provincial Electoral District(s): Parry Sound-Muskoka
Federal Electoral District(s): Parry Sound-Muskoka
Next Election: Oct. 2014 (4 year terms)
Council
Claude Doughty, Mayor
council@huntsville.ca
Fran Coleman, District & Town Councillor
Brian Thompson, District & Town Councillor
Scott Aitchison, District & Town Councillor
Tim Withey, Councillor, Ward(s): Brunel
John Davis, Councillor, Ward(s): Chaffey
Karin Terziano, Councillor, Ward(s): Huntsville
Det Schumacher, Councillor, Ward(s): Stisted/Stephenson/Port Sydney
Chris Zanetti, Councillor, Ward(s): Stisted/Stephenson/Port Sydney
Administration
Kathleen Gilchrist, Municipal Clerk, Administration
corporateservices@huntsville.ca
Kelly Pender, Chief Administrative Officer, Administration
Dianne Leeder, Treasurer, Administration
Brian Crozier, Director, Community Services, Administration
Mike Gooch, Director, Development Services, Administration
developmentservices@huntsville.ca
Steve Hernen, Director, Protective Services, Administration
fire.chief@huntsville.ca
Steve Keeley, Director, Public Works, Administration
publicworks@huntsville.ca
Colleen MacDonald, Manager, Parks, Cemeteries & Environment, Administration
Lisa Smith, Manager, Human Resources, Administration

Ingersoll
130 Oxford St.
Ingersoll, ON N5C 2V5
519-485-0120
Fax: 519-485-3543
clerks@ingersoll.ca
www.ingersoll.ca
Municipal Type: City
Area: 12.9 sq km
County or District: Oxford; *Population in 2006:* 11,760
Provincial Electoral District(s): Oxford
Federal Electoral District(s): Oxford
Next Election: Oct. 2014 (4 year terms)
Council
Ted J. Comiskey, Mayor
mayor@ingersoll.ca

Fred Freeman, Deputy Mayor & Councillor
ffreeman@ingersoll.ca
John F. Fortner, Councillor
Gord Lesser, Councillor
glesser@ingersoll.ca
Dave McLeod, Councillor
dmcleod@ingersoll.ca
Cathy Mott, Councillor
Kristy Van Kooten-Bossence, Councillor
kvankootenbossence@ingersoll.ca
Administration
Elaine Clark, Clerk, Administration
clerks@ingersoll.ca
James Timlin, Chief Administrative Officer, Administration
jtimlin@ingersoll.ca
Gary Seitz, Treasurer & Director, Finance, Administration
Gene McLaren, Director, Engineering Services, Administration
John Phillips, Director, Public Works, Administration
Bonnie Ward, Director, Recreation, Administration
Darell Parker, Fire Chief, Administration

Innisfil
2101 Innisfil Beach Rd.
Innisfil, ON L9S 1A1
705-436-3710
Fax: 705-436-7120
www.innisfil.ca
Municipal Type: City
Incorporated: 1850 *Area:* 284.18 sq km
County or District: Simcoe; *Population in 2006:* 31,175
Provincial Electoral District(s): York Simcoe
Federal Electoral District(s): York-Simcoe; Barrie
Next Election: Oct. 2014 (4 year terms)
Council
Barb Baguley, Mayor
bbaguley@innisfil.ca
Dan Davidson, Deputy Mayor & Councillor
ddavidson@innisfil.ca
Doug Lougheed, Councillor, Ward(s): 1
dlougheed@innisfil.ca
Richard Simpson, Councillor, Ward(s): 2
rsimpson@innisfil.ca
Ken Simpson, Councillor, Ward(s): 3
ksimpson@innisfil.ca
Rod Boynton, Councillor, Ward(s): 4
rboynton@innisfil.ca
Bill Lougheed, Councillor, Ward(s): 5
blougheed@innisfil.ca
Maria Baier, Councillor, Ward(s): 6
mbaierinnisfil.ca
Lynn Dollin, Councillor, Ward(s): 7
ldollin@innisfil.ca
Administration
John D. Leach, Clerk, Administration
Lawrence Allsion, Chief Administrative Officer, Administration
Ian Goodfellow, Treasurer, Administration
Kerry Columbus, Director, Community Services, Administration
Susan Downs, Director, Corporate Services & Chief Librarian, Administration
Robert McAuley, Director, Planning & Development, Administration
Michelle Collette, Manager, Human Resources, Administration
Ross Cotton, Manager, Planning, Administration
R. Wayne Young, Manager, Operational Services, Administration
Scott Griffith, Fire Chief, Administration

Kawartha Lakes
P.O. Box 9000
26 Francis St.
Lindsay, ON K9V 5R8
705-324-9411
Fax: 705-324-1750
Toll Free Phone: 1-888-822-2225
info@city.kawarthalakes.on.ca
www.city.kawarthalakes.on.ca
Municipal Type: City
Incorporated: Jan. 1, 2001 *Area:* 3,059.47 sq km
Population in 2006: 74,561
Provincial Electoral District(s): Haliburton-Kawartha Lakes-Brock
Federal Electoral District(s): Haliburton-Kawartha Lakes-Brock
Next Election: Oct. 2014 (4 year terms)
Note: Formerly the County of Victoria.

See blue tabs following this section for Municipal Waste Management and Water & Wastewater Treatment.

Municipal Governments / Ontario

Council
Ric McGee, Mayor
rmcgee@city.kawarthalakes.on.ca
John Macklem, Councillor, Ward(s): 1
jmacklem@city.kawarthalakes.on.ca
Emmett Yeo, Councillor, Ward(s): 2
eyeo@city.kawarthalakes.on.ca
David Hodgson, Councillor, Ward(s): 3
dhodgson@city.kawarthalakes.on.ca
Glenn Campbell, Councillor, Ward(s): 4
gcampbell@city.kawarthalakes.on.ca
Stephen Strangway, Councillor, Ward(s): 5
sstrangway@city.kawarthalakes.on.ca
Doug Elmslie, Councillor, Ward(s): 6
delmslie@city.kawarthalakes.on.ca
Brian Junkin, Councillor, Ward(s): 7
bjunkin@city.kawarthalakes.on.ca
Donna Villemaire, Councillor, Ward(s): 8
dvillemaire@city.kawarthalakes.on.ca
Andy Luff, Councillor, Ward(s): 9
aluff@city.kawarthalakes.on.ca
Pat Dunn, Councillor, Ward(s): 10
pdunn@city.kawarthalakes.on.ca
Patrick O'Reilly, Councillor, Ward(s): 11
poreilly@city.kawarthalakes.on.ca
Gord James, Councillor, Ward(s): 12
gjames@city.kawarthalakes.on.ca
Pat Warren, Councillor, Ward(s): 13
pwarren@city.kawarthalakes.on.ca
Ron Ashmore, Councillor, Ward(s): 14
rashmore@city.kawarthalakes.on.ca
Gerald McGregor, Councillor, Ward(s): 15
gmcgregor@city.kawarthalakes.on.ca
Heather Stauble, Councillor, Ward(s): 16
hstauble@city.kawarthalakes.on.ca
Administration
Judy Currins, Administration
Jane Reynolds, Chief Administrative Officer, Administration
jreynolds@city.kawarthalakes.on.ca
Rudy Huisman, Director, Financial Services, Administration
rhuisman@city.kawarthalakes.on.ca
Ken Becking, Director, Public Works, Administration
kbecking@city.kawarthalakes.on.ca
Richard Danziger, Director, Development Services, Administration
rdanziger@city.kawarthalakes.on.ca
Bob Knight, Director, Health & Social Services, Administration
bknight@city.kawarthalakes.on.ca
Janice Platt, Director, Human Resources, Administration
jplatt@city.kawarthalakes.on.ca
Kevin Williams, Director, Community Services, Administration
dguilbault@city.kawarthalakes.on.ca
David Guilbault, Fire Chief, Administration
dguilbault@city.kawarthalakes.on.ca

Kingston
City Hall
216 Ontario St.
Kingston, ON K7L 2Z3
613-546-4291
Fax: 613-546-5232
TTY: 613-546-4889
contactus@cityofkingston.ca
www.cityofkingston.ca
Municipal Type: City
Incorporated: Jan. 1, 1998 *Area:* 450.39 sq km
County or District: Frontenac; *Population in 2006:* 117,207
Provincial Electoral District(s): Kingston & the Islands
Federal Electoral District(s): Kingston & the Islands
Next Election: Oct. 2014 (4 year terms)
Council
Mark Gerretsen, Mayor
Rick Downes, Councillor, Ward(s): Cataraqui District
Lisa Osanic, Councillor, Ward(s): Collins-Bayridge District
Jeff Scott, Councillor, Ward(s): Countryside District
Rob Hutchinson, Councillor, Ward(s): King's Town District
Sandy Berg, Councillor, Ward(s): Kingscourt-Strathcona District
Dorothy Hector, Councillor, Ward(s): Lakeside District
Kevin George, Councillor, Ward(s): Loyalist-Cataraqui District
Brian Reitzel, Councillor, Ward(s): Pittsburgh District
Liz Schell, Councillor, Ward(s): Portsmouth District
Bill Glover, Councillor, Ward(s): Sydenham District
Bryan Paterson, Councillor, Ward(s): Trillium District
Jim Neill, Councillor, Ward(s): Williamsville District

Administration
Carolyn Downs, City Clerk, Administration
Gerard Hunt, Chief Administrative Officer, Administration
Desiree Kennedy, Director, Financial Services, Administration
Cynthia Beach, Commissioner, Sustainability & Growth, Administration
Denis Leger, Commissioner, Corporate Services, Administration
James de Hoop, Director, Community & Family Services, Administration
Lanie Hurdle, Director, Recreation & Leisure Services, Administration
Paul MacLatchy, Director, Strategy, Environment, & Communications, Administration
Malcolm Morris, Director, Transportation, Administration
Mark Van Buren, Director, Engineering, Administration
George Wallace, Director, Planning & Development, Administration
Damon Wells, Director, Public Works, Administration
Terry Willing, Director, Building & Licensing, Administration
Harold Tulk, Fire Chief, Administration
John Cross, Manager, Emergency Services, Administration
John Giles, Manager, Solid Waste, Administration

Kingsville
2021 Division Rd. North
Kingsville, ON N9Y 2Y9
519-733-2305
Fax: 519-733-8108
www.kingsville.ca
Municipal Type: City
Incorporated: 1874 *Area:* 246.84 sq km
County or District: Essex; *Population in 2006:* 20,908
Provincial Electoral District(s): Essex
Federal Electoral District(s): Essex
Next Election: Oct. 2014 (4 year terms)
Note: Incorporated as a town in 1901. Restructuring occurred in 1999.
Council
Nelson Santos, Mayor
nsantos@kingsville.ca
Tamara Stomp, Deputy Mayor & Councillor
Ron Colasanti, Councillor
Gord Queen, Councillor
pgordonqueen@msn.com
Bob Peterson, Councillor
rpeterson9@cogeco.ca
Sandi McIntyre, Councillor
Gail Stiffler, Councillor
Administration
Linda Burling, Clerk, Administration
lburling@kingsville.ca
Dan DiGiovanni, Chief Administrative Officer, Administration
ddigiovanni@kingsville.ca
Sandra Ingratta, Director, Financial Services, Administration
singratta@kingsville.ca
Andrew Plancke, C.E.T., Director, Municipal Services, Administration
aplancke@kingsville.ca
Michael Arthur, Chief Building Official, Administration
marthur@kingsville.ca
Bob Kissner, Fire Chief, Administration
bkissner@kingsville.ca
Ron Steinwender, Manager, Public Works, Administration
rsteinwender@kingsville.ca
Dan Wood, Manager, Parks & Recreation, Administration
dwood@kingsville.ca

Kitchener
City Hall
P.O. Box 1118
200 King St. West
Kitchener, ON N2G 4G7
519-741-2286
Fax: 519-741-2705
TTY: 1-866-969-9994
info@kitchener.ca
www.kitchener.ca
Municipal Type: City
Incorporated: June 9, 1912 *Area:* 136.89 sq km
County or District: Waterloo Regional Municipality; *Population in 2006:* 204,668
Provincial Electoral District(s): Kitchener Centre; Kitchener-Waterloo; Waterloo-Wellington
Federal Electoral District(s): Kitchener Centre; Kitchener-Waterloo; Kitchener-Conestoga
Next Election: Oct. 2014 (4 year terms)
Council
Carl Zehr, Mayor
carl.zehr@kitchener.ca
Scott Davey, Councillor, Ward(s): 1
Berry Vrbanovic, Councillor, Ward(s): 2
John Gazzola, Councillor, Ward(s): 3
Yvonne Fernandes, Councillor, Ward(s): 4
Kelly Galloway, Councillor, Ward(s): 5
Paul Singh, Councillor, Ward(s): 6
Bil Ioannidis, Councillor, Ward(s): 7
Zyg Janecki, Councillor, Ward(s): 8
Frank Etherington, Councillor, Ward(s): 9
Daniel Glenn-Graham, Councillor, Ward(s): 10
Administration
Carla Ladd, Chief Administrative Officer, Administration
519-741-2350, Fax: 519-741-2705
carla.ladd@kitchener.ca
Dan Chapman, City Treasurer & General Manager, Financial Services, Administration
519-741-2357
Pauline Houston, General Manager, Community Services, Administration
519-741-2646
Troy Speck, General Manager, Corporate Services, Administration
519-741-2279
Jeff Willmer, General Manager, Development & Technical Services, Administration
Grant Murphy, Director, Engineering Services, Administration
519-741-2410
Alain Pinard, Director, Planning, Administration
519-741-2426
Mike Seiling, Director, Building, Administration
519-741-2669
Tim Beckett, Fire Chief, Administration
519-741-2495

Lakeshore
419 Notre Dame Rd.
Belle River, ON N0R 1A0
519-728-2700
Fax: 519-728-9530
mmasse@lakeshore.ca
www.lakeshore.ca
Municipal Type: City
Incorporated: 1999 *Area:* 530.32 sq km
County or District: Essex; *Population in 2006:* 33,245
Provincial Electoral District(s): Essex
Federal Electoral District(s): Essex
Next Election: Oct. 2014 (4 year terms)
Note: Amalgamation of the former Town of Belle River & the former Townships of Maidstone, Rochester, Tilbury North & Tilbury West.
Council
Tom Bain, Mayor
tbain@lakeshore.ca
Al Fazio, Deputy Mayor & Councillor
afazio@lakeshore.ca
Len Janisse, Councillor, Ward(s): 1
ljanisse@lakeshore.ca
Dave Monk, Councillor, Ward(s): 2
dmonk@lakeshore.ca
Charles W. McLean, Councillor, Ward(s): 3
cmclean@lakeshore.ca
Steven Bezaire, Councillor, Ward(s): 4
sbezaire@lakeshore.ca
Dan Diemer, Councillor, Ward(s): 5
ddiemer@lakeshore.ca
Linda McKinlay, Councillor, Ward(s): 6
lmckinlay@lakeshore.ca
Administration
Mary Masse, Clerk, Administration
Ruth Coursey, Chief Administrative Officer, Administration
Sylvia Rammelaere, Director, Finance & Performance Service, Administration
Kirk Foran, Director, Corporate Services, Administration
kforan@lakeshore.ca
Lee Holling, Director, Community & Development Services, Administration
Dan Piescic, Director, Engineering & Infrastructure Services, Administration
Chuck Chevalier, Manager, Public Works, Administration
Kim Darroch, Manager, Development Services, Administration

See blue tabs following this section for Municipal Waste Management and Water & Wastewater Treatment.

Tony DiCiocco, Manager, Engineering Services, Administration
Tony Francisco, Manager, Environmental Services, Administration
Don Williamson, Fire Chief, Administration
Maureen Lesperance, Coordinator, Planning, Administration

LaSalle
5950 Malden Rd.
Lasalle, ON N9H 1S4
519-969-7770
Fax: 519-969-4469
webmaster@town.lasalle.on.ca
www.town.lasalle.on.ca
Municipal Type: City
Incorporated: 1924 *Area:* 65.25 sq km
County or District: Essex; *Population in 2006:* 27,652
Provincial Electoral District(s): Essex
Federal Electoral District(s): Essex
Next Election: Oct. 2014 (4 year terms)
Note: Dissolved into Township of Sandwich West in 1959. Status & name change to Town of LaSalle in 1991.
Council
Ken Antaya, Mayor
mayor@town.lasalle.on.ca
Mark Carrick, Deputy Mayor & Councillor
Marc Bondy, Councillor
mbondy@town.lasalle.on.ca
Terry Burns, Councillor
tburns@town.lasalle.on.ca
Sue Desjarlais, Councillor
sdesjarl@town.lasalle.on.ca
Crystal B. Meloche, Councillor
cmeloche@town.lasalle.on.ca
Ray Renaud, Councillor
rrenaud@town.lasalle.on.ca
Administration
Brenda Andreatta, Clerk, Administration
bandreat@town.lasalle.on.ca
Kevin Miller, Chief Administrative Officer, Administration
kmiller@town.lasalle.on.ca
Joe Milicia, Treasurer, Administration
jmilicia@town.lasalle.on.ca
Larry Silani, Director, Planning & Development Services, Administration
lsilani@town.lasalle.on.ca
Robert Hayes, P. Eng, Town Engineer, Administration
rhayes@town.lasalle.on.ca

Lincoln
4800 South Service Rd.
Beamsville, ON L0R 1B1
905-563-8205
Fax: 905-563-6566
info@lincoln.ca
www.lincoln.ca
Municipal Type: City
Incorporated: Jan. 1, 1970 *Area:* 162.86 sq km
County or District: Niagara Reg. Mun.; *Population in 2006:* 21,722
Provincial Electoral District(s): Niagara West-Glanbrook
Federal Electoral District(s): Niagara West-Glanbrook
Next Election: Oct. 2014 (4 year terms)
Note: Amalgamation of the Town of Beamsville, the Township of Clinton, & part of the Township of Louth.
Council
Bill Hodgson, Mayor
bhodgson@lincoln.ca
Dianne Rintjema, Councillor, Ward(s): 1
drintjema@lincoln.ca
Robert Foster, Councillor, Ward(s): 1
rfoster@lincoln.ca
John A. Kralt, Councillor, Ward(s): 2
jkralt@lincoln.ca
John D. Pachereva, Councillor, Ward(s): 2
jdpachereva@lincoln.ca
Robert Condotta, Councillor, Ward(s): 3
rcondotta@lincoln.ca
Dave A. Thomson, Councillor, Ward(s): 3
Geoffrey Barlow, Councillor, Ward(s): 4
gbarlow@lincoln.ca
Wayne MacMillan, Councillor, Ward(s): 4
wmacmillan@lincoln.ca
Administration
William J. Kolasa, Clerk & Director, Corporate Services, Administration
wkolasa@lincoln.ca
Anne Louise Heron, Chief Administrative Officer, Administration
aheron@lincoln.ca
Robert Spadoni, Director, Finance, Administration
bspadoni@lincoln.ca
Kathleen Dale, Director, Planning & Development, Administration
kdale@lincoln.ca
Doug Kerr, Director, Public Works, Administration
dkerr@lincoln.ca
Judy Pease, Director, Community Services, Administration
jpease@lincoln.ca
Scott Blake, Fire Chief, Administration
sblake@lincoln.ca
Andrew Greenaway, Chief Building Official, Administration
agreenaway@lincoln.ca
Greg Lancaster, Manager, Facilities & Parks, Administration
glancaster@lincoln.ca

London
City Hall
P.O. Box 5035
300 Dufferin Ave.
London, ON N6A 4L9
519-661-4500
Fax: 519-661-4892
webmaster@london.ca
www.london.ca
Municipal Type: City
Incorporated: 1855 *Area:* 420.57 sq km
County or District: Middlesex; *Population in 2006:* 352,395
Provincial Electoral District(s): London-Fanshawe; Elgin-Middlesex-London; London North Centre; London West
Federal Electoral District(s): London-Fanshawe; Elgin-Middlesex-London; London North Centre; London West
Next Election: Oct. 2014 (4 year terms)
Council
Joe Fontana, Mayor, Administration
Bud Polhill, Councillor, Ward(s): 1
Bill Armstrong, Councillor, Ward(s): 2
Joe Swan, Councillor, Ward(s): 3
Stephen Orser, Councillor, Ward(s): 4
Joni Baechler, Councillor, Ward(s): 5
Nancy Ann Branscombe, Councillor, Ward(s): 6
Matt Brown, Councillor, Ward(s): 7
Paul Hubert, Councillor, Ward(s): 8
Dale Henderson, Councillor, Ward(s): 9
Paul Van Meerbergen, Councillor, Ward(s): 10
Denise Brown, Councillor, Ward(s): 11
Harold Usher, Councillor, Ward(s): 12
Judy Bryant, Councillor, Ward(s): 13
Sandy White, Councillor, Ward(s): 14
Kevin Bain, City Clerk, Administration
Jeff Fielding, Chief Administrative Officer, Administration
Mike St. Amant, City Treasurer, Administration
Victor Cote, General Manager, Finance & Corporate Services, Administration
Ross Fair, General Manager, Community Services, Administration
Patrick McNally, P.Eng., General Manager, Environmental Engineering Services, Administration
Rob Panzer, General Manager, Planning & Development, Administration
William Coxhead, Director, Parks & Recreation, Administration
Karl Drysdale, Director, Technology Services, Administration
David Leckie, Director, Roads & Transportation, Administration
Veronica McAlea Major, Director, Human Resources, Administration
Ronald Standish, Director, Wastewater & Treatment, Administration
Jay Stanford, Director, Environmental Programs & Solid Waste, Administration

Markham
Markham Civic Centre
101 Town Centre Blvd.
Markham, ON L3R 9W3
905-477-7000
Fax: 905-479-7771
Language Phone Line: 905-477-5530 (150 languages)
customerservice@markham.ca; webmaster@markham.ca
www.markham.ca
Municipal Type: City
Incorporated: Jan. 1, 1971 *Area:* 212.58 sq km
County or District: York Reg. Mun.; *Population in 2006:* 261,573
Provincial Electoral District(s): Markham-Unionville; Oak Ridges-Markham; Thornhill
Federal Electoral District(s): Markham-Unionville; Oak Ridges-Markham; Thornhill
Next Election: Oct. 2014 (4 year terms)
Council
Frank Scarpitti, Mayor
905-475-4702
Jack Heath, Deputy Mayor & Regional Councillor
905-475-4872
Jim Jones, Regional Councillor
905-479-7757
Gordon Landon, Regional Councillor
905-415-7534
Joe Li, Regional Councillor
Valerie Burke, Councillor, Ward(s): 1
905-479-7747
Howard Shore, Councillor, Ward(s): 2
Don Hamilton, Councillor, Ward(s): 3
Carolina Moretti, Councillor, Ward(s): 4
905-479-7751
Colin Campbell, Councillor, Ward(s): 5
Alan Ho, Councillor, Ward(s): 6
Logan Kanapathi, Councillor, Ward(s): 7
905-479-7748
Alex Chiu, Councillor, Ward(s): 8
Administration
Kimberly Kitteringham, Town Clerk, Administration
905-475-4729
kkitteringham@markham.ca
John Livey, Chief Administrative Officer, Administration
905-479-7755
jlivey@markham.ca
Barbara Cribbett, Treasurer
905-475-4735
bcribbett@markham.ca
Jim Baird, Commissioner, Development Services, Administration
905-475-4875
Brenda Librecz, Commissioner, Community & Fire Services, Administration
905-479-7761
Andy Taylor, Commissioner, Corporate Services, Administration
905-475-4705
Nasir Kenea, Chief Information Officer, Administration
905-475-4733
Bill Snowball, Fire Chief, Fire & Emergency Services, Administration
905-305-5982
Alan Brown, Director, Engineering, Administration
905-415-7507
Sharon Laing, Director, Human Resources, Administration
905-475-4725
Peter Loukes, Director, Operations, Administration
905-475-4894
Valerie Shuttleworth, Director, Planning & Urban Design, Administration, Fax: 905-479-7768
John C. Wright, Director, Building Standards, Administration
905-475-4712
Jerry Klaus, General Manager, Waterworks, Administration
jklaus@markham.ca
Claudia Marsales, Manager, Waste Management, Administration
cmarsales@markham.ca

Midland
575 Dominion Ave.
Midland, ON L4R 1R2
705-526-4275
Fax: 705-526-9971
TTY: 705-526-4276, ext. 2824
info@midland.ca
www.midland.ca
Municipal Type: City
Area: 29.09 sq km
County or District: Simcoe; *Population in 2006:* 16,300
Provincial Electoral District(s): Simcoe North
Federal Electoral District(s): Simcoe North
Next Election: Oct. 2014 (4 year terms)
Council
Gordon A. McKay, Mayor
Stephan M. Kramp, Deputy Mayor & Councillor
Jim Attwood, Councillor, Ward(s): 1
Patricia A. File, Councillor, Ward(s): 1
Zena Pendlebury, Councillor, Ward(s): 1
Jack H. Charlebois, Councillor, Ward(s): 2

See blue tabs following this section for Municipal Waste Management and Water & Wastewater Treatment.

Municipal Governments / Ontario

Bob Jeffery, Councillor, Ward(s): 2
Mike Ross, Councillor, Ward(s): 2
Glen M. Canning, Councillor, Ward(s): 3
Administration
Andrea Fay, Clerk, Administration
clerks@midland.ca
Ted Walker, Chief Administrative Officer, Administration
Sue Gignac, Treasurer
treasury@midland.ca
Wes Crown, Director, Planning & Development, Administration
wcrown@midland.ca; townplan@midland.ca
Doug Baker, General Manager, Public Works, & Town Engineer, Administration
engineering@midland.ca
Suzanne Beatty, Manager, Human Resources, Administration
hr@midland.ca
Kevin Foster, Fire Chief, Administration
fire@midland.ca

Milton
150 Mary St.
Milton, ON L9T 6Z5
905-878-7252
Fax: 905-878-6995
info@milton.ca
www.milton.ca
Municipal Type: City
Incorporated: 1857 *Area:* 366.61 sq km
County or District: Halton Regional Municipality; *Population in 2006:* 53,939
Provincial Electoral District(s): Halton
Federal Electoral District(s): Halton
Next Election: Oct. 2014 (4 year terms)
Council
Gordon A. Krantz, Mayor
Tony Lambert, Local & Regional Councillor, Ward(s): South
Colin Best, Local & Regional Councillor, Ward(s): North
Sharon Barkley, Councillor, Ward(s): 1
Andrew Salmons, Councillor, Ward(s): 1
Greg Nelson, Councillor, Ward(s): 2
Mike Broughton, Councillor, Ward(s): 2
Cindy Lunau, Councillor, Ward(s): 3
Jan Mowbray, Councillor, Ward(s): 3
jan@janmowbray.ca
Rick Malboeuf, Councillor, Ward(s): 4
Paul Scherer, Councillor, Ward(s): 4
Arnold Huffman, Councillor, Ward(s): 5
Michael Bugala, Councillor, Ward(s): 5
Mike Cluett, Councillor, Ward(s): 6
Maqsood A. Soomro, Councillor, Ward(s): 6
Rick Di Lorenzo, Councillor, Ward(s): 7
Paul Virdo, Councillor, Ward(s): 7
Zeeshan Hamid, Councillor, Ward(s): 8
Jefferey C. Belo, Councillor, Ward(s): 8
Administration
Troy McHarg, Clerk, Administration
townclerk@milton.ca
W.F. Mann, P.Eng., Director, Planning & Development, Administration
James G. McQueen, Director, Corporate Services, Administration
Jennifer Reynolds, Director, Community Services, Administration
Brian Elsworth, P.Eng., Fire Chief, Administration

Mississauga
Civic Centre
300 City Centre Dr.
Mississauga, ON L5B 3C1
905-896-5000
Fax: 905-615-4081
TTY: 905-896-5151
public.info@mississauga.ca
www.mississauga.ca
Municipal Type: City
Incorporated: Jan. 1, 1974 *Area:* 288.53 sq km
County or District: Peel Reg. Mun.; *Population in 2006:* 668,549
Provincial Electoral District(s): Bramalea-Gore-Malton; Mississauga-Brampton South; Mississauga-Erindale; Mississauga East-Cooksville; Mississauga South; Mississauga-Streetsville
Federal Electoral District(s): Bramalea-Gore-Malton; Mississauga-Brampton South; Mississauga-Erindale; Mississauga East-Cooksville; Mississauga South; Mississauga-Streetsville
Next Election: Oct. 2014 (4 year terms)

Council
Hazel McCallion, Mayor
Jim Tovey, Councillor, Ward(s): 1
Patricia Mullin, Councillor, Ward(s): 2
Chris Fonseca, Councillor, Ward(s): 3
Frank Dale, Councillor, Ward(s): 4
Eve Adams, Councillor, Ward(s): 5
Ron Starr, Councillor, Ward(s): 6
Nando Iannicca, Councillor, Ward(s): 7
Katie Mahoney, Councillor, Ward(s): 8
Pat Saito, Councillor, Ward(s): 9
Sue McFadden, Councillor, Ward(s): 10
George Carlson, Councillor, Ward(s): 11
Administration
Crystal Greer, City Clerk, Administration
Janice Baker, City Manager & Chief Administrative Officer, Administration
city.manager@mississauga.ca
Brenda Breault, Commissioner, Corporate Services, & Treasurer, Administration
Paul Mitcham, Commissioner, Community Services, Administration
Martin Powell, Commissioner, Transportation & Works, Administration
Ed Sajecki, Commissioner, Planning & Building, Administration
Garry W. Morden, Fire Chief, Administration

Mississippi Mills
P.O. Box 400
3131 Old Perth Rd., RR#2
Almonte, ON K0A 1A0
613-256-2064
Fax: 613-256-4887
Toll Free Phone: 1-888-779-8666
town@mississippimills.ca
www.mississippimills.ca
Municipal Type: City
Incorporated: Jan. 1, 1998 *Area:* 509.05 sq km
County or District: Lanark; *Population in 2006:* 11,734
Provincial Electoral District(s): Carleton-Mississippi Mills
Federal Electoral District(s): Carleton-Mississippi Mills
Next Election: Oct. 2014 (4 year terms)
Note: Merger of the Town of Almonte with the townships of Ramsay & Pakenham.
Council
John Levi, Mayor
Garry Dalgity, Councillor, Ward(s): Almonte
garry.dalgity@sympatico.ca
Rick Minnille, Councillor, Ward(s): Almonte
garry.dalgity@sympatico.ca
Bernard Cameron, Councillor, Ward(s): Almonte
Alex Gillis, Councillor, Ward(s): Almonte
Duncan A. Abbott, Councillor, Ward(s): Pakenham
Denzil Ferguson, Councillor, Ward(s): Pakenham
John H. Edwards, Councillor, Ward(s): Ramsay
Shaun J. McLaughlin, Councillor, Ward(s): Ramsay
Paul J. Watters, Councillor, Ward(s): Ramsay
Val Wilkinson, Councillor, Ward(s): Ramsay
Administration
Cynthia Halcrow, Town Clerk, Administration
chalcrow@mississippimills.ca
Diane Smithson, Chief Administrative Officer, Administration
dsmithson@mississippimills.ca
Rhonda Whitmarsh, Treasurer, Administration
rwhitmarsh@mississippimills.ca
Tim Kocialek, Director, Roads & Public Work, Administration
tkocialek@mississippimills.ca
Rod Cameron, Manager, Operations, Administration
rcameron@mississippimills.ca
Art Brown, Fire Chief, Administration
abrown@mississippimills.ca
Paul Lemay, Chief Building Official, Administration
plemay@mississippimills.ca

New Tecumseth
Town Administration Centre
P.O. Box 910
10 Wellington St. East
Alliston, ON L9R 1A1
705-435-6219
Fax: 705-435-2873
Alternative Phone: 905-729-0057
www.town.newtecumseth.on.ca
Municipal Type: City
Incorporated: Jan. 1991 *Area:* 274.18 sq km

County or District: Simcoe; *Population in 2006:* 27,701
Provincial Electoral District(s): Simcoe-Grey
Federal Electoral District(s): Simcoe-Grey
Next Election: Oct. 2014 (4 year terms)
Council
Mike MacEachern, Mayor
mayor@town.newtecumseth.on.ca
Rick Milne, Deputy Mayor & Councillor
deputymayor@town.newtecumseth.on.ca
Bob Marrs, Councillor, Ward(s): 1
ward.1@town.newtecumseth.on.ca
Jamie Smith, Councillor, Ward(s): 2
ward.2@town.newtecumseth.on.ca
J.J. Paul Whiteside, Councillor, Ward(s): 3
ward.3@town.newtecumseth.on.ca
Fran Sainsbury, Councillor, Ward(s): 4
ward.4@town.newtecumseth.on.ca
Donna Jebb, Councillor, Ward(s): 5
ward.5@town.newtecumseth.on.ca
Richard Norcross, Councillor, Ward(s): 6
ward.6@town.newtecumseth.on.ca
Bruce Haire, Councillor, Ward(s): 7
ward.7@town.newtecumseth.on.ca
Jim Stone, Councillor, Ward(s): 8
ward.8@town.newtecumseth.on.ca
Administration
Gayla McDonald, Clerk & Manager, Administration, Administration
Terri Caron, Chief Administrative Officer, Administration
Mark Sirr, Treasurer & Manager, Finance, Administration
Eric Chandler, Manager, Planning, Administration
Joyce Epstein, Manager, Parks, Recreation & Culture, Administration
Chad Horan, Manager, Public Works, Administration
Hilary McCormack, Manager, Human Resources, Administration
John Miller, Manager, Building Standards & Chief Building Official, Administration
Rick Vatri, Manager, Engineering, Administration
Dan Heydon, Fire Chief, Administration

Newmarket
P.O. Box 328
395 Mulock Dr.
Newmarket, ON L3Y 4X7
905-895-5193
Fax: 905-953-5100
customerservice@newmarket.ca
www.newmarket.ca
Municipal Type: City
Incorporated: 1857 *Area:* 38.08 sq km
County or District: York Regional Municipality; *Population in 2006:* 74,295
Provincial Electoral District(s): Newmarket-Aurora
Federal Electoral District(s): Newmarket-Aurora
Next Election: Oct. 2014 (4 year terms)
Note: Incorporated as a town in 1880.
Council
Tony Van Bynen, Mayor
905-898-2876, Fax: 905-953-5102
mayor@newmarket.ca
John Taylor, Regional Councillor
jtaylor@newmarket.ca
Tom Vegh, Councillor, Ward(s): 1
tomvegh@gmail.com
Dave Kerwin, Councillor, Ward(s): 2
dkerwin@newmarket.ca
Jane Twinney, Councillor, Ward(s): 3
Tom Hempen, Councillor, Ward(s): 4
Joe Sponga, Councillor, Ward(s): 5
jsponga@newmarket.ca
Maddie Di Muccio, Councillor, Ward(s): 6
Chris Emanuel, Councillor, Ward(s): 7
cemanuel@newmarket.ca
Administration
Anita Moore, Town Clerk, Administration
clerks@newmarket.ca
Robert N. Shelton, Chief Administrative Officer, Administration
Mike Mayes, Treasurer, Administration
finance@newmarket.ca
Robert Dixon, Commissioner, Corporate & Financial Services, Administration
Robert Prentice, Commissioner, Community Services, Administration
Brian Jones, Director, Public Works Services, Administration

See blue tabs following this section for Municipal Waste Management and Water & Wastewater Treatment.

Jim Koutroubis, Director, Engineering Services, Administration
engineering@newmarket.ca
Ian McDougall, Director, Recreation & Culture Services, Administration
John Molyneaux, Director, Emergency Services, & Fire Chief, Administration
Rick Nethery, BES, MCIP, RPP, Director, Planning, Administration
905-953-5321, Fax: 905-953-5140
planning@newmarket.ca
Ron Tremblay, Director, Building & Bylaws, Administration
buildings@newmarket.ca
Wanda Bennett, Manager, Corporate Communications, Administration
communications@newmarket.ca
Lynn Georgeff, Manager, Human Resources, Administration

Niagara Falls
City Hall
P.O. Box 1023
4310 Queen St.
Niagara Falls, ON L2E 6X5
905-356-7521
Fax: 905-356-9083
www.niagarafalls.ca
Municipal Type: City
Incorporated: Jan. 1, 1904 *Area:* 209.58 sq km
County or District: Niagara Reg. Mun.; *Population in 2006:* 82,184
Provincial Electoral District(s): Niagara Falls
Federal Electoral District(s): Niagara Falls
Next Election: Oct. 2014 (4 year terms)
Council
Jim Diodati, Mayor
jdiodati@niagarafalls.ca
Wayne Thomson, City Councillor
wthomson@niagarafalls.ca
Victor Pietrangelo, City Councillor
vpietrangelo@niagarafalls.ca
Carolynn Ioannoni, City Councillor
ioannoni@niagarafalls.ca
Vince A. Kerrio, City Councillor
kerrio@overlookingthefalls.com s
Wayne Gates, City Councillor
Joyce Morocco, City Councillor
Janice Wing, City Councillor
jwing@niagarafalls.ca
Bart Maves, City & Regional Councillor
Barbara Greenwood, Regional Councillor
Selina Volpatti, Regional Councillor
Administration
Dean Iorfida, City Clerk & Director, Council Services, Administration
diorfida@niagarafalls.ca
Ken Todd, Chief Administrative Officer, Administration
ktodd@niagarafalls.ca
Ken Burden, Executive Director, Corporate Services, Administration
finance@niagarafalls.ca
Edward Dujlovic, Executive Director, Community Services, Administration
Serge Felicetti, Director, Business Development, Administration
sfelicetti@niagarafalls.ca
Alex Herlovitch, Director, Planning & Development, Administration
planning@niagarafalls.ca
Geoffrey Holman, Director, Municipal Works, Administration
Denyse Morrissey, Director, Parks, Recreation, & Culture, Administration
Lee Smith, Fire Chief, Administration

Niagara-on-the-Lake
P.O. Box 100
1593 Four Mile Creek Rd.
Virgil, ON L0S 1T0
905-468-3266
Fax: 905-468-2959
hdowd@notl.org
www.notl.org
Municipal Type: City
Area: 132.83 sq km
County or District: Niagara Reg. Mun.; *Population in 2006:* 14,587
Provincial Electoral District(s): Niagara Falls
Federal Electoral District(s): Niagara Falls
Next Election: Oct. 2014 (4 year terms)
Council
David Eke, Mayor
Gary Burroughs, Regional Councillor
Dennis Dick, Councillor
Terry Flynn, Councillor
Andrea Kaiser, Councillor
Jamie R. King, Councillor
Martin Mazza, Councillor
Gary Zalepa, Jr., Councillor
Maria Bau-Coote, Councillor
Jim Collard, Councillor
Administration
Holly Dowd, Town Clerk, Administration
hdowd@notl.org
Don Smith, Chief Administrative Officer, Administration
donsmith@notl.org
Scott Tipping, CMA, Director, Corporate Services, Administration
stipping@notl.org
S. Bedford, Director, Planning & Development, Administration
Clive Buist, Director, Parks & Recreation, Administration
cbuist@notl.org
E. Kuczera, Director, Public Works, Administration
ekuczera@notl.org
Ken Eden, Fire Chief, Administration
keden@notl.org
Larry Higgins, Supervisor, Water & Sewer, Administration
lhiggins@notl.org
J. Darren MacKenzie, Superintendent, Irrigation & Drainage, Administration
dmackenzie@notl.org

North Bay
City Hall
P.O. Box 360
200 McIntyre St. East
North Bay, ON P1B 8H8
705-474-0400
Fax: 705-495-4353
Toll Free Phone: 1-800-465-1882
info@cityofnorthbay.ca
www.city.north-bay.on.ca
Municipal Type: City
Incorporated: 1925 *Area:* 314.91 sq km
County or District: Nipissing District; *Population in 2006:* 53,966
Provincial Electoral District(s): Nipissing
Federal Electoral District(s): Nipissing-Timiskaming
Next Election: Oct. 2014 (4 year terms)
Council
Al McDonald, Mayor
Mayor@cityofnorthbay.ca
Peter Chirico, Councillor
Peter.Chirico@cityofnorthbay.ca
Mike Anthony, Councillor
Mike.Anthony@cityofnorthbay.ca
Mac Bain, Councillor
Mac.Bain@cityofnorthbay.ca
Sean Lawlor, Councillor
Sean.Lawlor@cityofnorthbay.ca
George Maroosis, Councillor
George.Maroosis@cityofnorthbay.ca
Judy Koziol, Councillor
Judy.Koziol@cityofnorthbay.ca
Chris Mayne, Councillor
Chris.Mayne@cityofnorthbay.ca
Dave Mendicino, Councillor
Dave.Mendicino@cityofnorthbay.ca
Daryl Vaillancourt, Councillor
Daryl.Vaillancourt@cityofnorthbay.ca
Tanya Vrebosch Merry, Councillor
Tanya.Vrebosch-Merry@cityofnorthbay.ca
Administration
Cathy Conrad, City Clerk, Administration
cathy.conrad@cityofnorthbay.ca
Dave Linkie, Chief Administration Officer, Administration
Brian Rogers, Chief Financial Officer, Administration
brian.rogers@cityofnorthbay.ca
Michael Burke, Managing Director, Corporate Services, Administration
Jerry Knox, Managing Director, Community Services, Administration
Alan Korell, Managing Director, Engineering, Environmental & Works, Administration
David Euler, Director, Sewer & Water, Administration
Jamie Houston, Director, Parks, Recreation, & Leisure Services, Administration
Bob McGrath, Director, Human Resources, Administration
Peter Bullock, Manager, Environmental Services, Administration
Dorothea Carvell, Manager, Transit, Administration
Joe Germano, Manager, Road & Traffic, Administration
Ian Kilgour, Manager, Planning Services, Administration
Shawn Killins, Chief Building Official, Administration
Grant Love, Fire Chief, Administration

North Perth
330 Wallace Ave. North
Listowel, ON N4W 1L3
519-291-2950
Fax: 519-291-1804
Toll Free Phone: 1-888-714-1993
town@northperth.ca
www.northperth.ca
Municipal Type: City
Incorporated: 1998 *Area:* 493.18 sq km
County or District: Perth; *Population in 2006:* 12,254
Provincial Electoral District(s): Perth-Wellington
Federal Electoral District(s): Perth-Wellington
Next Election: Oct. 2014 (4 year terms)
Note: Amalgamation of Elma Township, Town of Listowel & Wallace Township.
Council
Julie Behrns, Mayor
Council
Vince Judge, Deputy Mayor & Councillor
Doug Kellum, Councillor, Ward(s): Listowel
Warren Howard, Councillor, Ward(s): Listowel
Matt Richardson, Councillor, Ward(s): Listowel
Kenneth Buchanan, Councillor, Ward(s): Elma
David Ludington, Councillor, Ward(s): Elma
Matt Duncan, Councillor, Ward(s): Elma
Meredith Schneider, Councillor, Ward(s): Wallace
Paul Horn, Councillor, Ward(s): Wallace
Administration
Patricia Berfelz, Clerk, Administration
519-292-2062
PBerfelz@northperth.ca
Frances Hale, Treasurer & Director, Finance, Administration
519-292-2045, Fax: 519-291-5611
FHale@northperth.ca
Steve Hardie, Director, Parks & Recreation, Administration
519-292-2055
SHardie@northperth.ca
Gary Pipe, Director, Public Works & Superintendent, Drainage, Administration
519-292-2066, Fax: 519-291-9643
GPipe@northperth.ca
Ed Podniewicz, Chief Building Official & Administrator, Zoning, Administration
519-292-2058
Ed@northperth.ca
Ed Smith, Fire Chief, Administration
519-292-2053
ESmith@northperth.ca

Oakville
P.O. Box 310
1225 Trafalgar Rd.
Oakville, ON L6J 5A6
905-845-6601
Fax: 905-815-2025
TTY: 905-338-4200
publicinquiry@oakville.ca; communications@oakville.ca
www.oakville.ca
Municipal Type: City
Incorporated: May 27, 1857 *Area:* 138.56 sq km
County or District: Halton Regional Municipality; *Population in 2006:* 165,613
Provincial Electoral District(s): Halton; Oakville
Federal Electoral District(s): Halton; Oakville
Next Election: Oct. 2014 (4 year terms)
Council
Rob Burton, Mayor, Fax: 905-815-2001
mayor@oakville.ca
Alan Johnston, Town & Regional Councillor, Ward(s): 1
Ralph Robinson, Town Councillor, Ward(s): 1
Cathy Duddeck, Town & Regional Councillor, Ward(s): 2
Pam Damoff, Town Councillor, Ward(s): 2
F. Keith Bird, Town & Regional Councillor, Ward(s): 3
Dave Gittings, Town Councillor, Ward(s): 3

See blue tabs following this section for Municipal Waste Management and Water & Wastewater Treatment.

Municipal Governments / Ontario

Allan Elgar, Town & Regional Councillor, Ward(s): 4
Roger Lapworth, Town Councillor, Ward(s): 4
Jeff Knoll, Town & Regional Councillor, Ward(s): 5
Marc Grant, Town Councillor, Ward(s): 5
Tom Adams, Town & Regional Councillor, Ward(s): 6
Max Khan, Town Councillor, Ward(s): 6
Administration
Cathie Best, Town Clerk, Administration
clerks@oakville.ca; cbest@oakville.ca
Ray Green, Chief Administrative Officer, Administration
rgreen@oakville.ca
Patricia Elliott-Spencer, M.B.A., CMA, Treasurer & Director, Finance, Administration
pelliott-spencer@oakville.ca; finance@oakville.ca
David Bloomer, Commissioner, Infrastructure & Transportation Services, Administration
dbloomer@oakville.ca
Jane Clohecy, Commissioner, Planning & Development Services, Administration
jclohecy@oakville.ca; planning@oakville.ca
Gord Lalonde, Commissioner, Corporate Services, Administration
glalonde@oakville.ca
Domenic Lunardo, Commissioner, Community Services, Administration
dlunardo@oakville.ca
Elizabeth Bourns, Director, Human Resources, Administration
ebourns@oakville.ca; humanresources@oakville.ca
Barry Cole, Director, Transit Services, Administration
bcole@oakville.ca; transit@oakville.ca
Daniel Cozzi, P.Eng., Director, Roads & Works Operations, Administration
dcozzi@oakville.ca
Darnell Lambert, C.E.T., Director, Engineering & Construction, Administration
dlambert@oakville.ca
Chris Mark, Director, Parks & Open Space, Administration
cmark@oakville.ca; parks@oakville.ca
Cindy Toth, Director, Environmental Policy, Administration
ctoth@oakville.ca; environment@oakville.ca
Sheldon Switzer, Director, Building Services & Chief Building Official, Administration
sswitzer@oakville.ca; building@oakville.ca
John McNeil, Manager, Forestry & Cemetery Services, Administration
jmcneil@oakville.ca; forestry@oakville.ca
Richard Boyes, Fire Chief, Administration
rboyes@oakville.ca; fire@oakville.ca

Orangeville
87 Broadway St.
Orangeville, ON L9W 1K1
519-941-0440
Fax: 519-941-9033
Toll Free Phone: 1-866-941-0440; TTY: 519-943-0782
info@orangeville.ca
www.orangeville.ca
Municipal Type: City
Incorporated: Dec. 22, 1863 *Area:* 15.57 sq km
County or District: Dufferin; *Population in 2006:* 26,925
Provincial Electoral District(s): Dufferin-Caledon
Federal Electoral District(s): Dufferin-Caledon
Next Election: Oct. 2014 (4 year terms)
Note: Incorporated as a town on Dec. 15, 1873.
Council
Rob Adams, Mayor
radams@orangeville.ca
Warren Maycock, Deputy Mayor & Councillor
Sylvia Bradley, Councillor
Gail Campbell, Councillor
Mary Rose, Councillor
Jeremy Williams, Councillor
Scott Wilson, Councillor
Administration
Cheryl Johns, Clerk, Administration
cjohns@orangeville.ca
Rick Schwarzer, Chief Administrative Officer, Administration
rschwarzer@orangeville.ca
Karen Craggs, Deputy Treasurer, Administration
kcraggs@orangeville.ca
Vern Douglas, Director, Building & By-law Enforcement, Administration
vdouglas@orangeville.ca
Sonya Pritchard, Director, Parks & Recreation, Administration
spritchard@orangeville.ca

James Stiver, Director, Planning, Administration
jstiver@orangeville.ca
Jack Tupling, Director, Public Works, Administration
jtupling@orangeville.ca
Ed Gill, Managing Director, Operations & Transportation, Administration
egill@orangeville.ca
Doug Jones, Managing Director, Environmental & Development Services, Administration
djones@orangeville.ca
Jennifer Gohn, Manager, Human Resources, Administration
jgohn@orangeville.ca
Andy Macintosh, Fire Chief, Administration
amacintosh@orangeville.ca

Orillia
Administration Office
#300, 50 Andrew St. South
Orillia, ON L3V 7T5
705-325-1311
Fax: 705-325-5178
corporate@city.orillia.on.ca
www.city.orillia.on.ca
Municipal Type: City
Incorporated: 1867 *Area:* 28.61 sq km
County or District: Simcoe; *Population in 2006:* 30,259
Provincial Electoral District(s): Simcoe North
Federal Electoral District(s): Simcoe North
Next Election: Oct. 2014 (4 year terms)
Note: Incorporated as a town in 1875 & as a city in 1969.
Council
Angelo Orsi, Mayor
mayor@city.orillia.on.ca
Patrick F. Kehoe, Councillor, Ward(s): 1
Donald W. Jenkins, Councillor, Ward(s): 1
Linda Murray, Councillor, Ward(s): 2
Pete Bowen, Councillor, Ward(s): 2
Michael Fogarty, Councillor, Ward(s): 3
Paul Spears, Councillor, Ward(s): 3
Tony Madden, Councillor, Ward(s): 4
Andrew Hill, Councillor, Ward(s): 4
Administration
Gayle Jackson, City Clerk, Administration
clerks@city.orillia.on.ca
Ian C.R. Brown, City Manager, Administration
clerks@city.orillia.on.ca
Bob Ripley, City Treasurer, Administration
treas@city.orillia.on.ca
Lori Bolton, Director, Human Resources, Administration
Peter Dance, Director, Public Works, Administration
publicworks@city.orillia.on.ca
Ray Merkley, Director, Parks & Recreation, Administration
parks@city.orillia.on.ca
Craig Metcalf, Director, Culture & Heritage, Administration
parks@city.orillia.on.ca
Ian Sugden, Director, Planning & Development, Administration
planning@city.orillia.on.ca
Ralph Dominell, Fire Chief, Administration
ord@city.orillia.on.ca
Kelly Smith, Chief Building Official, Administration
Jack Green, Manager, Transportation, Administration
Andrew Schell, Manager, Environmental Services, Administration
Percival Thomas, Manager, Water & Wastewater Systems, Administration

Oshawa
City Hall
50 Centre St. South
Oshawa, ON L1H 3Z7
905-436-3311
Fax: 905-436-5642
Toll Free Phone: 1-800-667-4292; TTY: 905-436-5627
service@oshawa.ca
www.oshawa.ca
Municipal Type: City
Incorporated: March 8, 1924 *Area:* 145.67 sq km
County or District: Durham Reg. Mun.; *Population in 2006:* 141,590
Provincial Electoral District(s): Whitby-Oshawa; Oshawa
Federal Electoral District(s): Whitby-Oshawa; Oshawa
Next Election: Oct. 2014 (4 year terms)
Council
John Henry, Mayor
John Aker, Regional Councillor

Bob Chapman, Regional Councillor
Nancy Diamond, Regional Councillor
Amy England, Regional Councillor
Tito-Dante Marimpietri, Regional Councillor
John Neal, Regional Councillor
Nester Pidwerbecki, Regional Councillor
Roger Bouma, City Councillor
Mike Nicholson, City Councillor
Bruce Wood, City Councillor
Administration
Sandra Kranc, City Clerk, Administration, Fax: 905-436-5697
Bob Duignan, City Manager, Administration
905-436-5622, Fax: 905-436-5623
oshawae@oshawa.ca
Chris Brown, Director, Finance Services, Administration, Fax: 905-436-5664
finance@oshawa.ca
Stan Bertoia, Commissioner, Community Services Department, Administration
sbertoia@oshawa.ca
Tom Hodgins, Commissioner, Development Services Department, Administration
planning@oshawa.ca
Rick Stockman, Commissioner, Corporate Services Department, Administration
rstockman@oshawa.ca
Ron Foster, Auditor General, Administration
rfoster@oshawa.ca
Tracy Adams, Director, Corporate Communications & Marketing, Administration
marketing@oshawa.ca
Jamie Bronsema, Director, Strategic & Business Services, Administration
jbronsema@oshawa.ca
Dan Carnegie, Director, Human Resource Services, Administration
humanresources@oshawa.ca
Gary Carroll, Director, Engineering Services, Administration
engineering@oshawa.ca
Mary Creighton, Director, Recreation & Culture Services, Administration
recreation@oshawa.ca
Craig Kelly, Director, Works & Transportation Services, Administration
ckelly@oshawa.ca
Mike Molinari, Director, Parks & Environmental Services, Administration
Paul Ralph, Director, Planning Services, Administration
planning@oshawa.ca
Mike Leonard, Chief Building Official, Administration
buildings@oshawa.ca
Steve Meringer, Fire Chief, Administration
fire@oshawa.ca

Ottawa
City Hall
110 Laurier Ave. West
Ottawa, ON K1P 1J1
613-580-2400
Fax: 613-560-1380
Toll Free Phone: 1-866-261-9799; or 311
info@ottawa.ca
www.ottawa.ca
Municipal Type: City
Incorporated: Jan. 1, 1855 *Area:* 2,778.13 sq km
Population in 2006: 812,129
Provincial Electoral District(s): Glengarry-Prescott-Russell; Nepean-Carleton; Ottawa Centre; Ottawa South; Ottawa-Vanier; Ottawa West-Nepean; Ottawa-Orléans; Carleton-Mississippi Mills
Federal Electoral District(s): Glengarry-Prescott-Russell; Nepean-Carleton; Ottawa Centre; Ottawa South; Ottawa-Vanier; Ottawa West-Nepean; Ottawa-Orléans; Carleton-Mississippi Mills
Next Election: Oct. 2014 (4 year terms)
Council
Jim Watson, Mayor
Bob Monette, Councillor, Ward(s): 1 - Orléans
613-580-2471
Bob.Monette@ottawa.ca
Rainer Bloess, Councillor, Ward(s): 2 - Innes
613-580-2472
Rainer.Bloess@ottawa.ca

See blue tabs following this section for Municipal Waste Management and Water & Wastewater Treatment.

Jan Harder, Councillor, Ward(s): 3 - Barrhaven
613-580-2473
Jan.Harder@ottawa.ca
Marianne Wilkinson, Councillor, Ward(s): 4 - Kanata North
613-580-2474
Marianne.Wilkinson@ottawa.ca
Eli El-Chantiry, Councillor, Ward(s): 5 - West Carleton-March
613-580-2475
Eli.El-Chantiry@ottawa.ca
Shad Qadri, Councillor, Ward(s): 6 - Stittsville-Kanata West
613-580-2476
Shad.Qadri@ottawa.ca
Mark Taylor, Councillor, Ward(s): 7 - Bay
Rick Chiarelli, Councillor, Ward(s): 8 - College
613-580-2478
Rick.Chiarelli@ottawa.ca
Keith Egli, Councillor, Ward(s): 9 - Knoxdale-Merivale
Diane Deans, Councillor, Ward(s): 10 - Gloucester-Southgate
613-580-2480
Diane.Deans@ottawa.ca
Tim Tierney, Councillor, Ward(s): 11 - Beacon Hill-Cyrville
Mathieu Fleury, Councillor, Ward(s): 12 - Rideau-Vanier
Peter Clark, Councillor, Ward(s): 13 - Rideau-Rockcliffe
Diane Holmes, Councillor, Ward(s): 14 - Somerset
613-580-2484
Diane.Holmes@ottawa.ca
Katherine Hobbs, Councillor, Ward(s): 15 - Kitchissippi
Maria McRae, Councillor, Ward(s): 16 - River
613-580-2486
Maria.Mcrae@ottawa.ca
David Chernushenko, Councillor, Ward(s): 17 - Capital
Peter Hume, Councillor, Ward(s): 18 - Alta Vista
613-580-2488
Peter.Hume@ottawa.ca
Stephen Blais, Councillor, Ward(s): 19 - Cumberland
Doug Thompson, Councillor, Ward(s): 20 - Osgoode
613-580-2490
Doug.Thompson@ottawa.ca
Scott Moffatt, Councillor, Ward(s): 21 - Rideau-Goulbourn
Steve Desroches, Councillor, Ward(s): 22 - Gloucester-South
613-580-2751
Steve.Desroches@ottawa.ca
Allan Hubley, Councillor, Ward(s): 23 - Kanata South
Administration
M. Rick O'Connor, City Clerk & Solicitor, Administration
Kent Kirkpatrick, City Manager, Administration
Marian Simulik, City Treasurer, Administration
Steve Kanellakos, Deputy City Manager, Administration
Nancy Schepers, Deputy City Manager, Administration
Chris Day, Chief, Corporate Communications, Administration
Catherine Frederick, Director, Human Resources, Administration
Donna L. Gray, Director, Organizational Development & Performance, Administration
Guy Michaud, Director, Information Technology & Chief Information Officer, Administration
Johanne Levesque, Director, Community Sustainability, Administration
Wayne Newell, Director, Infrastructure Services, Administration
Aaron Burry, General Manager, Community & Social Services, Administration
Dan Chenier, General Manager, Parks, Recreation & Cultural Service, Administration
Susan Jones, General Manager, Emergency & Protective Services, Administration
John Manconi, General Manager, Public Works, Administration
Alain Mercier, General Manager, Transit Services, Administration
John Moser, General Manager, Planning & Growth Management, Administration
Dixon A. Weir, General Manager, Environmental Services, Administration
Isra Levy, Medical Officer of Health, Administration
Michel Chevalier, Manager, Wastewater & Drainage Operations, Administration
Felice Petti, Manager, Strategic & Environmental Services, Administration
Tammy Rose, Manager, Drinking Water Services, Administration

Owen Sound
City Hall
808 - 2nd Ave. East
Owen Sound, ON N4K 2H4
519-376-1440
Fax: 519-371-0511
cityadmin@e-owensound.com;
communityservices@e-owensound.com
www.owensound.ca
Municipal Type: City
Incorporated: Jan. 1, 2001 *Area:* 24.22 sq km
County or District: Grey; *Population in 2006:* 21,753
Provincial Electoral District(s): Bruce-Grey-Owen Sound
Federal Electoral District(s): Bruce-Grey-Owen Sound
Next Election: Oct. 2014 (4 year terms)
Council
Deborah Haswell, Mayor
David Adair, Councillor
dadair@e-owensound.com
Ian C. Boddy, Councillor
Jan Chamberlain, Councillor
Peter Lemon, Councillor
plemon@e-owensound.com
Jim McManaman, Councillor
jmcmanaman@e-owensound.com
Colleen Purdon, Councillor
Bill Twaddle, Councillor
Arlene Wright, City & County Councillor
awright@e-owensound.com
Administration
Marion Koepke, C.M.O., City Clerk, Administration
mkoepke@owensound.ca
Jim Harrold, City Manager, Administration
Wayne Ritchie, CGA, Director, Financial Services, Administration
writchie@e-owensound.com
Pam Coulter, Director, Community Services, Administration
pcoulter@e-owensound.com
Glen Henry, C.M.O., Director, Corporate Services, Administration
ghenry@owensound.ca
John D. Johnston, C.E.T., Director, Operations, Administration
jdjohnson@e-owensound.com
Steve Furness, Manager, Economic Development & Tourism, Administration
business@e-owensound.com
Chris Webb, P.Eng., Manager, Engineering Services, Administration
Ed Nowak, Fire Chief, Administration
enowak@e-owensound.com

Pelham
P.O. Box 400
20 Pelham Town Sq.
Fonthill, ON L0S 1E0
905-892-2607
Fax: 905-892-5055
www.pelham.ca
Municipal Type: City
Incorporated: 1970 *Area:* 126.42 sq km
County or District: Niagara Reg. Mun.; *Population in 2006:* 16,155
Provincial Electoral District(s): Niagara West-Glanbrook
Federal Electoral District(s): Niagara West-Glanbrook
Next Election: Oct. 2014 (4 year terms)
Council
Dave Augustyn, Mayor
mayordave@pelham.ca
Larry Clark, Councillor, Ward(s): 1
Debbie Urbanowicz, Councillor, Ward(s): 1
Gary Accursi, Councillor, Ward(s): 2
Catherine King, Councillor, Ward(s): 2
John Durley, Councillor, Ward(s): 3
jjdurley@sympatico.ca
Peter Papp, Councillor, Ward(s): 3
peter.papp@sympatico.ca
Administration
Cheryl Miclette, Clerk, Administration
clerks@pelham.ca
Martin Yamich, Chief Administrative Officer, Administration
myamich@pelham.ca
Cari Pupo, Director, Financial Services, Administration
cpupo@pelham.ca
Craig Larmour, Director, Planning Services, Administration
clarmour@pelham.ca
Kelly Walsh, P.Eng., Director, Community & Infrastructure Services, Administration
kwalsh@pelham.ca
Keegan Gennings, Chief Building Official, Administration
kgennings@pelham.ca
Scott McLeod, Fire Chief, Administration
fire@pelham.ca
Alan Mannell, Manager, Engineering, Administration
amannell@pelham.ca

Pembroke
1 Pembroke St. East
Pembroke, ON K8A 3J5
613-735-6821
Fax: 613-735-3660
pembroke@pembroke.ca
www.pembroke.ca
Municipal Type: City
Incorporated: 1877 *Area:* 14.35 sq km
County or District: Renfrew; *Population in 2006:* 13,930
Provincial Electoral District(s): Renfrew-Nipissing-Pembroke
Federal Electoral District(s): Renfrew-Nipissing-Pembroke
Next Election: Oct. 2014 (4 year terms)
Note: Incorporated as a city in 1971.
Council
Ed Jacyno, Mayor
Dan Callaghan, Councillor
Ronald Gervais, Councillor
Bob Hackett, Councillor
Patricia Lafreniere, Councillor
Terry O'Neill, Councillor
Les Scott, Councillor
Gary Severin, Councillor
Colonel Towriss, Councillor
Administration
Terry Lapierre, Chief Administrative Officer, Administration
L. Eckford, Treasurer & Deputy Clerk, Administration
S. Ellis, Manager, Economic Development, Recreation, & Tourism, Administration
T. Lapierre, Manager, Human Resources, Administration
Colleen Sauriol, Manager, Planning, Building, & Parking Authority, Administration
D. Sitland, Manager, Operations, Administration
D. Herback, Fire Chief, Administration
B. Hughes, Chief Building Official, Administration
R. Conroy, Supervisor, Parks & Facilities, Administration
B. Lewis, Supervisor, Roads & Fleet, Administration
C. Mick, Supervisor, Water & Sewer, Administration

Petawawa
1111 Victoria St.
Petawawa, ON K8H 2E6
613-687-5536
Fax: 613-687-5973
tspurrell@petawawa.ca (Executive Assistant)
www.petawawa.ca
Municipal Type: City
Incorporated: July 1, 1997 *Area:* 164.68 sq km
County or District: Renfrew; *Population in 2006:* 14,651
Provincial Electoral District(s): Renfrew-Nipissing-Pembroke
Federal Electoral District(s): Renfrew-Nipissing-Pembroke
Next Election: Oct. 2014 (4 year terms)
Note: Amalgamation of Petawawa Village & Petawawa Township.
Council
Robert Sweet, Mayor
mayor@petawawa.ca
Tom Mohns, Deputy Mayor & Councillor
James Carmody, Councillor
Frank Cirella, Councillor
Treena Lemay, Councillor
tlemay@petawawa.ca
Murray Rutz, Councillor
Theresa Sabourin, Councillor
tsabourin@petawawa.ca
Administration
Mitchell Stillman, Chief Administrative Officer & Clerk, Administration
mstillman@petawawa.ca
Daniel Scissons, Treasurer & Deputy Clerk, Administration
dscissons@petawawa.ca
Richard Bechamp, Chief Building Official, Administration
rbechamp@petawawa.ca
Steve Knott, Fire Chief, Administration
sknott@petawawa.ca
Tom Renaud, Supervisor, Public Works, Administration
works@petawawa.ca
Lynn Beatty, Coordinator, Economic Development, Administration
lbeatty@petawawa.ca

See blue tabs following this section for Municipal Waste Management and Water & Wastewater Treatment.

Karen Cronier, kcronier@petawawa.ca, Technician, Planning, Administration
kcronier@petawawa.ca

Peterborough
500 George St. North
Peterborough, ON K9H 3R9
705-742-7777
Fax: 705-742-4138
E-mail, Human Resources: hr@peterborough.ca
cityptbo@peterborough.ca; clerk@peterborough.ca
www.peterborough.ca
Municipal Type: City
Incorporated: 1850 *Area:* 58.40 sq km
County or District: Peterborough; *Population in 2006:* 74,898
Provincial Electoral District(s): Peterborough
Federal Electoral District(s): Peterborough
Next Election: Oct. 2014 (4 year terms)
Council
Daryl Bennett, Mayor
mayor@peterborough.ca
Dan McWilliams, Councillor, Ward(s): 1 - Otonabee
Lesley Parnell, Councillor, Ward(s): 1 - Otonabee
Henry Clarke, Councillor, Ward(s): 2 - Monaghan
hclarke@peterborough.ca
Jack Doris, Councillor, Ward(s): 2 - Monaghan
Bill J. Juby, Councillor, Ward(s): 3 - Town
Dean Pappas, Councillor, Ward(s): 3 - Town
dpappas@peterborough.ca
Keith G. Riel, Councillor, Ward(s): 4 - Ashburnham
Len Vass, Councillor, Ward(s): 4 - Ashburnham
lvass@peterborough.ca
Andrew Beamer, Councillor, Ward(s): 5 - Northcrest
Bob Hall, Councillor, Ward(s): 5 - Northcrest
bhall@peterborough.ca
Administration
Nancy Wright-Laking, City Clerk, Administration
nwright-laking@peterborough.ca
Linda Reed, Chief Administrative Officer, Administration
cao@peterborough.ca
Brian Horton, Senior Director, Corporate Services, Administration
bhorton@peterborough.ca
Ken Doherty, Director, Community Services, Administration
kdoherty@peterborough.ca
Malcolm Hunt, Director, Planning & Development Services, Administration
mhunt@peterborough.ca
Wayne Jackson, Director, Utility Services, Administration
wjackson@peterborough.ca
Trent Gervais, Fire Chief, Administration

Pickering
1 The Esplanade
Pickering, ON L1V 6K7
905-420-2222
Fax: 905-420-0515
Toll Free Phone: 1-866-683-2760; TTY: 905-420-1739
info@cityofpickering.com; customercare@cityofpickering.com
www.cityofpickering.com
Municipal Type: City
Incorporated: 1849 *Area:* 231.59 sq km
County or District: Durham Reg. Mun.; *Population in 2006:* 87,838
Provincial Electoral District(s): Ajax-Pickering; Pickering-Scarborough East
Federal Electoral District(s): Ajax-Pickering; Pickering-Scarborough East
Next Election: Oct. 2014 (4 year terms)
Note: Incorporated as a town in 1974 & as a city in 2000.
Council
Dave Ryan, Mayor
905-420-4600, Fax: 905-420-6064
mayor@cityofpickering.com
Jennifer O'Connell, Regional Councillor, Ward(s): 1
Kevin Ashe, City Councillor, Ward(s): 1
Bill McLean, Regional Councillor, Ward(s): 2
bmclean@cityofpickering.com
Doug Dickerson, City Councillor, Ward(s): 2
ddickerson@cityofpickering.com
Peter Rodrigues, Regional Councillor, Ward(s): 3
David Pickles, City Councillor, Ward(s): 3
dpickles@cityofpickering.com

Administration
Debi Wilcox, City Clerk, Administration
dwilcox@cityofpickering.com
Thomas J. Quinn, Chief Administrative Officer, Administration
905-420-4648, Fax: 905-420-6064
cao@cityofpickering.com
Gilles A. Paterson, Treasurer & Director, Corporate Services, Administration
905-420-4634, Fax: 905-420-5313
gpaterson@cityofpickering.com
Everett Buntsma, Director, Operations & Emergency Services, Administration
905-420-4624, Fax: 905-420-4650
ebuntsma@cityofpickering.com
Neil Carroll, Director, Planning & Development, Administration
905-420-4617, Fax: 905-420-7648
ncarroll@cityofpickering.com
Thomas E. Melymuk, Director, Office of Sustainability, Administration
905-420-4625, Fax: 905-420-4610
tmelymuk@cityofpickering.com
Richard W. Holborn, Division Head, Municipal Property & Engineering Division, Administration
90-542-0463, Fax: 905-420-4650
rholborn@cityofpickering.com
Jennifer Parent, Division Head, Human Resources, Administration
905-420-4627, Fax: 905-420-4638
hr@cityofpickering.com
Stephen Reynolds, Division Head, Culture & Recreation, Administration
905-420-4620, Fax: 905-420-2596
sreynolds@cityofpickering.com
William T. Douglas, Fire Chief, Administration
905-839-9968, Fax: 905-839-6327
fire@cityofpickering.com
Tim Moore, Chief Building Official, Administration
905-420-4617, Fax: 905-420-7648
tmoore@cityofpickering.com
Andrew C. Allison, City Solicitor, Administration
905-420-4626, Fax: 905-420-3534
aallison@cityofpickering.com

Port Colborne
66 Charlotte St.
Port Colborne, ON L3K 3C8
905-835-2900
Fax: 905-834-5746
www.portcolborne.ca
Municipal Type: City
Incorporated: 1870 *Area:* 121.97 sq km
County or District: Niagara Reg. Mun.; *Population in 2006:* 18,599
Provincial Electoral District(s): Welland
Federal Electoral District(s): Welland
Next Election: Oct. 2014 (4 year terms)
Note: Incorporated as a town in 1918 & as a city in 1966.
Council
Vance Badawey, Mayor, Fax: 905-835-2969
mayor@portcolborne.ca
David Barrick, Regional Councillor
David B. Elliott, Councillor, Ward(s): 1
Bill Steele, Councillor, Ward(s): 1
905-834-4483
billsteele@portcolborne.ca
Yvon A. Doucet, Councillor, Ward(s): 2
Angie Desmarais, Councillor, Ward(s): 2
Frank M. Danch, Councillor, Ward(s): 3
Bea Kenny, Councillor, Ward(s): 3
905-834-7685
beakenny@portcolborne.ca
Ron Bodner, Councillor, Ward(s): 4
Barbara Butters, Councillor, Ward(s): 4
905-834-4005
barbarabutters@portcolborne.ca
Administration
Janet Beckett, Clerk, Administration
janetbeckett@portcolborne.ca
Robert J. Heil, Chief Administrative Officer, Administration
cao@portcolborne.ca
Dan Aquilina, Director, Planning & Development, Administration
danaquilina@portcolborne.ca
Ron Hanson, Director, Engineering & Operations, Administration
hanson@portcolborne.cane.ca

Peter Sense, Director, Community & Corporate Services, Administration
petersenese@portcolborne.ca
Stephen Thompson, General Manager, Economic Development & Tourism, Administration
stephenthompson@portcolborne.ca
Thomas Cartwright, Fire Chief, Administration
firechief@portcolborne.ca
Ernie Cronier, Chief Building Official, Administration
erniecronier@portcolborne.ca
Tammy Morden, Coordinator, Human Resources, Administration
tammymorden@portcolborne.ca
Darlene Suddard, Coordinator, Water & Waste Water Compliance, Administration
darlenesuddard@portcolborne.ca
Martha Toscher, Coordinator, Health & Safety, Administration
marthatoscher@portcolborne.ca

Quinte West
P.O. Box 490
7 Creswell Dr.
Trenton, ON K8V 5R6
613-392-2841
Fax: 613-392-0714
Toll Free Phone: 1-866-485-2841
www.city.quintewest.on.ca
Municipal Type: City
Incorporated: Jan. 1, 1998 *Area:* 493.85 sq km
County or District: Hastings; *Population in 2006:* 42,697
Provincial Electoral District(s): Northumberland-Quinte West
Federal Electoral District(s): Northumberland-Quinte West
Next Election: Oct. 2014 (4 year terms)
Note: Amalgamation of the former municipalities of Trenton, Sidney, Murray & Frankford.
Council
John R. Williams, Mayor
866-987-2694, Fax: 613-392-5608
mayor@city.quintewest.on.ca
Sally Freeman, Councillor, Ward(s): 1 - Trenton
613-965-6769
Fred Kuypers, Councillor, Ward(s): 1 - Trenton
613-392-8588
Leslie Roseblade, Councillor, Ward(s): 1 - Trenton
Bob Wannamaker, Councillor, Ward(s): 1 - Trenton
613-392-8548
Doug Whitney, Councillor, Ward(s): 1 - Trenton
613-392-4779
Terry R.F. Cassidy, Councillor, Ward(s): 2 - Sidney
613-395-2031
Ron Hamilton, Councillor, Ward(s): 2 - Sidney
613-392-5369
Don Kuntze, Councillor, Ward(s): 2 - Sidney
613-962-6122
Paul Kyte, Councillor, Ward(s): 2 - Sidney
613-967-2134
Jim Alyea, Councillor, Ward(s): 3 - Murray
613-475-1519
Jim Harrison, Councillor, Ward(s): 3 - Murray
613-392-9437
Keith Reid, Councillor, Ward(s): 4 - Frankford
613-398-7991
Administration
Gary Dyke, CAO, City Clerk, & Manager, Corporate & Economic Development Svs., Administration
David Clazie, Treasurer & Director, Finance, Administration
Chris Angelo, Director, Public Works, Administration
613-392-7151
Charlie Murphy, Director, Planning & Development Services, Administration
613-392-7151
Tim Colasante, Manager, Engineering Services, Administration
Matt Tracey, Manager, Water & Wastewater, Administration
Cheryl Vandervoort, Manager, Human Resources, Administration
Ron Wardhaugh, Chief Building Official, Administration
John Whelan, Fire Chief, Administration
613-392-6567

Richmond Hill
225 East Beaver Creek Rd.
Richmond Hill, ON L4B 3P4
905-771-8800
Fax: 905-771-2502
info@richmondhill.ca
www.richmondhill.ca

See blue tabs following this section for Municipal Waste Management and Water & Wastewater Treatment.

Municipal Type: City
Incorporated: 1873 Area: 100.89 sq km
County or District: York Reg. Mun.; Population in 2006: 162,704
Provincial Electoral District(s): Richmond Hill; Oak Ridges-Markham
Federal Electoral District(s): Richmond Hill; Oak Ridges-Markham
Next Election: Oct. 2014 (4 year terms)
Council
Dave Barrow, Mayor, Fax: 905-771-2500
officemayor@richmondhill.ca
Brenda Hogg, Regional & Local Councillor
bhogg@richmondhill.ca
Vito Spatafora, Regional & Local Councillor
vspatafora@richmondhill.ca
Greg Beros, Councillor, Ward(s): 1
gberos@richmondhill.ca
Carmine Perrelli, Councillor, Ward(s): 2
Catro Liu, Councillor, Ward(s): 3
Lynn Foster, Councillor, Ward(s): 4
lfoster@richmondhill.ca
Nick Papa, Councillor, Ward(s): 5
npapa@richmondhill.ca
Godwin Chan, Councillor, Ward(s): 6
gchan@richmondhill.ca
Administration
D. McLarty, Town Clerk, Administration
clerks@richmondhill.ca
Joan Anderton, Chief Administrative Officer, Administration
905-771-2505, Fax: 905-771-2406
janderton@richmondhill.ca; cao@richmondhill.ca
David Dexter, Treasurer & Director, Financial Services, Administration
revenue@richmondhill.ca; budget@richmondhill.ca
A. Bassios, Commissioner, Planning, Administration
planning@richmondhill.ca
Italo Brutto, Commissioner, Engineering & Public Works, Administration
905-771-8830
epw@richmondhill.ca
D. Miller, Commissioner, Corporate & Financial Services, Administration
905-771-8830
epw@richmondhill.ca
J. DeVries, Director, Building Services, & Chief Building Official, Administration
D. Joslin, Director, Recreation & Culture, Administration
K. Kwan, Director, Development, Administration

St. Catharines
City Hall
P.O. Box 3012
50 Church St.
St Catharines, ON L2R 7C2
905-688-5600
Fax: 905-682-3631
clerks@stcatharines.ca; hr@stcatharines.ca (Human Resources)
www.stcatharines.ca
Municipal Type: City
Incorporated: 1876 Area: 96.11 sq km
County or District: Niagara Reg. Mun.; Population in 2006: 131,989
Provincial Electoral District(s): St. Catharines; Welland
Federal Electoral District(s): St. Catharines; Welland
Next Election: Oct. 2014 (4 year terms)
Council
Brian McMullan, Mayor
905-688-5600
bmcmullan@stcatharines.ca
Jeff Burch, Councillor, Ward(s): 1. Merritton
905-988-3695
Jennifer Stevens, Councillor, Ward(s): 1. Merritton
905-641-5744
Matthew J. Harris, Councillor, Ward(s): 2. St. Andrew's
Joseph Kushner, Councillor, Ward(s): 2. St. Andrew's
905-685-1817
Peter Secord, Councillor, Ward(s): 3. St. Georges
905-937-0044
Greg Washuta, Councillor, Ward(s): 3. St. Georges
905-938-5123
Mark Elliott, Councillor, Ward(s): 4. St. Patricks
Mathew D. Siscoe, Councillor, Ward(s): 4. St. Patricks
Dawn Dodge, Councillor, Ward(s): 5. Grantham
905-934-9138
Bill Phillips, Councillor, Ward(s): 5. Grantham
905-937-7752
Len Stack, Councillor, Ward(s): 6. Port Dalhousie
Bruce Williamson, Councillor, Ward(s): 6. Port Dalhousie
905-934-2787
Administration
Kenneth R. Todd, City Clerk & Director, Corporate Services, Administration
ktodd@stcatharines.ca
Colin Briggs, Chief Administrative Officer, Administration
cbriggs@stcatharines.ca
Shelley Chemnitz, Director, Financial Management Services, Administration
fms@stcatharines.ca
Paul Chapman, Director, Planning Services, Administration
ps@stcatharines.ca
Richard Lane, Director, Recreation & Community Services, Administration
rcs@stcatharines.ca
Mark Mehlenbacher, Director, Fire & Emergency Management Services, Administration
Paul Mustard, Director, Transportation & Environmental Services, Administration
tes@stcatharines.ca
David Oakes, Director, Economic Development & Tourism Services, Administration
edts@stcatharines.ca
Annette Poulin, City Solicitor, Administration
Diane Garrington, Coordinator, Communications, Administration
dgarrington@stcatharines.ca

St. Thomas
City Hall
P.O. Box 520
545 Talbot St.
St Thomas, ON N5P 3V7
519-631-1680
Fax: 519-633-9019
info@city.st-thomas.on.ca
www.city.st-thomas.on.ca
Municipal Type: City
Incorporated: March 4, 1881 Area: 35.48 sq km
County or District: Elgin; Population in 2006: 36,110
Provincial Electoral District(s): Elgin-Middlesex-London
Federal Electoral District(s): Elgin-Middlesex-London
Next Election: Oct. 2014 (4 year terms)
Council
Heather Jackson-Chapman, Mayor
mayor@city.st-thomas.on.ca
Lori Baldwin-Sands, Alderman, Council
loribaldwinsands@live.com
Gord Campbell, Alderman, Council
jcampbell384@rogers.com
Mark Cosens, Alderman, Council
mark@markyourx.com
Tom Johnston, Alderman, Council
tomjohnston@execulink.com
Jeff Kohler, Alderman, Council
jkohler67@live.com
David Warden, Alderman, Council
warden_dave@hotmail.com
Sam Yusuf, Alderman, Council
sam@samyusuf.ca
Administration
Wendell Graves, City Clerk, Administration
wgraves@city.st-thomas.on.ca
Bill Day, City Treasurer, Administration
bday@city.st-thomas.on.ca
Graham Dart, Director, Human Resources, Administration
gdart@city.st-thomas.on.ca
John Dewancker, Director, Environmental Services, & City Engineer, Administration
jdewancker@city.st-thomas.on.ca
Patrick Keenan, Director, Planning, Administration
pkeenan@city.st-thomas.on.ca
Brian Clement, Manager, Engineering, Administration
bclement@city.st-thomas.on.ca
Edward Soldo, Manager, Operations & Compliance, Administration
esoldo@city.st-thomas.on.ca
Ross Tucker, Manager, Parks & Recreation, Administration
rtucker@city.st-thomas.on.ca
Bob Barber, Fire Chief, Administration
rbarber@city.st-thomas.on.ca
Jeff Jilek, Chief Building Official, Administration
jjilek@city.st-thomas.on.ca
Chuck Fiddy, Supervisor, Water & Wastewater, Administration
cfiddy@city.st-thomas.on.ca
Dave White, Supervisor, Roads & Transportation, Administration
dwhite@city.st-thomas.on.ca

Sarnia
City Hall
P.O. Box 3018
255 North Christina St.
Sarnia, ON N7T 7N2
519-332-0330
Fax: 519-332-3995
TTY: 519-332-2664
clerks@sarnia.ca; bylaws@sarnia.ca; legal@sarnia.ca
www.sarnia.ca
Municipal Type: City
Incorporated: May 7, 1914 Area: 164.63 sq km
County or District: Lambton; Population in 2006: 71,419
Provincial Electoral District(s): Sarnia-Lambton
Federal Electoral District(s): Sarnia-Lambton
Next Election: Oct. 2014 (4 year terms)
Council
Mike Bradley, Mayor
mayor@sarnia.ca
Dave Boushy, City / County Councillor
d.boushy@cogeco.ca
Jim Foubister, City / County Councillor
jimfoubister@sarnia.ca
Anne Marie Gillis, City / County Councillor
annemariegillis@sarnia.ca
Bev MacDougall, City / County Councillor
bevmacdougall@ebtech.net
Andy Bruziewicz, City Councillor
andybruziewicz@hotmail.com
Terry Burrell, City Councillor
terry@terryburrell.ca
Mike Kelch, City Councillor
mjkelch@mac.com
Jon McEachran, City Councillor
jonmceachran@hotmail.com
Administration
Brian Knott, Clerk & Solicitor, Administration
bknott@sarnia.ca
Lloyd Fennell, City Manager, Administration
lfennell@sarnia.ca
Brian McKay, Director, Finance, Administration
finance@.sarnia.ca
Kim Bresee, Director, Planning & Building, Administration
planning@sarnia.ca; buildept@sarnia.ca
Ian Smith, Director, Community Services, Administration
comserv@city.sarnia.ca
Jim Stevens, Director, Transit, Administration
transit@sarnia.ca
Peter Hungerford, Manager, Economic Development & Corporate Planning, Administration
pbh.edcp@sarnia.ca
Kathy Meade, Manager, Human Resources, Administration
hr@sarnia.ca
David Fielding, City Engineer, Administration
engineer@sarnia.ca
Doug Robertson, Superintendent, Public Works Department, Administration
Pat Cayen, Fire Chief, Fire Rescue Services, Administration
firerescue@sarnia.ca

Saugeen Shores
P.O. Box 820
600 Tomlinson Dr.
Port Elgin, ON N0H 2C0
519-832-2008
Fax: 519-832-2140
www.saugeenshores.ca
Municipal Type: City
Area: 170.58 sq km
County or District: Bruce; Population in 2006: 11,720
Provincial Electoral District(s): Huron-Bruce
Federal Electoral District(s): Huron-Bruce
Next Election: Oct. 2014 (4 year terms)
Council
Mike Smith, Mayor
mayor@town.saugeenshores.on.ca
Luke Charbonneau, Deputy Mayor & Councillor
lcharbonneau@bmts.com

Municipal Governments / Ontario

Doug Gowanlock, Vice Deputy Mayor, Councillor
beaglerun@bmts.com
Marcel Legault, Councillor, Ward(s): Port Elgin
mlegaul@bmts.comcom
Fred Schildroth, Councillor, Ward(s): Port Elgin
schildrf@bmts.com
Gary R. Brown, Councillor, Ward(s): Saugeen
cargar@bmts.com
Taun Frosst, Councillor, Ward(s): Saugeen
sunset.taun@gmail.com
Diane Huber, Councillor, Ward(s): Southampton
dianehuber@bmts.com
Thead Seaman, Councillor, Ward(s): Southampton
t.j.seaman@bmts.com
Administration
Linda White, Clerk, Administration
whitel@town.saugeenshores.on.ca
Lawrence Allison, Chief Administrative Officer, Administration
allisonl@town.saugeenshores.on.ca
Lori Sweiger, Treasurer, Administration
sweigerl@town.saugeenshores.on.ca
Dave Burnside, Director, Engineering Services, Administration
burnsided@town.saugeenshores.on.ca
Bill Jones, Director, Public Works, Administration
jonesb@town.saugeenshores.on.ca
Mike Myatt, Director, Community Services, Administration
myattm@town.saugeenshores.on.ca
Lynn Worsley, Officer, Human Resources, Administration
worsleyl@town.saugeenshores.on.ca
Jim Bell, Chief Building Official, Administration
bellj@town.saugeenshores.on.ca
Phil Eagleson, Fire Chief, Administration
shores.fire@bmts.com
Cassie Coulson, Coordinator, Water & Sewer, Administration
coulsonc@town.saugeenshores.on.ca

Sault Ste. Marie
Civic Centre
P.O. Box 580
99 Foster Dr.
Sault Ste Marie, ON P6A 5N1
705-759-2500
Fax: 705-759-2310
webmaster@cityssm.on.
www.cityssm.on.ca
Municipal Type: City
Incorporated: 1912 *Area:* 221.71 sq km
County or District: Algoma District; *Population in 2006:* 74,948
Provincial Electoral District(s): Sault Ste. Marie
Federal Electoral District(s): Sault Ste. Marie
Next Election: Oct. 2014 (4 year terms)
Council
Debbie Amaroso, Mayor
705-759-7550
damaroso@shaw.ca
Steve Butland, Councillor, Ward(s): 1
s.butland@cityssm.on.ca
Paul Christian, Councillor, Ward(s): 1
paul.christian1@shaw.ca
Terry Sheehan, Councillor, Ward(s): 2
t.sheehan@cityssm.on.ca
Susan Myers, Councillor, Ward(s): 2
s.myers@cityssm.on.ca
Pat Mick, Councillor, Ward(s): 3
p.mick@cityssm.on.ca
Brian Watkins, Councillor, Ward(s): 3
brian@aoe.ca
Lou Turco, Councillor, Ward(s): 4
l.turco@cityssm.on.ca
Rick Niro, Councillor, Ward(s): 4
rick.niro@gmail.com
Frank Fata, Councillor, Ward(s): 5
f.fata@cityssm.on.ca
Marchy Bruni, Councillor, Ward(s): 5
Marchy_Bruni@hotmail.com
Frank Manzo, Councillor, Ward(s): 6
Joe Krmpotich, Councillor, Ward(s): 6
joekrmpotich@hotmail.com
Administration
Donna P. Irving, City Clerk, Administration
705-759-5388
cityclerk@cityssm.on.ca
Joseph M. (Joe) Fratesi, B.A., LL.B., Chief Administrative Officer, Administration
705-759-5347
j.fratesi@cityssm.on.ca
William Freiburger, Treasurer & Commissioner, Finance, Administration
705-759-5349
b.freiburger@cityssm.on.ca
Nicholas J. Apostle, Commissioner, Community Services, Administration
n.apostle@cityssm.on.ca
Jerry Dolcetti, Commissioner, Engineering & Planning, Administration
j.dolcetti@cityssm.on.ca
John R. Luszka, Commissioner, Human Resources, Administration
j.luszka@cityssm.on.ca
Patrick McAuley, P.Eng., Commissioner, Public Works & Transportation, Administration
p.mcauley@cityssm.on.ca
Kim Streich-Poser, Commissioner, Social Services, Administration
k.streich-poser@cityssm.on.ca
Lorie Bottos, City Solicitor, Administration
l.bottos@cityssm.on.ca
Marcel Provenzano, Fire Chief, Administration
m.provenzano@cityssm.on.ca

Stratford
City Hall
P.O. Box 818
1 Wellington St.
Stratford, ON N5A 6W1
519-271-0250
Fax: 519-273-5041
TTY: 519-271-5241
general@city.stratford.on.ca
www.city.stratford.on.ca
Municipal Type: City
Incorporated: 1854 *Area:* 25.28 sq km
County or District: Perth; *Population in 2006:* 30,461
Provincial Electoral District(s): Perth-Wellington
Federal Electoral District(s): Perth-Wellington
Next Election: Oct. 2014 (4 year terms)
Note: Incorporated as a city in 1886.
Council
Daniel Mathieson, Mayor
519-271-2783
dmathieson@city.stratford.on.ca
Brad Beatty, Councillor
George Brown, Councillor
gbrown@city.stratford.on.ca
Tom Clifford, Councillor
tclifford@city.stratford.on.ca
Keith Culliton, Councillor
kculliton@city.stratford.on.ca
Bonnie Henderson, Councillor
bhenderson@city.stratford.on.ca
Frank Mark, Councillor
fmark@city.stratford.on.ca
Kerry McManus, Councillor
Paul Nickel, Councillor
pnickel@city.stratford.on.ca
Martin Ritsma, Councillor
Karen Smythe, Councillor
ksmythe@city.stratford.on.ca
Administration
Joan Thomson, Clerk, Administration
clerks@city.stratford.on.ca
Ronald R. Shaw, Chief Administrative Officer, Administration
cao@city.stratford.on.ca
Larry Appel, Director, Economic Development, Administration
George Bowa, Director, Engineering & Public Works, Administration
Philip Buxton, Director, Corporate Services, Administration
Barbara Dembek, Director, Building & Planning, Administration
David St. Louis, Director, Community Services, Administration
Bill Tigert, Director, Social Services, Administration
Rick Young, Fire Chief, Administration
Jeff Bannon, City Planner, Administration
Randy Mattice, Economic Development Officer, Administration

Tecumseh
917 Lesperance Rd.
Tecumseh, ON N8N 1W9
519-735-2184
Fax: 519-735-6712
www.tecumseh.ca
Municipal Type: City
Incorporated: 1921 *Area:* 94.71 sq km
County or District: Essex; *Population in 2006:* 24,224
Provincial Electoral District(s): Windsor-Tecumseh
Federal Electoral District(s): Windsor-Tecumseh
Next Election: Oct. 2014 (4 year terms)
Note: Restructuring occurred in 1999.
Council
Gary McNamara, Mayor
519-735-6654
Cheryl M. Hardcastle, Deputy Mayor & Councillor
519-817-4864
Marcel (Pat) Blais, Councillor, Ward(s): 1
519-735-2686
Rita Ossington, Councillor, Ward(s): 1
519-735-8251
Guy Dorion, Councillor, Ward(s): 2
519-735-8580
Joe Bachetti, Councillor, Ward(s): 3
519-979-3339
Tania C. Jobin, Councillor, Ward(s): 4
519-735-9286
Administration
Laura Moy, Clerk & Director, Staff Services, Administration
Luc Gagnon, Treasurer & Director, Financial Services, Administration
George De Groot, Director, Public Works & Environmental Services, Administration
Shaun Fuerth, Director, Information Technology, Administration
Brian Hillman, Director, Planning & Building Services, Administration
Ken McMullen, Director, Fire Services, Administration
Denis Berthiume, Manager, Area Water Services, Administration
Casey Colthurst, Manager, Area Parks & Horticulture, Administration
Rob Filipov, Manager, Engineering Services, Administration
Kerri Rice, Manager, Area Recreation, Administration

Thorold
Thorold City Hall
P.O. Box 1044
3540 Schmon Pkwy.
Thorold, ON L2V 4A7
905-227-6613
Fax: 905-227-5590
E-mail, Deputy City Clerk: depclerk@thorold.com
secr@thorold.com (Administrative Assistant)
www.thorold.com
Municipal Type: City
Incorporated: 1798 *Area:* 83 sq km
County or District: Niagara Reg. Mun.; *Population in 2006:* 18,224
Provincial Electoral District(s): Welland
Federal Electoral District(s): Welland
Next Election: Oct. 2014 (4 year terms)
Note: Incorporated as a village in 1850, as a town in 1875, as a new town (amalgamating the Township of Thorold & the Town of Thorold) in 1970, & as a city in 1975.
Council
Ted Luciani, Mayor
mayor@thorold.com
Henry D'Angela, Regional Councillor
Arlene Arch, Councillor
Becky Day, Councillor
Jennifer Ferry, Councillor
Mike Murphy, Councillor
Norbert Preiner, Councillor
Tim Whalen, Councillor
twhalen1@cogeco.ca
Shawn Wilson, Councillor
shawn.wilson@thorold.com
Administration
Susan M. Daniels, AMCT, City Clerk, Administration
clerk@thorold.com
John Nicol, Chief Administrative Officer, Administration
adm@thorold.com
Maria J. Mauro, Director, Finance, Administration
finance@thorold.com
Adele Arbour, Director, Planning & Building Services, Administration
aarbour@thorold.com

See blue tabs following this section for Municipal Waste Management and Water & Wastewater Treatment.

Phillip Lambert, Director, Operations, Administration
905-227-3535, Fax: 905-227-3666
pubworks@thorold.com
Jeff Menard, A.Sc.T., B.Tech, Chief Building Official, Administration
jmenard@thorold.com
Dave Akrigg, Supervisor, Parks Operations, Administration
905-227-6544, Fax: 905-227-1149

Thunder Bay
City Hall
P.O. Box 800
500 Donald St. East
Thunder Bay, ON P7C 5K4
807-625-2230
Fax: 807-623-5468
TTY: 807-625-2230
cityinfo@thunderbay.ca
www.thunderbay.ca
Municipal Type: City
Incorporated: Jan 1, 1970 *Area:* 328.48 sq km
County or District: Thunder Bay District; *Population in 2006:* 109,140
Provincial Electoral District(s): Thunder Bay-Superior North; Thunder Bay-Atikokan
Federal Electoral District(s): Thunder Bay-Rainy River; Thunder Bay-Superior North
Next Election: Oct. 2014 (4 year terms)
Council
Keith Hobbs, Mayor
Iain Angus, Councillor at Large
Ken Boshcoff, Councillor at Large
Larry Hebert, Councillor at Large
Rebecca Johnson, Councillor at Large
Aldo. V. Ruberto, Councillor at Large
Andrew Foulds, Ward Councillor, Ward(s): Current River
Trevor Giertuga, Ward Councillor, Ward(s): McIntyre
Paul Pugh, Ward Councillor, Ward(s): McKellar
Linda Rydholm, Ward Councillor, Ward(s): Neebing
Mark Bentz, Ward Councillor, Ward(s): Northwood
Brian McKinnon, Ward Councillor, Ward(s): Red River
Joe Virdiramo, Ward Councillor, Ward(s): Westfort
Administration
John S. Hannam, City Clerk, Administration
807-623-2238, Fax: 807-623-5468
jhannam@thunderbay.ca
Tim Commisso, City Manager, Administration
807-625-2224, Fax: 807-623-1164
tcommisso@thunderbay.ca
Carol Busch, C.G.A., Treasurer & General Manager, Finance, Administration
807-625-2242
cbusch@thunderbay.ca
Greg Alexander, General Manager, Community Services, Administration
807-625-2315, Fax: 807-623-3292
galexander@thunderbay.ca
Rosalie Evans, General Manager, Corporate Services & City Solicitor, Administration
807-625-2405, Fax: 807-623-2256
revans@thunderbay.ca
Alan Fydirchuk, General Manager, Facililties & Fleet, Administration
807-684-2774, Fax: 807-345-1909
afydirchuk@thunderbay.ca
Darrell Matson, General Manager, Transportation & Works, Administration
807-625-2544, Fax: 807-625-2206
dmatson@thunderbay.ca
Mark Smith, General Manager, Development Services, Administration
807-625-2544, Fax: 807-625-2206
msmith@thunderbay.ca
Norm Gale, Chief, Emergency Medical Services, Administration
807-625-3259, Fax: 807-625-2698
ngale@thunderbay.ca
John Hay, Fire Chief, Administration
jhay@thunderbay.ca
Brad Loroff, Manager, Transit, Administration
807-684-2187
bloroff@thunderbay.ca
Alan Hjorth, Manager, Human Resources, Administration
807-625-2585, Fax: 807-625-3585
ahjorth@thunderbay.ca
Karen Lewis, Manager, Corporate Communications & Strategic Initiatives, Administration

807-625-3859, Fax: 807-625-0181
klewis@thunderbay.ca
Kerri Marshall, Manager, Environment, Administration
807-625-2836, Fax: 807-625-3588
kmarshall@thunderbay.ca
Pat Mauro, Manager, Engineering, Administration
807-625-3022, Fax: 807-625-3588
pmauro@thunderbay.ca

Tillsonburg
200 Broadway St., 2nd Fl.
Tillsonburg, ON N4G 5A7
519-842-6428
Fax: 519-842-9431
dmorris@town.tillsonburg.on.ca
www.tillsonburg.ca
Municipal Type: City
Incorporated: 1872 *Area:* 22.34 sq km
County or District: Oxford; *Population in 2006:* 14,822
Provincial Electoral District(s): Oxford
Federal Electoral District(s): Oxford
Next Election: Oct. 2014 (4 year terms)
Council
John Lessif, Mayor
Mark Renaud, Deputy Mayor & Councillor
Dave Beres, Councillor
Mel Getty, Councillor
Marty Klein, Councillor
Chris (Chrissy) Rosehart, Councillor
Brian Stephenson, Councillor
Administration
David C. Morris, CAO
Steve Lund, P.Eng., Director, Operations
slund@town.tillsonburg.on.ca
Cynthia Hildebrand, Director, Community Services
childebrand@town.tillsonburg.on.ca
Bryan Drinkwater, Manager, Operations Utility
bdrinkwater@town.tillsonburg.on.ca
Peter Fung, Manager, Engineering
pfung@town.tillsonburg.on.ca
Kelly Batt, Manager, Parks & Facilities
kbatt@town.tillsonburg.on.ca
Bob Parsons, Fire Chief
519-842-2905
bparsons@town.tillsonburg.on.ca

Timmins
220 Algonquin Blvd. East
Timmins, ON P4N 1B3
705-264-1331
Fax: 705-360-2674
www.timmins.ca
Municipal Type: City
Incorporated: 1973 *Area:* 2,961.58 sq km
County or District: Cochrane District; *Population in 2006:* 42,997
Provincial Electoral District(s): Timmins-James Bay
Federal Electoral District(s): Timmins-James Bay
Next Election: Oct. 2014 (4 year terms)
Council
Thomas B. Laughren, Mayor
mayor@timmins.ca
Gary Scripnick, Councillor, Ward(s): 1
John P. Curley, Councillor, Ward(s): 2
Noella C. Rinaldo, Councillor, Ward(s): 3
Pat Bamford, Councillor, Ward(s): 4
Steven L. Black, Councillor, Ward(s): 5
Michael J.J. Doody, Councillor, Ward(s): 5
Todd Lever, Councillor, Ward(s): 5
Andrew Marks, Councillor, Ward(s): 5
Administration
R. Jack Watson, Clerk, Administration
Joe Torlone, Chief Administrative Officer, Administration
Bernie Christian, City Treasurer, Administration
Luc Duval, Director, Public Works & Engineering, Administration
Rock Foy, Director, Human Resources, Administration
Mark B Jensen, BA, MPL, MCIP, RPP, Director, Community & Development Services, Administration
David Laneville, Director, Information Technology, Administration
Mike Pintar, Fire Chief, Administration

Toronto
City Hall
100 Queen St. West
Toronto, ON M5H 2N2

Fax: 416-338-0685
In Toronto: 311; 416-392-2489; TTY: 416-338-0889
accesstoronto@toronto.ca
www.toronto.ca
Municipal Type: City
Incorporated: March 6, 1834 *Area:* 630.18 sq km
Population in 2006: 2,503,281
Provincial Electoral District(s): Beaches-East York; To.-Danforth; Davenport; Don V. East; Don V. West; Eglinton-Lawrence; Etob. Centre; Etob.-Lakeshore; Etob. North; Parkdale-High Park; St. Paul's; Scarb.-Agincourt; Scarb. Centre; Scarb. Southwest; Scarb.-Guildwood; Scarb.-Rouge River; To. Centre; Trinity-Spadina; Willowdale; York Centre; York South-Weston; York West
Federal Electoral District(s): Beaches-East York; Davenport; Don V. East; Don V. West; Eglinton-Lawrence; Etob. Centre; Etob.-Lakeshore; Etob. North; Parkdale-High Park; St. Paul's; Scarb.-Agincourt; Scarb. Centre; Scarb. Southwest; Scarb.-Guildwood; Scarb.-Rouge River; To. Centre; To.-Danforth; Trinity-Spadina; Willowdale; York Centre; York South-Weston, York West
Next Election: Oct. 2014 (4 year terms)
Note: Incorporated as a city on Jan. 1, 1998, & comprising the 6 former municipalities of: Etobicoke; North York; York; East York; Scarborough; & Old Toronto
Council
Rob Ford, Mayor
Vincent Crisanti, Councillor, Ward(s): 1 - Etobicoke North
Doug Ford, Councillor, Ward(s): 2 - Etobicoke North
Doug Holyday, Councillor, Ward(s): 3 - Etobicoke Centre
councillor_holyday@toronto.ca
Gloria Lindsay Luby, Councillor, Ward(s): 4 - Etobicoke Centre
councillor_lindsay_luby@toronto.ca
Peter Milczyn, Councillor, Ward(s): 5 - Etobicoke-Lakeshore
councillor_milczyn@toronto.ca
Mark Grimes, Councillor, Ward(s): 6 - Etobicoke-Lakeshore
councillor_grimes@toronto.ca
Giorgio Mammoliti, Councillor, Ward(s): 7 - York West
councillor_mammoliti@toronto.ca
Anthony Perruzza, Councillor, Ward(s): 8 - York West
councillor_perruzza@toronto.ca
Maria Augimeri, Councillor, Ward(s): 9 - York Centre
councillor_augimeri@toronto.ca
James Pasternak, Councillor, Ward(s): 10 - York Centre
Frances Nunziata, Councillor, Ward(s): 11 - York South-Weston
councillor_nunziata@toronto.ca
Frank Di Giorgio, Councillor, Ward(s): 12 - York South-Weston
councillor_digiorgio@toronto.ca
Sarah Doucette, Councillor, Ward(s): 13 - Parkdale-High Park
Gord Perks, Councillor, Ward(s): 14 - Parkdale-High Park
councillor_perks@toronto.ca
Josh Colle, Councillor, Ward(s): 15 - Eglinton-Lawrence
Karen Stintz, Councillor, Ward(s): 16 - Eglinton-Lawrence
councillor_stintz@toronto.ca
Cesar Palacio, Councillor, Ward(s): 17 - Davenport
councillor_palacio@toronto.ca
Ana Bailao, Councillor, Ward(s): 18 - Davenport
Mike Layton, Councillor, Ward(s): 19 - Trinity-Spadina
Adam Vaughan, Councillor, Ward(s): 20 - Trinity-Spadina
councillor_vaughan@toronto.ca
Joe Mihevc, Councillor, Ward(s): 21 - St. Paul's
councillor_mihevc@toronto.ca
Josh Matlow, Councillor, Ward(s): 22 - St. Paul's
John Filion, Councillor, Ward(s): 23 - Willowdale
councillor_filion@toronto.ca
David Shiner, Councillor, Ward(s): 24 - Willowdale
councillor_shiner@toronto.ca
Jaye Robinson, Councillor, Ward(s): 25 - Don Valley West
John Parker, Councillor, Ward(s): 26 - Don Valley West
councillor_parker@toronto.ca
Kristyn Wong-Tam, Councillor, Ward(s): 27 - Toronto Centre-Rosedale
Pam McConnell, Councillor, Ward(s): 28 - Toronto Centre-Rosedale
councillor_mcconnell@toronto.ca
Mary Fragedakis, Councillor, Ward(s): 29 - Toronto-Danforth
Paula Fletcher, Councillor, Ward(s): 30 - Toronto-Danforth
councillor_fletcher@toronto.ca
Janet Davis, Councillor, Ward(s): 31 - Beaches-East York
councillor_davis@toronto.ca
Mary-Margaret McMahon, Councillor, Ward(s): 32 - Beaches-East York
Shelley Carroll, Councillor, Ward(s): 33 - Don Valley East
councillor_carroll@toronto.ca

See blue tabs following this section for Municipal Waste Management and Water & Wastewater Treatment.

Municipal Governments / Ontario

Denzil Minnan-Wong, Councillor, Ward(s): 34 - Don Valley East
councillor_minnan-wong@toronto.ca
Michelle Berardinetti, Councillor, Ward(s): 35 - Scarborough Southwest
Gary Crawford, Councillor, Ward(s): 36 - Scarborough Southwest
Michael Thompson, Councillor, Ward(s): 37 - Scarborough Centre
councillor_thompson@toronto.ca
Glenn De Baeremaeker, Councillor, Ward(s): 38 - Scarborough Centre
councillor_debaeremaeker@toronto.ca
Mike Del Grande, Councillor, Ward(s): 39 - Scarborough-Agincourt
councillor_delgrande@toronto.ca
Norm Kelly, Councillor, Ward(s): 40 - Scarborough-Agincourt
councillor_kelly@toronto.ca
Chin Lee, Councillor, Ward(s): 41 - Scarborough-Rouge River
councillor_lee@toronto.ca
Raymond Cho, Councillor, Ward(s): 42 - Scarborough-Rouge River
councillor_cho@toronto.ca
Paul Ainslie, Councillor, Ward(s): 43 - Scarborough East
councillor_ainslie@toronto.ca
Ron Moeser, Councillor, Ward(s): 44 - Scarborough East
councillor_moeser@toronto.ca
Administration
Ulli S. Watkiss, City Clerk, Administration
416-392-8010, Fax: 416-392-2980
Joseph Pennachetti, City Manager, Administration
416-392-3551, Fax: 416-392-1827
Cam Weldon, Chief Financial Officer & Deputy City Manager, Administration
416-392-8773, Fax: 416-397-5236
Richard Butts, Deputy City Manager, Administration
416-338-7200, Fax: 416-392-4540
Sue Corke, Deputy City Manager, Administration
416-338-7205, Fax: 416-395-0388
Bruce L. Anderson, Executive Director, Human Resources, Administration
416-397-4112, Fax: 416-392-1524
Ann Borooah, Executive Director, Toronto Building, & Chief Building Official, Administration
416-397-4446, Fax: 416-397-4383
Jim Hart, Executive Director, Municipal Licensing & Standards, Administration
416-392-8445, Fax: 416-397-5463
Gary Wright, Executive Director, City Planning, & Chief Planner, Administration
416-392-8772, Fax: 416-392-8115
Phil Brown, General Manager, Shelter, Support, & Housing Administration, Administration
416-392-7885, Fax: 416-392-0548
Lou Di Gironimo, General Manager, Toronto Water, Administration
416-392-8200, Fax: 416-302-4540
Bruce K. Farr, General Manager, Emergency Medical Services, & EMS Chief, Administration
416-397-9240, Fax: 416-392-2115
Heather MacVicar, General Manager, Employment & Social Services, Administration
416-392-8952, Fax: 416-392-4214
Brenda Patterson, General Manager, Parks, Forestry, & Recreation, Administration
416-392-8182, Fax: 416-392-8565
parks@toronto.ca
Geoff Rathbone, General Manager, Solid Waste Management Services, Administration
416-392-4715, Fax: 416-392-4754
William (Bill) Stewart, General Manager, Fire Services & Fire Chief, Administration
416-338-9051, Fax: 416-338-9060
Gary Welsh, General Manager, Transportation Services, Administration
416-392-8431, Fax: 416-392-4455
Anna Kinastowski, City Solicitor, Administration
416-392-0080, Fax: 416-397-5624
David McKeown, Medical Officer of Health, Administration
416-338-7820, Fax: 416-392-0713

Vaughan
2141 Major Mackenzie Dr.
Vaughan, ON L6A 1T1
905-832-2281
Fax: 905-832-8535
Phone (Automated): 905-832-8585
clerks@vaughan.ca; resume@vaughan.ca (Human Resources)
www.vaughan.ca
Municipal Type: City
Incorporated: Jan. 1, 1971 *Area:* 273.58 sq km
County or District: York Regional Municipality; *Population in 2006:* 238,866
Provincial Electoral District(s): Vaughan; Thornhill
Federal Electoral District(s): Vaughan; Thornhill
Next Election: Oct. 2014 (4 year terms)
Council
Maurizio Bevilacqua, Mayor
mayor@vaughan.ca
Michael Di Biase, Regional Councillor
Gino Rosati, Regional Councillor
gino.rosati@vaughan.ca
Deb Schulte, Regional Councillor
Marilyn Iafrate, Councillor, Ward(s): 1
Tony Carella, Councillor, Ward(s): 2
tony.carella@vaughan.ca
Rosanna Defrancesca, Councillor, Ward(s): 3
Sandra Yeung Racco, Councillor, Ward(s): 4
sandra.racco@vaughan.ca
Alan Shefman, Councillor, Ward(s): 5
alan.shefman@vaughan.ca
Administration
Jeffrey A. Abrams, City Clerk, Administration
jeffrey.abrams@vaughan.ca
Michael DeAngelis, City Manager, Administration
michael.deangelis@vaughan.ca
Clayton D. Harris, Deputy City Manager & Commissioner, Finance & Corporate Services, Administration
clayton.harris@vaughan.ca
Janet Atwood-Petkovski, Commissioner, Legal & Administrative Services, Administration
janice.atwood-petkovski@vaughan.ca
Marlon Kallideen, Commissioner, Community Services, Administration
marlon.kallideen@vaughan.ca
Bill Robinson, Commissioner, Engineering & Public Works, Administration
bill.robinson@city.vaughan.on.ca
John Zipay, Commissioner, Planning, Administration
commissionerofplanning@vaughan.ca
Marjie Fraser, Director, Parks & Forestry Operations, Administration
Jack Graziosi, Director, Engineering Services, Administration
jack.graziosi@vaughan.ca
Leo Grellette, Director, Building Standards, Administration
leo.grellette@vaughan.ca
Andrew D. Pearce, Director, Development & Transportation Engineering, Administration
andrew.pearce@vaughan.ca
Mary Reali, Director, Recreation & Culture, Administration
Madeline Zito, Director, Corporate Communications, Administration
madeline.zito@vaughan.ca
Gregory R. Senay, Fire Chief, Administration
firerescue@vaughan.ca

Wasaga Beach
30 Lewis St.
Wasaga Beach, ON L9Z 1A1
705-429-3844
Fax: 705-429-6732
cao@wasagabeach.com
www.wasagabeach.com
Municipal Type: City
Incorporated: 1947 *Area:* 58.43 sq km
County or District: Simcoe; *Population in 2006:* 15,029
Provincial Electoral District(s): Simcoe-Grey
Federal Electoral District(s): Simcoe-Grey
Next Election: Oct. 2014 (4 year terms)
Note: Incorporated as a village in 1951 & as a town in 1974.
Council
Cal Patterson, Mayor
mayor@wasagabeach.com
David Foster, Deputy Mayor & Councillor
Ron Anderson, Councillor
Morley Bercovitch, Councillor
Nina Bifolchi, Councillor
Connie Gray, Councillor
Stan Wells, Councillor
Administration
Audrey Johnstone, Clerk
clerk@wasagabeach.com
James A. McIntosh, Director, Public Works
705-429-2540, Fax: 705-429-8226
publicworks@wasagabeach.com
Gerry Reinders, Manager, Parks & Facilities
705-429-0412, Fax: 705-429-0413
parksandfac@wasagabeach.com
R. Kelso, Manager, Planning & Development
planning@wasagabeach.com
B. Smith, Economic Development Officer
705-429-3847
Donald Warden, Fire Chief
705-429-5281
fire@wasagabeach.com

Waterloo
City Hall
100 Regina St. South
Waterloo, ON N2J 4A8
519-886-1550
Fax: 519-747-8760
TTY Toll Free: 1-866-786-3942
elected@waterloo.ca (Elected Officials' Office)
www.city.waterloo.on.ca
Municipal Type: City
Incorporated: January 15, 1857 *Area:* 64.1 sq km
County or District: Waterloo Regional Municipality; *Population in 2006:* 97,475
Provincial Electoral District(s): Kitchener-Waterloo
Federal Electoral District(s): Kitchener-Waterloo
Next Election: Oct. 2014 (4 year terms)
Note: Incorporated as a town in 1876 & as a city on Jan 1, 1948.
Council
Brenda Halloran, Mayor
brenda.halloran@waterloo.ca
Scott Witmer, Councillor, Ward(s): 1
scott.witmer@waterloo.ca
Karen Scian, Councillor, Ward(s): 2
karen.scian@waterloo.ca
Angela Veith, Councillor, Ward(s): 3
angela.vieth@waterloo.ca
Diane Freeman, Councillor, Ward(s): 4
diane.freeman@waterloo.ca
Mark Whaley, Councillor, Ward(s): 5
mark.whaley@waterloo.ca
Jeff Henry, Councillor, Ward(s): 6
Melissa Durrell, Councillor, Ward(s): 7
Administration
Susan Greatrix, City Clerk, Administration
519-747-8705, Fax: 519-747-8510
Simon Farbrother, Chief Administrative Officer, Administration
519-747-8702, Fax: 519-747-8500
Bob Mavin, Chief Financial Officer, Administration
519-747-8722, Fax: 519-747-8541
David Calder, General Manager, Corporate Services, Administration
519-747-8542, Fax: 519-747-8553
Cameron Rapp, General Manager, Development Services, Administration
519-747-8763, Fax: 519-747-8523
David Smith, General Manager, Recreation & Leisure Services, Administration
519-747-8739, Fax: 519-747-8754
Mark Dykstra, Director, Environment & Parks Services, Administration
519-747-8611, Fax: 519-886-5788
Bill Garibaldi, Director, Water Services, Administration
519-747-8605, Fax: 519-886-5788
Phil Hewitson, Director, Transportation, Administration
519-747-8630, Fax: 519-886-5788
Patti McKague, Director, Corporate Communications, Administration
519-747-8748, Fax: 519-747-8646
Murray Kieswetter, Manager, Parks Operations, Administration
519-747-8607, Fax: 519-886-5788
Mary Thorpe, Manager, Human Resources, Administration
John DeHooge, Fire Chief, Administration

Welland
60 East Main St.
Welland, ON L3B 3X4
905-735-1700
Fax: 905-732-1919

See blue tabs following this section for Municipal Waste Management and Water & Wastewater Treatment.

E-mail, Bylaw Enforcement: bylaw_enforc@welland.ca
christine.mintoff@welland.ca (Communications Assistant)
www.welland.ca
Municipal Type: City
Incorporated: July 24, 1858 Area: 81.09 sq km
County or District: Niagara Regional Municipality; Population in 2006: 50,331
Provincial Electoral District(s): Welland
Federal Electoral District(s): Welland
Next Election: Oct. 2014 (4 year terms)
Note: Incorporated as a town on Jan. 1, 1878 & as a city on July 1, 1917.
Council
Barry Sharpe, Mayor
mayor@welland.ca
Mark Carl, Councillor, Ward(s): 1
Mary Ann Grimaldi, Councillor, Ward(s): 1
Frank Campion, Councillor, Ward(s): 2
David McLeod, Councillor, Ward(s): 2
Dan Fortier, Councillor, Ward(s): 3
Paul Grenier, Councillor, Ward(s): 3
Pat Chiocchio, Councillor, Ward(s): 4
Tony Dimarco, Councillor, Ward(s): 4
Rocky G. Létourneau, Councillor, Ward(s): 5
Michael Petrachenko, Councillor, Ward(s): 5
Jim Larouche, Councillor, Ward(s): 6
Bob Wright, Councillor, Ward(s): 6
Administration
Barbara Gallaccio, City Clerk, Administration
clerk@welland.ca
Craig A. Stirtzinger, City Manager, Administration
craig.stirtzinger@welland.ca
Bruno Silvestri, Treasurer & General Manager, Financial & Corporate Services, Administration
bruno.silvestri@welland.ca
Bill Fenwick, General Manager, Parks, Facilities, & Leisure Services, Administration
bill.fenwick@welland.ca
Sal Iannello, General Manager, Engineering, Public Works, & Transportation Svs., Administration
sal.iannello@welland.ca
Rosanne Mantesso, General Manager, Human Resources, Administration
rosanne.mantesso@welland.ca
Donald Thorpe, General Manager, Planning & Development Services, Administration
don.thorpe@welland.ca
Dan Degazio, Manager, Economic Development, Administration
Mike Mantessp, Chief Building Official, Administration
mike.mantesso@welland.ca
Denys Prevost, Fire Chief, Administration
denys.prevost@welland.ca

Whitby
575 Rossland Rd. East
Whitby, ON L1N 2M8
905-668-5803
Fax: 905-686-7005
TTY: 905-430-1942
info@whitby.ca
www.whitby.ca
Municipal Type: City
Incorporated: 1855 Area: 146.52 sq km
County or District: Durham Reg. Mun.; Population in 2006: 111,184
Provincial Electoral District(s): Whitby-Oshawa
Federal Electoral District(s): Whitby-Oshawa
Next Election: Oct. 2014 (4 year terms)
Council
Pat Perkins, Mayor
council@whitby.ca
Tracy Hanson, Councillor, Ward(s): 1 - North
Elizabeth Roy, Councillor, Ward(s): 2 - West
Michael G. Emm, Councillor, Ward(s): 3 - Centre
Ken Montague, Councillor, Ward(s): 4 - East
Lorne Earl Coe, Regional Councillor
Joe Drumm, Regional Councillor
Don Mitchell, Regional Councillor
Administration
Paul Jones, Town Clerk
clerks@whitby.ca
K.R. Nix, Acting CAO, Treasurer & Director, Corporate Services
Robert B. Short, Director, Planning
planning@whitby.ca

Peter LeBel, Director, Community & Marketing Services
ecdev@whitby.ca
Suzanne Beale, Acting Director, Public Works
engineering@whitby.ca
Jennifer Morrison, Manager, Economic Development
905-655-4571
ecdev@whitby.ca
C. Collier, Manager, Human Resources
hr@whitby.ca
Steve Edwards, Manager, Parks, Marina, Long Range Planning, Special Events & Tourism
K.W. MacKarl, Fire Chief
905-668-3312
fire@whitby.ca

Whitchurch-Stouffville
37 Sandiford Dr., 4th Fl.
Stouffville, ON L4A 7X5
905-640-1900
Fax: 905-640-7957
michele.kennedy@townofws.com
www.townofws.com
Municipal Type: City
Incorporated: 1877 Area: 206.74 sq km
County or District: York Reg. Mun.; Population in 2006: 24,390
Provincial Electoral District(s): Oak Ridges-Markham
Federal Electoral District(s): Oak Ridges-Markham
Next Election: Oct. 2014 (4 year terms)
Note: Incorporated as a town in 1971, with the amalgamation of Whitchurch Township & the Village of Stouffville.
Council
Wayne Emmerson, Mayor
Ken Ferdinands, Councillor, Ward(s): 1
Phil Bannon, Councillor, Ward(s): 2
Clyde Smith, Councillor, Ward(s): 3
Susanne Hilton, Councillor, Ward(s): 4
Richard Bartley, Councillor, Ward(s): 5
Rob Hargrave, Councillor, Ward(s): 6
Administration
Michele Kennedy, Clerk
Administration
Nick Kristoffy, Treasurer & Administrator
Tom Parry, Chief Building Official & Director, Development Services
tom.parry@townofws.com
Paul Whitehouse, Director, Public Works
paul.whitehouse@townofws.com
Rob Raycroft, Manager, Facilities & Parks
rob.raycroft@townofws.com
Denis Chartrand, Manager, Operations
denis.chartrand@townofws.com
Andrew McNeely, Manager, Planning Services
andrew.mcneely@townofws.com
Chris Powers, Fire Chief

Windsor
City Hall
P.O. Box 1607
350 City Hall Sq. West
Windsor, ON N9A 6S1
Fax: 519-255-6868
Phone: 311; Toll Free Phone: 1-877-746-4311
311@city.windsor.on.ca; hrdiv@city.windsor.on.ca (HR Dept.)
www.citywindsor.ca
Municipal Type: City
Incorporated: 1854 Area: 146.91 sq km
County or District: Essex; Population in 2006: 216,473
Provincial Electoral District(s): Windsor-Tecumseh; Windsor-West
Federal Electoral District(s): Windsor-Tecumseh; Windsor-West
Next Election: Oct. 2014 (4 year terms)
Note: Incorporated as a town in 1858 & as a city in 1892.
Council
Eddie Francis, Mayor
mayoro@city.windsor.on.ca
Drew Dilkens, Councillor, Ward(s): 1
ddilkens@city.windsor.on.ca
Ronald Jones, Councillor, Ward(s): 2
rjones@city.windsor.on.ca
Fulvio Valentinis, Councillor, Ward(s): 3
fvalentinis@city.windsor.on.ca
Alan Halberstadt, Councillor, Ward(s): 4
Ed Sleiman, Councillor, Ward(s): 5
Jo-Anne Gignac, Councillor, Ward(s): 6
Percy Hatfield, Councillor, Ward(s): 7

Bill (Biagio) Marra, Councillor, Ward(s): 8
Hilary Payne, Councillor, Ward(s): 9
Al Maghneih, Councillor, Ward(s): 10
Administration
Valerie Critchley, City Clerk, Administration
519-255-6868
clerks@city.windsor.on.ca
Helga Reidel, Chief Administrative Officer, Administration
519-255-6349
caodept@city.windsor.on.ca
Michael Duben, General Manager, Community & Protective Services, Administration
Dev Tyagi, General Manager, Public Works, Administration
pubwork@city.windsor.on.ca
Ronna Warsh, General Manager, Social & Health Services, Administration
socserv@city.windsor.on.ca
Thom Hunt, MCIP, RPP, City Planner, Administration
thunt@city.windsor.on.ca
Mario Sonego, P. Eng., City Engineer, Administration
engineeringdept@city.windsor.on.ca
David T. Fields, Fire Chief, Windsor Fire & Rescue Service, Administration
519-253-6573, Fax: 519-255-6832
Josette Eugeni, Manager, Transportation Planning, Administration
Bill Lacasse, Manager, Lou Romano Water Reclamation Plant, Administration
519-253-7217
Jack MacRae, Manager, Little River Pollution Control Plant, Administration
519-948-1751
Jim Yanchula, MCIP, RPP, Manager, Urban Design & Community Development, Administration
jyanchula@city.windsor.on.ca

Woodstock
City Hall
P.O. Box 1539
500 Dundas St.
Woodstock, ON N4S 7W5
519-539-1291
Fax: 519-539-7705
E-mail, Works Department: 519-539-2382, ext. 3104
aash@city.woodstock.on.ca (Assistant to Mayor & CAO)
www.city.woodstock.on.ca
Municipal Type: City
Incorporated: Jan. 1, 1851 Area: 43.79 sq km
County or District: Oxford; Population in 2006: 35,480
Provincial Electoral District(s): Oxford
Federal Electoral District(s): Oxford
Next Election: Oct. 2014 (4 year terms)
Note: Incorporated as a city on July 1, 1901.
Council
Pat Sobeski, Mayor
mayor@city.woodstock.on.ca
Deb A. Tait, City / County Councillor
519-421-7449
dtait@city.woodstock.on.ca
Sandra J. Talbot, City / County Councillor
519-788-0639
stalbot@city.woodstock.on.ca
Bill M. Bes, City Councillor
Ron Fraser, City Councillor
Jim Northcott, City Councillor
519-539-3698
jnorthcott@city.woodstock.on.ca
Paul D. Plant, City Councillor
Administration
Louise Gartshore, City Clerk, Administration
lgartshore@city.woodstock.on.ca
Paul Bryan-Pulham, Chief Administrative Officer, Administration
pbryan-pulham@city.woodstock.on.ca
Patrice Hilderley, Treasurer, Administration
philderley@city.woodstock.on.ca
Len Magyar, Commissioner, Development, Administration
lmagyar@city.woodstock.on.ca
Bob McFarland, Director, Community Services, Administration
bmcfarland@city.woodstock.on.ca
David Creery, City Engineer, Administration
dcreery@city.woodstock.on.ca
Harold deHaan, Engineer, Development, Administration
hdehaan@city.woodstock.on.ca
Sil Nadalin, Engineer, Design & Construction, Administration
snadalin@city.woodstock.on.ca

See blue tabs following this section for Municipal Waste Management and Water & Wastewater Treatment.

Municipal Governments / Ontario

Scott Tegler, Fire Chief, Administration
stegler@city.woodstock.on.ca
Terry Harrington, Manager, Water Department, Administration
tharrington@city.woodstock.on.ca
Tony Pihowich, Manager, Human Resources, Administration
tpihowich@city.woodstock.on.ca
Rick D'Entremont, Superintendent, Works, Administration
rdentremont@city.woodstock.on.ca
Dan Major, Supervisor, Parks, Administration
dmajor@city.woodstock.on.ca

Other Municipalities in Ontario

Adjala-Tosorontio
7855 Sideroad 30, RR#1
Alliston, ON L9R 1V1
705-434-5055
Fax: 705-434-5051
www.townshipadjtos.on.ca
Municipal Type: Township
Incorporated: Jan. 1, 1994 *Area:* 372.33 sq km
County or District: Simcoe; *Population in 2006:* 10,695
Provincial Electoral District(s): Simcoe-Grey
Federal Electoral District(s): Simcoe-Grey
Next Election: Oct. 2014 (4 year terms)
Note: Amalgamation of the former Township of Adjala & the former Township of Tosorontio.
Tom Walsh, Mayor
905-729-2132
Doug Little, Deputy Mayor & Councillor
705-435-9020
Jack Jordan, Deputy Mayor & Councillor, Ward(s): 1
519-941-6687
jack.jordan@sympatico.ca
Ray Wallace, Councillor, Ward(s): 2
905-936-3116
Mary Brett, Councillor, Ward(s): 3
519-941-5828
marysmallbrett@sympatico.ca
Joy Webster, Councillor, Ward(s): 4
705-434-0355
joywebster@sympatico.ca
Tom Cook, Councillor, Ward(s): 5
705-424-2065
tcook@drlogick.com
Barbara Kane, Clerk, Administration
bkane@townshipadjtos.on.ca
Dorthy Bulman, Treasurer & Deputy Clerk, Administration
dbulman@townshipadjtos.on.ca
Gerry Caterer, Director, Planning, Administration
gcaterer@townshipadjtos.on.ca
Eric Wargel, Director, Public Works & Deputy CAO, Administration
ewargel@townshipadjtos.on.ca

Alnwick-Haldimand
P.O. Box 70
10836 County Rd. No. 2
Grafton, ON K0K 2G0
905-349-2822
Fax: 905-349-3259
Phone, Roseneath Satellite Office: 905-352-3949
alnhald@eagle.ca
www.alnwickhaldimand.ca
Municipal Type: Township
Area: 398.08 sq km
County or District: Northumberland; *Population in 2006:* 6,435
Provincial Electoral District(s): Northumberland-Quinte West
Federal Electoral District(s): Northumberland-Quinte West
Next Election: Oct. 2014 (4 year terms)
Dalton McDonald, Mayor
905-349-2747
Terrence Korotki, B.A., A.M.C.T., Administrator-Clerk & Coordinator, Planning

Brock
P.O. Box 10
1 Cameron St. East
Cannington, ON L0E 1E0
705-432-2355
Fax: 705-432-3487
Toll Free Phone: 1-866-223-7668
brock@townshipofbrock.ca
www.townshipofbrock.ca
Municipal Type: Township
Incorporated: 1973 *Area:* 423.31 sq km
County or District: Durham Reg. Mun.; *Population in 2006:* 11,979
Provincial Electoral District(s): Haliburton-Kawartha Lakes-Brock
Federal Electoral District(s): Haliburton-Kawartha Lakes-Brock
Next Election: Oct. 2014 (4 year terms)
Larry O'Connor, Mayor
loconnor@townshipofbrock.ca
John Grant, Regional Councillor
Mike Manchester, Councillor, Ward(s): 1
Randy Skinner, Councillor, Ward(s): 2
Anthony Woodruff, Councillor, Ward(s): 3
David Marquis, Councillor, Ward(s): 4
W.E. Ted Ted Smith, Councillor, Ward(s): 5
Thomas G. Gettinby, MA, MCIP, RPP, CMO, Municipal Clerk, Administration
tgettinby@townshipofbrock.ca
Kathryn McCann, BAS, AMCT, Chief Administrative Officer, Administration
kmccann@townshipofbrock.ca
Michael Legge, Treasurer, Administration
mlegge@townshipofbrock.ca
Judith S. Avery, Director, Public Works, Administration
javery@townshipofbrock.ca
Joseph J. Bonura, Chief Building Offical, Administration
jbonura@townshipofbrock.ca
Rick Harrison, Chief, Fire, Administration
rharrison@townshipofbrock.ca

Central Elgin
450 Sunset Dr.
St Thomas, ON N5R 5V1
519-631-4860
Fax: 519-631-4036
dwilson@centralelgin.org
www.centralelgin.org
Municipal Type: Municipality
Area: 280.22 sq km
County or District: Elgin; *Population in 2006:* 12,723
Provincial Electoral District(s): Elgin-Middlesex-London
Federal Electoral District(s): Elgin-Middlesex-London
Next Election: Oct. 2014 (4 year terms)
Sylvia Hofhuis, Mayor
519-782-3541
shofhuis@centralelgin.org
T. Marks, Deputy Mayor & Councillor
S. Carr, Councillor
S. Marr, Councillor
S. Martyn, Councillor
R. Matthews, Councillor
G. Reu, Councillor
Donald N. Leitch, Chief Administrative Officer & Clerk, Administration
dleitch@centralelgin.org
Sharon Larmour, Treasurer & Director, Financial Services, Administration
Donald Crocker, Director, Fire & Rescue Services, Administration
Lloyd Perrin, Director, Physical Services, Administration

Centre Wellington
P.O. Box 10
1 MacDonald Sq.
Elora, ON N0B 1S0
519-846-9691
Fax: 519-846-2190
www.centrewellington.ca
Municipal Type: Township
Area: 407.33 sq km
County or District: Wellington; *Population in 2006:* 26,049
Provincial Electoral District(s): Wellington-Halton Hills
Federal Electoral District(s): Wellington-Halton Hills
Next Election: Oct. 2014 (4 year terms)
Joanne Ross-Zuj, Mayor
519-846-0213, Fax: 519-846-2825
mayor@centrewellington.ca
Shawn Watters, Councillor, Ward(s): 1
ward1@centrewellington.ca
Kirk McElwain, Councillor, Ward(s): 2
ward2@centrewellington.ca
Robert Foster, Councillor, Ward(s): 3
ward3@centrewellington.ca
Fred Morris, Councillor, Ward(s): 4
ward4@centrewellington.ca
Walt Visser, Councillor, Ward(s): 5
ward5@centrewellington.ca
Ron Hallman, Councillor, Ward(s): 6
ward6@centrewellington.ca
Marion Morris, Clerk, Administration
mmorris@centrewellington.ca
Michael K. Wood, Chief Administrative Officer, Administration
Wes Snarr, Chief Financial Officer & Treasurer, Administration
wsnarr@centrewellington.ca
Andrew Goldie, Director, Parks & Recreation, Administration
agoldie@centrewellington.ca
Brett Salmon, Director, Planning, Administration
bsalmon@centrewellington.ca
Brad Patton, Fire Chief, Administration
bpatton@centrewellington.ca
Ken Elder, Contact, Public Works, Administration
519-846-9801
kelder@centrewellington.ca

Chatham-Kent
Civic Centre
P.O. Box 640
315 King St. West
Chatham, ON N7M 5K8
519-360-1998
Fax: 519-436-3237
Toll Free Phone: 1-800-714-7497
CKinfo@chatham-kent.ca
www.chatham-kent.ca
Municipal Type: Municipality
Incorporated: Jan. 1, 1998 *Area:* 2,458.06 sq km
Population in 2006: 108,177
Provincial Electoral District(s): Chatham-Kent-Essex; Lambton-Kent-Middlesex
Federal Electoral District(s): Chatham-Kent-Essex; Lambton-Kent-Middlesex
Next Election: Oct. 2014 (4 year terms)
Note: Formerly the County of Kent.
Randy Hope, Mayor & Chief Executive Officer
519-436-3219, Fax: 519-436-3236
CKmayor@chatham-kent.ca
Bryon Fluker, Councillor, Ward(s): 1 - West Kent
Brian W. King, Councillor, Ward(s): 1 - West Kent
Karen Herman, Councillor, Ward(s): 2 - South Kent
Art Sterling, Councillor, Ward(s): 2 - South Kent
Frank Vercouteren, Councillor, Ward(s): 2 - South Kent
Jim Brown, Councillor, Ward(s): 3 - East Kent
Steve Pinsonneault, Councillor, Ward(s): 3 - East Kent
Joe Faas, Councillor, Ward(s): 4 - North Kent
Bill Weaver, Councillor, Ward(s): 4 - North Kent
Sheldon Parsons, Councillor, Ward(s): 5 - Wallaceburg
Tom McGregor, Councillor, Ward(s): 5 - Wallaceburg
Anne Gilbert, Councillor, Ward(s): 6 - Chatham
Larry Mansfield Robbins, Councillor, Ward(s): 6 - Chatham
Marjorie Crew, Councillor, Ward(s): 6 - Chatham
Don Clarke, Councillor, Ward(s): 6 - Chatham
Douglas Sulman, Councillor, Ward(s): 6 - Chatham
Steve Pickard, Councillor, Ward(s): 6 - Chatham
Elinor Mifflin, Clerk, Administration
Rob Browning, Chief Administrative Officer, Administration
Stuart Wood, CMA, Director, Financial Services & Treasurer, Administration
Lucy Brown, General Manager, Health & Family Services, Administration
lucyb@chatham-kent.ca
Leo Denys, General Manager, Infrastructure & Engineering Systems, Administration
Don Shropshire, General Manager. Community Development & Planning Services, Administration

Clarington
40 Temperance St.
Bowmanville, ON L1C 3A6
905-623-3379
Fax: 905-623-6506
Toll Free Phone: 1-800-563-1195
info@clarington.net; communications@clarington.net
www.clarington.net
Municipal Type: Municipality
Area: 611.1 sq km
County or District: Durham Reg. Mun.; *Population in 2006:* 77,820
Provincial Electoral District(s): Durham
Federal Electoral District(s): Durham
Next Election: Oct. 2014 (4 year terms)

See blue tabs following this section for Municipal Waste Management and Water & Wastewater Treatment.

Jim Abernethy, Mayor
mayor@clarington.net
Mary Novak, Regional Councillor, Ward(s): 1 & 2
mnovak@clarington.net
Charlie Trim, Regional Councillor, Ward(s): 3 & 4
ctrim@clarington.net
Adrian Foster, Local Councillor, Ward(s): 1
afoster@clarington.net
Ron Hooper, Local Councillor, Ward(s): 2
rhooper@clarington.net
Willie Woo, Local Councillor, Ward(s): 3
wwoo@clarington.net
Gord Robinson, Local Councillor, Ward(s): 4
grobinson@clarington.net
Patti L. Barrie, Municipal Clerk, Administration
pbarrie@clarington.net; clerks@clarington.net
Franklin Wu, Chief Administrative Officer, Administration
cao@clarington.net
Nancy Taylor, Treasurer & Director, Finance, Administration
ntaylor@clarington.net; finance@clarington.net
Tony Cannella, Director, Engineering Services, Administration
tcannella@clarington.net
Joseph Caruana, Director, Community Services, Administration
jcaruana@clarington.net
David Crome, Director, Planning Services, Administration
dcrome@clarington.net; planning@clarington.net
Fred Horvath, Director, Operations, Administration
fhorvath@clarington.net; operations@clarington.net
Marie Marano, Director, Corporate Services, Administration
mmarano@clarington.net
Gord Weir, Director, Emergency & Fire Services, Administration
gweir@clarington.net

Clearview
P.O. Box 200
217 Gideon St.
Stayner, ON L0M 1S0
705-428-6230
Fax: 705-428-0288
brenda.falls@clearview.ca (Administration)
www.clearviewtwp.on.ca
Municipal Type: Township
Area: 557.32 sq km
County or District: Simcoe; Population in 2006: 14,088
Provincial Electoral District(s): Simcoe-Grey
Federal Electoral District(s): Simcoe-Grey
Next Election: Oct. 2014 (4 year terms)
Ken Ferguson, Mayor
705-446-2323
kferguson@clearviewtwp.on.ca
Alicia Savage, Deputy Mayor & Councillor
asavage@clearviewtwp.on.ca
Doug Measures, Councillor, Ward(s): 1
dmeasures@clearviewtwp.on.ca
Orville Brown, Councillor, Ward(s): 2
obrown@clearviewtwp.on.ca
Mark Royal, Councillor, Ward(s): 3
mroyal@clearviewtwp.on.ca
Thom Paterson, Councillor, Ward(s): 4
tpaterson@clearviewtwp.on.ca
Robert Walker, Councillor, Ward(s): 5
rwalker@clearviewtwp.on.ca
Roger McGillvray, Councillor, Ward(s): 6
Rmcgillvray@clearviewtwp.on.ca
Shawn Davidson, Councillor, Ward(s): 7
sdavidson@clearviewtwp.on.ca
Bob Campbell, Clerk, Administration
bcampbell@clearview.ca
Susan McKenzie, Chief Administrative Officer, Administration
smckenzie@clearview.ca
Mitch Carruthers, Treasurer, Administration
mcarruthers@clearview.ca
Richard Spraggs, Director, Public Works, Administration
rspraggs@clearview.ca
Michael Wynia, Director, Planning & Development, Administration
mwynia@clearview.ca
Dave Carruthers, Fire Chief, Administration
dcarruthers@clearview.ca

Cochrane
Cochrane, ON
Municipal Type: District
Area: 141,247.30 sq km
Population in 2006: 82,503
David Landers, CAO, Cochrane District Social Services Administration Board
705-268-7722, Fax: 705-268-8290
CAO@cdssab.on.ca

Elizabethtown-Kitley
6544 New Dublin Rd., RR#2
Addison, ON K0E 1A0
613-345-7480
Fax: 613-345-7235
Toll Free Phone: 1-800-492-3175
mail@elizabethtown-kitley.on.ca
www.elizabethtown-kitley.on.ca
Municipal Type: Township
Area: 554.24 sq km
County or District: Leeds & Grenville; Population in 2006: 10,201
Provincial Electoral District(s): Leeds-Grenville
Federal Electoral District(s): Leeds-Grenville
Next Election: Oct. 2014 (4 year terms)
Jim Pickard, Mayor
613-342-5721
jimpickard@ripnet.com
John Johnston, Councillor
613-342-8952
Jim Miller, Councillor
613-924-9542
Eleanor Renaud, Councillor
613-275-2091
Earl F. Brayton, Councillor
613-345-2650
Susan Prettejohn, Councillor
613-498-2842
Herb Scott, Councillor
613-924-2133
Yvonne L. Robert, Administrator-Clerk, Administration
Melanie Kirkby, Director, Finance & Treasurer, Administration
Barbara Kalivas, Director, Planning & Development, Administration
Dale Kulp, Director, Public Works, Administration
Jim Donovan, Fire Chief, Administration
Ray Scissons, Chief Building Official, Administration

Essa
5786 County Rd. 21
Utopia, ON L0M 1T0
705-424-9770
Fax: 705-424-2367
TTY: 705-424-5302; Canine Control: 1-888-624-6455
info@essatownship.on.ca
www.essatownship.on.ca
Municipal Type: Township
Incorporated: 1850 Area: 279.57 sq km
County or District: Simcoe; Population in 2006: 16,901
Provincial Electoral District(s): Simcoe-Grey
Federal Electoral District(s): Simcoe-Grey
Next Election: Oct. 2014 (4 year terms)
David Guergis, Mayor
705-424-0698
Terry Dowdall, Deputy Mayor & Councillor
705-423-1154
Sandie Macdonald, Councillor
705-424-6844
Rick Newlove, Councillor
705-458-1337
Ron Henderson, Councillor
705-424-9752
Mike Galloway, CMO, Clerk, Administration
mgalloway@essatownship.on.ca
Greg Murphy, CMO, Chief Administrative Officer & Manager, Public Works, Administration
gmurphy@essatownship.on.ca
Julie Barrett, Treasurer & Deputy-Clerk, Administration
jbarrett@essatownship.on.ca
Colleen Healey, Manager, Planning & Development, Administration
chealey@essatownship.on.ca
Paul Macdonald, Fire Chief, Administration
fire@essatownship.on.ca
Heather Rutherford, Chief Building Official, Administration
hrutherford@essatownship.on.ca

Georgian Bluffs
177964 Grey Rd. 18, RR#3
Owen Sound, ON N4K 5N5
519-376-2729
Fax: 519-372-1620
office@georgianbluffs.on.ca
www.georgianbluffs.on.ca
Municipal Type: Township
Incorporated: Jan. 1, 2001 Area: 603.58 sq km
County or District: Grey; Population in 2006: 10,506
Provincial Electoral District(s): Bruce-Grey-Owen Sound
Federal Electoral District(s): Bruce-Grey-Owen Sound
Next Election: Oct. 2014 (4 year terms)
Note: Amalgamation of the Townships of Derby, Keppel & Sarawak.
Alan Barfoot, Mayor
Dwight Burley, Deputy Mayor & Councillor
Carol Barfoot, Councillor
Judy Gay, Councillor
Robert Lennox, Councillor
Ryan Thompson, Councillor
Tom Wiley, Councillor
Bruce Hoffman, Clerk, Administration
Bill White, Chief Administrative Officer, Administration
Holly Morrison, Treasurer, Administration
Rick Winters, Manager, Operations, Administration
Bill Klingenberg, Chief Building Official, Administration
Bev Nicolson, Planner, Administration
Martin Timmerman, Superintendent, Roads, Administration

Guelph-Eramosa
P.O. Box 700
8348 Wellington Rd. 124
Rockwood, ON N0B 2K0
519-856-9951
Fax: 519-856-2240
Toll Free Phone: 1-800-267-1465
general@get.on.ca
www.get.on.ca
Municipal Type: Township
Incorporated: Jan. 1, 1999 Area: 291.73 sq km
County or District: Wellington; Population in 2006: 12,066
Provincial Electoral District(s): Wellington-Halton Hills
Federal Electoral District(s): Wellington-Halton Hills
Next Election: Oct. 2014 (4 year terms)
Note: Amalgamation of the Townships of Guelph, Eramosa, Pilkington & Nichol.
Chris White, Mayor
whitecj@sympatico.ca
Meaghen Reid, Clerk
mreid@get.on.ca
Shawn Armstrong, Fire Chief
519-824-6590
Brad Roelofson, Manager, Property & Leisure Services
broelofson@get.on.ca
Ken Gagnon, Manager, Public Works
kgagnon@get.on.ca
Mark Thorpe, Officer, Bylaw Enforcement
mthorpe@get.on.ca
Mike Newark, Chief Building Official
mnewark@get.on.ca

Hamilton
P.O. Box 1060
8285 Majestic Hills Dr.
Cobourg, ON K9A 4W5
905-342-2810
Fax: 905-342-2818
info@hamiltontownship.ca
www.hamiltontownship.ca
Municipal Type: Township
Area: 256.11 sq km
County or District: Northumberland; Population in 2006: 10,972
Provincial Electoral District(s): Northumberland-Quinte West
Federal Electoral District(s): Northumberland-Quinte West
Next Election: Oct. 2014 (4 year terms)
Mark Lovshin, Deputy Mayor & Councillor
mlovshin@cogeco.ca
Isobel Hie, Mayor
oldhomestead1@gmail.com
Gary Woods, Councillor
woodsgj@gmail.com
Twila Marston, Councillor
tmarston@opseu.org

See blue tabs following this section for Municipal Waste Management and Water & Wastewater Treatment.

Municipal Governments / Ontario

Pat McCourt, Councillor
mccourt@eagle.ca
Betty McIntosh, Chief Administrative Officer, Clerk, & Treasurer, Administration
bmcintosh@hamiltontownship.ca
Doug Murray, Director, Public Works, Administration
dmurray@hamiltontownship.ca
Ken Clapperton, Fire Chief, Baltimore, Administration
baltimorefire@hamiltontownship.ca
Reg Jackson, Fire Chief, Bewdley, Administration
bewdleyfire@hamiltontownship.ca
Pete Staples, Fire Chief, Harwood, Administration
harwoodfire@hamiltontownship.ca
Scott Jibb, Chief Building Official, Administration
sjibb@hamiltontownship.ca
Sandra Stothart, Coordinator, Planning, Administration
sstothart@hamiltontownship.ca
Doug Thompson, Manager, Water Operations, Administration
dthompson@hamiltontownship.ca

Kenora
Kenora District Services Board Admin Office
#1, 211 Princess St.
Dryden, ON P8N 3L5

Municipal Type: District
Area: 407,192.66 sq km
Population in 2006: 64,419
Rory McMillan, Chair, Kenora District Services Board of Directors, & Councillor
807-468-4383
rmcmillan@kenora.ca
Sten S. Lif, Chief Administrative Officer, Kenora District Services Board
807-223-2100, Fax: 807-223-6500
kdsb@kdsb.on.ca; slif@kdsb.on.ca

Kincardine
1475 Conc. 5, RR#5
Kincardine, ON N2Z 2X6
519-396-3468
Fax: 519-396-8288
ssmith@kincardine.net
www.kincardine.net
Municipal Type: Municipality
Area: 537.65 sq km
County or District: Bruce; *Population in 2006:* 11,173
Provincial Electoral District(s): Huron-Bruce
Federal Electoral District(s): Huron-Bruce
Next Election: Oct. 2014 (4 year terms)
Larry Kraemer, Mayor
519-395-3130
mayor@kincardine.net
Laura Haight, Deputy Mayor & Councillor
519-396-5204
Kenneth Craig, Councillor at Large
519-396-8767
Ron Hewitt, Councillor at Large
519-395-2774
Marsha Leggett, Councillor at Large
519-368-7644
Guy Anderson, Councillor, Ward(s): 1
519-396-3529
Mike Leggett, Councillor, Ward(s): 1
519-396-4529
Gordon Campbell, Councillor, Ward(s): 2
519-396-8075
Randy Roppel, Councillor, Ward(s): 3
519-368-7792
Donna MacDougall, Clerk, Administration
clerk@kincardine.net
John deRosenroll, Chief Administrative Officer, Administration
519-396-3018
Brenda French, Treasurer, Administration
519-396-3468
Michele Barr, Manager, Building & Planning, Administration
buildings@kincardine.net
Jim O'Rourke, Manager, Public Works, Administration
pwcasual@kincardine.net
Jamie MacKinnon, Fire Chief, Administration
kinfire@bmts.com
Steve Murray, Coordinator, Economic Development, & Manager, Tourism, Administration
smurray@kincardine.net

Roberta Trelford, Coordinator, Community Emergency Management, & Health & Safety, Administration
kinfirecemc@bmts.com
Donna Hardman, Compliance Officer, Water & Waste Water Administration, Administration
519-396-4660, Fax: 519-396-4673
waterservice@bmts.com

King
2075 King Rd.
King City, ON L7B 1A1
905-833-5321
Fax: 905-833-2300
online@king.ca
www.king.ca
Municipal Type: Township
Incorporated: 1850 *Area:* 333.04 sq km
County or District: York Reg. Mun.; *Population in 2006:* 19,487
Provincial Electoral District(s): Oak Ridges-Markham; York-Simcoe
Federal Electoral District(s): Oak Ridges-Markham; York-Simcoe
Next Election: Oct. 2014 (4 year terms)
Cleve Mortelliti, Mayor
mayor@king.ca
Cleve Mortelliti, Councillor, Ward(s): 1
cleve@kingcentric.ca
Jeff Laidlaw, Councillor, Ward(s): 2
kingribbit@gmail.com
Linda Pabst, Councillor, Ward(s): 3
csomerville@king.ca
Bill Cober, Councillor, Ward(s): 4
billcober@aol.com
Jane Underhill, Councillor, Ward(s): 5
janeunderhill@sympatico.ca
Jack Rupke, Councillor, Ward(s): 6
csomerville@king.ca
Chris Somerville, Clerk, Administration
csomerville@king.ca
Scott Somerville, Chief Administrative Officer, Administration
Donald Young, Director, Finance, Administration
Robert Flindall, Director, Engineering & Public Works, Administration
Catherine Purcell, Director, Parks, Recreation, & Culture, Administration
Marilyn Loan, Manager, Human Resources, Administration
Gaspare Ritacca, Manager, Planning & Development, Administration
Bryan Burbidge, Fire Chief, Administration
Jamie Smyth, Economic Development Officer, Administration

Lambton Shores
P.O. Box 610
7883 Amtelecom Pkwy.
Forest, ON N0N 1J0
519-786-2335
Fax: 519-786-2135
administration@lambtonshores.ca
www.lambtonshores.ca
Municipal Type: Municipality
Incorporated: 2001 *Area:* 331.08 sq km
County or District: Lambton; *Population in 2006:* 11,150
Provincial Electoral District(s): Lambton-Kent-Middlesex
Federal Electoral District(s): Lambton-Kent-Middlesex
Next Election: Oct. 2014 (4 year terms)
Note: Amalgamation of the Towns of Bosanquet & Forest, & the Villages of Thedford, Arkona & Grand Bend.
Gord Minielly, Mayor
519-786-4629
gminielly@lambtonshores.ca
Carolyn Jamieson, Deputy Mayor & Councillor
519-296-5810
cjamieson@lambtonshores.ca
John Dehondt, Councillor, Ward(s): 1
jdehondt@lambtonshores.ca
Bill Weber, Councillor, Ward(s): 2
bweber@lambtonshores.ca
Mark Simpson, Councillor, Ward(s): 3
msimpson@lambtonshores.ca
Ruth Illman, Councillor, Ward(s): 4
rillman@lambtonshores.ca
Gerry Rupke, Councillor, Ward(s): 5
grupke@lambtonshores.ca
Ken Evans, Councillor, Ward(s): 6
kevans@lambtonshores.ca

Carol McKenzie, Clerk, Administration
cpmckenzie@lambtonshores.ca
John Byrne, Chief Administrative Officer, Administration
jbyrne@lambtonshores.ca
Janet Ferguson, Treasurer, Administration
jferguson@lambtonshores.ca
Peggy Van Mierlo-West, Director, Community Services, Administration
pvmwest@lambtonshores.ca
Venkat Ramani, Manager, Infrastructure, Administration
vramani@lambtonshores.ca
Allan Little, Superintendent, Drainage, & Construction Inspector, Administration
alittle@lambtonshores.ca

Leamington
38 Erie St. North
Leamington, ON N8H 2Z3
519-326-5761
Fax: 519-326-2481
info@leamington.ca
www.leamington.ca
Municipal Type: Municipality
Incorporated: 1874 *Area:* 261.92 sq km
County or District: Essex; *Population in 2006:* 28,833
Provincial Electoral District(s): Chatham-Kent-Essex
Federal Electoral District(s): Chatham-Kent-Essex
Next Election: Oct. 2014 (4 year terms)
Note: Incorporated as a town in 1890. Restructuring occurred in 1999.
John M. Adams, Mayor
councilmembers@leamington.ca
Rob Schmidt, Deputy Mayor & Councillor
Rick Atkin, Councillor
Bill Derbyshire, Councillor
Herb Enns, Councillor
Hilda MacDonald, Councillor
John Paterson, Councillor
Brian R. Sweet, B.A., LL.B, Municipal Clerk, Corporate Counsel & Director, Corporate Services, Administration
clerk@leamington.ca
William J. Marck, B.A., LL.B, Chief Administrative Officer, Administration
bmarck@leamington.ca
Cheryl L. Horrobin, B.Comm, CA, AMCT, Director, Finance & Business Services, Administration
Douglas Morrish, Director, Development Services, Administration
John Tofflemire, Director, Community Services, Administration
Robert R. Bradt, Manager, Fire Services & Fire Chief, Administration
Bechara Daher, Manager, Building Services, Administration
Arthur Glab, Manager, Engineering, Administration
Cameron McKay, Manager, Public Works, Administration
Tracey Pillon-Abbs, Manager, Planning Services, Administration
Gary Foisy, Superintendent, Water Services, Administration
Kit Woods, Superintendent, Pollution Control Centre, Administration
Pauline Russell, MEd., IPMA-CP, Officer, Human Resources, Administration

Leeds & Grenville
#100, 25 Central Ave. West
Brockville, ON K6V 4N6
613-342-3840
Fax: 613-342-2101
Toll Free Phone: 1-800-770-2170
www.uclg.ca
Municipal Type: United County
Area: 3,350.18 sq km
Population in 2006: 99,206
Next Election: Oct. 2014 (4 year terms)
Council
Vacant, Warden & Councillor
Herb Scott, Councillor, Ward(s): Athens Township
Mel Campbell, Councillor, Ward(s): Augusta Township
William Sloan, Councillor, Ward(s): Edwardsburgh/Cardinal Township
Jim Pickard, Councillor, Ward(s): Elizabethtown-Kitley Township
Roger Haley, Councillor, Ward(s): Front of Yonge Township
Bruce Bryan, Councillor, Ward(s): Leeds & The Thousand Islands
J. Douglas Struthers, Councillor, Ward(s): Merrickville-Wolford
David Gordon, Councillor, Ward(s): North Grenville Municipality
Ronald E. Holman, Councillor, Ward(s): Rideau Lakes Township
William (Bill) L. Thake, Councillor, Ward(s): Westport

See blue tabs following this section for Municipal Waste Management and Water & Wastewater Treatment.

Administration
Lesley Todd, Clerk, Administration
Steven Silver, Chief Administrative Officer, Administration
Nigel White, Treasurer & Director, Corporate Services, Administration
Leslie Shepherd, Director, Works, Planning Services, & Asset Management, Administration
Dorothy Theobald, Director, Human Services, Administration
James Alexander (Sandy) Hay, County Planner, Administration
Bob Cheetham, Manager, Economic Development, Administration
Dan Chevrier, Manager, Emergency Medical Services (EMS) Division, Administration
Kristen Hobbs, Manager, Human Resources, Administration
Geoff McVey, Manager, Forest, Administration

Loyalist
P.O. Box 70
263 Main St.
Odessa, ON K0H 2H0
613-386-7351
Fax: 613-386-3833
www.loyalisttownship.ca
Municipal Type: Township
Incorporated: 1998 *Area:* 340.02 sq km
County or District: Lennox & Addington; *Population in 2006:* 15,062
Provincial Electoral District(s): Lanark-Frontenac-Lennox & Addington
Federal Electoral District(s): Lanark-Frontenac-Lennox & Addington
Next Election: Oct. 2014 (4 year terms)
Note: Amalgamation of the Townships of Ernestown, Amherst Island & the Village of Bath.
Bill Lowry, Reeve
Bill Lowry, Deputy Reeve
Duncan Ashley, Councillor, Ward(s): 1 Amherst Island
Joe Hudacin, Councillor, Ward(s): 2 Bath
Carl Bresee, Councillor, Ward(s): 3 Ernestown
John Ibey, Councillor, Ward(s): 3 Ernestown
Ric Bresee, Councillor, Ward(s): 3 Ernestown
Brenda Hamilton, Township Clerk, Administration
Diane Pearce, Chief Administrative Officer, Administration
Alida Moffatt, Director, Finance, Administration
Cindy Lawson, Director, Recreation, Administration
David Thompson, Director, Engineering Services, Administration
Murray Beckel, Chief Building Official & Planner, Administration
Wayne Calver, Fire Chief, Administration
Bruce Hughson, Manager, Transportaton & Solid Waste, Administration
Lorie McFarland, Manager, Utilities, Administration
Brenda Martineau, Coordinator, Employee Relations, Administration

Manitoulin
Gore Bay, ON

Municipal Type: District
Area: 4,759.74 sq km
Population in 2006: 13,090
Provincial Electoral District(s): Algoma-Manitoulin
Federal Electoral District(s): Algoma-Manitoulin-Kapuskasing
Note: The District incorporates the towns of Gore Bay, & Northeastern Manitoulin & the Islands; communities in the townships of Assiginack, Barrie Isl., Billing, Burpe & Mills, Central Manitoulin, Cockburn Isl., Gordon, & Tehkummah; & 1st Nations reserves

Meaford
21 Trowbridge St. West
Meaford, ON N4L 1A1
519-538-1060
Fax: 519-538-5240
info@meaford.ca
www.meaford.ca
Municipal Type: Municipality
Incorporated: Jan. 1, 2001 *Area:* 588.47 sq km
County or District: Grey; *Population in 2006:* 10,948
Provincial Electoral District(s): Bruce-Grey-Owen Sound
Federal Electoral District(s): Bruce-Grey-Owen Sound
Next Election: Oct. 2014 (4 year terms)
Note: Formerly the Town of Georgian Highlands. Amalgamation of Sydenham, St. Vincent & Meaford.

Francis Richardson, Mayor
519-538-5998
frichardson@meaford.ca
Michael Traynor, Deputy Mayor & Councillor
519-376-8791
mtraynor@meaford.ca
Harley Greenfield, Councillor
519-538-2570
hgreenfield@meaford.ca
Cynthia Lemon, Councillor
519-376-1013
clemon@meaford.ca
Jim McPherson, Councillor
519-538-0859
jmcpherson@meaford.ca
Gerald Shortt, Councillor
519-538-2648
gshortt@meaford.ca
Lynda Stephens, Councillor
519-538-1189
lstephens@meaford.ca
Peggy Rouse, Clerk, Administration
prouse@meaford.ca
Frank Miele, Chief Administrative Officer, Administration
Robert Armstrong, Director, Planning & Building, Administration
Karen Davies, Director, Human Resources, Administration
Stephen Vokes, Director, Operations, Administration
Rick Carefoot, Chief Building Official, Administration
Chris Collyer, Chief Operator, Environmental Services, Administration
Steve Nickels, Fire Chief, Administration

Middlesex Centre
10227 Ilderton Rd., RR#2
Ilderton, ON N0M 2A0
519-666-0190
Fax: 519-666-0271
Toll Free Phone: 1-800-220-8968
cormans@middlesexcentre.on.ca
www.middlesexcentre.on.ca
Municipal Type: Township
Incorporated: Jan. 1, 1998 *Area:* 588.05 sq km
County or District: Middlesex; *Population in 2006:* 15,589
Provincial Electoral District(s): Lambton-Kent-Middlesex
Federal Electoral District(s): Lambton-Kent-Middlesex
Next Election: Oct. 2014 (4 year terms)
Note: Amalgamation of the former Townships of Delaware, Lobo, & London.
Council
Al Edmondson, Mayor
wa.edmondson@sympatico.ca
Clare Bloomfield, Deputy Mayor
Stephen Harvey, Councillor, Ward(s): 1
John Brennan, Councillor, Ward(s): 2
519-666-0549
Sharon McMillan, Councillor, Ward(s): 3
Aina DeViet, Councillor, Ward(s): 4
Frank Berze, Councillor, Ward(s): 5
fberze@rogers.com
Administration
Cathy Saunders, Chief Administrative Officer & Clerk, Administration
saunders@middlesexcentre.on.ca
Greg Watterton, Treasurer & Deputy Clerk, Administration
wattertg@middlesexcentre.on.ca
Maureen A. Looby, Director, Public Works & Engineering, Administration
loobym@middlesexcentre.on.ca
Arnie Marsman, Director, Planning & Development Svs., & Chief Building Official, Administration
marsmana@middlesexcentre.on.ca
John Elston, Fire Chief & Supervisor, Emergency Services, Administration
elstonj@middlesexcentre.on.ca
Jim Reeve, Superintendent, Drainage, Administration
reevej@middlesexcentre.on.ca
Mauro Castrilli, Coordinator, Transportation, Administration
castrilli@middlesexcentre.on.ca
Brian Hansen, Environmental Technologist, Administration
hansen@middlesexcentre.on.ca

Nipissing
District Social Services Administration Bd.
P.O. Box 750

200 McIntyre St. East
North Bay, ON P1B 8J8

Municipal Type: District
Area: 17,065.07 sq km
Population in 2006: 84,688
George Jupp, Chair, District of Nipissing Social Services Administration Board
877-829-5121, Fax: 705-474-0136
William A. White, CAO, District of Nipissing Social Services Administration Board
705-474-2151, Fax: 705-474-7155

North Dundas
P.O. Box 489
636 St. Lawrence St.
Winchester, ON K0C 2K0
613-774-2105
Fax: 613-774-5699
info@northdundas.com
www.northdundas.com
Municipal Type: Township
Incorporated: Jan. 1, 1998 *Area:* 503.18 sq km
County or District: Stormont, Dundas & Glengarry; *Population in 2006:* 11,095
Provincial Electoral District(s): Stormont-Dundas-South Glengarry
Federal Electoral District(s): Stormont-Dundas-South Glengarry
Next Election: Oct. 2014 (4 year terms)
Note: Amalgamation of the former Townships of Winchester & Mountain & the villages of Chesterville & Winchester.
Council
Eric Duncan, Mayor
Gerry Boyce, Deputy Mayor
Allan Armstrong, Councillor
alarmstrong@sympatico.ca
Tony Fraser, Councillor
John Thompson, Councillor
jthompsonelect@hotmail.com
Administration
Jo-Anne McCaslin, Clerk, Administration
jmccaslin@northdundas.com
Howard F. Smith, Chief Administrative Officer, Administration
hsmith@northdundas.com
John J. Gareau, CA, AMCT, Treasurer, Administration
jgareau@northdundas.com
Arden Carruthers, Director, Public Works, & Fire Chief, Morewood, Administration
acarruthers@northdundas.com
Mark Guy, Director, Recreation & Culture, Administration
mguy@northdundas.com
Calvin Pol, BES, MCIP, RPP, Director, Planning, Building, & Enforcement, Administration
cpol@northdundas.com
Angela Rutley, Manager, Water & Sewer Department, Administration
Doug Froats, Coordinator, Waste Management, Administration
dfroats@northdundas.com
Dan Kelly, Fire Chief, Winchester, Administration
Mike McMahon, Fire Chief, Chesterville, Administration
Scott Patterson, Fire Chief, Mountain, Administration

North Glengarry
P.O. Box 700
90 Main St. South
Alexandria, ON K0C 1A0
613-525-1110
Fax: 613-525-1649
www.northglengarry.ca
Municipal Type: Township
Area: 642.4 sq km
County or District: Stormont, Dundas & Glengarry; *Population in 2006:* 10,635
Provincial Electoral District(s): Glengarry-Prescott-Russell
Federal Electoral District(s): Glengarry-Prescott-Russell
Next Election: Oct. 2014 (4 year terms)
Council
Grant E. Crack, Mayor
Chris McDonell, Deputy Mayor & Councillor
Gary Shepherd, Councillor at Large
Jamie MacDonald, Councillor, Ward(s): Alexandria
Jim Picken, Councillor, Ward(s): Kenyon
Eric MacSweyn, Councillor, Ward(s): Lochiel
Carma Williams, Councillor, Ward(s): Maxville

Municipal Governments / Ontario

Administration
Terry Hart, Clerk Administrator, Administration
Johanna (Annie) Levac, Treasurer, Administration
André Bachand, Manager, Public Works, Administration
Gerry Murphy, Manager, Planning & By-law Enforcement, & Chief Building Official, Administration
Frank Flipsen, Fire Chief, Administration
Manson Barton, Superintendent, Drainage, Administration

North Grenville
P.O. Box 130
285 County Rd. 44
Kemptville, ON K0G 1J0
613-258-9569
Fax: 613-258-9620
www.northgrenville.ca
Municipal Type: MN
Incorporated: July 14, 2003 *Area:* 350.14 sq km
County or District: Leeds-Grenville; *Population in 2006:* 14,198
Provincial Electoral District(s): Leeds-Grenville
Federal Electoral District(s): Leeds-Grenville
Next Election: Oct. 2014 (4 year terms)
Council
David Gordon, Mayor
Terry Butler, Councillor
tbutler@can.rogers.com
Ken Finnerty
kfinnerty@northgrenville.on.ca
Tim Sutton, Councillor
tsutton@northgrenville.on.ca
Barb Tobin, Councillor
btobin@northgrenville.on.ca
Administration
Cahl Pominville, Clerk, Administration
cpominville@northgrenville.on.ca
Andy Brown, Chief Administrative Officer, Administration
abrown@northgrenville.on.ca
Sheila Kehoe, Treasurer, Administration
skehoe@northgrenville.on.ca
Karen Dunlop, Director, Public Works, Administration
Darren Patmore, Director, Parks, Recreation & Culture, Administration
Forbes Symon, Director, Planning & Development, Administration
Tim Bond, Fire Chief, Administration
Philip Gerrard, Chief Building Official, Administration
Jim Beeler, Chief Superintendent, Environmental Services, Administration
Gary Boal, Superintendent, Waste Site, Administration
Doug Scott, Superintendent, Roads, Administration
Jeff McEwen, Coordinator, Engineering, Administration
Gary Simser, Technician, Regulatory Water / Wastewater Compliance, Administration

Norwich
P.O. Box 100
210 Main St. East
Otterville, ON N0J 1R0
519-863-2709
Fax: 519-879-6385
Alternative Phone: 519-879-6568
www.twp.norwich.on.ca
Municipal Type: Township
Area: 431.28 sq km
County or District: Oxford; *Population in 2006:* 10,481
Provincial Electoral District(s): Oxford
Federal Electoral District(s): Oxford
Next Election: Oct. 2014 (4 year terms)
Council
Donald Doan, Mayor
ddoan@twp.norwich.on.ca
Pat Lee, Councillor, Ward(s): 1
plee@twp.norwich.on.ca
Lynne DePlancke, Councillor, Ward(s): 2
ldeplancke@twp.norwich.on.ca
Russell Jull, Councillor, Ward(s): 3
rjull@twp.norwich.on.ca
Susan Hampson, Councillor, Ward(s): 4
Administration
Michael Graves, Chief Administrativve Officer & Clerk, Administration
519-879-6568
mgraves@twp.norwich.on.ca
H. Roy Bauslaugh, Treasurer, Administration
rbauslaugh@twp.norwich.on.ca

Brian Reid, Chief Building Official, Property Standards, Administration
breid@twp.norwich.on.ca
Wray Ramsay, Superintendent, Drainage, Administration
519-879-6568
Ron Smith, Superintendent, Public Works, Administration
ronsmith@twp.norwich.on.ca
Ted Hunt, Officer, Economic Development, Administration
thunt@twp.norwich.on.ca

Oro-Medonte
P.O. Box 100
148 Line 7 South
Oro, ON L0L 2X0
705-487-2171
Fax: 705-487-0133
www.oro-medonte.ca
Municipal Type: Township
Area: 586.65 sq km
County or District: Simcoe; *Population in 2006:* 20,031
Provincial Electoral District(s): Simcoe North
Federal Electoral District(s): Simcoe North
Next Election: Oct. 2014 (4 year terms)
Council
Harry Hughes, Mayor
Ralph Hough, Deputy Mayor & Councillor
705-835-2770
Mel Coutanche, Councillor, Ward(s): 1
705-835-5728
Kelly Meyer, Councillor, Ward(s): 2
Marty Lancaster, Councillor, Ward(s): 3
John Crawford, Councillor, Ward(s): 4
705-487-3373
Dwight Evans, Councillor, Ward(s): 5
705-325-1653
Administration
Doug Irwin, Clerk & Director, Corporate Services, Administration
Robin Dunn, Chief Administrative Officer, Administration
Paul Gravelle, Treasurer, Deputy CAO, & Director, Finance, Administration
Jerry Ball, Director, Transportation & Environmental Services, Administration
Shawn Binns, Director, Recreation & Community Services, Administration
Andria Leigh, Director, Development Services, Administration
Richard Playfair, Director, Fire & Emergency Services, Administration
Kim Allen, Chief Building Official, Administration
Glenn White, Senior Planner, Administration
Tamara Obee, Officer, Human Resources, Administration

Oxford
P.O. Box 1614
21 Givins St.
Woodstock, ON N4S 7Y3
519-539-9800
Fax: 519-421-4712
www.oxfordcounty.ca
Municipal Type: Restructured County
Area: 2,039.46 sq km
Population in 2006: 102,756
Next Election: Oct. 2014 (4 year terms)
Council
Vacant, Warden & Councillor
Marion Wearn, Councillor, Ward(s): Blandford-Blenheim
Don E. McKay, Councillor, Ward(s): East Zorra-Tavistock
519-462-2697
Ted J. Comiskey, Councillor, Ward(s): Ingersoll
519-462-2697
Donald Doan, Councillor, Ward(s): Norwich
519-863-2709
David Mayberry, Councillor, Ward(s): South-West Oxford
John Lessif, Councillor, Ward(s): Tillsonburg
Pat Sobeski, Councillor, Ward(s): Woodstock
Deb A. Tait, Councillor, Ward(s): Woodstock
Sandra J. Talbot, Councillor, Ward(s): Woodstock
519-539-6685
Margaret E. Lupton, Councillor, Ward(s): Zorra
519-485-2490
Administration
Michael Bragg, Chief Administrative Officer & Clerk, Administration
Lynn Buchner, Director, Corporate Services, Administration
Mary Metcalfe, Director, Public Health & Emergency Services, Administration

Robert Walton, Director, Public Works, Administration
Margaret Misek-Evans, Corporate Manager, Community & Strategic Planning, Administration
Janice Kubiak, Corporate Manager, Human Resources, Administration
Margaret Misek-Evans, Corporate Manager, Community & Strategic Planning, Administration

Parry Sound
District Social Services Administration Bd.
76 Church St., 2nd Fl.
Parry Sound, ON P2A 1Z1
705-746-7777
Fax: 705-746-7783
Municipal Type: District
Area: 9,222.04 sq km
Population in 2006: 40,918
Rick Rick Zanussi, Chair, ezanussi@zeuter.com
Janet Patterson, Chief Administrative Officer, District Social Service Admin. Bd.
705-746-7777, Fax: 705-746-7783

Perth East
P.O. Box 455
25 Mill St. East
Milverton, ON N0K 1M0
519-595-2800
Fax: 519-595-2801
township@pertheast.on.ca
www.pertheast.on.ca
Municipal Type: Township
Area: 715.07 sq km
County or District: Perth; *Population in 2006:* 12,041
Provincial Electoral District(s): Perth-Wellinton
Federal Electoral District(s): Perth-Wellington
Next Election: Oct. 2014 (4 year terms)
Note: Amalgamation of North Easthope Township, South Easthope Township, Ellice Township, Village of Milverton & Mornington Township.
Council
Ian Forrest, Mayor
iforrest@pertheast.on.ca
Bob McMillan, Deputy Mayor & Councillor
Rhonda Ehgoetz, Councillor, Ward(s): Ellice
Jeremy Matheson, Councillor, Ward(s): Milverton
Don Brunk, Councillor, Ward(s): Mornington
Hugh McDermid, Councillor, Ward(s): North Easthope
Andrew MacAlpine, Councillor, Ward(s): South Easthope
Administration
Kerri Ann O'Rourke, Clerk, Administration
Glenn Schwendinger, Chief Administrative Officer, Administration
Rhonda Fischer, Treasurer, Administration
Wes Kuepfer, Manager, Public Works, Administration
Donna Chaffe, Coordinator, Human Resources, Administration
Bill Wilson, Coordinator, Operations, Administration
Darrell Reis, Fire Chief, Administration
Grant Schwartzentruber, Chief Building Official, Administration

Port Hope
56 Queen St.
Port Hope, ON L1A 3Z9
905-885-4544
Fax: 905-885-7698
admin@porthope.ca
www.porthope.ca
Municipal Type: Municipality
Incorporated: March 6, 1834 *Area:* 278.97 sq km
County or District: Northumberland; *Population in 2006:* 16,390
Provincial Electoral District(s): Northumberland-Quinte West
Federal Electoral District(s): Northumberland-Quinte West
Next Election: Oct. 2014 (4 year terms)
Council
Linda M. Thompson, Mayor
mayor@porthope.ca
Rick Austin, Councillor, Ward(s): 1
David Turck, Councillor, Ward(s): 1
dturck@porthope.ca
Jeff G. Lees, Councillor, Ward(s): 1
Greg W. Burns, Councillor, Ward(s): 2
Jeffrey S. Gilmer, Councillor, Ward(s): 2
Administration
Sue Dawe, Clerk & Director, Corporate Services, Administration
sdawe@porthope.ca
R. Carl Cannon, Chief Administrative Officer, Administration

See blue tabs following this section for Municipal Waste Management and Water & Wastewater Treatment.

Barbara Spry, Treasurer, Administration
bspry@porthope.ca
Peter Angelo, Director, Public Works, Administration
905-885-2431
publicworks@porthope.ca; pangelo@porthope.ca
Rob Collins, Director, Fire & Emergency Services, Administration
905-885-5323
rcollins@porthope.ca
Eugene Todd, Director, Parks, Recreation, & Culture, Administration
905-753-2230
etodd@porthope.ca
Ron Warne, Director, Planning & Development Services, Administration
905-885-2415
planning@porthope.ca
Ken Andrus, Chief Building Official, Administration
905-885-2415
cbo@porthope.ca
Gina Jackson, Manager, Human Resources, Administration
905-885-4544
gjackson@porthope.ca

Prescott & Russell
P.O. Box 304
59 Court St.
L'Orignal, ON K0B 1K0
613-675-4661
Fax: 613-675-2519
Toll Free Phone: 1-800-667-6307
support@prescott-russell.on.ca
www.prescott-russell.on.ca
Municipal Type: United County
Incorporated: 1820 *Area:* 2,001.18 sq km
Population in 2006: 80,184
Next Election: Oct. 2014 (4 year terms)
Council
Vacant, Warden & Councillor
Council
Stéphane P. Parisien, Chief Administrative Officer & Clerk, Administration
spparisien@prescott-russell.on.ca
Jean-Yves Lalonde, Councillor, Ward(s): Alfred & Plantagenet
Louise Lepage-Gareau, Treasurer, Administration
llgareau@prescott-russell.on.ca
Claude Levac, Councillor, Ward(s): Casselman
Michel Chrétien, Director, Emergency Services, Administration
Gary J. Barton, Councillor, Ward(s): Champlain
Marc Clermont, Director, Public Works, Administration
Marcel Guibord, Councillor, Ward(s): Clarence-Rockland
Louis Prevost, Director, Planning & Forestry, Administration
Robert Kirby, Councillor, Ward(s): East Hawkesbury
Elizabeth Gauthier, Manager, Human Resources, Administration
Rene Berthiaume, Councillor, Ward(s): Hawkesbury
François St. Amour, Councillor, Ward(s): The Nation
Jean-Paul Saint-Pierre, Councillor, Ward(s): Russell

Rainy River
District Social Services Administration Bd.
450 Scott St.
Fort Frances, ON P9A 1H2
807-274-5349
Toll Free Phone: 1-800-265-5349
Municipal Type: District
Area: 15,472.94 sq km
Population in 2006: 21,564
Michael Lewis, Chair, Rainy River District Social Services Administration Board
Donna Dittaro, CAO, Rainy River District Social Services Administration Board
donnad@rrdssab.on.ca

Russell
717 Notre Dame St.
Embrun, ON K0A 1W1
613-443-3066
Fax: 613-443-1042
ginettebertrand@russell.ca (Ginette Bertrand)
www.russell.ca
Municipal Type: Township
Area: 198.96 sq km
County or District: Prescott & Russell; *Population in 2006:* 13,883
Provincial Electoral District(s): Glengarry-Prescott-Russell
Federal Electoral District(s): Glengarry-Prescott-Russell
Next Election: Oct. 2014 (4 year terms)
Ken Hill, Mayor
kenhill@russell.ca
Lorraine Dicaire, Councillor
lorrainedicaire@russell.ca
Jamie Laurin, Councillor
jlaurin@russell.ca
Donald St. Pierre, Councillor
dstpierre@russell.ca
Jean-Paul St. Pierre, Councillor
jpstpierre@russell.ca
Ginette Bertrand, Municipal Clerk, Administration
ginettebertrand@russell.ca
Jean Leduc, Chief Administrative Officer, Administration
jeanleduc@russell.ca
Christiane B. Brault, Director, Finance, Administration
christianebrault@russell.ca
Millie Bourdeau, Director, Public Safety & Enforcement, Administration
milliebourdeau@russell.ca
Lawrence Gangur, Director, Environmental Services, Administration
lawrencegangur@russell.ca
Jacques Lortie, Director, Public Works, Parks, & Recreation, Administration
jacqueslortie@russell.ca
Dominique Tremblay, Director, Planning, Administration
dominiquetremblay@russell.ca
Bruce Armstrong, Fire Chief, Russell, Administration
brucearmstrong@russell.ca
Jean-Luc Bourgie, Fire Chief, Embrun, Administration
bourgie@rogers.com
Julia Tuff, Chief Building Official, Administration
juliatuff@russell.ca

St. Clair
Civic Centre
1155 Emily St.
Mooretown, ON N0N 1M0
519-867-2021
Fax: 519-867-5509
Toll Free Phone: 1-800-809-0301 (Sombra & Lambton)
webmaster@twp.stclair.on.ca
www.twp.stclair.on.ca
Municipal Type: Township
Area: 619.3 sq km
County or District: Lambton; *Population in 2006:* 14,649
Provincial Electoral District(s): Sarnia-Lambton
Federal Electoral District(s): Sarnia-Lambton
Next Election: Oct. 2014 (4 year terms)
Council
Steve Arnold, Mayor
519-867-3333
Peter Gilliland, Deputy Mayor & Councillor
519-862-3534
Jeff Agar, Councillor, Ward(s): 1
519-862-5062
Patricia Carswell-Alexander, Councillor, Ward(s): 1
519-864-4006
Jim DeGurse, Councillor, Ward(s): 1
519-677-5676
Steve Miller, Councillor, Ward(s): 2
519-677-5676
Darrell Randell, Councillor, Ward(s): 2
519-627-3764
Administration
John DeMars, Clerk & Director, Administration, Administration
J. Rodey, Chief Administrative Officer, Administration
C. Quenneville, Treasurer & Director, Finance, Administration
L. Burnham, Director, Public Works, Operations, & Engineering, Administration
R. Dewhirst, Director, Fire Services, Administration
G. Hackett, Director, Community Services, Administration

Scugog
P.O. Box 780
181 Perry St.
Port Perry, ON L9L 1A7
905-985-7346
Fax: 905-985-1931
mail@township.scugog.on.ca
www.scugog.ca
Municipal Type: Township
Area: 474.63 sq km
County or District: Durham Regional Municipality; *Population in 2006:* 21,439
Provincial Electoral District(s): Durham
Federal Electoral District(s): Durham
Next Election: Oct. 2014 (4 year terms)
Council
Chuck Mercier, Mayor
Bobbie Drew, Regional Councillor
Larry Corrigan, Councillor, Ward(s): 1
John Hancock, Councillor, Ward(s): 2
Jim Howard, Councillor, Ward(s): 3
Wilma Wotten, Councillor, Ward(s): 4
Howard Danson, Councillor, Ward(s): 5
Administration
Kim Coates, Administration
Bev Hendry, Chief Administrative Officer, Administration
Kathryn McCann, Commissioner, Corporate Services, Administration
Gene Chartier, Commissioner, Planning & Public Works, Administration
John Sellars, Director, Parks, Recreation, & Culture, Administration
Richard Miller, Fire Chief, Administration

Severn
P.O. Box 159
1024 Hurlwood Lane
Orillia, ON L3V 6J3
705-325-2315
Fax: 705-327-5818
severn@encode.com
www.townshipofsevern.com
Municipal Type: Township
Incorporated: Jan. 1, 1994 *Area:* 534.78 sq km
County or District: Simcoe; *Population in 2006:* 12,030
Provincial Electoral District(s): Simcoe North
Federal Electoral District(s): Simcoe North
Next Election: Oct. 2014 (4 year terms)
Council
Mike H. Burkett, Mayor
Judith Cox, Deputy Mayor & Councillor
Mark Taylor, Councillor, Ward(s): 1
Jane Dunlop, Councillor, Ward(s): 2
Ian Crichton, Councillor, Ward(s): 3
Ron Stevens, Councillor, Ward(s): 4
Rob Ferguson, Councillor, Ward(s): 5
Administration
Henry Sander, Clerk-Treasurer & Director, Corporate Services, Administration
Eric Peterson, Chief Administrative Officer, Administration
Clayton Cameron, Director, Public Works, Administration
Eric Dowell, Director, Fire & Emergency Services, Administration
David Parks, Director, Planning & Development, Administration

Smith-Ennismore-Lakefield
P.O. Box 270
1310 Centre Line, RR#4
Bridgenorth, ON K0L 1H0
705-292-9507
Fax: 705-292-8964
Toll Free Phone: 1-877-213-7419 (In 705 area code)
www.smithennismorelakefield.on.ca
Municipal Type: Township
Area: 318.77 sq km
County or District: Peterborough; *Population in 2006:* 17,413
Provincial Electoral District(s): Peterborough
Federal Electoral District(s): Peterborough
Next Election: Oct. 2014 (4 year terms)
Council
Mary Smith, Reeve
Andy Mitchell, Deputy Reeve
Donna Ballantyne, Councillor, Ward(s): Ennismore
dib1452@bell.net
Anita Locke, Councillor, Ward(s): Lakefield
anitalocke@anitalocke.ca; jasana@nexicom.net
Sherry Senis, Councillor, Ward(s): Lakefield
wssenis@sympatico.ca
Administration
Angela Chittick, Clerk, Administration
705-292-9507, Fax: 705-292-8964
Janice Lavalley, Chief Administrative Officer, Administration
R. Lane Vance, Treasurer & Manager, Financial Services, Administration
Ed Barber, Manager, Recreation, Administration
705-292-8774

Municipal Governments / Ontario

Stephen Crough, Manager, Public Works, Administration
705-292-8621
Robert Lamarre, Manager, Building & Planning, Administration
Gord Jopling, Fire Chief, Administration
705-292-7282
Karen McGee, Coordinator, Human Resources, Administration

South Dundas
P.O. Box 160
4296 County Rd. 31
Williamsburg, ON K0C 2H0
613-535-2673
Fax: 613-535-2099
Toll Free Phone: 1-800-265-0619
mail@southdundas.com
www.southdundas.com
Municipal Type: Township
Area: 519.98 sq km
County or District: Stormont, Dundas & Glengarry; *Population in 2006:* 10,535
Provincial Electoral District(s): Stormont-Dundas-South Glengarry
Federal Electoral District(s): Stormont-Dundas-South Glengarry
Next Election: Oct. 2014 (4 year terms)
Council
Steven J. Byvelds, Mayor
Jim Locke, Deputy Mayor & Councillor
Evonne Delegarde, Councillor
613-652-1388
evonne_delegarde@hotmail.com
Archie L. Mellan, Councillor
Jim Graham, Councillor
613-543-3588
del_jones@sympatico.ca
Administration
Brenda M. Brunt, Clerk, Administration
bbrunt@southdundas.com
Stephen McDonald, Chief Administrative Officer, Administration
smcdonald@southdundas.com
Shannon Geraghty, Treasurer, Administration
sgeraghty@southdundas.com
Hugh Garlough, Manager, Public Works, Administration
hgarlough@southdundas.com
Don J.W. Lewis, Manager, Planning & Enforcement, Administration
dlewis@southdundas.com
Linda Wilson, Officer, Economic Development, Administration
lwilson@southdundas.com
Bill Shearing, Coordinator, Emergency Management, Administration
bill.shearing@sympatico.ca

South Frontenac
P.O. Box 100
4432 George St.
Sydenham, ON K0H 2T0
613-376-3027
Fax: 613-376-6657
Toll Free Phone: 1-800-559-5862
admin@township.southfrontenac.on.ca
www.township.southfrontenac.on.ca
Municipal Type: Township
Incorporated: Jan. 1, 1998 *Area:* 941.28 sq km
County or District: Frontenac; *Population in 2006:* 18,227
Provincial Electoral District(s): Lanark-Frontenac-Lennox & Addington
Federal Electoral District(s): Lanark-Frontenac-Lennox & Addington
Next Election: Oct. 2014 (4 year terms)
Council
Gary C Davison, Mayor
davison4544@yahoo.ca
Del Stowe, Councillor, Ward(s): Bedford
delstowe@yahoo.com
Mark Tinlin, Councillor, Ward(s): Bedford
Allan G. McPhail, Councillor, Ward(s): Loughborough
mcphail@queensu.ca
Ron W. Vandewal, Councillor, Ward(s): Loughborough
lakevalley@kos.net
John R. McDougall, Councillor, Ward(s): Portland
Bill W.L. Robinson, Councillor, Ward(s): Portland
sfronten@kingston.net
Cam L. Naish, Councillor, Ward(s): Storrington
Larry W. York, Councillor, Ward(s): Storrington
blue@reztel.net

Administration
Wayne Orr, Clerk & Administrator, Administration
worr@township.southfrontenac.on.ca
Deb Bracken, Treasurer, Administration
dbracken@township.southfrontenac.on.ca
Mark Segsworth, Manager, Public Works, Administration
msegsworth@township.southfrontenac.on.ca
Lindsay Mills, Coordinator, Planning, Administration
lmills@township.southfrontenac.on.ca
Rick Chesebrough, Fire Chief, Administration
rchesebrough@township.southfrontenac.on.ca
Alan Revill, Chief Building Inspector, Administration
rchesebrough@township.southfrontenac.on.ca

South Glengarry
P.O. Box 220
6 Oak St.
Lancaster, ON K0C 1N0
613-347-1166
Fax: 613-347-3411
info@southglengarry.com
www.southglengarry.com
Municipal Type: Township
Incorporated: Jan. 1, 1998 *Area:* 604.91 sq km
County or District: Stormont, Dundas & Glengarry; *Population in 2006:* 12,880
Provincial Electoral District(s): Stormont-Dundas-South Glengarry
Federal Electoral District(s): Stormont-Dundas-South Glengarry
Next Election: Oct. 2014 (4 year terms)
Council
Jim McDonell, Mayor
jim.mcdonell@bell.ca
Ian McLeod, Deputy Mayor & Councillor
Trevor Bougie, Councillor
Joyce Gravelle, Councillor
gravelle@cnwl.igs.net
Bill McKenzie, Councillor
613-347-3254, Fax: 613-347-3119
Administration
Marilyn Lebrun, Clerk, Administration
marilyn@southglengarry.com
Derik Brandt, Chief Administrative Officer, Administration
derik@southglengarry.com
Michel Samson, Treasurer & Deputy Clerk, Administration
mike@southglengarry.com
Joanne Haley, General Manager, Community Services, Administration
jhaley@southglengarry.com
J. Ewen MacDonald, General Manager, Infrastructure Services, Administration
ewen@southglengarry.com
Dwane Crawford, Manager, Development, Administration
dwane@southglengarry.com
Shawn Killoran, Manager, Water & Wastewater Operations, Administration
shawnkilloran@on.aibn.com

South Huron
P.O. Box 759
322 Main St. South
Exeter, ON N0M 1S6
519-235-0310
Fax: 519-235-3304
Toll Free: 1-877-204-0747
info@southhuron.ca
www.southhuron.ca
Municipal Type: Municipality
Incorporated: 2001 *Area:* 425.35 sq km
County or District: Huron; *Population in 2006:* 9,982
Provincial Electoral District(s): Huron-Bruce
Federal Electoral District(s): Huron-Bruce
Next Election: Oct. 2014 (4 year terms)
George Robertson, Mayor
Michael Di Lullo, Clerk & Manager, Corporate Services
m.dilullo@southhuron.ca

South Stormont
P.O. Box 340
4949 Country Rd. 14
Ingleside, ON K0C 1M0
613-537-2362
Fax: 613-537-8113
Toll Free Phone: 1-800-265-3915

info@southstormont.ca; bylawofficer@southstormont.ca
www.southstormont.ca
Municipal Type: Township
Area: 447.46 sq km
County or District: Stormont, Dundas & Glengarry; *Population in 2006:* 12,520
Provincial Electoral District(s): Stormont-Dundas-South Glengarry
Federal Electoral District(s): Stormont-Dundas-South Glengarry
Next Election: Oct. 2014 (4 year terms)
Council
Bryan McGillis, Mayor
mayor@southstormont.ca
Tammy Hart, Deputy Mayor & Councillor
Barry Brownlee, Councillor
613-537-9753
Richard Waldroff, Councillor
Cindy Woods, Councillor
cindy_woods@xplornet.com
Administration
Betty de Haan, Chief Administrative Officer & Clerk, Administration
betty@southstormont.ca
Johanna Barkley, Treasurer, Administration
johanna@southstormont.ca
Dan Pilon, Manager, Public Works, Administration
dan@southstormont.ca
Hilton Cryderman, Chief Building Official & Administrator, Planning & Zoning, Administration
hilton@southstormont.ca
Roger Desjardins, Fire Chief, Administration
roger@southstormont.ca
Harry Hutchinson, Deputy Chief Building Official & Superintendent, Drainage, Administration
buildinginspector@southstormont.ca

Springwater
Simcoe County Administrative Centre
2231 Nursery Rd.
Minesing, ON L0L 1Y2
705-728-4784
Fax: 705-728-6957
info@springwater.ca; council@springwater.ca
www.springwater.ca
Municipal Type: Township
Incorporated: Jan. 1, 1994 *Area:* 536.3 sq km
County or District: Simcoe; *Population in 2006:* 17,456
Provincial Electoral District(s): Simcoe-Grey
Federal Electoral District(s): Simcoe-Grey
Next Election: Oct. 2014 (4 year terms)
Council
Linda Collins, Mayor
Dan McLean, Deputy Mayor & Councillor
Dan Clement, Councillor, Ward(s): 1
Perry Ritchie, Councillor, Ward(s): 2
Rick Webser, Councillor, Ward(s): 3
Sandy McConkey, Councillor, Ward(s): 4
Jack Hanna, Councillor, Ward(s): 5
Administration
John Daly, Clerk & Director, Corporate Services, Administration
Winanne Grant, Chief Administrative Officer, Administration
Laurie Kennard, Treasurer & Director, Finance, Administration
finance@springwater.ca
Ron Belcourt, Director, Recreation Services, Administration
recreation@springwater.ca
Brad Sokach, Director, Public Works, Administration
publicworks@springwater.ca
Nancy Tuckett, Director, Planning & Development, Administration
planning@springwater.ca
Tony Van Dam, Director, Fire & Emergency Services, Administration
fire@springwater.ca
Nick Ippolito, Chief Building Official, Administration
building@springwater.ca
Barb Fralick, Manager, Human Resources, Administration

Stormont, Dundas & Glengarry
26 Pitt St.
Cornwall, ON K6J 3P2
613-932-1515
Fax: 613-936-2913
Toll Free Phone: 1-800-267-7158
info@sdgcounties.ca
www.sdgcounties.ca

See blue tabs following this section for Municipal Waste Management and Water & Wastewater Treatment.

Municipal Type: United County
Area: 3,306.86 sq km
Population in 2006: 110,399
Next Election: Oct. 2014 (4 year terms)
Council
Eric Duncan, Mayor, Ward(s): North Dundas
Grant Crack, Mayor, Ward(s): North Glengarry
grantcrack@northglengarry.ca
Denis Fife, Mayor, Ward(s): North Stormont
fifeag@plantpioneer.com
Steven Byvelds, Mayor, Ward(s): South Dundas
Jim McDonell, Mayor, Ward(s): South Glengarry
jim.mcdonell@bell.ca
Bryan McGillis, Mayor, Ward(s): South Stormont
bryansouthstormont@hotmail.com
Administration
Helen Thomson, Clerk, Administration
hthomson@sdgcounties.ca
Michael S. Waddell, Chief Administrative Officer, Administration
mwaddell@sdgcounties.ca
Donald J. McDonald, County Engineer, Administration
Michael Otis, County Planner, Administration

Strathroy-Caradoc
52 Frank St.
Strathroy, ON N7G 2R4
519-245-1070
Fax: 519-245-6353
general@strathroy-caradoc.ca
www.strathroy-caradoc.ca
Municipal Type: Township
Incorporated: 2001 *Area:* 274.19 sq km
County or District: Middlesex; *Population in 2006:* 19,977
Provincial Electoral District(s): Lambton-Kent-Middlesex
Federal Electoral District(s): Lambton-Kent-Middlesex
Next Election: Oct. 2014 (4 year terms)
Note: Amalgamation of the Town of Strathroy & the Township of Caradoc.
Council
Joanne Vanderheyden, Mayor
Brad Richards, Deputy Mayor & Councillor
Marie Baker, Councillor, Ward(s): 1 - Strathroy
mbaker@strathroy-caradoc.caadoc.ca
John G. Brennan, Councillor, Ward(s): 1 - Strathroy
jbrennan@strathroy-caradoc.ca
Steve Pelkman, Councillor, Ward(s): 1 - Strathroy
spelkman@strathroy-caradoc.ca
Dave Cameron, Councillor, Ward(s): 1 - Strathroy
Steve Dausett, Councillor, Ward(s): 2 - Caradoc
sdausett@strathroy-caradoc.ca
Larry Cowan, Councillor, Ward(s): 2 - Caradoc
Neil Flegel, Councillor, Ward(s): 2 - Caradoc
Administration
Angela Toth, Clerk & Director, Corporate Services, Administration
atoth@strathroy-caradoc.ca
Jim Fairlie, Chief Administrative Officer, Administration
jfairlie@strathroy-caradoc.ca
Jane McPherson, Treasurer & Director, Financial Services, Administration
jmcpherson@strathroy-caradoc.ca
Bill Gibson, Director, Fire Services, & Fire Chief, Administration
bgibson@strathroy-caradoc.ca
Tim Hanna, Director, Recreation & Leisure Services, Administration
thanna@strathroy-caradoc.ca
Mark Harris, Director, Environmental Services, Administration
mharris@strathroy-caradoc.ca
Brad Dausett, Manager, Roads, Administration
bdausett@strathroy-caradoc.ca
Paul Hicks, Coordinator, Planning, Administration
dwalsh@strathroy-caradoc.ca
Andrew Meyer, Coordinator, Community Development, Administration
Leslie Pommer, Coordinator, Customer Services & Concession, Administration

Sudbury District
c/o Manitoulin-Sudbury District Services Bd
210 Mead Blvd.
Espanola, ON P5E 1R9
www.msdsb.net
Municipal Type: District
Area: 38,504.53 sq km
Population in 2006: 21,392

Provincial Electoral District(s): Algoma-Manitoulin; Nickel Belt
Federal Electoral District(s): Nickel Belt;
Algoma-Manitoulin-Kapuskasing
Note: Includes incorporated municipalities surrounding Greater Sudbury, unincorporated settlements, & First Nations reserves Chapleau 74A & 75, Duck Lake, Mattagami, Mountbatten, Whitefish Lake, & Whitefish River
J. Raymond (Ray) Chénier, Board Chair, Manitoulin-Sudbury District Services Board
705-862-7850
rchenier@msdsb.net
Fern Dominelli, Chief Administrative Officer, Manitoulin-Sudbury District Svs Bd
cao@msdsb.net

Tay
P.O. Box 100
450 Park St.
Victoria Harbour, ON L0K 2A0
705-534-7248
Fax: 705-534-4493
taytownship@tay.ca
www.tay.ca
Municipal Type: Township
Area: 138.93 sq km
County or District: Simcoe; *Population in 2006:* 9,748
Provincial Electoral District(s): Simcoe North
Federal Electoral District(s): Simcoe North
Next Election: Oct. 2014 (4 year terms)
Scott Warnock, Mayor
swarnock@tay.ca
Alison Thomas, Clerk
athomas@tay.ca
Wes Crown, Director, Planning
Herbert Proudley, Director, Public Works

Thames Centre
4305 Hamilton Rd.
Dorchester, ON N0L 1G3
519-268-7334
Fax: 519-268-3928
Toll Free Phone: 1-866-425-7306
inquiries@thamescentre.on.ca
www.thamescentre.on.ca
Municipal Type: Municipality
Incorporated: Jan. 1, 2001 *Area:* 433.8 sq km
County or District: Middlesex; *Population in 2006:* 13,085
Provincial Electoral District(s): Elgin-Middlesex-London
Federal Electoral District(s): Elgin-Middlesex-London
Next Election: Oct. 2014 (4 year terms)
Note: Amalgamation of the former Township of West Nissouri & the Township of North Dorchester.
Jim Maudsley, Mayor
jmaudsley@thamescentre.on.ca
Margaret Lewis, Clerk
Stewart M. Findlater, Director, Community Services & Development
sfindlater@thamescentre.on.ca
Steve McAuley, Director, Operations
smcauley@thamescentre.on.ca
Paul Hunter, Fire Chief
Dave Murray, Chief Building Official
Jarrod Craven, Area Superintendent, Water & Wastewater
Jarrod Craven, Superintendent, Environmental Services
Dennis Shand, Superintendent, Drainage
dshand@thamescentre.on.ca

The Nation
958 Rte. 500 West
Casselman, ON K0A 1M0
613-764-5444
Fax: 613-764-3310
mmccuaig@nationmun.ca
www.nationmun.ca
Municipal Type: Municipality
Incorporated: Jan. 1, 1998 *Area:* 657.16 sq km
County or District: Prescott & Russell; *Population in 2006:* 10,643
Provincial Electoral District(s): Glengarry-Prescott-Russell
Federal Electoral District(s): Glengarry-Prescott-Russell
Next Election: Oct. 2014 (4 year terms)
Note: Amalgamation of the Townships of Cambridge, South Plantagenet, Caledonia & the Village of St. Isidore.
François St. Amour, Mayor

Mary J. McCuaig, Clerk
mmccuaig@nationmun.ca
Guylain Laflèche, Municipal Planner
glafleche@nationmun.ca
Marc Legailt, Superintendent, Roads
marclegault@nationmun.ca
Charles Bray, Chief Building Official
cbray@nationmun.ca

Thunder Bay
Thunder Bay, ON

Municipal Type: District
Area: 103,706.27 sq km
Population in 2006: 149,063

Timiskaming
Haileybury, ON

Municipal Type: District
Area: 13,279.88 sq km
Population in 2006: 33,283

Trent Hills
P.O. Box 1030
66 Front St. South
Campbellford, ON K0L 1L0
705-653-1900
Fax: 705-653-5904
info@trenthills.ca
www.trenthills.ca
Municipal Type: Municipality
Area: 510.83 sq km
County or District: Northumberland; *Population in 2006:* 12,247
Provincial Electoral District(s): Northumberland-Quinte West
Federal Electoral District(s): Northumberland-Quinte West
Next Election: Oct. 2014 (4 year terms)
Hector MacMillan, Mayor
hecmacmillan@accel.net
Jim Peters, Director, Planning
jim.peters@trenthills.ca
Scott White, Manager, Water Operations
Shari Lang, Coordinator, Public Works
shari.lang@trenthills.ca
Joe Kelly, Manager, Wastewater
705-653-1480
Jim McIlmoyle, Manager, Roads
Shirley Preston, Deputy Clerk, Protective Services
shirley.preston@trenthills.ca
Tim Blake, Fire Chief, Campbellford/Seymour
705-653-1234
Bill Kelly, Fire Chief, Hastings & Warkworth
Margaret Montgomery, Clerk
marg.montgomery@trenthills.ca
Brenda Otto, Officer, Community Development
brenda.otto@trenthills.ca
David Rogers, Chief Building Official
dave.rogers@trenthills.ca

Uxbridge
P.O. Box 190
51 Toronto St. South
Uxbridge, ON L9P 1T1
905-852-9181
Fax: 905-852-9674
info@town.uxbridge.on.ca
www.town.uxbridge.on.ca
Municipal Type: Township
Incorporated: 1872 *Area:* 420.65 sq km
County or District: Durham Reg. Mun.; *Population in 2006:* 19,169
Provincial Electoral District(s): Durham
Federal Electoral District(s): Durham
Next Election: Oct. 2014 (4 year terms)
Note: Incorporated as a town in 1885, & town became part of Uxbridge Township in 1973.
Gerri Lynn O'Connor, Mayor
Debbie Leroux, Clerk & Officer, Lottery Licensing
dleroux@town.uxbridge.on.ca
Ron Mitchell, Treasurer
Alex Gant, Chief Administrator
agane@town.uxbridge.on.ca
Ben Kester, Director, Public Works
bkester@town.uxbridge.on.ca
Ingrid Svelnis, Director, Parks, Recreation & Culture
isvelnis@town.uxbridge.on.ca

See blue tabs following this section for Municipal Waste Management and Water & Wastewater Treatment .

Municipal Governments / Prince Edward Island

Simon Almond, Fire Chief
905-852-3393

Wellington North
P.O. Box 125
7490 Sideroad 7 West
Kenilworth, ON N0G 2E0
519-848-3620
Fax: 519-848-3228
Toll Free Phone: 1-866-848-3620
township@wellington-north.com
www.wellington-north.com
Municipal Type: Township
Incorporated: Jan. 1, 1999 *Area:* 524.38 sq km
County or District: Wellington; *Population in 2006:* 11,175
Provincial Electoral District(s): Perth-Wellington
Federal Electoral District(s): Perth-Wellington
Next Election: Oct. 2014 (4 year terms)
Note: Amalgamation of the Township of Arthur, Arthur Village, the Township of West Luther & the Town of Mount Forest.
Raymond T. Tout, Mayor
Lorraine (Lori) Heinbuch, Clerk
lheinbuch@wellington-north.com
Harold Knox, Chief Building Official
hknox@wellington-north.com
Gary Williamson, Superintendent, Works
garywil@wellington-north.com
Barry Trood, Foreman, Water & Sewer
519-848-5327
btrood@wellington-north.com
Melissa Irvine, Process/Compliance Analyst, Water & Sewer
Ronald MacEachern, Acting Fire Chief, Mount Forest
519-323-1441
Brent Barnes, Fire Chief, Arthur
519-848-3500

West Grey
402813 Grey Rd., RR#2
Durham, ON N0G 1R0
519-369-2200
Fax: 519-369-5962
Toll Free Phone: 1-800-538-9647
info@westgrey.com
www.westgrey.com
Municipal Type: Municipality
Incorporated: Jan 1, 2001 *Area:* 875.37 sq km
County or District: Grey; *Population in 2006:* 12,193
Provincial Electoral District(s): Bruce-Grey-Owen Sound
Federal Electoral District(s): Bruce-Grey-Owen Sound
Next Election: Oct. 2014 (4 year terms)
Note: Amalgamation of Bentinck, Glenelg, Normanby, Neustadt & Durham.
Kevin Eccles, Mayor
Christine Robinson, Chief Administrative Officer & Clerk
robinsonc@westgrey.com
Ken Gould, Manager, Public Works
kgould@westgrey.com
Ray Holliday, Chief Building Official
rholliday@westgrey.com
Phillip Schwartz, Fire Chief & Coordinator, Health & Safety
durhamstation@bmts.com

West Lincoln
P.O. Box 400
318 Canborough St.
Smithville, ON L0R 2A0
905-957-3346
Fax: 905-957-3219
Toll Free Phone: 1-800-350-3876
jscime@westlincoln.com
www.westlincoln.com
Municipal Type: Township
Incorporated: Jan. 1, 1970 *Area:* 387.72 sq km
County or District: Niagara Reg. Mun.; *Population in 2006:* 13,167
Provincial Electoral District(s): Niagara West-Glanbrook
Federal Electoral District(s): Niagara West-Glanbrook
Next Election: Oct. 2014 (4 year terms)
Note: Amalgamation of the former Townships of South Grimsby, Caistor, & Gainsborough.
Douglas Joyner, Mayor
Carolyn Langley, Clerk
carolynlangley@westlincoln.com
Stephanie Nagel, Treasurer & Director, Finance
snagel@westlincoln.com
Derrick Thomas, Chief Administrative Officer
dthomson@westlincoln.ca
Sue-Ellen Merritt, Chair, Planning, Building & Environmental Committee
Anthony Boncori, Chief Building Official
aboncori@westlincoln.com
John Ganann, Fire Chief
905-957-3361
Kathy Desjardins, Director, Planning
kathyd@westlincoln.com
Kathy Sipos, Manager, Public Works
ksipos@westlincoln.com
Gary Ricker, Supervisor, Water & Sewer
John Branco, Operator, Water & Sewer

West Nipissing
#101, 225 Holditch St.
Sturgeon Falls, ON P2B 1T1
705-753-2250
Fax: 705-753-3950
jbarbeau@municipality.westnipissing.on.ca
www.westnipissingouest.ca
Municipal Type: Municipality
Area: 1,989.57 sq km
County or District: Nipissing District; *Population in 2006:* 13,410
Provincial Electoral District(s): Timiskaming-Cochrane
Federal Electoral District(s): Nickel Belt
Next Election: Oct. 2014 (4 year terms)
Joanne Savage, Mayor
jsavage@municipality.westnipissing.on.ca
Melanie Ducharme, Municipal Clerk & Planner
705-753-2250
mducharme@westnipissing.ca
Roger Lachance, Director, Planning
rlachance@municipality.westnipissing.on.ca
Rachel Prudhomme, Director, Public Works
rprudhomme@municipality.westnipissing.on.ca
Richard Savage, Fire Chief
rsavage@wnfs.ca
Denis Lafreniere, Manager, Solid Waste
Peter Ming, Manager, Water/Wastewater Operations
Lynne Duhaime, Coordinator, Community Services
lduhaime@municipality.westnipissing.on.ca
Rheal Levac, Superintendent, Roads

Wilmot
60 Snyder's Rd. West
Baden, ON N3A 1A1
519-634-8444
Fax: 519-634-5522
Toll Free Phone: 1-800-469-5576
info@wilmot.ca
www.wilmot.ca
Municipal Type: Township
Area: 263.73 sq km
County or District: Waterloo Regional Municipality; *Population in 2006:* 17,097
Provincial Electoral District(s): Kitchener-Conestoga
Federal Electoral District(s): Kitchener-Conestoga
Next Election: Oct. 2014 (4 year terms)
Les Armstrong, Mayor
Barbara McLeod, Clerk
barb.mcleod@wilmot.ca
John A. Hacking, Treasurer
Grant Whittington, Chief Administrative Officer
grant.whittington@wilmot.ca
John Ritz, Fire Chief
john.ritz@wilmot.ca
Doug Robertson, Chief Building Official
Gary Charbonneau, Director, Public Works
gary.charbonneau@wilmot.ca
Harold O'Krafka, Director, Development Services
harold.okrafka@wilmot.ca
Geoff Dubrick, Manager, Parks/Facilities
geoff.dubrick@wilmot.ca
Andrew Martin, Planner & Officer, Economic Development
andrew.martin@wilmot.ca
Derek Wallace, Officer, By-law Enforcement
Ken Dietrich, Foreman, Roads
Sean Montgomery, Foreman, Utilities
sean.montgomery@wilmot.ca

Woolwich
P.O. Box 158
69 Arthur St. South
Elmira, ON N3B 2Z6
519-669-1647
Fax: 519-669-1820
woolwich.mail@woolwich.ca
www.woolwich.ca
Municipal Type: Township
Incorporated: Jan. 1, 1973 *Area:* 326 sq km
County or District: Waterloo Regional Municipality; *Population in 2006:* 19,658
Provincial Electoral District(s): Kitchener-Conestoga
Federal Electoral District(s): Kitchener-Conestoga
Next Election: Oct. 2014 (4 year terms)
Todd Cowan, Mayor
Christine Broughton, Clerk & Director, Council & Information Services
Dan Chapman, Treasurer
Rod Kruger, Manager, Engineering Operations
rkruger@township.woolwich.on.ca
Earl Wideman, Fire Chief
519-664-2237
Peter Vanderbeek, Chief Building Official
pvanderbeek@township.woolwich.on.ca

Prince Edward Island

The Prince Edward Island Department of Environment, Energy & Forestry is responsible for The Prince Edward Island Department of Environmental Protection Act.

The entire municipal population of 29 island communities is served by central wastewater treatment plants. Municipal wastewater includes household wastewater, waste from shopping malls, office buildings, hospitals, schools and some manufacturing plants. The central wastewater treatment system cleans the water until it is safe to return to the environment via rivers and harbours.

The Waste Resource Management Regulations are for the construction and operation of all facilities that handle solid waste in the province. This includes landfill sites and recycling facilities. Materials diverted from landfill sites are compost, paper, plastic, glass, cans and dry cell batteries. The entire province, including rural areas, has curbside recycling pickup. Solid waste that is not compostable or recyclable is sent to one of three landfill sites in the province. There is one incinerator in Charlottetown, which powers a hospital.

The Drinking Water Strategy is an updated action plan with new and tighter regulations, implemented summer of 2002. This provincial action plan ensures that PEI drinking water stays clear from the ground to the glass. In PEI, 57% of the population depends on private wells for drinking water and approximately 40% of the population has onsite sewage disposal systems for wastewater treatment.

Under the Renewable Energy Act, given Royal Assent in December 2004, the province established a guaranteed selling price for electricity supplied to the provincial utility from a community or cooperative wind system, and gave residents the opportunity to invest in local wind energy projects.

Under the federal government's New Deal for Cities, Prince Edward Island was allocated $37.5 million in federal gas tax funding between 2005 and 2010 for municipal infrastructure projects.

Major Municipalities in Prince Edward Island

Charlottetown
P.O. Box 90, 199 Queen St.
Charlottetown, PE C1A 4B7
902-566-5548
Fax: 902-566-4701
city@city.charlottetown.pe.ca
www.city.charlottetown.pe.ca
Municipal Type: City
Incorporated: 1855 *Area:* 44.33 sq km
County or District: Hillsborough; *Population in 2006:* 32,174
Provincial Electoral District(s): Charlottetown-Sherwood; Charlottetown-Parkdale; Charlottetown-Victoria Park; Charlottetown-Brighton; Charlottetown-Lewis Point
Federal Electoral District(s): Charlottetown
Next Election: Nov. 2010 (four year terms)

See blue tabs following this section for Municipal Waste Management and Water & Wastewater Treatment.

Council
Clifford J. Lee, Mayor
mayor@city.charlottetown.pe.ca
Kim Devine, B.A., Councillor, Ward(s): 1
kdevine@city.charlottetown.pe.ca
Daniel (Danny) J. Redmond, B.A., Councillor, Ward(s): 2
dredmond@city.charlottetown.pe.ca
Rob Lantz, B.Sc., Councillor, Ward(s): 3
rlantz@city.charlottetown.pe.ca
Mitchell G. Tweel, B.A., Councillor, Ward(s): 4
mitchell.tweel@pei.sympatico.ca
Sterling MacFadyen, Deputy Mayor & Councillor, Ward(s): 5
smacfadyen@city.charlottetown.pe.ca
David MacDonald, Councillor, Ward(s): 6
dmacdonald@city.charlottetown.pe.ca
Cecil F. Villard, Councillor, Ward(s): 7
cvillard@city.charlottetown.pe.ca
Peter F. McCloskey, Councillor, Ward(s): 8
pmccloskey@city.charlottetown.pe.ca
Melissa Hilton, B.A., Councillor, Ward(s): 9
mhilton@city.charlottetown.pe.ca
Terence H. Bernard, Councillor, Ward(s): 10
tbernard@city.charlottetown.pe.ca

Administration
Roy Main, Chief Administrative Officer
rmain@city.charlottetown.pe.ca
Joseph Coady, Director, Public Services
jcoady@city.charlottetown.pe.ca
Donna Waddell, Director, Corporate Services
dwaddell@city.charlottetown.pe.ca
Phil Handrahan, Director, Fiscal & Development Services
phandrahan@city.charlottetown.pe.ca
Craig Walker, Manager, Water & Sewer Utility
902-629-4014
cwalker@city.charlottetown.pe.ca
Bill Clair, Works Superintendent, Water & Sewer Utility
902-629-4015
bclair@city.charlottetown.pe.ca
Herman Van Omme, Superintendent, Waste Water Treatment Plant
902-628-6647, Fax: 902-628-6684
hvanomme@city.charlottetown.pe.ca
Ron Atkinson, Economic Development Officer, Economic Development, Tourism & Events
ratkinson@city.charlottetown.pe.ca
Dan Hughes, Manager, Human Resources
Don Poole, Manager of Planning, Planning & Development
dpoole@city.charlottetown.pe.ca
Vada Fernandez, Purchasing Officer, Finance
vfernandez@city.charlottetown.pe.ca
Mel Cheverie, Chief Building Inspector, Planning & Development
mcheverie@city.charlottetown.pe.ca
Jim Molyneux, Field Works Coordinator, Public Works
jmolyneux@city.charlottetown.pe.ca
Blair Kinch, Sr. Superintendent, Public Works
bkinch@city.charlottetown.pe.ca
Lance Jones, Streets Maintenance Supervisor, Public Works
ljones@city.charlottetown.pe.ca
Nancy McMinn, Parks Superintendent, Parks & Recreation
nmcminn@city.charlottetown.pe.ca
Scott Ryan, M.B.A., CMA, FCMA, Manager, Finance
sryan@city.charlottetown.pe.ca
Randy MacDonald, Fire Chief, Fire Services
rmacdonald@city.charlottetown.pe.ca
Paul Johnston, Manager, Public Works
902-894-5208
pjohnston@city.charlottetown.pe.ca
Sue Hendricken, Manager, Parks & Recreation
902-368-1025
shendricken@city.charlottetown.pe.ca
Paul Smith, Chief of Police
psmith@city.charlottetown.pe.ca

Summerside
275 Fitzroy St.
Summerside, PE C1N 1H9
902-432-1288
Fax: 902-436-9296
cityhall@city.summerside.pe.ca
www.city.summerside.pe.ca
Municipal Type: City
Incorporated: 1995 *Area:* 28.36 sq km
County or District: Egmont; *Population in 2006:* 14,500
Provincial Electoral District(s): Wilmot-Summerside; St. Eleanors-Summerside
Federal Electoral District(s): Egmont
Next Election: Nov. 2010 (four year terms)

Council
Basil L. Stewart, Mayor
mayor@city.summerside.pe.ca
Bruce MacDougall, Deputy Mayor & Councillor
bmacdougall@city.summerside.pe.ca
Cory Thomas, Councillor
cthomas@city.summerside.pe.ca
Brent Gallant, Councillor
bgallant@city.summerside.pe.ca
Ron Dowling, Councillor
rdowling@city.summerside.pe.ca
Garth Lyle, Councillor
glyle@city.summerside.pe.ca
Norma McColeman, Councillor
nmccoleman@city.summerside.pe.ca
Barry Chappell, Councillor
bchappell@city.summerside.pe.ca
Vance Bridges, Councillor
vbridges@pei.sympatico.ca

Administration
Terry Murphy, CAO
tmurphy@city.summerside.pe.ca
Malcolm Millar, Director, Financial Services
mmillar@city.summerside.pe.ca
David Morgan, Director, Community Services
dmorgan@city.summerside.pe.ca
James Peters, Director, Fire Services
jpeters@city.summerside.pe.ca
J. David Poirier, Director, Police Services
dpoirier@city.summerside.pe.ca
Gordon MacFarlane, Director, Human Resources
gmacfarlane@city.summerside.pe.ca
Michael Thususka, Director, Economic Development
miket@city.summerside.pe.ca
Aaron MacDonald, Director, Technical Services
aaronmac@city.summerside.pe.ca

Québec

Garbage collection is conducted by municipalities; recycling and waste management is carried out by municipalities and upper tier level governments. Water and wastewater treatment is similarly the responsibility of municipalities and upper tier level governments. Municipalities may enter into agreements with one another in the management & delivery of these services. With the exception of garbage collection, all the above services are subsidized in part by the provincial government.

Funding was made available to communities under the Strategy & Action Plan on Biological Diversity 2004-2007. Rural municipal infrastructure funding ($390 million) is a federal-provincial initiative.

Under the federal government's New Deal for Cities, Qu<130>bec was allocated $1.151 billion in federal gas tax funding between 2005 and 2010 for municipal infrastructure projects.

Major Municipalities in Québec

Alma
140, rue St-Joseph sud
Alma, QC G8B 3R1
418-669-5000
Fax: 418-669-5019
info@ville.alma.qc.ca
www.ville.alma.qc.ca
Municipal Type: City
Incorporated: 21 février 2001 *Area:* 202,10 km2
County or District: Lac-St-Jean-Est; *Population in 2006:* 29,998
Provincial Electoral District(s): Lac-Saint-Jean
Federal Electoral District(s): Jonquière-Alma
Next Election: 1er novembre 2013
Gérald Scullion, Maire
418-669-5005
gerald.scullion@ville.alma.qc.ca
Jean Paradis, Greffier
jean.paradis@ville.alma.qc.ca
Jean-Yves Lessard, Directeur, Travaux publics
jeanyves.lessard@ville.alma.qc.ca
Lucien Boily, Conseillers et Districts, Ward(s): 1
418-669-1070
lucien.boily@ville.alma.qc.ca
Jocelyn Fradette, Conseillers et Districts, Ward(s): 2
418-480-1359
jocelyn.fradette@ville.alma.qc.ca
Yves Thériault, Trésorier
yves.theriault@ville.alma.qc.ca
Guy Simard, Directeur général
guy.simard@ville.alma.qc.ca
Bernard Dallaire, Directeur, Prévention des incendies
418-669-5059
bernard.dallaire@ville.alma.qc.ca
Claude Garneau, Conseillers et Districts, Ward(s): 3
418-668-3694
claude.garneau@ville.alma.qc.ca
Frédéric Tremblay, Conseillers et Districts, Ward(s): 4
418-668-5014
frederic.tremblay@ville.alma.qc.ca
Jean-Rock Pedneault, Conseillers et Districts, Ward(s): 5
418-662-6223
jean-rock.pedneault@ville.alma.qc.ca
Sylvie Beaumont, Conseillers et Districts, Ward(s): 6
418-668-0919
sylvie.beaumont@ville.alma.qc.ca
Pascal Pilote, Conseillers et Districts, Ward(s): 7
418-480-1417
pascal.pilote@ville.alma.qc.ca
Marc Asselin, Conseillers et Districts, Ward(s): 8
418-668-8923
marc.asselin@ville.alma.qc.ca
Marcel Guérin, Directeur, Loisirs/culture
418-669-5111
marcel.guerin@ville.alma.qc.ca

Amos
182, 1e Rue est
Amos, QC J9T 2G1
819-732-3254
Fax: 819-727-9792
infos@ville.amos.qc.ca
www.ville.amos.qc.ca
Municipal Type: City
Incorporated: 17 janvier 1987 *Area:* 430,84 km2
County or District: Abitibi; *Population in 2009:* 12,729
Provincial Electoral District(s): Abitibi-Ouest
Federal Electoral District(s): Abitibi-Témiscamingue
Next Election: 1er novembre 2013
Alain Plante, Greffier
Ulrick Chérubin, Maire
Gérald Lavoie, Trésorier
Martin Brunet, Inspecteur municipal
Guy Nolet, Directeur général
Lucie Veillette, Responsable, Communications
Yvon Rioux, Directeur, Loisirs

Baie-Comeau
19, av Marquette
Baie-Comeau, QC G4Z 1K5
418-296-4931
Fax: 418-296-3759
vbc@ville.baie-comeau.qc.ca
www.ville.baie-comeau.qc.ca
Municipal Type: City
Incorporated: 23 juin 1982 *Area:* 371,69 km2
County or District: Manicouagan; *Population in 2006:* 22,554
Provincial Electoral District(s): René-Lévesque
Federal Electoral District(s): Manicouagan
Next Election: 1er novembre 2013
François Corriveau, Greffier
418-296-8109, Fax: 418-296-8194
greffebc@ville.baie-comeau.qc.ca
Danielle Bernatchez, Directrice, Finances
418-296-8128, Fax: 418-296-3759
dbernatchez@ville.baie-comeau.qc.ca
Paul Joncas, Directeur général
418-296-8104, Fax: 418-296-8121
jviens@ville.baie-comeau.qc.ca
Jacques Comeau, Directeur, Service des communications
418-296-8142, Fax: 418-296-3759
jcomeau@ville.baie-comeau.qc.ca
Ivo Di Piazza, Maire
418-296-8101
mairie@ville.baie-comeau.qc.ca
François Leblond, Directeur, Loisirs/sports/arts/culture/vie communautaire
418-296-8358, Fax: 418-296-8399
fleblond@ville.baie-comeau.qc.ca

Municipal Governments / Québec

Alain Larouche, Conseillers et Districts, Ward(s):
Saint-Sacrement
418-589-2107
Raymond Coulombe, Conseillers et Districts, Ward(s): Mgr Bélanger
418-589-8930
Christine Brisson, Conseillers et Districts, Ward(s): Trudel
418-295-2883
Carole Deschênes, Conseillers et Districts, Ward(s):
N.-A.-Labrie
418-589-8734
Jean Thériault, Conseillers et Districts, Ward(s): La Chasse
418-296-8637
Steve Ahern, Conseillers et Districts, Ward(s):
Saint-Nom-de-Marie
418-296-2245
Reina Savoie Jourdain, Conseillers et Districts, Ward(s):
Sainte-Amélie
418-296-5231
Yvon Boudreau, Conseillers et Districts, Ward(s): Saint-Georges
418-296-2672

Beaconsfield
303, boul Beaconsfield
Beaconsfield, QC H9W 4A7
514-428-4400
Fax: 514-428-4424
bob.benedetti@beaconsfield.ca
www.ville.montreal.qc.ca/bbdu/
Municipal Type: City
Incorporated: 1er janvier 2006 *Area:* 10,64 km2
Population in 2006: 19,194
Provincial Electoral District(s): Jacques-Cartier
Federal Electoral District(s): Communauté-Urbaine-de-Montréal
Next Election: 1er janvier 2012
Bob Benedetti, Maire
Helen Finn, Greffière

Beauharnois
#100, 660, rue Ellice
Beauharnois, QC J6N 1Y1
450-429-3546
Fax: 450-429-6663
manon.fortier@ville.beauharnois.qc.ca
www.ville.beauharnois.qc.ca
Municipal Type: City
Incorporated: 1er janvier 2002 *Area:* 73,05 km2
County or District: Beauharnois-Salaberry; *Population in 2006:* 11,918
Provincial Electoral District(s): Beauharnois
Federal Electoral District(s): Beauharnois-Salaberry
Next Election: 1er novembre 2013
Manon Fortier, Directrice générale (par intérim) & Greffière
manon.fortier@ville.beauharnois.qc.ca
Daniel Charlesbois, Maire
daniel.charlebois@ville.beauharnois.qc.ca

Bécancour
1295, av Nicolas-Perrot
Bécancour, QC G9H 1A1
819-294-6500
Fax: 819-294-6535
becancour@ville.becancour.qc.ca
www.becancour.net
Municipal Type: City
Incorporated: 17 octobre 1965 *Area:* 434,28 km2
County or District: Bécancour; *Population in 2009:* 11,171
Provincial Electoral District(s): Nicolet-Yamaska
Federal Electoral District(s): Bas-Richelieu-Nicolet-Bécancour
Next Election: 1er novembre 2013
France Leclerc, Greffière
Maurice Richard, Maire
Daniel Brunelle, Directeur, Finances
Gaston Bélanger, Directeur général

Beloeil
777, rue Laurier
Beloeil, QC J3G 4S9
450-467-2835
Fax: 450-464-5445
info@ville.beloeil.qc.ca
www.ville.beloeil.qc.ca
Municipal Type: City
Incorporated: 9 décembre 1903 *Area:* 24 km2
County or District: La Vallée-du-Richelieu; *Population in 2006:* 18,927
Provincial Electoral District(s): Borduas
Federal Electoral District(s): Chambly-Borduas
Next Election: 1er novembre 2013
Sylvie Piérard, Greffière
greffe@ville.beloeil.qc.ca
Réal Jeannotte, Maire
450-467-4679
rjeannotte@ville.beloeil.qc.ca
Nathalie Guérin, Directrice, Finances
finances@ville.beloeil.qc.ca
Martine Vallières, Directrice générale
direction@ville.beloeil.qc.ca
Réginald Gagnon, Conseillers et Districts, Ward(s): 1
514-569-4500
rgagnon@ville.beloeil.qc.ca
Jean-Guy Savard, Conseillers et Districts, Ward(s): 2
450-467-2545
jgsavard@ville.beloeil.qc.ca
Gilles Gaucher, Conseillers et Districts, Ward(s): 3
450-446-5576
ggaucher@ville.beloeil.qc.ca
Denis Corriveau, Conseillers et Districts, Ward(s): 4
450-464-2435
dcorriveau@ville.beloeil.qc.ca
Pierre Verret, Conseillers et Districts, Ward(s): 5
450-467-0630
pverret@ville.beloeil.qc.ca
Bernard Cardinal, Conseillers et Districts, Ward(s): 6
450-467-7127
bcardinal@ville.beloeil.qc.ca
Diane Lavoie, Conseillers et Districts, Ward(s): 7
450-464-3095
dlavoie@ville.beloeil.qc.ca
Jean-Yves Labadie, Conseillers et Districts, Ward(s): 8
450-446-0347
jylabadie@ville.beloeil.qc.ca

Blainville
1000, ch du Plan-Bouchard
Blainville, QC J7C 3S9
450-434-5200
Fax: 450-434-8295
accueil@ville.blainville.qc.ca
www.ville.blainville.qc.ca
Municipal Type: City
Incorporated: 1er juillet 1855 *Area:* 54,62 km2
County or District: Thérèse-De Blainville; Communauté métropolitaine de Montréal; *Population in 2009:* 48,821
Provincial Electoral District(s): Blainville
Federal Electoral District(s): Terrebonne-Blainville
Next Election: 1er novembre 2013
Claude Bertrand, Greffier
450-434-5215
servicesjuridiques@ville.blainville.qc.ca
François Cantin, Maire
450-434-5203
cabinetdumaire@ville.blainville.ca
Paul Allard, Directeur général
450-434-5209
directiongenerale@ville.blainville.qc.ca
Claude Perrotte, Directeur, Finances
450-434-5237
finances@ville.blainville.qc.ca
Michèle Murray, Conseillers et Districts, Ward(s): 1 Fontainebleau
Alain Portelance, Conseillers et Districts, Ward(s): 2
Côte-Saint-Louis
Serge Paquette, Conseillers et Districts, Ward(s): 3
Saint-Rédempteur
Guy Frigon, Conseillers et Districts, Ward(s): 4 Plan-Bouchard
Normand Dupont, Conseillers et Districts, Ward(s): 5
Notre-Dame-de-l'Assomption
Jeannette Lavoie, Conseillers et Districts, Ward(s): 6
Chante-Bois
Louis Lamarre, Conseillers et Districts, Ward(s): 7 Hirondelles
Richard Perreault, Conseillers et Districts, Ward(s): 8 Alençon
François Garand, Conseillers et Districts, Ward(s): 9
Renaissance
Marie-Claude Collin, Conseillers et Districts, Ward(s): 10
Blainvillier

Boisbriand
940, boul de la Grande-Allée
Boisbriand, QC J7G 2J7
450-435-1954
Fax: 450-435-6398
www.ville.boisbriand.qc.ca
Municipal Type: City
Incorporated: 1er janvier 1946 *Area:* 26,43 km2
County or District: Thérèse-De Blainville; Communauté métropolitaine de Montréal; *Population in 2009:* 26,674
Provincial Electoral District(s): Groulx
Federal Electoral District(s): Rivière-des-Mille-Iles
Next Election: 1er novembre 2013
Lucie Mongeau, Greffière
Sylvie St-Jean, Mairesse
sstjean@ville.boisbriand.qc.ca
Michel Lacasse, Directeur général
André Drainville, Directeur, Finances & Trésorerie
Lyne Levert, Conseillers et Districts, Ward(s): 1 Sanche
llevert@ville.boisbriand.qc.ca
Gilles Sauriol, Conseillers et Districts, Ward(s): 2 Du Gué
gsauriol@ville.broisbriand.qc.ca
Robert Frégeau, Conseillers et Districts, Ward(s): 3 Filion
rfregeau@ville.boisbriand.qc.ca
Patrick Thifault, Conseillers et Districts, Ward(s): 4 Dubois
pthifault@ville.boisbriand.qc.ca
Louise Gauthier, Conseillers et Districts, Ward(s): 5 Brosseau
lgauthier@ville.boisbriand.qc.ca
Louise Lemay, Conseillers et Districts, Ward(s): 6 Labelle
llemay@ville.boisbriand.qc.ca
Mario Lavallée, Conseillers et Districts, Ward(s): 7 Desjardins
mlavallee@ville.boisbriand.qc.ca
Marlene Cordato, Conseillers et Districts, Ward(s): 8 Dion
mcordato@ville.boisbriand.qc.ca

Candiac
100, boul Montcalm nord
Candiac, QC J5R 3L8
450-444-6000
Fax: 450-444-6009
info@ville.candiac.qc.ca
www.ville.candiac.qc.ca
Municipal Type: City
Incorporated: 31 janvier 1957 *Area:* 16,40 km2
County or District: Roussillon; Communauté métropolitaine de Montréal; *Population in 2009:* 16,825
Provincial Electoral District(s): La Prairie
Federal Electoral District(s): Brossard-La Prairie
Next Election: 1er novembre 2013
Carole Lemaire, Greffière
André J. Côté, Maire
Serge Drouin, Directeur général
Patrick Quirion, Trésorier

Chambly
56, rue Martel
Chambly, QC J3L 1V3
450-658-8788
Fax: 450-447-4525
information@ville.chambly.qc.ca
www.ville.chambly.qc.ca
Municipal Type: City
Incorporated: 26 octobre 1848 *Area:* 25,01 km2
County or District: La Vallée-du-Richelieu; *Population in 2006:* 22,608
Provincial Electoral District(s): Chambly
Federal Electoral District(s): Chambly-Borduas
Next Election: 1er novembre 2013
Louise Bouvier, Greffière
louise.bouvier@ville.chambly.qc.ca
Denis Lavoie, Maire
maire@ville.chambly.qc.ca
Jean Beauregard, Conseillers et Districts, Ward(s): Canton
450-658-2213
Cécile Ouellet, Conseillers et Districts, Ward(s): Bassin
450-658-2045
Normand Houle, Conseillers et Districts, Ward(s):
Charles-Michel-de Salaberry
450-658-0362
Richard Tetreault, Conseillers et Districts, Ward(s): La Petite Rivière
450-658-4282
Ken Moquin, Conseillers et Districts, Ward(s):
Antoine-Louis-Fréchette
450-658-8124
Daniel Monast, Conseillers et Districts, Ward(s): Louis-Franquet
514-978-5405

See blue tabs following this section for Municipal Waste Management and Water & Wastewater Treatment.

Jean Roy, Conseillers et Districts, Ward(s): Ruisseau
450-447-6152
Steeves Demers, Conseillers et Districts, Ward(s): Grandes Terres
514-250-9960
André Cholette, Directeur général
andre.cholette@ville.chambly.qc.ca
Annie Nepton, Directrice, Services des finances
finances@ville.chambly.qc.ca

Châteauguay
5, boul d'Youville
Châteauguay, QC J6J 2P8
450-698-3000
Fax: 450-698-3019
info@ville.chateauguay.qc.ca
www.ville.chateauguay.qc.ca
Municipal Type: City
Incorporated: 3 novembre 1975 *Area:* 35,37 km2
County or District: Roussillon; Communauté métropolitaine de Montréal; *Population in 2006:* 42,786
Provincial Electoral District(s): Châteauguay
Federal Electoral District(s): Châteauguay-St-Constant
Next Election: 1er novembre 2013
Paul G. Brunet, Greffier & Directeur général
Sergio Pavone, Maire
mairie@ville.chateauguay.qc.ca
Anthony Boffice, Conseillers et Districts, Ward(s): 1 La Noue
450-699-4613
Stephen Brisebois, Conseillers et Districts, Ward(s): 2 Filgate
514-914-4945
Daniel Kabasele, Conseillers et Districts, Ward(s): 3 Robutel
450-699-4883
Serge Dion, Conseillers et Districts, Ward(s): 4 Bumbray
450-691-6088
Marcel Deschamps, Conseillers et Districts, Ward(s): 5 Salaberry
450-699-1120
Mike Gendron, Conseillers et Districts, Ward(s): 6 Lang
514-829-1986
André St-Pierre, Conseillers et Districts, Ward(s): 7 Le Moyne
450-692-4979
Richard Motard, Conseillers et Districts, Ward(s): 8 D'Youville
450-699-6141

Cowansville
220, place Municipale
Cowansville, QC J2K 1T4
450-263-0141
Fax: 450-263-9357
hoteldeville@ville.cowansville.qc.ca
www.cowansville.org
Municipal Type: City
Incorporated: 1er janvier 1876 *Area:* 48,79 km2
County or District: Brome-Missisquoi; *Population in 2009:* 12,297
Provincial Electoral District(s): Brome-Missisquoi
Federal Electoral District(s): Brome-Missisquoi
Next Election: 1er novembre 2013
Joanne Skelling, Greffière
Arthur Fauteux, Maire
Pierre Bell, Trésorier

Deux-Montagnes
803, ch d'Oka
Deux-Montagnes, QC J7R 1L8
450-473-2796
Fax: 450-473-2417
www.ville.deux-montagnes.qc.ca
Municipal Type: City
Incorporated: 18 août 1921 *Area:* 5,82 km2
County or District: Deux-Montagnes; *Population in 2006:* 17,402
Provincial Electoral District(s): Deux-Montagnes
Federal Electoral District(s): Rivière-des-Mille-Iles
Next Election: 1er novembre 2013
Nicolas Bouchard, Directeur général
Marc Lauzon, Maire
450-473-8898
mlauzon@ville.deux-montagnes.qc.ca
Martin Bigras, Conseillers et Districts, Ward(s): Coteau
mbigras@ville.deux-montagnes.qc.ca
Nathalie Chayer, Conseillers et Districts, Ward(s): Gare
nchayer@ville.deux-montagnes.qc.ca
Denis Joannette, Conseillers et Districts, Ward(s): Olympia
djoannette@ville.deux-montagnes.qc.ca

Mario Saint-Charles, Conseillers et Districts, Ward(s): Lac
mst-charles@ville.deux-montagnes.qc.ca
Gilles Saint-Marseille, Conseillers et Districts, Ward(s): Golf
gst-marseille@ville.deux-montagnes.qc.ca
Sylvain Sauvageau, Conseillers et Districts, Ward(s): Grand-Moulin
ssauvageau@ville.deux-montagnes.qc.ca
Alexandre Verdy, Greffier
Marie-Josée Boissonneault, Directrice, Finances & Trésorerie

Dolbeau-Mistassini
1100, boul Wallberg
Dolbeau-Mistassini, QC G8L 1G7
418-276-0160
Fax: 418-276-8312
hotelville@ville.dolbeau-mistassini.qc.ca
www.ville.dolbeau-mistassini.qc.ca
Municipal Type: City
Incorporated: 17 décembre 1997 *Area:* 296,57 km2
County or District: Maria-Chapdelaine; *Population in 2009:* 14,474
Provincial Electoral District(s): Roberval
Federal Electoral District(s): Roberval-Lac-St-Jean
Next Election: 1er novembre 2013
André Côté, Greffier
Georges Simard, Maire
Frédéric Lemieux, Directeur général
Suzy Gagnon, Trésorière

Drummondville
CP 398
415, rue Lindsay
Drummondville, QC J2B 6W3
819-478-6550
communications@ville.drummondville.qc.ca
www.ville.drummondville.qc.ca
Municipal Type: City
Incorporated: 7 juillet 2004 *Area:* 249,80 km2
County or District: Drummond; *Population in 2006:* 67,392
Provincial Electoral District(s): Drummond
Federal Electoral District(s): Drummond
Next Election: 1er novembre 2013
Note: Effective July 7, 2004, the municipalities of St-Charles-de-Drummond & St-Joachim-de-Courval & the cities of St-Nicéphore & Drummondville regrouped to form the new city of Drummondville
Thérèse Cajolet, Greffière
819-478-6554, Fax: 819-478-3363
greffe@ville.drummondville.qc.ca
Francine Ruest Jutras, Mairesse
mairie@ville.drummondville.qc.ca
Claude Proulx, Directeur général
819-478-6557, Fax: 819-478-3363
direction@ville.drummondville.qc.ca
Gilles Bélisle, CGA, Trésorier
819-478-6559, Fax: 819-478-3164
tresor@ville.drummondville.qc.ca

Gaspé
25, rue de l'Hôtel-de-Ville
Gaspé, QC G4X 2A5
418-368-2104
Fax: 418-368-8532
direction.generale@ville.gaspe.qc.ca
www.ville.gaspe.qc.ca
Municipal Type: City
Incorporated: 1er janvier 1971 *Area:* 1446,95 km2
County or District: La Côte-de-Gaspé; *Population in 2009:* 14,958
Provincial Electoral District(s): Gaspé
Federal Electoral District(s): Gaspésie-Iles-de-la-Madeleine
Next Election: 1er novembre 2013
Sébastien Fournier, Greffier
François Roussy, Maire
Gaétan Lelièvre, Directeur général
Dave St-Croix, Trésorier

Gatineau
CP 1970 Hull
25, rue Laurier
Gatineau, QC J8X 3Y9
819-595-2002
info@gatineau.ca
www.gatineau.ca
Municipal Type: City
Incorporated: 1er janvier 2002 *Area:* 344,16 km2

Population in 2006: 242,124
Provincial Electoral District(s): Gatineau; Chapleau; Hull; Papineau; Pontiac
Federal Electoral District(s): Gatineau
Next Election: 1er novembre 2013
Marc Bureau, Maire
819-595-7100
maire@gatineau.ca
Roland Morin, Responsable, Travaux publics et environnement
Robert F. Weemaes, Directeur général
Suzanne Ouellet, Greffière
Marc Pageau, Directeur, Service des ressources humaines
André Langelier, Coordonnateur, Mesures d'urgence
André Bonneau, Directeur, Service d'incendie
Frank Thérien, Conseillers et Districts, Ward(s): Aylmer
therien.frank@gatineau.ca
Denis Tassé, Conseillers et Districts, Ward(s): Riverains
tasse.denis@gatineau.ca
Alain Riel, Conseillers et Districts, Ward(s): Deschênes
riel.alain@gatineau.ca
Joseph De Sylva, Conseillers et Districts, Ward(s): Versant
desylva.joseph@gatineau.ca
Alain Pilon, Conseillers et Districts, Ward(s): Val-Tétreau
pilon.alain@gatineau.ca
Luc Angers, Conseillers et Districts, Ward(s): Promenades
angers.luc@gatineau.ca
Richard Côté, Conseillers et Districts, Ward(s): Bellevue
cote.richard@gatineau.ca
Claude Millette, Conseillers et Districts, Ward(s): Orée-du-Parc
millette.claude@gatineau.ca
Yvon Boucher, Conseillers et Districts, Ward(s): Rivière-Blanche
boucher.yvon@gatineau.ca
Patrice Martin, Conseillers et Districts, Ward(s): Wright-Parc-de-la-Montagne
martin.patrice@gatineau.ca
Aurèle Desjardins, Conseillers et Districts, Ward(s): Lac-Beauchamp
desjardins.aurele@gatineau.ca
André Laframboise, Conseillers et Districts, Ward(s): Lucerne
laframboise.andre@gatineau.ca
Claude Doucet, Directeur, Urbanisme
Pierre Philion, Conseillers et Districts, Ward(s): Saint-Raymond-Vanier
philion.pierre@gatineau.ca
Denise Laferrière, Conseillers et Districts, Ward(s): Hull
laferriere.denise@gatineau.ca
Simon Racine, Conseillers et Districts, Ward(s): Limbour
racine.simon@gatineau.ca
Luc Montreuil, Conseillers et Districts, Ward(s): Masson-Angers
montreuil.luc@gatineau.ca
Jocelyne Houle, Conseillers et Districts, Ward(s): Buckingham
houle.jocelyne@gatineau.ca
André Barbeau, Trésorier, Finances & trésorerie
Nicole Dumoulin, Directrice, Communications
Mario Harel, Directeur et Chef, Police

Granby
87, rue Principale
Granby, QC J2G 2T8
450-776-8282
Fax: 450-776-8278
communication@ville.granby.qc.ca
www.ville.granby.qc.ca
Municipal Type: City
Incorporated: 1er janvier 2007 *Area:* 156,68 km2
County or District: La Haute-Yamaska; *Population in 2006:* 47,637
Provincial Electoral District(s): Shefford
Federal Electoral District(s): Shefford
Next Election: 1er novembre 2013
Catherine Bouchard, Greffière
450-776-8275, Fax: 450-776-8278
greffe@ville.granby.qc.ca
Richard Goulet, Maire
450-776-8228, Fax: 450-776-8383
mairie@ville.granby.qc.ca
Michel Pinault, Directeur général
450-776-8232, Fax: 450-776-8279
direction.generale@ville.granby.ca
Jean-Pierre Renaud, Trésorier
450-776-8287, Fax: 450-776-8384
tresorerie@ville.granby.qc.ca
André Jean, Directeur, Travaux publics
450-776-8366, Fax: 450-776-8370
travaux.publics@ville.granby.qc.ca

Municipal Governments / Québec

Pierre Lacombe, Directeur, Service d'incendie
450-776-8344, Fax: 450-776-8390
incendie@ville.granby.qc.ca
Louise Brodeur Comeau, Conseillers et Districts, Ward(s): 1
Claudette Hudon, Conseillers et Districts, Ward(s): 2
Pierre Breton, Conseillers et Districts, Ward(s): 3
Réal Bernard, Conseillers et Districts, Ward(s): 4
Denis Choinière, Conseillers et Districts, Ward(s): 5
Serges Ruel, Conseillers et Districts, Ward(s): 6
Jacques Gévry, Conseillers et Districts, Ward(s): 7
Guy Gaudor, Conseillers et Districts, Ward(s): 8
Yves Bélanger, Conseillers et Districts, Ward(s): 9
Michel Mailhot, Conseillers et Districts, Ward(s): 10
Patrice Faucher, Directeur, Loisir/arts/culture/vie communautaire
450-776-8824
pfaucher@ville.granby.qc.ca

Joliette
614, boul Manseau
Joliette, QC J6E 3E4
450-753-8000
Fax: 450-753-8199
greffier@ville.joliette.qc.ca
www.ville.joliette.qc.ca
Municipal Type: City
Incorporated: 12 novembre 1966 Area: 22,36 km2
County or District: Joliette; Population in 2006: 19,044
Provincial Electoral District(s): Joliette
Federal Electoral District(s): Joliette
Next Election: 1er novembre 2013
Pierrick Sylvestre, Greffier
René Laurin, Maire
Robert Pépin, Directeur/Chef, Brigade des pompiers
450-759-5222
service.incendies@ville.joliette.qc.ca
Renald Gravel, Coordonnateur, Mesures d'urgence
Gilles Montambault, Inspecteur municipal de voirie

L'Assomption
399, rue Dorval
L'Assomption, QC J5W 1A1
450-589-5671
Fax: 450-589-4512
information@ville.lassomption.qc.ca
www.ville.lassomption.qc.ca
Municipal Type: City
Incorporated: 1er juillet 2000 Area: 100,09 km2
County or District: L'Assomption; Population in 2006: 16,738
Provincial Electoral District(s): L'Assomption
Federal Electoral District(s): Repentigny
Next Election: 1er novembre 2013
Chantal Bédard, Greffière
greffe@ville.lassomption.qc.ca
Pierre Gour, Maire
Dominique Valiquette, CGA, OMA, Trésorier
tresorerie@ville.lassomption.qc.ca
Martin Lelièvre, Directeur général
directionenerale@ville.lassomption.qc.ca

La Prairie
#400, 170, boul Taschereau
La Prairie, QC J5R 5H6
450-444-6600
Fax: 450-444-6636
info@ville.laprairie.qc.ca
www.ville.laprairie.qc.ca
Municipal Type: City
Incorporated: 30 mars 1846 Area: 43,53 km2
County or District: Roussillon; Population in 2006: 21,763
Provincial Electoral District(s): La Prairie
Federal Electoral District(s): Brossard-La Prairie
Next Election: 1er novembre 2013
Manon Thériault, Greffière
450-444-6625
greffe@ville.laprairie.qc.ca
Lucie F. Roussel, Mairesse
450-444-6618
communications@ville.laprairie.qc.ca
Jean Bergeron, Directeur général
450-444-6619
communications@ville.laprairie.qc.ca
Nathalie Guérin, Trésorière
450-444-6603
finances@ville.laprairies.qc.ca
Donat Serres, Conseillers et Districts, Ward(s): 1 la Milice

Christian Caron, Conseillers et Districts, Ward(s): 2 Christ-Roi
Laurent Blais, Conseillers et Districts, Ward(s): 3 Vieux La Prairie
Yvon Brière, Conseillers et Districts, Ward(s): 5 La Clairière
Pierre Vocino, Conseillers et Districts, Ward(s): 6 La Magdeleine
Jacques Bourbonnais, Conseillers et Districts, Ward(s): 4 La Citière
Yves Senécal, Conseillers et Districts, Ward(s): 7 la Bataille
Suzanne Perron, Conseillers et Districts, Ward(s): 8 la Briqueterie

La Tuque
375, rue St-Joseph
La Tuque, QC G9X 1L5
819-676-5091
Fax: 819-523-5419
infoservice@ville.latuque.qc.ca
www.ville.latuque.qc.ca
Municipal Type: City
Incorporated: 26 mars 2003 Area: 28 421,48 km2
Population in 2009: 11,759
Provincial Electoral District(s): Laviolette
Federal Electoral District(s): St-Maurice-Champlain
Next Election: 1er novembre 2013
Note: Dès le 26 mars 2003, la nouvelle ville de La Tuque regroupe La Tuque, les municipalités de La Croche, La Bostonnais, & Lac-Édouard, le village de Parent, & 8 autres territoires.
Yves Tousignant, Directeur général
dirgeneral@ville.latuque.qc.ca
Réjean Gaudreault, Maire
Jean-Sébastien Poirier, Greffier
greffe@ville.latuque.qc.ca
Pierre Bouchard, Trésorier
pbouchard@ville.latuque.qc.ca

Lachute
380, rue Principale
Lachute, QC J8H 1Y2
450-562-3781
Fax: 450-562-1431
lachute@ville.lachute.qc.ca
www.ville.lachute.qc.ca
Municipal Type: City
Incorporated: 30 avril 1966 Area: 111,20 km2
County or District: Argenteuil; Population in 2009: 11,889
Provincial Electoral District(s): Argenteuil
Federal Electoral District(s): Argenteuil-Papineau-Mirabel
Next Election: 1er novembre 2013
Louise Beaulieu, Greffière
Daniel Mayer, Maire
Pierre Gionet, Directeur général
Jeannic D'Aoust, Trésorière

Laval
Hôtel de Ville
CP 422 St-Martin
1, Place du Souvenir
Laval, QC H7V 3Z4
450-978-2900
Fax: 450-978-6569
info@ville.laval.qc.ca
www.ville.laval.qc.ca
Municipal Type: City
Incorporated: 6 août 1965 Area: 245,40 km2
County or District: Communauté métropolitaine de Montréal; Population in 2009: 377,332
Provincial Electoral District(s): Chomedey; Fabre; Laval-des-Rapides; Mille-Iles; Vimont
Federal Electoral District(s): Laval; Marc-Aurèle-Fortin; Alfred-Pellan; Laval-Les Iles
Next Election: 1er novembre 2013
Richard Fleury, Directeur général
Robert Cadieux, Contentieux
450-978-5866
Ernest Lépine, Évaluation
450-978-8777
Suzanne Deshaies, Trésorière, Finances
450-978-5700
Guy Collard, Greffier
450-978-3950
Martin Fiset, Ressources humaines
450-978-6560

Paul Lemay, Directeur, Vie communautaire, culture & communications
450-662-4343
Jean-Pierre Gariépy, Directeur, Protection des citoyens
450-662-4242
Pierre Pelletier, Directeur, Travaux publics
450-662-4600
Gérard Poirier, Ingénierie
450-978-6888
Sylvain Dubois, Directeur, Urbanisme
450-978-6888
Gilles Vaillancourt, Maire
Jean-Jacques Lapierre, Conseillers, Ward(s): 6: Concorde-Bois-de-Boulogne
Basile Angelopoulos, Conseillers, Ward(s): 14: Chomedey
Norman Girard, Conseillers, Ward(s): 8: Vimont
Benoit Fradet, Conseillers, Ward(s): 7: Renaud
Pierre Cléroux, Conseillers, Ward(s): 16: Sainte-Dorothée
Michèle Des Trois Maisons, Conseillers, Ward(s): 4: Duvernay-Pont-Viau
André Boileau, Conseillers, Ward(s): 20: Fabreville
Jocelyne Guertin, Conseillers, Ward(s): 12: Souvenir-Labelle
Ginette Legault-Bernier, Conseillers, Ward(s): 13: Abord-à-Plouffe
Ginette Grisé, Conseillers, Ward(s): 11: Laval-des-Rapides
Jean-Jacques Beldié, Conseillers, Ward(s): 17: Laval-les-Îles
Robert Plante, Conseillers, Ward(s): 18: Orée-des-bois
Yvon Bromley, Conseillers, Ward(s): 19: Marc-Aurèle-Fortin
Yvon Martineau, Conseillers, Ward(s): 9: Saint-Bruno
Jacques St-Jean, Conseillers, Ward(s): 1: Saint-François
Denis Robillard, Conseillers, Ward(s): 21: Sainte-Rose
Lucie Hill Laroque, Conseillers, Ward(s): 10: Auteuil
Alexandre Duplessis, Conseillers, Ward(s): 15: Saint-Martin
Madeleine Sollazzo, Conseillers, Ward(s): 3: Val-des-Arbres
Sylvie Clermont, Conseillers, Ward(s): 2: Saint-Vincent-de-Paul
Francine Légaré, Conseillers, Ward(s): 5: Marigot
Denis Bertrand, Régime de rentes
450-978-5876
Paul Martell, Systèmes & technologies
Martine Lachambre, Vérificatrice générale
450-978-8715
Guy Courchesne, Environnement
450-978-6888

Lavaltrie
1370, rue Notre-Dame
Lavaltrie, QC J5T 1M5
450-586-2921
Fax: 450-586-3939
mairie@ville.lavaltrie.qc.ca
www.ville.lavaltrie.qc.ca
Municipal Type: City
Incorporated: 16 mai 2001 Area: 68,61 km2
County or District: D'Autray; Population in 2009: 12,514
Provincial Electoral District(s): Berthier
Federal Electoral District(s): Berthier-Maskinongé
Next Election: 1er novembre 2013
Madeleine Barbeau, Greffière
Norman Blackburn, Maire
Réjean Nantais, Trésorier
Yvon Mousseau, Directeur général
Simon Coulombe, Directeur, Travaux publics

Lévis
2175, ch du Fleuve
Saint-Romuald, QC G6W 7W9
418-839-2002
Fax: 418-839-5548
levis@ville.levis.qc.ca
www.ville.levis.qc.ca
Municipal Type: City
Incorporated: 1er janvier 2002 Area: 443,65 km2
Population in 2006: 130,006
Provincial Electoral District(s): Chutes-de-la-Chaudière; Lévis
Federal Electoral District(s): Lévis-Bellechasse; Lotbinière-Chutes-de-la-Chaudière
Next Election: 1er novembre 2013
Danielle Bilodeau, Directrice, Affaires juridiques & du greffe
418-839-2002
levis@ville.levis.qc.ca
Danielle Roy Marinelli, Mairesse
dmarinelli@ville.levis.qc.ca
Philippe Laberge, Conseillers et Districts, Ward(s): 1 Chutes-de-la-Chaudière-Ouest
plaberge@ville.levis.qc.ca

See blue tabs following this section for Municipal Waste Management and Water & Wastewater Treatment.

Dominique Maranda, Conseillers et Districts, Ward(s): 2
Chutes-de-la-Chaudière-Ouest
dmaranda@ville.levis.qc.ca
Anne Ladouceur, Conseillers et Districts, Ward(s): 3
Chutes-de-la-Chaudière-Ouest
aladouceur@ville.levis.qc.ca
Isabelle Demers, Conseillers et Districts, Ward(s): 4
Chutes-de-la-Chaudière-Ouest
idemers@ville.levis.qc.ca
Alain Lemaire, Conseillers et Districts, Ward(s): 5
Chutes-de-la-Chaudière-Est
alemaire@ville.levis.qc.ca
Nicole Larouche, Conseillers et Districts, Ward(s): 6
Chutes-de-la-Chaudière-Est
nlarouche@ville.levis.qc.ca
Guy Dumoulin, Conseillers et Districts, Ward(s): 7
Chutes-de-la-Chaudière-Est
gdumoulin@ville.levis.qc.ca
Jean-Pierre Bazinet, Conseillers et Districts, Ward(s): 8
Chutes-de-la-Chaudière-Est
jpbazinet@ville.levis.qc.ca
Jean-Luc Daigle, Conseillers et Districts, Ward(s): 9
Chutes-de-la-Chaudière-Est
jldaigle@ville.levis.qc.ca
Simon Théberge, Conseillers et Districts, Ward(s): 10 Desjardins
stheberge@ville.levis.qc.ca
Jean Girard, Conseillers et Districts, Ward(s): 11 Desjardins
jgirard@ville.levis.qc.ca
André Hamel, Conseillers et Districts, Ward(s): 12 Desjardins
ahamel@ville.levis.qc.ca
Robert Maranda, Conseillers et Districts, Ward(s): 13 Desjardins
rmaranda@ville.levis.qc.ca
Jean-Claude Bouchard, Conseillers et Districts, Ward(s): 14 Desjardins
jcbouchard@ville.levis.qc.ca
Ann Jeffrey, Conseillers et Districts, Ward(s): 15 Desjardins
ajeffrey@ville.levis.qc.ca
Sabin Tremblay, Directeur général adjoint
418-839-2002
levis@ville.levis.qc.ca
Marcel Rodrigue, Directeur, Finances & Services administratifs
418-839-2002
levis@ville.levis.qc.ca
Jean Dubé, Directeur général
418-839-2002
levis@ville.levis.qc.ca
Jean-François Roy, Directeur, Service de police
418-839-2002
levis@ville.levis.qc.ca
Christian Brière, Directeur, Communications
418-839-2002
levis@ville.levis.qc.ca
Claude Guérin, Directeur, Ressources humaines
418-839-2002
levis@ville.levis.qc.ca
René Tremblay, Directeur, Vie communautaire
418-839-2002
levis@ville.levis.qc.ca
Alain Francoeur, Directeur, Environnement & infrastructures
418-839-2002
levis@ville.levis.qc.ca
Dominique Fortin, Directeur, Sécurité incendie
418-839-2002
levis@ville.levis.qc.ca
Michel Bélanger, Vérificateur général
418-839-2002
levis@ville.levis.qc.ca
Robert Cooke, Directeur, Urbanisme & Arrondissements
418-839-2002
levis@ville.levis.qc.ca
Philippe Meurant, Directeur, Développement
418-839-2002
levis@ville.levis.qc.ca

Longueuil
4250, ch de la Savane
Saint-Hubert, QC J3Y 9G4
450-463-7000
Fax: 450-463-7403
information@ville.longueuil.qc.ca
www.longueuil.ca
Municipal Type: City
Incorporated: 1er janvier 2002 *Area:* 111,50 km2
County or District: Communauté métropolitaine de Montréal;
Population in 2006: 230,949

Provincial Electoral District(s): Marie-Victorin; Taillon; Laporte; Vachon
Federal Electoral District(s): Saint-Lambert; Brossard-LaPrairie; Longueuil-Pierre-Boucher; Saint-Bruno-Saint Hubert
Next Election: 1er novembre 2013
Claude Gladu, Maire
Michel Desjardins, Conseillers et Districts, Ward(s): 1 Vieux-Longueuil
Simon Crochetière, Conseillers et Districts, Ward(s): 2 Vieux-Longueuil
Claudette Tessier, Conseillers et Districts, Ward(s): 3 Vieux-Longueuil
Jacques Goyette, Conseillers et Districts, Ward(s): 4 Vieux-Longueuil
Robert Charland, Conseillers et Districts, Ward(s): 5 Vieux-Longueuil
Alain St-Pierre, Conseillers et Districts, Ward(s): 6 Vieux-Longueuil
Marie-Lise Sauvé, Conseillers et Districts, Ward(s): 7 Vieux-Longueuil
Manon D. Hénault, Conseillers et Districts, Ward(s): 8 Vieux-Longueuil
Nicole Lafontaine, Conseillers et Districts, Ward(s): 9 Vieux-Longueuil
Nicole Béliveau, Conseillers et Districts, Ward(s): 10 Vieux-Longueuil
Johane Fontaine-Deshaies, Conseillers et Districts, Ward(s): 11 Vieux-Longueuil
Normand Caisse, Conseillers et Districts, Ward(s): 12 Vieux-Longueuil
Gilbert Côté, Conseillers et Districts, Ward(s): 13 Vieux-Longueuil
Robert Gladu, Conseillers et Districts, Ward(s): 14 Vieux-Longueuil
Gilles Grégoire, Conseillers et Districts, Ward(s): 15 Vieux-Longueuil
Mireille Carrière, Conseillers et Districts, Ward(s): 16 Greenfield Park
Robert Myles, Conseillers et Districts, Ward(s): 17 Greenfield Park
Guy Benedetti, Directeur général
Diane Boileau, Directrice, Ressources humaines
Daniel Carrier, Directeur, Services juridiques
Pierre D. Poisson, Vérificateur général
Alain Bissonnette, Directeur, Finances/Trésorier
Bernard Constantini, Conseillers et Districts, Ward(s): 18 Greenfield Park
Jacques Lemire, Conseillers et Districts, Ward(s): 19 St-Hubert
Roger Roy, Conseillers et Districts, Ward(s): 20 St-Hubert
Jacques E. Poitras, Conseillers et Districts, Ward(s): 21 St-Hubert
Lise Bélisle Dutil, Conseillers et Districts, Ward(s): 22 St-Hubert
Stéphane Desjardins, Conseillers et Districts, Ward(s): 23 St-Hubert
Suzanne Charbonneau, Conseillers et Districts, Ward(s): 24 St-Hubert
Lorraine Guay-Boivin, Conseillers et Districts, Ward(s): 25 St-Hubert
Michel Latendresse, Conseillers et Districts, Ward(s): 26 St-Hubert
Pierre Archambault, Directeur, Ressources informationnelles & matérielles
Gilles Côté, Directeur général adjoint, Développement
François Laramée, Directeur, Communications & relations avec le citoyen
Marc St-Laurent, Directeur, Service de police
Jean-Pierre Lacombe, Directeur, Service de sécurité incendie
Michel Binet, Directeur, Travaux publics
Hélène Ladouceur, Directrice, Urbanisme
Michel Vallée, Directeur, Évaluation
André Lachapelle, Directeur général adjoint, Services administratifs

Magog
7, rue Principale est
Magog, QC J1X 1Y4
819-843-6501
Fax: 819-843-1091
info@ville.magog.qc.ca
www.ville.magog.qc.ca
Municipal Type: City
Incorporated: 9 octobre 2002 *Area:* 145,68 km2
County or District: Memphrémagog; *Population in 2006:* 23,880
Provincial Electoral District(s): Orford
Federal Electoral District(s): Brome-Missisquoi

Next Election: 1er novembre 2013
Note: Depuis le 9 oct., le canton de Magog, le village d'Omerville & la ville de Magog sont regroupés pour former la nouvelle ville de Magog.
Martine Savard, Greffière
greffe@ville.magog.qc.ca
Marc Poulin, Maire
819-843-2880
info@ville.magog.qc.ca
Anne Couturier, Trésorière
finances@ville.magog.qc.ca
Gilles Bertrand, Directeur général
819-843-2880
dg@ville.magog.qc.ca
Michel Bombardier, Conseillers et Districts, Ward(s): 1 La Rivière
mbom@cgocable.ca
Stéphane Simard, Conseillers et Districts, Ward(s): 2 Omerville
819-843-6389
Denise Poulin-Marcotte, Conseillers et Districts, Ward(s): 3 Des Sommets
819-843-1146
denisepmarcotte@hotmail.com
Alain Vanden Eynden, Conseillers et Districts, Ward(s): 4 Du Marais
819-843-1706
alain.eynden@cgocable.ca
Vicki May Hamm, Conseillers et Districts, Ward(s): 5 Canton Ouest
819-347-7409
vm.hamm@ville.magog.qc.ca
Jacques Laurendeau, Conseillers et Districts, Ward(s): 6 Des Pionniers
819-843-3244
info@ville.magog.qc.ca
Gilbert Kurt Boucher, Conseillers et Districts, Ward(s): 7 Centre
819-868-2006
info@ville.magog.qc.ca
Gilles Robinson, Conseillers et Districts, Ward(s): 8 Monseigneur Vel
819-843-2364
gilles.robinson@cgocable.ca
Serge Gosselin, Conseillers et Districts, Ward(s): 9 Des Marinas
819-843-8203
info@ville.magog.qc.ca
Jocelyne Mongrain, Conseillers et Districts, Ward(s): 10 Des Deux-lacs
819-847-1577
info@ville.magog.qc.ca

Mascouche
3034, ch Ste-Marie
Mascouche, QC J7K 1P1
450-474-4133
Fax: 450-474-6401
greffe@ville.mascouche.qc.ca
www.ville.mascouche.qc.ca
Municipal Type: City
Incorporated: 1er juillet 1855 *Area:* 107,95 km2
County or District: Les Moulins; Communauté métropolitaine de Montréal; *Population in 2009:* 35,755
Provincial Electoral District(s): Masson
Federal Electoral District(s): Montcalm
Next Election: 1er novembre 2013
Yvan Laberge, Greffier
Richard Marcotte, Maire
Luc Tremblay, Directeur général
Michel Gobeil, Directeur, Finances
Normand Pagé, Conseillers et Districts, Ward(s): 1 Louis-Hébert
450-966-6326
Lise Gagnon, Conseillers et Districts, Ward(s): 2 Laurier
450-474-4501
 Siège vacant, Conseillers et Districts, Ward(s): 3 Le Gardeur
Donald Mailly, Conseillers et Districts, Ward(s): 4 La Vérendrye
450-966-1413
Pierre Villeneuve, Conseillers et Districts, Ward(s): 5 Du Coteau
450-474-3626
Denise Cloutier, Conseillers et Districts, Ward(s): 6 Des Hauts-Bois
450-968-0325
Louise Fourtané Bordonado, Conseillers et Districts, Ward(s): 7 Du Rucher
450-474-0847
Denise Paquette, Conseillers et Districts, Ward(s): 8 Du Manoir
450-966-6044

Municipal Governments / Québec

Matane
230, av St-Jérôme
Matane, QC G4W 3A2
418-562-2333
Fax: 418-562-4869
mairie@ville.matane.qc.ca
www.ville.matane.qc.ca
Municipal Type: City
Incorporated: 26 septembre 2001 *Area:* 214,63 km2
County or District: Matane; *Population in 2006:* 14,742
Provincial Electoral District(s): Matane
Federal Electoral District(s): Haute-Gaspésie-La Mitis-Matane-Matapédia
Next Election: 1er novembre 2013
Dominique Tancrède, Greffière
d.tancrede@ville.matane.qc.ca
Linda Cormier, Mairesse
mairie@ville.matane.qc.ca
Marie Pelletier, Directrice, Services financiers
m.pelletier@ville.matane.qc.ca
Michel Barriault, Directeur général
m.barriault@ville.matane.qc.ca

Mirabel
14111, rue Saint-Jean
Mirabel, QC J7J 1Y3
450-475-8653
Fax: 450-475-7195
communications@ville.mirabel.qc.ca
www.ville.mirabel.qc.ca
Municipal Type: City
Incorporated: 1er janvier 1971 *Area:* 477,86 km2
County or District: Mirabel; *Population in 2006:* 34,626
Provincial Electoral District(s): Mirabel
Federal Electoral District(s): Argenteuil-Papineau-Mirabel
Next Election: 1er novembre 2013
Suzanne Mireault, Greffière
450-475-2002
s.mireault@ville.mirabel.qc.ca
Hubert Meilleur, Maire
Germain Paquette, Trésorier
450-475-2003
g.paquette@ville.mirabel.qc.ca
Bernard Poulin, Directeur, Communications
450-475-2001
b.poulin@ville.mirabel.qc.ca
Jean Gaudreault, Directeur, Loisirs/Culture/Vie communautaire
450-475-8656
j.gaudreault@ville.mirabel.qc.ca
Denis Maurice, Directeur, Service d'incendie
450-475-2010
d.maurice@ville.mirabel.qc.ca
Louis Prud'homme, Directeur général
450-475-2000, Fax: 450-475-2013
l.prud'homme@ville.mirabel.qc.ca
Michel Lauzon, Conseillers et Districts, Ward(s): 1
Gérald Forget, Conseillers et Districts, Ward(s): 2
Jean Bouchard, Conseillers et Districts, Ward(s): 3
Luc St-Jean, Conseillers et Districts, Ward(s): 4
Daniel Gauthier, Conseillers et Districts, Ward(s): 5
Pierre-Paul Meloche, Conseillers et Districts, Ward(s): 6
François Bélanger, Conseillers et Districts, Ward(s): 7
Guy Laurin, Conseillers et Districts, Ward(s): 8

Mont-Laurier
485, rue Mercier
Mont-Laurier, QC J9L 3N8
819-623-1221
Fax: 819-623-4840
mlaurier@lino.com
www.villemontlaurier.qc.ca
Municipal Type: City
Incorporated: 8 janvier 2003 *Area:* 590,64 km2
County or District: Antoine-Labelle; *Population in 2009:* 13,394
Provincial Electoral District(s): Labelle
Federal Electoral District(s): Laurentides-Labelle
Next Election: 1er novembre 2013
Note: Dès le 8 janvier 2003, la ville de Mont-Laurier regroupe les municipalités de Des Ruisseaux & Saint-Aimé-du-Lac-des-Iles.
Blandine Boulianne, Greffière
Michel Adrien, Maire
Jean-Yves Forget, Directeur général
Johanne Nantel, Trésorière

Mont-St-Hilaire
100, rue du Centre-Civique
Mont-Saint-Hilaire, QC J3H 3M8
450-467-2854
Fax: 450-467-6460
greffe@villemsh.ca
www.ville.mont-saint-hilaire.qc.ca
Municipal Type: City
Incorporated: 12 mars 1966 *Area:* 38,96 km2
County or District: La Vallée-du-Richelieu; Communauté métropolitaine de Montréal; *Population in 2009:* 16,177
Provincial Electoral District(s): Borduas
Federal Electoral District(s): Chambly-Borduas
Next Election: 1er novembre 2013
Estelle Simard, Greffière
Michel Gilbert, Maire
Patrick Savard, Directeur général
Carmel Constant, Trésorier
Pierre Bergeron, Directeur, Communications/Loisirs/Culture

Montmagny
134, rue St-Jean-Baptiste est
Montmagny, QC G5V 1K6
418-248-3361
Fax: 418-248-4870
info@ville.montmagny.qc.ca
www.ville.montmagny.qc.ca
Municipal Type: City
Incorporated: 2 avril 1966 *Area:* 125,76 km2
County or District: Montmagny; *Population in 2006:* 11,353
Provincial Electoral District(s): Montmagny-L'Islet
Federal Electoral District(s): Montmagny-L'Islet-Kamouraska-Riviére-du-Loup
Next Election: 1er novembre 2013
Félix Michaud, Greffier
felix.michaud@ville.montmagny.qc.ca
Jean-Guy Desrosiers, Maire
André Lévesque, CA, Directeur, Service des finances/Approvisionnement
418-248-3361, Fax: 418-248-8468
finances@ville.montmagny.qc.ca
Yves Chayer, Directeur, Service incendie
418-248-5813, Fax: 418-248-2266
yves.chayer@ville.montmagny.qc.ca
Bernard Létourneau, Directeur général
info@ville.montmagny.qc.ca

Montréal
Hôtel de Ville
275, rue Notre-Dame est
Montréal, QC H2Y 1C6
514-872-3142
Fax: 514-872-5655
www.ville.montreal.qc.ca
Municipal Type: City
Incorporated: 1er janvier 2002 *Area:* 363,52 km2
County or District: Communauté métropolitaine de Montréal; *Population in 2009:* 1,640,565
Provincial Electoral District(s): Acadie;Anjou;Bourassa-Sauvé;Bourget;Crémazie;D'Arcy McGee;Gouin;Hochelaga-Maisonneuve;Jeanne-Mance-Viger;La Fontaine;Laurier-Dorion;Marguerite-Bourgeoys;Mercier;Marquette;Mont-Royal;Nelligan;Notre-Dame-de-Grâce;Outremont;Pointe-aux-Trembles;Robert-Baldwin;Rosemont;St-Henri-Ste-Anne;St-Laurent;Ste-Marie -St-Jacques;Westmount-St-Louis;Verdun;Viau
Federal Electoral District(s): Ahuntsic; Bourassa; Hochelaga; Honoré-Mercier; Jeanne-Le Ber; Lac-Saint-Louis; LaSalle-Émard; Laurier-Ste-Marie; Mount Royal; Notre-Dame-de-Grâce-Lachine; Outremont; Papineau; Rosemont-La Petite-Patrie; Westmount-Ville-Marie; St-Laurent-Cartierville; St-Léonard-St-Michel; La Pointe-de-l'Ile; Pierrefonds-Dollard
Next Election: 1er novembre 2013
Gérald Tremblay, Maire
514-872-3101
Michel Labrecque, Conseiller de ville, Mile-End, Conseillers et Districts, Ward(s): Le Plateau-Mont-Royal
michellabrecque@ville.montreal.qc.ca
Noushig Eloyan, Conseillère, Bordeaux-Cartierville, Conseillers et Districts, Ward(s): Ahuntsic-Cartierville
neloyan@ville.montreal.qc.ca
Hasmig Belleli, Conseillère, Ahuntsic, Conseillers et Districts, Ward(s): Ahuntsic-Cartierville
hasmig.belleli@ville.montreal.qc.ca
Catherine Sévigny, Conseillère de ville, Peter-McGill, Conseillers et Districts, Ward(s): Ville-Marie
catherinesevigny@ville.montreal.qc.ca
Marcel Tremblay, Conseiller, Notre-Dame-de-Grâce, Conseillers et Districts, Ward(s): Côte-des-Neiges-N.-D.-de-Grâce
marcelgtremblay@ville.montreal.qc.ca
Frank Venneri, Conseiller, François-Perrault, Conseillers et Districts, Ward(s): Villeray St-Michel-Parc-Extens
mfvenneri@ville.montreal.qc.ca
Sylvain Lachance, Conseiller, Villeray, Conseillers et Districts, Ward(s): Villeray St-Michel-Parc-Extens
slachance@ville.montreal.qc.ca
Anie Samson, Mairesse d'arrondissement, Conseillers et Districts, Ward(s): Villeray St-Michel-Parc-Extens
asamson@ville.montreal.qc.ca
Mary Deros, Conseillère, Parc-Extension, Conseillers et Districts, Ward(s): Villeray St-Michel-Parc-Extens
mderos@ville.montreal.qc.ca
François Purcell, Conseiller, Saint-Édouard, Conseillers et Districts, Ward(s): Rosemont—La Petite-Patrie
fpurcell@ville.montreal.qc.ca
Dominic Perri, B.Sc., M.A., Conseiller de ville, St-Léonard-Ouest, Conseillers et Districts, Ward(s): Saint-Léonard
dperri@ville.montreal.qc.ca
Alain Tassé, Conseiller de ville, Desmarchais-Crawford, Conseillers et Districts, Ward(s): Verdun
alain.tasse@verdun.ca
Manon Barbe, Mairesse d'arrondissement/Conseillère de la ville, Conseillers et Districts, Ward(s): LaSalle
mbarbe@ville.montreal.qc.ca
Joe Magri, Conseiller de ville, Rivière-des-Prairies, Conseillers et Districts, Ward(s): Riv.-des-Prairies-Pte-aux-Trem
joemagri@ville.montreal.qc.ca
Claude Trudel, Maire d'arrondissement/Conseiller de ville, Conseillers et Districts, Ward(s): Verdun
claude.trudel@verdun.ca
Helen Fotopulos, Mairesse d'arrondissement, Conseillers et Districts, Ward(s): Le Plateau-Mont-Royal
hfotopulos@ville.montreal.qc.ca
Michel Prescott, Conseiller de ville, Jeanne-Mance, Conseillers et Districts, Ward(s): Le Plateau-Mont-Royal
mprescott@ville.montreal.qc.ca
Luis Miranda, Maire d'arrondissement/Conseiller de la ville, Conseillers et Districts, Ward(s): Anjou
lmiranda@ville.montreal.qc.ca
Lyn Thériault, Mairesse d'arrondissement, Conseillers et Districts, Ward(s): Mercier-Hochelaga-Maisonneuve
lyn.theriault@ville.montreal.qc.ca
Saulie Zajdel, Conseiller, Darlington, Conseillers et Districts, Ward(s): Côte-des-Neiges-N.-D.-de-Grâce
szajdel@ville.montreal.qc.ca
Marvin Rotrand, Conseiller, Snowdon, Conseillers et Districts, Ward(s): Côte-des-Neiges-N.-D.-de-Grâce
mrotrand@ville.montreal.qc.ca
Michael Applebaum, Maire d'arrondissement, Conseillers et Districts, Ward(s): Côte-des-Neiges-N.-D.-de-Grâce
mapplebaum@ville.montreal.qc.ca
Jean-François St-Onge, Conseiller, Sault-au-Récollet, Conseillers et Districts, Ward(s): Ahuntsic-Cartierville
jfstonge@ville.montreal.qc.ca
Francine Senécal, Conseillère, Côte-des-Neiges, Conseillers et Districts, Ward(s): Côte-des-Neiges-N.-D.-de-Grâce
fsenecal@ville.montreal.qc.ca
Alvaro Farinacci, Conseiller de ville, Cecil-P.-Newman, Conseillers et Districts, Ward(s): LaSalle
genesee@qc.aira.com
Line Hamel, Conseillère de ville, St-Henri-Petite-Bourgogne-Pte-St-Charles, Conseillers et Districts, Ward(s): Le Sud-Ouest
linehamel@ville.montreal.qc.ca
André Lavallée, Maire d'arrondissement, Conseillers et Districts, Ward(s): Rosemont—La Petite-Patrie
andrelavallee@ville.montreal.qc.ca
Richer Dompierre, Conseiller, Louis-Riel, Conseillers et Districts, Ward(s): Mercier-Hochelaga-Maisonneuve
rdompierre@ville.montreal.qc.ca
Marcel Parent, Maire d'arrondissement/Conseiller de la ville, Conseillers et Districts, Ward(s): Montréal-Nord
marcelmparent@ville.montreal.qc.ca
Jane Cowell-Poitras, Conseillère de ville, Conseillers et Districts, Ward(s): Lachine
Claire St-Arnaud, Conseillère, Maisonneuve-Longue-Pointe, Conseillers et Districts, Ward(s):

See blue tabs following this section for Municipal Waste Management and Water & Wastewater Treatment.

Municipal Governments / Québec

Mercier-Hochelaga-Maisonneuve
cstarnaud@ville.montreal.qc.ca
Ginette Marotte, Conseillère de ville,
Champlain-L'île-des-Soeurs, Conseillers et Districts, Ward(s): Verdun
ginette.marotte@verdun.ca
Richard Deschamps, Conseiller de ville, Sault-St-Louis, Conseillers et Districts, Ward(s): LaSalle
richarddeschamps@ville.montreal.qc.ca
Gaëtan Primeau, Conseiller, Tétreaultville, Conseillers et Districts, Ward(s): Mercier-Hochelaga-Maisonneuve
gaetanprimeau@ville.montreal.qc.ca
Claude Dauphin, Maire d'arrondissement, Conseillers et Districts, Ward(s): Lachine
Claude Léger, Directeur général
514-872-0589
claudeleger@ville.montreal.qc.ca
Yves Saindon, Greffier
514-872-3007
yvessaindon@ville.montreal.qc.ca
Christian G. Dubois, Conseiller de ville, Conseillers et Districts, Ward(s): Pierrefonds-Roxboro
christiangdubois@ville.montreal.qc.ca
Carole Du Sault, Conseillère, Étienne-Desmarteau, Conseillers et Districts, Ward(s): Rosemont—La Petite-Patrie
caroledusault@ville.montreal.qc.ca
Alan DeSousa, FCA, Maire d'arrondissement, Conseillers et Districts, Ward(s): Saint-Laurent
adesousa@ville.montreal.qc.ca
Benoît Labonté, Maire d'arrondissement, Conseillers et Districts, Ward(s): Ville-Marie
benoitlabonte@ville.montreal.qc.ca
Jean-Marc Gibeau, Conseiller de ville, Ovide-Clermont, Conseillers et Districts, Ward(s): Montréal-Nord
jgibeau@ville.montreal.qc.ca
James V. Infantino, Conseiller de ville, Marie-Clarac, Conseillers et Districts, Ward(s): Montréal-Nord
jinfantino@ville.montreal.qc.ca
Marie Cinq-Mars, Mairesse d'arrondissement/Conseillère de la ville, Conseillers et Districts, Ward(s): Outremont
mariecinq-mars@ville.montreal.qc.ca
Gilles Grondin, Conseiller, Vieux-Rosemont, Conseillers et Districts, Ward(s): Rosemont—La Petite-Patrie
ggrondinrosemont@ville.montreal.qc.ca
Nicolas Montmorency, Conseiller de ville, Pointe-aux-Prairies, Conseillers et Districts, Ward(s): Riv.-des-Prairies-Pte-aux-Trem
nicolasmontmorency@ville.montreal.qc.ca
Soraya Martinez, Conseillère, Saint-Michel, Conseillers et Districts, Ward(s): Villeray St-Michel-Parc-Extens
sorayamartinez@ville.montreal.qc.ca
Jacqueline Montpetit, Mairesse d'arrondissement, Conseillers et Districts, Ward(s): Le Sud-Ouest
jacquelinemontpetit@ville.montreal.qc.ca
Robert L. Zambito, Conseiller d'arrondissement, St-Léonard-Est, Conseillers et Districts, Ward(s): Saint-Léonard
rzambito@ville.montreal.qc.ca
Bertrand A. Ward, Conseiller de ville, Conseillers et Districts, Ward(s): Pierrefonds-Roxboro
bward@ville.montreal.qc.ca
Monique Worth, Mairesse d'arrondissement/Conseillère de la ville, Conseillers et Districts, Ward(s): Pierrefonds-Roxboro
mworth@ville.montreal.qc.ca
Jean-Yves Cartier, Conseiller de ville, Saint-Paul-Émard, Conseillers et Districts, Ward(s): Le Sud-Ouest
jeanyvescartier@ville.montreal.qc.ca
Elizabeth Verge, Conseillère d'arrondissement, Canal, Conseillers et Districts, Ward(s): Lachine
Andrée Hénault, Conseillère de ville, Conseillers et Districts, Ward(s): Anjou
ahenault@ville.montreal.qc.ca
Vincenzo Cesari, Conseiller d'arrondissement, Cecil-P.-Newman, Conseillers et Districts, Ward(s): LaSalle
Gilles Beaudry, Conseiller d'arrondissement, Anjou Ouest, Conseillers et Districts, Ward(s): Anjou
gillesbeaudry@ville.montreal.qc.ca
Eleni Fakotakis, Conseillère d'arrondissement, Mile-End, Conseillers et Districts, Ward(s): Le Plateau-Mont-Royal
elenifakotakis@ville.montreal.qc.ca
Maria Calderone, Conseillère d'arrondissement, Rivière-des-Prairies, Conseillers et Districts, Ward(s): Riv.-des-Prairies-Pte-aux-Trem
mariacalderone@ville.montreal.qc.ca
Bernard Blanchet, Conseiller d'arrondissement, J.-Émery-Provost, Conseillers et Districts, Ward(s): Lachine

Josée Lavigueur-Thériault, Conseillère d'arrondissement, Desmarchais-Crawford, Conseillers et Districts, Ward(s): Verdun
josee.lavigueur@verdun.ca
Catherine Clément-Talbot, Conseillère d'arrondissement, Conseillers et Districts, Ward(s): Pierrefonds-Roxboro
catherineclementtalbot@ville.montreal.qc.ca
Paul Beaupré, Conseiller d'arrondissement, Champlain-L'île-des-Soeurs, Conseillers et Districts, Ward(s): Verdun
paul.beaupre@verdun.ca
Pierre E. Fréchette, Conseiller d'arrondissmnt., St-Henri-Pte-Bourgogne-Pte-St-Charles, Conseillers et Districts, Ward(s): Le Sud-Ouest
pierreefrechette@ville.montreal.qc.ca
Suzanne Décarie, Conseillère d'arrondissement, Pointe-aux-Trembles, Conseillers et Districts, Ward(s): Riv.-des-Prairies-Pte-aux-Trem
suzannedecarie@ville.montreal.qc.ca
Ronald Bossy, Conseiller d'arrondissement, St-Paul-Émard, Conseillers et Districts, Ward(s): Le Sud-Ouest
ronaldbossy@ville.montreal.qc.ca
Ross Blackhurst, Conseiller d'arrondissement, Sault-St-Louis, Conseillers et Districts, Ward(s): LaSalle
Normand Fortin, Conseiller d'arrondissement, Ovide-Clermont, Conseillers et Districts, Ward(s): Montréal-Nord
nfortin@ville.montreal.qc.ca
Claude B. Piquette, Conseiller, Joseph-Beaubien, Conseillers et Districts, Ward(s): Outremont
claudebpiquette@ville.montreal.qc.ca
Marie Potvin, Conseillère, Robert-Bourassa, Conseillers et Districts, Ward(s): Outremont
marie.potvin@ville.montreal.qc.ca
Joseph Di Pietro, Conseiller d'arrondissement, Pointe-aux-Prairies, Conseillers et Districts, Ward(s): Riv.-des-Prairies-Pte-aux-Trem
josephdipietro@ville.montreal.qc.ca
Jean-François Cloutier, Conseiller d'arrondissement, Fort-Rolland, Conseillers et Districts, Ward(s): Lachine
Diane Gibb, Conseillère, Pierre-Foretier, Conseillers et Districts, Ward(s): L'île-Bizard—Ste-Geneviève
dianegibb@ville.montreal.qc.ca
Maurice Cohen, Conseiller d'arrondissement, Côte-de-Liesse, Conseillers et Districts, Ward(s): Saint-Laurent
mcohen@ville.montreal.qc.ca
Michèle D. Biron, Conseillère d'arrondissement, Norman-McLaren, Conseillers et Districts, Ward(s): Saint-Laurent
michelebiron@ville.montreal.qc.ca
Mario Battista, Conseiller d'arrondissement, St-Léonard-Ouest, Conseillers et Districts, Ward(s): Saint-Léonard
mbattista@ville.montreal.qc.ca
Josée Duplessis, Conseillère d'arrondissement, De Lorimier, Conseillers et Districts, Ward(s): Le Plateau-Mont-Royal
joseeduplessis@ville.montreal.qc.ca
Karim Boulos, Conseiller d'arrondissement, Peter-McGill, Conseillers et Districts, Ward(s): Ville-Marie
karimboulos@ville.montreal.qc.ca
Christopher Little, Conseiller, Denis-Benjamin-Viger, Conseillers et Districts, Ward(s): L'île-Bizard—Ste-Geneviève
littlechristopher@ville.montreal.qc.ca
Isabel Dos Santos, Conseillère d'arrondissement, Jeanne-Mance, Conseillers et Districts, Ward(s): Le Plateau-Mont-Royal
isabeldossantos@ville.montreal.qc.ca
Jacques Bergeron, Vérificateur général
Colombe Cliche, Directrice, Communications/Relations avec les citoyens
Pierre Reid, Directeur, Service du Capital humain
Robert Lamontagne, CA, MBA, Directeur, Finances & Trésorerie
Warren Allmand, Conseiller, Loyola, Conseillers et Districts, Ward(s): Côte-des-Neiges-N.-D.-de-Grâce
warrenallmand@ville.montreal.qc.ca
Marie-Andrée Beaudoin, Mairesse d'arrondissement, Conseillers et Districts, Ward(s): Ahuntsic-Cartierville
mabeaudoin@ville.montreal.qc.ca
Laurent Blanchard, Conseiller, Hochelaga, Conseillers et Districts, Ward(s): Mercier-Hochelaga-Maisonneuve
laurentblanchard@ville.montreal.qc.ca
Richard Bélanger, Maire d'arrondissement/Conseiller de la ville, Conseillers et Districts, Ward(s): L'île-Bizard—Ste-Geneviève
richardbelanger@ville.montreal.qc.ca
André Bélisle, Conseiller de ville, Pointe-aux-Trembles, Conseillers et Districts, Ward(s): Riv.-des-Prairies-Pte-aux-Trem
andrebelisle@ville.montreal.qc.ca

Jocelyn Ann Campbell, Conseillère, Saint-Sulpice, Conseillers et Districts, Ward(s): Ahuntsic-Cartierville
jacampbell@ville.montreal.qc.ca
Laval Demers, CA, Conseiller de ville, Côte-de-Liesse, Conseillers et Districts, Ward(s): Saint-Laurent
lavaldemers@ville.montreal.qc.ca
Pierre Mainville, Conseiller d'arrondissement, Ste-Marie-St-Jacques, Conseillers et Districts, Ward(s): Ville-Marie
pierremainville@ville.montreal.qc.ca
Louis Moffatt, Conseiller, Claude-Ryan, Conseillers et Districts, Ward(s): Outremont
louismoffatt@ville.montreal.qc.ca
Ana Nunes, Conseillère, Jeanne-Sauvé, Conseillers et Districts, Ward(s): Outremont
anunes@ville.montreal.qc.ca
Laura Palestini, Conseillère d'arrondissement, Sault-St-Louis, Conseillers et Districts, Ward(s): LaSalle
François Robert, Conseiller, Jacques-Bizard, Conseillers et Districts, Ward(s): L'île-Bizard—Ste-Geneviève
francoisrobert@ville.montreal.qc.ca
André Savard, Conseiller d'arrondissement, Desmarchais-Crawford, Conseillers et Districts, Ward(s): Verdun
andre.savard@ville.montreal.qc.ca
Clementina Teti-Tomassi, Conseillère d'arrondissement, Marie-Clarac, Conseillers et Districts, Ward(s): Montréal-Nord
clementinatetitomassi@ville.montreal.qc.ca
Rémy Tondreau, Conseiller d'arrondissement, Anjou Est, Conseillers et Districts, Ward(s): Anjou
remytondreau@ville.montreal.qc.ca
Marc Touchette, Conseiller d'arrondissement, Champlain-L'île-des-Soeurs, Conseillers et Districts, Ward(s): Verdun
marc.touchette.verdun.ca
Roger Trottier, Conseiller d'arrondissement, Conseillers et Districts, Ward(s): Pierrefonds-Roxboro
rogertrottier@ville.montreal.qc.ca
Philippe Voisard, Conseiller, Ste-Geneviève, Conseillers et Districts, Ward(s): L'île-Bizard—Ste-Geneviève
philippevoisard@ville.montreal.qc.ca
Michelle Zammit, Conseillère d'arrondissement, Anjou Centre, Conseillers et Districts, Ward(s): Anjou
mzammit@ville.montreal.qc.ca
Michael Vadacchino, Conseiller d'arrondissement, Cecil-P.-Newman, Conseillers et Districts, Ward(s): LaSalle
Richard Bergeron, Conseiller de ville, De Lorimier, Conseillers et Districts, Ward(s): Le Plateau-Mont-Royal
richardbbergeron@ville.montreal.qc.ca
Michel Bissonnet, Maire d'arrondissement, Conseillers et Districts, Ward(s): Saint-Léonard
Patricia Bittar, M.Sc., Conseillère de ville, Norman-McLaren, Conseillers et Districts, Ward(s): Saint-Laurent
patriciabittar@ville.montreal.qc.ca
Carle Bernier-Genest, Conseiller, Maire-Victorin, Conseillers et Districts, Ward(s): Rosemont—La Petite-Patrie
cbg@ville.montreal.qc.ca
Sammy Forcillo, Conseiller de ville, Ste-Marie-St-Jacques, Conseillers et Districts, Ward(s): Ville-Marie
sforcillo@ville.montreal.qc.ca
Cosmo Maciocia, Maire d'arrondissement, Conseillers et Districts, Ward(s): Riv.-des-Prairies-Pte-aux-Trem
cmaciocia@ville.montreal.qc.ca
Yvette Bissonnet, Conseillère de ville, Saint-Léonard, Conseillers et Districts, Ward(s): Saint-Léonard

Pincourt
919, ch Duhamel
Pincourt, QC J7V 4G8
514-453-8981
Fax: 514-453-8401
m.perrier@villepincourt.qc.ca
www.villepincourt.qc.ca
Municipal Type: City
Incorporated: 1er janvier 1950 *Area:* 8,36 km2
County or District: Vaudreuil-Soulanges; Communauté métropolitaine de Montréal; *Population in 2009:* 11,777
Provincial Electoral District(s): Vaudreuil
Federal Electoral District(s): Vaudreuil-Soulanges
Next Election: 1er novembre 2013
Michel Perrier, Directeur général
Michel Kandyba, Maire
Nicole Drouin, Greffière

See blue tabs following this section for Municipal Waste Management and Water & Wastewater Treatment.

Municipal Governments / Québec

Québec
Hôtel de Ville
CP 700 Haute-Ville
2, rue des Jardins
Québec, QC G1R 4S9
418-691-6010
Fax: 418-641-6357
renseignements@ville.quebec.qc.ca
www.ville.quebec.qc.ca
Municipal Type: City
Incorporated: 1er janvier 2002 *Area:* 451,79 km2
Population in 2006: 491,142
Provincial Electoral District(s):
Charlesbourg-Haute-Saint-Charles; Chauveau; Jean-Lesage; Jean-Talon; La Peltrie; Louis-Hébert; Montmorency; Taschereau; Vanier
Federal Electoral District(s): Québec; Louis-St-Laurent
Next Election: 1er novembre 2013
Louise Lapointe, Conseillers et Arrondissements, Ward(s): La Cité/Saint-Sauveur
François Picard, Conseillers et Arrondissements, Ward(s): Rivières/Lebourgneuf
Gérald Poirier, Conseillers et Arrondissements, Ward(s): Rivières/Saules
Jérôme Vaillancourt, Conseillers et Arrondissements, Ward(s): Ste-Foy-Sillery/Cité-univers.
Paul Shoiry, Conseillers et Arrondissements, Ward(s): Ste-Foy-Sillery/Sillery
Francine Bouchard, Conseillers et Arrondissements, Ward(s): Ste-Foy-Sillery/Pte-Sainte-Foy
Ralph Mercier, Conseillers et Arrondissements, Ward(s): Charlesbourg/Charlesbourg-Ctre
Jean-Marie Laliberté, Conseillers et Arrondissements, Ward(s): Charlesbourg/Monts
Michel Fecteau, Conseillers et Arrondissements, Ward(s): Charlesbourg/Sentiers
Poste vacant, Conseillers et Arrondissements, Ward(s): Rivières/Duberger
Lisette Lepage, Conseillers et Arrondissements, Ward(s): Beauport/Saint-Michel
Carol Bégin Giroux, Conseillers et Arrondissements, Ward(s): Beauport/Chute-Montmorency
Marc Simoneau, Conseillers et Arrondissements, Ward(s): Beauport/Vieux-Moulin
Alain Loubier, Conseillers et Arrondissements, Ward(s): Limoilou/Maizerets
Anne Beaulieu, Conseillers et Arrondissements, Ward(s): Limoilou/Vieux-Limoilou
Ginette Picard Lavoie, Conseillers et Arrondissements, Ward(s): Limoilou/Lairet
Jean-Marie Matte, Conseillers et Arrondissements, Ward(s): Laurentien/Val-Bélair
Guy Perrault, Conseillers et Arrondissements, Ward(s): Laurentien/Chauveau
Régis Labeaume, Maire
418-641-6434
Sylvain Ouellet, Greffier
418-641-6212
Alain Marcoux, Directeur général
directiongenerale@ville.quebec.qc.ca
Jacques Grantham, Directeur, Environnement
Annie Gaudreault, Directrice, Division du greffe de la cour municipale
Chantale Giguère, Directrice, Service des ressources humaines
Denis Deslauriers, Directeur, Service des technologies de l'information/télécomm.
418-641-6239
Rhonda Rioux, Directrice, Service de la culture
418-641-6181
Fernand Martin, Directeur, Service de l'aménagement du territoire
418-641-6160
Marcel Roy, Directeur, Service des travaux publics
418-641-6240
Pierre Huot, Directeur, Service de l'évaluation
418-641-6193
Guy Bélanger, Directeur, Service des loisirs, des sports & vie communautaire
Jean-Yves Tellier, Directeur, Service du développement économique
Daniel Lessard, Directeur, Service de l'ingénierie
Richard Poitras, Directeur, Service de protection contre l'incendie
418-641-6231
Serge Bélisle, Directeur, Service de la police
418-641-6292
Pierre Gignac, Directeur, Service des communications
418-641-6210
Daniel Maranda, Directeur, Service des approvisionnements
418-641-6164
Gabriel Savard, Directeur, Office du tourisme et des congrès
418-522-3511
Jacques Joli-Coeur, Conseillers et Arrondissements, Ward(s): La Cité/Samuel-de-Champlain
Anne Guérette, Conseillers et Arrondissements, Ward(s): La Cité/Montcalm
Yvon Bussières, Conseillers et Arrondissements, Ward(s): La Cité/Saint-Sacrement
Pierre Maheux, Conseillers et Arrondissements, Ward(s): La Cité/Faubourgs
Richard Côté, Conseillers et Arrondissements, Ward(s): Rivières/Vanier
Patrick Paquet, Conseillers et Arrondissements, Ward(s): Rivières/Neufchâtel
André Demers, Conseillers et Arrondissements, Ward(s): Ste-Foy-Sillery/Saint-Louis
Gérard Landry, Conseillers et Arrondissements, Ward(s): Ste-Foy-Sillery/Plateau
Denise Trudel, Conseillers et Arrondissements, Ward(s): Charlesbourg/Saint-Rodrigue
Gilles Marcotte, Conseillers et Arrondissements, Ward(s): Charlesbourg/Jean-Talon
Marie-France Trudel, Conseillers et Arrondissements, Ward(s): Beauport/Laurentides
André Letendre, Conseillers et Arrondissements, Ward(s): Beauport/Vieux-Bourg
Anne Létourneau, Conseillers et Arrondissements, Ward(s): Limoilou/Colisée
Steeve Verret, Conseillers et Arrondissements, Ward(s): Hte-St-Charles/Saint-Émile
Jacques Teasdale, Conseillers et Arrondissements, Ward(s): Hte-St-Charles/Lac-St-Charles
Raymond Dion, Conseillers et Arrondissements, Ward(s): Hte-St-Charles/Loretteville
Pierre Blouin, Conseillers et Arrondissements, Ward(s): Hte-Saint-Charles/Châtels
Conrad Verret, Conseillers et Arrondissements, Ward(s): Laurentien/Champigny
Denise Tremblay Blanchette, Conseillers et Arrondissements, Ward(s): Laurentien/Cap-Rouge
François Gagnon, Vérificateur général
Serge Giasson, Directeur, Affaires juridiques
Gilles Noël, Directeur général adjoint, Services de soutien
Suzanne Canac Marquis, Directrice générale adjointe, Développement culturel, touristique, sportif & social
Guy Renaud, Directeur général adjoint, Développement durable
Chantale Giguère, Directrice générale adjointe, Sécurité publique
Alain Thériault, Directeur général adjoint, Coordination des arrondissements
Yves Courchesne, Directeur, Services des finances
418-641-6203

Repentigny
435, boul Iberville
Repentigny, QC J6A 2B6
450-470-3000
Fax: 450-470-3082
communication@ville.repentigny.qc.ca
www.ville.repentigny.qc.ca
Municipal Type: City
Incorporated: 1er juin 2002 *Area:* 68,42 km2
County or District: L'Assomption; Communauté métropolitaine de Montréal; *Population in 2009:* 78,812
Provincial Electoral District(s): L'Assomption; Masson
Federal Electoral District(s): Montcalm; Repentigny; Terrebonne-Blainville
Next Election: 1er novembre 2013
Louis-André Garceau, Greffier
450-470-3130
greffe@ville.repentigny.qc.ca
Chantal Deschamps, Mairesse
450-470-3103
Daniel L'Écuyer, Directeur général
450-470-3110
direction-generale@ville.repentigny.qc.ca
Diane Pelchat, Trésorière
450-470-3200
finance@ville.repentigny.qc.ca
Michel Mailhot, Directeur, Ressources humaines
450-470-3700
ressources-humaines@ville.repentigny.qc.ca
Serge Daoust, Directeur, Police (Administration)
450-470-3600
securite-publique@ville.repentigny.qc.ca
David Legault, Directeur, Permis, inspections & urbanisme
450-470-3840
permis@ville.repentigny.qc.ca
Denis Larose, Directeur, Service d'incendie
450-470-3620
securite-publique@ville.repentigny.qc.ca
Sylvie Bouchard, Directrice, Travaux publics
450-470-3800
travaux-publics@ville.repentigny.qc.ca
Marlène Girard, Directrice, Communications
450-470-3140
communication@ville.repentigny.qc.ca
José Girard, Directeur, Transport collectif
450-470-3860
info@gortc.info
Sylviane DiFolco, Directrice, Loisirs, culture & vie communautaire
450-470-3400
loisirs@ville.repentigny.qc.ca
Ghislain Bélanger, Directeur, Développement économique & services techniques
450-470-3150
ingenierie@ville.repentigny.qc.ca
André Cyr, Conseillers et Districts, Ward(s): 1
450-585-3410
Georges Robinson, Conseillers et Districts, Ward(s): 2
450-654-9746
Denyse Peltier, Conseillers et Districts, Ward(s): 3
450-581-5733
Cécile Hénault, Conseillers et Districts, Ward(s): 4
450-654-3046
Patrice Peltier-Rivest, Conseillers et Districts, Ward(s): 5
450-657-1255
Daniel Labrecque, Conseillers et Districts, Ward(s): 6
450-841-2437
Raymond Hénault, Conseillers et Districts, Ward(s): 7
450-581-0319
Mario Morais, Conseillers et Districts, Ward(s): 8
450-654-4018
Jean Langlois, Conseillers et Districts, Ward(s): 9
450-585-4285
Jeannot Lemay, Conseillers et Districts, Ward(s): 10
450-585-6594
Francine Payer, Conseillers et Districts, Ward(s): 11
450-582-7711
Sylvie Langlois-Brouillette, Conseillers et Districts, Ward(s): 12
514-295-8376

Rimouski
CP 710
205, av de la Cathédrale
Rimouski, QC G5L 7C7
418-724-3108
Fax: 418-724-3183
communications@ville.rimouski.qc.ca
www.ville.rimouski.qc.ca
Municipal Type: City
Incorporated: 1er janvier 2002 *Area:* 254,16 km2
County or District: Rimouski-Neigette; *Population in 2006:* 42,240
Provincial Electoral District(s): Rimouski
Federal Electoral District(s):
Rimouski-Neigette-Témiscouata-Les Basques
Next Election: 1er novembre 2013
Marc Doucet, Greffier
418-724-3125, Fax: 418-724-9795
greffe@ville.rimouski.qc.ca
Éric Forest, Maire
418-724-3126
mairie@ville.rimouski.qc.ca
Jean Matte, Directeur général
418-724-3171, Fax: 418-724-3183
direction.generale@ville.rimouski.qc.ca
Jean-Charles Fournier, Directeur, Service des finances
418-724-3111, Fax: 418-724-3180
finances@ville.rimouski.qc.ca
Marc St-Laurent, Conseillers et Districts, Ward(s): 1
Sacré-Coeur
marc.st-laurent@ville.rimouski.qc.ca

See blue tabs following this section for Municipal Waste Management and Water & Wastewater Treatment.

Rodrigue Joncas, Conseillers et Districts, Ward(s): 2 Nazareth
rodrigue.joncas@ville.rimouski.qc.ca
Claude Mongrain, Conseillers et Districts, Ward(s): 3 Saint-Germain
claude.mongrain@ville.rimouski.qc.ca
Richard Caissy, Conseillers et Districts, Ward(s): 4 Rimouski-Est
richard.caissy@ville.rimouski.qc.ca
Raymond-Marie Murray, Conseillers et Districts, Ward(s): 5 Pointe-au-Père
raymond-marie.murray@ville.rimouski.qc.ca
Donald Bélanger, Conseillers et Districts, Ward(s): 6 Sainte-Odile
donald.belanger@ville.rimouski.qc.ca
Gisèle Saint-Pierre-Beaulieu, Conseillers et Districts, Ward(s): 7 Saint-Robert
gisele.st-pierre-beaulieu@ville.rimouski.qc.ca
Pierre Tourville, Conseillers et Districts, Ward(s): 8 Terrasse Arthur-Buies
pierre.tourville@ville.rimouski.qc.ca
Karol Francis, Conseillers et Districts, Ward(s): 9 Saint-Pie-X
karol.francis@ville.rimouski.qc.ca
Francis Proulx, Conseillers et Districts, Ward(s): 10 Sainte-Blanche/Mont-Lebel
francis.proulx@ville.rimouski.qc.ca

Rivière-du-Loup
CP 37
65, rue de l'Hôtel-de-Ville
Rivière-du-Loup, QC G5R 3Y7
418-867-6700
Fax: 418-862-2817
sylvie.roussel@ville.riviere-du-loup.qc.ca
www.ville.riviere-du-loup.qc.ca
Municipal Type: City
Incorporated: 30 décembre 1998 *Area:* 83,39 km2
County or District: Rivière-du-Loup; *Population in 2006:* 18,586
Provincial Electoral District(s): Rivière-du-Loup
Federal Electoral District(s): Montmagny-L'Islet-Kamouraska-Rivière-du-Loup
Next Election: 1er novembre 2013
Georges Deschênes, Greffier
418-867-6715
georges.deschenes@ville.riviere-du-loup.qc.ca
Michel Morin, Maire
418-867-6625
maire@ville.riviere-du-loup.qc.ca
Gérald Tremblay, Directeur, Travaux publics
418-862-2121, Fax: 418-867-6096
gerald.tremblay@ville.riviere-du-loup.qc.ca
Marie Lapointe, Directrice, Service finances & Trésorerie
418-867-6711
marie.lapointe@ville.riviere-du-loup.qc.ca
Jacques Poulin, Directeur général
418-867-6707
jacques.poulin@ville.riviere-du-loup.qc.ca
Éric Côté, Directeur, Environnement
418-867-6663
eric.cote@ville.riviere-du-loup.qc.ca
Claude Pelletier, Conseillers et Districts, Ward(s): la Rivière
Hervé Bouchard, Conseillers et Districts, Ward(s): Fraserville
Sylvie Vignet, Conseillers et Districts, Ward(s): la Plaine
Jacques Thériault, Conseillers et Districts, Ward(s): la Pointe
Gaétan St-Pierre, Conseillers et Districts, Ward(s): l'Estuaire
Denis Tardif, Conseillers et Districts, Ward(s): Saint-Patrice
Benoît Ouellet, Directeur, Loisirs, culture & vie communautaire
418-862-0906
benoit.ouellet@ville.riviere-du-loup.qc.ca

Roberval
851, boul St-Joseph
Roberval, QC G8H 2L6
418-275-0202
Fax: 418-275-5031
vroberval@ville.roberval.qc.ca
www.ville.roberval.qc.ca
Municipal Type: City
Incorporated: 23 décembre 1976 *Area:* 168,27 km2
County or District: Le Domaine-du-Roy; *Population in 2009:* 10,512
Provincial Electoral District(s): Roberval
Federal Electoral District(s): Roberval-Lac-St-Jean
Next Election: 1er novembre 2013
Jean-Guy Tardif, Greffier
Michel Larouche, Maire

Jeannot Gagnon, Directeur général
jeannotgagnon@ville.roberval.qc.ca
Nancy Boutin, Trésorière
nboutin@ville.roberval.qc.ca

Rosemère
100, rue Charbonneau
Rosemère, QC J7A 3W1
450-621-3500
Fax: 450-621-7601
info@ville.rosemere.qc.ca
www.ville.rosemere.qc.ca
Municipal Type: City
Incorporated: 1er janvier 1947 *Area:* 10,35 km2
County or District: Thérèse-De Blainville; Communauté métropolitaine de Montréal; *Population in 2009:* 14,284
Provincial Electoral District(s): Groulx
Federal Electoral District(s): Marc-Aurèle-Fortin
Next Election: 1er novembre 2013
Patrick St-Amour, Greffier
Hélène Daneault, Mairesse
Michel Gagné, Directeur général
Luce Jacques, Trésorière

Rouyn-Noranda
CP 220
100, rue Taschereau est
Rouyn-Noranda, QC J9X 5C3
819-797-7110
Fax: 819-797-7108
www.ville.rouyn-noranda.qc.ca
Municipal Type: City
Incorporated: 1er janvier 2002 *Area:* 6435,64 km2
Population in 2006: 39,924
Provincial Electoral District(s): Abitibi-Est; Rouyn-Noranda-Témiscamingue
Federal Electoral District(s): Abitibi-Témiscamingue
Next Election: 1er novembre 2013
Daniel Samson, Greffier
Poste vacant, Directeur, Finances
Mario Provencher, Maire
Denis Charron, Directeur général
Noël Lanouette, Directeur, Travaux publics & services techniques
Léo Boisvert, Conseillers et Districts, Ward(s): Noranda-Nord/Lac-Dufault
Sylvie Turgeon, Conseillers et Districts, Ward(s): Rouyn-Noranda Ouest
André Philippon, Conseillers et Districts, Ward(s): Dallaire
Mario Provencher, Conseillers et Districts, Ward(s): Centre-ville
Siège vacant, Conseillers et Districts, Ward(s): Vieux-Noranda
Bernard Duchesneau, Conseillers et Districts, Ward(s): l'Université
Marcel Loyer, Conseillers et Districts, Ward(s): Granada
Siège vacant, Conseillers et Districts, Ward(s): Des Pionniers
Siège vacant, Conseillers et Districts, Ward(s): Évain
Danielle Simard, Conseillers et Districts, Ward(s): Arntfield/Montbeillard/Rollet
Marcel Maheux, Conseillers et Districts, Ward(s): Bellecombe/Beaudry/Cloutier
Pierre Rodrigue, Conseillers et Districts, Ward(s): Alembert/Cléricy/Mt-Brun/Destr
Ronald Gaudet, Conseillers et Districts, Ward(s): McWatters
René Ducharme, Conseillers et Districts, Ward(s): Cadillac & T.N.O.

Saguenay
CP 129
201, rue Racine est
Chicoutimi, QC G7H 5B8
418-698-3000
Fax: 418-541-4524
info@ville.saguenay.qc.ca
www.ville.saguenay.qc.ca
Municipal Type: City
Incorporated: 18 février 2002 *Area:* 1,166 km2
Population in 2006: 143,692
Provincial Electoral District(s): Dubuc; Chicoutimi; Jonquière
Federal Electoral District(s): Chicoutimi-Le Fjord
Next Election: 1er novembre 2013
Jean Tremblay, Maire
418-698-3330, Fax: 418-541-4510
maire@ville.saguenay.qc.ca
Paul-Roger Cantin, Conseillers et Districts, Ward(s): 1 Jonquière
paul-roger.cantin@ville.saguenay.qc.ca

Réjean Laforest, Conseillers et Districts, Ward(s): 2 Jonquière
rejean.laforest@ville.saguenay.qc.ca
Sylvie Gaudreault, Conseillers et Districts, Ward(s): 3 Jonquière
sylvie.gaudreault@ville.saguenay.qc.ca
Georges Bouchard, Conseillers et Districts, Ward(s): 4 Jonquière
georges.bouchard@ville.saguenay.qc.ca
Bernard Noël, Conseillers et Districts, Ward(s): 5 Jonquière
bernard.noel@ville.saguenay.qc.ca
Raoul Simard, Conseillers et Districts, Ward(s): 6 Jonquière
raoul.simard@ville.saguenay.qc.ca
Claude Tremblay, Conseillers et Districts, Ward(s): 7 Jonquière
claude.tremblay@ville.saguenay.qc.ca
Fabien Hovington, Conseillers et Districts, Ward(s): 8 Jonquière
fabien.hovington@ville.saguenay.qc.ca
Jean-Yves Provencher, Conseillers et Districts, Ward(s): 9 Chicoutimi
jean-yves.provencher@ville.saguenay.qc.ca
Carl Savard, Conseillers et Districts, Ward(s): 10 Chicoutimi
carl.savard@ville.saguenay.qc.ca
Marina Larouche, Conseillers et Districts, Ward(s): 11 Chicoutimi
marina.larouche@ville.saguenay.qc.ca
Marcel Jean, Conseillers et Districts, Ward(s): 12 Chicoutimi
marcel.jean@ville.saguenay.qc.ca
Jacques Cleary, Conseillers et Districts, Ward(s): 13 Chicoutimi
jacques.cleary@ville.saguenay.qc.ca
Denis Dahl, Conseillers et Districts, Ward(s): 14 Chicoutimi
denis.dahl@ville.saguenay.qc.ca
Jacques Fortin, Conseillers et Districts, Ward(s): 15 Chicoutimi
jacques.fortin@ville.saguenay.qc.ca
Luc Blackburn, Conseillers et Districts, Ward(s): 16 Chicoutimi
luc.blackburn@ville.saguenay.qc.ca
Poste vacant, Conseillers et Districts, Ward(s): 17 La Baie
Marc-André Gagnon, Conseillers et Districts, Ward(s): 18 La Baie
marc-andre.gagnon@ville.saguenay.qc.ca
Jean-Eudes Simard, Conseillers et Districts, Ward(s): 19 La Baie
jean-eudes.simard@ville.saguenay.qc.ca
Jean-François Boivin, Directeur général
418-698-3320, Fax: 418-541-4524
directiongenerale@ville.saguenay.qc.ca
Serges Chamberland, Directeur général adjoint, Opérations
Francine Maltais, Directrice, Services des arts, culture, communautaire & bibliothèque
Daniel Larouche, Directeur, Arrondissement de Jonquière
arrondissementdejonquiere@ville.saguenay.qc.ca
André Martin, Directeur, Arrondissement de Chicoutimi
arrondissementdechicoutimi@ville.saguenay.qc.ca
Gaétan Bergeron, Directeur, Arrondissement de La Baie
arrondissementdelabaie@ville.saguenay.qc.ca
Pierre Brassard, Greffier
greffe@ville.saguenay.qc.ca
Christine Tremblay, Directrice, Trésorerie et Évaluation
tresorerie@ville.saguenay.qc.ca
Jeannot Allard, Directeur, Service des communications
communications@ville.saguenay.qc.ca
Sylvie Jean, Directrice, Service des approvisionnements
approvisionnements@ville.saguenay.qc.ca
Pierre A. Tremblay, Directeur, Service des ressources informationnelles
informatique@ville.saguenay.qc.ca
Robert Pépin, Directeur, Service des affaires juridiques & du greffe
affairesjuridiques@ville.saguenay.qc.ca
Denis Coulombe, Directeur, Aménagement du territoire & urbanisme
urbanisme@ville.saguenay.qc.ca
Claude Bouchard, Directeur, Hydro-Jonquière
hydrojonquiere@ville.saguenay.qc.ca
Jean Morneau, Directeur, Service des immeubles et équipements motorisés
equipements@ville.saguenay.qc.ca
Pierre Racine, Directeur, Service des sports & du plein air
Carol Girard, Directeur, Sécurité incendie
incendie@ville.saguenay.qc.ca
Mario Giroux, Directeur, Sécurité publique
police@ville.saguenay.qc.ca
Denis Simard, Directeur, Travaux publics
travauxpublics@ville.saguenay.qc.ca

Saint-Basile-le-Grand
204, rue Principale
Saint-Basile-le-Grand, QC J3N 1M1
450-461-8000
Fax: 450-461-8029

Municipal Governments / Québec

communications@ville.saint-basile-le-grand.qc.ca
www.ville.saint-basile-le-grand.qc.ca
Municipal Type: City
Incorporated: 15 juin 1871 *Area:* 34,82 km2
County or District: La Vallée-du-Richelieu; Communauté métropolitaine de Montréal; *Population in 2009:* 16,088
Provincial Electoral District(s): Chambly
Federal Electoral District(s): Chambly-Borduas
Next Election: 1er novembre 2013
Luce Doucet, Greffière
Michel Carrières, Maire
Normand Lalande, Trésorier
Jean-Marie Beaupré, Directeur général
Marc-André Lehoux, Directeur, Culture/Loisirs

Saint-Constant
147, rue St-Pierre
Saint-Constant, QC J5A 2G2
450-638-2010
Fax: 450-638-5919
communications@ville.saint-constant.qc.ca
www.ville.saint-constant.qc.ca
Municipal Type: City
Incorporated: 1er juillet 1855 *Area:* 56,58 km2
County or District: Roussillon; *Population in 2006:* 23,957
Provincial Electoral District(s): La Prairie
Federal Electoral District(s): Châteauguay-St-Constant
Next Election: 1er novembre 2013
Sophie Laflammme, Greffière
Gilles Pepin, Maire
Pierre Morin, Responsable, Travaux publics
Susan McKercher, Directrice générale
Jean Gariépy, Directeur et chef, Brigade des pompiers
Bernard Armand, Coordonnateur, Mesures d'urgence
Denise Poirier Rivard, Conseillers et Districts, Ward(s): 1
Raymond Létourneau, Conseillers et Districts, Ward(s): 2
Yvan Riendeau, Conseillers et Districts, Ward(s): 3
France Hébert, Conseillers et Districts, Ward(s): 4
André Sauvé, Conseillers et Districts, Ward(s): 5
Mignonne Pouliot, Conseillers et Districts, Ward(s): 6
Jean-François Ouellet, Conseillers et Districts, Ward(s): 7
Mario Arsenault, Conseillers et Districts, Ward(s): 8

Saint-Eustache
145, rue St-Louis
Saint-Eustache, QC J7R 1X9
450-974-5000
www.ville.saint-eustache.qc.ca
Municipal Type: City
Incorporated: 15 janvier 1972 *Area:* 70,61 km2
County or District: Deux-Montagnes; Communauté métropolitaine de Montréal; *Population in 2009:* 42,762
Provincial Electoral District(s): Deux-Montagnes
Federal Electoral District(s): Rivière-des-Mille-Iles
Next Election: 1er novembre 2013
Marc Tourangeau, Greffier
Christian Bellemare, Directeur général
450-974-5280, Fax: 450-974-5229
Yves Guillemette, Directeur général adjoint
Bastien Morin, Directeur, Services municipaux
450-974-5284, Fax: 450-974-5229
Sylvain Mallette, Conseillers et Districts, Ward(s): 1 Vieux-Saint-Eustache
450-472-2519
smallette@ville.saint-eustache.qc.ca
André Biard, Conseillers et Districts, Ward(s): 2 Carrefour
450-473-2214
abiard@ville.saint-eustache.qc.ca
Patrice Paquette, Conseillers et Districts, Ward(s): 3 Rivière-Nord
450-974-1120
ppaquette@ville.saint-eustache.qc.ca
Stéphanie Bouchard, Directrice, Communications
450-974-5220, Fax: 450-974-5223
communications@ville.saint-eustache.qc.ca
Ginette Lacoix, Directrice, Finances
450-974-5070, Fax: 450-974-5077
Daniel Goyer, Conseillers et Districts, Ward(s): 4 Des Érables
450-974-9104
dgoyer@ville.saint-eustache.qc.ca
Pierre Charron, Conseillers et Districts, Ward(s): 5 Clair Matin
450-473-8054
pcharron@ville.saint-eustache.qc.ca

Claude Carignan, Maire
450-974-5014, Fax: 450-974-5203
maire@ville.saint-eustache.qc.ca
Germain Lalonde, Conseillers et Districts, Ward(s): 6 la Seigneurie
450-472-5890
glalonde@ville.saint-eustache.qc.ca
Pauline Harrison, Conseillers et Districts, Ward(s): 7 Des Moissons
450-473-8141
pharrison@ville.saint-eustache.qc.ca
Raymond Tessier, Conseillers et Districts, Ward(s): 8 Des ×les
450-472-3951
rtessier@ville.saint-eustache.qc.ca
Nicole Carignan Lefebvre, Conseillers et Districts, Ward(s): 9 Plateau-des-Chênes
450-623-5730
ncarignan-lefebvre@ville.saint-eustache.qc.ca
Sylvie Cloutier, Conseillers et Districts, Ward(s): 10 Des Jardins
450-974-9379
scloutier@ville.saint-eustache.qc.ca

Saint-Félicien
CP 7000
1209, boul Sacré-Coeur
Saint-Félicien, QC G8K 2R5
418-679-0251
Fax: 418-679-1449
dir.general@ville.stfelicien.qc.ca
www.ville.stfelicien.qc.ca
Municipal Type: City
Incorporated: 12 juin 1996 *Area:* 359,69 km2
County or District: Le Domaine-du-Roy; *Population in 2006:* 10,477
Provincial Electoral District(s): Roberval
Federal Electoral District(s): Roberval-Lac-St-Jean
Next Election: 1er novembre 2013
Luc Bergeron, Directeur général
418-679-2100, Fax: 418-679-1449
luc.bergeron@ville.stfelicien.qc.ca
Gilles Potvin, Maire
maire@ville.stfelicien.qc.ca
Louise Ménard, Greffière
louise.menard@ville.stfelicien.qc.ca
Dany Coudé, Trésorier
tresorerie@ville.stfelicien.qc.ca
Olivier de Launière, Directeur, Sécurité incendie
418-679-0313, Fax: 418-679-8217
odelauniere@ville.stfelicien.qc.ca
Paul-René Doucet, Directeur, Aménagement & entretien du territoire
prdoucet@ville.stfelicien.qc.ca
Bertrand Boutin, Siège #1, Conseillers et Districts
Bernard Boivin, Siège #2, Conseillers et Districts
Dany Larochelle, Siège #3, Conseillers et Districts
Luc Gibbons, Siège #4, Conseillers et Districts
Sonia Boudreault, Siège #5, Conseillers et Districts
Michel Gagnon, Siège #6, Conseillers et Districts

Saint-Georges
11700, boul Lacroix
Saint-Georges, QC G5Y 1L3
418-228-5555
Fax: 418-228-3855
direction.generale@ville.saint-georges.qc.ca
www.ville.saint-georges.qc.ca
Municipal Type: City
Incorporated: 26 septembre 2001 *Area:* 199,51 km2
County or District: Beauce-Sartigan; *Population in 2006:* 29,616
Provincial Electoral District(s): Beauce-Sud
Federal Electoral District(s): Beauce
Next Election: 1er novembre 2013
Jean McCollough, Greffier
jean.mccollough@ville.saint-georges.qc.ca
Roger Carette, Maire
maire@ville.saint-georges.qc.ca
Marcel Grondin, Directeur général
marcel.grondin@ville.saint-georges.qc.ca
Serge Paquet, Conseillers et Districts, Ward(s): 1
Daniel Lessard, Conseillers et Districts, Ward(s): 2
Jean Perron, Conseillers et Districts, Ward(s): 3
Irma Quirion, Conseillers et Districts, Ward(s): 4
Régis Drouin, Conseillers et Districts, Ward(s): 5
Marie-Ôve Dutil, Conseillers et Districts, Ward(s): 6
Karen Hilchey, Conseillers et Districts, Ward(s): 7

Marcel Bérubé, Conseillers et Districts, Ward(s): 8
Clément Poulin, Directeur, Finances & Trésorerie
clement.poulin@ville.saint-georges.qc.ca

Saint-Hyacinthe
CP 10
700, av de l'Hôtel-de-Ville
Saint-Hyacinthe, QC J2S 5B2
450-778-8300
Fax: 450-778-5817
communications@ville.st-hyacinthe.qc.ca
www.ville.st-hyacinthe.qc.ca
Municipal Type: City
Incorporated: 27 décembre 2001 *Area:* 189,11 km2
County or District: Les Maskoutains; *Population in 2006:* 51,616
Provincial Electoral District(s): St-Hyacinthe
Federal Electoral District(s): St-Hyacinthe-Bagot
Next Election: 1er novembre 2013
Hélène Beauchesne, Notaire; OMA, Greffière
450-778-8317
helene.beauchesne@ville.st-hyacinthe.qc.ca
Louis Bilodeau, Directeur général
louis.bilodeau@ville.st-hyacinthe.qc.ca
Chantal Frigon, Directrice, Communications
450-778-8304
chantal.frigon@ville.st-hyacinthe.qc.ca
Claude Bernier, Maire
450-778-8302, Fax: 450-778-5800
claude.bernier@ville.st-hyacinthe.qc.ca
Patrice Furlan, Directeur, Service d'urbanisme
450-778-8320, Fax: 450-778-5820
patrice.furlan@ville.st-hyacinthe.qc.ca
Daniel Dubois, Directeur, Sécurité incendie
daniel.dubois@ville.st-hyacinthe.qc.ca
Johanne Delage, Conseillers et Districts, Ward(s): 1. Yamaska
johanne.delage@ville.st-hyacinthe.qc.ca
Rosaire Martin, Conseillers et Districts, Ward(s): 2. Saint-Joseph
rosaire.martin@ville.st-hyacinthe.qc.ca
Bernard Barré, Conseillers et Districts, Ward(s): 3. La Providence
bernard.barre@ville.st-hyacinthe.qc.ca
Sylvie Adam, Conseillers et Districts, Ward(s): 4. Cascades
sylvie.adam@ville.st-hyacinthe.qc.ca
Réal St-Pierre, Conseillers et Districts, Ward(s): 5. Notre-Dame
real.st-pierre@ville.st-hyacinthe.qc.ca
Nicole Dion-Audette, Conseillers et Districts, Ward(s): 6. Hertel
n.dion-audette@ville.st-hyacinthe.qc.ca
Siège vacant, Conseillers et Districts, Ward(s): 7. Douville
Ray-Marc Dumoulin, Conseillers et Districts, Ward(s): 8. Bois-Joli
rm.dumoulin@ville.st-hyacinthe.qc.ca
Huguette Corbeil, Conseillers et Districts, Ward(s): 9. Deux-Clochers
huguette.corbeil@ville.st-hyacinthe.qc.ca
Jean-Claude Patenaude, Conseillers et Districts, Ward(s): 10. Vanier
jc.patenaude@ville.st-hyacinthe.qc.ca
Léon Plante, Conseillers et Districts, Ward(s): 11. Sainte-Rosalie
leon.plante@ville.st-hyacinthe.qc.ca
Guylain Coulombe, Conseillers et Districts, Ward(s): 12. Saint-Thomas-d'Aquin
guylain.coulombe@ville.st-hyacinthe.qc.ca
Réjean Veilleux, Conseillers et Districts, Ward(s): 13. Ceinture-Verte
rejean.veilleux@ville.st-hyacinthe.qc.ca
Jean Bélisle, OMA, Directeur, Service des finances
450-778-8387
jean.belisle@ville.st-hyacinthe.qc.ca

Saint-Jean-sur-Richelieu
CP 1025
188, rue Jacques-Cartier nord
Saint-Jean-sur-Richelieu, QC J3B 7B2
450-357-2100
Fax: 450-357-2285
info@ville.saint-jean-sur-richelieu.qc.ca
www.ville.saint-jean-sur-richelieu.qc.ca
Municipal Type: City
Incorporated: 24 janvier 2001 *Area:* 225,61 km2
County or District: Le Haut-Richelieu; *Population in 2006:* 87,492
Provincial Electoral District(s): St-Jean; Iberville
Federal Electoral District(s): St-Jean
Next Election: 1er novembre 2013

See blue tabs following this section for Municipal Waste Management and Water & Wastewater Treatment.

François Lapointe, Greffier
450-357-2077, Fax: 450-357-2362
greffe@ville.saint-jean-sur-richelieu.qc.ca
Gilles Dolbec, Maire
450-357-2095, Fax: 450-357-2079
mairie@ville.saint-jean-sur-richelieu.qc.ca
Roch Arbour, Directeur, Travaux publics
450-357-2238, Fax: 450-357-2290
Philippe Lasnier, Conseillers et Districts, Ward(s): 1
450-347-1299
p.lasnier@ville.saint-jean-sur-richelieu.qc.ca
Michel Gauthier, Conseillers et Districts, Ward(s): 2
450-515-9846
m.gauthier@ville.saint-jean-sur-richelieu.qc.ca
Gaétan Gagnon, Conseillers et Districts, Ward(s): 3
450-347-3209
g.gagnon@ville.saint-jean-sur-richelieu.qc.ca
Jean Fontaine, Conseillers et Districts, Ward(s): 4
450-346-3063
j.fontaine@ville.saint-jean-sur-richelieu.qc.ca
Stéphane Legrand, Conseillers et Districts, Ward(s): 5
450-545-9515
s.legrand@ville.saint-jean-sur-richelieu.qc.ca
Germain Poissant, Conseillers et Districts, Ward(s): 6
450-347-8703
g.poissant@ville.saint-jean-sur-richelieu.qc.ca
Christiane Marcoux, Conseillers et Districts, Ward(s): 7
450-347-5277
c.marcoux@ville.saint-jean-sur-richelieu.qc.ca
Marco Savard, Conseillers et Districts, Ward(s): 8
450-349-0473
m.savard@ville.saint-jean-sur-richelieu.qc.ca
Yvan Berthelot, Conseillers et Districts, Ward(s): 9
450-349-0685
v.berthelot@ville.saint-jean-sur-richelieu.qc.ca
Jean Lamoureux, Conseillers et Districts, Ward(s): 10
450-348-5014
j.lamoureux@ville.saint-jean-sur-richelieu.qc.ca
Michelle Power, Conseillers et Districts, Ward(s): 11
514-449-9614
m.power@ville.saint-jean-sur-richelieu.qc.ca
Robert Cantin, Conseillers et Districts, Ward(s): 12
450-349-6661
r.cantin@ville.saint-jean-sur-richelieu.qc.ca
Daniel Desroches, Directeur général
450-357-2383, Fax: 450-357-2385
Michelle Hébert, Directrice générale adjointe
Serge Boulerice, Directeur, Service de police
450-359-2529
police@ville.saint-jean-sur-richelieu.qc.ca
Mario Verville, Directeur, Service de l'urbanisme
450-359-2400, Fax: 450-359-2407
urbanisme@ville.saint-jean-sur-richelieu.qc.ca
Harold Ellefsen, Directeur, Service des finances
finances@ville.saint-jean-sur-richelieu.qc.ca

Saint-Jérôme
#301, 10, rue St-Joseph
Saint-Jérôme, QC J7Z 7G7
450-436-1511
Fax: 450-436-6626
info@vsj.ca
www.vsj.ca
Municipal Type: City
Incorporated: 1er janvier 2002 Area: 89,37 km2
County or District: La Rivière-du-Nord; Population in 2006: 63,729
Provincial Electoral District(s): Prévost
Federal Electoral District(s): Rivière-du-Nord
Next Election: 1er novembre 2013
Marcel Bélanger, Greffier
Marc Gascon, Maire
Richard Bégin, Directeur, Travaux publics
Yves Legris, Conseillers et Districts, Ward(s): 5 Parent
450-438-1076
Robert Rioux, Conseillers et Districts, Ward(s): 13 Dumont
450-438-2057
Bernard Bougie, Conseillers et Districts, Ward(s): 4 Labelle
450-431-7227
Louise Bouchard, Conseillers et Districts, Ward(s): 1 Rolland
450-432-9625
Marcel Lachance, Conseillers et Districts, Ward(s): 2 Brière
450-432-4399
Guy Lalande, Conseillers et Districts, Ward(s): 3 Laviolette
450-438-2021

Sylvain Gagné, Conseillers et Districts, Ward(s): 11 Forget
450-436-5357
Manon Labrèche, Conseillers et Districts, Ward(s): 12 Schulz
450-432-2733
Robert Carrière, Conseillers et Districts, Ward(s): 6 Desjardins
450-432-5629
Michèle Céclier, Conseillers et Districts, Ward(s): 14 Paquette
450-438-1073
Benoît Delage, Conseillers et Districts, Ward(s): 7 Bouvrette
450-436-6134
Stéphane Piché, Conseillers et Districts, Ward(s): 8 Lamontagne
450-432-2791
Martin Pigeon, Conseillers et Districts, Ward(s): 9 Crispin
450-436-1787
François Boyer, Conseillers et Districts, Ward(s): 10 Richer
450-224-1148
Éric Lachapelle, Directeur général
René Lachance, Directeur, Finances
Pierre Bourgeois, Directeur, Service de police
Guy Meilleur, Directeur, Service de la sécurité incendie
Michel Larose, Directeur, Ressources humaines
Raymond Zizian, Directeur, Culture/Loisirs/Vie communautaire
Louis Parent, Directeur, Communications
Pierre Ratté, Directeur, Service de l'urbanisme

Saint-Lazare
1960, ch Ste-Angélique
Saint-Lazare, QC J7T 3A3
450-424-8000
Fax: 450-455-4712
info@ville.saint-lazare.qc.ca
www.ville.saint-lazare.qc.ca
Municipal Type: City
Incorporated: 29 décembre 1875 Area: 67,59 km2
County or District: Vaudreuil-Soulanges; Population in 2006: 17,016
Provincial Electoral District(s): Soulanges
Federal Electoral District(s): Vaudreuil-Soulanges
Next Election: 1er novembre 2013
Nathaly Rayneault, Greffière
Paul Carzoli, Maire
Ghislain Castonguay, Directeur, Travaux publics
gcastonguay@ville.saint-lazare.qc.ca
Lucie Gendron, Directrice générale
Paul Laflamme, Conseillers et Districts, Ward(s): 1
Gaétan Aubé, Conseillers et Districts, Ward(s): 2
Brigitte Asselin, Conseillers et Districts, Ward(s): 3
Michel St-Louis, Conseillers et Districts, Ward(s): 4
Gaétan Ménard, Conseillers et Districts, Ward(s): 5
Chico Levy, Conseillers et Districts, Ward(s): 6

Saint-Lin-Laurentides
900, 12e av
Saint-Lin-Laurentides, QC J5M 2W2
450-439-3130
Fax: 450-439-1525
s.martel@saint-lin-laurentides.com
saint-lin-laurentides.com
Municipal Type: City
Incorporated: 1er mars 2000 Area: 117,52 km2
County or District: Montcalm; Population in 2006: 14,159
Provincial Electoral District(s): Rousseau
Federal Electoral District(s): Montcalm
Next Election: 1er novembre 2013
Sylvain Martel, Trésorier, Finance et trésoire
André Auger, Maire
Richard Dufort, Greffier & Directeur général
André Héroux, Directeur, Travaux publics
Jean-Pierre Desjardins, Directeur, Service des incendies

Sainte-Anne-des-Plaines
139, boul Ste-Anne
Sainte-Anne-des-Plaines, QC J0N 1H0
450-478-0211
Fax: 450-478-5660
villesteannedesplaines@videotron.ca
www.ville.ste-anne-des-plaines.qc.ca
Municipal Type: City
Incorporated: 1er juillet 1855 Area: 92,22 km2
County or District: Thérèse-De Blainville; Communauté métropolitaine de Montréal; Population in 2006: 13,412
Provincial Electoral District(s): Blainville
Federal Electoral District(s): Terrebonne-Blainville
Next Election: 1er novembre 2013
Serge Lepage, Greffier & Directeur général

Catherine Collin, Mairesse
Christiane Joyal, Trésorière
Carl St-Louis, Directeur, Travaux publics

Sainte-Catherine
5465, boul Marie-Victorin
Sainte-Catherine, QC J5C 1M1
450-632-0590
Fax: 450-632-3298
directiongenerale@ville.sainte-catherine.qc.ca
www.ville.sainte-catherine.qc.ca
Municipal Type: City
Incorporated: 30 octobre 1937 Area: 9,06 km2
County or District: Roussillon; Communauté métropolitaine de Montréal; Population in 2009: 16,306
Provincial Electoral District(s): Châteauguay
Federal Electoral District(s): Châteauguay-St-Constant
Next Election: 1er novembre 2013
Carole Cousineau, Greffière
Jocelyne Bates, Mairesse
Danielle Chevrette, Directrice générale
Serge Courchesne, Trésorier

Sainte-Julie
1580, ch du Fer-à-Cheval
Sainte-Julie, QC J3E 2M1
450-922-7111
Fax: 450-922-7108
communications@ville.sainte-julie.qc.ca
www.ville.sainte-julie.qc.ca
Municipal Type: City
Incorporated: 1er juillet 1855 Area: 47,78 km2
County or District: Lajemmerais; Communauté métropolitaine de Montréal; Population in 2009: 29,561
Provincial Electoral District(s): Marguerite-D'Youville
Federal Electoral District(s): Verchères-Les Patriotes
Next Election: 1er novembre 2013
Jean-François Gauthier, MBA, OMA, Greffier
450-922-7050
greffe@ville.sainte-julie.qc.ca
Suzanne Roy, Mairesse, mairie@ville.sainte-julie.qc.ca
450-922-7053
Denyse Journault, Directrice, Communications
450-922-7092
communications@ville.sainte-julie.qc.ca
Pierre-Luc Blanchard, Directeur, Service de l'urbanisme
450-922-7142
urbanisme@ville.sainte-julie.qc.ca
Jean-Pierre Duplin, Trésorier
450-922-7062
finances@ville.sainte-julie.qc.ca
Claude Laperrière, Directeur général
450-922-7102
dirgen@ville.sainte-julie.qc.ca
Isabelle Poulet, Conseillers et Districts, Ward(s): 1 Belle-Rivière/Ringuet
André Lemay, Conseillers et Districts, Ward(s): 2 Moulin
Donald Savaria, Conseillers et Districts, Ward(s): 3 Vallée
Nicole Marchand, Conseillers et Districts, Ward(s): 4 Rucher
Mario Lemay, Conseillers et Districts, Ward(s): 5 Vieux-Village
Normand Varin, Conseillers et Districts, Ward(s): 6 Grand-Coteau
Henri Corbin, Conseillers et Districts, Ward(s): 7 Arc-en-Ciel
Lucie Bisson, Conseillers et Districts, Ward(s): 8 Montagne
Daniel Chagnon, Directeur, Service des loisirs
450-922-7122
loisirs@ville.sainte-julie.qc.ca

Sainte-Marie
270, av Marguerite-Bourgeoys
Sainte-Marie, QC G6E 3Z3
418-387-2301
Fax: 418-387-2454
administration@ville.sainte-marie.qc.ca
www.ville.sainte-marie.qc.ca
Municipal Type: City
Incorporated: 15 avril 1978 Area: 106,65 km2
County or District: La Nouvelle-Beauce; Population in 2009: 11,857
Provincial Electoral District(s): Beauce-Nord
Federal Electoral District(s): Beauce
Next Election: 1er novembre 2013
Hélène Gagné, Greffière
helene.gagne@ville.sainte-marie.qc.ca
Harold Guay, Maire

Municipal Governments / Québec

Jacques Boutin, Trésorier
Maurice Mercier, Directeur, Travaux publics
Louis Normand, Directeur général

Sainte-Thérèse
CP 100
6, rue de l'Église
Sainte-Thérèse, QC J7E 4H7
450-434-1440
Fax: 450-434-1499
info@sainte-therese.ca
www.ville.sainte-therese.qc.ca
Municipal Type: City
Incorporated: 1er juin 1849 *Area:* 8,62 km2
County or District: Thérèse-De Blainville; Communauté métropolitaine de Montréal; *Population in 2009:* 25,642
Provincial Electoral District(s): Groulx
Federal Electoral District(s): Marc-Aurèle-Fortin
Next Election: 1er novembre 2013
Jean-Luc Berthiaume, M.Sc., OMA, Greffier
jl.berthiaume@sainte-therese.ca
Sylvie Surprenant, Mairesse
mairie@sainte-therese.ca
Chantal Gauvreau, Directrice générale
c.gauvreau@sainte-therese.ca
Jean Pierre Gendron, Directeur, Finances
jp.gendron@sainte-therese.ca
Denise Perreault-Théberge, Conseillers et Districts, Ward(s): 1 De Sève
d.perreault-theberge@sainte-therese.ca
Patrick Morin, Conseillers et Districts, Ward(s): 2 Verschelden
p.morin@sainte-therese.ca
Marie-Andrée Petelle, Conseillers et Districts, Ward(s): 3 Morris
ma.petelle@sainte-therese.ca
Marie-Noëlle Closson Duquette, Conseillers et Districts, Ward(s): 4 Chapleau
mn.closson-duquette@sainte-therese.ca
Luc Vézina, Conseillers et Districts, Ward(s): 5 Lonergan
l.vezina@sainte-therese.ca
Anne Lauzon, Conseillers et Districts, Ward(s): 6 Ducharme
a.lauzon@sainte-therese.ca
Louis Lauzon, Conseillers et Districts, Ward(s): 7 Blanchard
l.lauzon@sainte-therese.ca
Vincent Arseneau, Conseillers et Districts, Ward(s): 8 Marie-Thérèse
v.arseneau@sainte-therese.ca

Salaberry-de-Valleyfield
61, rue Ste-Cécile
Salaberry-de-Valleyfield, QC J6T 1L8
450-370-4300
communications@ville.valleyfield.qc.ca
www.ville.valleyfield.qc.ca
Municipal Type: City
Incorporated: 24 avril 2002 *Area:* 100,96 km2
County or District: Beauharnois-Salaberry; *Population in 2006:* 39,672
Provincial Electoral District(s): Beauharnois
Federal Electoral District(s): Beauharnois-Salaberry
Next Election: 1er novembre 2013
Alain Gagnon, Greffier
450-370-4304, Fax: 450-370-4388
alain.gagnon@ville.valleyfield.qc.ca
Pierre Chevrier, Directeur général
450-370-4800, Fax: 450-370-4343
pierre.chevrier@ville.valleyfield.qc.ca
Denis Lapointe, Maire
450-370-4819, Fax: 450-370-4343
denis.lapointe@ville.valleyfield.qc.ca
Michel Ménard, Directeur, Sécurité incendie
450-370-4750, Fax: 450-370-4755
securiteincendie@ville.valleyfield.qc.ca
Denis Larochelle, Directeur, Eau/Environnement/Travaux publics
450-370-4820, Fax: 450-370-4370
gestionduterritoire@ville.valleyfield.qc.ca
Danielle Prieur, Coordonnatrice, Communications
450-370-4875, Fax: 450-370-4343
communications@ville.valleyfield.qc.ca
Jacques Lemieux, CA, OMA, Trésorier
450-370-4320, Fax: 450-370-4316
jacques.lemieux@ville.valleyfield.qc.ca
Denis Laître, Conseillers et Districts, Ward(s): 1 Grande-Île
450-373-0954
denis.laitre@ville.valleyfield.qc.ca
Jean-Marc Rochon, Conseillers et Districts, Ward(s): 2 Nitro
450-377-2774
jean-marc.rochon@ville.valleyfield.qc.ca
Siège vacant, Conseillers et Districts, Ward(s): 3 Georges-Leduc
Robert Savard, Conseillers et Districts, Ward(s): 4 Champlain
450-371-1173
robert.savard@ville.valleyfield.qc.ca
Jean-Jacques Leduc, Conseillers et Districts, Ward(s): 5 La Baie
450-371-5099
jean-jacques.leduc@ville.valleyfield.qc.ca
Jacques Smith, Conseillers et Districts, Ward(s): 6 Robert-Cauchon
450-371-4975
jacques.smith@ville.valleyfield.qc.ca
Pierre-Paul Messier, Conseillers et Districts, Ward(s): 7 Jules-Léger
450-373-5459
pierre-paul.messier@ville.valleyfield.qc.ca
Normand Amesse, Conseillers et Districts, Ward(s): 8 Saint-Timothée
450-371-6895
normand.amesse@ville.valleyfield.qc.ca
René Monette, Directeur, Service récréatif & communautaire
450-370-4390, Fax: 450-370-4888
src@ville.valleyfield.qc.ca

Sept-Îles
546, av De Quen
Sept-Îles, QC G4R 2R4
418-962-2525
Fax: 418-964-3213
info@ville.sept-iles.qc.ca
www.ville.sept-iles.qc.ca
Municipal Type: City
Incorporated: 12 février 2003 *Area:* 1 969,42 km2
County or District: Sept-Rivières; *Population in 2006:* 25,514
Provincial Electoral District(s): Duplessis
Federal Electoral District(s): Manicouagan
Next Election: 1er novembre 2013
Note: En 1970, Clarke City est fusionnée à Sept-Îles; le 12 fév., 2003, Moisie & Gallix sont fusionnées à Sept-Îles.
Valérie Haince, Greffière
418-964-3205
greffe@ville.sept-iles.qc.ca
Claude Bureau, Directeur général
418-964-3201
directiongenerale@ville.sept-iles.qc.ca
Ghislain Lévesque, Maire
maire@ville.sept-iles.qc.ca
Serge Gagné, Directeur, Finances
418-964-3215
finances@ville.sept-iles.qc.ca
Gervais Gagné, Conseillers et Districts, Ward(s): 1 Clarke
district1@ville.sept-iles.qc.ca
Poste vacant, Conseillers et Districts, Ward(s): 2 Ferland
district2@ville.sept-iles.qc.ca
Jean Masse, Conseillers et Districts, Ward(s): 3 L'Anse
district3@ville.sept-iles.qc.ca
Denis Miousse, Conseillers et Districts, Ward(s): 4 Vieux-Poste
district4@ville.sept-iles.qc.ca
Gaby Gauthier, Conseillers et Districts, Ward(s): 5 Vigneault
district5@ville.sept-iles.qc.ca
Lorraine Dubuc-Johnson, Conseillers et Districts, Ward(s): 6 Mgr-Blanche
district6@ville.sept-iles.qc.ca
Martial Lévesque, Conseillers et Districts, Ward(s): 7 Sainte-Famille
district7@ville.sept-iles.qc.ca
Serge Lévesque, Conseillers et Districts, Ward(s): 8 La Rive
district8@ville.sept-iles.qc.ca
Guylaine Lejeune, Conseillers et Districts, Ward(s): 9 Gallix
district9@ville.sept-iles.qc.ca
Claude Lessard, Conseillers et Districts, Ward(s): 10 Moisie
district10@ville.sept-iles.qc.ca

Shawinigan
CP 400
550, av de l'Hôtel-de-Ville
Shawinigan, QC G9N 6V3
819-536-7200
Fax: 819-536-7255
information@shawinigan.ca
www.shawinigan.qc.ca
Municipal Type: City
Incorporated: 1er janvier 2002 *Area:* 781,81 km2
Population in 2006: 51,904
Provincial Electoral District(s): St-Maurice; Laviolette
Federal Electoral District(s): Berthier-Maskinongé
Next Election: 1er novembre 2013
Note: 8 nouveaux districts seront en vigueur lors des élections municipal de nov/09.
Yves Vincent, Greffier
greffe@shawinigan.ca
Lise Landry, Mairesse
cabinetdumaire@shawinigan.ca
Benoît Fortier, Directeur, Service de l'aménagement & de l'environnement
urbanisme@shawinigan.ca
François St-Onge, Directeur, Communications
fstonge@shawinigan.ca
Pierre Godin, Directeur, Travaux publics
travauxpublics@shawinigan.ca
Gaétan Béchard, Directeur général
directiongenerale@shawinigan.ca
Réal Beauchamp, Directeur général adjoint
directiongenerale@shawinigan.ca
Robert Y. Desjardins, Directeur, Loisirs, culture & vie communautaire
loisirs@shawinigan.ca
Sylvie Lavoie, Directrice, Finances
servicesadministratifs@shawinigan.ca
François Garceau, Directeur, Ressources humaines
ressourceshumaines@shawinigan.ca
Sylvain Trudel, Conseillers et Districts, Ward(s): 1
strudel@shawinigan.ca
Alain Lord, Conseillers et Districts, Ward(s): 10
alord@shawinigan.ca
Yves Bordeleau, Conseillers et Districts, Ward(s): 3
ybordeleau@shawinigan.ca
Robert Dupont, Conseillers et Districts, Ward(s): 6
rdupont@shawinigan.ca
Steve Martin, Conseillers et Districts, Ward(s): 7
smartin@shawinigan.ca
Alain Beauparlant, Conseillers et Districts, Ward(s): 5
abeauparlant@shawinigan.ca
Gilles Marchand, Conseillers et Districts, Ward(s): 8
gmarchand@shawinigan.ca
Denis Lampron, Conseillers et Districts, Ward(s): 9
dlampron@shawinigan.ca
France Beaulieu, Conseillers et Districts, Ward(s): 2
fbeaulieu@shawinigan.ca
Josette Allard-Gignac, Conseillers et Districts, Ward(s): 4
jallard-gignac@shawinigan.ca
Claude Larocque, Directeur, Services techniques
servicestechniques@shawinigan.ca
François Lelièvre, Directeur, Service de sécurité incendie
incendie@shawinigan.ca

Sherbrooke
CP 610
191, rue du Palais
Sherbrooke, QC J1H 5H9
819-821-5969
Fax: 819-822-6131
mairie@ville.sherbrooke.qc.ca
www.ville.sherbrooke.qc.ca
Municipal Type: City
Incorporated: 1er janvier 2001 *Area:* 366,00 km2
Population in 2006: 147,427
Provincial Electoral District(s): St-François; Sherbrooke; Orford; Johnson
Federal Electoral District(s): Sherbrooke
Next Election: 1er novembre 2013
Marc Latendresse, Directeur, Services des loisirs, sports, culture et vie communautaire
services.recreatifs.communautaires@ville.sherbrook
Colette Ouellet, Directrice, Service des communications
819-821-5572, Fax: 819-823-5153
communications@ville.sherbrooke.qc.ca
Roger Vachon, Directeur, Service d'Hydro-Sherbrooke
819-821-5726, Fax: 819-822-6085
hydro.sherbrooke@ville.sherbrooke.qc.ca
Jean Perrault, Maire
819-821-5969, Fax: 819-822-6131
mairie@ville.sherbrooke.qc.ca
Jean-François Rouleau, Conseillers et Districts, Ward(s): Mont-Bellevue/Université
jean-francois.rouleau@ville.sherbrooke.qc.ca

See blue tabs following this section for Municipal Waste Management and Water & Wastewater Treatment.

Roger Labrecque, Conseillers et Districts, Ward(s): Fleurimont/Quatre-Saisons
labrecqueniro@videotron.ca
Pierre Boisvert, Conseillers et Districts, Ward(s): Mont-Bellevue/Croix-Lumineuse
pboisvert2005@sympatico.ca
Serge Paquin, Conseillers et Districts, Ward(s): Mont-Bellevue/Centre-Sud
mepaquin@pariseaucliche.com
Chantal L'Espérance, Conseillers et Districts, Ward(s): Jacques-Cartier/Domaine-Howard
chantal.lesperance@ville.sherbrooke.qc.ca
Louida Brochu, Conseillers et Districts, Ward(s): Fleurimont/Lavigerie
louida.brochu@ville.sherbrooke.qc.ca
Francis Gagnon, Conseillers et Districts, Ward(s): Fleurimont/Desranleau
francis.gagnon2@sympatico.ca
Bernard F. Tanguay, Conseillers et Districts, Ward(s): Fleurimont/Marie-Rivier
btanguay@notarius.net
Mariette Fugère, Conseillers et Districts, Ward(s): Fleurimont/Pin-Solitaire
mariette.fugere@sympatico.ca
Jacques Testulat, Conseillers et Districts, Ward(s): Jacques-Cartier/Beckett
mj.testulat@videotron.ca
Nicole Bergeron, Conseillers et Districts, Ward(s): Brompton
Dany Lachance, Conseillers et Districts, Ward(s): Jacques-Cartier/Carrefour
danylachance@notairedl.com
Sylvie Lapointe, Directrice générale
819-821-5618, Fax: 819-823-5121
direction.generale@ville.sherbrooke.qc.ca
François Poulette, Trésorier et Directeur, Service des finances
819-821-5490, Fax: 819-822-6091
finances@ville.sherbrooke.qc.ca
Isabelle Sauvé, Greffière, Services des affaires juridiques et corporatives
819-821-5500, Fax: 819-822-6064
servicesjuridiques@ville.sherbrooke.qc.ca
Jacques Leduc, Directeur, Ressources humaines
819-821-5677, Fax: 819-822-6086
ressources.humaines@ville.sherbrooke.qc.ca
Michel Richer, Directeur, Service de protection des incendies
819-821-5514, Fax: 819-821-5516
protection.incendies@ville.sherbrooke.qc.ca
Claude Marcoux, Directeur, Service de la planification et du développement urbain
819-821-5901, Fax: 819-822-6070
planification.travaux.publics@ville.sherbrooke.qc.
Douglas MacAulay, Conseillers et Districts, Ward(s): Lennoxville
douglas.macaulay@ville.sherbrooke.qc.ca
Robert Y. Pouliot, Conseillers et Districts, Ward(s): Mont-Bellevue/Ascot
Diane Délisle, Conseillers et Districts, Ward(s): Rock Forest-St-Élie-Deauville
ddelisle@abacom.com
Bernard Sévigny, Conseillers et Districts, Ward(s): Rock Forest-St-Élie-Deauville
bernard.sevigny@usherbrooke.ca
Serge Forest, Conseillers et Districts, Ward(s): Rock Forest-St-Élie-Deauville
serge.forest@videotron.ca
Julien Lachance, Conseillers et Districts, Ward(s): Rock Forest-St-Élie-Deauville
jlach@videotron.ca
Marc Denault, Conseillers et Districts, Ward(s): Jacques-Cartier/Montcalm
denaultm@abacom.com
Michel Caron, Directeur, Service des bâtiments et des équipements
819-821-5630, Fax: 819-821-5426
ressources.materielles@ville.sherbrooke.qc.ca
Louis Daigle, Directeur, Service des technologies de l'information
819-821-5623, Fax: 819-821-5470
informatique@ville.sherbrooke.qc.ca
Gaétan Labbé, Directeur, Service de police
819-821-5555
police@ville.sherbrooke.qc.ca
Benoît Dionne, Conseillers et Districts, Ward(s): Brompton/Beauvoir
dionneb@csrs.qc.ca

Michel Lamontagne, Conseillers et Districts, Ward(s): Brompton/Moulins
Thomas A. Allen, Conseillers et Districts, Ward(s): Lennoxville/Fairview
tallen@ubishops.ca
William Smith, Conseillers et Districts, Ward(s): Lennoxville/Uplands

Sorel-Tracy
CP 368
71, rue Charlotte
Sorel-Tracy, QC J3P 7K1
450-780-5600
Fax: 450-780-5625
info@ville.sorel-tracy.qc.ca
www.ville.sorel.qc.ca
Municipal Type: City
Incorporated: 15 mars 2000 *Area:* 56,58 km2
County or District: Pierre-De Saurel; *Population in 2009:* 34,308
Provincial Electoral District(s): Richelieu
Federal Electoral District(s): Bas-Richelieu-Nicolet-Bécancour
Next Election: 1er novembre 2013
René Chevalier, Greffier
Marcel Robert, Maire
Diane Robillard, Directrice, Finances & Trésorerie
Alain Rouleau, Directeur, Sécurité incendie
Mario Lazure, Directeur général
Michel Berthiaume, Conseillers et Districts, Ward(s): 1 Bourgchemin
450-742-0267
Yvon Bibeau, Conseillers et Districts, Ward(s): 3 Saint-Laurent
450-746-8987
Corina Bastiani, Conseillers et Districts, Ward(s): 4 Vieux-Sorel
450-743-8484
Marcel Lavallée, Conseillers et Districts, Ward(s): 5 Du Faubourg
450-742-3101
André Bélanger, Conseillers et Districts, Ward(s): 6 Des Gouverneurs
450-742-9587
Michèle Lacombe-Gauthier, Conseillers et Districts, Ward(s): 7 Des Patriotes
450-746-7710
Yves Bérard, Conseillers et Districts, Ward(s): 8 Pierre-De Saurel
450-746-8671
Denis Gagné, Conseillers et Districts, Ward(s): 2 Richelieu
450-742-6481

Terrebonne
775, rue St-Jean-Baptiste
Terrebonne, QC J6W 1B5
450-961-2001
information@ville.terrebonne.qc.ca
www.ville.terrebonne.qc.ca
Municipal Type: City
Incorporated: 27 juin 2001 *Area:* 155,44 km2
County or District: Les Moulins; Communauté métropolitaine de Montréal; *Population in 2009:* 98,459
Provincial Electoral District(s): Terrebonne; Masson
Federal Electoral District(s): Terrebonne-Blainville
Next Election: 1er novembre 2013
Denis Bouffard, Greffier
Jean-Marc Robitaille, Maire
Claude Lacasse, Conseillers et Districts, Ward(s): 1
Daniel L'Espérance, Conseillers et Districts, Ward(s): 2
Paul Asselin, Conseillers et Districts, Ward(s): 7
Marie-Claude Lamarche, Conseillers et Districts, Ward(s): 3
Réal Leclerc, Conseillers et Districts, Ward(s): 4
Michel Morin, Conseillers et Districts, Ward(s): 6
Denis Poitras, Conseillers et Districts, Ward(s): 5
Marie-Josée Beaupré, Conseillers et Districts, Ward(s): 8
Marc Campagna, Conseillers et Districts, Ward(s): 9
Frédéric Asselin, Conseillers et Districts, Ward(s): 10
Clermont Lévesque, Conseillers et Districts, Ward(s): 11
Jean-Luc Labrecque, Conseillers et Districts, Ward(s): 12
Sylvain Tousignant, Conseillers et Districts, Ward(s): 13
Michel Lefebvre, Conseillers et Districts, Ward(s): 14
Micheline Mathieu, Conseillers et Districts, Ward(s): 15
Jean-Guy Sénécal, Conseillers et Districts, Ward(s): 16
Raymond Champagne, Directeur, Finances
450-492-2433
Denis Lévesque, Directeur général
Guy Dubois, Chef de police
Réal Lanoue, Directeur, Service de l'incendie

Michel Sarrazin, Directeur, Entretien du territoire

Thetford Mines
CP 489
144, rue Notre-Dame ouest
Thetford Mines, QC G6G 5T3
418-335-2981
Fax: 418-335-7089
infos@ville.thetfordmines.qc.ca
www.ville.thetfordmines.qc.ca
Municipal Type: City
Incorporated: 17 octobre 2001 *Area:* 224,37 km2
County or District: Les Appalaches; *Population in 2009:* 16,124
Provincial Electoral District(s): Frontenac
Federal Electoral District(s): Mégantic-L'Érable
Next Election: 1er novembre 2013
Réjean Martin, Greffier
greffe@ville.thetfordmines.qc.ca
Luc Berthold, Maire
René Soucy, Directeur général
dirgen@ville.thetfordmines.qc.ca
Sylvain Tremblay, Directeur, Service des ressources financières
s.tremblay@ville.thetfordmines.qc.ca
François Gagnon, Directeur, Sécurité publique
secpub@ville.thetfordmines.qc.ca
Clément Boudreau, Conseillers et Districts, Ward(s): 1 Black Lake
418-423-2257
Renaud Legendre, Conseillers et Districts, Ward(s): 2 Black Lake-Mitchell/Lacs
418-423-2349
Ghyslain Cliche, Conseillers et Districts, Ward(s): 3 Thetford Mines
418-335-9267
Luc Champagne, Conseillers et Districts, Ward(s): 4 Thetford Mines
418-338-2812
Carmen Jalbert-Jacques, Conseillers et Districts, Ward(s): 5 Thetford Mines
418-338-1901
cjalbertjacques@sympatico.ca
Louis-Philippe Champagne, Conseillers et Districts, Ward(s): 6 Thetford Mines
418-335-7119
Marco Tanguay, Conseillers et Districts, Ward(s): 7 Thetford Mines
418-338-8819
Marc Vachon, Conseillers et Districts, Ward(s): 8 Thetford Mines
418-334-0340
Paul-André Marchand, Conseillers et Districts, Ward(s): 9 Thetford-Sud
418-335-9871
Gaétan Vachon, Conseillers et Districts, Ward(s): 10 Robertsonville/Pontbriand
418-335-9543

Trois-Rivières
CP 368
1325, place de l'Hôtel-de-Ville
Trois-Rivières, QC G9A 5H3
819-374-2002
Fax: 819-372-4674
info@v3r.net
www.v3r.net
Municipal Type: City
Incorporated: 1er janvier 2002 *Area:* 288,50 km2
Population in 2006: 129,100
Provincial Electoral District(s): Trois-Rivières; Maskinongé; Champlain
Federal Electoral District(s): Trois-Rivières
Next Election: 1er novembre 2013
Yves Lévesque, Maire
Michel Byette, Directeur général
819-372-4608, Fax: 819-372-4631
directiongenerale@v3r.net
Daniel Thibault, Directeur général adjoint
819-372-4649, Fax: 819-372-0125
directiongeneraleadjointe@v3r.net
Gilles Poulin, Directeur, Service du greffe/Services juridiques
819-372-4604, Fax: 819-372-4636
greffe@v3r.net
Alain Brouillette, Directeur, Finances et administration
819-372-4642, Fax: 819-374-1243
finances@v3r.net

See blue tabs following this section for Municipal Waste Management and Water & Wastewater Treatment.

Municipal Governments / Québec

Éric Chevalier, Directeur, Ressources humaines
819-372-4603, Fax: 819-374-9005
ressourceshumaines@v3r.net
Francis Gobeil, Directeur, Sécurité publique
819-370-6700, Fax: 819-374-3506
policeincendie@v3r.net
Michel Lemieux, Directeur, Loisirs & services communautaires
819-372-4621, Fax: 819-374-7133
Michel Jutras, Responsable, Arts et culture
Pierre Desjardins, Directeur, Aménagement, gestion & développement durable du territoire
819-372-4626, Fax: 819-375-5865
urbanisme@v3r.net
Jacques St-Laurent, Directeur, Développement
819-372-4642, Fax: 819-374-1243
directiondeveloppement@v3r.net
François Roy, Directeur, Communications
819-372-4602, Fax: 819-374-0210
relationspubliques@v3r.net
Ghislain Lachance, Directeur, Travaux publics
Vincent Fortier, Directeur, Services techniques
819-372-4627, Fax: 819-374-6646
Micheline Courteau, Conseillers et Districts, Ward(s): Ste-Marthe-du-Cap
Monique Leclerc, Conseillers et Districts, Ward(s): Châteaudun
Fernand Lajoie, Conseillers et Districts, Ward(s): Estacades
Denis Beaulieu, Conseillers et Districts, Ward(s): Sanctuaire
René Goyette, Conseillers et Districts, Ward(s): la Madeleine
Michel Bronsard, Conseillers et Districts, Ward(s): St-Louis-de-France
Joan Lefebvre, Conseillers et Districts, Ward(s): Plateaux
André Noël, Conseillers et Districts, Ward(s): Carmel
Sylvie Tardif, Conseillers et Districts, Ward(s): Marie de l'Incarnation
Guy Daigle, Conseillers et Districts, Ward(s): Laviolette
Claude Lacroix, Conseillers et Districts, Ward(s): Chavigny
Ginette Bellemare, Conseillers et Districts, Ward(s): Rigaud
Pierre A. Dupont, Conseillers et Districts, Ward(s): Ste-Marguerite
Yves Landry, Conseillers et Districts, Ward(s): Terrasses
Michel Veillette, Conseillers et Districts, Ward(s): Pointe-du-lac
Françoise H. Viens, Conseillers et Districts, Ward(s): Vieilles-Forges

Val-d'Or
CP 400
855, 2e av
Val-d'Or, QC J9P 4P4
819-824-9613
Fax: 819-825-6650
info@ville.valdor.qc.ca
www.ville.valdor.qc.ca
Municipal Type: City
Incorporated: 1er janvier 2002 *Area:* 3 958,13 km2
County or District: Vallée-de-l'Or; *Population in 2006:* 31,123
Provincial Electoral District(s): Abitibi-Est
Federal Electoral District(s): Abitibi-Baie-James-Nunavik-Eeyou
Next Election: 1er novembre 2013
Sophie Gareau, Greffière
Fernand Trahan, Maire
Guy Faucher, Directeur général
Réal Houle, Trésorier
Alain Cloutier, Directeur, Ressources humaines/Communications
Danny Burbridge, Directeur, Infrastructures urbaines
Robert Migué, Directeur, Service culturel
Suzanne Couture Bordeleau, Conseillers et Districts, Ward(s): 1 Lac Blouin-Centre-ville
Yvon Frenette, Conseillers et Districts, Ward(s): 2 Paquinville-Fatima
Yolette Lévy, Conseillers et Districts, Ward(s): 3 Belvédère
Céline Brindamour, Conseillers et Districts, Ward(s): 4 Sullivan
Gilles Bérubé, Conseillers et Districts, Ward(s): 5 Val-Senneville-Vassan
Francis Murphy, Conseillers et Districts, Ward(s): 6 Bourlamaque-Louvicourt
André Gilbert, Conseillers et Districts, Ward(s): 7 Lemoine-Baie-Carrière
Claudia Chaput, Conseillers et Districts, Ward(s): 8 Dubuisson

Varennes
CP 5000
175, rue Ste-Anne
Varennes, QC J3X 1T5
450-652-9888
Fax: 450-652-2655
general@ville.varennes.qc.ca
www.ville.varennes.qc.ca
Municipal Type: City
Incorporated: 26 août 1972 *Area:* 93,96 km2
County or District: Lajemmerais; *Population in 2006:* 20,950
Provincial Electoral District(s): Verchères
Federal Electoral District(s): Verchères-Les Patriotes
Next Election: 1er novembre 2013
Marc Giard, Greffier
Claude Provost, ing., Responsable, Travaux publics
Denis Marchand, Responsable, Environnement
Michel Tremblay, Maire
Denis Marchand, Directeur, Urbanisme
Gilles Lacroix, Conseillers et Districts, Ward(s): 1 La Guillaudière
Martin Damphousse, Conseillers et Districts, Ward(s): 2 La Sitière
Francis Rinfret, Conseillers et Districts, Ward(s): 3 Langloiserie
f.rinfret@videotron.ca
Denis Le Blanc, Conseillers et Districts, Ward(s): 4 Notre-Dame
Yves Tremblay, Conseillers et Districts, Ward(s): 5 Petite Prairie
yves.tremblay@videotron.ca
Gilles Lebrun, Conseillers et Districts, Ward(s): 6 Les Seigneuries
gilebrun@videotron.ca
Michel Lyons, Conseillers et Districts, Ward(s): 7 Saint-Charles
michel.lyons@videotron.ca
Brigitte Collin, Conseillers et Districts, Ward(s): 8 De Martigny
bcollin@videotron.ca

Vaudreuil-Dorion
#200, 2555, rue Dutrisac
Vaudreuil-Dorion, QC J7V 7E6
450-455-3371
Fax: 450-424-8540
courriel@ville.vaudreuil-dorion.qc.ca
www.ville.vaudreuil-dorion.qc.ca
Municipal Type: City
Incorporated: 16 mars 1994 *Area:* 73,18 km2
County or District: Vaudreuil-Soulanges; Communauté métropolitaine de Montréal; *Population in 2009:* 27,330
Provincial Electoral District(s): Vaudreuil
Federal Electoral District(s): Vaudreuil-Soulanges
Next Election: 1er novembre 2013
Jean St-Antoine, Greffier
greffe@ville.vaudreuil-dorion.qc.ca
Guy Pilon, Maire
Mona Dumouchel, Trésorière
450-424-8532
tresorerie@ville.vaudreuil-dorion.qc.ca
Luc Duval, Directeur, Travaux publics
450-455-7636, Fax: 450-424-8590
t.publics@ville.vaudreuil-dorion.qc.ca
Manon Bernard, Directrice générale
Claude Beaudoin, Conseillers et Districts, Ward(s): 1
François Séguin, Conseillers et Districts, Ward(s): 2
Robert A. Laurence, Conseillers et Districts, Ward(s): 3
Denis Vincent, Conseillers et Districts, Ward(s): 4
Rénald Gabriele, Conseillers et Districts, Ward(s): 5
Gabriel Parent, Conseillers et Districts, Ward(s): 6
Guylène Duplessis, Conseillers et Districts, Ward(s): 7
Paul Dumoulin, Conseillers et Districts, Ward(s): 8

Victoriaville
CP 370
1, rue Notre-Dame ouest
Victoriaville, QC G6P 6T2
819-204-1571
Fax: 819-758-9292
info@ville.victoriaville.qc.ca
www.ville.victoriaville.qc.ca
Municipal Type: City
Incorporated: 23 juin 1993 *Area:* 81,06 km2
County or District: Arthabaska; *Population in 2006:* 40,486
Provincial Electoral District(s): Arthabaska
Federal Electoral District(s): Richmond-Arthabaska
Next Election: 1er novembre 2013
Jean Poirier, Greffier
jean.poirier@ville.victoriaville.qc.ca
Roger Richard, Maire
819-758-1571
roger.richard@ville.victoriaville.qc.ca
Martin Lessard, Directeur général
martin.lessard@ville.victoriaville.qc.ca
Jean Mercier, Directeur, Service des ressources humaines
819-758-1571
jean.mercier@ville.victoriaville.qc.ca
André Charest, Directeur, Services des travaux publics
819-758-0651
andre.charest@ville.victoriaville.qc.ca
Jean Demers, Directeur, Gestion du territoire
819-758-1571
jean.demers@ville.victoriaville.qc.ca
Yves Fréchette, Directeur, Services administratifs
yves.frechette@ville.victoriaville.qc.ca
Bertrand Lambert, Conseillers et Districts, Ward(s): 1 Parc de l'Amitié
819-752-5388
bertrand.lambert@ville.victoriaville.qc.ca
Jacques Gagnon, Conseillers et Districts, Ward(s): 2 Parc-de-l'Île
819-758-8511
jacques.gagnon@ville.victoriaville.qc.ca
Jacques Nadeau, Conseillers et Districts, Ward(s): 3 Charles-Édouard-Mailhot
819-758-8530
jacques.nadeau@ville.victoriaville.qc.ca
Alexandre Côté, Conseillers et Districts, Ward(s): 4 Sainte-Famille
819-357-3272
alexandre.cote@ville.victoriaville.qc.ca
France Auger, Conseillers et Districts, Ward(s): 5 Parc-Terre-des-Jeunes
819-758-7330
france.auger@ville.victoriaville.qc.ca
Michel Allard, Conseillers et Districts, Ward(s): 7 Sainte-Victoire
819-752-6362
michel.allard@ville.victoriaville.qc.ca
Denis Morin, Conseillers et Districts, Ward(s): 8 Arthabaska-Nord
819-357-7821
denis.morin@ville.victoriaville.qc.ca
Donald Dumont, Conseillers et Districts, Ward(s): 9 Arthabaska-Ouest
819-758-9169
donald.dumont@ville.victoriaville.qc.ca
Christian Lettre, Conseillers et Districts, Ward(s): 10 Arthabaska-Est
819-357-8573
christian.lettre@ville.victoriaville.qc.ca
Siège vacant, Conseillers et Districts, Ward(s): 6 Parc-Victoria

Other Municipalities in Québec

Abitibi
CP 214
571, 1re Rue est
Amos, QC J9T 2H3
819-732-5356
Fax: 819-732-9607
mrc@mrcabitibi.qc.ca
www.mrcabitibi.qc.ca
Municipal Type: Regional County Municipality
Population in 2009: 24,060
Note: 17 municipalités & 2 autres territoires.
Michel Roy, Directeur général
michel.roy@mrcabitibi.qc.ca
Jacques Riopel, Préfet

Abitibi-Ouest
#105, 6, 8e Av est
La Sarre, QC J9Z 1N6
819-339-5671
Fax: 819-339-5400
mrcao@mrcao.qc.ca
mrc.ao.ca
Municipal Type: Regional County Municipality
Population in 2009: 20,929
Note: 21 municipalités & 2 autres territoires.
Nicole Breton, Directrice générale
Daniel Rancourt, Préfet
Ian Cameron, Directeur, Service à l'aménagement du territoire
Sylvie Grenier, Responsable, Forêt/Géomatique

Acton
CP 99
1037, rue Beaugrand
Acton Vale, QC J0H 1A0

See blue tabs following this section for Municipal Waste Management and Water & Wastewater Treatment.

Municipal Governments / Québec

450-546-3256
Fax: 450-546-0525
info@mrcacton.qc.ca
www.mrcacton.qc.ca
Municipal Type: Regional County Municipality
Population in 2006: 15,289
Yvan Talbot, Sec.-Trés. & Directeur général
Pascal Joly, Urbaniste, Services en géomatique

Antoine-Labelle
425, rue du Pont
Mont-Laurier, QC J9L 2R6
819-623-3485
Fax: 819-623-5052
administration@mrc-antoine-labelle.qc.ca
www.mrc-antoine-labelle.qc.ca
Municipal Type: Regional County Municipality
Population in 2009: 35,507
Note: 17 municipalités & 11 autres territoires.
Jacline Williams, Directrice générale
Roger Lapointe, Préfet

Argenteuil
430, rue Grace
Lachute, QC J8H 1M6
450-562-2474
Fax: 450-562-1911
mrc@argenteuil.qc.ca
www.argenteuil.qc.ca
Municipal Type: Regional County Municipality
Population in 2009: 30,267
Note: 9 municipalités.
Renée-Claude L'Allier, Greffière
rclallier@argenteuil.qc.ca
Daniel Beaulieu, Préfet
Marc Carrière, Directeur général
mcarriere@argenteuil.qc.ca

Arthabaska
40, rte de la Grande-Ligne
Victoriaville, QC G6T 0E6
819-752-2444
Fax: 819-752-3623
info@mrc-arthabaska.qc.ca
www.mrc-arthabaska.qc.ca
Municipal Type: Regional County Municipality
Population in 2009: 67,405
Note: 24 municipalités.
Frédérick Michaud, Directeur général
Lionel Fréchette, Préfet

Avignon
CP 128
470, rue Francoeur
Nouvelle, QC G0C 2E0
418-794-2221
Fax: 418-794-2076
info@mrcavignon.com
www.mrcavignon.com
Municipal Type: Regional County Municipality
Incorporated: 18 mars 1981
Population in 2009: 13,219
Note: 11 municipalités & 2 autres territoires.
Gaétan Bernatchez, Directeur général
Bertrand Berger, Préfet

Batiscan
395, rue Principale
Batiscan, QC G0X 1A0
418-362-2421
Fax: 418-362-3174
municipalite@batiscan.ca
www.batiscan.ca
Municipal Type: Municipality
Incorporated: 1er juillet 1855 *Area:* 44,02 km2
County or District: Les Chenaux; *Population in 2006:* 949
Provincial Electoral District(s): Champlain
Federal Electoral District(s): St-Maurice-Champlain
Next Election: 1er novembre 2013
Caroline Cyr, Sec.-Trés.
Christian Fortin, Maire

Beauce-Sartigan
2727, 6e Av
Saint-Georges, QC G5Y 3Y1
418-228-8418
Fax: 418-228-3709
mrcbsart@globetrotter.net
Municipal Type: Regional County Municipality
Population in 2009: 50,229
Note: 16 municipalités.
Éric Paquet, Directeur général
Luc Lemieux, Préfet

Beauharnois-Salaberry
#200, 660, rue Ellice
Beauharnois, QC J6N 1Y1
450-225-0870
Fax: 450-225-0872
info@mrc-beauharnois-salaberry.com
www.mrc-beauharnois-salaberry.com
Municipal Type: Regional County Municipality
Population in 2009: 61,531
Note: 7 municipalités.
Linda Phaneuf, Directrice générale
l.phaneuf@mrc-beauharnois-salaberry.com
Philippe Meunier, Coordonnateur, Aménagement & développement du territoire
p.meunier@mrc-beauharnois-salaberry.com
Yves Daoust, Préfet

Bécancour
#1, 3689, boul Bécancour
Bécancour, QC G9H 3W7
819-298-2070
Fax: 819-298-2041
info@mrcbecancour.qc.ca
Municipal Type: Regional County Municipality
Incorporated: 1 janvier 1982
Population in 2009: 18,816
Note: 12 municipalités.
Laval Dubois, Directeur général
Maurice Richard, Préfet

Bellechasse
100, rue Monseigneur-Bilodeau
Saint-Lazare-de-Bellechasse, QC G0R 3J0
418-883-3347
Fax: 418-883-2555
clement@mrcbellechasse.qc.ca
www.mrcbellechasse.qc.ca
Municipal Type: Regional County Municipality
Incorporated: 1 janvier 1982
Population in 2009: 33,792
Note: 20 municipalités.
Clément Fillion, Directeur général
Hervé Blais, Préfet

Bonaventure
CP 310
51, rue Notre-Dame
New Carlisle, QC G0C 1Z0
418-752-6601
Fax: 418-752-6657
mrcbonav@globetrotter.net
www.mrcbonaventure.com
Municipal Type: Regional County Municipality
Incorporated: 8 avril 1981
Population in 2009: 17,987
Note: 13 municipalités & 1 autre territoire.
Anne-Marie Flowers, Directrice générale
mrcbonavaflowers@globetrotter.net
Jean-Guy Poirier, Préfet

Brome-Missisquoi
749, rue Principale
Cowansville, QC J2K 1J8
450-266-4900
Fax: 450-266-6141
administration@mrcbm.qc.ca
www.brome-missisquoi.ca
Municipal Type: Regional County Municipality
Population in 2009: 47,127
Note: 20 municipalités.
Robert Desmarais, Directeur général
Arthur Fauteux, Préfet

Charlevoix
#201, 4, place de l'Église
Baie-Saint-Paul, QC G3Z 1T2
418-435-2639
Fax: 418-435-2666
mrc@charlevoix.net
www.mrc-charlevoix.com
Municipal Type: Regional County Municipality
Incorporated: 1 janvier 1982
Population in 2009: 13,228
Note: 6 municipalités & 1 autre territoire.
Karine Horvath, Directrice générale
Dominic Tremblay, Préfet

Charlevoix-Est
172, boul Notre-Dame
Clermont, QC G4A 1G1
418-439-3947
Fax: 418-439-2502
direction@mrccharlevoixest.ca
www.mrccharlevoixest.ca
Municipal Type: Regional County Municipality
Incorporated: 1 janvier 1982
Population in 2009: 16,347
Note: 7 municipalités & 2 autres territoires.
Pierre Girard, Directeur général
Jean-Luc Simard, Préfet

Coaticook
294, rue St-Jacques nord
Coaticook, QC J1A 2R3
819-849-9166
Fax: 819-849-4320
secretariat@mrcdecoaticook.qc.ca
www.mrcdecoaticook.qc.ca
Municipal Type: Regional County Municipality
Incorporated: 1 janvier 1982
Population in 2009: 18,680
Note: 12 municipalités.
Nancy Bilodeau, Greffière
greffe.archive@mrcdecoaticook.qc.ca
Sylvie Harvey, Directice générale
direction@mrcdecoaticook.qc.ca
Réjean Masson, Préfet

D'Autray
CP 1500
550, rue De Montcalm
Berthierville, QC J0K 1A0
450-836-7007
Fax: 450-836-1576
mrcautray@mrcautray.com
mrcautray.com
Municipal Type: Regional County Municipality
Population in 2009: 41,052
Note: 15 municipalités.
Danielle Joyal, Directrice générale
Norman Blackburn, Préfet

Deux-Montagnes
#301, 1, place de la Gare
Saint-Eustache, QC J7R 0B4
450-491-1818
Fax: 450-491-3040
info@mrc2m.qc.ca
www.clddm.com/mrc.php
Municipal Type: Regional County Municipality
Population in 2009: 90,638
Note: 7 municipalités.
Nicole Loiselle, Directrice générale
Marc Lauzon, Préfet

Drummond
436, rue Lindsay
Drummondville, QC J2B 1G6
819-477-2230
Fax: 819-477-8442
courriel@mrcdrummond.qc.ca
www.mrcdrummond.qc.ca
Municipal Type: Regional County Municipality
Population in 2009: 94,559
Note: 18 municipalités.
Michel Gagnon, Directeur général
mgagnon@mrcdrummond.qc.ca
Francine Ruest Jutras, Préfète (par intérim)

Joliette
632, rue De Lanaudière
Joliette, QC J6E 3M7

See blue tabs following this section for Municipal Waste Management and Water & Wastewater Treatment.

Municipal Governments / Québec

450-759-2237
Fax: 450-759-2597
info@mrcjoliette.qc.ca
www.mrcjoliette.qc.ca
Municipal Type: Regional County Municipality
Incorporated:
Population in 2009: 59,329
Note: 10 municipalités.
Line Laporte, Directrice générale
André Hénault, Préfet

Kamouraska
CP 1120
425, av Patry
Saint-Pascal, QC G0L 3Y0
418-492-1660
Fax: 418-492-2220
info@mrckamouraska.com
www.mrckamouraska.com
Municipal Type: Regional County Municipality
Incorporated: 1 janvier 1982
Population in 2009: 22,055
Note: 17 municipalités & 2 autres territoires.
Guy Lavoie, Directeur général
Jean-Guy Charest, Préfet

L'Assomption
300A, rue Dorval
L'Assomption, QC J5W 3A1
450-589-2288
Fax: 450-589-9430
mrcinfo@mrclassomption.qc.ca
www.mrclassomption.qc.ca
Municipal Type: Regional County Municipality
Population in 2009: 113,413
Note: 6 municipalités.
Michel C. Gagnon, Directeur général
Chantal Deschamps, Préfète

L'Érable
#300, 1783, av St-Édouard
Plessisville, QC G6L 3S7
819-362-2333
Fax: 819-362-9150
info@mrc-erable.qc.ca
www.mrc-erable.qc.ca
Municipal Type: Regional County Municipality
Incorporated: 1 janvier 1982
Population in 2009: 23,209
Note: 11 municipalités.
Rick Lavergne, Directeur général
Donald Langlois, Préfet

L'Islet
364, rue Verreault
Saint-Jean-Port-Joli, QC G0R 3G0
418-598-3076
Fax: 418-598-6880
administration@mrclislet.com
www.mrclislet.com
Municipal Type: Regional County Municipality
Incorporated: 1er janvier 1982 *Area:* 2 091,92 km2
Population in 2009: 19,010
Note: 14 municipalités.
Michel Pelletier, Directeur général
Réal Laverdière, Préfet

La Côte-de-Beaupré
3, rue de la Seigneurie
Château-Richer, QC G0A 1N0
418-824-3444
Fax: 418-824-3917
info@mrccotedebeaupre.qc.ca
Municipal Type: Regional County Municipality
Incorporated: 1 janvier 1982
Population in 2009: 23,675
Note: 9 municipalités & 2 autres territoires.
Chantal Hamel, Greffière
Jacques Pichette, Directeur général
Henri Cloutier, Préfet

La Côte-de-Gaspé
CP 57
187, boul Renard ouest
Rivière-au-Renard, QC G4X 5B1
418-269-7718
Fax: 418-269-5419
mrc@mrccotegaspe.net
Municipal Type: Regional County Municipality
Incorporated: 1 janvier 1982
Population in 2009: 18,060
Note: 5 municipalités & 2 autres territoires.
Pierre R. Charron, Directeur général
prcharron@mrccotegaspe.net
François Roussy, Préfet

La Haute-Côte-Nord
#101, 26, rue de la Rivière
Les Escoumins, QC G0T 1K0
418-233-2102
Fax: 418-233-3010
info@mrchcn.qc.ca
www.mrchcn.qc.ca
Municipal Type: Regional County Municipality
Incorporated: 1 janvier 1982
Population in 2009: 12,053
Note: 8 municipalités & 1 autre territoire.
Alain Tremblay, Directeur général
Jean-Marie Delaunay, Préfet

La Haute-Gaspésie
464, boul Ste-Anne ouest
Sainte-Anne-des-Monts, QC G4V 1T5
418-763-7791
Fax: 418-763-7737
mrc.haute-gaspesie@globetrotter.net
www.hautegaspesie.com
Municipal Type: Regional County Municipality
Incorporated: 18 mars 1981
Population in 2009: 12,233
Note: 8 municipalités & 2 autres territoires.
Jacques Paquin, Directeur général
Majella Émond, Préfet

La Haute-Yamaska
#100, 142, rue Dufferin
Granby, QC J2G 4X1
450-378-9975
Fax: 450-378-2465
mrc@haute-yamaska.ca
www.haute-yamaska.ca
Municipal Type: Regional County Municipality
Population in 2009: 87,405
Note: 9 municipalités.
Johanne Gaouette, Directrice générale
jgaouette@haute-yamaska.ca
Paul Sarrazin, Préfet
psarrazin@haute-yamaska.ca
Dominique Desmet, Directeur, Services techniques/Aménagement du territoire
ddesmet@haute-yamaska.ca

La Jacques-Cartier
60, rue St-Patrick
Shannon, QC G0A 4N0
418-844-2160
Fax: 418-844-2664
fbreton@mrc.lajacquescartier.qc.ca
www.mrc.lajacquescartier.qc.ca
Municipal Type: Regional County Municipality
Incorporated: 1 avril 1981
Population in 2009: 31,258
Note: 9 municipalités & 1 autre territoire.
Francine Breton, Directrice générale
Michel Giroux, Préfet

La Matapédia
#501, 123, rue Desbiens
Amqui, QC G5J 3P9
418-629-2053
Fax: 418-629-3195
administration@mrcmatapedia.qc.ca
www.lamatapedia.com/mrc
Municipal Type: Regional County Municipality
Incorporated: 1 janvier 1982
Population in 2009: 19,316
Note: 18 municipalités & 7 autres territoires.
Mario Lavoie, Directeur général
Georges Guénard, Préfet

La Mitis
300, av du Sanatorium
Mont-Joli, QC G5H 1V7
418-775-8445
Fax: 418-775-9303
mrcmitis@mitis.qc.ca
www.lamitis.ca
Municipal Type: Regional County Municipality
Incorporated: 1 janvier 1982
Population in 2009: 19,425
Note: 16 municipalités & 2 autres territoires.
Marcel Moreau, Directeur général
mmoreau@mitis.qc.ca
Jean-Clément Ouellet, Préfet
Paul Gingras, Directeur, Service d'aménagement
pgingras@mitis.qc.ca

La Nouvelle-Beauce
#B, 700, rue Notre-Dame nord
Sainte-Marie, QC G6E 2K9
418-387-3444
Fax: 418-387-7060
mrc@nouvellebeauce.com
www.nouvellebeauce.com
Municipal Type: Regional County Municipality
Incorporated: 1 janvier 1982
Population in 2009: 32,042
Note: 11 municipalités.
Mario Caron, Directeur général
mariocaron@nouvellebeauce.com
Richard Lehoux, Préfet
Gaston Lévesque, Directeur, Service de l'aménagement du territoire/Développement
gastonlevesque@nouvellebeauce.com
Carole Binet, Directrice générale adjointe
carolebinet@nouvellebeauce.com

La Rivière-du-Nord
#200, 161, rue de la Gare
Saint-Jérôme, QC J7Z 2B9
450-436-9321
Fax: 450-436-1977
info@mrcrivieredunord.qc.ca
www.mrcrivieredunord.qc.ca
Municipal Type: Regional County Municipality
Population in 2009: 105,087
Note: 5 municipalités.
Pierre Godin, Directeur général
pgodindg@mrcrivieredunord.qc.ca
Roland Charbonneau, Préfet
rcharbonneau@mrcrivieredunord.qc.ca

La Vallée-de-l'Or
42, place Hammond
Val-d'Or, QC J9P 3A9
819-825-7733
Fax: 819-825-4137
info@mrcvo.qc.ca
www.mrcvo.qc.ca
Municipal Type: Regional County Municipality
Population in 2009: 41,497
Note: 6 municipalités & 5 autres territoires.
Louis Bourget, Directeur général
Fernand Trahan, Préfet
Christian Riopel, Directeur, Service de l'environnement
Mario Sylvain, Directeur, Service de l'aménagement du territoire

La Vallée-de-la-Gatineau
CP 307
7, rue de la Polyvalente
Gracefield, QC J0X 1W0
819 463 3241
Fax: 819-463-3632
info@mrcvg.qc.ca
www.mrcvg.qc.ca
Municipal Type: Regional County Municipality
Incorporated: 1 janvieer 1983
Population in 2009: 19,264
Note: 17 municipalités & 5 autres territoires.
André Beauchemin, Directeur général
Pierre Rondeau, Préfet

La Vallée-du-Richelieu
#100, 255, boul Laurier
McMasterville, QC J3G 0B7

See blue tabs following this section for Municipal Waste Management and Water & Wastewater Treatment.

450-464-0339
Fax: 450-464-3827
mrcvr@vallee-du-richelieu.ca
www.vallee-du-richelieu.ca
Municipal Type: Regional County Municipality
Population in 2009: 109,996
Note: 13 municipalités.
Bernard Roy, Directeur général
Gilles Plante, Préfet

Lac-Saint-Jean-Est
625, rue Bergeron ouest
Alma, QC G8B 1V3
418-668-3023
Fax: 418-668-5112
sabin.larouche@mrclac.qc.ca
www.mrclacsaintjeanest.qc.ca
Municipal Type: Regional County Municipality
Population in 2009: 51,606
Note: 14 municipalités & 4 autres territoires.
Sabin Larouche, Directeur général
Léonard Côté, Préfet

Lajemmerais
609, rte Marie-Victorin
Verchères, QC J0L 2R0
450-583-3301
Fax: 450-583-3592
info@mrclajemmerais.qc.ca
www.mrclajemmerais.qc.ca
Municipal Type: Regional County Municipality
Population in 2009: 71,385
Note: 6 municipalités.
Sylvain Berthiaume, Directeur général
Suzanne Roy, Préfète

Le Domaine-du-Roy
901, boul St-Joseph
Roberval, QC G8H 2L8
418-275-5044
Fax: 418-275-4049
administration@mrcdomaineduroy.ca
www.domaineduroy.ca
Municipal Type: Regional County Municipality
Incorporated: 1 janvier 1983
Population in 2009: 30,346
Note: 9 municipalités & 1 autre territoire.
Denis Taillon, Directeur général
Bernard Généreux, Préfet

Le Fjord-du-Saguenay
3110, boul Martel
St. Honoré-de-Chicoutimi, QC G0V 1L0
418-673-1705
Fax: 418-673-7205
reception@mrc-fjord.qc.ca
www.mrc-fjord.qc.ca
Municipal Type: Regional County Municipality
Population in 2009: 20,312
Note: 13 municipalités & 3 autres territoires.
Christine Dufour, Directrice générale
christine.dufour@mrc-fjord.qc.ca
Jean-Marie Claveau, Préfet

Le Granit
5090, rue Frontenac
Lac-Mégantic, QC G6B 1H3
819-583-0181
Fax: 819-583-5327
administration@mrcgranit.qc.ca
www.mrcgranit.qc.ca
Municipal Type: Regional County Municipality
Incorporated: 26 mai 1982
Population in 2009: 22,527
Note: 20 municipalités.
Serge Bilodeau, Directeur général
Maurice Bernier, Préfet

Le Haut-Richelieu
380, 4e av
Saint-Jean-sur-Richelieu, QC J2X 1W9
450-346-3636
Fax: 450-346-8464
info@mrchr.qc.ca
www.mrchr.qc.ca

Municipal Type: Regional County Municipality
Incorporated: 1 janvier 1982
Population in 2009: 111,093
Note: 14 municipalités.
Joane Saulnier, Directrice générale
Gilles Dolbec, Préfet

Le Haut-St-François
85, rue du Parc
Cookshire, QC J0B 1M0
819-560-8400
Fax: 819-560-8479
direction.mrc@hsfqc.ca
www.mrchsf.com
Municipal Type: Regional County Municipality
Incorporated: 1 janvier 1982
Population in 2009: 22,181
Note: 14 municipalités.
Dominic Provost, Directeur général
dominic.provost@hsfqc.ca
Nicole Robert, Préfète

Le Haut-St-Laurent
#400, 10, rue King
Huntingdon, QC J0S 1H0
450-264-5411
Fax: 450-264-6885
mrchsl@mrchsl.com
www.mrchsl.com
Municipal Type: Regional County Municipality
Incorporated: 1 janvier 1982
Population in 2009: 21,829
Note: 13 municipalités.
François Landreville, Directeur général
Alain Castagner, Préfet

Le Rocher-Percé
CP 128
129, boul René-Lévesque ouest
Chandler, QC G0C 1K0
418-689-4313
Fax: 418-689-5807
mrc@rocherperce.qc.ca
www.rocherperce.qc.ca
Municipal Type: Regional County Municipality
Incorporated: 1 avril 1981
Population in 2009: 18,375
Note: 5 municipalités & 1 autre territoire.
Mario Grenier, Directeur général
Claude Cyr, Préfet

Le Val-St-François
810, montée du Parc
Richmond, QC J0B 2H0
819-826-6505
Fax: 819-826-3484
mrc@val-saint-francois.qc.ca
www.val-saint-francois.qc.ca
Municipal Type: Regional County Municipality
Incorporated: 26 mai 1982
Population in 2009: 29,335
Note: 18 municipalités.
Manon Fortin, Directrice générale
Gerald Badger, Préfet

Les Appalaches
3830, boul Frontenac ouest
Thetford Mines, QC G6H 2L8
418-423-2757
Fax: 418-423-5122
info@mrcdesappalaches.ca
www.mrcdesappalaches.ca
Municipal Type: Regional County Municipality
Population in 2009: 43,602
Note: 19 municipalités.
Alain Gravel, Directeur général
alain.gravel@mrcdesappalaches.ca
Hélène Faucher, Préfète
mun.adstock@globetrotter.net

Les Basques
#400, 2, rue Jean-Rioux
Trois-Pistoles, QC G0L 4K0
418-851-3206
Fax: 418-851-3171

mrc@mrcdesbasques.com
www.mrcdesbasques.com
Municipal Type: Regional County Municipality
Incorporated: 1 avril 1981
Population in 2009: 9,464
Note: 11 municipalités & 1 autre territoire.
François Gosselin, Directeur général
André Leblond, Préfet

Les Chenaux
630, rue Principale
Saint-Luc-de-Vincennes, QC G0X 3K0
819-840-0704
Fax: 819-295-5117
info@mrcdeschenaux.ca
www.mrcdeschenaux.ca
Municipal Type: Regional County Municipality
Incorporated: 1 janvier 2002
Population in 2009: 17,199
Note: 10 municipalités.
Pierre St-Onge, Directeur général
pierre.stonge@mrcdeschenaux.ca
Gérard Bruneau, Préfet

Les Collines-de-l'Outaouais
216, ch Old Chelsea
Chelsea, QC J9B 1J4
819-827-0516
Fax: 819-827-9272
gpoulin@mrcdescollines.com
www.mrcdescollines.com
Municipal Type: Regional County Municipality
Population in 2009: 43,358
Note: 7 municipalités.
Ghislain Poulin, Directeur général
Jean Perras, Préfet

Les Etchemins
1137, rte 277
Lac-Etchemin, QC G0R 1S0
418-625-9000
Fax: 418-625-9005
mrcetchemins@sogetel.net
www.mrcetchemins.qc.ca
Municipal Type: Regional County Municipality
Incorporated: 1 janvier 1982
Population in 2009: 17,613
Note: 13 muncipalités.
Fernand Heppell, Directeur général
Hector Provençal, Préfet

Les Jardins-de-Napierville
1767, rue Principale
Saint-Michel, QC J0L 2J0
450-454-0559
Fax: 450-454-0560
info@mrcjardinsdenapierville.ca
Municipal Type: Regional County Municipality
Population in 2009: 24,745
Provincial Electoral District(s): Huntington
Federal Electoral District(s): Beauharnois-Salaberry
Note: 11 municipalités.
Nicole Inkel, Directrice générale
Michel Lavoie, Préfet

Les Laurentides
1255, ch des Lacs
Saint-Faustin-Lac-Carré, QC J0T 1J2
819-425-5555
Fax: 819-688-6590
adm@mrclaurentides.qc.ca
www.mrclaurentides.qc.ca
Municipal Type: Regional County Municipality
Population in 2009: 43,467
Note: 20 municipalités.
Michel Bélanger, Directeur général
Ronald Provost, Préfet

Les Maskoutains
805, av du Palais
Saint-Hyacinthe, QC J2S 5C6
450-774-3141
Fax: 450-774-7161
admin@mrcmaskoutains.qc.ca
www.mrcmaskoutains.qc.ca

See blue tabs following this section for Municipal Waste Management and Water & Wastewater Treatment.

Municipal Type: Regional County Municipality
Population in 2009: 81,937
Note: 17 municipalités.
Francine Morin, Préfète
Gabriel Michaud, Directeur général

Les Moulins
148, rue St-André
Terrebonne, QC J6W 3C3
450-471-9576
Fax: 450-471-8193
info@mrclesmoulins.ca
www.mrclesmoulins.ca
Municipal Type: Regional County Municipality
Population in 2009: 134,214
Note: 2 municipalités.
Daniel Pilon, Directeur général
Jean-Marc Robitaille, Préfet

Les Pays-d'en-Haut
1014, rue Valiquette
Sainte-Adèle, QC J8B 2M3
450-229-6637
Fax: 450-229-5203
info@mrcpdh.org
www.mrcpdh.com
Municipal Type: Regional County Municipality
Incorporated: 1 janvier 1983
Population in 2009: 37,456
Note: 10 municipalités.
Yvan Genest, Directeur général
Charles Garnier, Préfet

Les Sources
309, rue Chassé
Asbestos, QC J1T 2B4
819-879-6661
Fax: 819-879-5188
mrcdessources@mrcdessources.com
www.mrcdessources.com
Municipal Type: Regional County Municipality
Population in 2009: 14,569
Note: 7 municipalités.
Yvan Provencher, Directeur général
Jacques Hémond, Préfet

Lotbinière
6375, rue Garneau
Sainte-Croix, QC G0S 2H0
418-926-3407
Fax: 418-926-3409
info@mrclotbiniere.org
www.mrclotbiniere.org
Municipal Type: Regional County Municipality
Incorporated: 1 janvier 1982
Population in 2009: 27,819
Note: 18 municipalités.
Daniel Patry, Directeur général
daniel.patry@mrclotbiniere.org
Maurice Sénécal, Préfet
Isabelle Fradette, Greffière
isabelle.fradette@mrclotbiniere.org

Manicouagan
768, rue Bossé
Baie-Comeau, QC G5C 1L6
418-589-9594
Fax: 418-589-6383
info@mrcmanicouagan.qc.ca
www.mrcmanicouagan.qc.ca
Municipal Type: Regional County Municipality
Incorporated: 1 avril 1981
Population in 2009: 33,689
Note: 8 municipalités & 1 autre territoire.
Patricia Huet, Directrice générale
patricia.huet@mrcmanicouagan.qc.ca
Ivo Di Piazza, Préfet

Maria-Chapdelaine
173, boul St-Michel
Dolbeau-Mistassini, QC G8L 4N9
418-276-2131
Fax: 418-276-7043
portail@mrcmaria.qc.ca
www.mrcdemaria-chapdelaine.ca

Municipal Type: Regional County Municipality
Population in 2009: 25,737
Note: 12 municipalités & 2 autres territoires.
Christian Bouchard, Directeur général
Gilbert Goulet, Préfet

Maskinongé
651, boul St-Laurent est
Louiseville, QC J5V 1J1
819-228-9461
Fax: 819-228-2193
mrcinfo@mrc-maskinonge.qc.ca
www.mrc-maskinonge.qc.ca
Municipal Type: Regional County Municipality
Incorporated: 1 janvier 1982
Population in 2009: 36,048
Note: 17 municipalités.
Janyse L. Pichette, Directrice générale
Robert Lalonde, Préfet

Matane
145, rue Soucy
Matane, QC G4W 2E1
418-562-6734
Fax: 418-562-7265
mrcmatane@mrcdematane.qc.ca
Municipal Type: Regional County Municipality
Incorporated: 1 janvier 1982
Population in 2009: 22,378
Note: 11 municipalités & 1 autre territoire.
Line Ross, Directrice générale
Donald Grenier, Préfet

Matawinie
3184, 1re Av
Rawdon, QC J0K 1S0
450-834-5441
Fax: 450-834-6560
administration@mrcmatawinie.qc.ca
www.matawinie.org
Municipal Type: Regional County Municipality
Population in 2009: 48,309
Note: 15 municipalités & 12 autres territoires.
Lyne Arbour, Directrice générale
lynearbour@matawinie.org
Gaétan Morin, Préfet
Hélène Fortin, Greffière
hfortin@matawinie.org
Gilles Locat, Directeur, Service d'aménagement
gilleslocat@matawinie.org

Mékinac
560, rue Notre-Dame
Saint-Tite, QC G0X 3H0
418-365-5151
Fax: 418-365-7377
mrcmekinac@mrcmekinac.com
www.regionmekinac.com
Municipal Type: Regional County Municipality
Incorporated: 1 janvier 1982
Population in 2009: 12,666
Note: 10 municipalités & 4 autres territoires.
Claude Beaulieu, Directeur général
Lucien Mongrain, Préfet

Memphrémagog
#200, 455, rue MacDonald
Magog, QC J1X 1M2
819-843-9292
Fax: 819-843-7295
info@mrcmemphremagog.com
www.mrcmemphremagog.com
Municipal Type: Regional County Municipality
Population in 2009: 46,041
Note: 17 municipalités.
Guy Jauron, Directeur général
Roger Nicolet, Préfet

Minganie
1303, rue de la Digue
Hâvre-Saint-Pierre, QC G0G 1P0
418-538-2732
Fax: 418-538-3711
info@mrc.minganie.org
www.mrc.minganie.org

Municipal Type: Regional County Municipality
Incorporated: 1 janvier 1982
Population in 2009: 5,167
Note: 8 municipalités & 2 autres territoires.
Nathalie de Grandpré, Directice générale
Pierre Cormier, Prèfet

Montcalm
1540, rue Albert
Sainte-Julienne, QC J0K 2T0
450-831-2182
Fax: 450-831-2647
info@mrcmontcalm.com
www.mrcmontcalm.com
Municipal Type: Regional County Municipality
Population in 2009: 44,201
Note: 11 municipalités.
Gaétan Hudon, Directeur général
Yves Prud'homme, Préfet

Montmagny
159, rue Saint-Louis
Montmagny, QC G5V 1N5
418-248-5985
Fax: 418-248-4624
mrc@montmagny.com
www.montmagny.com
Municipal Type: Regional County Municipality
Incorporated: 1 janvier 1982
Population in 2009: 23,155
Note: 14 municipalités.
Nancy Labrecque, Directrice générale
Marcel Catellier, Préfet

Nicolet-Yamaska
#257, 1, rue de Mgr-Courchesne
Nicolet, QC J3T 2C1
819-293-2997
Fax: 819-293-5367
mrcny@mrcnicolet-yamaska.qc.ca
www.mrcnicolet-yamaska.qc.ca
Municipal Type: Regional County Municipality
Incorporated: 1 janvier 1982
Population in 2009: 22,557
Note: 16 municipalités.
Donald Martel, Directeur général
Raymond Bilodeau, Préfet
Hélène Deveault, Greffière

Papineau
266, rue Viger
Papineauville, QC J0V 1R0
819-427-6243
Fax: 819-427-8318
info@mrcpapineau.com
www.mrcpapineau.com
Municipal Type: Regional County Municipality
Incorporated: 1 janvier 1983
Population in 2009: 21,895
Note: 24 municipalités.
Ghislain Ménard, Directeur général
menard@mrcpapineau.com
Paulette Lalande, Préfète
Roxanne Lauzon, Greffière
lauzon@mrcpapineau.com
Jean Perreault, Coordonnateur, Service de la planification/Aménagement du territoire
perreault@mrcpapineau.com

Pierre-De Saurel
50, rue du Fort
Sorel-Tracy, QC J3P 7X7
450-743-2703
Fax: 450-743-7313
mrc@pierredesaurel.com
www.mrcpierredesaurel.com
Municipal Type: Regional County Municipality
Incorporated: 1 janvier 1982
Population in 2009: 50,286
Note: 12 municipalités.
Denis Boisvert, Directeur général
Raymond Arel, Préfet

See blue tabs following this section for Municipal Waste Management and Water & Wastewater Treatment.

Municipal Governments / Québec

Pontiac
CP 460
602, rte 301
Campbell's Bay, QC J0X 1K0
819-648-5689
Fax: 819-648-5810
mrc@mrcpontiac.qc.ca
www.mrcpontiac.qc.ca
Municipal Type: Regional County Municipality
Incorporated: 1 janvier 1983 Area: 13 848,26 km2
Population in 2009: 14,608
Note: 18 municipalités & 1 autre territoire.
Rémi Bertrand, Directeur général
Michael McCrank, Préfet

Portneuf
185, rte 138
Cap-Santé, QC G0A 1L0
418-285-3744
Fax: 418-285-1703
portneuf@mrc-portneuf.qc.ca
www.portneuf.com
Municipal Type: Regional County Municipality
Population in 2009: 47,206
Note: 18 municipalités & 3 autres territoires.
Daniel Le Pape, Directeur général
Jacques Landry, Directeur, Aménagement du territoire/Urbanisme
jlandry@mrc-portneuf.qc.ca
Denis Langlois, Préfet

Régie d'aqueduc de Grand Pré
3000, Rang des chutes
Saint-Édouard-de-Maskinongé, QC J0K 2H0
819-228-0181
Fax: 819-228-0807
Municipal Type: Water Commission
Eve Masson, Sec.-Trés.
André Lahaye, Directeur, Opérations

Régie d'aqueduc intermunicipale des Moulins
775, rue St-Jean-Baptiste
Terrebonne, QC J6W 1B5
450-471-4192
Fax: 450-471-2594
Municipal Type: Water Commission
Claude Therrien, Operator

Régie d'aqueduc intermunicipale paroisse St-Pie et Notre-Dame-de-St-Hyacinthe
4740, rue Gouyn
Saint-Hyacinthe, QC J2S 1E1
450-773-3720
Fax: 450-773-5611
Municipal Type: Water Commission
Jean-Luc Giard, Sec.-Trés.

Régie d'aqueduc Richelieu-Centre
765A, rue St-Joseph
Saint-Louis, QC J0G 1K0
450-788-2544
Fax: 450-788-4003
rarc@mtic.qc.ca
Municipal Type: Water Commission
Ronald Jacques, Coordonateur

Régie d'assainissement des Coteaux
65, rte 338
Les Côteaux, QC J7X 1A2
450-763-0980
Fax: 450-763-1410
filt.coteau@qc.aira.com
Municipal Type: Water Commission
Jacques Legault, Agent de liaison

Régie d'assainissement des eaux de Chandler, Pabos et Pabos Mills
CP 459
35, rue Commerciale ouest
Chandler, QC G0C 1K0
418-689-2221
Fax: 418-689-4963
Municipal Type: Water Commission
Léandre Savoie, Sec.-Trés.

Régie d'assainissement des eaux de la région sherbrookoise
CP 610
555, rue des Grandes-Fourches sud, bloc
Sherbrooke, QC J1H 5H9
819-823-5562
Fax: 819-823-8207
info@raers.qc.ca
Municipal Type: Water Commission
André-P. Robert, Ing., dsa., Directeur-général, Assainissement des eaux uséee

Régie d'assainissement des eaux de la Vallée du Richelieu
300, ch Brunet
Mont-Saint-Hilaire, QC J3G 4S6
450-464-0041
Municipal Type: Water Commission
Jean Tremblay, Sec.-Trés.
Ghislain Bégin, Administrateur

Régie d'assainissement des eaux du bassin de la Prairie
5000, boul Marie-Victorin
Sainte-Catherine, QC J5C 1L9
450-638-2163
Fax: 450-638-6567
Municipal Type: Water Commission
Gilbert Samson, Sec.-Trés.

Régie d'assainissement des eaux du Haut-Richelieu
CP 1025
188, rue Jacques-Cartier nord
Saint-Jean-sur-Richelieu, QC J3B 7B2
450-348-2667
Fax: 450-357-2285
Municipal Type: Water Commission
Jacques Jutras, Secrétaire

Régie d'assainissement des eaux Richelieu/Saint-Laurent
390, boul Poliquin
Sorel, QC J3P 5N3
Fax: 450-743-4132
Municipal Type: Water Commission
Louis Cardin, Sec.-Trés.

Régie d'assainissement des eaux usées de Boischatel, L'Ange-Gardien, Château-Richer
9, côte de l'Eglise
Boischatel, QC G0A 1H0
418-822-4500
Fax: 418-822-4512
Municipal Type: Water Commission
Jacques Villeneuve, Sec.-Trés.
Ghislain Bergeron, Chef technicien

Régie d'assainissement des eaux usées de la Basse-Lièvre
CP 670
57, ch de Montréal est
Masson-Angers, QC J8M 1K7
Fax: 819-986-9539
Municipal Type: Water Commission
Pierre Hayes, Sec.-Trés.

Régie d'assainissement des eaux usées de Piedmont, St-Sauveur et St-Sauveur-des-Monts
2125, ch Jean Adam
Saint-Sauveur, QC J0R 1R2
450-227-2668
Fax: 450-227-8564
Municipal Type: Water Commission
Patrice Normand, Sec.-Trés.

Régie d'assainissement des eaux usées Rougemont/St-Césaire
#4, 1111, av St-Paul
Saint-Césaire, QC J0L 1T0
450-469-0651
Fax: 450-469-5275
regie1996@bellnet.ca
Municipal Type: Water Commission
Susie Dubois, Sec.-Trés.

Régie d'assainissement des eaux usées Terrebonne/Mascouche
199, ch de la Cabane Ronde
Mascouche, QC J7K 1P1
450-474-4133
Municipal Type: Water Commission
Luc Tremblay, Sec.-Trés.

Régie de l'eau de l'Ile Perrot
1244, boul Perrot
Notre-Dame-de-l'Ile-Perrot, QC J7V 7P2
514-425-2244
Fax: 514-425-2252
Municipal Type: Water Commission
Jacob Céline, Sec.-Trés.

Régie Intermunicipale Argenteuil-Deux-Montagnes
Complex Environnemental
651, ch Félix-Touchette
Lachute, QC J8H 2C5
450-562-0778
Fax: 450-562-8482
info@riadm.ca
Municipal Type: Waste Commission
Daniel Mayer, Président

Régie intermunicipale d'alimentation en eau potable du Bas-St-François
CP 429
39, rue Aly
Pierreville, QC J0G 1M0
450-568-7160
Fax: 450-568-7160
Municipal Type: Water Commission
Diane Précourt, Sec.-Trés.

Régie intermunicipale d'approvisionnement en eau potable de l'île centrale
CP 1170
1589, ch L'Étand-du-Nord
L'Étand-du-Nord, QC G0B 1E0

Municipal Type: Water Commission
Elphège LeBlanc, Sec.-Trés., Responsable de l'alimentation en eau potable

Régie intermunicipale d'approvisionnement en eau potable Henryville/Venise
559, rue Dussault
Saint-Sébastien, QC J0J 2C0
450-244-5813
Fax: 450-244-5813
Municipal Type: Water Commission
Suzanne Ouellet, Sec.-Trés.

Régie intermunicipale d'aqueduc de la vallée de Châteauguay
527, rang St-Joseph
Saint-Paul-de-Chateauguay, QC J0S 1V0
450-427-3703
Fax: 450-427-2548
Municipal Type: Water Commission
Léopold Vanier, Secrétaire

Régie intermunicipale d'aqueduc du Bas-Richelieu
737, ch des Patriotes
Saint-Denis-sur-Richelieu, QC J0H 1K0
450-787-2101
Fax: 450-787-3857
Municipal Type: Water Commission
Pierre Bélanger, Directeur-général

Régie intermunicipale d'aqueduc et d'égout de Lotbinière-Centre
121, rue St-André
Laurier-Station, QC G0S 1N0
418-728-3852
Fax: 418-728-4801
Municipal Type: Water Commission
Jean-Paul Lemay, Usine d'épuration des eaux
418-728-3976

See blue tabs following this section for Municipal Waste Management and Water & Wastewater Treatment.

Municipal Governments / Québec

Régie intermunicipale d'aqueduc Richelieu-Yamaska
517, ch Ste-Victoire
Sainte-Victoire-de-Sorel, QC J0G 1T0
450-782-3111
Fax: 450-782-2687
Municipal Type: Water Commission
Michel St-Martin, Sec.-Trés.

Régie intermunicipale d'assainissement de Daveluyville
CP 187
337, rue Principale
Daveluyville, QC G0Z 1C0
819-367-3395
Fax: 819-367-3395
Municipal Type: Water Commission
Gaston Bélanger, Sec.-Trés.

Régie intermunicipale d'assainissement de la Haute-Bécancour
144, rue Notre-Dame sud
Thetford Mines, QC G6G 5T3
418-423-2773
Fax: 418-335-7089
Municipal Type: Water Commission
Denise Veilleux, Secrétaire

Régie intermunicipale d'assainissement des eaux usées des Desjardins
225, côte du Passage
Lévis, QC G6V 5T4
418-838-4000
Municipal Type: Water Commission
Denis Fradette, Sec.-Trés.

Régie intermunicipale d'assainissement des eaux de Sainte-Thérèse et Blainville
500, rue Omer-deSerres
Blainville, QC J7C 5N6
450-435-9090
Fax: 450-435-8839
assainissement.stb@videotron.net
Municipal Type: Water Commission
Diane Dubé, Sec.-Trés.

Régie intermunicipale d'assainissement des eaux du Trois-Rivières Métropolitain
CP 368
1325, place de l'Hôtel-de-Ville
Trois-Rivières, QC G9A 5H3
819-374-3521
Fax: 819-372-4631
Municipal Type: Water Commission
Claude Doucet, Sec.-Trés.

Régie intermunicipale d'assainissement des eaux de Rosemère et de Lorraine
100, rue Charbonneau
Rosemère, QC J7A 3W1
450-621-3500
Fax: 450-621-7601
Municipal Type: Water Commission
Chantal Gauvreau, Sec.-Trés.

Régie intermunicipale d'assainissement du canton de Metgermette
CP 249
735, 15e rue
Saint-Zacharie, QC G0M 2C0
418-593-3185
Fax: 418-593-3085
Municipal Type: Water Commission
Sophie Fortin, Sec.-Trés.

Régie intermunicipale d'élimination de déchets solides de Brome-Missisquoi
2500 Rang St-Joseph
Cowansville, QC J2K 3G6
450-263-2351
Fax: 450-263-4977
info@riedsbm.ca
www.riedsbm.ca
Municipal Type: Waste Commission
Gaetan Martel, Directeur operations

Caroline Lasnier, Comptable
Brigitte Nadeau, ing., MBA, Directrice generale

Régie intermunicipale d'enfouissement sanitaire de Manicouagan
768, rue Bossé
Baie-Comeau, QC G5C 1L6
418-589-0762
Fax: 418-589-6450
Municipal Type: Waste Commission

Régie intermunicipale d'enfouissement sanitaire de Charlevoix-Est
119, ch Snigoll
Clermont, QC G4A 1B1
418-439-3051
Fax: 418-439-3051
Municipal Type: Waste Commission

Régie intermunicipale de gestion des déchets solides de Saint-Vianney et Saint-Tharcisius
CP 39
170, av Centrale
Saint-Vianney, QC G0J 3J0
418-629-4082
Fax: 418-629-4821
Municipal Type: Waste Commission
Adrien Beaupré, Sec.-Trés.

Régie intermunicipale de gestion des déchets solides des Etchemins
CP 10
167, route 204
Sainte-Justine, QC G0R 1Y0
418-383-5397
Fax: 418-383-5398
sjustine@sogetel.net
www.stejustine.net/
Municipal Type: Waste Commission
Marcel Morissette, Maire

Régie intermunicipale de gestion des déchets solides de la région de Coaticook
98, rue Norton
Coaticook, QC J1A 2S8
819-849-6668
Fax: 819-849-6668
Municipal Type: Waste Commission
Yves Morissette, Sec.-Trés.

Régie intermunicipale de gestion des déchets de la région Maskoutaine
#201, 2200, av Pratte
Saint-Hyacinthe, QC J2S 4B6
450-774-2350
Fax: 450-774-9737
rigdrm@ntic.qc.ca
www.regiedesdechets.qc.ca
Municipal Type: Waste Commission
Lynda Charest, Directrice générale

Régie intermunicipale de gestion des déchets de la Mauricie
1, boul de la Gabelle
Saint-Étienne-des-Grès, QC G0X 2P0
819-373-3130
Fax: 819-694-1004
Municipal Type: Waste Commission

Régie intermunicipale de gestion des déchets des Chutes-de-la-Chaudière
114, rue du Pont
Saint-Lambert-de-Lauzon, QC G0S 2W0
418-889-8662
Fax: 418-889-5157
rigdcc@chutes.chaudiere.com
www.chaudiere.com/regie-dechets
Municipal Type: Waste Commission
Lois Fleury, Sec.-Treas.

Régie intermunicipale de gestion des déchets de la Rive-Sud de Québec
259, ch des Iles
Saint-David, QC G6V 7M5

418-837-3361
Fax: 418-837-1103
Municipal Type: Waste Commission
Alexandre Faber, Sec.-Trés.

Régie intermunicipale de gestion des déchets de l'Islet-Sud
366, rue Principale
Sainte-Perpétue-de-l'Islet, QC G0R 3Z0
418-359-2966
Fax: 418-359-2707
Municipal Type: Waste Commission
Marie-Claude Chouinard, Sec.-Trés.

Régie intermunicipale de gestion des déchets solides de l'Anse-à-Gilles
284, boul Nilus-Leclerc, Local 2
L'Islet, QC G0R 2C0
418-247-3884
Fax: 418-247-3885
Municipal Type: Waste Commission
Martine Fortin, Secrétaire

Régie intermunicipale de gestion des déchets solides de New Richmond, Caplan et Maria
CP 338
99, place Suzanne-Guité
New Richmond, QC G0C 2B0
418-392-5602
Fax: 418-392-5331
Municipal Type: Waste Commission
Benoît Roussy, Sec.-Trés.

Régie intermunicipale de gestion des déchets solides des Anses
CP 939
108, rue de l'Hôtel-de-Ville
Grande-Rivière, QC G0C 1V0
418-385-2282
Fax: 418-385-2290
Municipal Type: Waste Commission
Denis Beaudin, Sec.-Trés.

Régie intermunicipale de gestion des déchets du Bas St-François
38, rue Notre-Dame
Saint-François-du-Lac, QC J0G 1M0
450-568-7013
Fax: 450-568-7015
Municipal Type: Waste Commission
Sylvie Gelly, Directrice générake

Régie intermunicipale de gestion intégrée des déchets Bécancour-Nicolet-Yamaska
8405, rue Desormeaux
Bécancour, QC G9H 2X3
819-294-2999
Fax: 819-294-2966
Municipal Type: Waste Commission
Manon Poliquin, Sec.-Trés.

Régie intermunicipale de l'aqueduc de Saint-Antoine
105, av Saint-Laurent
Louiseville, QC J5V 2L6

Municipal Type: Water Commission

Régie intermunicipale de l'eau de Deux-Montagnes
101, 26e av
Deux-Montagnes, QC J7R 5T3
450-473-4502
Municipal Type: Water Commission
Denis Berthellette, Directeur d'Exploitation

Régie intermunicipale de l'eau de la Vallée du Richelieu
1348, ch des Patriotes
Otterburn Park, QC J3H 2B3
450-464-0348
Fax: 450-464-3827
Municipal Type: Water Commission
Claude Giroux, Sec.-Trés.

See blue tabs following this section for Municipal Waste Management and Water & Wastewater Treatment.

Municipal Governments / Saskatchewan

Régie intermunicipale de l'eau potable Varennes, Ste-Julie, St-Amable
1870, boul Marie-Victorin
Varennes, QC J3X 1R3
450-652-2052
Fax: 450-652-3808
Municipal Type: Water Commission
Normand Massicotte, Sec.-Trés.

Régie intermunicipale de l'Est de Portneuf
212, rue Dupont est
Pont-Rouge, QC G3H 1A1
418-873-4481
Fax: 418-873-3494
Municipal Type: Waste Commission
Paul-Eugène Parent, Président

Régie intermunicipale de récuperation des Hautes-Laurentides
402, route 117 sud
Marchand, QC J0T 1T0
819-275-3516
Fax: 819-275-3925
Municipal Type: Waste Commission

Régie intermunicipale de traitement de l'eau potable Saint-Romuald/Saint-Jean
CP 43100
2175, ch du Fleuve
Saint-Romuald, QC G6W 7W9
418-839-4141
Fax: 418-839-5548
Municipal Type: Water Commission
Marcel Deslandes, Directeur
Denis Gosselin, Directeur, Travaux publics
Pierre Boulay, Directeur, Urbanisme

Régie intermunicipale de traitement des déchets de Matawinie
3184, 1e av
Rawdon, QC J0K 1S0
450-834-5441
Fax: 450-834-6560
Municipal Type: Waste Commission

Régie intermunicipale des déchets de CJLLR
CP 10
Sainte-Justine, QC G0R 1Y0
418-383-5397
Fax: 418-383-5398
Municipal Type: Waste Commission
Gilles Vézina, Sec.-Trés.

Régie intermunicipale des déchets de la Rouge
400 Route 117 Sud
Marchand, QC J0T 1T0
819-275-3205
Fax: 819-275-2139
ridrouge@lannon.qc.ca
Municipal Type: Waste Commission
Johanne Bock, Directrice-générale

Régie intermunicipale des déchets solides de la Lièvre
CP 160
1064, boul Industriel
Mont-Laurier, QC J9L 3G9
819-623-7382
Municipal Type: Waste Commission
Jimmy Brisebois, Directeur-général

Régie intermunicipale du comté de Beauce-Sud
695 rang St-Joseph
Saint-Côme Linière, QC G0M 1J0
418-685-2230
Fax: 418-685-3952
Municipal Type: Waste Commission
Roger Turcotte, Sec.-Trés.

Rimouski-Neigette
220, av de la Cathédrale
Rimouski, QC G5L 5J2
418-724-5154
Fax: 418-725-4567
administration@mrcrimouskineigette.qc.ca
Municipal Type: Regional County Municipality
Population in 2009: 53,878
Note: 10 municipalités & 1 autre territoire.
Louise Audet, Directrice générale
Gilbert Pigeon, Préfet

Rivière-du-Loup
310, rue St-Pierre
Rivière-du-Loup, QC G5R 3V3
418-867-2485
Fax: 418-867-3100
administration@mrc-riviere-du-loup.qc.ca
www.rivieredulou.ca
Municipal Type: Regional County Municipality
Incorporated: 1 janvier 1982 Area: 1 267,45 km2
Population in 2009: 33,947
Note: 13 municipalités.
Raymond Duval, Directeur général
Michel Lagacé, Préfet

Robert-Cliche
111A, 107e Rue
Beauceville, QC G5X 2P9
418-774-9828
Fax: 418-774-4057
www.beaucerc.com
Municipal Type: Regional County Municipality
Incorporated: 1 janvier 1982 Area: 829,03 km2
Population in 2009: 19,001
Note: 10 municipalités.
Gilbert Caron, Directeur général
gilbert.caron@beaucerc.com
André Labbé, Préfet

Roussillon
#200, 260, rue Saint-Pierre
Saint-Constant, QC J5A 2A5
450-638-1221
Fax: 450-638-4499
admin@mrcroussillon.qc.ca
www.mrcroussillon.qc.ca
Municipal Type: Regional County Municipality
Population in 2009: 153,382
Note: 11 municipalités.
Pierre Largy, Directeur général
p.largy@mrcroussillon.qc.ca
Jocelyne Bates, Préfète

Rouville
#100, 500 rue Desjardins
Marieville, QC J3M 1E1
450-460-2127
Fax: 450-460-7169
mrcrouville@on.aira.com
www.mrcrouville.qc.ca
Municipal Type: Regional County Municipality
Incorporated: 1 janvier 1982 Area: 484,99 km2
Population in 2009: 31,926
Note: 8 municipalités.
Francis Provencher, Coordonnateur, Aménagement
francis@mrcrouville.qc.ca
Rosaire Marcil, Directeur général
r.marcil@mrcrouville.qc.ca
Michel Picotte, Préfet

Saint-Charles-Borromée
525, rue de la Visitation
Saint-Charles-Borromée, QC J6E 4P2
450-759-4415
Fax: 450-759-3393
info@st-charles-borromee.org
www.st-charles-borromee.org
Municipal Type: Municipality
Incorporated: 1er juillet 1855 Area: 18,60 km2
County or District: Joliette; Population in 2009: 12,345
Provincial Electoral District(s): Joliette
Federal Electoral District(s): Joliette
Next Election: 1er novembre 2013
François Thériault, Directeur général
André Hénault, Maire
Denis Girard, Coordonnateur, Génie/Urbanisme
Jacques Fortin, Directeur, Services d'incendie/Protection civile

Sept-Rivières
#400, 106, rue Napoléon
Sept-×les, QC G4R 3L7
418-962-1900
Fax: 418-962-3365
mrcsept@globetrotter.net
Municipal Type: Regional County Municipality
Incorporated: 18 mars 1981 Area: 32 153,95 km2
Population in 2009: 32,823
Note: 2 municipalités & 2 autres territoires.
Alain Lapierre, Directeur général
Ghislain Lévesque, Préfet

Témiscamingue
#209, 21, rue Notre-Dame-de-Lourdes
Ville-Marie, QC J9V 1X8
819-629-2829
Fax: 819-629-3472
mrc@mrctemiscamingue.qc.ca
www.temiscamingue.net
Municipal Type: Regional County Municipality
Incorporated: 15 avril 1981 Area: 19 243,88 km2
Population in 2009: 16,218
Note: 20 municipalités & 2 autres territoires.
Denis Clermont, Directeur général
Jean-Pierre Charron, Préfet

Témiscouata
5, rue de l'Hôtel de Ville, 2e étage
Notre-Dame-du-Lac, QC G0L 1X0
418-899-6725
Fax: 418-899-2000
admin@mrctemis.ca
www.mrctemiscouata.qc.ca
Municipal Type: Regional County Municipality
Incorporated: 1 janvier 1982 Area: 3 920,90 km2
Population in 2009: 21,791
Note: 20 municipalités.
Jean-Pierre Laplante, Directeur général
Serge Fortin, Préfet

Thérèse-de-Blainville
479, boul Adolphe-Chapleau
Bois-des-Filion, QC J6Z 1J9
450-621-5546
Fax: 450-621-2628
reception@mrc-tdb.org
www.mrctheresedeblainville.qc.ca
Municipal Type: Regional County Municipality
Population in 2009: 147,403
Note: 7 municipalités.
Perrine Lapierre, Directrice générale
Paul Larocque, Préfet

Vaudreuil-Soulanges
420, av Saint-Charles
Vaudreuil-Dorion, QC J7V 2N1
450-455-5753
Fax: 450-455-0145
info@mrcvs.ca
www.mrcvs.ca
Municipal Type: Regional County Municipality
Population in 2009: 125,404
Note: 23 municipalités.
Guy-Lin Beaudoin, Directeur général
Gilles Farand, Préfet

Saskatchewan

Saskatchewan Environment's mandate is to manage, enhance and protect Saskatchewan's natural and environmental resources for conservation, recreation, social, and economic purposes and to ensure they are sustained for future generations.

The department regulates municipal or communal drinking water systems. Communities own and operate their own water treatment facilities. SaskWater is working with communities to provide a sustainable, reliable, safe and clean supply of drinking water. The Safe Drinking Water Strategy focuses on waterworks operator certification; assisting northern municipalities through the Northern Water & Sewer Program, Northern Emergency Water & Sewer Program. Municipal waterworks rate and capital investment bylaws were put in place July 1, 2006 to ensure that waterworks revenue covers expenses and capital debt payments. The Planning & Development Act required municipalities to have land use bylaws to protect watersheds.

There are over 600 waste disposal sites in Saskatchewan. Eight regional waste authorities have been created to consolidate and

See blue tabs following this section for Municipal Waste Management and Water & Wastewater Treatment.

Municipal Governments / Saskatchewan

streamline waste management. Eighty percent of $20 million in infrastructure funding from the federal and provincial governments went for green municipal projects in the province. In the department's Performance Plan for 2004-05, key actions are planned in the areas of developing a provincial strategy for municipal solid waste, developing and implementing recycling programs for electronics and new paint.

Sewage lagoons are designed and operated to treat sewage to a quality acceptable for release into the environment. Treated effluent from domestic sewage holding tanks or septic tanks is becoming a resource (fertilizer, source of moisture) rather than a pollutant. Where access to sewage systems or lagoons is unavailable, disposal of liquid sewage by haulers is an option.

The consumer pays a deposit for the container and an Environmental Handling Charge (EHC) on the refillable & non-refillable containers. When the refillable container is returned, the consumer receives a refund. EHCs are not refundable and help to fund the province-wide transportation, processing and marketing system. There are more than 70 recycling centres in the province. Recent reycling figures show the following recovery rates for selected categories: scrap tires (59%); beverage containers (89%); pesticide containers (64%); used oil (77%); used oil filters (82%).

Under the federal government's New Deal for Cities, Saskatchewan received $147 million in federal gas tax funding from 2005 to 2010 for municipal infrastructure projects.

Major Municipalities in Saskatchewan

Estevan
1102 - 4 St.
Estevan, SK S4A 0W7
306-634-1800
Fax: 306-634-9790
citymanager@estevan.ca
www.estevan.ca
Municipal Type: City
Incorporated: Nov. 2, 1899 *Area:* 17.56 sq km
Population in 2006: 10,084
Provincial Electoral District(s): Estevan
Federal Electoral District(s): Souris-Moose Mountain
Next Election: Oct. 2012 (3 year terms)
Note: Incorporated as city on March 1, 1957.
Council
Gary St. Onge, Mayor
Administration
Lyndon Stachoski, Clerk
administration@estevan.ca
Greg Wock, Manager, Engineering Services
306-634-1823
engman@estevan.ca
Rick Perry, Fire Chief
306-634-1850
rperry@estevan.ca
Jim Puffalt, City Manager
306-634-1803
Les Naka, Manager, Public Works Services
306-634-1818
Kevin Sutter, Manager, Water/Wastewater Treatment Services
wt.manager@estevan.ca
Rob Denys, Manager, Land Development Services
306-634-1821
Dan Chestney, Foreman, Roads & Drainage
306-634-1829

Lloydminster
City Hall
4420 - 50 Ave.
Lloydminster, SK T9V 0W2
306-875-6184
Fax: 306-871-8346
tomlysyk@telusplanet.net
www.lloydminster.ca
Municipal Type: City
Incorporated: Nov. 25, 1903 *Area:* 17.34 sq km
Population in 2006: 24,028
Provincial Electoral District(s): Lloydminster
Federal Electoral District(s): Battlefords-Lloydminster
Next Election: Oct. 2012 (3 year terms)
Note: Population figure represents both the Alberta & Saskatchewan populations. Incorporated as a city on Jan. 1, 1958.
Council
Ken Baker, Mayor
Administration
Tom Lysyk, City Clerk

Moose Jaw
228 Main St. North
Moose Jaw, SK S6H 3J8
306-694-4400
Fax: 306-694-4400
webmaster@moosejaw.ca
www.moosejaw.ca
Municipal Type: City
Incorporated: Jan. 19, 1884 *Area:* 46.82 sq km
Population in 2006: 32,132
Provincial Electoral District(s): Moose Jaw North; Moose Jaw Wakamow
Federal Electoral District(s): Palliser
Next Election: Oct. 2012 (3 year terms)
Note: Incorporated as a city on Nov. 20, 1903.
Council
Dale McBain, Mayor
Administration
Myron Gulka-Tiechko, Clerk

North Battleford
P.O. Box 460
North Battleford, SK S9A 2Y6
306-445-1700
Fax: 306-445-0411
jtoye@cityofnb.ca
www.cityofnb.ca
Municipal Type: City
Incorporated: March 21, 1906 *Area:* 33.55 sq km
Population in 2006: 13,190
Provincial Electoral District(s): The Battlefords
Federal Electoral District(s): Battlefords-Lloydminster
Next Election: Oct. 2012 (3 year terms)
Note: Proclaimed as a city on May 1, 1913.
Council
Julian Sadlowski, Mayor
jsadlowski@cityofnb.ca
Administration
Elaine Kostiuk, Clerk
ejkostiuk@cityofnb.ca
Tim LaFreniere, City Planner
tlafreniere@citynb.ca
Stewart Schafer, Director, Public Works & Engineering
sschafer@cityofnb.ca
Alan Parkin, Director, Parks & Recreation
306-445-1740
aparkin@cityofnb.ca
Pat MacIsaac, Chief, Fire
nbfire@citynb.ca

Prince Albert
City Hall
1084 Central Ave.
Prince Albert, SK S6V 7P3
306-953-4305
Fax: 306-953-4313
cskauge@citypa.com
www.citypa.ca
Municipal Type: City
Incorporated: Oct. 8, 1885 *Area:* 65.68 sq km
Population in 2006: 34,138
Provincial Electoral District(s): Prince Albert Carlton; Prince Albert Northcote
Federal Electoral District(s): Prince Albert
Next Election: Oct. 2012 (3 year terms)
Note: Incorporated as a city on Oct. 8, 1904.
Council
Jim Scarrow, Mayor
mayor@citypa.com
Administration
Cliff Skauge, Clerk
cskauge@citypa.com
Les Karpluk, Fire Chief
306-953-4200
lkarpluk@citypa.com
Robert Cotterill, City Manager
306-953-4300
rcotterill@citypa.com

Regina
City Hall
P.O. Box 1790
2476 Victoria Ave.
Regina, SK S4P 3C8
306-777-7000
Fax: 306-777-6809
www.regina.ca
Municipal Type: City
Incorporated: Dec. 1, 1883 *Area:* 118.87 sq km
Population in 2006: 179,246
Provincial Electoral District(s): Regina Elphinstone-Centre; Regina Coronation Park; Regina Dewdney; Regina Douglas Park; Regina Lakeview; Regina Northeast; Regina Qu'Appelle Valley; Regina Rosemont; Regina South; Regina Walsh Acres; Regina Wascana Plains
Federal Electoral District(s): Palliser; Regina-Lumsden-Lake Centre; Regina-Qu'Appelle; Wascana
Next Election: Oct. 2012 (3 year terms)
Note: Incorporated as a city on June 19, 1903.
Council
Pat Fiacco, Mayor
Louis Browne, B.A.(Hons.), LL.B., Councillor, Ward(s): 1
306-531-5151
Jocelyn Hutchinson, Councillor, Ward(s): 2
306-584-1739
Fred Clipsham, Councillor, Ward(s): 3
306-757-8212
Michael Fougere, B.A.(Hons.), M.Sc., Councillor, Ward(s): 4
306-789-5586
John Findura, Councillor, Ward(s): 5
306-536-4250
Wade Murray, Councillor, Ward(s): 6
306-596-1035
Sharron Bryce, R.N., Councillor, Ward(s): 7
306-949-5025
Mike O'Donnell, Councillor, Ward(s): 8
306-545-7300
Terry Hincks, Councillor, Ward(s): 9
306-949-9690
Chris Szarka, Councillor, Ward(s): 10
306-551-2766
Administration
Joni Swidnicki, City Clerk
306-777-7262
Glen Davies, B.A., M.A., City Manager
306-777-7314, Fax: 306-949-7210
Bonny Bryant, B.A., M.P.A., General Manager, Community & Protective Services
Dorian Wandzura, P.Eng., General Manager, Public Works Division
Brent Sjoberg, C.M.A., General Manager, Corporate Services
Rick McCullough, Director, Protective Services
Jason Carlston, B.A., M.A., General Manager, Planning & Development
Troy Hagen, Chief, Regina Police Service
306-777-6500, Fax: 306-757-5461
rps@police.regina.sk.ca
Jim Nicol, Chief of Staff, City Manager's Office

Saskatoon
City Hall
222 - 3rd Ave. North
Saskatoon, SK S7K 0J5
306-975-3200
Fax: 306-975-2784
city.clerks@saskatoon.ca
www.saskatoon.ca
Municipal Type: City
Incorporated: Nov. 16, 1901 *Area:* 170.83 sq km
Population in 2006: 202,340
Provincial Electoral District(s): Saskatoon Centre; Saskatoon Eastview; Saskatoon Fairview; Saskatoon Greystone; Saskatoon Massey Place; Saskatoon Meewasin; Saskatoon Northwest; Saskatoon Nutana; Saskatoon Riversdale; Saskatoon Silver Springs; Saskatoon Southeast; Saskatoon Sutherland
Federal Electoral District(s): Blackstrap; Saskatoon-Humboldt; Saskatoon-Rosetown-Biggar; Saskatoon-Wanuskewin
Next Election: Oct. 2012 (3 year terms)
Note: Incorporated as a city on May 26, 1906.
Council
Donald J. Atchison, Mayor
306-975-3202, Fax: 306-975-3144

See blue tabs following this section for Municipal Waste Management and Water & Wastewater Treatment.

Darren Hill, Councillor, Ward(s): 1
darren.hill@saskatoon.ca
Pat Lorje, B.A., M.A., Councillor, Ward(s): 2
pat.lorje@saskatoon.ca
Maurice (Moe) Neault, Councillor, Ward(s): 3
maurice.neault@saskatoon.ca
Myles Heidt, Councillor, Ward(s): 4
myles.heidt@saskatoon.ca
Gordon Wyant, B.A., LL.B., Councillor, Ward(s): 5
gordon.wyant@saskatoon.ca
Charlie Clark, B.Ed., M.E.S., Councillor, Ward(s): 6
charlie.clark@saskatcoon.ca
Bob Pringle, B.S.W., M.S.W., Councillor, Ward(s): 7
bob.pringle@saskatoon.ca
Glen Penner, B.Ed., M.Ed., Councillor, Ward(s): 8
glen.penner@saskatoon.ca
Tiffany Paulsen, B.A., LL.B., Councillor, Ward(s): 9
tiffany.paulsen@saskatoon.ca
Bev Dubois, Councillor, Ward(s): 10
bev.dubois@saskatoon.ca
Administration
Janice Mann, City Clerk
306-975-3240, Fax: 306-975-2784
Shelley Sutherland, Treasurer
Marlys Bilanski, General Manager, Corporate Services
306-975-3206, Fax: 306-975-7975
Gaston Gourdeau, General Manager, Infrastructure Services
Paul Gauthier, General Manager, Community Services
Murray Totland, City Manager
Lorne Sully, Manager, City Planning
Brian Bentley, General Manager, Fire & Protective Services
306-975-2575, Fax: 306-975-2689
fire.protective.services@city.saskatoon.sk.ca
Cal Sexsmith, Manager, Municipal Engineering
Wayne Briant, Manager, Parks
Gaston Gourdeau, Manager, Public Works
Pawel Kerc, Contact, Environmental Compliance
306-975-2486
Tim Sedgewick, Contact, Wastewater Treatment
Mark Keller, Contact, Water Treatment & Meters
Randy Grauer, Manager, Development Services
Clive Weighill, Police Chief
306-975-8300
police.service@city.saskatoon.sk.ca
Theresa Dust, City Solicitor
306-975-3270, Fax: 306-975-7828
Jeff Jorgenson, General Manager, Utility Services

Swift Current
P.O. Box 340
177 - 1st Ave. NE
Swift Current, SK S9H 3W1
306-778-2777
Fax: 306-773-2194
admin@swiftcurrent.ca; m.johnson@swiftcurrent.ca
www.swiftcurrent.ca
Municipal Type: City
Incorporated: Feb. 4, 1904 *Area:* 24.04 sq km
Population in 2006: 14,946
Provincial Electoral District(s): Swift Current
Federal Electoral District(s): Cypress Hills-Grasslands
Next Election: Oct. 2012 (3 year terms)
Note: Incorporated as a city on Jan. 15, 1914.
Council
Sandy Larson, Mayor
Administration
Dianne Hahn, Clerk
d.hahn@swiftcurrent.ca
Mac Forster, Director, Engineering
306-778-2740
eng@swiftcurrent.ca
Bob Rindahl, Fire Chief
306-778-2760
Andy Toth, Manager, Parks
306-778-2787
Greg Parsons, Manager, Public Works
Stuart Kyle, Superintendent, Streets & Transportation
306-778-2748
Tim Cox, Superintendent, Water & Wastewater Division
306-778-2748
Rudy Holland, Superintendent, Water Treatment
306-778-2755
Trevor Feicht, Manager, Engineering Services
Dean Robson, Director, Recreation & Parks

Yorkton
P.O. Box 400
Yorkton, SK S3N 2W3
306-786-1700
Fax: 306-786-6880
bschenher@yorkton.ca
www.yorkton.ca
Municipal Type: City
Incorporated: July 11, 1894 *Area:* 24.57 sq km
Population in 2006: 15,038
Provincial Electoral District(s): Yorkton
Federal Electoral District(s): Yorkton-Melville
Next Election: Oct. 2012 (3 year terms)
Note: Incorporated as a city on Feb. 1, 1928.
Council
Chris Whyatt, Mayor
Administration
Bonnie Schenher, City Clerk
Lonnie Kaal, Director, Finance
306-786-1721, Fax: 306-786-6880
lkaal@yorkton.ca
Roger Hunter, Director, Planning & Engineering
306-786-1730
Dean Clark, Fire Chief, Fire Protective Services
306-786-1795, Fax: 306-786-6588
dclark@yorkton.ca
Faisal Anwar, Officer, Economic Development
306-786-1747
econdev@yorkton.ca
Trent Mandzuk, Manager, Public Works
306-786-1760
tmanzuk@yorkton.ca
Michael Buchholzer, Manager, Water Works
306-786-1771, Fax: 306-782-4990
mbuchholzer@yorkton.ca
Maureen Berard, Manager, Building Services
306-786-1710, Fax: 306-786-6880
mberard@yorkton.ca
David Putz, CGA, City Manager
306-786-1703, Fax: 306-786-6880
dputz@yorkton.ca
Darcy McLeod, Director, Leisure Services
306-786-1750, Fax: 306-786-6880
dmcleod@yorkton.ca

Yukon Territory

The Yukon Environmental Protection & Assessment Branch is responsible for environment impact analysis, contaminated sites monitoring, permits for regulated activities/substances, recycling education and promotion, public education & awareness.

Municipalities are responsible for their own water quality, clean drinking water, waste management, water and wastewater treatment. There are seven water supply systems and nine sewage treatment facilities. The government has begun review and public consultation of proposed guidelines to facilitate construction and management practices for municipal wastewater treatment systems — a draft document was made available in July 2005. A Rural Drinking Water Strategy was also developed.

Most solid waste is deposited in one of the 26 waste disposal sites located near all Yukon communities. The Department of Community Services manages 19 sites, while incorporated municipalities manage the rest. Permits are required for designing, operating, maintaining and closing dumps and landfills. Burning garbage is still allowed, but not recommended, and an Air Emissions permit is required. All municipal and territorial waste disposal facilities were required to develop a 10-year Solid Waste Management Plan by 2002, describing their operation, upgrading, closure and post-closure plans.

The Yukon's Beverage Container Regulations are based on consumers paying a deposit when they purchase beverages and receiving a refund when the empty containers are returned to a registered recycling depot in the territory. Yukon beverage recycling program has been very successful at promoting high return rates on recyclable containers. Recycled containers are sold to recycling and re-use markets in southern Canada, while glass is re-used locally in road construction projects. A used tire management program has been set up.

Under the federal government's New Deal for Cities, the Yukon received $37.5 million in federal gas tax funding from 2005 to 2010 for municipal infrastructure projects.

Major Municipalities in Yukon Territory

Whitehorse
2121 Second Ave.
Whitehorse, YT Y1A 1C2
867-667-6401
Fax: 867-668-8384
council.services@whitehorse.ca
www.city.whitehorse.yk.ca
Municipal Type: City
Incorporated: June 1, 1950 *Area:* 416.43 sq km
Population in 2009: 25,690
Provincial Electoral District(s): Whitehorse Centre; Whitehorse West; Copperbelt; McIntyre-Takhini; Porter Creek Centre; Porter Creek North; Porter Creek South; Riverdale North; Riverdale South
Federal Electoral District(s): Yukon
Next Election: Oct. 2012 (3 year terms)
Council
Bev Buckway, Mayor
867-668-8626
bev.buckway@whitehorse.ca
Dave Austin, Councillor
dave.austin@whitehorse.ca
Doug Graham, Councillor
doug.graham@whitehorse.ca
Betty Irwin, Councillor
betty.irwin@whitehorse.ca
Florence Roberts, Councillor
florence.roberts@whitehorse.ca
Ranj Pillai, Councillor
ranj.pillai@whitehorse.ca
Dave Stockdale, Councillor
dave.stockdale@whitehorse.ca
Administration
Dennis Shewfelt, City Manager
867-668-8650, Fax: 867-668-8639
dennis.shewfelt@whitehorse.ca
Robert Fendrick, Director, Administrative Services
867-668-8612, Fax: 867-668-8384
robert.fendrick@whitehorse.ca
Brian Crist, Director, Operations
867-668-8301, Fax: 867-668-8386
brian.crist@whitehorse.ca
James D. MacLeod, Manager, Public Works
867-668-8351
james.mcleod@whitehorse.ca
Clive Sparks, Fire Chief
867-668-8383
clive.sparks@whitehorse.ca
George White, Manager, Maintenance & Safety Services
867-668-8345
george.white@whitehorse.ca
Mike Stevely, Manager, Information Systems
867-334-2100
mike.stevely@whitehorse.ca
Dave Muir, Manager, Transit
867-668-8391
dave.muir@whitehorse.ca
Sheila Dodd, Supervisor, Economic Development & Tourism
867-668-8660
sheila.dodd@whitehorse.ca
Sabine Schweiger, Co-Coordinator, Environmental Services
867-668-8312
environment@whitehorse.ca
John Taylor, Manager, Bylaw Services
867-668-8318
john.taylor@whitehorse.ca
Wayne Tuck, Manager, Engineering & Environmental Services
867-668-8306
wayne.tuck@whitehorse.ca
Linda Rapp, Manager, Parks & Recreation
867-668-8325, Fax: 867-668-8675
parks.recreation@whitehorse.ca
Mike Gau, Manager, Planning & Development Services
867-668-8333, Fax: 867-668-8395
planning.services@whitehorse.ca
Pippa McNeil, Co-Coordinator, Environmental Services
867-668-8312
environment@whitehorse.ca
Ray Osborne, Supervisor, Utility Stations
867-668-8669
ray.osborne@whitehorse.ca

See blue tabs following this section for Municipal Waste Management and Water & Wastewater Treatment.

Municipal Waste Management and Water & Wastewater Treatment

Alberta

Airdrie, page 670
Waste Management:
Hauled by contractor & disposed of at Calgary landfills.
Solid Waste Disposal Fees: Transfer site fee $20/ truckload (3/4 tonne)
Clean Fill Fee: No
Transfer Station(s): Yes
Recycling: ; Located at 15 East Lake Hill. Compost, grass & plant clippings accepted in the spring
Hazardous Waste Depot or Facility: Toxic Roundup May 1 to Sept 30
Composters subsidized: Yes
Other Initiatives:
Use-pay garbage collection system; Airdrie Environmental Education Centre.

Alberta Capital Region Wastewater Commission, page 757
Water & Wastewater Treatment:
Responsible only for wastewater transmission & treatment for cities of St. Albert, Leduc, Spruce Grove & Fort Saskatchewan, towns of Morinville, Stony Plain, Beaumont, Bon Accord & Gibbons, counties of Strathcona, Leduc & Parkland, & Sturgeon.

Big Country Waste Management Commission, page 757
Waste Management:
Members include Special Areas 2, 3, & 4, Towns of Hanna & Oyen, Villages of Cereal, Consort, Empress, Veteran & Youngstown; Youngstown regional landfill, 403/779-3890
Composters subsidized: No

Brooks, page 671
Water & Wastewater Treatment:
Town of Brooks Water Treatment System
Other Initiatives:
Surface irrigation system supplies untreated water, pumped through a piped network to homes & parks to reduce consumption of treated water for irrigation; WTP treated storage & high-lift design & construction.

Calgary, page 671
Waste Management:
Number of landfill sites: 3; *Landfill Capacity:* 45 years
Solid Waste Disposal Fees: $33.50/tonne
Recycling: ; 44 residential depot locations
Special Bans/by-laws: Sewer service by-law; waste by-law; unsightly premises by-law
Hazardous Waste Depot or Facility: 3 landfill sites; 5 fire stations
Compost Sites: Yes *Composters subsidized:* Yes
Water & Wastewater Treatment:
Bonnybrook Water Treatment Plant; Fish Creek Water Treatment Plant
Other Initiatives:
Fleet & Supply Management Services, golf courses & the Calgary Fire Dept. achieved ISO 14001 certification in 2001. City of Calgary Climate Change Action Plan includes emission reduction initiatives, such as streetlight & traffic signal head retrofitting. Mayor's Environmental Expo, an environmental forum & community outreach opportunity, is hosted annually by the city.

Camrose, page 671
Waste Management:
Waste collection contracted to Waste Services Inc., 780/679-0409
Number of landfill sites: 1
Solid Waste Disposal Fees: $24.00/tonne
Clean Fill Fee:
Recycling: Depot; Centra Cam Recycling Depot, 4402 - 51 Ave., Camrose.
Hazardous Waste Depot or Facility: Alberta Special Waste Management Facility, near Swan Hills
Compost Sites: Yes *Composters subsidized:* Yes
Water & Wastewater Treatment:
Camrose Water Treatment Plant; Camrose Wastewater Treatment Plant
Other Initiatives:
Composting workshop each spring; Emergency Clothing & Furniture Depot, 780/672-9282; Tire Recycling Management Association, 1-880-999-8767; Hazardous Waste Round-Up & Paint Exchange twice each year

Canmore, page 671
Waste Management:
Number of landfill sites: 1
Solid Waste Disposal Fees: Varies
Clean Fill Fee: Yes; Varies
Recycling: Depot; 2 depots located at 115 Boulder Cres. & Sobeys; Canmore Bottle Depot located at 103 Boulder Cres.
Special Bans/by-laws: Waste Control Bylaw
Water & Wastewater Treatment:
Managed by EPCOR Water Services, Phone 403/609-6400.
Other Initiatives:
Francis Cooke Regional Class III Landfill Site, operated by Bow Valley Waste Management Commission; Animal Proof Waste Handling System (no curbside waste collection); Residential toxic round-up & paint exchange events; Community Clean Up; eWaste Recycling Program at Boulder Recycling Depot; Leaf & Grass Collection Program

Capital Region Northeast Water Services Commission, page 757
Water & Wastewater Treatment:
Member areas: County of Strathcona #20, Municipal District of Sturgeon #90, Towns of Redwater, Gibbons, Fort Saskatchewan & Bon Accord

Capital Region Parkland Water Services, page 757
Water & Wastewater Treatment:
Capital Region Parkland Water Services serves the following municipalities: County of Parkland No. 31, Town of Spruce Grove & Town of Stony Plain; Water supplied from Epcor Water Services Inc.

Capital Region Vegreville Corridor Water Services Commission, page 757
Water & Wastewater Treatment:
Water is purchased & transported via pipeline from Edmonton to the counties of Lamont & Strathcona, towns of Bruderheim, Lamont, Mundare & Vegreville, & the village of Chipman.

Clearwater County, page 669
Water & Wastewater Treatment:
Nordegg water treatment plant plus sewer systems in Nordegg, Leslieville & Condor maintained by county public works department
Other Initiatives:
Green zone development

Cochrane, page 671
Waste Management:
Waste collection is contracted out & transported to a landfill site in Calgary.
Recycling: ; Town of Cochrane Recycling Plant. 413/932-2742
Water & Wastewater Treatment:
Town of Cochrane Water Treatment Plant. Six sewage lift stations in operation in town, with a pipeline to the Bonnybrook Wastewater Treatment plant in Calgary.
Other Initiatives:
Residents are restricted to 3 bags of garbage per week; Toxic-Round-Up

Cold Lake, page 672
Waste Management:
Waste Management of Canada Corp., 1-800-648-3433
Number of landfill sites: 1; *Landfill Capacity:* 2.5 years
Solid Waste Disposal Fees: $40/tonne
Recycling: Depot; North: 8th Ave./13th St.; South: west of curling rink; 4 Wing: MFRC building
Compost Sites: Yes *Composters subsidized:* No
Water & Wastewater Treatment:
Regional water plant, 780/639-3604; Water treatment, 102 - 10th St. NW; Cold Lake Regional Utilities Services Commission
Other Initiatives:
Toxic Round-Up; Undertaking a water treatment plant improvement, expansion & lagoon upgrade to conform to Alberta legislation; Toxic waste roundup June; Beginning transition to regional waste management model by 2007.

Cold Lake Regional Utility, page 757
Water & Wastewater Treatment:
Member areas: City of Cold Lake, Cold Lake Indian Reserve #149, Cold Lake Armed Forces Base, Municipal District of Bonnyville #87

Edmonton, page 672
Waste Management:
Half of waste collection contracted to Waste Services Inc., 780/464-9400 & other half to City crews, 780/496-5678. Automated collection BFI, FM & WSI. Weekly (special winter collection schedule) pickup of waste & recyclables.
Number of landfill sites: 2; *Landfill Capacity:* 5 years each, Cloverbar Landfill (city), Waste Management Landfill
Solid Waste Disposal Fees: $42/tonne for Cloverbar Landfill; $60/tonne Waste Management Landfill
Clean Fill Fee: Yes; $5/tonne, city owned landfill
Transfer Station(s): 1
Recycling: Both Curbside & Depot; 20 depot locations throughout the city
Hazardous Waste Depot or Facility: Year-round Eco stations accept household hazardous wastes & other recyclables, 2 depot locations; *Composte site(s):* Yes; *Composters subsidized:* Yes
Compost Sites: Yes *Composters subsidized:* Yes
Water & Wastewater Treatment:
Rosedale Water Treatment Plant in city centre; E.L. Smith Water Treatment Plant on western outskirts; Gold Bar Waste Water Treatment Plant in east
Other Initiatives:
Brownfield redevelopment grant pilot project, $500,000 to be used for development of 5 sites to encourage redevelopment & cleanup of contaminated sites in Edmonton. Blue Bag program serves 156,904 single family residents (84% participation rate). 20 community recycling depots for multi-dwelling residents. A new direct recycling collection for the multi-family sector (approx. 126,087 households) began March, 2002. Master Composter/Recycler Program trains 30 community volunteers per year. Approximately 20-30,000 Christmas trees collected003—the first of its kind in Canada. Edmonton Composting Facility opened in March 2000 & has a capacity of accepting 22,500 dewatered tonnes of bio-solids & 200,000 tonnes of municipal solid waste. Materials Recovery Facility opened in April, 1999 & has processing capabilities of 40,000 tonnes per year. Various public education programs & events, garbage fairs. Energy Management Program in place for over 10 years with a $5 million revolving fund in place to finance energy retrofit projects. Energy & water use tracked & reported for all city-owned facilities. Administration working closely with the Alberta Clean Air Strategic Alliance (CASA) process in developing air quality management initiatives for the Edmonton area. Water treatment pilot plant used to test innovative treatment processes. North Saskatchewan River Valley lands protected by by-law. An environmental impact assessment is required prior to development. Policy developed for protection of other environmentally sensitive & natural areas. Environmental Strategic Plan developed & approved by City Council in July, 1999. eEdmonton's first Report on Environmental Performance was published in May, 2001. Second report was published in October 2002. The third published in March 2004. The reports provide an accounting of the implementation of the City's Environmental Strateigc Plan, summarizing the City's environmental mission & vision. Greenhouse Gas Emissions Reduction Plan for City Operations developed & approved by Council in October, 1999. Community-wide Greenhouse Gas Reducation & Energy Strategy was developed with many external stake-holders. The strategy was approved by City Council in December, 2001. A 10-year strategy to develop a 62-kilometre network of multi-use trail corridors was approved by City Council in March, 2002. The trail corridor network will be a

Page numbers refer to full profile.

Municipal Waste Management and Water & Wastewater Treatment / Alberta

comprehensive system for self-propelled transportation through the City that links residential districts with the downtown, University & the river valley.

Foothills No. 31, page 669
Waste Management:
Number of landfill sites: 1
Solid Waste Disposal Fees: $39/tonne (over 200 kg); $58/tonne (hard to handle garbage)
Transfer Station(s): Priddis - 264 St. West & 178 Ave.; Black Diamond/Turner Valley - 168 St. West & 402 Ave.
Recycling: Depot; Foothills Regional Waste Management Facility, Secondary Hwy. 783, south of Okotoks
Hazardous Waste Depot or Facility: Foothills Regional Waste Management Facility, 403/938-5224
Composters subsidized: Yes
Water & Wastewater Treatment:
Aldersyde, Blackie & Cayley Waterworks Systems
Other Initiatives:
Salvage Centre for reusable items at Regional Waste Management Facility, solidwaste@platinum.ca

Foothills Regional Services, page 757
Waste Management:
Number of landfill sites: 1; *Landfill Capacity:* 80 years
Solid Waste Disposal Fees: $33/tonne
Clean Fill Fee: No
Recycling: Depot; Depots located in area's towns
Hazardous Waste Depot or Facility: Depots in each town
Composters subsidized: Yes
Water & Wastewater Treatment:
Responsible for municipal district of Foothills & towns & hamlets of Blackie, Cayley & Aldersyde.

Fort Saskatchewan, page 672
Waste Management:
Garbage disposal, 780/992-6248; Recycling/Waste Transfer station, 780/992-6152; There is a regional landfill centre; Waste collection contracted to Waste Services Inc., 780/464-9401
Recycling: Depot; Recycling/Waste Transfer Station, 8609 - 111 St.
Compost Sites: Yes *Composters subsidized:* Yes
Water & Wastewater Treatment:
Water is purified at the Capital Region Northeast Water Services Commission, 780/992-6229; Wastewater is processed at the Alberta Capital Regional Wastewater Commission, 780/467-8655
Other Initiatives:
Diversion of grass clippings & yard waste from landfill to produce compost, which is marketed to the general public; Annual Toxic Round-Up

Grande Prairie, page 672
Waste Management:
Waste management responsibility of Aquatera Utilites Inc., a regional utility corporation, 780/538-0452; Waste collection contracted by Aquatera to Waste Management, waste@aquatera.ca
Water & Wastewater Treatment:
Water & wastewater treatment responsibility of Aquatera Utilities Inc., 780/538-0348

Grande Prairie No. 1, page 669
Waste Management:
Waste collection contracted to Prairie Disposal, 780/539-5950
Number of landfill sites: 4
Solid Waste Disposal Fees: $52/tonne (county commercial & non-county)
Recycling: Depot; 6 recycle bin locations at LaGlace, Teepee Creek, Bezanson, Clairmont, Elmworth & Valhalla
Other Initiatives:
Electronics recycling program at regional landfill

Henry Kroeger Regional Water Services Commission, page 757
Water & Wastewater Treatment:
Members include towns of Hanna & Oyen, villages of Youngstown, Cereal & Delia, Starland County & Special Areas 2, 3, & 4.

Highway 43 East Waste Commission Services, page 757
Waste Management:
Members include Lac Ste. Anne County, Villages of Alberta Beach, Onoway & Sangudo, Town of Mayerthorpe, Summer Villages of Birch Cove, Castle Island, Nakamun Park, Ross Haven, Sandy Beach, Silver Sands, South View, Sunrise Beach, Sunset Point, Val Quentin, West Cove & Yellowstone.

Lacombe County, page 669
Waste Management:
Waste management responsibility of Lacombe Regional Solid Waste Authority, 403/782-6601; Daily operations of Authority responsibility of county public works department
Number of landfill sites: 1
Solid Waste Disposal Fees: $20/tonne (dry rubble)
Transfer Station(s): Bentley, Spruceville, Prentice, Eckville, Blackfalds & Alix/Mirror transfer stations
Other Initiatives:
Environmental program to assist agricultural producers; Household hazardous waste roundup; Electronics recycling accepted at Prentiss transfer station

Leduc, page 673
Waste Management:
Waste collection contracted to Canadian Waste; Leduc & District Regional Landfill, 780/986-4202
Number of landfill sites: 1
Recycling: Both Curbside & Depot; Recycling depot located at 61 Ave. & 46 St., Leduc, 780/986-9494
Hazardous Waste Depot or Facility: Materials Recovery Facility, Leduc & District Regional Landfill Site
Composters subsidized: Yes
Water & Wastewater Treatment:
Capital Region Southwest Water Services Commission provides water service to city
Other Initiatives:
Limit of 4 bags/cans of garbage each pickup; Large item collection each spring; Yard waste pickup each spring & fall; Christmas tree collection program; Annual residential toxic waste round-up held in Sept.; Composting sites at the recycling depot & Lede Park

Leduc County, page 669
Waste Management:
Number of landfill sites: 1; *Landfill Capacity:* 14+ years
Solid Waste Disposal Fees: $27/tonne (regular residential waste)
Clean Fill Fee: No
Transfer Station(s): New Sarepta; Rollyview; Looma; Thorsby; Mission Beach; Sunnybrook; Warburg; St. Francis
Recycling: Depot; Materials Recovery Facility at Leduc & District Regional Landfill
Hazardous Waste Depot or Facility: Materials Recovery Facility at Leduc & District Regional Landfill
Water & Wastewater Treatment:
Capital Region Southwest Water Services Commission provides water service to the county
Other Initiatives:
Agricultural Services Dept. provides the following services: weed control, pest control, water management, sustainable agriculture & soil conservation information

Lethbridge, page 673
Waste Management:
City responsible for waste collection, 403/320-3850; For landfill fees, recycling depot locations, hazardous waste disposal locations & composting, contact 403/329-7367
Number of landfill sites: 1; *Landfill Capacity:* 23 years
Solid Waste Disposal Fees: $37-52/tonne
Clean Fill Fee: Yes; $0-27/load
Recycling: Depot; 7 depot locations
Hazardous Waste Depot or Facility: 1430 - 33 St. North
Compost Sites: Yes
Water & Wastewater Treatment:
For information about water & wastewater treatment, contact 403/320-3850
Other Initiatives:
Sponsors "Environment Week"; Cleanup projects such as "Toxic Roundup" are very effective; "Spring Cleanup", door-to-door spring pick up of bulky waste; Christmas tree recycling; Initiated an electronics recycling program

Lethbridge Regional Waste Management Services, page 757
Waste Management:
Commission serves the following municipalities: County of Lethbridge, Town of Picture Butte & Village of Nobleford; City of Lethbridge Regional Landfill is used
Transfer Station(s): Picture Butte; Nobleford; Coaldale; Iron Springs

Lloydminster, page 673
Waste Management:
Waste collection contracted to Quik Pick Waste Disposal, 780/875-4100; Blue box recycling contracted to Bea Fisher Enterprises, 306/825-9777
Number of landfill sites: 1
Solid Waste Disposal Fees: $10/tonne
Recycling: Both Curbside & Depot; Depot located at 1215 - 50 Ave.
Special Bans/by-laws: Boulevard tree planting (Bylaw 21-2002); Cardboard ban at landfill (Bylaw 24-2001); Higher tire disposal fees at landfill (Bylaw 09-2002)
Composters subsidized: Yes
Water & Wastewater Treatment:
Lloydminster Water Treatment Plant, 4701 - 67 St., 306/625-2437
Other Initiatives:
Hazardous household waste roundup; Computer recycling program; Pitch-in week

Medicine Hat, page 673
Waste Management:
Recycling program operated in partnership with REDI Recycle, 403/504-1322; Residential yard waste in biodegradable paper bags or marked containers is picked up with regular garbage from April to October; Composting facility is operated at City landfill site, 403/527-1718
Number of landfill sites: 1; *Landfill Capacity:* 15-30 years
Solid Waste Disposal Fees: $15/tonne
Recycling: Depot; 4 depots
Hazardous Waste Depot or Facility: City Landfill site
Composters subsidized: Yes
Water & Wastewater Treatment:
City operated

Mountain View County, page 669
Waste Management:
Waste management responsibility of Mountain View Regional Waste Management Commission, Email: wastemgmt@mountainview-ab.com
Solid Waste Disposal Fees: $100/tonne
Transfer Station(s): Olds, Sundre, Water Valley, Reed Ranch & Carstairs
Recycling: Depot; Recycle Centres located at Village of Cremona, Town of Carstairs, Town of Didsbury, Town of Olds (2), Town of Sundre & Eagle Hill
Hazardous Waste Depot or Facility: Eco Site Centres located at Olds, Sundre, Water Valley & Didsbury MVRWMC Landfill
Water & Wastewater Treatment:
Water services responsibility of Mountain View Regional Water Services Commission
Other Initiatives:
Environmental farm plan workshops

North Forty Mile Regional Waste Management Services Commission, page 758
Waste Management:
Commission serves the following municipalities: Town of Bow Island & County of Forty Mile
Number of landfill sites: 1

Okotoks, page 674
Waste Management:
Okotoks Operations Dept. responsible for waste collection, composting & recycling; Waste disposal at Municipality of Foothills Landfill; Email: solidwaste@okotoks.ca; Phone: 403/938-8054
Recycling: Both Curbside & Depot; Recycling Depot 3730 - 32 St., Okotoks, 403/938-2652
Water & Wastewater Treatment:
Okotoks Wastewater Treatment Plant; Water services handled by EPCOR Water Services, Inc.
Other Initiatives:
Town operates a drop off center for composting of grass & leaves; Toxic round-up drop-off locations are Okotoks Fire Station or the regional landfill

Parkland County, page 670
Waste Management:
Number of landfill sites: 3
Clean Fill Fee: No
Transfer Station(s): 3
Hazardous Waste Depot or Facility: Yes
Water & Wastewater Treatment:
Water systems: Acheson Industrial Area Water Distribution System, Big Lake Water Distribution System, Entwistle Water

Page numbers refer to full profile.

Treatment & Distribution System. Wastewater systems: Acheson Industrial Area Sanitary Sewer System, Big Lake Water Sanitary Sewer System, Tomahawk Sanitary Sewer System, Duffield Sanitary Sewage System, Regional Sewage Transfer Stations, Entwistle Sewage Collection System & Lagoon.
Other Initiatives:
Development of a municipal based conservation plan.

Red Deer, page 674
Waste Management:
Number of landfill sites: 1
Recycling: Curbside; Blue Box program in effect
Special Bans/by-laws: 5-unit limit on residential garbage collection
Hazardous Waste Depot or Facility: Waste Management Facility, 1709 - 40 Ave., Red Deer, 403/340-2583
Compost Sites: No *Composters subsidized:* Yes
Water & Wastewater Treatment:
Water & wastewater treatment plants operated by city
Other Initiatives:
Parks Department administers biological pest control; Habitat conservation; Backyard composting; Naturalization of park trees; Tree planting; Office paper recycling depot located at 5420 - 47 St., Red Deer, 403/340-2583; Yard waste collection program in effect; Electronics recycling

Red Deer County, page 670
Waste Management:
Waste management responsibility of Central Alberta Regional Waste Commission
Transfer Station(s): Horne Hill, Kevisville, Lousana & Innisfail Solid Waste Transfer Stations
Recycling: Depot; Burnt Lake Business Park, Spruce View, Bowden, Delburne & Innisfail Recycling Depots
Special Bans/by-laws: Land Use Bylaw
Water & Wastewater Treatment:
County has a utility management agreement with EPCOR to operate water & wastewater systems in the following 5 communities: Springbrook, Spruce View, Benalto, South Hills & Lousana
Other Initiatives:
Reeve's Task Force on Land Use Planning & Sustainable Agriculture; County partnered with Alberta Environmentally Sustainable Agriculture to provide farmers & ranchers with a conservation program; Household hazardous waste roundup

Rocky View No. 44, page 670
Waste Management:
Municipality operates 4 transfer sites. There are no landfill sites in the municipality. Residents may use City of Calgary landfill sites. Hazardous waste is not accepted at transfer stations.
Solid Waste Disposal Fees: No
Recycling: ; Facility locations: Wintergreen Road NE., Bragg Creek, AB, Railway Ave., Langdon AB, Range Rd. 33, Springbank, AB
Water & Wastewater Treatment:
Wastewater collection & treatment utility, Hamlet of Langdon, administered by Municipality; Domestic water co-ops & private water distribution companies own & operate distribution systems.
Other Initiatives:
62 Environmental reserve parcels protected under municipal government act.

Roseridge Waste Management Services Commission, page 758
Waste Management:
Number of landfill sites: 1
Solid Waste Disposal Fees: $38.50/tonne
Recycling: Depot; at landfill site

St. Albert, page 674
Waste Management:
Waste collection contracted to Canadian Waste Management, 780/440-1700; St. Albert residents may use Northwest ECOstation in Edmonton
Recycling: Depot; St. Albert Recycling depot located at 7 Chevigny St. Campbell Industrial Park, 780/459-1557
Special Bans/by-laws: No open air burning of waste
Hazardous Waste Depot or Facility: Eco Station, 40 Bellrose Dr., St. Albert
Composters subsidized: Yes
Other Initiatives:
Establishment of Environment Advisory Committee; "Pay-as-you-throw" waste management system subscription; Annual "Take It or Leave It" event in June to dispose of unwanted usable items; Residents may pick up free compost material in spring & fall; Christmas tree collection in January; 2 bottle depots; Green cart pick up in summer months; St. Albert Compost Depot located on Veness Rd.; St. Albert residents may also use Eco Stations in Edmonton for household hazardous waste; Expansion of the Lacombe Park Water Reservoir

Spruce Grove, page 674
Waste Management:
Waste collection contracted to Waste Management of Canada Corporation, 780-440-1700
Transfer Station(s): 10 Alberta Ave., Spruce Grove, 780/962-9383
Recycling: Depot; Recycling Centre located at 10 Alberta Ave., Spruce Grove, 780/962-9383, operated by KC Environmental Group Ltd.
Water & Wastewater Treatment:
Water services handled by Capital Region Parkland Water Services Commission; Town Public Works department responsible for system maintenance
Other Initiatives:
Organic collection program; Spring toxic roundup; Electronic (e-waste) recycling program; Rechargeable Battery Recycling program; Annual fall home & yard clean up pickup; Business BEST (Building an Environmental & Social Trust), a program where businesses commit to environmental & community considerations in their operations; Partners for Climate Protection program; Urban forest management; Sale of compost from Spruce Grove Recycling Centre

Strathcona County, page 670
Waste Management:
Waste disposal handled by City of Edmonton Waste Management Centre's Clover Bar Landfill; Waste transfer handled by City of Fort Saskatchewan's Transfer Station & Beaver Regional Waste Commission's Lindbrook Transfer Station
Recycling: Both Curbside & Depot; Streambank Avenue Recycling Centre, 420 Streambank Ave., Sherwood Park; Baseline Rd. Recycling Station, 624 Bethel Dr., Sherwood Park; Josephburg Recycling Station, Moyer Recreation Centre; Ardrossan Recycling Station, Ardrossan Recreation Complex; South Cooking Lake Recycling Station, Fire Hall
Compost Sites: Yes *Composters subsidized:* Yes
Water & Wastewater Treatment:
Water treatment handled by EPCOR Water which operates 2 water treatment plants in Edmonton; Wastewater treatment handled by Alberta Capital Region Wastewater Commission
Other Initiatives:
Freecycle program in Sherwood Park

Sturgeon County, page 670
Waste Management:
Landfill site is the Roseridge Landfill, Roseridge Waste Management Services Commission; Free permits are issued to county residents to use the landfill
Number of landfill sites: 1; *Landfill Capacity:* 100 years
Solid Waste Disposal Fees: $58.50/tonne
Recycling: Depot; Landfill site
Special Bans/by-laws: Each household is permitted 8,000 kg of garbage per year; If limit is exceeded, fee is $30/tonne
Water & Wastewater Treatment:
Water supply attained via City of Edmonton or municipal treated water; Capital Region Wastewater Sewer Commission
Other Initiatives:
Agricultural services include conservation programs, pest & weed control & water management.

Wetaskiwin, page 674
Waste Management:
Waste management handled by Wetaskiwin Operational Services dept.; Landfill site is Wetaskiwin Regional Sanitary Landfill.
Number of landfill sites: 1
Solid Waste Disposal Fees: $53/tonne for residents, $95/tonne for non-residents.
Clean Fill Fee: No
Recycling: Depot; Recycling depot located at 5707-51st St., Wetaskiwin, 780/361-4431
Composters subsidized: Yes
Water & Wastewater Treatment:
Water Treatment Plant located in Coal Lake, AB, 780/361-4415; Sewage treatment provided by a series of lagoons
Other Initiatives:
User pay approach to waste handling; Spring & fall clean-up; Annual household toxic round-up; E-waste drop-off at recycling depot

Wetaskiwin County No. 10, page 670
Waste Management:
Landfill is serviced by the West Dried Meat Lake Regional Landfill, located within the County of Camrose
; *Landfill Capacity:* 100 years
Water & Wastewater Treatment:
2 independent water systems serving the Hamlet of Winfield & Mulhurst Bay's Lakeview subdivision are serviced by the county; Wastewater systems are Gwynne, Falun, Mulhurst Bay, Winfield & Alder Flats Wastewater System

Wood Buffalo, page 670
Waste Management:
Landfill & composting is at the Fort McMurray Regional Landfill site; Regional landfill design for 6-8 communities; Contracted to Fort McMurray, Conklin & Janvier; Contract for hamlet waste collection; First Nations & industry responsible for their waste management & sewage treatment facilities
Number of landfill sites: 7; *Landfill Capacity:* 4-10 years
Solid Waste Disposal Fees: $21.21 - 64/tonne (household refuse & commercial waste); $50/tonne (waste requiring special handling)
Transfer Station(s): Shift to transfer stations for hamlets
Recycling: Depot; Depots located at Timberlea, Thickwood, Downtown: Planning 6 more in 2008
Special Bans/by-laws: Animal waste in residential collection; Natural oil in Oilsands; Hydro-carbon contaminations
Hazardous Waste Depot or Facility: Fort McMurray Landfill
Compost Sites: Yes *Composters subsidized:* Yes
Water & Wastewater Treatment:
Water treatment plants located at Conklin, Chard, Anzac, Fort McMurray, Fort McKay, Fort Chipewyan
Other Initiatives:
Fort McMurray water treatment plant optimization; Trunkline water supply designed for Anzac; Membrane treatment for Fort MacKay; BNR sewage treatment designed for Fort McMurray; New truck fill at McMurray, phase II Fort McMurray Intake; Fort McKay LIFTS station; Conklin water treatment expansion

British Columbia

Abbotsford, page 679
Waste Management:
Waste hauled to Cache Creek landfill; Hazardous household wastes handled by Product Care association
Transfer Station(s): Matsqui Transfer Station, 33621 Valley Rd., operated under contract with the Greater Vancouver Regional District.
Recycling: Both Curbside & Depot; Abbotsford/Mission Recycling Depot, 33670 Valley Rd.
Compost Sites: No *Composters subsidized:* Yes
Water & Wastewater Treatment:
Wastewater treatment responsibility of Fraser Valley Regional District; Small urban area serviced by Clearbrook Waterworks, a private utility
Other Initiatives:
Preparation of "Abbotsford Charter of Sustainability: Principles for Sustainable Community Development."

Alberni-Clayoquot, page 676
Waste Management:
Number of landfill sites: 2
Solid Waste Disposal Fees: $65/tonne (residential); $82.50/tonne (land clearing debris)
Composters subsidized: Yes

Bulkley-Nechako, page 676
Waste Management:
Operates landfill sites & transfer stations for the Regional District.
Number of landfill sites: 7
Recycling: ; Depot locations: Smithers/Telkwa Transfer Station, Landfills: Knockholt, Granisle, Burns Lake, Fraser Lake, Fort Fraser, Fort St. James, Vanderhoof, Southside Transfer Station
Special Bans/by-laws: Ban on tires in landfill
Hazardous Waste Depot or Facility: Smithers/Telkiva Transfer Station.
Composters subsidized: Yes
Other Initiatives:
Implementation of noxious weed control program; Re-use sheds for public use.

Municipal Waste Management and Water & Wastewater Treatment / British Columbia

Burnaby, page 679
Waste Management:
Waste collection responsibility of city; Disposal responsibility of Greater Vancouver Regional District
Transfer Station(s): Still Creek, Burnaby
Recycling: Both Curbside & Depot; Depot located at Still Creek
Special Bans/by-laws: Watercourse bylaw prohibits fouling, destructing or impeding watercourses in Burnaby; Pesticide notification bylaw
Hazardous Waste Depot or Facility: Still Creek Depot, Burnaby
Compost Sites: Yes *Composters subsidized:* Yes
Water & Wastewater Treatment:
Water provided by Greater Vancouver Regional District & distributed by the City; Wastewater collection by the city, treatment by Greater Vancouver Regional District
Other Initiatives:
Alternative stormwater management approaches; watershed-based planning initiatives/stormwater management plans (Brunette Basin, Byrne Creek, Stoney Creek); management/area plans & OPCs with comprehensive environmental sections; "streamkeepers" projects; urban noise remediation; State of the Environment Report; integrated pest management; Environment & Waste Management Committee

Campbell River, page 679
Waste Management:
Waste collection contracted to International Paper Industries (250/286-0211); Recycling & landfill responsibility of Comox Strathcona Regional District
Number of landfill sites: 1
Solid Waste Disposal Fees: Schedule depending on type of waste (from no fee to $350/tonne)
Clean Fill Fee: No
Recycling: Depot; Private & regional district depots
Special Bans/by-laws: Restrictions on burning; sanitary sewer source control by-law; cardboard disposal surcharge
Hazardous Waste Depot or Facility: Privately run depot
Composters subsidized: Yes
Water & Wastewater Treatment:
One re-chlorination station; Two wastewater treatment plants: Industrial Park Treatment Plant (lagoon); Norm Wood Environmental Centre (two secondary oxidation ditches with secondary clarifiers)
Other Initiatives:
Biosolids reuse project; Hybrid poplar plantation on land at Norm Wood Environmental Centre; 2005 plan changes to water bylaw to place more emphasis on water conservation

Capital Regional District, page 676
Waste Management:
Collection of recyclables contracted to International Paper Industries Ltd.; For more information contact CRD Recycling hotline 250/360-3030, or Email: hotline@crd.bc.ca.
Number of landfill sites: 1
Solid Waste Disposal Fees: $82/tonne (general refuse)
Recycling: Both Curbside & Depot; Hartland Recyling Area, Hartland Landfill, north of Victoria; Depots under contract to the CRD, Southern Gulf Islands & Salt Spring Island
Special Bans/by-laws: Landfill restricted wastes: aggregate, asphalt, biomedical waste, clean soil, concrete, corrugated cardboard, directories, lead acid batteries, PCBs, drywall, hazardous wastes, liquids, radioactive & reactive waste, ignitable wastes, motor vehicle bodies & farm implements, scrap metal, tires, white goods
Hazardous Waste Depot or Facility: Hartland Landfill Recyling Area, Hartland Ave., north of Victoria
Composters subsidized: Yes
Water & Wastewater Treatment:
Water treatment plants: Japan Gulch Treatment Plant; Charters Creek Treatment Plant; Wastewater treatment plants: Saanich Peninsula Treatment Plant; Port Renfrew Treatment Plant, Vancouver Island; Ganges Harbour Treatment Plant, Salt Spring Island; Maliview Treatment Plant, Salt Spring Island; Schooner Way Treatment Plant, Pender Island; Cannon Crescent Treatment Plant, Pender Island; For more information contact water@crd.bc.ca
Other Initiatives:
Environmental education & awareness through publications & promotional campaigns; Composting initiatives; Liquid waste management plan; Stewardship intiatives; Air quality working group; Stormwater, harbours & watersheds program; Sooke reservoir expansion

Cariboo, page 677
Waste Management:
Cities of Quesnel & Williams Lake operate their landfills
Number of landfill sites: 14
Transfer Station(s): 15 transfer stations
Recycling: Curbside; Depot locations: 100 Mile House, Williams Lake, Quesnel
Water & Wastewater Treatment:
Cities within the region are responsible for their own water & wastewater treatment; regional district is responsible for the following water systems: Alexis Creek, Lac La Hache, Forest Grove & 108 Mile
Other Initiatives:
Institutional, commercial & industrial waste exchange program; landfill & transfer station upgrading program; wood waste management program

Central Kootenay, page 677
Waste Management:
Waste collection responsibility of member areas
Number of landfill sites: 4
Solid Waste Disposal Fees: Yes
Transfer Station(s): 9 transfer stations in the region
Recycling: Depot; 28 recycling depots in the region
Water & Wastewater Treatment:
8 water systems in the region

Central Okanagan, page 677
Waste Management:
Waste collection contracted to OK Environmental Waste Systems, 250/868-3211 & Waste Management, 250/861-8788; Recycling collection contracted to Canadian Waste Services
Number of landfill sites: 2
Solid Waste Disposal Fees: $50/tonne
Transfer Station(s): Westside Rd.; Whiteman Creek Forest Service Rd.
Recycling: Both Curbside & Depot; Depots: Kirschner Rd. Recycling, 1988 Kirschner Rd.; Metro Materials Recovery Recycling Depot, 144 Cambro Rd.; Glenmore Landfill, Glenmore Dr.; Westside Landfill, Asquith Rd.
Special Bans/by-laws: Bylaw to reduce emissions from open burning, camp fires, & wood burning appliances to ensure good air quality
Composters subsidized: Yes
Water & Wastewater Treatment:
Westside Regional Waste Water Treatment Plant, south end of Gellatly Rd.; Regional district administers 8 water distribution systems
Other Initiatives:
Residential grasscycling promotion; Composting workshops & education garden; Technical assistance in starting up recycling & waste reduction programs at home & work; Recycling directories for residential, commercial & construction, demolition & renovation; Spring & fall yard waste pick-up; Annual household hazardous waste round-up; Private depots collect pesticides, oil, flammable liquids, batteries, paint & computers; Recycling at work program, 250/846-6250, recycle@cord.bc.ca; Joe Rich Creek Watershed Restoration; Protection of enviro

Central Saanich, page 686
Waste Management:
Responsibility of Capital Regional District.
Water & Wastewater Treatment:
Responsibility of Capital Regional District.

Chilliwack, page 680
Waste Management:
Municipality responsible for waste management. Waste collection contracted to Waste Management of Canada Corp. Household hazardous waste handled by BC Product Care Association at Chilliwack Bottle Depot.
Number of landfill sites: 1
Solid Waste Disposal Fees: $73/tonne; $115/tonne (for gypsum)
Recycling: Depot; Municipal Recycling Depot; Green Bin Recycling Depots
Hazardous Waste Depot or Facility: Annual household hazardous waste day
Compost Sites: Yes *Composters subsidized:* Yes
Water & Wastewater Treatment:
Water Pollution Control Plant, 44280 Wolfe Rd.
Other Initiatives:
Adopt a River & Adopt a Road programs; Christmas Tree Disposal & Spring Pitch-In campaigns

Columbia-Shuswap, page 677
Waste Management:
Regional landfills located in the following areas: Golden, Revelstoke, Salmon Arm, Sicamous & Skimikin
Number of landfill sites: 5
Solid Waste Disposal Fees: $60/tonne
Transfer Station(s): Falkland; Glenemma; Scotch Creek; Seymour Arm; Malakwa; Trout Lake; Parson
Recycling: Depot; 17 depots located throughout region
Special Bans/by-laws: Land Use
Water & Wastewater Treatment:
Community waterworks at Cedar Heights, Eagle Bay Estates & Falkland
Other Initiatives:
Elimination of small disposal sites in rural areas; Implementation of refuse disposal fees

Colwood, page 680
Waste Management:
Responsibility of Capital Regional District
Recycling: Curbside
Water & Wastewater Treatment:
Responsibility of Capital Regional District

Comox, page 680
Waste Management:
Waste collection & collection of recyclables responsibility of town; Compost site located at town's Public Works Yard; Waste disposal responsibility of Comox-Strathcona Regional District; Pidgeon Lake Regional Landfill is used
Recycling: Curbside
Composters subsidized: Yes
Water & Wastewater Treatment:
Responsibility of Comox-Strathcona Regional District
Other Initiatives:
Comox Return Centre for beverage containers & paint & paint products

Comox Valley, page 677
Waste Management:
Number of landfill sites: 4
Solid Waste Disposal Fees: $65/tonne
Transfer Station(s): Cortes Island, Gold River, Hornby Island
Recycling: Depot; 16 depots throughout the region
Special Bans/by-laws: Water Conservation Bylaw, Noise Control Bylaw, Noxious Weed Bylaw, Fire Control Bylaws, Floodplain Management Bylaw
Compost Sites: Yes *Composters subsidized:* Yes
Water & Wastewater Treatment:
Comox Valley Water Pollution Control Centre
Other Initiatives:
Compost education centres in Comox Valley & Campbell River; E-waste drop-off events; School & youth recycling education programs; Liquid waste management planning; Pesticide awareness & pesticide disposal at Campbell River Refund Centre; Promotion & education about household hazardous waste provincial programs

Coquitlam, page 680
Waste Management:
Responsibility of Greater Vancouver Regional District; Collection contracted to International Paper Industries (IPI)
Solid Waste Disposal Fees: $65/tonne
Compost Sites: Yes
Water & Wastewater Treatment:
Responsibility of Greater Vancouver Regional District

Courtenay, page 680
Waste Management:
Responsibility of the Regional District of Comox Strathcona; Collection contracted to West Coast Waste, 250/336-2172
Recycling: Curbside
Water & Wastewater Treatment:
Responsibility of the Regional District of Comox Strathcona
Other Initiatives:
Tree management & protection; Weekly garbage limit is a 121 litre can

Cowichan Valley, page 677
Waste Management:
Waste transported from transfer station to Cache Creek Landfill, near Kamloops
Solid Waste Disposal Fees: $110/tonne
Transfer Station(s): Bings Creek Waste Transfer Station
Recycling: Both Curbside & Depot; Depot locations: Peerless Road Recycling Drop-off Depot, Ladysmith; Meade Creek

Recycling Drop-off Depot, Lake Cowichan; Bings Creek Solid Waste Management Complex, North Cowichan; 9 CVRD multi-product neighbourhood bin locations; For more information contact CVRD Recycling Hotline, 1-800-665-3955
Special Bans/by-laws: Waste stream management licensing bylaw
Water & Wastewater Treatment:
Region responsible for collection & disposal of sewage for the following sewer systems: Shawnigan Beach Estates, Maple Hills, Cowichan Bay, Eagle Heights, Mesachie Lake, Kerry Village & Creekside Resort; Engineering department maintains operations of the following water systems: Shawnigan Lake North, Cherry Point Estates, Honeymoon Bay, Mesachie Lake, Saltair Water System, Lakeside Estates, Kerry Village & Youbou Water System

Cranbrook, page 680
Waste Management:
Responsibility of the Regional District of East Kootenay
Water & Wastewater Treatment:
Cranbrook Water Treatment Plant

Dawson Creek, page 680
Waste Management:
Waste collection contracted to Canadian Waste, 250/782-6488; Landfill the responsibility of the Peace River Regional District; Recycling handled by Recycle Plus
Water & Wastewater Treatment:
City of Dawson Creek Water Treatment Plant; Wastewater treatment plant

Delta, page 686
Waste Management:
Waste collection contracted to Remple Disposal, 604/580-3379
Recycling: Curbside
Special Bans/by-laws: Two-can limit on curbside garbage collection
Water & Wastewater Treatment:
Responsibility of Greater Vancouver Regional District
Other Initiatives:
Annual Spring Clean-up; Christmas tree chipping; Various drop off locations throughout area for household hazardous waste & recyclables; Streamside & tree protection; Watershed creek restoration; Agricultural land stewardship

East Kootenay, page 677
Waste Management:
Number of landfill sites: 2
Solid Waste Disposal Fees: No charge for household refuse; User fees apply at staffed facilities on most other loads
Transfer Station(s): 4 covered transfer stations, Cranbrook, Kimberley, Sparwood & Elkford; 15 rural transfer stations, across the region
Recycling: Depot; Yellow bin program for mixed recyclables; Glass recycling program; Blue bin program for household plastics; Elkford, Sparwood & Fernie have their own programs
Hazardous Waste Depot or Facility: Consumer Stewardship Program depot: Purcell Recycling, 125 Slater Rd., Cranbrook
Water & Wastewater Treatment:
Region manages sewage collection & disposal systems at Holland Creek (Kinbasket Sewage Treatment Plant), Edgewater; Region operates water systems in Elko, Moyie, Windermere, Timber Ridge, Holland Creek & Edgewater
Other Initiatives:
Paint & used oil depots across the region

Esquimalt, page 686
Waste Management:
Waste collection responsibility of Township; Collection of recyclables responsibility of Capital Regional District; CRD Recycling Hotline: 250/360-3030; Waste management responsibility of Capital Regional District; Hartland Landfill is used
Composters subsidized: Yes
Water & Wastewater Treatment:
Design, inspection & technical supervision of water distribution systems responsibility of City of Victoria; Maintenance & upgrading of sewer system & sewage pump stations responsibility of Township; Sewage treatment responsibility of Capital Regional District
Other Initiatives:
Canteen Composting located at 605 Canteen Rd.; Phone: 250/386-3343

Fort St. John, page 681
Waste Management:
Waste management responsibility of Peace River Regional District; Waste collection responsibility of City
Water & Wastewater Treatment:
South Sewage Treatment Lagoons; North Sewage Treatment Lagoons; Fort St. John Water Treatment Plant & Bulk Water Station, West Bypass Rd.
Other Initiatives:
Creation of Liquid Waste Management Plan

Fraser Valley, page 677
Waste Management:
Waste collection & recycling services in electoral areas A, B, C, F & G & several First Nations Reserves responsibility of region; Collection of recyclables in certain areas contracted to R&R Recycling, 604/869-3328
Number of landfill sites: 1
Solid Waste Disposal Fees: $163.50/tonne (residents outside Electoral Area A)
Transfer Station(s): Sunshine Valley Station; Harrison Mills Station, 14050 Chehalis Forest Service Rd.; Hemlock Valley Station, Laurel Rd.; Sylve
Recycling: Both Curbside & Depot; Depots: Chaumox Landfill, North Bend, Electoral Area A; Sunshine Valley Transfer Station, Electoral Area B; Harrison Mills Transfer Station, 14050 Chehalis Forest Service Rd., Electoral Area C; Sylvester Rd. Transfer Station, Electoral Area F
Composters subsidized: Yes
Water & Wastewater Treatment:
Operataion of 10 water systems & 3 sewer systems responsibility of region's engineering services department
Other Initiatives:
Free stores at 3 transfer stations for exchange of used items; Air quality monitoring

Fraser-Fort George, page 678
Waste Management:
Responsibility of the regional district; municipalities (Prince George, MacKenzie, McBride & Valemount) carry out the waste collection.
Number of landfill sites: 6
Solid Waste Disposal Fees: $42/tonne
Recycling: ; Depot locations: Prince George, MacKenzie, McBride, Dunster & Valemount
Hazardous Waste Depot or Facility: Household depot location Product Care Assn. Depot, 1922 First Ave., Prince George.
Composters subsidized: Yes
Other Initiatives:
Upgrading or closing of landfill sites. "Swap Shed" waste exchange areas. Industrial, commercial & institutional recycling processing plant, 1015 Great St., Prince George is operated by Metro Materials. Developed "Prince George Air Quality Management Plan."

Kamloops, page 681
Waste Management:
Number of landfill sites: 3
Solid Waste Disposal Fees: $25/tonne (loads greater than 250 kgs)
Clean Fill Fee: No
Recycling: Depot; Mission Flats Recycling Service; Recycling bins located throughout city
Special Bans/by-laws: Backyard burning ban
Hazardous Waste Depot or Facility: Mission Flats landfill site, Consumer Product Stewardship Program
Composters subsidized: Yes
Water & Wastewater Treatment:
Kamloops Centre for Water Quality water treatment plant; Kamloops Wastewater Treatment Centre
Other Initiatives:
Partners for Climate Protection Program; TravelSmart Plan; WaterSmart Program

Kelowna, page 681
Waste Management:
Waste collection contracted to Waste Management of Canada Inc., 250/861-8788
Number of landfill sites: 2
Solid Waste Disposal Fees: $50/tonne
Recycling: Depot; Depots located at Kirschner Road Depot, 1988 Kirchner Rd.; Glenmore Landfill, 2105 Glenmore Rd.; Westside Landfill, Asquith Rd.; Metro Materials Recovery Inc. Depot, 144 Cambro Rd.
Water & Wastewater Treatment:
Kelowna Joint Water Committee includes city's 5 major water suppliers, 250/861-4200; Kelowna Wastewater Treatment Facility, Raymer Ave., 250/469-8502; Bardenpho Wastewater Treatment Facility
Other Initiatives:
Ogogrow composing program; Christmas tree drop-off; Water smart program, watersmart@look.ca; Wetland protection; Environmental education & events

Kitimat, page 687
Waste Management:
Number of landfill sites: 1
Recycling: Depot; 316 Railway Ave.; Depot operated by Kitimat Understanding the Environment (KUTE), 250/632-6633
Water & Wastewater Treatment:
Kitimat Pollution Control Centre

Kitimat-Stikine, page 678
Waste Management:
Number of landfill sites: 6; *Landfill Capacity:* 5-30 years
Solid Waste Disposal Fees: $12.50 - $50.00 (truck volume)
Special Bans/by-laws: Special wastes, waste oil, ozone-depleting substances & tires banned from landfill
Hazardous Waste Depot or Facility: Terrace Bottle Depot, Terrace BC
Composters subsidized: Yes
Water & Wastewater Treatment:
Thornhill Water System; Queensway Sewage System
Other Initiatives:
Re-use area at landfill where items such as lawnmowers, bicycles, small engines etc. are available for others to salvage; "Help Minimize Waste", "Making Compost" brochures on RDKS url, www.rdks.bc.ca; Kelse Lake/Jackpine Flats liquid waste management plan

Kootenay Boundary, page 678
Waste Management:
Collection responsibility of the member municipalities; regional district responsible for recycling & disposal
Number of landfill sites: 5
Solid Waste Disposal Fees: $60/tonne or $9/cubic metre; fees in effect at all sites
Recycling: Both Curbside & Depot; 16 depots across the district
Special Bans/by-laws: Ban on cardboard, paper fibre, beverage containers, all recyclable glass, metal, plastics, compostable yard & garden waste in effect
Hazardous Waste Depot or Facility: Trail, Grand Forks, Greenwood, Beaverdell
Composters subsidized: Yes
Water & Wastewater Treatment:
Water & wastewater treatment contracted to City of Trail's Columbia Pollution Control Centre, 250/368-3822
Other Initiatives:
Increase in tipping fees in 2006

Langford, page 681
Waste Management:
Waste collectors hired by property owners; Waste management responsibility of Capital Regional District
Water & Wastewater Treatment:
Sewer construction & maintenance responsibility of City Engineering Department; Water & wastewater treatment responsibility of Capital Regional District

Langley, page 681
Waste Management:
Responsibility of the Greater Vancouver Regional District; waste collection contracted to Canadian Waste Services, 604/520-7800.
Transfer Station(s): Langley Transfer Station, 1070 - 272 St., Aldergrove
Recycling: Curbside; Depots at City of Langley Works Yard, 5713 - 198 St.; Langley Transfer Station; Willowbrook Recycling, 6001 - 196A St.; Masonville Plastics, 19402 - 56 Ave.; Aldergrove Landfill, 1070 - 272 St.; Enviro Wood Waste, 2460 - 192 St.
Hazardous Waste Depot or Facility: JR Bottle Depot, #224, 9640 - 201 St.; Langley Bottle Depot, 20137 Industrial Ave.
Water & Wastewater Treatment:
Responsibility of the Greater Vancouver Regional District.

Langley, page 687
Waste Management:
Responsibility of Greater Vancouver Regional District, contracted to International Paper Industries, 604/530-3939
Solid Waste Disposal Fees: $65/tonne

Page numbers refer to full profile.

Municipal Waste Management and Water & Wastewater Treatment / British Columbia

Recycling: Curbside
Hazardous Waste Depot or Facility: Depot locations in Langley, through the Paint & Consumer Product Stewardship Program
Compost Sites: Yes
Water & Wastewater Treatment:
Water treatment is the responsiblity of the Greater Vancouver Regional District, Aldergrove Water Treatment Plant, 27540 - 28 Ave.; Wastewater treatment is the responsibility of the Greater Vancouver Regional District & the Fraser Valley Regional District

Maple Ridge, page 687
Waste Management:
Responsibility of the Greater Vancouver Regional District
Transfer Station(s): Maple Ridge Transfer Station, 236th & River Rd.
Recycling: Both Curbside & Depot; Maple Ridge
Special Bans/by-laws: Bylaws on soil deposit, tree preservation, water preservation, watercourse protection
Composters subsidized: Yes
Water & Wastewater Treatment:
2 reservoirs on the Greater Vancouver Regional District system
Other Initiatives:
Green waste drop-off program; Community compost demonstration garden; Collection of flammable liquids, pesticides & gasoline at recycling depot

Metro Vancouver, page 678
Waste Management:
One mass burn MSW incinerator with energy recovery
Number of landfill sites: 2; *Landfill Capacity:* 5-10 & 30+ years
Solid Waste Disposal Fees: $65/tonne
Transfer Station(s): Six waste transfer facilities
Special Bans/by-laws: Disposal bans on gypsum, used oil filters, corrugated cardboard; voluntary Code of Practice for source separation of designated recyclable materials, waste audits & waste reduction plans for all businesses
Hazardous Waste Depot or Facility: No
Water & Wastewater Treatment:
District operates 5 wastewater treatment plants

Mission, page 687
Waste Management:
Waste collection contracted to Smithrite Disposal Ltd., 604/299-4030.
Number of landfill sites: 1
Solid Waste Disposal Fees: $60/tonne
Recycling: Both Curbside & Depot; No collection for rural residents; 6 depots
Water & Wastewater Treatment:
Responsibility of the Central Fraser Valley Water Commission.

Mount Waddington, page 678
Waste Management:
Contracted to 4B Enterprises
Number of landfill sites: 1; *Landfill Capacity:* 20 years
Solid Waste Disposal Fees: $2/can or bag (residential), $80/tonne (construction, demolition, woodwaste)
Clean Fill Fee: Yes; $5/tonne
Recycling: Depot; Depot 7-Mile Landfill & Recycling Facility
Hazardous Waste Depot or Facility: Household waste 7-Mile Landfill & Recycling; BC Paint Care Drop-Off & Exchange.
Water & Wastewater Treatment:
Region administers sewer & water services in rural communities. Sewage collection & treatment are provided in: Coal Harbour, Quatsino First Nation, Sointula, Woss, Quatse Lake. Contracted to PG Enterprises 250/949-7075.
Other Initiatives:
Biosolids composted & reused. Sale of reusable items & construction materials at 7-Mile site.

Nanaimo, page 681
Waste Management:
Operation of regional landfill responsibility of Regional District of Nanaimo; Waste collection responsibility of City of Nanaimo
Recycling: Both Curbside & Depot; Collection contracted to Waste Services Inc., 250/758-5360; Depot located at centralized recycling facility, operated by Nanaimo Recycling Exchange, 2477 Kenworth Rd.
Special Bans/by-laws: Tree Protection By-law
Water & Wastewater Treatment:
Water treatment responsibility of city; Chlorine & treatment plants, located in the Village of South West Extension & the City of Nanaimo
Other Initiatives:
Water quality protection program; Watershed management; Wise use of water program; Reuse rendezvous

Nanaimo, page 678
Waste Management:
Number of landfill sites: 1
Solid Waste Disposal Fees: $95/tonne (solid waste); $190/tonne (controlled waste)
Transfer Station(s): Church Road Transfer Station, 860 Church Rd., Parksville
Recycling: Both Curbside & Depot
Composters subsidized: Yes
Water & Wastewater Treatment:
Region operates the following Water Local Service Areas: Nanoose, Fairwinds, Arbutus Park, West Bay, Driftwood, Madrona, Wall Beach, San Pareil, Decourcey, Englishman River, Melrose Terrace, Surfside & French Creek; Wastewater treatment plants in the region: Greater Nanaimo Water Pollution Control Centre, French Creek Water Pollution Control Centre, Nanoose Water Pollution Control Centre, Duke Point Water Pollution Control Centre
Other Initiatives:
Garbage limitations; Landfill project to reduce greenhouse gases; Food waste diversion program; Organics diversion strategy; Directory available of recycling depots throughout region

New Westminster, page 682
Waste Management:
Responsibility of Greater Vancouver Regional District.
Recycling: Both Curbside & Depot; New Westminster Recycling Depot at 6th Ave. & McBride Blvd.
Water & Wastewater Treatment:
Responsibility of Greater Vancouver Regional District.
Other Initiatives:
Development of greenways.

North Cowichan, page 687
Waste Management:
Responsibility of Cowichan Valley Regional District; collection & recycling programs responsibility of the municipality.
Recycling: Both Curbside & Depot; Collection is contracted to Active Disposal & Recycling; Depot located at Bing's Creek Depot, Drinkwater Rd., 250/701-0092; Multi-product bins provided by regional district
Water & Wastewater Treatment:
Chemainus Waste Treatment Treatment Plant, 9575 Bare Point Rd., Chemainus; Crofton Wastewater Treatment Plant, 1575 Chaplin St., Crofton; North Cowichan-Duncan Joint Utilities Sewage Lagoons Wastewater Treatment Plant.

North Okanagan, page 678
Waste Management:
Number of landfill sites: 4
Solid Waste Disposal Fees: $57/tonne; $22.25/cubic metre compacted; $7.40/cubic metre loose
Transfer Station(s): King Fisher at Mabel Lake & Silver Star Mountain
Recycling: Both Curbside & Depot; Recycling & Disposal Facilities in Greater Vernon, Armstrong/Spallumcheen, Lumby & Cherryville
Special Bans/by-laws: Recyclable Materials Separation Bylaw; Open Burning/Fire Regulation Bylaw
Hazardous Waste Depot or Facility: Chasers Bottle Depot, 4612 - 27 St., Vernon
Composters subsidized: Yes
Water & Wastewater Treatment:
Silver Star Water Utility; Whitevale Water Utility; Grinwold Water Utility
Other Initiatives:
Recyclable glass program; Bagged organics programs; Annual household hazardous waste round-up

North Vancouver, page 688
Waste Management:
Waste management responsibility of Greater Vancouver Regional District; Waste collection responsibility of District's Solid Waste Dept.
Transfer Station(s): 30 Riverside Dr., North Vancouver
Recycling: Both Curbside & Depot; North Shore Recycling Program, 604/984-9730; North Shore Recycling Drop-off Depot, 75 Riverside Dr., North Vancouver
Special Bans/by-laws: Environmental Protection & Preservation By-law; Regulations regarding water courses, trees, soils, sloping land
Hazardous Waste Depot or Facility: Drop off at transfer station
Compost Sites: Yes *Composters subsidized:* Yes
Water & Wastewater Treatment:
Responsibility of Greater Vancouver Regional District
Other Initiatives:
Sediment & erosion control; Stream & waterfront setbacks

North Vancouver, page 682
Waste Management:
Waste collection responsibility of city; Waste disposal responsibility of Greater Vancouver Regional District
Transfer Station(s): North Shore Transfer Station, 30 Riverside Dr., North Vancouver
Recycling: Both Curbside & Depot; Collection contracted to Waste Management of Canada, 604/929-3416; North Shore Recycling Drop-off Depot, 29 Riverside Dr., North Vancouver
Hazardous Waste Depot or Facility: North Shore Transfer Station Hazardous Household Waste Collection Depot
Compost Sites: Yes *Composters subsidized:* Yes
Water & Wastewater Treatment:
Responsibility of Greater Vancouver Regional District
Other Initiatives:
Environmental Protection Program; Curbside yard trimmings collection; Pesticide Management Plan; Parks & Greenways Strategic Plan

Oak Bay, page 688
Waste Management:
Waste management responsibility of the Capital Regional District; Waste collection responsibility of the municipality
Recycling: Curbside
Special Bans/by-laws: Land development & tree protection
Water & Wastewater Treatment:
Responsibility of Capital Regional District
Other Initiatives:
Regulation totes & blue boxes; Annual garden refuse pickup; Sale of compost

Okanagan-Similkameen, page 678
Waste Management:
Collection of recyclables contracted to OK Environmental, 250/492-4707; Waste collection contracted to Canadian Waste, 250/492-0089
Number of landfill sites: 4
Solid Waste Disposal Fees: $43/tonne
Recycling: Both Curbside & Depot; Main recycling depots at the following landfill sites: Campbell Mountain, Okanagan Falls, Keremeos, Oliver
Water & Wastewater Treatment:
Region responsible for the following water systems: Apex; Faulder; Naramato
Other Initiatives:
User pay principle for garbage collection services; Environmental education programs; Okanagan Falls landfill in process of becoming a Regional Service Area Centre for demolition, land clearing & construction waste

Parksville, page 682
Waste Management:
Responsibility of Nanaimo Regional District
Water & Wastewater Treatment:
Responsibility of Nanaimo Regional District
Other Initiatives:
Wood chipping program

Peace River, page 678
Waste Management:
Contracted to Canadian Waste, 250/262-7183 & DC Waste Disposal, 250/784-3333
Number of landfill sites: 4; *Landfill Capacity:* 8 years
Solid Waste Disposal Fees: $30/tonne or $2/cubic metre
Clean Fill Fee: No
Recycling: Depot; Depots at Dawson Creek, Fort St. John, Chetwynd, Tumbler Ridge
Hazardous Waste Depot or Facility: No
Water & Wastewater Treatment:
Wastewater treatment plants: Kelly Lake, Rolla, Fort St. John Airport Water & Sewer Utility, Charlie Lake Sewer Utility, Chilton Subdivision Sewer Utility
Other Initiatives:
Solid waste management plan; implementation of a regional disposal & reduction system

Penticton, page 682
Waste Management:
Waste management responsibility of Regional District of Okanagan-Similkameen; Waste collection responsibility of city; Waste collection contracted to Waste Services Inc., 250/490-3888

Page numbers refer to full profile.

Water & Wastewater Treatment:
City of Penticton Water Treatment Plant, 1900 Penticton Ave., 250/490-2560, Email: wtp@city.penticton.bc.ca; Advanced Wastewater Treatment Plant, 459 Waterloo Ave., 250/490-2550, Email:wwtp@city.penticton.bc.ca
Other Initiatives:
Upgrades to Advanced Wastewater Treatment Plant; Updates to Liquid Waste Management Plan; Yard waste pickup, 4 times/yr.

Pitt Meadows, page 683
Waste Management:
Waste collection contracted to Canadian Waste Services, 604/520-7806
Recycling: Curbside
Composters subsidized: Yes
Water & Wastewater Treatment:
Maintenance of water supply system & wastewater system responsibility of District Municipality's Operations Centre; Water & wastewater treatment responsibility of Greater Vancouver Regional District
Other Initiatives:
Agricultural Land Reserve; Watercourse & tree preservation; Ongoing education to reduce, reuse & recycle; Compost site located at 18020 Kennedy Rd., 604/465-1311; Hazardous waste handled by BC Recycling

Port Alberni, page 683
Waste Management:
Alberni-Clayoquot Regional district responsible for waste disposal; municipality responsible for collection
Water & Wastewater Treatment:
Chlorination stations: Bainbridge Pumpstation, Johnston Pumpstation & Somass Pump/Intake; Sewage Treatment Facility: aeration Lagoon, south side of Somass River
Other Initiatives:
Developing a liquid waste management plan with Associated Engineering & the Ministry of the Environment

Port Coquitlam, page 683
Waste Management:
Waste management responsibility of Greater Vancouver Regional District.; Waste collection responsibility of city
Recycling: Curbside
Hazardous Waste Depot or Facility: Biggar Bottle Depot, 2577 Kingsway Ave.
Water & Wastewater Treatment:
Water treatment responsibility of Greater Vancouver Regional District; Maintenance of watermain & sewer system responsibility of city
Other Initiatives:
Tree bylaw; Waterways protection; Reduction of road salt; Anti-idling program; Watershed management plan; Water conservation; Pitch in for PoCo pride; Seasonal green waste collection

Port Moody, page 683
Waste Management:
Waste disposal responsibility of Greater Vancouver Regional District; Collection contracted by the City to International Paper industries, 604/520-3157
Recycling: Curbside
Compost Sites: Yes
Water & Wastewater Treatment:
Responsibility of Greater Vancouver Regional District
Other Initiatives:
"Environmentally Sensitive Areas Management Strategy"; Creeks & streams stewardship; Composting & Rain Collection Program

Powell River, page 683
Waste Management:
Recycling: Both Curbside & Depot; Augusta Recyclers Depot, 7346 Hwy. 101, Powell River
Water & Wastewater Treatment:
Westview Sewage Treatment Plant; Wildwood Sewage Lagoon Plant; Halsam Lake System (chlorinating, screening); Powell Lake System (chlorinating), townsite sewage treatment
Other Initiatives:
Bag & tag system in place for all curbside collection

Powell River, page 679
Other Initiatives:
Myrtle Pond Water Study; Texada Island Shoreline Hazards Study; Savary Island Dune & Shoreline Study

Prince George, page 683
Waste Management:
Waste management, including operation of the Foothills Blvd. Regional Landfill, drop-depot recycling system & composting, responsibility of Regional District of Fraser Fort George; Waste collection responsibility of city
Transfer Station(s): 18th & Quinn Streets; Vanway Firehall
Special Bans/by-laws: Clean Air Bylaw
Water & Wastewater Treatment:
Waste Water Treatment Centre, 250/562-4578
Other Initiatives:
Air Quality Management Plan prepared by the Prince George Airshed Technical Management Committee; Stream stewardship; Spring clean up; Urban forest management & stewardship plan; Water conservation plan

Prince Rupert, page 684
Waste Management:
Waste collection responsibility of City; Recycling & waste management responsibility of Skeena-Queen Charlotte Regional District
Number of landfill sites: 1
Solid Waste Disposal Fees: $85/tonne
Other Initiatives:
Adopt a Green Space & Adopt a Trail programs

Quesnel, page 688
Waste Management:
Residential, commercial & industrial waste collection responsibility of city
Number of landfill sites: 1
Solid Waste Disposal Fees: $15/1 ton truck
Transfer Station(s): Carson Pitt Rd., 250/992-3817
Recycling: Depot; City of Quesnel Landfill Site & Recycling Depot, Carson Pitt Rd., 250/992-2426
Other Initiatives:
Quesnel Air Quality Roundtable; Community Action on Energy Efficiency

Richmond, page 684
Waste Management:
Disposal responsibility of Greater Vancouver Regional District; Waste collection contracted to International Paper Industries, 604/599-8151
Number of landfill sites: 1; *Landfill Capacity:* 25 years; private site, owned by Ecowaste Industries
Solid Waste Disposal Fees: $65/tonne
Transfer Station(s): Yes
Recycling: Both Curbside & Depot; Depot at 5555 Lynas Lane
Special Bans/by-laws: Solid waste & recycling regulation bylaw; ESA bylaw; storm sewer bylaw; pollution prevention
Hazardous Waste Depot or Facility: paint, pesticides & solvents only to depot at 5555 Lynas Lane.
Compost Sites: Yes *Composters subsidized:* Yes
Water & Wastewater Treatment:
Responsibility of Greater Vancouver Regional District
Other Initiatives:
Programs include: Advisory Committee on Environment; Environmental Purchasing Policy & Guideline; Partners for Beautification; State of Environment Report; Environmental Project Handbook; Partners for Climate Protection

Saanich, page 688
Waste Management:
Capital Regional District responsible for waste disposal & recycling; Saanich responsible for collection
Special Bans/by-laws: Watercourse; tree preservation; deposit of fill; floodplane development permit area; streamside development permit area; urban outdoor burning ban
Water & Wastewater Treatment:
Responsibility of Capital Regional District
Other Initiatives:
Production of an environmentally significant areas atlas; Saanich Native Plant Salvage Program; Curbside Pickup program; Paint can & garden waste drop off; Transportation demand management; Environmental management plan; Garry Oak Restoration Program; LEED Gold or Silver rating for new municipal buildings; Pesticide Reduction Initiative

Salmon Arm, page 684
Waste Management:
Responsibility of the Columbia Shuswap Regional District
Water & Wastewater Treatment:
Water sources are East Canoe Creek & Shuswap Lake; Storage & distribution form pump stations & 11 reservoirs; Sewage treatment at Waste Water Treatment Plant, 250/832-3500

Other Initiatives:
SCADA computer program to monitor water & sewer systems

Sidney, page 684
Waste Management:
Waste collection & composting pickup contracted to Evergreen Industries (Alpine Disposal), 250/474-5145; Waste management & recycling responsibility of Capital Regional District
Special Bans/by-laws: Tree Preservation Bylaw; Backyard burning ban
Water & Wastewater Treatment:
Responsibility of the Capital Regional District

Skeena-Queen Charlotte, page 679
Waste Management:
All aspects of waste management on the Queen Charlotte Islands & recycling in all areas responsibility of the regional district
Number of landfill sites: 1
Transfer Station(s): 3 island transfer stations
Recycling: Depot; Depot locations: Prince Rupert Envirocenter, Port Edward Drop-Off station, 2 mainland urban drop-off stations, 3 island drop-off locations with limited recycling
Other Initiatives:
Waste management user fees policies; Waste collection limit for each island household; Agricultural Land Reserve, Queen Charlotte Islands; Recycling education & training

Squamish, page 688
Waste Management:
Waste collection contracted to Carney's Waste Systems, 604/892-5604
Number of landfill sites: 1
Solid Waste Disposal Fees: $80/tonne
Recycling: Both Curbside & Depot
Water & Wastewater Treatment:
Water source is Powerhouse Springs; Mashiter Creek & Stawamus River are emergency water sources; Water treatment includes chlorination; Wastewater treatment at Mamquam & Central plants, operated & maintained by municipal crews
Other Initiatives:
Water conservation strategy; Expansion of Mamquam (wastewater) plant; Squamish estuary management plan

Squamish-Lillooet, page 679
Waste Management:
Number of landfill sites: 3
Solid Waste Disposal Fees: $65-80/tonne & $10/cubic metre
Clean Fill Fee: Yes
Transfer Station(s): 3 sites
Water & Wastewater Treatment:
Devine Water System, D'Arcy; Pemberton North Water System, Pemberton; Bralorne Water System, Bralorne Sewage System, Bralorne; Furry Creek Water & Sewage System, Furry Creek.
Other Initiatives:
Squamish Coast demonstration garden; Subsidized vermibins, with training session; 3Rs educator community workshops, plus composting & household hazardous waste community outreach programs; Composting facility feasibility study for southern region; Study to reduce construction & demolition waste; Application to construct new transfer station & recycling centre, south of Pemberton

Summerland, page 689
Waste Management:
Number of landfill sites: 1
Solid Waste Disposal Fees: $55/tonne
Recycling: Depot; Depot at 9119 Peach Orchard Rd.
Composters subsidized: Yes
Water & Wastewater Treatment:
Trout Creek Chlorinator; Garnett Valley Chlorinator; Wastewater Treatment Plant, Trout Creek
Other Initiatives:
Establishment of Agricultural Advisory Committee, committee@summerland.ca

Sunshine Coast, page 679
Waste Management:
SCRD contracts for residential garbage collection
Number of landfill sites: 2
Solid Waste Disposal Fees: $60/tonne
Recycling: Depot; Sechelt & Pender Harbour Landfills offer recycling programs
Water & Wastewater Treatment:
Region operates & maintains sewage treatment facilities in West Howe Sound, Elphinstone, Halfmoon Bay & Pender Harbour;

Page numbers refer to full profile.

Municipal Waste Management and Water & Wastewater Treatment / Manitoba

Water purification & treatment facilities are at Chapman Creek & Gray Creek
Other Initiatives:
1 garbage can/household/week; Fee for extra garbage; After July 2002 all toilets installed in SCRD water service area meet low-flow requirements; Water Efficiency Award Program for non-residential buildings; Free mulch available from yard waste drop off at landfills; Paint Care Depot & Product Care Depot at Sechelt Landfill site; Sharesheds at Sechelt & Pender Harbour Landfills; Annual Spring Cleanup program

Surrey, page 684
Waste Management:
Waste management responsibility of Greater Vancouver Regional District; Collection of garbage, recyclables & yard waste responsibility of city; Waste collection contracted to Waste Management Inc., 604/520-7800
Solid Waste Disposal Fees: $65/tonne
Transfer Station(s): Surrey Transfer Station, 9770 - 192 St., Surrey; Coquitlam Transfer Station, 1200 United Blvd., Coquitlam; Waste trucked to C
Recycling: Both Curbside & Depot
Hazardous Waste Depot or Facility: Metro Material Recovery; International Paper Industries; Willowbrook Recycling Depot
Water & Wastewater Treatment:
Water treatment responsibility of Greater Vancouver Regional District; Maintenance & operation of sanitary sewer system responsibility of city
Other Initiatives:
Environmental education programs; Large item collections; Water conservation; Protection of environmentally sensitive areas; Adopt a street neighbourhood litter stewardship program; Partners in Parks programs; Releaf program tree planting initiative; Stream restoration projects; Reduction in use of chemical fertilizers, pesticides & herbicides

Terrace, page 685
Waste Management:
Disposal responsibility of the regional district. Waste collection contracted to Residential City Collection, 250/635-6311.
Number of landfill sites: 1
Recycling: Depot; Terrace Bottle Depot, 3098 Kofoed Dr
Hazardous Waste Depot or Facility: Paint & Consumer Product Stewardship Program; Terrace Bottle Depot, 250/635-6909
Composters subsidized: Yes
Water & Wastewater Treatment:
Sewage treatment plant, 5123 Graham Ave.; fluoridation & chlorination water treatment facilities.
Other Initiatives:
Curbside collection of compost; free spring & fall cleanup collection; re-use area at Terrace Landfill, Kalum Lake Dr.; water conservation program, including publication of household guide to water efficiency.

Thompson-Nicola, page 679
Waste Management:
Responsible for waste management in the regional district, except for the City of Kamloops. Region has 32 container sites. Five of the landfill sites & twelve of the container sites are controlled access.
Number of landfill sites: 5
Solid Waste Disposal Fees: $31-$103/load, depending on size of load (demolition & land clearing debris only)
Special Bans/by-laws: Landfills not authorized to accept special wastes, biomedical wastes, waste oil or raw sewage

Vancouver, page 685
Waste Management:
Number of landfill sites: 1; *Landfill Capacity:* 40 years
Solid Waste Disposal Fees: $65/tonne
Transfer Station(s): Vancouver South Transfer Station, 377 West Kent Ave. North, Vancouver
Recycling: Both Curbside & Depot; Depots located at Vancouver South Transfer Station; Recycling Depot & Yard Trimmings Drop Off, 377 West Kent Ave. North
Special Bans/by-laws: Gypsum ban; paper products; garbage collection limit is 2 bags or cans per week; city stickers available for purchase for extra garbage
Hazardous Waste Depot or Facility: Go Green Depot & Recycling, East Van Bottle Depot, Joe's Bottle Depot
Compost Sites: Yes *Composters subsidized:* Yes
Water & Wastewater Treatment:
Iona Island Sewage Treatment Plant, owned & operated by Greater Vancouver Sewage & Drainage District
Other Initiatives:
Keep Vancouver Spectacular annual cleanup campaign; annual leaf removal program; apartment recycling service; sale of compost from Yard & Garden Trimmings Composting Facility at Vancouver landfill; rain barrel program; demonstration gardens to promote water conservation, backyard composting, worm bins; industrial water conservation programs; automating garbage & yard trimmings collection; landfill gas cogeneration system 5.5 megawatts, heats tomato green house; automated garbage & yard trimmings in various sized containers, fee based on

Vernon, page 685
Waste Management:
Disposal responsibility of North Okanagan Regional District; Waste collection contracted to O.K. Environmental Waste System Ltd., 250/549-3234
Recycling: ; Collection contracted to Alson Waste Systems, 1-888-547-6961
Water & Wastewater Treatment:
City of Vernon Water Reclamation Plant, 2400 - 43 St., Vernon, 250/542-9825; Greater Vernon Water Utility oversees supply & distribution, 250/542-8410; City's utilities division is responsible for wastewater treatment
Other Initiatives:
Two-bag non-recyclable garbage limit per week; Spring chipping program; Spring & fall collection of leaves & garden refuse; Christmas Tree Disposal

Victoria, page 685
Waste Management:
Residential collecion by the City of Victoria; Commercial waste collection contracted out by owners of property
Number of landfill sites: 1; *Landfill Capacity:* 44 years, Hartland Landfill
Solid Waste Disposal Fees: $82/tonne
Recycling: Both Curbside & Depot; Pickup by Ellice Recycle; Depots at Hartland Landfill & Ellise Recycle
Special Bans/by-laws: Stormwater quality
Hazardous Waste Depot or Facility: Hartland Landfill & Ellice Recycle
Composters subsidized: Yes
Water & Wastewater Treatment:
Responsibility of Capital Regional District
Other Initiatives:
Victoria Harbour Environmental Protection Plan; Pilot program in conjunction with Capital Regional District to enhance composting by removing kitchen waste

West Vancouver, page 689
Waste Management:
Collection & disposal responsibility of municipality's Engineering & Transportation Division
Solid Waste Disposal Fees: Yes
Recycling: Both Curbside & Depot; North Shore Recyling Drop-off Depot
Composters subsidized: Yes
Water & Wastewater Treatment:
Responsibility of Greater Vancouver Regional District
Other Initiatives:
Opening of Citrus Wynd Wastewater Treatment Plant; Product Care organization responsible for collection of hazardous waste; East Lake Micro-generation Project

White Rock, page 686
Waste Management:
Waste collection responsibility of city operations department; Collection of recyclables for multi-family & commercial properties contracted to Encorp Pacific (Canada), 604/473-2400
Recycling: Both Curbside & Depot; Four cardboard recycling depots
Water & Wastewater Treatment:
Responsibility of Epcor White Rock Water Inc., 604/536-7556
Other Initiatives:
Branch chipping, rubbish removal & collection of green waste for fee; Tree management

Williams Lake, page 686
Waste Management:
Waste management responsibility of Cariboo Regional District
Transfer Station(s): Central Cariboo Transfer Station, 5025 Frizzi Rd., 250/392-6379
Recycling: Curbside
Special Bans/by-laws: Water Management Bylaw
Water & Wastewater Treatment:
Water management responsibility of City Municipal Services Dept., Water & Sewer Division

Other Initiatives:
Share Shed

Manitoba

Brandon, page 689
Waste Management:
Number of landfill sites: 1; *Landfill Capacity:* 50 years
Solid Waste Disposal Fees: $34/tonne
Clean Fill Fee: Yes; $1.30/tonne
Recycling: Both Curbside & Depot; Depot locations, 1st St & Richmond Ave., Rideau Park, Canada Games Sportsplex, 34th St. & Victoria Ave., Westridge Community Centre, Capitol Theatre, Brandon Shoppers Mall, Material Recovery Facility, Eastview Landfill Site, 3000 Victoria Ave. E.
Special Bans/by-laws: Pesticide Use Bylaw
Hazardous Waste Depot or Facility: twice yearly, pending available funding
Compost Sites: No *Composters subsidized:* Yes
Water & Wastewater Treatment:
City of Brandon Water Treatment Plant, 108 - 26th St. North, 204/729-2190,.; Municipal Wastewater Treatment Facility, 4040 Victoria Ave. East; Industrial Wastewater Treatment Facility, Richmond Ave. E.; email: wwtp@brandon.ca
Other Initiatives:
Implementation of City's Green Space Master Plan; Two hazardous waste days/year in May & Oct. at Civic Works Complex; Spring & Fall Clean Up; Community Clean-up events; Methane gas recovery; Bio-Diesel program; Vegetable (Grocer) Composting

Hanover, page 690
Waste Management:
Number of landfill sites: 1
Recycling: Both Curbside & Depot
Composters subsidized: No
Water & Wastewater Treatment:
Region owns & operates water systems in Grunthal & Kleefeld Co-Op

Portage La Prairie, page 689
Waste Management:
Waste collection contracted to International Paper Industries.
Number of landfill sites: 1; *Landfill Capacity:* 40 years
Solid Waste Disposal Fees: $25/tonne
Recycling: Both Curbside & Depot; Depot located at 700 Phillips St., 204/239-8346. Operation of recycling depot contracted to Portage & District Recycling Inc.
Special Bans/by-laws: User pay waste collection; two-bag limit per five-day cycle, extra bags must have a $1.00 waste collection tag
Hazardous Waste Depot or Facility: Yes
Compost Sites: Yes *Composters subsidized:* Yes
Water & Wastewater Treatment:
Responsibility of the city; Water pollution control facility at 400 River Rd.; Water treatment plant at 120 - 130 Yellowquill Trail; Water Pollution Control, 204/239-8360, Fax: 204/239-8364; Water Treatment Plant, 204/239-8374, Fax: 204/239-8371
Other Initiatives:
Tree disposal site; Christmas Tree collection program; Annual household hazardous waste day; Annual spring & fall curbside yard waste pickup

St. Andrews, page 690
Waste Management:
Number of landfill sites: 2
Recycling: ; Depot locations: Earl Grey Road Landfill, Clandeboye (Bell Road) Landfill, Harry's Foods, Hwy 9 & St. Andrews Rd.)

Springfield, page 690
Waste Management:
Contracted to BI (204/633-9730), Canadian Waste (204/956-6360) & G.H. Sanitation (204/866-3200)
Solid Waste Disposal Fees: $22.50/tonne
Recycling: Both Curbside & Depot; Hillside & Oakwood transfer stations
Water & Wastewater Treatment:
Oakbank & Dugald water treatment stations

Thompson, page 690
Waste Management:
Waste disposal site is owned & operated by the local government district of Mystery Lake; Waste collection responsibility of city

Recycling: Both Curbside & Depot; Thompson Recycling Centre, 204/677-7991, Fax: 204/778-7844; Several depots throughout the city
Water & Wastewater Treatment:
Water treatment plant is owned & operated by Inco Ltd.; Water distribution responsibility of city; City of Thompson Sewage Treatment Plant, Nelson Rd.
Other Initiatives:
Spring Cleanup Program

Winnipeg, page 690
Waste Management:
Number of landfill sites: 1
Solid Waste Disposal Fees: $22.50/tonne
Recycling: Both Curbside & Depot; 6 depot locations, Customer Service Centre: 204/986-5858
Hazardous Waste Depot or Facility: Collection depot at 65 Trottier Bay, 204/925-9615 (Miller Environmental Corp.)
Composters subsidized: Yes
Water & Wastewater Treatment:
Wastewater treatment plants: North End, West End, & South End Water Pollution Control Centres; New water treatment plant being built at Deacon Reservoir
Other Initiatives:
Septic waste hauler licensing & monitoring; Abandoned landfill monitoring; Bio-solid application service offered to agricultural land holders; Ozone-depleting substance appliance collection & disposal; Christmas tree, bulk metal & used tire recycling programs; Flood control education; Land drainage collection; Dead animal collection & disposal

New Brunswick

Bathurst, page 690
Waste Management:
Waste collection responsibility of city above ground operational services department; Waste management responsibility of the Commission des déchets solides de Nepisiguit-Chaleur
Water & Wastewater Treatment:
Water treatment plant & waste water treatment plant operations responsibility of city utilities department

Commission de gestion des déchets solides de la péninsule Acadienne (COGEDES), page 758
Waste Management:
Responsible for the municipalities of Caraquet, Tracadie-Sheila, St-Isidore, Shippagan, Lamèque, Maisonnette, Grande-Anse, Bas-Caraquet, Paquetville, Saint-Léolin & Bertrand; Waste is transported to Red Pine landfill in Allardville, in Nepisiguit-Chaleur Solid Waste Commission region
Transfer Station(s): Station operated by MDI
Other Initiatives:
Special household hazardous waste collection days

Commission de gestion enviro ressources du Nord-Ouest (COGERNO), page 758
Waste Management:
Number of landfill sites: 1
Solid Waste Disposal Fees: Yes
Recycling: Depot; 30 recycling depots throughout the region
Other Initiatives:
Annual household hazardous waste day

Dieppe, page 691
Waste Management:
Waste management responsibility of Westmorland-Albert Solid Waste Corporation; Waste collection responsibility of city
Special Bans/by-laws: Water conservation bylaw; Backwater valver bylaw
Water & Wastewater Treatment:
Management, operation & maintenance of water distribution responsibility of city public works department; Maintenance of sanitary & storm sewer components responsibility of city
Other Initiatives:
Three special waste collections & two hazardous waste collections each year; Construction of second water reservoir; Increased pump capacity & pumping station improvements in 2005

Edmundston, page 691
Waste Management:
Waste collection contracted to Gallant Entreprises Ltée, 506/739-9390.
Hazardous Waste Depot or Facility: Fire & Rescue Dept., 7 Canada Rd.

Water & Wastewater Treatment:
Wastewater treatment lagoon
Other Initiatives:
Special collections each month

Fredericton, page 691
Waste Management:
Responsibility of Fredericton Region Solid Waste Commission
Number of landfill sites: 1
Solid Waste Disposal Fees: $61/tonne (household, ICI); $30.50/tonne (segregated construction & demolition waste)
Recycling: Both Curbside & Depot; Beverage container redemption centres; Recycling Hotline: 506/453-9938
Hazardous Waste Depot or Facility: Depot at Fredericton Landfill, Alison Blvd.; HHW Info: 506/453-9938
Water & Wastewater Treatment:
Water Treatment Plant, off Woodstock Rd., operated by the city's water & sewer division; Barker St. Treatment Plant is operated by Fredericton Area Pollution Control Commission; City's water & sewer division also operates 2 sewage treatment facilities
Other Initiatives:
Backyard Composting Display Site at Fredericton Region Sanitary Landfill, 1775 Alison Blvd., Fredericton

Fredericton Region Solid Waste Commission, page 758
Waste Management:
Serves the following areas: Fredericton Junction, Nackawic, Millville, Keswick, Dumfries, New Maryland, Chipman, Estey Bridge, Stanley, Cambridge Narrows, Lincoln, Oromocto, Tracy, Gagetown, Fredericton, Minto.
Number of landfill sites: 1
Solid Waste Disposal Fees: $59/tonne (residential/ICI); $29.50/tonne (construction/demolition material)
Recycling: Both Curbside & Depot; 5 depots in Oromocto, Minto, Stanley, Cambridge-Narrows, Fredericton
Hazardous Waste Depot or Facility: Depot at Fredericton landfill, 790 Wilsey Rd. South
Other Initiatives:
Recycling at Work program in the Fredericton & Oromocto areas.

Fundy Region Solid Waste Commission, page 758
Waste Management:
Commission serves the following municipalities: Saint John, Grand Bay-Westfield, Hampton, Quispamsis, Rothesay, St. Martins, plus 10 parishes
Number of landfill sites: 1
Solid Waste Disposal Fees: $108/tonne (municipal & commerical waste); $28/tonne (construction & demolition waste); $45/tonne (compostable material)
Recycling: Depot; 23 recycling depots located throughout the region
Hazardous Waste Depot or Facility: Crane Mountain Landfill, 10 Crane Mountain Rd., Saint John
Composters subsidized: Yes
Other Initiatives:
Sale of compost

Kent County Solid Waste Commission, page 758
Waste Management:
Waste is transported to the Westmorland-Albert Regional Wet/Dry Processing Facility & Sanitary Landfill, Berry Mills.
Transfer Station(s): Located at Bouctouche, operated by Tiru NB, Inc.
Recycling: ; Westmorland-Albert Solid Waste Corporation Dry plant
Hazardous Waste Depot or Facility: WASWC Household Hazardous Waste Depot
Composters subsidized: Yes
Other Initiatives:
Compost (wet waste) is sent to the WASWC Wet plant; Recycling wet/dry program; WASWC Mobile Household Hazardous Waste Unit

Kings County Region Solid Waste Commission, page 758
Waste Management:
Waste from transfer station is transported to the Westmorland-Albert Solid Waste Corporation's sanitary landfill site
Transfer Station(s): Yes

Miramichi, page 691
Waste Management:
Responsibility of the Northumberland Waste Commission; waste

collection responsibility of the city; waste is transported to the Red Pine Solid Waste Disposal Site in Allardville
Water & Wastewater Treatment:
Water & Wastewater treatment plants
Other Initiatives:
Consulting Engineers of Canada Award of Merit for the Paul J. Hayes Wastewater Treatment Plant project

Moncton / Ville de Moncton, page 691
Waste Management:
Responsibility of the Westmorland Albert Solid Waste Corporation.
Number of landfill sites: 1; *Landfill Capacity:* 100 years
Solid Waste Disposal Fees: $53.60/tonne
Hazardous Waste Depot or Facility: Westmorland Albert Solid Waste Corporation sponsors events twice per year
Composters subsidized: Yes
Water & Wastewater Treatment:
Responsibility of the Greater Moncton Sewerage Commission, Riverview NB; Construction of a new water treatment plant under consideration.
Other Initiatives:
Annual spring clean-up week; Christmas tree mulching program.

Nepisiguit-Chaleur Solid Waste Commission, page 758
Waste Management:
NCSWC operates the Red Pine landfill at Red Pine Station which accepts waste from the following commissions: Nepisiguit-Chaleur Solid Waste Commission, Northumberland Solid Waste Commission, COGEDES Transfer Station, Restigouche Solid Waste Corporation
Number of landfill sites: 1

Northumberland Solid Waste Commission, page 758
Waste Management:
Waste is transported to the Red Pine Sanitary Landfill in the Nepisiguit-Chaleur Solid Waste Commission region
Recycling: Depot
Other Initiatives:
Paper, cardboard, plastic & metal can recyclying program, with depots located in the city of Miramichi & throughout Northumberland County

Quispamsis, page 692
Waste Management:
Town issues licenses to private collectors for waste collection. Town supports recycling & composting programs of the Fundy Region Solid Waste Commission. Fundy Region Solid Waste Commission serves town through operation of the Crane Mountain Landfill, 506/738-1200, Fax: 506/738-1207.
Water & Wastewater Treatment:
Responsibility of the municipality; 13 wastewater pumping stations; 1 expanded & enlarged wastewater treatment plant

Restigouche Solid Waste Corporation, page 758
Waste Management:
Waste from the Restigouche Transfer Station is transported to the Red Pine landfill site in Allard
Transfer Station(s): Transfer station operated by MDI
Recycling: Depot; 9 recycling depots throughout region for cardboard & paper

Riverview, page 692
Waste Management:
Serviced by Westmoreland-Albert Solid Waste Corporation
Other Initiatives:
Spring & Fall Clean Ups; Christmas Tree Pick Up

Rothesay, page 692
Waste Management:
Waste collection contracted to Dominion Refuse, 506/633-8986; Waste management responsibility of Fundy Region Solid Waste Commission, which manages Crane Mountain Landfill, 506/738-1212, Fax: 506/738-1207.
Water & Wastewater Treatment:
Water Treatment Plant; Two wastewater treatment lagoons & 11 wastewater pumping stations; Water operations monitoring is contracted to Rutter Engineering & Automation Inc. & Zenon Environmental Inc.
Other Initiatives:
Curbside collection of compost

Saint John, page 692
Waste Management:
City issues licenses to waste collectors; Fundy Region Solid

Municipal Waste Management and Water & Wastewater Treatment / Newfoundland & Labrador

Waste Commission serves the city through the operation of the Crane Mountain landfill, a recycling depot program & a community composting program (506/738-1200; Fax: 506/738-1207)

South West Solid Waste Commission, page 759
Waste Management:
Commission serves the following: Blacks Harbour, St. Andrews, St. George, St. Stephen, Grand Manan, Canterbury, Harvey, McAdam, Meductic, Charlotte County, York County, Carleton County. Waste collection contracted to private companies. Contracting is the responsibility of the municipality or local municipal services representative.
Number of landfill sites: 1
Solid Waste Disposal Fees: $68.50/tonne (household waste); $20/tonne (construction/demolition material)
Recycling: Depot; 12 locations
Hazardous Waste Depot or Facility: Hemlock Knoll Landfill Site Lawrence Station
Composters subsidized: Yes
Other Initiatives:
Compost demonstration site, at Hemlock Knoll landfill site. Construction of new recycling plant.

Valley Solid Waste Commission, page 759
Waste Management:
Waste disposal with two NB landfills & 1 transfer station contracted to commission
Recycling: Depot; Several community recycling depots
Other Initiatives:
Household hazardous waste round-up events

Westmorland-Albert Solid Waste Corporation, page 759
Waste Management:
Serves the following areas: Alma, Cap-Péle, Dieppe, Dorchester, Hillsborough, Moncton, Memramcook, Petitcodiac, Port Elgin, Riverside-Albert, Riverview, Sackville, Salisbury, Shediac; Waste collection is the responsibility of municipalities
Number of landfill sites: 1
Solid Waste Disposal Fees: $53.58/tonne (mixed waste); $20/tonne (construction & demolition waste)
Transfer Station(s): Yes
Hazardous Waste Depot or Facility: Mobile HHW recovery unit operates in the spring & fall
Other Initiatives:
Christmas tree mulching; Wet/dry source separation program includes curbside collection & transportation to WASWC Waste Management Facility; Electronic recycling program; Rechargeable battery recycling program

Newfoundland & Labrador

Conception Bay South, page 693
Waste Management:
Waste collection contracted to Bishop's Service Ltd.
Water & Wastewater Treatment:
Topsail sewage treatment plant, Goodland Rd.
Other Initiatives:
Bulk garbage bins at Topsail Treatment Plant

Corner Brook, page 693
Waste Management:
Waste collection is contracted to Murphy Bros. Ltd., 709/634-3345
Number of landfill sites: 1; *Landfill Capacity:* 11 years
Solid Waste Disposal Fees: Schedule as per type of vehicle & cubic meters
Recycling: Both Curbside & Depot; Depot at Scotia Recycling
Special Bans/by-laws: Voluntary pesticide ban
Water & Wastewater Treatment:
Treatment contracted to City of Cornerbrook, 709/637-1595; Chlorine treatment plants located in Trout Pond, Second Pond, Burnt Pond
Other Initiatives:
Annual "Clean Up" period each spring; Special household hazardous waste collection days, with collection site designated, in cooperation with Island Waste Management; Annual Earth "Car Free" day; New solid waste collection, contact A-1 Transportation

Gander, page 694
Waste Management:
Number of landfill sites: 1
Solid Waste Disposal Fees: No
Clean Fill Fee: No
Recycling: Depot
Special Bans/by-laws: Municipal wildlife stewardship agreement
Compost Sites: Yes
Water & Wastewater Treatment:
Beaverwood Sewage Treatment Plant, Navy Rd.; Gander Bay Road Wastewater Treatment Plant, Gander Bay Rd.
Other Initiatives:
Household hazardous waste day; Cleanup Week

Grand Falls-Windsor, page 694
Waste Management:
Trans Canada Hwy. Landfill closed; New Bay Rd. Regional Landfill site, managed by Exploits Regional Services Board, now serves the town
Recycling: Curbside
Other Initiatives:
Spring Clean-up; Household Hazardous Waste Collection program handled by the Multi-Materials Stewardship Board

Mount Pearl, page 694
Waste Management:
Recycling: Curbside
Hazardous Waste Depot or Facility: 59 Clyde Ave.
Water & Wastewater Treatment:
Mt. Pearl's water supplied by Bay Bulls Big Pond Water Treatment Plant; Regional water system administered by Regional Water Authority
Other Initiatives:
Water conservation program; Energy management control system for major city facilities; Household hazardous waste collection twice a year; Adopt-a-Park; Slam Dunk your Junk; Community clean-ups; Bulk garbage collection; Construction of sewage treatment plant for Mount Pearl, St. John's & Paradise

St. John's, page 694
Waste Management:
Recycling provided by Scotia Recycling (1990) Ltd.
Number of landfill sites: 1; *Landfill Capacity:* 30+ years
Solid Waste Disposal Fees: $23/tonne
Clean Fill Fee: No
Special Bans/by-laws: Cardboard ban
Composters subsidized: No
Water & Wastewater Treatment:
Bay Bulls Big Pond Regional Water Facility, 709/745-1870; Windsor Lake Water Treatment Facility, 709/576-8391
Other Initiatives:
Storm drain marking program; Household hazardous waste day; Christmas tree mulching; Leaf recycling; "Blue Thumb" program

Northwest Territories

Yellowknife, page 695
Waste Management:
Waste collection contracted to Kavanaugh Bros Ltd. Waste Removal Services, 403/873-2811
Number of landfill sites: 1
Solid Waste Disposal Fees: $15/tonne (regular domestic waste); $22/tonne (construction & demolition waste)
Clean Fill Fee: No
Recycling: Depot; Depot locations: Solid Waste Management Facility; Co-op parking lot; Pool/Arena parking lot; Schooldraw Ave. & Franklin Ave.
Water & Wastewater Treatment:
City's Department of Public Works & Engineering responsible for water treatment & sewage disposal facilities
Other Initiatives:
Used motor oil collected at baling facility at the Solid Waste Management Facility; Annual spring & fall clean up; Adopt-A-Street; Environmental Spill Line, 867/820-8130; Community energy plan

Nova Scotia

Annapolis County, page 696
Waste Management:
Waste collection & disposal responsibility of Valley Waste Resource Management Authority
Water & Wastewater Treatment:
Water supply & sewer systems responsibility of municipality's engineering services

Antigonish County, page 696
Waste Management:
Number of landfill sites: 1

Solid Waste Disposal Fees: $45/tonne
Clean Fill Fee: No
Recycling: Curbside

Cape Breton, page 695
Waste Management:
Incinerator, off Sydney Port Access Rd., 902/563-5592
Recycling: Both Curbside & Depot; Green Island Recycling Facility, Sydport Industrial Park
Compost Sites: Yes
Water & Wastewater Treatment:
The municipality manages 10 water treatment & pumping facilities at the following locations: Sydney, Glace Bay, New Waterford, North Sydney, Louisbourg, Birch Grove, Port Morien, Donkin, Former Radar Base & Coxheath; Water Treatment: 902/562-5509
Other Initiatives:
Water conservation program; Mandatory blue bag recycling program; 5 garbage bag limit per household

Chester District, page 697
Waste Management:
For information about waste collection contact G.E.'s All Trucking, 1-866-303-1103
Number of landfill sites: 1
Recycling: Curbside
Hazardous Waste Depot or Facility: Kaizer Meadow Landfill, 450 Kaizer Meadow Rd.
Other Initiatives:
Adopt-a-Highway; Environment Week; Green Cart program for organics; Composting/Recycling Workshops; Plant-a-Row; Grow & Row; Derelict Vehicle Removal

Colchester County, page 697
Waste Management:
Number of landfill sites: 1; *Landfill Capacity:* 70 years (Regional Balefill & Composting Facility, Kemptown)
Solid Waste Disposal Fees: $60/tonne (mixed garbage)
Recycling: Both Curbside & Depot; Enviro-Depot locations: John Ross & Sons, Truro; Subway Bottle Exchange, Bible Hill; TNT Recycling, Stewiacke; Tatamagouche Recycling, Tatamagouche; Colchester Materials Recovery Facility, Kemptown
Hazardous Waste Depot or Facility: Clean Harbours, 640 McElmon Rd., Debert
Compost Sites: Yes *Composters subsidized:* Yes
Water & Wastewater Treatment:
Wastewater treatment facility handles wastewater from central region areas of Truro, Valley, Salmon River, Bible Hill, Hilden, Lower Truro, Truro Heights & part of Onslow; County also maintains wastewater treatment plants in Tatamagouche, Great Village & Brookfield; Wastewater treatment information, 902/897-3175; Municipality manages only the Tatamagouche Water Utility
Other Initiatives:
Free compost for residents; Spring & Fall clean ups; Christmas tree collection; Free annual removal of derelict vehicles for recycling; Residents are supplied with green carts & small mini-bins for composting; Backyard earth machines are also for sale; In vessel composting program at Waste Management Park in Kemptown; Educational programs

Cumberland County, page 697
Waste Management:
Cumberland Central Landfill operated by Cumberland Joint Services Management Authority, 902/667-5141
Number of landfill sites: 1
Transfer Station(s): Yes
Recycling: Depot; Cumberland Central Recycling Facility, 2052 Littleforks Rd., Littleforks, NS
Special Bans/by-laws: Open Burning Bylaw
Compost Sites: Yes *Composters subsidized:* Yes
Water & Wastewater Treatment:
Amherst Marsh Ultra Violet Treatment Building; Pugwash Sewage Treatment Plant
Other Initiatives:
Enviro-Depots for beverage container refunds, unused paint & automotive batteries; Scheduled collections for household hazardous waste

Halifax Regional Municipality, page 695
Waste Management:
Household hazardous waste depot located behind Material Recycling Facility, Bayers Lake Park; No curbside pickup
Number of landfill sites: 1; *Landfill Capacity:* 22 years
Solid Waste Disposal Fees: $115/tonne
Recycling: Both Curbside & Depot; 23 Enviro-Depots in

Page numbers refer to full profile.

municipality. Material Recycling Facility, 50 Chain Lake Dr., Bayers Lake Park, 902/490-6640
Special Bans/by-laws: Pesticides, solid waste, construction & demolition materials recycling & disposal.
Hazardous Waste Depot or Facility: 50 Chain Link Drive; Bayers Lake Industrial Park, Halifax
Compost Sites: Yes *Composters subsidized:* Yes
Water & Wastewater Treatment:
Wastewater Treatment Division of Environmental Management Services operates & maintains the following municipal facilities: Water Pollution Control Plants at Eastern Passage, Mill Cove, Lakeside/Timberlea, Lockview-MacPherson, Springfield Lake, Middle Musquodoboit, North Preston, Uplands Park & Aerotech; Sewage treatment plants at Steeves Subdivision, Frame Subdivision, Lively Subdivision, Leachate Treatment Facility, Aerotech Water Treatment Plant & Aerotech Biosolids Lagoon; 2004 contract sign
Other Initiatives:
"Streets for Cycling" initiative to improve air quality; "Traffic Demand Management" initiatives, pedestrian facility enhancements, transit incentives, ride sharing programs, road policy & vehicle restrictions; Water resources management study; Halifax Harbour Solutions Project will provide 3 additional advanced-primary treatment plants around the harbour to treat sewage; Construction of new Otter Lake Waste Management Facility, comprising end processor, waste stabilization facility & residual disposal facility; New multi-ye

Hants East District, page 697
Waste Management:
Solid waste collection & transportation contracted to Miller Waste Systems, 902/883-4561
Number of landfill sites: 1
Solid Waste Disposal Fees: Yes
Water & Wastewater Treatment:
2 water utilities & 3 sewage collection & treatment systems are operated by the municipality's public works department for the following communities: Enfield, Elmsdale, Lantz, Milford & Shubenacadie
Other Initiatives:
Water conservation program; Household hazardous waste & paint events; Christmas tree collection; Derelict vehicle removal program; Compost give-away events; Community clean-ups

Hants West District, page 697
Waste Management:
Waste collection contracted to Waste Management of Canada Corp., 902/798-0910
Number of landfill sites: 1; *Landfill Capacity:* .5 year
Solid Waste Disposal Fees: $40/tonne
Clean Fill Fee: No
Recycling: Curbside
Hazardous Waste Depot or Facility: Cogmagun Landfill, 1379 Walton Woods Rd.
Compost Sites: Yes
Water & Wastewater Treatment:
Wastewater treatment plant, Falmouth Water Treatment Plant, 242 Eldridge Rd., Falmouth, NS
Other Initiatives:
Public/private partnership for solid waste disposal

Inverness County, page 697
Waste Management:
Contracted to Leo S. Bourgeois Inc., c/o Terry Bennett, 902/224-1600
Solid Waste Disposal Fees: $75/tonne
Clean Fill Fee: Yes; $30/tonne
Recycling: Curbside
Compost Sites: Yes *Composters subsidized:* Yes
Water & Wastewater Treatment:
Inverness, Judique, Mabour, Port Hood, Whycocomagh
Other Initiatives:
New regional sewage treatment plant & wastewater collection system, replacing two sewage treatment plants in Port Hawkesbury & Port Hastings

Kings County, page 696
Waste Management:
Waste management handled by Valley Waste Resource Management, 902/679-1325, Toll free 1-877/927-8300
Water & Wastewater Treatment:
Public Works operates & maintains the Greenwood Water Utility (supplier to village of Greenwood & an area of Aylesford); Wastewater treatment plants: Hants Border, Avonport, Canning, Aldershot, New Minas, Waterville, Aylesford, Greenwood

Lunenburg District, page 697
Waste Management:
Number of landfill sites: 1
Solid Waste Disposal Fees: $110/tonne
Recycling: Both Curbside & Depot; Lunenburg Regional Recycling & Composting Facility, 908 Mullock Rd., Whynott's Settlement, 902/543-2991, Email: recycle@lunrecycle.ns.ca
Hazardous Waste Depot or Facility: Lunenberg Regional Recycling & Composting Facility
Composters subsidized: Yes
Water & Wastewater Treatment:
Municipality collected septage & treatment system, located at Lunenburg Regional Recycling & Composting Facility; Sewage treatment plants, located at New Germany & Conquerall Bank; Public community sewer system at Hebbville is connected to Town of Bridgewater sewage treatment plant
Other Initiatives:
Closure of landfill at Lunenburg Regional Recycling & Composting Facility; New landfill to be located in Chester; Transfer station at Recycling & Composting Facility to operate in 2006

Pictou County, page 698
Waste Management:
Number of landfill sites: 1
Solid Waste Disposal Fees: $75/metric tonne; $55/tonne organics
Recycling: Both Curbside & Depot; Enviro-Depot locations: Johns Bottle & Recycling Depot, Pictou; Bill Stewart Metal & Bottle, New Glasgow; Golden Penney, New Glasgow
Hazardous Waste Depot or Facility: Mount William Landfill Site, Mount William, NS
Composters subsidized: Yes
Water & Wastewater Treatment:
Central Sewage Treatment Plant (part of East River Pollution Abatement System)

Richmond County, page 698
Waste Management:
Sorting of recyclables responsibility of Green Island Recycling Ltd.
Number of landfill sites: 1
Solid Waste Disposal Fees: $35/tonne (sorted material); $70/tonne (unsorted material)
Recycling: Curbside
Water & Wastewater Treatment:
Arichat/Petit de Grat Water Treatment Plant; Evanston Sewage Treatment Plant; Petit de Grat Sewage Treatment Plant; Operation & maintenance of the municipality's water & sewer services responsibility of county public works department
Other Initiatives:
Free curbside collection of "heavy collection" in May & Sept.

Truro, page 696
Waste Management:
Responsibility shared by Truro & Colchester County
Number of landfill sites: 1; *Landfill Capacity:* 35 years
Water & Wastewater Treatment:
Victoria Park Water Treatment Plant; Central Colchester Wastewater Treatment Plant
Other Initiatives:
Spring Clean-up

Yarmouth District, page 698
Waste Management:
Landfill sites have been closed & municipal waste is now deposited at the transfer station, to be shipped to Queens Co., located in the Municipality of the District of Yarmouth; Waste collection is contracted to Wasteco Ltd., 902/742-7707
Solid Waste Disposal Fees: $100/tonne; $79/tonne for compost; $9,118/month for handling recyclables
Water & Wastewater Treatment:
Water & wastewater treatment plant in Port Maitland, Yarmouth County

Nunavut

Iqaluit, page 698
Waste Management:
City's Public Works Dept. responsible for waste collection & management of the municipal landfill in the West 40
Number of landfill sites: 1
Solid Waste Disposal Fees: $5/half ton pick-up truck
Recycling: Both Curbside & Depot
Special Bans/by-laws: Noise by-law; All-terrain vehicle by-law

Water & Wastewater Treatment:
Utilidor responsible for maintenance of Water Treatment Plant & Sewage Treatment Facility, Phone: 867/979-5648, Fax: 867/979-4166

Ontario

Adjala-Tosorontio, page 724
Waste Management:
Waste collection, management & recycling responsibility of County of Simcoe
Water & Wastewater Treatment:
Water & wastewater treatment responsibility of township public works department, water sector; Township's water systems include Colgan, Everett, Hockley, Lisle, Loretto Heights, Rosemont & Weca

Ajax, page 705
Waste Management:
Responsibility of Regional Municipality of Durham, 905/579-5264, 1-800-667-5671
Recycling: Both Curbside & Depot
Hazardous Waste Depot or Facility: Yes
Water & Wastewater Treatment:
Responsibility of Region of Durham
Other Initiatives:
Anti-Idling policy applies to all town staff when using town equipment/vehicles (2 min. idle time), Scott Glew, Fleet Manager, 905/683-3949; Plant health care program, minimize/eliminate use of selective herbicides through aggressive aeration, over seeding/top dragging program, Jeff Stewart, Parks, 905/683-2957

Amherstburg, page 705
Waste Management:
Contracted to D.W. Crowder Trucking
Water & Wastewater Treatment:
Amherstburg Water Treatment Plant; Boblo Island Water Treatment Plant
Other Initiatives:
Yard Waste Depot, 512 Sandwich St. South

Aurora, page 706
Waste Management:
Waste collection contracted to Miller Waste Systems, 1-800-465-5914; Waste management responsibility of York Region
Recycling: Curbside
Water & Wastewater Treatment:
Water & wastewater treatment responsibility of York Region

Barrie, page 706
Waste Management:
Garbage, recyclable & yard waste collection contracted to Frith Regional Waste, 705/733-1200
Number of landfill sites: 1; *Landfill Capacity:* 10 years
Solid Waste Disposal Fees: $105/tonne; $52.50/tonne (leaf & yard waste)
Recycling: Curbside; For occasional & scrap metals only
Hazardous Waste Depot or Facility: HHW Depot at Barrie's Environmental Centre, 272 Ferndale Dr. North
Compost Sites: No *Composters subsidized:* Yes
Water & Wastewater Treatment:
13 wells; 3 reservoirs, 3 water towers & 5 booster stations in 5 pressure zones; Water Pollution Control Centre, 249 Bradford St. Barrie
Other Initiatives:
Low flow toilet rebate program; 1 garbage container limit, cost for additional containers; Organics collection to all single family residences

Belleville, page 706
Waste Management:
Household hazardous waste disposal responsibility of Quinte Waste Solutions, 613/394-6266
Number of landfill sites: 2
Solid Waste Disposal Fees: $99/tonne
Recycling: Curbside; Recyclable collection contracted to Quinte Waste Solutions
Hazardous Waste Depot or Facility: 75 Wallbridge Cres.
Water & Wastewater Treatment:
Belleville Water Distribution & Services, 195 College St. West, PO Box 939, Belleville, 613/966-3651, Fax: 613/969-1944; Belleville Water Treatment, 2 Sidney St., Belleville
Other Initiatives:

Special collections for leaf & yard waste; User-pay garbage system

Bracebridge, page 706
Waste Management:
Operation of domestic waste collection & landfill site responsibility of District of Muskoka
Water & Wastewater Treatment:
Water & sewer operations responsibility of the District of Muskoka

Bradford West Gwillimbury, page 706
Waste Management:
Waste management is the responsibility of the County of Simcoe
Water & Wastewater Treatment:
7 municipal wells plus pump house treatment facilities; Waste water treatment, 225 Dissette St., Bradford
Other Initiatives:
Leaf & yard waste collection; Fall brush collection

Brampton, page 706
Waste Management:
Responsibility of the Regional Municipality of Peel
Water & Wastewater Treatment:
Responsibility of the Regional Municipality of Peel
Other Initiatives:
"Harvest Cleanup" in Oct.; "Spring Cleanup" in April

Brant, page 698
Waste Management:
Recycling & waste collection contracted to Abco Waste Services, 519/751-4599
Number of landfill sites: 1
Solid Waste Disposal Fees: $71.50/tonne
Recycling: Both Curbside & Depot; Paris Recycling Transfer Station; Biggars Lane Landfill
Water & Wastewater Treatment:
St. George Water Supply System, 60 Church St.; Cainsville Distribution System (Brantford WTP); Brant County Airport Water Works, 9 Airport Rd.; Mt. Pleasant Water Supply System, 320 Maple Ave.; Paris Water Supply System, 319 Grand River St. North, 166 West River Rd. & 57 Schuyler St.
Other Initiatives:
5 garbage bag limit; Household hazardous waste day event

Brantford, page 707
Waste Management:
Waste collection contracted to Capital Environmental, 519/756-4444; Recycling processing & WSI
Number of landfill sites: 1; *Landfill Capacity:* 60 years
Solid Waste Disposal Fees: $60/tonne; $140/tonne for mixed loads of wood, metal, cardboard, house
Recycling: Both Curbside & Depot
Special Bans/by-laws: Recently enacted bylaw for maximum of $1,000 financial assistance to rectify private drain cross connections where current home owner not responsible & original builder/developer not available to correct
Hazardous Waste Depot or Facility: Landfill site
Compost Sites: Yes *Composters subsidized:* Yes
Water & Wastewater Treatment:
Water treatment plant operated by city staff after PUC amalgamation; New pre-treatment system for raw water in 1998; New residual management facility added in 2003; Brantford Water Pollution Control Plant owned by city & operated by Ontario Clean Water Agency; 2006 Water rate is 68 cents/cubic metre; 2006 Sewage rate is 65 cents/cubic metre with residential bill capped at 30 cubic metres/month

Brock, page 724
Waste Management:
Responsibility of Regional Municipality of Durham
Water & Wastewater Treatment:
Responsibility of Regional Municipality of Durham

Brockville, page 707
Waste Management:
Waste collection contracted to Waste Services Inc., 613/345-2442
Transfer Station(s): Refuse Transfer Station, 4800 Development Dr., Brockville, 613/345-2442
Recycling: Both Curbside & Depot
Compost Sites: Yes *Composters subsidized:* Yes
Water & Wastewater Treatment:
City of Brockville Water Treatment Plant, 20 Rivers Ave., Brockville; City of Brockville Water Pollution Control Centre, 1807 Hwy. 2 East, Brockville

Other Initiatives:
Annual household hazardous waste collection days; 1 container/week refuse limit

Bruce, page 698
Waste Management:
County responsible for waste management planning; Member municipalities responsible for waste diversion & disposal
Water & Wastewater Treatment:
Responsibility of member municipalities

Burlington, page 707
Waste Management:
Responsibility of Regional Municipality of Halton
Water & Wastewater Treatment:
Responsibility of Regional Municipality of Halton
Other Initiatives:
Preparation of environmental management plan for the city; Adoption of Halton Public Sector Smog Response Plan; Development of a healthy green spaces strategy for public land; Maintenance of tree protection standards; Reduction of road salt & pesticide usage; Use of natural creek channel design; EnerGuide for houses program; Partners for climate protection; Idling awareness campaign

Caledon, page 707
Waste Management:
Responsibility of Regional Municipality of Peel
Special Bans/by-laws: Healthy Horticultural Landscapes By-Law
Water & Wastewater Treatment:
Responsibility of Regional Municipality of Peel
Other Initiatives:
Environmental Progress Office to develop & promote environmental initiatives; Membership in Partners for Climate Protection Program; Smog Response Strategy; Wind Solutions Business Case Committee; Salt & chloride management

Cambridge, page 707
Waste Management:
Responsibility of Regional Municipality of Waterloo
Water & Wastewater Treatment:
Responsibility of Regional Municipality of Waterloo
Other Initiatives:
City Green Strategy is a community action plan for environmental initiatives; Establishment of Cambridge Trails Advisory Committee, which reviews riverbank & greenbelt development; Groundwater Guardian is a volunteer-led groundwater education initiative; Cambridge Environmental Advisory Committee established to advise council

Central Elgin, page 724
Waste Management:
Waste & recyclable collection contracted to Green Lane Environmental Group Ltd.
Recycling: Curbside
Water & Wastewater Treatment:
Belmont Water System; Water treatment lagoons, Belmont

Centre Wellington, page 724
Waste Management:
Responsibility of Wellington County
Water & Wastewater Treatment:
Enviro-Test Laboratories Ltd. performs & analyzes samples collected by the township from Elora & Fergus water supply systems
Other Initiatives:
Leaf collection & Christmas tree pick-up by township's Public Works Department

Chatham-Kent, page 724
Waste Management:
Collection of recyclables by contractor
Solid Waste Disposal Fees: $80/tonne (Ridge Landfill); $55/tonne (Blenheim Landfill)
Transfer Station(s): Yes
Recycling: Both Curbside & Depot
Composters subsidized: Yes
Water & Wastewater Treatment:
The following Sewage Treatment Plants are located in Chatham-Kent: Chatham, Dresden, Ridgetown, Thamesville, Wallaceburg & Wheatley; For further information, contact Chatham-Kent Public Utilities Commission, 325 Grand Ave., East, Chatham, Phone: 519/436-0119, Email: CKpuc@chatham-kent.ca
Other Initiatives:

Annual household hazardous waste days; Leaf & yard waste collection plus 7 depots

Clarence-Rockland, page 708
Waste Management:
Number of landfill sites: 1
Solid Waste Disposal Fees: $70/1-7 ton truck
Transfer Station(s): Industrielle St., Rockland
Recycling: Curbside
Special Bans/by-laws: Watering By-law
Hazardous Waste Depot or Facility: Landfill site, 2335 Lalonde Rd., Bourget
Composters subsidized: Yes
Water & Wastewater Treatment:
Rockland Water Treatment Plant, Edwards St., Rockland; Sewage treatment facility, Industrielle St., Rockland.; Sewage treatment facility operated by Ontario Clean Water Agency
Other Initiatives:
Tags for additional refuse over 3 containers; Spring & fall clean-ups

Clarington, page 724
Waste Management:
Operations Dept. administers waste disposal & recycling contracts
Water & Wastewater Treatment:
Responsibility of Regional Municipality of Durham

Clearview, page 725
Waste Management:
Responsibility of the County of Simcoe
Water & Wastewater Treatment:
Township owns & manages 6 water systems & 6 community center water systems; Water systems with well supplies include Stayner, Creemore, New Lowell, Buckingham Woods, Colling-Woodlands & McKean

Cobourg, page 708
Waste Management:
Responsibility of the County of Northumberland
Water & Wastewater Treatment:
Operation of the water system contracted by the town to Lakefront Utility Services Inc., 207 Division St., Cobourg; Town of Cobourg Water Treatment Plant; Town responsible for wastewater treatment; Water Pollution Control Plant #1, end of University Ave., west shore of Cobourg Creek; Water Pollution Control Plant #2 - Lucas Point, west side of Normar Rd., on shore of Lake Ontario

Collingwood, page 708
Waste Management:
Waste management responsibility of Simcoe County
Water & Wastewater Treatment:
Raymond A. Barker Ultra-Filtration Water Treatment Plant, 2 Raglan St.; Ted Carmichael Reservoir; Water facilities operated by Collingwood Public Utilities

Cornwall, page 708
Waste Management:
Curbside solid waste & recycling contracted to HGC Management Inc., 613/936-6072
Number of landfill sites: 1; *Landfill Capacity:* 35 years
Solid Waste Disposal Fees: $50/tonne (regular waste, scrap metal & white goods)
Recycling: Both Curbside & Depot; Recycling Plant, located at City of Cornwall Landfill site, 613/933-6953
Hazardous Waste Depot or Facility: City of Cornwall Landfill & Household Special Waste Facility, 2590 Cornwall Centre Rd. W.; *Composters subsidized:* Yes
Water & Wastewater Treatment:
Cornwall Water Purification Plant, 861 Second St. West; Cornwall Wastewater Treatment Plant, 2800 Montreal Rd. East
Other Initiatives:
Autumn collection of leaf & yard waste; Hazardous waste days; Christmas tree collection; White goods collection for fee; Free compost

Dufferin, page 699
Waste Management:
Member municipalities responsible for waste management
Other Initiatives:
Organization of household hazardous waste days in partnership with local municipalities; Annual Dufferin Environment Day features litter clean-up of roads & community areas; County awarded consulting contract, in 2002, for the Dufferin County Alternative Waste Diversion & Disposal Plan; Waste

Management Forum & Roundtable discussions organized; Pilot project in process - Dufferin Composts; Weigh our Waste program initiated

Durham, page 699
Waste Management:
Region responsible for disposal of residential solid waste, waste reduction programs, operation of five waste management facilities including a recycling processing centre, as well as blue box collection & marketing of recyclables; Area municipalities responsible for garbage & yard waste collection
Number of landfill sites: 1; *Landfill Capacity:* 25 years
Solid Waste Disposal Fees: $90/tonne for garbage & mixed loads; No charge for source-separated blue box materials & HHW
Recycling: Both Curbside & Depot; 4 depots
Special Bans/by-laws: Regional sewer use
Hazardous Waste Depot or Facility: Oshawa, Port Perry & Brock; Hazardous waste/paint exchange site at Oshawa waste management
Compost Sites: Yes
Water & Wastewater Treatment:
Water supply plants: Ajax, Bowmanville, Newcastle, Oshawa & Whitby; Water pollution control plants: Corbett Creek, Duffin Creek, Newcastle, Harmony Creek, Pringle Creek, Port Darlington & Lake Simcoe
Other Initiatives:
Region operates a 34,000 tonne/year recycling centre; Spring & Fall Newsletter "Durham Works"; Daily radio messages on local stations to promote 3Rs; Mall displays & tours of recycling centres; Electronics recycling; Blue box sales events; Compost giveaways; Wellhead protection program for groundwater supply systems

East Gwillimbury, page 708
Waste Management:
Waste management is the responsibility of the Regional Municipality of York; Waste collection contracted to LaRue's, 905/478-1940
Compost Sites: Yes
Water & Wastewater Treatment:
Responsibility of the Regional Municipality of York
Other Initiatives:
Garbage bag/can limit; Annual clean-up green-up day

Elgin, page 699
Waste Management:
Responsibility of member municipalities
Water & Wastewater Treatment:
Responsibility of member municipalities

Elizabethtown-Kitley, page 725
Waste Management:
Number of landfill sites: 1
Solid Waste Disposal Fees: $22.50/quarter to half ton truck or 8 foot trailer
Recycling: Depot; Located at waste disposal site, 8468 County Rd. 7
Water & Wastewater Treatment:
Township of Elizabethtown-Kitley Water Distribution System; City of Brockville Water Treatment Plant, 20 Rivers Ave., Brockville, serves a portion of Elizabethtown-Kitley
Other Initiatives:
User-pay waste collection & disposal services; Upgrades to water treatment plant; Pitch-In Elizabeth-Kitley Program to clean up roadside garbage

Elliot Lake, page 709
Waste Management:
Number of landfill sites: 1
Water & Wastewater Treatment:
Water treatment plant on Spine Rd., Elliot Lake; Wastewater treatment plant on Scott Rd., Elliot Lake

Erin, page 709
Waste Management:
Responsibility of the County of Wellington
Special Bans/by-laws: Nutrient Management for Certain Livestock Operations

Essa, page 725
Waste Management:
Responsibility of County of Simcoe, 705/735-6901
Water & Wastewater Treatment:
Water treatment contracted to Ontario Clean Water Agency, 1-866-775-7712

Essex, page 709
Waste Management:
Responsibility of the Essex-Windsor Solid Waste Authority (519/776-6441), an agency created by the County of Essex & the City of Windsor
Water & Wastewater Treatment:
Operation of the Union Water Treatment Plant & the Harrow/Colchester South Water Treatment Plant contracted to Ontario Clean Water Agency

Essex, page 699
Waste Management:
Waste management responsibility of Essex-Windsor Solid Waste Authority, Fax: 519/776-6370, Email: info@ewswa.org; Waste collection responsibility of member municipalities
Number of landfill sites: 1
Solid Waste Disposal Fees: $48.50-$54.50/tonne (industrial, commercial & institutional); $7.80/100 kg (residential)
Transfer Station(s): 3460 North Service Rd. East, Windsor; 2021 County Rd. 31, Municipality of Kingsville
Recycling: Both Curbside & Depot; Recycling Centre, 3560 North Service Rd. East, Windsor
Special Bans/by-laws: Pallets, radioactive, biomedical & chemical waste, yard waste, white goods (metal items), tires
Hazardous Waste Depot or Facility: 3450 North Service Rd. East, Windsor; County Rd. 31, Municipality of Kingsville
Composters subsidized: Yes
Water & Wastewater Treatment:
Responsibility of member municipalities
Other Initiatives:
Public education programs; Waste reduction programs; White goods collection & recycling; Reuse Centre, 3450 North Service Rd. East, Windsor; Compost sales; Christmas tree recycling

Fort Erie, page 709
Waste Management:
Responsibility of the Region of Niagara
Water & Wastewater Treatment:
Responsibility of the Region of Niagara
Other Initiatives:
Transportation environmental study report

Frontenac, page 699
Waste Management:
Responsibility of member municipalities
Water & Wastewater Treatment:
Responsibility of member municipalities

Georgian Bluffs, page 725
Waste Management:
Waste collection contracted to Bruce Service Sales & Rentals, 519/363-3811; Recycling collection contracted to Miller Waste Services, 519/373-1855
Number of landfill sites: 1
Solid Waste Disposal Fees: $70/tonne (sorted domestic, commercial & industrial materials); $95/tonne (unsorted)
Recycling: Curbside
Water & Wastewater Treatment:
Responsibility of Veolia Water Canada, 519/376-4640
Other Initiatives:
2005 Environmental Study Report for provision of expanded municipal water supply system; Residential energy efficiency program; 2 bag garbage limit; Bale wrap recycling program for farmers

Georgina, page 709
Waste Management:
Waste management responsibility of the Regional Municipality of York; Waste & blue box collection contracted to Miller Waste Limited, 1-800-465-5914
Water & Wastewater Treatment:
Responsibility of the Regional Municipality of York

Gravenhurst, page 709
Waste Management:
Responsibility of District of Muskoka
Water & Wastewater Treatment:
Responsibility of District of Muskoka

Greater Napanee, page 709
Waste Management:
Garbage & recycling collection contracted to Waste Management, Canadian Waste, 613/549-7100
Number of landfill sites: 3
Solid Waste Disposal Fees: $10/utility trailers, cars, 1/2 & 3/4 ton trucks

Recycling: Curbside
Other Initiatives:
Waste Reduction Week

Greater Sudbury / Grand Sudbury, page 710
Waste Management:
Number of landfill sites: 4
Solid Waste Disposal Fees: $60/tonne
Recycling: Both Curbside & Depot; Recycling Centre, 1825 Frobisher St.
Hazardous Waste Depot or Facility: 1853 Frobisher St.
Composters subsidized: Yes
Water & Wastewater Treatment:
10 wastewater treatment plants; 4 sewage treatment lagoons; David Street Water Treatment Plant; Wanapitei Water Treatment Plant; For more information, 705/560-2022
Other Initiatives:
Adopt-a-road; Derelict motor vehicle removal & recycling program; Annual clean-up blitz; Waste optimization study; Leaf & yard trimmings collection; Garbage bag limit; Landfill diversion areas for items such as scrap metal & white goods, reusable cloth items & electronic waste; Land reclamation program

Grey, page 700
Waste Management:
Waste long-term management strategy responsibility of county
Other Initiatives:
Grey-Owen Sound Waste Management Plan Study carried out by county & city of Owen Sound; Grey County Forest Stewardship Network, established to encourage wise use of forests & natural resources

Grimsby, page 710
Waste Management:
Responsibility of Region of Niagara, 1-800-594-5542 or 905/687-9595
Water & Wastewater Treatment:
Grimsby Water Treatment Plant, 905/945-2840; Maintenance & operation of drinking water distribution system & wastewater collection system responsibility of town environmental services department

Guelph, page 710
Waste Management:
Number of landfill sites: 1
Solid Waste Disposal Fees: $70/tonne
Recycling: Both Curbside & Depot; Waste Resource Innovation Centre, 110 Dunlop Dr.
Hazardous Waste Depot or Facility: Waste Resource Innovation Centre, 110 Dunlop Dr.
Composters subsidized: Yes
Water & Wastewater Treatment:
F.M. Woods Pumping Station, 29 Waterworks Place, waterworks@guelph.ca; Wastewater Treatment Plant, 530 Wellington St., wastewater@guelph.ca
Other Initiatives:
User-pay bulky item collection program; Formation of an environmental advisory committee & pesticide review committee; Outside water use program; City of Guelph Green Plan; Waste Reduction Week; Formation of anti-litter team; Paint plus reuse program; Recycling programs for industries & apartments; Air quality monitoring station; Natural heritage strategy

Guelph-Eramosa, page 725
Waste Management:
Responsibility of County of Wellington, wasteinfo@county.wellington.on.ca
Special Bans/by-laws: Water Use Bylaw; Nutrient Management Bylaw
Water & Wastewater Treatment:
Operation of Rockwood water system (2 wells, a pumping station & standpipe) & Hamilton hamlet water system (3 wells, 3 pumping stations & standpipe) responsibility of township; Wastewater system, with a pre-treatment plant, operated in Rockwood, with further treatment at City of Guelph treatment plant

Haldimand, page 700
Waste Management:
Waste collection contracted to HGC Management
Number of landfill sites: 1
Solid Waste Disposal Fees: $55/1-100 tonnes/month
Transfer Station(s): Canborough Transfer Station
Recycling: Curbside
Water & Wastewater Treatment:
County's Environmental Services Division administers contracts

for water & wastewater; Water treatment plants are the responsibility of Ontario Clean Water Agency; Nanticoke Water Treatment Plant; Dunnville Water Treatment Plant; City of Hamilton supplies Caledonia & Cayuga with treated water; Wastewater treatment responsibility of Veolia Water Canada
Other Initiatives:
Household hazardous waste days; Electronic equipment recycling at Tom Howe Landfill

Haliburton, page 700
Waste Management:
Special Bans/by-laws: Tree Cutting By-Law enforces sustainable, low impact harvesting operations
Other Initiatives:
Adopt-a-Road; Wetland assessment project; Groundwater/source protection project

Halton, page 700
Waste Management:
Waste collection responsibility of region; Waste & recyclables collection contracted to Halton Recycling Limited, 1-888-403-3333
Number of landfill sites: 1; *Landfill Capacity:* 38 years
Solid Waste Disposal Fees: $98/tonne
Clean Fill Fee: Yes; $98/tonne
Special Bans/by-laws: Landfill ban on all blue box materials as well as drywall, tires, scrap metal & hazardous waste
Hazardous Waste Depot or Facility: Halton Waste Management Site
Composters subsidized: Yes
Water & Wastewater Treatment:
Water purification plants: Burlington (3249 Lakeshore Rd.), Georgetown (241 Maple Ave.), Oakville (21 Kerr St.), Kelso (Tremaine Rd./3rd Side Rd.); Wastewater treatment plants: Burlington (1125 Lakeshore Rd.), Acton (202 Churchill Rd. S.), Georgetown (275 Mountainview Rd. S.), Oakville (2195 North Service Rd., 2497 Lakeshore Rd. E., 1385 Lakeshore Rd. W.), Milton (161 Fulton St.)
Other Initiatives:
Construction of new Burloak Water Purification Plant; Development of a blueprint for the Halton Durable Plan: Building our Future; Implementation of the initiatives identified in the new 2006-2010 Halton Waste Management Strategy; Water conservation

Halton Hills, page 710
Waste Management:
Responsibility of the Regional Municipality of Halton
Special Bans/by-laws: Smoking Bylaw
Water & Wastewater Treatment:
Responsibility of the Regional Municipality of Halton
Other Initiatives:
Adopt A Road program; Community Clean Up Days; Water resource management

Hamilton, page 711
Waste Management:
Email: wastemanagement@city.hamilton.on.ca
Number of landfill sites: 1
Recycling: Both Curbside & Depot; Depots located at Dundas Transfer Station, Mountain Transfer Station
Hazardous Waste Depot or Facility: Contract with Hotz Environmental Services Inc., 239 Lottridge St. North
Composters subsidized: Yes
Water & Wastewater Treatment:
The following are owned by the city: Woodward Ave. Water Treatment Facility, 700 Woodward Ave.; Wastewater Treatment Facility, King St.; Wastewater Treatment Facility, Dundas; Main St. Wastewater Treatment Facility, Waterdown; For more information, Email: water-quality@hamilton.ca

Hamilton, page 725
Waste Management:
Responsibility of Northumberland County, 905/372-3329
Special Bans/by-laws: Outside water use restrictions
Water & Wastewater Treatment:
Town of Cobourg Water Treatment Plant; Camborne Water Treatment Plant; Creighton Heights Water Treatment Plant

Hastings, page 700
Waste Management:
Responsibility of member municipalities
Water & Wastewater Treatment:
Responsibility of member municipalities

Hawkesbury, page 711
Water & Wastewater Treatment:
Water pollution control plant, located on Main St. East, is operated by the Ontario Clean Water Agency; Town manages water filtration plant, located at 670 Main St. West
Other Initiatives:
Major upgrade to water pollution control plant

Huntsville, page 711
Waste Management:
Responsibility of District Municipality of Muskoka, 905/645-6764
Water & Wastewater Treatment:
Water & wastewater treatment responsibility of District Municipality of Muskoka

Huron, page 701
Waste Management:
County responsible for waste management planning
Special Bans/by-laws: Forestry Conservation By-law
Water & Wastewater Treatment:
Responsibility of member municipalities
Other Initiatives:
Household hazardous waste disposal program; Water Protection Steering Committe; Huron Clean Water Project; Aggregates Strategy

Ingersoll, page 711
Waste Management:
Waste management responsibility of the County of Oxford
Recycling: Curbside
Water & Wastewater Treatment:
Responsibility of Oxford County, Public Works Department
Other Initiatives:
Annual Special Waste Day for household hazardous waste; Collections for spring rubbish, leaves & Christmas trees

Innisfil, page 711
Waste Management:
All aspects of waste management responsibility of Simcoe County
Recycling: Curbside
Water & Wastewater Treatment:
Water treatment facilities owned & operated by town: Lakeshore Water Filtration Plant, 2155 - 25th Sideroad, Innisfil ON L9S 4V3; Wastewater treatment plant, 1578 St. John's Rd., Innisfil ON L9S 4T9
Other Initiatives:
Two-bag garbage limit, extra bags require $1.25 tags; Special collection for yard waste, brush, large items & Christmas trees

Kawartha Lakes, page 711
Waste Management:
Waste collection contracted to National Waste Services, 1-866-344-1544
Number of landfill sites: 5; *Landfill Capacity:* 25 years
Solid Waste Disposal Fees: $85/tonne
Recycling: Curbside
Hazardous Waste Depot or Facility: Household Hazardous Waste Depot, Fenelon Waste Facility, 341 Mark Rd.
Compost Sites: Yes *Composters subsidized:* Yes
Water & Wastewater Treatment:
The city operates water treatment facilities in Birch Point, Highview Acres, Kinmount, Lindsay, Norland, Palmina, Sonya, Southview Estates, Springdale Gardens, Sturgeon Park & Western Trent; Ontario Clean Water Agency (OCWA) operates water treatment facilities in Bobcaygeon, Canadiana Shores, Fenelon Falls, Janetville, King's Bay, Manorview/Bethany, Mariposa Estates, Oakwood Estates, Omemee, Pinewood/Pontypool, Pleasant Point, Sandwood, Sunny Acres, Victoria Place, Woodfield, Woods of Manilla &
Other Initiatives:
Reuse Centre plus Electronics Recycling Depot, located at Fenelon Waste Facility

Kincardine, page 726
Waste Management:
Waste collection is contracted to Bruce Area Solid Waste Recycling, 1-800-794-9770
Number of landfill sites: 3
Recycling: Curbside
Water & Wastewater Treatment:
Municipality of Kincardine & Ontario Clean Water Agency responsible for Kincardine Water Treatment Plant & sewage treatment plants
Other Initiatives:
Upgrades to 8 municipal water systems

King, page 726
Waste Management:
Waste collection handled by Sandhill Disposal & Recycling Services, 905/505-5252; Region of York provides waste management services for township
Number of landfill sites: 1
Solid Waste Disposal Fees: $5/vehicle
Water & Wastewater Treatment:
Responsibility of Region of York

Kingston, page 712
Waste Management:
Number of landfill sites: 1; *Landfill Capacity:* 2 years
Solid Waste Disposal Fees: $110/tonne
Transfer Station(s): Yes
Recycling: Both Curbside & Depot; Kingston Area Recycling Centre, 196 Lappan's Lane
Hazardous Waste Depot or Facility: 196 Lappan's Lane
Compost Sites: Yes *Composters subsidized:* Yes
Water & Wastewater Treatment:
Kingston Central Water Treatment Plant, 302 King St. West; Kingston West Water Treatment Plant, 80 Sunny Acres Rd.; Ravensview Water Pollution Control Plant, Hwy. #2; Kingston West Water Pollution Control Plant, Days Rd.

Kingsville, page 712
Waste Management:
Waste management responsibility of Essex County; Public Works Dept. is responsible for waste collection
Water & Wastewater Treatment:
Ontario Clean Water Agency operates the Lakeshore West Wastewater Treatment Plant & the Waste Treatment Lagoon
Other Initiatives:
Special collections for grass clippings, brush, leaves & Christmas trees

Kitchener, page 712
Waste Management:
Responsibility of the Regional Municipality of Waterloo
Other Initiatives:
Environmental Strategic Plan: identifying a number of issues & initiatives in the areas of water resources, waste management, growth management, energy systems, resource consumption, natural areas, education & public awareness

Lakeshore, page 712
Waste Management:
Waste management responsibility of Essex-Windsor Solid Waste Authority, 1-800-563-3377
Recycling: Curbside
Water & Wastewater Treatment:
Belle River Water Treatment Plant, 493 Lakeview Dr.; Stoney Point Water Treatment Plant, 6011 St. Clair Rd.; Wheatley Water Treatment Plant (supplier to the Lighthouse Cove Water Distribution system, through an agreement with the Municipality of Chatham-Kent for water supply); Tecumseh Water Treatment Plant, 9725 Riverside Dr. Windsor (supplier to the Tecumseh Water Service Area, through an agreement with the Town of Tecumseh for water supply); Union Water Treatment Plant, Kingsville; Belle Rive
Other Initiatives:
Monthly collection of white goods; Organic waste collection

Lambton, page 701
Waste Management:
County responsible for waste disposal; Member municipalities responsible for composting, recycling & collection; Waste disposal contracted to Canadian Waste Services Inc.
Number of landfill sites: 6; *Landfill Capacity:* County contracts with 2 active private landfills
Solid Waste Disposal Fees: $35/tonne
Clean Fill Fee: No
Hazardous Waste Depot or Facility: Clean Harbours Facility
Water & Wastewater Treatment:
Responsibility of member municipalities
Other Initiatives:
6 household Hazardous Waste collection events; Adopt-a-County Road program

Lambton Shores, page 726
Waste Management:
Waste management responsibility of Lambton County; Waste collection responsibility of City's Community Services Dept.; Recycling handled by Bluewater Recycling Association, 519/228-6678
Composters subsidized: Yes

Water & Wastewater Treatment:
Water & wastewater services managed, operated & maintained by Operations Management International Canada Inc.

Lanark, page 701
Waste Management:
Local municipalities responsible for their own waste & recycling
Water & Wastewater Treatment:
Responsibility of local municipalities

LaSalle, page 713
Waste Management:
Waste management responsibility of Essex-Windsor Solid Waste Authority, 519/776-6441; Waste collection provided by Windsor Disposal, 519/944-8009
Water & Wastewater Treatment:
Water received from ENWIN Utilities Ltd., 519/255-2727

Leamington, page 726
Waste Management:
Waste management responsibility of Essex-Windsor Solid Waste Authority, 1-800-563-3377; Waste collection responsibility of Operations Deptartment
Clean Fill Fee:
Water & Wastewater Treatment:
Leamington is a member municipality of the Union Water Treatment Plant, 1615 Union Ave., Ruthven, operated by the Ontario Clean Water Agency; Leamington Pollution Control Centre

Leeds & Grenville, page 726
Waste Management:
Member municipalities without active landfills have private waste disposal agreements
Water & Wastewater Treatment:
Responsibility of area municipalities
Other Initiatives:
County-wide groundwater management study

Lennox & Addington, page 701
Waste Management:
Responsibility of area municipalities

Lincoln, page 713
Waste Management:
Responsibility of Region of Niagara
Water & Wastewater Treatment:
Responsibility of Region of Niagara

London, page 713
Water & Wastewater Treatment:
The city operates the following Water Pollution Control Plants: Greenway, Pottersburg, Vauxhall, Adelaide, Oxford, Westminster & Lambeth (Southland Park)

Loyalist, page 727
Waste Management:
Waste collection contracted to Canadian Waste Services, 613/549-7100; Recycling services contracted to Kingston Area Recycling Centre, operated by the City of Kingston
Number of landfill sites: 2
Solid Waste Disposal Fees: $105/tonne
Recycling: Both Curbside & Depot
Special Bans/by-laws: Open air burning restrictions; Lawn watering restrictions
Hazardous Waste Depot or Facility: 70 Lappan's Lane, Kingston
Composters subsidized: Yes
Water & Wastewater Treatment:
Fairfield Water Treatment Plant, servicing Amhertsview, Odessa, Harewood & Brooklands; Bath Water Treatment Plant; Bath Water Pollution Control Plant; Amhertsview Water Pollution Control Plant; Odessa Waste Water Treatment Plant, owned & operated by the township
Other Initiatives:
Pay-as-you-throw bag tag program; Large item & free drop-off days at Violet Landfill & Amherst Island Landfill sites; Spring & fall yard waste collections; Disposal of CFC units, subsidized composters; Transit Services (Amhertsview to City of Kingston)

Markham, page 713
Waste Management:
Waste collection responsibility of city waste management division; Waste management responsibility of the Region of York
Recycling: Both Curbside & Depot; Depot locations: Unionville Recycling Depot, Thornhill Recycling Depot, Markham Recycling Depot & Milliken Mills Drop-Off Centre

Water & Wastewater Treatment:
City receives treated water from 4 plants owned & operated by the City of Toronto

Meaford, page 727
Waste Management:
Waste collection contracted to North Grey Sanitation Services, 519/376-0440
Number of landfill sites: 1; *Landfill Capacity:* 9 years
Solid Waste Disposal Fees: $48-78/tonne
Clean Fill Fee: Yes; $48-48/tonne
Recycling: Both Curbside & Depot; Miller St. depot
Hazardous Waste Depot or Facility: 20th St. East, Owen Sound
Compost Sites: Yes *Composters subsidized:* Yes
Water & Wastewater Treatment:
Meaford Water Treatment Plant, 574 Grandview Dr.; Leith Water Treatment Plant, 359466 Bayshore Rd.; Meaford Wastewater Treatment Plant, 35 Grant Ave., Meaford; Wastewater contracted to OCWA, 519/538-3311

Middlesex, page 701
Waste Management:
Responsibility of area municipalities
Special Bans/by-laws: Woodlands Conservation By-law; Liquid Manure Transfer
Other Initiatives:
Clean Water Program, a rural water quality initiative; County residents use City of London Household Hazardous Waste Drop-off Depot

Middlesex Centre, page 727
Waste Management:
Township public works & engineering department responsible for recycling, waste collection & waste disposal; Waste collection contracted to Bluewater Recycling Association, 1-800-265-9799
Recycling: Curbside
Composters subsidized: Yes
Water & Wastewater Treatment:
Operation of all township water & sewer systems responsibility of Ontario Clean Water Agency, 519/641-2116
Other Initiatives:
Hazardous waste & clean-up days

Midland, page 713
Waste Management:
Responsibility of County of Simcoe
Water & Wastewater Treatment:
Water distribution system, including wells, booster pumping stations, storage reservoir sites & a lift station operated & maintained by town; Sewage treatment facility operated by town

Milton, page 714
Waste Management:
Responsibility of Regional Municipality of Halton

Mississauga, page 714
Waste Management:
Responsibility of Regional Municipality of Peel
Special Bans/by-laws: Erosion & sediment control bylaw; Storm sewer use bylaw; Noise bylaw; Debris bylaw; Tree permit bylaw
Water & Wastewater Treatment:
Responsibility of Regional Municipality of Peel
Other Initiatives:
Tree preservation; Leaf collection service; Street tree planting & management of woodlands; Ecological restoration; Parkland naturalization of parks & open spaces; Natural areas survey; Integrated turf management/pesticide reduction program; Bicycle pathways program; City plan environmental policies; Energy management plan; Stormwater channel stabilization & erosion control monitoring; Subwatershed plans; Earth Days & Litter Not campaign; Displays of city & community environmental programs

Mississippi Mills, page 714
Waste Management:
Waste collection contracted to Topps Waste Management, Carleton Place, 613/257-2955 or 1-800-387-5710
Number of landfill sites: 1
Solid Waste Disposal Fees: $80/tonne
Recycling: Both Curbside & Depot; Recycling Transfer Station, Pakenham Landfill Site
Hazardous Waste Depot or Facility: Carleton Place depot
Compost Sites: Yes
Water & Wastewater Treatment:
Ontario Clean Water Agency operates the sewage lagoon & 5 wells

Muskoka, page 702
Waste Management:
Waste management responsibility of the district municipality
Number of landfill sites: 3
Solid Waste Disposal Fees: $95/tonne
Transfer Station(s): Lake of Bays Township: Baysville, Dorset, Sinclair, Dwight; Muskoka Lakes Township: Eveleigh Road; Georgian Bay Township: Tow
Recycling: Curbside
Hazardous Waste Depot or Facility: Hazardous waste day services provided by Brendar Environmental Inc.
Water & Wastewater Treatment:
District municipality's water & sewer operations division is responsible for operation & maintenance of water & sewage treatment plants; Kirby's Beach Water Treatment Plant, Bracebridge Water Works; Gravenhurst Water Treatment Plant, Gravenhurst Water Works; Highway 60 Water Treatment Plant, Huntsville Water Works; Clarke Crescent Well Water System, Port Sydney Water Works; Ferndale Water Treatment Plant, Port Carling Water Works; Beech Avenue Water Treatment Plant, MacTier Water Works; Bala Wat
Other Initiatives:
Household hazardous waste depots: Town of Bracebridge Landfill, Town of Huntsville Madill Church Works Yard, Township of Lake of Bays Dwight Transfer Site, Town of Gravenhurst Landfill, Township of Muskoka Lakes Eveleigh Road Transfer Site, Township of Georgian Bay Baxter Transfer Site; Reuse buildings at most landfills & transfer stations

New Tecumseth, page 714
Waste Management:
Responsibility of County of Simcoe
Water & Wastewater Treatment:
Town provides water & sewer services for the Alliston Water System & the Hillcrest Water System; Wastewater treatment facilities: Sir Frederick Banting WPCP, Regional WPCP, Tottenham WPCP; Contracted to Town of New Tecumseh 705/435-3900

Newmarket, page 714
Waste Management:
Waste management responsibility of the Regional Municipality of York; Waste collection responsibility of Town
Recycling: Curbside
Water & Wastewater Treatment:
Responsibility of the Regional Municipality of York
Other Initiatives:
Yard waste collection; Ccurbside give-away days; Eestablishment of Environmental Advisory Committee with the following subcommittees: education, outreach & stewardship, terrestrial planning & policy, & atmospheric; Green series seminars; Reduction in road salting; Identification of green space areas; Appliance collection

Niagara, page 702
Waste Management:
Waste collection contracted to Canada Waste Services, 905/687-6687; Modern Corporation, 905/262-6000; Household hazardous waste permanent location: Niagara Road 12 Landfill Site, West Lincoln; 7 temporary household hazardous waste locations: Niagara Falls, St. Catharines, Port Colborne, Welland, Fort Erie, Wainfleet & Niagara-on-the-Lake
Number of landfill sites: 5; *Landfill Capacity:* 6-25 years, various sites
Solid Waste Disposal Fees: $60/tonne
Clean Fill Fee:
Recycling: Both Curbside & Depot; Depot locations: Bridge Street Landfill, Fort Erie; Elm Street, Port Colborne; Niagara Road 12, West Lincoln; Humberstone Landfill, Welland; Residential Waste Drop-Off Depot, Walker Industries, Thorold; Niagara Recycling, Niagara Falls
Hazardous Waste Depot or Facility: Niagara Road 12; temporary depots
Compost Sites: Yes *Composters subsidized:* Yes
Water & Wastewater Treatment:
Water & Wastewater Division operates the following water treatment plants: Niagara Falls Water Treatment Plant, 3599 Macklem St., Niagara Falls; Port Colborne Water Treatment Plant, 323 King St., Port Colborne; Grimsby Water Treatment Plant, 300 N. Service Rd., Grimsby; Wastewater treatment plants: Niagara Falls Water Pollution Control Plant (WPCP), 3450 Stanley Ave., Niagara Falls; Port Dalhousie WPCP, 40 Lighthouse Rd., St. Catharines; Port Weller WPCP, 27 Lombardy St., St. Catharines; Welland

Page numbers refer to full profile.

Municipal Waste Management and Water & Wastewater Treatment / Ontario

Other Initiatives:
Organics curbside residential collection

Niagara Falls, page 715
Waste Management:
Responsibility of Regional Municipality of Niagara
Water & Wastewater Treatment:
Responsibility of Regional Municipality of Niagara
Other Initiatives:
Woodlot study to promote stewardship

Niagara-on-the-Lake, page 715
Waste Management:
Waste management responsibility of Regional Municipality of Niagara, 1-800-594-5542
Water & Wastewater Treatment:
Responsibility of the Regional Municipality of Niagara
Other Initiatives:
Reduction in salt use in winter control operations

Norfolk, page 702
Waste Management:
100% of waste collection is contracted to Norfolk Disposal, 519/443-8022
Number of landfill sites: 2; *Landfill Capacity:* 12 years
Solid Waste Disposal Fees: $55/tonne
Transfer Station(s): 2 sites
Recycling: Both Curbside & Depot; Material Recovery Facility, 28 Grigg Dr., Simcoe
Special Bans/by-laws: Leaves & Christmas trees banned from landfill
Hazardous Waste Depot or Facility: yearly from 4 depots
Compost Sites: Yes *Composters subsidized:* Yes
Water & Wastewater Treatment:
Water & wastewater facilities in Simcoe, Waterford, Port Dover, Delhi, Port Rowan & Courtland; Contracted to Veolia, 519/583-0612
Other Initiatives:
Curbside bulky pickup tri-annually

North Bay, page 715
Waste Management:
Waste collection contracted to Miller Waste Systems
Number of landfill sites: 1
Solid Waste Disposal Fees: $20/minimum load; $45/tonne (ICI)
Clean Fill Fee: No
Recycling: Both Curbside & Depot; Recycling Centre, 112 Patton St.; Organic drop-off area
Special Bans/by-laws: Household hazardous waste, corrugated cardboard, tires, liquid waste, pathological waste banned from Merrick landfill; ban on grass collection
Hazardous Waste Depot or Facility: Facility at 112 Patton St.
Water & Wastewater Treatment:
North Bay WPCP, 650 Memorial Dr.; Water treatment plant, 248 Lakeside Dr.; Both facilities are operated by the Ontario Clean Water Agency

North Dundas, page 727
Waste Management:
Number of landfill sites: 2
Solid Waste Disposal Fees: $10/cubic yard
Recycling: Curbside
Water & Wastewater Treatment:
Chesterville Water System; Winchester Water System; Ontario Clean Water Agency, 613-448-3098, inspects new service
Other Initiatives:
Hazardous Household Waste Days

North Glengarry, page 727
Waste Management:
Number of landfill sites: 2
Solid Waste Disposal Fees: $50/ton, commercial & industrial waste
Recycling: Depot; Alexandria Recycling (R.A.R.E. Plant), 265 Industrial Blvd., Alexandria
Special Bans/by-laws: Bonfire By-law

North Grenville, page 728
Waste Management:
Number of landfill sites: 1
Recycling: Curbside; Depot at Kemptville Landfill Site, 190 County Rd. 44
Water & Wastewater Treatment:
Municipality of North Grenville Wastewater Treatment Plant, Hwy. 43, 613/258-7400
Other Initiatives:
Oxford Mills Brush Depot, 699 Crozier Rd.; Leaf & yard waste depot, Ferguson Forest Centre County Rd. 43

North Perth, page 715
Waste Management:
Recycling handled by Bluewater Recycling Association, 1-800-265-9799
Number of landfill sites: 3
Solid Waste Disposal Fees: $50/1 ton truck, household waste
Recycling: Both Curbside & Depot; Listowel Landfill, 905 Louise Ave. North, accepts some recyclables
Water & Wastewater Treatment:
Bowman, Gowanstown, Listowel & Smith drinking water systems owned by town
Other Initiatives:
User pay system for waste

Northumberland, page 702
Waste Management:
Responsibility of county; Collection of waste & recyclables contracted to National Waste Services; Waste & Recycling Hot Line: 1-866-293-8379
Number of landfill sites: 2
Solid Waste Disposal Fees: $85/tonne
Transfer Station(s): Bewdley Transfer Station; Hope Transfer Station
Recycling: Both Curbside & Depot; Depot is the County of Northumberland Material Recovery Facility, Edwardson Rd., Grafton
Special Bans/by-laws: Tree Conservation By-law
Hazardous Waste Depot or Facility: Cobourg HHW Depot; Bewdley HHW Depot; Seymour HHW Depot; Brighton HHW Depot
Compost Sites: Yes *Composters subsidized:* Yes
Water & Wastewater Treatment:
Responsibility of the area municipalities
Other Initiatives:
Maintenance of 6 closed landfills; Electronics waste disposal; Large item disposal program; Sale of compost; Northumberland Forest Users Committee; Weed control; Salt management

Norwich, page 728
Waste Management:
Responsibility of County of Oxford
Water & Wastewater Treatment:
Responsiblity of County of Oxford
Other Initiatives:
Household hazardous waste day; White goods & scrap metal collection depots; Large article collection

Oakville, page 715
Waste Management:
Responsibility of Regional Municipality of Halton
Water & Wastewater Treatment:
Responsibility of Regional Municipality of Halton
Other Initiatives:
The following programs have been initiated: Doors Closed Campaign, 20/20 The Way to Clean Air, Rain Water Barrels, Purchase Hybrid Vehicles & LED Traffic Signal Replacement

Orangeville, page 716
Waste Management:
Solid Waste Disposal Fees: $85/tonne
Recycling: Curbside; Depot at Dufferin Transfer & Recycling Facility, County Rd. 11
Special Bans/by-laws: Residents may have up to 3 bags per week for curbside collection, additional waste is charged $1 per bag
Hazardous Waste Depot or Facility: Yes
Compost Sites: Yes
Water & Wastewater Treatment:
Water Pollution Control Plant operated by Ontario Clean Water Agency

Orillia, page 716
Waste Management:
Number of landfill sites: 1
Recycling: Both Curbside & Depot; Depot located at Recycling Depot, Waste Diversion Site, 100 Kitchener St., Orillia
Hazardous Waste Depot or Facility: Depot at 100 Kitchener St., Orillia
Composters subsidized: Yes
Water & Wastewater Treatment:
Water Filtration Plant at 200 Bay St., Orillia; Wastewater Treatment Centre at 40 Kitchener St., Orillia
Other Initiatives:
Garbage tag program; Compostable waste collected year-round; Paint reuse depot; Tree planting rebate; Water efficiency rebate program; Upgrades to Water Filtration Plant

Oro-Medonte, page 728
Waste Management:
Responsibility of Simcoe County
Water & Wastewater Treatment:
Water systems in 11 locations are owned & operated by the municipality

Oshawa, page 716
Waste Management:
Waste diversion & management responsiblity of Durham Region; Waste collection responsibility of city's public works services
Water & Wastewater Treatment:
Responsibility of Durham Region
Other Initiatives:
Christmas tree, yard waste & green bin collection programs; Forestry & environmental stewardship programs

Ottawa, page 716
Waste Management:
Waste collection responsibility of city & private contractors
Number of landfill sites: 2; *Landfill Capacity:* 30 years
Solid Waste Disposal Fees: $73/tonne
Clean Fill Fee: Yes; $20/tonne
Composters subsidized: Yes
Water & Wastewater Treatment:
Lemieux Island Water Purification Plant; Britannia Water Purification Plant; Robert O. Pickard Environmental Centre, a wastewater treatment facility
Other Initiatives:
Plasma gasification pilot project (75 tonnes of MSW converted to electrical energy), start-up at end 2006; Travelwise, a program to promote healthier alternatives to driving; Take it Back, a program to return hazardous waste products to participating retailers; Reduction of pesticide/herbicide use; Sewer Use Program, in conjunction with the sewer use by-law, to protect water through pollution prevention; Air Quality & Climate Change Management Plan; One day household hazardous waste depots; Natural areas protection; Sub-watershed planni

Owen Sound, page 717
Waste Management:
Number of landfill sites: 1
Solid Waste Disposal Fees: $47.50/tonne, domestic waste; $70/tonne, commercial or industrial general waste
Clean Fill Fee:
Recycling: Both Curbside & Depot; Depot: Miller Waste Yard Drop-off, 2125 - 20 St. East
Hazardous Waste Depot or Facility: Occasional temporary site on designated days; Owen Sound Public Works Facility, HHW Depot
Compost Sites: Yes
Water & Wastewater Treatment:
Richard H. Neath Water Treatment Plant, 2600 - 3rd Ave. East, Owen Sound
Other Initiatives:
Owen Sound Leaf & Yard Waste Composting Site; Hazardous waste events on specified days; Recyclable electronics accepted at Electronics Depot, Miller Waste Facility, 2125 - 20 St. East; User pay garbage, Bag Tag program

Oxford, page 728
Waste Management:
County responsible for all waste management (waste collection & recycling); Area municipalities look after some customer service associated with waste management
Number of landfill sites: 1; *Landfill Capacity:* 18 years
Solid Waste Disposal Fees: $45/tonne
Recycling: Curbside
Special Bans/by-laws: Water Use; Sewer Use; Water Rate
Hazardous Waste Depot or Facility: Special hazardous waste days; Woodstock-WPCP; Ingersoll - Cami Auto; Tillsonburg - Public
Compost Sites: Yes *Composters subsidized:* Yes
Water & Wastewater Treatment:
County responsible for all water systems & wastewater treatment facilities, including planning, design & construction, maintenance, monitoring & operations; Wastewater systems in Drumbo, Ingersoll, Norwich, Plattsville, Tavistock, Thamesford, Tillsonburg & Woodstock; Water treatment plants in Beachville-Loweville, Bright, Brownsville, Dereham Centre, Drumbo, Embro, Hickson-King, Ingersoll, Innerkip, Lakeside, Mount Elgin, Norwich, Otterville, Plattsville, Princeton,

Page numbers refer to full profile.

Springford, Sweaburg-Oxford
Other Initiatives:
Thornton/Tabor Well Field Study; Groundwater Pilot Project.

Peel, page 703
Waste Management:
Collection contracted to Sandhill Waste Collection & Recycling (rural collection); Waste haulage & disposal contracted to Wilson Logistic Inc.; Republic Service Inc. contracted to haul waste to Michigan for disposal; Information about waste management Wasteline, 905/791-9499
Number of landfill sites: 1
Recycling: Both Curbside & Depot; Depot locations: Bolton Community Recycling Centre, Caledon Public Waste & Recycling Depot, Brampton Community Recycling Centre, Britannnia Public Waste & Recycling Depot, Mississauga
Hazardous Waste Depot or Facility: Brampton CRC, 395 Chrysler Dr.; Caledon Public Waste & Recycling Depot, 1795 Quarry Dr.
Compost Sites: Yes *Composters subsidized:* Yes
Water & Wastewater Treatment:
Public Works Dept. operates & maintains 2 water treatment plants, 2 wastewater treatment plants & 80 pumping stations
Other Initiatives:
"Three Bag Standard" for garbage collection; "Environment Days" for drop off of unwanted materials; Outdoor water efficiency kits & rain barrels available from the Region; Organics demonstration project; Reuse stores at Bolton CRC; Electronics recycling program; Peel Odour Management Strategy; Water Smart Peel conservation program; Algonquin Power Energy from waste facility; Expansion of Lakeview Wastewater Treatment Facility, Clarkson Wastewater Treatment Facility & Lakeview Water Treatment Facility by 2006

Pelham, page 717
Waste Management:
Responsibility of the Regional Municipality of Niagara
Water & Wastewater Treatment:
Responsibility of the Regional Municipality of Niagara

Pembroke, page 717
Waste Management:
Responsibility of City of Pembroke, in partnership with the Township of Laurentian Valley, the Town of Petawawa, the Township of North Algoma-Wilberforce & the Township of Bonnechere Valley; Landfill site located on Woito Station Rd., Pembroke
Number of landfill sites: 1
Solid Waste Disposal Fees: $65.87/tonne
Recycling: Both Curbside & Depot; Material Recovery Facility at Ottawa Valley Waste Recovery Centre, 900 Woito Station Rd., Pembroke
Hazardous Waste Depot or Facility: Ottawa Valley Waste Recovery Centre, 900 Woito Station Rd., Pembroke
Composters subsidized: Yes
Water & Wastewater Treatment:
Water Purification Plant, 1 Riverside Dr., Pembroke, 613/735-0309; Pollution Control Plant, 98 Rankin St. Pembroke, 613/735-0409
Other Initiatives:
Upgrades to Water Purification Plant & Pollution Control Plant; Spring & fall special garbage collection

Perth, page 703
Waste Management:
Responsibility of area municipalities
Special Bans/by-laws: Bylaw to regulate nutrient management for certain livestock operations; Bylaw to restrict & regulate destruction of trees
Water & Wastewater Treatment:
Responsibility of area municipalities
Other Initiatives:
Perth County groundwater study

Perth East, page 728
Waste Management:
Number of landfill sites: 2
Water & Wastewater Treatment:
Township's public works dept. operates 2 water supply systems in Milverton & Shakespeare, plus 1 wastewater treatment system in Milverton

Petawawa, page 717
Waste Management:
Responsibility of the Town of Petawawa, in partnership with the Township of Laurentian Valley, the City of Pembroke, the Township of North Algona-Wilberforce & the Township of Bonnechere Valley; Landfill site located at 1076 Woito Station Rd., in the township of Laurentian Valley
Number of landfill sites: 1
Hazardous Waste Depot or Facility: Ottawa Valley Waste Recovery Centre, 900 Woito Station Rd, Twp of Laurentian Valley, 613/7
Water & Wastewater Treatment:
Town of Petawawa Water Pollution Control Plant & water treatment plant, operated by Ontario Clean Water Agency, 613/687-7512

Peterborough, page 718
Waste Management:
Handled by the city
Number of landfill sites: 1; *Landfill Capacity:* 25 years
Solid Waste Disposal Fees: $70/tonne
Recycling: Both Curbside & Depot; Depots: Materials Recycling Facility, Peterborough; Peterborough County/City Landfill site; Electronics Drop-Off Depot, Peterborough
Special Bans/by-laws: Garbage limit 2/household/week, 4/business/week; Following items banned from Peterborough County/City landfill site: blue box recyclables, tires, green wastes, hazardous materials, biomedical wastes, radioactive wastes, liquid wastes, materials from outside County of Peterborough
Hazardous Waste Depot or Facility: 400 Pido Rd., Peterborough
Composters subsidized: Yes
Water & Wastewater Treatment:
City of Peterborough Wastewater Treatment Plant, 425 Kennedy Rd., Peterborough; City of Peterborough Water Treatment Plant, 1230 Water St. North, Peterborough
Other Initiatives:
Clean Stream Waste Management Program; Curbside collection of household food wastes; Hope to expand the organics collection to all households

Peterborough, page 703
Waste Management:
Recycling: Both Curbside & Depot; County provides recycling depots at all waste depots & transfer stations; Recycling information 705/743-0380, ext.777, Email: rrr@county.peterborough.on.ca
Hazardous Waste Depot or Facility: Belmont Transfer Stn, Anstruther Lake, City/Cty HHW facility, Buckhorn Landfill, Bobcaygeo
Compost Sites: No
Water & Wastewater Treatment:
Responsibility of individual member municipalities
Other Initiatives:
Adopt-A-Road program; Free reuse area at household waste depots for paints & stains; Annual White Goods Days, when unwanted appliances & scrap metal are accepted for re-use or recycling; Drop-off locations for Christmas trees

Pickering, page 718
Waste Management:
Responsibility of Regional Municipality of Durham, waste@region.durham.on.ca
Special Bans/by-laws: Waste management by-law; Anti-idling by-law
Water & Wastewater Treatment:
Responsibility of Regional Municipality of Durham

Port Colborne, page 718
Waste Management:
Responsibility of the Regional Municipality of Niagara
Water & Wastewater Treatment:
Responsibility of the Regional Municipality of Niagara

Port Hope, page 728
Waste Management:
Responsibility of Northumberland County
Water & Wastewater Treatment:
Water purification plant, Marsh St. Port Hope; Sewage treatment plant, 100 Lake St., Port Hope
Other Initiatives:
Construction of new water treatment plant, www.porthopewatertreatment.ca

Prescott & Russell, page 729
Waste Management:
Responsibility of area municipalities
Water & Wastewater Treatment:
Responsibility of area municipalities

Quinte West, page 718
Waste Management:
Waste management in the Frankford ward responsibility of city's public works department; Waste management contracts in the Murray, Sidney & Trenton wards overseen by city's public works department
Number of landfill sites: 1
Recycling: Curbside; Administered by Centre & South Hastings Waste Services Board
Water & Wastewater Treatment:
Water treatment & distribution plus sewage collection & treatment responsibility of city's public works department; Treatment plants include: Trenton Water Treatment Plant, 20 Chester Rd.; Trenton Ward Wastewater Treatment Plant, Bay St.; Bayside Water Treatment Plant, Aikins Rd.; Frankford Water & Sewage Treatment Plant, North Trent St.; Batawa Water & Sewage Treatments Plants, Batawa
Other Initiatives:
Bag tag garbage program; Information about recycling, household hazardous waste disposal & composting, contact Quinte Waste Solutions, 613/394-6266; Yard waste site, Frankford Landfill; Designated depots for disposal of large & bulky items

Renfrew, page 704
Water & Wastewater Treatment:
Responsibility of area municipalities
Other Initiatives:
Adopt-a-road program; Forest operating plan; Regional groundwater & aquifer study

Richmond Hill, page 718
Waste Management:
Town is responsible for collection of garbage & recyclables; Regional Municipality of York is responsible for household hazardous waste depot & compost facility; Waste disposal handled by Region of York & City of Toronto transfer stations
Recycling: Curbside
Compost Sites: Yes
Water & Wastewater Treatment:
Water supply from Lake Ontario is treated by City of Toronto Metro Works; Regional Municipality of York accepts the water from the City of Toronto; Town is responsible for maintenance of the water distribution system; Town is responsible for maintenance & operation of sewage collection system; Durham & York Region sewage systems treat sewage
Other Initiatives:
Clean air initiatives include the following programs: walk to school day, clean air local business award, telework, & development of sustainable transportation policies; Lake Wilcox remediation strategy; Planting of native trees & plants; Natural heritage strategy; Yard waste & Christmas tree collection; No clear plastic bags accepted for yard waste; Introduction of green bins for organic waste; Spring clean-up program; Salt management plan; Water conservation practices

Russell, page 729
Waste Management:
Contracted to Malex Waste Systems, 819/778-5237
Number of landfill sites: 1; *Landfill Capacity:* 20 years
Solid Waste Disposal Fees: $12.50/cu metre
Clean Fill Fee: Yes; $12.50/cu metre
Recycling: Curbside
Hazardous Waste Depot or Facility: Depot at the landfill site
Composters subsidized: Yes
Water & Wastewater Treatment:
Township of Russell, Utilities Services, 851 Rte. 400, Embrun, ON, K0A 1W1

St. Catharines, page 719
Waste Management:
Responsibility of Regional Municipality of Niagara, 905/356-4141
Water & Wastewater Treatment:
Responsibility of Regional Municipality of Niagara
Other Initiatives:
Flood alleviation program; Green Ribbon Trail Eco-Tour

St. Clair, page 729
Waste Management:
Waste collection responsibility of township public works & operations department; Collection of yard waste in urbanized areas; Collection of recyclables contracted to Halton Recycling; Waste management responsibility of County of Lambton
Recycling: Curbside
Special Bans/by-laws: Water restrictions
Compost Sites: Yes

Municipal Waste Management and Water & Wastewater Treatment / Ontario

Water & Wastewater Treatment:
St. Clair Distribution System operated by township; Majority of water supply from Lambton Area Water Supply System

St. Thomas, page 719
Waste Management:
Waste collection contracted to Green Lane Environmental Group Ltd., 519/631-7970
Recycling: Curbside
Water & Wastewater Treatment:
St. Thomas Secondary Water System is operated by American Water Services Canada Corp., under contract to St. Thomas Secondary Water Board; Elgin-Middlesex Pumping Station treatment facility, Lot 9, Concession 9, Former township of Yarmouth
Other Initiatives:
Curbside composting

Sarnia, page 719
Waste Management:
Waste collection contracted to Marcotte Disposal, 519/339-9988; Recycling services contracted to Halton Recycling, 1-866-628-0735
Recycling: Curbside
Composters subsidized: Yes
Water & Wastewater Treatment:
Water supplied to the city by the Lambton Area Water Supply System, operated by the Ontario Clean Water Agency; Water distribution system is maintained by the City of Sarnia Engineering & Public Works Dept.
Other Initiatives:
Household Hazardous Waste Days provided by the County of Lambton

Saugeen Shores, page 719
Waste Management:
Bruce Solid Waste Recycling Association responsible for recycling pickup
Number of landfill sites: 2
Recycling: Depot; Services provided by Bruce Area Solid Waste Recycling, 519/797-5557.
Water & Wastewater Treatment:
Sewage treatment plant, Lehnen St.; Southhampton Water Treatment Plant
Other Initiatives:
Goods Exchange Days; Hazardous Waste Disposal Day; Leaf Collection

Sault Ste. Marie, page 720
Waste Management:
Industrial, commercial & institutional waste collection & disposal provided by Sault Ste. Marie Disposals, 705/945-7554 & Canadian Waste Services, 705/254-5050
Number of landfill sites: 1
Solid Waste Disposal Fees: $27.50/tonne; $55/tonne
Recycling: Curbside; Depot located at Sault Ste. Marie Recycling Depot, McNabb St. Operated by Canadian Waste Services, 705/254-5050
Hazardous Waste Depot or Facility: Household Special Waste Depot, 115 Industrial Pk., Cres.

Scugog, page 729
Waste Management:
Responsibility of Regional Municipality of Durham
Water & Wastewater Treatment:
Responsibility of Regional Municipality of Durham

Severn, page 729
Waste Management:
Responsibility of County of Simcoe
Special Bans/by-laws: Littering By-law; Clean & Clear Yards By-law
Water & Wastewater Treatment:
The following municipal drinking water systems & water treatment plants are owned and operated by the township: Bass Lake Woodlands Well Supply & Distribution; Coldwater Well Supply & Distribution; Sandcastle Estates Water Treatment Plant; Severn Estates Well Supply & Distribution; Washago Water Treatment Plant; Westshore Water Treatment Plant
Other Initiatives:
Westshore Water & Sewer Project completed in 2006

Simcoe, page 704
Waste Management:
Waste collection, recycling & operation of several waste disposal facilities responsibility of county

Number of landfill sites: 8
Transfer Station(s): North Simcoe Transfer Station, 1700 Golflink Rd., Tiny Twp.; New Tecumseth Transfer Station, 5917 - 7th Line, New Tecumseth
Recycling: Curbside
Hazardous Waste Depot or Facility: Nottawasaga Landfill Site, 5715 - 30/31 Sideroad; North Simcoe & New Tecumseth Transfer St
Water & Wastewater Treatment:
Water & wastewater treatment responsibility of member municipalities
Other Initiatives:
Household hazardous waste days; Curbside organics collection pilot program; Leaf, yard waste & metal item special collections; Management of closed landfills; Forest management, including tree cutting bylaw

Smith-Ennismore-Lakefield, page 729
Waste Management:
Waste collection is contracted to Capital Environmental, 705/742-4268; County of Peterborough is responsible for recycling & disposal of hazardous waste
Number of landfill sites: 2
Solid Waste Disposal Fees: Yes
Composters subsidized: Yes
Water & Wastewater Treatment:
Township has agreement with Peterborough Utilities Services Inc. to maintain operations of Lakefield Water Works & Woodland Acres Water Works; Private wells & septic systems serve other areas
Other Initiatives:
Major appliances & large household furniture day at Smith Landfill Site

South Dundas, page 730
Waste Management:
Collection of waste & recyclables plus waste disposal responsibility of township public works department
Number of landfill sites: 2
Solid Waste Disposal Fees: $10/ 1/2 or 3/4 ton pick-up; $50/construction material
Recycling: Curbside
Composters subsidized: Yes
Water & Wastewater Treatment:
St. Lawrence River is township water source; Regional water treatment facility; Sewage treatment facilities
Other Initiatives:
Limit of 2 bags of garbage/week; Stickers for additional bags of garbage cost $1.25 each; Participation with township of North Dundas in its household hazardous waste program; Landfill sites are located in Williamsburg & Matilda wards; Upgrades to water distribution system

South Frontenac, page 730
Waste Management:
Landfills/waste disposal sites located in Bedford, Loughborough, Portland & Storrington
Solid Waste Disposal Fees: Yes
Recycling: Both Curbside & Depot; Depots at the following waste disposal sites: Bradshaw, Green Bay, Salem & Massassauga
Other Initiatives:
Hazardous waste disposal tickets may be purchased & turned into the City of Kingston Hazardous Waste Disposal Site; Garbage bag limits

South Glengarry, page 730
Waste Management:
Recycling handled by R.A.R.E. Recycling
Number of landfill sites: 2
Solid Waste Disposal Fees: $10/van, pickup truck, private car, utility trailer; $50/1 ton vehicle
Water & Wastewater Treatment:
Glen Walter Water Treatment Plant, 18352 County Rd.2, in Glen Walter
Other Initiatives:
Adopt-a-Road program; Household hazardous waste day

South Huron, page 730
Waste Management:
Blue Water Recycling, 519/228-6678
Number of landfill sites: 1; *Landfill Capacity:* 100 years
Solid Waste Disposal Fees: $75.00/tonne
Recycling: Curbside; Recycling handled by Bluewater Recycling Assoc.
Hazardous Waste Depot or Facility: 82 Nelson St., Exeter
Water & Wastewater Treatment:

Lake Huron Water Plant, Hwy. 21, 683 South Huron
Other Initiatives:
Special pick-up for brush, furniture, fixtures, appliances & compostable garden waste; User pay system for garbage; Special depots, at certain times for household hazardous waste

South Stormont, page 730
Waste Management:
Number of landfill sites: 1
Solid Waste Disposal Fees: $5/car; $15/pick up truck; $20/1 ton truck; $30/white goods containing freon; $22/tractor & loader tires; $15/large truck tire; $5/car & light truck t
Recycling: Curbside
Water & Wastewater Treatment:
Township's Public Works Dept. responsible for waterworks at Ingleside & Long Sault (South Stormont Regional Water Treatment Plant), Rosedale/St. Andrews, Newington & Osnabruck Centre; Wastewater handled at Ingleside & Long Sault
Other Initiatives:
Household garbage limit; Household hazardous waste accepted at City of Cornwall Landfill Site on specific dates; Water system upgrades

Springwater, page 730
Waste Management:
Responsibility of the County of Simcoe
Water & Wastewater Treatment:
Township's Public Works Dept. is responsible for the operation of water systems in the following areas: Anten Mills, Elmvale, Hillsdale, Midhurst, Midhurst - Carson Rd., Minesing, Snow Valley, Vespra Downs & Sunnidale Rd.; Systems include the following: wells, pumping stations, towers, reservoirs, booster stations, generator sets, watermain & metered units; Operation of the Elmvale Sewage Treatment Plant & 2 pumping stations is contracted to the Ontario Clean Water Agency
Other Initiatives:
Environmental assessment regarding a municipal water system to serve Phelpston

Stormont, Dundas & Glengarry, page 730
Waste Management:
Responsibility of area municipalities; County involved in waste management planning only
Water & Wastewater Treatment:
Responsibility of area municipalities
Other Initiatives:
Designation of open spaces in urban settlement areas; Adopt-a-road program; Designation of agricultural resource lands for protection; Policies to control operational impacts of extractive resouce lands; Designation of provincially significant wetlands

Stratford, page 720
Waste Management:
Waste collection contracted to BFI, 519/681-4040
Number of landfill sites: 1
Solid Waste Disposal Fees: $58/tonne
Recycling: Both Curbside & Depot; Recycling Depot at Stratford Landfill, 777 Romeo St. South
Hazardous Waste Depot or Facility: Household Hazardous Waste Depot at Stratford Landfill, 777 Romeo St. South
Composters subsidized: Yes
Water & Wastewater Treatment:
Water Pollution Control Plant, West Gore St., owned by the city & operated by Ontario Clean Water Agency
Other Initiatives:
Pay as You Waste garbage system

Strathroy-Caradoc, page 731
Waste Management:
Garbage collection contracted to Bluewater Recycling Association, 1-800-265-9799
Recycling: Curbside
Water & Wastewater Treatment:
Strathroy-Caradoc Wastewater Treatment Plant, Pike Rd., Strathroy

Thames Centre, page 731
Waste Management:
Waste collection & collection of recyclables contracted to Halton Recycling, 519/690-2796
Number of landfill sites: 1
Solid Waste Disposal Fees: $100/tonne, oversized non-recyclable waste; $20/recyclable waste
Clean Fill Fee: No

Page numbers refer to full profile.

Municipal Waste Management and Water & Wastewater Treatment / Ontario

Recycling: Both Curbside & Depot; Landfill Site, 2015 Crampton Dr.
Special Bans/by-laws: Water use restictions
Composters subsidized: Yes
Water & Wastewater Treatment:
Dorechester Water Treatment Facility; Thorndale Well Supply System
Other Initiatives:
Garbage bag tag system; Township residents can use the City of London Household Special Waste Drop-Off Depot; Open air burning regulated

The Nation, page 731
Waste Management:
Waste removal contracted to Mike's Waste Disposal; Household waste is hauled to the Lafleche Environmental Site in the Township of North Stormont
Number of landfill sites: 3; *Landfill Capacity:* 50 years
Recycling: Curbside
Water & Wastewater Treatment:
Limoges Water Treatment Plant; St.Isidore Water Treatment Plant; Ontario Clean Water Agency, 613/443-2195

Thorold, page 720
Waste Management:
Responsibility of the Regional Municipality of Niagara, 905/356-4141
Water & Wastewater Treatment:
Responsibility of the Regional Municipality of Niagara, www.regional.niagara.on.ca

Thunder Bay, page 721
Waste Management:
Number of landfill sites: 1
Solid Waste Disposal Fees: $34.65/tonne
Recycling: Both Curbside & Depot; Collection provided by Recool Canada Inc., 807/577-0411; Depots: Mountdale Ave., Front St., John St. Landfill site
Special Bans/by-laws: Refrigeration units containing CFCs not accepted at depots
Hazardous Waste Depot or Facility: John St. Landfill site, opened Saturdays only between May & October.
Composters subsidized: Yes
Water & Wastewater Treatment:
Water treatment plants: RR#13 Bare Point Rd., 807/683-8141 & Loch Lomond Rd.; Water Pollution Control plant at 901 Atlantic Ave., 807/625-3370
Other Initiatives:
Spring & fall leaf & yard collection; St. John Landfill site composting facility

Tillsonburg, page 721
Waste Management:
Responsibility of County of Oxford
Water & Wastewater Treatment:
Responsibility of County of Oxford
Other Initiatives:
Town's public works department is responsible for leaf collection; Leaf, grass, concrete & asphalt recycling; Transfer station operation

Timmins, page 721
Waste Management:
Recycling: Both Curbside & Depot; Depot locations: Deloro Landfill Site; Tisdale Landfill Site; German Township Disposal Site
Water & Wastewater Treatment:
City of Timmins Water Filtration Plant, 15 Feldman Rd.; Whitney & Tisdale Waste Water Treatment Plant, 6th Ave., Porcupine, serves South Porcupine & Porcupine; Mattagami River Waste Water Treatment Plant, 837 Airport Rd., serves Timmins, Mountjoy & Schumacher
Other Initiatives:
Upgrades to operational & maintenance systems at Water Filtration Plant; Waste container limit

Toronto, page 721
Waste Management:
Waste from transfer stations transported to Carlton Farms Landfill in Michigan
Solid Waste Disposal Fees: Yes
Transfer Station(s): Bermondsey; Commissioners; Disco; Ingram, Scarborough; Victoria Park
Recycling: Both Curbside & Depot; Bermondsey, 188 Bermondsey Rd., 416/392-3133; Dufferin, 35 Vanley Cres., 416/392-3161 (tires only); Ingram, 50 Ingram Dr., 416/392-5592; Scarborough, 1 Transfer Pl., 416/392-3019; Victoria Park, 3350 Victoria Park Ave., 416/392-3025
Hazardous Waste Depot or Facility: Bermondsey; Commissioners; Disco; Ingram; Scarborough; Victoria Park
Compost Sites: Yes *Composters subsidized:* Yes
Water & Wastewater Treatment:
Wastewater treatment plants: Highland Creek, Ashbridges Bay, North Toronto, Humber Bay; Water filtration plants: R.C. Harris, R.L. Clark, Frank J. Horgan, Island
Other Initiatives:
City run composting demonstration sites; Green bin program for organics collection, greenbin@toronto.ca; Yellow bag program, a waste management program for commercial customers, yellowbag@toronto.ca; Establishment of the Energy Efficient Office, 416/392-1110; Toxics Taxi will pick up more than 10 litres of hazardous waste from a residence, 416/392-4330; HHW Reuse Centres at Bermondsey, Disco, Ingram & Scarborough Depots; Computer drop-off at Commissioners, Disco, Ingram, Scarborough & Victoria Park depots; Adopt-a-bin program; Leaf management facility

Trent Hills, page 731
Waste Management:
Waste & recycling collection & management responsibility of County of Northumberland, Department of Transportation & Waste Office, 905/372-3329
Water & Wastewater Treatment:
Water treatment responsibility of town; Campbellford Water Treatment Plant; Hastings Water Treatment Plant; Warkworth Water Treatment Plant; Trentview Estates Water Distribution System; Wastewater treatment contracted to Ontario Clean Water Agency; Campbellford Wastewater Treatment Plant; Hastings Wastewater Treatment Plant

Uxbridge, page 731
Waste Management:
Responsibility of Region of Durham
Water & Wastewater Treatment:
Responsibility of Region of Durham
Other Initiatives:
Established Uxbridge Brook Watershed Committee to enhance & protect water resources

Vaughan, page 722
Waste Management:
Responsibility of the Regional Municipality of York
Water & Wastewater Treatment:
Majority of water supply & treatment by City of Toronto; Well water supply & treatment in Kleinberg area responsibility of Regional Municipality of York; Sewage treatment responsibility of Dufferin Creek Treatment Plant
Other Initiatives:
Adopt-a-park program; Free mulch day; Greening Vaughan programs, including organics (green bin) collection, greeningvaughan@vaughan.ca; Anti-idling program; Vaughan manufacturers' sustainability program

Wasaga Beach, page 722
Waste Management:
Responsibility of Simcoe County
Water & Wastewater Treatment:
Powerline Road Water Plant/Water Pollution Control Plant & Janetta Well Site, operated by Ontario Clean Water Agency

Waterloo, page 722
Waste Management:
Responsibility of the Regional Municipality of Waterloo
Water & Wastewater Treatment:
Responsibility of the Regional Municipality of Waterloo; Waterloo Utilities is responsible for operation of the water distribution & wastewater collection systems
Other Initiatives:
Partners in Parks program; Environmental Lands Acquisition & Maintenance Policy; Protective measures for trees; Green space naturalization & rehabilitation; Watershed monitoring program; Adopt-a-Road program; Storm water management; Waste reduction with all city facilities; Energy & water conservation; Reduction of road salt use; Pesticide reduction campaign; Green roof project

Waterloo, page 704
Waste Management:
Waste disposal & recycling responsibility of regional municipality
Number of landfill sites: 2; *Landfill Capacity:* 30 years (Waterloo), 8 years (Cambridge Waste Management Centre)
Solid Waste Disposal Fees: Commercial $50/tonne; Residential $65/tonne
Clean Fill Fee: Yes; first 50 kg free & $3/100 kg therea
Transfer Station(s): Elmira, Ayr, Wilmot, Wellesley
Hazardous Waste Depot or Facility: Waterloo & Cambridge landfill sites
Compost Sites: Yes *Composters subsidized:* Yes
Water & Wastewater Treatment:
Water treatment responsibility of the Region; Water & wastewater treatment contracted to Ontario Clean Water Agency, 1-800-667-OCWA; Mannheim Water Treatment Plant, 2069 Ottawa St. South, Kitchener
Other Initiatives:
Currently undertaking a comprehensive ground & surface water protection strategy; Evaluating long-term water supply; Water conservation devices easily available region-wide (ie., toilet replacement program, using six-litre ultra-low flush unit); Area municipalities required to enact by-laws for lawn watering regulation; Environmental sampling/testing

Welland, page 722
Waste Management:
Waste management responsibility of Region of Niagara
Water & Wastewater Treatment:
Responsibility of Region of Niagara; City's Public Works Division maintains sewers & waterworks

Wellington, page 705
Waste Management:
The City of Guelph operates its own recycling, disposal & transfer facilities
Number of landfill sites: 3
Solid Waste Disposal Fees: $60/tonne
Transfer Station(s): 3 transfer stations
Recycling: Both Curbside & Depot; Drop off locations Aberfoyle, Riverstown, Harriston, Rothsay, Belwood, Elora, Hillsburgh
Special Bans/by-laws: Tree cutting by-law
Hazardous Waste Depot or Facility: Guelph Household Hazardous Waste Depot, 110 Dunlop Dr., Guelph.
Other Initiatives:
Curbside user pay garbage program; Household hazardous waste event days; Curbside Christmas tree collection; Adopt-A-Road program; Tire recycling; Appliance collection areas at landfill sites & transfer stations; Wood & brush diversion programs; Pilot Reuse Center at Aberfoyle Landfill site

Wellington North, page 732
Waste Management:
Responsibility of County of Wellington
Special Bans/by-laws: Nutrient Management By-Law
Water & Wastewater Treatment:
Kenilworth Well Water Supply System; Damascus Hall Well Water Supply System; Operation of Arthur Wastewater Treatment Plant & Mount Forest Wastewater Treatment Plant contracted to Ontario Clean Water Agency
Other Initiatives:
Annual tree planting; Brush collection; Salt management plan

West Grey, page 732
Waste Management:
Number of landfill sites: 3
Recycling: Curbside
Other Initiatives:
Waste bag tag system; Goods exchange day; Household hazardous waste program through Owen Sound Public Works Depot

West Lincoln, page 732
Waste Management:
Waste management responsibility of the Regional Municipality of Niagara
Water & Wastewater Treatment:
Water & wastewater treatment responsibility of the Regional Municipality of Niagara

West Nipissing, page 732
Waste Management:
Municipality administers landfill sites owned by Field, Caldwell, Sturgeon Falls & the Ministry of Natural Resources
Number of landfill sites: 7
Water & Wastewater Treatment:
Sturgeon Falls & Cache Bay Water Treatment Facility, 705/753-5287; Verner Water Treatment Facility, 705/594-2763; Sturgeon Falls, Cache Bay & Field Sewage Treatment Facility/Pumping Station, 705/753-3210; Verner Sewage Treatment Facility/Pumping Station, 705/753-2763

Page numbers refer to full profile.

Whitby, page 723
Waste Management:
Waste disposal responsibility of Durham Region; Whitby's Public Works Dept. responsible for waste, compost & special collections; Recyclables collected by Miller Waste Systems
Water & Wastewater Treatment:
Responsibility of Durham Region
Other Initiatives:
Garbage Bag Tag program, 4 item (bag/can) limit; Use of kraft bags for leaf & yard waste collection; Fee for special collection for items containing CFCs

Whitchurch-Stouffville, page 723
Waste Management:
Waste collection contracted to Miller Waste Systems, 905/475-6356; Composting facilities responsibility of York Region Waste Management Division, 1-877-464-4675, ext.5717
Recycling: Both Curbside & Depot; Whitchurch-Stouffville Recycling Depot, off Burkholder St.
Special Bans/by-laws: Waste collection limit of 3 containers; Waste stickers available at $2.00 for each bag above three & up to a maximum of six
Water & Wastewater Treatment:
Treatment responsibility of the Region of York; Operation & maintenance of water distribution & sewer collection systems responsibility of town
Other Initiatives:
Large article, yard waste & Christmas tree collection

Wilmot, page 732
Waste Management:
Responsibility of Regional Municipality of Waterloo
Water & Wastewater Treatment:
Responsibility of Regional Municipality of Waterloo

Windsor, page 723
Waste Management:
Number of landfill sites: 1
Solid Waste Disposal Fees: $53/tonne (garbage & household waste); $38.50/tonne (yard waste)
Recycling: Both Curbside & Depot; Public Drop Off Depot, E.C. Row & Central Ave., 519/974-1010
Special Bans/by-laws: Various sewer usage by-laws
Hazardous Waste Depot or Facility: Household Chemical Waste Depot & Reuse Centre, C.C. Row & Central Ave.
Water & Wastewater Treatment:
Lou Romano Water Reclamation Plant, 519/253-7217; Little River Pollution Control Plant, 519/948-1751; City's Environmental Services also maintains 32 pumping stations
Other Initiatives:
Adopt-A-Street

Woodstock, page 723
Waste Management:
Waste & recycling collection responsibility of city
Special Bans/by-laws: By-law #7138-94 makes recycling mandatory for certain items; Waste limit 3 bags/week/residence; Extra bags will not be collected
Composters subsidized: Yes
Water & Wastewater Treatment:
Water Pollution Control Plant, 519/537-8351
Other Initiatives:
Paint Swap; Appliance Drop-Off Day; Household Hazardous Waste days

Woolwich, page 732
Waste Management:
Responsibility of the Regional Municipality of Waterloo
Water & Wastewater Treatment:
Regional Municipality of Waterloo responsible for water & wastewater treatment; Township responsible for collection & local distribution

York, page 705
Waste Management:
Waste from transfer stations is transported to the Green Lane Landfill in southwestern Ontario & the Onyx Arbor Hills Landfill & Carleton Farms Landfill in Michigan; Contact: garbage@region.york.on.ca
Solid Waste Disposal Fees: $70/tonne (residential); $86/tonne (industrial, commercial & institutional)
Clean Fill Fee: Yes; $7/load (up to 500 kg)
Transfer Station(s): Georgina Waste Transfer Station (Household Hazardous Waste & Recycling Depot), 23068 Warden Ave., Town of Georgina
Recycling: Both Curbside & Depot; York Region Waste Management Centre (Household Hazardous Waste & Recycling Depot), 100 Garfield Wright Blvd., East Gwillimbury; York Region Waste Transfer Station (Household Hazardous Waste & Recycling Depot), 23068 Warden Ave., Georgina; Contact: recycling@region.york.on.ca
Hazardous Waste Depot or Facility: Georgina (Warden); Markham (Rodick Rd); East Gwillimbury (Garfield Wright)
Composters subsidized: Yes
Water & Wastewater Treatment:
City of Toronto supplies water from its water treatment plants to urban areas of Markham, Richmond Hill & Vaughan; Water treatment plants owned & operated by the region: Georgina, Keswick; Wastewater treatment plants owned & operated by region: Stouffville, Mount Albert, Holland Landing, Schomberg, Kleinburg, Keswick, Sutton; York Durham Sewage System: Duffin Creek Water Pollution Control Plant in Pickering serves Newmarket, Aurora, Richmond Hill, Vaughan & Markham
Other Initiatives:
In addition to the region's Georgina Waste Transfer Station, waste is accepted at City of Toronto transfer stations & Miller Waste Systems' Transfer Station (a private facility); In addition to the region's 2 recycling locations, Markham, Aurora & Whitchurch-Stouffville operate their own recycling depots

Prince Edward Island

Charlottetown, page 732
Waste Management:
Waste collection services provided by Island Waste Management Commission, 902/894-0330, URL: www.iwmc.pe.ca, Email: info@iwmc.pe.ca
Special Bans/by-laws: Tree maintenance bylaws
Water & Wastewater Treatment:
Water sources include the Brackley, Suffolk & Union main wellfields & the smaller Brookdale & Hunter Green systems; Malpeque pumping station is a water supply used as required; Sewage treatment facilities include the Riverside Drive Treatment Plant, East Royalty Lagoon & sewer pumping stations at Dorchester Street, Navy Quay, West Royalty & West Royalty Industrial Park
Other Initiatives:
Establishment of Department of Urban Beautification & Forestry

Summerside, page 733
Waste Management:
Waste collection responsibility of Waste Management Commission

Québec

Abitibi, page 746
Waste Management:
Many contractors
Number of landfill sites: 12
Recycling: Curbside; 80% of households have collection
Hazardous Waste Depot or Facility: 50% of households have collection

Abitibi-Ouest, page 746
Other Initiatives:
Plan de gestion des matières résiduelles; service de collecte et traitement des boues des fosses septiques

Acton, page 746
Waste Management:
Several centers & organizations accept recyclable materials, composting materials & hazardous waste
Recycling: Both Curbside & Depot
Water & Wastewater Treatment:
7 centres to treat sludge
Other Initiatives:
Plan conjoint de gestion des matiSres résiduelles des MRC d'Acton et Maskoutains; 3 collections: regular household waste, recyclable waste, organic materials

Alma, page 733
Waste Management:
Recycling: Both Curbside & Depot

Amos, page 733
Waste Management:
Contracted to Sanimos Inc., 819/732-8833
Solid Waste Disposal Fees: $60.00
Recycling: Both Curbside & Depot; Depot centre is for three regions

Special Bans/by-laws: Institutions, businesses & plants are required to recycle materials using blue & grey boxes
Hazardous Waste Depot or Facility: Sorting area with the materials forwarded to specialized centres
Water & Wastewater Treatment:
Drinking water from well #1 & #2 purified through a filter system

Argenteuil, page 747
Water & Wastewater Treatment:
Responsibility of MRC
Other Initiatives:
Implementation of Plan de gestion des matières résiduelles

Baie-Comeau, page 733
Waste Management:
Recycling: Curbside

Beauharnois, page 734
Waste Management:
Recycling: Both Curbside & Depot

Beauharnois-Salaberry, page 747
Waste Management:
Number of landfill sites: 1
Composters subsidized: Yes
Water & Wastewater Treatment:
Responsibility of MRC
Other Initiatives:
Implementation of Plan de gestion des matières résiduelles; Automated collection of recyclable materials; Promotion of composting; New garbage containers for household waste

Bécancour, page 734
Water & Wastewater Treatment:
Centrale de traitement d'eau, (155, av. Godefroy), 819/233-2147

Bellechasse, page 747
Waste Management:
Waste management responsibiltiy of MRC de Bellechasse; Garbage trucks belong to the MRC; Collection handled by Campor inc. for MRC de Bellechasse, Montmagny & Les Etchemins; Landfill site in Armagh

Beloeil, page 734
Waste Management:
Recycling: Both Curbside & Depot

Blainville, page 734
Waste Management:
Waste collection contracted to Entreprise Sanitaire F.A. Ltée, 514/661-5080; Recyclables collection contracted to La Régie Intermunicipale d'Argenteuil Deux-Montagnes, 450/562-0778; Dry material depot: 60, boul de la Seigneurie Est, Blainville, 450/434-5348
Transfer Station(s): Corporation régionale de Centre de Tri-CFER, 450/562-4488
Hazardous Waste Depot or Facility: 60, boul de la Seigneurie
Water & Wastewater Treatment:
Responsibility of the city of Ste-Thérèse

Boisbriand, page 734
Waste Management:
Waste collection responsibility of Régie intermunicipale Argenteuil Deux Montagnes; Treatment under CFER Lachute
Water & Wastewater Treatment:
Responsibliity of town of Ste-Thérèse

Bonaventure, page 747
Water & Wastewater Treatment:
All municipal water responsibility of MRC

Brome-Missisquoi, page 747
Waste Management:
Landfill operated by Régie Intermunicipale d'Élimination de Déchets Solides de Brome-Missisquoi
Other Initiatives:
Implementation of Plan de gestion des matières résiduelles; Publications: Guide pratique de la récupération, Prendre en main nos déchets, Dépliant sur l'herbicyclage

Candiac, page 734
Waste Management:
Responsibility of the MRC (Roussillon)
Recycling: Both Curbside & Depot
Water & Wastewater Treatment:
Water treatment plant located at 62, Marie-Victorin, operated by Ville de Candiac, 450/444-6000

Page numbers refer to full profile.

Municipal Waste Management and Water & Wastewater Treatment / Québec

Chambly, page 734
Waste Management:
Waste collection contracted to Intersan; Chambly residents can drop off construction debris at a dry materials site located at 2400, boul Industriel
Number of landfill sites: 1
Hazardous Waste Depot or Facility: Yes
Water & Wastewater Treatment:
Water treatment contracted to SECTEAU, 514/658-1112
Other Initiatives:
Collection of leaves & yard waste for composting

Charlevoix, page 747
Waste Management:
Waste management responsibility of the MRC; Landfill operated by the MRC

Châteauguay, page 735
Waste Management:
Recycling: Curbside
Water & Wastewater Treatment:
Wastewater Treatment Plant located in Saint-Bernard; Pumping stations: Jean-Louis Chèvrefils, Joseph-Chèvrefils, Marchard & Alonzo-Béliveau
Other Initiatives:
Household hazardous waste collected annually

Coaticook, page 747
Waste Management:
Number of landfill sites: 1; *Landfill Capacity:* 30 years
Recycling: Curbside
Other Initiatives:
Implementation of an Eco-centre; Septic tank policy for municipalities; Implementation of Plan de gestion des matières résiduelles; Environmental brochures; Metal containers for paint cans

Cowansville, page 735
Waste Management:
Responsible for waste collection; Collection of toxic materials
Hazardous Waste Depot or Facility: Landfill stie, 2500, rang St-Joseph, Cowansville, 450/263-2351
Other Initiatives:
Pick-up of composting materials

D'Autray, page 747
Waste Management:
Landfill owned by Groupe EBI
Other Initiatives:
Implementation of Plan de gestion des matières résiduelles; Septic tank policy; Collection of composting materials

Deux-Montagnes, page 735
Waste Management:
Recycling: Curbside

Drummond, page 747
Other Initiatives:
Implementation of Plan de gestion des matières résiduelles: En vert et avec tous; No new landfill will be authorized; Reuse & recycle 65% of solid waste

Drummondville, page 735
Waste Management:
Recycling: Both Curbside & Depot
Water & Wastewater Treatment:
Water treatment plant at 60, rue Poirier, 819/478-6576, Fax: 819/474-8824, Email: ute@cgocable.ca
Other Initiatives:
Pick-up of composting materials

Gaspé, page 735
Waste Management:
Waste collection & management responsibility of the city; Some contracts are undertaken by private companies under the supervision of the public works superintendent

Gatineau, page 735
Waste Management:
Waste collection responsibility of the city
Recycling: Both Curbside & Depot
Other Initiatives:
Composting materials pick-up in Aylmer & Hull region in 2007 & other regions in 2008

Granby, page 735
Waste Management:
Recycling: Curbside
Water & Wastewater Treatment:
Station d'épuration des eaux usées, 1250, boul Industriel; Centrale de traitement d'eau potable, 91, rue Robitaille

L'Assomption, page 736
Waste Management:
Construction materials collected through Groupe EBI, 450/836-2546
Recycling: Curbside
Hazardous Waste Depot or Facility: 134, ch des Commissaires
Water & Wastewater Treatment:
Jean Perreault Water Treatment Plant, 450, boul l'Ange-Gardien; Wastewater pumping stations at Thouin & St-Ours; 8 pumping stations; Directeur: Christian Sauvageau

L'Assomption, page 748
Other Initiatives:
Implementation of Plan de gestion des matières résiduelles; High waste recovery objectives; Promotion of recycling & composting

L'Érable, page 748
Other Initiatives:
Implementation of Plan de gestion des matières résiduelles; Reclaim 65% of recoverable residual material; Promote recycling, reusing, reducing & composting; Establish a waste sorting & recovery centre

La Haute-Yamaska, page 748
Water & Wastewater Treatment:
Water management responsibility of MRC
Other Initiatives:
Implementaion of Plan de gestion des matières résiduelles; Reduce the use of landfills by 60% through reuse, recycling & composting

La Mitis, page 748
Waste Management:
MRC responsible for landfill used by 11 municipalities
Other Initiatives:
Centre de formation en entreprise et récupération (CFER) managed by MRC

La Nouvelle-Beauce, page 748
Waste Management:
CRGD (Centre de récupération et de gestion des déchets), 418/397-5402; Info-environnement: 418/387-3441

La Prairie, page 736
Waste Management:
Recycling: Both Curbside & Depot
Water & Wastewater Treatment:
Filtration plant, 310, rue Ignace, La Prairie J5R 1E5, 450/444-6694

La Vallée-de-l'Or, page 748
Other Initiatives:
Implementation of Plan de gestion des matières résiduelles, Vert un mode de vie; Reduce waste by 65%, through waste reduction, recycling, reuse, composting & special collections; Septic tanks policies

La Vallée-de-la-Gatineau, page 748
Water & Wastewater Treatment:
Sludge from septic tanks is treated at Kazabazua purification plant, responsibility of MRC
Other Initiatives:
Implementation of Plan de gestion des matières résiduelles; Reduce use of landfills by 60% through recycling, reducing & composting

La Vallée-du-Richelieu, page 748
Water & Wastewater Treatment:
All waters on territory managed by the MRC

Lachute, page 736
Waste Management:
Wastewater plant, 550, boul de l'Aéroparc
Water & Wastewater Treatment:
Water filtration plant, 1950, ch Thomas-Gore, 450-562-9302

Lajemmerais, page 749
Waste Management:
Garage municipal de Contrecoeur, 4884, rang du Ruisseau

Water & Wastewater Treatment:
Plant: 533, rue de l'Aqueduc; All waters under the jurisdiction of the MRC
Other Initiatives:
Collection of recyclable & green materials; Promotion of composting; Publications: Guide pratique de la récupération domestique; Water conservation; Pesticides policies

Laval, page 736
Waste Management:
Waste collection contracted to Intersan, Clément Riberdy, 450/438-5604; Recyclables collection contracted to Rebuts Solides Canadiens, Michel Leboeuf, 514/593-8555
Solid Waste Disposal Fees: $33.72/tonne
Clean Fill Fee: No
Transfer Station(s): Yes
Recycling: Curbside
Hazardous Waste Depot or Facility: Collection days
Compost Sites: No *Composters subsidized:* Yes
Water & Wastewater Treatment:
Water treatment plants: Usine Chomedey, 3810, boul Lévesque; Usine Pont-Viau, 45, rue St-Hubert; Usine Ste-Rose, 4, rue Hotte; Wastewater treatment plants: Station d'épuration Fabreville, 3985, rue Séguin; Station d'épuration Auteuil, 8985, boul des Laurentides; Station d'épuration Lapinière, 1133, Montée Masson
Other Initiatives:
First 3 streams collection system in Québec, carts & composting; Distribution of 9,000 subsidized household composters; Household composting demonstration site; Christmas tree collection; Waste education programs; Water-use education program; Lawn watering control; Wastewater sludge agricultural utilization after drying & granulation; Leaf collection & composting pilot program; Collects 3 streams from 6,000 households - garbage, recyclables & compostables; Herbicylage program; Ecological landscaping demonstration area

Le Haut-Richelieu, page 749
Other Initiatives:
Partnership with Comp-Haut-Richelieu; Recycling information: www.compo-haut-richelieu.qc.ca/cgi-bin/index.cgi

Le Haut-St-François, page 749
Other Initiatives:
Establish a waste sorting and recovery centre; Collection of hazardous waste; Promote composting; Public awareness program

Le Val-St-François, page 749
Waste Management:
All waste management, including landfill management, by the Société de gestion, d'élimination et de mise en valeur des matières résiduelles du Val-Saint-François

Les Appalaches, page 749
Other Initiatives:
Implementation of Plan de gestion des matières résiduelles; Reduce waste by 65% through waste reduction, recycling, composting, increased collections, waste sorting & recovery centres

Les Chenaux, page 749
Waste Management:
Régie de gestion des matières résiduelles de la Mauricie
Water & Wastewater Treatment:
All waters on the territory responsibility of the MRC
Other Initiatives:
Implementation of Plan de gestion des matières résiduelles managed by Régie de gestion des matières résiduelles de la Mauricie

Les Collines-de-l'Outaouais, page 749
Water & Wastewater Treatment:
Septic tank program in collaboration with municipalities
Other Initiatives:
Implementation of Plan de gestion des matières résiduelles; Waste sorting & recovery centre managed by Cascades Récupération; Reclaim 65% of recoverable residual material; Initiate composting program

Les Laurentides, page 749
Waste Management:
Managed by Régie intermunicipale de Récupération des Hautes-Laurentides & Régie intermunicipale des déchets de la Rouge for 13 municipalities
Other Initiatives:

Page numbers refer to full profile.

Municipal Waste Management and Water & Wastewater Treatment / Québec

Implementation of Plan de gestion des matières résiduelles; Reclaim 65% of recoverable residual material; Establish a Complexe interrégional de traitement & an éco-centre; Composting program; Special attention given to tourist areas

Les Maskoutains, page 749
Waste Management:
Managed by the Régie intermunicipale de gestion des déchets de la région maskoutaine
Other Initiatives:
Implementation of Plan de gestion des matières résiduelles in collaboration with MRC d'Acton; Use of 3 containers: green (recyclable materials); grey (household refuse); brown (organic matter)

Les Pays-d'en-Haut, page 750
Water & Wastewater Treatment:
MRC responsible for all waters on its territory
Other Initiatives:
Implementation of Plan de gestion des matières résiduelles; Recover 65% of residual materials that can be recuperated; Promotion of reduce, reuse, recycle & compost; Increase efficiency of green waste collection

Les Sources, page 750
Other Initiatives:
Implementation of La Brigade verte: mrcasbestos.com/brigadeverte/index.htm

Lévis, page 736
Waste Management:
Incinérateur municipal: 259, ch des Iles; Déchetterie de St-Lambert: 517, rue St-Aimé, St-Lambert-de-Lauzon
Recycling: Both Curbside & Depot
Water & Wastewater Treatment:
Four filtration plants (Charny, Lévis, Lauzon, St-Romuald)

Longueuil, page 737
Waste Management:
Recycling: Curbside
Hazardous Waste Depot or Facility: Yes
Water & Wastewater Treatment:
Filtration plant Le Royer (Brossard, Greenfield Park, St-Lambert-Le Moyne); Water/wastewater treatment plant Rive-Sud (Saint-Hubert); 3 plants in Longueuil
Other Initiatives:
Leaf drop-off bins

Lotbinière, page 750
Water & Wastewater Treatment:
Site d'enfouissement, 1450, rang Pointe-du-Jour, 418/728-5554, Fax: 418/728-5554

Magog, page 737
Waste Management:
Recycling: Both Curbside & Depot
Water & Wastewater Treatment:
Wastewater treatment plant, 819/843-0215, Fax: 819/843-9036

Mascouche, page 737
Waste Management:
Recycling: Both Curbside & Depot

Matane, page 738
Waste Management:
Landfill at 330, rue des Goélands, 418-562-5023
Number of landfill sites: 1
Recycling: Both Curbside & Depot

Matawinie, page 750
Waste Management:
Responsibility of the municipalities

Memphrémagog, page 750
Other Initiatives:
Septic tank policies; Regulations for protection of lake waters from pleasure boat waste & sewage discharges; Implementation of Plan de gestion des matières résiduelles; Recovery of residual material; Promote reduce, reuse & recycle; Composting program; Public awareness campaigns; Promote composting; Regulations for pesticide use; Forestry preservation plan

Minganie, page 750
Waste Management:
Responsibility of member municipalities
Other Initiatives:
Septic tank waste treatment

Mirabel, page 738
Waste Management:
4 Écocentres: St-Justin, St-Canut, St-Janvier, Ste-Scholastique
Recycling: Both Curbside & Depot

Mont-St-Hilaire, page 738
Waste Management:
Recycling: Both Curbside & Depot
Other Initiatives:
Collection & composting of leaves; Annual collection of household hazardous waste

Montcalm, page 750
Waste Management:
Contracted to EBI in St-Thomas-de-Joliette
Recycling: Curbside; Contracted to EBI
Hazardous Waste Depot or Facility: Sainte-Julienne
Water & Wastewater Treatment:
Not the responsibility of the MRC

Montmagny, page 750
Other Initiatives:
Implementation of Plan de gestion des matières résiduelles; Reclaim 65% of recoverable residual material

Montréal, page 738
Waste Management:
Complexe environmental Saint-Michel (CESM) 2235, rue Michel-Jurdant, 514/872-1226
Water & Wastewater Treatment:
Station d'épuration 12001, Maurice Duplessis; 514/280-4400; Fax: 514/280-4387
Other Initiatives:
Guide du réemploi de Montréal: guide pratique permet de trouver des moyens pour contribuer à la protection de l'environnement en diminuant la quantité de matières acheminées vers les sites d'enfouissement.

Nicolet-Yamaska, page 750
Waste Management:
Waste collection outsourced to several organizations, but managed by Régie intermunicipale de gestion intégrée des déchets Bécancour Nicolet-Yamaska & Bas-St-François
Other Initiatives:
Implementation of Plan de gestion des matières résiduelles; Increase services offered; Public awareness campaigns

Papineau, page 750
Other Initiatives:
Implementation of Plan de gestion des matières résiduelles; Recycling residual materials from forestry industry

Pierre-De Saurel, page 750
Waste Management:
Waste collection contracted to Conporec Inc., 514/746-9996
Other Initiatives:
Implementation of Plan de gestion des matières résiduelles; Reclaim 65% of recoverable residual material; Provide a waste sorting & recovery centre; Promote recycling, reusing & composting; Increase collections & number of containers per household

Pincourt, page 739
Waste Management:
Responsibility of the MRC (Vaudreil-Soulanges), 450/455-5753
Recycling: Curbside
Special Bans/by-laws: Pesticide ban in effect for the months of July & August; Water restrictions
Water & Wastewater Treatment:
Usine de Pincourt, 707, Cardinal-Léger, Pincourt QC J7V 6W9, 514/425-2622
Other Initiatives:
Household hazardous waste collection every 2 years

Portneuf, page 751
Waste Management:
Waste collections done by Service sanitaire Donat Pagé, Services sanitaires NGCDA & Services Matrec; Landfill managed by Régie intermunicipale de l'Est de Portneuf
Other Initiatives:
Septic tank policies; Implementation of Plan de gestion des matières résiduelles; Increase recycling initiatives & green waste collections; Inform & educate citizens on source reduction & reuse of residual materials; Establish a waste sorting & recovery centre; Increase household containers capacity

Québec, page 740
Waste Management:
Dry waste drop-off site: 336, rue Charles-Marchand; Paint: Centre de rénovation Prud'homme, 444, rue Notre-Dame
Recycling: Both Curbside & Depot
Water & Wastewater Treatment:
Water treatment: 535, rue La Traverse, 450-470-3870; Wastewater plant: 45, rue Lebel, 450-470-3880

Régie d'assainissement des eaux de la région sherbrookoise, page 759
Water & Wastewater Treatment:
Responsible for the treatment of wastewater only; Wastewater treatment is contracted to Jean-Francois Audet, Aquatech, 819/566-1150, poste 202

Régie d'assainissement des eaux usées de Boischatel, L'Ange-Gardien, Château-Ric, page 759
Waste Management:
Waste collection contracted to C.S. Matrec, 418/628-8666
Composters subsidized: Yes
Water & Wastewater Treatment:
Water treatment at Regie d'assainissement des eaux usees, 66010, boul Ste-Anne, L'Ange-Guardien, G0A 2K0

Régie d'assainissement des eaux usées Rougemont/St-Césaire, page 759
Water & Wastewater Treatment:
Water management contracted to Aquatech Inc., 450/646-5270; Station d'épuration inter-municipale, 1372, rte 112, Rougemont, QC

Régie intermunicipale d'assainissement des eaux de Sainte-Thérèse et Blainville, page 760
Water & Wastewater Treatment:
Régie intermunicipale d'assainissement des eaux usées de Sainte-Thérese et Blainville; Contracted to Simo Management, 514/281-1010

Régie intermunicipale d'assainissement des eaux de Rosemère et de Lorraine, page 760
Water & Wastewater Treatment:
Centrale de traitement de l'eau de Rosemère; Usine d'épuration de Rosemère et de Lorraine

Régie intermunicipale de gestion des déchets solides des Etchemins, page 760
Waste Management:
Responsibility of the Régie des déchets de CJLLR, 418/383-5397
Water & Wastewater Treatment:
Not the responsibility of the Régie

Régie intermunicipale de l'eau de Deux-Montagnes, page 760
Water & Wastewater Treatment:
Responsible for water treatment for the municipalities of Deux-Montagnes, St-Marthe-sur-le-Lac, St-Joseph-du-Lac, & Pointe-Calumet since the formation of the Régie in 1987

Régie intermunicipale de l'eau potable Varennes, Ste-Julie, St-Amable, page 760
Water & Wastewater Treatment:
Responsible for water treatment for Varennes, Sainte-Julie & Saint-Amable; Usine de filtration, 1870 Marie-Victorin, Varennes; usine d'épuration, 2630 Ste-Anne, Varennes

Régie intermunicipale des déchets de la Rouge, page 761
Waste Management:
Waste collection contracted to Intersan & Service environnementaux Lachute
Number of landfill sites: 1; *Landfill Capacity:* 5 years
Solid Waste Disposal Fees: $35/tonne
Hazardous Waste Depot or Facility: Landfill site

Régie intermunicipale des déchets solides de la Lièvre, page 761
Waste Management:
Waste collection contracted to Laidlaw & Service environnementaux Lachute

Régie intermunicipale du comté de Beauce-Sud, page 761
Waste Management:
Contracted to SSDF Inc., 418/228-7877
Number of landfill sites: 1
Solid Waste Disposal Fees: $100/tonne
Clean Fill Fee: Yes; $100/tonne
Hazardous Waste Depot or Facility: Let St. Couric Liniec
Water & Wastewater Treatment:
Regie intermunicipale du comite du Beauce Sud

Repentigny, page 740
Waste Management:
Transfer Station(s): 139, de la rue Louvain
Hazardous Waste Depot or Facility: 134, ch des Commissaires, L'Assomption
Composters subsidized: Yes
Water & Wastewater Treatment:
Water treatment at 535, rue de la Traverse, 450/654-2369; Wastewater treatment at 428, rue Notre-Dame, 450/654-2468
Other Initiatives:
Dye or paint products can be dropped off at Centre de rénovation Prud-homme, 444, rue Notre-Dame

Rimouski, page 740
Waste Management:
Contracted to Sanibelle Inc., 418/724-6447
Number of landfill sites: 2; *Landfill Capacity:* 50 years
Solid Waste Disposal Fees: $38.30/capita
Recycling: Both Curbside & Depot; Colisee depot
Special Bans/by-laws: Pesticide ban, water restrictions
Hazardous Waste Depot or Facility: Annual collection
Water & Wastewater Treatment:
Household water is treated
Other Initiatives:
New Eco-centre; New landfill

Rivière-du-Loup, page 741
Waste Management:
Sanibele, 418/862-9017
Number of landfill sites: 1; *Landfill Capacity:* 50 years
Solid Waste Disposal Fees: $43.50/tonne
Hazardous Waste Depot or Facility: No
Compost Sites: Yes *Composters subsidized:* No
Water & Wastewater Treatment:
Usine de filtration, eau potable, 100, rue Delage; E'tangs aérés, 300, Bellevue

Robert-Cliche, page 753
Other Initiatives:
Implementation of Plan de gestion des matières résiduelles; Increase services throughout the region; Update infrastructure; Increase capacity of household containers; Promote composting; Establish a waste sorting and recovery centre; Educate citizens

Roberval, page 741
Water & Wastewater Treatment:
Water treatment: Usine d'eau potable, 770, boul de la Traversée, Roberval; Wastewater: Usine de prétraitement, 201, rue Côté, Roberval

Rosemère, page 741
Waste Management:
Waste collection contracted to Entr. Sanitaire F.A. Ltée., 514/661-5080
Solid Waste Disposal Fees: $23/tonne
Special Bans/by-laws: Regulations on pesticide use; drinking water, runoff.
Hazardous Waste Depot or Facility: 190, rue Charbonneau
Water & Wastewater Treatment:
Water treatment plant, 450/621-6630; Wastewater treatment plant, Rosemère-Lorraine, 450/621-6630

Roussillon, page 753
Waste Management:
Services Matrec, Boucherville
Other Initiatives:
Publication: Journal La Vie d'ange; 16 schools participate in composting program

Rouville, page 753
Waste Management:
Waste management responsibility of MRC; Waste management contracted to Matrec/Transvick Inc., 514/641-3070
Composters subsidized: Yes
Water & Wastewater Treatment:
Wastewater treatment plant located in Ange-Gardien
Other Initiatives:
Implementation of Plan de gestion des matières résiduelles; Green waste collections; Paint disposal program in collaboration with local businesses; Used oil program in collaboration with Canadian Tire

Rouyn-Noranda, page 741
Waste Management:
Large items accepted at Éco-centre; Motor oil accepted at Canadian Tire; Fluorescents accepted at Norama Industries; Batteries accepted at La Sources; Expired drugs accepted at pharmacies
Recycling: Both Curbside & Depot
Hazardous Waste Depot or Facility: Éco-centre Arthur Gagnon, 210, av Marcel Baril
Water & Wastewater Treatment:
Water filtration plant located at 2, 9e rue
Other Initiatives:
Opération grand nettoyage in the fall

Saguenay, page 741
Waste Management:
Waste collection contracted to Matrec, 418/549-8074 & Service Sanitaire R. Bonneau, 1-800-590-2615
Solid Waste Disposal Fees: $66/tonne
Recycling: ; 5 depots
Hazardous Waste Depot or Facility: No
Compost Sites: Yes *Composters subsidized:* Yes
Water & Wastewater Treatment:
Water filtration plants at Chicoutimi, Arvida & Jonquière; Wastewater plants at Chicoutimi, Jonquière & La Baie
Other Initiatives:
Plan de gestion des matieres residuelles sera mis á jour dans les proclaires mors

Saint-Basile-le-Grand, page 741
Waste Management:
Recycling: Both Curbside & Depot

Saint-Charles-Borromée, page 753
Water & Wastewater Treatment:
Water treatment at 1020, rue de la Visitation

Saint-Constant, page 742
Waste Management:
Éco-centre: 25, montée Lasaline
Recycling: Depot
Other Initiatives:
Bac roulant de 360 litres

Saint-Eustache, page 742
Waste Management:
Waste collection cntracted to Rebus Canada, 514/648-8815
Solid Waste Disposal Fees: $23/tonne
Clean Fill Fee: Yes; $5/cubic metre
Hazardous Waste Depot or Facility: Garage municipal
Compost Sites: Yes
Water & Wastewater Treatment:
Wastewater treatment plant at 50, 25e av; Filtration plant at 45, rue Chénier; Water treatment contracted to Simo Management Inc., 514/384-5660

Saint-Georges, page 742
Waste Management:
Responsibility of the Régie intermunicipale du comté de Beauce-Sud; Collection contracted to GS Gestion des déchets
Recycling: Curbside
Water & Wastewater Treatment:
Water treatment contracted to Aquatech, 418/228-6640; Water treatment plant, 14800, 1ère av, St-Georges, 418/228-6640; Wastewater treatment plant, 400, av Chaudière, St-Georges, 418/228-4841

Saint-Hyacinthe, page 742
Waste Management:
Recycling: Both Curbside & Depot
Water & Wastewater Treatment:
Sewage & wastewater treatment plant, Email: usine-epuration@ville.st.-hyacinthe.qc.ca; Water filtration plant, 450/778-8373, Email: usine-filtration@ville.st.-hyacinthe.qc.ca

Saint-Jérôme, page 743
Waste Management:
Écocentre, rue Lajeunesse & de l'Industrie; Tricentris, 601, ch Félix-Touchette, Lachute J8H 2C5, 450-562-4488
Recycling: Both Curbside & Depot
Other Initiatives:
Cèdres Recyclés (cedar trees pick up); Composting program

Saint-Lazare, page 743
Waste Management:
Recycling: Both Curbside & Depot
Other Initiatives:
Since Nov. 2000, the Town of St. Lazare prohibits the use of pesticides for cosmetic purposes. Since that time, residents dealing with major infestation problems must apply for a temporary spraying permit with the town's Urban Planning & Zoning departments.

Saint-Lin-Laurentides, page 743
Waste Management:
Construction material drop-off, Ste-Sophie (1-800-267-1251), Service fee
Recycling: Both Curbside & Depot
Hazardous Waste Depot or Facility:

Sainte-Anne-des-Plaines, page 743
Water & Wastewater Treatment:
Water treatment at 3, boul Ste-Anne, 450/478-5373; Municipal aqueduct at 146, rue Chaumont, 450/478-0414

Sainte-Julie, page 743
Waste Management:
Contact: 100, rue de Murano
Other Initiatives:
Computer information, c/o Club informatique, 450-653-4871

Sainte-Thérèse, page 744
Waste Management:
Recycling: Curbside
Compost Sites: Yes
Water & Wastewater Treatment:
111, boul Curé-Labelle, Rosemère J7A 4C1
Other Initiatives:
No pesticides/herbicides allowed - free consulting service

Salaberry-de-Valleyfield, page 744
Waste Management:
Contact: 978 & 1000 boul Cadieux, 450-370-4230
Recycling: Both Curbside & Depot
Water & Wastewater Treatment:
Water treatment plant: 64, av du Centenaire

Sept-Iles, page 744
Waste Management:
Recycling: Both Curbside & Depot

Sept-Rivières, page 753
Waste Management:
Responsibility of the Ville de Sept-Iles & Ville de Port-Cortice

Shawinigan, page 744
Waste Management:
La Ressourcerie, 2132, av de la Transmission, 819-537-8737; Éco-centre
Recycling: Both Curbside & Depot

Sherbrooke, page 744
Water & Wastewater Treatment:
Water & wastewater treatment plant operated by Régie intermunicipale des eaux usées, 2275, Claude Giffard, Sherbrooke, 819/823-5562, Email: info@raers.qc.ca

Sorel-Tracy, page 745
Waste Management:
Construction materials: c/o Conporec, 746-9996, service fee
Other Initiatives:
Implementation of wheeled containers for garbage

Témiscamingue, page 753
Waste Management:
Waste collection contracted to Transport Larouche et Beauregard
Number of landfill sites: 19
Recycling: Depot; 21 dépôts in Ville-Marie
Water & Wastewater Treatment:
Wastewater treatment plant at Ville-Marie

Terrebonne, page 745
Other Initiatives:
Environmental policy: Plan vert

Page numbers refer to full profile.

Municipal Waste Management and Water & Wastewater Treatment / Saskatchewan

Thetford Mines, page 745
Waste Management:
Transport ordurier de la région de L'Amiante; 2951 2076 Québec inc.; Services Sanitaires Denis Fortier
Recycling: Curbside
Other Initiatives:
Centre de tri: Récupération Frontenac inc., 418/338-8551

Val-d'Or, page 746
Waste Management:
Recycling: Both Curbside & Depot
Water & Wastewater Treatment:
Usine d'épuration, 1500, chemin des Eaux-Nettes, Val-d'Or, QC, J9P 4N7, phone & fax: 819/874-8722
Other Initiatives:
Info-Récup, 819/874-8378

Varennes, page 746
Waste Management:
Waste collection responsibility of the MRC de Lajemmerais; Waste collection contracted to Services Matrec Inc.
Hazardous Waste Depot or Facility: 1850 Marie-Victorin (once a year)
Water & Wastewater Treatment:
Water treatment responsibility of the Régie intermunicipale de l'eau potable Varennes - Sainte-Julie - Saint-Amable, 514/652-2052; Usine de filtration, 1870 boul Marie-Victorin, Varennes; Wastewater treatment responsibility of the city

Vaudreuil-Dorion, page 746
Waste Management:
Contact: 325, rue Marie-Curie
Water & Wastewater Treatment:
Contact: 2530, ch Paul-Gérin-Lajoie, 450-424-7802

Vaudreuil-Soulanges, page 753
Waste Management:
Waste collection done by Rebuts Solides Canadiens & Robert Daoust; Waste processing outside the MRC
Other Initiatives:
Implementation of Plan de gestion des matières résiduelles; Improve existing collection services; Increase reduce, reuse & recycle practices; Establish a composting site

Victoriaville, page 746
Waste Management:
Contact: 350, rue de la Bulstrode, 819-357-8666
Recycling: Both Curbside & Depot
Water & Wastewater Treatment:
Usine d'épuration des eaux Achille-Gagnon, 555, boul Jutras ouest
Other Initiatives:
3 containers: green (recyclable materials), brown (organic matters), grey (solid waste)

Saskatchewan

Estevan, page 754
Waste Management:
City's Engineering Services Division manages third party contracts for residential waste collection
Number of landfill sites: 1
Water & Wastewater Treatment:
City of Estevan Water Treatment Plant, River Rd., 306/634-1822; City of Estevan Wastewater Treatment Plant, southern city limits
Other Initiatives:
Paint recycle program

Moose Jaw, page 754
Waste Management:
Number of landfill sites: 1
Recycling: Depot; EcoCentre Recycling, sanitary landfill site, northeastern city limits
Hazardous Waste Depot or Facility: Hazardous Waste Collection Site, sanitary landfill site, northeastern city limits
Water & Wastewater Treatment:
Advanced Waste Water Treatment & Disposal Project, Baildon Irrigation Area; Buffalo Pound Water Treatment Plant
Other Initiatives:
Community Clean Up Week; Annual household hazardous waste collection day; Paint exchange day; Municipal Advisory Committee on the Environment; Parks & Recreation Dept. green space & urban forest area maintenance

North Battleford, page 754
Waste Management:
Waste collection contracted to K&B Construction, 306/445-3900.
Number of landfill sites: 1; *Landfill Capacity:* 50 years
Solid Waste Disposal Fees: $40/tonne
Recycling: Depot; 2 main & 35 paper only depots
Hazardous Waste Depot or Facility: Various depots
Composters subsidized: Yes
Water & Wastewater Treatment:
City owns: #1 Water Treatment Plant, FE Holliday Water Treatment Plant & a Wastewater Treatment Plant, 306/445-1766
Other Initiatives:
Newly renovated water treatment plants with UV; New wastewater plant with UV; Impressed current trial for well maintenance; Recycling & water conservation education programs

Prince Albert, page 754
Waste Management:
Number of landfill sites: 1; *Landfill Capacity:* 100 years
Solid Waste Disposal Fees: $30/tonne
Recycling: Both Curbside & Depot; Depots throughout the city
Composters subsidized: Yes
Water & Wastewater Treatment:
Water treatment plant, 655 River St. West, Prince Albert; Wastewater treatment plant, J.W. Oliver Pollution Control Centre, 2100 1st St., Prince Albert
Other Initiatives:
Composting facility in operation at landfill; Annual Paint Recycling Day; Hazardous Waste Collection Day

Regina, page 754
Waste Management:
Number of landfill sites: 1
Water & Wastewater Treatment:
Buffalo Pound Water Treatment Plant, northeast of Moose Jaw, co-owned & operated by cities of Regina & Moose Jaw; City of Regina sewage treatment plant, Engineer, 306/777-7440; Supervisor, 306/777-7692
Other Initiatives:
Big Blue Bin program features big blue recycling bins in 12 city neighbourhoods; Waste paper from bins is transported to city's Paper Recycling Depot, operated by organization under contract with the city; Cool Down the City program, encourages reduction of greenhouse gas emissions, Program Coordinator, 306/777-7639, Email: ksare@cituregina.com; Paint it Recycled program collects & recycles paint & paint cans; Tinsel Mulch Christmas Tree Recycling & Tinsel Mulch Give-Away programs; Water Conservation Program includes a Xeriscape Demonstllange for workers to use green modes of transportation

Saskatoon, page 754
Waste Management:
Number of landfill sites: 1

Solid Waste Disposal Fees: $25/tonne
Clean Fill Fee: No
Water & Wastewater Treatment:
Water treatment plant at 1030 Ave. H South; Wastewater treatment plant, 470 Whiteswan Dr.
Other Initiatives:
Paint exchange program; Cosmo Bins for newspaper & magazine recycling & Can-Man bins for tin can recycling, located throughout city; Eco Centre, located at Saskatoon landfill, offers recycling opportunities; Christmas tree drop-off locations open each January

Swift Current, page 755
Waste Management:
Waste collection contracted to Waste Management
Number of landfill sites: 1
Solid Waste Disposal Fees: $20/tonne
Recycling: Depot; Green Stop recycling depots locations: Wheatland Mall, Swift Current Mall, Fairview Arena, Civic Centre, 10th St. NW & Chaplin St., & North Railway St. East
Composters subsidized: Yes
Water & Wastewater Treatment:
Water source is Duncairn Dam; Swift Current Water Treatment Plant; Swift Current Wastewater Treatment Plant
Other Initiatives:
Community composting program, including compost collection; Household hazardous waste day; Christmas tree pickup program; 2006 litter campaign; Water conservation program, including sale of water saving devices; Renovations & upgrades to water treatment plant

Yorkton, page 755
Waste Management:
Waste collection contracted to Ottenbriet Waste Systems Ltd., 306/783-3867
Number of landfill sites: 1
Solid Waste Disposal Fees: Yes
Clean Fill Fee:
Recycling: Depot; Sask. Abilities Council, 162 Ball Rd., 306/782-7844
Special Bans/by-laws: Smoking in public & work places within the city of Yorkton
Water & Wastewater Treatment:
City owns & operates the H.M. Bailey Water Pollution Control Plant, secondary wastewater treatment facility, located east of Hwy. 9, 1 km north of the city, 306/786-1774; City owns & operates 3 water treatment plants, which are being upgraded; Contact Michael Buchholzer, 306/786-1771

Yukon Territory

Whitehorse, page 755
Waste Management:
Waste collection responsibility of city's public works department
Number of landfill sites: 1
Solid Waste Disposal Fees: $5.00/pick-up truck load
Recycling: Both Curbside & Depot; Whitehorse Landfill, Alaska Hwy.; 3 privately operated depots
Special Bans/by-laws: All-terrain vehicle bylaw; Snowmobile bylaw; Limit of 4 garbage bags collected per household per curbside collection
Water & Wastewater Treatment:
Water & sewer systems responsibility of the city; One main lagoon system, plus one minor lagoon system to serve Crestview
Other Initiatives:
Habitat conservation & stewardship program; Compostables may be dropped off at Whitehorse Landfill, Alaska Hwy., 867/668-1621

Waste & Water Commissions

Alberta

Other Municipalities in Alberta

Alberta Capital Region Wastewater Commission
23262 Township Rd. 540
Fort Saskatchewan, AB T8L 4A2
780-467-8655 Fax: 780-467-5398
Municipal Type: Water Commission
Gordon Thompson, General Manager
gthompson@acrwc.ab.ca

Athabasca Regional Waste Management Services Commission
P.O. Box 90
Athabasca, AB T9S 2A2
780-675-1117 Fax: 780-675-8881
arwmsc@telusplanet.net
Municipal Type: Water Commission
Robert Smith, Manager

Beaver Regional Waste Management Services Commission
P.O. Box 322
Ryley, AB T0B 4A0
780-663-2038 Fax: 780-663-2006
brwmsccc@telusplanet.net
www.brwmsc.com
Municipal Type: Waste Commission
Forrest Wright, CAO
Owen Ligard, Director, Operations
owen.ligard@brwmsc.com

Beaver River Regional Waste Management Commission
Bag 1010
Bonnyville, AB T9N 2J7
780-826-3951 Fax: 780-826-5064
Municipal Type: Water Commission
Marco Schroeninger, Manager
marco@md.bonnyville.ab.ca

Big Country Waste Management Commission
P.O. Box 1906
Hanna, AB T0J 1P0
403-854-5600 Fax: 403-854-5527
Municipal Type: Waste Commission
Greg R. Sheppard, Operations Manager

Bow Valley Waste Management Commission
Wild Earth Associates Inc.
185 Carey
Canmore, AB T1W 2R7
403-609-7229 Fax: 403-609-0320
bvwmc@wildearth.ab.ca
Municipal Type: Water Commission
John Stutz, Chair
jstutz@telusplanet.net

Capital Region Northeast Water Services Commission
10005 - 102 St.
Fort Saskatchewan, AB T8L 2C5
780-992-6207 Fax: 780-992-1375
Municipal Type: Water Commission
Dave Worman, Manager
dworman@fortsask.ca

Capital Region Parkland Water Services
c/o 315 Jesperson Ave.
Spruce Grove, AB T7X 3E8
780-962-2611
Municipal Type: Water Commission

Capital Region Southwest Water Services Commission
#101, 1101 - 5 St.
Nisku, AB T9E 2X3
780-955-3555 Fax: 780-955-3444
Municipal Type: Water Commission
Darryl Rubis, Manager
darryl@leduc-county.com

Capital Region Vegreville Corridor Water Services Commission
P.O. Box 176
Chipman, AB T0B 0W0
780-363-3982 Fax: 780-363-2386
chipmanab@primus.ca
Municipal Type: Waste Commission
Pat Tomkow, Manager

Central Peace Regional Waste Management Commission
c/o Saddle Hills County
P.O. Box 69
Spirit River, AB T0H 3G0
780-864-3760 Fax: 780-864-3904
Municipal Type: Water Commission
Cliff Travis, Chair

Cold Lake Regional Utility
5513 - 48 Ave.
Cold Lake, AB T9M 1A1
780-594-4494 Fax: 780-594-3480
Municipal Type: Water Commission

Evergreen Regional Waste Management Services Commission
5015 - 49 Ave.
St Paul, AB T0A 3A4
780-645-3301 Fax: 780-645-3104
Municipal Type: Water Commission
Dennis Bergheim, Manager

Foothills Regional Services
P.O. Box 5605
High River, AB T1V 1M7
403-652-2341 Fax: 403-652-7880
Municipal Type: Waste Commission
Bill Robinson, Sec.-Treas.
wrobins@mdfoothills.com
Irv Cherneski, Chair

Greenview Regional Waste Management Commission
P.O. Box 115
Valleyview, AB T0H 3N0
780-524-7601 Fax: 780-524-4432
Municipal Type: Water Commission
Gordon Frank, Acting Administrator

Henry Kroeger Regional Water Services Commission
P.O. Box 25
Youngstown, AB T0J 3P0
403-779-3904 Fax: 403-779-2279
Municipal Type: Waste Commission
Evelyn Manion, Manager

Highway 14 Regional Water Services
P.O. Box 322
Ryley, AB T0B 4A0
780-663-2039 Fax: 780-663-2006
brwmsccc@telusplanet.net
Municipal Type: Water Commission
Forrest Wright, CAO
brwmscfw@telusplanet.net

Highway 43 East Waste Commission Services
P.O. Box 219
Sangudo, AB T0E 2A0
780-785-3411 Fax: 780-785-2359
bweldon@vennercs.com
Municipal Type: Waste Commission
Ron Kidd, Chair
Mark Anker, Manager
780-454-9414

Kneehill Regional Water Services Commission
P.O. Box 592
Acme, AB T0M 2A0
403-546-3783 Fax: 403-546-3014
vacme@telus.net
Municipal Type: Water Commission
John Van Doesburg, Manager

Lakeland Regional Waste Management Services Commission
P.O. Box 387
Lac La Biche, AB T0A 2C0
780-623-4323 Fax: 780-623-3510
townlib@telusplanet.net
Municipal Type: Water Commission
Gordon Elliott, Chair

Lamont County Regional Solid Waste Commission
General Delivery
Lamont, AB T0B 2R0
780-895-2233 Fax: 780-895-7404
Municipal Type: Water Commission
John Stribling, Chair

Lesser Slave Lake Regional Waste Management Services Commission
P.O. Box 722
Slave Lake, AB T0G 2A0
780-369-2590 Fax: 780-369-2599
md124@md124.ca
www.md124.ca
Municipal Type: Water Commission
George Snider, Interim Manager

Lethbridge Regional Waste Management Services
P.O. Box 1594
Lethbridge, AB T1J 4K3
403-732-4722 Fax: 403-732-4328
rsnowdon@county.lethbridge.ab.ca
Municipal Type: Waste Commission
Eugene Wauters, Chair
Larry Thomson, Vice-Chair
Sandy Trocakstad, Sec.-Treas.

Lethbridge Regional Water Services Commission
c/o County of Lethbridge
#100, 905 - 4 Ave. South
Lethbridge, AB T1J 4E4
403-328-5525 Fax: 403-328-5602
rrobinson@county.lethbridge.ab.ca
Municipal Type: Water Commission
Rick Robinson, Commission Manager
Duncan Lloyd, Chair

Long Lake Regional Waste Management Commission
P.O. Box 178
Grimshaw, AB T0H 1W0
780-971-2200 Fax: 780-971-2200
llrwmsc@telusplanet.net
Municipal Type: Waste Commission
Elzina Vance, Acting Manager
May Rowe, Chair

Mackenzie Regional Waste Management Commission
9813 - 102 St.
High Level, AB T0H 1Z0
780-926-2201 Fax: 780-926-2899
landfill@highlevel.ca
Municipal Type: Water Commission
Ron Pelensky, Manager
Pat Kulscar, Chair

Mountain View Regional Waste Management Commission
1230
Didsbury, AB T0M 0W0
403-335-2005 Fax: 403-335-8132
nrkivell@telusplanet.net

Waste & Water Commissions / New Brunswick

Municipal Type: Water Commission
Dave Derksen, Chair

Mountain View Regional Water Services
Site 22, Box 1, RR#1
Innisfail, AB T4G 1T6
403-227-5828 Fax: 403-227-5831
mtnwater@telusplanet.net
Municipal Type: Water Commission
John Van Doesburg, Administrator

North 43 Lagoon Commission
14403 - 110 Ave.
Edmonton, AB T5N 1J7
780-454-9414 Fax: 780-452-2322
Municipal Type: Water Commission
Mark Anker, Manager

North Forty Mile Regional Waste Management Services Commission
P.O. Box 276
Bow Island, AB T0K 0G0
403-833-3805
Municipal Type: Waste Commission
Bill Ressler, Chair
Ron Lane, Vice-Chair
Roselyn Pahl, Sec.-Treas.

North Peace Regional Landfill Commission
P.O. Box 2654
Fairview, AB T0H 1L0
780-835-2576 Fax: 780-835-2579
info@nprlandfill.com
www.nprlandfill.com
Municipal Type: Water Commission
Darren Lubeck, Manager
Brent Dechant, Chair

North Red Deer River Water Services Commission
5432 - 56 Ave.
Lacombe, AB T4L 1E9
403-391-0270
Municipal Type: Water Commission
Judy Gordon, Chair

Northeast Pigeon Lake Regional Services Commission
P.O. Box 6960
Wetaskiwin, AB T9A 2G5
780-352-3321 Fax: 780-352-3486
fcoutney@telusplanet.net
Municipal Type: Water Commission
Frank Coutney, Manager
Ralph B. Johnston, Chair

Roseridge Waste Management Services Commission
P.O. Box 19
Site 1, RR#1
Morinville, AB T8R 1P4
780-939-5678 Fax: 780-939-4788
sbberry@sturgeoncounty.ab.ca
Municipal Type: Water Commission
Susan Berry, Manager
Vic Pasay, Chair

Smoky River Regional Waste Management Commission
P.O. Box 155
Falher, AB T0H 1M0
780-837-2247 Fax: 780-837-2647
tnfalher@telusplanet.net
Municipal Type: Water Commission
Carmen Ewing, Chair

Smoky River Regional Water Management Commission
P.O. Box 155
Falher, AB T0H 1M0
780-837-2247 Fax: 780-837-2647
Municipal Type: Water Commission
Margaret Tardif, Chair

South Forty Waste Services Commission
P.O. Box 307
Foremost, AB T0K 0X0

403-867-3530 Fax: 403-867-2242
Municipal Type: Water Commission
Lynden Hutchinson, Chair
lhutch@telusplanet.net

Thorhild Regional Waste Management Services Commission
P.O. Box 10
Thorhild, AB T0A 3J0
780-398-3741 Fax: 780-398-3748
Municipal Type: Water Commission
Debbie Hamilton, Acting Commission Manager
debbie@thorhild.com

Thorhild Regional Water Services Commission
P.O. Box 310
Thorhild, AB T0A 3J0
780-398-3688 Fax: 780-398-2100
dhamilton@telusplanet.net
Municipal Type: Water Commission
Debbie Hamilton, Manager

Tri Village Regional Sewage Services
Box 16, Site 1, RR#2
Carvel, AB T0E 0H0
780-963-4211 Fax: 780-963-4260
Municipal Type: Water Commission
Don Boudreaux, Chair

Two Hills Regional Waste Management Commission
P.O. Box 8
Two Hills, AB T0B 4K0
780-567-2016
Municipal Type: Water Commission
Darren Banack, Operations Manager

Vulcan District Waste Commission
P.O. Box 180
Vulcan, AB T0L 2B0
403-485-2241 Fax: 403-482-2920
countyadmin@vulcancounty.ab.ca
www.vulcancounty.ab.ca
Municipal Type: Water Commission
Merle Wyatt, Chair

Westend Regional Sewage Services
P.O. Box 330
Turner Valley, AB T0L 2A0
403-933-4744 Fax: 403-933-5377
Municipal Type: Water Commission
Sharlene Brown, Chair

Westlock Regional Waste Management Commission
10336 - 106 St.
Westlock, AB T7P 2G1
780-349-3346 Fax: 780-349-2012
Municipal Type: Water Commission
Vacant, Manager

Willow Creek Regional Waste Management Services Commission
P.O. Box 2820
Claresholm, AB T0L 0T0
403-687-2603 Fax: 403-287-2602
wcrwmsc@telusplanet.net
Municipal Type: Water Commission
Gerry McGueire, Chair

New Brunswick

Other Municipalities in New Brunswick

Commission de gestion des déchets solides de la péninsule Acadienne (COGEDES)
#4, 149, boul St-Pierre ouest
Caraquet, NB E1W 1B6
506-726-2911 Fax: 506-726-2912
cogedes@nbnet.nb.ca
www.cogedes.com
Municipal Type: Waste Commission
Jean-Marie Gionet, Chair
Gary LeBlanc, General Manager

Commission de gestion enviro ressources du Nord-Ouest (COGERNO)
248, ch Clément Roy
Rivière-Verte, NB E7C 2W7
506-263-3470 Fax: 506-263-3476
jean@nbnet.nb.ca
www.cogerno.com
Municipal Type: Water Commission
Jean A. Bourque, General Manager
Pierre Michaud, Chair

Fredericton Region Solid Waste Commission
P.O. Box 21 A
Fredericton, NB E3B 4Y2
506-453-9930 Fax: 506-453-9933
swc99@nbnet.nb.ca
www.frswc.ca
Municipal Type: Water Commission
Gordon Wilson, General Manager
506-444-0960
gordon@frswc.ca
Pierre Theriault, Operations Manager
506-453-9932
John Bigger, Chair

Fundy Region Solid Waste Commission
P.O. Box 3032
Grand-Bay Westfield, NB E5K 4V3
506-738-1212 Fax: 506-738-1207
hotline@fundyrecycles.com
www.fundyrecycles.com
Municipal Type: Water Commission
Jack Keir, General Manager
Rob Dean, Site Operations Supervisor, Crane Mountain Landfill
Ron Nelson, Environmental Coordinator
Chris Harned, Supervisor, Waste Diversion
Catherine Doucette, Officer, Public Education
Brenda MacCallum, Public Education Officer

Kent County Solid Waste Commission
2249 Rte. 134
Lakeville-Westmorland, NB E1H 1P3
506-384-9195 Fax: 506-384-6029 Toll Free Phone: 1-877-588-1125
Municipal Type: Water Commission
Roland Fougère, Chair
Florence Babineau, General Manager
fbabineau@rogers.com

Kings County Region Solid Waste Commission
P.O. Box 4861
Sussex, NB E4E 5L9
506-433-6502 Fax: 506-432-6435
kcrswc@nbnet.nb.ca
Municipal Type: Waste Commission
Garth Long, Chair
506-433-1341
gplong@nbnet.nb.ca

Nepisiguit-Chaleur Solid Waste Commission
1300, rte 360
Allardville, NB E8L 1H5
506-725-2402 Fax: 506-725-2410
redpine@nb.sympatico.ca
Municipal Type: Waste Commission
Raymond Bryar, General Manager
Graham Wiseman, Chair

Northumberland Solid Waste Commission
505 Old King George Hwy.
Miramichi, NB E1V 1J8
506-778-6646 Fax: 506-778-6642
info@nswc-cdsn.ca
www.nswc-cdsn.ca
Municipal Type: Waste Commission
Marie LeBlanc, Manager, Administration
Scotty Bernard, Chair
April Conroy, Coordinator, Waste Reduction

Restigouche Solid Waste Corporation
P.O. Box 93
162B Water St.
Campbellton, NB E3N 3G1
506-789-2111 Fax: 506-789-2111
Municipal Type: Waste Commission

Ian Comeau, General Manager
comeai@nbnet.nb.ca
Jean Perron, Chair

South West Solid Waste Commission
P.O. Box 243
St Stephen, NB E3L 2X2
506-466-7830 Fax: 506-466-7833
crww@nbnet.nb.ca
www.swswc.com
Municipal Type: Waste Commission
Ken Landmaid, Chair, Managed Forest Committee
Glenn Greenlaw, Chair, Technical Committee
Peter Fenety, Chair, Environmental Monitoring Committee

Valley Solid Waste Commission
P.O. Box 880
Hartland, NB E7P 3K4
506-375-3040 Fax: 506-375-3043 Toll Free Phone:
1-866-312-8800
vswc@nb.sympatico.ca
www.valleysolidwaste.com
Municipal Type: Water Commission
Denise Brown, Office Administrator

Westmorland-Albert Solid Waste Corporation
P.O. Box 1397
Moncton, NB E1C 8T6
506-877-1050 Fax: 506-877-1060
www.westmorlandalbert.com
Municipal Type: Waste Commission
Bill Slater, General Manager
Norman H. Crossman, Chair
Christa Methot, Coordinator, Community Relations
Yvon Gautreau, Vice-Chair
Greg Martin, Corporate Secretary
Trina Davidson, Supervisor, Site Operations

Québec

Other Municipalities in Québec

Régie d'aqueduc de Grand Pré
3000, Rang des chutes
Saint-Édouard-de-Maskinongé, QC J0K 2H0
819-228-0181 Fax: 819-228-0807
Municipal Type: Water Commission
Eve Masson, Sec.-Trés.
André Lahaye, Directeur, Opérations

Régie d'aqueduc intermunicipale des Moulins
775, rue St-Jean-Baptiste
Terrebonne, QC J6W 1B5
450-471-4192 Fax: 450-471-2594
Municipal Type: Water Commission
Claude Therrien, Operator

Régie d'aqueduc intermunicipale paroisse St-Pie et Notre-Dame-de-St-Hyacinthe
4740, rue Gouyn
Saint-Hyacinthe, QC J2S 1E1
450-773-3720 Fax: 450-773-5611
Municipal Type: Water Commission
Jean-Luc Giard, Sec.-Trés.

Régie d'aqueduc Richelieu-Centre
765A, rue St-Joseph
Saint-Louis, QC J0G 1K0
450-788-2544 Fax: 450-788-4003
rarc@mtic.qc.ca
Municipal Type: Water Commission
Ronald Jacques, Coordonateur

Régie d'assainissement des Coteaux
65, rte 338
Les Côteaux, QC J7X 1A2
450-763-0980 Fax: 450-763-1410
filt.coteau@qc.aira.com
Municipal Type: Water Commission
Jacques Legault, Agent de liaison

Régie d'assainissement des eaux de Chandler, Pabos et Pabos Mills
CP 459
35, rue Commerciale ouest
Chandler, QC G0C 1K0
418-689-2221 Fax: 418-689-4963
Municipal Type: Water Commission
Léandre Savoie, Sec.-Trés.

Régie d'assainissement des eaux de la région sherbrookoise
CP 610
555, rue des Grandes-Fourches sud, bloc
Sherbrooke, QC J1H 5H9
819-823-5562 Fax: 819-823-8207
info@raers.qc.ca
Municipal Type: Water Commission
André-P. Robert, Ing., dsa., Directeur-général, Assainissement des eaux usée

Régie d'assainissement des eaux de la Vallée du Richelieu
300, ch Brunet
Mont-Saint-Hilaire, QC J3G 4S6
450-464-0041
Municipal Type: Water Commission
Jean Tremblay, Sec.-Trés.
Ghislain Bégin, Administrateur

Régie d'assainissement des eaux du bassin de la Prairie
5000, boul Marie-Victorin
Sainte-Catherine, QC J5C 1L9
450-638-2163 Fax: 450-638-6567
Municipal Type: Water Commission
Gilbert Samson, Sec.-Trés.

Régie d'assainissement des eaux du Haut-Richelieu
CP 1025
188, rue Jacques-Cartier nord
Saint-Jean-sur-Richelieu, QC J3B 7B2
450-348-2667 Fax: 450-357-2285
Municipal Type: Water Commission
Jacques Jutras, Secrétaire

Régie d'assainissement des eaux Richelieu/Saint-Laurent
390, boul Poliquin
Sorel, QC J3P 5N3
Fax: 450-743-4132
Municipal Type: Water Commission
Louis Cardin, Sec.-Trés.

Régie d'assainissement des eaux usées de Boischatel, L'Ange-Gardien, Château-Richer
9, côte de l'Eglise
Boischatel, QC G0A 1H0
418-822-4500 Fax: 418-822-4512
Municipal Type: Water Commission
Jacques Villeneuve, Sec.-Trés.
Ghislain Bergeron, Chef technicien

Régie d'assainissement des eaux usées de la Basse-Lièvre
CP 670
57, ch de Montréal est
Masson-Angers, QC J8M 1K7
Fax: 819-986-9539
Municipal Type: Water Commission
Pierre Hayes, Sec.-Trés.

Régie d'assainissement des eaux usées de Piedmont, St-Sauveur et St-Sauveur-des-Monts
2125, ch Jean Adam
Saint-Sauveur, QC J0R 1R2
450-227-2668 Fax: 450-227-8564
Municipal Type: Water Commission
Patrice Normand, Sec.-Trés.

Régie d'assainissement des eaux usées Rougemont/St-Césaire
#4, 1111, av St-Paul
Saint-Césaire, QC J0L 1T0
450-469-0651 Fax: 450-469-5275
regie1996@bellnet.ca

Municipal Type: Water Commission
Susie Dubois, Sec.-Trés.

Régie d'assainissement des eaux usées Terrebonne/Mascouche
199, ch de la Cabane Ronde
Mascouche, QC J7K 1P1
450-474-4133
Municipal Type: Water Commission
Luc Tremblay, Sec.-Trés.

Régie de l'eau de l'Ile Perrot
1244, boul Perrot
Notre-Dame-de-l'Ile-Perrot, QC J7V 7P2
514-425-2244 Fax: 514-425-2252
Municipal Type: Water Commission
Jacob Céline, Sec.-Trés.

Régie Intermunicipale Argenteuil-Deux-Montagnes
Complex Environnemental
651, ch Félix-Touchette
Lachute, QC J8H 2C5
450-562-0778 Fax: 450-562-8482
info@riadm.ca
Municipal Type: Waste Commission
Daniel Mayer, Président

Régie intermunicipale d'alimentation en eau potable du Bas-St-François
CP 429
39, rue Aly
Pierreville, QC J0G 1M0
450-568-7160 Fax: 450-568-7160
Municipal Type: Water Commission
Diane Précourt, Sec.-Trés.

Régie intermunicipale d'approvisionnement en eau potable de l'île centrale
CP 1170
1589, ch L'Étand-du-Nord
L'Étand-du-Nord, QC G0B 1E0

Municipal Type: Water Commission
Elphège LeBlanc, Sec.-Trés., Responsable de l'alimentation en eau p

Régie intermunicipale d'approvisionnement en eau potable Henryville/Venise
559, rue Dussault
Saint-Sébastien, QC J0J 2C0
450-244-5813 Fax: 450-244-5813
Municipal Type: Water Commission
Suzanne Ouellet, Sec.-Trés.

Régie intermunicipale d'aqueduc de la vallée de Châteauguay
527, rang St-Joseph
Saint-Paul-de-Chateauguay, QC J0S 1V0
450-427-3703 Fax: 450-427-2548
Municipal Type: Water Commission
Léopold Vanier, Secrétaire

Régie intermunicipale d'aqueduc du Bas-Richelieu
737, ch des Patriotes
Saint-Denis-sur-Richelieu, QC J0H 1K0
450-787-2101 Fax: 450-787-3857
Municipal Type: Water Commission
Pierre Bélanger, Directeur-général

Régie intermunicipale d'aqueduc et d'égout de Lotbinière-Centre
121, rue St-André
Laurier-Station, QC G0S 1N0
418-728-3852 Fax: 418-728-4801
Municipal Type: Water Commission
Jean-Paul Lemay, Usine d'épuration des eaux
418-728-3976

Régie intermunicipale d'aqueduc Richelieu-Yamaska
517, ch Ste-Victoire
Sainte-Victoire-de-Sorel, QC J0G 1T0
450-782-3111 Fax: 450-782-2687
Municipal Type: Water Commission
Michel St-Martin, Sec.-Trés.

Waste & Water Commissions / Québec

Régie intermunicipale d'assainissement de Daveluyville
CP 187
337, rue Principale
Daveluyville, QC G0Z 1C0
819-367-3395 Fax: 819-367-3395
Municipal Type: Water Commission
Gaston Bélanger, Sec.-Trés.

Régie intermunicipale d'assainissement de la Haute-Bécancour
144, rue Notre-Dame sud
Thetford Mines, QC G6G 5T3
418-423-2773 Fax: 418-335-7089
Municipal Type: Water Commission
Denise Veilleux, Secrétaire

Régie intermunicipale d'assainissement des eaux usées des Desjardins
225, côte du Passage
Lévis, QC G6V 5T4
418-838-4000
Municipal Type: Water Commission
Denis Fradette, Sec.-Trés.

Régie intermunicipale d'assainissement des eaux de Sainte-Thérèse et Blainville
500, rue Omer-deSerres
Blainville, QC J7C 5N6
450-435-9090 Fax: 450-435-8839
assainissement.stb@videotron.net
Municipal Type: Water Commission
Diane Dubé, Sec.-Trés.

Régie intermunicipale d'assainissement des eaux du Trois-Rivières Métropolitain
CP 368
1325, place de l'Hôtel-de-Ville
Trois-Rivières, QC G9A 5H3
819-374-3521 Fax: 819-372-4631
Municipal Type: Water Commission
Claude Doucet, Sec.-Trés.

Régie intermunicipale d'assainissement des eaux de Rosemère et de Lorraine
100, rue Charbonneau
Rosemère, QC J7A 3W1
450-621-3500 Fax: 450-621-7601
Municipal Type: Water Commission
Chantal Gauvreau, Sec.-Trés.

Régie intermunicipale d'assainissement du canton de Metgermette
CP 249
735, 15e rue
Saint-Zacharie, QC G0M 2C0
418-593-3185 Fax: 418-593-3085
Municipal Type: Water Commission
Sophie Fortin, Sec.-Trés.

Régie intermunicipale d'élimination de déchets solides de Brome-Missisquoi
2500 Rang St-Joseph
Cowansville, QC J2K 3G6
450-263-2351 Fax: 450-263-4977
info@riedsbm.ca
www.riedsbm.ca
Municipal Type: Waste Commission
Gaetan Martel, Directeur operations
Caroline Lasnier, Comptable
Brigitte Nadeau, ing., MBA, Directrice generale

Régie intermunicipale d'enfouissement sanitaire de Manicouagan
768, rue Bossé
Baie-Comeau, QC G5C 1L6
418-589-0762 Fax: 418-589-6450
Municipal Type: Waste Commission

Régie intermunicipale d'enfouissement sanitaire de Charlevoix-Est
119, ch Snigoll
Clermont, QC G4A 1B1
418-439-3051 Fax: 418-439-3051
Municipal Type: Waste Commission

Régie intermunicipale de gestion des déchets solides de Saint-Vianney et Saint-Tharcisius
CP 39
170, av Centrale
Saint-Vianney, QC G0J 3J0
418-629-4082 Fax: 418-629-4821
Municipal Type: Waste Commission
Adrien Beaupré, Sec.-Trés.

Régie intermunicipale de gestion des déchets solides des Etchemins
CP 10
167, route 204
Sainte-Justine, QC G0R 1Y0
418-383-5397 Fax: 418-383-5398
sjustine@sogetel.net
www.stejustine.net/
Municipal Type: Waste Commission
Marcel Morissette, Maire

Régie intermunicipale de gestion des déchets solides de la région de Coaticook
98, rue Norton
Coaticook, QC J1A 2S8
819-849-6668 Fax: 819-849-6668
Municipal Type: Waste Commission
Yves Morissette, Sec.-Trés.

Régie intermunicipale de gestion des déchets de la région Maskoutaine
#201, 2200, av Pratte
Saint-Hyacinthe, QC J2S 4B6
450-774-2350 Fax: 450-774-9737
rigdrm@ntic.qc.ca
www.regiedesdechets.qc.ca
Municipal Type: Waste Commission
Lynda Charest, Directrice générale

Régie intermunicipale de gestion des déchets de la Mauricie
1, boul de la Gabelle
Saint-Étienne-des-Grès, QC G0X 2P0
819-373-3130 Fax: 819-694-1004
Municipal Type: Waste Commission

Régie intermunicipale de gestion des déchets des Chutes-de-la-Chaudière
114, rue du Pont
Saint-Lambert-de-Lauzon, QC G0S 2W0
418-889-8662 Fax: 418-889-5157
rigdcc@chutes.chaudiere.com
www.chaudiere.com/regie-dechets
Municipal Type: Waste Commission
Lois Fleury, Sec.-Treas.

Régie intermunicipale de gestion des déchets de la Rive-Sud de Québec
259, ch des Iles
Saint-David, QC G6V 7M5
418-837-3361 Fax: 418-837-1103
Municipal Type: Waste Commission
Alexandre Faber, Sec.-Trés.

Régie intermunicipale de gestion des déchets de l'Islet-Sud
366, rue Principale
Sainte-Perpétue-de-l'Islet, QC G0R 3Z0
418-359-2966 Fax: 418-359-2707
Municipal Type: Waste Commission
Marie-Claude Chouinard, Sec.-Trés.

Régie intermunicipale de gestion des déchets solides de l'Anse-à-Gilles
284, boul Nilus-Leclerc, Local 2
L'Islet, QC G0R 2C0
418-247-3884 Fax: 418-247-3885
Municipal Type: Waste Commission
Martine Fortin, Secrétaire

Régie intermunicipale de gestion des déchets solides de New Richmond, Caplan et Maria
CP 338
99, place Suzanne-Guité
New Richmond, QC G0C 2B0
418-392-5602 Fax: 418-392-5331
Municipal Type: Waste Commission
Benoît Roussy, Sec.-Trés.

Régie intermunicipale de gestion des déchets solides des Anses
CP 939
108, rue de l'Hôtel-de-Ville
Grande-Rivière, QC G0C 1V0
418-385-2282 Fax: 418-385-2290
Municipal Type: Waste Commission
Denis Beaudin, Sec.-Trés.

Régie intermunicipale de gestion des déchets du Bas St-François
38, rue Notre-Dame
Saint-François-du-Lac, QC J0G 1M0
450-568-7013 Fax: 450-568-7015
Municipal Type: Waste Commission
Sylvie Gelly, Directrice générake

Régie intermunicipale de gestion intégrée des déchets Bécancour-Nicolet-Yamaska
8405, rue Desormeaux
Bécancour, QC G9H 2X3
819-294-2999 Fax: 819-294-2966
Municipal Type: Waste Commission
Manon Poliquin, Sec.-Trés.

Régie intermunicipale de l'aqueduc de Saint-Antoine
105, av Saint-Laurent
Louiseville, QC J5V 2L6

Municipal Type: Water Commission

Régie intermunicipale de l'eau de Deux-Montagnes
101, 26e av
Deux-Montagnes, QC J7R 5T3
450-473-4502
Municipal Type: Water Commission
Denis Berthellette, Directeur d'Exploitation

Régie intermunicipale de l'eau de la Vallée du Richelieu
1348, ch des Patriotes
Otterburn Park, QC J3H 2B3
450-464-0348 Fax: 450-464-3827
Municipal Type: Water Commission
Claude Giroux, Sec.-Trés.

Régie intermunicipale de l'eau potable Varennes, Ste-Julie, St-Amable
1870, boul Marie-Victorin
Varennes, QC J3X 1R3
450-652-2052 Fax: 450-652-3808
Municipal Type: Water Commission
Normand Massicotte, Sec.-Trés.

Régie intermunicipale de l'Est de Portneuf
212, rue Dupont est
Pont-Rouge, QC G3H 1A1
418-873-4481 Fax: 418-873-3494
Municipal Type: Waste Commission
Paul-Eugène Parent, Président

Régie intermunicipale de récuperation des Hautes-Laurentides
402, route 117 sud
Marchand, QC J0T 1T0
819-275-3516 Fax: 819-275-3925
Municipal Type: Waste Commission

Régie intermunicipale de traitement de l'eau potable Saint-Romuald/Saint-Jean
CP 43100
2175, ch du Fleuve
Saint-Romuald, QC G6W 7W9
418-839-4141 Fax: 418-839-5548
Municipal Type: Water Commission
Marcel Deslandes, Directeur
Denis Gosselin, Directeur, Travaux publics
Pierre Boulay, Directeur, Urbanisme

Régie intermunicipale de traitement des déchets de Matawinie
3184, 1e av
Rawdon, QC J0K 1S0

Waste & Water Commissions / Québec

450-834-5441 Fax: 450-834-6560
Municipal Type: Waste Commission

Régie intermunicipale des déchets de CJLLR
CP 10
Sainte-Justine, QC G0R 1Y0
418-383-5397 Fax: 418-383-5398
Municipal Type: Waste Commission
Gilles Vézina, Sec.-Trés.

Régie intermunicipale des déchets de la Rouge
400 Route 117 Sud
Marchand, QC J0T 1T0

819-275-3205 Fax: 819-275-2139
ridrouge@lannon.qc.ca
Municipal Type: Waste Commission
Johanne Bock, Directrice-générale

Régie intermunicipale des déchets solides de la Lièvre
CP 160
1064, boul Industriel
Mont-Laurier, QC J9L 3G9
819-623-7382
Municipal Type: Waste Commission
Jimmy Brisebois, Directeur-général

Régie intermunicipale du comté de Beauce-Sud
695 rang St-Joseph
Saint-Côme Linière, QC G0M 1J0
418-685-2230 Fax: 418-685-3952
Municipal Type: Waste Commission
Roger Turcotte, Sec.-Trés

Intergovernmental Offices & Councils

Arctic Council
Foreign Affairs & International Trade Canada, 125 Sussex Dr., Ottawa ON K1A 0G2
Tel: 613-944-4000; *Fax:* 613-996-9709; *Toll-Free* 800-267-8376
URL: www.arctic-council.org
Chief Officer(s):
Sheila Riordon, Director General
sheila.riordon@international.gc.ca
Description: Intergovernmental forum for addressing common concerns & challenges by the member states of Canada, Denmark (including Greenland & the Faroe Islands), Finland, Iceland, Norway, the Russian Federation, Sweden & the U.S. Its objective is to be a regional forum for sustainable development mandated to address environmental, social & economic issues. The scientific work of the Council is carried out in six expert working groups focusing on such issues as monitoring, assessing & preventing pollution in the Arctic, climate change, biodiversity conservation & sustainable use, emergency preparedness & prevention. The six working groups are: Sustainable Development Working Group; Arctic Monitoring & Assessment Programme; Protection of the Marine Environment; Conservation of Arctic Flora & Fauna; Emergency, Prevention, Preparedness & Response; Arctic Contaminants Action Program. The Council meets every two years; the secretariat rotates among the member states.

Arctic Goose Joint Venture
e-mail: agjv@ec.gc.ca
URL: www.agjv.ca

Black Duck Joint Venture
URL: www.blackduckjv.org
Contact:
Brigitte Collins
Coordinator, BDJV
Environment Canada
Canadian Wildlife Service
335 River Road
Ottawa, Ontario K1A0H3
613-949-8254
brigitte.collins@ec.gc.ca

Patrick Devers
Science Coordinator, BDJV
U.S. Fish and Wildlife Service
11410 American Holly Drive
Laurel, MD 20708
301-497-5549
patrick_devers@fws.gov

Canada-Newfoundland Offshore Petroleum Board
TD Place, 140 Water St., 5th Fl., St. John's NL A1C 6H6
Tel: 709-778-1400; *Fax:* 709-778-1473
e-mail: postmaster@cnlopb.nl.ca
URL: www.cnlopb.nl.ca
Chief Officer(s):
Max Ruelokke, P.Eng, Chair & CEO
Dave Burley, Manager, Environmental Affairs, 709-778-1403
dburley@cnlopb.nf.ca
Description: The Canada-Newfoundland Offshore Petroleum Board manages the petroleum resources in the Nlfd. offshore area on behalf of the Government of Canada & the Government of N.L. The Board's authority is derived from the legislation implementing the 1985 Atlantic Accord between the two governments. The Environmental Affairs department ensures that offshore oil & gas industrial activities proceed in an environmentally acceptable manner & evaluates the effect of the offshore environment upon the safety of offshore activities & by ensuring protection of the environment during the conduct of these activities. Working in close consultation with the Operations & Safety department, Environmental Affairs assesses the effects of environmental conditions, such as winds, waves & ice conditions, in the Nlfd. offshore area upon the safety of operations. Environmental Affairs reviews operators' plans for collecting the weather, oceanographic & ice data that they are required to measure at offshore drilling & production sites. The Board reviews proposals for all physical activities offshore to identify their potential effects upon the natural environment or upon other users of that environment, such as the fishery. It evaluates measures that are proposed to prevent or mitigate these effects. This activity includes reviewing operators' contingency plans for environmental emergencies, especially oil spills, to ensure there are adequate response measures.

Canada-Nova Scotia Offshore Petroleum Board
TD Centre, 1791 Barrington St., 6th Fl., Halifax NS B3J 3K9
Tel: 902-422-5588; *Fax:* 902-422-1799
e-mail: postmaster@cnsopb.ns.ca
URL: www.cnsopb.ns.ca
Chief Officer(s):
Stuart Pinks, CEO
Keith Landra, Manager, Environment
Eric Theriault, Advisor, Environmental Affairs
etheriault@onsopb.ns.ca
Description: CNSOPB is responsible for protection of the environment during all phases of offshore petroleum activities, from initial exploration to abandonment. The Board is a Federal Authority under the Canadian Environmental Assessment Act. The environmental assessment process starts at the Call for Bids stage. At this stage, a strategic or broad environmental assessment is conducted which identifies environmental concerns or issues. All subsequent projects, including seismic programs & exploratory wells, must undergo an environmental assessment prior to approval by the CNSOPB. The Board also uses class screenings or generic assessments to streamline the regulatory process. These more in-depth environmental assessments, usually jointly funded by a number of petroleum companies, provide more detailed overviews of potential environmental effects, research priorities & mitigation measure than can be accomplished in a single project-specific environmental assessment. Applications from the petroleum industry for work authorizations must include an environmental assessment, environmental contingency plan & spill contingency plan. The Board consults with FEAC on environmental & fisheries-related matters. The Board is also involved in initiatives led by the Department of Fisheries & Oceans (DFO) related to marine protected areas & integrated management planning under the Oceans Act. The Board has signed memorandums of understanding with both the DFO & Environment Canada.

Canadian Council of Forest Ministers (CCFM) / Conseil canadien des ministres des forêts
c/o Secretariat, Claude Léger, Senior Advisor, National Departmental Relations Division, Canadian Forest Service, Natural Resources Canada, 2934 Baseline Rd., Tower B, Ottawa ON K2H 7T3
Tel: 613-900-5822; *Fax:* 613-947-9033
e-mail: cleger@nrcan.gc.ca
URL: www.ccfm.org
Chief Officer(s):
Claude Léger, Senior Advisor, Federal-Provincial Relations & Secretariat Contact
cleger@nrcan.gc.ca
Description: The Canadian Council of Ministers (CCFM) was established in 1985 to give sufficient attention to forest issues. CCFM stimulates the development of policies & initiatives for strengthening the forest sector, including the forest resource & its use. It provides leadership, addresses national & international issues & sets the direction for stewardship & sustainable management of Canada's forests. The CCFM is composed of the fourteen federal, provincial & territorial ministers responsible for forests. The CCFM undertakes activities primarily through ad hoc fora, committees & working groups. At present there are 9 committees. CCFM initiatives include: International Forest Issues Working Group; International Forestry Partnerships Program; Sustainable Forest Management Working Group; Canadian Wildland Fire Strategy; National Forest Information System; National Forestry Database Program; Science & Technology Working Group; Forest Communities Working Group. The Council also cooperates with the Canadian Wildland Fire Strategy Declaration, a federal-provincial-territorial initiative to address the management of wildland fires. National Forestry Database Program: nfdp.ccfm.org/; National Forest Information System: nfis.org

Canadian Council of Ministers of the Environment (CCME) / Conseil canadien des ministres de l'environnement
#360, 123 Main St., Winnipeg MB R3C 1A3
Tel: 204-948-2090; *Fax:* 204-948-2125
Toll-Free: 800-805-3025
e-mail: info@ccme.ca
URL: www.ccme.ca
Chief Officer(s):
J. Michael Miltenberger, President
Gary Bohnet, Secretariat
John MacQuarrie, Environmental Planning & Protection Committee
Finances: *Annual Operating Budget:* $1.5 Million-$3 Million; *Funding Sources:* Federal, provincial & territorial governments
Staff: 8 staff member(s)
Membership: 1-99; *Committees:* Environmental Planning & Protection
Description: CCME is comprised of the environment ministers from the federal, provincial and territorial governments. These 14 ministers normally meet at least once a year to discuss national environmental priorities and determine work to be carried out under the auspices of CCME. The Council seeks to achieve positive environmental results, focusing on issues that are national in scope and that require collective attention by a number of governments. CCME aims to assist its members to meet their mandate of protecting Canada's environment. As with any association, each member can accomplish more by working together than by working alone. CCME serves as a principal forum for members to develop national strategies, norms, and guidelines that each environment ministry across the country can use. Since environment is constitutionally speaking an area of shared jurisdiction, it makes sense to work together to promote effective results. CCME is not another level of government regulator, but a council of government ministers holding similar responsibilities.

Canadian Intergovernmental Conference Secretariat (CICS) / Secrétariat des conférences intergouvernementales canadiennes
PO Box 488, Stn. A, Ottawa ON K1N 8V5
Location/Deliveries: 222 Queen St. 10th Fl., Ottawa ON K1P 5V9
Tel: 613-995-2341; *Fax:* 613-996-6091
e-mail: info@scics.gc.ca
URL: www.scics.gc.ca
Chief Officer(s):
André McArdle, Secretary, 613-995-2344
SMacKinnon@scics.gc.ca
Description: CICS was established in 1973 by the First Ministers as an agency of the federal & provincial governments. Governments recognized a need for a mechanism to serve on a continuing basis, conferences of First Ministers & a growing number of intergovernmental meetings. CICS serves federal-provincial First Ministers' meetings, the Annual Premiers' Conference, the Eastern Canadian Premiers' & New England Governors' Conference & the Western Premiers' Conference. The core of the Secretariat's work is providing services to multilateral meetings of Ministers & Deputy Ministers in virtually every sector of government activity. The Secretariat's services are available to federal, provincial & territorial departments that are called upon to organize & chair such meetings. The agency's mandate & sole program are designed to relieve its clients of the numerous & various technical & administrative tasks associated with the planning & conduct of senior level intergovernmental conferences. The CICS maintains through its Information Services section, a document archives for the use of governments & the general public. Containing over 25,000 conference-related documents spanning every sector of conference activity, this collection is unique. The information contained in the archives is made available, as appropriate, to government institutions at the federal, provincial & territorial levels while unclassified material is also available to the public on request.

Commission for Environmental Cooperation (CEC) / Commission Coopération Environnementale
Secretariat, #200, 393 rue St-Jacques ouest, Montréal QC H2Y 1N9
Tel: 514-350-4300; *Fax:* 514-350-4314
e-mail: info@cec.org
URL: www.cec.org
Chief Officer(s):
Evan Lloyd, Executive Director
Dane Ratliff, Director, Submission on Enforcement Matters Unit, 514-350-4332

Marco Antonio Heredia Fragoso, Head, Environmental Law, 514-350-4302
maheredia@cec.org
Orlando Cabrera-Rivera, Program Manager, Air Quality & PRTR, 514-350-4323
ocabrera@cec.org
Ned T. Brooks, Program Manager, Chemicals Management, 514-350-4372
nbrooks@cec.org
Description: The Commission for Environmental Cooperation (CEC) is an international organization created by Canada, Mexico & the United States under the North American Agreement on Environmental Cooperation (NAAEC). The CEC was established to address regional environmental concerns, help prevent potential trade & environmental conflicts & to promote the effective enforcement of environmental law. The Agreement complements the environmental provisions of the North American Free Trade Agreement (NAFTA).

Commission for Sustainable Development
#DC2-2220, 2 United Nations Plaza, New York NY 10017 USA
Tel: 212-963-8102; *Fax:* 212-963-4260
e-mail: dsd@un.org
URL: www.un.org/esa/dsd/csd/csd_index.shtml
Chief Officer(s):
Mr. Sha Zukang, Secretary-General for 2012
Member Profile: Permanent Mission of Canada to the UN: 1 Dag Hammarskjold Plaza, New York NY 10017 212/848-1100; Fax: 212/848-1195; Email: canada@un.it
Description: Functional commission of the UN Economic & Social Council, composed of members elected for terms of office for three years. An intergovernmental body, members are elected by the Economic & Social Council from member states of the United Nations & its specialized agencies. The Commission meets annually; a multi-year (2004-2017) program of work outlines seven two-year cycles, with each two-year cyle focused on themes. For 2010-2011, the themes centre on poverty eradication, changing unsustainable patterns of consumption and production, protecting and managing the natural resource base of economic and social development, sustainable development in a globalizing world, health and sustainable development, sustainable development of SIDS, sustainable development for Africa, other regional initiatives, means of implementation, institutional framework for sustainable development, gender equality, and education. The role of the Commission as a high level forum on sustainable development, includes reviewing progress at the international, regional & national levels in the implementation of recommendations & commitments contained in Agenda 21 & the Rio Declaration on Environment & Development; elaborates policy & options for future activities to follow up the Johannesburg Plan of Implementation & achieve sustainable development; promotes dialogue & builds partnerships for sustainable development with governments, the international community & the major groups who have a role to play in the transition towards sustainable development, including women, youth, indigenous peoples, non-governmental organizations, local authorities, workers & trade unions, business & industry, the scientific community & farmers.

Conference of New England Governors & Eastern Canadian Premiers
Eastern Canadian Secretariat, PO Box 2044, Halifax NS B3J 2Z1
Tel: 902-424-7590; *Fax:* 902-424-8976
e-mail: info@cap-cpma.ca
URL: www.cap-cpma.ca
Chief Officer(s):
Don Osmond, Secretary, Council of Atlantic Premiers
Description: Established in 1973, & is composed of the premiers of the Atlantic provinces, Québec & governors of six New England States. Initiatives include the expansion of economic ties among the states & provinces; the fostering of energy exchanges; the forceful advocacy of environmental issues & sustainable development; & the coordination of numerous policies & programs in such areas as transportation, forest management, tourism, small-scale agriculture & fisheries. At annual conferences the Governors & Premiers discuss issues of common interest & concern, & enact policy resolutions that call on actions by the state & provincial governments, as well as by the two national governments. During the year, the Conference convenes meetings of state & provincial officials, organizes roundtables & workshops, & prepares reports & studies of issues of regional import. The Committee on the Environment adopted an acid rain action plan & a mercury action plan. The Northeast International Committee on Energy monitors & acts on common issues in the northeast region, such as electric restructuring; natural gas developments; resource & infrastructure development;collaboration with environmental departments & agencies; new technologies. At its most recent meeting, Aug. 2006, the conference resolved to create an Oceans Working Committee for ocean management, to develop a long term strategy to explore regional governance issues, to mitigate future growth in energy, increase amount of new renewable energy.

Council of Atlantic Premiers (CAP)
Council Secretariat, PO Box 2044, #1006, 5161 George St., Halifax NS B3J 2Z1
Tel: 902-424-7590; *Fax:* 902-424-8976
e-mail: info@cap-cpma.ca
URL: www.cap-cpma.ca
Chief Officer(s):
Don Osmond, Secretary to Council, 902-424-7600
Description: The mandate of the Council is also to promote Atlantic Canadian interests on national issues. To accomplish this, the Council seeks to establish common views & positions to ensure that Atlantic Canadians & their interests are well represented in national debates. The work of the Council of Atlantic Premiers builds on the ongoing work of the Council of Maritime Premiers & the Conference of Atlantic Premiers. The premiers are committed to work together on behalf of Atlantic Canadians to strengthen the economic competitiveness of the region, improve the quality of public services to Atlantic Canadians and/or improve the cost-effectiveness of delivering public services to Atlantic Canadians. In June 2005, CAP released their Atlantic Action Plan 2005-2008. Environmental priorities include establishing a Council of Atlantic Ministers of the Environment to better communicate & collaborate on issues, collaborate on pest management education initiatives through the Atlantic Working Group in Pest Management Education & Training Standards, explore extended producer responsibility programs to address common solid waste resource management issues. The Atlantic Energy Ministers Forum commits to developing an energy efficiency awareness campaign & a regional electricity sector approach which takes into account energy efficiency & renewable energy technologies. The Forum will also examine developing regional air emissions reduction models applicable to sulphur dioxides & nitrous oxides.

Eastern Habitat Joint Venture
Eastern Habitat Joint Venture (Ontario) Project Officer
Canadian Wildlife Service – Ontario, Environment Canada, 335 River Road, Ottawa ON K1A 0H3
Tel: (613) 949-8264
Biodiversity Section, Ontario Ministry of Natural Resources, P.O. Box 7000, 300 Water Street, Peterborough ON K9J 8M5
Tel: (705) 755-1960

Federal House in Order
e-mail: FHIO-IFPPE@ec.gc.ca
Chief Officer(s):
Jim Comtois, Natural Resources Canada, 613-943-0225
Jim Mohninger, Environment Canada, 819-953-4080
Description: The Federal House in Order (FHIO) initiative is the federal government's plan for reducing greenhouse gas emissions (GHGs) within its own operations in line with the National Implementation Strategy on Climate Change. Under Action Plan 2000 on Climate Change & the National Implementation Strategy, both announced in October 2000, a total federal commitment of $1.1 billion over 5 years has been made to take action to reduce greenhouse gas emissions from all sectors of the Canadian economy. Of this investment, $44.2 million has been allocated to FHIO which includes $30 million for the purchase of electricity from renewable resources. Through the Federal House in Order initiative, the eleven departments & agencies which account for 95 percent of GHG emissions have agreed to collectively meet a target of reducing greenhouse gases within their operations by 31% from 1990 levels to 2010. From 1990 to 2002, a total reduction in greenhouse gas emissions of 24% has been achieved within federal government operations through reductions in floor space and fleet size, a switch to less carbon-intensive energy sources, improvements in energy efficiency & fuel switching. Of the remaining 7%, half of the target will be achieved through central purchases of emerging renewable electricity & the other half will be met by energy efficiency & fuel switching in buildings & fleets.

Great Lakes Commission / Commission des Grands Lacs
Eisenhower Corporate Park, #100, 2805 S. Industrial Way, Ann Arbor MI 48104-6791 USA
Tel: 734-971-9135; *Fax:* 734-971-9150
URL: www.glc.org
Chief Officer(s):
Tim Elder, Executive Director
teder@glc.org
Description: The Great Lakes Commission is a binational public agency dedicated to the use, management & protection of water, land & other natural resources of the Great Lakes-St. Lawrence system. In partnership with 8 Great Lakes states & provinces of Ontario & Québec, the Commission applies sustainable development principles addressing issues of resource management, environmental protection, transportation & sustainable development. The Commission provides accurate & objective information on public policy issues; an effective forum for developing & coordinating public policy; & a unified, system wide voice to advocate member interests.

Greening Government
Tel: 416-512-5700; *Toll-Free:* 800-622-6232
e-mail: ecologisation.greening@tpsgc-pwgsc.gc.ca
URL:
http://www.tpsgc-pwgsc.gc.ca/ecologisation-greening/index-eng.html
Description: GreeningGovernment is an electronic information system developed by the Government of Canada for the internet. It is designed to provide a one-window access to sustainable development in government operations knowledge in the Government of Canada. This web site was developed to support the Sustainable Development in Government Operations (SDGO) initiative, whose purpose is to coordinate the federal effort to green government operations & encourage the report of concrete results among the departments & agencies that prepare Sustainable Development Strategies (SDSs). There are seven priority areas of operations: Energy Efficiency/Buildings, Human Resources Management, Land Use Management, Procurement, Vehicle Fleet Management, Waste Management & Water Conservation & Wastewater Management.

Gulf of Maine Council on the Marine Environment
c/o New Brunswick Dept. Of Agriculture, Fisheries & Aquaculture, PO Box 6000, 850 Lincoln Rd., Fredericton NB E3B 5H1
Tel: 506-453-2253; *Fax:* 506-453-5210
URL: www.gulfofmaine.org
Chief Officer(s):
Robert Capozi, New Brunswick Contact
NB Department of Environment
PO Box 6000
Fredericton, NB E3B 5H1
Tel: 506.457.8946
Fax: 506.457.7823
robert.capozi@gnb.ca
Justin Huston, Nova Scotia Contact
NS Department of Fisheries and Aquaculture
1741 Brunswick St • 3rd Fl
PO Box 2223
Halifax, NS B3J 3X8
Tel: 902.424.2996
hustonje@gov.ns.ca
Member Profile: Nova Scotia Department of Environment & Labour, PO Box 442, 5151 Terminal Road, Halifax, Nova Scotia, Canada B3J 2P8
Tel (Halifax): 902-424-3600
Fax: 902-424-0503
Description: A U.S.-Canadian partnership of government & non-government organizations working to maintain & enhance environmental quality in the Gulf of Maine to allow for sustainable resource use. The Council organizes conferences & workshops; offers grants & recognition awards; conducts environmental monitoring; provides science translation to management; raises public awareness about the Gulf. The secretariat rotates annually among the member jurisdictions. Initiatives include Gulf of Maine Mapping Initiative (GOMMI), comprehensive seafloor imaging, mapping & biological & geological surveys; habitat restoration grants program (U.S. only); Action Plan grants program; annual recognition awards; Gulf of Maine Times, a quarterly newspaper; Gulfwatch Monitoring Program, which helps to assess the fate & impacts of toxic contaminants in the Gulf of Maine.

North American Bird Conservation Initiative Canada (NABCI)
NAWCC (Canada) Secretariat Wetlands Office, Place Vincent Massey, 7th floor, 351 St. Joseph Boulevard, Gatineau, Quebec, Canada, K1A 0H3.
Tel: 819-934-6034; *Fax:* 819-934-6017

e-mail: nawmp@ec.gc.ca
URL: www.nabci.net
Chief Officer(s):
Michele Brenning, Chair, Environment Canada
Description: The NABCI is a coordinated effort among Canada, the United States & Mexico to maintain the diversity & abundance of all North American birds. National coordination of this effort in Canada occurs through the NABCI Canada Council, chaired by the Asst. Deputy Minister of Environment Canada's Environmental Conservation Service. Council members include representatives from provincial governments, non-government organizations, four bird plans (waterfowl, landbirds, shorebirds, waterbirds), & habitat joint ventures. In Canada, the joint venture conservation projects has three habitat joint ventures (Pacific Coast, Prairie Habitat, Eastern Habitat) & three species (Arctic Goose, Black Duck, Sea Duck).

North American Waterfowl Management Plan (NAWMP) / Le plan nord-américain de gestion de la sauvagine
c/o Canadian Wildlife Service, Place Vincent Massey, 16th fl., 351, boul St. Joseph, Hull QC K1A 0H3
Tel: 819-934-6034; *Fax:* 819-934-6017
e-mail: nabci@ec.gc.ca
URL: www.nawmp.ca
Description: The North American Waterfowl Management Plan is an international action plan to conserve migratory birds throughout the continent. The Plan's goal is toreturn waterfowl populations to their 1970's levels by conserving wetland and upland habitat. Canada & the United States signed the Plan in 1986 in reaction to critically low numbers of waterfowl. Mexico joined in 1994 making it a truly continental effort. The Plan is a partnership of federal, provincial/state & municipal governments, non-governmental organizations, private companies & many individuals, all working towards achieving better wetland habitat for the benefit of migratory birds, other wetland-associated species & people. The Plan's unique combination of biology, landscape conservation & partnerships comprise its exemplary conservation legacy. Plan projects are international in scope, but implemented at regional levels. These projects contribute to the protection of habitat & wildlife species across the North American landscape. In fact, the North American Waterfowl Management Plan is considered one of the most successful conservation initiatives in the world.

Pacific States/British Columbia Oil Spill Task Force
Environmental Emergencies Branch, BC Ministry of Environment
P. O. Box 9377 Stn. Prov. Govt, Victoria, BC, Canada V8W 9M6
Tel: 250-356-9302; *Fax:* 250-356-0742
URL: www.oilspilltaskforce.org
Chief Officer(s):
Jean R. Cameron, Executive Coordinator, 503-392-5860
JeanRCameron@oregoncoast.com
Graham Knox, Coordinating Committee Member, Provincial Representative, 250-356-8383, Fax: 250-387-9935
Description: The Pacific States/British Columbia Oil Spill Task Force was authorized by a Memorandum of Cooperation signed in 1989 by the Governors of Alaska, Washington, Oregon, and California and the Premier of British Columbia following the Nestucca and Exxon Valdez oil spills. These events highlighted their common concerns regarding oil spill risks and the need for cooperation across shared borders. In June 2001 a revised Memorandum of Cooperation was adopted to include the State of Hawaii and expand our focus to spill preparedness and prevention needs of the 21st century. Now in our second decade, we provide a forum where Task Force Members can work with stakeholders from the Western US and Canada to implement regional initiatives that protect 56,660 miles of coastline from Alaska to California and the Hawaiian archipelago. The Task Force Members are senior executives from the environmental agencies with oil spill regulatory authority in the states of Alaska, Washington, Oregon, California and Hawaii and the Province of British Columbia. Oil spill program managers from each member agency comprise the Task Force's Coordinating Committee, which oversees activities and projects as authorized by the Members when they adopt a Five Year Strategic Plan and Annual Work Plans. The Coordinating Committee convenes four times a year. The Task Force Members hold their Annual Meetings each summer, rotating locations among member jurisdictions.

Prairie Habitat
c/o Prairie & Northern Region, CWS, #200, 4999 - 98 Ave., Edmonton AB T6B 2X3
Tel: 780-951-8652; *Fax:* 780-495-2615
Contact:
Diana Ghikas, Environment Canada, Canadian Wildlife Service, Prairie and Northern Region, 200, 4999 98 Avenue, Edmonton, AB, T6B 2X3
diana.ghikas@ec.gc.ca

Environmental Trade Representatives Abroad

People's Democratic Republic of Algeria
Canadian Embassy, PO Box 48, Alger-Gare, 16035 Algeria
011-213-7008-3000, Fax: 011-213-7008-3070,
alger@international.gc.ca
www.international.gc.ca/world/embassies/algeria/
Kristine Randall, Second Secretary (Commercial & Development), Trade Commissioner, Environmental Industries

Argentine Republic
Canadian Embassy, Casilla de Correo 1598, Correa Central, Buenos Aires, C1000WAP Argentine
011-54-11-4808-1000, Fax: 011-54-11-4808-111,
bairs-webmail@international.gc.ca
www.buenosaires.gc.ca
Paula Solari, Trade Commissioner, Environmental Industries

Commonwealth of Australia
Canadian High Commission, Commonwealth Ave., Canberra, ACT 2600 Australia
61-2-6270-4000, Fax: 61-2-6270-3585,
cnbra@international.gc.ca
www.canada.org.au
Sarah Powles, Trade Commissioner
Ilsa Stuart-Muirk, Trade Commissioner

Republic of Austria
Canadian Embassy, Laurenzerberg 2, Vienna, A-1010 Austria
43-1-531-38-3321, Fax: 43-1-531-38-3910,
vienn@international.gc.ca
www.dfait-maeci.gc.ca/canadaeurope/austria
Roland Rossi, Trade Commissioner, Environmental Industries, roland.rossi@international.gc.ca

People's Republic of Bangladesh
Canadian High Commission, GPO Box 569, Dhaka, 1212 Bangladesh
88-2-988-7091, Fax: 88-2-882-3043,
dhaka@international.gc.ca
www.bangladesh.gc.ca
Mortoza Tarafder, Sr. Trade Commissioner, Environmental Industries, mortoza.tarafder@international.gc.ca

Barbados
Canadian High Commission, PO Box 404, Bridgetown, Barbados
246-429-3550, Fax: 246-429-3780,
bdgtn@international.gc.ca
Tammy Griffith, Trade Commissioner, Environmental Industries

Kingdom of Belgium
Canadian Embassy, 2, av de Tervuren, Brussels, 1040 Belgium
32-2-741-0611, Fax: 32-2-741-0643,
bru@international.gc.ca
www.ambassade-canada.be
Fabienne De Kimpe, Trade Commissioner, Environmental Industries, fabienne.de-kimpe@international.gc.ca

Republic of Bolivia
See: Republic of Peru
Jillian Senkiw, Third Secretary & Trade Commissioner, Environmental Industries, jillian.senkiw@international.gc.ca

Brunei Darussalam
Canadian High Commission, PO Box 2808, Bandar Seri Begawan, BS8675 Brunei Darussalam
673-2-220-043, Fax: 673-2-220-040,
bsbgn@international.gc.ca
www.dfait-maeci.gc.ca/brunei
Celestina Leong, Trade Commissioner, celestina.leong@international.gc.ca

Republic of Bulgaria
See: Republic of Romania c/o Republic of Romania, Consulate of Canada, 9, Moskovska str., Sofia, Bulgaria
(011-359-2)969-9719, Fax: (011-359-2)981-6081,
bucst-td@international.gc.ca
Magdalena Goranova, Trade Commissioner, Environmental Industries

Republic of Cameroon
Canadian High Commission, Immeuble SCI-TOM (formerly Stamatiades), PO Box 572, Yaoundé, Cameroon
011-237-2223-2311, Fax: 011-237-2222-1090,
yunde@international.gc.ca

Jude Bijingsi, Trade Commissioner, Environmental Industries, jude.bijingsi@international.gc.ca

Republic of Chile
Canadian Embassy, Cassilla 139, Correo 10, Santiago, Chile
56-2-652-3800, Fax: 56-2-652-3912,
stago@international.gc.ca
www.chile.gc.ca
Margot Edwards, Trade Commissioner, Environmental Industries

People's Republic of China
Canadian Embassy, 19 Dong Zhi Men Wai St., Chao Yang Dist., Beijing, 100600 China
011-86-10-5139-4000, Fax: 011-86-10-5139-4454,
bejing@international.gc.ca
www.beijing.gc.ca
Owen Teo, Senior Trade Commissioner, Environmental Industries

Republic of Colombia
Canadian Embassy, Apartado Aereo 110067, Bogota, Colombia
57-1-657-9800, Fax: 57-1-657-9912,
bgota@international.gc.ca
www.bogota.gc.ca
Claudia Paola Gutierrez Chaves, Trade Commissioner

Republic of Costa Rica
Canadian Embassy, Apartado Postal 351-1007 Centro Colon, San José, Costa Rica
506-2242-4400, Fax: 506-2242-4410,
sjcra@international.gc.ca
www.costarica.gc.ca
Adolfo Quesada, Trade Commissioner, Environmental Industries, adolfo.quesada@international.gc.ca

Republic of Croatia
Prilaz Gjure Dezelica #4, Zagreb, 10 000 Croatia
385-1-488-1200, Fax: 385-1-488-1230,
zagrb@international.gc.ca
Synthia Dodig, Trade Commissioner, Environmental Industries, synthia.dodig@international.gc.ca

Republic of Cuba
Canadian Embassy, Calle 30, No. 518, Esquina 7a, Miramar, Havana, Cuba
53-7-204-2516, Fax: 53-7-204-9772,
havan@international.gc.ca
www.dfait-maeci.gc.ca/cuba
Francisco Rodriguez, Trade Commissioner, Environmental Industries

Republic of Cyprus
See: Republic of Romania c/o Republic of Romania, PO Box 22125, Consulate of Canada c/o The Canadian Embassy, Nicosia, 1517 Cyprus (00-357-22) 775-508,
Fax: (00-357-22) 779-905, info@consulcanada.com.cy
Rhea Pelides, Trade Commissioner, Environmental Industries

Czech Republic
Canadian Embassy, Muchova 6, 160 00, Prague, 6 Czech Republic
420 272 101 800, Fax: 420 272 101 898,
prgue@dfait-maeci.gc.ca
www.canada.cz
Jitka Hoskova, Trade Commissioner, Environmental Industries, jitka.hoskova@international.gc.ca

Kingdom of Denmark
Canadian Embassy, Kr. Bernikows Gade 1, Copenhagen, DK-1105 Denmark
45-33-48-32-00, Fax: 45-33-48-32-20,
copen@international.gc.ca
www.denmark.gc.ca
Suzanne Steensen, Trade Commissioner, Environmental Industries

Dominican Republic
Canadian Embassy, PO Box 2054, Santo Domingo, Dominican Republic
809-685-1136, Fax: 809-682-2691,
sdmgo@international.gc.ca
www.santodomingo.gc.ca

Regis Batista-Lemaire, Trade Commissioner, Environmental Industries, regis.barista@international.gc.ca

Republic of Ecuador
PO Box 17-11-6512, Quito, Ecuador
593-2-2455-499, Fax: 593-2-2277-672,
quito@international.gc.ca
www.ecuador.gc.ca
Ryan Kuffner, Trade Commissioner, Environmental Industries

Republic of El Salvador
Canadian Embassy, Edificio Centro Financiero Gigante, Alameda Roosevelt y 63 Avenida Sur, Nivel Lobby 2, Loca, San Salvador, El Salvador
503-2279-4655, Fax: 503-2279-0765,
ssal@international.gc.ca
www.sansalvador.gc.ca
Romeo Calderon, Trade Commissioner, Environmental Industries, romeo.calderon@international.gc.ca

Federal Democratic Republic of Ethiopia
Canadian Embassy, PO Box 1130, Addis Ababa, Ethiopia
251-1-71-30-22, Fax: 251-1-71-30-33,
addis@international.gc.ca
Richard Le Bars, Second Secretary & Vice-Consul & Sr. Trade Commissioner, Environmental Industries, richard.lebars@international.gc.ca

Republic of Finland
Canadian Embassy, PO Box 779, Helsinki, FIN-00101 Finland
358-9-228-530, Fax: 358-9-601-060,
hsnki@international.gc.ca
www.canada.fi
Seppo Vihersaari, Trade Commissioner, Environmental Industries, seppo.vihersaari@international.gc.ca

French Republic
Canadian Embassy, 35 - 37, av Montaigne, Paris, 75008 France
33-1-44-43-29-00, Fax: 33-1-44-43-29-99,
paris@international.gc.ca
www.international.gc.ca/canada-europa/france
Musto Mitha, Trade Commissioner, Environmental Industries

Gabonese Republic
Canadian Embassy, PO Box 4037, Libreville, Gabon
241-73-73-54, Fax: 241-73-73-88,
lbrve@international.gc.ca
François Coté, Trade Commissioner, Environmental Industries, francois.cote@international.gc.ca

Federal Republic of Germany
Canadian Embassy, Leipziger Platz 17, Berlin, 10117 Germany
41-30-20-312-0, Fax: 49-30-20-312-590,
brlin@international.gc.ca
www.dfait-maeci.gc.ca/canada-europa/germany
Dr. Steffen Preusser, Trade Commissioner, Environmental Industries, steffen.preusser@international.gc.ca

Hellenic Republic
Canadian Embassy, 4 Ioannou Ghennadiou St., Athens, 115 21 Greece
30-210-727-3400, Fax: 30-210-727-3480,
athns@international.gc.ca
www.dfait-maeci.gc.ca/canadaeuropa/greece/
Marguerita Niada, Trade Commissioner, Environmental Industries, marguerita.niada@international.gc.ca

Republic of Guatemala
Canadian Embassy, PO Box 400, Guatemala City, 1001 Guatemala
502-2363-4348, Fax: 502-2365-1210,
gtmla@international.gc.ca
www.guatemala.gc.ca
Christine Luttmann, Trade Commissioner, Environmental Industries

Republic of Guyana
Canadian High Commission, PO Box 10880, Georgetown, Guyana
592-227-2081, Fax: 592-225-8380,
grgtn@international.gc.ca
www.guyana.gc.ca
Lyris Primo, Commercial Officer, lyris.primo@international.gc.ca

Environmental Trade Representatives Abroad

Republic of Hungary
Canadian Embassy, Ganz U. 12-14, Budapest, 10 1027 Hungary
36-1-392-3360, Fax: 36-1-392-3390,
bpest@international.gc.ca
www.canadaeuropa.gc.ca/hungary
Zsuzsanna Matyus, Trade Commissioner, Environmental Industries, zsuzsanna.matyus@international.gc.ca

Republic of Iceland
PO Box 1510, Reykjavik, 121 Iceland
354-575-6500, Fax: 354-575-6501,
rkjvk@international.gc.ca
www.canada.is
Kristbjorg Agustsdottir, Trade Commissioner, Environmental Industries, kristbjorg.agustsdottir@international.gc

Republic of India
Canadian High Commission, PO Box 5208, New Delhi, 110021 India
91-11-4178-2000, Fax: 91-11-4178-2020,
delhi@international.gc.ca
www.india.gc.ca
Viney Gupta, Trade Commissioner, Environmental Industries, delhi.commerce@international.gc.ca

Republic of Indonesia
Canadian Embassy, PO Box 8324/JKS.MP, Jakarta, 12083 Indonesia
62-21-2550-7800, Fax: 62-21-2550-7811,
jkrta@international.gc.ca
www.jakarta.gc.ca
Dian Martosoebroto, Trade Commissioner, Environmental Industries

Republic of Ireland
Canadian Embassy, 7-8 Wilton Terrace, Dublin 2, Ireland
353-1-234-4000, Fax: 353-1-234-4101,
dubln@international.gc.ca
www.canada.ie
Gerry Mongey, Trade Commissioner, Environmental Industries, gerry.mongey@international.gc.ca

State of Israel
Canadian Embassy, PO Box 9442, 3 Nirim St., 4th Fl., Tel Aviv, 67060 Israel
011-972-3-636-3300, Fax: 011-972-3-636-3380,
taviv@international.gc.ca
www.dfait-maeci.gc.ca/telaviv/
Mona Ashkar, Trade Commissioner, Environmental Industries

Italian Republic
Canadian Embassy, Villa Grazioli, Via Salaria 243, Rome, 00199 Italy
39-06-85444-1, Fax: 39-06-85444-3947,
rome@international.gc.ca
www.canada.it
Patrizia Giuliotti, Trade Commissioner, Environmental Industries

Republic of Ivory Coast
Canadian Embassy, Immeuble Trade Centre, 23, av Nogues, 6th & 7th Fls., Le Plateau, Abidjan, 01 Ivory Coast
225-20 30 07 00, Fax: 225-20 30 07 20,
abdjn@international.gc.ca
www.dfait-maeci.gc.ca/abidjan
Jean-Claude Diplo, Trade Commissioner, Environmental Services, jean-claude.diplo@international.gc.ca

Jamaica
Canadian High Commission, PO Box 1500, Kingston, 10 Jamaica
876/926-1500-7, Fax: 876/511-3494,
kngtn-cs@international.gc.ca
www.kingston.gc.ca
Yasmin Chong, Trade Commissioner, Environmental Industries, yasmin.chong@international.gc.ca

Hashemite Kingdom of Jordan
Canadian Embassy, PO Box 815403, Amman, 11180 Jordan
962-6-520-3300, Fax: 962-6-520-3390,
amman@international.gc.ca
www.amman.gc.ca
Wafa Herzallah, Trade Commissioner, Environmental Industries, wafa.herzallah@international.gc.ca

Republic of Kazakhstan
Canadian Embassy, 34 Karasai Batir St., Almaty, 050010 Kazakhstan
73-27-250-11-51, Fax: 73-27-258-24-93,
almat@international.tc.ca
www.infoexport.gc.ca/kz
David Mallette, Trade Commissioner

Republic of Korea
Canadian Embassy, 16-1 Jeong-dong, Jung-gu, Seoul, Korea
82-2-3783-6000, Fax: 82-2-3783-6239,
seoul@international.gc.ca
www.korea.gc.ca
Yon-Ho Choi, Trade Commissioner, Environmental Industries, yon-ho.cho@international.gc.ca

State of Kuwait
Canadian Embassy, PO Box 25281, Safat, Kuwait City, 13113 Kuwait
965-2256-3025, Fax: 965-2256-0173,
kwait@international.gc.ca
www.infoexport.gc.ca/kw
Martin Barratt, Sr. Trade Commissioner, martin.barratt@international.gc.ca

Republic of Latvia
Canadian Embassy, 20/22 Baznicas St., 6th Fl., Riga, LV-1010 Latvia
371-6781-3945, Fax: 371-6781-3960,
riga@international.gc.ca
www.balticstates.gc.ca
Irena Cirpuse, Trade Commissioner, Environmental Industries, irena.cirpuse@international.gc.ca

Lebanese Republic
Canadian Embassy, 43 Autostrade Jal El Dib, Beirut, Lebanon
961-4-713-900, Fax: 961-4-710-595,
berut@international.gc.ca
www.dfait-maeci.gc.ca/beirut/
Grace Dib, Trade Commissioner, Environmental Industries, grace.dib@international.gc.ca

Socialist People's Libyan Arab Jamahiriya
PO Box 93392, Al-Fateh Tower, 7th Fl., Tripoli, Libya
218-21-335-1633, Fax: 218-21-335-1630,
trpli@international.gc.ca
www.dfait-maeci.gc.ca/world/embassies/libya/
Hesham Ganem, Trade Commissioner, Environmental Industries, hesham.ganem@international.gc.ca

Federation of Malaysia
Canadian High Commission, PO Box 10990, Kuala Lumpur, Malaysia
60-3-2718-3333, Fax: 60-3-2718-3399,
klmpr@international.gc.ca
www.international.gc.ca/missions/malaysia-mala isie/
Mia Yen, Second Secretary (Commercial) & Trade Commissioner, Environmental Industries, mia.yen@international.gc.ca

Republic of Mali
Canadian Embassy, PO Box 198, Route de Koulikoro, Immeuble séméga, Bamako, Mali
223-2021-2236, Fax: 223-2021-4362,
bmako@international.gc.ca
www.bamako.gc.ca
Ernest Akpoue, Trade Commissioner, Environmental Industries, ernest.akpoue@international.gc.ca

United Mexican States
Canadian Embassy, Apartado Postal 105-05, Mexico City, 11580 Mexico
52-57-24-7900, Fax: 52-57-24-7980,
mxico@international.gc.ca
www.mexico.gc.ca
Other information: Emergency: 1-800-703-2900
Paula Caldwell, Senior Trade Commissioner,
mexico.commerce@international.gc.ca
Rosalba Cruz, Trade Commissioner, Environmental Industries, mexico.commerce@international.gc.ca

Kingdom of Morocco
Canadian Embassy, PO Box 709, Rabat-Agdal, Morocco
212-37-68-74-00, Fax: 212-37-68-74-30,
rabat@international.gc.ca
www.rabat.gc.ca
Asmae Amrouche, Trade Commissioner, Environmental Industries

Republic of Mozambique
Canadian High Commission, PO Box 1578, 1138, Kenneth Kaunda Ave., Maputo, Mozambique
258-21-492-623, Fax: 258-21-492-667,
mputo@international.gc.ca
Lurdes Magneli, Trade Commissioner, Environmental Industries

Kingdom of the Netherlands
Canadian Embassy, Sophialaan 7, The Hague, 2514 JP The Netherlands
31-70-311-1600, Fax: 31-70-311-1620,
hague@international.gc.ca
www.canada.nl
Judith Baguley, Trade Commissioner, Environmental Industries

Kingdom of Norway
Canadian Embassy, Wergelandsveien 7, Oslo, 0244 Norway
47-2299-5300, Fax: 47-2299-5301,
oslo@international.gc.ca
www.canada.no
John Winterbourne, Trade Commissioner, Environmental Industries, john.winterbourne@international.gc.ca

Republic of Panama
Apartado Postal 0832-2446, Estafata World Trade Centre, Panama City, Panama
011-507-264-9731, Fax: 011-507-263-8083,
panam@international.gc.ca
www.panama.gc.ca
Luis Cedeno, Trade Commissioner, Environmental Industries, luis.cedeno@international.gc.ca

Republic of Peru
Canadian Embassy, Calle Bolognesi 228, Miraflores, Lima, Peru
511-319-3200, Fax: 511-446-4912,
lima@international.gc.ca
Alexandra Laverdure, Trade Commissioner, Environmental Industries, lima.commerce@international.gc.ca

Republic of the Philippines
PO Box 2098, Makati Central Post Office, Makati City, 1200 Philippines
63-2-857-9000, Fax: 63-2-843-1082,
manil@international.gc.ca
www.dfait-maeci.gc.ca/manila/
Ramon Yazon, Trade Commissioner, Environmental Industries, ramon.yazon@international.gc.ca

Republic of Poland
Canadian Embassy, ul. Jana Matejiki 1/5, Warsaw, 00-481 Poland
48-22-584-3100, Fax: 48-22-584-3192,
wsaw@international.gc.ca
www.canada.pl
Ewa Gawron-Dobroczynska, Trade Commissioner, Environmental Industries

Portuguese Republic
Canadian Embassy, Avenida da Liberdade, 196-200, 3rd Fl., Lisbon, 1269-121 Portugal
351-21-316-4600, Fax: 351-21-316-4691,
lsbon@international.gc.ca
www.portugal.gc.ca
Carlos Lindo da Silva, Trade Commissioner, Environmental Industries

Republic of Romania
Canadian Embassy, 1-3 Tuberozelor Str., Bucharest, 011411 Romania
40-21-307-5000, Fax: 40-21-307-5010,
bucst@international.gc.ca
www.dfait-maeci.gc.ca/bucharest
Octavian Bonea, Trade Commissioner, Environmental Industries

Russian Federation
Canadian Embassy, 23 Starokonyushenny Pereulok, Moscow, 119002 Russian Federation
7-495-925-6000, Fax: 7-495-925-6025,
mosco@international.gc.ca
Lilya Panova, Trade Commissioner, Environmental Industries, lilya.panova@international.gc.ca

Kingdom of Saudi Arabia
Canadian Embassy, PO Box 94321, Riyadh, 11693 Saudi Arabia
966-1-488-2288, Fax: 966-1-488-1997,
ryadh@international.gc.ca
Mazen El-Khatib, Trade Commissioner, Environmental Industries, mazen.el-khatib@international.gc.ca

Republic of Senegal
Canadian Embassy, PO Box 3373, Dakar, Senegal

Environmental Trade Representatives Abroad

221-33-889-4700, Fax: 221-33-889-4720,
dakar@international.gc.ca
www.dakar.gc.ca
Aminata Ly Faye, Trade Commissioner, Environmental Industries, aminata.ly@international.gc.ca

Republic of Singapore
Canadian High Commission, PO Box 845, Singapore, 901645 Singapore
65 68545900, Fax: 65 68545930,
spore@international.gc.ca
www.dfait-maeci.gc.ca/singapore/
Fumiko Kitano, Second Secretary (Commercial) & Trade Commissioner

Slovak Republic
Embassy of Canada, Mostova 2, Bratislava, 811 02 Slovak Republic
421-259-204-031, Fax: 421-254-434-227,
brtsv@international.gc.ca
www.ocanada.sk
Ambassador resides in Prague, Czech Republic
M. Calcott, Ambassador

Kingdom of Spain
Canadian Embassy, Apartado 587, Madrid, 28080 Spain
34-9-423-3250, Fax: 34-9-423-3251,
mdrid@international.gc.ca
www.spain.gc.ca
Amaya Jauregui, Trade Commissioner, Environmental Industries

Democratic Socialist Republic of Sri Lanka
Canadian High Commission, PO Box 1006, Colombo, 7 Sri Lanka
94-11-522-6232, Fax: 94-11-522-6299,
clmbo@international.gc.ca
Sanjeeva Sellahewe, Trade Commissioner, Environmental Industries, sanjeeva.sellahewe@international.gc.ca

Kingdom of Sweden
Canadian Embassy, PO Box 16129, Stockholm, 103 23 Sweden
46-8-453-3000, Fax: 46-8-453-3016,
stkhm@international.gc.ca
www.canadaeuropa.gc.ca/sweden
Inga-Lill Olsson, Trade Commissioner, Environmental Industries

Swiss Confederation
Canadian Embassy, Kirchenfeldstrasse 88, Bern, CH-3005 Switzerland
41-31-357-3200, Fax: 41-31-357-3210,
bern@international.gc.ca
www.switzerland.gc.ca
Werner Naef, Trade Commissioner, Environmental Industries, werner.naef@international.gc.ca

Syrian Arab Republic
Canadian Embassy, PO Box 3394, Damascus, Syria
963-11-611-6692, Fax: 963-11-611-4000,
dmcus@international.gc.ca
www.international.gc.ca/syria
Stéphane Beaulieu, Counsellor (Commercial) & Sr. Trade Commissioner, stephane.beaulieu@international.gc.ca

United Republic of Tanzania
Canadian High Commission, PO Box 1022, Dar-es-Salaam, Tanzania
255-22-216-3300, Fax: 255-22-211-6897,
dslam@international.gc.ca
www.dfait-maeci.gc.ca/tanzania
Noel Amos, Trade Commissioner, Environmental Industries, noel.amos@international.gc.ca

Kingdom of Thailand
Canadian Embassy, PO Box 2090, Bangkok, 10501 Thailand
66-2-636-0540, Fax: 66-2-636-0566,
bngkk@international.gc.ca
www.thailand.gc.ca
Orawan Chandrangsu, Trade Commissioner, Environmental Industries

Republic of Trinidad & Tobago
Canadian High Commission, PO Box 1246, Port of Spain, Trinidad
868-622-6232, Fax: 868-628-2581,
pspan@international.gc.ca
www.trinidadandtobago.gc.ca
Michaeline Narcisse, Trade Commissioner, Environmental Industries, michaeline.narcisse@international.gc.ca

Republic of Tunisia
Canadian Embassy, PO Box 31, Tunis, 1002 Tunisia
216-71-104-000, Fax: 216-71-104-191,
tunis@international.gc.ca
www.dfait-maeci.gc.ca/tunisia
Lassaad Bourguiba, Trade Commissioner, Environmental Industries, lassaad.bourguiba@international.gc.ca

Republic of Turkey
Canadian Embassy, Cinnah Caddesi 58, Cankaya, Ankara, 06690 Turkey
90-312-409-2700, Fax: 90-312-312-409-2810,
ankra@international.gc.ca
www.dfait-maeci.gc.ca/canadaeuropa/turkey/menu -en.asp
Akin Kosetorunu, Trade Commissioner, Environmental Industries, akin.kosetorunu@international.gc.ca

Ukraine
Canadian Embassy, 31 Yaroslaviv Val, Kyiv, 1901 Ukraine

380-44-590-3100, Fax: 380-44-590-3109,
kyiv@international.gc.ca
www.kyiv.gc.ca
Yury Mardak, Trade Commissioner, Environmental Industries, yury.mardak@international.gc.ca

United Arab Emirates
The Canadian Embassy, PO Box 6970, Abu Dhabi, United Arab Emirates
971-2-694-0300, Fax: 971-2-694-0399,
abdbi@international.gc.ca
www.uae.gc.ca
Imad Arafat, Trade Commissioner, Environmental Industries, imad.arafat@international.gc.ca

United Kingdom of Great Britain & Northern Ireland
Canadian High Commission, MacDonald House, One Grosvenor Sq., London, W1K 4AB United Kingdom
44-20-7258-6600, Fax: 44-20-7258-6384,
ldn@international.gc.ca
www.london.gc.ca
Sushma Gera, Trade Commissioner, Environmental Industries

Eastern Republic of Uruguay
Canadian Embassy, #102, Plaza Independencia 749, C.P. 11100, Montevideo, Uruguay
598-2-902-2030, Fax: 598-2-902-2029,
mvdeo@international.gc.ca
www.montevideo.gc.ca
Patricia Wilson, Trade Commissioner, Environmental Industries

Republic of Venezuela
Canadian Embassy, Apartado Postal 62302, Caracas, 1060A Venezuela
58-212-600-3000, Fax: 58-212-263-8326,
crcas@international.gc.ca
www.caracas.gc.ca
Daniela Oyague, Trade Commissioner, Environmental Industries

Socialist Republic of Vietnam
Canadian Embassy, 31 Huong Vuong St., Hanoi, Vietnam
84-4-3734-5000, Fax: 84-4-3734-5049,
hanoi@international.gc.ca
www.vietnam.gc.ca
Dang-Anh Thu, Trade Commissioner, Environmental Industries, dang-anh.thu@international.gc.ca

Republic of Zambia
Canadian High Commission, PO Box 31313, Lusaka, 10101 Zambia
260-1-25-08-33, Fax: 260-1-25-41-76,
lsaka@international.gc.ca
www.international.gc.ca/world/embassies/zambia /
Solomon Milimbo, Trade Commissioner, Environmental Industries, solomon.milimbo@international.gc.ca

SECTION 4

Environmental Resources

Included in this section:
- *Associations Subject Index* 773
- *Associations Acronym Index* 800
- *Associations Publications Index* 807
- Associations/Organizations 813

- *Educational Programs Index* 1027
- Educational Programs 1029

- *Foundations & Grants Index* 1037
- Foundations & Grants 1039

- *Law Firms Index* 1047
- Law Firms 1049

- *Libraries & Resource Centres Index* 1093
- Libraries & Resource Centres 1099

- Publications
   - Non-government 1193
   - Government Distribution Centres 1195

- *Research Centres Index* 1197
- Research Centres 1199

- Websites 1213

Associations Subject Index

A.I.
See Artificial Intelligence

Aboriginal Peoples
See Native Peoples

Academic Medicine
See Medical Schools

Accident Prevention
See also Fire Protection & Prevention; Occupational Health & Safety; Safety; Safety Engineering
Association paritaire pour la santé et la sécurité du travail - Affaires municipales, 840
Association paritaire pour la santé et la sécurité du travail - Imprimerie et activités connexes, 840
Association paritaire pour la santé et la sécurité du travail - Mines et services miniers, 841
Association paritaire pour la santé et la sécurité du travail - Administration provinciale, 840
Association paritaire pour la santé et la sécurité du travail - Services automobiles, 841
Association paritaire pour la santé et la sécurité du travail - Affaires sociales, 840
Association paritaire pour la santé et la sécurité du travail - Produits en métal et électriques, 841
Association paritaire pour la santé et la sécurité du travail - Habillement, 840
Association sectorielle - Fabrication d'équipement de transport et de machines, 842
Canadian Centre for Occupational Health & Safety, 862
Industrial Accident Victims Group of Ontario, 930
Institut de recherche Robert-Sauvé en santé et en sécurité du travail, 932
Ontario Industrial Fire Protection Association, 975
Safe Workplace Promotion Services Ontario, 997
World Safety Organization, 1023

Accommodation
See Housing

Accountants, Chartered
Canadian Institute of Chartered Accountants, 873

Acculturation
See Cross-Cultural Communication

Acid Rain
See also Air Pollution; Water Pollution
Association pour la prévention de la contamination de l'air et du sol, 841
Environmental Protection UK, 912

Acoustics
See also Architectural Acoustics
Acoustical Association Ontario, 813
Canadian Acoustical Association, 854

Acquired Immune Deficiency Syndrome
See AIDS

Active Living
See Recreation

Administrative Law
See Law

Administrative Management
See Management

Administrative Sciences
See also Business Education; Management
Association canadienne des sciences régionales, 830

Adolescence
See Youth

Advanced Industrial Materials
See Industrial Materials, Advanced

Advanced Manufacturing
See Industrial Materials, Advanced

Advanced Technology
See High Technology

Adventure Activities, Outdoor
See Recreation

Adventure Travel
See Travel Industry

Advertising
See also Direct Marketing; Marketing
Canadian Marketing Association, 877

Advocates
See Lawyers

Aeronautics
See also Aviation
Canadian Aeronautics & Space Institute, 854

Aerospace Industries
See also Space Sciences
Aerospace Industries Association of Canada, 813

Affordable Housing
See Housing

Aggregate Industry
See also Granite; Marble; Quarrying Industry; Stone
Aggregate Producers' Association of Ontario, 813

Agribitions
See Agricultural Exhibitions

Agricultural Biomass
See Biomass Energy

Agricultural Cooperatives
Canadian Co-operative Wool Growers Ltd., 864

Agricultural Economics
Alberta Agricultural Economics Association, 815
Canadian Agricultural Economics Society, 854
International Association of Agricultural Economists, 935

Agricultural Engineering
See also Sustainable Development
Canadian Society for Bioengineering, 885
International Commission of Agricultural & Biosystems Engineering, 937

Agricultural Equipment & Machinery
See also Equipment & Machinery
AMC - Agricultural Manufacturers of Canada, 822
Association of Equipment Manufacturers - Canada, 835
British Columbia Farm Machinery & Agriculture Museum Association, 847
Canada East Equipment Dealers' Association, 852
International Commission of Agricultural & Biosystems Engineering, 937
Prairie Agricultural Machinery Institute, 988

Agricultural Exhibitions
See also Exhibitions & Fairs
Association des expositions agricoles du Québec, 832
British Columbia Association of Agricultural Fairs & Exhibitions, 847
Lloydminster Agricultural Exhibition Association, 949
Norfolk County Agricultural Society, 964
Ontario Association of Agricultural Societies, 971
Royal Agricultural Winter Fair Association, 996

Agricultural Geography
See Geography

Agriculturalists
See Agronomists

Agriculture
See also Agricultural Cooperatives; Agricultural Engineering; Agricultural Equipment & Machinery; Agricultural Exhibitions; Agriculture & Youth; Agrologists; Agronomists; Farms & Farming; Horticulture; Seeds; Soil Science; Sustainable Development
Agricultural Alliance of New Brunswick, 813
Agricultural Groups Concerned About Resources & the Environment, 814
Agricultural Institute of Canada, 814
Agricultural Institute of Canada Foundation, 814
Agricultural Producers Association of Saskatchewan, 814
Alameda Agricultural Society, 815
Alberta Association of Agricultural Societies, 815
Alberta Conservation Tillage Society II, 816
Alberta Institute of Agrologists, 817
Alliance for Sustainability, 821
American Farmland Trust, 823
Association des technologues en agroalimentaire, 833
Association of Alberta Agricultural Fieldmen, 834
Barrie Agricultural Society, 844
Bengough Agricultural Society, 845
Binbrook Agricultural Society, 845
British Columbia Agriculture Council, 846
Canadian Agricultural Safety Association, 854
Canadian Agri-Marketing Association (Alberta), 855
Canadian Agri-Marketing Association (Manitoba), 855
Canadian Animal Health Institute, 855
Canadian Federation of Agriculture, 867
Canadian Hay Association, 870
The Canadian National Committee for Irrigation & Drainage, 879
Canadian Organic Growers Inc., 880
Carp Agricultural Society, 892
Consultative Group on International Agricultural Research, 902
Creelman Agricultural Society, 905
Ecological Agriculture Projects, 908
Expo agricole de Chicoutimi, 914
FarmFolk/CityFolk Society, 914
Hanley & District Agricultural Society, 927
Henry A. Wallace Center for Agricultural & Environmental Policy at Winrock International, 929
Heritage Agricultural Society, 929
Indian Agricultural Program of Ontario, 930
Integrated Vegetation Management Association of British Columbia, 934
International Federation of Organic Agriculture Movements, 939
International Peat Society - Canadian National Committee, 941
International Plant Propagators Society, Inc., 942
Keystone Agricultural Producers, 947
Melfort Agricultural Society, 953
Melville & District Agri-Park Association Inc., 953
Middlesex Federation of Agriculture, 954
Millarville Racing & Agricultural Society, 954
National Sunflower Association of Canada, 958
New Brunswick Soil & Crop Improvement Association, 961
Newfoundland & Labrador Federation of Agriculture, 962
Norfolk County Agricultural Society, 964
Nova Scotia Federation of Agriculture, 968
Ontario Agricultural Training Institute, 970
Ontario Agri-Food Education Inc., 970
Ontario Association of Agricultural Societies, 971
Ontario Corn Producers' Association, 972
Ontario Federation of Agriculture, 973
Ontario Soil & Crop Improvement Association, 979
Ontario Soybean Growers, 979
Ontario Vegetation Management Association, 981
Pesticide Action Network North America, 985
Prairie Fruit Growers Association, 988
Prince Edward Island Federation of Agriculture, 988
Research & Development Institute for the Agri-Environment, 994
Resource Efficient Agricultural Production, 995
Richmond Agricultural Society, 995
The Rocky Mountain Institute, 996
Saltcoats Agricultural Society, 998
Saskatchewan Association of Agricultural Societies & Exhibitions, 999
Saskatchewan Soil Conservation Association, 1001
SeCan Association, 1003
Swift Current Agricultural & Exhibition Association, 1011
Union des producteurs agricoles, 1014
Vanscoy & District Agricultural Society, 1016
Weed Science Society of America, 1018
Weyburn Agricultural Society, 1019
Wild Rose Agricultural Producers, 1020

Agriculture & Youth
Association des jeunes ruraux du Québec, 832
Canadian 4-H Council, 854
International Agricultural Exchange Association, 934
Junior Farmers' Association of Ontario, 947

Associations Subject Index

Québec 4-H, 991

Agrochemicals
See also **Pest Management**
Croplife International, 906
Integrated Vegetation Management Association of British Columbia, 934
Northwest Coalition for Alternatives to Pesticides, 966
Ontario Vegetation Management Association, 981
Weed Science Society of America, 1018

Agroforestry
World Agroforestry Centre, 1021

Agrologists
See also **Agronomists**
Alberta Institute of Agrologists, 817
British Columbia Institute of Agrologists, 848
Canadian Consulting Agrologists Association, 863
Manitoba Institute of Agrologists, 951
New Brunswick Institute of Agrologists, 961
Newfoundland & Labrador Institute of Agrologists, 963
Nova Scotia Institute of Agrologists, 968
Ontario Institute of Agrologists, 975
Ordre des agronomes du Québec, 981
Prince Edward Island Institute of Agrologists, 989

Agronomists
See also **Horticulture**
Canadian Society of Agronomy, 886
Ordre des agronomes du Québec, 981

AIDS
CUSO-VSO, 906
Panos Canada, 984
Panos London, 984
Panos Washington, 984

Air & Waste Management
See **Waste Management**

Air Ambulance
See **Emergency Services; Search & Rescue**

Air Conditioning
See also **Heating; Refrigeration; Ventilation**
American Society of Heating, Refrigerating & Air Conditioning Engineers, 824
Heating, Refrigeration & Air Conditioning Contractors Association Atlantic, 928
Heating, Refrigeration & Air Conditioning Institute of Canada, 928
Ontario Refrigeration & Air Conditioning Contractors Association, 978
Refrigeration & Air Conditioning Contractors Association of British Columbia, 993
Refrigeration & Air Conditioning Contractors Association of Manitoba, 993
Sheet Metal & Air Conditioning Contractors' National Association, 1003
Sheet Metal Contractors Association of Alberta, 1003
Thermal Environmental Comfort Association, 1012

Air Freight
See **Freight Services**

Air Pollution
See also **Acid Rain**
Air & Waste Management Association, 814
Association pour la prévention de la contamination de l'air et du sol, 841
Clean Air Foundation, 896
Clean Air Strategic Alliance, 896
Environmental Protection UK, 912

Air Quality Testing
See **Laboratories; Testing**

Air Rescue
See **Search & Rescue**

Air Search
See **Search & Rescue**

Air Transportation
See also **Freight Services**
Air Transport Association of Canada, 814
Association québécoise du transport aérien, 842
International Air Transport Association, 934

Aircraft Industry
See **Aerospace Industries**

Allergies
See also **Respiratory Allergies**
AllerGen NCE Inc., 820
Allergy Asthma Information Association, 821
Allergy, Asthma & Immunology Society of Ontario, 821
Association des Allergologues et Immunologues du Québec, 831
Canadian Society of Allergy & Clinical Immunology, 886
Environmental Health Association of Ontario, 912

Alpine Skiing
See **Skiing**

Alternate Therapy
See **Therapy**

Alternative Agriculture
See **Organic Farming & Gardening**

Alternative Energy
See **Energy Conservation; Renewable Energy Resources**

Aluminum
The Aluminum Association, 821

Amazon Rainforest
See **Rainforests**

Angling
See **Fishing & Angling**

Animal Experimentation
See **Animal Welfare**

Animal Feed Industry
See also **Pet Industry**
Animal Nutrition Association of Canada, 827
Ontario Agri Business Association, 970

Animal Health
See **Animal Science; Veterinary Medicine**

Animal Rights Movement
See also **Animal Welfare**
Animal Alliance of Canada, 827
Animal Defence & Anti-Vivisection Society of BC, 827
Animal Defence League of Canada, 827
Friends of Animals, 920
Fur-Bearer Defenders, 922
Lifeforce Foundation, 949
People for the Ethical Treatment of Animals, 985
Sea Shepherd Conservation Society, 1002
Sea Shepherd Conservation Society - USA, 1002

Animal Science
See also **Poultry Science; Veterinary Medicine**
Canadian Association for Laboratory Animal Science, 856
Canadian Society of Animal Science, 886
International Council for Laboratory Animal Science, 937
National Horse Protection League, 958

Animal Welfare
See also **Animal Rights Movement**
Action Volunteers for Animals, 813
Animal Welfare Foundation of Canada, 827
ARK II, 829
Canadian Association for Humane Trapping, 855
Canadian Association of Animal Health Technologists & Technicians, 856
Canadian Association of Swine Veterinarians, 859
Canadian Council on Animal Care, 865
Canadian Farm Animal Care Trust, 867
Canadian Federation of Humane Societies, 868
Canadians for Ethical Treatment of Food Animals, 892
Elsa Wild Animal Appeal of Canada, 909
Friends of Abandoned Pets, 920
Hope for Wildlife Society, 930
International Fund for Animal Welfare Canada, 939
International Primate Protection League, 942
The Kindness Club, 947
National Horse Protection League, 958
Saint John Animal Rescue League, 998
Société québécoise pour la défense des animaux, 1006
Wildlife Haven Rehabilitation Centre, 1020
Wildlife Rescue Association of British Columbia, 1020
World Society for the Protection of Animals, 1023
ZOOCHECK Canada Inc., 1025

Anthropology & Ethnology
See also **Archaeology**
International Council for Archaeozoology, 937

Anti-Semitism
See **Race Relations**

Anti-Smoking
See **Smoking**

Anti-Vivisection
See **Animal Rights Movement; Animal Welfare**

Antiquities
See also **Archaeology**
Archaeological Institute of America, 828

Apparel Industry
See **Clothing**

Apples
See **Fruit & Vegetables**

Applied Sciences
See **Engineering**

Appraisal
See also **Building Inspection; Home Inspection; Real Estate**
Canadian General Standards Board, 869

Apprenticeship
See **Staff Training & Development; Vocational & Technical Education**

Aquaculture
See also **Fish; Fisheries; Fisheries Science; Salmon; Trout**
Alberta Aquaculture Association, 815
American Fisheries Society, 823
Aquaculture Association of Canada, 828
Aquaculture Association of Nova Scotia, 828
AquaNet - Network in Aquaculture, 828
British Columbia Salmon Farmers Association, 849
Canadian Aquaculture Industry Alliance, 855
Canadian Centre for Fisheries Innovation, 861
Groundfish Enterprise Allocation Council, 926
New Brunswick Salmon Growers Association, 961
Newfoundland Aquaculture Industry Association, 963
Northern Ontario Aquaculture Association, 966
Prince Edward Island Aquaculture Alliance, 988
Prince Edward Island Finfish Growers Association, 988
World Aquaculture Society, 1021

Aquariums
American Zoo & Aquarium Association, 827
Canadian Association of Zoos & Aquariums, 859

Aquatic Biology
See **Fisheries Science**

Aquatic Biomass
See **Biomass Energy**

Aquatic Habitat, Conservation of
See **Conservation of Natural Resources**

Aquatic Monitoring
See **Laboratories; Testing**

Aquatic Sports
Manitoba Underwater Council, 952

Arboreta
See **Horticulture**

Arboriculture
See also **Agroforestry**
Christmas Tree Farmers of Ontario, 895
International Society of Arboriculture, 943
Manitoba Christmas Tree Grower Association, 950
Northern Interior Vegetation Management Association, 966
Ontario Urban Forest Council, 980
Prince Edward Island Forest Improvement Association, 988
Royal Botanical Gardens, 996
Western Silvicultural Contractors' Association, 1019
World Agroforestry Centre, 1021

Archaeology
See also **Anthropology & Ethnology; Antiquities; Industrial Archaeology; Underwater Archaeology**
Archaeological Institute of America, 828

Associations Subject Index

Canadian Archaeological Association, 855
Explorer's Club (Canadian Chapter), 914
International Council for Archaeozoology, 937

Archaeozoology
See Archaeology

Architectural Conservation
See also Conservation of Historic & Artistic; Heritage; Preservation Technology
The Architectural Conservancy of Ontario, 828
Architectural Heritage Society of Saskatchewan, 828
Conseil des monuments et sites du Québec, 900
ICOMOS Canada, 930
International Council on Monuments & Sites, 938

Architecture
See also Architectural Acoustics; Architectural Conservation; Structural Engineering
Heritage Canada Foundation, 929
Union internationale des architectes, 1014

Arctic Region
See also Northern Canada
Arctic Institute of North America, 829
ArcticNet Inc., 829
Association of Canadian Universities for Northern Studies, 834
Canadian Circumpolar Institute, 862
International Arctic Science Committee, 934

Arms Control
See also Disarmament
Canadian Coalition for Nuclear Responsibility, 862

Artificial Intelligence
Communications & Information Technology Ontario, 898

Artistic Works, Conservation of
See Conservation of Historic & Artistic

Asbestos Industry
See also Building Materials; Mining
Chrysotile Institute, 895

Assessment
See Appraisal

Asthma
See also Respiratory Allergies; Respiratory Therapy
Allergy Asthma Information Association, 821
Allergy, Asthma & Immunology Society of Ontario, 821
Canadian Society of Allergy & Clinical Immunology, 886

Astronautical Sciences
See Space Sciences

Astronomy
See also Planetariums
H.R. MacMillan Space Centre Society, 930

Atlantic Provinces
See also Acadians; Labrador
Acadian Entomological Society, 813
Québec-Labrador Foundation (Canada) Inc., 991
Seagull Foundation, 1003

Atmosphere
Association québécoise de lutte contre la pollution atmosphérique, 841

Atomic Energy
See Nuclear Energy

Attorneys
See Lawyers

Authors
See Writers

Automation
See High Technology

Automobile Industry
See Automotive Industry

Automobiles
See also Antique Automobiles & Trucks; Automobile Clubs; Automobile Dealers; Automobile Racing; Automotive Industry; Automotive Services; Driver Education; Motor Vehicles; Sports Cars
AUTO21 - The Automobile of the 21st Century, 844

Automotive Industry
Association of International Automobile Manufacturers of Canada, 836
Automotive Industries Association of Canada, 844
Automotive Parts Manufacturers' Association, 844
Ontario Automotive Recyclers Association, 971

Avian Pathology
See Poultry Science

Aviation
See also Aeronautics; Air Force; Air Safety; Air Shows; Air Sports; Air Traffic Control; Aircraft; Airlines; Airports; Pilots
Aerospace Industries Association of Canada, 813
Explorer's Club (Canadian Chapter), 914
International Flying Farmers, 939

Aviculture
See Birds

Backpacking
See Camping; Hiking; Orienteering

Bags
See Containers; Packaging

Banking Industry
See Banks

Banks
See also Credit Unions & Bureaux; Finance; Financial Services Industry
Environmental Bankers Association, 911

Bar Associations
See Law

Barristers
See Lawyers

Bears
See also Wildlife Conservation
International Association for Bear Research & Management, 934

Bed & Breakfast Accommodations
See Hospitality Industry

Beef
See Meat

Beef Cattle
See Livestock

Bigotry
See Race Relations

Biochemistry
See also Biophysics; Physiology
Association des médecins biochimistes du Québec, 833
Canadian Association of Medical Biochemists, 857
The Canadian Society of Biochemistry, Molecular & Cellular Biology, 886

Biodiversity
ETC Group, 913
Falls Brook Centre, 914
International Union of Biological Sciences, 945
Rare Breeds Canada, 992

Biodynamic Farming
See Farms & Farming

Bioenergetic Analysis
See Science

Bioethics
See also Genetic Engineering; Medical Ethics
Canadian Bioethics Society, 860
Joint Centre for Bioethics, 947

Biogeography
See Geography

Biology
See also Biochemistry; Biophysics; Chemistry; Microbiology
Alberta Society of Professional Biologists, 819
American Society of Plant Biologists, 826
Association of Professional Biology, 837
Coastal Ecosystems Research Foundation, 897
College of Applied Biology British Columbia, 897
Council of Science Editors, 905
Institut de recherche en biologie végétale, 932
International Federation for Medical & Biological Engineering, 939
International Union of Biological Sciences, 945
Society for Conservation Biology, 1006
The Waterbird Society, 1018

Biomass Energy
Canadian Renewable Fuels Association, 884

Biomedical Engineering
See also Genetic Engineering
Canadian Medical & Biological Engineering Society, 877
International Federation for Medical & Biological Engineering, 939

Biomedical Research
Canadian Association of Medical Biochemists, 857

Biometeorology
See Meteorology

Bioorganic Chemistry
See Chemistry

Biophysics
See also Biochemistry
Biophysical Society of Canada, 845

Biotechnology
See also Biomedical Engineering; Biomedical Research; Genetic Engineering; Medical Research; Medical Technology
AllerGen NCE Inc., 820
BIOQuébec, 845
BIOTECanada, 845
Canadian Society of Microbiologists, 887
International Society for Environmental Biotechnology, 942
International Society for Evolutionary Protistology, 943
LifeSciences British Columbia, 949
Stem Cell Network, 1010
Toronto Biotechnology Initiative, 1012

Birds
See also Ducks; Fish & Game; Hawks; Poultry; Poultry Science
Alberta Falconry Association, 816
American Birding Association, 822
American Ornithologists' Union, 824
The Avian Preservation Foundation, 844
Avicultural Advancement Council of Canada, 844
Beaverhill Bird Observatory, 845
Bird Studies Canada, 845
British Columbia Waterfowl Society, 850
Club des ornithologues de Québec inc., 896
Durham Avicultural Society of Ontario, 907
Grand Manan Whale & Seabird Research Station, 924
Hawk Migration Association of North America, 927
Jack Miner Migratory Bird Foundation, Inc., 946
National Audubon Society, Inc., 957
Ontario Field Ornithologists, 973
Pembroke Area Field Naturalists, 985
Regroupement QuébecOiseaux, 994
Society of Canadian Ornithologists, 1007
Toronto Ornithological Club, 1012
The Waterbird Society, 1018
Wild Bird Care Centre, 1020

Bison
See Livestock

Blue Box Program
See Recycling

Boating
See also Aquatic Sports; Boats; Canoeing & Rafting; Housebeating; Kayaking; Rowing; Sailing
British Columbia Marine Trades Association, 849
National Marine Manufacturers Association Canada, 958
Ontario Marine Operators Association, 975

Boats
See also Marinas; Ships
National Marine Manufacturers Association, 958

Boring
See Drilling

Botanical Gardens
See Horticulture

CANADIAN ENVIRONMENTAL RESOURCE GUIDE 2011-2012

Associations Subject Index

Botany
See also Botanic Medicine; Horticulture
American Association of Botanical Gardens & Arboreta, 822
American Society of Plant Biologists, 826
Canadian Botanical Association, 860
Canadian Phytopathological Society, 882
Canadian Society of Plant Physiologists, 887
Center for Plant Conservation, 893
Field Botanists of Ontario, 916
International Plant Propagators Society, Inc., 942
International Society for Plant Pathology, 943
VanDusen Botanical Garden Association, 1016

Bottled Water
Association des embouteilleurs d'eau du Québec, 831
Canadian Bottled Water Association, 860
International Bottled Water Association, 936

Boxes
See Containers

Breast Cancer
See Cancer

Breeding
See also Artificial Insemination (Animal); Cattle; Foxes; Fur Trade; Goats; Livestock; Mink; Rabbits; Sheep; Swine
Canadian Cattle Breeders' Association, 861
Rare Breeds Canada, 992
Saskatchewan Stock Growers Association, 1001

British Isles
British Council - Canada, 851

Budget Preparation
See Finance

Building Inspection
See also Appraisal; Home Inspection
World Organization of Building Officials, 1022

Building Maintenance
See also Property Management
World Organization of Building Officials, 1022

Building Materials
See also Brick Industry; Construction Industry; Fibreboard Industry
Building Supply Industry Association of British Columbia, 851
Cement Association of Canada, 893
Independent Lumber Dealers Co-operative, 930
Lumber & Building Materials Association of Ontario, 949
Ontario Lumber Manufacturers' Association, 975
Western Retail Lumber Association, 1019
World Organization of Building Officials, 1022

Building Trades
See also Building & Construction Trades Coun; Construction Industry; Renovation; Roofing Trade
Association provinciale des constructeurs d'habitations du Québec inc., 841
National Building Envelope Council, 957

Built Heritage
See Architectural Conservation; Conservation of Historic & Artistic; Heritage

Bus Transport
See also Motor Vehicles
Canadian Bus Association, 860

Business
See also Business Economics; Business Education; Business Forms; Commerce; Corporate Planning; Home-Based Business; Small Business; Women in Business, Industry & Trade
Asia Pacific Foundation of Canada, 829
Business Council of British Columbia, 852
Canadian Council of Chief Executives, 864
SHAD Valley International, 1003
Strategic Leadership Forum, The Toronto Society for Strategic Management, 1010
Yukon Tourism Education Council, 1024

Business Aviation
See Aviation

Business Valuators
See Appraisal

Business, Small
See Small Business

Butterflies
See Entomology

Cage Birds
See Birds

Camping
See also Hiking; Orienteering
Alberta Camping Association, 816
British Columbia Camping Association, 847
British Columbia Lodging & Campgrounds Association, 848
Campground Owners Association of Nova Scotia, 852
Camping Québec, 852
Canadian Camping Association, 860
Fédération québécoise de camping et de caravaning inc., 916
Fédération québécoise du canot et du kayak, 916
Manitoba Camping Association, 950
Newfoundland & Labrador Camping Association, 962
Ontario Camps Association, 971
Recreation New Brunswick, 992
Saskatchewan Camping Association, 999

Canada & Canadian Studies
See also Arctic Region; Atlantic Provinces; Great Lakes; Northern Canada; Québec
The Canadian Institute, 872

Canadian Charter of Rights & Freedo
See Human Rights

Canadian Unity
See Canada & Canadian Studies

Canals
See Locks & Canals

Cancer
See also Chemotherapy; Leukemia; Oncology
Breast Cancer Action, 846
Breast Cancer Society of Canada, 846
Canadian Cancer Society, 861
Canadian Cancer Society Research Institute, 861
Cancer Research Society, 892
Fondation québécoise du cancer, 917

Canoeing & Rafting
See also Boating; Kayaking
Fédération québécoise du canot et du kayak, 916
Outward Bound Canada, 983
Paddle Canada, 984
Wilderness Canoe Association, 1020

Canola
Alberta Canola Producers Commission, 816

Cans
See Containers

Cape Breton
See Atlantic Provinces

Caravanning
See Camping

Career Colleges
See Universities & Colleges

Career Training
See Staff Training & Development

Cargo Handling
See Freight Services; Shipping

Carrying Capacity
See also Populations
Carrying Capacity Network, 892
Earth Voice, 907

Cars
See Automobiles

Cartography
See Maps

Casual Employment
See Labour

Catalogue Shopping
See Direct Marketing

Cattle
See also Breeding; Livestock
Alberta Beef Producers, 815
American Association of Bovine Practitioners, 822
British Columbia Cattlemen's Association, 847
Canadian Cattle Breeders' Association, 861
Canadian Cattlemen's Association, 861
Manitoba Cattle Producers Association, 950
Nova Scotia Cattle Producers, 967
Ontario Cattlemen's Association, 971
Prince Edward Island Cattle Producers, 988
Saskatchewan Stock Growers Association, 1001

Caulking
See Building Trades

Caves
See Speleology

CEGEPS
See Universities & Colleges

Cellular Biology
See Microbiology

Cement
See also Concrete
Cement Association of Canada, 893

Census
See Populations; Statistics

Central Labour Congresses
See Labour Unions

Centres of Excellence (Ontario)
See also Networks of Centres of Excellence
Communications & Information Technology Ontario, 898
Materials & Manufacturing Ontario, Division of OCE Inc., 952
Ontario Centre of Excellence for Photonics, 971
Ontario Centres of Excellence - Centre for Earth & Environmental Technologies, 972

Certified Administrative Managers
See Management

Cetaceans
See Marine Mammals

CFCs
See Air Conditioning; Refrigeration

Chambers of Commerce
See also Boards of Trade
The Canadian Chamber of Commerce, 862
Pigeon Lake Regional Chamber of Commerce, 986

Chambers of Mines
See also Mining; Prospecting
Alberta Chamber of Resources, 816
Association for Mineral Exploration British Columbia, 833
Chamber of Mineral Resources of Nova Scotia, 894
Chamber of Mines of Eastern British Columbia, 894
East Kootenay Chamber of Mines, 907
NWT & Nunavut Chamber of Mines, 969
Yukon Chamber of Mines, 1024

Charter Boats
See Boats

Charter of Rights & Freedoms
See Human Rights

Chartered Accountants
See Accountants, Chartered

Chemical Engineering
Chemical Institute of Canada, 894

Chemical Feedstocks, Conversion
See Biomass Energy

Chemical Industry
See also Agrochemicals; Chemical Engineering; Chemistry
Alberta Sulphur Research Ltd., 820
Canadian Association of Agri-Retailers, 856
Canadian Association of Chemical Distributors, 857
Canadian Chemical Producers' Association, 862
Canadian Consumer Specialty Products Association, 863
Croplife International, 906
National Association of the Chemistry Industry, 957

Society of Chemical Industry - Canadian Section, 1008

Chemistry
See also Biochemistry; Chemical Engineering; Chemical Industry; Geochemistry
Association of the Chemical Profession of Alberta, 840
Chemical Institute of Canada, 894
International Association of Environmental Analytical Chemistry, 935
International Confederation for Thermal Analysis & Calorimetry, 937
International Union of Pure & Applied Chemistry, 945
Ontario Centre of Excellence for Photonics, 971
Society of Environmental Toxicology & Chemistry, 1008

Chemists
See also Pharmacists
Association of the Chemical Profession of Ontario, 840
Canadian Society of Clinical Chemists, 886
Ordre des chimistes du Québec, 981

Chest Disorders & Diseases
See Lung Disorders & Diseases

Chickens
See Poultry

Children
See also Child Welfare; Children - Death; Children - Diseases; Exceptional Children; Gifted Children; Youth
The Kindness Club, 947

Chlorofluorocarbons
See Air Conditioning; Refrigeration

Christians & Christianity
See also Anglicans; Baptists; Bible; Catholics & Catholicism; Christian Education; Churches; Clergy; Ecumenism; Mennonites; Missions & Missionaries; Orthodox Church; United Church of Canada
Lifewater Canada, 949

Christmas
Manitoba Christmas Tree Grower Association, 950

Cities & Towns
See Community Planning; Municipal Government; Single Industry Communities; Sustainable Cities; Urban Planning

Citizens' Groups
CIVICUS: World Alliance for Citizen Participation, 896
Environmental Defence, 911
Pickering & Ajax Citizens Together for the Environment, 986
Toronto Environmental Alliance, 1012

City Planning
See Urban Planning

Civil Aviation
See Aviation

Civil Engineering
Canadian Society for Civil Engineering, 885

Civil Liberties
See Human Rights

Civil Rights
See Human Rights

Clean Air
See Air Pollution

Clean Water
See Water Pollution

Climate
See also Global Warming; Meteorology; Ozone Layer Depletion
Canadian Foundation for Climate & Atmospheric Sciences, 869
Climate Action Network - Canada, 896
Climate Institute, 896
Executive Forum on Climate Change, 914
International Institute for Energy Conservation, 940
International Society of Biometeorology, 943
World Meteorological Organization, 1022

Climate Change
See Climate

Clinical Chemistry
See Chemistry

Clinical Medicine
See Medicine

Clothing
See also Bridal Industry; Fashion Design; Footwear; Protective Clothing; Textiles
Association paritaire pour la santé et la sécurité du travail - Habillement, 840
The Fur Council of Canada, 922

Clothing Banks
See Emergency Services

Coal
See also Mining
Canadian Carbonization Research Association, 861
Canadian Clean Power Coalition, 862
World Coal Institute, 1022

Coatings
See Paint

Coke
See Coal

Cold Regions
See Arctic Region

Colleges
See Universities & Colleges

Commercial Art
See Advertising; Graphic Arts & Design

Communications
See also Advertising; Broadcasting; Captioning, Closed; Computer Networks; Media; Radio Broadcasting; Telecommunications
BIOTECanada, 845
Ceta-Research Inc., 894
Communications & Information Technology Ontario, 898

Community Colleges
See Universities & Colleges

Community Development
See also Community Planning; Economic Development; Social Planning Councils
Arusha Centre Society, 829
Canadian Institute of Planners, 875
Federation of Calgary Communities, 915
Federation of Canadian Municipalities, 915
Ordre des urbanistes du Québec, 982
World Society for Ekistics, 1023
Youth Challenge International, 1024

Community Development Corporations
See Economic Development

Community Education
See Education

Community Foundations
See Foundations

Community Health
See Public Health

Community Land Trusts
See Environment

Community Legal Education
See Legal Education

Community Living Associations
See Developmentally Disabled Persons

Community Planning
See also Community Development; Economic Development; Regional Planning; Social Planning Councils; Urban Planning
Association of Professional Community Planners of Saskatchewan, 838
Institute of Urban Studies, 934

Community Theatre
See Theatre

Commuter
Smart Commute, 1004

Commuter Rail
See Railroads & Railways

Comparative Literature
See Literature

Compensation, Workers'
See Workers' Compensation

Composting
See also Recycling
Compost Council of Canada, 899

Computer Hardware
See Computers

Computer Languages
See Computers

Computer Literacy
See Computers

Computer Programmes
See Computers

Computers
See also Computer Networks; Computer Software; Computer User Groups; Data Base Management; Information Technology
Urban & Regional Information Systems Association, 1015

Concrete
See also Cement
British Columbia Ready Mixed Concrete Association, 849
Canadian Concrete Pipe Association, 863
Canadian Precast / Prestressed Concrete Institute, 883
Ontario Concrete Pipe Association, 972

Conference Facilities
See Meetings & Conventions

Congress Organizers
See Meetings & Conventions

Conservation Education
See Environmental & Outdoor Education

Conservation of Historic & Artistic
See also Architectural Conservation; Heritage; Preservation Technology
Heritage Canada Foundation, 929
International Institute for Conservation of Historic & Artistic Works, 940
Ontario Heritage Trust, 974
Save Ontario Shipwrecks, 1002

Conservation of Natural Resources
See also Ecology; Energy Conservation; Forestry; Renewable Energy Resources; Water Resources; Wilderness; Wildlife Conservation
Action to Restore a Clean Humber, 813
African Wildlife Foundation, 813
Agricultural Groups Concerned About Resources & the Environment, 814
Alberta Conservation Association, 816
Alberta Conservation Tillage Society II, 816
Alliance for the Wild Rockies, 821
Amalgamated Conservation Society, 821
American Cave Conservation Association, 822
American Rivers, 824
American Wildlands, 827
Ausable Bayfield Conservation Foundation, 844
Barrow Bay & District Sports Fishing Association, 844
Big Rideau Lake Association, 845
British Columbia Conservation Foundation, 847
British Columbia Spaces for Nature, 850
Carrying Capacity Network, 892
Castle-Crown Wilderness Coalition, 892
Clean Annapolis River Project, 896
Clubs 4-H du Québec, 897
Conseil régional de l'environnement de la Gaspésie et des Iles-de-la-Madeleine, 901
Conservation International, 901
The Cousteau Society, 905
EAGLE (Environmental-Aboriginal Guardianship through Law & Education), 907
Earthwatch Europe, 907
FarmFolk/CityFolk Society, 914
Forest Action Network, 918
Foundation for Environmental Conservation, 919
Friends of Clayoquot Sound, 920
Friends of Mount Revelstoke & Glacier, 921
Friends of the Earth International, 921

Associations Subject Index

Grand River Conservation Foundation, 924
International Peat Society - Canadian National Committee, 941
International Union for Conservation of Nature, 944
International Wildlife Coalition, 946
Jack Miner Migratory Bird Foundation, Inc., 946
Kamloops Wildlife Park Society, 947
The Ladies of the Lake, 947
Lake Simcoe Region Conservation Foundation, 948
Meewasin Valley Authority, 953
MiningWatch Canada, 955
Montréal Field Naturalists Club, 955
Muskoka Lakes Association, 956
National Audubon Society, Inc., 957
National Parks Conservation Association, 958
National Wildlife Federation, 958
Newfoundland & Labrador Forest Protection Association, 962
Nunavut Harvesters Association, 969
The Ocean Conservancy, 969
Ontario Federation of Anglers & Hunters, 973
Ontario Streams, 979
Ottawa Duck Club, 983
Partners FOR the Saskatchewan River Basin, 985
Prairie Conservation Forum, 988
Prince George Recycling & Environmental Action Planning Society, 989
Protected Areas Association of Newfoundland & Labrador, 990
Rainforest Action Network, 992
Réseau environnement, 994
Salmon Arm Bay Nature Enhancement Society, 998
Saskatchewan Soil Conservation Association, 1001
SEEDS Foundation, 1003
Society for Conservation Biology, 1006
Soil & Water Conservation Society, 1009
Soil Conservation Council of Canada, 1009
Sustainable Forestry Initiative, 1011
The Township of Muskoka Lakes Ratepayers' Association, 1013
UNEP - World Conservation Monitoring Centre, 1014
Union mondiale pour la nature - Bureau de Montréal, 1014
Upper Thames River Conservation Authority, 1015
Uxbridge Conservation Association, 1016
World Association of Industrial & Technological Research Organizations, 1021
World Blue Chain for the Protection of Animals & Nature, 1021
World Resources Institute, 1023
World Wildlife Fund - USA, 1023
WWF International, 1024

Conservation, Architectural
See Architectural Conservation

Construction Industry
See also Building & Construction Trades Coun; Building Materials; Building Trades; Contractors; Heavy Construction; Renovation; Roads & Roadbuilding; Roofing Trade
Alberta Building Envelope Council (South), 816
Alberta Construction Association, 816
British Columbia Construction Association, 847
Canadian Construction Association, 863
Canadian Home Builders' Association, 871
Canadian Home Builders' Association - British Columbia, 871
Canadian Steel Construction Council, 889
Construction Association of New Brunswick Inc., 902
Construction Association of Prince Edward Island, 902
Construction Specifications Canada, 902
Council of Ontario Construction Associations, 905
National Building Envelope Council, 957
Newfoundland & Labrador Construction Association, 962
Northwest Territories Construction Association, 967
Pipe Line Contractors Association of Canada, 987
Saskatchewan Construction Safety Association Inc., 999
Vancouver Regional Construction Association, 1016
Western Retail Lumber Association, 1019
World Organization of Building Officials, 1022

Consultants & Consulting
Association of Consulting Engineering Companies - Canada, 835
Association of Consulting Engineering Companies - New Brunswick, 835
Canadian Consulting Agrologists Association, 863
Consulting Engineers of Alberta, 902
Consulting Engineers of British Columbia, 903
Consulting Engineers of Manitoba Inc., 903
Consulting Engineers of Nova Scotia, 903
Consulting Engineers of Ontario, 903
Consulting Engineers of Saskatchewan, 903
Consulting Engineers of Yukon, 903
Consulting Foresters of British Columbia, 903
Mining Suppliers, Contractors & Consultants Association of BC, 955

Consumer Protection
See also Better Business Bureau; Standards; Testing
Consumers International, 903
Consumers' Association of Canada, 904
Association pour la protection des intérêts des consommateurs de la C, 0

Containers
See also Packaging
Alliance of Foam Packaging Recyclers, 821
Association of Postconsumer Plastic Recyclers, 837
Canadian Wood Pallet & Container Association, 892
Glass Packaging Institute, 923
National Association for PET Container Resources, 957

Continuing Legal Education
See Legal Education

Contractors
See also Construction Industry
Canadian Association of Geophysical Contractors, 857
Mining Suppliers, Contractors & Consultants Association of BC, 955
Refrigeration & Air Conditioning Contractors Association of British Columbia, 993
Sheet Metal & Air Conditioning Contractors' National Association, 1003
Western Silvicultural Contractors' Association, 1019

Convention Planning
See Meetings & Conventions

Cooperative Education
See Education

Cooperative Learning
See Education

Cooperative Movement
See also Agricultural Cooperatives; Cooperative Housing
Canadian Association for Studies in Co-operation, 856
International Cooperative Alliance, 937

Corrugated Packaging
See Packaging

Corrugated Steel Pipe
See Pipes

Cottages
Federation of Ontario Cottagers' Associations, 915
Muskoka Lakes Association, 956

Country Vacations
See Vacation Industry

Criminal Justice
See Law

Criminal Lawyers
See Lawyers

Crop Protection
See Agriculture; Farms & Farming; Soil Science; Sustainable Development

Cross-Country Skiing
See Skiing

Cross-Cultural Communication
See also Developing Countries; Development Education; International Relations
Canadian Council for International Co-operation, 864
Coady International Institute, 897
CUSO-VSO, 906
Kawartha World Issues Centre, 947

Crown Attorneys
See Lawyers

Crude Oil
See Oil

Cruelty to Animals
See Animal Welfare

Crystallography
See Mineralogy

Cultural Geography
See Geography

Culture
See also Arts Councils; Cultural Affairs; The Arts
Société de conservation de la Baie de l'Isle-Verte, 1005

Curriculum Development
See Education

Dairy Industry
See also Cheese; Ice Cream; Milk
Alberta Milk, 818
Atlantic Dairy Council, 843
Ontario Creamerymen's Association, 972
Ontario Dairy Council, 972

Dams
American Rivers, 824
Canadian Dam Association, 865
Probe International, 989

Data Base Management
Public Petroleum Data Model Association, 991

Data Retrieval
See Computers

Database Management
See Data Base Management

Debt Counselling
See Finance

Demographics
See Populations

Developing Countries
Canadian Council for International Co-operation, 864
CODE, 897
CUSO-VSO, 906
Farm Radio International, 914
International Development Research Centre, 938
Probe International, 989
United Nations Conference on Trade & Development, 1015
WaterCan, 1018
Youth Challenge International, 1024

Development Education
See also Cross-Cultural Communication; International Cooperation; International Relations
Coady International Institute, 897
CODE, 897
CUSO-VSO, 906
Kawartha World Issues Centre, 947
Pacific Peoples Partnership, 983
Société de coopération pour le développement international, 1005

Development Officers
See Economic Development; Industrial Development

Developmentally Disabled Persons
See also Disabled Persons; Learning Disabilities
Saskatchewan Association of Rehabilitation Centres, 999

Developmentally Handicapped Persons
See Developmentally Disabled Persons

Diamond Drilling
See Drilling

Direct Marketing
See also Marketing; Telemarketing
Canadian Marketing Association, 877
Direct Marketing Association, 906
Direct Sellers Association of Canada, 906

Disabled Artists
See Disabled Persons

Disabled Children
See Disabled Persons

Disabled Persons
See also Developmentally Disabled Persons; Housing for the Physically Disabled; Sports for the Disabled
Lansdowne Outdoor Recreational Development Association, 948

Disarmament
See also Arms Control; Peace
Canadian Coalition for Nuclear Responsibility, 862

Disaster Relief
See Emergency Services; International Relief

Discrimination, Racial
See Race Relations

Diseases
See also Disorders
Canadian Genetic Diseases Network, 869

Diving
See also Skin Diving; Swimming
Manitoba Underwater Council, 952

Doctors, Medical
See Physicians; Surgeons

Dolphins
See Marine Mammals

Drainage
See Irrigation

Dresses
See Clothing

Drilling
Alberta Water Well Drilling Association, 820
Association des enterprises spécialiseés en eau du Québec, 832
British Columbia Ground Water Association, 848
Canadian Association of Drilling Engineers, 857
Canadian Association of Oilwell Drilling Contractors, 858
Canadian Ground Water Association, 870
Nova Scotia Ground Water Association, 968

Drinking Water
See also Bottled Water; Water Resources
Lifewater Canada, 949

Ducks
See also Wildlife Conservation
Ducks Unlimited Canada, 906
Ducks Unlimited Inc., 907
Ottawa Duck Club, 983

Early Childhood Education
See also Child Care
Concerned Educators Allied for a Safe Environment, 899

Earth Sciences
See Geology; Geophysics; Mineralogy; Paleontology

Eco-Tourism
See Tourism

Ecological Urban Planning
See Urban Planning

Ecology
See also Conservation of Natural Resources; Limnology; Rivers & Streams
Antarctic & Southern Ocean Coalition, 828
Bruce Peninsula Environment Group, 851
Canadian Council on Ecological Areas, 865
Conservation Council of New Brunswick, 901
Conservation Council of Ontario, 901
Conservation Halton Foundation, 901
Credit Valley Conservation Foundation, 905
David Suzuki Foundation, 906
Earth Voice, 907
Earthroots, 907
Ecoforestry Institute Society, 908
Ecological Agriculture Projects, 908
Ecological Farmers Association of Ontario, 908
Ecological Society of America, 908
Ecology Action Centre, 908
Fédération des sociétés d'horticulture et d'écologie du Québec, 915
Friends of Ecological Reserves, 920
Friends of the Delta Marsh Field Station, 921
Friends of the Earth Canada, 921
Groupe de recherche en écologie sociale, 926
International Association for Ecology, 934
International Federation of Organic Agriculture Movements, 939
International Society for Ecological Economics, 942
International Society for Ecological Modelling, 942
International Union for Conservation of Nature, 944

International Union of Biological Sciences, 945
Lifeforce Foundation, 949
Lynn Canyon Ecology Centre, 950
Meewasin Valley Authority, 953
The Nature Conservancy of Canada, 959
Niagara Peninsula Conservation Foundation, 964
Oakville Community Centre for Peace, Ecology & Human Rights, 969
Partners FOR the Saskatchewan River Basin, 985
Québec-Labrador Foundation (Canada) Inc., 991
Réseau québécois des groupes écologistes, 994
Sierra Club, 1003
Sierra Club of British Columbia, 1004
Sierra Club of Canada, 1004
Sierra Club of Canada - Ontario Chapter, 1004
Sierra Club of Canada - Prairie Chapter, 1004
Sierra Youth Coalition, 1004
Society for Ecological Restoration International, 1007
Society for Socialist Studies, 1007
Society Promoting Environmental Conservation, 1009
Stanley Park Ecology Society, 1010
Thames Region Ecological Association, 1012
Union mondiale pour la nature - Bureau de Montréal, 1014
The Waterbird Society, 1018
World Agroforestry Centre, 1021
World Wildlife Fund - Canada, 1023
Yukon Conservation Society, 1024

Economic Development
See also Community Development; Developing Countries; Foreign Aid; Industrial Development; Native Development Corporations; Regional Development
Association canadienne des sciences régionales, 830
Institute for Research on Public Policy, 932
Native Investment & Trade Association, 959
Organization for Economic Cooperation & Development, 982
Pacific NorthWest Economic Region, 983
Société de développement économique du Saint-Laurent, 1005

Economic Geography
See Geography

Economics
See also Agricultural Economics; Business Economics
Canadian Association for Health Services & Policy Research, 855
Canadian Centre for Policy Alternatives, 862
C.D. Howe Institute, 893
The Conference Board of Canada, 899
Connexions Information Sharing Services, 900
International Institute for Applied Systems Analysis, 940
International Institute of Fisheries Economics & Trade, 940
Social Investment Organization, 1004

Ecosystems Conservation
See Ecology

Editors
See also Newspapers; Publishing
Council of Science Editors, 905

Education
See also Adult Education; Boards of Education; Christian Education; Development Education; Distance Education; Early Childhood Education; Educational Media; Schools; Students; Teaching; Universities & Colleges; Vocational & Technical Education
Association of University Forestry Schools of Canada, 840
Canadian Institute for Energy Training, 872
The Canadian Network for Environmental Education & Communication, 879
Council of Canadian Fire Marshals & Fire Commissioners, 904
Earthwatch Europe, 907
Ecological Farmers Association of Ontario, 908
International Association of Educators for World Peace, 935
International Centre for Conservation Education, 936
International Council of Associations for Science Education, 938
International Ocean Institute, 941
The Jane Goodall Institute of Canada, 946
National Council for Science & the Environment, 957
Ontario Agri-Food Education Inc., 970
SEEDS Foundation, 1003
The W. Garfield Weston Foundation, 1017

Educational Exchange Programmes
See Student Exchanges

Electric Power
See also Nuclear Energy; Public Utilities
Association of Major Power Consumers in Ontario, 836
Canadian Association of Members of Public Utility Tribunals, 857
Canadian Clean Power Coalition, 862
Canadian Hydropower Association, 872
Electricity Distributors Association, 909
Electro-Federation Canada Inc., 909
Independent Power Producers Association of British Columbia, 930
Independent Power Producers Society of Alberta, 930

Electric Railways
See Railroads & Railways

Electric Vehicles
See Motor Vehicles

Electrical Engineering
See also Electronics Industry; Lighting
Conseil Canadien des Électrotechnologies, 900
Institute of Electrical & Electronics Engineers Inc. - Canada, 932
Institute of Electrical & Electronics Engineers Inc., 932
Maintenance & Engineering Society of The Canadian Institute of Mining, Metallurgy & Petroleum, 950
Ontario Centre of Excellence for Photonics, 971

Electrical Industry
Association paritaire pour la santé et la sécurité du travail - Produits en métal et électriques, 841
Electro-Federation Canada Inc., 909
Ontario Electrical League, 972

Electrical Maintenance
See Electrical Industry

Electronic Engineering
Institute of Electrical & Electronics Engineers Inc., 932
Institute of Electrical & Electronics Engineers Inc. - Canada, 932

Electronics Industry
British Columbia Technology Industries Association, 850
Electronics Product Stewardship Canada, 909

Emergency Services
See also Ambulance Service; Citizens' Band Radio; Emergency Housing; Fire Fighting; Food Banks; Lifesaving; Search & Rescue
Canadian Avalanche Association, 859
Canadian Centre for Emergency Preparedness, 861

Emerging Nations
See Developing Countries

Employment Agencies
See Human Resources

Endangered Species (Flora & Fauna)
See Botany; Wildlife Conservation

Energy
See also Biomass Energy; Gas; Nuclear Energy; Oil; Renewable Energy Resources; Solar Energy; Wood Energy
Alberta Cogenerators Council, 816
Association of Major Power Consumers in Ontario, 836
Association of Power Producers of Ontario, 837
Association québécoise pour la maîtrise de l'énergie, 842
Canadian Centre for Energy Information, 861
Canadian District Energy Association, 866
Canadian Electricity Association, 866
Canadian Energy Efficiency Alliance, 866
Canadian Energy Research Institute, 866
Canadian GeoExchange Coalition, 869
Canadian Institute for Energy Training, 872
Canadian Institute of Energy, 873
Canadian Wind Energy Association Inc., 891
Communications, Energy & Paperworkers Union of Canada, 899
Earth Energy Society of Canada, 907
Energy Action Council of Toronto, 909
Energy Council of Canada, 909
Energy Probe Research Foundation, 910
Independent Power Producers Association of British Columbia, 930
Independent Power Producers Society of Alberta, 930
Institut de l'énergie et de l'environnement de la Francophonie, 931
International Energy Foundation, 938
Offshore Energy Environmental Research Association, 970

Associations Subject Index

Ontario Energy Association, 973
Ontario Sustainable Energy Association, 980
Planetary Association for Clean Energy, Inc., 987
The Rocky Mountain Institute, 996
SEEDS Foundation, 1003
Warmer Bulletin - Residua Ltd., 1017
World Coal Institute, 1022
World Energy Council, 1022
World Fuel Cell Council, 1022
World Nuclear Association, 1022
World Petroleum Congress, 1023

Energy Conservation
American Council for an Energy-Efficient Economy, 823
Elora Environment Centre, 909
Energy Action Council of Toronto, 909
Energy Council of Canada, 909
Energy Probe Research Foundation, 910
Foundation for Environmental Conservation, 919
International Institute for Energy Conservation, 940
National Energy Conservation Association Inc., 957
World Energy Council, 1022

Engineering
See also Aerospace Engineering; Biomedical Engineering; Chemical Engineering; Electrical Engineering; Electronic Engineering; Industrial Engineering; Marine Engineering; Mechanical Engineering; Structural Engineering
American Association for the Advancement of Science, 822
American Society of Heating, Refrigerating & Air Conditioning Engineers, 824
American Society of Mining & Reclamation, 825
Applied Science Technologists & Technicians of British Columbia, 828
Association des ingénieurs municipaux du Québec, 832
Association des ingénieurs-conseils du Québec, 832
Association des ingénieurs-professeurs des sciences appliquées, 832
Association of Certified Engineering Technicians & Technologists of Prince Edward Island, 835
Association of Consulting Engineering Companies - Canada, 835
Association of Consulting Engineering Companies - New Brunswick, 835
Association of Engineering Technicians & Technologists of Newfoundland & Labrador, 835
Association of Environmental Engineering & Science Professors, 835
Association of Professional Engineers & Geoscientists of British Columbia, 838
Association of Professional Engineers & Geoscientists of New Brunswick, 838
Association of Professional Engineers & Geoscientists of Saskatchewan, 838
Association of Professional Engineers & Geoscientists of Manitoba, 838
Association of Professional Engineers of Nova Scotia, 838
Association of Professional Engineers of Prince Edward Island, 839
Association of Professional Engineers of the Yukon Territory, 839
Association of Professional Engineers, Geologists & Geophysicists of the Northwest Territories & Nunavut, 839
Association of Professional Engineers, Geologists & Geophysicists of Alberta, 839
The Association of Science and Engineering Technology Professionals of Alberta, 840
Association professionnelle des ingénieurs du gouvernement du Québec (ind.), 841
Canadian Academy of Engineering, 854
Canadian Associated Air Balance Council, 855
Canadian Association of Drilling Engineers, 857
Canadian Federation of Engineering Students, 868
Certified Technicians & Technologists Association of Manitoba, 894
Commonwealth Engineers' Council, 898
Conseil Canadien des Électrotechnologies, 900
Consulting Engineers of Alberta, 902
Consulting Engineers of British Columbia, 903
Consulting Engineers of Manitoba Inc., 903
Consulting Engineers of Nova Scotia, 903
Consulting Engineers of Ontario, 903
Consulting Engineers of Saskatchewan, 903
Consulting Engineers of Yukon, 903
The Engineering Institute of Canada, 910
Engineers Canada, 910

Engineers Without Borders, 910
Institute of Power Engineers, 933
Institute of Transportation Engineers, 933
International Association for Earthquake Engineering, 934
International Society for Rock Mechanics, 943
International Society for Soil Mechanics & Geotechnical Engineering, 943
Maintenance & Engineering Society of The Canadian Institute of Mining, Metallurgy & Petroleum, 950
Municipal Engineers Association, 955
NACE International, 956
New Brunswick Society of Certified Engineering Technicians & Technologists, 961
NSERC/Petro-Canada Chair for Women in Science & Engineering, 969
Ontario Association of Certified Engineering Technicians & Technologists, 971
Ontario Society of Professional Engineers, 979
Ordre des ingénieurs du Québec, 981
Ordre des ingénieurs forestiers du Québec, 981
Pan American Center for Sanitary Engineering & Environmental Sciences, 984
Professional Engineers & Geoscientists Newfoundland & Labrador, 989
Professional Engineers Ontario, 990
Refrigeration Service Engineers Society (Canada), 994
Saskatchewan Applied Science Technologists & Technicians, 998
Society of Fire Protection Engineers, 1008
Society of Petroleum Engineers, 1008
Society of Professional Engineers & Associates, 1008
TechNova, 1011
Tunnelling Association of Canada, 1014
World Federation of Ukrainian Engineering Societies, 1022

Engineering, Biomedical
See Biomedical Engineering

Engineering, Chemical
See Chemical Engineering

Engineering, Civil
See Civil Engineering

Engineering, Electrical
See Electrical Engineering

Engineering, Electronic
See Electronic Engineering

Engineering, Human
See Ergonomics

Engineering, Mechanical
See Mechanical Engineering

Engineering, Medical
See Medical Engineering

Engineering, Sanitation
See Sanitary Engineering

Engraving
See Printing Industries

Entomology
Acadian Entomological Society, 813
Association des entomologistes amateurs du Québec inc., 832
Entomological Society of Alberta, 910
Entomological Society of British Columbia, 910
Entomological Society of Manitoba Inc., 910
Entomological Society of Ontario, 911
Entomological Society of Saskatchewan, 911
Société d'entomologie du Québec, 1005
Toronto Entomologists Association, 1012

Entrepreneurship
See Business

Environment
See also Conservation of Natural Resources; Environment Industry; Environmental & Outdoor Education; Environmental Compensation; Environmental Design; Environmental Health; Environmental Law; Environmental Management; Environmental Policy; Pollution; Sustainable Development; Wildlife
Acadia Environmental Society, 813
Action to Restore a Clean Humber, 813
Action: Environment, 813

Agricultural Groups Concerned About Resources & the Environment, 814
Alberta Environmental Network, 816
Alberta Institute of Agrologists, 817
Algoma Manitoulin Environmental Awareness, 820
American Society for Environmental History, 824
American Society of Mining & Reclamation, 825
Les AmiEs de la Terre de Québec, 827
Atlantic Canada Centre for Environmental Science, 842
Ausable Bayfield Conservation Foundation, 844
Bedeque Bay Environmental Management Association, 845
Big Rideau Lake Association, 845
British Columbia Environmental Network, 847
British Columbia Spaces for Nature, 850
Bruce Peninsula Environment Group, 851
BurlingtonGreen Environmental Association, 852
Burrard Inlet Environmental Action Program & Fraser River Estuary Management Program, 852
California Institute of Public Affairs, 852
Canadian Association of Physicians for the Environment, 858
Canadian Council of Ministers of the Environment, 865
Canadian Environmental Grantmakers' Network, 867
Canadian Environmental Network, 867
The Canadian Network for Environmental Education & Communication, 879
Carolinian Canada Coalition, 892
Castle-Crown Wilderness Coalition, 892
Centre for Indigenous Environmental Resources, 893
Citizens for a Safe Environment, 895
Citizens' Environment Watch, 895
Citizens' Opposed to Paving the Escarpment, 895
Clubs 4-H du Québec, 897
Concerned Educators Allied for a Safe Environment, 899
Connexions Information Sharing Services, 900
Conseil régional de l'environnement de la Gaspésie et des Iles-de-la-Madeleine, 901
Conservation Council of Ontario, 901
Conservation Foundation, 901
Conserver Society of Hamilton & District, 902
Cumulative Environmental Management Association, 906
CUSO-VSO, 906
David Suzuki Foundation, 906
Earth Day Canada, 907
Earth First! Journal, 907
Earth Island Institute, 907
Earthsave Canada, 907
Ecology Action Centre, 908
EcoPerth, 908
EcoSource Mississauga, 908
Elora Environment Centre, 909
Enviro-Accès Inc., 911
Environmental Action Barrie, 911
Environmental Careers Organization of Canada, 911
The Environmental Coalition of PEI, 911
Environmental Defence, 911
Environmental Defense, 911
Environmental Information Association, 912
Environmental Studies Association of Canada, 913
Environmental Youth Alliance, 913
Environmentalists For Nuclear Energy (Canada) Inc., 913
Environnement jeunesse, 913
FarmFolk/CityFolk Society, 914
First Nations Environmental Network, 916
Fondation Hydro-Québec pour l'environnement, 917
Fondation québécoise en environnement, 918
Friends of Clayoquot Sound, 920
Friends of Mount Revelstoke & Glacier, 921
Friends of Oak Hammock Marsh, 921
Friends of the Earth Canada, 921
Friends of the Earth International, 921
Go for Green, 924
Grand River Conservation Foundation, 924
Greenpeace Canada, 926
Greenpeace International HQ, 926
Greenpeace USA, 926
Greenspace Alliance of Canada's Capital, 926
Groupe de recherche en écologie sociale, 926
Habitat Acquisition Trust, 927
Harmony Foundation of Canada, 927
Institute for Local Self-Reliance, 932
Intergovernmental Committee on Urban & Regional Research, 934
International Association for Impact Assessment, 935
International Council for Local Environmental Initiatives, 937
International Society for Environmental Biotechnology, 942

Associations Subject Index

International Society for Environmental Ethics, 943
International Society of Indoor Air Quality & Climate, 943
Island Nature Trust, 946
Jasper Environmental Association, 947
Kamloops Wildlife Park Society, 947
The Kindness Club, 947
Lambton Wildlife Incorporated, 948
Land Trust Alliance, 948
London Regional Resource Centre for Heritage & the Environment, 949
Macleod Institute, 950
Manitoba Eco-Network Inc., 950
Montréal Field Naturalists Club, 955
National Council for Science & the Environment, 957
National Parks Conservation Association, 958
The Nature Conservancy of Canada, 959
Nature Trust of New Brunswick, 960
New Brunswick Environmental Network, 960
Niagara Peninsula Conservation Foundation, 964
Nipissing Environmental Watch, 964
Northwatch, 966
Northwest Territories Association of Landscape Architects, 967
Nova Scotia Environmental Network, 967
Nova Scotia Nature Trust, 968
Ontario Environmental Network, 973
Ontario Public Health Association, 977
Ontario Streams, 979
Panos Canada, 984
Panos London, 984
Panos Washington, 984
Peace & Environment Resource Centre, 985
Peace Valley Environment Association, 985
The Pembina Institute, 985
Petroleum Tank Management Association of Alberta, 986
Planetary Association for Clean Energy, Inc., 987
The Pollution Probe Foundation, 987
Prince Edward Island Eco-Net, 988
Prince George Recycling & Environmental Action Planning Society, 989
Protected Areas Association of Newfoundland & Labrador, 990
Rainforest Action Network, 992
Réseau environnement, 994
Réseau québécois des groupes écologistes, 994
Rideau Environmental Action League, 995
Ruiter Valley Land Trust, 997
St. John's Clean & Beautiful, 998
Salmon Arm Bay Nature Enhancement Society, 998
Sarnia-Lambton Environmental Association, 998
Sarnia-Lambton Environmental Association, 998
Saskatchewan Eco-Network, 999
Saskatchewan Environmental Society, 1000
Severn Sound Environmental Association, 1003
Sierra Club, 1003
Sierra Club of British Columbia, 1004
Sierra Club of Canada, 1004
Sierra Club of Canada - Ontario Chapter, 1004
Sierra Club of Canada - Prairie Chapter, 1004
Society of Environmental Toxicology & Chemistry, 1008
Society Promoting Environmental Conservation, 1009
Stockholm Environment Institute, 1010
TD Friends of the Environment Foundation, 1011
Tellus Institute, 1011
Temiskaming Environmental Action Committee, 1012
Toronto Environmental Alliance, 1012
Upper Thames River Conservation Authority, 1015
Uxbridge Conservation Association, 1016
The W. Garfield Weston Foundation, 1017
World Resources Institute, 1023
Worldwatch Institute, 1023
Youth Challenge International, 1024
Yukon Environmental Network, 1024

Environment Industry
See also **Hazardous Wastes; Waste Management**
Alliance of Foam Packaging Recyclers, 821
Associated Environmental Site Assessors of Canada, 829
Association of Environmental Engineering & Science Professors, 835
Association of Postconsumer Plastic Recyclers, 837
British Columbia Environment Industry Association, 847
Canadian Association of Recycling Industries, 858
Canadian Centre for Energy Information, 861
Canadian Environmental Technology Advancement Corporation - West, 867
Canadian Hydrogen & Fuel Cell Association, 871
Canadian Polystyrene Recycling Alliance, 882
Conseil patronal de l'environnement du Québec, 901
Environmental Abatement Council of Ontario, 911
Environmental Bankers Association, 911
Environmental Industry Associations, 912
Environmental Services Association of Alberta, 912
Environmental Services Association of Nova Scotia, 913
GLOBE Foundation, 924
Green Roofs for Healthy Cities, 926
Hamilton Incubator of Technology, 927
Hamilton Industrial Environmental Association, 927
Institute of Scrap Recycling Industries, Inc., 933
International Geosynthetics Society, 940
Manitoba Environmental Industries Association Inc., 951
National Association of Environmental Professionals, 957
New Brunswick Environment Industry Association, 960
Newfoundland & Labrador Environmental Industry Association, 962
North American Recycled Rubber Association, 965
ONEIA - Ontario Environment Industry Association, 970
Ontario Environment Industry Association, 973
Ontario Pollution Control Equipment Association, 977
Saskatchewan Environmental Industry & Managers' Association, 999
The Vinyl Institute, 1017

Environmental & Outdoor Education
Australian Association for Environmental Education, 844
Citizen Scientists, 895
Clubs 4-H du Québec, 897
Coalition for Education in the Outdoors, 897
Council of Outdoor Educators of Ontario, 905
Environmental Educators' Provincial Specialist Association, 912
Evergreen, 914
Falls Brook Centre, 914
FortWhyte Alive, 919
Global, Environmental & Outdoor Education Council, 924
The Green Brick Road, 925
Green Communities Canada, 925
Green Kids Inc., 925
Greenest City, 926
Inside Education, 931
International Centre for Conservation Education, 936
LEAD Canada Inc., 948
National Association for Environmental Education (UK), 956
North American Association for Environmental Education, 964
Northwest Wildlife Preservation Society, 967
Ontario Association for Geographic & Environmental Education, 971
Ontario Society for Environmental Education, 978
Peterborough Field Naturalists, 985
Saskatchewan Outdoor & Environmental Education Association, 1001
Seagull Foundation, 1003
Strathcona Park Lodge & Outdoor Education Centre, 1010
VanDusen Botanical Garden Association, 1016
Whole Village, 1019

Environmental Analysis
See **Laboratories; Testing**

Environmental Auditing
Auditing Association of Canada, 844

Environmental Biology
Canadian Society of Environmental Biologists, 887

Environmental Compliance Regulation
See **Environmental Law**

Environmental Databases
Atlantic Canada Centre for Environmental Science, 842
Resources for Global Sustainability, 995

Environmental Design
Canada Green Building Council, 853
Society for Environmental Graphic Design, 1007
U.S. Green Building Council, 1016

Environmental Education
See **Environmental & Outdoor Education**

Environmental Health
American Industrial Hygiene Association, 823
Environmental Health Association of Ontario, 912
Environmental Health Foundation of Canada, 912
Green Roofs for Healthy Cities, 926
International Institute of Concern for Public Health, 940
International Society for Environmental Epidemiology, 942
National Environmental Health Association, 957

Environmental Law
Asia-Pacific Centre for Environmental Law, 829
Canadian Environmental Law Association, 867
Canadian Institute for Environmental Law & Policy, 872
Canadian Institute of Resources Law, 875
Centre québécois du droit de l'environnement, 894
Commission for Environmental Cooperation, 898
EAGLE (Environmental-Aboriginal Guardianship through Law & Education), 907
Ecojustice Canada, 908
The Environmental Law Centre (Alberta) Society, 912
Environmental Law Institute, 912
Foundation for International Environmental Law & Development, 919
International Council of Environmental Law, 938
International Society for Environmental Ethics, 943
Ottawa Environmental Law Clinic, 983
West Coast Environmental Law Research Foundation, 1018

Environmental Management
Alberta Lake Management Society, 818
Burrard Inlet Environmental Action Program & Fraser River Estuary Management Program, 852
Environmental Services Association of Alberta, 912
Green Communities Canada, 925
International Network for Environmental Management, 941
National Association for Environmental Management, 956
Ontario Society for Environmental Management, 978
Ontario Sustainable Energy Association, 980
Research & Development Institute for the Agri-Environment, 994
Saskatchewan Environmental Industry & Managers' Association, 999

Environmental Policy
Canadian Environmental Certification Approvals Board, 866
Canadian Institute for Environmental Law & Policy, 872
Consumer Policy Institute, 903
Council on Hemispheric Affairs, 905
Greenest City, 926
INFORM Inc., 931
International Institute for Applied Systems Analysis, 940
Nova Scotia Public Interest Research Group, 968
Ontario Public Interest Research Group, 978
Peace Valley Environment Association, 985
Québec Public Interest Research Group - McGill, 991
United Nations Environment Programme, 1015

Environmental Pollution
See **Pollution**

Environmental Science
See **Science**

Environology
See **Ergonomics**

Equality in Accommodation
See **Housing; Human Rights**

Equipment & Machinery
See also **Agricultural Equipment & Machinery; Heavy Equipment Industry; Industrial Equipment; Machine Tools**
AMC - Agricultural Manufacturers of Canada, 822
Association of Equipment Manufacturers - Canada, 835
Association sectorielle - Fabrication d'équipement de transport et de machines, 842
Canadian Association of Equipment Distributors, 857
Canadian Association of Mining Equipment & Services for Export, 858
Municipal Equipment & Operations Association (Ontario) Inc., 955
Ontario Pollution Control Equipment Association, 977

Ergonomics
See also **Environmental Design; Occupational Health & Safety; Quality of Working Life**
Association of Canadian Ergonomists, 834
Commonwealth Human Ecology Council, 898
International Ergonomics Association, 938

Erosion Control
See **Soil Science**

Ethical Treatment of Animals
See **Animal Welfare**

Associations Subject Index

Ethics
See also Bioethics; Medical Ethics
Canadian Society for the Study of Practical Ethics, 886
Centre for Medicine, Ethics & Law, 893
International Society for Environmental Ethics, 943

Ethnobotany
See Botany

Ethnobusiness
See Business

Ethnology
See Anthropology & Ethnology

Evaluation
See Standards

Evolutionary Botany
See Botany

EVs
See Motor Vehicles

Excavation
See Tunnelling

Exchanges, Student
See Student Exchanges

Exhibitions & Fairs
See also Agricultural Exhibitions; Festivals
Battlefords Agricultural Society, 845
British Columbia Association of Agricultural Fairs & Exhibitions, 847
Richmond Agricultural Society, 995
Royal Agricultural Winter Fair Association, 996

Exotic Pet Trade
See Animal Rights Movement; Animal Welfare

Export Trade
See also Free Trade; Import Trade; International Trade
Canada Beef Export Federation, 852
Canadian Association of Mining Equipment & Services for Export, 858
Canadian Manufacturers & Exporters, 876
Canadian Swine Exporters Association, 889
Saskatchewan Trade & Export Partnership Inc., 1002

Expositions
See Exhibitions & Fairs

Extension
See Agriculture

Extinct Species
See Wildlife Conservation

Factory Farming
See Animal Rights Movement; Animal Welfare

Fairs
See Agricultural Exhibitions; Exhibitions & Fairs

Family Enterprise
See Business

Family Foundations
See Foundations

Family Physicians
See Physicians

Farm Animals
See Farms & Farming; Livestock

Farm Machinery
See Agricultural Equipment & Machinery

Farm Management
See Agricultural Economics

Farm Vacations
See Vacation Industry

Farms & Farming
See also Agriculture; Agriculture & Youth; Fertilizer Industry; Horticulture; Livestock; Organic Farming & Gardening; Rural Living
Alberta Conservation Tillage Society II, 816
Alberta Farm Fresh Producers Association, 816
Alberta Farmers' Market Association, 817
American Farmland Trust, 823
Association des fermières de l'Ontario, 832
Association des jeunes ruraux du Québec, 832
Canadian Farm Writers' Federation, 867
Christian Farmers Federation of Ontario, 895
Ecological Farmers Association of Ontario, 908
Farm Radio International, 914
International Federation of Organic Agriculture Movements, 939
International Flying Farmers, 939
Junior Farmers' Association of Ontario, 947
National Farmers Union, 958
Québec Farmers' Association, 991
Union des cultivateurs franco-ontariens, 1014

Feed
See Animal Feed Industry

Feminism
See Women

Ferry Boats
See Boats

Fertilizer Industry
Canadian Association of Agri-Retailers, 856
Canadian Fertilizer Institute, 868
International Plant Nutrition Institute, 942

Fiction
See Literature; Writers

Field Botanists
See Naturalists

Field Naturalists
See Naturalists

Finance
See also Banks; Credit Counselling; Financial Services Industry; Treasury Management
Social Investment Organization, 1004

Fire Fighting
Association des chefs en sécurité incendie du Québec, 831
Canadian Association of Fire Chiefs, 857
International Association of Fire Fighters (AFL-CIO/CLC), 935
Ontario Fire Buff Associates, 973
Ontario Professional Fire Fighters Association, 977

Fire Protection & Prevention
See also Accident Prevention; Fire Prevention Equipment Industry
Canadian Fire Safety Association, 868
Council of Canadian Fire Marshals & Fire Commissioners, 904
Fire Prevention Canada, 916
Ontario Industrial Fire Protection Association, 975
Society of Fire Protection Engineers, 1008
World Safety Organization, 1023

Firemen
See Fire Fighting

First Nations
See Native Peoples

Fish
See also Aquaculture; Aquariums; Fisheries; Salmon; Seafood; Shellfish; Trout
Association of Fish & Wildlife Agencies, 835
Groundfish Enterprise Allocation Council, 926
Ontario Commercial Fisheries' Association, 972

Fish & Game
See also Hunting; Wildlife
Alberta Fish & Game Association, 817
Association chasse et pêche du Lac Brébeuf, 830
Association de chasse et pêche nordique, inc., 831
Fort Saskatchewan Fish & Game Association, 919
Fredericton Fish & Game Association, 919
Newfoundland & Labrador Outfitters Association, 963
Nova Scotia Swordfish Fishermen's Association, 969
Rimbey Fish & Game Association, 996
Salmon Preservation Association for the Waters of Newfoundland, 998
Vulcan & District Fish & Game Club, 1017
Whitecourt Fish & Game Association, 1019
Yukon Fish & Game Association, 1024

Fish Farming
See Aquaculture

Fisheries
See also Aquaculture; Fisheries Science; Fishermen; Seafood; Sustainable Development
American Fisheries Society, 823
Association québécoise de l'industrie de la pêche, 841
Atlantic Salmon Federation, 843
Canadian Council of Professional Fish Harvesters, 865
Council of the Haida Nation - Haida Fisheries Program, 905
Fish Harvesters Resource Centres, 917
Fisheries Council of Canada, 917
Fisheries Council of Canada - British Columbia Representative, 917
Freshwater Fisheries Society of British Columbia, 920
International Coalition of Fisheries Associations, 936
International Institute of Fisheries Economics & Trade, 940
Nova Scotia Fish Packers Association, 968
Nova Scotia Mackerel Association, 968
Nova Scotia Salmon Association, 969
Nova Scotia Swordfish Fishermen's Association, 969
Pacific Urchin Harvesters Association, 984
Prince Edward Island Cultured Mussel Growers Association, 988

Fisheries Science
See also Aquaculture; Sustainable Development
Alberta Aquaculture Association, 815
American Fisheries Society, 823
Aquaculture Association of Nova Scotia, 828
Canadian Centre for Fisheries Innovation, 861
Fishermen and Scientists Research Society, 917
World Aquaculture Society, 1021

Fishermen
Fishermen and Scientists Research Society, 917
Northern Native Fishing Corporation, 966
Prince Edward Island Fishermen's Association, 988

Fishing & Angling
See also Fish & Game
Barrow Bay & District Sports Fishing Association, 844
Ontario Federation of Anglers & Hunters, 973

Flatwater Canoeing
See Canoeing & Rafting

Flax
Flax Canada 2015, 917
Flax Council of Canada, 917

Flower Gardening
See Flowers

Flowers
See also Gladioli; Horticulture; Nursery Trades; Orchids; Roses; Seeds
African Violet Society of Canada, 813
Aldergrove Daylily Society, 820
British Columbia Fuchsia & Begonia Society, 848
Canadian Hemerocallis Society, 871
Canadian Iris Society, 876
Canadian Rose Society, 884
Central Ontario Orchid Society, 893
Eastern Canada Orchid Society, 907
Flowers Canada, 917
The Garden Clubs of Ontario, 922
Greater Toronto Rose & Garden Society, 925
International Lilac Society, 941
Manitoba Regional Lily Society, 951
North American Native Plant Society, 965
Nova Scotia Daylily Society, 967
Nova Scotia Wild Flora Society, 969
Ontario Daylily Society, 972
Ontario Delphinium Club, 972
The Ontario Greenhouse Alliance, 974
Ottawa Orchid Society, 983
Rhododendron Society of Canada, 995
Société des roses du Québec, 1005
Société québécoise des hostas et des hémérocalles, 1006
Société québécoise du dahlia, 1006
Southern Ontario Orchid Society, 1010
Victoria Orchid Society, 1017

Fluid Power
Canadian Fluid Power Association, 868

Fly Fishing
See Fishing & Angling

Flying
See Aviation

Associations Subject Index

Foam Packaging
See Packaging

Food Cooperatives
See Agricultural Cooperatives

Food Industry
See also Agriculture; Catering Industry; Fast Food Industry; Grocery Trade; Kosher Food; Natural Products Industry; Snack Food Industry
Conseil de la transformation agroalimentaire et des produits de consommation, 900
Food & Consumer Products of Canada, 918
Food Processors of Canada, 918
Foodservice & Packaging Institute, 918
Ontario Agri-Food Education Inc., 970
Ontario Food Processors Association, 973

Food Science
Advanced Foods & Materials Network, 813
British Columbia Food Technolgists, 847
Canadian Council of Food & Nutrition, 864
Canadian Institute of Food Science & Technology, 874
Canadian Meat Science Association, 877
Institute of Food Technologists, 932
International Commission of Agricultural & Biosystems Engineering, 937
International Union of Food Science & Technology, 945

Foreign Affairs
See Developing Countries; International Relations

Foreign Policy
See International Relations

Foreign Trade
See Export Trade; Free Trade; Import Trade; International Trade

Forest Biomass
See Biomass Energy

Forest Industries
See also Logging; Lumber Industry; Pulp & Paper Industry
Alberta Forest Products Association, 817
American Forest & Paper Association, 823
Central British Columbia Railway & Forest Industry Museum Society, 893
Communications, Energy & Paperworkers Union of Canada, 899
Conseil de l'industrie forestière du Québec, 900
Council of Forest Industries, 905
Forest Products Association of Canada, 918
Forest Products Association of Nova Scotia, 919
New Brunswick Forest Products Association Inc., 961
Ontario Forest Industries Association, 974
Prince George Regional Forest Exhibition Society, 989

Forestry
See also Agroforestry; Arboriculture; Forest Industries
Alberta Centre for Boreal Studies, 816
Alberta Forest Products Association, 817
Alberta Forestry Association, 817
Association of British Columbia Forest Professionals, 834
Association of Registered Professional Foresters of New Brunswick, 839
Association of University Forestry Schools of Canada, 840
Bas-Saint-Laurent Model Forest, 845
Canadian Forestry Association, 868
Canadian Forestry Association of New Brunswick, 869
Canadian Institute of Forestry, 874
Coalition to Save the Elms, 897
College of Alberta Professional Foresters, 897
Commonwealth Forestry Association - Canadian Chapter, 898
Conseil de la recherche forestière du Québec, 900
Consulting Foresters of British Columbia, 903
Earthroots, 907
Eastern Ontario Model Forest, 908
Ecoforestry Institute Society, 908
Fédération québécoise des coopératives forestières, 916
Foothills Research Institute, 918
Fored BC, 918
Forest Products Association of Nova Scotia, 919
FPInnovations, 919
Friends of the Forestry Farm House Inc., 921
Fundy Model Forest, 922
International Union of Forest Research Organizations, 945
Lake Abitibi Model Forest, 948
Manitoba Forestry Association Inc., 951
Manitoba Model Forest, 951
McGregor Model Forest, 952
Model Forest of Newfoundland and Labrador, 955
National Aboriginal Forestry Association, 956
Newfoundland & Labrador Forest Protection Association, 962
North Shore Forest Products Marketing Board, 966
Northern Interior Vegetation Management Association, 966
Nova Forest Alliance, 967
Nova Scotia Forest Technicians Association, 968
Nova Scotia Forestry Association, 968
Office de vente des produits forestiers du Madawaska, 970
Ontario Forestry Association, 974
Ontario Professional Foresters Association, 977
Ordre des ingénieurs forestiers du Québec, 981
Prince Albert Model Forest Association Inc., 988
Prince Edward Island Forest Improvement Association, 988
Rainforest Action Network, 992
Registered Professional Foresters Association of Nova Scotia, 994
Regroupement des associations forestières régionales du Québec, 994
Saskatchewan Forestry Association, 1000
Sustainable Forestry Initiative, 1011
Waswanipi Cree Model Forest, 1017
World Agroforestry Centre, 1021

Fossil Fuels
See Coal; Oil

Foundations
African Wildlife Foundation, 813
Agricultural Institute of Canada Foundation, 814
Alberta Historical Resources Foundation, 817
Animal Welfare Foundation of Canada, 827
Asia Pacific Foundation of Canada, 829
Association of World Citizens & World Citizens Foundation, 840
Ausable Bayfield Conservation Foundation, 844
The Avian Preservation Foundation, 844
British Columbia Conservation Foundation, 847
Canadian Foundation for Climate & Atmospheric Sciences, 869
Canadian Ornamental Plant Foundation, 881
Clean Nova Scotia, 896
Coastal Ecosystems Research Foundation, 897
Conservation Foundation, 901
Conservation Halton Foundation, 901
Credit Valley Conservation Foundation, 905
David Suzuki Foundation, 906
Edmonton Space & Science Foundation, 909
Energy Probe Research Foundation, 910
Evergreen, 914
Fondation des partenaires de la Biosphère de Montréal, 917
Fondation Hydro-Québec pour l'environnement, 917
Fondation québécoise en environnement, 918
Foundation for Educational Exchange Between Canada & the United States of America, 919
Foundation for International Environmental Law & Development, 919
GLOBE Foundation, 924
Grand River Conservation Foundation, 924
Harmony Foundation of Canada, 927
Heritage Canada Foundation, 929
Heritage Foundation of Newfoundland & Labrador, 929
International Energy Foundation, 938
Jack Miner Migratory Bird Foundation, Inc., 946
Lake Simcoe Region Conservation Foundation, 948
Lifeforce Foundation, 949
Marmot Recovery Foundation, 952
Niagara Peninsula Conservation Foundation, 964
The Pollution Probe Foundation, 987
Québec-Labrador Foundation (Canada) Inc., 991
Quetico Foundation, 992
Quidi Vidi Rennie's River Development Foundation, 992
Richard Ivey Foundation, 995
Science Alberta Foundation, 1002
Seagull Foundation, 1003
SEEDS Foundation, 1003
Smoking & Health Action Foundation, 1004
TD Friends of the Environment Foundation, 1011
Trans Canada Trail Foundation, 1013
Tree Canada Foundation, 1013
The W. Garfield Weston Foundation, 1017
Waterloo Regional Heritage Foundation, 1018
West Coast Environmental Law Research Foundation, 1018

Founding
See also Metal Industries; Molding (Founding); Pattern-Making; Tool & Die Industry
Canadian Foundry Association, 869

Foundry Industry
See Founding

Four-Wheel Drive
See Motor Vehicles

Francophones in Canada
See also Acadians; Bilingualism; French Immersion Programs; French Language; Québec
Association francophone pour le savoir, 833
Union des cultivateurs franco-ontariens, 1014

Free Expression
See Human Rights

Free Speech
See Human Rights

Freelance Editors
See Editors

Freelance Writers
See Writers

Freestyle Skiing
See Skiing

Freight Services
See also Air Transportation; Railroads & Railways; Shipping; Trucks & Trucking
Freight Carriers Association of Canada, 920

French Canadians
See Francophones in Canada

French Language
See also Bilingualism; French Immersion Programs; French Media
Institut de l'énergie et de l'environnement de la Francophonie, 931

Freshwater Ecosystems
See Ecology; Limnology; Rivers & Streams

Friends of Groups
Friends of Abandoned Pets, 920
The Friends of Algonquin Park, 920
Friends of Animals, 920
The Friends of Awenda Park, 920
The Friends of Bon Echo Park, 920
The Friends of Bonnechere Parks, 920
The Friends of Charleston Lake Park, 920
Friends of Clayoquot Sound, 920
Friends of Devonian Botanic Garden, 920
Friends of Ecological Reserves, 920
Friends of Ferris, 920
The Friends of Frontenac Park, 920
The Friends of Killarney Park, 920
The Friends of MacGregor Point, 920
Friends of Mashkinonje Park, 921
Friends of Mount Revelstoke & Glacier, 921
The Friends of Nancy Island Historic Site & Wasaga Beach Park, 921
Friends of Nature Conservation Society, 921
Friends of Oak Hammock Marsh, 921
The Friends of Pinery Park, 921
The Friends of Presqu'ile Park, 921
The Friends of Rondeau Park, 921
The Friends of Sandbanks Park, 921
Friends of Short Hills Park, 921
The Friends of Sleeping Giant, 921
Friends of the Delta Marsh Field Station, 921
Friends of the Earth Canada, 921
Friends of the Earth International, 921
Friends of the Forestry Farm House Inc., 921
Friends of the Oldman River, 921
Friends of the Stikine Society, 921
Friends of the Trent-Severn Waterway, 922
The Friends of West Kootenay Parks Society, 922
Niijkiwenhwag - Friends of Lake Superior Park, 964

Frozen Foods
See Food Industry

Fruit & Vegetables
See also Marketing Boards & Commissions

Associations Subject Index

Alberta Greenhouse Growers Association, 817
British Columbia Fruit Growers' Association, 848
Canadian Sugar Beet Producers' Association Inc., 889
Horticulture Nova Scotia, 930
International Society of Citriculture, 943
New Brunswick Fruit Growers Association Inc., 961
Nova Scotia Fruit Growers' Association, 968
Ontario Fruit & Vegetable Growers' Association, 974
The Ontario Greenhouse Alliance, 974
Ontario Tender Fruit Producers, 980
Prairie Fruit Growers Association, 988
Vegetable Growers' Association of Manitoba, 1016

Fuel
See Coal; Energy; Natural Gas; Oil

Fungicides
See Agrochemicals

Fur Trade
See also Breeding; Chinchilla; Foxes; Mink; Wildlife
Alberta Trappers' Association, 820
Canadian Association for Humane Trapping, 855
The Fur Council of Canada, 922
Fur Institute of Canada, 922
Fur-Bearer Defenders, 922
Furriers Guild of Canada, 922

Futurism
World Future Society, 1022

Galvanizing
See Metal Industries

Game & Fish
See Fish & Game

Game Farming
See Breeding

Garbage
See Waste Management

Gardening
See Horticulture

Garment Manufacturers
See Clothing; Textiles

Gas
See also Hydrocarbon Processing Industry; Natural Gas
Association québécoise du gaz naturel, 842
Canadian Association of Drilling Engineers, 857
Canadian Association of Petroleum Producers, 858
Canadian Petroleum Law Foundation, 882
Compressed Gas Association, Inc., 899
Enform: The Safety Association for the Upstream Oil & Gas Industry, 910
Gas Processing Association Canada, 922
Industrial Gas Users Association Inc., 930
NOIA, 964
Ontario Petroleum Institute Inc., 976
Pipe Line Contractors Association of Canada, 987
Propane Gas Association of Canada Inc., 990
Society of Petroleum Engineers, 1008
World Petroleum Congress, 1023

Gas Emissions Testing
See Laboratories; Testing

Gems
See also Jewellery; Mineralogy
Bancroft Gem & Mineral Club, 844
Brantford Lapidary & Mineral Society Inc., 846
Gem & Mineral Club of Scarborough, 922
Kingston Lapidary & Mineral Club, 947
Montréal Gem & Mineral Club, 955
Oxford County Geological Society, 983
Sudbury Rock & Lapidary Society, 1011
Victoria Lapidary & Mineral Society, 1017

Genetics
See also Genetic Counselling; Genetic Diseases & Disorders; Genetic Engineering; Medical Genetics
AllerGen NCE Inc., 820
Canadian Genetic Diseases Network, 869
Genetics Society of Canada, 922
International Genetics Federation, 939

Genomics
Genome Canada, 923

Geochemistry
See also Geophysics
Association of Applied Geochemists, 834
Geochemical Society, 923
Geological Association of Canada, 923

Geography
See also Land Use; Maps; Remote Sensing
Association of American Geographers, 834
Association professionnelle des géographes du Québec, 841
Canadian Association of Geographers, 857
Canadian Cartographic Association, 861
Commonwealth Geographical Bureau, 898
International Geographic Union, 939
International Geographical Union - Canadian Committee, 939
Ontario Association for Geographic & Environmental Education, 971
The Royal Canadian Geographical Society, 996

Geology
See also Gems; Geochemistry; Geophysics; Geoscience; Geotechnique; Hydrogeology; Mineralogy; Paleontology; Permafrost
The American Association of Petroleum Geologists, 822
Association of Professional Engineers, Geologists & Geophysicists of the Northwest Territories & Nunavut, 839
Association of Professional Engineers, Geologists & Geophysicists of Alberta, 839
Canadian Rock Mechanics Association, 884
Canadian Society of Petroleum Geologists, 887
Explorer's Club (Canadian Chapter), 914
Geological Association of Canada, 923
Hamilton Geological Society, 927
International Association for Earthquake Engineering, 934
International Association of Sedimentologists, 936
International Permafrost Association, 941
International Society for Rock Mechanics, 943
International Society for Soil Mechanics & Geotechnical Engineering, 943
Mineralogical Association of Canada, 954
Niagara Peninsula Geological Society, 964
Oxford County Geological Society, 983

Geomatics
Canadian Institute of Geomatics, 874
Canadian Remote Sensing Society, 884
Geomatics for Informed Decisions Network, 923
Geomatics Industry Association of Canada, 923

Geophysics
See also Geochemistry
Association of Professional Engineers, Geologists & Geophysicists of Alberta, 839
Association of Professional Engineers, Geologists & Geophysicists of the Northwest Territories & Nunavut, 839
Canadian Association of Geophysical Contractors, 857
Canadian Federation of Earth Sciences, 867
Canadian Geophysical Union, 869
Canadian Society of Exploration Geophysicists, 887
European Association of Geoscientists & Engineers, 913
European Geosciences Union, 913
Geological Association of Canada, 923
International Permafrost Association, 941
International Union of Geodesy & Geophysics, 945

Geoscience
See also Geochemistry
Association of Professional Engineers & Geoscientists of New Brunswick, 838
Association of Professional Engineers & Geoscientists of British Columbia, 838
Association of Professional Engineers & Geoscientists of Saskatchewan, 838
Association of Professional Engineers of Nova Scotia, 838
Association of Professional Geoscientists of Nova Scotia, 839
Association of Professional Geoscientists of Ontario, 839
Canadian Federation of Earth Sciences, 867
Geological Association of Canada, 923
Professional Engineers & Geoscientists Newfoundland & Labrador, 989

Geotechnique
See also Geology
Geotechnical Society of Edmonton, 923
International Geosynthetics Society, 940

Geothermal Power
See Energy Conservation

Glass
See also Stained Glass
Glass Packaging Institute, 923

Global Education
See Cross-Cultural Communication

Global Governance
See also Government; Human Rights
Association of World Citizens & World Citizens Foundation, 840
World Federalist Movement, 1022
Worldwatch Institute, 1023

Global Warming
See also Ozone Layer Depletion
Climate Institute, 896

Government
See also Civil Service Employees; Global Governance; Municipal Government; Parliament; Public Administration; Public Service Employees
Alberta Development Officers Association, 816
Association professionnelle des ingénieurs du gouvernement du Québec (ind.), 841
Canadian Council of Ministers of the Environment, 865
Federation of Calgary Communities, 915
North Central Local Government Association, 965
The Public Affairs Association of Canada, 990
Southern Interior Local Government Association, 1010

Grains
Animal Nutrition Association of Canada, 827
Canadian Ports Clearance Association, 882
Grain Elevator & Processing Society, 924
Ontario Agri Business Association, 970
Seeds of Diversity Canada, 1003

Grants
See also Awards, Honours, Prizes
Canadian Environmental Grantmakers' Network, 867

Great Lakes
See also Limnology
Association of Great Lakes Outdoor Writers, 835
Citizens' Environment Alliance of Southwestern Ontario, 895
Council of Great Lakes Governors, 905
Great Lakes Institute for Environmental Research, 925
The Great Lakes Research Consortium, 925
Great Lakes United, 925
International Association for Great Lakes Research, 935

Green Transportation Modes
See Transportation Sustainability

Greenhouse Gases
See Global Warming

Greenhouse Products
See Fruit & Vegetables

Grocery Trade
Canadian Council of Grocery Distributors, 864
Canadian Federation of Independent Grocers, 868
Food & Consumer Products of Canada, 918

Ground Water
See Drilling; Water Supply; Wells

Guide Outfitters
See Camping; Hiking; Orienteering

Guided Missile Industries
See Aerospace Industries

Habitat Protection
See Conservation of Natural Resources; Ecology

Habitat, Wildlife
See Conservation of Natural Resources; Wildlife Conservation

Handicapped Housing
See Housing

Handicapped Persons
See Disabled Persons

Harbours & Ports
See also Marine Trades; Shipping
Association of Canadian Port Authorities, 834

Associations Subject Index

Hardware, Computer
See Computers

Hawks
Hawk Migration Association of North America, 927

Hazardous Substances in the Workpla
See Occupational Health & Safety

Hazardous Wastes
See also Environment Industry; Industrial Waste; Waste Management
Air & Waste Management Association, 814
Center for Health, Environment & Justice, 893
Dangerous Goods Advisory Council, 906
The New Directions Group, 962
Ontario Waste Management Association, 981
Toxics Watch Society of Alberta, 1013

Health
See also Health Care Facilities; Infection Control; Medicine; Mental Health; Public Health; Telehealth; Women & Health
Action on Smoking & Health, 813
Association of Local Public Health Agencies, 836
Canadian Association for Health Services & Policy Research, 855
Canadian Council for Tobacco Control, 864
Canadian Horticultural Therapy Association, 871
Canadian Society for International Health, 885
Canadian Society for Medical Laboratory Science, 886
Consumer Health Organization of Canada, 903
Council for a Smoke-Free PEI, 904
Health & Safety Conference Society of Alberta, 927
Health Sciences Association of Alberta, 928
Health Sciences Association of Saskatchewan, 928
Healthy Indoors Partnership, 928
Manitoba Tobacco Reduction Alliance, 952
Ontario Healthy Communities Coalition, 974
The Regional Health Authorities of Manitoba, 994
Saskatchewan Coalition for Tobacco Reduction, 999
Smoke-Free Nova Scotia, 1004
World Health Organization, 1022

Health Food
See Natural Products Industry

Health Libraries
See Medical Libraries

Heat Insulation
See Insulation

Heating
See also Air Conditioning; Mechanical Contractors; Refrigeration
American Society of Heating, Refrigerating & Air Conditioning Engineers, 824
Canadian Institute of Plumbing & Heating, 875
Canadian Oil Heat Association, 880
Heating, Refrigeration & Air Conditioning Contractors Association Atlantic, 928
Heating, Refrigeration & Air Conditioning Institute of Canada, 928
Thermal Environmental Comfort Association, 1012

Herbicides
See Agrochemicals

Herbs
British Columbia Herb Growers Association, 848
Herb Society of Manitoba, 929
Saskatchewan Herb & Spice Association, 1000

Heritage
See also Architectural Conservation; Archives; Genealogy; Historical Re-enactment; History; Museums; Preservation Technology
Alberta Historical Resources Foundation, 817
Architectural Heritage Society of Saskatchewan, 828
Canadian Association of Professional Heritage Consultants, 858
Canadian Parks Partnership, 881
Cole Harbour Rural Heritage Society, 897
Conseil des monuments et sites du Québec, 900
Conservation Foundation, 901
Federation of Nova Scotian Heritage, 915
Heritage Association of Antigonish, 929
Heritage Canada Foundation, 929
L'Héritage canadien du Québec, 929
Heritage Foundation of Newfoundland & Labrador, 929
Héritage Montréal, 929
Heritage Society of British Columbia, 929
Heritage Trust of Nova Scotia, 929
Heritage Winnipeg Corp., 930
Lethbridge & District Japanese Garden Society, 948
London Regional Resource Centre for Heritage & the Environment, 949
Ontario Heritage Trust, 974
Save Ontario Shipwrecks, 1002
Waterloo Regional Heritage Foundation, 1018

Heritage Seeds
See Seeds

High Technology
See also Robotics
Advanced Foods & Materials Network, 813
Canadian Institute for Photonics Innovations, 873
Communications & Information Technology Ontario, 898
Geomatics for Informed Decisions Network, 923
Hamilton Incubator of Technology, 927
Ontario Centre of Excellence for Photonics, 971

High-Efficiency Electric Generation
See Energy

Highways
See Roads & Roadbuilding

Hiking
See also Camping; Orienteering; Walking
The Bruce Trail Conservancy, 851
Ganaraska Hiking Trail Association, 922
Hike Ontario, 930
Musquodoboit Trailways Association, 956
Ontario Trails Council, 980
Rideau Trail Association, 995
Trans Canada Trail Foundation, 1013
Voyageur Trail Association, 1017

Historic Works, Conservation of
See Conservation of Historic & Artistic

Historical Geography
See Geography

History
See also Archives; Conservation of Historic & Artistic; Folklore; Genealogy; Heritage; Historical Re-enactment; Oral History
Alberta Historical Resources Foundation, 817
American Society for Environmental History, 824
Friends of the Forestry Farm House Inc., 921
Heritage Canada Foundation, 929
L'Héritage canadien du Québec, 929
North American Society for Oceanic History, 965
Société de conservation de la Baie de l'Isle-Verte, 1005

History, Natural
See Natural History

HIV Virus
See AIDS

Holiday Exchange
See Vacation Industry

Home Building
See Construction Industry

Home Environmentalists
See Environment

Home Shopping
See Direct Marketing

Horses
See also Equestrian Sports & Activities; Horse Racing
National Horse Protection League, 958

Horticulture
See also Agronomists; Flowers; Landscape Architecture; Nursery Trades; Seeds
Alpine Garden Club of BC, 821
American Association of Botanical Gardens & Arboreta, 822
Les Amis du Jardin botanique de Montréal, 827
Brampton Horticultural Society, 846
Calgary Horticultural Society, 852
Canadian Botanical Conservation Network, 860
Canadian Horticultural Council, 871
Canadian Horticultural Therapy Association, 871
Canadian Nursery Landscape Association, 880
Canadian Ornamental Plant Foundation, 881
Canadian Society for Horticultural Science, 885
Center for Plant Conservation, 893
City Farmer - Canada's Office of Urban Agriculture, 895
Conserver Society of Hamilton & District, 902
Expo agricole de Chicoutimi, 914
Fédération des sociétés d'horticulture et d'écologie du Québec, 915
Friends of Devonian Botanic Garden, 920
The Garden Clubs of Ontario, 922
Garden Institute of Alberta, 922
Greater Toronto Water Garden & Horticultural Society, 925
Integrated Vegetation Management Association of British Columbia, 934
International Plant Propagators Society, Inc., 942
Landscape Alberta Nursery Trades Association, 948
Lethbridge & District Japanese Garden Society, 948
Manitoba Regional Lily Society, 951
Newfoundland Horticultural Society, 963
Ontario Horticultural Association, 974
Ontario Rock Garden Society, 978
Ontario Vegetation Management Association, 981
Ottawa Valley Rock Garden & Horticultural Society, 983
Royal Botanical Gardens, 996
Seeds of Diversity Canada, 1003
Société de protection des plantes du Québec, 1005
VanDusen Botanical Garden Association, 1016
Weed Science Society of America, 1018

Hospitality Industry
See also Bars & Taverns; Catering Industry; Hotels & Motels; Resorts; Restaurants
Ontario Farm & Country Accommodations Association, 973

Hotels & Motels
See also Hospitality Industry; Resorts; Tourism
British Columbia Lodging & Campgrounds Association, 848

House Construction
See Construction Industry

Houseboats
See Boats

Housing
See also Apartments; Condominiums; Cooperative Housing; Emergency Housing; Housing for the Physically Disabled; Landlords; Social Housing; Tenants
Canadian Association for Studies in Co-operation, 856
Intergovernmental Committee on Urban & Regional Research, 934
International Federation for Housing & Planning, 939

Human Engineering
See Ergonomics

Human Factors
See Ergonomics

Human Immunodeficiency Virus
See AIDS

Human Resources
See also Employee Counselling; Employment; Staff Training & Development
BIOTECanada, 845
Canadian Council of Professional Fish Harvesters, 865
Canadian Plastics Sector Council, 882
Environmental Careers Organization of Canada, 911
Mining Industry Human Resources Council, 955
Petroleum Human Resources Council of Canada, 986
Wood Manufacturing Council, 1021
Yukon Tourism Education Council, 1024

Human Rights
See also Constitutional Law; Democracy; Global Governance; Law; Patients' Rights; Political Prisoners
Canadian Council for International Co-operation, 864
CUSO-VSO, 906
Nova Scotia Public Interest Research Group, 968
Oakville Community Centre for Peace, Ecology & Human Rights, 969
Ontario Public Interest Research Group, 978
Québec Public Interest Research Group - McGill, 991

Humane Societies
See Animal Welfare

Associations Subject Index

Humanism
The Royal Society of Canada, 996

Humanities
See also Classical Studies; History; Learned Societies
American Society for Environmental History, 824

Hunting
See also Archery; Fish & Game; Fishing & Angling; Shooting Sports
Alberta Professional Outfitters Society, 819
Ontario Federation of Anglers & Hunters, 973

Hydraulics
See Fluid Power

Hydrocarbon Processing Industry
See also Gas
Gas Processing Association Canada, 922

Hydroelectric Dams
See Dams

Hydroelectric Power
See Electric Power; Public Utilities

Hydrogen
Canadian Hydrogen & Fuel Cell Association, 871

Hydrogeology
International Association of Hydrogeologists, 935
International Association of Hydrogeologists - Canadian National Chapter, 936

Hydrography
Canadian Hydrographic Association, 871
Canadian Institute of Geomatics, 874
International Federation of Hydrographic Societies, 939

Hydrology
World Meteorological Organization, 1022

Ice
See also Snow
Salt Institute, 998

Ichthyology
African Coelacanth Ecosystem Programme, 813

Immunology
Allergy, Asthma & Immunology Society of Ontario, 821
Association des Allergologues et Immunologues du Québec, 831
Canadian Society of Allergy & Clinical Immunology, 886

Impact Assessment
Association québécoise pour l'évaluation d'impacts, 842
International Association for Impact Assessment - Western & Northern Canada, 935
International Association for Impact Assessment, 935
Ontario Association for Impact Assessment, 971

Implements
See Agricultural Equipment & Machinery; Equipment & Machinery

Import Trade
See also Export Trade; International Trade
Association of International Automobile Manufacturers of Canada, 836

Incentive Travel
See Travel Industry

Independent Power Production
See Energy

Indigenous Peoples
See Native Peoples

Indoor Air Quality
Healthy Indoors Partnership, 928
International Society of Indoor Air Quality & Climate, 943

Industrial Accident Victims
See Injured Workers; Workers' Compensation

Industrial Accidents
See Accident Prevention; Workers' Compensation

Industrial Chemistry
See Chemistry

Industrial Development
See also Economic Development; Regional Development

Canadian Innovation Centre, 872
United Nations Industrial Development Organization, 1015

Industrial Engineering
See also CAD/CAM; Computer Integrated Manufacturings
Canadian Society for Industrial Engineering, 885
Institute of Industrial Engineers, 933
Plant Engineering & Maintenance Association of Canada, 987

Industrial Equipment
See also Equipment & Machinery
Canadian Process Control Association, 883

Industrial Geography
See Geography

Industrial Materials, Advanced
Canadian Advanced Technology Alliance, 854

Industrial Research
See Biomedical Research; Research

Industrial Safety
See Occupational Health & Safety

Industrial Trucks
See Trucks & Trucking

Industrial Waste
See also Environment Industry
Air & Waste Management Association, 814
American Industrial Hygiene Association, 823
Center for Health, Environment & Justice, 893
Ontario Waste Management Association, 981

Industry
See Manufacturing

Infectious Diseases
See Diseases; Disorders

Information Management
See Data Base Management

Information Science
See also Computers; Library Science
Healthcare Information & Management Systems Society, 928
Urban & Regional Information Systems Association, 1015

Information Technology
See also Computer Software
British Columbia Technology Industries Association, 850
Communications & Information Technology Ontario, 898
Newfoundland & Labrador Association of Technology Companies, 962

Inhalation Therapy
See Respiratory Therapy

Injured Workers
See also Workers' Compensation
Canadian Injured Workers Alliance, 872
Industrial Accident Victims Group of Ontario, 930

Inland Water Ecosystems
See Limnology

Innkeepers
See Hotels & Motels

Innovation Technology
See Technology

Insects
See Entomology

Insulation
Association d'isolation du Québec, 831
Canadian Urethane Foam Contractors Association, 890
Master Insulators' Association of Ontario Inc., 952
Thermal Insulation Association of Alberta, 1012

Intensive Farming
See Breeding

Intercultural Communication
See Cross-Cultural Communication

Intercultural Education
See Cross-Cultural Communication

Intergenerational Projects
See Senior Citizens; Volunteers

Intermediate Teachers
See Teaching

Internal Medicine
See Medical Specialists

International Business
See International Trade

International Cooperation
See also International Relations
Association québécoise des organismes de coopération internationale, 842
Canadian Council for International Co-operation, 864
CUSO-VSO, 906
Earthwatch Europe, 907
European Solidarity Towards Equal Participation of People, 913
Foundation for International Environmental Law & Development, 919
Manitoba Council for International Cooperation, 950
Société de coopération pour le développement international, 1005
United Nations Environment Programme, 1015
World Federalist Movement, 1022

International Law
Canadian Council on International Law, 865
International Law Association - Canadian Branch, 940

International Relations
See also International Cooperation
Canadian International Council, 876
Connexions Information Sharing Services, 900
Council on Hemispheric Affairs, 905
Institut de l'énergie et de l'environnement de la Francophonie, 931
International Labour Organization, 940
United Nations Association in Canada, 1015

International Relief
See also Economic Assistance (International); Foreign Aid; Red Cross
Canadian Association for Mine & Explosive Ordnance Security, 856
Engineers Without Borders, 910
Lifewater Canada, 949
Probe International, 989

International Trade
See also Export Trade; Free Trade; Import Trade
Asia Pacific Foundation of Canada, 829
Canadian Council of Chief Executives, 864
Can-Am Border Trade Alliance, 892
Council on Hemispheric Affairs, 905
United Nations Conference on Trade & Development, 1015

Internet
Canadian Association for Renewable Energies, 856

Interns, Medical
See Medicine

Intramural Recreation
See Recreation

Invertebrate Ecology
See Ecology

Investigative Journalism
See Journalism

Investigative Medicine
See Medicine

Investment
See also Financial Services Industry; Mutual Funds; Securities; Stock Exchange; Venture Capital
Native Investment & Trade Association, 959
Social Investment Organization, 1004

Iris
See also Flowers
Canadian Iris Society, 876

Iron
American Iron & Steel Institute, 823

Iron Work
See Metal Industries

Irrigation
Alberta Irrigation Projects Association, 818

Associations Subject Index

The Canadian National Committee for Irrigation & Drainage, 879
International Commission on Irrigation & Drainage, 937

Jeans
See Clothing

Journalism
See also Book Trade; Ethnic Press; Media; Newspapers; Periodicals & Magazines; Publishing
Canadian Farm Writers' Federation, 867

Jurists
See Lawyers

Kayaking
See also Canoeing & Rafting
Paddle Canada, 984
Wilderness Canoe Association, 1020

Labelling
See Packaging

Laboratories
Canadian Association for Laboratory Accreditation Inc., 856
Canadian Council of Independent Laboratories, 864
Canadian Society for Medical Laboratory Science, 886

Laboratory Medicine
See also Laboratories; Medical Research
International Council for Laboratory Animal Science, 937

Labour
See also Employment; Equal Opportunity Employment; Labour Councils; Labour Legislation; Labour Relations; Labour Unions
International Labour Organization, 940

Labour Unions
See also Employees; Employers; Employment; Employment Standards; Labour Relations
Association professionnelle des ingénieurs du gouvernement du Québec (ind.), 841
Canadian Labour Congress, 876
Communications, Energy & Paperworkers Union of Canada, 899
Health Sciences Association of Alberta, 928
Health Sciences Association of Saskatchewan, 928
International Association of Fire Fighters (AFL-CIO/CLC), 935
Natural Resources Union, 959
Ontario Professional Fire Fighters Association, 977

Lakes
See Great Lakes; Limnology; Rivers & Streams; Water Resources

Land Economics
See Land Use

Land Mines
Canadian Association for Mine & Explosive Ordnance Security, 856

Land Reclamation
American Society of Mining & Reclamation, 825
Canadian Land Reclamation Association, 876
Canadian Society of Soil Science, 888
Federation of Saskatchewan Surface Rights Association, 916
International Soil Reference & Information Centre, 944

Land Surveying
Alberta Land Surveyors' Association, 818
Association of British Columbia Land Surveyors, 834
Association of Canada Lands Surveyors, 834
Association of Manitoba Land Surveyors, 836
Association of New Brunswick Land Surveyors, 837
Association of Newfoundland Land Surveyors, 837
Association of Nova Scotia Land Surveyors, 837
Association of Ontario Land Surveyors, 837
Association of Prince Edward Island Land Surveyors, 837
Canadian Council of Land Surveyors, 864
Canadian Institute of Geomatics, 874
Commonwealth Association of Surveying & Land Economy, 898
International Federation of Surveyors, 939
Ordre des arpenteurs-géomètres du Québec, 981
Saskatchewan Land Surveyors' Association, 1000

Land Trusts, Community
See Environment

Land Use
See also Land Reclamation; Landscape Architecture
American Farmland Trust, 823
American Society of Mining & Reclamation, 825
American Wildlands, 827
Association of Ontario Land Economists, 837
Canadian Land Reclamation Association, 876
Canadian Society of Soil Science, 888
Commonwealth Association of Surveying & Land Economy, 898
International Soil Reference & Information Centre, 944
Land Improvement Contractors of Ontario, 948
Land Trust Alliance, 948
Urban Development Institute of Canada, 1016

Landfill
See Waste Management

Landscape Architecture
See also Horticulture
Alberta Association of Landscape Architects, 815
Association des architectes paysagistes du Québec, 831
Atlantic Provinces Association of Landscape Architects, 843
British Columbia Society of Landscape Architects, 850
Canadian Society of Landscape Architects, 887
International Federation of Landscape Architects, 939
Manitoba Association of Landscape Architects, 950
Newfoundland & Labrador Association of Landscape Architects, 962
Northwest Territories Association of Landscape Architects, 967
Ontario Association of Landscape Architects, 971
Saskatchewan Association of Landscape Architects, 999
Saskatchewan Nursery Landscape Association, 1001

Lapidary
See Gems; Jewellery; Mineralogy

Lasers
Ontario Centre of Excellence for Photonics, 971

Law
See also Constitutional Law; Courts; Environmental Law; Human Rights; International Law; Judges; Law Libraries; Lawyers; Legal Clinics; Maritime Law; Petroleum Law
Canadian Council on International Law, 865
Canadian Law & Society Association, 876
Carleton County Law Association, 892
Centre for Medicine, Ethics & Law, 893
International Bar Association, 936

Law of the Sea
See Maritime Law

Lawyers
See also Legal Assistants
Canadian Bar Association, 860

Learned Societies
See also Humanities
Archaeological Institute of America, 828
Canadian Association for Studies in Co-operation, 856
The Royal Society of Canada, 996
Society for Socialist Studies, 1007

Learning Materials
See Education

Legal Education
People's Law School, 985
Public Legal Education Association of Saskatchewan, Inc., 991
Public Legal Information Association of Newfoundland, 991
Yukon Public Legal Education Association, 1024

Legislature
See Government; Parliament

Leisure
See Recreation

Lifestyle
Commonwealth Human Ecology Council, 898

Limnology
See also Ecology; Great Lakes; Microbiology; Rivers & Streams; Toxicology; Water Resources
International Society of Limnology, 944

Lingerie
See Clothing

Literacy
See also Reading
CODE, 897

Literature
See also Book Trade; Children's Literature; Humanities; Learned Societies; Poetry
Canadian Science Writers' Association, 884

Litigation
See Law

Livestock
See also Breeding; Cattle; Meat
Canadian Animal Health Institute, 855
Canadian Bison Association, 860
Canadian Council on Animal Care, 865
Canadian Organic Livestock Association, 881
Canadians for Ethical Treatment of Food Animals, 892
Ontario Cattlemen's Association, 971
The Ontario Farm Animal Council, 973
Rare Breeds Canada, 992
Saskatchewan Livestock Association, 1000
Saskatchewan Stock Growers Association, 1001

Local Government
See Municipal Government

Local History
See History

Locks & Canals
Friends of the Trent-Severn Waterway, 922

Locomotives
See Railroads & Railways

Logging
See also Forest Industries; Lumber Industry
Association de la santé et de la sécurité des pâtes et papiers et des industries de la forêt du Québec, 831
Canadian Well Logging Society, 891
Central Interior Logging Association, 893

Logistics
Canadian Institute of Traffic & Transportation, 875

Loungewear
See Clothing

Lumber Industry
See also Forest Industries; Logging
Association de la santé et de la sécurité des pâtes et papiers et des industries de la forêt du Québec, 831
Canadian Lumbermen's Association, 876
Coast Forest Products Association, 897
Conseil de l'industrie forestière du Québec, 900
Independent Lumber Dealers Co-operative, 930
Lumber & Building Materials Association of Ontario, 949
New Brunswick Federation of Woodlot Owners Inc., 961
Ontario Lumber Manufacturers' Association, 975
Ontario Woodlot Association, 981
Truck Loggers Association, 1014
Western Red Cedar Lumber Association, 1019
Western Retail Lumber Association, 1019
Wood Manufacturing Council, 1021

Lung Disorders & Diseases
See also Respiratory Disorders; Respiratory Therapy; Smoking; Tuberculosis
Alberta & Northwest Territories Lung Association, 815
American Lung Association, 823
British Columbia Lung Association, 848
Canadian Lung Association, 876
Canadian Respiratory Health Professionals, 884
Manitoba Lung Association, 951
New Brunswick Lung Association, 961
Newfoundland & Labrador Lung Association, 963
Nova Scotia Lung Association, 968
Ontario Lung Association, 975
Ontario Respiratory Care Society, 978
Prince Edward Island Lung Association, 989
Québec Lung Association, 991
Saskatchewan Lung Association, 1000

Machinery & Equipment
See Equipment & Machinery

Mail Order
See Direct Marketing

Management
See also Administrative Sciences; Associations; Employers; Environmental Management; Executives;

Associations Subject Index

Facility Management; Management Consultants; Project Management
Association des Aménagistes Régionaux du Québec, 831
The Conference Board of Canada, 899
Innovation Management Association of Canada, 931
Strategic Leadership Forum, The Toronto Society for Strategic Management, 1010

Management, Waste
See Waste Management

Manufactured Housing
See Housing

Manufacturing
See also Industrial Development; Industrial Equipment; Industrial Materials, Advanced; Women in Business, Industry & Trade
AMC - Agricultural Manufacturers of Canada, 822
Association of International Automobile Manufacturers of Canada, 836
British Columbia Paint Manufacturers' Association, 849
Canadian Manufacturers & Exporters, 876
Canadian Printing Ink Manufacturers Association, 883
Materials & Manufacturing Ontario, Division of OCE Inc., 952
National Marine Manufacturers Association, 958

Maps
See also Geography; Map Libraries
Canadian Cartographic Association, 861
Canadian Institute of Geomatics, 874

Marathon Canoeing
See Canoeing & Rafting

Mariculture
See Aquaculture

Marine Aquariums
See Aquariums

Marine Archaeology
See Underwater Archaeology

Marine Biology
See also Fisheries Science; Oceanography
Canadian Meteorological & Oceanographic Society, 878
Coastal Ecosystems Research Foundation, 897
Explorer's Club (Canadian Chapter), 914
Grand Manan Whale & Seabird Research Station, 924
International Ocean Institute, 941

Marine Ecology
See Ecology

Marine Mammals
See also Wildlife Conservation
Antarctic & Southern Ocean Coalition, 828
Ceta-Research Inc., 894
Grand Manan Whale & Seabird Research Station, 924
International Whaling Commission, 946
Marmot Recovery Foundation, 952
Sea Shepherd Conservation Society, 1002
Sea Shepherd Conservation Society - USA, 1002

Marine Search & Rescue
See Search & Rescue

Marine Trades
See also Fisheries; Harbours & Ports; Shipping
British Columbia Marine Trades Association, 849
Comité maritime international, 898
Council of Marine Carriers, 905
International Maritime Organization, 941
National Marine Manufacturers Association, 958
National Marine Manufacturers Association Canada, 958
NOIA, 904
Shipbuilding Association of Canada, 1003

Maritime Heritage
See Heritage

Maritime Industries
See Marine Trades

Maritime Law
Canadian Maritime Law Association, 877

Market Gardening
See Farms & Farming

Marketing
See also Advertising; Direct Marketing; Market Research; Marketing Boards & Commissions; Telemarketing
Alberta Farmers' Market Association, 817
Canadian Agri-Marketing Association (Alberta), 855
Canadian Agri-Marketing Association (Manitoba), 855
Canadian Marketing Association, 877

Marketing Boards & Commissions
See also Agriculture; Fruit & Vegetables; Marketing
British Columbia Farm Industry Review Board, 847
Office de vente des produits forestiers du Madawaska, 970
Ontario Soybean Growers, 979
Ontario Wheat Producers' Marketing Board, 981
Potatoes NB, 987

Mass Communications
See Communications

Material Culture
See Conservation of Historic & Artistic; Heritage

Meat
Canada Beef Export Federation, 852
Canadian Bison Association, 860
Canadian Meat Council, 877

Mechanical Contractors
See also Air Conditioning; Heating; Refrigeration
Mechanical Contractors Association of Alberta, 953
Mechanical Contractors Association of British Columbia, 953
Mechanical Contractors Association of Canada, 953
Mechanical Contractors Association of Manitoba, 953
Mechanical Contractors Association of New Brunswick, 953
Mechanical Contractors Association of Newfoundland & Labrador, 953
Mechanical Contractors Association of Nova Scotia, 953
Mechanical Contractors Association of Ontario, 953
Mechanical Contractors Association of Prince Edward Island, 953
Mechanical Contractors Association of Saskatchewan Inc., 953

Mechanical Engineering
American Society of Mechanical Engineers, 824
AUTO21 - The Automobile of the 21st Century, 844
Canadian Society for Mechanical Engineering, 885
Corporation des maîtres mécaniciens en tuyauterie du Québec, 904
Institution of Mechanical Engineers, 934
Maintenance & Engineering Society of The Canadian Institute of Mining, Metallurgy & Petroleum, 950
Ontario Plumbing Inspectors Association, 977

Medical Engineering
See also Biomedical Engineering; Biotechnology; Genetic Engineering
International Federation for Medical & Biological Engineering, 939

Medical Laboratories
See Laboratory Medicine

Medical Libraries
See also Health Records
Canadian Health Libraries Association, 870
Golden Horseshoe Health Libraries Association, 924
Health Libraries Association of British Columbia, 928
London Area Health Libraries Association, 949
Manitoba Association of Health Information Providers, 950
Maritimes Health Libraries Association, 952
Newfoundland & Labrador Health Libraries Association, 963
Northern Alberta Health Libraries Association, 966
Northern Lights Health Library Association, 966
Northwestern Ontario Health Libraries Association, 967
Ottawa Valley Health Libraries Association, 983
Saskatchewan Health Libraries Association, 1000
Southern Alberta Health Libraries Association, 1010
Toronto Health Libraries Association, 1012

Medical Reform
See Medicine

Medical Research
See also Biotechnology; Genetic Engineering; Research
Canadian Genetic Diseases Network, 869

Medical Residents
See Medicine

Medical Schools
The Michener Institute for Applied Health Sciences, 954

Medical Specialists
Association des Allergologues et Immunologues du Québec, 831
Association des médecins biochimistes du Québec, 833

Medication
See Pharmaceuticals

Medicine
See also Aerospace Medicine; Alternative Medicine; Botanic Medicine; Health; Health Professionals; Legal Medicine; Medical Schools; Medical Specialists; Medical Technology; Nuclear Medicine; Veterinary Medicine; Women & Health
Alberta Medical Association, 818
American Medical Association, 823
Association médicale du Québec, 833
British Columbia Medical Association, 849
Canadian Medical Association, 877
Centre for Medicine, Ethics & Law, 893
Doctors Manitoba, 906
Doctors Nova Scotia, 906
Medical Society of Prince Edward Island, 953
Natural Health Practitioners of Canada, 959
New Brunswick Medical Society, 961
Newfoundland & Labrador Medical Association, 963
Occupational & Environmental Medical Association of Canada, 969
Ontario Medical Association, 975
Saskatchewan Medical Association, 1001

Meetings & Conventions
See also Business Travel; Hospitality Industry; Speakers
GLOBE Foundation, 924

Mental Retardation
See Developmentally Disabled Persons

Mentally Handicapped
See Developmentally Disabled Persons

Merchants
See Business

Metal Industries
See also Aluminum; Brass; Copper; Founding; Iron; Magnesium; Metallurgy; Molding (Founding); Pattern-Making; Sheet Metal; Steel Industry; Tool & Die Industry
Association paritaire pour la santé et la sécurité du travail - Produits en métal et électriques, 841
International Titanium Association, 944
Nickel Institute, 964
Western Employers Labour Relations Association, 1019

Metal Trades
See Metal Industries

Metallurgy
See also Metal Industries
Canadian Institute of Mining, Metallurgy & Petroleum, 874
International Titanium Association, 944
Metallurgy & Materials Society of the Canadian Institute of Mining, Metallurgy & Petroleum, 954

Metalwork
See Metallurgy; Sheet Metal

Meteorology
See also Climate; Global Warming; Ozone Layer Depletion
Canadian Meteorological & Oceanographic Society, 878
Climate Institute, 896
International Society of Biometeorology, 943
World Meteorological Organization, 1022

Microbiology
See also Biotechnology; Limnology; Mycology
Association des microbiologistes du Québec, 833
Canadian Society of Microbiologists, 887
International Federation for Cell Biology, 939
International Union of Microbiological Societies, 945

Microcomputers
See also Computer Software; Computers; Desktop Publishing
Urban & Regional Information Systems Association, 1015

Associations Subject Index

Microwave Communication
See Communications

Middle Management
See Management

Migration, Birds
See Birds

Military Vehicles
See Motor Vehicles

Military Weapons
See also Arms Control; Disarmament
Canadian Association for Mine & Explosive Ordnance Security, 856

Mineral Exploration
See Chambers of Mines; Mining; Prospecting

Mineral Extraction
See Mining

Mineral Resources, Chambers of
See Chambers of Mines

Mineralogy
See also Gems; Geology; Jewellery
Bancroft Gem & Mineral Club, 844
Canadian Micro-Mineral Association, 879
Canadian Mineral Society, 879
Canadian Rock Mechanics Association, 884
Central Canadian Federation of Mineralogical Societies, 893
Geological Association of Canada, 923
Hamilton Geological Society, 927
International Council for Applied Mineralogy, 937
International Titanium Association, 944
Kingston Lapidary & Mineral Club, 947
Mineral Society of Manitoba, 954
Mineralogical Association of Canada, 954
Niagara Peninsula Geological Society, 964
Oxford County Geological Society, 983
Sudbury Rock & Lapidary Society, 1011

Mining
See also Asbestos Industry; Chambers of Mines; Coal; Mineralogy; Prospecting
Alberta Chamber of Resources, 816
American Society of Mining & Reclamation, 825
Association de l'exploration minière de Québec, 831
Association minière du Québec, 834
Association of Applied Geochemists, 834
Association paritaire pour la santé et la sécurité du travail - Mines et services miniers, 841
Canadian Association of Mining Equipment & Services for Export, 858
Canadian Institute of Mining, Metallurgy & Petroleum, 874
Canadian Land Reclamation Association, 876
Canadian Mineral Analysts, 879
Canadian Mining Industry Research Organization, 879
European Association of Geoscientists & Engineers, 913
Kamloops Exploration Group, 947
Klondike Placer Miners' Association, 947
Maintenance & Engineering Society of The Canadian Institute of Mining, Metallurgy & Petroleum, 950
Mineralogical Association of Canada, 954
Mines & Aggregates Safety & Health Association, 954
Mining Association of British Columbia, 954
Mining Association of Canada, 955
Mining Association of Manitoba Inc., 955
Mining Industry Human Resources Council, 955
Mining Society of Nova Scotia, 955
Mining Suppliers, Contractors & Consultants Association of BC, 955
MiningWatch Canada, 955
New Brunswick Mining Association, 961
Ontario Mining Association, 976
Saskatchewan Mining Association, 1001

Modelling of Aquatic Ecosystems
See Ecology

Molecular Biology
The Canadian Society of Biochemistry, Molecular & Cellular Biology, 886

Montessori Education
See Education

Monuments & Sites, Conservation of
See Architectural Conservation

Motels
See Hotels & Motels

Moths
See Entomology

Motor Coach Industry
See Bus Transport

Motor Vehicles
See also All-Terrain Vehicles; Antique Automobiles & Trucks; Automobiles; Bus Transport; Motorcycles; Recovery Vehicles; Trucks & Trucking
Canadian Bus Association, 860
Electric Vehicle Council of Ottawa Inc., 909
Electric Vehicle Society of Canada, 909
Vancouver Electric Vehicle Association, 1016

Motorboating
See Boating

Mountaineering
Fédération québécoise de la montagne et de l'escalade, 916

Municipal Government
Alberta Association of Municipal Districts & Counties, 815
Alberta Development Officers Association, 816
Alberta Rural Municipal Administrators Association, 819
Alberta Urban Municipalities Association, 820
Association des Aménagistes Régionaux du Québec, 831
Association des directeurs généraux des municipalités du Québec, 831
Association des ingénieurs municipaux du Québec, 832
Association of Manitoba Municipalities, 836
Association of Municipal Administrators of New Brunswick, 836
Association of Municipal Administrators, Nova Scotia, 836
Association of Municipalities of Ontario, 836
Association of Yukon Communities, 840
Association paritaire pour la santé et la sécurité du travail - Affaires municipales, 840
Corporation des officiers municipaux agréés du Québec, 904
Federation of Canadian Municipalities, 915
Federation of Northern Ontario Municipalities, 915
Federation of Prince Edward Island Municipalities Inc., 915
Fédération Québécoise des Municipalités, 916
Local Government Management Association of British Columbia, 949
Manitoba Municipal Administrators' Association Inc., 951
Municipalities Newfoundland & Labrador, 956
National Centre for Small Communities, 957
Northwest Territories Association of Communities, 967
Northwestern Ontario Municipal Association, 967
Ontario Municipal Human Resources Association, 976
Ontario Municipal Management Institute, 976
Ontario Small Urban Municipalities, 978
Rural Municipal Administrators' Association of Saskatchewan, 997
Saskatchewan Association of Rural Municipalities, 999
Saskatchewan Urban Municipalities Association, 1002
Union des municipalités du Québec, 1014
Union of British Columbia Municipalities, 1014
Union of Nova Scotia Municipalities, 1015
Urban & Regional Information Systems Association, 1015
Urban Municipal Administrators' Association of Saskatchewan, 1016

Municipal Waste
See Waste Management

Municipal Waste Recycling
See Recycling; Waste Management

Museums
See also Archives; Art Galleries; Heritage; History
British Columbia Farm Machinery & Agriculture Museum Association, 847
Central British Columbia Railway & Forest Industry Museum Society, 893

Mussels
See Shellfish

Native Development Corporations
Native Investment & Trade Association, 959

Native Peoples
See also Inuit; Métis; Native Communications; Native Development Corporations; Native Friendship Centres; Native Women; Tribal Councils
Alberta Trappers' Association, 820
Assembly of First Nations, 829
Centre for Indigenous Environmental Resources, 893
Council of the Haida Nation - Haida Fisheries Program, 905
EAGLE (Environmental-Aboriginal Guardianship through Law & Education), 907
Indian Agricultural Program of Ontario, 930
National Aboriginal Forestry Association, 956
Native Investment & Trade Association, 959
Northern Native Fishing Corporation, 966

Natural Gas
Canadian Gas Association, 869

Natural History
See also Naturalists
Natural History Society of Newfoundland & Labrador, 959
Nature Saskatchewan, 960
Nature Vancouver, 960
Société Provancher d'histoire naturelle du Canada, 1006
Victoria Natural History Society, 1017
Waterton Natural History Association, 1018

Natural Products Industry
See also Organic Farming & Gardening
Canadian Health Food Association, 870
Canadian Organic Growers Inc., 880
Canadian Organic Livestock Association, 881
International Federation of Organic Agriculture Movements, 939
Organic Crop Producers & Processors Ontario Inc., 982
Organic Verification Organization of North America, 982

Natural Resource Management
See Environmental Management

Natural Resources, Conservation of
See Conservation of Natural Resources

Naturalists
See also Natural History
Alberni Valley Outdoor Club, 815
Alouette Field Naturalists, 821
Annapolis Field Naturalist Society, 828
Arrowsmith Naturalists, 829
Blomidon Naturalists Society, 846
Bowen Nature Club, 846
Brereton Field Naturalists' Club Inc., 846
British Columbia Nature (Federation of British Columbia Naturalists), 849
Buffalo Lake Naturalists Club, 851
Bulkley Valley Naturalists, 851
Burke Mountain Naturalists, 851
Calgary Field Naturalists' Society, 852
Central Okanagan Naturalists Club, 893
Central Valley Naturalists, 893
Cercles des jeunes naturalistes, 894
Chilliwack Field Naturalists, 895
Cole Harbour Rural Heritage Society, 897
Cowichan Valley Naturalists' Society, 905
Explorer's Club (Canadian Chapter), 914
Federation of Alberta Naturalists, 915
Field Botanists of Ontario, 916
Friends of Mount Revelstoke & Glacier, 921
Grasslands Naturalists, 925
Halifax Field Naturalists, 927
Hamilton Naturalists' Club, 927
Ingersoll District Nature Club, 931
Kamloops Naturalist Club, 947
Kennebecasis Naturalists' Society, 947
Kingston Field Naturalists, 947
Kitchener-Waterloo Field Naturalists, 947
Kitimat Valley Naturalists, 947
Langley Field Naturalists Society, 948
Lethbridge Naturalists' Society, 948
McIlwraith Field Naturalists, 953
Mitlenatch Field Naturalists Society, 955
Montréal Field Naturalists Club, 955
Nanaimo Field Naturalists, 956
National Audubon Society, Inc., 957
Nature Canada, 959
Nature Manitoba, 959
Nature NB, 960
Nature Nova Scotia (Federation of Nova Scotia Naturalists), 960

Associations Subject Index

Nature Québec, 960
Niagara Falls Nature Club, 964
Norfolk Field Naturalists, 964
North Okanagan Naturalists Club, 965
North Shuswap Naturalists, 966
Nova Scotia Wild Flora Society, 969
Oliver-Osoyoos Naturalists, 970
Ontario Field Ornithologists, 973
Ontario Nature, 976
Ottawa Field-Naturalists' Club, 983
Peace Parkland Naturalists, 985
Pembroke Area Field Naturalists, 985
Pender Island Field Naturalists, 985
Peninsula Field Naturalists, 985
Peterborough Field Naturalists, 985
Pickering Naturalists, 986
Prince George Backcountry Recreation Society, 989
Prince George Naturalists, 989
Quesnel Naturalists, 992
Red Deer River Naturalists, 993
Richmond Hill Naturalists, 995
Rideau Valley Field Naturalists, 995
Rocky Mountain Naturalists, 996
Royal Botanical Gardens, 996
Royal City Field Naturalists, 996
Saint John Naturalists' Club, 998
Sault Naturalists, 1002
Seniors for Nature Canoe Club, 1003
Shuswap Naturalists, 1003
Similkameen Naturalist Club, 1004
Skeena Valley Naturalists, 1004
Somenos Marsh Wildlife Society, 1009
South Lake Simcoe Naturalists, 1010
South Peel Naturalists' Club, 1010
Sydenham Field Naturalists, 1011
Thunder Bay Field Naturalists, 1012
Timberline Trail & Nature Club, 1012
Toronto Entomologists Association, 1012
Toronto Field Naturalists, 1012
Toronto Ornithological Club, 1012
Vermilion Forks Field Naturalists, 1016
Vermilion River Naturalist Club, 1016
West Elgin Nature Club, 1018
West Kootenay Naturalists Association, 1018
Williams Lake Field Naturalists, 1020
Willow Beach Field Naturalists, 1020
Windfall Ecology Centre, 1021
Woodstock Field Naturalists, 1021

Needle Trades
See Clothing

Networks of Centres of Excellence
See also Centres of Excellence (Ontario)
Advanced Foods & Materials Network, 813
AquaNet - Network in Aquaculture, 828
ArcticNet Inc., 829
AUTO21 - The Automobile of the 21st Century, 844
Canadian Genetic Diseases Network, 869
Canadian Institute for Photonics Innovations, 873
Canadian Network for Vaccines & Immunotherapeutics, 879
Canadian Pulp & Paper Network for Innovation in Education & Research, 883
Canadian Water Network, 890
Geomatics for Informed Decisions Network, 923
Stem Cell Network, 1010
Sustainable Forestry Initiative, 1011

Neurodegenerative Diseases
See Diseases; Disorders

Nickel
Nickel Institute, 964

Non-Prescription Drugs
See Pharmaceuticals

Non-Utility Generation
See Energy

Nondestructive Testing
See Testing

Nordic Combined Skiing
See Skiing

Northern Canada
See also Arctic Region
Arctic Institute of North America, 829
Association of Canadian Universities for Northern Studies, 834
Canadian Circumpolar Institute, 862

Noxious Animals & Plants, Control o
See Pest Management

Nuclear Arms Control
See Arms Control

Nuclear Energy
See also Uranium
Canadian Coalition for Nuclear Responsibility, 862
Canadian Nuclear Association, 879
Canadian Nuclear Society, 880
Environmentalists For Nuclear Energy (Canada) Inc., 913
International Atomic Energy Agency, 936
Nuclear Information & Resource Service, 969
Organization of CANDU Industries, 982
World Nuclear Association, 1022

Nuclear Law
International Nuclear Law Association, 941

Nuclear Power
See Electric Power; Nuclear Energy

Nuclear Weapons
See also Arms Control; Disarmament; Peace
Canadian Coalition for Nuclear Responsibility, 862

Numeracy
See Literacy

Nursery Trades
See also Horticulture; Landscape Architecture; Lawn and Garden Equipment
British Columbia Landscape & Nursery Association, 848
Canadian Nursery Landscape Association, 880
Flowers Canada, 917
Landscape Alberta Nursery Trades Association, 948
Landscape Newfoundland & Labrador, 948
Landscape Nova Scotia, 948
Landscape Ontario Horticultural Trades Association, 948
Saskatchewan Nursery Landscape Association, 1001

Nutrition
See also Dietitians & Nutritionists; Vegans; Vegetarians
Alberta Milk, 818
Canadian Council of Food & Nutrition, 864
International Union of Nutritional Sciences, 945
Ontario Society of Nutrition Professionals in Public Health, 979

Occasional Teachers
See Teaching

Occupational Health & Safety
See also Public Health; Safety Engineering
Alberta Occupational Health Nurses Association, 818
Association de la santé et de la sécurité des pâtes et papiers et des industries de la forêt du Québec, 831
Association paritaire pour la santé et la sécurité du travail - Affaires municipales, 840
Association paritaire pour la santé et la sécurité du travail - Administration provinciale, 840
Association paritaire pour la santé et la sécurité du travail - Imprimerie et activités connexes, 840
Association paritaire pour la santé et la sécurité du travail - Produits en métal et électriques, 841
Association paritaire pour la santé et la sécurité du travail - Mines et services miniers, 841
Association paritaire pour la santé et la sécurité du travail - Services automobiles, 841
Association paritaire pour la santé et la sécurité du travail - Affaires sociales, 840
Association paritaire pour la santé et la sécurité du travail - Habillement, 840
Association québécoise pour l'hygiène, la santé et la sécurité du travail, 842
Association sectorielle - Fabrication d'équipement de transport et de machines, 842
Board of Canadian Registered Safety Professionals, 846
Canadian Agricultural Safety Association, 854
Canadian Centre for Occupational Health & Safety, 862
Canadian Society of Safety Engineering, Inc., 888
Industrial Accident Victims Group of Ontario, 930
Institut de recherche Robert-Sauvé en santé et en sécurité du travail, 932
Institute for Work & Health, 932
International Commission on Occupational Health, 937
International Occupational Safety & Health Information Centre, 941
Mines & Aggregates Safety & Health Association, 954
Occupational & Environmental Medical Association of Canada, 969
Occupational Health Clinics for Ontario Workers, 969
Occupational Health Nurses of British Columbia, 969
Occupational Hygiene Association of Ontario, 969
Ontario Occupational Health Nurses Association, 976
Safe Workplace Promotion Services Ontario, 997
World Safety Organization, 1023

Occupational Health Libraries
See Medical Libraries

Occupational Safety
See Occupational Health & Safety

Occupational Training
See Staff Training & Development

Oceanography
See also Fisheries Science; Marine Biology
Canadian Meteorological & Oceanographic Society, 878
The Oceanography Society, 970

Oceans
See also Marine Biology; Marine Engineering; Oceanography; Underwater Archaeology
Antarctic & Southern Ocean Coalition, 828
International Ocean Institute, 941
International Oceans Institute of Canada, 941
NOIA, 964
The Ocean Conservancy, 969
Ocean Net, 970

Oil
See also Petroleum Law
The American Association of Petroleum Geologists, 822
Canadian Association of Drilling Engineers, 857
Canadian Association of Oilwell Drilling Contractors, 858
Canadian Association of Petroleum Landmen, 858
Canadian Association of Petroleum Producers, 858
Canadian Heavy Oil Association, 871
Canadian Institute of Mining, Metallurgy & Petroleum, 874
Canadian Oil Heat Association, 880
Canadian Petroleum Law Foundation, 882
Canadian Society of Petroleum Geologists, 887
Enform: The Safety Association for the Upstream Oil & Gas Industry, 910
NOIA, 964
NORA, An Association of Responsible Recyclers, 964
Ontario Petroleum Institute Inc., 976
Petroleum Human Resources Council of Canada, 986
Petroleum Research Atlantic Canada, 986
Petroleum Services Association of Canada, 986
Petroleum Society of CIM, 986
Petroleum Tank Management Association of Alberta, 986
Petroleum Technology Alliance Canada, 986
Public Petroleum Data Model Association, 991
Society of Petroleum Engineers, 1008
World Petroleum Congress, 1023

Old Age
See Senior Citizens

Optical Engineering
See Engineering

Orchids
See also Flowers
Central Ontario Orchid Society, 893
Eastern Canada Orchid Society, 907
Native Orchid Conservation Inc., 959
Ottawa Orchid Society, 983
Southern Ontario Orchid Society, 1010
Victoria Orchid Society, 1017

Organic Chemistry
See Chemistry

Organic Farming & Gardening
See also Natural Products Industry
Alberta Organic Producers Association, 818
Atlantic Canadian Organic Regional Network, 843
Bio-dynamic Agricultural Society of British Columbia, 845
Boundary Organic Producers Association, 846
British Columbia Association for Regenerative Agriculture, 846

Associations Subject Index

Canadian Organic Growers Inc., 880
Canadian Organic Livestock Association, 881
Certified Organic Associations of British Columbia, 894
Ecological Agriculture Projects, 908
Ecological Farmers Association of Ontario, 908
Fédération d'agriculture biologique du Québec, 914
Henry A. Wallace Center for Agricultural & Environmental Policy at Winrock International, 929
International Federation of Organic Agriculture Movements, 939
International WWOOF Association, 946
Islands Organic Producers Association, 946
North Okanagan Organic Association, 965
Northeast Organic Farming Association, 966
Organic Crop Improvement Association - New Brunswick, 982
Organic Crop Improvement Association - Québec & Ontario, 982
Organic Crop Improvement Association (International), 982
Organic Crop Producers & Processors Ontario Inc., 982
Organic Producers Association of Manitoba Co-operative Inc., 982
Organic Trade Association, 982
Organic Verification Organization of North America, 982
Similkameen Okanagan Organic Producers Association, 1004
Society for Organic Urban Land Care, 1007
WWOOF Canada, 1024

Organization Development
See Management

Ornithology
See Birds

Outdoor Adventure Activities
See Recreation

Outdoor Advertising
See Advertising

Outdoor Measurement
See Advertising

Outdoor Recreation
See Recreation

Outerwear
See Clothing

Ozone Layer Depletion
See also Global Warming
Climate Institute, 896
Manitoba Ozone Protection Industry Association, 951

Pacific Islands
Pacific Peoples Partnership, 983

Packaging
See also Containers
Alliance of Foam Packaging Recyclers, 821
Association of Independent Corrugated Converters, 836
Association of Postconsumer Plastic Recyclers, 837
Foodservice & Packaging Institute, 918
Institute of Packaging Professionals, 933
North American Packaging Association - Canada, 965
Packaging Association of Canada, 984
Paper Packaging Canada, 984
Polystyrene Packaging Council, 987
World Packaging Organization, 1023

Paddling
See Canoeing & Rafting

Paint
See also Painting & Decorating
British Columbia Paint Manufacturers' Association, 849
Canadian Paint & Coatings Association, 881

Paleolimnology
See Limnology

Paleontology
See also Geology
Niagara Peninsula Geological Society, 964
Oxford County Geological Society, 983

Pallets (Shipping, Storage, etc.)
See also Containers
Canadian Pallet Council, 881
Canadian Wood Pallet & Container Association, 892

Palynology
Canadian Association of Palynologists, 858

Paper
See Pulp & Paper Industry; Stationery

Paralegals
See Law

Parallel Generation
See Energy

Parking
See Automobiles

Parks
See also Camping; Recreation; Zoos
Alberta Recreation & Parks Association, 819
Association des jardineries du Québec, 832
Association des jardins du Québec, 832
Association for Mountain Parks Protection & Enjoyment, 833
British Columbia Recreation & Parks Association, 849
Canadian Association of Zoos & Aquariums, 859
Canadian Parks & Recreation Association, 881
Canadian Parks & Wilderness Society, 881
Canadian Parks Partnership, 881
Conservation Ontario, 901
The Friends of Algonquin Park, 920
The Friends of Awenda Park, 920
The Friends of Bon Echo Park, 920
The Friends of Bonnechere Parks, 920
The Friends of Charleston Lake Park, 920
Friends of Ferris, 920
The Friends of Frontenac Park, 920
The Friends of Killarney Park, 920
The Friends of MacGregor Point, 920
Friends of Mashkinonje Park, 921
The Friends of Nancy Island Historic Site & Wasaga Beach Park, 921
The Friends of Pinery Park, 921
The Friends of Presqu'ile Park, 921
The Friends of Rondeau Park, 921
The Friends of Sandbanks Park, 921
Friends of Short Hills Park, 921
The Friends of Sleeping Giant, 921
Jasper Environmental Association, 947
National Parks Conservation Association, 958
Niijkiwenhwag - Friends of Lake Superior Park, 964
Okanagan Similkameen Parks Society, 970
Ontario Parks Association, 976
Parks & Recreation Ontario, 984
Protected Areas Association of Newfoundland & Labrador, 990
Quetico Foundation, 992
Recreation New Brunswick, 992
Recreation Newfoundland & Labrador, 992
Saskatchewan Parks & Recreation Association, 1001

Parties, Political
See Political Organizations

Pathology, Plant
See Botany

Payments
See Finance

PCB Waste
See Hazardous Wastes

Peace
See also Arms Control; Disarmament; International Cooperation; International Relations; Nuclear Weapons
Concerned Educators Allied for a Safe Environment, 899
International Association of Educators for World Peace, 935
Oakville Community Centre for Peace, Ecology & Human Rights, 969
Peace & Environment Resource Centre, 985
World Federalist Movement, 1022

Peat
See also Nursery Trades
Canadian Sphagnum Peat Moss Association, 888
International Peat Society, 941
International Peat Society - Canadian National Committee, 941

Permafrost
International Permafrost Association, 941

Personal Computers
See Computers

Personal Property Appraisal
See Appraisal

Personnel
See Human Resources

Pest Management
See also Agrochemicals
Association québécoise de la gestion parasitaire, 841
Atlantic Pest Control Association, 843
Canadian Association of Physicians for the Environment, 858
Canadian Pest Management Association, 882
CropLife Canada, 905
Croplife International, 906
Integrated Vegetation Management Association of British Columbia, 934
National Coalition Against the Misuse of Pesticides, 957
Northern Interior Vegetation Management Association, 966
Northwest Coalition for Alternatives to Pesticides, 966
Ontario Vegetation Management Association, 981
Pest Management Association of Alberta, 985
Pesticide Action Network North America, 985
Pesticide Education Network, 985
Structural Pest Management Association of Ontario, 1010
Structural Pest Management Association of British Columbia, 1010
Urban Pest Management Council of Canada, 1016
Weed Science Society of America, 1018

Pesticides
See Pest Management

Petrochemical Industry
See Chemical Industry

Petroleum
See Gas; Oil

Petroleum Law
Canadian Petroleum Law Foundation, 882

Petrology
See Geology; Mineralogy

Pharmaceuticals
Canada's Research-Based Pharmaceutical Companies (Rx&D), 853

Photogrammetry
See Remote Sensing

Photonics
Canadian Institute for Photonics Innovations, 873

Physical Geography
See Geography

Physically Challenged Persons
See Disabled Persons

Physically Disabled
See Disabled Persons

Physically Handicapped
See Disabled Persons

Physicians
See also Medical Specialists; Surgeons
Canadian Association of Physicians for the Environment, 858
Ontario Medical Association, 975
Physicians for a Smoke-Free Canada, 986

Physics
See also Biophysics
Ontario Centre of Excellence for Photonics, 971

Physiology
See also Anatomists; Neurophysiology; Pharmacology; Toxicology
Canadian Physiological Society, 882
Society of Toxicology of Canada, 1009

Phytopathology
See Botany

Pickup Trucks
See Trucks & Trucking

Pigeons
See Birds

Pigs
See Swine

Pioneers
See Heritage; History

Associations Subject Index

Pipe Smoking
See Smoking

Pipelines
See also Gas; Oil
Canadian Energy Pipeline Association, 866

Pipes
See also Valves
Canadian Concrete Pipe Association, 863
Corporation des maîtres mécaniciens en tuyauterie du Québec, 904
Corrugated Steel Pipe Institute, 904
Ontario Concrete Pipe Association, 972
Ontario Pipe Trades Council, 977

Placement Agencies
See Human Resources

Planetariums
See also Astronomy
H.R. MacMillan Space Centre Society, 930

Planetary Sciences
See Space Sciences

Planning
See also Community Development; Community Planning; Corporate Planning; Family Planning; Regional Planning; Urban Planning
American Planning Association, 824
Atlantic Planners Institute, 843
Canadian Association for Studies in Co-operation, 856
Canadian Institute of Planners, 875
Manitoba Professional Planners Institute, 951
Ontario Professional Planners Institute, 977
Planning Institute of British Columbia, 987
Strategic Leadership Forum, The Toronto Society for Strategic Management, 1010

Plant Engineering
See Industrial Engineering

Plant Growth Regulators
See Agrochemicals

Plant Oils
See Agriculture

Plant Pathology
See Botany

Plants (Botanical)
See Botany

Plastic Film
See Plastics

Plastics
See also Plastics As Art Material; Vinyl
Alberta Plastics Recycling Association, 818
American Plastics Council, 824
Association of Postconsumer Plastic Recyclers, 837
Bureau of International Recycling, 851
Canadian Plastics Industry Association, 882
Canadian Plastics Sector Council, 882
Canadian Polystyrene Recycling Alliance, 882
Film & Bag Federation, 916
National Association for PET Container Resources, 957
Plastic Loose Fill Council, 987
Society of the Plastics Industry, Inc., 1008

Plumbing
See also Pipes; Valves
American Society of Plumbing Engineers, 826
Canadian Institute of Plumbing & Heating, 875
Corporation des maîtres mécaniciens en tuyauterie du Québec, 904
Ontario Plumbing Inspectors Association, 977

Political Geography
See Geography

Political Organizations
Alberta Greens, 817
Green Party of British Columbia, 926
Green Party of Canada, 926
The Green Party of Manitoba, 926
Green Party of New Brunswick, 926
The Green Party of Ontario, 926
Parti Vert du Québec, 985

Pollen & Spores
See Palynology

Pollution
See also Acid Rain; Air Pollution; Hazardous Wastes; Noise Pollution; Waste Management; Water Pollution
Action to Restore a Clean Humber, 813
Association québécoise de lutte contre la pollution atmosphérique, 841
Canadian Centre for Pollution Prevention, 862
Clean North, 896
Earth Voice, 907
Environmental Protection UK, 912
Friends of the Earth International, 921
Green Calgary, 925
National Coalition Against the Misuse of Pesticides, 957
Ocean Net, 970
Ontario Clean Air Alliance, 972
Ontario Pollution Control Equipment Association, 977
The Pollution Probe Foundation, 987

Polystyrene
See also Plastics
Canadian Polystyrene Recycling Alliance, 882
Polystyrene Packaging Council, 987

Ponies
See Horses

Populations
See also Birth Control; Carrying Capacity; Childbirth; Family Planning; Fertility & Infertility (Human)
Carrying Capacity Network, 892
Foundation for Environmental Conservation, 919
Population Connection, 987

Porpoises
See Marine Mammals

Ports
See Harbours & Ports

Post-Secondary Education
See Universities & Colleges

Potash
International Plant Nutrition Institute, 942

Potatoes
Horticulture Nova Scotia, 930
Potatoes NB, 987

Poultry
See also Poultry Science; Ratites
The Ontario Farm Animal Council, 973

Poultry Science
Rare Breeds Canada, 992

Pound Seizure (Animals)
See Animal Rights Movement; Animal Welfare

Power
See Energy

Prejudice
See Race Relations

Prescription Drugs
See Pharmaceuticals

Press
See Journalism

Prevention of Cruelty to Animals
See Animal Welfare

Preventive Health Care Services
See Medicine

Primates
International Primate Protection League, 942
The Jane Goodall Institute for Wildlife Research, Education & Conservation, 946
The Jane Goodall Institute of Canada, 946

Printing Industries
See also Desktop Publishing; Graphic Arts & Design; Printing Trades Councils; Publishing
Association paritaire pour la santé et la sécurité du travail - Imprimerie et activités connexes, 840
Canadian Printing Industries Association, 883
Canadian Printing Ink Manufacturers Association, 883
Ontario Printing & Imaging Association, 977

Privacy, Right to
See Human Rights

Produce
See Fruit & Vegetables

Product Certification
See Standards

Product Development
See Research

Product Testing
See Laboratories; Testing

Professional Development
See also Professions; Staff Training & Development
Council of Canadian Fire Marshals & Fire Commissioners, 904

Promotional Marketing
See Marketing

Propane
Propane Gas Association of Canada Inc., 990

Property Assessment
See Appraisal

Prosecutors
See Lawyers

Prospecting
See also Chambers of Mines; Mining
Alberta Chamber of Resources, 816
Association de l'exploration minière de Québec, 831
Association of Applied Geochemists, 834
Canadian Institute of Mining, Metallurgy & Petroleum, 874
European Association of Geoscientists & Engineers, 913
Mineralogical Association of Canada, 954
New Brunswick Mining Association, 961
Northern Prospectors Association, 966
Ontario Prospectors Association, 977
Prospectors & Developers Association of Canada, 990

Public Administration
See also Government; Municipal Government; Public Policy
Alberta Rural Municipal Administrators Association, 819
California Institute of Public Affairs, 852
Intergovernmental Committee on Urban & Regional Research, 934
The Public Affairs Association of Canada, 990

Public Affairs
See Government; Public Administration

Public Appraisers
See Appraisal

Public Health
See also Occupational Health & Safety; Safety
Alberta Public Health Association, 819
Association des médecins spécialistes en santé communautaire du Québec, 833
Association of Supervisors of Public Health Inspectors (Ontario), 840
Association pour la santé publique du Québec, 841
Canadian Institute of Public Health Inspectors, 875
Canadian Public Health Association, 883
Canadian Public Health Association - NB/PEI Branch, 883
Canadian Public Health Association - NWT/Nunavut Branch, 883
Environmental Health Foundation of Canada, 912
International Institute of Concern for Public Health, 940
Manitoba Public Health Association, 951
Newfoundland & Labrador Public Health Association, 963
Ontario Public Health Association, 977
Ontario Society of Nutrition Professionals in Public Health, 979
Public Health Association of British Columbia, 990
Public Health Association of Nova Scotia, 991
Saskatchewan Public Health Association Inc., 1001
World Safety Organization, 1023
Yukon Public Health Association, 1024

Public Land Policy Reform
See Land Use

Public Legal Education
See Legal Education

Associations Subject Index

Public Participation
International Association for Public Participation, 935

Public Policy
See also Government; Municipal Government; Public Administration
Canadian Centre for Policy Alternatives, 862
Canadian Council of Chief Executives, 864
C.D. Howe Institute, 893
The Conference Board of Canada, 899
Couchiching Institute on Public Affairs, 904
Institute for Research on Public Policy, 932
Ontario Municipal Management Institute, 976
Pacific NorthWest Economic Region, 983

Public Safety
See Safety

Public Utilities
See also Electric Power; Gas
American Public Works Association, 824
Canadian Association of Members of Public Utility Tribunals, 857
Canadian Public Works Association, 883
Electricity Distributors Association, 909
Municipal Equipment & Operations Association (Ontario) Inc., 955
Ontario Municipal Water Association, 976

Public Works
American Public Works Association, 824
Canadian Public Works Association, 883

Pulmonary Diseases
See Lung Disorders & Diseases

Pulp & Paper Industry
See also Forest Industries
Bureau of International Recycling, 851
Canadian Pulp & Paper Network for Innovation in Education & Research, 883
Forest Products Association of Canada, 918
Forest Products Association of Nova Scotia, 919
Pulp & Paper Technical Association of Canada, 991

Pure Chemistry
See Chemistry

Quality of Drinking Water
See Drinking Water

Quality of Working Life
See also Equal Opportunity Employment; Ergonomics; Occupational Health & Safety; Sexual Harassment
Institute for Work & Health, 932

R & D
See Research

Race Relations
See also Human Rights
Arusha Centre Society, 829

Racial Discrimination
See Race Relations

Racism
See Race Relations

Radar
See Remote Sensing

Radiation
See also Food Irradiation; Medical Radiation; Nuclear Energy; Nuclear Weapons
Canadian Radiation Protection Association, 883
International Commission on Radiological Protection, 937
Radiation Safety Institute of Canada, 992

Radio Broadcasting
See also Citizens' Band Radio; Multicultural Broadcasting; Radio Operators; Radio, Amateur
Farm Radio International, 914

Radon Testing
See Laboratories; Testing

Rafting
See Canoeing & Rafting

Rail Transit
See Railroads & Railways

Rail Transportation
See Freight Services; Railroads & Railways

Railroads & Railways
See also Freight Services; Transportation
Central British Columbia Railway & Forest Industry Museum Society, 893
International Heavy Haul Association, 940

Rainforests
Conservation International, 901
Forest Action Network, 918
Friends of Clayoquot Sound, 920
Rainforest Action Network, 992
Rainforest Alliance, 992

Rainwear
See Clothing

Rapeseed
See Canola

Ratepayers
See Residents & Ratepayers

Reactors
See Nuclear Energy

Ready-Mixed Concrete
See Concrete

Real Estate Appraisal
See Appraisal

Real Estate Development
See also Real Estate
Urban Development Institute of Canada, 1016

Recreation
See also Arenas; Environmental & Outdoor Education; Parks; Resorts; Sports
Alberta Recreation & Parks Association, 819
British Columbia Marine Trades Association, 849
British Columbia Recreation & Parks Association, 849
Canadian Parks & Recreation Association, 881
Fédération québécoise de la montagne et de l'escalade, 916
Lansdowne Outdoor Recreational Development Association, 948
National Marine Manufacturers Association Canada, 958
Northwest Territories Recreation & Parks Association, 967
Ontario Trails Council, 980
Outward Bound Canada, 983
Parks & Recreation Ontario, 984
Recreation New Brunswick, 992
Recreation Newfoundland & Labrador, 992
Saskatchewan Camping Association, 999
Saskatchewan Parks & Recreation Association, 1001
Strathcona Park Lodge & Outdoor Education Centre, 1010
Trans Canada Trail Foundation, 1013

Recreational Canoeing
See Canoeing & Rafting

Recreational Geography
See Geography

Recruitment - Employment
See Human Resources

Recycled Paper
See Recycling

Recycling
See also Composting; Environment Industry; Waste Management
Alberta Bottle Depot Association, 816
Alberta Plastics Recycling Association, 818
Alliance of Foam Packaging Recyclers, 821
The Aluminum Association, 821
Association of Postconsumer Plastic Recyclers, 837
Bluewater Recycling Association, 846
British Columbia Bottle Depot Association, 847
Bureau of International Recycling, 851
Canadian Association of Recycling Industries, 858
Canadian Polystyrene Recycling Alliance, 882
Center for Health, Environment & Justice, 893
Centre de formation en entreprise et récupération, 893
Clean Nova Scotia, 896
Conserver Society of Hamilton & District, 902
DRS Earthwise Society, 906
Earth Voice, 907
Éco Entreprises Québec, 908
Ecology North, 908
Electronics Product Stewardship Canada, 909
The Environmental Coalition of PEI, 911
Environmental Education Ontario, 912
Green Action Centre, 925
INFORM Inc., 931
Institute for Local Self-Reliance, 932
Institute of Scrap Recycling Industries, Inc., 933
Municipal Waste Association, 955
NAID Canada, 956
National Association for Information Destruction, 956
National Association for PET Container Resources, 957
National Recycling Coalition, 958
NORA, An Association of Responsible Recyclers, 964
North American Recycled Rubber Association, 965
Ontario Automotive Recyclers Association, 971
Pitch-In Alberta, 987
Pitch-In Canada, 987
Prince George Recycling & Environmental Action Planning Society, 989
Recycling Council of Alberta, 993
Recycling Council of British Columbia, 993
Recycling Council of Ontario, 993
Resource Recycling Inc., 995
Rubber Manufacturers Association, 997
Saskatchewan Waste Reduction Council, 1002
Société québécoise de récupération et de recyclage, 1006
Steel Recycling Institute, 1010
Thames Region Ecological Association, 1012
The Vinyl Institute, 1017
Warmer Bulletin - Residua Ltd., 1017
Whitchurch-Stouffville Recycling Group, 1019

Reduce, Reuse, Recycle
See Recycling

Reduction, Waste
See Recycling

Reforestation
Tree Canada Foundation, 1013

Refrigeration
See also Air Conditioning; Heating; Mechanical Contractors
American Society of Heating, Refrigerating & Air Conditioning Engineers, 824
Corporation des entreprises de traitement de l'air et du froid, 904
Heating, Refrigeration & Air Conditioning Contractors Association Atlantic, 928
Heating, Refrigeration & Air Conditioning Institute of Canada, 928
Ontario Refrigeration & Air Conditioning Contractors Association, 978
Refrigeration & Air Conditioning Contractors Association of British Columbia, 993
Refrigeration & Air Conditioning Contractors Association of Manitoba, 993
Refrigeration Service Engineers Society (Canada), 994

Refuse Disposal
See Waste Management

Refuse Handling
See Waste Management

Regional Development
See also Industrial Development
Association canadienne des sciences régionales, 830

Regional Planning
See also Community Planning; Regional Development; Urban Planning
Association des Aménagistes Régionaux du Québec, 831
International Federation for Housing & Planning, 939

Rehabilitation
See also Occupational Therapy; Offenders (Criminal) & Ex-Offenders; Vocational Rehabilitation
Saskatchewan Association of Rehabilitation Centres, 999

Relief, International
See International Relief

Remote Sensing
See also Geography
Canadian Institute of Geomatics, 874
Canadian Remote Sensing Society, 884

Associations Subject Index

Renewable Energy Resources
See also Biomass Energy; Energy Conservation; Solar Energy
Association of Power Producers of Ontario, 837
Canadian Association for Renewable Energies, 856
Canadian Renewable Fuels Association, 884
Canadian Wind Energy Association Inc., 891
Citizens For Renewable Energy, 895
Energy Action Council of Toronto, 909
Energy Council of Canada, 909
Energy Probe Research Foundation, 910
Fédération des producteurs de cultures commerciales du Québec, 915
Institute for Local Self-Reliance, 932
International Solar Energy Society, 944
Ontario Corn Producers' Association, 972
Ontario Soybean Growers, 979
Ontario Wheat Producers' Marketing Board, 981
Renewable Natural Resources Foundation, 994
Solar & Sustainable Energy Society of Canada Inc., 1009
Warmer Bulletin - Residua Ltd., 1017

Rent Controls
See Housing

Rental Housing
See Housing

Reporters
See Journalism; Media

Reproductive Biotechnology
See Breeding

Reproductive Health
See Health

Rescue Services
See Emergency Services; Search & Rescue

Research
See also Market Research; Medical Research; Operations Research; Psychical Research; Science
Advanced Foods & Materials Network, 813
Alberta Sulphur Research Ltd., 820
AquaNet - Network in Aquaculture, 828
ArcticNet Inc., 829
Atlantic Turfgrass Research Foundation, 843
AUTO21 - The Automobile of the 21st Century, 844
Canadian Association for Health Services & Policy Research, 855
Canadian Association for Research in Nondestructive Evaluation, 856
Canadian Association on Water Quality, 859
Canadian Carbonization Research Association, 861
Canadian Centre for Fisheries Innovation, 861
Canadian Centre for Policy Alternatives, 862
Canadian Circumpolar Institute, 862
Canadian Energy Research Institute, 866
Canadian Institute for Photonics Innovations, 873
Canadian Mining Industry Research Organization, 879
Canadian Network for Vaccines & Immunotherapeutics, 879
Canadian Pulp & Paper Network for Innovation in Education & Research, 883
Canadian Transportation Research Forum, 889
Canadian Water Network, 890
C.D. Howe Institute, 893
Coastal Ecosystems Research Foundation, 897
Communications & Information Technology Ontario, 898
Conseil de la recherche forestière du Québec, 900
Consultative Group on International Agricultural Research, 902
Earthwatch Europe, 907
Fishermen and Scientists Research Society, 917
FPInnovations, 919
Geomatics for Informed Decisions Network, 923
Grand Manan Whale & Seabird Research Station, 924
The Great Lakes Research Consortium, 925
Groupe de recherche en écologie sociale, 926
INFORM Inc., 931
Innovation Management Association of Canada, 931
Institut de recherche Robert-Sauvé en santé et en sécurité du travail, 932
Institute for Risk Research, 932
Intergovernmental Committee on Urban & Regional Research, 934
International Association for Bear Research & Management, 934
International Association for Great Lakes Research, 935
International Development Research Centre, 938
International Institute for Applied Systems Analysis, 940
International Research Group on Wood Protection, 942
International Society for Evolutionary Protistology, 943
International Union of Forest Research Organizations, 945
The Jane Goodall Institute for Wildlife Research, Education & Conservation, 946
The Jane Goodall Institute of Canada, 946
Macleod Institute, 950
Materials & Manufacturing Ontario, Division of OCE Inc., 952
National Council for Science & the Environment, 957
Nova Scotia Public Interest Research Group, 968
Offshore Energy Environmental Research Association, 970
Ontario Centre of Excellence for Photonics, 971
Ontario Public Interest Research Group, 978
Petroleum Research Atlantic Canada, 986
Québec Public Interest Research Group - McGill, 991
Society for Research on Nicotine & Tobacco, 1007
Stem Cell Network, 1010
Stockholm Environment Institute, 1010
Tellus Institute, 1011
World Agroforestry Centre, 1021
World Association of Industrial & Technological Research Organizations, 1021

Research & Development
See Research

Research, Biomedical
See Biomedical Research

Residential Facilities
See Housing

Residents & Ratepayers
The Township of Muskoka Lakes Ratepayers' Association, 1013

Residents, Medical
See Medicine

Resorts
British Columbia Lodging & Campgrounds Association, 848

Resource Geography
See Geography

Resources Law
See Environmental Law

Resources, Chambers of
See Chambers of Mines

Respiratory Disorders
See also Asthma; Lung Disorders & Diseases; Respiratory Allergies; Respiratory Therapy; Smoking
Canadian Respiratory Health Professionals, 884
International Primary Care Respiratory Group, 942
Ontario Lung Association, 975
Ontario Respiratory Care Society, 978

Respiratory Therapy
International Primary Care Respiratory Group, 942
Ontario Lung Association, 975
Ontario Respiratory Care Society, 978

Restoration, Architectural
See Architectural Conservation

Retail Trade
See also Direct Marketing; Lord's Day Legislation; Wholesale Trade
Canada East Equipment Dealers' Association, 852
The Fur Council of Canada, 922
Retail Council of Canada, 995
Western Retail Lumber Association, 1019

Retardation
See Developmentally Disabled Persons

Retraining
See Staff Training & Development

River Rafting
See Canoeing & Rafting

Rivers & Streams
See also Limnology
Black Creek Conservation Project, 845
Friends of the Oldman River, 921
Friends of the Stikine Society, 921
Friends of the Trent-Severn Waterway, 922
Grand River Conservation Foundation, 924
Meewasin Valley Authority, 953
Partners FOR the Saskatchewan River Basin, 985
Quidi Vidi Rennie's River Development Foundation, 992
St Mary's River Association, 998

Roads & Roadbuilding
See also Heavy Construction
Ontario Good Roads Association, 974
Salt Institute, 998
Trans Canada Yellowhead Highway Association, 1013

Rock Climbing
See Mountaineering

Rock Mechanics
See Geology

Rocketry
See Space Sciences

Rocks
See Gems; Geology; Mineralogy

Rodenticides
See Pest Management

Romance Writers
See Writers

Roses
Canadian Rose Society, 884
Greater Toronto Rose & Garden Society, 925
Société des roses du Québec, 1005

Rubber
North American Recycled Rubber Association, 965
The Rubber Association of Canada, 997

Rural Living
Alberta Rural Municipal Administrators Association, 819
British Columbia Women's Institutes, 850
Cole Harbour Rural Heritage Society, 897
Fédération des agricultrices du Québec, 914
National Farmers Union, 958
Saskatchewan Association of Rural Municipalities, 999

Safety
See also Accident Prevention; Air Safety; Electronic Security Industry; Fire Protection & Prevention; Occupational Health & Safety; Safety Engineering; Traffic Injury; Water Safety
Alberta Motor Transport Association, 818
Alberta Safety Council, 819
American Industrial Hygiene Association, 823
Association de la santé et de la sécurité des pâtes et papiers et des industries de la forêt du Québec, 831
Board of Canadian Registered Safety Professionals, 846
Canada Safety Council, 853
Canadian Centre for Occupational Health & Safety, 862
Canadian Dam Association, 865
Canadian Fire Safety Association, 868
Canadians for Responsible & Safe Highways, 892
Enform: The Safety Association for the Upstream Oil & Gas Industry, 910
Fire Prevention Canada, 916
Health & Safety Conference Society of Alberta, 927
Institut de recherche Robert-Sauvé en santé et en sécurité du travail, 932
Mines & Aggregates Safety & Health Association, 954
Newfoundland & Labrador Safety Council, 963
Nova Scotia Safety Council, 968
Ontario Industrial Fire Protection Association, 975
Ontario Safety League, 978
Ontario Traffic Conference, 980
Ottawa Safety Council, 983
Radiation Safety Institute of Canada, 992
Safety Services Manitoba, 997
Safety Services New Brunswick, 997
Saskatchewan Safety Council, 1001
World Safety Organization, 1023

Safety Engineering
See also Occupational Health & Safety
American Society of Safety Engineers, 826
Canadian Society of Safety Engineering, Inc., 888

Sales
See Marketing; Retail Trade

Associations Subject Index

Salespeople
See Retail Trade

Salmon
See also Fish; Fisheries
Atlantic Salmon Federation, 843
British Columbia Salmon Farmers Association, 849
Fédération québécoise pour le saumon atlantique, 916
Nepisiguit Salmon Association, 960
New Brunswick Salmon Council, 961
New Brunswick Salmon Growers Association, 961
Northumberland Salmon Protection Association, 966
Nova Scotia Salmon Association, 969
Prince Edward Island Salmon Association, 989
Salmon Preservation Association for the Waters of Newfoundland, 998

Salt
Salt Institute, 998

Sanitary Engineering
See also Waste Management
Pan American Center for Sanitary Engineering & Environmental Sciences, 984

Sanitation Supply Industry
Canadian Sanitation Supply Association, 884
International Sanitary Supply Association, Inc., 942

Scholarly Societies
See Learned Societies

School Buses
See Bus Transport

Science
See also Research
American Association for the Advancement of Science, 822
Association francophone pour le savoir, 833
Association of Professional Geoscientists of Nova Scotia, 839
Atlantic Provinces Council on the Sciences, 843
Canadian Association of Palynologists, 858
Canadian Science Writers' Association, 884
Earthwatch Europe, 907
International Association of Hydrogeologists, 935
International Association of Science & Technology for Development, 936
International Council of Associations for Science Education, 938
International Union of Biological Sciences, 945
Nova Scotian Institute of Science, 969
NSERC/Petro-Canada Chair for Women in Science & Engineering, 969
Pan American Center for Sanitary Engineering & Environmental Sciences, 984
Science Alberta Foundation, 1002
Society for Canadian Women in Science & Technology, 1006

Science, Applied
See Engineering

Science, Social
See Social Science

Science, Soil
See Soil Science

Scrap Recycling
See Recycling

Scriptwriting
See Writers

Scuba Diving
See Aquatic Sports; Diving

Seafood
See also Shellfish
Fisheries Council of Canada, 917
Fisheries Council of Canada - British Columbia Representative, 917
International Institute of Fisheries Economics & Trade, 940
Prince Edward Island Cultured Mussel Growers Association, 988

Search & Rescue
Canadian Avalanche Association, 859

Sedimentology
See Geology

Seeds
Canadian Seed Growers' Association, 884
Canadian Seed Trade Association, 884
National Sunflower Association of Canada, 958
SeCan Association, 1003
Seeds of Diversity Canada, 1003

Senior Citizens
See also Geriatric Nurses; Pensions & Benefits; Retirement; Seniors Centres
Lansdowne Outdoor Recreational Development Association, 948

Sewage Disposal
See Waste Management

Sewerage
See Waste Management

Sheep
See also Wool
Canadian Sheep Breeders' Association, 885
Saskatchewan Katahdin Sheep Association Inc., 1000

Sheet Metal
Bureau of International Recycling, 851
Sheet Metal & Air Conditioning Contractors' National Association, 1003
Sheet Metal Contractors Association of Alberta, 1003
Toronto Sheet Metal Contractors Association, 1013

Shellfish
See also Clams; Oysters; Seafood
British Columbia Shellfish Growers Association, 849

Shelters, Animal
See Animal Welfare

Shipbuilding
Shipbuilding Association of Canada, 1003

Shipping
See also Containers; Freight Services; Harbours & Ports; Longshoremen; Marine Trades; Pallets (Shipping, Storage, etc.); Transportation
Association of Canadian Port Authorities, 834
Canadian Ports Clearance Association, 882
International Maritime Organization, 941

Silicosis
See Occupational Health & Safety

Silviculture
See Arboriculture

Skiing
Fédération québécoise de la montagne et de l'escalade, 916

Skilled Labour
See Labour

Small Business
See also Home-Based Business
Hamilton Incubator of Technology, 927

Smelting
See Iron

Smoking
See also Lung Disorders & Diseases; Respiratory Disorders; Tobacco Industry
Action on Smoking & Health, 813
Airspace Action on Smoking & Health, 814
Canadian Council for Tobacco Control, 864
Conseil québécois sur le tabac et la santé, 901
Council for a Smoke-Free PEI, 904
Manitoba Tobacco Reduction Alliance, 952
Non-Smokers' Rights Association, 964
Physicians for a Smoke-Free Canada, 986
Saskatchewan Coalition for Tobacco Reduction, 999
Smoke-Free Nova Scotia, 1004
Smoking & Health Action Foundation, 1004

Snorkelling
See Diving

Social Geography
See Geography

Social Investment
See Economics; Investment

Social Rehabilitation
See Rehabilitation

Social Science
See also Psychology; Social Work; Sociology
Society for Socialist Studies, 1007

Socialism
Society for Socialist Studies, 1007

Sod
See Nursery Trades

Soft Drinks Industry
See also Bottling Industry
Refreshments Canada, 993

Soil Mechanics
See Geology

Soil Science
See also Agriculture
Alberta Conservation Tillage Society II, 816
Bedeque Bay Environmental Management Association, 845
Canadian Society of Soil Science, 888
International Erosion Control Association, 938
International Society for Soil Mechanics & Geotechnical Engineering, 943
International Soil Reference & Information Centre, 944
International Union of Soil Sciences, 945
New Brunswick Soil & Crop Improvement Association, 961
Ontario Soil & Crop Improvement Association, 979
Saskatchewan Soil Conservation Association, 1001
Soil & Water Conservation Society, 1009
Soil Conservation Council of Canada, 1009
Weed Science Society of America, 1018

Solar Energy
Canadian Solar Industries Association Inc., 888
Énergie Solaire Québec, 909
International Solar Energy Society, 944
Solar & Sustainable Energy Society of Canada Inc., 1009

Solar Power
See Solar Energy

Solid Waste Management
See Waste Management

Source Separation
See Recycling

South Pacific
See Pacific Islands

Space Sciences
See also Aerospace Industries
Canadian Aeronautics & Space Institute, 854
Canadian Space Society, 888
Edmonton Space & Science Foundation, 909
European Geosciences Union, 913
European Space Agency, 913
H.R. MacMillan Space Centre Society, 930
Institute of Space & Atmospheric Studies, 933

SPCAs
See Animal Welfare

Special Education
See Education

Specialists, Medical
See Medical Specialists

Specialty Foods
See Food Industry

Specifications
See Standards

Spectroscopy
Canadian Society for Analytical Sciences & Spectroscopy, 885

Speleology
Alberta Speleological Society, 820
American Cave Conservation Association, 822
Société québécoise de spéléologie, 1006

Sphagnum Peat
See Peat

Spices
Saskatchewan Herb & Spice Association, 1000

Spores & Pollen
See Palynology

Associations Subject Index

Sportsfishing
See Fishing & Angling

Sportsmen's Clubs
See Fish; Fish & Game; Fishing & Angling; Hunting

Sportswear
See Clothing

Sportswriters
See Writers

Staff Management Relations
See Human Resources; Labour Relations

Staff Training & Development
See also Skills Education; Vocational & Technical Education
Ontario Municipal Management Institute, 976

Standards
See also Consumer Protection; Employment Standards; Testing
Auditing Association of Canada, 844
Canadian General Standards Board, 869
Canadian Standards Association, 888
Consumers International, 903
Consumers' Association of Canada, 904
International Organization for Standardization, 941
Association pour la protection des intérêts des consommateurs de la Côte-Nord, 841

Statistics
Alberta Society of Surveying & Mapping Technologies, 819
Canadian Institute for Health Information, 872
Council of Canadian Fire Marshals & Fire Commissioners, 904

Steel Industry
American Iron & Steel Institute, 823
Canadian Institute of Steel Construction, 875
Canadian Sheet Steel Building Institute, 885
Canadian Steel Construction Council, 889
Canadian Steel Partnership Council, 889
Canadian Steel Producers Association, 889
Steel Recycling Institute, 1010

Steel, Structural
See Steel Industry

Stem Cells
Stem Cell Network, 1010

Stereology
See Biophysics

Stewardship
See Environment

Stock Growers
See Breeding; Cattle; Livestock

Stocks & Bonds
See Investment

Strategic Management
See Management

Structural Steel
See Steel Industry

Student Exchanges
Foundation for Educational Exchange Between Canada & the United States of America, 919

Sulphur
See also Chemical Industry
Alberta Sulphur Research Ltd., 820

Surface Mining
See Mining

Surface Rights
See Land Reclamation

Surveying, Land
See Land Surveying

Surveys, Statistical
See Statistics

Sustainable Cities
See also Community Development; Urban Planning
BurlingtonGreen Environmental Association, 852
EcoPerth, 908

EcoSource Mississauga, 908
International Centre for Sustainable Cities, 936
Rideau Environmental Action League, 995
Severn Sound Environmental Association, 1003
Sustainable Urban Development Association, 1011
Sustainable Urban Development Association, 1011
Toronto Environmental Alliance, 1012
Urban Development Institute of Canada, 1016

Sustainable Development
See also Agricultural Engineering; Agriculture; Farms & Farming; Soil Science
African Wildlife Foundation, 813
Alliance for Sustainability, 821
American Farmland Trust, 823
American Fisheries Society, 823
Bas-Saint-Laurent Model Forest, 845
Burrard Inlet Environmental Action Program & Fraser River Estuary Management Program, 852
Citizens' Opposed to Paving the Escarpment, 895
David Suzuki Foundation, 906
Earth Voice, 907
Eastern Ontario Model Forest, 908
Ecological Agriculture Projects, 908
Evergreen, 914
Foothills Research Institute, 918
Friends of the Earth Canada, 921
Fundy Model Forest, 922
Greenspace Alliance of Canada's Capital, 926
Groupe de recherche en écologie sociale, 926
Henry A. Wallace Center for Agricultural & Environmental Policy at Winrock International, 929
Institute of Urban Studies, 934
Intergovernmental Committee on Urban & Regional Research, 934
International Centre for Conservation Education, 936
International Commission of Agricultural & Biosystems Engineering, 937
International Institute for Applied Systems Analysis, 940
International Institute for Sustainable Development, 940
International Institute of Fisheries Economics & Trade, 940
International Society for Ecological Economics, 942
International Union for Conservation of Nature, 944
Lake Abitibi Model Forest, 948
LEAD Canada Inc., 948
Manitoba Model Forest, 951
McGregor Model Forest, 952
Model Forest of Newfoundland and Labrador, 955
New Brunswick Soil & Crop Improvement Association, 961
Nunavut Harvesters Association, 969
Ontario Sustainable Energy Association, 980
Pacific Peoples Partnership, 983
Panos Canada, 984
Panos London, 984
Panos Washington, 984
The Pembina Institute, 985
Prince Albert Model Forest Association Inc., 988
Resource Efficient Agricultural Production, 995
The Rocky Mountain Institute, 996
Saskatchewan Soil Conservation Association, 1001
Society for Ecological Restoration International, 1007
Sustainable Buildings Canada, 1011
Sustainable Development Technology Canada, 1011
UNEP - World Conservation Monitoring Centre, 1014
Union mondiale pour la nature - Bureau de Montréal, 1014
United Nations Development Program, 1015
United Nations Environment Programme, 1015
Waswanipi Cree Model Forest, 1017
Whole Village, 1019
Wildlife Habitat Canada, 1020
World Business Council for Sustainable Development, 1021

Swine
See also Livestock; Pork
Canadian Association of Swine Veterinarians, 859
Canadian Swine Breeders' Association, 889
Canadian Swine Exporters Association, 889

Teacher Education
See Education

Teaching
See also Language Teaching; Music Teachers; Professors; Schools
Association des ingénieurs-professeurs des sciences appliquées, 832
Environmental Educators' Provincial Specialist Association, 912

Technical Writing
See Writers

Technicians & Technologists
Applied Science Technologists & Technicians of British Columbia, 828
Association des technologues en agroalimentaire, 833
Association of Certified Engineering Technicians & Technologists of Prince Edward Island, 835
Association of Engineering Technicians & Technologists of Newfoundland & Labrador, 835
The Association of Science and Engineering Technology Professionals of Alberta, 840
British Columbia Food Technolgists, 847
Canadian Council of Technicians & Technologists, 865
Canadian Society for Medical Laboratory Science, 886
Certified Technicians & Technologists Association of Manitoba, 894
Institute of Food Technologists, 932
New Brunswick Society of Certified Engineering Technicians & Technologists, 961
Ontario Association of Certified Engineering Technicians & Technologists, 971
Ordre des technologues professionnels du Québec, 982
Saskatchewan Applied Science Technologists & Technicians, 998
TechNova, 1011

Technology
See also Biotechnology; High Technology; Industrial Materials, Advanced; Medical Technology; Research; Technicians & Technologists
Alberta Sulphur Research Ltd., 820
American Association for the Advancement of Science, 822
British Columbia Technology Industries Association, 850
Canadian Advanced Technology Alliance, 854
Canadian Environmental Technology Advancement Corporation - West, 867
Canadian Innovation Centre, 872
Canadian Institute of Food Science & Technology, 874
International Association of Science & Technology for Development, 936
International Union of Food Science & Technology, 945
Materials & Manufacturing Ontario, Division of OCE Inc., 952
Newfoundland & Labrador Association of Technology Companies, 962
SHAD Valley International, 1003
Society for Canadian Women in Science & Technology, 1006

Telephone Sales
See Direct Marketing

Tender Fruit
See Fruit & Vegetables

Terrestrial Ecology
See Ecology

Testing
See also Laboratories; Standards
Association des consultants et laboratoires experts, 831
Canadian Associated Air Balance Council, 855
Canadian Institute for NDE, 872

The Elderly
See Senior Citizens

The Three Rs
See Recycling

Theatre
See also Actors; Drama; Musical Theatre; Performing Arts; Playwriting
Green Kids Inc., 925

Therapy
See also Art Therapy; Chemotherapy; Counselling; Family Therapy; Occupational Therapy; Respiratory Therapy; Sex Therapy
Canadian Horticultural Therapy Association, 871

Therapy, Respiratory
See Respiratory Therapy

Thermal Insulation
See Insulation

Thermal Power
See Energy

Associations Subject Index

Third World
See Developing Countries

Thoracic Health
See Lung Disorders & Diseases

Thoroughbred Horses
See Horses

Threatened Species
See Wildlife Conservation

Timber Management
See Forest Industries; Forestry

Timesharing
See Vacation Industry

Tires
Ontario Tire Dealers Association, 980
Rubber Manufacturers Association, 997
Tire Stewardship BC Association, 1012
Western Canada Tire Dealers Association, 1018

Tour Organizers
See Meetings & Conventions

Tourism
See also Business Travel; Hospitality Industry; Hotels & Motels; Resorts; Travel Industry
Association for Mountain Parks Protection & Enjoyment, 833
Green Tourism Association, 926
Ontario Farm & Country Accommodations Association, 973
Wilderness Tourism Association, 1020
Yukon Tourism Education Council, 1024

Tourist Trade
See Tourism

Town Planning
See Community Planning; Urban Planning

Towns & Townships
See Municipal Government; Single Industry Communities; Urban Planning

Toxic Wastes
See Hazardous Wastes

Toxicology
See also Physiology; Poison
Canadian Network of Toxicology Centres, 879
Society of Environmental Toxicology & Chemistry, 1008
Society of Toxicology, 1008
Society of Toxicology of Canada, 1009

Trade
See also Boards of Trade; Commerce; Export Trade; Free Trade; Import Trade; International Trade
Canadian Council of Chief Executives, 864
Can-Am Border Trade Alliance, 892
International Institute of Fisheries Economics & Trade, 940
Saskatchewan Trade & Export Partnership Inc., 1002
United Nations Conference on Trade & Development, 1015

Trade Shows
See Exhibitions & Fairs

Trade Unions
See Labour Unions

Trade, Export
See Export Trade

Trade, Import
See Import Trade

Trade, International
See International Trade

Traffic
See Transportation

Trails
See Hiking

Training
See Staff Training & Development; Vocational & Technical Education

Transport
See Transportation

Transportation
See also Harbours & Ports; Transportation Sustainability; Trucks & Trucking
Air Transport Association of Canada, 814
Alberta Motor Transport Association, 818
Association québécoise du transport et des routes inc., 842
Canadian Automobile Association, 859
Canadian Bus Association, 860
Canadian Council of Motor Transport Administrators, 865
Canadian Industrial Transportation Association, 872
Canadian Institute of Traffic & Transportation, 875
Canadian Transportation Research Forum, 889
Canadian Urban Transit Association, 889
Canadians for Responsible & Safe Highways, 892
Chartered Institute of Logistics and Transport in North America, 894
Electric Vehicle Council of Ottawa Inc., 909
Electric Vehicle Society of Canada, 909
Freight Carriers Association of Canada, 920
Industrial Truck Association, 931
Institute of Transportation Engineers, 933
International Heavy Haul Association, 940
Ontario Community Transit Association, 972
Ontario Good Roads Association, 974
Ontario Traffic Conference, 980
Ontario Trucking Association, 980
Private Motor Truck Council of Canada, 989
Saskatchewan Trucking Association, 1002
Toronto Transportation Society, 1013
Transport Action Canada, 1013
Transportation Association of Canada, 1013
The Van Horne Institute for International Transportation & Regulatory Affairs, 1016
Western Transportation Advisory Council, 1019

Transportation Sustainability
INFORM Inc., 931

Trapping
See Fur Trade

Travel Agents
See Travel Industry

Travel Industry
See also Tourism; Vacation Industry
Canadian Automobile Association, 859

Travel Writers
See Writers

Tree Planting
See Arboriculture; Forestry

Trial Lawyers
See Lawyers

Trolleys
See Transportation

Tropical Diseases
See Diseases

Tropical Forests
See Rainforests

Tropical Medicine
See Medicine

Trout
Prince Edward Island Finfish Growers Association, 988
Trout Unlimited Canada, 1013

Trucks & Trucking
See also Antique Automobiles & Trucks; Freight Services; Transportation
Alberta Motor Transport Association, 818
Association du camionnage du Québec inc., 833
Atlantic Provinces Trucking Association, 843
British Columbia Trucking Association, 850
Canadian Trucking Alliance, 889
Canadians for Responsible & Safe Highways, 892
Industrial Truck Association, 931
Manitoba Trucking Association, 952
Ontario Trucking Association, 980
Private Motor Truck Council of Canada, 989
Saskatchewan Trucking Association, 1002

Tunnelling
Tunnelling Association of Canada, 1014

Turkeys
See Poultry

Typography
See Printing Industries

U.N.
See United Nations

Underwater Archaeology
Alberta Underwater Council, 820
Save Ontario Shipwrecks, 1002
Underwater Archaeological Society of British Columbia, 1014

Underwater Sports
See Aquatic Sports

Unions
See Labour Unions

United Kingdom
See British Isles

United Nations
United Nations Association in Canada, 1015
United Nations Conference on Trade & Development, 1015
United Nations Development Program, 1015
United Nations Environment Programme, 1015
United Nations Industrial Development Organization, 1015

Unity, Canadian
See Canada & Canadian Studies

Universities & Colleges
See also Deans; Faculty & Staff Associations; Graduate Studies; Professors; Students; University & College Libraries
Association of Canadian Universities for Northern Studies, 834
Association of University Forestry Schools of Canada, 840

Uranium
See also Nuclear Energy
World Nuclear Association, 1022

Urban Agriculture
See Horticulture

Urban Development
See Community Development; Urban Planning

Urban Geography
See Geography

Urban Planning
See also Community Planning; Regional Planning; Sustainable Cities
Association québécoise d'urbanisme, 841
Canadian Institute of Planners, 875
Institute of Urban Studies, 934
Intergovernmental Committee on Urban & Regional Research, 934
International Centre for Sustainable Cities, 936
International Federation for Housing & Planning, 939
International Society of City & Regional Planners, 943
Ordre des urbanistes du Québec, 982
Urban Development Institute of Canada, 1016
World Society for Ekistics, 1023

Urban Policy
See Community Development; Municipal Government; Urban Planning

Urethane
See also Insulation
Canadian Urethane Manufacturers Association, 890

Utilities
See Public Utilities

Vacation Industry
See also Cottages; Hotels & Motels; Resorts; Tourism; Travel Industry
British Columbia Lodging & Campgrounds Association, 848
Ontario Farm & Country Accommodations Association, 973

Vaccine
Canadian Network for Vaccines & Immunotherapeutics, 879

Valuation
See Appraisal

Vegetarians
See also Vegans

Associations Subject Index

Earthsave Canada, 907

Vehicles
See Automobiles; Motor Vehicles

Veterinary Medicine
See also Animal Science
American Association of Bovine Practitioners, 822
Canadian Animal Health Institute, 855
Canadian Association of Animal Health Technologists & Technicians, 856
Canadian Association of Swine Veterinarians, 859
Canadian Veterinary Medical Association, 890
International Council for Laboratory Animal Science, 937

Victims, Industrial Accident
See Injured Workers; Workers' Compensation

Vintage Locomotives
See Railroads & Railways

Vintage Radio
See Radio Broadcasting

Vinyl
See also Plastics
The Vinyl Institute, 1017

Visitors & Convention Bureaus
See Meetings & Conventions; Tourism

Visual Merchandising
See Advertising

Vivisection
See Animal Welfare

Volunteer Firemen
See Fire Fighting

Waste Management
See also Environment Industry; Hazardous Wastes; Industrial Waste; Recycling; Water & Wastewater
Action: Environment, 813
Air & Waste Management Association, 814
Alberta Plastics Recycling Association, 818
Atlantic Canada Water & Wastewater Association, 842
British Columbia Water & Waste Association, 850
Center for Health, Environment & Justice, 893
Centre de formation en entreprise et récupération, 893
Citizens for a Safe Environment, 895
Citizens' Clearinghouse on Waste Management, 895
Clean Nova Scotia, 896
Ecology Action Centre, 908
Electronics Product Stewardship Canada, 909
Environmental Action Barrie, 911
The Environmental Coalition of PEI, 911
Environmental Education Ontario, 912
Film & Bag Federation, 916
Green Action Centre, 925
International Solid Waste Association, 944
Municipal Waste Association, 955
National Solid Wastes Management Association, 958
Ontario Waste Management Association, 981
Pickering & Ajax Citizens Together for the Environment, 986
Pitch-In Alberta, 987
Pitch-In Canada, 987
Recycling Council of Alberta, 993
Recycling Council of British Columbia, 993
Société québécoise de récupération et de recyclage, 1006
Solid Waste Association of North America, 1009
Warmer Bulletin - Residua Ltd., 1017

Waste Reduction
See Recycling

Wastewater
See Water & Wastewater

Water & Wastewater
See also Pumps
Alberta Water & Wastewater Operators Association, 820
Atlantic Canada Water & Wastewater Association, 842
British Columbia Water & Waste Association, 850
Canadian Water & Wastewater Association, 890
Canadian Water Network, 890
Canadian Water Quality Association, 890
International Solid Waste Association, 944
IRC International Water & Sanitation Centre, 946
Manitoba Water & Wastewater Association, 952

New Brunswick Ground Water Association, 961
Ontario Sewer & Watermain Construction Association, 978
Water Environment Association of Ontario, 1017
Water Environment Federation, 1017
Western Canada Water, 1019

Water Chemistry
See Chemistry

Water Pollution
See also Acid Rain
American Water Works Association, 826
Bonn Agreement, 846
Canadian Association on Water Quality, 859
Clean Water Action, 896
International Water Association, 946
Ontario Municipal Water Association, 976
Ontario Water Works Association, 981
OSPAR Commission, 983
Société québécoise d'assainissement des eaux, 1006
Water Environment Association of Ontario, 1017
Water Environment Federation, 1017
WaterCan, 1018

Water Resources
See also Hydrogeology; Hydrology; Limnology; Rivers & Streams
Alberta Irrigation Projects Association, 818
Alberta Lake Management Society, 818
Alberta Water Council, 820
Alberta Water Well Drilling Association, 820
American Water Resources Association, 826
Canadian Water & Wastewater Association, 890
Canadian Water Network, 890
Canadian Water Resources Association, 891
Elora Environment Centre, 909
Fédération des associations pour la protection de l'environnement des lacs inc., 914
International Association for Environmental Hydrology, 935
International Water Association, 946
IRC International Water & Sanitation Centre, 946
National Ground Water Association, 958
North Saskatchewan Watershed Alliance, 966
Northeast Avalon ACAP, Inc., 966
Ontario Ground Water Association, 974
Ontario Water Works Association, 981
Soil & Water Conservation Society, 1009
Swift Current Creek Watershed Stewards, 1011
Water Environment Federation, 1017
WaterCan, 1018
World Association of Industrial & Technological Research Organizations, 1021

Water Sports
See Aquatic Sports

Water Supply
See also Wells
American Water Works Association, 826
Atlantic Canada Water & Wastewater Association, 842
Bedeque Bay Environmental Management Association, 845
British Columbia Water & Waste Association, 850
Canadian Ground Water Association, 870
IRC International Water & Sanitation Centre, 946
Manitoba Water Well Association, 952
Newfoundland/Labrador Ground Water Association, 964
Ontario Ground Water Association, 974
Ontario Municipal Water Association, 976
Ontario Water Works Association, 981
Prince Edward Island Ground Water Association, 988
Saskatchewan Ground Water Association, 1000
Water Environment Federation, 1017

Water, Bottled
See Bottled Water

Water-Borne Contaminants
See Water & Wastewater

Waterfowl
See Ducks; Wildlife; Wildlife Conservation

Waterfront
See Harbours & Ports

Watermains
See Water & Wastewater

Watershed & Reservoir Management
See Great Lakes; Limnology; Rivers & Streams; Water Resources

Waterways
See Locks & Canals

Weeds
See Horticulture

Wellness
See Health

Wells
See also Drilling; Water Resources; Water Supply
Association des enterprises spécialiseés en eau du Québec, 832
British Columbia Ground Water Association, 848
Canadian Ground Water Association, 870
Manitoba Water Well Association, 952
New Brunswick Ground Water Association, 961
Newfoundland/Labrador Ground Water Association, 964
Nova Scotia Ground Water Association, 968
Ontario Ground Water Association, 974
Prince Edward Island Ground Water Association, 988
Saskatchewan Ground Water Association, 1000

Wetlands, Conservation of
See Conservation of Natural Resources; Limnology

Whales
See Marine Mammals

Wharfs
See Harbours & Ports

Wheat
Ontario Wheat Producers' Marketing Board, 981

Whitewater Canoeing
See Canoeing & Rafting

Whitewater Rafting
See Canoeing & Rafting

Wilderness
See also Conservation of Natural Resources; Parks; Rainforests
Alberta Native Plant Council, 818
Alberta Wilderness Association, 820
American Wildlands, 827
Canadian Parks & Wilderness Society, 881
Conservation International, 901
Earthroots, 907
Outward Bound Canada, 983
Quetico Foundation, 992
Sierra Club, 1003
Sierra Club of British Columbia, 1004
Sierra Club of Canada, 1004
Sierra Club of Canada - Ontario Chapter, 1004
Sierra Club of Canada - Prairie Chapter, 1004
Sierra Youth Coalition, 1004
Valhalla Wilderness Society, 1016
Western Canada Wilderness Committee, 1019
Wilderness Tourism Association, 1020

Wilderness Gardeners
See Horticulture

Wildflowers
See Flowers

Wildlife
See also Animal Welfare; Fish & Game; Fur Trade; Wildlife Conservation; Zoos
African Wildlife Foundation, 813
Association of Fish & Wildlife Agencies, 835
British Columbia Waterfowl Society, 850
Canadian Association for Humane Trapping, 855
Canadian Wildlife Federation, 891
Ducks Unlimited Canada, 906
East African Wild Life Society, 907
Fédération québécoise des chasseurs et pêcheurs, 916
Fondation de la faune du Québec, 917
Fur-Bearer Defenders, 922
Grand Manan Wildlife Association, 924
Hope for Wildlife Society, 930
International Wildlife Coalition, 946
Lambton Wildlife Incorporated, 948
Manitoba Wildlife Federation, 952
Moose Jaw Wildlife Federation, 955

Associations Subject Index

National Wildlife Federation, 958
New Brunswick Wildlife Federation, 962
Newfoundland & Labrador Wildlife Federation, 963
Prince Edward Island Wildlife Federation, 989
Regina Wildlife Federation, 994
Saskatchewan Wildlife Federation, 1002
Saskatoon Wildlife Federation, 1002
Weyburn Wildlife Federation, 1019
Wildlife Habitat Canada, 1020
Wildlife Rescue Association of British Columbia, 1020

Wildlife Conservation
African Coelacanth Ecosystem Programme, 813
American Wildlands, 827
American Zoo & Aquarium Association, 827
Animal Alliance of Canada, 827
Animal Defence League of Canada, 827
Annapolis Field Naturalist Society, 828
Association of Fish & Wildlife Agencies, 835
Ducks Unlimited Canada, 906
Earthroots, 907
East African Wild Life Society, 907
Elsa Wild Animal Appeal of Canada, 909
Foundation for Environmental Conservation, 919
Friends of Nature Conservation Society, 921
Friends of the Delta Marsh Field Station, 921
Friends of the Earth International, 921
Hope for Wildlife Society, 930
International Association for Bear Research & Management, 934
International Primate Protection League, 942
International Union for Conservation of Nature, 944
International Whaling Commission, 946
International Wildlife Rehabilitation Council, 946
The Jane Goodal Institute of Canada, 946
The Jane Goodall Institute for Wildlife Research, Education & Conservation, 946
The Jane Goodall Institute of Canada, 946
Northwest Wildlife Preservation Society, 967
Nunavut Harvesters Association, 969
Ottawa Duck Club, 983
Sea Shepherd Conservation Society, 1002
Sea Shepherd Conservation Society - USA, 1002
Sierra Club, 1003
Sierra Club of British Columbia, 1004
Sierra Club of Canada, 1004
Sierra Club of Canada - Ontario Chapter, 1004
Sierra Club of Canada - Prairie Chapter, 1004
Sierra Youth Coalition, 1004
Société québécoise pour la défense des animaux, 1006
Sunshine Coast Natural History Society, 1011
Toronto Zoo, 1013
Union mondiale pour la nature - Bureau de Montréal, 1014
Wild Bird Care Centre, 1020
Wildlife Preservation Canada, 1020
Wildlife Rescue Association of British Columbia, 1020
World Blue Chain for the Protection of Animals & Nature, 1021
World Society for the Protection of Animals, 1023
World Wildlife Fund - Canada, 1023
World Wildlife Fund - USA, 1023
WWF International, 1024
ZOOCHECK Canada Inc., 1025
Zoological Society of Montréal, 1025

Wind Energy
See Wind Engineering

Wind Engineering
Canadian Wind Energy Association Inc., 891

Windmills
See Wind Engineering

Wire Services
See Journalism

Women
See also Native Women; Religious Orders of Women; Violence Against Women; Women & Health; Women & Politics; Women & Religion; Women & the Arts; Women & the Environment; Women in Business, Industry & Trade; Women in Professions; Women in Sports; Women in the Mass Media
Association des fermières de l'Ontario, 832
Breast Cancer Action, 846
Fédération des agricultrices du Québec, 914

Women & Health
Panos Canada, 984
Panos London, 984
Panos Washington, 984

Women & the Environment
British Columbia Women's Institutes, 850
The Ladies of the Lake, 947
Women's Environment & Development Organization, 1021
Women's Healthy Environments Network, 1021

Women in Professions
See also Women in Business, Industry & Trade
NSERC/Petro-Canada Chair for Women in Science & Engineering, 969
Society for Canadian Women in Science & Technology, 1006

Women in the Mass Media
See also Women & the Arts
Panos Canada, 984
Panos London, 984
Panos Washington, 984

Wood
See also Building Materials; Forest Industries; Lumber Industry; Wood Energy
American Forest & Paper Association, 823
British Columbia Wood Specialities Group Association, 851
Canadian Federation of Woodlot Owners, 868
Canadian Plywood Association, 882
Canadian Wood Council, 891
Canadian Wood Preservers Bureau, 892
La Fédération des producteurs de bois du Québec, 914
International Research Group on Wood Protection, 942
Wood Preservation Canada, 1021

Wood Energy
Wood Energy Technology Transfer Inc., 1021

Wood Industry
See Lumber Industry

Wood Pallets
See Pallets (Shipping, Storage, etc.)

Woodlots
See Lumber Industry

Woods, Biomass
See Biomass Energy

Wool
See also Sheep
Canadian Co-operative Wool Growers Ltd., 864

Work Place Environment
See Quality of Working Life

Workers' Compensation
See also Injured Workers; Occupational Health & Safety
Industrial Accident Victims Group of Ontario, 930
Institute for Work & Health, 932

World Development
See Developing Countries; International Cooperation

World Trade
See International Trade

World Wide Web
See Internet

Writers
See also Crime Writers; Journalism; Playwriting; Publishing
Association of Great Lakes Outdoor Writers, 835
Canadian Farm Writers' Federation, 867
Canadian Science Writers' Association, 884
Outdoor Writers of Canada, 983

Yachts
See Boats

Youth
See also Agriculture & Youth; Children; Streetkids; Students
Canadian 4-H Council, 854
Cercles des jeunes naturalistes, 894
Environmental Youth Alliance, 913
Environnement jeunesse, 913
Sierra Youth Coalition, 1004
Youth Challenge International, 1024

Zoology
See also Zoos
Canadian Society of Zoologists, 888
International Council for Archaeozoology, 937
Société des établissements de plein air du Québec, 1005

Zoos
See also Parks
American Zoo & Aquarium Association, 827
Calgary Zoological Society, 852
Canadian Association of Zoos & Aquariums, 859
Jardin zoologique du Québec, 946
Toronto Zoo, 1013
ZOOCHECK Canada Inc., 1025
Zoological Society of Manitoba, 1025
Zoological Society of Montréal, 1025

Associations Acronym Index

A

A&WMA - Air & Waste Management Association, 814
AAAF - Association of Alberta Agricultural Fieldmen, 834
AAAS - Alberta Association of Agricultural Societies, 815
AAAS - American Association for the Advancement of Science, 822
AABGA - American Association of Botanical Gardens & Arboreta, 822
AABP - American Association of Bovine Practitioners, 822
AAC - Animal Alliance of Canada, 827
AAC - Auditing Association of Canada, 844
AAC - Aquaculture Association of Canada, 828
AACC - Avicultural Advancement Council of Canada, 844
AAEA - Alberta Agricultural Economics Association, 815
AAEE - Australian Association for Environmental Education, 844
AAG - Association of American Geographers, 834
AAIA - Allergy Asthma Information Association, 821
AALA - Alberta Association of Landscape Architects, 815
AAMD&C - Alberta Association of Municipal Districts & Counties, 815
AANB - Agricultural Alliance of New Brunswick, 813
AANS - Aquaculture Association of Nova Scotia, 828
AAO - Acoustical Association Ontario, 813
AAPG - The American Association of Petroleum Geologists, 822
AAPQ - Association des architectes paysagistes du Québec, 831
AARQ - Association des Aménagistes Régionaux du Québec, 831
ABA - American Birding Association, 822
ABCFP - Association of British Columbia Forest Professionals, 834
ABCLS - Association of British Columbia Land Surveyors, 834
ABDA - Alberta Bottle Depot Association, 816
ABEC - Alberta Building Envelope Council (South), 816
ABP - Alberta Beef Producers, 815
ACA - Alberta Construction Association, 816
ACA - Alberta Camping Association, 816
ACA - Alberta Conservation Association, 816
ACCA - American Cave Conservation Association, 822
ACCES - Atlantic Canada Centre for Environmental Science, 842
ACE - Association of Canadian Ergonomists, 834
ACEC - Association of Consulting Engineering Companies - Canada, 835
ACEC-NB - Association of Consulting Engineering Companies - New Brunswick, 835
ACEEE - American Council for an Energy-Efficient Economy, 823
ACEP - African Coelacanth Ecosystem Programme, 813
ACETTPEI - Association of Certified Engineering Technicians & Technologists of Prince Edward Island, 835
ACFAS - Association francophone pour le savoir, 833
ACLE - Association des consultants et laboratoires experts, 831
ACO - The Architectural Conservancy of Ontario, 828
ACORN - Atlantic Canadian Organic Regional Network, 843
ACPA - Association of Canadian Port Authorities, 834
ACPA - Association of the Chemical Profession of Alberta, 840
ACPC - Alberta Canola Producers Commission, 816
ACPO - Association of the Chemical Profession of Ontario, 840
ACQ - Association du camionnage du Québec inc., 833
ACS - Amalgamated Conservation Society, 821
ACSIQ - Association des chefs en sécurité incendie du Québec, 831
ACSR - Association canadienne des sciences régionales, 830
ACTS - Alberta Conservation Tillage Society II, 816
ACUNS - Association of Canadian Universities for Northern Studies, 834
ACWWA - Atlantic Canada Water & Wastewater Association, 842
ADAV - Animal Defence & Anti-Vivisection Society of BC, 827
ADC - Atlantic Dairy Council, 843
ADLC - Animal Defence League of Canada, 827
AEAQ - Association des expositions agricoles du Québec, 832
AEAQ - Association des entomologistes amateurs du Québec inc., 832
AEEQ - Association des embouteilleurs d'eau du Québec, 831
AEESP - Association of Environmental Engineering & Science Professors, 835
AEG - Association of Applied Geochemists, 834
AEM-Canada - Association of Equipment Manufacturers - Canada, 835
AEMQ - Association de l'exploration minière de Québec, 831
AEN - Alberta Environmental Network, 816
AES - Acadian Entomological Society, 813
AESAC - Associated Environmental Site Assessors of Canada, 829
AETTNL - Association of Engineering Technicians & Technologists of Newfoundland & Labrador, 835
AF&PA - American Forest & Paper Association, 823
AFFPA - Alberta Farm Fresh Producers Association, 816
AFGA - Alberta Fish & Game Association, 817
AFMA - Alberta Farmers' Market Association, 817
AFN - Alouette Field Naturalists, 821
AFN - Assembly of First Nations, 829
AFNS - Annapolis Field Naturalist Society, 828
AFO - Association des fermières de l'Ontario, 832
AFPA - Alberta Forest Products Association, 817
AFPR - Alliance of Foam Packaging Recyclers, 821
AFS - American Fisheries Society, 823
AFT - American Farmland Trust, 823
AGGA - Alberta Greenhouse Growers Association, 817
AGLOW - Association of Great Lakes Outdoor Writers, 835
AHRF - Alberta Historical Resources Foundation, 817
AHSS - Architectural Heritage Society of Saskatchewan, 828
AIA - Archaeological Institute of America, 828
AIAC - Aerospace Industries Association of Canada, 813
AIAC - Automotive Industries Association of Canada, 844
AIAMC - Association of International Automobile Manufacturers of Canada, 836
AIC - Agricultural Institute of Canada, 814
AICF - Agricultural Institute of Canada Foundation, 814
AICQ - Association des ingénieurs-conseils du Québec, 832
AIHA - American Industrial Hygiene Association, 823
AIMQ - Association des ingénieurs municipaux du Québec, 832
AINA - Arctic Institute of North America, 829
AIPA - Alberta Irrigation Projects Association, 818
AIPSA - Association des ingénieurs-professeurs des sciences appliquées, 832
AIQ - Association d'isolation du Québec, 831
AISI - American Iron & Steel Institute, 823
AJQ - Association des jardineries du Québec, 832
AJRQ - Association des jeunes ruraux du Québec, 832
ALA - American Lung Association, 823
ALMS - Alberta Lake Management Society, 818
ALPHA - Association of Local Public Health Agencies, 836
ALSA - Alberta Land Surveyors' Association, 818
AMANB - Association of Municipal Administrators of New Brunswick, 836
AMANS - Association of Municipal Administrators, Nova Scotia, 836
AMEA - Algoma Manitoulin Environmental Awareness, 820
AMEBC - Association for Mineral Exploration British Columbia, 833
AMM - Association of Manitoba Municipalities, 836
AMO - Association of Municipalities of Ontario, 836
AMPCO - Association of Major Power Consumers in Ontario, 836
AMPPE - Association for Mountain Parks Protection & Enjoyment, 833
AMQ - Association médicale du Québec, 833
AMQ - Association des microbiologistes du Québec, 833
AMQ - Association minière du Québec, 834
AMSSCQ - Association des médecins spécialistes en santé communautaire du Québec, 833
AMTA - Alberta Motor Transport Association, 818
ANAC - Animal Nutrition Association of Canada, 827
ANBLS - Association of New Brunswick Land Surveyors, 837
ANPC - Alberta Native Plant Council, 818
ANSLS - Association of Nova Scotia Land Surveyors, 837
AOHNA - Alberta Occupational Health Nurses Association, 818
AOLS - Association of Ontario Land Surveyors, 837
AOPA - Alberta Organic Producers Association, 818
AOU - American Ornithologists' Union, 824
APA - American Planning Association, 824
APALA - Atlantic Provinces Association of Landscape Architects, 843
APAO - Aggregate Producers' Association of Ontario, 813
APAS - Agricultural Producers Association of Saskatchewan, 814
APB - Association of Professional Biology, 837
APC - American Plastics Council, 824
APCAS - Association pour la prévention de la contamination de l'air et du sol, 841
APCEL - Asia-Pacific Centre for Environmental Law, 829
APCHQ - Association provinciale des constructeurs d'habitations du Québec inc., 841
APCO - Atlantic Pest Control Association, 843
APCS - Atlantic Provinces Council on the Sciences, 843
APEGBC - Association of Professional Engineers & Geoscientists of British Columbia, 838
APEGGA - Association of Professional Engineers, Geologists & Geophysicists of Alberta, 839
APEGM - Association of Professional Engineers & Geoscientists of Manitoba, 838
APEGNB - Association of Professional Engineers & Geoscientists of New Brunswick, 838
APEGS - Association of Professional Engineers & Geoscientists of Saskatchewan, 838
APEILS - Association of Prince Edward Island Land Surveyors, 837
APENS - Association of Professional Engineers of Nova Scotia, 838
APEPEI - Association of Professional Engineers of Prince Edward Island, 839
APEY - Association of Professional Engineers of the Yukon Territory, 839
APF - The Avian Preservation Foundation, 844
APFC - Asia Pacific Foundation of Canada, 829
APGNS - Association of Professional Geoscientists of Nova Scotia, 839
APGO - Association of Professional Geoscientists of Ontario, 839
APGQ - Association professionnelle des géographes du Québec, 841
APHA - Alberta Public Health Association, 819
API - Atlantic Planners Institute, 843
APIGQ - Association professionnelle des ingénieurs du gouvernement du Québec (ind.), 841
APMA - Automotive Parts Manufacturers' Association, 844
APOS - Alberta Professional Outfitters Society, 819
APPrO - Association of Power Producers of Ontario, 837
APR - Association of Postconsumer Plastic Recyclers, 837
APRA - Alberta Plastics Recycling Association, 818
APSAM - Association paritaire pour la santé et la sécurité du travail - Affaires municipales, 840
APSM - Association paritaire pour la santé et la sécurité du travail - Mines et services miniers, 841
APTA - Atlantic Provinces Trucking Association, 843
APWA - American Public Works Association, 824
AQEI - Association québécoise pour l'évaluation d'impacts, 842
AQGN - Association québécoise du gaz naturel, 842
AQGP - Association québécoise de la gestion parasitaire, 841
AQHSST - Association québécoise pour l'hygiène, la santé et la sécurité du travail, 842
AQIP - Association québécoise de l'industrie de la pêche, 841
AQLPA - Association québécoise de lutte contre la pollution atmosphérique, 841
AQME - Association québécoise pour la maîtrise de l'énergie, 842
AQOCI - Association québécoise des organismes de coopération internationale, 842
AQSA - Association of Quantity Surveyors of Alberta, 839
AQTA - Association québécoise du transport aérien, 842
AQTR - Association québécoise du transport et des routes inc., 842
AQU - Association québécoise d'urbanisme, 841
ARC - Automotive Recyclers of Canada, 844
ARCH - Action to Restore a Clean Humber, 813
ARPA - Alberta Recreation & Parks Association, 819
ARPFNB - Association of Registered Professional Foresters of New Brunswick, 839
ASEH - American Society for Environmental History, 824
ASET - The Association of Science and Engineering Technology Professionals of Alberta, 840
ASF - Atlantic Salmon Federation, 843
ASFETM - Association sectorielle - Fabrication d'équipement de transport et de machines, 842
ASH - Action on Smoking & Health, 813
ASHRAE - American Society of Heating, Refrigerating & Air Conditioning Engineers, 824
ASME - American Society of Mechanical Engineers, 824
ASMR - American Society of Mining & Reclamation, 825
ASOC - Antarctic & Southern Ocean Coalition, 828
ASPB - Alberta Society of Professional Biologists, 819
ASPB - American Society of Plant Biologists, 826
ASPE - American Society of Plumbing Engineers, 826
ASPHIO - Association of Supervisors of Public Health Inspectors (Ontario), 840
ASPQ - Association pour la santé publique du Québec, 841
ASRL - Alberta Sulphur Research Ltd., 820
ASS - Alberta Speleological Society, 820
ASSE - American Society of Safety Engineers, 826
ASSIFQ-ASSPPQ - Association de la santé et de la sécurité des pâtes et papiers et des industries de la forêt du Québec, 831
ASSMT - Alberta Society of Surveying & Mapping Technologies, 819
ASTTBC - Applied Science Technologists & Technicians of British Columbia, 828
ATA - Association des technologues en agroalimentaire, 833
ATAC - Air Transport Association of Canada, 814
ATQ - Les AmiEs de la Terre de Québec, 827
ATRC - Atlantic Turfgrass Research Foundation, 843
AUC - Alberta Underwater Council, 820
AUFSC - Association of University Forestry Schools of Canada, 840
AUMA - Alberta Urban Municipalities Association, 820
AVA - Action Volunteers for Animals, 813
AWA - Alberta Wilderness Association, 820
AWC - Association of World Citizens & World Citizens Foundation, 840

800 GUIDE DES RESSOURCES ENVIRONNEMENTALES CANADIENNES 2011-2012

Associations Acronym Index

AWF - Animal Welfare Foundation of Canada, 827
AWF - African Wildlife Foundation, 813
AWL - American Wildlands, 827
AWR - Alliance for the Wild Rockies, 821
AWRA - American Water Resources Association, 826
AWWA - American Water Works Association, 826
AWWDA - Alberta Water Well Drilling Association, 820
AWWOA - Alberta Water & Wastewater Operators Association, 820
AYC - Association of Yukon Communities, 840
AZA - American Zoo & Aquarium Association, 827

B

BAS - Battlefords Agricultural Society, 845
BAS - Binbrook Agricultural Society, 845
BBEMA - Bedeque Bay Environmental Management Association, 845
BBO - Beaverhill Bird Observatory, 845
BCA - Breast Cancer Action, 846
BCARA - British Columbia Association for Regenerative Agriculture, 846
BCBDA - British Columbia Bottle Depot Association, 847
BCCA - British Columbia Construction Association, 847
BCCA - British Columbia Cattlemen's Association, 847
BCCF - British Columbia Conservation Foundation, 847
BCEIA - British Columbia Environment Industry Association, 847
BCEN - British Columbia Environmental Network, 847
BCFIRB - British Columbia Farm Industry Review Board, 847
BCGWA - British Columbia Ground Water Association, 848
BCHGA - British Columbia Herb Growers Association, 848
BCIA - British Columbia Institute of Agrologists, 848
BCLA - British Columbia Lung Association, 848
BCLCA - British Columbia Lodging & Campgrounds Association, 848
BCLNA - British Columbia Landscape & Nursery Association, 848
BCMA - British Columbia Medical Association, 849
BCMTA - British Columbia Marine Trades Association, 849
BCOHN - Occupational Health Nurses of British Columbia, 969
BCPMA - British Columbia Paint Manufacturers' Association, 849
BCRPA - British Columbia Recreation & Parks Association, 849
BCRSP - Board of Canadian Registered Safety Professionals, 846
BCSEA - British Columbia Sustainable Energy Association, 850
BCSFA - British Columbia Salmon Farmers Association, 849
BCSGA - British Columbia Shellfish Growers Association, 849
BCSLA - British Columbia Society of Landscape Architects, 850
BCTA - British Columbia Trucking Association, 850
BCTF - British Columbia Food Technolgists, 847
BCTIA - British Columbia Technology Industries Association, 850
BCWI - British Columbia Women's Institutes, 850
BCWWA - British Columbia Water & Waste Association, 850
BFN - Brereton Field Naturalists' Club Inc., 846
BIEAP/FREMP - Burrard Inlet Environmental Action Program & Fraser River Estuary Management Program, 852
BIR - Bureau of International Recycling, 851
BLMS - Brantford Lapidary & Mineral Society Inc., 846
BNS - Blomidon Naturalists Society, 846
BONN - Bonn Agreement, 846
BOPA - Boundary Organic Producers Association, 846
BPEG - Bruce Peninsula Environment Group, 851
BRA - Bluewater Recycling Association, 846
BRLA - Big Rideau Lake Association, 845
BSC - Bird Studies Canada, 845
BSC - Biophysical Society of Canada, 845
BSIA of BC - Building Supply Industry Association of British Columbia, 851

C

C2P2 - Canadian Centre for Pollution Prevention, 862
CAA - Canadian Automobile Association, 859
CAA - Canadian Archaeological Association, 855
CAA - Canadian Avalanche Association, 859
CAABC - Canadian Associated Air Balance Council, 855
CAAHTT - Canadian Association of Animal Health Technologists & Technicians, 856
CAAR - Canadian Association of Agri-Retailers, 856
CAC - Cement Association of Canada, 893
CAC - Consumers' Association of Canada, 904
CAC - Canadian Airports Council, 855
CACD - Canadian Association of Chemical Distributors, 857
CADE - Canadian Association of Drilling Engineers, 857
CAE - Canadian Academy of Engineering, 854
CAED - Canadian Association of Equipment Distributors, 857
CAES - Canadian Agricultural Economics Society, 854
CAFC - Canadian Association of Fire Chiefs, 857
CAG - Canadian Association of Geographers, 857
CaGBC - Canada Green Building Council, 853
CAGC - Canadian Association of Geophysical Contractors, 857
CAHI - Canadian Animal Health Institute, 855
CAHSPR - Canadian Association for Health Services & Policy Research, 855
CAHT - Canadian Association for Humane Trapping, 855
CAIA - Canadian Aquaculture Industry Alliance, 855
CALA - Canadian Association for Laboratory Accreditation Inc., 856
CALAS - Canadian Association for Laboratory Animal Science, 856
CAMA - Canadian Agri-Marketing Association (Alberta), 855
CAMB - Canadian Association of Medical Biochemists, 857
CAMEO - Canadian Association for Mine & Explosive Ordnance Security, 856
CAMESE - Canadian Association of Mining Equipment & Services for Export, 858
CAMIRO - Canadian Mining Industry Research Organization, 879
CAMPUT - Canadian Association of Members of Public Utility Tribunals, 857
CANB - Construction Association of New Brunswick Inc., 902
CANCID - The Canadian National Committee for Irrigation & Drainage, 879
CanREA - Canadian Renewable Energy Association, 884
CanSIA - Canadian Solar Industries Association Inc., 888
CanWEA - Canadian Wind Energy Association Inc., 891
CAODC - Canadian Association of Oilwell Drilling Contractors, 858
CAP - Council of Atlantic Premiers, 904
CAP - Canadian Association of Palynologists, 858
CAPE - Canadian Association of Physicians for the Environment, 858
CAPEI - Construction Association of Prince Edward Island, 902
CAPHC - Canadian Association of Professional Heritage Consultants, 858
CAPL - Canadian Association of Petroleum Landmen, 858
CAPP - Canadian Association of Petroleum Producers, 858
CARE - Canadian Association for Renewable Energies, 856
CARI - Canadian Association of Recycling Industries, 858
CARMA - Canadian Rock Mechanics Association, 884
CARNDE - Canadian Association for Research in Nondestructive Evaluation, 856
CARP - Clean Annapolis River Project, 896
CASA - Canadian Agricultural Safety Association, 854
CASA - Clean Air Strategic Alliance, 896
CASC - Canadian Association for Studies in Co-operation, 856
CASI - Canadian Aeronautics & Space Institute, 854
CASLE - Commonwealth Association of Surveying & Land Economy, 898
CASV - Canadian Association of Swine Veterinarians, 859
CATA Alliance - Canadian Advanced Technology Alliance, 854
CAWQ - Canadian Association on Water Quality, 859
CAZA - Canadian Association of Zoos & Aquariums, 859
CBA - Canadian Botanical Association, 860
CBA - Canadian Bar Association, 860
CBA - Canadian Bison Association, 860
CBA - Canadian Bus Association, 860
CBCN - Canadian Botanical Conservation Network, 860
CBS - Canadian Bioethics Society, 860
CBWA - Canadian Bottled Water Association, 860
CCA - Canadian Cartographic Association, 861
CCA - Canadian Construction Association, 863
CCA - Canadian Cattlemen's Association, 861
CCA - Canadian Camping Association, 860
CCAA - Canadian Consulting Agrologists Association, 863
CCAC - Canadian Council on Animal Care, 865
CCBA - Canadian Cattle Breeders' Association, 861
CCCE - Canadian Council of Chief Executives, 864
CCE - Conseil Canadien des Électrotechnologies, 900
CCEA - Canadian Council on Ecological Areas, 865
CCEP - Canadian Centre for Emergency Preparedness, 861
CCFI - Canadian Centre for Fisheries Innovation, 861
CCFM - Canadian Council of Forest Ministers, 864
CCFMFC - Council of Canadian Fire Marshals & Fire Commissioners, 904
CCFMS - Central Canadian Federation of Mineralogical Societies, 893
CCFN - Canadian Council of Food & Nutrition, 864
CCGD - Canadian Council of Grocery Distributors, 864
CCHL - Canadian College of Health Leaders, 863
CCI - Canadian Circumpolar Institute, 862
CCIC - Canadian Council for International Co-operation, 864
CCIL - Canadian Council on International Law, 865
CCIL - Canadian Council of Independent Laboratories, 864
CCLA - Carleton County Law Association, 892
CCLS - Canadian Council of Land Surveyors, 864
CCME - Canadian Council of Ministers of the Environment, 865
CCMTA - Canadian Council of Motor Transport Administrators, 865
CCN - Carrying Capacity Network, 892
CCNB - Conservation Council of New Brunswick, 901
CCNR - Canadian Coalition for Nuclear Responsibility, 862
CCO - Conservation Council of Ontario, 901
CCOHS - Canadian Centre for Occupational Health & Safety, 862
CCPA - Canadian Centre for Policy Alternatives, 862
CCPA - Canadian Chemical Producers' Association, 862
CCPA - Canadian Concrete Pipe Association, 863
CCPC - Canadian Clean Power Coalition, 862
CCPFH - Canadian Council of Professional Fish Harvesters, 865
CCRA - Canadian Carbonization Research Association, 861
CCS - Canadian Cancer Society, 861
CCSPA - Canadian Consumer Specialty Products Association, 863
CCTC - Canadian Council for Tobacco Control, 864
CCTT - Canadian Council of Technicians & Technologists, 865
CCWC - Castle-Crown Wilderness Coalition, 892
CCWG - Canadian Co-operative Wool Growers Ltd., 864
CCWM - Citizens' Clearinghouse on Waste Management, 895
CDA - Canadian Dam Association, 865
CDEA - Canadian District Energy Association, 866
CEA - Citizens' Environment Alliance of Southwestern Ontario, 895
CEA - Consulting Engineers of Alberta, 902
CEA - Canadian Electricity Association, 866
CEASE - Concerned Educators Allied for a Safe Environment, 899
CEBC - Consulting Engineers of British Columbia, 903
CEC - Commonwealth Engineers' Council, 898
CEC - Commission for Environmental Cooperation, 898
CEC - Commission for Environmental Cooperation, 898
CECAB - Canadian Environmental Certification Approvals Board, 866
CEEA - Canadian Energy Efficiency Alliance, 866
CEEDA - Canada East Equipment Dealers' Association, 852
CEGN - Canadian Environmental Grantmakers' Network, 867
CELA - Canadian Environmental Law Association, 867
CEM - Consulting Engineers of Manitoba Inc., 903
CEMA - Cumulative Environmental Management Association, 906
CENS - Consulting Engineers of Nova Scotia, 903
CEO - Consulting Engineers of Ontario, 903
CEP - Communications, Energy & Paperworkers Union of Canada, 899
CEPA - Canadian Energy Pipeline Association, 866
CEPIS - Pan American Center for Sanitary Engineering & Environmental Sciences, 984
CERI - Canadian Energy Research Institute, 866
CES - Consulting Engineers of Saskatchewan, 903
CETAC - Canadian Environmental Technology Advancement Corporation - West, 867
CETAF - Corporation des entreprises de traitement de l'air et du froid, 904
CETFA - Canadians for Ethical Treatment of Food Animals, 892
CEW - Citizens' Environment Watch, 895
CEY - Consulting Engineers of Yukon, 903
CFA - Canadian Federation of Agriculture, 867
CFA - Canadian Forestry Association, 868
CFA - Canadian Foundry Association, 869
CFA - Commonwealth Forestry Association - Canadian Chapter, 898
CFANB - Canadian Forestry Association of New Brunswick, 869
CFCAS - Canadian Foundation for Climate & Atmospheric Sciences, 869
CFES - Canadian Federation of Earth Sciences, 867
CFES - Canadian Federation of Engineering Students, 868
CFFO - Christian Farmers Federation of Ontario, 895
CFHS - Canadian Federation of Humane Societies, 868
CFI - Canadian Fertilizer Institute, 868
CFIG - Canadian Federation of Independent Grocers, 868
CFNS - Calgary Field Naturalists' Society, 852
CFPA - Canadian Fluid Power Association, 868
CFPA - Coast Forest Products Association, 897
CFRE - Citizens For Renewable Energy, 895
CFSA - Canadian Fire Safety Association, 868
CFTO - Christmas Tree Farmers of Ontario, 895
CFWF - Canadian Farm Writers' Federation, 867
CGA - Compressed Gas Association, Inc., 899
CGA - Canadian Gas Association, 869
CGB - Commonwealth Geographical Bureau, 898
CGC - Canadian GeoExchange Coalition, 869
CGDN - Canadian Genetic Diseases Network, 869
CGIAR - Consultative Group on International Agricultural Research, 902
CGLG - Council of Great Lakes Governors, 905
CGSA - Canadian Golf Superintendents Association, 870
CGSB - Canadian General Standards Board, 869
CGU - Canadian Geophysical Union, 869
CGWA - Canadian Ground Water Association, 870
CHA - Canadian Hydrographic Association, 871
CHA - Canadian Hydropower Association, 872
CHA - Canadian Hay Association, 870
CHBA - Canadian Home Builders' Association, 871
CHBA BC - Canadian Home Builders' Association - British Columbia, 871
CHC - Canadian Horticultural Council, 871
CHEC - Commonwealth Human Ecology Council, 898
CHEJ - Center for Health, Environment & Justice, 893
CHFA - Canadian Health Food Association, 870
CHFCA - Canadian Hydrogen & Fuel Cell Association, 871
CHLA - Canadian Health Libraries Association, 870
CHNC - Community Health Nurses of Canada, 899

Environmental Resources

Associations Acronym Index

CHOA - Canadian Heavy Oil Association, 871
CHOC - Consumer Health Organization of Canada, 903
CHRHS - Cole Harbour Rural Heritage Society, 897
CHS - Calgary Horticultural Society, 852
CI - The Canadian Institute, 872
CI - Consumers International, 903
CI - Conservation International, 901
CIC - Canadian International Council, 876
CIC - Chemical Institute of Canada, 894
CIC - Canadian Innovation Centre, 872
CICA - Canadian Institute of Chartered Accountants, 873
CICS - Canadian Intergovernmental Conference Secretariat, 875
CIE - Canadian Institute of Energy, 873
CIELAP - Canadian Institute for Environmental Law & Policy, 872
CIER - Centre for Indigenous Environmental Resources, 893
CIET - Canadian Institute for Energy Training, 872
CIFQ - Conseil de l'industrie forestière du Québec, 900
CIFST - Canadian Institute of Food Science & Technology, 874
CIG - Canadian Institute of Geomatics, 874
CIHI - Canadian Institute for Health Information, 872
CII - Coady International Institute, 897
CILA - Central Interior Logging Association, 893
CILT - Chartered Institute of Logistics and Transport in North America, 894
CIM - Canadian Institute of Mining, Metallurgy & Petroleum, 874
CIP - Canadian Institute of Planners, 875
CIPA - Couchiching Institute on Public Affairs, 904
CIPA - California Institute of Public Affairs, 852
CIPH - Canadian Institute of Plumbing & Heating, 875
CIPHI - Canadian Institute of Public Health Inspectors, 875
CIPI - Canadian Institute for Photonics Innovations, 873
CIRL - Canadian Institute of Resources Law, 875
CIS - Canadian Iris Society, 876
CISC - Canadian Institute of Steel Construction, 875
CITA - Canadian Industrial Transportation Association, 872
CITO - Communications & Information Technology Ontario, 898
CITT - Canadian Institute of Traffic & Transportation, 875
CIWA - Canadian Injured Workers Alliance, 872
CJN - Cercles des jeunes naturalistes, 894
CLA - Canadian Lumbermen's Association, 876
CLA - Canadian Lung Association, 876
CLC - Canadian Labour Congress, 876
CLRA - Canadian Land Reclamation Association, 876
CLSA - Canadian Law & Society Association, 876
CMA - Canadian Marketing Association, 877
CMA - Canadian Medical Association, 877
CMA - Canadian Mineral Analysts, 879
CMBES - Canadian Medical & Biological Engineering Society, 877
CMC - Canadian Meat Council, 877
CME - Canadian Manufacturers & Exporters, 876
CMI - Comité maritime international, 898
CMMTQ - Corporation des maîtres mécaniciens en tuyauterie du Québec, 904
CMOS - Canadian Meteorological & Oceanographic Society, 878
CMRNS - Chamber of Mineral Resources of Nova Scotia, 894
CMS - Canadian Mineral Society, 879
CMSA - Canadian Meat Science Association, 877
CMSQ - Conseil des monuments et sites du Québec, 900
CNA - Canadian Nuclear Association, 879
CNLA - Canadian Nursery Landscape Association, 880
CNS - Canadian Nuclear Society, 880
CNS - Clean Nova Scotia, 896
CNTC - Canadian Network of Toxicology Centres, 879
COABC - Certified Organic Associations of British Columbia, 894
COANS - Campground Owners Association of Nova Scotia, 852
COCA - Council of Ontario Construction Associations, 905
COEO - Council of Outdoor Educators of Ontario, 905
COFI - Council of Forest Industries, 905
COG - Canadian Organic Growers Inc., 880
COHA - Canadian Oil Heat Association, 880
COHA - Council on Hemispheric Affairs, 905
COLA - Canadian Organic Livestock Association, 881
COMAQ - Corporation des officiers municipaux agréés du Québec, 904
CONC - Central Okanagan Naturalists Club, 893
COOS - Central Ontario Orchid Society, 893
COPE - Citizens' Opposed to Paving the Escarpment, 895
COPF - Canadian Ornamental Plant Foundation, 881
COQ - Club des ornithologues de Québec inc., 896
CPAWS - Canadian Parks & Wilderness Society, 881
CPC - Canadian Pallet Council, 881
CPCA - Canadian Paint & Coatings Association, 881
CPCA - Canadian Process Control Association, 883
CPCI - Canadian Precast / Prestressed Concrete Institute, 883
CPEQ - Conseil patronal de l'environnement du Québec, 901
CPHA - Canadian Public Health Association, 883
CPI - Consumer Policy Institute, 903
CPIA - Canadian Printing Industries Association, 883

CPIA - Canadian Plastics Industry Association, 882
CPIMA - Canadian Printing Ink Manufacturers Association, 883
CPMA - Canadian Pest Management Association, 882
CPP - Canadian Parks Partnership, 881
CPRA - Canadian Polystyrene Recycling Alliance, 882
CPRA - Canadian Parks & Recreation Association, 881
CPS - Canadian Phytopathological Society, 882
CPS - Canadian Physiological Society, 882
CPSC - Canadian Plastics Sector Council, 882
CPSI - Canadian Patient Safety Institute, 881
CPWA - Canadian Public Works Association, 883
CQDE - Centre québécois du droit de l'environnement, 894
CRASH - Canadians for Responsible & Safe Highways, 892
CREGIM - Conseil régional de l'environnement de la Gaspésie et des Iles-de-la-Madeleine, 901
CRFA - Canadian Renewable Fuels Association, 884
CRFQ - Conseil de la recherche forestière du Québec, 900
CRHP - Canadian Respiratory Health Professionals, 884
CRPA - Canadian Radiation Protection Association, 883
CRS - Coalition of Rail Shippers, 897
CRS - Canadian Rose Society, 884
CRS - Cancer Research Society, 892
CRSS - Canadian Remote Sensing Society, 884
CSA - Canadian Standards Association, 888
CSACI - Canadian Society of Allergy & Clinical Immunology, 886
CSAS - Canadian Society of Animal Science, 886
CSASI - Canadian Society of Air Safety Investigators, 886
CSBA - Canadian Sheep Breeders' Association, 885
CSBA - Canadian Swine Breeders' Association, 889
CSBE - Canadian Society for Bioengineering, 885
CSBPA - Canadian Sugar Beet Producers' Association Inc., 889
CSC - Canada Safety Council, 853
CSC - Construction Specifications Canada, 902
CSCC - Canadian Steel Construction Council, 889
CSCC - Canadian Society of Clinical Chemists, 886
CSCE - Canadian Society for Civil Engineering, 885
CSE - Citizens for a Safe Environment, 895
CSEA - Canadian Swine Exporters Association, 889
CSEB - Canadian Society of Environmental Biologists, 887
CSEG - Canadian Society of Exploration Geophysicists, 887
CSGA - Canadian Seed Growers' Association, 884
CSHS - Canadian Society for Horticultural Science, 885
CSIE - Canadian Society for Industrial Engineering, 885
CSIH - Canadian Society for International Health, 885
CSLA - Canadian Society of Landscape Architects, 887
CSM - Canadian Society of Microbiologists, 887
CSME - Canadian Society for Mechanical Engineering, 885
CSMLS - Canadian Society for Medical Laboratory Science, 886
CSPA - Canadian Steel Producers Association, 889
CSPC - Canadian Steel Partnership Council, 889
CSPG - Canadian Society of Petroleum Geologists, 887
CSPI - Corrugated Steel Pipe Institute, 904
CSPMA - Canadian Sphagnum Peat Moss Association, 888
CSPP - Canadian Society of Plant Physiologists, 887
CSS - Canadian Space Society, 888
CSSA - Canadian Sanitation Supply Association, 884
CSSBI - Canadian Sheet Steel Building Institute, 885
CSSE - Canadian Society of Safety Engineering, Inc., 888
CSSPE - Canadian Society for the Study of Practical Ethics, 886
CSSS - Canadian Society of Soil Science, 888
CSTA - Canadian Seed Trade Association, 884
CSWA - Canadian Science Writers' Association, 884
CSZ - Canadian Society of Zoologists, 888
CTA - Canadian Trucking Alliance, 889
CTAC - Conseil de la transformation agroalimentaire et des produits de consommation, 900
CTRF - Canadian Transportation Research Forum, 889
CTTAM - Certified Technicians & Technologists Association of Manitoba, 894
CUFCA - Canadian Urethane Foam Contractors Association, 890
CUMA - Canadian Urethane Manufacturers Association, 890
CUTA - Canadian Urban Transit Association, 889
CVMA - Canadian Veterinary Medical Association, 890
CVNS - Cowichan Valley Naturalists' Society, 905
CWC - Canadian Wood Council, 891
CWF - Canadian Wildlife Federation, 891
CWLS - Canadian Well Logging Society, 891
CWN - Canadian Water Network, 890
CWPCA - Canadian Wood Pallet & Container Association, 892
CWQA - Canadian Water Quality Association, 890
CWRA - Canadian Water Resources Association, 891
CWWA - Canadian Water & Wastewater Association, 890

D

DAS - Durham Avicultural Society of Ontario, 907
DMA - Direct Marketing Association, 906
DSA - Direct Sellers Association of Canada, 906

DSF - David Suzuki Foundation, 906
DU - Ducks Unlimited Inc., 907
DUC - Ducks Unlimited Canada, 906

E

EAC - Ecology Action Centre, 908
EACO - Environmental Abatement Council of Ontario, 911
EAGE - European Association of Geoscientists & Engineers, 913
EAP - Ecological Agriculture Projects, 908
EAWLS - East African Wild Life Society, 907
EBA - Environmental Bankers Association, 911
ECOS - Eastern Canada Orchid Society, 907
EDA - Electricity Distributors Association, 909
EDC - Earth Day Canada, 907
EECOM - The Canadian Network for Environmental Education & Communication, 879
EEON - Environmental Education Ontario, 912
EEPSA - Environmental Educators' Provincial Specialist Association, 912
EEQ - Éco Entreprises Québec, 908
EESC - Earth Energy Society of Canada, 907
EF! - Earth First! Journal, 907
EFAO - Ecological Farmers Association of Ontario, 908
EFC - Electro-Federation Canada Inc., 909
EGS - European Geosciences Union, 913
EHA Ontario - Environmental Health Association of Ontario, 912
EHFC - Environmental Health Foundation of Canada, 912
EIA - Environmental Industry Associations, 912
EIC - The Engineering Institute of Canada, 910
EII - Earth Island Institute, 907
EIS - Ecoforestry Institute Society, 908
ELC - The Environmental Law Centre (Alberta) Society, 912
EMABC - Environmental Managers Association of British Columbia, 912
EnerACT - Energy Action Council of Toronto, 909
EPRF - Energy Probe Research Foundation, 910
ESA - European Space Agency, 913
ESA - Ecological Society of America, 908
ESA - Entomological Society of Alberta, 910
ESAA - Environmental Services Association of Alberta, 912
ESAC - Environmental Studies Association of Canada, 913
ESANS - Environmental Services Association of Nova Scotia, 913
ESBC - Entomological Society of British Columbia, 910
ESC - Earthsave Canada, 907
ESM - Entomological Society of Manitoba Inc., 910
ESO - Entomological Society of Ontario, 911
ESS - Entomological Society of Saskatchewan, 911
ESSF - Edmonton Space & Science Foundation, 909
EVCO - Electric Vehicle Council of Ottawa Inc., 909
EVS - Electric Vehicle Society of Canada, 909
EWB - Engineers Without Borders, 910
EYA - Environmental Youth Alliance, 913

F

FABQ - Fédération d'agriculture biologique du Québec, 914
FAN - Federation of Alberta Naturalists, 915
FAN - Forest Action Network, 918
FAPEL - Fédération des associations pour la protection de l'environnement des lacs inc., 914
FAQ - Fédération des agricultrices du Québec, 914
FBCN - British Columbia Nature (Federation of British Columbia Naturalists), 849
FBD - Fur-Bearer Defenders, 922
FBO - Field Botanists of Ontario, 916
FC - Flowers Canada, 917
FCA - Freight Carriers Association of Canada, 920
FCC - Federation of Calgary Communities, 915
FCC - Fisheries Council of Canada, 917
FCC - The Fur Council of Canada, 922
FCM - Federation of Canadian Municipalities, 915
FCPC - Food & Consumer Products of Canada, 918
FEC - Foundation for Environmental Conservation, 919
FER - Friends of Ecological Reserves, 920
FF/CF - FarmFolk/CityFolk Society, 914
FFFH - Friends of the Forestry Farm House Inc., 921
FFGA - Fredericton Fish & Game Association, 919
FFQ - Fondation de la faune du Québec, 917
FFSBC - Freshwater Fisheries Society of British Columbia, 920
FIC - Fur Institute of Canada, 922
FIELD - Foundation for International Environmental Law & Development, 919
FNSH - Federation of Nova Scotian Heritage, 915
FoA - Friends of Animals, 920
FOCA - Federation of Ontario Cottagers' Associations, 915
FOCS - Friends of Clayoquot Sound, 920
FoE - Friends of the Earth Canada, 921

Associations Acronym Index

FoEI - Friends of the Earth International, 921
FONOM - Federation of Northern Ontario Municipalities, 915
FOR - Friends of the Oldman River, 921
FOS - Friends of the Stikine Society, 921
FPAC - Forest Products Association of Canada, 918
FPANS - Forest Products Association of Nova Scotia, 919
FPBQ - La Fédération des producteurs de bois du Québec, 914
FPC - Food Processors of Canada, 918
FPC - Fire Prevention Canada, 916
FPCCQ - Fédération des producteurs de cultures commerciales du Québec, 915
FPEIM - Federation of Prince Edward Island Municipalities Inc., 915
FPI - Foodservice & Packaging Institute, 918
FQCC - Fédération québécoise de camping et de caravaning inc., 916
FQCF - Fédération québécoise des coopératives forestières, 916
FQCK - Fédération québécoise du canot et du kayak, 916
FQM - Fédération Québécoise des Municipalités, 916
FQME - Fédération québécoise de la montagne et de l'escalade, 916
FQSA - Fédération québécoise pour le saumon atlantique, 916
FRC - Fish Harvesters Resource Centres, 917
FSHÉQ - Fédération des sociétés d'horticulture et d'écologie du Québec, 915
FSRS - Fishermen and Scientists Research Society, 917
FSSRA - Federation of Saskatchewan Surface Rights Association, 916
FTSW - Friends of the Trent-Severn Waterway, 922
FWKP - The Friends of West Kootenay Parks Society, 922

G

GAC - Geological Association of Canada, 923
GBR - The Green Brick Road, 925
GCC - Green Communities Canada, 925
GCO - The Garden Clubs of Ontario, 922
GEAPS - Grain Elevator & Processing Society, 924
GEOEC - Global, Environmental & Outdoor Education Council, 924
GHTA - Ganaraska Hiking Trail Association, 922
GIAC - Geomatics Industry Association of Canada, 923
GLIER - Great Lakes Institute for Environmental Research, 925
GLRC - The Great Lakes Research Consortium, 925
GLU - Great Lakes United, 925
GMCS - Gem & Mineral Club of Scarborough, 922
GMWSRS - Grand Manan Whale & Seabird Research Station, 924
GN - Grasslands Naturalists, 925
GPAC - Gas Processing Association Canada, 922
GPBC - Green Party of British Columbia, 926
GPC - Green Party of Canada, 926
GPI - Glass Packaging Institute, 923
GPO - The Green Party of Ontario, 926
GRESOC - Groupe de recherche en écologie sociale, 926
GRHC - Green Roofs for Healthy Cities, 926
GSC - Genetics Society of Canada, 922

H

HAT - Habitat Acquisition Trust, 927
HCF - Heritage Canada Foundation, 929
HCQ - L'Héritage canadien du Québec, 929
HFN - Halifax Field Naturalists, 927
HFP - Council of the Haida Nation - Haida Fisheries Program, 905
HIEA - Hamilton Industrial Environmental Association, 927
HIMSS - Healthcare Information & Management Systems Society, 928
HIP - Healthy Indoors Partnership, 928
HIT - Hamilton Incubator of Technology, 927
HLABC - Health Libraries Association of British Columbia, 928
HM - Héritage Montréal, 929
HMANA - Hawk Migration Association of North America, 927
HNC - Hamilton Naturalists' Club, 927
HNS - Horticulture Nova Scotia, 930
HRAI - Heating, Refrigeration & Air Conditioning Institute of Canada, 928
HRMSC - H.R. MacMillan Space Centre Society, 930
HSAA - Health Sciences Association of Alberta, 928
HSAS - Health Sciences Association of Saskatchewan, 928
HSCSA - Health & Safety Conference Society of Alberta, 927
HW - Heritage Winnipeg Corp., 930

I

IAAE - International Association of Agricultural Economists, 935
IAEA - International Atomic Energy Agency, 936
IAEAC - International Association of Environmental Analytical Chemistry, 935
IAEE - International Association for Earthquake Engineering, 934
IAEH - International Association for Environmental Hydrology, 935
IAEWP Canada - International Association of Educators for World Peace, 935
IAFF - International Association of Fire Fighters (AFL-CIO/CLC), 935
IAGLR - International Association for Great Lakes Research, 935
IAH - International Association of Hydrogeologists, 935
IAH-CNC - International Association of Hydrogeologists - Canadian National Chapter, 936
IAIA - International Association for Impact Assessment, 935
IAP2 - International Association for Public Participation, 935
IAPO - Indian Agricultural Program of Ontario, 930
IAS - International Association of Sedimentologists, 936
IASC - International Arctic Science Committee, 934
IASTED - International Association of Science & Technology for Development, 936
IATAL - International Society of Limnology, 944
IAVGO - Industrial Accident Victims Group of Ontario, 930
IBA - International Bar Association, 936
IBA - International Association for Bear Research & Management, 934
IBWA - International Bottled Water Association, 936
ICA - International Cooperative Alliance, 937
ICAM - International Council for Applied Mineralogy, 937
ICASE - International Council of Associations for Science Education, 938
ICAZ - International Council for Archaeozoology, 937
ICCE - International Centre for Conservation Education, 936
ICEL - International Council of Environmental Law, 938
ICFA - International Coalition of Fisheries Associations, 936
ICID - International Commission on Irrigation & Drainage, 937
ICLAS - International Council for Laboratory Animal Science, 937
ICLEI - International Council for Local Environmental Initiatives, 937
ICOH - International Commission on Occupational Health, 937
ICOMOS - International Council on Monuments & Sites, 938
ICRP - International Commission on Radiological Protection, 937
ICSC - International Centre for Sustainable Cities, 936
ICTAC - International Confederation for Thermal Analysis & Calorimetry, 937
ICURR - Intergovernmental Committee on Urban & Regional Research, 934
IDRC - International Development Research Centre, 938
IDSA - Infectious Diseases Society of America, 931
IECA - International Erosion Control Association, 938
IEEE - Institute of Electrical & Electronics Engineers Inc., 932
IEF - International Energy Foundation, 938
IEPF - Institut de l'énergie et de l'environnement de la Francophonie, 931
IFAW - International Fund for Animal Welfare Canada, 939
IFCB - International Federation for Cell Biology, 939
IFF - International Flying Farmers, 939
IFHP - International Federation for Housing & Planning, 939
IFLA - International Federation of Landscape Architects, 939
IFMBE - International Federation for Medical & Biological Engineering, 939
IFOAM - International Federation of Organic Agriculture Movements, 939
IFS - International Federation of Surveyors, 939
IFT - Institute of Food Technologists, 932
IGF - International Genetics Federation, 939
IGS - International Geosynthetics Society, 940
IGU - International Geographic Union, 939
IGUA - Industrial Gas Users Association Inc., 930
IHHA - International Heavy Haul Association, 940
IIASA - International Institute for Applied Systems Analysis, 940
IIC - International Institute for Conservation of Historic & Artistic Works, 940
IICPH - International Institute of Concern for Public Health, 940
IIE - Institute of Industrial Engineers, 933
IIEC - International Institute for Energy Conservation, 940
IIFET - International Institute of Fisheries Economics & Trade, 940
IISD - International Institute for Sustainable Development, 940
ILDC - Independent Lumber Dealers Co-operative, 930
ILO - International Labour Organization, 940
ILSR - Institute for Local Self-Reliance, 932
IMAC - Innovation Management Association of Canada, 931
IMechE - Institution of Mechanical Engineers, 934
IMO - International Maritime Organization, 941
INEM - International Network for Environmental Management, 941
INLA - International Nuclear Law Association, 941
INT - Island Nature Trust, 946
INTECOL - International Association for Ecology, 934
IOI - International Ocean Institute, 941
IOIC - International Oceans Institute of Canada, 941
IOPA - Islands Organic Producers Association, 946
IoPP - Institute of Packaging Professionals, 933
IPA - International Permafrost Association, 941
IPCRG - International Primary Care Respiratory Group, 942
IPE - Institute of Power Engineers, 933
IPNI - International Plant Nutrition Institute, 942
IPPL - International Primate Protection League, 942
IPPS - International Plant Propagators Society, Inc., 942
IPPSA - Independent Power Producers Society of Alberta, 930
IPS - International Peat Society, 941
IRBV - Institut de recherche en biologie végétale, 932
IRDA - Research & Development Institute for the Agri-Environment, 994
IRG - International Research Group on Wood Protection, 942
IRR - Institute for Risk Research, 932
IRSST - Institut de recherche Robert-Sauvé en santé et en sécurité du travail, 932
ISAS - Institute of Space & Atmospheric Studies, 933
ISB - International Society of Biometeorology, 943
ISC - International Society of Citriculture, 943
ISEB - International Society for Environmental Biotechnology, 942
ISEE - International Society for Ecological Economics, 942
ISEE - International Society for Environmental Ethics, 943
ISEE - International Society for Environmental Epidemiology, 942
ISEM - International Society for Ecological Modelling, 942
ISEP - International Society for Evolutionary Protistology, 943
ISES - International Solar Energy Society, 944
ISIAQ - International Society of Indoor Air Quality & Climate, 943
ISO - International Organization for Standardization, 941
ISRI - Institute of Scrap Recycling Industries, Inc., 933
ISRIC - International Soil Reference & Information Centre, 944
ISRM - International Society for Rock Mechanics, 943
ISSA - International Sanitary Supply Association, Inc., 942
ISSMGE - International Society for Soil Mechanics & Geotechnical Engineering, 943
ISWA - International Solid Waste Association, 944
ITA - Industrial Truck Association, 931
ITA - International Titanium Association, 944
ITE - Institute of Transportation Engineers, 933
IUBS - International Union of Biological Sciences, 945
IUCN - International Union for Conservation of Nature, 944
IUFoST - International Union of Food Science & Technology, 945
IUFRO - International Union of Forest Research Organizations, 945
IUGG - International Union of Geodesy & Geophysics, 945
IUPAC - International Union of Pure & Applied Chemistry, 945
IUS - Institute of Urban Studies, 934
IUSS - International Union of Soil Sciences, 945
IVMA - Integrated Vegetation Management Association of British Columbia, 934
IWA - International Water Association, 946
IWC - International Whaling Commission, 946
IWC - International Wildlife Coalition, 946
IWH - Institute for Work & Health, 932
IWRC - International Wildlife Rehabilitation Council, 946

J

JEA - Jasper Environmental Association, 947
JFAO - Junior Farmers' Association of Ontario, 947
JGI - The Jane Goodall Institute of Canada, 946
JZQ - Jardin zoologique du Québec, 946

K

KAP - Keystone Agricultural Producers, 947
KFN - Kingston Field Naturalists, 947
KNC - Kamloops Naturalist Club, 947
KWIC - Kawartha World Issues Centre, 947

L

LAEA - Lloydminster Agricultural Exhibition Association, 949
LAHLA - London Area Health Libraries Association, 949
LANS - Nova Scotia Lung Association, 968
LANTA - Landscape Alberta Nursery Trades Association, 948
LBMAO - Lumber & Building Materials Association of Ontario, 949
LFN - Langley Field Naturalists Society, 948
LGMA - Local Government Management Association of British Columbia, 949
LNL - Landscape Newfoundland & Labrador, 948
LOHTA - Landscape Ontario Horticultural Trades Association, 948
LORDA - Lansdowne Outdoor Recreational Development Association, 948
LTA - Land Trust Alliance, 948
LWI - Lambton Wildlife Incorporated, 948

M

MABC - Mining Association of British Columbia, 954
MAC - Mineralogical Association of Canada, 954
MAC - Mining Association of Canada, 955
MAHIP - Manitoba Association of Health Information Providers, 950
MALA - Manitoba Association of Landscape Architects, 950
MAMI - Mining Association of Manitoba Inc., 955
MASHA - Mines & Aggregates Safety & Health Association, 954
MCA - Manitoba Camping Association, 950

Associations Acronym Index

MCABC - Mechanical Contractors Association of British Columbia, 953
MCAC - Mechanical Contractors Association of Canada, 953
MCAM - Mechanical Contractors Association of Manitoba, 953
MCAO - Mechanical Contractors Association of Ontario, 953
MCAS - Mechanical Contractors Association of Saskatchewan Inc., 953
MCIC - Manitoba Council for International Cooperation, 950
MCPA - Manitoba Cattle Producers Association, 950
MEA - Municipal Engineers Association, 955
MEIA - Manitoba Environmental Industries Association Inc., 951
MEN - Manitoba Eco-Network Inc., 950
MetSoc - Metallurgy & Materials Society of the Canadian Institute of Mining, Metallurgy & Petroleum, 954
MFA - Middlesex Federation of Agriculture, 954
MFNL - Model Forest of Newfoundland and Labrador, 955
MHLA - Maritimes Health Libraries Association, 952
MIA - Manitoba Institute of Agrologists, 951
MMO - Materials & Manufacturing Ontario, Division of OCE Inc., 952
MNS - Nature Manitoba, 959
MOPIA - Manitoba Ozone Protection Industry Association, 951
MPHA - Manitoba Public Health Association, 951
MPPI - Manitoba Professional Planners Institute, 951
MRAS - Millarville Racing & Agricultural Society, 954
MSCCA - Mining Suppliers, Contractors & Consultants Association of BC, 955
MSM - Mineral Society of Manitoba, 954
MSPEI - Medical Society of Prince Edward Island, 953
MUC - Manitoba Underwater Council, 952
MVA - Meewasin Valley Authority, 953
MWA - Municipal Waste Association, 955
MWF - Manitoba Wildlife Federation, 952
MWWA - Manitoba Water Well Association, 952
MWWA - Manitoba Water & Wastewater Association, 952

N

NAAEE - North American Association for Environmental Education, 964
NABCI - North American Bird Conservation Initiative Canada, 965
NACE - NACE International, 956
NAEE - National Association for Environmental Education (UK), 956
NAEM - National Association for Environmental Management, 956
NAEP - National Association of Environmental Professionals, 957
NAFA - National Aboriginal Forestry Association, 956
NAIA - Newfoundland Aquaculture Industry Association, 963
NAID - National Association for Information Destruction, 956
NANPS - North American Native Plant Society, 965
NAPCOR - National Association for PET Container Resources, 957
NAPEGG - Association of Professional Engineers, Geologists & Geophysicists of the Northwest Territories & Nunavut, 839
NARRA - North American Recycled Rubber Association, 965
NAS - National Audubon Society, Inc., 957
NASOH - North American Society for Oceanic History, 965
NAWMP - North American Waterfowl Management Plan, 965
NBEIA - New Brunswick Environment Industry Association, 960
NBEN - New Brunswick Environmental Network, 960
NBFPA - New Brunswick Forest Products Association Inc., 961
NBIA - New Brunswick Institute of Agrologists, 961
NBMS - New Brunswick Medical Society, 961
NBSC - New Brunswick Salmon Council, 961
NBSCETT - New Brunswick Society of Certified Engineering Technicians & Technologists, 961
NBSCIA - New Brunswick Soil & Crop Improvement Association, 961
NBSGA - New Brunswick Salmon Growers Association, 961
NBWF - New Brunswick Wildlife Federation, 962
NCAMP - National Coalition Against the Misuse of Pesticides, 957
NCAP - Northwest Coalition for Alternatives to Pesticides, 966
NCC - The Nature Conservancy of Canada, 959
NCLGA - North Central Local Government Association, 965
NCSC - National Centre for Small Communities, 957
NCSE - National Council for Science & the Environment, 957
NECA - National Energy Conservation Association Inc., 957
NEHA - National Environmental Health Association, 957
NEIA - Newfoundland & Labrador Environmental Industry Association, 962
NEW - Nipissing Environmental Watch, 964
NFN - Norfolk Field Naturalists, 964
NFNC - Nanaimo Field Naturalists, 956
NFNC - Niagara Falls Nature Club, 964
NFU - National Farmers Union, 958
NGWA - National Ground Water Association, 958
NHA - Nunavut Harvesters Association, 969
NHPC - Natural Health Practitioners of Canada, 959
NIRS - Nuclear Information & Resource Service, 969
NITA - Native Investment & Trade Association, 959
NIVMA - Northern Interior Vegetation Management Association, 966
NLALA - Newfoundland & Labrador Association of Landscape Architects, 962
NLATC - Newfoundland & Labrador Association of Technology Companies, 962
NLCA - Newfoundland & Labrador Construction Association, 962
NLHLA - Newfoundland & Labrador Health Libraries Association, 963
NLIA - Newfoundland & Labrador Institute of Agrologists, 963
NLLA - Newfoundland & Labrador Lung Association, 963
NLMA - Newfoundland & Labrador Medical Association, 963
NLOA - Newfoundland & Labrador Outfitters Association, 963
NLPHA - Newfoundland & Labrador Public Health Association, 963
NMMA - National Marine Manufacturers Association, 958
NMMA - National Marine Manufacturers Association Canada, 958
NNFC - Northern Native Fishing Corporation, 966
NOFA - Northeast Organic Farming Association, 966
NOHLA - Northwestern Ontario Health Libraries Association, 967
NOMA - Northwestern Ontario Municipal Association, 967
NONC - North Okanagan Naturalists Club, 965
NOOA - North Okanagan Organic Association, 965
NORA - NORA, An Association of Responsible Recyclers, 964
NPA - Northern Prospectors Association, 966
NPCA - National Parks Conservation Association, 958
NPCF - Niagara Peninsula Conservation Foundation, 964
NPGS - Niagara Peninsula Geological Society, 964
NRU - Natural Resources Union, 959
NSA - Nepisiguit Salmon Association, 960
NSAC - National Sunflower Association of Canada, 958
NSCP - Nova Scotia Cattle Producers, 967
NSEN - Nova Scotia Environmental Network, 967
NSFA - Nova Scotia Federation of Agriculture, 968
NSFA - Nova Scotia Forestry Association, 968
NSFGA - Nova Scotia Fruit Growers' Association, 968
NSFPA - Nova Scotia Fish Packers Association, 968
NSFTA - Nova Scotia Forest Technicians Association, 968
NSGWA - Nova Scotia Ground Water Association, 968
NSIA - Nova Scotia Institute of Agrologists, 968
NSIS - Nova Scotian Institute of Science, 969
NSNT - Nova Scotia Nature Trust, 968
NSPIRG - Nova Scotia Public Interest Research Group, 968
NSRA - Non-Smokers' Rights Association, 964
NSSA - Nova Scotia Salmon Association, 969
NSWMA - National Solid Wastes Management Association, 958
NTNB - Nature Trust of New Brunswick, 960
NW - Northwatch, 966
NWF - National Wildlife Federation, 958
NWLF - Newfoundland & Labrador Wildlife Federation, 963
NWPS - Northwest Wildlife Preservation Society, 967
NWTAC - Northwest Territories Association of Communities, 967
NWTALA - Northwest Territories Association of Landscape Architects, 967
NWTCA - Northwest Territories Construction Association, 967
NWTRPA - Northwest Territories Recreation & Parks Association, 967

O

OAAS - Ontario Association of Agricultural Societies, 971
OABA - Ontario Agri Business Association, 970
OACETT - Ontario Association of Certified Engineering Technicians & Technologists, 971
OAFE - Ontario Agri-Food Education Inc., 970
OAGEE - Ontario Association for Geographic & Environmental Education, 971
OAGQ - Ordre des arpenteurs-géomètres du Québec, 981
OAIA - Ontario Association for Impact Assessment, 971
OALA - Ontario Association of Landscape Architects, 971
OAQ - Ordre des agronomes du Québec, 981
OARA - Ontario Automotive Recyclers Association, 971
OATI - Ontario Agricultural Training Institute, 970
OCA - Ontario Cattlemen's Association, 971
OCA - Ontario Camps Association, 971
OCAA - Ontario Clean Air Alliance, 972
OCE-ETech - Ontario Centres of Excellence - Centre for Earth & Environmental Technologies, 972
OCFA - Ontario Commercial Fisheries' Association, 972
OCI - Organization of CANDU Industries, 982
OCIA - Organic Crop Improvement Association (International), 982
OCIA-NB - Organic Crop Improvement Association - New Brunswick, 982
OCPA - Ontario Concrete Pipe Association, 972
OCPA - Ontario Corn Producers' Association, 972
OCPP - Organic Crop Producers & Processors Ontario Inc., 982
OCQ - Ordre des chimistes du Québec, 981
OCSC - Ottawa Safety Council, 983
OCTA - Ontario Community Transit Association, 972
ODC - Ontario Dairy Council, 972
ODC - Ottawa Duck Club, 983
ODS - Ontario Daylily Society, 972
OECD - Organization for Economic Cooperation & Development, 982
OEER - Offshore Energy Environmental Research Association, 970
OEL - Ontario Electrical League, 972
OEMAC - Occupational & Environmental Medical Association of Canada, 969
OEN - Ontario Environmental Network, 973
OFA - Ontario Federation of Agriculture, 973
OFA - Ontario Forestry Association, 974
OFAC - The Ontario Farm Animal Council, 973
OFAH - Ontario Federation of Anglers & Hunters, 973
OFBA - Ontario Fire Buff Associates, 973
OFCA - Ontario Farm & Country Accommodations Association, 973
OFIA - Ontario Forest Industries Association, 974
OFNC - Ottawa Field-Naturalists' Club, 983
OFO - Ontario Field Ornithologists, 973
OFPA - Ontario Food Processors Association, 973
OFVGA - Ontario Fruit & Vegetable Growers' Association, 974
OGGO - Office of Greening Government Operations, 970
OGRA - Ontario Good Roads Association, 974
OGWA - Ontario Ground Water Association, 974
OHA - Ontario Hospital Association, 975
OHA - Ontario Horticultural Association, 974
OHAO - Occupational Hygiene Association of Ontario, 969
OHCC - Ontario Healthy Communities Coalition, 974
OHCOW - Occupational Health Clinics for Ontario Workers, 969
OHT - Ontario Heritage Trust, 974
OIA - Ontario Institute of Agrologists, 975
OIFPA - Ontario Industrial Fire Protection Association, 975
OIFQ - Ordre des ingénieurs forestiers du Québec, 981
OIQ - Ordre des ingénieurs du Québec, 981
OLA - Ontario Lung Association, 975
OLMA - Ontario Lumber Manufacturers' Association, 975
OMA - Ontario Medical Association, 975
OMA - Ontario Mining Association, 976
OMHRA - Ontario Municipal Human Resources Association, 976
OMMI - Ontario Municipal Management Institute, 976
OMOA - Ontario Marine Operators Association, 975
OMWA - Ontario Municipal Water Association, 976
ONEIA - Ontario Environment Industry Association, 973
OOHNA - Ontario Occupational Health Nurses Association, 976
OPA - Ontario Parks Association, 976
OPAM - Organic Producers Association of Manitoba Co-operative Inc., 982
OPCEA - Ontario Pollution Control Equipment Association, 977
OPFA - Ontario Professional Foresters Association, 977
OPFFA - Ontario Professional Fire Fighters Association, 977
OPHA - Ontario Public Health Association, 977
OPI - Ontario Petroleum Institute Inc., 976
OPIA - Ontario Plumbing Inspectors Association, 977
OPIA - Ontario Printing & Imaging Association, 977
OPIRG - Ontario Public Interest Research Group, 978
OPPI - Ontario Professional Planners Institute, 977
ORAC - Ontario Refrigeration & Air Conditioning Contractors Association, 978
ORCS - Ontario Respiratory Care Society, 978
OSCIA - Ontario Soil & Crop Improvement Association, 979
OSEA - Ontario Sustainable Energy Association, 980
OSEM - Ontario Society for Environmental Management, 978
OSL - Ontario Safety League, 978
OSNPPH - Ontario Society of Nutrition Professionals in Public Health, 979
OSPAR - OSPAR Commission, 983
OSPE - Ontario Society of Professional Engineers, 979
OSPS - Okanagan Similkameen Parks Society, 970
OSUM - Ontario Small Urban Municipalities, 978
OSWCA - Ontario Sewer & Watermain Construction Association, 978
OTA - Ontario Trucking Association, 980
OTA - Organic Trade Association, 982
OTC - Ontario Traffic Conference, 980
OTPQ - Ordre des technologues professionnels du Québec, 982
OUFC - Ontario Urban Forest Council, 980
OUQ - Ordre des urbanistes du Québec, 982
OVHLA - Ottawa Valley Health Libraries Association, 983
OVMA - Ontario Vegetation Management Association, 981
OVONO US - Organic Verification Organization of North America, 982
OWMA - Ontario Waste Management Association, 981
OWPMB - Ontario Wheat Producers' Marketing Board, 981
OWWA - Ontario Water Works Association, 981

P

PAA - Protected Areas Association of Newfoundland & Labrador, 990
PAAC - The Public Affairs Association of Canada, 990
PAC - Packaging Association of Canada, 984
PACE - Planetary Association for Clean Energy, Inc., 987
PACT - Pickering & Ajax Citizens Together for the Environment, 986
PAFN - Pembroke Area Field Naturalists, 985
PAMF - Prince Albert Model Forest Association Inc., 988
PAMI - Prairie Agricultural Machinery Institute, 988

804 GUIDE DES RESSOURCES ENVIRONNEMENTALES CANADIENNES 2011-2012

Associations Acronym Index

PANNA - Pesticide Action Network North America, 985
PAPTAC - Pulp & Paper Technical Association of Canada, 991
PC - Paddle Canada, 984
PC - Population Connection, 987
PDAC - Prospectors & Developers Association of Canada, 990
PEG-NL - Professional Engineers & Geoscientists Newfoundland & Labrador, 989
PEIAA - Prince Edward Island Aquaculture Alliance, 988
PEICMGA - Prince Edward Island Cultured Mussel Growers Association, 988
PEICP - Prince Edward Island Cattle Producers, 988
PEIEN - Prince Edward Island Eco-Net, 988
PEIFA - Prince Edward Island Federation of Agriculture, 988
PEIFA - Prince Edward Island Fishermen's Association, 988
PEIFIA - Prince Edward Island Forest Improvement Association, 988
PEIIA - Prince Edward Island Institute of Agrologists, 989
PEISA - Prince Edward Island Salmon Association, 989
PEMAC - Plant Engineering & Maintenance Association of Canada, 987
PEO - Professional Engineers Ontario, 990
PETA - People for the Ethical Treatment of Animals, 985
PFGA - Prairie Fruit Growers Association, 988
PFN - Peninsula Field Naturalists, 985
PFN - Peterborough Field Naturalists, 985
PFSRB - Partners FOR the Saskatchewan River Basin, 985
PGAC - Propane Gas Association of Canada Inc., 990
PGBRS - Prince George Backcountry Recreation Society, 989
PGNC - Prince George Naturalists, 989
PHABC - Public Health Association of British Columbia, 990
PHANS - Public Health Association of Nova Scotia, 991
PHRCC - Petroleum Human Resources Council of Canada, 986
PI - Probe International, 989
PIA - Pitch-In Alberta, 987
PIBC - Planning Institute of British Columbia, 987
PIC - Pitch-In Canada, 987
PLCAC - Pipe Line Contractors Association of Canada, 987
PLEA Sask. - Public Legal Education Association of Saskatchewan, Inc., 991
PLFC - Plastic Loose Fill Council, 987
PLIAN - Public Legal Information Association of Newfoundland, 991
PLRCC - Pigeon Lake Regional Chamber of Commerce, 986
PMAA - Pest Management Association of Alberta, 985
PMTC - Private Motor Truck Council of Canada, 989
PNWER - Pacific NorthWest Economic Region, 983
PPDM - Public Petroleum Data Model Association, 991
PPEC - Paper & Paperboard Packaging Environmental Council, 984
PPF - The Pollution Probe Foundation, 987
PPP - Pacific Peoples Partnership, 983
PRAC - Petroleum Research Atlantic Canada, 986
PRO - Parks & Recreation Ontario, 984
PSAC - Petroleum Services Association of Canada, 986
PSPC - Polystyrene Packaging Council, 987
PTAC - Petroleum Technology Alliance Canada, 986
PTMAA - Petroleum Tank Management Association of Alberta, 986
PUHA - Pacific Urchin Harvesters Association, 984
PVEA - Peace Valley Environment Association, 985
PVQ - Parti Vert du Québec, 985

Q

QFA - Québec Farmers' Association, 991
QLA - Québec Lung Association, 991
QLF (Canada) - Québec-Labrador Foundation (Canada) Inc., 991
QVRRDF - Quidi Vidi Rennie's River Development Foundation, 992

R

RA - Rainforest Alliance, 992
RAC - The Rubber Association of Canada, 997
RACCA-BC - Refrigeration & Air Conditioning Contractors Association of British Columbia, 993
RAN - Rainforest Action Network, 992
RAWF - Royal Agricultural Winter Fair Association, 996
RBC - Rare Breeds Canada, 992
RBG - Royal Botanical Gardens, 996
RCA - Recycling Council of Alberta, 993
RCBC - Recycling Council of British Columbia, 993
RCC - Retail Council of Canada, 995
RCEN - Canadian Environmental Network, 867
RCGS - The Royal Canadian Geographical Society, 996
RCM - Green Action Centre, 925
RCO - Recycling Council of Ontario, 993
RDLC - Regina & District Labour Council, 994
RDRN - Red Deer River Naturalists, 993
REAL - Rideau Environmental Action League, 995
REAP Canada - Resource Efficient Agricultural Production, 995
REAPS - Prince George Recycling & Environmental Action Planning Society, 989
RGS - Resources for Global Sustainability, 995
RHAM - The Regional Health Authorities of Manitoba, 994
RHN - Richmond Hill Naturalists, 995
RMA - Rubber Manufacturers Association, 997
RMAA - Rural Municipal Administrators' Association of Saskatchewan, 997
RMI - The Rocky Mountain Institute, 996
RNRF - Renewable Natural Resources Foundation, 994
RPFANS - Registered Professional Foresters Association of Nova Scotia, 994
RQGE - Réseau québécois des groupes écologistes, 994
RSC - The Royal Society of Canada, 996
RSC - Rhododendron Society of Canada, 995
RSES Canada - Refrigeration Service Engineers Society (Canada), 994
RTA - Rideau Trail Association, 995
RVCA - Rideau Valley Conservation Authority, 995
RVFN - Rideau Valley Field Naturalists, 995
RVLT - Ruiter Valley Land Trust, 997
RWF - Regina Wildlife Federation, 994

S

SAASE - Saskatchewan Association of Agricultural Societies & Exhibitions, 999
SABNES - Salmon Arm Bay Nature Enhancement Society, 998
SAHLA - Southern Alberta Health Libraries Association, 1010
SALA - Saskatchewan Association of Landscape Architects, 999
SARC - Saskatchewan Association of Rehabilitation Centres, 999
SARM - Saskatchewan Association of Rural Municipalities, 999
SASTT - Saskatchewan Applied Science Technologists & Technicians, 998
SBC - Sustainable Buildings Canada, 1011
SCA - Saskatchewan Camping Association, 999
SCB - Society for Conservation Biology, 1006
SCBC - Sierra Club of British Columbia, 1004
SCC - Sierra Club of Canada, 1004
SCCC - Soil Conservation Council of Canada, 1009
SCCWS - Swift Current Creek Watershed Stewards, 1011
SCI - Society of Chemical Industry - Canadian Section, 1008
SCN - Stem Cell Network, 1010
SCNHS - Sunshine Coast Natural History Society, 1011
SCO - Society of Canadian Ornithologists, 1007
SCSA - Saskatchewan Construction Safety Association Inc., 999
SCTR - Saskatchewan Coalition for Tobacco Reduction, 999
SCWIST - Society for Canadian Women in Science & Technology, 1006
SDTC - Sustainable Development Technology Canada, 1011
SEA - Southeast Environmental Association, 1010
SEGD - Society for Environmental Graphic Design, 1007
SEI - Stockholm Environment Institute, 1010
SEIMA - Saskatchewan Environmental Industry & Managers' Association, 999
SEN - Saskatchewan Eco-Network, 999
SEPAQ - Société des établissements de plein air du Québec, 1005
SEQ - Société d'entomologie du Québec, 1005
SER - Society for Ecological Restoration International, 1007
SES - Saskatchewan Environmental Society, 1000
SESCI - Solar & Sustainable Energy Society of Canada Inc., 1009
SETAC - Society of Environmental Toxicology & Chemistry, 1008
SFA - Saskatchewan Forestry Association, 1000
SFN - Sydenham Field Naturalists, 1011
SFPE - Society of Fire Protection Engineers, 1008
SGWA - Saskatchewan Ground Water Association, 1000
SHLA - Saskatchewan Health Libraries Association, 1000
SILGA - Southern Interior Local Government Association, 1010
SIO - Social Investment Organization, 1004
SJCAB - St. John's Clean & Beautiful, 998
SKSA - Saskatchewan Katahdin Sheep Association Inc., 1000
SLA - Saskatchewan Livestock Association, 1000
SLEA - Sarnia-Lambton Environmental Association, 998
SLF - Strategic Leadership Forum, The Toronto Society for Strategic Management, 1010
SLSA - Saskatchewan Land Surveyors' Association, 1000
SMA - Saskatchewan Medical Association, 1001
SMA - Saskatchewan Mining Association, 1001
SMACNA - Sheet Metal & Air Conditioning Contractors' National Association, 1003
SMCAA - Sheet Metal Contractors Association of Alberta, 1003
SMRA - St Mary's River Association, 998
SNLA - Saskatchewan Nursery Landscape Association, 1001
SNRT - Society for Research on Nicotine & Tobacco, 1007
SOCODEVI - Société de coopération pour le développement international, 1005
SoDC - Seeds of Diversity Canada, 1003
SODES - Société de développement économique du Saint-Laurent, 1005
SOEEA - Saskatchewan Outdoor & Environmental Education Association, 1001
SOOPA - Similkameen Okanagan Organic Producers Association, 1004
SOS - Save Ontario Shipwrecks, 1002
SOSN - Southern Ontario Seismic Network, 1010
SOT - Society of Toxicology, 1008
SPAWN - Salmon Preservation Association for the Waters of Newfoundland, 998
SPE - Society of Petroleum Engineers, 1008
SPEA - Society of Professional Engineers & Associates, 1008
SPEC - Society Promoting Environmental Conservation, 1009
SPES - Stanley Park Ecology Society, 1010
SPHNC - Société Provancher d'histoire naturelle du Canada, 1006
SPI - Society of the Plastics Industry, Inc., 1008
SPMABC - Structural Pest Management Association of British Columbia, 1010
SPMAO - Structural Pest Management Association of Ontario, 1010
SPNC - South Peel Naturalists' Club, 1010
SPRA - Saskatchewan Parks & Recreation Association, 1001
SQAE - Société québécoise d'assainissement des eaux, 1006
SQDA - Société québécoise pour la défense des animaux, 1006
SQHH - Société québécoise des hostas et des hémérocalles, 1006
SQS - Société québécoise de spéléologie, 1006
SRI - Steel Recycling Institute, 1010
SRLS - Sudbury Rock & Lapidary Society, 1011
SSCA - Saskatchewan Soil Conservation Association, 1001
SSCS - Sea Shepherd Conservation Society, 1002
SSCS - Sea Shepherd Conservation Society - USA, 1002
SSEA - Severn Sound Environmental Association, 1003
SSGA - Saskatchewan Stock Growers Association, 1001
SSM - Safety Services Manitoba, 997
SSNB - Safety Services New Brunswick, 997
SSS - Society for Socialist Studies, 1007
STA - Saskatchewan Trucking Association, 1002
STC - Society of Toxicology of Canada, 1009
STEP - Saskatchewan Trade & Export Partnership Inc., 1002
SUDA - Sustainable Urban Development Association, 1011
SUMA - Saskatchewan Urban Municipalities Association, 1002
SWANA - Solid Waste Association of North America, 1009
SWCS - Soil & Water Conservation Society, 1009
SWF - Saskatchewan Wildlife Federation, 1002
SWPSO - Safe Workplace Promotion Services Ontario, 997
SWRC - Saskatchewan Waste Reduction Council, 1002

T

TAC - Transportation Association of Canada, 1013
TAC - Tunnelling Association of Canada, 1014
TBFN - Thunder Bay Field Naturalists, 1012
TBI - Toronto Biotechnology Initiative, 1012
TCF - Tree Canada Foundation, 1013
TCS - The Cousteau Society, 905
TCTF - Trans Canada Trail Foundation, 1013
TCYHA - Trans Canada Yellowhead Highway Association, 1013
TEA - Toronto Entomologists Association, 1012
TEA - Toronto Environmental Alliance, 1012
TEAC - Temiskaming Environmental Action Committee, 1012
TECA - Thermal Environmental Comfort Association, 1012
TFN - Toronto Field Naturalists, 1012
THLA - Toronto Health Libraries Association, 1012
TLA - Truck Loggers Association, 1014
TMLRA - The Township of Muskoka Lakes Ratepayers' Association, 1013
TOC - Toronto Ornithological Club, 1012
TOGA - The Ontario Greenhouse Alliance, 974
TREA - Thames Region Ecological Association, 1012
TREC - Toronto Renewable Energy Co-operative, 1013
TSBC - Tire Stewardship BC Association, 1012
TSMCA - Toronto Sheet Metal Contractors Association, 1013
TTS - Toronto Transportation Society, 1013
TUC - Trout Unlimited Canada, 1013
TWS - Toxics Watch Society of Alberta, 1013

U

UASBC - Underwater Archaeological Society of British Columbia, 1014
UCA - Uxbridge Conservation Association, 1016
UCFO - Union des cultivateurs franco-ontariens, 1014
UDI - Urban Development Institute of Canada, 1016
UIA - Union internationale des architectes, 1014
UICN - Union mondiale pour la nature - Bureau de Montréal, 1014
UMAAS - Urban Municipal Administrators' Association of Saskatchewan, 1016
UMQ - Union des municipalités du Québec, 1014
UNAC - United Nations Association in Canada, 1015

Environmental Resources

CANADIAN ENVIRONMENTAL RESOURCE GUIDE 2011-2012 805

Associations Acronym Index

UNCTAD - United Nations Conference on Trade & Development, 1015
UNDP - United Nations Development Program, 1015
UNEP - United Nations Environment Programme, 1015
UNEP-WCMC - UNEP - World Conservation Monitoring Centre, 1014
UNIDO - United Nations Industrial Development Organization, 1015
UNSM - Union of Nova Scotia Municipalities, 1015
UPA - Union des producteurs agricoles, 1014
URISA - Urban & Regional Information Systems Association, 1015

V

VBGA - VanDusen Botanical Garden Association, 1016
VEVA - Vancouver Electric Vehicle Association, 1016
VGAM - Vegetable Growers' Association of Manitoba, 1016
VI - The Vinyl Institute, 1017
VLMS - Victoria Lapidary & Mineral Society, 1017
VRCA - Vancouver Regional Construction Association, 1016
VWS - Valhalla Wilderness Society, 1016

W

WAITRO - World Association of Industrial & Technological Research Organizations, 1021
WAS - World Aquaculture Society, 1021
WBCC - Wild Bird Care Centre, 1020
WBCSD - World Business Council for Sustainable Development, 1021
WBEA - Wood Buffalo Environmental Association, 1021
WBFN - Willow Beach Field Naturalists, 1020
WCA - Wilderness Canoe Association, 1020
WCEL - West Coast Environmental Law Research Foundation, 1018
WCI - World Coal Institute, 1022
WCSC - Western Canadian Shippers' Coalition, 1019
WCTD - Western Canada Tire Dealers Association, 1018
WCWC - Western Canada Wilderness Committee, 1019
WCWWA - Western Canada Water, 1019
WEAO - Water Environment Association of Ontario, 1017
WEC - World Energy Council, 1022
WEDO - Women's Environment & Development Organization, 1021
WEF - Water Environment Federation, 1017
WESTAC - Western Transportation Advisory Council, 1019
WETT - Wood Energy Technology Transfer Inc., 1021
WFM - World Federalist Movement, 1022
WFS - World Future Society, 1022
WFUES - World Federation of Ukrainian Engineering Societies, 1022
WHC - Wildlife Habitat Canada, 1020
WHO - World Health Organization, 1022
WMC - Wood Manufacturing Council, 1021
WMO - World Meteorological Organization, 1022
WNA - World Nuclear Association, 1022
WNHA - Waterton Natural History Association, 1018
WOBO - World Organization of Building Officials, 1022
WPC - Wood Preservation Canada, 1021
WPC - Canadian Wood Preservers Bureau, 892
WPC - World Petroleum Congress, 1023
WPC - Wildlife Preservation Canada, 1020
WPO - World Packaging Organization, 1023
WRA - Wildlife Rescue Association of British Columbia, 1020
WRCLA - Western Red Cedar Lumber Association, 1019
WRHF - Waterloo Regional Heritage Foundation, 1018
WRI - World Resources Institute, 1023
WRLA - Western Retail Lumber Association, 1019
WSCA - Western Silvicultural Contractors' Association, 1019
WSE - World Society for Ekistics, 1023
WSO - World Safety Organization, 1023
WSPA - World Society for the Protection of Animals, 1023
WSSA - Weed Science Society of America, 1018
WTA - Wilderness Tourism Association, 1020
WWF - WWF International, 1024
WWF-Canada - World Wildlife Fund - Canada, 1023
WWF-USA - World Wildlife Fund - USA, 1023
WWOOF Canada - WWOOF Canada, 1024

Y

YCI - Youth Challenge International, 1024
YCM - Yukon Chamber of Mines, 1024
YCS - Yukon Conservation Society, 1024
YFGA - Yukon Fish & Game Association, 1024
YPHA - Yukon Public Health Association, 1024
YPLEA - Yukon Public Legal Education Association, 1024
YTEC - Yukon Tourism Education Council, 1024

Associations Publications Index

A

AAAS [American Association for the Advancement of Science] Annual Report, 822
AAAS [American Association for the Advancement of Science] Advances, 822
AAAS [American Association for the Advancement of Science] Policy Alert, 822
AASB Update [a publication of the Canadian Institute of Chartered Accountants], 873
Accident Prevention, 997
Across the Fence [a publication of the Alberta Association of Agricultural Societies], 815
ACWWA [Atlantic Canada Water & Wastewater Association] Newsletter, 842
Adaptive Management of Stream Corridors in Ontario, 901
Advisory Practice Bulletins [publications of the Association of Professional Biology], 837
Advocacy Link [a publication of the Canadian Institute of Plumbing & Heating], 875
Affiliates Council Guide [a publication of the National Association for Environmental Management], 956
Affinity Group of National Associations (AGNA) Newsletter, 896
Ag Buyer's Guide [a publication of the Ontario Federation of Agriculture], 973
Agenda [a publication of AllerGen NCE Inc.], 820
Agricultural Engineering International: The CIGR Journal of Scientific Research & Development, 937
AgriView [a publication of Newfoundland & Labrador Federation of Agriculture], 962
Agro Solutions / Revue Agrosolutions [a publication of the Research & Development Institute for the Agri-Environment], 994
AIA [Alberta Institute of Agrologists] Bulletin, 817
Air & Waste Management Association Membership Directory, 814
Air Transport Association of Canada Annual Report, 814
The Airport Voice: News & Views, 855
Airwaves - The Newsletter of the Canadian Respiratory Health Professionals, 884
AirWays [a publication of AllerGen NCE Inc.], 820
Alberta & Northwest Territories Lung Association Annual Report, 815
Alberta Association of Agricultural Societies Membership Directory, 815
Alberta Association of Landscape Architects Newsletter, 815
Alberta Greenhouse Growers Association Newsletter, 817
Alberta Milk Annual Report, 818
Alberta Milk Producer Handbook, 818
Alberta Native Plant Council Guidelines, 818
Alberta Organic Producers Association Chapter Binder, 818
Alberta Plastics Recycling Association News, 818
Alberta Post-Consumer Plastics Recycling Strategy, Recycled Plastic Audit, 818
Alberta Recreation & Parks Association Recreation Buyers Guide, 819
Alberta Utility Operator Newsletter, 820
Alchemist Digest: The CMA / SMA [Canadian Mineral Analysts / Analystes des minéraux canadiens] Newsletter, 879
AllerGen NCE Inc. Annual Report, 820
AllerGen Network Newsletter, 820
Allergy Asthma Information Association Newsletter, 821
Allergy, Asthma & Clinical Immunology: Official Journal of the Canadian Society of Allergy & Clinical Immunology, 886
American Association of Bovine Practitioners Newsletter, 822
American Association of Bovine Practitioners Annual Membership Directory, 822
American Caves, 822
American Industrial Hygiene Association Member Directory, 823
American Journal of Archaeology, 828

American Water Works Association Officers & Committee Directory, 826
AMO Watch File e-Newstter, 836
Animal Welfare in Focus, 868
Annual Report of the Municipal Engineers Association Administrative & Standing Committees, 955
Annual Service Continuity Report on Distribution System Performance in Electrical Utilities, 866
AOPA [Alberta Organic Producers Association] Newsletter, 818
APEGBC [Association of Professional Engineers & Geoscientists of British Columbia] Membership Directory, 838
APEGBC [Association of Professional Engineers & Geoscientists of British Columbia] Professional Practice Guidelines, 838
Applied Mechanics Reviews, 824
APPrO [Association of Power Producers of Ontario] Conference Proceedings, 837
Aquaculture Canada Abstracts, 828
Aquaculture Canada Proceedings of Contributed Papers, 828
Archaeology, 828
ArcticNet Inc. Annual Report, 829
ArcticNet Newsletter, 829
The Ark [a publication of The Nature Conservancy of Canada], 959
ARL [Animal Rescue League] Shelter Speak, 998
Arts Revision Report: Renewables Without Limits [a publication of the Ontario Sustainable Energy Association], 980
ASEH [American Society for Environmental History] News, 824
ASHRAE [American Society of Heating, Refrigerating & Air Conditioning Engineers] Journal, 824
ASME [American Society of Mechanical Engineers] Capitol Update, 824
ASPB [American Society of Plant Biologists] News, 826
Association of Municipalities of Ontario Annual Report, 836
Association of Professional Engineers & Geoscientists of British Columbia Report on Members' Compensation & Benefits, 838
Association of Professional Engineers & Geoscientists of British Columbia Annual Report, 838
Association of Professional Engineers & Geoscientists of British Columbia Technical Bulletins, 838
Association of Professional Engineers of Yukon Newsletter, 839
Association of Professional Engineers, Geologists & Geophysicists of Alberta Annual Report, 839
Association of Professional Engineers, Geologists & Geophysicists of Alberta Business Plan, 839
Association of Professional Geoscientists of Ontario Annual Report, 839
Association of Quantity Surveyors of Alberta Newsletter, 839
Association of the Chemical Profession of Alberta Newsletter, 840
Asthma Action, 975
At the Source [a publication of the Canadian Centre for Pollution Prevention], 862
@ATAC [Air Transport Association of Canada] Newsletter, 814
AtlanTECH News, 835
Atlantic Salmon Federation Annual Report, 843
Atlantic Salmon Federation Newsletter, 843
Atlantic Salmon Journal, 843
Atmosphere-Ocean, 878
Au Courant [a publication of the Canadian Council for International Co-operation], 864
The Auk [a publication of the American Ornithologists' Union], 824
Autobiography of John Macoun, Canadian Explorer & Naturalist, 1831-1920, 983
Avalanche Accidents in Canada, 859
avalanche.ca, 859
L'avantage 4-H Advantage, 854

Avian Conservation & Ecology, 1007
AWWA [American Water Works Association] Standards, 826
AWWA [American Water Works Association] Streamlines, 826
AWWA Wastewater Operator Field Guide, 842
AWWA Water Operator Field Guide, 842

B

Basin Research, 936
BC Homes Magazine, 871
BC Nature Magazine, 849
BC Occupational Health Nurses PPG Newsletter, 969
BC Organic Grower, 894
BCHGA [British Columbia Herb Growers Association] Newsletter, 848
Beef Business, 1001
Beef In BC, 847
Beef Newsletter, 988
Behind the Headlines [a publication of the Canadian International Council], 876
Beneficial Management Practices: Envrionmental Manual for Alberta Cow/Calf Producers, 815
The Benefits Catalogue, 881
Best Practices for Multi-Family Food Scraps Collection, 993
Better Farming, 973
Between Friends [a publication of Friends of Mount Revelstoke & Glacier], 921
B.I.D.S. (Business Initiative Development Service), 912
Biology & Conservation of Forest Birds, 1007
Biology International, 945
BioNews [a publication of the Association of Professional Biology], 837
BIOS [a publication of the Alberta Society of Professional Biologists], 819
Biosolids Technical Bulletin [a publication of the Water Environment Federation], 1017
Biosphère [a publication of the Canadian Wildlife Federation], 891
A Birder's Checklist of Ottawa, 983
Birding, 822
The Birds of Manitoba, 959
Blazing Star [a publication of the North American Native Plant Society], 965
The Blue Heron, 846
Blue Jay, 960
Boating Ontario: Marinas & Destination Guide, 975
Botany, 860
The Bovine Practitioner, 822
Breast Cancer Society of Canada Newsletter, 846
Breathworks, 975
Breathworks: COPD Newsletter, 1000
Bringing it Back: A Restoration Framework for the Castle Wilderness, 892
British Columbia Cattlemen's Association Newsletter, 847
British Columbia Farm Industry Review Board Strategic Plan, 847
British Columbia Forest Industry Fact Book, 905
British Columbia Ground Water Association Newsletter, 848
British Columbia Herb Growers Association Annual Report, 848
British Columbia Herb Growers Association Directory, 848
British Columbia Lung Association Annual Report, 848
British Columbia Recreation & Parks Association Annual Report, 849
BSIA e-news, 851
BSIA News Magazine, 851
Building a Dialogue with Aboriginal Communities: A Guide for Junior Exploration Companies & Prospectors, 977
Building a Fishery that Works: Ottawa Update, 917
Building Bridges [a publication of the International Union for Conservation of Nature], 944

Building Supply Industry Association of British Columbia Directory, 851
Building Supply Industry Association of British Columbia Retail Product Buying Guide, 851
Bullet [a publication of the Consulting Engineers of Alberta], 902
The Bulletin, 821
Le Bulletin de l'association pulmonaire du Québec, 991
The Bulletin of Canadian Petroleum Geology, 887
Bulletin of the Aquaculture Association of Canada, 828
BurlingtonGreen Environmental Association Newsletter, 852
BurlingtonGreen Youth Network Bulletin, 852
Business Law International, 936
A Buyers' Guide to Canada's Sustainable Forest Products, 918
Bylaws of the Association [a publication of the Association of Professional Engineers & Geoscientists of British Columbia], 838
By-Laws of the Nova Scotia Environmental Network (NSEN), 967

C

CA Alert / Alerte CA [a publication of the Canadian Institute of Chartered Accountants], 873
CA Magazine [a publication of the Canadian Institute of Chartered Accountants], 873
CA Practice Advantage [a publication of the Canadian Institute of Chartered Accountants], 873
CAA [Canadian Archaeological Association] Newsletter / Bulletin de l'ACA [Association d'archéologie canadienne-, 855
CAAR [Canadian Association of Agri-Retailers] Communicator, 856
CAAR [Canadian Association of Agri-Retailers] Roster, 856
CADEnews [a publication of the Canadian Association of Drilling Engineers], 857
CAED [Canadian Association of Equipment Distributors] - Ontario Membership Newsletter, 857
The CAG [Canadian Association of Geographers] Annual Directory, 857
The CAG [Canadian Association of Geographers] Newsletter, 857
CAHI [Canadian Animal Health Institute] Resource Directory, 855
CAHSPR [Canadian Association for Health Services & Policy Research] Newsletter, 855
The CAHT [Canadian Association for Humane Trapping] Bulletin, 855
Calgary Zoological Society eMagazine, 852
CAMA [Canadian Agri-Marketing Association] Membership Directory, 855
CAMESE [Canadian Association of Mining Equipment & Services for Export] Bulletin, 858
Camp Health Issues, 971
Canada Energy Law Service, 875
Canada ePestWorld, 882
Canadian 4-H Council Annual Report, 854
Canadian Academy of Engineering Newsletter / Communiqué, 854
Canadian Acoustics, 854
Canadian Aeronautics & Space Journal (CASJ), 854
Canadian Agricultural Economics Society Newsletter, 854
The Canadian Airports Council Annual Report, 855
Canadian Association for Laboratory Accreditation Inc. Annual Report, 856
Canadian Association for Laboratory Animal Science Members' Magazine, 856
Canadian Association of Animal Health Technologists & Technicians Annual Report, 856
Canadian Association of Fire Chiefs Directory of Members, 857
Canadian Association of Professional Heritage Consultants Forum, 858
Canadian Association of Recycling Industries Membership Directory, 858

Associations Publications Index

Canadian Association of Zoos & Aquariums Membership Directory, 859
Canadian Association on Water Quality Annual Report, 859
Canadian Bioethics Society Newsletter, 860
Canadian Biosystems Engineering Journal / Le Journal de la Société Canadienne de Génie Agroalimentaire et de Bioingénierie, 885
Canadian Cancer Statistics, 861
Canadian Capabilities Guide: Canada's Hydrogen & Fuel Cell Industry, 871
Canadian Cattlemen's Association By-laws, 861
Canadian Cattlemen's Association Policy Manual, 861
Canadian Circumpolar Institute Occasional Publications Series, 862
Canadian Civil Engineer (CCE), 885
Canadian College of Health Service Executives Membership Directory, 863
Canadian College of Health Service Executives Annual Report, 863
Canadian Construction Association National Review, 863
Canadian Council of Professional Fish Harvesters Newsletter, 865
Canadian Council on Animal Care Workshop Proceedings, 865
Canadian Dam Association Bulletin, 865
Canadian Drilling Activity Forecast, 986
Canadian Federation of Humane Societies Factsheets, 868
Canadian Forestry Association Teaching Kit User Guide, 868
Canadian Forestry Association Teaching Kit, Volume 1: Canada's Forests - Learning from the Past, Building for the Future, 868
Canadian Forestry Association Teaching Kit, Volume 2: Canada's Forests - A Breath of Fresh Air, 868
Canadian Forestry Association Teaching Kit, Volume 3: Canada's Forests - All Things Big & Small, 868
Canadian Forestry Association Teaching Kit, Volume 4: Canada's Forests - Source of Life, 868
Canadian Forestry Association Teaching Kit, Volume 5: Canada's Forest - A Fine Balance, 868
Canadian Forestry Association Teaching Kit, Volume 6: Canada's Forests & Wetlands - Our Natural Water Filters, 868
Canadian Forestry Association Teaching Kit, Volume 7: The Boreal Forest - A Global Legacy, 868
Canadian Forestry Association Teaching Kit, Volume 8: Canada's Boreal Forest - Tradition & Transition, 868
Canadian Forests: A Primer, 974
Canadian Fuel Cell Commercialization Roadmap Update: Progress of Canada's Hydrogen & Fuel Cell Industry, 871
Canadian Gas Association Market Updates, 869
Canadian Gas Association Membership Directory, 869
The Canadian Geographer (TCG) / Le Géographe canadien (LGC), 857
Canadian Geographic, 996
The Canadian Ground Water Journal, 870
Canadian Health Food Association Annual Report, 870
Canadian Health Food Association e-News, 870
Canadian Health Food Association Member Bulletins, 870
Canadian Health Magazine, 877
Canadian Home Builders' Association Builders' Manual, 871
Canadian Hydrogen & Fuel Cell Association Newsletter, 871
Canadian Hydrogen & Fuel Cell Sector Profile, 871
Canadian Institute for Health Information Annual Report, 872
Canadian Institute of Forestry Annual Report, 874
Canadian Institute of Forestry E-news, 874
Canadian Institute of Plumbing & Heating Member Directory, 875
Canadian Institute of Public Health Inspectors National Newsletter, 875
Canadian Journal of Agricultural Economics / Revue Canadienne d'Agroéconomie, 854
Canadian Journal of Archaeology / Journal canadien d'archéologie, 855
Canadian Journal of Civil Engineering (CJCE), 885
Canadian Journal of Electrical & Computer Engineering, 932
Canadian Journal of Infection Control, 899
Canadian Journal of Law & Society / La Revue Canadienne Droit et Société (CJLS / RCDS), 876
Canadian Journal of Medical Laboratory Science, 886
Canadian Journal of Plant Pathology / Revue canadienne de phytopathologie, 882
Canadian Journal of Plant Science (CJPS), 885
The Canadian Journal of Public Health, 883
Canadian Journal of Remote Sensing (CJRS), 854
Canadian Journal of Remote Sensing (CJRS) / Journal canadien de télédétection (JCT), 884
Canadian Journal of Soil Science, 888
Canadian Journal of Surgery (CJS), 877
Canadian Journal of Veterinary Research, 890
Canadian Land Reclamation Association Annual Meeting Proceedings, 876
Canadian Lung Association Annual Report, 876
Canadian Marketing Association Membership Directory & Buyers' Guide, 877
Canadian Meat Council Members Bulletin, 877
Canadian Meat Science Association Membership Directory, 877
Canadian Medical & Biological Engineering Society Conference Proceedings & Abstracts, 877
Canadian Medical & Biological Engineering Society Career Booklet, 877
Canadian Medical Association Complete Home Medical Guide, 877
Canadian Medical Association Conference Updates, 877
Canadian Medical Association Journal (CMAJ), 877
Canadian Metallurgical Quarterly: The Canadian Journal of Metallurgy & Materials Science, 954
Canadian Meteorological & Oceanographic Society Annual Review, 878
Canadian Meteorological & Oceanographic Society Annual Congress Program & Abstracts, 878
The Canadian Mineralogist: The Journal of the Mineralogical Association of Canada, 954
Canadian Municipal Water News & Review, 890
Canadian Natural Gas Magazine, 869
Canadian Nuclear Society Bulletin, 880
Canadian Nuclear Society Proceedings, 880
The Canadian Organic Grower, 880
Canadian Parks & Recreation Association Annual Report, 881
Canadian Parks & Recreation Association Research Reports, 881
Canadian Perspectives on Integrated Water Resources Management, 891
Canadian Plant Disease Survey / Inventaire des maladies des plantes au Canada, 882
Canadian Plastics Industry Association Executive Summary, 882
Canadian Power Directory, 837
Canadian Printing Ink Manufacturers Association Technical Bulletins, 883
Canadian Public Health Association Annual Report, 883
Canadian Pulp & Paper Network for Innovation in Education & Research Newsletter, 883
Canadian Reclamation, 876
Canadian Renewable Energy Guide, 1009
The Canadian Retail Food Safety Manual, 868
Canadian Sanitation Supply Association Bulletin, 884
Canadian Sanitation Supply Association Update, 884
Canadian Science Writers' Association Membership Directory, 884
Canadian Society for Bioengineering Annual Meeting Papers, 885
Canadian Society for Civil Engineering Annual Report, 885
Canadian Society for Civil Engineering Conference Proceedings, 885
Canadian Society for Civil Engineering E-Bulletin, 885
Canadian Society for Civil Engineering President's E-Letter, 885
Canadian Society of Air Safety Investigators Proceedings, 886
Canadian Society of Air Safety Investigators Newsletter, 886
Canadian Society of Clinical Chemists Member Handbook, 886
Canadian Society of Exploration Geophysicists Annual Report, 887
Canadian Society of Microbiologists Call for Abstracts, 887
Canadian Society of Microbiologists Graduate Studies & Membership Directory, 887
Canadian Society of Microbiologists Programme & Abstracts, 887
Canadian Society of Petroleum Geologists Calendar, 887
Canadian Society of Plant Physiologists Membership List, 887
Canadian Society of Zoologists / Société canadienne de zoologie Bulletin, 888
Canadian Solar Industries Association Inc. Membership Directory, 888
Canadian Space Gazette, 888
Canadian Standards Association Annual Report, 888
Canadian Standards for Nursery Stock, 880
Canadian Transit Forum, 889
Canadian Urban Transit Association's Buyer's Guide, 889
Canadian Veterinary Journal, 890
Canadian Water & Wastewater Association Conference Proceedings, 890
Canadian Water Resources Association Conference Proceedings, 891
Canadian Water Resources Journal, 891
Canadian Wilderness, 881
Canadian Wildlife [a publication of the Canadian Wildlife Federation], 891
Canadian Wood Council Awards Book, 891
Canadian Wood Council Technical Publications, 891
Canadian Wood, Renewable by Nature, Sustainable by Design, 918
CanWEA Members Directory, 891
CAODC [Canadian Association of Oilwell Drilling Contractors] Oil Driller, 858
CAP [Canadian Association of Palynologists] Newsletter, 858
CAPE [Canadian Association of Physicians for the Environment] News, 858
CAPEI [Construction Association of Prince Edward Island] Project Newsletter, 902
CAPHC [Canadian Association of Professional Heritage Consultants] Membership Directory, 858
CAPL [Canadian Association of Petroleum Landmen] Annual Report, 858
A Carbon Offsetting Primer, 896
CareerVision [a publication of the Canadian Institute of Chartered Accountants], 873
Cartographica, 861
Cartouche, 861
CASA [Canadian Agricultural Safety Association] / ACSA [Association canadienne de sécurité agricole] Liaison, 854
CASI [Canadian Aeronautics & Space Institute] Clipper, 854
CASI [Canadian Aeronautics & Space Institute] Log, 854
The Castle Wilderness Environmental Inventory, 892
Castle Wilderness News, 892
Catalyst, 862
Cattle Country: The Voice of Manitoba's Cattle Industry, 950
CAZA [Canadian Association of Zoos & Aquariums] News, 859
CAZA [Canadian Association of Zoos & Aquariums] Annual Report, 859
CBA [Canadian Botanical Association] / ABC [Association botanique du Canada] Bulletin, 860
CBCN [Canadian Botanical Conservation Network] Newsletter, 860
CCA [Canadian Cattlemen's Association] Annual Report, 861
CCA [Canadian Cattlemen's Association] Monthly Report, 861
CCA [Canadian Cattlemen's Association] News, 861
CCA [Canadian Construction Association] Committee Bulletins, 863
CCA [Canadian Construction Association] National Newsletter, 863
CCAA [Canadian Consulting Agrologists Association] Member Directory, 863
CCAA [Canadian Consulting Agrologists Association] Newsletter, 863
CCAC [Canadian Council on Animal Care] Annual Report, 865
CCAC [Canadian Council on Animal Care] Guide to the Care & Use of Experimental Animals, 865
CCAC [Canadian Council on Animal Care] Guidelines, 865
CCEP [Canadian Centre for Emergency Preparedness] Newsletter, 861
CCLA [Carleton County Law Association] Bulletin, 892
The CCLS / CCAG Forum, 864
CCMTA [Canadian Council of Motor Transport Administrators] News, 865
CCMTA [Canadian Council of Motor Transport Administrators] Directory, 865
The CCPA Monitor, 862
CE [Consulting Engineers] News, 835
The CEA [Canadian Electricity Association] Member Directory, 866
CEA [Consulting Engineers of Alberta] Annual Report, 902
CEA [Consulting Engineers of Alberta] Progress Report on Salaries, 902
Central Okanagan Naturalist Newsletter, 893
CFCAS [Canadian Foundation for Climate & Atmospheric Sciences] News, 869
CFES [Canadian Federation of Engineering Students] eBulletin, 868
CFHS [Canadian Federation of Humane Societies] Annual Report, 868
CFIG's [Canadian Federation of Independent Grocers] Crisis Communication & Pandemic Planning Manual, 868
CGDN [Canadian Genetic Diseases Network] Annual Report, 869
CGSA [Canadian Golf Superintendents Association] Membership Directory, 870
Chatter, 813
Checklist of the Birds of Manitoba, 959
Checklist of the Butterflies of the Ottawa District, 983
The Chemunicator, 857
CHLA [Canadian Health Libraries Association] / ABSC Directory & Membership List, 870
CHOA [Canadian Heavy Oil Association] Handbook, 871
CICA [Canadian Institute of Chartered Accountants] Standards & Guidance Collection, 873
CICA [Canadian Institute of Chartered Accountants] Annual Report, 873
CIGR [Commission Internationale du Genie Rural] Newsletter / Bulletin de la CIGR, 937
CIHI [Canadian Institute for Health Information] Directions ICIS [Institut canadien d'information sur la santé], 872
CIM [Canadian Institute of Mining, Metallurgy & Petroleum] Magazine, 874
CIM [Canadian Institute of Mining, Metallurgy & Petroleum] Directory, 874
CIM [Canadian Institute of Mining, Metallurgy & Petroleum] Reporter, 874
CINDE [Canadian Institute for NDE] Journal, 872
CIPH [Canadian Institute of Plumbing & Heating] EconoLink, 875
CIPH [Canadian Institute of Plumbing & Heating] Wholesalers Sales Statistics, 875
The Circular, 989
Circumpolar Research Series, 862
CIRL [Canadian Institute of Resources Law] Annual Report, 875
A Civil Society - A brief personal history of the CSCE [Canadian Society for Civil Engineering], 885
Civil Society Index (CSI) Newsletter, 896
Civil Society Watch (CSW) Monthly Bulletin, 896
CLA [Canadian Lumbermen's Association] Membership Directory, 876
CLA [Canadian Lumbermen's Association] News, 876
The CLA [Canadian Lumbermen's Association] Story - 100 Years of Service, 876
Clean & Green Newsletter, 896
Clean Nova Scotia Annual Report, 896
Clean Nova Scotia Strategic Plan, 896
ClimaPresse, 904
Climate Alert, 896
Clinical Biochemistry, 886
Clinical Engineering Standards of Practice [a publication of the Canadian Medical & Biological Engineering Society], 877
Clinical Infectious Diseases, 931
The CLSA / ACDS Bulletin, 876
CMA [Canadian Marketing Association] Fundraiser's Handbook, 877

808 GUIDE DES RESSOURCES ENVIRONNEMENTALES CANADIENNES 2011-2012

Associations Publications Index

CMA [Canadian Marketing Association] Guide to E-mail Marketing, 877
CMA [Canadian Medical Association] Bulletin, 877
CMA [Canadian Medical Association] Complete Book of Mother & Baby Care, 877
CMA [Canadian Medical Association] Driver's Guide: Determining Medical Fitness to Operate Motor Vehicles, 877
CMA [Canadian Medical Association] Leadership Series: MD Pulse, 877
CMA [Canadian Medical Association] Leadership Series: Primary Care Reform, 877
CMA [Canadian Medical Association] Leadership Series: Elder Care - Issues & Options, 877
CMA [Canadian Medical Association] Leadership Series: Women's Health - Research & Practice Issues for Canadian Physicians, 877
CMBES [Canadian Medical & Biological Engineering Society Inc.] Newsletter, 877
CME [Canadian Manufacturers & Exporters] Newsletter, 876
CMOS [Canadian Meteorological & Oceanographic Society] Bulletin SCMO [Société canadienne de météorologie et d'océanographie], 878
CMSA [Canadian Meat Science Association] News, 877
CNLA [Canadian Nursery Landscape Association] Newsbrief, 880
CNLA [Canadian Nursery Landscape Association] Membership Directory, 880
CNTC [Canadian Network of Toxicology Centres] News, 879
CNTC [Canadian Network of Toxicology Centres] Science Briefs, 879
CNTC [Canadian Network of Toxicology Centres] Annual Report, 879
CNTC [Canadian Network of Toxicology Centres] Annual Symposium Report, 879
Code of Ethics for Members of the Canadian College of Health Service Executives, 863
COFI [Council of Forest Industries] News: Month in Review, 905
COHA [Canadian Oil Heat Association] Directory, 880
Cold Harvester, 963
Come To Our Farm Guide, 816
The Communicator [a publication of the Alberta Development Officers Association], 816
Communiqué [a publication of the Canadian College of Health Leaders], 863
Communiqué [a publication of the Canadian Water Quality Association], 890
Communiqué [a publication of the Prospectors & Developers Association of Canada], 990
Communiqué [a publication of the Society of Toxicology], 1008
Community & Hospital Infection Control Association Canada Annual Member & Source Guide, 899
Community Atlas Initiative [a publication of the Canadian Parks & Wilderness Society], 881
Community Health Nurses of Canada Newsletter, 899
Community Health Nursing Standards of Practice, 899
Community Health Nursing Standards Toolkit, 899
Community Health Nursing Vision 2020: Shaping the Future, 899
Community Power Financing Guidebook, 980
The Community Power Guidebook, 980
Compendium of Canadian Mining Suppliers, 858
Competition Law International, 936
Compost Matters, 899
Comprehensive Reviews in Food Science & Food Safety, 932
Connecting Canadians to Nature: Strategic Plan [a publication of the Canadian Association of Zoos & Aquariums, 859
Connecting with Customers [a publication of the Canadian Home Builders' Association], 871
Connections [a publication of the Global, Environmental & Outdoor Education Council], 924
Connections [a publication of the Natural Health Practitioners of Canada], 959
Connections E-news [a publication of the Association of Professional Engineers & Geoscientists of British Columbia], 838
Connector [a publication of the Recycling Council of Alberta], 993
Conservation, 1006
Conservation Biology, 1006
Conservation Education & Outreach Techniques, 964
Conservation Letters, A Journal of the Society for Conservation Biology, 1006
Conservation Made Clear, 944
Conservation Ontario Annual Report, 901
Conservation Ontario E-Bulletin, 901
Conservator, 906
Construction Association of Prince Edward Island Membership Directory, 902
Construction Law International, 936
Consultants Directory [a publication of the Association of Quantity Surveyors of Alberta], 839
Consultants' Directory [a publication of the Ontario Professional Planners Institute], 977
Consultants' Listing [a publication of the Ontario Water Works Association], 981
Consulting Engineers of Alberta Directory of Members, 902
Consulting Engineers of British Columbia Annual Report, 903
Consulting Engineers Rate Guidelines, 902
Context Sensitive Solutions in Designing Major Urban Thoroughfares for Walkable Communities, 933
Contractor News [a publication of the Ontario Electrical League], 972
Contractor Newsbrief [a publication of the Ontario Electrical League], 972
Control & Intelligent Systems, 936
Convergence [a publication of the International Bar Association], 936
Cost Benefit Analysis of Agricultural Source Water Protection Beneficial Management Practices, 901
Council of Forest Industries Annual Report, 905
Councillor Development Resource Manual, 976
Councillors Handbook: Stewardship Responsibilities Under the Safe Drinking Water Act, 976
The Counsellor [a publication of the Private Motor Truck Council of Canada], 989
Country Guide, 973
CPAWS [Canadian Parks & Wilderness Society] Annual Report, 881
CPAWS [Canadian Parks & Wilderness Society] Research Reports, 881
CPC [Canadian Pallet Council] Communiqué, 881
CPCI [Canadian Precast / Prestressed Concrete Institute] Imagineering, 883
CPHA [Canadian Public Health Association] Health Digest, 883
CPIA [Canadian Plastics Industry Association] Annual Report, 882
CPIA [Canadian Plastics Industry Association] Membership Directory, 882
CPIA [Canadian Plastics Industry Association] Plastics Machinery & Moulds Export Directory, 882
CPRA [Canadian Parks & Recreation Association] E-News, 881
CPRA [Canadian Parks & Recreation Association] Tool Kits, 881
CPSC [Canadian Plastics Sector Council] Newsletter / Bulletin du CCSP [Conseil canadien sectoriel des plastiques], 882
Crop Advances: Field Crop Reports, 979
CRPA [Canadian Radiation Protection Association] Bulletin, 883
The CRS Comm Poster, 884
CSACI [Canadian Society of Allergy & Clinical Immunology] Newsletter / Bulletin CSAIC, 886
CSBMCB [The Canadian Society of Biochemistry, Molecular & Cellular Biology] Bulletin, 886
The CSCC [Canadian Society of Clinical Chemists] News, 886
CSEB [Canadian Society of Environmental Biologists] National Newsletter / Bulletin, 887
The CSEG / CSPG Geophysical Atlas of Western Canadian Hydrocarbon Pools, 887
CSHS [Canadian Society for Horticultural Science] Newsletter, 885
CSHS [Canadian Society for Horticultural Science] Membership Directory, 885
CSLA [Canadian Society of Landscape Architects] Bulletin, 887
CSLA [Canadian Society of Landscape Architects] Membership Directory, 887
CSLA [Canadian Society of Landscape Architects] Annual Report, 887
CSM [Canadian Society of Microbiologists] Newsletter, 887
CSME [Canadian Society for Mechanical Engineering] Bulletin, 885
CSPP [Canadian Society of Plant Physiologists] / SCPV [Société canadienne de physiologie végétale] Bulletin, 887
CSSE [Canadian Society of Safety Engineering, Inc.] Contact, 888
CSSS [Canadian Society of Soil Science] Newsletter, 888
CUTA Membership Directory, 889
The CWC [Canadian Wood Council] Newsletter, 891
CWLS [Canadian Well Logging Society] Annual Report, 891
CWLS [Canadian Well Logging Society] InSite, 891
CWLS [Canadian Well Logging Society] Journal, 891
CWRA [Canadian Water Resources Association] Water News, 891
CWWA [Canadian Water & Wastewater Association] Membership Directory, 890
CWWA [Canadian Water & Wastewater Association] Bulletin, 890
CWWA Members' Briefing Book: Current National Issues & Topics Concerning Water & Wastewater Management in Canada, 890

D

Daily News [a publication of the Mining Association of British Columbia], 954
Dam Safety Guidelines, 865
Dams in Canada, 865
Dandelion Recipes: 34 great recipes for salads, jellies, beverages, & appetizers!, 818
Dialogue [a publication of the Ontario Electrical League], 972
Digital Atlas: Geological Atlas of the Western Canada Sedimentary Basin, 887
The Digital Office, 928
Direct Currents [a publication of the Alberta Farm Fresh Producers Association], 816
Direct Seeding Manual, 1001
Direct Seeding Manual: A Farming System for the New Millennium, 988
Directors Source News [a publication of the Canadian Institute of Chartered Accountants], 873
Directory of CEBC [Consulting Engineers of British Columbia] Member Firms, 903
Directory of ESAC [Environmental Studies Association of Canada] Members, 913
Directory of Sources of Contaminants Entering Municipal Sewer Systems, 890
Disaster Management Canada (DMC), 861
Diseases & Pests of Vegetable Crops in Canada, 882
Diseases of Field Crop Crops in Canada, 882
Dispute Resolution International, 936
Ducks Unlimited Canada Annual Report, 906
Ducks Unlimited Magazine, 907

E

Earth First!, 907
Earth: The Sequel - The Race to Reinvent Energy and Stop Global Warming, 911
Eat Your Words, 932
e-CIVICUS [a publication of CIVICUS: World Alliance for Citizen Participation], 896
Eco-Connections [a publication of the Nova Scotia Environmental Network], 967
Ecoforestry, 908
Ecological Restoration, 1007
eCOMoS [a publication of the ICOMOS Canada], 930
The Edmonton Tornado & Hailstorm: A Decade of Research, 878
EE News [a publication of the North American Association for Environmental Education], 964
EECOM News, 879
Electric Vehicle Conversion Manual: A Workshop Guide for High Schools, 909
Electricity Annual, 866
Elementary School Teachers' Beliefs About Teaching Environmental Education, 964
Elements Magazine [a publication of the Geochemical Society], 923
Elements: An International Magazine of Mineralogy, Geochemistry, & Petrology, 954
Elements: The Newsletter of the Canadian Geophysical Union / Le Bulletin de l'union géophysique canadienne, 869
EM, The Magazine for Environmental Managers, 814
Emergency Food Recall Registry, 868
Energy Research & Innovation Directory, 861
E-news [a publication of the Canadian Federation of Independent Grocers], 868
L'Entre-Presse, 904
Enviro Boater, 975
Enviro Business Guide, 993
Environmental Association of Alberta Annual Report, 912
Environmental Awareness Training for Ozone Depleting Substances (ODS) & Other Halocarbons, 951
Environmental Education at the Early Childhood Level, 964
Environmental Education in the Schools: Creating a Program That Works!, 964
Environmental Education Research, Special Issue on Significant Life Experiences, 964
Environmental Education Undergraduate & Graduate Programs & Faculty in the United States, 964
Environmental Education: Academia's Response, 964
Environmental Ethics Syllabus Project, 943
Environmental Health Review, 875
Environmental History, 824
Environmental Literacy in the United States: What Should Be...What Is...Getting from Here to There, 964
Environmental Management Resource Manual [a publication of the Canadian Golf Superintendents Association], 870
Environmental Product & Services Directory, 847
Environmental Toxicology & Chemistry, 1008
Envisage [a publication of the Saskatchewan Outdoor & Environmental Education Association], 1001
E-PEG, 839
Epidemiology, 942
The ESAA [Environmental Services Association of Alberta] Weekly News, 912
Evaluating Your Environmental Education Programs: A Workbook for Practitioners, 964
An Evaluation of Water Resource Monitoring Efforts in Support of Agricultural Stewardship in Watersheds of the Great Lakes, 901
EVSurge [a publication of the Electric Vehicle Society of Canada], 909
Examining the Waste-to-Energy Option, 993
Exchange, 949
Exploration & Development Highlights, 990
The Explorationist [a publication of the Northern Prospectors Association & the Ontario Prospectors Association], 977
The Explorationist [a publication of the Northern Prospectors Association & the Ontario Prospectors Association], 966
Express Connect, 932
EXPRESSions, 889

F

Famille Avertie, 853
The Farm Journalist: Newsletter of the Canadian Farm Writers' Federation, 867
FAST-Line [a publication of the Petroleum Services Association of Canada], 986
Federation of Canadian Municipalities Annual Report, 915
Federation of Ontario Cottagers' Associations Report to Members, 915
Field Botanists of Ontario Newsletter, 916
Field Checklist of Ontario Birds, 973
A Field Guide to Environmental Literacy: Making Strategic Investments in Environmental Education, 964
Field Notes: Association of Professional Geoscientists of Ontario Newsletter, 839
Financial Edge, 928
Finding Birds in Southern Manitoba, 959
Finishing the Coal Phase Out: An Historic Opportunity for Climate Leadership, 972
Fire Chief Magazine, 857
Firewatch, 975

Environmental Resources

CANADIAN ENVIRONMENTAL RESOURCE GUIDE 2011-2012 809

Associations Publications Index

Fisheries, 823
Fisheries Council of Canada Annual Fish & Seafood Products & Services Directory, 917
Flightplan, 814
Food Technology, 932
Forced Outage Performance of Transmission Equipment [a publication of the Canadian Electricity Association], 866
Foreign Policy for Canada's Tomorrow, 876
Forest Certification in Canada: The Programs, Similarities, & Achievements, 918
Forest Products Association of Canada Annual Report, 918
Forest Products Association of Nova Scotia Newsletter, 919
Forest Steward [a publication of the Registered Professional Foresters Association of Nova Scotia], 994
The Forestry Chronicle: The Official Journal of the Canadian Institute of Forestry, 874
The Formulator [a publication of the Canadian Consumer Specialty Products Association], 863
Forum: Canada's National Municipal Magazine, 915
FPAC [Forest Products Association of Canada] Sustainability Report, 918
From Steam to Space. . . Contributions of Mechanical Engineering to Canadian Development, 885
Frozen Ground: The News Bulletin of the International Permafrost Association, 941
Future Practice, 877
Future Survey, 1022
Future Times, 1022
Futures Research Quarterly, 1022
Futurist Update, 1022
The Futurist, 1022
FYI [a publication of the Canadian Institute of Chartered Accountants], 873

G

Gatineau Park: A Threatened Treasure, 881
GCA: Geochimica et Cosmochimica Acta, 923
G-Cubed (Geochemistry, Geophysics, Geosystems), 923
Geminews, 955
General Policies of the Nova Scotia Environmental Network (NSEN), 967
Generation Equipment Status [a publication of the Canadian Electricity Association], 866
Geochemical News, 923
Geochemical Society Special Publication Series, 923
géographica, 996
Geolog, 923
Geological Association of Canada Membership Directory, 923
Geomatica, 874
Geoscience Canada, 923
Global News [a publication of the International Solid Waste Association], 944
GLOBE-Net Environmental Business E-Newsletter, 924
Green Building, 882
Green Community News, 925
Green Energy ACTion Kit, 980
Green Teacher, 1001
Green TIPS Guide, 956
Greening Tips, 852
GreenMaster, 870
Greenmatter E-News [a publication of the Canadian Golf Superintendents Association], 870
Greenprint: Towards a Sustainable New Brunswick, 960
The Griffin [a publication of the Heritage Trust of Nova Scotia], 929
Guide to Conservation Areas, 901
A Guide to Energy Efficiency for Religious Buildings in Nova Scotia, 896
Guide to International Opportunities in Landscape Architecture, Education & Internships, 939
A Guide to the Geology of the Gatineau-Lièvre District, 983
A Guide to the Geology of the Ottawa District, 983
Guidelines for Snow Avalanche Risk Determination & Mapping in Canada, 859
Guidelines To Best Practices For Heavy Haul Railway Operations - Infrastructure Construction & Maintenance Issues, 940
Guidelines To Best Practices For Heavy Haul Railway Operations - Wheel & Rail Interface Issues, 940

H

The Health & Safety Report, 862
Health Libraries Association of British Columbia Directory, 928
Healthcare Governance Update, 975
Healthcare IT News, 928
Healthcare Management FORUM, 863
Healthcare Policy, 855
Highlights [a publication of the Canadian Injured Workers Alliance], 872
HIMSS [Healthcare Information & Management Systems Society] Weekly Insider, 928
HIMSS [Healthcare Information & Management Systems Society] Conference Proceedings, 928
HIMSS [Healthcare Information & Management Systems Society] Clinical Informatics Insights, 928
HIMSS [Healthcare Information & Management Systems Society] Pulse on Public Policy, 928
HIMSS [Healthcare Information & Management Systems Society] HIELights, 928
History & Heritage Newsletter [a publication of the American Society of Mechanical Engineers], 824
History of the Canadian Medical Association, 1954-94, 877
Home on the Range [a publication of Wildlife Preservation Canada], 1020
Honour Due: the Story of Dr. Leonora Howard King, 877
Hospital Perspectives, 975
How to be a Camp Counsellor . . . The Best Job in the World!, 971
How to Manage Risk: A Canadian Home Builders' Association Guide for New Home Builders & Renovators, 871
HSAA Challenger, 928
Hydroscan: Airborne Laser Mapping of Hydrological Features & Resources, 891

I

IDA Journal on Desalination & Water Reuse [a publication of the American Water Works Association], 826
Ideas for a More Effective Environmental Movement in Canada, 867
IDSA [Infectious Diseases Society of America] News, 931
IEEE [Institute of Electrical & Electronics Engineers Inc.] Canada Newsletter / Bulletin de IEEE Canada, 932
IEEE [Institute of Electrical & Electronics Engineers Inc.] Canadian Review / La revue canadienne de l'IEEE, 932
IFHP [International Federation for Housing & Planning] Membership List & Directory, 939
IFLA Journal, 939
IGU [International Geographic Union] Newsletter, 939
Incidence & Impacts of Escaped Farmed Atlantic Salmon "Salmo Salar" in Nature, 843
Increasing Productivity & Moving Towards a Renewable Future: A New Electricity Strategy for Ontario, 972
Independent Grocer Newsmagazine, 868
Indoor Air: The International Journal of Indoor Environment & Health, 943
Indoor Environment Connections, 912
Industrial Wastewater [a publication of the Water Environment Federation], 1017
Influents [a publication of the Ontario Pollution Control Equipment Association], 077
INFLUENTS [a publication of the Water Environment Association of Ontario], 1017
Inforum [a publication of the Canadian Animal Health Institute], 855
The In-House Perspective [a publication of the International Bar Association-, 936
Innovation [a publication of the Association of Professional Engineers & Geoscientists of British Columbia], 838
Innovation [a publication of the Canadian Council of Technicians & Technologists], 865
Innovations in Water Management, 901
Input [a publication of the Canadian Association of Agri-Retailers], 856
Inside EIA [Environmental Information Association], 912
Insolvency & Restructuring International, 936
Institute of Food Technologists Annual Meeting & Food Expo Preview, 932
Institute of Food Technologists Annual Meeting & Food Expo Wrap-up, 932
Integrated Environmental Assessment & Management, 1008
International Bar News, 936
International Bear News, 934
International Fire Fighter, 935
International Heavy Haul Association Conference Proceedings, 940
International Insights, 876
International Journal, 876
International Journal of Computational Bioscience, 936
International Journal of Computers and Applications, 936
International Journal of Modelling and Simulation, 936
International Journal of Power and Energy Systems, 936
International Journal of Robotics and Automation, 936
International Journal of Rock Mechanics & Mining Sciences, 943
International Manual of Planning Practice (IMPP), 943
International Society for Environmental Epidemiology Directory of Members, 942
International Society for Environmental Ethics Newsletter, 943
International Society of City & Regional Planners Annual Congress Report, 943
International Society of Indoor Air Quality & Climate Conference Proceedings, 943
International Society of Indoor Air Quality & Climate Task Force Reports, 943
International Society of Indoor Air Quality & Climate Newsletter, 943
International Solid Waste Association Annual Report, 944
International Solid Waste Association Conference Proceedings, 944
International Union of Food Science & Technology Scientific Information Bulletins, 945
The Investigative & Forensic Accounting (CA-IFA) Media Directory, 873
IPPSO FACTO: Magazine of the Association of Power Producers of Ontario, 837
IRIS: The Alberta Native Plant Council Newsletter, 818
ISASI Forum, 886
ISC [International Society of Citriculture] Proceedings, 943
ISOCARP [International Society of City & Regional Planners] NET, 943
ISOCARP [International Society of City & Regional Planners] Review, 943
ISRM [International Society for Rock Mechanics] News Journal, 943
ISRM [International Society for Rock Mechanics] Newsletter, 943
Issues in Focus [a publication of the North Central Local Government Association], 965
IUFoST Newsline, 945
IWA's Water 21, 859

J

Jane Goodall Institute of Canada eNewsletter, 946
Jobs & Environment: Moving British Columbia into the 21st Century, 850
Journal AWWA [American Water Works Association], 826
Journal of Applied Mechanics, 824
Journal of Biomechanical Engineering, 824
Journal of Computational & Nonlinear Dynamics, 824
Journal of Computing & Information Science in Engineering, 824
Journal of Dynamic Systems, Measurement, & Control, 824
Journal of Electronic Packaging, 824
Journal of Energy & Natural Resources Law, 936
Journal of Energy Resources Technology, 824
Journal of Engineering for Gas Turbines & Power, 824
Journal of Engineering Materials & Technology, 824
Journal of Environmental Health, 957
Journal of Environmental Hydrology, 935
Journal of Fluids Engineering, 824
Journal of Food Science, 932
Journal of Food Science Education, 932
Journal of Fuel Cell Science & Technology, 824
Journal of Healthcare Information Management, 928
Journal of Heat Transfer, 824
Journal of Infectious Diseases, 931
Journal of Manufacturing Science & Engineering, 824
Journal of Mechanical Design, 824
Journal of Mechanisms & Robotics, 824
Journal of Medical Devices, 824
Journal of Nanotechnology in Engineering & Medicine, 824
Journal of Occupational & Environmental Hygiene, 823
Journal of Offshore Mechanics & Arctic Engineering, 824
Journal of Petroleum Geology, 936
Journal of Pressure Vessel Technology, 824
Journal of Pulp and Paper Science (JPPS), 991
Journal of Rock Mechanics & Rock Engineering, 943
Journal of Solar Energy Engineering, 824
The Journal of the Acadian Entomological Society, 813
Journal of the Air & Waste Management Association, 814
Journal of the Canadian Health Libraries Association / Journal de l'association des bibliothèques de la santé du Canada, 870
Journal of the Canadian Heavy Oil Association, 871
Journal of the Entomological Society of Ontario, 911
Journal of Thermal Science & Engineering Applications, 824
Journal of Tribology, 824
Journal of Turbomachinery, 824
Journal of Vibration & Acoustics, 824

K

Keeping the Special in Special Management Zones: A Citizens Guide [a publication of British Columbia Spaces for Nature], 850
Klinaklini Resource Analysis [a publication of British Columbia Spaces for Nature], 850

L

Lake Stewards Newsletter, 915
Land Managers Guide for Snow Avalanche Hazards in Canada, 859
The Land Surveyor, 834
Landscapes / Paysages, 887
Legal Information for Environmental Groups, 960
Lessons Learned: Reflections of Canadian Physician Leaders, 877
Liaison [a publication of the Canadian Centre for Occupational Health & Safety], 862
Liaison [a publication of the Occupational & Environmental Medical Association of Canada], 969
Lichens of the Ottawa Region, 983
Lighthouse: The Journal of the Canadian Hydrographic Association, 871
The Link, 834
Living Architecture Monitor, 926
Living Safety, 853
Local Government Elections Manual, 949
Local Government Management Association of British Columbia Annual Report, 949
Local Government Management Association of British Columbia Guide for Approving Officers, 949
Local Government Management Association of British Columbia Records Management Manual for Local Government, 949
Lumber Grading 101 Student Manual, 876
Lung Association of Saskatchewan Annual Report, 1000

M

Manitoba Environmental Industries Association Inc. Members' Directory, 951
Manitoba Farmers' Voice, 947

Manitoba Lung Association Annual Report, 951
Manitoba Ozone Protection Industry Association Annual Report, 951
Manitoba Water Well Association Newsletter, 952
Marina News, 975
Market Express, 817
The Marketing Advantage: A Guide For Professional Home Renovators, 871
MarketNews [a publication of the Canadian Agri-Marketing Association], 855
MD Lounge, 877
ME Today [a publication of the American Society of Mechanical Engineers], 824
MEIA [Manitoba Environmental Industries Association Inc.] Information Bulletin, 951
Member Savvy [a publication of the American Society of Mechanical Engineers], 824
Membership that Matters! [a publication of the Canadian Health Food Association], 870
Mercury . . . A Public Concern, including Analysis of Mercury Emissions from Coal-Fired Power Plants & Canada-Wide Standards, 867
Mercury - A Global Toxin: Perspectives on Initiatives & Programs on Coal-Fired Power Plants & Mercury Emissions, 867
Meters Made Easy: A Guide to the Economic Appraisal of Alternative Metering Investment Strategies, 890
MIA [Manitoba Institute of Agrologists] Bulletin, 951
Microgram [a publication of the Canadian Consumer Specialty Products Association], 863
Milestones [a publication of the Ontario Good Roads Association], 974
Milking Times, 818
The Mineral Vein: The Mineral Society of Manitoba Newsletter, 954
Mires & Peat, 941
mLink: The The Electronic Newsletter of the METSOC of CIM, 954
The Monograph Editor, 971
MOPIA [Manitoba Ozone Protection Industry Association] E-Bulletin, 951
More Than Trees: A Citizen's Guide to Making Conservation a Bigger Part of Forest Management, 881
Municipal Engineers Association Members Directory, 955
Municipal Water & Wastewater Rate Manual, 890
Municipal Water & Wastewater Rates Primer, 890

N

NAAEE [North American Association for Environmental Education] Communicator, 964
NAEM [National Association for Environmental Management] Network E-News, 956
Nahanni: Protected Forever, 881
The National [a publication of the Canadian Home Builders' Association], 871
National Water Works Operator Training Manuals, 890
Native Agri Update, 930
Native Plant Source List, 818
The Natural Voice [a publication of the Canadian Health Food Association], 870
Nature & Natural Areas in Canada's Capital, 983
The Nature Conservancy of Canada Annual Report to our Donors, 959
Nature Manitoba News, 959
The Nature Nation, 959
Nature Niagara News, 964
Nature Nova Scotia Annual Report, 960
Nature Views, 960
Naturescape Manitoba, 959
Navigating Ontario's Future: A Water Budget Overview for Ontario, 901
Navigating Ontario's Future: Overview of Integrated Watershed Management in Ontario, 901
Navigating Ontario's Future: Water Management Framework, 901
The Negotiator: The Magazine of the Canadian Association of Petroleum Landmen, 858
Net News [a publication of the Environmental Information Association], 912
New Brunswick Environment Industry Association Newsletter, 960
New Brunswick Soil & Crop Improvement Association Newsletter, 961

New Crops, Old Challenges: Tips & Tricks for Managing New Crops!, 979
The New Face of the Canadian Forest Industry: The Emerging Bio-revolution (The Bio-pathways Project), 918
Newfoundland & Labrador Construction Association Weekly Bulletin, 962
Newfoundland & Labrador Construction Association Membership Directory, 962
Newfoundland & Labrador Lung Association Newsletter, 963
Newfoundland & Labrador Public Health Association Newsletter, 963
Newfoundland Aquaculture Industry Association Member Directory, 963
News & Activities [a publication of the Prospectors & Developers Association of Canada], 990
News for Ewes, 1000
News Update [a publication of the Alberta Institute of Agrologists], 817
NewsBriefs [a publication of the Private Motor Truck Council of Canada], 989
Nickel Basin Rockhound, 1011
Nicotine & Tobacco Research: The Journal of SRNT [Society for Research on Nicotine & Tobacco], 1007
Nightly Nezzz Newsletter, 1000
North American Association for Environmental Education Conference Proceedings, 964
Northern Hunter-Gatherers Research Series, 862
Northern Reference Series [publications of the Canadian Circumpolar Institute], 862
Nova Scotia Environmental Network Annual Activity Report, 967
N.S.C.Action [a publication of Nova Scotia Cattle Producers], 967
NSWMA [National Solid Wastes Management Association] e-News, 958
Nuclear Canada, 879
Nuclear Canada Yearbook, 879
Nuclear Energy Handbook, 879
Numerical Methods in Atmospheric & Oceanic Modelling: The André J. Robert Memorial Volume, 878
Nutraraceutical Newsletter, 932

O

Observation Guidelines & Recording Standards for Weather, Snowpack, & Avalanches (OGRS), 859
OCA [Ontario Camps Association] Bulletin, 971
OCA [Ontario Camps Association] Camps Guide, 971
OCA [Ontario Camps Association] Crisis Response & Management Plan, 971
OCA [Ontario Cattlemen's Association] Weekly Update, 971
Occupational Health & Safety Policy & Procedures Manual, 851
Oceanography, 970
OEN [Ontario Environmental Network] Announcements, 973
Off the Shelf [a publication of the International Union for Conservation of Nature], 944
OFO [Ontario Field Ornithologists] News, 973
OHA [Ontario Hospital Association] Executive Report, 975
On the Edge [a publication of Wildlife Preservation Canada], 1020
On the Road to Zero Waste: Priorities for Local Governments, 993
Ontario Beef, 971
Ontario Birds, 973
Ontario Camps Association's Guidelines for Accreditation, 971
Ontario Cattlemen's Association Production Guides, 971
Ontario Clean Air Alliance E-Bulletin, 972
Ontario Drinking Water Stewardship Program Outreach & Education Toolkit, 901
Ontario Electrical League Chapter Newsletter, 972
Ontario Environmental Directory, 973
Ontario Federation of Agriculture Policy Handbook, 973
Ontario Good Roads Association Annual Report, 974
Ontario Hospital Association Annual Report, 975
Ontario Landowner's Guide to Wind Energy, 980
Ontario Medical Review, 975

Ontario Mining & Exploration Directory, 977
Ontario Municipal Water Association Members' Handbook, 976
Ontario Petroleum Institute Annual Conference & Trade Show Proceedings, 976
Ontario Pipeline, 981
Ontario Planning Journal, 977
The Ontario Power Authority's Coal Phase-Out Strategy: A Critical Review, 972
The Ontario Prospector, 977
Ontario Public Health Association E-Bulletin, 977
Ontario Soil & Crop Improvement Association Newsletter, 979
The Ontario Steakholder, 971
Ontario Sustainable Energy Association E-Bulletin, 980
Ontario Tire Dealers Association Membership Directory, 980
Ontario's Coal Phase-Out: A Major Climate Accomplishment Within Our Grasp, 972
Ontario's Green Future: How We Can Build a 100% Renewable Electricity Grid by 2027, 972
OPA [Ontario Parks Association] Playability Tool Kit: Building Accessible Playspaces, 976
OPCEA [Ontario Pollution Control Equipment Association] Membership Directory & Buyers Guide, 977
Operator Certification Study Guide [a publication of the Atlantic Canada Water & Wastewater Association], 842
Opflow [a publication of the American Water Works Association], 826
OPI [Ontario Petroleum Institute Inc.] Newsletter, 976
OPPI [Ontario Professional Planners Institute] Members Update, 977
OPTA [Ontario Community Transit Association] News, 972
ORCS [Ontario Respiratory Care Society] Update, 978
Organic Statistics, 880
Organics Working Group Report: Recommendations for Residential Collection, 993
Ornithology in Ontario, 973
OSEA [Ontario Sustainable Energy Association] Member Directory, 980
Ottawa & Eastern Ontario Lawyers' Directory, 892
Ottawa Safety Council Newsletter, 983
Our Schools / Our Selves, 862
Outdoor Edge [a publication of the Manitoba Wildlife Federation], 952
Outdoor Edge [a publication of the Saskatchewan Wildlife Federation], 1002
Outdoor Edge [a publication of the Yukon Fish & Game Association], 1024
Oxygen, 975

P

Parking Generation: An ITE Informational Report, 933
Participating in Federal Public Policy: A Guide for the Voluntary Sector, 867
Patient Safety Matters: The CPSI Newsletter, 881
PDAC [Prospectors & Developers Association of Canada] Activities, 990
PDAC [Prospectors & Developers Association of Canada] in Brief, 990
Peat News, 941
Peatlands International, 941
PEI Cattle Producers Annual Report with Financial Statements, 988
Permafrost & Periglacial Processes, 941
Permitting & Approvals Processes for CP Projects [a publication of the Ontario Sustainable Energy Association], 980
Perspectives [a publication of the Canadian Council of Chief Executives], 864
Perspectives [a publication of the Canadian Standards Association], 888
Perspectives: The Newsletter of CSBE [Canadian Society for Bioengineering] / Les Nouvelles de SCGAB, 885
Pest Gazette, 882
The Pest Management Research Report (PMRR), 882
PestWorld, 882
Pet Talk, 920

Petroleum Services Association of Canada Annual Report, 986
Petroleum Services Association of Canada Membership Directory, 986
Petroleum Services News, 986
Picoides: Bulletin of the Society of Canadian Ornithologists / Bulletin de la Société des Ornithologistes du Canada, 1007
The Pink Dolomite Saddle Bulletin, 964
Pipeline, 875
Planning by Design: A Healthy Communities Handbook, 977
The Plant Cell, 826
Plant Collection Guidelines, 818
Plant Physiology, 826
PMI [Physician Management Institute] Newsletter: Leadership for Physicians, 877
Powerful Options: A Review of Ontario's Options for Replacing Aging Nuclear Plants, 972
Powering Ontario Communities: Proposed Policy for Projects up to 10mw, 980
Practical Skills Handbooks, 880
Practice Advice [a publication of the Canadian Institute of Chartered Accountants], 873
Prairie Soils & Crops eJournal, 1001
Prairie Steward, 1001
Précis [a publication of the Canadian Council of Grocery Distributors], 864
Predictions in Ungauged Basins, 891
Preliminary Program [a publication of the Society of Toxicology], 1008
Preparing Effective Environmental Educators, 964
Primary Care Respiratory Journal, 942
PrimePlus [a publication of the Canadian Institute of Chartered Accountants], 873
Prince Edward Island Nitrate Report, 843
Privacy Guide [a publication of the Canadian Federation of Independent Grocers], 868
Proceedings, 941
Proceedings of the American Association of Bovine Practitioners Annual Conference, 822
Proceedings of the Canadian Mineral Analysts / Analystes des minéraux canadiens Annual Meeting, 879
Proceedings of the International Conferences on Permafrost, 941
The Professional Geographer, 834
Profofessional Safety, 826
Program & Abstracts of the CSHS [Canadian Society for Horticultural Science] Annual Conference, 885
Project [a publication of the Canadian Federation of Engineering Students], 868
The Prompt [a publication of the Canadian Association of Recycling Industries], 858
Proposal for a Green Energy Act for Ontario, 980
Protecting People & Property: A Business Case for Investing in Flood Prevention & Control, 901
The Protector [a publication of the Soil Conservation Council of Canada], 1009
PSAB Bulletin [a publication of the Public Sector Accounting Board], 873
The Public Garden, 822
Public Health Nursing Competencies, 899
Public Health Nursing Practice in Canada: A Review of the Literature, 899
Public Health Pulse, 836
Public Health Today, 977
The Pulse [a publication of the Canadian Association of Recycling Industries], 858

Q

QC / QA Manual [a publication of the Canadian Mineral Analysts], 879
Quarterly Stumpage Update [a publication of the Council of Forest Industries], 905

R

The Rancher's Guide to Elk & Bison Handling Facilities, 988
Le Rapport annuel de l'association pulmonaire du Québec, 991
RCBC [Recycling Council of British Columbia] Backgrounder: Degradable Plastic Bags, 993
RCEN [Canadian Environmental Network] Annual Report, 867

Associations Publications Index

RCEN [Canadian Environmental Network] e-Bulletin, 867
RCEN [Canadian Environmental Network] Youth Friendly Guide: Youth Guide to Policy Change for Intergenerational Partnerships, 867
RCO [Recycling Council of Ontario] Highlights the Headlines, 993
ReAction [a publication of AllerGen NCE Inc.], 820
Reclamation Newsletter, 876
Recommendations for Procuring Sustainable Energy: An Addendum to Renewables Without Limits, 980
Recommended Code of Practice for the Care & Handling of Farm Animals: Beef Cattle Edition, 815
REConnect [a publication of the Alberta Recreation & Parks Association], 819
Recorder, 887
Recreation & Parks BC, 849
Recycling Council of British Columbia Annual Report, 993
Recycling Council of Ontario Annual Report, 993
Recycling Council of Ontario e-Newsletter, 993
Recycling Council of Ontario Member Bulletin, 993
Reflections on Water: CWRA 1947 - 1997, 891
Refocus Weekly [a publication of the Canadian Association for Renewable Energies], 856
Regional Crop Reports, 817
The Regulatory Review [a publication of the Environmental Services Association of Alberta], 912
Renewable Energy Focus, 856
Répertoire Cabinets CA Firm Directory [a publication of the Canadian Institute of Chartered Accountants], 873
Report on Industry (ROI) [a publication of the Canadian Institute of Chartered Accountants], 873
Research & Development Institute for the Agri-Environment Annual Report, 994
Research & Development Institute for the Agri-Environment Scientific Activity Report, 994
Research & Your Health, 870
Research Connection [a publication of the Canadian Cancer Society Research Institute], 861
Research Monitor [a publication of the Canadian Institute of Chartered Accountants], 873
Research Review [a joint publication of the Ontario Respiratory Care Society & the Ontario Thoracic Society], 978
Reservoir [a publication of the Canadian Society of Petroleum Geologists], 887
Resource [a publication of the Canadian Society for Bioengineering], 885
Resource Recycling, 995
Resource: The Newsletter of the Canadian Council on Animal Care (CCAC), 865
Resources [a publication of the Canadian Institute of Resources Law], 875
Restoration Ecology, 1007
Restore [a publication of the Society for Ecological Restoration International], 1007
Retail Job Descriptions Handbook, 851
Retailer Wage Survey [a publication of the Canadian Association of Agri-Retailers], 856
RHEIG [Respiratory Health Educators Interest Group] Connections, 978
Rhizome [a publication of the Environmental Studies Association of Canada], 913
The RHN [Richmond Hill Naturalists] Bulletin, 995
Rideau Trail Association E-Letter, 995
Rideau Trail Association Newsletter, 995
The Rideau Trail Guidebook, 995
The RIO Report [a publication of the Sierra Club of Canada], 1004
Risk Alert [a publication of the Canadian Institute of Chartered Accountants], 873
Royal Canadian Geoographical Society Annual Report, 996
Roots & Shoots Canada eNewsletter, 946
The Rosarian, 884
The Rose Annual, 884
Rubber Manufacturers Association Member Directory, 997
Rural Councillor, 999

S

Safety Advocate Newsletter, 999
Safety Lines, 968
Saint John Naturalists' Club Bulletin, 998
Saskatchewan Applied Science Technologists & Technicians Salary Survey, 998
Saskatchewan Directory of Camps, 999
Saskatchewan Environmental Industry & Managers' Association Member Directory & Buyer's Guide, 999
Saskatchewan Environmental Industry & Managers' Association Newsletter, 999
Saskatchewan Environmental Society Newsletter, 1000
Saskatchewan Katahdin Sheep Association Membership Directory, 1000
Saskatchewan's Green Directory, 999
SASTT [Saskatchewan Applied Science Technologists & Technicians] Journal, 998
SCAN - Sierra Club of Canada Activist News, 1004
SCAN: The Saskatchewan Camping Association Newsletter, 999
SCB [Society for Conservation Biology] Newsletter, 1006
Science [a publication of the American Association for the Advancement of Science], 822
Science Books & Films [a publication of the American Association for the Advancement of Science], 822
Science Link [a publication of the Canadian Science Writers' Association], 884
Science Roundup [a publication of the American Association for the Advancement of Science], 822
Science Signaling [a publication of the American Association for the Advancement of Science], 822
Science Translational Medicine [a publication of the American Association for the Advancement of Science], 822
Sedimentology, 936
segdDESIGN: The International Journal of Environmental Graphic Design, 1007
SEN [Saskatchewan Eco-Network] Bulletin, 999
Sensitivity Mapping & Local Watershed Assessments for Climate Change Detection & Adaptation Monitoring, 901
Showcase Newsletter: News from the Canadian Association of Equipment Distributors, 857
SLSA [Saskatchewan Land Surveyors' Association] Corner Post, 1000
SMA [Saskatchewan Medical Association] News, 1001
Socialist Studies: Journal of the Society for Socialist Studies, 1007
Society for Ecological Restoration International Newsletter, 1007
Society for Environmental Graphic Design Membership Directory, 1007
Society for Research on Nicotine & Tobacco Annual Meeting Abstracts, 1007
Society of Environmental Toxicology & Chemistry Annual Report, 1008
Society of Toxicology Membership Directory, 1008
SOL [a publication of the Solar & Sustainable Energy Society of Canada Inc.], 1009
Solar Energy, 944
Solar PV Community Action Manual, 980
Solar Thermal Community Action Manual, 980
Solstice Series [publications of the Canadian Circumpolar Institute], 862
SOLutions [a publication of the Canadian Solar Industries Association Inc.], 888
The Source [a publication of the Ontario Ground Water Association], 974
The Source: The Voice of Business in the Canadian Seismic Industry, 857
SPECTRUM [a publication of the Society Promoting Environmental Conservation], 1009
Spike [a publication of the Ottawa Orchid Society], 983
SRNT [Society for Research on Nicotine & Tobacco] Newsletter, 1007
SRNT [Society for Research on Nicotine & Tobacco] Membership Directory, 1007
Standards & Certification Update [a publication of the American Society of Mechanical Engineers], 824
Standards for Library & Information Services in Canadian Healthcare Facilities, 870
The State of the Castle Wilderness: Annual Report, 892
State of the Population - Atlantic Salmon, 843
STEP Global Newsletter, 1002
The Stockman's Guide to Range Livestock Watering from Surface Sources, 988
Stormy Weather 101 - Solutions to Global Climate Change, 867
Strata Data: GMCS [Gem & Mineral Club of Scarborough] Newsletter, 922
Strategic Datalink [a publication of the Canadian International Council], 876
The Streak Plate: The Kingston Lapidary & Mineral Club Newsletter, 947
Sudden & Disruptive Climate Change: Exploring the Real Risks & How We Can Avoid Them, 896
Surveyor-In-Training Manual, 837
Sustainable Development at Risk: Ignoring the Past, 945
Sustainable Development Technology Canada Annual Report, 1011
Sustainable Development Technology Canada Corporate Plan, 1011
Sustainable Forestry Initiative Newsletter, 1011
The Synergist, 823
Synergy Online, 885

T

Tackle Climate Change, Use Wood, 918
Taproot, 897
Tech Talk: The British Columbia Food Technolgists Newsletter, 847
TechLife [a publication of the Canadian Association of Animal Health Technologists & Technicians], 856
1075news bytes [a publication of the Propane Gas Association of Canada Inc.], 990
1075news talk [a publication of the Propane Gas Association of Canada Inc.], 990
The Textbook of Food Science & Technology, 945
Titanium Update Newsletter, 944
To the Rescue [a publication of the Wildlife Rescue Association of British Columbia], 1020
Today's Oilheat Newsletter, 880
Toronto Field Naturalist, 1012
Total Compensation Survey [a publication of the Petroleum Services Association of Canada], 986
ToxExpo Directory, 1008
ToxSci Journal, 1008
Tracker, 1018
Traffic Engineering Handbook, 933
Traffic Signal Timing Manual, 933
Trail & Landscape, 983
Transactions of the Canadian Society for Mechanical Engineering, 885
Transforming Canada's Forest Products Industry: Summary of Findings from the Future Bio-Pathways Project, 918
Transit Vision 2040, 889
Transportation Impact Analyses for Site Development: An ITE Proposed Recommended Practice, 933
Transportation Planning Handbook, 933
TreeLines [a publication of the Saskatchewan Forestry Association], 1000
Trends [a publication of the Ontario Tire Dealers Association], 980
Trends in Food Science & Technology, 945
Trip Generation: An ITE Informational Report, 933
20/20: Canada's Industry Association Magazine, 876

U

UNFCCC Newsletter, 944
The Urban Imperative: Urban Outreach Strategies for Protected Area Agencies, 852
Urban Parks in Ontario, 976
Urban Street Geometric Design Handbook, 933
Ursus [a publication of the International Association for Bear Research & Management], 934
Using a Logic Model to Review & Analyze an Environmental Education Program, 964
Using Food Science & Technology to Improve Nutrition & Promote National Development: Selected Case Studies, 945
Utility Executive [a publication of the Water Environment Federation], 1017

V

Victoria Lapidary & Mineral Society Newsletter, 1017
Vocabulary of the Indoor Air Sciences, 943

W

Walk Softly, 1024
Walkerton Inquiry, 901
Waste Management & Research, 944
Waste Management World, 944
WasteWatch, 1002
Wastewater Operator Certification Study Guide, 842
The Water Dictionary: A Comprehensive Reference of Water Terminology, 826
Water Environment & Technology [a publication of the Water Environment Federation], 1017
Water Environment Laboratory Solutions [a publication of the Water Environment Federation], 1017
Water Environment Regulation Watch, 1017
Water Environment Research [a publication of the Water Environment Federation], 1017
Water Practice [a publication of the Water Environment Federation], 1017
Water Quality Research Journal of Canada, 859
Water Resources Information Project, 901
Water Safety Plans for Municipal Drinking Water Systems, 890
Water Treatment Principles & Applications, 890
Waterbirds, 1018
Watermark, 850
The Watermark [a publication of the Aquaculture Association of Canada], 828
WaterPower, 860
The Weekly Newsletter, 932
WEF [Water Environment Federation] Highlights, 1017
Well Cost Study, 986
West Chilcotin Demonstration Project [a publication of British Columbia Spaces for Nature], 850
Western Canada Highway News, 952
Western Canada Water, 1019
Western Canada Water Member Newsletter, 1019
The Wetlands Observer, 921
What's Fair Got To Do With It: Diversity Cases from Environmental Educators, 964
What's New in P2, 862
Who's Who in International Development, 864
Wild [a publication of the Canadian Wildlife Federation], 891
Wildlife Preservation Canada Annual Report, 1020
WindLink, 891
WindSight, 891
Wood Design & Building, 891
Wood WORKS!, 891
Woodland Caribou Recovery: Audit of Operatinig Practices & Mitigation Measures Employed within Woodland Caribou Ranges, 918
Working for You [a publication of the Construction Association of Prince Edward Island], 902
Workload Measurement Systems: A Guide for Libraries, 870
World Conservation, 944
The World of Food Science, 932
World Water, 1017

Y

The YardStick [a publication of the Western Retail Lumber Association], 1019
You & Your Local Government, 976
Your Big Backyard, 891
Your Health, 848
Yukon Tourism Education Council Newsletter, 1024
Yukon Tourism Education Council Newsletter, 839

Associations/Organizations

Académie canadienne du génie *See* Canadian Academy of Engineering

Acadia Environmental Society
c/o Acadia Students' Union, PO Box 1269, Wolfville NS B0P 1Z0
Tel: 902-585-2150
e-mail: aes@acadiau.ca
Overview: A small local organization founded in 1989
Chief Officer(s):
James Patterson, Coordinator
Finances: *Annual Operating Budget:* Less than $50,000; *Funding Sources:* Acadia Students' Union
Committees: Events Coordination; Fundraising & Membership; Finance; Education & Networking
Mission: To provide an information resource on environmental issues; to encourage & help the Acadia community to adopt & maintain environmentally sound & sustainable practices

Acadian Entomological Society (AES)
Natural Resources Canada, Canadian Forest Service, PO Box 4000, Atlantic Forestry Centre, 1350 Regent St., Fredericton NB E3B 597
URL: www.acadianes.org/aes.html
Overview: A small local organization founded in 1915
Finances: *Annual Operating Budget:* Less than $50,000; *Funding Sources:* Membership dues; Entomological Society of Canada
Staff: 5 volunteer(s)
Membership: 50; *Fees:* Annual - Regular: $10; Student: $6; **Committees:** Archives; Memberships; Pest Management; Public Education
Publications: *The Journal of the Acadian Entomological Society Editor:* Don Ostaff *ISSN:* 1710-4033
Mission: To bring about a close association of entomologists & those interested in entomology in the four Atlantic provinces & the neighbouring New England States; to cooperate with, & to support the Entomological Society of Canada; *Affiliation(s):* Entomological Society of Canada

Acoustical Association Ontario (AAO)
32 Vancho Cres., Toronto ON M9A 4Z2
Tel: 905-738-1733; *Fax:* 416-240-1465
e-mail: aao@bellnet.ca
URL: www.aao-online.ca
Overview: A small provincial organization founded in 1963
Chief Officer(s):
Joseph De Caria, Executive Secretary
Membership: 55; *Member Profile:* Unionized contractors engaged in interior finishing construction
Mission: The Acoustical Association Ontario (AAO) is an association representing unionized employers engaged in Acoustic and Drywall construction in the Industrial, Commercial and Institutional sector of the construction industry in the Province of Ontario.

Action Nord Terre
535, 4e Rue, Chibougamau QC G8P 1S4
Tél: 418-748-7056
Aperçu: Dimension: petite; *Envergure:* locale
Membre(s) du bureau directeur:
André Naud, Président

Action on Smoking & Health (ASH)
#1101, 10080 Jasper Ave., Edmonton AB T5J 1V9
Tel: 780-426-7867; *Fax:* 780-426-7872
e-mail: website@ash.ca
URL: www.ash.ca
Overview: A small national organization founded in 1979
Chief Officer(s):
Roger Hodkinson, Honorary Chair
Finances: *Annual Operating Budget:* $100,000-$250,000
Staff: 2 staff member(s); 20 volunteer(s)
Membership: 300; *Fees:* Corporate: $100; 3-year Household: $65; 1-year Household: $25
Activities: *Speaker Service:* Yes
Mission: To reduce & prevent tobacco use

Action to Restore a Clean Humber (ARCH)
21 Taysham Cres., Toronto ON M9V 1X1
Tel: 416-326-0726
e-mail: archnow@interlog.com
Overview: A small local organization founded in 1991

Chief Officer(s):
Luciano Martin, Executive Director
Mission: To clean up & conserve the Humber watersheds

Action Volunteers for Animals (AVA)
PO Box 64578, Unionville ON L3R 0M9
Tel: 416-439-8770
e-mail: actionvolunteers@yahoo.com
URL: www.actionvolunteersforanimals.com
Overview: A medium-sized local charitable organization founded in 1972
Finances: *Annual Operating Budget:* $50,000-$100,000
Staff: 20 volunteer(s)
Membership: 600; *Fees:* $25; *Committees:* Stray Animals; Vet Fund; Anti-Fur; Fundraising
Activities: Meetings, demonstrations, membership parties, lectures, fundraising events; *Library:* AVA Library; Open to public
Mission: To abolish all cruelty against & suffering of non-human animals

Action: Environment
38 Tobin Cres., St. John's NL A1A 2J3
Tel: 709-722-1925
Overview: A small provincial organization founded in 1989
Chief Officer(s):
Majorie Evans, Contact
Finances: *Funding Sources:* Membership dues
Staff: 2 volunteer(s)
Fees: $10; *Member Profile:* Individuals interested in environmental issues; *Committees:* NL Environmental Network
Mission: To take an active role in protecting, restoring & enhancing the environment; committed to taking an advocacy & activist role in our community; *Member of:* Canadian Environmental Network; Newfoundland & Labrador Environmental Network

Advanced Foods & Materials Network / Réseau des aliments et des matériaux d'avant-garde
#215, 150 Research Lane, Guelph ON N1G 4T2
Tel: 519-822-6253; *Fax:* 519-824-8453
URL: www.afmnet.ca
Also Known As: AFMNet
Overview: A medium-sized national organization
Chief Officer(s):
Ron Woznow, Executive Director, 519-822-6253 Ext. 56524
ron.woznow@afmnet.ca
Rickey Yada, Ph.D., Scientific Director, 519-824-4120 Ext. 58915, Fax: 519-824-6631
rickey.yada@afmnet.ca
Member of: Networks of Centres of Excellence

Aerospace Industries Association of Canada (AIAC) / Association des industries aérospatiales du Canada
#1200, 60 Queen St., Ottawa ON K1P 5Y7
Tel: 613-232-4297; *Fax:* 613-232-1142
e-mail: info@aiac.ca
URL: www.aiac.ca
Previous Name: Air Industries Association of Canada
Overview: A large national organization founded in 1962
Membership: 400; *Committees:* Airworthiness; International Exhibition; Technology Council; Defence Procurement Council; Suppliers Council; Space Council
Mission: To promote & facilitate the continued success & growth of this strategic industry; to establish & maintain a public policy environment that enables sustained aerospace industry growth; to strengthen the international competitiveness of all aerospace firms in Canada; to strengthen Canadian aerospace SME capabilities & position them as "suppliers of choice"; to represent & involve the full range of aerospace companies that operate in Canada

African Coelacanth Ecosystem Programme (ACEP)
Somerset St., Private Bag 1015, Eastern Cape, Grahamstown 6140 South Africa
Tel: 27-46-636-1002; *Fax:* 27-46-622-2403
URL: www.acep.co.za
Overview: A medium-sized international organization founded in 2002
Chief Officer(s):

Melanie Darlow, Coordinator
m.darlow@ru.ac.za
Activities: Multidisciplinary project of South Africa, Mozambique, Tanzania, Kenya, the Comoros, the Seychelles & Madagascar, that uses science to explore the deep unknown & develop sustainability, & to benefit people
Member of: South African Institute for Aquatic Biodiversity; *Affiliation(s):* Canadian Centre of Excellence on Biotelemetry (University of British Columbia); Vancouver Aquarium

African Violet Society of Canada
c/o 349 Hyman Dr., Dollard-des-Ormeaux QC H9B 1L5
e-mail: info@avsc.ca
URL: www.avsc.ca
Overview: A small national organization
Chief Officer(s):
Bill Price, President
Membership: 400+; *Fees:* $15 annual
Publications: *Chatter*
Type: Magazine *Frequency:* Quarterly

African Wildlife Foundation (AWF)
#120, 1400 Sixteenth St. NW, Washington DC 20036 USA
Tel: 202-939-3333; *Fax:* 202-939-3332
Toll-Free: 888-494-5354
e-mail: africanwildlife@awf.org
URL: www.awf.org
Social Media: www.facebook.com/group.php?gid=5583020690
Overview: A large international organization
Chief Officer(s):
Patrick J. Bergin, PhD, President/CEO
Gregg Mitchell, Vice-President, Philanthropy & Marketing
Jeff Chrisfield, CFO
Mission: To promote conservation of Africa's wildlife & natural resources; to promote belief that the survival of African wildlife lies in a working knowledge of the relationship between man, his economics & his environment; to promote, establish & support grassroots & institutional programs in conservation education, wildlife management & training, & management of threatened conservation areas; to manage projects aimed at saving endangered species (eg. the African Elephant, Mountain Gorilla, Rhinoceros)

Agence internationale de l'énergie atomique *See* International Atomic Energy Agency

Agence spatiale européenne *See* European Space Agency

Aggregate Producers' Association of Ontario (APAO)
#2, 365 Brunel Rd., Mississauga ON L4Z 1Z5
Tel: 905-507-0711; *Fax:* 905-507-0717
e-mail: mmiller@apao.com
URL: www.apao.com
Overview: A medium-sized provincial organization founded in 1956
Finances: *Annual Operating Budget:* $250,000-$500,000; *Funding Sources:* Membership dues
Staff: 7 staff member(s)
Membership: 200+ corporate

Agricultural Alliance of New Brunswick (AANB) / Alliance agricole du Nouveau-Brunswick
Parent: Canadian Federation of Agriculture
#303, 259 Brunswick St., Fredericton NB E3B 1G8
Tel: 506-452-8101; *Fax:* 506-452-1085
e-mail: alliance@fermenbfarm.ca
URL: www.fermenbfarm.ca
Previous Name: New Brunswick Federation of Agriculture
Overview: A medium-sized provincial charitable organization founded in 1876
Finances: *Annual Operating Budget:* $100,000-$250,000; *Funding Sources:* Membership fees
Staff: 3 staff member(s); 12 volunteer(s)
Membership: 1,200 individual; *Fees:* $150-500; *Member Profile:* Farmers maintaining specified level of specific commodity; *Committees:* Training; Sustainable Agriculture; Farm Safety; Farm Finance
Activities: *Speaker Service:* Yes; *Library:* Yes
Mission: To promote & advance the social & economic conditions of those engaged in agricultural pursuits; to formulate

Associations/Organizations / Agricultural Groups Concerned About Resources & the Environment

& promote agricultural policies to meet changing economic conditions; *Member of:* Atlantic Farmers Council

Agricultural Groups Concerned About Resources & the Environment
Ontario AgriCentre, #106, 100 Stone Rd. West, Guelph ON N1G 5L3
Tel: 519-837-1326; *Fax:* 519-837-3209
e-mail: agcare@agcare.org
URL: www.agcare.org
Also Known As: AGCare
Overview: A medium-sized provincial organization
Lilian Schaer, Executive Director
Heather Hargrave, Coordinator, Communications
Finances: *Funding Sources:* Funded by all major Ontario farm organizations involved in crop production
Membership: 45,000 Ontario horticultural & field crop producers
Activities: Our Farm Environmental Agenda (drafted by a coalition of AGCare, the Christian Farmers' Federation of Ontario, the Ontario Farm Animal Council & the Ontario Federation of Agriculture) outlines the strong commitment of farmers, through Environmental Farm Plans, to document present environmental conditions on their farms, develop a strategy for making appropriate changes, document actual farm practices & use that data for the development of new farm environmental initiatives
Affiliation(s): Christian Farmers' Federation of Ontario; Federated Women's Institutes of Ontario; Ontario Beekeepers' Association; Ontario Canola Growers' Association; Ontario Soybean Growers; Ontario Fruit & Vegetable Growers' Association; Ontario Corn Producers' Association; Ontario Wheat Producers' Marketing Board; Ontario Potato Board; Ontario Processing Vegetable Growers; Ontario Bean Producers' Marketing Board; Ontario Seed Growers' Association; Ontario Soil & Crop Improvement Association; Ontario Federation of Agriculture; Flowers Canada (Ontario); Ontario Flue-Cured Tobacco Growers' Marketing Board

Agricultural Institute of Canada (AIC) / Institut agricole du Canada
#900, 9 Corvus Crt., Ottawa ON K2E 7Z4
Tel: 613-232-9459; *Fax:* 613-594-5190
Toll-Free: 888-277-7980
e-mail: office@aic.ca
URL: www.aic.ca
Social Media: www.facebook.com/group.php?gid=14076387524
Overview: A large national organization founded in 1920
Finances: *Annual Operating Budget:* $100,000-$250,000; *Funding Sources:* Membership fees
Staff: 8 staff member(s)
Membership: 9 provincial institutes + 8 agriculture-related scientific societies; *Fees:* $125 individual; $500 corporate; $1,000 association
Activities: News service; international program
Mission: To provide the voice for national knowledge & expertise; To promote the creation, production, & delivery of safe foods & sustainable use of related national resources in Canada & beyond; **Affiliation(s):** Canadian Agricultural Economics; Canadian Consulting Agrologists' Association; Canadian Society of Agronomy; Canadian Society of Animal Science; Canadian Society for Horticultural Science; Canadian Society of Soil Science; Canadian Society of Agrometeorology; British Columbia Institute of Agrologists; Alberta Institute of Agrologists; Saskatchewan Institute of Agrologists; Manitoba Institute of Agrologists; Ontario Institute of Agrologists; New Brunswick Institute of Agrologists; Nova Scotia Institute of Agrologists; PEI Institute of Agrologists; Newfoundland/Labrador Institute of Agrologists

Agricultural Institute of Canada Foundation (AICF)
#900, 9 Corvus St., Ottawa ON K2E 7Z4
Tel: 613-232-9459; *Fax:* 613-594-5190
Toll-Free: 888-277-7980
e-mail: office@aic.ca
URL: www.aic.ca
Overview: A large national charitable organization founded in 1988
Chief Officer(s):
Myles Frosst, CEO, 613-232-9459 Ext. 302, Fax: 613-594-5190 mfrosst@aic.ca
Susan Simpson, MBA, P.Ag., President
Sandy Todd, P.Ag., Treasurer
Finances: *Annual Operating Budget:* Less than $50,000; *Funding Sources:* Personal donations; corporate sponsorship
Staff: 1 staff member(s)

Mission: To enhance agriculture & the role it plays in providing Canadians with a safe, affordable, nutritious food supply; **Affiliation(s):** Agricultural Institute of Canada

Agricultural Producers Association of Saskatchewan (APAS)
Parent: Canadian Federation of Agriculture
#100, 2400 College Ave., Regina SK S4P 1C8
Tel: 306-789-7774; *Fax:* 306-789-7779
e-mail: info@apas.ca
URL: www.apas.ca
Overview: A medium-sized provincial organization
Chief Officer(s):
Nial Kuyek, General Manager
Membership: 114 rural municipalities; *Member Profile:* Producers in rural municipalities of Saskatchewan
Mission: To provide farmers & ranchers with a democratically elected, grassroots, non-partisan producer organization based on rural municipal boundaries

Agricultural Technologists Association Inc. *Voir* Association des technologues en agroalimentaire

Air & Waste Management Association (A&WMA) / Association pour la prévention de la contamination de l'air et du sol
One Gateway Center, 420 Fort Duquesne Blvd., 3rd Fl., Pittsburgh PA 15222-1435 USA
Tel: 412-232-3444; *Fax:* 412-232-3450
Toll-Free: 800-270-3444
e-mail: info@awma.org
URL: www.awma.org
Social Media: www.facebook.com/group.php?gid=33499462923
Previous Name: Air Pollution Control Association
Overview: A large international organization founded in 1907
Membership: 8,000+ in 65 countries; *Fees:* $40 students; $75 emeritus members; $105 young professional members; $200 individuals; $480 primary organizational members; *Member Profile:* Environmental professionals
Awards: S. Smith Griswold Outstanding Air Pollution Control Official Award (Award)
Frank A. Chambers Excellence in Air Pollution Control Award (Award)
Awarded to individuals who make an exceptional contribution to any technical aspect of air pollution control
Richard Beatty Mellon Environmental Stewardship Award (Award)
Presented to a person who has made a civic contribution to a field related to the mission & objectives of the association
Charles W. Gruber Association Leadership Award (Award)
Lyman A. Ripperton Environmental Educator Award (Award)
Presented to teachers who inspire students to achieve excellence in professional & social endeavours; recipients are educators from some field related to the mission & objectives of the association
J. Deane Sensenbaugh Environmental Technology Award (Award)
Presented every year to a firm, company, or corporation that has made outstanding achievements in air pollution control or waste management; the recipient's contribution to the state of the art must be one that has been recognized & accepted in the field
Waste Management Award (Award)
Honorary A&WMA Membership (Award)
Fellow A&WMA Membership (Award)
Outstanding Young Professional Award (Award)
Milton Feldstein Memorial Scholarship (Scholarship)
Jacqueline Shields Memorial Scholarship (Scholarship)
Richard Stessel Memorial Scholarship (Scholarship)

Meetings/Conferences:
For more information see Trade Shows, Conferences and Seminars Chapter
Air & Waste Management Association 104th Annual Conference & Exhibition
June 2011 Orlando, FL
Air & Waste Management Association 105th Annual Conference & Exhibition
June 2012 San Antonio, TX
Publications: *Journal of the Air & Waste Management Association*
Type: Journal *Frequency:* m. *Editor:* Tim Keener
Profile: Peer reviewed, technical environmental journal
EM, The Magazine for Environmental Managers
Type: Magazine *Frequency:* m. *Accepts Advertising :* Yes *Price:* $180 individuals; $265 nonprofit organization & government agencies; $405 all others
Profile: Management, policy, & regulatory perspective

Air & Waste Management Association Membership Directory
Type: Directory
Profile: Contact information for members
Mission: To improve environmental knowledge & decisions; To assist members in critical environmental decision making & professional development; To provide a neutral forum for exchanging information & developing networking opportunities; To increase public education & outreach; *Member of:* International Union of Air Pollution Prevention & Environmental Protection Associations; **Affiliation(s):** Canadian Prairie & Northern Section (www.cpans.org); Ontario Section (www.awma.on.ca); Québec Section (www.apcas.qc.ca); Ottawa Valley Chapter (www.awma-ovc.ca)
Environmental Activity: Promoting global environmental responsibility

Air Industries Association of Canada *See* Aerospace Industries Association of Canada

Air Pollution Control Association *See* Air & Waste Management Association

Air Transport Association of Canada (ATAC) / Association du transport aérien du Canada
#700, 255 Albert St., Ottawa ON K1P 6A9
Tel: 613-233-7727; *Fax:* 613-230-8648
e-mail: atac@atac.ca
URL: www.atac.ca
Overview: A medium-sized national organization founded in 1934
Chief Officer(s):
John McKenna, President & Chief Executive Officer
jmckenna@atac.ca
Bill Boucher, Vice-President, Flight Operations
bboucher@atac.ca
Wayne Gouveia, Vice-President, Commercial General Aviation
wgouveia@atac.ca
Cedric Paillard, Vice-President, Communications & Marketing
cpaillard@atac.ca
Mike Skrobica, Vice-President, Industry Monetary Affairs
mikes@atac.ca
Brian Whitehead, Vice-President, Technical Operations
bwhitehead@atac.ca
Membership: 200; *Member Profile:* Operators; Associates; Affiliates
Activities: Engaging in lobbying activities; *Speaker Service:* Yes
Meetings/Conferences:
For more information see Trade Shows, Conferences and Seminars Chapter
Air Transport Association of Canada 2011 77th Annual General Meeting & Trade Show
November 2011 Montréal, QC
Air Transport Association of Canada 2012 Annual Spring Event
Other Conferences in 2012 2012
Air Transport Association of Canada 2012 78th Annual General Meeting & Trade Show
Other Conferences in 2012 2012
Air Transport Association of Canada 2013 Annual Spring Event
Other Conferences in 2013 2013
Publications: *Flightplan*
Type: Magazine *Price:* Free with Air Transport Association of Canada membership
Air Transport Association of Canada Annual Report
Type: Magazine *Frequency:* a.
Mission: To advance the issues that affect members from the commercial aviation & flight training industries as well as aviaation industry suppliers
Environmental Activity: Working to reduce emissions, as part of Canada's commitment to the International Civil Aviation Organization goal of achieving carbon neutral growth by 2020

Air Waste Management Association - Québec Section *Voir* Association pour la prévention de la contamination de l'air et du sol

Airspace Action on Smoking & Health
Delta BC V4L 2M4
Tel: 604-943-6789
Toll-Free: 888-245-7722
e-mail: airspace@airspace.bc.ca
URL: airspace.bc.ca
Previous Name: AIRSPACE Non-Smokers' Rights Society
Overview: A medium-sized provincial organization founded in 1981
Finances: *Funding Sources:* Membership dues

Associations/Organizations / Alameda Agricultural Society

Staff: 9 volunteer(s)
Membership: 1,700; *Fees:* $20 individual; $25 family; $125 individual lifetime; $130 family; *Committees:* Newsletter Publication; Smoke-Free Restaurant List; Demonstrations; Letter-Writing Campaigns
Activities: *Internships:* Yes; *Speaker Service:* Yes; *Library:* Yes, Open to public
Mission: To educate non-smokers on the effects that smoking has on them & of their legal right to smoke-free air; to help establish laws to protect the comfort, safety & health of non-smokers; to help reduce the number of future smokers; Affiliation(s): Non-Smokers' Rights Association; Canadian Council on Smoking & Health

AIRSPACE Non-Smokers' Rights Society *See* Airspace Action on Smoking & Health

Alameda Agricultural Society
PO Box 103, Alameda SK S0C 0A0
Tel: 306-489-4415
Overview: A small local organization
Member of: Saskatchewan Association of Agricultural Societies & Exhibitions

Alberni Valley Outdoor Club
c/o Ursula Knoll, 3941 - 9th Ave., Port Alberni BC V9Y 4V1
Tel: 250-723-6883
e-mail: uschik@telus.net
URL: www.albernivalleyoutdoorclub.org
Overview: A small local organization
Chief Officer(s):
Harold Carlson, Chairperson
willow@alberni.net
Fees: Annual - Single: $25; Family: $45; Associate: $5
Member of: Federation of Mountain Clubs of British Columbia

Alberta & Northwest Territories Lung Association
Parent: Canadian Lung Association
PO Box 4500, Stn. South, #208, 17420 Stony Plain Rd., Edmonton AB T5E 6K2
Tel: 780-488-6819; *Fax:* 780-488-7195
Toll-Free: 888-566-5864
e-mail: info@ab.lung.ca
URL: www.ab.lung.ca
Social Media:
www.facebook.com/group.php?gid=192015860715
Overview: A medium-sized provincial charitable organization founded in 1939
Finances: *Funding Sources:* Donations; Fundraising; Sponsorships
Fees: $25
Activities: Providing indepth information about asthma, COPD, sleep apnea, tuberculosis, & other lung conditions, as well as smoking & clean air; Organizing & promoting events about lung health to support the association; Funding medical research; *Awareness Events:* Radon Awareness Campaign; Northwest Territories Asthma & Allergies Door-to-Door Campaign, May
Meetings/Conferences:
For more information see Trade Shows, Conferences and Seminars Chapter
Alberta & Northwest Territories Lung Association 2012 3rd Annual Tobacco Stakeholders Workshop
Other Conferences in 2012 2012
Alberta & Northwest Territories Lung Association 2012 8th Annual Alberta Sleep Forum
Other Conferences in 2012 2012
Alberta & Northwest Territories Lung Association 2012 Annual General Meeting
Other Conferences in 2012 2012
Publications: *Alberta & Northwest Territories Lung Association Annual Report*
Type: Yearbook *Frequency:* a.
Profile: Highlights of fundraising activities, advocacy activities, & patient support programs
Mission: To educate the public & medical professionals about lung health

Alberta Agricultural Economics Association (AAEA)
Dept. of Rural Economy, University of Alberta, 515 General Services Bldg., Edmonton AB T6G 2H1
Tel: 780-422-3122
e-mail: info@aaea.ab.ca
URL: www.aaea.ab.ca
Overview: A small provincial charitable organization
Chief Officer(s):
Diane McCann-Hiltz, Secretary, 780-422-6081
diane.mccann-hiltz@gov.ab.ca
Sean Cash, President, 780-492-4562
sean.cash@ualberta.ca
Finances: *Annual Operating Budget:* Less than $50,000
Membership: 200; *Fees:* Annual - $30
Activities: Annual 'Visions' Conference in May; regional seminars & luncheon speakers; newsletter; undergraduate & graduate scholarships in agricultural economics at University of Alberta
Mission: To provide an opportunity for communication among those interested in the agricultural & rural social sciences; to provide a forum for the discussion of issues affecting the rural economy; to encourage research & dissemination of research results & other information relating to Alberta's rural economy & to provide avenues for continuing education & professional upgrading

Alberta Aquaculture Association
PO Box 26, Site 3, RR#1, Red Deer AB T4N 5E1
Tel: 403-342-5206; *Fax:* 403-342-2646
e-mail: info@affa.ab.ca
URL: www.affa.ab.ca
Previous Name: Alberta Fish Farmers Association
Overview: A small local organization
Chief Officer(s):
Dan Menard, Treasurer
rdmenard@telusplanet.net
Victoria Page, Sec.-Treas.
Fees: $10 Assoc.; $100 Full; $250 Corporate; $250 Ed. Inst.
Mission: To support the pursuit of aquaculture promotion & education; *Member of:* Canadian Aquaculture Producers' Council

Alberta Association of Agricultural Societies (AAAS)
J.G. O'Donoghue Building, #200, 7000 - 113 St., Edmonton AB T6H 5T6
Tel: 780-427-2174; *Fax:* 780-422-7755
e-mail: aaas@gov.ab.ca
URL: www.albertaagsocieties.ca
Overview: A medium-sized provincial organization founded in 1947
Chief Officer(s):
Tim Carson, Chief Executive Officer
tim.carson@xplornet.com
Lisa Hardy, Executive Director
lisa.hardy@gov.ab.ca
Monica Bradley, Treasurer
monica.bradley@shaw.ca
Membership: 294+; *Fees:* $150 service membership; $200 agricultural societies; *Member Profile:* Agricultural societies & communities in Alberta
Activities: Presenting education programs; Lobbying government; Providing information; Facilitating networking
Meetings/Conferences:
For more information see Trade Shows, Conferences and Seminars Chapter
Alberta Association of Agricultural Societies 2012 Annual Meeting & Convention
Other Conferences in 2012 2012, AB
Alberta Association of Agricultural Societies 2012 Regional Meetings
Other Conferences in 2012 2012, AB
Publications: *Across the Fence [a publication of the Alberta Association of Agricultural Societies]*
Type: Newsletter *Frequency:* q. *Accepts Advertising* : Yes *Price:* Free with Alberta Association of Agricultural Societies membership
Profile: Contents include the chief executive officer's message, industry topics, conventions, awards, grant opportunities, & regional issues
Alberta Association of Agricultural Societies Membership Directory
Type: Directory *Price:* Free access on request, with Alberta Association of Agricultural Societies membership
Mission: To preserve & enhance the viability of agricultural societies in Alberta
Environmental Activity: Encouraging environmental responsibility

Alberta Association of Landscape Architects (AALA)
PO Box 21052, Edmonton AB T6R 2V4
Tel: 780-435-9902; *Fax:* 780-413-0076
e-mail: aala@aala.ab.ca
URL: www.aala.ab.ca
Overview: A medium-sized provincial organization founded in 1970
Chief Officer(s):
Mark Nolan, Registrar, 780-428-4000
mnolan7@hotmail.com
Brian Charanduk, Treasurer, 780-917-7219
brian.charanduk@stantec.com
Finances: *Funding Sources:* Membership dues; Sponsorships
Fees: $50; *Committees:* Registration; Discipline & Practice Review; Website; Grievance; Promotions; Continuing Education; Examining Board; Calgary; Edmonton
Activities: Offering a continuing education program; *Internships:* Yes; *Library:* Alberta Association of Landscape Architects Resource Library
Meetings/Conferences:
For more information see Trade Shows, Conferences and Seminars Chapter
Alberta Association of Landscape Architects 2012 Annual General Meeting
Other Conferences in 2012 2012, AB
Alberta Association of Landscape Architects 2012 12th Annual Erosion & Sediment Control Course
Other Conferences in 2012 2012, AB
Publications: *Alberta Association of Landscape Architects Newsletter*
Type: Newsletter
Profile: Association activities & forthcoming events
Mission: To advance the quality of the professional practice of landscape architecture in Alberta; *Member of:* Canadian Society of Landscape Architects
Environmental Activity: Teaching about environmental construction; Promoting the planning, designing, & managing of land to protect the natural environment

Alberta Association of Municipal Districts & Counties (AAMD&C)
2510 Sparrow Dr., Nisku AB T9E 8N5
Tel: 780-955-3639; *Fax:* 780-955-3615
e-mail: aamdc@aamdc.com
URL: www.aamdc.com
Overview: A medium-sized provincial organization founded in 1909
Finances: *Annual Operating Budget:* $500,000-$1.5 Million
Staff: 13 staff member(s)
Membership: 68 regular; 650 associate; *Member Profile:* Rural municipalities, counties & municipal districts in Alberta
Meetings/Conferences:
For more information see Trade Shows, Conferences and Seminars Chapter
Alberta Association of Municipal Districts & Counties Fall 2011 Convention
November 2011, AB
Alberta Association of Municipal Districts & Counties Spring 2012 Convention & Trade Show
March 2012, AB
Alberta Association of Municipal Districts & Counties Fall 2012 Convention
November 2012, AB
Member of: Federation of Canadian Municipalities

Alberta Beef Producers (ABP)
#320, 6715 - 8th St. NE, Calgary AB T2E 7H7
Tel: 403-275-4400; *Fax:* 403-274-0007
e-mail: abpfeedback@albertabeef.org
URL: www.albertabeef.org
Previous Name: Alberta Cattle Commission
Overview: A medium-sized provincial organization founded in 1969
Chief Officer(s):
Rich Smith, General Manager, 403-451-1183
RichS@albertabeef.org
Lori Creech, Manager, Communications, 403-451-1179
loric@albertabeef.org
Barb Sweetland, Manager, Promotions, 403-451-1178
BarbS@albertabeef.org
Fred Hays, Policy Analyst, 403-451-1181
fredh@albertabeef.org
Membership: 15,000-49,999
Activities: Influencing government policy; Improving the beef industry's public image; Engaging in research activities; Providing landowners with information on rangeland health
Awards: Environmental Stewardship Award (Award) Presented annually to the beef producer who best exemplifies environmentally sustainable cattle production
Publications: *Beneficial Management Practices: Envrionmental Manual for Alberta Cow/Calf Producers*

Associations/Organizations / Alberta Bottle Depot Association

Price: Free to all Alberta cattle producers
Profile: Developed in partnership with Alberta Beef Producers (ABP) & Alberta Agriculture, Food, & Rural Development *Recommended Code of Practice for the Care & Handling of Farm Animals: Beef Cattle Edition*
Type: Booklet *Price:* Free
Mission: To strengthen the sustainability & competitiveness of the beef industry; To produce beef in an environmentally sustainable manner; To support responsible animal care & handling; *Member of:* Canadian Cattlemen's Association (CCA)
Environmental Activity: Promoting beneficial environmental management practices; Supporting policies, programs, & educational efforts related to environmental stewardship; Recognizing producers who have incorporated environmental protection into their management strategy

Alberta Bottle Depot Association (ABDA)
#202, 17850 - 105 Ave., Edmonton AB T5S 2H5
Tel: 780-454-0400; *Fax:* 780-454-0424
e-mail: abdasdeb@yahoo.com
URL: www.albertadepot.ca
Overview: A small provincial organization
Chief Officer(s):
Tamara Janzen, Contact
Jeff Linton, Executive Director
abda.jeff@telusplanet.net
Finances: Funding Sources: Membership dues
Staff: 2 staff member(s); 14 volunteer(s)
Membership: 184
Activities: Library: Yes, Not open to the public
Mission: To educate about industry & to standardize the practices for depot operation

Alberta Building Envelope Council (South) (ABEC)
PO Box 61152, Stn. Kensington, Calgary AB T2N 4S6
Tel: 403-246-4500; *Fax:* 403-246-4220
URL: www.abecsouth.org
Overview: A small provincial organization founded in 1983
Finances: Annual Operating Budget: Less than $50,000; *Funding Sources:* Membership dues
Staff: 8 volunteer(s)
Membership: 148; *Fees:* Individual: $48; Corporate: $65; Student: $10
Activities: The link between architects, building owners, engineers & contractors; *Speaker Service:* Yes
Mission: ABEC is interested in design, construction, performance, evaluation, testing, renovation, restoration and maintenance of building envelopes.; *Member of:* National Building Envelope Council

Alberta Camping Association (ACA)
Parent: Canadian Camping Association
Percy Page Centre, 11759 Groat Rd., Edmonton AB T5M 3K6
Tel: 780-427-6605; *Fax:* 780-427-6695
e-mail: info@albertacamping.com
URL: www.albertacamping.com
Overview: A medium-sized provincial charitable organization founded in 1949
Chief Officer(s):
Laureen Wray, President
Scott Lister, Treasurer
Finances: Annual Operating Budget: $50,000-$100,000; *Funding Sources:* Lotteries; community development; recreation; Parks & Wildlife Foundation
Staff: 1 staff member(s); 18 volunteer(s)
Membership: 20 corporate + 400 individual + 100 camps; *Fees:* $15 student; $35 general; $150 camps; $100 commercial; *Committees:* Conference & Education; Marketing & Fundraising; Standards; Research & Development; Newsletter
Activities: Speaker Service: Yes; *Rents Mailing List:* Yes; *Library:* ACA Resource Centre; Open to public
Mission: To promote & coordinate organized camping in Alberta by providing camp information & leadership direction as well as promoting high standards of camp programs & activities for all populations; to take a leading role in the recognition & promotion of professional standards for organized camps in Alberta

Alberta Canola Producers Commission (ACPC)
#170, 14315 - 118 Ave., Edmonton AB T5L 4S6
Tel: 780-454-0844; *Fax:* 780-465-5473
Toll-Free: 800-551-6652
e-mail: acpc@canola.ab.ca
URL: www.canola.ab.ca
Overview: A medium-sized provincial organization founded in 1989
Finances: Annual Operating Budget: $500,000-$1.5 Million
Staff: 3 staff member(s)

Membership: 26,000; *Fees:* Based on sale of canola seed; *Committees:* Administration & Finance; Market Development; Member Relation & Extension; Research
Activities: Speaker Service: Yes
Mission: To provide leadership in a vibrant canola industry for the benefit of Alberta canola producers; to strive to improve the long-term profitability of Alberta canola producers; *Member of:* Canola Council of Canada; Food Safety Info Society; Agriculture Education Network; *Affiliation(s):* Canadian Canola Growers Association

Alberta Cattle Commission *See* Alberta Beef Producers

Alberta Centre for Boreal Studies
PO Box 52031, 8210 - 109 St., Edmonton AB T6G 2T5
e-mail: contact@borealcentre.ca
URL: www.borealcentre.ca
Overview: A small provincial organization
Chief Officer(s):
Richard Schneider, Executive Director
Mission: To promote the involvement & effectiveness of the public in decision-making on boreal issues, enabling them to promote the conservation of biodiversity more effectively

Alberta Chamber of Resources
#1940, 10180 - 101 St., Edmonton AB T5J 3S4
Tel: 780-420-1030; *Fax:* 780-425-4623
e-mail: acr-mail@acr-alberta.com
URL: www.acr-alberta.com
Overview: A medium-sized provincial organization

Alberta Cogenerators Council
Postal Bag 1020, Grande Prairie AB T8V 3A9
Tel: 403-539-8069; *Fax:* 403-539-8597
Toll-Free: 866-953-0530
e-mail: kim.logan@weyerhaeuser.com
Overview: A small provincial organization
Chief Officer(s):
Kim Logan

Alberta Conservation Association (ACA)
#101, 9 Chippewa Rd., Sherwood Park AB T8A 6J7
Tel: 780-410-1999; *Fax:* 780-464-0990
Toll-Free: 877-969-9091
e-mail: info@ab-conservation.com
URL: www.ab-conservation.com
Overview: A medium-sized provincial charitable organization founded in 1997
Chief Officer(s):
Todd Zimmerling, President/CEO
Finances: Funding Sources: Alberta conservationists: Hunters; Anglers; corporate partners
Staff: 75 staff member(s)
Membership: 1-99
Activities: Speaker Service: Yes
Mission: To envision an Alberta where citizens understand & support good stewardship of natural biological resources, & where future generations can value, enjoy & use these natural biological resources
Environmental Activity: Maintaining habitat integrity; Encouraging government, business, & citizens to work together for nature conservation

Alberta Conservation Tillage Society II (ACTS)
#211, 2 Athabasca Ave., Sherwood Park AB T8A 4E3
Tel: 780-416-6046; *Fax:* 780-416-8915
e-mail: admin@areca.ab.ca
URL: www.areca.ab.ca/site/acts
Overview: A medium-sized provincial organization founded in 1978
Chief Officer(s):
Val Blize, Contact
Finances: Annual Operating Budget: $500,000-$1.5 Million; *Funding Sources:* Government; industry; membership dues
Staff: 1 staff member(s); 16 volunteer(s)
Membership: 400 + 4,000 associate; *Fees:* $30; *Member Profile:* Interest in soil conservation
Activities: Alberta Reduced Tillage Initiative; Reduced Tillage Courses; Direct Seeding Demonstration Days; Farm Tours; *Speaker Service:* Yes; *Rents Mailing List:* Yes; *Library:* Yes, Open to public, open by appointment
Awards: Provincial Conservation Farm Family Award (Award)
Mission: To protect & enhance soil productivity by promoting environmentally responsible conservation farming systems; to address soil & related water conservation resource concerns including government policy & programming, research,

environmental & food safety issues, public awareness, & education; *Member of:* Soil Conservation Council of Canada

Alberta Construction Association (ACA)
Parent: Canadian Construction Association
18012, 107 Ave., Edmonton AB T5S 1M1
Tel: 780-455-1122; *Fax:* 780-451-2152
e-mail: info@abconst.org
URL: www.abconst.org
Overview: A medium-sized provincial organization founded in 1958
Finances: Annual Operating Budget: $250,000-$500,000; *Funding Sources:* Membership dues
Staff: 3 staff member(s); 120 volunteer(s)
Membership: 1,663
Activities: Speaker Service: Yes; *Rents Mailing List:* Yes

Alberta Development Officers Association
6807 - 104 St., Edmonton AB T6H 2L5
Tel: 780-913-4214; *Fax:* 780-452-7718
e-mail: adoa@telus.net
URL: www.adoa.net
Overview: A small provincial organization founded in 1984
Membership: 301; *Fees:* $75; *Member Profile:* Development Officers from rural & urban municipalities in Alberta; Municipal & independent planners; Engineers; Surveyors
Activities: Establishing a certified training course through the University of Alberta
Publications: The Communicator [a publication of the Alberta Development Officers Association]
Editor: Carol-Lynn Gilchrist
Profile: Association activities, conferences, training, & articles

Alberta Environmental Network (AEN)
Parent: Canadian Environmental Network
#2, 6328A - 104 St. NW, Edmonton AB T6H 2K9
Tel: 780-439-1916; *Fax:* 780-433-3792
e-mail: aen@web.ca
URL: www.aenweb.ca
Overview: A medium-sized provincial organization founded in 1987
Finances: Annual Operating Budget: $100,000-$250,000
Staff: 2 staff member(s)
Membership: 70; *Fees:* $30-$200; *Member Profile:* Alberta Environmental NGOs; *Committees:* Clean Air/Energy; Forest; Waste Avoidance/Toxics
Activities: Rents Mailing List: Yes
Mission: To facilitate communication & cooperation among environmental groups in Alberta in order to contribute to the enhancement & protection of the environment

Alberta Falconry Association
22 Chilcotin Way West, Lethbridge AB T1K 7L8
e-mail: info@albertafalconry.com
URL: www.albertafalconry.com
Overview: A small local organization founded in 1965
Chief Officer(s):
Alex Stokes, Contact
Membership: 35; *Fees:* $70; $35 renewal
Mission: In addition to providing guidance for any Alberta resident who is interested in falconry & the care of falcons, the aims of the association are to promote the conservation of raptors and their prey, & to perpetuate the highest standards of the practice.

Alberta Farm Fresh Producers Association (AFFPA)
PO Box 56, Kelsey AB T0B 2K0
Tel: 780-373-2503; *Fax:* 780-373-2297
Toll-Free: 800-661-2642
e-mail: jag@syban.net
URL: www.albertafarmfresh.com
Overview: A small provincial organization
Chief Officer(s):
Jim Hill, President, 403 887 3778, Fax: 403-887-3768
hillj@telusplanet.net
Nelson Boychuk, Vice-President, 780-398-2123, Fax: 780-398-2123
rrlc@telus.net
Don Gregorwich, Secretary, 780-373-2503, Fax: 780-373-2297
dgregorwich@syban.net
Grace Fedak, Treasurer, 403-934-2412
fedakg@telus.net
Joan Gregorwich, Contact, Administration, 780-373-2503
dgregorwich@syban.net
Membership: 162; *Fees:* $145; *Member Profile:* Agri-preneuers in Alberta

Activities: Promoting the farm direct market industry; Providing educational opportunities, such as courses & workshops; Supporting horticultural research; Collaborating with industry partners & government; Arranging insurance; Branding Alberta products from members; Offering networking opportunities with growers acrossAlberta
Publications: *Come To Our Farm Guide*
Type: Guide *Price:* Free
Profile: Contact & product information about Alberta Farm Fresh Producers Association members
Direct Currents [a publication of the Alberta Farm Fresh Producers Association]
Type: Newsletter *Frequency:* q. *Accepts Advertising* : Yes *Price:* Free with Alberta Farm Fresh Producers Association membership
Profile: Association updates
Mission: To develop a sustainable & profitable farm direct marketing industry; To support the production of farm direct market vegetable, berry, & fruit crops, perennials, herbs, flowers, & bedding plants, meat, poulty, & eggs, & other specialty items; To contribute to the health & economic well-being of Albertans

Alberta Farmers' Market Association (AFMA)
#201, 7000 - 113 St., Edmonton AB T6H 5T6
Tel: 780-644-5377; *Fax:* 780-422-7755
e-mail: director@albertamarkets.com
URL: www.albertamarkets.com
Overview: A small provincial organization founded in 1994
Chief Officer(s):
Darlene Cavanaugh, Director, 780-644-5377
director@albertamarkets.com
Becky Lipton, Coordinator, Training & Communications, 780-427-6403
becky@albertamarkets.com
Member Profile: Alberta Approved Farmers' Markets in Alberta; Vendors; Managers; Boards; Sponsors; Persons who support the principles by which farmers' markets operate
Activities: Promoting Alberta's farmers' markets; Providing education for members, such as regional workshops & market manager training; Offering networking opportunities; Funding & establishing surveys; Advising government organizations regarding guidelines for markets; Arranging market & vendor group liability insurance; *Awareness Events:* Alberta Farmers' Market Awareness Week
Publications: *Market Express*
Type: Newsletter *Frequency:* q.
Profile: Feature articles, recipes, & reports from executive members, committess, & regional directors
Mission: To provide direction & support to members; To assist Alberta Approved Farmers' Markets in playing a major role in the establishment of vibrant communities; To advocate for farmers' markets in Alberta; *Member of:* Alberta Farm Fresh Producers Association; Growing Alberta; Dine Alberta; Alberta Association of Agricultural Societies; GO Organic; *Affiliation(s):* Alberta Farmers' Market Program; Alberta Agriculture & Rural Development; RBC Agencies/The Cooperators; Times Two Gifts & Promotions; Whyteaspace

Alberta Fish & Game Association (AFGA)
Parent: Canadian Wildlife Federation
6924 - 104 St., Edmonton AB T6H 2L7
Tel: 780-437-2342; *Fax:* 780-438-6872
e-mail: office@afga.org
URL: www.afga.org
Overview: A medium-sized provincial organization
Chief Officer(s):
Conrad Fennema, President
Martin Sharren, Executive Vice-President
Sandie Buwalda, Coordinator, Programs
Brad Fenson, Coordinator, Habitats
Kerry Grisley, Co-Manager, Operation Grassland Community
Susan Skinner, Co-Manager, Operation Grassland Community
Finances: *Funding Sources:* Membership fees; Donations
Membership: 20,000 members in 100+ clubs; *Fees:* $35 individuals; $55 families; *Committees:* Finance; Environment; Fishing; Hunting; Programs
Activities: Providing educational programs; Liaising with government, industry, & other organizations
Meetings/Conferences:
For more information see Trade Shows, Conferences and Seminars Chapter
Alberta Fish & Game Association 2012 Annual General Meeting
Other Conferences in 2012 2012, AB
Mission: To ensure fish & wildlife habitat & resources in Alberta
Environmental Activity: Promoting conservation & utilization of fish & wildlife

Alberta Fish Farmers Association *See* Alberta Aquaculture Association

Alberta Forest Products Association (AFPA)
#500, 10709 Jasper Ave., Edmonton AB T5J 3N3
Tel: 780-452-2841; *Fax:* 780-455-0505
e-mail: info@albertforestproducts.ca
URL: www.albertaforestproducts.ca
Overview: A medium-sized provincial licensing organization founded in 1942
Chief Officer(s):
Brady Whittaker, President & Chief Executive Officer
Norm Dupuis, Director, Grade Bureau, 780-452-2841 Ext. 235
Brock Mulligan, Director, Communications, 780-452-2841 Ext. 229
Keith Murray, Director, Policy & Regulation, 780-452-2841 Ext. 227
Carola von Sass, Director, Health & Safety, 780-452-2841 Ext. 237
Finances: *Funding Sources:* Membership fees; Sponsorships
Member Profile: Manufacturers of pulp & paper, lumber, panelboard, & secondary manufactured wood products in Alberta
Meetings/Conferences:
For more information see Trade Shows, Conferences and Seminars Chapter
Alberta Forest Products Association 2011 69th Annual General Meeting & Conference
September 2011 Jasper, AB
Alberta Forest Products Association 2011 Lumber Grading School
November 2011 Edmonton, AB
Alberta Forest Products Association 2012 70th Annual General Meeting & Conference
Other Conferences in 2012 2012, AB
Mission: To represent companies that manufacture forest products throughout Alberta
Environmental Activity: Providing members with services & information in the areas of forestry, the environment, health & safety, transportation, & lumber grading; Increasing public awareness of environmental & social values

Alberta Forestry Association
Parent: Canadian Forestry Association
4331 - 114B St., Edmonton AB T6J 1N8
Tel: 780-432-3683; *Fax:* 780-430-8349
e-mail: jimmefc@telusplanet.net
Overview: A medium-sized provincial organization founded in 1970
Finances: *Funding Sources:* Grants; memberships; donations; events
Membership: 180; *Member Profile:* Growers; harvesters; conservationists & environmentalists; foresters; hunters; birders; recreationists; private sector forest industry managers; government planners; citizens with interest in forests; *Committees:* Membership; Education; Newsletter
Mission: To maintain Alberta's forests as a productive & renewable resource; to increase public awareness, school education & natural appreciation of forests; to bring about better understanding of forests to people of all ages & backgrounds

Alberta Greenhouse Growers Association (AGGA)
#200, 10331 - 178 St., Edmonton AB T5S 1R5
Tel: 780-489-1991; *Fax:* 780-444-2152
e-mail: info@landscape-alberta.com
URL: www.agga.ca
Overview: A small provincial organization
Chief Officer(s):
Robert VanDam, President, 403-548-8139
John Bouw, Vice-President, 403-309-7700
Nick Savidov, Secretary, 403-362-1312
Dietrich Kuhlmann, Treasurer, 780-475-7500
Fees: $27.30 students; $54.60 associates & individuals; $168 growers; $180.60 allied trades people; *Member Profile:* Growers; Allied trades people; Educators; Students; Individuals with an interest in horticulture
Activities: Promoting the greenhouse growing industry in Alberta; Providing workshops & seminars; Conducting research; Liaising with related organizations, such as the Canadian Horticultural Council & the Alberta Professional Horticultural Growers Congress Foundation; Increasing cooperation; Assisting members in marketing
Awards: Alberta Greenhouse Growers Association Scholarship (Scholarship)
Eligibility: Awarded to the child of an AGGA grower member

Award Amount: $500 *Contact:* Rob Veno *Contact Detail:* Phone: 866-783-4038; Fax: 866-783-4038
Publications: *Alberta Greenhouse Growers Association Newsletter*
Type: Newsletter *Frequency:* q. *Editor:* Peter Johnston-Berresford
Profile: Association activities, & greenhouse growing industry research, developments, & policy
Regional Crop Reports
Mission: To strengthen the greenhouse growing industry in Alberta; to act as the voice of the industry, in areas such as taxation, natural gas rebates, disaster relief, & electricity costs

Alberta Greens
Parent: Green Party of Canada
PO Box 61251, Stn. Brentwood, Calgary AB T2L 2K6
Tel: 403-282-4788; *Fax:* 403-289-6658
e-mail: secretary@albertagreens.ca
URL: albertagreens.ca
Also Known As: The Green Party of Alberta
Overview: A small provincial organization founded in 1990
Finances: *Annual Operating Budget:* Less than $50,000; *Funding Sources:* Donations; membership
Staff: 20 volunteer(s)
Membership: 1,000+; *Fees:* $10; *Member Profile:* Environmentally & socially concerned Albertans; *Committees:* Membership & Newsletter; Communications; Administration; Strategy & Policy
Activities: Organizing for provincial elections; education; raising awareness of issues; *Speaker Service:* Yes
Mission: To encourage the development of an attitude that everyone is part of the land; to encourage strict control of all forms of pollution; to promote programs teaching consensus & facilitation; to facilitate the process of all interested community members becoming involved in education, both learning & teaching, guided by the long-term sustainability of the Earth community; to create the opportunity for Albertans to become involved in the strategic planning process; *Affiliation(s):* Green Alternatives Institute of Alberta

Alberta Historical Resources Foundation (AHRF)
8820 - 112 St., Edmonton AB T6G 2P8
Tel: 780-431-2300; *Fax:* 780-427-5598
URL: culture.alberta.ca/ahrf/default.aspx
Overview: A medium-sized provincial organization founded in 1976
Chief Officer(s):
David Link, Director
Finances: *Annual Operating Budget:* $3 Million-$5 Million; *Funding Sources:* Alberta Lotteries
Staff: 3 staff member(s)
Committees: Geographical Names
Activities: Alberta Main Street Programme; Heritage Preservation Grants; Heritage Awareness Grants
Awards: Heritage Awards (Award)
Established in 1981 to stimulate awareness & recognize outstanding contributions to the preservation of Alberta's past
Roger Soderstrom Scholarship in Historical Preservation (Scholarship)
Encourages professional development & advanced studies in the field of heritage conservation in Alberta; for university students at the graduate level in disciplines relating to heritage preservation & research, focussing on Alberta; includes studies in architectural restoration; area conservation & research preservation planning &/or interpretive development of archaeological, historical or palaeontological sites in the province, as well as related thematic work *Eligibility:* Canadian citizen or landed immigrant & a resident of Alberta for at least six months prior to applying *Deadline:* Feb. 1; Sept. 1 *Award Amount:* up to $3,000 *Contact:* Community Resources Officer
Mission: To assist in the preservation of Alberta's historic sites, buildings & objects; to encourage & promote public awareness of the province's past; grants are awarded in the spring & fall at each year to a wide variety of community-based heritage initiatives

Alberta Institute of Agrologists
Parent: Agricultural Institute of Canada
#249, 2055 Premier Way, Sherwood Park AB T8H 0G2
Tel: 780-464-9797; *Fax:* 780-464-1171
e-mail: info@aia.ab.ca
URL: www.aia.ab.ca
Overview: A small provincial licensing organization founded in 1947
Finances: *Funding Sources:* Membership fees

Associations/Organizations / Alberta Irrigation Projects Association

Membership: 1,500; *Member Profile:* Professional Agrologists (P.Ag.); Articling Agrologists (A.Ag.)
Activities: In-training programs;
Awards: Distinguished Agrologist Award (Award)
$1000/year to a University of Saskatchewan agrology student
Outstanding Young Agrologist Award (Award)
Professional Recognition Award (Award)
Honorary Member Award (Award)
Publications: *News Update [a publication of the Alberta Institute of Agrologists]*
Type: Newsletter
Profile: Update on Institute issues
AIA [Alberta Institute of Agrologists] Bulletin
Profile: Events of interest to Agrologists
Mission: AIA serves as a regulatory body within the province for matters related to agrology.

Alberta Irrigation Projects Association (AIPA)
#909, 400 - 4 Ave. South, Lethbridge AB T1K 7H5
Tel: 403-328-3063; *Fax:* 403-327-1043
e-mail: info@aipa.org
URL: www.aipa.org
Overview: A medium-sized provincial organization founded in 1946
Chief Officer(s):
Ron McMullin, Executive Director, 403-328-3063, Fax: 403-327-1043
ron.mcmullin@aipa.org
Vicky Kress, Administrator, 403-328-3063, Fax: 403-327-1043
vicky.kress@aipa.org
Member Profile: Incorporated Irrigation Districts in Alberta; Associate members; Honorary members
Activities: Participating in education & outreach activities; Developing policy; Researching; Providing information to federal, provincial, & local government officials, departments & agencies, water management stakeholders, members, the public, & the media; Promoting the benefits of Alberta's irrigations infrastructure; Developing partnerships
Meetings/Conferences:
For more information see Trade Shows, Conferences and Seminars Chapter
Alberta Irrigation Projects Association 2011 Irrigation Technical Conference
June 2011 Lethbridge, AB
Alberta Irrigation Projects Association 2011 Directors' Meeting
September 2011 Magrath, AB
Alberta Irrigation Projects Association 2011 Conference
November 2011 Lethbridge, AB
Alberta Irrigation Projects Association 2011 Annual General Meeting
December 2011 Lethbridge, AB
Mission: To advance understanding of the value of irrigation to Alberta; To promote progressive water management practices; *Affiliation(s):* Canadian Water Resources Association
Environmental Activity: Ensuring water conservation; Monitoring water quality; Publishing reports on collaborative decision making, conservation, efficiency, & productivity, & the value of water

Alberta Lake Management Society (ALMS)
PO Box 4283, Edmonton AB T6E 4T3
Tel: 780-702-2567; *Fax:* 501-423-6381
e-mail: info@alms.ca
URL: www.alms.ca
Also Known As: Lakewatch
Overview: A small provincial charitable organization founded in 1991
Chief Officer(s):
Stephanie Neufeld, President
Finances: *Annual Operating Budget:* Less than $50,000; *Funding Sources:* Government; workshops
Staff: 16 volunteer(s)
Membership: 100+, *Fees:* $50 associations, $25 individual, $15 student; *Member Profile:* Private citizens; municipalities; government organizations
Activities: Water sampling; conservation & lake management; *Speaker Service:* Yes; *Library:* ALMS Library; open by appointment
Mission: To promote understanding & comprehensive management of lakes & reservoirs & their watersheds; *Member of:* North American Lake Management Society

Alberta Land Surveyors' Association (ALSA)
Parent: Canadian Council of Land Surveyors
#1000, 10020 - 101A Ave., Edmonton AB T5J 3G2
Tel: 780-429-8805; *Fax:* 780-429-3374
Toll-Free: 800-665-2572
e-mail: info@alsa.ab.ca
URL: www.alsa.ab.ca
Overview: A medium-sized provincial organization founded in 1910
Finances: *Funding Sources:* Membership fees; products
Staff: 9 staff member(s)
Activities: *Library:* Yes
Mission: The ALSA is a self-governing professional association which regulates the practice of land surveying.

Alberta Medical Association
Parent: Canadian Medical Association
12230 - 106 Ave. NW, Edmonton AB T5N 3Z1
Tel: 780-482-2626; *Fax:* 780-482-5445
Toll-Free: 800-272-9680
e-mail: amamail@albertadoctors.org
URL: www.albertadoctors.org/home
Overview: A medium-sized provincial organization founded in 1905
Finances: *Annual Operating Budget:* $3 Million-$5 Million
Membership: 4,400
Activities: *Library:* Yes, Not open to the public
Mission: To advocate on behalf of its physician members; to provide leadership & support for their role in the provision of quality health care

Alberta Milk
1303 - 91 St. SW, Edmonton AB T6X 1H1
Tel: 780-453-5942; *Fax:* 780-455-2196
Toll-Free: 877-361-1231
e-mail: cblatz@albertamilk.com
URL: www.albertamilk.com
Previous Name: Dairy Nutrition Council of Alberta
Overview: A small provincial organization founded in 2002
Member Profile: Milk producers of Alberta; *Committees:* Executive; Animal Health & Environment Advisory; Canadian Milk Supply Management; Corporate Affairs; Dairy Advisory; Dairy Farmers of Canada; Finance; Market Development Advisory; Milk Quality, Component & Measurement Advisory; Research & Extension Advisory; Transportation Advisory; Western Milk Pool Coordinating
Activities: Providing industry-specific information to producers, such as Canadian Quality Milk & production reports; Offering nutritional & educational resources to the public; Supporting research
Publications: *Alberta Milk Annual Report*
Type: Yearbook *Frequency:* a.
Milking Times
Type: Newsletter *Frequency:* m. *Accepts Advertising* : Yes
Number of Pages: 12
Profile: Information for Alberta's dairy producers & their industry partners
Alberta Milk Producer Handbook
Type: Handbook
Mission: To promote the sustainability of the dairy industry in Alberta; *Affiliation(s):* Dairy Farmers of Canada

Alberta Motor Transport Association (AMTA)
Parent: Canadian Trucking Alliance
3660 Blackfoot Trail SE, Calgary AB T2G 4E6
Tel: 403-243-4161; *Fax:* 403-243-4610
Toll-Free: 800-267-1003
e-mail: amtamsc@amta.ca
URL: www.amta.ca
Merged from: Alberta Trucking Industry Safety Association; Alberta Trucking Association
Overview: A medium-sized provincial organization
Chief Officer(s):
Mayne Root, Executive Director
mayner1@amta.ca
Richard Warnock, President
rwarnock@westfreight.com
Membership: 12,000; *Member Profile:* All sectors of the highway transportation industry; *Committees:* Injury Reduction & Training; Compliance & Regulatory Affairs; Member Services
Activities: Six regional meetings
Mission: To take a leadership role in fostering a healthy, vibrant industry. PUBLICATIONS: Quaterly Newsletter; Annual Source Book; Western Canada Highway News Magazine.; *Member of:* Canadian Council of Motor Transport Administrators

Alberta Native Plant Council (ANPC)
PO Box 52099, Stn. Garneau Postal Outlet, Edmonton AB T6G 2T5
e-mail: info@anpc.ab.ca
URL: www.anpc.ab.ca
Overview: A small provincial organization founded in 1987
Fees: $10 students & seniors; $15 individuals; $25 families; $50 corporate memberships; $500 lifetime memberships; *Member Profile:* Individuals interested in ecology, natural history, conservation, photography, drawing, & hiking; *Committees:* Education & Information; Rare Plants; Reclamation & Horticulture; Conservation Action
Activities: Preserving plant species & habitats in Alberta; Supporting legislation to protect native plants; Promoting awareness of native plant issues; Organizing field trips & species counts; Developing collection, salvage & management guidelines; Providing information about uses for native plants; Awarding grants
Publications: *IRIS: The Alberta Native Plant Council Newsletter*
Type: Newsletter *Frequency:* 3-4 pa *Price:* Free with Alberta Native Plant Council membership
Profile: ANPC activities, articles, & plant happenings
Dandelion Recipes: 34 great recipes for salads, jellies, beverages, & appetizers!
Plant Collection Guidelines
Profile: Topics include plant collection guidelines for horticultural use of native plants; researchers, students, & consultants, & wildcrafters
Alberta Native Plant Council Guidelines
Profile: Topics include rare plant surveys in Alberta & the purchase & use of wildflower seed mixes
Native Plant Source List
Mission: To increase knowledge of native plants in Alberta among individuals, government, & industry; to conserve Alberta's native plant species

Alberta Natural History Society *See* Red Deer River Naturalists

Alberta Occupational Health Nurses Association (AOHNA)
c/o College & Association of Registered Nurses of Alberta (CARNA), 11620 - 168 St., Edmonton AB T5M 4A6
Tel: 403-506-8171
e-mail: aohna@telusplanet.net
URL: www.aohna.ab.ca
Overview: A small provincial organization founded in 1977
Fees: $75 active memberships; $40 associate memberships; *Member Profile:* Occupational health nurses employed in Alberta
Activities: Protecting the health of workers; Preventing occupational injuries & illnesses; Providing educational & networking opportunities; *Awareness Events:* North American Occupational Safety & Health (NAOSH) Week, May
Mission: To promote healthy work environments; *Member of:* College & Association of Registered Nurses of Alberta (CARNA); *Affiliation(s):* Canadian Occupational Health Nurses Association

Alberta Organic Producers Association (AOPA)
RR#1, Morinville AB T8R 1P4
Tel: 780-939-5808; *Fax:* 780-939-6738
e-mail: aopa@cruzinternet.com
URL: www.albertaorganicproducers.org
Previous Name: Organic Crop Improvement Association - Alberta Chapter #1
Overview: A small local organization founded in 1990
Fees: $50; *Member Profile:* Individuals interested in the production, processing, marketing, & consumption of organic products in Alberta
Activities: Offering a certificate to producers who meet the special organic criteria; Providing workshops & seminars
Publications: *Alberta Organic Producers Association Chapter Binder*
Type: Manual
Profile: Information for first time organic producers, with examples of forms & documents
AOPA [Alberta Organic Producers Association] Newsletter
Type: Newsletter
Profile: Association updates & upcoming events
Affiliation(s): Organic Crop Improvement Association International (OCIA) Inc.

Alberta Plastics Recycling Association (APRA)
Mission Hill Plaza, PO Box 65066, St Albert AB T8N 5Y3
Tel: 780-939-2386
e-mail: plasticsrecyc@lincsat.com
URL: www.recycleyourplastic.ca
Overview: A medium-sized provincial organization founded in 1991
Chief Officer(s):

Grant Cameron, Executive Director
Dave Schwass, President
Otto Parets, Vice-President
Member Profile: Plastics resin producers; Plastic manufacturers, fabricators, & converters; Packagers & fillers of plastic products; Wholesalers & retailers of plastic products & products in plastics packaging; Plastics recyclers & the recycling community; Industry associations; Interested members of the public
Activities: Collaborating with industry, environmental interest groups, & all levels of government; Providing resources to companies, groups, & individuals
Publications: *Alberta Plastics Recycling Association News*
Type: Newsletter
Profile: Highlights & accomplishments of the Alberta Plastics Recycling Association
Alberta Post-Consumer Plastics Recycling Strategy, Recycled Plastic Audit
Number of Pages: 36
Profile: An initiative of the Alberta Plastics Recycling Association in partnership with Alberta Environment
Mission: To minimize plastic waste to landfill in Alberta; Affiliation(s): Environment and Plastics Industry Council (EPIC)
Environmental Activity: Developing sustainable programs to manage plastics waste

Alberta Professional Outfitters Society (APOS)
#103, 6030 - 88 St., Edmonton AB T6E 6G4
Tel: 780-414-0249; *Fax:* 780-465-6801
e-mail: info@apos.ab.ca
URL: www.apos.ab.ca
Previous Name: Professional Outfitters Association of Alberta
Overview: A small provincial organization founded in 1997
Chief Officer(s):
Bob Byers, President
bob.byers@xplornet.com
Alan Steel, Managing Director
alan@apos.ab.ca
Finances: *Annual Operating Budget:* $500,000-$1.5 Million
Staff: 3 staff member(s); 30 volunteer(s)
Membership: 400; *Fees:* OG permit $107
Activities: Provides all administrative services to the industry; government liaison; cooperative marketing; disciplinary function
Mission: To provide leadership & direction in the continuing development of Alberta's outfitter-hunting industry; strives for long term sustainability in its approach to wildlife management, business opportunities & global competitiveness; Affiliation(s): Safari Club International; Foundation for North American Wild Sheep; Rocky Mountain Elk Foundation

Alberta Public Health Association (APHA)
Parent: **Canadian Public Health Association**
c/o ACICR, 4075 RTF, 8308 - 114th St., Edmonton AB T6G 2E1
Tel: 780-492-6014; *Fax:* 780-492-7154
e-mail: info@apha.ab.ca
URL: www.apha.ab.ca
Overview: A medium-sized provincial charitable organization founded in 1943
Finances: *Annual Operating Budget:* $100,000-$250,000;
Funding Sources: Membership dues; annual conference; charitable donations; grants
Staff: 1 staff member(s); 15 volunteer(s)
Membership: 300; *Fees:* $50 regular; student/retired $22;
Member Profile: Public health practitioners; professionals from NGOs; educators, government & citizens interested in advocating for, promoting & protecting the health of the public;
Committees: Conference; Program; Communications; Membership
Awards: Dr. Jean C. Nelson Foundation Award (Award)
Dr. John Waters Award (Award)
Mission: To promote & protect the health of the public through advocacy, partnerships, & education

Alberta Recreation & Parks Association (ARPA)
Parent: **Canadian Parks & Recreation Association**
11759 Groat Rd., Edmonton AB T5M 3K6
Tel: 780-415-1745; *Fax:* 780-451-7915
Toll-Free: 877-544-1747
e-mail: arpa@arpaonline.ca
URL: www.arpaonline.ca
Social Media: www.facebook.com/arpaonline;
www.twitter.com/#!/arpaonline
Overview: A medium-sized provincial charitable organization
Chief Officer(s):
Rick Curtis, Executive Director, 780-415-1745
rcurtis@arpaonline.ca

Steve Allan, Manager, Finance & Operations
sallan@arpaonline.ca
Carol Petersen, Manager, Recreation & Community Development
cpetersen@arpaonline.ca
Lisa Tink, Manager, Children & Youth Programs
ltink@arpaonline.ca
Mandi Wise, Coordinator, Communications
mwise@arpaonline.ca
Membership: 1,300+; *Member Profile:* Students; Municipal elected officials, staff, volunteers & stakeholders; Business staff, suppliers & clients; Eductional institution staff; Non-profit association & government agency elected officials, staff, volunteers & stakeholders; Individuals interested in or working in areas of recreation, parks, leisure, & tourism
Activities: Providing leadership to Alberta's recreation & parks industry; Facilitating communication & information networking; Maximizing human & financial resources for recreation & parks services; Establishing relations with the provincial government; Advocating recreational safety, fair play & gender equity; Increasing public awareness of recreation & active lifestyles; Monitoring development of formal post-secondary educational opportunities for recreation & parks; Research & preparing position papers on various issues; *Awareness Events:* Recreation & Parks Month, June; Communities in Bloom; Community Choosewell Challenge
Awards: Alberta Recreation & Parks Association Merit Award (Award)
Wild Rose Award (Award)
A.V. Pettigrew Award (Award)
Excellence in Youth Development Award (Award)
Parks Excellence Award (Award)
Halladay Memorial Scholarship (Scholarship)
Alberta Advisory Board on Recreation for the Disabled (AABRD) Legacy Award (Award)
Alberta Advisory Board on Recreation for the Disabled (AABRD) Undergraduate & Graduate Scholarships (Scholarship)
Meetings/Conferences:
For more information see Trade Shows, Conferences and Seminars Chapter
Alberta Recreation & Parks Association 2011 National Recreation Summit (co-hosted by Alberta Tourism, Parks & Recreation)
October 2011 Lake Louise, AB
Alberta Recreation & Parks Association 2011 Annual Conference & Energize Workshop: Recreation & Parks - Bringing Quality to Life
October 2011 Lake Louise, AB
Alberta Recreation & Parks Association 2012 Annual Conference & Energize Workshop
Other Conferences in 2012 2012, AB
Alberta Recreation & Parks Association 2012 Biennial Youth Development Through Recreation Services Symposium
Other Conferences in 2012 2012 Banff, AB
Alberta Recreation & Parks Association 2012 Provincial Dialogue
Other Conferences in 2012 2012, AB
Alberta Recreation & Parks Association 2013 Annual Conference & Energize Workshop
Other Conferences in 2013 2013, AB
Alberta Recreation & Parks Association 2013 Parks Forum
Other Conferences in 2013 2013, AB
Alberta Recreation & Parks Association 2014 Biennial Youth Development Through Recreation Services Symposium
Other Conferences in 2014 2014 Banff, AB
Alberta Recreation & Parks Association 2015 Parks Forum
Other Conferences in 2015 2015, AB
Publications: *REConnect [a publication of the Alberta Recreation & Parks Association]*
Type: Newsletter *Frequency:* m.
Profile: News about recreation & parks related issues in Alberta
Alberta Recreation & Parks Association Recreation Buyers Guide
Type: Booklet *Accepts Advertising:* Yes
Profile: Advertisements with contact information
Mission: To promote accessibility to recreation & parks & their benefits to Albertans; To work toward economic sustainability, natural resource protection, & conservation within provincial parks & natural environments
Environmental Activity: Working to build healthy environments & citizens throughout Alberta

Alberta Registered Professional Foresters Association *See* College of Alberta Professional Foresters

Alberta Rural Municipal Administrators Association
6027 - 4 St. NE, Calgary AB T2K 4Z5
Tel: 403-275-0622; *Fax:* 403-275-8179
e-mail: d_vschmaltz@shaw.ca
URL: www.armaa.ca
Overview: A medium-sized provincial organization founded in 1922
Finances: *Annual Operating Budget:* Less than $50,000;
Funding Sources: Membership dues; grant
Membership: 95; *Fees:* $120; *Member Profile:* Rural municipal administrator; *Committees:* Various Ad Hoc

Alberta Safety Council
4831 - 93 Ave. NW, Edmonton AB T6B 3A2
Tel: 780-462-7300; *Fax:* 780-462-7318
Toll-Free: 800-301-6407
URL: www.safetycouncil.ab.ca
Overview: A medium-sized provincial organization founded in 1946
Finances: *Annual Operating Budget:* $1.5 Million-$3 Million
Staff: 12 staff member(s); 100 volunteer(s)
Membership: 200; *Fees:* $175 corporate/group; $40 individual;
Member Profile: Companies, organizations, agencies which promote safety
Activities: *Speaker Service:* Yes; *Library:* Yes, Open to public
Mission: To create awareness & provide educational & training programs to citizens of Alberta on how to maintain a safe environment at home, in traffic, at work & at play; Affiliation(s): Canada Safety Council; National Safety Council

Alberta Society of Engineering Technologists *See* The Association of Science and Engineering Technology Professionals of Alberta

Alberta Society of Petroleum Geologists *See* Canadian Society of Petroleum Geologists

Alberta Society of Professional Biologists (ASPB)
PO Box 21104, Edmonton AB T6R 2V4
Tel: 780-434-5765; *Fax:* 780-413-0076
e-mail: pbiol@aspb.ab.ca
URL: www.aspb.ab.ca
Overview: A medium-sized provincial organization founded in 1975
Chief Officer(s):
P. Ross Bradford, Executive Director, 780-469-6196
Executivedirector@aspb.ab.ca
Bette Beswick, Registrar, 403-560-4357
bette_beswick@golder.com
Monika Burak, Coordinator, Finance, 780-434-5765
monika@managewise.ca
Shauna Prokopchuk, Coordinator, Membership & Communications, 780-434-5765
shauna@managewise.ca
Joy Sager, Coordinator, Association & Events, 780-434-5765
joy@managewise.ca
Fees: $25 student biologists; $50 biologists in training; $250 professional biologists; *Member Profile:* Persons from all disciplines of biology, such as aquatic biology, botany, ecology, genetics, biotechnology, entomology, physiology, & zoology; Student Members; *Committees:* Discipline, Practice Review; Communications
Activities: Upholding the code of ethics; Organizing seminars for practitioners; Offering a mentorship program
Meetings/Conferences:
For more information see Trade Shows, Conferences and Seminars Chapter
Alberta Society of Professional Biologists 2012 Annual Conference & General Meeting
Other Conferences in 2012 2012, AB
Alberta Society of Professional Biologists 2013 Annual Conference & General Meeting
Other Conferences in 2013 2013, AB
Publications: *BIOS [a publication of the Alberta Society of Professional Biologists]*
Type: Newsletter *Frequency:* 3 pa *Editor:* Linda Zimmerling (lindazim@shaw.ca)
Profile: Articles to inform & educate members of the society & the public
Mission: To promote excellence in the practice of biology; To provide a voice for professional biologists in Alberta

Alberta Society of Surveying & Mapping Technologies (ASSMT)
PO Box 68168, 28 Crowfoot Terrace N.W., Calgary AB T3G 3N8

Associations/Organizations / Alberta Speleological Society

Tel: 403-244-3732; *Fax:* 403-244-2260
e-mail: manager@assmt.ab.ca
URL: www.assmt.ab.ca
Overview: A medium-sized provincial organization founded in 1970
Chief Officer(s):
Wayne Latam, Executive Manager
Finances: *Annual Operating Budget:* Less than $50,000
Staff: 1 staff member(s); 15 volunteer(s)
Membership: 30 student; 250 individual; 10 associate; *Fees:* $75 individual; $40 associate; students free; *Committees:* Legislation; Education; Membership; Publication; Nominating
Activities: Regional meetings; Annual general meeting; certification
Awards: SAIT/NAIT (Award)
Award Amount: $300 Bursary
OLS College (Award)
Award Amount: $300 Bursary
Mission: To promote the knowledge, skill & proficiency of technicians & technologists involved in the field of surveying & mapping in Alberta; Affiliation(s): Alberta Land Surveyors' Association

Alberta Special Waste Services Association See
Environmental Services Association of Alberta

Alberta Speleological Society (ASS)
#6309, 315 Southampton Dr. SW, Calgary AB T2W 2T6
e-mail: info@caving.ab.ca
URL: www.caving.ab.ca
Overview: A medium-sized provincial organization founded in 1968
Finances: *Funding Sources:* Membership fees
Fees: $15 individual; $18.75 family
Activities: Periodic field trips, occasional expeditions (Canadian & foreign) for cave/karst research & exploration; *Library:* Yes, open by appointmentNot open to the public
Mission: To promote cave/karst conservation; to facilitate cave/karst explorations primarily in the Canadian Rockies, with some activities throughout Western Canada & internationally; *Member of:* Federation of Alberta Naturalists

Alberta Sulphur Research Ltd. (ASRL)
Center for Applied Catalysts & Industrial Sulfur Chemistry, #6, 3535 Research Rd. NW, Calgary AB T2L 2K8
Tel: 403-220-5346; *Fax:* 403-284-2054
e-mail: asrinfo@ucalgary.ca
URL: www.chem.ucalgary.ca/asr
Overview: A small international organization founded in 1964
Finances: *Annual Operating Budget:* $500,000-$1.5 Million; *Funding Sources:* Membership research contributions
Staff: 15 staff member(s)
Membership: 56; *Member Profile:* Sulphur producer/user; *Committees:* Technical Advisory; Planning; Executive
Activities: *Library:* Yes, open by appointmentNot open to the public
Mission: Provides technological support for producers & users of sulfur; research & technology training through seminars & courses; provides contact between industry & academia for applied catalysis & industrial sulfur chemistry; examination of the chemistry & technology of sulfur & its compunds; emphasis on research relevant to sour gas, sulfur & refining industries; Affiliation(s): Chemistry Dept., Univ. of Calgary

Alberta Trappers' Association
#2, 9919 - 106 St., Westlock AB T7P 2K1
Tel: 780-349-6626; *Fax:* 780-349-6634
e-mail: info@albertatrappers.com
URL: www.albertatrappers.com
Overview: A small provincial organization
Chief Officer(s):
Gordy Klassen, President
trappergord@telus.net
Fees: Annual - Regular/Associate: $35; Corporate: $535;

Alberta Underwater Council (AUC)
Percy Page Centre, 11759 Groat Rd. NW, Edmonton AB T5M 3K6
Tel: 780-427-9125; *Fax:* 780-427-8139
Toll-Free: 888-307-8566
e-mail: info@albertaunderwatercouncil.com
URL: www.albertaunderwatercouncil.com
Overview: A medium-sized local organization founded in 1962
Finances: *Annual Operating Budget:* $250,000-$500,000; *Funding Sources:* Alberta Gaming; Alberta Sport Recreation Parks & Wildlife Foundation
Staff: 1 staff member(s)
Membership: 600 individual; *Fees:* $15; *Member Profile:* Snorkel, scuba divers, underwater sports
Activities: Underwater Outreach; Safety; Lake Clean-Ups; *Awareness Events:* Divescapes
Mission: To represent responsible participation in & awareness of underwater activities while seeking to preserve the aquatic environment; Affiliation(s): Canadian Federation of Underwater Activities; Alberta Underwater Archaeology Society; Canadian Underwater Games Association

Alberta Urban Municipalities Association (AUMA)
10507 Saskatchewan Dr. NW, Edmonton AB T6E 4S1
Tel: 780-433-4431; *Fax:* 780-433-4454
Toll-Free: 800-310-2862
e-mail: main@auma.ca
URL: www.auma.ca
Overview: A medium-sized provincial organization founded in 1905
Finances: *Funding Sources:* Membership dues
Staff: 23 staff member(s)
Membership: 284 municipalities; *Fees:* $474 + GST affiliate/associate; *Committees:* 15 Committees & Task Forces
Activities: *Rents Mailing List:* Yes; *Library:* Yes
Meetings/Conferences:
For more information see Trade Shows, Conferences and Seminars Chapter
Alberta Urban Municipalities Association 2011 Annual Convention
September 2011 Calgary, AB
Mission: To provide leadership in advocating local government interests to the provincial government & other organizations, & to provide services that address the needs of its membership

Alberta Water & Wastewater Operators Association (AWWOA)
11810 Kingsway Ave., Edmonton AB T5G 0X5
Tel: 780-454-7745; *Fax:* 780-451-6451
Toll-Free: 877-454-7745
e-mail: awwoa@telus.net
URL: www.awwoa.ab.ca
Overview: A small provincial organization founded in 1976
Chief Officer(s):
Del Morrison, Executive Director, Fax: 780-451-6451
awwoa1@telus.net
Cathie Monson, Coordinator, Training Program, Fax: 780-454-7748
awwoa@telus.nett
Laura Selcho, Course Registrar, Fax: 780-454-7758
awwoa2@telus.net
Activities: Providing manuals to operators
Awards: Alberta Water & Wastewater Operator's Association Bursary (Scholarship)
Available to students entering the Water & Wastewater Technician program at the Northern Alberta Institute of Technology; awarded on the basis of municipal sponsorship & academic achievement *Award Amount:* up to $3,000
Meetings/Conferences:
For more information see Trade Shows, Conferences and Seminars Chapter
Alberta Water & Wastewater Operators Association 2012 37th Annual Operators Seminar
Other Conferences in 2012 2012, AB
Publications: *Alberta Utility Operator Newsletter*
Type: Newsletter *Frequency:* 3 pa *Editor:* Gayle Sacuta
Profile: Information about Alberta's water & wastewater operations, new technologies, research, & regulatory changes
Mission: To contribute to the training & upgrading of persons employed in the water & wastewater field in Alberta; To encourage the best possible operation of water & wastewater facilities; Affiliation(s): Western Canada Water & Wastewater Association
Environmental Activity: SponsoringAlberta Environment training programs

Alberta Water Council
Petroleum Plaza, South Tower, #1400, 9915 - 108 St., Edmonton AB T5K 2G8
Tel: 780-644-7380
URL: www.albertawatercouncil.ca
Overview: A medium-sized provincial organization
Chief Officer(s):
Gord Edwards, Executive Director
g.edwards@awchome.ca
Membership: 24 institutional
Mission: The Alberta Water Council is a stakeholder partnership that provides leadership, expertise and advocacy, to engage and empower individuals, organizations, business and governments to achieve the outcomes of the Water for Life strategy.

Alberta Water Well Drilling Association (AWWDA)
Parent: Canadian Ground Water Association
PO Box 130, Lougheed AB T0B 2V0
Tel: 780-386-2335; *Fax:* 780-386-2344
e-mail: awwda@telusplanet.net
URL: www.awwda.com
Overview: A medium-sized provincial organization founded in 1958
Mission: The AWWDA is a non-profit, non-sectarian organization with certain objectives including: assisting, promoting, encouraging, and supporting the interest and welfare of the water well industry in all of its phases; fostering aid and promote scientific education, standard research, and technique in order to improve methods of well construction and development and advance the science of groundwater in the province of Alberta.

Alberta Wilderness Association (AWA)
455 - 12 St. NW, Calgary AB T2N 1Y9
Tel: 403-283-2025; *Fax:* 403-270-2743
Toll-Free: 866-313-0713
e-mail: awa@shaw.ca
URL: albertawilderness.ca
Overview: A large provincial charitable organization founded in 1965
Finances: *Annual Operating Budget:* $250,000-$500,000; *Funding Sources:* Provincial grants; fundraising events; membership fees; donations
Staff: 4 staff member(s); 250 volunteer(s)
Membership: 2,500 individual + 110 organizations; *Fees:* $25 single; $30 family; *Committees:* Bow Corridor; Bull Trout; Cypress Hills; Game Ranching; Helicopter Access; Milk River Ecological Reserve; Northern Forests; Prairie Conservation Forum; Provincial Recreation & Parks; Public Lands; Special Places 2000; Three Rivers (Oldman) Dam; Wetlands; Wildlands Project; Wild Rivers; Wilderness Dependent Wildlife; Yellowstone-to-Yukon
Activities: Research on wilderness issues; wildlands cleanups, trips, hikes, lectures; *Awareness Events:* Climb the Calgary Tower for Wilderness, April; *Speaker Service:* Yes; *Library:* Wilderness Resource Centre; Open to public
Mission: AWA is a non-profit, federally registered, charitable society that: promotes the protection of Alberta's rivers & wildlands areas; works to restore the natural ecosystems of Alberta; educates Albertans on wilderness conservation & sustainable use of natural lands & waters.; *Member of:* Alberta Environment Network; Environmental Law Centre; Calgary & Area Outdoor Council; Volunteer Centre of Calgary; Affiliation(s): Environmental Resource Centre

Aldergrove Daylily Society
24642 - 51 Ave., Langley BC V2Z 1H9
Tel: 604-856-5758
e-mail: pamela1@istar.ca
URL: www.distinctly.on.ca/chs/aldergrove.html
Overview: A small local organization founded in 1991
Chief Officer(s):
Pam Erikson, President
Fees: $10 individual; $15 family

Algoma Manitoulin Environmental Awareness (AMEA)
RR#1, Kagawong ON P0P 1J0
Tel: 705-282-2886
Previous Name: Manitoulin Environmental Awareness
Overview: A small local organization
Chief Officer(s):
Ed Burt, Contact
Mission: To promote citizen participation in environmental matters, & to provide public exchange in RAP's, & environmental advocacy in regional watershed plans, & mines management

AllerGen NCE Inc.
Michael DeGroote Centre for Learning & Discovery, McMaster University, #3120, 1200 Main St. West, Hamilton ON L8N 2A5
Tel: 905-525-9140; *Fax:* 905-524-0611
e-mail: info@allergen-nce.ca
URL: www.allergen-nce.ca
Overview: A medium-sized national organization founded in 2004
Chief Officer(s):

Judah Denburg, CEO & Scientific Director, 905-525-9140 Ext. 26502
Diana Royce, Chief Operating Officer & Managing Director, 905-525-9140 Ext. 26502
Mark Mitchell, Manager, Research & Partnerships, 905-525-9140 Ext. 26092
Marta Rudyk, Manager, Communications & Coordinator, Knowledge Mobilization, 905-525-9140 Ext. 26641
Allison Brown, Coordinator, Research, 905-525-9140 Ext. 26553
Michelle Harkness, Coordinator, Highly Qualified Personnel & Events, 905-525-9140 Ext. 26633
Finances: *Funding Sources:* Government of Canada, through the Networks of Centres of Excellence (NCE) Program
Meetings/Conferences:
For more information see Trade Shows, Conferences and Seminars Chapter
AllerGen NCE Inc. 2012 7th Annual Conference
Other Conferences in 2012 2012
Publications: *AllerGen NCE Inc. Annual Report*
Type: Yearbook *Frequency:* a.
Profile: Highlights of the year & a financial overview
ReAction [a publication of AllerGen NCE Inc.]
Type: Newsletter
Profile: Partnership, training, & networking opportunities
AllerGen Network Newsletter
Type: Newsletter *Frequency:* q.
Profile: Information about the management of the network for board & committee members & investigators
Agenda [a publication of AllerGen NCE Inc.]
Type: Newsletter
Profile: An overview of research, training, partnerships, & networking
AirWays [a publication of AllerGen NCE Inc.]
Type: Newsletter
Profile: News about training & professional development opportunities
Mission: To support research, capacity building activities, & networking regarding allergic disease in Canada; To reduce the morbidity, mortality & socio-economic impacts of allergy, asthma, & related immune diseases
Environmental Activity: Conducting research programs in the areas of gene-environment interactions, diagnostics & therapeutics, & public health, ethics, policy, & society

Allergie Asthme association d'information *See* Allergy Asthma Information Association

Allergy & Environmental Health Association *See* Environmental Health Association of Ontario

Allergy Asthma Information Association (AAIA) / Allergie Asthme association d'information
#118, 295 The West Mall, Toronto ON M9C 4Z4
Tel: 416-621-4571; *Fax:* 416-621-5034
Toll-Free: 800-611-7011
e-mail: admin@aaia.ca
URL: www.aaia.ca
Overview: A large national charitable organization founded in 1964
Chief Officer(s):
Mary Allen, Chief Executive Officer, 866-694-0679 quebec@aaia.ca
Louis Isabella, Treasurer
Finances: *Funding Sources:* Donations; Corporate partnerships *Fees:* $35
Activities: Providing education; Raising money for research; Working with related organizations, government, & the food industry; Engaging in advocacy activities; Offering food allergy summer camps; *Awareness Events:* Walk to Axe Anaphylaxis
Publications: *Allergy Asthma Information Association Newsletter*
Type: Newsletter *Frequency:* q.
Profile: Information for persons affected by allergy, asthma, & anaphylaxis
Mission: To create a safer environment for Canadians with allergies, asthma, & anaphylaxis; To assist persons coping with allergies; To act as a national voice for individuals affected by allergy, asthma, & anaphylaxis; *Affiliation(s):* Canadian Society of Allergy & Immunology

Allergy, Asthma & Immunology Society of Ontario
2 Demaris Ave., Toronto ON M3N 1M1
Tel: 416-633-2215
e-mail: inquiry@allergyasthma.on.ca
URL: www.allergyasthma.on.ca
Previous Name: Ontario Allergy Society

Overview: A small provincial organization founded in 1958
Member Profile: Practicing physicians
Activities: *Speaker Service:* Yes
Mission: To strive to provide high quality medical services to the public, through consultation by referral from other physicians, as well as through public service education

Alliance agricole du Nouveau-Brunswick *See* Agricultural Alliance of New Brunswick

Alliance animale du Canada *See* Animal Alliance of Canada

L'Alliance canadienne des victimes d'accidents et de maladies du travail *See* Canadian Injured Workers Alliance

L'Alliance canadienne du camionnage *See* Canadian Trucking Alliance

Alliance de l'industrie canadienne de l'aquiculture *See* Canadian Aquaculture Industry Alliance

Alliance for Sustainability
Hillel Centre, 1521 University Ave. SE, Minneapolis MN 55414 USA
Tel: 612-331-1099; *Fax:* 612-379-9004
e-mail: iasa@mtn.org
URL: www.afors.org
Also Known As: International Alliance for Sustainable Agriculture
Overview: A medium-sized international charitable organization founded in 1983
Finances: *Annual Operating Budget:* Less than $50,000; *Funding Sources:* Membership; foundations; donors; corporations; religious groups; fundraising; revenue from public speaking, sale of publications, shirts, & buttons
Staff: 1 staff member(s); 5 volunteer(s)
Membership: 800; *Fees:* $25; *Member Profile:* Farmers; consumers; business & government leaders; environmentalists; educators & scientists
Activities: Natural Step Network meetings; introductory presentations; slide shows; seminars; support projects overseas; *Internships:* Yes; *Speaker Service:* Yes; *Library:* Sustainability Resource Center; Open to public
Mission: Supporting ecologically sound, economically viable, socially just & humane projects on a personal, organizational & planetary level

Alliance for the Wild Rockies (AWR)
PO Box 505, Helena MT 59624 USA
Tel: 406-459-5936
e-mail: awr@wildrockiesalliance.org
URL: www.wildrockiesalliance.org
Overview: A medium-sized international organization founded in 1988
Chief Officer(s):
Michael T. Garrity, Executive Director
Finances: *Annual Operating Budget:* $250,000-$500,000; *Funding Sources:* Membership dues; fundraising; donations; foundations
Staff: 2 staff member(s); 10 volunteer(s)
Membership: 3,500 individual + 1,000 organizational; *Fees:* (USD) Habitat Sponsor: $25; Watershed Sponsor: $50; Ecosystem Sponsor: $100; Bioregion Sponsor: $1000
Activities: *Internships:* Yes; *Library:* Ecosystem Defense; Open to public
Mission: To protect wildlands & wildlife habitat in the Wild Rockies Bioregion, containing parts of Alberta, British Columbia, Montana, Idaho, Wyoming, Oregon, Washington; to protect threatened, endangered & sensitive species; to promote sound ecosystem protection & sustainable economic development; to promote ecosystem-based land management based on scientific principles

Alliance of Foam Packaging Recyclers (AFPR)
#201, 1298 Cronson Blvd., Crofton MD 21114 USA
Tel: 410-451-8340; *Fax:* 410-451-8343
e-mail: info@epscentral.org
URL: www.epspackaging.org
Overview: A small international organization founded in 1991
Finances: *Annual Operating Budget:* $100,000-$250,000; *Funding Sources:* Manufacturers of expanded polystyrene packaging
Staff: 4 staff member(s)
Membership: 45; *Fees:* $1,000-$36,000
Mission: AFPR supports & provides leadership to the EPS foam packaging industry through activities that promote the development of recycling. It maintains a network for the collection, reprocessing and reuse of foam packaging.; *Member of:* Institute of Packaging Professionals

Alliance of Manufacturers & Exporters Canada *See* Canadian Manufacturers & Exporters

Alouette Field Naturalists (AFN)
12554 Grace St., Maple Ridge BC V2X 5N2
Tel: 604-463-8743
Overview: A small local organization founded in 1973
Membership: 30-35; *Fees:* $16-30; *Committees:* Pitt Polder Preservation Society; Blue Mountain-Kanata Creek Conservation Committee
Activities: Rivers Day, Nature Day, with displays; hiking, camping, birding, botanizing, mycologizing; *Awareness Events:* Earth Day, April
Mission: To promote the enjoyment of nature through environmental appreciation & conservation; to encourage wise use & conservation of natural resources & environmental protection; *Member of:* Federation of BC Naturalists

Alpine Garden Club of BC
c/o 14776 - 90th Ave., Surrey BC V3R 1A4
Tel: 604-580-3219
URL: www.agc-bc.ca
Overview: A small local organization
Chief Officer(s):
Linda Verbeek, President, 604-526-6656
Membership: 500; *Fees:* $25
Activities: Seed exchange; open gardens; field trips; plants sales; *Library:* Yes, Not open to the public
Publications: *The Bulletin*
Type: newsletter *Frequency:* quarterly
Mission: To promote the propagation & display of plants suitable for the alpine garden & alpine house, rare & unusual species of hardy plants, trees, shrubs & ferns, plants suitable for the art of bonsai; to promote an interest in the native plants of British Columbia & their preservation; *Member of:* North American Rock Garden Society

The Aluminum Association
#600, 1525 Wilson Blvd., Arlington VA 22209 USA
Tel: 703-358-2960; *Fax:* 703-358-2961
URL: www.aluminum.org
Previous Name: Aluminum Recycling Association
Overview: A small national organization
Chief Officer(s):
J. Stephen Larkin, President
Member Profile: Producers of primary aluminum, recyclers & semi-fabricated aluminum products, as well as suppliers to the industry
Mission: To enhance aluminum's position in a world of proliferating materials, increase its use as the "material of choice" remove impediments to its fullest use & assist in achieving the industry's environmental, societal, & economic objectives

Aluminum Recycling Association *See* The Aluminum Association

Amalgamated Conservation Society (ACS)
PO Box 8741, Victoria BC V8W 3S3
Tel: 250-382-8502
e-mail: kimibbotson@shaw.ca
Previous Name: Amalgamated Lower Islands Sportsmen's Association
Overview: A small local organization founded in 1963
Finances: *Annual Operating Budget:* Less than $50,000; *Funding Sources:* Donations; government grants
Staff: 3 volunteer(s)
Membership: 8 organizations representing 3,000 individuals; *Fees:* $30; *Member Profile:* Membership restricted to associations with similar objectives; *Committees:* Projects
Activities: Salmonid Enhancement Projects; *Speaker Service:* Yes
Mission: To promote the conservation of fish, game & natural resources; to provide the machinery necessary to put up a united front to combat any program by which the democratic rights of individuals may be threatened; to provide a permanent council through which such joint action may be directed

Amalgamated Construction Association of British Columbia *See* Vancouver Regional Construction Association

Associations/Organizations / AMC - Agricultural Manufacturers of Canada

Amalgamated Lower Islands Sportsmen's Association See Amalgamated Conservation Society

AMC - Agricultural Manufacturers of Canada
PO Box 636, Stn. Main, Regina SK S4P 3A3
Tel: 306-522-2710; *Fax:* 306-781-7293
Toll-Free: 800-959-7462
e-mail: amc@a-m-c.ca
URL: www.a-m-c.ca
Previous Name: Prairie Implement Manufacturers Association; PIMA - Agricultural Manufacturers of Canada
Overview: A medium-sized local licensing charitable organization founded in 1970
Finances: *Annual Operating Budget:* $250,000-$500,000; *Funding Sources:* Membership fees; special projects
Staff: 9 staff member(s)
Membership: 200 regular + 5 affiliate + 300 associate; *Fees:* Schedule available; *Member Profile:* Regular - manufacturer of farm & ranch equipment; associate - supplier of goods & services; *Committees:* Legislative; Export; Taxation; Agriculture; Standards; History; Insurance; Quality Assurance
Mission: To foster & promote the growth & development of the agricultural equipment manufacturing industry; to identify industry problems & take remedial action; to encourage governments to enact legislation & offer programs that enhance the growth potential of industry; to provide a forum for members to exchange ideas & discuss their industry as it relates to the national & international economy

American Association for the Advancement of Science (AAAS)
1200 New York Ave. NW, Washington DC 20005 USA
Tel: 202-326-6440
e-mail: membership@aaas.org; media@aaas.org; development@aaas.org
URL: www.aaas.org
Overview: A large national organization founded in 1848
Chief Officer(s):
Peter C. Agre, Chair
Alice S. Huang, President
Alan I. Leshner, Chief Executive Officer
David E. Shaw, Treasurer
Member Profile: Open to all
Activities: Offering international programs; Providing science education; Publishing books & reports; Promoting the integrity of science & its responsible use in public policy; Facilitating communication among scientists, engineers, & the public; Raising public engagement with science & technology
Awards: AAAS Philip Hauge Abelson Prize
AAAS Award for International Scientific Cooperation
AAAS Award for Public Understanding of Science and Technology
AAAS Mentor Award
AAAS Scientific Freedom and Responsibility Award
AAAS Science Journalism Award
Meetings/Conferences:
For more information see Trade Shows, Conferences and Seminars Chapter
American Association for the Advancement of Science 2012 Annual Meeting
February 2012 Vancouver, BC
American Association for the Advancement of Science 2013 Annual Meeting
February 2013 Boston, MA
Publications: *Science [a publication of the American Association for the Advancement of Science]*
Type: Journal *Frequency:* w. *Editor:* Bruce Alberts
Profile: Original scientific research & global news
Science Translational Medicine [a publication of the American Association for the Advancement of Science]
Type: Journal *Editor:* Katrina L. Kelner, Ph.D.
Profile: Information for basic translational, & clinical research practitioners & trainees
Science Signaling [a publication of the American Association for the Advancement of Science]
Type: Journal *Frequency:* w. *Editor:* Michael B. Yaffe, M.D., Ph.D *ISSN:* 1937-9145
Profile: Information for experts & novices in cell signaling
AAAS [American Association for the Advancement of Science] Annual Report
Type: Yearbook *Frequency:* a.
Science Books & Films [a publication of the American Association for the Advancement of Science]
Type: Journal

Profile: A critical review journal of educational materials for science teachers
AAAS [American Association for the Advancement of Science] Advances
Type: Newsletter
Profile: A members only newsletter with updates on American Association for the Advancement of Science research
Science Roundup [a publication of the American Association for the Advancement of Science]
Type: Newsletter
Profile: A members only newsletter with updates on American Association for the Advancement of Science research & programs
AAAS [American Association for the Advancement of Science] Policy Alert
Type: Newsletter *Frequency:* w.
Profile: News about science policy
Mission: To advance science, engineering, & innovation around the world to benefit all people; To provide a voice for science on societal issues; Affiliation(s): 262 affiliated societies & academies of science

American Association of Botanical Gardens & Arboreta (AABGA)
#614, 100 - 10th St. West, Wilmington DE 19801 USA
Tel: 302-655-7100; *Fax:* 302-655-8100
URL: www.publicgardens.org
Overview: A medium-sized international organization founded in 1940
Chief Officer(s):
Daniel J. Stark, Executive Director
dstark@publicgardens.org
Finances: *Annual Operating Budget:* $250,000-$500,000; *Funding Sources:* Membership dues; meetings; publication sales
Staff: 8 staff member(s)
Membership: 2,400; *Fees:* $65-80 regular; $35 student; $50 library subscription; institutional dues based on operating budget; *Member Profile:* Anyone who works or volunteers for public gardens, zoos, horticultural societies, arboreta or historic house gardens
Activities: *Internships:* Yes; *Rents Mailing List:* Yes; *Library:* Yes, open by appointment
Publications: *The Public Garden*
Profile: Quarterly Magazine
Mission: To support North American botanical gardens & arboreta, public horticultural organizations, their staff & trustees by: promoting the value of botanical gardens, arboreta & public horticultural organizations involved in the display, study & conservation of plants for public benefit; setting, promoting & recognizing professional standards; facilitating the exchange of information; advocating the collective interests of the association's members; promoting membership services

American Association of Bovine Practitioners (AABP)
PO Box 3610, #802, 3320 Skyway Dr., Auburn AL 36831-3610 USA
Tel: 334-821-0442; *Fax:* 334-821-9532
e-mail: aabphq@aabp.org
URL: www.aabp.org
Overview: A medium-sized international organization
Chief Officer(s):
Roger Saltman, President
M. Gatz Riddell, Executive Vice-President
mgriddell@aabp.org
Member Profile: International veterinarians engaged in the general field of bovine medicine or those who are interested in bovine medicine; Honorary members are persons who have made outstanding contributions to bovine practice; Veterinary students; *Committees:* Amstutz Scholarship; Animal Welfare; Beef Production Management; Biological Risk Management & Preparedness; Bovine Respiratory Disease; Food Quality, Safety, & Security; Distance Education; Information Management; Lameness; Milk Quality & Udder Health; Membership; Nutrition; Pharmaceutical & Biological Issues; Reproduction
Activities: Offering continuing education programs; Providing networking opportunities with fellow veterinarians; Improving career opportunities in bovine medicine; Increasing awareness of issues in the cattle industry; Promoting leadership on critical issues in the cattle business
Meetings/Conferences:
For more information see Trade Shows, Conferences and Seminars Chapter
The American Association of Bovine Practitioners 2011 Annual Conference
September 2011 St. Louis, MO
The American Association of Bovine Practitioners 2012 Annual Conference
September 2012 Montréal, QC
The American Association of Bovine Practitioners 2013 Annual Conference
September 2013 Milwaukee, WI
The American Association of Bovine Practitioners 2014 Annual Conference
September 2014 Albuquerque, NM
Publications: *American Association of Bovine Practitioners Newsletter*
Type: Newsletter *Frequency:* m. *Price:* Free with American Association of Bovine Practitioners membership
Profile: Updates from the association
The Bovine Practitioner
Type: Journal *Frequency:* s-a. *Accepts Advertising* : Yes *Price:* Free with American Association of Bovine Practitioners membership
Proceedings of the American Association of Bovine Practitioners Annual Conference
Type: Yearbook *Frequency:* a. *Price:* Free with American Association of Bovine Practitioners membership
American Association of Bovine Practitioners Annual Membership Directory
Type: Directory *Frequency:* a. *Price:* Free with American Association of Bovine Practitioners membership
Mission: To enhance the professional lives of international veterinarians; To improve the well-being of cattle; To help the economic success of cattle owners

The American Association of Petroleum Geologists (AAPG)
PO Box 979, 1444 South Boulder, Tulsa OK 74101-0979 USA
Tel: 918-584-2555; *Fax:* 918-560-2665
Toll-Free: 800-364-2274
e-mail: postmaster@aapg.org
URL: www.aapg.org
Overview: A small national organization
Chief Officer(s):
Richard (Rick) D. Fritz, Executive Director
Scott W. Tinker, President
Awards: Grants-in-Aid (Scholarship)
Postgraduate research projects leading to the M.S. degree in geology, geophysics, engineering, environmental studies, earth sciences, chemistry, mineralogy or science for Canadian, landed immigrant or visa students *Award Amount:* $2,000 maximum
Affiliation(s): Canadian Society of Petroleum Geologists

American Birding Association (ABA)
#200, 4945 North 30th St., Colorado Springs CO 80919 USA
Tel: 719-578-9703; *Fax:* 719-578-1480
Toll-Free: 800-850-2473
e-mail: member@aba.org
URL: www.americanbirding.org
Social Media: www.facebook.com/group.php?gid=22934255714
Overview: A large national organization founded in 1969
Chief Officer(s):
Carol Wallace, Association Secretary, 719-578-9703
cwallace@aba.org
Richard H. Payne, President/CEO
Finances: *Annual Operating Budget:* $500,000-$1.5 Million
Staff: 18 staff member(s)
Membership: 22,000; *Fees:* US$55 individual; US$63 family
Activities: Youth Education; Conservation Programs; *Rents Mailing List:* Yes; *Library:* Yes, Open to public
Publications: *Birding*
Editor: Ted Floyd
Profile: Bi-monthly Magazine
Mission: To provide leadership to field birders by increasing their knowledge, skills & enjoyment of birding & by contributing to bird conservation; *Member of:* Partners in Flight; American Bird Conservancy; Bird Conservation Alliance

American Cave Conservation Association (ACCA)
PO Box 409, 119 Main St. East, Horse Cave KY 42749 USA
Tel: 270-786-1466; *Fax:* 270-786-1467
URL: www.cavern.org
Also Known As: American Cave & Karst Center
Overview: A small international organization founded in 1977
Chief Officer(s):
David G. Foster, Executive Director
acca@cavern.org
Finances: *Annual Operating Budget:* $250,000-$500,000
Staff: 7 staff member(s)

Membership: 500; Fees: Regular: $25-30; Student: $25; Family: $35, Supporter: $50; Sustainer: $100; Guarantor: $200; Benefactor: $500; Patron: $1000
Activities: Operates National Cave Management Training program & The American Cave Museum; provides outreach educational programs; constructs cave gates; Library: Yes, open by appointmentNot open to the public
Publications: American Caves
Mission: To protect & preserve caves, karstlands & groundwater; to bring together information about cave & karst resources from across the nation & make it available to those who are working to protect these resources

American Council for an Energy-Efficient Economy (ACEEE)
#600, 529 14th Street NW, Washington DC 20045-1000 USA
Tel: 202-507-4000; Fax: 202-429-2248
e-mail: info@aceee.org
URL: www.aceee.org
Overview: A medium-sized national organization founded in 1980
Chief Officer(s):
Steven Nadel, Executive Director
Activities: Library: Yes
Mission: To advance energy-conserving technology & policies; to assist utilities & regulators to implement cost-effective conservation programs; to support the adoption of comprehensive new policies for increasing energy efficiency; to show how energy efficiency improvements can protect the environment; to analyse & promote technologies & policies for increasing vehicle fuel efficiency & reducing vehicle use; to help developing & Eastern European countries undertake energy efficiency programs

American Farmland Trust (AFT)
#800, 1200 - 18th St. NW, Washington DC 20036 USA
Tel: 202-331-7300; Fax: 202-659-8339
e-mail: info@farmland.org
URL: www.farmland.org
Social Media: www.facebook.com/AmericanFarmland
Overview: A large national charitable organization founded in 1980
Chief Officer(s):
John Winthrop, Chair
Membership: 20,000; Fees: $25
Activities: Public education; technical assistance in policy development; direct farmland protection projects; sustainable agriculture projects
Mission: To stop the loss of productive farmland & to promote farming practices that lead to a healthy environment

American Fisheries Society (AFS)
5410 Grosvenor Lane, Bethesda MD 20814-2199 USA
Tel: 301-897-8616; Fax: 301-897-8096
e-mail: main@fisheries.org
URL: www.fisheries.org
Social Media: www.facebook.com/group.php?gid=39804224812
Overview: A large international organization founded in 1870
Chief Officer(s):
Bill Franzin, President
Ghassan N. Rassam, Executive Director
Finances: Annual Operating Budget: $1.5 Million-$3 Million; Funding Sources: Donations; Grants; Membership fees; Publication sales
Staff: 24 staff member(s)
Membership: 8,500+ fisheries & aquatic science professionals & students; Fees: Regular: $76; Student: $19; Young Professional/Retired: $38; Lifetime: $1000-1737; Member Profile: Open to anyone interested in the progress of fisheries science & education & the conservation & management of fisheries resources; Committees: Arrangements; Award of Excellence; Board of Appeals; Board of Professional Certification; Budget & Finance; Continuing Education; Mail Ballot Tally; Membership; Membership Concerns; Names of Fishes; Names of Aquatic Invertebrates; Nominating; Program; Publications Overview; Resolutions; Resource Policy; Time & Place
Activities: Rents Mailing List: Yes
Awards: The Meritorious Service Award (Award)
Given to an individual for loyalty, dedication & meritorious service to the society over a long period of time, & for exceptional commitment to the society's programs, ideals, objectives, & long-term goals
The Distinguished Service Award (Award)
Given in recognition of outstanding service to the society

The AFS Award of Excellence (Award)
Given to recognize outstanding scientists in the fields of fisheries & aquatic biology
The Carl R. Sullivan Fisheries Conservation Award (Award)
Given annually to an individual or organization, professional or non-professional, for outstanding contributions to the conservation of fishery resources
Award for Excellence in Fisheries Education (Award)
Presented annually to an individual to recognize excellence in organized teaching & advising in a field of fisheries
J. Frances Allen Scholarship (Scholarship)
Awarded annually to a female Ph.D. student whose research emphasis is in an area of fisheries science Eligibility: Must be an AFS member
Honourary Membership (Award)
Awarded to individuals who have achieved outstanding professional or other attainments or have given outstanding service to the Society
Presidents' Fishery Conservation Award (Award)
Presented annually, one or more awards if warranted, in one of two categories: (1) an AFS individual or unit or (2) a non-AFS individual or entity, for a singular accomplishment or activity that advancces aquatic resource conservation at the regional or Society level
William E. Ricker Resource Conservation Award (Award)
Given to any entity for a singular accomplishment or activity in resource conservation that is significant at the U.S., continental, or international level
Excellence in Public Outreach (Award)
Awarded annually to an AFS member who goes "the extra mile" in sharing the value of fisheries science/research with the general public through the popular media & other communication channels
Fish Culture Hall of Fame (Award)
Inductees will have made significant contributions to the advancement of fish culture in the United States
Publications: Fisheries
Profile: Monthly Magazine
Mission: To advance fisheries science & the conservation of renewable aquatic resources; To promote & evaluate the educational, scientific, & technological development & advancement of all branches of fisheries science & practice, including aquatic biology, engineering, economics, fish culture, limnology, oceanography, & technology; To gather & disseminate technical & other information on fish, fishing, fisheries, & all phases of fisheries science & practice; To encourage the teaching of all phases of fisheries science

American Forest & Paper Association (AF&PA)
#800, 1111 - 19th St. NW, Washington DC 20036 USA
Tel: 202-463-2700
Toll-Free: 800-878-8878
e-mail: info@afandpa.org; membership@afandpa.org
URL: www.afandpa.org
Previous Name: American Paper Institute
Overview: A large international organization founded in 1993
Chief Officer(s):
F. Colin Moseley, Chair
Donna A. Harman, President & Chief Executive Officer
Jan Poling, Vice-President, General Counsel & Secretary
Membership: 157; Member Profile: Companies & associations that produce forest, paper, & wood products; Committees: North American Forest Carbon Standards; Environment Resource; Energy Resource; Air Quality; Printing-Writing; Timber Purchasers
Activities: Providing advice & counsel about the forest products industry; Operating a statistics program in the paper & packaging industry
Mission: To act as a leading voice for the forest products industry
Environmental Activity: Advancing policies that promote a sustainable forest products industry, such as recycling, clean air, & clean water

American Industrial Hygiene Association (AIHA)
#250, 2700 Prosperity Ave., Fairfax VA 22031 USA
Tel: 703-849-8888; Fax: 703-207-3561
e-mail: infonet@aiha.org
URL: www.aiha.org
Overview: A medium-sized international organization founded in 1939
Chief Officer(s):
Peter J. O'Neil, CAE, Executive Director, 703-846-0760
Mary Ellen Brennan, Director, Human Resources, 703-846-0760

Mary Ann Latko, Director, Scientific & Technical Initiatives, 703-846-0786
mlatko@aiha.org
Cheryl Morton, Director, Laboratory Quality Assurance Programs, 703-846-0789
cmorton@aiha.org
Connie Paradise, CAE, Director, Communications & Product Development, 703-846-0742
cparadise@aiha.org
Aaron Trippler, Director, Government Affairs, 703-846-0730
atrippler@aiha.org
Vicky Yobp, CAE, Director, Member Services & Special Interest Groups, 703-846-0769
vyobp@aiha.org
Membership: 10,460; Member Profile: International occupational & environmental health & safety professionals, who practise industrial hygiene in industry, academic institutions, government, & independent organizations
Activities: Administering education programs; Operating laboratory accreditation programs based on high international standards; Providing networking opportunities; Engaging in advocacy activities
Meetings/Conferences:
For more information see Trade Shows, Conferences and Seminars Chapter
American Industrial Hygiene Conference & Exposition 2013
May 2013 Montréal, QC
Publications: Journal of Occupational & Environmental Hygiene
Type: Journal Accepts Advertising : Yes Editor: Sheila Brown
Profile: A peer-reviewed publication to enhance the knowledge & practice of occupational & environmental hygiene & safety
The Synergist
Type: Magazine Frequency: m. Accepts Advertising : Yes Editor: Ed Rutkowski
Profile: Information about the occupational & environmental health & safety fields & the industrial hygiene profession, including industry trends, government activities, technical information, & association news
American Industrial Hygiene Association Member Directory
Type: Directory
Mission: To serve the needs of occupational & environmental health professionals; To achieve high professional standards; To promote certification of industrial hygienists

American Iron & Steel Institute (AISI)
#705, 1140 Connecticut Ave. NW, Washington DC 20036 USA
Tel: 202-452-7100; Fax: 202-463-6573
e-mail: webmaster@steel.org
URL: www.steel.org
Overview: A small international organization
Chief Officer(s):
Ward J. Timken Jr., Chair
Member Profile: Producer companies - including integrated, electric furnace & reconstituted mills; associate companies - suppliers to or customers of the industry; affiliate organizations - downstream steel producers of products such as cold rolled strip, pipe & tube, coated sheet
Mission: To advance steel as the material of choice and to enhance the competitiveness of member companies and the North American steel industry.

American Lung Association (ALA)
Washington Office, #900, 1150 - 18th St. N.W., Washington DC 20036 USA
Tel: 202-785-3355; Fax: 202-452-1805
Toll-Free: 800-732-9339
e-mail: alaw@alaw.org
URL: www.lungusa.org
Overview: A large national charitable organization founded in 1904
Chief Officer(s):
Stephen J. Nolan, Esq., Chair
Finances: Annual Operating Budget: Greater than $5 Million; Funding Sources: Donations; Grants
Staff: 105 staff member(s)
Membership: 130,000 volunteers
Mission: To prevent lung disease & promote lung health; Affiliation(s): American Thoracic Society

American Medical Association
515 North State St., Chicago IL 60610 USA
Tel: 312-464-5000; Fax: 312-464-5443
Toll-Free: 800-621-8335
URL: www.ama-assn.org
Overview: A large national organization founded in 1847
Chief Officer(s):

Associations/Organizations / American Ornithologists' Union

Michael D. Maves, MD, MBA, Exec. Vice President & CEO
Fees: Physician: $84-420; Intern/Resident/Fellow: $45-160; Student: $20-68
Activities: Council on Scientific Affairs - major contributions in the area of environmental health; Dept. of Environmental, Public & Occupational Health (these responsibilities are now with the Dept. of Risk Assessment in the Division of Biomedical Science)

American Ornithologists' Union (AOU)
#402, 1313 Dolley Madison Blvd., McLean VA 22101 USA
Tel: 505-326-1579
e-mail: aou@aou.org
URL: www.aou.org
Overview: A medium-sized national organization founded in 1883
Chief Officer(s):
Edward H. Burtt, President
aoupresident@aou.org
Sara R. Morris, Secretary
aousecretary@aou.org
Membership: 4,500; *Fees:* Regular: $85; Student: $27; Lifetime: $2550
Activities: Supporting individual research projects; Providing funds for graduate students to attend annual meetings; Presenting several annual awards for excellence in research; *Rents Mailing List:* Yes
Awards: William Brewster Memorial Award
Elliott Coues Award
Ned K. Johnson Young Investigator Award
Ralph W. Schreiber Conservation Award
Marion Jenkinson AOU Service Award
Publications: The Auk [a publication of the American Ornithologists' Union]
Type: Journal *Frequency:* q.
Profile: A journal of ornithology
Mission: To be devoted to the scientific study of birds in North America

American Paper Institute *See* American Forest & Paper Association

American Planning Association (APA)
#400, 1776 Massachusetts Ave. NW, Washington DC 20036-1904 USA
Tel: 202-872-0611; *Fax:* 202-872-0643
e-mail: customerservice@planning.org
URL: www.planning.org
Overview: A large national organization founded in 1909
Chief Officer(s):
Paul Farmer, FAICP, Executive Director
Robert B. Hunter, FAICP, President
Finances: Annual Operating Budget: $3 Million-$5 Million
Staff: 66 staff member(s)
Membership: 29,000
Activities: Environment, Natural Resources & Energy Division - to bring sound planning principles to the protection, management or conservation of environmental, natural & energy resources, as well as national forests & public lands; Small town & Rural Planning Division - oriented toward improving the quality & extent of planning in small communities & rural areas with a focus on protection of natural resources; *Rents Mailing List:* Yes
Mission: To provide members with systematic ways to work on problems in common & to affect national planning policies

American Plastics Council (APC)
#800, 1300 Wilson Blvd., Arlington VA 22209 USA
Tel: 703-741-5000
Toll-Free: 800-243-5790
URL: www.plasticsresource.com
Overview: A medium-sized national organization
Chief Officer(s):
Ron Krebs, Director, Communications
Activities: Technical Assistance Program (TAP); research & development
Mission: To demonstrate the benefits of plastic products & the contributions of the plastics industry to the society we serve; to demonstrate that plastics are an efficient use of natural resources & that plastics & the plastics industry are part of the solution to the public's environmental performance expectations

American Public Works Association (APWA)
#700, 2345 Grand Blvd., Kansas City MO 64108-2625 USA
Tel: 816-472-6100; *Fax:* 816-472-1610
Toll-Free: 800-848-2792
e-mail: apwa@apwa.net
URL: www.apwa.net

Overview: A medium-sized international organization founded in 1938
Chief Officer(s):
Peter King, Executive Director, 202-218-6700
pking@apwa.net
Kaye Sullivan, Deputy Executive Director/COO, 816-595-5233
ksullivan@apwa.net
Finances: Annual Operating Budget: Greater than $5 Million; *Funding Sources:* Membership dues; Federal grants; Products
Staff: 50 staff member(s); 250+ volunteer(s)
Membership: 26,000; *Fees:* Schedule available; *Member Profile:* Public agencies, private sector companies, & individuals engaged in public works services; *Committees:* Transportation; Solid Waste; Water Resources; Engineering & Technology; Management & Leadership; Emergency Management; Fleet Services; Facilities & Grounds; Utility & Public Right of Way
Mission: To provide high quality public works goods & services

American Rivers
#1400, 1101 - 14th St. NW, Washington DC 20005 USA
Tel: 202-347-7550; *Fax:* 202-347-9240
e-mail: amrivers@americanrivers.org
URL: www.americanrivers.org
Previous Name: American Rivers Conservation Council
Overview: A medium-sized national organization founded in 1973
Chief Officer(s):
Edward B. Whitney, Chair
Finances: Annual Operating Budget: $1.5 Million-$3 Million
Staff: 25 staff member(s); 7 volunteer(s)
Fees: $20
Activities: Policy manuals; *Internships:* Yes; *Speaker Service:* Yes
Mission: To preserve & restore America's river systems; to foster a river stewardship ethic

American Rivers Conservation Council *See* American Rivers

American Society for Environmental History (ASEH)
Interdisciplinary Arts & Sciences Program, University of Washington, PO Box 358436, 1900 Commerce St., Tacoma WA 98402-3100 USA
Tel: 206-465-0630
e-mail: director@aseh.net
URL: www.aseh.net
Overview: A small international charitable organization founded in 1977
Chief Officer(s):
Harriet Ritvo, President
ritvo@mit.edu
Lisa Mighetto, Executive Director
Committees: Executive; Nominating; Diversity; Outreach; Conference Site Selection; Publications; Education; Conference Program; Conference Local Arrangements; George Perkins Marsh Prize; Alice Hamilton Prize; Rachel Carson Prize; Leopold-Hidy Prize; H-Evironment
Awards: Leopold-Hidy Prize for Best Article in Environmental History (Award)
Alice Hamilton Prize for Best Article, Outside the journal, Environmental History (Award)
Rachel Carson Prize for Best Dissertation in Environmental History (Award)
George Perkins March Prize for Best Book in Environmental History (Award)
Publications: ASEH [American Society for Environmental History] News
Type: Newsletter *Frequency:* q.
Environmental History
Type: Journal
Profile: Published jointly with the Forest History Society
Mission: To promote interdisciplinary study of past environmental change; to promote the study of environmental history in all disciplines; *Member of:* American Council of Learned Societies; *Affiliation(s):* International Consortium of Environmental History Organizations

American Society of Heating, Refrigerating & Air Conditioning Engineers (ASHRAE)
1791 Tullie Circle NE, Atlanta GA 30329 USA
Tel: 404-636-8400; *Fax:* 404-321-5478
Toll-Free: 800-527-4723
e-mail: ashrae@ashrae.org
URL: www.ashrae.org
Social Media: facebook.com/pages/ashrae/106136469528
Overview: A medium-sized international organization founded in 1894
Membership: 50,000; *Fees:* Regular/Student: $165; Associate: $165; Affiliate: $40
Awards: ASHRAE Engineers Grant-in-Aid (Scholarship)
Graduate level studies in the areas of heating, cooling, refrigeration, air conditioning, energy conservation, air quality *Deadline:* Feb. 16 *Award Amount:* $6,000 US; 12 awards available Contact: Manager of Research, ASHRAE, 1791 Tullie Cir.
Publications: ASHRAE [American Society of Heating, Refrigerating & Air Conditioning Engineers] Journal
Type: Journal *Frequency:* m.
Mission: ASHRAE is an international organization with a mission of advancing heating, ventilation, air conditioning & refrigeration. It promotes a sustainable environment through research, standards writing, publishing & continuing education.

American Society of Mechanical Engineers (ASME)
3 Park Ave., New York NY 10016-5990 USA
Tel: 800-843-2763 *Tel:* 973-882-1170
e-mail: infocentral@asme.org
URL: www.asme.org
Overview: A large international organization founded in 1880
Finances: Funding Sources: Publications; Meetings; Standards accreditation
Membership: 120,000+ in 150+ countries; *Fees:* Schedule available; *Member Profile:* Students; Engineers; Technical professionals; Researchers; Project managers; Academic leaders; Corporate executives
Activities: Promoting multidisciplinary engineering & allied science throughout the world; Engaging in research; Liaising with government; Enabling knowledge sharing; Offering continuing education & professional development in mechanical engineering; Maintaining codes & standards; Promoting the technical competency of members; Offering a mentoring program; *Library:* American Society of Mechanical Engineers e-Library; Not open to the public
Meetings/Conferences:
For more information see Trade Shows, Conferences and Seminars Chapter
American Society of Mechanical Engineers 2011 Turbo Expo
June 2011 Vancouver, BC
American Society of Mechanical Engineers 2011 Emergency Operations & Hoistway Committee Meetings
June 2011 Québec, QC
American Society of Mechanical Engineers 2011 Gas Transmission & Distribution Piping System Meeting
June 2011 St. Louis, MO
American Society of Mechanical Engineers 2011 Annual Meeting
June 2011 Dallas, TX
American Society of Mechanical Engineers 2011 Wind Turbine Project Team Meeting
June 2011 Toronto, ON
American Society of Mechanical Engineers 2011 Escalator & Moving Walk Committee Meeting
June 2011 Montréal, QC
Ocean, Offshore, & Arctic Engineering 2011 30th International Conference
June 2011 Rotterdam
American Society of Mechanical Engineers 2011 Summer Bioengineering Conference
June 2011
American Society of Mechanical Engineers Power 2011
July 2011 Denver, CO
American Society of Mechanical Engineers 2011 Pressure Vessels & Piping Conference: Pressure Vessel Technologies - A Look Ahead into the Next Decade
July 2011 Baltimore, MD
American Society of Mechanical Engineers 2011 5th International Conference on Energy Sustainability
August 2011 Washington, DC
American Society of Mechanical Engineers 2011 9th Fuel Cell Science, Engineering, & Technology Conference
August 2011 Washington, DC
American Society of Mechanical Engineers / NRC 2011 Pump & Valve Symposium
August 2011 Rockville, MD
American Society of Mechanical Engineers 2011 International Design Engineering Technical Conference
August 2011 Washington, DC
American Society of Mechanical Engineers 2011 Computers & Information in Engineering Conference
August 2011 Washington, DC
American Society of Mechanical Engineers 2011 Conference on Smart Materials, Adaptive Structures, & Intelligent Systems
September 2011 Scottsdale, AZ

American Society of Mechanical Engineers 2011 14th International Conference on Environmental Remediation & Radioactive Waste Management
September 2011 Reims
American Society of Mechanical Engineers 2011 6th Frontiers in Biomedical Devices Conference & Exhibition
September 2011 Irvine, CA
American Society of Mechanical Engineers 2011 Small Modular Reactors Symposium
September 2011 Washington, DC
American Society of Mechanical Engineers 2011 Nuclear Quality Assurance Meeting
October 2011 St. Petersburg, FL
American Society of Mechanical Engineers 2011 International Offshore Pipeline Forum
October 2011 Houston, TX
American Society of Mechanical Engineers 2011 Committee on Fiber-Reinforced Plastic Pressure Vessels Meeting
October 2011 Las Vegas, NV
American Society of Mechanical Engineers 2011 Program
October 2011 Houston, TX
American Society of Mechanical Engineers 2011 International Mechanical Engineering Congress & Exposition: Energy & Water Scarcity
November 2011 Denver, CO
American Society of Mechanical Engineers 2011 Program
November 2011 Orlando, FL
American Society of Mechanical Engineers 2011 Committee on Operation and Maintenance of Nuclear Power Plants Meeting
December 2011 Clearwater, FL
American Society of Mechanical Engineers 2012 Annual Meeting
June 2012 Montréal, QC
American Society of Mechanical Engineers 2012 57th Turbo Expo
June 2012 Copenhagen
American Society of Mechanical Engineers 2012 Pressure Vessels & Piping Conference
July 2012 Toronto, ON
American Society of Mechanical Engineers 2012 International Mechanical Engineering Congress & Exposition
November 2012 Houston, TX
Ocean, Offshore, & Arctic Engineering 2012 31st International Conference
Other Conferences in 2012 2012 Rio de Janeiro
American Society of Mechanical Engineers 2013 58th Turbo Expo
Other Conferences in 2013 2013
Ocean, Offshore, & Arctic Engineering 2013 32nd International Conference
Other Conferences in 2013 2013 Nantes
Publications: *History & Heritage Newsletter [a publication of the American Society of Mechanical Engineers]*
Type: Newsletter Frequency: s-a.
Profile: Notable accomplishments in mechanical engineering history
ME Today [a publication of the American Society of Mechanical Engineers]
Type: Newsletter Frequency: q.
Profile: Information of interest to early career engineers
Member Savvy [a publication of the American Society of Mechanical Engineers]
Type: Newsletter Frequency: m.
Profile: The benefits of membership in the American Society of Mechanical Engineer
ASME [American Society of Mechanical Engineers] Capitol Update
Type: Newsletter Frequency: w.
Profile: Legislative & regulatory news of interest to the engineering community
Standards & Certification Update [a publication of the American Society of Mechanical Engineers]
Type: Newsletter Frequency: q.
Profile: Information about American Society of Mechanical Engineers standards & certification activities, including new publications, professional development, & conformity assessment
Applied Mechanics Reviews
Type: Journal Frequency: bi-m. Editor: J.N. Reddy ISSN: 0003-6900
Profile: An international review journal featuring topics such as heat transfer, vibration, & dynamics
Journal of Applied Mechanics
Type: Journal Frequency: bi-m. Editor: Robert M. McMeeking ISSN: 0021-8936
Profile: Peer-reviewed research papers covering subjects such as wave propagation, turbulence, stress analysis, structures, hydraulics, & flow & fracture
Journal of Biomechanical Engineering
Type: Journal Frequency: m. Editor: Michael S. Sacks ISSN: 0148-0731
Profile: Research papers on topics such as cellular mechanics, the design & control of biological systems, bioheat transfer, biomaterials, & biomechanics
Journal of Computational & Nonlinear Dynamics
Type: Journal Frequency: q. Editor: Ahmed A. Shabana, Ph.D. ISSN: 1555-1415
Profile: Technical briefs & research papers cover bio-mechanical dynamics, design & design optimization dynamical analysis & method, vehicular dynamics, stability, & aerospace applications
Journal of Computing & Information Science in Engineering
Type: Journal Frequency: q. Editor: Bahram Ravani ISSN: 1530-9827
Profile: Research papers & technical briefs about virtual environments & haptics, tolerance mondeling & computational metrology, reverse engineering, & internet-aided design, manufacturing, & commerce
Journal of Dynamic Systems, Measurement, & Control
Type: Journal Frequency: bi-m. Editor: Suhada Jayasuriya ISSN: 0022-0434
Profile: Articles on design innovation, research papers, & technical briefs address aerospace systems, energy systems & control, manufacturing technology, power systems, production systems, signal processing, & transportation
Journal of Electronic Packaging
Type: Journal Frequency: q. Editor: Bahgat Sammakia ISSN: 1043-7398
Profile: Papers to address mechanical, materials, & reliability problems encountered in the design, manufacturing, & operation of electronic, optoelectronic, & photonic systems
Journal of Energy Resources Technology
Type: Journal Frequency: q. Editor: Andrew K. Wojtanowicz ISSN: 0195-0738
Profile: Research on topics such as extraction of energy from natural resources, enerty resource recovery from biomass & solid wastes, technology for energy generations, offshore & deepwater mechanics, petroleum engineering, natural gas technology, & rock & material mechanics for energy resources
Journal of Engineering for Gas Turbines & Power
Type: Journal Frequency: m. Editor: Dilip R. Ballal ISSN: 0742-4795
Profile: Technical briefs & research examime nuclear engineering, coal, biomass & alternative fuels, energy production & conversion, & oil & gas applications
Journal of Engineering Materials & Technology
Type: Journal Frequency: q. Editor: Hussein M. Zbib ISSN: 0094-4289
Profile: Topics include environmental effects, fatigue, fracture, high temperature creep, & phase transformations in materials
Journal of Fluids Engineering
Type: Journal Frequency: m. Editor: Malcolm J. Andrews ISSN: 0098-2202
Profile: Contents include cavitation erosion, flow in biolgical systems, fluid transients & wave motion, naval hydrodynamics, pumps, pipelines, turbines, propulsion systems, & water hammers
Journal of Fuel Cell Science & Technology
Type: Journal Frequency: bi-m. Editor: Nigel M. Sammes ISSN: 1550-624X
Profile: Subjects include durability & damage tolerance, aging, system design & manufacturing, & fuel cell applications
Journal of Heat Transfer
Type: Journal Frequency: m. Editor: Terrence W. Simon ISSN: 0022-1481
Profile: Featuring research on environmental issues, low temperature & the Arctic, aircraft, & energy technology & systems
Journal of Manufacturing Science & Engineering
Type: Journal Frequency: bi-m. Editor: Kornel F. Ehmann ISSN: 1087-1357
Profile: Subjects include rail transportation, inspection & quality control, material removal by machining, production systems optimization, textile production, & sensors
Journal of Mechanical Design
Type: Journal Frequency: m. Editor: Panos Y. Papalambros ISSN: 1050-0472
Profile: Technical briefs & research papers address design theory & methodology, design automation, & design of direct contact systems
Journal of Mechanisms & Robotics
Type: Journal Frequency: q. Editor: J. Michael McCarthys ISSN: 1942-4302
Profile: Research covers the theory, algorithms, & applications for robotic & machine systems
Journal of Medical Devices
Type: Journal Frequency: q. Editor: Arthur G. Erdman; Gerald E. Miller ISSN: 1932-6181
Profile: Design innovation articles & research papers focus upon new medical devices or instrumentation that improve diagnostic interventional & therapeutic treatments
Journal of Nanotechnology in Engineering & Medicine
Type: Journal Frequency: q. Editor: Vijay K. Varadan ISSN: 1949-2944
Profile: The impact of nanotechnology upon medicine & the direction of research & development
Journal of Offshore Mechanics & Arctic Engineering
Type: Journal Frequency: q. Editor: Solomon C. Yim ISSN: 0892-7219
Profile: Articles highlight Arctic exploration & drilling, permafrost engineering & Arctic thermal design, offshore structures, ice structure interaction, & marine geotechnique
Journal of Pressure Vessel Technology
Type: Journal Frequency: bi-m. Editor: G. E. Otto Widera ISSN: 0094-9930
Profile: Technology reviews & research papers cover codes & standards, pressure vessel & piping, fatigue & fracture prediction, elevated temperature analysis & design, lifeline earthquake engineering, & safety & reliability
Journal of Solar Energy Engineering
Type: Journal Frequency: q. Editor: Gilles Flamant ISSN: 0199-6231
Profile: Research papers & technical information about solar collectors, solar optics, solar chemistry & bioconversion, solar thermal power, energy storage, conservation, solar buildings, solar space applications, wind energy, emerging technologies, & energy policy
Journal of Thermal Science & Engineering Applications
Type: Journal Frequency: q. Editor: Michael Jensen ISSN: 1948-5085
Profile: Subjects addressed include applications in areas such as defense systems, aerospace systems, energy systems, refrigeration & air conditioning, petrochemical processing, combustion systems, & medical systems
Journal of Tribology
Type: Journal Frequency: q. Editor: Michael D. Bryant ISSN: 0742-4787
Profile: Technical information & research cover tribological systems, bearing design & technology, gears, seals, & friction & wear
Journal of Turbomachinery
Type: Journal Frequency: q. Editor: David Wisler ISSN: 0889-504X
Profile: Research papers examine fluid dynamics & heat transfer phenomena in compressor & turbine components
Journal of Vibration & Acoustics
Type: Journal Frequency: bi-m. Editor: Noel C. Perkins ISSN: 1048-9002
Profile: Subjects include areas such as machinery dynamics & noise, structural acoustics, acoustic emission, noise control, & vibration suppression
Mission: To promote the art, science, & practice of multidisciplinary engineering; To focus on the technical, educational, & research issues of the engineering & technology community; To help the engineering community develop solutions to improve the quality of life
Environmental Activity: Promoting environmental engineering to help make the land, air, & water safer for humans

American Society of Mining & Reclamation (ASMR)
3134 Montavesta Rd., Lexington KY 40502-3548 USA
Tel: 859-351-9032; Fax: 859-335-6529
e-mail: asmr@insightbb.com
URL: ces.ca.uky.edu/asmr
Overview: A medium-sized international charitable organization founded in 1983
Chief Officer(s):
Vern Pfannenstiel, President
Finances: *Annual Operating Budget:* $50,000-$100,000; *Funding Sources:* Membership dues
Staff: 1 staff member(s); 1 volunteer(s)
Membership: 400; *Fees:* $100 sustaining; $50 regular; $10-25 student; *Member Profile:* Sustaining - agency, department, organization, corporation, or individual representation; regular - individual representation; student - full-time students at accredited colleges; *Committees:* Publication Policy & Review Board; Awards; National Meeting; Membership; Memorial

Associations/Organizations / American Society of Plant Biologists

Scholarship Fund; National Register of Research & Demonstration
Activities: Small independent professional groups affiliated with the Society have been organized to concentrate on a particular aspect of surface mining or reclamation: International Tailings Reclamation, Landscape Architecture, Soil & Overburden, Ecology, Geotechnical Engineering, Meter Management, Forestry & Wildlife
Awards: Reclamation Researcher of the Year (Award)
Awarded to research scientists who have made substantive contributions to the advancement of reclamation science &/or technology, or contributed meaningful information relating to the economic, social, environmental or ecological effects of surface mining
William T. Plass Award (Award)
Awarded irregularly; recognizes outstanding contributions in the areas of mining, teaching, research, &/or regulating authority as they relate to land reclamation. Those nominated should be recognized nationally & internationally for their contibutions covering a significant portion of their career
Reclamationist of the Year (Award)
Awarded to individuals demonstrating outstanding accomplishments in the practical application or evaluation of reclamation technology
Mission: To encourage any agency, institution, organization, or individual in their efforts to protect, re-establish or enhance the surface resources of land disturbances associated with mineral extraction; to promote, support & assist in research & studies; to encourage communication between the research scientist, regulatory agencies, organizations & others who seek assistance; to promote & support related educational programs; **Affiliation(s):** International Affiliation of Land Reclamationists

American Society of Plant Biologists (ASPB)
15501 Monona Dr., Rockville MD 20855-2768 USA
Tel: 301-251-0560; *Fax:* 301-279-2996
e-mail: info@aspb.org
URL: www.aspb.org
Overview: A medium-sized international organization founded in 1924
Chief Officer(s):
Crispin Taylor, Executive Director
ctaylor@aspb.org
Kim Kimnach, Executive Director
kKimnach@aspb.org
Gordon Gordon, Manager, Executive & Governance Affairs
dgordon@aspb.org
Member Profile: Plant biology researchers, educators, & students from any nation; Any person concerned with the physiology, molecular biology, environmental biology, cell biology, & biophysics of plants; *Committees:* Awards; Constitution & Bylaws; Education; Executive; International; Membership; Minority Affairs; Nominating; Operations Subcommittee; Program; Public Affairs; Publications; Women in Plant Biology
Meetings/Conferences:
For more information see Trade Shows, Conferences and Seminars Chapter
Plant Biology 2011
August 2011 Minneapolis, MN
Publications: *The Plant Cell*
Type: Journal *Frequency:* m. *Accepts Advertising*: Yes *Editor:* John Long *ISSN:* 1040-4651
Profile: Primary research in the plant sciences
Plant Physiology
Type: Journal *Frequency:* m. *Accepts Advertising*: Yes *Editor:* John Long *ISSN:* 0032-0889
Profile: Physiology, biochemistry, cellular & molecular biology, genetics, biophysics, & environmental biology of plants
ASPB [American Society of Plant Biologists] News
Type: Newsletter *Frequency:* bi-m. *Price:* Free for American Society Of Plant Biologists members; $30 non-members
Mission: To advance the plant sciences; To promote the development & outreach of plant biology as a pure & applied science

American Society of Plumbing Engineers (ASPE)
#1007, 8614 Catalpa Ave., Chicago IL 60656-1116 USA
Tel: 773-693-2773; *Fax:* 773-695-9007
e-mail: info@aspe.org
URL: www.aspe.org
Overview: A medium-sized international organization founded in 1964
Chief Officer(s):
Stanley Wolfson, Executive Director
aspeexdir@aol.com
Membership: 6,500

American Society of Safety Engineers (ASSE)
1800 East Oakton St., Des Plaines IL 60018-2187 USA
Tel: 847-699-2929; *Fax:* 847-768-3434
e-mail: customerservice@asse.org
URL: www.asse.org
Overview: A large international organization founded in 1911
Chief Officer(s):
Fred J. Fortman, Executive Director
Membership: 30,000; *Fees:* Regular: $160; Student: $135
Activities: Providing a Professional Development Conference & Exposition; Offering continuing education & training seminars; Presenting technical publications & audio-visual training courses; *Awareness Events:* National Safety Week, June; *Rents Mailing List:* Yes
Publications: *Profofessional Safety*
Profile: Monthly journal
Mission: To promote the advancement of the safety profession & to foster the technical, scientific, managerial & ethical knowledge, skills & competency of safety professionals; **Affiliation(s):** Canadian Society of Safety Engineering, Inc.

American Water Resources Association (AWRA)
PO Box 1626, 4 Federal St. West, Middleburg VA 20118-1626 USA
Tel: 540-687-8390; *Fax:* 540-687-8395
e-mail: info@awra.org
URL: www.awra.org
Overview: A large national organization founded in 1964
Chief Officer(s):
Jerry Selhke, President Elect
Finances: *Annual Operating Budget:* $500,000-$1.5 Million
Staff: 8 staff member(s)
Membership: 3,000 worldwide; *Fees:* Schedule available; *Member Profile:* Regular - persons interested in any aspect of water resources; student - full-time student engaged in study of any aspect of water resources at a college or university; institutional - universities, governmental agencies & institutions; corporate - consulting firms & business concerns
Activities: Technical Committees provide a focus for special interests; *Rents Mailing List:* Yes
Mission: To advance research, planning, management, development & education in water resources; provides a focal point for the collection, organization & dissemination of ideas & information in the physical, biological, economic, social, political, legal & engineering aspects of water-related problems; to provide a forum for communication among disciplines with a common interest in water supply, quality, use, development & conservation

American Water Works Association (AWWA)
6666 West Quincy Ave., Denver CO 80235 USA
Tel: 303-794-7711; *Fax:* 303-347-0804
Toll-Free: 800-926-7337
e-mail: custsvc@awwa.org
URL: www.awwa.org
Social Media: www.facebook.com/pages/American-Water-Works-Association/210194499809
Overview: A large international organization founded in 1881
Chief Officer(s):
David B. LaFrance, Executive Director
dlafrance@awwa.org
Susan Franceschi, Chief Membership Officer
sfranceschi@awwa.org
Bob Huff, Chief Information Officer
bhuff@awwa.org
Kevin Mann, Chief Financial Officer
kmann@awwa.org
April DeBaker, Director, Conferences & Events
adebaker@awwa.org
Liz Haigh, Director, Publishing
lhaigh@awwa.org
Tania Haskins, Director, Administration
thaskins@awwa.org
Jane Johnson, Director, Sales & Research
jjohnson@awwa.org
Roy Martinez, Director, Engineering & Technical Services
rmartinez@awwa.org
Membership: 60,000+; *Fees:* Schedule available; *Member Profile:* Treatment plant operators & managers; Scientists; Environmentalists; Manufacturers; Academics; Regulators; Others interested in water supply & public health
Activities: Providing information about the water industry; *Library:* American Water Works Association Water Library

Meetings/Conferences:
For more information see Trade Shows, Conferences and Seminars Chapter
American Water Works Association 2011 130th Annual Conference & Exposition
June 2011 Washington, DC
American Water Works Association 2011 Distribution Systems Symposium & Exposition & Water Security Conference
September 2011 Nashville, TN
American Water Works Association 2011 Financial Management Seminar: The Cost of Service Rate Making
September 2011 Las Vegas, NV
American Water Works Association 2011 Water Quality Technology Conference & Exposition
November 2011 Phoenix, AZ
American Water Works Association & The Water Environment Federation 2012 Utility Management Conference
January 2012 Miami, FL
American Water Works Association & The American Membrane Technology Association 2012 Membrane Technology Joint Conference & Exposition
February 2012 Glendale, AZ
American Water Works Association 2012 Customer Service & Information Management Conference & Exposition
March 2012 Atlanta, GA
American Water Works Association 2012 Sustainable Water Management Conference & Exposition
March 2012 Portland, OR
American Water Works Association 2012 131st Annual Conference & Exposition
June 2012 Dallas, TX
American Water Works Association 2013 132nd Annual Conference & Exposition
June 2013 Denver, CO
American Water Works Association 2014 133rd Annual Conference & Exposition
June 2014 Boston, MA
American Water Works Association 2015 134th Annual Conference & Exposition
June 2015 Anaheim, CA
American Water Works Association 2016 135th Annual Conference & Exposition
June 2016 Chicago, IL
American Water Works Association 2017 136th Annual Conference & Exposition
June 2017 Philadelphia, PA
American Water Works Association 2018 137th Annual Conference & Exposition
June 2018 Las Vegas, NV
American Water Works Association 2019 138th Annual Conference & Exposition
June 2019 Denver, CO
American Water Works Association 2020 139th Annual Conference & Exposition
June 2020 Orlando, FL
American Water Works Association 2021 140th Annual Conference & Exposition
Other Conferences in 2021 2021
Publications: *Journal AWWA [American Water Works Association]*
Type: Journal *Frequency:* m. *Editor:* Marcia Lacey (mlacey@awwa.org) *ISSN:* 1551-8833 *Price:* Free with individual, utility, & service provider membership in AWWA
Profile: Peer-reviewed information about water quality, resources, & supply, in addition to professional & scholarly articles about the management & operation of water utilities
Opflow [a publication of the American Water Works Association]
Type: Magazine *Frequency:* m. *Accepts Advertising*: Yes *Editor:* John Hughes (jhughes@awwa.org) *ISSN:* 1551-8701 *Price:* Free with individual, utility, & service provider membership in AWWA
Profile: Practical publication for water supply operators
IDA Journal on Desalination & Water Reuse [a publication of the American Water Works Association]
Type: Journal *Frequency:* q. *Accepts Advertising*: Yes *Editor:* John Hughes (jhughes@awwa.org)
Profile: Co-published by the International Desalination Association (IDA) & the American Water Works Association, the journal offers peer-reviewed, technical literature about desalination
AWWA [American Water Works Association] Streamlines
Type: Newsletter *Frequency:* bi-weekly *Price:* Free with individual, utility, & service provider membership in AWWA
Profile: Information about regulatory & legislative developments,

research, new technologies, industry trends, utility practices, plus American Water Works Association activities & resources
The Water Dictionary: A Comprehensive Reference of Water Terminology
Type: Book *Number of Pages:* 716 *Editor:* Nancy McTigue
ISSN: 978-1-58321-741-2
Profile: Definitions for 15,000 water-related words, acronyms, & formulas
AWWA [American Water Works Association] Standards
Profile: A print set of the current standards of the American Water Works Association
American Water Works Association Officers & Committee Directory
Type: Directory
Profile: Director, trustee, officer, & staff management information, plus the AWWA strategic plan & statements of policy
Mission: To advance public health & safety through the improvement of water quality & supply throughout North America & beyond; To provide standards for the design, manufacturing, installation, & performance of water industry products; To advance & protect the interests of the water industry
Environmental Activity: Advocating to improve the quality & supply of water in North America & beyond

American Wilderness Alliance *See* American Wildlands

American Wildlands (AWL)
PO Box 6669, #418, 321 East Main St., Bozeman MT 59771 USA
Tel: 406-586-8175; *Fax:* 406-586-8242
e-mail: info@wildlands.org
URL: www.wildlands.org
Previous Name: American Wilderness Alliance
Overview: A medium-sized international organization founded in 1977
Chief Officer(s):
Tom Skeele, Executive Director
Finances: *Annual Operating Budget:* $250,000-$500,000
Staff: 6 staff member(s); 6 volunteer(s)
Membership: 2,500; *Fees:* $40
Activities: *Internships:* Yes; *Speaker Service:* Yes; *Rents Mailing List:* Yes
Mission: To insure the responsible management & protection of forests, wildlife, wilderness, wetlands, watersheds, rivers & fisheries

American Zoo & Aquarium Association (AZA)
#710, 8403 Colesville Rd., Silver Spring MD 20910-3314 USA
Tel: 301-562-0777; *Fax:* 301-562-0888
URL: www.aza.org
Overview: A medium-sized national organization founded in 1924
Chief Officer(s):
Jim Maddy, President & CEO
Finances: *Annual Operating Budget:* $500,000-$1.5 Million
Staff: 20 staff member(s)
Membership: 5,500; *Fees:* Associate: $70; Affiliate: $95; Fellow: $195; *Member Profile:* Comprises zoological institutions, related organizations, societies, zoological staff employees, commercial concerns that provide products & services to zoological facilities & other interested individuals; open to anyone interested in animal welfare, protection of wildlife & the development of better zoos & aquariums for the good of animals & people; *Committees:* Accreditation; Animal Data Information Systems; Animal Health; Animal Welfare; Aquatic Advisory; Board of Regents; Charter & Bylaws; Conference; Conservation Education; Diversity; Ethics; Field Conservation; Finance & Investments; Government Affairs; Honors & Awards; Information Trends; Marketing; Membership; National Awareness Campaign; Nominating; Operations; Public Relations; Wildlife Conservation & Management
Activities: Species Survival Plan - a strategy for the long-term survival of certain endangered species; International Species Information System (ISIS) - to promote healthy gene pools; computerized inventory of over 60,000 living animals in order to enable zoos to locate the best individuals for their breeding programs; *Rents Mailing List:* Yes
Mission: To help preserve the world's rare & endangered species; to advance zoological parks & aquariums through conservation, education, scientific studies & recreation; to cooperate with government agencies & international conservation groups in matters dealing with the health & welfare of wildlife in captivity; *Affiliation(s):* World Wildlife Fund - USA; Species Survival Commission of IUCN - World Conservation Union; Captive Breeding Specialist Group; International Species Information System; Wildlife Conservation International; American Committee for International Conservation; Centre for Marine Conservation; International Union of Directors of Zoological Gardens; International Association of Zoo Educators

Les Ami(e)s de la Terre Canada *See* Friends of the Earth Canada

Les AmiEs de la Terre de Québec (ATQ)
Centre Frédéric-Back Culture et Environnement, #210, 870, rue Salaberry, Québec QC G1R 2T9
Tél: 418-524-2744
Courriel: info@atquebec.org
URL: www.atquebec.org
Aperçu: *Dimension:* petite; *Envergure:* locale; *Organisme sans but lucratif; fondée en* 1978
Finances: *Budget de fonctionnement annuel:* Moins de $50,000
Membre: 250; *Montant de la cotisation:* 10$ travailleur; 5$ non-travailleur; *Comités:* Paix; Environnement et mondialisation; Écologie et santéEau; Forêt
Activités: RadioTerre; émission hebdomadaire d'écologie politique diffusée sur les ondes de CKIA FM (Québec); une conférence par mois sur des thèmes reliés à l'écologie; *Service de conférenciers:* Oui; *Bibliothèque:* Centre documentation des ATQ
Mission: Conscientiser la population à la crise écologique mondiale versus le droit de tous à un environnement sain; éduquer les gens à leur propre prise en charge personnelle et collective face à cette crise; améliorer les communications entre écologistes aussi bien qu'entre ceux-ci et la population qu'ils desservent; renforcer la qualité de la vie associative chez-nous aussi bien qu'ailleurs dans la région et au Québec; *Membre de:* Réseau Québécois des Groupes Écologistes (RQGE); Regroupement d'éducation populaire en action communautaire (Répac)

Les Amis du Jardin botanique de Montréal / Friends of the Montréal Botanical Garden
#A-206, 4101, rue Sherbrooke est, Montréal QC H1X 2B2
Tél: 514-872-1493; *Téléc:* 514-872-3765
URL: www.amisjardin.qc.ca
Nom précédent: Société d'animation du Jardin et de l'Institut botanique
Aperçu: *Dimension:* moyenne; *Envergure:* locale; *Organisme sans but lucratif; fondée en* 1975
Membre(s) du bureau directeur:
Michèle-E. Hogue, Directrice générale
xhogumi@ville.montreal.qc.ca
Paule Lamontagne, Présidente
Finances: *Budget de fonctionnement annuel:* $250,000-$500,000
Personnel: 70 bénévole(s)
Membre: 8 500; *Montant de la cotisation:* 45$ individu; 60$ familial; 30$ étudiant/ainé$180 corporatif
Activités: Cours et ateliers donnés par des spécialistes; conférences; visites guidées et excursions; voyages
Mission: Promouvoir une culture scientifique et une culture générale concernant la nature, l'environnement et la botanique; supporter, par des actions concrètes, le Jardin botanique dans sa mission afin d'assurer son développement; informer les membres, de façon privilégiée, des plus récents progrès scientifiques; présenter au public les différentes composantes du Jardin botanique et en vulgariser le rôle, les actions et le contenu; valoriser la flore mondiale, particulièrement celle du Québec et promouvoir la conservation de la nature; représenter le grand public auprès des instances du Jardin; *Membre de:* Fédération des sociétés d'horticulture et d'écologie du Québec (FSHEQ); Flora Québec

Les Amis du Parc Awenda *See* The Friends of Awenda Park

Analystes des minéraux canadiens *See* Canadian Mineral Analysts

Animal Alliance of Canada (AAC) / Alliance animale du Canada
#101, 221 Broadview Ave., Toronto ON M4M 2G3
Tel: 416-462-9541; *Fax:* 416-462-9647
e-mail: info@animalalliance.ca
URL: www.animalalliance.ca
Overview: A medium-sized national organization founded in 1990
Finances: *Funding Sources:* Private donations; garage sales; merchandise; information & displays
Staff: 5 staff member(s); 130 volunteer(s)
Membership: 20,000

Activities: Promoting cruelty-free, environmentally friendly biodegradable products; currently involved in working to ban pound seizure; information displays; National Wolf Campaign; Endangered Species Campaign; working to end the destruction of over 1,000,000 companion animals (abandoned & unwanted pets) in Canada each year through legislation, spay/neuter programs & public education; working to ban the keeping of exotic animals as pets; *Awareness Events:* "Literary Lions" annual literary benefit; "Animal Magnetism" annual music benefit; *Library:* Animal Alliance Resource Centre
Mission: To preserve & protect all animals; to promote harmonious relationship between people, animals & the environment; to address issues including pound seizure, cosmetic & product testing, puppy mills, pet overpopulation, exotic pet trade, the fur trade, sport hunting, factory farming, animals as "entertainment"

Animal Defence & Anti-Vivisection Society of BC (ADAV)
PO Box 391, Stn. A, Vancouver BC V6C 2N2
URL: www.animalvoices.org/adav/
Overview: A small provincial organization
Finances: *Funding Sources:* Private
Staff: 6 staff member(s)
Membership: 200; *Fees:* $5 student/senior; $10 individual; $50 lifetime

Animal Defence League of Canada (ADLC)
PO Box 3880, Stn. C, Ottawa ON K1Y 4M5
Tel: 613-233-6117; *Fax:* 613-233-6117
Overview: A medium-sized national organization founded in 1958
Finances: *Annual Operating Budget:* $50,000-$100,000; *Funding Sources:* Donations; membership fees
Membership: 2,250; *Fees:* $50 lifetime; $10 individual; $5 senior/student; *Committees:* Companion Animals; Food Animals; Experimentation; Wildlife Protection
Activities: *Speaker Service:* Yes; *Library:* Yes, Open to public
Mission: To promote animal welfare/rights; to work to end animal exploitation, cruelty & suffering; *Member of:* World Society for the Protection of Animals

Animal Nutrition Association of Canada (ANAC) / Association de nutrition animale du Canada
#1301, 150 Metcalfe St., Ottawa ON K2P 1P1
Tel: 613-241-6421; *Fax:* 613-241-7970
e-mail: info@anacan.org
URL: www.anacan.org
Previous Name: Canadian Feed Industry Association
Overview: A large national organization founded in 1929
Finances: *Funding Sources:* Membership fees
Staff: 3 staff member(s)
Membership: 180 organizations; *Fees:* Variable; *Member Profile:* Manufacturers & suppliers of animal nutrition products to Canada's livestock & poultry industries; *Committees:* FFA; GMP; Certification
Activities: Canadian Feed Industry Advisor Certification Program; Canadian Feed Technology Seminar; Canadian Feed Industry Commodity Supplier Course; promotion of environment & animal care issues, & regulations & legislation pertaining to feed products, manufacturing, food safety & salmonella control; monitors regulations pertaining to agricultural trade & international & interprovincial import & export;
Mission: ANAC advocates on behalf of the livestock & poultry feed industry with government regulators & policy-makers, & works to maintain high standards of feed & food safety.; *Affiliation(s):* Canola Council of Canada; Canada Grains Council; Canadian Egg Marketing Agency; Canadian Chicken Marketing Agency; Canadian Turkey Marketing Agency

Animal Welfare Foundation of Canada (AWF) / Fondation du bien-être animal du Canada
#343, 300 Earl Grey Dr., Ottawa ON K2T 1C1
e-mail: info@awfc.ca
URL: www.awfc.ca
Overview: A small national charitable organization founded in 1965
Chief Officer(s):
Ian Duncan, Ph.D, President & Chair
Frances Rodenberg, Honorary Secretary
Finances: *Annual Operating Budget:* $100,000-$250,000
Staff: 14 volunteer(s)
Activities: *Speaker Service:* Yes
Mission: The Animal Welfare Foundation of Canada is a registered charity, supported by donors and administered by a volunteer Board of Directors. The Foundation seeks to improve the quality of life for animals in this country. Since the 1960s the

Associations/Organizations / Annapolis Field Naturalist Society

Foundation, an independent watchdog organization, has been at the forefront of issues of humane care of animals in Canada.; Affiliation(s): World Society for the Protection of Animals

Annapolis Field Naturalist Society (AFNS)
PO Box 576, Annapolis Royal NS B0S 1A0
Tel: 902-532-5129
e-mail: info@natureannapolis.ca
URL: www.natureannapolis.ca
Overview: A small local organization founded in 1988
Chief Officer(s):
Wilmer Horsfall, Treasurer
Jon Percy, President
Andi Rierden, Vice-President
Finances: *Annual Operating Budget:* Less than $50,000; *Funding Sources:* Membership fees; Recreation department grants
Staff: 20 volunteer(s)
Membership: 90+; *Fees:* $12 individual; $18 family; *Member Profile:* Naturalists; *Committees:* Program; Environment
Activities: Regular monthly meetings; regular field trips
Mission: To encourage in all age groups a greater appreciation & understanding of Nova Scotia's natural history, both within the membership & in the general public; to promote the protection of the environment & the conservation of Nova Scotia's natural resources; *Member of:* Federation of Nova Scotia Naturalists; Affiliation(s): Canadian Nature Federation

Antarctic & Southern Ocean Coalition (ASOC)
1630 Connecticut Ave., 3rd Fl., Washington DC 20009 USA
Tel: 202-234-2480; *Fax:* 202-387-4823
e-mail: antarctica@igc.org
URL: www.asoc.org
Also Known As: Secretariat, The Antarctica Project
Overview: A medium-sized international organization founded in 1977
Finances: *Annual Operating Budget:* $250,000-$500,000; *Funding Sources:* Foundation grants; membership dues
Staff: 9 staff member(s); 2 volunteer(s)
Membership: 235
Activities: Conducts legal & policy research & analysis; testifies at Congressional hearings; produces educational materials; works with the key users of Antarctica, including scientists, tourists, & governments, to ensure that activities have a minimal environmental impact; attends all Antarctic Treaty Consultative Meetings & all CCAMLR meetings; *Library:* Yes, open by appointment
Mission: To protect the biological diversity & pristine wilderness of Antarctica, including its oceans & marine life; to work for the passage of strong measures which protect the marine ecosystem from the harmful effects of overfishing; to ensure that the integrity of the southern ocean whale sanctuary is maintained & internationally respected; Affiliation(s): World Wildlife Fund Canada; World Society for the Protection of Animals; Friends of the Earth; Greenpeace; Sierra Club

Anti-Tuberculosis Society See British Columbia Lung Association

Applied Science Technologists & Technicians of British Columbia (ASTTBC)
Parent: Canadian Council of Technicians & Technologists
10767 - 148 St., Surrey BC V3R 0S4
Tel: 604-585-2788; *Fax:* 604-585-2790
e-mail: techinfo@asttbc.org
URL: www.asttbc.org
Previous Name: Society of Engineering Technologists of BC
Overview: A large provincial organization founded in 1958
Finances: *Annual Operating Budget:* $500,000-$1.5 Million; *Funding Sources:* Membership dues; accreditation; member services; advertising; education
Staff: 14 staff member(s); 250 volunteer(s)
Membership: 8,600; *Fees:* $255
Activities: Foundation FEAT; *Internships:* Yes; *Rents Mailing List:* Yes
Awards: 25 Year Membership Award (Award)

Retiring Presidents Award (Award)
Peter Allan AScT Leadership Award (Award)
Advanced Technology Award (Award)
Certificate of Appreciation (Award)
Life Member (Award)
Professional Achievement (Award)
R. Littledale Memorial Award (Award)
Service Award (Award)

Special Award (Award)
Honorary Member (Award)
Mission: To advance the profession of applied science technology & the professional recognition of applied science technologists, certified technicians & other members in a manner that serves & protects the public interest

Aquaculture Association of Canada (AAC) / Association Aquacole du Canada
16 Lobster Lane, St. Andrews NB E5B 3T6
Tel: 506-529-4766; *Fax:* 506-529-4609
e-mail: aac@dfo-mpo.gc.ca
URL: www.aquacultureassociation.ca
Overview: A medium-sized national charitable organization founded in 1984
Chief Officer(s):
Susan Waddy, Manager, Association Office, 506-529-4766
Susan.Waddy@dfo-mpo.gc.ca
Tim Jackson, President, 506-636-3728, Fax: 506-636-3479
timothy.jackson@nrc-cnrc.gc.ca
Joy Wade, Vice-President, 250-754-6884
joy2004wade@yahoo.ca
Shelley King, Secretary, 902-421-5646, Fax: 902-421-2733
sking@genomeatlantic.ca
Caroline Graham, Treasurer
cpgraham@rogers.com
Finances: *Funding Sources:* Donations
Membership: 900+; *Member Profile:* Students; Educators; Producers; Suppliers; Scientists; Government representatives; *Committees:* Election; Finance; Rules; Time & Place; Arrangements; Program; Publications; Awards; Student Affairs; Membership; Business Development
Activities: Promoting the study of aquaculture & related sciences; Providing scientific & technical information related to aquaculture; Increasing public awareness & understanding of aquaculture; Liaising with goverment & industry; Providing networking opportunities; Conducting seminars
Meetings/Conferences:
For more information see Trade Shows, Conferences and Seminars Chapter
Aquaculture Canada 2012: The Aquaculture Association of Canada's Annual Conference & General Meeting
May 2012 Charlottetown, PE
Aquaculture Canada 2013: The Aquaculture Association of Canada's Annual Conference & General Meeting
Other Conferences in 2013 2013
Aquaculture Canada 2014: The Aquaculture Association of Canada's Annual Conference & General Meeting
Other Conferences in 2014 2014
Aquaculture Canada 2015: The Aquaculture Association of Canada's Annual Conference & General Meeting
Other Conferences in 2015 2015
Publications: *The Watermark [a publication of the Aquaculture Association of Canada]*
Type: Newsletter *Frequency:* 3 pa *Editor:* Gregor Reid; Candace Durston
Profile: Aquaculture Association of Canada updates, such as donations, awards, & meetings
Bulletin of the Aquaculture Association of Canada
Type: Newsletter
Profile: Topics have included sea-urchin aquaculture, application of genome science to sustainable aquaculture, proceedings of the scallop aquaculture session, fish health, aquaculture public awareness & education, water movement & aquatic animal health, aquaculture biotechnology, & progress in cod farming
Aquaculture Canada Abstracts
Profile: Conference program guides, featuring conference sessions
Aquaculture Canada Proceedings of Contributed Papers
Profile: Proceedings of the contributed papers of the annual meetings of the Aquaculture Association of Canada
Mission: To foster an aquaculture industry in Canada; To encourage & support the educational, technological, & scientific advancement of aquaculture
Environmental Activity: Promoting sustainable aquaculture

Aquaculture Association of Nova Scotia (AANS)
c/o Starlite Gallery, #215, 7071 Bayers Rd., Halifax NS B3L 2C2
Tel: 902-422-6234; *Fax:* 902-422-6248
e-mail: bmuiseaans@eastlink.ca
URL: www.aansonline.ca
Overview: A small provincial organization founded in 1977
Finances: *Funding Sources:* Membership fees
Staff: 3 staff member(s)
Membership: 40; *Fees:* Producers $500-10,000; Suppliers/Processors $375-10,000; Friends $150; Students $25;

Member Profile: Not-for-profit association of growers, suppliers & industry supporters
Member of: Canadian Aquaculture Industry Alliance

AquaNet - Network in Aquaculture
Ocean Sciences Centre, Memorial University of Newfoundland, St. John's NL A1C 5S7
Tel: 709-737-3245; *Fax:* 709-737-3500
e-mail: info@aquanet.ca
URL: www.aquanet.ca
Overview: A medium-sized national organization
Chief Officer(s):
Scott McKinley, Executive Scientific Director
Mission: To foster a sustainable aquaculture sector in Canada through high quality research & education; *Member of:* Networks of Centres of Excellence

Archaeological Institute of America (AIA) / Institut Archéologique d'Amérique
656 Beacon St., Boston MA 02215-2006 USA
Tel: 617-353-9361; *Fax:* 617-353-6550
e-mail: aia@aia.bu.edu
URL: www.archaeological.org
Overview: A large international charitable organization founded in 1879
Chief Officer(s):
C. Brian Rose, President
Finances: *Annual Operating Budget:* Greater than $5 Million; *Funding Sources:* Membership dues; donations; subscription income
Staff: 25 staff member(s)
Membership: 9,000; *Fees:* Schedule available
Activities: Provides over 250 lectures within the US each year; *Speaker Service:* Yes; *Rents Mailing List:* Yes
Awards: The Harriet Pomerance Fellowship (Scholarship)
Given to a resident of the US or Canada for travel to the Mediterranean area to pursue a scholarly project in Aegean Bronze Age archaeology
The Olivia James Traveling Fellowship (Scholarship)
Provides funds to citizens or permanent residents of the US for travel & study in Greece, the Aegean Islands, Sicily, Southern Italy, Turkey, or Iraq
Colburn Fellowship (Scholarship)
S. Woodruff Fellowship (Scholarship)
Publications: *Archaeology*
Editor: Peter A. Young
Profile: Bi-monthly magazine
American Journal of Archaeology
Editor: Naomi Norman
Profile: Quarterly academic journal
Mission: To encourage & support archaeological research & publication; to encourage protection of world's cultural heritage; *Member of:* American Council of Learned Societies; Affiliation(s): Fédération internationale des associations d'études classiques

The Architectural Conservancy of Ontario (ACO)
#403, 10 Adelaide St. East, Toronto ON M5C 1J3
Tel: 416-367-8075; *Fax:* 416-367-8630
Toll-Free: 877-264-8937
e-mail: manager@arconserv.ca
URL: www.arconserv.ca
Overview: A medium-sized provincial charitable organization founded in 1933
Finances: *Annual Operating Budget:* $100,000-$250,000; *Funding Sources:* Donations; government grants; membership dues; fundraising activities
Staff: 2 staff member(s); 81 volunteer(s)
Membership: 1,025 + 25 branches & groups; *Fees:* $35; *Committees:* Advisory Board & various Planning Committees
Activities: Technical consulting service for property owners, groups & municipalities; neighbourhood & garden tours; conferences & workshops; capital fundraising for repair & restoration work; architectural research; property acquisition
Mission: To preserve buildings & structures of architectural merit & places of natural beauty or interest; Affiliation(s): Ontario Heritage Alliance

Architectural Heritage Society of Saskatchewan (AHSS)
202 - 1275 Broad St., Regina SK S4R 1Y2
Tel: 306-359-0933; *Fax:* 306-359-3899
e-mail: sahs@sasktel.net
URL: www.ahsk.ca
Overview: A small provincial organization founded in 1987
Finances: *Annual Operating Budget:* $50,000-$100,000; *Funding Sources:* Private & public sector funding
Staff: 1 staff member(s)

Membership: 230; Fees: $20; Committees: Membership; Finance; Administration; Policy
Mission: To promote, support & facilitate the preservation, conservation, restoration & reuse of distinct architectural & historical heritage properties (designated or potential) throughout the province, ensuring that our built heritage is maintained for present & future citizens to appreciate the contributions & craftsmanship of past generations; to enhance the current social, economic & environmental quality of life; Member of: Saskatchewan Council of Cultural Organizations; Canadian Heritage Network; National Preservation Trust

Arctic Council
Foreign Affairs Canada, 125 Sussex Dr., Ottawa ON K1A 0G2
Tel: 613-992-6700; Fax: 613-644-1852
URL: www.arctic-council.org
Chief Officer(s):
Jack Anawak, Ambassador for Circumpolar Affairs
jack.anawak@international.gc.ca
Member Profile: Member states include Canada, Denmark (including Greenland & the Faroe Islands), Finland, Iceland, Norway, the Russian Federation, Sweden & the United States
Activities: Five working groups are as follows: Sustainable Development Working Group; Arctic Monitoring & Assessment Programme; Protection of the Marine Environment; Conservation of Arctic Flora & Fauna; Emergency, Prevention, Preparedness & Response
Mission: To operate as an intergovernmental forum; To address common concerns & challenges by the member states of Canada, Denmark (including Greenland & the Faroe Islands), Finland, Iceland, Norway, the Russian Federation, Sweden & the United States; To address environmental, social & economic issues; To carry out scientific work in five expert working groups, focusing on such issues as monitoring, assessing & preventing pollution in the Arctic, climate change, biodiversity conservation & sustainable use, emergency preparedness, & prevention; To meet every two years, with the secretariat rotating among the member states
Environmental Activity: Acting as a a regional forum for sustainable development

Arctic Institute of North America (AINA)
University of Calgary, 2500 University Dr. NW, Calgary AB T2N 1N4
Tel: 403-220-7515; Fax: 403-282-4609
e-mail: arctic@ucalgary.ca
URL: www.arctic.ucalgary.ca
Overview: A medium-sized local organization founded in 1945
Membership: 1,000-4,999
Awards: Jennifer Robinson Memorial Scholarship (Scholarship) For Master's or Ph.D. students; must submit a brief statement of research objectives Deadline: Dec. 1 Award Amount: $5,000
Lorraine Allison Scholarship (Scholarship) Granted on the basis of academic standing, commitment to northern Canadian research & benefit to Northerners; Master's or Ph.D. students from the Yukon & NWT are encouraged to apply Deadline: 1-May Award Amount: $2,000
Mission: To encourage & support scientific research pertaining to the polar regions; Affiliation(s): The University of Alaska

ArcticNet Inc.
Pavillon Alexandre-Vachon, Université Laval, #4081, 1045, av de la Médecine, Québec QC G1V 0A6
Tel: 418-656-5830; Fax: 418-656-2334
e-mail: arcticnet@arcticnet.ulaval.ca
URL: www.arcticnet-ulaval.ca
Overview: A medium-sized national organization founded in 2003
Chief Officer(s):
Martin Fortier, Executive Director, 418-656-5233
martin.fortier@arcticnet.ulaval.ca
Louis Fortier, Scientific Director, 418-656-5646
louis.fortier@bio.ulaval.ca
Réal Choquette, Administrative Director, 418-656-2445
real.choquette@arcticnet.ulaval.ca
Jean-Luc Bernier, Officer, Communications, 418-656-7106
jean-luc.bernier@arcticnet.ulaval.ca
Keith Levesque, Coordinator, Ship-based Research, 418-656-3071
keith.levesque@arcticnet.ulaval.ca
Josée Michaud, Coordinator, Data, 418-656-2411
Josee.Michaud@arcticnet.ulaval.ca
Finances: Funding Sources: Government of Canada, through the Networks of Centres of Excellence programs
Membership: 1-99; Member Profile: Educational institutions; Committees: Executive; Communications; Audit & Finance;

Environmental Review; Industrial Partnership; Inuit Partnership; Research Management; Inuit Advisory
Activities: Conducting Integrated Regional Impact Studies on marine & terrestrial coastal ecosystems & societies in the Eastern Canadian Arctic, the Canadian High Arctic & in Hudson Bay; Disseminating knowledge; Facilitating networking opportunities
Publications: ArcticNet Inc. Annual Report
Type: Yearbook Frequency: a.
ArcticNet Newsletter
Type: Newsletter Frequency: .
Mission: To study the impacts of climate change in the coastal Canadian Arctic; To engage Inuit organizations, northern communities, universities, research institutes, industry, government, & international agencies as partners in the scientific process; Member of: Network of Centres of Excellence of Canada
Environmental Activity: Formulating strategies to face the impacts of climate change & globalization in the Arctic

ARK II
PO Box 687, Stn. Q, Toronto ON M4T 2N5
Tel: 416-536-2308
e-mail: info@ark-ii.com
URL: www.ark-ii.com
Also Known As: Animal Rights Kollective
Overview: A small local charitable organization
Fees: Annual: $10; Lifetime: $50
Activities: Anti-fur campaigns, Veganism/Vegetarianism promotion, Anti-animal experimentation campaigns
Mission: To promote & protect the rights of all animals & foster their individual liberties through direct action, political action, & public awareness campaigns

Arrowsmith Natural History Society See Arrowsmith Naturalists

Arrowsmith Naturalists
PO Box 1542, Parksville BC V9P 2H4
Tel: 250-752-0445
URL: members.shaw.ca/arrowsmithnaturalists/index.htm
Previous Name: Arrowsmith Natural History Society
Overview: A small local organization founded in 1970
Finances: Annual Operating Budget: Less than $50,000
Membership: 110; Fees: $20 individual; $30 couple; Member Profile: Interest in nature; Committees: Botany; Birds; Outings
Mission: To further the understanding & conservation of nature; Member of: Federation of BC Naturalists

Arusha Centre Society
The Old "Y" Bldg., #106, 223 - 12 Ave. SW, Calgary AB T2R 0G6
Tel: 403-270-3200; Fax: 403-270-8832
e-mail: arusha@arusha.org
URL: www.arusha.org
Overview: A small local charitable organization founded in 1972
Finances: Annual Operating Budget: $250,000-$500,000; Funding Sources: Federal & provincial government; donations; United Way
Staff: 7 staff member(s); 75 volunteer(s)
Membership: 225; Fees: $10; Member Profile: Calgary community; Committees: Finance; Fundraising; Membership; Programming; Marketing
Activities: Library: Resource Centre; Open to public,
Mission: To provide opportunities for, & remove barriers to, individual & community participation, self-determination & empowerment, especially for those who have been marginalized; to acknowledge, respect & actively value diversity, based on the belief in inherent human dignity; to challenge unjust internal & external assumptions & structures & work toward socially just alternatives; to connect social, economic & ecological issues, both locally & globally; to create a meaningful partnership that fosters social justice internally & externally; Member of: Volunteer Centre of Calgary; Parklands Institute

Asia Pacific Foundation of Canada (APFC) / Fondation Asie Pacifique du Canada
#220, 890 West Pender St., Vancouver BC V6C 1J9
Tel: 604-684-5986; Fax: 604-681-1370
e-mail: info@asiapacific.ca
URL: www.asiapacific.ca
Also Known As: APF Canada
Overview: A medium-sized international organization founded in 1984
Chief Officer(s):

Yuen Pau Woo, President & Co-CEO
president@asiapacific.ca
Paul Evans, Co-CEO & Chair
president@asiapacific.ca
Melinda Czerwinski, Coordinator, Communications
Finances: Annual Operating Budget: $1.5 Million-$3 Million; Funding Sources: Federal & provincial government
Staff: 30 staff member(s)
Activities: Business; media; education; public policy; research; Internships: Yes
Mission: Independent think tank on Canada's relations with Asia; to bring together people & knowledge to provide the most current & comprehensive research, analysis & information on Canada's transpacific relations; to promote dialogue on economic, security, political & social issues, helping to influence public policy & foster informed decision-making in the Canadian public, private & non-governmental sectors

Asia-Pacific Centre for Environmental Law (APCEL)
Faculty of Law, Ntl. University of Singapore, Eu Tong Sen Bldg., 469G Bukit Timah Rd., Singapore 259776 Singapore
Tel: 65-6516-6246; Fax: 65-6872-1937
e-mail: lawapcel@nus.edu.sg
URL: law.nus.edu.sg/apcel/
Overview: A small international organization
Chief Officer(s):
Koh Kheng-Lian, Director
Shirley Mak, Secretary
lawmaksy@nus.edu.sg

Asociación Nacional de la Industria Química, A.C See National Association of the Chemistry Industry

Assemblée des Premières Nations See Assembly of First Nations

Assembly of First Nations (AFN) / Assemblée des Premières Nations (APN)
Trebla Building, 473 Albert St., Ottawa ON K1R 5B4
Tel: 613-241-6789; Fax: 613-241-5808
Toll-Free: 866-869-6789
e-mail: imcleod@afn.ca
URL: www.afn.ca
Previous Name: National Indian Brotherhood
Overview: A large national organization
Chief Officer(s):
Shawn Atleo, National Chief
Finances: Funding Sources: Federal grants
Staff: 100 staff member(s)
Membership: 633 First Nations in Canada
Mission: The AFN Secretariat acts as an advocate for First Nations on many issues, including Aboriginal & Treaty Rights, economic development, education, languages & literacy, health, housing, social development, justice, land claims & the environment

Associated Environmental Site Assessors of Canada (AESAC)
PO Box 490, Fenelon Falls ON K0M 1N0
Toll-Free: 877-512-3722
e-mail: info@aesac.ca
URL: www.aesac.ca
Overview: A small national organization founded in 1992
Chief Officer(s):
Bruno Luzak, President
Mission: Dedicated to providing services to assist site assessors in meeting the needs of potential clients such as lenders & major property owners; an inter-disciplinary organization that assists practitioners from many different professional backgrounds in identifying & maintaining appropriate standards for conducting site assessments

Association Aquacole du Canada See Aquaculture Association of Canada

Association botanique du Canada See Canadian Botanical Association

Association canadienne d'acoustique See Canadian Acoustical Association

Association canadienne d'énergie éolienne See Canadian Wind Energy Association Inc.

Association canadienne d'énergie fluide See Canadian Fluid Power Association

L'Association canadienne d'ergonomie See Association of Canadian Ergonomists

Associations/Organizations / Association canadienne des sciences régionales

Association canadienne d'études environnementales *See* Environmental Studies Association of Canada

Association canadienne d'experts-conseils en patrimoine *See* Canadian Association of Professional Heritage Consultants

Association canadienne d'hydrographie *See* Canadian Hydrographic Association

Association canadienne de cartographie *See* Canadian Cartographic Association

Association canadienne de droit et société *See* Canadian Law & Society Association

Association canadienne de droit maritime *See* Canadian Maritime Law Association

Association canadienne de l'autobus *See* Canadian Bus Association

Association canadienne de l'électricité *See* Canadian Electricity Association

Association canadienne de l'emballage *See* Packaging Association of Canada

Association canadienne de l'hydroélectricité *See* Canadian Hydropower Association

Association canadienne de l'imprimerie *See* Canadian Printing Industries Association

Association canadienne de l'industrie de la peinture et du revêtement *See* Canadian Paint & Coatings Association

Association canadienne de l'industrie des boissons gazeuses *See* Refreshments Canada

Association canadienne de l'industrie des plastiques *See* Canadian Plastics Industry Association

Association canadienne de l'industrie du bois *See* Canadian Lumbermen's Association

Association canadienne de l'industrie du caoutchouc *See* The Rubber Association of Canada

Association canadienne de la construction *See* Canadian Construction Association

Association canadienne de la gestion de l'innovation *See* Innovation Management Association of Canada

Association canadienne de la gestion parasitaire *See* Canadian Pest Management Association

Association canadienne de la médecine du travail et de l'environnement *See* Occupational & Environmental Medical Association of Canada

Association canadienne de méchanique des roches *See* Canadian Rock Mechanics Association

Association canadienne de radioprotection *See* Canadian Radiation Protection Association

Association canadienne de recherches en évaluation non-destructive *See* Canadian Association for Research in Nondestructive Evaluation

Association canadienne de réhabilitation des sites dégradés *See* Canadian Land Reclamation Association

Association canadienne de santé publique *See* Canadian Public Health Association

Association canadienne de sécurité agricole *See* Canadian Agricultural Safety Association

Association canadienne de technologie de pointe *See* Canadian Advanced Technology Alliance

Association canadienne de transport industriel *See* Canadian Industrial Transportation Association

Association canadienne des agronomes-conseils *See* Canadian Consulting Agrologists Association

Association canadienne des aliments de santé *See* Canadian Health Food Association

Association canadienne des automobilistes *See* Canadian Automobile Association

Association canadienne des barrages *See* Canadian Dam Association

Association canadienne des carburants renouvelables *See* Canadian Renewable Fuels Association

Association canadienne des chefs de pompiers *See* Canadian Association of Fire Chiefs

Association canadienne des constructeurs d'habitations *See* Canadian Home Builders' Association

Association canadienne des distributeurs de produits chimiques *See* Canadian Association of Chemical Distributors

Association canadienne des eaux potables et usées *See* Canadian Water & Wastewater Association

Association canadienne des eaux souterraines *See* Canadian Ground Water Association

L'Association canadienne des éleveurs de porcs *See* Canadian Swine Breeders' Association

Association canadienne des embouteilleurs d'eau *See* Canadian Bottled Water Association

Association canadienne des entrepreneurs en mousse de polyuréthane *See* Canadian Urethane Foam Contractors Association

Association canadienne des entreprises de géomatique *See* Geomatics Industry Association of Canada

Association canadienne des exportateurs d'équipement et services miniers *See* Canadian Association of Mining Equipment & Services for Export

Association canadienne des fabricants de produits chimiques *See* Canadian Chemical Producers' Association

Association canadienne des fabricants de tuyaux de béton *See* Canadian Concrete Pipe Association

Association canadienne des fournisseurs de produits sanitaires *See* Canadian Sanitation Supply Association

Association canadienne des géographes *See* Canadian Association of Geographers

Association canadienne des industries du recyclage *See* Canadian Association of Recycling Industries

Association canadienne des laboratoires d'essais *Voir* Association des consultants et laboratoires experts

Association canadienne des manufacturiers de palettes et contenants *See* Canadian Wood Pallet & Container Association

Association canadienne des médecins vétérinaires *See* Canadian Veterinary Medical Association

Association canadienne des membres des tribunaux d'utilité publique *See* Canadian Association of Members of Public Utility Tribunals

Association canadienne des palynologues *See* Canadian Association of Palynologists

Association canadienne des parcs et loisirs *See* Canadian Parks & Recreation Association

Association canadienne des producteurs d'acier *See* Canadian Steel Producers Association

Association canadienne des producteurs de semences *See* Canadian Seed Growers' Association

Association canadienne des producteurs pétroliers *See* Canadian Association of Petroleum Producers

Association canadienne des prospecteurs & entrepreneurs *See* Prospectors & Developers Association of Canada

Association canadienne des rédacteurs scientifiques *See* Canadian Science Writers' Association

Association canadienne des réseaux thermiques *See* Canadian District Energy Association

Association canadienne des ressources hydriques *See* Canadian Water Resources Association

Association canadienne des sciences géomatiques *See* Canadian Institute of Geomatics

Association canadienne des sciences régionales (ACSR) / Canadian Regional Science Association (CRSA)
a/s INRS-Urbanisation, 3465, rue Durocher, Montréal QC H2X 2C6
Tél: 514-499-4052; *Téléc:* 514-499-4065
Courriel: Richard_Shearmur@inrs-urb.uquebec.ca
URL: eratos.erin.utoronto.ca/crsa-acsr/home_fr.htm
Aperçu: Dimension: petite; Envergure: nationale; fondée en 1977
Membre(s) du bureau directeur:
K. Bruce Newbold, Président
newbold@mcmaster
Richard Shearmur, Vice-président
richard.shearmur@ucs.inrs.ca
Finances: Budget de fonctionnement annuel: Moins de $50,000
Membre: 245; Montant de la cotisation: 60$ individuel; 25$ étudiant/sans emploi
Activités: *Listes de destinataires:* Oui
Mission: Favoriser la circulation des idées et promouvoir les études canadiennes portant sur les régions en se servant d'instruments, de méthodes et de cadres théoriques; propos aux sciences régionales comme ceux mis en avant par les diverses sciences, sociales ou autres; *Membre de:* Humanities & Social Sciences Federation of Canada

Association canadienne des surintendants de golf *See* Canadian Golf Superintendents Association

Association canadienne des techniciens et technologistes en santé animale *See* Canadian Association of Animal Health Technologists & Technicians

Association Canadienne des Travaux Publics *See* Canadian Public Works Association

Association canadienne des tunnels *See* Tunnelling Association of Canada

Association Canadienne des Vétérinaires Porcins *See* Canadian Association of Swine Veterinarians

Association canadienne du bison *See* Canadian Bison Association

Association canadienne du camionnage d'entreprise *See* Private Motor Truck Council of Canada

Association canadienne du ciment *See* Cement Association of Canada

Association canadienne du commerce des semences *See* Canadian Seed Trade Association

Association canadienne du droit de l'environnement *See* Canadian Environmental Law Association

Association canadienne du gaz *See* Canadian Gas Association

Association canadienne du gaz propane inc. *See* Propane Gas Association of Canada Inc.

Association canadienne du marketing *See* Canadian Marketing Association

Association canadienne du transport urbain *See* Canadian Urban Transit Association

Association canadienne française pour l'avancement des sciences *Voir* Association francophone pour le savoir

Association canadienne pour la recherche sur les services et les politiques de la santé *See* Canadian Association for Health Services & Policy Research

Association canadienne pour les énergies renouvelables *See* Canadian Association for Renewable Energies

Association canadienne pour les études sur la coopération *See* Canadian Association for Studies in Co-operation

Association canadienne pour les Nations-Unies *See* United Nations Association in Canada

Association canadienne sur la qualité de l'eau *See* Canadian Association on Water Quality

Association canadienne Tourbe de Sphaigne *See* Canadian Sphagnum Peat Moss Association

Association chasse et pêche du Lac Brébeuf
247, ch du Lac Brébeuf, Saint-Félix-d'Otis QC G0V 1M0

Tél: 418-544-4884
Aperçu: *Dimension:* petite; *Envergure:* locale
Finances: *Budget de fonctionnement annuel:* $100,000-$250,000; *Fonds:* Gouvernement provincial
Personnel: 4 membre(s) du personnel; 10 bénévole(s)
Membre: 400 individu; *Montant de la cotisation:* 22$ & 25$ individu
Mission: S'occupe de ce territoire protégé et contrôlé de chasse, de pêche et de villégiature; *Affiliation(s):* Regroupement régional de gestionnaires de Zec

Association d'archéologie canadienne *See* Canadian Archaeological Association

Association d'isolation du Québec (AIQ)
#102, 4099, boul St-Jean-Baptiste, Montréal QC H1B 5V3
Tél: 514-354-9877; Téléc: 514-354-7401
Ligne sans frais: 800-711-2381
Courriel: info@isolation-aiq.ca
URL: www.isolation-aiq.ca
Nom précédent: Association des entrepreneurs en isolation de la Province de Québec
Aperçu: *Dimension:* petite; *Envergure:* provinciale; *fondée en 1959*
Montant de la cotisation: 700 $ - 1 073.24 $; *Critères d'admissibilite:* Entrepreneurs; fabricants; distributeurs
Mission: L'AIQ fait la promotion du respect des règles de l'art du métier et de l'utilisation dans les secteurs commerciaux, industriels et institutionnels.

Association de chasse et pêche nordique, inc.
148, St-Marcellin ouest, Les Escoumins QC G0T 1K0
Tél: 418-233-3062; Téléc: 418-233-3083
Aperçu: *Dimension:* petite; *Envergure:* locale; *fondée en 1978*
Membre(s) du bureau directeur:
Marc St-Pierre, Président
Finances: *Budget de fonctionnement annuel:* $100,000-$250,000; *Fonds:* Gouvernement régional
Membre: 600; *Montant de la cotisation:* 12$
Affiliation(s): Fédération québécoise des gestionnaires de Zec

L'Association de l'efficacité énergétique du Canada *See* Canadian Energy Efficiency Alliance

Association de l'exploration minière de Québec (AEMQ)
#203, 132, avenue du Lac, Rouyn-Noranda QC J9X 4N5
Tél: 819-762-1599; Téléc: 819-762-1522
Courriel: aemq@aemq.org
URL: www.aemq.org
Nom précédent: Association des prospecteurs du Québec
Aperçu: *Dimension:* moyenne; *Envergure:* provinciale; *fondée en 1975*
Membre(s) du bureau directeur:
Ghislain Poirier, Président
Mélissa Desrochers, Vice-présidente, Communications
Finances: *Budget de fonctionnement annuel:* $100,000-$250,000
Personnel: 2 membre(s) du personnel; 20 bénévole(s)
Membre: 1 510 membres individuels, incluant 184 entreprises; *Montant de la cotisation:* 20$ étudiant - 2 000$ entreprises; *Critères d'admissibilite:* Oeuvrer en exploration minière
Mission: Développer, défendre et promouvoir l'exploration minière au Québec

Association de la construction navale du Canada *See* Shipbuilding Association of Canada

Association de la santé et de la sécurité des pâtes et papiers et des industries de la forêt du Québec (ASSIFQ-ASSPPQ)
Place Iberville II, #210, 1175, av Lavigerie, Sainte-Foy QC G1V 4P1
Tél: 418-657-2267; Téléc: 418-651-4622
Ligne sans frais: 888-632-9326
Courriel: info@santesecurite.org
URL: www.santesecurite.org
Aperçu: *Dimension:* moyenne; *Envergure:* provinciale; *fondée en 2010*
Finances: *Budget de fonctionnement annuel:* $1.5 Million-$3 Million
Personnel: 35 membre(s) du personnel
Membre: 600 entreprises; *Montant de la cotisation:* Barème; *Critères d'admissibilite:* Oeuvrer dans le domaine des industries de la forêt ou des pâtes et papiers
Activités: Information; formation; expertise-conseil et impartition; mutuelles de prévention; activités régionales; *Stagiaires:* Oui; *Bibliothèque:* Oui

Mission: A pour mission de soutenir et d'accompagner les entreprises dans l'amélioration continue de la santé et de la sécurité du travail; *Affiliation(s):* Association des entrepreneurs en travaux sylvicoles du Québec; Association des fabricants des meubles du Québec; Association des manufacturiers de palettes et contenants du Québec; Conseil de l'industrie forestière du Québec; Fédération québécoise des coopératives forestières; Regroupement des sociétés d'aménagement du Québec; Commission de la santé et de la sécurité du travail

Association de nutrition animale du Canada *See* Animal Nutrition Association of Canada

Association de ventes directes du Canada *See* Direct Sellers Association of Canada

Association des administrateurs municipaux du Nouveau-Brunswick *See* Association of Municipal Administrators of New Brunswick

Association des affaires publiques du Canada *See* The Public Affairs Association of Canada

Association des Allergologues et Immunologues du Québec
Parent: Fédération des médecins spécialistes du Québec
CP 216, Succ. Desjardins, #3000, 2, Complexe Desjardins, Montréal QC H5B 1G8
Tél: 514-350-5101; Téléc: 514-350-5146
Courriel: jdelisle@fmsq.org
URL: www.allerg.qc.ca
Aperçu: *Dimension:* moyenne; *Envergure:* provinciale
Membre: Fédération des medecins spéialistes du Québec

Association des Aménagistes Régionaux du Québec (AARQ)
#105, 870, av de Salaberry, Québec QC G1R 2T9
Tél: 418-524-4666; Téléc: 418-524-3666
Ligne sans frais: 888-771-4559
Courriel: secretariat@aarq.qc.ca
URL: www.aarq.qc.ca
Aperçu: *Dimension:* petite; *Envergure:* provinciale; *Organisme sans but lucratif; fondée en 1983*
Membre(s) du bureau directeur:
Marie-Josée Casaubon, Présidente
Finances: *Budget de fonctionnement annuel:* $50,000-$100,000
Personnel: 1 membre(s) du personnel; 12 bénévole(s)
Membre: 120; *Montant de la cotisation:* 195$; *Critères d'admissibilite:* Aménagiste travaillant au sein d'une M.R.C.
Activités: Lieu d'échange entre les professionnels de l'aménagement du territoire oeuvrant au sein des municipalités régionales de comté (M.R.C.)

Association des architectes paysagistes du Canada *See* Canadian Society of Landscape Architects

Association des architectes paysagistes du Québec (AAPQ)
4655, De Lorimier, Montréal QC H2H 2B4
Tél: 514-990-7731; Téléc: 877-990-7731
Courriel: info@aapq.org
URL: www.aapq.org
Aperçu: *Dimension:* petite; *Envergure:* provinciale; *fondée en 1965*
Finances: *Budget de fonctionnement annuel:* $50,000-$100,000
Membre: 100-499; *Montant de la cotisation:* Barème; *Comités:* Admission; Nomination; Affaires légales et éthique professionelle; Promotion; Formation continue; Pratique privée; Action - réaction; Bulletin
Mission: Promouvoir la création et la valorisation du paysage en milieu naturel et construit dans le but de constituer un cadre de vie sain, fonctionnel, esthétique, axé sur les besoins de la population et répondant aux exigences écologiques; *Affiliation(s):* Association des Architectes Paysagistes du Canada

Association des arpenteurs des terres du Canada *See* Association of Canada Lands Surveyors

Association des arpenteurs-géomètres du Nouveau-Brunswick *See* Association of New Brunswick Land Surveyors

Association des bibliothèques de la santé des Maritimes *See* Maritimes Health Libraries Association

Association des bibliothèques de la santé du Canada *See* Canadian Health Libraries Association

Association des bibliothèques de santé de la Vallée d'Outaouais *See* Ottawa Valley Health Libraries Association

Association des camps du Canada *See* Canadian Camping Association

Association des chefs de services d'incendie du Québec *Voir* Association des chefs en sécurité incendie du Québec

Association des chefs en sécurité incendie du Québec (ACSIQ) / Québec Association of Fire Chiefs
5, rue Dupré, Beloeil QC J3G 3J7
Tél: 450-464-6413; Téléc: 450-467-6297
Ligne sans frais: 888-464-6413
URL: www.acsiq.qc.ca
Nom précédent: Association des chefs de services d'incendie du Québec
Aperçu: *Dimension:* moyenne; *Envergure:* provinciale; *Organisme sans but lucratif; fondée en 1968*
Finances: *Budget de fonctionnement annuel:* $250,000-$500,000
Personnel: 3 membre(s) du personnel
Membre: 1 000; *Montant de la cotisation:* 195$; *Critères d'admissibilite:* Chefs de service incendie de municipalités ou de brigade en industries; *Comités:* Mise en candidature; vérification des politiques; évaluation du rendement du directeur général; finances; consultatif; comités ad hoc; prévention; consultatif en sécurité incendie
Activités: *Evénements de sensibilisation:* Congrès annuel
Mission: Regroupe les personnes détanant un poste de commande dans le domaine de la prévention et de la lutte contre les incendies

Association des consommateurs du Canada *See* Consumers' Association of Canada

Association des consommateurs industriels de gaz *See* Industrial Gas Users Association Inc.

Association des consultants et laboratoires experts (ACLE)
#211, 6360, rue Jean-Talon Est, Saint-Léonard QC H1S 1M8
Tél: 514-253-2878; Téléc: 514-253-6825
Courriel: info@acle.qc.ca
URL: www.acle.qc.ca
Nom précédent: Association canadienne des laboratoires d'essais
Aperçu: *Dimension:* moyenne; *Envergure:* nationale; *Organisme sans but lucratif; fondée en 1959*
Finances: *Budget de fonctionnement annuel:* $50,000-$100,000
Personnel: 1 membre(s) du personnel
Membre: 90 firmes, laboratoires associés et succursales; *Critères d'admissibilite:* Entreprises indépendants réparties en trois divisions - Ingénierie des Sols et Matériaux; Services Analytiques et Environnement; Toiture et Étanchéité
Mission: Developper, promouvoir et sauvegarder les intérêts techniques et commerciaux communs des membres et de leurs clients

Association des directeurs généraux des municipalités du Québec
#129, 10, rue Hugues-Pommier, Beauport QC G1E 4T9
Tél: 418-660-7591; Téléc: 418-660-0848
Courriel: adgmq@adgmq.qc.ca
URL: www.adgmq.qc.ca/
Aperçu: *Dimension:* moyenne; *Envergure:* provinciale; *fondée en 1973*
Membre: 200; *Montant de la cotisation:* 365$; *Critères d'admissibilite:* Directeur général d'une municipalité gérée par la loi des cités et villes
Mission: Permettre l'amélioration des connaissances et du statut de ses membres et la promotion de la formule de gestion conseil/directeur général

Association des eaux souterraines du Québec *Voir* Association des enterprises spécialiseés en eau du Québec

Association des écoles forestières universitaires du Canada *See* Association of University Forestry Schools of Canada

Association des embouteilleurs d'eau du Québec (AEEQ) / Québec Water Bottlers' Association
#102, 200, rue MacDonald, Saint-Jean-sur-Richelieu QC J3B 8J6
Tél: 450-349-1521; Téléc: 450-349-6923
Courriel: info@conseiltac.com
URL: www.aeeq.org

Associations/Organizations / Association des enterprises spécialiseés en eau du Québec

Aperçu: *Dimension:* moyenne; *Envergure:* provinciale; fondée en 1975
Membre(s) du bureau directeur:
Daniel Colpron, Président
Pierre Gagné, Vice-président
Membre: 24; *Montant de la cotisation:* 1000$ régulier; 1,500$ privilégié*Critères d'admissibilite:* Entreprises spécialisées dans le commerce de l'eau embouteillée; fournisseurs de services et d'équipments
Mission: L'association des embouteilleurs d'eau du Québec (AEEQ) est le porte-parole de l'industrie québécoise de l'embouteillage de l'eau de source et de l'eau minérale; *Membre de:* Canadian Bottled Water Federation

Association des enterprises spécialiseés en eau du Québec
Parent: Canadian Ground Water Association
5930, boul Louis-H. Lafontaine, Montréal QC H1M 1S7
Tél: 514-353-9960; *Téléc:* 514-353-3393
Ligne sans frais: 800-468-8160
Courriel: contact@aeseq.com
URL: www.aeseq.com
Nom précédent: Association des eaux souterraines du Québec
Aperçu: *Dimension:* moyenne; *Envergure:* provinciale
Membre: 148; *Critères d'admissibilite:* Entrepreneurs puisatiers; entrepreneurs en installation de pompe, ou en assainissement autonome, ou en traitement d'eau potable; fournisseurs d'équipement et de matériaux; consultants; organismes publics et parapublics
Mission: L'AESEQ est la seule association qui regroupe les entrepreneurs de construction oeuvrant dans tous les secteurs du cycle de l'eau décentralisé au Québec

Association des entomologistes amateurs du Québec inc. (AEAQ)
302, rue Gabrielle Roy, Varennes QC J3X 1L8
Courriel: info@aeaq.ca
URL: www.aeaq.ca
Aperçu: *Dimension:* petite; *Envergure:* provinciale; Organisme sans but lucratif; fondée en 1973
Membre(s) du bureau directeur:
Claude Chantal, Président
Finances: *Budget de fonctionnement annuel:* Moins de $50,000
Personnel: 10 bénévole(s)
Membre: 200; *Montant de la cotisation:* 30$ régulière, Canada
Mission: Promouvoir l'entomologie comme loisir scientifique; favoriser l'échange d'informations entre les membres lors des réunions; publier les travaux et les observations entomologiques des membres; veiller à la protection et à la conservation de l'entomofaune et du patrimoine entomologique du Québec; initier les nouveaux membres à l'étude des insectes à l'aide de séances d'identification, d'excursions et de rencontres avec des spécialistes; *Affiliation(s):* Société d'entomologie du Québec; Corporation Entomofaune du Québec; Amis de l'Insectarium de Montréal

Association des entrepreneurs en isolation de la Province de Québec *Voir* Association d'isolation du Québec

Association des entrepreneurs en mécanique du Canada *See* Mechanical Contractors Association of Canada

Association des entrepreneurs en mécanique du N.-B. *See* Mechanical Contractors Association of New Brunswick

Association des expositions agricoles du Québec (AEAQ)
CP 547, 23, av Ste-Brigitte nord, Montmagny QC G5V 3S9
Tél: 418-248-8824; *Téléc:* 418-248-0407
Ligne sans frais: 800-267-2579
Courriel: aeaq@globetrotter.net
URL: expoduquebec.com
Aperçu: *Dimension:* petite; *Envergure:* provinciale; fondée en 1940
Membre(s) du bureau directeur:
Benoît Boulanger, Secrétaire
Finances: *Budget de fonctionnement annuel:* $500,000-$1.5 Million
Membre: 41; *Montant de la cotisation:* 50$
Mission: D'offrir aux agriculteurs et aux éleveurs des événements professionnels spécialisés et bien organisés; et de présenter au grand public des événements populaires, éducatifs, divertissants et sécuritaires.

Association des fabricants internationaux d'automobiles du Canada *See* Association of International Automobile Manufacturers of Canada

Association des fermières de l'Ontario (AFO)
CP 190, 5095, rue Fatima, Saint-Eugène ON K0B 1P0
Tél: 613-674-2035; *Téléc:* 613-674-1176
Courriel: cerclefermieres@cnwl.igs.net
Aperçu: *Dimension:* moyenne; *Envergure:* provinciale; Organisme sans but lucratif; fondée en 1969
Finances: *Budget de fonctionnement annuel:* Moins de $50,000
Personnel: 10 bénévole(s)
Membre: 300; *Montant de la cotisation:* 6$; *Critères d'admissibilite:* Femme de 20 ans (en moyenne) et plus, interessée à sa santé, bien-être, culture (artisanat), connaissances générales, économie, loi etc.
Activités: Exposition artisanale annuelle; *Service de conférenciers:* Oui
Mission: Travailler aux intérêts des femmes et jeunes filles dans les paroisses, en artisanat, au progrès spirituel, social, culturel, économique et technique; *Affiliation(s):* Association canadienne-française de l'Ontario

Association des fonderies canadiennes *See* Canadian Foundry Association

Association des forestiers agréés du Nouveau-Brunswick *See* Association of Registered Professional Foresters of New Brunswick

L'Association des fruiticulteurs et des maraîchers de l'Ontario *See* Ontario Fruit & Vegetable Growers' Association

Association des industries aérospatiales du Canada *See* Aerospace Industries Association of Canada

Association des industries CANDU *See* Organization of CANDU Industries

Association des industries de l'automobile du Canada *See* Automotive Industries Association of Canada

L'Association des industries de l'environnement du Nouveau-Brunswick *See* New Brunswick Environment Industry Association

Association des industries solaires du Canada inc. *See* Canadian Solar Industries Association Inc.

Association des ingénieurs et géoscientifiques du Nouveau-Brunswick *See* Association of Professional Engineers & Geoscientists of New Brunswick

Association des ingénieurs municipaux du Québec (AIMQ) / Association of Québec Municipal Engineers
CP 792, Succ. B, Montréal QC H3B 3K5
Tél: 514-845-5303
Courriel: aimg.rlamarche@videotron.ca
URL: www.aimq.net
Aperçu: *Dimension:* moyenne; *Envergure:* provinciale; fondée en 1963
Finances: *Budget de fonctionnement annuel:* $100,000-$250,000
Personnel: 15 bénévole(s)
Membre: 200; *Montant de la cotisation:* 225.75$; *Critères d'admissibilite:* Membre de l'Ordre des ingénieurs du Québec; employé d'une administration municipale ou régionale
Activités: Séminaire de formation annuel; *Listes de destinataires:* Oui
Mission: Améliorer les connaissances et le statut de l'ingénieur municipal par l'échange d'information, la coopération entre ingénieurs municipaux et avec d'autres associations professionnelles et la promotion des intérêts communs des membres de l'Association

Association des ingénieurs-conseils du Québec (AICQ) / Consulting Engineers of Québec
Parent: Association of Consulting Engineering Companies - Canada
#030, 1440, rue Ste-Catherine ouest, Montréal QC H3G 1R8
Tél: 514-871-2229; *Téléc:* 514-871-9903
Courriel: info@aicq.qc.ca
URL: www.aicq.qc.ca
Aperçu: *Dimension:* grande; *Envergure:* provinciale; fondée en 1974
Finances: *Budget de fonctionnement annuel:* $250,000-$500,000
Personnel: 5 membre(s) du personnel; 100 bénévole(s)
Membre: 280 bureaux
Activités: *Listes de destinataires:* Oui; *Bibliothèque:* Oui; rendez-vous
Mission: Promouvoir et développer l'industrie du génie-conseil en regroupant des membres qui offrent des services de qualité

Association des ingénieurs-professeurs des sciences appliquées (AIPSA)
c/o Université de Sherbrooke, 2500, boul Université, Sherbrooke QC J1K 2R1
Tél: 819-821-7929; *Téléc:* 819-821-7955
Courriel: aipsa@usherbrooke.ca
Aperçu: *Dimension:* petite; *Envergure:* locale; Organisme sans but lucratif; fondée en 1970
Finances: *Budget de fonctionnement annuel:* Moins de $50,000
Personnel: 6 membre(s) du personnel
Membre: 95; *Montant de la cotisation:* 0.75% du salaire régulier annuel; *Critères d'admissibilite:* Membre de l'ordre des ingénieurs du QC; salarié affecté à une tâche d'enseignement ou de recherche à l'Université de Sherbrooke
Mission: Négocier la convention collective des ingénieur-professeurs; représenter les ingénieur-professeurs au sens du code du travail

Association des jardineries du Québec (AJQ)
#300, 3230, rue Sicotte ouest, Saint-Hyacinthe QC J2S 7B3
Tél: 450-774-2228; *Téléc:* 450-774-3556
Courriel: fihoq@fihoq.qc.ca
URL: www.fihoq.qc.ca
Aperçu: *Dimension:* petite; *Envergure:* provinciale; Organisme sans but lucratif; fondée en 1992
Membre(s) du bureau directeur:
Lise Gauthier, Présidente
floriculture.gauthier@cgocable.ca
Finances: *Budget de fonctionnement annuel:* Moins de $50,000
Membre: 99; *Montant de la cotisation:* 225$; *Critères d'admissibilite:* Centre-jardin
Activités: Colloque conjoint AJQ-AQPP; formation
Mission: Les principaux objectifs de l'Association sont de favoriser le développement des jardineries du Québec, d'encourager le dialogue entre les membres et d'assurer la défense des membres au niveau gouvernemental ou d'autres institutions.; *Affiliation(s):* Fédération Interdisciplinaire de l'horticulture ornementale du Québec

Association des jardins du Québec / Québec Gardens Association
82, Grande-Allée ouest, Québec QC G1R 2G6
Tél: 418-692-0886
Courriel: info@jardinsduquebec.com
URL: www.jardinsduquebec.com
Aperçu: *Dimension:* petite; *Envergure:* provinciale
Membre: 20
Mission: L'Association des jardins du Québec a comme mission de regrouper en corporation les jardins du Québec ouverts au public afin d'aider à leur développement et à leur promotion et de souligner leur apport à la culture et au patrimoine québécois

Association des jeunes ruraux du Québec (AJRQ)
65, rang 3 est, Princeville QC G6L 4B9
Tél: 819-364-5606; *Téléc:* 819-364-5006
Courriel: info@ajrq.qc.ca
URL: www.ajrq.qc.ca
Aperçu: *Dimension:* moyenne; *Envergure:* provinciale; fondée en 1974
Membre(s) du bureau directeur:
Josiane Chabot, Présidente
Annie Chabot, Directrice générale
Finances: *Budget de fonctionnement annuel:* $100,000-$250,000
Personnel: 2 membre(s) du personnel; 300 bénévole(s)
Membre: 1 200; *Montant de la cotisation:* 5$
Activités: *Stagiaires:* Oui; *Listes de destinataires:* Oui
Mission: Promouvoir la formation auprès de nos membres; soutenir leur sentiment d'appartenance au milieu rural; *Membre de:* Regroupement Loisir Québec; *Affiliation(s):* Conseil des 4-H du Canada

Association des manufacturiers de bois de sciage de l'Ontario *See* Ontario Lumber Manufacturers' Association

Association des manufacturiers de bois de sciage du Québec *Voir* Conseil de l'industrie forestière du Québec

Association des manufacturiers de produits alimentaires du Québec *Voir* Conseil de la transformation agroalimentaire et des produits de consommation

Association des médecins biochimistes du Canada *See* Canadian Association of Medical Biochemists

Association des médecins biochimistes du Québec
Parent: Fédération des médecins spécialistes du Québec
#3000, 2, Complexe Desjardins, Montréal QC H5B 1G8
Tél: 514-350-5105; Téléc: 514-350-5151
Courriel: ambq@fmsq.org
URL: www.ambq.med.usherbrooke.ca
Aperçu: Dimension: petite; *Envergure:* provinciale
Mission: Promouvoir l'utilisation optimale des tests de laboratoire au Québec en offrant, au professionnel de la santé et au patient, les meilleurs services de diagnostic et de dépistage de maladies grâce à des techniques biochimiques et immunologiques

Association des médecins spécialistes en santé communautaire du Québec (AMSSCQ)
Parent: Fédération des médecins spécialistes du Québec
#3000, 2, Complexe Desjardins, Montréal QC H5B 1G8
Tél: 514-350-5138; Téléc: 514-350-5151
Courriel: amsscq@fmsq.org
URL: www.amsscq.org
Aperçu: Dimension: petite; *Envergure:* provinciale; *fondée en* 1982
Mission: L'association a pour rôle de promouvoir les intérêts professionnels et économiques de ses membres

Association des microbiologistes du Québec (AMQ)
5094A, av. Charlemagne, Montréal QC H1X 3P3
Tél: 514-728-1087; Téléc: 514-374-3988
Courriel: amq@microbiologistes.ca
URL: www.microbiologistes.ca
Aperçu: Dimension: moyenne; *Envergure:* provinciale; *fondée en* 1975
Finances: Budget de fonctionnement annuel: Moins de $50,000
Personnel: 7 bénévole(s)
Membre: 500; *Montant de la cotisation:* Barème; *Critères d'admissibilité:* 30 crédits universitaires en microbiologie
Mission: L'association regroupe les microbiologistes du Québec oeuvrant principalemtn en environnement, en alimentaire et en pharmaceutique. Elle a pour but d'étudier, de protéger et de développer les intérêts économiques, sociaux et professionnels des microbiologistes et de promouvoir l'essor de la microbiologie en général; est impliquée au niveau de l'accréditation des laboratoires d'analyses microbiologiques et elle est représentée au sein de plusieurs comités ou associations.

Association des mines de métaux du Québec inc. *Voir* Association minière du Québec

Association des pompiers professionnels de l'Ontario (ind.) *See* Ontario Professional Fire Fighters Association

Association des produits forestiers du Canada *See* Forest Products Association of Canada

L'Association des produits forestiers du Nouveau-Brunswick *See* New Brunswick Forest Products Association Inc.

Association des prospecteurs du Québec *Voir* Association de l'exploration minière de Québec

Association des sciences de la santé de l'Alberta (ind.) *See* Health Sciences Association of Alberta

Association des sciences de la santé de la Saskatchewan (ind.) *See* Health Sciences Association of Saskatchewan

Association des spécialistes en extermination du Québec *Voir* Association québécoise de la gestion parasitaire

Association des technologistes agro-alimentaires inc. *Voir* Association des technologues en agroalimentaire

Association des technologues en agroalimentaire (ATA) / Agricultural Technologists Association Inc.
a/s Ordre des technologues professionnels du Québec, #720, 1265, rue Berri, Montréal QC H2L 4X4
Tél: 514-845-3247; Téléc: 514-845-3643
Ligne sans frais: 800-561-3459
URL: www.otpq.qc.ca
Nom précédent: Association des technologistes agro-alimentaires inc.
Aperçu: Dimension: moyenne; *Envergure:* provinciale; Organisme sans but lucratif; *fondée en* 1964

Finances: Budget de fonctionnement annuel: Moins de $50,000
Personnel: 1 membre(s) du personnel; 5 bénévole(s)
Membre: 300; *Montant de la cotisation:* 396.68$
Mission: Défense des intérêts professionnels; promouvoir la profession et le perfectionnement des membres; *Membre de:* Ordre des technologues professionnels du Québec

Association des terrains de camping du Québec *Voir* Camping Québec

Association des transports du Canada *See* Transportation Association of Canada

Association des zoos et aquariums du Canada *See* Canadian Association of Zoos & Aquariums

Association du barreau canadien *See* Canadian Bar Association

Association du barreau du comté de Carleton *See* Carleton County Law Association

Association du camionnage du Québec inc. (ACQ) / Québec Trucking Association Inc.
Parent: Canadian Trucking Alliance
#200, 6450, rue Notre Dame ouest, Montréal QC H4C 1C4
Tél: 514-932-0377; Téléc: 514-932-1358
Ligne sans frais: 800-361-5813
Courriel: info@carrefour-acq.org
URL: www.carrefour-acq.org
Aperçu: Dimension: moyenne; *Envergure:* provinciale; Organisme sans but lucratif; *fondée en* 1951
Finances: Budget de fonctionnement annuel: $500,000-$1.5 Million
Personnel: 13 membre(s) du personnel
Membre: 600 sociétés + 251 associés; *Critères d'admissibilite:* transporteurs et locateurs publics & privés
Activités: Stagiaires: Oui
Mission: Favoriser l'amélioration des normes de sécurité, d'efficacité et d'éthique dans l'industrie du camionnage; maintenir un contact avec l'autorité gouvernementale, les usagers des services de camionnage et le public en général; soutenir le perfectionnement professionnel; soutenir les entreprises dans la défense de leurs intérêts.; *Affiliation(s):* Union Internationale des Transports Routiers - Genève; American Trucking Association - Washington, DC

L'Association du saumon Nepisiguit *See* Nepisiguit Salmon Association

Association du transport aérien du Canada *See* Air Transport Association of Canada

Association du transport aérien international *See* International Air Transport Association

Association for Canadian Registered Safety Professionals *See* Board of Canadian Registered Safety Professionals

Association for Mineral Exploration British Columbia (AMEBC)
#800, 889 Pender St. West, Vancouver BC V6C 3B2
Tel: 604-689-5271; Fax: 604-681-2363
e-mail: info@amebc.ca
URL: www.amebc.ca
Previous Name: British Columbia & Yukon Chamber of Mines
Overview: A medium-sized provincial organization founded in 1912
Finances: Annual Operating Budget: $250,000-$500,000; *Funding Sources:* Membership dues
Staff: 6 staff member(s)
Membership: 3,605 individual + 179 corporate; *Fees:* $50 individual; *Member Profile:* Member of mining community; *Committees:* Many-Land Use; Mining Law; Safety
Activities: Library: Charles S. Ney Library; Open to public
Mission: To promote & assist development & growth of mining of mineral exploration in BC; *Affiliation(s):* Mining Association of Canada; Mining Association of BC

Association for Mountain Parks Protection & Enjoyment (AMPPE)
PO Box 2999, Banff AB T1L 1C7
Tel: 403-762-3800; Fax: 403-762-3828
e-mail: info@amppe.org
URL: www.amppe.org
Overview: A small provincial organization founded in 1994
Chief Officer(s):
Richard Leavens, Executive Director

Fees: $50
Mission: We champion & promote sustainable tourism, a vibrant mountain economy & responsible human use in our mountain parks

Association forestière canadienne *See* Canadian Forestry Association

Association forestière canadienne du Nouveau-Brunswick *See* Canadian Forestry Association of New Brunswick

Association forestière de l'Ontario *See* Ontario Forestry Association

Association francophone pour le savoir (ACFAS)
425, rue de la Gauchetière est, Montréal QC H2L 2M7
Tél: 514-849-0045; Téléc: 514-849-5558
Courriel: acfas@acfas.ca
URL: www.acfas.ca
Nom précédent: Association canadienne française pour l'avancement des sciences
Aperçu: Dimension: moyenne; *Envergure:* nationale; *fondée en* 1923
Finances: Budget de fonctionnement annuel: $500,000-$1.5 Million
Personnel: 8 membre(s) du personnel
Membre: 8 000 individu; 40 institutionnel; *Montant de la cotisation:* 45$
Prix, Bouses: Prix J.-Armand-Bombardier (Bourse d études)
Award for technological innovation *Award Amount:* $2,500
Prix Léo-Pariseau (Bourse d études)
Award for biological or health sciences *Award Amount:* $2,500
Prix Marcel-Vincent (Bourse d études)
Award for social sciences; sponsored by Bell Canada *Award Amount:* $2,500
Prix Urgel-Archambault (Bourse d études)
Award for physics, mathematics or engineering; sponsored by Alcan *Award Amount:* $2,500
Prix Desjardins d'excellence étudiants-chercheurs (Bourse d études)
For master's or doctoral students; sponsored by the Fondation Desjardins *Award Amount:* Three awards of $2,500
Prix Bernard-Belleau (Bourse d études)
Award for doctoral student in health or pharmaceuticals *Award Amount:* $2,500
Prix Michel-Jurdant (Bourse d études)
Award recognizes research in environmental sciences; sponsored by Hydro-Québec *Award Amount:* $2,500
Mission: Promouvoir et soutenir la science et la technologie pour encourager le développement culturel et économique de la société

Association géologique du Canada *See* Geological Association of Canada

Association internationale des pompiers (FAT-COI/CTC) *See* International Association of Fire Fighters (AFL-CIO/CLC)

Association internationale du droit nucléaire *See* International Nuclear Law Association

Association médicale canadienne *See* Canadian Medical Association

Association médicale du Québec (AMQ) / Québec Medical Association (QMA)
Parent: Canadian Medical Association
#3200, 380, rue Saint-Antoine ouest, Montréal QC H2Y 3X7
Tel: 514-866-0660; Fax: 514-866-0670
Toll-Free: 800-363-3932
e-mail: admin@amq.ca
URL: www.amq.ca
Overview: A medium-sized provincial charitable organization founded in 1922
Membership: 8 500; *Fees:* 110-620, schedule; *Member Profile:* Etre médecin et être membre de la Corporation professionnelle des médecins du Québec; *Committees:* Soins et promotion de la santéÉconomique et politique de la santéÉducation; Éthique; Mises en candidatures; Finances
Mission: Rassembler et soutenir les médecins du Québec afin de garantir à la population québécoise des conditions et des soins de santé de qualité

Association minéralogique du Canada *See* Mineralogical Association of Canada

Association minière du Canada *See* Mining Association of Canada

Associations/Organizations / Association minière du Québec

L'Association minière du Nouveau-Brunswick *See* New Brunswick Mining Association

Association minière du Québec (AMQ) / Québec Mining Association
Parent: Mining Association of Canada
Place de la Cité - Tour Belle Cour, #720, 2590, boul Laurier, Québec QC G1V 4M6
Tél: 418-657-2016; *Téléc:* 418-657-2154
Courriel: mines@amq-inc.com
URL: www.amq-inc.com
Nom précédent: Association des mines de métaux du Québec inc.
Aperçu: *Dimension:* grande; *Envergure:* provinciale; Organisme sans but lucratif; fondée en 1936
Finances: *Budget de fonctionnement annuel:* $500,000-$1.5 Million
Personnel: 9 membre(s) du personnel
Membre: 1-99; *Critères d'admissibilite:* Toutes les compagnies opérant dans le secteur minier ou dans un secteur connexe; *Comités:* Environnement; Prévention des accidents; SantéRelations publiques; FiscalitéContrôle de terrain; Sauvetage minier (catamine); Entretien
Mission: Promouvoir le développement de l'industrie des mines, de la métallurgie et des industries connexes; défendre les intérêts généraux de ses membres; soutenir les efforts de ses membres quant au bien-être, à la sécurité et à la prévention des accidents au travail

Association nationale pour la conservation de l'énergie *See* National Energy Conservation Association Inc.

Association nucléaire canadienne *See* Canadian Nuclear Association

Association of Alberta Agricultural Fieldmen (AAAF)
c/o Municipal District of Rocky View, 911 - 32nd Ave. NE, Calgary AB T2E 6X6
Tel: 403-230-1401
e-mail: info@aaaf.ab.ca
URL: www.aaaf.ab.ca
Overview: A small provincial organization
Chief Officer(s):
Pat Dirk, President, 403-362-4343
dirkp@countyofnewell.ab.ca
Kim Butler, Supervisor, Agricultural Services
kbutler@rockyview.ca
Finances: *Annual Operating Budget:* Less than $50,000
Membership: 107; *Fees:* $125; *Member Profile:* Agricultural fieldmen develop, implement, and control programs that adhere to the priorities and policies set by the Agricultural Service Board across the province.; *Committees:* Education; Policy; Soils; Weed Control
Mission: Committed to the enhancement, promotion & protection of the agricultural resources of Alberta

Association of American Geographers (AAG)
1710 - 16 St. NW, Washington DC 20009-3198 USA
Tel: 202-234-1450; *Fax:* 202-234-2744
e-mail: gaia@aag.org
URL: www.aag.org
Overview: A medium-sized national organization founded in 1904
Chief Officer(s):
Douglas Richardson, Executive Director
Finances: *Annual Operating Budget:* $1.5 Million-$3 Million
Staff: 10 staff member(s)
Membership: 7,100 individual + 800 institutional; *Fees:* Schedule available; *Member Profile:* Members include students & professionals with backgrounds in a wide variety of geographic subfields such as urban geography, geographic information systems, cartography, remote sensing, historical geography, geomorphology, political geography, planning, environmental studies, & area studies
Activities: Specialty groups (comprised of geographers who share a professional interest in a systematic or topical specialty or in a major region of the world) sponsor sessions at the annual meetings, publish newsletters or other communications, & develop workshops & other projects to advance their professional interests; AAG manages several funded projects; AAG supports special symposia; *Internships:* Yes; *Rents Mailing List:* Yes
Publications: *The Professional Geographer*
Editor: Sharmistha Bagchi-Sen
Profile: Annual journal
Mission: To advance professional studies in geography & to encourage the application of geographic research in education, government & business; to promote discussion among its members & with scholars in related fields; to support the publication of scholarly studies; *Member of:* American Council of Learned Societies

Association of Applied Geochemists (AEG)
PO Box 26099, 72 Robertson Rd., Nepean ON K2H 9R0
Tel: 613-828-0199; *Fax:* 613-828-9288
e-mail: office@appliedgeochemists.org
URL: www.appliedgeochemists.org
Previous Name: Association of Exploration Geochemists
Overview: A medium-sized international organization founded in 1970
Finances: *Annual Operating Budget:* $50,000-$100,000; *Funding Sources:* Membership dues; publisher rebates
Staff: 2 staff member(s); 70 volunteer(s)
Membership: 650; *Fees:* US$100
Activities: *Speaker Service:* Yes
Mission: To promote interest in the applications of geochemistry to mineral & petroleum exploration, resource evaluation & related fields

Association of British Columbia Forest Professionals (ABCFP)
#1030, 1188 Georgia St. West, Vancouver BC V6E 4A2
Tel: 604-687-8027; *Fax:* 604-687-3264
e-mail: info@abcfp.ca
URL: www.abcfp.ca
Previous Name: Association of British Columbia Professional Foresters
Overview: A medium-sized provincial licensing organization founded in 1947
Finances: *Annual Operating Budget:* $500,000-$1.5 Million; *Funding Sources:* Membership dues
Staff: 12 staff member(s); 300 volunteer(s)
Membership: 5,300; *Fees:* $300-330 + GST; *Member Profile:* Individual - membership is mandatory for all who practise professional forestry in the province of British Columbia; *Committees:* ABCFP Forestrust
Activities: Policy review seminars; Professional Foresters' Network; Forest Capital of BC
Awards: Honorary Membership (Award)
Non-members, nominated by the membership
Distinguished Forest Professional Award (Award)
Eligibility: BC registered professional foresters, nominated by their peers
Forester of the Year Award (Award)
Eligibility: BC registered professional foresters, nominated by their peers
Mission: To protect the public interest in the practice of professional forestry by ensuring the competence, independence & integrity of its members; to ensure that every person practising professional forestry is accountable to the association & to the public; *Member of:* Canadian Federation of Professional Foresters Association

Association of British Columbia Land Surveyors (ABCLS)
Parent: Canadian Council of Land Surveyors
#301, 2400 Bevan Ave., Sidney BC V8L 1W1
Tel: 250-655-7222; *Fax:* 250-655-7223
e-mail: office@abcls.ca
URL: www.abcls.ca
Also Known As: British Columbia Land Surveyors
Overview: A medium-sized provincial licensing organization founded in 1905
Activities: Conducting examining for admission; Performing legal surveys in British Columbia; Providing professional development opportunities
Meetings/Conferences:
For more information see Trade Shows, Conferences and Seminars Chapter
Association of British Columbia Land Surveyors 2012 Annual General Meeting
Other Conferences in 2012 2012, BC
Publications: *The Link*
Type: Magazine *Frequency:* 3 pa *Accepts Advertising* : Yes
Profile: Information distributed to all British Columbia land surveyors
The Land Surveyor
Type: Newsletter *Editor:* Janice Henshaw
Profile: Articles about land surveying in British Columbia
Mission: To set educational requirements for land surveyors; To regulate professional land surveyors in British Columbia

Association of British Columbia Professional Foresters *See* Association of British Columbia Forest Professionals

Association of Canada Lands Surveyors / Association des arpenteurs des terres du Canada
100E, 900 Dynes Rd., Ottawa ON K2C 3L6
Tel: 613-723-9200; *Fax:* 613-723-5558
e-mail: admin@acls-aatc.ca
URL: www.acls-aatc.ca
Previous Name: Canadian Institute of Surveying
Overview: A medium-sized national organization
Chief Officer(s):
Jean-Claude Tétreault, Executive Director
jctetreault@acls-aatc.ca
Mission: To establish & maintain standards of qualification for Canada Lands Surveyors; to regulate Canada Lands Surveyors; to establish & maintain standards of conduct, knowledge & skill among members of the Association & permit holders; to govern the activities of members of the Association & permit holders; to cooperate with other organizations for the advancement of surveying; & to perform the duties & exercise the powers that are imposed or conferred on the Association by the Act

Association of Canadian Ergonomists (ACE) / L'Association canadienne d'ergonomie
#1003, 105-150 Crowfoot Cres. NW, Calgary AB T3G 3T2
Tel: 403-219-4001; *Fax:* 403-451-1503
Toll-Free: 888-432-2223
e-mail: info@ace-ergocanada.ca
URL: www.ace-ergocanada.ca
Previous Name: Human Factors Association of Canada
Overview: A small national organization founded in 1968
Finances: *Annual Operating Budget:* $100,000-$250,000; *Funding Sources:* Membership dues; annual conference
Staff: 2 staff member(s)
Membership: 600 individuals; *Fees:* $150 full; $75 affiliate; $34 student; *Member Profile:* Engineers; medical practitioners; safety specialists; research scientists; architects; designers; educators; managers; consultants; kinesiologists; psychologists; ergonomists
Activities: *Speaker Service:* Yes
Awards: Student Paper Awards
Award Amount: $250
Mission: To advance human factors/ergonomics through encouraging a high quality of practice, education & research; to facilitate communication among members; to represent the discipline; to increase awareness of human factors/ergonomics; to identify resources; *Member of:* International Ergonomics Association

Association of Canadian Port Authorities (ACPA)
#1502, 85 Albert St., Ottawa ON K1P 6A4
Tel: 613-232-2036; *Fax:* 613-232-9554
e-mail: leroux@acpa-ports.net
URL: www.acpa-ports.net
Previous Name: Canadian Port & Harbour Association
Overview: A medium-sized national organization founded in 1958
Finances: *Annual Operating Budget:* $50,000-$100,000; *Funding Sources:* Membership fees; seminars
Staff: 1 staff member(s)
Membership: 18 corporate + 17 associate; *Fees:* $750 associate & affiliate; $100 individual; *Committees:* Constitution; Finance & Administration; Marketing; Public Relations; Operations & Environment; Past Presidents; Real Property Management
Activities: Annual conferences where papers are given by experts in the field of port operations & where members inspect the host port's dock & industrial facilities; port-related research; special seminars; *Speaker Service:* Yes
Mission: To encourage, mentor & stimulate the development of excellence within Canadian ports; *Affiliation(s):* American Association of Port Authorities

Association of Canadian Universities for Northern Studies (ACUNS) / Association universitaire canadienne d'études nordiques
Parent: Association of Universities & Colleges of Canada
#405, 17 York St., Ottawa ON K1N 9J6
Tel: 613-562-0515; *Fax:* 613-562-0533
e-mail: office@acuns.ca
URL: www.acuns.ca
Social Media: twitter.com/acunsaucen
Overview: A small national charitable organization founded in 1977
Finances: *Annual Operating Budget:* $100,000-$250,000; *Funding Sources:* University dues

Staff: 1 staff member(s)
Membership: 32 universities/colleges; *Fees:* $1,082
Activities: Maintaining a network of circumpolar contacts; providing education & public awareness programs; triennial Student Conference on Northern Studies
Awards: Caribou Research Award (Award)
Awarded to students enrolled in a recognized Canadian community college or university pursuing studies that will contribute to the understanding of the Beverly & Qamanirjuaq Barren Ground Caribou (& their habitat) in Canada *Deadline:* Jan. 31 *Award Amount:* Up to $1,500
Studentships in Northern Studies (Scholarship)
Research culminating in a thesis or similar document involving direct northern experience; for students enrolled in graduate & undergraduate degree programs or other courses of study recognized at a Canadian university with special relevance to Canada's northern territories & adjacent regions *Deadline:* Jan. 31 *Award Amount:* $10,000
Cooperative Award (Award)
Awarded to a student whose studies will contribute to the understanding & development of cooperatives in NWT; applicants who are not northern residents must be full-time students at the Cooperative College of Canada, a recognized Canadian community college, or a Canadian university *Deadline:* Jan. 31 *Award Amount:* $2,000
Research Support Opportunity in Arctic Environmental Studies (Award)
Preference is given to environmental research proposals in the physical &/or biological sciences for which location at the High Arctic Weather Stations would be advantageous; graduate level studies *Deadline:* Jan. 31 *Award Amount:* Logistical support
Canadian Northern Studies Polar Commission Scholarship (Award)
Mission: The Association encourages the government & private sector to support polar scholarship, fostering programs to increase public awareness of polar sciences & research. It represents its member universities & colleges, encouraging the establishment of funds & resources to ensure a network of trained researchers, regional managers & educators.

Association of Certified Engineering Technicians & Technologists of Prince Edward Island (ACETTPEI)
Parent: **Canadian Council of Technicians & Technologists**
PO Box 1436, 92 Queen St., Charlottetown PE C1A 7N1
Tel: 902-892-8324
e-mail: info@acettpei.ca
URL: www.acettpei.ca
Previous Name: Prince Edward Island Society of Certified Engineering Technologists
Overview: A small provincial organization founded in 1972
Activities: Certifying engineering / applied science technicians & technologists; Conferring the designations C.Tech., C.E.T., & A.Sc.T.; *Awareness Events:* Career Options Day, Nov.; National Skilled Trades Day, Nov.; National Technology Week, Nov.
Publications: AtlanTECH News
Type: Newsletter
Profile: Information for technology professionals in New Brunswick, Prince Edward Island, & Newfoundland & Labrador
Mission: To benefit society by advancing the professions of applied science & engineering technology in Prince Edward Island

Association of Consulting Engineering Companies - Canada (ACEC)
#420, 130 Albert St., Ottawa ON K1P 5G4
Fax: 613-236-6193
Toll-Free: 800-565-0569
e-mail: info@acec.ca
URL: www.acec.ca
Previous Name: Association of Consulting Engineers of Canada
Overview: A large national organization founded in 1925
Finances: *Annual Operating Budget:* $500,000-$1.5 Million
Staff: 6 staff member(s); 35+ volunteer(s)
Membership: 600 independent consulting engineering companies & 11 provincial and territorial member organizations; *Fees:* Based on annual revenue; *Member Profile:* Firms which have passed a thorough membership screening process: proven technical capability, necessary experience as consultants, adherence to rules of ethical practice & professional responsibility; membership is voluntary & is limited to those firms primarily engaged in providing independent consulting engineering services to the public
Activities: Federal government lobbying on major public policy issues; Negotiations with government departments re: contracting-out of public work, selection of consultants & remuneration; Negotiations with other industry organizations re: establishment of guidelines for contracts; International market development; *Speaker Service:* Yes; *Rents Mailing List:* Yes; *Library:* Yes, Open to public
Awards: Public Service Awards (Award), Canadian Consulting Engineering Awards
Shreyer Award (Award), Canadian Consulting Engineering Awards
Awards of Excellence & Merit (Award), Canadian Consulting Engineering Awards
Mission: To assist in promoting satisfactory business relations between its Member Firms & their clients; To promote cordial relations among the various consulting engineering firms in Canada & to foster the interchange of professional, management & business experience & information among them; To safeguard the interest of the consulting engineer; To further the maintenance of high professional standards in the consulting engineering profession; *Member of:* International Federation of Consulting Engineers

Association of Consulting Engineering Companies - New Brunswick (ACEC-NB)
Parent: **Association of Consulting Engineering Companies - Canada**
183 Hanwell Rd., Fredericton NB E3B 2R2
Tel: 506-470-9211; *Fax:* 506-451-9629
e-mail: info@acec-nb.ca
URL: www.cenb.nb.ca
Overview: A medium-sized provincial organization founded in 1983
Chief Officer(s):
John Fudge, P.Eng, Executive Director
David McAllister, P.Eng, President
Christy Cunningham, Secretary
Karen Robichaud, Treasurer
Activities: Advocating for consulting engineering companies in New Brunswick; Providing training opportunities
Awards: CENB Showcase Awards (Award)
Includes the following awards: Benefit to Society Award, Innovation Award, Technical Excellence Award, & Sustainability Award
Meetings/Conferences:
For more information see Trade Shows, Conferences and Seminars Chapter
Association of Consulting Engineering Companies - New Brunswick 2012 5th Annual Deputy Ministers' Dinner & Information Session
Other Conferences in 2012 2012, NB
Association of Consulting Engineering Companies - New Brunswick 2012 15th Annual General Meeting, Trade Show, Conference, & Awards Gala
Other Conferences in 2012 2012, NB
Publications: CE [Consulting Engineers] News
Type: Newsletter *Language:* B *Frequency:* bi-m.
Profile: Information for Association of Consulting Engineering Companies - New Brunswick members
Mission: To develop & support member firms; To improve the business environment for member firms & their clients; To further the professional standards of the consulting engineering profession

Association of Consulting Engineers of Canada See
Association of Consulting Engineering Companies - Canada

Association of Consulting Engineers of Saskatchewan See
Consulting Engineers of Saskatchewan

Association of Engineering Technicians & Technologists of Newfoundland & Labrador (AETTNL)
Parent: **Canadian Council of Technicians & Technologists**
Donovan's Industrial Park, PO Box 790, 22 Sagona Ave., Mount Pearl NL A1N 2Y2
Tel: 709-747-2868; *Fax:* 709-747-2869
Toll-Free: 888-238-8600
e-mail: aettnl@aettnl.com
URL: www.aettnl.com
Overview: A small provincial organization founded in 1968
Finances: *Annual Operating Budget:* Less than $50,000
Membership: 1200; *Fees:* Schedule available; *Committees:* Certification/Registration Board; Constitution/Bylaws; Accreditation Board; Act; Public Relations
Mission: AETTNL's mission is to advance the profession of Applied Science/Engineering Technology & the professional recognition of Certified Technicians & Technologists. It regulates the standards of training & practice, & protects the interests of its members & the public.

Association of Environmental Engineering & Science Professors (AEESP)
2303 Naples Ct., Champaign IL 61822-3510 USA
Tel: 217-398-6969; *Fax:* 217-355-9232
e-mail: joanne@aeesp.org
URL: www.aeesp.org
Overview: A medium-sized international organization founded in 1963
Chief Officer(s):
Amy Childress, President
Joanne Fetzner, Manager, Business Office
Finances: *Annual Operating Budget:* $50,000-$100,000
Membership: 700; *Fees:* $15 student; $75 professor
Activities: *Rents Mailing List:* Yes
Mission: To assist members in the development & dissemination of knowledge in environmental engineering & science; to strengthen & advance the environmental field through cooperation amongst academic & other communities

Association of Equipment Manufacturers - Canada (AEM-Canada)
World Exchange Plaza, PO Box 81067, #880, 111 Albert St., Ottawa ON K1P 1B1
Tel: 613-566-4568; *Fax:* 613-566-2026
URL: www.aem.org
Previous Name: Canadian Farm & Industrial Equipment Institute
Overview: A small national organization founded in 1966
Membership: 750 companies; *Fees:* Based on sales; *Member Profile:* Manufacturers & distributors of equipment, & those who offer services, in the agriculture, construction, forestry, mining & utility industries.
Mission: The Association acts as a voice for its members to the public & on a governmental level. It is also a regulatory body setting standars for safety, offering a variety of educational programs & seminars. AEM also serves as a disseminating body providing it members with current information & news on the industry.

Association of Exploration Geochemists See Association of Applied Geochemists

Association of Fish & Wildlife Agencies
#725, 444 North Capitol St. NW, Washington DC 20001 USA
Tel: 202-624-7890; *Fax:* 202-624-7891
e-mail: info@fishwildlife.org
URL: www.fishwildlife.org
Previous Name: International Association of Fish & Wildlife Agencies
Overview: A small international organization founded in 1902
Finances: *Annual Operating Budget:* $500,000-$1.5 Million
Staff: 25 staff member(s)
Member Profile: Conservationists; Governments & government agencies; Regional associations; Organizations with similar objectives or supportive of the Association; Sportsmen; Individuals with varied backgrounds
Activities: All bird conservation; Agency information database; Automated wildlife data systems; Conservation education; Conservation Leadership Institute; Farm Bill program; Furbearer management; International relations; Legislation; National Fish Habitat Action Plan; Science & Research; Teaming with wildlife; Wildlife conflict
Mission: The Association works cooperatively to guide its members toward long term conservation of renewable natural resources by employing conservation science & research.

Association of Great Lakes Outdoor Writers (AGLOW)
PO Box 35, Benld IL 62009 USA
Toll-Free: 877-472-4569
e-mail: edir@AGLOW.INFO
URL: www.aglow.info
Overview: A small local organization founded in 1954
Chief Officer(s):
Curt Hicken, Executive Director
Bob Whitehead, President
OGMBOBW@aol.com
Finances: *Annual Operating Budget:* Less than $50,000; *Funding Sources:* Membership dues; fundraising
Staff: 2 staff member(s)
Membership: 330; *Fees:* $45-135

Associations/Organizations / Association of Independent Corrugated Converters

Mission: Dedicated to communicating the outdoor experience in word & image

Association of Heritage Consultants *See* Canadian Association of Professional Heritage Consultants

Association of Independent Corrugated Converters
PO Box 73063, Stn. White Shields, 2300 Lawrence Ave. East, Toronto ON M1P 4Z5
Tel: 905-727-9405; *Fax:* 905-727-1061
e-mail: info@aicc11.com
URL: www.aiccbox.org
Also Known As: AICC Canada
Overview: A small national organization founded in 1975
Finances: *Annual Operating Budget:* $50,000-$100,000; *Funding Sources:* Membership fees
Staff: 2 staff member(s); 10 volunteer(s)
Membership: 65 regular + 35 associate; *Fees:* Levels based on gross sales or total number of staff; *Member Profile:* Sheet plant owners & associated members; *Committees:* Education, Program, Hall of Fame, Golf Tournament, Industry Lobby Committee
Mission: To provide a forum for the independent corrugated converter on legitimate matters of mutual interest; to enhance the level of professionalism of the independent converter in the operation of his/her business; to implement democratically determined goals on matters civil & governmental which have a positive effect on all independent corrugated converters; *Member of:* AICC International - Alexandria, Virginia
Environmental Activity: Member of the Paper & Paperboard Packaging Environmental Council (PPEC)

Association of International Automobile Manufacturers of Canada (AIAMC) / Association des fabricants internationaux d'automobiles du Canada
Parent: The Canadian Association of Importers & Exporters
PO Box 5, #1804, 2 Bloor St. West, Toronto ON M4W 3E2
Tel: 416-595-8251; *Fax:* 416-595-2864
e-mail: auto@aiamc.com
URL: www.aiamc.com
Previous Name: Automobile Importers of Canada
Overview: A medium-sized national organization founded in 1973
Finances: *Annual Operating Budget:* $500,000-$1.5 Million; *Funding Sources:* Membership dues
Staff: 1 staff member(s); 100 volunteer(s)
Membership: 25; *Member Profile:* Distributing light-duty vehicles in Canada; headquartered outside North America; *Committees:* Executive; Consumer Relations; Custom; Finance & Taxation; Financial Services; Government Relations; Legal; Logistics; Parts; Show Exhibitors; Statistical; Technical
Activities: *Library:* Yes, Open to public
Mission: To represent before federal, provincial & territorial governments the interests of members engaged in the manufacturing, importation, distribution & servicing of light-duty vehicles

Association of Local Official Health Agencies (ALOHA) *See* Association of Local Public Health Agencies

Association of Local Public Health Agencies (ALPHA)
#1306, 2 Carlton St., Toronto ON M5G 1T6
Tel: 416-595-0006; *Fax:* 416-595-0030
e-mail: info@alphaweb.org
URL: www.alphaweb.org
Previous Name: Association of Local Official Health Agencies (ALOHA)
Overview: A medium-sized provincial organization founded in 1986
Membership: 30 health units; *Member Profile:* Board of health members of health units in Ontario; Medical & associate medical officers of health; *Committees:* Advocacy
Activities: Advocating for public health policies, programs, & services
Meetings/Conferences:
For more information see Trade Shows, Conferences and Seminars Chapter
Association of Local Public Health Agencies 2011 Fall Symposium
October 2011, ON
Association of Local Public Health Agencies 2012 Winter Symposium
February 2012, ON
Association of Local Public Health Agencies 2012 Annual Conference
June 2012, ON
Association of Local Public Health Agencies 2012 Fall Symposium
October 2012, ON
Publications: *Public Health Pulse*
Type: Newsletter *Frequency:* q. *Editor:* Tannisha Lambert
Profile: Association activities, affiliate information, conference highlights, & upcoming events
Mission: To provide leadership in public health management to health units in Ontario; To assist local public health units in the provision of efficient & effective services; *Affiliation(s):* ANDSOOHA - Public Health Nursing Management; Association of Ontario Public Health Business Administrators; Association of Public Health Epidemiologists in Ontario; Association of Supervisors of Public Health Inspectors of Ontario; Health Promotion Ontario; Ontario Association of Public Health Dentistry; Ontario Society of Nutrition Professionals in Public Health
Environmental Activity: Providing information on issues related to public health

Association of Major Power Consumers in Ontario (AMPCO)
Sterling Tower, 372 Bay St., Toronto ON M5H 2W9
Tel: 416-260-0280; *Fax:* 416-260-0442
e-mail: info@ampco.org
URL: www.ampco.org
Overview: A large provincial organization founded in 1975
Finances: *Funding Sources:* Membership fees
Staff: 1 staff member(s)
Membership: 42; *Fees:* Based on electrical energy usage; *Member Profile:* Companies that are major manufacturers, employers, & power consumers (represents key industries - mining, pulp & paper, automobile manufacturing, petro-chemicals, metals, consumer products, steel, etc.); *Committees:* Transition Issues; Executive
Mission: To represent Ontario's electricity-intensive companies; to ensure reliability of power supply to support the economy of Ontario & to advocate a fair & equitable pricing system for electricity; to present views on energy matters to such groups as the Ontario Energy Board, the Ontario Government, Ontario Hydro, the news media, & the general public; to provide decision makers with recommendations on resolving issues

Association of Manitoba Land Surveyors
Parent: Canadian Council of Land Surveyors
#202, 83 Gary St., Winnipeg MB R3C 4J9
Tel: 204-943-6972; *Fax:* 204-957-7602
e-mail: amls@mts.net
URL: www.amls.ca
Overview: A medium-sized provincial licensing organization founded in 1881
Finances: *Annual Operating Budget:* $100,000-$250,000; *Funding Sources:* Membership fees
Membership: 10 student + 13 lifetime + 64 individual; *Fees:* Schedule available; *Member Profile:* Commissioned land surveyor in Manitoba; *Committees:* Board of Examiners; Continuing Education; Executive Council; Legislation; Nominating; Professional Standards & Ethics; Public Relations; Restoration
Activities: *Internships:* Yes; *Speaker Service:* Yes; *Rents Mailing List:* Yes; *Library:* Yes, Open to public, open by appointment
Mission: To license qualified persons becoming commissioned land surveyors; to protect public interests concerning land boundary matters; *Affiliation(s):* Canadian Institute of Surveying & Mapping; Western Canadian Board of Examiners for Land Surveyors

Association of Manitoba Municipalities (AMM)
1910 Saskatchewan Ave. West, Portage la Prairie MB R1N 0P1
Tel: 204-857-8666; *Fax:* 204-856-2370
e-mail: amm@amm.mb.ca
URL: www.amm.mb.ca
Merged from: Union of Manitoba Municipalities; Manitoba Association of Urban Municipalities
Overview: A medium-sized provincial organization founded in 1905
Chief Officer(s):
Joe Masi, Executive Director, 204-856-2360
Ron Bell, President
Finances: *Annual Operating Budget:* $500,000-$1.5 Million; *Funding Sources:* Membership fees
Staff: 6 staff member(s)
Membership: 165 municipalities
Activities: *Library:* Yes, Not open to the public
Meetings/Conferences:
For more information see Trade Shows, Conferences and Seminars Chapter
Municipal Officials Seminar & MTCML Trade Show 2012
April 2012 Brandon, MB
Mission: To provide communications link between municipalities; to lobby for municipal governments with senior levels of government; *Member of:* Federation of Canadian Municipalities

Association of Municipal Administrators of New Brunswick (AMANB) / Association des administrateurs municipaux du Nouveau-Brunswick (AAMNB)
PO Box 30044, Stn. Prospect Plaza RPO, Fredericton NB E3B 0H8
Tel: 506-453-4229; *Fax:* 506-444-5452
e-mail: amanb@nb.aibn.com
URL: www.amanb-aamnb.ca
Overview: A medium-sized provincial organization founded in 1977
Finances: *Annual Operating Budget:* Less than $50,000
Staff: 1 staff member(s)
Membership: 226 municipal + 23 associate; *Committees:* Legislation; Education; Membership
Mission: To promote & advance status of persons employed in field of municipal administration; to advance quality of administration of municipal services; to encourage closer official & personal relationship among members to facilitate interchange of ideas & experience; to establish & maintain standards of performance for members; to assist in provision of formal training & educational facilities

Association of Municipal Administrators, Nova Scotia (AMANS)
#1106, 1809 Barrington St., Halifax NS B3J 3K8
Tel: 902-423-2215; *Fax:* 902-425-5592
e-mail: amans@eastlink.ca
URL: www.amans.ca
Overview: A medium-sized provincial organization founded in 1970
Finances: *Annual Operating Budget:* $50,000-$100,000; *Funding Sources:* Membership dues; conference surplus
Staff: 1 staff member(s)
Membership: 165; *Fees:* $175
Mission: To improve the quality of local government in Nova Scotia through the development of educational programs; to provide a forum for the exchange of ideas; to provide a resource to municipal officials; to provide service to members to improve their professional capabilities

Association of Municipal Recycling Coordinators *See* Municipal Waste Association

Association of Municipalities of Ontario (AMO)
#801, 200 University Ave., Toronto ON M5H 3C6
Tel: 416-971-9856; *Fax:* 416-971-6191
Toll-free: 877-426-6527
e-mail: amo@amo.on.ca; municom@amo.on.ca; policy@amo.on.ca
URL: www.amo.on.ca
Overview: A medium-sized provincial organization founded in 1899
Finances: *Funding Sources:* Membership fees; Sales of services & products; Sponsorships
Membership: 100-499; *Fees:* Free for affiliate members; $339 districts; $678 associates; $1,323.23 non-profit organizations; $2,644.20 commercial & government organizations; *Member Profile:* Ontario municipalities; Related non-profit organizations & private corporations
Activities: Developing policy positions; Reporting on issues; Liaising with the Ontario provincial government; Informing & educating the media & the public; Marketing services to the municipal sector; *Library:* Association of Municipalities of Ontario Resource Centre; open by appointment
Meetings/Conferences:
For more information see Trade Shows, Conferences and Seminars Chapter
Association of Municipalities of Ontario 2011 Heads of Council Training
August 2011 London, ON
Association of Municipalities of Ontario 2011 Heads of Council Forum
August 2011 London, ON

Association of Municipalities of Ontario 2011 Annual Conference
August 2011 London, ON
Association of Municipalities of Ontario 2011 Counties, Regions, & Single Tiers Conference
Other Conferences in 2011 2011, ON
Association of Municipalities of Ontario 2012 Annual Conference
August 2012, ON
Association of Municipalities of Ontario 2012 Counties, Regions, & Single Tiers Conference
Other Conferences in 2012 2012, ON
Association of Municipalities of Ontario 2013 Annual Conference
August 2013, ON
Publications: *Association of Municipalities of Ontario Annual Report*
Type: Yearbook *Frequency:* a.
AMO Watch File e-Newstter
Type: Newsletter
Mission: To support & enhance strong & effective municipal government in Ontario; To represent almost all of Ontario's 444 municipal governments; *Member of:* Federation of Canadian Municipalities

Association of New Brunswick Land Surveyors (ANBLS) / Association des arpenteurs-géomètres du Nouveau-Brunswick (AA-GN-B)
Parent: Canadian Council of Land Surveyors
#312, 212, Queen St., Fredericton NB E3B 1A8
Tel: 506-458-8266; *Fax:* 506-458-8267
e-mail: anbls@nbnet.nb.ca
URL: www.anbls.nb.ca
Overview: A small provincial licensing organization founded in 1954
Membership: 140; *Member Profile:* Individuals who comply with the requirements as specified in the New Brunswick Land Surveyors Act, 1986, & By-Laws
Activities: Increasing public awareness of the role of the association; Liaising with other professional organizations
Publications: *Surveyor-In-Training Manual*
Type: Manual
Mission: To regulate & govern the practice of land surveying in New Brunswick; To develop & maintain standards of knowledge, skill, & professional ethics

Association of Newfoundland Land Surveyors
Parent: Canadian Council of Land Surveyors
#203, 62-64 Pippy Pl., St. John's NL A1B 4H7
Tel: 709-722-2031; *Fax:* 709-722-4104
e-mail: anls@nf.aibn.com
URL: www.surveyors.nf.ca
Overview: A small provincial licensing organization founded in 1953
Committees: Annual General Meeting; Archives; Board of Examiners; By-laws & Regulations; Discipline; Executive Directory; Finance; Land Surveyors Act; Liability Insurance; Liaison; Nominating; Professional Development; Regional Representatives; Representatives
Activities: Advancing & protecting the interests of members; Improving the knowledge & skill of members; Liaising with other professional organizations
Mission: To establish & maintain standards of knowledge, skill, & professional conduct in the practice of land surveying, in order to serve & protect the public interest in Newfoundland; to regulate & govern the practice of land surveying in the province

Association of Nova Scotia Land Surveyors (ANSLS)
Parent: Canadian Council of Land Surveyors
325A Prince Albert Rd., Dartmouth NS B2Y 1N5
Tel: 902-469-7962; *Fax:* 902-469-7963
e-mail: ansls@accesswave.ca
URL: www.ansls.ca
Overview: A medium-sized provincial licensing organization founded in 1951
Finances: *Funding Sources:* Membership dues
Staff: 3 staff member(s); 30 volunteer(s)
Membership: 172 regular + 19 life + 39 retired + 24 student; *Fees:* $800 regular; $120 retired; $80 student; *Member Profile:* Examinations & apprenticeship; licensed professionals
Activities: *Internships:* Yes; *Speaker Service:* Yes; *Library:* Yes, Not open to the public
Awards: J.E.R. March Prize (Award)
J.A.H. Church Prize (Award)
G.T. Bates Scholarship (Scholarship)
Mission: To establish & maintain standards of professional ethics among its members, student members & holders of a certificate of authorization, in order that the public interest may be served & protected; & knowledge & skills among its members, student members & holders of a certificate of authorization; to regulate the practice of professional land surveying & govern the profession in accordance with the Act, the regulations & the by-laws; & to communicate & cooperate with other professional organizations for the advancement of the best interests of the surveying profession

Association of Ontario Land Economists
PO Box 97510, 364 Old Kingston Rd., Toronto ON M1C 4Z1
Tel: 416-283-0440; *Fax:* 416-283-1399
URL: aole.org
Overview: A medium-sized provincial organization founded in 1962
Finances: *Annual Operating Budget:* Less than $50,000
Staff: 1 staff member(s)
Membership: 215; *Fees:* $144.45; *Member Profile:* Architects; Certified Property Managers; Economists; Land Use Planners; Management Consultants; Mortgage Brokers; Municipal Assessors; Ontario Land Surveyors; Engineers; Property Tax Agents; Quantity Surveyors; Real Estate Brokers; Real Property Appraisers
Mission: To continue attracting membership-quality professionals engaged in land economics pursuits; to broaden & enrich the professional development of members; to promote & maintain high ethical work standards throughout our membership; to make submissions to government for improvements in law & public administration bearing on land economics

Association of Ontario Land Surveyors (AOLS)
Parent: Canadian Council of Land Surveyors
1043 McNicoll Ave., Toronto ON M1W 3W6
Tel: 416-491-9020; *Fax:* 416-491-2576
Toll-Free: 800-268-0718
e-mail: blain@aols.org
URL: www.aols.org
Overview: A medium-sized provincial licensing organization founded in 1892
Finances: *Funding Sources:* Membership fees
Staff: 8 staff member(s)
Membership: 500-999; *Fees:* $56.50 associate; *Member Profile:* Individuals with a degree in Geomatics from an accredited university program, followed bu a term of articles & professional examinations
Activities: Providing continuing education; *Speaker Service:* Yes
Mission: AOLS is responsible for the licensing and governance of professional land surveyors, in accordance with the Surveyors Act. The self-governing association ensures that public interest is paramount.

Association of Postconsumer Plastic Recyclers (APR)
#500 west, 1001 - G St. NW, Washington DC 20001 USA
Tel: 202-316-3046
e-mail: info@plasticsrecycling.org
URL: www.plasticsrecycling.org
Overview: A small national organization founded in 1992
Chief Officer(s):
Steve Alexander, Executive Director
salexander@cmrgroup4.com
Finances: *Annual Operating Budget:* $100,000-$250,000; *Funding Sources:* Related associations; membership dues
Staff: 1 staff member(s)
Membership: 103; *Fees:* $800-3,500; *Member Profile:* PCR reclaimers; *Committees:* Market Development; Technical; Executive
Activities: Design for Recyclability Programs; Champions for Change
Mission: The Association represents companies who acquire, reprocess & sell post-consumer plastic. It strives to enhance the plastics recycling industry by promoting cooperative testing for the development of new packaging, improving the quality of plastics, encouraging better recycling guidelines, & presenting awards for advancements in the industry.

Association of Power Producers of Ontario (APPrO)
PO Box 1084, Stn. F, #1602, 25 Adelaide St. East, Toronto ON M5C 3A1
Tel: 416-322-6549; *Fax:* 416-481-5785
e-mail: appro@appro.org; marketing@appro.org
URL: www.appro.org
Previous Name: Independent Power Producers Society of Ontario (IPPSO)
Overview: A medium-sized provincial organization founded in 1986
Chief Officer(s):
Jake Brooks, Executive Director
jake.brooks@appro.org
David Butters, President
david.butters@appro.org
Carole Kielly, Manager, Sales & Marketing, 416-322-6549 Ext. 222
carole.kielly@appro.org
Soraya Rivera, Manager, Registration & Data
soraya.rivera@appro.org
Karla Martinez, Manager, Office
karla.martinez@appro.org
Membership: 100+; *Member Profile:* Companies involved in the generation of electricity in Ontario, including suppliers of services & consulting services
Activities: Advocating for generators; Offering resources to assist business, government, utilities, & researchers; Organizing educational programs
Meetings/Conferences:
For more information see Trade Shows, Conferences and Seminars Chapter
Association of Power Producers of Ontario 2011: 23rd Annual Canadian Power Conference & Power Networking Centre
November 2011 Toronto, ON
Association of Power Producers of Ontario 2012: 24th Annual Canadian Power Conference
Other Conferences in 2012 2012, ON
Association of Power Producers of Ontario 2013: 25th Annual Canadian Power
Other Conferences in 2013 2013, ON
Association of Power Producers of Ontario 2014: 26th Annual Canadian Power Conference & Power Networking Centre
Other Conferences in 2014 2014, ON
Publications: *IPPSO FACTO: Magazine of the Association of Power Producers of Ontario*
Type: Magazine *Frequency:* bi-m. *Accepts Advertising* : Yes
Price: Free with Association of Power Producers of Ontario membership
Profile: Ontario, national, international, & regulatory news
APPrO [Association of Power Producers of Ontario] Conference Proceedings
Type: Yearbook *Frequency:* a. *Price:* $40
Canadian Power Directory
Type: Directory
Profile: Contact information for organizations involved in all aspects of electricity generation in Canada, such as developers, equipment & service suppliers, utilities, & resource groups
Mission: To act as the voice of electricity generators in Ontario; To support a reliable & secure electricity supply in Ontario
Environmental Activity: Promoting use of renewable energy generation

Association of Prince Edward Island Land Surveyors (APEILS)
Parent: Canadian Council of Land Surveyors
PO Box 20100, Charlottetown PE C1A 9E3
Tel: 902-566-9966
Overview: A small provincial licensing organization

Association of Professional Biology (APB)
#300, 1095 McKenzie Ave., Victoria BC V8P 2L5
Tel: 250-483-4283; *Fax:* 250-483-3439
e-mail: apbbc@apbbc.bc.ca
URL: www.apbbc.bc.ca
Overview: A medium-sized provincial organization founded in 1980
Chief Officer(s):
Megan Hanacek, Managing Director & Registrar
managingdirector@apbbc.bc.ca; registrar@apbbc.bc.ca
Committees: Constitution & By-law; Legislation & Policy; Nominations; Communications & Networking; Mentorship; Awards & Scholarships; Conference; AGM Resolutions; Practice Advisory
Activities: Providing continuing education
Awards: Ian McTaggart-Cowan Award for Excellence in Biology (Award)
To recognize significant contribution to the biological sciences in British Columbia Contact: Debbi Stanyer, R.P.Bio., Chair, Awards *Contact Detail:* #300, 1095 McKenzie Ave., Victoria, BC, V8P 2L5
W. Young Award for Integrated Resource Management (Award)
Sponsored jointly with the Association of BC Forest Professionals Contact: Debbi Stanyer, R.P.Bio., Chair, Awards *Contact Detail:* #300, 1095 McKenzie Ave., Victoria, BC, V8P 2L5

Associations/Organizations / Association of Professional Community Planners of Saskatchewan

Biology Professional of the Year Award (Award)
To honour contributions to biological science & the application of biology in a local or regional area Contact: Debbi Stanyer, R.P.Bio., Chair, Awards *Contact Detail: #300, 1095 McKenzie Ave., Victoria, BC, V8P 2L5*
Meritorious Service Awards (Award)
To recognize members of the Association of Professional Biology for outstanding contributions to the association Contact: Debbi Stanyer, R.P.Bio., Chair, Awards *Contact Detail: #300, 1095 McKenzie Ave., Victoria, BC, V8P 2L5*
Fellowship in Association of Professional Biology (Award)
A designation reserved for members who bring distinction to the profession through inspiration & mentorship to others Contact: Association of Professional Biology Office *Contact Detail: Phone: 250-483-4283, Fax: 250-483-3439, E-mail: apbbc@apbbc.bc.ca*
Meetings/Conferences:
For more information see Trade Shows, Conferences and Seminars Chapter
Association of Professional Biology 2012 Annual Applied Biology Conference & Trade Show & Annual General Meeting
Other Conferences in 2012 2012, BC
Association of Professional Biology 2013 Annual Applied Biology Conference & Trade Show & Annual General Meeting
Other Conferences in 2013 2013, BC
Publications: *Advisory Practice Bulletins [publications of the Association of Professional Biology]*
Profile: Topics include principles of stewardship, professional behaviour, & the code of ethics interpretive notes
BioNews [a publication of the Association of Professional Biology]
Type: Newsletter *Frequency:* q. *Editor:* Megan Hanacek; Barb Faggetter
Profile: Featuring a summary of the meetings of the association's board of directors & other information of interest to members
Mission: To promote & assist professional practitioners of applied biology
Environmental Activity: Advancing the application of sound biological principles to manage & conserve British Columbia's natural resources; Raising public awareness of the impact of human activities on natural resources

Association of Professional Community Planners of Saskatchewan
Parent: Canadian Institute of Planners
3803 Lakeview Ave., Regina SK S4S 1H3
e-mail: president@apcps.ca
URL: www.apcps.ca
Overview: A medium-sized provincial organization founded in 1963
Finances: *Annual Operating Budget:* Less than $50,000
Staff: 8 volunteer(s)
Membership: 24 student + 78 individual + 11 non-resident; *Committees:* Program; Education; Membership
Activities: *Speaker Service:* Yes; *Rents Mailing List:* Yes
Mission: To promote & maintain professionalism in planning field

Association of Professional Engineers & Geoscientists of British Columbia (APEGBC)
Parent: Canadian Council of Professional Engineers
#200, 4010 Regent St., Burnaby BC V5C 6N2
Tel: 604-430-8035; *Fax:* 604-430-8085
Toll-Free: 888-430-8035
e-mail: apeginfo@apeg.bc.ca; communication@apeg.bc.ca
URL: www.apeg.bc.ca
Overview: A large provincial licensing organization founded in 1920
Committees: Audit; Branches; Discipline; Executive; Geoscience; Registration; Structural Qualifications Bd.; Applications; Bd. of Examiners; Registration Task Force; Professional Renewal Task Force; ABCPF/APEGBC Joint Practice Bd.; Building Codes; Building Envelope; Consulting Practice; Environment; Investigation; Practice Review; Sustainability; Continuing Professional Dev.; Editorial Bd.; Mentoring; Standing Awards; Div. for Advancement of Woman in Engineering & Geoscience; Div. of Engineers & Geoscientists in the Resource Sector; Municipal Engineers Div.; Div. of Environmental Professionals
Activities: Maintaining practice standards; Upholding the code of ethics; Publishing brochures, position papers, & other association documents; Promoting the professions; Protecting members' interests; Establishing the Engineers Benevolent Fund to assist members; Setting up Foundation Trustees to support education through scholarships & bursaries & to promote professional development opportunities
Meetings/Conferences:
For more information see Trade Shows, Conferences and Seminars Chapter
Association of Professional Engineers & Geoscientists of British Columbia Seminar: Hydraulic Network Modeling of Sanitary Sewer Collection Systems
June 2011 Vancouver, BC
Association of Professional Engineers & Geoscientists of British Columbia 2011 Conference & Annual General Meeting: Growing the Professional Community
October 2011 Kelowna, BC
Association of Professional Engineers & Geoscientists of British Columbia 2012 Conference & Annual General Meeting
Other Conferences in 2012 2012, BC
Association of Professional Engineers & Geoscientists of British Columbia 2013 Conference & Annual General Meeting
Other Conferences in 2013 2013, BC
Publications: *APEGBC [Association of Professional Engineers & Geoscientists of British Columbia] Membership Directory*
Type: Directory
Profile: Rosters of professional engineers & professional geoscientists with contact information & scope of practice
Association of Professional Engineers & Geoscientists of British Columbia Report on Members' Compensation & Benefits
Profile: Compensation survey results
Innovation [a publication of the Association of Professional Engineers & Geoscientists of British Columbia]
Type: Magazine *Frequency:* bi-m. *Accepts Advertising:* Yes
Editor: Melinda Lau (mlau@apeg.bc.ca)
Profile: Information circulated to more than 26,000 British Columbia registered professional engineers & geoscientists, industry & government reporesentatives, educational institutions, as well as the general public
Connections E-news [a publication of the Association of Professional Engineers & Geoscientists of British Columbia]
Type: Newsletter *Frequency:* m.
Profile: Currents happenings in the association & in the professions of engineers & geoscientists in British Columbia
Association of Professional Engineers & Geoscientists of British Columbia Annual Report
Type: Yearbook *Frequency:* a.
Profile: A yearly review, featuring reports from the association's executive director & president, as well as the auditor
Bylaws of the Association [a publication of the Association of Professional Engineers & Geoscientists of British Columbia]
Type: Booklet
Profile: Information about items such as conduct of meetings, election of council, finances, & membership
APEGBC [Association of Professional Engineers & Geoscientists of British Columbia] Professional Practice Guidelines
Type: Guides
Profile: Examples of guidelines are as follows: APEGBC/CEBC Budget Guidelines for Engineering Services; Guidelines for Terrain Stability Assessments in the Forest Sector; & Guidelines for Legislated Landslide Assessments for Proposed Residential Development in British Columbia
Association of Professional Engineers & Geoscientists of British Columbia Technical Bulletins
Type: Bulletins
Profile: Examples of technical bulletins are as follows: Assessment of Seismic Slope Stability; Engineering Modifications to Fire Tested & Listed Assemblies; & Addressing Smoke & CO Control in Elevator Machine Rooms
Mission: To protect the public interest in matters related to geoscience & engineering; To regulate & govern the professions of professional engineers & geoscientists in British Columbia, according to the Engineers & Geoscientists Act; To strive for professional excellence, by establishing academic, experience, & professional practice standards
Environmental Activity: Establishing an Environment Committee to provide advice on environmental matters

Association of Professional Engineers & Geoscientists of Manitoba (APEGM)
Parent: Canadian Council of Professional Engineers
850A Pembina Hwy., Winnipeg MB R3M 2M7
Tel: 204-474-2736; *Fax:* 204-474-5960
Toll-Free: 866-227-9600
e-mail: apegm@apegm.mb.ca
URL: www.apegm.mb.ca
Overview: A large provincial organization founded in 1920
Finances: *Annual Operating Budget:* $500,000-$1.5 Million
Staff: 8 staff member(s)
Membership: 3,500; *Fees:* $218
Mission: To serve & protect the public interest by governing & advancing the practice of engineering in accordance with the Engineering Profession Act of Manitoba
Environmental Activity: Sustainable Development Task Force

Association of Professional Engineers & Geoscientists of New Brunswick (APEGNB) / Association des ingénieurs et géoscientifiques du Nouveau-Brunswick (AINB)
Parent: Canadian Council of Professional Engineers
183 Hanwell Rd., Fredericton NB E3B 2R2
Tel: 506-458-8083; *Fax:* 506-451-9629
e-mail: info@apegnb.com
URL: www.apegnb.com
Overview: A large provincial licensing organization founded in 1920
Finances: *Funding Sources:* Membership fees
Staff: 8 staff member(s)
Membership: 3,400; *Fees:* $216; *Committees:* Executive; Councillors; Admissions; Board of Examiners; Discipline; Internship; Legislation; Nominating; Professional Condut
Activities: *Awareness Events:* Fellowship Awards Dinner
Mission: To establish, maintain & develop standards of knowledge & skill, qualification & practice, & professional ethics; to promote public awareness of the role of the association

Association of Professional Engineers & Geoscientists of Newfoundland See Professional Engineers & Geoscientists Newfoundland & Labrador

Association of Professional Engineers & Geoscientists of Saskatchewan (APEGS)
Parent: Canadian Council of Professional Engineers
#104, 2255 - 13 Ave., Regina SK S4P 0V6
Tel: 306-525-9547; *Fax:* 306-525-0851
Toll-Free: 800-500-9547
e-mail: apegs@apegs.sk.ca
URL: www.apegs.sk.ca
Overview: A large provincial licensing organization founded in 1930
Finances: *Annual Operating Budget:* $500,000-$1.5 Million; *Funding Sources:* Membership dues
Staff: 8 staff member(s); 125 volunteer(s)
Membership: 3,070; *Committees:* Education Board (Professional Development, Student Development, Innovators Planning); Governance Board (Consulting Practice, Discipline, Investigation, Professional Liability Insurance, Registration, Act Awareness); Image & Identity Board (Communications & Public Relations, Internal Affairs, Professional Edge, Women in Engineering); Issues Management Board (Forward Planning, Issues Management, Legislative Review)
Activities: *Internships:* Yes; *Speaker Service:* Yes
Mission: To achieve a safe & prosperous future through engineering & geoscience

Association of Professional Engineers of Nova Scotia (APENS)
Parent: Canadian Council of Professional Engineers
PO Box 129, 1355 Barrington St., Halifax NS B3J 2M4
Tel: 902-429-2250; *Fax:* 902-423-9769
Toll-Free: 888-802-7367
e-mail: info@apens.ns.ca
URL: www.apens.ns.ca
Overview: A medium-sized provincial licensing organization founded in 1920
Finances: *Annual Operating Budget:* $500,000-$1.5 Million; *Funding Sources:* Membership dues
Staff: 7 staff member(s); 230 volunteer(s)
Membership: 4,300; *Fees:* $167; *Committees:* Public Relations; Student Affairs; Awards; Building; Professional Development; Professional Practice; Construction; Consulting Practice; Zones; Engineering Week; Finance; Publications; Information Highway; Salary; Employee Engineers
Activities: Board of Examiners; Discipline of Members; Act Enforcement; Environment Committee; *Awareness Events:* National Engineering Week, 1st week in March; *Internships:* Yes; *Speaker Service:* Yes
Mission: To establish, maintain & develop standards of knowledge & skill, standards of qualification & practice, standards of professional ethics; to promote public awareness of the role of the association

Association of Professional Engineers of Ontario See Professional Engineers Ontario

Association of Professional Engineers of Prince Edward Island (APEPEI)
Parent: Canadian Council of Professional Engineers
549 North River Rd., Charlottetown PE C1E 1J6
Tel: 902-566-1268; *Fax:* 902-566-5551
e-mail: info@engineerspei.com
URL: www.engineerspei.com
Also Known As: Engineers PEI
Overview: A small provincial licensing charitable organization founded in 1955
Finances: *Annual Operating Budget:* $100,000-$250,000; *Funding Sources:* Membership dues
Staff: 2 staff member(s); 35 volunteer(s)
Membership: 275; *Fees:* $200; *Member Profile:* Open to those with B.Sc. (Engineering) from an accredited institution & four years acceptable engineering experience
Activities: Bridge Building Contest for students, grades 5-12; *Awareness Events:* National Engineering Month, March; *Internships:* Yes
Awards: Friend of the Profession Award (Award)
Honorary Life Members (Award)
Engineering Award for Excellence (Award)
Young Engineer Achievement Award (Award)
Community Service Award (Award)
The Ralph L. Woodside Memorial Award for Service to the Profession (Award)
Mission: Engineers PEI regulates the practice of professional engineering in the province, with authority over members, licensees, engineers-in-training, & holders of certificates of authorization.

Association of Professional Engineers of the Government of Québec (Ind.) *Voir* Association professionnelle des ingénieurs du gouvernement du Québec (ind.)

Association of Professional Engineers of the Yukon Territory (APEY)
Parent: Canadian Council of Professional Engineers
312B Hanson St., Whitehorse YT Y1A 1Y6
Tel: 867-667-6727; *Fax:* 867-668-2142
e-mail: staff@apey.yk.ca
URL: www.apey.yk.ca
Overview: A medium-sized provincial licensing organization founded in 1955
Finances: *Funding Sources:* Membership fees
Fees: $240 + $45 for a stamp + GST, Registered Professional Engineer; $72.50 + GST Engineer in Training; *Member Profile:* Persons with a degree in engineering from an accredited university & 4 years of experience
Activities: Annual Bridge Building Competition; Professional development; National Secondary Professional Liability Insurance Program; *Awareness Events:* Engineering Week
Awards: APEY Educational Award (Scholarship)
Publications: *Association of Professional Engineers of Yukon Newsletter*
Type: Newsletter *Frequency:* 3 pa
Mission: To establish, maintain & develop standards of knowledge & skill, standards of qualification & practice & standards of professional ethics; to promote public awareness of the role of the association

Association of Professional Engineers, Geologists & Geophysicists of Alberta (APEGGA)
Parent: Canadian Council of Professional Engineers
Scotia One, #1500, 10060 Jasper Ave. NW, Edmonton AB T5J 4A2
Tel: 780-426-3990; *Fax:* 780-426-1877
Toll-Free: 800-661-7020
e-mail: email@apegga.org
URL: www.apegga.org
Overview: A large provincial licensing organization founded in 1920
Membership: 58,000+
Activities: Determining disciplinary actions, when necessary, for members; Providing continuing professional development activities; Offering networking opportunities; Raising awareness of achievements in engineering & geoscience, as well as science, math, & technology, during National Engineering & Geoscience Week; Conducting salary surveys
Awards: Teacher Awards Program (Award)
Recognizing excellence in the teaching of science & math
Awards & Scholarships Program (Award)
Funding Alberta engineering & geoscience education
Summit Awards (Award)
Recognizing personal & professional contributions

Meetings/Conferences:
For more information see Trade Shows, Conferences and Seminars Chapter
Association of Professional Engineers, Geologists & Geophysicists of Alberta 2012 Annual Conference & Annual General Meeting
April 2012, AB
Association of Professional Engineers, Geologists & Geophysicists of Alberta 2013 Annual Conference & Annual General Meeting
April 2013, AB
Publications: *E-PEG*
Type: Newsletter *Frequency:* m. *Editor:* George Lee (glee@apegga.org)
Profile: Updates on APEGGA events & news
Association of Professional Engineers, Geologists & Geophysicists of Alberta Annual Report
Type: Yearbook *Frequency:* a.
Profile: A review of activities, plus financial information
Association of Professional Engineers, Geologists & Geophysicists of Alberta Business Plan
Type: Yearbook *Frequency:* a.
Profile: Information about strategic & operational priorities & core activities for the forthcoming year
Mission: To register & set practice standards & coes of professional conduct & ethics for professional engineers, geologists, & geophysicists in Alberta, according to The Engineering, Geological and Geophysical Professions Act

Association of Professional Engineers, Geologists & Geophysicists of the Northwest Territories & Nunavut (NAPEGG)
Parent: Canadian Council of Professional Engineers
#201, 4817 - 49 St., Yellowknife NT X1A 3S7
Tel: 867-920-4055; *Fax:* 867-873-4058
e-mail: napegg@tamarack.nt.ca
URL: www.napegg.nt.ca
Overview: A medium-sized provincial licensing organization founded in 1978
Finances: *Annual Operating Budget:* $250,000-$500,000; *Funding Sources:* Membership fees & dues
Staff: 3 staff member(s); 100 volunteer(s)
Membership: 397 + 781 Licensees; *Fees:* $300 registration; $220 annual dues; *Member Profile:* Accredited degree in engineering, geology or geophysics followed by 4 years of directly related experience in practice of engineering, geology & geophysics; must pass Association's Professional Practice Examination; *Committees:* Council; Executive; Discipline; Membership/Enforcement; Professional Development; Public Relations; Newsletter; Professional Practice; Nominating; Planning; Environment; Finance
Activities: *Awareness Events:* National Engineering Week, March; National Science & Technology Week, Oct.
Mission: To regulate the practices of our professions; to establish & maintain standards in order to serve & protect the public

Association of Professional Geoscientists of Nova Scotia (APGNS)
PO Box 8541, Halifax NS B3K 5M3
Tel: 902-420-9928
e-mail: nkeeping@dal.ca
URL: www.apgns.ns.ca
Overview: A small provincial organization
Chief Officer(s):
Howard Donohoe, P.Geo, Executive Director & Registrar
howarddonohoe@eastlink.ca
Fees: $200 Member-in-Training; $400 License to Practice; $450 Member;
Publications: *Yukon Tourism Education Council Newsletter*
Type: Newsletter *Frequency:* irreg.
Mission: To ensure high standards of practice within the geoscience community; To promote & advance the profession; To work with associated organizations across Canada to facilitate the registration of APGNS members in other provinces

Association of Professional Geoscientists of Ontario (APGO)
#913, 60 St. Clair Ave. East, Toronto ON M4T 1N5
Tel: 416-203-2746
Toll-Free: 877-557-2746
e-mail: info@apgo.net
URL: www.apgo.net
Overview: A small provincial organization founded in 2000
Chief Officer(s):
Andrea Y. Waldie, P.Geo., APGO Executive Director & Registrar

Greg Finn, Ph.D., P.Geo., President
Stephen Wilson, P.Geo., Vice-President
Kristin E. Hansen, M.Sc., P. Geo.,, Treasurer
Finances: *Funding Sources:* Sponsorships
Membership: 1,389 practising members + 12 temporary members + 10 limited members + 12 non-practising members + 60 geoscientists in training + 24 student members; *Committees:* Discipline; Complaints; Registration; Executive; Finance; Nomination; Non-Member Appointment; Insurance Advisory; Governance; Professional Practice; Enforcement & Compliance; Communications & Public Awareness
Activities: Reporting to Ontario's Minister of Northern Development & Mines; Accepting registration for the licensure to practice professional geoscience in Ontario; Disciplining members for professional misconduct; Organizing continuing professional development programs
Publications: *Field Notes: Association of Professional Geoscientists of Ontario Newsletter*
Type: Newsletter *Frequency:* bi-m. *Editor:* Wendy Diaz, M.Sc., P.Geo.
Profile: Association reports, meetings, awards, & news for all APGO members
Association of Professional Geoscientists of Ontario Annual Report
Type: Yearbook *Frequency:* a.
Mission: To govern the practice of professional geoscience in Ontario, in accordance with The Professional Geoscientists Act, 2000, in order to protect the public & investors; to develop standards of knowledge & skills for association members; *Affiliation(s):* Canadian Council of Professional Geoscientists; Canadian Geoscience Standards Board; National Professional Practice & Ethics Exam Advisory Committee; CCPG Licensure Compliance Committee

Association of Quantity Surveyors of Alberta (AQSA)
Kingsway Mall, PO Box 34062, Edmonton AB T5G 3G4
Tel: 780-628-7324
e-mail: info@aqsa.ca
URL: www.aqsa.ca
Overview: A small provincial organization founded in 1979
Member Profile: Professional Quantity Surveyors (PQS) & Construction Estimator Certifieds (CEC), from areas such as construction companies, private practice, & government organizations, in the provinces of Alberta, Saskatchewan, & Manitoba, as well as the Northwest Territories & Nunavut
Activities: Offering continuing professional development programs; Facilitating networking opportunities & the exchange of knowledge; Providing professional costing, value, & estimating advice; Disciplining members; Collaborating with other organizations;
Publications: *Association of Quantity Surveyors of Alberta Newsletter*
Type: Newsletter *Price:* Free with association membership
Profile: Association reports, chapter news, forthcoming events, & Canadian Institute of Quantity Surveyors (CIQS) updates
Consultants Directory [a publication of the Association of Quantity Surveyors of Alberta]
Type: Directory
Profile: Listing of firms, with one or more principals who are Professional Quantity Surveyors (PQS) &, which are operating in private practice in Alberta, Saskatchewan, Manitoba, the Northwest Territories, or Nunavut
Mission: To promote & advance the professional status of quantity surveyors & certified cost estimators; to establish & maintain high standards of professional competence; *Member of:* International Cost Engineering Council; Pacific Association of Quantity Surveyors; *Affiliation(s):* Canadian Institute of Quantity Surveyors (CIQS); Australian Institute of Quantity Surveyors (Reciprocal Agreement); Canadian Construction Association (Reciprocal Agreement); Appraisal Institute of Canada (Memoranda of Understanding); Royal Institution of Chartered Surveyors - Canada (Memoranda of Understanding)

Association of Québec Municipal Engineers *Voir* Association des ingénieurs municipaux du Québec

Association of Registered Professional Foresters of New Brunswick (ARPFNB) / Association des forestiers agréés du Nouveau-Brunswick (AFANB)
#221, 1350 Regent St., Fredericton NB E3C 2G6
Tel: 506-452-6933; *Fax:* 506-450-3128
e-mail: info@arpfnb.ca
URL: www.arpfnb.ca
Overview: A small provincial organization founded in 1937

Associations/Organizations / The Association of Science and Engineering Technology Professionals of Alberta

Membership: 300; *Member Profile:* Registered Professional Foresters eligible to practice Forestry in New Brunswick, including forestry consultants, & federal & provincial public servants
Activities: Improving forestry practice in New Brunswick; Increasing understanding of forestry issues; Promoting the knowledge & skill of association members
Mission: To manage the forest resources of New Brunswick for the sustained development of these resources; to assure the proficiency & competency of Registered Professional Foresters in New Brunswick; Affiliation(s): Canadian Federation of Professional Foresters Association (CFPFA)

The Association of Science and Engineering Technology Professionals of Alberta (ASET)
Parent: Canadian Council of Technicians & Technologists
Phipps-McKinnon Building, #1630, 10020 - 101A Ave., Edmonton AB T5J 3G2
Tel: 780-425-0626; *Fax:* 780-424-5053
Toll-Free: 800-272-5619
e-mail: asetadmin@aset.ab.ca
URL: www.aset.ab.ca
Previous Name: Alberta Society of Engineering Technologists
Overview: A large provincial organization founded in 1963
Finances: *Annual Operating Budget:* $500,000-$1.5 Million
Staff: 11 staff member(s)
Membership: 16,800
Activities: Engineering Technology Scholarship Foundation of Alberta (ETSFA) scholarships; *Speaker Service:* Yes
Mission: To benefit the public & the profession by regulating & promoting safe, high quality professional technology practice; focus is on the engineering technology, applied science & information technology fields; issues credentials to qualified individuals & accredits training programs

Association of Supervisors of Public Health Inspectors (Ontario) (ASPHIO)
c/o Durham Region Health Dept., 101 Consumers Dr., 2nd Fl., Whitby ON L1N 1C4
Tel: 905-723-3818; *Fax:* 905-666-1887
e-mail: Ken.Gorman@region.durham.on.ca
Overview: A medium-sized provincial organization founded in 1982
Chief Officer(s):
Ted Devine, Secretary
ted.devine@smdhu.org
Joe LaMarca, Treasurer
Joe.Lamarca@york.ca
Ken Gorman, President
Finances: *Annual Operating Budget:* Less than $50,000; *Funding Sources:* Membership fees
Staff: 4 volunteer(s)
Membership: 116; *Fees:* $75; *Member Profile:* Persons immediately responsible for giving direction to Public Health Inspection Programs of Local Health Agencies in Ontario; voting privileges will be restricted to one vote per local official agency
Activities: *Speaker Service:* Yes; *Rents Mailing List:* Yes
Mission: To provide a recognized organization which can bring together persons immediately responsible for public health inspection programs for discussion on matters of public interest; to promote public health inspection programs affecting the Ministry of Health, other ministers & local health agencies; to represent all members in liaison with other associations or societies; to provide regular updates of information on the activities of the association to each of the directors of member health units; to act as a resource group on all matters that fall within the competence of the association; *Member of:* Ontario Public Health Association; Affiliation(s): Association of Local Official Health Agencies (alPHa)

Association of the Chemical Profession of Alberta (ACPA)
PO Box 21017, Edmonton AB T6R 2V4
Tel: 780-413-0004; *Fax:* 780-413-0076
e-mail: ACPAoffice2004@pchem.ca
URL: www.pchem.ca
Overview: A small national organization founded in 1992
Chief Officer(s):
Roger Cowles, President
Fees: $150 Professional Chemist; $75 Chemist-in-Training; $50 Retired Member. Associate Member; Student Members free
Publications: Association of the Chemical Profession of Alberta Newsletter
Type: Newsletter *Frequency:* irreg.

Mission: To provides a legal definition of chemistry; To promote & increase the knowledge, skills, & proficiency of members in all things relating to chemistry

Association of the Chemical Profession of Ontario (ACPO)
#1801, 1 Yonge St., Toronto ON M5E 1W7
Tel: 416-364-4609; *Fax:* 416-369-0515
Toll-Free: 800-260-0992
e-mail: info@acpo.on.ca
URL: www.acpo.on.ca/
Overview: A medium-sized provincial organization founded in 1958
Finances: *Annual Operating Budget:* Less than $50,000
Membership: 1,200; *Fees:* $40-$140; *Member Profile:* Honours degree with work experience deemed acceptable by the association; 3-year chemistry degree with 5 years experience; 6 years experience & written examinations set by the association; *Committees:* Professional Affairs; Membership; Environmental
Activities: *Speaker Service:* Yes
Mission: To promote & increase the knowledge, skills & proficiency of its members in all things relating to chemistry & to establish standards of chemical practice for its members; provides a legal definition of chemistry & of those practising chemistry in Ontario

Association of University Forestry Schools of Canada (AUFSC) / Association des écoles forestières universitaires du Canada
Parent: Association of Universities & Colleges of Canada
c/o School of Forestry, Lakehead University, 955 Oliver Rd., Thunder Bay ON P7B 5E1
Tel: 807-343-8511
Overview: A medium-sized national organization
Membership: 9

Association of World Citizens & World Citizens Foundation (AWC)
#224, 55 New Montgomery St., San Francisco CA 94105 USA
Tel: 415-541-9610; *Fax:* 650-745-0640
e-mail: info@worldcitizens.org
URL: www.worldcitizens.org
Previous Name: World Citizens Assembly
Overview: A large international organization founded in 1975
Chief Officer(s):
Douglas Mattern, President
Martha Killebrew, Treasurer
Finances: *Annual Operating Budget:* Less than $50,000
Staff: 15 volunteer(s)
Membership: 5,000; 130 World Citizen Centres in 50 countries; *Fees:* US$25; *Committees:* Commissions on - Environment Education; Global Security; Human Rights & Alternative Economics
Activities: *Internships:* Yes; *Speaker Service:* Yes; *Library:* Yes
Mission: To abolish war & build a world community; to promote global consciousness

Association of Yukon Communities (AYC)
#15, 1114 - 1st Ave., Whitehorse YT Y1A 1A3
Tel: 867-668-4388; *Fax:* 867-668-7574
e-mail: ayc@northwestel.net
URL: www.ayc.yk.ca
Previous Name: Association of Yukon Municipalities
Overview: A medium-sized provincial organization founded in 1974
Finances: *Annual Operating Budget:* $100,000-$250,000; *Funding Sources:* Membership dues; government
Staff: 1 staff member(s)
Membership: 52; *Fees:* Schedule available; *Member Profile:* Yukon communities & elected officials; *Committees:* Energy; Municipal Act Review
Mission: To further the establishment of responsible government at the community level; to provide a united approach to issues affecting local governments; to advance ambitions & goals of member communities by developing a shared common vision of the future; to represent members in matters affecting them & the welfare of their communities; to provide programs & services of common interest & benefit to members; Affiliation(s): Federation of Canadian Municipalities

Association of Yukon Municipalities *See* Association of Yukon Communities

Association ontarienne des éleveurs de bovins *See* Ontario Cattlemen's Association

Association paritaire pour la santé et la sécurité du travail - Administration provinciale
#10, 1220, boul Lebourgneuf, Québec QC G2K 2G4
Tél: 418-624-4801; *Téléc:* 418-624-4858
Courriel: apssap@apssap.qc.ca
URL: www.apssap.qc.ca
Aperçu: *Dimension:* moyenne; *Envergure:* provinciale
Mission: L'Association a pour mission de supporter la prise en charge paritaire de la prévention en matière de santé, de sécurité et d'intégrité physique des personnes du secteur de l'Administration provinciale.

Association paritaire pour la santé et la sécurité du travail - Affaires municipales (APSAM)
#710, 715, carré Victoria, Montréal QC H2Y 2H7
Tél: 514-849-8373; *Téléc:* 514-849-8873
Ligne sans frais: 800-465-1754
Courriel: info@apsam.com
URL: www.apsam.com
Aperçu: *Dimension:* moyenne; *Envergure:* provinciale; *fondée en* 1985
Finances: *Budget de fonctionnement annuel:* $500,000-$1.5 Million
Membre: 3 000
Activités: *Service de conférenciers:* Oui; *Listes de destinataires:* Oui; *Bibliothèque:* Oui, rendez-vous
Mission: Développer et promouvoir les moyens nécessaires pour protéger la santé et la sécurité des personnes à l'emploi des municipalités et des organismes qui y sont reliés, dans l'ensemble du Québec; fournir aux employeurs et travailleurs des municipalités du Québec des services de formation, d'information, de recherche et de conseil

Association paritaire pour la santé et la sécurité du travail - Affaires sociales
#950, 5100, rue Sherbrooke est, Montréal QC H1V 3R9
Tél: 514-253-6871; *Téléc:* 514-253-1443
Ligne sans frais: 800-361-4528
Courriel: info@asstsas.qc.ca
URL: www.asstsas.qc.ca
Aperçu: *Dimension:* moyenne; *Envergure:* provinciale
Mission: Une association sectorielle paritaire vouée exclusivement à la prévention en santé et en sécurité du travail dans le secteur de la santé et des services sociaux

Association paritaire pour la santé et la sécurité du travail - Habillement
#301, 2271, boul Fernand-Lafontaine, Longueuil QC J4G 2R7
Tél: 450-651-4348; *Téléc:* 450-442-2332
Courriel: info@aspme.org
URL: www.asp-habillement.org/
Également appelé: ASP Habillement
Aperçu: *Dimension:* grande; *Envergure:* provinciale; *Organisme sans but lucratif; fondée en* 1986
Membre(s) du bureau directeur:
Alain Plourde, Directeur général
Finances: *Budget de fonctionnement annuel:* $500,000-$1.5 Million
Personnel: 7 membre(s) du personnel
Activités: *Stagiaires:* Oui; *Service de conférenciers:* Oui
Mission: Specializes in the prevention of work-related injuries in the apparel sector.

Association paritaire pour la santé et la sécurité du travail - Imprimerie et activités connexes
#450, 7450, boul Galeries d'Anjou, Anjou QC H1M 3M3
Tél: 514-355-8282; *Téléc:* 514-355-6818
URL: www.aspimprimerie.qc.ca
Également appelé: ASP Inprimerie
Aperçu: *Dimension:* moyenne; *Envergure:* provinciale; *Organisme sans but lucratif; fondée en* 1983
Finances: *Budget de fonctionnement annuel:* $500,000-$1.5 Million
Personnel: 8 membre(s) du personnel
Membre: 1-99
Activités: Formations de groupe: Action sur les machines: Évacuation en cas d'incendie; Introduction à la prévention; Superviser avec diligence; Enquête accident; Formateur chariot; Formation de formateurs SIMDUT; *Stagiaires:* Oui; *Bibliothèque:* Oui, rendez-vous
Mission: Fournir aux employeurs et aux travailleurs du secteur imprimerie et activités connexes des services d'information, de formation, de conseil et de recherche pour favoriser la prise en charge de la prévention dans les entreprises

Association paritaire pour la santé et la sécurité du travail - Mines et services miniers (APSM)
#570, 979, av de Bourgogne, Sainte-Foy QC G1W 2L4
Tél: 418-653-1933; *Téléc:* 418-653-7726
Courriel: info@apsam.com
URL: www.apsam.com
Aperçu: Dimension: moyenne; *Envergure: provinciale; fondée en 1986*
Finances: Budget de fonctionnement annuel: $500,000-$1.5 Million
Membre: 100; *Montant de la cotisation:* .13$/100$ de masse salariale;

Association paritaire pour la santé et la sécurité du travail - Produits en métal et électriques
#301, 2271, boul Fernand-Lafontaine, Longueuil QC J4G 2R7
Tél: 450-442-7763; *Téléc:* 450-442-2332
Courriel: jarsenault@aspme.org
URL: www.aspme.org
Aperçu: Dimension: moyenne; *Envergure: provinciale*

Association paritaire pour la santé et la sécurité du travail - Services automobiles
#150, 8, rue de la Place-Du-Commerce, Brossard QC J4W 3H2
Tél: 450-672-9330; *Téléc:* 450-672-4835
Ligne sans frais: 800-363-2344
Courriel: info@autoprevention.qc.ca
URL: www.autoprevention.qc.ca
Également appelé: Auto Prévention
Aperçu: Dimension: moyenne; *Envergure: provinciale*
Mission: Depuis 1983, Auto Prévention aide les travailleurs et les employeurs du secteur des services automobiles à prendre en charge la santé et la sécurité au travail, afin d'éliminer les risques d'accidents et de maladies professionnelles.

Association pour l'amélioration des cultures biologiques (international) *See* Organic Crop Improvement Association (International)

Association pour l'amélioration des sols et des récoltes de l'Ontario *See* Ontario Soil & Crop Improvement Association

Association pour l'amélioration du sol et des cultures du Nouveau-Brunswick *See* New Brunswick Soil & Crop Improvement Association

Association pour l'enseignement de la géographie et de l'environnement en Ontario *See* Ontario Association for Geographic & Environmental Education

Association pour la prévention de la contamination de l'air et du sol (APCAS) / Air Waste Management Association - Québec Section
CP 49527, 5122, Côte des Neiges, Montréal QC H3T 2A5
Tél: 514-355-2675; *Téléc:* 514-355-4159
Courriel: apcas@apcas.qc.ca
URL: www.apcas.qc.ca
Aperçu: Dimension: petite; *Envergure: provinciale*
Finances: Budget de fonctionnement annuel: Moins de $50,000
Membre: 100-499
Mission: La formation professionnelle dans les domaines de la qualité et du traitement de l'air, de la gestion des matières résiduelles, des sols contaminés

Association pour la prévention de la contamination de l'air et du sol *See* Air & Waste Management Association

Association pour la prévention des infections à l'hôpital et dans la communauté - Canada *See* Community & Hospital Infection Control Association Canada

Association pour la protection des intérêts des consommateurs de la Côté-Nord
872, rue Depuyjalon, 2e étage, Baie-Comeau QC G5C 1N1
Tél: 418-589-7324; *Téléc:* 418-589-7088
Courriel: apic@globetrotter.net
Également appelé: APIC Côte-Nord
Aperçu: Dimension: petite; *Envergure: locale; Organisme sans but lucratif; fondée en 1978*
Finances: Budget de fonctionnement annuel: $50,000-$100,000
Personnel: 2 membre(s) du personnel; 12 bénévole(s)
Membre: 1199; *Montant de la cotisation:* 5$ individu
Activités: Aide de planification budgétaire; ateliers; centre de documentation; traitement des plaintes; informations;
Bibliothèque: Oui
Mission: Promouvoir les intérêts des consommateurs dans tous les aspects de la consommation; grouper les consommateurs de la région Côte-Nord; *Membre de:* Coalition des associations de consommateurs du Québec

Association pour la santé publique de l'Ontario *See* Ontario Public Health Association

Association pour la santé publique du Québec (ASPQ) / Québec Public Health Association
Parent: Canadian Public Health Association
#200, 4126, rue St-Denis, Montréal QC H2W 2M5
Tél: 514-528-5811; *Téléc:* 514-528-5590
Courriel: info@aspq.org
URL: www.aspq.org
Aperçu: Dimension: moyenne; *Envergure: provinciale; Organisme sans but lucratif; fondée en 1943*
Membre(s) du bureau directeur:
Lucie Granger, Directrice Générale, 514-528-5811 Ext. 225
Martine Deschênes, Adjointe administrative
Finances: Budget de fonctionnement annuel: $100,000-$250,000
Personnel: 2 membre(s) du personnel
Membre: 450; *Montant de la cotisation:* 46-110 régulier; 12-29 étudiant; 144-691 corptatif
Prix, Bouses: Prix Jean-Pierre Bélanger (Prix)
Mission: Préserver, améliorer et maintenir la santé publique: en identifiant les problèmes de santé publique; en initiant, participant et promouvant la recherche en santé publique; en vulgarisant les pratiques et principes tendant à préserver, améliorer et maintenir la santé publique; en participant à l'élaboration de politiques opérationnelles; en incitant et aidant au perfectionnement des membres; en publiant pour les membres des travaux scientifiques ou autres destinés à améliorer leur compétence; en informant les membres des derniers développements et découvertes en santé publique

Association pour les droits des non-fumeurs *See* Non-Smokers' Rights Association

Association professionnelle des géographes du Québec (APGQ)
Dept. de géographie - UQAM, CP 8888, Succ. Centre-Ville, Montréal QC H3C 3P8
Tél: 514-987-3000; *Téléc:* 514-987-6784
Courriel: apgq@uqam.ca
Aperçu: Dimension: petite; *Envergure: provinciale; fondée en 1962*
Membre(s) du bureau directeur:
Guy Mercier, Président
Guy.Mercier@ggr.ulaval.ca
Montant de la cotisation: 85$ (membre régulier); *Comités:* Scientifique; Environnement; Affaires internationales; Recrutement
Activités: Représentation auprès des gouvernements et des entreprises privées; bottin des membres; colloque annuel, congrès
Mission: Promouvoir la géographie comme discipline de même que la pratique professionnelle de ses membres

Association professionnelle des ingénieurs du gouvernement du Québec (ind.) (APIGQ) / Association of Professional Engineers of the Government of Québec (Ind.)
Complexe Iberville, #600, 2954, boul Laurier, Sainte-Foy QC G1V 4T2
Tél: 418-683-3633; *Téléc:* 418-683-6878
Courriel: lepont@apigq.qc.ca
URL: www.apigq.qc.ca
Aperçu: Dimension: moyenne; *Envergure: provinciale; fondée en 1986*
Membre(s) du bureau directeur:
Michel Gagnon, ing., Président
Finances: Budget de fonctionnement annuel: $250,000-$500,000
Personnel: 2 membre(s) du personnel
Membre: 1 000; *Critères d'admissibilite:* Ingénieur; *Comités:* CE (Comité exécutif); CRS (Conseil des représentants de section)
Mission: Association professionnelle des ingénieurs du Gouvernement du Québec.

Association provinciale des constructeurs d'habitations du Québec inc. (APCHQ) / Provincial Association of Home Builders of Québec
5930, boul Louis-H.-Lafontaine, Anjou QC H1M 1S7
Tél: 514-353-9960; *Téléc:* 514-353-4825
Ligne sans frais: 800-468-8160
URL: www.apchq.com
Aperçu: Dimension: moyenne; *Envergure: provinciale; fondée en 1950*
Membre(s) du bureau directeur:
Marc Savard, Directeur général
nsavard@apchqmontreal.ca
Frédéric Birtz, Directeur des opérations
fbirtz@apchqmontreal.ca
Membre: 3 600
Mission: Depuis 1997, l'APCHQ est la plus importante gestionnaire de mutuelles de prévention du domaine de la construction. Étant le seul agent négociateur patronal des relations de travail dans le secteur résidentiel, elle défend les intérêts de quelque 12 000 employeurs et 25 000 travailleurs

Association pulmonaire du Canada *See* Canadian Lung Association

Association pulmonaire du Nouveau-Brunswick *See* New Brunswick Lung Association

Association pulmonaire du Québec *See* Québec Lung Association

Association québécoise d'urbanisme (AQU)
CP 655, Succ. Saint-Jacques, Montréal QC H3C 2T8
Tél: 514-277-0228; *Téléc:* 514-277-0093
Courriel: info@aqu.qc.ca
URL: www.aqu.qc.ca
Aperçu: Dimension: petite; *Envergure: provinciale; Organisme sans but lucratif; fondée en 1978*
Membre(s) du bureau directeur:
Noël Pelletier, Président
Finances: Budget de fonctionnement annuel: Moins de $50,000
Personnel: 1 membre(s) du personnel; 1 bénévole(s)
Membre: 700; *Montant de la cotisation:* 35$ étudiant; 100$ individuel; 370$ collectif
Mission: La promotion de l'urbanisme et de l'aménagement du territoire

Association québécoise de l'industrie de la pêche (AQIP) / Québec Fish Processor Association
#843, 2600, boul Laurier, Sainte-Foy QC G1V 4W2
Tél: 418-654-1831; *Téléc:* 418-654-1376
Courriel: aqip@quebectel.com
URL: www.quebecweb.com/aqip/
Aperçu: Dimension: moyenne; *Envergure: provinciale; fondée en 1978*
Finances: Budget de fonctionnement annuel: $250,000-$500,000
Membre: 40 industriels; *Montant de la cotisation:* 1 000-3 000$; *Comités:* Comité sur la rationalisation des usines; Comité sur les approvisionnements extérieurs; Comité sur le transport des produits marins
Activités: Négociations des plans conjoints
Mission: Défendre les intérêts professionnels des industries québécoises de la transformation des produits marins; travailler au développement des services; aider à l'amélioration de la productivité en usines; *Membre de:* CRCD Gaspésie des Iles

Association québécoise de la gestion parasitaire (AQGP)
CP 32, #410, 7400, boul Les Galeries d'Anjou, Anjou QC H1M 3M2
Tél: 514-355-3757; *Téléc:* 514-355-4159
Ligne sans frais: 800-663-2730
Courriel: aqgp@spg.qc.ca
URL: www.spg.qc.ca/aqgp/index.php
Nom précédent: Association des spécialistes en extermination du Québec
Aperçu: Dimension: petite; *Envergure: provinciale; fondée en 1968*
Membre(s) du bureau directeur:
Nathalie Juteau, Présidente
service@parasitech.com
Pierre St-Louis, Vice-président
pierrestlouis@videotron.ca
Membre: 125
Mission: Promouvoir le professionnalisme de ses membres - en les représentant auprès des instances régissant l'industrie de l'extermination et du public en général; en s'assurant de la conformité de ses membres par l'élaboration de normes et de règlements spécifiques; en contribuant à l'accroissement de leurs connaissances techniques et scientifiques par l'accès à l'information et l'élaboration de programmes de formation adaptés; *Membre de:* Canadian Pest Management Association

Association québécoise de lutte contre la pollution atmosphérique (AQLPA)
CP 26, 489A, rue Principale, Saint-Léon-de-Standon QC G0R 4L0

Associations/Organizations / Association québécoise des organismes de coopération internationale

Tél: 418-642-1322; Téléc: 418-642-1323
Ligne sans frais: 888-819-7330
Courriel: info@aqlpa.com
URL: www.aqlpa.com
Aperçu: Dimension: petite; *Envergure:* provinciale; *fondée en 1982*
Membre(s) du bureau directeur:
André Belisle, Président
andre.belisle@aqlpa.com
Membre: 415
Mission: L'Association québécoise de lutte contre la pollution atmosphérique (AQLPA) est un organisme qui s'est donnée pour mandat de contribuer à la protection de l'air et de l'atmosphère entourant notre planète, à la fois pour la santé des humains et des écosystèmes qu'elle abrite

Association québécoise des groupes d'ornithologues *Voir* Regroupement QuébecOiseaux

Association québécoise des organismes de coopération internationale (AQOCI) / Québec Association of International Cooperation
#540, 1001, rue Sherbrooke Est, Montréal QC H2L 1L3
Tél: 514-871-1086; Téléc: 514-871-9866
Courriel: aqoci@aqoci.qc.ca
URL: www.aqoci.qc.ca
Aperçu: Dimension: moyenne; *Envergure:* internationale; *fondée en 1976*
Membre(s) du bureau directeur:
Maria-Luisa Monreal, Directrice générale
Brian Barton, Président
Finances: *Budget de fonctionnement annuel:* $250,000-$500,000
Personnel: 5 membre(s) du personnel
Membre: 68; *Montant de la cotisation:* Selon revenu; *Critères d'admissibilite:* Regroupements d'organismes de coopération internationale; *Comités:* Comité québécois femmes et développement (CQFD)
Activités: *Stagiaires:* Oui; *Service de conférenciers:* Oui
Mission: Soutenir le travail des membres afin de permettre leur développement en s'inspirant des principes de solidarité et de coopération; favoriser l'échange pour mieux coordonner les actions communautaires; regrouper des organismes de coopération et d'éducation à la solidarité oeuvrant au Québec; *Membre de:* Canadian Council for International Cooperation; Conseil canadien pour la coopération internationale; *Affiliation(s):* Réseau québécois sur l'intégration continentale; Conseil canadien pour la coopération internationale

Association québécoise des techniques de l'environnement *Voir* Réseau environnement

Association québécoise du gaz naturel (AQGN)
#207, 560, boul. Henri-Bourassa Ouest, Montréal QC H3L 1P4
Tél: 514-339-9399; Téléc: 514-339-9353
Courriel: aqgn@aqgn.com
URL: www.aqgn.com
Aperçu: Dimension: petite; *Envergure:* provinciale
Membre(s) du bureau directeur:
Ginette Gamache, Directrice générale
Montant de la cotisation: 450$ régulier; 2 500$ aviseur
Mission: L'Association Québécoise du Gaz Naturel regroupe les gens d'affaires intéressés par le développement de l'industrie du gaz naturel au Québec

Association québécoise du transport aérien (AQTA)
Aéroport international Jean-Lesage, 600, 6e av de l'Aéroport, Québec QC G2G 2T5
Tél: 418-871-4635; Téléc: 418-871-8189
Courriel: aqta@aqta.ca
URL: www.aqta.ca
Aperçu: Dimension: moyenne; *Envergure:* provinciale; *Organisme sans but lucratif; fondée en 1975*
Membre: 130; *Montant de la cotisation:* Barème; *Critères d'admissibilité:* Transporteurs aériens et fournisseurs de produits et services liés à l'aviation
Mission: Voué à la défense et la promotion des intérêts de tous les secteurs du transport aérien

Association québécoise du transport et des routes inc. (AQTR)
#200, 1255, rue University, Montréal QC H3B 3B2
Tél: 514-523-6444; Téléc: 514-523-2666
Courriel: info@aqtr.qc.ca
URL: www.aqtr.qc.ca
Aperçu: Dimension: grande; *Envergure:* provinciale; *fondée en 1965*
Finances: *Budget de fonctionnement annuel:* $500,000-$1.5 Million
Personnel: 7 membre(s) du personnel; 100+ bénévole(s)
Membre: 950; *Montant de la cotisation:* 270 $; *Critères d'admissibilité:* Secteur privé - Ingénieur conseils; Entrepreneurs; Fournisseurs et manufacturiers; Laboratoires; Transporteurs; Architectes et urbanistes; Étudiants; Spécialistes en environnement; Secteur public et parapublic - Ministères; Municipalités; Maisons d'enseignement; Sociétés de transport; Autres sociétés, départements et services publics; *Comités:* Directions techniques - Infrastructures de transport; Transport des personnes; Circulation; Sécurité dans les transports; Transport aérien; Recherche et développement; Comités - Transport des marchandises; Environnement; Revue; Congrès; Activités municipales
Activités: Regrouper les personnes impliquées dans les techniques du transport; encourager les échanges multidisciplinaires et favoriser la collaboration entre différents secteurs; recommander toute mesure permettant de développer des techniques du transport; *Listes de destinataires:* Oui
Mission: Assumer un leadership technique; définir des règles en matière de sécurité et d'environnement; favoriser l'échange international des expertises; promouvoir la recherche et le développement des expertises et des produits en transport; promouvoir la formation dans le domaine des transports; assumer la représentativité de l'AQTR par la participation aux principaux forums sur les transports; contribuer à servir la société par l'éducation et l'information du grand public.

Association québécoise pour l'évaluation d'impacts (AQEI)
CP 785, Succ. Place d'Armes, Montréal QC H2Y 3J2
Tél: 514-990-2193
Courriel: mondorf@aqei.qc.ca
URL: www.aqei.qc.ca
Aperçu: Dimension: moyenne; *Envergure:* provinciale
Membre(s) du bureau directeur:
Françoise Mondor, Coordonnatrice
Montant de la cotisation: Barème
Mission: Regrouper toute personne, professionnelle ou non, intéressée par l'évaluation d'impacts et à son utilisation dans le processus de planification et de prise de décision; *Affiliation(s):* International Association for Impact Assessment

Association québécoise pour l'hygiène, la santé et la sécurité du travail (AQHSST)
#410, 7400, boul. Les Galeries d'Anjou, Ville d'Anjou QC H1M 3M2
Tél: 514-335-3830; Téléc: 514-355-4159
Courriel: info@aqhsst.qc.ca
URL: www.aqhsst.qc.ca
Aperçu: Dimension: moyenne; *Envergure:* provinciale; *Organisme sans but lucratif; fondée en 1978*
Membre(s) du bureau directeur:
Carolyne Perras, Présidente
presidence@aqhsst.qc.ca
Mario Saucier, Vice-président
vicepresidence@aqhsst.qc.ca
Montant de la cotisation: 30$ membre étudiant; 115$ membre individuel; 325$ membre corporatif
Activités: *Bibliothèque:* UNF Library; Bibliothèque publique
Prix, Bouses: Prix Antoine-Aumont de l'AQHSST (Prix)
Prix Méritas (Prix)
Bourse 3M (Brouse)
Bourse Levitt sécurité Ltée (Brouse)
Mission: Promouvoir les connaissances relatives à l'hygiène industrielle par l'échange et la vulgarisation de l'information; faire la promotion des connaissances dans des domaines connexes pouvant avoir un impact sur la santé et la sécurité du travail tels la sécurité, l'ergonomie et l'environnement; étudier les législations portinentes et toute action gouvernementale relatives à ses champs d'activités et faire les représentations qu'elle juge à propos; encourager la reconnaissance de la compétence de ses membres

Association québécoise pour la maîtrise de l'énergie (AQME) / Québec Association of Energy Managers (QAEM)
#750, 255, boul. CréMazie est, Montréal QC H2M 1L5
Tél: 514-866-5584; Téléc: 514-874-1272
Courriel: info@aqme.org
URL: www.aqme.org
Aperçu: Dimension: moyenne; *Envergure:* provinciale; *Organisme sans but lucratif; fondée en 1985*
Membre(s) du bureau directeur:
Jean Lacroix, Président/directeur général
jlacroix@aqme.org
Finances: *Budget de fonctionnement annuel:* $500,000-$1.5 Million
Personnel: 5 membre(s) du personnel; 100 bénévole(s)
Membre: 700; *Montant de la cotisation:* 160$; *Critères d'admissibilité:* Utilisateur ou fournisseur d'énergie; *Comités:* Bâtiment; MunicipalitéIndustrie
Activités: Congrès annuel, concours Énergia, party homards, tournois de golf; *Stagiaires:* Oui; *Bibliothèque:* Oui, rendez-vous
Mission: Contribuer à la promotion de la maîtrise de l'énergie au Québec pour une utilisation et une exploitation optimale des ressources et pour le respect de l'environnement

Association scientifique canadienne de la viande *See* Canadian Meat Science Association

Association SeCan *See* SeCan Association

Association sectorielle - Fabrication d'équipement de transport et de machines (ASFETM) / Sectorial Association - Transportation Equipment & Machinery Manufacturing (SATEMM)
#202, 3565, rue Jarry est, Montréal QC H1Z 4K6
Tél: 514-729-6961; Téléc: 514-729-8628
Ligne sans frais: 888-527-3386
Courriel: info@asfetm.com
URL: www.asfetm.com
Aperçu: Dimension: grande; *Envergure:* provinciale; *Organisme sans but lucratif; fondée en 1983*
Membre(s) du bureau directeur:
Arnold Dugas, Directeur général
Suzanne Ready, Chargée de l'information
Finances: *Budget de fonctionnement annuel:* $500,000-$1.5 Million
Personnel: 20 membre(s) du personnel
Membre: 8 groupes corporatifs - 3 patronaux + 5 syndicaux; *Critères d'admissibilité:* Etre une association patronale ou syndicale du secteur
Activités: Programme d'action annuel (30 projets); journées de sessions et de formation; colloques; *Bibliothèque:* Centre de documentation; rendez-vousNot open to the public
Mission: Aider les employeurs et les travailleurs à prévenir les accidents du travail et les maladies professionnelles, en faisant pour eux de la recherche, en leur dispensant de l'information, de la formation et de l'assistance technique qui visent essentiellement à rendre impossibles les accidents et les maladies au travail, et en privilégiant, à cette fin, l'élimination de cette possibilité à sa source même selon un processus de participation paritaire; *Membre de:* National Safety Council (USA); Association du camionnage du Québec

Association technique des pâtes et papiers du Canada *See* Pulp & Paper Technical Association of Canada

Association universitaire canadienne d'études nordiques *See* Association of Canadian Universities for Northern Studies

Atlantic Canada Centre for Environmental Science (ACCES)
Saint Mary's University, 923 Robie St., Halifax NS B3H 3C3
URL: www.smu.ca
Overview: A medium-sized local organization founded in 1991
Chief Officer(s):
G. Pe-Piper, Contact, 902-420-5744, Fax: 902-496-8104
gpiper@smu.ca
Member Profile: Saint Mary's University faculty members; Professionals interested in environmental science
Mission: TO foster interdisciplinary research related to the environment
Environmental Activity: Conducting research in areas such as climate change, geothermal energy, pollution, impacts of mining, coastal zone management, fisheries management, & conservation

Atlantic Canada Water & Wastewater Association (ACWWA)
PO Box 41002, Dartmouth NS B2Y 4P7
Tel: 902-434-6002; Fax: 902-435-7796
e-mail: acwwa@hfx.andara.com
URL: www.acwwa.ca
Overview: A medium-sized local organization
Chief Officer(s):
Ensor Nicholson, P.Eng, Chair
ensor.nicholson@moncton.org
Willard D'Eon, MPH, P.Eng, Secretary-Treasurer
willardd@cbcl.ca

Darrell Fisher, P.Eng, Director, Communications
dfisher@adi.ca
Membership: 430+; *Member Profile:* Water professionals in Atlantic Canada, from areas such as service provision, contracting, utility management, operations, system design, consulting, & academia; *Committees:* Education; Membership; Newsletter; Technical Papers; CWWA & CAC; Cross Connection Control; Young Professionals; Water for People; Government Affairs; Conference; Operator Involvement; Volunteers; Website
Activities: Providing training & information about the water & wastewater industry to members; Enhancing government relations; Offering networking opportunities
Meetings/Conferences:
For more information see Trade Shows, Conferences and Seminars Chapter
Atlantic Canada Water & Wastewater Association 2012 65th Annual Conference
Other Conferences in 2012 2012 Charlottetown, PE
Atlantic Canada Water & Wastewater Association 2013 66th Annual Conference
Other Conferences in 2013 2013 Halifax, NS
Atlantic Canada Water & Wastewater Association 2014 67th Annual Conference
Other Conferences in 2014 2014, NB
Atlantic Canada Water & Wastewater Association 2015 68th Annual Conference
Other Conferences in 2015 2015
Publications: ACWWA *[Atlantic Canada Water & Wastewater Association] Newsletter*
Type: Newsletter
Profile: Association activities
Operator Certification Study Guide [a publication of the Atlantic Canada Water & Wastewater Association]
Type: Booklet *Price:* $75
Profile: Information for water treatment & water distribution operators
AWWA Water Operator Field Guide
Type: Booklet *Price:* $55
Profile: Information for water treatment plant operators & water distribution operators
AWWA Wastewater Operator Field Guide
Type: Booklet *Price:* $55
Profile: Information used daily by wastewater system operators
Wastewater Operator Certification Study Guide
Type: Booklet *Price:* $75
Profile: Sample questions & answer for wastewater operator certification exams
Mission: To improve drinking water in Atlantic Canada; *Member of:* American Water Works Association (AWWA); Water Environment Federation (WEF)

Atlantic Canadian Organic Regional Network (ACORN) / Réseau régional du l'industrie biologique du Canada atlantique
PO Box 6343, 43 Main St., Sackville NB E4L 1G6
Tel: 506-536-2867; *Fax:* 506-536-0221
Toll-Free: 866-322-2676
e-mail: admin@acornorganic.org
URL: www.acornorganic.org
Social Media:
www.facebook.com/group.php?gid=153617164641
Overview: A medium-sized local organization founded in 2000
Chief Officer(s):
Beth McMahon, Executive Director
Membership: 300; *Fees:* $30
Mission: Voice of organics in Atlantic Canada; *Member of:* Volunteer Canada; Organic Materials Review Institute; Affiliation(s): Canadian Organic Growers

Atlantic Dairy Council (ADC)
PO Box 9410, Stn. A, #700, 6009 Quinpool Rd., Halifax NS B3K 5S3
Tel: 902-425-2445; *Fax:* 902-425-2441
e-mail: info@adcrecycles.com
URL: www.adcrecycles.com
Overview: A medium-sized local organization
Membership: 80
Mission: To maintain good relations among those engaged in dairy processing & distribution industries; to provide opportunities for industry training courses; & to enable united action on any matter concerning the welfare of the dairy trade

Atlantic Pest Control Association (APCO)
Bedford Industrial Park, 51 Duke St., Bedford NS B4A 2Z2
Tel: 902-835-2304; *Fax:* 902-835-0953
Overview: A small local organization

Member of: Canadian Pest Management Association

Atlantic Planners Institute (API) / Institut des Urbanistes de l'atlantique (IVA)
Parent: Canadian Institute of Planners
57 Parkside Dr., Charlottetown PE C1E 1N1
Tel: 902-892-3684
Toll-Free: 800-207-2138
e-mail: krlewis@pei.eastlink.ca
URL: www.atlanticplanners.org
Overview: A medium-sized provincial organization
Finances: *Annual Operating Budget:* Less than $50,000; *Funding Sources:* Membership fees
Membership: 100-499; *Member Profile:* Professional planner in the four Atlantic Provinces of Canada; New Brunswick, Newfoundland and Labrador, Nova Scotia, and Prince Edward Island.
Mission: Represents professional planners in New Brunswick, Prince Edward Island, Nova Scotia, Newfoundland & Labrador. They provide the processing of membership applications, maintenance of the membership roster, production of a regularly-scheduled newsletter, funding guarantess for the annual conference organizing committee.; Affiliation(s): Canadian Institute of Planners

Atlantic Provinces Association of Landscape Architects (APALA)
PO Box 653, Stn. Halifax CRO, Halifax NS B3J 2Z1
e-mail: info@apala.ca
URL: www.apala.ca
Overview: A medium-sized local organization
Membership: 56
Mission: To promote, improve & advance the profession; to maintain standards of professional practice & conduct consistent with the need to serve & to protect the public interest; to support improvement &/or conservation of the natural, cultural, social & built environment

Atlantic Provinces Council on the Sciences (APCS) / Conseil des provinces atlantiques pour les sciences (CPAS)
1390 Le Marchant St., Halifax NS B3H 3P9
Tel: 902-494-3421; *Fax:* 902-494-6643
e-mail: apics@dal.ca
URL: www.apics.dal.ca
Previous Name: Atlantic Provinces Inter-University Committee on the Sciences
Overview: A medium-sized local organization founded in 1962
Finances: *Funding Sources:* Membership dues
Staff: 2 staff member(s)
Membership: 17
Mission: To advance science & technology through education & public awareness & the promotion of scientific literacy education & research throughout the region

Atlantic Provinces Inter-University Committee on the Sciences See Atlantic Provinces Council on the Sciences

Atlantic Provinces Trucking Association (APTA)
Parent: Canadian Trucking Alliance
#400, 725 Champlain St., Dieppe NB E1A 1P6
Tel: 506-855-2782; *Fax:* 506-853-7424
Toll-Free: 866-866-1679
e-mail: apta@apta.ca
URL: www.apta.ca
Overview: A medium-sized local organization founded in 1950
Membership: 400 corporate & individual; *Member Profile:* Open to anyone having an interest in the trucking industry in Atlantic Canada, including common carriers, owner-operators & private fleets; *Committees:* Accident Review; Associated Trades Council; Broker; Common Carrier; Group Insurance; Marine; Membership; New Brunswick Legislative; Newfoundland Legislative; Nova Scotia Legislative; Prince Edward Island Legislative; Safety Council; Workers Compensation
Activities: Infrastructure improvements; complete twinning of the highway between Halifax & Saint John; elimination of motor carrier plates & fees; simplification of multiple registration & other tax collection systems in North America to allow for "one-stop shipping"; establishment of training programs; Annual Meeting & Convention; Atlantic Truck Show; Spring Maintenance Seminar; *Rents Mailing List:* Yes
Awards: Safety to Motor Transporation (Award)
Sponsored by Laurentian General Insurance Company; presented to an individual actively involved in promoting road & safety in the trucking industry

Service to Industry Award (Award)
Sponsored by Trailmobile Canada; awarded to the person who has made the greatest contribution to the industry in the past year
Atlantic Driver of the Year (Award)
Sponsored by Volvo GM Canada Heavy Truck Corporation; recognizes all-round distinction in driving, courtesy, safety & community activity
Mission: To promote an efficient, safe & environmentally sound trucking industry in Atlantic Canada. PUBLICATIONS: Atlantic Trucking Magazine (quaterly); Atlantic Report Newsletter (monthly) (only to members).

Atlantic Salmon Federation (ASF) / Fédération du saumon atlantique
PO Box 5200, St Andrews NB E5B 3S8
Tel: 506-529-4581; *Fax:* 506-529-4438
e-mail: savesalmon@asf.ca
URL: www.asf.ca
Overview: A large international charitable organization founded in 1948
Finances: *Funding Sources:* Donations from individuals, corporations, & foundations
Activities: Sharing knowledge with adults & children about wild Atlantic salmon; Conducting scientific research
Awards: Olin Fellowships (Scholarship)
Presented annually to individuals who seek to improve their knowledge & skills while searching for solutions to challenges in Atlantic salmon biology, conservation, & management *Deadline:* March 15 *Award Amount:* $1000-3000 Contact: Olin Fellowships, Atlantic Salmon Federation *Contact Detail:* PO Box 5200, St. Andrews, NB, EOG 2X0
T.B. (Happy) Fraser Award (Award)
Presented annually to an individual who has made outstanding contributions to wild Atlantic salmon conservation at a regional or national level
Lee Wulff Conservation Award (Award)
Presented annually to an individual who has made outstanding contributions to wild Atlantic salmon conservation
Atlantic Salmon Federation Roll Of Honor (Award)
Presented annually to individuals who demonstrate outstanding commitment to wild Atlantic salmon conservation at the grass-roots level
Affiliate of the Year Award (Award)
To recognize outstanding leadership in wild Atlantic salmon conservation within the Atlantic Salmon Federation's affiliate structure
Publications: *Atlantic Salmon Federation Newsletter*
Type: Newsletter
Profile: Updates on activities of the Federation
Atlantic Salmon Journal
Type: Journal *Accepts Advertising:* Yes *Editor:* Martin Silverstone
Profile: Issues surrounding wild Atlantic salmon, including protection of the species
State of the Population - Atlantic Salmon
Type: Report
Profile: A backgrounder on the Atlantic salmon population, featuring statistics, tables, & graphs
Prince Edward Island Nitrate Report
Type: Report
Profile: The problem of nitrates entering streams & lakes
Incidence & Impacts of Escaped Farmed Atlantic Salmon "Salmo Salar" in Nature
Type: Report *Number of Pages:* 114 *Author:* Eva B. Thorstad et al.
Profile: The impacts of escaped farmed salmon
Atlantic Salmon Federation Annual Report
Type: Yearbook *Frequency:* a.
Profile: Information about the federation's current projects that impact Atlantic salmon restoration plus future strategies
Mission: To protect, conserve, & restore wild Atlantic salmon & their ecosystems
Environmental Activity: Encouraging stewardship of watersheds

Atlantic Turfgrass Research Foundation (ATRC)
Nova Scotia Agricultural College, 20 Rock Garden Rd., Truro NS B2N 5E3
URL: www.turfgrass.ca/atrc.htm
Overview: A small provincial organization founded in 1992
Chief Officer(s):
Barry Stone, Chair
Gorden Horsman, Secretary
Steve Lowe, Treasurer

Associations/Organizations / Auditing Association of Canada

Activities: Researching turfgrass systems, in areas such as irrigation efficiency & water conservation & management
Mission: To advance the turfgrass industry in Atlantic Canada

Auditing Association of Canada (AAC)
#262, 610 Ford Dr., Oakville ON L6J 7W4
Fax: 519-488-3655
Toll-Free: 866-582-9595
e-mail: admin@auditingcanada.com
URL: www.auditingcanada.com
Previous Name: Canadian Environmental Auditing Association
Overview: A medium-sized international organization founded in 1991
Guy Brisebois, Executive Director
Finances: *Annual Operating Budget:* $100,000-$250,000; *Funding Sources:* Membership dues; seminars/conferences; application fees
Staff: 2 staff member(s); 50 volunteer(s)
Membership: 375; *Fees:* $195 individual; $25 student; $1000-$10,000 corporate; *Member Profile:* Practitioners of auditing; *Committees:* Member Services; Management; Certification; Nominations; Marketing; Discipline
Mission: To represent, support and promote our chosen auditing professions and to enable our members in the environmental, health and safety, and related areas to provide the highest quality services, and through our work to advance the public interest.

Ausable Bayfield Conservation Foundation
71108 Morrison Line, RR#3, Exeter ON N0M 1S5
Tel: 519-235-2610; *Fax:* 519-235-1963
Toll-Free: 888-286-2610
e-mail: info@abca.on.ca
URL: www.abca.on.ca
Overview: A small local organization founded in 1974
Chief Officer(s):
Tom Prout, Secretary/General Manager
Finances: *Annual Operating Budget:* Less than $50,000
Staff: 2 staff member(s); 9 volunteer(s)
Membership: 1-99
Activities: Conservation Dinner Auction;
Mission: Raising funds for conservation, preservation & protection of the natural landscapes of the Ausable River, Bayfield River & Packhill Creek watersheds

Australian Association for Environmental Education (AAEE)
PO Box 560, Bellingen 2454 Australia
Tel: 61-2-6655-1865
e-mail: admin@aaee.org.au
URL: www.aaee.org.au
Overview: A small national organization founded in 1980
Chief Officer(s):
Phil Smith, President
rephilled@hotmail.com
Finances: *Annual Operating Budget:* $50,000-$100,000; *Funding Sources:* Fees; grants; sponsorship; subsidies
Staff: 1 staff member(s); 30 volunteer(s)
Membership: 500; *Fees:* $90-$99 individual; $120 family; $240 corporate; $140 school/NGO; $896-$985 lifetime; *Member Profile:* Professionals; *Committees:* Special interest groups
Mission: To promote environmental education

AUTO21 - The Automobile of the 21st Century
754 California Ave., Windsor ON N9B 2Z2
Tel: 519-253-3000; *Fax:* 519-971-3626
e-mail: info@auto21.ca
URL: www.auto21.ca
Overview: A medium-sized national organization
Chief Officer(s):
Sandra Bortolotti, Operations Manager
sandra.bortolotti@auto21.ca
Stephanie Campeau, Communications Manager
stephanie.campeau@auto21.ca
Member of: Networks of Centres of Excellence

Automobile Importers of Canada *See* Association of International Automobile Manufacturers of Canada

Automotive Industries Association of Canada (AIAC) / Association des industries de l'automobile du Canada
1272 Wellington St. West, Ottawa ON K1Y 3A7
Fax: 613-728-6021
Toll-Free: 800-808-2920
e-mail: info.aia@aiacanada.com
URL: www.aiacanada.com
Overview: A large national organization founded in 1964
Finances: *Funding Sources:* Membership dues
Staff: 14 staff member(s); 300 volunteer(s)
Membership: 1,400 organizations; *Fees:* Dues based on the confirmed sales volumes of the individual members; *Member Profile:* Open to wholesalers, warehouse distributors, mass merchandizers, specialty groups & oil company headquarters, manufacturers, rebuilders, national distributors, manufacturers' agents, international exporters, allied organizations that supply goods &/or services to members of the association not for resale to warehouse distributors or wholesalers
Activities: Correspondence courses (parts specialist training; sales training; jobber management; dangerous goods, WHMIS & hazardous waste); AIA seminars; insurance services (benefits & pensions); scholarships; market research; public & government relations; *Awareness Events:* Car Care Month, May; Car Safety Month, Oct.; *Speaker Service:* Yes
Awards: Marion Roberts Memorial Scholarship Award (Scholarship)
Available to children of AIA member-company employees pursuing a post-secondary education
Automotive Scholarship (Scholarship)
5 scholarships (one in each of 4 regions in Canada, & one for students of the Canadian Automotive Institute) awarded to qualified candidates who are pursuing training in an program that will lead to a career in the aftermarket industry
Mission: A national trade association representing the automotive aftermarket industry in Canada & with a mandate to promote, educate & represent members

Automotive Parts Manufacturers' Association (APMA)
#801, 10 Four Seasons Pl., Toronto ON M9B 6H7
Tel: 416-620-4220; *Fax:* 416-620-9730
e-mail: info@apma.ca
URL: www.apma.ca
Overview: A large national organization founded in 1952
Membership: 400+ corporate; *Fees:* Schedule available; *Member Profile:* Canadian producers of parts, components, systems, tools, equipment & services for the automotive & truck manufacturing industries worldwide; 3 categories: Regular - manufacturers in Canada independent of vehicle companies; Canadian manufacturers which are divisions or affiliates of vehicle companies; International associates - manufacturers outside Canada interested or involved in the Canadian market & industry; Other associates - not manufacturers but interested in keeping in touch with industry trends & developments; *Committees:* Environmental Issues; Trade Policy; Annual Meeting; Human Resources Management; Legal/Bylaws; Technology; Membership; Nominating
Activities: Emissions survey; waste water analysis & reduction project
Mission: To promote the manufacture in Canada of automotive parts, systems, components, materials, tools, equipment & supplies, & also the provision of services used in the automotive industry & in particular for the original equipment market; to engage in activities in support of the welfare of the members of the Association

Automotive Recyclers of Canada (ARC)
134 Langarth St. E., London ON N6C 1Z5
Tel: 519-858-8761
e-mail: info@autorecyclers.ca
URL: www.autorecyclers.ca
Overview: A large national organization founded in 1997
Membership: 7; *Member Profile:* Automotive recycling associations
Mission: To act as the national voice for provincial member automotive recycling associations

The Avian Preservation Foundation (APF)
PO Box 123, Chemainus BC V0R 1K0
Tel: 250-246-4803; *Fax:* 250-246-4912
e-mail: exec@aacc.ca
URL: www.aacc.ca
Overview: A medium-sized national charitable organization
Chief Officer(s):
Mark S. Curtis, Executive Director
Finances: *Annual Operating Budget:* Less than $50,000
Staff: 12 volunteer(s)
Membership: 250; *Fees:* $35
Mission: To support recognized expert aviculturists who are endeavouring to breed rare & endangered avian species; to establish a Canadian breeding centre for rare & endangered avian species; to establish a monitoring body for captive avian stocks in Canada through surveys & computer software; to create & maintain a breeding program throughout Canada for avian species currently listed as endangered; to create a captive preservation program for rare & endangered species within zoos, bird parks & sanctuaries where re-introduction into the natural habitat is not possible or practical; *Member of:* Avicultural Advancement Council of Canada

Avicultural Advancement Council of Canada (AACC)
PO Box 123, Chemainus BC V0R 1K0
Tel: 250-246-4803; *Fax:* 250-246-4912
e-mail: exec@aacc.ca
URL: www.aacc.ca
Overview: A medium-sized national licensing organization founded in 1972
Finances: *Annual Operating Budget:* Less than $50,000; *Funding Sources:* Membership dues; donations
Staff: 12 volunteer(s)
Membership: 300 individual + 40 institutional; *Fees:* $30 individual; $70 club; *Member Profile:* Breeders, exhibitors & fanciers of birds; clubs who subscribe to the principles of association
Activities: *Library:* Yes, Not open to the public
Mission: To establish & maintain a national association of interested societies & individuals to promote the advancement of aviculture in Canada; to represent the Canadian avicultural community internationally; to disseminate information; to support recognized expert aviculturalists; to assist all levels of government in preparing informed legislation & policy relating to aviculture; to establish standards for the exhibition of birds in Canada; to provide a national identification leg band registry; to establish an avian species preservation program in Canada; *Affiliation(s):* American Singer Canary Club of Canada; Assoc. des amateurs d'oiseaux de la Mauricie; Assoc. des éleveurs d'oiseaux de Montréal; BC Avicultural Society; BC Exotic Bird Society; Budgerigar & Foreign Bird Society; Cage Bird Society of Hamilton; Calgary Canary Club; Canadian Dove Assoc.; Canadian Gloster Club; Cowichan Valley & Upper Island Cage Bird Club; Durham Avicultural Society; Edmonton Avicultural Association; Essex-Kent Cage Bird Society; Feather Fanciers Club; Golden Triangle Parrot Club; Kamloops Aviculturalist Society; London & District Cage Bird Society; Manitoba Canary & Finch Club

Bancroft Gem & Mineral Club
PO Box 1749, Bancroft ON K0L 1C0
Tel: 613-332-1611
Overview: A small local charitable organization
Chief Officer(s):
Chris Fouts, Contact
Dick Farmery, Contact
dfarmery@nexicom.net
Activities: Hosting monthly meetings at The Door Next Door Cafe; Organizing field trips
Mission: To foster an interest in the earth sciences & related lapidary arts; *Member of:* Central Canadian Federation of Mineralogical Societies

Barrie Agricultural Society
PO Box 217, Barrie ON L4M 4T2
Tel: 705-737-3670; *Fax:* 705-737-2581
e-mail: info@eventcentre.ca
URL: www.eventcentre.ca
Also Known As: Event Centre
Overview: A small local charitable organization founded in 1853
Chief Officer(s):
John Madden, President
Kim Sarmiento, General Manager
Finances: *Annual Operating Budget:* $250,000-$500,000; *Funding Sources:* Sponsors; Rental revenue; Barrie Fair
Staff: 4 staff member(s); 150 volunteer(s)
Membership: 1,000-4,999; *Fees:* $5
Mission: To encourage an awareness of agriculture; promote improvements in the quality of life for persons living in our community, rural & urban; organize & operate the Barrie Fair & other similar events; provides a venue which exhibitors can showcase, compete & market their products, crops or livestock

Barrow Bay & District Sports Fishing Association
PO Box 987, Lions Head ON N0H 1W0
Fax: 519-793-3363
e-mail: barrowbayfishing@hotmail.com
URL: www.bltg.com/bbdsfa/
Overview: A small local organization founded in 1993
Chief Officer(s):
Bill Howe, Vice-President

Jim Halliday, Sec.-Treas.
Don Huehn, President
Finances: *Annual Operating Budget:* $50,000-$100,000; *Funding Sources:* Membership dues; fundraising; government grants
Staff: 35 volunteer(s)
Membership: 142; *Fees:* $40 adult; $50 family; *Member Profile:* Local sport fishers & environmentalists
Member of: Ontario Federation of Anglers & Hunters

Bas-Saint-Laurent Model Forest / La Forêt modèle du Bas-Saint-Laurent
#J463, 300, Allée des Ursulines, Rimouski QC G5L 3A1
Tél: 418-722-7211; Téléc: 418-721-5630
Courriel: foretmodele@fmodbsl.qc.ca
URL: wwwforet.fmodbsl.qc.ca
Aperçu: Dimension: petite; *Envergure:* locale
Membre de: Canadian Model Forest Network

Bâtiments Durables Canada See Sustainable Buildings Canada

Battlefords Agricultural Society (BAS)
PO Box 668, North Battleford SK S9A 2Y9
Tel: 306-445-2024; Fax: 306-445-3352
e-mail: b.agsociety@sasktel.net
URL: agsociety.com
Previous Name: Battlefords Exhibition Association
Overview: A small local charitable organization founded in 1884
Finances: *Annual Operating Budget:* $500,000-$1.5 Million
Staff: 4 staff member(s); 130 volunteer(s)
Membership: 125; *Fees:* $15; *Member Profile:* Families, ages 16-85
Activities: Trade shows, quarter horse shows, raffles, chuckwagon races, 4H Regional Show, children's festival
Mission: To promote improvements in agriculture & community development; to provide facilities for educational & leisure programs; *Member of:* Saskatchewan Association of Agricultural Societies & Exhibitions

Battlefords Exhibition Association See Battlefords Agricultural Society

BC Biotech See LifeSciences British Columbia

BC Motels, Campgrounds, Resorts Association See British Columbia Lodging & Campgrounds Association

BC Motor Transport Association See British Columbia Trucking Association

Bear Biology Association See International Association for Bear Research & Management

Beaverhill Bird Observatory (BBO)
PO Box 1418, Edmonton AB T5J 2N5
e-mail: webmaster@beaverhillbirds.com
URL: www.beaverhillbirds.com
Overview: A small local charitable organization
Chief Officer(s):
Charles Priestley, Chair
charles@ualberta.ca
Member Profile: Biologists; Nature lovers
Activities: Documenting & monitoring changes in the avian species that utilize the Beaverhill area; Promoting an interest in the conservation of birds; Encouraging nature activities
Mission: To promote study of resident & migratory birds & other aspects of natural history at Beaverhill Lake & elsewhere
Environmental Activity: Acting as a steward of the Beaverhill Natural Area

Bedeque Bay Environmental Management Association (BBEMA)
PO Box 8310, Emerald PE C0B 1M0
Tel: 902-886-3211
URL: www.bbema.ca
Overview: A small local organization founded in 1992
Mission: To provide a framework for citizen-based education and action that reduced soil erosion, maintained water quality and improved the ecosystem.

Bengough Agricultural Society
PO Box 411, Bengough SK S0C 0K0
Tel: 306-268-2855
e-mail: benagsoc@hotmail.com
Overview: A small local charitable organization founded in 1915
Finances: *Annual Operating Budget:* Less than $50,000
Staff: 12 volunteer(s)
Membership: 60 individual; *Fees:* $3; *Member Profile:* Area residents striving to promote our community through education & entertainment
Activities: Horse show & fair; trade show; farmers market;
Awards: Bengough Agricultural Society Agricultural Scholarship (Scholarship)
To any Bengough high school student for post-secondary education studying agriculture *Award Amount:* $200
Mission: To improve agriculture & the quality of life in the community by educating members & the community; to provide a community forum for discussing agricultural issues; to foster community development & community spirit; to help provide markets for Saskatchewan products; to encourage conservation of natural resources, including soil conservation, reforestation, rural & urban beautification; *Member of:* Saskatchewan Association of Agricultural Societies & Exhibitions

Big Rideau Lake Association (BRLA)
PO Box 93, Hwy. 15, Portland ON K0G 1V0
Tel: 613-272-3629
e-mail: brla@brla.on.ca
URL: www.brla.ca
Overview: A medium-sized local organization founded in 1911
Chief Officer(s):
Peter Copestake, President
Fees: $60
Mission: The Big Rideau Lake Association (BRLA) is a non-profit organization committed to long-term environmental protection and service to all who use Big Rideau Lake and share its resources.
Environmental Activity: Water testing; Wildlife monitoring

Binbrook Agricultural Society (BAS)
PO Box 244, 2600, R.R. #56, Binbrook ON L0R 1C0
Tel: 905-692-4003; Fax: 905-692-1434
e-mail: info@binbrookagriculturalsociety.org
URL: www.binbrookagriculturalsociety.org
Overview: A small local organization founded in 1854
Chief Officer(s):
Ruth Mitchell, Sec.-Treas.
Finances: *Annual Operating Budget:* Less than $50,000; *Funding Sources:* Regional government
Staff: 1 staff member(s); 140 volunteer(s)
Membership: 175 individual; 18 associate; *Fees:* $5 individual; $5 associate
Activities: Annual Fall Fair; agricultural education & awareness programs
Affiliation(s): Ontario Association of Agricultural Societies; Canadian Association of Exhibitions

Bio-dynamic Agricultural Society of British Columbia
7, 776 Townline Rd., Abbotsford BC V2T 6C9
Tel: 604-859-5959; Fax: 604-859-5959
e-mail: bdcertification@yahoo.ca
Overview: A small provincial organization
Chief Officer(s):
Mary Forstbauer, President
Affiliation(s): Certified Organic Associations of BC

Biophysical Society of Canada (BSC) / La société de biophysique du Canada
Parent: Canadian Federation of Biological Societies
a/s Dept. de chimie-biologie, Univ. du Québec à Trois-Rivières, CP 500, Trois-Rivières QC G9A 5H7
Tel: 819-376-5011; Fax: 819-376-5057
e-mail: fragata@uqtr.ca
URL: www.uqtr.ca/sbc/
Overview: A medium-sized national organization founded in 1985
Finances: *Annual Operating Budget:* Less than $50,000; *Funding Sources:* Membership dues
Staff: 10 volunteer(s)
Membership: 80; *Fees:* $84.20
Activities: Speaker Service: Yes
Awards: Student Poster Award (Award)
Mission: To promote biophysical research & education; to encourage cross-feeding of ideas between the physical & biological sciences; to foster & support scientific meetings, workshops & discussions in biophysics; to represent Canadian biophysics & biophysicists

BIOQuébec / Québec Bio-Industries Business Network
#300, 381, rue Notre-Dame ouest, Montréal QC H2Y 1V2
Tél: 514-733-8411; Téléc: 514-733-8272
Courriel: reception@bioquebec.com
URL: www.bioquebec.com
Nom précédent: Conseil des bio-industries du Québec; Association québécoise des bio-industries
Aperçu: Dimension: moyenne; *Envergure:* provinciale; *Organisme sans but lucratif; fondée en* 1997
Membre(s) du bureau directeur:
Bertrand Bolduc, Président
Perry Niro, M.Sc., Directeur général et chef de la dir
Finances: *Budget de fonctionnement annuel:* $500,000-$1.5 Million; *Fonds:* Federal Office of Regional Development - Québec; membership fees; Laval Technopole
Personnel: 1 membre(s) du personnel; 4 bénévole(s)
Membre: 240 companies; *Montant de la cotisation:* 385$ (corporatif 1-5 employés); *Comités:* Environnement d'affaires; Conseil de l'innovation biopharmaceutique
Activités: Colloques, conférences, expositions;
Prix, Bouses: Genesis Awards (Prix)
Mission: Ôtre le porte-parole des entreprises biotechnologiques du Québec; favoriser le développement et la mise en valeur des biotechnologies et des bioindustries québécoises, et ce au bénéfice de ses membres; To promote the development & the upgrading of biotechnologies; to supply strategic information of technical & economical content as well as carry out projects, events & activities; to stimulate collaboration between private industry, governments & universities; to stimulate the growth of structuring economical activities in this field; to act as a spokesman for the bio-industry in Québec

The Biosphere of Montréal Partner's Foundation Voir Fondation des partenaires de la Biosphère de Montréal

BIOTECanada
#420, 130 Albert St., Ottawa ON K1P 5G4
Tel: 613-230-5585; Fax: 613-563-8850
e-mail: info@biotech.ca
URL: www.biotech.ca
Previous Name: Canadian Institute of Biotechnology; Industrial Biotechnology Association of Canada
Overview: A medium-sized national organization
Chief Officer(s):
Peter Brenders, President & CEO, 613-230-5585 Ext. 229
peter.brenders@biotech.ca
Finances: *Annual Operating Budget:* $1.5 Million-$3 Million; *Funding Sources:* Membership dues; government; sponsorship
Staff: 10 staff member(s)
Membership: 110 institutional; *Fees:* Schedule available; *Member Profile:* Biotechnology industry & regional groups; *Committees:* Agriculture; Human Health Care; Environment; Finance; Intellectual Property; Ethics; Communications; Government Relations; Science
Activities: Policy & regulatory advocacy; communications; human resources; *Rents Mailing List:* Yes
Mission: To provide a unified voice fostering an environment that responds to the needs of the biotechnology industry & research community, both nationally & internationally

Bird Studies Canada (BSC)
PO Box 160, Port Rowan ON N0E 1M0
Fax: 519-586-3532
Toll-Free: 888-448-2473
e-mail: generalinfo@bsc-eoc.org
URL: www.bsc-eoc.org
Previous Name: Long Point Bird Observatory
Overview: A small provincial charitable organization founded in 1960
Finances: *Annual Operating Budget:* $1.5 Million-$3 Million
Staff: 34 staff member(s)
Membership: 5,000-14,999; *Fees:* $25 student; $35 individual; $50 family; $100 contributing; $175 sustaining; $1000 lifetime; $2500 patron
Activities: *Internships:* Yes; *Library:* Yes, open by appointment
Mission: To advance the understanding, appreciation & conservation of wild birds & their habitats, in Canada & elsewhere, through studies that engage the skills, enthusiasm, & support of its members volunteers, staff & the interested public; *Member of:* Federation of Ontario Naturalists; **Affiliation(s):** Ontario Bird Banding Association; James L. Baillie Memorial Fund

Black Creek Conservation Project
PO Box 324, Stn. A, Toronto ON M3M 3A6
Tel: 416-661-6000; Fax: 416-667-6523

Associations/Organizations / Blomidon Naturalists Society

Previous Name: Black Creek Project of Toronto Inc.
Overview: A small local organization founded in 1982
Finances: *Annual Operating Budget:* $50,000-$100,000; *Funding Sources:* Government; private
Staff: 1 staff member(s); 80 volunteer(s)
Membership: 45; *Fees:* $15
Activities: Tree planting; garbage clean-up; environmental lectures; erosion control; wetland creation
Mission: To preserve & rehabilitate the Black Creek watershed; To support a healthy, diverse, & sustainable ecosystem; *Member of:* Federation of Ontario Naturalists

Black Creek Project of Toronto Inc. *See* Black Creek Conservation Project

Blomidon Naturalists Society (BNS)
PO Box 2350, Wolfville NS B4P 2N5
e-mail: bluebird.o@ns.sympatico.ca
URL: www.blomidonnaturalists.ca
Overview: A small local charitable organization founded in 1974
Chief Officer(s):
Rick Whitman, President
rick.whitman@ns.sympatico.ca
Helen Archibald, Secretary
hfarchibald@ns.sympatico.ca
Finances: *Annual Operating Budget:* $50,000-$100,000; *Funding Sources:* Membership dues
Staff: 15 volunteer(s)
Membership: 250; *Fees:* $20 adult, family; $1 Junior
Activities: Monthly meetings, field trips, bird counts, astronomy sessions
Awards: Robie Tufts Young Naturalist Award (Award)
Mission: To encourage & develop an understanding & appreciation of nature; *Member of:* Nature Nova Scotia, Nature Canada

Bluewater Recycling Association (BRA)
415 Canada Avenue, Huron Park ON N0M 1Y0
Tel: 519-228-6678; *Fax:* 519-228-6656
e-mail: bluebox@bra.org
URL: www.bra.org
Overview: A small local organization founded in 1989
Chief Officer(s):
Francis Veilleux, President
Finances: *Annual Operating Budget:* Greater than $5 Million
Staff: 55 staff member(s)
Membership: 21; *Fees:* Schedule available; *Member Profile:* Municipalities
Activities: *Speaker Service:* Yes
Mission: To provide ethical, innovative, effective resource-management services; to carry out our mission efficiently, safely & in an environmentally responsible manner, ultimately enabling our members to meet their environmental commitments

Board of Canadian Registered Safety Professionals (BCRSP) / Conseil canadien des professionnels en securité agréés
6519B Mississauga Rd., Mississauga ON L5N 1A6
Tel: 905-567-7198; *Fax:* 905-567-7191
Toll-Free: 888-279-2777
e-mail: bcrsp@sympatico.ca
URL: www.bcrsp.ca
Previous Name: Association for Canadian Registered Safety Professionals
Overview: A medium-sized national licensing organization founded in 1976
Finances: *Annual Operating Budget:* $250,000-$500,000; *Funding Sources:* Membership dues
Staff: 5 staff member(s); 130 volunteer(s)
Membership: 2,000; *Fees:* $125; *Member Profile:* Successfully completed high school or equivalency; three years of continuous safety experience & current employment of at least 50% in a safety practitioners role
Activities: CRSP designation (the Board evaluates qualifications of candidates & members against established standards)
Mission: To protect & promote occupational health & safety, environmental safety, & public safety, through the registration of qualified health & safety professionals committed to a code of ethics

Bonn Agreement (BONN)
New Court, 48 Carey St., London WC2A 2JQ United Kingdom

Tel: 44-20-7430-5200; *Fax:* 44-20-7430-5225
e-mail: secretariat@bonnagreement.org
URL: www.bonnagreement.org
Overview: A small international organization founded in 1969
Membership: 9 European & EU countries; *Fees:* Annual contribution
Mission: To provide a cooperation forum for dealing with accidental marine pollution of the North Sea & marine pollution aerial surveillance

Boreal Institute for Northern Studies (1960-1990) *See* Canadian Circumpolar Institute

Boundary Organic Producers Association (BOPA)
PO Box 675, Grand Forks BC V0H 1H0
Tel: 250-442-4247
Overview: A small local organization
Chief Officer(s):
Owen Broad, President
Danna O'Donnell, COABC Representative
May Lungle, Administrator
Finances: *Annual Operating Budget:* Less than $50,000
Staff: 1 staff member(s)
Membership: 10-15 certified organic operators & associate members; *Fees:* $25; *Member Profile:* Organic producers & processors; *Committees:* Certification
Activities: Organic certification of producers & processors
Affiliation(s): Certified Organic Associations of BC

Bowen Nature Club
RR#1, CL-27, Bowen Island BC V0N 1G0
Tel: 604-947-9562
e-mail: foreverlyn@telus.net
Overview: A small local organization founded in 1985
Fees: $18 individual; $22 family
Mission: To promote the enjoyment of nature through environmental appreciation & conservation; to encourage wise use & conservation of natural resources & environmental protection; *Member of:* Federation of BC Naturalists

Brampton Horticultural Society
PO Box 92546, 160 Main St. South, Brampton ON L6W 4R1
e-mail: bramhort@hotmail.com
Overview: A small local charitable organization founded in 1895
Chief Officer(s):
Fran Caldwell, President
Wendy Lovegrove, Secretary
Fees: $19 single; $26 family; $14 senior single; $20 senior family; $2.50 junior

Brantford Lapidary & Mineral Society Inc. (BLMS)
c/o Woodman Community Centre, 491 Grey St., Brantford ON N3S 7L7
Tel: 519-753-4711
Overview: A small local organization founded in 1964
Chief Officer(s):
Marie Mellick, Secretary
Activities: Offering lapidary training; Providing equipment access
Awards: Brantford Lapidary and Mineral Society Inc. Awards (Award)
Eligibility: Presented annually to students enrolled in an Earth Sciences program in the Faculty of Science at the University of Waterloo who have achieved a minimum overall average of 75%
Award Amount: $1,000 each
Mission: To increase interest in the earth sciences & related lapidary arts; *Member of:* Central Canadian Federation of Mineralogical Societies

Breast Cancer Action (BCA) / Sensibilisation au cancer du sein
Riverside Mall, 739A Ridgewood Ave., Ottawa ON K1V 6M8
Tel: 613-736-5921; *Fax:* 613-736-8422
e-mail: info@bcaott.ca
URL: www.bcaott.ca
Overview: A medium-sized local charitable organization founded in 1993
Chief Officer(s):
Diane Ryan, President
Finances: *Annual Operating Budget:* $100,000-$250,000; *Funding Sources:* Private donations; fundraisers
Staff: 2 staff member(s); 50 volunteer(s)
Membership: 400; *Fees:* $40
Activities: *Awareness Events:* Annual Walk/Fun Run, June; *Library:* Yes, Open to public

Mission: To advocate establishment of a national resource office, directed by women affected by breast cancer, to serve as clearinghouse for information about treatment, legislative action, access to treatments & support services; to advocate for a designated centre for excellence to accelerate research; to advocate greater emphasis on developing earlier detection; to promote increased survivor participation in cancer care planning & policy making; to promote better education of family physicians & women in early detection & follow-up

Breast Cancer Society of Canada / Société du cancer du sein du Canada
420 East St. North, Sarnia ON N7T 6Y5
Tel: 519-336-0746; *Fax:* 519-336-5725
Toll-Free: 800-567-8767
e-mail: bcsc@bcsc.ca
URL: www.bcsc.ca
Social Media: www.facebook.com/breastcancersocietyofcanada
Overview: A large national charitable organization founded in 1991
Chief Officer(s):
Marsha Davidson, Executive Director
Dawn Hamilton, Coordinator, Fund Development
Bunny Caughlin, Officer, Operations
Johanne Deschamps, Officer, Communications
Finances: *Funding Sources:* Donations; Fundraising
Activities: *Awareness Events:* Scotiabank Toronto Waterfront Marathon; Pam Greenaway-Kohlmeier Memorial Golf Tournament; Cruise for the Cure
Publications: *Breast Cancer Society of Canada Newsletter*
Type: Newsletter
Profile: Recent information about the society & research endeavours
Mission: To support research into the prevention, detection, & treatment of breast cancer

Brereton Field Naturalists' Club Inc. (BFN)
PO Box 1084, Barrie ON L4M 5E1
URL: www.breretonfieldnaturalists.org
Overview: A small local charitable organization founded in 1951
Chief Officer(s):
Brian Gibbon, Contact, 705-726-8969
bwg@backland.net
Finances: *Annual Operating Budget:* Less than $50,000; *Funding Sources:* Membership fees
Staff: 95 volunteer(s)
Membership: 125; *Fees:* $10 student; $15 corresponding; $25 individual; $30 family; *Committees:* Conservation; Education; Field Trips; Newsletter; Program
Activities: Bird-watching outings; nature strolls; lunches; *Speaker Service:* Yes; *Library:* BFN Library; open by appointmentNot open to the public
Publications: *The Blue Heron*
Type: newsletter *Frequency:* annual
Mission: To acquire & disseminate knowledge of natural history; to protect & preserve wildlife; to stimulate public interest in nature & its preservation; *Affiliation(s):* Federation of Ontario Naturalists

British Columbia & Yukon Chamber of Mines *See* Association for Mineral Exploration British Columbia

British Columbia Agriculture Council
Parent: Canadian Federation of Agriculture
#230, 32160 South Fraser Way, Abbotsford BC V2T 1W5
Tel: 604-854-4454; *Fax:* 604-854-4485
Toll-Free: 866-522-3477
e-mail: bcac@bcagcouncil.com
URL: www.bcac.bc.ca
Overview: A medium-sized provincial organization founded in 1997
Chief Officer(s):
Andy Dolborg, Executive Director
andy@bcac.bc.ca
Mission: To provide leadership in representing, promoting, & advocating the collective interests of all agriculture producers in the province of British Colombia; To foster cooperation & a collective response to matters affecting the future of agriculture in the province; To facilitate programs & service delivery for a number of programs that benefit the industry

British Columbia Association for Regenerative Agriculture (BCARA)
PO Box 1601, Aldergrove BC V4W 2V1
Tel: 604-322-1215; *Fax:* 604-793-9225
e-mail: bcara.admin@gmail.com

Overview: A small provincial organization
Chief Officer(s):
Sarah Davidson, Administrator
Susan Davidson, President
Membership: 100-499
Affiliation(s): Certified Organic Associations of BC

British Columbia Association of Agricultural Fairs & Exhibitions
18231 60th Avenue, Surrey BC V3S 1V7
Tel: 778-574-4082; *Fax:* 778-574-4082
e-mail: jbshaw@shaw.ca
URL: www.bcfairs.ca
Overview: A small provincial organization
Chief Officer(s):
Janine B. Saw, Executive Director
Fees: $150

British Columbia Bottle Depot Association (BCBDA)
9850 King George Hwy., Surrey BC V3T 4Y3
Tel: 604-930-0003; *Fax:* 604-930-0060
e-mail: bcbda@telus.net
URL: www.bcbda.com; www.mydepot.ca
Overview: A small provincial organization founded in 1997
Chief Officer(s):
Corinne Atwood, Executive Director
Grant Robertson, Chair
grobertson@bcbda.com
Kulbir Rana, Secretary-Treasurer
krana@bcbda.com
Finances: *Funding Sources:* Membership fees
Member Profile: Bottle depots in British Columbia
Activities: Liaising with government & industry partners; Assisting the public by maintaining a website with information about depot locations, sales, & what each depot accepts for recycling
Mission: To further the interests of association members through representation; to support a healthy environment by promoting recycling programs

British Columbia Camping Association
Parent: Canadian Camping Association
c/o Sasamat Outdoor Centre, 3302 Senkler Rd., Belcarra BC V3H 4S3
Tel: 604-931-6449; *Fax:* 604-939-8522
e-mail: info@bccamping.org
URL: www.bccamping.org
Overview: A medium-sized provincial organization
Chief Officer(s):
Hart Banack, President
Activities: *Rents Mailing List:* Yes
Mission: To facilitate the development of organized camping in order to provide educational, character-building & constructive recreational experiences for all people; to develop awareness & appreciation of the natural environment

British Columbia Cattlemen's Association (BCCA)
#4, 10145 Dallas Dr., Kamloops BC V2C 6T4
Tel: 250-573-3611; *Fax:* 250-573-5155
Toll-Free: 877-688-2333
e-mail: info@cattlemen.bc.ca
URL: www.cattlemen.bc.ca
Also Known As: BC Cattlemen
Overview: A medium-sized provincial organization founded in 1929
Finances: *Funding Sources:* Sponsorships
Membership: 1,300; *Fees:* $101; *Member Profile:* Cattle producers in British Columbia; *Committees:* Land Stewardship & Aboriginal Affairs; Environmental Stewardship; Public Affairs, Education & Research; Livestock Industry Protection; Finance & Taxation
Activities: Providing input on government regulations related to ranching; Advocating for cattle producers; Liaising with local, provincial, & federal government officials; Sponsoring courses at the Rangeland Management School; Providing industry information; Increasing awarenss of the beef industry & its issues; Offering various programs, such as the Dam Inspection Program & the BC Highways Fencing Program; Researching; Collaborating with the Canadian Beef Export Federation to expand foreign markets; Protecting landowner rights
Awards: Environmental Stewardship Award (Award)
To recognize a ranching family for outstanding commitment to environmental stewardship
Brigadier W.N. Bostock Memorial Research Grant (Grant)
To recognize those whose research benefits the beef cattle industry in British Columbia *Award Amount:* $2,000
Martin Riedemann Annual Bursary (Grant)
To assist worthy students, especially those from rural areas *Award Amount:* $1,000
Gung Loy Jim Scholarships (Scholarship)
To assist worthy students from British Columbia, especially those from rural areas *Award Amount:* $2,000
RBC Dominion Securities Bursary (Grant)
To assist worthy students, especially those from rural areas *Award Amount:* $1,000
British Columbia Cattlemen's Association Bursary (Grant)
Eligibility: Applicants must be a child or grandchild of a British Columbia Cattlemen's Association member *Award Amount:* $1,000
Publications: Beef In BC
Type: Magazine *Frequency:* 7 pa *Accepts Advertising* : Yes
Editor: Diane Edstrom *Price:* $24 Canada; $34 USA
Profile: Association reports & articles about issues important to the cattle production industry
British Columbia Cattlemen's Association Newsletter
Type: Newsletter *Frequency:* m.
Mission: To develop & protect the cattle industry in British Columbia; To act as the official voice of the beef cattle industry in British Columbia; To act in an environmentally responsible manner; To provide quality beef products to consumers;
Affiliation(s): Canadian Cattlemen's Association
Environmental Activity: Providing the the Environmental Farm Planning Program; Offering the Farmland-Riparian Interface Stewardship Program to assist ranchers to achieve best management practices; Promoting environmental stewardship

British Columbia Conservation Foundation (BCCF)
#206, 17564 - 56A Ave., Surrey BC V3S 1G3
Tel: 604-576-1433; *Fax:* 604-576-1482
e-mail: hoffice@bccf.com
URL: www.bccf.com
Overview: A medium-sized provincial organization founded in 1969
Membership: 30
Activities: Four regional offices
Mission: The British Columbia Conservation Foundation (BCCF) was founded and incorporated under the Society Act of British Columbia in 1969, by the Directors of the BC Wildlife Federation, to contribute significantly to the perpetuation and expansion of fish and wildlife populations through the efficient implementation of projects in the field. They are a federally registered charity dedicated to the conservation and stewardship of British Columbia's ecosystems and species.

British Columbia Construction Association (BCCA)
Parent: Canadian Construction Association
#210, 174 Wilson St., Victoria BC V9A 7N6
Tel: 250-475-1077; *Fax:* 250-475-1078
e-mail: bcca@bccassn.com
URL: www.bccassn.com
Overview: A large provincial organization founded in 1969
Finances: *Funding Sources:* Membership dues; group benefit plan; industry forms & publications
Staff: 5 staff member(s); 13 volunteer(s)
Membership: 1,800 individual + 4 regional associations
Activities: Apprenticeship Task Force; Design - Build Task Force; BC Construction Forum; Bid Depository Committee
Mission: To provide excellence in the representation of & service to British Columbia's construction industry

British Columbia Environment Industry Association (BCEIA)
#400, 602 West Hastings St., Vancouver BC V6B 1P2
Tel: 604-683-2751; *Fax:* 604-677-5960
e-mail: info@bceia.com
URL: www.bceia.com
Previous Name: Canadian Environment Industry Association - British Columbia Chapter
Overview: A medium-sized provincial organization founded in 1992
Chief Officer(s):
Bob Symington, President
Frank Came, Vice-President
Jeff Eltom, Executive Director
Michael Lyons, Secretary-Treasurer
Member Profile: Engineering & environmental service companies; Research organizations; Technology providers; Disaster response organizations; Environmental law firms; Environmental analysts & consultants; Government agencies; *Committees:* Contaminated sites; Hazardous waste; Enertech; International relations; Executive; Ethics
Activities: Networking within the environmental industry; Engaging in advocacy activities; Providing market & regulatory information; Offering professional development seminars on environmental related topics;
Publications: Environmental Product & Services Directory
Type: Directory
Profile: Comprehensive listings available to British Columbia Environment Industry Association members
British Columbia Environment Industry Association Newsletter
Type: Newsletter
Profile: Association announcements & upcoming events
Mission: To develop the environmental industry in British Columbia; To promote technological development
Environmental Activity: Increasing awareness of the environmental industry

British Columbia Environmental Network (BCEN)
Parent: Canadian Environmental Network
#461, 1755 Robson St., Vancouver BC V6G 3B7
Tel: 604-515-1969
e-mail: editor@ecobc.ca
URL: www.ecobc.org
Overview: A medium-sized provincial organization founded in 1979
Finances: *Annual Operating Budget:* $50,000-$100,000
Staff: 2 staff member(s); 15 volunteer(s)
Membership: 419 groups; *Fees:* $40 for groups under 100 individuals; $80 for groups over 100 individuals; *Member Profile:* Open to non-profit environmental groups promoting environmental integrity; *Committees:* Steering
Activities: *Speaker Service:* Yes; *Rents Mailing List:* Yes
Mission: To facilitate communication among environmental groups & individuals so that ecological sustainability & economic stability prevail, & biological diversity & human health remain viable

British Columbia Farm Industry Review Board (BCFIRB)
PO Box 9129, Stn. Prov. Govt., 1007 Fort St., 3rd Fl., Victoria BC V8W 9B5
Tel: 250-356-8945; *Fax:* 250-356-5131
e-mail: firb@gov.bc.ca
URL: www.firb.gov.bc.ca
Previous Name: British Columbia Marketing Board (BCMB)
Merged from: British Columbia Marketing Board (BCMB) & The Farm Practices Board (FPB)
Overview: A medium-sized provincial organization founded in 1934
Chief Officer(s):
Richard Bullock, Chair
Sandi Ulmi, Vice-Chair
Jim Collins, General Manager
Andy Dolberg, Manager, Issues & Planning
Activities: Studying & reporting on farm practices in British Columbia; Promoting cooperation between urban & agricultural interests; Meeting regularly with commodity boards
Publications: British Columbia Farm Industry Review Board Strategic Plan
Mission: To act in accordance with the Natural Products Marketing (BC) Act, the Agricultural Produce Grading Act, & the Farm Practices Protection (Right to Farm) Act; to supervise regulated marketing boards; to hear complaints regarding agriculture or aquaculture operations; to hear appeals from those who have had grading licenses refused, suspended, or revoked; to serve & protect the public interest

British Columbia Farm Machinery & Agriculture Museum Association
9131 King St., Fort Langley BC V1M 2R9
Tel: 604-888-2273
e-mail: bcfarm@vcn.bc.ca
URL: www.bcfma.com
Overview: A small provincial charitable organization founded in 1958
Activities: Operating a museum with a collection of farm artifacts, such as carriages, wagons, & tractors, a sawmill, & a blacksmith shop; *Library:* British Columbia Farm Machinery & Agriculture Museum Library; Open to public
Member of: British Columbia Museums Association

British Columbia Food Technolgists (BCTF)
Parent: Canadian Institute of Food Science & Technology
c/o Nealanders International Inc., #201, 7950 Huston Rd., Delta BC V4G 1C2

Associations/Organizations / British Columbia Fruit Growers' Association

Tel: 604-940-4181
e-mail: info@bcft.ca; membership@bcft.ca; newsletter@bcft.ca
URL: www.bcft.ca
Overview: A small provincial organization
Chief Officer(s):
Peter Taylor, Chair
taylor58@telus.net
Reena Mistry, Secretary
Thu Pham, Treasurer
Kim Mayes, Chair, Membership & Program Committee
membership@bcft.ca
Nancy Ross, Chair, Banquet & Program Committee
info@foodquality.ca
Nilmini Wijewickreme, Chair, Advertising
nwijiwickreme@maxxam.ca; advertisements@bcft.ca
Member Profile: Scientists & technologists from government, academia, & industry; *Committees:* Advertising; Banquet; Membership; Program
Activities: Engaging in advocacy activities; Offering networking opportunities
Meetings/Conferences:
For more information see Trade Shows, Conferences and Seminars Chapter
British Columbia Food Technolgists Meeting: Banquet & Golf Tournament
June 2011 Richmond, BC
Publications: *Tech Talk: The British Columbia Food Technolgists Newsletter*
Type: Newsletter *Frequency:* 9 pa *Accepts Advertising* : Yes
Editor: Brian Jang (bjang@maxxam.ca)
Profile: Association information, meetings, & food-related activities on the local & international scene, for persons involved in areas such as food processing, research, product development, quality control, sales, & management
Mission: To advance food science & technology in British Columbia; *Member of:* Canadian Institute of Food Science & Technology; Institute of Food Technologists; Affiliation(s): Packaging Association of British Columbia; British Columbia Food Protection Association; British Columbia Nutraceutical Network
Environmental Activity: Promoting the quality & safety of the food supply by applying science & technology

British Columbia Fruit Growers' Association
1473 Water St., Kelowna BC V1Y 1J6
Tel: 250-762-5226; Fax: 250-861-9089
e-mail: info@bcfga.com
URL: www.bcfga.com
Overview: A medium-sized provincial organization
Member Profile: Fruit growers in British Columbia
Activities: Lobbying the government for positive change to risk management programs, such as crop insurance & the Net Income Stablization Program; Providing services & products to growers
Mission: To represent fruit growers' interests in British Columbia

British Columbia Fuchsia & Begonia Society
c/o #17, 910 Fort Fraser Rise, Port Coquitlam BC V3C 6K3
e-mail: info@bcfuchsiasociety.com
URL: www.bcfuchsiasociety.com
Overview: A small provincial organization founded in 1961
Chief Officer(s):
Fran Carter, President
Lorna Herchenson, Int'l Corresponding Secretary
lherchenson@telus.net
Diane Rudd, Membership Contact
Finances: *Annual Operating Budget:* Less than $50,000;
Funding Sources: Membership dues; plant sales; raffles
Staff: 185 volunteer(s)
Membership: 185; *Fees:* $18 single; $23 family
Activities: Meetings; workshops; plant sales; speaking to the community & other garden clubs; *Awareness Events:* Annual Show & Competition; *Speaker Service:* Yes; *Library:* Yes, Not open to the public
Mission: The Society encourages the cultivation & promotion of fuchsias, begonias, ferns, gesneriads & all other shade-loving plants.; *Member of:* BC Council of Garden Clubs

British Columbia Grain Shippers Clearance Association; Lake Shippers Clearance Association See Canadian Ports Clearance Association

British Columbia Ground Water Association (BCGWA)
Parent: Canadian Ground Water Association
c/o Office Of The Secretary, 1708 - 197A St., Langley BC V2Z 1K2
Tel: 604-530-8934; Fax: 604-530-8934
e-mail: secretary@bcgwa.org
URL: www.bcgwa.org
Overview: A small provincial organization
Chief Officer(s):
Remi Allard, President, 250-860-8424, Fax: 250-860-9874
rallard@golder.com
Tim Oster, Vice-President, 604-534-4108
Dave Mellis, Treasurer, 604-534-1115
Joan Perry, Secretary
Member Profile: Corporations that employ persons who work in water well contracting, manufacturing or supplying materials & equipment, or consulting in the groundwater industry; Individuals employed by a company or who belong to an association affiliated with the ground water industry
Activities: Offering workshops & seminars; Promoting research & standards in water well construction; Liaising with government agencies
Publications: *British Columbia Ground Water Association Newsletter*
Type: Newsletter *Frequency:* q.
Mission: To advance the ground water industry, through professional & technical leadership; to promote the responsible development & use of ground water resources in British Columbia; to protect the underground water supply; Affiliation(s): Canadian Ground Water Association

British Columbia Herb Growers Association (BCHGA)
998 Skeena Dr., Kelowna BC V1V 2K7
Tel: 604-764-1263
e-mail: info@bcherbgrowers.com
URL: www.bcherbgrowers.com
Overview: A small provincial organization founded in 1997
Chief Officer(s):
Herbert Strobl, Contact
Finances: *Funding Sources:* Sponsorships
Membership: 50; *Fees:* $50 individuals; $75 foreign memberships; $125 corporations; *Member Profile:* Individuals & corporations involved in the herb business, such asresearchers, educators, growers, manufacturers, processors, buyers, distributors, retailers, & service providers
Activities: Facilitating research; Providing networking opportunities; Offering market information; Organizing workshops; Supporting herb marketing
Publications: *BCHGA [British Columbia Herb Growers Association] Newsletter*
Type: Newsletter *Frequency:* q. *Accepts Advertising* : Yes
Profile: Upcoming meetings, trade shows, & educational opportunities, association reports, & articles
British Columbia Herb Growers Association Annual Report
Type: Yearbook *Frequency:* a.
British Columbia Herb Growers Association Directory
Type: Directory
Profile: Listing of association members with contact information
Mission: To promote & enhance herb growing in British Columbia; to represent herb growers

British Columbia Institute of Agrologists (BCIA)
Parent: Agricultural Institute of Canada
#205, 733 Johnson St., Victoria BC V8W 3C7
Tel: 250-380-9292; Fax: 250-380-9233
Toll-Free: 877-855-9291
e-mail: p.ag@bcia.com
URL: www.bcia.com
Overview: A medium-sized provincial licensing organization founded in 1947
Finances: *Annual Operating Budget:* $250,000-$500,000;
Funding Sources: Membership dues
Staff: 2 staff member(s); 20 volunteer(s)
Membership: 950; *Fees:* $150; *Member Profile:* Professional agrologists
Activities: *Internships:* Yes

British Columbia Landscape & Nursery Association (BCLNA)
Parent: Canadian Nursery Landscape Association
#102, 5783 - 176A St., Surrey BC V3S 6S6
Tel: 604-574-7772; Fax: 604-574-7773
Toll-Free: 800-421-7963
e-mail: info@bclna.com
URL: www.bclna.com
Previous Name: British Columbia Nursery Trades Association
Overview: A medium-sized provincial organization founded in 1953
Finances: *Annual Operating Budget:* $1.5 Million-$3 Million;
Funding Sources: Membership dues; CanWest Horticultural Show
Staff: 10 staff member(s)
Membership: 800; *Fees:* $370-$980, based on gross sales;
Member Profile: Nurserymen, garden centre operators, landscape & maintenance contractors, sod growers, arborists & suppliers from across British Columbia
Activities: Educational seminars; certification programs
Mission: To work together to improve quality & standards of the industry; *Member of:* BC Agriculture Council

British Columbia Lodging & Campgrounds Association (BCLCA)
#209, 3003 St. John's St., Port Moody BC V3H 2C4
Tel: 604-945-7676; Fax: 604-945-7606
Toll-Free: 888-923-4678
e-mail: info@bclca.com
URL: www.bclca.com
Previous Name: BC Motels, Campgrounds, Resorts Association
Overview: A medium-sized provincial organization founded in 1944
Chief Officer(s):
Joss Penny, Executive Director
jpenny@bclca.com
Finances: *Annual Operating Budget:* $250,000-$500,000
Staff: 3 staff member(s)
Membership: 625; *Fees:* $280; *Member Profile:* Motels; resorts; campgrounds
Activities: Marketing & promotion; group purchasing discounts; lobbying; education & industry standards
Mission: To promote the public's utilization of member lodging & campground businesses; to monitor & make representation to governments on legislation affecting the interests of British Columbia's lodging & campground businesses; to speak for the membership on matters of general or specific interest; to encourage members to strive for excellence in accommodation & service

British Columbia Lung Association (BCLA)
Parent: Canadian Lung Association
2675 Oak St., Vancouver BC V6H 2K2
Tel: 604-731-5864; Fax: 604-731-5810
Toll-Free: 800-665-5864
e-mail: info@bc.lung.ca
URL: www.bc.lung.ca
Social Media:
www.facebook.com/home.php?#!/BCLungAssociation
Previous Name: Anti-Tuberculosis Society
Overview: A medium-sized provincial charitable organization founded in 1906
Finances: *Funding Sources:* Donations; Sponsorships; Fundraising
Committees: Executive; Medical Advisory
Activities: Providing money to physicians & scientists doing research in British Columbia on lung diseases; Offering breathing test events; *Awareness Events:* The Staircimb for Clean Air, February; The Bicycle Trek for Life and Breath, September
Meetings/Conferences:
For more information see Trade Shows, Conferences and Seminars Chapter
British Columbia Lung Association 2012 Annual General Meeting
Other Conferences in 2012 2012, BC
British Columbia Lung Association 2012 9th Annual Air Quality & Health Workshop
Other Conferences in 2012 2012, BC
Publications: *British Columbia Lung Association Annual Report*
Type: Yearbook *Frequency:* a.
Your Health
Type: Magazine *Frequency:* s-a. *Editor:* Katrina van Bylandt, Destin Haynes
Profile: Health information for medical & health promoters, educators, donors to the Lung Association, & persons interested in respiratory health
Mission: To support lung health research, education, prevention, & advocacy; To help people manage respiratory diseases, including asthma, COPD (chronic bronchitis and emphysema), lung cancer, sleep apnea, & tuberculosis
Environmental Activity: Providing information on lung health & air quality issues

British Columbia Marine Trades Association (BCMTA)
#300, 1275 West 6th Ave., Vancouver BC V6H 1A6
Tel: 604-683-5191; *Fax:* 604-893-8808
e-mail: mta@bcmta.com
URL: www.bcmta.com
Overview: A medium-sized provincial organization
Finances: *Annual Operating Budget:* $50,000-$100,000
Membership: 300 corporate; *Fees:* $295-395
Mission: The voice of the BC recreational marine industry

British Columbia Marketing Board (BCMB) *See* British Columbia Farm Industry Review Board

British Columbia Medical Association (BCMA)
Parent: Canadian Medical Association
#115, 1665 West Broadway, Vancouver BC V6J 5A4
Tel: 604-736-5551; *Fax:* 604-736-4566
Toll-Free: 800-665-2262
e-mail: communications@bcma.bc.ca
URL: www.bcma.org
Overview: A medium-sized provincial organization founded in 1900
Membership: 11,000; *Committees:* Environmental Health
Activities: Programs to explore & articulate concerns regarding environmental health issues in a fashion which will best enable an informed public to participate in an open, valid, scientifically based analysis of issues involved; to assist society in development of policies dealing with environmental health issues; to enhance public health & harmony between humans & nature; Waste Management; Water Quality; Air Quality; *Internships:* Yes; *Speaker Service:* Yes; *Rents Mailing List:* Yes; *Library:* Yes
Mission: To promote a social, economic & political climate in which members can provide the citizens of British Columbia with the highest standard of health care while achieving maximum professional satisfaction & fair economic reward.

British Columbia Nature (Federation of British Columbia Naturalists) (FBCN)
c/o Parks Heritage Centre, 1620 Mount Seymour Rd., North Vancouver BC V7G 2R9
Tel: 604-985-3057
e-mail: manager@bcnature.ca
URL: www.bcnature.ca
Previous Name: Nature Council of British Columbia
Overview: A medium-sized provincial organization founded in 1969
Chief Officer(s):
Betty Davison, Office Manager, 604-985-3057
manager@bcnature.ca
Rosemary Fox, Chair, Conservation
foxikrj@bulkley.net
Joan Snyder, Chair, Education
snowdance@columbiawireless.ca
Pat Westheuser, Chair, Awards
hughwest@shaw.ca
Finances: *Funding Sources:* Membership fees; Donations; Fundraising
Membership: 50+ local nature clubs; *Fees:* $20; *Member Profile:* Naturalists, biologists, academics, environmentalists, nature experts, local natural history groups, & nature clubs throughout British Columbia; *Committees:* Conservation; Education; Awards
Activities: Providing educational opportunities; Coordinating stewardship projects
Meetings/Conferences:
For more information see Trade Shows, Conferences and Seminars Chapter
British Columbia Nature (Federation of British Columbia Naturalists) 2011 Manning Park Bird Blitz
June 2011, BC
British Columbia Nature (Federation of British Columbia Naturalists) 2011 Exploratory Trip
July 2011 Nuit Range, BC
British Columbia Nature (Federation of British Columbia Naturalists) 2011 Summer Camp (in cooperation with the Comox Valley Naturalists)
July 2011 Strathcona Park, BC
British Columbia Nature (Federation of British Columbia Naturalists) 2011 Exploratory Trip
July 2011 South Chilcotins, BC
British Columbia Nature (Federation of British Columbia Naturalists) 2011 Nature Conference & Fall General Meeting
September 2011 Delta, BC
British Columbia Nature (Federation of British Columbia Naturalists) 2012 Nature Conference & Annual General Meeting
Other Conferences in 2012 2012, BC
British Columbia Nature (Federation of British Columbia Naturalists) 2013 Nature Conference & Annual General Meeting
Other Conferences in 2013 2013, BC
British Columbia Nature (Federation of British Columbia Naturalists) 2014 Nature Conference & Fall General Meeting
Other Conferences in 2014 2014, BC
Publications: *BC Nature Magazine*
Type: Magazine *Frequency:* q. *Accepts Advertising* : Yes *Price:* Free with membership in the British Columbia Nature (Federation of BC Naturalists)
Profile: Club news, conservation information, & book reviews
Mission: To protect biodiversity, species at risk, & natural areas throughout British Columbia; To present a unified voice on conservation & environmental issues
Environmental Activity: Implementing conservation & stewardship project; Fostering awareness & understanding of the natural environment; Providing a means of communication between British Columbia naturalists; Offering field trips, such as birding & marine biology outings

British Columbia Nursery Trades Association *See* British Columbia Landscape & Nursery Association

British Columbia Oyster Growers' Association *See* British Columbia Shellfish Growers Association

British Columbia Paint Manufacturers' Association (BCPMA)
c/o Cloverdale Paint Inc., 6950 King George Hwy., Surrey BC V3W 4Z1
Tel: 604-596-6261; *Fax:* 604-597-2677
URL: www.bcpma.bc.ca
Overview: A small provincial organization founded in 1933
Membership: 1-99; *Member Profile:* Paint manufacturing companies in British Columbia
Activities: Engaging in advocacy activities related to the paint manufacturing industry in British Columbia; Liaising with various levels of government
Mission: To act as the voice of paint manufacturers in British Columbia; to promote the welfare of association members

British Columbia Ready Mixed Concrete Association
Parent: Canadian Ready Mixed Concrete Association
26162 - 30A Ave., Aldergrove BC V4W 2W5
Tel: 604-626-4141; *Fax:* 604-626-4143
e-mail: ccampbell@bcrmca.bc.ca
URL: www.bcrmca.bc.ca
Overview: A medium-sized provincial organization
Chief Officer(s):
Carolyn Campbell, Executive Director
Mission: To work cooperatively with all levels of government to ensure the ready-mix concrete industry operates with a focus on the communities & the environment

British Columbia Recreation & Parks Association (BCRPA)
Parent: Canadian Parks & Recreation Association
#101, 4664 Lougheed Hwy., Burnaby BC V5C 5T5
Tel: 604-629-0965; *Fax:* 604-629-2651
Toll-Free: 866-929-0965
e-mail: bcrpa@bcrpa.bc.ca; registration@bcrpa.bc.ca
URL: www.bcrpa.bc.ca
Overview: A medium-sized provincial charitable organization founded in 1958
Chief Officer(s):
Dean Gibson, President
Suzanne Allard Strutt, Chief Executive Officer
sstrutt@bcrpa.bc.ca
Holly-Ann Burrows, Manager, Communication
hburrows@bcrpa.bc.ca
Sandra Couto, Manager, Finance
scouto@bcrpa.bc.ca
Kara Misra, Manager, Parks & Recreation
kmisra@bcrpa.bc.ca
Misty Thomas, Manager, Fitness Program
mthomas@bcrpa.bc.ca
Finances: *Funding Sources:* Membership fees; Donations
Fees: Free, 1st year students; $60 individual goverment members; $245 individual independent members; Schedule based on population for local governments; *Member Profile:* Local governments, such as municipalities & regional districts; Corporations or commercial organizations; Not-for-profit organizations & educational institutions, connected to park, recreation, & cultural sectors; Individuals who work for or who are connected to a local government member; Students
Activities: Advocating accessibility & inclusiveness to recreation & physical activity; Providing training & resources; Distributing manuals on topics such as fitness theory, aquatic fitness group fitness, weight training, & yoga fitness
Meetings/Conferences:
For more information see Trade Shows, Conferences and Seminars Chapter
British Columbia Recreation & Parks Association 2011 37th Leisure Development Course
June 2011, BC
British Columbia Recreation & Parks Association 2011 Ripple Effects Provincial Aquatics Conference
October 2011, BC
British Columbia Recreation & Parks Association 2012 Symposium
May 2012 Victoria, BC
British Columbia Recreation & Parks Association 2012 35th Annual ProvincialParks & Grounds Spring Training Conference
Other Conferences in 2012 2012, BC
British Columbia Recreation & Parks Association 2013 36th Annual ProvincialParks & Grounds Spring Training Conference
Other Conferences in 2013 2013, BC
British Columbia Recreation & Parks Association 2013 Symposium
Other Conferences in 2013 2013, BC
British Columbia Recreation & Parks Association 2013 Provincial Aquatics Conference
Other Conferences in 2013 2013, BC
Publications: *British Columbia Recreation & Parks Association Annual Report*
Type: Yearbook
Recreation & Parks BC
Type: Magazine *Frequency:* q.
Profile: Happenings in the parks & recreation sector
Mission: To establish & sustain healthy lifestyles & communities in British Columbia
Environmental Activity: Fostering economic & environmental sustainability

British Columbia Salmon Farmers Association (BCSFA)
#302, 871 Island Hwy., Campbell River BC V9W 2C2
Tel: 250-286-1636; *Fax:* 250-286-1574
Toll-Free: 800-661-7256
e-mail: info@salmonfarmers.org
URL: www.salmonfarmers.org
Overview: A small provincial organization founded in 1984
Chief Officer(s):
Mary Ellen Walling, Executive Director
Finances: *Annual Operating Budget:* $500,000-$1.5 Million; *Funding Sources:* Membership fees; government
Staff: 6 staff member(s)
Membership: 50; *Fees:* $375 sustaining; $1500 associate
Activities: Oyster River Enhancement & others; *Speaker Service:* Yes
Mission: To promote the interests of persons, firms & corporations growing & selling farmed salmon in BC; *Member of:* Canadian Aquaculture Producers' Council; Canadian Aquaculture Industry Alliance; BC Federation of Agriculture; Salmon Health Consortium

British Columbia Shellfish Growers Association (BCSGA)
2002 Comox Ave., Unit F, Comox BC V9M 3M6
Tel: 250-890-7561; *Fax:* 250-890-7563
e-mail: roberta@bcsga.ca
URL: www.bcsga.ca
Previous Name: British Columbia Oyster Growers' Association
Overview: A small provincial organization founded in 1949
Finances: *Annual Operating Budget:* $100,000-$250,000; *Funding Sources:* Membership fees
Staff: 2 staff member(s)
Membership: 181; *Fees:* $500
Activities: Advocacy; research & development; marketing; member services; *Library:* Yes, Not open to the public
Mission: Advancing the sustainable growth & prosperity of the BC shellfish industry in a global economy by providing leadership & advocacy to members & stakeholders while maintaining the integrity of the marine environment; *Member of:* Canadian Aquaculture Industry Alliance; Aquaculture Association of Canada

Associations/Organizations / British Columbia Society of Landscape Architects

British Columbia Society of Landscape Architects (BCSLA)
#110, 355 Burrard St., Vancouver BC V6C 2G8
Tel: 604-682-5610; *Fax:* 604-681-3394
e-mail: admin@bcsla.org
URL: www.bcsla.org
Overview: A medium-sized provincial licensing organization founded in 1964
Finances: *Funding Sources:* Membership dues; special events; sponsors
Staff: 1 staff member(s); 13 volunteer(s)
Membership: 370; *Fees:* $550 landscape architect; $159 associate; $36 student; *Member Profile:* Must have university degree in landscape architecture followed by two years experience working for registered landscape architect; must complete series of exams.; *Committees:* Urban Issues; Membership; Ethics; Standards; Annual General Meeting; Promotion; Continuing Education
Activities: *Internships:* Yes
Mission: To promote, improve & advance the profession; to maintain standards of professional practice & conduct consistent with the need to serve & protect the public interest; to support the improvement &/or conservation of the natural, cultural, social & built environment.; *Member of:* Canadian Society of Landscape Architects

British Columbia Spaces for Nature
PO Box 673, Gibsons BC V0N 1V0
e-mail: bcspaces@spacesfornature.org
URL: www.spacesfornature.org
Overview: A medium-sized provincial charitable organization founded in 1989
Chief Officer(s):
Robert Ballantyne, Executive Member
Chloe O'Loughlin, Executive Member
Loretta Woodcock, Executive Member
Activities: Leading campaigns to protect wilderness areas throughout British Columbia; *Library:* British Columbia Spaces for Nature Library
Publications: *Jobs & Environment: Moving British Columbia into the 21st Century*
Type: Report *Number of Pages:* 74
Profile: Policy options & recommendations for British Columbia's future
Keeping the Special in Special Management Zones: A Citizens Guide [a publication of British Columbia Spaces for Nature]
Type: Report *Number of Pages:* 143
Profile: Information about special management zones, or government designated land use planning areas, where conservation is emphasized in management decisions
West Chilcotin Demonstration Project [a publication of British Columbia Spaces for Nature]
Type: Report *Number of Pages:* 73
Profile: Collaboration between First Nations, the local community, the tourism industry, & the forest industry to create a sustainable future for the West Chilcotin
Klinaklini Resource Analysis [a publication of British Columbia Spaces for Nature]
Type: Report *Number of Pages:* 87
Profile: Suggestions for safeguarding the biodiversity of this interior-to-coastal watershed
Mission: To protect British Columbia's wilderness resource
Environmental Activity: Providing education about caring for nature & conservation issues in British Columbia; Implementing the Tourism Zonation System, a land use planning approach that allows tourism in an environmentally sensitive & economically viable manner

British Columbia Sustainable Energy Association (BCSEA)
#5, 4217 Glanford Ave., Victoria BC V8Z 4B9
Tel: 250-744-2720
e-mail: info@bcsea.org
URL: www.bcsea.org
Social Media: www.facebook.com/BCSEA
Overview: A medium-sized provincial organization founded in 2004
Finances: *Funding Sources:* Donations
Fees: Schedule available; *Member Profile:* Individuals & organizations
Activities: Providing education through programs & webinars
Mission: To empower British Columbians to build a clean, renewable energy future; *Member of:* Canadian Renewable Energy Alliance; Canadian Solar Industries Ass'n; Canadian Wind Energy Ass'n; Climate Action Network Canada; KyotoPLUS; Livable Region Coalition; Oil Free Coast Alliance; Organizing for Change: Priorities for Environmental Leadership
Environmental Activity: Offering the SolarBC project, Climate Change Showdown program, Clean Energy Classroom progject, & the Green Landlords program

British Columbia Technology Industries Association (BCTIA)
#900, 1188 West Georgia St., Vancouver BC V6E 4A2
Tel: 604-683-6159; *Fax:* 604-683-3879
e-mail: info@bctia.org
URL: www.bctia.org
Also Known As: BC Technology Industries Association
Previous Name: Technologies Industry Association of BC
Overview: A medium-sized provincial organization founded in 1994
Chief Officer(s):
Pascal E. Spothelfer, President & CEO, 604-602-5230
pspothelfer@bctia.org
Membership: 200 companies; *Member Profile:* Full Voting Membership - companies deriving at least 50% of their revenue from technology products or services; Associate Membership - organizations which do not qualify for full membership, yet have an interest in technology industries; Agency Membership - government agencies & departments, crown corporations, educational institutes & other associations; *Committees:* Executive; Finance & Administration; Government Relations; Information Resource; Members' Services; Membership; Programs; Publicity & Marketing; Publications; Training & Human Resources
Activities: Technology Net Project seeks to overcome barriers to using the Internet by developing online business resources, new interfaces & database tools; also includes "Technopedia", an online interactive encyclopedia of BC technology companies; holds regular dinner events with speakers, special trade exhibits & industry roundtables; TIA Education Series features technical & marketing seminars
Mission: To provide the opportunity for executives & staff of member companies to enhance their leadership, management & technical skills through networking, educational programs, special interest groups & distribution of information; to promote linkages between member & other companies; to provide publicity to increase awareness of the success & importance of advanced technology industries to BC employment & economic activity; Affiliation(s): Information Technology Association of Canada

British Columbia Trucking Association (BCTA)
Parent: **Canadian Trucking Alliance**
#100, 20111 - 93A Ave., Langley BC V1M 4A9
Tel: 604-888-5319; *Fax:* 604-888-2941
Toll-Free: 800-565-2282
e-mail: bcta@bctrucking.com
URL: www.bctrucking.com
Previous Name: BC Motor Transport Association
Overview: A large provincial organization founded in 1913
Finances: *Annual Operating Budget:* $500,000-$1.5 Million; *Funding Sources:* Membership dues
Staff: 8 staff member(s)
Membership: 1,000 corporate; *Fees:* $325-$400; *Member Profile:* Trucking company operating in BC or supplier to trucking industry; *Committees:* Convention; Insurance; International; Labour; Freight Claims & Hazardous Goods; Safety; Truxpo; Vehicle Standards
Activities: *Speaker Service:* Yes; *Rents Mailing List:* Yes; *Library:* Yes, open by appointment
Mission: To act as the recognised voice of the commercial road transportation industry in British Columbia, by consulting & communicating with the industry, government & the public; to promote a prosperous, safe, efficient & responsible road transportation industry; to provide programs & services to members

British Columbia Water & Waste Association (BCWWA)
#221, 8678 Greenall Ave., Burnaby BC V5J 3M6
Tel: 604-433-4389; *Fax:* 604-433-9859
Toll-Free: 877-433-4389
e-mail: contact@bcwwa.org
URL: www.bcwwa.org
Social Media: www.facebook.com/group.php?gid=21435804125
Overview: A medium-sized provincial organization founded in 1964
Finances: *Funding Sources:* Membership fees; Courses; Seminars; Annual conference
Fees: $25 students; $35 operators; $60 full members; *Member Profile:* British Columbia & Yukon professionals & students in the water & wastewater fields; *Committees:* Membership; Communications; Conference; Young Professionals; Climate Change; Cross Connection Control; Decentralized Wastewater Management; Drinking Water; Energy Management; Infrastructure Management; Residuals Management; Small Water Systems; SCADA & Information Technology; Vancouver Island; Wastewater Collection; Wastewater Management; Wastewater Source Control; Water Sustainability; Watershed (Stormwater) Management; Yukon; Small Wastewater Systems; Small Water Systems; Wastewater Treatment; Water Distribution; Water Treatment; Awards; Elections; Governance; Nominations; Leadership Council
Activities: Promoting dialogue & information dissemination on environmental matters; Offering operator education & training opportunities; Providing networking opportunities; *Speaker Service:* Yes; *Library:* British Columbia Water & Waste Association Library
Awards: Stanley S. Copp Award (Award)
Personal Recognition Award (Award)
Corporate Recognition Award (Award)
Bridge Building Award (Award)
Small Water Systems Award (Award)
Victor M. Terry Award (Award)
Water for People Kenneth J. Miller Award (Award)
Okanagan College Bursary (Grant)
UBC Bursary (Grant)
Meetings/Conferences:
For more information see Trade Shows, Conferences and Seminars Chapter
British Columbia Water & Waste Association 2012 40th Annual Conference & Trade Show
Other Conferences in 2012 2012, BC
British Columbia Water & Waste Association 2013 41st Annual Conference & Trade Show
Other Conferences in 2013 2013, BC
British Columbia Water & Waste Association 2014 42nd Annual Conference & Trade Show
Other Conferences in 2014 2014, BC
British Columbia Water & Waste Association 2015 43rd Annual Conference & Trade Show
Other Conferences in 2015 2015, BC
Publications: *Watermark*
Type: Magazine *Frequency:* q. *Accepts Advertising*: Yes *Editor:* Carol Campbell
Profile: Calendar of events, product listings, new member listings, employment opportunities, informative articles, & reports on the annual conference, technical seminars & symposia
Mission: Safeguarding public health & the environment by sharing skills, knowledge, & experience with water & wastewater industry workers in British Columbia & the Yukon; To act a voice for the water & waste community in British Columbia & the Yukon; *Member of:* American Water Works Association (AWWA); Water Environment Federation (WEF)

British Columbia Waterfowl Society
5191 Robertson Rd., RR#1, Delta BC V4K 3N2
Tel: 604-946-6980; *Fax:* 604-946-6980
URL: www.reifelbirdsanctuary.com
Also Known As: Reifel Bird Sanctuary
Overview: A medium-sized provincial charitable organization founded in 1961
Finances: *Annual Operating Budget:* $100,000-$250,000
Staff: 2 staff member(s); 40 volunteer(s)
Membership: 2,000; *Fees:* $20 single; $40 family; $500 life; *Committees:* Conservation; Publicity & Promotion; Operations; Membership Services
Activities: *Awareness Events:* Snow Goose Festival, Nov.; *Speaker Service:* Yes; *Library:* Yes, Not open to the public
Mission: To encourage conservation of wetlands; to spur public awareness on importance of conservation of estuaries; to operate George C. Reifel Migratory Bird Sanctuary.

British Columbia Women's Institutes (BCWI)
Parent: **Federated Women's Institutes of Canada**
#203B, 750 Cottonwood Ave., Kamloops BC V2B 3X2
Tel: 250-554-5406; *Fax:* 250-554-5406
e-mail: info@bcwi.org
URL: www.bcwi.org
Overview: A medium-sized provincial charitable organization founded in 1909
Finances: *Annual Operating Budget:* $50,000-$100,000; *Funding Sources:* Membership dues; grants
Staff: 1 staff member(s)
Membership: 1,800; *Fees:* $15

Activities: *Awareness Events:* Women's Institutes Week, Feb.; *Speaker Service:* Yes; *Library:* Yes, Open to public, open by appointment
Mission: To help discover, stimulate & develop leadership among women; to assist, encourage & support women to become knowledgeable & responsible citizens; to ensure basic human rights for women & to work towards their equality; to be a strong voice through which matters of utmost concern can reach the decision makers; to network with organizations sharing similar objectives; to promote the improvement of agricultural & other rural communities & to safeguard the environment; *Member of:* Associated Country Women of the World; *Affiliation(s):* BC Federation of Agriculture

British Columbia Wood Specialities Group Association
#200, 9292 - 200th St., Langley BC V1M 3A6
Tel: 604-882-7100; *Fax:* 604-882-7300
Toll-Free: 877-422-9663
e-mail: info@bcwood.com
URL: www.bcwood.com
Also Known As: BC Wood
Overview: A medium-sized provincial charitable organization founded in 1989
Chief Officer(s):
Brian Hawrysh, CEO
Finances: *Annual Operating Budget:* $1.5 Million-$3 Million; *Funding Sources:* Membership dues; provincial government; federal government
Staff: 12 staff member(s)
Membership: 260; *Fees:* $500-$2,000; *Member Profile:* Manufacturers of value-added wood products in BC; *Committees:* Marketing
Activities: *Speaker Service:* Yes; *Library:* BC Wood Resource Library; open by appointment
Mission: To assist BC manufacturers of value-added products achieve global competitiveness by providing essential marketing services to capitalize on new market opportunities

British Council - Canada
80 Elgin St., Ottawa ON K1P 5K7
Tel: 613-364-6236; *Fax:* 613-569-1478
e-mail: education.enquiries@ca.britishcouncil.org
URL: www.britishcouncil.org/canada
Overview: A small international charitable organization
Chief Officer(s):
Martin Rose, Director
Jocelyne Sauvé, Administrative Assistant
Activities: Education, arts, science & information
Awards: Arts Grants (Grant)
UK/Canada Collaborative Programme (Scholarship)
British Chevening Scholarships (Award)
One year's postgraduate study at a British university in disciplines including: environmental studies, science, international relations, engineering
Mission: To encourage cultural, scientific, technological & educational cooperation between Britain & Canada

Bruce Peninsula Environment Group (BPEG)
PO Box 1072, Lions Head ON N0H 1W0
e-mail: info@bpeg.ca
URL: www.bpeg.ca
Overview: A small local organization founded in 1989
Chief Officer(s):
Tony Barton, Chair, 519-534-2355
Finances: *Annual Operating Budget:* Less than $50,000; *Funding Sources:* Membership fees; donations
Staff: 8 volunteer(s)
Membership: 125; *Fees:* $25 family, $15 single; *Member Profile:* Residents of the Bruce Peninsula; *Committees:* Alternate Energy; Dark Sky; Media; Recycling; Sustainable Forestry
Activities: Earth Day; energy tour; monthly meetings; tree planting; road clean-ups; recycling; environmental awards; *Awareness Events:* Energy Tour, June 4; *Library:* Yes, open by appointment
Awards: Bruce Peninsula Environment Group Award for Excellence (Award)
Mission: BPEG is a group of people concerned about the environment & committed to preserving the unique ecology of the Bruce Peninsula. It promotes awareness of the region's diverse flora, fauna, geology & cultural history, & monitors human impact on them. It has planted trees, helped with water quality issues on farmland, encouraged wildlife with habitat improvement, & has been active in legislating for better forestry practices.; *Member of:* Great Lakes United; Ontario Environment Network; Durham Nuclear Awareness; Canadian Environmental Network; Grey-Bruce Power Council

The Bruce Trail Association *See* The Bruce Trail Conservancy

The Bruce Trail Conservancy
PO Box 857, Hamilton ON L8N 3N9
Tel: 905-529-6821; *Fax:* 905-529-6823
Toll-Free: 800-665-4453
e-mail: info@brucetrail.org
URL: www.brucetrail.org
Social Media:
www.facebook.com/group.php?gid=111645892194726
Previous Name: The Bruce Trail Association
Overview: A medium-sized provincial charitable organization founded in 1963
Finances: *Annual Operating Budget:* $250,000-$500,000; *Funding Sources:* Memberships; donations; sales
Staff: 14 staff member(s); 1050 volunteer(s)
Membership: 8,500; *Fees:* $50
Activities: Land conservation; trail management & development; environmental hikes; *Awareness Events:* Bruce Trail Day, Oct.; *Speaker Service:* Yes; *Library:* Yes, open by appointment
Mission: To secure, develop & manage the Bruce Trail as a public footpath along the Niagara Escarpment from Queenston to Tobermory, thereby promoting preservation of the escarpment's ecological & cultural integrity & fostering an appreciation of its natural beauty. The Bruce Trail, designated as a UNESCO World Biosphere Reserve, is Canada's oldest and longest footpath.; *Member of:* Hike Ontario; *Affiliation(s):* Ontario Trails Council; Coalition on the Niagara Escarpment; Federation of Ontario Naturalists; Hike Ontario

Buffalo Lake Naturalists Club
PO Box 1802, Stettler AB T0C 2L0
Tel: 403-747-2221
e-mail: clipskic@rttinc.com
Overview: A small local organization founded in 1973
Finances: *Annual Operating Budget:* Less than $50,000; *Funding Sources:* Membership fees
Staff: 26 volunteer(s)
Membership: 30; *Fees:* $10 single; *Committees:* Environmental Protection; Program; Trail
Activities: Bird, plant & butterfly identification field trips; community projects; park planning & cleanup; *Library:* Yes
Mission: To promote the enjoyment of nature through environmental appreciation & conservation; to encourage wise use & conservation of natural resources & environmental protection; *Member of:* Federation of Alberta Naturalists

Building Supply Industry Association of British Columbia (BSIA of BC)
#2, 19299 - 94th Ave., Surrey BC V4N 4E6
Tel: 604-513-2205; *Fax:* 604-513-2206
Toll-Free: 888-711-5656
URL: www.bsiabc.ca
Overview: A medium-sized provincial organization founded in 1938
Fees: $169 wholesale branches; $199 retail stores & manufacturer's agents; $399 associates & retail & wholesale head offices; *Member Profile:* Manufacturers; Wholesalers; Suppliers; Retailers who operate lumber yards, hardware stores, & home centres
Activities: Promoting the building supply industry in British Columbia; Liaising with government; Addressing concerns within the industry; Providing information to members; Hosting product knowledge evenings at the BSIA office
Meetings/Conferences:
For more information see Trade Shows, Conferences and Seminars Chapter
Westcoast Building & Hardware Show 2012
Other Conferences in 2012 2012, BC
Westcoast Building & Hardware Show 2013
Other Conferences in 2013 2013, BC
Publications: *Building Supply Industry Association of British Columbia Directory*
Type: Directory *Frequency:* a. *Accepts Advertising* : Yes *Price:* Free with membership in the Building Supply Industry Association of British Columbia
Profile: An alphabetical & city listing of British Columbia's building material & hardware retailers & suppliers
BSIA News Magazine
Type: Magazine *Frequency:* 5 pa *Accepts Advertising* : Yes *Price:* Free with membership in the Building Supply Industry Association of British Columbia
Profile: A 40 to 60 page magazine, featuring association activities & in-depth articles for building supply dealers & suppliers throughout British Columbia, who retail a wide range of home improvement supplies & materials
Building Supply Industry Association of British Columbia Retail Product Buying Guide
Type: Guide *Frequency:* a. *Accepts Advertising* : Yes *Price:* Free with membership in the Building Supply Industry Association of British Columbia
Profile: Information about industry related vendors & suppliers
BSIA e-news
Type: Newsletter *Frequency:* m. *Accepts Advertising* : Yes *Price:* Free with membership in the Building Supply Industry Association of British Columbia
Profile: Industry & association news
Occupational Health & Safety Policy & Procedures Manual
Type: Manual *Price:* Free with membership in the BSIA of British Columbia; $19.95 non-members
Profile: A generic guide to the development of a specific manual for each business
Retail Job Descriptions Handbook
Type: Handbook
Mission: To act as the official voice of the building supply industry in British Columbia; To provide services to members
Environmental Activity: Addressing environmental issues affecting the building supply industry in British Columbia; Providing information about health & safety in the workplace; Printing & distributing the Occupational Health & Safety Policy & Procedures Manual

Bulkley Valley Naturalists
PO Box 4209, Smithers BC V0J 2N0
Tel: 250-847-3727
e-mail: hoekjh@mail.bulkley.net
Overview: A small local organization
Fees: $15 individual; $20 family
Activities: Participating in Christmas bird count and midwinter Bald Eagle count; participating on advisory committees on land use; developing nature education programs, field trips for schools
Mission: To promote the enjoyment of nature through environmental appreciation & conservation; to encourage wise use & conservation of natural resources & environmental protection.; *Member of:* Federation of BC Naturalists; *Affiliation(s):* Federation of BC Naturalists.

Bureau canadien de reconnaissance professionnelle des spécialistes de l'environnement *See* Canadian Environmental Certification Approvals Board

Bureau d'assurance du Canada *See* Insurance Bureau of Canada

Bureau of International Recycling (BIR)
24, av Franklin Roosevelt, Brussels B-1050 Belgium
Tel: 32-2-627-5770; *Fax:* 32-2-627-5773
e-mail: bir@bir.org
URL: www.bir.org
Overview: A medium-sized international organization founded in 1948
Fees: î1460-1820
Mission: To promote recycling & a recyclability, thereby conserving natural resources, protecting the environment, & facilitating free trade of recyclables in an environmentally sound manner

Burke Mountain Naturalists
PO Box 52540, Stn. Coquitlam Centre, Coquitlam BC V3B 7J4
Tel: 604-937-3483; *Fax:* 604-937-3483
e-mail: burkemtnnats@gmail.com
URL: www.bmn.bc.ca
Overview: A small local charitable organization founded in 1989
Chief Officer(s):
Ian McArthur, President, 604-939-4039
imcart@telus.net
Carole Edwards, Treasurer, 604-461-3864
caroleedwards@shaw.ca
Membership: 450; *Fees:* $25 single; $30 family/group
Activities: Monthly meetings; field trips & hikes; recording bird/flora sightings; preparing natural history brochures
Mission: The group is a non-profit society that promotes the enjoyment of nature through environmental appreciation & conservation. It advocates accessibility & maintenance of natural areas, particularly local ones. It is a registered charity, BN: 873847966RR0001.; *Member of:* BC Nature

BurlingtonGreen Environmental Association
3281 Myers Lane, Burlington ON L7N 1K6
Tel: 905-466-2171
URL: www.burlingtongreen.org
Social Media: www.facebook.com/burlington.green.environment
Overview: A medium-sized local organization
Chief Officer(s):
Amy Schnurr, Executive Director
Finances: *Funding Sources:* Membership fees; Donations
Fees: $5 students; $20 individuals; $25 families; *Member Profile:* Citizens for a greener community
Activities: Establishing the BurlingtonGreen Youth Network which meets monthly; *Awareness Events:* BurlingtonGreen Eco-Film Festival
Publications: *BurlingtonGreen Environmental Association Newsletter*
Type: Newsletter *Frequency:* a.
Profile: Information, eco-event listings, stories, & special bulletins
Greening Tips
Type: Newsletter *Frequency:* m.
BurlingtonGreen Youth Network Bulletin
Type: Newsletter
Profile: Information about volunteering, events, competitions, & scholarships
Mission: To advocate for local environmental issues
Environmental Activity: Hosting events on eco-topics; Providing information to the public about environmental issues

Burrard Inlet Environmental Action Program & Fraser River Estuary Management Program (BIEAP/FREMP)
#501, 5945 Kathleen Ave., Burnaby BC V5H 4J7
Tel: 604-775-5756; *Fax:* 604-775-5198
e-mail: mail@bieapfremp.org
URL: bieapfremp.org
Overview: A small local organization founded in 1985
Chief Officer(s):
Michelle Gaudry, Policy Coordinator
Finances: *Annual Operating Budget:* $250,000-$500,000; *Funding Sources:* Federal, provincial & regional government
Staff: 3 staff member(s)
Mission: To establish a management framework to facilitate activities to protect & improve the environmental quality of Burrard Inlet & the Fraser River Estuary; to promote the balance between the environment & the economy

Business Council of British Columbia
#810, 1050 Pender St. West, Vancouver BC V6E 3S7
Tel: 604-684-3384; *Fax:* 604-684-7957
e-mail: info@bcbc.com
URL: www.bcbc.com
Previous Name: Employers' Council of BC
Overview: A large provincial organization founded in 1966
Finances: *Annual Operating Budget:* $500,000-$1.5 Million; *Funding Sources:* Membership fees
Staff: 10 staff member(s)
Membership: 260 organizations; *Fees:* Schedule available; *Committees:* Occupational Health & Safety; Aboriginal Issues; Economic Policy; Environmental Policy; Government & Public Affairs Forum; Education & Skills Development; Employee Relations
Mission: To build a competitive & growing economy that provides opportunities for all who invest, work & live in British Columbia.

Business Council on National Issues *See* Canadian Council of Chief Executives

Calgary Field Naturalists' Society (CFNS)
Parent: Federation of Alberta Naturalists
PO Box 981, Stn. M, Calgary AB T2P 2K4
Tel: 403-239-6444
e-mail: naturecalgary@cfns.fanweb.ca
URL: cfns.fanweb.ca
Also Known As: Nature Calgary
Overview: A small local charitable organization founded in 1955
Finances: *Annual Operating Budget:* Less than $50,000; *Funding Sources:* Membership dues; donations; publications sale
Staff: 185 volunteer(s)
Membership: 100-499; *Fees:* $20 regular; $25 family; *Committees:* Bird Study; Botany & Fungi Study; Nature Photography; Endangered Species; Natural Areas
Activities: 35 slide shows/presentations & over 100 field trips a year; *Speaker Service:* Yes; *Library:* Yes, open by appointmentNot open to the public
Awards: President's Award, Honorary Life Memberships (Award)
Mission: To promote enjoyment of nature through environmental appreciation & conservation; to encourage wise use & conservation of natural resources & environmental protection; *Member of:* Calgary Area Outdoor Council; Alberta Environmental Network

Calgary Horticultural Society (CHS)
208 - 50 Ave. SW, Calgary AB T2S 2S1
Tel: 403-287-3469; *Fax:* 403-287-6986
e-mail: office@calhort.org
URL: www.calhort.org
Overview: A medium-sized provincial organization founded in 1907
Chief Officer(s):
Christina Smith, President
Elizabeth Jolicoeur, General Manager
Finances: *Annual Operating Budget:* $250,000-$500,000; *Funding Sources:* Membership fees; committee activities
Staff: 5 staff member(s); 650 volunteer(s)
Membership: 5,000+; *Fees:* $37 individual; $50 family; $200 corporate; *Committees:* Advertising; Books & Library; Bus Tours; CHS Book Committee; Clinics; Finance; Flower Show; Fundraising; Garden Competition; Garden Design Competition; Garden Viewing (Open Gardens); Home Show; Membership; Newsletter; Plant Exchange; Programs; Properties; Public Relations; Research & Development; Social; Volunteers
Activities: Gardeners Fair; garden competition; plant exchanges; *Speaker Service:* Yes; *Library:* Yes, Not open to the public
Mission: To educate, promote & encourage gardening in the Calgary area; *Affiliation(s):* Royal Horticultural Society

Calgary Zoological Society
1300 Zoo Rd. NE, Calgary AB T2E 7V6
Tel: 403-232-9300; *Fax:* 403-237-7582
Toll-Free: 800-588-9993
e-mail: comments@calgaryzoo.ab.ca; guestrelations@calgaryzoo.ab.ca
URL: www.calgaryzoo.org
Social Media: www.facebook.com/thecalgaryzoo
Overview: A large provincial charitable organization founded in 1929
Finances: *Funding Sources:* Donations; Sponsorships; Admission
Activities: Offering educational programs; Providing the Calgary Zoo's Endangered Species Reintroduction Research program
Meetings/Conferences:
For more information see Trade Shows, Conferences and Seminars Chapter
Calgary Zoological Society 2012 Annual General Meeting
Other Conferences in 2012 2012, AB
Publications: *Calgary Zoological Society eMagazine*
Frequency: q.
Mission: To operate the Calgary Zoo, Botanical Garden & Prehistoric Park To advocate on behalf of animals; *Member of:* Canadian Association of Zoos & Aquariums (CAZA); Association of Zoos & Aquariums (AZA)
Environmental Activity: Conserving endangered species, habitats, & ecosystems in Canada & throughout the world; Conducting scientific research in zoos & in the wild through The Calgary Zoo's Centre for Conservation Research; Participatign in Species Survival Plans

California Institute of Public Affairs (CIPA)
PO Box 189040, Sacramento CA 95818 USA
Tel: 916-442-2472; *Fax:* 916-442-2478
e-mail: info@interenvironment.org
URL: www.interenvironment.org/cipa
Overview: A small international organization founded in 1969
Chief Officer(s):
Thaddeus C. Trzyna, President
Elisabeth K. Kersten, Senior Associate
Finances: *Annual Operating Budget:* $100,000-$250,000
Staff: 3 staff member(s)
Publications: *The Urban Imperative: Urban Outreach Strategies for Protected Area Agencies*
Number of Pages: 168 *Editor:* Ted Trzyna *Price:* $35
Mission: To promote lateral communication & cooperation across professions, academic disciplines, governmental agencies & other sectors of society; to help define the public interest by bringing together people with disparate interests to find common ground; serves as the headquarters of the International Center for the Environment & Public Policy (ICEP), established in 1993 to provide a focus for CIPA international activities that started in 1972; *Affiliation(s):* Claremont Graduate School; IUCN - The World Conservation Union

Campground Owners Association of Nova Scotia (COANS)
Parent: Canadian Camping Association
c/o Arm of Gold Campground, 24 Church Rd., Little Bras d'Or, Cape Breton NS B1Y 2Y2
Tel: 902-736-6671
e-mail: info@campingnovascotia.com
URL: www.campingnovascotia.com
Previous Name: Camping Association of Nova Scotia
Overview: A medium-sized provincial organization founded in 1941
Chief Officer(s):
John Brennick, President, 902-736-6671
camp@armofgoldcamp.com
Chris Miller, Vice-President
campshubie@ns.sympatico.ca
Finances: *Annual Operating Budget:* Less than $50,000; *Funding Sources:* Membership dues; conferences; government grants
Staff: 10 volunteer(s)
Membership: 69; *Committees:* Membership; Newsletter; Marketing & Promotion; Nomination; Publication
Awards: Betty Campbell Camper Award (Award)
Mission: To provide the best camping experience possible throughout our diverse province; to improve standards at all the province's campgrounds; to provide leadership to this important segment of the provincial economy.

Camping Association of Nova Scotia *See* Campground Owners Association of Nova Scotia

Camping Québec
#700, 2001, rue de la Metropole, Longueuil QC J4G 1S9
Tél: 450-651-7396; *Téléc:* 450-651-7397
Ligne sans frais: 800-363-0457
URL: www.destinationcamping.ca
Nom précédent: Association des terrains de camping du Québec
Aperçu: *Dimension:* moyenne; *Envergure:* provinciale; *fondée en 1962*
Membre(s) du bureau directeur:
Maryse Catellier, Vice-président exécutif
Finances: *Budget de fonctionnement annuel:* $500,000-$1.5 Million
Personnel: 4 membre(s) du personnel
Membre: 430; *Montant de la cotisation:* 400$; *Critères d'admissibilite:* Exploitants de terrains de camping
Prix, Bouses: Prix de l'Excellence (Prix)
Mission: Défendre les intérêts de nos membres; offrir des services de publications et promotion, des activitées, des escomptes sur achats et programmes divers.

Canada Beef Export Federation
#235, 6715 - 8th St. NE, Calgary AB T2E 7H7
Tel: 403-274-0005; *Fax:* 403-274-7275
e-mail: canada@cbef.com
URL: www.cbef.com
Overview: A medium-sized national organization founded in 1989
Chief Officer(s):
Ted Haney, President
canada@cbef.com
Gib Drury, Chairman
Mission: The Canada Beef Export Federation facilitates the expansion of strategic global markets for Canadian beef products and identifies and develops key export markets to increase the sale of Canadian beef products. Their objective revolves around securing and increasing markets outside the USA for Canadian beef products in order to decrease export dependence on the United States.

Canada East Equipment Dealers' Association (CEEDA)
64 Temperance St., Aurora ON L4G 2P8
Tel: 905-841-6888; *Fax:* 905-841-1214
e-mail: info@orfeda.com
URL: www.orfeda.com
Previous Name: Ontario Retail Farm Equipment Dealers' Association

Overview: A medium-sized provincial organization founded in 1945
Member Profile: Farmstead, agricultural, powersport, & outdoor power equipment dealers from Ontario & the Maritimes
Activities: Liaising with educational institutions, equipment manufacturers, & provincial & federal governments; Providing training seminars; Collecting industry statistics; Disseminating timely information; Offering insurance counselling; Promoting safety
Meetings/Conferences:
For more information see Trade Shows, Conferences and Seminars Chapter
Canada East Equipment Dealers' Association 2012 Annual Meeting & Convention
February 2012
Mission: To promote the welfare of equipment trade retailers in the Maritimes & Ontario; To represent dealer interests in government legislation & regulation; To foster cooperation among manufacturers & distributors; To promote high standards for the retail equipment industry; Affiliation(s): North American Equipment Dealers' Association (NAEDA)

Canada Green Building Council (CaGBC) / Conseil du bâtiment durable du Canada (CBDCa)
#202, 47 Clarence St., Ottawa ON K1N 9K1
Tel: 613-241-1184; Fax: 613-241-4782
Toll-Free: 866-941-1184
e-mail: info@cagbc.org; education@cagbc.org
URL: www.cagbc.org
Social Media:
www.facebook.com/pages/CaGBC/168202776539520;
www.twitter.com/#!/CaGBC
Overview: A small national organization founded in 2002
Chief Officer(s):
Lisa Bate, Chair
Joanne Weir, Secretary
Anthony Exposti, Treasurer
Finances: *Funding Sources:* Sponsorships
Activities: Developing best design practices; Providing educational materials for members
Meetings/Conferences:
For more information see Trade Shows, Conferences and Seminars Chapter
Canada Green Building Council 2011 Green Associate Study Course
June 2011 Calgary, AB
Canada Green Building Council 2011 Green Associate Study Course
June 2011 Moncton, NB
Canada Green Building Council 2011 Annual General Meeting
June 2011 Toronto, ON
Canada Green Building Council 2011 LEED Canada Documentation Course
June 2011 Ottawa, ON
Canada Green Building Council 2011 Course: Design Installation & Management of Rainwater Harvesting Systems
June 2011 Woodbridge, ON
Canada Green Building Council 2011 Building Tour
June 2011 Ottawa, ON
Canada Green Building Council 2011 Workshop: LEED Canada for Existing Buildings, Operations & Maintenance
June 2011 Vancouver, BC
Canada Green Building Council 2011 Workshop: LEED Canada for New Construction 2009, Technical Review
June 2011 Edmonton, AB
Canada Green Building Council 2011 Green Associate Study Course
June 2011 Toronto, ON
Canada Green Building Council 2011 Green Associate Study Course
June 2011 Victoria, BC
Canada Green Building Council 2011 Living Building Challenge
June 2011 Edmonton, AB
Canada Green Building Council 2011 Workshop: Solar Energy, Best Practices for Residential Buildings
June 2011 Woodbridge, ON
Greenbuild 2011 International Conference & Expo (hosted by the Canada Green Building Council)
October 2011 Toronto, ON
Greenbuild 2012 International Conference & Expo
November 2012 San Francisco, CA
Canada Green Building Council 2012 Annual General Meeting
Other Conferences in 2012 2012
Canada Green Building Council 2012 National Symposium
Other Conferences in 2012 2012
Greenbuild 2013 International Conference & Expo
November 2013 Philadelphia, PA
Greenbuild 2014 International Conference & Expo
November 2014 New Orleans, LA
Greenbuild 2015 International Conference & Expo
November 2014 Washington, DC
Mission: To create buildings, homes, & communities across Canada that are environmentally responsible & high-performing; To advocate for green buildings
Environmental Activity: Promoting sustainable building across Canada; Encouraging energy efficiency; Offering in formaton about the LEED Canada program, Green Up program, Smart Growth program, & the Living Building Challenge

Canada Nature *See* **Nature Canada**

Canada Safety Council (CSC) / Conseil canadien de la sécurité (CCS)
1020 Thomas Spratt Pl., Ottawa ON K1G 5L5
Tel: 613-739-1535; Fax: 613-739-1566
e-mail: canadasafetycouncil@safety-council.org
URL: www.safety-council.org
Social Media: www.facebook.com/canada.safety
Overview: A large national charitable organization founded in 1968
Finances: *Annual Operating Budget:* $1.5 Million-$3 Million; *Funding Sources:* Programs; sponsors; contributions
Staff: 9 staff member(s)
Membership: 300 corporate + 200 individual; *Fees:* $50 individual; $250-$1,000 corporate
Activities: National Farm Safety Week, March; National Summer Safety Week, May; National Road Safety Week, May; National School Safety Week, Oct.; National Community Safety & Crime Prevention Week, Nov.; National Seniors' Safety Week, Nov.; National Home Fire Safety Week, Nov.; National Safe Driving Week, Dec.; *Speaker Service:* Yes; *Rents Mailing List:* Yes
Publications: *Living Safety*
Type: Magazine Language: E Frequency: q. Price: $11.25
Profile: CSC news, CSC initiatives, & traffic, occupational & public safety
Famille Avertie
Language: F Frequency: q.
Mission: To exercise leadership in a national effort to prevent death, injury & economic loss caused by accidents in the traffic, occupational & public environments; focus is on safety education & support of safety legislation

Canada's Research-Based Pharmaceutical Companies (Rx&D) / Les companies de recherche pharmaceutique du Canada
#1220, 55 Metcalfe St., Ottawa ON K1P 6L5
Tel: 613-236-0455; Fax: 613-236-6861
e-mail: info@canadapharma.org
URL: www.canadapharma.org
Previous Name: Pharmaceutical Manufacturers Association of Canada
Overview: A medium-sized national organization founded in 1914
Membership: 23,000 Canadians who work for 54 companies
Activities: Administers Rx&D Health Research Foundation
Awards: Post-Doctoral Fellowships in Pharmacy (Scholarship), PMAC Health Research Foundation
Provides highly-qualified individuals the opportunity to undertake post-graduate research & research training in the area of therapeutics or drug evaluation; the four annual awards are tenable only at Canadian faculties of pharmacy for two years
Research Career Awards in Medicine (Scholarship), PMAC Health Research Foundation
Provides protected time for independent investigators in the fields of clinical pharmacology, therapeutics or drug evaluation; tenable for a five-year period
Research Studentships in Pharmacology (Scholarship), PMAC Health Research Foundation
Provides the opportunity for students to undertake research in either basic or clinical pharmacology; tenable only at the faculties of medicine at the University of Calgary & McMaster University
Summer Student Research Scholarships in Pharmacy (Scholarship), PMAC Health Research Foundation
Provides the opportunity for students to undertake research in the fields of medicine & therapeutics during the summer; tenable only at Canadian faculties of pharmacy; two scholarships per faculty are available
Graduate Research Scholarships in Pharmacy (Scholarship), PMAC Health Research Foundation
Provides the opportunity for graduate students to undertake research training in the fields of medicine & therapeutics; tenable only at Canadian schools of pharmacy for two years
Summer Student Research Scholarships in Medicine (Scholarship), PMAC Health Research Foundation
Provides promising students the opportunity to undertake research in either basic or clinical pharmacology during the summer; tenable only at Canadian faculties of medicine (the University of Calgary & McMaster University excepted)
Medal of Honour (Award)
Established 1945; awarded periodically when an individual has made an invaluable contribution to the advancement of science
Mission: To discover new medicines that improve the quality of health care available for every Canadian; *Member of:* Canadian Institute of Biotechnology
Environmental Activity: Programs researching disposal of hazardous waste materials

Canada-Newfoundland Offshore Petroleum Board
TD Place, 140 Water St., 5th Fl., St. John's NL A1C 6H6
Tel: 709-778-1400; Fax: 709-778-1473
e-mail: postmaster@cnlopb.nl.ca
URL: www.cnlopb.nl.ca
Chief Officer(s):
Max Ruelokke, P.Eng, Chair & CEO
Dave Burley, Manager, Environmental Affairs, 709-778-1403
dburley@cnlopb.nf.ca
Mission: The Canada-Newfoundland Offshore Petroleum Board manages the petroleum resources in the Nlfd. offshore area on behalf of the Government of Canada & the Government of N.L. The Board's authority is derived from the legislation implementing the 1985 Atlantic Accord between the two governments. The Environmental Affairs department ensures that offshore oil & gas industrial activities proceed in an environmentally acceptable manner & evaluates the effect of the offshore environment upon the safety of offshore activities & by ensuring protection of the environment during the conduct of these activities. Working in close consultation with the Operations & Safety department, Environmental Affairs assesses the effects of environmental conditions, such as winds, waves & ice conditions, in the Nfld. offshore area upon the safety of operations. Environmental Affairs reviews operators' plans for collecting the weather, oceanographic & ice data that they are required to measure at offshore drilling & production sites. The Board reviews proposals for all physical activities offshore to identify their potential effects upon the natural environment or upon other users of that environment, such as the fishery. It evaluates measures that are proposed to prevent or mitigate these effects. This activity includes reviewing operators' contingency plans for environmental emergencies, especially oil spills, to ensure there are adequate response measures.

Canada-Nova Scotia Offshore Petroleum Board
TD Centre, 1791 Barrington St., 6th Fl., Halifax NS B3J 3K9
Tel: 902-422-5588; Fax: 902-422-1799
e-mail: postmaster@cnsopb.ns.ca
URL: www.cnsopb.ns.ca
Chief Officer(s):
Stuart Pinks, CEO
Keith Landra, Manager, Environment
Eric Theriault, Advisor, Environmental Affairs
etheriault@onsopb.ns.ca
Mission: CNSOPB is responsible for protection of the environment during all phases of offshore petroleum activities, from initial exploration to abandonment. The Board is a Federal Authority under the Canadian Environmental Assessment Act. The environmental assessment process starts at the Call for Bids stage. At this stage, a strategic or broad environmental assessment is conducted which identifies environmental concerns or issues. All subsequent projects, including seismic programs & exploratory wells, must undergo an environmental assessment prior to approval by the CNSOPB. The Board also uses class screenings or generic assessments to streamline the regulatory process. These more in-depth environmental assessments, usually jointly funded by a number of petroleum companies, provide more detailed overviews of potential environmental effects, research priorities & mitigation measure than can be accomplished in a single project-specific environmental assessment. Applications from the petroleum industry for work authorizations must include an environmental assessment, environmental contingency plan & spill contingency plan. The Board consults with FEAC on environmental & fisheries-related matters. The Board is also involved in initiatives led by the Department of Fisheries & Oceans (DFO) related to marine protected areas & integrated management planning

under the Oceans Act. The Board has signed memorandums of understanding with both the DFO & Environment Canada

Canadian 4-H Council / Conseil des 4-H du Canada
Central Experimental Farm, #26, 930 Carling Ave., Ottawa ON K1A 0C6
Tel: 613-234-4448; *Fax:* 613-234-1112
URL: www.4-h-canada.ca
Social Media: www.facebook.com/4HCanada; twitter.com/4HCanada
Previous Name: Canadian Council on 4-H Clubs
Overview: A large national charitable organization founded in 1933
Finances: *Funding Sources:* Memberhip fees; Sponsorships; Donations; Wills & Bequests
Activities: Offering exchanges & scholarships which focus on citizenship; Providing leadership development opportunities
Publications: *L'avantage 4-H Advantage*
Type: Magazine Frequency: s-a. Price: Free
Profile: Coverage of national programs & 4-H activities across Canada
Canadian 4-H Council Annual Report
Type: Yearbook Frequency: a.
Profile: Annual Report of the Canadian 4-H Council & Canadian 4-H Foundation
Mission: To inspire youth across Canada to become contributing leaders in their communities; To support the development of Canada's rural youth

Canadian Academy of Engineering (CAE) / Académie canadienne du génie (ACG)
#1100, 180 Elgin St., Ottawa ON K2P 2K3
Tel: 613-235-9056; *Fax:* 613-235-6861
e-mail: info@acad-eng-gen.ca
URL: www.acad-eng-gen.ca
Overview: A medium-sized national charitable organization founded in 1987
Finances: *Funding Sources:* Sponsorships
Membership: 304 active members + 111 emeritus members + 3 honorary members; *Member Profile:* Accomplished engineers, nominated & elected by their peers
Activities: Increasing awareness of engineering in society; Promoting industrial competitiveness & environmental preservation; Advising on engineering education, research, & innovation; Developing relations with other professional engineering organizations
Publications: *Canadian Academy of Engineering Newsletter / Communiqué*
Type: Newsletter Frequency: q.
Profile: Reports, updates, upcoming events, & activities of the Academy & its Fellows
Mission: To ensure that Canadian engineering expertise is applied to the benefit of all Canadians; *Member of:* International Council of Academies of Engineering & Technological Sciences (CAETS); *Affiliation(s):* Council of Canadian Academies

Canadian Acoustical Association / Association canadienne d'acoustique
c/o National Research Council of Canada, Institute for Research in Construction, Ottawa ON K1A 0R6
Tel: 613-993-7985; *Fax:* 613-954-1495
e-mail: secretary@caa-aca.ca
URL: www.caa-aca.ca
Overview: A large national charitable organization
Finances: *Annual Operating Budget:* $50,000-$100,000; *Funding Sources:* Membership; subscriptions; conference fees
Staff: 20+ volunteer(s)
Membership: 300 individuals + 80 organizations; *Fees:* $80 individual; $25 student; *Member Profile:* Students; professors; consultants; government
Activities: *Awareness Events:* Canadian Acoustics Week Annual Conference, Oct.
Awards: Student Presentation Awards (Scholarship)
Awarded annually to undergraduate or graduate students making the best presentations during the technical sessions of Canadian Acoustics Week Eligibility: Application must be made at the time of submission of the abstract Award Amount: Three awards of $500 each
Alexander Graham Bell Graduate Student Prize in Speech Communication and Hearing (Scholarship)
Eligibility: For a graduate student enrolled in a Canadian academic institution & conducting research in the field of speech communication or behavioural acoustics; applicants must submit an application form & supporting documentation before the end of February of the year the award is to be made Award Amount: $800
Fessenden Student Prize in Underwater Acoustics (Scholarship)
Awarded every two years Eligibility: For a graduate student enrolled at a Canadian university & conducting research in underwater acoustics or in a branch of science closely connected to underwater acoustics; applicants must submit an application & supporting documentation before the end of February of the year the award is to be made Award Amount: $400
Eckel Student Prize in Noise Control (Scholarship)
Awarded annually for a graduate student pursuing studies in any discipline of acoustics & conducting research related to the advancement of the practice of noise control Award Amount: $500
Directors' Awards (Award)
Three awards are made annually to the authors of the best papers published in Canadian Acoustics Eligibility: The first author must study or work in Canada; all papers reporting new results, as well as review & tutorial papers are eligible; technical notes are not eligible Award Amount: $500 to a graduate student author; $500 to professional authors Contact: Chantal Laroche
Edgar & Millicent Shaw Postdoctoral Prize in Acoustics (Scholarship)
Eligibility: For full-time research for 12 months for a highly qualified candidate holding a Ph.D. degree or the equivalent, who has completed all formal academic research training & who wishes to acquire up to two years supervised research training in an established setting; the proposed research must be related to some area of acoustics, psychoacoustics, speech communication or noise; applicants must submit an application form & supporting documentation Award Amount: $3,000
Publications: *Canadian Acoustics*
Type: Journal Frequency: q. Price: Free to CAA members
Profile: Refereed articles, research, reviews, activities, new products, & news about acoustics & vibration
Mission: To foster communication among people working in all areas of acoustics in Canada; to promote the growth & practical application of knowledge in acoustics; to encourage education, research & employment in acoustics

Canadian Advanced Technology Alliance (CATA Alliance) / Association canadienne de technologie de pointe
#416, 207 Bank St., Ottawa ON K2P 2N2
Tel: 613-236-6550
e-mail: info@cata.ca; cmalette@cata.ca (Membership)
URL: www.cata.ca
Social Media: facebook.com/group.php?gid=5391503953; http://twitter.com/CATAAlliance
Overview: A large national organization founded in 1978
Member Profile: Corporations with Canadian offices, engaged in research & development activities; international corporations in a collaboration with CATA; user industries; service companies
Activities: Engaging in advocacy activities; providing original & timely information for members & stakeholders; supporting research projects
Awards: Innovation & Leadership Awards (Award)
To recognize expertise, innovation, & leadership in the Canadian high-technology sector
Sara Kirke Award (Award)
To recognize woman entrepreneurship, including outstanding technological innovation & corporate leadership
Mission: CATA Alliance provides its members with a network to establish partnerships, to match up with global business opportunities. It offers communication & advocacy services, notably in dealing with the government, working to ensure that policies are favourable to Cdn. technology companies. It maintains a research repository where members can access information to advance their agendas. The ultimate goal is to give members a competitve edge.

Canadian Aeronautical Institute (CAI) See Canadian Aeronautics & Space Institute

Canadian Aeronautics & Space Institute (CASI) / Institut aéronautique et spatial du Canada
#104, 350 Terry Fox Dr., Ottawa ON K2K 2W5
Tel: 613-591-8787; *Fax:* 613-591-7291
e-mail: casi@casi.ca; membership@casi.ca
URL: www.casi.ca
Previous Name: Canadian Aeronautical Institute (CAI)
Merged from: Institute of Aircraft Technicians; Ottawa Aeronautical Society; US Institute of Aeronautical Science
Overview: A medium-sized national licensing organization founded in 1954
Membership: 1,600; *Fees:* $36.75 juniors; $63 seniors; $94.50 associates & individuals
Activities: Facilitating communications among the Canadian aeronautics & space community; Developing members' skills
Awards: Trans-Canada (McKee) Trophy (Award)
The McCurdy Award (Award)
To recognize outstanding achievement in the science & creative aspects of engineering
The C.D. Howe Award (Award)
To honour achievements in the fields of planning & policy making, plus leadership
The Romeo Vachon Award (Award)
To recognize an outstanding display of initiative & practical skills in the solution of a particular problem
The Alouette Award (Scholarship)
To celebrate an outstanding contribution to advancement in space technology, science, engingeering, & application
Publications: *CASI [Canadian Aeronautics & Space Institute] Clipper*
Frequency: bi-weekly
Profile: Information about the aeronautics, space, & remote sensing communities, produced & distributed to members & corporate partners
CASI [Canadian Aeronautics & Space Institute] Log
Type: Newsletter
Profile: Information about events & branches, produced & distributed to members & corporate partners
Canadian Aeronautics & Space Journal (CASJ)
Type: Journal Frequency: 4 pa Accepts Advertising : Yes Editor: Dr. Steven Zan Price: Free to members & corporate
Profile: Fundamental & applied research, new technologies, & developments in the aerospace sciences & related fields
Canadian Journal of Remote Sensing (CJRS)
Type: Journal Frequency: 6 pa Accepts Advertising : Yes Editor: Nicholas Coops Price: Free to members & corporate partners
Profile: Technical research articles, notes, & review papers on topics such as information processing methods, data acquisition, & applications
Mission: To advance the art, science, engineering, & applications of aeronautics & associated technologies in Canada; to promote Canadian competence & international competitiveness; *Affiliation(s):* Canadian Air Cushion Technology Society; Canadian Navigation Society; Canadian Remote Sensing Society

Canadian Agricultural Economics & Farm Management Society See Canadian Agricultural Economics Society

Canadian Agricultural Economics Society (CAES) / Société canadienne d'agroéconomie (SCAE)
University Of Victoria, PO Box 1700, Stn. CSC, Rm. 360, Business & Economics Bldg., Victoria BC V8W 2Y2
e-mail: caes@aganalysis.com
URL: www.caes.ca
Previous Name: Canadian Agricultural Economics & Farm Management Society
Overview: A medium-sized national organization
Membership: 488; *Fees:* Schedule available; *Member Profile:* Individuals with interest in agricultural economics
Publications: *Canadian Agricultural Economics Society Newsletter*
Type: Newsletter
Profile: CAES news & activities
Canadian Journal of Agricultural Economics / Revue Canadienne d'Agroéconomie
Type: Journal Frequency: 4 pa Price: Free to members
Profile: International peer-reviewed journal about agricultural & resource economics
Mission: To address problems related to the economics of food production & marketing & the quality of rural life through extension, research, teaching, & policy making in government & private industry; *Affiliation(s):* Agricultural Institute of Canada

Canadian Agricultural Safety Association (CASA) / Association canadienne de sécurité agricole (ACSA)
#5A, 1325 Markham Rd., Winnipeg MB R3T 4J6
Tel: 204-452-2272; *Fax:* 204-261-5004
e-mail: info@casa-acsa.ca
URL: www.casa-acsa.ca
Overview: A medium-sized national organization founded in 1993
Chief Officer(s):
Marcel L. Hacault, Executive Director
Fees: $50 personal, not-profit; $250 academia, producer, government, service/supply industry

Publications: CASA [Canadian Agricultural Safety Association] / ACSA [Association canadienne de sécurité agricole] Liaison
Type: Newsletter **Frequency:** q.
Profile: News for members & interested individuals
Mission: Addresses problems of illness, injuries & accidental death in farmers, their families & agricultural workers; improve health & safety conditions of those that live or work on Canadian farms

Canadian Agri-Marketing Association (Alberta) (CAMA)
PO Box 4520, Stn. C, Calgary AB T2T 5N3
URL: www.cama.org
Also Known As: CAMA Alberta
Overview: A medium-sized provincial organization founded in 1978
Fees: $140
Activities: Offering professional development seminars; Providing networking opportunities
Publications: CAMA [Canadian Agri-Marketing Association] Membership Directory
Type: Directory
Profile: Contact information for CAMA members throughout Canada
MarketNews [a publication of the Canadian Agri-Marketing Association]
Type: Newsletter **Frequency:** 5 pa
Profile: Association events & industry information for members
Mission: To increase knowledge of ideas related to agri-marketing; to promote high professional standards of agricultural marketing; **Affiliation(s):** National Agri-Marketing Association (NAMA); CAMA Saskatchewan; CAMA Manitoba; CAMA Ontario; CAMA Québec

Canadian Agri-Marketing Association (Manitoba)
210 - 1600 Kenaston Blvd., Winnipeg MB R3P 0Y4
Tel: 204-799-2019; **Fax:** 204-257-5651
e-mail: camamb@mts.net
URL: www.cama.org/manitoba/ManitobaHome.aspx
Also Known As: CAMA Manitoba
Overview: A small provincial organization founded in 1985
Chief Officer(s):
David Lazarnko, President
dlazarenko@bcg.ca
Finances: Annual Operating Budget: Less than $50,000
Staff: 1 staff member(s); 12 volunteer(s)
Membership: 125 individual; **Fees:** $100 individual; $25 student
Mission: To promote excellence in agrimarketing; **Affiliation(s):** CAMA Ontario; CAMA Alberta; CAMA Saskatchewan

Canadian Airports Council (CAC) / Conseil des aéroports du Canada
#706, 350 Sparks St., Ottawa ON K1R 7S8
Tel: 613-560-9302; **Fax:** 613-560-6599
e-mail: sharon.redden@cacairports.ca
URL: www.cacairports.ca
Overview: A medium-sized national organization founded in 1991
Chief Officer(s):
Jim Facette, President/CEO, 613-560-9302 Ext. 11
Daniel-Robert Gooch, Director, Communications
daniel.gooch@cacairports.ca
Finances: Funding Sources: Sponsorships
Membership: 48; **Member Profile:** Canadian airports (CAC members are also members of Airports Council International - North America)
Activities: Preparing submissions to governmental bodies & agencies
Publications: The Airport Voice: News & Views
Type: Newsletter
Profile: National & international news affecting Canadian airports
The Canadian Airports Council Annual Report
Type: Yearbook **Frequency:** a.
Profile: Significant developments at the CAC & in the industry during the year
Mission: To act as the voice for Canadian airports on a great range of important issues; **Member of:** Airports Council International - North America (ACI-NA); **Affiliation(s):** Air Transport Association of Canada (ATAC); Canadian International Freight Forwarders Association (CIFFA); Canadian Chamber of Commerce; Canadian Tourism Commission; Tourism Industry Association of Canada (TIAC)

Canadian Animal Health Institute (CAHI) / Institut canadien de la santé animale
#102, 160 Research Lane, Guelph ON N1G 5B2
Tel: 519-763-7777; **Fax:** 519-763-7407
e-mail: cahi@cahi-icsa.ca
URL: www.cahi-icsa.ca
Overview: A medium-sized national organization founded in 1968
Finances: Annual Operating Budget: $250,000-$500,000; Funding Sources: Membership dues
Staff: 3 staff member(s)
Membership: 60 organizations
Awards: Industry Leadership Award (Award)
Publications: CAHI [Canadian Animal Health Institute] Resource Directory
Type: Directory **Frequency:** biennial
Profile: Listings of CAHI members, veterinary associations, government agencies related to animal health, commodity organizations, & CAHI's foreign sister organizations
Inforum [a publication of the Canadian Animal Health Institute]
Type: Newsletter **Frequency:** 4 pa
Profile: Distributed to Canadian veterinarians in the Canadian Veterinary Journal
Mission: To work closely with allied industry groups for the betterment of Canadian agriculture; to foster & maintain a regulatory & legislative climate which will encourage member companies to develop & market useful animal health products & services; to promote the proper use of animal health & nutrition products by livestock & poultry farmers through user education information programs; to develop a public information program which enhances appreciation of the contributions the animal health & nutrition industry makes to the economy & society

Canadian Aquaculture Industry Alliance (CAIA) / Alliance de l'industrie canadienne de l'aquiculture
PO Box 81100, Stn. World Exchange Plaza, #705, 116 Albert St., Ottawa ON K1P 1B1
Tel: 613-239-0612; **Fax:** 613-239-0619
e-mail: info@aquaculture.ca
URL: www.aquaculture.ca
Social Media: @CDNaquaculture
Overview: A medium-sized national organization founded in 1987
Chief Officer(s):
Ruth Salmon, Executive Director, 613-239-0612, Fax: 613-239-0619
ruth.salmon@aquaculture.ca
Sherry Sadler, Coordinator, Projects
sherry.sadler@aquaculture.ca
Member Profile: Aquaculture operators; Feed companies; Suppliers; Provincial shellfish & finfish aquaculture associations
Activities: Advocating for Canadian aquaculture issues; Fostering cooperation among various aquaculture interests; Promoting a positive image of the Canadian aquaculture industry; Encouraging the consumption of aquaculture products from Canada
Mission: To represent the interests of aquaculture operators, feed companies, suppliers, & provincial finfish & shellfish aquaculture associations on both the national & international scenes; To ensure the international competitiveness of the Canadian aquaculture industry

Canadian Archaeological Association (CAA) / Association d'archéologie canadienne
c/o Jack Brink, Royal Alberta Museum, 12845 - 102 Ave., Edmonton AB T5N 0M6
Tel: 780-453-9151
e-mail: president@canadianarchaeology.com
URL: www.canadianarchaeology.com
Overview: A small national charitable organization founded in 1968
Chief Officer(s):
Jack Brink, President
Eric Damkjar, Vice-President
vicepresident@canadianarchaeology.com
Jeff Hunston, Secretary-Treasurer
secretary-treasurer@canadianarchaeology.com
Member Profile: Professional, avocational, & student archaeologists; General public; **Committees:** Heritage & Legislation Policy; Aboriginal Heritage; Public Communications Awards; Comité du Prix Weetaluktuk Award Committee; Financial Advisory; Cultural Resource Management
Activities: Fostering cooperation with aboriginal groups; Promoting activities advantageous to archaeology; Advocating nationally
Awards: Daniel Weetaluktuk Award (Award)
Public Communications Award (Award)
Margaret & James F. Pendergast Award (Award)
Smith Wintenberg Award (Award)
Publications: Canadian Journal of Archaeology / Journal canadien d'archéologie
Type: Journal **Frequency:** s-a. **Editor:** Dr. Gerry Oetelaar
Profile: Documents the processes & results of Canadian archaeology
CAA [Canadian Archaeological Association] Newsletter / Bulletin de l'ACA [Association d'archéologie canadienne-
Type: Newsletter **Frequency:** s-a. **Editor:** Colin Varley
Mission: To publish & disseminate archaeological knowledge in Canada; to encourage archaeological research & conservation efforts; to promote cooperation among archaeological societies & agencies

Canadian Associated Air Balance Council (CAABC)
c/o President, 4043 Carling Ave., Ottawa ON K2K 2A4
Tel: 613-592-4991; **Fax:** 613-592-0867
URL: www.caabc.org
Overview: A small national organization founded in 1970
Chief Officer(s):
Marc Desjardins, President
kab@on.aibn.com
Finances: Funding Sources: Membership fees
Staff: 1 staff member(s); 18 volunteer(s)
Membership: 20; **Fees:** $3,000; **Committees:** Membership; Technical; Standards
Mission: To promote independent testing & balancing of mechanical systems; to produce standards to advance the industry; **Affiliation(s):** Associated Air Balance Council

Canadian Association for Health Services & Policy Research (CAHSPR) / Association canadienne pour la recherche sur les services et les politiques de la santé (ACRSPS)
292 Somerset St. West, Ottawa ON K2P 0J6
Tel: 613-235-7180; **Fax:** 613-235-5451
e-mail: cahspr@cahspr.ca
URL: www.cahspr.ca
Previous Name: Canadian Health Economics Research Association
Overview: A small national organization founded in 1982
Chief Officer(s):
Kevin Barclay, Executive Director
Renaldo Battista, President
Marcel Saulnier, Secretary
Eric Latimer, Treasurer
Finances: Funding Sources: Membership dues
Membership: 100-499; **Fees:** $150 individual; $750 university; $35 student; **Member Profile:** Health services & policy researchers; Decision makers; Practitioners; Students; Users of research from organizations & industry; Representatives from sponsor organizations; **Committees:** Conference Planning; Communications; Development; Membership; Nominating; Strategic Planning
Publications: Healthcare Policy
Type: Journal **Frequency:** q.
CAHSPR [Canadian Association for Health Services & Policy Research] Newsletter
Type: Newsletter **Frequency:** w.
Profile: CAHSPR activities & upcoming events, career opportunities, links to course materials for student members, research & policy items of interest to members
Mission: To improve the quality, relevance, & application of health services & policy research

Canadian Association for Humane Trapping (CAHT)
PO Box 7115, Stn. Maplehurst, Burlington ON L7T 4J8
Tel: 905-637-9623; **Fax:** 905-637-3912
e-mail: caht1@cogeco.ca
URL: www.caht.ca
Overview: A medium-sized national charitable organization founded in 1954
Finances: Annual Operating Budget: $50,000-$100,000; Funding Sources: Membership fees; Bequests; Donations
Staff: 1 staff member(s)
Membership: 750; **Fees:** $10; **Committees:** Trap research & development
Activities: Speaker Service: Yes
Publications: The CAHT [Canadian Association for Humane Trapping] Bulletin
Type: Newsletter **Number of Pages:** 16
Mission: To reduce & eliminate suffering of animals trapped for whatever reason; to work with governments, trappers, the commercial fur industry, animal welfare organizations & the public-at-large to bring about actual trapping improvements; **Member of:** World Conservation Union; Fur Institute of Canada;

Associations/Organizations / Canadian Association for Laboratory Accreditation Inc.

World Wildlife Fund; Canadian Nature Federation; Canadian Federation of Humane Societies

Canadian Association for Laboratory Accreditation Inc. (CALA)
#310, 1565 Carling Ave., Ottawa ON K1Z 8R1
Tel: 613-233-5300; *Fax:* 613-233-5501
e-mail: ecummins@cala.ca
URL: www.cala.ca
Overview: A medium-sized national organization founded in 1989
Fees: $15 students; $35 associates; $45 individual (voting) members; $400 institutional (voting) members; *Member Profile:* Individuals, consultants, institutions, industrial organizations, regulatory agencies, laboratory equipment suppliers, & user groups interested in the work of environmental analytical laboratories
Activities: Advocating for change in protecting public health & safety; Educating the public & raising awareness of laboratory accreditation; Offering training opportunities, such as workshops & web-based education; Conducting site audits & proficiency testing to evaluate the performance of laboratories; Granting accreditation to laboratories, based on decisions of the CALA Accreditation Council
Publications: *Canadian Association for Laboratory Accreditation Inc. Annual Report*
Type: Yearbook *Frequency:* a.
Mission: To provide internationally-recognized accreditation services; To assist laboratories in the achievement of high levels of scientific & management excellence; To improve environmental quality & public health & safety; *Member of:* Asia Pacific Laboratory Accreditation Cooperation; International Laboratory Accreditation Cooperation

Canadian Association for Laboratory Animal Science (CALAS)
#640, 144 Front St., Toronto ON M5J 2L7
Tel: 416-593-0268; *Fax:* 416-979-1819
e-mail: office@calas-acsal.org; membership@calas-acsal.org
URL: www.calas-acsal.org
Overview: A small national organization founded in 1962
Finances: *Funding Sources:* Membership fees; Sponsorships
Membership: 1,000; *Member Profile:* Veterinarians; Physicians; Researchers; Technicians; Administrators; Students; Institutions; *Committees:* Awards; Marketing; Membership; Educational; Regional Chapter; Symposium; Continuing Education
Activities: Providing information about the animal science industry; Offering networking opportunities; Providing continuing education to advance the knowledge & skills of persons who work with laboratory animals
Publications: *Canadian Association for Laboratory Animal Science Members' Magazine*
Type: Magazine *Frequency:* bi-m. *Price:* Free with membership in the Canadian Association for Laboratory Animal Science
Mission: To elevate standards of laboratory animal science; To promote excellence in research; To eliminate inhumane & unnecessary use of animals in research; To enhance animal welfare

Canadian Association for Mine & Explosive Ordnance Security (CAMEO)
1009 Oak Cres., Cornwall ON K6J 2N2
Tel: 613-937-0686; *Fax:* 613-937-4643
e-mail: frank.jewsbury@rogers.com
URL: www.cameo.org
Also Known As: CAMEO Landmine Clearance
Overview: A small international charitable organization
Chief Officer(s):
James D. McGill, P.Eng., Executive Director
megill@cameo.org
Membership: 100-499
Activities: Landmine clearance in Southern Sudan; *Speaker Service:* Yes
Mission: To engage in humanitarian mine clearance; to engage in humanitarian explosive ordnance disposal; to engage in live-firing area clearance & environmental clean-up; to engage in land mine & explosive ordnance awareness training; to engage in land mine & battle area surveys; to provide training & assistance to others in the carrying out of all of the above activities

Canadian Association for Renewable Energies (CARE) / Association canadienne pour les énergies renouvelables
7885 Jock Trail, Ottawa ON K0A 2Z0
Fax: 613-822-4987
e-mail: eggertson@renewables.ca
URL: www.renewables.ca
Also Known As: we c.a.r.e
Overview: A small national organization founded in 1998
Chief Officer(s):
Bill Eggertson, CAE, Executive Director
Finances: *Funding Sources:* Membership fees
Fees: $214 personal; $321 corporate; $1,070 institutional;
Member Profile: Supporters of renewable energies
Activities: Undertaking research to optimize renewable energy technologies
Publications: *Refocus Weekly [a publication of the Canadian Association for Renewable Energies]*
Type: Newsletter *Frequency:* w. *Accepts Advertising* : Yes
Profile: News, reports, & events from around the world
Renewable Energy Focus
Type: Magazine *Accepts Advertising* : Yes
Profile: Debate & dialogue between industry, research, government agencies, & financial organizations throughout the world on topics such as biomass, biogass, hydroelectricity, wind, waves, solar architecture, & fuel cells
Mission: To promote feasible applications of renewable energies

Canadian Association for Research in Nondestructive Evaluation (CARNDE) / Association canadienne de recherches en évaluation non-destructive (ACREND)
75, boul de Montagne, Boucherville QC J4B 6Y4
Tel: 450-641-5252; *Fax:* 450-641-5106
e-mail: jean.bussiere@nrc.ca
URL: www.nrc.ca
Overview: A small national organization founded in 1987
Chief Officer(s):
Jean Bussière, Research Editor
Membership: 100; *Member Profile:* Open to applied scientists & engineers who have a professional interest in conductor application of research in NDE
Activities: *Rents Mailing List:* Yes
Mission: To foster, coordinate & disseminate results of research, development & application of new or advanced NDE techniques in Canada; to promote technology transfer by encouraging collaboration between universities, research organizations & industrial or governmental users; to raise the profile of NDE research in Canada by publicizing the need for & economic benefits arising from advances in NDE

Canadian Association for Studies in Co-operation (CASC) / Association canadienne pour les études sur la coopération (ACEC)
c/o C. Leviten-Reid, Ctr for the Study of Co-operatives, U of SK, 101 Diefenbaker Pl., Saskatoon SK S7N 5B8
Tel: 306-966-8509; *Fax:* 306-966-8517
e-mail: casc@coopresearch.coop
URL: www.coopresearch.coop
Overview: A small national organization founded in 2000
Chief Officer(s):
Catherine Leviten-Reid, Ph.D., President
casc_pres@coopresearch.coop
Robin Puga, Vice-President
casc_vp@coopresearch.coop
Member Profile: Researchers, scholars, & practitioners working in the area of co-operatives
Awards: Lemaire Co-operative Studies Award (Scholarship)
Postgraduate & undergraduate awards to encourage students to undertake studies which will help them to contribute to the development of co-operatives in Canada or elsewhere; disciplines include: housing, planning, environmental studies, engineering, geography, science, architecture *Award Amount:* $1,000 - $3,000
Alexander Fraser Laidlaw Fellowship (Scholarship)
Postgraduate award for students in: housing, environmental studies, planning, geography, science, architecture, civil engineering, engineering; the fellowship is awarded on the basis of the applicant's academic record & the importance of the proposed research activities to the development of the co-operative movement in Canada or elsewhere *Award Amount:* $1,000
Amy & Tim Dauphinee Scholarships for Studies in Co-operation (Scholarship)
For graduate students in the following disciplines: cooperatives, housing, planning, environmental studies, geography, science, architecture, civil engineering, engineering; awards based on the applicant's academic records & on the importance of the proposed research activities to the development of the co-operative movement in Canada or abroad *Award Amount:* $3,000
Mission: To promote research on co-operatives in Canada

The Canadian Association for the Prevention of Consumption & Other Forms of Tuberculosis; The Canadian Tuberculosis & Respiratory Disease Associa *See* Canadian Lung Association

Canadian Association of Aerial Surveyors *See* Geomatics Industry Association of Canada

Canadian Association of Agri-Retailers (CAAR)
#107, 1090 Waverley St., Winnipeg MB R3T 0P4
Tel: 204-989-9300; *Fax:* 204-989-9306
Toll-Free: 800-463-9323
e-mail: info@caar.org
URL: www.caar.org
Previous Name: Western Fertilizer & Chemical Dealers Association
Overview: A medium-sized national organization founded in 1978
Member Profile: Canadian agricultural retailer members, who provide farmers with the products & services required for agricultural production; Canadian suppliers, who manufacture the products sold by retailers; *Committees:* Executive Council; Finance; Membership Development & Services; Facility & Transport Logistics; Convention; Communication & Public Relations; Stewardship & Agronomy; Government Affairs & Industry Relations
Activities: Liaising with provincial & national governments; Engaging in advocacy actitivities; Offering networking opportunities for agricultural suppliers & retailers; Providing information & training events
Awards: Operator of the Year (Award)
Retailer of the Year (Award)
Award Amount: $2,000
Retailer Hall of Fame (Award)
Award Amount: $2,000
Meetings/Conferences:
For more information see Trade Shows, Conferences and Seminars Chapter
Canadian Association of Agri-Retailers 2012 17th Annual Convention & Trade Show
Other Conferences in 2012 2012
Publications: *CAAR [Canadian Association of Agri-Retailers] Communicator*
Type: Magazine
Input [a publication of the Canadian Association of Agri-Retailers]
Type: Newsletter
CAAR [Canadian Association of Agri-Retailers] Roster
Type: Directory
Retailer Wage Survey [a publication of the Canadian Association of Agri-Retailers]
Mission: To represent & protect the interests of Canadian agricultural retailers

Canadian Association of Animal Health Technologists & Technicians (CAAHTT) / Association canadienne des techniciens et technologistes en santé animale (ACTTSA)
339 Booth St., Ottawa ON K1R 7K1
Tel: 800-567-2862
e-mail: info@caahtt-acttsa.ca
URL: www.caahtt-acttsa.ca
Overview: A medium-sized national organization founded in 1989
Chief Officer(s):
Michele Moroz, President
Chantal Cormier, Vice-President
Finances: *Funding Sources:* Provincial association fees; Corporate sponsorship
Committees: Professional Development; Veterinary Technician Testing; CVMA Animal Health Technology / Veterinary Technician Program Accreditation; CVMA Professional Development
Activities: Facilitating communication links; Providing informational updates; Lobbying to protect & promote the profession; Coordinating national & provincial activities; Promoting Doggone Safe, a national dog bit prevention program; *Awareness Events:* Veterinary Technician Week; Animal Health Week

Awards: Canadian AHT/VT of the Year Award (Award) Awarded to a technician who exemplifies the definition of an outstanding individual in the profession of AHT/VT CAAHTT/ACTTSA Recognition Award: "Making a Difference" (Award) Formally recognizes the contribution of an individual AHT/VT & their contribution to their national association
Meetings/Conferences:
For more information see Trade Shows, Conferences and Seminars Chapter
Canadian Association of Animal Health Technologists & Technicians 2011 22nd Annual General Meeting: Best Medicine Practices - Timely Topics
July 2011 Halifax, NS
Canadian Association of Animal Health Technologists & Technicians 2012 23rd Annual General Meeting
Other Conferences in 2012 2012 Montréal, QC
Canadian Association of Animal Health Technologists & Technicians 2013 24th Annual General Meeting
July 2013 Victoria, BC
Publications: *TechLife [a publication of the Canadian Association of Animal Health Technologists & Technicians]*
Type: Journal
Profile: Continuing education publication for animal health technicians
Canadian Association of Animal Health Technologists & Technicians Annual Report
Type: Yearbook *Frequency:* a.
Mission: To provide coordination & resources to support members in the delivery of animal health care services; *Member of:* International Veterinary Nurses & Technicians Association (IVNTA); *Affiliation(s):* Canadian Veterinary Medical Association; National Association of Veterinary Technicians in America (NAVTA)

Canadian Association of Chemical Distributors (CACD) / Association canadienne des distributeurs de produits chimiques (ACDPC)
349 Davis Rd., #A, Oakville ON L6J 2X2
Tel: 905-844-9140; *Fax:* 905-844-5706
URL: www.cacd.ca
Overview: A medium-sized national organization founded in 1986
Membership: 52; *Member Profile:* Chemical distributing companies; *Committees:* Financial Reporting; Operations & Logistics; Regulatory Affairs; Responsible Distribution
Activities: Collaborating with government to establish policies
Meetings/Conferences:
For more information see Trade Shows, Conferences and Seminars Chapter
Canadian Association of Chemical Distributors 2011 25th Annual General Meeting
June 2011 St. John's, NL
Canadian Association of Chemical Distributors 2011 Semi Annual Meeting
October 2011
Canadian Association of Chemical Distributors 2012 26th Annual General Meeting
June 2012 Whistler, BC
Canadian Association of Chemical Distributors 2013 27th Annual General Meeting
Other Conferences in 2013 2013
Publications: *The Chemunicator*
Type: Magazine *Frequency:* 3 pa *Accepts Advertising* : Yes
Editor: C. Wieckowska (catherine@cacd.ca)
Profile: Canadian Association of Chemical Distributors reports, plus news & information for the chemical distribution industry
Mission: To speak for the distribution sector of the Canadian chemical industry, reflecting the collective views of members, in dealing with governments, allied associations, & the public; To provide members of the association with services which assist them in the conduct of their business; To ensure adherence by members to a Code of Practice for Responsible Distribution
Environmental Activity: Serving & supporting ethical, safe, & responsible operations in the Canadian chemical distribution industry; Meeting regularly with Environment Canada, Health Canada, & Industry Canada

Canadian Association of Drilling Engineers (CADE)
#800, 540 - 5 Ave. SW, Calgary AB T2P 0M2
Tel: 403-264-4311; *Fax:* 403-263-3796
e-mail: info@cade.ca
URL: www.cade.ca
Overview: A medium-sized national organization founded in 1974

Finances: *Annual Operating Budget:* $50,000-$100,000; *Funding Sources:* Membership dues
Staff: 11 volunteer(s)
Membership: 620 corporate + 2 institutional + 8 student + 8 senior/lifetime; *Fees:* Student - $10; Retiree - $47.50; Full Member - $95; *Member Profile:* Open to those who work in the petroleum industry
Publications: *CADEnews [a publication of the Canadian Association of Drilling Engineers]*
Type: Newsletter *Editor:* Glenn Mencer
Mission: To provide a forum for the exchange of technical drilling knowledge & expertise; *Affiliation(s):* Canadian Association of Oilwell Drilling Contractors

Canadian Association of Equipment Distributors (CAED)
4531 Southclark Pl., Ottawa ON K1T 3V2
Tel: 613-822-8861; *Fax:* 613-822-8862
e-mail: mswan@caed.org
URL: www.caed.org
Overview: A small national organization founded in 1943
Finances: *Funding Sources:* Sponsorships
Membership: 1,500; *Member Profile:* Canadian firms that provide equipment to the construction, forestry, mining, marine, & oil &-gas industries across Canada & throughout the world; Other organizations, such as manufacturers, trade media, financial organizations, & specialized service firms, are allied members
Activities: Liaising with federal & provincial governments & other industry associations; Implementing & harmonizing regulations; Facilitating communication among members; Offering learning materials
Publications: *Showcase Newsletter: News from the Canadian Association of Equipment Distributors*
Type: Newsletter *Frequency:* m.
Profile: CAED reports, industry news, & forthcoming events
CAED [Canadian Association of Equipment Distributors] - Ontario Membership Newsletter
Type: Newsletter
Profile: Articles of interest to Ontario chapter members
Mission: To represent the equipment industry in Canada; to promote cooperation between distributors & manufacturers; to encourage environmentally sound business practices; *Affiliation(s):* Associated Equipment Distributors (USA)
Environmental Activity: Establishing an industry focused Environment, Health, & Safety committee to promote best practices

Canadian Association of Fire Chiefs (CAFC) / Association canadienne des chefs de pompiers (ACCP)
#702, 280 Albert St., Ottawa ON K1P 5G8
Tel: 613-270-9138; *Fax:* 613-233-9138
e-mail: info@cafc.ca
URL: www.cafc.ca
Overview: A medium-sized national organization
Finances: *Annual Operating Budget:* $100,000-$250,000
Staff: 1 staff member(s)
Membership: 1,000; *Fees:* $190 + GST
Activities: *Rents Mailing List:* Yes; *Library:* Fire Services Resource Centre; Open to public
Publications: *Fire Chief Magazine*
Type: Magazine *Frequency:* q.
Profile: Important issues about fire services
Canadian Association of Fire Chiefs Directory of Members
Type: Directory *Frequency:* a.
Profile: Includes CAFC leadership listings & updated bylaws
Mission: To lead & represent the Canadian Fire Service on public safety issues with the vision of being nationally recognized as the fire service voice of authority; *Affiliation(s):* International Association of Fire Chiefs

Canadian Association of Geographers (CAG) / Association canadienne des géographes
Department of Geography, McGill University, #425, 805, rue Sherbrooke ouest, Montréal QC H3A 2K6
Tel: 514-398-4946; *Fax:* 514-398-7437
e-mail: valerie.shoffey@cag-acg.ca (Executive Secretary)
URL: www.cag-acg.ca
Overview: A medium-sized national organization founded in 1951
Member Profile: Practicing geographers from the public & private sectors & universities across Canada & internationally; Students

Activities: Promoting geographic education; Disseminating geographic research; Collaborating with other national & international geographic organizations
Meetings/Conferences:
For more information see Trade Shows, Conferences and Seminars Chapter
Canadian Association of Geographers 2012 Annual Meeting & Conference (with the Canadian Federation for the Humanities & Social Sciences)
Other Conferences in 2012 2012 Waterloo, ON
Canadian Association of Geographers 2013 Annual Meeting & Conference
Other Conferences in 2013 2013 Whitehorse, YK
Canadian Association of Geographers 2014 Annual Meeting & Conference
Other Conferences in 2014 2014 Toronto, ON
Canadian Association of Geographers 2015 Annual Meeting & Conference
Other Conferences in 2015 2015
Publications: *The Canadian Geographer (TCG) / Le Géographe canadien (LGC)*
Type: Journal *Language:* B *Frequency:* q. *Editor:* Ian MacLachlan *Price:* Free with membership in the Canadian Association of Geographers
Profile: Philosophical, theoretical, & methodological subjects of interest to scholars & geographers in Canada & worldwide
The CAG [Canadian Association of Geographers] Newsletter
Type: Newsletter *Language:* B *Frequency:* q. *Editor:* Valerie Shoffey *Price:* Free with membership in the Canadian Association of Geographers
Profile: News about members, employment opportunities & announcements, technical features, Statistics Canada news, research highlights, & student information
The CAG [Canadian Association of Geographers] Annual Directory
Type: Directory *Frequency:* a. *Editor:* Kim Falcigno (kimfalcigno@shaw.ca) *Price:* Free with membership in the Canadian Association of Geographers
Profile: Listings of CAG members, academic staff, research activities, & current publications of Canadian university geography departments & government agencies
Mission: To promote the discipline of geography in Canada & internationally; *Member of:* Humanities & Social Science Federation of Canada; Canadian Federation of Earth Sciences; International Geographical Union; *Affiliation(s):* L'l'association professionelle des géographes du Québec; Association of American Geographers; Institute of British Geographers

Canadian Association of Geophysical Contractors (CAGC)
#1045, 1015 - 4 St. SW, Calgary AB T2R 1J4
Tel: 403-265-0045; *Fax:* 403-265-0025
e-mail: info@cagc.ca
URL: www.cagc.ca
Overview: A small national organization founded in 1977
Activities: Working with governments, stakeholders, & communities; Promoting hight ethical standards throughout the geophysical industry; Providing health & safety training
Publications: *The Source: The Voice of Business in the Canadian Seismic Industry*
Type: Magazine *Frequency:* q.
Profile: Canadian Association of Geophysical Contractors membership news, awards, & upcoming events
Mission: To act as the voice of business in the Canadian seismic industry; To promote the Canadian geophysical industry
Environmental Activity: Promoting the protection of the natural environment in geophysical operations

Canadian Association of Medical Biochemists (CAMB) / Association des médecins biochimistes du Canada (AMBC)
774 Echo Dr., Ottawa ON K1S 5N8
Tel: 613-730-8177; *Fax:* 613-730-1116
Toll-Free: 800-668-3740
e-mail: camb@rcpsc.edu
URL: www.camb-ambc.ca
Overview: A small national organization founded in 1975
Fees: $100 ordinary members; $15 emeritus & student members

Canadian Association of Members of Public Utility Tribunals (CAMPUT) / Association canadienne des membres des tribunaux d'utilité publique
#646, 200 North Service Rd. West, Oakville ON L6M 2Y1

Associations/Organizations / Canadian Association of Mining Equipment & Services for Export

Tel: 905-827-5139; *Fax:* 905-827-3260
e-mail: info@camput.org
URL: www.camput.org
Previous Name: Canadian Association of Utility Commissioners
Overview: A small national organization founded in 1976
Member Profile: Federal, provincial, & territorial boards & commissions which regulate electric, water, gas, & pipeline utilities in Canada; *Committees:* Regulatory Affairs; Education
Activities: Educating & training commissioners & staff of public utility tribunals; Communicating with members; Liaising with parallel regulatory organizations;
Mission: To improve public utility regulation in Canada

Canadian Association of Mining Equipment & Services for Export (CAMESE) / Association canadienne des exportateurs d'équipement et services miniers
#101, 345 Renfrew Dr., Markham ON L3R 9S9
Tel: 905-513-0046; *Fax:* 905-513-1834
e-mail: minesupply@camese.org
URL: www.camese.org
Overview: A medium-sized international organization founded in 1981
Fees: Schedule available; *Member Profile:* Organizations, with an office or employee in Canada, which seek to export goods & services to the global mining industry; Organizations which assist others to export goods & services; *Committees:* Member Services; Information & Communication; International Market Development
Activities: Providing selling advice to members; Participating in international mining trade exhibitions; Networking with other firms in the mining sector; Researching target makets for member firms
Publications: *Compendium of Canadian Mining Suppliers*
Type: Yearbook *Frequency:* a. *Editor:* Bonnie Toews
CAMESE [Canadian Association of Mining Equipment & Services for Export] Bulletin
Type: Newsletter *Frequency:* s-m.
Profile: Market conditions, export sales opportunities, & upcoming events in the mining sector
Mission: To advocate for the mining supply sector to the Canadian government, the mining industry, & the Canadian public; to support Canadian mining suppliers in global marketing; to help foreign buyers to locate Canadian sources for mining equipment & services

Canadian Association of Oilwell Drilling Contractors (CAODC)
#800, 540 - 5 Ave. SW, Calgary AB T2P 0M2
Tel: 403-264-4311; *Fax:* 403-263-3796
e-mail: info@caodc.ca
URL: www.caodc.ca
Overview: A large national organization founded in 1949
Membership: 252; *Member Profile:* Upstream Canadian petroleum drilling contractors (land-based & offshore) service rig contractors & associate companies; *Committees:* Accounting & Taxation; Drilling & Completions; Engineering & Technical; Scholarship; Environment; Executive Advisory; Forecasting; Government & Public Relations; Health, Safety & Environment; Legal & Contracts; Membership; Petroleum Safety Council; Service Rig Safety & Technical; Service Rig Transportation & Environment; Human Relations & Training; Trades & Apprenticeship
Activities: *Awareness Events:* Annual BBQ; *Library:* Yes, Open to public, open by appointment
Publications: *CAODC [Canadian Association of Oilwell Drilling Contractors] Oil Driller*
Type: Magazine *Frequency:* 3 pa *Accepts Advertising* : Yes
Editor: Cindy Soderstrom
Profile: Reports on issues about Canada's oil industry. drilling forecasts, & CAODC committee updates
Mission: To represent drilling rig contractors; to provide ongoing means of communication between drilling & well servicing contractors, governments, other industry sector participants, & the general public; to improve standards for safety & training, equipment & technical procedures; to coordinate programs between government bodies & contractors; oversees the Rig Technician Trade & Apprenticeship Program in Alberta, British Columbia & Saskatchewan

Canadian Association of Palynologists (CAP) / Association canadienne des palynologues
c/o Dr. Mary A. Vetter, Luther College, University of Regina, Regina SK S4S 0A2
URL: www.scirpus.ca/cap/cap.shtml
Overview: A small national organization founded in 1979

Chief Officer(s):
Matthew Peros, President
mperos@uottawa.ca
Mary A. Vetter, Secretary-Treasurer
mary.vetter@uregina.ca
Terri Lacourse, Editor, CAP Newsletter
tlacours@uvic.ca
Finances: *Funding Sources:* Membership dues
Membership: 57; *Fees:* $10; *Member Profile:* Palynologists from universities, government agencies, & industries; Persons with an interest in Canadian palynology
Activities: Promoting cooperation between palynologists & persons in related fields of study; *Library:* CAP Library
Awards: Canadian Association of Palynologists Annual Student Research Award (Award)
To recognize students' contributions to palynological research
Contact: Matthew Peros *Contact Detail: E-mail:* mperos@uottawa.ca
Publications: *CAP [Canadian Association of Palynologists] Newsletter*
Type: Newsletter *Frequency:* s-a. *Editor:* Dr. Terri Lacourse
Price: Free with membership in the Canadian Association of Palynologists
Profile: Reports about fieldwork, analytical methods, & research in Canadian palynology, plus essays & conference information
Mission: To advance all aspects of palynology in Canada; *Affiliation(s):* International Federation of Palynological Societies (IFPS)

Canadian Association of Petroleum Landmen (CAPL)
#350, 500 - 5 Ave. SW, Calgary AB T2P 3L5
Tel: 403-237-6635; *Fax:* 403-263-1620
e-mail: dgrieve@landman.ca
URL: www.landman.ca
Overview: A small national organization founded in 1948
Finances: *Funding Sources:* Sponsorships
Activities: Communicating with members; Providing professional development opportunities
Publications: *The Negotiator: The Magazine of the Canadian Association of Petroleum Landmen*
Type: Magazine *Frequency:* 10 pa *Accepts Advertising* : Yes
Editor: T. Hunter, C. Kendrick, & M. Graham
Profile: Feature articles, CAPL conference information, CAPL news & events
CAPL [Canadian Association of Petroleum Landmen] Annual Report
Type: Yearbook *Frequency:* a.
Mission: To enhance all facets of the land profession; *Affiliation(s):* American Association of Professional Landmen

Canadian Association of Petroleum Producers (CAPP) / Association canadienne des producteurs pétroliers
#2100, 350 - 7 Ave. SW, Calgary AB T2P 3N9
Tel: 403-267-1100; *Fax:* 403-261-4622
e-mail: communication@capp.ca; membership@capp.ca; publications@capp.ca
URL: www.capp.ca
Merged from: Canadian Petroleum Association; Independent Petroleum Association of Canada
Overview: A large national organization founded in 1992
Membership: 100+ producer members + 150 associate members; *Member Profile:* Producer members range from two person operations to internationally recognized corporations employing thousands; Associate members provide services, such as drilling, baniking, & computing, for Canada's oil & gas industry
Activities: Reviewing, analyzing, & recommending industry policy positions; Participating in regulatory change dialogues; Representing the industry on multi-sector international, federal, & provincial consultation bodies; Communicating with governments, regulators, stakeholders, & the public; Offering seminars & workshops; Providing industry trends, statistics, & research information; Informing members of industry standards & guidelines; Monitoring pipeline expansions; Improving coordinated land use planning processes
Mission: To represent companies that produce Canada's natural gas & crude oil; To enhance the economic sustainability of the Canadian upstream petroleum industry; To ensure work is conducted in a safe & environmentally & socially responsible manner; To work with government to develop regulatory requirements
Environmental Activity: Offering Energy in Action, with activities that bring industry & communities together to care for the environment; Facilitating development of performance

measures for environmental stewardship; Maintaining environmental operating guidelines

Canadian Association of Physicians for the Environment (CAPE)
#301, 130 Spadina Ave., Toronto ON M5V 2L4
Tel: 416-306-2273; *Fax:* 416-960-9392
e-mail: webmaster@cape.ca; info@cape.ca
URL: www.cape.ca
Overview: A small national organization founded in 1994
Chief Officer(s):
Kapil Khatter, President
John Howard, Chair
Finances: *Funding Sources:* Membership fees; Donations
Fees: $50 - $200; *Member Profile:* Physicians; Health care workers; Citizens across Canada
Activities: Providing educational opportunities; Liaising with other national & international organizations; Designing the online resource, Children's Environmental Health Project; Advocating for laws, standards, & policies to promote health & protect the environment
Publications: *CAPE [Canadian Association of Physicians for the Environment] News*
Type: Newsletter
Profile: Association news & information on the health implications of environmental issues
Mission: To act as a national voice of physicians on issues surrounding health & the environment; to address issues of environmental degradation to protect & promote human health; *Affiliation(s):* International Society of Doctors for the Environment (ISDE)

Canadian Association of Professional Heritage Consultants (CAPHC) / Association canadienne d'experts-conseils en patrimoine (ACECP)
George Brown House, #211, 50 Baldwin St., Toronto ON M5T 1L4
Tel: 416-515-7450; *Fax:* 416-515-0961
e-mail: admin@caphc.ca
URL: www.caphc.ca
Previous Name: Association of Heritage Consultants
Overview: A medium-sized national organization founded in 1987
Membership: 210; *Fees:* $50; *Member Profile:* Practitioners active in either private or public sector in fields allied to heritage conservation; *Committees:* Advocacy; Professional Conduct & Ethics; Communications; Membership Services; Strategic Business Development
Activities: Members offer the following range of services: archaeology, anthropology, conservation, curation, design & planning, education, heritage administration, history, landscape design, photography, illustration & recording, restoration, trade, craft
Publications: *CAPHC [Canadian Association of Professional Heritage Consultants] Membership Directory*
Type: Directory *Accepts Advertising* : Yes
Canadian Association of Professional Heritage Consultants Forum
Type: Newsletter *Accepts Advertising* : Yes
Profile: Articles on conservation, CAPHC / ACECP news & events
Mission: To represent & further the professional interests of heritage consultants active in both the private & public sectors; to establish & maintain principles & standards of practice for heritage consultants; to enhance awareness & appreciation of heritage resources, & the contribution of heritage consultants; to foster communication among private practitioners, public agencies, & the public at large in matters related to heritage conservation; *Affiliation(s):* ICOMOS International (International Council on Monuments & Sites); ICOMOS Canada - English-Speaking Committee

Canadian Association of Recycling Industries (CARI) / Association canadienne des industries du recyclage (ACIR)
#1, 682 Monarch Ave., Ajax ON L1S 4S2
Tel: 905-426-9313; *Fax:* 905-426-9314
URL: www.cari-acir.org
Overview: A medium-sized national organization founded in 1941
Membership: 260+; *Member Profile:* Canadian companies in the recycling sector, from small scrap yards to large processing plants
Activities: Providing information on government legislation, environment & safety regulations, & new technology; Organizing networking events; Working to solve scrap metal theft;

Developing cost cutting services for members; *Speaker Service:* Yes
Meetings/Conferences:
For more information see Trade Shows, Conferences and Seminars Chapter
Canadian Association of Recycling Industries (CARI) 2011 70th Annual General Meeting & Convention: Beyond North America
June 2011 Whistler, BC
Canadian Association of Recycling Industries (CARI) 2011 14th Annual Consumers' Night
October 2011 Toronto, ON
Canadian Association of Recycling Industries (CARI) 2012 71st Annual General Meeting & Convention
Other Conferences in 2012 2012
Canadian Association of Recycling Industries (CARI) 2012 15th Annual Consumers' Night
Other Conferences in 2012 2012,
Publications: *Canadian Association of Recycling Industries Membership Directory*
Type: Directory *Frequency:* a.
Profile: Listings of contact information for the recycling industry
The Pulse [a publication of the Canadian Association of Recycling Industries]
Type: Newsletter *Frequency:* m. *Accepts Advertising*: Yes
Profile: Information for CARI members & industry leaders concerning recycling industry issues & opportunities, including market trends, governmental legislation, & technology advancements
The Prompt [a publication of the Canadian Association of Recycling Industries]
Type: Newsletter *Accepts Advertising*: Yes
Profile: Information about business opportunities & forthcoming events
Mission: To address issues facing the recycling industry in Canada & internationally; To promote commercial recycling activities
Environmental Activity: Advocating on behalf of Canada's recycling industry; Promoting the recycling industry to the public & the government

Canadian Association of Swine Veterinarians (CASV) / Association Canadienne des Vétérinaires Porcins (ACVP)
Tel: 519-273-7170
e-mail: gcharbon@swineservices.ca
URL: www.casv-acvp.ca
Overview: A small national organization founded in 2003
Chief Officer(s):
John Harding, Chair, 306-966-7070
john.harding@usask.ca
George Charbonneau, President, 519-273-7170
gcharbon@swineservices.ca
Member Profile: Canadian veterinarians who have a special interest in swine; Persons in industry, academia, & government
Activities: Facilitating networking opportunities; Encouraging professional development; Promoting communications among organizations with similar interests
Mission: To support members; To discuss issues affecting members; To offer a nation voice on issues that affect pork production; To enhance knowledge of animal welfare, herd health management, & food safety

Canadian Association of Utility Commissioners *See* Canadian Association of Members of Public Utility Tribunals

Canadian Association of Zoological Parks & Aquariums *See* Canadian Association of Zoos & Aquariums

Canadian Association of Zoos & Aquariums (CAZA) / Association des zoos et aquariums du Canada (AZAC)
#400, 280 Metcalfe St., Ottawa ON K2P 1R7
Tel: 613-567-0099; *Fax:* 613-233-5438
Toll-Free: 888-822-2907
e-mail: info@caza.ca
URL: www.caza.ca
Previous Name: Canadian Association of Zoological Parks & Aquariums
Overview: A medium-sized national charitable organization founded in 1975
Chief Officer(s):
Robin Hale, President
rhale@torontozoo.ca
Bill Peters, National Director, 613-567-0099 Ext. 242
bpeters@caza.ca
Greg Tarry, Manager, Special Projects
gtarry@caza.ca
Serge Lussier, Secretary-Treasurer
slussier@lionsafari.com
Finances: *Funding Sources:* Donations
Member Profile: Zoo & aquarium professionals; *Committees:* Executive; Nominating; Ethics; Awards; Conservation & Education; National Awareness; Policy; Accreditation; Business Development; Government Relations; Membership Services; Finance; Arctic Biodiversity; Conference
Activities: Administering the CAZA Accreditation Program; Upholding the CAZA Code of Professional Ethics; Promoting education; Offering a mentoring program for institutions
Meetings/Conferences:
For more information see Trade Shows, Conferences and Seminars Chapter
Canadian Association of Zoos & Aquariums 2011 Annual Conference
September 2011 Golden, BC
Canadian Association of Zoos & Aquariums 2012 Annual Conference
Other Conferences in 2012 2012
Publications: *CAZA [Canadian Association of Zoos & Aquariums] News*
Type: Newsletter *Frequency:* bi-m. *Editor:* G. Tarry *Price:* Free with Canadian Association of Zoos & Aquariums membership
CAZA [Canadian Association of Zoos & Aquariums] Annual Report
Type: Yearbook *Frequency:* a.
Connecting Canadians to Nature: Strategic Plan [a publication of the Canadian Association of Zoos & Aquariums
Type: Report *Number of Pages:* 16
Canadian Association of Zoos & Aquariums Membership Directory
Type: Directory
Profile: A listing of institutional, commercial, & affiliate members of the Canadian Association of Zoos & Aquariums
Mission: To promote the welfare of animals; To provide input into legislative matters & government policy affecting the zoo & aquarium industry; *Member of:* IUCN, International Union for Conservation of Nature; The World Association of Zoos & Aquariums; Canadian Museums Association
Environmental Activity: Encouraging the advancement of conservation & science; Initiating a national awareness campaign about the preservation of biodiversity in the Arctic; Increasing awareness about endangered species in Canada & throughout the world

Canadian Association on Water Pollution Research & Control *See* Canadian Association on Water Quality

Canadian Association on Water Quality (CAWQ) / Association canadienne sur la qualité de l'eau (ACQE)
PO Box 5050, 867 Lakeshore Rd., Burlington ON L7R 4A6
Tel: 905-336-6291; *Fax:* 905-336-4877
URL: www.cawq.ca
Also Known As: Canadian National Committee of the International Association on Water Quality
Previous Name: Canadian Association on Water Pollution Research & Control
Overview: A medium-sized national charitable organization founded in 1967
Finances: *Funding Sources:* Membership fees; subscriptions; grants
Membership: 10 corporate + 210 individual; *Fees:* Schedule available; *Member Profile:* Joint or individual - engaged in water quality & pollution research & control; corporate - organizations engaged in water quality & pollution research & control; sustaining - individuals & organizations interested in support & results of water quality & pollution research & control; joint or student - students engaged in full-time study on water quality & pollution research & control
Publications: *Water Quality Research Journal of Canada*
Type: Journal *Frequency:* q. *Price:* Free for individual CAWQ members; $250 Canada & USA; $295 International
Profile: Peer-reviewed scholarly & review articles & original research on topics such as the impact of pollutants & contaminants on aquatic ecosystems, aquatic species at risk, water treatment & quality, conservation, & water pollution policies
IWA's Water 21
Type: Newsletter *Frequency:* bi-m.
Canadian Association on Water Quality Annual Report
Frequency: a.
Mission: To promote research on scientific, technological, legal & administrative aspects of water pollution research & control; To further the exchange of information & the practical application of such research for public benefit; *Member of:* International Association on Water Quality

Canadian Automobile Association (CAA) / Association canadienne des automobilistes
National Office, #200, 1145 Hunt Club Rd., Ottawa ON K1V 0Y3
Tel: 613-247-0117; *Fax:* 613-247-0118
e-mail: info@national.caa.ca
URL: www.caa.ca
Overview: A large national organization founded in 1913
Finances: *Funding Sources:* Membership dues
Staff: 25 staff member(s)
Membership: 5+million; *Member Profile:* CAA British Columbia; Alberta Motor Association; CAA Saskatchewan; CAA Manitoba; CAA Mid-Western Ontario; CAA South Central Ontario; CAA Niagara; CAA Central Ontario; CAA North & East Ontario; CAA Québec; CAA Maritimes
Activities: *Speaker Service:* Yes; *Library:* Yes
Mission: To promote, develop & implement programs & information relating to the rights, responsibilities & needs of the motorist as a consumer; *Affiliation(s):* Alliance internationale de tourisme; Fédération internationale de l'automobile; Federacion interamericana de touring y automovil-clubes; Commonwealth Motoring Conference; American Automobile Association

Canadian Avalanche Association (CAA)
PO Box 2759, 110 MacKenzie Ave., Revelstoke BC V0E 2S0
Tel: 250-837-2435; *Fax:* 250-837-4624
Toll-Free: 800-667-1105
e-mail: info@avalanche.ca
URL: www.avalanche.ca
Overview: A medium-sized national organization founded in 1982
Chief Officer(s):
Ian Tomm, Executive Director
itomm@avalanche.ca
Mary Clayton, Director, Communications
mclayton@avalanche.ca
Kristin Anthony-Malone, Manager, Operations
kmalone@avalanche.ca
Emily Grady, Manager, Industry Training Program
egrady@avalanche.ca
Finances: *Funding Sources:* Donations
Activities: Establishing technical standards; Providing technical training courses for professional avalanche workers, wilderness guiding operations, government programs (Parks Canada & provincial parks), & highway, railway, mining, forestry, & construction operations
Meetings/Conferences:
For more information see Trade Shows, Conferences and Seminars Chapter
Canadian Avalanche Association 2011 Course: Introduction to Snow Avalanche Mapping
September 2011 Golden, BC
Canadian Avalanche Association 2011 Course: Introduction to Weather Skills for Avalanche Workers
September 2011, BC
Canadian Avalanche Association 2011 Course: Introduction to Snow Avalanche Mapping
September 2011 Nelson, BC
Canadian Avalanche Association 2011 Course: Advanced Weather Skills for Avalanche Workers
September 2011, BC
Canadian Avalanche Association 2011 Course: AvSAR Response
November 2011 Revelstoke, BC
Canadian Avalanche Association 2011 Course: Avalanche Control Blasting
November 2011 Fernie, BC
Canadian Avalanche Association 2012 Course: Resource & Transportation Avalanche Management
January 2012 Nelson, BC
Publications: *avalanche.ca*
Type: Journal *Frequency:* q. *Accepts Advertising*: Yes *Price:* $30 Canada; $40 USA; $45 international
Profile: Research, reports from alpine countries, publication & product reviews, plus techniques, tools, & tips for avalanche safety
Land Managers Guide for Snow Avalanche Hazards in Canada
Type: Guide *Price:* $20
Profile: A guide to help land managers & consultants recognize & mitigate potential snow avalanche hazards

Associations/Organizations / Canadian Bar Association

Observation Guidelines & Recording Standards for Weather, Snowpack, & Avalanches (OGRS)
Type: Guide
Profile: A technical guide for professional avalanche safety operations & research in Canada
Guidelines for Snow Avalanche Risk Determination & Mapping in Canada
Type: Guide *Price:* $20
Profile: A technical reference for avalanche consultants & others, featuring concepts for the determination of avalanche risks, plus guidelines for avalanche mapping & acceptable risks
Avalanche Accidents in Canada
Profile: Volume 1 - 1955 to 1976; Volume 2 - 1943 to 1978; Volume 3 - 1978 to 1984; Volume 4 - 1984 to 1996; Volume 5 - 1996 to 2007
Mission: To foster & support a professional environment for avalanche safety operations in Canada; To represent the avalanche community to stakeholders
Environmental Activity: Operating as a repository for snow science & avalanche research

Canadian Bar Association (CBA) / Association du barreau canadien
#500, 865 Carling Ave., Ottawa ON K1S 5S8
Tel: 613-237-2925; *Fax:* 613-237-0185
Toll-Free: 800-267-8860
e-mail: info@cba.org
URL: www.cba.org
Overview: A large national organization founded in 1921
Finances: *Annual Operating Budget:* Greater than $5 Million
Staff: 70 staff member(s)
Membership: 37,000; *Member Profile:* Open to lawyers, notaries, judges, law students, persons with a recognized law degree but not licensed to practise or retired from active practice of law, law administrators; membership is voluntary in all but British Columbia & New Brunswick; *Committees:* Awards; Communications; Continuing Legal Education; Equality; Ethics & Professional Issues; International Development; Judicial Compensation & Benefits Commitee; Law Day; Legal Aid; Legislation & Law Reform; Membership; Resolutions, Constitution & ByLaws; Supreme Court of Canada
Activities: Law for the Future Fund; legal aid; law reform initiatives; insurance & financial services for members; advocacy; Canadian Bar Foundation; *Awareness Events:* National Law Day, April
Awards: Pro Bono Award (Award)

Justica Award (Award)
CBA President's Award (Award)
The Douglas Miller Award (Award)
The Louis St-Laurent Award of Excellence (Award)
PAJLO Student Essay Contest (Award)
Ramon John Hnatyshyn Award for Law (Award)
Viscount Bennett Fellowship (Scholarship)
Meetings/Conferences:
For more information see Trade Shows, Conferences and Seminars Chapter
Canadian Bar Association Canadian Legal Conference & Expo 2011
August 2011 Halifax, NS
Canadian Bar Association Mid-Winter Meeting of Council 2012
February 2012 Mayan Riviera
Canadian Bar Association Canadian Legal Conference & Expo 2012
August 2012 Vancouver, BC
Mission: To promote improvements in the law; to promote improvements in the administration of justice; to promote individual lawyer training; to advocate in the public interest; to represent the profession on a national & international level; to promote the interests of the CBA; to promote equality in the profession; *Affiliation(s):* Canadian Association of Law Teachers; Canadian Law Information Council; Commonwealth Bar Association; Inter-American Bar Association; International Bar Association; Union internationale des avocats

Canadian Biochemical Society *See* The Canadian Society of Biochemistry, Molecular & Cellular Biology

Canadian Bioethics Society (CBS) / Société canadienne de bioéthique
561 Rocky Ridge Bay NW, Calgary AB T3G 4E7
Tel: 403-208-8027
e-mail: lmriddell@shaw.ca
URL: www.bioethics.ca

Merged from: Canadian Society of Bioethic; Société canadienne de la bioéthique médicale
Overview: A small national organization founded in 1988
Chief Officer(s):
Patricia Rodney, RN, PhD, President, 604-822-7507
rodney@nursing.ubc.ca
Bashir Jiwani, Treasurer, 604-587-4632
basher.jiwani@fraserhealth.ca
Stacey Page, PhD, Officer, Communications, 403-220-2763
sapage@ucalgary.ca
Finances: *Funding Sources:* Donations
Membership: 600+; *Fees:* $80 regular members; $35 student & under or unemployed members; $40 emeritus members; $250 institutions; *Member Profile:* Professional individuals & institutions interested in ethics & health research & practice
Activities: Promoting teaching of bioethics
Publications: *Canadian Bioethics Society Newsletter*
Type: Newsletter *Language:* B *Accepts Advertising*: Yes *Editor:* Stacey Page
Profile: Articles. book reviews, CBS activities, & upcoming events of interest to CBS members
Mission: To facilitate knowledge sharing related to bioethics; to discover solutions to bioethical problems by promotion of research & dissemination of information

Canadian Bison Association (CBA) / Association canadienne du bison
PO Box 3116, #200, 1660 Pasqua St., Regina SK S4P 3G7
Tel: 306-522-4766; *Fax:* 306-522-4768
URL: www.canadianbison.ca
Overview: A medium-sized national licensing charitable organization founded in 1984
Finances: *Funding Sources:* Membership fees; convention; show & sale
Staff: 3 staff member(s); 10 volunteer(s)
Membership: 1,300 active + 100 associate; *Fees:* Schedule available; *Member Profile:* Active - own bison; associate - interest in bison industry; *Committees:* Research; Promotions; Disease; Grading; Food Safety
Activities: Bison Show & Sale; Annual Convention
Mission: To develop the bison industry; to maintain the production of bison in a natural state (no growth hormones, chemicals, feed lots, free-range management); to be the voice for commercial breeders; to assist in the formation of regulations & guidelines in commercial production & management of Canadian Plains Bison & to promote the product & awareness of the bison industry; *Member of:* Canadian Livestock Records Corp.; *Affiliation(s):* National Bison Association - USA; BC Interior Bison Association; Peace Country Bison Association; Alberta, Saskatchewan, Manitoba, Ontario Bison Association; Québec Bison Union

Canadian Botanical Association (CBA) / Association botanique du Canada (ABC)
PO Box 160, Aberdeen SK S0K 0A0
Tel: 613-364-4074; *Fax:* 613-364-4027
e-mail: lconsaul@mus-nature.ca
URL: www.cba-abc.ca
Overview: A small national organization founded in 1965
Finances: *Annual Operating Budget:* Less than $50,000; *Funding Sources:* Membership
Fees: $55 regular; $25 student & retired; *Member Profile:* Professional botanists; academics; research scientists; *Committees:* Conservation; Science Policy; Development; Membership
Activities: Ecology; Mycology; Structure & development; Systematics & phytogeography; Teaching; *Library:* Yes, Not open to the public
Awards: Iain & Sylvia Taylor Award (Award)
Mary E. Elliott Service Award (Award)
Lionel Cinq-Mars Award (Award)
John Macoun Travel Bursary (Scholarship)
Undergraduate Student Regional Awards (Award)

Lawson Medal (Award)
Publications: *Botany*
Type: Journal *Frequency:* m. *Editor:* Cecily Pearson *ISSN:* 1480-3305
CBA [Canadian Botanical Association] / ABC [Association botanique du Canada] Bulletin
Type: Bulletin *Frequency:* 3 pa *Editor:* Christine D. Maxwell
Mission: Representing Canadian Botany & botanists nationally & internationally, the Association responds quickly & professionally on matters that are of concern to Canadian botanists.; *Affiliation(s):* Botanical Society of America

Canadian Botanical Conservation Network (CBCN) / Le Réseau canadien pour la conservation de la flore
c/o Science Department, Royal Botanical Gardens, PO Box 399, Hamilton ON L8N 3H8
Tel: 905-527-1158; *Fax:* 905-577-0375
e-mail: dgalbraith@rbg.ca
URL: www.rbg.ca/cbcn/
Overview: A small national organization founded in 1994
Chief Officer(s):
David A. Galbraith, Executive Director
dgalbraith@rbg.ca
Member Profile: Individuals & organizations with an interest in conservation of plant diversity
Activities: Promoting preservation of native plant species, wild habitats, & ecosystems through education & conservation programs; *Library:* CBCN Library
Publications: *CBCN [Canadian Botanical Conservation Network] Newsletter*
Type: Newsletter *Frequency:* q. *Editor:* Dr. David A. Galbraith *ISSN:* 1480-8218
Profile: Plant conservation & biodiversity news, CNCN member news, & upcoming events
Mission: To preserve the biological diversity of Canada's rare & endangered native plant species, wild habitats & ecosystems

Canadian Bottled Water Association (CBWA) / Association canadienne des embouteilleurs d'eau
#337-24, 155 East Beaver Creek Rd., Richmond Hill ON L4B 2N1
Tel: 905-886-6928; *Fax:* 905-886-9531
e-mail: info@cbwa.ca
URL: www.cbwa.ca
Overview: A medium-sized national licensing organization founded in 1992
Chief Officer(s):
Elizabeth Griswold, Executive Director
griswold@cbwa.ca
Fees: CBWA dues formula; *Member Profile:* Canadian bottled water companies that meet federal standards & the association's requirements for the production and sale of bottled water; Equipment manufacturers; Distributors; Suppliers
Activities: Education & training seminars
Awards: Lifetime Achievement Award (Award)
Publications: *WaterPower*
Type: Magazine *Frequency:* s-a. *Accepts Advertising*: Yes
Mission: Committed to environmentally responsible practices, CBWA supports & promotes bottled water as a healthy, safe & convenient food product. Dialogue is encourage between industry, government, consumers, & other stakeholders.; *Member of:* International Council of Bottled Water Associations

Canadian Bottlers of Carbonated Beverages; Canadian Soft Drink Association *See* Refreshments Canada

Canadian Bus Association (CBA) / Association canadienne de l'autobus
c/o #2001, 45 O'Connor St., Ottawa ON K1P 1A4
Tel: 613-238-1800; *Fax:* 613-241-4936
e-mail: mresnick@rothwellgroup.ca
Previous Name: Canadian Motor Coach Association
Overview: A medium-sized national organization founded in 1936
Membership: 100 companies
Awards: Canadian Bus Driver of the Year Award (Award)
Mission: To act as the national voice of the Canadian bus industry; to act as a national forum for the discussion of bus-related issues & the establishment of positions in relation to industry-wide areas of concern; to function as a technical & operational information gathering & exchange mechanism; to further the objectives of safety, convenience & quality of the motor coach industry.

Canadian Camping Association (CCA) / Association des camps du Canada (ACC)
2494, rte 125 sud, St-Donat QC J0T 2C0
Tel: 819-424-2662; *Fax:* 819-424-2662
Toll-Free: 877-427-6958
e-mail: info@ccamping.org
URL: www.ccamping.org
Overview: A large national charitable organization founded in 1936
Chief Officer(s):
Jeff Bradshaw, President
jeff@campwenonah.com

Membership: 9 provincial camping associations, representing more than 700 camps throughtout Canada; *Member Profile:* Provincial camping associations
Activities: Providing information about camping developments & regulations; Engaging in advocacy activities; Guiding camping leaders
Awards: Ron Johnstone Lifetime Achievement Award (Award) Jack Pearse Award of Honour (Award) CCA / ACC Awards of Excellence (Award)
Mission: To develop & promote organized camping for all populations across Canada; To further the interests & welfare of children, youth, & adults through camping; To encourage high standards in camping

Canadian Cancer Society (CCS) / Société canadienne du cancer
National Office, #200, 10 Alcorn Ave., Toronto ON M4V 3B1
Tel: 416-961-7223; *Fax:* 416-961-4189
Toll-Free: 888-939-3333
e-mail: ccs@cancer.ca; info@cis.cancer.ca
URL: www.cancer.ca
Social Media: www.facebook.com/canadiancancersociety
Overview: A large national charitable organization founded in 1938
Finances: *Funding Sources:* Donations
Staff: 1200 staff member(s); 170, volunteer(s)
Activities: Advocating for social & political change to control & reduce cancer; promoting methods of prevention; providing the Cancer Information Service; *Awareness Events:* Daffodil Month, April; Childhood, Men's, & Ovarian Cancer Awareness Month, September; Breast Cancer Awareness Month, October
Publications: *Canadian Cancer Statistics*
Frequency: a.
Profile: Report of cancer incidence & mortality in Canada
Mission: The Society collects donations to fund cancer research in Canada. It disseminates information on cancer prevention & treatments, advocating for healthy environment & lifestyle to reduce the incidence of cancer, and also offers individual & group support programs for caregivers, family & friends of cancer patients. It is a registered charity, BN: 118829803RR0001.; Affiliation(s): National Cancer Institute of Canada; Canadian Breast Cancer Research Alliance; Canadian Prostate Cancer Research Initiative; Canadian Tobacco Control Research Initiative; Canadian Association of Provincial Cancer Agencies

Canadian Cancer Society Research Institute
#200, 10 Alcorn Ave., Toronto ON M4V 3B1
Tel: 416-961-7223; *Fax:* 416-961-4189
e-mail: ccsri@cancer.ca; research@cancer.ca; agiorgi@cancer.ca (Media)
URL: www.cancer.ca/research
Previous Name: National Cancer Institute of Canada
Overview: A medium-sized national organization founded in 2009
Activities: Funding promising cancer research; Sponsoring clinical trials to test new drugs; Offering programs to train, develop, & support cancer researchers; Establishing peer review panels to review applications to conduct studies; Presenting awards; Collaborating with other research organizations, such as the Canadian Breast Cancer Research Alliance & the Canadian Tobacco Control Research Initiative
Publications: *Research Connection [a publication of the Canadian Cancer Society Research Institute]*
Type: Newsletter
Profile: News for cancer researchers, including information about research grants
Mission: To act as a strong voice in the cancer research community; To support a broad range of projects that involve Canadian investigators across the spectrum of cancer research

Canadian Carbonization Research Association (CCRA)
PO Box 2460, Burlington ON L8N 3J5
Tel: 905-548-4796
URL: www.cancarb.ca
Overview: A small national organization founded in 1965
Finances: *Annual Operating Budget:* $500,000-$1.5 Million; *Funding Sources:* Membership fees
Membership: 6 corporate; *Member Profile:* Coal producer, coke producer or related to coal/coke products; *Committees:* Technical
Mission: To fund coke & coal research in Canada for benefit of member companies

Canadian Cartographic Association (CCA) / Association canadienne de cartographie
c/o Department of Geography, University of Victoria, PO Box 3050, Stn. CSC, Victoria BC V8W 3P5
e-mail: awood@mun.ca
URL: www.cca-acc.org
Overview: A small national organization founded in 1975
Fees: $45 students, retired members, & institutions; $90 regular members; $110 family membership; $200 corporate; *Member Profile:* Individuals with an interest in mapping
Activities: Facilitating the exchange of information; Organizing a biannual exhibit of Canadian cartography; Collaborating with sister organizations
Publications: *Cartographica*
Type: Journal *Frequency:* q. *ISSN:* 0317-7173 *Price:* Free with CCA membership
Profile: Cartographica also appears as a monograph on a single topic
Cartouche
Type: Newsletter *Frequency:* q. *Editor:* Patricia Connor Reid
Price: Free with CCA membership
Profile: Association activities, forthcoming events, articles, products, & news
Mission: To promote interest in cartographic materials; To encourage research in the field of cartography; To advance education in cartography; Affiliation(s): International Cartographic Association

Canadian Cattle Breeders' Association (CCBA) / Société des éleveurs de bovins canadiens (SEBC)
4865, boul Laurier ouest, Saint-Hyacinthe QC J2S 3V4
Tel: 450-774-2775; *Fax:* 450-774-9775
e-mail: info@cqrl.org
URL: www.clrc.ca/canadiancattle.shtml
Overview: A medium-sized national organization founded in 1895
Finances: *Annual Operating Budget:* $50,000-$100,000; *Funding Sources:* Membership dues, casino
Staff: 1 staff member(s)
Membership: 93; *Fees:* $40 regular; $15 supportive; *Committees:* Genetic Classification

Canadian Cattlemen's Association (CCA)
#310, 6715 - 8 St. NE, Calgary AB T2E 7H7
Tel: 403-275-8558; *Fax:* 403-274-5686
e-mail: feedback@cattle.ca
URL: www.cattle.ca
Overview: A large national organization founded in 1932
Finances: *Funding Sources:* Fee assessments to provincial cattle organization members; National Check-off Agency
Committees: Environment; Animal Care; Animal Health & Meat Inspection; Value Creation & Competitiveness; Foreign Trade; Domestic Ag-Policy & Regulations; Convention; Executive & Finance
Activities: Collaborating with other agricultural sectors & food industries on matters of mutual concern; Providing a mentorship program
Meetings/Conferences:
For more information see Trade Shows, Conferences and Seminars Chapter
Canadian Cattlemen's Association 2011 Semi-Annual Meeting & Convention
August 2011 Calgary, AB
Canadian Cattlemen's Association 2012 Annual General Meeting
Other Conferences in 2012 2012
Canadian Cattlemen's Association 2012 Semi-Annual Meeting & Convention
Other Conferences in 2012 2012
Publications: *CCA [Canadian Cattlemen's Association] Monthly Report*
Type: Report *Frequency:* m.
Profile: CCA news & information about the beef producing industry
CCA [Canadian Cattlemen's Association] Annual Report
Frequency: a.
Profile: Executive, division, committee, provincial association, & financial reports
Canadian Cattlemen's Association By-laws
Number of Pages: 20
Canadian Cattlemen's Association Policy Manual
Type: Manual *Number of Pages:* 26
Profile: Topics include animal care, animal health, meat inspection, environment, finance, foreign trade, value creation, & competitiveness

CCA [Canadian Cattlemen's Association] News
Type: Newsletter *Frequency:* s-m. *Price:* Free
Profile: Recent association & industry information
Mission: To act as the national voice of beef producers across Canada; To produce high-quality beef products; To maintain a profitable Canadian beef industry; To use management practices that protect the health of the animal & protect the environment
Environmental Activity: Administering the Greenhouse Gas Mitigation Program for Canadian Agriculture with three other national organizations; Promoting environmental stewardship; Presenting the Environmental Stewardship Award; Participating in the protection of birds

Canadian Centre for Creative Technology See SHAD Valley International

Canadian Centre for Emergency Preparedness (CCEP)
#210, 860 Harrington Ct., Burlington ON L7N 3N4
Tel: 905-331-2552; *Fax:* 905-331-1641
e-mail: info@ccep.ca
URL: www.ccep.ca
Overview: A small national organization founded in 1993
Chief Officer(s):
Adrian Gordon, President & Chief Executive Officer
agordon@ccep.ca
Gary Mohr, Executive Vice-President
gemohr@ccep.ca
Mary-Ellen Heiman, Director, Development & Funding
meheiman@ccep.ca
Richard Kinchlea, Director, Operations
rkinchlea@ccep.ca
Activities: Advocating for disaster resilient communities; Liaising with all levels of government; Providing information & emergency preparedness programs; Sharing knowledge with international disaster management organizations
Publications: *Disaster Management Canada (DMC)*
Type: Magazine *Frequency:* q. *Accepts Advertising :* Yes *Price:* Free to qualified disaster management professionals with Canadian addresses
Profile: Timely, practical information from across the disaster management spectrum for emergency management & business continuity readers
CCEP [Canadian Centre for Emergency Preparedness] Newsletter
Type: Newsletter *Frequency:* q. *Price:* Free
Mission: To develop a disaster resilient Canada; To prepare small businesses, non-profit organizations, & disaster management professionals; To foster the establishment & maintenance of professional standards & certification for the disaster management community
Environmental Activity: Encouraging the balance of environmental, social, & economic considerations in formulating government policy

Canadian Centre for Energy Information / Centre info-énergie
#1600, 800 - 6th Ave. SW, Calgary AB T2P 3G3
Tel: 403-263-7722; *Fax:* 403-237-6286
Toll-Free: 877-606-4636
URL: www.centreforenergy.com
Also Known As: Centre for Energy
Overview: A medium-sized national organization founded in 2002
Chief Officer(s):
Pierre Alvarez, Chair
Thomas Cotter, Secretary
David Luff, Treasurer
Activities: Raising awareness & understanding about the Canadian energy system; Providing learning resources for teachers & students; *Speaker Service:* Yes
Publications: *Energy Research & Innovation Directory*
Type: Directory
Profile: Highlights of energy research projects, developed in partnership with the Department of Foreign Affairs & International Trade
Mission: To provide information about the Canadian energy system & energy-related issues

Canadian Centre for Fisheries Innovation (CCFI) / Centre canadien d'innovations des pêches
PO Box 4920, Stn. C, Ridge Rd., St. John's NL A1C 5R3
Tel: 709-778-0517; *Fax:* 709-778-0516
e-mail: ccfi@mi.mun.ca
URL: www.ccfi.ca
Previous Name: Centre for Fisheries Innovation

Associations/Organizations / Canadian Centre for Occupational Health & Safety

Overview: A medium-sized national organization founded in 1989
Activities: Efforts of the Centre are concentrated in four main areas: aquaculture, harvesting, processing & equipment development; the pursuit of excellence in these areas is addressed through demonstration projects, & research & development projects which pool the expertise of industry, educational institutions & governments; the Centre plays a leading role in technology transfer & information dissemination initiatives so that the fishing industry may benefit from scientific discoveries & state-of-the-art equipment
Mission: To work with the fishing industry to improve productivity & profitability of fishery through science & technology; *Member of:* Newfoundland Ocean Industries Association; Aquaculture Association of Canada; Fisheries Council of Canada; St. John's Board of Trade; Affiliation(s): Memorial University of Newfoundland; Marine Institute

Canadian Centre for Occupational Health & Safety (CCOHS) / Centre canadien d'hygiène et de sécurité au travail (CCHST)
135 Hunter St. East, Hamilton ON L8N 1M5
Tel: 905-572-2981; *Fax:* 905-572-2206
Toll-Free: 800-668-4284
e-mail: clientservices@ccohs.ca
URL: www.ccohs.ca
Social Media: www.facebook.com/CCOHS
Overview: A large national charitable organization founded in 1978
Finances: *Annual Operating Budget:* Greater than $5 Million; *Funding Sources:* Government & revenue from product sales
Staff: 85 staff member(s)
Fees: Optional membership packages at $100, $200 & $400; customized membership packages can include consulting, customized training, database development
Activities: Provides occupational health & safety information through a free & confidential Inquiries Service, publications, & CCINFO (its computerized information service); computerized information is available both online & on CD-ROM (CCINFOdisc); information services include over 50 databases containing information on chemicals of environmental concern (CESARS), pure chemicals (CHEMINFO), Agriculture Canada's information on pest control & MSD Database chemical trade name products; over 300 publications; *Speaker Service:* Yes; *Library:* Documentation Resources; open by appointment
Publications: *The Health & Safety Report*
Type: Newsletter *Frequency:* m. *Price:* Free
Profile: Workplace health & safety news, plus information & tips
Liaison [a publication of the Canadian Centre for Occupational Health & Safety]
Type: Newsletter *Frequency:* bi-m.
Profile: CCOHS developments, resources, & initiatives
Mission: To promote health & safety in the workplace, & the physical & mental health of working people in Canada

Canadian Centre for Policy Alternatives (CCPA) / Centre canadien de politique alternative
#205, 75 Albert St., Ottawa ON K1P 5E7
Tel: 613-563-1341; *Fax:* 613-233-1458
e-mail: ccpa@policyalternatives.ca
URL: www.policyalternatives.ca
Overview: A medium-sized national organization founded in 1980
Finances: *Annual Operating Budget:* $500,000-$1.5 Million
Staff: 15 staff member(s)
Membership: 3,600 individual + 150 organizations; *Fees:* $1000 director's circle; $500 editor's circle; $300 sponsor; $100 sustaining; $35 student/low income; *Member Profile:* open
Activities: Publishes research reports & books; organizes public symposiums & conferences
Publications: *The CCPA Monitor*
Type: Magazine *Frequency:* m. *Price:* Free to CCPA members
Profile: Research articles
Our Schools / Our Selves
Type: Journal *Frequency:* q.
Profile: Articles on educational issues such as social justice, action, pedagogy, & educational content
Mission: To promote research on economic & social issues facing Canada; to monitor current developments in economy & study important trends that affect Canadians; to demonstrate thoughtful alternatives to the limited perspectives of business, research institutes & government agencies; to put forward research that reflects concerns of women & men, labour & business, churches, cooperatives & voluntary agencies, governments, minorities, disadvantaged & fortunate individuals

Canadian Centre for Pollution Prevention (C2P2) / Centre canadien pour la prévention de la pollution
#134, 215 Spadina Ave., Toronto ON M5T 2C7
Tel: 905-822-4133; *Fax:* 416-979-3936
Toll-Free: 800-667-9790
e-mail: info@c2p2online.com
URL: www.c2p2online.com
Overview: A small national organization founded in 1992
Chief Officer(s):
Fred Granek, Chief Operating Officer, 905-822-4133 Ext. 224
fred@c2p2online.com
Leah Nielsen, Coordinator, Projects
Shari Russell, Coordinator, Projects
Activities: Providing training opportunities; Sharing knowledge with governments, businesses, academia, & organizations
Meetings/Conferences:
For more information see Trade Shows, Conferences and Seminars Chapter
Canadian Pollution Prevention 2012 16th Annual Roundtable
Other Conferences in 2012 2012
Publications: *At the Source* [a publication of the Canadian Centre for Pollution Prevention]
Type: Newsletter *Frequency:* 3 pa
Profile: Highlights of pollution prevention activities
What's New in P2
Type: Newsletter *Frequency:* m.
Profile: National & international pollution prevention news, upcoming conferences, & recent publications
Mission: To shape the future of production & consumption; To catalyze behavioural change in order to increase sustainable practices, a healthier environment, & competitiveness
Environmental Activity: Applying sound pollution prevention technologies, methods, & practices

The Canadian Chamber of Commerce / La Chambre de commerce du Canada
#420, 360 Albert St., Ottawa ON K1R 7X7
Tel: 613-238-4000; *Fax:* 613-238-7643
e-mail: info@chamber.ca
URL: www.chamber.ca
Overview: A large national organization founded in 1925
Membership: 175,000 businesses across Canada; *Committees:* Biotechnology Task Force; Competition Law & Policy; Economic Policy; Electronic Commerce & Telecommunications; Environment; Intellectual Property; International Affairs; Ottawa Liaison; Taxation; Transportation
Mission: To create a climate for competitiveness, profitability & job creation for enterprises of all sizes in all sectors across Canada. Offices in Ottawa, Toronto, Montreal & Calgary

Canadian Chemical Producers' Association (CCPA) / Association canadienne des fabricants de produits chimiques
#805, 350 Sparks St., Ottawa ON K1R 7S8
Tel: 613-237-6215; *Fax:* 613-237-4061
e-mail: glaurin@ccpa.ca
URL: www.ccpa.ca
Overview: A medium-sized national organization founded in 1962
Chief Officer(s):
Richard Paton, President & CEO
Michael Bourque, Vice-President, Public Affairs
David Podruzny, Vice-President, Business & Economics
Gordon Lloyd, Vice-President, Technical Affairs
Brian Wastle, Vice-President, Responsible Care
Membership: 60+; *Member Profile:* Companies that manufacture or formulate chemicals, with a commitment to ethics & codes; Companies that directly manage chemicals; Companies that supply goods or services to the chemical industry; Responsible care partnership associations & responsible care supporting associations
Activities: Communicating values & concerns of the chemcial producing industry to member companies, governments, & the public; Supporting & sharing successful practices; Promoting improved safety & environmental performance; *Library:* Canadian Chemical Producers' Association Library
Publications: *Catalyst*
Frequency: q. *Accepts Advertising*: Yes *Editor:* Michael Bourque
Profile: Feature articles & departments about the management of chemicals throughout their life cycle
Mission: To represent the interests of chemical manufacturers; to promote the ethic, "Responsible Care"; to act responsibly, with accountability & openness

Canadian Circumpolar Institute (CCI) / Institut circumpolaire canadien
University of Alberta, #1-42, Pembina Hall, Edmonton AB T6G 2H8
Tel: 780-492-4512; *Fax:* 780-492-1153
URL: www.uofaweb.ualberta.ca/CCI
Previous Name: Boreal Institute for Northern Studies (1960-1990)
Overview: A small international organization founded in 1990
Chief Officer(s):
Marianne S. Douglas, Director, 780-492-0055, Fax: 780-492-1153
marianne.douglas@ualberta.ca
Anita Dey Nuttall, Associate Director, Research Advancement, 780-492-9089, Fax: 780-492-1153
anitad@ualberta.ca
Lindsay Johnston, Circumpolar Librarian & Public Service Mgr, Cameron Library, 780-492-5946
lindsay.johnston@ualberta.ca
Elaine L. Maloney, Managing Editor, CCI Press, 780-492-4999, Fax: 780-492-1153
elaine.maloney@ualberta.ca
Finances: *Funding Sources:* Grants; Donations
Membership: 500-999
Activities: Developing & facilitating interdisciplinary circumpolar research & education; Facilitating communication among northern researchers; Awarding grants & scholarships; Providing outreach programs; Publishing three to five titles each year in subject areas related to the north; Disseminating information about circumpolar areas; *Library:* The Canadian Circumpolar Collection (CCC), U of Alberta Library; Open to public
Publications: *Circumpolar Research Series*
Type: Monographs *Editor:* Elaine L. Maloney, CCI Press *ISSN:* 0838-133X
Profile: Scholarly research on circumpolar situations & concerns
Canadian Circumpolar Institute Occasional Publications Series
Type: Monographs *Editor:* Elaine L. Maloney, CCI Press *ISSN:* 0068-0303
Profile: Conference proceedings & collections of papers
Northern Reference Series [publications of the Canadian Circumpolar Institute]
Editor: Elaine L. Maloney, CCI Press *ISSN:* 1192-5620
Profile: Bibliographies, literature reviews, annotated bibliographies, & review papers
Northern Hunter-Gatherers Research Series
Editor: Elaine L. Maloney, CCI Press *ISSN:* 1707-522X
Profile: Interdisciplinary research about the hunting & gathering peoples of arctic, boreal, & sub-arctic regions
Solstice Series [publications of the Canadian Circumpolar Institute]
Editor: Elaine L. Maloney, CCI Press *ISSN:* 1709-5824
Profile: Case studies & community-based models
Mission: To promote & support research, education, & training related to the boreal & circumpolar regions of the Arctic & Antactica; To enhance awareness of polar environments; *Member of:* University of Alberta
Environmental Activity: Promoting sustainability of circumpolar areas, including northern Canada, the Arctic, & Antarctic

Canadian Clean Power Coalition (CCPC)
c/o Bob Stobbs, Executive Director, 2901 Powerhouse Dr., Regina SK S4N 0A1
URL: www.canadiancleanpowercoalition.com
Overview: A medium-sized national organization
Chief Officer(s):
Bob Stobbs, Executive Director, 306-566-3326
bstobbs@saskpower.com
David Lewin, Chair, 780-412-3196
dlewin@epcor.ca
Member Profile: Canadian coal & coal-fired electricity producers
Activities: Addressing environmental issues with governments & stakeholders
Mission: To secure a future for coal-fired electricity generation, along with a mix of fuels such as solar, wind, hydro, & nuclear; to research & develop clean coal technology

Canadian Coalition for Nuclear Responsibility (CCNR) / Regroupement pour la surveillance du nucléaire (RSN)
PO Box 236, Stn. Snowdon, Montréal QC H3X 3T4
Fax: 514-489-5118
e-mail: ccnr@web.ca
URL: www.ccnr.org
Overview: A small national organization founded in 1975
Finances: *Annual Operating Budget:* Less than $50,000

Mission: Dedicated to education and research on all issues related to nuclear energy, whether civilian or military — including non-nuclear alternatives — especially those pertaining to Canada.; *Affiliation(s):* Environment Liaison Centre - International; Friends of the Earth - Canada; Canadian Peace Alliance; Abolition 2000

Canadian College of Health Leaders (CCHL) / Collège canadien des leaders en santé
292 Somerset St. West, Ottawa ON K2P 0J6
Tel: 613-235-7218; *Fax:* 613-235-5451
Toll-Free: 800-363-9056
e-mail: info@cchl-ccls.ca; communications@cchse.org
URL: www.cchl-ccls.ca
Social Media:
www.facebook.com/group.php?gid=154324094612698; twitter.com/CCHL_CCLS
Previous Name: Canadian College of Service Executives
Overview: A large national organization founded in 1970
Finances: *Funding Sources:* Membership dues; Advertising; Sponsorships
Membership: 3,000 individuals + 80 corporate members; *Member Profile:* Individuals & corporations from all health sectors throughout Canada; Students; Retired members
Activities: Offering a competency-based certification program; Advocating for the profession; Providing professional development resources & opportunities; Preparing position papers on topics such as pandemic planning & patient safety; Offering a forum for the exchange of best practices
Awards: 3M Health Care Quality Team Awards (Award)
To recognize innovation, quality, & teamwork Contact: Cindy MacBride, Manager Awards & Sponsorships *Contact Detail:* Phone: 613-235-7218, ext. 13, E-mail: cmacbride@cchl-ccls.ca
College Honorary Life Member Award (Award)
To honour longstanding College members who have contributed significantly to Canada's health system Contact: Cindy MacBride, Manager Awards & Sponsorships *Contact Detail:* Phone: 613-235-7218, ext. 13, E-mail: cmacbride@cchl-ccls.ca
Chair's Award for Distinguished Service (Award)
To recognize individual or corporate members for significant contribution to the College Contact: Cindy MacBride, Manager Awards & Sponsorships *Contact Detail:* Phone: 613-235-7218, ext. 13, E-mail: cmacbride@cchl-ccls.ca
Chapter Awards for Distinguished Service (Award)
To honour an individual or corporate member who has made a significant contribution to their chapter Contact: Cindy MacBride, Manager Awards & Sponsorships *Contact Detail:* Phone: 613-235-7218, ext. 13, E-mail: cmacbride@cchl-ccls.ca
CHE Self-directed Learning Paper Award (Award)
An award for high quality papers submitted as a component of the Certified Health Executive (CHE) program Contact: Cindy MacBride, Manager Awards & Sponsorships *Contact Detail:* Phone: 613-235-7218, ext. 13, E-mail: cmacbride@cchl-ccls.ca
Energy & Environmental Stewardship Award (Award)
Awarded to a health care organization that has implemented programs that demonstrate environmental responsibility, such as the preservation of natural resources, the reducion of energy usage, & effective waste diversion solutions Contact: Cindy MacBride, Manager Awards & Sponsorships *Contact Detail:* Phone: 613-235-7218, ext. 13, E-mail: cmacbride@cchl-ccls.ca
Health Care Safety Award (Award)
To recognize individuals or teams that improve workplace & patient safety Contact: Cindy MacBride, Manager Awards & Sponsorships *Contact Detail:* Phone: 613-235-7218, ext. 13, E-mail: cmacbride@cchl-ccls.ca
Innovation Award for Health Care Leadership (Award)
Awarded to a senior executive for innovation in their organization Contact: Cindy MacBride, Manager Awards & Sponsorships *Contact Detail:* Phone: 613-235-7218, ext. 13, E-mail: cmacbride@cchl-ccls.ca
Mentorship Award (Award)
Presented to a leader who is committed to mentoring & inspiring health care leadership Contact: Cindy MacBride, Manager Awards & Sponsorships *Contact Detail:* Phone: 613-235-7218, ext. 13, E-mail: cmacbride@cchl-ccls.ca
Nursing Leadership Award (Award)
To honour persons committed to excellence in patient centered care & leadership Contact: Cindy MacBride, Manager Awards & Sponsorships *Contact Detail:* Phone: 613-235-7218, ext. 13, E-mail: cmacbride@cchl-ccls.ca
President's Award for Outstanding Corporate Membership in the College (Award)
Presented to a corporate member who has helped the College achieve its mission Contact: Cindy MacBride, Manager Awards & Sponsorships *Contact Detail:* Phone: 613-235-7218, ext. 13, E-mail: cmacbride@cchl-ccls.ca
Quality of Life Award (Award)
Awarded to persons who improve the lives of patients & families & the community Contact: Cindy MacBride, Manager Awards & Sponsorships *Contact Detail:* Phone: 613-235-7218, ext. 13, E-mail: cmacbride@cchl-ccls.ca
The Robert Wood Johnson Award (Award)
Awarded to one student from each of the six Canadian universities offering graduate programs in health services administration Contact: Cindy MacBride, Manager Awards & Sponsorships *Contact Detail:* Phone: 613-235-7218, ext. 13, E-mail: cmacbride@cchl-ccls.ca
The Robert Zed Young Health Leader Award (Award)
To recognize a Canadian health care leader who has demonstrated leadership in improving the effectiveness & sustainability of the nation's health system Contact: Cindy MacBride, Manager Awards & Sponsorships *Contact Detail:* Phone: 613-235-7218, ext. 13, E-mail: cmacbride@cchl-ccls.ca
Meetings/Conferences:
For more information see Trade Shows, Conferences and Seminars Chapter
Canadian College of Health Leaders 2011 Annual General Meeting
June 2011 Whistler, BC
Canadian College of Health Leaders 2011 National Awards Gala
June 2011 Whistler, BC
Canadian College of Health Leaders & the Canadian Healthcare Association's 2011 National Healthcare Leadership Conference
June 2011 Whistler, BC
Publications: *Communiqué [a publication of the Canadian College of Health Leaders]*
Type: Newsletter *Frequency:* m. Accepts Advertising : Yes *Price:* Free with membership in the Canadian College of Health Service Executives
Profile: College & member news, initiatives in health care, & career opportunities for members
Canadian College of Health Service Executives Membership Directory
Type: Directory
Healthcare Management FORUM
Type: Journal *Frequency:* q. Accepts Advertising : Yes *Editor:* Laurie Wilson (editor@sympatico.ca) *ISSN:* 0840-4704 *Price:* Free for active members of the College; $90 individuals in Canada; $175 institutions
Profile: Peer-reviewed articles about Canadian health services management issues, theory, & practice
Canadian College of Health Service Executives Annual Report
Type: Yearbook *Frequency:* a.
Code of Ethics for Members of the Canadian College of Health Service Executives
Price: Free with membership in the Canadian College of Health Service Executives
Profile: A guide for professional & personal behaviour
Mission: To advance excellence in health leadership; To act as a collective voice for the profession; *Member of:* Health Action Lobby; Coalition for Public Health in the 21st Century
Environmental Activity: Presenting the Energy & Environmental Stewardship Award to organizations that implement programs, such as reducing energy usage, diverting waste, & preserving natural resources; Recognizing individuals or teams for improving workplace safety

Canadian College of Service Executives *See* Canadian College of Health Leaders

Canadian Concrete Pipe Association (CCPA) / Association canadienne des fabricants de tuyaux de béton (ACTB)
205 Miller Dr., Halton Hills ON L7G 6G4
Tel: 905-877-5369; *Fax:* 905-877-5369
e-mail: info@ccpa.com
URL: www.ccpa.com
Social Media:
www.facebook.com/group.php?gid=106265401921
Overview: A medium-sized national organization founded in 1992
Chief Officer(s):
John Greer, Chair
Finances: *Annual Operating Budget:* Less than $50,000; *Funding Sources:* Membership dues; research grants
Staff: 2 staff member(s); 30 volunteer(s)
Membership: 35; *Member Profile:* Manufacturers of concrete pipes & related products; suppliers to manufacturers
Activities: Software development; product development; market research; *Speaker Service:* Yes; *Library:* Data Centre; Open to public
Mission: To coordinate research & development, promotion, education & federal government relations programs pertaining to the marketing of high quality precast concrete waste water & storm drainage products in Canada.; *Member of:* Federation of Canadian Municipalities; *Affiliation(s):* Ontario Concrete Pipe Association; Tubecon; American Concrete Pipe Association

Canadian Construction Association (CCA) / Association canadienne de la construction (ACC)
#400, 75 Albert St., Ottawa ON K1P 5E7
Tel: 613-236-9455; *Fax:* 613-236-9526
e-mail: cca@cca-acc.com
URL: www.cca-acc.com
Overview: A large national organization founded in 1918
Membership: 20,000 firms; *Committees:* Canadian Design-Build Institute; Construction Opportunities On-Line Network; Environment; Exports; Gold Seal; Research & Innovation Task Force; TRIP Canada
Publications: *Canadian Construction Association National Review*
Type: Magazine *Frequency:* a.
CCA [Canadian Construction Association] National Newsletter
Type: Newsletter *Frequency:* q.
CCA [Canadian Construction Association] Committee Bulletins
Profile: Updates & analysis on important industry issues
Mission: CCA, the national voice of the construction industry, serves, promotes, & enhances the construction industry by acting on behalf of its members in matters of national concern.

Canadian Consulting Agrologists Association (CCAA) / Association canadienne des agronomes-conseils
502 - 45 St. West, 2nd Fl., Saskatoon SK S7L 6H2
Tel: 306-933-2974; *Fax:* 306-244-4497
e-mail: info@ccaa.bz
URL: www.ccaa.bz
Overview: A small national organization founded in 1973
Fees: Schedule available; *Member Profile:* Professional agrology consultants who offer consulting services to agricultural sectors around the world
Activities: Promoting certification; Offering professional development & networking opportunities; Advocating for the profession of agricultural consulting; Promoting member services to national & international agricultural sectors
Awards: Lifetime Achievement Award (Award)
Distinguished Certified Agricultural Consultant (Award)
CCAA Fellow Award (Award)
Publications: *CCAA [Canadian Consulting Agrologists Association] Member Directory*
Type: Directory
CCAA [Canadian Consulting Agrologists Association] Newsletter
Type: Newsletter *Frequency:* q.
Profile: Current industry practices & trends & professional development
Mission: To provide excellence in agricultural consulting; to promote standards of competency; to maintain Standards of Ethical Conduct

Canadian Consumer Specialty Products Association (CCSPA)
#800, 130 Albert St., Ottawa ON K1P 5G4
Tel: 613-232-6616; *Fax:* 613-233-6350
e-mail: assoc@ccspa.org
URL: www.ccspa.org
Previous Name: Canadian Manufacturers of Chemical Specialties Association
Overview: A medium-sized national organization founded in 1958
Finances: *Annual Operating Budget:* $250,000-$500,000
Staff: 6 staff member(s)
Membership: 60+ corporate; *Committees:* Technical: Soap & Detergent; Antimicrobial Chemicals; Pest Control Products; Waxes & Polishes; Occupational Health & Safety; Pesticides; Automotive Chemicals; Aerosols; Environmental; Non-Technical: Executive; Public Relations; Membership Recruitment; Ontario Golf
Activities: *Rents Mailing List:* Yes
Awards: Chevalier Award (Scholarship)
Publications: *The Formulator [a publication of the Canadian Consumer Specialty Products Association]*
Type: Magazine *Frequency:* a. *Editor:* Ali Mintenko
Profile: Feature articles & CCSPA information

Associations/Organizations / Canadian Co-operative Wool Growers Ltd.

Microgram [a publication of the Canadian Consumer Specialty Products Association]
Type: Newsletter Frequency: q.
Profile: CCSPA new for members only
Mission: Represents the specialty chemical & formulated products industry; promotes the interests of member companies by providing a national voice, encouraging ethical practices, negotiating with government, & fostering industry cooperation

Canadian Co-operative Wool Growers Ltd. (CCWG)
PO Box 130, 142 Franktown Rd., Carleton Place ON K7C 3P3
Tel: 613-257-2714; *Fax:* 613-257-8896
Toll-Free: 800-488-2714
e-mail: ccwghq@wool.ca
URL: www.wool.ca
Overview: A medium-sized national organization founded in 1918
Membership: 1,200
Awards: Certificate of Merit, Commercial Wool Production in Canada (Award)
Honorary Knights of the Golden Fleece (Award)
Mission: To operate as a producer-owned wool marketing cooperative; To collect, grade, & market, the majority of the Canadian wool clip to the global market; To retail farm supplies & animal health & identification products

Canadian Council for Human Resources in the Environment Industry *See* Environmental Careers Organization of Canada

Canadian Council for International Co-operation (CCIC) / Conseil canadien pour la coopération internationale
#300, 1 Nicholas St., Ottawa ON K1N 7B7
Tel: 613-241-7007; *Fax:* 613-241-5302
e-mail: info@ccic.ca
URL: www.ccic.ca
Overview: A large national organization founded in 1968
Finances: *Annual Operating Budget:* $1.5 Million-$3 Million; *Funding Sources:* Federal government through CIDA
Staff: 22 staff member(s); 4 volunteer(s)
Membership: 100 organizations; *Member Profile:* Non-profit organizations working in Canada & overseas, including religious & secular development groups, professional associations, & labour unions; these work with NGOs, cooperatives, & citizens' groups in Africa, Asia, & Latin America to meet basic needs for food, shelter, education, health, & sanitation; many groups conduct policy research & campaign with their southern partners for fair trade, global security, children's rights, biodiversity, or the forgiveness of multilateral debt; some members work exclusively in Canada, designing education materials for use in classrooms & resource centres; all members must adhere to a Code of Ethics which governs their financial management, communications with the public, & administration
Activities: Monitors & analyzes federal policies on foreign affairs, aid, trade, debt & defence, & communicates its findings to members & the public; engages Canadians in a collective search for development alternatives; *Internships:* Yes; *Speaker Service:* Yes
Publications: *Au Courant [a publication of the Canadian Council for International Co-operation]*
Type: Newsletter Frequency: s-a. Editor: Katia Gianneschi & Ann Simpson ISSN: 118-604X
Profile: News, analysis, & opinion about domestic & international economic policy, development aid, & foreign policy
Who's Who in International Development
Type: Directory
Profile: Listing of CCIC members working to end global poverty
Mission: A coalition of Canadian voluntary sector organizations working globally to achieve sustainable human development; CCIC seeks to end global poverty, & to promote social justice & human dignity for all

Canadian Council for Tobacco Control (CCTC) / Conseil canadien pour le contrôle du tabac
192 Bank St., Ottawa ON K2P 1W8
Tel: 613-567-3050; *Fax:* 613-567-2730
Toll-Free: 800-267-5234
e-mail: infoservices@cctc.ca
URL: www.cctc.ca
Previous Name: Canadian Council on Smoking & Health
Overview: A medium-sized national charitable organization founded in 1974
Chief Officer(s):
Robert Walsh, Executive Director
rwalsh@cctc.ca

L. Dubernet, Administrative Assistant
ldubernet@cctc.ca
Finances: *Annual Operating Budget:* $500,000-$1.5 Million; *Funding Sources:* Federal & provincial governments
Staff: 7 staff member(s)
Fees: $40 student; $75 individual; $500 Organizational up to 10 members
Activities: *Awareness Events:* National Non-Smoking Week/Weedless Wednesday, Jan.; *Speaker Service:* Yes; *Library:* National Clearing House for Tobacco & Health; Not open to the public
Awards: Award of Excellence (Award)
Mission: To envision a strong & effective tobacco control movement; To diminish the adverse impact to the health of Canadians caused by tobacco industry products; To increase the effectiveness & capacity of individuals & organizations involved in tobacco control, to achieve a smoke free society in Canada; To prevent tobaccco use; To persuade & help smokers to stop using tobacco products; To educate Canadians about the marketing strategies & tactics of the tobacco industry & the adverse effects tobacco products have on the health of Canadians
Environmental Activity: Striving to eliminate exposure to second-hand smoke

Canadian Council of Chief Executives (CCCE) / Conseil canadien des chefs d'entreprise
#1001, 99 Bank St., Ottawa ON K1P 6B9
Tel: 613-238-3727; *Fax:* 613-236-8679
e-mail: leaders@ceocouncil.ca
URL: www.ceocouncil.ca
Previous Name: Business Council on National Issues
Overview: A large national organization founded in 1976
Membership: 100-499; *Member Profile:* Business leaders from 150 Canadian corporations
Activities: Working on national issues, such as taxation, fiscal & monetary policy, corporate governance, & competitiveness; Preparing presentations & reports
Publications: *Perspectives [a publication of the Canadian Council of Chief Executives]*
Language: B Editor: Ross Laver
Profile: Articles about globalization challenges, sustainable growth, corporate responsibiliy, & strengthening Canadian competitiveness
Mission: To engage in policy work in Canada, North America, & the world

Canadian Council of Engineering Technicians and Technologists (CCETT) *See* Canadian Council of Technicians & Technologists

Canadian Council of Food & Nutrition (CCFN) / Conseil canadien des aliments et de la nutrition
2810 Matheson Blvd. East, 1st Fl., Mississauga ON L4W 4X7
Tel: 905-625-5746; *Fax:* 905-265-9372
e-mail: info@ccfn.ca
URL: www.ccfn.ca
Previous Name: Canadian Institute of Food & Nutrition; Canadian Food Information Council
Overview: A medium-sized national organization founded in 2004
Chief Officer(s):
Francey Pillo-Blocka, President & CEO
Finances: *Annual Operating Budget:* $250,000-$500,000
Staff: 1.5 staff member(s)
Membership: 30 active members; *Fees:* based on annual sales active; patron national $2,500, provincial $1,350; *Member Profile:* Active members from agri-food industry corporations; patron members from agri-food trade associations & marketing boards, pharma, retail grocery, pr firms.
Activities: *Library:* Resource Centre; Not open to the public
Mission: The multi-sectoral trusted voice for science-based food & nutrition policy & information in Canada.

Canadian Council of Forest Ministers (CCFM) / Conseil canadien des ministres des forêts
c/o Science and Policy Integration, Natural Resources Canada, 580 Booth St., 11th Fl., Ottawa ON K1A 0E4
Tel: 613-947-9099; *Fax:* 613-947-9033
URL: www.ccfm.org
Chief Officer(s):
Claude Léger, Senior Advisor, Federal-Provincial Relations & Secretariat Contact
cleger@nrcan.gc.ca
Mission: The Canadian Council of Ministers (CCFM) was established in 1985 to give sufficient attention to forest issues.

CCFM stimulates the development of policies & initiatives for strengthening the forest sector, including the forest resource & its use. It provides leadership, addresses national & international issues & sets the direction for stewardship & sustainable management of Canada's forests. The CCFM is composed of the fourteen federal, provincial & territorial ministers responsible for forests. The CCFM undertakes activities primarily through ad hoc fora, committees & working groups. At present there are 9 committees. CCFM initiatives include: International Forest Issues Working Group; International Forestry Partnerships Program; Sustainable Forest Management Working Group; Canadian Wildland Fire Strategy; National Forest Information System; National Forestry Database Program; Science & Technology Working Group; Forest Communities Working Group. The Council also cooperates with the Canadian Wildland Fire Strategy Declaration, a federal-provincial-territorial initiative to address the management of wildland fires. National Forestry Database Program: nfdp.ccfm.org/; National Forest Information System: nfis.org

Canadian Council of Grocery Distributors (CCGD) / Conseil canadien de la distribution alimentaire (CCDA)
#402, 6455, rue Jean-Talon est, Montréal QC H1S 3E8
Tel: 514-982-0267
URL: www.ccgd.ca
Previous Name: Canadian Wholesale Grocers Association
Overview: A medium-sized national organization founded in 1919
Finances: *Funding Sources:* Membership dues; Sponsorships
Member Profile: Retail & wholesale operations; Foodservice distributors, including Canada's major retail grocery distributors regional distributors, & locally-based grocery firms; Allied members who provide products & services to the industry
Activities: Developing high standards; Promoting best practices; Enhancing competitveness; Providing early warning on issues to members; Creating an international data source of non-proprietary business information; Protecting the industry's profile; Collaborating with governments, non-governmental organizations, & other industry associations; Publishing industry reports to raise awareness & discussion among stakeholders & policy-makers
Awards: Canadian Grand Prix New Product Awards (Award)
To recognize new product development & innovation
Meetings/Conferences:
For more information see Trade Shows, Conferences and Seminars Chapter
Canadian Council of Grocery Distributors 2012 National Grocery Conference
May 2012
Publications: *Précis [a publication of the Canadian Council of Grocery Distributors]*
Type: Newsletter Frequency: m.
Profile: For Canadian Council of Grocery Distributors members
Mission: To advance & promote the Canadian grocery & foodservice distribution industry at regional & national levels; To act as the voice for the grocery industry in Canada, on policies such as labour laws, & environment initiatives; Affiliation(s): Retail Council of Canada
Environmental Activity: Seeking innovation & best practices in product development, energy efficiency, & waste diversion & reduction

Canadian Council of Independent Laboratories (CCIL) / Conseil canadien des laboratoires indépendants
PO Box 41027, Ottawa ON K1G 5K9
Tel: 613-746-3919; *Fax:* 613-746-4324
e-mail: ccil@magma.ca
URL: www.ccil.com
Overview: A medium-sized national licensing organization founded in 1993
Chief Officer(s):
Alnoor Nathoo, P.Eng., Vice-President; Secretary-Treasurer
David Hope, President
Membership: 51
Activities: *Speaker Service:* Yes

Canadian Council of Land Surveyors (CCLS) / Conseil Canadien des arpenteurs-géomètres
#100E, 900 Dynes Rd., Ottawa ON K2C 3N6
Tel: 613-226-5110; *Fax:* 613-723-5558
Toll-Free: 800-241-7200
e-mail: admin@ccls-ccag.ca
URL: www.ccls-ccag.ca

Overview: A medium-sized national organization founded in 1976
Finances: *Funding Sources:* Membership fees
Staff: 2 staff member(s)
Membership: 10 provincial & 1 federal associations; *Fees:* $40
Activities: Accreditation of three Canadian universities offering surveying engineering
Awards: Champlain Award (Award)
Publications: *The CCLS / CCAG Forum*
Type: Newsletter *Language:* B
Profile: Current initiatives, developments, & opportunities for councils, executive, & committees of member associations & CCLS.
Mission: To represent the disciplines of cadastral, geodetic, hydrographic, & photogrammetric surveying & land information management; To provide proactive leadership to its member associations; To provide national strategies, & national & international representation for land surveyors within the geomatics profession

Canadian Council of Ministers of the Environment (CCME) / Conseil canadien des ministres de l'environnement
#360, 123 Main St., Winnipeg MB R3C 1A3
Tel: 204-948-2090; *Fax:* 204-948-2125
Toll-Free: 800-805-3025
e-mail: info@ccme.ca
URL: www.ccme.ca
Finances: *Annual Operating Budget:* $1.5 Million-$3 Million; *Funding Sources:* Federal, provincial & territorial governments
Staff: 8 staff member(s)
Membership: 1-99; *Committees:* Environmental Planning & Protection
Mission: CCME is comprised of the environment ministers from the federal, provincial and territorial governments. These 14 ministers normally meet at least once a year to discuss national environmental priorities and determine work to be carried out under the auspices of CCME. The Council seeks to achieve positive environmental results, focusing on issues that are national in scope and that require collective attention by a number of governments. CCME aims to assist its members to meet their mandate of protecting Canada's environment. As with any association, each member can accomplish more by working together than by working alone. CCME serves as a principal forum for members to develop national strategies, norms, and guidelines that each environment ministry across the country can use. Since environment is constitutionally speaking an area of shared jurisdiction, it makes sense to work together to promote effective results. CCME is not another level of government regulator, but a council of government ministers holding similar responsibilities

Canadian Council of Motor Transport Administrators (CCMTA) / Conseil canadien des administrateurs en transport motorisé (CCATM)
2323 St. Laurent Blvd., Ottawa ON K1G 4J8
Tel: 613-736-1003; *Fax:* 613-736-1395
e-mail: ccmta-secretariat@ccmta.ca
URL: www.ccmta.ca
Overview: A medium-sized national charitable organization founded in 1940
Finances: *Funding Sources:* Member assessments; special projects; membership fees
Membership: 100-499; *Member Profile:* Members include representatives of provincial, territorial, & federal governments, & associate members from transportation related organizations.; *Committees:* Drivers & Vehicles; Compliance & Regulatory Affairs; Road Safety Research & Policies
Activities: Developing strategies & programs; Managing a communications network, called the Interprovincial Record Exchange system; *Rents Mailing List:* Yes
Awards: CCMTA-Police Partnership Award (Award)
Associate Member Award (Award)
Government Member Award (Award)
Distinguished Service Award (Award)
Award of Distinction (Award)
President's Award (Award)
Publications: *CCMTA [Canadian Council of Motor Transport Administrators] News*
Type: Newsletter *Frequency:* s-a.
Profile: Current projects & activities of CCMTA
CCMTA [Canadian Council of Motor Transport Administrators] Directory
Type: Directory *Language:* B
Profile: Bilingual list of names, addresses, telephone & fax numbers, & email addresses of over 600 contacts

Mission: CCMTA coordinates operational matters dealing with the administration, regulation, & control of motor vehicle transportation & highway safety.

Canadian Council of Professional Engineers *See* Engineers Canada

Canadian Council of Professional Fish Harvesters (CCPFH) / Conseil canadien des pêcheurs professionnels (CCPP)
#712, 1 Nicholas St., Ottawa ON K1N 7B7
Tel: 613-235-3474; *Fax:* 613-231-4313
e-mail: fish@ccpfh-ccpp.org
URL: www.ccpfh-ccpp.org
Overview: A medium-sized national organization founded in 1995
Chief Officer(s):
John Sutcliffe, Executive Director
Earle McCurdy, President
Ronnie Heighton, Vice-President
Daniel Landry, Secretary
O'Neil Cloutier, Treasurer
Member Profile: Fish harvesters; captains & crew members
Publications: *Canadian Council of Professional Fish Harvesters Newsletter*
Type: Newsletter *Frequency:* q.
Profile: News & information from the council & industry
Mission: To represent the interests of professional fish harvesters across Canada in their dealings with the federal, provincial & territorial governments on national issues of common concern; to provide organizational structure & leadership for the development of a program of professionalization for fish harvesters in collaboration with the organizations representing professional fishers across Canada; to act as a national industry sector council to plan & implement training & adjustment programs for the fish harvesting industry in Canada

Canadian Council of Technicians & Technologists (CCTT) / Conseil canadien des techniciens et technologues
#295, 1101 Prince Of Wales Dr., Ottawa ON K2C 3W7
Tel: 613-238-8123; *Fax:* 613-238-8822
Toll-Free: 800-891-1140
e-mail: cctadm@cctt.ca; fq@cctt.ca (foreign qualification assessment)
URL: www.cctt.ca
Social Media: www.twitter.com/#!/CCTTCanada
Previous Name: Canadian Council of Engineering Technicians and Technologists (CCETT)
Overview: A large national organization founded in 1973
Chief Officer(s):
Isidore J. LeBlond, Director, Program Development
ileblond@cctt.ca
Rick Tachuk, Director, Communications
rtachuk@cctt.ca
Darlene Pilon, Manager, Finance & Events Management
dpilon@cctt.ca
Valery Vidershpan, Manager, Database Development
vvidershpan@cctt.ca
Activities: *Awareness Events:* National Technology Week
Publications: *Innovation [a publication of the Canadian Council of Technicians & Technologists]*
Type: Newsletter *Frequency:* m.
Profile: News for technology professionals across Canada, including credential information, awards, & awareness activities
Mission: To advocate on behalf of Canada's certified technicians & technologists; To establish & maintain national competency standards

Canadian Council on 4-H Clubs *See* Canadian 4-H Council

Canadian Council on Animal Care (CCAC) / Conseil canadien de protection des animaux (CCPA)
#1510, 130 Albert St., Ottawa ON K1P 5G4
Tel: 613-238-4031; *Fax:* 613-238-2837
e-mail: ccac@ccac.ca
URL: www.ccac.ca
Overview: A medium-sized national organization founded in 1968
Finances: *Annual Operating Budget:* $250,000-$500,000
Staff: 12 staff member(s)
Membership: 22 organizations; *Committees:* Planning & Priorities; Finance; Guidelines; Education & Training; Assessments

Activities: *Library:* Yes, Open to public, open by appointment
Publications: *CCAC [Canadian Council on Animal Care] Annual Report*
Frequency: a.
Resource: The Newsletter of the Canadian Council on Animal Care (CCAC)
Type: Newsletter *Frequency:* s-a. *Editor:* Clément Gauthier, PhD
ISSN: 0700-5237
Profile: Articles about laboratory animal science; news about current issues & events related to the CCAC
CCAC [Canadian Council on Animal Care] Guidelines
Frequency: irreg.
Profile: Topics include procurement of animals used in science, laboratory animal facilities, the care and use of wildlife, antibody production, institutional animal user training, transgenic animals, & animal use protocol review
CCAC [Canadian Council on Animal Care] Guide to the Care & Use of Experimental Animals
Canadian Council on Animal Care Workshop Proceedings
Mission: To act on behalf of the people of Canada to ensure, through programs of education, assessment & persuasion that the use of animals in Canada, where necessary for research, teaching & testing, employs physical & psychological care according to acceptable scientific standards, & to promote an increased level of knowledge, awareness & sensitivity to the relevant ethical principles

Canadian Council on Ecological Areas (CCEA)
c/o Environmental Stewardship Branch, Environment Canada, #3, 351, boul St. Joseph, Gatineau QC K1A 0H3
Tel: 819-934-6064; *Fax:* 819-994-4445
e-mail: mark.richardson@ec.gc.ca
URL: www.ccea.org
Overview: A small national organization founded in 1982
Chief Officer(s):
Mark Richardson, Sec.-Manager
Mission: To facilitate the establishment of a comprehensive network of protected areas which are linked together in a system that will protect Canada's terrestrial & aquatic diversity in perpetuity

Canadian Council on Electrotechnologies *Voir* Conseil Canadien des Électrotechnologies

Canadian Council on International Law (CCIL) / Conseil canadien de droit international (CCDI)
275 Bay St., Ottawa ON K1R 5Z5
Tel: 613-235-0442; *Fax:* 613-232-8228
e-mail: info@ccil-ccdi.ca
URL: www.ccil-ccdi.ca
Overview: A small international charitable organization founded in 1972
Finances: *Annual Operating Budget:* $50,000-$100,000; *Funding Sources:* Membership fees, donations, government project funding
Staff: 1 staff member(s); 24 volunteer(s)
Membership: 400; *Fees:* $85 individual; $45 student; *Member Profile:* Leading scholars; students of international law; government & practising lawyers from both public & private sectors
Activities: Speakers series; *Speaker Service:* Yes; *Library:* Yes;
Awards: John E. Read Medal (Award)
Mission: To bring together scholars of international law & organizations engaged in teaching & research at Canadian universities; to encourage & conduct studies in international law with a view to its progressive development & codification; to foster the study of legal aspects of Canada's international problems & to advocate their solution in accordance with existing or developing principles of international law.; *Affiliation(s):* Société québécoise de droit international; American Society of International Law; Japanese Association of International Law

Canadian Council on Smoking & Health *See* Canadian Council for Tobacco Control

Canadian Dam Association (CDA) / Association canadienne des barrages (ACB)
PO Box 2281, Moose Jaw SK S6TH 7W6
URL: www.cda.ca
Merged from: Canadian National Committee on Large Dams
Overview: A small national organization founded in 1989
Chief Officer(s):
Wayne Phillips, Executive Director
Finances: *Funding Sources:* Membership fees; Conferences; Advertising

Associations/Organizations / Canadian District Energy Association

Fees: $5 students; $40 individuals; $350 corporate members; $700 corporate sponsors; *Member Profile:* Individuals, students, & corporations with an interest in dam safety, such as dam owners, engineers, technologists, researchers, government agencies, hydro companies, & equipment manufacturers & suppliers
Activities: Promoting the adoption of regulatory policies & safety guidelines for dams & reservoirs in Canada; Fostering inter-provincial cooperation; Offering education & outreach about dams
Awards: Inge Anderson Award of Merit (Award)
Contact: Tony Bennett, Awards Committee Chair *Contact Detail: Phone:* 905-262-2667
Gary Salmon Memorial Scholarship (Scholarship)
Contact: Tony Bennett, Awards Committee Chair *Contact Detail: Phone:* 905-262-2667
Peter Halliday Award for Service (Award)
Contact: Tony Bennett, Awards Committee Chair *Contact Detail: Phone:* 905-262-2667
Published Paper Award of Excellence (Award)
Contact: Tony Bennett, Awards Committee Chair *Contact Detail: Phone:* 905-262-2667
Research Award (Award)
Contact: Tony Bennett, Awards Committee Chair *Contact Detail: Phone:* 905-262-2667
Student Achievement Award (Award)
Contact: Tony Bennett, Awards Committee Chair *Contact Detail: Phone:* 905-262-2667
Meritorious Achievement Award (Award)
Contact: Tony Bennett, Awards Committee Chair *Contact Detail: Phone:* 905-262-2667
Meetings/Conferences:
For more information see Trade Shows, Conferences and Seminars Chapter
Canadian Dam Association 2011 Annual Conference
October 2011 Fredericton, NB
Canadian Dam Association 2012 Annual Conference
Other Conferences in 2012 2012
Canadian Dam Association 2013 Annual Conference
Other Conferences in 2013 2013
Canadian Dam Association 2014 Annual Conference
Other Conferences in 2014 2014
Publications: *Canadian Dam Association Bulletin*
Type: Magazine *Language:* B *Frequency:* q. *Accepts Advertising*: Yes *Editor:* A. Kirkham (allan.kirkham@opg.com) *Price:* Free with membership in the Canadian Dam Association
Profile: Information from the Canadian Dam Association to help members remain informed about the association, the board, awards, conferences, & suppliers & buyers
Dam Safety Guidelines
Type: Guidelines *Language:* B *Number of Pages:* 82 *Price:* $60 each, plus GST, for CDA members; $100 each, plus GST, for non-members
Profile: A Canadian Dam Association publication, with a companion series of English language technical bulletins (235 pages)
Dams in Canada
Type: CD *Language:* B *Price:* $60 each, plus GST, for CDA members; $100 each, plus GST, for non-members
Profile: Featuring chapters, with photographs, drawings, & text, on water resources, water supply, irrigation, hydroelectric dams, & flood control dams, plus the Dams in Canada Register, with information about over 900 dams
Mission: To monitor the technical, environmental, social, economic, legal, & administrative aspects of dams in Canada; To ensure the safe operation of dams across Canada; *Member of:* Society of the Engineering Institute of Canada; International Commission on Large Dams
Environmental Activity: Providing for the exchange of ideas & experiences regarding dam safety, public safety, & the protection of the environment in Canada; Monitoring coastal zone & shoreline protection

Canadian Direct Marketing Association *See* Canadian Marketing Association

Canadian District Energy Association (CDEA) / Association canadienne des réseaux thermiques
PO Box 612, #402, 555 Richmond St. West, Toronto ON M5V 3B1
Tel: 416-365-0765; *Fax:* 416-365-0650
e-mail: cdea@canurb.com
URL: www.cdea.ca
Overview: A small national organization founded in 1994

Membership: 66; *Fees:* $1,200 owner/operator; $900 goods or service supplier; $300 associate; $90 full time student or professor
Mission: The Canadian District Energy Association (CDEA) is an industry association representing member utilities, government agencies, building owners, consulting engineers, suppliers, developers, bankers, and investors who share a common interest in promoting the growth of district energy in Canada.

Canadian Earth Energy Association *See* Earth Energy Society of Canada

Canadian Electricity Association (CEA) / Association canadienne de l'électricité (ACE)
#1100, 350 Sparks St., Ottawa ON K1R 7S8
Tel: 613-230-9263; *Fax:* 613-230-9326
e-mail: info@electricity.ca
URL: www.electricity.ca
Overview: A medium-sized national organization founded in 1891
Chief Officer(s):
Pierre Guimond, President & Chief Executive Officer, 613-230-4762
Francis Bradley, Vice-President, Policy Development, 613-230-5027
Sandra Schwartz, Vice-President, Policy Advocacy, 613-230-9876
Louisa Hood, Director, Communications, 613-688-2954
Angela Macleod, Corporate Secretary, 613-230-7384
Richard Lussier, Controller, 613-688-2065
Member Profile: Members generate, transmit, & distribute electrical energy to residential, commercial, institutional, & industrial customers throughout Canada
Activities: Analyzing national & international business issues; Providing a national forum for the electricity business; Advocating industry views; Helping companies in evolving markets; Communicating findings about concerns such as mercury emissions & electric & magnetic fields
Meetings/Conferences:
For more information see Trade Shows, Conferences and Seminars Chapter
Smart Grid Interoperability 2011 2nd Annual Summit
June 2011 Toronto, ON
Smart Grid Interoperability 2012 3rd Annual Summit
Other Conferences in 2012 2012
Annual Smart Grid Interoperability 2013 4th Annual Summit
Other Conferences in 2013 2013
Publications: *Forced Outage Performance of Transmission Equipment [a publication of the Canadian Electricity Association]*
Type: Yearbook *Frequency:* a.
Profile: Produced by the Performance Excellence & Benchmarking program of the Canadian Electricity Association, the report addresses the performance of transmission equipment in Canada
Generation Equipment Status [a publication of the Canadian Electricity Association]
Type: Yearbook *Frequency:* a.
Profile: Produced by the Performance Excellence & Benchmarking program of the Canadian Electricity Association, the report features information on the performance of electrical generating units in Canada
Annual Service Continuity Report on Distribution System Performance in Electrical Utilities
Type: Yearbook *Frequency:* a.
Profile: Produced by the Performance Excellence & Benchmarking program of the Canadian Electricity Association, the report contains information about industry standard metrics for electricity distribution, including system average interruption frequency index & the system average interruption duration index
Electricity Annual
Type: Yearbook *Frequency:* a.
Profile: The Canadian Electricity Association's yearly industry review
The CEA [Canadian Electricity Association] Member Directory
Type: Directory *Frequency:* a. *Price:* $15 members; $65 non-members
Profile: Contact information for the Canadian electricity industry's major players, in addition to information about the operations of the Canadian Electricity Association's member companies
Mission: To act as the voice of the Canadian electricity business
Environmental Activity: Implementing Sustainable Electricity, an industry-wide intitiative

Canadian Energy Efficiency Alliance (CEEA) / L'Association de l'efficacité énergétique du Canada
#402, 2800 Skymark Ave., Mississauga ON L4W 5A6
Tel: 905-614-1641
Toll-Free: 866-614-1641
e-mail: alliance@energyefficiency.org
URL: www.energyefficiency.org
Overview: A medium-sized national organization founded in 1995
Chief Officer(s):
Ken Elsey, President/CEO
kenelsey@energyefficiency.org
Finances: *Annual Operating Budget:* $250,000-$500,000; *Funding Sources:* Membership dues & projects
Staff: 14 volunteer(s)
Membership: 40; *Fees:* $1,500 corporate; $15,000 leader; *Committees:* Codes & Standards; Executive; Government Relations
Activities: Establishing a National Energy Efficiency Centre to be North America's energy technology showcase; promoting/advocating energy efficiency; breakfast policy updates; annual meeting
Mission: To become the leading energy efficiency advocate in Canada; to work in partnership with industry, environmental & consumer leaders to promote energy efficiency programs & policies that will move Canada toward a more sustainable future; *Affiliation(s):* Canadian Energy Efficiency Centre

Canadian Energy Pipeline Association (CEPA)
#1860, 205 - 5th Ave. SW, Calgary AB T2P 2V7
Tel: 403-221-8777; *Fax:* 403-221-8760
e-mail: info@cepa.com
URL: www.cepa.com
Overview: A medium-sized national organization founded in 1993
Chief Officer(s):
Brenda Kenny, President
Myra Paul, Administrative Assistant
Awards: Environmental Management Award (Award)
Environmental Achievement Award (Award)
Spill Prevention Award (Award)
Mission: The Canadian Energy Pipeline Association (CEPA) represents Canada's trasmissions pipeline companie. Their members transport 97% of Canada's daily crude oil and natural gas production from producing regions to markets throughout Canada and the United States.

Canadian Energy Research Institute (CERI)
#150, 3512 - 33 St. NW, Calgary AB T2L 2A6
Tel: 403-282-1231; *Fax:* 403-284-4181
e-mail: ceri@ceri.ca
URL: www.ceri.ca
Overview: A medium-sized national organization founded in 1975
Membership: 150
Activities: Recent study topics include: world oil market, natural gas market, demand side management & electric utilities, Canadian oil replacement costs, economics of conventional Alberta oil supply, world trade in natural gas, transportation demand management, electric vehicles; *Speaker Service:* Yes; *Library:* I.N. McKinnon Memorial Library
Mission: To provide the public, industry & the government with information concerning all aspects of energy

Canadian Environment Industry Association - British Columbia Chapter *See* British Columbia Environment Industry Association

Canadian Environment Industry Association - Ontario Chapter *See* ONEIA - Ontario Environment Industry Association

Canadian Environmental Auditing Association *See* Auditing Association of Canada

Canadian Environmental Certification Approvals Board (CECAB) / Bureau canadien de reconnaissance professionnelle des spécialistes de l'environnement
#200, 308 - 11th Ave. SE, Calgary AB T2G 0Y2
Tel: 403-233-7484; *Fax:* 403-264-6240
e-mail: certification@eco.ca
URL: www.cecab.org
Overview: A small national licensing organization founded in 1998

Chief Officer(s):
Lou Locatelli, Vice Chair
Finances: *Annual Operating Budget:* $250,000-$500,000; *Funding Sources:* Industry; HRDC; CCHREI
Staff: 3 staff member(s)
Membership: 700+; *Fees:* CEDIT $50; CCEP $150-300; *Member Profile:* Environmental practitioners from all provinces & territories, representing all disciplines.; *Committees:* Certification; Discipline; Ethics; Professional Development
Mission: CECAB is a professional autonomous body providing national certification for Canadian environmental practitioners.

Canadian Environmental Defence Fund *See* Environmental Defence

Canadian Environmental Grantmakers' Network (CEGN) / Réseau canadien des subventionneurs en environnement (RCSE)
#360, 215 Spadina Ave., Toronto ON M5T 2C7
Tel: 416-961-1273; *Fax:* 416-979-3936
e-mail: pegi_dover@cegn.org
URL: www.cegn.org
Overview: A medium-sized national organization
Chief Officer(s):
Pegi Dover, Executive Director
Member Profile: Private, community, public & corporate foundations; government & corporate funding programs that give grants in support of Canadian environment
Mission: Works to develop an effective network of environmental grantmakers in Canada by facilitating information-sharing, collaboration, training & professional development, research, & communications

Canadian Environmental Law Association (CELA) / Association canadienne du droit de l'environnement
#301, 130 Spadina Ave., Toronto ON M5V 2L4
Tel: 416-960-2284; *Fax:* 416-960-9392
e-mail: millers@cela.ca
URL: www.cela.ca
Overview: A medium-sized national organization founded in 1970
Finances: *Annual Operating Budget:* $250,000-$500,000; *Funding Sources:* Legal Aid Ontario
Staff: 12 staff member(s); 1 volunteer(s)
Membership: 23
Activities: *Library:* Resource Library for the Environment & the Law; open by appointment
Mission: To advocate for environmental law reform; To act in court or during hearings on behalf of citizens' groups & individuals who would otherwise be unable to afford legal assistance

Canadian Environmental Law Research Foundation *See* Canadian Institute for Environmental Law & Policy

Canadian Environmental Network (RCEN) / Réseau canadien de l'environnement
39 McArthur Ave., Level 1-1, Ottawa ON K1L 8L7
Tel: 613-728-9810; *Fax:* 613-728-2963
e-mail: info@cen-rce.org
URL: www.cen-rce.org
Social Media:
www.facebook.com/CanadianEnvironmentalNetwork;
www.twitter.com/#!/RCEN
Overview: A large national organization founded in 1977
Membership: 600+ organizations; *Member Profile:* Canadian non-profit, non-governmental organizations with a focus on environmental concerns; *Committees:* Atmosphere & Energy; Agriculture; Biodiversity; Environmental Planning & Assessment; Health; International Program; Mining; Toxics; Water, Fisheries & Oceans; Youth
Activities: Providing communication & networking services for members; *Awareness Events:* Environment Week, June
Meetings/Conferences:
For more information see Trade Shows, Conferences and Seminars Chapter
Canadian Environmental Network / Réseau canadien de l'environnement 2012 Annual Conference on the Environment
Other Conferences in 2012 2012
Publications: *RCEN [Canadian Environmental Network] e-Bulletin*
Type: Newsletter *Frequency:* w.
Profile: Up-to-date information about RCEN activities & news of interest for RECEN members

RCEN [Canadian Environmental Network] Annual Report
Type: Yearbook *Frequency:* a.
Profile: A review of the network's activities & audited financial statements
Participating in Federal Public Policy: A Guide for the Voluntary Sector
Type: Guide
Profile: A resource to assist voluntary organizations participate in the federal public policy development process
RCEN [Canadian Environmental Network] Youth Friendly Guide: Youth Guide to Policy Change for Intergenerational Partnerships
Type: Guide
Profile: A guidebook of interest to organizations wanting to make their operations youth-friendly
Stormy Weather 101 - Solutions to Global Climate Change
Author: Guy Dauncey; Patrick Mazza *Editor:* Maggie Paquet
Price: $27.95
Profile: Suggestions for making a positive difference
Mercury . . . A Public Concern, including Analysis of Mercury Emissions from Coal-Fired Power Plants & Canada-Wide Standards
Number of Pages: 198 *Author:* Anna Tilman
Profile: Government Programs-Mercury; Canada-wide Standards for Mercury Electric Power Generating Sector; Mercury Data from Coal-Fired Plants; Cumulative Emissions-The True Loading Picture; U.S. Regulatory Action on Mercury & Coal-Fired Plants; Recommendations for Canada-wide Standards for Mercury
Mercury - A Global Toxin: Perspectives on Initiatives & Programs on Coal-Fired Power Plants & Mercury Emissions
Number of Pages: 114 *Author:* Anna Tilman
Profile: Coal-fired Power Plants - Mercury Emissions; Canada-wide Standards for Mercury Electric Power Generating Sector; Strategies & Control Technologies for Reducing Mercury Emissions; Mercury Emission Trading; U.S. Regulatory Action on Mercury & Coal-Fired Plants; Global Initiatives on Mercury
Ideas for a More Effective Environmental Movement in Canada
Number of Pages: 17 *Author:* Jerry DeMarco
Mission: To promote ecologically sound ways of life; To enhance members' work to restore, protect, & promote a clean & sustainable environment
Environmental Activity: Working with organizations & citizens to protect, preserve, & restore the environment; Affecting how people think about environmental issues; Coordinating projects to strengthen the environmental movement across Canada

Canadian Environmental Technology Advancement Corporation - West (CETAC)
Research Park, Univ. of Calgary, 3608 - 33rd St. NW, Calgary AB T2L 2A6
Tel: 403-777-9595; *Fax:* 403-777-9599
e-mail: cetac@cetacwest.com
URL: www.cetacwest.com
Also Known As: CETAC-West
Overview: A medium-sized national organization founded in 1994
Chief Officer(s):
Joe Lukacs, President/CEO
jlukacs@cetacwest.com
Margaret Kelly, Vice-President, Alberta
mkelly@cetacwest.com
Finances: *Funding Sources:* Provincial & federal government
Staff: 8 staff member(s)
Activities: Specialist advisors provide technical research assistance, regulatory counsel & a range of consulting & referral services; focuses on technologies for natural resource conservation, pollution prevention & control, waste reductions & management, & environmental protection & remediation
Mission: Established by Environment Canada, CETAC-West is a private sector, not-for-profit corporation committed to helping small & medium-sized enterprises that are engaged in the development & commercialization of new environmental technologies. To this end, it has created a network of technology producers, industry experts, & investment sources.

Canadian Farm & Industrial Equipment Institute *See* Association of Equipment Manufacturers - Canada

Canadian Farm Animal Care Trust
#306, 92 Caplan Ave., Barrie ON L4N 0Z7
Tel: 705-436-5776; *Fax:* 705-436-3551
e-mail: canfact@rogers.com
URL: www.canfact.ca
Also Known As: CANFACT

Overview: A small national charitable organization founded in 1989
Finances: *Annual Operating Budget:* $50,000-$100,000
Staff: 15 volunteer(s)
Activities: *Speaker Service:* Yes
Mission: To encourage the development & use of systems that subject farm animals to the minimum amount of stress, distress or injury in the rearing, transportation & slaughter of these animals

Canadian Farm Writers' Federation (CFWF)
PO Box 250, Ormstown QC J0S 1K0
Fax: 450-829-2226
Toll-Free: 877-782-6456
e-mail: hugh@quanglo.ca
URL: www.cfwf.ca
Overview: A small national organization founded in 1955
Chief Officer(s):
John Greig, President
jgreig@bowesnet.com
Myrna Stark Leader, Vice-President
m.starkleader@sasktel.net
Hugh Maynard, Secretary-Treasurer
Membership: 380+; *Member Profile:* Agricultural journalists, such as editors, reporters, & broadcasters; Journalists in business & government who are responsible for agricultural communications
Activities: Providing networking opportunities; Offering professional development
Publications: *The Farm Journalist: Newsletter of the Canadian Farm Writers' Federation*
Type: Newsletter *Frequency:* bi-m. *Editor:* Connie Duivenvoorden
Profile: News for farm journalists, information sources, events, launches, awards, & professional development information
Mission: To serve the interests of agricultural journalists;
Affiliation(s): International Federation of Agricultural Journalist (IFAJ); British Columbia Farm Writers' Association (BCFWA); Alberta Farm Writers' Association (AFWA); Saskatchewan Farm Writers' Association (SFWA); Manitoba Farm Writers' & Broadcasters' Association; Eastern Canada Farm Writers' Association (ECFWA)

Canadian Federation of Agriculture (CFA) / Fédération canadienne de l'agriculture
21 Florence St., Ottawa ON K2P 0W6
Tel: 613-236-3633; *Fax:* 613-236-5749
e-mail: info@cfafca.ca
URL: www.cfa-fca.ca
Overview: A large national organization founded in 1935
Finances: *Annual Operating Budget:* $500,000-$1.5 Million; *Funding Sources:* Membership fees
Staff: 8 staff member(s)
Membership: 23 provincial farm organizations, national/regional commodity organizations; *Member Profile:* Farm organization or farmer co-op; *Committees:* Trade; Safety Nets; Environment; Food Safety
Activities: *Internships:* Yes; *Library:* Yes, open by appointment
Mission: To coordinate the efforts of agricultural producer organizations throughout Canada for the purpose of promoting their common interests through collective action; to promote & advance the social & economic conditions of those engaged in agricultural pursuits; to assist in formulating & promoting national agricultural policies to meet changing national & international conditions; *Member of:* International Federation of Agriculture Producers; *Affiliation(s):* BC Agriculture Council; Keystone Agricultural Producers (Manitoba); Ontario Federation of Agriculture; L'Union des producteurs agricoles (Québec); Coopérative fédérée de Québec; NS Federation of Agriculture; PEI Federation of Agriculture; Agriculture Producers Assoc. of New Brunswick; Newfoundland & Labrador Federation of Agriculture; Dairy Farmers of Canada; Canadian Egg Marketing Agency; Chicken Farmers of Canada; Canadian Turkey Marketing Agency; Canadian Broiler Hatching Egg Marketing Agency; Canadian Sugar Beet Producers' Assoc.; Canadian Pork Council; Wild Rose Agricultural Producers

Canadian Federation of Earth Sciences (CFES) / Fédération canadienne des sciences de la Terre
c/o Managing Director, 210 Main St., Wolfville NS B4P 1C4
Tel: 902-542-6125
e-mail: cfes@magma.ca
URL: www.geoscience.ca
Previous Name: Canadian Geoscience Council
Overview: A medium-sized national organization founded in 1972

Associations/Organizations / Canadian Federation of Engineering Students

Finances: Annual Operating Budget: $100,000-$250,000; *Funding Sources:* Geological Survey of Canada; member societies
Membership: 20,000 individuals + 13 societies + 5 associate organizations
Mission: To promote coordination & cooperation in activities in Canadian geoscientific education; to advise on science policy involving the earth sciences; to provide an informed opinion to the public of Canada on matters of public concern.

Canadian Federation of Engineering Students (CFES) / Fédération canadienne des étudiants et étudiantes en génie
c/o Engineers Canada, #1100, 180 Elgin St., Ottawa ON K2P 2K3
Toll-Free: 866-600-7067
e-mail: info@cfes.ca
URL: www.cfes.ca
Overview: A medium-sized national organization founded in 1969
Chief Officer(s):
Kyle Ruttan, CFES President
kyle.ruttan@cfes.ca
Evan Singer, Vice-President, Finances & Administration
vpfa@cfes.ca
Eamon McDermott, Vice-President, Communications
vpcomm@cfes.ca
Finances: Funding Sources: Sponsorships
Membership: 60,000; *Member Profile:* Engineering students across Canada; *Committees:* Education; Official Languages; Information Technology; Outreach
Activities: Facilitating the exchange of information between members; Recognizing student achievements; Supporting an all-encompassing education for engineering students; Offering complementary education courses
Publications: Project [a publication of the Canadian Federation of Engineering Students]
Type: Magazine *Language:* B *Frequency:* s-a. *Accepts Advertising* : Yes *Editor:* Shaunvir Sidhu *Price:* Distributed to schools for engineering students
Profile: Relevant articles for engineering students across Canada
CFES [Canadian Federation of Engineering Students] eBulletin
Type: Newsletter
Profile: Federation activities, commissioner reports, & upcoming events
Mission: To act as a unified voice for engineering students both nationally & internationally; to assist engineering students in both personal & professional growth; to be aware of & communicate changes in society which affect the engineering profession & engineering students; Affiliation(s): BEST (Board of European Students of Technology)

Canadian Federation of Humane Societies (CFHS) / Fédération des sociétés canadiennes d'assistance aux animaux
#102, 30 Concourse Gate, Ottawa ON K2E 7V7
Tel: 613-224-8072; *Fax:* 613-723-0252
Toll-Free: 888-678-2347
e-mail: info@cfhs.ca
URL: www.cfhs.ca
Overview: A large national charitable organization founded in 1957
Finances: Annual Operating Budget: $250,000-$500,000; *Funding Sources:* Donations
Staff: 5 staff member(s)
Membership: 38 organizations; *Member Profile:* Any society devoted to the prevention of cruelty to or suffering of animals; *Committees:* Farm Animal; Companion Animal; Member Services; Bills & Legislation; Wildlife & Habitat
Activities: Library: Yes, Open to public, open by appointment
Publications: Animal Welfare in Focus
Type: Newsletter *Frequency:* s-a. *Editor:* Tanya O'Callaghan *Price:* Free for CFHS member societies, donors, & the public upon request
Profile: Up-to-date information about the CFHS & member societies, & animal welfare news from Canada & abroad
Canadian Federation of Humane Societies Factsheets
Price: Free
Profile: Information about companion animals, wildlife, & farm animal welfare issues
CFHS [Canadian Federation of Humane Societies] Annual Report
Type: Yearbook *Frequency:* a.
Mission: As the national voice of societies and SPCAs, the CFHS supports its member animal welfare organizations across Canada in promoting respect & humane treatment toward all animals; Affiliation(s): American Humane Association; World Society for the Protection of Animals; Canadian Nature Federation; Delta Society

Canadian Federation of Independent Grocers (CFIG) / Fédération canadienne des épiciers indépendants
#902, 2235 Sheppard Ave. East, Toronto ON M2J 5B5
Tel: 416-492-2311; *Fax:* 416-492-2347
Toll-Free: 800-661-2344
e-mail: info@cfig.ca
URL: www.cfig.ca
Overview: A large national organization founded in 1962
Membership: 4,000+; *Member Profile:* Independent, franchised, & specialty grocery retailers throughout Canada
Activities: Providing educational & training programs; Offering information about the food industry
Awards: Canadian Independent Grocer of the Year Awards (Award)
Contact: Kimberley Kwo, Manager, Member Services *Contact Detail:* kkwo@cfig.ca
Canadian Master Merchandiser Awards (Award)
Contact: Kimberley Kwo, Manager, Member Services *Contact Detail:* kkwo@cfig.ca
National Scholarship Programs (Scholarship)
Contact: Kimberley Kwo, Manager, Member Services *Contact Detail:* kkwo@cfig.ca
Spirit of the Independent Award (Award)
Contact: Kimberley Kwo, Manager, Member Services *Contact Detail:* kkwo@cfig.ca
Meetings/Conferences:
For more information see Trade Shows, Conferences and Seminars Chapter
Grocery Showcase West 2011
Other Conferences in 2011 2011
Grocery Innovations Canada 2011
Other Conferences in 2011 2011
Publications: Independent Grocer Newsmagazine
Type: Magazine *Frequency:* 5 pa *Accepts Advertising* : Yes
Profile: CFIG programs, activities, & member achievements, & industry & government updates, for CFIG members only
The Canadian Retail Food Safety Manual
Type: Manual *Price:* $175 members; $375 non-members
Profile: Retail food safety practices & procedures, produced in collaboration with the Canadian Council of Grocery Distributors
CFIG's [Canadian Federation of Independent Grocers] Crisis Communication & Pandemic Planning Manual
Type: Manual *Price:* $30 members; $300 non-members
Privacy Guide [a publication of the Canadian Federation of Independent Grocers]
Price: Free to CFIG members
Profile: Available to CFIG members
E-news [a publication of the Canadian Federation of Independent Grocers]
Type: Newsletter *Frequency:* w.
Profile: Headlines plus highlights of government policies, available to CFIG members
Emergency Food Recall Registry
Profile: Current food re-calls & government announcements available to CFIG members
Mission: To equip & enable independent, franchised, & specialty grocers for sustainable success; To act as a united voice for independent grocers across Canada

Canadian Federation of Mayors & Municipalities *See* Federation of Canadian Municipalities

Canadian Federation of Woodlot Owners
#304, 259 Brunswick St., Fredericton NB E3B 1G8
Tel: 506-459-2990; *Fax:* 506-459-3515
e-mail: nbfwo@nbnet.nb.ca
Overview: A medium-sized national organization founded in 1989
Chief Officer(s):
Peter de Marsh, President

Canadian Feed Industry Association *See* Animal Nutrition Association of Canada

Canadian Fertilizer Institute (CFI) / Institut canadien des engrais
#802, 350 Sparks St., Ottawa ON K1R 7S8
Tel: 613-230-2600; *Fax:* 613-230-5142
e-mail: fertilizer@cfi.ca
URL: www.cfi.ca

Overview: A medium-sized national organization
Membership: 70 organizations

Canadian Fire Safety Association (CFSA)
#310, 2175 Sheppard Ave. East, Toronto ON M2J 1W8
Tel: 416-492-9417; *Fax:* 416-491-1670
e-mail: cfsa@taylorenterprises.com
URL: www.canadianfiresafety.com
Overview: A medium-sized national organization founded in 1971
Finances: Funding Sources: Membership fees
Staff: 10 volunteer(s)
Membership: 350; *Fees:* $390-$1290 corporate; $80 individual; *Member Profile:* Membership represents a broad cross-section of government, business & education including architects, engineers, fire officials, building officials, fire protection consultants, manufacturers, the insurance industry, teachers & students.
Mission: To promote fire safety through seminars, safety training courses, scholarships & regular meetings.

Canadian Fisheries Association *See* Fisheries Council of Canada

Canadian Fluid Power Association (CFPA) / Association canadienne d'énergie fluide
#310, 2175 Sheppard Ave. East, Toronto ON M2J 1W8
Tel: 416-499-1416; *Fax:* 416-491-1670
e-mail: info@cfpa.ca
URL: www.cfpa.ca
Overview: A medium-sized national organization founded in 1974
Finances: Annual Operating Budget: Less than $50,000; *Funding Sources:* Membership fees; Sponsorships
Staff: 1 staff member(s); 10 volunteer(s)
Membership: 80 corporate; *Fees:* $588.50 large corporation; $401.25 small corporation; $160.50 individual; *Member Profile:* Open to manufacturers, distributors, assemblers, educators, consultants & designers of fluid power components, systems & services; *Committees:* Communications; Membership
Activities: Committees involved in standardization, statistics, education & legislation; CFPA represents the fluid power industry on the Canadian advisory committee with regard to the drafting of international standards; represents the fluid power industry in the formulation of applicable national standards; list of fluid power educational materials & sources is available to all colleges & universities; bursary program will present an award to deserving students; *Speaker Service:* Yes
Mission: To build public awareness of fluid power technology; to provide a forum for the exchange of information & opinion; to represent the Canadian fluid power industry to government, educational institutions & other organizations; to ensure that members' concerns are known to those in government; to ensure that students are able to be properly prepared for careers in the fluid power industry; to ensure that members are kept abreast of the latest developments in the fluid power industry; *Member of:* National Fluid Power Association

Canadian Forestry Association (CFA) / Association forestière canadienne
#200, 1027 Pembroke St., Pembroke ON K8A 3M4
Tel: 613-732-2917; *Fax:* 613-732-3386
Toll-Free: 866-441-4006
e-mail: dlemkay@bell.net (GM);
teachingkits@canadianforestry.com
URL: www.canadianforestry.com
Overview: A large national charitable organization founded in 1900
Activities: Advising the federal government of forest policy; Increasing public awareness about the protection of forests; *Awareness Events:* National Forest Week, September
Publications: Canadian Forestry Association Teaching Kit, Volume 1: Canada's Forests - Learning from the Past, Building for the Future
Type: Kit *Number of Pages:* 32
Profile: A tool for educators to help young people in junior to senior grades understand the importance of protecting & conserving forests
Canadian Forestry Association Teaching Kit, Volume 2: Canada's Forests - A Breath of Fresh Air
Type: Booklet *Number of Pages:* 40
Profile: An exploration of climate change & its effects on Canadian forests
Canadian Forestry Association Teaching Kit, Volume 3: Canada's Forests - All Things Big & Small
Type: Booklet *Number of Pages:* 40

Profile: An examination of biodiversity in Canada's forests for the junior to intermediate grade levels
Canadian Forestry Association Teaching Kit, Volume 4: Canada's Forests - Source of Life
Type: Booklet *Number of Pages:* 48
Profile: Information about forest sustainability for students from grade 4 to 7
Canadian Forestry Association Teaching Kit, Volume 5: Canada's Forest - A Fine Balance
Type: Booklet *Number of Pages:* 44
Profile: Information & activities about the decline of wildlife habitat & species at risk, for students from grade 4 to grade 12
Canadian Forestry Association Teaching Kit, Volume 6: Canada's Forests & Wetlands - Our Natural Water Filters
Type: Booklet *Number of Pages:* 40
Profile: Forest, wetland, & water issues presented for children in grades 5 to 8
Canadian Forestry Association Teaching Kit, Volume 7: The Boreal Forest - A Global Legacy
Type: Booklet *Number of Pages:* 48
Profile: A teaching kit about the boreal forest intended for students from age 5 to 18
Canadian Forestry Association Teaching Kit, Volume 8: Canada's Boreal Forest - Tradition & Transition
Type: Booklet *Number of Pages:* 44
Profile: An exploration of the boreal forest & the interdependence that exists between the forest & Canadians
Canadian Forestry Association Teaching Kit User Guide
Type: Guide
Profile: Activities for the entire class, group activities, activities for partners, games, outdoor activities, research, student presentations, & activities with Aboriginal content
Mission: To advocate for the wise use & protection of Canada's forest, water, & wildlife resources; To nurture economic & environmental health, through the management & conservation of forest resources; To provide a national voice for provincial forestry agencies
Environmental Activity: Promoting sustainable forest development, management, & conservation; Coordinatign the Logging for Wildlife program; Administering tree planting programs

Canadian Forestry Association of BC; British Columbia Forestry Association *See* Fored BC

Canadian Forestry Association of New Brunswick (CFANB) / Association forestière canadienne du Nouveau-Brunswick (AFCNB)
Parent: Canadian Forestry Association
Maritime College of Forest Technology, #248, 1350 Regent St., Fredericton NB E3C 2G6
Tel: 506-452-1339; *Fax:* 506-452-7950
Toll-Free: 866-405-7000
e-mail: info@cfanb.ca
URL: www.cfanb.ca
Also Known As: The Tree House
Overview: A medium-sized provincial charitable organization founded in 1939
Finances: *Annual Operating Budget:* $100,000-$250,000; *Funding Sources:* Membership fees; Government grants; Foundation support
Staff: 3 staff member(s); 20 volunteer(s)
Membership: 75; *Fees:* Schedule available; Individual membership $25; *Member Profile:* Open
Activities: Fall Colours information service; *Awareness Events:* National Forest Week, last week of Sept.; Arbor Day, 3rd Thu. of May
Mission: Champions trees & forests of NB; explains their importance in people's lives; promotes environmental, commercial, recreational & inspirational benefits; underlying principle is stewardship & understanding that an inter-dependency exists among all parts of the environment; encourages conservation & wise use of natural resources

Canadian Foundation for Climate & Atmospheric Sciences (CFCAS) / Fondation canadienne pour les sciences du climat et de l'atmosphère (FCSCA)
#901, 350 Sparks St., Ottawa ON K1R 7S8
Tel: 613-238-2223; *Fax:* 613-238-2227
e-mail: conway@cfcas.org
URL: www.cfcas.org
Overview: A medium-sized national charitable organization founded in 2000
Chief Officer(s):
Dawn Conway, Executive Director

Irenka Farmilo, Officer, Communications
Farmilo@cfcas.org
Tim Aston, Officer, Science
aston@cfcas.org
Finances: *Annual Operating Budget:* Greater than $5 Million
Activities: Responding to national needs or scientific imperatives; Providing grants;
Publications: *CFCAS [Canadian Foundation for Climate & Atmospheric Sciences] News*
Type: Newsletter
Profile: Foundation happenings, research news, & grant information
Mission: To fund university-based research on climate, & atmospheric & related oceanic work in Canada

Canadian Foundry Association (CFA) / Association des fonderies canadiennes
#1500, 1 Nicholas St., Ottawa ON K1N 7B7
Tel: 613-789-4894; *Fax:* 613-789-5957
e-mail: judy@foundryassociation.ca
URL: www.foundryassociation.ca
Overview: A medium-sized national organization founded in 1975
Finances: *Annual Operating Budget:* $100,000-$250,000
Staff: 1 staff member(s)
Membership: 50 organizations; *Fees:* Fees based on sales volume; *Member Profile:* Pour metal castings or supplier to the industry; *Committees:* Education; Environment; Membership; Occupational Health & Safety
Activities: *Rents Mailing List:* Yes
Mission: To assist & represent the membership in dealing with government on industry specific issues; to communicate information to the industry, which will assist its members in strengthening their own competitive position & ensuring a strong Canadian foundry industry; *Member of:* Canadian Society of Association Executives

Canadian Gas Association (CGA) / Association canadienne du gaz
#809, 350 Sparks St., Ottawa ON K1R 7S8
Tel: 613-748-0057; *Fax:* 613-748-9078
e-mail: info@cga.ca
URL: www.cga.ca
Overview: A large national organization founded in 1907
Chief Officer(s):
Timothy M. Egan, President & Chief Executive Officer
tegan@cga.ca
Paula Dunlop, Director, Public Affairs & Strategy
pdunlop@cga.ca
Bryan Gormely, Director, Policy, Economics, & Information
bgormley@cga.ca
Jim Tweedie, Director, Operations, Safety, & Integrity Management
jtweedie@cga.ca
Valerie Prokop, Manager, Finance & Corporate Services
vprokop@cga.ca
Member Profile: Equipment manufacturers; Distribution companies; Transmission companies; Service providers
Activities: Advancing policy positions with federal & provincial decision makers; Developing educational information
Meetings/Conferences:
For more information see Trade Shows, Conferences and Seminars Chapter
Canadian Gas Association 2011 Gas Measurement School
June 2011 Winnipeg, MB
Canadian Gas Association 2011 Biennial Technical Symposium: Industrial Application of Gas Turbines
October 2011 Banff, AB
Canadian Gas Association 2013 Biennial Technical Symposium
Other Conferences in 2013 2013
Publications: *Canadian Natural Gas Magazine*
Type: Magazine *Language:* B *Frequency:* s-a. *Accepts Advertising :* Yes *Editor:* Suzy Richardson
Profile: CGA news, feature articles, & a buyers' guide for the natural gas distribution industry in Canada
Canadian Gas Association Membership Directory
Type: Directory
Profile: Available for current CGA members
Canadian Gas Association Market Updates
Language: B
Profile: Topics include natural gas markets pre-heating season, post-heating season, supply, & demographics
Mission: To act as the voice of the natural gas distribution industry in Canada
Environmental Activity: Promoting natural gas as a clean, safe, & reliable energy choice

Canadian Gas Processors Association *See* Gas Processing Association Canada

Canadian General Standards Board (CGSB) / Office des normes générales du Canada (ONGC)
CGSB, #6B1, Place Du Portage III, Gatineau QC K1A 1G6
Tel: 819-956-0425; *Fax:* 819-956-1634
Toll-Free: 800-665-2472
e-mail: ncr.cqsb-onqc@pwgsc.gc.ca
URL: www.ongc-cgsb.gc.ca
Previous Name: Canadian Government Specifications Board
Overview: A medium-sized national organization founded in 1934
Chief Officer(s):
Terrence Davies, Acting Director
Finances: *Annual Operating Budget:* $3 Million-$5 Million
Staff: 53 staff member(s); 5000 volunteer(s)
Membership: 1,000-4,999
Activities: *Library:* Sales Centre; Open to public
Mission: To develop standards, through accreditation with the Standards Council of Canada; To offer conformity assessment services, including product certification & registration of quality & environmental management systems, conforming to ISO standards; *Member of:* American Society for Quality; Business Forms Management Association; Canadian Safe Boating Council; Standards Engineering Society; Affiliation(s): Standards Council of Canada; National Standards Authority of Ireland; Standards & Industrial Research Institute of Malaysia; Business & Institutional Furniture Manufacturers' Association; American Society for Testing & Materials; Canadian Centre for Occupational Health & Safety; Information Handling Services; Canadian International Development Agency; Canadian Society for Nondestructive Testing, Inc.; Techstreet; Provincial Territorial Committee on Building Standards; Canadian Council of Fire Marshals & Fire Commissioners

Canadian Genetic Diseases Network (CGDN) / Réseau canadien sur les maladies génétiques (RCMG)
#201, 2150 Western Pkwy., Vancouver BC V6T 1Z4
Tel: 604-221-7300; *Fax:* 604-221-0778
e-mail: info@cgdn.ca
URL: www.cgdn.ca
Overview: A medium-sized national organization founded in 1990
Chief Officer(s):
Rob Abbott, CEO
Finances: *Annual Operating Budget:* $3 Million-$5 Million; *Funding Sources:* Federal government; industry; foundations
Staff: 8 staff member(s); 1 volunteer(s)
Membership: 58; *Committees:* Board of Directors; Priority & Planning
Publications: *CGDN [Canadian Genetic Diseases Network] Annual Report*
Type: Yearbook *Frequency:* a.
Mission: A nation-wide consortium of Canada's top investigators & core-technology facilities in human genetics, partnered with colleagues from industry to conduct leading-edge research within an "Institute without Walls"; to achieve international competitiveness in scientific research with social & economic benefits

Canadian GeoExchange Coalition (CGC) / Coalition canadienne de l'énergie géothermique
#405, 1030, rue Cherrier, Montréal QC H2L 1H9
Tel: 514-807-7559; *Fax:* 514-807-8221
URL: www.geo-exchange.ca
Overview: A medium-sized national organization
Committees: Training; Technology
Activities: Providing information, training, & certification; Increasing public awareness; Working with stakeholders to foster the growth of the Canadian geoexchange industry; Liaising with provincial ministries of energy in Canada
Mission: To develop industry standards; To expand the market for geoexchange technology in Canada; *Member of:* Energy Dialogue Group

Canadian Geophysical Union (CGU) / Union géophysique canadienne (UGC)
c/o Dept. of Geology & Geophysics, University of Calgary, ES #278, 2500 University Dr. NW, Calgary AB T2N 1N4
Tel: 403-220-2794; *Fax:* 403-284-0074
e-mail: cgu@ucalgary.ca
URL: www.cgu-ugc.ca
Overview: A medium-sized national organization founded in 1973

Associations/Organizations / Canadian Golf Superintendents Association

Finances: *Annual Operating Budget:* Less than $50,000
Staff: 1 staff member(s); 12 volunteer(s)
Membership: 500; *Fees:* $30 full; $15 associate
Publications: *Elements: The Newsletter of the Canadian Geophysical Union / Le Bulletin de l'union géophysique canadienne*
Type: Newsletter *Frequency:* s-a. *Accepts Advertising* : Yes
Editor: Ed S. Krebes *Price:* Free to CGU members
Profile: CGU information, announcements, events, awards, officers, & section & committee news
Mission: To bring together & promote the geophysical sciences; To provide a focus for geophysicists at Canadian universities, government agencies, & industry in fields of study encompassing the composition & processes of the whole earth, including hydrology, space studies, & geology

Canadian Geoscience Council *See* Canadian Federation of Earth Sciences

Canadian Golf Superintendents Association (CGSA) / Association canadienne des surintendants de golf
#205, 5520 Explorer Dr., Mississauga ON L4W 5L1
Tel: 905-602-8873; *Fax:* 905-602-1958
Toll-Free: 800-387-1056
e-mail: cgsa@golfsupers.com
URL: www.golfsupers.com
Social Media: www.facebook.com/group.php?gid=151227228150
Overview: A medium-sized national organization founded in 1966
Finances: *Funding Sources:* Sponsorships
Membership: 1,600; *Fees:* $421 superintendents & course management; $330 assistant superintendents; $199 golf course maintenance; $179 equipment technicians; $61 students; *Member Profile:* Golf course superintendents & turfgrass specialists in Canada; *Committees:* Environment; Communications, Marketing, & Public Relations; Professional Development & Research; Conference & Events; Member Services; Equipment Technicians Advisory
Activities: Providing continuing professional development opportunities for members; Sponsoring research projects; Establishing the Master Superintendent Designation Program; Offering networking opportunities; *Library:* CGSA Office Library
Meetings/Conferences:
For more information see Trade Shows, Conferences and Seminars Chapter
Canadian International Turfgrass 2012 45th Annual Conference & Trade Show
March 2012
Publications: *GreenMaster*
Type: Magazine *Frequency:* bi-m. *Price:* Free with Canadian Golf Superintendents Association membership
Profile: Informative articles of interest to golf course superintendents
Greenmatter E-News [a publication of the Canadian Golf Superintendents Association]
Type: Newsletter *Frequency:* m.
Profile: Current issues, regional news, & product information
CGSA [Canadian Golf Superintendents Association] Membership Directory
Type: Directory *Frequency:* a. *Price:* Free with Canadian Golf Superintendents Association membership
Profile: Listings of CGSA members, members' clubs, & industry affiliates, for members only
Environmental Management Resource Manual [a publication of the Canadian Golf Superintendents Association]
Type: Manual
Mission: To promote excellence in golf course management & environmental responsibility; To uphold the Canadian Golf Superintendents Association Principles Of Professional Practice & Code of Ethics & Conduct

Canadian Government Specifications Board *See* Canadian General Standards Board

Canadian Ground Water Association (CGWA) / Association canadienne des eaux souterraines
#100-409, 1600 Bedford Hwy., Bedford NS B4A 1E8
Tel: 902-845-1885; *Fax:* 902-845-1886
e-mail: info@cgwa.org
URL: www.cgwa.org
Previous Name: Canadian Water Well Association
Overview: A medium-sized national organization founded in 1976
Chief Officer(s):
Wayne C. MacRae, Executive Officer, 902-845-1885, Fax: 902-845-1886
cgwa@ns.sympatico.ca
John Freisen, President, 204-326-2485, Fax: 204-326-2483
john@friesendrillers.com
Finances: *Funding Sources:* Sponsorships
Activities: Promoting the development of ground water guidelines & strategies; Providing education about ground water for members & the public
Meetings/Conferences:
For more information see Trade Shows, Conferences and Seminars Chapter
Canadian Ground Water Association CanWell 2012: Canada's National Ground Water Symposium
May 2012 Hamilton, ON
Canadian Ground Water Association CanWell 2014: Canada's National Ground Water Symposium
Other Conferences in 2014 2014
Canadian Ground Water Association CanWell 2016: Canada's National Ground Water Symposium
Other Conferences in 2016 2016
Publications: *The Canadian Ground Water Journal*
Type: Journal *Frequency:* q. *Accepts Advertising* : Yes
Profile: Readership includes engineering & consulting companies, geo-thermal companies, certified drillers, certified pump installers, & decision-makers in the drilling & ground water market
Mission: To act as the national voice of the ground water industry in Canada; To encourage the management & protection of ground water
Environmental Activity: Serving as stewards of the Canadian ground water resource

Canadian Hay Association (CHA)
1274 - 3rd Ave. South, Lethbridge AB T1J 0J9
Tel: 403-320-2727; *Fax:* 403-320-2855
e-mail: info@canadianhay.com
URL: www.canadianhay.com/index.shtml
Overview: A small national organization founded in 1987
Chief Officer(s):
Marc Lavoie, President, 780-624-2850
John van Hierden, Vice-President, 403-327-9941
Albert VanGenderen, Secretary Treasurer, 403-380-6667
Finances: *Annual Operating Budget:* $50,000-$100,000;
Funding Sources: Membership service fee & dues
Staff: 1 staff member(s); 8 volunteer(s)
Membership: 154; *Fees:* $150 (voting); $50 (non-voting); $300 (corporate); *Member Profile:* Producers, processor companies, marketers & brokers, & industry suppliers such as equipment manufacturers, seed companies, chemical companies
Mission: To promote the development of Canada's hay industry for the benefit of its members

Canadian Health Economics Research Association *See* Canadian Association for Health Services & Policy Research

Canadian Health Food Association (CHFA) / Association canadienne des aliments de santé
#302, 235 Yorkland Blvd., Toronto ON M2J 4Y8
Tel: 416-497-6939; *Fax:* 905-479-3214
Toll-Free: 800-661-4510
e-mail: info@chfa.ca
URL: www.chfa.ca
Social Media: www.facebook.com/group.php?gid=12940324924
Previous Name: Health Food Dealers Association
Overview: A medium-sized national organization founded in 1964
Chief Officer(s):
Deborah Callbreath, Chair, 416-497-6939 Ext. 501
board@chfa.ca
Natalie Cajic, Specialist, Communications
ncajic@chfa.ca
Membership: 1,000+; *Member Profile:* Suppliers of natural products &/or organics; Retailers of natural health products &/or health foods; Associate members, such as farmers, organic certification providers, health practitioners, gyms, industry consultants, & media
Activities: Supporting & empowering members; Seeking scientific advice from the Expert Scientific Advisory Panel; Engaging in advocacy & outreach activities; Offering education; Providing networking opportunities
Awards: Hall of Fame Award (Award)
Meetings/Conferences:
For more information see Trade Shows, Conferences and Seminars Chapter
Canadian Health Food Association (CHFA) Expo East 2011
October 2011 Toronto, ON
Canadian Health Food Association (CHFA) Expo West 2012
April 2012 Vancouver, BC
Canadian Health Food Association (CHFA) Québec 2012
Other Conferences in 2012 2012
Publications: *The Natural Voice [a publication of the Canadian Health Food Association]*
Type: Newsletter *Frequency:* q. *Price:* Free with membership in the Canadian Health Food Association
Profile: Association & industry news
Canadian Health Food Association e-News
Type: Newsletter *Frequency:* w. *Price:* Free with membership in the Canadian Health Food Association
Profile: Latest developments in the natural health & organic products industry
Canadian Health Food Association Member Bulletins
Type: Newsletter *Frequency:* irregular *Price:* Free with membership in the Canadian Health Food Association
Profile: Recent news in the natural health & organic products industry
Research & Your Health
Type: Newsletter *Frequency:* q. *Number of Pages:* 8 *Price:* Free with membership in the Canadian Health Food Association
Profile: Abstracts about the value of natural health products
Canadian Health Food Association Annual Report
Type: Yearbook *Frequency:* a.
Profile: Activities of the association during the past year.
Membership that Matters! [a publication of the Canadian Health Food Association]
Type: Newsletter *Price:* Free with membership in the Canadian Health Food Association
Profile: Information for members to help their businesses prosper
Mission: To act as the voice of the natural products industry; To promote natural & organic products as an integral part of health & well-being; To ensure the growth of the natural & organic industry

Canadian Health Libraries Association (CHLA) / Association des bibliothèques de la santé du Canada (ABSC)
39 River St., Toronto ON M5A 3P1
Tel: 416-646-1600; *Fax:* 416-646-9460
e-mail: chla-absc.ca; pr@chla-absc.ca (Public Relations)
URL: www.chla-absc.ca
Overview: A large national organization founded in 1976
Fees: $40 students & retired persons; $100 regular members; $200 institutions; *Member Profile:* Health librarian; Institutions; Students
Activities: Facilitating the transfer of knowledge in health sciences; Offering professional development events; Providing grants for members to attend continuing education events; Engaging in advocacy activities; Providing networking opportunities; *Rents Mailing List:* Yes
Meetings/Conferences:
For more information see Trade Shows, Conferences and Seminars Chapter
Canadian Health Libraries Association (CHLA) / Association des bibliothèques de la santé du Canada (ABSC) 2012 36th Annual Conference
Other Conferences in 2012 2012 Hamilton, ON
Canadian Health Libraries Association (CHLA) / Association des bibliothèques de la santé du Canada (ABSC) 2013 37th Annual Conference
Other Conferences in 2013 2013 Saskatoon, SK
Canadian Health Libraries Association (CHLA) / Association des bibliothèques de la santé du Canada (ABSC) 2014 38th Annual Conference
Other Conferences in 2014 2014
Canadian Health Libraries Association (CHLA) / Association des bibliothèques de la santé du Canada (ABSC) 2015 39th Annual Conference
Other Conferences in 2015 2015 Vancouver, BC
Publications: *CHLA [Canadian Health Libraries Association] / ABSC Directory & Membership List*
Type: Directory
Profile: For members only
Journal of the Canadian Health Libraries Association / Journal de l'association des bibliothèques de la santé du Canada
Type: Journal *Language:* B *Frequency:* q. *Accepts Advertising* : Yes *ISSN:* 1708-6892
Profile: Feature articles, book reviews, & news
Standards for Library & Information Services in Canadian Healthcare Facilities

Type: Monograph *ISBN:* 0-9692171-4-5 *Price:* $30 Canadian Health Libraries Association; $35 Non-members
Workload Measurement Systems: A Guide for Libraries
Type: Monograph *ISBN:* 0-9692171-3-7 *Price:* $30 Canadian Health Libraries Association; $40 Non-members
Mission: To lead health librarians towards excellence

Canadian Heavy Oil Association (CHOA)
#400, 500 - 5th Ave. SW, Calgary AB T2P 3L5
Tel: 403-269-1755; *Fax:* 403-453-0179
e-mail: office@choa.ab.ca
URL: www.choa.ab.ca
Overview: A medium-sized national organization
Finances: *Funding Sources:* Membership fees; Sponsorships
Membership: 1,200+; *Fees:* $25 plus GST students; $100 plus GST regular members; *Member Profile:* Individuals employed in heavy oil exploration & production, service & supply, consulting, & government; Students
Activities: Providing continuing education; Offering networking opportunities with industry peers; *Library:* Canadian Heavy Oil Association Library; open by appointmentNot open to the public
Awards: CHOA Scholarships (Scholarship)
Award Amount: $2,000
CHOA Bursary Program (Grant)
To support students with financial needs to pursue programs that mat lead to work in the heavy oil industry Contact: K.C. Yeung, Education Committee Chair *Contact Detail: E-mail:* office@choa.ab.ca
Meetings/Conferences:
For more information see Trade Shows, Conferences and Seminars Chapter
Canadian Heavy Oil Association Technical Event: Drilling & Completions
June 2011 Calgary, AB
Canadian Heavy Oil Association 2011 Fall Conference
November 2011
Publications: *CHOA [Canadian Heavy Oil Association] Handbook*
Type: Handbook *Price:* $60
Profile: Topics include markets & logistics, environment & regulatory best management practices, geology & geophysics, geostatistics, geomechanics, reservoir & wellbore simulation, drilling & completions, field testing, bitumen / heavy oil upgrading, & heavy oil research
Journal of the Canadian Heavy Oil Association
Type: Journal *Accepts Advertising* : Yes *Editor:* Deborah Jaremko
Profile: Feature articles, technology information, news from the association, scholarship winners, volunteer recognition, & sponsor information
Mission: To provide a technical, educational, & social forum for people employed in, or associated with, the oil sands & heavy oil industries

Canadian Hemerocallis Society
16 Douville Ct., Toronto ON M5A 4E7
Tel: 416-362-1682
URL: www.distinctly.on.ca/chs
Also Known As: National Daylily Society of Canada
Overview: A small national organization
Chief Officer(s):
John P. Peat, President
jpeat@distinctly.on.ca
Fees: $25
Mission: To promote, encourage & foster the development & improvement of the genus Hemerocallis

The Canadian Heritage of Québec *Voir* L'Héritage canadien du Québec

Canadian Home Builders' Association (CHBA) / Association canadienne des constructeurs d'habitations
#500, 150 Laurier Ave. West, Ottawa ON K1P 5J4
Tel: 613-230-3060; *Fax:* 613-232-8214
e-mail: chba@chba.ca
URL: www.chba.ca
Previous Name: Housing & Urban Development Association of Canada
Overview: A large national organization founded in 1943
Member Profile: New home builders; renovators; trade contractors; leading manufacturers; suppliers; warranty program providers; government housing agents; service people; professionals
Activities: Promoting the interests of housing consumers; liaising with all levels of government; working to influence decision-makers on issues such as taxation & regulatory reform; developing courses & workshops; distributing industry news;
Awareness Events: Renovation Month, October
Publications: *Canadian Home Builders' Association Builders' Manual*
Type: Book *Number of Pages:* 400 *Price:* $65
Profile: A guide to building energy-efficient housing
Connecting with Customers [a publication of the Canadian Home Builders' Association]
Type: Book *Price:* $15
Profile: Practical information & strategies for new home builders to sell homes, including market research & marketing plans
The Marketing Advantage: A Guide For Professional Home Renovators
Type: Book *Price:* $15
Profile: Advice for home renovators, including information on advertising & presentations
How to Manage Risk: A Canadian Home Builders' Association Guide for New Home Builders & Renovators
Type: Book *Price:* $15
Profile: Featuring topics such as main insurance coverages & financial assurance instruments
The National [a publication of the Canadian Home Builders' Association]
Type: Newspaper *Frequency:* q. *Editor:* Kerry Gibbens
Profile: Current events in the housing industry
Mission: To assist its members in serving the needs & meeting the aspirations of Canadians for housing; to be the voice of the residential construction industry in Canada; to achieve an environment in which members can operate profitably; to promote affordability & choice in housing for all Canadians; to support the professionalism of members

Canadian Home Builders' Association - British Columbia (CHBA BC)
Parent: Canadian Home Builders' Association
c/o Bldg. NW5, British Columbia Institute of Technology Campus, 3700 Willingdon Ave., Burnaby BC V5G 3H2
Tel: 604-432-7112; *Fax:* 604-432-9038
Toll-Free: 800-933-6777
e-mail: info@chbabc.org; sales@bchomesmag.com; circulation@bchomesmag.com
URL: www.chbabc.org
Overview: A medium-sized provincial organization founded in 1967
Committees: Renovation Council; Technical Council; Education & Training
Activities: Liaising with the provincial government on province-wide initiatives; offering courses for Master Builder credential; providing government information & reference materials; offering technical support services; *Library:* CHBA BC Technical & Video Library
Awards: Georgie Awards (Award)
To celebrate excellence in home building
Publications: *BC Homes Magazine*
Type: Magazine *Frequency:* bi-m. *Accepts Advertising* : Yes
Editor: Scott Whitemarsh
Profile: Issue in British Columbia's housing industry
Mission: To act as the voice of British Columbia's residential construction industry; to foster an environment for effectiveness & professionalism in the industry; to maintain affordability & profitability in British Columbia's housing industry
Environmental Activity: Launching the Built Green BC program, an energy efficiency & sustainability program for residential housing

Canadian Horticultural Council (CHC) / Conseil canadien de l'horticulture
9 Corvus Ct., Ottawa ON K2E 7Z4
Tel: 613-226-4880; *Fax:* 613-226-4497
e-mail: webmaster@hortcouncil.ca
URL: www.hortcouncil.ca
Overview: A large national organization founded in 1922
Finances: *Annual Operating Budget:* $500,000-$1.5 Million
Staff: 10 staff member(s)
Membership: 116 organizations; *Fees:* Amount based on national farm cash receipts; *Member Profile:* Organizations promoting development of horticultural industry; horticultural commodity organizations; federal & provincial government agriculture departments; *Committees:* Apple & Fruit; Crop, Plant Protection & Environment; Finance & Marketing; Human Resources; Potato; Research & Technology; Trade & Industry Standards; Vegetable
Activities: *Library:* Yes
Mission: To improve horticultural & allied industries including production, grading, packing, transportation, storage & marketing

Canadian Horticultural Therapy Association
100 Westmount Rd., Guelph ON N1H 5H8
Tel: 519-822-9842
e-mail: admin@chta.ca
URL: www.chta.ca
Overview: A small national organization
Chief Officer(s):
Ann Kent, Chair
chair@chta.ca
Fees: $25 student; $55 individual; $75 corporate; *Member Profile:* Professionals such as occupational therapists, physiotherapists, recreation therapists, social workers, nurses, psychologists, landscape architects & designers, horticulturists, & people who have a passion for gardening
Mission: To promote the use & awareness of horticulture as a therapeutic modality; horticultural therapy is a process which uses plants, horticultural activities, & the natural world to promote awareness & well-being by improving the body, mind, & spirit

Canadian Hydrogen & Fuel Cell Association (CHFCA)
4250 Wesbrook Mall, Vancouver BC V6T 1W5
Tel: 604-822-9178; *Fax:* 604-822-8106
e-mail: info@chfca.ca
URL: www.chfca.ca
Merged from: Canadian Hydrogen Association (CHA) & Hydrogen & Fuel Cells Canada (H2FCC)
Overview: A small national organization founded in 2009
Chief Officer(s):
John W. Tak, President & Chief Executive Officer
Terry Kimmel, Vice-President, 613-230-8484
tkimmel@chfea.ca
Michael Dujardin, Controller, 604-822-0170
mdujardin@chfca.ca
Javis Lui, Manager, Communications & Member Relations, 604-822-9178
jlui@chfca.ca
Sarah Richards, Manager, Conferences & Workshops, 604-822-1736
srichards@chfca.ca
Membership: 70 organizations; *Fees:* Schedule available, based upon number of employees; *Member Profile:* Hydrogen & fuel cell technology & component firms; Fuelling system organizations; Fuel storage services; Engineering firms; Financial services
Activities: Increasing awareness of the economic, environmental, & social benefits of hydrogen & fuel cells; Supporting the development of regulations, codes, & standards; Facilitating demonstration projects, such as Hydrogen Village & the Hydrogen Highway; Supporting the safe & widespread application & commercialization of hydrogen & fuel cell products; Engaging in advocacy activities; Liasing with government stakeholders; Providing information to governments, media & the pubblic; Offering networking opportunities for members;
Publications: *Canadian Capabilities Guide: Canada's Hydrogen & Fuel Cell Industry*
Type: Guide
Profile: Profiles & critical information about companies & organizations in Canada's hydrogen & fuel cell sector
Canadian Hydrogen & Fuel Cell Association Newsletter
Type: Newsletter *Frequency:* q.
Profile: Association member news & successes
Canadian Hydrogen & Fuel Cell Sector Profile
Type: Guide *Language:* B
Profile: Statistics about Canada's hydrogen & fuel cell sector
Canadian Fuel Cell Commercialization Roadmap Update: Progress of Canada's Hydrogen & Fuel Cell Industry
Type: Guide *Language:* B
Profile: ISSN: 978-1-100-10468-360537E
Mission: To act as the collective voice of the hydrogen & fuel cell technologies & products sector; To support Canadian corporations, educational institutions, & governments which develop & deploy hydrogen & fuel cell products & services in Canada

Canadian Hydrographic Association (CHA) / Association canadienne d'hydrographie
867 Lakeshore Rd., Burlington ON L7R 4A6
Tel: 905-336-4491
URL: www.hydrography.ca
Overview: A small national organization founded in 1966
Finances: *Funding Sources:* Membership dues; Conferences & seminars; Sponsorships
Membership: 200+; *Fees:* $40 individual; $150 corporate; $20 student; *Member Profile:* Hydrographers; Workers in associated

Associations/Organizations / Canadian Hydropower Association

disciplines; persons interested in hydrography & marine cartography
Activities: Operating a Student Award Program; *Library:* Gerry Wade Memorial Library; open by appointment
Awards: Canadian Hydrographic Association Award (Award) Awarded to a student at any Canadian university or technological college who must be continuing into second year of a program in one of the following fields of study: hydrography, cartography, geomatics, survey sciences; award based on 70% or better GPA & financial need *Award Amount:* $2,000 scholarship
Publications: *Lighthouse: The Journal of the Canadian Hydrographic Association*
Type: Journal *Frequency:* s-a. *Number of Pages:* 60 *Price:* $20 Canada; $25 international
Profile: Timely scientific, technical, & non-technical articles about hydrography in Canada, news from the industry, & CHA activities & events
Mission: The scientific & technical group has the following objectives: to advance the development of hydrography & associated activities in Canada; to further the knowledge & professional development of members; to enhance & demonstrate the public need for hydrography; & to help the development of hydrographic sciences in developing countries; & to embrace the disciplines of marine cartography, hydrographic surveying, offshore exploration, marine geodesy, & tidal studies.; *Member of:* International Federation of Hydrographic Societies; *Affiliation(s):* Canadian Institute of Geomatics (formal affiliation); The Hydrographic Society (informal affiliation)

Canadian Hydropower Association (CHA) / Association canadienne de l'hydroélectricité
#1300, 340 Albert St., Ottawa ON K1R 7Y9
Tel: 613-751-6655; *Fax:* 613-751-4465
e-mail: info@canhydropower.org
URL: www.canhydropower.org
Overview: A small national organization founded in 1998
Membership: 16 generators; 21 industry; 8 associate; *Member Profile:* Hydroelectric generation; hydroelectric industry; Associated associations and organizations
Mission: To provide leadership for the responsible growth & prosperity of the Canadian hydropower industry

Canadian Industrial Transportation Association (CITA) / Association canadienne de transport industriel (ACTI)
#405, 580 Terry Fox Dr., Ottawa ON K2L 4C2
Tel: 613-599-3283; *Fax:* 613-599-1295
e-mail: info@cita-acti.ca
URL: www.cita-acti.ca
Overview: A medium-sized national organization
Finances: *Annual Operating Budget:* $250,000-$500,000; *Funding Sources:* Membership dues
Staff: 3 staff member(s)
Membership: 400 major shippers
Activities: Advocacy; education; *Speaker Service:* Yes; *Library:* Yes, Not open to the public
Mission: CITA-ACTI actively promotes a competitive and cost effective North American transportation system serving Canada and its NAFTA allies. Their vision is to be recognized as the "National Voice" of industrial transportation in Canada through increased membership and member representation in all regions of the county.

Canadian Injured Workers Alliance (CIWA) / L'Alliance canadienne des victimes d'accidents et de maladies du travail (ACVAMT)
PO Box 10098, 1201 Jasper Dr., Thunder Bay ON P7B 6T6
Tel: 807-345-3429; *Fax:* 807-344-8683
Toll-Free: 877-787-7010
e-mail: ciwa@vianet.ca
URL: www.ciwa.ca
Overview: A medium-sized national organization founded in 1990
Chief Officer(s):
Phil Brake, National Coordinator
Finances: *Annual Operating Budget:* $100,000-$250,000
Staff: 3 staff member(s); 20 volunteer(s)
Membership: 8; *Member Profile:* Provincial injured workers organizations
Activities: Offering conferences & workshops; Providing leadership training; Conducting a survey on the re-employment of injured workers; Engaging in research; *Speaker Service:* Yes; *Library:* Resource Centre; Not open to the public

Publications: *Highlights [a publication of the Canadian Injured Workers Alliance]*
Type: Newsletter *Frequency:* q. *Price:* $5 injured worker & unemployed; $10 individual; $15 organization
Profile: Information about provincial & national developments, government policies, & CIWA projects for injured workers' groups
Mission: To support & strengthen the work of local & provincial groups by providing a forum for exchanging information & experiences; To provide training & educational resources in partnership with these groups to ensure that injured workers maintain control over their destinies & that the groups themselves be democratically controlled by the workers

Canadian Innovation Centre (CIC)
c/o Waterloo Research & Technology Park, #15, 295 Hagey Blvd., Waterloo ON N2L 6R5
Tel: 519-885-5870; *Fax:* 519-513-2421
Toll-Free: 800-265-4559
e-mail: info@innovationcentre.ca
URL: www.innovationcentre.ca
Overview: A medium-sized national organization founded in 1981
Chief Officer(s):
Ted Cross, Chair & CEO
Activities: *Library:* Yes, open by appointment
Awards: Market Research Services (Grant)
Assists individuals & established companies in commercializing their technologies & business ventures; will conduct preliminary & detailed market research, evaluate commercial potential, manage development & testing, assist in venture planning, provide training & education programs, & promote international technologies available for license *Eligibility:* Individual entrepreneurs, inventors/innovators & small businesses
The Inventor's Assistance Program (Grant)
Provides an objective evaluation of a new idea which considers technical feasibility, available legal protection & market competition *Eligibility:* Individual entrepreneurs, inventors/innovators or small businesses
Mission: To advance innovation by helping our clients make better business decisions through information, education & commercialization.

The Canadian Institute (CI) / L'Institut canadien
1329 Bay St., Toronto ON M5R 2C4
Tel: 416-927-7936; *Fax:* 416-927-1563
Toll-Free: 877-927-7936
e-mail: customerservice@canadianinstitute.com
URL: www.canadianinstitute.com
Overview: A small national organization
Finances: *Funding Sources:* Sponsorships; Conference fees
Activities: Organizing conferences, executive briefings, & summits for senior delegates; Publishing materials for conferences
Mission: To monitor trends in public policy, the law, & major industry sectors; To provide business intelligence for Canadian decision-makers; *Affiliation(s):* American Conference Institute (New York); C5 (London, UK)

Canadian Institute for Energy Training (CIET) / Institut canadien de formation de l'énergie
PO Box 21007, 150 First St., Orangeville ON L9W 4S7
Tel: 519-856-0051; *Fax:* 519-856-0061
Toll-Free: 800-461-7618
e-mail: dtripp@cietcanada.com
URL: www.cietcanada.com
Overview: A medium-sized national organization founded in 1994
Chief Officer(s):
Douglas Tripp, P.Eng., President
Finances: *Annual Operating Budget:* $250,000-$500,000; *Funding Sources:* Fees for service
Staff: 1 staff member(s)
Activities: Energy & water efficiency training programs & workshops offered on a public subscription basis or by contract as customized solutions
Mission: A private, international training organization (division of Sustainable Development Consulting Associates Inc.), recognized as an educational institution by Human Resources Development Canada; To focus on the advancement of energy efficiency in industrial, commercial, & public sector organizations; To provide effective training solutions for the incorporation of energy management into organizational management priorities; *Member of:* Association of Energy Engineers; *Affiliation(s):* Engineering Institute of Canada; The Energy Institute (UK)

Canadian Institute for Environmental Law & Policy (CIELAP) / Institut canadien du droit et de la politique de l'environnement
#305, 130 Spadina Ave., Toronto ON M5V 2L4
Tel: 416-923-3529; *Fax:* 416-923-5949
e-mail: cielap@cielap.org
URL: www.cielap.org
Previous Name: Canadian Environmental Law Research Foundation
Overview: A medium-sized national charitable organization founded in 1970
Finances: *Annual Operating Budget:* $250,000-$500,000; *Funding Sources:* Foundations; fee for services; sales; governments; donors
Staff: 3 staff member(s); 8 volunteer(s)
Membership: 500; *Fees:* $100 individual; $1,000 association; *Committees:* Communications & Fund Development; Research; Knowledge Cluster
Activities: Analysis of current environmental policy issues; identification of emerging issues facing Canada & the world; research into, & the evaluation of, legal & economic policy options for public & private sector responses; communication of research results to lay & professional audiences; conferences, presentations, publications; *Internships:* Yes; *Speaker Service:* Yes
Mission: To provide leadership in the research & development of environmental law & policy which promotes the public interest & sustainability; *Affiliation(s):* Canadian Environmental Network; Ontario Environmental Network, Great Lakes United

Canadian Institute for Health Information (CIHI) / Institut canadien d'information sur la santé (ICIS)
#600, 495 Richmond Rd., Ottawa ON K2A 4H6
Tel: 613-241-7860; *Fax:* 613-241-8120
e-mail: communications@cihi.ca; help@cihi.ca
URL: www.cihi.ca
Overview: A small national organization founded in 1994
Chief Officer(s):
John Wright, President & Chief Executive Officer, 613-694-6500 JWright@cihi.ca
Louis Barré, Vice-President, Strategy, Planning & Outreach LBarre@cihi.ca
Jean-Marie Berthelot, Vice-President, Programs JBerthelot@cihi.ca
Anne McFarlane, Vice-President, Western Canada & Developmental Initiatives AMcFarlane@cihi.ca
Louise Ogilvie, Vice-President, Corporate Services LOgilvie@cihi.caca
Jeremy Veillard, Vice-President, Research & Analysis JVeillard@cihi.ca
Finances: *Funding Sources:* Federal, provincial, & territorial governments
Activities: Maintaining health databases, measurements, & standards; Developing reports; Raising awareness about services; *Speaker Service:* Yes
Publications: *Canadian Institute for Health Information Annual Report*
Type: Yearbook *Frequency:* a.
CIHI [Canadian Institute for Health Information] Directions ICIS [Institut canadien d'information sur la santé]
Type: Newsletter *ISSN:* 1201-0383
Mission: To collect, analyze, & provide information about the health system in Canada & the health of Canadians; To support persons who use data for health & health-services research

Canadian Institute for NDE
135 Fennell Ave. West, Hamilton ON L8N 3T2
Tel: 905-387-1655; *Fax:* 905-574-6080
Toll-Free: 800-964-9488
e-mail: info@cinde.ca
URL: www.cinde.ca
Also Known As: CINDE
Merged from: Canadian Society for Nondestructive Testing; NDE Institute of Canada
Overview: A medium-sized national organization founded in 1964
Finances: *Annual Operating Budget:* $100,000-$250,000
Staff: 1 staff member(s)
Membership: 50 corporate + 20 associate + 20 student + 20 senior/lifetime + 1,000 individual + 50 subscriptions; *Fees:* $60 individual; $160 sustaining; $475 corporate
Publications: *CINDE [Canadian Institute for NDE] Journal*
Type: Journal *Frequency:* bi-m. *Accepts Advertising:* Yes *Price:* Free with Canadian Institute for NDE membership; $80 Canada; $110 USA; $135 overseas

Profile: Canadian Institute for NDE chapter reports, conferences, members, & board of directors, industry & international news, business directory, & new products supplies & services
Mission: To advance scientific, engineering, technical knowledge in the field of nondestructive testing; to gather & disseminate information relating to nondestructive testing useful to individuals & beneficial to the general public; to promote nondestructive testing through courses of instruction, lectures, meetings, publications, conferences, etc.; *Member of:* NDE Institute of Canada

Canadian Institute for Photonics Innovations (CIPI)
Université Laval, Pavillion d'optique-photonique, #2111, 2375 rue de la Terrasse, Québec QC G1V 0A6
Tel: 418-656-3013; *Fax:* 418-656-2995
e-mail: cipi@cipi.ulaval.ca
URL: www.cipi.ulaval.ca
Overview: A medium-sized national organization
Chief Officer(s):
Robert Corriveau, President
robert.corriveau@cipi.ulaval.ca
Mission: Photonics - science of generating, manipulating, transmitting & detecting light; *Member of:* Networks of Centres of Excellence

Canadian Institute for Radiation Safety *See* Radiation Safety Institute of Canada

Canadian Institute of Biotechnology; Industrial Biotechnology Association of Canada *See* BIOTECanada

Canadian Institute of Chartered Accountants (CICA) / Institut canadien des comptables agréés
277 Wellington St. West, Toronto ON M5V 3H2
Tel: 416-977-3222; *Fax:* 416-977-8585
URL: www.cica.ca
Also Known As: Chartered Accountants of Canada
Overview: A large national licensing organization founded in 1902
Activities: Providing continuing education opportunities
Awards: National Post Annual Reports Awards (Award) Sponsored by The National Post; In 1993 awards for environmental reporting were added to these annual awards & cover environmental reports in: mining; oil & gas; paper & forest products, & industrial products Contact: Mi Mi Tsui, Awards Manager
Meetings/Conferences:
For more information see Trade Shows, Conferences and Seminars Chapter
Canadian Institute of Chartered Accountants 2011 Income Tax Brief: The Changing Tax Landscape Faced By High Net Worth Individuals
June 2011 Toronto, ON
Canadian Institute of Chartered Accountants 2011 In-depth GST/HST Course
June 2011 Niagara-on-the-Lake, ON
Canadian Institute of Chartered Accountants 2011 In-depth Course on GHG Emissions - Risk, Reporting, & Assurance
June 2011 Calgary, AB
Canadian Institute of Chartered Accountants 2011 Workshop: IFRS Implementation for the Mining Industry
June 2011 Vancouver, BC
Canadian Institute of Chartered Accountants 2011 Financial Services Course
June 2011 Toronto, ON
Canadian Institute of Chartered Accountants 2011 Practice Management Workshop for SME Advisors
July 2011 Blue Mountains, ON
Canadian Institute of Chartered Accountants 2011 Workshop: IFRS Implementation for the Mining Industry
July 2011 Toronto, ON
Canadian Institute of Chartered Accountants 2011 Practice Management Workshop for SME Advisors
August 2011 Whistler, BC
Canadian Institute of Chartered Accountants 2011 IFRS Immersion 2 Course
August 2011 Halifax, NS
Canadian Institute of Chartered Accountants 2011 In-depth Tax Course (Part 3)
August 2011 Whistler, BC
Canadian Institute of Chartered Accountants 2011 In-depth Brokers & Investment Dealers Course
September 2011 Toronto, ON
Canadian Institute of Chartered Accountants 2011 IFRS Immersion 1 Course
September 2011 Toronto, ON
Canadian Institute of Chartered Accountants 2011 Commodity Tax Symposium
September 2011 Ottawa, ON
Canadian Institute of Chartered Accountants 2011 Annual Financial Reporting & Accounting Conference (IFRS & ASPE)
September 2011 Toronto, ON
Canadian Institute of Chartered Accountants 2011 Conference on Environmental, Social, & Governance Issues
October 2011 Vancouver, BC
Canadian Institute of Chartered Accountants 2011 Public Sector & Not-for-Profit Financial Reporting Conference
October 2011 Ottawa, ON
Canadian Institute of Chartered Accountants 2011 National Conference on Income Taxes
October 2011 Toronto, ON
Canadian Institute of Chartered Accountants 2011 IFRS Immersion 1 Course
October 2011 Calgary, AB
Canadian Institute of Chartered Accountants 2011 Investigative & Forensic Accounting
October 2011 Montréal, QC
Canadian Institute of Chartered Accountants 2011 Advanced Tax Course: Corporate Reorganizations
November 2011 Whistler, BC
Canadian Institute of Chartered Accountants 2011 Advanced Personal Financial Planning Conference & Showcase
November 2011 Toronto, ON
Canadian Institute of Chartered Accountants 2011 Advanced Tax Issues for the Owner-managed Business Tax Course
November 2011 Niagara-on-the-Lake, ON
Canadian Institute of Chartered Accountants 2011 Course: Income Tax Practice
November 2011 Collingwood, ON
Canadian Institute of Chartered Accountants 2011 Conference for Audit Committees
November 2011 Toronto, ON
Canadian Institute of Chartered Accountants 2011 Business & Industry Conference
November 2011 Toronto, ON
Canadian Institute of Chartered Accountants 2011 IFRS Immersion 2 Course
December 2011 Toronto, ON
Publications: CA Magazine *[a publication of the Canadian Institute of Chartered Accountants]*
Type: Magazine *Language:* B *Frequency:* 10 pa *Accepts Advertising :* Yes *Editor:* Christian Bellavance *ISSN:* 0317-6878
Price: $28 members & non-members; $25 students; $4.75 single issue
Profile: An information resource for Canadian chartered accountants & financial executives
AASB Update *[a publication of the Canadian Institute of Chartered Accountants]*
Type: Newsletter *Frequency:* irreg.
Profile: Activities of the CICA Auditing & Assurance Standards Board
CA Practice Advantage *[a publication of the Canadian Institute of Chartered Accountants]*
Type: Newsletter *Frequency:* q. *Price:* Free
Profile: For chartered accountants in public practice
CareerVision *[a publication of the Canadian Institute of Chartered Accountants]*
Type: Newsletter *Frequency:* m. *Accepts Advertising :* Yes *Editor:* Janice Turner *Price:* Free
Profile: Career & recruitment-related articles, research, trends, & job postings for chartered accountants & those who hire chartered accountants
Directors Source News *[a publication of the Canadian Institute of Chartered Accountants]*
Type: Newsletter *Frequency:* bi-m. *Editor:* Janice Turner *Price:* Free
Profile: Timely information about best practices in governance, legal issues, regulatory changes & professional development opportunities
FYI *[a publication of the Canadian Institute of Chartered Accountants]*
Type: Newsletter *Frequency:* bi-m. *Editor:* Harry Klompas, CA
Profile: Highlights of the Canadian Accounting Standards Board & staff
PSAB Bulletin *[a publication of the Public Sector Accounting Board]*
Type: Newsletter *Frequency:* irreg.
Profile: Information about decision-making & accountability, published by the Public Sector Accounting Board
Practice Advice *[a publication of the Canadian Institute of Chartered Accountants]*
Type: Newsletter
Profile: Review & compilation services for chartered accountants
PrimePlus *[a publication of the Canadian Institute of Chartered Accountants]*
Type: Newsletter *Frequency:* irreg.
Profile: Resources, strategies, & solutions
Report on Industry (ROI) *[a publication of the Canadian Institute of Chartered Accountants]*
Type: Newsletter *Frequency:* q. *Price:* Free
Profile: Synopses of information, news, trends, best practices, research, standards & regulations, human resources, events, information technology, & recent publications for chartered accountants in industry
Research Monitor *[a publication of the Canadian Institute of Chartered Accountants]*
Type: Newsletter *Frequency:* bi-m. *Price:* Free
Profile: Summaries of, & links to, research reports on the web, of interest to chartered accountants
Risk Alert *[a publication of the Canadian Institute of Chartered Accountants]*
Type: Newsletter *Frequency:* a.
Profile: For chartered accountants who perform audits & reviews
The Investigative & Forensic Accounting (CA-IFA) Media Directory
Type: Directory
Profile: Listing of investigative & forensic accountants, with subject areas about which they would be willing to speak
CA Alert / Alerte CA *[a publication of the Canadian Institute of Chartered Accountants]*
Type: Newsletter *Frequency:* irregular
Profile: Updates on matters of importance to the CA profession
CICA *[Canadian Institute of Chartered Accountants]* Standards & Guidance Collection
Profile: Includes the CICA Handbook - Accounting, CICA Handbook - Assurance, CICA Public Sector Accounting Handbook, Management's Discussion & Analysis, Criteria of Control Publications, & Risk Management & Governance Collection
Répertoire Cabinets CA Firm Directory *[a publication of the Canadian Institute of Chartered Accountants]*
Type: Directory
CICA *[Canadian Institute of Chartered Accountants]* Annual Report
Type: Yearbook *Frequency:* a.
Profile: A summary of the year's activities
Mission: To foster public confidence in the chartered accountant profession; To assist members to excel
Environmental Activity: Offering conferences on environmental, social, & governance issues, featuring environmental business risks, opportunities, & strategies; Recognizing the business, accounting, & financial reporting implications of climate change

Canadian Institute of Energy (CIE)
987 Devon Rd., North Vancouver BC V7R 1V8
Tel: 604-904-5777; *Fax:* 604-987-3073
e-mail: info@cienergy.org
URL: www.cienergy.org
Overview: A medium-sized national organization founded in 1979
Finances: *Annual Operating Budget:* Less than $50,000; *Funding Sources:* Membership fees
Staff: 6 volunteer(s)
Membership: 500; *Fees:* $60; *Member Profile:* Professionally involved in all aspects of energy, whether in exploring for sources, conducting energy research, converting or using energy, or in energy planning
Activities: *Speaker Service:* Yes; *Rents Mailing List:* Yes
Awards: Energy Scholarship Award (Award)
Energy Research & Development Award (Award)
Applied Energy Innovation Award (Award)
Mission: To provide a Canadian perspective on energy technology, business & policy, nationally & internationally, for those affected professionally or personally by energy issues; to encourage energy research, education & dissemination of topical information; to provide an unbiased forum for discussion & debate

Canadian Institute of Food & Nutrition; Canadian Food Information Council *See* Canadian Council of Food & Nutrition

Associations/Organizations / Canadian Institute of Food Science & Technology

Canadian Institute of Food Science & Technology (CIFST) / Institut canadien de science et technologie alimentaires (ICSTA)
#1311, 3-1750 The Queensway, Toronto ON M9C 5H5
Tel: 905-271-8338; *Fax:* 905-271-8344
e-mail: cifst@cifst.ca
URL: www.cifst.ca
Overview: A medium-sized national organization founded in 1951
Finances: *Funding Sources:* Sponsorships
Membership: 1,200+; *Member Profile:* Food industry professionals from across Canada, such as scientists & technologists in industry, academia, & government; *Committees:* Awards; Executive; National Symposium; Conference; International Liaison; Membership; Nominations; Fellow Selection
Activities: Exchanging scientific, educational, & business information; Engaging in advocacy activities; Liaising with related national & international organizations, such as Agriculture & Agri-Food Canada (AAFC) & the International Union of Food Science & Technology (IUFoST); Promoting professional development; Establishing Subject Interest Divisions, such as food process engineering, functional foods, government & regulatory affairs, microbiology, nutrition, packaging, & sensory evaluation
Mission: To advance food science & technology; To act as a voice for scientific issues related to the Canadian food industry; *Affiliation(s):* British Columbia Food Technolgists
Environmental Activity: Promoting the quality & safety of the food supply by applying science & technology

Canadian Institute of Forestry / Institut forestier du Canada
c/o The Canadian Ecology Centre, PO Box 430, 6905 Hwy. 17 West, Mattawa ON P0H 1V0
Tel: 705-744-1715; *Fax:* 705-744-1716
e-mail: admin@cif-ifc.org; questions@cif-ifc.org
URL: www.cif-ifc.org
Previous Name: Canadian Society of Forest Engineers
Overview: A large national organization founded in 1908
Finances: *Funding Sources:* Membership dues; Sponsorships
Membership: 2,200; *Fees:* $39.55 students; $67.80 retired members; $50 sustaining individuals; $111.87 active members & spousal; $192.10 current active members; *Member Profile:* Foresters; Forest technicians & technologists; Educators; Scientists, such as biologists & ecologists; Students; Others with a professional interest in forestry; *Committees:* National board of Directors; Executive; Awards; Silver Ring Accreditation
Activities: Providing national leadership in forestry; Promoting competence & knowledge of forestry for professionals; Presenting a national electronic lecture series; Providing workshops & seminars; Fostering public awareness & understanding of forestry issues; Presenting rings to graduates of Canadian forest technical & forestry baccalaureate programs; Offering field tours; Establishing demonstration forests; Providing networking opportunities; Liaising with the Canadian Council of Forest Ministers; *Speaker Service:* Yes
Awards: International Forestry Achievement Award (Award)
To recognize outstanding achievement in international forestry
James M. Kitz Award (Award)
To honour contributions of forest practitioners who are new to the profession
Canadian Forest Management Group Achievement Award (Award)
To honour outstanding achievement by teams & groups of natural resource managers, researchers, & NGO groups in the field of forest resource related activities in Canada
Canadian Forestry Achievement Award (Award)
To recognize outstanding achievement in forestry in Canada
Canadian Forestry Scientific Achievement Award (Award)
To honour unique achievement in forestry research in Canada
Presidential Award (Award)
Presented to individuals who have made significant or consistent contributions to the practice & profession of forestry
Section of the Year Award (Award)
Awarded to sections that exemplify the objects of the Canadian Institute of Forestry
Tree of Life Award (Award)
To honour persons who have made superior contributions to forest renewal, sustainable forest resource management, or sustained yield integrated management of the forest & its intrinsic resources
Gold Medal (Award)
For graduating students, selected by the head of each school, from each forestry baccalaureate school & each forestry diploma school in Canada
Honourary Members (Award)
For a non-member who has made outstanding contributions to the advancement of forestry
J. Michael Waldram Memorial Model Forest Fellowship (Scholarship)
For a Canadian Aboriginal youth enrolled in at least their second year in either a degree or diploma program in natural resource management at a Canadian university or college
Fellows of the Institute (Award)
To recognize a member or ex-member who has made outstanding contributions to the advancement of forestry or to the Candian Institute of Forestry
Meetings/Conferences:
For more information see Trade Shows, Conferences and Seminars Chapter
Canadian Institute of Forestry / Institut forestier du Canada 2011 103rd Annual General Meeting & Conference
September 2011 Huntsville, ON
Canadian Institute of Forestry / Institut forestier du Canada 2012 104th Annual General Meeting & Conference
Other Conferences in 2012 2012
Publications: *Canadian Institute of Forestry E-news*
Type: Newsletter *Frequency:* bi-m.
Profile: Information about the Institute, such as conferences, section updates, & member resources
Canadian Institute of Forestry Annual Report
Type: Yearbook *Frequency:* a.
The Forestry Chronicle: The Official Journal of the Canadian Institute of Forestry
Type: Journal *Frequency:* bi-m. *Accepts Advertising:* Yes *Editor:* Brian Haddon *Price:* $100 personal electronic & print; $300 multi-users electronic & print
Profile: Practical & applied science & information for forest management planning & operations
Mission: To act as the national voice of forest practitioners; *Member of:* International Union of Societies of Foresters
Environmental Activity: Advancing the stewardship of Canada's forest resources; Examining topics such as biodiversity & species at risk & climate change adaptation; Presenting the Tree of Life Award for contributions to forest renewal & sustainable forest management

Canadian Institute of Geomatics (CIG) / Association canadienne des sciences géomatiques
#100D, 900 Dynes Rd., Ottawa ON K2C 3L6
Tel: 613-224-9851; *Fax:* 613-224-9577
e-mail: admincig@magma.ca
URL: www.cig-acsg.ca
Overview: A medium-sized national organization founded in 1882
Chief Officer(s):
Jean Thie, Executive Director
exdircig@magma.ca
Lucie Lebrun-Ginn, Office Administrator
admincig@magma.ca
Finances: *Annual Operating Budget:* $100,000-$250,000; *Funding Sources:* Membership fees; events; contributions
Staff: 3 staff member(s); 30 volunteer(s)
Membership: 1,500; *Fees:* $95 member; $500 sustaining; $40 student; *Committees:* Cartography; Education; Engineering & Mining; Geodesy; Geospatial Data Infrastructures; Hydrography; GPS; Land Surveying; Land Information Management; Photogrammetry; Remote Sensing; Urban Regional Information; Annual Conferences
Activities: Geographical information systems (GIS); global positioning systems & remote sensing as tools & techniques in environmental monitoring & planning (ie. sustainable development); *Library:* Yes, open by appointment
Awards: Intermap Award (Award)
Jim Jones Award (Award)
John Carroll Geodesy Award (Award)
Triathlon Award (Award)
CIG Student Membership Award (Award)
Hans Klinkenberg Memorial Scholarship Fund (Scholarship)
Publications: *Geomatica*
Type: Journal *Frequency:* q. *Accepts Advertising:* Yes *Price:* $275
Profile: Formerly the CISM Journal ACSGC, the surveying & mapping publication features both scientific & practical information, conferences, reviews, industry news, & new products
Mission: Geomatics is commonly defined as a "discipline aimed at managing geographic data by means of the science & technology used to acquire, store, process, display & distribute them"; to advance the development of geomatics sciences in Canada; to enhance & demonstrate the public usefulness of geomatics; to further the professional development of its members; to foster cooperation between & promote unity of purpose among Canadian geomatics organizations; to represent & promote Canadian interests in geomatics internationally; *Affiliation(s):* International Federation of Surveyors; International Society for Photogrammetry & Remote Sensing; International Cartographic Association; Commonwealth Association of Canada Lands Surveyors; Canadian Council of Land Surveyors; Canadian Hydrographic Association

Canadian Institute of International Affairs / Institut canadien des affaires internationales *See* Canadian International Council

Canadian Institute of Mining & Metallurgy *See* Canadian Institute of Mining, Metallurgy & Petroleum

Canadian Institute of Mining, Metallurgy & Petroleum (CIM) / Institut canadien des mines, de la métallurgie et du pétrole
CIM National Office, #1250, 3500, boul de Maisonneuve ouest, Westmount QC H3Z 3C1
Tel: 514-939-2710; *Fax:* 514-939-2714
e-mail: cim@cim.org
URL: www.cim.org
Previous Name: Canadian Institute of Mining & Metallurgy
Overview: A large national organization founded in 1898
Membership: 12,000+; *Member Profile:* Professionals in the Canadian minerals, metals, materials, & energy sectors, from industry, government, & academia; *Committees:* Central Publications; Audit; Bulletin; By-Laws; CIM Valuation of Mineral Properties; Education; Estimation Guidelines; Human Resources; International Advisory Liaison; Membership; President Elect Nominating; Public Affairs; Special Volumes
Activities: Providing technical forums & professional networking opportunities; Offering continuing education; Recognizing excellent programs; *Speaker Service:* Yes; *Library:* Canadian Institute of Mining, Metallurgy & Petroleum Library
Awards: CIM Awards (Award)
The institute administers 27 awards recognizing achievement in mining, metallurgy & petroleum industries
CIM Journalism Awards (Award)
Established 1985; presented to print, radio & television journalists in Canada for balanced & technically accurate news reporting, feature writing, radio & television broadcasting that best enhance public understanding of the minerals industry & its contribution to the economic & social well-being of Canada
Award Amount: $500 first prizes
Medals for Bravery (Award)
Established 1933; medals are awarded in recognition of great valour displayed to save life in mines or plants of Canadian mining companies; an award is made only in a case where a person knowingly risks his/her life in attempting to rescue a fellow worker
The Order of Santa Barbara (Award)
Established 1968; a silver medal is awarded to any woman who has made a significant contribution to the welfare of a mining community in Canada
Meetings/Conferences:
For more information see Trade Shows, Conferences and Seminars Chapter
Canadian Institute of Mining, Metallurgy & Petroleum 2011 Smart Learning Seminar: Health Safety Mining Innovations - People & Practice
September 2011
Canadian Institute of Mining, Metallurgy & Petroleum 2012 Annual Conference & Exhibition (in conjunction with the Canadian Rock Mechanics Symposium)
May 2012 Edmonton, AB
Canadian Institute of Mining, Metallurgy & Petroleum MASSMIN 2012: 6th Intl Conference & Exhibition on Mass Mining: Advancing the State-of-the-Art
June 2012 Sudbury, ON
Canadian Institute of Mining, Metallurgy & Petroleum 2013 Annual Conference & Exhibition
Other Conferences in 2013 2013
Publications: *CIM [Canadian Institute of Mining, Metallurgy & Petroleum] Magazine*
Type: Magazine *Frequency:* 7 pa *Accepts Advertising:* Yes
ISSN: 1718-4177 *Price:* Free for members; $160 non-members in Canada

Profile: Editorials, technical information, industry events, & industry information
CIM [Canadian Institute of Mining, Metallurgy & Petroleum] Directory
Type: Directory *Frequency:* a.
Profile: Listing of individual & corporate CIM members
CIM [Canadian Institute of Mining, Metallurgy & Petroleum] Reporter
Frequency: a.
Profile: Official publication of the annual CIM Conference & Exhibition, for all registered delegates & visitors
Mission: To act as a source of leadership for its members, by offering conferences & courses, liaising with government departments, commissioning special volumes & reports, & publishing technical papers

Canadian Institute of Planners (CIP) / Institut canadien des urbanistes (ICU)
#1112, 141 Laurier Ave. West, Ottawa ON K1P 5J3
Tel: 613-237-7526; *Fax:* 613-237-7045
Toll-Free: 800-207-2138
e-mail: general@cip-icu.ca
URL: www.cip-icu.ca
Overview: A medium-sized national organization founded in 1919
Finances: *Annual Operating Budget:* $250,000-$500,000; *Funding Sources:* Membership fees
Staff: 3 staff member(s)
Membership: 7,000; *Member Profile:* Professional community & regional planners employed in the private sector in the consulting & land development industries & in the public sector at all levels of government.
Activities: *Awareness Events:* World Town Planning Day, Nov. 8; *Internships:* Yes; *Rents Mailing List:* Yes
Mission: To advance professional planning excellence, through the delivery of membership & public services in Canada & abroad; Affiliation(s): Alberta Association, Canadian Institute of Planners; Association of Professional Community Planners of Saskatchewan; Atlantic Planners Institute; Manitoba Professional Planners Institute; Ontario Professional Planners Institute; Ordre des urbanistes du Québec; Planning Institute of British Columbia

Canadian Institute of Plumbing & Heating (CIPH) / Institut canadien de plomberie et de chauffage
#330, 295 The West Mall, Toronto ON M9C 4Z4
Tel: 416-695-0447; *Fax:* 416-695-0450
Toll-Free: 800-639-2474
e-mail: info@ciph.com
URL: ww.ciph.com
Overview: A large national organization founded in 1933
Member Profile: Companies throughout Canada that manufacture, sell, & distribute plumbing, heating, hydronic, PVF, & waterworks products & services; *Committees:* Executive / Finance; Nominating; Membership; Government Affairs; Region Hydronics; Charity Committee for Habitat for Humanity Canada; Manufacturers' Agents; Wholesalers' Division; Manufacturers' Division; Education & Training Council; Plumbing Industry Advisory Council; Canadian Hydronics Council; Industrial Pipe, Valve, & Fittings Council
Activities: Liaising with governments & organizations; Influencing the development of standards & codes; Raising awareness of safety; Providing education; Offering networking opportunities to share best practices
Meetings/Conferences:
For more information see Trade Shows, Conferences and Seminars Chapter
Canadian Institute of Plumbing & Heating 2011 Annual Business Conference
June 2011 Victoria, BC
CIPHEX Roadshow
October 2011
CMX CIPHEX 2012
March 2012 Toronto, ON
Canadian Institute of Plumbing & Heating 2012 Annual General Meeting
June 2012 Montebello, QC
Canadian Institute of Plumbing & Heating 2013 Annual Business Conference
Other Conferences in 2013 2013
Publications: *Canadian Institute of Plumbing & Heating Member Directory*
Type: Directory
Profile: Listing of members by head office, plus further information such as sales offices & contacts

Pipeline
Type: Newsletter *Frequency:* 3-4 pa
Profile: Information about the hydronics, plumbing, & PVF industries, educational products, trade shows, & association activities for Canadian Institute of Plumbing & Heating members, industry stakeholders, & government
Advocacy Link [a publication of the Canadian Institute of Plumbing & Heating]
Type: Newsletter
Profile: A summary of information about the Canadian Institute of Plumbing & Heating. the Industrial Pipes, Valves, & Fittings Council, & the Canadian Hydronics Council, involving code & standards, public safety, & education
CIPH [Canadian Institute of Plumbing & Heating] EconoLink
Profile: Results from surveys
CIPH [Canadian Institute of Plumbing & Heating] Wholesalers Sales Statistics
Frequency: m. *Price:* $325
Profile: A summary of sales survey results in six regions by product groups
Mission: To act as a unified voice for plumbing, heating, hydronic, PVF, & waterworks across Canada
Environmental Activity: Promoting clean technologies

Canadian Institute of Public Health Inspectors (CIPHI) / Institut Canadien des inspecteurs en santé publique (ICISP)
#720, 999 West Broadway Ave., Vancouver BC V5Z 1K5
Tel: 604-739-8180; *Fax:* 604-738-4080
Toll-Free: 888-245-8180
e-mail: questions@ciphi.ca; office@ciphi.ca
URL: www.ciphi.ca
Previous Name: Canadian Institute of Sanitary Inspectors
Overview: A medium-sized national licensing organization founded in 1934
Membership: 1,000-4,999; *Fees:* Schedule available; *Member Profile:* Canadian public health inspectors; Environmental health officers
Activities: Providing professional development opportunities; *Awareness Events:* Environmental Public Health Week (EPHW), January; *Speaker Service:* Yes
Meetings/Conferences:
For more information see Trade Shows, Conferences and Seminars Chapter
Canadian Institute of Public Health Inspectors 77th Annual Educational Conference: Strengthening Collaboration, Strengthening the Profession
June 2011 Halifax, NS
Canadian Institute of Public Health Inspectors 2012 78th Annual Educational Conference
Other Conferences in 2012 2012
Publications: *Environmental Health Review*
Frequency: q. *Editor:* Domenic Losito *Price:* Free for Canadian Institute of Public Health Inspectors members
Canadian Institute of Public Health Inspectors National Newsletter
Type: Newsletter
Mission: To protect the health of all Canadians; To advance the environmental & health sciences; To enhance the field of public health inspection through certification, information, & advocacy; Affiliation(s): National Environmental Health Association (NEHA)
Environmental Activity: Ensuring food protection, drinking water quality, indoor air quality, tobacco reduction, & on-site wastewater disposal, plus other environmental health initiatives

Canadian Institute of Resources Law (CIRL) / Institut canadien du droit des ressources
Murray Fraser Hall, University of Calgary, #3353, 2500 University Dr. NW, Calgary AB T2N 1N4
Tel: 403-220-3200; *Fax:* 403-282-6182
e-mail: cirl@ucalgary.ca
URL: www.cirl.ca
Overview: A small national charitable organization founded in 1979
Finances: *Funding Sources:* Alberta Law Foundation
Activities: Sponsoring conferences & courses on aspects of resources law
Publications: *Canada Energy Law Service*
Profile: Looseleaf guide to the regulatory regimes administered by the National Energy Board & the Alberta Energy & Utilities Board
Resources [a publication of the Canadian Institute of Resources Law]
Type: Newsletter *Frequency:* q. *ISSN:* 0714-5918 *Price:* Free
Profile: Commentary on matters of concern in natural resources law & policy, developments in resources case & statute law, & CIRL new publications, courses, & conferences
CIRL [Canadian Institute of Resources Law] Annual Report
Type: Yearbook *Language:* B *Frequency:* a.
Mission: To conduct legal & policy research for Canadian federal, provincial, & territorial departments, as well as domestic & international organizations; Affiliation(s): International Bar Association, Section on Energy & Resources Law

Canadian Institute of Sanitary Inspectors *See* Canadian Institute of Public Health Inspectors

Canadian Institute of Steel Construction (CISC) / Institut canadien de la construction en acier (ICCA)
#200, 3760 - 14th Ave., Markham ON L3R 3T7
Tel: 905-946-0864; *Fax:* 905-946-8574
e-mail: info@cisc-icca.ca
URL: www.cisc-icca.ca
Overview: A medium-sized national organization founded in 1942
Membership: 448
Activities: *Speaker Service:* Yes; *Library:* Yes, open by appointment
Mission: To promote good design & safety, together with efficient & economical use of steel as a means of expanding the construction markets for structural steel, joists & platework; *Member of:* Standards Council of Canada; Canadian Standards Association; Canadian Welding Bureau; Welding Institute of Canada; Canadian Steel Trade & Employment Congress; Canadian Construction Association; Construction Specifications Canada; Transportation Association of Canada; Affiliation(s): Canadian Steel Construction Council; Steel Structures Education Foundation

Canadian Institute of Surveying *See* Association of Canada Lands Surveyors

Canadian Institute of Traffic & Transportation (CITT) / Institut canadien du trafic et du transport
#400, 10 King St. East, Toronto ON M5C 1C3
Tel: 416-363-5696; *Fax:* 416-363-5698
e-mail: info@citt.ca
URL: www.citt.ca
Social Media:
www.facebook.com/group.php?gid=148552441716
Overview: A medium-sized national organization founded in 1958
Membership: 2,000; *Fees:* $275; *Member Profile:* Members must complete course of study to hold the designation, CITT
Activities: Offers the CITT Diploma Program
Mission: Designation granting body in logistics management.

Canadian Institute of Treated Wood *See* Wood Preservation Canada

Canadian Intergovernmental Conference Secretariat (CICS) / Secrétariat des conférences intergouvernementales canadiennes
PO Box 488, Stn. A, 222 Queen St., 10th Fl., Ottawa ON K1N 8V5
Tel: 613-995-2341; *Fax:* 613-996-6091
e-mail: info@scics.gc.ca
URL: www.scics.gc.ca
Chief Officer(s):
André McArdle, Secretary, 613-995-2344
Mission: CICS was established in 1973 by the First Ministers as an agency of the federal & provincial governments. Governments recognized a need for a mechanism to serve on a continuing basis, conferences of First Ministers & a growing number of intergovernmental meetings. CICS serves federal-provincial First Ministers' meetings, the Annual Premiers' Conference, the Eastern Canadian Premiers' & New England Governors' Conference & the Western Premiers' Conference. The core of the Secretariat's work is providing services to multilateral meetings of Ministers & Deputy Ministers in virtually every sector of government activity. The Secretariat's services are available to federal, provincial & territorial departments that are called upon to organize & chair such meetings. The agency's mandate & sole program are designed to relieve its clients of the numerous & various technical & administrative tasks associated with the planning & conduct of senior level intergovernmental conferences. The CICS maintains through its Information Services section, a document archives for the use of governments & the general public. Containing over 25,000

Associations/Organizations / Canadian International Council

conference-related documents spanning every sector of conference activity, this collection is unique. The information contained in the archives is made available, as appropriate, to government institutions at the federal, provincial & territorial levels while unclassified material is also available to the public on request

Canadian International Council (CIC) / Conseil international du Canada
PO Box 210, 45 Willcocks St., Toronto ON M5S 1C7
Tel: 416-977-9000; Fax: 416-946-7319
Toll-Free: 800-668-2442
e-mail: mailbox@canadianinternationalcouncil.org
URL: www.canadianinternationalcouncil.org
Previous Name: Canadian Institute of International Affairs / Institut canadien des affaires internationales
Overview: A medium-sized international charitable organization founded in 1928
Finances: Funding Sources: Private supporters
Fees: $75 regular members; $35 students; Member Profile: Individuals & organizations interested in international affairs
Activities: Conducting policy research; Offering a fellowship program (fellowship@canadianinternationalcouncil.org); Presenting seminars, discussions, & study groups
Awards: Globalist of the Year Award (Award)
Publications: International Journal
Type: Journal Editor: Rima Berns-McGown
Profile: Scholarly articles on international relations
Behind the Headlines [a publication of the Canadian International Council]
Editor: Robert Johnstone Price: Free for CIC members
Profile: Articles on international issues, with an emphasis on their implications for Canada
International Insights
Profile: Canada's role in international security issues
Foreign Policy for Canada's Tomorrow
Profile: Preliminary papers to outline critical issues which have not yet been peer reviewed
Strategic Datalink [a publication of the Canadian International Council]
Profile: Analytical paper on a timely, policy-relevant international security issue
Mission: To strengthen Canada's role in international affairs; To advance research & dialogue on international affairs

Canadian Iris Society (CIS)
c/o Ed Jowett, 1960 Sideroad 15, RR#2, Tottenham ON L0G 1W0
Tel: 905-936-9941
e-mail: cdn-iris@rogers.com
URL: www.cdn-iris.ca
Overview: A small national organization founded in 1946
Chief Officer(s):
Ed Jowett, President
ed.jowett@hotmail.com
Ann Granatier, Secretary, 519-647-9746
ann@trailsendiris.com
Finances: Funding Sources: Membership dues; iris auctions
Membership: 600; Fees: $15; Member Profile: Amateur gardeners; gardening experts; horticulturists
Activities: June Iris Shows: Royal Botanical Gardens, Hamilton; Iris sales & auctions; Awareness Events: June Iris Shows
Mission: To encourage, improve & extend the cultivation of the Iris & to collaborate with other societies for this purpose, as well as to regulate the nomenclature & colour classification of this flower.

Canadian Labour Congress (CLC) / Congrès du travail du Canada (CTC)
National Headquarters, 2841 Riverside Dr., Ottawa ON K1V 8X7
Tel: 613-521-3400; Fax: 613-521-4655
URL: www.canadianlabour.ca
Social Media: www.facebook.com/clc.ctc
Overview: A large national licensing organization founded in 1956
Chief Officer(s):
Ken Georgetti, President
Barbara Byers, Executive Vice-President
Marie Clarke Walker, Executive Vice-President
Hassan Yussuff, Secretary-Treasurer
Karl Flecker, Director, Anti-Racism & Human Rights, 613-521-3400 Ext. 236
Andrew Jackson, Director, Social & Economic Policy, 613-521-3400 Ext. 262
Daniel Mallett, Director, Political Action, 613-521-3400 Ext. 322
Lucien Royer, Director, International, 613-521-3400 Ext. 270
Colleen Kilty, Manager, Human Resources, 613-521-3400 Ext. 325
Dennis Gruending, Contact, Communications, Media Calls, 613-526-7431
Membership: 3,000,000+; Member Profile: Affiliated workers in various occupations throughout Canada
Activities: Lobbying politicians; Organizing campaigns & rallies; Representing the Canadian labour movement when dealing with the media & business
Meetings/Conferences:
For more information see Trade Shows, Conferences and Seminars Chapter
Canadian Labour Congress 2014 National Convention
May 2014
Mission: To represent the interests of affiliated workers across Canada; To act as an umbrella organization for affiliated regional labour councils, provincial federations, Canadian unions, & international unions

Canadian Land Reclamation Association (CLRA) / Association canadienne de réhabilitation des sites dégradés (ACRSD)
PO Box 61047, RPO Kensington, Calgary AB T2N 4S6
Tel: 403-289-9435; Fax: 403-289-9435
e-mail: clra@telusplanet.net; aquila7@telusplanet.net (Magazine)
URL: www.clra.ca
Overview: A small national organization founded in 1975
Finances: Funding Sources: Membership fees; Sponsorships
Fees: $15 full-time students & retirees; $50 regular members; $200 corporate members; Member Profile: Individuals & corporations interested in or engaged in reclamation activities
Activities: Facilitating the exchange of information & experience; Encouraging education in the field of land reclamation
Awards: William E. Coates Student Awards (Scholarship)
Award Amount: $500
Dr. Edward M. Watkin Award (Award)
To recognize contributions that advance the progress of reclamation or the association
Noranda Land Reclamation Award (Award)
To recognize outstanding achievement in land reclamation in Canada
Meetings/Conferences:
For more information see Trade Shows, Conferences and Seminars Chapter
Centre for Land Reclamation & the Australian Centre for Geomechanics 2011 6th Annual International Conference on Mine Closure
September 2011 Lake Louise, AB
Publications: Reclamation Newsletter
Type: Newsletter Frequency: s-a. Editor: Linda Jones
Profile: Articles & updates on all aspects of reclamation
Canadian Reclamation
Type: Magazine Frequency: s-a. Accepts Advertising : Yes
Editor: Tracy Patterson
Profile: Articles & illustrations
Canadian Land Reclamation Association Annual Meeting Proceedings
Type: Yearbook Frequency: a.
Mission: To rehabilitate disturbed lands & waterways; Member of: International Affiliation of Land Reclamationists

Canadian Law & Society Association (CLSA) / Association canadienne de droit et société (ACDS)
c/o Journals Division, University of Toronto Press, 5201 Dufferin St., Toronto ON M3H 5T8
Tel: 416-667-7810; Fax: 416-667-7881
Toll-Free: 800-221-9985
URL: www.acds-clsa.org
Overview: A small national organization founded in 1985
Member Profile: Scholars from many disciplines, with an interst in the place of law in economic political, cultural, social life
Activities: Awaring prizes for scholarship
Publications: Canadian Journal of Law & Society / La Revue Canadienne Droit et Société (CJLS / RCDS)
Type: Journal Language: B Frequency: s-a. Accepts Advertising : Yes Editor: D. Moore, M. Valverde, & M. Coutu ISSN: 0829-3201 Price: Free with CLSA / ACDS membership; $90 Canada; $110 International
Profile: Original academic research in the field of law & society scholarship
The CLSA / ACDS Bulletin
Type: Newsletter Language: B Frequency: s-a. Editor: Kimberley White Price: Free with CLSA / ACDS membership
Profile: Forum for for CLSA members to share information on developments & issues affecting Canadian law & society research
Mission: To encourage socio-legal inquiry both domestically & internationally; Member of: Canadian Federation for the Humanities & Social Sciences

Canadian Lumbermen's Association (CLA) / Association canadienne de l'industrie du bois (ACIB)
#200, 30 Concourse Gate, Ottawa ON K2E 7V7
Tel: 613-233-6205; Fax: 613-233-1929
e-mail: info@cla-ca.ca
URL: www.canadianlumbermen.com
Overview: A large national organization founded in 1908
Membership: 300 organizations
Publications: CLA [Canadian Lumbermen's Association] News
Type: Newsletter
Profile: CLA directors & personnel, convention information, awards, & activities
The CLA [Canadian Lumbermen's Association] Story - 100 Years of Service
Price: Free for CLA members; $10 non-members
CLA [Canadian Lumbermen's Association] Membership Directory
Type: Directory Language: B Price: Free for CLA members; $10 non-members
Profile: Listing of member firms & their products & services
Lumber Grading 101 Student Manual
Price: $15 members; $20 non-members
Mission: To promote the interests & conserve the rights of those engaged in lumbering operations or in the manufacture, sale or distribution of lumber & other related products

Canadian Lung Association (CLA) / Association pulmonaire du Canada
#300, 1750 Courtwood Cres., Ottawa ON K2C 2B5
Tel: 613-569-6411; Fax: 613-569-8860
Toll-Free: 800-566-5864
e-mail: info@lung.ca
URL: www.lung.ca
Previous Name: The Canadian Association for the Prevention of Consumption & Other Forms of Tuberculosis; The Canadian Tuberculosis & Respiratory Disease Association
Overview: A large national charitable organization founded in 1900
Finances: Funding Sources: Donations; Fundraising; Sponsorships
Activities: Advocating for improvements to care for lung disease patients; Providing lung health information to governments & the public; Funding medical research; Coordinating the Christmas Seal campaign; Awareness Events: Lung Cancer Month, November; COPD Awareness Week, November; National Non-Smoking Week, January
Meetings/Conferences:
For more information see Trade Shows, Conferences and Seminars Chapter
Canadian Respiratory Conference 2012
April 2012 Vancouver, BC
Publications: Canadian Lung Association Annual Report
Type: Yearbook Frequency: a.
Mission: To improve & promote lung health across Canada
Environmental Activity: Informing the public about the health effects of air pollution; Encouraging laws & policies that promote clean air

Canadian Manufacturers & Exporters (CME) / Manufacturiers et Exportateurs Canada
#1500, 1 Nicholas St., Ottawa ON K1N 7B7
Tel: 613-238-8888; Fax: 613-563-9218
e-mail: national@cme-mec.ca
URL: www.cme-mec.ca
Previous Name: Alliance of Manufacturers & Exporters Canada
Merged from: Canadian Manufacturers' Association (1871); Canadian Exporters' Association (1943)
Overview: A large national organization founded in 1996
Finances: Annual Operating Budget: Greater than $5 Million; Funding Sources: Membership fees; publication sales; services
Staff: 75 staff member(s)
Membership: 5,000-14,999; Fees: Schedule available; Member Profile: Manufacturers, exporters, exporting companies, businesses & institutions servicing the manufacturing & exporting sectors; Committees: Environmental Quality; Export Financing; Insurance; Export Issues Roundtable; Export Promotion; Development Aid; Legislation; Market Access & Customs; Science & Technology; Service Exporters; Standards; Taxation & Financial Issues; Transportation

Activities: *Awareness Events:* Canadian Manufacturing Week, 2nd week of Oct.; *Speaker Service:* Yes; *Library:* Yes, Open to public
Publications: *20/20: Canada's Industry Association Magazine*
Type: Magazine *Frequency:* bi-m. *Accepts Advertising* : Yes
Editor: Marie Morden
Profile: Information for Canadian industry to compete in the global economy, on subjects such as global competitiveness, workforce capability, energy, environment & efficiency, financial services, logistics, innovation, & CME strategy
CME [Canadian Manufacturers & Exporters] Newsletter
Type: Newsletter
Mission: Canada's leading business network; to continuously improve the competitiveness of Canadian industry & to expand export business by: aggressive, effective advocacy to government at all levels; delivering timely, relevant information, programs & support of superior quality & value; providing opportunities for education, learning & professional growth; & promoting the development & implementation of advanced technology

Canadian Manufacturers of Chemical Specialties Association *See* Canadian Consumer Specialty Products Association

Canadian Marine Manufacturers Association *See* National Marine Manufacturers Association Canada

Canadian Maritime Industries Association *See* Shipbuilding Association of Canada

Canadian Maritime Law Association / Association canadienne de droit maritime
#4600, 800, place Victoria, Montréal QC H4Z 1H6
Tel: 514-849-4161; *Fax:* 514-849-4167
e-mail: cmla@cmla.org
URL: www.cmla.org
Overview: A medium-sized national organization founded in 1951
Finances: *Funding Sources:* Membership fees
Membership: 318 individual + 20 organizations; *Fees:* $105 individual; $500 organization; *Member Profile:* Individual, association, or corporate body resident in Canada; *Committees:* Executive; Liaison; Limitation of Liability; Marine Insurance; Special Liaison; Tanker Safety
Mission: To represent all Canadian commercial maritime interests for the uniform development of Canadian & international maritime law affecting marine transportation & related aspects; *Member of:* Comité maritime international

Canadian Marketing Association (CMA) / Association canadienne du marketing (ACM)
#607, 1 Concorde Gate, Toronto ON M3C 3N6
Tel: 416-391-2362; *Fax:* 416-441-4062
e-mail: info@the-cma.org
URL: www.the-cma.org
Social Media: facebook.com/group.php?gid=68638569592#!/cdnmarketing
Previous Name: Canadian Direct Marketing Association
Overview: A large national organization founded in 1967
Finances: *Annual Operating Budget:* $1.5 Million-$3 Million; *Funding Sources:* Membership dues; events
Staff: 28 staff member(s); 400 volunteer(s)
Membership: 800 corporate; 1,200 total; *Member Profile:* Membership includes corporations & organizations which encompass Canada's major business sectors & which represent the integration & convergence of all marketing disciplines, channels & technologies; supports 480,000 jobs & generates more than $51 billion in overall annual sales; *Committees:* Special Interest Councils - Branding & Strategic Planning; Customer Relationship Management; Database & Marketing Technology; Integrated Marketing Communications; Not-for-Profit; Contact Centre; Direct Mail; E-Marketing
Activities: Responds to public policy issues; participates in a variety of government-led task forces & working groups on issues such as privacy, electronic commerce, consumer protection, the prevention of telemarketing fraud, & unsolicited bulk e-mail; forms internal task forces to develop self-regulatory policies on standards of business practice, ethics, privacy, & marketing to children & teenagers; enforces Code of Ethics & Standards of Practice & Privacy Code; *Rents Mailing List:* Yes
Awards: CMA Awards (Award)
20 categories; direct response campaigns from all media are considered
Publications: *Canadian Marketing Association Membership Directory & Buyers' Guide*
Type: Directory *Accepts Advertising* : Yes
Profile: Listing of companies & their services
CMA [Canadian Marketing Association] Guide to E-mail Marketing
Type: Guide
Profile: Theory, best practices & practical advice, for marketers
CMA [Canadian Marketing Association] Fundraiser's Handbook
Type: Handbook *Number of Pages:* 35 *Price:* $15 members; $25 non-members
Profile: A guide to measurement & evaluation
Mission: To be the pre-eminent marketing association in Canada representing the integration & convergence of all marketing disciplines, channels & technologies; *Affiliation(s):* European Direct Marketing Association; Direct Marketing Association - USA

Canadian Meat Council (CMC) / Conseil des viandes du Canada
#305, 955 Green Valley Cres., Ottawa ON K2C 3V4
Tel: 613-729-3911; *Fax:* 613-729-4997
e-mail: info@cmc-cvc.com
URL: www.cmc-cvc.com
Previous Name: Meat Packers Council of Canada
Overview: A medium-sized national organization founded in 1919
Finances: *Funding Sources:* Membership dues
Membership: 1-99; *Member Profile:* Federally inspected packers & processors of meat; *Committees:* Beef, Veal and Lamb; Pork; Technical, Processed Meats, Environment; Foodservice; Special Events; Annual Conference; Administrative Committees
Activities: Responding to members' needs; Contributing to the competitiveness of the industry at both domestic & international levels; Providing a forum for members to discuss & consider matters relating to government regulations & activities, competitiveness, & dealings with other national trade associations; Working towards a free and expanding market environment; *Speaker Service:* Yes; *Library:* Council Library
Publications: *Canadian Meat Council Members Bulletin*
Type: Newsletter
Mission: The Council expresses the views of the membership with government, all elements of the food industry, consumer organizations, the research & academic community, & the media. High standards of industry integrity, & a vast range of wholesome, nutritional meat products are fostered by the Council.

Canadian Meat Science Association (CMSA) / Association scientifique canadienne de la viande (ASCB)
Dept. of Agricultural, Food & Nutritional Science, Univ. of Alberta, #4-10, Agriculture / Forestry Centre, Edmonton AB T6G 2P5
Tel: 780-492-3239; *Fax:* 780-492-4265
e-mail: cindy.rowles@ualberta.ca
URL: cmsa-ascv.ca/default.htm
Overview: A medium-sized national organization
Chief Officer(s):
Frances Nattress, President, 403-782-8140
nattressf@agr.gc.ca
Cindy Delaloye, Sec.-Treas., 403-274-0301
cbga@telusplanet.net
Membership: 100-499; *Member Profile:* Members include individuals & corporations with an interest in the science of meat & meat products.; *Committees:* Promotion & Membership; Education; Newsletter; Nominations & Elections; Symposium; Website & Electronic Communications
Activities: Providing forums & networking opportunities for discussion & dissemination of information; Promoting recognition of peoplee engaged in meat science
Awards: Percy Gitelman Memorial Scholarship (Scholarship)
CMC Associate Members Scholarship (Scholarship)
Publications: *Canadian Meat Science Association Membership Directory*
Type: Directory *Frequency:* a.
CMSA [Canadian Meat Science Association] News
Type: Newsletter *Frequency:* q.
Profile: Activities of the meat sector & the association for CMSA members
Mission: CMSA promotes the application of science & technology to the production, processing, packaging, distribution, preparation, evaluation, & utilization of all meat & meat products. Useful, coordinated research, educational techniques, & service activities are developed & promoted.

Canadian Medical & Biological Engineering Society (CMBES) / Société canadienne de génie biomédical inc. (SCGB)
1485 Laperrière Ave., Ottawa ON K1Z 7S8
Tel: 613-728-1759
e-mail: secretariat@cmbes.ca
URL: www.cmbes.ca
Overview: A medium-sized national organization founded in 1965
Chief Officer(s):
Murat Firat, MSc., President
murat.firat@uhn.on.ca
Mike Capuano, Chair, Professional Affairs
capuamik@hhsc.ca
Tim J. Zakutney, MHSc, PEng, CCE, Chair, Awards
tzakutney@ottawaheart.ca
Martin Poulin, M.Eng., P.Eng., Treasurer
martin.poulin@viha.ca
Melanie Chayra, Secretariat, 613-728-1759
secretariat@cmbes.ca
Membership: 100-499; *Fees:* $35 students; $130 full members; $150 student institutional; Schedule for corporate members, based upon number of members per group
Activities: Offering continuing education; Providing networking opportunities; *Awareness Events:* Biomedical / Clinical Engineering Appreciation Week
Meetings/Conferences:
For more information see Trade Shows, Conferences and Seminars Chapter
Canadian Medical & Biological Engineering Society 2011 34th Annual National Conference
June 2011 Toronto, ON
Canadian Medical & Biological Engineering Society 2012 35th Annual National Conference
Other Conferences in 2012 2012 Halifax, NS
Canadian Medical & Biological Engineering Society 2013 36th Annual National Conference
Other Conferences in 2013 2013
Publications: *CMBES [Canadian Medical & Biological Engineering Society Inc.] Newsletter*
Type: Newsletter *Editor:* Dr. Gnahoua Zoabli; Pamela Wilson
ISSN: 1499-4089
Profile: Society activities, conferences, events, awards, chapters, & events
Clinical Engineering Standards of Practice [a publication of the Canadian Medical & Biological Engineering Society]
Type: Guide *Language:* B *Price:* Free with Cdn. Medical & Biological Engineering Society membership; $50 non-members
Profile: Criteria for health care institutions on the management of medical devices, the education & certification requirements for clinical engineers & biomedical engineering technologists & technicians & the promotion of professional development
Canadian Medical & Biological Engineering Society Conference Proceedings & Abstracts
Canadian Medical & Biological Engineering Society Career Booklet
Type: Booklet
Profile: Information for guidance counselors & employment centers
Mission: To advance the theory & practice of medical device technology; To advance individuals who are engaged in interdisciplinary work involving medicine, engineering, & the life sciences; To represent the interests of biomedical & clinical engineering to government agencies; *Affiliation(s):* International Federation for Medical and Biological Engineering (IFMBE)

Canadian Medical Association (CMA) / Association médicale canadienne (AMC)
1867 Alta Vista Dr., Ottawa ON K1G 5W8
Tel: 613-731-8610; *Fax:* 613-236-8864
Toll-Free: 888-855-2555
e-mail: cmamsc@cma.ca; cmatechsupport@cma.ca (technical support)
URL: www.cma.ca
Social Media: www.twitter.com/CMA_Docs
Overview: A large national organization founded in 1867
Membership: Over 50,000; *Member Profile:* Practising physicians; Residents; Retired physicians; Students; *Committees:* Ethics; Political Action; Health Care & Promotion; Health Policy & Economics; Education & Professional Development
Activities: Providing national & provincial advocacy; Offering practice management solutions; Providing courses through the CMA's Physician Management Institute, a leadership

Associations/Organizations / Canadian Meteorological & Oceanographic Society

development program designed for physicians in the Canadian health care system
Awards: Medal of Honour (Award)
Contact: Chair, Committee on Archives & Awards *Contact Detail:* Phone: 1-800-663-7336, ext. 2243, E-mail: Julie.perron@cma.ca
Medal of Service (Award)
Contact: Chair, Committee on Archives & Awards *Contact Detail:* Phone: 1-800-663-7336, ext. 2243, E-mail: Julie.perron@cma.ca
May Cohen Award for Women Mentors (Award)
Contact: Chair, Committee on Archives & Awards *Contact Detail:* Phone: 1-800-663-7336, ext. 2243, E-mail: Julie.perron@cma.ca
Sir Charles Tupper Award for Political Action (Award)
Contact: Chair, Committee on Archives & Awards *Contact Detail:* Phone: 1-800-663-7336, ext. 2243, E-mail: Julie.perron@cma.ca
F.N.G. Starr Award (Award)
Contact: Chair, Committee on Archives & Awards *Contact Detail:* Phone: 1-800-663-7336, ext. 2243, E-mail: Julie.perron@cma.ca
Award for Excellence in Health Promotion (Award)
Contact: Chair, Committee on Archives & Awards *Contact Detail:* Phone: 1-800-663-7336, ext. 2243, E-mail: Julie.perron@cma.ca
Awards for Young Leaders (Award)
Contact: Chair, Committee on Archives & Awards *Contact Detail:* Phone: 1-800-663-7336, ext. 2243, E-mail: Julie.perron@cma.ca
Dr. William Marsden Award in Medical Ethics (Award)
Contact: Chair, Committee on Archives & Awards *Contact Detail:* Phone: 1-800-663-7336, ext. 2243, E-mail: Julie.perron@cma.ca
Physician Misericordia Award (Award)
Contact: Chair, Committee on Archives & Awards *Contact Detail:* Phone: 1-800-663-7336, ext. 2243, E-mail: Julie.perron@cma.ca
Meetings/Conferences:
For more information see Trade Shows, Conferences and Seminars Chapter
Canadian Medical Association Physician Management Institute 2011 Course: Strategic Influence - Advocacy, Alliances, & Accountability
June 2011 Mississauga, ON
Canadian Medical Association 2011 144th Annual Meeting
August 2011 St. John's, NL
Canadian Medical Association Physician Management Institute 2011 Course: Dollars & Sense - Finance & Economics for the Health Care Leader
September 2011 Montebello, QC
Canadian Medical Association Physician Management Institute 2011 Course: Negotiation & Conflict Management - Vital Skills for Success
September 2011 Vancouver, BC
Canadian Medical Association Physician Management Institute 2011 Course: Disruptive Behaviour - Resolving Personalized Conflict
September 2011 Vancouver, BC
Canadian Medical Association Physician Management Institute 2011 Course: Self-Awareness & Effective Leadership
October 2011 Toronto, ON
Canadian Medical Association Physician Management Institute 2011 Course: Engaging Others
October 2011 Toronto, ON
Canadian Conference on Physician Health 2011
October 2011 Toronto, ON
Canadian Medical Association Physician Management Institute 2011 Course: Strategic Planning - From Vision to Action
November 2011 Vancouver, BC
Canadian Medical Association Physician Management Institute 2011 Course: Management Dynamics - Understanding Hospital Performance
November 2011 Vancouver, BC
Canadian Medical Association Physician Management Institute 2011 Course: Leading Change & Innovation
November 2011 Vancouver, BC
Canadian Medical Association 2012 145th Annual Meeting
August 2012 Yellowknife, NT
Canadian Medical Association 2013 146th Annual Meeting
August 2013 Calgary, AB
Canadian Medical Association 2014 147th Annual Meeting
August 2014 Ottawa, ON
Canadian Medical Association 2015 148th Annual Meeting
Other Conferences in 2015 2015
Publications: CMA [Canadian Medical Association] Bulletin
Type: Newsletter *Frequency:* s-m. *Editor:* Patrick Sullivan; Steve Wharry
Profile: A communication from the Canadian Medical Association, with news stories of interest to Canadian physicians, inserted in the Canadian Medical Association Journal
Canadian Medical Association Journal (CMAJ)
Type: Journal *Frequency:* s-m. *Accepts Advertising* : Yes *Editor:* Paul C. Hébert (pubs@cmaj.ca) *ISSN:* 0820-3946 *Price:* $35 / issue Canadian; $40 / issue USA
Profile: Peer-reviewed original research, review articles, practice updates, drug alerts, health news, & commentaries for clinicians, available online & in print
CMA [Canadian Medical Association] Driver's Guide: Determining Medical Fitness to Operate Motor Vehicles
Type: Guide *Price:* Free for Canadian Medical Association members
Profile: Examples of sections include the following: Functional assessment - emerging emphasis; Reporting - when & why; Driving cessation; Aging; Vision; Respiratory diseases; Psychiatric illness; Cardiovascular diseases; Seat belts & air bags; Motorcycles & off-road vehicles; Aviation; Railway; & Appendices
Canadian Journal of Surgery (CJS)
Type: Journal *Frequency:* bi-m. *Accepts Advertising* : Yes *Editor:* E.J. Harvey, MD; G.L. Warnock, MD *ISSN:* 0008-428X *Price:* $35 Canadian students & residents; $175 Canadian individuals; $270 institutions
Profile: Continuing medical education for Canadian surgical specialists
MD Lounge
Type: Magazine *Editor:* Dr. Francine Lemire et al.
Profile: Information & advice to strengthen relations between general practitioners, family physicians, & other specialists, published by the Canadian Medical Association in partnership with The Royal College of Physicians & Surgeons of Canada & the College of Family Physicians of Canada
Future Practice
Type: Magazine *Frequency:* irreg. *Editor:* Pat Rich
Profile: Information for physicians about health information technology in Canada
Canadian Health Magazine
Type: Magazine *Frequency:* q. *Accepts Advertising* : Yes *Editor:* Diana Swift *Price:* $12 / year
Profile: A health & wellness resource for patients in a physician's waiting room
CMA [Canadian Medical Association] Leadership Series: MD Pulse
Type: Magazine *Price:* $8.95 / copy members; $14.95 nonmembers
Profile: Results of the National Physician Survey, prepared by the Canadian Medical Association in collaboration with the College of Family Physicians of Canada & the Royal College of Physicians & Surgeons of Canada
CMA [Canadian Medical Association] Leadership Series: Primary Care Reform
Type: Magazine *Editor:* Dr. Albert Schumacher
Profile: An outline of primary care reform initiatives throughout Canada
CMA [Canadian Medical Association] Leadership Series: Elder Care - Issues & Options
Type: Magazine *Price:* $8.95 / copy members; $14.95 nonmembers
Profile: An examination of the medical, social, & ethical dimensions of care for older patients
CMA [Canadian Medical Association] Leadership Series: Women's Health - Research & Practice Issues for Canadian Physicians
Type: Magazine *Price:* $8.95 / copy members; $14.95 nonmemebers
Profile: Published by the Canadian Medical Association in partnership with the Centre for Research in Women's Health
CMA [Canadian Medical Association] Complete Book of Mother & Baby Care
Type: Book *Number of Pages:* 264 *Editor:* Anne Biringer MD, CCFP,FCFP *ISBN:* 978-1-55363-154-5 *Price:* $24 members
Profile: Care for a mother & her baby, from conception to age three
Canadian Medical Association Complete Home Medical Guide
Type: Book *ISSN:* 1-55363-054-8 *Price:* $51.95 members
Profile: An 1104 page authoritative & user-friendly resource for physicians to recommend to patients
History of the Canadian Medical Association, 1954-94
Type: Book *Number of Pages:* 388 *Author:* John Sutton Bennett, MD *ISBN:* 0-920169-83-X *Price:* $19.95 members
Profile: A comprehensive account of important events that continue to affect medicine in Canada
Honour Due: the Story of Dr. Leonora Howard King
Type: Book *Number of Pages:* 236 *Author:* Margaret I. Negodaeff-Tomsik *ISBN:* 0-920169-33-3 *Price:* $19.95 members
Profile: The story of the first Canadian to work as a physician in China
Lessons Learned: Reflections of Canadian Physician Leaders
Type: Book *Number of Pages:* 123 *Editor:* Chris Carruthers, MD *ISBN:* 978-1-897490-09-9 *Price:* $16.95 members
Canadian Medical Association Conference Updates
Profile: The latest news from major clinical meetings
PMI [Physician Management Institute] Newsletter: Leadership for Physicians
Type: Newsletter
Profile: Information about leadership theories & techniques
Mission: To act as the national voice of physicians in Canada; To serve the Canadian medical community; To promote the highest standards of health & health care; *Member of:* World Medical Association; *Affiliation(s):* Assn. of Cdn. Medical Colleges; Cdn. Anesthesiologists' Soc.; Cdn. Assn. of Medical Biochemists; Cdn. Assn. of Physicians with Disabilities; Cdn. Assn. of Physicians for the Environment; Cdn. Assn. of Radiation Oncologists; Cdn. Fedn. of Medical Students; Cdn. Infectious Disease Soc.; Cdn. Neurological/Neurosurgical/Clinical Neurophysiologists Societies; Cdn. Ophthalmological Soc.; Cdn. Orthopaedic Assn.; Cdn. Paediatric Soc.; Cdn. Psychiatric Assn; Cdn. Rheumatology Assn.; Cdn. Soc. of Addiction Medicine; Cdn. Soc. of Internal Medicine; Cdn. Soc. of Nuclear Medicine; Cdn. Soc. of Otolaryngoly
Environmental Activity: Protecting & promoting health, through the Office for Public Health, by addressing the environmental, physical, & mental health concerns of the population

Canadian Meteorological & Oceanographic Society (CMOS) / Société canadienne de météorologie et d'océanographie (SCMO)
PO Box 3211, Stn. D, Ottawa ON K1P 6H7
Tel: 613-990-0300; Fax: 613-990-1617
e-mail: communications@cmos.ca; accounts@cmos.ca; publications@cmos.ca
URL: www.cmos.ca
Previous Name: Canadian Meteorological Society
Overview: A large national charitable organization founded in 1967
Finances: *Funding Sources:* Membership fees; Donations
Membership: 500-999; *Member Profile:* Meteorologists & oceanographers; Persons interested in meteorology & oceanography; Corporations & institutions; Government organizations; Students; *Committees:* Accreditation; Ad hoc Student Committee; External Relations; Fellows; Finance & Investment; Ad hoc Flight Service Specialist Accreditation Committee; Membership; Private Sector; Prizes & Awards; Scientific; University & Professional Education; Weathercaster Endorsement
Activities: Participating in School Science Fairs; Accrediting consultants in meteorology & oceanography; Providing advice & suggestions to government & its departments on meteorological & oceanographic issues; *Speaker Service:* Yes
Awards: Postgraduate Scholarship (Scholarship)
Undergraduate Scholarship (Scholarship)
Tertia M.C. Hughes Memorial Prize (Award)
The J.P. Tully Medal in Oceanography (Award)
May be awarded each year to a person whose scientific contributions have had a significant impact on Canadian oceanography
The President's Prize (Award)
May be awarded each year to a member or members of the Society for a recent paper or book of special merit in the fields of meteorology or oceanography. *Eligibility:* Paper must have been published in Atmosphere-Ocean, The CMOS bulletin, SCMO or another referred journal
The Prize in Applied Oceanography (Award)
May be awarded each year to a member or members of the Society for an outstanding contribution to the application of oceanography in Canada
The Rube Hornstein Medal in Operational Meteorology (Award)
May be awarded each year to an individual for outstanding operational meteorological service. The work for which the prize is granted may be cumulative over a period of years or may be a single notable achievement
The Dr. Andrew Thomson Prize (Award)
May be awarded each year to a member or members of the Society for an outstanding contribution to the application of meteorology in Canada
Meetings/Conferences:
For more information see Trade Shows, Conferences and Seminars Chapter
Canadian Meteorological & Oceanographic Society Congress 2011 45th Annual Congress: Ocean, Atmosphere & The

Changing Pacific
June 2011 Victoria, BC
Canadian Meteorological & Oceanographic Society Congress 2012 46th Annual Congress
Other Conferences in 2012 2012
Publications: *Atmosphere-Ocean*
Type: Journal *Language:* B *Frequency:* q. *ISSN:* 0705-5900 *Price:* $50 individual; $125 institutions
Profile: Scientific journal with original research, survey articles, & comments on published papers in the fields of atmospheric, oceanographic, & hydrological sciences
CMOS [Canadian Meteorological & Oceanographic Society] Bulletin SCMO [Société canadienne de météorologie et d'océanographie]
Frequency: bi-m. *Accepts Advertising* : Yes *Editor:* Paul-André Bolduc *Price:* Free with CMOS / SCMO membership; $80 non-members & institutions
Profile: Technical articles, conferences, & events related to meteorology, oceanography, climatology, & meteorological & oceanographic history
Canadian Meteorological & Oceanographic Society Annual Review
Frequency: a. *Price:* Free with Canadian Meteorological & Oceanographic Society membership
Profile: Summaries of the Canadian Meteorological & Oceanographic Society yearly activities & the audited financial statement
Canadian Meteorological & Oceanographic Society Annual Congress Program & Abstracts
Type: Yearbook *Frequency:* a. *Price:* Free with CMOS membership; $50 non-members & institutions
Profile: Guide to the Canadian Meteorological & Oceanographic Society Annual Congress sessions & abstracts of papers to be presented
Numerical Methods in Atmospheric & Oceanic Modelling: The André J. Robert Memorial Volume
Number of Pages: 634 *Editor:* C. Lin, R. Laprise, & H. Ritchie *ISBN:* 0-9698414-4-2 *Price:* $39.95
Profile: Refereed papers by scientists on the art & science of numerical modelling, for students & researchers
The Edmonton Tornado & Hailstorm: A Decade of Research
Author: R. Charlton, B. Kachman, L. Wojtiw *Price:* $10
Mission: To advance meteorology & oceanography in Canada

Canadian Meteorological Society *See* Canadian Meteorological & Oceanographic Society

Canadian Micro-Mineral Association
21 Hathway Dr., Toronto ON M1P 4L4
Tel: 416-438-8908
e-mail: bill.lechner@rogers.com
URL: canadianmicrominerals.ca
Overview: A small national organization founded in 1964
Chief Officer(s):
Bill Lechner, President
Membership: 1-99; *Fees:* $15
Activities: Micro Symposium; Micro Workshop
Mission: To promote education & interest in micromineralogy & to encourage fellowship & goodwill among its members; *Member of:* Gem & Mineral Federation of Canada

Canadian Mineral Analysts (CMA) / Analystes des minéraux canadiens
444 Harold Ave. West, Winnipeg MB R2C 2E2
Tel: 204-224-1443
e-mail: jgregorchuk@shaw.ca
URL: www.canadianmineralanalysts.com
Overview: A small national organization founded in 1969
Chief Officer(s):
John Gregorchuk, Managing Secretary, 204-224-1443 jgregorchuk@mts.net
Sean Murry, Treasurer, 604-270-2252 smurry@anachemia.com
Eric Arseneault, Executive Secretary, 506-522-7143 EArseneault@xstrata.com
Fees: $25 students & retired individuals; $40 new & renewing members; $1000 corporate members; *Member Profile:* Analysts employed in the mineral industry; Technical personnel connected with the provision of analyses
Activities: Providing educational opportunities; Assisting in the development of methods for element analysis; Compiling methods manuals for members; Liaising with laboratories of the Canadian mining industry; Supporting the Certified Assayers Foundation of British Columbia

Awards: Canadian Mineral Analysts Scholarships (Scholarship) Awarded for courses in mineral sciences & chemical technology at Canadian colleges
Publications: *Alchemist Digest: The CMA / SMA [Canadian Mineral Analysts / Analystes des minéraux canadiens] Newsletter*
Type: Newsletter *Editor:* Mark Lewis *Price:* Free with CMA / SMA membership
Proceedings of the Canadian Mineral Analysts / Analystes des minéraux canadiens Annual Meeting
Type: Yearbook *Frequency:* a. *Price:* Free with CMA / SMA membership
QC / QA Manual [a publication of the Canadian Mineral Analysts]
Type: Manual *Price:* $30
Mission: To promote communication among analysts in the mining industry & persons engaged in analytical procedures & the development of methods

Canadian Mineral Society (CMS) / Société canadienne de Minéralogie
e-mail: editor@canadianrockhound.ca
URL: www.canadianrockhound.ca/cms/
Overview: A small national organization founded in 1998
Member Profile: Professional & avocational collectors of Canadian & worldwide mineral specimens
Mission: To promote the collection, preservation, & appreciation of Canadian minerals, & minerals in general; to promote & appreciate the aesthetic beauty of mineral specimens; to provide a suitable environment in which to promote the above; to provide collectors a means to find other collectors in Canada & around the world; to promote the sharing or exchange of knowledge with other collectors; & provide a means for collectors to increase their knowledge of minerals, & to advance their skills in mineral collecting

Canadian Mining Industry Research Organization (CAMIRO)
935 Ramsey Lake Rd., Sudbury ON P3E 2C6
Tel: 705-673-6595; *Fax:* 705-671-6606
e-mail: info@camiro.org
URL: www.camiro.org
Overview: A small national organization
Member Profile: Corporations & organizations who wish to further the objects of the association
Activities: Initiating applied research
Mission: To manage collaborative mining research in the divisions of exploration, mining, & metallurgical processing; to contribute to the safety, growth, & competitiveness of the Canadian mineral industry

Canadian Motor Coach Association *See* Canadian Bus Association

The Canadian National Committee for Irrigation & Drainage (CANCID)
c/o Canadian Water Resources Association (CWRA), #900, 280 Albert St., Ottawa ON K1P 5G8
Tel: 613-237-9363; *Fax:* 613-594-5190
URL: www.cwra.org/branches/CANCID/Default.aspx
Previous Name: International Commission on Irrigation & Drainage - Canadian National Committee
Overview: A small international organization
Activities: Disseminating news about technical information & CANCID & ICID activities; Liaising with other ICID committees & related organizations
Mission: To promote research, development, & application of technology among those interested in irrigation, drainage, & flood control; *Affiliation(s):* Canadian Water Resources Association (CWRA); International Commission on Irrigation & Drainage (ICID)

Canadian Nature Federation *See* Nature Canada

The Canadian Network for Environmental Education & Communication (EECOM) / Réseau canadien d'éducation et de communication relatives à l'environnement
c/o 336 Rosedale Ave., Winnipeg MB R3L 1L8
e-mail: nswayze@eecom.org
URL: www.eecom.org
Overview: A small national charitable organization founded in 1993
Chief Officer(s):
Natalie Swayzer, Executive Director, 204-221-2007

Grant Gardner, Chair, 709-737-8155
Rick Wishart, Treasurer, 204-467-3254
Finances: *Funding Sources:* Donations
Fees: $10 associates; $20 students; $40 individuals; $115 not-for-profit organizations; $280 corporations & government; *Member Profile:* Environmental educators, practitioners, researchers, scientists, administrators, & business representatives
Activities: Offering networking opportunities; Providing professional development resources & activities; Liaising with other organizations
Awards: EECom Awards for Excellence in Environmental Education (Award)
Publications: *EECOM News*
Type: Newsletter *Frequency:* bi-m. *Editor:* Sue Wallace *Price:* Free with Canadian Network for Environmental Education & Communication membership
Profile: Conferences, members, regional reports, awards, & announcements
Mission: To advance environmental learning in Canada; to promote environmental literacy & environmental stewardship; to contribute to a sustainable future

Canadian Network for Vaccines & Immunotherapeutics
#790, 5160, boul Décarie, Montréal QC H3X 2H9
Tel: 514-343-6111; *Fax:* 514-343-7854
e-mail: michel.klein@canvac.ca
URL: www.canvac.ca
Also Known As: CANVAC
Overview: A medium-sized national organization
Chief Officer(s):
Michel Klein, Executive Director
Member of: Networks of Centres of Excellence

Canadian Network of Toxicology Centres (CNTC) / Réseau canadien des centres de toxicologie
Bovey Bldg., 2nd Fl., Gordon St., Guelph ON N1G 2W1
Tel: 519-824-4120; *Fax:* 519-837-3861
e-mail: dwarner@uoguelph.ca
URL: www.uoguelph.ca/cntc/
Overview: A medium-sized national organization founded in 1983
Finances: *Annual Operating Budget:* $1.5 Million-$3 Million; *Funding Sources:* Environment Canada; grants from government & industrial companies & associations
Staff: 4 staff member(s)
Activities: 4 themes - Human Health & Environmental Risk Assessment; Metal Speciation at the Biological Interface; Endocrine Disrupters & Reproductive/Endocrines Toxicology; Immunotoxicology; also conducts research on a contract basis for government or industry, develops educational materials on toxicology for secondary school programs across Canada; risk assessments of complex mixtures
Publications: *CNTC [Canadian Network of Toxicology Centres] News*
Type: Newsletter
Profile: Communication among CNTC member scientists & the public to increase education about toxicology
CNTC [Canadian Network of Toxicology Centres] Science Briefs
Type: Newsletter
CNTC [Canadian Network of Toxicology Centres] Annual Report
Type: Yearbook *Language:* B *Frequency:* a.
CNTC [Canadian Network of Toxicology Centres] Annual Symposium Report
Type: Yearbook *Frequency:* a.
Mission: To be recognized & respected for excellence in research, training, analysis & communication of information focused on critical toxicology issues for ecosystem & human health; to achieve this through innovative, multi-disciplinary teamwork & partnerships between the public & private sector; *Affiliation(s):* Metals in the Environment Research Network

Canadian Nuclear Association (CNA) / Association nucléaire canadienne
#1610, 130 Albert St., Ottawa ON K1P 5G4
Tel: 613-237-4262; *Fax:* 613-237-0989
e-mail: lindsayj@cna.ca
URL: www.cna.ca
Overview: A large national organization founded in 1960
Finances: *Annual Operating Budget:* $1.5 Million-$3 Million; *Funding Sources:* Membership fees
Staff: 6 staff member(s)
Membership: 112; *Fees:* Based on company size & activity; *Member Profile:* Industries & enterprises interested in the development & application of nuclear energy for peaceful

Associations/Organizations / Canadian Nuclear Society

purposes including uranium producers, reactor manufacturers, electrical utilities, engineering companies, banks, employee unions, departments of federal & provincial governments, educational establishments; *Committees:* Communications; Regulatory Affairs; Climate Change
Activities: Public advertising; Conferences; Electronic & print publications; *Library:* Yes
Publications: *Nuclear Canada Yearbook*
Type: Yearbook *Frequency:* a.
Profile: Information about the Canadian nuclear industry & a buyers' guide of nuclear products & services
Nuclear Energy Handbook
Profile: Basic & factual information about nuclear energy
Nuclear Canada
Type: Newsletter *Editor:* Colin G. Hunt
Profile: CNA activities & news about nuclear energy in Canada
Mission: To promote the orderly & sound development of nuclear energy for peaceful purposes in Canada & abroad; to promote & foster an environment favourable to the healthy growth of the uses of nuclear energy & radioisotopes; to encourage cooperation between various industries, utilities, educational institutions, government departments & agencies, which may have a common interest in the development of economic nuclear power & the uses of radioisotopes; to provide a forum for the discussion & resolution of problems which are of concern to the members, the industry, or the Canadian public; to stimulate cooperation with other associations with similar objectives & purposes

Canadian Nuclear Society (CNS) / Société nucléaire canadienne (SNC)
655 Bay St., 17th Fl., Toronto ON M5G 2K4
Tel: 416-977-7620; *Fax:* 416-977-8131
e-mail: cns-snc@on.aibn.com
URL: www.cns-snc.ca
Previous Name: The technical society of the Canadian Nuclear Association (CNA)
Overview: A medium-sized national organization founded in 1979
Finances: *Funding Sources:* Sponsorships
Fees: $27.81 students; $48.41 retirees; $82.40 regular members; *Member Profile:* Individuals directly involved with nuclear technology; Students; Persons interested in nuclear topics; *Committees:* Program; CNA Interface; WIN Interface; COG Interface; OCI Interface; Branch Affairs; Education & Communication; Membership; Bulletin; Finance; Past Presidents'; Climate Change, The Nuclear Future, & Communication Advisory; Fusion; Honours & Awards; Universities / UNENE; Inter-society Relations; Young Generation; Representative to PAGSE
Activities: Providing education; Offering opportunities to network with colleagues in Canada & internationally
Awards: W.B. Lewis Medal (Award), Canadian Nuclear Society
Contact: The Chair, Honours & Awards Committee *Contact Detail:* 655 Bay St., 17th Fl. Toronto, ON M5G 2K4
Ian McRae Award of Merit (Award), Canadian Nuclear Society
Contact: The Chair, Honours & Awards Committee *Contact Detail:* 655 Bay St., 17th Fl. Toronto, ON M5G 2K4
Outstanding Contribution Award (Award), Canadian Nuclear Society
Contact: The Chair, Honours & Awards Committee *Contact Detail:* 655 Bay St., 17th Fl. Toronto, ON M5G 2K4
Innovative Achievement Award (Award), Canadian Nuclear Society
Contact: The Chair, Honours & Awards Committee *Contact Detail:* 655 Bay St., 17th Fl. Toronto, ON M5G 2K4
Fellows of the Canadian Nuclear Society (Award), Canadian Nuclear Society
Contact: The Chair, Honours & Awards Committee *Contact Detail:* 655 Bay St., 17th Fl. Toronto, ON M5G 2K4
John S. Hewitt Team Achievement Award (Award), Canadian Nuclear Society
Contact: The Chair, Honours & Awards Committee *Contact Detail:* 655 Bay St., 17th Fl. Toronto, ON M5G 2K4
Education & Communication Award (Award), Canadian Nuclear Society
Contact: The Chair, Honours & Awards Committee *Contact Detail:* 655 Bay St., 17th Fl. Toronto, ON M5G 2K4
R.E. Jervis Award (Award), Canadian Nuclear Society
Contact: The Chair, Honours & Awards Committee *Contact Detail:* 655 Bay St., 17th Fl. Toronto, ON M5G 2K4
CNA International Award (Award), Canadian Nuclear Society
Contact: The Chair, Honours & Awards Committee *Contact Detail:* 655 Bay St., 17th Fl. Toronto, ON M5G 2K4
CNS President's Award (Award), Canadian Nuclear Society
Contact: Chair, Honours & Awards Committee *Contact Detail:* 655 Bay St., 17th Fl. Toronto, ON M5G 2K4
Meetings/Conferences:
For more information see Trade Shows, Conferences and Seminars Chapter
Real-Time Measurement, Instrumentation & Control 2011 2nd International Workshop (Sponsored by the Canadian Nuclear Society)
June 2011 Oshawa, ON
Canadian Nuclear Society 2011 32nd Annual Conference & 35th Annual CNS / CNA Student Conference
June 2011 Niagara Falls, ON
Canadian Nuclear Society 2011 2nd Annual Workshop on Nuclear Education & Outreach: Lighting Our Way to The Future
June 2011 Niagara Falls, ON
Radioecology & Environmental Radioactivity International Conference: Environment & Nuclear Renaissance (Sponsored by the Canadian Nuclear Society)
June 2011 Hamilton, ON
Waste Management, Decommissioning, & Environmental Restoration for Canada's Nuclear Activities: Current Practices & Future Needs
September 2011 Toronto, ON
Nuclear Reactor Thermalhydraulics 14th International Topical Meeting: Helping the Environment with Advances in Thermalhydraulics
September 2011 Toronto, ON
Global 2011: Innovative Nuclear Energy Systems Toward 2030 & Beyond
September 2011
The Future of Heavy Water Reactors 2011 International Conference (HWR - Future)
October 2011 Ottawa, ON
Canadian Nuclear Society 2011 9th International Conference on CANDU Maintenance: Industry Performance - Getting a Grip
December 2011 Toronto, ON
Canadian Nuclear Society 2012 33rd Annual Conference & 36th Annual CNS / CNA Student Conference
June 2012 Saskatoon, SK
Canadian Nuclear Society 2012 3rd Annual Workshop on Nuclear Education & Outreach
Other Conferences in 2012 2012
Canadian Nuclear Society 2013 34th Annual Conference & 37th Annual CNS / CNA Student Conference
Other Conferences in 2013 2013
Canadian Nuclear Society 2014 35th Annual Conference & 38th Annual CNS / CNA Student Conference
Other Conferences in 2014 2014
Publications: *Canadian Nuclear Society Bulletin*
Type: Journal *Frequency:* q. *Editor:* Ric Fluke *Price:* Free with Canadian Nuclear Society membership
Profile: Society news, conference reports, technical papers, articles, & letters
Canadian Nuclear Society Proceedings
Profile: Information from Canadian Nuclear Society conferences or symposia
Mission: To promote the exchange of information about nuclear science & technology & its applications; To foster the beneficial utilization of nuclear science; *Member of:* Engineering Institute of Canada (EIC)
Environmental Activity: Encouraging information exchange on topics such as uranium mining & refining, the management of radioactive wastes, used fuel, & environmental & occupational radiation protection

Canadian Nursery Landscape Association (CNLA)
7856 Fifth Line South, Milton ON L9T 2X8
Tel: 905-875-1399; *Fax:* 905-875-1840
Toll-Free: 888-446-3499
e-mail: info@canadanursery.com
URL: www.canadanursery.com
Previous Name: Canadian Nursery Trades Association; Landscape Canada
Overview: A medium-sized national organization founded in 1968
Finances: *Annual Operating Budget:* $500,000-$1.5 Million; *Funding Sources:* Membership dues; publications; management fees
Staff: 8 staff member(s); 21 volunteer(s)
Membership: 3,210; *Fees:* $115.23; *Member Profile:* Must be a supplier, active or associate member of one of the provincial organizations; *Committees:* Certification; Garden Centres; Growers; Human Resources; Insurance; Landscape
Awards: Award of Excellence for Landscape Construction/Installation (Award)
Award of Excellence for Landscape Maintenance (Award)
Publications: *CNLA [Canadian Nursery Landscape Association] Newsbrief*
Type: Newsletter *Frequency:* bi-m. *Price:* Free with CNLA membership
Profile: National news about the industry & the association
CNLA [Canadian Nursery Landscape Association] Membership Directory
Type: Directory *Frequency:* a. *Price:* Free with CNLA membership
Canadian Standards for Nursery Stock
Price: Free with CNLA membership
Profile: A set of minimum professional standards for for the nursery industry
Mission: To coordinate provincial member groups in the Canadian horticultural industry; to set national standards; to work with government; to develop national priorities; *Affiliation(s):* Flowers Canada; Canadian Ornamental Plant Foundation; Associated Landscape Contractors of America; International Garden Centres Association; North American Plant Protection Organization; American Nursery & Landscape Association; International Ornamental Growers Association; Canadian Plant Protection Advisory Committee; Canadian Horticultural Council

Canadian Nursery Trades Association; Landscape Canada
See Canadian Nursery Landscape Association

Canadian Oil Heat Association (COHA)
#202, 115 Apple Creek Blvd., Markham ON L3R 6C9
Tel: 905-946-0264; *Fax:* 905-946-0316
Toll-Free: 800-257-1593
e-mail: oilheat@coha.ca
URL: www.coha.ca
Overview: A small national organization founded in 1983
Chief Officer(s):
Veronica Yu, President & CEO
Finances: *Annual Operating Budget:* $250,000-$500,000
Staff: 3 staff member(s)
Membership: 400; *Fees:* $300 - $18,000; *Member Profile:* Oil companies; HVAC manufacturers & suppliers; service contractors; *Committees:* Technical Development & Education; Marketing; Membership; Certification & Training
Activities: Promoting the benefits of residential fuel oil to the consumer public
Publications: *Today's Oilheat Newsletter*
Type: Newsletter
COHA [Canadian Oil Heat Association] Directory
Type: Directory
Profile: Listing of equipment wholesalers & manufacturers, fuel oil suppliers, & service contractors
Mission: A voluntary membership organization, COHA serves as the industry's voice to provincial and federal regulators and government decision makers on matters of policy, safety, and certification. COHA works with government and other stakeholders to foster a sustainable business environment for its members.; *Member of:* Canadian Association Executives

Canadian Organic Growers Inc. (COG)
323 Chapel St., Ottawa ON K1N 7Z2
Tel: 613-216-0741; *Fax:* 613-236-0743
Toll-Free: 888-375-7383
e-mail: office@cog.ca
URL: www.cog.ca
Social Media:
www.facebook.com/pages/Canadian-Organic-Growers/277231516329
Overview: A medium-sized national charitable organization founded in 1975
Finances: *Annual Operating Budget:* $250,000-$500,000; *Funding Sources:* Membership dues; Publications sale; Foundations; Governments
Staff: 5 staff member(s); 20 volunteer(s)
Membership: 2,000; *Fees:* $40-250; *Member Profile:* Farmers; Gardeners; Consumers; Environmentalists; Writers; Wholesale marketers
Activities: *Library:* Mail-Lending Library; Not open to the public
Awards: Mary Perlmutter Scholarship (Scholarship)
Awarded annually to a graduate student whose work within a recognized research institution is deemed beneficial to organic growers
Publications: *The Canadian Organic Grower*
Type: Journal *Frequency:* q. *Accepts Advertising* : Yes *Editor:*

Janet Wallace *Price:* Free with COG membership; $35 individual; $40 institution; $50 international
Profile: Information for farmers, gardeners, & consumers
Organic Statistics
Profile: Statistical overview of the Canadian organic sector for Canada & by province
Practical Skills Handbooks
Profile: Resources for organic, transitioning, & conventional farmers on topics such as organic field crops & organic livestock
Mission: To conduct research into alternatives to traditional chemical & energy-intensive food growing practices; To provide a resource base & a forum open to all farmers & food growers interested in alternative agriculture; To foster the goals of a decentralized, bio-regionally-based food system; To endorse practices which promote & maintain long-term soil fertility, reduce fossil fuel uses, reduce pollution, recycle wastes & conserve non-renewable resources; To assist the farmer, grower, food processor & consumer, through education & demonstration, in understanding the value of organic foods; *Member of:* Canadian Environmental Network; *Affiliation(s):* International Federation of Organic Agriculture Movements; Organic Trade Association

Canadian Organic Livestock Association (COLA)
PO Box 396, Kelvington SK S0A 1W0
Tel: 306-327-4753; *Fax:* 306-327-5759
e-mail: jclowndes@sasktel.net
URL: www.colabeef.ca
Overview: A small national organization founded in 1998
Chief Officer(s):
Pat Godhe, President
Darrell Wotherspoon, Vice-President
Carol Lowndes, Secretary-Treasurer
Activities: Promoting the benefits of the organic livestock industry; Developing sustainable agriculture
Mission: To promote the Canadian organic beef sector; to raise standards of beef production; *Affiliation(s):* COLA-Beef Marketing Inc. (CBM)

Canadian Ornamental Plant Foundation (COPF) / Fondation canadienne des plantes ornementales
5A - #218, 975 McKeown Ave., North Bay ON P1B 9P2
Tel: 705-495-2563; *Fax:* 705-495-1449
Toll-Free: 800-265-1629
e-mail: info@copf.org
URL: www.copf.org
Overview: A small national organization founded in 1964
Finances: *Annual Operating Budget:* $100,000-$250,000
Staff: 7 staff member(s); 12 volunteer(s)
Membership: 650; *Fees:* Schedule available
Activities: *Rents Mailing List:* Yes
Mission: To encourage new plant development by strengthening relations between growers & breeders for the benefit of the horticulture industry; *Member of:* Canadian Horticultural Council; International Plant Propagators Society

Canadian Paint & Coatings Association (CPCA) / Association canadienne de l'industrie de la peinture et du revêtement
#1200, 170 Laurier Ave. West, Ottawa ON K1P 5V5
Tel: 613-231-3604; *Fax:* 613-231-4908
e-mail: cpca@cdnpaint.org
URL: www.cdnpaint.org
Overview: A medium-sized national organization founded in 1913
Finances: *Annual Operating Budget:* $500,000-$1.5 Million
Staff: 5 staff member(s)
Membership: 105 organizations
Activities: Seminars; annual convention; government relations
Mission: To represent the paint industry among the provincial, federal & municipal governments

Canadian Pallet Council (CPC) / Conseil des palettes du Canada
239 Division St., Cobourg ON K9A 3P9
Tel: 905-372-1871; *Fax:* 905-373-0230
e-mail: info@cpcpallet.com
URL: www.cpcpallet.com
Overview: A medium-sized national organization founded in 1977
Finances: *Funding Sources:* Membership fees; royalties
Staff: 3 staff member(s)
Membership: 1,300+; *Fees:* $485-$5,665
Publications: *CPC [Canadian Pallet Council] Communiqué*
Type: Newsletter *Frequency:* bi-m. *Price:* Free with CPC membership
Profile: Pallet issues & topics of interest for members

Canadian Paper Box Manufacturers' Association Inc *See* North American Packaging Association - Canada

Canadian Parks & Recreation Association (CPRA) / Association canadienne des parcs et loisirs
PO Box 83069, 1180 Walkley Rd., Ottawa ON K1V 2M5
Tel: 613-523-5315
e-mail: info@cpra.ca
URL: www.cpra.ca
Overview: A large national charitable organization founded in 1945
Membership: 2,600+; *Member Profile:* Parks & recreation professionals; *Committees:* Finance; Strategic Development; Communications; Awards
Activities: Influencing policy direction; Promoting the benefits of parks & recreation; Providing information to members; Offering professional development opportunities; *Awareness Events:* Recreation & Parks Month, June
Awards: Claude Langelier Award for Young Professionals (Award)
Award of Merit (Award)
Citation of Outstanding Achievement (Award)
Honourary Life Membership (Award)
Boothman Bursary (Scholarship)
Award of Excellence for Innovation (Award)
Publications: *CPRA [Canadian Parks & Recreation Association] E-News*
Type: Newsletter *Frequency:* q. *Price:* Free with CPRA membership
Profile: CPRA activities, conferences, awards, news, resources, initiatives, & research
The Benefits Catalogue
Type: Catalogue *Number of Pages:* 200
Profile: Research outlining why parks, recreation, fitness, arts, & culture are important to the development of healthy individuals & communities
Canadian Parks & Recreation Association Annual Report
Type: Yearbook *Frequency:* a.
CPRA [Canadian Parks & Recreation Association] Tool Kits
Type: Kit
Profile: Topics of tool kits include Making All Recreation Safe, Relevant Recreation, & Everybody Gets to Play
Canadian Parks & Recreation Association Research Reports
Profile: Topics include A Workbook on Child Health & Poverty: A Shared Vision for Health Children; Recreation & Children & Youth Living in Poverty: Barriers, Benefits & Success Stories; & Bridging the Recreation Divide: Listening to Youth & Parents from Low-income Families across Canada
Mission: To advocate on the benefits of parks & recreation services
Environmental Activity: Contributing to healthy communities; Collaborating with environmental & public health organizations

Canadian Parks & Wilderness Society (CPAWS) / Société pour la nature et les parcs du Canada (SNAP)
#506, 250 City Centre Ave., Ottawa ON K1R 6K7
Tel: 613-569-7226; *Fax:* 613-569-7098
Toll-Free: 800-333-9453
e-mail: info@cpaws.org
URL: www.cpaws.org
Social Media: www.facebook.com/cpaws; www.twitter.com/#!/cpaws
Previous Name: National & Provincial Parks Association (NPPAC)
Overview: A medium-sized national charitable organization founded in 1963
Finances: *Funding Sources:* Donations; Fundraising
Staff: 50+ staff member(s)
Membership: 20,000
Activities: Increasing awareness & understanding of ecological principles; Providing educational programs; Liaising with government, First Nations, business, & other organizations
Awards: J.B. Harkin Medal (Award)
To honour individuals who have made a significant contribution to the conservation of Canada's parks & wilderness
Meetings/Conferences:
For more information see Trade Shows, Conferences and Seminars Chapter
Canadian Parks & Wilderness Society 2011 Annual General Meeting
November 2011
Publications: *Canadian Wilderness*
Type: Newsletter *Frequency:* s-a. *Price:* Free with Canadian Parks & Wilderness Society membership
Profile: Wilderness conservation news & views from across Canada for Canadian Parks & Wilderness Society members
CPAWS [Canadian Parks & Wilderness Society] Annual Report
Type: Yearbook *Frequency:* a.
Profile: CPAWS yearly highlights & financial information
CPAWS [Canadian Parks & Wilderness Society] Research Reports
Frequency: irreg.
Profile: Conservation biology scientific report topics include Grizzly Challenge; Special Marine Areas in Newfoundland & Labrador; Ontario's Timber Harvesting Levels: Science or Wishful Thinking?; The State of the Alberta Parks & Protected Areas; & Uncertain Future: Woodland Caribou & Canada's Boreal Forest
Community Atlas Initiative [a publication of the Canadian Parks & Wilderness Society]
Profile: CPAWS works with communities near national parks to produce atlases about land use & the natural environment, such as the Gulf Islands Community Atlas, the Riding Mountain Community Atlas, the St. Lawrence Islands Atlas, & the Bruce Penninsula Community Atlas
Nahanni: Protected Forever
Type: Booklet *Number of Pages:* 16
Profile: The expansion of the Nahanni National Park Reserve
Gatineau Park: A Threatened Treasure
Type: Booklet *Number of Pages:* 28
Profile: Information to ensure a sustainable future for Gatineau Park & its ecosystems
More Than Trees: A Citizen's Guide to Making Conservation a Bigger Part of Forest Management
Type: Guide *Number of Pages:* 91 *Editor:* Chris Henschel; Dave Pearce
Profile: A guide featuring advice fact sheets, compliance checklists, & the forest guardians reporting form
Mission: To act as the Canadian voice for public wilderness protection
Environmental Activity: Creating protected areas in Canada; Conducting research in conservation biology

Canadian Parks Partnership (CPP) / Partenaires des parcs canadiens
#360, 1414 - 8th St. SW, Calgary AB T2R 1J6
Tel: 613-567-0099
e-mail: nature@canadianparkspartnership.com
Overview: A medium-sized national organization founded in 1986
Chief Officer(s):
Bruce Livingston, Chair
Finances: *Annual Operating Budget:* Less than $50,000
Staff: 3 staff member(s)
Membership: Over 60 associations across Canada which work on an individual level with their partner national & provincial park or historic site
Activities: Direct Volunteer Support Program - to help cooperating associations to be strong & effective partners to their local national/provincial parks & historic sites & other protected area sites across Canada; National Education Programs - reaching beyond the park gate to encourage public awareness, appreciation of & involvement in supporting our special places; Canadian Parks Partnership Fund - was established in 1992 to act as a community foundation; *Speaker Service:* Yes; *Rents Mailing List:* Yes; *Library:* Yes, Not open to the public
Mission: To support the overall enhancement of Canada's parks, historic sites & canals system & to foster public awareness, appreciation, understanding of & involvement in the system

Canadian Patient Safety Institute (CPSI) / Institut canadien pour la sécurité des patients
#1414, 10235 - 101 St., Edmonton AB T5J 3G1
Tel: 780-409-8090; *Fax:* 780-409-8098
Toll-Free: 866-421-6933
e-mail: info@cpsi-icsp.ca
URL: www.patientsafetyinstitute.ca
Overview: A small national organization founded in 2003
Chief Officer(s):
Doug Cochrane, Chair
Hugh MacLeod, CEO
hmacleod@cpsi-icsp.ca
Cecilia Bloxom, Director, Communications
cbloxom@cpsi-icsp.ca
Finances: *Funding Sources:* Health Canada
Activities: Providing resources about patient safety; Identifying patient safety practices; Developing safety competencies; Promoting integration of patient safety practices into educational

Associations/Organizations / Canadian Pest Management Association

& training programs; *Awareness Events:* Canadian Patient Safety Week; *Library:* Canadian Patient Safety Institute Library; *Publications: Patient Safety Matters: The CPSI Newsletter*
Type: Newsletter
Profile: Institute updates, courses, appointments, profiles, funding, & upcoming events
Mission: To work with patients, healthcare providers, organizations, regulatory bodies, & governments to provide safer healthcare for Canadians; To promote leading practices for patient safety within Canada's health system

Canadian Pest Control Association *See* Canadian Pest Management Association

Canadian Pest Management Association (CPMA) / Association canadienne de la gestion parasitaire (ACGP)
PO Box 1748, Moncton NB E1C 9X5
Fax: 866-957-7378
Toll-Free: 866-630-2762
e-mail: cpma@pestworld.org
URL: www.pestworldcanada.org
Previous Name: Canadian Pest Control Association
Overview: A medium-sized national organization founded in 1943
Chief Officer(s):
Bill Melville, President
bmelville@orkincanada.com
Karen Furgiuele-Percy, Director, Business Development
kfurgiuele@gardexinc.com
Randy Hobbs, Director, Government Affairs
rhobbs@braemargroup.ca
Sean Rollo, Treasurer
srollo@pcocanada.com
Member Profile: Members of provincial & regional pest management associations; Suppliers
Activities: Offering training & networking opportunities; Conducting research; Offering assistance to consumers seeking a professional pest control company
Meetings/Conferences:
For more information see Trade Shows, Conferences and Seminars Chapter
Pest Management Canada 2012
March 2012 Vancouver, BC
Publications: *Canada ePestWorld*
Type: Newsletter *Frequency:* m. *Price:* Free with Canadian Pest Management Association membership
Profile: Timely national industry news & happenings, membership bulletins, & articles
PestWorld
Type: Newsletter *Frequency:* bi-m. *Price:* Free with Canadian Pest Management Association membership
Profile: Business techniques & tips, analysis of the pest management industry, field stories, technical updates, & legislative news
Pest Gazette
Type: Newsletter *Frequency:* q. *Number of Pages:* 4
Profile: Educational information about seasonal pests for pest management consumers
Mission: To provide pest management information; To act as the voice of the pest management industry throughout Canada; Upholding the association's Code of Ethics; *Affiliation(s):* National Pest Management Association; Leadership Development Group; Minorities in Pest Management; Professional Women in Pest Management
Environmental Activity: Speaking with legislators & formulators to ensure the industry has environmentally friendly legislation & tools

Canadian Petroleum Law Foundation
PO Box 4143, Stn. C, Calgary AB T2T 5M9
Tel: 403-237-2423
e-mail: lara.h.pella@esso.ca
URL: www.cplf.org
Overview: A small national organization founded in 1963
Chief Officer(s):
Ben Rogers, President
ben.rogers@blakes.com
Miles Pittman, Treasurer
miles.pittman@fmc-law.com
Mission: To study oil & gas laws

Canadian Physiological Society (CPS) / Société canadienne de physiologie
Parent: Canadian Federation of Biological Societies
c/o Dr. Melanie Woodin, Dept. of Cell & Systems Biology, U. of Toronto, 25 Harbord St., Toronto ON M5S 3G5
URL: www.cpsscp.ca
Overview: A medium-sized national charitable organization founded in 1935
Chief Officer(s):
Melanie Woodin, Secretary, 416-978-8646, *Fax:* 416-978-8532
m.woodin@utoronto.ca
Fees: $25 students; $65 associates; $100 regular; *Committees:* Nominating; Web Resources
Activities: Encouraging reseaerch in the physiological sciences; Fostering communication within the scientific community in Canada
Meetings/Conferences:
For more information see Trade Shows, Conferences and Seminars Chapter
Canadian Physiological Society 2012 Annual Winter Meeting
Other Conferences in 2012 2012
Canadian Physiological Society 2013 Annual Winter Meeting
Other Conferences in 2013 2013
Mission: To disseminate & discuss scientific information of interest to researchers in physiology & biological sciences

Canadian Phytopathological Society (CPS) / Société Canadienne de Phytopathologie (SCP)
c/o Crop Protection & Food Research Ctr Agriculture & Agri-Food Canada, 1391 Sandford St., London ON N5V 4T3
e-mail: connk@agr.gc.ca
URL: www.cps-scp.ca
Overview: A medium-sized national organization founded in 1929
Finances: *Funding Sources:* Membership fees
Meetings/Conferences:
For more information see Trade Shows, Conferences and Seminars Chapter
Canadian Phytopathological Society 2011 Joint Annual Meeting & Conference with Plant Canada
July 2011, NS
Publications: *Canadian Journal of Plant Pathology / Revue canadienne de phytopathologie*
Type: Journal *Language:* B *Frequency:* q. *Editor:* Zamir K. Punja
ISSN: 0706-0661 *Price:* $85 Canada individuals; $140 Canada institutions; $95-$105 international individuals
Profile: Scientific research, reviews & information about plant pathology
Canadian Plant Disease Survey / Inventaire des maladies des plantes au Canada
Editor: Dr. Robin Morrall, Coordinator
Profile: Records of plant diseases in Canada & assessments of losses from disease
The Pest Management Research Report (PMRR)
Language: B *Editor:* Andrea Labaj
Profile: Information about integrated pest management (IPM) for researchers & advisors
Diseases of Field Crop Crops in Canada
Number of Pages: 304 *Editor:* Bailey, Gossen, Gugel & Morrall
ISBN: 0-9691627-6-6 *Price:* $35
Profile: Thorough, illustrated guide to identifying diseases of forage, pulse, oilseed, cereal, & specialty crops
Diseases & Pests of Vegetable Crops in Canada
Number of Pages: 554 *Editor:* R. Howard, J. Garland, & W. Seaman
Profile: Joint publication of the Canadian Phytopathological Society & the Entomological Society of Canada
Mission: To encourage & support research, education, & dissemination of knowledge on the nature, cause, & control of plant diseases; To promote communication among plant pathologists; To broaden educational opportunities for members

Canadian Plastics Industry Association (CPIA) / Association canadienne de l'industrie des plastiques
#712, 5915 Airport Rd., Mississauga ON L4V 1T1
Tel: 905-678-7748; *Fax:* 905-678-0774
e-mail: national@cpia.ca
URL: www.cpia.ca
Previous Name: Society of the Plastics Industry of Canada
Overview: A large national organization founded in 1997
Finances: *Funding Sources:* Membership fees
Staff: 30 staff member(s)
Membership: 500; *Member Profile:* Companies involved in Canadian plastics industry; *Committees:* Composites; Construction; EH&S; EPIC; Machinery; Mould Makers; Natural Composites; Plastic Film Manufacturers Assn of Canada; Vinyl
Activities: P3 Sustainability Management Program; *Speaker Service:* Yes; *Rents Mailing List:* Yes; *Library:* Technical Information Resource Centre; Open to public, open by appointment
Publications: *CPIA [Canadian Plastics Industry Association] Annual Report*
Type: Yearbook *Frequency:* a.
Canadian Plastics Industry Association Executive Summary
Type: Newsletter
Profile: Internal newsletter of the CPIA President & CEO for CPIA members only
Green Building
Type: Newsletter
Profile: Publication of the Green Building Task Force of the Canadian Plastics Industry Association
CPIA [Canadian Plastics Industry Association] Membership Directory
Type: Directory
CPIA [Canadian Plastics Industry Association] Plastics Machinery & Moulds Export Directory
Type: Directory
Mission: To advance the prosperity & international competitiveness of the Canadian plastics industry in an environmentally & socially responsible manner

Canadian Plastics Sector Council (CPSC) / Conseil canadien sectoriel des plastiques
#1, 200 Colonnade Rd., Ottawa ON K2E 7M1
Tel: 613-231-4470; *Fax:* 613-231-3775
e-mail: info@cpsc-ccsp.ca
URL: www.cpsc-ccsp.ca
Overview: A small national organization founded in 2000
Chief Officer(s):
Amelia Siva, Executive Director
Finances: *Annual Operating Budget:* $500,000-$1.5 Million
Staff: 4 staff member(s)
Publications: *CPSC [Canadian Plastics Sector Council] Newsletter / Bulletin du CCSP [Conseil canadien sectoriel des plastiques]*
Type: Newsletter *Language:* B *Frequency:* 3 pa *Editor:* Jérôme Bourgault
Profile: Feature articles & CPSC activities
Mission: To explore & address emerging human resources issues in the plastics processing industry

Canadian Plumbing & Mechanical Contractors Association, BC Branch *See* Mechanical Contractors Association of British Columbia

Canadian Plywood Association
735 - 15 St. West, North Vancouver BC V7M 1T2
Tel: 604-981-4190; *Fax:* 604-985-0342
e-mail: info@canply.org
URL: www.canply.org
Also Known As: CANPLY
Overview: A medium-sized national organization
Chief Officer(s):
Judy White, Office Manager
James F. Shaw, President
Finances: *Annual Operating Budget:* $1.5 Million-$3 Million
Staff: 14 staff member(s)
Membership: 1-99
Mission: Canadian plywood organization.

Canadian Polystyrene Recycling Alliance (CPRA)
260 Peter St., Port Hope ON L1A 3V6
URL: www.cpracanada.ca
Overview: A medium-sized national organization founded in 1989
Chief Officer(s):
Sam Alavy, President & Chief Executive Officer
Mission: To operate a vertically integrated polystyrene recycling facility to recycle polystyrene into picture frames & mouldings

Canadian Port & Harbour Association *See* Association of Canadian Port Authorities

Canadian Portland Cement Association *See* Cement Association of Canada

Canadian Ports Clearance Association
#500, 101 Syndicate Ave. North, Thunder Bay ON P7C 3V4
Tel: 807-623-8491; *Fax:* 807-623-2676

Previous Name: British Columbia Grain Shippers Clearance Association; Lake Shippers Clearance Association
Overview: A small national organization
Mission: Shipping agent

Canadian Precast / Prestressed Concrete Institute (CPCI) / Institut canadien du béton préfabriqué et précontraint
#100, 196 Bronson Ave., Ottawa ON K1R 6H4
Tel: 613-232-2619; *Fax:* 613-232-5139
Toll-Free: 877-937-2724
e-mail: info@cpci.ca
URL: www.cpci.ca
Overview: A medium-sized national organization founded in 1961
Finances: *Annual Operating Budget:* $500,000-$1.5 Million
Staff: 3 staff member(s)
Membership: 250 individual + 50 institutional
Activities: *Library:* Yes, Open to public
Publications: *CPCI [Canadian Precast / Prestressed Concrete Institute] Imagineering*
Type: Magazine *Accepts Advertising* : Yes *Editor:* Cydney Keith
Profile: Feature articles, industry updates, member directory, "tech talk", marketing information, president's messages
Mission: To stimulate & advance the common interests & general welfare of the structural precast/prestressed concrete industry, the architectural precast concrete industry & the post-tensioned concrete industry in Canada

Canadian Printing Industries Association (CPIA) / Association canadienne de l'imprimerie (ACI)
#1110, 151 Slater St., Ottawa ON K1P 5H3
Tel: 613-236-7208; *Fax:* 613-232-1334
e-mail: info@cpia-aci.ca
URL: www.cpia-aci.ca
Previous Name: Graphic Arts Industries Association; Canadian Printing & Imaging Association
Overview: A medium-sized national organization founded in 1939
Finances: *Annual Operating Budget:* $250,000-$500,000; *Funding Sources:* Membership dues
Staff: 2 staff member(s); 25 volunteer(s)
Membership: 600; *Member Profile:* Owners/senior executives of companies in pre-press, press, bindery & allied industries; *Committees:* Government Affairs; Membership
Activities: *Library:* Yes, Not open to the public
Mission: To advance the quality of management in the printing & allied trades; to offer services through a network of local & related organizations including representations to various sectors; to enhance the image & profile of the industry; **Affiliation(s):** Graphic Arts Technical Foundation; Printing Industries of America

Canadian Printing Ink Manufacturers Association (CPIMA)
52 Palmer Rd., Grimsby L3M 5L4
Tel: 905-309-5883; *Fax:* 905-309-5838
e-mail: cpima@sympatico.ca
URL: www.cpima.org
Overview: A medium-sized national organization founded in 1936
Chief Officer(s):
Shiona Finlayson, President
Finances: *Annual Operating Budget:* Less than $50,000; *Funding Sources:* Membership dues
Staff: 1 staff member(s)
Membership: 5; *Fees:* Based on sales; *Member Profile:* Canadian ink manufacturers; *Committees:* Management; Technical
Awards: The Jim Glynn Award (Award)
Publications: *Canadian Printing Ink Manufacturers Association Technical Bulletins*
Type: Newsletter *Frequency:* irreg.
Profile: Topics include environmental issues, printing inks & food packaging, scrap ink, & UV inks health & saftey
Mission: To exchange information that will be of benefit to members, the ink industry, & the printing industry; **Affiliation(s):** Society of British Ink Manufacturers; National Association of Printing Ink Manufacturers

Canadian Process Control Association (CPCA)
2100 Banbury Cres., Oakville ON L6H 5P6
Tel: 905-844-6822; *Fax:* 905-901-9913
e-mail: cpca@cpca-assoc.com
URL: www.cpca-assoc.com
Previous Name: Industrial Instrument Manufacturers Association

Overview: A medium-sized national organization
Finances: *Annual Operating Budget:* Less than $50,000
Membership: 52 corporate;
Mission: To promote the industry & its members to customers, academia, & public bodies; To provide a forum to exchange technical, industry, & regulatory information; To develop industry statistics; To encourage professional & ethical behaviour & quality standards among members

Canadian Public Health Association (CPHA) / Association canadienne de santé publique (ACSP)
#400, 1565 Carling Ave., Ottawa ON K1Z 8R1
Tel: 613-725-3769; *Fax:* 613-725-9826
e-mail: info@cpha.ca
URL: www.cpha.ca
Social Media:
www.facebook.com/group.php?gid=159289860285?ref
Overview: A large national charitable organization founded in 1910
Finances: *Funding Sources:* Membership fees; Donations
Membership: 2,000; *Fees:* $88 students, retired persons, & low income individuals; $107 international students; $165 regular members; $170 regular international members; *Member Profile:* Individuals who support Canadian Public Health Association objectives, & who are engaged or interested in community or public health activities, such as professionals in public health practice, researchers, professors, & government workers
Activities: Advising decision-makers about public health system reform; Liaising with provincial & territorial public health associations & national & international agencies & organizations; Publishing & disseminating research results; *Speaker Service:* Yes
Awards: Aventis Pasteur International Award (Award)
Ron Draper Health Promotion Award (Award)
Certificate of Merit (Award)
Student Award (Award)
Honorary Life Membership (Award)
Awarded for exceptional excellence as an educator, researcher or practitioner in the field of public health, as demonstrated by achievements, valuable & outstanding research or distinguished service in the advancement of public health knowledge & practice
Defries Award (Award)
The highest honour granted by the association; presented to the CPHA members who have made outstanding contributions in the broad field of public health; preference is given to Canadian contributions & individuals who have substantially supported the objectives of the association; the award carries with it an honorary life membership
Janssen-Ortho Inc. Award (Award)
Presented to the candidate who has significantly advanced the cause, legitimized & stressed the responsibility & state of the art of public health
Publications: *The Canadian Journal of Public Health*
Type: Journal *Frequency:* bi-m. *Accepts Advertising* : Yes *Editor:* Debra Lynkowski *Price:* Free with membership in the Canadian Public Health Association
Profile: Articles on public health, including epidemiology, nutrition, family health, environmental health, sexually transmitted diseases, gerontology, behavioural medicine, rural health, health promotion, & public health policy
CPHA [Canadian Public Health Association] Health Digest
Frequency: q. *Editor:* Debra Lynkowski *ISBN:* 0703-5624 *Price:* Free with membership in the Canadian Public Health Association
Profile: Incorporates the international newsletter, Partners Around the World, plus articles from across Canada & around the world
Canadian Public Health Association Annual Report
Type: Yearbook *Frequency:* a.
Mission: To represent public health in Canada; To support universal & equitable access to the necessary conditions to achieve health for all Canadians; To provide links to the international public health community; **Affiliation(s):** World Health Organization; World Federation of Public Health Associations
Environmental Activity: Guiding intitiatives to safeguard the personal & community health of Canadians

Canadian Public Health Association - NB/PEI Branch
Parent: Canadian Public Health Association
#34, 2865 Rothesay Rd., Rothesay NB E3B 4P2
Tel: 506-847-0311; *Fax:* 506-847-0311
Overview: A small provincial organization founded in 1952
Chief Officer(s):
Cristin Muecke, President
Ann Harling, Secretary-Treasurer

Canadian Public Health Association - NWT/Nunavut Branch
Parent: Canadian Public Health Association
PO Box 1000, Stn. 1000, Iqaluit NU X0A 0H0
Tel: 867-975-5774; *Fax:* 867-975-5755
e-mail: isobol@gov.nu.ca
Overview: A small provincial organization
Chief Officer(s):
Isaac Sobol, President

Canadian Public Works Association (CPWA) / Association Canadienne des Travaux Publics
#191, 253 College St., Toronto ON M5T 1R5
Tel: 202-408-9541; *Fax:* 202-408-9542
e-mail: cpwa@cpwa.net
URL: www.cpwa.net
Overview: A medium-sized national organization founded in 1938
Membership: 1,800
Mission: Their mission statement is to be recognized as the "voice of public works" in Canada; to create a forum for public works professionals in Canada to exchange inforamtion, develop ideas, and share skills, knowledge, and technologies on issues unique to Canada; to increase membership and participation.

Canadian Pulp & Paper Association *See* Forest Products Association of Canada

Canadian Pulp & Paper Association - Technical Section *See* Pulp & Paper Technical Association of Canada

Canadian Pulp & Paper Network for Innovation in Education & Research / Réseau canadien de pâtes et papiers pour l'innovation en éducation et en recherche
570, boul St-Jean, Pointe-Claire QC H9R 3J9
Tel: 514-630-4100; *Fax:* 514-630-4107
e-mail: papier@paprican.ca
URL: www.papiernet.ca
Also Known As: Papier
Previous Name: Mechanical Wood-Pulps Network
Overview: A large national organization founded in 1990
Chief Officer(s):
Patrice Mangin, Chair
Richard Kerekes, Director
kerekes@chbe.ubc.ca
Membership: 100; *Member Profile:* Canadian university faculty involved in teaching & research for the pulp & paper industry
Activities: Collaborating with similar international organizations
Publications: *Canadian Pulp & Paper Network for Innovation in Education & Research Newsletter*
Type: Newsletter *Frequency:* s-a.
Profile: Papier's recent activities, such as meetings & award presentations
Mission: To act as the voice of Canadian university faculty involved in teaching & research for the pulp & paper industry

Canadian Radiation Protection Association (CRPA) / Association canadienne de radioprotection (ACRP)
PO Box 83, Carleton Place ON K7C 3P3
Tel: 613-253-3779; *Fax:* 888-551-0712
e-mail: secretariat2007@crpa-acrp.ca
URL: www.crpa-acrp.ca
Overview: A small national organization founded in 1982
Fees: $485 corporate members; $120 full or associate members; $20 students; *Member Profile:* Individuals with training who are engaged in the science & practice of radiation protection
Activities: Promoting educational opportunities
Publications: *CRPA [Canadian Radiation Protection Association] Bulletin*
Type: Newsletter *Language:* B *Frequency:* q.
Profile: For Canadian Radiation Protection Association members only
Mission: To develop scientific knowledge for protection from the harmful effects of radiation; to encourage research; to assist in the development of professional standards in the discipline; **Affiliation(s):** International Radiation Protection Association (IRPA).

Canadian Recreational Canoeing Association *See* Paddle Canada

Canadian Regional Science Association *Voir* Association canadienne des sciences régionales

Associations/Organizations / Canadian Remote Sensing Society

Canadian Remote Sensing Society (CRSS) / Société canadienne de télédétection
1750 Courtlandt Cres., Ottawa ON K2C 2B5
Tel: 613-234-0191; *Fax:* 613-234-9039
e-mail: casi@casi.ca
URL: www.casi.ca/canadianremotesensingsociety.aspx
Overview: A small national organization founded in 1978
Chief Officer(s):
Derek R. Peddle, Chair
derek.peddle@uleth.ca
Monique Bernier, Vice-Chair
Anne Smith, Secretary-Treasurer
Activities: Disseminating technical remote sensing information; Developing a program for certification of remote sensing scientists & mapping scientists in GIS & photogrammetry
Publications: *Canadian Journal of Remote Sensing (CJRS) / Journal canadien de télédétection (JCT)*
Type: Journal *Language:* B *Frequency:* bi-m. *Accepts Advertising:* Yes *Editor:* Nicholas Coops *Price:* $211.68 Canada; $206.30 USA; $217.20 International
Profile: Research articles & notes, technical notes, & review papers on topics such as information processing methods, data acquisition, & applications
Mission: To advance the art, science, engineering, & application of remote sensing in Canada; to uphold the Society's Code of Ethics; *Member of:* Canadian Aeronautics & Space Institute (CASI)

Canadian Renewable Energy Association (CanREA)
URL: www.canrea.ca
Overview: A large national organization
Membership: 16; *Member Profile:* Registered and incorporated not-for-profit organizations which actively promote renewable energy policy and implementation and are in good standing under applicable laws
Activities: Conferences
Mission: CanREA is an alliance of Canadian non-profit/voluntary organizations with a common interest in promoting a global transition to energy conservation and efficiency, and the use of renewable energy. A founding member of the North American Alliance for Renewable Energy, CanREA and its members advocate to all levels of government and work with like-minded organizations worldwide to recommend new policy directions and practical strategies. Members: The BC Sustainable Energy Association; The David Suzuki Foundation; Ecology Action Centre, Nova Scotia; EcoPEI; The Falls Brook Centre, New Brunswick; Green Communities Canada; Greenpeace Canada; Nova Scotia Cooperative Council; The Ontario Sustainable Energy Association; One Sky - The Canadian Institute for Sustainable Living, BC; The Pembina Institute; Pollution Probe; Sierra Club Canada; The Saskatchewan Environmental Society; Toronto Renewable Energy Co-operative; and The Windfall Ecology Centre, Ontario.

Canadian Renewable Fuels Association (CRFA) / Association canadienne des carburants renouvelables
#605, 350 Sparks St., Ottawa ON K1R 7S8
Tel: 613-594-5528; *Fax:* 613-594-3076
URL: www.greenfuels.org
Overview: A medium-sized national organization founded in 1984
Finances: *Funding Sources:* Membership dues
Membership: 1-99; *Fees:* Schedule available based upon company's litres of pro; *Member Profile:* Representatives from all levels of the ethanol & biodiesel industries
Activities: Liaising with government; Promoting policy initiatives advantageous to ethanol & biodiesel fuel development; Increasing awareness of ethanol & biodiesel; Conducting research
Meetings/Conferences:
For more information see Trade Shows, Conferences and Seminars Chapter
Canadian Renewable Fuels 2011 8th Annual Summit: Growing Our Energy Diversity
November 2011 Calgary, AB
Canadian Renewable Fuels 2012 9th Annual Summit: Growing Our Energy Diversity
Other Conferences in 2012 2012
Mission: To promote renewable fuel development & usage
Environmental Activity: Providing information about the development & use of renewable fuel

Canadian Research Management Association *See* Innovation Management Association of Canada

Canadian Respiratory Health Professionals (CRHP)
Parent: Canadian Lung Association
#300, 1750 Courtwood Cres., Ottawa ON K2C 2B5
Tel: 613-569-6411; *Fax:* 613-569-8860
e-mail: crhpinfo@lung.ca
URL: www.lung.ca/crhp
Merged from: Cdn Nurses Respiratory, Cdn Physiotherapy Cardio-Respiratory, & Respiratory Therapy Societies
Overview: A small national organization founded in 2004
Fees: $30 associate member; $45 full member; *Member Profile:* A multidisciplinary health professional section of The Canadian Lung Association, consisting of respiratory therapists, cardio-pulmonary physiotherapists, nurses, pharmacists, & other health professionals who work in the respiratory field
Activities: Advising the Canadian Lung Association on scientific matters, as well as professional & public education; Administering a research & fellowship program; Facilitating interprofessional collaboration
Meetings/Conferences:
For more information see Trade Shows, Conferences and Seminars Chapter
Canadian Respiratory Health Professionals 2012 Annual General Meeting
Other Conferences in 2012 2012
Publications: *Airwaves - The Newsletter of the Canadian Respiratory Health Professionals*
Type: Newsletter *Price:* Free with CRHP membership
Profile: Information for Canadian Respiratory Health Professionals members
Mission: To promote lung health & the prevention of lung disease; *Affiliation(s):* Canadian Thoracic Society

Canadian Rock Mechanics Association (CARMA) / Association canadienne de méchanique des roches
c/o Civil Engineering Department, University of Toronto, 35 St. George St., Toronto ON M5S 1A4
e-mail: giovanni.grasselli@utoronto.ca
URL: www.carma-rocks.ca
Overview: A medium-sized national organization founded in 1980
Membership: 165
Awards: John Franklin Award (Award)
Recognizes an individual who has recently made an outstanding and published technical contribution in the fields of rock mechanics or rock engineering in Canada and/or internationally. Given biannually
Mission: To represent Canada to the international community of engineers working in the mining & civil engineering aspects of rock mechanics engineering; *Member of:* Canadian Geotechnical Society; Canadian Institute of Mining & Metallurgy; *Affiliation(s):* International Society for Rock Mechanics

Canadian Rose Society (CRS)
c/o #504, 334 Queen Mary Rd., Kingston ON K7M 7E7
e-mail: info@canadianrosesociety.org
URL: www.canadianrosesociety.org
Previous Name: Rose Society of Ontario
Overview: A medium-sized national charitable organization founded in 1955
Membership: 500-999; *Fees:* $30 regular; $35 family, affiliate society, nursery, institute, & U.S.A. members; $50 foreign
Activities: *Speaker Service:* Yes; *Library:* Rose Book Library & Rose Slide Library
Publications: *The CRS Comm Poster*
Type: Newsletter *Frequency:* 5 pa *Editor:* Marilynn Mitchener
The Rose Annual
Type: Yearbook *Frequency:* a.
Profile: Informative articles, colour illustrations, & comments on new roses
The Rosarian
Type: Magazine *Frequency:* s-a.
Profile: Current developments & practical tips about rose growing
Mission: To provide information about rose growing, speakers, judges, nurseries & suppliers, & rose shows; To correspond with people with similar interests throughout Canada & around the world; *Member of:* World Federation of Rose Societies; *Affiliation(s):* World Federation of Rose Societies

Canadian Sanitation Standards Association *See* Canadian Sanitation Supply Association

Canadian Sanitation Supply Association (CSSA) / Association canadienne des fournisseurs de produits sanitaires
PO Box 10009, 910 Dundas St. West, Whitby ON L1P 1P7
Tel: 905-665-8001; *Fax:* 905-430-6418
Toll-Free: 866-684-8273
e-mail: info@cssa.com
URL: www.cssa.com
Previous Name: Canadian Sanitation Standards Association
Overview: A large national organization founded in 1957
Finances: *Annual Operating Budget:* $250,000-$500,000
Staff: 1 staff member(s); 10 volunteer(s)
Membership: 395 corporate + 10 associate + 15 senior/lifetime; *Fees:* Schedule available; *Member Profile:* Manufacturer or distributor of sanitation products & services; *Committees:* Long Range Planning; Government Liaison
Activities: *Library:* Yes, open by appointment
Publications: *Canadian Sanitation Supply Association Update*
Type: Newsletter *Price:* Free with CSSA membership
Profile: CSSA activities, awards, chapter news, & events
Canadian Sanitation Supply Association Bulletin
Type: Newsletter *Price:* Free with CSSA membership
Profile: Information for CSSA members important to their business
Mission: To provide a high degree of professionalism, technical knowledge & business ethics within the membership; to promote greater public awareness, appreciation & understanding of the sanitation industry

Canadian Science Writers' Association (CSWA) / Association canadienne des rédacteurs scientifiques
PO Box 75, Stn. A, Toronto ON M5W 1A2
Toll-Free: 800-796-8595
e-mail: office@sciencewriters.ca
URL: www.sciencewriters.ca
Overview: A small national organization founded in 1971
Membership: 450+; *Fees:* $75 regular members; $35 students; *Member Profile:* Professional science communicators in all media, who communicate science & technology to non-specialist audiences
Activities: Providing networking opportunities for communications officers in science & technology institutions, media professionals, educators, & technical writers; Offering workshops & public meetings; Encouraging awareness of the need for science coverage
Awards: Science in Society Book Awards (Award)
Science in Society Journalism Awards (Award)
Medal For Excellence In Health Research Journalism (Award)
L'Oreal Excellence In Science Journalism Award (Award)
Yves Fortier Earth Science Journalism Award (Award)
Publications: *Science Link [a publication of the Canadian Science Writers' Association]*
Type: Newsletter *Editor:* Peter McMahon
Profile: Information for CSWA / ACRS members
Canadian Science Writers' Association Membership Directory
Type: Directory
Profile: For CSWA / ACRS members
Mission: To foster excellence in science communication; to increase public awareness of Canadian science & technology

Canadian Seed Growers' Association (CSGA) / Association canadienne des producteurs de semences
PO Box 8455, #202, 240 Catherine St., Ottawa ON K1G 3T1
Tel: 613-236-0497; *Fax:* 613-563-7855
e-mail: seeds@seedgrowers.ca
URL: www.seedgrowers.ca
Overview: A medium-sized national organization founded in 1904
Membership: 4,300

Canadian Seed Trade Association (CSTA) / Association canadienne du commerce des semences (ACCS)
#505, 39 Robertson Rd., Ottawa ON K2H 8R2
Tel: 613-829-9527; *Fax:* 613-829-3530
e-mail: csta@cdnseed.org
URL: www.cdnseed.org
Overview: A medium-sized national organization founded in 1923
Finances: *Funding Sources:* Membership fees
Staff: 2 staff member(s)
Mission: The Canadian Seed Trade Association (CSTA) is committed to fostering an environment conducive to research, developing, distributing, and trading seed and associated

technologies; with the goal of bettering the choices and successes of our members and their customers. Their five key goals are as follows; fostering innovation; support for a science based regulatory system; increase the use of pedigreed seed; support the understanding and use of indentity preserved systems; improve market access and understanding for the trade of seed

Canadian Sheep Breeders' Association (CSBA) / La société canadienne des éleveurs de moutons
c/o Cathy Gallivan, 1489 Route 560, Deerville NB E7K 1W7
Fax: 506-328-8165
Toll-Free: 866-956-1116
e-mail: office@sheepbreeders.ca
URL: www.sheepbreeders.ca
Overview: A medium-sized national organization
Membership: 1,100; *Fees:* $20

Canadian Sheet Steel Building Institute (CSSBI) / Institut canadien de la tôle d'acier pour le bâtiment (ICTAB)
#2A, 652 Bishop St. North, Cambridge ON N3H 4V6
Tel: 519-650-1285; *Fax:* 519-650-8081
e-mail: info@cssbi.ca
URL: www.cssbi.ca
Overview: A medium-sized national organization founded in 1961
Membership: 27 corporate; *Member Profile:* Producers, fabricators & associates involved in the structural sheet steel industry;
Mission: The CSSBI's vision statement is to make steel the material of choice for building construction in Canada.

Canadian Society for Analytical Sciences & Spectroscopy
PO Box 46122, 2339 Ogilvie Rd., Ottawa ON K1J 9M7
Fax: 204-954-5984
URL: www.csass.org
Previous Name: Spectroscopy Society of Canada
Overview: A medium-sized national organization founded in 1957
Finances: *Annual Operating Budget:* $50,000-$100,000
Staff: 25 volunteer(s)
Membership: 500; *Fees:* Schedule available; *Committees:* National Executive
Mission: To organize programs of scientific & general interest for the educational benefit of members & the public; to organize annual scientific conferences & workshops on various aspects of pure & applied spectroscopy in the chemical, biological, geochemical & metallurgical sciences; *Affiliation(s):* Society for Applied Spectroscopy - USA; Colloquium Spectroscopicum Internationale; Chemical Institute of Canada; Canadian Society of Forensic Science

Canadian Society for Bioengineering (CSBE) / Société canadienne de génie agroalimentaire et de bioingénierie (SCGAB)
PO Box 23101, Stn. McGillivray, Winnipeg MB R3T 5S3
Tel: 204-233-1881; *Fax:* 204-231-8282
e-mail: bioeng@shaw.ca
URL: www.bioeng.ca
Previous Name: Canadian Society for Engineering in Agricultural, Food & Biological Systems
Overview: A medium-sized national organization founded in 1958
Finances: *Annual Operating Budget:* Less than $50,000; *Funding Sources:* Annual dues
Staff: 1 staff member(s); 17 volunteer(s)
Membership: 500 full + 200 students; *Fees:* Schedule available
Activities: Canadian Society for Bioengineering Foundation
Awards: John Turnbull Award (Award)
John Clark Award (Award)
Glenn Downing Award (Award)
Jim Beamish Award (Award)
Maple Leaf Award (Award)
Industrial Award (Award)
CSBE Fellow Award (Award)
Publications: *Perspectives: The Newsletter of CSBE [Canadian Society for Bioengineering] / Les Nouvelles de SCGAB*
Type: Newsletter *Language:* B
Profile: Canadian Society for Bioengineering / Société canadienne de génie agroalimentaire et de bioingénierie activities, awards, chapter news, job opportunities, & events
Canadian Biosystems Engineering Journal / Le Journal de la Société Canadienne de Génie Agroalimentaire et de Bioingénierie
Type: Journal *Language:* B *Editor:* Ranjan Sri Ranjan *Price:* $50

Canada non-members; $30 Canada CSBE / SCGAB members
Profile: Peer-reviewed papers
Resource [a publication of the Canadian Society for Bioengineering]
Type: Magazine *Accepts Advertising* : Yes
Profile: Industry news & trends
Canadian Society for Bioengineering Annual Meeting Papers
Frequency: a.
Profile: Presentations from conferences
Mission: To provide expertise in the areas of farm power & machinery, structures & environment, soil & water & electrical power & processing; *Affiliation(s):* American Society of Agricultural & Biological Engineers

Canadian Society for Civil Engineering (CSCE) / Société canadienne de génie civil
Parent: The Engineering Institute of Canada
4877, rue Sherbrooke ouest, Montréal QC H3Z 1G9
Tel: 514-933-2634; *Fax:* 514-933-3504
e-mail: info@csce.ca; membership@csce.ca
URL: www.csce.ca
Overview: A medium-sized national organization founded in 1887
Chief Officer(s):
Doug Salloum, Executive Director
doug.salloum@csce.ca
Mahmoud Lardjane, Manager, Programs
mahmoud@csce.ca
Louise Newman, Manager, Communications
louise@csce.ca
Andrea Grimaud, Officer, Membership Liaison
membership@csce.ca
Fees: Schedule available; *Committees:* Infrastructure Renewal; Innovations & IT; International Affairs; Sustainable Development; Career Development; Honours & Fellowships; History
Activities: Offering continuing education & networking opportunities; Working with sister organizations; Promoting civil engineering
Meetings/Conferences:
For more information see Trade Shows, Conferences and Seminars Chapter
Canadian Society for Civil Engineering 2011 Annual General Meeting & Conference: Engineers - Advocates for Future Policy
June 2011 Ottawa, ON
Canadian Society for Civil Engineering 2011 Executives / Board Workshop
June 2011 Ottawa, ON
Canadian Society for Civil Engineering 2012 Annual General Meeting & Conference
June 2012 Edmonton, AB
Canadian Society for Civil Engineering 2013 Annual General Meeting & Conference
May 2013 Montréal, QC
Publications: *Canadian Civil Engineer (CCE)*
Type: Magazine *Frequency:* 5 pa *Accepts Advertising* : Yes
Editor: Louise Newman *ISSN:* 9825-7515 *Price:* $35 Canada & U.S.A.; $45 other countries
Profile: Technical activity reports, technical articles, corporate & personal achievement items, & networking news
Canadian Journal of Civil Engineering (CJCE)
Type: Journal
Profile: Technical journal featuring scholarly papers devoted to civil engineering
Canadian Society for Civil Engineering Annual Report
Type: Yearbook *Frequency:* a.
Profile: Reports from executives such as the president, the president-elect, the executive director, vice-president, committees, & the CSCE Foundation, in addition to the auditor's report & financial statements
Canadian Society for Civil Engineering E-Bulletin
Type: Newsletter *Frequency:* m. *Accepts Advertising* : Yes
Profile: Featuring current industry & society news, trends, & forthcoming events of interest to over 7,000 subscribers
Canadian Society for Civil Engineering President's E-Letter
Type: Newsletter *Frequency:* m.
Profile: Information for members of the Canadian Society for Civil Engineering, including forthcoming programs & conferences
Canadian Society for Civil Engineering Conference Proceedings
Type: Yearbook *Frequency:* a.
Profile: Proceedings usually include an abstract book & CD-ROM with details of the society's annual conference
A Civil Society - A brief personal history of the CSCE [Canadian Society for Civil Engineering]
Mission: To develop & maintain high standard of civil engineering practice in Canada; To enhance the public image of

the civil engineering profession
Environmental Activity: Establishing environmental & transportation technical divisions; Providing leadership in sustainable infrastructure

Canadian Society for Engineering in Agricultural, Food & Biological Systems See Canadian Society for Bioengineering

Canadian Society for Horticultural Science (CSHS) / Société canadienne de science horticole
#1112, 141 Laurier Ave. West, Ottawa ON K1P 5J3
Tel: 613-232-9459; *Fax:* 613-594-5190
e-mail: services@aic.ca
URL: www.cshs.ca
Overview: A small national organization founded in 1956
Member Profile: Scientists; Educators; Extension agents; Industry personnel; Students
Activities: Providing professional development opportunities; Organizing an annual conference & scientific meeting
Publications: *CSHS [Canadian Society for Horticultural Science] Newsletter*
Type: Newsletter *Frequency:* q.
Profile: Society activities, issues, & events
CSHS [Canadian Society for Horticultural Science] Membership Directory
Type: Directory *Frequency:* a.
Profile: Listings of Society members, plus information about governance, committees, & awards
Program & Abstracts of the CSHS [Canadian Society for Horticultural Science] Annual Conference
Type: Yearbook *Frequency:* a.
Profile: The latest horticultural research
Canadian Journal of Plant Science (CJPS)
Type: Journal *Frequency:* q. *Editor:* Vaino Poysa
Profile: Shared with the Canadian Society of Agronomy (CSA)
Mission: To advance research, teaching, information, & technology related to all horticultural crops

Canadian Society for Industrial Engineering (CSIE) / Société canadienne de génie industriel (SCGI)
PO Box 92016, Stn. Portobello, Brossard QC J4W 3K8
Tel: 450-672-8599
e-mail: info@scgi-csie.qc.ca
URL: www.scgi-csie.qc.ca
Previous Name: Institute of Industrial Engineers
Overview: A medium-sized national organization founded in 1960

Canadian Society for International Health (CSIH) / Société canadienne de la santé internationale
#1105, 1 Nicholas St., Ottawa ON K1N 7B7
Tel: 613-241-5785; *Fax:* 613-241-3845
e-mail: csih@csih.org
URL: www.csih.org
Previous Name: Canadian Society for Tropical Medicine & International Health
Overview: A medium-sized international charitable organization founded in 1977
Finances: *Annual Operating Budget:* $1.5 Million-$3 Million; *Funding Sources:* Membership fees; Contracts; CIDA; Competitive bids
Staff: 11 staff member(s); 30 volunteer(s)
Membership: 400; *Fees:* $50; *Member Profile:* Persons with interest in health development, tropical medicine, health systems strengthening, & capacity building; *Committees:* Communication; Advocacy; Research
Activities: *Internships:* Yes; *Library:* Yes
Publications: *Synergy Online*
Type: Newsletter *Frequency:* m.
Profile: International health & development information, news bulletins, awards, conference information, & job listings
Mission: To promote international health & development through mobilization of Canadian resources; To advocate & facilitate research, education, & service activities in international health; To further Canadian strengths of progressive health policy & programming in all fields where global & domestic health concerns meet; To contribute to the evolving global understanding of health & development; *Member of:* Canadian Coalition for Global Health Research

Canadian Society for Mechanical Engineering (CSME) / Société canadienne de génie mécanique (SCGM)
Parent: The Engineering Institute of Canada
1295 Hwy. 2 East, Kingston ON K7L 4V1

Associations/Organizations / Canadian Society for Medical Laboratory Science

Tel: 613-547-5989; *Fax:* 613-547-0195
e-mail: csme@cogeco.ca
URL: www.csme-scgm.ca
Overview: A medium-sized national charitable organization founded in 1970
Chief Officer(s):
Rama B. Bhat, Ph.D, FCSME, President
Fees: $15 students; $45 retired members; $85 first year membership; $115 professional affiliate; $125 full membership; *Member Profile:* Mechnical engineering personnel; Engineers in other disciplines who are interested in mechanical engineering; *Committees:* Executive; Regional Vice Presidents; Chairs Special; Chairs Standing; Chairs Technical
Activities: Providing continuing education; Arranging networking opportunities
Meetings/Conferences:
For more information see Trade Shows, Conferences and Seminars Chapter
Canadian Society for Mechanical Engineering 2011 23rd Biennial Canadian Congress of Applied Mechanics (CANCAM) June 2011 Vancouver, BC
Canadian Society for Mechanical Engineering 2012 Forum Other Conferences in 2012 2012
Canadian Society for Mechanical Engineering 2013 24th Biennial Canadian Congress of Applied Mechanics (CANCAM) Other Conferences in 2013 2013
Canadian Society for Mechanical Engineering 2014 Forum Other Conferences in 2014 2014
Canadian Society for Mechanical Engineering 2015 25th Biennial Canadian Congress of Applied Mechanics (CANCAM) Other Conferences in 2015 2015,
Publications: *From Steam to Space. . . Contributions of Mechanical Engineering to Canadian Development Number of Pages:* 400 *Editor:* Andrew H. Wilson *Price:* $25 softcover; $50 hardcover
Profile: Essays, memoirs, & photographs
Transactions of the Canadian Society for Mechanical Engineering
Type: Journal *Frequency:* q. *Editor:* Paul J. Zsombor-Murray
ISSN: 0315-8977 *Price:* $40 / year for members of the Canadian Society for Mechanical Engineering
Profile: Scholarly papers of a reference or archival nature in the field of mechanical engineering or related disciplines
CSME [Canadian Society for Mechanical Engineering] Bulletin
Type: Newsletter *Frequency:* 3 pa *Editor:* Kamran Siddiqui, PhD
Price: Free with membership in the Canadian Society for Mechanical Engineering
Profile: News & articles of a general technical nature, covering all aspects of the practice of mechanical engineering
Mission: To benefit Canada & the world by fostering excellence in the practice of mechanical engineering; To support members; *Affiliation(s):* Engineering Institute of Canada

Canadian Society for Medical Laboratory Science (CSMLS) / Société canadienne de science de laboratoire médical
PO Box 2830, Stn. LCD 1, 33 Wellington Ave. North, Hamilton ON L8N 3N8
Tel: 905-528-8642; *Fax:* 905-528-4968
URL: www.csmls.org
Previous Name: Canadian Society of Laboratory Technologists
Overview: A large national licensing organization founded in 1937
Finances: *Funding Sources:* Membership dues
Membership: 15,000-49,999; *Fees:* $142 active & affiliate; $85 inactive; $62 certified retired; $112 laboratory assistant; $78-$102 student; *Member Profile:* Certified medical laboratory technologists; *Committees:* Marketing & Communications; Professional Development; Council on National Certification; National Advocacy Council; National Regulatory Council
Activities: Develops competency profiles; conducts examinations across Canada & issues certificates of qualification; offers certification in general medical laboratory technology, cytology & clinical genetics; *Awareness Events:* National Medical Laboratory Week, 3rd week of April
Awards: CSMLS Student Scholarship Program (Award)
Awarded to the best students who are enrolled in general medical laboratory technology, cytotechnology, or cytogenetics studies *Deadline:* Nov. 1 *Award Amount:* Five scholarships of $500 each
E.V. Booth Scholarship Award (Award)
Awarded to certified medical laboratory technologists who are enrolled in studies leading to a degree in medical laboratory science *Award Amount:* Two awards of $500
Honorary Awards & Fellowship Awards (Award)

Publications: *Canadian Journal of Medical Laboratory Science*
Type: Journal *Frequency:* bi-m.
Profile: Articles on trends in medical laboratory science & other professional issues, book reviews, & a regular column on laboratory safety
Mission: To promote & maintain a nationally accepted standard of medical laboratory technology; to promote, maintain, & protect professional identity & interests of medical laboratory technologists; *Member of:* International Federation of Biomedical Laboratory Science; *Affiliation(s):* International Association of Medical Laboratory Technologists; Intersociety Council of Laboratory Medicine; Conjoint Council on Accreditation of Allied Programs in Health Care

Canadian Society for the Study of Allergy; Canadian Academy of Allergy See Canadian Society of Allergy & Clinical Immunology

Canadian Society for the Study of Practical Ethics (CSSPE) / Société canadienne pour l'étude de l'éthique appliquée (SCEEA)
c/o Dept. of Philosophy, #618, Jorgenson Hall, Ryerson Univ., 350 Victoria St., Toronto ON M5B 2K3
Tel: 416-979-5000; *Fax:* 416-979-5362
URL: www.csspe.ca
Overview: A small national organization founded in 1987
Chief Officer(s):
Philip MacEwen, President
pmacewen@yorku.ca
Sandra Tomsons, Vice-President
stomsons@mts.net
Angela White, Secretary-Treasurer
awhite33@uwo.ca
Member Profile: Persons interested in practical ethics, from a variety of fields, such as academia, business, & the civil service
Activities: Addressing ethical issues which arise in areas of learning & activitiy, such as the social sciences & professions
Mission: To study all areas of practical ethics, including environmental ethics, health care ethics, bioethics, & business ethics

Canadian Society for Tropical Medicine & International Health See Canadian Society for International Health

Canadian Society of Agronomy
S.C. Sheppard, PO Box 637, Pinawa MB R0E 1L0
Tel: 204-753-2747; *Fax:* 204-753-8478
e-mail: sheppards@ecomatters.com
URL: www.agronomycanada.com
Overview: A medium-sized national organization
Membership: 300
Mission: The mission of The Canadian Society of Agronomy is dedicated to enhancing cooperation and coorindation among agronomists, to recognizing significant achievements in agronomy and to providing the oppourtunity to report and evaluate information pertinent to agronomy in Canada. The goals and objects include networking; external relations and awareness; and internal communications and coordination.; *Member of:* Agricultural Institute of Canada

Canadian Society of Air Safety Investigators (CSASI)
139 West 13th Ave., Vancouver BC V5Y 1V8
e-mail: avsafe@rogers.com
Overview: A small international organization founded in 1975
Fees: $100 annual fee; $65 initiation fee; $25 student annual fee; $20 student initiation fee; *Member Profile:* Canadian aircraft accident investigators; Students
Publications: *Canadian Society of Air Safety Investigators Proceedings*
Price: Free with CSASA membership
Profile: Papers presented at each seminar
ISASI Forum
Frequency: q. *Price:* Free with CSASA membership
Canadian Society of Air Safety Investigators Newsletter
Type: Newsletter *Price:* Free with CSASA membership
Mission: To ensure air safety through investigation; *Affiliation(s):* International Society of Air Safety Investigators

Canadian Society of Allergy & Clinical Immunology (CSACI) / Société canadienne d'allergie et d'immunologie clinique
774 Echo Dr., Ottawa ON K1S 5N8
Tel: 613-730-6272; *Fax:* 613-730-1116
e-mail: csaci@rcpsc.edu
URL: www.csaci.ca

Previous Name: Canadian Society for the Study of Allergy; Canadian Academy of Allergy
Overview: A small national organization founded in 1945
Chief Officer(s):
Charles Frankish, President
Richard Warrington, Vice-President
Stuart Carr, Secretary-Treasurer
Finances: *Funding Sources:* Donations; Sponsorships
Activities: Conducting research; Engaging in advocacy activities; Offering continuing professional development; Providing education to the public
Publications: *Allergy, Asthma & Clinical Immunology: Official Journal of the Canadian Society of Allergy & Clinical Immunology*
Type: Journal *Frequency:* q.
CSACI [Canadian Society of Allergy & Clinical Immunology] Newsletter / Bulletin CSAIC
Type: Newsletter *Frequency:* bi-m.
Profile: CSACI activities, events, & awards
Mission: To ensure optimal patient care by advancing the knowledge & practice of allergy, clinical immunology, & asthma

Canadian Society of Animal Science (CSAS) / Société canadienne de science animale
c/o Agriculture & Agri-Food Canada Research Station, CP 90, #2000, rte 108 est, Sherbrooke QC J1M 1Z3
Tél: 819-565-9171; *Téléc:* 819-564-5507
Courriel: info@aic.ca
URL: www.csas.net
Aperçu: *Dimension:* moyenne; *Envergure:* nationale; *fondée en 1951*
Membre: 500-999; *Critères d'admissibilite:* Membership is open to persons currently or previously employed in research, teaching, administration, extension, production, marketing, or otherwise interested in any field pertaining to the animal industry. There are three categories for membership; regular, retired, or student members (undergraduate or graduate).; *Comités:* Awards; Membership
Prix, Bouses: Honorary Life Memberships (Prix)
Young Scientist Award (Prix)
Fellowship Award (Prix)
Award for Excellence in Nutrition & Meat Sciences (Prix)
Animal Industries Award in Extension & Public Service (Prix)
Award for Technical Innovation in Enhancing Production of Safe Affordable Food (Prix)
Mission: To provide opportunities to discuss the problems of the Canadian animal & poultry industries, with the objective of furthering advancements in these industries; To assist in the coordination of research, teaching & technology transfer related to the animal & poultry industries; To encourage publication of scientific information; To provide an annual forum for professionals in the agricultural industry to meet & discuss the most recent technological advancements in the field of animal & poultry science; *Membre de:* Agricultural Institute of Canada

The Canadian Society of Biochemistry, Molecular & Cellular Biology / Société canadienne de biochimie et de biologie moléculaire et cellulaire
Parent: Canadian Federation of Biological Societies
c/o Department of Biochemistry, University of Toronto, Medical Sciences Bldg., 1 King's College Circle, Toronto ON M5S 1A8
Tel: 416-978-0774
e-mail: rob.reedijk@utoronto.ca
URL: www.csbmcb.ca
Previous Name: Canadian Biochemical Society
Overview: A medium-sized national organization founded in 1958
Finances: *Annual Operating Budget:* $100,000-$250,000; *Funding Sources:* Membership fees
Staff: 12 volunteer(s)
Membership: 100 student + 50 senior/lifetime + 650 other; *Member Profile:* Demonstrated interest in biochemistry research
Activities: *Internships:* Yes; *Rents Mailing List:* Yes
Publications: *CSBMCB [The Canadian Society of Biochemistry, Molecular & Cellular Biology] Bulletin*
Type: Newsletter
Profile: CSBMCB activites, meeting minutes, lectures, awards, & news from member departments

Canadian Society of Clinical Chemists (CSCC) / Société canadienne des clinico-chimistes
PO Box 1570, #310, 4 Cataraqui St., Kingston ON K7L 5C8
Tel: 613-531-8899; *Fax:* 613-531-0626
URL: www.cscc.ca
Overview: A medium-sized national organization founded in 1965

Member Profile: Clinical biochemists throughout Canada
Activities: Providing leadership, education, & research in the practice of clinical biochemistry & clinical laboratory medicine; Liaising with goverment, industry, & healthcare associations; Engaging in advocacy activities
Publications: *Clinical Biochemistry*
Type: Journal *Editor:* Edgard E. Delvin *ISSN:* 0009-9120
Profile: Analytical & clinical investigative articles related to molecular biology, chemistry, biochemistry, immunology, clinical investigation, diagnosis, therapy, & monitoring human disease, for chemists, immunologists, biologists, & biochemists
The CSCC [Canadian Society of Clinical Chemists] News
Type: Newsletter
Profile: Society activities & information for CSCC members
Canadian Society of Clinical Chemists Member Handbook
Type: Yearbook *Frequency:* a.
Mission: To establish standards for diagnostic services in the practice of clinical biochemistry & clinical laboratory medicine

Canadian Society of Environmental Biologists (CSEB) / Société canadienne des biologistes de l'environnement
PO Box 962, Stn. F, Toronto ON M4Y 2N9
e-mail: cseb_on@hotmail.com
URL: www.cseb-scbe.org
Overview: A medium-sized national charitable organization founded in 1943
Finances: *Annual Operating Budget:* Less than $50,000; *Funding Sources:* Membership dues
Staff: 2 staff member(s); 30 volunteer(s)
Membership: 500; *Fees:* $35; *Member Profile:* Regular - graduate from college or university in discipline of biological sciences, professionally engaged in teaching, management or research related to natural resources & the environment; Student - persons enrolled in accredited college or university in discipline of biological sciences & preparing themselves for professional work in teaching, management or research related to natural resources; Associate - supporters in general
Activities: *Speaker Service:* Yes; *Rents Mailing List:* Yes
Publications: *CSEB [Canadian Society of Environmental Biologists] National Newsletter / Bulletin*
Type: Newsletter *Frequency:* q. *Accepts Advertising* : Yes *Editor:* Gary Ash *ISSN:* 0318-5133 *Price:* Free with Canadian Society of Environmental Biologists membership
Profile: CSEB activities, & national & regional news, for members
Mission: To further the conservation of natural resources of Canada & to promote the prudent management of these resources so as to minimize adverse environmental effects; to ensure high professional standards in education, research & management related to resources & environment; to advance the education of the public & to protect public interest on matters pertaining to the use of natural resources & the protection & management of the environment; to undertake environmental research & education programs; to assess & evaluate administrative & legislative policies having ecological significance in terms of conservation of resources & quality of the environment; to develop & promote policies that seek to achieve balance among resource management & utilization, protection of the environment & quality of life; to foster liaison among environmental biologists working within governmental, industrial & educational frameworks across Canada

Canadian Society of Exploration Geophysicists (CSEG)
#600, 640 - 8th Ave. SW, Calgary AB T2P 1G7
Tel: 403-262-0015
e-mail: cseg.office@shaw.ca
URL: www.cseg.ca
Overview: A medium-sized national organization founded in 1949
Finances: *Funding Sources:* Membership fees
Membership: 1,800; *Member Profile:* Geophysicists involved in hydrocarbon exploration; Geologists; Field specialists; Technical specialists; Academics; Interested industry personnel; Corporate members
Activities: Offering a mentorship program; Exchanging technical information; Providing networking activities
Meetings/Conferences:
For more information see Trade Shows, Conferences and Seminars Chapter
Canadian Society of Exploration Geophysicists, Canadian Society of Petroleum Geologists & Canadian Well Logging Society 2012 Joint Annual Convention
Other Conferences in 2012 2012
Canadian Society of Exploration Geophysicists, Canadian Society of Petroleum Geologists & Canadian Well Logging Society 2013 Joint Annual Convention
Other Conferences in 2013 2013
Canadian Society of Exploration Geophysicists, Canadian Society of Petroleum Geologists & Canadian Well Logging Society 2014 Joint Annual Convention
Other Conferences in 2014 2014
Publications: *Canadian Society of Exploration Geophysicists Annual Report*
Type: Yearbook *Frequency:* a.
Recorder
Type: Magazine *Frequency:* m. *Accepts Advertising* : Yes
Profile: Canadian Society of Exploration Geophysicists membership news, & events, plus articles related to geophysics
The CSEG / CSPG Geophysical Atlas of Western Canadian Hydrocarbon Pools
Type: Atlas *Editor:* Leonard V. Hills
Mission: To promote the science of geophysics; *Affiliation(s):* Society of Exploration Geophysicists (USA); European Association of Geoscientists & Engineers

Canadian Society of Forest Engineers *See* Canadian Institute of Forestry

Canadian Society of Laboratory Technologists *See* Canadian Society for Medical Laboratory Science

Canadian Society of Landscape Architects (CSLA) / Association des architectes paysagistes du Canada (AAPC)
PO Box 13594, Ottawa ON K2K 1X6
Tel: 866-781-9799; *Fax:* 866-871-1419
e-mail: info@csla.ca
URL: www.csla.ca
Overview: A medium-sized national organization founded in 1934
Finances: *Annual Operating Budget:* $100,000-$250,000; *Funding Sources:* Membership dues
Staff: 40 volunteer(s)
Membership: 1,250 individuals; *Fees:* $115; *Member Profile:* Qualified & experienced landscape architects who practise their profession by providing a variety of services ranging from advice, consultation & design to preparing working drawings, contract documents & supervising the implementation of various size construction projects;
Publications: *Landscapes / Paysages*
Type: Journal *Frequency:* q. *Accepts Advertising* : Yes
Profile: Articles about the professional practice of landscape architecture in Canada, related to culture, design, & the environment
CSLA [Canadian Society of Landscape Architects] Bulletin
Type: Newsletter *Language:* B *Frequency:* m.
Profile: News & events related to landscape architecture in Canada
CSLA [Canadian Society of Landscape Architects] Membership Directory
Type: Directory
CSLA [Canadian Society of Landscape Architects] Annual Report
Type: Yearbook *Frequency:* a.
Mission: To support the improvement &/or conservation of the natural, cultural, social & built environment; to promote visibility, recognition, acceptance & understanding of the profession by communicating its value in relation to that of the public good; *Affiliation(s):* International Federation of Landscape Architects; Landscape Alliance

Canadian Society of Microbiologists (CSM) / Société canadienne des microbiologistes
CSM-SCM Secretariat, #305, 1750 Courtwood Cres., Ottawa ON K2C 2B5
Tel: 613-225-8889; *Fax:* 613-225-9621
e-mail: info@csm-scm.org
URL: www.csm-scm.org
Overview: A medium-sized national organization founded in 1958
Finances: *Annual Operating Budget:* $100,000-$250,000
Staff: 2 staff member(s)
Membership: 450; *Fees:* $75; *Member Profile:* open; *Committees:* Education; Manpower Placement; Science Policy; Regulatory Issues
Publications: *CSM [Canadian Society of Microbiologists] Newsletter*
Type: Newsletter *Frequency:* 3 pa
Canadian Society of Microbiologists Call for Abstracts
Type: Booklet *Frequency:* a.
Profile: Published in advance of the Annual General Meeting in November / December
Canadian Society of Microbiologists Programme & Abstracts
Frequency: a.
Profile: Published for the Annual General Meeting each May
Canadian Society of Microbiologists Graduate Studies & Membership Directory
Type: Directory *Frequency:* biennial
Mission: To advance microbiology in all its aspects; to facilitate interchange of ideas between microbiologists; *Affiliation(s):* Youth Science Foundation; International Union of Microbiological Societies

Canadian Society of Petroleum Geologists (CSPG)
#600, 640 - 8th Ave. SW, Calgary AB T2P 1G7
Tel: 403-264-5610; *Fax:* 403-264-5898
e-mail: cspg@cspg.org
URL: www.cspg.org
Previous Name: Alberta Society of Petroleum Geologists
Overview: A medium-sized national organization founded in 1929
Finances: *Annual Operating Budget:* $250,000-$500,000; *Funding Sources:* Membership dues; publications; programs; trust fund
Staff: 3 staff member(s); 300+ volunteer(s)
Membership: 3,500; *Fees:* $65; $20 students; $500 corporate
Activities: Education trust fund; member programs
Awards: CSPG Graduate Scholarships (Scholarship)
Three scholarships available (Atlantic, Ontario/Québec & Western) in petroleum geology, one in marine geoscience; awarded to a second year graduate student *Deadline:* 1-May *Award Amount:* $1,500
Publications: *Reservoir [a publication of the Canadian Society of Petroleum Geologists]*
Type: Magazine *Frequency:* 11 pa *Accepts Advertising* : Yes *Editor:* Heather Tyminski *Price:* $60 Canada; $70 USA; $80 International
Profile: Industry articles & commentaries, conferences, upcoming events, & awards of interest to CSPG members
The Bulletin of Canadian Petroleum Geology
Type: Journal *Frequency:* q. *Accepts Advertising* : Yes *Editor:* Denise Then *ISSN:* 0007-4802 *Price:* $120 Canada; $140 USA; $170 International
Profile: Peer-reviewed scientific articles, technical papers, book reviews, & debates of interest to the Canadian petroleum geoscience community
Digital Atlas: Geological Atlas of the Western Canada Sedimentary Basin
Profile: Created by CSPG & the Alberta Geologic Survey (AGS)
Canadian Society of Petroleum Geologists Calendar
Frequency: a.
Profile: Photographs & CSPG, CSEG, APEGGA, & CWLS events
Mission: To advance the science of geology, especially as it relates to petroleum, natural gas & other fossil fuels; to promote the technology of exploration for finding & producing these resources; to foster the spirit of scientific research; to develop a sense of pride & community among Canadian Petroleum Geologists; to provide the means to ensure that the Canadian Petroleum Geologist is the best trained, best supported & most skillful practitioner in the world

Canadian Society of Plant Physiologists (CSPP) / Société canadienne de physiologie végétale (SCPV)
c/o Dr. Harold Weger, Department of Biology, University of Regina, 3737 Wascana Pkwy., Regina SK S4S 0A2
e-mail: treasurer@cspp-scpvca.ca
URL: www.cspp-scpv.ca
Overview: A small national organization founded in 1958
Member Profile: Plant scientists in Canada; Retired members; Students; Persons who live outside Canada are eligible for corresponding membership; *Committees:* Society (Gold) Medal Award; C.D. Nelson Award; David J. Gifford Tree Physiology Award; Gleb Krotkov Award; Ann Oaks Scholarship; Ragai Ibrahim Award; Communications; Education; Meeting Site; Nominating; Auditors
Activities: Facilitating the exchange of information; Promoting the importance of research in plant sciences; Liaising with other educational, non-profi, or governmental agencies or organizations to develop the science of plant physiology
Awards: C.D. Nelson Award (Award)
To honour outstanding research contributions to plant physiology
Gleb Krotkov Award of the CSPP (Award)
To honour outstanding service to the Society

The Gold Medal Award (The CSPP Medal) (Award)
To recognize either outstanding published contributions or distinguished service to plant physiology
David J. Gifford Award in Tree Physiology (Award)
To recognize outstanding research contributions in tree physiology
The President's Awards (Award)
To recognize the best student oral & poster presentations at the Annual General Meeting
The Regional Directors' Awards (Award)
To recognize the best student oral & poster presentations at the Eastern and Western Regional Meetings
Ragai Ibrahim Award (Award)
To recognize the best student paper
Publications: *CSPP [Canadian Society of Plant Physiologists] / SCPV [Société canadienne de physiologie végétale] Bulletin*
Type: Newsletter Frequency: s-a. Editor: Gordon Gray ISSN: 1183-9597
Profile: Issues related to plant biology, & CSPP / SCPV events, activites, awards, & financial information, of interest to society members
Canadian Society of Plant Physiologists Membership List
Mission: To promote the teaching & public awareness of plant physiology in Canada

Canadian Society of Safety Engineering, Inc. (CSSE) / Société canadienne de la santé et de la sécurité, inc.
39 River St., Toronto ON M5A 3P1
Tel: 416-646-1600; Fax: 416-646-9460
e-mail: wglover@associationsfirst.com
URL: www.csse.org
Previous Name: Ontario Society of Safety Engineering
Overview: A medium-sized national organization founded in 1949
Finances: *Annual Operating Budget:* $250,000-$500,000; *Funding Sources:* Membership dues; educational programs
Staff: 7 staff member(s); 50 volunteer(s)
Membership: 30 associate + 100 student + 45 senior/lifetime + 2,000 individual; *Fees:* $150; *Member Profile:* Open to those employed full-time in occupational health, safety & environment work
Activities: Certification program for Health & Safety Consultant; *Awareness Events:* Canadian Occupational Health & Safety Week, 1st week of June; *Speaker Service:* Yes; *Rents Mailing List:* Yes
Publications: *CSSE [Canadian Society of Safety Engineering, Inc.] Contact*
Type: Newsletter Frequency: q. Price: Free with CSSE membership; $100 non-members
Mission: To be the voice of safety in Canada; *Affiliation(s):* American Society of Safety Engineers

Canadian Society of Soil Science (CSSS) / Société canadienne de la science du sol
Business Office, PO Box 637, Pinawa MB R0E 1L0
Tel: 204-753-2747; Fax: 204-753-8478
e-mail: sheppards@ecomatters.com
URL: www.csss.ca
Overview: A medium-sized national charitable organization
Finances: *Funding Sources:* Membership dues
Membership: 100-499; *Member Profile:* Open to those concerned with farming practices as they affect soil quality & the development of soil conserving cropping practices, or those concerned with non-agricultural uses of soils, including forestry, engineering, & reclamation
Activities: *Speaker Service:* Yes
Publications: *Canadian Journal of Soil Science*
Type: Journal Frequency: q. Editor: Dr. F.J. Larney
Profile: International peer-reviewed original research related to the development, structure, use, & management of soils
CSSS [Canadian Society of Soil Science] Newsletter
Type: Newsletter Frequency: 3 pa Price: Free with CSSS membership
Profile: CSSS activities, awards, events, & reports
Mission: To be actively engaged in land use, soils research, & classification; *Member of:* Agricultural Institute of Canada; *Affiliation(s):* International Union of Soil Science

Canadian Society of Zoologists (CSZ) / Société canadienne de zoologie (SCZ)
c/o Fisheries & Oceans Canada, 531 Brandy Cove Rd., St Andrews NB E5B 2L9
Tel: 506-529-5889; Fax: 506-529-5862
e-mail: martelldj@mar.dfo-mpo.gc.ca
URL: www.csz-scz.ca
Overview: A medium-sized national organization founded in 1961
Finances: *Annual Operating Budget:* Less than $50,000; *Funding Sources:* Membership fees
Staff: 23 volunteer(s)
Membership: 373; *Fees:* $80 regular; $20 student, associate, & emeritus; *Member Profile:* Working in zoology; *Committees:* Membership; Recognition; Science Policy; Biodiversity; Animal Care Advisory; Collections Advisory; Outstanding Ph.D. Thesis; Communications; Nominating
Awards: CSZ Public Awarensss Award - Public Education Prize (Award)
Intended to recognize excellent in public education about zoology Award Amount: $300
Helen Battle Award (Award)
Cash prize & scroll, given for the best student poster at the Annual Conference Award Amount: $200
Leo Margolis Scholarship (Scholarship)
Presented to a Canadian who is registered in a graduate studies program at a Canadian university, whose research is in the field of fisheries biology Award Amount: $500
CSZ Student Research Grant (Grant)
To assist students & post-doctoral fellows from Canadian Universities to conduct zoological research Award Amount: Up to $500
CSZ Public Awareness Award; Best issue driven popular press article (Award)
Cash prize & scroll, intended to encourage & stimulate members to increase public awarenss of zoology through articles in the popular press Award Amount: $500
Fry Award - Outstanding Biologist of the Year (Award)
Receives the Fry Medal, delivers the Fry Lecture at the AGM, full travel expenses are reimbursed
Fry Award & Medal - Outstanding Zoologist of the Year (Award)
Recipient receives the Fry Medal, delivers the Fry Lecture at the Annual Meeting
CSZ Distinguished Service Medal (Award)
Scroll & medal, presented at the AGM; recognizing members who have contributed to the well being of zoology in Canada, by working hard for the CSZ
T.W.M. Cameron Outstanding Ph.D. Thesis Award (Award)
Recipient is invited to present a lecture of their dissertation to the AGM
Hoar Award (Award)
Cash prize & scroll given for the best student paper presented orally at the Annual Conference Award Amount: $500
CSZ New Investigator Award (Award)
Scroll & cash award to an individual, who since professional appointment, has made a significant contribution to zoology & may be considered a 'rising star' in their field Award Amount: Up to $500
Publications: *Canadian Society of Zoologists / Société canadienne de zoologie Bulletin*
Type: Newsletter Language: B Frequency: 3 pa Editor: Sally Leys ISSN: 0319-6674 Price: Free with CSZ / SCZ membership
Profile: CSZ / SCZ reports, events, articles, & interviews
Mission: To promote advancement & public awareness of zoology; to facilitate sharing of knowledge & ideas among all persons interested in science & practice of zoology; to organize discussions & debates of general interest; *Affiliation(s):* Canadian Council on Animal Care; Canadian Federation of Biological Societies

Canadian Solar Industries Association Inc. (CanSIA) / Association des industries solaires du Canada inc.
#208, 2378 Holly Lane, Ottawa ON K1V 7P1
Tel: 613-736-9077; Fax: 613-736-8938
Toll-Free: 866-522-6742
e-mail: info@cansia.ca
URL: www.cansia.ca
Merged from: Canadian Photovoltaic Industries Association
Overview: A medium-sized national organization founded in 1978
Finances: *Annual Operating Budget:* $50,000-$100,000; *Funding Sources:* Government contracts; membership fees; fees for service
Staff: 3 staff member(s); 10 volunteer(s)
Membership: 110 corporate; *Fees:* $250 corporate; $75 associate; *Member Profile:* Professional people involved in the solar industry, who promote solar energy on a daily basis; those who lobby the governments, educate the public & inform the media
Activities: *Library:* Yes
Publications: *Canadian Solar Industries Association Inc. Membership Directory*
Type: Directory Frequency: a. Accepts Advertising : Yes
SOLutions [a publication of the Canadian Solar Industries Association Inc.]
Type: Magazine Frequency: s-a. Accepts Advertising : Yes
Mission: To establish programs & activities to develop greater understanding of & acceleration of the use of solar energy; to enhance the growth & effectiveness of the industry & its individual members; to advance the contributions of the members; to ensure government has an understanding of the contribution a viable solar equipment industry base can make to Canada; to coordinate activities with regard to product standards, with emphasis on safety, performance, & economic impact; to collect statistics, to carry on research, experiments, conferences & publications that advance the membership; to develop working relationship with other national & international associations; to aid those engaged in or having an interest in the furthering any objectives; to promote the welfare of the Canadian solar industry to the public & governments

Canadian Space Society (CSS) / La société canadienne de l'espace
Parc Downsview Park, 65 Carl Hall Rd., Toronto ON M3K 2E1
URL: www.css.ca
Overview: A small national organization founded in 1983
Chief Officer(s):
Kevin Shortt, President
president@css.ca
Vivian Lee, Coordinator, Membership
membership@css.ca
Fees: $40 regular members; $15 students; *Member Profile:* Professionals & individuals interested in the exploration of the solar system, including engineers, teachers, environmentalists, & writers
Activities: Increasing knowledge of space & space-related technologies among members & the public; Providing feedback to the government on legislation that impacts Canadian space development
Publications: *Canadian Space Gazette*
Frequency: q. Accepts Advertising : Yes
Profile: Current affairs in space development & exploration of interest to the Canadian space community
Mission: To conduct technical & outreach projects; to promote the involvement of Canadians in space development

Canadian Sphagnum Peat Moss Association (CSPMA) / Association canadienne Tourbe de Sphaigne
#2208, 13 Mission Ave., St Albert AB T8N 1H6
Tel: 780-460-8280; Fax: 780-459-0939
e-mail: cspma@peatmoss.com
URL: www.peatmoss.com
Overview: A medium-sized national organization founded in 1988
Finances: *Annual Operating Budget:* $250,000-$500,000; *Funding Sources:* Membership dues
Staff: 2 staff member(s)
Membership: 18 producers; *Member Profile:* Producer/broker of Canadian peat moss; supplier to industry
Mission: To promote the benefits of peat moss to horticulturists and home gardeners throughout North America.; *Member of:* Canadian Society of Association Executives
Environmental Activity: Restoration & restoration research

Canadian Standards Association (CSA)
#100, 5060 Spectrum Way, Mississauga ON L4W 5N6
Tel: 416-747-4000; Fax: 416-747-2473
Toll-Free: 800-463-6727
e-mail: member@csa.ca; sales@csa.ca; seminars@csa.ca; elearning@csa.ca
URL: www.csa.ca
Overview: A medium-sized national organization
Chief Officer(s):
Bonnie Rose, President
Finances: *Funding Sources:* Sponsorships
Activities: Presenting e-learning, seminars, & training opportunities, through the CSA Learning Centre, to assist people to understand standards; Reviewing & considering adopted & adapted standards from other organizations & countries
Meetings/Conferences:
For more information see Trade Shows, Conferences and Seminars Chapter
Canadian Standards Association 2011 Annual Conference & Committee Week
June 2011 Victoria, BC

Canadian Standards Association 2012 Annual Conference & Committee Week
Other Conferences in 2012 2012
Canadian Standards Association 2013 Annual Conference & Committee Week
Other Conferences in 2013 2013
Publications: *Canadian Standards Association Annual Report*
Type: Yearbook Frequency: a.
Profile: A review of the association's activities for the past year
Perspectives [a publication of the Canadian Standards Association]
Type: Newsletter Editor: James Harrison
Profile: Current information about standards development initiatives for members
Mission: To develop new standards & codes to meet needs, such as public health & safety & the facilitation of trade; To contribute to the global harmonization of standards; To serve government, industry, business, & consumers in Canada & the worldwide marketplace; Member of: CSA Group
Environmental Activity: Establishing standards which will help to preserve the environment

Canadian Steel Construction Council (CSCC) / Conseil canadien de la construction en acier
#300, 201 Consumers Rd., Toronto ON M2J 4G8
Tel: 416-491-9898; Fax: 416-491-6461
e-mail: hakrentz@telus.net
Previous Name: Canadian Steel Industries Construction Council
Overview: A medium-sized national organization founded in 1960
Membership: 9; Committees: Codes & Standards; Fire Protection
Activities: Speaker Service: Yes; Library: Yes,
Mission: To represent the manufacturers of steel products, including: open-web steel joists, steel platework, corrugated steel pipe, sheet steel, & steel fasteners; to promote the use of steel in construction through research & engineering; Affiliation(s): Canadian Institute of Steel Construction; Steel Structures Education Foundation

Canadian Steel Industries Construction Council *See* Canadian Steel Construction Council

Canadian Steel Partnership Council (CSPC)
#407, 350 Sparks St., Ottawa ON K1R 7S8
Tel: 613-238-6049; Fax: 613-238-1832
Overview: A small national organization
Chief Officer(s):
Ron Watkins, President, CSPA
Mission: To address the global competitiveness & sustainability of the Canadian steel industry; Affiliation(s): Canadian Steel Producers Association

Canadian Steel Producers Association (CSPA) / Association canadienne des producteurs d'acier (ACPA)
#906, 350 Sparks St., Ottawa ON K1R 7S8
Tel: 613-238-6049; Fax: 613-238-1832
e-mail: info@canadiansteel.ca
URL: www.canadiansteel.ca
Overview: A medium-sized national organization founded in 1986
Finances: Annual Operating Budget: $500,000-$1.5 Million; Funding Sources: Membership dues
Staff: 4 staff member(s)
Membership: 17; Committees: Communications; Environment; Climate Change; Statistics; Trade; Research & Development
Mission: To represent the steel producers that melt & pour steel in Canada

Canadian Sugar Beet Producers' Association Inc. (CSBPA)
Parent: Canadian Federation of Agriculture
4900 - 50 St., Taber AB T1G 1T3
Tel: 403-223-1110; Fax: 403-223-1022
e-mail: sugarmb@telusplanet.net
Overview: A medium-sized national organization founded in 1943
Chief Officer(s):
Bruce Webster, General Manager
sugarmb@telusplanet.net
Finances: Annual Operating Budget: $250,000-$500,000
Staff: 2 staff member(s)
Membership: 470; Member Profile: Member must be sugar beet grower.; Committees: Executive

Mission: To represent interests of Canadian sugar beet growers on provincial & federal government levels & on an international level through the World Association of Beet & Cane Growers; to raise public profile of the beet sugar industry.; Affiliation(s): World Association of Beet & Cane Growers

Canadian Swine Breeders' Association (CSBA) / L'Association canadienne des éleveurs de porcs
Bldg 54, Central Experiemental Farm, 930 Carling Ave., Ottawa ON K1A 0C6
Tel: 613-731-5531; Fax: 613-233-8903
e-mail: canswine@canswine.ca
URL: www.canswine.ca
Previous Name: Purebred Swine Breeders' Association of Canada
Overview: A medium-sized national organization founded in 1889
Finances: Annual Operating Budget: $100,000-$250,000
Staff: 3 staff member(s)
Membership: 120; Fees: Schedule available; Member Profile: Four classes: honorary, life, annual, non-resident; Committees: Promotion
Mission: To improve & promote Canadian purebred swine; to lobby on behalf of purebred swine breeders in Canada; to direct & regulate purebred swine industry; to be involved in registration & transfer of following breeds: Berkshire, British Saddleback, Chester White, Duroc, Hampshire, Large Black, Pietrain, Poland China, Spotted, Tamworth, Welsh, Yorkshire, Landrace, Lacombe, Red Wattle (registration forms can be obtained from Canadian Livestock Records Corporation).

Canadian Swine Exporters Association (CSEA)
Tel: 519-421-0997; Fax: 519-421-0887
e-mail: csea@rogers.com
URL: www.canadianswine.com
Overview: A small national organization
Chief Officer(s):
Rosemary Smart, Intl Marketing Programs Coordinator
Membership: 19; Member Profile: Represents the top exporters from Canada
Mission: To assist the Canadian swine industry promote & market swine genetics worldwide

Canadian Transport Tariff Bureau Association *See* Freight Carriers Association of Canada

Canadian Transportation Research Forum (CTRF) / Groupe de recherches sur les transports au Canada
PO Box 23033, Woodstock ON N4T 1R0
Tel: 519-421-9701; Fax: 519-421-9319
e-mail: feedback@ctrf.ca, cawoudsma@ctrf.ca
URL: www.ctrf.ca
Overview: A medium-sized national charitable organization founded in 1967
Finances: Annual Operating Budget: Less than $50,000
Staff: 21 volunteer(s)
Membership: 320; Fees: $129; Member Profile: Open to anyone interested in any aspect of transportation; membership is individual rather than corporate; present membership is drawn from carriers, shippers, consultants & suppliers in the commercial sector, the policy, regulatory, planning & research environments at all levels of government, students & professors at universitites & community colleges
Awards: Scholarships for Graduate Study in Transportation (Scholarship)
In cooperation with several other organizations, offers up to five scholarships; field of study may be in business administration, civil engineering, economics, geography, law, planning, or other fields Deadline: Feb. 28 Award Amount: $4,000
Student Research Paper Competition (Award)
Prizes awarded annually for student papers dealing with transportation; prizes are awarded for the best undergraduate papers, the best papers at the master's level, & the best papers at the doctorate level
Mission: To promote the development of research in transportation & related fields; to publish research papers through media & through national & regional forum meetings.

Canadian Trucking Alliance (CTA) / L'Alliance canadienne du camionnage (ACC)
324 Somerset St. West, Ottawa ON K2P 0J9
Tel: 613-236-9426; Fax: 866-823-4076
e-mail: info@cantruck.ca
URL: www.cantruck.com
Overview: A medium-sized national organization founded in 1937

Member Profile: Motor carriers & associated trades
Activities: Speaker Service: Yes
Mission: To promote business excellence in trucking; to participate in the development of public policy which supports the economic growth, safety & prosperity of the industry; to provide services, including research, development, products & information to meet the needs of the industry.
PUBLICATIONS: Dangerous Goods: A Trucker's Guide; Crossing International Borders:A Trucker's Guide; National Safety Code: A Trucker's Guide.

Canadian University Service Overseas *See* CUSO-VSO

Canadian Urban Transit Association (CUTA) / Association canadienne du transport urbain (ACTU)
#1401, 55 York St., Toronto ON M5J 1R7
Tel: 416-365-9800; Fax: 416-365-1295
e-mail: transit@cutaactu.ca
URL: www.cutaactu.ca
Overview: A large national organization founded in 1904
Membership: 503; Member Profile: Transit systems; Manufacturers & suppliers of transit equipment; Federal, provincial, & municipal government agencies; Consultants; Affiliated individuals & companies; Committees: Business Members; Communications & Public Affairs; Human Resources; Technical Services; Transit Board Members
Activities: Conducting research & preparing statistics; Providing technical & operational information; Liaising with government; Partnering with other transportation associations & community development stakeholders; Engaging in advocacy activities; Raising public awareness of transit's contributions to communities; Library: Canadian Urban Transit Association Library; Not open to the public
Meetings/Conferences:
For more information see Trade Shows, Conferences and Seminars Chapter
Canadian Urban Transit Association Training Course: Transit Planning
June 2011 Abbotsford, BC
Canadian Urban Transit Association Training Course: SmartDRIVER Train the Trainer
September 2011 Burlington, ON
Canadian Urban Transit Association Training Course: Transit Ambassador Train the Trainer
September 2011 Victoria, BC
Canadian Urban Transit Association Training Course: Scheduling & Runcutting
September 2011 Parksville, BC
Canadian Urban Transit Association Training Course: SmartDRIVER Train the Trainer
October 2011 Halifax, NS
Canadian Urban Transit Association Training Course: Transit Ambassador Train the Trainer
October 2011 Calgary, AB
Canadian Urban Transit Association Training Course: Transit Maintenance & Asset Management
October 2011 Red Deer, AB
Canadian Urban Transit Association 2011 Fall Conference & Trans-Expo
November 2011 Toronto, ON
Canadian Urban Transit Association Training Course: Transit Ambassador Train the Trainer
November 2011 Brampton, ON
Canadian Urban Transit Association Training Course: Advanced Scheduling & Runcutting
November 2011 Oakville, ON
Canadian Urban Transit Association Training Course: Transit Ambassador Advanced Train the Trainer - Using the Additional Customer Service Modules
November 2011 Kitchener, ON
Canadian Urban Transit Association 2012 Annual Conference
May 2012 Victoria, BC
Canadian Urban Transit Association 2012 Fall Conference & Trans-Expo
November 2012 Québec, QC
Canadian Urban Transit Association 2013 Annual Conference
Other Conferences in 2013 2013 St. John's, NL
Canadian Urban Transit Association 2013 Fall Conference & Trans-Expo
November 2013 Calgary, AB
Canadian Urban Transit Association 2014 Annual Conference
Other Conferences in 2014 2014
Canadian Urban Transit Association 2014 Fall Conference & Trans-Expo
November 2014

Associations/Organizations / Canadian Urethane Foam Contractors Association

Canadian Urban Transit Association 2015 Annual Conference
Other Conferences in 2015 2015
Canadian Urban Transit Association 2015 Fall Conference & Trans-Expo
November 2015
Canadian Urban Transit Association 2016 Annual Conference
Other Conferences in 2016 2016
Canadian Urban Transit Association 2016 Fall Conference & Trans-Expo
November 2016
Publications: *Canadian Transit Forum*
Type: Magazine Frequency: Y
Profile: Transit industry news in Canada, plus special conference issues in May/June & November/December
EXPRESSions
Type: Newsletter Frequency: s-m.
Profile: Association activities & forthcoming events
CUTA Membership Directory
Type: Directory Frequency: a. Accepts Advertising : Yes Price: $50
Profile: Specific contact details for transit systems, suppliers, government agencies, consultants, & affiliate members
Canadian Urban Transit Association's Buyer's Guide
Type: Guide
Profile: Products & services organized by categories
Transit Vision 2040
Number of Pages: 74
Profile: An industry vision of the role of public transit in Canada
Mission: To represent the public transit community throughout Canada; To strengthen the industry
Environmental Activity: Strengthening public transit's contributions to the environment & health

Canadian Urethane Foam Contractors Association (CUFCA) / Association canadienne des entrepreneurs en mousse de polyuréthane
PO Box 3214, Winnipeg MB R3C 4E7
Tel: 204-956-5888; Fax: 204-956-5819
Toll-Free: 866-467-7729
e-mail: cufca@cufca.ca
URL: www.cufca.ca
Overview: A small national licensing organization founded in 1985
Fees: $500 general membership & contractors; $3,500 manufacturers; *Member Profile:* Manufacturers; Contractors
Activities: Liaising with government agencies; Encouraging professional development; Providing a quality assurance program; Promoting use of ray polyurethane foam; Facilitating research; Publishing; Implementing standards for materials
Mission: To champion the polyurethane foam industry in Canada; to maintain high standards in the industry; to ensure the professionalism & profitability of the industry

Canadian Urethane Manufacturers Association (CUMA)
151 Briarcliffe Cres., Waterloo ON N2L 5T6
Tel: 519-884-2855; Fax: 519-884-0653
URL: www.cumahome.org
Overview: A medium-sized national organization founded in 1974
Finances: Annual Operating Budget: Less than $50,000
Membership: 45 corporate; *Fees:* $375; *Member Profile:* Urethane processors & suppliers; *Committees:* Health; Safety; Environmental

Canadian Veterinary Medical Association (CVMA) / Association canadienne des médecins vétérinaires (ACMV)
339 Booth St., Ottawa ON K1R 7K1
Tel: 613-236-1162; Fax: 613-236-9681
e-mail: admin@cvma-acmv.org
URL: www.canadianveterinarians.net
Overview: A medium-sized national organization founded in 1948
Finances: Annual Operating Budget: $1.5 Million-$3 Million
Staff: 17 staff member(s)
Member Profile: Graduate in veterinary medicine; *Committees:* National Issues; Animal Welfare; Pet Food Certification; Professional Development; National Examining Board; Marketing; Communications & Public Relations; Business Management
Activities: *Awareness Events:* Animal Health Week, Oct.
Awards: CVMA Industry Award (Award)
Hill's Public Relations Award (Award)
CVMA Award (Award)
Established 1966; awarded annually to a veterinary student in the third year at each of the four Canadian veterinary colleges; the recipient is selected by his/her classmates on the basis of achievement & leadership in student affairs
R.V.L. Walker Award (Award)
Established 1986; awarded to an undergraduate student in one of the four veterinary colleges in Canada who has made the greatest contribution in promoting student interest in the Association; the recipient should have demonstrated active interest in student & college affairs & have a satisfactory student record
The Schering Veterinary Award (Award)
Established 1985 to enhance progress in large animal medicine & surgery; award made to a veterinarian whose work in large animal practice, clinical research or basic sciences is judged to have contributed significantly to the advancement of large animal medicine, surgery & theriogenology, including herd health management; $1,000 & a plaque awarded
CVMA Pet Food Certification & Nutrition Award (Award)
The Small Animal Practitioner Award (Award)
Established 1987 to encourage progress in the field of small animal medicine & surgery; awarded to a veterinarian whose work in small animal practice, clinical research or basic sciences is judged to have contributed significantly to the advancement of small animal medicine, surgery, or the management of small animal practice, including the advancement of the public's knowledge of the responsibilities of pet ownership; $1,000 & a plaque awarded
The CVMA Humane Award (Award)
Established 1986 to encourage care & well-being of animals; awarded to an individual (veterinarian or non-veterinarian) whose work is judged to have contributed significantly to the welfare & well-being of animals; $1,000 & a plaque awarded
Publications: *Canadian Veterinary Journal*
Type: Journal Frequency: m.
Canadian Journal of Veterinary Research
Type: Journal Frequency: q.
Mission: To represent the interests of the veterinary profession in Canada; commits to excellence within the profession & to the well-being of animals; promotes public awareness of the contribution of animals & veterinarians to society

Canadian Water & Wastewater Association (CWWA) / Association canadienne des eaux potables et usées (ACEPU)
#11, 1010 Polytek Rd., Ottawa ON K1J 9H9
Tel: 613-747-0524; Fax: 613-747-0523
e-mail: tdellison@cwwa.ca
URL: www.cwwa.ca
Overview: A medium-sized national organization founded in 1986
Member Profile: Utility members are owners or operators of municipal infrastructure or services; Associate members are the private sector & academics; Subscription members are federal, provincial, or territorial government departments or agencies; *Committees:* Wastewater & Stormwater; National Water Efficiency; Drinking Water Quality; Water Protection Information; Biosolids; Energy
Activities: Monitoring policies, legislation, & standards; Liaising with federal & interprovincial organizations; Hosting workshops; Facilitating networking opportunities; Increasing & improving public awareness; Cooperating with regional water & wastewater associations;
Awards: Steve Bonk Scholarship (Scholarship)
Meetings/Conferences:
For more information see Trade Shows, Conferences and Seminars Chapter
Drinking Water 2012 15th Biennial Canadian National Conference
Other Conferences in 2012 2012
Wastewater Management 2013 5th Biennial Canadian National Conference
Other Conferences in 2013 2013
Water Efficiency & Conservation 2013 5th Biennial Conference
Other Conferences in 2013 2013
Drinking Water 2014 16th Biennial Canadian National Conference
Other Conferences in 2014 2014
Wastewater Management 2015 6th Biennial Canadian National Conference
Other Conferences in 2015 2015
Water Efficiency & Conservation 2015 6th Biennial Conference
Other Conferences in 2015 2015
Publications: *CWWA [Canadian Water & Wastewater Association] Membership Directory*
Type: Directory Accepts Advertising : Yes
Profile: Directory acts as association information as well as a buyers' guide
CWWA [Canadian Water & Wastewater Association] Bulletin
Type: Newsletter Frequency: 10 pa
Profile: National information on water & wastewater developments, for CWWA members
Canadian Municipal Water News & Review
Type: Magazine Frequency: s-a.
Water Safety Plans for Municipal Drinking Water Systems
Profile: Hazard Analysis & Critical Control Points (HACCP) Plan for the source, treatment, & distribution of drinking water in Canada
CWWA Members' Briefing Book: Current National Issues & Topics Concerning Water & Wastewater Management in Canada
Frequency: q.
Profile: Briefing notes on current management topics that are national in nature, to assist managers & operators
Canadian Water & Wastewater Association Conference Proceedings
National Water Works Operator Training Manuals
Type: Manual
Meters Made Easy: A Guide to the Economic Appraisal of Alternative Metering Investment Strategies
Type: Guidebook
Profile: A tool to assist system owners & operators determine whether the introduction of meters will produce long-term savings in their community
Municipal Water & Wastewater Rate Manual
Type: Manual
Profile: New & alternative approaches to traditional & current rate setting methods
Municipal Water & Wastewater Rates Primer
Type: Monograph
Profile: An overview of topics on rate setting
Water Treatment Principles & Applications
Directory of Sources of Contaminants Entering Municipal Sewer Systems
Type: Directory
Profile: Aid in identifying industrial, commercial, & institutional sources of contaminants entering municipal sewage treatment plants
Mission: To represent the common interests of Canadian municipal water & wastewater systems to federal & interprovincial bodies; *Member of:* Canadian National Committee for the International Water Association
Environmental Activity: Addressing Canadian water & wastewater issues at the national level

Canadian Water Network (CWN) / Réseau canadien de l'eau
University of Waterloo, 200 University Ave. West, Waterloo ON N2L 3G1
Tel: 519-888-4567; Fax: 519-883-7574
e-mail: info@cwn-rce.ca
URL: www.cwn-rce.ca
Overview: A medium-sized national organization founded in 2001
Chief Officer(s):
Bernadette Conant, Director of Programs, 519-888-4567
bconant@cwn-rce.ca
Mark Servos, Scientific Director, 519-888-4567 Ext. 36034
mservos@uwaterloo.ca
David Cotter, Director of Communications, 519-888-4567 Ext. 37709
dcotter@cwn-rce.ca
Finances: Annual Operating Budget: $3 Million-$5 Million
Staff: 8 staff member(s)
Membership: 48 industrial, 65 government, 120 researchers, 200 students; *Fees:* None
Activities: Research funding, student development, national networking; *Internships:* Yes
Mission: To create a national partnership in innovation that promotes environmentally responsible stewardship & opportunities with respect to Canada's water resources resulting in sustained prosperity & improved quality of life for Canadians.; *Member of:* Networks of Centres of Excellence

Canadian Water Quality Association (CWQA)
#330, 295 The West Mall, Toronto ON M9C 4Z4
Tel: 416-695-3068; Fax: 416-695-2945
Toll-Free: 866-383-7617
e-mail: k.wong@cwqa.com
URL: www.cwqa.com
Overview: A medium-sized national organization founded in 1967

Chief Officer(s):
Kevin Wong, Executive Director
Membership: 106 dealers/distributors + 16 manufacturers/suppliers + 10 associates; *Fees:* $355 associate; Based on volume for dealer/distributor & manufacturer/supplier
Publications: *Communiqué [a publication of the Canadian Water Quality Association]*
Frequency: 11 pa.
Mission: To promote the individual right to quality water; To educate water quality professionals; To promote the growth of the water quality improvement industry; To serve as a unified voice in government & public relations; To provide a role in consumer education

Canadian Water Resources Association (CWRA) / Association canadienne des ressources hydriques (ACRH)
c/o Membership Office, 9 Covus Crt., Ottawa ON K2E 7Z4
Tel: 613-237-9363; *Fax:* 613-594-5190
e-mail: services@aic.ca
URL: www.cwra.org
Overview: A large national charitable organization founded in 1948
Member Profile: Individuals & organizations interested in the management of Canada's water resources, including private & public sector water resource managers, administrators, scientists, academics, students, & users
Activities: Increasing awareness & understanding of Canada's water resources; Providing a forum for the exchange of information; Participating with appropriate agencies in international water management activities;
Meetings/Conferences:
For more information see Trade Shows, Conferences and Seminars Chapter
Canadian Water Resources Association 2011 Water, Agriculture, & the Environment Conference: Supply, Quality, Management
June 2011 Lethbridge, ON
Canadian Water Resources Association 2011 Ontario Branch Symposium & Annual General Meeting
June 2011 Toronto, ON
Canadian Water Resources Association, Alberta Branch, 2011 Future of Water Workshop Series: Developing Better Leaders
June 2011 Canmore, AB
Canadian Water Resources Association 2011 64th National Conference: Our Water, Our Life - The Most Valuable Resource
June 2011 St. John's, NL
Canadian Water Resources Association, Alberta Branch, 2011 Course: Applied Fluvial Geomorphology, Level 1
August 2011 Calgary, AB
Publications: *Canadian Water Resources Journal*
Type: Journal *Frequency:* q. *Editor:* Paul H. Whitfield *ISSN:* 0701-1784
Profile: Research articles, technical notes, & review papers
CWRA [Canadian Water Resources Association] Water News
Type: Newsletter *Frequency:* q. *Editor:* F.A. (Rick) Ross
Profile: National & branch activities, international water resource information, a technical supplement, & a profile article
Canadian Water Resources Association Conference Proceedings
Hydroscan: Airborne Laser Mapping of Hydrological Features & Resources
Type: Book *Editor:* Chris Hopkinson et al. *Price:* $15
Predictions in Ungauged Basins
Type: Book *Editor:* C. Spence et al. *Price:* $15
Canadian Perspectives on Integrated Water Resources Management
Type: Book *Number of Pages:* 123 *Editor:* Dan Shrubsole *Price:* $23
Reflections on Water: CWRA 1947 - 1997
Type: Book *Author:* B. Mitchell; Robert de Loe *Price:* $20
Mission: To encourage recognition of the high priority & value of water; Affiliation(s): Canadian Water & Wasterwater Association; International Water Resources Association; American Water Resources Association; British Hydological Society; American Institute of Hydrology
Environmental Activity: Promoting effective water management

Canadian Water Well Association *See* Canadian Ground Water Association

Canadian Well Logging Society (CWLS)
Scotia Centre, #2200, 700 - 2nd St. SW, Calgary AB T2P 2W1

Tel: 403-269-9366; *Fax:* 403-269-2787
e-mail: roy_benteau@eogresources.com
URL: www.cwls.com
Overview: A medium-sized national organization founded in 1957
Finances: *Annual Operating Budget:* Less than $50,000; *Funding Sources:* Membership fees; corporate sponsors
Membership: 500; *Fees:* $40; *Member Profile:* Oil industry petrophysical interests
Publications: *CWLS [Canadian Well Logging Society] InSite*
Type: Newsletter *Frequency:* q. *Accepts Advertising* : Yes *Editor:* Tyler Maksymchuk & Kelly Skuce *Price:* Free with CWLS membership
Profile: Short articles, & upcoming events to inform CWLS members
CWLS [Canadian Well Logging Society] Journal
Type: Journal *Frequency:* biennial *Price:* Free with CWLS membership
Profile: Formal papers for people interested in formation evaluation
CWLS [Canadian Well Logging Society] Annual Report
Type: Yearbook *Frequency:* a. *Price:* Free with Canadian Well Logging Society membership

Canadian Wholesale Grocers Association *See* Canadian Council of Grocery Distributors

Canadian Wildflower Society *See* North American Native Plant Society

Canadian Wildlife Federation (CWF) / Fédération canadienne de la faune
350 Michael Cowpland Dr., Kanata ON K2M 2W1
Tel: 613-599-9594; *Fax:* 613-599-4428
Toll-Free: 800-563-9453
e-mail: info@cwf-fcf.org
URL: www.cwf-fcf.org
Overview: A large national charitable organization founded in 1961
Finances: *Annual Operating Budget:* Greater than $5 Million; *Funding Sources:* Membership fees; sales of merchandise; donations
Staff: 33 staff member(s)
Membership: 300,000; *Fees:* $25; *Committees:* Affiliate; Associate Member; Audit; Awards; Constitution; Credentials; Energy; Environment; Fisheries; Forestry; Native Affairs; Nominating; Parks; Resolutions; Wildlife
Activities: Educational programs - National Wildlife Week, Project WILD (Wildlife in Learning Design), Endangered Species, Habitat 2000 (a wildlife habitat improvement program for young people); Conservation Action programs - sponsor of the National Inquiry into Freshwater Fisheries, leading the development of a new Canadian Recreational Fisheries Program, sponsor of World Conservation Strategy Conference; advocate on national & international conservation & environmental issues, such as acid rain & International Caribou Agreement; *Awareness Events:* National Wildlife Week, 1st full week of April; Canadian Rivers Day, June; *Speaker Service:* Yes; *Rents Mailing List:* Yes; *Library:* Yes, Open to public, open by appointment
Awards: Doug Clarke Memorial Award (Award), Canadian Conservation Achievement Awards Program
Presented annually to a Canadian Wildlife Federation affiliate for the most outstanding conservation project completed during the previous year by the affiliate or its clubs or members Contact: Sandy Baugartner
Stan Hodgkiss Outdoorsman of the Year Award (Award), Canadian Conservation Achievement Awards Program
Presented annually to an outdoorsperson who has demonstrated an active commitment to conservation in Canada
Roland Michener Conservation Award (Award), Canadian Conservation Achievement Awards Program
A trophy is given annually in recognition of an individual's outstanding achievement in the field of conservation in Canada
Roderick Haig-Brown Memorial Award (Award), Canadian Conservation Achievement Awards Program
Awarded annually to an individual who has made a significant contribution to furthering the sport of angling &/or conservation & wise use of Canada's recreational fisheries resources
Past Presidents' Canadian Legislator Award (Award), Canadian Conservation Achievement Awards Program
Presented annually to an elected provincial, territorial or federal legislator in recognition of a significant contribution toward the conservation of wildlife in Canada Contact: Sandy Baugartner

Publications: *Canadian Wildlife [a publication of the Canadian Wildlife Federation]*
Type: Magazine *Language:* E *Frequency:* bi-m.
Profile: Stories about Canadian & international wildlife, plus CWF news & reports, for young adults & adults
Biosphère [a publication of the Canadian Wildlife Federation]
Language: F *Frequency:* bi-m.
Profile: French language edition of Canadian Wildlife, for young adults & adults
Wild [a publication of the Canadian Wildlife Federation]
Type: Magazine *Frequency:* 8 pa
Profile: Educational information & games, for children between the ages of 6 & 12
Your Big Backyard
Type: Magazine *Frequency:* m.
Profile: Easy-to-read nature information, puzzles, & games, for children between the ages of 3 & 5
Mission: To promote the conservation of fish & wildlife, wildlife habitat & quality aquatic environments; to foster an understanding of natural processes; to ensure adequate stocks of wildlife for the use & enjoyment of all Canadians; to sponsor research; to cooperate with legislators, government & non-government agencies in achieving conservation objectives; *Member of:* World Conservation Union

Canadian Wind Energy Association Inc. (CanWEA) / Association canadienne d'énergie éolienne
#810, 170 Laurier Ave. West, Ottawa ON K1P 5V5
Tel: 613-234-8716; *Fax:* 613-234-5642
Toll-Free: 800-922-6932
e-mail: info@canwea.ca
URL: www.canwea.ca
Social Media: twitter.com/canwindenergy
Overview: A small national organization founded in 1984
Finances: *Funding Sources:* Membership fees; Conference & workshop fees
Membership: 420; *Member Profile:* Organizations & individuals who are involved in the development & application of wind energy technology, products, & services in Canada
Activities: Providing information about wind energy; Offering networking opportunities for all stakeholders; Facilitating research; Forming strategic alliances; *Library:* Canadian Wind Energy Association Library; open by appointment
Publications: *WindLink*
Type: Newsletter *Frequency:* s-m.
Profile: Issues & events that affect the Canadian wind energy for CanWEA members, policymakers, & the public
WindSight
Type: Magazine *Frequency:* q.
Profile: Detailed articles on Canadian wind energy projects & policy
CanWEA Members Directory
Type: Directory
Profile: Contact information & a profile of each CanWEA member
Mission: To promote the social, economic, & environmental benefits of wind energy in Canada; To encourage the appropriate development & application of wind energy; To create suitable environmental policy
Environmental Activity: Advocating for the responsible & sustainable growth of wind energy; Developing policy with different levels of government; Providing education, such as Wind Matters seminars

Canadian Wood Council (CWC) / Conseil canadien du bois (CCB)
#400, 99 Bank St., Ottawa ON K1P 6B9
Tel: 613-747-5544; *Fax:* 613-747-6264
Toll-Free: 800-463-5091
e-mail: admin@cwc.ca
URL: www.cwc.ca
Overview: A large national organization founded in 1959
Finances: *Annual Operating Budget:* $3 Million-$5 Million
Staff: 15 staff member(s)
Membership: 15 corporate; *Fees:* Schedule available; *Member Profile:* Manufacturers of Canadian wood products used in construction; *Committees:* Management: Audit, Finance & Risk Management; Membership; HR; Nominating. Operations: U.S. Affairs; Lumber Properties Steering Committee; Market Development; Fire & Structural Design; Canadian Wood Industries Forum on Market Access; Canadian Sustainable Building Partnership. Other: WoodWORKS!; Advisory Groups; Chairmen's Club
Activities: *Awareness Events:* Annual Wood WORKS! Awards Gala; Wood Solutions Fairs; *Library:* Yes, open by appointment

Associations/Organizations / Canadian Wood Pallet & Container Association

Publications: *Wood Design & Building*
Type: Magazine *Frequency:* q. *Accepts Advertising* : Yes *Editor:* Bernadette Johnson *Price:* $24
Profile: Wood use in architecture & construction
Canadian Wood Council Awards Book
Type: Yearbook *Frequency:* a.
Profile: Compilation of best projects submitted to the Wood Design Awards program
Canadian Wood Council Technical Publications
Profile: Topics include the Wood Design Manual, Span Books, & Engineering Guides
The CWC [Canadian Wood Council] Newsletter
Type: Newsletter *Frequency:* w.
Profile: Trends & events that affect the wood products industry
Wood WORKS!
Type: Newsletter *Frequency:* m.
Profile: Resources for technical support, training opportunities, & educational events
Mission: To represent Canadian manufacturers of wood products use in construction, the council role of insuring market access for wood products accomplished through codes standards, the production & communication of technical information & in educational programs for students & construction professionals

Canadian Wood Pallet & Container Association (CWPCA) / Association canadienne des manufacturiers de palettes et contenants
#201, 2141 Thurston Dr., Ottawa ON K1G 6C9
Tel: 613-521-6468; *Fax:* 613-521-1835
Toll-Free: 877-224-3555
e-mail: info@canadianpallets.com
URL: www.canadianpallets.com
Overview: A small national organization founded in 1967
Finances: *Annual Operating Budget:* $100,000-$250,000
Staff: 2 staff member(s)
Membership: 300; *Fees:* $595 corporate; $525 associate;
Member Profile: Active manufacturers & suppliers within wood pallet & container industry; *Committees:* Wood Waste Standards; Workers Compensation; Education
Activities: *Speaker Service:* Yes; *Library:* Yes, Open to public
Mission: To promote the general welfare of the wooden pallet & container manufacturing industry; to improve services directly or otherwise; to cooperate with officers of government & business in any program considered essential to the national welfare or economy; to engage in any other lawful activities & enjoy powers, rights & privileges granted or conferred upon associations of a similar nature.; *Affiliation(s):* National Wooden Pallet & Container Association; Western Pallet Association
Environmental Activity: National Packaging Protocol

Canadian Wood Preservers Bureau (WPC) / Préservation du bois Canada
#202, 2141 Thurston Dr., Ottawa ON K1G 6C9
Tel: 613-737-4337; *Fax:* 613-247-0540
e-mail: info@woodpreservation.ca
URL: www.woodpreservation.ca
Previous Name: Canadian Wood Preservers Bureau
Overview: A small national organization founded in 1988
Finances: *Annual Operating Budget:* Less than $50,000; *Funding Sources:* Membership dues
Staff: 1 staff member(s); 7 volunteer(s)
Membership: 11 corporate + 4 institutional; *Member Profile:* Treated wood producers; consumer groups
Mission: To provide a quality assurance program for the treated wood industry

Canadian Wood Preservers Bureau *See* Canadian Wood Preservers Bureau

Canadians for Ethical Treatment of Food Animals (CETFA)
PO Box 18024, 2225 - 41 Ave. West, Vancouver BC V6M 4L3
e-mail: care@cetfa.com
URL: www.cetfa.com
Social Media: facebook.com/cetfa.news
Overview: A medium-sized national organization founded in 1990
Chief Officer(s):
Patricia Oswald, President
Twyla Francois, Head, Investigation, 204-296-1375
twyla.1@mts.net
Fees: $10
Mission: CETFA is an investigation-based, farm animal advocacy organization that promotes the humane treatment of animals raised for food. It works to educate the public about Canada's food industry by providing information on factory farming practices.

Canadians for Responsible & Safe Highways (CRASH)
PO Box 1042, Stn. B, Ottawa ON K1P 5R1
Tel: 613-860-0529; *Fax:* 613-567-6204
Toll-Free: 800-530-9945
Overview: A small national organization
Chief Officer(s):
Harry Gow, President
Mission: CRASH strives to ensure that safety, environmental & economic concerns are fully considered by governments when the latter establish & administer regulations pertaining to trucking operations on public highways.

Can-Am Border Trade Alliance
PO Box 929, Lewiston NY 14092 USA
Tel: 716-754-8824; *Fax:* 716-754-8824
e-mail: canambta@aol.com
URL: www.canambta.org
Overview: A medium-sized international organization
Chief Officer(s):
James D. Phillips, President & CEO
Mission: To maximize global commercial activity and ensure continued growth of two-way cross border trade along the entire common U.S./Canadian border and assure efficient, productive border crossing capabilities; and also to provide unified leadership for border concern, operations and needs and to act as an effective, proactive and focused border issues resource.

Canards Illimités Canada *See* Ducks Unlimited Canada

Cancer Research Society (CRS) / Société de recherche sur le cancer
#402, 625, av Président-Kennedy, Montréal QC H3A 3S5
Tel: 514-861-9227; *Fax:* 514-861-9220
Toll-Free: 866-343-2262
e-mail: info@src-crs.ca
URL: src-crs.ca
Overview: A large national charitable organization founded in 1945
Chief Officer(s):
Mario Chevrette, President
Andy Chabot, Executive Director
achabot@src-crs.ca
Finances: *Annual Operating Budget:* Greater than $5 Million; *Funding Sources:* Donations
Staff: 9 staff member(s)
Membership: 1,000; *Fees:* $500 life; $250 Governor; $200 executive; $100 benefactor; $50 patron; $25 general
Activities: *Awareness Events:* The Cancer Research Society Golf Classic, June; Step Up for the Cure; The Crossing of Hope
Awards: Grants (Grant)
Institutional grants, fellowships, general research grants, award grants & special grants
Mission: CRS is a not-for-profit organization that supports basic cancer research through funding & seed money. Grants & fellowships are allocated to universities & hospitals involved in research across Canada. It is a registered charity, BN: 119153229RR0001.

Carleton County Law Association (CCLA) / Association du barreau du comté de Carleton
Ottawa Courthouse, #2004, 161 Elgin St., Ottawa ON K2P 2K1
Tel: 613-233-7386; *Fax:* 613-238-3788
Toll-Free: 866-637-3888
e-mail: info@ccla.ottawa.on.ca
URL: www.ccla.ottawa.on.ca
Overview: A small local organization founded in 1888
Chief Officer(s):
Rick Haga, B.Sc., Executive Director
rick.haga@ccla.ottawa.on.ca
Wanda Walters, Administrator, Finance & Membership
wanda.walters@ccla.ottawa.on.ca
Jennifer Walker, B.A.H., B.Ed.,,, Head Librarian
jennifer.walker@ccla.ottawa.on.ca
Fees: $52.50 - $309.75; *Member Profile:* Ottawa & Eastern Ontario lawyers
Activities: Offering continuing education programs; Providing networking opportunities; *Library:* County of Carleton Law Association Ottawa Courthouse Law Library
Publications: *Ottawa & Eastern Ontario Lawyers' Directory*
Type: Directory *Frequency:* a. *Accepts Advertising* : Yes *Price:* $55 - $65

CCLA [Carleton County Law Association] Bulletin
Type: Newsletter *Frequency:* bi-m.
Profile: Updated policies & procedures for CCLA members
Mission: To advance the interests of it members; to promote the administration of justice

Carolinian Canada Coalition
Grosvenor Lodge, 1017 Western Rd., London ON N6G 1G5
Tel: 519-433-7077; *Fax:* 519-913-2449
e-mail: info@carolinian.org
URL: www.carolinian.org
Overview: A medium-sized local organization
Chief Officer(s):
Gordon Nelson, Chair
Fees: $20 individual; $50 organization
Mission: To promote the protection and conservation of the Carolinian Life Zone of Southwestern Ontario.

Carp Agricultural Society
PO Box 188, Carp ON K0A 1L0
Tel: 613-839-2172; *Fax:* 613-839-1961
URL: www.carpfair.ca
Overview: A medium-sized local charitable organization founded in 1863
Finances: *Annual Operating Budget:* $500,000-$1.5 Million
Staff: 300 volunteer(s)
Membership: 1,000 senior/lifetime; *Fees:* $5
Mission: To improve agriculture & the quality of life in the community by educating members & the community; to provide a community forum for discussing agricultural issues; to foster community development & community spirit; to help provide markets for Ontario products; to encourage conservation of natural resources, including soil conservation, reforestation, rural & urban beautification

Carrying Capacity Network (CCN)
PO Box 18221, #310, 2000 P St. NW, Washington DC 20036 USA
Tel: 202-296-4548; *Fax:* 202-296-4609
Toll-Free: 800-466-4866
e-mail: info@carryingcapacity.org
URL: www.carryingcapacity.org
Overview: A large international organization founded in 1989
Finances: *Annual Operating Budget:* $500,000-$1.5 Million
Staff: 8 staff member(s)
Fees: $20 senior/student; $25 adult; $40 sustaining; $100 major; $250 sponsor; $500 benefactor; $1,000 patron
Activities: Resource Bank (a catalogue of resources to aid participants in their search for information); Speakers/Writers Bureau (a database of individuals & organizations that would speak or write on the wide range of carrying capacity issues); *Speaker Service:* Yes
Mission: "Carrying Capacity" refers to the number of individuals who can be supported without degrading the physical, ecological, cultural & social environment (ie without reducing the ability of the environment to sustain the desired quality of life over the long term); CCN functions as a clearinghouse of information for participants, a forum for discussion of controversial issues & as a catalyst for cooperation among diverse groups involved in carrying capacity issues; CCN's objective is to facilitate the understanding of the crucial linkages between population & the environment by exchanging information, disseminating news & encouraging cooperation among environmental, resource conservation, growth control & population stabilization organizations & activists

Castle-Crown Wilderness Coalition (CCWC)
Box 2621, Pincher Creek AB T0K 1W0
Tel: 403-627-5059
e-mail: office@ccwc.ab.ca
URL: www.ccwc.ab.ca
Overview: A small local organization founded in 1989
Chief Officer(s):
Gordon Petersen, President & Treasurer
Judy Huntley, Exective Director
James Tweedie, Director, Conservation
james@ccwc.ab.ca
Finances: *Funding Sources:* Membership fees; Donations; Conservation organizations; Fisheries & Oceans Canada
Membership: 500+; *Fees:* $10 individuals; $15 families; $25 groups; $110 supporting members; $250 life members
Activities: Sponsoring a stewardship program to monitor & restore the Castle Wilderness; Conducting hikes to raise awareness of the area
Publications: *The State of the Castle Wilderness: Annual Report*
Type: Yearbook *Frequency:* a.

Castle Wilderness News
Type: Newsletter Frequency: q. Editor: Judy Huntley
The Castle Wilderness Environmental Inventory
Bringing it Back: A Restoration Framework for the Castle Wilderness
Mission: To restore & maintain the Castle Wilderness within the Crown of the Continent Ecosystem

C.D. Howe Institute / Institut C.D. Howe
#300, 67 Yonge St., Toronto ON M5E 1J8
Tel: 416-865-1904; Fax: 416-865-1866
e-mail: cdhowe@cdhowe.org
URL: www.cdhowe.org
Overview: A medium-sized international organization founded in 1973
Finances: Annual Operating Budget: $1.5 Million-$3 Million; Funding Sources: Membership dues
Staff: 18 staff member(s)
Membership: 215 corporate + 50 institutional; Fees: Schedule available; Member Profile: Participation in & support of its activities from business, organized labor, associations, professions & interested individuals; Committees: British-North American; North-American
Activities: Speaker Service: Yes; Library: Yes, open by appointment
Mission: Research & educational institute identifying current & emerging economic & social policy issues facing Canadians; to recommend particular policy options; to communicate conclusions of research to domestic & international audiences.

Cement Association of Canada (CAC) / Association canadienne du ciment
#502, 350 Sparks St., Ottawa ON K1R 7S8
Tel: 613-236-9471; Fax: 613-563-4498
e-mail: headquarters@cement.ca
URL: www.cement.ca
Previous Name: Canadian Portland Cement Association
Overview: A medium-sized national organization
Membership: 10 companies; Member Profile: 100% of the manufacturers of Portland cement in Canada
Mission: Represents all of Canada's cement producers; aims to improve & extend the uses of cement & concrete through market development, engineering, research, education, & public affairs work

Center for Health, Environment & Justice (CHEJ)
PO Box 6806, Falls Church VA 22040-6806 USA
Tel: 703-237-2249; Fax: 703-237-8389
e-mail: chej@chej.org
URL: www.chej.org
Previous Name: Citizens Clearinghouse for Hazardous Wastes
Overview: A medium-sized national charitable organization founded in 1981
Chief Officer(s):
Lois Marie Gibbs, Executive Director/Founder
Sharon Franklin, Finance/Administrative Director
Finances: Annual Operating Budget: $500,000-$1.5 Million; Funding Sources: Membership dues; donations
Staff: 14 staff member(s)
Membership: 25,000 individual + 7,500 groups; Fees: $30 individual; $100 group
Activities: Provides science, organizing & technical assistance to citizens concerned with dioxin, toxic waste, chemical poisons, etc. in their communities; site visits by staff; 130+ self-help guides & fact packs; campaigns: Stop Dioxin Exposure; childproofing communities; BESAFE; Awareness Events: March into Spring, March; Internships: Yes; Speaker Service: Yes; Library: Yes, Open to public
Mission: To help communities win environmental justice

Center for Marine Conservation; Center for Environmental Education See The Ocean Conservancy

Center for Plant Conservation
PO Box 299, St. Louis MO 63166-0299 USA
Tel: 314-577-9450; Fax: 314-577-9465
e-mail: cpc@mobot.org
URL: www.centerforplantconservation.org
Overview: A medium-sized international organization founded in 1984
Chief Officer(s):
Kathryn Kennedy, Ph.D, President & Executive Director
Activities: The National Collection of Endangered Species consists of living plant materials collected from the wild, representing to the greatest extent possible the genetic diversity found in natural populations; Participating Institutions - affiliated botanical gardens & arboreta around the US; Priority Regions - areas facing a major plant extinction crisis; Integrated Conservation; Conservation Research; Information & Data Systems; Economic Plant Research; International Conservation
Mission: To create a systematic, comprehensive national program of plant conservation, research & education within existing institutions, as a complement to the preservation of genetic diversity through habitat protection; to strengthen its collaborative ties with countries contiguous to the US & its territories - Canada, Mexico & nations of the Greater Antilles; to develop & maintain comprehensive & broadly accessible information systems, national networks & databases concerning the biology, horticulture & conservation status of all nationally endangered native plants of the US

Central British Columbia Railway & Forest Industry Museum Society
850 River Rd., Prince George BC V2L 5S8
Tel: 250-563-7351; Fax: 250-563-3697
e-mail: trains@pgrfm.bc.ca
URL: www.pgrfm.bc.ca
Also Known As: Railway & Forestry Museum
Overview: A small local charitable organization founded in 1983
Chief Officer(s):
Laura Williams, General Manager
Finances: Annual Operating Budget: $50,000-$100,000
Staff: 6 staff member(s); 15 volunteer(s)
Membership: 75; Fees: $15-$40
Activities: Awareness Events: Steam Day; Forester Day; Family Carnival; Library: Canfor Library; open by appointment
Mission: Administers Prince George Railway & Forest Industry Museum; Member of: Canadian Railway Historical Association; Canadian Museum Association; British Columbia Museum Association; American Railway Museum Association

Central Canadian Federation of Mineralogical Societies (CCFMS)
c/o Bill Plavac, 626 Simcoe St., Niagara-on-the-Lake ON L0S 1J0
URL: www.ccfms.ca
Overview: A medium-sized national organization founded in 1969
Chief Officer(s):
Robert Beckett, President, 705-748-0178
rbeckett@cogeco.ca
Jim Glen, Vice-President
jrglen@sympatico.ca
Bill Plavac, Secretary, 905-468-5393
wplavac@cogeco.ca
Don Oliver, Treasurer, 905-336-1206
geminiofburl@cogeco.ca
Membership: 25 clubs; Member Profile: Rock, mineral, & lapidary clubs for hobbyists in central Canada
Activities: Promoting the earth sciences; Encouraging exchange of information between societies, federations, & institutions; Educating rock & mineral collectors; Protecting collecting sites; Speaker Service: Yes
Mission: To act as the voice for amateur rock, mineral, & lapidary clubs in central Canada

Central Interior Logging Association (CILA)
#201, 850 River Rd., Prince George BC V2L 5S8
Tel: 250-562-3368; Fax: 250-563-3697
e-mail: cila@pgonline.com
URL: www.cila.bc.ca/index.html
Previous Name: Prince George & District Truck Loggers Association
Overview: A medium-sized local charitable organization founded in 1966
Fees: $413.40-$3174.70; Member Profile: Companies & individuals directly or indirectly engaged in logging or log hauling; manufacturers & suppliers of goods &/or services to the logging industry
Mission: To present the views of members to all levels of government, its agencies, & the corporate sector

Central Okanagan Naturalists Club (CONC)
PO Box 21128, Stn. Orchard Park, Kelowna BC V1Y 9N8
Tel: 250-768-3334
e-mail: guilds@telus.net
URL: www.okanagannature.org
Overview: A small local charitable organization founded in 1962
Finances: Annual Operating Budget: Less than $50,000
Staff: 9 staff member(s); 70 volunteer(s)
Membership: 200; Fees: $14 student; $30 single; $42 family; Member Profile: Retirees; Committees: Education; Ecological Reserves; Forestry
Activities: Hiking; skiing; botany; ornithology; participating with City of Kelowna in environmental events; conservation; Library: CONC Library; Not open to the public
Publications: *Central Okanagan Naturalist Newsletter*
Type: Newsletter Language: E Frequency: 10 per year Editor: Teresa Smith
Mission: To promote the enjoyment of nature through environmental appreciation & conservation; to encourage wise use & conservation of natural resources & environmental protection.; Member of: Federation of BC Naturalists

Central Ontario Orchid Society (COOS)
PO Box 40074, 75 King St. South, Waterloo ON N2J 4V1
e-mail: jerry@uwaterloo.ca
URL: www.coos.ca
Overview: A small local organization founded in 1985
Chief Officer(s):
Judy Sparkes, Secretary
judysparkes@sympatico.ca
Rennie Taylor, President
paph008@rogers.com
Finances: Annual Operating Budget: Less than $50,000
Membership: 80; Fees: $15 individual; $20 family
Activities: Promote & train people about growing orchids; Speaker Service: Yes; Library: Yes, Not open to the public
Mission: To promote & train people about growing orchids

Central Valley Naturalists
PO Box 612, Abbotsford BC V2T 6Z8
Tel: 604-853-4283
e-mail: haroos@shaw.ca
URL: www.centralvalleynaturalists.org
Overview: A small local organization
Chief Officer(s):
Hank Roos, President
Membership: 120; Fees: $30 individual; $35 family
Affiliation(s): Federation of BC Naturalists

Centre canadien d'hygiène et de sécurité au travail See Canadian Centre for Occupational Health & Safety

Centre canadien d'innovations des pêches See Canadian Centre for Fisheries Innovation

Centre canadien de politique alternative See Canadian Centre for Policy Alternatives

Centre canadien pour la prévention de la pollution See Canadian Centre for Pollution Prevention

Centre de formation en entreprise et récupération
605, rue Notre-Dame est, Victoriaville QC G6P 6Y9
Tél: 819-758-4789; Téléc: 819-752-3488
Courriel: cfer@csbf.qc.ca
Aperçu: Dimension: moyenne; Envergure: provinciale
Membre(s) du bureau directeur:
Marie-France Provencher, Présidente
Yves Couture, Directeur
Mission: Offrir aux jeunes en difficultés une formation préparatoire au marché du travail; initier les enfants du primaire aux grandes problématiques environnementales; développer une conscience environnementale chez les jeunes

Centre de recherche sur la vie marine de Grand Manan See Grand Manan Whale & Seabird Research Station

Centre de recherches pour le développement international See International Development Research Centre

Centre for Environmental Law & Development See Foundation for International Environmental Law & Development

Centre for Fisheries Innovation See Canadian Centre for Fisheries Innovation

Centre for Indigenous Environmental Resources (CIER)
245 McDermot Ave., 3rd Fl., Winnipeg MB R3B 0S6
Tel: 204-956-0660; Fax: 204-956-1895
e-mail: earth@cier.ca
URL: www.cier.ca
Overview: A small national organization
Chief Officer(s):
Merrell-Anne Phare, Executive Director

Centre for Medicine, Ethics & Law
McGill University, #201, 3690, rue Peel, Montréal QC H3A 1W9

Associations/Organizations / Centre québécois du droit de l'environnement

Tel: 514-398-7400; *Fax:* 514-398-4668
e-mail: cmel@falaw.mcgill.ca
Overview: A small national organization
Chief Officer(s):
M.A. Somerville, Director

Centre info-énergie *See* Canadian Centre for Energy Information

Centre international d'informations de sécurité et de santé au travail *See* International Occupational Safety & Health Information Centre

Centre québécois du droit de l'environnement (CQDE) / Québec Environmental Law Centre
454, av Laurier Est, Montréal QC H2J 1E7
Tél: 514-861-7022
Courriel: info@cqde.org
URL: www.cqde.org
Aperçu: *Dimension:* petite; *Envergure:* provinciale; *Organisme sans but lucratif; fondée en* 1989
Membre(s) du bureau directeur:
Jean-François Girard, Président
Anna-Léa Scollan, Vice-présidente
Anne-Marie Robichaud, Secrétaire
Finances: *Budget de fonctionnement annuel:* $100,000-$250,000
Membre: 120; *Montant de la cotisation:* 10$ étudiant; 20$ membre individuel; 50$ entreprise
Activités: *Service de conférenciers:* Oui; *Bibliothèque:* Oui, Bibliothèque publique, rendez-vous
Mission: Promouvoir le droit de l'environnement comme outil de protection de la santé publique et du patrimoine collectif

Le Cercle Saint-François *See* The Kindness Club

Cercles des jeunes naturalistes (CJN)
Jardin botanique de Montréal, #262, 4101, rue Sherbrooke est, Montréal QC H1X 2B2
Tél: 514-252-3023; *Téléc:* 514-254-8744
Courriel: info@jeunesnaturalistes.org
URL: www.jeunesnaturalistes.org
Aperçu: *Dimension:* grande; *Envergure:* nationale; *Organisme sans but lucratif; fondée en* 1931
Membre(s) du bureau directeur:
Laure Bouchard, Administratrice
Christine Presseau, Président
Monique Bouchard, Administratrice
Finances: *Fonds:* Gouvernement provincial pour la gestion du Siège social
Personnel: 2 membre(s) du personnel; 4 bénévole(s)
Membre: 1300 membres; 135 animateurs bénévoles; *Montant de la cotisation:* 35$ individuel; 50$ famille
Activités: Camps nature; animations dans les cercles avec les Jeunes Naturalistes sur les sciences de la nature; activités parascolaires et dans les écoles; formation pour animateurs; trousses d'animations; festival provincial annuel; *Bibliothèque:* Oui, Not open to the public
Mission: Nous initions les jeunes à l'étude des sciences de la nature et à la protection de l'environnement; *Membre de:* Regroupement Loisir Québec

Certified Organic Associations of British Columbia (COABC)
#202, 3002 - 32nd Ave., Vernon BC V1T 2L7
Tel: 250-260-4429; *Fax:* 250-260-4436
e-mail: office@certifiedorganic.bc.ca
URL: www.certifiedorganic.bc.ca
Overview: A medium-sized provincial organization founded in 1994
Chief Officer(s):
Sarah Clark, Administrator
Kristy Wipperman, Office Manager
Activities: Cyber-Help; Canadian Organic Initiative; Organic Environmental Farm Program; Organic Harvest Awards; Organic Sector Development Program; Standards
Publications: *BC Organic Grower*
Frequency: q.
Mission: To maintain a credible set of organic production & processing standards

Certified Technicians & Technologists Association of Manitoba (CTTAM)
Parent: Canadian Council of Technicians & Technologists
#602, 1661 Portage Ave., Winnipeg MB R3J 3T7
Tel: 204-784-1088; *Fax:* 204-784-1084
e-mail: admin@cttam.com
URL: www.cttam.com
Previous Name: Manitoba Society of Certified Engineering Technicians & Technologists Inc.
Overview: A medium-sized provincial organization founded in 1965
Finances: *Annual Operating Budget:* $100,000-$250,000; *Funding Sources:* Membership fees
Staff: 3 staff member(s)
Membership: 2,600; *Fees:* $155; *Member Profile:* Open to those employed in all aspects of engineering technology (civil, mechanical, electrical, electronic, computer, instrumentation, surveying, design & drafting, structural, construction) provided they meet the academic requirements
Activities: *Internships:* Yes
Awards: Scholarships (Scholarship)
Award Amount: Three $600 scholarships
Mission: To advance the professional recognition & development of certified applied science technicians & technologists in a manner that serves the public interest; *Member of:* Science & Technology Awareness Network

Ceta-Research Inc.
PO Box 10, Trinity NL A0C 2S0
Tel: 709-464-3269; *Fax:* 709-464-3700
e-mail: beamish@oceancontact.com
URL: www.oceancontact.com/research/research.html
Overview: A medium-sized local organization founded in 1990
Chief Officer(s):
Peter Beamish, Co-Director
Christine Beamish, Co-Director
Finances: *Annual Operating Budget:* $100,000-$250,000
Staff: 30 staff member(s)
Membership: 5,000 individual
Mission: To undertake the rescue of entrapped whales & dolphins; to conduct research on whales; responsible for organizing a discovery in animal communication using Rhythm Bases Communication

La Chaine bleue mondiale *See* World Blue Chain for the Protection of Animals & Nature

Chamber of Mineral Resources of Nova Scotia (CMRNS)
PO Box 2171, Windsor NS B0N 2T0
Tel: 902-798-0187; *Fax:* 902-798-2141
e-mail: terry.daniels@ns.sympatico.ca
Overview: A medium-sized provincial organization founded in 1981
Finances: *Annual Operating Budget:* Less than $50,000
Membership: 150
Activities: *Awareness Events:* Mining Week; *Library:* Yes, open by appointment
Mission: To ensure Nova Scotia is recognized internationally as having mineral resources worthy of investment; to develop mineral deposits; to work for government policies that provide a framework for a competitive mining industry within the global marketplace; to promote mining as a corporate industry creating wealth & long-term stable employment, with responsible environmental & social attitudes; *Affiliation(s):* Mining Association of Canada

Chamber of Mines of Eastern British Columbia
215 Hall St., Nelson BC V1L 5X4
Tel: 250-352-5242; *Fax:* 250-352-7227
e-mail: chamberofminesebc@netidea.com
URL: www.cmebc.com
Overview: A medium-sized provincial organization founded in 1921
Chief Officer(s):
Jack Denny, President
Dennis Llewellyn, Chamber Manager
Finances: *Annual Operating Budget:* Less than $50,000
Staff: 1 staff member(s)
Membership: 175; *Fees:* $40 individual; $100-$500 corporate
Activities: *Library:* Yes
Mission: To act as advocate for the mining industry in British Columbia; to provide a collective voice on behalf of prospectors & miners; to provide information on exploration & mining; to educate the public through accessibility to mineral museum & library.; *Member of:* BC Mining Association; BC/Yukon Chamber of Mines

La Chambre de commerce du Canada *See* The Canadian Chamber of Commerce

Chartered Institute of Logistics and Transport in North America (CILT) / Institut agréé de la logistique et des transports Amérique du Nord
#900, 275 Slater St., Ottawa ON K1P 5H9
Tel: 613-688-1438; *Fax:* 613-688-0966
e-mail: ghonima@ciltna.com
URL: www.ciltna.com
Also Known As: CILT in North America
Previous Name: Chartered Institute of Transport in Canada
Overview: A medium-sized international organization founded in 1919
Chief Officer(s):
Gilles Legault, FCILT, Chair
Hazem Ghonima, FCILT, CEO
Donald McKnight, FCILT Executive Director
Sam Barone, FCILT Treasurer
Mike Paré, FCILT Secretary
Finances: *Funding Sources:* Membership fees
Staff: 1 staff member(s); 15 volunteer(s)
Membership: 460; *Member Profile:* Individuals with experience, interest & education in the transportation field.; *Committees:* Regional
Mission: To promote, encourage, coordinate study & advancement of science & art of transportation.; *Member of:* Chartered Institute of Transport

Chartered Institute of Transport in Canada *See* Chartered Institute of Logistics and Transport in North America

Chemical Institute of Canada (CIC) / Institut de chimie du Canada
#550, 130 Slater St., Ottawa ON K1P 6E2
Tel: 613-232-6252; *Fax:* 613-232-5862
Toll-Free: 888-542-2242
e-mail: info@cheminst.ca
URL: www.cheminst.ca
Overview: A large national organization founded in 1945
Finances: *Annual Operating Budget:* $500,000-$1.5 Million; *Funding Sources:* Membership fees
Staff: 9 staff member(s)
Membership: 6,000; *Fees:* Schedule available; *Member Profile:* Open to those interested in chemistry/chemical technology & engineering with appropriate background
Activities: *Awareness Events:* National Chemistry Week; *Speaker Service:* Yes; *Rents Mailing List:* Yes
Awards: The Chemical Institute of Canada Award for Environmental Improvement (Award)
A plaque & certificate & up to $500 travel assistance awarded to a company, individual, team or organization in Canada for a significant achievement in pollution prevention, treatment or remediation in Canada Contact: Awards Manager, Email: awards@cheminst.ca
The Catalysis Award (Award)
Awarded biennially to an individual who has made a distinguished contribution to the field of catalysis; sponsored by the Canadian Catalysis Foundation *Award Amount:* A rhodium-plated silver medal & travel expense to present the award lecture
Chemical Institute of Canada Awards (Award)
The institute administers several awards & scholarships in chemistry, chemical engineering, & macromolecular science or engineering
The Macromolecular Science & Engineering Lecture Award (Award)
Established 1989; awarded annually to an individual who has made a distinguished contribution to macromolecular science & engineering *Award Amount:* $1,500 & a framed scroll provided by Novacor Chemicals Ltd.
Pestcon Graduate Scholarship (Scholarship)
For M.Sc. or Ph.D. students for research into alternate pest control strategies *Deadline:* 1-Mar *Award Amount:* $3,000
Union Carbide Award for Chemical Education (Award)
Established 1961; awarded annually to recognize an individual who has made outstanding contributions in Canada to education at any level in the field of chemistry or chemical engineering *Award Amount:* $1,000, a scroll & up to $400 in travel expenses if required
Polysar Awards of the CIC for High School Chemistry Teachers (Award)
Two awards a year recognizing excellence in the teaching of chemistry at the secondary level in Canada *Award Amount:* $500, a scroll & membership in the CIC
Sarnia Chemical Engineering Community Scholarship (Scholarship)
Awarded to an undergraduate student about to enter the final

Associations/Organizations / Chilliwack Field Naturalists

year of studies at a Canadian university in chemical engineering; based on academic excellence & demonstrated contributions to the Canadian Society for Chemical Engineering *Award Amount:* $1,000
The Chemical Institute of Canada Medal (Award)
Established 1951; a palladium medal is awarded as a mark of distinction & recognition to a person who has made an outstanding contribution to the science of chemistry or chemical engineering in Canada
The Montreal Medal (Award)
Established 1956; awarded annually as a mark of distinction & honour to a resident of Canada who has shown significant leadership in or has made an outstanding contribution to the profession of chemistry or chemical engineering in Canada *Award Amount:* A medal & up to $300 travel expenses if required
Mission: To maintain all branches of the professions of chemical sciences & chemical engineering in their proper status among other learned & scientific professions; to encourage original research & develop & maintain high standards in profession; to enhance usefulness of profession to the public; *Affiliation(s):* Canadian Society for Chemical Engineering; Canadian Society for Chemical Technology; Canadian Society for Chemistry

Chilliwack Field Naturalists
#216, 45598 McIntosh Dr., Chilliwack BC V2P 1J3
Tel: 604-796-9182
e-mail: postmaster@chilliwackfieldnaturalists.com
URL: www.chilliwackfieldnaturalists.com
Overview: A small local organization founded in 1970
Membership: 60 individual; *Fees:* $25 individual; $35 family; *Committees:* Conservation; Education
Activities: Field trips; meetings & speakers; education; *Library:* Yes, Not open to the public
Mission: To promote the enjoyment of nature through environmental appreciation & conservation; to encourage wise use & conservation of natural resources & environmental protection; *Member of:* Federation of BC Naturalists

Christian Farmers Federation of Ontario (CFFO)
7660 Mill Rd., RR#4, Guelph ON N1H 6J1
Tel: 519-837-1620; *Fax:* 519-824-1835
e-mail: cffomail@christianfarmers.org
URL: www.christianfarmers.org
Overview: A large provincial organization founded in 1954
Finances: *Annual Operating Budget:* $500,000-$1.5 Million; *Funding Sources:* Membership fees
Staff: 5 staff member(s)
Membership: 4,172; *Fees:* $157.50; *Member Profile:* Full-time commercial family farm entrepreneurs; part-time, hobby & lifestyle farmers; all those who have directed their farm organization fee to CFFO when they register with the Ontario Ministry of Agriculture, Food & Rural Affairs as part of the farm business registration process; *Committees:* Supply Management; Pork Producers; Sheep Producers; Stewardship & Policy East; Stewardship & Policy West
Activities: Our Farm Environmental Agenda (drafted by a coalition of Christian Farmers Federation of Ontario, AGCare, Ontario Federation of Agriculture, & the Ontario Farm Animal Council) outlines the strong commitment of farmers, through farm plans, to document present environmental conditions on their farms, develop a strategy for making appropriate changes, document actual farm practices & use that data for the development of new farm environmental initiatives; *Speaker Service:* Yes
Mission: A professional organization for Christian family farm entrepreneurs; a general farm organization with an interest in a broad range of agricultural, rural & social issues that impact upon the quality of the family life & family businesses of members; as a professional organization, committed to enabling members as producers, as marketers & as citizens, developing both the entrepreneurial & community leadership of members; through involvement in public policy, promotes a family farm & stewardship perspective; as a confessional organization, committed to being upfront about the Christian value system that motivates members, in order to make the wisdom of the Christian faith available to farm practice & farm policy; *Affiliation(s):* AG Care; Christian Farmers Federation of Alberta; Christian Environmental Council; Rural Development Advisory Committee

Christmas Tree Farmers of Ontario (CFTO)
#1, 9251 County Rd., Palgrave ON L0N 1P0
Fax: 905-729-0548
Toll-Free: 800-661-3530

e-mail: ctfo@christmastrees.on.ca
URL: www.christmastrees.on.ca
Overview: A small provincial organization founded in 1950
Membership: 200; *Fees:* Member $195; Senior member $250; Plus member $360; Associate member $130; Subscriber $80; *Member Profile:* Christmas tree farmers; *Committees:* Public Relations; Membership
Mission: CFTO is an association devoted to farmers who specialize in Christmas tree growing.; *Member of:* Canadian Christmas Tree Growers Association

Chrysotile Institute
#1640, 1200, av McGill College, Montréal QC H3B 4G7
Tel: 514-877-9797; *Fax:* 514-877-9717
e-mail: info@chrysotile.com
URL: www.chrysotile.com/
Overview: A medium-sized national organization founded in 1984
Activities: Participates in international missions by providing information, consultation, or training of a technical, medical & scientific nature for processors & users in other countries; gathers & disseminates medical, scientific & technical data about asbestos & substitute fibres; *Library:* Yes, open by appointment
Mission: To promote the implementation & enforcement of effective regulations, standards, work practices & techniques for the safe use of asbestos.

Citizen Scientists
c/o Rouge Valley Conservation Centre, 1749 Meadowvale Rd., Toronto ON M1B 5W8
e-mail: info@citizenscientists.ca
URL: www.citizenscientists.ca
Social Media: www.facebook.com/group.php?gid=2259994028
Overview: A medium-sized local organization founded in 2001
Membership: 11 institutional
Mission: To monitor local watersheds, foster local environmental stewardship, and educate volunteers and the public.

Citizens Clearinghouse for Hazardous Wastes See Center for Health, Environment & Justice

Citizens for a Safe Environment (CSE)
Tel: 416-461-1092
e-mail: info@csetoronto.org
URL: www.csetoronto.org
Overview: A medium-sized local organization founded in 1983
Activities: *Awareness Events:* Green Tea Parties; *Speaker Service:* Yes
Mission: To promomote waste management practices that protect the health of Toronto citizens, their communities and the environment.; *Member of:* Ontario Environmental Network
Environmental Activity: School Programs

Citizens For Renewable Energy (CFRE)
462 East Rd., RR#4, Lions Head ON N0H 1W0
Tel: 519-795-7725
e-mail: cfre@web.ca
URL: www.cfre.ca
Overview: A small national organization founded in 1996
Chief Officer(s):
Vitold Kreutzer, President
Annette Verhagen, Vice-President
Peter McIllwraith, Secretary
S. (Ziggy) Kleinau, Coordinator
Finances: *Annual Operating Budget:* Less than $50,000; *Funding Sources:* Membership fees; private donations
Staff: 20 volunteer(s)
Membership: 1,100; *Fees:* $15 individual; $8 student/senior; $25 sustaining; $40 three-year membership; *Member Profile:* Ontario/Canadian residents
Activities: Quarterly newsletter; annual general meeting; workshops; *Speaker Service:* Yes
Mission: To accelerate the introduction & use of clean renewable energy, thereby speeding up the phase-out of polluting fossil & nuclear energy production; *Member of:* Great Lakes United; Ontario Environmental Network; World Renewable Energy Council; Ontario Sustainable Energy Association; Ontario Clean Air Alliance; *Affiliation(s):* Canadian Solar Energy Society; Ecological Farmers Association

Citizens' Clearinghouse on Waste Management (CCWM)
17 Major St., Kitchener ON N2H 4R1
URL: www.citizenswasteinfo.org
Overview: A small national organization founded in 1989

Chief Officer(s):
John Jackson, Coordinator
jjackson@web.net
Mission: To help citizens gain access to information that will help them solve waste management problems in their communities and across Ontario.

Citizens' Environment Alliance of Southwestern Ontario (CEA)
1950 Ottawa St., Windsor ON N8Y 1R7
Tel: 519-973-1116; *Fax:* 519-973-8360
e-mail: ceaadmin@cogeco.net
URL: www.citizensenvironmentalliance.org
Social Media: facebook.com/group.php?gid=4417742199
Previous Name: Citizens' Environment Alliance of Southwestern Ontario
Overview: A small local charitable organization founded in 1985
Finances: *Annual Operating Budget:* $50,000-$100,000
Staff: 20 volunteer(s)
Membership: 100-499; *Fees:* Donations; *Committees:* Endangered Species; Toxic Trackers; Air Quality; Area Clean-up Team
Activities: "State of the Detroit River" boat tour; annual "Weenie Award" night; endangered natural spaces; toxic trackers; air quality; Detroit River clean-up; waste management; *Speaker Service:* Yes; *Rents Mailing List:* Yes; *Library:* Environmental & Resource Library; Open to public
Mission: CEA is a non-profit, grass-roots, international, education & research organization that aims to protect, restore & enhance the quality of the local environment in the Detroit-St. Clair Rivers corridor & in the Essex-Kent regions of the Great Lakes Basin; educate the public about environmental problems & solutions as they relate to the Great Lakes ecosystems & in particular to Southwestern Ontario. It is a registered charity, BN: 899837850RR0001.; *Member of:* Canadian Environmental Network; Ontario Environment Network; Environmental Action Ontario; *Affiliation(s):* Canadian Environmental Network (RCEN); Ontario Environmental Network (OEN); Lake Erie Millennium Network (LEMN); Ontario Water Conservation Alliance

Citizens' Environment Alliance of Southwestern Ontario See Citizens' Environment Alliance of Southwestern Ontario

Citizens' Environment Watch (CEW)
#204, 147 Spadina Ave., Toronto ON M5V 2L7
Tel: 647-258-3280; *Fax:* 416-637-2717
e-mail: info@citizensenvironmentwatch.org
URL: www.citizensenvironmentwatch.org
Overview: A medium-sized national organization founded in 1996
Chief Officer(s):
Meredith Cochrane, Executive Director
Finances: *Annual Operating Budget:* $250,000-$500,000; *Funding Sources:* Government, Foundations
Staff: 4 staff member(s)
Mission: To provide communities the tools for education, monitoring and influencing positive change and to encourage people to take an active role in restoring and sustaining nature.

Citizens' Opposed to Paving the Escarpment (COPE)
PO Box 40548, Stn. Upper Brant, Burlington ON L7P 4W1
e-mail: mail@cope-nomph.org
URL: www.cope-nomph.org
Overview: A large local organization
Membership: 1000+; *Fees:* Donations of $10 or more
Mission: To preserve the Niagara Escarpment, by ensuring that no new highway corridors are paved across the Niagara Escarpment & that all viable alternatives to the proposed Mid-Peninsula Highway are fully considered; *Affiliation(s):* Coalition on the Niagara Escarpment; Sierra Club

City Farmer - Canada's Office of Urban Agriculture
PO Box 74567, Stn. Kitsilano, Vancouver BC V6K 4P4
Tel: 604-685-5832
e-mail: cityfarm@interchange.ubc.ca
URL: www.cityfarmer.org
Social Media: cityfarmer.info
Overview: A small national organization founded in 1978
Activities: Research Garden functions as the City of Vancouver's Compost Demonstration Garden & site of the Compost Hotline: 604-736-2250
Mission: City Farmer encourages gardening in an urban environment. The website carries information for communities & schools about organic farming, composting, pest control.

Associations/Organizations / CIVICUS: World Alliance for Citizen Participation

CIVICUS: World Alliance for Citizen Participation
Stn. 933, 24 Gwigwi Mrwebi St., Johannesburg 2135 South Africa
Tel: +27 11 833 5959; *Fax:* +27 11 833 7997
e-mail: info@civicus.org; membership@civicus.org
URL: www.civicus.org
Overview: A small international organization
Chief Officer(s):
Ingrid Srinath, Secretary General
Katsuji Imata, Deputy Secretary General, Programs
Sebastian Njagi Runguma, Manager, Planning & Learning
Sandra Pires, Manager, Membership
Devendra Tak, Manager, Communications & Media
Membership: 450+; *Member Profile:* Citizens from 110 countries, including individuals, youth, business associates, citizen organizations, & nongovernmental grantmaking organizations
Activities: Advocating for citizen participation; Amplifying the opinions of ordinary people; Increasing the effectiveness of civil society organizations
Meetings/Conferences:
For more information see Trade Shows, Conferences and Seminars Chapter
CIVICUS: World Alliance for Citizen Participatio 10th World Assembly - Acting Together for a Just World
August 2011 Montréal, QC
CIVICUS: World Alliance for Citizen Participation 11th World Assembly - Acting Together for a Just World
August 2012 Montréal, QC
Publications: *Affinity Group of National Associations (AGNA) Newsletter*
Type: Newsletter
Civil Society Index (CSI) Newsletter
Type: Newsletter *Frequency:* q.
Profile: Project updates
Civil Society Watch (CSW) Monthly Bulletin
Type: Newsletter *Frequency:* m.
e-CIVICUS [a publication of CIVICUS: World Alliance for Citizen Participation]
Type: Newsletter *Frequency:* w.
Profile: Developments in civil society organizations around the world
Mission: To strengthen citizen action & civil society around the globe towards a more just & equitable world; To promote the rights of citizens to organize & act collectively; To foster interaction between civil society & other institutions

Clean Air Foundation
#201, 1216 Yonge St., Toronto ON M4T 1W1
Tel: 416-922-9038; *Fax:* 416-922-1028
URL: www.cleanairfoundation.org
Overview: A small national organization
Chief Officer(s):
Ersilia Serafini, Executive Director
eserafini@cleanairfoundation.org
Activities: Offering Car Heaven, Mow Down Pollution, Keep Cool, Switch Out, Energy Smarts, & Cool Shops
Mission: To develop, implement, & manage public engagement programs & other strategic approaches that lead to measurable emission reductions, to improve air quality & protect the climate
Environmental Activity: Reducing emissions; Improving air quality

Clean Air Strategic Alliance (CASA)
10035 - 108 St., 10th Fl., Edmonton AB T5J 3E1
Tel: 780-427-9793; *Fax:* 780-422-3127
e-mail: casa@casahome.org
URL: www.casahome.org
Social Media: www.facebook.com/group.php?gid=38613321574
Overview: A medium-sized provincial organization founded in 1994
Chief Officer(s):
Kerra Chomlak, Executive Director
Finances: *Annual Operating Budget:* $500,000-$1.5 Million; *Funding Sources:* Industry; Government; Donations
Staff: 200 volunteer(s)
Mission: To manage strategic issues of air quality in Alberta; To represent three levels of government, as well as industry & NGOs; To plan for, organize, & commit resources related to air quality in Alberta; Operating the Comprehensive Air Quality Management System (CAMS)
Environmental Activity: Working towards a vision of air that will be odourless, tasteless, look clear, & have no measurable short- or long-term adverse effects on people, animals, or the environment

Clean Annapolis River Project (CARP)
PO Box 395, Annapolis Royal NS B0S 1A0
Tel: 902-532-7533; *Fax:* 902-532-3038
Toll-Free: 888-547-4344
e-mail: carp@annapolisriver.ca
URL: www.annapolisriver.ca
Overview: A medium-sized local charitable organization founded in 1990
Finances: *Annual Operating Budget:* $250,000-$500,000; *Funding Sources:* Private & public
Staff: 12 staff member(s); 60 volunteer(s)
Membership: 100; *Fees:* $5 student; $7 individual; $10 family; $25 NGO; $100 lifetime
Activities: Environment monitoring; habitat restoration; climate change issues; water quality issues; public awareness;
Internships: Yes; *Speaker Service:* Yes; *Library:* Yes, open by appointment
Mission: To promote, encourage & assist with the wise use of the resources of the Annapolis Watershed; Water quality monitoring program

Clean Calgary Association *See* Green Calgary

Clean North
736A Queen St. East, Sault Ste Marie ON P6A 2A9
Tel: 705-945-1573
e-mail: info@cleannorth.org
URL: www.cleannorth.org
Also Known As: The Sault & District Recycling Association
Overview: A small provincial organization founded in 1989
Finances: *Annual Operating Budget:* $50,000-$100,000; *Funding Sources:* Membership dues; fundraising; foundations; grants
Staff: 210 volunteer(s)
Membership: 350; *Fees:* $10 & $15
Activities: Recycling phone books; dry cells; Christmas trees; *Internships:* Yes; *Speaker Service:* Yes; *Library:* Environmental Resource Room; Open to public
Mission: This citizens' group promotes environmental protection through reduction, reuse & recycling of residential & industrial waste in Sault Ste. Marie & the Algoma District.; *Member of:* Northwatch; Ontario Environmental Network; Affiliation(s): Ontario Environment Network; Northwatch
Environmental Activity: Planting trees

Clean Nova Scotia (CNS)
126 Portland St., Dartmouth NS B2Y 1H8
Tel: 902-420-3474; *Fax:* 902-424-5334
e-mail: cns@clean.ns.ca
URL: www.clean.ns.ca
Social Media: www.facebook.com/group.php?gid=8509319491
Previous Name: The Clean Nova Scotia Foundation
Overview: A medium-sized provincial charitable organization founded in 1988
Finances: *Funding Sources:* Donations; Sponsorships
Member Profile: Persons & businesses committed to the creation of a sustainable & healthy environment in Nova Scotia
Activities: Providing environmental education & information; *Awareness Events:* Commuter Challenge
Publications: *Clean Nova Scotia Annual Report*
Type: Yearbook *Frequency:* a.
Clean Nova Scotia Strategic Plan
Profile: A direction for the organization's activities during the next three to five years
A Carbon Offsetting Primer
Author: Gina Patterson
A Guide to Energy Efficiency for Religious Buildings in Nova Scotia
Type: Guide *Number of Pages:* 50
Profile: Sections of the guide include getting started, the walk-through audit, how to do a greenhouse gas inventory, youth group engagement, energy efficiency improvements, a case study, a master checklist, resources for churches, & references
Clean & Green Newsletter
Type: Newsletter *ISSN:* 1715-7897 *Price:* Free with Clean Nova Scotia membership
Profile: Environmental articles & tips, plus a list of interesting websites
Mission: To inspire positive environmental change in Nova Scotia
Environmental Activity: Effecting change in air quality, climate change, waste, water, energy, & health

The Clean Nova Scotia Foundation *See* Clean Nova Scotia

Clean Water Action
#1100, 1010 Vermont Ave. NW, Washington DC 20005-4918 USA
Tel: 202-895-0420; *Fax:* 202-895-0438
e-mail: dcjobs@cleanwater.org
URL: www.cleanwateraction.org
Overview: A large international organization founded in 1971
Membership: 1,200,000
Mission: a national organization of diverse people and groups working together for clean water, protection of health, creation of jobs and making democracy work for environmental causes.

Clear Hamilton of Pollution (CHOP) *See* Conserver Society of Hamilton & District

Climate Action Network - Canada
#412, 1 Nicholas St., Ottawa ON K1N 7B7
Tel: 613-241-4413
Toll-Free: 866-373-2990
e-mail: info@climateactionnetwork.ca
URL: www.climateactionnetwork.ca
Overview: A small national organization
Chief Officer(s):
David Coon, Chair
Fees: $40
Mission: To support & empower Canada's governments, private sector, labour & civil society by designing, developing & implementing effective strategies to reduce greenhouse gas emissions at international, national & local levels, & to prevent dangerous levels of human interference with the global climate system

Climate Institute
1785 Massachusetts Ave., NW, Washington DC 20036 USA
Tel: 202-547-0104; *Fax:* 202-547-0111
e-mail: info@climate.org
URL: www.climate.org
Overview: A medium-sized international charitable organization founded in 1986
Chief Officer(s):
John C. Topping Jr., President/CEO
Crispin Tickell, Chair (Emeritus)
Finances: *Annual Operating Budget:* $500,000-$1.5 Million; *Funding Sources:* Foundation; US government; Corporations
Staff: 8 staff member(s)
Membership: 1,500; *Fees:* $95 member; $200 associate; $1,000 patron; $2,500 sponsor; $5,000 benefactor; *Member Profile:* Scientists & environmentalists of many nationalities; *Committees:* Leadership Council
Activities: *Internships:* Yes; *Speaker Service:* Yes; *Library:* Yes, open by appointment
Publications: *Sudden & Disruptive Climate Change: Exploring the Real Risks & How We Can Avoid Them*
Type: Book *Editor:* Michael C. MacKracken et al.
Profile: An outline of the risks of & solutions to climate change
Climate Alert
Editor: Corrine Kisner
Profile: Quarterly Newsletter
Mission: To help maintain the balance between climate & life on earth; To strive to be a source of objective, reliable information & a trustworthy facilitator of dialogue among scientists, policy makers, business executives, & citizens
Environmental Activity: Conducting projects on energy efficiency & cities, climate change in developing countries, & environmental refugees

Le Club de gemmologie et de minérlogie de Montréal *See* Montréal Gem & Mineral Club

Club de naturalistes de Prince George *See* Prince George Naturalists

Club des ornithologues de Québec inc. (COQ)
Domaine de Maizerets, 2000, boul Montmorency, Québec QC G1J 5E7
Tél: 418-661-3544
Courriel: coq@coq.qc.ca
URL: www.coq.qc.ca
Aperçu: *Dimension:* petite; *Envergure:* provinciale; Organisme sans but lucratif; fondée en 1955
Membre(s) du bureau directeur:
Marguerite Larouche, Vice-président
Dany Cloutier, Trésorier
Louis Messely, Secrétaire
Norbert Lacroix, Président
Finances: *Budget de fonctionnement annuel:* Moins de $50,000

Personnel: 2 membre(s) du personnel; 25 bénévole(s)
Membre: 713; *Montant de la cotisation:* 22$ individus; 30$ organisme ou famille; *Critères d'admissibilité:* Toute personne qui aime les oiseaux et qui prend plaisir à se promener en pleine nature; *Comités:* Guide des Sites; Anniversaires du Club; Kiosques
Activités: Excursions; conférences; événements ornithologiques; cours ornithologiques; kiosques; observations ornithologiques; receusement de Noël; *Stagiaires:* Oui; *Service de conférenciers:* Oui
Mission: Organiser des excursions, camps, conférences, etc.; publier, imprimer des livres ou toute publication destinés à faire connaître les oiseaux; contribuer à encourager la conservation des milieux naturels propices aux oiseaux; *Affiliation(s):* Association québécoise des groupes d'ornithologues

Clubs 4-H du Québec
#224, 1040, av Belvédère, Sillery QC G1S 3G3
Tél: 418-529-4705; *Téléc:* 418-529-3021
Courriel: 4h.bc@qc.aira.com
URL: www.clubs4h.qc.ca
Aperçu: *Dimension:* moyenne; *Envergure: provinciale; fondée en 1942*
Membre(s) du bureau directeur:
Manon Fortier, Présidente
Finances: *Budget de fonctionnement annuel:* $100,000-$250,000
Personnel: 4 membre(s) du personnel; 300 bénévole(s)
Membre: 30 institutionnel; 1 000 individu; *Montant de la cotisation:* $100/club
Activités: *Evénements de sensibilisation:* Mois de l'arbre et des forêts, mai
Mission: Susciter et développer, chez le jeune, une préoccupation active pour la conservation de l'arbre, du milieu forestier et de l'environnement; développer le sens des autres, le sens des responsabilités, l'esprit d'initiative, la créativité, le sens de l'émerveillement et le respect pour tout ce qui vit; contribuer à répandre dans le public une mentalité de conservation envers l'environnement, en posant des gestes concrets pour l'amélioration de la qualité de la vie; *Membre de:* Regroupement Loisir Québec; Conseil québécois du loisir

Coady International Institute (CII)
St. Francis Xavier University, PO Box 5000, Antigonish NS B2G 2W5
Tel: 902-867-3960; *Fax:* 902-867-3907
Toll-Free: 866-820-7835
e-mail: coady@stfx.ca
URL: www.coady.stfx.ca
Overview: A large international charitable organization founded in 1959
Finances: *Annual Operating Budget:* $1.5 Million-$3 Million
Staff: 28 staff member(s)
Committees: University Advisory
Activities: Publishes occasional papers; *Awareness Events:* Coady Celebrates, Nov 1; *Internships:* Yes; *Library:* Marie Michael Library; Open to public
Mission: Promotes learning in individuals & organizations engaged in community-driven action to achieve wellbeing, global justice, peace & participating democracy; *Member of:* Canadian Council for International Cooperation
Environmental Activity: Environment & Development course taught as part of 6-month diploma course in Social Development

Coalition canadienne de l'énergie géothermique *See* Canadian GeoExchange Coalition

Coalition des communautés en santé de l'Ontario *See* Ontario Healthy Communities Coalition

Coalition for Education in the Outdoors
PO Box 2000, S.U.N.Y. Cortland, Cortland NY 13045 USA
Tel: 607-753-4971; *Fax:* 607-753-5982
e-mail: info@outdooredcoalition.org
URL: www.outdooredcoalition.org
Overview: A medium-sized international organization founded in 1987
Finances: *Annual Operating Budget:* Less than $50,000
Staff: 2 staff member(s)
Membership: 70 affiliates; *Fees:* $60-$250; *Member Profile:* A network of agencies, institutions, associations, centres, businesses & organizations linked & communicating in support of the broad purposes of education in, for, & about the outdoors
Activities: *Speaker Service:* Yes
Publications: *Taproot*
Profile: Quarterly Journal

Mission: To assist in identifying the networking needs of its affiliates & to seek ways to meet those needs

Coalition Jeunesse Sierra *See* Sierra Youth Coalition

Coalition of Rail Shippers (CRS)
#405, 580 Terry Fox Dr., Ottawa ON K2L 4C2
Tel: 613-599-3283; *Fax:* 613-599-1295
Overview: A medium-sized national organization founded in 2005
Member Profile: Shipping industry associations
Mission: CRS provides input to government on matters affecting Canadian, rail freight transportation.

Coalition to Save the Elms
1539 Waverley St., Winnipeg MB R3T 4V7
Tel: 204-832-7188; *Fax:* 204-986-4050
e-mail: elms@mts.net
URL: www.savetheelms.mb.ca
Overview: A medium-sized local charitable organization founded in 1992
Chief Officer(s):
Samantha Mutchmor, Executive Director
Finances: *Annual Operating Budget:* $50,000-$100,000
Staff: 1 staff member(s)
Membership: 10,000; *Fees:* $25 preferred; $15 regular/renewal
Activities: Public Workshops; treebanding program; *Awareness Events:* Arbor Day, June; Adopt-a-Tree Program; *Speaker Service:* Yes
Mission: To protect, preserve & promote the urban forest & environment

Coast Forest & Lumber Association *See* Coast Forest Products Association

Coast Forest Products Association (CFPA)
#1200, 1090 Pender St. West, Vancouver BC V6E 2N7
Tel: 604-891-1237; *Fax:* 604-682-8641
e-mail: info@coastforest.org
URL: www.coastforest.org
Also Known As: Coast Forest
Previous Name: Coast Forest & Lumber Association
Overview: A medium-sized international organization founded in 1994
Chief Officer(s):
Rick Jeffrey, President/CEO
Finances: *Annual Operating Budget:* $3 Million-$5 Million; *Funding Sources:* Coast Forest Industry; Partnership funding for lumber promotion in Japan & China
Staff: 3 staff member(s)
Membership: 20; *Fees:* Production related; *Member Profile:* Logging companies &/or lumber manufacturing companies
Activities: User-pay menu programs; log security; Japan & China lumber promotion;
Mission: To promote the interests & protect the rights of those engaged in the coast forest industry in BC; *Member of:* Canadian Wood Council; Business Council of BC; Vancouver Board of Trade

Coastal Ecosystems Research Foundation
General Delivery, Dawson's Landing BC V0N 1M0
Tel: 44-0-7745-730873; *Fax:* 815-327-0173
e-mail: info@cerf.bc.ca
URL: www.cerf.bc.ca
Overview: A small local organization founded in 1995
Chief Officer(s):
William Megill, Ph.D, Research Director
megillw@cerf.bc.ca
Finances: *Annual Operating Budget:* $50,000-$100,000; *Funding Sources:* Provincial & national government
Staff: 4 staff member(s)
Membership: 120
Activities: Week-long "research adventure" in which people can participate in all aspects of our research while living a wilderness adventure along the southern Central Coast of British Columbia; this program almost completely funds our research focused on grey & humpback whales studies of the subtidal intertidal & coastal forest zones;
Mission: To fund ecological research through eco-tourism

CODE
321 Chapel St., Ottawa ON K1N 7Z2
Tel: 613-232-3569; *Fax:* 613-232-7435
Toll-Free: 800-661-2633
e-mail: codehq@codecan.org
URL: www.codecan.org

Also Known As: Canadian Organization for Development through Education
Overview: A large international charitable organization founded in 1959
Finances: *Annual Operating Budget:* $1.5 Million-$3 Million; *Funding Sources:* Individual; corporate donations; CIDA
Staff: 15 staff member(s); 4500 volunteer(s)
Membership: 30; *Fees:* $20; *Committees:* Governance; Audit; Human Resources
Activities: Project Love - global education project held in Canadian schools every Feb.; students pack kits of school supplies for children in developing countries; Adopt a Library - support a community library in Tanzania, Ethiopia or Malawi; Code Cabinet - social networking to help raise awareness & funds for CODE programs
Mission: To enable people to learn by developing partnerships that provide resources for learning, to promote awareness & understanding & to encourage self-reliance; to support training for teachers & librarians; to coordinate books donations from North American publishers to schools & libraries in the developing world; *Member of:* Canadian Council for International Cooperation; *Affiliation(s):* International Book Bank; CODE Europe; CODE Inc.; CODE Foundation

Cole Harbour Rural Heritage Society (CHRHS)
471 Poplar Dr., Dartmouth NS B2W 4L2
Tel: 902-434-0222
e-mail: farm.museum@ns.aliantzinc.ca
URL: www.coleharbourfarmmuseum.ca/chrhs.html
Overview: A small local charitable organization founded in 1973
Finances: *Funding Sources:* Community support
Fees: $10 individuals; $15 families; $25 supporting members
Activities: Administering the Cole Harbour Rural Heritage Farm Museum, a community museum that preserves & interprets the agricultural history of Cole Harbour; Preserving the former Methodist Chapel, now known as the Cole Harbour Meeting House; Advocating for the protection of natural history in the Cole Harbour area; Providing education about the ecosystem of the region; Promoting careful use of sensitive lands around Cole Harbour
Mission: To protect & increase awareness of the natural history & cultural resources of Cole Harbour & the surrounding area; To foster appreciation & respect for the resources of the Cole Harbour region

Collège canadien des leaders en santé *See* Canadian College of Health Leaders

College of Alberta Professional Foresters
#209, 10544 - 106 St., Edmonton AB T5H 2X6
Tel: 780-432-1177; *Fax:* 780-432-7046
e-mail: office@capf.ca
URL: www.capf.ca
Previous Name: Alberta Registered Professional Foresters Association
Overview: A medium-sized provincial licensing organization founded in 1988
Chief Officer(s):
Ted Gooding, President
Finances: *Funding Sources:* Membership fees
Staff: 1 staff member(s); 14 volunteer(s)
Membership: 630+; *Fees:* $285 Registered Professional Forester (RPF); $261 Forester-in-Training (FIT); $52 retired; $142.50 non-resident; $52 Syllabus member; *Member Profile:* B.Sc. in Forestry + professional examination + 2 yr. Forester-in-Training period; *Committees:* Executive; Discipline; Competence; Registration; Policy, Act, Regulation & Bylaws; Finance; Nominating
Awards: Frank Appleby Professional Award (Award)
Mission: To maintain an accurate register of registered professional foresters in Alberta; To set standards of professional conduct & competence for members; To administer the title, Registered Professional Forester (RPF); *Member of:* Canadian Federation of Professional Foresters Associations; *Affiliation(s):* Alberta Forest Technologists Association; Canadian Institute of Forestry

College of Applied Biology British Columbia
#205, 733 Johnson St., Victoria BC V8W 3C7
Tel: 250-383-3306; *Fax:* 250-383-2400
e-mail: cab@cab-bc.org
URL: www.cab-bc.org
Overview: A small provincial licensing organization
Chief Officer(s):
Paul McElligott, RPBio., President
Linda Michaluk, RPBio., Executive Director
Finances: *Annual Operating Budget:* $250,000-$500,000

Associations/Organizations / Comité maritime international

Staff: 4 staff member(s); 30 volunteer(s)
Membership: 1,500
Mission: To uphold & protect the public interest by: preserving & protecting the scientific methods & principles that are the foundation of the applied bilogical sciences; upholding the principles of stewardship of aquatic & terrestrial ecosystems & biological resources; ensuring the integrity, objectivity & expertise of its members

Colonial Waterbird Society *See* The Waterbird Society

Comité canadien des Électrotechnologies *Voir* Conseil Canadien des Électrotechnologies

Comité intergouvernemental de recherches urbaines et régionales *See* Intergovernmental Committee on Urban & Regional Research

Comité maritime international (CMI) / International Maritime Committee
Everdijstraat 43, Antwerpen B-2000 Belgium
Tel: 32-3-227-3526; *Fax:* 32-3-227-3528
e-mail: admini@cmi-imc.org
URL: www.comitemaritime.org
Overview: A medium-sized international organization founded in 1897
Membership: 50 associations
Activities: *Library:* CMI-Secretariat; Open to public, open by appointment
Mission: To contribute by all appropriate means & activities to the unification of maritime law; *Affiliation(s):* Canadian Maritime Law Association

Commission Coopération Environnementale *See* Commission for Environmental Cooperation

Commission de coopération environnementale *See* Commission for Environmental Cooperation

Commission des Grands Lacs *See* Great Lakes Commission

Commission for Environmental Cooperation (CEC) / Commission Coopération Environnementale
Secrétariat, #200, 393, rue St-Jacques ouest, Montréal QC H2Y 1N9
Tel: 514-350-4300; *Fax:* 514-350-4314
e-mail: info@cec.org
URL: www.cec.org
Chief Officer(s):
Evan Lloyd, Acting Executive Director
Dane Ratliff, Director, Submission on Enforcement Matters Unit, 514-350-4332
José Carlos Fernández Ugalde, Manager, Environment & Trade Program, 514-350-4348
jcfernandez@cec.org
Hans Hermann, Senior Manager, Biodiversity, 514-350-4340
hhermann@cec.org
Marco Antonio Heredia Fragoso, Head, Environmental Law, 514-350-4302
maheredia@cec.org
Orlando Cabrera-Rivera, Program Manager, Air Quality & PRTR, 514-350-4323
ocabrera@cec.org
Luke Trip, Program Manager, Chemicals Management, 514-350-4372
ltrip@cec.org
Keith Channon, Program Manager, Pollutants & Health, 514-350-4323
kchannon@cec.org
Mission: The Commission for Environmental Cooperation (CEC) is an international organization created by Canada, Mexico & the United States under the North American Agreement on Environmental Cooperation (NAAEC). The CEC was established to address regional environmental concerns, help prevent potential trade & environmental conflicts & to promote the effective enforcement of environmental law. The Agreement complements the environmental provisions of the North American Free Trade Agreement (NAFTA)

Commission for Environmental Cooperation (CEC) / Commission de coopération environnementale (CCE)
#200, 393, rue St-Jacques ouest, Montréal QC H2Y 1N9
Tel: 514-350-4300; *Fax:* 514-350-4314
e-mail: info@cec.org
URL: www.cec.org

Overview: A medium-sized international organization founded in 1995
Chief Officer(s):
José Carlos Fernández Ugalde, Program Manager, Environment & Trade
Hans Hermann, Senior Program Manager, Conservation of Biodiversity
Felipe Adrián Vázquez-Gálvez, Executive Director
Finances: *Annual Operating Budget:* Greater than $5 Million; *Funding Sources:* Three NAFTA governments, Canada, Mexico, United States
Staff: 55 staff member(s)
Membership: 1-99
Activities: *Internships:* Yes; *Library:* Yes
Mission: Created by Canada, Mexico & the United States to address regional environmental concerns; to help prevent potential trade & environmental conflicts, & to promote the effective enforcement of environmental law

Commission for Sustainable Development
#DC2-2220, 2 United Nations Plaza, New York NY 10017 USA
Tel: 212-963-8102; *Fax:* 212-963-4260
e-mail: dsd@un.org
URL: www.un.org/esa/dsd/csd/csd_index.shtml
Chief Officer(s):
Patricia Chaves, Secretartiat
Member Profile: Members of the intergovernmental body are elected by the Economic & Social Council from memberstates of the United Nations & its specialized agencies
Activities: Promoting dialogue & building partnerships for sustainable development with governments, the international community, & the major groups who have a role to play in the transition towards sustainable development, including women, youth, indigenous peoples, non-governmental organizations, local authorities, workers & trade unions, business & industry, the scientific community, & farmers
Mission: To operate as a functional commission of the UN Economic & Social Council, composed of members elected for terms of office for three years; To meet annually; To be guided by a multi-year (2004-2017) program of work which outlines seven two-year cycles, with each two-year cyle focused on themes; To review progress at the international, regional, & national levels in the implementation of recommendations & commitments contained in Agenda 21 & the Rio Declaration on Environment & Development

Commission internationale de la santé au travail *See* International Commission on Occupational Health

Commission internationale des irrigations & du drainage *See* International Commission on Irrigation & Drainage

Commission Internationale du Genie Rural *See* International Commission of Agricultural & Biosystems Engineering

Committee for the National Institutes for the Environment *See* National Council for Science & the Environment

Committee on Nutrition in the Commonwealth *See* Commonwealth Human Ecology Council

Commonwealth Association of Surveying & Land Economy (CASLE)
c/o Faculty of the Built Environment, Univ. of West England, Coldharbour Lane, Bristol BS16 1QY United Kingdom
Tel: 44-117-750440; *Fax:* 44-117-750440
e-mail: sspedding@rics.org.uk
URL: www.casle.org
Overview: A medium-sized international organization founded in 1969
Finances: *Annual Operating Budget:* $50,000-$100,000
Membership: 40 societies; *Member Profile:* Open to leading society in each surveying discipline in each Commonwealth country; *Committees:* Management Board
Activities: Conferences/seminars; research into sustainable development
Mission: To maintain & strengthen professional links between Commonwealth countries, with the aim of assisting each country to achieve the scale, quality & integrity of surveying services that it requires; to foster the establishment of professional societies in countries where none exists & to promote their usefulness for the public advantage

Commonwealth Engineers' Council (CEC)
The Institution of Civil Engineers, One Great George St., London SW1P 3AA United Kingdom

Tel: 44-20-7665-2156; *Fax:* 44-20-7223-1806
e-mail: bridget.tracy@ice.org.uk
URL: www.ice.org.uk/cec/
Overview: A small international organization founded in 1946
Finances: *Funding Sources:* Membership fees; Commonwealth Foundation
Staff: 3 staff member(s)
Membership: 42
Member of: World Federation of Engineering Organizations; *Affiliation(s):* Canadian Council of Professional Engineers

Commonwealth Forestry Association - Canadian Chapter (CFA)
c/o Faculty of Forestry, University of BC, #2045, 2424 Main Mall, Vancouver BC V6T 1Z4
Tel: 604-822-6761; *Fax:* 604-822-9106
URL: www.cfa-international.org
Overview: A small international organization founded in 1921
Chief Officer(s):
John Innes, Professor, Regional Director, The Americas
john.innes@ubc.ca
Finances: *Annual Operating Budget:* Less than $50,000
Staff: 1 volunteer(s)
Membership: 60; *Fees:* $108; *Member Profile:* Professional foresters
Mission: To promote the conservation and sustainable management of the world's forests and the contribution they make to peoples' livelihoods; *Member of:* Commonwealth Forestry Association, UK

Commonwealth Geographical Bureau (CGB)
c/o Dept. of Geography, 1 Arts Link, National Univ. of Singapore, Singapore 117570 Singapore
Tel: 65-6874-3855; *Fax:* 65-6777-3091
URL: www.commonwealthgeography.org
Overview: A small international organization founded in 1968
Finances: *Annual Operating Budget:* Less than $50,000; *Funding Sources:* Commonwealth Foundation
Staff: 4 volunteer(s)
Membership: 5,000-14,999; *Member Profile:* Commonwealth geographers; *Committees:* Management; Small Island Development
Activities: Organizing workshops
Mission: CGB promotes the study & practice of geography at all levels within the Commonwealth, especially in developing countries. It aims to disseminate information to Commonwealth geographers & effect the exchange of staff between member countries.; *Affiliation(s):* International Geographical Union

Commonwealth Human Ecology Council (CHEC)
Church House, Newton Rd., Bayswater, London W2 5LS United Kingdom
Tel: 44 (0) 207 7925934; *Fax:* 44 (0) 207 7925948
e-mail: chec@btopenworld.com
URL: www.checinternational.org
Previous Name: Committee on Nutrition in the Commonwealth
Overview: A medium-sized international charitable organization founded in 1969
Finances: *Annual Operating Budget:* $100,000-$250,000; *Funding Sources:* Commonwealth Foundation; UK Government; UK Lottery; Comic Relief
Staff: 4 staff member(s); 2 volunteer(s)
Membership: 500; *Fees:* £20 individual; £50 corporate; *Member Profile:* Government; non-government; professionals; cross section of communities & civil society; *Committees:* Executives; Finance; Governing Board; Projects
Mission: CHEC is a human ecology network with links in many Commonwealth countries. The Council challenges governments to create policies in support of ecological & sustainable communities, & has successfully implemented projects in countries as diverse as Kenya, Bangladesh, Hong Kong, Malta, New Zealand, India, Canada, Guyana, Barbados, Sierra Leone, Pakistan, Nigeria, Australia, & Sri Lanka. It promotes discussion & action programmes with emphasis on the joint responsibilities of government, civil society & the individual to alleviate poverty. It is recognized in Britain as an international charity.; *Affiliation(s):* In consultative status with UN ECOSOC (Economic & Social Council)

Communications & Information Technology Ontario (CITO)
#200, 2625 Queensview Dr., Ottawa ON K2B 8K2
Tel: 613-726-3420; *Fax:* 613-726-3424
Toll-Free: 566-759-6014
Also Known As: Centre for Communications & Information Technology
Previous Name: Information Technology Research Centre

Merged from: Telecommunications Research Institute of Ontario
Overview: A small provincial organization
Finances: *Annual Operating Budget:* $1.5 Million-$3 Million; *Funding Sources:* Provincial government; industry
Staff: 10 staff member(s)
Membership: 56; *Fees:* $300-$2,000; *Member Profile:* Communications or information technology service provider, developer or user
Activities: *Library:* Yes, Not open to the public
Mission: To be a catalyst for innovation & entreprenership in Ontario's communications & information technology industry; to promote the interchange of people, ideas & technologies between industry & universities by advancing university-based research & supporting universities in graduating students in communications & information technology; *Member of:* Ontario Centres of Excellence

Communications, Energy & Paperworkers Union of Canada (CEP) / Syndicat canadien des communications, de l'énergie et du papier (SCEP)
301 Laurier Ave. West, Ottawa ON K1P 6M6
Tel: 613-230-5200; *Fax:* 613-230-5801
Toll-Free: 877-230-5201
e-mail: info@cep.ca
URL: www.cep.ca
Overview: A large national organization founded in 1992
Chief Officer(s):
Gaétan Ménard, Sec.-Treas.
Dave Coles, President
Finances: *Annual Operating Budget:* Greater than $5 Million; *Funding Sources:* Membership dues
Staff: 150 staff member(s)
Membership: 167,470 + 853 locals; *Committees:* Health & Safety; Pensions; Women's; Special Committees
Activities: Education Program; *Library:* Yes
Meetings/Conferences:
For more information see Trade Shows, Conferences and Seminars Chapter
Communication, Energy & Paperworkers Union of Canada 2012 Convention
October 2012 Québec, QC
Mission: To improve pay & working conditions through collective bargaining & to represent members at grievance hearings; to present a common front with other unions & community groups to governments on issues that affect all workers, from minimum wage to medicare; Affiliation(s): Canadian Labour Congress

Community & Hospital Infection Control Association Canada / Association pour la prévention des infections à l'hôpital et dans la communauté - Canada
PO Box 46125, RPO Westdale, Winnipeg MB R3R 3S3
Tel: 204-897-5990; *Fax:* 204-895-9595
Toll-Free: 866-999-7111
e-mail: chicacda@mts.net
URL: www.chica.org
Also Known As: CHICA-Canada
Overview: A medium-sized national charitable organization founded in 1976
Chief Officer(s):
Marion Yetman, President, 709-729-3287, Fax: 709-729-0730
MarionYetman@gov.nl.ca
Activities: Education; Communication; Standards; Research; Consumer awareness; *Library:* Yes
Publications: *Canadian Journal of Infection Control*
Type: Journal *Language:* B *Frequency:* q. *Editor:* Pat Piaskowski, RN, HBScN, CIC *Price:* Free with CHICA-Canada membership
Profile: Information relevant to the practice of infection control in hospitals & communities
Community & Hospital Infection Control Association Canada Annual Member & Source Guide
Type: Yearbook *Frequency:* a. *Price:* Free with CHICA-Canada membership
Mission: To promote excellence in the practice of infection prevention & control; to employ evidence based practice & application of epidemiological principles to improve the health of Canadians; *Member of:* International Federation of Infection Control (IFIC)

Community Health Nurses of Canada (CHNC) / Infirmières et infirmiers en santé communautaire au Canada
182 Clendenan Ave., Toronto ON M6P 2X2
Tel: 647-239-9554; *Fax:* 416-426-7280
e-mail: info@chnc.ca
URL: www.chnc.ca
Overview: A medium-sized provincial organization founded in 1987
Chief Officer(s):
Kate Thompson, BScN, MSc, CCHN, President
kate_chnc@rogers.com
Evelyn Butler, RN, BN, MPA, Administrative Manager
evelyn.cbutler@gmail.com
Ruth Schofield, RN, MSc(T), Secretary
schofir@mcmaster.ca
Anne Clarotto, RN, BN, MHS, Treasurer
anne.clarotto@interiorhealth.ca
Yvette Laforet-Fliesser, RN, BScN, MScN,, Officer, Communications
yvette.laforetfliesser@mlhu.on.ca
Member Profile: Community health nurses throughout Canada; Provincial & territorial community health nursing interest groups; *Committees:* Bylaws, Constitution, & Annual General Meeting; Certification, Standards, & Competencies; Communication / Membership; Education / Professional Development; Political Action / Advocacy
Activities: Facilitating communication among community health nurses throughout Canada; Developing standards of practice & a community health nursing certification process
Publications: *Community Health Nurses of Canada Newsletter*
Type: Newsletter *Price:* Free with Community Health Nurses of Canada membership
Profile: Association communications to members
Public Health Nursing Competencies
Community Health Nursing Standards of Practice
Community Health Nursing Vision 2020: Shaping the Future
Public Health Nursing Practice in Canada: A Review of the Literature
Community Health Nursing Standards Toolkit
Profile: A resource to facilitate use of standards
Mission: To act as the voice of community health nurses across Canada; To respond to issues which affect community health nurses; *Member of:* Canadian Nurses Association (CNA); Affiliation(s): Registered Nurses Association Community Health Nurses Initiatives Group
Environmental Activity: Promoting the health of communities & community health nursing

Les companies de recherche pharmaceutique du Canada
See Canada's Research-Based Pharmaceutical Companies (Rx&D)

Compost Council of Canada / Conseil canadien du compost
16 Northumberland St., Toronto ON M6H 1P7
Tel: 416-535-0240; *Fax:* 416-536-9892
Toll-Free: 877-571-4769
e-mail: info@compost.org
URL: www.compost.org
Social Media:
www.facebook.com/people/Compost-Council/100001137258465
Overview: A medium-sized national organization founded in 1991
Chief Officer(s):
Susan Antler, Executive Director
Activities: Providing resources for the Canadian compost industry; *Awareness Events:* Compost Week, May
Meetings/Conferences:
For more information see Trade Shows, Conferences and Seminars Chapter
Compost Council of Canada 2011 21st Annual National Compost Conference
September 2012 Charlottetown, PE
Compost Council of Canada 2012 22nd Annual National Compost Conference
Other Conferences in 2012 2012
Compost Council of Canada 2012 Regional Workshop: Compost Matters!
Other Conferences in 2012 2012
Compost Council of Canada 2012 Compost Garden Party
Other Conferences in 2012 2012
Compost Council of Canada 2013 23rd Annual National Compost Conference
Other Conferences in 2013 2013
Publications: *Compost Matters*
Type: Newsletter
Profile: Information for members of the Compost Council of Canada, such as regulations, members, grants, workshops, conferences, & awareness events
Mission: To advance organics residuals recycling & compost use; To contribute to environmental sustainability
Environmental Activity: Advocating for organics residuals recycling; Offering composting & other greening advice; Promoting composting & compost usage; Developing a greenhouse gas protocol for centralized costing facilities in Canada

Compressed Gas Association, Inc. (CGA)
4221 Walney Rd., 5th Fl., Chantilly VA 20151-2923 USA
Tel: 703-788-2700; *Fax:* 703-961-1831
e-mail: cga@cganet.com
URL: www.cganet.com
Overview: A small international organization founded in 1913
Finances: *Funding Sources:* Membership dues
Staff: 14 staff member(s)
Membership: 150; *Fees:* Schedule available
Awards: Compressed Gas Association Safety Awards
Mission: To promote, develop & coordinate technical & standardization activities in compressed gas industries in interest of public safety

Concerned Educators Allied for a Safe Environment (CEASE)
55 Frost St., Cambridge MA 2140 USA
Tel: 617-661-8347
e-mail: info@peaceeducators.org
URL: www.peaceeducators.org
Overview: A small national organization founded in 1979
Chief Officer(s):
Lucy Stroock
Susan Hopkins
Chris Lamm
Lucy Stroock, Sec.-Treas.
Finances: *Annual Operating Budget:* Less than $50,000; *Funding Sources:* Subscriptions; membership dues; donations
Staff: 6 volunteer(s)
Membership: 1,000; *Fees:* $10; $5 student; *Member Profile:* Early childhood educators & trainers
Activities: Workshops; seminars
Mission: To create safe world for children; to seek to end the violence in society & remove the root causes of violence by advocating for peace, justice & economic opportunity; *Member of:* Survival Education Fund; Affiliation(s): National Association for the Education of Young Children

Le Conference Board du Canada *See* The Conference Board of Canada

The Conference Board of Canada / Le Conference Board du Canada
255 Smyth Rd., Ottawa ON K1H 8M7
Tel: 613-526-3280; *Fax:* 613-526-4857
Toll-Free: 866-711-2262
e-mail: contactcboc@conferenceboard.ca
URL: www.conferenceboard.ca
Overview: A medium-sized national organization founded in 1954
Finances: *Funding Sources:* Fees for service to the public & private sectors
Activities: The Business & Environment Research Program provides research & networking facilities for business & government in the economics, business management & public policy aspects of environmental issues. Other activities include conferences, publishing & disseminating research, & facilitating networking & training for leadership; *Library:* Information Centre; open by appointment
Awards: National Awards in Governance (Award)
Awarded to boards of directors that have demonstrated excellence in governance & have implemented successful innovations in their governance practices; overall award for innovation & sector specific awards for public, private & not for profit sectors
National Awards for Excellence in Business-Education Partnership (Award)
Awarded to partnerships that have a demonstrated record of success in promoting the importance of science, technology &/or mathematics; linking education & the world of work, promoting teacher development, encouraging students to stay in school, expanding vocational &/or apprenticeship training Contact: Mary Ann McLaughlin
Mission: To be dedicated to applied research, notably in public policy, economic trends, & organizational performance

Conférence des coopératives forestières du Québec *Voir* Fédération québécoise des coopératives forestières

Associations/Organizations / Conference of New England Governors & Eastern Canadian Premiers

Conférence des Nations Unies sur le commerce et le développement See United Nations Conference on Trade & Development

Conference of New England Governors & Eastern Canadian Premiers
Eastern Canadian Secretariat, PO Box 2044, Halifax NS B3J 2Z1
Tel: 902-424-7590; Fax: 902-424-8976
e-mail: info@cap-cpma.ca
URL: www.cap-cpma.ca
Chief Officer(s):
Don Osmond, Secretary, Council of Atlantic Premiers
Member Profile: Premiers of the Atlantic provinces & Québec; Governors of six New England States
Activities: Hosting conferences of the Premiers & Governors to discuss issues of common interest; Convening meetings of state & provincial officials; Organizing workshops & roundtables; Preparing reports & studies; Monitoring & acting on common issues in the northeast region, such as electric restructuring
Mission: To expand economic ties among the Atlantic provinces, Québec, & six New England states; To foster energy exchanges; To coordinate numerous policies & programs, in areas such as transportation, forest management, tourism, small-scale agriculture & fisheries; To enact policy resolutions that call on actions by the state & provincial governments, as well as by the two national governments; To promote natural gas, resource, & infrastructure development
Environmental Activity: Advocating for environmental issues & & sustainable development; Adopting an acid rain action plan & a mercury action plan; Collaborating with environmental departments & agencies

Congrès du travail du Canada See Canadian Labour Congress

Congrès mondiaux du pétrole See World Petroleum Congress

Connexions Information Sharing Services
#305, 489 College St., Toronto ON M6G 1A5
Tel: 416-964-1511
URL: www.connexions.org
Overview: A small national organization founded in 1975
Finances: Annual Operating Budget: Less than $50,000
Staff: 3 staff member(s); 12 volunteer(s)
Activities: Internships: Yes; Speaker Service: Yes; Rents Mailing List: Yes; Library: Yes, open by appointment
Mission: To link people striving to create positive solutions to social, environmental, economic & international problems; to encourage development of a more just & democratic society; to disseminate information & ideas that contribute to this goal;
Member of: Ontario Environment Network

Conseil canadien de droit international See Canadian Council on International Law

Conseil canadien de l'énergie See Energy Council of Canada

Conseil canadien de l'horticulture See Canadian Horticultural Council

Conseil canadien de la construction en acier See Canadian Steel Construction Council

Conseil canadien de la distribution alimentaire See Canadian Council of Grocery Distributors

Conseil canadien de la fourrure See The Fur Council of Canada

Conseil canadien de la lutte antiparasitaire en milieu urbain See Urban Pest Management Council of Canada

Conseil canadien de la sécurité See Canada Safety Council

Conseil canadien de protection des animaux See Canadian Council on Animal Care

Conseil canadien des administrateurs en transport motorisé See Canadian Council of Motor Transport Administrators

Conseil canadien des aliments et de la nutrition See Canadian Council of Food & Nutrition

Conseil Canadien des arpenteurs-géomètres See Canadian Council of Land Surveyors

Conseil canadien des chefs d'entreprise See Canadian Council of Chief Executives

Conseil canadien des directeurs provinciaux et des commissaires des incendies See Council of Canadian Fire Marshals & Fire Commissioners

Conseil Canadien des Électrotechnologies (CCE) / Canadian Council on Electrotechnologies (CCE)
600, av de la Montagne, Shawinigan QC G9N 7N5
Tél: 819-539-1560; Téléc: 819-539-1558
Nom précédent: Comité canadien des Électrotechnologies
Aperçu: Dimension: moyenne; Envergure: nationale; fondée en 1986
Membre: 20; Montant de la cotisation: 500$; Critères d'admissibilite: Industriels, ingénieurs, chercheurs, professeurs, producteurs et distributeurs d'électricité
Activités: Groupes technologie, éducation, information; Service de conférenciers: Oui; Bibliothèque: Oui, Bibliothèque publique, rendez-vous
Mission: Transfert technologique en vue de l'utilisation rationnelle et optimale de l'électricité

Conseil canadien des laboratoires indépendants See Canadian Council of Independent Laboratories

Conseil canadien des ministres de l'environnement See Canadian Council of Ministers of the Environment

Conseil canadien des ministres des forêts See Canadian Council of Forest Ministers

Conseil canadien des pêcheurs professionnels See Canadian Council of Professional Fish Harvesters

Conseil canadien des professionnels en sécurité agréés See Board of Canadian Registered Safety Professionals

Conseil canadien des techniciens et technologues See Canadian Council of Technicians & Technologists

Conseil canadien du bois See Canadian Wood Council

Conseil canadien du commerce de détail See Retail Council of Canada

Conseil canadien du compost See Compost Council of Canada

Conseil canadien pour la coopération internationale See Canadian Council for International Co-operation

Conseil canadien pour le contrôle du tabac See Canadian Council for Tobacco Control

Conseil canadien sectoriel des plastiques See Canadian Plastics Sector Council

Conseil de conservation de l'Ontario See Conservation Council of Ontario

Conseil de l'industrie forestière du Québec (CIFQ) / Québec Forestry Industry Council (QFIC)
#200, 1175, av Lavigerie, Sainte-Foy QC G1V 4P1
Tél: 418-657-7916; Téléc: 418-657-7971
Courriel: info@cifq.qc.ca
URL: www.cifq.qc.ca
Nom précédent: Association des manufacturiers de bois de sciage du Québec
Aperçu: Dimension: grande; Envergure: provinciale
Membre: 200 compagnies; Critères d'admissibilite: Membres réguliers - compagnies possédant une ou des usines de sciage ou de rabotage ou papetière; membres remanufacturiers - compagnies dont la fonction consiste à transformer le bois en provenance d'une autre; membres associés - grossistes, manufacturiers d'équipements, consultants, sociétés financières dont les activités sont reliées à celles des membres réguliers
Activités: Listes de destinataires: Oui
Mission: Représente la très grande majorité des entreprises de sciage résineux, de pâtes, papiers, cartons et panneaux oeuvrant au Québec; se consacre à la défense des intérêts de ces entreprsies, à la promotion de leur contribution au développement socio-économique, à la gestion intégrée et à l'aménagement durable des forêts, de même qu'à l'utilisation optimale des ressources naturelles; oeuvre auprès des instances gouvernementales, des organismes publics et parapublics, des organisations et de la population; encourage un comportement responsable de ses membres en regard des dimensions environnementales, économiques et sociales de leurs activités.
Environmental Activity: Comité Environnement

Conseil de la conservation du Nouveau-Brunswick See Conservation Council of New Brunswick

Conseil de la recherche forestière du Québec (CRFQ) / Québec Forest Research Council
#203, 1175, av Lavigerie, Sainte-Foy QC G1V 4P1
Tél: 418-656-6041; Téléc: 418-657-7971
Courriel: info@crfq.qc.ca
URL: www.crfq.qc.ca
Aperçu: Dimension: moyenne; Envergure: provinciale; Organisme sans but lucratif; fondée en 1988
Membre(s) du bureau directeur:
Jacques Gauvin, Président
Finances: Budget de fonctionnement annuel: $100,000-$250,000
Personnel: 2 membre(s) du personnel; 28 bénévole(s)
Membre: 10; Montant de la cotisation: 23,50$; Critères d'admissibilite: Associations, ministères et universités; Comités: Coordonation de la recherche forestière
Mission: Orienter, coordonner et faire la promotion de la recherche forestière au Québec

Conseil de la transformation agroalimentaire et des produits de consommation (CTAC) / Council of Food Processing & Consumer Products
#102, 200, rue MacDonald, Saint-Jean-sur-Richelieu QC J3B 8J6
Tél: 450-349-1521; Téléc: 450-349-6923
Courriel: info@conseiltac.com
URL: www.conseiltac.com
Nom précédent: Association des manufacturiers de produits alimentaires du Québec
Merged from: Conseil de la boulangerie du Québec; Association des abattoirs avicoles du Québec
Aperçu: Dimension: moyenne; Envergure: provinciale; Organisme sans but lucratif; fondée en 1954
Finances: Budget de fonctionnement annuel: $500,000-$1.5 Million
Personnel: 5 membre(s) du personnel
Membre: 400; Critères d'admissibilite: Fabricants; fournisseurs; distributeurs; Comités: Activités sociales; Agriculture; Environnement; Mise en marchéNégociations; Nomination; Recrutement; Santé et sécurité du travail; Travail
Mission: Le porte-parole officiel des manufacturiers de produits alimentaires du Québec qui s'y regroupent à titre de membres fabricants; canalise les représentations des manufacturiers, en particulier auprès des gouvernements; coordonne l'action des membres en vue de promouvoir leurs intérêts économiques, sociaux et professionnels; suscite l'éducation des consommateurs sur les valeurs d'une bonne alimentation; favorise la promotion des produits fabriqués par les membres; établit des liaisons entre les manufacturiers, les producteurs, les fournisseurs, les distributeurs, les consommateurs et les autres maillons de la chaîne alimentaire; encourage la recherche dans les domaines de l'agriculture, de l'alimentation et du marketing

Conseil de sécurité d'Ottawa See Ottawa Safety Council

Conseil des 4-H du Canada See Canadian 4-H Council

Conseil des aéroports du Canada See Canadian Airports Council

Conseil des bio-industries du Québec; Association québécoise des bio-industries Voir BIOQuébec

Conseil des fabricants de bois See Wood Manufacturing Council

Conseil des monuments et sites du Québec (CMSQ)
82, Grande-Allée ouest, Québec QC G1R 2G6
Tél: 418-647-4347; Téléc: 418-647-6483
Ligne sans frais: 800-494-4347
Courriel: cmsq@cmsq.qc.ca
URL: www.cmsq.qc.ca
Aperçu: Dimension: petite; Envergure: provinciale; fondée en 1975
Finances: Budget de fonctionnement annuel: $100,000-$250,000
Personnel: 10 membre(s) du personnel; 100 bénévole(s)
Membre: 2 000; Montant de la cotisation: 25$ étudiant; 40$ membre régulier; 50$ membre associé75$ institution; Critères d'admissibilite: Ouvert à toute personne intéressée par la sauvegarde et la mise en valeur du patrimoine du Québec
Activités: Evénements de sensibilisation: Réseau des intérieurs et des jardins anciens de Québec; Listes de destinataires: Oui; Bibliothèque: Oui
Mission: Oeuvrer à valoriser et faire connaître les monuments et les sites aux autorités et à la population du Québec; rassembler les individus, organismes et groupes partageant sa

Associations/Organizations / Conseil patronal de l'environnement du Québec

mission; entreprendre les actions appropriées à la mise en valeur et à la sauvegarde des éléments patrimoniaux

Conseil des palettes du Canada See Canadian Pallet Council

Conseil des provinces atlantiques pour les sciences See Atlantic Provinces Council on the Sciences

Conseil des viandes du Canada See Canadian Meat Council

Conseil du bâtiment durable du Canada See Canada Green Building Council

Conseil du Manitoba pour la coopération internationale See Manitoba Council for International Cooperation

Conseil du recyclage de l'Ontario See Recycling Council of Ontario

Conseil international des Monuments et des Sites See International Council on Monuments & Sites

Conseil international des sciences de l'animal de laboratoire See International Council for Laboratory Animal Science

Conseil international du Canada See Canadian International Council

Conseil Mondial de l'Energie See World Energy Council

Conseil patronal de l'environnement du Québec (CPEQ)
#206, 640, rue Saint-Paul ouest, Montréal QC H3C 1L9
Tél: 514-393-1122; Téléc: 514-393-1146
Courriel: info@cpeq.qc.ca
URL: www.cpeq.qc.ca
Aperçu: Dimension: moyenne; Envergure: provinciale
Membre(s) du bureau directeur:
Hélène Lauzon, Présidente
Mission: To promote the interests of industry & business in environmental matters

Conseil québécois sur le tabac et la santé / Québec Council on Tobacco & Health
#302, 4126, rue St-Denis, Montréal QC H2W 2M5
Tél: 514-948-5317; Téléc: 514-948-4582
Courriel: info@cqts.qc.ca
URL: www.cqts.qc.ca
Aperçu: Dimension: moyenne; Envergure: provinciale; Organisme sans but lucratif; fondée en 1976
Membre(s) du bureau directeur:
Mario Bujold, Directeur général
Finances: Budget de fonctionnement annuel: $250,000-$500,000
Membre: 600
Activités: Evénements de sensibilisation: Semaine québécoise pour un avenir sans tabac
Mission: Promouvoir la santé du fumeur et du non-fumeur; faire le lien entre les associations, groupes bénévoles et autres intéressés à la santé publique; trouver des approches et des moyens pour améliorer l'éducation face à l'usage du tabac;
Membre de: Conseil canadien pour le contrôle du tabac

Conseil régional de l'environnement de la Gaspésie et des Iles-de-la-Madeleine (CREGIM)
#103, 106-A, Port Royal, Bonaventure QC G0C 1E0
Tél: 418-534-4498
Ligne sans frais: 877-534-4498
Courriel: cregim@globetrotter.net
URL: www.cregim.org
Aperçu: Dimension: petite; Envergure: locale; fondée en 1995
Membre(s) du bureau directeur:
Caroline Duchesne, Directrice
caroline.cregim@globetrotter.net
Maryèvette Charland-Lallier, Présidente
Monette Bujold, Secrétaire adjointe-administrative
monette.cregim@globetrotter.net
Finances: Budget de fonctionnement annuel:
$50,000-$100,000; Fonds: Gouvernement provincial; gouvernement régional; gouvernement municipal
Personnel: 4 membre(s) du personnel; 9 bénévole(s)
Membre: 119; Montant de la cotisation: 100$ institutionnel; 10$ individu; 30$ associé
Mission: Regrouper et représenter des organismes proenvironnementaux et des individus voués à la protection et la mise en valeur de l'environnement, auprès de toutes les instances concernées; favoriser la concertation et assurer l'établissement de priorités et de suivi en matière d'environnement; favoriser et promouvoir des stratégies d'actions concertées; agir à titre d'organisme ressource aux services des intervenants régionaux; Affiliation(s): Regroupement national des Conseils régionaux en environnement

Conservation Council of New Brunswick (CCNB) / Conseil de la conservation du Nouveau-Brunswick
180 St. John St., Fredericton NB E3B 4A9
Tel: 506-458-8747; Fax: 506-458-1047
e-mail: info@conservationcouncil.ca
URL: www.conservationcouncil.ca
Overview: A medium-sized provincial charitable organization founded in 1969
Finances: Annual Operating Budget: $100,000-$250,000; Funding Sources: Enterprise activities; special events; contracts for special projects
Staff: 3 staff member(s)
Membership: 550; Fees: Schedule available
Activities: Speaking engagements, educational publications, displays & demonstration projects; direct representation to government, industry & the media; forest conservation program; marine conservation program; toxics in the environment program; global climate change; Rents Mailing List: Yes; Library: Yes
Mission: To generate awareness of the ecological foundations of our quality of life; to promote public policies with respect to the integrity of natural systems & to contribute to a sustainable society; to advocate appropriate remedies to pressing environmental problems such as ground water contamination & hazardous wastes.; Member of: New Brunswick Environmental Network; Canadian Environmental Networks; Affiliation(s): Friends of the Earth Canada

Conservation Council of Ontario (CCO) / Conseil de conservation de l'Ontario
215 Spadina Ave., Toronto ON M5T 2C7
Tel: 416-533-1635
e-mail: cco@web.ca
URL: www.greenontario.org/cco/index.html
Overview: A medium-sized provincial charitable organization founded in 1951
Membership: 44 organizations + 62 individuals; Member Profile: Organizations & individuals dedicated to conservation & a healthy environment
Activities: Increasing public awareness; Promoting conservation solutions; Provision of meetings, workshops, & conferences about ideas & issues of concern
Mission: To build a strong province-wide conservation movement

Conservation de la faune au Canada See Wildlife Preservation Canada

Conservation Foundation
5 Shoreham Dr., Toronto ON M3N 1S4
Tel: 416-667-6279; Fax: 416-667-6275
e-mail: fdn@trca.on.ca
URL: www.trca.on.ca
Previous Name: The Metropolitan Toronto & Region Conservation Foundation; The Conservation Foundation of Greater Toronto
Overview: A small local charitable organization founded in 1961
Chief Officer(s):
Linda Craib, Admin Coordinator & Sr. Researcher
lcraib@trca.on.ca
David Love, Executive Director
dlove@trca.on.ca
Finances: Annual Operating Budget: $250,000-$500,000; Funding Sources: Donors include businesses, industries, other foundations, estates, conservation organizations & individuals
Staff: 20 volunteer(s)
Membership: 20; Committees: Board; Campaign; Executive; Members
Activities: Tree For Life Program; Kortright Centre for Conservation; Conservation Education Field Centres (conservation education schools at Albion Hills, Cold Creek & Claremont Conservation Areas); conservation libraries & scholarships; Don River; Greenspace Strategy (the authority's conservation vision for the 21st century - urges greater cooperation between the authority, the province & the municipalities in managing the regional watershed; also advocates protection of the Oak Ridges Moraine complex
Mission: To acquire & manage regional greenspace & watershed conservation lands; To support watershed management, reforestation, wildlife habitats, public access & recreation, historic sites, & environmental rehabilitation of natural spaces; Affiliation(s): The Toronto & Region Conservation Authority

Conservation Halton Foundation
2596 Britannia Rd., RR#2, Milton ON L9T 2X6
Tel: 905-336-1158; Fax: 905-336-7014
e-mail: admin@hrca.on.ca
URL: www.conservationhalton.on.ca
Previous Name: Halton Foundation
Overview: A small local charitable organization
Chief Officer(s):
Brian Penman, Chair
John Vice, Vice-Chair
Finances: Annual Operating Budget: $100,000-$250,000
Mission: To raise funds for Conservation Halton projects & programs that protect & enhance the natural environment

Conservation International (CI)
#500, 2011 Crystal Drive, Arlington VA 22202 USA
Tel: 703-341-2400
Toll-Free: 800-429-5660
e-mail: newmember@conservation.org
URL: www.conservation.org
Overview: A large international charitable organization founded in 1987
Chief Officer(s):
Matthew Costello, Secretary, Board of Directors
Russell A. Mittermeier, President
Peter Seligmann, Chair & CEO
Barbara DiPietro, Vice-President, Finance & Administration
Finances: Annual Operating Budget: Greater than $5 Million; Funding Sources: Private; government; agencies; foundations
Staff: 1200 staff member(s)
Membership: 5,000; Fees: $35; Member Profile: Scientists; economists; communicators; educators; conservation professionals
Activities: Center for Applied Biodiversity Science; Critical Ecosystem Partnership Fund; Global Conservation Fund; Center for Environmental Leadership in Business; Field Support; Resources & Communications; Internships: Yes; Library: Yes, Not open to the public
Mission: To conserve the Earth's living natural heritage, our global biodiversity, & to demonstrate that human societies are able to live harmoniously with nature

Conservation Ontario
Box 11, 120 Bayview Pkwy., Newmarket ON L3R 4W3
Tel: 905-895-0716; Fax: 905-895-0751
e-mail: info@conservationontario.ca
URL: www.conservation-ontario.on.ca
Social Media:
www.facebook.com/home.php?sk=group_33621230329
Also Known As: Association of Conservation Authorities of Ontario
Overview: A medium-sized provincial organization founded in 1946
Finances: Funding Sources: Levies provided by the conservation authorities
Membership: 36 organizations; Member Profile: Ontario's conservation authorities; Community-based watershed management agencies
Activities: Developing programs to protect life & property from natural hazards, such as erosion & flooding; Encouraging watershed stewardship practices; Promoting teh expertise of conservation authorities in managing Ontario's environment
Publications: Conservation Ontario Annual Report
Type: Yearbook Frequency: a.
Conservation Ontario E-Bulletin
Type: Newsletter
Profile: Information & updates on issues about conservation authorities
Guide to Conservation Areas
Type: Guide Number of Pages: 64
Profile: A guide to 261 conservation areas among 36 conservation authorities in Ontario
Sensitivity Mapping & Local Watershed Assessments for Climate Change Detection & Adaptation Monitoring
Type: Report Number of Pages: 77
Profile: Topics include Ontario sensitivity assessment using GIS mapping, climate change detection monitoring, & climate change adaptation monitoring
Protecting People & Property: A Business Case for Investing in Flood Prevention & Control
Type: Report Number of Pages: 56 Author: M. Fortin
Profile: Subjects addressed include the evolution of flood

Associations/Organizations / Conserver Society of Hamilton & District

management, accomplishments, flood frequency & severity, responding to future risks, & costs & benefits of improvements
Navigating Ontario's Future: Overview of Integrated Watershed Management in Ontario
Type: Report *Number of Pages:* 122
Navigating Ontario's Future: Water Management Framework
Type: Report *Number of Pages:* 32
Profile: Contents include the need for a framework, developing the water management framework, the use of the framework in Ontario, & next steps
Navigating Ontario's Future: A Water Budget Overview for Ontario
Type: Report *Number of Pages:* 36
Adaptive Management of Stream Corridors in Ontario
Type: Report
Profile: A planning & design guide
An Evaluation of Water Resource Monitoring Efforts in Support of Agricultural Stewardship in Watersheds of the Great Lakes
Type: Report
Profile: Produced by Conservation Ontario in partnership with the Ontario Ministry of Agriculture, Food & Rural Affairs
Water Resources Information Project
Type: Report
Profile: The current state of water information in Ontario
Innovations in Water Management
Type: Report
Profile: Place-based environmental management approaches
Cost Benefit Analysis of Agricultural Source Water Protection Beneficial Management Practices
Type: Report
Profile: Agricultural beneficial management practices such as plant buffers, soile testing, crop covers, & crop rotation to protect the quality & supply of water
Walkerton Inquiry
Type: Report
Profile: A summary of Conservation Ontario's participation in part II of the Walkerton Inquiry, including a position paper entitled "The Importance of Watershed Management in Protecting Ontario's Drinking Water Supplies"
Ontario Drinking Water Stewardship Program Outreach & Education Toolkit
Type: Kit
Profile: A communication toolkit for each Source Protection Region & Source Protection Area in Ontario
Mission: To represent & support a network of community-based environmental organizations; To ensure conservation, restoration, & responsible management of Ontario's wetlands, woodlands, & natural habitat
Environmental Activity: Raising awareness of the importance of healthy watersheds; Delivering watershed-based ecosystem resources & services; Conducting a water resources information project; Ensuring that rivers, lakes, & streams are properly safeguarded

Conserver Society of Hamilton & District
PO Box 89002, 991 King St. West, Hamilton ON L8S 4R5
e-mail: contact@conserversociety.ca
URL: www.conserversociety.ca
Previous Name: Clear Hamilton of Pollution (CHOP)
Overview: A small local organization founded in 1969
Chief Officer(s):
Warren Beacham, Treasurer
Alison Healing, President
Finances: *Annual Operating Budget:* Less than $50,000
Staff: 50 volunteer(s)
Membership: 200+; *Fees:* $20 individual; $30 family; $40 group
Activities: Tree planting; Land use advocacy
Mission: To promote solutions for a sustainable environment, through education, community action, advocacy, & collaboration; Affiliation(s): Ontario Environment Network
Environmental Activity: Recycling; Composting; Promoting the reduction of air pollution & the use of pesticides

Construction Association of New Brunswick Inc. (CANB)
Parent: Canadian Construction Association
59 Avonlea Ct., Fredericton NB E3C 1N8
Tel: 506-459-5770; *Fax:* 506-457-1913
e-mail: canb1@nbnet.nb.ca
URL: www.constructnb.ca
Overview: A small provincial organization founded in 1971
Mission: CANB is designed to perform a co-ordinating function for reaching consensus to effectively present the Industry's collective views to various client groups, partic-ularly to relevant departments and agencies of the provincial government.

Construction Association of Prince Edward Island (CAPEI)
Parent: Canadian Construction Association
PO Box 728, #223, 40 Enman Cres., Charlottetown PE C1E 1E6
Tel: 902-368-3303; *Fax:* 902-894-9757
e-mail: admin@capei.ca
URL: www.capei.ca
Overview: A medium-sized provincial organization
Publications: *Construction Association of Prince Edward Island Membership Directory*
Type: Directory
Profile: Guide for public of CAPEI members' company information
Working for You [a publication of the Construction Association of Prince Edward Island]
Type: Newsletter
CAPEI [Construction Association of Prince Edward Island] Project Newsletter
Type: Newsletter *Frequency:* w.
Mission: To foster, promote & advance the interests & efficiency of Prince Edward Island's construction industry

Construction Specifications Canada (CSC) / Devis de construction Canada
#312, 120 Carlton St., Toronto ON M5A 4K2
Tel: 416-777-2198; *Fax:* 416-777-2197
e-mail: info@csc-dcc.ca
URL: www.csc-dcc.ca
Previous Name: Specification Writers Association of Canada
Overview: A large national organization founded in 1954
Finances: *Annual Operating Budget:* $500,000-$1.5 Million; *Funding Sources:* Sale of technical documents; membership fees
Staff: 4 staff member(s)
Membership: 650 specifier architects & engineers + 750 industrial manufacturers, suppliers & contractors; *Fees:* $210; $50 student; *Member Profile:* Interested & involved in the dissemination of construction specifications & related documentation; incorporates specifiers, architects, engineers, construction product manufacturers & distributors, general & trade contractors; chapter-based association with chapters in Halifax, Québec, Montréal, Ottawa, Toronto, Hamilton/ Niagara, Grand Valley, London, Winnipeg, Regina, Saskatoon, Edmonton, Calgary & Vancouver; *Committees:* Awards; Conferences; Executive; Finance; French Language Publications; Legislative; Professional Development & Education; Technical Studies
Activities: National education programs consists of Technical Documents Programs including Home Study Course for Architectural Specifiers, & courses leading to the Registered Specification Writer (RSW) designation; *Speaker Service:* Yes; *Rents Mailing List:* Yes
Awards: CSC Awards
Awards of merit, National and Chapter
Mission: To improve communication, contract documentation, & technical information in the construction industry; Affiliation(s): Construction Specification Foundation; Construction Specifications Canada/Alberta Section Training Trust Fund; Construction Specifications Institute; Canadian Standards Assoc.; Mechanical Contractors Assoc. of Canada; Ontario Bid Depository Council; Alberta Building Envelope Council; Alberta Roofing Contractor's Assoc.; Canadian Institute of Plumbing & Heating; Assoc. of Professional Engineers of Canada; Royal Architectural Institute of Canada; Canadian Construction Assoc.; Toronto Construction Assoc.; Society of the Plastics Industry of Canada; Thermal Insulation Assoc. of Canada

Consultative Group on International Agricultural Research (CGIAR)
Secretariat, 1818 H St. NW, MSN-G6-601, Washington DC 20433 USA
Tel: 202-473-8951; *Fax:* 202-473-8110
e-mail: cgiar@cgiar.org
URL: www.cgiar.org
Overview: A medium-sized international organization founded in 1971
Chief Officer(s):
Ren Wang, Director
Finances: *Annual Operating Budget:* Greater than $5 Million
Membership: 64
Activities: *Library:* Information Center; open by appointment
Mission: To achieve sustainable food security and reduce poverty in developing countries through scientific research and research-related activities in the fields of agriculture, forestry, fisheries, policy, and environment.

Consulting Engineers of Alberta (CEA)
Parent: Association of Consulting Engineering Companies - Canada
Phipps-McKinnon Building, #870, 10020 - 101A Ave., Edmonton AB T5J 3G2
Tel: 780-421-1852; *Fax:* 780-424-5225
e-mail: info@cea.ca
URL: www.cea.ca
Overview: A medium-sized provincial organization founded in 1978
Chief Officer(s):
Gord Johnston, P.Eng., President
gord.johnston@stantec.com
Ken Pilip, Registrar
Sharon Moroskat, Manager, Finance & Administration
smoroskat@cea.ca
Hiju Song, Manager, Events & Communications
hsong@cea.ca
Finances: *Funding Sources:* Membership fees; Sponsorships
Committees: Board of Directors; Buildings; City of Calgary Liaison; City of Edmonton Liaison; Environmental; Industrial; Municipal Liaison; Small Firm; Transportation; Transportation Conference; Young Professionals' Group
Activities: Protecting legislative & regulatory interests; Offering a forum to exchange ideas; Providing training programs & information; *Speaker Service:* Yes
Meetings/Conferences:
For more information see Trade Shows, Conferences and Seminars Chapter
SustainaBUILD 2011 2nd Annual Conference
June 2011 Calgary, AB
Consulting Engineers of Alberta Young Professionals' Group 2011 Speaker Series: Liability 101 for YPs
June 2011 Edmonton, AB
Consulting Engineers of Alberta 2011 Business Professional Development for Engineers Program: Information Technology Risk Management
June 2011 Edmonton, AB
Consulting Engineers of Alberta 2011 Business Professional Development for Engineers Program: Engage Everyone - Project Leadership
June 2011 Edmonton, AB
Consulting Engineers of Alberta 2011 Business Professional Development for Engineers Program: Building an Effective Client Consultant Team
June 2011 Edmonton, AB
Consulting Engineers of Alberta 2011 Infrastructure Partners Conference
November 2011 Edmonton, AB
Consulting Engineers of Alberta 2012 34th Annual General Meeting
Other Conferences in 2012 2012, AB
Consulting Engineers of Alberta 2012 15th Annual Transportation Conference & Trade Show
Other Conferences in 2012 2012, AB
Consulting Engineers of Alberta 2012 Infrastructure Partners Conference
Other Conferences in 2012 2012, AB
Consulting Engineers of Alberta 2012 Annual Luncheon with the City of Edmonton Council
Other Conferences in 2012 2012, AB
SustainaBUILD 2012 3rd Annual Conference
Other Conferences in 2012 2012, AB
Consulting Engineers of Alberta 2012 4th Annual Young Professionals' Forum
Other Conferences in 2012 2012, AB
Consulting Engineers of Alberta 2013 35th Annual General Meeting
Other Conferences in 2013 2013, AB
Consulting Engineers of Alberta 2013 16th Annual Transportation Conference & Trade Show
Other Conferences in 2013 2013, AB
Consulting Engineers of Alberta 2013 Annual Luncheon with the City of Edmonton Council
Other Conferences in 2013 2013, AB
Publications: *CEA [Consulting Engineers of Alberta] Progress Report on Salaries*
Frequency: a.
Profile: Salary recommendations
Consulting Engineers Rate Guidelines
Profile: Standard hourly rates for engineers, technicians, & technologists in Alberta
CEA [Consulting Engineers of Alberta] Annual Report
Type: Yearbook *Frequency:* a.

Associations/Organizations / Consulting Engineers of British Columbia

Consulting Engineers of Alberta Directory of Members
Type: Directory
Profile: Listing of members, including location & size of firms
Bullet [a publication of the Consulting Engineers of Alberta]
Type: Newsletter
Profile: Information for Consulting Engineers of Alberta, such as forthcoming meetings, sponsorship opportunities, & social events
Mission: To provide leadership to foster a positive business environment for the consulting engineering firms in Alberta; To promote the engineering industry; To enhance interests & opportunities of CEA members; To provide society with high standards of engineering design & safety
Environmental Activity: Working to make significant contributions to the environment, society, & the economy; Establishing an environmental committee to provide further information on items such as the Alberta Water Act & its effect upon the work of engineers

Consulting Engineers of British Columbia (CEBC)
Parent: **Association of Consulting Engineering Companies - Canada**
#1258, 409 Granville St., Vancouver BC V6C 1T2
Tel: 604-687-2811; *Fax:* 604-688-7110
e-mail: info@cebc.org
URL: www.cebc.org
Overview: A medium-sized provincial organization founded in 1976
Chief Officer(s):
Glenn Martin, Executive Director
glenn@cebc.org
Jack Lee, President
Alla Samusevich, Coordinator, Accounting & Events
alla@cebc.org
Member Profile: Consulting engineering firms across British Columbia that provide services to the built & natural environment; *Committees:* Building Engineering; Municipal Engineering; Resource & Energy; Transportation; Business Practice; Membership Affairs; Young Professsionals' Group; Okanagan/Thompson Liaison; Vancouver Island Liaison
Activities: Lobbying to policymakers in districts, provincial & municipal governments, & private sector clients; Coordinating a common industry approach to issues; Promoting CEBC members' consulting services; Providing networking, educational, & professional development opportunities
Awards: Awards for Engineering Excellence (Award) To honour outstanding achievements in engineering
Meetings/Conferences:
For more information see Trade Shows, Conferences and Seminars Chapter
Consulting Engineers of British Columbia 2011 Annual General Meeting
June 2011 Vancouver, BC
Consulting Engineers of British Columbia 2012 Annual General Meeting
Other Conferences in 2012 2012, BC
Consulting Engineers of British Columbia 2012 Annual Transportation Conference
Other Conferences in 2012 2012, BC
Consulting Engineers of British Columbia 2012 Member / Industry Dinner
Other Conferences in 2012 2012, BC
Consulting Engineers of British Columbia 2012 Awards Gala
Other Conferences in 2012 2012, BC
Consulting Engineers of British Columbia 2012 Client Mixers
Other Conferences in 2012 2012, BC
Consulting Engineers of British Columbia 2012 Government Relations Day
Other Conferences in 2012 2012, BC
Consulting Engineers of British Columbia 2012 Young Professionals' Group Seminar
Other Conferences in 2012 2012, BC
Consulting Engineers of British Columbia 2013 Annual General Meeting
Other Conferences in 2013 2013, BC
Consulting Engineers of British Columbia 2013 Annual Transportation Conference
Other Conferences in 2013 2013, BC
Consulting Engineers of British Columbia 2013 Awards Gala
Other Conferences in 2012 2012, BC
Publications: *Directory of CEBC [Consulting Engineers of British Columbia] Member Firms*
Type: Directory
Profile: Listings of Consulting Engineers of British Columbia members, available for the public

Consulting Engineers of British Columbia Annual Report
Type: Yearbook *Frequency:* a.
Profile: The association's profile, reports from the president, executive director, treasurer, & the committees, the minutes from the annual general meeting, awards, & events
Mission: To improve the commercial environment for consulting engineering firms
Environmental Activity: Hosting conferences to address issues such as reducing greenhouse gas & adapting to climate change

Consulting Engineers of Manitoba Inc. (CEM)
Parent: **Association of Consulting Engineering Companies - Canada**
PO Box 1547, Stn. Main, Winnipeg MB R3C 2Z4
Tel: 204-774-5258; *Fax:* 204-779-0788
e-mail: cemca@shaw.ca
URL: www.cemanitoba.com
Overview: A medium-sized provincial organization founded in 1978
Finances: *Annual Operating Budget:* $50,000-$100,000; *Funding Sources:* Membership dues
Membership: 31 firms; *Member Profile:* Offer primarily consulting engineering services to public; *Committees:* City of Winnipeg; First Nations; Golf Tournament; MWSB/PFRA; Private Industry Liasion; Public Relations; Transportation
Activities: *Speaker Service:* Yes
Mission: To promote & enhance the business interests of the consulting engineers of Manitoba; to lead in the application of technology for the benefit of society.; *Affiliation(s):* Association of Professional Engineers of Manitoba; International Federation of Consulting Engineers; Manitoba Association of Architects

Consulting Engineers of Nova Scotia (CENS)
Parent: **Association of Consulting Engineering Companies - Canada**
PO Box 613, Stn. M, Halifax NS B3J 2R7
Tel: 902-461-1325; *Fax:* 902-461-1321
e-mail: cens@eastlink.ca
URL: www.cens.org
Previous Name: Nova Scotia Consulting Engineers Association
Overview: A medium-sized provincial organization founded in 1973
Membership: 50 companies; *Member Profile:* Nova Scotia based companies in the business of engineering & related services
Activities: Maintaining high professional standards in the industry; Increasing awareness about the work & employment of consulting engineers
Mission: To enable the consulting engineering industry in Nova Scotia to capitalize on opportunities to grow; To promote employment of member firms

Consulting Engineers of Ontario (CEO)
Parent: **Association of Consulting Engineering Companies - Canada**
#405, 10 Four Seasons Pl., Toronto ON M9B 6H7
Tel: 416-620-1400; *Fax:* 416-620-5803
e-mail: staff@ceo.on.ca
URL: www.ceo.on.ca
Overview: A medium-sized provincial organization founded in 1975
Finances: *Annual Operating Budget:* $250,000-$500,000
Staff: 4 staff member(s)
Membership: 250 firms
Activities: Co-sponsor "Living Earth" exhibit at Ontario Science Centre; *Speaker Service:* Yes
Mission: To further the maintenance of high professional standards in consulting engineering profession; to promote cordial relations among various consulting firms in Ontario; to foster interchange of professional management & business experience & information among consulting engineers; to develop regional representation & participation in affairs of the association.

Consulting Engineers of Québec *Voir* Association des ingénieurs-conseils du Québec

Consulting Engineers of Saskatchewan (CES)
Parent: **Association of Consulting Engineering Companies - Canada**
#12, 2010 - 7 Ave., Regina SK S4R 1C2
Tel: 306-359-3338; *Fax:* 306-522-5325
e-mail: ces@sasktel.net
URL: www.ces.sk.ca
Previous Name: Association of Consulting Engineers of Saskatchewan
Overview: A small provincial organization founded in 1977

Finances: *Annual Operating Budget:* $50,000-$100,000
Membership: 49 firms + 9 associates
Mission: To further the maintenance of high professional standards in consulting engineering profession; to promote cordial relations among various consulting firms in Saskatchewan; to foster interchange of professional management & business experience & information among consulting engineers; to develop regional representation & participation in affairs of the association

Consulting Engineers of Yukon (CEY)
Parent: **Association of Consulting Engineering Companies - Canada**
c/o EBA Engineering Consultants Ltd., #6, 151 Industrial Rd., Whitehorse YT Y1A 2V3
Tel: 867-668-3068; *Fax:* 867-668-4349
e-mail: cey@eba.ca
URL: www.cey.ca
Overview: A small provincial organization founded in 1983
Membership: 21 firms
Mission: To maintain high professional standards in the consulting engineering profession; to promote cordial relations among various consulting firms in the Yukon; to foster interchange of professional management & business experience & information among consulting engineers; to develop regional representation & participation in affairs of the association

Consulting Foresters of British Columbia
PO Box 98, Pender Island BC V0N 2M0
Tel: 250-656-8818
e-mail: info@cfbc.bc.ca
URL: www.cfbc.bc.ca
Overview: A small provincial organization founded in 1968
Membership: 80; *Fees:* $200-$1000
Mission: To maintain high professional standards in forestry consulting; To advance contact between its members, client groups, & the public at large

Consumer Health Organization of Canada (CHOC)
#1901, 355 St. Clair Ave. West, Toronto ON M5P 1N5
Tel: 416-924-9800; *Fax:* 416-924-6404
e-mail: info@consumerhealth.org
URL: www.consumerhealth.org
Overview: A medium-sized national organization founded in 1975
Membership: 3,000; *Fees:* $45
Activities: *Speaker Service:* Yes
Mission: To encourage the prevention of all kinds of illness through knowledge; to help the individual, the family & the community to enjoy the benefits of a more wholesome lifestyle; to promote harmony & cooperation between like-minded groups.; *Affiliation(s):* National Health Federation in US

Consumer Policy Institute (CPI)
225 Brunswick Ave., Toronto ON M5S 2M6
Tel: 416-964-9223; *Fax:* 416-964-8239
e-mail: cpi@eprf.ca
URL: www.c-p-i.org/cpi/index.cfm
Overview: A small local organization founded in 1980
Chief Officer(s):
Lawrence Solomon, Executive Director
lawrence.solomon@nextcity.com
Mission: A project of the Energy Probe Research Foundation (EPRF), CPI focuses on the force of the individual consumer, the empowerment of the general public brought about by the communications revolution & trade liberalization, circumstances that are eroding the power of traditional authorities in society. CPI understands this individual empowerment must be rooted in a sense of responsibility to other people & to the environment. The Institute is activly involved in a number of campaigns, covering a wide range of such fields as health care, tranportation, economic policy, automobile insurance & airports. EPRF is a registered charity, BN: 107305146RR0001.

Consumers International (CI)
24 Highbury Cres., London N5 1RX United Kingdom
Tel: 44-20-7226-6663; *Fax:* 44-20-7354-0607
e-mail: consint@consint.org
URL: www.consumersinternational.org
Overview: A medium-sized international organization founded in 1960
Finances: *Annual Operating Budget:* $1.5 Million-$3 Million; *Funding Sources:* Membership fees; Project funding
Staff: 80 staff member(s)
Membership: links the activities of more than 220 consumer groups in 115 countries; *Fees:* Schedule available

Associations/Organizations / Consumers' Association of Canada

Activities: Special services available only to IOCU members, volunteers, correspondents, networks & participants of like-minded organizations: Consumer Alert (a hazard notification issued by the Consumer Interpol; Consumer Interpol seeks to protect consumers from hazardous products, technologies & wastes); Consumer Interpol Memo (disseminates news on health & safety issues); Pesticide Monitor (disseminates information on the work of the Pesticide Action Network, a global network which aims to curb indiscriminate use; *Internships:* Yes; *Speaker Service:* Yes
Mission: To protect consumer interests worldwide through institution building, education, research & lobbying of international decision making bodies

Consumers' Association of Canada (CAC) / Association des consommateurs du Canada
PO Box 9300, 436 Gilmour St., 3rd Fl., Ottawa ON K1G 3T9
Tel: 613-238-2533; *Fax:* 613-238-2538
e-mail: info@consumer.ca
URL: www.consumer.ca
Overview: A large national organization founded in 1947
Finances: *Funding Sources:* Membership fees; project grants; donations
Staff: 6 staff member(s); 350 volunteer(s)
Membership: 16,000; *Fees:* $25; *Member Profile:* Open; *Committees:* Financial Services; Communications; Food & Agriculture - Supply Management Task Force & Biotechnology Task Force; Health; Marketplace Issues - Standards, Environment Network, Energy Network
Activities: Consumer literacy program; consumer referral, information, education, consumer representation - standards development & implementation, multi-stakeholder working groups & advisory committees, special purpose task forces; *Speaker Service:* Yes
Mission: To represent & articulate the best interests of Canadian consumers to all levels of government & to all sectors of society by continually earning recognition as the trusted voice of the consumer on a national basis; to inform & educate consumers on marketplace issues; work with government & industry to solve marketplace problems; focuses its work in the areas of food, health, trade, standards, financial services, communications industries & other marketplace issues as they emerge

Corporation des agronomes du Québec *Voir* Ordre des agronomes du Québec

Corporation des entreprises de traitement de l'air et du froid (CETAF) / Corporation of Air Treatment & Cold Processing Enterprises
#301, 6525, boul Décarie, Montréal QC H3W 3E3
Tél: 514-735-1131; *Téléc:* 514-735-3509
Ligne sans frais: 866-402-3823
Courriel: cetaf@cetaf.qc.ca
URL: www.cetaf.qc.ca
Aperçu: *Dimension:* moyenne; *Envergure:* provinciale; *Organisme sans but lucratif; fondée en 1964*
Finances: *Budget de fonctionnement annuel:* $250,000-$500,000
Personnel: 3 membre(s) du personnel; 16 bénévole(s)
Membre: 300 entreprises; *Montant de la cotisation:* 660$; *Critères d'admissibilite:* Détenir une licence de la RBQ #4230.1, 4230.2, 4230.3, 4234, 4250.4 ou 4509
Activités: Mecanex-Climatex: Exposition commerciale - le carrefour annuel des professionnels de l'installation, de la vente et du service, dans l'industrie du traitement de l'air et du froid; séminaires; programme de formation et de perfectionnement; tournoi de golf annuel; *Bibliothèque:* Oui, rendez-vousNot open to the public
Publications: *ClimaPresse*
Profile: Une revue technique et professionnelle d'expression française, publiée 6 fois l'an
Mission: Représenter et défendre les intérêts de ses membres; règlementer leur discipline et leur conduite professionnelle; favoriser et encourager la formation permanente

Corporation des maîtres mécaniciens en tuyauterie du Québec (CMMTQ) / Corporation of Master Pipe Mechanics of Québec
8175, boul St-Laurent, Montréal QC H2P 2M1
Tél: 514-382-2668; *Téléc:* 514-382-1566
Ligne sans frais: 800-465-2668
URL: www.cmmtq.org
Aperçu: *Dimension:* moyenne; *Envergure:* provinciale; *Organisme sans but lucratif; fondée en 1949*

Finances: *Budget de fonctionnement annuel:* $500,000-$1.5 Million
Personnel: 21 membre(s) du personnel
Membre: 2 200; *Montant de la cotisation:* 660$; *Critères d'admissibilite:* Entrepreneur en mécanique du bâtiment
Activités: Mécanex
Publications: *L'Entre-Presse*
Type: Newsletter *Frequency:* bi-weekly
Mission: Augmenter la compétence et l'habilité de ses membres en vue d'assurer au public une plus grande sécurité et protection au point de vue de l'hygiène et de la santé*Membre de:* Heating, Refrigeration & Air Conditioning Institute of Canada

Corporation des officiers municipaux agréés du Québec (COMAQ) / Corporation of Chartered Municipal Officers of Québec
Édifice Lomer-Gouin, #R02, 575, rue Saint-Amable, Québec QC G1R 2G4
Tél: 418-527-1231; *Téléc:* 418-527-4462
Ligne sans frais: 800-305-1031
Courriel: info@comaq.qc.ca
URL: www.comaq.qc.ca
Aperçu: *Dimension:* moyenne; *Envergure:* provinciale; fondée en 1968
Finances: *Budget de fonctionnement annuel:* $250,000-$500,000
Personnel: 2 membre(s) du personnel; 100+ bénévole(s)
Membre: 600 officiers municipaux; *Montant de la cotisation:* 405$; *Critères d'admissibilite:* Gestionnaires municipaux; *Comités:* Comité de formation professionnelle, des communications, des retraités, des technologies de l'information, de législation et scrutins, des finances et fiscalité municipales
Activités: Cours aménagement et urbanisme; scrutins municipaux; rédaction d'articles - information; étude des lois municipales des cités et villes; *Listes de destinataires:* Oui
Mission: Regrouper les cadres municipaux des cités et villes du Québec; promouvoir la formation professionnelle par l'organisation de cours; protéger les intérêts sociaux-économiques des membres.

Corporation of Air Treatment & Cold Processing Enterprises *Voir* Corporation des entreprises de traitement de l'air et du froid

Corporation of Chartered Municipal Officers of Québec *Voir* Corporation des officiers municipaux agréés du Québec

Corporation of Master Pipe Mechanics of Québec *Voir* Corporation des maîtres mécaniciens en tuyauterie du Québec

Corporation professionnelle des technologues professionnelles du Québec *Voir* Ordre des technologues professionnels du Québec

Corrugated Steel Pipe Institute (CSPI) / Institut pour tuyaux de tôle ondulée
#2A, 652 Bishop St. North, Cambridge ON N3H 4V6
Tel: 519-650-8080; *Fax:* 519-650-8081
e-mail: info@cspi.ca
URL: www.cspi.ca
Overview: A medium-sized national organization
Membership: 9 active (manufacturers) + 4 associate (materials) + 2 affiliate (non-domestic) + 1 special (equipment)
Activities: *Library:* Yes, Open to public
Mission: To promote & encourage general & wider use of corrugated steel pipe for drainage & other uses across Canada; to initiate & support research, marketing, promotion, public relations & advertising programs designed to broaden the markets for CSP products; to cooperate with public & private agencies engaged in the formulation of specifications & designs for drainage & other underground structures; to provide the industry & the public with documented experience & up-to-date technical information on CSP products & their proper use & application; to enhance, through responsible public relations practices, the reputation & image of the Canadian CSP industry; to cooperate with allied industry & government authorities; to encourage & participate in educational endeavours in colleges & universities.

Couchiching Institute on Public Affairs (CIPA)
#301, 250 Consumers Rd., Toronto ON M2J 4V6
Tel: 416-642-6374; *Fax:* 416-495-8723
Toll-Free: 866-647-6374
e-mail: couch@couch.ca
URL: www.couch.ca
Overview: A small international charitable organization founded in 1931

Finances: *Annual Operating Budget:* $100,000-$250,000; *Funding Sources:* Charitable, corporate, personal & government donations; membership & conference fees
Staff: 6 staff member(s)
Membership: 350 individual; *Fees:* $100 family; $75 individual; $25 student; *Member Profile:* Individuals interested in public affairs; *Committees:* Program; Communications; Membership; Fundraising; Youth
Awards: Couchiching Award for Public Policy Leadership (Award)
Mission: To bring together interested Canadians to discuss important public policy issues with experts & other members of the general public

Council for a Smoke-Free PEI
c/o PEI Lung Association, #2, 1 Rochford St., Charlottetown PE C1A 9L2
Tel: 902-566-4007
Overview: A small provincial organization
Chief Officer(s):
Dawn Binns, Contact
Finances: *Annual Operating Budget:* Less than $50,000; *Funding Sources:* Membership fees
Staff: 15 volunteer(s)
Membership: 16; *Fees:* $25 individual; $75 organization; *Committees:* National Non-Smoking Week; Legislation
Activities: *Awareness Events:* National Non-Smoking Week; *Speaker Service:* Yes
Mission: To promote a tobacco-free society

Council for a Tobacco-Free Manitoba *See* Manitoba Tobacco Reduction Alliance

Council of Atlantic Premiers (CAP)
Council Secretariat, PO Box 2044, #1006, 5161 George St., Halifax NS B3J 2Z1
Tel: 902-424-7590; *Fax:* 902-424-8976
e-mail: info@cap-cpma.ca
URL: www.cap-cpma.ca
Chief Officer(s):
Don Osmond, Secretary to Council, 902-424-7600
Mission: The mandate of the Council is also to promote Atlantic Canadian interests on national issues. To accomplish this, the Council seeks to establish common views & positions to ensure that Atlantic Canadians & their interests are well represented in national debates. The work of the Council of Atlantic Premiers builds on the ongoing work of the Council of Maritime Premiers & the Conference of Atlantic Premiers. The premiers are committed to work together on behalf of Atlantic Canadians to strengthen the economic competitiveness of the region, improve the quality of public services to Atlantic Canadians and/or improve the cost-effectiveness of delivering public services to Atlantic Canadians. In June 2005, CAP released their Atlantic Action Plan 2005-2008. Environmental priorities include establishing a Council of Atlantic Ministers of the Environment to better communicate & collaborate on issues, collaborate on pest management education initiatives through the Atlantic Working Group in Pest Management Education & Training Standards, explore extended producer responsibility programs to address common solid waste resource management issues. The Atlantic Energy Ministers Forum commits to developing an energy efficiency awareness campaign & a regional electricity sector approach which takes into account energy efficiency & renewable energy technologies. The Forum will also examine developing regional air emissions reduction models applicable to sulphur dioxides & nitrous oxides

Council of Biology Editors *See* Council of Science Editors

Council of Canadian Fire Marshals & Fire Commissioners (CCFMFC) / Conseil canadien des directeurs provinciaux et des commissaires des incendies
c/o 491 McLeod Hill Rd., Fredericton NB E3A 6H6
Tel: 506-453-1208; *Fax:* 506-457-0793
e-mail: philippag@rogers.com
URL: www.ccfmfc.ca
Overview: A medium-sized national organization founded in 1921
Chief Officer(s):
Ben Laroche, President
Christopher Jones, Vice-President
Philippa Gourley, Secretary-Treasurer
Activities: Advising on & promoting legislation, policies, & procedures; Participating in the development of standards &

codes; Arranging national fire loss statistics; Supporting professional development of the Canadian fire service; Identifying trends related to the causes of fire; Providing a forum for the exchange of information on fire safety matters; Offering advice to accredited agencies involved in the testing & certification of fire protection equipment
Mission: To contribute to a reduction in the number of fire deaths
Environmental Activity: Promoting fire safety awareness

Council of Food Processing & Consumer Products Voir
Conseil de la transformation agroalimentaire et des produits de consommation

Council of Forest Industries (COFI)
Pender Place I Business Building, #1501, 700 Pender St. West, Vancouver BC V6C 1G8
Tel: 604-684-0211; *Fax:* 604-687-4930
e-mail: info@cofi.org
URL: www.cofi.org
Also Known As: Canadian Forest Industries Council
Overview: A medium-sized provincial organization
Member Profile: Companies that operate production facilities in forest dependent communities in the interior of British Columbia
Activities: Advocating for British Columbia's forest industry; Liaising with government about the development & implementation of policies related to British Columbia's forest sector; Increasing public awareness about the importance of the forest sector
Meetings/Conferences:
For more information see Trade Shows, Conferences and Seminars Chapter
Council of Forest Industries 2011 Annual Convention
September 2011 Prince George, BC
Council of Forest Industries 2012 Annual Convention
Other Conferences in 2012 2012, BC
Publications: COFI [Council of Forest Industries] News: Month in Review
Type: Newsletter
Profile: Council of Forest Industries events & British Columbia forest industry news
Quarterly Stumpage Update [a publication of the Council of Forest Industries]
Profile: Including British Columbia stumpage parameters & average stumpage prices
Council of Forest Industries Annual Report
Type: Yearbook *Frequency:* a.
Profile: A review of operations & the financial report
British Columbia Forest Industry Fact Book
Type: Book
Profile: Sections include the world's forests & forest industry; Canada's forests & forest industry; competitiveness; land use, forest management, & the environment; & British Columbia forest industry statistical tables
Mission: To be the voice of the British Columbia interior forest industry; To offer member companies services in areas such as international market & trade development, community relations, public affairs, quality control, & forest policy
Environmental Activity: Preserving sensitive ecosystems, through old growth conservation, a limited working forest, regulated & limited logging, & full restoration

Council of Great Lakes Governors (CGLG)
#301, 121 Richmond St. West, Toronto ON M5H 2K1
Tel: 416-368-6956; *Fax:* 416-368-2547
e-mail: trade@cglg-canada.com
URL: www.cglg-canada.com
Also Known As: Canadian Trade Liaison Office
Overview: A small international organization founded in 1990
Chief Officer(s):
Nancy Ward, Director
Activities: Trade office for the states of Indiana, Wisconsin, Pennsylvania & Michigan; *Internships:* Yes
Member of: Council of American States in Canada

Council of Marine Carriers
#200, 1575 Georgia St. West, Vancouver BC V6G 2V3
Tel: 604-687-9677; *Fax:* 604-687-1788
e-mail: cmc@comc.cc
URL: www.comc.cc
Overview: A small national organization founded in 1972
Chief Officer(s):
Phillip J. Nelson, President

Council of Ontario Construction Associations (COCA)
#2001, 180 Dundas St. West, Toronto ON M5G 1Z8
Tel: 416-968-7200; *Fax:* 416-968-0362
e-mail: info@coca.on.ca
URL: www.coca.on.ca
Overview: A large provincial organization founded in 1974
Membership: 32 organizations; *Committees:* Labour Legislation; Environment; WSIB; Taxation; Occupational Health & Safety; Employment Practices; Human Resources
Activities: *Speaker Service:* Yes
Mission: To contribute to the long-term growth & profitability of the construction industry in Ontario; to speak with a unified voice to government, the industry & the public.

Council of Outdoor Educators of Ontario (COEO)
3 Concorde Gate, Toronto ON M3C 3N7
e-mail: info@coeo.org
URL: www.coeo.org
Overview: A medium-sized provincial charitable organization founded in 1969
Finances: *Annual Operating Budget:* Less than $50,000
Staff: 20 volunteer(s)
Membership: 30 student + 10 senior/lifetime + 200 individual; *Fees:* $35 student; $50 individual; $60 family
Activities: *Speaker Service:* Yes
Mission: To promote outdoor education in a safe manner; to develop environmental awareness of the outdoors; to act as a professional body for outdoor educators in Ontario; *Member of:* North American Association of Environmental Educators

Council of Science Editors
#304, 10200 W. 44th Ave., Wheat Ridge CO 80033 USA
Tel: 720-881-6046; *Fax:* 303-422-8894
e-mail: cse@councilscienceeditors.org
URL: www.councilscienceeditors.org
Social Media:
www.facebook.com/CouncilofScienceEditors?ref=ts
Previous Name: Council of Biology Editors
Overview: A small international organization
Chief Officer(s):
David Stumph, Executive Director
Membership: 1,200; *Fees:* $164; $43 student
Mission: To improve communications in the life sciences; to educate authors, editors & publishers; to promote effective communication practices in primary & secondary publishing in any form

Council of the Haida Nation - Haida Fisheries Program (HFP)
PO Box 87, 2143 Collison Ave., Old Masset BC V0T 1M0
Tel: 250-626-3302; *Fax:* 250-626-3309
Toll-Free: 888-638-7778
e-mail: hfpm.reception@haidanation.net
URL: www.haidanation.ca/Pages/Programs/Fish/Fish.html
Overview: A small local organization
Chief Officer(s):
Marvin Collison, Receptionist
Activities: Pallant Creek hatchery; Integrated Marine Use Plan; abalone stewardship
Mission: The Program provides advice to the Council of the Haida Nation about actions, political or otherwise, on the marine habitat & environment. It assesses all commerical/recreational fisheries & any plans affecting marine resources. Its priority is the protection of Aboriginal rights & title of the Haida people.

Council on Hemispheric Affairs (COHA)
#1C, 1250 Connecticut Ave. NW, Washington DC 20036 USA
Tel: 202-223-4975; *Fax:* 202-223-4979
Toll-Free: 888-922-9261
e-mail: coha@coha.org
URL: www.coha.org
Overview: A medium-sized international organization founded in 1975
Chief Officer(s):
Larry Birns, Director
Finances: *Annual Operating Budget:* $100,000-$250,000; *Funding Sources:* Subscription revenue; private donations
Staff: 4 staff member(s); 25 volunteer(s)
Membership: 1,500; *Fees:* $100
Activities: Issue press releases, submit op-eds to national newspapers for publication; publish biweekly Washington Report on the Hemisphere; provide congressional testimony & media resource; representatives frequently appear on radio & tv programs to analyze news stories; *Internships:* Yes; *Speaker Service:* Yes; *Library:* Yes
Mission: To monitor US-Canadian-Latin American relations in the areas of economics, politics, human rights, trade & diplomacy through public statements, critical analyses & media appearances

The Cousteau Society (TCS) / Société Cousteau
710 Settlers Landing Rd., Hampton VA 23669 USA
Tel: 757-722-9300; *Fax:* 757-722-8185
Toll-Free: 800-441-4395
e-mail: cousteau@cousteausociety.org
URL: www.cousteausociety.org
Overview: A large international charitable organization founded in 1973
Chief Officer(s):
Francine Cousteau, President
Finances: *Annual Operating Budget:* Greater than $5 Million; *Funding Sources:* Membership fees; production contracts
Staff: 32 staff member(s); 5 volunteer(s)
Membership: 50,000 worldwide including sister organization Equipe Cousteau; *Fees:* $30 individual; $40 family
Activities: Produces television films, filmstrips & books on important environmental concerns for the general public
Mission: Dedicated to the protection & wise management of natural resources & the improvement of life for present & future generations; to promote an increased awareness & knowledge of the beauty & fragility of the planet's resources

Cowichan Valley Naturalists' Society (CVNS)
PO Box 361, Duncan BC V9L 3X5
Tel: 250-746-6141
e-mail: cvns@naturecowichan.net
URL: www.island.net/~cvns/
Overview: A small local organization founded in 1962
Chief Officer(s):
John Scull, Vice-President
Finances: *Annual Operating Budget:* Less than $50,000; *Funding Sources:* Membership fees; donations
Membership: 100; *Fees:* $25 individual; $30 family; *Member Profile:* Interest in nature; *Committees:* Conservation; Evening Programs; Coffee House; Publicity; Botany; Marine Biology; Outings
Activities: Stream stewardship; ecological reserve maintenance; outings; summer picnics
Mission: To promote the enjoyment of nature through environmental appreciation & conservation; to encourage wise use & conservation of natural resources & environmental protection; *Member of:* Federation of BC Naturalists; *Affiliation(s):* BC Environmental Network; Cowichan Watershed Council

Credit Valley Conservation Foundation
1255 Old Derry Rd. West, Mississauga ON L5N 6R4
Tel: 905-670-1615; *Fax:* 905-670-2210
Toll-Free: 800-668-5557
e-mail: cvc@creditvalleycons.com
URL: www.creditvalleycons.com
Overview: A small local organization
Chief Officer(s):
Pat Mullin, Chair
Robert Shirley, Vice-Chair
Finances: *Funding Sources:* 67% from member municipalities; 20% generated by Credit Valley Conservation Foundation
Activities: Publishing a coffee table book; raising funds for the development of the Elora Cataract Trailway & Glassford Arboretum Trail; provides an annual bursary to a student at the University of Guelph & University of Toronto (Erindale)
Mission: To raise funds & awareness in support of Credit Valley Conservation's goal of an environmentally healthy river for economically & socially healthy communities

Creelman Agricultural Society
PO Box 46, Creelman SK S0G 0X0
Tel: 306-433-2062
e-mail: reallan@sasktel.net
Overview: A small local organization
Mission: To improve agriculture & the quality of life in the community by educating members & the community; to provide a community forum for discussion of agricultural issues; to encourage conservation of natural resources; *Member of:* Saskatchewan Association of Agricultural Societies & Exhibitions

Crop Protection Institute of Canada See CropLife Canada

CropLife Canada
#627, 21 Four Seasons Pl., Toronto ON M9B 6J8
Tel: 416-622-9771
URL: www.croplife.ca
Previous Name: Crop Protection Institute of Canada
Overview: A medium-sized national organization founded in 1952
Finances: *Funding Sources:* Sponsorships

Associations/Organizations / Croplife International

Member Profile: Developers, manufacturers, & distributors of plant science innovations
Activities: Conducting research; Promoting the code of conduct
Meetings/Conferences:
For more information see Trade Shows, Conferences and Seminars Chapter
Climate Change & the Implications for Plant Science 2011 Symposium (hosted by CropLife Canada & the University of Guelph)
June 2011 Guelph, ON
Grow Canada 2011 Conference: Invested, Innovative
November 2011 Winnipeg, MB
Mission: To represent Canada's plant science industry; To foster the development of the industry; To build Canadians' trust & appreciation for plant science innovations; *Member of:* CropLife International
Environmental Activity: Protecting human health & the environment through safe & effective technology; Supporting innovative & sustainable agriculture in Canada; Offering Stewardship First initiatives, including Biotech Stewardship, Urban Stewardship & Chemistry Stewardship

Croplife International
PO Box 35, 326, av Louise, Brussels 1050 Belgium
Tel: 32-2-542-0410; *Fax:* 32-2-542-0419
e-mail: croplife@croplife.org
URL: www.croplife.org
Previous Name: Global Crop Protection Federation; International Group of National Associations of Manufacturers of Agrochemical Products
Overview: A medium-sized international charitable organization
Chief Officer(s):
Christian Verschueren, Director General
Membership: 1-99; *Member Profile:* Regional crop protection associations
Mission: To act as an ambassador for the pan science industry, encouraging understanding & dialogue whilst promoting agricultural technology in the context of sustainable development

Cumulative Environmental Management Association (CEMA)
Morrison Center, #214, 9914 Morrison St., Fort McMurray AB T9H 4A4
Tel: 780-799-3947; *Fax:* 780-714-3081
e-mail: info@cemaonline.ca
URL: www.cemaonline.ca
Overview: A medium-sized national organization founded in 2000
Chief Officer(s):
Glen Semenchuk, Executive Director
glen.semenchuk@cemaonline.ca
Membership: 44 institutional
Mission: To study the cumulative environmental effects of industrial development in the region and produce guidelines and management frameworks.

CUSO-VSO
44 Eccles St., Ottawa ON K1R 6S4
Tel: 613-829-7445; *Fax:* 613-829-7996
Toll-Free: 888-434-2876
e-mail: questions@cuso-vso.org
URL: www.cuso-vso.org
Social Media: www.facebook.com/cusovso
Previous Name: Canadian University Service Overseas
Overview: A large international charitable organization founded in 1961
Finances: Annual Operating Budget: Greater than $5 Million; *Funding Sources:* Largest donor is Canadian International Development Agency (CIDA)
Staff: 140 staff member(s); 400 volunteer(s)
Activities: Works in over 40 countries, Canada's largest volunteer-sending agency; *Internships:* Yes; *Speaker Service:* Yes
Mission: CUSO-VSO is a non-profit development agency that works through skilled volunteers to aid global social justice; to address poverty, human rights violations, HIV/AIDS, inequity & environmental degradation; to give Canadians information, the experiences & the tools they need to become active global citizens.; *Member of:* VSO International; Canadian Council for International Cooperation; Global Campaign for Education (GCE); Global Citizens for Change Coalition; Canadian Make Poverty History Campaign; *Affiliation(s):* CJEO Youth Avenue Internationale; El Salvador Cultural Partnership; International Model Forest Partnership; Canadian Community Economic Development Network (CCEDNet); Marbek Resource Consultants

---

Dairy Nutrition Council of Alberta See Alberta Milk

Dangerous Goods Advisory Council
#740, 1100 H St. NW, Washington DC 20005 USA
Tel: 202-289-4550; *Fax:* 202-289-4074
e-mail: info@dgac.org
URL: www.hmac.org
Also Known As: Hazardous Materials Advisory Council
Overview: A medium-sized international organization founded in 1978
Chief Officer(s):
Mike Morrissette, President
Loretta Saunders, Office Manager
Fees: Schedule available; *Member Profile:* Shippers; carriers; container manufacturers & reconditioners; emergency response/waste clean-up companies; trade associations
Mission: To promote improvement in the safe transportation of hazardous materials/dangerous goods globally by providing education, assistance & information to the private & public sectors, through our unique status with regulatory bodies, & the diversity & technical strengths of our membership; *Affiliation(s):* Canadian Government

David Suzuki Foundation (DSF)
#219, 2211 - 4th Ave. West, Vancouver BC V6K 4S2
Tel: 604-732-4228; *Fax:* 604-732-0752
Toll-Free: 800-453-1533
e-mail: contact@davidsuzuki.org
URL: www.davidsuzuki.org
Social Media: www.facebook.com/DavidSuzuki; twitter.com/DavidSuzukiFDN
Overview: A small national organization founded in 1991
Chief Officer(s):
Tara Cullis, President
David Suzuki, Chair
Peter Robinson, CEO
Membership: 45,000
Mission: To seek out & commission the best, most up-to-date research to help reveal ways we can live in balance with nature; to support the implementation of ecologically sustainable models - from local projects, such as habitat restoration, to international initiatives, such as better frameworks for economic decisions; to ensure the solutions developed through research & application to reach the widest possible audience, & help mobilize broadly supported change; to urge decision makers to adopt policies which encourage & guide individuals & businesses, so their daily decisions reflect the need to act within nature's constraints; *Member of:* Canadian Renewable Energy Alliance

Defense environmentale See Environmental Defence

Delta Recycling Society See DRS Earthwise Society

Developing Countries Farm Radio Network See Farm Radio International

Devis de construction Canada See Construction Specifications Canada

Direct Marketing Association (DMA)
1120 Avenue of the Americas, New York NY 10036-6700 USA
Tel: 212-768-7277; *Fax:* 212-302-6714
e-mail: customerservice@the-dma.org
URL: www.the-dma.org/
Overview: A large international organization
Finances: Funding Sources: Membership dues
Staff: 120 staff member(s)
Membership: 3,600
Activities: Rents Mailing List: Yes; *Library:* Yes, open by appointment

Direct Sellers Association of Canada (DSA) / Association de ventes directes du Canada
#250, 180 Attwell Dr., Toronto ON M9W 6A9
Tel: 416-679-8555; *Fax:* 416-679-1568
e-mail: info@dsa.ca
URL: www.dsa.ca
Overview: A small national organization founded in 1954
Membership: 48
Mission: The Association represents companies that manufacture & distribute goods & services through independent sales contractors, away from a fixed retail location; encourages strong consumer protection, through Codes of Ethics & Business Practices; engages in discussion with government & industry; acts as the voice of the direct selling industry to government in pursuit of better business opportunities for Canadian entrepreneurs.

Division de l'Atlantique de l'association Canadienne des Géographes See Canadian Association of Geographers

Doctors Manitoba
Parent: Canadian Medical Association
20 Desjardins Dr., Winnipeg MB R3X 0E8
Tel: 204-985-5888; *Fax:* 204-985-5844
Toll-Free: 888-322-4242
URL: www.docsmb.org
Previous Name: Manitoba Medical Association
Overview: A medium-sized provincial organization founded in 1908
Finances: Annual Operating Budget: $1.5 Million-$3 Million; *Funding Sources:* Membership dues
Staff: 16 staff member(s)
Membership: 2,272; *Member Profile:* Manitoba physicians, medical students & residents; *Committees:* Public Health Issues; Aboriginal Health; Ethics; Insurance
Mission: To advocate for Manitoba physicians, representing their professional & economic interests.

Doctors Nova Scotia
Parent: Canadian Medical Association
25 Spectacle Lake Dr., Dartmouth NS B3B 1X7
Tel: 902-468-1866; *Fax:* 902-468-6578
e-mail: webmaster@doctorsns.com
URL: www.doctorsns.com
Previous Name: Medical Society of Nova Scotia
Overview: A medium-sized provincial organization founded in 1862
Membership: 2,200 physicians + 700 medical students & residents; *Member Profile:* Doctors, medical students, & residents in Nova Scotia
Activities: Educating the public on healthy lifestyle choices; Partnering with organizations; Offering the Youth Running for Fun Program; Voicing physician concerns with the health-care system; Advising on health-related policies & legislation
Mission: To maintain the integrity of the medical profession; To represent members; To promote high quality health care & disease prevention in Nova Scotia; *Member of:* Canadian Medical Association

DRS Earthwise Society
6400 Delta Avenue, Delta BC V4L 1B1
Tel: 604-946-9828; *Fax:* 604-946-3823
e-mail: info@drsociety.bc.ca
URL: www.drsociety.bc.ca
Previous Name: Delta Recycling Society
Overview: A small local organization
Chief Officer(s):
Duane Laird, President

Ducks Unlimited Canada (DUC) / Canards Illimités Canada
PO Box 1160, Stonewall MB R0C 2Z0
Fax: 204-467-9028
Toll-Free: 800-665-3825
e-mail: webfoot@ducks.ca; volunteer@ducks.ca; member@ducks.ca
URL: www.ducks.ca
Also Known As: DU Canada
Overview: A large national charitable organization founded in 1937
Finances: Funding Sources: Donations; Fundraising; Corporate partners
Activities: Conducting wetland & waterfowl research to guide conservation work; *Library:* Ducks Unlimited Film & Video Library
Publications: Conservator
Type: Magazine *Frequency:* 5 pa *Accepts Advertising* : Yes
Editor: D. Morrison (d_morrison@ducks.ca)
Profile: Feature articles from the world of wetland & waterfowl conservation
Ducks Unlimited Canada Annual Report
Type: Yearbook *Frequency:* a.
Profile: A yearly tracking of Ducks Unlimited Canada's scientific research, conservation programs, partnerships, volunteers, & supporters
Mission: To conserve, restore, & manage wetlands & associated habitats, for the benefit of waterfowl, which in turn provide healthy environments for wildlife & people; *Affiliation(s):* North American Waterfowl Management Plan (NAWMP)
Environmental Activity: Working to change policy in favour of wetland & habitat conservation; Delivering environmental

education programs; Working with landowners to make land use more sustainable

Ducks Unlimited Inc. (DU)
1 Waterfowl Way, Memphis TN 38120 USA
Tel: 901-758-3825
Toll-Free: 800-459-8257
e-mail: webmaster@ducks.org
URL: www.ducks.org
Overview: A medium-sized international organization founded in 1937
Chief Officer(s):
Don A. Young, Executive Vice-President
Publications: *Ducks Unlimited Magazine*
Editor: Tom Fulgham
Profile: Bimonthly magazine
Mission: To fulfill the annual life cycle needs of North American waterfowl by protecting, enhancing, restoring & managing important wetlands & associated uplands

Durham Avicultural Society of Ontario (DAS)
c/o Marg Bonenfant, 21 Birmingham Ave., Bowmanville ON L1C 4Z6
Tel: 905-697-7775
e-mail: secretary@birdclub.ca
URL: www.birdclub.ca
Overview: A small local organization founded in 1977
Membership: 150; *Fees:* $35 individual/family; $25 senior
Mission: To serve breeders in Durham & surrounding area; to improve fellowship among breeders & between clubs; to exchange ideas & educate members for betterment of the fancy through breeding & exhibiting; to encourage members to deal fairly with fellow breeders; to keep birds in good physical condition & not overextend breeding; *Member of:* Avicultural Advancement Council of Canada

EAGLE (Environmental-Aboriginal Guardianship through Law & Education)
6520 Salish Dr., Vancouver BC V6N 2C7
Tel: 604-536-6261; *Fax:* 604-536-6221
e-mail: eagle@eaglelaw.org
URL: www.eaglelaw.org
Overview: A small national charitable organization
Chief Officer(s):
Gibby Jacob, Chair
Deanie Kolybabi, Executive Director
dkolybabi@eaglelaw.org
Activities: Litigation Program; Education Program
Mission: EAGLE is a national organization that assists Aboriginal Peoples in protecting & restoring the natural environment. It also promotes the understanding of Aboriginal Rights & responsibilities as cultural stewards of the land.

Earth Day Canada (EDC) / Jour de la terre Canada
#503, 111 Peter St., Toronto ON M5V 2H1
Tel: 416-599-1991; *Fax:* 416-599-3100
Toll-Free: 888-283-2784
e-mail: info@earthday.ca; donate@earthday.ca; communications@earthday.ca
URL: www.earthday.ca
Overview: A medium-sized national charitable organization founded in 1991
Chief Officer(s):
Jed Goldberg, President
jgoldberg@earthday.ca
Keith Treffry, Director, Communications
keith@earthday.ca
Paul Bubelis, Chair
Finances: *Funding Sources:* Sponsorships; Donations
Membership: 5,000 organizations
Activities: Coordinating & promoting Earth Day; Circulating educational materials; Initiating & coordinating environmental projects; Offering programs, such as EcoKids; *Awareness Events:* Earth Day, April; Earth Month
Mission: To improve the state of the environment by motivating & helping Canadians to achieve local solutions; *Affiliation(s):* Earth Day Network; 3,500 community-based organizations

Earth Energy Society of Canada (EESC) / Société canadienne de l'énergie du sol
Fax: 613-822-4987
e-mail: info@earthenergy.ca
URL: www.earthenergy.ca
Previous Name: Canadian Earth Energy Association
Overview: A medium-sized national organization founded in 1987

Member Profile: Members of the ground-source / geothermal heat pump industry
Activities: Developing & delivering training for practitioners
Mission: To represent the domestic earth energy industry; To promote installations & earth energy technology as an economic & environmental option

Earth First! Journal (EF!)
PO Box 3023, Tucson AZ 85702-3023 USA
Tel: 520-620-6900
e-mail: collective@earthfirstjournal.org
URL: www.earthfirstjournal.org
Overview: A small international organization founded in 1979
Finances: *Annual Operating Budget:* $50,000-$100,000; *Funding Sources:* Subscriptions; merchandise sales; grants; donations
Staff: 4 staff member(s); 30 volunteer(s)
Activities: *Internships:* Yes; *Speaker Service:* Yes
Publications: *Earth First!*
Price: $25-$75, depending on location and delivery method
Profile: Journal, published six times annually

Earth Island Institute (EII)
#460, 2150 Allston Way, Berkeley CA 94704-1375 USA
Tel: 510-859-9100; *Fax:* 510-859-9091
URL: www.earthisland.org
Overview: A large international organization founded in 1982
Chief Officer(s):
Martha Davis, President
Finances: *Annual Operating Budget:* $3 Million-$5 Million; *Funding Sources:* Membership dues; grants; contributions
Staff: 65 staff member(s); 25 volunteer(s)
Membership: 15,000; *Fees:* US$25
Activities: Earth Island Projects include: Baikal Watch; Borneo Project; Brower Fund; Campaign to Safeguard America's Waters; Centre for Safe Energy; Global Service Corps; International Marine Mammal Project; Tibetan Plateau Project; *Library:* Yes, open by appointment
Mission: To develop innovative projects for the conservation, preservation & restoration of the global environment

Earth Voice
2100 L St. NW, Washington DC 20037 USA
Tel: 202-778-6146; *Fax:* 202-778-6134
e-mail: earthvoice@earthvoice.org
URL: www.earthvoice.org
Overview: A small international organization
Chief Officer(s):
Jan A. Hartke, Executive Director
Mission: To preserve the biological support systems upon which all life depends, including but not limited to forests, topsoils, coral reefs & wetlands; to promote attitudes & policies which will seek to prevent the abuse & suffering of all living creatures & protect them from becoming threatened or endangered; to stabilize the growth of human population so that it will not exceed the carrying capacity of the land or displace other forms of life; to choose a renewable energy path that will not destroy the forests, pollute the waters, degrade the atmosphere, or endanger wildlife; to support an agricultural system that is sustainable, equitable & humane; to promote pollution prevention by reusing, repairing & recycling wherever possible

Earthroots
#410, 401 Richmond St. West, Toronto ON M5V 3A8
Tel: 416-599-0152; *Fax:* 416-340-2429
e-mail: info@earthroots.org
URL: www.earthroots.org; www.wolvesontario.org; www.oakridgesmoraine.c
Previous Name: Earthroots Coalition; Temagami Wilderness Society
Overview: A medium-sized local organization founded in 1986
Chief Officer(s):
Amber Ellis, Executive Director
Josh Garfinkel, Campaign Director
Finances: *Annual Operating Budget:* $250,000-$500,000; *Funding Sources:* Individual donors
Staff: 5 staff member(s); 40 volunteer(s)
Membership: 12,000; *Fees:* $40 donation
Activities: Works to protect wilderness, wildlife & watersheds through research, education & action; *Library:* Yes, open by appointment
Mission: To preserve Ontario's ancient forests & other threatened ecosystems; *Affiliation(s):* Temagami Wilderness Society

Earthroots Coalition; Temagami Wilderness Society *See* Earthroots

Earthsave Canada (ESC) / SauveTerre
2150 Maple St., Vancouver BC V6J 3T3
Tel: 604-731-5885; *Fax:* 604-731-5805
e-mail: office@earthsave.bc.ca
URL: www.earthsave.bc.ca
Overview: A small national charitable organization founded in 1990
Chief Officer(s):
Dave Way, President
Finances: *Annual Operating Budget:* $100,000-$250,000; *Funding Sources:* BC Gaming; Individual donations; Memberships; Retail sales
Staff: 2 staff member(s); 250 volunteer(s)
Membership: 500; *Fees:* $24 senior; $36 individual; $48 family; $96 corporate; $12 youth/student; *Committees:* Events; Healthy School Lunch Program; Taste of Health
Activities: Wellness Show; Healthy Living Expo; monthly potlucks; monthly dine-outs; Healthy School Lunch Program; Taste of Health; Vegetarian Food Festival; *Awareness Events:* Taste of Health, Vegetarian Food Festival, Oct.; *Library:* Yes, Open to public
Mission: To promote awareness of the health, ethical & environmental consequences of our food choices; to advocate transition to a plant-based diet for better health, a cleaner environment & a more compassionate world; *Affiliation(s):* EarthSave International

Earthwatch Europe
256 Banbury Rd., Oxford OX2 7DE United Kingdom
Tel: 44-1865-318-838; *Fax:* 44-1865-311-383
e-mail: info@earthwatch.org.uk
URL: www.earthwatch.org/europe
Overview: A large international charitable organization
Chief Officer(s):
Nigel Winser, Executive Director
Finances: *Annual Operating Budget:* Greater than $5 Million
Staff: 50 staff member(s); 5 volunteer(s)
Membership: 5,000-14,999
Activities: *Internships:* Yes; *Speaker Service:* Yes
Mission: To engage people worldwide in scientific field research & education
Environmental Activity: Promoting the understanding & actions necessary for a sustainable environment

East African Wild Life Society (EAWLS)
PO Box 20110-00200, Nairobi 00200 Kenya
Tel: 254-2-574-145; *Fax:* 254-2-570-335
e-mail: info@eawildlife.org
URL: www.eawildlife.org
Overview: A medium-sized international organization founded in 1956
Nigel Derek Hunter, Executive Director
Finances: *Funding Sources:* Membership fees; shop fund; donations
Staff: 40 staff member(s); 7 volunteer(s)
Membership: 5,500; *Fees:* Schedule available; *Committees:* Conservation; Fundraising; Executive
Activities: Education & awareness; advocacy; monitoring of species; field projects; *Speaker Service:* Yes; *Library:* Yes, open by appointment
Mission: To promote the conservation & wise use of wildlife & the environment in East Africa; *Member of:* World Conservation Union

East Kootenay Chamber of Mines
#201, 12 - 11th Avenue South, Cranbrook BC V1C 2P1
Tel: 250-489-2255; *Fax:* 250-426-8755
URL: www.ekcm.org/chamber2
Overview: A small local organization
Chief Officer(s):
Ross Stanfield, President

Eastern Canada Orchid Society (ECOS)
699, rue Cardinal, Mont-Saint-Hilaire QC J3H 3Z5
Tel: 514-684-3904
e-mail: info@ecosorchids.ca
URL: www.ecosorchids.ca
Overview: A small national organization founded in 1953
Chief Officer(s):
Brian Dunbar, President
Fees: $25 individual; $30 couple
Activities: Orchidfête; *Library:* Yes, Not open to the public
Mission: ECOS is a non-profit group of orchid hobbyists dedicated to promoting the art, science & culture of raising

Associations/Organizations / Eastern Ontario Model Forest

orchids in the Montréal area.; *Affiliation(s):* Canadian Orchid Congress; American Orchid Society

Eastern Ontario Model Forest
PO Box 2111, Kemptville ON K0G 1J0
Tel: 613-258-8241; *Fax:* 613-258-8363
e-mail: modelforest@eomf.on.ca
URL: www.eomf.on.ca
Overview: A small local organization
Chief Officer(s):
Brian Barkley, General Manager
Mission: To demonstrate how partners, representing a diversity of forest values, can work together to achieve sustainable forest management using innovative, region-specific approaches; *Member of:* Canadian Model Forest Network

Eau Vive *See* WaterCan

Éco Entreprises Québec (EEQ)
#600, 1600, boul René-Lévesque ouest, Montréal QC H3H 1P9
Tél: 514-987-1491; *Téléc:* 514-987-1598
Courriel: service@ecoentreprises.qc.ca
URL: www.ecoentreprises.qc.ca
Aperçu: Dimension: petite; *Envergure:* provinciale; fondée en 2003
Membre(s) du bureau directeur:
Maryse Vermette, B.Sc., MBA, Présidente-directrice générale
mvermette@ecoentreprises.qc.ca
Marie-Andrée Prénoveau, Directrice, Affaires corporatives, relations externes et communications
mprenoveau@ecoentreprises.qc.ca
Prix, Bouses: Prix Phénix (Prix)
Mission: Organisme privé sans but lucratif; représenter les entreprises assujetties à la Loi sur la qualité de l'environnement qui mettent sur le marché québécois des contenants et emballages et des imprimés.

Ecoforestry Institute Society (EIS)
PO Box 5070, Stn. B, Victoria BC V8R 6N3
Tel: 604-595-0655
e-mail: journal@ecoforestry.ca
URL: www.ecoforestry.ca
Overview: A small national charitable organization founded in 1992
Chief Officer(s):
Irv Penner, Journal Chair
Finances: *Annual Operating Budget:* $50,000-$100,000; *Funding Sources:* Foundations; donations; subscriptions
Staff: 1 staff member(s); 12 volunteer(s)
Membership: 250; *Fees:* $10
Activities: Provides community outreach through conferences, videos & publications; helps community watershed & land trusts set up ecoforestry programs; *Speaker Service:* Yes
Publications: *Ecoforestry*
Editor: Davd Martin *Price:* $30 Subscription
Profile: Quarterly Journal
Mission: To provide ecologically sound alternatives to current ruinous industrial forestry practices; to support preservation of ancient & natural forests; to encourage restoration of plantation tree farms to natural forest status; *Member of:* BC Environmental Network; Forest Stewardship Council

Ecojustice Canada
#214, 131 Water St., Vancouver BC V6B 4M3
Tel: 604-685-5618; *Fax:* 604-685-7813
Toll-Free: 800-926-7744
e-mail: cmcdonald@ecojustice.ca
URL: www.ecojustice.ca
Previous Name: Sierra Legal Defence Fund
Overview: A medium-sized national organization founded in 1990
Chief Officer(s):
Carol McDonald, Director, Administration & Human Resources
Finances: *Annual Operating Budget:* $1.5 Million-$3 Million; *Funding Sources:* Individual donors; private foundations
Staff: 49 staff member(s); 10 volunteer(s)
Membership: 5,000-14,999
Activities: Free legal services; litigation; *Internships:* Yes
Mission: To provide legal representation to environmental groups that cannot afford to go to court against large institutions when important wilderness values are at stake; to bring selected cases with the ultimate goal of establishing an aggregate of strong legal precedents that recognize environmental values; to provide professional advice on the development of environmental legislation

Ecological Agriculture Projects (EAP) / Projets pour une agriculture écologique (PAE)
Macdonald Campus of McGill University, Sainte-Anne-de-Bellevue QC H9X 3V9
Tel: 514-398-7771; *Fax:* 514-398-7621
e-mail: ecological.agriculture@mcgill.ca
URL: www.eap.mcgill.ca
Overview: A small national organization founded in 1974
Finances: *Annual Operating Budget:* $100,000-$250,000
Staff: 1 staff member(s)
Fees: $40 individual; $60 organization; $500 sustaining; $1,250 organization
Activities: *Speaker Service:* Yes; *Library:* Yes, Open to public, open by appointment
Mission: To facilitate the establishment of nutritional, just, & sustainable food systems worldwide; *Affiliation(s):* International Federation of Organic Agriculture Movements

Ecological Farmers Association of Ontario (EFAO)
5420 Hwy. 6 North, RR#5, Guelph ON N1H 6J2
Tel: 519-822-8606; *Fax:* 519-822-5681
Toll-Free: 877-822-8606
e-mail: info@efao.ca
URL: www.efao.ca
Overview: A medium-sized provincial charitable organization founded in 1979
Chief Officer(s):
Karen Maitland, Coordinator
Finances: *Annual Operating Budget:* Less than $50,000; *Funding Sources:* Membership fees; donations
Staff: 1 staff member(s); 30 volunteer(s)
Membership: 400+; *Fees:* $45/year; $120/3 years; *Member Profile:* Farmers; *Committees:* Membership; Promotion; Education
Activities: Offers two-day course "An Introduction to Ecological Agriculture"; annual symposium; courses; farm tours; kitchen table meetings; *Library:* EFAO Lending Library; Not open to the public
Mission: To educate farmers to adopt ecologically sound management practices; *Affiliation(s):* Canadian Organic Growers

Ecological Society of America (ESA)
#700, 1990 M St. NW, Washington DC 20036 USA
Tel: 202-833-8773; *Fax:* 202-833-8775
e-mail: esahq@esa.org
URL: www.esa.org
Overview: A medium-sized international organization founded in 1915
Chief Officer(s):
Katherine S. McCarter, Executive Director
ksm@esa.org
Finances: *Annual Operating Budget:* $3 Million-$5 Million
Staff: 30 staff member(s)
Membership: 7,800; *Fees:* Schedule available
Activities: Maintains sections for ecologists with special needs & interests: Paleoecology, Aquatic, Physiological, Statistical, Applied Ecology, Vegetation, Education, Long-Term Studies; Professional Certification (constitutes recognition by the Society that an applicant meets the minimum educational experience & ethical standards adopted by ESA for professional ecologists); *Internships:* Yes; *Rents Mailing List:* Yes
Awards: The Mercer Award (Award)
Given for outstanding paper published by a young ecologist
The MacArthur Award (Award)
Given for outstanding research contributions by an established ecologist
The Cooper Award (Award)
Given for the best paper in geobotany, physiographic ecology, etc.
The Whittaker Travel Fellowship (Award)
Brings a leading foreign scientist to America
The E. Lucy Braun Award (Award)
The Murray F. Buell Award (Award)
Outstanding paper presented orally at the ESA Annual meeting by an undergraduate
Eminent Ecologist Award (Award)
Given to senior ecologist for distinguished contributions
Corporate Award (Award)
Given to a corporation, business, program or individual of a company for incorporating sound ecological concepts in operating procedures
Mission: To stimulate & publish research on the interrelations of organisms & their environment; to facilitate an exchange of ideas among those interested in ecology; to instill ecological principles in the decision-making of society at large; provides Professional Certification which constitutes recognition by the Society that an applicant meets the minimum educational, experience & ethical standards adopted by ESA for professional ecologists; *Affiliation(s):* American Association for the Advancement of Science; American Institute of Biological Sciences; National Resources Council; National Research Council; Council of Scientific Society Presidents; Renewable Natural Resources Foundation

Écologistes pour l'énergie nucléaire (CANADA) inc. *See* Environmentalists For Nuclear Energy (Canada) Inc.

Ecology Action Centre (EAC)
2705 Fern Lane, Halifax NS B3K 4L3
Tel: 902-429-2202; *Fax:* 902-405-3716
e-mail: info@ecologyaction.ca
URL: www.ecologyaction.ca
Social Media: www.facebook.com/EcologyActionCentre
Overview: A medium-sized provincial organization founded in 1971
Finances: *Funding Sources:* Membership dues; Donations
Staff: 30 staff member(s); 200 volunteer(s)
Membership: 1,000+; *Committees:* Marine Issues; Transportation; Wilderness Issues; Coastal Issues; Energy Issues; Food Action; Built Environment; Climate Change
Activities: Communication; education and programming; research; advocacy; *Awareness Events:* Annual Awards
Mission: To act as a voice for Nova Scotia's environment; to build a healthier, more sustainable Nova Scotia.; *Member of:* Canadian Renewable Energy Alliance

Ecology North
5013 - 51 St. St., Yellowknife NT X1A 2N4
Tel: 867-873-6019; *Fax:* 867-873-6149
e-mail: admin@ecologynorth.ca
URL: www.ecologynorth.ca
Overview: A small local organization
Chief Officer(s):
John Carr, Contact
Finances: *Annual Operating Budget:* $50,000-$100,000
Staff: 2 staff member(s)
Membership: 200; *Committees:* Recycling; Botanical Gardens/Volunteer Development; Endangered Species
Activities: Participates in environmental hearings; reviews legislation & policy; sponsors a wide range of activities such as bird walks & nature hikes; public education seminars on various aspects of the northern environment; community recycling programs; *Awareness Events:* Christmas Bird Count; *Library:* Recycling Resource Centre
Mission: To promote appreciation & protection of the natural environment of the Northwest Territories; to foster public awareness through seminars & outdoor activities; to provide a forum for communication of ideas on environmental issues between the scientific community, government & the peoples of the Northwest Territories; *Member of:* Canadian Environmental Network

EcoPerth
2196 Old Brooke Rd., RR#2, Maberry ON K0H 2B0
Tel: 613-267-6463; *Fax:* 613-268-2907
e-mail: info@ecoperth.on.ca
URL: www.ecoperth.on.ca
Overview: A small local organization
Chief Officer(s):
Bob Argue, Executive Director
bob@ecoperth.on.ca
Mission: To promote local projects that are environmentally sustainable and economically efficient in the Perth, Ontario area.

EcoSource Mississauga
Clarke Hall, 161 Lakeshore Rd. West, 2nd Fl., Mississauga ON L5H 1G3
Tel: 905-274-6222; *Fax:* 905-274-4387
e-mail: ecosource@ecosource.ca
URL: www.ecosource.ca
Overview: A small local charitable organization founded in 1979
Chief Officer(s):
Rick Holden, President
Lea Ann Mallett, Executive Director
Finances: *Annual Operating Budget:* $100,000-$250,000
Staff: 4 staff member(s); 30 volunteer(s)
Activities: 3Rs education program offered to elementary schools; volunteer community outreach program; public workshops; educational displays (consumer shows, malls, businesses, libraries, etc.); resource centre for 3Rs information; participation in environmental events; 3Rs publications, fact sheets, surveys & public awareness programs; assistance for

community based projects; Earth Days; Renaissance Craft Fair; *Internships:* Yes; *Speaker Service:* Yes
Mission: To promote improvement of the environment through public education on waste reduction & conservation of our natural resources; to move public attitudes & perceptions about environmental issues toward responsible personal action; *Member of:* Recycling Council of Ontario; Canadian Environmental Network; Ontario Environmental Network

Edmonton Association of Sheet Metal & Air Conditioning Contractors *See* Sheet Metal Contractors Association of Alberta

Edmonton Space & Science Foundation (ESSF)
11211 - 142 St., Edmonton AB T5M 4A1
Tel: 780-452-9100; *Fax:* 780-455-5882
e-mail: info@telusworldofscienceedmonton.com
URL: www.telusworldofscience.com/edmonton
Also Known As: Telus World of Science - Edmonton
Overview: A small local organization founded in 1978
Finances: *Annual Operating Budget:* $3 Million-$5 Million; *Funding Sources:* Revenue; donations; grants
Staff: 82 staff member(s); 265 volunteer(s)
Membership: 7,950; *Fees:* $122.95 family; $53.50 adult; $43 senior/student/child
Activities: Community courses; Mobile Astronomy program; Challenger Missions; Summer camps; *Library:* Yes, open by appointment
Mission: To inspire & motivate people to learn about & contribute to science & technology advances that strengthen themselves, their family & community

Electric Vehicle Council of Ottawa Inc. (EVCO)
PO Box 4044, Stn. E, Ottawa ON K1S 5B1
e-mail: info@evco.ca
URL: www.evco.ca
Overview: A small local organization founded in 1980
Finances: *Annual Operating Budget:* Less than $50,000; *Funding Sources:* Memberships
Membership: 80; *Fees:* $5 student; $25 electronic; $30 paper
Mission: To provide information about electric road vehicles, in Canada & worldwide

Electric Vehicle Society of Canada (EVS)
21 Burritt Rd., Toronto ON M1R 3S5
Tel: 416-755-4324; *Fax:* 416-755-4324
e-mail: info@evsociety.ca
URL: www.evsociety.ca
Overview: A medium-sized national organization founded in 1991
Chief Officer(s):
Howard W. Hutt, President
hhutt@rogers.com
Joel Clemens, Treasurer
Emile Stevens, Contact, Membership
Robert Weekley, Editor, EVSurge
editor@evsociety.ca
Fees: $20 students, spouses, & seniors; $30 adults; $50 families; $100 corporations; *Member Profile:* Engineers; Environmentalists; Enthusiasts for electric energy for propulsion
Activities: Providing a forum for member discussions; Examining modes of electric transportation
Meetings/Conferences:
For more information see Trade Shows, Conferences and Seminars Chapter
Electric Vehicle Society of Canada & Toronto Hybrid Group 2011 EV Festival
Other Conferences in 2011 2011 Toronto, ON
Electric Vehicle Society of Canada 2011 Meeting June 2011 Toronto, ON
Electric Vehicle Society of Canada 2011 Meeting September 2011 Toronto, ON
Electric Vehicle Society of Canada 2011 Meeting October 2011 Toronto, ON
Electric Vehicle Society of Canada 2011 Meeting November 2011 Toronto, ON
Publications: *Electric Vehicle Conversion Manual: A Workshop Guide for High Schools*
Type: Manual *Number of Pages:* 85 *Author:* Neil Gover et al.
Profile: Contents include the move to sustainable transportation, getting started, basics of electrical energy & electricity, starting the conversion, & EV performance & evaluation
EVSurge [a publication of the Electric Vehicle Society of Canada]
Type: Newsletter *Frequency:* bi-m. *Editor:* Robert Weekley *Price:* Free with Electric Vehicle Society of Canada membership

Profile: Electric Vehicle Society of Canada events, membership information, & articles about activities in the EV world
Mission: To investigate & promote clean transportation technologies
Environmental Activity: Encouraging electric vehicle conversions

Electricity Distributors Association (EDA)
#1100, 3700 Steeles Ave. West, Vaughan ON L4L 8K8
Tel: 905-265-5300; *Fax:* 905-265-5301
Toll-Free: 800-668-9979
e-mail: email@eda-on.ca
URL: www.eda-on.ca
Previous Name: Municipal Electric Association
Overview: A large provincial organization founded in 1986
Finances: *Annual Operating Budget:* Greater than $5 Million; *Funding Sources:* Membership dues
Staff: 18 staff member(s); 100 volunteer(s)
Membership: 256; *Fees:* $750 commercial member; *Member Profile:* Public & privately owned electricity distributors
Mission: To be the voice of Ontario's electricity distributors, the publicly & privately owned companies that deliver electricity to Ontario homes, businesses & public institutions. Focus is on advocacy & representation to government, analysis of legislation & market regulations, communication & networking among members & industry colleagues

Electro-Federation Canada Inc. (EFC)
#200, 5800 Explorer Dr., Mississauga ON L4W 5K9
Tel: 905-602-8877; *Fax:* 905-602-5686
Toll-Free: 866-602-8877
e-mail: info@electrofed.com
URL: www.electrofed.com
Overview: A medium-sized national organization founded in 1995
Chief Officer(s):
Milos Jancik, President/CEO
mjancik@electrofed.com
Ken Frankum, Chair
Harald Henze, Treasurer
Larry Moore, Vice-President, Consumer Councils
lmoore@electrofed.com
Joseph Neu, Vice-President, Engineering, Codes & Standards
jneu@electrofed.com
Membership: 300 companies; *Member Profile:* Companies that manufacture, distribute, & service electrical, electronics, & telecommunications products; *Committees:* Canadian Appliance Manufacturers Association; Consumer Electronics Marketers of Canada; Electrical Equipment Manufacturers Association of Canada; Supply & Manufacturers' Reps Councils; Installation Maintenance & Repair Sector Council & Trade Association; Electro-Federation Canada Alumni Association
Activities: Collecting & disseminating market data; Providing networking opportunities; Hosting annual conferences; Researching; Offering educational programs; Communicating with members; Promoting the industry; Conducting surveys
Mission: To represent members provincially, federally, & internationally on issues affecting the electro-technical business

Electronics Product Stewardship Canada
#600, 15 Allstate Parkway, Markham ON L3R 5B4
Tel: 905-415-4591
e-mail: info@epsc.ca
URL: www.epsc.ca
Overview: A medium-sized national organization founded in 2003
Chief Officer(s):
Shelagh Kerr, President/CEO
Nathan B. MacDonald, Director, Environmental Programs
nathan@epsc.ca
Membership: 16 leading electronics manufacturers
Mission: To design, promote & implement sustainable solutions for electronics waste

Elora Centre for Environmental Excellence *See* Elora Environment Centre

Elora Environment Centre
PO Box 1100, 75 Melville St., 2nd Fl., Elora ON N0B 1S0
Tel: 519-846-8464; *Fax:* 519-846-8464
Toll-Free: 866-865-7337
e-mail: info@eloraenvironmentcentre.ca
URL: www.ecee.on.ca
Previous Name: Elora Centre for Environmental Excellence
Overview: A small local charitable organization founded in 1993
Chief Officer(s):

Jennifer McLellan, Chair
Lynda Bausinger, Acting General Manager
wellaware@eloraenvironmentcentre.ca
Finances: *Annual Operating Budget:* $50,000-$100,000; *Funding Sources:* Fees from clients; Natural Resources Canada
Staff: 7 staff member(s)
Activities: Home energy evaluations; NeighbourWoods tree steward program; *Speaker Service:* Yes
Mission: The Centre a not-for-profit organization focused on providing leadership in community-based environmental initiatives for both urban & rural communities. Areas of experience include: energy efficiency, greenhouse gas reduction, water efficiency, sustainable transportation, environmental education. It is a registered charity, BN: 138373196RR0001.; *Member of:* Green Communities Canada; *Affiliation(s):* Ontario Environmental Network; Centre for Applied Renewable Energy; GreenPathways; several municipal governments & hydro-electric companies

Elsa Wild Animal Appeal of Canada
PO Box 45051, 2482 Yonge St., Toronto ON M4P 3E3
Tel: 416-489-8862; *Fax:* 416-489-4769
e-mail: info@elsacanada.com
URL: www.elsacanada.com
Also Known As: Elsa Canada
Overview: A small national charitable organization founded in 1971
Finances: *Annual Operating Budget:* Less than $50,000; *Funding Sources:* Donations; membership fees; fundraising
Staff: 15 volunteer(s)
Membership: 150; *Fees:* $25
Mission: To help save endangered wildlife species in Canada

Employers' Council of BC *See* Business Council of British Columbia

Énergie Solaire Québec
CP 540, Succ. St-Laurent, Ville St-Laurent QC H4L 4V7
Tél: 514-392-0095
Courriel: info@esq.qc.ca
URL: www.esq.qc.ca/
Aperçu: *Dimension:* petite; *Envergure:* provinciale
Membre(s) du bureau directeur:
Benoit Perron, Président
Montant de la cotisation: 40$ individuel
Activités: Souper solaire; clinique solaire; concours Cocktail Transport
Mission: Promouvoir l'utilisation de l'énergie solaire au Québec

Energy Action Council of Toronto (EnerACT)
#401, 401 Richmond St. West, Toronto ON M5V 3A8
Tel: 416-488-3966; *Fax:* 416-977-2157
e-mail: info@eneract.org
URL: www.eneract.org
Overview: A small local organization
Fees: Schedule available
Mission: To accelerate the change in society's usage of energy away from environmentally inappropriate forms towards conservation & renewable energy; to encourage the further application of technologies which contribute to energy conservation & the wider use of renewable energy; to broaden society's understanding of the relationship between energy & the environment & the potential for meeting society's energy needs through conservation & renewable energy technologies; to assist in the development of public policies which encourage energy conservation & the use of renewable energy

Energy Council of Canada / Conseil canadien de l'énergie
#608, 350 Sparks St., Ottawa ON K1R 7S8
Tel: 613-232-8239; *Fax:* 613-232-1079
e-mail: krystal.piamonte@energy.ca
URL: www.energy.ca
Previous Name: World Energy Council - Canadian Member Committee
Overview: A medium-sized national organization founded in 1924
Chief Officer(s):
Murray J. Stewart, President
murray.stewart@energy.ca
Brigitte Svarich, Director, Operations
brigitte.svarich@energy.ca
Membership: 75+; *Member Profile:* Representatives from all facets of Canada's energy sector
Activities: Providing networking opportunities; Sponsoring forums & conferences; Disseminating current energy reports &

Associations/Organizations / Energy Probe Research Foundation

information; Contributing to the development of the Canadian energy policy
Mission: To foster a greater understanding of energy issues; To enhance the effectiveness of the Canadian energy strategy; *Member of:* World Energy Council

Energy Probe Research Foundation (EPRF)
225 Brunswick Ave., Toronto ON M5S 2M6
Tel: 416-964-9223; *Fax:* 416-964-8239
e-mail: webadmin@eprf.ca
URL: www.eprf.ca
Overview: A large national charitable organization founded in 1980
Finances: Annual Operating Budget: $1.5 Million-$3 Million; *Funding Sources:* Donations
Staff: 15 staff member(s); 10 volunteer(s)
Membership: 50,000 supporters
Activities: Policy research & education; *Internships:* Yes; *Speaker Service:* Yes; *Library:* Yes, Open to public
Awards: The Margaret Laurence Fund (Grant)
Grants & scholarships are made to foster an understanding of peace & the environment upon which the fate of the planet rests
Eligibility: Recipients of the grants & scholarships are limited to students, authors, researchers, & publishers, working with the foundation in collaborative projects approved by the directors
Mission: To educate Canadians about the benefits of conservation & renewable energy; to help Canada secure long-term energy self-sufficiency in the shortest possible time with the fewest disruptive effects & with the greatest societal, environmental & economic benefits; to provide business, government & the public with information on energy & energy-related issues; to help Canada contribute to global harmony & prosperity; recipient of the 1990 Lieutenant Governor's Conservation Award, the first time that an environmental organization has been so honoured; divisions include Energy Probe, Probe International, Environment Probe, Margaret Laurence Fund, Consumer Policy Institute, Environmental Bureau of Investigations, Urban Renaissance Institute; *Affiliation(s):* Energy Probe; Probe International; Environment Probe; Consumer Policy Institute; Urban Renaissance Institute; Environmental Bureau of Investigation; Three Gorges Probe; Canadian Environmental News Network

Enform: The Safety Association for the Upstream Oil & Gas Industry
Head Office, 1538 - 25th Ave. NE, Calgary AB T2E 8Y3
Tel: 403-250-9606; *Fax:* 403-250-1289
Toll-Free: 800-667-5557
URL: www.enform.ca
Previous Name: Petroleum Industry Training Service
Overview: A large national licensing charitable organization founded in 2005
Chief Officer(s):
Dennis Miller, Chair
dgmiller@telusplanet.net
Wallace E. Baer, President, 403-250-0875
wbaer@enform.ca
W. Wetmore, Senior Vice-President, Training & Workforce Development
L. Harman, Vice-President
R. Ogilvie, Vice-President
Activities: Providing training courses; Offering saftey information; Promoting shared safety practices in the Canadian oil & gas industry; Providing the Small Employers Certificate of Recognition (SECOR), the Certificate of Recognition (COR), & the Petroleum Competency Program
Mission: To improve the Canadian upstream oil & gas industry's safety performance; To prevent work-related injuries in the upstream oil & gas industry in Canada; *Affiliation(s):* Canadian Association of Geophysical Contractors (CAGC); Canadian Association of Oilwell Drilling Contractors (CAODC); Canadian Association of Petroleum Producers (CAPP); Canadian Energy Pipeline Association (CEPA); Petroleum Services Association of Canada (PSAC); Small Explorers & Producers Association of Canada (SEPAC)
Environmental Activity: Offering training programs in environmental management

The Engineering Institute of Canada (EIC) / L'Institut canadien des ingénieurs (ICI)
1295 Hwy. 2 East, Kingston ON K7L 4V1
Tel: 613-547-5989; *Fax:* 613-547-0195
e-mail: jplant1@cogeco.ca
URL: www.eic-ici.ca
Overview: A large national charitable organization founded in 1887

Finances: Annual Operating Budget: $100,000-$250,000; *Funding Sources:* Membership fees; sustaining members
Staff: 1 staff member(s); 20-3 volunteer(s)
Membership: 12 member societies; *Fees:* $325-$5,400 Sustaining; *Member Profile:* Join one of the member societies: Canadian Society for Civil Engineering; Canadian Society for Mechanical Engineering; Canadian Geotechnical Society; Canadian Society for Engineering in Management; IEEE - Canada; Canadian Society for Chemical Engineering;
Committees: Professional Development; Honours & Awards; History & Archives; Life Members Organization
Activities: Promotes the creation, exchange & dissemination of technical information; organizes conferences & symposia & promotes continuing education for engineers; supports engineering student advancement; maintains an official Registry of Continuing Education Units & Professional Development Activities; *Awareness Events:* National Engineering Week
Awards: K.Y.L.O. Medal (Award)
The Julian C. Smith Medal (Award)
The John B. Stirling Medal (Award)
Established in 1987 in honour of Dr. John B. Stirling, a past president of the EIC & an outstanding engineer; medal is awarded in recognition of leadership & distinguished service at the national level within the institute &/or its member societies
Canadian Pacific Rail Engineering Medal (Award)
Established 1987 in appreciation of CP Rail's contribution to the development of Canada; awarded in recognition of leadership & distinguished service at the local level within the institute &/or its member societies
The Sir John Kennedy Medal (Award)
Established in 1927 in commemoration of the great services rendered in the field of engineering by Sir John Kennedy, a past president of the EIC; medal is awarded every two years by the council in recognition of outstanding merit in the profession or of noteworthy contributions to the science of engineering or to the benefit of the institute
Mission: To further the development of engineering in Canada; to stimulate the advancement of the quality & scope of Canadian engineering; to meet regularly with other engineering organizations & industries to promote understanding & improvement of the profession, the diffusion of engineering information & to provide Canadian representation in specialized engineering fields; to interact with government agencies & departments for the purpose of influencing decision making on matters relating to engineering & technology; to cooperate with the provincial engineering licensing bodies, The Canadian Council of Professional Engineering, The Association of Consulting Engineers of Canada, The Canadian Academy of Engineering & other engineering organizations in matters of common interest; to promote interaction with specific interest groups; to collaborate with universities & educational institutions; *Affiliation(s):* Engineers Canada; Association of Canadian Engineering Companies; Canadian Academy of Engineering; International Association for Continuing Education & Training (IACET); Internation Association for Continuing Engineering Education (IACEE)

Engineers Canada / Ingénieurs Canada
#1100, 180 Elgin St., Ottawa ON K2P 2K3
Tel: 613-232-2474; *Fax:* 613-230-5759
e-mail: info@ccpe.ca
URL: www.ccpe.ca
Previous Name: Canadian Council of Professional Engineers
Overview: A large national organization founded in 1936
Finances: Funding Sources: Membership dues
Staff: 16 staff member(s)
Membership: 10 provincial + 2 territorial associations representing 160,000 professional engineers; *Committees:* Canadian Engineering Accreditation Board (CEAB); Canadian Engineering Qualifications Board (CEQB); Canadian Engineering Human Resources Board (CEHRB)
Activities: Awareness Events: National Engineering Week, 1st week of March
Awards: National Award for Exceptional Engineering Achievement (Award)
For outstanding engineering projects or achievements by an engineering team in which Canadian engineers were involved
The Professional Service Award (Award)
For outstanding contribution to a professional, consulting or technical engineering association or society in Canada
The Community Service Award (Award)
Awarded for exemplary voluntary contribution to a community organization or humanitarian endeavour

The Young Engineer Achievement Award (Award)
Awarded for outstanding contribution in a field of engineering by an engineer 35 years of age or younger
Medal for Distinction in Engineering Education (Scholarship)
Awarded for exemplary contribution to engineering teaching at a Canadian University
Gold Medal Award (Award)
Awarded for exceptional individual achievement & distinction in a field of engineering
Mission: To establish & maintain a common bond between constituent associations & assist them to meet their common needs & those of their members by coordinating standards, procedures & programs across Canada, by representing the engineering profession with respect to national & international affairs & generally by increasing the profile & prestige of the engineering profession; *Affiliation(s):* World Federation of Engineering Organizations

Engineers Without Borders (EWB) / Ingénieurs sans Frontières (ISF)
#601, 366 Adelaide St. West, Toronto ON M5V 1R9
Tel: 416-481-3696; *Fax:* 416-352-5360
Toll-Free: 866-481-3696
e-mail: info@ewb.ca
URL: www.ewb.ca
Overview: A small international organization
Chief Officer(s):
Parker Mitchell, Co-CEO
parkermitchell@ewb.ca
George Roter, Co-CEO
georgeroter@ewb.ca
Brenna Donoghue, Director of Operations
brennadonoghue@ewb.ca
Mission: To promote human development through access to technology

Entomological Society of Alberta (ESA)
Agriculture & Agri-Food Canada, Lethbridge Research Centre, PO Box 3000, 5403 - 1st Ave. South, Lethbridge AB T1J 4B1
Tel: 403-317-3404; *Fax:* 403-382-3156
e-mail: llumley@ualberta.ca
URL: www.biology.ualberta.ca/courses.hp/esa/esa.htm
Overview: A small provincial organization founded in 1952
Chief Officer(s):
Lisa Lumey, Treasurer
Rose De Clerck-Floate, President
Finances: Annual Operating Budget: Less than $50,000
Membership: 108; *Fees:* $10
Mission: To foster the advancement, exchange & dissemination of the knowledge of insects in relation to their importance in agriculture, forestry, public health & industry; *Member of:* Entomological Society of Canada

Entomological Society of British Columbia (ESBC)
c/o BC Ministry of Forests And Range, 515 Columbia Street, Kamloops BC V2C 2T7
Tel: 250-828-4179; *Fax:* 250-828-4154
e-mail: lorraine.maclauchlan@gov.bc.ca
URL: www.sfu.ca/biology/esbc
Overview: A small provincial organization founded in 1902
Chief Officer(s):
Maclauchlan Lorraine, Sec.-Treas.
Membership: 230; *Fees:* $20; *Member Profile:* Professional; amateur; student entomologists
Activities: Library: Pacific Forestry Centre
Awards: Student Research Presentation Awards (Award)
Graduate Student Travel Grants (Grant)
Member of: Entomological Society of Canada

Entomological Society of Manitoba Inc. (ESM)
Agriculture Canada, Research Station, 195 Dafoe Rd., Winnipeg MB R3T 2M9
Tel: 204-983-1450; *Fax:* 204-983-4604
e-mail: iwise@agr.gc.ca
URL: home.cc.umanitoba.ca/~fieldspg
Overview: A small provincial charitable organization founded in 1945
Chief Officer(s):
David Ostermann, Secretary
Finances: Annual Operating Budget: Less than $50,000; *Funding Sources:* Donations; membership fees; interest income; fundraising
Staff: 25-3 volunteer(s)
Membership: 106; *Fees:* $25; *Member Profile:* Professional & amateur entomologists

Activities: Scientific paper symposia; public education presentations on entomology; *Library:* Agriculture & Agrifood Canada Resource Centre; Not open to the public
Awards: ESM Scholarship (Scholarship)
ESM Student Award (Award)
SWAT Award (Award)
Mission: To encourage & promote the field of entomology; to provide a forum to enable individuals with an interest in entomology to acquire & share information; *Affiliation(s):* Entomological Society of Canada

Entomological Society of Ontario (ESO)
Vista Centre, PO Box 83025, 1830 Bank St., Ottawa ON K1V 1A3
Tel: 603-736-3393; *Fax:* 613-736-3964
URL: www.entsocont.ca
Overview: A small provincial organization founded in 1863
Chief Officer(s):
Bruce Gill, President, 613-759-1842, Fax: 613-759-6938
bruce.gill@inspection.gc.ca
Nicole McKenzie, Secretary
nicole_mckenzie@hc-sc.gc.ca
Finances: *Annual Operating Budget:* Less than $50,000
Membership: 253; *Fees:* $30/yr. regular; free for retired, students, amateurs in Canada; *Member Profile:* Amateurs & professionals
Activities: photo contests; journal; *Library:* Yes
Publications: *Journal of the Entomological Society of Ontario*
Type: Journal *Frequency:* a.
Mission: The Society fosters interest in entomology by providing a network for members & interested parties. Since 1906, its headquarters has been located at the Ontario Agricultural College in Guelph. Currently its library & archives are also housed in the Library there.

Entomological Society of Saskatchewan (ESS)
c/o Agriculture & Agri-Food Canada, 107 Science Pl., Saskatoon SK S7N OX2
Tel: 306-956-7287; *Fax:* 306-956-7247
URL: www.usask.ca/biology/ess/ess.html
Overview: A small provincial organization founded in 1952
Chief Officer(s):
Ruwandi Andrahennadi, President
ruwandi.andra@usask.ca
Finances: *Annual Operating Budget:* Less than $50,000
Fees: $20; $5 student; *Member Profile:* Amateurs & professionals
Activities: North American butterfly count; insect inventory of endangered/protected ecosystems; talks & presentations; displays at schools; *Speaker Service:* Yes; *Rents Mailing List:* Yes; *Library:* Yes
Mission: The Society promotes the significance of entomology to the general public & provides a forum for those interested in the field to communicate. It also works in conjunction with other similar societies.; *Member of:* Entomological Society of Canada

Enviro-Accès Inc.
Place Andrew-Paton, #150, 85, rue Belvédère nord, Sherbrooke QC J1H 4A7
Tél: 819-823-2230; *Télec:* 819-823-6632
Courriel: enviro@enviroaccess.ca
URL: www.enviroaccess.ca
Également appelé: Centre pour l'avancement des technologies environnementales
Aperçu: Dimension: moyenne; Envergure: provinciale; fondée en 1993
Membre(s) du bureau directeur:
Manon Laporte, Présidente-directrice générale
mlaporte@enviroaccess.ca
Finances: *Budget de fonctionnement annuel:* $1.5 Million-$3 Million
Personnel: 10 membre(s) du personnel
Membre: 1-99
Mission: Supporter les petites et moyennes entreprises qui oeuvrent dans le domaine de l'environnement en leur offrant les services professionnels nécessaires au développement de leurs projets et de leurs affaires.

Environmental & Outdoor Education Council of Alberta *See* Global, Environmental & Outdoor Education Council

Environmental Abatement Council of Ontario (EACO)
70 Leek Cres., Richmond Hill ON L4B 1H1
Tel: 416-499-4000; *Fax:* 416-499-8752
e-mail: mthorburn@tcanetworks.com
URL: www.eacoontario.com
Previous Name: Ontario Asbestos Removal Contractors Association
Overview: A medium-sized provincial organization founded in 1992
Chief Officer(s):
Mary Thorburn, Secretary/Manager
Finances: *Annual Operating Budget:* Less than $50,000; *Funding Sources:* Membership dues
Staff: 10 staff member(s); 30 volunteer(s)
Membership: 25 corporate; *Fees:* $625 general/contractor; $75 associate
Mission: To collect, generate & disseminate information concerning environmental abatement & other hazardous environmental health issues

Environmental Action Barrie
34 Ross St., Barrie ON L4N 1E9
Tel: 705-734-2877; *Fax:* 705-734-2651
e-mail: info@livinggreen.info
URL: www.livinggreen.info
Also Known As: Living Green
Overview: A small local charitable organization founded in 1990
Chief Officer(s):
Annette Cutler, Secretary
Finances: *Annual Operating Budget:* $50,000-$100,000
Staff: 3 staff member(s); 50 volunteer(s)
Membership: 100; *Fees:* $5; *Committees:* Board of Directors; Pesticide Action
Activities: Environmental Action Centre; EnerGuide for Houses; Alternative Recycling Depot; Ecology Garden; letterwriting campaign; *Speaker Service:* Yes; *Library:* Yes
Mission: To work towards a healthy environment through community involvement; *Member of:* Green Communites Association; Ontario Environment Network

Environmental Bankers Association (EBA)
#410, 510 King St., Alexandria VA 22314 USA
Tel: 703-549-0977; *Fax:* 703-548-5945
e-mail: eba@envirobank.org
URL: www.envirobank.org
Overview: A medium-sized international organization founded in 1994
Chief Officer(s):
Beth Gray, President
beth.gray1@wachovia.com
D. Jeff Telego, Co-Executive Director
jefftelego@envirobank.org
Tacy Telego, Co-Executive Director
Tacytelego@envirobank.org
Dan Richardson, General Counsel
drichardson@llw-law.com
Rick Plewa, Secretary & Communication Officer
rjplewa@comerica.com
Membership: 1-99; *Fees:* Schedule available based upon asset size of financial; *Member Profile:* Members of the financial services industry, such as bank & non-bank financial institutions, asset management firms, insurers, & those who provide services to them; Environmental consultants, appraisers, environmental attorneys, & environmental information management firms; *Committees:* Policy; Finance & Budget; Communications & Programs; Business Development & Membership; Legal & ASTM; Trust; Risk Management; Global Issues; Technical
Activities: Facilitating networking opportunities
Mission: To assist the financial services industry in developing environmental risk management policies & procedures
Environmental Activity: Responding to the need for due diligence policies & procedures, sustainable development, & environmental risk management in financial institutions

Environmental Careers Organization of Canada / L'Organisation pour les carrières en environnement du Canada
#200, 308 - 11th Ave. SE, Calgary AB T2G 0Y2
Tel: 403-233-0748; *Fax:* 403-269-9544
e-mail: info@eco.ca; techsupport@eco.ca
URL: www.eco.ca
Also Known As: ECO Canada
Previous Name: Canadian Council for Human Resources in the Environment Industry
Overview: A medium-sized national organization founded in 1992
Chief Officer(s):
Jon Ogryzlo, Sec.-Treas.
Grant S. Trump, President/CEO
Michael Kerford, Vice-President
Janelle Thomlinson, Director, Marketing & Communications
Finances: *Funding Sources:* Government of Canada's Sector Council Program
Activities: Providing career information & a job board; Recruiting; Offering ECO Canada internships; Providing professional development opportunities to practitioners; Offering employee retention strategies to employers; Providing tools for career change & career development; Disseminating human resource statistics & trends; Increasing Aboriginal employment in the environment sector through career awareness, training, & employment resources
Mission: To provide services to all participants in the environmental sector, including educators, students, practitioners, & employers

The Environmental Coalition of PEI
126 Richmond St., Charlottetown PE C1A 1H9
Tel: 902-566-4696; *Fax:* 902-566-4037
e-mail: energy@ecopei.ca
URL: www.ecopei.ca
Also Known As: ECO-PEI
Overview: A medium-sized provincial organization founded in 1988
Chief Officer(s):
Kate McDonald, Energy Coordinator
Finances: *Annual Operating Budget:* $100,000-$250,000
Staff: 15 volunteer(s)
Membership: 150; *Fees:* $10
Awards: Environmental Awards (Award)
Awarded to Islanders who have demonstrated their dedication to preserving & enhancing the PEI environment; categories include individual, industry, citizen group or organization, & education
Mission: To preserve & enhance the environment for all living things; *Member of:* PEI Environmental Network; Canadian Environmental Network

Environmental Data Research Institute *See* Resources for Global Sustainability

Environmental Defence / Defense environmentale
#705, 317 Adelaide St. West, Toronto ON M5V 1P9
Tel: 416-323-9521; *Fax:* 416-323-9301
Toll-Free: 877-399-2333
e-mail: info@environmentaldefence.ca
URL: www.environmentaldefence.ca
Previous Name: Canadian Environmental Defence Fund
Overview: A medium-sized national charitable organization founded in 1985
Chief Officer(s):
Rick Smith, Executive Director
Finances: *Annual Operating Budget:* $500,000-$1.5 Million
Staff: 25 volunteer(s)
Mission: To protect the environment & human health; To research, educate, & initiate action in the courts when necessary; *Member of:* Canadian Environmental Network
Environmental Activity: Ensuring clean air, safe food, & thriving ecosystems nationwide

Environmental Defense
257 Park Ave. South, 17th Fl., New York NY 10010 USA
Tel: 212-505-2100; *Fax:* 212-505-2375
Toll-Free: 800-684-3322
e-mail: members@environmentaldefense.org
URL: www.environmentaldefense.org
Previous Name: Environmental Defense Fund
Overview: A large international organization founded in 1967
Chief Officer(s):
Fred Krupp, President
David Yarnold, Executive Director
Finances: *Annual Operating Budget:* Greater than $5 Million; *Funding Sources:* Membership dues; foundations
Staff: 250 staff member(s)
Membership: 300,000+; *Fees:* $24 individual; $35 family; $50 contributor; $100 associate; $250 donor; $500 patron; $1,000 benefactor
Publications: *Earth: The Sequel - The Race to Reinvent Energy and Stop Global Warming*
Number of Pages: 256 *Author:* Fred Krupp, Miriam Horn *Price:* $24.95
Mission: To protect environmental rights for all people — clean air, clean water, healthy food, & flourishing ecosystems; To work to create practical solutions, guided by science, that win lasting political, economic & social support

Associations/Organizations / Environmental Education Ontario

Environmental Activity: Initiating legal action on environmental matters; Conducting educational campaigns

Environmental Defense Fund *See* Environmental Defense

Environmental Education Ontario (EEON)
32 Springdale Dr., Kitchener ON N2K 1P9
Tel: 519-579-3097
e-mail: admin@eeon.org
URL: www.eeon.org
Social Media: facebook.com/group.php?gid=103171483071910&ref=ts
Overview: A small local charitable organization founded in 2000
Finances: *Annual Operating Budget:* Less than $50,000; *Funding Sources:* Federal & provincial governments; foundations
Staff: 12 volunteer(s)
Member Profile: Environmental & ecological educators, concerned citizens, parents, & representatives from non-governmental organizations & government agencies; *Committees:* Fundraising; Research; Education; Tracking
Activities: *Listserv;* meetings; representations; *Speaker Service:* Yes
Mission: EEON promotes in Ontario the facilitation, development & implementation of education on sustainable environments. It is a registered charity, BN: 864934617RR0001.; *Member of:* Education Alliance for a Sustainable Ontario

Environmental Educators' Provincial Specialist Association (EEPSA)
c/o British Columbia Teachers' Federation, #100, 550 - 6th Ave. West, Vancouver BC V5Z 4P2
Tel: 604-871-2283
e-mail: pabrobo@shaw.ca
URL: www.bctf.ca/eepsa
Overview: A medium-sized provincial organization founded in 1972
Finances: *Funding Sources:* Membership dues
Membership: 200; *Fees:* $15 student; $25 BCTF members; $45.68 associate
Mission: To promote, through public education, greater awareness, understanding & appreciation of the environment & to encourage global citizenship through the development of active decision making; *Member of:* BC Teachers' Federation

Environmental Health Association of Ontario (EHA Ontario)
PO Box 33023, Ottawa ON K2C 3Y9
Tel: 613-860-2342
e-mail: helpline@ehaontario.ca
URL: www.ehaontario.ca
Previous Name: Allergy & Environmental Health Association
Overview: A small national charitable organization founded in 1975
Finances: *Funding Sources:* Donations; Membership fees
Membership: 300; *Fees:* $28 new member; $25 pa renewal; *Member Profile:* Individuals with environmental sensitivities & their families; *Committees:* Membership; Newsletter
Activities: *Library:* AEHA-Ottawa Library; Not open to the public
Mission: EHA Ontario is a volunteer, not-for-profit, self-help organization for persons with chemical & environmental allergies. It promotes awareness of environmental conditions that may be harmful to human health, & advocates less-contaminated sources of food, water, clothing, personal & home care products, home furnishings & building materials. It also disseminates information to its members, as well as the general public concerning allergies & environmental health-related issues. It is a registered charity, BN 132737099RR0001.; *Member of:* Human Ecology Foundation of Canada; Affiliation(s): EHA Nova Scotia; EHA Québec; EHA Alberta; EHA BC

Environmental Health Foundation of Canada (EHFC)
Parent: Canadian Institute of Public Health Inspectors
Stn. #720, 999 West Broadway Ave., Vancouver BC V5Z 1K5
URL: www.ehfc.ca
Overview: A small national charitable organization founded in 1989
Chief Officer(s):
Tim Roark, Treasurer
Member Profile: Members of the environmental public health profession; industry representatives; educational institutions; government
Mission: The research & educational arm of the Canadian Institute of Public Health Inspectors; Dedicated to advancing environmental health in Canada through the development & implementation of education & research initiatives

Environmental Industry Associations (EIA)
#300, 4301 Connecticut Ave., Washington DC 20008-2304 USA
Tel: 202-244-4700; *Fax:* 202-966-4818
Toll-Free: 800-424-2869
URL: www.envasns.org
Overview: A medium-sized national organization
Chief Officer(s):
Bruce J. Parker, President & CEO
bparker@nswma.org

Environmental Information Association
#306, 6935 Wisconsin Ave., Chevy Chase MD 20815-6112 USA
Tel: 301-961-4999; *Fax:* 301-961-3094
Toll-Free: 888-343-4342
e-mail: info@eia-usa.org
URL: www.eia-usa.org
Previous Name: National Asbestos Council
Overview: A small international organization
Chief Officer(s):
Michael Breu, President
michaelbreu@hotmail.com
Brent Kynoch, Managing Director
bkynoch@eia-usa.org
Mike Schrum, Secretary
mwschrum@terracon.com
Kevin Cannan, Treasurer
ktc@aac-contracting.com
Kim Goodman, Manager, Membership & Marketing
kgoodman@kynoch.com
Kelly Ruttman, Manager, Development & Communications
krutt@kynoch.com
Fees: $1,000 executive; $500 organization; $125 individual; *Committees:* Conference; Membership / Marketing; Publications; Strategic Planning; Training; Asbestos; EMS / ESA; Indoor Air Quality; Lead Paint; Sampling & Analysis
Activities: Offering professional development opportunities; Providing networking events
Publications: *Inside EIA [Environmental Information Association]*
Type: Newsletter *Accepts Advertising :* Yes *Price:* Free with Environmental Information Association membership
Indoor Environment Connections
Type: Newsletter *Price:* Free with Environmental Information Association membership
Net News [a publication of the Environmental Information Association]
Type: Newsletter *Frequency:* w. *Price:* Free with Environmental Information Association membership
Mission: To protect public health & safety; To provide information about environmental health hazards to occupants of buildings, industrial sites, & other facility operations

The Environmental Law Centre (Alberta) Society (ELC)
#800, 10025 - 106 Street, Edmonton AB T5J 1G4
Tel: 780-424-5099; *Fax:* 780-424-5133
Toll-Free: 800-661-4238
e-mail: elc@elc.ab.ca
URL: www.elc.ab.ca
Overview: A small provincial charitable organization founded in 1981
Chief Officer(s):
Cindy Chiasson, Executive Director
Finances: *Annual Operating Budget:* $500,000-$1.5 Million; *Funding Sources:* Funded in part by the Alberta Law Foundation & through public support
Staff: 9 staff member(s)
Membership: 13
Activities: *Speaker Service:* Yes; *Rents Mailing List:* Yes; *Library:* Yes
Awards: Sir John A. Mactaggart Essay Prize (Scholarship) Open to undergraduate & graduate students attending a recognized law school in Canada; prizes will be awarded for essays of high quality which address an issue in environmental law which is orginal, significant & relevant to Canada *Award Amount:* First prize is $500 plus a bound volume of the author's choice from Carswell; winning essay will als
Mission: To conduct research in environmental & natural resources law, policy & procedure; to educate the public on environmental law; to operate an environmental law information & referral service for the benefit of the public; to monitor relevant municipal, provincial & federal environmental laws, policies & procedures, & make recommendations for reform; *Member of:* Alberta Environmental Network

Environmental Law Institute
#620, 2000 L St. NW, Washington DC 20036 USA
Tel: 202-939-3800; *Fax:* 202-939-3868
e-mail: law@eli.org
URL: www.eli.org
Overview: A medium-sized international organization
Chief Officer(s):
Leslie Carothers, President
Finances: *Annual Operating Budget:* Greater than $5 Million; *Funding Sources:* Subscriptions; fees; grants
Staff: 52 staff member(s)
Membership: 1,000-4,999
Activities: *Internships:* Yes; *Speaker Service:* Yes; *Library:* Yes
Mission: To advance environmental protection by improving law, policy & management; to research pressing problems; to educate professionals & citizens about the nature of these issues; to convene all sectors in forging effective solutions; to achieve society's goals for improving the health of the biosphere & its inhabitants

Environmental Managers Association of British Columbia (EMABC)
PO Box 3741, Vancouver BC V6B 3Z8
Tel: 604-998-2226; *Fax:* 604-998-2226
e-mail: info@emaofbc.com
URL: www.emaofbc.com
Overview: A medium-sized provincial organization
Chief Officer(s):
Patrick Novak, President
Krista Hennebury, Executive Director
Membership: 67 corporate; *Fees:* $450
Mission: To encourage education, share knowledge among members and create a forum for environmental management issues in the industrial, commercial and institutional sectors, serve as a key resource of environmental information for members and explore existing and emerging environmental issues.

Environmental Protection UK
44 Grand Parade, Brighton BN2 9QA United Kingdom
Tel: 01273 878770; *Fax:* 01273 606626
e-mail: admin@environmental-protection.org.uk
URL: www.environmental-protection.org.uk
Previous Name: National Society for Clean Air
Overview: A medium-sized international organization founded in 1898
Finances: *Funding Sources:* Funded by members' subscriptions, donations, & money raised by activities
Staff: 10 staff member(s)
Membership: 344 individuals; *Member Profile:* Open to local authorities, universities & colleges, professional & learned institutions, the energy industries, industrial companies & private individuals; *Committees:* Noise; Technical; Finance & Administration; Conference & Promotions
Activities: *Rents Mailing List:* Yes; *Library:* Yes, Open to public, open by appointment
Mission: To bring together organisations across the public, private & voluntary sectors to promote a balanced & innovative approach to understanding & solving environmental problems

Environmental Services Association of Alberta (ESAA)
#102, 2528 Ellwood Dr. SW, Edmonton AB T6X 0A9
Tel: 780-429-6363; *Fax:* 780-429-4249
Toll-Free: 800-661-9278
e-mail: info@esaa.org
URL: www.esaa.org
Previous Name: Alberta Special Waste Services Association
Overview: A medium-sized provincial organization founded in 1987
Chief Officer(s):
Craig Robertson, President
Randy Neumann, Secretary
Skip Kerr, Treasurer
Joe Barraclough, Director, Industry & Government Relations, 780-429-6363 Ext. 224
Joe Chowaniec, Director, Program & Event Development, 780-429-6363 Ext. 223
chowaniec@esaa.org
Membership: 200+ organizations; *Fees:* $475
Activities: Communicating with all levels of government; Providing networking opportunities; Offering market & industry information

Meetings/Conferences:
For more information see Trade Shows, Conferences and Seminars Chapter
Remediation Technologies 2012 Symposium
Other Conferences in 2012 2012 Banff, AB
Publications: *Environmental Association of Alberta Annual Report*
Type: Yearbook *Frequency:* a.
The ESAA [Environmental Services Association of Alberta] Weekly News
Type: Newsletter *Frequency:* w. *Accepts Advertising* : Yes
Profile: Association happenings, such as conferences & job opportunities, for Environmental Services Association of Alberta members
B.I.D.S. (Business Initiative Development Service)
Type: Newsletter *Frequency:* w.
Profile: Environmental business opportunities, news, & marketing information for the buyers & sellers of environmental goods & services
The Regulatory Review [a publication of the Environmental Services Association of Alberta]
Frequency: m.
Profile: Current information on environmental policies & law, produced by the Environmental Services Association of Alberta & the Environmental Law Center
Mission: To act as the voice of Alberta's environment industry
Environmental Activity: Monitoring & informing members of changes in environmental regulations

Environmental Services Association of Nova Scotia (ESANS)
Woodside Industrial Park, #211-2, 1 Research Dr., Dartmouth NS B2Y 4M9
Tel: 902-463-3538; *Fax:* 902-466-6889
e-mail: contact@esans.ca
URL: www.esans.ca
Also Known As: Nova Scotia Environmental Business Network
Overview: A medium-sized provincial organization founded in 1994
Chief Officer(s):
Adam Cooney, P.Eng., President
Finances: *Annual Operating Budget:* $100,000-$250,000; *Funding Sources:* Membership; projects; government
Staff: 1 staff member(s)
Membership: 100-499; *Fees:* Schedule available; *Member Profile:* Individuals & companies/organizations involved in the environmental industry; *Committees:* Communications; Membership; Business Development; Government Liaison; Finance; Nominating
Activities: *Awareness Events:* Membership Appreciation Social; *Internships:* Yes; *Rents Mailing List:* Yes
Mission: ESANS is a province-wide business organization dedicated to the promotion of environmental products, services & organizations within the environmental industry.

Environmental Studies Association of Canada (ESAC) / Association canadienne d'études environnementales
c/o Dean's Office, Faculty of Environmental Studies, Univ. of Waterloo, Waterloo ON N2L 3G1
Tel: 519-888-4442; *Fax:* 519-746-0292
e-mail: esac@fes.uwaterloo.ca
URL: www.thegreenpages.ca/esac
Overview: A small national organization founded in 1993
Chief Officer(s):
Tim Quick, President & Director, Membership
timquick@yorku.ca
Patricia Ballamingie, Vice-President
Patricia_Ballamingie@carleton.ca
Windibank Erin, Treasurer
rogo2156@wlu.ca
Fees: $40 student & unwaged; $30 - $75 small NGOs; $85 faculty & professional; $110 institutional; *Member Profile:* Members include individuals, who are interested in social science & humanities approaches to environmental issues, from educational institutions, government agencies, & private sector & non-profit organizations.
Publications: *Rhizome [a publication of the Environmental Studies Association of Canada]*
Type: Newsletter *Editor:* Angela Waldie
Profile: Information about conferences, research projects, events, new publications, & teaching materials
Directory of ESAC [Environmental Studies Association of Canada] Members
Type: Directory *Frequency:* a.

Profile: Listing of ESAC members, with their areas of interest & research
Mission: To to advance research & teaching activities in areas related to environmental studies in Canada

Environmental Youth Alliance (EYA)
PO Box 3601, Stn. Terminal, #517, 119 Pender St. West, Vancouver BC V6B 1S5
Tel: 604-689-4446; *Fax:* 604-689-4242
e-mail: info@eya.ca
URL: www.eya.ca
Overview: A small local organization founded in 1989
Finances: *Annual Operating Budget:* $100,000-$250,000; *Funding Sources:* Federal, provincial & municipal government; foundations
Staff: 2 staff member(s); 25 volunteer(s)
Membership: 10,000
Activities: Stewardship of urban sites; *Speaker Service:* Yes; *Library:* Yes, open by appointment
Mission: To save the earth through non-violent means; to promote change by educating people on our interconnectedness with Nature & involving youth in action projects; to create a youth movement that is activist-oriented & works towards environmental respect & protection.

Environmentalists For Nuclear Energy (Canada) Inc. / Écologistes pour l'énergie nucléaire (CANADA) inc.
1940 Hill 60 Rd., RR#5, Cobourg ON K9A 4J8
Tel: 905-372-2410; *Fax:* 905-372-6274
e-mail: nuc-ca@ecolo.org
URL: www.ecolo.org/base/baseca.htm
Also Known As: EFN Canada
Overview: A small national organization
Chief Officer(s):
Rodney Anderson, Founding President
Patrick Moore, Honorary Chair
Fees: $50-$200
Activities: Publication of books, pamphlets & CD-ROM's; lectures to the public; contribution of scientific, technical, & educational communications to the media; creation, operation & maintenance of multilingual internet sites; professional fairs & exhibitions
Mission: To provide complete & straightforward information about energy & the environment; to make known the advantages of nuclear energy, & especially the environmental benefits; to bring together persons favouring the use of nuclear energy for peaceful purposes with respect for the environment & with proper management of nuclear waste

Environnement jeunesse
454, rue Laurier est, Montréal QC H2J 1E7
Tél: 514-252-3016; *Téléc:* 514-254-5873
Ligne sans frais: 866-377-3016
Courriel: infoenjeu@enjeu.qc.ca
URL: www.enjeu.qc.ca
Également appelé: ENJEU
Aperçu: *Dimension:* moyenne; *Envergure:* provinciale; fondée en 1979
Membre(s) du bureau directeur:
Jérôme Normand, Directeur général
Finances: *Budget de fonctionnement annuel:* $250,000-$500,000
Personnel: 5 membre(s) du personnel; 40 bénévole(s)
Membre: 400 individu; 300 associations
Activités: Tient une assemblée générale annuelle; organise un colloque annuel, La Bise D'Automne; tient des comités inter-groupes; réalise L'Écologie en Action, un vaste projet d'éducation et d'action relatifs à l'environnement; offre un Service d'Activités en Formation et en Éducation Relatives à l'Environnement; produit une panoplie d'outils de qualité visant à soutenir l'action des groupes membres; participe à des processus de consultation publique; *Service de conférenciers:* Oui
Mission: Promouvoir la conservation et l'amélioration de la qualité de l'environnement; développer chez les jeunes les qualités favorisant leur implication sociale.; *Affiliation(s):* Réseau québécois des groupes écologistes; Association québécoise pour la promotion de l'éducation relative à l'environnement

ETC Group
431 Gilmour St., 2nd Fl., Ottawa ON K2P 0R5
Tel: 613-241-2267; *Fax:* 613-241-2506
e-mail: etc@etcgroup.org
URL: www.etcgroup.org
Also Known As: Action Group on Erosion, Technology & Concentration
Previous Name: Rural Advancement Foundation International

Overview: A small international organization founded in 1985
Chief Officer(s):
Pat Roy Mooney, Executive Director
Finances: *Annual Operating Budget:* $500,000-$1.5 Million
Staff: 8 staff member(s); 2 volunteer(s)
Activities: *Library:* Resource Library; open by appointment
Mission: To promote the sustainable improvement of agricultural biodiversity & the socially responsible development of technologies useful to rural societies
Environmental Activity: To conserve agricultural biodiversity

European Association of Geoscientists & Engineers (EAGE)
PO Box 59, Houten 3990 DB Netherlands
Tel: 31-30-635-4055; *Fax:* 31-30-634-3524
e-mail: eage@eage.org
URL: www.eage.nl
Overview: A medium-sized international organization founded in 1951
Chief Officer(s):
Phil Christie, President
Membership: 6,000; *Fees:* 50 euros general; 25 euros student; *Committees:* Technical Program; Awards; Publications; Executive
Activities: *Speaker Service:* Yes; *Library:* Yes, open by appointment
Mission: To promote exploration geophysics; to foster fellowship & cooperation among those working, studying, or being otherwise interested in the field; comprised of EAEG Division (formerly European Association of Exploration Geophysicists) & EAPG Division (formerly European Association of Petroleum Geoscientists & Engineers); *Affiliation(s):* Society of Exploration Geophysicists

European Geophysical Union *See* European Geosciences Union

European Geosciences Union (EGS)
5, rue René Descartes, Strasbourg 67084 France
Tel: 33-3-88450191; *Fax:* 33-3-88603887
e-mail: egu@eost.u-strasbg.fr
URL: www.egu.eu
Previous Name: European Geophysical Union
Overview: A medium-sized international organization founded in 2002
Membership: 6,000; *Fees:* Schedule available; *Member Profile:* Scientists
Activities: Organization of conferences; meetings & workshops; publication of scientific journals & books
Mission: To promote geophysics including planetary & space sciences by assisting cooperation among scientists, laboratories, institutes & individual research workers; *Affiliation(s):* Canadian Geophysical Union

European Solidarity Towards Equal Participation of People / Solidarité européenne pour une égale participation des peuples
115, rue Stévin, Brussels B-1000 Belgium
Tel: 32-2-231-1659; *Fax:* 32-2-230-3780
e-mail: admin@eurostep.org
URL: www.eurostep.org
Also Known As: EUROSTEP
Overview: A small international organization founded in 1990
Chief Officer(s):
Simon Stocker, Director
Finances: *Annual Operating Budget:* $250,000-$500,000
Activities: *Internships:* Yes
Mission: To co-ordinate the policy work of its members at European level & to influence the policy & practice of the European Union; with a focus on the EU's cooperation with other countries, particularly in Africa, Asia, & Latin America, Eurostep uses its membership base in 15 European countries & the secretariat located in Brussels to present common policy approaches to the European Commission, European Parliament & Member States governments

European Space Agency (ESA) / Agence spatiale européenne
8-10, rue Mario Nikis, Paris 75738 France
Tel: 33-1-5369-7654; *Fax:* 33-1-5369-7560
e-mail: contactesa@esa.int
URL: www.esa.int
Social Media: twitter.com/esa
Merged from: European Space Research Organization (ESRO); European Organization for the Development & Constructio

Associations/Organizations / Evergreen

Overview: A large international organization founded in 1975
Finances: *Annual Operating Budget:* $1.5 Million-$3 Million
Staff: 2000 staff member(s)
Membership: 18 member states
Mission: To provide for & to promote, for exclusively peaceful purposes, cooperation among European States in space research & technology & their space applications, with a view to their being used for scientific purposes & for operational space applications systems; *Affiliation(s):* Canadian Space Agency

Evergreen
355 Adelaide St. West, 5th Fl., Toronto ON M5V 1S2
Tel: 416-596-1495; *Fax:* 416-596-1443
Toll-Free: 888-426-3138
e-mail: info@evergreen.ca; donate@evergreen.ca
URL: www.evergreen.ca
Previous Name: The Evergreen Foundation
Overview: A medium-sized national charitable organization founded in 1991
Chief Officer(s):
Geoff Cape, Executive Director
gcape@evergreen.ca
Matthew Church, Director, Marketing & Communications
mchurch@evergreen.ca
Finances: *Funding Sources:* Donations; Sponsorships
Activities: Creating innovative resources; Transforming school grounds & home landscapes; Conserving publicly accessible land; Hosting conferences; *Library:* Yes;
Mission: To bring communities & nature together for the benefit of both; To create sustaining, healthy, dynamic outdoor spaces by engaging people & encouraging local stewardship

The Evergreen Foundation *See* Evergreen

Executive Forum on Climate Change / Forum de la grande entreprise sur les changements climatiques
e-mail: efcc@policyingenuity.org
Overview: A small international organization
Chief Officer(s):
Louise Comeau, 819-682-0794
Alexander Christen, 514-848-8151

Explorer's Club (Canadian Chapter)
171 Brentwood Rd. North, Toronto ON M8X 2C8
Tel: 416-239-8840
e-mail: explorersclubcanada@hotmail.com
URL: www.explorersclub.ca; www.explorers.org
Overview: A medium-sized national organization founded in 1979
Chief Officer(s):
Jason Schoonover, Communications Director
Joseph G. Frey, Chair
Finances: *Annual Operating Budget:* Less than $50,000
Staff: 11 staff member(s)
Membership: 110; 3,000 worldwide; *Fees:* US$120-450;
Member Profile: Field scientists; *Committees:* Exploration; Student Recruitment; Events; Membership; Communications; Executive; Regional
Activities: *Speaker Service:* Yes
Mission: To promote field sciences & exploration of land, sea, air & space; *Affiliation(s):* Explorer's Club (New York)

Expo agricole de Chicoutimi
CP 622, 350, boul Université est, Chicoutimi QC G7H 5C8
Tél: 418-545-8597; *Téléc:* 418-545-9243
Courriel: info@expoagricoledechicoutimi.com
URL: www.expoagricoledechicoutimi.com
Nom précédent: Société d'agriculture de Chicoutimi
Aperçu: Dimension: petite; *Envergure:* locale
Membre(s) du bureau directeur:
Louis-Joseph Jean, Directeur général
Finances: *Budget de fonctionnement annuel:* $100,000-$250,000; *Fonds:* Gouvernement régional
Personnel: 1 membre(s) du personnel; 6 bénévole(s)
Membre: 70 individu; 5 associé*Montant de la cotisation:* 10$ individu; 100$ associé
Activités: Exposition agricole
Mission: Encourager l'amélioration de l'agriculture, de l'horticulture, de la sylviculture, de l'apiculture, de l'acériculture et de tous les autres domaines qui s'adonnent à l'agriculture par la tenue d'une exposition annuelle et par tout autres moyens; *Affiliation(s):* Association des expositions agricoles du Québec

Fabricants de produits alimentaires du Canada *See* Food Processors of Canada

Falls Brook Centre
125 South Knowlesville Rd., Knowlesville NB E7L 1B1
Tel: 506-375-8143; *Fax:* 506-375-4221
e-mail: ja@fallsbrookcentre.ca
URL: www.fallsbrookcentre.ca
Overview: A small local organization
Chief Officer(s):
Jean Arnold, Executive Director
Activities: Education and Outreach; Community Development; International Work; workshops and workbees
Mission: Situated on 400 acres of rural forest and farmland, the Centre is a sustainable community demonstration and training centre. On-site activities and features include solar and wind energy systems, organic gardening, forest trails, herbariums and tree nurseries, and a conference centre. The Centre promotes sustainability and collaborates with the community to provide alternatives.; *Member of:* Canadian Renewable Energy Alliance; *Affiliation(s):* Canadian Coalition for Biodiversity
Environmental Activity: Forest Stewardship; Organic Agriculture; Appropriate Technology

Farm Radio International / Radios Rurales Internationales
1404 Scott St., Ottawa ON K1Y 4M8
Tel: 613-761-3650; *Fax:* 613-798-0990
Toll-Free: 888-773-7717
e-mail: info@farmradio.org
URL: www.farmradio.org
Previous Name: Developing Countries Farm Radio Network
Overview: A medium-sized international charitable organization founded in 1979
Finances: *Annual Operating Budget:* $250,000-$500,000;
Funding Sources: Private donations; government grants; CIDA
Staff: 6 staff member(s); 10 volunteer(s)
Membership: 500; *Fees:* Free to rural radio stations in developing countries; *Member Profile:* Rural radio broadcasters in developing countries;
Mission: To increase food supplies & to improve the nutrition, health & quality of life of small-scale farmers in developing countries through a coordinating network of broadcasters & others who exchange information about simple, practical sustainable farming techniques & health practices; to support broadcasters to strengthen small scale farmers & rural life; *Member of:* Canadian Centre for Philanthropy; Ontario Council for International Cooperation; Canadian Council for International Cooperation

FarmFolk/CityFolk Society (FF/CF) / Société des gens de ferme et des gens de ville
1937 - 2nd West Ave., Vancouver BC V6J 1J2
Tel: 604-730-0450; *Fax:* 604-730-0451
Toll-Free: 877-730-0452
e-mail: info@ffcf.bc.ca
URL: www.ffcf.bc.ca
Overview: A small local charitable organization founded in 1993
Chief Officer(s):
Heather Pritchard, Execxutive Director
Finances: *Annual Operating Budget:* $100,000-$250,000;
Funding Sources: Foundations; memberships; donations
Staff: 4 staff member(s); 80 volunteer(s)
Membership: 15 institutional; 200 student; 200 individual; 20 associate; *Fees:* $500+ corporate; $100 farm; $50 family; $30 individual; *Member Profile:* Not-for-profit, charitable organization
Activities: Events, projects, education; *Awareness Events:* "Feast of Fields" Fundraiser, Sept.; *Library:* FarmFolk/CityFolk Resource Library; Open to public
Mission: To work with others for a local, sustainable food system; to make connection between farm & city, producer & consumer, grower & eater that creates sustainable communities; to protect foodlands, support farmers & food producers, & connect communities

FaunENord
313, 3e Rue, 2e étage, Chibougamau QC G8P 1N4
Tél: 418-748-4441; *Téléc:* 418-748-1110
URL: www.faunenord.icr.qc.ca
Aperçu: Dimension: petite; *Envergure:* locale
Membre(s) du bureau directeur:
Justine Desmeules
jdesmeules.faunenord.lino.com
Mission: Une entreprise vouée à la promotion & à l'aménagement durable des ressources fauniques & des écosystèmes

Fédération canadienne de l'agriculture *See* Canadian Federation of Agriculture

Fédération canadienne de la faune *See* Canadian Wildlife Federation

Fédération canadienne des épiciers indépendants *See* Canadian Federation of Independent Grocers

Fédération canadienne des étudiants et étudiantes en génie *See* Canadian Federation of Engineering Students

Fédération canadienne des municipalités *See* Federation of Canadian Municipalities

Fédération canadienne des sciences de la Terre *See* Canadian Federation of Earth Sciences

Fédération d'agriculture biologique du Québec (FABQ)
#100, 555, boul Roland-Therrien, Longueuil QC J4H 3Y9
Tél: 450-679-0530; *Téléc:* 450-670-4867
Courriel: fabq@upa.qc.ca
URL: www.fabqbio.ca
Aperçu: Dimension: petite; *Envergure:* provinciale; fondée en 1989
Membre(s) du bureau directeur:
Gérard Bouchard, Président
Finances: *Budget de fonctionnement annuel:* $50,000-$100,000
Personnel: 1 membre(s) du personnel; 7 bénévole(s)
Membre: 200; *Montant de la cotisation:* 125$; *Critères d'admissibilite:* Producteurs agricoles biologiques
Activités: Promotion générique; développement de marchés; information
Mission: Promouvoir l'étude, la défense et le développement des intérêts économiques, sociaux et moraux de ses membres; administrer tout le programme de la mise en marché étudier les problèmes relatifs à la production; coopérer à la vulgarisation des techniques de production biologique; renseigner le producteur sur la production et la vente de produits biologiques certifiés

Fédération de la faune du Nouveau-Brunswick *See* New Brunswick Wildlife Federation

Fédération des agricultrices du Québec (FAQ)
555, boul Roland-Therrien, Longueuil QC J4H 4E7
Tél: 450-679-0530; *Téléc:* 450-463-5228
Courriel: info@agricultrices.com
URL: www.agricultrices.com
Aperçu: Dimension: moyenne; *Envergure:* provinciale; Organisme sans but lucratif; fondée en 1987
Membre: 1,000-4,999; *Critères d'admissibilite:* Agricultrice, membre de soutien
Mission: Valoriser la profession; créer un réseau entre les femmes; avoir une force politique capable de défendre les intérêts des agricultrices; prodiguer de la formation; *Membre de:* L'Union des producteurs agricoles

Fédération des associations pour la protection de l'environnement des lacs inc. (FAPEL)
CP 51128, Succ. Centre, Montréal QC H1N 3T8
Tél: 514-254-5361
Courriel: fapel@fapel.org
URL: fapel.org
Aperçu: Dimension: grande; *Envergure:* provinciale; fondée en 1976
Membre: 650 sociétés;

La Fédération des producteurs de bois du Québec (FPBQ)
#565, 555, boul Roland-Therrien, Longueuil QC J4H 4E7
Tél: 450-679-0530; *Téléc:* 450-679-4300
Courriel: bois@upa.qc.ca
URL: www.fpbq.qc.ca
Aperçu: Dimension: moyenne; *Envergure:* provinciale; fondée en 1970
Membre(s) du bureau directeur:
Jean-Pierre Dansereau, Directeur
jpdansereau@upa.qc.ca
Finances: *Budget de fonctionnement annuel:* $500,000-$1.5 Million
Personnel: 9 membre(s) du personnel
Mission: Défendre les intérêts de l'ensemble des propriétaires de boisés du Québec ainsi que l'élaboration et la promotion des politiques souhaitables et nécessaires pour atteindre cet objectif; représenter les propriétaires de boisés privés auprès des pouvoirs publics et des autres groupes de la société au niveau provincial et national; coordonner l'ensemble des activités des Syndicats et Offices de producteurs de bois ainsi que l'établissement, le maintien et le développement entre eux d'une

étroite collaboration; Affiliation(s): Union des producteurs agricoles

Fédération des producteurs de cultures commerciales du Québec (FPCCQ)
#505, 555, boul Roland-Therrien, Longueuil QC J4H 3Y9
Tél: 450-679-0540; Téléc: 450-679-6372
Courriel: fpccq@fpccq.qc.ca
URL: www.fpccq.qc.ca
Aperçu: Dimension: petite; Envergure: provinciale; fondée en 1975
Membre(s) du bureau directeur:
Christian Overbeek, Président
Membre: 11 syndicats
Affiliation(s): Union des producteurs agricoles (UPA)

Fédération des propriétaires de lots boisés du Nouveau-Brunswick inc. See New Brunswick Federation of Woodlot Owners Inc.

Fédération des sociétés canadiennes d'assistance aux animaux See Canadian Federation of Humane Societies

Fédération des sociétés d'horticulture et d'écologie du Québec (FSHÉQ)
CP 1000, Succ. M, 4545, av Pierre-de-Coubertin, Montréal QC H1V 3R2
Tél: 514-252-3010; Téléc: 514-251-8038
Courriel: fsheq@fsheq.com
URL: www.fsheq.com
Aperçu: Dimension: moyenne; Envergure: provinciale; Organisme sans but lucratif; fondée en 1978
Membre(s) du bureau directeur:
Thérèse Tourigny, Directrice générale
Finances: Budget de fonctionnement annuel: $50,000-$100,000
Personnel: 3 bénévole(s)
Membre: 280; Montant de la cotisation: 90$; Critères d'admissibilite: Sociétés d'horticulture
Activités: Service de conférenciers: Oui
Mission: Regrouper tous les organismes voués à l'horticulture; faire la promotion de l'horticulture.

Fédération du saumon atlantique See Atlantic Salmon Federation

Fédération internationale des Amis de la Terre See Friends of the Earth International

Fédération internationale des architectes paysagistes See International Federation of Landscape Architects

Fédération Internationale des Associations de Professeurs de Sciences See International Council of Associations for Science Education

Fédération internationale des géomètres See International Federation of Surveyors

Fédération internationale des mouvements d'agriculture biologique See International Federation of Organic Agriculture Movements

Fédération internationale pour l'habitation, l'urbanisme et l'aménagement des territoires See International Federation for Housing & Planning

Federation of Alberta Naturalists (FAN)
11759 Groat Rd., Edmonton AB T5M 3K6
Tel: 780-427-8124; Fax: 780-422-2663
e-mail: info@fanweb.ca
URL: www.fanweb.ca
Overview: A medium-sized provincial charitable organization founded in 1970
Finances: Annual Operating Budget: $50,000-$100,000; Funding Sources: Donations; grants; projects
Staff: 3 volunteer(s)
Membership: 5,000 individual + 42 clubs; Fees: $20
Awards: Loran L. Goulden Memorial Award (Award)
Mission: To encourage Albertans to increase knowledge & understanding of natural history & ecological processes; to provide a unified voice for naturalists on conservation issues; to organize field meetings, conferences, nature camps, research symposia, & other activities.; Member of: Canadian Nature Federation

Federation of Calgary Communities (FCC)
#301, 1609 - 14 St. SW, Calgary AB T3C 1E4
Tel: 403-244-4111; Fax: 403-244-4129
e-mail: fcc@calgarycommunities.com
URL: www.calgarycommunities.com
Overview: A small local licensing organization founded in 1961
Finances: Annual Operating Budget: $100,000-$250,000
Staff: 1 staff member(s); 25 volunteer(s)
Membership: 114
Activities: Rents Mailing List: Yes; Library: Yes, Open to public
Mission: To enhance Calgary communities

Federation of Canadian Municipalities (FCM) / Fédération canadienne des municipalités
24 Clarence St., Ottawa ON K1N 5P3
Tel: 613-241-5221; Fax: 613-241-7440
e-mail: federation@fcm.ca
URL: www.fcm.ca
Previous Name: Canadian Federation of Mayors & Municipalities
Overview: A large national organization founded in 1901
Finances: Funding Sources: Membership fees; advertising; trade show; market research
Membership: 1,600+; Fees: Schedule available based on population; Member Profile: Members include Canada's cities, small urban & rural communities, & provincial & territorial municipal associations.; Committees: Standing Committees: Increasing Women's Participation in Municipal Government; Community Safety & Crime Prevention; Environmental Issues & Sustainable Development; International Relations; Municipal Finance & Intergovernmental Arrangements; Municipal Infrastructure & Transportation Policy; Northern Forum; Rural Forum; Social Economic Development
Activities: Promoting strong, effective, & accountable municipal government; Rents Mailing List: Yes
Awards: Race Relations Awards (Award)
FCM/CH2M Hill Canada Awards (Award)
The Roll of Honour (Award)
Outstanding International Volunteer Contribution Awards (Award)
Meetings/Conferences:
For more information see Trade Shows, Conferences and Seminars Chapter
Federation of Canadian Municipalities 2011 74th Annual Conference & Municipal Expo
June 2011 Halifax, NS
Federation of Canadian Municipalities 2012 75th Annual Conference & Municipal Expo
June 2012 Saskatoon, SK
Publications: Forum: Canada's National Municipal Magazine
Type: Magazine Frequency: bi-m. Accepts Advertising : Yes
Editor: Robert Ross
Profile: Recent municipal-sector developments
Federation of Canadian Municipalities Annual Report
Type: Yearbook Frequency: a.
Mission: FCM is the national voice of municipal government that represents the interests of municipalities on policy & program matters that fall within federal jurisdiction. Its goal in serving elected municipal officials is the improvement of the quality of life in all communities.

Federation of Northern Ontario Municipalities (FONOM)
PO Box 2175, Stn. A, Sudbury ON P3A 4S1
Tel: 705-586-9120; Fax: 705-586-9195
e-mail: fonom@eastlink.ca
URL: www.fonom.org
Overview: A medium-sized local organization founded in 1960
Finances: Funding Sources: Membership fees; Provincial grants; Sponsorships
Membership: 111; Member Profile: Municipal governments from the following districts: Cochrane, Algoma, Manitoulin, Nipissing, Parry Sound, Sudbury, & Timiskaming
Meetings/Conferences:
For more information see Trade Shows, Conferences and Seminars Chapter
Federation of Northern Ontario Municipalities 2012 52nd Annual Conference
Other Conferences in 2012 2012, ON
Mission: To act as the voice for the people of northeastern Ontario communities; To work for the betterment of municipal government by striving for improved legislation respecting local government in northern Ontario; Member of: Association of Municipalities of Ontario

Federation of Nova Scotia Naturalists See Nature Nova Scotia (Federation of Nova Scotia Naturalists)

Federation of Nova Scotian Heritage (FNSH)
1113 Marginal Rd., Halifax NS B3H 4P7
Tel: 902-423-4677; Fax: 902-422-0881
Toll-Free: 800-355-6873
e-mail: fnsh@hfx.andara.com
Overview: A medium-sized provincial organization founded in 1976
Membership: 50 organizational + 25 individual + 1 student + 2 lifetime; Fees: $50 organizational; $25 individual; $15 student
Activities: Training & Education Program; Heritage Studies Certificate; applied learning workshops; seminars
Awards: President's Award (Award)
Dr. Phyllis R. Blakeley Lifetime Achievement Award (Award)
Outstanding Exhibit Award/Outstanding Promotion Award (Award)
Mission: To support, promote & link NS heritage groups; to be a leader in heritage issues; to promote heritage awareness in Nova Scotia; to coordinate professional & volunteer development.; Affiliation(s): Heritage Canada; Canadian Museums Association; Association for State & Local History

Federation of Ontario Cottagers' Associations (FOCA)
#201, 159 King St., Peterborough ON K9J 2R8
Tel: 705-749-3622; Fax: 705-749-6522
e-mail: info@foca.on.ca
URL: www.foca.on.ca
Overview: A medium-sized provincial organization founded in 1963
Finances: Funding Sources: Membership fees; Sponsorships; Donations
Membership: 550+; Fees: $37.50 individuals; $75 associations; Member Profile: Ontario cottagers' associations; Individuals, such as waterfront property owners
Activities: Providing information about issues that affect cottage properties; Offering networking opportunities
Meetings/Conferences:
For more information see Trade Shows, Conferences and Seminars Chapter
Federation of Ontario Cottagers' Associations 2011 Fall Seminar
Other Conferences in 2011 2011, ON
Federation of Ontario Cottagers' Associations 2012 Spring Annual General Meeting
Other Conferences in 2012 2012, ON
Publications: Federation of Ontario Cottagers' Associations Report to Members
Type: Newsletter Price: Free with Federation of Ontario Cottagers' Associations membership
Profile: Federation activities
Lake Stewards Newsletter
Type: Newsletter Frequency: a. Price: Free with Federation of Ontario Cottagers' Associations membership
Mission: To ensure a healthy future for waterfront Ontario; To support the interests of Ontario's cottagers
Environmental Activity: Engaging in freshwater advocacy activities; Promoting sustainable waterfront communities; Encouraging environmental stewardship

Federation of Ontario Naturalists See Ontario Nature

Federation of Prince Edward Island Municipalities Inc. (FPEIM)
1 Kirkdale Rd., Charlottetown PE C1E 1R3
Tel: 902-566-1493; Fax: 902-566-2880
e-mail: info@fpeim.ca
URL: www.fpeim.ca
Overview: A large provincial organization founded in 1957
Finances: Annual Operating Budget: $100,000-$250,000; Funding Sources: Small government grant; membership fees
Staff: 2 staff member(s); 13 volunteer(s)
Membership: 43 municipalities; Fees: Per capita fee; Member Profile: Incorporated municipality; Committees: Finance; Resolutions; Constitution; Annual Meeting; Semi-Annual Meeting; Transportation
Activities: Monthly board meetings; 2 full membership meetings per year; bi-monthly information updates to membership; liaising with provincial municipal associations across Canada as well as provincial & federal government departments; Awareness Events: Municipal Government Week; Library: Yes, open by appointment
Awards: The Gilbert C. Bell Memorial Award (Scholarship)
Presented annually to a full-time undergraduate student who exemplifies an interest in a career in Public Administration by obtaining the highest mark in Public Administration Course #311 - Public Policy & Administration 1, in that academic year
Municipal Achievement Award (Award)
Awarded annually to a municipality that has demonstrated a

commitment to improving the quality of life of its residents through innovative local projects & activities; two awards presented each year: one award to a municipality with a population of 1,500 & under; one award to a municipality with a population over 1,500; open to FPEI Municipalities members
Mission: To represent the interests of the cities, towns & communities within PEI; to secure united action for the protection of individual municipalities & municipal interests as a whole; to act as a clearing house for the collection, exchange & dissemination of information of concern & interest to member municipalities; to provide training, education & development opportunities for elected & appointed municipal officials; *Member of:* Federation of Canadian Municipalities; *Affiliation(s):* Association of Municipal Administrators, PEI

Federation of Saskatchewan Surface Rights Association (FSSRA)
PO Box 53, Lone Rock SK S0M 1K0
Tel: 306-387-6650; *Fax:* 306-387-6650
Overview: A small provincial organization founded in 1982
Membership: 1-99; *Member Profile:* Farmers
Activities: *Speaker Service:* Yes
Mission: To aid in reclamation concerns in land, gas lines, rail lines, compensation, environmental issues & legislation; *Affiliation(s):* Alberta Surface Rights Federation

Federation of Sewage Works Associations; Federation of Sewage & Industrial Wastes Associations; Water Pollution Control Federation *See* Water Environment Federation

Fédération québécoise de camping et de caravaning inc. (FQCC)
CP 100, 1560, rue Eiffel, Boucherville QC J4B 5Y1
Tél: 450-650-3722; *Téléc:* 450-650-3721
Ligne sans frais: 877-650-3722
Courriel: info@fqcc.ca
URL: www.fqcc.ca
Aperçu: *Dimension:* grande; *Envergure:* provinciale; fondée en 1967
Membre(s) du bureau directeur:
Louise Saindon, Présidente
Claude Cournoyer, Trésorier
Finances: *Budget de fonctionnement annuel:* $500,000-$1.5 Million
Personnel: 10 membre(s) du personnel
Membre: 45 000 familles membres; *Montant de la cotisation:* 45$
Activités: *Service de conférenciers:* Oui
Mission: Unir les adeptes du camping et du caravaning; entreprendre et coordonner des actions relatives au camping et au caravaning.; *Membre de:* Fédération internationale de camping et de caravaning

Fédération québécoise de la faune *Voir* Fédération québécoise des chasseurs et pêcheurs

Fédération québécoise de la montagne et de l'escalade (FQME)
CP 1000, Succ. M, 4545, av Pierre-de-Coubertin, Montréal QC H1V 3R2
Tél: 514-252-3004; *Téléc:* 514-252-3201
Ligne sans frais: 866-204-3763
Courriel: fqme@fqme.qc.ca
URL: www.fqme.qc.ca
Aperçu: *Dimension:* petite; *Envergure:* provinciale; Organisme sans but lucratif; fondée en 1969
Finances: *Budget de fonctionnement annuel:* $100,000-$250,000
Membre: 2 000; *Montant de la cotisation:* 30$ adulte; 10$ jeune; *Comités:* Formation; Site; Expédition
Activités: Amateur d'activités montagnes; *Stagiaires:* Oui; *Bibliothèque:* Centre de documentation; rendez-vous
Mission: Regrouper les adeptes de l'escalade et de l'alpinisme au Québec; promouvoir l'escalade (rocher et glace) et le ski de l'alpinisme et de randonnée en montagne; promouvoir une pratique sécuritaire de ces activités; protéger et rendre accessibles les différents sites d'escalade et de grande randonnée à skis au Québec; *Membre de:* Canadian Avalanche Association; Outdoor Recreation Coalition of America (ORCA); *Affiliation(s):* Union internationale des associations d'alpinisme

Fédération québécoise des chasseurs et pêcheurs
Parent: Canadian Wildlife Federation
#109, 6780, 1re av, Québec QC G1H 2W8
Tél: 418-626-6858; *Téléc:* 418-622-6168
Ligne sans frais: 888-523-2863
Courriel: info@fedecp.qc.ca
URL: www.fqf.qc.ca
Nom précédent: Fédération québécoise de la faune
Aperçu: *Dimension:* moyenne; *Envergure:* provinciale; fondée en 1946
Membre: 200 associations; *Montant de la cotisation:* 39,95$ membre individuel; *Critères d'admissibilite:* Chasseurs, pêcheurs
Mission: Contribuer, dans le respect de la faune et de ses habitats, à la gestion du développement et à la perpétuation de la chasse et de la pêche comme activités traditionnelles et sportives

Fédération québécoise des coopératives forestières (FQCF)
#200, 3188, ch Sainte-Foy, Québec QC G1X 1R4
Tél: 418-651-0388; *Téléc:* 418-651-3860
Courriel: cathyg@fqcf.coop
URL: www.fqcf.coop
Nom précédent: Conférence des coopératives forestières du Québec
Aperçu: *Dimension:* moyenne; *Envergure:* provinciale; fondée en 1985
Membre(s) du bureau directeur:
Jocelyn Lessard, Directeur général
j.lessard@fqcf.coop
Finances: *Budget de fonctionnement annuel:* $500,000-$1.5 Million
Personnel: 4 membre(s) du personnel
Membre: 44
Mission: La Fédération québécoise des coopératives forestières (FQCF) regroupe et représente dans des domaines d'intérêts communs l'ensemble des coopératives forestières de travailleurs, les coopératives de travailleurs actionnaires et les coopératives de solidarité actives dans le milieu forestier, et ce dans toutes les régions du Québec

Fédération Québécoise des Municipalités (FQM)
#560, 2954, boul Laurier, Sainte-Foy QC G1V 4T2
Tél: 418-651-3343; *Téléc:* 418-651-1127
Courriel: fqm@fqm.ca
URL: www.fqm.ca
Nom précédent: Union des municipalités régionales de comté et des municipalités locales du Québec
Aperçu: *Dimension:* moyenne; *Envergure:* provinciale; fondée en 1944
Membre(s) du bureau directeur:
Bernard Généreux, Président
Membre: 1000 municipalités et presque la totalité des MRC; *Critères d'admissibilite:* Municipalités
Activités: *Service de conférenciers:* Oui
Mission: Etre la porte-parole des régions; défendre les intérêts de ses membres

Fédération québécoise du canot camping inc *Voir* Fédération québécoise du canot et du kayak

Fédération québécoise du canot et du kayak (FQCK)
CP 1000, Succ. M, 4545, av Pierre-de-Coubertin, Montréal QC H1V 3R2
Tél: 514-252-3001; *Téléc:* 514-252-3091
Courriel: info@canot-kayak.qc.ca
URL: www.canot-kayak.qc.ca
Nom précédent: Fédération québécoise du canot camping inc
Aperçu: *Dimension:* moyenne; *Envergure:* provinciale; Organisme sans but lucratif; fondée en 1976
Finances: *Budget de fonctionnement annuel:* $250,000-$500,000
Personnel: 2 membre(s) du personnel; 15 bénévole(s)
Membre: 4 000; *Montant de la cotisation:* 40$; *Comités:* Cartographie; Formation
Activités: Affilié au Canot-camping La Vérendrye; *Stagiaires:* Oui; *Service de conférenciers:* Oui
Mission: Regrouper les organismes et individus intéressés à la pratique du canotage récréatif et du canot-camping et de promouvoir la pratique de ces activités en utilisant le canot ouvert de type amérindien autrement appelé Canot Canadien
Environmental Activity: Fonds de préservation des rivières

Fédération québécoise pour le saumon atlantique (FQSA)
42B, rue Racine, Loretteville QC G2B 1C6
Tél: 418-847-9191; *Téléc:* 418-847-9279
Ligne sans frais: 888-728-6667
Courriel: secretariat@saumon-fqsa.qc.ca
URL: www.saumon-fqsa.qc.ca
Aperçu: *Dimension:* moyenne; *Envergure:* provinciale; fondée en 1984
Membre(s) du bureau directeur:
Michel Jean, Directeur général
mjean@saumon-fqsa.qc.ca
Membre: 1 000; *Montant de la cotisation:* 40$
Mission: Organisme à but non lucratif dont la raison d'être est d'unir et de représenter les intérêts de l'ensemble des saumoniers du Québec

FEESA - An Environmental Education Society *See* Inside Education

Fiducie du patrimoine ontarien *See* Ontario Heritage Trust

Fiducie foncière Vallée de Ruiter *See* Ruiter Valley Land Trust

Field Botanists of Ontario (FBO)
c/o W.D. McIlveen, RR#1, Acton ON L7J 2L7
e-mail: wmcilveen@sympatico.ca
URL: aww.trentu.ca/fbo
Social Media:
www.facebook.com/group.php?gid=7783788221#!/group.php?gid=7783788221
Overview: A small provincial organization founded in 1983
Membership: 300; *Fees:* $15 individuals; $18 families; $250 life memberships; *Member Profile:* Amateur & professional botanists of all ages
Activities: Offering field trips; Providing education & workshops; Offering botanical expertise; Encouraging the exchange of botanical information; Facilitating networking opportunities
Meetings/Conferences:
For more information see Trade Shows, Conferences and Seminars Chapter
Field Botanists of Ontario 2011 Annual General Meeting
Other Conferences in 2011 2011, ON
Publications: *Field Botanists of Ontario Newsletter*
Type: Newsletter *Frequency:* q. *Editor:* Cheryl Hendrickson
Profile: Articles, meeting information, & field trip reports
Mission: To increase documentation of the flora of Ontario; To encourage interest in botany & conservation in the province of Ontario
Environmental Activity: Promoting conservation

Film & Bag Federation
#1000, 1667 K St. NW, Washington DC 20006 USA
Tel: 202-974-5218; *Fax:* 202-296-7675
URL: www.plasticbag.com
Previous Name: Plastic Bag Association; Plastic Bag Information Clearing House
Overview: A small national organization
Chief Officer(s):
Donna Dempsey, Executive Director
ddempsey@socplas.org

Fire Prevention Canada (FPC)
PO Box 47037, Ottawa ON K1B 5P9
Tel: 613-749-3844; *Fax:* 613-749-0109
Toll-Free: 877-906-6651
e-mail: info@fiprecan.ca
URL: www.fiprecan.ca
Also Known As: Fiprecan
Overview: A medium-sized national charitable organization
Mission: Working with the public & private sectors to achieve fire safety through education.

First Nations Environmental Network
Parent: Canadian Environmental Network
PO Box 394, Tofino BC V0R 2Z0
Tel: 250-726-5265; *Fax:* 250-725-2357
e-mail: councilfire@hotmail.com
URL: www.fnen.org
Overview: A small national organization
Chief Officer(s):
Steve Lawson, Coordinator
wolf@lincsat.com
Mission: The First Nations Environmental Network is a circle of First Nations people committed to protecting, defending, and restoring the balance of all life by honouring traditional Indigenous values and the path of our ancestors. We encourage the work of protecting, defending and healing Mother Earth. We desire and need to link grassroots Indigenous people nationally and internationally to support each other on environmental struggles and concerns. We are obligated to leave footprints for

our children to follow by striving to live our life with traditional values.

Fish Harvesters Resource Centres (FRC)
PO Box 1242, Stn. C, 2 Steers Cove, St. John's NL A1C 5M9
Tel: 709-576-0292; *Fax:* 709-576-0339
URL: www.frc.nf.ca
Overview: A small provincial organization founded in 1993
Chief Officer(s):
Richard Moores, Executive Director
rmoores@frc.nf.ca
Rose Walsh, Program Coordinator
rwalsh@frc.nf.ca
Mission: The Centres assist & support the restructuring of the Newfoundland & Labrador fishing industry by providing information & resources to fish harvesters in the province. They offer business counselling & technical assistance to encourage entrepreneurship among harvesters.; *Affiliation(s):* FFAW/CAW Fish; Food & Allied Workers Union; Atlantic Canada Opportunities Agency (ACOA)

Fisheries Council of British Columbia *See* Fisheries Council of Canada - British Columbia Representative

Fisheries Council of Canada (FCC)
#900, 170 Laurier Ave. West, Ottawa ON K1P 5V5
Tel: 613-727-7450; *Fax:* 613-727-7453
e-mail: info@fisheriescouncil.org
URL: www.fisheriescouncil.ca
Previous Name: Canadian Fisheries Association
Overview: A large national organization founded in 1915
Fees: $600 associate members; $5000 special purpose associations; *Member Profile:* Enterprises & associations that harvest, handle, process, distribute, & market fish & seafood; Associate institutions & firms that provide a product or service to the fish & seafood industry
Activities: Developing an economically sound & competitive industry; Liaising with government departments & agencies
Meetings/Conferences:
For more information see Trade Shows, Conferences and Seminars Chapter
Fisheries Council of Canada 2011 66th Annual Conference Other Conferences in 2011 2011
Fisheries Council of Canada 2012 67th Annual Conference Other Conferences in 2012 2012
Publications: *Building a Fishery that Works: Ottawa Update*
Type: Newsletter *Frequency:* m.
Profile: Updates on the Council's activities, environmental issues, Canadian & international fisheries issues, & market reports
Fisheries Council of Canada Annual Fish & Seafood Products & Services Directory
Type: Directory *Frequency:* a.
Profile: Listings to promote members' products & services
Mission: To represent Canada's fish & seafood industry
Environmental Activity: Conserving fishing resources to ensure a sustainable future for the fishing industry; Providing information on environmental issues such as species at risk & ocean use; Promoting a healthy resource; Protecting the marine environment

Fisheries Council of Canada - British Columbia Representative
4214 - 199A St., Langley BC V3A 4V6
Tel: 604-530-7258; *Fax:* 604-530-2015
e-mail: gjconsult@telus.net
Previous Name: Fisheries Council of British Columbia
Overview: A medium-sized provincial organization
Member of: Fisheries Council of Canada

Fishermen and Scientists Research Society (FSRS)
PO Box 25125, Halifax NS B3M 4H4
Tel: 902-876-1160; *Fax:* 902-876-1320
URL: www.fsrs.ns.ca
Overview: A medium-sized provincial organization
Chief Officer(s):
Patricia King, General Manager
Member Profile: Fishermen; Research scientists
Mission: To establish and maintain a network of fishermen and scientific personnel that are concerned with the long-term sustainability of the marine fishing industry in the Atlantic Region.

Flax Canada 2015
#465, 167 Lombard Ave., Winnipeg MB R3B 0T6
Tel: 204-942-2115; *Fax:* 204-942-1841
e-mail: kelley@fc2015.ca
URL: www.fc2015.ca
Overview: A small national organization
Chief Officer(s):
Kelley C. Fitzpatrick, Director
Mission: To position flax as one of the main drivers of the Canadian bio-economy by the year 2015; To develop health care strategies based on flaxseed; To increase research & commercialization of new products from flax; To ensure utilization of value-added components from seed & straw; To develop a "branding strategy" for flax; To capture opportunities provided by the multiple end-uses of flax to increase net farm income; To improve agricultural sustainability & to enhance Canada's rural communities

Flax Council of Canada
#465, 167 Lombard Ave., Winnipeg MB R3B 0T6
Tel: 204-982-2115; *Fax:* 204-942-1841
e-mail: flax@flaxcouncil.ca
URL: www.flaxcouncil.ca
Overview: A medium-sized national organization founded in 1985
Finances: *Annual Operating Budget:* $500,000-$1.5 Million
Membership: 60 corporate; *Fees:* $200; *Committees:* Communications; Market Development; Research & Technical
Activities: *Library:* Yes, Open to public
Mission: To provide a central focus for industry, producers, government, research institutions & marketing organizations; to promote flax worldwide through crop, market & product development.

Fleurs Canada *See* Flowers Canada

Flowers Canada (FC) / Fleurs Canada
Retail & Distribution Sector, #305, 99 Fifth Ave., Ottawa ON K1S 5P5
Fax: 866-671-8091
Toll-Free: 800-447-5147
e-mail: flowers@flowerscanada.org
URL: www.flowerscanada.org
Also Known As: Association of the Canadian Floral Industry
Overview: A medium-sized national organization founded in 1897
Chief Officer(s):
Arman Patel, Executive Director
Membership: 1,000; *Fees:* $200 associates; $265 retailers; $500 distributors & wholesalers; *Member Profile:* Flower growers; Distributors; Retailers; Educators; Associates
Activities: Establishing partnerships; Researching; Developing consumers; Taking legislative action; Encouraging professional accreditation; Providing education; Offering business services; Giving sales & marketing support; Organizing conferences; Communicating with members; Developing standards; Conducting research; Identifying & sharing best practices; Promoting e-business; Presenting awards; *Library:* Yes, Not open to the public
Mission: To act as the voice of the Canadian floriculture industry; To improve the Canadian floriculture industry

Foire agricole royale d'hiver *See* Royal Agricultural Winter Fair Association

Fondation Asie Pacifique du Canada *See* Asia Pacific Foundation of Canada

Fondation canadienne de l'arbre *See* Tree Canada Foundation

Fondation canadienne des plantes ornementales *See* Canadian Ornamental Plant Foundation

Fondation canadienne pour les sciences du climat et de l'atmosphère *See* Canadian Foundation for Climate & Atmospheric Sciences

Fondation de la faune du Québec (FFQ)
#420, 1175, av Lavigerie, Québec QC G1V 4P1
Tél: 418-644-7926; *Téléc:* 418-643-7655
Ligne sans frais: 877-639-0742
Courriel: ffq@fondationdelafaune.qc.ca
URL: www.fondationdelafaune.qc.ca
Aperçu: *Dimension:* moyenne; *Envergure:* provinciale; Organisme sans but lucratif; fondée en 1985
Membre(s) du bureau directeur:
André Martin, Président-directeur général
direction@fondationdelafaune.qc.ca
Finances: *Budget de fonctionnement annuel:* $3 Million-$5 Million
Personnel: 17 membre(s) du personnel
Membre: 4 500; *Montant de la cotisation:* 20$
Activités: Programmes de subvention: amélioration de la qualité des habitats aquatiques; faire connaître nos habitats fauniques; programme d'aide à la protection des habitats; pêche en herbe, faune en danger; programme de mise en valeur des cours d'eau en milieu agricole
Mission: Promouvoir la conservation et la mise en valeur de la faune et de son habitat

Fondation des amis de l'environnement TD *See* TD Friends of the Environment Foundation

Fondation des partenaires de la Biosphère de Montréal / The Biosphere of Montréal Partner's Foundation
160, ch Tour-de-l'Isle - Ile Ste-Hélène, Montréal QC H3C 4G8
Tél: 514-496-8300; *Téléc:* 514-283-5021
Courriel: info@fondationbiosphere.org
Aperçu: *Dimension:* petite; *Envergure:* internationale; fondée en 1994
Membre(s) du bureau directeur:
André Turmel, Président
Finances: *Budget de fonctionnement annuel:* $100,000-$250,000
Personnel: 10 bénévole(s)
Membre: 10
Mission: Supporter la Biosphère de Montréal dans la réalisation de ses objectifs qui sont de favoriser l'émergence d'un nouveau rapport individuel et collectif à l'environnement de façon plus particulière à l'eau "source de vie" et à l'écosystème Saint-Laurent - Grands Lacs

Fondation du bien-être animal du Canada *See* Animal Welfare Foundation of Canada

Fondation du sentier transcanadien *See* Trans Canada Trail Foundation

Fondation Harmonie du Canada *See* Harmony Foundation of Canada

Fondation Héritage Canada *See* Heritage Canada Foundation

Fondation Hydro-Québec pour l'environnement / Hydro-Québec Foundation for the Environment
740, rue Notre-Dame Ouest, 8e étage, Montréal QC H3C 3X6
Tél: 514-289-5384; *Téléc:* 514-289-2079
Courriel: fondation_environnement@hydro.qc.ca
URL: www.hydroquebec.com/fondation_environnement
Aperçu: *Dimension:* petite; *Envergure:* provinciale
Membre(s) du bureau directeur:
Marie-José Nadeau, Présidente
Mission: Promouvoir la conservation, la restauration et la mise en valeur de la faune, de la flore et des habitats naturels; soutenir les besoins locaux en matière de prise en charge de l'environnement; contribuer à l'utilisation responsable et durable des ressources naturelles

Fondation pour la conservation de l'environnement *See* Foundation for Environmental Conservation

Fondation pour la protection des sites naturels du Nouveau-Brunswick *See* Nature Trust of New Brunswick

Fondation Québec Labrador du (Canada) inc. *See* Québec-Labrador Foundation (Canada) Inc.

Fondation québécoise du cancer
2075, rue de Champlain, Montréal QC H2L 2T1
Tél: 514-527-2194; *Téléc:* 514-527-1943
Ligne sans frais: 877-336-4443
Courriel: cancerquebec.mtl@fqc.qc.ca
URL: www.fqc.qc.ca
Aperçu: *Dimension:* petite; *Envergure:* provinciale; Organisme sans but lucratif; fondée en 1979
Membre(s) du bureau directeur:
Michel Gélinas, Président-fondateur
Finances: *Budget de fonctionnement annuel:* $500,000-$1.5 Million
Personnel: 30 membre(s) du personnel; 100 bénévole(s)
Membre: 1-99; *Montant de la cotisation:* 25$; *Comités:* scientifique
Activités: *Stagiaires:* Oui; *Bibliothèque:* Oui, Bibliothèque publique
Mission: Vouée à l'amélioration de la condition de la personne atteinte de cancer et de ses proches; offrir des services

Associations/Organizations / Fondation québécoise en environnement

d'hôtellerie, d'écoute et d'information pour gens atteints du cancer; améliorer la qualité de vie des patients et celle de leurs proches.

Fondation québécoise en environnement / Québec Environment Foundation
#706, 1255 carré Phillips, Montréal QC H3B 3G1
Tél: 514-849-3323; *Téléc:* 514-849-0028
Ligne sans frais: 800-361-2503
Courriel: info@fqe.qc.ca
URL: www.fqe.qc.ca
Aperçu: Dimension: moyenne; *Envergure:* provinciale; Organisme sans but lucratif; fondée en 1987
Membre(s) du bureau directeur:
Louis-Paul Allard, Président
Claude Hill, Directeur général
chill@fge.qc.ca
Finances: Budget de fonctionnement annuel: $500,000-$1.5 Million
Personnel: 5 membre(s) du personnel; 35 bénévole(s)
Membre: 210 membres; 10 000 ami(e)s; *Montant de la cotisation:* 25$; *Comités:* Environnement
Activités: Journées éducatives, colloques, conférences, plantations d'arbres; *Service de conférenciers:* Oui
Mission: Sensibiliser les Québécoises et les Québécois à l'égard de l'environnement par l'information et l'éducation; créer une synergie entre l'économie et l'écologie; favoriser la recherche et la mise en place de solutions concrètes et efficaces

Fonds international pour la protection des animaux *See* International Fund for Animal Welfare Canada

Fonds mondial pour la nature *See* World Wildlife Fund - USA

Fonds mondial pour la nature *See* World Wildlife Fund - Canada

Food & Consumer Products of Canada (FCPC) / Produits alimentaires et de consommation du Canada (PACC)
#301, 885 Don Mills Rd., Toronto ON M3C 1V9
Tel: 416-510-8024; *Fax:* 416-510-8043
e-mail: info@fcpc.ca
URL: www.fcpc.ca
Previous Name: Grocery Products Manufacturers of Canada; Food & Consumer Products Manufacturers of Canada
Overview: A large national organization founded in 1959
Chief Officer(s):
Nancy Croitoru, President & Chief Executive Officer
Lesley McKeever, Senior Vice-President, Industry Affairs & Membership
Errol Cerit, Senior Director, Industry Affairs
Rachel Kagan, Senior Director, Environment & Sustainability Policy
Janice Emery-Carter, Manager, Education Centre
Linda Saunby, Coordinator, Public Affairs
Heather Spencer, Coordinator, Member Services
Heather.Spencer@fcpc.ca
Jami Nirenberg, Coordinator, Events
Member Profile: Companies that make & market retailer & national brands
Activities: Offering educational opportunities; Engaging in advocacy activities; Advising members about government policy changes; Offering networking opportunities
Meetings/Conferences:
For more information see Trade Shows, Conferences and Seminars Chapter
Food & Consumer Products of Canada 2011 Sodexo Executive Foodservice Breakfast
June 2011 Mississauga, ON
Food & Consumer Products of Canada 2011 Giant Tiger Executive Trade Breakfast
June 2011 Toronto, ON
Food & Consumer Products of Canada 2011 CEO Executive Conference: Growing in a Changing World
October 2011 Rosseau, ON
Mission: To represent the food & consumer products industry, from small privately-owned companies to big glboal multinationals
Environmental Activity: Working with government, regulatory bodies, & retail & foodservice partners on issues such as food safety; Providing environmental & safety issue information

Food Institute of Canada *See* Food Processors of Canada

Food Processors of Canada (FPC) / Fabricants de produits alimentaires du Canada
350 Sparks St., Ottawa ON K1R 7S8
Tel: 613-722-1000; *Fax:* 613-722-1404
e-mail: fpc@foodprocessors.ca; conferences@foodprocessors.ca
URL: www.foodprocessors.ca
Previous Name: Food Institute of Canada
Overview: A medium-sized national organization founded in 1989
Member Profile: Canadian food industry executives who own or manage food processing companies
Activities: Maintaining relationships with government departments to affect policies, programs, & regulations; Organizing conferences; Providing networking opportunities
Mission: To provide professional services & advice to members on matters such as manufacturing, trade, & commerce

Foodservice & Packaging Institute (FPI)
#204, 150 Washington St. South, Falls Church VA 22046 USA
Tel: 703-538-2800; *Fax:* 703-538-2187
e-mail: fpi@fpi.org
URL: www.fpi.org
Overview: A small national organization founded in 1933
Chief Officer(s):
John Burke, President
Beth Phillips, Director, Member Services & Administration
Lynn Rosseth, Director, Market Development & Programs
Finances: Annual Operating Budget: $500,000-$1.5 Million; *Funding Sources:* Membership fees
Staff: 3 staff member(s)
Membership: 25; *Fees:* Varies by sales; *Member Profile:* Serves the single-use foodservice packaging industry; is the material-neutral trade association for manufacturers, suppliers & distributors of single-use foodservice packaging products; *Committees:* Market Development; Marketing & Communicaitions; Public Affairs; Safety Management; Technical; Standards Council
Activities: Market development; marketing & communications; member services; public affairs & technical programs

Foothills Model Forest *See* Foothills Research Institute

Foothills Research Institute
PO Box 6330, Hinton AB T7V 1X6
Tel: 780-865-8330; *Fax:* 780-865-8331
e-mail: fmf@fmf.ab.ca
URL: www.fmf.ab.ca
Previous Name: Foothills Model Forest
Overview: A small local organization founded in 1992
Chief Officer(s):
Tom Archibald, General Manager
Finances: Annual Operating Budget: $3 Million-$5 Million
Membership: 1-99; *Member Profile:* Industry, government, environmental non-governmental offices, academics, aboriginals, researchers
Mission: Plays a key role in establishing Alberta & Canada's reputation as a world leader in sustainable forest management; *Member of:* Canadian Model Forest Network

Fored BC
Parent: Canadian Forestry Association
#213, 4438 - 10th Ave. West, Vancouver BC V6R 4R8
Tel: 604-737-8555; *Fax:* 604-737-8598
Toll-Free: 888-288-7337
e-mail: info@foredbc.org; education@foredbc.org; admin@foredbc.org
URL: www.landscapesmag.com
Previous Name: Canadian Forestry Association of BC; British Columbia Forestry Association
Overview: A medium-sized provincial charitable organization founded in 1925
Finances: Funding Sources: Donations
Activities: Offering field service programs; Providing information resources about sustainability; Supporting youth volunteer groups; Providing community participation models for First Nations; Increasing public awareness about conservation, stewardship, economic diversification, & volunteerism; Providing resource packages to community groups, youth leaders, teachers, & volunteers involved in environmental activities; Giving workshops; Consulting with communities & youth groups; *Awareness Events:* National Forest Week, Sept.
Mission: To provide education to lifelong learners in all segments of society about the environment & its resources to achieve better environmental decisions & health outcomes; To engage citizens, communities, & volunteers to rehabilitate, protect, & enhance the environment

Forest Action Network (FAN)
PO Box 625, Bella Coola BC V0T 1C0
Tel: 250-799-5800; *Fax:* 250-604-677
e-mail: forest@fanweb.org
URL: www.fanweb.org
Overview: A small local organization founded in 1993
Finances: Annual Operating Budget: Less than $50,000
Membership: 100-499
Activities: Public education & civil disobedience against clearcutting & other industrial deforestation;
Mission: To campaign to save British Columbia's coastal temperate rainforest & other ancient forests

Forest Engineering Research Institute of Canada, A Division of FPInnovations *See* FPInnovations

Forest Products Association of Canada (FPAC) / Association des produits forestiers du Canada
#410, 99 Bank St., Ottawa ON K1P 6B9
Tel: 613-563-1441; *Fax:* 613-563-4720
e-mail: ottawa@fpac.ca; customercentre@fpac.ca
URL: www.fpac.ca
Previous Name: Canadian Pulp & Paper Association
Overview: A medium-sized national organization founded in 1913
Chief Officer(s):
Avrim Lazar, President & Chief Executive Officer
Andrew Casey, Vice-President, Public Affairs & International Trade
Catherine Cobden, Vice-President, Economics & Regulatory Affairs
Isabelle Des Chênes, Vice-President, Market Relations & Communications
Mark Hubert, Vice-President, Climate Change Leadership
Susan Murray, Executive Director, Public Relations, 613-563-1441 Ext. 313
smurray@fpac.ca
David Church, Director, Transportation & Recycling
Roger Cook, Director, Environment
Andrew DeVries, Director, Conservation Biology & Aboriginal Affairs
Jon Flemming, Director, Ecomonics & Trade Policy
Paul Lansbergen, Director, Energy, Economics, & Climate Change
Joel Neuheimer, Director, Market Affairs
Étienne Bélanger, Manager, Forestry Issues
George Wamala, Manager, Government Relations & Policy
Member Profile: Canadian producers of forest products, with third-party certification of member companies' forest practices
Activities: Liaising with governments, non-governmental organizations (NGOs), & multi-stakeholder groups; Conducting advertising campaigns; *Library:* Forest Products Association of Canada Resource Centre
Publications: Transforming Canada's Forest Products Industry: Summary of Findings from the Future Bio-Pathways Project
Type: Report
Profile: Forest Products Association of Canada investigators & their partner, FPInnovations, examine traditional & emerging bio-industries to assess how wood fibre can create bio-products such as bio-energy & bio-chemicals
The New Face of the Canadian Forest Industry: The Emerging Bio-revolution (The Bio-pathways Project)
Type: Report
Profile: An examination of the market potential of emerging bio-energy, bio-chemical, & bio-products
Forest Products Association of Canada Annual Report
Type: Yearbook *Frequency:* a.
Woodland Caribou Recovery: Audit of Operatinig Practices & Mitigation Measures Employed within Woodland Caribou Ranges
Type: Report *Author:* Golder Associates
Profile: An audit commissioned by the Forest Products Association of Canada & the Caribou Landscape Management Association
A Buyers' Guide to Canada's Sustainable Forest Products
Type: Guide *Number of Pages:* 32
Profile: Contents include sustainable procurement, key issues related to sustainable procurement, sample forest products procurement, green building with Canada's forest products, FPAC member companies, a glossary, useful links, reference guides, & standards, & environmental performance data

Tackle Climate Change, Use Wood
Type: Report *Number of Pages:* 22
Profile: Managing forests to mitigate climate change
Canadian Wood, Renewable by Nature, Sustainable by Design
Type: Report *Number of Pages:* 22
Profile: Information about sustainable forest management in Canada
FPAC [Forest Products Association of Canada] Sustainability Report
Type: Report *Frequency:* biennial
Forest Certification in Canada: The Programs, Similarities, & Achievements
Type: Report *Number of Pages:* 26
Profile: Contents include an introduction to certification, Canada, a world leader in forest certification, & key elements of certification programs
Mission: To be the voice of Canada's wood, pulp & paper producers nationally & internationally in the areas of government, trade, & environmental affairs; To advance the Canadian forest products industry's global competitiveness & sustainable stewardship; To operate in a mannner which is economically viable, environmentally responsible, & socially desirable
Environmental Activity: Regenerating harvested areas; Participating in recovery & recycling; Promoting carbon neutrality; Reducing greenhouse gas emissions in the pulp & paper industry; Operating according to government-approved forest management plans

Forest Products Association of Nova Scotia (FPANS)
PO Box 696, Truro NS B2N 5E5
Tel: 902-895-1179; *Fax:* 902-893-1197
URL: www.fpans.ca
Previous Name: Nova Scotia Forest Products Association
Overview: A medium-sized provincial organization founded in 1934
Chief Officer(s):
Steve Talbot, Executive Director
stalbot@fpans.ca
Jeff Bishop, Coordinator, Communications
jbishop@fpans.ca
Membership: 500-999; *Fees:* Schedule available; *Member Profile:* Representatives from the logging sector of the trucking industry; Pulp & paper manufacturers; Sawmill operators; Forest equipment operators; Woodlot owners; Small & large landowners; Maple product producers; Silviculture & harvesting contractors; Christmas tree producers; *Committees:* Forest management; Gas tax access road; Annual meeting; Communications; Energy; Environment; Safety training & worker's compensation; Transportation; Ad hoc gypsy moth
Activities: Enhancing training standards; Providing educational programs in schools; *Awareness Events:* National Forest Week
Meetings/Conferences:
For more information see Trade Shows, Conferences and Seminars Chapter
Forest Products Association of Nova Scotia 2012 Annual Meeting
Other Conferences in 2012 2012, NS
Publications: *Forest Products Association of Nova Scotia Newsletter*
Type: Newsletter
Profile: Updates for association members
Mission: To act as the voice of the forest industry in Nova Scotia; To cooperate with industry, federal, provincial, & municipal governments, & other stakeholders to ensure adherence to forest management & stewardship policies; To promote sustainable management & viability of the forest industry
Environmental Activity: Offering programs in forest stewardship; Supporting forest sustainability, wildlife habitat, & watercourse protection regulations; Presenting the Don Eldridge Memorial Award for sustainable forest stewardship practices

La Forêt modèle du Bas-Saint-Laurent *Voir*
Bas-Saint-Laurent Model Forest

Fort Saskatchewan Fish & Game Association
PO Box 3038, Fort Saskatchewan AB T8L 2T1
Tel: 780-895-7799
Overview: A small local organization founded in 1958
Finances: *Funding Sources:* Fundraising
Staff: 500 volunteer(s)
Membership: 500; *Fees:* $25

Activities: Monthly club meetings; various events for members & families; *Awareness Events:* Kid's Ice Fishing Derby, March; Fishing Derby, June; Family Fun Day & Fishing Derby, Dec.
Mission: To promote through education, lobbying & programs the conservation & utilization of fish & wildlife; protect & enhance the habitat they depend on; *Member of:* Alberta Fish & Game Association

FortWhyte Alive
1961 McCreary Rd., Winnipeg MB R3P 2K9
Tel: 204-989-8355; *Fax:* 204-895-4700
e-mail: info@fortwhyte.org
URL: www.fortwhyte.org
Social Media:
www.facebook.com/pages/FortWhyte-Alive/471614835647?ref=ts
Previous Name: Wildlife Foundation of Manitoba; Fort Whyte Centre for Environmental Education
Overview: A small local organization founded in 1966
Chief Officer(s):
Bill Elliott, President/CEO
Membership: 2,000; *Fees:* Schedule available
Mission: FortWhyte Alive is dedicated to providing programming, natural settings and facilities for environmental education and outdoor recreation. In so doing, FortWhyte promotes awareness and understanding of the natural world and actions leading to sustainable living.

Forum de la grande entreprise sur les changements climatiques *See* Executive Forum on Climate Change

Foundation for Educational Exchange Between Canada & the United States of America
#2015, 350 Albert St., Ottawa ON K1R 1A4
Tel: 613-688-5540; *Fax:* 613-237-2029
e-mail: info@fulbright.ca
URL: www.fulbright.ca
Also Known As: Canada-U.S. Fulbright Program
Overview: A medium-sized international charitable organization founded in 1990
Chief Officer(s):
Michael K. Hawes, Executive Director
mhawes@fulbright.ca
Sandy Hanna, Sr. Program Officer
shanna@fulbright.ca
Finances: *Funding Sources:* Department of Foreign Affairs and International Trade Canada; United States Department of State; Public sector partners; Private sector partners
Activities: Presenting grants & scholarships to Canadian & American scholars, post-doctoral researchers, experienced professionals, junior professionals, executives of the Government of Canada, & Canadian & American teachers; *Internships:* Yes
Mission: To support outstanding graduate students, faculty, professionals, & independent researchers in order to enhance understanding between the people of Canada & the United States

Foundation for Environmental Conservation (FEC) / Fondation pour la conservation de l'environnement
1148 Moiry, Switzerland
Fax: 41-21-8666-6616
e-mail: envcons@ncl.ac.uk
URL: www.ncl.ac.uk/icef
Overview: A small international organization founded in 1975
Committees: Awards
Activities: International Conferences on Environmental Future (ICEFs); specialist workshops
Mission: To undertake, in cooperation with appropriate individuals, organizations & other groups, all possible activities to further environmental conservation & global sustainability

Foundation for International Environmental Law & Development (FIELD)
3 Endsleigh St., London WC1H 0DD United Kingdom
Tel: 44-20-7872-7200; *Fax:* 44-20-7388-2826
e-mail: field.org@field.org.uk
URL: www.field.org.uk
Previous Name: Centre for Environmental Law & Development
Overview: A small international organization founded in 1989
Chief Officer(s):
Joy Hyvarinen, Director
Finances: *Annual Operating Budget:* $500,000-$1.5 Million; *Funding Sources:* Foundations; Consultancy work
Staff: 13 staff member(s); 8 volunteer(s)
Member Profile: Public international lawyers
Activities: *Internships:* Yes

Mission: To help vulnerable countries, communities, & campaigners negotiate for fairer international environmental laws

FPInnovations
580, boul Saint-Jean, Pointe-Claire QC H9R 3J9
Tel: 514-694-1140; *Fax:* 514-694-4351
e-mail: admin@fpinnovations.ca
URL: www.feric.ca
Previous Name: Forest Engineering Research Institute of Canada, A Division of FPInnovations
Overview: A medium-sized national organization founded in 1975
Finances: *Funding Sources:* Forestry companies; Government of Canada; Provincial & territorial governments
Staff: 100+ staff member(s)
Member Profile: Forestry companies; Canadian forestry equipment manufacturers & distributors (CFEMD); *Committees:* Strategic Advisory; Advisory Committeeon Forest Engineering Research; Advisory Committee on Wildland Fire Operations Research
Activities: Researching, in consultation with members & partners, which focuses on silvicultural operations, harvesting, wildland fire operations, transportation & roads, & precision forestry; Providing Feric workshops & seminars; *Library:* FERIC Library
Mission: To develop & assist with the implementation of innovative & safe forest operational solutions, which encompass areas such as the engineering, environmental, & human aspects of forestry & wildland fire operations; To improve sustainable forest operations in Canada; To provide members with knowledge & technology, based on research, to conduct cost-competitive, quality forest operations

Fraser Valley Labour Council
Parent: British Columbia Federation of Labour
#202, 9292 - 200th St., Langley BC V1M 3A6
Tel: 604-314-9867; *Fax:* 604-430-6762
e-mail: bharder@usw.ca
URL: www.fvlc.ca
Social Media:
www.facebook.com/group.php?gid=242003131602&ref=mf
Overview: A small local organization founded in 2007
Chief Officer(s):
Brian Harder, President
bharder@usw.ca
Pamela Willingshofer, Secretary
kidogo@shaw.ca
Karen Porter, Treasurer
kporter64@shaw.ca
Membership: 12,000; *Member Profile:* Members of unions from the Fraser Valley region of British Columbia, such as Chilliwack, Hope, Abbotsford, Mission, Lytton, & Harrison
Activities: Lobbying governments about worker's issues; Providing labour education; Conducting campaigns to support the issues of working families; Supporting local organizations, such as the United Way
Meetings/Conferences:
For more information see Trade Shows, Conferences and Seminars Chapter
Fraser Valley Labour Council 2012 Annual General Meeting January 2012, BC
Fraser Valley Labour Council 2013 Annual General Meeting January 2013, BC
Mission: To advance the economic, social, & political life of persons in British Columbia's Fraser Valley; To act as the unified voice for workers to ensure workers' rights, such as fair wages & safe working conditions
Environmental Activity: Working to ensure a sustainable environment

Fredericton Fish & Game Association (FFGA)
PO Box 1083, Stn. A, Fredericton NB E3B 5C2
Tel: 506-474-0458
e-mail: fjwilson@nbnet.nb.ca
URL: www.freewebs.com/fishandgame
Overview: A small local organization founded in 1924
Chief Officer(s):
Frank Wilson, President
Finances: *Annual Operating Budget:* Less than $50,000
Staff: 30+ volunteer(s)
Membership: 140; *Fees:* $25 single; $40 family; *Member Profile:* Individuals concerned about natural resources & willing to assist in conservation; *Committees:* Jr. Branch; Education; Environment; Conservation Lottery; Wildlife; Newsletter
Activities: Adopt-A-Stream; Youth Fishing Tournament; Fishing & Hunting Enhancement Project; education & speakers

Associations/Organizations / Freight Carriers Association of Canada

Mission: To foster sound management & wise use of natural resources so that economic, recreational & aesthetic values may continue to benefit future generations; *Member of:* New Brunswick Wildlife Federation

Freight Carriers Association of Canada (FCA)
#3-4, 427 Garrison Rd., Fort Erie ON L2A 6E6
Tel: 905-994-0560; *Fax:* 905-994-0117
Toll-Free: 800-559-7421
e-mail: info@fca-natc.org
URL: www.fca-natc.org
Previous Name: Canadian Transport Tariff Bureau Association
Overview: A medium-sized national organization founded in 1939
Finances: *Annual Operating Budget:* $1.5 Million-$3 Million; *Funding Sources:* Membership fees; sales of publications & software
Staff: 17 staff member(s)
Membership: 100; *Fees:* Based on revenues; *Member Profile:* For-hire motor carriers; *Committees:* Tariff Advisory; Québec Comité Consultatif
Activities: Carrier meetings; seminars; research; info gathering & dissemination; *Speaker Service:* Yes
Mission: To provide quality information, products & services to users, providers & third parties involved in motor carrier transportation. PUBLICATIONS: Fuel Price and Surcharge Information Bulletin (weekly); Currency Exchange Bulletin (2X/month -14th and last day of the month).; *Affiliation(s):* North American Transportation Council

Freshwater Fisheries Society of British Columbia (FFSBC)
#101, 80 Regatta Landing, Victoria BC V9A 7S2
Tel: 250-414-4200; *Fax:* 250-414-4211
Toll-Free: 888-601-4200
e-mail: fish@gofishbc.com
URL: www.gofishbc.com
Overview: A medium-sized provincial organization
Chief Officer(s):
Evert Van Eerden, Chair
Rob Adkin, Secretary-Treasurer
Activities: Providing information related to freshwater fishing & freshwater ecosystems in British Columbia; Partnering with organizations such as the Ministry of Environment to offer the Go Fish program so that children can experience fishing & foster an appreciation for the environment
Mission: To stock eggs & fish into lakes & streams across British Columbia; To support sturgeon & steelhead recovery programs; To operate hatcheries & visitor's centres
Environmental Activity: Restoring & conserving wild fish populations; Working with the Ministry of Environment to create fisheries & to manage existing fisheries

Friends of Abandoned Pets
PO Box 67052, Ottawa ON K2A 4E4
Tel: 613-729-9820
e-mail: information@foap.on.ca
URL: www.foap.on.ca
Overview: A small local organization founded in 1992
Chief Officer(s):
Berni Conn, President
Membership: 400 individual; *Fees:* $30 individual; $50 family
Publications: *Pet Talk*
Type: Newsletter *Frequency:* s-a *Editor:* Pat Winter, Jean Burns
Mission: To prevent cruelty to animals by caring for stray & abandoned animals

The Friends of Algonquin Park
PO Box 248, Whitney ON K0J 2M0
Tel: 613-637-2828; *Fax:* 613-637-2138
URL: www.algonquinpark.on.ca/friends
Overview: A small local charitable organization founded in 1983
Chief Officer(s):
Lee Pauzé, General Manager
Finances: *Annual Operating Budget:* $500,000-$1.5 Million
Staff: 7 staff member(s); 197 volunteer(s)
Membership: 3,000; *Fees:* $7 student; $12 individual; $17 family
Activities: *Speaker Service:* Yes
Mission: To further the educational & interpretive programs in Algonquin Park; *Affiliation(s):* Canadian Parks Partnership; Ontario Parks

Friends of Animals (FoA)
#205, 777 Post Rd., Darien CT 06820 USA
Tel: 203-656-1522; *Fax:* 203-656-0267
e-mail: info@friendsofanimals.org
URL: www.friendsofanimals.org
Overview: A large national charitable organization founded in 1957
Chief Officer(s):
Priscilla Feral, President
Finances: *Annual Operating Budget:* $3 Million-$5 Million; *Funding Sources:* Membership dues; bequests; grants; donations
Staff: 23 staff member(s); 185 volunteer(s)
Membership: 200,000; *Fees:* $25 USA; $30 international
Activities: Low-cost spay/neuter program; anti-fur, anti-wolf & anti-ivory campaigns; opposes all hunting & & international animal trade; supports marine mammal protection; assists & supports programs in Africa for chimpanzees & other animals; anti-vivisection; advocates vegan, plant-based diets
Mission: To free animals from cruelty & institutionalized exploitation around the world; works to cultivate a respectful view of nonhuman animals, free-living & domestic. Branch offices in New York, Washington, and Victoria, BC.
Environmental Activity: Protects national wildlife refuges & public lands

The Friends of Awenda Park / Les Amis du Parc Awenda
c/o Awenda Provincial Park, PO Box 5004, Penetanguishene ON L9M 2G2
Tel: 705-549-2231
e-mail: awenda@csolve.net
URL: www.awendapark.ca
Overview: A small local organization founded in 1991
Mission: Dedicated to the preservation, understanding & interpretation of Awenda's biological, geological & cultural treasurers

The Friends of Bon Echo Park
16151 Highway 41, RR#1, Cloyne ON K0H 1K0
Tel: 613-336-0830; *Fax:* 613-336-2712
e-mail: fobecho@mazinaw.on.ca
URL: www.mazinaw.on.ca/fobecho
Overview: A small local charitable organization
Chief Officer(s):
E. Helen Yanch, Operations Manager
Finances: *Annual Operating Budget:* $100,000-$250,000
Staff: 90 volunteer(s)
Membership: 200; *Fees:* $10 individual; $15 family; $25 corporate; $100 life
Activities: Annual Art Show & Sale, July
Mission: To preserve the natural & cultural heritage of Bon Echo Provincial Park

The Friends of Bonnechere Parks
RR#5, Killaloe ON K0J 2A0
Tel: 613-732-9273
e-mail: bettyb@nrtco.net
URL: www.bonnecherepark.on.ca
Overview: A small local organization founded in 1992
Chief Officer(s):
Betty Biesenthal, Director of Publicity
Mission: To encourage & support programs for interpretive, educational, scientific, historical, protection & preservation purposes related to the natural & historic resources of the Little Bonnechere River in the Ottawa Valley

The Friends of Charleston Lake Park
148 Woodvale Rd., RR#4, Lansdowne ON K0E 1L0
e-mail: info@friendsofcharlestonlake.ca
URL: www.friendsofcharlestonlake.ca
Overview: A small local organization
Mission: To help people enjoy Charleston Lake Park, this unique & beautiful place & to help keep it that way

Friends of Clayoquot Sound (FOCS)
PO Box 489, 331 Neill St., Tofino BC V0R 2Z0
Tel: 250-725-4218; *Fax:* 250-725-2527
e-mail: info@focs.ca
URL: www.focs.ca
Overview: A medium-sized local charitable organization founded in 1979
Finances: *Annual Operating Budget:* $100,000-$250,000; *Funding Sources:* Individual donors; foundation grants
Staff: 4 staff member(s)
Membership: 3,000; *Fees:* $25
Activities: *Speaker Service:* Yes; *Library:* FOCS Resource Centre
Mission: To be peaceful & courageous advocates for the earth, air & waters of Clayoquot Sound & all temperate rainforests; to dramatically reduce economic reliance upon raw resource extraction by developing sustainability in rural & urban cultures; to oppose logging on ancient temperate rainforests, as well as the export of raw (unprocessed) logs; to support ecoforestry in second growth forest; to promote reduced wood & paper consumption & support the use of ecologically sustainable, tree-free alternatives to wood & wood-fibre products; to advocate taking fish farms out of wild waters & putting them in on-land closed containment systems; *Member of:* BC Environmental Network; Coastal Alliance for Aquaculture Reform (CAAR); *Affiliation(s):* Greenpeace; Sierra Club; Natural Resources Defence Council; Western Canada Wilderness Committee (WCWC)

Friends of Devonian Botanic Garden
University of Alberta, Edmonton AB T6G 2R3
Tel: 780-987-3054; *Fax:* 780-987-4141
e-mail: friends@ualberta.ca
URL: www.devonian.ualberta.ca
Overview: A medium-sized local charitable organization founded in 1971
Finances: *Annual Operating Budget:* $50,000-$100,000; *Funding Sources:* Membership fees; donations
Staff: 14 staff member(s); 300 volunteer(s)
Membership: 800; *Fees:* $50 families; $45 individuals; $35 seniors/students
Activities: Sponsors lectures, courses, papers, seminars, publishes material on botanical & horticultural matters; promotes & finances construction of gardens, path, signs, structures & other facilities; raises funds for projects of the society; *Library:* Yes, Open to public, open by appointment

Friends of Ecological Reserves (FER)
PO Box 8477, Stn. Central, Victoria BC V8W 3S1
Tel: 250-361-1694
e-mail: ecoreserves@hotmail.com
URL: www.ecoreserves.bc.ca
Overview: A small local organization founded in 1982
Chief Officer(s):
Michael Fenger, President
Finances: *Annual Operating Budget:* $50,000-$100,000
Membership: 250; *Fees:* $20 individuals; $25 family/institution; $15 seniors/students; *Member Profile:* Biologists; birders; conservationists; naturalists
Activities: Field trips; volunteer warden program; illustrated lecture series; research scholarship program; *Internships:* Yes
Mission: To promote the interests of the BC Ecological Reserve Program (138 ecological reservations in BC) & concept through land acquisition, support for research in ecological reserves & protected areas; to work for the protection of threatened & endangered ecosystems & study of ecosystems for use in long-term measurement of the impacts of development in similar ecosystems; to protect gene pools; *Member of:* BC Environmental Network; The Land Conservancy of BC

Friends of Ferris
PO Box 504, Campbellford ON K0L 1L0
Tel: 705-653-3575
e-mail: info@friendsofferris.ca
URL: www.friendsofferris.ca
Overview: A small local organization founded in 1994
Chief Officer(s):
Doreen Sharpe, President
Fees: $10 individual; $17 family
Mission: The Friends of Ferris is a non-profit group of volunteers who are hard at work, constantly bringing to Ferris special events and promotions unique to the Provincial Park.

The Friends of Frontenac Park
PO Box 2237, Kingston ON K7L 5J8
e-mail: frontenacpark@frontenacpark.ca
URL: www.frontenacpark.ca
Overview: A small local organization

The Friends of Killarney Park
c/o Killarney Provincial Park, Killarney ON P0M 2A0
Tel: 705-287-2800; *Fax:* 705-287-2922
URL: friendsofkillarneypark.ca
Overview: A small local organization founded in 1986
Mission: To enhance the interpretive, educational & recreational objectives of Killarney Park

The Friends of MacGregor Point
c/o MacGregor Point Provincial Park, RR#1, Port Elgin ON N0H 2C5

Tel: 519-389-6232; Fax: 519-389-2444
e-mail: fompp@bmts.com
URL: www.friendsofmacgregor.org
Overview: A small local organization
Fees: $15 individual; $20 family; $30 corporate
Mission: To supplement & enhance the interpretive & educational programs in the park; to stimulate community interest in & understanding of the park & its resources; to support research of the park's natural & cultural resources

Friends of Mashkinonje Park
Site 8, Box 1, 99 Langs Landing, Monetville ON P0M 2K0
e-mail: mashkinonje@hotmail.com
URL: www.mashkinonje.com
Overview: A small local organization founded in 2000
Chief Officer(s):
Angela Martin, President
Fees: $15 individual; $25 family; $50 organization
Publications: The Wetlands Observer
Type: Newsletter Frequency: s-a
Mission: To maintain & share the beauty of this unique area of scenic shorelines & wonderful wetlands

Friends of Mount Revelstoke & Glacier
PO Box 2992, #301B, 3rd St. West, Revelstoke BC V0E 2S0
Tel: 250-837-2010; Fax: 250-837-2050
e-mail: fmrg@telus.net
URL: www.friendsrevglacier.com
Overview: A small local charitable organization founded in 1987
Chief Officer(s):
A. Neills Kristensen, Executive Director
Finances: Annual Operating Budget: $100,000-$250,000
Staff: 4 staff member(s); 30 volunteer(s)
Membership: 78 individual; 52 family; 17 associate; 56 lifetime; 3 corporate; 1 non-profit; Fees: $15 individual; $10 associate; $25 family; $150 lifetime; Committees: Naturalist & Environment; Mountain Club; Volunteer & Membership; Marketing
Activities: Education program, hiking, interpretation, speaker evenings; Speaker Service: Yes; Library: Yes
Publications: Between Friends [a publication of Friends of Mount Revelstoke & Glacier]
Type: Newsletter Frequency: s-a
Mission: To promote the protection, appreciation, enjoyment & understanding of Mount Revelstoke & Glacier National Parks; Affiliation(s): Canadian Parks Partnership

The Friends of Nancy Island Historic Site & Wasaga Beach Park
11 - 22nd St. North, Wasaga Beach ON L9Z 2V9
Tel: 705-429-2516; Fax: 705-429-7983
e-mail: nancyisland@wasagabeachpark.com
URL: www.wasagabeachpark.com
Overview: A small local organization
Mission: To further the educational & interpretive programs of Wasaga Beach Provincial Park & Nancy Island Historic Site

Friends of Nature Conservation Society
PO Box 281, Chester NS B0J 1J0
Tel: 902-275-3361
Overview: A small local organization founded in 1968
Finances: Annual Operating Budget: Less than $50,000
Membership: 100-499
Mission: To preserve the balance of nature for the mutual benefit of people & their plant & animal friends; Affiliation(s): Canadian Nature Federation

Friends of Oak Hammock Marsh
PO Box 1160, 1 Snow Goose Bay Hwy. 220, Stonewall MB R0C 2Z0
Tel: 204-467-3300; Fax: 204-467-3311
Toll-Free: 204-506-2774
e-mail: ohmic@ducks.ca
URL: www.oakhammockmarsh.ca
Overview: A small local organization founded in 1990
Membership: 200+
Mission: To promote public awareness of issues involving Oak Hammock Marsh; Member of: Manitoba Eco-Network

The Friends of Pinery Park
RR#2, Grand Bend ON N0M 1T0
Tel: 519-243-1521
URL: www.pinerypark.on.ca/friends.html
Overview: A small local organization founded in 1989
Mission: Dedicated to the development of interpretive, educational, historical & scientific projects & programs to ensure that Pinery Provincial Park's natural legacy will remain for future generations

The Friends of Presqu'ile Park
RR#4, Brighton ON K0K 1H0
Tel: 613-475-1688
e-mail: friends_presquile@hotmail.com
URL: www.friendsofpresquile.on.ca
Overview: A small local organization
Mission: To enhance the educational, interpretive, & scientific research programs at Presqu'ile Provincial Park

The Friends of Rondeau Park
RR#1, Morpeth ON N0P 1X0
Tel: 519-674-1777
e-mail: for@msni.net
URL: www.rondeauprovincialpark.ca
Overview: A small local organization
Mission: To raise funds on a continuing basis in order to encourage & support programs for interpretive, educational, scientific, historical, protection & preservation purposes related to the natural & historical resources of Rondeau Provincial Park & other Ontario Provincial Parks

The Friends of Sandbanks Park
PO Box 20007, 219 Main St., Picton ON K0K 3V0
URL: www.pec.on.ca/friends/
Overview: A small local organization
Mission: To protect & preserve the natural & cultural history of provincial park through interpretation, education, & scientific & historic research

Friends of Short Hills Park
PO Box 236, Fonthill ON L0S 1E0
URL: www.friendsofshorthillspark.ca
Overview: A small local organization
Fees: $20
Mission: To preserve the cultural & natural integrity of Short Hills Provincial Park through liaison with Ontario Parks, volunteer work, public education & fundraising activities

The Friends of Sleeping Giant
PO Box 29031, Thunder Bay ON P7B 6P9
e-mail: lyndasisco@tbaytel.net
URL: www.thefriendsofsleepinggiant.ca
Overview: A small local organization founded in 1993
Mission: To assist in conserving & fostering an appreciation for Sleeping Giant Provincial Park

Friends of the Delta Marsh Field Station
c/o University Field Station, University of Manitoba, 239 Machray Hall, Winnipeg MB R3T 2N2
Tel: 204-474-9297
e-mail: delta_marsh@umanitoba.ca
URL: www.umanitoba.ca/faculties/science/delta_marsh/friends
Previous Name: Friends of the Field Station (Delta Marsh)
Overview: A small local organization
Chief Officer(s):
Harry Duckworth, President
Finances: Annual Operating Budget: Less than $50,000
Staff: 3 staff member(s); 10 volunteer(s)
Membership: 1-99; Fees: $15 individual; $25 family
Mission: To further the development & use of the University of Manitoba field stations

Friends of the Earth Canada (FoE) / Les Ami(e)s de la Terre Canada
#300, 260 St. Patrick St., Ottawa ON K1N 5K5
Tel: 613-241-0085; Fax: 613-241-7998
Toll-Free: 888-385-4444
e-mail: foe@foecanada.org
URL: www.foecanada.org
Overview: A large international charitable organization founded in 1978
Finances: Annual Operating Budget: $250,000-$500,000;
Funding Sources: 52% individuals; 19% corporate; 5% foundation; 11% government; 13% earned income/merchandise
Staff: 6 staff member(s); 10 volunteer(s)
Membership: 1,000-4,999; Committees: Campaigns: Stop Global Warming; Universal Water Security; Stop Devils Lake Outlet; Environmental Justice
Activities: Speaker Service: Yes
Mission: To serve as a national voice for the environment, working with others to inspire the renewal of our communities & the earth, through research, education, advocacy & cooperation; Member of: Friends of the Earth International; Canadian Council for International Cooperation; Affiliation(s): Canadian Environmental Network

Friends of the Earth International (FoEI) / Fédération internationale des Amis de la Terre
International Secretariat, PO Box 19199, Amsterdam 1000 GD Netherlands
Tel: 31-20-622-1369; Fax: 31-20-639-2181
e-mail: foei@foei.org
URL: www.foei.org
Also Known As: Amigos de la Tierra
Overview: A medium-sized international organization founded in 1971
Finances: Annual Operating Budget: $250,000-$500,000;
Funding Sources: Fees; Donations; Subsidies
Staff: 12 staff member(s); 4 volunteer(s)
Membership: Over 50,000; Member Profile: Comprises 71 member organizations, with a combined membership of nearly one million; the European member groups have formed FoE European Coordination with its own structure & offices in Brussels; each country member group is an autonomous body responsible for their own funding & campaigning strategies
Activities: Workshops on specific campaigns; Political lobbying; Information distribution
Mission: To promote that environmental problems do not respect geographical & political boundaries; To cooperate with other organizations; To raise awareness that environmental, social, economic & political issues are interdependent; To encourage positive alternatives to policies & practices which cause ecological degradation; Member of: International Union for the Conservation of Nature; Affiliation(s): International Rivers Network; Rainforest Action Network; Rainforest Information Centre; EcoPeace; Action for Solidarity, Equality Environment & Development Europe
Environmental Activity: Creating networks of environmental, consumer, & human rights organizations worldwide

Friends of the Environment Foundation See TD Friends of the Environment Foundation

Friends of the Field Station (Delta Marsh) See Friends of the Delta Marsh Field Station

Friends of the Forestry Farm House Inc. (FFFH)
1903 Forestry Farm Drive, Saskatoon SK S7N 1G9
Tel: 306-249-1315
e-mail: bernie.fffh@sasktel.net
URL: www.fffh.ca
Overview: A small local charitable organization founded in 1996
Chief Officer(s):
Bernie Cruikshank, President
Finances: Annual Operating Budget: Less than $50,000;
Funding Sources: Saskatchewan Heritage Foundation; City of Saskatoon Heritage Conservation Program
Staff: 3 staff member(s); 20 volunteer(s)
Membership: 1-99; Fees: $10
Activities: Historical walking tour brochure Victoria Day High Tea; Haunted House Program; Old Fashioned Christmas Party; Speaker Service: Yes
Mission: To restore the superintendent's residence of the Sutherland Forest Nursery Station which, from 1913 to 1965, distributed millions of trees to prairie farmers, who planted these trees on their land to create the miles of shelterbelts; Affiliation(s): Saskatoon Tourism; Saskatchewan Tourism

Friends of the Montréal Botanical Garden Voir Les Amis du Jardin botanique de Montréal

Friends of the Oldman River (FOR)
615 Deer Croft Way SE, Calgary AB T2J 5V4
Tel: 403-271-1408
e-mail: for@shaw.ca
Overview: A small local organization founded in 1987
Finances: Annual Operating Budget: Less than $50,000;
Funding Sources: Membership dues; donations
Staff: 8 volunteer(s)
Membership: 1,000; Fees: $5
Activities: Sustainable community/watershed project in Cameroon; legal actions on water issues; Speaker Service: Yes
Mission: To defend the Oldman River from environmentally destructive activities; to protect the Oldman River & decommission the Oldman Dam; Member of: Alberta Environmental Network; Affiliation(s): Canadian Environmental Network

Friends of the Stikine Society (FOS)
#502, 620 View St., Victoria BC V8W 1J6

Associations/Organizations / Friends of the Trent-Severn Waterway

Tel: 250-383-5677
e-mail: stikine@islandnet.com
Overview: A small local organization founded in 1981
Finances: *Annual Operating Budget:* Less than $50,000; *Funding Sources:* Membership fees; donations
Staff: 3 volunteer(s)
Membership: 100; *Fees:* $35
Activities: *Speaker Service:* Yes
Mission: To maintain a free-flowing Stikine; to protect the integrity of the Stikine watershed & her peoples & the biodiversity of life & habitats within it; to achieve Canadian Heritage River status for the entire mainstream Stikine River; Affiliation(s): BC Environmental Network; Environmental Mining Council of BC; Outdoor Recreation Council of BC; Canadian Nature Federation; Canadian Environmental Network

Friends of the Trent-Severn Waterway (FTSW)
PO Box 572, Peterborough ON K9J 6Z6
Tel: 705-742-2251; *Fax:* 705-742-9644
Toll-Free: 800-663-2628
e-mail: info@ftsw.com
Overview: A small local organization founded in 1982
Finances: *Annual Operating Budget:* $50,000-$100,000
Staff: 1 staff member(s); 50 volunteer(s)
Membership: 275; *Fees:* $20 family; $50 corporate; *Committees:* Volunteer; Selection; Publicity; Trust; Environment; Marine Safety; Speakers Bureau; Tourism
Activities: *Speaker Service:* Yes
Mission: To assist Parks Canada to protect, preserve & interpret the natural historical, recreational & cultural resources of the Trent Severn Waterway; to encourage awareness & appreciation, develop & support programs to further enhance awareness; *Member of:* Canadian Parks Partnership

The Friends of West Kootenay Parks Society (FWKP)
PO Box 212, Nelson BC V1L 5P9
e-mail: contactus@fwkp.kics.bc.ca
URL: www.fwkp.kics.bc.ca
Overview: A small local organization founded in 1988
Chief Officer(s):
Bill Bryce, Chair
Fees: $10
Activities: Kokanee Glacier Alpine Campaign; advocacy for parks; construction projects; fundraising; publicizing parks issues
Mission: To promote conservationist & recreational use of British Columbia parks in the West Kootenay area

Frontline Associates Conference Coordinators
676 Borebank St., Winnipeg MB R3N 1G2
Tel: 204-489-2739
Overview: A small local organization

Fundy Model Forest
#2, 701 Main St., Sussex NB E4E 7H7
Tel: 506-432-7575; *Fax:* 506-432-7562
e-mail: info@fundymodelforest.net
URL: www.fundymodelforest.net
Overview: A small local organization
Chief Officer(s):
Nairn Hay, General Manager
Membership: 30
Member of: Canadian Model Forest Network

The Fur Council of Canada (FCC) / Conseil canadien de la fourrure
#1270, 1435, rue Saint-Alexandre, Montréal QC H3A 2G4
Tel: 514-844-1945; *Fax:* 514-844-8593
e-mail: info@furcouncil.com
URL: www.furcouncil.com
Overview: A medium-sized national organization founded in 1964
Activities: Public education; fashion promotion & advertising; market development
Mission: To promote all aspects of the fur trade

Fur Institute of Canada (FIC) / Institut de la fourrure du Canada (IFC)
#701, 331 Cooper St., Ottawa ON K2P 0G5
Tel: 613-231-7099; *Fax:* 613-231-7940
e-mail: info@fur.ca
URL: www.fur.ca
Overview: A medium-sized national organization founded in 1983
Chief Officer(s):
Robert B. Cahill, Executive Director
rcahill@fur.ca

Bruce Williams, Chair
Mary Baskin, Manager, Corporate & Communications
mbaskin@fur.ca
Finances: *Funding Sources:* Membership dues; Donations
Member Profile: Trappers; Fur Farmers; Wholesale Fur Dealers; Fur Manufacturers & Processors; Fur Retailers; Aboriginal Organizations; Conservation Organizations; Animal Welfare Associations; Support Industries; Government of Canada; Provincial & Territorial Governments; *Committees:* Trap Research & Development; National Communications; Aboriginal Communications; External Communications
Activities: Coordinating the implementation of the Agreement on International Humane Trapping Standards in Canada; Presenting awards; Offering programs such as trap research & testing, conservation, international relations, communication, aboriginal communications, & funding; Researching; Promoting conservation efforts
Mission: To promote the sustainable & wise use of Canadian fur resources; *Member of:* International Fur Trade Federation; World Conservation Union; International Association of Fish & Wildlife Agencies

Fur-Bearer Defenders (FBD)
#101, 225 - 17th Ave. East, Vancouver BC V5V 1A6
Tel: 604-435-1850; *Fax:* 604-435-1840
e-mail: fbd@banlegholdtraps.com
URL: www.banlegholdtraps.com; www.dogcatfur.com
Also Known As: Association for the Protection of Fur-Bearing Animals
Previous Name: The Fur-Bearers
Overview: A medium-sized national charitable organization founded in 1944
Finances: *Funding Sources:* Donations; Membership dues
Fees: $10/yr.; $100 lifetime
Activities: Providing information to government, media, activists, & the public; Launching campaigns to create awareness
Mission: To stop trapping cruelty & protect fur-bearing animals

The Fur-Bearers *See* Fur-Bearer Defenders

Furriers Guild of Canada
#211, 4174 Dundas St. West, Toronto ON M8X 1X3
Tel: 416-234-9494; *Fax:* 416-234-2244
e-mail: furriersguildca@ica.net
Merged from: Fur Trade Association of Canada (Ontario) Inc.; Retail Furriers Guild of Canada
Overview: A medium-sized national organization
Member Profile: Canadian fur retailers
Activities: Providing programs such as community outreach
Mission: To promote Canadian fur retailers

Ganaraska Hiking Trail Association (GHTA)
PO Box 693, 12 King St., Orillia ON L3V 6K7
Tel: 705-487-6457; *Fax:* 705-487-6459
e-mail: admin@ganaraska-hiking-trail.ca
URL: www.ganaraska-hiking-trail.ca
Overview: A small local charitable organization founded in 1969
Finances: *Annual Operating Budget:* Less than $50,000; *Funding Sources:* Membership dues; donations
Staff: 120 volunteer(s)
Membership: 500; *Fees:* $20; *Committees:* Landowners; Trail; Guidebook
Activities: On the edge of the Laurentian Shield, within reach of Ontario's major cities, the trail forms a vital link in the National Trail network (500 km)
Mission: To construct & maintain a hiking trail from Port Hope to Glen Huron; to encourage recreational hiking & respect for the environment; *Member of:* Hike Ontario; Ontario Nature

The Garden Clubs of Ontario (GCO)
RR#2, 593 Balmy Beach Rd., Owen Sound ON N4K 5N4
Overview: A small provincial organization founded in 1954
Chief Officer(s):
Janice Middleton, Contact
Finances: *Annual Operating Budget:* $50,000-$100,000
Staff: 15 volunteer(s)
Membership: 1,500 individual; *Committees:* Archives; Judges; National & International Liaison
Activities: Coordinates activities of 12 Garden Clubs in Ontario; Tour of Summer Gardens
Mission: To stimulate knowledge & love of gardening amongst amateurs; to aid in the protection of native plants, trees, birds & soil; to encourage civic planning; *Member of:* Ontario Horticultural Association; World Association of Flower Arrangers

Garden Institute of Alberta
#1406, 5328 Calgary Trail, Edmonton AB T6H 4J8
Tel: 780-705-9958; *Fax:* 780-469-6314
e-mail: slrempel@shaw.ca
Overview: A small provincial organization founded in 1997
Chief Officer(s):
Nancy Finlayson, Founder
Sharon Rempel, Founder & Project Manager
oldwheat@shaw.ca
Finances: *Annual Operating Budget:* $50,000-$100,000; *Funding Sources:* Fundraising projects
Membership: 1-99
Activities: *Speaker Service:* Yes
Mission: To promote organic urban agriculture & gardening

Gas Processing Association Canada (GPAC)
#505, 900 - 6th Ave. SW, Calgary AB T2P 3K2
Tel: 403-705-0223; *Fax:* 403-263-6886
e-mail: info@gpacanada.com
URL: www.gpacanada.com
Previous Name: Canadian Gas Processors Association
Overview: A medium-sized national organization founded in 1960
Finances: *Annual Operating Budget:* Less than $50,000; *Funding Sources:* Membership dues
Staff: 17 volunteer(s)
Membership: 450 individual; *Fees:* $75 Regular, $9 Retired; *Member Profile:* Open to those employed in companies processing gaseous & liquid hydrocarbons; *Committees:* Safety; Research; Environment; Membership; Publications
Activities: *Library:* Yes
Mission: To promote interaction & exchange of ideas & technology that will add value to those who are involved with or affected by the hydrocarbon processing industry; Affiliation(s): Gas Processors Association (USA)

Gem & Mineral Club of Scarborough (GMCS)
#1B, 10 Chichester Pl., Toronto ON M1T 1G5
Tel: 416-284-9797
e-mail: rbruce@can.rogers.com
URL: www.scarbgemclub.ca
Overview: A small local organization founded in 1963
Chief Officer(s):
Russ Bruce, President
Fees: $15 single members; $20 families
Activities: Hosting monthly meetings; Organizing exhibits; Presenting auctions; Planning mineral & fossil collecting field trips; Providing workshops
Publications: *Strata Data: GMCS [Gem & Mineral Club of Scarborough] Newsletter*
Type: Newsletter *Frequency:* 10 pa
Profile: Upcoming events & articles about the hobby
Mission: To promote collecting & studying rocks, minerals, fossils, & lapidary work; *Member of:* Central Canadian Federation of Mineralogical Societies (CCFMS); SCRIBE

Genetics Society of Canada (GSC) / Société de génétique du Canada
c/o The Snider's Web, 59 Aulac Rd., Aulac NB E4L 2V6
Tel: 506-536-1768; *Fax:* 902-484-5694
e-mail: gsc@thesnidersweb.com
URL: life.biology.mcmaster.ca/GSC/
Overview: A medium-sized national charitable organization founded in 1956
Finances: *Annual Operating Budget:* Less than $50,000; *Funding Sources:* Membership dues
Staff: 13+ volunteer(s)
Membership: 392; *Fees:* Schedule available; *Member Profile:* Regular - scientific interest in any field of genetics or cytology; student - graduate or senior undergraduate students in Canada & graduate students outside Canada who provide evidence of status; emeritus - regular member in good standing at age of 70 years, or reaching compulsory retirement; life - honour bestowed by the Society upon member in recognition of outstanding contributions to society & science of genetics; *Committees:* Annual Meetings; Archivist; Auditors; Awards; Bursaries; Constitution & Bylaws; Education; Elections; Evolution; Executive; Executive Finance; Gene Resources; New Initiatives; Nominations; Publications Policy; Science Policy
Activities: *Speaker Service:* Yes
Mission: To provide means of liaison between geneticists for coordination & development of genetics & science policy in Canada; to promote facilities for reporting, exchanging & disseminating knowledge related to genetics & to make known theSociety's views on genetic knowledge which is of direct concern to the Canadianpublic.; Affiliation(s): Canadian

Federation of Biological Sciences; International Genetics Federation

Genome Canada
#2100, 150 Metcalfe St., Ottawa ON K2P 1P1
Tel: 613-751-4460; *Fax:* 613-751-4474
e-mail: info@genomecanada.ca
URL: www.genomecanada.ca
Overview: A medium-sized national organization
Chief Officer(s):
Karen Dewar, Director, National Genomics Programs
kdewar@genomecanada.ca
Hélène Meilleur, Director, Communications & Events
hmeilleur@genomecanada.ca
Mission: To develop & implement a national strategy in genomics & proteomics research for the benefit of all Canadians; to enable Canada to become a world leader in genomics & proteomics research in key selected areas as agriculture, environment, fisheries, forestry & health

Geochemical Society
c/o Earth & Planetary Sciences Department, Washington University, #CB 11691, Brookings Dr., St. Louis MO 63130-4899 USA
Tel: 314-935-4131; *Fax:* 314-935-4121
e-mail: gsoffice@geochemsoc.org
URL: www.geochemsoc.org
Overview: A medium-sized international organization
Chief Officer(s):
Martin Goldhaber, President
mgold@usgs.gov
Samuel Mukasa, Vice-President
mukasa@umich.edu
Neil Sturchio, Secretary
sturchio@uic.edu
Louise Criscenti, Treasurer
ljcrisc@sandia.gov
Seth Davis, Manager, Business
seth.davis@geochemsoc.org
Member Profile: An international membership with interests in fields such as high & low-temperature geochemistry, fluid-rock interaction, organic geochemistry, petrology, isotope geochemistry, & meteoritics; *Committees:* Joint Publications; Nominations; Program; V.M. Goldschmidt Award; F.W. Clarke Award; C.C. Patterson Award; Geochemical Fellows; OGD Executive; Alfred Treibs Award; OGD Best Paper Award; AAAS Liaison
Meetings/Conferences:
For more information see Trade Shows, Conferences and Seminars Chapter
Goldschmidt Conference 2011
June 2011 Prague
Goldschmidt Conference 2012
June 2012 Montréal, QC
Publications: *Geochemical News*
Type: Newsletter *Frequency:* q. *Editor:* Stephen Komor
Profile: News of the Geochemical Society
Elements Magazine [a publication of the Geochemical Society]
Type: Journal *Frequency:* bi-m. *Price:* Free with membership in the Geochemical Society
Profile: Theme issues with peer-reviewed invited papers related to the mineral & geochemical sciences
GCA: Geochimica et Cosmochimica Acta
Type: Journal *Frequency:* bi-weekly *Editor:* Dr. Frank Podosek
Profile: Scientific contributions related to geochemistry & cosmochemistry
G-Cubed (Geochemistry, Geophysics, Geosystems)
Type: Journal
Profile: Research papers on the chemistry, physics, & biology of earth & planetary processes
Geochemical Society Special Publication Series
Profile: Scientifically significant collections of related, original papers on topics such as magmatic processes, fluid-mineral interactions, stable isotope geochemistry, mineral spectroscopy, mantle petrology, & volcanic, geothermal, & ore-forming fluids
Mission: To encourage the application of chemistry to the solution of geological & cosmological problems; *Affiliation(s):* American Association for the Advancement of Science; International Union of Geological Sciences; Council of Scientific Society Presidents; Geological Society of America

Geological Association of Canada (GAC) / Association géologique du Canada (AGC)
Department of Earth Sciences, Memorial University of Newfoundland, #ER4063, Alexander Murray Bldg., St. John's NL A1B 3X5
Tel: 709-737-7660; *Fax:* 709-737-2532
e-mail: gac@mun.ca; gacpublications@mun.ca (GEOLOG newsmagazine)
URL: www.gac.ca
Overview: A large national organization founded in 1947
Finances: *Funding Sources:* Membership fees; Publication sales
Membership: 1,000-4,999; *Fees:* $10 students & teachers; $20 spousal; $70 - $80 seniors & unemployed; $105 - $120 full members; $250 universities; $500 supporters; $1000 sponsors; *Committees:* Science Program; Finance; Publications; Communications
Activities: Providing professional development opportunities for members; Disseminating information about geoscience; Offering networking opportunities; *Internships:* Yes; *Speaker Service:* Yes
Awards: Logan Medal (Award)
To honour an individual for sustained distinguished achievement in Canadian earth science Contact: Stephen Johnston *Contact Detail: E-mail: stj@uvic.ca*
W.W. Hutchison Medal (Award)
To recognize a young person for exceptional advances in Canadian earth science research Contact: Daniel Lebel *Contact Detail: E-mail: Daniel.lebel@ec.gc.ca*
E.R. Ward Neale Medal (Award)
To honour an individual for sustained outstanding efforts in sharing earth science with Canadians Contact: Tim Corkery *Contact Detail: E-mail: timothy.corkery@gov.mb.ca*
J. Willis Ambrose Medal (Award)
To recognize a person for dedicated service to the Canadian earth science community Contact: Stephen Rowins *Contact Detail: E-mail: stephen.rowins@gov.bc.ca*
Yves O. Fortier Earth Science Journalism Award (Award)
To honour excellence in journalistic presentation of earth science in the newsprint media Contact: Eileen van der Flier-Keller *Contact Detail: E-mail: fkeller@uvic.ca*
CJES Best Paper Award (Award)
Presented jointly by the Geological Association of Canada & the National Research Council Press for the best paper published in the Canadian Journal of Earth Sciences
Distinguished Member Award (Award)
A service award of the Geological Association of Canada Contact: Carolyn Relf *Contact Detail: Phone: 867-667-8892; E-mail: carolyn.relf@gov.yk.ca*
Distinguished Service Award (Award)
To recognize outstanding contributions to the Geological Association of Canada through volunteer work Contact: Tim Corkery *Contact Detail: Phone: 204-945-6554; E-mail: timothy.corkery@gov.mb.ca*
Voluntary Service Award (Award)
Awarded to members or non-members for significant voluntary contributions to the Geological Association of Canada Contact: Tim Corkery *Contact Detail: Phone: 204-945-6554; E-mail: timothy.corkery@gov.mb.ca*
Honorary Life Members (Award)
To honour individuals for long-term distinguished service to the Geological Association of Canada Contact: Tim Corkery *Contact Detail: Phone: 204-945-6554; E-mail: timothy.corkery@gov.mb.ca*
Certificate of Appreciation (Award)
To recognize both members of the Geological Association of Canada & non-members for voluntary service to the association
Mary-Claire Ward Geoscience Award (Award)
Awarded to a graduate student at a Canadian university whose thesis incorporates geoscience mapping Contact: Lisa McDonald *Contact Detail: E-mail: lmcdonald@pdac.ca*
Jerome H. Remick Poster Awards (Award)
Awards & certificates of merit given to outstanding poster presenters at each Geological Association of Canada Annual Meeting
Meetings/Conferences:
For more information see Trade Shows, Conferences and Seminars Chapter
Geological Association of Canada (GAC) & the Mineralogical Association of Canada (MAC) 2012 Joint Annual Meeting: At The Geoscience Edge
May 2012 St. John's, NL
Geological Association of Canada (GAC) & the Mineralogical Association of Canada (MAC) 2013 Joint Annual Meeting
May 2013 Winnipeg, MB
Geological Association of Canada (GAC) & the Mineralogical Association of Canada (MAC) 2014 Joint Annual Meeting
Other Conferences in 2014 2014
Publications: *Geoscience Canada*
Type: Journal *Frequency:* q. *Accepts Advertising:* Yes *Editor:* R.A. Wilson (reg.wilson@gnb.ca) *Price:* Free with membership in the Geological Association of Canada
Profile: A general interest, earth-science journal featuring review papers, topical articles, conference reports, book reviews, & commentary
Geolog
Type: Magazine *Frequency:* q. *Accepts Advertising:* Yes *Price:* Free with membership in the Geological Association of Canada
Profile: News items & short articles of interest to Geological Association of Canada members
Geological Association of Canada Membership Directory
Type: Directory
Mission: To advance the wise use of geoscience in academic, professional, & public circles; *Member of:* Canadian Federation of Earth Sciences; *Affiliation(s):* American Geophysical Union; Atlantic Geoscience Society; Canadian Geophysical Union; Canadian Quaternary Association; Canadian Society of Petroleum Geologists; Toronto Geological Discussion Group

Geomatics for Informed Decisions Network
#3732, Pavillon Casault, Université Laval, Québec QC G1V 0A6
Tel: 418-656-7758; *Fax:* 418-656-2611
e-mail: info@geoide.ulaval.ca
URL: www.geoide.ulaval.ca
Also Known As: GEOIDE
Overview: A medium-sized national organization
Chief Officer(s):
Réal Choquette, Network Manager
Mark Zacharias, Executive Director
Member of: Networks of Centres of Excellence

Geomatics Industry Association of Canada (GIAC) / Association canadienne des entreprises de géomatique
Covent Glen, PO Box 62009, 6491 Jeanne D'Arc Blvd., Ottawa ON K1C 2S0
Fax: 613-851-1256
e-mail: dhtessier@giac.ca
URL: www.giac.ca
Previous Name: Canadian Association of Aerial Surveyors
Overview: A medium-sized national organization founded in 1961
Finances: *Annual Operating Budget:* $100,000-$250,000; *Funding Sources:* Membership fees
Staff: 2 staff member(s)
Membership: 100 firms; *Committees:* Export
Mission: To strengthen business climate; to maintain cooperative relations with government; to promote expanded role for members in provision of geomatics products & services; to encourage adoption by governments of improved policies & practices for procurement of geomatics products & services; to promote member firms as source of high quality, professional services; to promote Canadian geomatics industry abroad.; *Member of:* Alliance of Manufacturers & Exporters Canada

Geotechnical Society of Edmonton
c/o City of Edmonton, Engineering Services Section, 11404 - 60 Ave., 2nd Fl., Edmonton AB T6H 1J5
Tel: 780-496-6773; *Fax:* 780-944-7653
e-mail: gse@geotechnical.ca
URL: www.geotechnical.ca
Overview: A small local organization founded in 1969
Chief Officer(s):
Sean Birch, President
Membership: 190; *Fees:* $15

Glass Packaging Institute (GPI)
#510, 700 North Fairfax St., Alexandria VA 22314 USA
Tel: 703-684-6359; *Fax:* 703-299-1543
e-mail: info@gpi.org
URL: www.gpi.org
Overview: A medium-sized national organization
Chief Officer(s):
Joseph J. Cattaneo, President
jcattaneo@gpi.org
Awards: Clear Choice Awards, Glass Packaging Institute Awards for consumer product goods manufacturers who expand the fronteirs of glass packaging design my using glass containers in innovatibe ways Contact: Kristen LeKander *Contact Detail: kristen@lindberggrp.com; 703/778-7644*

Global Crop Protection Federation; International Group of National Associations of Manufacturers of Agrochemical Products See Croplife International

Global, Environmental & Outdoor Education Council (GEOEC)
c/o Barnett House, Alberta Teachers' Association, 11010 - 142 St. NW, Edmonton AB T5N 2R1
Tel: 780-987-7315; *Fax:* 780-455-6481
Toll-Free: 800-232-7208
e-mail: info@geoec.org
URL: www.geoec.org
Previous Name: Environmental & Outdoor Education Council of Alberta
Overview: A small provincial organization founded in 1976
Chief Officer(s):
Rita Poruchny, President, 403-949-3444
reporuchny@cbe.ab.ca
Chenoa Marcotte, Secretary
chenoamarcotte@hotmail.com
Karen Whitehead, Treasurer
kuntzhead@shaw.ca
Fees: $12.50 students; $25 regular & life memberships; $30 subscription; *Member Profile:* Active members of the Alberta Teachers' Association; Students members of the Alberta Teachers' Association; Individuals or corporations ineligible for active or associate membership in the Alberta Teachers' Association, such as teaching assistants, parents, & libraries
Activities: Providing workshops
Awards: Appreciation of Serivce (Award)
Award of Merit (Award)
Distinguished Service (Award)
Publications: Connections [a publication of the Global, Environmental & Outdoor Education Council]
Type: Newsletter *Frequency:* q. *Editor:* Noel Jantzie *Price:* Free with membership in the Global, Environmental & Outdoor Education Council
Profile: Articles & features related to global, environmental, & outdoor education
Mission: To encourage professional development for teachers in the area of global, environmental, & outdoor education; *Member of:* Alberta Teachers' Association

GLOBE Foundation
World Trade Centre, #578, 999 Canada Pl., Vancouver BC V6C 3E1
Tel: 604-695-5001; *Fax:* 604-695-5019
Toll-Free: 800-274-6097
e-mail: info@globe.ca
URL: www.globe.ca
Overview: A medium-sized national organization founded in 1993
Chief Officer(s):
John D. Wiebe, President & Chief Executive Officer
ceo@globe.ca
Freddie Frankling, Vice-President, International Relations
freddie.frankling@globe.ca
Nancy Wright, Vice-President, Marketing
nancy.wright@globe.ca
Cindy Leung, Director, Finance & Administration
cindy.leung@globe.ca
John Gough, Manager, Information Technology
john.gough@globe.ca
Zahida Kanani, Manager, Registration & Database
zahida.kanani@globe.ca
Finances: *Funding Sources:* Sponsorships
Activities: Researching & consulting; Managing projects; Providing opportunities for communication; Developing partnerships
Awards: The GLOBE Awards for Environmental Excellence: The Award for Corporate Environmental Excellence (Award)
Presented to a Canadian corporation with a record of environmental stewardship & sustainability practices Contact: Carine Vindeirinho, GLOBE Awards Coordinator *Contact Detail: Phone:* 604-695-5002, *Fax:* 604-695-5019, *E-mail:* carine@globe.ca
The GLOBE Awards for Environmental Excellence: The Award for Technology Innovation & Application (Award)
Awarded to a Canadian company or group of companies that have developed or applied an innovative technology with a significant environmental application Contact: Carine Vindeirinho, GLOBE Awards Coordinator *Contact Detail: Phone:* 604-695-5002, *Fax:* 604-695-5019, *E-mail:* carine@globe.ca
The GLOBE Awards for Environmental Excellence: The Award for Excellence in Urban Sustainability (Award)
To honour a local government, private sector company, or consortium that has developed & applied beneficial urban sustainability principles Contact: Carine Vindeirinho, GLOBE Awards Coordinator *Contact Detail: Phone:* 604-695-5002, *Fax:* 604-695-5019, *E-mail:* carine@globe.ca
The GLOBE Awards for Environmental Excellence: The Award for Best Green Consumer Product (Award)
To recognize a Canadian company or group of companies that is pursing new & emerging technologies, or has advanced current environmental technologies Contact: Carine Vindeirinho, GLOBE Awards Coordinator *Contact Detail: Phone:* 604-695-5002, *Fax:* 604-695-5019, *E-mail:* carine@globe.ca
The GLOBE Awards for Environmental Excellence: The Finance Award for Sustainability (Award)
To recognize a North American fund manager, a global fund manager, a commercial bank, an investment bank, a private bank, an investment broker, an asset management company, a venture capital firm, or an investment advisor who developed portfolios, investment instruments, analytical tools, or funds for Canadian environmental markets Contact: Carine Vindeirinho, GLOBE Awards Coordinator *Contact Detail: Phone:* 604-695-5002, *Fax:* 604-695-5019, *E-mail:* carine@globe.ca
Meetings/Conferences:
For more information see Trade Shows, Conferences and Seminars Chapter
GLOBE Costa Rica 2011: Accelerating the Shift Towards a Low Carbon Economy in Latin America
June 2011 San Jose
GLOBE 2012 12th Biennial Conference & Trade Fair on Business & the Environment: Driving Economic Performance Through Sustainability
March 2012 Vancouver, BC
GLOBE Foundation 2012 6th Annual EPIC Sustainable Living Expo
Other Conferences in 2012 2012
GLOBE Foundation 2013 7th Annual EPIC Sustainable Living Expo
Other Conferences in 2013 2013
GLOBE 2014 13th Biennial Conference & Trade Fair on Business & the Environment
Other Conferences in 2014 2014
Publications: GLOBE-Net Environmental Business E-Newsletter
Type: Newsletter *Frequency:* w.
Mission: To strive to find practical business-oriented solutions to environmental problems; To assist companies & individuals realize the value of economically viable environmental business opportunities
Environmental Activity: Promoting the business case for sustainable development

Go for Green
#16, 5480 Canoteck Rd., Gloucester ON K1J 9H6
Tel: 613-748-1800; *Fax:* 613-748-0357
e-mail: info@goforgreen.ca
URL: www.goforgreen.ca
Overview: A medium-sized national organization
Chief Officer(s):
Johanne Lacombe, Executive Director
Activities: National programs: Commuter Challenge; Active Transportation; TrailsCanada; Gardening for Life; Active & Safe Routes to School; Winter Green; *Awareness Events:* International Walk to School Day, Oct.
Mission: To encourage Canadians to pursue healthy, outdoor physical activities that protect, enhance & restore the environment; to aim to inform Canadians about healthy, active lifestyle choices; to nurture commitment & action to improve personal health & the health of the environment

Golden Horseshoe Health Libraries Association
Parent: Canadian Health Libraries Association
c/o BCHS Resource Library, 200 Terrace Hill St., Brantford ON N3R 1G9
Tel: 905-519-5544
URL: www.chla-absc.ca/?q=en/node/71
Overview: A small local organization
Chief Officer(s):
Barbara Gray, President
bgray1@bchsys.org
Mission: The Association's mission is to improve health and health care by promoting excellence in access to information.; *Member of:* Canadian Health Libraries Association

Government Refuse Collection & Disposal Association *See* Solid Waste Association of North America

Grain Elevator & Processing Society (GEAPS)
4248 Park Glen Road, Minneapolis MN 55416 USA
Tel: 952-928-4640; *Fax:* 952-929-1318
e-mail: info@geaps.com
URL: www.geaps.com
Overview: A medium-sized international organization founded in 1937
Chief Officer(s):
David Krejci, Executive Vice-President
Finances: *Annual Operating Budget:* $500,000-$1.5 Million; *Funding Sources:* Membership dues; publications
Staff: 7 staff member(s)
Membership: 2,500 individual; *Fees:* US$185; *Member Profile:* Individuals across the grain operations industry worldwide; *Committees:* Grain Handling & Storage, Facility Design; Safety & Health; Environmental Responsibility
Activities: Publications; education & training; trade shows; conferences; *Awareness Events:* International Technical Conference & Expositions; *Speaker Service:* Yes; *Rents Mailing List:* Yes
Mission: To provide a forum for the analysis & exchange of information affecting the industries; to advance educational & professional qualifications of the members; to represent the interests of the members in governmental activities; to foster good business ethics & social responsibility throughout the membership; to communicate with the trade media & general public concerning the issues of interest to the members & the industries; to provide technical information on grain handling & storage

Grand Manan Whale & Seabird Research Station (GMWSRS) / Centre de recherche sur la vie marine de Grand Manan
24 Rte. 776, Grand Manan NB E5G 1A1
Tel: 506-662-3804; *Fax:* 506-662-9804
e-mail: info@gmwsrs.org
URL: www.gmwsrs.org
Overview: A small local charitable organization founded in 1981
Chief Officer(s):
Laurie Murison, Managing Director, 506-662-8316
Finances: *Annual Operating Budget:* $50,000-$100,000
Staff: 4 volunteer(s)
Activities: *Speaker Service:* Yes; *Library:* Gaskin Memorial Library; open by appointment
Mission: To conduct research on the Bay of Fundy ecosystem, concentrating on marine mammals & seabirds; to operate a public display of Bay of Fundy Marine Fauna; *Member of:* New Brunswick Environmental Network

Grand Manan Wildlife Association
PO Box 926, 212 Ingalls Head Rd., Grand Manan NB E5G 4M1
Tel: 506-662-3508; *Fax:* 506-662-3508
Overview: A small local organization founded in 1975
Membership: 75; *Fees:* $30
Member of: New Brunswick Wildlife Federation

Grand River Conservation Foundation
400 Clyde Rd., Cambridge ON N1R 5W6
Tel: 519-621-2761; *Fax:* 519-621-4844
Toll-Free: 877-294-7263
e-mail: foundation@grandriver.ca
URL: www.grandriver.ca
Previous Name: Grand River Foundation
Overview: A small local charitable organization founded in 1965
Chief Officer(s):
David Hales, President
Finances: *Annual Operating Budget:* Less than $50,000; *Funding Sources:* Individuals, groups & corporations
Staff: 1 staff member(s); 22 volunteer(s)
Membership: 1-99; *Committees:* Endowment; Marketing; Outdoor Education
Activities: *Speaker Service:* Yes
Awards: S.C. Johnson & Son Ltd. Environmental Scholarship (Scholarship)
Annual award for a student enrolled in an environmental sciences program with an emphasis on manufacturing, eocnomics, business, chemistry or related applications at a university in the Grand River watershed area *Award Amount:* $1,500
Mission: To provide leadership & support within the community of the Valley of the Grand River for the protection, conservation, responsible use & management of its natural resources, in response to the needs & wishes & for the ongoing enjoyment of its residents, as well as of the broader community of our province & country

Grand River Foundation *See* Grand River Conservation Foundation

Graphic Arts Industries Association; Canadian Printing & Imaging Association *See* Canadian Printing Industries Association

Grasslands Naturalists (GN)
Police Point Park Nature Centre, PO Box 2491, Police Point Dr NE, Medicine Hat AB T1A 8G8
Tel: 403-529-6225; *Fax:* 403-526-6408
e-mail: mhip@natureline.info
URL: natureline.info
Also Known As: Society of Grasslands Naturalists
Overview: A small local charitable organization founded in 1991
Chief Officer(s):
Dawn Dickinson, Contact
Finances: *Annual Operating Budget:* $50,000-$100,000
Staff: 1 staff member(s); 25 volunteer(s)
Membership: 140; *Fees:* $20 individual; $25 family; *Committees:* Land; Wildlife
Activities: Conservation projects; environmental consulting; education; environmental research; field trips; monthly speaker series; bi-weekly newspaper column; *Library:* Police Point Interpretive Centre, Resource Centre
Mission: The society manages the Medicine Hat Interpretive Program which offers nature activties to the public year round. The group encourages the study, conservation & protection of all components of the natural world & provides curriculum-based, educational opportunities to schools. It also assists in the collection & provision of species data. It is a registered charity, BN: 130725922RR0001.; *Member of:* Federation of Alberta Naturalists; Affiliation(s): Canadian Nature Federation

Great Lakes Commission / Commission des Grands Lacs
Eisenhower Corporate Park, #100, 2805 S. Industrial Way, Ann Arbor MI 48104-6791 USA
Tel: 734-971-9135; *Fax:* 734-971-9150
URL: www.glc.org
Chief Officer(s):
James M. Tierney, Chair
Tim A. Eder, Executive Director
teder@glc.org
Mission: The Commission is a binational, public agency dedicated to the use, management & protection of water, land & other natural resources of the Great Lakes-St. Lawrence system. In partnership with 8 Great Lakes states & provinces of Ontario & Québec, the Commission applies sustainable development principles addressing issues of resource management, environmental protection, transportation & sustainable development. The Commission provides information on public policy issues; a forum for developing & coordinating public policy; & a unified, system-wide voice to advocate member interests.

Great Lakes Institute for Environmental Research (GLIER)
University of Windsor, 401 Sunset Ave., Windsor ON N9B 3P4
Tel: 519-253-3000; *Fax:* 519-971-3616
e-mail: glier@uwindsor.ca
URL: cronus.uwindsor.ca/glier
Overview: A small local organization founded in 1981

The Great Lakes Research Consortium (GLRC)
SUNY College of Environmental Science & Forestry, 253 Baker Labs, 1 Forestry Drive, Syracuse NY 13210 USA
Tel: 315-470-6720; *Fax:* 315-470-6970
e-mail: glrc@esf.edu
URL: www.esf.edu/glrc
Overview: A medium-sized international organization founded in 1986
Chief Officer(s):
Richard Smardon, Co-Director
Greg Boyer, Ph.D, Executive Director
Edward Mills, Ph.D., Research Director
Finances: *Annual Operating Budget:* $100,000-$250,000
Staff: 2 staff member(s)
Membership: 18 institutional; *Fees:* $500-1,000 per campus; *Member Profile:* New York State colleges & universities + 9 Ontario universities
Activities: Speakers exchange; task forces; small grants program; annual student/faculty conferences; *Speaker Service:* Yes
Mission: To facilitate research & scholarship on Great Lakes problems; to provide opportunities for training & education of students; to disseminate important information & research findings

Great Lakes United (GLU) / Union Saint Laurent/Grands Lacs
3388 rue Adam, Montréal QC H1W 1Y1
Tel: 514-396-3333; *Fax:* 514-396-0297
e-mail: usgl@glu.org
URL: www.glu.org
Overview: A small international charitable organization founded in 1982
Chief Officer(s):
Derek Stack, Executive Director
Hélène Godmaire, Director, Québec Operations
Finances: *Annual Operating Budget:* $500,000-$1.5 Million
Membership: 100-499; *Fees:* $50-$75 individual; $35-$125 organization; $20 student
Activities: H20 Levels, H20 Quality; *Internships:* Yes; *Rents Mailing List:* Yes
Mission: To preserve the Great Lakes - St. Lawrence ecosystem; Affiliation(s): Canadian Institute for Environmental Law & Policy
Environmental Activity: Restoring the Great Lakes - St. Lawrence ecosystem

Greater Hamilton Technology Enterprise Centre *See* Hamilton Incubator of Technology

Greater Toronto Rose & Garden Society
Parent: Ontario Horticultural Association
9 Tarlton Rd., Toronto ON M5P 2M5
Tel: 416-485-5907
e-mail: GTRoses@aol.com
URL: www.gardenontario.org/site.php/rosegarden
Also Known As: Toronto Rose
Previous Name: York Rose & Garden Society
Overview: A small local organization founded in 1979
Chief Officer(s):
Christine Moore, Contact
Membership: 150; *Fees:* $10 regular; $15 family
Activities: Annual "Roses" garden tour; lectures; public meetings
Mission: Dedicated to cultivation & enjoyment of roses; *Member of:* Canadian Rose Society, American Rose Society, Ontario Horticultural Association

Greater Toronto Water Garden & Horticultural Society
4691 Hwy. 7A, RR#1, Nestleton Station ON L0B 1L0
e-mail: info@onwatergarden.com
URL: www.onwatergarden.com
Previous Name: Ontario Water Garden Society
Overview: A small provincial organization
Chief Officer(s):
Laura Grant, Contact, 416-422-2164, *Fax:* 416-422-2820
Joachim G. Doehler, President
Peter Poot, Secretary
Fees: $20 single; $25 family

Green Action Centre (RCM)
303 Portage Ave., 3rd Fl., Winnipeg MB R3B 2B4
Tel: 204-925-3777; *Fax:* 204-942-4207
Toll-Free: 866-394-8880
e-mail: info@resourceconservation.mb.ca
URL: www.resourceconservation.mb.ca
Social Media: www.facebook.com/group.php?gid=1347608132229244
Previous Name: Recycling Council of Manitoba; Resource Conservation Manitoba Inc.
Overview: A medium-sized provincial organization founded in 1985
Chief Officer(s):
Randall McQuaker, Executive Director, 204-925-3770
Finances: *Annual Operating Budget:* $100,000-$250,000; *Funding Sources:* 3 levels of government; corporate; private foundations; membership dues
Staff: 11 staff member(s); 20 volunteer(s)
Membership: 200; *Committees:* Membership; Policy
Activities: Public Infoline; Environmental Speaker's Bureau; The R-Report; Public Forums; Green Commuting Program; Composting Education Program; *Speaker Service:* Yes; *Library:* Resource Centre
Mission: To promote ecological sustainability by developing alternatives to currently unsustainable practices; our principal activity is environmental education; our partners & clients include businesses, schools, non-profit groups, governments, recyclers, home gardeners & general public; *Member of:* Canadian Environment Network; Manitoba Eco-Network; Manitoba Environmental Industries Association

The Green Brick Road (GBR)
#408, 429 Danforth Ave., Toronto ON M4K 1P1
Tel: 416-421-9816; *Fax:* 416-537-7518
Toll-Free: 800-473-3638
e-mail: gbr@look.ca
Overview: A small local organization founded in 1990
Chief Officer(s):
John Tersigni, Executive Director
Mission: To distribute teaching materials related to environmental & global education for all grade levels

Green Calgary
809 - 4th Ave. SW, Calgary AB T2P 0K5
Tel: 403-230-1443; *Fax:* 403-230-1458
e-mail: info@greencalgary.org
URL: www.greencalgary.org
Previous Name: Clean Calgary Association
Overview: A medium-sized local charitable organization founded in 1978
Finances: *Annual Operating Budget:* $250,000-$500,000; *Funding Sources:* Municipal government; corporate; casino; goods & services
Staff: 8 staff member(s); 125 volunteer(s)
Membership: 90; *Fees:* $15 low-income/student; $50 individual; $75 non-profit; $200 business; *Member Profile:* Concern for environment & positive, proactive programs
Activities: Waste reduction & water conservation; *Speaker Service:* Yes
Mission: To provide educational programs which assist Calgarians to develop an environmentally friendly lifestyle; *Member of:* Alberta Environmental Network; Ecotrust; City of Calgary Environment Advisory Committee

Green Communities Association *See* Green Communities Canada

Green Communities Canada (GCC)
PO Box 928, 416 Chambers St., 2nd Fl., Peterborough ON K9J 7A5
Tel: 705-745-7479; *Fax:* 705-745-7294
e-mail: info@greencommunitiescanada.org
URL: www.gca.ca
Previous Name: Green Communities Association
Overview: A small national organization founded in 1995
Chief Officer(s):
Clifford Maynes, Executive Director, 705-745-7479 Ext. 118
Beth Jones, Associate Director & Manager, EcoDriver, 705-745-7479 Ext. 152
Jacky Kennedy, Director, Walking Programs, 416-488-7263, *Fax:* 416-488-2296
Bhim Subba, Director, Home Energy, 705-745-9183
Heather Kirby, Manager, Well Aware, 705-745-7479 Ext. 114
Bruce Roxburgh, Manager, Green Information Technology, 705-745-7479 Ext. 117
Fees: $500 full membership; $250 associate membership; *Member Profile:* Non-profit community-based organizations that deliver environmental programs
Activities: Sharing information & resources; joint member projects; Water Programs; Energy Programs; Walking Programs/Safe Routes to School; Green IT
Publications: *Green Community News*
Type: Newsletter *Frequency:* w.
Profile: Association activities, resources, & events
Mission: To support member organizations in achieving environmental sustainability; *Member of:* Canadian Renewable Energy Alliance

Green Kids Inc.
#670, 776 Corydon Ave., Winnipeg MB R3M 0Y1
Tel: 204-940-4745; *Fax:* 204-289-4066
Toll-Free: 800-441-6751
e-mail: jeff@greenkids.com
URL: www.greenkids.com
Overview: A small national charitable organization founded in 1991
Chief Officer(s):
Daina Leitold, Tour Manager
Finances: *Annual Operating Budget:* $100,000-$250,000
Staff: 5 staff member(s); 4 volunteer(s)
Activities: Educates children (K-8) about environmental issues in schools using interactive theatre
Mission: To empower children to take positive action & change the world

Associations/Organizations / Green Party of British Columbia

Green Party of British Columbia (GPBC)
Parent: Green Party of Canada
Dominion Bldg., PO Box 2827, Stn. Terminal, #610, 207 West Hastings St., Vancouver BC V6B 3X2
Tel: 604-687-1199; *Fax:* 604-909-4722
Toll-Free: 888-473-3686
e-mail: info@greenparty.bc.ca
URL: www.greenparty.bc.ca
Also Known As: BC Greens
Overview: A medium-sized provincial charitable organization founded in 1983
Finances: *Funding Sources:* Donations
Membership: 4,000; *Fees:* Donation; *Member Profile:* Residents of British Columbia, fourteen years of age & older, who are not members of any other provincial political party; *Committees:* Fundraising; Administration; Media; Organizing; Membership
Mission: To form healthy communities with diverse economies by involving the citizens of British Columbia in the political process; To offer voters in British Columbia fiscal responsibility, socially progressive policies, & environmental sustainability

Green Party of Canada (GPC) / Parti vert du Canada
PO Box 997, Stn. B, #204, 396 Cooper St., Ottawa ON K1P 5R1
Tel: 613-562-4916; *Fax:* 613-482-4632
Toll-Free: 888-868-3447
e-mail: info@greenparty.ca
URL: www.greenparty.ca
Social Media: www.twitter.com/canadiangreens
Overview: A medium-sized national organization founded in 1983
Finances: *Annual Operating Budget:* $50,000-$100,000; *Funding Sources:* Individual contributions
Staff: 1 staff member(s); 40 volunteer(s)
Membership: 4,000; *Fees:* $10+; *Committees:* Election Coordinating; Officer/Functionary Review; Finance/Administration; Green Convenors
Activities: *Speaker Service:* Yes
Mission: To promote a platform that includes debt reduction, eco-jobs, saving Canada's forests, supporting small business, use of soft energies, sovereignty for First Nations, & a guarantee of full rights for women; *Member of:* CanAmex; World Greens Coordination

The Green Party of Manitoba
Parent: Green Party of Canada
PO Box 26023, Stn. Maryland, Winnipeg MB R3C 3R3
Tel: 204-488-2831; *Fax:* 204-992-2712
Toll-Free: 866-742-4292
e-mail: info@greenparty.mb.ca
URL: www.greenparty.mb.ca
Overview: A medium-sized provincial organization founded in 1996
Chief Officer(s):
James Beddome, President
Fees: $5

Green Party of New Brunswick
Parent: Green Party of Canada
PO Box 3723, Stn. B, Fredericton NB E3A 5L8
Tel: 506-447-8499; *Fax:* 506-447-8489
Toll-Free: 888-662-8683
e-mail: info@greenpartynb.ca
URL: www.greenpartynb.ca
Overview: A small provincial organization
Chief Officer(s):
Jack MacDougall, Leader

The Green Party of Ontario (GPO) / Parti Vert d'Ontario
Parent: Green Party of Canada
PO Box 1132, Stn. F, Toronto ON M4Y 2T8
Tel: 416-977-7476; *Fax:* 416-977-5476
Toll-Free: 888-647-3366
e-mail: admin@gpo.ca
URL: www.gpo.ca
Previous Name: The Ontario Greens
Overview: A small provincial organization founded in 1983
Finances: *Funding Sources:* Membership dues
Staff: 1 staff member(s); 900 volunteer(s)
Membership: 1,000; *Fees:* $25; *Committees:* Policy; Candidate Facilitation
Activities: Annual Fall Meeting; *Library:* Yes, open by appointment

Green Party of Québec *Voir* Parti Vert du Québec

Green Roofs for Healthy Cities (GRHC)
406 King St. East, Toronto ON M5A 1L4
Tel: 416-971-4494; *Fax:* 416-971-9844
URL: www.greenroofs.org
Overview: A medium-sized international organization founded in 1999
Chief Officer(s):
Jeffrey Bruce, Chair
Steven Peck, President
speck@greenroofs.org
Dan Slone, Secretary
Rick Buist, Treasurer
Member Profile: Corporate suppliers & manufacturers; Individuals who practise the art of living architecture; Supporters (LAM subscribers); *Committees:* Research; Policy; Membership; Training & Accreditation; Corporate Members; Technical; GreenSave Calculator; Conference; Green Walls; Integrated Building Water Management; Growing Medium
Activities: Increasing awareness of the environmental, economic, & social benefits of green roofs & green walls; Providing education; Offering networking opportunities
Publications: *Living Architecture Monitor*
Type: Magazine *Frequency:* q. *Accepts Advertising* : Yes *Editor:* Caroline Nolan
Profile: For Green Roofs for Healthy Cities members only
Mission: To promote the green roof industry throughout North America

Green Tourism Association
850 Coxwell Ave., 2nd Fl., Toronto ON M4Y 2J4
Tel: 416-392-1288; *Fax:* 416-392-0071
Overview: A small local organization founded in 1993
Chief Officer(s):
Shari Simpson Campbell, Director
Sharon L. Meade, Event Coordinator
Membership: 100; *Fees:* $75-100
Activities: Ecotourism; responsible tourism/sustainable tourism development; sustainable transportation; green accommodation initiatives; greening our business/environment; *Library:* On-line Resource Centre
Mission: To develop & cultivate a green tourism industry within the Toronto region

Greenest City
#120, 215 Spadina Ave., Toronto ON M5T 2C7
Tel: 647-438-0038
e-mail: info@greenestcity.net
URL: www.greenestcity.net
Overview: A small local organization
Chief Officer(s):
Sandi Trillo, Secretary
Activities: Walk to School Day; Active & Safe Routes to School; Walking School Bus; projects & campaigns embrace community diversity & engage people in finding locally appropriate solutions to global environmental problems
Mission: To reduce pollution; to regenerate urban life; to promote social equity

Greenpeace Canada
33 Cecil St., Toronto ON M5T 1N1
Tel: 416-597-8408; *Fax:* 416-597-8422
Toll-Free: 800-320-7183
e-mail: supporter.ca@greenpeace.org
URL: www.greenpeacecanada.org
Social Media: facebook.com/greenpeace.canada
Overview: A large international charitable organization founded in 1971
Finances: *Annual Operating Budget:* $1.5 Million-$3 Million; *Funding Sources:* Donations; shop sales
Staff: 35 staff member(s)
Membership: 100,000+ in Canada + over 2.5 million internationally; *Fees:* $30
Activities: Communications; e-news; reports; Greenpeace Magazine; *Speaker Service:* Yes; *Library:* Information Office; Open to public
Mission: Greenpeace is an independent, non-profit organization best known for non-violent direct actions to raise awareness on issues such as biodiversity, pollution of the Earth, nuclear threats & disarmament; it brings public opinion to bear on decisions makers. Public protest is only one of many Greenpeace strategies; it conducts scientific, economic & political research, publicizes environmental problems, recommends environmentally sound solutions & lobbies for change.; *Member of:* Greenpeace International; Canadian Renewable Energy Alliance
Environmental Activity: Campaigns: Climate Change; Tar Sands; Nuclear Power; Boreal Forest; Great Bear Rainforest; Marine Fish; GMO Foods

Greenpeace International HQ
Ottho Heldringstraat 5, Amsterdam 1066 AZ Netherlands
Tel: 31-20-718-2000; *Fax:* 31-20-514-8151
e-mail: supporter.services@int.greenpeace.org
URL: www.greenpeace.org
Overview: A large international organization founded in 1971
Finances: *Annual Operating Budget:* $1.5 Million-$3 Million
Membership: 5 million
Mission: To protect the environment from the threats of pollution, global warming, & the depletion of natural resources; To protect endangered species, such as whales, dolphins, & seals

Greenpeace USA
702 H St. NW, Washington DC 20001 USA
Tel: 202-462-1177
Toll-Free: 800-326-0959
e-mail: info@wdc.greenpeace.org
URL: www.greenpeaceusa.org
Overview: A large international charitable organization founded in 1971
Chief Officer(s):
Phil Radford, Executive Director
Finances: *Annual Operating Budget:* Greater than $5 Million
Membership: 4 million; *Fees:* $30
Activities: *Internships:* Yes; *Speaker Service:* Yes; *Rents Mailing List:* Yes
Mission: To use non-violent confrontation to expose global environmental problems & to promote solutions essential to a green & peaceful future; to protect biodiversity in all its forms; to end the nuclear threat & promote global disarmament; *Affiliation(s):* Greenpeace International

Greenspace Alliance of Canada's Capital
PO Box 55085, 240 Sparks St., Ottawa ON K1P 1A1
e-mail: greenspace@greenspace-alliance.ca
URL: www.greenspace-alliance.ca
Overview: A medium-sized local organization founded in 1997
Chief Officer(s):
Cheryl Doran, Chair
Fees: $15 group; $5 student; $30 associate
Mission: To preserve green spaces in the National Capital area.

Grocery Products Manufacturers of Canada; Food & Consumer Products Manufacturers of Canada *See* Food & Consumer Products of Canada

Groundfish Enterprise Allocation Council
1362 Revell Road, Manotick ON K4M K84
Tel: 613-692-8249; *Fax:* 613-692-8250
e-mail: bchapman@sympatico.ca
URL: www.geaconline.com
Overview: A medium-sized national organization founded in 1997
Chief Officer(s):
Bruce Chapman, Executive Director
Mission: To generally promote the common interests of its members; to promote the wise use, development & conservation of the Atlantic Canadian groundfish resource; to provide an organization that permits Atlantic groundfish enterprise allocation license holders to speak with a unified voice to the general public & all levels of government on matters of broad concern to the members; to provide an organization that permits groundfish enterprise allocation license holders to interface with similar organizations in Canada; to conduct research that has the potential to produce information & data that will be helpful or useful to the members; to monitor regional, national & international corporate & political activities which have a bearing on the members; to provide a platform for the views of members with regard to these activities

Groupe de recherche d'intérêt public de l'Ontario *See* Ontario Public Interest Research Group

Groupe de recherche d'intérêt public du Québec - McGill *Voir* Québec Public Interest Research Group - McGill

Groupe de recherche en écologie sociale (GRESOC) / Social Ecology Research Group (SERG)
Dépt. de Sociologie, Université de Montréal, CP 6128, Montréal QC H3C 3J7
Tél: 514-343-5959; *Téléc:* 514-343-5722
Courriel: jean.guy.vaillancourt@umontreal.ca

Aperçu: Dimension: petite; *Envergure:* locale; *Organisme sans but lucratif; fondée en 1978*
Finances: *Budget de fonctionnement annuel:* Moins de $50,000; *Fonds:* Hydro-Québec; Agence de l'éfficacité energétique; étalez votre science
Personnel: 2 bénévole(s)
Membre: 25; *Critères d'admissibilite:* Chercheurs universitaires
Activités: *Stagiaires:* Oui; *Bibliothèque:* Oui, Not open to the public
Mission: Le GRESOC est constitué de chercheurs universitaires qui s'intéressent à l'écologie sociale, à l'écosociologie et à la sociologie de l'environnement; les recherches en cours portent sur le mouvement vert (écologisme et environnementalisme), le développement durable, les pluies acides, les déchets, et les aspects sociaux des changements environnementaux globaux; plusieurs rapports de recherches, livres, chapitres et articles ont été publiés; *Membre de:* Réseau des Groupes Écologistes Québécois; Conseil Régional de l'Environnement de Montréal

Groupe de recherches sur les transports au Canada *See* Canadian Transportation Research Forum

Gulf of Maine Council on the Marine Environment
c/o New Brunswick Dept. Of Agriculture & Aquaculture, PO Box 6000, 850 Lincoln Rd., Fredericton NB E3B 5H1
Tel: 506-453-2666; *Fax:* 506-453-7170
e-mail: daa-maa@gnb.ca
URL: www.gulfofmaine.org
Chief Officer(s):
Robert Capozi, New Brunswick Contact
robert.capozi@gnb.ca
Justin Huston, Nova Scotia Contact
hustonje@gov.ns.ca
Member Profile: Nova Scotia Department of Environment & Labour, Terminal Bldg., Terminal Rd., Halifax NS B3J 2T8; 902/424-6345; Fax: 902/424-0501
Mission: This U.S.-Canadian partnership of government & non-government organizations works to maintain & enhance environmental quality in the Gulf of Maine to allow for sustainable resource use. The Council organizes conferences & workshops; offers grants & recognition awards; conducts environmental monitoring; provides science translation to management; raises public awareness about the Gulf. The secretariat rotates annually among the member jurisdictions. Initiatives include: Gulf of Maine Mapping Initiative (GOMMI), comprehensive seafloor imaging, mapping & biological & geological surveys; habitat restoration grants program (U.S. only); Action Plan grants program; Gulf of Maine Times, a quarterly newspaper; Gulfwatch Monitoring Program, which helps to assess the fate & impacts of toxic contaminants in the Gulf of Maine.; *Affiliation(s):* ME State Planning Office; NB Department of Environment; naturesource communications, NH; NH Department of Environmental Services; NS Department of Fisheries & Aquaculture

Habitat Acquisition Trust (HAT)
PO Box 8552, Victoria BC V8W 3S2
Tel: 250-995-2428; *Fax:* 250-920-7975
e-mail: hatmail@hat.bc.ca
URL: www.hat.bc.ca
Overview: A small local charitable organization founded in 1996
Jennifer Eliason, Executive Director
Finances: *Annual Operating Budget:* $100,000-$250,000; *Funding Sources:* Private; foundations; government
Staff: 4 staff member(s); 100+ volunteer(s)
Membership: 100-499; *Fees:* $30; $20 student; $45 family; $100 corporate
Activities: Land purchase; conservation covenants (easements); environmental education; *Library:* Bob Ogilvie Bioregional Resource Library; Open to public, open by appointment
Mission: To promote the preservation of the natural environment on Southern Vancouver Island & the Southern Gulf Island by: conserving habitats by acquisition, conservation coverants or other legal mechanisms; & promoting habitat stewardship, education & research; *Member of:* Land Trust Alliance of British Columbia; *Affiliation(s):* Victoria Natural History Society

Habitat faunique Canada *See* Wildlife Habitat Canada

Halifax Field Naturalists (HFN)
c/o Nova Scotia Museum of Natural History, 1747 Summer St., Halifax NS B3H 3A6
e-mail: ip-hfn@chebucto.ns.ca
URL: www.halifaxfieldnaturalists.ca/hfnWP

Overview: A small local charitable organization founded in 1975
Chief Officer(s):
Allan Robertson, President
Finances: *Annual Operating Budget:* Less than $50,000; *Funding Sources:* Membership dues; sales; donations
Membership: 120; *Fees:* $15 individual; $20 family; $25 supporting; $5 Federation of N.S.; *Committees:* Membership; Newsletter
Activities: Presentations, field trips; *Speaker Service:* Yes
Mission: To promote the enjoyment & preservation of Nova Scotia's history & natural areas through education, discussion & fellowship; *Member of:* Federation of Nova Scotia Naturalists; *Affiliation(s):* Canadian Nature Federation; Canadian Parks & Wilderness Society; The Nature Conservancy of Canada

Halton Foundation *See* Conservation Halton Foundation

Hamilton Geological Society
McMaster University, PO Box 59, Hamilton ON L8S 1C0
Tel: 905-527-7646
Overview: A small local organization
Chief Officer(s):
K. Kaiser, Secretary
Fees: $13.50
Activities: Meetings 3rd Tuesday of every month except July & August
Mission: To foster an interest in the earth sciences & related lapidary arts; *Member of:* Central Canadian Federation of Mineralogical Societies

Hamilton Incubator of Technology (HIT)
#200, 7 Innovation Dr., Flamborough ON L9H 7H9
Tel: 905-689-2400; *Fax:* 905-689-2200
e-mail: pgardine@hamilton.ca
URL: www.hitcentre.ca
Previous Name: Greater Hamilton Technology Enterprise Centre
Overview: A small local organization founded in 1977
Chief Officer(s):
Penny Gardiner, Facilities Director
Finances: *Annual Operating Budget:* $250,000-$500,000; *Funding Sources:* City of Hamilton
Staff: 2 staff member(s)
Activities: Incubating, mentoring & coaching tech business start-ups
Mission: To create wealth-generating jobs by helping form & grow technology-focussed business; *Member of:* City of Hamilton

Hamilton Industrial Environmental Association (HIEA)
PO Box 35545, Hamilton ON L8H 7S6
Tel: 905-561-4432
e-mail: info@hiea.org
URL: www.hiea.org
Overview: A medium-sized local organization
Chief Officer(s):
Jim Stirling, Chair
Membership: 15 companies
Mission: To improve the local environment - air, land and water - through joint and individual activities, and by partnering with the community to enhance future understanding of environmental issues and help establish priorities for action.

Hamilton Naturalists' Club (HNC)
PO Box 89052, Hamilton ON L8S 4R5
Tel: 905-381-0329
e-mail: info@hamiltonnature.org
URL: www.hamiltonnature.org
Overview: A small local charitable organization founded in 1919
Finances: *Annual Operating Budget:* Less than $50,000; *Funding Sources:* Donations; membership dues; grants
Staff: 80 volunteer(s)
Membership: 500; *Fees:* $30 senior/student; $35 individual/institution; $40 family; $750 lifetime; *Committees:* Bird Study Group; Conservation; Hamilton Bird Records; Education; Sanctuary; Newsletter; Plant Study Group
Activities: Monthly public meetings from Sept.-May; public hikes; *Speaker Service:* Yes
Mission: To promote the enjoyment of nature through environmental appreciation & conservation; to foster public interest & education in the appreciation & study of nature; to encourage wise use & conservation of natural resources; to promote environmental protection; *Member of:* Federation of Ontario Naturalists; *Affiliation(s):* Canadian Nature Federation

Hanley & District Agricultural Society
PO Box 172, c/o 320 Walter Scott St., Hanley SK S0G 2E0
Overview: A small local organization founded in 1982
Finances: *Annual Operating Budget:* Less than $50,000
Staff: 30 volunteer(s)
Activities: Agricultural & domestic displays; beef show; light horse show; co-ed slow pitch; men's fastball; children's activities
Mission: The Society works to improve agriculture & the quality of life in the community by providing a forum for discussion of agricultural issues. It also encourages conservation of natural resources.; *Member of:* Saskatchewan Association of Agricultural Societies & Exhibitions

Harmony Foundation of Canada / Fondation Harmonie du Canada
PO Box 50022, #15, 1594 Fairfield Rd., Victoria BC V8S 1G1
Tel: 250-380-3001; *Fax:* 250-380-0887
e-mail: harmony@islandnet.com
URL: www.harmonyfdn.ca
Overview: A medium-sized international charitable organization founded in 1985
Finances: *Funding Sources:* Donations; Sponsorships
Activities: Working with organizations & individuals around the world through the Building Sustainable Societies Program; Improving environmental practices in workplaces; Providing community service opportunities for young people; Publishing action guides for homes, workplaces, & communities; Implementing training programs; Forming partnerships to establish meaningful results around environment & development issues; Educating about sustainable development & global change
Mission: To encourage development which is socially & environmentally sustainable; To strive towards ecological stability, long-term prosperity, & social harmony

Hawk Migration Association of North America (HMANA)
C/O John Weeks, Membership Secretary, 51 Pheasant Run, North Granby CT 06060 USA
URL: www.hmana.org
Overview: A medium-sized international organization founded in 1974
Chief Officer(s):
Iain MacLeod, Chair
Finances: *Annual Operating Budget:* Less than $50,000
Membership: 900; *Fees:* US$25; family US$40; club US$50; benefactor US$100; corporate US$250; life US$500
Activities: *Speaker Service:* Yes
Mission: To conserve raptor populations through the scientific study, enjoyment & appreciation of hawk migration

Health & Safety Conference Society of Alberta (HSCSA)
PO Box 38009, Calgary AB T3K 5G9
Tel: 403-236-2225; *Fax:* 403-206-7099
e-mail: info@hsconference.com
URL: www.hsconference.com
Overview: A small provincial organization
Chief Officer(s):
Diane Radnoff, President
Jerald Richelhoff, Vice-President
Dianne Paulson, Secretary
Justin DeGagne, Treasurer
Finances: *Funding Sources:* Sponsorships
Membership: 1-99; *Member Profile:* Health & safety associations; Professional societies; Employer associations
Activities: Hosting an annual multi-partner conference; Providing health & safety education
Meetings/Conferences:
For more information see Trade Shows, Conferences and Seminars Chapter
Alberta Health & Safety 2011 10th Annual Conference & Trade Fair
November 2011 Calgary, AB
Alberta Health & Safety 2012 11th Annual Conference & Trade Fair
November 2012 Edmonton, AB
Mission: To promote the importance of health & safety for safer workplaces

Health Food Dealers Association *See* Canadian Health Food Association

Associations/Organizations / Health Libraries Association of British Columbia

Health Libraries Association of British Columbia (HLABC)
Parent: Canadian Health Libraries Association
c/o Devon Greyson, UBC Centre for Health Services & Policy Research, #201, 2206 East Mall, Vancouver BC V6T 1Z3
Tel: 604-822-7353; *Fax:* 604-822-5690
e-mail: devon-at-chspr.ubc.ca (President)
URL: www.hlabc.bc.ca
Social Media: www.facebook.com/group.php?gid=2347253553
Overview: A small provincial organization founded in 1980
Chief Officer(s):
Devon Greyson, President
devon-at-chspr.ubc.ca
Brooke Ballantyne-Scott, Vice-President, 604-520-4755
brooke.scott-at-fraserhealth.ca
Elisheba Muturi, Secretary, 604-660-1616
elisheba.muturi-at-gov.bc.ca
Anne Allgaier, Treasurer & Contact, Membership, 250-565-2219
Anne.allgaier-at-northernhealth.ca
Fees: $25 regular members; $15 students (after free first year); **Member Profile:** Librarians working in health services throughout British Columbia
Activities: Delivering continuing education programs for librarians
Publications: *Health Libraries Association of British Columbia Directory*
Type: Directory
Profile: Detailed listing of association members
Mission: To support the work of health librarians throughout British Columbia

Health Sciences Association of Alberta (HSAA) / Association des sciences de la santé de l'Alberta (ind.)
10212 - 112 St., Edmonton AB T5K 1M4
Tel: 780-488-0168; *Fax:* 780-488-0534
Toll-Free: 800-252-7904
URL: www.hsaa.ca
Overview: A medium-sized provincial organization founded in 1971
Chief Officer(s):
Elisabeth Ballermann, President
elisabethb@hsaa.ca
Patricia Heffel, Director, Administrative Services
patriciah@hsaa.ca
Lynette McAvoy, Director, Labour Relations
lynettem@hsaa.ca
Roni Hermanutz, Manager, Human Resources
ronih@hsaa.ca
Joanne Monro, Officer, Occupational Health & Safety
joannem@hsaa.ca
Scott Pattison, Officer, Communications, 780-405-4684
scottpat@hsaa.ca
Finances: *Funding Sources:* Membership dues; Merchandise sales
Membership: 17,000; **Member Profile:** Professional, paramedical technical, general support, & EMS employees in the public & private health care sectors of Alberta; *Committees:* Bylaws & Resolutions; Community Relations; Elections/Credentials; EMAC; Environmental; Finance; Human Rights & Equality; Labour Relations Appeals; Members' Benefits; OHS&W; Political Action / Education
Activities: Offering educational workshops; Awarding bursaries
Awards: Barb Mikulin Award (Award)
To honour an HSAA member who has made extraordinary efforts to improve the world
Meetings/Conferences:
For more information see Trade Shows, Conferences and Seminars Chapter
Health Sciences Association of Alberta 2011 40th Annual General Meeting
June 2011 Edmonton, AB
Health Sciences Association of Alberta Executive Meeting & Retirement Dinner
June 2011 Edmonton, AB
Health Sciences Association of Alberta Board / Governance Session, Board & Staff Golf Retreat, & Board Meeting
June 2011 Edmonton, AB
Health Sciences Association of Alberta Board Retreat & Stategic Planning
September 2011, AB
Health Sciences Association of Alberta Chairs Conference
September 2011 Edmonton, AB
Health Sciences Association of Alberta 2012 41st Annual General Meeting
May 2012, AB
Health Sciences Association of Alberta 2013 42nd Annual General Meeting
Other Conferences in 2013 2013, AB
Publications: *HSAA Challenger*
Type: Magazine *Frequency:* q. *Accepts Advertising:* Yes *Editor:* Scott Pattison (scottpat@hsaa.ca)
Profile: Feature articles, labour relations updates, HSAA activities, affiliate & member news, forthcoming workshops & events
Mission: To conduct activities as a labour union to enhance the quality of life for HSAA members & society

Health Sciences Association of Saskatchewan (HSAS) / Association des sciences de la santé de la Saskatchewan (ind.)
#42, 1736 Quebec Ave., Saskatoon SK S7K 1V9
Tel: 306-955-3399; *Fax:* 306-955-3396
Toll-Free: 888-565-3399
e-mail: hsasstoon@sasktel.net; hsasregina@sasktel.net
URL: www.hsa-sk.com
Overview: A medium-sized provincial organization founded in 1972
Chief Officer(s):
Bill Craik, Executive Director, 306-585-7757
bill.hsas@sasktel.net
Chris Driol, President
Cathy Dickson, Vice-President
diet.hsas@sasktel.net
Mary Spurr, Secretary
ot.hsas@sasktel.net
Karen Wasylenko, Treasurer
slp.hsas@sasktel.net
Membership: 2,900+; *Member Profile:* Health professionals from all health regions in Saskatchewan; *Committees:* Annual Convention; Constitutional; Emergency Fund; Grievance; Charitable Donations / Professional Contributions; Communications; Education Fund; Regional Council Development; Provincial Negotiating; Finance
Activities: Conducting public relations campaigns to increase public awareness about the profession; Presenting bursaries & scholarships
Mission: To conduct activities as an independent union representing its members who are health sciences professionals in Saskatchewan

Healthcare Information & Management Systems Society (HIMSS)
#500, 230 East Ohio St., Chicago IL 60611-3270 USA
Tel: 312-664-4467; *Fax:* 312-664-6143
e-mail: himss@himss.org; suggestions@himss.org; advocacy@himss.org
URL: www.himss.org
Overview: A large international organization
Chief Officer(s):
Barry P. Chaiken, MD, Chair
H. Stephen Lieber, CAE, President & Chief Executive Officer
slieber@himss.org
Dave Garets, FHIMSS, Executive VP & President/CEO, HIMSS Analytics
dgarets@himss.org
R. Norris Orms, FACHE, CAE, Exec. VP & COO & Executive Director, HIMSS Foundation
norms@himss.org
Carla Smith, NCMN, FHIMSS, Executive Vice-President
csmith@himss.org
Jeremy Bonfini, Global Services
jbonfini@himss.org
Membership: 20,000+
Publications: *Journal of Healthcare Information Management*
Type: Journal *Frequency:* q. *Accepts Advertising:* Yes *Editor:* M.A. Annecharico, Exec. Director *Price:* Free with HIMSS membership
Profile: Peer-reviewed journal for healthcare information & management systems professionals
HIMSS [Healthcare Information & Management Systems Society] Weekly Insider
Type: Newsletter *Frequency:* w. *Price:* Free with HIMSS membership
Profile: Current news from HIMSS, member profiles, & interviews
Healthcare IT News
Type: Newspaper *Frequency:* m. *Price:* Free with HIMSS membership
Profile: Features the HIMSS Insider newsletter, plus information about advocacy, education, & HIMSS happenings
HIMSS [Healthcare Information & Management Systems Society] Conference Proceedings
Frequency: a.
Profile: Proceedings from the annual HIMSS conference & exhibition
HIMSS [Healthcare Information & Management Systems Society] Clinical Informatics Insights
Type: Newsletter *Frequency:* m. *Price:* Free with HIMSS membership
Profile: Comprehensive articles about informatics across the continuum of care
Financial Edge
Type: Newsletter *Frequency:* m. *Price:* Free with HIMSS membership
Profile: HIMSS' financial systems e-newsletter, with current issues & trends related to financial systems & other technologies in healthcare
HIMSS [Healthcare Information & Management Systems Society] Pulse on Public Policy
Type: Newsletter *Frequency:* m. *Price:* Free with HIMSS membership
Profile: Information for HIMSS members, policymakers, regulators, & interested stakeholders
The Digital Office
Type: Newsletter *Frequency:* m. *Price:* Free with HIMSS membership
Profile: Information about health information technology & electronic medical records
HIMSS [Healthcare Information & Management Systems Society] HIELights
Type: Newsletter *Frequency:* m. *Price:* Free with HIMSS membership
Profile: Issues pertaining to health information exchange & regional health information organizations
Mission: To provide worldwide leadership in the optimal use of healthcare information technology & management systems in order to improve healthcare

Healthy Indoors Partnership (HIP) / Partenariat pour des environnements intérieurs sains
61 Forest Hills Avenue, Ottawa ON K2C 1P7
Tel: 613-224-3800
e-mail: mail@cullbridge.com
URL: www.cullbridge.com/Projects/Healthy_Indoors.htm
Overview: A small national organization
Chief Officer(s):
Jay Kassirer, President
kassirer@healthyindoors.com
Fees: $100
Mission: To involve private, public & not-for-profit organizations & individuals in the development, implementation & financing of a broad range of collaborative actions to improve indoor environments in Canada

Heating, Refrigeration & Air Conditioning Contractors Association Atlantic
Tel: 902-425-0475
Also Known As: HRAC Atlantic
Overview: A medium-sized provincial organization
Chief Officer(s):
John Sutherland, Contact
Dallas McDonald, Contact

Heating, Refrigeration & Air Conditioning Institute of Canada (HRAI) / Institut canadien du chauffage, de la climatisation et de la réfrigération (ICCCR)
Bldg. 1, #201, 2800 Skymark Ave., Mississauga ON L4W 5A6
Tel: 905-602-4700; *Fax:* 905-602-1197
Toll-Free: 800-267-2231
e-mail: hraimail@hrai.ca
URL: www.hrai.ca
Overview: A large national organization founded in 1969
Finances: *Annual Operating Budget:* $1.5 Million-$3 Million; *Funding Sources:* Membership dues; education programs
Staff: 24 staff member(s)
Membership: 900 corporate; *Member Profile:* Voting members divided into three divisions based on industry sector - manufacturers, wholesalers & contractors; Associate members include utilities, municipalities, manufacturers' agents & distributors, builders, educational institutions, building maintenance, other associations, & consultants; *Committees:* C.M.X. Show; Technical; Education
Activities: Owns the Canadian Mechanicals Exposition (C.M.X.), a national trade show held every two years in Toronto

at the end of March; educational programs provide industry members with the technical & management competence required to design & install HVAC systems & operate successful HVAC businesses
Mission: To serve the HRAI membership & HVACR industry in Canada by facilitating industry solutions, coordinating a strong national membership, representing the industry to their publics, conducting accountable association activities, providing quality member/customer services, & educating & training industry members

Henry A. Wallace Center for Agricultural & Environmental Policy at Winrock International
#1200, 1621 Kent St. North, Arlington VA 22209-2134 USA
Tel: 703-525-9430; *Fax:* 703-525-1744
e-mail: wallacecenter@winrock.org
URL: www.winrock.org/wallace; www.wallacecenter.org
Also Known As: Wallace Center
Previous Name: Institute for Alternative Agriculture
Overview: A small national charitable organization founded in 1983
Chief Officer(s):
Erin Caricofe, Program Assistant
John Fisk, Director
Finances: *Annual Operating Budget:* $500,000-$1.5 Million
Staff: 10 staff member(s)
Membership: 995; *Fees:* US$16 individual; *Member Profile:* Farmers, researchers, Extension personnel, policy makers & consumers
Activities: Research; policy analysis & development; education & outreach; scientific & general audience publications; symposia
Mission: To serve as publisher of reliable scientific information on alternative agriculture; to sponsor research & education outreach programs; to be a voice for alternative agriculture; to act as a contact for farmers & others who seek information on diversified, sustainable farming systems; to encourage & facilitate the adoption of low-cost, resource-conserving & environmentally sound farming methods

Herb Society of Manitoba
15 Conservatory Dr., Winnipeg MB R3P 2N5
Tel: 204-785-8690
e-mail: herbsocietymb@mts.net
URL: www.herbsocietymb.com
Overview: A small national organization founded in 1995
Chief Officer(s):
Shelley Kaptein, President
Fees: $20 single; $25 family; $100 business
Activities: *Awareness Events:* International Herb Day, Oct. 14
Mission: To promote knowledge, use & enjoyment of herbs through education, programs, research & sharing the experience of its members with the community

Heritage Agricultural Society
PO Box 2188, 5411 - 51 St., Stony Plain AB T7Z 1X7
Tel: 780-963-2777; *Fax:* 780-963-0233
URL: www.multicentre.org
Also Known As: Multicultural Heritage Centre
Overview: A small local charitable organization founded in 1974
Finances: *Annual Operating Budget:* $500,000-$1.5 Million; *Funding Sources:* Alberta Museums Association
Staff: 20 staff member(s); 180 volunteer(s)
Membership: 250; *Fees:* $10
Activities: Tours; school programs for classes K-12; farm demonstrations; farmers' market; *Library:* Wild Rose Library; Open to public
Mission: The Society is a non-profit organization dedicated to the preservation of the region's cultural heritage. It acts as custodian to the Multicultural Heritage Centre, a living museum of 2 historic buildings which reflect local history & Western Canadian pioneer life. The Society is a registered charity, BN: 107478760RR0001.

Heritage Association of Antigonish
20 East Main St., Antigonish NS B2G 2E9
Tel: 902-863-6160
e-mail: antheritage@parl.ns.ca
Overview: A small local organization founded in 1982
Membership: 60; *Fees:* $7 individual; $10 family
Member of: Federation of the Nova Scotian Heritage

Heritage Canada Foundation (HCF) / Fondation Héritage Canada
5 Blackburn Ave., Ottawa ON K1N 8A2
Tel: 613-237-1066; *Fax:* 613-237-5987
Toll-Free: 866-964-1066
e-mail: heritagecanada@heritagecanada.org
URL: www.heritagecanada.org
Overview: A large national charitable organization founded in 1973
Finances: *Annual Operating Budget:* $250,000-$500,000; *Funding Sources:* Grants; individuals; corporate; endowment
Staff: 20 staff member(s); 3 volunteer(s)
Membership: 2,400 voting members; 100,000 network members; *Fees:* $35 individual; $25 student; $70 family; $150 organization
Activities: *Awareness Events:* Heritage Day, 3rd Monday of Feb.; National Flag of Canada Day, Feb. 15; *Internships:* Yes; *Speaker Service:* Yes; *Library:* Yes, open by appointment
Awards: Prince of Wales Prize (Award)
Established in 1999, awarded annually to a municipal government which has shown exemplary commitment to heritage preservation within its jurisdiction
The Heritage Canada Journalism Prize (Award)
Awarded annually to a journalist, working in either the print or electronic media, whose coverage of heritage issues is judged to be outstanding
Heritage Canada Corporate Prize (Award)
Presented annually to any incorporated business, sale proprietorship or partnership, that demonstrates outstanding stewardship of its built heritage
Gabrielle Léger Award (Award)
Recognizes outstanding work in architectural conservation in Canada; this is an annual national award to an individual who has contributed outstanding community service in the cause of heritage conservation
Achievement Awards (Award)
Established 1989, these awards recognize individuals or groups for achievements in the conservation of heritage in the natural or cultural environments; designed to be presented jointly by Heritage Canada & established provincial or territorial umbrella groups or associations that are members of Heritage Canada & that have juried awards programs & awards ceremonies; each group or association, called a partner, will be fully responsible for choosing its candidate within prescribed criteria & eligibility rules; in this way, Heritage Canada also recognizes these partners for their dedication & commitment to excellence in heritage preservation
Lieutenant Governor's Award (Award)
Established 1979 to recognize outstanding work in architectural conservation on a provincial level by an individual or group
Eligibility: It must be demonstrated that the applicant's continuous efforts in the field of heritage conservation have benefited the province where the foundation's annual meeting is being held; applicants must be sponsored by an organized heritage group &/or elected officials at any level of government
Mission: To foster & ensure the understanding, protection & sustainable evolution of Canada's heritage buildings & historic places; Affiliation(s): Canadian Heritage Network

L'Héritage canadien du Québec (HCQ) / The Canadian Heritage of Québec (CHQ)
1181, rue de la Montagne, Montréal QC H3G 1Z2
Tél: 514-393-1417; *Téléc:* 514-393-9444
Courriel: chq@total.net
URL: www.hcq-chq.org/french/
Aperçu: *Dimension:* petite; *Envergure:* provinciale; fondée en 1960
Finances: *Budget de fonctionnement annuel:* $250,000-$500,000
Personnel: 1 membre(s) du personnel
Membre: 250; *Montant de la cotisation:* $50 (Ami/Amie)
Mission: Organisme qui se consacre à la préservation des terrains & des constructions revêtant une valeur historique/architecturale dans la province du Québec

Heritage Foundation of Newfoundland & Labrador
PO Box 5171, 1 Springdale St., St. John's NL A1C 5V5
Tel: 709-739-1892; *Fax:* 709-739-5413
Toll-Free: 888-739-1892
e-mail: info@heritagefoundation.ca
URL: www.heritagefoundation.ca
Overview: A small provincial charitable organization founded in 1984
Finances: *Annual Operating Budget:* $100,000-$250,000; *Funding Sources:* Provincial government; private
Staff: 3 staff member(s)
Membership: 11; *Member Profile:* Appointed Board by Lt. Governor in council; *Committees:* Buildings; Grants; Finance; Public Relations; Policy
Activities: Education & advisory service in restoration of older structures; *Library:* Yes, open by appointment
Mission: To stimulate an understanding of & appreciation for the architectural heritage of Newfoundland & Labrador; to support & contribute to the preservation, maintenance & restoration of buildings of architectural or historical significance; to designate buildings & structures as Registered Heritage Structures; may make grants for purpose of preservation, maintenance, or restoration (Deadline for submitting grant application is Mar. 1 & Sept. 1 of each year); *Member of:* Heritage Canada; Newfoundland & Labrador Homebuilders Association; Heritage Coalition of Newfoundland & Labrador; Newfoundland Historic Trust

Héritage Montréal (HM)
#0500, 100, rue Sherbrooke est, Montréal QC H2X 1C3
Tél: 514-286-2662; *Téléc:* 514-286-1661
URL: www.heritagemontreal.org
Également appelé: Fondation Héritage Montréal
Aperçu: *Dimension:* moyenne; *Envergure:* locale; Organisme sans but lucratif; fondée en 1975
Membre(s) du bureau directeur:
Marie Senécal-Tremblay, Directrice générale (par intérim)
Finances: *Budget de fonctionnement annuel:* $250,000-$500,000
Personnel: 5 membre(s) du personnel; 30 bénévole(s)
Membre: 700; *Montant de la cotisation:* 50$ (individuel); 125-500 (corporatif); *Comités:* Patrimoine et aménagement
Activités: Promenades architecturales; cours de rénovation; conférences; recherches; publications; *Bibliothèque:* Oui, Bibliothèque publique
Mission: Encourager auprès des décideurs publics et privés la transformation des attitudes et favoriser l'introduction et la mise en oeuvre des méthodes et des stratégies permettant la conservation du patrimoine urbain architectural de Montréal, le patrimoine naturel, les espaces publics ainsi que l'environnement culturel et social; *Membre de:* Forum québécois du patrimoine; Conseil régional de l'environnement de Montréal; Affiliation(s): International Council on Monuments & Sites

Heritage Society of British Columbia
914 Garthland Pl. West, Victoria BC V9A 4J5
Tel: 250-384-4840
e-mail: hsbc@islandnet.com
URL: www.heritagebc.ca
Also Known As: Dogwood Heritage Society of British Columbia
Overview: A medium-sized provincial organization founded in 1981
Chief Officer(s):
Rick Goodacre, Executive Director
Jonathan Yardley, President
yardleyj@telus.net
Leslie Gilbert, Sec.-Treas.
leslie.gilbert@cityofportmoody.com
Activities: Presenting awards; Organizing conferences; Preserving historical sites, such as trails; Restoring the built environment; Funding community participation in workshops; *Awareness Events:* Heritage Week, Feb.
Mission: To represent groups involved with heritage projects & issues; Affiliation(s): Heritage Canada

Heritage Trust of Nova Scotia
PO Box 36111, Stn. RPO Spring Garden, 1588 Barrington St., Halifax NS B3J 3S9
Tel: 902-423-4807; *Fax:* 902-423-3977
e-mail: heritage.trust@ns.sympatico.ca
URL: www.htns.ca
Overview: A medium-sized provincial charitable organization founded in 1959
Finances: *Annual Operating Budget:* $50,000-$100,000
Membership: 450; *Fees:* $5 student; $15 single; $20 family; $10 senior; $15 senior couple; $25 institutions; $500 life membership; *Member Profile:* Individuals & groups who are committed to the protection & rehabilitation of Nova Scotia's heritage; *Committees:* Membership; Programme (Lectures); Programme (Tours); Projects; Research; Property Management; Publications; Publicity; Finance; Communities; Awards; Newsletter
Activities: Providing a public lecture series; Offering input on legislative policy at the municipal & provincial levels; *Speaker Service:* Yes; *Library:* Yes, Open to public
Awards: Heritage Trust of Nova Scotia Built Heritage Award (Award)
Presented for outstanding contribution to building restoration
Contact: Joyce McCulloch, HTNS Awards Chair
Publications: *The Griffin* [a publication of the Heritage Trust of Nova Scotia]

Associations/Organizations / Heritage Winnipeg Corp.

Type: Newsletter *Frequency:* q. *Price:* Free with Heritage Trust of Nova Scotia membership
Mission: To promote interest in the preservation of historic structures & sites in Nova Scotia; *Member of:* Federation of the Nova Scotian Heritage; *Affiliation(s):* Heritage Canada

Heritage Winnipeg Corp. (HW)
#509, 63 Albert St., Winnipeg MB R3B 1G4
Tel: 204-942-2663; *Fax:* 204-942-2094
e-mail: info@heritagewinnipeg.com
URL: www.heritagewinnipeg.com
Overview: A small local charitable organization founded in 1978
Finances: Annual Operating Budget: Less than $50,000;
Funding Sources: Private donations; provincial government; city of Winnipeg; membership dues; fundraisers
Staff: 1 staff member(s); Dec- volunteer(s)
Membership: 170; *Fees:* $20 individual; $15 student/senior; $30 family/organization; corporate $100-$1,000; *Committees:* Public Service & Information; Legal & Economic Instruments; Advocacy; Preservation Awards; Education
Activities: Museum & Heritage Exposition; heritage auctions; annual preservation awards; school presentations; walking tours; Manitoba Day events; heritage fairs; Doors Open Winnipeg; *Awareness Events:* Heritage Preservation Awards; Doors Open Winnipeg; 3rd Mon. in Feb.; *Speaker Service:* Yes; *Library:* Yes, Open to public, open by appointment
Awards: Architectural Conservation Award (Award)
Institutional Architectural Conservation Award (Award)
Residential Architectural Conservation Award (Award)
Distinguished Service Award (Award)
Youth Awards (Award)
Mission: To promote & encourage preservation of historic sites & structures in Winnipeg; to educate the public on heritage issues & make them aware of the richness of their material culture; to advocate & lobby on behalf of heritage related issues; *Member of:* Heritage Canada; Manitoba Historical Society; St. Boniface Historical Society; Manitoba Heritage Federation; *Affiliation(s):* Downtown Biz; Exchange Biz, Destination Winnipeg; Parks Canada; City of Winnipeg; Province of Manitoba

Hike Ontario
#400, 165 Dundas St. West, Mississauga ON L5B 2N6
Tel: 905-277-4453
Toll-Free: 800-894-7249
e-mail: info@hikeontario.com
URL: www.hikeontario.com
Overview: A medium-sized provincial charitable organization founded in 1974
Finances: Funding Sources: Membership dues; Grants; Sponsorships; Donations
Member Profile: Not-for-profit trail building & hiking organizations; Individuals; Corporations, government agencies, & organizations other than hiking or trail building organizations
Activities: Providing hiking information & services throughout Ontario; Offering the Hike Leader Certification Program & the Young Hikers Program; Supporting trails across the province; Advocating for clubs; Liaising with government; Promoting research & education into the health benefits of walking & hiking; Presenting awards to celebrate dedicated hikers; *Awareness Events:* Ontario Hiking Week, Sept.
Meetings/Conferences:
For more information see Trade Shows, Conferences and Seminars Chapter
Hike Ontario 2011 Annual Summit
October 2011, ON
Mission: To act as the voice for hikers & walkers in Ontario; To encourage hiking, walking & trail development in Ontario; To promote trail maintenance. best practices, & safe hiking; To enhance environmental awareness, conservation & sustainable trails; *Affiliation(s):* Ontario Trails Council (OTC); Hike Canada En Marche

Hope for Wildlife Society
PO Box 1, 5909 Hwy. 207, #14 R.R.#2, Head of Chezzetcook NS B0J 1N0
Tel: 902-452-3339
e-mail: info@hopeforwildlife.net
URL: www.hopeforwildlife.net
Overview: A small provincial organization founded in 1997
Chief Officer(s):
Hope Swinimer, CVPM, Founder & Director
Mission: Specializing in the care, treatment and rehabilitation of injured or orphaned native fur bearing mammals, sea birds and songbirds both indigenous to the Nova Scotia area as well as non-indigenous species and pets.

Horticulture Nova Scotia (HNS)
Kentville Agricultural Centre, 32 Main St., Kentville NS B4N 1J5
Tel: 902-678-9335; *Fax:* 902-678-1280
e-mail: hortns@ns.sympatico.ca
URL: www.hortns.com
Previous Name: Vegetable & Potato Producers' Association of Nova Scotia
Overview: A small provincial organization founded in 1998
Finances: Annual Operating Budget: $50,000-$100,000;
Funding Sources: Membership fees
Staff: 1 staff member(s); 8 volunteer(s)
Membership: 100+; *Fees:* Scale based on acreage & gross income; *Member Profile:* Vegetable & berry growers; agribusiness; *Committees:* Research; Human Resources; Agriculture Awareness; Marketing; Conference
Activities: Administers NS Potato Marketing Board & NS Processing Pea & Bean Growers Marketing Board
Mission: To enhance collaborative efforts among members which will strengthen & provide leadership to the horticultural industry; *Affiliation(s):* NS Federation of Agriculture; Canadian Horticultural Council

Housing & Urban Development Association of Canada *See* Canadian Home Builders' Association

H.R. MacMillan Space Centre Society (HRMSC)
1100 Chestnut St., Vancouver BC V6J 3J9
Tel: 604-738-7827; *Fax:* 604-736-5665
e-mail: info@spacecentre.ca
URL: www.hrmacmillanspacecentre.com
Also Known As: H.R. MacMillan Planetarium
Previous Name: Pacific Space Centre Society
Overview: A medium-sized local charitable organization founded in 1968
Finances: Annual Operating Budget: $1.5 Million-$3 Million;
Funding Sources: Government; foundations; corporate sponsors; individuals; admissions to facility
Staff: 40 staff member(s)
Membership: 1,000-4,999; *Fees:* $30 individual; $55 couple; $80 family
Activities: New star show productions; teacher workshops; classroom activities; community astronomy; Starlab; video-conferences
Mission: To educate, inspire & evoke a sense of wonder about the universe, our planet & space exploration; *Member of:* Canadian Association of Science Centres; *Affiliation(s):* Canadian Museums Association

Human Factors Association of Canada *See* Association of Canadian Ergonomists

Hydrographic Society *See* International Federation of Hydrographic Societies

Hydro-Québec Foundation for the Environment *Voir* Fondation Hydro-Québec pour l'environnement

ICOMOS Canada
PO Box 737, Stn. B, Ottawa ON K1P 5P8
Tel: 613-749-0971
e-mail: canada@icomos.org
URL: www.canada.icomos.org
Also Known As: International Council on Monuments & Sites Canada
Overview: A medium-sized international organization founded in 1975
Finances: Annual Operating Budget: Less than $50,000
Staff: 1 staff member(s)
Membership: 500; *Fees:* $85 individual; $30 students & friends; institutional available; *Member Profile:* Conservation professionals & advocates concerned with developing & promoting, through international exchange, the highest professional standards of practice in the conservation of the built environment; *Committees:* National Committees which bring together professionals in each country
Activities: Researching; Communicating; Providing professional services
Publications: eCOMoS [a publication of the ICOMOS Canada]
Type: Newsletter
Mission: To further the conservation, protection, rehabilitation, & enhancement of monuments, groups of buildings & sites; To encourage primary research in many important fields; *Affiliation(s):* UNESCO; International Centre for the Study of the Preservation & Restoration of Cultural Property (ICCROM)

Independent Lumber Dealers Co-operative (ILDC)
#100, 596 Kingston Rd. West, Ajax ON L1T 3A2
Tel: 905-428-0700; *Fax:* 905-428-0690
e-mail: ildc@idirect.com
URL: www.ildc.com
Overview: A small local organization founded in 1964
Finances: Annual Operating Budget: $250,000-$500,000
Membership: 22; *Member Profile:* Independent home improvement chains
Member of: SPANCAN

Independent Power Producers Association of British Columbia
#26, 181 Ravine Dr., Port Moody BC V3H 4T3
Tel: 604-461-4778; *Fax:* 604-469-3717
e-mail: steve.davis@ippbc.com
URL: www.ippbc.com
Overview: A small provincial organization
Chief Officer(s):
Steve Davis, President
Mission: To develop a viable independent power industry in British Columbia that serves the public interest by providing cost-effective electricity through the efficient & environmentally responsible development of the Province's energy resources

Independent Power Producers Society of Alberta (IPPSA)
#400, 505 - 8th Ave. SW, Calgary AB T2P 1G2
Tel: 403-282-8811; *Fax:* 403-256-8342
e-mail: Evan.Bahry@ippsa.com
URL: www.ippsa.com
Overview: A small provincial organization
Chief Officer(s):
Evan Bahry, Executive Director
Membership: 185; *Fees:* $250-$10,000; *Member Profile:* Power suppliers, retailers & supporting industries;

Independent Power Producers Society of Ontario (IPPSO)
See Association of Power Producers of Ontario

Indian Agricultural Program of Ontario (IAPO)
PO Box 100, 220 North St., Stirling ON K0K 3E0
Tel: 613-395-5505; *Fax:* 613-395-5510
Toll-Free: 800-363-0329
e-mail: iapo-lambeth@on.aibn.com
URL: www.indianag.on.ca
Overview: A small provincial organization founded in 1984
Chief Officer(s):
William J. Brant, Chair
Beth Wismer, General Manager
beth@indianag.on.ca
Member Profile: Status Indians registered in Ontario with businesses on or off reserve
Activities: Loans program; agriculture advisory service; seminars; conferences
Publications: Native Agri Update
Type: Newsletter *Frequency:* m.
Mission: IAPO is a non-profit corporation that fosters sustainable economic growth of Ontario First Nations People through agricultural programs involved in all sectors, including dairy, beef, swine, poultry, crops, farm retail, repair, & agri-forestry.

Industrial Accident Victims Group of Ontario (IAVGO)
#203, 489 College St., Toronto ON M6G 1A5
Tel: 416-924-6477
Toll-Free: 877-230-6311
URL: www.iavgo.org
Overview: A medium-sized provincial charitable organization founded in 1975
Finances: Annual Operating Budget: $100,000-$250,000
Staff: 8 staff member(s)
Fees: $10
Activities: Library: Yes, open by appointment
Mission: Our community legal clinic provides free services to injured workers in Ontario including legal advice, legal representation, public legal education, advocacy training and community development.

Industrial Gas Users Association Inc. (IGUA) / Association des consommateurs industriels de gaz (ACIG)
#1201, 99 Metcalfe St., Ottawa ON K1P 6L7
Tel: 613-236-8021; *Fax:* 613-230-9531
URL: www.igua.ca

Overview: A medium-sized national organization founded in 1973
Finances: *Annual Operating Budget:* $500,000-$1.5 Million; *Funding Sources:* Membership dues
Staff: 3 staff member(s)
Membership: 39 corporate; *Fees:* Based on gas consumption, $1,200-$36,099; *Member Profile:* Open to end users of natural gas
Mission: To provide a coordinated & effective voice for industrial firms depending on natural gas as fuel or feedstock; to represent industrial users of natural gas before regulatory boards & governments

Industrial Instrument Manufacturers Association *See* Canadian Process Control Association

Industrial Truck Association (ITA)
#460, 1750 K St. NW, Washington DC 20006 USA
Tel: 202-296-9880; *Fax:* 202-296-9884
URL: www.indtrk.org
Overview: A medium-sized international organization
Finances: *Annual Operating Budget:* $1.5 Million-$3 Million
Staff: 5 staff member(s)
Membership: 100; *Fees:* Varies; *Member Profile:* Manufacturers of forklifts & suppliers
Mission: Represents the manufacturers of lift trucks & their suppliers who do business in Canada, the United States or Mexico

l'Industrie forestière de l'Ontario *See* Ontario Forest Industries Association

Infectious Diseases Society of America (IDSA)
#300, 1300 Wilson Blvd., Arlington VA 22209 USA
Tel: 703-299-0200; *Fax:* 703-299-0204
e-mail: membership@idsociety.org
URL: www.idsociety.org
Overview: A large international organization
Chief Officer(s):
Anne Gershon, MD, FIDSA, President
James M. Hughes, MD, FIDSA, Vice-President
William Schaffner, MD, FIDSA, Secretary
Barbara E. Murray, MD, FIDSA, Treasurer
Member Profile: Physicians; Scientists; Health care professionals who specialize in infectious diseases
Publications: *IDSA [Infectious Diseases Society of America] News*
Type: Newsletter
Profile: Society activities, education, research, & prevention & treatment advances
Clinical Infectious Diseases
Type: Journal
Profile: State-of-the-art clinical articles, medical & legal issues, review articles, & studies in infectious disease research
Journal of Infectious Diseases
Type: Journal
Profile: Original research about the pathogenesis, diagnosis, & treatment of infectious diseases
Mission: To improve the health of individuals, communities, & society; To promote excellence in education, research, public health, prevention, & patient care

Infirmières et infirmiers en santé communautaire au Canada *See* Community Health Nurses of Canada

INFORM Inc.
5 Hanover Sq., 19th Fl., New York NY 10004 USA
Tel: 212-361-2400; *Fax:* 212-361-2412
e-mail: inform@informinc.org
URL: www.informinc.org
Overview: A medium-sized international charitable organization founded in 1974
Chief Officer(s):
Virginia Ramsey, President
Julia J. Mair, Director, Foundation & Corporate Relations
Sophie Cardona, Manager, Communications & Operations
Finances: *Annual Operating Budget:* $1.5 Million-$3 Million; *Funding Sources:* Individual donors; Foundations; Government; Corporate contributions; Book sales
Staff: 25 staff member(s); 5-10 volunteer(s)
Membership: 1,000; *Fees:* $35
Activities: Researching strategies to prevent chemical hazards & to develop sustainable products & practices; *Internships:* Yes; *Speaker Service:* Yes
Mission: To examine the effects of business practices on the environment & human health; *Member of:* Earthshare

Environmental Activity: Identifying ways of doing business that ensure environmentally sustainable economic growth

Information Technology Research Centre *See* Communications & Information Technology Ontario

Ingénieurs Canada *See* Engineers Canada

Ingénieurs sans Frontières *See* Engineers Without Borders

Ingersoll District Nature Club
RR#1, Salford ON N0J 1W0
URL: www.ingersollnature.ca
Overview: A small local charitable organization
Finances: *Annual Operating Budget:* Less than $50,000
Membership: 45; *Fees:* $10 youth; $15 single; $25 family
Mission: To promote the enjoyment of nature through environmental appreciation & conservation; to encourage wise use & conservation of natural resources; to promote environmental protection; *Member of:* Federation of Ontario Naturalists

L'Initiative torontoise de biotechnologie *See* Toronto Biotechnology Initiative

Innovation Management Association of Canada (IMAC) / Association canadienne de la gestion de l'innovation (ACGI)
c/o CATAAlliance, #416, 207 Bank St., Ottawa ON K2P 2N2
Tel: 613-236-6550; *Fax:* 613-236-8189
e-mail: info@cata.ca
URL: www.cata.ca/imac/
Previous Name: Canadian Research Management Association
Overview: A small national organization founded in 1996
Finances: *Annual Operating Budget:* $50,000-$100,000
Membership: 240; *Fees:* $225 individual; *Member Profile:* Research, technology management & innovation leaders; *Committees:* Program; Research Practices
Mission: To enhance the productivity & effectiveness of Canadian research development & technology-based innovations

Inside Education
#200, 10235 - 124 St., Edmonton AB T5N 1P9
Tel: 780-421-1497; *Fax:* 780-425-4506
Toll-Free: 888-421-1497
e-mail: info@insideeducation.ca
URL: www.insideeducation.ca
Previous Name: FEESA - An Environmental Education Society
Overview: A medium-sized provincial charitable organization founded in 1985
Chief Officer(s):
Steve McIsaac, Executive Director
Finances: *Annual Operating Budget:* $500,000-$1.5 Million; *Funding Sources:* Industry 50%; government 40%; private/users 10%
Staff: 9 staff member(s); 1000 volunteer(s)
Membership: 300 associates; 18 members (Board); *Fees:* $15 student; $25 individual; $50 institution; $250 corporate
Activities: Promotion of environmental education in formal & public education areas; presentations, conferences & conventions; coordination & development of education resources that focus on a variety of environmental & educational needs; teacher-training institutes focusing on a variety of environmental issues; *Awareness Events:* Environment Week, 1st week of June
Mission: To empower all Albertans to make informed choices about the environment by providing bias-balanced environmental education; to communicate, coordinate & initiate the development & support of bias-balanced environmental education in Alberta through a variety of programs & services; to ensure that the views of business, industry, government, the environment & community sector are represented in any programming or communication; *Member of:* Environmental Outdoor Education Council; Alberta Environmental Network; Canadian Environmental Network; *Affiliation(s):* North American Association for Environmental Education; EECOM

Institut aéronautique et spatial du Canada *See* Canadian Aeronautics & Space Institute

Institut agréé de la logistique et des transports Amérique du Nord *See* Chartered Institute of Logistics and Transport in North America

Institut agricole du Canada *See* Agricultural Institute of Canada

Institut Archéologique d'Amérique *See* Archaeological Institute of America

L'Institut canadien *See* The Canadian Institute

Institut canadien d'information sur la santé *See* Canadian Institute for Health Information

Institut canadien de formation de l'énergie *See* Canadian Institute for Energy Training

Institut canadien de la construction en acier *See* Canadian Institute of Steel Construction

Institut canadien de la santé animale *See* Canadian Animal Health Institute

Institut canadien de la tôle d'acier pour le bâtiment *See* Canadian Sheet Steel Building Institute

Institut canadien de plomberie et de chauffage *See* Canadian Institute of Plumbing & Heating

Institut canadien de science et technologie alimentaires *See* Canadian Institute of Food Science & Technology

Institut canadien des comptables agréés *See* Canadian Institute of Chartered Accountants

Institut canadien des engrais *See* Canadian Fertilizer Institute

L'Institut canadien des ingénieurs *See* The Engineering Institute of Canada

Institut Canadien des inspecteurs en santé publique *See* Canadian Institute of Public Health Inspectors

Institut canadien des mines, de la métallurgie et du pétrole *See* Canadian Institute of Mining, Metallurgy & Petroleum

Institut canadien des urbanistes *See* Canadian Institute of Planners

Institut canadien du béton préfabriqué et précontraint *See* Canadian Precast / Prestressed Concrete Institute

Institut canadien du chauffage, de la climatisation et de la réfrigération *See* Heating, Refrigeration & Air Conditioning Institute of Canada

Institut canadien du droit des ressources *See* Canadian Institute of Resources Law

Institut canadien du droit et de la politique de l'environnement *See* Canadian Institute for Environmental Law & Policy

Institut canadien du trafic et du transport *See* Canadian Institute of Traffic & Transportation

Institut canadien pour la sécurité des patients *See* Canadian Patient Safety Institute

Institut C.D. Howe *See* C.D. Howe Institute

Institut circumpolaire canadien *See* Canadian Circumpolar Institute

Institut de chimie du Canada *See* Chemical Institute of Canada

Institut de développement urbain du Canada *See* Urban Development Institute of Canada

Institut de l'énergie et de l'environnement de la Francophonie (IEPF)
56, rue St-Pierre, 3e étage, Québec QC G1K 4A1
Tél: 418-692-5727; *Télec:* 418-692-5644
Courriel: iepf@iepf.org
URL: www.iepf.org
Aperçu: *Dimension:* moyenne; *Envergure:* internationale; Organisme sans but lucratif; fondée en 1988
Membre(s) du bureau directeur:
Fatimata Dia Touré, Directrice
Finances: *Budget de fonctionnement annuel:* $3 Million-$5 Million
Personnel: 17 membre(s) du personnel
Activités: *Bibliothèque:* Service information et documentation
Mission: Contribuer au renforcement des capacités nationales et au développement des partenariats dans les domaines de l'énergie et de l'environnement; *Membre de:* Agence de la Francophonie

Institut de la fourrure du Canada *See* Fur Institute of Canada

Associations/Organizations / Institut de recherche en biologie végétale

Institut de radioprotection du Canada *See* Radiation Safety Institute of Canada

Institut de recherche en biologie végétale (IRBV) / Plant Biology Research Institute (PBRI)
4101, rue Sherbrooke est, Montréal QC H1X 2B2
Tél: 514-343-2121
Courriel: irbv@irbv.umontreal.ca
URL: www.irbv.umontreal.ca
Aperçu: Dimension: petite; *Envergure: locale; Organisme sans but lucratif; fondée en 1990*
Membre(s) du bureau directeur:
Anne Bruneau, Directrice
Finances: *Budget de fonctionnement annuel:* $1.5 Million-$3 Million
Personnel: 100 membre(s) du personnel
Membre: 1-99
Activités: *Service de conférenciers:* Oui; *Bibliothèque:* Oui, Not open to the public
Mission: To develop a centre of excellence in plant biology; both in fundamental research and its applicaitons; train students in plant biology at the master, doctoral, and post-doctoral levels; further training and knowledge of its researchers and technical personnel; promote the technological transfer of its scientific research results to users; provide complementary services to the community in fields relevant to plant biology, where expertise in the field is lacking.

Institut de recherche en politiques publiques *See* Institute for Research on Public Policy

Institut de recherche et de développement en agroenvironnement *See* Research & Development Institute for the Agri-Environment

Institut de recherche Robert-Sauvé en santé et en sécurité du travail (IRSST) / Robert Sauvé Occupational Health & Safety Research Institute
505, boul de Maisonneuve ouest, 15e étage, Montréal QC H3A 3C2
Tél: 514-288-1551; *Téléc:* 514-288-7636
Courriel: communications@irsst.qc.ca
URL: www.irsst.qc.ca
Aperçu: Dimension: moyenne; *Envergure: provinciale; fondée en 1980*
Finances: *Budget de fonctionnement annuel:* Plus de $5 Million *Fonds:* Près de 85 % des revenus proviennent d'une subvention de la Commission de la santé et de la sécurité du travail du Québec (CSST)
Personnel: 130 membre(s) du personnel
Activités: *Bibliothèque:* Oui, Bibliothèque publique
Mission: Contribuer par la recherche et le développement à l'amélioration de la santé et de la sécurité des travailleurs et plus spécifiquement, à l'élimination à la source des dangers pour leur santé, leur sécurité et leur intégrité physique ainsi qu'à la réadaptation des travailleurs victimes d'accidents ou de maladies professionnelles; fournir au Réseau public québécois de la prévention en santé et en sécurité du travail - composé de CSST, des Centres locaux de services communautaires, des Régies de la santé et des services sociaux et des associations sectorielles paritaires - les services et l'expertise nécessaires à leur action; diffuser les connaissances issues de ces recherches et de ces expertises auprès des milieux de travail et en favoriser le transfert; accorder des bourses d'études supérieures en santé et en sécurité du travail; agir comme laboratoire de référence au Québec, dans le domaine de l'hygiène industrielle.; *Affiliation(s):* International Occupational Safety & Health Information Centre

Institut de recherche sur le travail et la santé *See* Institute for Work & Health

L'Institut des agronomes du Nouveau-Brunswick *See* New Brunswick Institute of Agrologists

Institut des planificateurs professionnels de l'Ontario *See* Ontario Professional Planners Institute

Institut des Urbanistes de l'atlantique *See* Atlantic Planners Institute

Institut forestier du Canada *See* Canadian Institute of Forestry

Institut international de l'ocean *See* International Ocean Institute

Institut international du développement durable *See* International Institute for Sustainable Development

Institut pour tuyaux de tôle ondulée *See* Corrugated Steel Pipe Institute

Institute for Alternative Agriculture *See* Henry A. Wallace Center for Agricultural & Environmental Policy at Winrock International

Institute for Local Self-Reliance (ILSR)
927 - 15th St. NW, 4th Fl., Washington DC 20005 USA
Tel: 202-898-1610; *Fax:* 202-898-1612
e-mail: info@ilsr.org
URL: www.ilsr.org
Overview: A medium-sized international organization founded in 1974
Chief Officer(s):
Neil Seldman, President
David Morris, Vice President
Finances: *Funding Sources:* Foundations; individuals; speaking; technical assistance
Staff: 11 staff member(s); 1 volunteer(s)
Activities: *Internships:* Yes; *Speaker Service:* Yes
Mission: Provides innovative strategies & models to support environmentally sound community development; works with citizens & policymakers to meet local needs; provides the tools to increase economic effectiveness, to reduce waste & decrease impacts on the environment, & provide for local ownership in infrastructure & resources; *Affiliation(s):* Healthy Building Network; Black Environment Justice Network; GrassRoots Recycling Network

Institute for Research on Public Policy / Institut de recherche en politiques publiques
#200, 1470, rue Peel, Montréal QC H3A 1T1
Tel: 514-985-2461; *Fax:* 514-985-2559
e-mail: irpp@irpp.org
URL: www.irpp.org
Overview: A medium-sized national organization founded in 1972
Activities: *Library:* Yes, Not open to the public
Mission: Independent, nonprofit research institution seeking to improve public policy in Canada by generating research, providing insight and sparking debate that will contribute to the public policy decision-making process and strengthen the quality of public policy decisions made by Canadian governments, citizens, institutions and organizations.

Institute for Risk Research (IRR)
University of Waterloo, 200 University Ave. West, Waterloo ON N2L 3G1
Tel: 519-888-4567; *Fax:* 519-725-4834
e-mail: irr-neram@uwaterloo.ca
URL: www.irr-neram.ca
Overview: A small local organization founded in 1982
Chief Officer(s):
John Shortreed, Director
Finances: *Funding Sources:* Corporations; government grants & contracts
Staff: 3 staff member(s)
Membership: 185; *Fees:* $25
Activities: Includes Environmental Risk Management shortcourse; environmental conferences; *Speaker Service:* Yes; *Library:* Yes, Open to public, open by appointment
Mission: To promote safety for Canadians by improving the understanding of risk & risk policy decisions

Institute for Work & Health (IWH) / Institut de recherche sur le travail et la santé
#800, 481 University Ave., Toronto ON M5G 2E9
Tel: 416-927-2027; *Fax:* 416-927-4167
e-mail: info@iwh.on.ca
URL: www.iwh.on.ca
Previous Name: Ontario Workers' Compensation Institute
Overview: A medium-sized provincial organization founded in 1990
Chief Officer(s):
Cameron Mustard, President & Senior Scientist
Roland Hosein, Chair
Finances: *Annual Operating Budget:* $3 Million-$5 Million; *Funding Sources:* Public & private sector; research grants
Staff: 75 staff member(s)
Activities: *Awareness Events:* Alf Nachemson Memorial Lecture; *Library:* Yes, Not open to the public
Awards: Mustard Fellowship in Work Environment & Health (Scholarship)
Deadline: 1-Apr
Mission: To conduct & share research with workers, labour, employers, clinicians & policy-makers to promote, protect & improve the health of working people

Institute of Electrical & Electronics Engineers Inc. (IEEE)
445 Hoes Lane, Piscataway NJ 8855 USA
Tel: 732-981-0060; *Fax:* 732-981-9667
e-mail: customer-service@ieee.org
URL: www.ieee.org
Overview: A large international organization founded in 1884
Membership: 365,000 worldwide; 39 technical societies; 4 councils; *Fees:* Schedule available
Activities: Has published more than 130 transactions, magazines & journals; global network of over 90 branches worldwide, providing local focus for engineering, including events, lectures & company visits; *Internships:* Yes; *Library:* Yes
Mission: The world's largest technical professional society; to advance theory & practice of electrical engineering, electronics, radio & allied branches of engineering & related arts & sciences; to publish documents in order to enhance the quality of life for all peoples through improved public awareness of the influences & applications of its technologies; to advance the standing of the engineering profession & its members; to provide leadership in areas ranging from aerospace, computers & communications to biomedical technology, electric power & consumer electronics

Institute of Electrical & Electronics Engineers Inc. - Canada
PO Box 63005, Stn. Uuniversity PO, Shoppers Drug Mart #742, 102 Plaza Dr., Dundas ON L9H 4H0
Tel: 905-628-9554; *Fax:* 905-628-9554
e-mail: admin@ieee.ca
URL: www.ieee.ca
Also Known As: IEEE Canada
Overview: A medium-sized national charitable organization founded in 1884
Finances: *Funding Sources:* Membership dues; Publications; Sponsorship; Sale of products & services
Membership: 13,000; *Member Profile:* Professional engineers or technologists; *Committees:* Awards; Conferences; Membership; Publications; Professional Activities; Student Activities; Educational Activites; Industry Relations; Other Societies; Sections/Chapter Support; GOLD (Graduates of the Last Decade); Life Members; Women in Engineering; Standards
Activities: Sponsoring technical conferences, symposia & local meetings worldwide; Providing resources to assist members in increasing their professional skills; Facilitating networking capabilities
Awards: A.G.L. McNaughton Gold Medal (Award)
R.A. Fessenden Award (Award)
Power Engineering Award (Award)
Computer Award (Award)
Outstanding Engineer Award (Award)
Outstanding Engineering Educator Award (Award)
W.S. Read Outstanding Service Award (Award)
J.J. Archambault Eastern Canada Merit Award (Award)
M.B. Broughton Central Canada Merit Award (Award)
E.F. Glass Western Canada Merit Award (Award)
RAB Achievement Award (Award)
RAB Innovation Award (Award)
RAB Leadership Award (Award)
RAB Larry K. Wilson Transnational Award (Award)
RAB GOLD Achievement Award (Award)
William W. Middleton Distinguished Service Award (Award)
Friend of IEEE Regional Activities Award (Award)
RAB Section Recognition Awards (Award)
Publications: *IEEE [Institute of Electrical & Electronics Engineers Inc.] Canada Newsletter / Bulletin de IEEE Canada*
Type: Newsletter *Frequency:* m. *Editor:* Alex Bot
Profile: IEEE activities & industry trends
IEEE [Institute of Electrical & Electronics Engineers Inc.] Canadian Review / La revue canadienne de l'IEEE
Type: Magazine *Frequency:* 3 pa *Accepts Advertising* : Yes
Editor: Eric Holdrinet *ISSN:* 1481-2002 *Price:* Free to members in Canada; $35 non-members; $37.50 corporations & libraries
Canadian Journal of Electrical & Computer Engineering
Type: Journal *Frequency:* q. *Editor:* Witold Kinsner; Xavier Maldague *ISSN:* 0840-8688 *Price:* $30 IEEE member; $60 other individual; $90 institution
Profile: Refereed scientific papers in all areas of electrical & computer engineering
Mission: IEEE Canada advances the theory & practice of electrical, electronics & computer engineering & computer science.; *Member of:* Institute of Electrical and Electronics Engineers (IEEE); *Affiliation(s):* The Engineering Institute of Canada

Institute of Food Technologists (IFT)
#1000, 525 West Van Buren, Chicago IL 60607

Associations/Organizations / Institute of Industrial Engineers

Tel: 312-782-8424; Fax: 312-782-8348
Toll-Free: 800-438-3663
e-mail: info@ift.org; sales@ift.org
URL: www.ift.org
Social Media: www.facebook.com/group.php?gid=51107253017; www.twitter.com/IFT
Overview: A large international organization founded in 1939
Chief Officer(s):
Robert Gravani, PhD, President
Kelley Ahuja, Chief Administrative Officer
kahuja@ift.org
Mark Barenie, Chief Financial Officer
mbarenie@ift.org
Tina Marie Wehmeir, Chief Development Officer & Senior VP
twehmeir@ift.org
Jerry Bowman, Vice-President, Communications & Media Relations
jmbowman@ift.org
Will Fisher, Vice-President, Science & Policy Initiatives
wfisher@ift.org
Finances: *Funding Sources:* Membership fees; Sponsorships
Member Profile: Food science & technology professionals from over 90 countries
Activities: Engaging in advocacy activities; Fostering technology development & supporting innovation in food science; Facilitating the exchange of information & ideas among the food community; Offering professional development activities; Increasing the understanding & application of the science of food; Publishing science reports of interest to members, government officials, scientific constituencies, government officials, the media, & the public; Publishing books through IFT Press, a joint publishing venture with Wiley-Blackwell
Meetings/Conferences:
For more information see Trade Shows, Conferences and Seminars Chapter
Institute of Food Technologists 2011 Pre-Annual Meeting Short Courses
June 2011 New Orleans, LA
Institute of Food Technologists 2011 Annual Meeting & Food Expo
June 2011 New Orleans, LA
Institute of Food Technologists 2012 Annual Wellness Conference
March 2012
Institute of Food Technologists 2012 Annual Meeting & Food Expo
June 2012 Las Vegas, NV
Institute of Food Technologists 2013 Annual Wellness Conference
March 2013
Institute of Food Technologists 2013 Annual Meeting & Food Expo
July 2013 Chicago, IL
Institute of Food Technologists 2014 Annual Wellness Conference
March 2014
Institute of Food Technologists 2014 Annual Meeting & Food Expo
June 2014 New Orleans, LA
Institute of Food Technologists 2015 Annual Meeting & Food Expo
July 2015 Chicago, IL
Publications: *Food Technology*
Type: Magazine *Frequency:* m. *Accepts Advertising* : Yes *Editor:* Bob Swientek (bswientek@ift.org)
Profile: Industry news, research developments, consumer product innovations, & professional opportunities
Journal of Food Science
Type: Journal *Frequency:* 9 pa *Editor:* Daryl B. Lund (dlund@cals.wisc.edu)
Profile: A peer-reviewed journal, featuring original research, & reviews of all aspects of food science
Journal of Food Science Education
Type: Journal *Editor:* Daryl B. Lund (dlund@cals.wisc.edu)
Profile: Information of interest to persons in the field of food science education at all levels, including primary, secondary, undergraduate & graduate, continuing, & workplace education
Comprehensive Reviews in Food Science & Food Safety
Type: Journal *Frequency:* bi-m. *Editor:* Daryl B. Lund (dlund@cals.wisc.edu)
Profile: A peer-reviewed journal, covering topics such as nutrition, physiology, microbiology, engineering, & regulations
The Weekly Newsletter
Type: Newsletter *Frequency:* w.

Profile: Industry news & highlights from the food science, technology, & regulatory sectors
Nutraceutical Newsletter
Type: Newsletter
Profile: News & current research from the nutraceutical & functional foods sector
Institute of Food Technologists Annual Meeting & Food Expo Preview
Type: Newsletter *Frequency:* a.
Profile: A preview of the annual educational event, which attracts food scientists, technologists, sellers, & buyers from around the globe
Institute of Food Technologists Annual Meeting & Food Expo Wrap-up
Type: Newsletter *Frequency:* a.
Profile: A review of the annual event, which features over 21,500 attendees, as well as more than 900 exhibitors who present recent products & innovations in the food industry
Express Connect
Type: Newsletter *Frequency:* m.
Profile: Happenings at the Institute of Food Technologists, for members only
Eat Your Words
Type: Newsletter *Frequency:* m.
Profile: Food science & technology stories for new professionals in the industry
The World of Food Science
Type: Journal *Editor:* Ken Buckle (k.buckle@unsw.edu.au)
Profile: A publication of current research on sensors & biosensors & its potential application in the food & technology industry, presented to readers by the Institute of Food Technologists & the International Union of Food Science & Technology
Mission: To advance food & health through science
Environmental Activity: Striving to ensure a safe & abundant food supply to contribute to health & wellness

Institute of Industrial Engineers (IIE)
#200, 3577 Parkway Lane, Norcross GA 30092 USA
Tel: 770-449-0461; Fax: 770-441-3295
e-mail: cs@iienet.org
URL: www.iienet2.org
Overview: A large national licensing organization founded in 1948
Finances: *Annual Operating Budget:* $3 Million-$5 Million
Staff: 35 staff member(s)
Membership: 24,000 internationally in 200 senior & 140 university chapters; *Fees:* $30-$139 USD; *Committees:* Divisions: Energy, Environment & Plant Engineering; Engineering Economy; Ergonomics; Facilities Planning & Design; Financial Services; Industrial & Labour Relations; Operations Research; Quality Control & Reliability; Utilities; Work Measurement & Methods Engineering; Interest Groups: Computer & Information Systems; Consultants; Electronics Industry; Engineering Design; Government; Maintenance; Process Industries; Production & Inventory Control; Retail; Transportation & Distribution
Activities: Provides continuing education opportunities through professional trade books, periodicals, journals, technical publications, conferences, seminars & workshops; Conferences: International Industrial Engineering, Industrial Engineering Research & International Maintenance; Material Handling Management Course; Management, Maintenance, Quality & Manufacturing Seminars; *Speaker Service:* Yes; *Rents Mailing List:* Yes; *Library:* Yes, open by appointment
Mission: To advance the technical & managerial excellence of industrial engineers, concerned with the design, installation & improvement of integrated systems of people, material, information, equipment & energy; Affiliation(s): Organized into three societies: Society for Health Systems (SHS); Society for Engineering & Management Systems (SEMS); Aerospace & Defense Society (ADS)

Institute of Industrial Engineers *See* Canadian Society for Industrial Engineering

Institute of Packaging Professionals (IoPP)
#101, 1601 North Bond St., Naperville IL 60563 USA
Tel: 630-544-5050; Fax: 630-544-5055
e-mail: info@iopp.org
URL: www.iopp.org
Overview: A medium-sized national organization
Chief Officer(s):
Edwin O. Landon, Executive Director
Finances: *Funding Sources:* Corporate sponsors

Membership: 5,000; *Fees:* $150; *Member Profile:* Packaging professionals
Mission: Dedicated to creating networking and educational opportunities that help packaging professionals succeed.

Institute of Power Engineers (IPE)
PO Box 878, Burlington ON L7R 3Y7
Tel: 905-333-3348; Fax: 905-333-9328
e-mail: ipenat@nipe.ca
URL: www.nipe.ca
Overview: A medium-sized national organization founded in 1940
Chief Officer(s):
Lorne Shewfelt, National President
Jude Rankin, 1st National Vice President
Don Purser, National Secretary
Finances: *Annual Operating Budget:* $50,000-$100,000
Staff: 1400 volunteer(s)
Membership: 1,420; *Fees:* $60; *Member Profile:* Persons holding certificates of qualification as recognized by the Institute; persons enrolled in recognized power engineering courses; persons engaged in any pursuit identified or allied with power engineering
Mission: To promote business relations, social activities & mutual understanding among power engineers.

Institute of Scrap Recycling Industries, Inc. (ISRI)
#600, 1615 I St. NW, Washington DC 20036-5610 USA
Tel: 202-662-8500; Fax: 202-626-0900
URL: www.isri.org
Overview: A medium-sized national organization
Chief Officer(s):
Robin K. Wiener, President
Membership: 1,250; 21 chapters across the US; *Fees:* Schedule available; *Member Profile:* North American companies that process, broker & consume srap commodities; associate memberships available for international members outside Canada, Mexico & the US, as well as to equipment & service providers of the scrap recycling industry
Activities: *Internships:* Yes; *Speaker Service:* Yes
Mission: To provide education, advocacy, compliance training; to promote public awareness of the value & importance of recycling to the produciton of the world's goods & services

Institute of Space & Atmospheric Studies (ISAS)
University of Saskatchewan, 116 Science Pl., Saskatoon SK S7N 5E2
Tel: 306-966-6401; Fax: 306-966-6428
e-mail: isas.office@usask.ca
URL: www.usask.ca/physics/isas/
Overview: A small national organization
Chief Officer(s):
Alan Manson, ISAS Secretary
Membership: 1-99; *Member Profile:* Professors, research associates, post-doctoral fellow, research engineers
Mission: Focus is on space & atmospheric studies, solar terrestrial physics, space weather, & atmospheric change

Institute of Transportation Engineers (ITE)
#300, 1099 - 14th St. NW, Washington DC 20005-3438 USA
Tel: 202-289-0222; Fax: 202-289-7722
e-mail: ite_staff@ite.org
URL: www.ite.org
Overview: A large international organization founded in 1930
Membership: 4,300; *Member Profile:* Transportation professionals with the responsibilities for meeting mobility & safety needs, such as transportation educators, researchers, consultants, planners, & engineers
Activities: Promoting professional development; Supporting education; Encouraging research; Increasing public awareness; Exchanging professional information
Meetings/Conferences:
For more information see Trade Shows, Conferences and Seminars Chapter
Institute of Transportation Engineers 2011 Annual Meeting & Exhibit
August 2011 St. Louis, MO
Institute of Transportation Engineers 2012 Technical Conference & Exhibit
March 2012 Pasadena, CA
Institute of Transportation Engineers 2012 Annual Meeting & Exhibit
August 2012 Atlanta, GA
Institute of Transportation Engineers 2013 Annual Meeting & Exhibit
August 2013 Boston, MA

Institute of Transportation Engineers 2014 Annual Meeting & Exhibit
August 2014 Seattle, WA
Institute of Transportation Engineers 2015 Technical Conference & Exhibit
March 2015 Tucson, AZ
Institute of Transportation Engineers 2015 Annual Meeting & Exhibit
August 2015 Hollywood, FL
Institute of Transportation Engineers 2016 Annual Meeting & Exhibit
August 2016 Anaheim, CA
Institute of Transportation Engineers 2017 Annual Meeting & Exhibit
July 2017 Toronto, ON
Publications: *Traffic Engineering Handbook*
Traffic Signal Timing Manual
Transportation Planning Handbook
Trip Generation: An ITE Informational Report
Urban Street Geometric Design Handbook
Transportation Impact Analyses for Site Development: An ITE Proposed Recommended Practice
Parking Generation: An ITE Informational Report
Context Sensitive Solutions in Designing Major Urban Thoroughfares for Walkable Communities
Profile: An ITE Proposed Recommended Practice
Mission: To facilitate the application of technology & scientific principles for modes of ground transportation

Institute of Urban Studies (IUS)
University of Winnipeg, #103, 520 Portage Ave., Winnipeg MB R3C 0G2
Tel: 204-982-1140; Fax: 204-943-4695
e-mail: ius@uwinnipeg.ca
URL: ius.uwinnipeg.ca
Overview: A medium-sized national organization founded in 1969
Chief Officer(s):
Jino Distasio, Director
j.distasio@uwinnipeg.ca
Finances: *Funding Sources:* University of Winnipeg; contracts
Staff: 5 staff member(s)
Activities: Areas of expertise include: housing, planning, urban Aboriginal issues, sustainable development, municipal government & finance, & socio-economic & demographic analysis; Research services include: trend analysis, market analysis, cost/benefit analysis, database development, survey & data analysis, community needs assessment, program/policy development & evaluation, community consultation & consensus building, & literature search & review, bibliography development; conference, workshop & publishing services; *Library:* Yes, open by appointment
Mission: To undertake policy-oriented research in the field of Urban Studies; to serve as a resource centre for the community; to provide educational services to the University community & the community-at-large.; *Member of:* National Housing Research Committee

Institution of Mechanical Engineers (IMechE)
1 Birdcage Walk, London SW1H 9JJ United Kingdom
Tel: 44-(0)20-7222-7899; Fax: 44-(0)20-7222-4557
e-mail: International@imeche.org
URL: www.imeche.org.uk
Overview: A medium-sized international organization founded in 1847
Chief Officer(s):
William M. Banks, President
Finances: *Annual Operating Budget:* $3 Million-$5 Million; *Funding Sources:* Subscriptions & earnings
Staff: 180 staff member(s)
Membership: 75,000+
Activities: *Speaker Service:* Yes; *Library:* Yes, open by appointment
Mission: To educate, train & promote the professional development of engineers; to act as an international centre for technology transfer in mechanical engineering

Insurance Council of Canada *See* Insurance Bureau of Canada

Integrated Vegetation Management Association of British Columbia (IVMA)
#720, 999 West Broadway, Vancouver BC V5Z 1K5
e-mail: reception@ivma.com
URL: www.ivma.com
Overview: A small provincial organization
Chief Officer(s):
Peter Mohammed, President
Member Profile: Independent contractors, consultants, manufacturers, suppliers
Mission: The organization is dedicated to the responsible practice of all aspects of vegetation management

Intergovernmental Committee on Urban & Regional Research (ICURR) / Comité intergouvernemental de recherches urbaines et régionales (CIRUR)
#206, 40 Wynford Dr., Toronto ON M3C 1J5
Tel: 416-973-5629; Fax: 416-973-1375
URL: www.muniscope.ca
Overview: A medium-sized national organization founded in 1967
Finances: *Funding Sources:* Canadian Mortgage & Housing Corporation
Staff: 6 staff member(s)
Activities: Information exchange & research; *Rents Mailing List:* Yes; *Library:* Yes
Mission: ICURR supports local and regional governments, as well as private and non-profit companies through subsidized information and networking services. Muniscope is Canada's national resource on municipal issues, with subscription-based research and library services available on economic development, finance and taxation, housing and infrastructure, transportation, planning, and sustainability.

International Agricultural Exchange Association
#202A, 300 Merganser Dr., Chestermere AB T1X 1L6
Tel: 403-255-7799; Fax: 403-255-6024
Toll-Free: 800-263-1827
e-mail: canada@agriventure.com
URL: www.agriventure.com
Overview: A small international organization
Membership: 5,000 in 14 countries
Mission: To administer agricultural exchange for young people

International Air Transport Association / Association du transport aérien international
PO Box 113, 800, Place Victoria, Montréal QC H4Z 1M1
Tel: 514-874-0202; Fax: 514-874-9632
URL: www.iata.org
Overview: A small international organization founded in 1945
Committees: Avionics & Telecommunications; Engineering & Environment; Airports; Flight Operations; Medical; Security; Air Law; Financial; Traffic Coordination; Traffic Services
Mission: To promote safe, regular & economical air transport for the benefit of the peoples of the world; to foster air commerce; to study the problems connected with air transport; to provide a means for collaboration among the air transport enterprises engaged directly or indirectly in international air transport service; to cooperate with the International Civil Aviation Organization & other international organizations; to furnish for governments a forum for developing industry working standards &, as appropriate, coordinating international fares & rates; to simplify the travelling process for the general public; Affiliation(s): International Civil Aviation Organization

International Arctic Science Committee (IASC)
Secretariat, PO Box 50003, Stockholm 104 05 Sweden
Tel: 468-673-9613
e-mail: iasc@iasc.se
URL: www.arcticportal.org/iasc
Overview: A large international organization founded in 1990
Chief Officer(s):
Kristjáan Kristjáansson, President
Dieter Fütterer, Vice-President
Volker Rachold, Executive Secretary
Finances: *Annual Operating Budget:* $250,000-$500,000; *Funding Sources:* Government of Norway: the IASC Secretariat
Staff: 2 staff member(s); 150 volunteer(s)
Membership: 18 countries; *Fees:* $7,000-9,000; *Member Profile:* Significant arctic research for a period of at least 5 years
Activities: Circum-Arctic research planning; 12 project groups; Developing Arctic EIA Guidelines under the Arctic Environmental Protection Strategy & International Arctic Environmental Data Directory; *Awareness Events:* Arctic Science Summit Week; *Internships:* Yes
Mission: To encourage & facilitate cooperation in all aspects of arctic research, in all countries engaged in arctic research & in all areas of the arctic region; to provide scientific advice on arctic issues including environmental & technological matters; Affiliation(s): Canadian Polar Commission

International Association for Bear Research & Management (IBA)
c/o Terry While, USGS-SAFL, University of Tennessee, 274 Ellington Hall, Knoxville TN 37996 USA
Fax: 865-974-3555
e-mail: tdwhite@utk.edu
URL: www.bearbiology.com
Also Known As: IUCN/SSC Bear Specialist Group
Previous Name: Bear Biology Association
Overview: A small international charitable organization founded in 1968
Chief Officer(s):
Frank van Manen, President
vanmanen@utk.edu
Harry Reynolds, Vice-President, Americas
hreynolds@reynoldsalaska.com
Diana Doan-Crider, Secretary
d-crider@tamu.edu
Cecily Costello, Treasurer
ccostello@bresnan.net
Membership: 550+ from 50+ countries; *Member Profile:* Professional biologists with an interest in bears; Wildlife managers; Others dedicated to the conservation of all bear species; *Committees:* Conference; Publications; Membership; Website
Activities: Encouraging communication & collaboration across scientific disciplines; Increasing public awareness & understanding of bear ecology; Maintaining high standards of professional ethics; Building an endowment & a future funding base; Sponsoring workshops & conferences on bear ecology, management, & biology;
Awards: Research & Conservation Grants (Grant)
Contact: Dr. Frederick C. Dean *Contact Detail:* deansfs@alaska.net
Experience & Exchange Grants (Grant)
Contact: Ole Jakob Sorensen *Contact Detail:* ole.j.sorensen@hint.no
Meetings/Conferences:
For more information see Trade Shows, Conferences and Seminars Chapter
International Association for Bear Research & Management 2011 International Conference & Exhibition
July 2011 Ottawa, ON
Advancing Bear Care 2011
October 2011 Banff, AB
Publications: *International Bear News*
Type: Newsletter *Frequency:* q. *Editor:* Tanya Rosen *ISSN:* 1064-1564 *Price:* Free for members of the International Association for Bear Research & Management
Profile: Articles about biology, conservation, & management of the world's eight bear species, plus reviews of books on bears
Ursus [a publication of the International Association for Bear Research & Management]
Type: Journal *Frequency:* s-a. *Editor:* Richard B. Harris *Price:* Free for members of the International Association for Bear Research & Management
Profile: A peer-reviewed journal with articles on all aspects of bear management & research worldwide
Mission: To support the scientific management of bears & their habitats, through research & distribution of information
Environmental Activity: Promoting the conservation & restoration of the world's bears; Supporting innovative solutions to bear conservation; Developing sound stewardship through population & habitat management

International Association for Earthquake Engineering (IAEE)
Central Office, Ken chiku-kaikan Bldg., 3rd Fl., Minatoku Shiba 5, Chome 26-20, Tokyo 108-0014 Japan
Fax: 81-3-3453-0428
e-mail: secretary@iaee.or.jp
URL: www.iaee.or.jp
Overview: A medium-sized international organization founded in 1963
Chief Officer(s):
Manabu Yoshimura, Secretary General
Tsuneo Katayama, President
Membership: 54 countries
Mission: To promote international cooperation among scientists, engineers & other professionals in the broad field of earthquake engineering through interchange of knowledge, ideas, results of research & practical experience

International Association for Ecology (INTECOL)
Dean of Faculty of Pure Science, Dept. of Animal & Plant Sciences, Univ. of Sheffield, Sheffield S10 2TN United Kingdom

e-mail: j.a.lee@sheffield.ac.uk
URL: www.intecol.net
Overview: A medium-sized international organization founded in 1967
Membership: 1,000; *Fees:* $25
Mission: To promote the development of the science of ecology & the application of ecological principles to global needs; to collect, evaluate & disseminate information about ecology; to promote international actions in ecological research; *Member of:* Union of Biological Societies

International Association for Environmental Hydrology (IAEH)
2607 Hopeton Dr., San Antonio TX 78230 USA
Tel: 201-984-7593; *Fax:* 201-564-8581
e-mail: hydroweb@gmail.com
URL: www.hydroweb.com
Overview: A medium-sized international organization founded in 1991
Finances: *Annual Operating Budget:* Less than $50,000
Staff: 2 staff member(s)
Membership: 450; *Fees:* US$75
Activities: Publish Hydrokit, CD-ROM of Environmental Modeling Programs
Publications: *Journal of Environmental Hydrology*
Type: Journal Frequency: m *ISSN:* 1058-3912
Mission: To provide a place to share technical information & exchange ideas, & to provide a source of inexpensive tools for the environmental hydrologist, especially hydrologists & water resource engineers in developing countries

International Association for Great Lakes Research (IAGLR)
4840 South State Rd., Ann Arbor MI 48108 USA
Tel: 734-665-5303; *Fax:* 734-741-2055
e-mail: office@iaglr.org
URL: www.iaglr.org
Overview: A small international organization
Chief Officer(s):
Wendy Foster, Business Manager
Matt F. Simcik, President
Membership: 1,000; *Fees:* $70 individual; $37 student; $200 library; $1,000 life
Activities: Annual four-day Conference on Great Lakes Research to exchange information on all aspects of research applicable to the understanding of large lakes of the world & to the human societies surrounding them
Awards: IAGLR Scholarship (Scholarship)
To a M.Sc or PhD student whose proposed research topic is relevant to large lake research *Award Amount:* US$2,000
Norman S. Baldwin Fishery Science Scholarship (Scholarship) *Award Amount:* US$1,000
Chandler-Misener Award (Award)
Presented annually to the author(s) of the paper in the current volume of the peer reviewed Journal of Great Lakes Research judged to be "most notable"
Anderson-Everett Award (Award)
Recognizes important & continued contributions to the Association
Editor's Award (Award)
Presented for outstanding support of the Journal's review process
IAGLR-Hydrolab Student Paper & Poster Awards (Award)
Offered for the best oral & poster presentations given by students at the annual conference; co-sponsored by Hydrolab Inc. *Award Amount:* US$250 & one year membership in association
Paul W. Rodgers Scholarship (Scholarship)
Awarded annually to senior undergraduate, masters or doctoral student who wishes to pursue a future in research, conservation, education, communication, management or other knowledge-based activity pertaining to the Great Lakes *Award Amount:* US$2,000
Mission: To promote all aspects of Great Lakes research & the dissemination of research information through publications & meetings

International Association for Impact Assessment (IAIA)
1330 - 23rd St. South, #C, Fargo ND 58103-3705 USA
Tel: 701-297-7908; *Fax:* 701-297-7917
e-mail: info@iaia.org
URL: www.iaia.org
Overview: A small international organization founded in 1980
Finances: *Annual Operating Budget:* $500,000-$1.5 Million; *Funding Sources:* Membership fees; meeting registration

Staff: 4 staff member(s)
Membership: 1,600 in more than 120 countries; *Fees:* $US110 individual (base rate); $55 student; *Member Profile:* Corporate planners & managers; public interest advocates; government planners & administrators; private consultants & policy analysts; college teachers; students; *Committees:* Awards; Financial Affairs; Program; Board Nominations; Publications; Training & Professional Development; Conferences; Affiliates; Editorial Board; Conference Sponsorship
Activities: Presentation of papers, posters, plenary sessions, exhibits, technical tours, pre-meeting training courses; *Internships:* Yes
Awards: Corporate (Award)
Best Poster (Award)
Global Environment (Award)
Regional (Award)
Institutional (Award)
Individual (Award)
IAPA Best Paper (Award)
Outstanding Service to IAIA (Award)
Rose-Hulman Award (Award)
Mission: To be a forum for advancing innovation, development & communication of best practice in impact assessment; to promote the development of local & global capacity for the application of environmental assessment in which sound science & full public participation provide a foundation for equitable & sustainable development; *Affiliation(s):* Netherlands Association for Environmental Professionals; Association Argentina de Geologia Aplicada a la Ingenieria; International Society of City & Regional Planners; Environment Institute of Australia & New Zealand; South Asian Regional Environment Assessment Association; Japan Society for Impact Assessment; Chinese Association of Environmental Protection Industry

International Association for Impact Assessment - Western & Northern Canada
PO Box 2619, Stn. Bankview, 14 Street S.W., Calgary AB T2T 5X6
Tel: 403-245-6404
e-mail: IAIA-WNC@praxis.ca
URL: www.iaiawnc.org
Overview: A small local organization
Chief Officer(s):
Alan Ehrlich, President
aehrlich@mveirb.nt.ca

International Association for Public Participation (IAP2)
3030 W. 81st Ave., Westminster CO 80031 USA
Tel: 303-458-5945; *Fax:* 303-458-0002
Toll-Free: 800-644-4273
e-mail: iap2hq@iap2.org
URL: www.iap2.org
Previous Name: International Association of Public Participation Practitioners
Overview: A medium-sized international organization founded in 1990
Chief Officer(s):
Dina Alengi Storz, Administrator
Membership: 1,100; *Fees:* $975 individual; *Member Profile:* Public participation designers & facilitators; policymakers; project managers; representatives from government agencies; members of advocacy groups & professional organizations; trainers; mediators; citizen activists
Mission: To serve the learning needs of members through events, publications & communication technology; to advocate for public participation throughout the world; to promote research; to provide technical assistance

International Association of Agricultural Economists (IAAE)
#1100, 555 East Wells St., Milwaukee WI 53202 USA
Tel: 414-918-3199; *Fax:* 414-276-3349
e-mail: iaae@execinc.com
URL: www.iaae-agecon.org
Overview: A medium-sized international organization founded in 1929
Finances: *Annual Operating Budget:* $50,000-$100,000
Membership: 1,700; *Fees:* US$60-US$175; *Member Profile:* A worldwide confederation of agricultural economists & others concerned with agricultural economic problems
Activities: *Rents Mailing List:* Yes
Mission: To foster the application of agricultural economics to improve rural economic & social conditions; to advance knowledge of agriculture's economic organization; to facilitate communication & information exchange among those concerned

with rural welfare; *Affiliation(s):* Canadian Council - International Association of Agricultural Economists

International Association of Educators for World Peace (IAEWP Canada)
#100-209, 2 Bloor St. West, Toronto ON M4W 3E2
Tel: 416-924-4449; *Fax:* 416-924-4094
e-mail: mgold@homeplanet.org
URL: www.homeplanet.org
Overview: A large international organization founded in 1969
Chief Officer(s):
Mitchell Gold, Executive Director
Finances: *Annual Operating Budget:* $50,000-$100,000; *Funding Sources:* Programs; grants
Staff: 1 staff member(s); 200 volunteer(s)
Membership: 35,000 worldwide; *Fees:* $50
Activities: Regional workshops; exchanges; community outreach projects; UNESCO clubs; lectures; seminars; Home Planet Alliance; TOPS Program; *Awareness Events:* Vision Changer Project; *Speaker Service:* Yes
Mission: To promote peace through education; to promote a universal declaration of human rights & responsibilities; to promote global citizenship; to promote World Water Day; to promote the Vision Changer Project, TOPS Program & homeplanet.org; *Affiliation(s):* NGO status with UNESCO, UNICEF, UNDPI, UNCED & United Nations

International Association of Environmental Analytical Chemistry (IAEAC)
Secretariat M. Frei, Postfach 46, Allschwil CH-4123 Switzerland
Tel: 41-61-481-2789; *Fax:* 41-61-482-0805
e-mail: iaeac@dplanet.ch
URL: www.iaeac.ch
Overview: A small international organization founded in 1977
Membership: 110-130; *Fees:* SFR 110-300
Mission: To support regular exchange of experiences between experts in the field of analytical chemistry of pollutants & related areas; to orient its members about recent advances in the field; to address relevant problems of environmental analysis & on questions related to environmental protection & control

International Association of Fire Fighters (AFL-CIO/CLC) (IAFF) / Association internationale des pompiers (FAT-COI/CTC)
#300, 1750 New York Ave. NW, Washington DC 20006-5395 USA
Tel: 202-737-8484; *Fax:* 202-737-8418
URL: www.iaff.org
Overview: A small international organization founded in 1918
Chief Officer(s):
Harold A. Schaitberger, General President
Membership: 298,000 +; *Member Profile:* full-time professional fire fighters & paramedics
Publications: *International Fire Fighter*
Type: magazine *Frequency:* 5 x yr.
Mission: IAFF has established professional standards for the North American fire service with active political & legislative programs, & with experts in the fields of occupational health & safety, fire-based emergency medical services & hazardous materials training. It provides a voice in the development & implementation of new training & equipment, & has worked to ensure the staffing of fire & EMS departments.

International Association of Fish & Wildlife Agencies *See* Association of Fish & Wildlife Agencies

International Association of Geochemistry & Cosmochemistry *See* International Association of GeoChemistry

International Association of Hydrogeologists (IAH)
PO Box 4130, Stn. Goring, Reading RG8 6BJKOA 1L0 United Kingdom
Tel: +44 870 762 4462; *Fax:* +44 870 762 8462
URL: www.iah.org
Overview: A medium-sized international organization founded in 1956
Chief Officer(s):
John Chilton, Executive Manager, IAH Secretariat
jchilton@iah.org
Membership: 4,000 in 135 countries; 300 in Canada
Mission: To advance the science of hydrogeology & exchange hydrogeologic information internationally; *Affiliation(s):* UNESCO; International Union of Geological Sciences

Associations/Organizations / International Association of Hydrogeologists - Canadian National Chapter

International Association of Hydrogeologists - Canadian National Chapter (IAH-CNC)
c/o WESA, 3108 Carp Rd., Carp ON K0A 1L0
Tel: 613-839-3053
URL: www.iah.ca
Overview: A medium-sized national organization founded in 1972
Chief Officer(s):
Nell van Walsum, Secretary
secretary1@iah.ca
Finances: *Annual Operating Budget:* Less than $50,000
Membership: 300 across Canada; *Fees:* $120; schedule
Activities: Speaker Service: Yes
Mission: To advance the science of hydrogeology & exchange hydrogeologic information internationally; *Member of:* Canadian Geoscience Council; Affiliation(s): International Union of Geological Congresses

International Association of Public Participation Practitioners See International Association for Public Participation

International Association of Science & Technology for Development (IASTED)
Bldg B6, #101, 2509 Dieppe Ave. SW, Calgary AB T3E 7J9
Tel: 403-288-1195; *Fax:* 403-247-6851
e-mail: calgary@iasted.com
URL: www.iasted.org
Overview: A medium-sized international organization founded in 1977
Finances: *Annual Operating Budget:* $500,000-$1.5 Million
Staff: 3 staff member(s); 100 volunteer(s)
Membership: 250; *Fees:* US$110 individual; US$190 corporate
Activities: Interchange & circulation of information on science & technology; organizing international conferences, symposia, courses
Publications: *Control & Intelligent Systems*
Type: Journal *Frequency:* q *Editor:* Prof. Clarence W. de Silva
International Journal of Computers and Applications
Type: Journal *Frequency:* q *Editor:* Dr. L. Monticone
International Journal of Power and Energy Systems
Type: Journal *Frequency:* q *Editor:* Dr. A/ Domijan, Jr.
International Journal of Modelling and Simulation
Type: Journal *Frequency:* q *Editor:* Prof. A. Houshyar
International Journal of Robotics and Automation
Type: Journal *Frequency:* q
International Journal of Computational Bioscience
Type: Journal *Frequency:* q *Editor:* Dr. L. Elnitski; Prof. L.R. Welch
Mission: To further economic development by promoting science & technology.

International Association of Sedimentologists (IAS)
c/o Instituto Geológico y Minero de Espa¤a, c/ Ríos Rosas 23, Madrid 28003 Spain
e-mail: info@iasnet.org
URL: www.iasnet.org
Overview: A medium-sized international organization founded in 1952
Chief Officer(s):
José-Pedro Calvo Sorando, General Secretary
jpc@igme.es
Finn Surlyk, President, University of Copenhagen
finns@geol.ku.dk
Patric Jacobs, Treasurer, Ghent University, Belgium
patric.jacobs@ugent.be
Finances: *Annual Operating Budget:* $500,000-$1.5 Million; *Funding Sources:* Membership dues; sales of books
Staff: 1 staff member(s)
Membership: 1,700; *Fees:* EUR 30 full member; EUR 15 student
Publications: *Sedimentology*
Type: Journal
Profile: Published by Blackwell
Basin Research
Type: Journal
Profile: Published by Blackwell
Journal of Petroleum Geology
Type: Journal
Profile: Published by Blackwell
Mission: To promote the study of sedimentology by publication, discussion & comparison of research results; to encourage the interchange of research, particularly where international cooperation is desirable; to promote integration with other disciplines. Canadian Correspondent: Dr. A. Guy Plint, Dept. of Earth Sciences, University of Western Ontario, London, ON N6A 5B7, email gplint@uwo.ca; *Member of:* International Union of Geological Sciences

International Association of Theoretical and Applied Limnology; Societas Internationalis Limnologiae, SIL See International Society of Limnology

International Association on Water Quality; International Association on Water Pollution Research & Control See International Water Association

International Atomic Energy Agency (IAEA) / Agence internationale de l'énergie atomique
PO Box 100, Wagramer Strasse 5, Vienna A-1400 Austria
Tel: 43-1 2600-21273; *Fax:* 43-1 2600-29610
e-mail: info@iaea.org
URL: www.iaea.org
Overview: A large international organization founded in 1957
Finances: *Annual Operating Budget:* Greater than $5 Million; *Funding Sources:* Member states contributions
Staff: 2307 staff member(s)
Membership: 140 sovereign states; *Fees:* Percentage of share of regular budget is fixed by UN General Assembly; *Member Profile:* Intergovernmental organization; *Committees:* Board of Governors of 35 member states
Activities: Verification in framework of Nuclear Non-Proliferation Treaty (NPT) that over 1,000 nuclear facilities in over 60 non-nuclear weapon states are used for peaceful purposes only; *Library:* Yes, open by appointment
Mission: An independent intergovernmental organization within the UN system; to accelerate & enlarge the contribution of atomic energy to peace, health & prosperity throughout the world; to ensure that assistance provided is not used to further any military purpose; Affiliation(s): United Nations

International Bar Association (IBA)
1 Stephen St., 10th Fl., London W1T 1AT United Kingdom
Tel: 44-20-7691-6868; *Fax:* 44-20-7691-6544
e-mail: member@int-bar.org
URL: www.ibanet.org
Overview: A large international organization founded in 1947
Membership: 30,000 individual lawyers + 195 bar associations & law societies; *Member Profile:* International legal practitioners; Bar associations; Law societies
Activities: Providing members with access to timely information; Establishing & operating IBA institutions such as the Bar Issues Commission, the Human Rights Institute, the Southern Africa Litigation Centre, & the International Legal Assistance Consortium; Supporting the independence of the judiciary & human rights for lawyers;
Publications: *International Bar News*
Type: Magazine *Frequency:* bi-m. *ISSN:* 0143 7453 *Price:* $198 non-members
Profile: Articles about legal & business issues, IBA initiatives & activities
Business Law International
Type: Journal *Frequency:* 3 pa *Editor:* J. William Rowley, QC
ISSN: 1467632X *Price:* $390 non-members
Profile: Issues of interest to the international commercial, legal, & academic community
Journal of Energy & Natural Resources Law
Type: Journal *Frequency:* q. *Editor:* Professor Nigel Bankes
ISSN: 0264-6811 *Price:* $620
Convergence [a publication of the International Bar Association]
Type: Journal *Frequency:* s-a. *Editor:* Robyn Durie *ISSN:* 1817-5694 *Price:* $240 non-members; $180 members
Profile: Journal of the Intellectual Property, Communications & Technology Section of the International Bar Association
Competition Law International
Type: Journal *Frequency:* 3 pa *Editor:* Dave Poddar; Jose Regazzini *ISSN:* 1817-5708 *Price:* $240 non-members; $160 members
Profile: Journal of the Antitrust & Trade Law Section of the IBA
The In-House Perspective [a publication of the International Bar Association-
Type: Magazine *Frequency:* q. *ISSN:* 1814 0408 *Price:* $198 non-members; $150 members
Profile: Magazine of the IBA Corporate Counsel Forum
Construction Law International
Type: Magazine *Frequency:* q. *Price:* $198 non-members; $150 members
Profile: Magazine of the IBA International Construction Projects Committee
Dispute Resolution International
Type: Journal *Frequency:* s-a. *Editor:* Andrew Foyle *Price:* $240 non-members; $180 members
Profile: Journal of the Dispute Resolution Section of the Legal Practice Division of the IBA
Insolvency & Restructuring International
Type: Journal *Editor:* Bart de Man; Derrick Tay *Price:* $198 non-members; $150 members
Profile: Issues of interest to the international legal business community
Mission: The development of international law reform is influenced by the IBA. The organization also shapes the future of the legal profession throughout the world. It is divided into the Legal Practice Division & the Public & Professional Interest Division.; Affiliation(s): Canadian Bar Association

International Bottled Water Association (IBWA)
#650, 1700 Diagonal Rd., Alexandria VA 22314 USA
Tel: 703-683-5213; *Fax:* 703-683-4074
Toll-Free: 800-928-3711
e-mail: ibwainfo@bottledwater.org
URL: www.bottledwater.org
Overview: A large international organization founded in 1958
Chief Officer(s):
Joseph K. Doss, President
Membership: 1,200; *Fees:* Schedule available
Activities: IBWA works closely with its member companies & with government officials; takes active role at all levels of local, state & federal governments to assist in the development of regulations for bottled water
Mission: To assure that safe, clean, good-tasting bottled water is produced & marketed to consumers

International Centre for Conservation Education (ICCE)
Brocklebank, Butts Lane, Woodmancote, Cheltenham GL52 9QH United Kingdom
Tel: 44-1242-674-839
e-mail: icce@brocklebank.plus.com
URL: www.icce.org.uk
Overview: A small international organization founded in 1984
Chief Officer(s):
Mark Boulton, Honorary Director
Finances: *Annual Operating Budget:* Less than $50,000; *Funding Sources:* Earned income; some charitable funds
Activities: Produces wide range of educational materials; distributes audiovisual presentations worldwide; manages an environmental photolibrary; undertakes conservation education consultancy services; provides EE Consultancy services worldwide; *Internships:* Yes
Mission: To promote greater understanding of conservation, the environment & sustainable development through education & communication, placing particular emphasis on the needs of Africa; *Member of:* World Conservation Union (IUCN)

International Centre for Research in Agroforestry (ICRAF) See World Agroforestry Centre

International Centre for Sustainable Cities (ICSC)
#415, 1788 West 5th Ave., Vancouver BC V6J 1P2
Tel: 604-666-0061; *Fax:* 604-666-0009
e-mail: info@icsc.ca
URL: www.icsc.ca
Overview: A small international charitable organization founded in 1993
Chief Officer(s):
Nola Kate Seymour, President & CEO
Finances: *Annual Operating Budget:* $500,000-$1.5 Million; *Funding Sources:* Projects
Staff: 5 staff member(s); 2 volunteer(s)
Membership: 36; *Committees:* Sustainable Cities Foundation; ICSC Management
Activities: Supports sustainable urban development demonstration projects in India, China, Columbia, Thailand, SE Asia (Thailand, Indonesia, Philippines), Turkey, Poland, Slovakia, Hungary: Plus-30 Network; *Internships:* Yes; *Library:* Yes, open by appointmentNot open to the public
Mission: To support sustainable city projects around the world through demonstration projects using Canadian experience & expertise

International Coalition of Fisheries Associations (ICFA)
#700, 7918 Jones Branch Dr., McLean VA 22102 USA

Tel: 703-752-8880
e-mail: contact@icfa.net
URL: www.icfa.net
Overview: A small international organization founded in 1988
Membership: 1,000
Mission: To provide a unified voice for the world's commercial fishing industries in international forums; to preserve & maintain the oceans as a major source of food for the people of the world; **Affiliation(s):** Fisheries Council of Canada

International Commission of Agricultural & Biosystems Engineering / Commission Internationale du Genie Rural (CIGR)
c/o Dr. Takaaki Maekawa, School of Life & Environmental Sciences, 1-1-1 Tennodai, University of Tsukuba, Tsukuba, Ibaraki Japan
Tel: +81-29-875-6380; Fax: +81-29-875-6381
e-mail: biopro@sakura.cc.tsukuba.ac.jp
URL: www.cigr.org
Overview: A medium-sized international organization
Chief Officer(s):
Soren Pedersen, President
Takaaki Maekawan, Secretary General
biopro@sakura.cc.tsukuba.ac.jp
Yutaka Kitamura, Secretary
kitamura@sakura.cc.tsukuba.ac.jp
Member Profile: National organizations, such as the Canadian Society for Bioengineering; Regional organizations; Individuals; Corporations
Activities: Providing networking opportunities for regional & national societies of agricultural engineering, as well as for private & public companies & individuals throughout the world
Meetings/Conferences:
For more information see Trade Shows, Conferences and Seminars Chapter
International Commission of Agricultural & Biosystems Engineering 3rd International Conference of Agricultural Engineering
July 2012 Valencia
International Commission of Agricultural & Biosystems Engineering XVIII 2014 World Congress
September 2014 Beijing
Publications: CIGR [Commission Internationale du Genie Rural] Newsletter / Bulletin de la CIGR
Type: Newsletter *Frequency:* q.
Profile: Available in English, French, Arabic, Chinese, Russian, & Spanish
Agricultural Engineering International: The CIGR Journal of Scientific Research & Development
Type: Journal *Editor:* Fedro S. Zazueta Ranahan
Mission: To ensure food security & the sustainable use of natural resources, through the application of principles of technology & engineering science

International Commission on Irrigation & Drainage (ICID) / Commission internationale des irrigations & du drainage
48 Nyaya Marg, Chanakyapuri, New Delhi 110021 India
Tel: 1191-11-301-6837; Fax: 1191-11-301-5962
e-mail: icid@icid.org
URL: www.icid.org
Overview: A small international organization founded in 1950
Membership: 107 countries
Activities: *Library:* Yes
Mission: To stimulate & promote development & application of arts, sciences & techniques of engineering, agriculture, economics, ecology & social science in managing water & land resources for irrigation, drainage, flood control & river training &/or for research in a more comprehensive manner adopting up-to-date techniques; to help produce more food from irrigated agriculture on a global basis to alleviate want & hunger without disturbing the environment adversely; **Affiliation(s):** International Commission on Irrigation & Drainage - Canadian National Committee
Environmental Activity: Working Group on Environmental Impacts of Irrigation, Drainage & Flood Control Porjects

International Commission on Irrigation & Drainage - Canadian National Committee *See* The Canadian National Committee for Irrigation & Drainage

International Commission on Occupational Health (ICOH) / Commission internationale de la santé au travail (CIST)
ISPESL, National Institute for Occupational Safety & Prevention, Via Fontana Candida 1, Monteporzio Catone, Rome I-00040 Italy
Tel: 39-06-941-814-07; Fax: 39-06-941-815-56
e-mail: icoh@ispesl.it
URL: www.icohweb.org
Overview: A small international organization founded in 1906
Finances: *Annual Operating Budget:* $100,000-$250,000
Staff: 2 staff member(s)
Membership: 1,900 individual + 19 sustaining + 31 affiliate (in 93 countries); *Member Profile:* Individual & collective members; sustaining - organization, society, industry, or enterprise; affiliate - professional organization or a scientific society; *Committees:* 36 scientific committees & working groups
Activities: International congresses; special meetings; collaboration with international & national bodies & societies having similar aims
Mission: To foster scientific progress, knowledge & development of occupational health & safety in all its aspects; **Affiliation(s):** International Association of Agricultural Medicine & Rural Health; International Federation of Associations of Specialists in Occupational Safety & Industrial Hygiene; International Social Security Association; ISSA International Section on Prevention of Occupational Risks in the Iron & Metal Industry

International Commission on Radiological Protection (ICRP)
PO Box 1046, Stn. B, 280 Slater St., Ottawa ON K1P 5S9
Tel: 613-947-9750
e-mail: admin@icrp.org
URL: www.icrp.org
Overview: A small international charitable organization founded in 1928
Finances: *Annual Operating Budget:* $250,000-$500,000; *Funding Sources:* Grants from intergovernmental/governmental organizations & national sources
Staff: 2 staff member(s); 100 volunteer(s)
Membership: 1-99; *Committees:* Radiation Effects; Doses from Exposures; Protection in Medicine; Application of the Commission's Recommendations; Radiological Protection of the Environment
Mission: To advance for the public benefit the science of radiological protection, in particular by providing recommendations & guidance on all aspects of protection against ionisary radiation

International Confederation for Thermal Analysis & Calorimetry (ICTAC)
SONY Inst. of Higher Education, Dept. of Informatics & Media Tech., Atsugi, Kanagawa 243-8501 Japan
Tel: 81-46-247-3131; Fax: 81-46-250-8936
e-mail: help@ictac.org
URL: www.ictac.org
Overview: A large international organization founded in 1965
Finances: *Annual Operating Budget:* Less than $50,000
Staff: 6 volunteer(s)
Membership: 500 full + 5,000 affiliate; *Fees:* US$16 student; US$80 individual; US$160 corporate; US$256 affiliate with less than 100 members; US$384 affiliate with more than 100 members; *Member Profile:* Open to scientists & technicians who are involved in thermal analysis; *Committees:* Standardization; Nomenclature; Awards; Kinetics; Education; Geo-Sciences; Publications; Liaison; Reactivity of Solids; Organizing of International Congresses; Working Groups: Polymers; Modulated Calorimetry; Sample Controlled Thermal Analysis; Sustainability & Environmental Protection; Thermoanalytical Procedures for Pharmaceuticals; Thermochemistry
Activities: Scientific congress every four years
Mission: To promote the use of thermal analysis in science & technology; to strengthen the collaboration between scientists & technicians from different parts of the world; *Member of:* International Union of Pure & Applied Chemistry

International Cooperative Alliance (ICA)
15, route des Morillons, Grand Saconnex, Geneva 1218 Switzerland
Tel: 41-22-929-8838; Fax: 41-22-798-4122
e-mail: ica@ica.coop
URL: www.coop.org
Overview: A small international organization founded in 1895
Chief Officer(s):
Ivano Barberini, President

Membership: 233 national & international cooperative
Mission: To unite, represent & serve cooperatives worldwide

International Council for Applied Mineralogy (ICAM)
Federal Institute for Geosciences & Natural Resources, B4.22 Petrology, Mineral Residues, Stilleweg 2, Hannover D-30655 Germany
Tel: 49-511-643-2565; Fax: 49-511-643-3685
e-mail: icam2000@bgr.de
URL: www.bgr.de/icam
Overview: A small international organization founded in 1981
Finances: *Annual Operating Budget:* Less than $50,000; *Funding Sources:* Meeting registrations; donations
Membership: 20; *Member Profile:* Professionals in the field
Mission: To promote scientific & technical interests of applied mineralogy by providing an international forum for exchange of ideas; **Affiliation(s):** National Mineralogical Association - USA, Australia, South Africa, Europe, Brazil, South America, Poland; International Mineralogical Association

International Council for Archaeozoology (ICAZ)
c/o University Of Sheffield, Department of Archaeology, Northgate House, West St., Sheffield S1 4ET England
e-mail: u.albarella@sheffield.ac.uk
URL: www.alexandriaarchive.org
Overview: A small international charitable organization founded in 1976
Finances: *Annual Operating Budget:* Less than $50,000; *Funding Sources:* Membership fees
Membership: 383; *Fees:* US$15; *Member Profile:* University staff; museums; freelance; *Committees:* Working Groups; Fish Remains; Bird Remains; Archaeozoology of Southwestern Asia & Adjacent Areas; Camelid; Animal Pathology; Worked Bone; North Atlantic Bioarchaeological Organization
Mission: To develop & stimulate archaeozoological research; to strengthen cooperation among archaeozoologists; to foster cooperation with archaeologists & scientists working in related fields; to promote high ethical & scientific standards for archaeozoological work; **Affiliation(s):** International Union of Prehistoric & Protohistoric Sciences

International Council for Laboratory Animal Science (ICLAS) / Conseil international des sciences de l'animal de laboratoire
PO Box 296, Stn. 1900, La Plata Argentina
Tel: 54-221-421-1276; Fax: 54-221-421-1276
e-mail: ccarbone@fcv.unlp.edu.ar
URL: www.iclas.org
Overview: A small international organization founded in 1956
Fees: Schedule available; *Committees:* Communications & Publications; Complementary Methods; Constitution & By-Laws; Education & Training; Finance; Historical; International Genetics; Nominations Reference & Monitoring Centers; Regional Assistance: Europe, French-speaking Africa, English-speaking Africa, InterAmerica, Australia, Oceania & India
Activities: Scientific meetings; reference & monitoring centres; training courses; publications
Mission: To promote the humane use of animals in research through recognition of ethical principles & scientific responsibilities; to be an advocate for the advancement of laboratory animal science & biological research resources throughout the world; to promote international collaboration as a worldwide resource of knowledge in laboratory animal science; to promote the production & monitoring of high-quality laboratory animals by establishing standards & providing support resources; **Affiliation(s):** Canadian Association for Laboratory Animal Science

International Council for Local Environmental Initiatives (ICLEI)
World Secretariat, 16th Fl., West Tower, City Hall, 100 Queen St. West, Toronto ON M5H 2N2
Tel: 416-392-1462; Fax: 416-392-1478
e-mail: iclei@iclei.org
URL: www.iclei.org
Overview: A small international organization founded in 1990
Chief Officer(s):
David Cadman, President
Finances: *Annual Operating Budget:* Greater than $5 Million; *Funding Sources:* Membership dues; project funding
Staff: 50 staff member(s)
Membership: 360; *Fees:* Schedule available
Activities: *Library:* Yes, open by appointment
Mission: To build & serve a worldwide movement of local governments to achieve tangible improvements in global environmental & sustainable development conditions through

cumulative local actions; Affiliation(s): International Union of Local Authorities

International Council of Associations for Science Education (ICASE) / Fédération Internationale des Associations de Professeurs de Sciences (FIAPS)

c/o Centre for Education, University of Tartu, Vanemuise 46, 226, Tartu 51014 Estonia
Fax: 372-7-375-082
e-mail: info@icaseonline.net
URL: www.icaseonline.net
Overview: A small international organization founded in 1973
Finances: *Annual Operating Budget:* Less than $50,000; *Funding Sources:* Membership fees
Staff: 1 staff member(s); 14 volunteer(s)
Membership: 155 organizations; *Fees:* Schedule available; *Member Profile:* Organization involved in science education
Activities: Project 2000+, providing appropriate science & technology education for all; exchange of teaching resources; science education research & its application in teaching; exchanges of science teaching personnel
Mission: To improve science education worldwide by assisting member organizations; Affiliation(s): Canadian Association for Science Education

International Council of Environmental Law (ICEL)

Godbergerallee 108-112, Bonn D-53175 Germany
Tel: 49-228-2692-240; *Fax:* 49-228-2692-251
e-mail: icel@intlawpol.org
URL: www.i-c-e-l.org
Overview: A small international organization founded in 1969
Finances: *Funding Sources:* Donations
Membership: 340
Activities: ICEL Reference to Environmental Policy & Law Literature; Bulletin online; *Library:* Yes, open by appointment
Mission: Promoting the exchange of information on the legal, administrative and policy aspects of environmental conservation and sustainable development, to support new initiatives in this field, and to encourage advice and assistance through its network.; *Member of:* The World Conservation Union

International Council on Monuments & Sites (ICOMOS) / Conseil international des Monuments et des Sites

#49, 51, rue de la Fédération, Paris 75015 France
Tel: 33-1-45-67-67-70; *Fax:* 33-1-45-66-06-22
e-mail: secretariat@icomos.org
URL: www.icomos.org
Overview: A medium-sized international organization founded in 1965
Membership: 9,500 worldwide; *Member Profile:* Architects & specialists in the conservation & renovation of built heritage
Activities: *Library:* UNESCO-ICOMOS Documentation Centre; Open to public
Mission: ICOMOS works for the conservation and protection of cultural heritage places, with a focus on the application of theory, methodology and scientific techniques for conservation.

International Development Research Centre (IDRC) / Centre de recherches pour le développement international

PO Box 8500, 150 Kent St., Ottawa ON K1G 3H9
Tel: 613-236-6163; *Fax:* 613-238-7230
e-mail: info@idrc.ca
URL: www.idrc.ca
Overview: A large international organization founded in 1970
Finances: *Annual Operating Budget:* Greater than $5 Million
Staff: 408 staff member(s)
Activities: Environment & natural resource management; social & economic equity; information & communication technologies for development; innovation, policy & science; *Internships:* Yes; *Library:* IDRC Library; Open to public
Awards: AGROPOLIS-Farming in the City (Scholarship)
Awards programme that supports innovative master's & doctoral level research. It aims to add to the body of knowledge of urban & peri-urban agriculture, & thereby to support interventions that address critical areas in the industry *Eligibility:* Award intended primarily for researchers from developing countries, including those studying in a developed country & returning to the South after their studies. However, up to a third of all awards may be granted to citizens or permanent residents of a developed country (currently only Canada). The research must be for a master's or a doctoral thesis. Researchers must be registered at a university-in the South or the North-that *Deadline:* Dec. 31 *Award Amount:* Maximum of $20,000 per year Contact: AGROPOLIS International & Graduate Research *Contact Detail: 613/236-6163; Fax: 567-7749; Email AGROPOLIS@idrc.ca*
Ecosystem Approaches to Human Health Training Awards (Award)
Supports research that focuses on ecosystem management interventions leading to the improvement of human health & well-being while simultaneously maintaining or improving the condition of the ecosystem as a whole. Awards will be granted for training & research linked to the Ecosystem Approaches to Human Health Program Initiatives of the Centre. Priority will be give to proposals for research on ecosystems that are stressed through agriculture, urbanization or mining activities *Eligibility:* Citizens of developing countries &/or Canadian citizens or landed immigrants students currently enrolled in a graduate programme at a recognized university in Canada or in a developing country. Relevant language proficiency for site of study *Deadline:* 31-May *Award Amount:* Up to 6 awards for a maximum of $15,000 Contact: Centre Training & Awards Unit *Contact Detail: 613/236-6163 ext 2098; Fax: 563-0815; Email: cta@idrc.da*
IDRC Doctoral Research Awards (IDRA) (Scholarship)
Supports the field research of Canadian graduate students enrolled in a Canadian university for doctoral research on a topic of relevance to sustainable & equitable development *Eligibility:* Applicants must hold Canadian citizenship or permanent residency status; be registered at a Canadian university; research proposal is for a doctoral thesis; provide evidence of affiliation with an institution or organization in the region in which the research will take place; have completed course work & passed comprehensive examinations by the time of award tenure *Deadline:* 14-May *Award Amount:* Maximum of $20,000 per year Contact: Centre Training & Awards Unit *Contact Detail: 613/236-6163 ext 2098; Fax: 613/563-0815; Email: cta@irdc.ca*
John G. Bene Fellowship: Community Forestry, Trees & People (Award)
Contributes to the expenses of Canadian graduate students undertaking field research in social forestry in a developing country *Eligibility:* Applicants must be Canadian citizens or hold permanent residency status; be registered in a Canadian university at the master's or doctoral level; have an academic background that combines forestry or agroforestry with social sciences. Applicants from interdisciplinary programs (e.g. environmental studies) may also be eligible, provided their programs contain the specified elements *Deadline:* 1-Mar *Award Amount:* $15,000 per year Contact: Centre Training & Awards Unit *Contact Detail: 613/236-6163 ext. 2098; Fax: 613/563-0815; Emails cta@irdc.ca*
Canadian Window on International Development Awards (Scholarship)
Award offered for doctoral research that explores the relationship between Canadian aid, trade, immigration & diplomatic policy, & international development & the alleviation of global policy *Eligibility:* Applicants must hold Canadian citizenship or permanent residency status; be registered at a Canadian university; be conducting the proposed research for a doctoral dissertation & have completed course work & passed comprehensive examinations by the time of the award tenure *Deadline:* 2-Apr *Award Amount:* $20,000 per year Contact: Centre Training & Awards Unit *Contact Detail: 613/236-6163 ext 2098; Fax: 613/563-0815; Email: cta@idrc.ca*
Bentley Fellowship: Use of Fertility Enhancing Food, Forage & Cover Crops in Sustainably Managed Agroecosystems (Award)
Supports applied research of Canadian graduate students on how increased use of forage crops in cropping systems can improve agricultural production by farmers in developing countries *Eligibility:* Applicants must be Canadian citizens or hold permanent residency status; be registered in a Canadian university at the master's or doctoral level; have an academic background in agriculture or biology undertaking research on the role of forage crops in improved sustainable tropical farming. Applicants from interdisciplinary programs (e.g. environmental studies) may be eligible provided their programs contain the specified elements *Deadline:* Oct. 2 *Award Amount:* $20,000 per year Contact: Centre Training & Awards Unit *Contact Detail: 613/236-6163 ext 2098; Fax: 613/563-0815; Email: cta@idrc.ca*
Mission: To help scientists in developing countries identify long-term, practical solutions to pressing development problems; support is given directly to scientists in universities, private enterprise, government & non-profit organizations; priority given to equitable & sustainable development; projects are designed to maximize the use of local materials & to strengthen human & institutional capacity; research is undertaken by Third World recipients independently or in collaboration with Canadian partners; Affiliation(s): Regional offices in Asia & Africa

International Energy Foundation (IEF)

Clear Mountain Estates, PO Box 64, Site 8, RR#1, Okotoks AB T1S 1A1
Tel: 403-938-6210; *Fax:* 403-938-6210
e-mail: chairman@ief-energy.org
URL: www.ief-energy.org
Overview: A medium-sized international charitable organization founded in 1989
Chief Officer(s):
Peter J. Catania, PhD, P.Eng., Chair
Finances: *Annual Operating Budget:* $100,000-$250,000; *Funding Sources:* Contributions, donations, subventions, aids & grants made by donors & benefactors; fees for membership
Staff: 50 volunteer(s)
Membership: fellows in 49 countries, committee members in 175 countries; *Member Profile:* Open to all professionals, educational institutes, industries, governmental or quasi-governmental bodies operating in the field of energy; *Committees:* Constitution & Bylaws; External Administrative Centres; External & Internal Meetings; Finance; Goals & Objectives; Membership; Publications & Public Relations
Activities: Conferences, symposiums, workshops; *Speaker Service:* Yes
Mission: To facilitate the transfer of research & technology in all areas of energy with special emphasis on developing countries; interested in better ways to produce, transmit & conserve energy; to sponsor & conduct research studies, surveys & state-of-the-art studies; to undertake consulting projects & organize training programs for the interchange of knowledge & expertise amongst the international community; to provide scholarships for the education of students in fields of interest consistent with the objectives of the Foundation; to administer awards for the purpose of recognition & encouragement of outstanding achievement in areas of study consistent with objectives of the Foundation; to recommend standards to existing national & international associations & promote adoption of such approved standards for energy consumption, production & conservation; *Member of:* International Standards Organization

International Ergonomics Association

Department of Industrial Engineering, National Tsing Hua University, 101, Sec. 2 Guang Fu Rd., Hsinchu 30013 Taiwan
Tel: 886-3-574-2649; *Fax:* 886-3-572-6153
URL: www.iea.cc
Overview: A small international organization
Chief Officer(s):
Eric Min-yang Wang, Secretary General
mywang@ie.nthu.edu.tw
Committees: Policy & Planning; Professional Standards & Education; Science, Technology & Practice; Communications & Public Relations; Industrially Developing Countries; Awards
Awards: K.U. Smith Student Paper Award (Award)
IEA/Liberty Mutual Prize in Occupational Safety & Ergonomics (Award)
IEA Fellow Award (Award)
Distinguished Service Award (Award)
Outstanding Educators Award (Award)
Award for Promotion of Ergonomics in Industrially Developing Countries (Award)
Ergonomics Development Award (Award)
President's Award (Award)
Mission: To elaborate & advance ergonomics science & practice & to improve the quality of life by expanding its scope of application & contribution to society

International Erosion Control Association (IECA)

#3500, 3401 Quebec St., Denver CO 80207 USA
Fax: 866-308-3087
Toll-Free: 800-455-4322
e-mail: ecinfo@ieca.org
URL: www.ieca.org
Overview: A medium-sized international organization founded in 1972
Chief Officer(s):
Michael Chase, President
Finances: *Annual Operating Budget:* $500,000-$1.5 Million; *Funding Sources:* Membership dues; conferences; courses; publications
Staff: 10 staff member(s)
Membership: 3,500 members in 52 countries; *Fees:* Schedule available; *Member Profile:* 17 Professional Fields of Practice: Academic, Consultant, Contractor, Developer, Engineer, Government Agency, Landscape Architect, Library, Mining, Non-Profit, Publisher, Ski Industry, Supplier, Utility Company, & Other

Activities: Professional development courses; field trips & tours throughout the world; training bureau; scholarship program; research grant program & an erosion control material standards program; *Speaker Service:* Yes
Mission: Serves as a global resource for environmental education & exchange of information; represents, leads & unifies a diverse group of people worldwide who share a common responsibility for the causes, prevention & control of erosion

International Federation for Cell Biology (IFCB)
URL: www.ifcbiol.org
Overview: A medium-sized international organization founded in 1972
Membership: 15 member organizations representing 60 nations; *Fees:* US$200
Mission: To promote cooperation & to contribute to the advancement of cell biology in all its branches; Affiliation(s): International Union of Biological Sciences; International Cell Research Organization

International Federation for Housing & Planning (IFHP) / Fédération internationale pour l'habitation, l'urbanisme et l'aménagement des territoires (FIHUAT)
43 Wassenaarseweg, 2596 CG, The Hague 2596 CG Netherlands
Tel: 31-70-324-4557; *Fax:* 31-70-328-2085
e-mail: info@ifhp.org
URL: www.ifhp.org
Previous Name: International Garden Cities & Town Planning Association
Overview: A medium-sized international organization founded in 1913
Membership: 500-999; *Member Profile:* Organizations or individuals who support the aims & objectives of IFHP, & who wish to participate in a worldwide network
Activities: Offering conferences, seminars, symposia, & study tours; Organizing student & film & video competitions
Publications: *IFHP [International Federation for Housing & Planning] Membership List & Directory*
Type: Directory *Number of Pages:* 77 *Price:* Free for members only
Mission: To plan & organize activities; To create opportunities for an exchange of professional knowledge & experience

International Federation for Medical & Biological Engineering (IFMBE)
e-mail: office@ifmbe.org
URL: www.ifmbe.org
Overview: A medium-sized international organization founded in 1959
Membership: 48 countries; *Fees:* Schedule available; *Committees:* Finance; Constitution & Bylaws; Secretaries; Working Groups: Asian Pacific Activities; Developing Countries; European Activities; Women in MBE; Regional Liaisons; International Liaisons; Nominating; Publication & Publicity; Federation Journal
Mission: To reflect the interests & initiatives of national affiliated organizations; to generate & disseminate information of interest to the medical & biological engineering community & international organizations; to provide an international forum for the exchange of ideas & concepts; to encourage & foster research & application of medical & biological engineering knowledge & techniques in support of life quality & cost-effective health care; to stimulate international cooperation & collaboration on medical & biological engineering matters; to encourage educational programs that develop scientific & technical expertise in medical & biological engineering. IFMBE Secretariat currently located in Stockholm, Sweden.; Affiliation(s): International Union of Physical & Engineering Sciences in Medicine; International Organization for Medical Physics

International Federation of Hydrographic Societies
PO Box 103, Plymouth PL4 7YP United Kingdom
Tel: 44-175-222-3512; *Fax:* 44-175-222-3512
e-mail: helen@hydrographicsociety.org
URL: www.hydrographicsociety.org
Previous Name: Hydrographic Society
Overview: A small international charitable organization founded in 1972
Finances: *Annual Operating Budget:* $100,000-$250,000
Staff: 1 staff member(s); 10 volunteer(s)
Membership: From over 70 countries; *Fees:* Available on application; *Member Profile:* Individuals & organizations with an interest in any aspect of surveying afloat; *Committees:* Educational Award Scheme
Activities: Publications, conferences, seminars, workshops

Mission: To promote the science of surveying afloat & related sciences; to promote better education & training of persons engaged or intending to engage in the study of hydrography & related sciences; to accumulate, extend & disseminate information, knowledge & expertise

International Federation of Landscape Architects (IFLA) / Fédération internationale des architectes paysagistes
Kaceni 6, Olomouc CZ-77200 Czech Republic
Tel: 420-585-207-778; *Fax:* 420-257-324-124
e-mail: info@iflaonline.org
URL: www.iflaonline.org
Also Known As: IFLA
Overview: A small international charitable organization founded in 1948
Membership: 1-99; *Member Profile:* National associations of professional landscape architects, individuals & corporations; *Committees:* Executive; Finance; Foundation
Activities: Offering world congresses, regional conferences, symposia & seminars; Organizing an international student design competition & educational programs
Publications: *Guide to International Opportunities in Landscape Architecture, Education & Internships*
Profile: Listing of international opportunities sorted by country
IFLA Journal
Type: Journal *Editor:* Thomas Jakob
Profile: Selected articles from landscape architecture magazines from around the world
Mission: To develop the profession of landscape architecture; To assist in identifying & preserving the intricate balance of ecological systems; To promote education & encourage scientific research in landscape architecture; To assist all levels of government in establishing & improving legislation connected with the profession of landscape architecture

International Federation of Organic Agriculture Movements (IFOAM) / Fédération internationale des mouvements d'agriculture biologique
Charles-de-Gaulle-Str.5, Bonn 53113 Germany
Tel: 49-228-926-5010; *Fax:* 49-228-926-5099
e-mail: headoffice@ifoam.org
URL: www.ifoam.org
Overview: A small international charitable organization founded in 1972
Finances: *Annual Operating Budget:* $500,000-$1.5 Million
Staff: 10 staff member(s)
Membership: 750 member organizations & corporate associates in 105 countries; *Fees:* Schedule available; *Committees:* Standards; Third World; Accreditation; Criteria Revision
Activities: *Internships:* Yes; *Speaker Service:* Yes; *Library:* Yes, open by appointment
Mission: To lead, assist, & unite the organic movement in its full diversity; To promote the worldwide adoption of ecologically, socially, & economically sound systems that are based on the principles of organic agriculture; *Member of:* Consumers Choice Council; Affiliation(s): Association interprofessionnelle pour le développement agrobiologique; Canadian Organic Growers; International Development Research Center; Ecological Agriculture Projects; Université écologique internationale; Mouvement pour l'agriculture biologique au Québec

International Federation of Surveyors (IFS) / Fédération internationale des géomètres (FIG)
Kalvebod Brygge 31-33, Copenhagen 1780 Denmark
Tel: 45 3886 1081; *Fax:* 45 3886 0252
e-mail: FIG@fig.net
URL: www.fig.net
Overview: A medium-sized international organization founded in 1878
Membership: 200,000
Mission: To ensure that the disciplines of surveying and all who practise them meet the needs of the markets and communities that they serve.; Affiliation(s): Canadian Institute of Surveying and Mapping

International Flying Farmers (IFF)
#490, 105 S. Broadway, Wichita KS 67202 USA
Tel: 316-943-4234; *Fax:* 800-266-5415
e-mail: flyingfarmers@sbcglobal.net
URL: www.flyingfarmers.org
Overview: A medium-sized international organization founded in 1944
Chief Officer(s):
Don Leis, President
Membership: 1,100; *Fees:* US$60 per family

Mission: To provide a personalized, unique & economical opportunity to experience agriculture & aviation in a family environment in Canada & the United States

International Fund for Animal Welfare Canada (IFAW) / Fonds international pour la protection des animaux
#612, 1 Nicholas St., Ottawa ON K1N 7B7
Tel: 613-241-8996; *Fax:* 613-241-0641
Toll-Free: 888-500-4329
URL: www.ifaw.org
Overview: A small international organization founded in 1969
Chief Officer(s):
Fred O'Regan, President
Olivier Bonnet, Canadian Director
Finances: *Annual Operating Budget:* $500,000-$1.5 Million
Staff: 12 staff member(s)
Membership: 45,000
Activities: Campaigns against the commercial seal hunt in Canada, supporting anti-cruelty legislations for Canada
Mission: Works to improve the welfare of wild & domestic animals throughout the world by reducing the commercial exploitation of animals, protecting wildlife habitats & assisting animals in distress; seeks to motivate the public to prevent cruelty to animals; promotes animal welfare & conservation policies that advance the well-being of animals & people

International Garden Cities & Town Planning Association
See International Federation for Housing & Planning

International Genetics Federation (IGF)
Dept. of Evolution & Ecology, University of California - Davis, 1 Shields Ave., Davis CA 95616-8554 USA
Tel: 530-752-4085; *Fax:* 530-752-1449
e-mail: chlangley@ucdavis.edu
URL: www.intergenetics.org
Overview: A small international organization founded in 1968
Membership: 63 national genetics societies
Mission: To promote the advancement of the science of genetics; *Member of:* International Union of Biological Sciences; Affiliation(s): Genetics Society of Canada

International Geographic Union (IGU) / Union géographique internationale
2246N Pollard St., Arlington VA 22207-3805 USA
Fax: 703-527-3227
e-mail: rabler@aag.org
URL: www.igu-net.org
Overview: A small international organization founded in 1922
Membership: 1-99
Activities: *Library:* Archives, Royal Geographical Society in London;
Awards: Planet & Humanity Medal (Award)
Laureat d'Honneur de l'IGU (Award)
Publications: *IGU [International Geographic Union] Newsletter*
Type: Newsletter *Frequency:* q. *Editor:* Ronald F. Abler
Profile: Announcements, information, calls for participation in scientific events, programs, & projects
Mission: The IGU has the following objectives: to promote the study of geographical problems; to initiate & coordinate geographical research; to provide for the participation of geographers in the work of international organizations; to facilitate the collection & diffusion of geographical data & documentation; & to promote international standardization or compatibility of methods, nomenclature & symbols employed in geography.; *Member of:* International Social Science Council; Affiliation(s): International Council of Science

International Geographical Union - Canadian Committee
Simon Fraser Univ., Dept. of Geography, 8888 University Dr., Burnaby BC V5A 1S6
Tel: 604-291-3321; *Fax:* 604-291-5841
e-mail: agill@sfu.ca
URL: www.igu-net.org/uk/what_is_igu/nationalcommittees.html
Overview: A small national organization
Finances: *Annual Operating Budget:* Less than $50,000; *Funding Sources:* National Research Council; SSHRCC
Staff: 10 volunteer(s)
Mission: To promote international programs in geography within Canada; to promote activities within IGU programs relevant to Canada & to coordinate Canadian participation; to formulate Canadian position & advise the National Research Council on Canadian participation in IGU activities

Associations/Organizations / International Geosynthetics Society

International Geosynthetics Society (IGS)
Secretariat, PO Box 347, Easley SC 29641-0347 USA
Tel: 864-855-0504; *Fax:* 864-859-1698
e-mail: igssec@geosyntheticssociety.org
URL: www.geosyntheticssociety.org
Overview: A medium-sized international organization founded in 1984
Chief Officer(s):
Fumio Tatsuoka, President
Finances: *Annual Operating Budget:* $100,000-$250,000; *Funding Sources:* Membership dues
Staff: 1 staff member(s); 10 volunteer(s)
Membership: 31 chapters; 2,279 individuals; 128 corporate members from 68 countries; 156 student members; *Fees:* Schedule available; *Member Profile:* Geosynthetics professionals; *Committees:* Awards; Chapters; Corporate; Education; Technical
Mission: Dedicated to the scientific & engineering development of geotextiles, geomembranes, related products & associated technologies

International Heavy Haul Association (IHHA)
2808 Forest Hills Crt., Virginia Beach 23454-1236 USA
Tel: 757-496-9384; *Fax:* 757-496-2622
URL: www.ihha.net
Overview: A large international organization
Chief Officer(s):
W. Scott Lovelace, Chief Executive Officer, 757-496-8288, Fax: 757-496-2622
ihha@cox.net
Finances: *Funding Sources:* Membership fees; Sponsorships
Member Profile: Railway organizations; National & state organizations; Private railway systems; Advocates for the world's heavy haul rail operations
Activities: Organizing specialist seminars & specialist technical sessions; Offering networking opportunities
Meetings/Conferences:
For more information see Trade Shows, Conferences and Seminars Chapter
International Heavy Haul Association 2011 Specialist Technical Session: Railroading in Extreme Environments
June 2011 Calgary, AB
International Heavy Haul Association 2013 International Conference
Other Conferences in 2013 2013
International Heavy Haul Association 2015 Specialist Technical Session
Other Conferences in 2015 2015
International Heavy Haul Association 2017 International Conference
Other Conferences in 2017 2017
Publications: *Guidelines To Best Practices For Heavy Haul Railway Operations - Infrastructure Construction & Maintenance Issues*
Price: $125
Guidelines To Best Practices For Heavy Haul Railway Operations - Wheel & Rail Interface Issues
Price: $80
International Heavy Haul Association Conference Proceedings
Mission: To pursue excellence in heavy haul railway operations, engineering, technology & maintenance

International Institute for Applied Systems Analysis (IIASA)
Schlossplatz 1, Laxenburg A-2361 Austria
Tel: 43-2236-807-0; *Fax:* 43-2236-71-313
e-mail: info@iiasa.ac.at
URL: www.iiasa.ac.at
Overview: A medium-sized international organization founded in 1972
Finances: *Annual Operating Budget:* Greater than $5 Million
Staff: 180 staff member(s)
Membership: 16; *Member Profile:* International & national research & policy institutes, organizations, & universities; *Committees:* Executive; Finance; Program; Membership; Advisory; Science; Steering
Activities: Policy-relevant research carried out by international, interdisciplinary teams, based on the following related themes: 1. Energy & Technology, including studies of environmentally compatible energy strategies, economic transition & integration, decision analysis & support, dynamic systems, & risk, modeling & policy; 2. Natural Resources & the Environment, including modeling land-use & land-cover changes in Europe & Northern Asia, sustainable boreal forest resources, transboundary air pollution, & adaptive dynamics; *Library:* Yes, open by appointment
Awards: Young Scientists Summer Program (Award)
Young Postdoctoral Fellows Program (Award)
Peccei & Mikhalevich Scholarship (Award)
Luis Donaldo Colosio Fellowship (Award)
Mission: To initiate & support individual & collaborative research on problems associated with social, economic, technological & environmental change, & thereby assist scientific, industrial & policy communities throughout the world in tackling such problems; current principal focus: scientific study of sustainability & the human dimensions of global change; to bring together scientists from various countries & disciplines to conduct research in a setting that is non-political & scientifically rigorous; to provide policy-oriented research results that deal with issues transcending national boundaries; to coordinate research projects, working in collaboration with worldwide networks of researchers, policy makers & research organizations; *Member of:* International Council for Science; International Federation of Institutes for Advanced Study; Affiliation(s): Canadian Committee for IIASA

International Institute for Conservation of Historic & Artistic Works (IIC)
6 Buckingham St., London WC2N 6BA United Kingdom
Tel: 44-20-7839-5975; *Fax:* 44-20-7976-1564
e-mail: iic@iiconservation.org
URL: www.iiconservation.org
Overview: A medium-sized international organization founded in 1950
Chief Officer(s):
Graham Voce, Executive Secretary
Valerie Compton-Taylor, Membership Secretary
membership@iiconservation.org
Fees: £49 individual; £19 student; £70 fellow; £170 institution; *Member Profile:* Restorers; Conservators; Conservation scientists; Educators; Students; Architects; Collection managers; Curators; Art historians; Cultural heritage professionals
Mission: The Instiute coordinates & improves the knowledge, methods & working standards needed to protect, preserve & maintain the condition & integrity of historic & artistic works.

International Institute for Energy Conservation (IIEC)
#100, 10005 Leamoore Lane, Vienna VA 22181 USA
Tel: 703-281-7263; *Fax:* 703-938-5153
e-mail: iiec@iiec.org
URL: www.iiec.org
Overview: A medium-sized international organization founded in 1984
Chief Officer(s):
Nitin Pandit, Ph.D., President
Mission: To bring the power of sustainable energy solutions to developing countries & economies in transition; these solutions include energy efficiency, renewable energy, & integrated transport planning; 8 offices worldwide.

International Institute for Sustainable Development (IISD) / Institut international du développement durable (IIDD)
161 Portage Ave. East, 6th Fl., Winnipeg MB R3B 0Y4
Tel: 204-958-7700; *Fax:* 204-958-7710
e-mail: info@iisd.ca
URL: www.iisd.org
Overview: A large international organization founded in 1990
Chief Officer(s):
David Runnalls, President/CEO
William H. Glanville, Vice-President & COO
Finances: *Annual Operating Budget:* Greater than $5 Million; *Funding Sources:* Federal & provincial government; government of other countries; philanthropic foundations
Staff: 80 staff member(s)
Activities: Trade & sustainable development; community adaptation & sustainable livelihoods; greening national budgets; business & industry accountability; Great Plains Sustainable Development; sustainable development measurement & indicators; *Internships:* Yes; *Speaker Service:* Yes; *Library:* Yes, Open to public, open by appointment
Awards: IISD Scholar (Scholarship)
To assist post-secondary students (up to the Ph.D. level) studying issues related to sustainable development *Award Amount:* $5,000
Mission: To promote sustainable development in decision-making in Canada & abroad by undertaking sustainable development research, advising government, business & organizations, analyzing & reporting on issues & events, & publishing & disseminating sustainable development information. Offices in Winnipeg, Ottawa, New York, & Geneva.

International Institute for Transportation & Ocean Policy Studies; Oceans Institute of Canada
See International Oceans Institute of Canada

International Institute of Concern for Public Health (IICPH)
PO Box 80523, Stn. RPO White Shield, 2300 Lawrence Ave. East, Toronto ON M1P 4Z5
Tel: 416-786-6128
e-mail: info@iicph.org
URL: www.iicph.org
Overview: A medium-sized international charitable organization founded in 1984
Chief Officer(s):
Rosalie Bertell, PhD., Founder
Finances: *Annual Operating Budget:* Less than $50,000; *Funding Sources:* Private donations
Staff: 7 volunteer(s)
Activities: *Speaker Service:* Yes
Mission: To engage in advocacy on health issues; to assist in promoting & protecting people in their work & living environment in Ontario; to provide expertise on health, scientific & environmental issues; *Member of:* Ontario Environment Network; Earth Appeal; Nuclear Waste Watch

International Institute of Fisheries Economics & Trade (IIFET)
Agricultural & Resource Economics, Oregon State University, 220 Ballard Hall, Corvallis OR 97331-3601 USA
Tel: 541-737-1416; *Fax:* 541-737-2563
e-mail: iifet@oregonstate.edu
URL: www.oregonstate.edu/Dept/IIFET/
Overview: A small international charitable organization founded in 1982
Membership: 100-499; *Fees:* $75 regular; $25 student; $500 corporate/institutional; *Member Profile:* International Fisheries Economists; *Committees:* Executive
Activities: *Rents Mailing List:* Yes
Mission: To promote discussion of factors which affect international trade in seafoods & fisheries policy questions

International Labour Organization (ILO)
4, route des Morillons, Geneva CH-1211 Switzerland
Tel: 41-22-799-6111; *Fax:* 41-22-798-8685
e-mail: ilo@ilo.org
URL: www.ilo.org
Overview: A large international organization founded in 1919
Finances: *Annual Operating Budget:* Greater than $5 Million
Staff: 2528 staff member(s)
Membership: 183 member states + worker & employer organizations; *Committees:* Freedom of Association; Application of Standards
Activities: Setting international labour standards; technical cooperation; publications & research; *Internships:* Yes; *Speaker Service:* Yes; *Library:* Yes, Open to public
Mission: To bring governments, employers & trade unions together for united action in the cause of social justice & better living conditions everywhere; supports efforts by the international community & by individual nations to achieve full employment, raise living standards, share the fruits of progress fairly, protect the life & health of workers, & to promote cooperation between workers & employers in order to improve production & working conditions; the ILO employs a tripartite structure (dialogue among governments, workers' & employers' organizations) in order to interpret the aims & aspirations of each country, reflect its preoccupations & reach realistic decisions based on the social & economic situations of the countries concerned; the ILO cooperates with other organizations of the international community
Environmental Activity: The International Occupational Safety & Health Information Centre (CIS) is a unit of ILO; CIS offers a unique service in covering OSH information from around the world; CIS is bilingual (English/French)

International Law Association - Canadian Branch
c/o Bloomfield & Associés, #1720, 1080, Côte du Beaver Hall Hill, Montréal QC H2Z 1S8
Tel: 514-871-9571; *Fax:* 514-397-0816
e-mail: ila@fieldbloom.com
URL: www.ila-canada.ca
Overview: A medium-sized national organization founded in 1967
Chief Officer(s):
Miles Barutciski, President
Mario J. Choueiri
Committees: International Committees

Activities: *Awareness Events:* Biennial Conference
Mission: Is a body for the study and advancement of international law in all its forms, commercial and interpersonal. Membership of the Association which is at present over 3,500 is spread among 50 Branches in every continent.

International Lilac Society
1510, rue Pine, Mascouche QC J7L 2M4
Tel: 450-477-3797
e-mail: info@lilacs.freeservers.com
URL: lilacs.freeservers.com
Overview: A small international organization
Chief Officer(s):
Frank Moro, Executive Vice-President, Canada
Mission: To promote & stimulate interest in the genus Syringa

International Maritime Committee *See* Comité maritime international

International Maritime Organization (IMO) / Organisation maritime internationale
4 Albert Embankment, London SE1 7SR United Kingdom
Tel: 44-20-7735-7611; *Fax:* 44-20-7587-3210
e-mail: info@imo.org
URL: www.imo.org
Overview: A large international organization founded in 1948
Chief Officer(s):
Lee Adamson, Manager, Public Information
Efthimios E. Mitropoulos, Secretary General
Finances: *Annual Operating Budget:* Greater than $5 Million; *Funding Sources:* Government
Staff: 300 staff member(s)
Membership: 166 governments; *Fees:* Based on shipping fleet tonnage; *Committees:* Maritime Safety; Marine Environment Protection; Legal; Technical Cooperation; Facilitation
Activities: *Library:* Yes, open by appointment
Awards: International Maritime Prize (Award)
Award Amount: US$1,000 + travel expenses
Mission: To encourage the adoption of high standards in matters concerning maritime safety, security, efficiency of navigation & control of marine pollution from ships
Environmental Activity: Oil Pollution Co-ordination Centre

International Network for Environmental Management (INEM)
Osterstrasse 58, Hamburg 20259 Germany
Tel: 49-89-18935-200; *Fax:* 49-89-18935-199
e-mail: l.karg@inem.org
URL: www.inem.org
Overview: A small international organization founded in 1991
Chief Officer(s):
Ludwig Karg, Chair
Member Profile: Autonomous & non-profit business associations concerned with environmental management
Mission: To be committed to the implementation of environmental management in businesses worldwide, including small- & medium-sized enterprises; To promote clean technologies

International Nuclear Law Association (INLA) / Association internationale du droit nucléaire
Square de Meeus 29, Brussels B-1000 Belgium
Tel: 32-2-547-5841; *Fax:* 32-2-503-0440
e-mail: info@aidn.inla.be
URL: www.aidn-inla.be
Overview: A small international organization founded in 1970
Membership: 500; *Committees:* Safety and Regulation; Nuclear Liability and Inurance; International Nuclear Trade; Radiological Protection; Waste Management; Radioisotopes
Mission: To promote international studies of legal problems related to the peaceful use of nuclear energy

International Occupational Safety & Health Information Centre / Centre international d'informations de sécurité et de santé au travail
International Labour Office/CIS, Geneva CH-1211 Switzerland
Tel: 41-22-799-67-40; *Fax:* 41-22-799-85-16
e-mail: cis@ilo.org
URL: www.ilo.org/cis/
Also Known As: Centro Internacional de Informacion sobre Seguridad y Salud en el Trabajo
Overview: A small international organization founded in 1959
Finances: *Annual Operating Budget:* $1.5 Million-$3 Million
Staff: 12 staff member(s)
Membership: 183 national centres; *Fees:* CHF 26-315
Activities: CIS Information Service (personalized searches on any OSH topic); CIS factual microcomputer databases (covering important OSH topics); CIS Information Sheets (chemical, medical, technical, ergonomic); CIS microfiche service (reproduction of abstracted documents no longer obtainable from original sources); Directory of OSH Institutions (complete international OSH contact information); CIS Glossary of OSH Terms (OSH words & expressions: English, French, Spanish, German, Russian); CIS Bibliographies; *Library:* Yes, Open to public
Mission: To collect & disseminate world information that can contribute to the prevention of occupational accidents & diseases; *Affiliation(s):* Canadian Centre for Occupational Health & Safety; Canada Safety Council; Institut de recherche en santé et en sécurité de travail - Québec

International Ocean Institute (IOI) / Institut international de l'ocean
PO Box 3, Gzira GZR 01 Malta
Tel: 356-21-346-529; *Fax:* 356-21-346-502
e-mail: ioihq@ioihq.org.mt
URL: www.ioinst.org
Overview: A small international organization founded in 1972
Finances: *Annual Operating Budget:* $1.5 Million-$3 Million; *Funding Sources:* Donations; UN & government funding agencies; private foundations; endowment fund
Staff: 35 staff member(s); 200 volunteer(s)
Membership: 25 operational centres worldwide; *Committees:* Directors; Governing Board
Activities: Policy research; training; advisory services; *Speaker Service:* Yes; *Library:* IOI, Malta HQ Library; Not open to the public
Mission: To promote education, training & research to enhance the peaceful uses of ocean space & its resources, their management & regulation as well as the protection & conservation of the marine environment, guided by the principle of the common heritage of mankind

International Oceans Institute of Canada (IOIC)
c/o Dalhousie Univ., 1226 LeMarchant St., Halifax NS B3H 3P7
Tel: 902-494-6918; *Fax:* 902-494-1334
e-mail: ioi@dal.ca
URL: internationaloceaninstitute.dal.ca
Previous Name: International Institute for Transportation & Ocean Policy Studies; Oceans Institute of Canada
Overview: A small national organization founded in 1976
Membership: 50
Activities: Services of the institute are available nationally & internationally for governments, organizations & private sector concerns, including industry, special interest groups & foundations; services include project development & management, policy development, education & training, conference & workshop coordination, research & information
Mission: To promote responsible management of the world's oceans & sustainable development of marine resources; to protect the integrity of the ocean environment; to promote sustainable resource development; to improve the quality of ocean-dependent human life, including health & safety of maritime communities; to further these objectives, all aspects of the ocean environment are pursued - resource management & development, marine environmental quality, ocean law & policy, high seas management, coastal zone management, marine transportation, ocean science & technology, tourism & recreation, ocean industries & maritime boundary delimitation; *Affiliation(s):* International Oceans Institute; Atlantic Coastal Zone Information Steering Committee

International Organization for Standardization (ISO) / Organisation internationale de normalisation
PO Box 56, 1, Voie-Creuse, Geneva 20 1211 Switzerland
Tel: 41-22-749-01-11; *Fax:* 41-22-749-71-08
e-mail: central@iso.org
URL: www.iso.org
Overview: A small international organization founded in 1947
Finances: *Funding Sources:* 62% member bodies + 38% subscriptions + publications income + other services
Staff: 154 staff member(s)
Membership: 162; *Member Profile:* National body, representative of standardization in its country; *Committees:* 192 technical committees which develop international standards in a wide range of technological areas; the secretariat for a number of committees is held by the ISO member body for Canada (Standards Council of Canada, Ottawa)
Activities: *Library:* Reference Library; Open to public
Mission: To promote the development of standardization & related activities in the world with a view to facilitating the international exchange of goods & services; developing cooperation in the spheres of intellectual, scientific, technological & economic activity; the results of ISO's technical work are published as "International Standards"; *Affiliation(s):* Standards Council of Canada

International Peat Society (IPS)
Vapaudenkatu 12, Jyväskylä FI-40100 Finland
Tel: 358-14-3385-440; *Fax:* 358-14-3385-410
e-mail: ips@peatsociety.org
URL: www.peatsociety.org
Overview: A small international organization founded in 1968
Membership: 1,300 from 38 countries; *Fees:* Schedule available; *Member Profile:* Scientific, industrial, commercial, & other organizations; Individuals interested in the study, conservation, & utilization of peat & peatlands
Activities: Organizing congresses, symposia & workshops; Publishing scientific publications; *Library:* Yes
Awards: Wim Tonnis Peat Award (Award)
Meetings/Conferences:
For more information see Trade Shows, Conferences and Seminars Chapter
Peatlands in Balance: 14th International Peat Congress
June 2012 Stockholm
Publications: *Peat News*
Type: Newsletter *Frequency:* m. *Editor:* Susann Warnecke
Peatlands International
Type: Magazine *Frequency:* s-a. *Accepts Advertising* : Yes
Number of Pages: 60 *Price:* Free for members
Profile: Background reports on peat & peatlands, reviews of conferences & books, research findings, business reports, & internal information about the IPS
Mires & Peat
Type: Journal *Editor:* Dr. Olivia Bragg; Prof. Jack Rieley
Profile: A joint scientific journal of the International Peat Society & the International Mire Conservation Group, featuring peer-reviewed academic papers on research related to mires, peatlands, & peat throughout the world
Proceedings
Profile: Proceedings of IPS conferences, symposia, & workshops
Mission: IPS works toward the advancement & communication of scientific, technical, & social knowledge for the wise use of peatlands & peat.; *Affiliation(s):* UNESCO

International Peat Society - Canadian National Committee
c/o Coastal Zones Research Institute, 232B, av de l'Eglise, Shippagan NB E8S 1J2
Tel: 506-336-6600; *Fax:* 506-336-6601
e-mail: jydaigle@umcs.ca
URL: www.peatsociety.org
Overview: A small national organization founded in 1970
Finances: *Annual Operating Budget:* Less than $50,000; *Funding Sources:* Membership fees
Membership: 41 institutional/corporate + 3 senior/lifetime + 11 individual; *Fees:* $200 institutional/corporate; $30 individual
Activities: *Rents Mailing List:* Yes
Mission: Dedicated to fostering the advancement, exchange and communication of scientific, technical and social knowledge and understanding for the wise use of peatlands and peat.; *Affiliation(s):* International Peat Society

International Permafrost Association (IPA)
c/o H. Lantuit, Alfred Wegener Institute for Polar & Marine Research, Telefrafenberg A43, Potsdam 14473 Germany
Tel: +49-331-288-2162; *Fax:* +49-331-288-2188
e-mail: contact@ipa-permafrost.org
URL: ipa.arcticportal.org
Social Media: twitter.com/ipapermafrost
Overview: A medium-sized international organization founded in 1983
Committees: Standing Committee on Data, Information & Communications; International Advisory Committee for ICOP
Activities: Assembling the following working groups: Antarctic Permafrost & Periglacial Environments; Coastal & Offshore Permafrost Dynamics; Cryosol; Glaciers & Permafrost Hazards in High Mountain Slopes; Isotopes & Geochemistry of Permafrost; Periglacial Landforms, Processes & Climate; Permafrost & Climate; Planetary Permafrost & Astrobiology; Permafrost Engineering
Meetings/Conferences:
For more information see Trade Shows, Conferences and Seminars Chapter
Permafrost: 10th International Conference
June 2012 Tyumen
Publications: *Frozen Ground: The News Bulletin of the International Permafrost Association*

Associations/Organizations / International Plant Nutrition Institute

Type: Yearbook *Frequency:* a. *ISSN:* 2076-7463
Profile: Member news, current events, working group & task force reports, calendar, & publications
Permafrost & Periglacial Processes
Type: Journal *Frequency:* s-a.
Profile: Reports from the International Permafrost Association
Proceedings of the International Conferences on Permafrost
Type: Yearbook *Frequency:* a.
Profile: Peer-reviewed conference proceedings
Mission: To disseminate knowledge concerning permafrost; To promote cooperation among persons & national or international organizations engaged in scientific investigation & enginering work on permafrost; Affiliation(s): International Union of Geological Science

International Plant Nutrition Institute (IPNI)
#550, 3500 Parkway Lane, Norcross GA 30092 USA
Tel: 770-447-0335; *Fax:* 770-448-0439
e-mail: info@ipni.net
URL: www.ppi-ppic.org
Previous Name: Potash & Phosphate Institute/Potash & Phosphate Institute of Canada
Overview: A medium-sized international organization founded in 1935
Finances: Annual Operating Budget: Greater than $5 Million;
Funding Sources: North American potash & phosphate producers; Government of Saskatchewan
Staff: 6 staff member(s)
Membership: 16 corporate; 6 affiliate companies; *Member Profile:* North American potash or phosphate producer
Activities: Library: Yes, Open to public
Awards: Robert E. Wagner Award (Award)
J. Fielding Reed PPI Fellowship (Scholarship)
Mission: To assist in the design & implementation of agronomic research; to obtain scientific facts & education programs to tell those facts about balanced fertilization, particularly in relation to agricultural production systems; to conduct & provide on-site support of field experiments worldwide

International Plant Propagators Society, Inc. (IPPS)
615 Willams Grove Rd., Mechanicsburg PA 17955-7512 USA
Tel: 717-691-8898; *Fax:* 717-691-5440
e-mail: Secretary@ipps.org
URL: www.ipps.org
Overview: A medium-sized international organization founded in 1951
Finances: Annual Operating Budget: $100,000-$250,000;
Funding Sources: Membership dues
Membership: 3,200 individual; *Fees:* Varies with region;
Member Profile: Open to individuals for commercial purposes or to those involved in research, teaching or extension activities
Mission: To seek & share information about the art & science of plant propagation

International Primary Care Respiratory Group (IPCRG)
c/o S. Louw, Ctr. of Academic Primary Care, Foresterhill Health Ctr., Westburn Rd., Aberdeen, Scotland AB25 2AY United Kingdom
Tel: + 44 1224 552427; *Fax:* + 44 1224 550683
e-mail: sam.knowles@abdn.ac.uk
URL: www.theipcrg.org
Overview: A medium-sized international organization
Chief Officer(s):
Siân Williams, Executive Officer
Activities: Engaging in collaborative research; Disseminating best practice information; Providing educational opportunities
Publications: Primary Care Respiratory Journal
Type: Journal
Profile: Original research papers, review, & discussion papers on respiratory conditions commonly found in primary & community settings in countries around the world
Mission: To represent international primary care perspectives in respiratory medicine; To raise standards of care worldwide

International Primate Protection League (IPPL)
PO Drawer 766, Summerville SC 29484 USA
Tel: 843-871-2280; *Fax:* 843-871-7988
e-mail: info@ippl.org
URL: www.ippl.org
Overview: A medium-sized international charitable organization founded in 1973
Finances: Annual Operating Budget: $500,000-$1.5 Million;
Funding Sources: Membership dues; foundation grants; bequests
Staff: 7 staff member(s); 4 volunteer(s)

Membership: 15,000 in over 60 countries; *Fees:* $20 regular; $10 student; $50 sustaining; $100 patron
Mission: To encourage & contribute to a better understanding of matters relating to the conservation of non-human primates & their habitats; to promote relevant training & educational activities with reference to non-human primates; to promote & enhance the welfare of non-human primates; to support primate protection projects; to investigate smuggling of primates; *Member of:* Monitor Consortium; Summit for the Animals; International Union for Conservation of Nature; Civicus

International Reference Centre for Community Water Supply & Sanitation *See* IRC International Water & Sanitation Centre

International Research Group on Wood Protection (IRG)
IRG Secretariat, PO Box 5609, Stockholm SE-114 86 Sweden
Tel: 46-8-101-453; *Fax:* 46-8-108-081
e-mail: irg@sp.se
URL: www.irg-wp.com
Overview: A small international organization founded in 1969
Finances: Annual Operating Budget: $100,000-$250,000;
Funding Sources: Membership & conference fees; sponsorships
Membership: 350; *Fees:* 900 SEK (Swedish Kroner) - regular; 450 SEK - student; *Member Profile:* Open to all persons with appropriate qualifications or research experience who are active or interested in wood protection research; *Committees:* Executive; Finance; Scientific Program; Membership; Ron Cockcroft Award; IRG Travel Awards; Electronic Communications
Activities: 4-day conference; workshops; plenary meetings; *Rents Mailing List:* Yes; *Library:* Yes, open by appointment
Awards: IRG Travel Awards (Grant)
Ron Cockcroft Award (Grant)
Travel grant for younger scientists, PhD students to attend annual meeting
Mission: To promote research throughout the world on the subject of wood protection; to facilitate collaborative research projects; to promote the exchange of technical information on wood protection

International Sanitary Supply Association, Inc. (ISSA)
7373 Lincoln Ave. North, Lincolnwood IL 60712-1799 USA
Tel: 847-982-0800; *Fax:* 847-982-1012
Toll-Free: 800-225-4772
e-mail: info@issa.com
URL: www.issa.com
Previous Name: National Sanitary Supply Association
Overview: A large international organization founded in 1923
Chief Officer(s):
John P. Garfinkel, Executive Director
Barbara Bornmann, Executive Assistant
barbara@issa.com
Finances: Annual Operating Budget: Greater than $5 Million; *Funding Sources:* Convention revenue; membership dues; educational materials
Staff: 24 staff member(s); 15 volunteer(s)
Membership: 5,700 companies in 83 countries; *Fees:* Schedule available; *Member Profile:* Firms which have been continuously engaged in the manufacture &/or distribution of cleaning & maintenance supplies & related products & services; classes of membership are distributor, wholesaler, manufacturer, associate, manufacturer representative, publisher
Activities: Awareness Events: Operation Clean Sweep; *Library:* Yes
Mission: To link resources & expertise of everyone in the cleaning & maintenance products industry through an ongoing program of training & education, regional & national conferences, publications & the industry's largest annual trade show; to act as one voice before government agencies; to increase product quality, service & value to the customer; to promote the highest standards of public health & sanitation

International Society for Ecological Economics (ISEE)
PO Box 44194, West Allis WI 53214 USA
Tel: 414-453-0030
e-mail: secretariat@ecoeco.org
URL: www.ecoeco.org
Social Media: www.facebook.com/iseeorg
www.twitter.com/ISEEORG
Overview: A medium-sized international organization founded in 1988
Finances: Annual Operating Budget: $100,000-$250,000;
Funding Sources: Membership fees; grants

Staff: 4 staff member(s)
Membership: 2,008; *Fees:* $15-$130; *Committees:* Curriculum Development; Policy
Mission: To extend & integrate the study & management of "nature's household" (ecology) & "humankind's household" (economics)

International Society for Ecological Modelling (ISEM)
PMB 255, 550 M Ritchie Hwy., Severna Park MD 21146 USA
e-mail: dmauriello@isemna.org
URL: www.isemna.org
Overview: A small international organization founded in 1975
Fees: $10 student; $20 individual; $100 institution
Mission: To promote the international exchange of ideas, scientific results, & general knowledge in the area of the application of systems analysis & simulation in ecology & natural resource management

International Society for Environmental Biotechnology (ISEB)
ISEB Secretariat, Dept. of Chemical Engineering, U. of Waterloo, Waterloo ON N2L 3G1
Fax: 519-746-4979
e-mail: iseb@cape.uwaterloo.ca
URL: www.iseb-web.org
Overview: A small international organization
Chief Officer(s):
William A. Anderson, Sec.-Treas.
Mission: To facilitate the development & promotion of environmental biotechnology worldwide

International Society for Environmental Epidemiology (ISEE)
c/o ISEE Secretariat, JSI Research & Training Institute, 44 Farnsworth St., Boston MA 2210 USA
Tel: 617-482-9485; *Fax:* 617-482-0617
e-mail: iseepi@jsi.org
URL: www.iseepi.org
Overview: A small international organization founded in 1989
Chief Officer(s):
Carol Rougvie, Secretariat
Daniel Wartenberg, President
dew@eohsi.rutgers.edu
Francine Laden, Sec.-Treas.
francine.laden@channing.harvard.edu
Membership: 500-999; *Fees:* US$220 full member; US$145 basic; US$55 developing country & student; *Member Profile:* Members include epidemiologists, toxicologists, exposure analysts & others with an interest in environmental epidemiology, from academia, local, state & federal government, industry, & community organizations.; *Committees:* Nominations; Annual Conference; Awards; Membership; Communications; Ethics & Philosophy; Capacity Building in Developing Countries
Activities: Rents Mailing List: Yes
Awards: The ISEE Research Integrity Award (Award)
Recognizes those who have remained true to the core values of the profession by maintaining objectivity in protecting the public health interest above any other interest Contact: Daniel Wartenberg, Chair, Awards Committee *Contact Detail:* dew@eohsi.rutgers.edu
Rebecca James Baker Memorial Prize (Award)
Eligibility: Graduate level students & new investigators who are within three years of completing their degree Contact: Irva Hertz-Picciotto, Co-Chair *Contact Detail:* ihp@ucdavis.edu
John Goldsmith Award for Outstanding Conributions to Environmental Epidemiology (Award)
Recognizes environmental epidemiologist who seve as models of excellence in research, unwavering promotion of environmental health, & integrity *Deadline:* March Contact: Daniel Wartenberg, Chair, Awards Committee *Contact Detail:* dew@eohsi.rutgers.edu
Publications: Epidemiology
Type: Journal *Frequency:* bi-m. *Editor:* Allen J. Wilcox *ISSN:* 1044-3983
Profile: A peer-reviewed scientific journal featuring original research on the full spectrum of epidemiologic topics
International Society for Environmental Epidemiology Directory of Members
Type: Directory
Profile: Includes all ISEE members
Mission: To provide a forum for the discussion of problems unique to the study of health & the environment, such as environmental exposures, health effects, methodology, environment-gene interactions, & ethics & law; *Member of:* International Society of Exposure Analysis

International Society for Environmental Ethics (ISEE)
c/o Mark Woods, Philosophy Department, University of San Diego, 5998 Alcala Park, San Diego CA 92110
URL: www.cep.unt.edu/ISEE.html
Overview: A small international organization founded in 1990
Chief Officer(s):
Emily Brady, President
Emily.Brady@ed.ac.uk
Philip J. Cafaro, Vice-President, 970-491-2061, Fax: 970-491-4900
philip.cafaro@colostate.edu
Mark Woods, Secretary, 619-260-6865, Fax: 619-260-7950
mwoods@sandiego.edu
Marion Hourdequin, Treasurer, 719-227-8331
marion.hourdequin@coloradocollege.edu
Fees: $25 regular membership (US); $15 students (US); $25 regular international member
Activities: Providing information about environmental ethics; Maintaining a bibliography on environmental ethics; Offering educational events
Publications: *International Society for Environmental Ethics Newsletter*
Frequency: 3 pa Editor: Mark Woods Price: Free with International Society for Environmental Ethics membership
Profile: Society activities & announcements, plus articles
Environmental Ethics Syllabus Project
Editor: Robert Hood ISSN: 1564-001
Profile: Information about courses in environmental philosophy & environmental ethics

International Society for Evolutionary Protistology (ISEP)
c/o Patrick Keeling, President, Botany Department, University of British Columbia, Vancouver BC V6T 1Z4
Tel: 604-822-4906; Fax: 604-822-6089
URL: www.isepsociety.com
Overview: A small international organization
Fees: $35 per 2-year period

International Society for Plant Pathology
c/o Secretary General, PO Box 412, Jamison ACT 2612 Australia
Tel: 61-2-62515658
URL: www.isppweb.org
Overview: A small international charitable organization founded in 1968
Chief Officer(s):
M. Lodovica Gullino, President
issp.president@isppweb.org
Thomas Evans, Treasurer
ispp.treasurer@isppweb.org
Member Profile: Open to persons interested in or involved in plant pathology
Mission: To promote the worldwide development of plant pathology & the dissemination of knowledge about plant diseases & plant health management; Member of: International Union of Biological Sciences; International Union of Microbiological Sciences

International Society for Rock Mechanics (ISRM)
c/o Laboratório Nacional de Engenharia Civil, 101 Av. do Brasil, Lisbon 1700-066 Portugal
Tel: 351-21-844-3419; Fax: 351-21-844-3021
e-mail: secretariat.isrm@lnec.pt
URL: www.isrm.net
Overview: A medium-sized international organization founded in 1962
Finances: Funding Sources: Membership fees; Grants that do not impair the Society's free action
Membership: 5,000 members + 46 national groups; Member Profile: Rock mechanics practitioners & corporations;
Committees: Joint Technical Committee on Landslides & Engineered Slopes; Joint Technical Committee on Representation of Geo-engineering Data in Electronic Form; Joint Technical Committee on Education & Training; Joint Technical Committee on Professional Practice; Joint Technical Committee on Sustainable Use of Underground Space; Joint Technical Committee on Ancient Monuments & Historical Sites; Joint Technical Committee on Soft Rocks & Indurated Soils
Activities: Encouraging teaching, research, & advancement of knowledge in rock mechanics; Operating commissions for studying scientific & technical matters; Sponsoring international & regional symposia;; Library: Yes, open by appointment
Awards: Rocha Medal (Award)
For an outstanding doctoral thesis
Müller Award (Award)
For distinguished contributions to the profession of rock mechanics and rock engineering
Meetings/Conferences:
For more information see Trade Shows, Conferences and Seminars Chapter
International Society for Rock Mechanics 12th International Congress on Rock Mechanics: Harmonising Rock Mechanics & the Environment
October 2011 Beijing
Publications: *ISRM [International Society for Rock Mechanics] News Journal*
Type: Journal
Profile: Information about technology related to rock mechanics, news on activities in the rock mechanics community
ISRM [International Society for Rock Mechanics] Newsletter
Type: Newsletter
International Journal of Rock Mechanics & Mining Sciences
Type: Journal
Journal of Rock Mechanics & Rock Engineering
Type: Journal
Mission: The non-profit scientific association encourages & coordinates international cooperation in the area of rock mechanics. It maintains liaison with other organizations dealing with fields of science related to rock mechanics, such as geology, geophysics, soil mechanics, mining engineering, petroleum engineering & civil engineering.; Member of: International Union of Geological Societies; Affiliation(s): Canadian Rock Mechanics Association; Canadian Geotechnical Society

International Society for Soil Mechanics & Foundation Engineering
See International Society for Soil Mechanics & Geotechnical Engineering

International Society for Soil Mechanics & Geotechnical Engineering (ISSMGE) / Société Internationale de Mécanique des Sols et de la Géotechnique (SIMSG)
City University, Northampton Square, London EC1V 0HB United Kingdom
Tel: 44-20-7040-8154; Fax: 44-20-7040-8832
e-mail: secretariat@issmge.org
URL: www.issmge.org
Previous Name: International Society for Soil Mechanics & Foundation Engineering
Overview: A medium-sized international organization
Finances: Annual Operating Budget: $250,000-$500,000
Membership: 15,000-49,999; Committees: 25 active international Technical Committees working in various specialist areas of geotechnics
Affiliation(s): International Society for Soil Mechanics & Geotechnical Engineering - Canadian Section; Canadian Geotechnical Society

International Society of Arboriculture
PO Box 3129, Champaign IL 61821-3129 USA
Tel: 217-355-9411; Fax: 217-355-9516
e-mail: isa@isa-arbor.com
URL: www.isa-arbor.com
Overview: A medium-sized international organization founded in 1924
Chief Officer(s):
Tim Gamma, President
tgammatree@aol.com
Jim Skiera, Executive Director
jskiera@isa-arbor.com
Mission: To foster research & education that promotes the care & the benefits of trees; office located at 2101 West Park Court, Champaign IL

International Society of Biometeorology (ISB) / Société internationale de biométéorolgy
Secretariat, Dept. of Geography, Univ. of Wisconsin-Milwaukee, Milwaukee WI 53201-0413 USA
Tel: 414-229-3740; Fax: 414-229-3981
URL: www.biometeorology.org
Overview: A small international organization founded in 1956
Chief Officer(s):
Paul Beggs, President
paul.beggs@mq.edu.au
Mark D. Schwartz, Secretary
mds@uwm.edu
Finances: Annual Operating Budget: Less than $50,000; Funding Sources: Membership fees
Membership: 240; Fees: US$85; Committees: Standing; Membership; Nomination; Election; Finance; Publication
Activities: Library: ISB Archive
Mission: To promote international collaboration of physicists, biologists, meteorologists & other scientists & the development of the field of meteorology in relation to humans, animals & plants

International Society of Citriculture (ISC)
Botany & Plant Sciences, University of California, Riverside CA 92521-0124 USA
Tel: 951-827-4663; Fax: 951-827-4437
e-mail: iscucr@ucr.edu
URL: www.crec.ifas.ufl.edu/societies/ISC/index.htm
Overview: A large international organization founded in 1976
Finances: Funding Sources: Membership dues; Sales of congress proceedings
Membership: 1,000-4,999; Fees: US$30/4 years; Member Profile: Any individual, corporation, unincorporated association, or organization interested in an aspect of citrus culture, handling, marketing, processing, transportation, research, or education
Publications: *ISC [International Society of Citriculture] Proceedings*
Profile: Papers presented at previous meetings
Mission: To promote & encourage research, exchange of information & education, in all aspects of citrus production, harvesting, handling, & distribution of both fresh fruit & products; Affiliation(s): International Society for Horticultural Science

International Society of City & Regional Planners
PO Box 983, The Hague 2501 CZ Netherlands
Tel: 31-70-346-2654; Fax: 31-70-361-7909
e-mail: isocarp@isocarp.org
URL: www.isocarp.org
Also Known As: ISOCARP
Overview: A small international licensing organization founded in 1965
Finances: Funding Sources: Membership fees
Membership: 100-499; Fees: Schedule available; Member Profile: Professional planners; Stakeholders involved in the development & maintenance of the built environment
Activities: Promoting the planning profession; Facilitating exchange between planners from different countries; Providing information on major planning issues; Evaluating developments & trends in planning practice
Awards: Gerd Albert Award (Award)
Routledge Prize (Award)
Poster congress prize
Publications: *ISOCARP [International Society of City & Regional Planners] NET*
Type: Newsletter Editor: Judy van Hemert
International Society of City & Regional Planners Annual Congress Report
Type: Yearbook Frequency: a.
Profile: Final report of each congress
International Manual of Planning Practice (IMPP)
Editor: Judith Ryser; Teresa Franchini
Profile: Reference guide to the key features of the spatial planning systems
ISOCARP [International Society of City & Regional Planners] Review
Profile: Complement to the research efforts prepared for the annual ISOCARP Congresses
Mission: To improve cities & territories through planning practice, training, education, & research; Affiliation(s): UNESCO; Council of Europe; UN/ECOSOC; UNCHS/Habitat

International Society of Indoor Air Quality & Climate (ISIAQ)
c/o Gina Bendy, 2548 Empire Grade, Santa Cruz CA 95060 USA
Tel: 831-426-0148; Fax: 831-426-6522
e-mail: info@isiaq.org
URL: www.isiaq.org
Overview: A medium-sized international organization founded in 1992
Chief Officer(s):
Richard Shaughnessy, President
rjstulsau@aol.com
Anne Hyvärinen, Secretary
anne.hyvarinen@thl.fi
Carl-Gustaf Bornehag, Treasurer
carl-gustaf.bornehag@kau.se
Finances: Funding Sources: Membership fees; Donations; Sponsorships

Associations/Organizations / International Society of Limnology

Fees: US $15 - $30 /year students; US $135 / year individuals; US $700 / year corporate members; *Member Profile:* Individuals, such as scientist involved in indoor air quality research, occupational health professionals, government & regulatory professionals, & architects; Corporations; Students; *Committees:* Task force on the control of moisture & mould problems in cold climate; Task force on the vocabulary of the indoor air sciences; Task force on the IAQ & climate in cultural & heritage collections; Task force on the criteria for cleaning of air handling systems; Task force on the performance of portable air cleaners; Task force on the education for healthier buildings; Task force on the effect of the indoor environment on productivity in offices; Task force on indoor air research & building practice
Activities: Facilitating international & interdisciplinary communication; Liaising with governments & other agencies with interests in indoor environment
Meetings/Conferences:
For more information see Trade Shows, Conferences and Seminars Chapter
Indoor Air 2011
June 2011 Austin, TX
Healthy Buildings 2012
July 2012 Brisbane
Indoor Air 2014: The Triennial Conference of the International Society of Indoor Air Quality and Climate (ISIAQ)
Other Conferences in 2014 2014
Publications: Indoor Air: The International Journal of Indoor Environment & Health
Type: Journal *Frequency:* bi-m. *Accepts Advertising* : Yes *Editor:* Jan Sundell; William Nazaroff *Price:* Free with International Society of Indoor Air Quality & Climate membership
Profile: Original research about indoor environments
Vocabulary of the Indoor Air Sciences
International Society of Indoor Air Quality & Climate Conference Proceedings
Profile: Proceedings of Healthy Buildings & Indoor Air conferences
International Society of Indoor Air Quality & Climate Task Force Reports
International Society of Indoor Air Quality & Climate Newsletter
Type: Newsletter *Accepts Advertising* : Yes *Price:* Free with International Society of Indoor Air Quality & Climate membership
Profile: Society activities
Mission: To support the establishment of healthy, productivity-encouraging indoor environments
Environmental Activity: Providing information about the latest developments in indoor air quality & climate; Developing guidelines to improve indoor air quality & climate

International Society of Limnology (IATAL) / Societas Internationalis Limnologiae (SIL)
c/o Denise L. Johnson, GSGPH, 135 Dauer Dr., ESE, 148 Rosenau Hall, University of North Carolina, Chapel Hill NC 27599-7431 USA
Tel: 336-376-9362; *Fax:* 336-376-8825
e-mail: denisej@email.unc.edu
URL: www.limnology.org
Previous Name: International Association of Theoretical and Applied Limnology; Societas Internationalis Limnologiae, SIL
Overview: A medium-sized international organization founded in 1922
Fees: US$55 regular; US$110 institutional; *Member Profile:* Open to those with an interest in limnology, the study of inland water ecosystems (rivers, lakes, streams, reservoirs, fish ponds, aquifers, & bogs); Members have varied interests which include physics of water movements, water chemistry, plankton & water plants, invertebrate ecology, fish & fisheries, watershed & reservoir management, pollution of inland waters, & modelling of aquatic ecosystems; *Committees:* Baldi Memorial; Conservation; International; Kilham Memorial; Limnology in Developing Countries; Naumann-Thienemann Medal; Nominating; Publication Advisory; Tonolli Memorial; Working Groups
Mission: The Society promotes communication between limnologists of all countries & all disciplines to increase understanding of inland aquatic ecosystems & their management.; *Affiliation(s):* Canadian Society of Limnology

International Society of Soil Science *See* International Union of Soil Sciences

International Soil Reference & Information Centre (ISRIC)
PO Box 353, 9 Duivendaal, Wageningen 6700 AJ Netherlands

Tel: 31-317-471-711; *Fax:* 31-317-471-700
e-mail: soil.isric@wur.nl
URL: www.isric.org
Overview: A small international organization founded in 1966
Finances: Annual Operating Budget: $500,000-$1.5 Million; *Funding Sources:* Dutch government, international/bilateral project donor organizations
Staff: 25 staff member(s)
Membership: 1-99
Activities: Library: Yes, Open to public, open by appointment
Mission: To contribute to the challenge of providing sufficient food for the growing world populations while preserving the biophysical potential of natural resources & minimizing environmental degradation; *Member of:* World Data Centres of International Council of Sciences; World Data Centre for Soils; *Affiliation(s):* Wageningen University & Research Centre

International Solar Energy Society (ISES)
International Headquarters, Villa Tannheim, Wiesentalstrasse 50, Freiburg 79115 Germany
Tel: 49-761-459-06-0; *Fax:* 49-761-459-06-99
e-mail: hq@ises.org
URL: www.ises.org
Overview: A medium-sized international charitable organization founded in 1954
Chief Officer(s):
Eduardo A. Rincón Mejía, Secretary, (Mexico)
rinconsolar@hotmail.com
Monica V. Oliphant, President, (Australia)
oliphant@adam.com.au
Membership: 4,000; *Fees:* Schedule available; *Member Profile:* Persons engaged in the research development & utilisation of solar energy & persons who have an interest in advancing the purposes of the society
Activities: All aspects of solar energy, including characteristics, effects & methods of use; international congresses on solar energy
Awards: Achievement through Action Award (Award)
Monetary, biennial; awarded to an individual, a group, or corporate body that has made an important contribution to the harnessing of solar energy for practical use or is proposing a new concept, development or product for the same purpose
Farrington Daniel Award (Award)
Recognition for outstanding intellectual leadership in the field of solar energy
Publications: Solar Energy
Type: Journal *Frequency:* m *Editor:* Dr. D. Yogi Goswami
Mission: A United Nations accredited NGO, with members in 50+ countries worldwide; goals include the promotion of renewable energy, with solar energy being a focus, sustainable development, and research; *Member of:* International Renewable Energy Alliance

International Solid Waste Association (ISWA)
Auerspergstrasse 15, Top 41, Vienna 1080 Austria
Tel: +43 1 253 6001; *Fax:* +43 1 523 6001 99
e-mail: iswa@iswa.dk
URL: www.iswa.org
Social Media:
www.facebook.com/group.php?gid=123367611068687
Overview: A medium-sized international organization founded in 1931
Chief Officer(s):
Hermann Koller, Managing Director
hkoller@iswa.org
Gerfried Habenicht, Manager, Communications
Alfred Holzschuster, Manager, Finance & Member Services
Rachael Williams, Technical Manager
Finances: Funding Sources: Sponsorships
Member Profile: Non-profit waste management associations representing the waste management industry in a particular country; Organizations or companies associated with or working in the field of waste management
Activities: Promoting professionalism; Supporting developing countries
Meetings/Conferences:
For more information see Trade Shows, Conferences and Seminars Chapter
International Solid Waste Association 2011 Annual Congress
October 2011 Daegu City
International Solid Waste Association 2012 Annual Congress
September 2012 Florence
Publications: Waste Management & Research
Type: Journal *Frequency:* m. *Editor:* Jens Aage Hansen
Profile: The theory & practice of waste management & research

Waste Management World
Type: Magazine *Frequency:* bi-m. *Accepts Advertising* : Yes
Editor: Tom Freyberg
Profile: Incorporates the International Directory of Solid Waste Management, with a listing of ISWA members & waste management companies
Global News [a publication of the International Solid Waste Association]
Type: Newsletter
Profile: Contents include news from the association president, conference information, awards, news from around the world, & forthcoming events
International Solid Waste Association Conference Proceedings
Type: Yearbook *Frequency:* a.
Profile: Information from the International Solid Waste Association Annual Congress, the Beacon Conference, & other conferences organized by the association
International Solid Waste Association Annual Report
Type: Yearbook *Frequency:* a.
Mission: To promote efficiency in environmental practice
Environmental Activity: Advancing waste management through training

International Titanium Association (ITA)
#300, 2655 West Midway Blvd., Broomfield CO 80020-7186 USA
Tel: 303-404-2221; *Fax:* 303-404-9111
e-mail: ita@titanium.org
URL: www.titanium.org
Overview: A large international organization founded in 1984
Chief Officer(s):
Jennifer Simpson, Executive Director
jsimpson@titanium.org
tTacey Blicker, Contact, Member Services
sblicker@titanium.org
Membership: 195 companies; *Committees:* Applications; Safety; Statistics; Nominating; Titanium Achievement Award; Conference; Grant; Membership
Activities: Offering titanium literature; Sponsoring educational workshops & seminars
Meetings/Conferences:
For more information see Trade Shows, Conferences and Seminars Chapter
International Titanium Association's 27th Annual Conference & Exhibition
October 2011 San Diego, CA
Publications: Titanium Update Newsletter
Type: Newsletter *Price:* Free
Profile: Titanium news, awards, & membership information
Mission: To connect the public with titanium specialists throughout the world, who can offer technical & sales assistance

International Union for Conservation of Nature (IUCN)
28, rue Mauverney, Gland 1196 Switzerland
Tel: 41-22-999-0000; *Fax:* 41-22-999-0002
e-mail: mail@iucn.org.
URL: www.iucn.org
Previous Name: The World Conservation Union; International Union for Conservation of Nature & Natural Resources
Overview: A large international organization founded in 1948
Finances: Funding Sources: Member organizations; Governments; Foundations; Bilateral & multilateral agencies; Corporations
Staff: 1000 staff member(s)
Membership: 1,000+ government organizations & NGOs + 11,000 volunteer scientist from over 160 countries; *Member Profile:* Government organizations; NGOs; Volunteer scientists
Activities: Supporting scientific research; Managing field projects; Coordinatingpersons & organization to develop & implement policies, laws, & best practices; Publishing over 150 books, reports, documents, & guidelines each year
Meetings/Conferences:
For more information see Trade Shows, Conferences and Seminars Chapter
International Union for Conservation of Nature World Conservation Congress 2012
September 2012 Jeju
Publications: Conservation Made Clear
Type: Newsletter *Frequency:* m.
Profile: Information about environmental issues & sustainable solutions
World Conservation
Type: Magazine *Frequency:* 2 - 3 pa

Profile: An examinations of conservation, development, economics, & society
Off the Shelf [a publication of the International Union for Conservation of Nature]
Type: Newsletter *Frequency:* m.
Profile: International Union for Conservation of Nature's latest & most notable publications
Building Bridges [a publication of the International Union for Conservation of Nature]
Type: Newsletter *Frequency:* q.
Profile: Conservation & the private sector
UNFCCC Newsletter
Type: Newsletter *Frequency:* s-a.
Profile: International Union for Conservation of Nature's contributions to the UN Framework Convention on Climate Change
Mission: To find solutions to environment & development challenges; To conserve the integrity & diversity of nature; To ensure the use of natural resources is equitable & ecologically sustainable
Environmental Activity: Promoting the value & conservation of nature; Providing authoritative information on the environment & sustainable development

International Union of Architects *See* Union internationale des architectes

International Union of Biological Sciences (IUBS) / Union internationale des sciences biologiques
Secretariat, Bat 442 Université Paris-Sud 11, Orsay cedex, Paris 91 405 France
Tel: 33 1 69 15 50 27; *Fax:* 33 1 69 15 79 47
e-mail: secretariat@iubs.org
URL: www.iubs.org
Overview: A medium-sized international charitable organization founded in 1919
Membership: 44 ordinary + 80 scientific (associations, societies or commissions); *Fees:* Schedule available; *Member Profile:* National science academies; International scientific organizations
Activities: *Speaker Service:* Yes
Publications: *Biology International*
Type: Journal *Frequency:* q
Mission: To promote the study of biological sciences; to initiate, facilitate & coordinate research & other scientific activities that require international cooperation; to ensure the discussion & dissemination of the results of cooperative research; to promote the organization of international conferences & to assist in the publication of their reports

International Union of Food Science & Technology (IUFoST)
International Union of Food Science & Technology Secretariat, PO Box 61021, #19, 511 Maple Grove Dr., Oakville ON L6J 6X0
Tel: 905-815-1926; *Fax:* 905-815-1574
e-mail: secretariat@iufost.org; Newslinks@iufost.org (Newsline)
URL: www.iufost.org
Overview: A large international organization
Chief Officer(s):
Geoffrey Campbell-Platt, President
Judith Meech, Secretary-General & Treasurer
Rick Yada, Chair, Scientific Council
Member Profile: Food scientists, technologists, & engineers from around the world
Activities: Promoting training in food science & technology; Sponsoring international conferences & workshops; Fostering the international exchange of knowledge in the food science & technology community
Meetings/Conferences:
For more information see Trade Shows, Conferences and Seminars Chapter
International Union of Food Science & Technology 12th ASEAN Food Conference 2011: Food Innovation - Key to Creative Economy
June 2011 Bitek, Bangkok
Publications: *International Union of Food Science & Technology Scientific Information Bulletins*
Type: Bulletin
Profile: Food science issues, presented by scientific experts & reviewed & approved by the IUFoST Scientific Council, for members of IUFoST adhering bodies, legislators, food scientists & technologists, & consumers
IUFoST Newsline
Type: Newsletter *Frequency:* irreg.
Profile: The official newsletter of the International Union of Food Science & Technology, featuring activities of the General Assembly, the Board, the Governing Council, the International Academy, & adhering bodies, for adhering bodies in more than 100 countries around the world
Trends in Food Science & Technology
Type: Journal *ISSN:* 0924-2244
Profile: A peer-reviewed journal, featuring critical synopses of advances in food research
Using Food Science & Technology to Improve Nutrition & Promote National Development: Selected Case Studies
Type: Book *Editor:* Gordon Robertson & John Lupien *ISBN:* 978-0-9810247-0-7
Profile: A handbook about the application of food science & technology to improve nutrition & promote national development in developing countries
The Textbook of Food Science & Technology
Type: Book *Editor:* Geoffrey Campbell-Platt
Profile: Chapters from international industry researchers, experts, & teachers, written for students, teachers, & professionals in the food industry
Sustainable Development at Risk: Ignoring the Past
Type: Book *Author:* Robert D. Reichert *ISBN:* 9788175965218
Profile: The challenge of improving third world nations, while conserving critical resources & protecting the environment
Mission: To improve the distribution & conservation of the world's food supply; To promote international cooperation among food technologists & scientists

International Union of Forest Research Organizations (IUFRO) / Union internationale des instituts de recherches forestières
IUFRO Secretariat, Mariabrunn (BFW), Hauptstrasse 7, Vienna A-1140 Austria
Tel: 43-1-877-01-510; *Fax:* 43-1-877-01-5150
e-mail: office@iufro.org
URL: www.iufro.org
Overview: A medium-sized international organization founded in 1892
Membership: 15,000 scientists in 700 member organizations in 110 countries worldwide; *Fees:* Schedule available; *Member Profile:* Open to organizations conducting research related to forestry, including government agencies, universities, private institutions, natural resource associations; associate - individuals
Activities: Environmental change; forests in sustainable mountain development; internet resources; sustainable forest management; management & conservation of forest gene resources; water & forests; on-line reference library; *Library:* Yes, Open to public
Awards: Student Award for Excellence in Forest Service (Award)
Distinguished Service Award (Award)
Honorary Membership (Award)
Scientific Achievement Award (Award)
Outstanding Doctoral Research Award (Award)
Mission: To promote international cooperation in scientific studies embracing the whole field of research related to forestry & forest products by facilitating exchanges of ideas, methods, data & results among researchers throughout the world

International Union of Geodesy & Geophysics (IUGG) / Union géodésique et géophysique internationale
University Of Karlsruhe, Geophysical Institute, Hertzstrasse 16 Geb. 06.36, Karlsruhe 76187 Germany
URL: www.iugg.org
Overview: A medium-sized international organization founded in 1919
Membership: 67 member countries; *Member Profile:* 8 member associations: International Assn of Cryospheric Sciences; International Assn of Geodesy; International Assn of Geomagnetism & Aeronomy; International Assn of Hydrological Sciences; International Assn of Meteorology & Atmospheric Sciences; International Assn of the Physical Sciences of the Ocean; International Assn of Seismology & Physics of the Earth's Interior; and International Assn of Volcanology & Chemistry of the Earth's Interior
Mission: To promote & coordinate studies of the Earth & its environment in space

International Union of Microbiological Societies
Centralbureau voor Schimmelcultures, PO Box 85167, Utrecht 3508AD Netherlands
Tel: 31-30-21-22-600; *Fax:* 31-30-251-2097
e-mail: samson@cbs.knaw.nl
URL: www.iums.org
Overview: A small international organization
Member Profile: National & international societies & other organizations having a common interest in microbiological sciences
Meetings/Conferences:
For more information see Trade Shows, Conferences and Seminars Chapter
International Union of Microbiological Societies Congress 2011
September 2011 Sapporo
International Union of Microbiological Societies 2014 XIV Congress
July 2014 Montréal, QC
Affiliation(s): International Council of Scientific Unions

International Union of Nutritional Sciences
c/o UCLA School of Public Health, PO Box 951772, Los Angeles CA 90095-1772 USA
Tel: 310-206-9639; *Fax:* 310-794-1805
e-mail: info@iuns.org
URL: www.iuns.org
Overview: A medium-sized international organization founded in 1948
Chief Officer(s):
Richard Uauy, President
ricardo.uauy@lshtm.ac.uk
Osman Galal, Secretary General
ogalal@ucla.edu
Suzanne Murphy, Treasurer
suzanne@crch.hawaii.edu
Finances: *Annual Operating Budget:* Less than $50,000; *Funding Sources:* International Council of Scientific Unions; UNESCO; membership
Membership: 81 adhering bodies + 15 affiliated bodies
Mission: To accomplish extensive international cooperation among scientists in nutrition-related research & education

International Union of Pure & Applied Chemistry (IUPAC)
IUPAC Secretariat, Bldg. 19, PO Box 13757, 104 T.W. Alexander Park, Research Triangle Park NC 27709-3757 USA
Tel: 919-485-8700; *Fax:* 919-485-8706
e-mail: secretariat@iupac.org
URL: www.iupac.org
Overview: A small international organization founded in 1919
Finances: *Annual Operating Budget:* $1.5 Million-$3 Million
Staff: 6 staff member(s); 1000 volunteer(s)
Membership: 49 National Adhering Organizations which represent the chemists of different member countries; *Fees:* Variable - min. US$1,400; *Member Profile:* Adhering organizations are the members of the Union & they may be a national chemical council, a national society representing chemistry, a national academy of science, or any institution or association of institutions representative of national chemical interests; *Committees:* Divisions: Physical & Biophysical, Inorganic, Organic & Biomolecular, Polymer, Analytical, Chemistry & the Environment, Chemistry & Human Health, Chemical Nomenclature & Structure Representation; Standing Committees: Chemical Research Applied to World Needs, Chemistry Education, Chemistry & Industry, Printed & Electronic Publications, Terminology Nomenclature & Symbols, Finance, Project, Evaluation
Awards: Financial Support for Symposia & Conferences in Scientifically Emerging Regions (Award)
IUPAC Prize for Young Chemists (Award)
Mission: To advance the worldwide aspects of the chemical sciences & to contribute to the application of chemistry in the service of mankind; *Member of:* International Council of Scientific Unions; Affiliation(s): World Health Organization; UN Food & Agricultural Organization; United Nations Education, Scientific & Cultural Organization; International Organization for Standardization; Organization internationale de métrologie légale

International Union of Soil Sciences (IUSS) / Union internationale de la science du sol
c/o Dept. of Soil Science, Univ. of Reading, PO Box 233, Stn. Whiteknights, Reading RG6 6DW United Kingdom
Tel: 44 (0) 118378 6559; *Fax:* 44 (0) 118378 6666
e-mail: iuss@reading.ac.uk
URL: www.iuss.org
Previous Name: International Society of Soil Science
Overview: A medium-sized international charitable organization founded in 1924
Finances: *Annual Operating Budget:* $50,000-$100,000; *Funding Sources:* Membership fees
Staff: 1 staff member(s); 3 volunteer(s)
Membership: 50,000 in 146 countries; *Fees:* According to number of members in national societies; *Member Profile:*

National soil science societies; *Committees:* Soil Physics; Soil Zoology; World Soils & Terrain Digital Data Base; Committee on Statute & Structure
Activities: Rents Mailing List: Yes; *Library:* Yes
Member of: International Council of Scientific Unions; Affiliation(s): Canadian Society of Soil Science

International Water Association (IWA)
Alliance House, 12 Caxton St., London SW1H 0QS United Kingdom
Tel: 44-20-7654-5500; *Fax:* 44-20-7654-5555
e-mail: water@iwahq.org.uk
URL: www.iwahq.org
Previous Name: International Association on Water Quality; International Association on Water Pollution Research & Control
Overview: A large international organization founded in 1999
Finances: *Annual Operating Budget:* $250,000-$500,000
Staff: 20 staff member(s)
Membership: 9,000; *Committees:* Executive; Program; Scientific & Technical; Management & Policy; Publications
Activities: Wastewater treatment processes; hazardous wastes & source control; impacts of pollutants on receiving waters; environmental restoration
Mission: To advance the science & practice of water management internationally

International Whaling Commission (IWC)
The Red House, 135 Station Rd., Impington, Cambridge CB4 9NP United Kingdom
Tel: 441-223-233-971; *Fax:* 441-223-232-876
e-mail: secretariat@iwcoffice.org
URL: www.iwcoffice.org
Overview: A medium-sized international organization founded in 1946
Membership: 88 whaling governments; *Member Profile:* Open to any country in the world that formally adheres to the 1946 Convention; *Committees:* Scientific; Technical; Finance & Administration
Activities: *Speaker Service:* Yes; *Library:* Yes, Open to public, open by appointment
Mission: To keep under review & revise as necessary those measures which provide for the complete protection of certain species of whales; to designate specified areas as whale sanctuaries; to set limits on the maximum numbers of whales which may be taken in one season; to prescribe open & closed seasons & areas for whaling; to set limits on the size of whales that may be killed; to prohibit the capture of suckling calves & female whales accompanied by calves; to encourage, coordinate & fund whale research; to publish results of research & other scientific research; to promote studies into related matters. Canada is not currently a member.

International Wildlife Coalition (IWC)
70 Falmouth Hwy. East, Falmouth MA 2536 USA
Tel: 508-548-8328; *Fax:* 508-457-1988
Overview: A medium-sized international charitable organization founded in 1982
Finances: *Annual Operating Budget:* $250,000-$500,000
Staff: 5 staff member(s)
Activities: *Internships:* Yes; *Rents Mailing List:* Yes
Mission: To prevent cruelty & killing of animals & the destruction of wildlife habitat; Affiliation(s): Canadian Federation of Humane Societies

International Wildlife Rehabilitation Council (IWRC)
PO Box 8187, San Jose CA 95155 USA
Tel: 408-271-2685; *Fax:* 408-271-9285
Toll-Free: 866-871-1869
e-mail: info@iwrc-online.org
URL: www.iwrc-online.org
Overview: A small international charitable organization founded in 1972
Chief Officer(s):
Dody Wyman, President
Finances: *Annual Operating Budget:* $250,000-$500,000; *Funding Sources:* Membership dues; course fees; private donations; sales of literature; annual conference
Staff: 3 staff member(s); 12 volunteer(s)
Membership: 1,850; *Fees:* $49 individual; $59 family; $75 organization; $32 library; *Member Profile:* Individual - persons actively working in the field of wildlife rehabilitation in administration, conservation, management, education, research, humane work, or veterinary or allied professional practice; Family - two or more active rehabilitators residing at the same address; Organizational/Institutional - non-profit corporations or public agencies affiliated with a branch of local, state, or federal government actively supporting or operating wildlife rehabilitation programs; Affiliate/Corporate - small & large businesses or foundations that are not actively involved in wildlife rehabilitation but wish to provide financial support for IWRC programs; Library/Agency: Accredited library or government, state, provincial agency
Activities: Nationwide certification program which includes a series of hands-on training seminars in state-of-the-art wildlife rehabilitation techniques, from beginner through advanced levels;
Mission: To further knowledge & experience in the field of wildlife rehabilitation, through education, networking, & professional standards of review; to preserve our wildlife & its habitat

International WWOOF Association
PO Box 2675, Lewes BN7 1RB United Kingdom
URL: www.wwoof.org
Also Known As: World-Wide Opportunities on Organic Farms
Overview: A small international organization
Chief Officer(s):
Sally Antill, Administrator
Mission: To help those who would like to volunteer on organic farms internationally

IRC International Water & Sanitation Centre
PO Box 2869, Delft 2601 CW Netherlands
Tel: 31-15-219-2939; *Fax:* 31-15-219-0955
e-mail: general@irc.nl
URL: www.irc.nl
Previous Name: International Reference Centre for Community Water Supply & Sanitation
Overview: A small international organization founded in 1968
Finances: *Annual Operating Budget:* $1.5 Million-$3 Million
Staff: 38 staff member(s)
Activities: *Internships:* Yes; *Library:* Yes, open by appointment
Mission: The IRC helps people in developing countries to get the best water & sanitation services they can afford

Island Nature Trust (INT)
PO Box 265, Charlottetown PE C1A 7K4
Tel: 902-566-9150; *Fax:* 902-628-6331
e-mail: intrust@isn.net
URL: www.islandnaturetrust.ca
Also Known As: Prince Edward Island Nature Trust
Overview: A small provincial charitable organization founded in 1979
Chief Officer(s):
Bruce Smith, Executive Director
Finances: *Annual Operating Budget:* $100,000-$250,000; *Funding Sources:* Donations; fundraising; contract work
Staff: 4 staff member(s); 100+ volunteer(s)
Membership: 350; *Fees:* $10; *Committees:* Acquisition; Fundraising; Program Development
Activities: Educational programs; acquisition, protection & management of natural areas; *Speaker Service:* Yes
Mission: To acquire & manage natural areas on PEI; *Member of:* Tourism Industry Association of PEI; Affiliation(s): Canadian Nature Federation; Tree Canada Foundation

Islands Organic Producers Association (IOPA)
3490 Glenora Rd., Duncan BC V9L 6S2
Tel: 250-748-2791; *Fax:* 250-748-2741
e-mail: lmime@telus.net
URL: www.iopa.ca
Overview: A small local organization founded in 1990
Finances: *Funding Sources:* Membership fees
Staff: 30 volunteer(s)
Membership: 60; *Member Profile:* Organic farmers
Affiliation(s): Certified Organic Associations of BC

Jack Miner Migratory Bird Foundation, Inc.
PO Box 39, Kingsville ON N9Y 2E8
Tel: 519-733-4034
Toll-Free: 877-289-8328
e-mail: info@jackminer.com
URL: www.jackminer.com
Overview: A small local charitable organization founded in 1904
Finances: *Funding Sources:* Private
Staff: 3 staff member(s); 12 volunteer(s)
Mission: The sanctuary provides food, shelter & protection to migratory water fowl, tags birds & tracks migration patterns

The Jane Goodal Institute of Canada (JGI)
PO Box 309, Stn. P, #711, 170 St. George St., Toronto ON M5S 2S8
Tel: 416-978-3711; *Fax:* 416-978-3713
Toll-Free: 888-882-4467
e-mail: info@janegoodall.ca; roots_shoots@janegoodall.ca
URL: www.janegoodall.ca/roots-shoots.php
Also Known As: Roots & Shoots
Overview: A small local organization founded in 1994
Chief Officer(s):
Jane Lawton, Executive Director
Jane Goodall, DBE, Founder
Barbara Cartwright, Chair
Louis Sapi, Secretary - Treasurer
Finances: *Funding Sources:* Donations
Activities: Providing training in environmental & humanitarian education; Raising awareness of endangered animals; Promoting activities to aid the well-being of wild & captive chimpanzees
Publications: *Jane Goodall Institute of Canada eNewsletter*
Type: Newsletter
Profile: Canadian news, news from the field, & ways to become involved
Roots & Shoots Canada eNewsletter
Type: Newsletter
Profile: Events, activities, parnerships, & resources
Mission: To support wildlife research, education, & conservation

The Jane Goodall Institute for Wildlife Research, Education & Conservation
#600, 4245 North Fairfax Dr., Arlington VA 22203 USA
Tel: 703-682-9220; *Fax:* 703-682-9312
URL: www.janegoodall.org
Overview: A small international organization founded in 1977
Chief Officer(s):
Robert G. Menzi, CFO & Executive Vice-President
Bill Johnston, President
Activities: Gombe Stream Research Centre; ChimpanZoo Project; reforestation projects; conservation centres; educational & communcation resources
Mission: To increase primate habitat conservation; to increase awareness of, support for & training in issues related to our relationship with each other, the environment & other animals (leading to behaviour change); to expand non-invasive research program on chimpanzees & other primates; to promote activities that ensure the well-being of chimpanzees, other primates & animal welfare activities in general

The Jane Goodall Institute of Canada
#711, 170 St. George St., Toronto ON M5R 2M8
Tel: 416-978-3711; *Fax:* 416-978-3713
Toll-Free: 888-882-4467
e-mail: info@janegoodall.ca
URL: www.janegoodall.ca
Overview: A small national charitable organization founded in 1994
Chief Officer(s):
Jane Lawton, Executive Director
Finances: *Annual Operating Budget:* $250,000-$500,000; *Funding Sources:* Private donations; lecture honorariums
Staff: 5 staff member(s); 32 volunteer(s)
Membership: 550; *Fees:* $40
Activities: Chimp Guardian Program - sponsor orphan chimpanzees; Roots & Shoots - Jane Goodall Institute's global environmental & humanitarian program; *Awareness Events:* Earth Day, April 22; Peace Day, Sept. 21; *Internships:* Yes
Mission: To support wildlife research, education & conservation; to promote informed & compassionate action to improve the environment shared by all Earth's living creatures; Affiliation(s): The Jane Goodall Institute - USA; The Jane Goodall Institute - UK

Jardin zoologique du Québec (JZQ)
9300, rue de la Faune, Charlesbourg QC G1G 5H9
Tél: 418-622-0312; *Téléc:* 418-646-9239
Courriel: spsnq@spsnq.qc.ca
Aperçu: *Dimension:* moyenne; *Envergure:* provinciale; fondée en 1931
Finances: *Budget de fonctionnement annuel:* $1.5 Million-$3 Million
Personnel: 25 membre(s) du personnel; 140 bénévole(s)
Activités: *Stagiaires:* Oui; *Service de conférenciers:* Oui; *Listes de destinataires:* Oui; *Bibliothèque:* Oui
Mission: Contribuer à l'étude, à la mise en valeur et à la conservation de la faune et de son environnement.; *Membre de:* Société des musées québécois
Environmental Activity: Activités éducatives, programmes de recherche et de conservation

Les jardins botaniques royaux *See* Royal Botanical Gardens

Jasper Environmental Association (JEA)
PO Box 2198, Jasper AB T0E 1E0
Tel: 780-852-4152; *Fax:* 780-852-4152
e-mail: jea2@telus.net
URL: www.jasperenvironmental.org
Overview: A medium-sized local organization
Fees: $5
Mission: To support Parks Canada in administering Jasper National Park in accordance with Canadian legislation, Parks Canada principles and policies and the wishes of the Canadian public.

Joint Centre for Bioethics
University of Toronto, 88 College St., Toronto ON M5G 1L4
Tel: 416-978-2709; *Fax:* 416-978-1911
e-mail: jcb.info@utoronto.ca
URL: www.utoronto.ca/jcb
Overview: A small national organization
Chief Officer(s):
Rhonda Martin, Executive Assistant

Jour de la terre Canada *See* Earth Day Canada

Junior Farmers' Association of Ontario (JFAO)
Ontario AgriCentre, #206, 100 Stone Rd. West, Guelph ON N1G 5L3
Tel: 519-780-5326; *Fax:* 519-821-8810
e-mail: info@jfao.on.ca
URL: www.jfao.on.ca
Social Media: www.facebook.com/group.php?gid=2212763210
Overview: A medium-sized provincial organization founded in 1944
Membership: 1,700 in 43 countries
Mission: To build future rural leaders through self-help & community betterment

Kamloops Exploration Group
#1100, 235 First Ave., Kamloops BC V2C 3J4
Tel: 250-828-2585
e-mail: info@keg.bc.ca
URL: www.keg.bc.ca
Overview: A small local organization
Chief Officer(s):
Mike Cathro, President
Mission: To generally promote the interests of mining & prospecting for minerals, metals, & petroleum to the general public; to further the member's knowledge of mineral exploration & mining by offering informational lectures to members & the general public; to hold prospecting classes & promote other educational projects in connection with mining & prospecting;to further the general public's knowledge on the subject of Geoscience

Kamloops Naturalist Club (KNC)
Parent: **Federation of BC Naturalists**
PO Box 625, Kamloops BC V2C 5L7
Tel: 250-554-1285
e-mail: marggraham@shaw.ca
URL: www.kamloopsnaturalist.ca
Overview: A small local charitable organization founded in 1981
Finances: *Annual Operating Budget:* Less than $50,000;
Funding Sources: Membership fees; grants; raffles
Membership: 1-99; *Fees:* $25 single; $35 family; *Member Profile:* All ages, but predominately retired
Activities: Field trips; workshops; monthly meetings; speakers
Mission: To promote the enjoyment of nature through environmental appreciation & conservation; to encourage wise use & conservation of natural resources & environmental protection; *Member of:* Canadian Nature Federation; Affiliation(s): Nature Canada

Kamloops Wildlife Park Society
9077 Dallas Dr., Kamloops BC V2C 6V1
Tel: 250-573-3242; *Fax:* 250-573-2406
e-mail: info@bczoo.org
URL: www.bczoo.org
Also Known As: BC Wildlife Park
Overview: A small local charitable organization founded in 1965
Chief Officer(s):
Glenn Grant, Operations Manager
glenn@bczoo.org
Mary Ann Milobar, President
Finances: *Annual Operating Budget:* $500,000-$1.5 Million; *Funding Sources:* Regional government; self-generated revenue
Staff: 15 staff member(s); 200 volunteer(s)
Membership: 2,000; *Fees:* $16 adults; $14 youths/seniors; $8 children; *Member Profile:* Families from Kamloops region

Activities: Captive breeding for release endangered Burrowing Owls; *Awareness Events:* BC Hydro Wildlights, Dec.-Jan.; Family Farm, May-Sept.; BC Wildlife Day, lst Mon. in Aug.; *Internships:* Yes; *Speaker Service:* Yes; *Library:* Yes, open by appointment
Mission: To encourage the appreciation of & respect for BC's wildlife; to assist in preserving biodiversity through education, research, captive breeding & rehabilitation service; Affiliation(s): Canadian Association of Zoos & Aquariums

Kawartha World Issues Centre (KWIC)
PO Box 895, Peterborough ON K9J 7A2
Tel: 705-748-1680; *Fax:* 705-748-1681
e-mail: kwic@trentu.ca
URL: www.trentu.ca/kwic
Overview: A small international charitable organization founded in 1988
Chief Officer(s):
Julie Cosgrove, Coordinator
Finances: *Funding Sources:* Public donations; Trent student donations; CIDA; special grants
Staff: 1 staff member(s); 50 volunteer(s)
Membership: 150; *Fees:* $20 individual; $20 - $50 group; $100 institutional
Activities: Public Programming on global issues; skills training; networking; special projects: Person's Day Breakfast, International Development Week; One World (Vegetarian) Dinner; Global Youth Day, Volunteer Recruitment & Training, Annual Secondary School Symposium; *Speaker Service:* Yes; *Library:* Yes, Open to public
Mission: To further an understanding of global issues; to create links between global & local community development; to promote analysis & action for positive social change; *Member of:* Eastern Ontario Coalition of Internationally-Minded NGOs; Ontario Council for International Cooperation

Kennebecasis Naturalists' Society
c/o Ms. H. Folkins, 827 Main St., Sussex NB E4E 2N1
e-mail: belliot@nbnet.nb.ca
URL: www.macbe.com/kns/
Overview: A small local organization
Chief Officer(s):
Gart Bishop, Chair
Membership: 80
Activities: Field trips

Keystone Agricultural Producers (KAP)
Parent: **Canadian Federation of Agriculture**
#203, 1700 Ellice Ave., Winnipeg MB R3H 0B1
Tel: 204-697-1140; *Fax:* 204-697-1109
e-mail: kap@kap.mb.ca
URL: www.kap.mb.ca
Previous Name: Manitoba Farm Bureau
Overview: A medium-sized provincial organization founded in 1985
Finances: *Annual Operating Budget:* $250,000-$500,000
Staff: 5 staff member(s)
Membership: 5,000; *Fees:* $150 per farm unit
Publications: *Manitoba Farmers' Voice*
Type: Journal *Frequency:* q
Mission: To be a democratic & effective policy organization, promoting the social, economic & physical well-being of all Manitoban agricultural producers

The Kindness Club / Le Cercle Saint-François
65 Brunswick St., Fredericton NB E3B 1G5
Tel: 506-459-3379; *Fax:* 506-450-3703
e-mail: kindness@nb.aibn.com
URL: www.kindnessclub.nb.ca
Overview: A small international charitable organization founded in 1959
Finances: *Annual Operating Budget:* $50,000-$100,000; *Funding Sources:* Donations; interest from small capital
Staff: 2 staff member(s); 6 volunteer(s)
Membership: 2,300; *Fees:* $5 child; $10 adult
Activities: Essay contest for students, grades 4-8; pet shows; displays; weekly column in 6 New Brunswick newspapers; liaison teacher program; *Library:* Yes
Mission: To educate children to be kind to animals & people & to respect the environment; *Member of:* Canadian Federation of Humane Societies; Affiliation(s): Canadian Nature Federation; Zoocheck Canada; New Brunswick Naturalists

Kingston Field Naturalists (KFN)
PO Box 831, Kingston ON K7L 4X6

Tel: 613-389-8338
e-mail: info@kingstonfieldnaturalists.org
URL: kingstonfieldnaturalists.org
Overview: A small local charitable organization founded in 1949
Finances: *Annual Operating Budget:* Less than $50,000;
Funding Sources: Membership fees
Membership: 500; *Fees:* $30 individual; $32 family; $20 young adult/junior; $800 life; *Committees:* Conservation; Education; Bird Records; Field Trips; Nature Reserves
Activities: Junior naturalists club (6-12); bird counts; Helen Quillam Sanctuary; Amherst Island Reserve; teen naturalists (13-17); habitat protection projects; *Awareness Events:* Spring/Fall Leisure Shows - Kingston
Awards: Scholarship (Scholarship)
For junior members to attend camp
Mission: To acquire, record & disseminate knowledge of natural history; to stimulate public interest in nature & in the protection & preservation of wildlife; *Member of:* Ontario Nature; Affiliation(s): Canadian Nature Federation; Thousand Islands-Frontenac Arch Biosphere Reserve Network

Kingston Lapidary & Mineral Club
c/o J.K. Tett Bldg., PO Box 9, 370 King St. West, Kingston ON K7L 2X4
URL: www.mineralclub.ca
Overview: A small local organization founded in 1962
Chief Officer(s):
Paul Blaney, President, 613-544-5138
paulrichardblaney@hotmail.com
Eileen Moss, Vice-President, emoss@cogeco.net
Alan Howie, Secretary
a_howie@cogeco.ca
Fees: $10 junior; $15 adult; $20 family; *Member Profile:* Rockhounds; Lapidary enthusiasts; Silversmiths
Activities: Hosting meetings & workshops; Organizing field trips; *Library:* Kingston Lapidary & Mineral Club Library
Publications: *The Streak Plate: The Kingston Lapidary & Mineral Club Newsletter*
Type: Newsletter *Frequency:* 5 pa *Editor:* John Casnig
Profile: Upcoming events & articles about the hobby
Mission: To encourage the growth of silversmithing work, & mineral, fossil, & crystal collecting; *Member of:* The Central Canadian Federation of Mineralogical Societies (CCFMS)

Kitchener-Waterloo Field Naturalists
317 Highland Rd. East, Kitchener ON N2M 3W6
Tel: 519-741-8272
e-mail: mave@microverse.on.ca
URL: www.sentex.net/~tntcomm/kwfn
Overview: A small local charitable organization founded in 1934
Finances: *Annual Operating Budget:* Less than $50,000
Membership: 250; *Fees:* $20
Activities: Walks; speakers; social; photography; plant study; *Library:* Yes, Not open to the public
Mission: To promote the enjoyment of nature through environmental appreciation & conservation; to encourage wise use & conservation of natural resources; *Member of:* Federation of Ontario Naturalists

Kitimat Valley Naturalists
12 Farrow St., Kitimat BC V8C 1E2
Tel: 250-632-7632; *Fax:* 250-632-2543
e-mail: aprilmac@monarch.net
Overview: A small local organization
Chief Officer(s):
April Macleod

Klondike Placer Miners' Association
3151B Third Ave., Whitehorse YT Y1A 1G1
Tel: 867-667-2267; *Fax:* 867-668-7127
e-mail: kpma@kpma.ca
URL: www.kpma.ca
Overview: A small provincial organization
Chief Officer(s):
Mike McDougall, President
Fees: $159-$3210

The Ladies of the Lake
Tel: 905-476-4045
e-mail: ladies@lakeladies.ca
URL: www.lakeladies.ca
Overview: A small local organization founded in 2005
Chief Officer(s):
Jane Meredith, Contact
Member Profile: Women of all ages, from Lake Simcoe watershed
Activities: Calendar; "Naked Truth" series of events

Associations/Organizations / Lake Abitibi Model Forest

Mission: To promote a greater sense of connection with Lake Simcoe; to get people involved in what the future brings - both in terms of the lake itself & for those who share it; to offer a set of possible actions to restore the Lake to health for the communities around the Lake & watershed

Lake Abitibi Model Forest
PO Box 129, 143 - 3rd St., Cochrane ON P0L 1C0
Tel: 705-272-7800; Fax: 705-272-2744
e-mail: office@lamf.net
URL: www.lamf.net
Overview: A small local organization
Chief Officer(s):
Jacynthe Peever, Business Administrator
Wayne D. Young, General Manager
Member of: Canadian Model Forest Network

Lake Simcoe Region Conservation Foundation
PO Box 282, 120 Bayview Pkwy., Newmarket ON L3Y 4X1
Tel: 905-895-1281
e-mail: foundation@lsrca.on.ca
URL: www.lsrca.on.ca/Foundation/index.html
Social Media: apps.facebook.com/causes/99249
Overview: A small local organization
Chief Officer(s):
Kimberley Mackenzie, Executive Director
k.mackenzie@lsrca.on.ca
Activities: Undertaken a million dollar fundraising campaign to help restore the lake
Mission: The Lake Simcoe Conservation Foundation (LSCF) invests in projects designed to protect and restore Lake Simcoe. Working in partnership with the Lake Simcoe Region Conservation Authority (LSRCA), watershed municipalities and other partners, they enable vital work to be done that maintains the natural environment, and in many places return the land and the rivers and the streams to a natural state.

Lambton Industrial Society: An Environmental Co-operative
See Sarnia-Lambton Environmental Association

Lambton Wildlife Incorporated (LWI)
PO Box 681, Sarnia ON N7T 7J7
Tel: 519-542-7914
e-mail: info@lambtonwildlife.com
URL: www.lambtonwildlife.com
Overview: A small local charitable organization founded in 1966
Finances: *Annual Operating Budget:* Less than $50,000;
Funding Sources: Membership fees; donations
Staff: 75 volunteer(s)
Membership: 210; *Fees:* $20 individual; $25 family; *Committees:* Adopt-a-Highway; Arbor Week; Ausable Trail; Binational Public Advisory; Bluebird Nesting; Conservation; Education; Environment; Indoor; Mandaumin Woods; Outdoor; Rural Lambton Stewardship; Wawanosh Wetlands Management; Wildlife Inventory; Woodlot Protection; Howard Watson Nature Trail; Port Franks Property Management
Activities: Education programs in environmental studies & natural history; lectures in natural history at Lambton County schools & other organizations; special public lectures; regular field trips; sponsors the annual Audubon Christmas Bird census in Lambton area; purchase & management of Mandaumin Woods Nature Reserve; establishment of Ausable Trail; sponsorship of the World Wildlife studies of the Port Franks Karner Blue Butterfly & the Walpole Island Life Science Inventory;
Mission: To preserve our natural heritage for present & future generations; particularly concerned with the natural history of Lambton County & the establishment & care of conservation areas & wildlife sanctuaries therein; *Member of:* Federation of Ontario Naturalists; *Affiliation(s):* Canadian Nature Federation

Land Improvement Contractors of Ontario
231 Dimson Rd., Guelph ON N1G 3C7
Tel: 519-836-1386; Fax: 519-836-4059
e-mail: john.johnston@gto.net
URL: www.drainage.org
Overview: A small provincial organization founded in 1995
Chief Officer(s):
Chris Groot, President
John Johnston, Sec.-Treas.
Finances: *Annual Operating Budget:* Less than $50,000
Mission: An association of professional contractors, suppliers of drainage pipe and equipment, engineers and municipal drainage superintendents principally concerned with agriculture and the land drainage industry of Ontario, Canada.

Land Trust Alliance (LTA)
#1100, 1660 L St. NW, Washington DC 20036 USA
Tel: 202-638-4725; Fax: 202-638-4730
e-mail: info@lta.org
URL: www.lta.org
Overview: A large international organization founded in 1982
Chief Officer(s):
Peter Hausmann, Chair
Jean Nelson, Secretary
Ted Ladd, Treasurer
Finances: *Annual Operating Budget:* $3 Million-$5 Million
Staff: 32 staff member(s)
Membership: 1,000
Activities: *Awareness Events:* National Land Trust Rally; *Internships:* Yes
Awards: Allen Morgan Award for Excellence in Membership Development (Award)
Mission: To strengthen the land trust movement & ensure that land trusts have the information, skills & resources they use to save land

Landscape Alberta Nursery Trades Association (LANTA)
Parent: **Canadian Nursery Landscape Association**
#200, 10331 - 178 St., Edmonton AB T5S 1R5
Tel: 780-489-1991; Fax: 780-444-2152
Toll-Free: 800-378-3198
e-mail: info@landscape-alberta.com
URL: www.landscape-alberta.com
Overview: A medium-sized provincial organization founded in 1957
Finances: *Annual Operating Budget:* $100,000-$250,000; *Funding Sources:* Membership fees; fundraising programs
Staff: 4 staff member(s)
Membership: 350; *Fees:* Schedule available; *Member Profile:* Must be engaged in the horticultural industry or a supplier
Mission: To advance the Alberta ornamental horticulture industry through unity, education & professionalism; *Affiliation(s):* Saskatchewan Nursery Landscape Association

Landscape Newfoundland & Labrador (LNL)
Parent: **Canadian Nursery Landscape Association**
PO Box 8062, St. John's NL A1B 3M9
Tel: 709-726-5651; Fax: 709-726-8441
e-mail: davek@nl.rogers.com
URL: www.landscapenf.org
Overview: A small provincial organization founded in 1992
Chief Officer(s):
David Kiell, Executive Director
Membership: 75; *Fees:* $50 individual; $125 affiliated; $310 associate/active
Mission: Our vision is one that promotes professionalism at all levels of the Industry, and achieves the highest standards of excellence in delivery of services and products across all sectors of our industry.

Landscape Nova Scotia
Parent: **Canadian Nursery Landscape Association**
Executive Plus Business Centre, #44, 201 Brownlow Ave., Dartmouth NS B3B 1W2
Tel: 902-463-0519; Fax: 902-463-6308
Toll-Free: 877-567-4769
e-mail: info@landscapenovascotia.ca
URL: www.landscapenovascotia.ca
Overview: A medium-sized provincial organization
Chief Officer(s):
Scott Mosher, President
Mission: Landscape Nova Scotia's mission is to promote high standards in product quality, professional service and conduct in the landscape and horticulture industry. We have been a voice for the landscape and horticultural industry for more than 20 years in Nova Scotia, and are committed to providing consumers with options to make informed decisions.

Landscape Ontario Horticultural Trades Association (LOHTA)
Parent: **Canadian Nursery Landscape Association**
7856 Fifth Line South, RR#4, Milton ON L9T 2X8
Tel: 905-875-1805; Fax: 905-875-3942
Toll-Free: 800-265-5656
URL: www.horttrades.com
Overview: A medium-sized provincial organization founded in 1973
Finances: *Annual Operating Budget:* $1.5 Million-$3 Million; *Funding Sources:* Membership dues; congress
Staff: 23 staff member(s)
Membership: 2,100 members in 9 chapters; *Fees:* $470 active; $281 interim; $572 associate; $150 horticultural; *Member Profile:* Active - firms with at least 3 years experience in the field; Interim/Active - firms with at least 1 year but less than 3 years experience in the field; Associate - suppliers to the industry & the association
Activities: *Speaker Service:* Yes
Awards: The Landscape Awards Program (Award)
Mission: To be a leader in representing, promoting & fostering a favourable environment for the advancement of the horticultural industry in Ontario; *Affiliation(s):* Horticultural Human Resource Council

Langley Field Naturalists Society (LFN)
PO Box 56052, Stn. Valley Centre, Langley BC V3A 8B3
Tel: 604-534-4314
e-mail: Langleyfieldnaturalists@shaw.ca
URL: www.langleyfieldnaturalists.org
Overview: A small local organization founded in 1973
Finances: *Annual Operating Budget:* Less than $50,000; *Funding Sources:* Langley Arts Council Grant; membership fees
Membership: 60-70; *Fees:* $25 single; $30 family; *Committees:* Conservation education; Watson nature reserve
Activities: Monthly field trips from Sept.-June, weekly walks July-Aug.; Maintenance of Brydan Lagoon & Irene Pearce Trail; *Awareness Events:* Rivers Day; Earth Day; Campbell Valley Country Celebration
Mission: To promote the enjoyment of nature; to learn about natural history; to promote preservation of the environment through active participation in conservation projects; *Member of:* The Federation of BC Naturalists; Canadian Nature Federation

Lansdowne Outdoor Recreational Development Association (LORDA)
PO Box 591, Westville NS B0K 2A0
Tel: 902-396-4470; Fax: 902-396-1399
e-mail: contact@lorda.org
URL: www.lorda.org
Overview: A small local organization
Chief Officer(s):
Dave Leese, Contact
dave@lorda.org
Activities: Operates senior citizen & disabled persons park; facilities: fishing ponds, nature trails, bocce court, trailer parking, picnic benches, screened gazebo, croquet court, tenting area

LEAD Canada Inc.
PO Box 250, 3202 Tullochgorum, Ormstown QC J0S 1K0
Toll-Free: 866-532-3539
e-mail: president@leadcanada.net
URL: www.leadcanada.net
Also Known As: Leadership for Environment & Development Canada
Overview: A small national organization
Chief Officer(s):
Carole Therrien, President
Fees: $35

Lethbridge & District Japanese Garden Society
PO Box 751, Lethbridge AB T1J 3Z6
Tel: 403-328-3511; Fax: 403-328-0511
e-mail: info@nikkayuko.com
URL: www.nikkayuko.com
Also Known As: Nikka Yuko Japanese Garden
Overview: A small local organization founded in 1965
Finances: *Annual Operating Budget:* $100,000-$250,000
Staff: 15 staff member(s); 29 volunteer(s)
Membership: 700; *Fees:* $25 single; $35 family; *Committees:* Budget; Personnel; Strategic Planning; Fundraising; Marketing; Gardening
Mission: To acquaint visitors with cultural & historical background; to create support for garden philosophy of authenticity & meditative/contemplative setting; to create a unique attraction drawing large numbers to foster economic betterment of the community; to contribute to education fields such as arts, botany & general gardening; *Member of:* Lethbridge Chamber of Commerce; *Affiliation(s):* Chinook Tourist Association; Community Volunteer Centre

Lethbridge Naturalists' Society
PO Box 1691, Stn. Main, Lethbridge AB T1J 4K4
Tel: 403-328-8977
e-mail: info@lethbridgenaturalistssociety.com
Overview: A small local organization founded in 1970
Finances: *Annual Operating Budget:* Less than $50,000; *Funding Sources:* Membership fees
Fees: $10 family/individual; $6 student

Activities: Winter programs; summer field trips
Mission: To encourage knowledge & appreciation of natural history & understanding of ecological processes; to organize lectures, visual presentations & field trips; to conduct research on natural history; to become involved in environmental issues relating to conservation of the natural environment; *Member of:* Federation of Alberta Naturalists

Lifeforce Foundation
PO Box 3117, Vancouver BC V6B 3X6
Tel: 604-649-5258
e-mail: lifeforcesociety@hotmail.com
URL: www.lifeforcefoundation.org
Also Known As: Lifeforce
Overview: A small international charitable organization founded in 1981
Finances: *Annual Operating Budget:* Less than $50,000; *Funding Sources:* Donations; membership fees; bequests
Staff: 1 staff member(s)
Membership: 500; *Fees:* $25 individual; $15 seniors/students; $50 family; $250 business; *Committees:* Ecology Issues
Activities: Whale & dolphin hotline; Orca research; Lifewatch program distributes whale watching regulations & stops boaters who harass marine mammals; Marine Wildlife Rescue; educational materials & displays; all animal rights & issues
Mission: Dedicated to raising public awareness of the interrelationship of human, animal & environmental problems; to urge society to address & solve problems by taking into consideration the long-term effects on all parts of the ecosystem

LifeSciences British Columbia
#900, 1188 West Georgia St., Vancouver BC V6E 4A2
Tel: 604-669-9909; *Fax:* 604-669-9912
URL: www.lifesciencebc.ca
Previous Name: BC Biotech
Overview: A medium-sized provincial organization founded in 1991
Chief Officer(s):
Barry Gee, Director, Operations & Communications
Karimah Es Sabar, President
Finances: *Annual Operating Budget:* $250,000-$500,000; *Funding Sources:* Membership fees
Staff: 4 staff member(s)
Membership: 260; *Fees:* $50 students; $250 individuals; $750+ corporations, depending on membership categories; *Member Profile:* Producers & users of biotechnology, including companies, colleges & universities, government agencies & students; *Committees:* Communications; Finance; Human Resources; Public Policies; Research & Development
Awards: Annual BC Biotechnology Awards (Award)
Mission: To improve the climate in which the business of biotechnology is conducted in BC; to be an advocate for the industry; to improve the level of awareness & understanding of biotechnology

Lifewater Canada
#194, 307 Euclid Ave., Thunder Bay ON P7E 6G6
Tel: 807-622-4848; *Fax:* 807-577-9798
Toll-Free: 888-543-3426
e-mail: gehrelji@yahoo.com
URL: www.lifewater.ca
Overview: A small international organization
Chief Officer(s):
Jim Gehrels, President
Member Profile: Hydrogeologists, well drillers, educators, engineers, environmental scientists, businessmen & many other people with diverse skills & training
Mission: Christian organization dedicated to ensuring that people everywhere have access to adequate supplies of safe water; to train & equip Nationals with drill rigs & hand pumps so they can solve their own water problems; to place as many technical documents on-line as possible so they can benefit people everywhere, regardless of affiliation

Ligue de sécurité de l'Ontario *See* Ontario Safety League

Lloydminster Agricultural Exhibition Association (LAEA)
PO Box 690, 5521 - 49 Ave., Lloydminster SK S9V 0Y7
Tel: 306-825-5571; *Fax:* 306-825-7017
e-mail: lloydexh@lloydexh.com
URL: www.lloydexh.com
Overview: A small local charitable organization founded in 1904
Finances: *Annual Operating Budget:* $1.5 Million-$3 Million
Staff: 15 staff member(s); 300 volunteer(s)
Membership: 100-499; *Fees:* $10 with $40 on demand

Activities: Agricultural activities; rentals; seminars; livestock sales & shows; social receptions;
Mission: Dedicated in continuing to foster and develop the tourism industry of Lloydminster, and providing support to the business, social and cultural sectors of the reason.; *Member of:* Saskatchewan Association of Agricultural Societies & Exhibitions; *Affiliation(s):* Alberta Association of Agricultural Associations; Canadian Association of Fairs & Exhibitions; International Association of Fairs & Exhibitions

Local Government Management Association of British Columbia (LGMA)
Central Building, 620 View St., 7th Fl., Victoria BC V8W 1J6
Tel: 250-383-7032; *Fax:* 250-384-4879
e-mail: office@lgma.ca; editor@lgma.ca (magazine); ads@lgma.ca
URL: www.lgma.ca
Previous Name: Municipal Officers' Association of British Columbia
Overview: A medium-sized provincial organization founded in 1919
Finances: *Funding Sources:* Membership dues; Conference fees; Workshop fees; Sponsorships
Fees: $125 retired; $275 regular; $325 affiliate; fee for corporate membership based on number of members; *Member Profile:* Municipal & regional district managers, administrators, clerks, treasurers, & other local government officials in the province of British Columbia; Persons with an interest in local government administration may be affiliate members; *Committees:* Operations & Member Services; Education; Special Initiatives & External Relations; LGMA Policy 004
Activities: Providing educational programs for local government professionals to encourage fellowship & networking; Offering career transition counselling services; Providing personal pension & retirement planning counselling services for members
Meetings/Conferences:
For more information see Trade Shows, Conferences and Seminars Chapter
Local Government Management Association of BC Professional Development Program: Municipal Administration Training Institute - Leadership Program
June 2011 Squamish, BC
Local Government Management Association of BC Professional Development Program: Municipal Administration Training Institute - Foundations Program
August 2011 Victoria, BC
Local Government Management Association of BC Professional Development Program: Municipal Administration Training Institute - Community Planning
October 2011 Kelowna, BC
Local Government Management Association of British Columbia 2011 Clerks & Corporate Officers Forum
October 2011, BC
Local Government Management Association of BC Professional Development Program: Municipal Administration Training Institute - Advanced Communications
April 2012 Bowen Island, BC
Local Government Management Association of BC Professional Development Program: Municipal Administration Training Institute - Managing People
May 2012 Bowen Island, BC
Local Government Management Association of British Columbia 2012 Annual General Meeting & Conference
May 2012 Victoria, BC
Local Government Management Association of British Columbia 2012 Women in Leadership Forum
May 2012, BC
Local Government Management Association of BC Professional Development Program: Municipal Administration Training Institute - Foundations Program
August 2012 Victoria, BC
Local Government Management Association of British Columbia 2012 Clerks & Corporate Officers Forum
October 2012, BC
Local Government Management Association of British Columbia 2012 Annual CAO (Chief Administrative Officers) Forum
Other Conferences in 2012 2012, BC
Local Government Management Association of British Columbia 2012 Administrative Professionals Conference
Other Conferences in 2012 2012, BC
Local Government Management Association of British Columbia 2013 Annual General Meeting & Conference
June 2013 Kelowna, BC

Local Government Management Association of British Columbia 2013 CAO (Chief Administrative Officers) Forum
Other Conferences in 2013 2013, BC
Local Government Management Association of British Columbia 2013 Administrative Professionals Conference
Other Conferences in 2013 2013, BC
Local Government Management Association of British Columbia 2014 Annual General Meeting & Conference
Other Conferences in 2014 2014 Vancouver, BC
Local Government Management Association of British Columbia 2015 Annual General Meeting & Conference
Other Conferences in 2015 2015, BC
Publications: *Exchange*
Type: Magazine *Frequency:* q. *Accepts Advertising :* Yes
Profile: A magazine, featuring best practices, ideas, & professional development, distributed to more than 1,000 local government managers, mayors, & regional district chairs throughout British Columbia, as well as business affiliates
Local Government Management Association of British Columbia Annual Report
Type: Yearbook *Frequency:* a.
Profile: A review of the year's activities, including chapter reports & financial statements
Local Government Elections Manual
Type: Manual *Price:* $175
Profile: Ready-to-use forms, plus a CD ROM with sample bylaws
Local Government Management Association of British Columbia Guide for Approving Officers
Type: Manual *Price:* $150 CD ROM; $225 print version, including the CD ROM
Profile: An updated edition to reflect new & amended legislation & court decisions
Local Government Management Association of British Columbia Records Management Manual for Local Government
Type: Manual *Price:* $150 CD ROM; $225 print version, including the CD ROM
Profile: Standards & best practices for records management
Mission: To promote professional management & leadership excellence in local government; To create awareness of local government officers' roles in the community

London Area Health Libraries Association (LAHLA)
Parent: Canadian Health Libraries Association
c/o South Huron Hospital, Shared Library Services, 24 Huron St. West, Exeter ON N0M 1S2
Tel: 519-235-5168; *Fax:* 519-235-4476
e-mail: linda.wilcox@shha.on.ca
Overview: A small local organization
Chief Officer(s):
Linda Wilcox, President
Membership: 36; *Fees:* $20; *Member Profile:* Health libraries

London Regional Resource Centre for Heritage & the Environment
1017 Western Rd., London ON N6G 1G5
Tel: 519-645-2845; *Fax:* 519-645-0981
e-mail: info@grosvenorlodge.com
URL: www.heritagelondonfoundation.org/IndexGrosvenor.htm
Also Known As: Grosvenor Lodge
Overview: A small local organization founded in 1992
Chief Officer(s):
Jan Dickinson, Executive Director
Mission: To promote heritage & environmental activities & organizations in the London area; *Member of:* Heritage London Foundation

Long Point Bird Observatory *See* Bird Studies Canada

Lower Mainland Wildlife Rescue Association *See* Wildlife Rescue Association of British Columbia

Lumber & Building Materials Association of Ontario (LBMAO)
#27, 5155 Spectrum Way, Mississauga ON L4W 5A1
Tel: 905-625-1084; *Fax:* 905-625-3006
Toll-Free: 888-365-2626
e-mail: dwcampbell@lbmao.on.ca
URL: www.lbmao.on.ca
Previous Name: Ontario Retail Lumber Dealers Association
Overview: A medium-sized provincial organization founded in 1917
Member Profile: Manufacturers; Distributors; Purchasing organizations; Wholesalers; Service firm
Activities: Providing educational opportunities; Offering support services; Engaging in advocacy activities

Associations/Organizations / Lynn Canyon Ecology Centre

Mission: To promote the welfare of members so that they are able to build a competitive advantage & remain at the leading edge of the lumber & building materials industry

Lynn Canyon Ecology Centre
3663 Park Rd., North Vancouver BC V7J 3G3
Tel: 604-990-3755
e-mail: ecocentre@dnv.org
URL: www.dnv.org/ecology/
Overview: A small local organization founded in 1971
Chief Officer(s):
S.A. Kissinger
D. Robertson
Finances: *Funding Sources:* District of North Vancouver
Staff: 3 staff member(s); 12 volunteer(s)
Membership: 1,000-4,999; *Committees:* Stream Keepers - Maplewood Conservation Area
Activities: School & public education program; displays; leaflets
Mission: To educate people about ecology

Macleod Institute
223, 20 Coachway Road SW, Calgary AB T3H 1E6
Tel: 403-240-2573; *Fax:* 403-246-1852
Toll-Free: 866-204-6123
e-mail: macleod@macleodinstitute.com
URL: www.macleodinstitute.com
Previous Name: Macleod Institute for Environmental Analysis
Overview: A small national organization
Chief Officer(s):
Elaine McCoy, QC, President
Finances: *Annual Operating Budget:* $100,000-$250,000; *Funding Sources:* Contract
Staff: 5 staff member(s)
Membership: 1-99
Mission: To provide impartial advice on regulatory & environmental issues; *Affiliation(s):* University of Calgary

Macleod Institute for Environmental Analysis *See* Macleod Institute

Madawaska Forest Products Marketing Board *Voir* Office de vente des produits forestiers du Madawaska

Maintenance & Engineering Society of The Canadian Institute of Mining, Metallurgy & Petroleum
Parent: Canadian Institute of Mining, Metallurgy & Petroleum
c/o Chair, Brad Kingston, Wardrop Engineering Inc., 725 Hewitson St., Thunder Bay ON P7B 6B5
Tel: 807-345-5453
e-mail: brad.kingston@wardrop.com
URL: www.cim.org/med
Previous Name: Mechanical-Electrical Division of The Canadian Institute of Mining, Metallurgy & Petroleum
Overview: A medium-sized national organization
Chief Officer(s):
Brad Kingston, Chair, 807-345-5453
brad.kingston@wardrop.com
Mel Harju, Director, Energy & Membership
mel.harju@sympatico.ca
Jacek Paraszczak, Director, Education, Student Papers, & Scholarships
jacek.paraszczak@gmn.ulaval.ca
Ed Patton, Secretary
emptech@sympatico.ca
R.A. (Dick) McIvor, Treasurer
dmcivor@sympatico.ca
Activities: Facilitating the exchange of information & data on electrical & mechanical subjects; Publishing technical papers; Providing educational assistance; Promoting methods & devices to increase safety
Awards: The McParland Memorial Medal (Award)

JD (Pat) Patterson Memorial Scholarship (Scholarship)
The CIM Fellow-ship Award (Award)
Centennial Scholarship (Scholarship)
Distinguished Lecturer (Award)
Meetings/Conferences:
For more information see Trade Shows, Conferences and Seminars Chapter
Maintenance & Engineering Society of The Canadian Institute of Mining, Metallurgy & Petroleum 2011 Maintenance Engineering/Mine Operators' Conference
November 2011 Saskatoon, SK
Maintenance & Engineering Society of The Canadian Institute of Mining, Metallurgy & Petroleum 2013 Maintenance Engineering/Mine Operators' Conference
Other Conferences in 2013 2013
Maintenance & Engineering Society of The Canadian Institute of Mining, Metallurgy & Petroleum 2015 Maintenance Engineering/Mine Operators' Conference
Other Conferences in 2015 2015
Mission: To advance the theory & practice of electrical & mechanical arts & sciences in the mining industry; To improve mechanical-electrical standards
Environmental Activity: Offering an information interchange service to mine designers, engineers, suppliers, & operating personnel for the sound operation & maintenance of projects, mines, & facilities

Manitoba Association of Health Information Providers (MAHIP)
Parent: Canadian Health Libraries Association
c/o J.W. Crane Memorial Library, University of Manitoba, 2109 Portage Ave., Winnipeg MB R3J 0L3
Tel: 204-831-2107
e-mail: angela_osterreicher@umanitoba.ca
URL: www.chla-absc.ca/?q=en/node/75
Previous Name: Manitoba Health Libraries Association
Overview: A small provincial organization founded in 1979
Chief Officer(s):
Angela Osterreicher, President
Membership: 50
Mission: To promote the provision of quality library service to the health community in Manitoba by communication & mutual assistance.

Manitoba Association of Landscape Architects (MALA)
131 Callum Cres., Winnipeg MB R2G 2C7
Tel: 204-663-4863; *Fax:* 204-668-5662
e-mail: malaoffice@shaw.ca
URL: www.mala.net
Overview: A medium-sized provincial organization founded in 1973
Finances: *Annual Operating Budget:* Less than $50,000
Staff: 1 staff member(s)
Membership: 49 individual + 5 honorary + 28 associate + 40 student affiliates + 4 friend; *Committees:* CSLA Awards/Annual Symposium; Communications; Examining Board; Ethics; University Liaison
Activities: *Internships:* Yes; *Rents Mailing List:* Yes
Mission: To promote, improve & advance the profession; to maintain standards of professional practice & conduct consistent with the need to serve & protect public interest; to support improvement &/or conservation of the natural, cultural, social & built environment; *Member of:* Canadian Society of Landscape Architects

Manitoba Camping Association (MCA)
Parent: Canadian Camping Association
#302, 960 Portage Ave., Winnipeg MB R3G 0R4
Tel: 204-784-1134; *Fax:* 204-784-4177
e-mail: info@mbcamping.ca; sunshinefund@mbcamping.ca
URL: www.mbcamping.ca
Overview: A medium-sized provincial organization founded in 1937
Chief Officer(s):
Bryan Ezako, Executive Director
executivedirector@mbcamping.ca
Laura-Ann Peterson, Coordinator, General Office Administration & Sunshine Fund Program, 204-784-1130
Finances: *Funding Sources:* Donations; Membership dues
Member Profile: Organizations & individuals who support organized childrens & family camps & the mission of the MCA
Activities: Developing standards for organized camping in Manitoba; Communicating information about regulations & developments that affect organized camping; Representing member camps to government agencies & to the public; Administering the Winnipeg Free Press Sunshine Fund which allows financially disadvantaged children to attend camps; Offering workshops; Providing networking opportunities; *Awareness Events:* Manitoba Parade of Camps
Mission: To act as a coordinating body for organized camping in Manitoba; To promote organized camping as an educational and recreational experience; *Member of:* Canadian Camping Association

Manitoba Cattle Producers Association (MCPA)
154 Paramount Rd., Winnipeg MB R2X 2W3
Tel: 204-772-4542; *Fax:* 204-774-3264
Toll-Free: 800-772-0458
e-mail: feedback@mcpa.net
URL: www.mcpa.net
Social Media: twitter.com/ManitobaBeef
Overview: A medium-sized provincial organization
Member Profile: Cattle producers in Manitoba; *Committees:* Executive; Animal Health; Annual Meeting; APF; Communications; Crown Lands; Environment; Finance; Production Management; Quality Starts Here; Research; Resolutions
Activities: Engaging in advocacy activities; Researching; Providing education; *Awareness Events:* Manitoba Beef Week
Awards: Environmental Stewardship Award (Award)
Publications: Cattle Country: The Voice of Manitoba's Cattle Industry
Type: Magazine *Frequency:* 8 pa *Accepts Advertising:* Yes
Editor: Karen Emilson *Price:* Free
Profile: Information for cattle producers & industry supporters in Manitoba & eastern Saskatchewan
Mission: To act as the voice of the cattle industry in Manitoba; To ensure a sustainable future for the industry; *Member of:* Canadian Cattlemen's Association

Manitoba Christmas Tree Grower Association
900 Corydon Ave., Winnipeg MB R3M 0Y4
Tel: 204-453-7105; *Fax:* 204-477-5765
e-mail: mctga@realchristmastrees.mb.ca
URL: www.realchristmastrees.mb.ca
Overview: A small provincial organization
Chief Officer(s):
Cliff Freund, President
Patricia Pohrebniuk, Program Administrator
Fees: $50
Mission: To assist membership in promoting benefits of Christmas trees

Manitoba Council for International Cooperation (MCIC) / Conseil du Manitoba pour la coopération internationale
#302, 280 Smith St., Winnipeg MB R3C 1K2
Tel: 204-987-6420; *Fax:* 204-956-0031
e-mail: info@mcic.ca; mcic@web.ca
URL: www.mcic.ca
Overview: A medium-sized international charitable organization founded in 1974
Finances: *Funding Sources:* Donations; Member agencies; MB Gov't Matching Grant Program; MB Education, Citizenship & Youth, Gov't of MB; Canadian International Development Agency
Activities: Administering funds for international development; Supporting overseas projects; Providing development education in Manitoba; Increasing public awareness of international issues; Fostering member interaction
Awards: Paul LeJeune Volunteer Service Award (Award)
Mission: To promote international development that protects the environment; To coordinate the development work of member agencies; *Member of:* Canadian Council for International Cooperation (CCIC)

Manitoba Eco-Network Inc. (MEN) / Réseau écologique du Manitoba inc.
Parent: Canadian Environmental Network
#3, 303 Portage Ave., Winnipeg MB R3B 2B4
Tel: 204-947-6511; *Fax:* 204-989-8476
e-mail: info@mbeconetwork.org
URL: www.mbeconetwork.org
Also Known As: Manitoba Environmental Network
Overview: A small provincial charitable organization founded in 1988
Finances: *Annual Operating Budget:* $100,000-$250,000; *Funding Sources:* Project work; donations; membership dues; grants
Staff: 6 staff member(s); 10 volunteer(s)
Membership: 55 groups; *Fees:* $50 organizations, agencies, government departments & corporation; *Member Profile:* Open to any non-profit non-governmental group which has as one of its objectives the enhancing or furthering of environmental quality, protecting the environment or environmental education
Activities: Sponsors public forums, speakers, workshops on a broad variety of issues; operates projects regarding climate change, water issues & organic lawn care; offers GIS & mapping services to environmental projects; meets regularly with officials of the provincial government; *Speaker Service:* Yes; *Library:* Alice Chambers Memorial Library; Open to public
Awards: Annual Environmental Awards (Award)
Mission: To educate the public on environmental issues; to conduct research on environmental issues; to facilitate

Associations/Organizations / Manitoba Environmental Industries Association Inc.

communications between environmental groups & the general public

Manitoba Environmental Industries Association Inc. (MEIA)
#100, 62 Albert St., Winnipeg MB R3B 1E9
Tel: 204-783-7090; *Fax:* 204-783-6501
e-mail: admin@meia.mb.ca
URL: www.meia.mb.ca
Overview: A medium-sized provincial organization founded in 1991
Chief Officer(s):
John Fjeldsted, Executive Director
Vaughn Bullough, President
Rosemary Deans, Coordinator, Education & Training
Deb Tardiff, Coordinator, Education & Training
Sheldon McLeod, Secretary
John Pikel, Treasurer
Finances: *Funding Sources:* Membership fees; Sponsorships
Fees: Schedule available, based upon number of employees &; *Member Profile:* Professionals, companies, & organizations in Manitoba who practise in the area of environment & sustainable development; *Committees:* Executive; Member Services; Legislation & Regulation; Programs Development
Activities: Providing professional development training, including courses, MEIA learning sessions, & environment industry workshops; Collaborating with other organizations; Providing networking opportunities
Meetings/Conferences:
For more information see Trade Shows, Conferences and Seminars Chapter
Manitoba Environmental Industries Association Inc. 2012 Annual General Meeting
Other Conferences in 2012 2012, MB
Manitoba Environmental Industries Association Inc. 2012 Conference: Emerging Issues
Other Conferences in 2012 2012, MB
Manitoba Environmental Industries Association Inc. 2012 Conference: Remediation & Prevention
Other Conferences in 2012 2012, MB
Publications: *MEIA [Manitoba Environmental Industries Association Inc.] Information Bulletin*
Type: Newsletter *Frequency:* bi-weekly
Profile: Information for Manitoba Environmental Industries Association Inc. members about events, technology updates, & emerging regulatory & policy issues
Manitoba Environmental Industries Association Inc. Members' Directory
Type: Directory
Profile: Contact information for association members
Mission: To assist members in the business of the environment; To connect business, government, & stakeholders with environmental issues
Environmental Activity: Liaising with the government to develop environmental policies, regulations, & standards; Increasing awareness of environmental practices & initiatives; Communicating with members regarding environmental developments

Manitoba Farm Bureau *See* Keystone Agricultural Producers

Manitoba Forestry Association Inc.
Parent: **Canadian Forestry Association**
900 Corydon Ave., Winnipeg MB R3M 0Y4
Tel: 204-453-3182; *Fax:* 204-477-5765
e-mail: mfainc@mts.net
URL: www.mbforestryassoc.ca
Previous Name: Prairie Provinces Forestry Association
Overview: A medium-sized provincial charitable organization founded in 1972
Finances: *Annual Operating Budget:* $100,000-$250,000; *Funding Sources:* Government; industry; individuals
Staff: 5 staff member(s); 34 volunteer(s)
Membership: 286 individual + 115 corporate; *Fees:* Individuals - $25 member; $50 contributing; $100 sustaining; Companies - $125 general; $250 contributing; $500 sustaining; *Committees:* Education & Public Information; Fundraising; Membership; National Forest Week; Special Events
Activities: School programs; forest centres; Private Land Forests Program; operates Forest Museum; conservation kits for use by teachers; wildfire prevention campaigns; *Awareness Events:* National Forest Week, May; *Speaker Service:* Yes; *Library:* Yes, Not open to the public
Awards: Alan B. Beaven Forestry Scholarship (Scholarship) Manitoba resident; must be a recent graduate of high school,

entering a Canadian university or technical school in forestry or an allied field *Deadline:* 31-Jul *Award Amount:* $500
Mission: To promote the wise use & management of all natural renewable resources, with emphasis on forests; to promote the planting of trees; to promote private land forestry (woodlots); to act as liaison among government, industry & the general public.

Manitoba Health Libraries Association *See* Manitoba Association of Health Information Providers

Manitoba Health Organizations *See* The Regional Health Authorities of Manitoba

Manitoba Institute of Agrologists (MIA)
Parent: **Agricultural Institute of Canada**
#201, 38 Dafoe Ave., Winnipeg MB R3T 2N2
Tel: 204-275-3721; *Fax:* 204-474-7521
e-mail: mia@mts.net
URL: www.mia.mb.ca
Overview: A small provincial organization founded in 1950
Member Profile: Agricultural professionals in Manitoba
Activities: Licensing agrologists; Promoting high standards in research; Improving conditions in the agricultural industry; Advancing the professional status of members; Providing educational & networking opportunities
Publications: *MIA [Manitoba Institute of Agrologists] Bulletin*
Type: Newsletter
Profile: Institute activities, member news, & events
Mission: To act in accordance with the Agrologists Act of Manitoba; To regulate the practice of agrology in Manitoba; To ensure the knowledge, competence, & integrity of institute members, in order to protect the public interest; To act as the voice of the agrology profession

Manitoba Lung Association
Parent: **Canadian Lung Association**
629 McDermot Ave., Winnipeg MB R3A 1P6
Tel: 204-774-5501; *Fax:* 204-772-5083
Toll-Free: 888-566-5864
e-mail: info@mb.lung.ca
URL: www.mb.lung.ca
Overview: A small provincial charitable organization founded in 1904
Finances: *Funding Sources:* Donations; Fundraising; Sponsorships
Activities: Providing information about lung health; Supporting & promoting research; Offering education programs in areas such as asthma, chronic obstructive pulmonary disease (COPD), & air quality
Publications: *Manitoba Lung Association Annual Report*
Type: Yearbook *Frequency:* a.
Mission: To improve lung health
Environmental Activity: Providing information about pollution & air quality

Manitoba Medical Association *See* Doctors Manitoba

Manitoba Model Forest
PO Box 6500, Pine Falls MB R0E 1M0
Tel: 204-367-5232; *Fax:* 204-367-8897
e-mail: miette@granite.mb.ca
URL: www.manitobamodelforest.net
Overview: A small provincial organization founded in 1992
Chief Officer(s):
Brian Kotak, General Manager
Member of: Canadian Model Forest Network

Manitoba Municipal Administrators' Association Inc.
533 Buckingham Rd., Winnipeg MB R3R 1B9
Tel: 204-255-4883; *Fax:* 204-255-2623
e-mail: mmaa@mts.net
URL: www.mmaa.mb.ca
Overview: A medium-sized provincial organization
Mission: The Manitoba Municipal Administrators' Association (MMAA) is a dynamic, action-orientated organization for Municipal Employees. The MMAA focusses on the needs of our membership and are committed to their professional development.

Manitoba Ozone Protection Industry Association (MOPIA)
1980B Main St., Winnipeg MB R2V 2B6
Tel: 204-338-0804; *Fax:* 204-338-0810
Toll-Free: 888-667-4203

e-mail: mopia@mts.net
URL: www.mopia.ca
Overview: A medium-sized provincial organization
Chief Officer(s):
Mark E. Miller, Executive Director
George Kurowski, Chair
John Kub, Secretary
Laverne Dalgleish, Treasurer
Activities: Liaising with industry, interest groups, & Manitoba Environment; Raising public awareness of the impact of ozone depleting substances
Meetings/Conferences:
For more information see Trade Shows, Conferences and Seminars Chapter
Manitoba Environmental Certification & Regulation Awareness 2011 Training Course
Other Conferences in 2011 2011, MB
Manitoba Ozone Protection Industry Association 2012 18th Annual General Meeting
March 2012, MB
Manitoba Ozone Protection Industry Association 2013 19th Annual General Meeting
Other Conferences in 2013 2013, MB
Publications: *MOPIA [Manitoba Ozone Protection Industry Association] E-Bulletin*
Type: Newsletter *Frequency:* m. *Editor:* Mark Miller; Vanessa Krahn
Profile: Information for Manitoba Ozone Protection Industry Association members & select stakeholders
Environmental Awareness Training for Ozone Depleting Substances (ODS) & Other Halocarbons
Type: Manual *Price:* $45
Profile: A training manual for persons working on refrigeration or air conditioning equipment that contains a regulated substance
Manitoba Ozone Protection Industry Association Annual Report
Type: Yearbook *Frequency:* a.
Profile: Featuring messages from the Chair of the Board of Directors & the Executive Director, reports from the treasurer & auditor, as well as highlights of the year
Mission: To work towards protection of the stratospheric ozone layer; To control, reduce, & eventually eliminate emissions of ozone depleting substances
Environmental Activity: Implementing the MOPIA Atmosphere Protection Program; Offering environmental certification training to persons in the air conditioning & refrigeration industry

Manitoba Professional Planners Institute (MPPI)
Parent: **Canadian Institute of Planners**
137 Bannatyne Ave., 2nd Fl., Winnipeg MB R3B 0R3
Tel: 204-943-3637; *Fax:* 204-925-4624
e-mail: mjohnson@mts.net
URL: www.mppi.mb.ca
Overview: A medium-sized provincial organization
Mission: MPPI is responsible for handling membership applications and services, and for the enforcement of the Code of Professional Conduct. MPPI, along with the Association of Community Planners of Saskatchewan, jointly publishes the membership newsletter SCENARIO and sponsors workshops and seminars for the purpose of informing the membership of relevant developments and issues in the planning field.; *Affiliation(s):* Canadian Institute of Planners (CIP)

Manitoba Public Health Association (MPHA)
Parent: **Canadian Public Health Association**
c/o Klinic Community Health Centre, 870 Portage Ave., Winnipeg MB R3G 0P1
e-mail: manitobapha@mts.net
URL: www.manitobapha.ca
Overview: A small provincial organization founded in 1940
Chief Officer(s):
Barb Wasilewski, President
manitobapha@mts.net
Fees: $67 MPHA / CPHA memberships for students, & retired & low-income people; $140 regular MPHA / CPHA memberships
Activities: Advocating for healthy public policies; Liaising with community & professional associations & the government
Mission: To influence health, social, environmental, & economic policy decisions, in order to improve the well-being of people in Manitoba; to ensure that health promotion, health protection, & disease protection are part of services; *Member of:* Canadian Public Health Association (CPHA)

Manitoba Regional Lily Society
PO Box 846, Neepawa MB R0J 1H0
e-mail: nigel@lilynook.mb.ca
URL: www.manitobalilies.ca

Associations/Organizations / Manitoba Tobacco Reduction Alliance

Overview: A small provincial organization
Chief Officer(s):
Nigel Strohman, President
Mission: To promote the growing and care of lillies in Manitoba.

Manitoba Safety Council *See* Safety Services Manitoba

Manitoba Society of Certified Engineering Technicians & Technologists Inc. *See* Certified Technicians & Technologists Association of Manitoba

Manitoba Tobacco Reduction Alliance
194B Sherbrook St., Winnipeg MB R3C 2B6
Tel: 204-784-7030; *Fax:* 204-784-7039
e-mail: admin@mantrainc.ca
URL: www.mantrainc.ca
Also Known As: ManTRA
Previous Name: Council for a Tobacco-Free Manitoba
Overview: A small provincial organization founded in 1977
Chief Officer(s):
Dhali Dhaliwal, MD, Chair
Finances: *Annual Operating Budget:* Less than $50,000
Membership: 14; *Fees:* $45; *Member Profile:* Open to organizations which are interested in achieving a tobacco-free society for Manitobans; associate - available for those who wish to receive minutes only at a reduced fee
Activities: *Awareness Events:* National Non-Smoking Week
Mission: Voluntary group of agencies dedicated to achieving a tobacco-free society for Manitobans; to encourage & support legislation to restrict smoking in public places & workplaces; to maintain awareness of the hazards of tobacco consumption to identified high-risk target groups; *Member of:* Canadian Council on Smoking & Health

Manitoba Trucking Association
Parent: Canadian Trucking Alliance
25 Bunting St., Winnipeg MB R2X 2P5
Tel: 204-632-6600; *Fax:* 204-694-7134
e-mail: info@trucking.mb.ca
URL: www.trucking.mb.ca
Overview: A medium-sized provincial organization founded in 1932
Finances: *Funding Sources:* Membership dues & fundraising through services
Staff: 5 staff member(s)
Membership: 350 organizations; *Member Profile:* PSV Carriers; City Transportation; Private Fleet; Household Goods Carriers; Associated Trades; Vehicle Maintenance; *Committees:* Associated Trades (Members, Executive); Vehicle Maintenance Council; Maintenace Council Executive
Activities: *Library:* Yes, open by appointment
Awards: MTA Scholarships (Scholarship)
Open to employees & dependants of member companies
Driver of the Month Award (Award)
Provincial & National Driver of the Year Awards (Award)
Trailmobile Service to Industry Award (Award)
Maxim Transportation Services Associate of the Year Award (Award)
Publications: *Western Canada Highway News*
Type: Journal *Frequency:* q
Mission: Serves the needs of the trucking industry & its interested parties by promoting a healthy business environment & advocating safety, education, & responsibility.; *Affiliation(s):* Canadian Trucking Alliance; Canadian Council of Motor Transport Administrators; Canadian Trucking Human Resource Council; Winnipeg Chamber of Commerce; Manitoba Chamber of Commerce; Infrastructure Council of Manitoba; Employers' Task Force on Workers' Compensation; Manitoba Employers' Council

Manitoba Underwater Council (MUC)
PO Box 711, Winnipeg MB R3C 2K3
Tel: 204-632-8508
e-mail: info@manunderwater.com
URL: www.manunderwater.com
Overview: A medium-sized provincial charitable organization founded in 1962
Finances: *Annual Operating Budget:* Less than $50,000; *Funding Sources:* Provincial Government & membership fees
Staff: 10 staff member(s); 10 volunteer(s)
Membership: 27 institutional + 150 individual; *Fees:* $20; *Member Profile:* Certified scuba divers, divers in training
Activities: Spear fishing competition, pumpkin dive, super dive, underwater football competition

Mission: To coordinate, preserve, support & promote sport diving clubs & associations; to promote safety in diving; to exchange & disseminate information concerning the sport of skin & scuba diving & to foster conservation; *Member of:* Sport Manitoba

Manitoba Water & Wastewater Association (MWWA)
PO Box 1600, Portage la Prairie MB R1N 3P1
Tel: 204-239-6868; *Fax:* 204-239-6872
Toll-Free: 866-396-2549
e-mail: mwwa@mts.net
URL: www.mwwa.net
Overview: A small provincial organization founded in 1975
Chief Officer(s):
Iva Last, Executive Director
Fees: $50
Mission: To provide members with educational opportunities; To promote operator certification & facility classification; *Member of:* Western Canada Water & Wastewater Association
Environmental Activity: To be dedicated to the stewardship of the environment & public health

Manitoba Water Well Association (MWWA)
Parent: Canadian Ground Water Association
PO Box 1648, Winnipeg MB R3C 2Z6
Tel: 204-479-3777
e-mail: info@mwwa.ca
URL: www.mwwa.ca
Overview: A medium-sized provincial organization founded in 1958
Chief Officer(s):
Jeff Bell, President
Lynn Giersch, Business Manager
Marilyn Schneider, Secretary-Treasurer
Member Profile: Manufacturers; Technicians; Suppliers; Contractors
Activities: Offering workshops & seminars; Providing networking opportunities; Fostering & promoting scientific education, research, & standards
Meetings/Conferences:
For more information see Trade Shows, Conferences and Seminars Chapter
Manitoba Water Well Association 2011 Annual General Meeting
Other Conferences in 2011 2011, MB
Manitoba Water Well Association 2012 Annual General Meeting
Other Conferences in 2012 2012, MB
Publications: *Manitoba Water Well Association Newsletter*
Type: Newsletter *Frequency:* q
Profile: Featuring the president's report, membership information
Mission: To promote & support the water well industry in Manitoba
Environmental Activity: Encouraging cooperation between association members & government agencies for the protection & management of the underground water supply in Manitoba

Manitoba Wildlife Federation (MWF)
Parent: Canadian Wildlife Federation
70 Stevenson Rd., Winnipeg MB R3H 0W7
Tel: 204-633-5967; *Fax:* 204-632-5200
e-mail: info@mwf.mb.ca; vpHunting@mwf.mb.ca;
vpPrograms@mwf.mb.ca
URL: www.mwf.mb.ca
Overview: A medium-sized provincial charitable organization founded in 1944
Chief Officer(s):
Reid Woods, President
President@mwf.mb.ca
Lori Thomas, Director, Administration
Rachelle Aime, Vice-President, Education
vpAngling@mwf.mb.ca
Ken MacMaster, Vice-President, Membership
vpMembership@mwf.mb.ca
Larry Millan, Vice-President, Environment & Habitat
vpEnvironment@mwf.mb.ca
Reg Wiebe, Coordinator, Hunter Education
Finances: *Funding Sources:* Membership fees; Donations; Sponsorships
Membership: 14,000; *Fees:* $7.50 youth (12 to 17 years of age); $25 individuals; $35 families; *Member Profile:* Anglers; Hunters; Outdoor enthusiasts; *Committees:* Education; Hunting; Environment & Habitat; Angling; Publicity; Program Coordination; Membership; Legislation Review; Internal Services
Activities: Offering hunting skills & firearms training programs; Developing the Hunters Sharing the Harvest program; Supporting the MWF Habitat Foundation

Publications: *Outdoor Edge [a publication of the Manitoba Wildlife Federation]*
Type: Magazine *Frequency:* bi-m. *Price:* Free with Manitoba Wildlife Federation membership
Profile: Information for Manitoba's hunters & anglers
Mission: To devote members to the causes of conservation & the participation in the wise use of natural resources; To encourage the propagation of game & fish; To promote the enforcement of game laws; To cooperate with government departments
Environmental Activity: Educating members & the public, especially about conservation & safety; Supporting research on diseases in fish & wildlife; Acting as a voice for the progressive management of Manitoba's natural resources; Cleaning up rivers & streams

Manitoba Wildlife Rehabilitation Organization *See* Wildlife Haven Rehabilitation Centre

Manitoulin Environmental Awareness *See* Algoma Manitoulin Environmental Awareness

Manufacturiers et Exportateurs Canada *See* Canadian Manufacturers & Exporters

Maritimes Health Libraries Association (MHLA) / Association des bibliothèques de la santé des Maritimes (ABSM)
Parent: Canadian Health Libraries Association
c/o W.K. Kellogg Health Sciences Library, Tupper Medical Building, PO Box 2100, 5850 College St., Halifax NS B3H 1X5
Tel: 902-494-2483
URL: www.chla-absc.ca/mhla/
Overview: A medium-sized local organization
Fees: $20; *Member Profile:* Health library specialists in the maritime provinces
Activities: Advocating for the value of health library specialists & health libraries; Providing educational opportunities; Communicating with members
Mission: To support members in the provision of quality information services for the health care community in the maritime provinces; *Member of:* Canadian Health Libraries Association / Association des bibliothèques de la santé du Canada

Marmot Recovery Foundation
PO Box 2332, Stn. A, Nanaimo BC V9R 6X6
Tel: 250-753-8080; *Fax:* 250-753-8070
Toll-Free: 877-462-7668
e-mail: marmot@islandnet.com
URL: www.marmots.org
Overview: A small local organization founded in 1998
Chief Officer(s):
Jim Walker, Chair
Mission: To manage the recovery effort for one of North America's most endangered mammals: the Vancouver Island marmot (Marmota vancouverensis); *Affiliation(s):* Vancouver Island Marmot Recovery Team

Master Insulators' Association of Ontario Inc.
Building 1, #101, 2600 Skymark Ave., Mississauga ON L4W 5B2
Tel: 905-279-6426; *Fax:* 905-279-6422
e-mail: manager@miaontario.org
URL: www.miaontario.org
Overview: A small provincial organization founded in 1942

Materials & Manufacturing Ontario, Division of OCE Inc. (MMO)
#250, 2655 North Sheridan Way, Mississauga ON L5K 2P8
Tel: 905-823-2020; *Fax:* 905-823-4141
Overview: A medium-sized provincial organization
Chief Officer(s):
Bob Civak, Managing Director
Membership: 1,700
Affiliation(s): Ontario Centres of Excellence

McGregor Model Forest
PO Box 2640, Prince George BC V2N 4T5
Tel: 250-612-5840; *Fax:* 250-612-5848
URL: www.mcgregor.bc.ca
Overview: A small local organization
Chief Officer(s):
Al Gorley, President
Dan Adamson, General Manager
dan.adamson@mcgregor.bc.ca
Member of: Canadian Model Forest Network

McIlwraith Field Naturalists
PO Box 24008, London ON N6H 5C4
Tel: 519-457-4593
e-mail: info@mcilwraith.ca
URL: www.mcilwraith.ca
Overview: A small local organization founded in 1890
Finances: *Annual Operating Budget:* $50,000-$100,000
Membership: 5 institutional + 400 individual; *Fees:* $30 individual; $10 student; $50 contributing; $100 sustaining; *Member Profile:* Interest in natural world; *Committees:* Conservation; Education; Birding; Junior Naturalists
Activities: Field trips; tree & wild flower plantings; nature reserve; life science inventories; *Speaker Service:* Yes
Mission: To promote the enjoyment of nature through environmental appreciation & conservation; to encourage wise use & conservation of natural resources; to promote environmental protection; *Affiliation(s):* Canadian Nature Federation; Federation of Ontario Naturalists

Meat Packers Council of Canada *See* Canadian Meat Council

Mechanical Contractors Association of Alberta
Parent: Mechanical Contractors Association of Canada
#204, 2725 - 12 St. NE, Calgary AB T2E 7J2
Tel: 403-250-7237; *Fax:* 403-291-0551
Toll-Free: 800-251-0620
URL: www.mcaalberta.com
Overview: A small provincial organization
Finances: *Annual Operating Budget:* $250,000-$500,000
Staff: 3 staff member(s)
Membership: 100-499; *Fees:* $530 contractor; $424 affiliate
Mission: To promote plumbing & mechanical contractors; to provide educational programs to foster improved management & productivity in mechanical contracting; to represent mechanical contractors with their various publics - governments, design authorities, labour; to foster professional advancement & profitability of the plumbing, heating & mechanical contracting industry through its member services

Mechanical Contractors Association of British Columbia (MCABC)
Parent: Mechanical Contractors Association of Canada
#223, 3989 Henning Dr., Burnaby BC V5C 6N5
Tel: 604-205-5058; *Fax:* 604-205-5075
Toll-Free: 800-663-8473
URL: www.mcabc.org
Previous Name: Canadian Plumbing & Mechanical Contractors Association, BC Branch
Overview: A medium-sized provincial organization founded in 1905
Finances: *Annual Operating Budget:* $250,000-$500,000
Staff: 3 staff member(s)
Membership: 14 senior/lifetime + 142 general + 63 associate; *Committees:* Contractor-Engineer; Joint Apprenticeship; Management Education
Activities: *Speaker Service:* Yes; *Library:* Yes
Mission: To encourage, support & promote the advancement of the mechanical contracting industry; to provide leadership, assistance & training to members.

Mechanical Contractors Association of Canada (MCAC) / Association des entrepreneurs en mécanique du Canada
#601, 280 Albert St., Ottawa ON K1P 5G8
Tel: 613-232-0492; *Fax:* 613-235-2793
e-mail: mcac@mcac.ca
URL: www.mcac.ca
Overview: A medium-sized national organization founded in 1895
Membership: 800
Mission: To promote plumbing & mechanical contractors; to provide educational programs to foster improved management & productivity in mechanical contracting; to represent mechanical contractors to their various publics - governments, design authorities, labour.; *Affiliation(s):* Council of Construction Trade Associations

Mechanical Contractors Association of Manitoba (MCAM)
Parent: Mechanical Contractors Association of Canada
#1, 860 Bradford St., Winnipeg MB R3H 0N5
Tel: 204-774-2404; *Fax:* 204-772-0233
e-mail: mcam@mts.net
URL: www.mca-mb.com
Overview: A medium-sized provincial organization founded in 1970
Mission: To continually improve mechanical industry standards while providing a high level of value performance & customer service for our members

Mechanical Contractors Association of New Brunswick / Association des entrepreneurs en mécanique du N.-B.
Parent: Mechanical Contractors Association of Canada
c/o Moncton Northeast Construction Association, 297 Collishaw St., Moncton NB E1C 9R2
Tel: 506-857-4128; *Fax:* 506-857-8861
e-mail: info@mneca.ca
URL: www.mneca.ca
Also Known As: MCA New Brunswick Inc.
Previous Name: Plumbing & Mechanical Contractors Association of New Brunswick
Overview: A small provincial organization founded in 1976
Finances: *Annual Operating Budget:* $100,000-$250,000; *Funding Sources:* Membership fees
Staff: 1 staff member(s)
Membership: 28; *Fees:* $1,017 contractor/sub-contractor/supplier; $491.55 associate; *Member Profile:* Open to individual firms engaged in plumbing & related trades
Mission: To provide leadership & service to members; to act on behalf of members in labour relations matters, including collective bargaining; to advance & develop the industry, primarily in New Brunswick; to endeavour to improve legislation affecting the industry; to promote sound labour relations; *Affiliation(s):* Canadian Construction Association

Mechanical Contractors Association of Newfoundland & Labrador
Parent: Mechanical Contractors Association of Canada
PO Box 745, Mount Pearl NL A1N 2Y2
Tel: 709-747-5577; *Fax:* 709-368-5342
e-mail: ddawe@nfld.net
Overview: A small provincial organization

Mechanical Contractors Association of Nova Scotia
Parent: Mechanical Contractors Association of Canada
c/o Construction Association of Nova Scotia, #3, 260 Brownlow Ave., Dartmouth NS B3B 1V9
Tel: 902-468-2267; *Fax:* 902-468-2470
e-mail: cans@cans.ns.ca
URL: www.cans.ns.ca
Also Known As: Mechanical Contractors Section of The Construction Association of Nova Scotia (CANS)
Overview: A small provincial organization

Mechanical Contractors Association of Ontario (MCAO)
Parent: Mechanical Contractors Association of Canada
#103, 10 Director Ct., Woodbridge ON L4L 7E8
Tel: 905-856-0342; *Fax:* 905-856-0385
e-mail: mcao@mcao.org
URL: www.mcao.org
Overview: A medium-sized provincial organization

Mechanical Contractors Association of Prince Edward Island
Parent: Mechanical Contractors Association of Canada
c/o Association of Commercial & Industrial Contractors of PEI, PO Box 1685, Charlottetown PE C1A 7N4
Tel: 902-566-3456; *Fax:* 902-368-2754
e-mail: wmm@wmm93.pe.ca
Overview: A small provincial organization

Mechanical Contractors Association of Saskatchewan Inc. (MCAS)
Parent: Mechanical Contractors Association of Canada
Heritage Business Park, #105, 2750 Faithfull Ave., Saskatoon SK S7K 6M6
Tel: 306-664-2154; *Fax:* 306-653-7233
e-mail: mca-sask@mca-sask.com
URL: www.mca-sask.com
Overview: A small provincial organization founded in 1919
Finances: *Funding Sources:* Membership fees
Staff: 1 staff member(s)
Membership: 150; *Fees:* $350; *Member Profile:* Mechanical contractors
Mission: MCAS is a provincial non-profit, trade association that represents plumbing & heating contractors in relation to the construction industry, legislative departments of municipal & provincial government & other industry-related bodies.; *Affiliation(s):* Mechanical Contractors Association of Canada

Mechanical Wood-Pulps Network *See* Canadian Pulp & Paper Network for Innovation in Education & Research

Mechanical-Electrical Division of The Canadian Institute of Mining, Metallurgy & Petroleum *See* Maintenance & Engineering Society of The Canadian Institute of Mining, Metallurgy & Petroleum

Médecins pour un Canada sans fumée *See* Physicians for a Smoke-Free Canada

Medical Society of Nova Scotia *See* Doctors Nova Scotia

Medical Society of Prince Edward Island (MSPEI)
Parent: Canadian Medical Association
2 Myrtle St., Stratford PE C1B 2W2
Tel: 902-368-7303; *Fax:* 902-566-3934
Toll-Free: 888-368-7303
URL: www.mspei.org
Overview: A medium-sized provincial organization founded in 1855
Finances: *Annual Operating Budget:* $100,000-$250,000; *Funding Sources:* Membership dues
Staff: 6 staff member(s)
Membership: 352 physicians; *Member Profile:* Individuals licensed to practise medicine in PEI
Activities: *Internships:* Yes; *Library:* Yes, open by appointment
Mission: To promote health & improvement of medical services; to prevent disease; to represent members at national bodies & government; to consider all matters concerning the professional welfare of members.

Meewasin Valley Authority (MVA)
402 - 3rd Ave. South, Saskatoon SK S7K 3G5
Tel: 306-665-6887; *Fax:* 306-665-6117
e-mail: meewasin@meewasin.com
URL: www.meewasin.com
Overview: A small local organization
Chief Officer(s):
Susan Lamb, CEO
Committees: Community Advisory
Activities: Clean-up Campaign; Stewardship Program; Dragon Boat Races
Mission: To ensure a healthy & vibrant river valley with a balance between human use & conservation by: providing leadership in the management of its resources; promoting understanding, conservation & beneficial use of the valley; undertaking programs & projects in river valley development & conservation for the benefit of present & future generations

Melfort Agricultural Society
PO Box 816, Melfort SK S0E 1A0
Tel: 306-752-2240
Overview: A small local charitable organization founded in 1906
Finances: *Annual Operating Budget:* $100,000-$250,000; *Funding Sources:* Bingo; flea markets; exhibition; grants
Staff: 1 staff member(s); 101 volunteer(s)
Membership: 101; *Fees:* $5
Mission: To improve agriculture & the quality of life in the community by educating members & the community; to provide a community forum for discussing agricultural issues; to foster community development & community spirit; to help provide markets for Saskatchewan products; to encourage conservation of natural resources, including soil conservation, reforestation, rural & urban beautification; *Member of:* Saskatchewan Association of Agricultural Societies & Exhibitions; Canadian Association of Fairs & Exhibitions

Melville & District Agri-Park Association Inc.
PO Box 2678, Melville SK S0A 2P0
Tel: 306-728-5277; *Fax:* 306-728-4544
e-mail: agripark@sasktel.net
URL: www.melvilleagripark.com
Also Known As: Melville Agri-Park

Overview: A small local organization founded in 1981
Finances: Annual Operating Budget: $50,000-$100,000
Staff: 1 staff member(s); 100 volunteer(s)
Membership: 200 senior/lifetime; *Fees:* $100; *Committees:* 4-H Organization; Horse Show; Showstoppers ATV; Archery Club; Homecrafts; Horse Racing; Rodeo; Cattle; Team Roping; Barrel Racing
Activities: *Internships:* Yes; *Rents Mailing List:* Yes
Mission: To promote agriculture events in Melville & surrounding district; *Member of:* Saskatchewan Association of Agricultural Societies & Exhibitions; Canadian Association of Exhibitions; Saskatchewan Horse Federation

Metal Industries Association *See* Western Employers Labour Relations Association

Metallurgy & Materials Society of the Canadian Institute of Mining, Metallurgy & Petroleum (MetSoc)
Parent: Canadian Institute of Mining, Metallurgy & Petroleum
#1250, 3500, boul de Maisonneuve ouest, Montréal QC H3Z 3C1
Tel: 514-939-2710
URL: www.metsoc.org
Social Media: www.facebook.com/group.php?gid=77992627143
Overview: A medium-sized national organization founded in 1967
Chief Officer(s):
Greg Richards, President
greg.richards@teck.com
Brigitte Farah, Manager, Administration & Meetings, 514-939-2710 Ext. 1329, Fax: 514-939-2714
bfarah@cim.org
Ronona Saunders, Contact, Publications, Web, & Marketing, 514-939-2710 Ext. 1327, Fax: 514-939-2714
rsaunders@cim.org
Member Profile: Persons involved in the development & application of technologies for the extraction, fabrication, & utilization of metals & materials in Canada; *Committees:* CIM Journal; Student Activities; Historical Metallurgy; Membership Services; Publications; Trustees
Activities: Providing information to the government & the public; Offering continuing education; Recognizing excellence; Providing networking opportunities
Meetings/Conferences:
For more information see Trade Shows, Conferences and Seminars Chapter
Metallurgy & Materials Society of the Canadian Institute of Mining, Metallurgy & Petroleum COM 2011: 50th Annual Conference of Metallurgists
October 2011 Montréal, QC
Metallurgy & Materials Society of the Canadian Institute of Mining, Metallurgy & Petroleum World Gold 2011 3rd International Conference
September 2011 Montréal, QC
Metallurgy & Materials Society of the Canadian Institute of Mining, Metallurgy & Petroleum COM 2012: 51st Annual Conference of Metallurgists
September 2012 Niagara Falls, ON
Metallurgy & Materials Society of the Canadian Institute of Mining, Metallurgy & Petroleum COM 2013: 52nd Annual Conference of Metallurgists
October 2013 Montréal, QC
Metallurgy & Materials Society of the Canadian Institute of Mining, Metallurgy & Petroleum World Gold 2013 4th International Conference
Other Conferences in 2013 2013
Metallurgy & Materials Society of the Canadian Institute of Mining, Metallurgy & Petroleum COM 2014: 53rd Annual Conference of Metallurgists
Other Conferences in 2014 2014
Metallurgy & Materials Society of the Canadian Institute of Mining, Metallurgy & Petroleum COM 2015: 54th Annual Conference of Metallurgists
Other Conferences in 2015 2015
Metallurgy & Materials Society of the Canadian Institute of Mining, Metallurgy & Petroleum World Gold 2015 5th International Conference
Other Conferences in 2015 2015
Publications: *Canadian Metallurgical Quarterly: The Canadian Journal of Metallurgy & Materials Science*
Type: Journal *Frequency:* q. *Accepts Advertising* : Yes *Editor:* Doug Boyd *ISSN:* 0008-4433
Profile: Research in the areas of mineral processing, extraction, synthesis, processing, characterization properties, & performance of metals & materials
mLink: The The Electronic Newsletter of the METSOC of CIM
Type: Newsletter
Profile: News for members & students about MetSoc meetings & publications
Mission: To expand the professional horizons of society members in order to serve the metals & materials industry
Environmental Activity: Serving members, society, & researchers involved in the development of technologies for the environmentally responsible extraction, fabrication, utilization, & recycling of metals & materials

The Metropolitan Toronto & Region Conservation Foundation; The Conservation Foundation of Greater Toronto *See* Conservation Foundation

Metropolitan Toronto Sewer & Watermain Contractors Association *See* Ontario Sewer & Watermain Construction Association

The Michener Institute for Applied Health Sciences
222 St. Patrick St., Toronto ON M5T 1V4
Tel: 416-596-3101; *Fax:* 416-596-3180
Toll-Free: 800-387-9066
e-mail: info@michener.ca
URL: www.michener.on.ca
Previous Name: Toronto Institute of Medical Technology
Overview: A medium-sized national organization founded in 1967
Chief Officer(s):
Cathy Fooks, Chair
Paul Gamble, Secretary/President & CEO
Finances: *Annual Operating Budget:* Greater than $5 Million; *Funding Sources:* Ontario Ministry of Health
Staff: 97 staff member(s)
Activities: *Library:* Yes, open by appointment
Mission: To design, develop & deliver the best educational programs, products & services in applied health sciences; *Affiliation(s):* 170 hospitals, labs, & clinics across Canada

Middlesex Federation of Agriculture (MFA)
Parent: Ontario Federation of Agriculture
PO Box 820, Mount Brydges ON N0L 1W0
Tel: 519-457-8444; *Fax:* 519-264-9173
e-mail: mfa@odyssey.on.ca
URL: www.ofa.on.ca/middlesex
Overview: A small local organization founded in 1939
Chief Officer(s):
Steve Fonger, President
Finances: *Annual Operating Budget:* $50,000-$100,000
Staff: 1 staff member(s); 50 volunteer(s)
Membership: 2500; *Committees:* Education; Communication; Special Events; Political Awareness
Mission: To advance agriculture & the rural community through partnerships, education & advocacy

Millarville Racing & Agricultural Society (MRAS)
Box 68, Millarville AB T0L 1K0
Tel: 403-931-3411; *Fax:* 403-931-3485
e-mail: mras@millarville.net
URL: www.millarville-ab.com
Overview: A small local organization founded in 1907
Chief Officer(s):
Barb Castell, Staff
Don Stewart, President
Finances: *Annual Operating Budget:* $250,000-$500,000
Staff: 3 staff member(s); 300 volunteer(s)
Membership: 500; *Fees:* $40 general; $325 family; $225 individual
Activities: Organizing rodeos, races, farmers' markets, & fairs
Mission: To build a strong community; *Member of:* Alberta Association of Agricultural Societies

Mineral Society of Manitoba (MSM)
c/o The Manitoba Museum, 190 Rupert Ave., Winnipeg MB R3B 0N2
e-mail: ysearle@mts.net
URL: www.umanitoba.ca/geoscience/mineralsociety/index.htm
Overview: A small provincial organization founded in 1971
Chief Officer(s):
Yvonne Searle, President, 204-663-6637
Jack Bauer, Vice-President, 204-632-6934
Evelyn Bauer, Treasurer, 204-632-6934
Fees: $10 individuals; $15 families
Activities: Hosting monthly meetings at the Manitoba Museum; Organizing field trips; Planning educational exhibits
Publications: *The Mineral Vein: The Mineral Society of Manitoba Newsletter*
Type: Newsletter *Frequency:* 9 pa *Editor:* Tony Smith
Profile: Upcoming events, presentation summaries, & articles about rockhounding & mineralogy
Mission: To promote the study of minerals, rocks, & fossils for both scientific & recreational purposes

Mineralogical Association of Canada (MAC) / Association minéralogique du Canada
490, rue de la Couronne, Québec QC G1K 9A9
Tel: 418-653-0333; *Fax:* 418-653-0777
e-mail: office@mineralogicalassociation.ca
URL: www.mineralogicalassociation.ca
Overview: A medium-sized national charitable organization founded in 1955
Member Profile: Individuals or organizations engaged or interested in mineralogy, crystallography, petrology, geochemistry, & economic geology
Activities: Organizing annual meetings & symposia; Providing short courses; Disseminating information about mineralogy; Providing reference books & textbooks in the mineral sciences; Presenting awards & scholarships; Increasing public awareness of science
Publications: *The Canadian Mineralogist: The Journal of the Mineralogical Association of Canada*
Type: Journal *Frequency:* bi-m. *Editor:* Robert F. Martin
Profile: Subjects include mineralogy, mineral deposits, petrology, crystallography, & geochemistry
Elements: An International Magazine of Mineralogy, Geochemistry, & Petrology
Type: Magazine *Frequency:* bi-m. *Accepts Advertising* : Yes *Editor:* Pierrette Tremblay *ISSN:* 1811-5209 *Price:* Free with membership in the Mineralogical Association of Canada
Profile: An international magazine published by organizations such as the Mineralogical Association of Canada, the Mineralogical Society of America, the Mineralogical Society of Great Britain & Ireland, the European Association of Geochemistry, the Clay Minerals Society, & the Geochemical Society
Mission: To promote & advance knowledge of mineralogy & the allied disciplines of petrology, crystallography, mineral deposits, & geochemistry

Mines & Aggregates Safety & Health Association (MASHA)
PO Box 2050, Stn. Main, North Bay ON P1B 9P1
Tel: 705-474-7233; *Fax:* 705-472-5800
e-mail: info@masha.on.ca
URL: www.masha.on.ca
Overview: A small provincial organization founded in 1998
Chief Officer(s):
Jean Chadbourn, Administrative Assistant, Field Services
Finances: *Annual Operating Budget:* $3 Million-$5 Million
Staff: 34 staff member(s)
Membership: 500-999; *Member Profile:* Underground & surface mining companies, exploration, diamond drilling, mine contractors, pits & quarries
Activities: Consulting, training, research, providing information; annual mining health & safety conference; *Library:* Yes, Not open to the public
Mission: To contribute to the continuous improvement of health & safety in the mining & aggregates industry; *Member of:* Workplace Safety & Insurance Board

Mines Alerte Canada *See* MiningWatch Canada

Mining Association of British Columbia (MABC)
Parent: Mining Association of Canada
#900, 808 West Hastings St., Vancouver BC V6C 2X4
Tel: 604-681-4321; *Fax:* 604-681-5305
e-mail: mabcinfo@mining.bc.ca
URL: www.mining.bc.ca
Overview: A medium-sized provincial organization founded in 1901
Member Profile: Members include corporate members with producing operations within BC, service & supply organizations, institutions, & non-profit organizations.
Activities: Liaising with government legislators; Lobbying for regulatory advancement; Promoting the economic & social value of mining; Updating members on regulatory change; Facilitating exchange of information among members
Publications: *Daily News [a publication of the Mining Association of British Columbia]*
Type: Newsletter *Frequency:* daily

Profile: Mining related news, on provincial, national, & international levels, for members
Mission: To speak on behalf of mineral producers; To represent the interests of British Columbia's mining industry; To communicate with senior government decision-makers, communities, NGOs, First Nations, & the media; To act as the industry's voice regarding issues such as environmental regulations, taxation, infrastructure demands, labour issues, health & safety, & international trade

Mining Association of Canada (MAC) / Association minière du Canada
#1105, 350 Sparks St., Ottawa ON K1R 7S8
Tel: 613-233-9391; *Fax:* 613-233-8897
e-mail: info@mining.ca
URL: www.mining.ca
Overview: A large national organization founded in 1935
Finances: *Annual Operating Budget:* $1.5 Million-$3 Million; *Funding Sources:* Membership dues
Staff: 10 staff member(s)
Membership: 55
Activities: *Awareness Events:* National Mining Week, May; Mining Weeks in Canada, April - June
Mission: To represent the interests of member companies engaged in mineral exploration, extraction & refining; to work with governments on public policy pertaining to minerals
Environmental Activity: Environmental Policy & Guidelines; Environmental Research

Mining Association of Manitoba Inc. (MAMI)
Parent: Mining Association of Canada
#700, 305 Broadway Ave., Winnipeg MB R3C 3J7
Tel: 204-989-1890
e-mail: pmarsden@mines.ca
URL: www.mines.ca
Overview: A medium-sized provincial organization founded in 1940
Finances: *Funding Sources:* Membership dues
Staff: 1 staff member(s)
Membership: 16; *Member Profile:* Mining companies with more than 50 employees; *Committees:* Environment; Exploration; Tax
Activities: *Speaker Service:* Yes; *Library:* Yes, open by appointment
Mission: To represent mining & exploration companies in Manitoba.

Mining Industry Human Resources Council
#102, 260 Hearst Way, Kanata ON K2L 3H1
Tel: 613-270-9696; *Fax:* 613-270-9399
e-mail: info@mihr.ca
URL: www.mitac.ca
Overview: A medium-sized national organization
Chief Officer(s):
Paul Hébert, Executive Director
Mission: Contributes to the strength, competitiveness & sustainability of the Canadian mining industry by collaborating with all communities of interest in the development & implementation of solutions to the industry's national human resource challenges

Mining Society of Nova Scotia
Parent: Mining Association of Canada
88 Leeside Dr., Sydney NS B1R 1S6
Tel: 902-567-2147; *Fax:* 902-567-2147
e-mail: florence@ns.sympatico.ca
Overview: A small provincial organization founded in 1887
Membership: 250; *Fees:* $90
Affiliation(s): Canadian Institute of Mining, Metallurgy & Petroleum

Mining Suppliers, Contractors & Consultants Association of BC (MSCCA)
#900, 808 West Hastings St., Vancouver BC V6C 2X4
Tel: 604-681-4321; *Fax:* 604-681-5305
e-mail: tmulligan@mining.bc.ca
URL: www.mscca.com
Overview: A medium-sized provincial licensing organization founded in 1986
Chief Officer(s):
Terry B. Mulligan, Executive Director
Finances: *Annual Operating Budget:* $100,000-$250,000; *Funding Sources:* Membership dues; special events
Staff: 1 staff member(s); 3 volunteer(s)
Membership: 225 companies; *Fees:* Based on sales to BC mining
Activities: Networking functions with the mining industry

Mission: To promote the development of a sustainable mining industry in BC; *Affiliation(s):* Mining Association of British Columbia

MiningWatch Canada / Mines Alerte Canada
#508, 250 City Centre Ave., Ottawa ON K1R 6K7
Tel: 613-569-3439; *Fax:* 613-569-5138
e-mail: info@miningwatch.ca
URL: www.miningwatch.ca
Overview: A small national organization founded in 1999
Chief Officer(s):
Catherine Coumans, Ph.D., Research Coordinator
Membership: 19; *Fees:* Sliding scale; *Member Profile:* Aboriginal, labour, environmental, international groups
Activities: Annual meeting; workshops; conferences
Mission: To address the urgent need for a coordinated public interest response to the threats to public health, water & air quality, fish & wildlife habitat & community interests posed by irresponsible mineral policies & practices in Canada & around the world; *Member of:* Canadian Environmental Network; Canadian Council for International Cooperation; Halifax Initiative

Mitlenatch Field Naturalists Society
PO Box 105, Quathiaski Cove BC V0P 1H0
Tel: 250-285-3570
Overview: A small local organization founded in 1970
Membership: 40; *Fees:* $17
Mission: To promote the enjoyment of nature through environmental appreciation & conservation; to encourage wise use & conservation of natural resources & environmental protection.; *Member of:* Federation of BC Naturalists

Model Forest of Newfoundland and Labrador (MFNL)
PO Box 68, Corner Brook NL A2H 6C3
Tel: 709-637-7300; *Fax:* 709-634-0255
e-mail: glendagarnier@mfnl.com
URL: www.wnmf.com
Previous Name: Western Newfoundland Model Forest
Overview: A small local organization
Chief Officer(s):
Muhammad Nazir, President
Mission: The Model Forest is a not-for-profit corporation formed as a partnership of organizations and individuals working on the implementation of activities that advance their abilities to practice sustainable forest management and community-based economic development utilizing our forest resources; *Member of:* Canadian Model Forest Network

Montréal Field Naturalists Club
42, av Ballantyne nord, Montréal QC H4X 2B8
Tel: 514-484-5664
e-mail: raymond.murphy@sympatico.ca
Overview: A small local organization founded in 1971
Chief Officer(s):
Raymond Murphy, President
Membership: 150 individual; *Fees:* $15 individual
Mission: To increase knowledge of nature through outdoor & indoor activities; to act when nature seems to be threatened, by expressing protests, participating in meetings

Montréal Gem & Mineral Club / Le Club de gemmologie et de minérlogie de Montréal
PO Box 1717, Stn. B, 2445 ch Lucern, Mont-Royal QC H3R 2K5
Tel: 514-878-9110
e-mail: geminews@canada.com
URL: www.montrealgemmineralclub.ca
Overview: A small local organization founded in 1957
Chief Officer(s):
Mike Rooney, Contact
Fees: $20 individual; $30 family; *Member Profile:* Jewelers; Lapidaries; Rockhounds; Collectors
Activities: Organizing programs & field trips; Planning workshops; *Library:* Montréal Gem & Mineral Club Library
Publications: Geminews
Type: Newsletter *Frequency:* m. *Price:* Free for Montréal Gem & Mineral Club members
Profile: Club activities & forthcoming events
Mission: To provide information about gems & minerals; *Member of:* Central Canadian Federation of Mineralogical Societies

Moose Jaw Wildlife Federation
1396 - 3rd NE, Moose Jaw SK S6H 0A1
Tel: 306-693-4047
Overview: A small local organization
Member of: Saskatchewan Wildlife Federation

Mouvement féderalist mondial *See* World Federalist Movement

Municipal Electric Association *See* Electricity Distributors Association

Municipal Engineers Association (MEA)
#2, 6355 Kennedy Rd., Mississauga ON L5T 2L5
Tel: 905-795-2555; *Fax:* 905-795-2660
e-mail: info@municipalengineers.on.ca
URL: www.municipalengineers.on.ca
Overview: A medium-sized provincial organization founded in 1974
Chief Officer(s):
Rick A. Kester, P.Eng, President, 905-795-2555, Fax: 905-795-2660
J. David Shantz, Executive Director
Member Profile: Public sector professional engineers in full time employment of municipalities, who perform functions in the field of municipal engineering; *Committees:* Administrative & Seconded; Municipal Transportation Advisory; MEA/CEO Liaison; Development Engineering; MEA/MNR/CO Liaison; MEA Training; MEA/MOE Liaison; Ontario Works Network; Tri-Committee Board
Activities: Organizing training events; Advocating for sound municipal engineering; Championing positions on municipal engineering issues; Recognizing achievements of municipal engineers
Meetings/Conferences:
For more information see Trade Shows, Conferences and Seminars Chapter
Municipal Engineers Association 2011 Annual General Meeting & Workshop
November 2011
Municipal Engineers Association 2012 Annual General Meeting & Workshop
November 2012
Municipal Engineers Association 2013 Annual General Meeting & Workshop
November 2013
Publications: *Annual Report of the Municipal Engineers Association Administrative & Standing Committees*
Type: Yearbook *Frequency:* a.
Profile: A review of the year's activities
Municipal Engineers Association Members Directory
Type: Directory
Mission: To provide focus & unity for licensed engineers employed by municipalities in Ontario; To address issues of common concern to members; To facilitate the dissemination of information

Municipal Equipment & Operations Association (Ontario) Inc.
38 Summit Ave., Kitchener ON N2M 4W5
Tel: 519-741-2780; *Fax:* 519-741-2750
e-mail: admin@meoa.org
URL: www.meoa.org
Overview: A medium-sized provincial organization
Membership: 270
Mission: A network of individuals working directly with equipment & operations, to exchange information, promote high standards in the field & cost effective public service in Ontario.

Municipal Officers' Association of British Columbia *See* Local Government Management Association of British Columbia

Municipal Waste Association (MWA)
#100, 127 Wyndham St. North, Guelph ON N1H 4E9
Tel: 519-823-1990; *Fax:* 519-823-0084
e-mail: carrie@municipalwaste.ca
URL: www.municipalwaste.ca
Previous Name: Association of Municipal Recycling Coordinators
Overview: A medium-sized provincial organization founded in 1987
Chief Officer(s):
Vivian De Giovanni, Executive Director
vivian@municipalwaste.ca
Sherry Arcaro, Chair
Finances: *Annual Operating Budget:* $100,000-$250,000; *Funding Sources:* Membership fees; project sponsorship
Staff: 3 staff member(s); 1 volunteer(s)
Membership: 110 municipal; 45 corporate; 50 associate; *Fees:* $85 - $995, based on population; *Committees:* Household

Associations/Organizations / Municipalities Newfoundland & Labrador

Hazardous Waste; Markets Operation & Contracts; Organic Waste Diversion; Policy & Program
Activities: One-day seminars/workshops provide coordinators with in-depth coverage of important program trends & issues; *Speaker Service:* Yes; *Library:* Yes, open by appointment
Mission: To expedite the flow of information regarding 3R programs to municipalities & other community & government groups; to act as an information forum for municipal recycling coordinators; allows member municipalities to act as a unified voice in promoting progressive waste reduction & recycling alternatives; *Member of:* Recycling Council of Ontario

Municipalities Newfoundland & Labrador
460 Torbay Rd., St. John's NL A1A 5J3
Tel: 709-753-6820; *Fax:* 709-738-0071
Toll-Free: 800-440-6536
e-mail: mnl@municipalitiesnl.com
URL: www.municipalitiesnl.com
Previous Name: Newfoundland & Labrador Federation of Municipalities
Overview: A medium-sized provincial charitable organization founded in 1951
Finances: *Annual Operating Budget:* $250,000-$500,000
Membership: 281 municipalities; *Fees:* Sliding scale based on population; *Member Profile:* Incorporated municipal governments in Newfoundland
Activities: *Internships:* Yes; *Rents Mailing List:* Yes
Mission: To assist communities in their endeavour to achieve & sustain strong & effective local government thereby improving the quality of life for all the people of this province.; *Member of:* Federation of Canadian Municipalities

Muskoka Lakes Association
PO Box 289, 65 Joseph St., Port Carling ON P0B 1J0
Tel: 705-765-5723; *Fax:* 705-765-3203
e-mail: info@mla.on.ca
URL: www.mla.on.ca
Overview: A medium-sized local organization founded in 1894
Chief Officer(s):
Brian McElwain, President
Membership: 2,975 members; *Fees:* $95 family; *Member Profile:* Permanent & seasonal residents of the Muskoka Lakes & area; anyone interested in the preservation & safety of the lakes
Mission: To represent the interests of lakeshore residents in preserving the unique beauty of Muskoka

Musquodoboit Trailways Association
PO Box 336, Musquodoboit Harbour NS B0J 2L0
Tel: 902-889-3447
e-mail: pmcpers@eastlink.ca
URL: www.mta-ns.ca
Overview: A small local organization founded in 1997
Chief Officer(s):
Peter McInroy, Chair
Fees: $10 individual; $15 family; $25 corporate
Activities: Manages & maintains 40 kms of non-motorized trails
Mission: To provide world-class hiking & cycling trails while preserving the ecosystem & wildlife habitats of the area; *Member of:* Nova Scotia Regional Trails Federation; Trans Canada Trail

NACE International (NACE)
1440 South Creek Dr., Houston TX 77084-4906 USA
Tel: 281-228-6200; *Fax:* 281-228-6300
Toll-Free: 800-797-6223
e-mail: firstservice@nace.org
URL: www.nace.org
Previous Name: The National Association of Corrosion Engineers
Overview: A large international licensing charitable organization founded in 1943
Finances: *Annual Operating Budget:* Greater than $5 Million; *Funding Sources:* Membership dues; registration fees; publication sales
Staff: 65 staff member(s)
Membership: 19,000 members in 100 countries; *Fees:* $130; *Member Profile:* Engineers & others involved in corrosion prevention & control
Activities: Technical training & certification; technical conferences; standards, publications & software; *Speaker Service:* Yes; *Rents Mailing List:* Yes; *Library:* Yes, Open to public
Mission: To protect people, assets & the environment from the effects of corrosion. Northern Area sections include: Atlantic Canada, B.C., Calgary, Canadian National Capital Section, Edmonton, Montreal, Saskatchewan & Toronto

NAID Canada
#301, 250 The Esplanade, Toronto ON M5A 1J2
Tel: 416-203-3701; *Fax:* 416-360-1353
e-mail: info@naidcanada.org
URL: www.naidcanada.org
Also Known As: National Association for Information Destruction Canada
Overview: A small national organization
Chief Officer(s):
Joseph Bozic, Chair
joseph.bozic@dataxile.com
Member Profile: Companies that specialize in secure information & document destruction
Mission: To raise awareness & understanding of the importance of secure information & document destruction; to ensure that private personal & business information is not used for purposes other than originally intended; to develop & implement industry standards & certification; to provide a range of member services which include advocacy, communication, education & professional development; *Member of:* National Association for Information Destruction in United States

Nanaimo Field Naturalists (NFNC)
PO Box 125, Nanaimo BC V9R 5K4
Tel: 250-753-0008
e-mail: john-lyn@shaw.ca
Overview: A small local organization founded in 1972
Finances: *Annual Operating Budget:* Less than $50,000; *Funding Sources:* Membership fees; civic & provincial grants for projects; sale of articles
Membership: 1-99; *Fees:* $32 individual; $36 family; *Member Profile:* Amateur & professional naturalists/biologists
Mission: To promote the enjoyment of nature through environmental appreciation & conservation; to encourage wise use & conservation of natural resources & environmental protection.; *Affiliation(s):* Federation of BC Naturalists

National & Provincial Parks Association (NPPAC) *See* Canadian Parks & Wilderness Society

National Aboriginal Forestry Association (NAFA)
#300, 396 Cooper St., Ottawa ON K2P 2H7
Tel: 613-233-5563; *Fax:* 613-233-4329
e-mail: hbombay@nafaforestry.org
URL: www.nafaforestry.org
Overview: A medium-sized national organization founded in 1989
Chief Officer(s):
Harry M. Bombay, Executive Director
hbombay@nafaforestry.org
Peggy Smith, RPF, Senior Advisor
Janet Pronovost, Office Manager
janet@nafaforestry.org
Fees: Schedule available
Mission: To promote & support increased Aboriginal involvement in forest management & related commercial opportunities; to assist Aboriginal communities in their quest to achieve a standard of land care which is balanced, sustainable & reflective of the traditional knowledge & forest values of Aboriginal peoples; to facilitate capacity-building in forest management through the development of human resource strategies & models for increased participation in natural resource decision making; to address the need for Aboriginal forest land rehabilitation & increased Aboriginal control over forest resources through the development of appropriate policy & programming

National Asbestos Council *See* Environmental Information Association

National Association for Environmental Education (UK) (NAEE)
University of Wolverhampton, Walsall Campus, Gorway Rd., Walsall WS1 3BD United Kingdom
Tel: 44-922-631-200; *Fax:* 44-922-631-200
e-mail: mail@naee.org.uk
URL: www.naee.org.uk
Overview: A medium-sized international charitable organization founded in 1965
Chief Officer(s):
Gabrielle Back, Vice-Chair
Finances: *Annual Operating Budget:* Less than $50,000; *Funding Sources:* Dept. of Environment grant; membership dues; publication sales
Staff: 2 staff member(s)
Membership: 1,000; *Fees:* 50 Pounds overseas; 40 Pounds Europe; 30 Pounds UK; *Member Profile:* Educationalists
Activities: Conferences & courses which attempt to further environmental education in both its natural & human setting; seminars on current topics; publications; *Speaker Service:* Yes; *Library:* Yes, Not open to the public
Mission: To promote environmental education for sustainability in the formal education sector by teachers for teachers; *Member of:* Council for Environmental Education

National Association for Environmental Management (naem)
#1002, 1612 K St. NW, Washington DC 20006 USA
Tel: 202-986-6616; *Fax:* 202-530-4408
Toll-Free: 800-391-6236
e-mail: programs@naem.org
URL: www.naem.org
Social Media: www.facebook.com/NAEM.org; www.twitter.com/#!/thegreentie
Overview: A large international organization founded in 1990
Chief Officer(s):
Carol Singer Neuvelt, Executive Director
csinger@naem.org
Virginia Hoekenga, Deputy Director
Virginia@naem.org
Mike Mahanna, Manager, Programs
mike@naem.org
Elizabeth Ryan, Manager, Interactive Media & Communications
elizabeth@naem.org
Member Profile: Corporate environmental, health & safety, & sustainability decision-makers
Activities: Conducting research; Creating a knowledge sharing network; Offering educational webinars
Meetings/Conferences:
For more information see Trade Shows, Conferences and Seminars Chapter
National Association for Environmental Management 2011 Conference: EHS Compliance Excellence & Best Practices
July 2011 Minneapolis, MN
National Association for Environmental Management 2011 19th Annual EHS Management Forum: EHS & Sustainability Success in the New Economic Era
October 2011 Tuscon, AZ
National Association for Environmental Management 2012 20th Annual EHS Management Forum
October 2012 Naples, FL
National Association for Environmental Management 2013 21st Annual EHS Management Forum
October 2013 Montréal, QC
National Association for Environmental Management 2014 22nd Annual EHS Management Forum
October 2014 Austin, TX
Publications: *NAEM [National Association for Environmental Management] Network E-News*
Type: Newsletter *Frequency:* bi-weekly
Profile: Relevant news for environmental, health & safety, & sustainability professionals
Green TIPS Guide
Type: Guide
Profile: A resource to engage others about a company's sustainability goals
Affiliates Council Guide [a publication of the National Association for Environmental Management]
Type: Guide
Profile: A guide to finding a service provider or consultant
Mission: To promote global sustainability; To advance environmental stewardship; To establish safe & healthy workplaces

National Association for Information Destruction (NAID)
#350, 1951 W Camelback Rd., Phoenix AZ 85015 USA
Tel: 602-788-6243; *Fax:* 602-788-4144
e-mail: info@naidonline.org
URL: www.naidonline.org
Overview: A small international organization
Chief Officer(s):
Robert Johnson, Executive Director
rjohnson@naidonline.org
Fees: Schedule available; *Member Profile:* Includes 50+ Canadian companies
Mission: NAID is the international, non-profit trade association of the information destruction industry. Its members are companies and individuals involved in providing information destruction services. NAID's mission is to educate business, industry and government of the importance of destroying

discarded information and the value of contract destruction services

National Association for PET Container Resources (NAPCOR)
PO Box 1327, Sonoma CA 95476 USA
Tel: 707-996-4207; *Fax:* 707-935-1998
Toll-Free: 800-762-7267
e-mail: information@napcor.com
URL: www.napcor.com
Overview: A small national organization founded in 1987
Chief Officer(s):
Mike Schedler, Technical Advisor
Dennis Sabourin, Executive Director
Finances: *Funding Sources:* Membership dues
Membership: 13; *Member Profile:* PET bottle manufacturers & suppliers to the PET industry
Mission: To promote the usage of PET packaging & to facilitate the collection of PET plastic containers

The National Association of Corrosion Engineers *See* NACE International

National Association of Environmental Professionals (NAEP)
c/o Bower Management Services, LLC, PO Box 460, Collingswood NJ 08108 USA
Tel: 856-283-7816; *Fax:* 856-210-1619
e-mail: tbower@bowermanagementservices.com
URL: www.naep.org
Overview: A medium-sized national organization founded in 1975
Chief Officer(s):
Tim Bower, CAE, NAEP Headquarters
Ron Deverman, President
deverman415@comcast.net
Finances: *Annual Operating Budget:* $100,000-$250,000
Staff: 2 staff member(s); 30 volunteer(s)
Membership: 2,000; *Fees:* US$150 general membership; *Committees:* Working Groups: NEPA Working Group; Education Research & Science Working Group; Transportation Working Group; Sustainable Systems Working Group; Utility Working Group; Health Impact Assessment Working Group; committees include membership, publications, external relations, & career development...
Activities: *Rents Mailing List:* Yes
Awards: NAEP Presidential Award For Excellence (Award)
Mission: To promote a code of ethics & standard of practice among environmental professionals

National Association of Sanitarians *See* National Environmental Health Association

National Association of the Chemistry Industry / Asociación Nacional de la Industria Química, A.C (ANIQ)
Angel Urraza No. 505, Col del Valle, Mexico 03100 DF Mexico
Tel: 52-55-5230-5100; *Fax:* 52-55-5230-5107
e-mail: anavarrete@aniq.org.mx
URL: www.aniq.org.mx
Overview: A medium-sized national organization
Chief Officer(s):
Miguel Benedetto Alexanderson, President
Finances: *Annual Operating Budget:* $500,000-$1.5 Million; *Funding Sources:* Membership fees & services
Staff: 50 staff member(s)
Membership: 223; *Member Profile:* Chemical producers & distributors; *Committees:* International Trade; Human Resources; Logistics & Transportation; Environment; Safety & Health; Communication & Information
Activities: National Forum of the Chemical Industry; *Internships:* Yes; *Speaker Service:* Yes; *Rents Mailing List:* Yes; *Library:* ANIQ's Information Centre; Open to public
Mission: To promote the sustainable development of the chemical sector, in harmony with the environment that surrounds it, as well as to look for joint solutions to common problems by dialogue & agreement, under strict rules of ethics & supported by specialized services, consulting, information, negotiation & diffusion

National Audubon Society, Inc. (NAS)
225 Varick St., 7th Fl., New York NY 10014 USA
Tel: 212-979-3000; *Fax:* 212-979-3188
e-mail: education@audubon.org
URL: www.audubon.org
Social Media: twitter.com/AudubonSociety
Overview: A large national organization founded in 1905
Chief Officer(s):
John Flicker, President/CEO
Brian Rutledge, Executive Director
Membership: 500,000; *Fees:* $20 USA; $45 Canada; $50 international
Activities: Seminars, educational events & workshops on various conservation topics
Mission: To conserve & restore natural ecosystems, focusing on birds, other wildlife & their habitats for the benefit of humanity & the earth's biological diversity

National Building Envelope Council
c/o 5041 Regent St., Burnaby BC V5C 4H4
Tel: 604-473-9587
Overview: A small national organization
Mission: To pursue excellence in the design, construction & performance of the building envelope

National Cancer Institute of Canada *See* Canadian Cancer Society Research Institute

National Centre for Small Communities (NCSC)
#397, 444 North Capitol St. NW, Washington DC 20001-1202 USA
Tel: 717-763-0930; *Fax:* 717-763-9732
e-mail: ncsc@sso.org
URL: www.smallcommunities.org/ncsc
Overview: A large national organization founded in 1977
Chief Officer(s):
G. Jeffrey Haber, President
Finances: *Annual Operating Budget:* $500,000-$1.5 Million
Staff: 5 staff member(s)
Membership: 13,000; *Fees:* US$100 active; US$200 affiliate; US$250 associate; *Member Profile:* Small, generally rural, communities
Activities: Offers technical assistance, educational services & public policy support to local government officials from small communities across the USA; conducts research & develops public policy recommendations through National Center for Small Communities; *Awareness Events:* America's Town Meeting, 1st week Sept.
Mission: To help improve the quality of life for rural people
Environmental Activity: Guidebooks on waste & drinking water; lobbying

National Coalition Against the Misuse of Pesticides (NCAMP)
#200, 701 East St. SE, Washington DC 20003 USA
Tel: 202-543-5450; *Fax:* 202-543-4791
e-mail: info@beyondpesticides.org
URL: www.beyondpesticides.org
Overview: A medium-sized national organization founded in 1981
Chief Officer(s):
Jay Feldman, Executive Director
jfeldman@beyondpesticides.org
Finances: *Annual Operating Budget:* $250,000-$500,000
Staff: 4 staff member(s); 1 volunteer(s)
Membership: 1,400
Activities: *Speaker Service:* Yes; *Library:* Yes
Mission: To address the issue of hazards of pesticide use; to provide the public with clearinghouse of information on pesticides & pesticides issues; to promote alternative forms of pest management

National Council for Science & the Environment (NCSE)
#250, 1101 17th St. NW, Washington DC 20036 USA
Tel: 202-530-5810; *Fax:* 202-628-4311
e-mail: info@ncseonline.org
URL: www.ncseonline.org
Previous Name: Committee for the National Institutes for the Environment
Overview: A medium-sized national organization founded in 1990
Chief Officer(s):
A. Karim Ahmed, Ph.D., Sec.-Treas.
ahmed@ncseonline.org
Peter D. Saundry, Ph.D., Executive Director
peter@ncseonline.org
Finances: *Annual Operating Budget:* $500,000-$1.5 Million
Staff: 12 staff member(s); 10 volunteer(s)
Member Profile: Open to any concerned individual or organization
Activities: National Conference on Science Policy & the Environment; education & outreach programs; *Library:* National Library for the Environment
Mission: Improving the scientific basis for environmental decision making; Affiliation(s): Council of Environmental Deans & Directors; National Commission on Science for Sustainable Forestry

National Energy Conservation Association Inc. (NECA) / Association nationale pour la conservation de l'énergie
250 McDermot Ave., Winnipeg MB R3B 0S5
Tel: 204-956-5888; *Fax:* 204-956-5819
Toll-Free: 800-263-5974
e-mail: neca@neca.ca
URL: www.neca.ca
Previous Name: National Insulation & Energy Conservation Contractors Association
Overview: A medium-sized national organization founded in 1983
Chief Officer(s):
Ryan Dalgleish, Contact, Business Development
Mission: To promote energy efficiency in the building sector; To work towards a sustainable future
Environmental Activity: Encouraging the use of energy efficient technology in existing & new buildings; Working with government agencies & utilities to develop energy conservation programs; Providing training in energy conservation & construction

National Environmental Health Association (NEHA)
#1000N, 720 South Colorado Blvd., Denver CO 80246 USA
Tel: 303-756-9090; *Fax:* 303-691-9490
Toll-Free: 866-956-2258
e-mail: staff@neha.org
URL: www.neha.org
Previous Name: National Association of Sanitarians
Overview: A medium-sized national charitable organization founded in 1937
Chief Officer(s):
Nelson Fabian, Executive Director
nfabian@neha.org
Jill Cruickshank, Manager, Marketing & Communications
jcruickshank@neha.org
Dawn Parks, Manager, Programs & Customer Service
dparks@neha.org
Larry Marcum, Manager, Research, Development, Government Affairs, & Radon Program
lmarcum@neha.org
Membership: 4,500+; *Member Profile:* Environmental health practitioners in both the public & private sectors; Academia; Uniformed services, employed mainly by health departments; *Committees:* Air / Land; Children's Environmental Health; Drinking Water Quality / Water Pollution; Emerging Pathogens / Vector Control & Zoonotic Diseases; Environmental Health Leadership Development; Environmental Health Research; Environmental Health Tracking & Informatics; Food Safety & Protection; General Environmental Health; Hazardous Materials & Toxic Substances; Injury Prevention / Occupational Health; Institutions & Schools Environmental Health; Onsite Wastewater Systems; & Terrorism & All-Hazards Preparedness
Activities: Providing national credential programs; Advocating for the profession; Offering networking opportunities; Working cooperatively with other national professional societies & government agencies
Meetings/Conferences:
For more information see Trade Shows, Conferences and Seminars Chapter
National Environmental Health Association 2011 75th Annual Conference & Exhibition
June 2011 Columbus, OH
National Environmental Health Association 2012 76th Annual Conference & Exhibition
Other Conferences in 2012 2012
Publications: Journal of Environmental Health
Type: Journal Frequency: 10 pa Accepts Advertising : Yes
Editor: Nelson Fabian
Profile: Current issues, peer-reviewed research, products, & services in the area or environmental health
Mission: To advance the environmental health & protection professional, in order to improve the environment throughout the world & provide a more healthful quality of life for all
Environmental Activity: Developing positions on serious environmental health concerns

Associations/Organizations / National Farmers Union

National Farmers Union (NFU) / Syndicat national des cultivateurs
2717 Wentz Ave., Saskatoon SK S7K 4B6
Tel: 306-652-9465; *Fax:* 306-664-6226
e-mail: nfu@nfu.ca
URL: www.nfu.ca
Overview: A large national organization founded in 1969
Finances: *Annual Operating Budget:* $500,000-$1.5 Million; *Funding Sources:* Membership dues; fundraising
Staff: 7 staff member(s); 300 volunteer(s)
Membership: 10,329; *Fees:* $150 family; $40 youth; *Committees:* Women's Advisory; Youth Advisory; International Policy
Activities: *Speaker Service:* Yes; *Library:* Yes
Mission: To improve economic & social well-being of rural people & rural communities; *Member of:* Rural Dignity of Canada; *Affiliation(s):* Action Canada Network

National Ground Water Association (NGWA)
601 Dempsey Rd., Westerville OH 43081 USA
Tel: 614-898-7791; *Fax:* 614-898-7786
Toll-Free: 800-551-7379
e-mail: ngwa@ngwa.org
URL: www.ngwa.org
Overview: A medium-sized international organization founded in 1948
Chief Officer(s):
Kevin McCray, Executive Director
kmmcray@ngwa.org
Paul Humes, Vice President, Operations
Finances: *Annual Operating Budget:* Greater than $5 Million
Staff: 34 staff member(s); 220 volunteer(s)
Membership: 13,000; *Fees:* Schedule available; *Member Profile:* Ground water scientists & engineers; water well drillers; pump installers; suppliers & manufacturers; *Committees:* Numerous committees, subcommittees & task forces
Activities: *Awareness Events:* Ground Water Awareness Week, March; *Speaker Service:* Yes; *Library:* National Ground Water Information Centre
Awards: Outstanding Project in Ground Water Protection Award (Award)
Outstanding Project in Ground Water Remediation Award (Award)
Life Member Awards (Award)

M. King Hubbert Award (Award)
Oliver Award (Award)
Outstanding Project in Ground Water Supply Award (Award)
Robert Storm Interdivisional Cooperation Award (Award)
Mission: Dedicated to advancing the expertise of all ground water professionals & furthering ground water awareness & protection through education & outreach; *Member of:* American Association for the Advancement of Science; Geological Society of America; Geoenvironmental Forum; Geothermal Heat Pump Consortium; Groundwater Foundation

National Horse Protection Coalition *See* National Horse Protection League

National Horse Protection League
PO Box 318, Chappaqua NY 10514 USA
Tel: 202-293-0570
e-mail: info@horse-protection.org
URL: www.horse-protection.org
Previous Name: National Horse Protection Coalition
Overview: A medium-sized national organization
Finances: *Annual Operating Budget:* $250,000-$500,000

National Indian Brotherhood *See* Assembly of First Nations

National Insulation & Energy Conservation Contractors Association *See* National Energy Conservation Association Inc.

National Marine Manufacturers Association (NMMA)
#5100, 200 E. Randolph Dr., Chicago IL 60601 USA
Tel: 312-946-6200
URL: www.nmma.org
Overview: A medium-sized international organization
Chief Officer(s):
Thomas Dammrich, President, 312-946-6220
Linda Waddell, Vice President, Northern Shows, 905-951-4051
Finances: *Funding Sources:* Membership fees & shows
Staff: 5 staff member(s)

Membership: 1,400 corporate; *Member Profile:* Canadian/American manufacturer, distributor, or retailer of boating-related products
Activities: *Internships:* Yes
Mission: NMMA is dedicated to creating, promoting and protecting an environment where members can achieve financial success through excellence in manufacturing, in selling, and in servicing their customers.; *Affiliation(s):* National Association of Boat Manufacturers; National Association of Marine Products & Services; Association of Marine Engine Manufacturers

National Marine Manufacturers Association Canada (NMMA)
#8, 14 McEwan Dr., Bolton ON L7E 1H1
Tel: 905-951-0009; *Fax:* 905-951-0018
e-mail: sanghel@nmma.org
URL: www.cmma.ca
Also Known As: NMMA Canada
Previous Name: Canadian Marine Manufacturers Association
Overview: A medium-sized national organization
Chief Officer(s):
Rick Layzell, Chair
rick_layzell@yamaha-motor.ca
Member Profile: Marine industry
Mission: The CMMA is committed to being a leader; in promoting boating, advocacy with government and providing value added services to foster the financial success of the marine industry.

National Oil Recyclers Association *See* NORA, An Association of Responsible Recyclers

National Parks Conservation Association (NPCA)
#300, 1300 - 19th St. NW, Washington DC 20036 USA
Tel: 202-223-6722; *Fax:* 202-659-0650
Toll-Free: 800-628-7275
e-mail: npca@npca.org
URL: www.npca.org
Overview: A large national organization founded in 1919
Chief Officer(s):
Thomas C. Kiernan, President
Tom Martin, Executive Vice-President
Finances: *Annual Operating Budget:* Greater than $5 Million
Membership: 460,000; *Fees:* $25; $18 students
Mission: America's only private, non-profit advocacy organization dedicated to protecting, preserving & enhancing the National Park system; to protect & improve the quality of parks & to promote an understanding of, appreciation for, & sense of personal commitment to parklands

National Recycling Coalition
#425, 805 15th St. NW, Washington DC 20005 USA
Tel: 202-789-1430; *Fax:* 202-789-1431
e-mail: info@nrc-recycle.org
URL: www.nrc-recycle.org
Overview: A small national organization founded in 1978
Chief Officer(s):
Ed Skernolis, Executive Director
eskernolis@nrc-recycle.org
Membership: 5,000+
Activities: *Internships:* Yes
Mission: To advance & improve recycling, source reduction, composting & reuse by providing technical information, education, training, outreach & advocacy services to its members in order to conserve resources & benefit the environment; *Affiliation(s):* California Resource Recovery Association; Northern California Recycling Association; Recycling Council of Alberta; Indiana Recycling Coalition; North Carolina Recycling Association; Oklahoma Recycling Association; Association of Oregon Recyclers; Pennsylvania Resources Council; Arizona Recycling Coalition; Arkansas Recycling Coalition; RECARIBE; Colorado Association for Recycling; Connecticut Recyclers Coalition; Recycle Florida Today; Illinois Recycling Association; Iowa Recycling Association; Kansas Recyclers Association; Louisiana Recycling Association

National Sanitary Supply Association *See* International Sanitary Supply Association, Inc.

National Society for Clean Air *See* Environmental Protection UK

National Solid Wastes Management Association (NSWMA)
#300, 4301 Connecticut Ave. NW, Washington DC 20008 USA
Tel: 202-244-4700; *Fax:* 202-966-4824
Toll-Free: 800-424-2869
URL: www.nswma.org
Social Media:
www.facebook.com/group.php?gid=130041787022156
Overview: A medium-sized international organization founded in 1962
Chief Officer(s):
Bruce J. Parker, President & Chief Executive Officer
bparker@nswma.org
David Biderman, General Counsel & Director, Safety
davidb@nswma.org
Christine Hutcherson, Director, Member Services
chutcherson@nswma.org
Alice Jacobsohn, Director, Education
alicej@nswma.org
Thom Metzger, Director, Communications & Public Affairs
tmetzger@nswma.org
Ed Repa, Director, Environmental Programs
erepa@nswma.org
Catherine Maimon, Manager, Meetings
cmaimon@nswma.org
Member Profile: For-profit companies in North America that provide solid, hazardous, & medical waste collection, recycling, & disposal services; Companies that provide professional & consulting services to the waste services industry
Activities: Offering educational & training opportunities; Engaging in research; Facilitating networking; *Library:* National Solid Wastes Management Association Library
Meetings/Conferences:
For more information see Trade Shows, Conferences and Seminars Chapter
National Solid Wastes Management Association 2011 Safety Seminar
July 2011 Independence, OH
National Solid Wastes Management Association 2011 Southeast Annual Conference
September 2011 Amelia Island, FL
National Solid Wastes Management Association 2011 South Central Annual Conference
September 2011 San Antonio, TX
National Solid Wastes Management Association 2011 Heartland Annual Conference
September 2011 Lone Wolf, OK
National Solid Wastes Management Association 2011 Mid-Atlantic Annual Conference
October 2011 Asheville, NC
National Solid Wastes Management Association 2011 Executive Roundtable Conference
October 2011 Naples, FL
WasteExpo 2012 44th Conference & Tradeshow
April 2012 Las Vegas, NV
Publications: NSWMA [National Solid Wastes Management Association] e-News
Type: Newsletter
Profile: Timely information to help businesses make decisions
Mission: To promote the environmentally responsible, efficient, profitable, & ethical management of waste

National Sunflower Association of Canada (NSAC)
PO Box 1269, 38 - 4th Ave. N.E., Carman MB R0G 0J0
Tel: 204-745-6776; *Fax:* 204-745-6122
e-mail: info@canadasunflower.com
URL: www.canadasunflower.com
Overview: A small national organization founded in 1996
Chief Officer(s):
Blair Woods, President
bwoods@westman.wave.ca
Darcelle Graham, Executive Director
Membership: 950; *Fees:* $50 producers; $500 corporate
Mission: To ensure the profitability and long term growth of the sunflower crop through industry wide leadership

National Wildlife Federation (NWF)
11100 Wildlife Center Dr., Reston VA 20190-5362 USA
Tel: 703-438-6000; *Fax:* 703-438-6035
Toll-Free: 800-822-9919
URL: www.nwf.org
Overview: A large national organization founded in 1936
Chief Officer(s):
Larry J. Schweiger, President & CEO

Finances: *Annual Operating Budget:* Greater than $5 Million;
Funding Sources: Memberships; donations; bequests; magazine subscriptions; sales of nature education materials
Staff: 600 staff member(s)
Membership: Over 4 million members & supporters + 46 affiliated organizations + 11 field office locations; *Fees:* $15+
Activities: *Awareness Events:* National Wildlife Week; *Internships:* Yes; *Rents Mailing List:* Yes; *Library:* Yes
Awards: The National Conservation Achievement Awards (Award)
Program that recognizes outstanding individual & group achievements in conservation
Mission: NWF advances common-sense conservation policies through advocacy, education & litigation in concert with affiliate groups & other like-minded organizations across the country & around the world; efforts focus on the conservation of wildlife & wild places & the health of the environment upon which we all depend, with special emphasis on wetlands, water quality, endangered habitats, land stewardship & sustainable communities

Native Investment & Trade Association (NITA)
6520 Salish Dr., Vancouver BC V6N 2C7
Tel: 604-275-6670; *Fax:* 604-275-0307
Toll-Free: 800-337-7743
e-mail: nita@express.ca
URL: www.native-invest-trade.com
Overview: A small national licensing organization founded in 1989
Chief Officer(s):
Calvin Helin, President
ch@native-invest-trade.com
Finances: *Annual Operating Budget:* $250,000-$500,000; *Funding Sources:* Registration fees
Staff: 10 staff member(s); 2 volunteer(s)
Activities: Online business directory; conferences; scholarships; business products and services; *Library:* NITA Resource Library
Mission: To promote, establish & maintain trade/investment opportunities in Native communities; encourages free enterprise solutions to economic & social problems confronting Native communities, but remains sensitive to their special cultural heritage, needs, requirements; views non-governmental business involvement with First Nations as a vital step towards greater self-reliance; fosters business ventures with high employment potential; promotes projects with potential for sustainable economic growth; conducts research into innovative approaches to economic development of Native communities

Native Orchid Conservation Inc.
117 Morier Ave., Winnipeg MB R2M 0C8
Tel: 204-947-9707
e-mail: adames@mts.net
URL: www.nativeorchid.org
Overview: A small local organization
Chief Officer(s):
Doris Ames, President
Fees: $10 individual; $25 group
Mission: To protect unique mini-ecosystems & their plant communities

Natural Health Practitioners of Canada (NHPC) / Praticiens de la santé naturelle du Canada (PSNC)
#600, 10339 - 124 St., Edmonton AB T5N 3W1
Tel: 780-484-2010; *Fax:* 780-484-3605
Toll-Free: 888-711-7701
e-mail: growingtogether@nhpcanada.org
URL: www.nhpcanada.org
Social Media:
www.facebook.com/group.php?gid=142729347410
Overview: A medium-sized national organization
Chief Officer(s):
Colleen MacDougall, Executive Director & Registrar
Publications: *Connections [a publication of the Natural Health Practitioners of Canada]*
Type: Magazine *Frequency:* q.
Mission: To provide programs, services and products for members in the service of public wellness and to serve the public by promoting and advocating the wellness professions.

Natural History Society of Manitoba; Manitoba Naturalists Society *See* Nature Manitoba

Natural History Society of Newfoundland & Labrador
c/o The Osprey, PO Box 1013, Stn. C, St. John's NL A1C 5M3
Tel: 709-754-0455
e-mail: nhs@nhs.nf.ca
URL: www.nhs.nf.ca
Overview: A small provincial charitable organization founded in 1963
Chief Officer(s):
Allan Stein, Acting Vice-President, 709-895-2056
arstein@mun.ca
Don Steele, Secretary
dsteele@mun.ca
Finances: *Annual Operating Budget:* Less than $50,000; *Funding Sources:* Membership fees; donations
Membership: 175; *Fees:* $25
Activities: Field trips; monthly meetings;
Awards: Wild Things Scholarship (Scholarship)
Mission: The Natural History Society is a province-wide organization with a primary interest in promoting the enjoyment and protection of all wildlife and natural history resources in the Province of Newfoundland and Labrador and surrounding waters.; *Member of:* Canadian Nature Federation

Natural Resources Union (NRU)
Parent: Public Service Alliance of Canada (CLC)
#600, 233 Gilmour St., Ottawa ON K2P 0P2
Tel: 613-560-4378; *Fax:* 613-233-7012
e-mail: info@nru-srn.com
URL: www.nru-srn.com
Previous Name: Union of Energy, Mines & Resources Employees
Overview: A medium-sized national organization founded in 1978
Chief Officer(s):
Claudia Thompson, National President
thompsonc@nru-srn.com
Finances: *Annual Operating Budget:* $250,000-$500,000
Staff: 2 staff member(s)
Membership: 1,600 + 20 locals; *Member Profile:* Government employees, Natural Resources Canada, Canadian Space Agency & various other agencies & boards; *Committees:* Occupational Safety & Health; Equal Opportunities; Labour Management Consultation

Nature Canada / Canada Nature
#300, 75 Albert St., Ottawa ON K1P 5E7
Tel: 613-562-3447; *Fax:* 613-562-3371
Toll-Free: 800-267-4088
e-mail: info@naturecanada.ca
URL: www.naturecanada.ca
Social Media: www.facebook.com/NatureCanada; www.twitter.com/#!/NatureCanada
Previous Name: Canadian Nature Federation
Overview: A large national charitable organization founded in 1971
Finances: *Funding Sources:* Donations
Membership: 350+ organizations + 40,000 supporters; *Member Profile:* Natualist organizations across Canada; Individual supporters
Activities: Offering outreach & educational programs; Organizing action campaigns for nature
Awards: Affiliate Award (Award)
To recognize conservation efforts of a partner organization that support Nature Canada's conservation initiatives or mission
Charles Labatiuk Volunteer Award (Award)
To recognize individuals who have made outstanding contributions to Canadian conservation *Deadline:* March 31
Volunteer Award (Award)
To honour individuals who contribute to a Nature Canada project
Charles Labatiuk Scholarship (Scholarship)
Eligibility: Any student enrolled in an entrance level course or program at an accredited college or university in Canada, in the interdisciplinary study of natural environmental systems *Award Amount:* $2000
Meetings/Conferences:
For more information see Trade Shows, Conferences and Seminars Chapter
Nature Canada 2011 Annual General Meeting
June 2011 Oak Hammock Marsh, MB
Nature Canada 2012 Annual General Meeting
Other Conferences in 2012 2012
Publications: *The Nature Nation*
Type: Newsletter *Frequency:* m.
Profile: Action alerts, reports, polls, reading suggestions, & upcoming events
Mission: To protect & conserve wildlife & habitats throughout Canada
Environmental Activity: Advocating on behalf of nature; Encouraging the development of parks & protected areas; Promoting biodiversity in Canada & abroad; Conserving bird habitat

The Nature Conservancy of Canada (NCC) / Société canadienne pour la conservation de la nature
#400, 36 Eglinton Ave. West, Toronto ON M4R 1A1
Tel: 416-932-3202; *Fax:* 416-932-3208
Toll-Free: 800-465-0029
e-mail: nature@natureconservancy.ca
URL: www.natureconservancy.ca
Social Media: www.twitter.com/NatureConsCDA
Overview: A large national charitable organization founded in 1962
Finances: *Funding Sources:* Donations
Committees: Executive; Governance & Nominating; Audit; Investment; Conservation
Activities: Partnering with landowners & corporations to protect Canada's natural areas
Publications: *The Nature Conservancy of Canada Annual Report to our Donors*
Type: Yearbook *Frequency:* a.
Profile: The year in review for each region of Canada
The Ark [a publication of The Nature Conservancy of Canada]
Type: Newsletter *Frequency:* 3 pa *Price:* A donation of $20+
Profile: A national newsletter, with updates on featured projects & properties, stewardship work, & threatened or vulnerable species
Mission: To protect Canada's biodiversity through long-term stewardship & property securement
Environmental Activity: Purchasing, acquiring by donation, or placing conservation easements on ecologically significant lands

Nature Council of British Columbia *See* British Columbia Nature (Federation of British Columbia Naturalists)

Nature Manitoba (MNS)
Hammond Building, #401, 63 Albert St., Winnipeg MB R3B 1G4
Tel: 204-943-9029; *Fax:* 204-943-9029
e-mail: info@naturemanitoba.ca; editor@naturemanitoba.ca (Newsletter)
URL: www.naturemanitoba.ca
Social Media:
www.facebook.com/pages/Nature-Manitoba/67945358869
Previous Name: Natural History Society of Manitoba; Manitoba Naturalists Society
Overview: A medium-sized provincial charitable organization founded in 1920
Finances: *Funding Sources:* Donations; Nature Manitoba Store
Fees: $20 students; $35 seniors; $40 individuals; $55 families; *Member Profile:* Manitobans who share a passion for nature
Activities: Conducting research; Engaging in advocacy activities; Offering educational & recreational programs & field trips to observe botany, butterflies, & birds; *Library:* Nature Manitoba Library;
Meetings/Conferences:
For more information see Trade Shows, Conferences and Seminars Chapter
Nature Manitoba's Birding for Beginners
June 2011, MB
Nature Manitoba's Mantario Wilderness Education Centre 2011 Training
June 2011 Whiteshell Prov. Park, MB
Nature Manitoba Habitat Committee's 2011 Annual Spurge Purge & Plant Walk
June 2011, MB
Nature Manitoba 2011 Natural Garden Tour
July 2011, MB
Nature Manitoba 2012 Annual General Meeting
Other Conferences in 2012 2012, MB
Publications: *Nature Manitoba News*
Type: Newsletter *Frequency:* bi-m. *Accepts Advertising* : Yes
Editor: Tommy Allen *Price:* Free with membership in Nature Manitoba
Profile: Information about Nature Manitoba's meetings & workshops, activities, members, & nature in the news
The Birds of Manitoba
Type: Book *Price:* $63.95
Profile: Information about & illustrations & photographs of the 382 species of birds known in Manitoba
Finding Birds in Southern Manitoba
Type: Guide *Price:* $20
Profile: A birding guide for southern Manitoba, featuring photographs & maps

Associations/Organizations / Nature NB

Checklist of the Birds of Manitoba
Price: $1
Profile: A checklist of 391 confirmed species in Manitoba
Naturescape Manitoba
Type: Book *Number of Pages:* 200 *Price:* $24.95
Profile: A source book about native planting & water conservation for the Prairies Ecozone of Manitoba
Mission: To foster the popular & scientific study of nature; To preserve the natural environment; To act as a voice for people interested in the outdoors & natural history
Environmental Activity: Providing programs to enhance awareness, understanding & appreciation for the natural environment; Working for environmental protection

Nature NB
#110, 924 Prospect St., Fredericton NB E3B 2T9
Tel: 506-459-4209; *Fax:* 506-459-4209
e-mail: nbfn@nb.aibn.com
URL: www.naturenb.ca
Previous Name: New Brunswick Federation of Naturalists
Overview: A medium-sized provincial charitable organization founded in 1979
Membership: 1,000-4,999; *Fees:* $25 individual; $30 family membership; *Member Profile:* 13 federated nature clubs
Mission: To preserve wildlife & protect its natural habitat; to promote a public interest in & a knowledge of natural history; to promote, encourage & cooperate with organizations & individuals who have similar interests & objectives; to consider matters of environmental concern.; *Member of:* Nature Canada

Nature Nova Scotia (Federation of Nova Scotia Naturalists)
c/o Nova Scotia Museum of Natural History, 1747 Summer St., Halifax NS B3H 3A6
Tel: 902-582-7176
e-mail: doug@fundymud.com
URL: www.naturens.ca
Previous Name: Federation of Nova Scotia Naturalists
Overview: A medium-sized provincial charitable organization founded in 1990
Chief Officer(s):
Bob Bancroft, President, 902-386-2501
Sue Abbot, Vice-President, 902-453-0435
Doug Linzey, Secretary, 902-582-7176
Jean Gibson, Treasurer, 902-678-4725
Finances: *Funding Sources:* Donations
Fees: $5 students & seniors; $20 single adults & families; *Member Profile:* Naturalists clubs & organizations within Nova Scotia; Members-at-large
Activities: Providing educational opportunities; Hosting field trips; Conducting research; Serving on committees & advisory boards involving issues that affect the health of the natural environment
Meetings/Conferences:
For more information see Trade Shows, Conferences and Seminars Chapter
Nature Nova Scotia 2011 Annual General Meeting & Conference (in partnership with the Bras d'Or Stewardship Society)
June 2011 St. Anne's, Cape Breton, NS
Nature Nova Scotia 2012 Annual General Meeting & Conference
Other Conferences in 2012 2012, NS
Publications: *Nature Nova Scotia Annual Report*
Type: Yearbook *Frequency:* a.
Profile: A summary of Nature Nova Scotia's yearly activities
Mission: To support the interests of naturalists clubs; To represent naturalists clubs throughout Nova Scotia; *Member of:* Nature Conservancy of Canada (NCC); Canadian Parks & Wilderness Society (CPAWS); *Affiliation(s):* Nature Canada
Environmental Activity: Establishing protected natural areas; Conserving species & spaces; Promoting the sustainable use of resources; Developing policies on issues such as ATVs, tidal power, & wind power

Nature Québec
#207, 870, av de Salaberry, Québec QC G1R 2T9
Tél: 418-648-2104; *Téléc:* 418-648-0991
Courriel: conservons@naturequebec.org
URL: www.naturequebec.org
Également appelé: UQCN
Nom précédent: Union québécoise pour la conservation de la nature
Aperçu: *Dimension:* moyenne; *Envergure:* provinciale; *Organisme sans but lucratif; fondée en 1981*
Membre(s) du bureau directeur:
Christian Simard, Directeur général, 418-648-2104 Ext. 2071
christian.simard@naturequebec.org

Finances: *Budget de fonctionnement annuel:* $500,000-$1.5 Million
Personnel: 8 membre(s) du personnel
Membre: 112 institutionnel; 5 000 individu; *Montant de la cotisation:* 25$
Activités: *Stagiaires:* Oui
Mission: Regrouper les individus et les sociétés oeuvrant en sciences naturelles et en environnement; maintenir des processus écologiques essentiels; préserver la diversité génétique; utiliser soutenablement des espèces et des écosystèmes; *Membre de:* World Conservation Union; World Wildlife Federation; Fédération canadienne de la nature

Nature Saskatchewan
#206, 1860 Lorne St., Regina SK S4P 2L7
Tel: 306-780-9273; *Fax:* 306-780-9263
Toll-Free: 800-667-4668
e-mail: info@naturesask.ca
URL: www.naturesask.ca
Also Known As: Saskatchewan Natural History Society
Overview: A medium-sized provincial charitable organization founded in 1949
Finances: *Funding Sources:* Membership fees; Donations; Sponsorships
Membership: 1,300; *Fees:* $15 students; $20 seniors; $25 individuals; $30 families, institutions, & foreign members; $600 lifetime members; *Member Profile:* Naturalists in Saskatchewan
Activities: Conducting research; Providing education; Producing special publications, such as Birds of the Saskatoon Area, The Great Sand Hills: A Prairie Oasis, & Prairie Phoenix: The Red Lily (Lilium philadelphicum) in Saskatchewan; *Library:* Nature Saskatchewan Resource Centre
Awards: Volunteer of the Year Award (Award)
Cliff Shaw Award (Award)
Fellows Award (Award)
Larry Morgotch Memorial Award (Award)
Conservation Award (Award)
Meetings/Conferences:
For more information see Trade Shows, Conferences and Seminars Chapter
Nature Saskatchewan 2011 Fall Meeting
Other Conferences in 2011 2011, SK
Publications: *Blue Jay*
Type: Journal *Accepts Advertising*: Yes *Editor:* Chris Somers; Vicky Kjoss *Price:* $25 / year
Profile: Conservation, nature, & scientific research news, plus artwork & poetry
Nature Views
Type: Newsletter *Frequency:* q. *Accepts Advertising*: Yes *Editor:* Robert Warnock; Angela Dohms *Price:* Free with Nature Saskatchewan membership
Profile: Discussions of environmental issues, contributions from well known naturalists, & forthcoming events
Mission: To foster appreciation & understanding for the natural environment; To document & protect the biological diversity of Saskatchewan; To preserve the natural eco-systems of the province
Environmental Activity: Promoting conservation; Engaging in stewardship projects, such as Operation Burrowing Owl, Rare Plant Rescue, & Shrubs for Shrikes

Nature Trust of New Brunswick (NTNB) / Fondation pour la protection des sites naturels du Nouveau-Brunswick
PO Box 603, Stn. A, 404 Queen St., 3rd Fl., Fredericton NB E3B 5A6
Tel: 506-457-2398; *Fax:* 506-450-2137
e-mail: ntnb@nbnet.nb.ca
URL: www.naturetrust.nb.ca
Overview: A small provincial charitable organization founded in 1987
Chief Officer(s):
Margo Sheppard, Executive Director
Ken Hirtle, President
John St. Pierre, Treasurer
Don Dennison, Vice-President
Finances: *Annual Operating Budget:* $100,000-$250,000;
Funding Sources: Donations; government grants
Staff: 1 staff member(s)
Membership: 275; *Fees:* $25 individual; $35 family/group; $75 supporting; $150 sponsoring; *Committees:* Property; Scientific Advisory; Education; Membership; Fundraising
Mission: To identify, classify & preserve natural areas which are outstanding for their biological, geological or aesthetic value; to foster in the people of New Brunswick an awareness of their natural heritage & to educate persons in connection therewith

Nature Vancouver
PO Box 3021, Vancouver BC V6B 3X5
Tel: 604-737-3074
e-mail: a-grantduff@shaw.ca
URL: www.naturevancouver.ca
Previous Name: Vancouver Natural History Society
Overview: A small local charitable organization founded in 1918
Finances: *Annual Operating Budget:* $50,000-$100,000;
Funding Sources: Membership fees
Staff: 750 volunteer(s)
Membership: 50 institutional + 10 junior + 50 lifetime + 700 single + 300 family; *Fees:* $40 individual; $50 family; $20 student; *Committees:* Conservation; Birding; Discovery (Publication); Field Trips; Botany
Activities: Marsh & bog restoration; bird & plant survey; conservation - briefs, forums & public information meetings; monthly speakers; annual summer camp to allow participants to learn about a special wilderness area in the province; *Speaker Service:* Yes
Mission: To promote the enjoyment of nature; to foster public interest & education in appreciation & study of nature; to encourage wise use & conservation of natural resources; to work for complete protection of endangered species & ecosystems; to promote access to & maintenance of natural areas in vicinity of Vancouver; *Member of:* The Federation of BC Naturalists; *Affiliation(s):* Nature Canada

Nepisiguit Salmon Association (NSA) / L'Association du saumon Nepisiguit
789 Riverside Dr., Bathurst NB E2A 2M8
Tel: 506-546-5279
Overview: A small local organization founded in 1976
Chief Officer(s):
J. Robert Chaisson, Vice-President
Bob Baker, President
Finances: *Annual Operating Budget:* $50,000-$100,000;
Funding Sources: Donations; grants; programs; fundraising
Membership: 300+; *Fees:* $10; $100 life member; *Member Profile:* Anglers & those interested in salmon conservation
Activities: Salmon enchancement program
Mission: To enhance & preserve Atlantic Salmon in general & in the Nepisiguit river in particular; to educate the public as to the value of this unique, renewable, natural resource; *Member of:* Atlantic Salmon Federation; *Affiliation(s):* New Brunswick Salmon Council; Nepisiguit Watershed Management Committee

New Brunswick Environment Industry Association (NBEIA) / L'Association des industries de l'environnement du Nouveau-Brunswick (AIENB)
PO Box 637, Stn. A, Fredericton NB E3B 5B3
Tel: 506-455-0212; *Fax:* 506-452-0213
e-mail: nbeia@nbnet.nb.ca
URL: www.nbeia.nb.ca
Overview: A medium-sized provincial organization founded in 1994
Chief Officer(s):
Pierre Landry, President
Eric Cook, Secretary-Treasurer
Membership: 130+; *Member Profile:* Companies & individuals from the environment sector, including manufacturing, engineering, technology development, laboratories, education, & consultation
Activities: Offering marketing & networking opportunities; Providing professional development for practitioners in the environmental sector
Publications: *New Brunswick Environment Industry Association Newsletter*
Type: Newsletter *Language:* B *Frequency:* q. *Accepts Advertising*: Yes *Editor:* Carol Tibbitts; Amy Brown
Profile: Environmental news, plus information about members' products & services
Mission: To promote the growth of environmental business in New Brunswick
Environmental Activity: Promoting high standards for environmental products & services

New Brunswick Environmental Network (NBEN) / Réseau environnemental du Nouveau-Brunswick (RENB)
Parent: Canadian Environmental Network
167 Creek Rd., Waterford NB E4E 4L7
Tel: 506-433-6101; *Fax:* 506-433-6111
e-mail: nben@nben.ca
URL: www.nben.ca
Social Media:
www.facebook.com/pages/NBEN-RENB/134259049952351

Overview: A medium-sized provincial organization founded in 1991
Chief Officer(s):
Mary Ann Coleman, Executive Director
Joanna Brown, Coordinator, Youth Outreach & Events
Raissa Marks, Coordinator, Education & Outreach Programs
Finances: *Funding Sources:* Environment Canada; Health Canada; NB Dept. of Environment; NB Dept. of Health; NB Dept. of Intergovernmental Affairs; NB Dept. of Natural Resources
Member Profile: Non-profit environmental organizations
Activities: Providing educational opportunities
Meetings/Conferences:
For more information see Trade Shows, Conferences and Seminars Chapter
New Brunswick Environmental Network 2012 Annual General Meeting
Other Conferences in 2012 2012, NB
Publications: *Greenprint: Towards a Sustainable New Brunswick*
Type: Report *Number of Pages:* 16
Profile: Lead organizations include the New Brunswick Environmental Network, Canadian Parks & Wilderness Society - New Brunswick Chapter, Conservation Council of New Brunswick, Falls Brook Centre, Meduxnekeag River Association Inc., & Petitcodiac Riverkeeper
Legal Information for Environmental Groups
Type: Guide *Number of Pages:* 20
Profile: Topics include civil disobedience, property law, endangered species, & international law
Mission: To strengthen the environmental movement throughout New Brunswick; To promote ecologically sound ways of life; Affiliation(s): Canadian Environmental Network
Environmental Activity: Improving cooperation among environmental groups, industry, & government

New Brunswick Federation of Agriculture *See* Agricultural Alliance of New Brunswick

New Brunswick Federation of Naturalists *See* Nature NB

New Brunswick Federation of Woodlot Owners Inc. / Fédération des propriétaires de lots boisés du Nouveau-Brunswick inc.
#304, 259 Brunswick St., Fredericton NB E3B 1G8
Tel: 506-459-2990; *Fax:* 506-459-3515
e-mail: nbfwo@nbnet.nb.ca
URL: www.nbwoodlotowners.ca
Overview: A small provincial organization founded in 1965
Mission: To advocate for woodlot owners; To direct government policy as it affects private woodlots

New Brunswick Forest Products Association Inc. (NBFPA) / L'Association des produits forestiers du Nouveau-Brunswick (APFNB)
Hugh John Flemming Forestry Centre, 1350 Regent St., Fredericton NB E3C 2G6
Tel: 506-452-6930; *Fax:* 506-450-3128
e-mail: info@nbforestry.com
URL: www.nbforestry.com
Overview: A small provincial organization founded in 1959
Membership: 110 organizations;
Mission: The New Brunswick Forest Products Association is a non-government, non-profit organization that represents its forest industry members by serving as a common voice in relations with the government and the public, promoting a healthy New Brunswick forest, raising public awareness of sustainable forest management practices, and providing a forum for the exchange of information, ideas, and concerns.

New Brunswick Fruit Growers Association Inc.
#302, 259 Brunswick St., Fredericton NB E3B 1G8
Tel: 506-452-8100; *Fax:* 506-452-1625
e-mail: nbapple@nbnet.nb.ca
Overview: A small provincial organization founded in 1904

New Brunswick Ground Water Association
Parent: Canadian Ground Water Association
31 Gray Rd., Penobsquis NB E4E 5S7
Tel: 506-433-6767; *Fax:* 506-432-6888
e-mail: nbgwa@nb.sympatico.ca
URL: www.nbgwa.ca
Overview: A small provincial organization
Chief Officer(s):
Roger Roy, President
Terry Burpee, Sec.-Treas.

Finances: *Annual Operating Budget:* Less than $50,000; *Funding Sources:* Membership dues
Membership: 42; *Fees:* $300
Mission: Mission statement is based around preserving and protecting New Brunswick's "most precious and natural resource": water. They aim to promote education of its members and the public and to promote the development of ground water guidelines and strategies.

New Brunswick Institute of Agrologists (NBIA) / L'Institut des agronomes du Nouveau-Brunswick (IANB)
Parent: Agricultural Institute of Canada
PO Box 3479, Stn. B, Fredericton NB E3B 5H2
Tel: 506-459-5536; *Fax:* 506-454-7837
e-mail: nbia@nbagrologists.nb.ca
URL: www.nbagrologists.nb.ca
Overview: A small provincial organization founded in 1960
Membership: 200; *Fees:* $25; *Member Profile:* Professional agrologists in New Brunswick, with a degree in agriculture from a recognized university, plus three or more years of training or experience in the field; Individuals with a degree accepted by the Council; Articling agrologists; *Committees:* Admissions; Act / Bylaws; Scholarship; Professional Development; NBIA Strategy; Communication; Discipline; Complaints; Nominating; Executive
Activities: Participating in programs to benefit the agriculture & food industry; Analyzing issues & making recommendations to organizations; Improving standards of research; Providing professional development & networking opportunities; Offering information for members, the farming industry, & the public; Promoting the profession of agrology to farmers
Mission: To maintain high competency & professional standards for those practicing agrology in New Brunswick; to uphold the NBIA Code of Ethics; to offer advice to the public about agriculture & related areas; to formulate policies & improve the agriculture & food industry

New Brunswick Lung Association / Association pulmonaire du Nouveau-Brunswick
Parent: Canadian Lung Association
65 Brunswick St., Fredericton NB E3B 1G5
Tel: 506-455-8961; *Fax:* 506-462-0939
Toll-Free: 800-565-5864
e-mail: nblung@nbnet.nb.ca
URL: www.nb.lung.ca
Overview: A small provincial charitable organization
Finances: *Funding Sources:* Donations; Sponsorships; Fundraising
Activities: Engaging in advocacy activities; Offering education about respiratory health; Providing resources such as fact sheets, booklets, & audio-visual & program resources; Supporting respiratory research; Organizing fundraising events to support children & adults with lung disease; *Awareness Events:* Asthma Month, March; Sleep Apnea Week, March; Clean Air Month, June; *Library:* NB Lung Associations' Environment & Health Public Resource Svs.; Open to public
Mission: To promote wellness throughout New Brunswick & prevent lung disease
Environmental Activity: Providing health & environment resources & programs to the public in New Brunswick

New Brunswick Medical Society (NBMS) / Société médicale du Nouveau-Brunswick
Parent: Canadian Medical Association
176 York St., Fredericton NB E3B 3N7
Tel: 506-458-8860; *Fax:* 506-458-9853
e-mail: nbms@nbnet.nb.ca
URL: www.nbms.nb.ca
Overview: A medium-sized provincial organization founded in 1867
Finances: *Annual Operating Budget:* $250,000-$500,000
Staff: 8 staff member(s)
Membership: 20 student + 40 senior/lifetime + 1,100 individual; *Fees:* Schedule available; *Member Profile:* Licensed physician by College of Physicians & Surgeons of NB; *Committees:* Economics; Health Care; Medical Education; Communications
Activities: *Internships:* Yes; *Speaker Service:* Yes; *Rents Mailing List:* Yes
Mission: To advance medical science in all its branches; to promote improvement of medical services; to prevent disease in cooperation with health officers & all others engaged in such work; to maintain high scientific & professional status for its members; to promote medical science & related arts & sciences

New Brunswick Mining Association / L'Association minière du Nouveau-Brunswick
Parent: Mining Association of Canada
#312, 236 St. George Blvd., Moncton NB E1C 1W1
Tel: 506-857-3056; *Fax:* 506-857-3059
Overview: A small provincial organization

New Brunswick Potato Agency *See* Potatoes NB

New Brunswick Safety Council Inc. *See* Safety Services New Brunswick

New Brunswick Salmon Council (NBSC)
PO Box 533, Stn. A, Fredericton NB E3B 5A6
Tel: 506-452-1875; *Fax:* 506-454-0336
e-mail: thenbsc@nbnet.nb.ca
URL: www.nbsalmoncouncil.com
Overview: A small provincial organization
Affiliation(s): Atlantic Salmon Federation

New Brunswick Salmon Growers Association (NBSGA)
226 Limekiln Rd., Letang NB E5C 2A8
Tel: 506-755-3526; *Fax:* 506-755-6237
e-mail: info@nbsga.com
URL: www.nbsga.com
Overview: A small provincial organization founded in 1987
Chief Officer(s):
Pamela Parker, Executive Director
Sybil Smith, Director, Operations
Betty House, Coordinator, Research & Development
Jim Hanley, Manager, Wharf
Member Profile: Salmon farming producers in New Brunswick; Companies & organizations that support the industry
Activities: Liaising with governments; Promoting fish health & welfare & social responsibility; Developing training programs; Fostering a positive image for finfish aquaculture in Atlantic Canada; Participating in management & research initiatives with related organizations, such as the Aquaculture Association of Canada, the National Fish Health Working Group, the Bay of Fundy Marine Resource Planning, & the Musquash Marine Protected Area Steering Committee
Mission: To act as the voice of New Brunswick's salmon farming industry; To implement fish health initiatives to produce high-quality finfish; Affiliation(s): Atlantic Canada Aquaculture Industry Research & Development Network (ACAIRDN)
Environmental Activity: Promoting environmental stewardship; Supporting research to ensure sustainability of the aquaculture industry in Atlantic Canada; Collaborating with conservation organizations, such as the North Atlantic Salmon Conservation Organization

New Brunswick Society of Certified Engineering Technicians & Technologists (NBSCETT) / Société des techniciens et des technologues agréés du génie du Nouveau-Brunswick (STTAGN-B)
Parent: Canadian Council of Technicians & Technologists
#2, 385 Wilsey Rd., Fredericton NB E3B 5N6
Tel: 506-454-6124; *Fax:* 506-452-7076
Toll-Free: 800-665-8324
e-mail: nbscett@nbscett.nb.ca
URL: www.nbscett.nb.ca
Overview: A medium-sized provincial organization founded in 1968
Finances: *Annual Operating Budget:* $100,000-$250,000; *Funding Sources:* Membership dues
Staff: 3 staff member(s)
Membership: 1,600; *Fees:* Schedule available; *Member Profile:* Certified - in field of engineering, applied science, technology & meets requirements for certification; Technology graduate in training - meet all of academic requirements for certification; Associate - employed in engineering technology field; *Committees:* Accreditation; Certification & Review; Finance; Human Resources
Activities: Awards; Scholarships; *Awareness Events:* Annual Awards; *Internships:* Yes; *Speaker Service:* Yes; *Library:* Yes, Open to public
Mission: To grant certification to applied science & engineering technology technicians & technologists; to protect titles & powers of discipline for its members

New Brunswick Soil & Crop Improvement Association (NBSCIA) / Association pour

Associations/Organizations / New Brunswick Wildlife Federation

l'amélioration du sol et des cultures du Nouveau-Brunswick
16 Gilks Rd., Maugerville NB E3A 8N4
Tel: 506-454-1736; Fax: 506-472-4718
e-mail: nbscia@nbnet.nb.ca
URL: www.nbscia.ca
Overview: A small provincial organization founded in 1978
Chief Officer(s):
Susannah Banks, General Manager
John Robinson, President, 506-432-6473
Fees: $20 provincial membership
Activities: Promoting environmental & economical agricultural practices in New Brunswick; Organizing field days & tours; Distributing educational information to New Brunswick farmers; Conducting research projects; Sponsoring research projects & new farming techniques; Liaising with government
Publications: New Brunswick Soil & Crop Improvement Association Newsletter
Type: Newsletter Frequency: q. Price: Free with New Brunswick Soil & Crop Improvement Association membership
Mission: To improve soil & crop sustainability in New Brunswick; to encourage research & innovation to advance the agricultural industry throughout the province; Affiliation(s): Agricultural Alliance of New Brunswick; Eastern Soil & Water Conservation Centre; Soil Conservation Council of Canada

New Brunswick Wildlife Federation (NBWF) / Fédération de la faune du Nouveau-Brunswick
Parent: Canadian Wildlife Federation
576, rue Principale, St. Leonard NB E7E 2H5
URL: www.nbwildlifefederation.org
Overview: A medium-sized provincial organization founded in 1924
Finances: Annual Operating Budget: $100,000-$250,000
Membership: 44 clubs + 10,000 individual; Fees: $40 individual; $400 max. per club; Committees: Adopt-a-Stream; Constitution & By-Laws; Environment; Fisheries; Forestry; Master Angler; Membership; Memorial Cards, Merchandise & Prints; Outdoor Heritage Camps; Resolutions; Wildlife & Hunter Education; Fundraising; Becoming an Outdoors-Woman
Activities: Speaker Service: Yes
Mission: To foster sound management & wise use of the renewable & non-renewable natural resources of New Brunswick; to assist & encourage the enforcement of those game laws which are in keeping with the objectives of the Federation & to strive for better management & game laws where & when necessary; to educate membership & the public, with particular emphasis upon conservation & safety; to represent the interests & concerns of New Brunswick sportsmen; to cooperate with government departments & all related groups, where interests are mutual.; Member of: New Brunswick Salmon Council; Fur Institute of Canada

The New Directions Group
PO Box 8105, Canmore AB T1W 2T8
Tel: 403-678-9956
e-mail: info@newdirectionsgroup.org
URL: www.newdirectionsgroup.org
Overview: A small national organization
Chief Officer(s):
Paul Griss, Co-ordinator
Activities: The New Directions Action Plan focuses first on the need for detailed knowledge about the nature & quantities of the substances being released into the Canadian environment (a national emissions inventory) & second on the call for targeted reductions & eliminations (involves the phasing out or "sunsetting" of selected substances & a reduction of emissions from all sources); the Plan lays out five main steps for proceeding with this process
Mission: To use cooperative, non-adversarial methods of identifying & providing leadership in addressing significant environment-economy issues; to choose to address the philosophy of zero discharge of toxic substances; to carry out the Action Plan within the context of four principles that guide the thinking of the New Directions Group: the goal of sustainable development, a commitment to a pollution prevention approach, a crossmedia approach (air, water, land, biota) to reduction not just shifting toxic substances from one medium to another & a commitment to public participation in decision-making

Newfoundland & Labrador Association of Landscape Architects (NLALA)
PO Box 5262, Stn. C, St. John's NL A1C 5W1
Tel: 709-579-5855; Fax: 709-579-5844
e-mail: info@tract.nf.net
URL: www.nlala.com
Overview: A medium-sized provincial organization
Membership: 12; Member Profile: Landscape architects & firms

Newfoundland & Labrador Association of Technology Companies (NLATC)
#5, 391 Empire Ave., St. John's NL A1E 1W6
Tel: 709-772-8324; Fax: 709-757-6284
e-mail: info@nati.net
URL: www.nati.net
Previous Name: Newfoundland Alliance of Technical Industries
Overview: A medium-sized provincial organization
Chief Officer(s):
Paul Dubé, Chief Executive Officer
paul.dube@nati.net
Finances: Annual Operating Budget: $500,000-$1.5 Million; Funding Sources: Membership dues; government
Staff: 10 staff member(s); 30 volunteer(s)
Membership: 200; Fees: $130-$695
Activities: Leadership; corporate development; market development; networking & communications; Library: NATI Library; Open to public
Mission: To act collectively for technical organizations in Newfoundland industry in cooperation with educational & public sectors to promote the growth of innovative technical industries in Newfoundland & Labrador & the rest of Canada; Affiliation(s): Canadian Advanced Technology Association; Information Technology Association of Canada

Newfoundland & Labrador Camping Association
Parent: Canadian Camping Association
PO Box 50846, SS#3, St. John's NL A1B 4M2
Tel: 709-576-6198; Fax: 709-576-8146
e-mail: malcolmcturner@gmail.com
Overview: A medium-sized provincial organization
Chief Officer(s):
Malcolm C. Turner
Mission: To facilitate the development of organized camping in order to provide educational, character-building & constructive recreational experiences for all people; to develop awareness & appreciation of the natural environment

Newfoundland & Labrador Construction Association (NLCA)
Parent: Canadian Construction Association
#201, 333 Pippy Pl., St. John's NL A1B 3X2
Tel: 709-753-8920; Fax: 709-754-3968
e-mail: info@nfld.com
URL: www.nlca.ca
Overview: A small provincial organization founded in 1968
Fees: Schedule available, based upon volume of construction; Member Profile: Contractors, builders, & suppliers in Newfoundland & Labrador's construction industry; Committees: Standard Practices; Safety; Membership; Education & Training; Conference Planning; Golf
Activities: Promoting safety practices in the workplace; Facilitating networking opportunities; Offering the Electronic Plans Room for members; Providing the Gold Seal Certification program; Selling CCA / CCDC construction documents & guides; Providing educational programs & seminars; Developing standard tendering & contractual practices & procedures; Awarding scholarships & bursaries; Speaker Service: Yes
Meetings/Conferences:
For more information see Trade Shows, Conferences and Seminars Chapter
Newfoundland & Labrador Construction Association 2012 Annual Awards Gala
Other Conferences in 2012 2012, NL
Newfoundland & Labrador Construction Association 2012 Annual Conference & Annual General Meeting
Other Conferences in 2012 2012
Newfoundland & Labrador Construction Association 2012 General Membership Meeting
Other Conferences in 2012 2012, NL
Newfoundland & Labrador Construction Association 2012 2nd Annual Construction Career Expo & Opportunities Fair
Other Conferences in 2012 2012, NL
Publications: Newfoundland & Labrador Construction Association Weekly Bulletin
Type: Newsletter Frequency: w.
Profile: Updates for NLCA members
Newfoundland & Labrador Construction Association Membership Directory
Type: Directory
Profile: Featuring a Trade Classification Section
Mission: To act as the voice of the construction industry in Newfoundland & Labrador; To enhance the professionalism & productivity of members through the development of policies; Member of: Canadian Construction Association

Newfoundland & Labrador Environmental Industry Association (NEIA)
Parsons Bldg., #101, 90 O'Leary Ave., St. John's NL A1B 2C7
Tel: 709-772-3333; Fax: 709-772-3213
e-mail: info@neia.org
URL: www.neia.org
Overview: A medium-sized provincial organization founded in 1992
Chief Officer(s):
Linda Bartlett, Executive Director
linda@neia.org
Bill Scott, President
wascott@nl.rogers.com
Finances: Funding Sources: Government; luncheons; seminars
Staff: 4 staff member(s); 20 volunteer(s)
Membership: 173; Member Profile: Full - commercial enterprises that provide environmental products & services in Newfoundland & Labrador; associate - individuals & organizations supportive of the aims & objectives of NEIA; Committees: Policy; Programs; Membership/Communications; Trade Development; Finance
Mission: To promote the growth & development of the environmental industry of Newfoundland & Labrador; to promote ethical behavior & high standards for environmental products & services; to provide a strong, unified voice toward all private sector, government & non-profit entities involved in the Newfoundland environmental industry.

Newfoundland & Labrador Federation of Agriculture
Parent: Canadian Federation of Agriculture
PO Box 1045, 308 Brookfield Rd., Bldg. 4, Mount Pearl NL A1N 3C9
Tel: 709-747-4874; Fax: 709-747-8827
e-mail: info@nlfa.ca
URL: www.nlfa.ca
Overview: A medium-sized provincial organization
Chief Officer(s):
Paul Connors, Executive Director
paul@nlfa.ca
Matthew Carlson, Officer, Communications
mcarlson@nlfa.ca
Jamie Warren, Officer, Industry Development
jamie@nlfa.ca
Gerry Sullivan, Coordinator, Agriculture Awareness & Agri-Tourism
gerry@nlfa.ca
Christa Wright, Coordinator, Agriculture in the Classroom
christa@nlfa.ca
Finances: Funding Sources: Membership fees; Federal or provincial government programs
Fees: Schedule available, based upon farm gate revenue; Member Profile: Farmers & farmer groups in Newfoundland & Labrador
Activities: Assisting in the formulation of agricultural policies; Providing information about the state of the industry
Meetings/Conferences:
For more information see Trade Shows, Conferences and Seminars Chapter
Newfoundland & Labrador Federation of Agriculture 2012 Annual General Meeting
Other Conferences in 2012 2012, NL
Publications: AgriView [a publication of Newfoundland & Labrador Federation of Agriculture]
Type: Newsletter Frequency: s-a. Accepts Advertising : Yes
Editor: Matthew Carlson (mcarlson@nlfa.ca) ISSN: 1911-2297
Price: Free with Newfoundland & Labrador Federation of Agriculture membership
Profile: Feature articles, news, forthcoming events, & safety information
Mission: To act as the united voice of farmers in Newfoundland & Labrador; To improve the agricultural industry in Newfoundland & Labrador; To advance the economic & social conditions of those in the agricultural industry

Newfoundland & Labrador Federation of Municipalities See
Municipalities Newfoundland & Labrador

Newfoundland & Labrador Forest Protection Association
Parent: Canadian Forestry Association
PO Box 728, Mount Pearl NL A1N 2C2

Tel: 709-729-1012; Fax: 709-368-2740
e-mail: nlfpa@nfld.com
URL: www.nlfpa.nfol.ca
Overview: A medium-sized provincial organization founded in 1910
Finances: Annual Operating Budget: Less than $50,000
Committees: Public Education
Activities: Awareness Events: National Forest Week, May; Speaker Service: Yes
Mission: To maintain Newfoundland's forests as a productive & renewable resource;to increase public awareness, school education & natural appreciation of forests; to bring about better understanding of forests to people of all ages & backgrounds.

Newfoundland & Labrador Health Libraries Association (NLHLA)
Parent: Canadian Health Libraries Association
c/o Health Sciences Library, Memorial Univ. of Newfoundland, St. John's NL A1B 3V6
Tel: 709-737-6676; Fax: 709-737-6866
e-mail: lbarnett@mun.ca
URL: www.infonet.st-johns.nf.ca/nlhla/
Overview: A medium-sized provincial organization founded in 1979
Chief Officer(s):
Linda Barnett, Secretary
lbarnett@mun.ca
Alison Reid, President
alisonr@mun.ca
Finances: Annual Operating Budget: Less than $50,000
Membership: 35; Fees: $10; Member Profile: People who work in hospital & other health-related libraries & resource centres throughout Newfoundland & Labrador
Activities: NLHLA Lifeline (internet newsletter); initiate & coordinate projects to improve library services & information access in the health care field in Newfoundland
Mission: To promote the provision of a high quality library service to the health community in Newfoundland & Labrador through mutual assistance & communication; to provide professional support to the membership by offering continuing education opportunities; Affiliation(s): Canadian Health Libraries Association

Newfoundland & Labrador Institute of Agrologists (NLIA)
Parent: Agricultural Institute of Canada
PO Box 978, Mount Pearl NL A1N 3C9
Tel: 709-772-4170
URL: www.aic.ca/agrology/nlia.cfm
Overview: A small provincial licensing organization founded in 1988
Chief Officer(s):
Gary Bishop, P.Ag, President/Treasurer
gary.bishop@agr.gc.ca
Samir Debnath, P.Ag., Registrar
Finances: Annual Operating Budget: Less than $50,000
Membership: 40; Fees: $110
Mission: Dedicated to the professional aspects of Canadian agriculture.

Newfoundland & Labrador Lung Association (NLLA)
Parent: Canadian Lung Association
Carnell Building, PO Box 13457, Stn. A, 15 Pippy Pl., 2nd Fl., St. John's NL A1B 4B8
Tel: 709-726-4664; Fax: 709-726-2550
Toll-Free: 888-566-5864
e-mail: info@nf.lung.ca; health@nf.lung.ca
URL: www.nf.lung.ca
Overview: A small provincial charitable organization founded in 1944
Finances: Funding Sources: Donations; Fundraising; Sponsorships
Activities: Organizing fundraisers; Supporting research; Providing education; Offering support groups in areas such asthma, COPD, & smoking cessation; Engaging in advocacy activities; Awareness Events: Idle Free School Program; Retire Your Ride
Publications: Newfoundland & Labrador Lung Association Newsletter
Type: Newsletter
Mission: To achieve healthy breathing for the people of Newfoundland & Labrador
Environmental Activity: Increasing awareness of the link between air pollution & respiratory illness

Newfoundland & Labrador Medical Association (NLMA)
Parent: Canadian Medical Association
164 MacDonald Dr., St. John's NL A1A 4B3
Tel: 709-726-7424; Fax: 709-726-7525
Toll-Free: 800-563-2003
e-mail: nlma@nlma.nf.ca
URL: www.nlma.nf.ca
Overview: A medium-sized provincial organization founded in 1924
Finances: Annual Operating Budget: $500,000-$1.5 Million; Funding Sources: Membership dues
Staff: 11 staff member(s); 60 volunteer(s)
Membership: 1,600; Fees: $1,394; Member Profile: Physicians; medical students; residents; retired physicians
Mission: To represent & support physicians in Newfoundland & Labrador; provide leadership in the promotion of good health & the provision of quality health care to the people of the province

Newfoundland & Labrador Outfitters Association (NLOA)
PO Box 149, #8, 23 Stentaford Ave., Pasadena NL A0L 1K0
Tel: 709-686-6350; Fax: 709-686-2081
Toll-Free: 866-470-6562
e-mail: info@nloa.ca
URL: www.nloa.ca
Overview: A small provincial organization
Chief Officer(s):
Melissa Byrne, Coordinator, Project Support
melissa@nloa.ca
Membership: 84; Member Profile: Hunting & fishing outfitters in Newfoundland & Labrador, licensed by the licensing body of the Government of Newfoundland & Labrador
Activities: Liaising with government departments & organizations; Providing information to members; Offering professional development opportunities
Mission: To uphold the Code of Ethics for outfitters; to advocate on issues affecting the outfitting industry; Affiliation(s): Canadian Federation of Outfitters Association (CFOA)

Newfoundland & Labrador Parks & Recreation Association
See Recreation Newfoundland & Labrador

Newfoundland & Labrador Public Health Association (NLPHA)
Parent: Canadian Public Health Association
PO Box 8172, St. John's NL A1B 3M9
Overview: A small provincial organization founded in 1978
Chief Officer(s):
Fay Matthews, President, 709-759-3359
fay.matthews@easternhealth.ca
Elizabeth Wright, Secretary
Pat Murray, Treasurer
Finances: Funding Sources: Donations
Fees: $20 direct NLPHA membership; $150 regular conjoint CPHA & NLPHA membership; $98 student conjoint CPHA & NLPHA membership; Member Profile: Individuals in Newfoundland & Labrador who are interested in public health & community activities, such as health & community service workers, researchers, & educators
Activities: Raising awareness of public health issues; Addressing public health issues, such as school nutrition, food security, mental health services, family life education, fetal alcohol syndrome, primary health care, & low level flying; Providing education; Offering prevention programming; Liaising with partners & community organizations to strengthen community health; Offering monthly business & educational teleconferences
Publications: Newfoundland & Labrador Public Health Association Newsletter
Type: Newsletter Editor: Douglas Howse
Mission: To advocate for the physical, emotional, social, & environmental well-being of Newfoundland & Labrador's people & communities; Member of: Canadian Public Health Association (CPHA)

Newfoundland & Labrador Safety Council
Regatta Plaza II, #84, 86 Elizabeth Ave., 2nd Fl., St. John's NL A1A 1W7
Tel: 709-754-0210; Fax: 709-754-0010
e-mail: info@safetycouncil.net
Overview: A medium-sized provincial organization
Mission: The Newfoundland and Labrador Safety Council is dedicated to the prevention of injuries and fatalities; represents all the major sectors of the province's industry, business, government departments, volunteer organizations and many individuals who have a personal interest in safety, both on and off the job.; Affiliation(s): Canada Safety Council

Newfoundland & Labrador Water Well Corporation *See* Newfoundland/Labrador Ground Water Association

Newfoundland & Labrador Wildlife Federation (NWLF)
Parent: Canadian Wildlife Federation
15 Conran St., St. John's NL A1E 5L8
Tel: 709-368-6180
e-mail: ward.sampson@nf.sympatico.ca
URL: www.nlwf.ca
Overview: A medium-sized provincial organization founded in 1962
Member Profile: Clubs or organizations; Individuals; Associate members; Honorary members
Activities: Liaising with government agencies & organizations with similar goals; Conducting educational programs in conservation
Mission: To foster awareness & enjoyment of the natural world; To promote the sustainable use of natural resources; To protect wildlife & its habitat through conservation & effective wildlife management; Affiliation(s): Over 15 affiliated conservation groups, including the Canadian Wildlife Federation (CWF), & Rod & Gun Clubs from St. John's, Bay Of Islands, Green Bay, Baie d'Espoir, Marystown, South East Placentia, & Grand Falls
Environmental Activity: Undertaking & sponsoring research related to wildlife & the environment; Recommending legislative changes for the benefit of wildlife & its habitat; Increasing understanding of the impact of human activities on the environment

Newfoundland Alliance of Technical Industries *See* Newfoundland & Labrador Association of Technology Companies

Newfoundland Aquaculture Industry Association (NAIA)
PO Box 23176, 20 Mount Scio Pl., St. John's NL A1B 4J9
Tel: 709-754-2854; Fax: 709-754-2981
URL: www.naia.ca
Overview: A small provincial organization
Chief Officer(s):
Miranda Pryor, Executive Director
miranda@naia.ca
Job Halfyard, President, 709-675-2511
Robert Barry, Secretary, 709-576-7292
Jennifer Caines, Treasurer, 709-665-3168
Fees: $400 regular members; $200 associate members; Member Profile: Finfish & shellfish farmers in Newfoundland; Primary & secondary processors; Hatcheries producers; Supply & service companies; Academic institutions
Activities: Liaising with government; Offering training & advice; Providing business intelligence; Awareness Events: Aquaculture Week, June
Publications: Cold Harvester
Type: Magazine Frequency: q.
Profile: Information about the successes & challenges of the aquaculture industry for Newfoundland Aquaculture Industry Association members
Newfoundland Aquaculture Industry Association Member Directory
Type: Directory
Mission: To facilitate the commercial development of aquaculture in Newfoundland; to strive towards excellence in quality, safety, environmental sustainability, & profitability; to act as the voice of the industry in the province; Member of: Canadian Aquaculture Industry Alliance (CAIA); National Seafood Sector Council (NSSC)

Newfoundland Horticultural Society
PO Box 28086, Stn. Avalon Mall, St. John's NL A1B 4J8
e-mail: NHSweb@nl.rogers.com
URL: trenchfoot.2y.net/nfldhort
Overview: A small provincial organization founded in 1963
Chief Officer(s):
Frank Rose, Treasurer
Finances: Annual Operating Budget: Less than $50,000; Funding Sources: Membership fees
Membership: 104; Fees: $20
Activities: Monthly meetings; garden visits in summer; Awareness Events: Garden Show, August

Mission: To encourage an interest in all aspects of gardening as related to Newfoundland conditions; Affiliation(s): Royal Horticultural Society

Newfoundland/Labrador Ground Water Association
Parent: Canadian Ground Water Association
PO Box 160, Doyles NL A0N 1J0
Tel: 709-955-2561; Fax: 709-955-3402
e-mail: gwater@nf.sympatico.ca
Previous Name: Newfoundland & Labrador Water Well Corporation
Overview: A small provincial organization
Activities: Increasing public awareness about ground water protection
Mission: To promote the protection & management of ground water in Newfoundland & Labrador

Niagara Falls Nature Club (NFNC)
PO Box 901, Niagara Falls ON L2E 6V8
e-mail: rick.y@sympatico.ca
URL: niagaranatureclub.tripod.com
Overview: A small local charitable organization founded in 1967
Chief Officer(s):
Win Laar, Contact, 905-262-5057
Fees: $15 students; $25 single members; $35 families
Activities: Arranging programs & field trips; Conducting regular meetings at the Niagara Falls Public Library
Awards: R.W. Sheppard Award (Award)
To honour an individual or organization for their contribution, through education, conservation or research, in the field of nature
Publications: Nature Niagara News
Type: Newsletter Editor: Margaret Pickles ISSN: 0829-1241
Profile: Articles about local nature
Mission: To promote awareness, understanding, preservation, & protection of the natural habitat of the Niagara area

Niagara Peninsula Conservation Foundation (NPCF)
250 Thorold Rd. West, 3rd Fl., Welland ON L3C 3W2
Tel: 905-788-3135; Fax: 905-788-1121
e-mail: mcdougall@conservation-niagara.on.ca
URL: www.conservation-niagara.on.ca
Also Known As: Conservation Niagara Foundation
Overview: A small local charitable organization founded in 1969
Chief Officer(s):
Terry McDougall, Executive Director
Finances: Annual Operating Budget: $100,000-$250,000;
Funding Sources: Donations; bequests; grants
Staff: 1 staff member(s)
Membership: 15; Member Profile: Member must be approved by conservation authority
Activities: Annual golf tournament; elimination draw & dinner;
Awareness Events: Golf Tournament, June; Elimination Draw & Dinner, Nov.
Mission: To assist the Niagara Peninsula Conservation Authority in the cultivation & advancement of conservation by actively seeking support for conservation projects & programs through fundraising efforts & by serving as the custodian for these donations & gifts; Member of: Canadian Centre for Philanthropy

Niagara Peninsula Geological Society (NPGS)
120 South Dr., St Catharines ON L2R 4V9
e-mail: npgs@ccfms.ca
URL: www.ccfms.ca/Clubs/NPGS
Overview: A small local organization founded in 1962
Chief Officer(s):
Sharon Groen, President
Helen Kerekes, Vice-President
Barry Douglas, Treasurer
Fees: $15 individuals; $20 families; Member Profile: Individuals interested in collecting rocks, minerals, & fossils & in jewellery making
Activities: Hosting monthly meetings at Brock University; Arranging collecting field trips; Providing children's workshops
Publications: The Pink Dolomite Saddle Bulletin
Type: Newsletter Frequency: 10 pa Editor: John Tordiff Price: Free with NPGS membership; $10 non-members
Profile: Upcoming regional events, club activities, & general interest articles
Member of: Central Canadian Federation of Mineralogical Societies

Nickel Development Institute See Nickel Institute

Nickel Institute
#1801, 55 University Ave., Toronto ON M5J 2H7
Tel: 416-591-7999; Fax: 416-591-7987
e-mail: ni_toronto@nickelinstitute.org
URL: www.nickelinstitute.org
Previous Name: Nickel Development Institute
Overview: A large national organization founded in 1984
Finances: Annual Operating Budget: Greater than $5 Million
Staff: 9 staff member(s)
Membership: 15 corporate; Member Profile: Nickel miner, smelter, refiner; Committees: Technical Program; Advisory
Activities: Library: Yes
Mission: Market development & applications oriented non-profit research organization of international nickel industry; to provide information for nickel users, designers, specifiers, educators & others interested in nickel-containing materials & their applications

Niijkiwenhwag - Friends of Lake Superior Park
c/o Lake Superior Provincial Park, PO Box 267, Wawa ON P0S 1K0
e-mail: info@lakesuperiorpark.ca
URL: www.lakesuperiorpark.ca
Overview: A small local organization founded in 1993
Chief Officer(s):
Joel Cooper, Chair
Christina Speer, Chair
Fees: $10 individual; $15 family
Mission: To achieve public awareness, knowledge & appreciation of the park's natural & cultural heritage; to coordinate special events & projects related to the park's theme; to support the development of park interpretive programs; to provide supplementary funds to complement park educational & scientific research projects

Nipissing Environmental Watch (NEW)
PO Box 1543, North Bay ON P1B 8K6
Tel: 705-494-8935
e-mail: info@nipissingenvironmentalwatch.org
URL: www.nipissingenvironmentalwatch.org
Overview: A small local organization
Mission: A local, independent, non-profit, environmental group serving the Nipissing District

NOIA
Atlantic Place, #602, 215 Water St., St. John's NL A1C 6C9
Tel: 709-758-6610; Fax: 709-758-6611
URL: www.noianet.com
Also Known As: Newfoundland & Labrador Oil & Gas Industries Association
Overview: A medium-sized provincial organization founded in 1977
Chief Officer(s):
Robert Cadigan, President & CEO
Finances: Annual Operating Budget: $500,000-$1.5 Million;
Funding Sources: Membership fees; conferences, seminars & special events
Staff: 10 staff member(s); 100 volunteer(s)
Membership: 450; Fees: Schedule available; Member Profile: Those who develop, manufacture & market products & services in the oil & gas industry, both offshore & onshore; Committees: Board of Directors; Petroleum Research & Information; Membership Services & Internal Communications; External Relations; Finance & Human Resources; Policy & Positions
Activities: Promotes development of East Coast Canada's hydrocarbon resources & facilitates its membership's participation in oil & gas industries; Library: Yes, open by appointment
Awards: NOIA Hibernia Commemorative Scholarship (Award)
Eligibility: Newfoundland post-secondary students planning to pursue a career in a petroleum-related field
Mission: To assist, promote & facilitate the participation of members in ocean industries, with particular emphasis on oil & gas, to enhance their growth & development; to promote the growth of ocean industry; to act as a focal point for representations to government bodies & agencies; to act as a source of information & education for members

Non-Smokers' Rights Association (NSRA) / Association pour les droits des non-fumeurs
#221, 720 Spadina Ave., Toronto ON M5S 2T9
Tel: 416-928-2900; Fax: 416-928-1860
e-mail: toronto@nsra-adnf.ca
URL: www.nsra-adnf.ca
Overview: A medium-sized national organization founded in 1974
Finances: Funding Sources: Membership fees

Fees: $29 individual; $36 family; $18 student or person over age 65; $47 institution
Activities: Advocating for tobacco-control efforts in Canada & throughout the world; Liaising with national, provincial, & local health organizatons & community groups
Mission: To promote public health by stopping illness & death due to tobacco, including second-hand smoke; Affiliation(s): Smoking & Health Action Foundation (SHAF)

NORA, An Association of Responsible Recyclers (NORA)
5965 Amber Ridge Rd., Haymarket VA 20169 USA
Tel: 703-753-4277; Fax: 703-733-2445
URL: www.noranews.org
Previous Name: National Oil Recyclers Association
Overview: A medium-sized national licensing organization founded in 1984
Chief Officer(s):
Scott D. Parker, Executive Director
sparker@noranews.org
Finances: Annual Operating Budget: $250,000-$500,000
Staff: 4 staff member(s)
Membership: 200 companies; Fees: Based on company type; Member Profile: Liquid recyclers & vendors; Committees: Membership; Marketing; Conference; Governmental Affairs; Parts cleanin; Chemical Recycling; Used Oil Recycling; Ethics/Standards; Strategic Planning; Associate Advisory
Activities: Rents Mailing List: Yes
Member of: American Society of Association Executives

Norfolk County Agricultural Society
172 South Dr., Simcoe ON N3Y 1G6
Tel: 519-426-7280; Fax: 519-426-7286
URL: www.norfair.com
Overview: A small local organization
Chief Officer(s):
Karen Matthews, General Manager
kmatthews@norfolkcountyfair.com

Norfolk Field Naturalists (NFN)
PO Box 995, Simcoe ON N3Y 5B3
Tel: 519-586-2603
e-mail: info@norfolkfieldnaturalists.org
URL: www.norfolkfieldnaturalists.org
Overview: A small local organization founded in 1962
Finances: Annual Operating Budget: Less than $50,000;
Funding Sources: Membership dues; donations; LPBO Birdathon
Staff: 10 volunteer(s)
Membership: 150; Fees: $20 single; $30 family; Committees: Local Environmental Protection; Waste Management
Activities: Field trips for birding; free identification; nature appreciation; local natural heritage sites; Speaker Service: Yes
Mission: Dedicated to the acquisition & extension of knowledge of natural history & appreciation, enjoyment & stewardship of natural environment, especially within the region of Haldimand-Norfolk; Member of: Federation of Ontario Naturalists; Long Point Bird Observatory; Carolinian Canada

Nornet-Yukon See Yukon Environmental Network

North American Association for Environmental Education (NAAEE)
#540, 2000 P St. NW, Washington DC 20036 USA
Tel: 202-419-0412; Fax: 202-419-0415
e-mail: bredy@naaee.org
URL: www.naaee.org
Overview: A medium-sized international organization founded in 1971
Chief Officer(s):
Brian A. Day, Executive Director
brian@naaee.org
Finances: Funding Sources: Donations
Member Profile: Practitioners in the fields of environmental education, outdoor education, & conservation education; Students in the field of environmental education
Activities: Providing professional development events; Offering networking opportunities
Publications: Evaluating Your Environmental Education Programs: A Workbook for Practitioners
Author: J.A. Ernst; M.C. Monroe; B. Simmons
Profile: Case sudies & application exercises
Conservation Education & Outreach Techniques
Number of Pages: 496 Author: S. Jacobson; M. McDuff; M.C. Monroe ISBN: 0-19-856772-3
Profile: Case sudies & application exercises

What's Fair Got To Do With It: Diversity Cases from Environmental Educators
Number of Pages: 119 **Editor:** Tania J. Madfes **ISBN:** 0-914409-20-4
Using a Logic Model to Review & Analyze an Environmental Education Program
Type: Monograph **Number of Pages:** 72 **Editor:** Thomas C. Marcinkowski **ISBN:** 1-884008-86-0
Preparing Effective Environmental Educators
Type: Monograph **Number of Pages:** 89 **Editor:** Dr. Bora Simmons **ISBN:** 1-884008-88-7
A Field Guide to Environmental Literacy: Making Strategic Investments in Environmental Education
Number of Pages: 110 **Author:** J.L. Elder **ISBN:** 1-884008-87-9
North American Association for Environmental Education Conference Proceedings
Environmental Education Undergraduate & Graduate Programs & Faculty in the United States
Author: Michaela Zint; Aimee Giles **ISBN:** 1-884008-79-B
Elementary School Teachers' Beliefs About Teaching Environmental Education
Number of Pages: 48 **Author:** S. Middlestadt; R. Ledsky **ISBN:** 1-884008-76-3
Environmental Education: Academia's Response
Number of Pages: 96 **Author:** E. Kormondy; P.B. Corcoran **ISBN:** 1-884008-51-8
Environmental Education at the Early Childhood Level
Number of Pages: 126 **Editor:** R. Wilson **ISBN:** 1-884008-14-3
Environmental Education in the Schools: Creating a Program That Works!
Number of Pages: 500 **Author:** J. Braus; D. Wood **ISBN:** 1-884008-08-9
Environmental Education Research, Special Issue on Significant Life Experiences
Number of Pages: 114 **Editor:** T. Tanner **ISBN:** 1350-4622
Environmental Literacy in the United States: What Should Be...What Is...Getting from Here to There
Number of Pages: 80 **Editor:** T. Volk; W. McBeth **ISBN:** 1-884008-73-9
EE News [a publication of the North American Association for Environmental Education]
Type: Newsletter
NAAEE [North American Association for Environmental Education] Communicator
Type: Newsletter
Mission: To promote education about environmental issues
Environmental Activity: Supporting the work of environmental educators

North American Bird Conservation Initiative Canada (NABCI)
c/o Canadian Wildlife Service-Environment Canada, 351, boul. St-Joseph, 3e étage, Gatineau QC K1A 0H3
Tel: 819-994-0512; **Fax:** 819-994-4445
e-mail: nabci@ec.gc.ca
URL: www.nabci.net
Chief Officer(s):
Cynthia Wright, Chair, NABCI Canada Council
Mission: The NABCI is a coordinated effort among Canada, the United States & Mexico to maintain the diversity & abundance of all North American birds. National coordination of this effort in Canada occurs through the NABCI Canada Council, chaired by the Asst. Deputy Minister of Environment Canada's Environmental Conservation Service. Council members include representatives from provincial governments, non-government organizations, four bird plans (waterfowl, landbirds, shorebirds, waterbirds), & habitat joint ventures. In Canada, the joint venture conservation projects has three habitat joint ventures (Pacific Coast, Prairie Habitat, Eastern Habitat) & three species (Arctic Goose, Black Duck, Sea Duck).

North American Native Plant Society (NANPS)
PO Box 84, Stn. D, Toronto ON M9A 4X1
Tel: 416-631-4438
e-mail: nanps@nanps.org
URL: www.nanps.org
Previous Name: Canadian Wildflower Society
Overview: A medium-sized provincial charitable organization founded in 1984
Fees: $20/year
Activities: Members-only seed exchange; Native Garden Award; Native Plant Sale
Publications: *Blazing Star [a publication of the North American Native Plant Society]*
Type: Journal **Frequency:** q.

Mission: Dedicated to the study, conservation & cultivation of North America's wild flora.; **Member of:** Federation of Ontario Naturalists

North American Packaging Association - Canada
#400, 701 Evans Ave., Toronto ON M9C 1A3
Tel: 416-626-7056; **Fax:** 416-626-7054
e-mail: info@paperbox.org
URL: www.paperbox.org
Previous Name: Canadian Paper Box Manufacturers' Association Inc
Merged from: Canadian Paperboard Packaging Association; North American Packaging Association
Overview: A large national organization
Finances: *Annual Operating Budget:* $250,000-$500,000; *Funding Sources:* Membership fees
Staff: 2 staff member(s)
Membership: 100-499
Activities: *Speaker Service:* Yes
Mission: The Canadian Paperboard Packaging Association merged with the North American Packaging Association in September, 2006. NAPA is an international trade association representing paperboard packaging converters & industry suppliers

North American Recycled Rubber Association (NARRA)
#24, 1621 McEwen Dr., Whitby ON L1N 9A5
Tel: 905-433-7769; **Fax:** 905-433-0905
e-mail: narra@oix.com
URL: www.recycle.net/recycle/assn/narra
Overview: A small national organization founded in 1994
Chief Officer(s):
Diane Sarracini, Office Manager
Finances: *Annual Operating Budget:* $100,000-$250,000; *Funding Sources:* Membership dues; research
Staff: 1 staff member(s); 1 volunteer(s)
Membership: 100; *Fees:* $350
Activities: Provides specialized training & feasibility studies; annual convention (March) & newsletter; *Speaker Service:* Yes; *Library:* Rubber Recycling Library; open by appointmentNot open to the public
Mission: The Association provides a unified voice, as well as a communication network & research facility, for issues of concern to those involved in rubber recycling across North America.; **Member of:** Canadian Environment Industry Association; Ontario Automotive Recyclers Association; International Tire & Rubber Association

North American Society for Oceanic History (NASOH)
Texas Christian University, Department Of History, PO Box 297260, Fort Worth TX 76129 USA
URL: www.nasoh.org
Overview: A small international organization founded in 1974
Finances: *Annual Operating Budget:* Less than $50,000
Membership: 220; *Fees:* $65 US individual/corporate; $18 US student
Awards: John Lyman Book Awards (Award)
Jack Bauer Award (Award)
Mission: To provide a forum for maritime history; To study & promote naval & maritime history; To promote exchange of information among its members & others interested in history of seas, lakes & inland waterways; To call attention to books, articles, other publications & documents pertinent to naval & maritime history; to work with local, regional, national & international organizations as well as appropriate government agencies towards goal of fostering a more general awareness & appreciation for North America's naval & maritime heritage

North American Waterfowl Management Plan (NAWMP) / Le plan nord-américain de gestion de la sauvagine
c/o Canadian Wildlife Service, Place Vincent Massey, 351, boul St. Joseph, 7th Fl., Gatineau QC K1A 0H3
Tel: 819-934-6034; **Fax:** 819-934-6017
e-mail: nawmp@ec.gc.ca
URL: www.nawmp.ca
Chief Officer(s):
Steve Wendt, Director, Canadian Wildlife Service
Awards: Great Blue Heron Award (Award)
Recognizes primary participants in the Plan who have made major, long-term national contributions that result in benefits to waterfowl & other bird populations of North America; for US nominations - Executive Director, N. American Waterfowl & Wetlands Office, US Fish & Wildlife Service, Rm.110, 4401 N. Fairfax Dr., Arlington VA 22203, ph. 703/358-1784; for Mexican nominations - Humberto Berlanga, Instituto Nacional de Ecolgis, Avenida Revoluclon 1425-19, Colonia Tlacopoc San Angel, Mexico D.F.01040, ph.(52-56)24-33-09-09; for Canadian nomination contact above address *Eligibility:* Nominees must demonstrate protection, maintenance, restoration or improvement of habitat for waterfowl & migratory bird populations; or initiation of legislation or major corporate or public policy that helped attain goals of the plan, & benefit waterfowl & migratory bird populations; or donation of a gift valued at $10,000 or more to any plan partner; for fostering of cooperation & coordination that contributes to plan goals *Deadline:* Feb. 1 *Award Amount:* A carving of a Great Blue Heron & a certificate
International Canvasback Award (Award)
For individuals, corporations, & organizations who have made substantial, long-term international contributions to the implementation & continuation of the plan throughout North America *Eligibility:* Same as above *Deadline:* Feb. 1 *Award Amount:* An original decoy carving of a Canvasback & a certificate Contact: Canadian, Mexican, US addresses as above
Mission: The North American Waterfowl Management Plan is an international action plan to conserve migratory birds throughout the continent. The Plan's goal is toreturn waterfowl populations to their 1970's levels by conserving wetland and upland habitat. Canada & the United States signed the Plan in 1986 in reaction to critically low numbers of waterfowl. Mexico joined in 1994 making it a truly continental effort. The Plan is a partnership of federal, provincial/state & municipal governments, non-governmental organizations, private companies & many individuals, all working towards achieving better wetland habitat for the benefit of migratory birds, other wetland-associated species & people. The Plan's unique combination of biology, landscape conservation & partnerships comprise its exemplary conservation legacy. Plan projects are international in scope, but implemented at regional levels. These projects contribute to the protection of habitat & wildlife species across the North American landscape. In fact, the North American Waterfowl Management Plan is considered one of the most successful conservation initiatives in the world.

North Central Local Government Association (NCLGA)
c/o Executive Director, #206, 155 George St., Prince George BC V2L 1P8
Tel: 250-564-6585; **Fax:** 250-564-6514
e-mail: kmarshall@nclga.ca (Executive Assistance)
URL: ncma.enorthernbc.com
Overview: A small local organization
Chief Officer(s):
Maxine Koppe, Executive Director
mkoppe@nclga.ca
Karen Goodings, Chair
Mike Bernier, First Vice President
Art Kaehn, Second Vice President
Membership: 40 municipalities; *Member Profile:* Elected officials from member regional municipalities, districts, cities, towns, & villages in the north area of British Columbia
Publications: *Issues in Focus [a publication of the North Central Local Government Association]*
Type: Newsletter **Frequency:** 8 pa
Mission: To address the issues of local governments; To mobilize initiatives to benefit member governments

North Okanagan Naturalists Club (NONC)
PO Box 473, Vernon BC V1T 6M4
Tel: 250-545-0490
URL: www.nonc.ca
Overview: A small local charitable organization founded in 1951
Finances: *Annual Operating Budget:* Less than $50,000; *Funding Sources:* Dues; social activities; club sales
Staff: 3 volunteer(s)
Membership: 180; *Fees:* $28 adults; $38 family; *Committees:* Conservation; Education; Land Stewardship; Socials; Trips; Ways & Means
Activities: *Awareness Events:* Annual Field & Dinner Day, May
Awards: James Grant Memorial Award (Award)
Mission: To foster an interest in nature; to record data & sightings of flora & fauna; to educate young people; to hold land; **Member of:** The Federation of BC Naturalists; Canadian Nature Federation

North Okanagan Organic Association (NOOA)
C76 Cedar Hill Road, RR#1, Vernon BC V0E 1W0
Tel: 250-540-2557
e-mail: northorganics@gmail.com
URL: www.certifiedorganic.bc.ca

Associations/Organizations / North Saskatchewan Watershed Alliance

Overview: A small local licensing organization
Chief Officer(s):
Cara Nunn
Finances: *Annual Operating Budget:* Less than $50,000
Membership: 101; *Fees:* $325; *Committees:* Certification; Standards
Activities: Certification of members' food products; monthly meeting for information on organic practices; *Library:* Yes, open by appointment
Mission: To encourage the practice of soil regeneration & sustainable food production, through the use of organic methods as per the Canadian definition; to certify members' food products that are organically grown in accordance with the association's guidelines; Affiliation(s): Certified Organic Associations of BC

North Saskatchewan Watershed Alliance
0504 - 49 St., Edmonton AB T6B 2M9
Tel: 780-442-6363; *Fax:* 780-495-0610
e-mail: water@nswa.ab.ca
URL: www.nswa.ab.ca
Overview: A small local organization founded in 2000
Chief Officer(s):
David Trew, Executive Director, 780-496-3474
Tom Cottrell, IWMP Coordinator, 780-496-6962
tom.cottrell@edmonton.ca
Finances: *Annual Operating Budget:* $50,000-$100,000; *Funding Sources:* Industry; government; grants
Staff: 6 staff member(s)
Membership: 140
Activities: State of watershed reporting; watershed planning; education & awareness; stewardship; *Library:* Yes, open by appointment
Mission: To protect & improve water quality & ecosystem functioning in the North Saskatchewan Watershed within Alberta

North Shore Forest Products Marketing Board
PO Box 386, Bathurst NB E2A 3Z3
Tel: 506-522-2246; *Fax:* 506-522-0230
e-mail: nsfpmb@nbnet.nb.ca
URL: www.forestrysyndicate.com
Overview: A small local organization founded in 1973
Chief Officer(s):
Patrick Doucet, Sylviculture Manager
Finances: *Annual Operating Budget:* Greater than $5 Million; *Funding Sources:* Regional Government
Staff: 10 staff member(s); 10 volunteer(s)
Membership: 2,000 individual
Activities: *Rents Mailing List:* Yes
Mission: To negotiate with industry & government on behalf of the private wood producers of the regulated area for fair prices for the products of the woodlots & to promote improved forest management; Affiliation(s): NB Forest Products Commission

North Shuswap Naturalists
Parent: Federation of BC Naturalists
Comp. 110, Site 11, RR#1, Chase BC V0E 1M0
Tel: 250-679-8763
Overview: A small local charitable organization
Finances: *Annual Operating Budget:* Less than $50,000; *Funding Sources:* Membership fees
Membership: 21; *Fees:* $20; *Member Profile:* Mostly seniors
Activities: Monthly meetings (Sept.-June); summer field trips
Mission: To promote the enjoyment of nature through environmental appreciation & conservation; to encourage wise use & conservation of natural resources & environmental protection.

Northeast Avalon ACAP, Inc.
PO Box 1027, Stn. C, 172 Military Rd., St. John's NL A1C 5M3
Tel: 709-726-9673; *Fax:* 709-726-2764
e-mail: info@naacap.ca
URL: www.naacap.ca
Also Known As: Atlantic Coastal Action Program
Previous Name: St. John's Harbour ACAP
Overview: A small local organization
Chief Officer(s):
Cal Baker, Chair
Patrick Wells, Secretary
Finances: *Annual Operating Budget:* $100,000-$250,000
Staff: 2 staff member(s); 25 volunteer(s)
Membership: 1-99
Activities: *Library:* Yes, Open to public, open by appointment
Member of: NL Environmental Industries Association; NL Environment Network

Northeast Organic Farming Association (NOFA)
Massachusetts Chapter, 411 Sheldon Rd., Barre MA 1005 USA
Tel: 978-355-2853; *Fax:* 978-355-4046
e-mail: nofa@nofamass.org
URL: www.nofamass.org
Overview: A small local charitable organization founded in 1982
Chief Officer(s):
Julie Rawson, Executive Director
Finances: *Annual Operating Budget:* $250,000-$500,000; *Funding Sources:* Private donations; membership dues; conference fees
Staff: 17 staff member(s); 50 volunteer(s)
Membership: 865; *Fees:* US$30 individual; US$20 low income; US$40 family/institution; US$150 supporting
Activities: Educational conferences & workshops; videos on organic growing; information about apprenticeship programs matching farms seeking workers with people wanting to learn organic methods; Organic Food Guide map listing organic farmers in Massachusetts; bulk order of soil amendments; genetic engineering awareness; *Speaker Service:* Yes
Mission: To educate members & the general public about the benefits of local organic systems based on complete cycles, natural materials & minimal waste for the health of individual beings, communities & the living planet

Northern Alberta Health Libraries Association
Parent: Canadian Health Libraries Association
c/o J.W. Scott Health Sciences Library, University of Alberta, 2K3.28 Walter MacKenzie Ctr., Edmonton AB T6G 2R7
e-mail: nahla@nahla.ca
URL: www.chla-absc.ca/nahla
Overview: A small local organization founded in 1984
Chief Officer(s):
Thane Chambers, President
Finances: *Annual Operating Budget:* Less than $50,000
Membership: 38; *Fees:* $25 regular; $12 student; *Member Profile:* librarians, library technicians and others interested in health libraries and health information.
Mission: This chapter of NAHLA exists to provide a forum for networking among libarianans, library technicians and other interested in health libraries and health information.; *Member of:* Canadian Health Libraries Association

Northern Interior Vegetation Management Association (NIVMA)
PO Box 460, Prince George BC V2L 4S6
Tel: 250-564-4115
e-mail: manager@nivma.bc.ca
Overview: A small local organization founded in 1988
Chief Officer(s):
Naomi Donat, Manager
Finances: *Annual Operating Budget:* $100,000-$250,000
Staff: 1 staff member(s)
Membership: 16; *Fees:* Based on harvest levels; *Member Profile:* Forest industry & government, northern BC & Alberta
Mission: To use common protocols & databases to adaptively & cost-effectively deliver defensible, effective, & ecologically sound practices that contribute to sustainable forest management

Northern Lights Health Library Association
Parent: Canadian Health Libraries Association
c/o Sault Area Hospital, 969 Queen Street East, Sault Ste Marie ON P6A 2C4
Tel: 705-759-3434; *Fax:* 705-759-3847
e-mail: aslettk@sah.on.ca
Overview: A small local organization
Chief Officer(s):
Kim Aslett, President
Finances: *Annual Operating Budget:* Less than $50,000; *Funding Sources:* Grants; Self funded
Membership: 15; *Member Profile:* Members who work in health or academic libraries in the northeast region; *Committees:* Education

Northern Native Fishing Corporation (NNFC)
344A 2nd Avenue W, Prince Rupert BC V8J 1G6
Tel: 250-627-8486; *Fax:* 250-624-6627
Toll-Free: 888-672-1804
Overview: A small local organization founded in 1982
Chief Officer(s):
Corinne McKay, General Manager
Mission: To preserve & enhance for individual native fishermen the economic opportunity to harvest & market marine resources by creating & ensuring access to the resources

Northern Ontario Aquaculture Association
PO Box 124, 13 Worthington St., Little Current ON P0P 1K0
Tel: 705-368-1345; *Fax:* 705-368-0685
e-mail: lori.noaa@manitoulin.net
URL: www.ontarioaquaculture.com
Overview: A small local organization
Chief Officer(s):
Mike Meeker, President
Karen Tracey, Executive Director
noaa@manitoulin.net
Membership: 30; *Fees:* Non-voting members: $100 associate. Voting members: $500 supporting; $1,000 corporate; $4,000 patron; $2,000 sustaining
Mission: The voice of Ontario's sustainable fish farming industry

Northern Prospectors Association (NPA)
PO Box 535, Kirkland Lake ON P2N 3J5
Tel: 705-642-1982; *Fax:* 705-567-4426
e-mail: ravenr@nt.net
URL: www.ontarioprospectors.com/northern/index.htm
Overview: A small local organization founded in 1971
Chief Officer(s):
Garry Clark, Contact
Member Profile: Members of the mining exploration community in the Kirkland Lake area, including prospectors & geologists
Activities: Offering courses on topics such as geology & geophysics; Hosting NPA gold panning events for tourists
Publications: *The Explorationist [a publication of the Northern Prospectors Association & the Ontario Prospectors Association]*
Type: Newsletter *Frequency:* 10 pa *Price:* Free with Northern Prospectors Association membership
Profile: Land use issues, the environment, & mining law, published in association with the Ontario Prospectors Association
Mission: To act as a strong voice for the prospecting & mining industry; Affiliation(s): Ontario Prospectors Association

Northumberland Salmon Protection Association
#11042, Rte 430, Trout Brook NB E9E 1R4
Tel: 506-622-8834; *Fax:* 506-622-7691
Overview: A small local organization
Chief Officer(s):
Debbie Norton, President
Membership: 200
Member of: Atlantic Salmon Federation

Northwatch (NW)
PO Box 282, North Bay ON P1B 8H2
Tel: 705-497-0373; *Fax:* 705-476-7060
e-mail: northwatch@onlink.net
URL: www.northwatch.org
Overview: A small local organization founded in 1988
Chief Officer(s):
B. Lloyd, Coordinator
Finances: *Annual Operating Budget:* Less than $50,000
Staff: 2 staff member(s); 100 volunteer(s)
Membership: 20 organizations; *Fees:* $10 individual; $25 group/supporting; *Committees:* Forest; Mining; Energy; Waste; Water
Activities: Advocacy; public education; regional meetings; workshops; tours; *Internships:* Yes; *Speaker Service:* Yes; *Library:* Yes, open by appointment
Mission: To act as a representative body & to provide support to local citizens groups addressing environmental issues such as energy use, generation & conservation, forest conservation & wild areas protection, waste management & water quality issues, mining & militarization as well as other environmental concerns; to improve forest management, promote community involvement in mine monitoring & management & to prevent northeastern Ontario from becoming the receiving ground for foreign wastes, including Toronto's garbage, Ontario's biomedical waste, Canada's nuclear reactor fuel waste & PCBs from around the world; *Member of:* Canadian Environmental Network

Northwest Coalition for Alternatives to Pesticides (NCAP)
PO Box 1393, Eugene OR 97440-1393 USA
Tel: 541-344-5044; *Fax:* 541-344-6923
e-mail: info@pesticide.org
URL: www.pesticide.org
Overview: A medium-sized local charitable organization founded in 1977
Chief Officer(s):
Aria Seligmann, Communications Coordinator
Norma Grier, Executive Director
Finances: *Annual Operating Budget:* $250,000-$500,000; *Funding Sources:* Grants; donations
Staff: 9 staff member(s); 10 volunteer(s)

Membership: 2,300; *Fees:* $25; $15 limited income; $50 associate
Activities: Clean water for salmon; public education; sustainable agriculture; pesticide free parks; inert ingredient disclosure; *Internships:* Yes; *Library:* Yes, Open to public
Mission: Works to protect the health of people & the environment by advancing alternatives to pesticides

Northwest Territories Association of Communities (NWTAC)
Finn Hansen Bldg., #200, 5105 - 50th St., Yellowknife NT X1A 1S1
Tel: 867-873-8359; *Fax:* 867-873-3042
Toll-Free: 866-973-8359
URL: www.nwtac.com
Overview: A medium-sized provincial organization founded in 1967
Chief Officer(s):
Yvette Gonzalez, CEO
yvette@nwtac.com
Mission: To promote the exchange of information amongst the community governments of the Northwest Territories and to provide a united front for the realization of goals.; *Member of:* Federation of Canadian Municipalities

Northwest Territories Association of Landscape Architects (NWTALA)
PO Box 1394, Yellowknife NT X1A 2P1
Tel: 867-920-2986; *Fax:* 867-920-2986
e-mail: atborow@internorth.com
Overview: A medium-sized provincial organization founded in 1991
Member Profile: Landscape architects in the Northwest Territories
Mission: To represent landscape architects in the Northwest Territories; *Affiliation(s):* Canadian Society of Landscape Architects (CSLA)

Northwest Territories Chamber of Mines *See* NWT & Nunavut Chamber of Mines

Northwest Territories Construction Association (NWTCA)
Parent: Canadian Construction Association
PO Box 2277, 4921 - 49th St., 3rd Fl., Yellowknife NT X1A 2P7
Tel: 867-873-3949; *Fax:* 867-873-8366
e-mail: director@nwtca.ca
URL: www.nwtca.ca
Overview: A medium-sized provincial organization founded in 1976
Fees: $250; *Member Profile:* Construction-related businesses in the Northwest Territories & Nunavut
Activities: Lobbying governments on behalf of the construction industry
Mission: To act as a voice for construction-related business in the Northwest Territories & Nunavut

Northwest Territories Recreation & Parks Association (NWTRPA)
Parent: Canadian Parks & Recreation Association
PO Box 841, Yellowknife NT X1A 2N6
Tel: 867-873-5340; *Fax:* 867-669-6791
e-mail: admin@nwtrpa.org
URL: www.nwtrpa.org
Overview: A small provincial organization founded in 1989
Chief Officer(s):
Robin Langille, President, 867-777-8627
Geoff Ray, Executive Director
gray@nwtrpa.org
Finances: Annual Operating Budget: $50,000-$100,000; *Funding Sources:* Federal, territorial government
Staff: 6 staff member(s)
Membership: 100; *Fees:* $35 individual; $75 municipal or recreation committee; *Committees:* Executive; Corporate; Sponsorship
Activities: Recreation Code of Ethics; Recreation & Parks Resource Binder; Awards Program; Corporate Sponsorship; Active Living
Mission: To increase public awareness of recreation & parks; to enhance the quality of life of residents of the NWT through fostering the development of recreation & parks services; *Affiliation(s):* Sport North

Northwest Wildlife Preservation Society (NWPS)
#203, 5066 Kingsway, Burnaby BC V5H 2E7
Tel: 604-568-9160; *Fax:* 604-568-6152
e-mail: info@northwestwildlife.com
URL: www.northwestwildlife.com
Overview: A small local organization founded in 1987
Chief Officer(s):
Ann Peters, Executive Director
Finances: Annual Operating Budget: $1.5 Million-$3 Million; *Funding Sources:* Donations; grants; honoria
Staff: 2 staff member(s); 60 volunteer(s)
Membership: 100+; *Fees:* $35 family; $20 individual; $15 senior/student; $100 corporate; *Committees:* Fundraising; Volunteer
Activities: Ongoing education programs; *Library:* NWPS Wildlife Library; open by appointment
Mission: To ensure that healthy wildlife populations are preserved for their own sake & for the appreciation of all; to develop & provide educational, research & advisory services which can advance the public's awareness & knowledge about wildlife & wildlife systems in northwest North America; *Member of:* BC Endangered Species Coalition; Vancouver Urban Wildlife Committee; BC Environmental Network

Northwestern Ontario Health Libraries Association (NOHLA)
Parent: Canadian Health Libraries Association
c/o S. Regalado, Librarian, SJCG Library Svs., St. Joseph's Care Group, PO Box 2930, 580 Algoma St. North, Thunder Bay ON P7B 5G4
Tel: 807-343-4362; *Fax:* 807-343-4306
e-mail: regalados@tbh.net; cmackenzie@hscn.on.ca
Overview: A small local organization
Chief Officer(s):
Sophie M. Regalado, MISt, MA, Chair
Membership: 1-99; *Member Profile:* Health librarians in Northwestern Ontario
Activities: Organizing regular meetings; Exchanging information on topical issues in northwestern Ontario's health libraries; Conducting workshops; Providing networking opportunities; Collaborating with other libraries in the region
Member of: Canadian Health Libraries Association / Association des bibliothèques de la santé du Canada

Northwestern Ontario Municipal Association (NOMA)
PO Box 10308, Thunder Bay ON P7B 6T8
Tel: 807-683-6662
e-mail: admin@noma.on.ca
URL: www.noma.on.ca
Overview: A medium-sized local organization founded in 1946
Finances: Funding Sources: Operating subsidy from the Ministry of Northern Development & Mines; Membership fees
Membership: 100-499; *Fees:* $250 not-for-profit organizations; $500 businesses; *Member Profile:* Membership is attained from the Corporation of the City of Thunder Bay, the Kenora District Municipal Association, the Rainy River District Municipal Association, & the Thunder Bay District Municipal League; Associate membership is comprised of not-for-profit organizations & businesses
Activities: Advocating for northwestern Ontario's regional interests; Acting on matters where municipal rights may be affected; Promoting municipal interests; Offering opportunities for education & discussion to advance the standards of municipal government
Meetings/Conferences:
For more information see Trade Shows, Conferences and Seminars Chapter
Northwestern Ontario Municipal Association 2011 Annual Regional Conference
September 2011, ON
Northwestern Ontario Municipal Association 2012 Annual General Meeting
April 2012, ON
Northwestern Ontario Municipal Association 2012 Annual Regional Conference
Other Conferences in 2012 2012, ON
Northwestern Ontario Municipal Association 2013 Annual General Meeting & Conference
April 2013, ON
Northwestern Ontario Municipal Association 2013 Annual Regional Conference
Other Conferences in 2013 2013, ON
Mission: To consider matters of interest to municipalities in northwestern Ontario; To procure enactment of legislation which may be advantageous to northwestern Ontario's municipalities; *Member of:* Association of Municipalities of Ontario

Not Far From The Tree
90 Croatia St., Toronto ON M6H 1K9
Tel: 416-363-6441
e-mail: info@notfarfromthetree.org
URL: www.notfarfromthetree.org
Overview: A small local organization
Mission: The group operates a residential, fruit-picking program where teams of volunteers are dispatched to harvest fruit from trees that the owners would otherwise let go to waste. The fruit is divided equally among the owners, volunteers & a local, community food distribution organization who can make good use of it.

Nova Forest Alliance
PO Box 208, 285 George St., Stewiacke NS B0N 2J0
Tel: 902-639-2921; *Fax:* 902-639-2981
e-mail: info@novaforestalliance.com
URL: www.novaforestalliance.com
Overview: A small provincial organization

Nova Scotia Cattle Producers (NSCP)
#201, 332 Willow St., Truro NS B2N 5A5
Tel: 902-893-7455; *Fax:* 902-893-3397
e-mail: office@nscattle.ca
URL: www.nscattle.ca
Previous Name: Nova Scotia Cattlemen's Association
Overview: A medium-sized provincial organization founded in 2004
Membership: 1,300; *Member Profile:* Persons involved in Nova Scotia's beef & dairy production industry
Activities: Providing information about beef production & marketing; Promoting the beef industry in Nova Scotia; Monitoring & responding to issues in the industry; Advocating on behalf of producers
Publications: N.S.C.Action [a publication of Nova Scotia Cattle Producers]
Type: Newsletter
Mission: To assist in the sustainable development of the beef production industry in Nova Scotia; *Member of:* Canadian Cattlemen's Association; *Affiliation(s):* National Check-off Agency; The Beef Cattle Research Agency; Beef Information Centre; Nappan Beef Research Committee; Maritime Beef Council; Maritime Beef Testing Society; The Nova Scotia Federation of Agriculture Council of Leaders
Environmental Activity: Focussing on food safety, environmental farm planning, animal welfare, & SRM disposal

Nova Scotia Cattlemen's Association *See* Nova Scotia Cattle Producers

Nova Scotia Consulting Engineers Association *See* Consulting Engineers of Nova Scotia

Nova Scotia Council on Smoking & Health *See* Smoke-Free Nova Scotia

Nova Scotia Daylily Society
Newport RR#3 999 McKay Rd., Hants Co NS B0N 2A0
Tel: 902-757-2057
e-mail: cgharvey@eastlink.ca
URL: www.nsdaylilysociety.com
Overview: A small provincial organization founded in 2003
Chief Officer(s):
Carla Heggie, President
heggiens@yahoo.ca
Membership: 110; *Fees:* $10

Nova Scotia Environmental Network (NSEN)
Parent: Canadian Environmental Network
3115 Veith St., Halifax NS B3K 3G9
Tel: 902-454-6846; *Fax:* 902-453-3633
e-mail: nsen@cen-rce.org; board_nsen@cen-rce.org
URL: www.nsen.ca
Overview: A medium-sized provincial organization founded in 1991
Finances: Funding Sources: Fundraising; Donations
Fees: Schedule available, based upon annual budget range; *Member Profile:* Non-profit groups, agencies, educational institutions, & individuals in Nova Scotia who share Nova Scotia Environmental Network's mission
Activities: Liaising with government at the provincial, national, & international levels; Organizing roundtables & conferences; Providing networking opportunities; Supporting members; Facilitating information exchange; Providing educational

Associations/Organizations / Nova Scotia Federation of Agriculture

activities; *Internships:* Yes; *Library:* Nova Scotia Environmental Network Library
Meetings/Conferences:
For more information see Trade Shows, Conferences and Seminars Chapter
Nova Scotia Environmental Network 2011 Workshop: Moving Water
June 2011 New Germany, NS
Nova Scotia Environmental Network 2011 Workshop: Fundraising 101
June 2011 Halifax, NS
Nova Scotia Environmental Network 2011 20th Anniversary Annual Gathering
October 2011 Tatamagouche, NS
Nova Scotia Environmental Network 2012 Annual General Meeting
Other Conferences in 2012 2012, NS
Nova Scotia Environmental Network 2012 Annual Roundtable
Other Conferences in 2012 2012, NS
Nova Scotia Environmental Network 2012 Annual Book Club
Other Conferences in 2012 2012, NS
Publications: *Eco-Connections [a publication of the Nova Scotia Environmental Network]*
Type: Newsletter *Frequency:* m. *Price:* Free with Nova Scotia Environmental Network membership
Profile: A bulletin about Nova Scotia Environmental Network's activities & environmental actions
Nova Scotia Environmental Network Annual Activity Report
Type: Yearbook *Frequency:* a.
Profile: A report of activities plus financial statements for the Canadian Environmental Network
By-Laws of the Nova Scotia Environmental Network (NSEN)
General Policies of the Nova Scotia Environmental Network (NSEN)
Profile: Topics include membership, the duties of the board, delegate selection, purchasing, the newsletter, mailing lists, meeting protocol, rights & responsibilities of general members, duties of the executive director, the caucus, working groups, & duties of the member representative
Mission: To conserve & enhance the natural environment; To achieve a sustainable future for Nova Scotia; To connect environmental & health organizations; Affiliation(s): Canadian Environmental Network (CEN)
Environmental Activity: Increasing community awareness of environmental conservation; Promoting sustainability; Presenting Eco-Hero awards; Networking with other environmental & health organizations in Nova Scotia

Nova Scotia Federation of Agriculture (NSFA)
Parent: Canadian Federation of Agriculture
Covington Place, 332 Willow St., 2nd Fl., Truro NS B2N 5A5
Tel: 902-893-2293; *Fax:* 902-893-7063
e-mail: info@nsfa-fane.ca
URL: www.nsfa-fane.ca
Overview: A medium-sized provincial organization founded in 1895
Membership: 1,800+; *Member Profile:* Individual farm businesses in Nova Scotia which represent all aspects of primary agriculture; Corporations
Activities: Reviewing legislative & regulatory issues & lobbying for change; Developing & delivering programs to meet the needs of the farm community, such a environmental farm planning services
Mission: To act as the voice for the agricultural community in Nova Scotia; To ensure a competitive & sustainable future for agriculture in Nova Scotia; To build financially viable, ecologically sound, & socially responsible farm businesses in the province; *Member of:* Canadian Federation of Agriculture

Nova Scotia Fish Packers Association (NSFPA)
38B John St., Yarmouth NS B5A 3H2
Tel: 902-742-6168; *Fax:* 902-742-1620
e-mail: fishpackers@klis.com
URL: www.fishpackers.com
Previous Name: Southwestern Nova Scotia Fish Packers Association
Overview: A small local organization founded in 1972
Finances: *Annual Operating Budget:* $50,000-$100,000
Staff: 1 staff member(s)
Membership: 44; *Fees:* $950-$2300 plus HST; $400 associate; *Member Profile:* Fish processing companies dealing with a wide variety of seafood for Canadian & export sales
Mission: To ensure the survival of a competitive seafood processing industry in Nova Scotia; to provide leadership on industry issues, effective representation with government, R&D, project management, & volume discount purchases

Nova Scotia Forest Products Association *See* Forest Products Association of Nova Scotia

Nova Scotia Forest Technicians Association (NSFTA)
164 Forest Hills Drive, Truro NS B2N 2B7
e-mail: nsfta@nsfta.com
URL: www.nsfta.ca
Overview: A small provincial organization
Chief Officer(s):
Lloyd Morgan, President
Finances: *Annual Operating Budget:* Less than $50,000
Staff: 12 volunteer(s)
Membership: 200 individual; *Fees:* $35 regular; $70 certified; *Member Profile:* Forest technicians; technologists
Activities: *Library:* Yes, Open to public

Nova Scotia Forestry Association (NSFA)
Parent: Canadian Forestry Association
PO Box 6901, Port Hawkesbury NS B9A 2W2
Tel: 902-625-2935
e-mail: dwaycott@nsfa.ca
URL: www.nsfa.ca
Overview: A medium-sized provincial charitable organization founded in 1959
Finances: *Funding Sources:* Sponships
Activities: Conducting programs in schools, such as Envirothon; Advocating for the full development, utilization, & protection of forests in Nova Scotia; Promoting reforestation; *Awareness Events:* Arbor Day, Sept.
Mission: To conserve Nova Scotia's forests; To promote the wise use & management of forest resources

Nova Scotia Fruit Growers' Association (NSFGA)
Kentville Agricultural Centre, 32 Main St., Kentville NS B4N 1J5
Tel: 902-678-1093; *Fax:* 902-679-1567
URL: www.nsapples.com
Overview: A small provincial organization founded in 1863
Finances: *Annual Operating Budget:* $100,000-$250,000
Staff: 10 staff member(s); 16 volunteer(s)
Membership: 220; *Fees:* $225.60-$1,804.84
Mission: To serve the interests of tree fruit growers in Nova Scotia; *Member of:* Canadian Horticulture Council; *Affiliation(s):* Nova Scotia Federation of Agriculture

Nova Scotia Ground Water Association (NSGWA)
Parent: Canadian Ground Water Association
#417, 3 - 644 Portland St., Dartmouth NS B2W 2M3
Fax: 902-435-0089
Toll-Free: 888-242-4440
e-mail: nsgwa@ns.aliantzinc.ca
URL: www.nsgwa.ca
Previous Name: Nova Scotia Well Drillers Association
Overview: A medium-sized provincial organization
Fees: $175; *Member Profile:* Well drillers; Well diggers; Pump installers; Manufacturers; Suppliers; Technicians
Activities: Increasing public awareness; Encouraging partnerships; Providing continuing education; Presenting awards
Mission: To act as the voice of the industry to all levels of government; To encourage the management & protection of ground water; *Member of:* Canadian Ground Water Association

The Nova Scotia Highway Safety Council *See* Nova Scotia Safety Council

Nova Scotia Institute of Agrologists (NSIA)
Parent: Agricultural Institute of Canada
PO Box 550, 35 Tower Rd., Truro NS B2N 5E3
Tel: 902-893-6520; *Fax:* 902-893-6393
e-mail: nsagrologists@eastlink.ca
URL: www.nsagrologists.ca
Overview: A medium-sized provincial licensing organization founded in 1953
Finances: *Annual Operating Budget:* Less than $50,000; *Funding Sources:* Membership dues
Staff: 15 volunteer(s)
Membership: 300; *Fees:* $110
Activities: *Internships:* Yes; *Speaker Service:* Yes; *Library:* Yes, Not open to the public
Awards: Outstanding Farmer (Award)
Outstanding Young Agrologist (Award)
Distinguished Life Member (Award)
Distinguished Agrologist (Award)
NSIA Scholarship (Scholarship)
Award Amount: $1,000

Honourary Member (Award)
C.A. Douglas Award (Award)
NSIA 50th Anniversary Scholarship (Scholarship)
Award Amount: $1,000

Nova Scotia Lung Association (LANS)
Parent: Canadian Lung Association
6331 Lady Hammond Rd., Halifax NS B3K 2S2
Tel: 902-443-8141; *Fax:* 902-445-2573
Toll-Free: 888-566-5864
e-mail: info@ns.lung.ca
URL: www.ns.lung.ca
Overview: A small provincial charitable organization founded in 1909
Finances: *Funding Sources:* Donations; Fundraising; Sponsorships
Activities: Offering education to Nova Scotians; Supporting research; Engaging in advocacy activities; Providing information & peer support to help people with COPD; Offering a camp for children with asthma; *Library:* Nova Scotia Lung Association Resource Library; Open to public
Mission: To control & prevent lung disease in Nova Scotia; To help people who live with lung disease
Environmental Activity: Providing tobacco control & environmental information

Nova Scotia Mackerel Association
PO Box 34, RR#2, Hubbards NS B0J 1T0
Tel: 902-857-3619
Overview: A small provincial organization founded in 1992
Chief Officer(s):
Robert Conrad, President

Nova Scotia Nature Trust (NSNT)
PO Box 2202, 2085 Maitland St., Halifax NS B3J 3C4
Tel: 902-425-5263; *Fax:* 902-429-5263
Toll-Free: 877-434-5263
e-mail: nature@nsnt.ca
URL: www.nsnt.ca
Overview: A medium-sized provincial organization founded in 1994
Chief Officer(s):
Nil d'Entremont, President
Bonnie Sutherland, Executive Director
Mission: To protect Nova Scotia's outstanding natural legacy through land conservation.

Nova Scotia Public Interest Research Group (NSPIRG)
#314, 6136 University Ave., Halifax NS B3H 4J2
Tel: 902-494-6662; *Fax:* 902-494-5185
e-mail: nspirg@is2.dal.ca
URL: www.nspirg.org
Overview: A medium-sized local organization
Chief Officer(s):
Jayme Melrose, Contact
Asaf Rashid, Contact
Finances: *Annual Operating Budget:* Less than $50,000
Membership: 5,000-14,999; *Fees:* $4; *Member Profile:* Dalhousie University students
Activities: Working Groups: Economic Justice; Eco Action; Food Co-Op; Animal Rights; Women's Health; Community Garden; Peace Action; Humans Against Homophobia; Education Network; *Speaker Service:* Yes; *Library:* Resource Library
Mission: To link research with social justice & environmental action

Nova Scotia Safety Council
Vantage Point 3, #3F, 110 Chain Lake Dr., Halifax NS B3S 1A9
Tel: 902-454-9621; *Fax:* 902-454-6027
URL: www.nssafety.ns.ca
Previous Name: The Nova Scotia Highway Safety Council
Overview: A small provincial organization founded in 1958
Finances: *Funding Sources:* Membership; courses; provincial government
Fees: $99 personal; $375 company; $655 enhanced corporate; $2200 partner in safety; *Member Profile:* Members include Nova Scotian businesses, government departments, charitable agencies, families, & hospital & police services.
Activities: Informing members of injury trends, new legislation, or anything that may affect the health & safety of members, their coworkers, family, & friends; *Library:* Yes
Publications: *Safety Lines*
Type: Newsletter *Frequency:* q.
Mission: The Safety Council develops & provides quality safety & health services, education & training programs to improve the

Associations/Organizations / Nova Scotia Salmon Association

quality of life of Nova Scotians.; Affiliation(s): Canada Safety Council

Nova Scotia Salmon Association (NSSA)
PO Box 396, Chester NS B0J 1J0
e-mail: nssalmo@yahoo.ca
URL: www.novascotiasalmon.ns.ca
Overview: A medium-sized provincial charitable organization founded in 1963
Chief Officer(s):
Carl Purcell, President, 902-466-3024
c.purcell@ns.sympatico.ca
Finances: *Funding Sources:* Donations
Fees: $20; $5 junior; *Member Profile:* Individuals with an interest in the welfare of salmon & trout; Affiliate associations
Activities: Increasing public awareness; Offering educational activities; Conducting & supporting research; Administering programs, such as Adopt-A-Stream;
Mission: To further the conservation & wise management of wild Atlantic salmon & trout; *Member of:* Atlantic Salmon Federation

Nova Scotia Swordfish Fishermen's Association
#9, 155 Chain Lake Dr., Halifax NS B3S 1B3
Tel: 902-875-2052; *Fax:* 902-875-1573
Overview: A small provincial organization
Chief Officer(s):
George Rennehan, Vice-President

Nova Scotia Well Drillers Association *See* Nova Scotia Ground Water Association

Nova Scotia Wild Flora Society
c/o Nova Scotia Museum, 1747 Summer St., Halifax NS B3H 3A6
Tel: 902-423-7032
URL: www.chebucto.ns.ca/~nswfs
Overview: A small provincial organization founded in 1990
Chief Officer(s):
Heather Drope, Sec.-Treas.
Finances: *Annual Operating Budget:* Less than $50,000; *Funding Sources:* Membership dues
Staff: 2 volunteer(s)
Membership: 50; *Fees:* $15 individual; $20 family
Member of: Federation of Nova Scotia Naturalists; *Affiliation(s):* Canadian Wildflower Society

Nova Scotian Institute of Science (NSIS)
Science Services, Killam Library, Dalhousie Univ., 6225 University Ave., Halifax NS B3H 4H8
Tel: 902-494-3621; *Fax:* 902-494-2062
e-mail: nsis@chebucto.ns.ca
URL: www.chebucto.ns.ca/Science/NSIS
Overview: A medium-sized provincial organization founded in 1862
Fees: $20 regular; $10 student; $300 life members; *Member Profile:* Individual with an amateur or professional interest in science
Activities: Conducting the NSIS Student Essay Competition; Providing a public lecture series; *Library:* Killam Library, Dalhousie University, Halifax, NS
Mission: To provide a forum for scientists & those interested in science

NSERC/Petro-Canada Chair for Women in Science & Engineering
c/o Faculty of Engineering & Applied Sciences, Memorial University, St. John's NL A1B 3X5
Tel: 709-737-7960; *Fax:* 709-737-7658
e-mail: cwse@morgan.ucs.mun.ca
URL: www.mun.ca/cwse/
Overview: A medium-sized national organization founded in 1977
Chief Officer(s):
Carolyn J. Emerson, Chair, Atlantic Region
Finances: *Annual Operating Budget:* Less than $50,000
Membership: 360; *Fees:* $250 corporate; $40 full; $25 associate; $10 student; $20 information (receives newsletter)
Activities: Speaker Service: Yes
Mission: To encourage women in Canada to enter careers in science, engineering, mathematics & computer sciences; to encourage women in Canada to attain high levels of professional achievement in these fields; to serve as an information centre for & about women in these fields; to make people aware of Canadian women scientists & engineers & of career opportunities available to them; to provide a forum for discussion of subjects of interest to members

Nuclear Information & Resource Service (NIRS)
#340, 6930 Carroll St., Tacoma Park MD 20912 USA
Tel: 301-270-6477; *Fax:* 301-270-4291
e-mail: nirsnet@nirs.org
URL: www.nirs.org
Overview: A small international organization founded in 1978
Chief Officer(s):
Don Keesing, Administrative Coordinator
Michael Mariotte, Executive Director
Finances: *Annual Operating Budget:* $500,000-$1.5 Million
Staff: 8 staff member(s)
Activities: *Internships:* Yes; *Speaker Service:* Yes; *Library:* Yes, open by appointment
Affiliation(s): Nuclear Awareness Project

Nunavut Harvesters Association (NHA)
c/o Brian Zawadski, PO Box 249, Rankin Inlet NU X0C 0G0
Tel: 867-645-3170; *Fax:* 867-645-3755
e-mail: brian@ndcorp.nu.ca
URL: www.harvesters.nu.ca
Overview: A small provincial organization
Chief Officer(s):
Brian Zawadski, Executive Director, 867-645-3170
brian@ndcorp.nu.ca
Activities: Promoting conservation of wildlife & natural resources in Nunavut; Administering & delivering the Agriculture & Agri-Food Canada program, entitled Advancing Canadian Agriculture & Agri-Food
Mission: To develop & promote the sustainable harvesting of natural resources & wildlife in Nunavut

NWT & Nunavut Chamber of Mines
PO Box 2818, Yellowknife NT X1A 2R1
Tel: 867-873-5281; *Fax:* 867-920-2145
e-mail: nwtmines@ssimicro.com
URL: www.miningnorth.com
Previous Name: Northwest Territories Chamber of Mines
Overview: A medium-sized provincial organization founded in 1967
Finances: *Annual Operating Budget:* $100,000-$250,000; *Funding Sources:* Membership fees
Staff: 2 staff member(s); 25 volunteer(s)
Membership: 200 corporate + 600 individual + 9 senior/lifetime; *Fees:* Schedule available; *Member Profile:* Persons & corporations interested in, or associated with, mining industry in NWT & Nunavut
Activities: *Awareness Events:* Mining Week, June; GeoScience Forum, Nov.; *Library:* Yes, open by appointmentNot open to the public
Mission: To promote & assist the development & growth of mining & mineral exploration in NWT & Nunavut; *Affiliation(s):* Mining Association of Canada; Canadian Institute of Mining, Metallurgy & Petroleum

Oakville Community Centre for Peace, Ecology & Human Rights
PO Box 52007, Oakville ON L6J 7N5
Tel: 905-849-5501
e-mail: info@oakvillepeacecentre.org
URL: www.oakvillepeacecentre.org
Overview: A small local organization
Chief Officer(s):
Stephen Dankowich, Executive Director

Occupational & Environmental Medical Association of Canada (OEMAC) / Association canadienne de la médecine du travail et de l'environnement (ACMTE)
#1430, 1101 Upper Middle Rd. East, Oakville ON L6H 5Z9
Tel: 905-849-9925; *Fax:* 905-338-8523
e-mail: oemac@oemac.org
URL: www.oemac.org
Overview: A medium-sized national organization founded in 1983
Finances: *Annual Operating Budget:* $50,000-$100,000; *Funding Sources:* Membership fees
Staff: 1 staff member(s); 12 volunteer(s)
Membership: 30 senior/lifetime + 282 individual; *Fees:* $250; *Member Profile:* Licensed physicians with an interest in occupational medicine
Activities: Exchanging scientific & professional information
Publications: Liaison [a publication of the Occupational & Environmental Medical Association of Canada]
Type: Newsletter *Frequency:* q
Mission: To act as the voice of the Canadian occupational & environmental medicine sector; *Affiliation(s):* Canadian Medical Association; Canadian Board of Occupational Medicine; Royal College of Physicians & Surgeons of Canada

Occupational Health Clinics for Ontario Workers (OHCOW)
#601, 15 Gervais Dr., Toronto ON M3C 1Y8
Tel: 416-510-8713; *Fax:* 416-443-9132
Toll-Free: 877-817-0336
e-mail: info@ohcow.on.ca
URL: www.ohcow.on.ca
Overview: A medium-sized provincial organization
Chief Officer(s):
Lyle Hargrove, President
Mission: To prevent work-related illnesses & injuries; to improve workers' physical, mental & social well-being

Occupational Health Nurses of British Columbia (BCOHN)
c/o Elise Kobylanski, 4473 Gerrard Pl., Richmond BC V7E 6S6
URL: www.bcohn.ca
Also Known As: British Columbia Occupational Health Nurses Professional Practice Group (BCOHNPPG)
Overview: A small provincial organization founded in 1961
Chief Officer(s):
Margaret Smithson, President
president@bcohn.ca
Fees: $20 retired members; $65 all other members; *Member Profile:* Occupational health nurses in British Columbia, who are responsible for safe & healthy work environments, work practices, & workers
Activities: Providing information about occupational issues encountered by British Columbia's occupational health nurses;
Publications: BC Occupational Health Nurses PPG Newsletter
Type: Newsletter
Member of: CRNBC College of Registered Nurses Association of British Columbia

Occupational Hygiene Association of Ontario (OHAO)
6519B Mississauga Rd., Mississauga ON L5N 1A6
Tel: 905-567-7196; *Fax:* 905-567-7191
e-mail: office@ohao.org
URL: www.ohao.org
Overview: A medium-sized provincial organization founded in 1984
Chief Officer(s):
Jason Hoffman, President
Richard Quenneville, Sec.-Treas.
Peter Fletcher, Executive Manager
Finances: *Annual Operating Budget:* $50,000-$100,000; *Funding Sources:* Membership dues; seminars
Staff: 10 volunteer(s)
Membership: 300; *Fees:* $84 individual; $26.25 student; *Committees:* Education; Program; Membership; Public Affairs
Activities: Regional meetings; *Awareness Events:* Technical Symposia; *Speaker Service:* Yes; *Rents Mailing List:* Yes
Awards: Hugh Nelson Award (Award)
Presented to an individual who has made a significant long-term contribution to the advancement of occupational hygiene in Ontario
Mission: To protect people's health from hazards arising in or from the workplace; to develop & promote the profession of occupational hygiene; to sponsor professional development, training & research; to provide public education

The Ocean Conservancy
1300 19th St. NW, 8th Fl., Washington DC 20036 USA
Tel: 202-429-5609; *Fax:* 202-872-0619
Toll-Free: 800-519-1541
e-mail: info@oceanconservancy.org
URL: www.oceanconservancy.org
Previous Name: Center for Marine Conservation; Center for Environmental Education
Overview: A large international organization founded in 1972
Chief Officer(s):
Vikki N. Spruill, President & CEO
vspruill@oceanconservancy.org
Finances: *Annual Operating Budget:* $3 Million-$5 Million; *Funding Sources:* Bequests; contributions; grants
Staff: 40 staff member(s)
Membership: 110,000; *Fees:* Schedule available
Activities: Policy oriented research; promotion of public awareness through education; *Internships:* Yes
Mission: To protect ocean ecosystems & conserve the global abundance & diversity of marine wildlife

Associations/Organizations / Ocean Net

Ocean Net
276 Water St., St. John's NL A1C 1B7
Tel: 709-753-3680
e-mail: info@oceannet.ca
URL: www.oceannet.ca
Overview: A small provincial organization
Chief Officer(s):
Robert O'Brien, Founder/Chair
Fees: $20 individual; $25 family; $30 association; $150 corporate
Mission: To help reverse the polluting of the world's ocean's

The Oceanography Society
PO Box 1931, Rockville MD 20849-1931 USA
Tel: 301-251-7708; *Fax:* 301-251-7709
e-mail: info@tos.org
URL: www.tos.org
Overview: A small international organization founded in 1988
Chief Officer(s):
Jennifer Ramarui, Executive Director
Publications: *Oceanography*
Editor: Dr. Ellen Kappel *ISSN:* 1042-8275
Profile: Monthly magazine; peer reviewed

Office de vente des produits forestiers du Madawaska / Madawaska Forest Products Marketing Board
CP 5, 870, rue Canada, Edmundston NB E3V 3X3
Tél: 506-739-9585; *Téléc:* 506-739-0859
Également appelé: Office de vente du Madawaska
Aperçu: *Dimension:* petite; *Envergure:* locale; *Organisme sans but lucratif;* fondée en 1962
Membre(s) du bureau directeur:
Claude A. Pelletier, Directeur général
Finances: *Budget de fonctionnement annuel:* $100,000-$250,000
Personnel: 7 membre(s) du personnel
Membre: 2 200 individu; 400 associé
Mission: Mise en marché des produits forestiers bruts; encourager les bonnes pratiques d'aménagement forestier; *Membre de:* La Fédération des Propriétaires de Lots Boisés du Nouveau Brunswick

Office des normes générales du Canada *See* Canadian General Standards Board

Office of Greening Government Operations (OGGO)
Toll-Free: 800-622-6232
URL: www.greeninggovernment.ca
Chief Officer(s):
Nigel Marsh, Contact, 416-241-4000 Ext. 221
nigel.marsh@govpages.ca
Mission: Greening Government is an electronic information system developed by the Government of Canada for the internet. It is designed to provide a one-window access to sustainable development in government operations knowledge in the Government of Canada. This website was developed to support the Sustainable Development in Government Operations (SDGO) initiative, whose purpose is to coordinate the federal effort to green government operations & encourage the report of concrete results among the departments & agencies that prepare Sustainable Development Strategies (SDSs). There are seven priority areas of operations: Energy Efficiency/Buildings, Human Resources Management, Land Use Management, Procurement, Vehicle Fleet Management, Waste Management & Water Conservation & Wastewater Management

Offshore Energy Environmental Research Association (OEER)
Bank of Montreal Building, PO Box 2664, #400, 5151 George St., Halifax NS B3J 3P7
Tel: 902-424-8479; *Fax:* 902-424-0528
Toll-Free: 888-257-8688
e-mail: oeer@offshoreenergyresearch.ca
URL: www.offshoreenergyresearch.ca
Overview: A medium-sized provincial organization
Chief Officer(s):
Wayne St-Amour, Executive Director
w.st-amour@offshoreenergyresearch.ca
Finances: *Funding Sources:* Grants, Provincial government, Universities
Membership: 4 institutional
Mission: To build research capacity in Nova Scotia and to assess the potential impacts of: petroleum exploration, development and production and renewable energy technologies (ocean currents, wind, tides and waves) on the marine environment.
Environmental Activity: Research projects

Okanagan Mainline Municipal Association; Okanagan Valley Municipal Association; Okanagan Valley Mayors & Reeves Association *See* Southern Interior Local Government Association

Okanagan Similkameen Parks Society (OSPS)
PO Box 787, Summerland BC V0H 1Z0
Tel: 250-494-8996; *Fax:* 250-494-3131
e-mail: anglerem@telus.net
Overview: A small local charitable organization founded in 1965
Finances: *Annual Operating Budget:* Less than $50,000; *Funding Sources:* Donations; membership fees; bequests; Penticton Foundation
Membership: 273; *Fees:* $10 single; $15 couple/family; $20 organization; *Member Profile:* Interest in parks; land & wildlife stewardship/conservation; historic trails; forestry practices; watershed protection; urban green spaces
Activities: Monthly meetings; special events; seminars; workshops; film; brochures & booklets; *Awareness Events:* Meadowlark Festival, Penticton - May
Member of: West Coast Environmental Law; Sierra Club; *Affiliation(s):* Friends of Stikine; Friends of Strathcona Park; Creston Wildlife; Okanagan Naturalists

Oliver-Osoyoos Naturalists
PO Box 1181, Osoyoos BC V0H 1V0
Tel: 250-495-6907
e-mail: hwbking@telus.net
Overview: A small local organization founded in 1973
Finances: *Annual Operating Budget:* Less than $50,000
Membership: 75; *Fees:* $20 individual; $25 family; *Member Profile:* People interested in nature & the environment
Activities: Walks; hiking; bird watching; outdoor education; caretaking of two ecological reserves; environmental restoration; "clean-up" projects.
Mission: To cooperate and communicate with other naturalists. To foster an awareness, appreciation and understanding of our natural environment so that it may be wisely used and maintained for future generations.; *Member of:* The Federation of BC Naturalists

One Sky: Canadian Institute of Sustainable Living
PO Box 3352, 3768 2nd Ave., Smithers BC V0J 1N0
Tel: 250-877-6030
URL: www.onesky.ca
Overview: A medium-sized national organization
Finances: *Funding Sources:* Donations
Fees: $10
Activities: Current projects include: GO2 Carshare Cooperative; Leading from Within - Integral Leadership for Sustainable Development; Fire and Ice; Athletes for Africa
Mission: A not-for-profit, non-governmental organization dedicated to a vision of an environmentally sustainable and socially just world, and the promotion of sustainable living globally. It seeks to inspire and promote solutions, provide practical solutions, and network across sectors with like-minded organizations.; *Member of:* Canadian Renewable Energy Alliance; *Affiliation(s):* BC Sustainable Energy Association

ONEIA - Ontario Environment Industry Association
2395 Speakman Drive, Mississauga ON L5K 1B3
Tel: 416-531-7884; *Fax:* 905-855-0406
e-mail: info@oneia.ca
URL: www.oneia.ca
Also Known As: Ontario Environmental Industry Association
Previous Name: Canadian Environment Industry Association - Ontario Chapter
Overview: A medium-sized provincial organization founded in 1991
Chief Officer(s):
Shai Spetgang, Manager, Membership Recruitment and Sponsor Relations
sspetgang@oneia.ca
Alex Gill, Executive Director
Finances: *Annual Operating Budget:* $100,000-$250,000; *Funding Sources:* Membership dues; projects
Staff: 1 staff member(s); 12 volunteer(s)
Membership: 167; *Fees:* $395-$1,375; *Member Profile:* Ontario-based companies, business associations & organizations which actively provide environmental technologies & services that help protect or improve the environment & that help achieve sustainable development; *Committees:* Advocacy; Business Development; Member Services
Activities: Has been an active participant in a number of initiatives - the Green Industry Strategy for Ontario led by the Ministry of Energy in collaboration with MOE & MITT; the 3R's Municipal Infrastructure Task Force to implement the MOE's Waste Management Initiative; the CCME Task Force for a National Waste Management Strategy; the Canadian-American Environmental Marketing Council to establish a facilitation office in Washington DC for Canadian companies pursuing the USA environmental market; *Library:* Yes, open by appointment
Mission: To promote the growth of environment business in Ontario; *Member of:* Canadian Environmental Auditing Association; CRESTech; Retail Council of Canada; *Affiliation(s):* Canadian Standards Association; Cements Association of Canada; Ontario Concrete Pipe Association; Ontario Sewer & Watermain Constructions Association; Ontario Environmental Training Consortium; Ontario Centre for Environmental Technology Advancement

Ontario Agri Business Association (OABA)
#104, 160 Research Lane, Guelph ON N1G 5B2
Tel: 519-822-3004; *Fax:* 519-822-8862
e-mail: info@oaba.on.ca
URL: www.oaba.on.ca
Merged from: Ontario Grain & Feed Association; Fertilizer Institute of Ontario
Overview: A medium-sized provincial organization founded in 1965
Finances: *Funding Sources:* Annual membership dues from regular, branch, &c associate members
Member Profile: Country grain elevators in Ontario; Ontario crop input supply businesses; Feed manufacturing facilities in the province; Associated businesses that provide products & services to the crop input, grain, & feed industry
Activities: Delivering products, programs, & services to members; Promoting the crop input, grain, & feed industry; Coordinating services of member sectors in areas such as food safety & environmental stewardship; Providing educational opportunities; Liaising with stakeholders, consumers, & government; Studying legislation affecting members; Disseminating information to members; Engaging in & sponsoring research
Mission: To serve & represent firms engaged in the crop inputs, country grain elevator, & feed & farm supply industy, plus related agricultural businesses operating within Ontario; *Member of:* Canadian Fertilizer Institute; Animal Nutrition Association of Canada

Ontario Agricultural Training Institute (OATI)
#101, 450 Speedvale Ave. West, Guelph ON N7M 7Y6
Tel: 519-763-3160; *Fax:* 519-763-9585
Overview: A medium-sized provincial organization founded in 1989
Chief Officer(s):
Ian Barrett, Executive Director
Carolyn Pletsch, Project Director
Finances: *Annual Operating Budget:* $500,000-$1.5 Million
Membership: 1-99
Activities: Training & development; administer provincial segment of federal government program; *Internships:* Yes; *Speaker Service:* Yes; *Library:* Yes
Mission: To strengthen rural communities by providing superior, specialized, accessible training & development activities

Ontario Agri-Food Education Inc. (OAFE)
PO Box 460, 8560 Tremaine Rd., Milton ON L9T 4Z1
Tel: 905-878-1510; *Fax:* 905-878-0342
e-mail: info@oafe.org
URL: www.oafe.org
Overview: A small provincial organization founded in 1991
Chief Officer(s):
Colleen Smith-Robinson, Executive Director
Fees: $50 individual
Mission: To build awareness & understanding of the importance of an agriculture & food sector; to provide high quality, objective & relevant agriculture & food related learning materials & services for Ontario educators to enhance the learning experiences of students in Ontario classrooms

Ontario Allergy Society *See* Allergy, Asthma & Immunology Society of Ontario

Ontario Asbestos Removal Contractors Association *See* Environmental Abatement Council of Ontario

Associations/Organizations / Ontario Association for Geographic & Environmental Education

Ontario Association for Geographic & Environmental Education (OAGEE) / Association pour l'enseignement de la géographie et de l'environnement en Ontario (AEGEO)
#202, 10 Morrow Ave., Toronto ON M6R 2J1
URL: www.oagee.org
Overview: A small provincial organization founded in 1949
Chief Officer(s):
Mark Lowry, President
Shawn Hughes, Vice-President, Membership Services, 705-742-9221
shawn_hughes@kprdsb.ca
Joe Maurice, Vice-President, Communications
Paul VanZant, Vice-President, Curriculum
Jennifer Farrell-Cordon, Secretary
Lew French, Treasurer
Fees: $25 university students & faculty; $30 retired members; $50 individuals; *Member Profile:* Teachers of geography from across Ontario
Activities: Providing information & resources to elementary & secondary school teachers of geography & environmental education
Meetings/Conferences:
For more information see Trade Shows, Conferences and Seminars Chapter
Ontario Association for Geographic & Environmental Education 2011 Fall Conference
Other Conferences in 2011 2011, ON
Publications: *The Monograph Editor*
Type: Journal *Frequency:* q. *Editor:* Gary Birchall *Price:* Free with Ontario Association of Geographic & Environmental Education membership
Profile: Lesson plans & activities, for geography courses, designed by teachers

Ontario Association for Impact Assessment (OAIA)
PO Box 2727, Stn. D, Ottawa ON K1P 5W7
e-mail: info@oaia.on.ca
URL: www.oaia.on.ca
Overview: A medium-sized provincial organization
Chief Officer(s):
John McCauley, President
Fees: $40 regular; $10 student

Ontario Association of Agricultural Societies (OAAS)
PO Box 189, Glencoe ON N0L 1M0
Tel: 519-287-3553; *Fax:* 519-287-2000
e-mail: oaas@bellnet.ca
URL: www.ontariofairs.com
Overview: A medium-sized provincial organization founded in 1900
Chief Officer(s):
Harry Emmott, President
Finances: *Annual Operating Budget:* $50,000-$100,000
Staff: 3 staff member(s)
Membership: 234; *Fees:* Depends on size of fair; *Member Profile:* Open to agricultural fair or service manager
Mission: To provide education, information & leadership to members & to act as a single voice when dealing with members, media, public & government; *Member of:* Canadian Association of Fairs & Exhibitions; International Association of Fairs & Expositions

Ontario Association of Certified Engineering Technicians & Technologists (OACETT)
#404, 10 Four Seasons Pl., Toronto ON M9B 6H7
Tel: 416-621-9621; *Fax:* 416-621-8694
e-mail: info@oacett.org
URL: www.oacett.org
Overview: A small provincial organization founded in 1957
Finances: *Annual Operating Budget:* $1.5 Million-$3 Million
Staff: 18 staff member(s); 300 volunteer(s)
Fees: Schedule available
Activities: *Internships:* Yes; *Speaker Service:* Yes
Mission: To advance the profession of applied science & engineering technology through standards for society's benefit.; *Member of:* Canadian Council of Technicians & Technologists

Ontario Association of Landscape Architects (OALA)
#407, 3 Church St., Toronto ON M5E 1M2
Tel: 416-231-4181; *Fax:* 416-231-2679
e-mail: oala@oala.ca
URL: www.oala.ca
Overview: A medium-sized provincial licensing organization founded in 1968
Finances: *Annual Operating Budget:* $3 Million-$5 Million; *Funding Sources:* Membership dues
Staff: 2 staff member(s); 100 volunteer(s)
Membership: 690 full + 250 associate + 20 affiliate; *Fees:* $696.25 full; $150 associate; $141.75 affiliate; *Member Profile:* Professional landscape architects; *Committees:* Ethics; Honours, Awards & Protocol; Discipline; Continuing Education; Marketing
Activities: *Internships:* Yes; *Library:* Yes, Not open to the public
Awards: Emeritus & Honorary Award (Award)
Honorary members being non-landscape architects appointed by Council, nominated by another member
Public Practice Award (Award)
Recognizes the outstanding leadership of a member of the profession in public practice who promotes & enhances landscape architecture by working for improved understanding & appreciation of the work of landscape architects in both public & private practice
Carl Borgstrom Award for Service to the Environment (Award)
Given to an individual landscape architect or landscape architectural group, organization or agency to recognize & encourage a special or unusual contribution to the sensitive, sustainable design for human use of the environment
OALA Award for Service to the Environment (Award)
Given to a non-landscape architectural individual, group, organization or agency to recognize & encourage a special or unusual contribution to the sensitive, sustainable design for human use of the environment
Pinnacle Award for Landscape Architectural Excellence (Award)
Recognizes an OALA member and their professional work
David Erb Memorial Award (Award)
Recognizes an OALA member who has made an exemplary voluntary contribution to the work of the association
Mission: To promote, improve & advance the profession; to maintain standards of professional practice & conduct consistent with the need to serve & to protect the public interest; to support improvement &/or conservation of the natural, cultural, social & built environment; *Member of:* Canadian Society of Landscape Architects; Council of Landscape Architectural Registration Boards; *Affiliation(s):* American Society of Landscape Architects

Ontario Automotive Recyclers Association (OARA)
Parent: **Automotive Recyclers of Canada**
#1, 1447 Upper James Street, Hamilton ON L8W 3J6
Tel: 905-383-9788; *Fax:* 905-383-1904
Toll-Free: 800-390-8743
e-mail: admin@oara.com
URL: www.oara.com
Overview: A small provincial organization founded in 1992
Chief Officer(s):
Steve Fletcher, Executive Director
Finances: *Funding Sources:* Membership fees
Staff: 3 staff member(s)
Membership: 170; *Fees:* $150-$500; *Member Profile:* Automotove recyclers; Direct Members must demonstrate compliance with the Ontario Certified Auto Recylcers Program; *Committees:* Government Affairs; Health & Safety; Meetings; Membership; Salvage & Licencing; Transportation; Budget & Audit; Nominations
Activities: *Rents Mailing List:* Yes
Mission: The association is the voice of the automotive recycling industry in Ontario. OARA works to improve recycling industry practices, and to promote the benefits of responsbile auto recycling to the general public, to stakeholders, and to local and provincial governments.

Ontario Beef Improvement Association *See* **Ontario Cattlemen's Association**

Ontario Camping Association *See* **Ontario Camps Association**

Ontario Camps Association (OCA)
Parent: **Canadian Camping Association**
#403, 250 Merton St., Toronto ON M4S 1B1
Tel: 416-485-0425; *Fax:* 416-485-0422
e-mail: info@ontariocamps.ca
URL: www.ontariocamps.ca
Previous Name: Ontario Camping Association
Overview: A medium-sized provincial organization founded in 1937
Chief Officer(s):
Rick Howard, President
Aruna Ogale, Executive Director
aruna@ontariocamps.ca
Member Profile: Ontario camps which meet the association's standards; Individuals; Like-minded organizations & agencies
Activities: Enforcing camp standards, through inspections, in order to ensure sound camp operation & administration & safe camping experiences; Sharing information & ideas; Supporting training seminars & workshops; Informing the public about the benefits of camping & the role of the association; Conducting research, through the OCA Educational Research Task Force
Publications: *OCA [Ontario Camps Association] Camps Guide*
Type: Directory *Frequency:* a. *Accepts Advertising :* Yes
Profile: Listings & descriptions of accredited camps in Ontario
OCA [Ontario Camps Association] Bulletin
Type: Newsletter
Ontario Camps Association's Guidelines for Accreditation
Price: $15
Profile: Addressing aspects of a day or residential camp's operations, such as health & safety, facilities, & leadership
Camp Health Issues
Price: $20
Profile: Articles about health & safety issues at camps
OCA [Ontario Camps Association] Crisis Response & Management Plan
Price: $10.50
Profile: Information about managing a crisis, plus forms for camps to use, such as a crisis response log, & a parent / guardian call form
How to be a Camp Counsellor . . . The Best Job in the World!
Author: Catherine Ross *Price:* $19.95
Profile: Tips & tools to become a summer camp counsellor, such as leadership styles, teaching techniques, & behaviour management
Mission: To promote youth camping throughout Ontario; To maintain high standards for organized camping; To advocate on issues which impact members

Ontario Cattlemen's Association (OCA) / Association ontarienne des éleveurs de bovins
130 Malcolm Rd., Guelph ON N1K 1B1
Tel: 519-824-0334; *Fax:* 519-824-9101
e-mail: ontbeef@cattle.guelph.on.ca
URL: www.cattle.guelph.on.ca
Previous Name: Ontario Beef Improvement Association
Overview: A medium-sized provincial organization founded in 1963
Member Profile: Cattle producers in Ontario; *Committees:* Cow / Calf; Feedlot; Research
Activities: Providing education & information to Ontario cattlemen; Engaging in advocacy activities on behalf of the Ontario beef industry; Liaising with government; Initiating studies, programs, & reviews; Encouraging economically sustainable production methods; Promoting Quality Starts Here programs to beef producers across Ontario; Developing domestic & export markets Promoting beef
Awards: The Environmental Stewardship Award (Award)
Meetings/Conferences:
For more information see Trade Shows, Conferences and Seminars Chapter
Ontario Cattlemen's Association 2012 Annual Convention
Other Conferences in 2012 2012, ON
Publications: *Ontario Beef*
Type: Magazine *Frequency:* 5 pa *Accepts Advertising* : Yes
Editor: Lianne Appleby *Price:* Free for members of the Ontario Cattlemen's Association
Profile: Information for producers, featuring articles of interest in the beef industry, research, market information, producer profiles, & current policy issues
OCA [Ontario Cattlemen's Association] Weekly Update
Type: Newsletter *Frequency:* w. *Editor:* Lianne Appleby
The Ontario Steakholder
Type: Newsletter *Frequency:* irregular *Editor:* Lianne Appleby
Profile: A timely publication for Ontario's MPs & MPPs to connect them with Ontario's beef farmers
Ontario Cattlemen's Association Production Guides
Type: Guide
Profile: Production information of a wide variety of topics
Mission: To foster a sustainable & profitable beef industry in Ontario; To provide programs & serivces to support local cattlemen's associations & provincial cattlemen in general; To lobby on issues at the provincial & national level; *Member of:* Canadian Cattlemen's Association
Environmental Activity: Encouraging environmentally sustainable production methods; Analyzing government regulations related to water quality issues; Evaluating & advising on nutrient management legislation; Conducting research on environmental issues

Ontario Centre of Excellence for Photonics
#200, 156 Front St. West, Toronto ON M5J 2L6

Associations/Organizations / Ontario Centres of Excellence - Centre for Earth & Environmental Technologies

Tel: 416-861-1092; *Fax:* 416-971-7164
Toll-Free: 866-759-6014
e-mail: don.wilford@oce-ontario.org
URL: www.oce-ontario.org/Pages/COEPhotonics.aspx
Overview: A medium-sized provincial organization
Chief Officer(s):
Donald Wilford, Managing Director
Marc Nantel, Director, Business Development, 416-861-1092 Ext. 1025
marc.nantel@oce-ontario.org
Activities: Establishing regional & international collaborations with companies that advance photonic technologies in a number of areas; Assisting Ontario firms and organizations; co-investing in the research & development of technologies
Mission: To create new photonics technology & knowledge; to enhance applications & commercialization of scientific discoveries; *Member of:* Ontario Centres for Excellence (OCE)

Ontario Centres of Excellence - Centre for Earth & Environmental Technologies (OCE-ETech)
#200, 156 Front St. West, Toronto ON M5J 2L6
Tel: 416-861-1092; *Fax:* 416-971-7164
Toll-Free: 866-759-6014
e-mail: anne.wettlaufer@oce-ontario.org
URL: www.oce-ontario.org
Overview: A large provincial organization founded in 1987
Chief Officer(s):
Tom Corr, President & CEO
tom.corr@oce-ontario.org
Tanya Dunn, Executive Assistant, Office of President
tanya.dunn@oce-ontario.org
Awards: Martin Walmsley Fellowship for Technological Entrepreneurship (Award)
Annual Media Award (Award)
Mission: ETech engages firms, clients & academic partners in the following areas: clean water technologies, resource management, sustainable agricultue & agri-food, sustainable infrastructure, clean air technologies, waste management & sustainable infrastrucutre; organizations & academics are encouraged to contact ETech to find out how to access the broad range of services available

Ontario Clean Air Alliance (OCAA)
#300, 160 John St., Toronto ON M5V 2E5
Tel: 416-260-2080; *Fax:* 416-598-9520
e-mail: contact@cleanairalliance.org
URL: www.cleanairalliance.org
Overview: A medium-sized provincial organization founded in 1997
Chief Officer(s):
Jack Gibbons, Chair, 416-260-2080 Ext. 2
jack@cleanairalliance.org
Angela Bischoff, Director, Outreach, 416-260-2080 Ext. 1
Angela@cleanairalliance.org
Finances: *Funding Sources:* Donations
Member Profile: Organizations & individuals who work for cleaner air through a coal phase-out & a move to a renewable electricity future
Publications: *Finishing the Coal Phase Out: An Historic Opportunity for Climate Leadership*
Type: Report
Profile: A review of the Government of Ontario's coal phase-out to reduce greenhouse gas emission
Powerful Options: A Review of Ontario's Options for Replacing Aging Nuclear Plants
Type: Report *Number of Pages:* 18
Profile: A presentation of options for replacing nuclear plants that are less expensive than building new nuclear reactors
Ontario's Green Future: How We Can Build a 100% Renewable Electricity Grid by 2027
Type: Report *Number of Pages:* 32 *Author:* Jack Gibbons
Profile: An Ontario Clean Air Alliance report with recommendations
Ontario Clean Air Alliance E-Bulletin
Type: Newsletter *Frequency:* s-m.
Profile: The most recent news & reports about energy issues & air quality
Ontario's Coal Phase-Out: A Major Climate Accomplishment Within Our Grasp
Type: Report *Number of Pages:* 10
Profile: A review of the coal phase-out's progress
The Ontario Power Authority's Coal Phase-Out Strategy: A Critical Review
Type: Report *Number of Pages:* 13

Increasing Productivity & Moving Towards a Renewable Future: A New Electricity Strategy for Ontario
Type: Report *Number of Pages:* 60 *Author:* Jack Gibbons
Mission: To ensure that Ontario's electricity needs are met by ecologically sustainable renewable sources
Environmental Activity: Advocating for the phase-out of coal-fired power plants in Ontario in order to reduce greenhouse gas; Promoting energy conservation & efficiency & green power; Campaigning for a renewable electricity future in Ontario

Ontario Commercial Fisheries' Association (OCFA)
PO Box 2129, 45 James St., Blenheim ON N0P 1A0
Tel: 519-676-0488; *Fax:* 519-676-0944
Toll-Free: 800-461-7890
e-mail: ocfa@ocfa.on.ca
URL: www.ocfa.on.ca
Overview: A medium-sized provincial organization founded in 1945
Chief Officer(s):
Peter Meisenheimer, Executive Director
Finances: *Annual Operating Budget:* $500,000-$1.5 Million; *Funding Sources:* Membership dues; Contractual programs
Staff: 22 staff member(s); 19 volunteer(s)
Membership: 267; *Fees:* $150; *Member Profile:* Licensed Ontario commercial fishing license holders; Federal registered processing plants
Activities: Maintaining a code of conduct for responsible fishing practices; Hosting an annual convention
Mission: To be dedicated to the growth & continued strength of a responsible, competitive, & sustainable licensed commercial fishery in Ontario; To represent the industry's interests & its view to government, the media, & consumers

Ontario Community Transit Association (OCTA)
#306, 4141 Yonge St., Toronto ON M2P 2A8
Tel: 416-229-6222; *Fax:* 416-229-6281
URL: www.octa.on.ca
Previous Name: Ontario Urban Transit Association
Overview: A medium-sized provincial organization founded in 1997
Fees: Annual fees for transportation service providers & suppliers based on transportation operating budget or net sales; $160 non-profit organizations; *Member Profile:* Representatives of public transit systems; Health & social service agency transportation providers; Government representatives; Suppliers to the industry; Consultants
Activities: Engaging in advocacy activities; Sharing information
Publications: *OPTA [Ontario Community Transit Association] News*
Type: Newsletter *Frequency:* q.
Profile: Association activities & upcoming events
Mission: To strengthen & improve public transit services in Ontario; To ensure excellence & sustainability in public transit

Ontario Concrete Pipe Association (OCPA)
5045 South Service Rd., 1st Fl., Burlington ON L7L 5Y7
Tel: 905-631-9696; *Fax:* 905-631-1905
Toll-Free: 800-435-0116
e-mail: info@ocpa.com
URL: www.ocpa.com
Overview: A medium-sized provincial organization founded in 1957
Finances: *Annual Operating Budget:* $250,000-$500,000; *Funding Sources:* Membership dues
Staff: 2 staff member(s); 30 volunteer(s)
Membership: 40; *Member Profile:* Manufacturers of precast concrete pipe & associated products; *Committees:* Prequalification; Public Relations & Communications; Technical
Activities: *Awareness Events:* Construct Canada; Ontario Good Roads; *Speaker Service:* Yes; *Library:* Yes, open by appointment
Mission: To represent the concrete pipe & maintenance hole industry throughout Ontario; to promote engineered concrete products of permanence; *Member of:* Canadian Standards Association; *Affiliation(s):* Municipal Engineers Association; Canadian Concrete Pipe Association; Tubecon; American Concrete Pipe Association; Canadian Portland Cement Association; Water Environment Association of Ontario; Canadian Public Works Association; Ontario Sewer & Watermain Construction Association; Consulting Engineers of Ontario

Ontario Corn Producers' Association (OCPA)
#201, 100 Stone Rd. West, Guelph ON N1G 5L3
Tel: 519-837-1660; *Fax:* 519-837-1674
e-mail: ontcorn@ontariocorn.org
URL: www.ontariocorn.org

Overview: A medium-sized provincial organization
Chief Officer(s):
Brenda Miller-Sanford, Business Operations Manager
Finances: *Annual Operating Budget:* $1.5 Million-$3 Million; *Funding Sources:* Producer check-off
Staff: 8 staff member(s)
Membership: 21,000; *Member Profile:* Ontario commercial grain corn farmers; *Committees:* Safety Nets; Grain, Trade & Marketing; Research & Technology; Communications; Market Development; Farm Finance
Activities: Advance Payment for Crops; Gross Revenue Insurance Plan; Net Income Stabilization Account; corn research; ethanol
Member of: Ontario Agricultural Commodity Council; Ontario Federation of Agriculture

Ontario Creamerymen's Association
26 Dominion St., Alliston ON L9R 1L5
Tel: 705-435-6751; *Fax:* 705-435-6797
e-mail: allistoncreamery1@bellnet.ca
Overview: A small provincial organization founded in 1935
Finances: *Annual Operating Budget:* Less than $50,000; *Funding Sources:* Membership dues
Staff: 3 volunteer(s)

Ontario Dairy Council (ODC)
6533D Mississauga Rd., Mississauga ON L5N 1A6
Tel: 905-542-3620; *Fax:* 905-542-3624
Toll-Free: 866-542-3620
e-mail: info@ontariodairies.ca
URL: www.ontariodairies.ca
Overview: A medium-sized provincial organization founded in 1971
Finances: *Annual Operating Budget:* $500,000-$1.5 Million; *Funding Sources:* Membership fees
Staff: 3 staff member(s)
Membership: 40 corporate + 50 associate; *Fees:* Schedule available; *Member Profile:* Licensed processor, marketer or distributor; *Committees:* Technical; Advisory; Environment; Policy & Technical
Activities: *Library:* Yes, open by appointment
Mission: To represent interests of dairy product processors, marketers & distributors in Ontario; *Affiliation(s):* International Dairy Federation

Ontario Daylily Society (ODS)
6798 9th Line, R R#2, Beeton ON L0G 1A0
Tel: 905-729-2718
e-mail: cgharvey@eastlink.ca
URL: www.nsdaylilysociety.com
Overview: A small provincial organization founded in 1997
Chief Officer(s):
Faye Collins, President
president@ontariodaylily.on.ca
Fees: $8 youth; $20 individual; $25 family

Ontario Delphinium Club
c/o Christine Gill, 4691 Hwy. 7A, RR#1, Nestleton Station ON L0B 1L0
Tel: 905-986-0310
e-mail: ontdelphs@yahoo.ca
URL: www.ondelphiniums.com
Overview: A small provincial organization
Fees: $10 family

Ontario Electrical League (OEL)
#300, 180 Attwell Dr., Toronto ON M9W 6A9
Tel: 905-238-1382; *Fax:* 905-238-1420
e-mail: communications@oel.org
URL: www.oel.org
Overview: A medium-sized provincial organization founded in 1966
Membership: 21 chapters, with 2,500+ members; *Member Profile:* Educators; Electricians; Electrical contractors; Electrical inspectors; Manufacturers; Consulting engineers; Distributors
Activities: Promoting Ontario's electrical industry; Providing educational opportunities
Awards: EFC / OEL Scholarship (Scholarship)
A post-secondary school scholarship, for enrollment in an electrical or related program, for members of the Ontario Electrical League & their families
Publications: *Dialogue [a publication of the Ontario Electrical League]*
Type: Magazine *Frequency:* q. *Accepts Advertising :* Yes *Price:* Free with membership in the Ontario Electrical League
Profile: League activities, member news, plus updates about industry & government issues

Contractor Newsbrief [a publication of the Ontario Electrical League]
Type: Newsletter
Profile: Contractor Committee activities, for Ontario Electrical League contractor members
Contractor News [a publication of the Ontario Electrical League]
Type: Newsletter Frequency: m.
Profile: Update on industry news, plus issues that affect contractors & their businesses
Ontario Electrical League Chapter Newsletter
Type: Newsletter
Profile: Chapter committee update
Mission: To represent & strengthen the electrical industry in Ontario

Ontario Energy Association
#409, 45 Sheppard Avenue E, Toronto ON M2N 5W9
Tel: 416-961-2339; Fax: 416-961-1173
e-mail: oea@energyontario.ca
URL: www.energyontario.ca
Overview: A small provincial organization
Chief Officer(s):
Shane Pospisil, President & CEO

Ontario Environment Industry Association (ONEIA)
#218, 330 Adelaide St. West, Toronto ON M5V 1R4
Tel: 416-531-7884
e-mail: info@oneia.ca
URL: www.oneia.ca
Overview: A large provincial organization founded in 1991
Chief Officer(s):
Alex Gill, Executive Director
Membership: 175 corporate; *Fees:* $395-$1375
Mission: To represent the interests of the environmental industry in Ontario; To promote environmental business to industry & government in Ontario

Ontario Environmental Network (OEN)
Parent: Canadian Environmental Network
PO Box 1412, Stn. Main, North Bay ON P1B 8K6
Tel: 705-840-2888; Fax: 705-840-5862
e-mail: oen@oen.ca
URL: www.oen.ca
Overview: A large provincial organization founded in 1981
Membership: 700+ environmental groups; *Fees:* $15 individuals; $30 government agencies & businesses; $40 organizations; *Member Profile:* Non-government, not-for-profit organizations in Ontario concerned with the preservation of the environment; Government agencies; Businesses; Individuals
Activities: Facilitating communication among environmental organizations; Maintaining a database of Ontario's environmental groups; Increasing awareness of environmental organizations
Meetings/Conferences:
For more information see Trade Shows, Conferences and Seminars Chapter
Ontario Environmental Network 2012 Annual General Meeting Other Conferences in 2012 2012, ON
Ontario Environmental Network 2013 Annual General Meeting Other Conferences in 2013 2013, ON
Publications: *OEN [Ontario Environmental Network] Announcements*
Type: Newsletter Frequency: s-m. Accepts Advertising : Yes
Price: Free with Ontario Environmental Network membership
Profile: Ontario Environment Network updates, events, & action alerts sent to member groups & subscribers
Ontario Environmental Directory
Type: Directory Editor: Peter Blanchard Price: Free with Ontario Environmental Network membership
Profile: Comprehensive information about Ontario environmental organizations & agencies
Mission: To encourage discussions of ways to protect the environment; To increase environmental awareness throughout Ontario; To serve the environmental non-profit, non-governmental community in Ontario; Affiliation(s): Canadian Environmental Network
Environmental Activity: Researching environmental matters; Providing envionmental education; Offering reference & referral services for environmentally-related inquiries; Establishing caucuses that work on issues such as energy, forest, & waste

Ontario Farm & Country Accommodations Association (OFCA)
8724 Wellington Rd. 18, RR#5, Belwood ON N0J 1J0
Tel: 519-787-0346; Fax: 519-787-0946
e-mail: paul.faires@sympatico.ca
URL: www.countryhosts.com
Overview: A small provincial organization founded in 1967
Chief Officer(s):
Lore Schafer, President
Paul Faires, Secretary
Finances: *Annual Operating Budget:* Less than $50,000
Staff: 1390 volunteer(s)
Membership: 50; *Fees:* $230
Activities: *Speaker Service:* Yes; *Rents Mailing List:* Yes
Mission: To be a self-supporting, accredited association whose members provide warm hospitality, country accommodations & farm tours, for guests seeking a unique getaway with the opportunity to experience rural culture, farming & the environment

The Ontario Farm Animal Council (OFAC)
#106, 100 Stone Rd. West, Guelph ON N1G 5L3
Tel: 519-837-1326; Fax: 519-837-3209
e-mail: info@ofac.org
URL: www.ofac.org
Overview: A medium-sized provincial organization founded in 1988
Chief Officer(s):
John Maaskant, Chairman
Crystal Mackay, Executive Director
Finances: *Annual Operating Budget:* $250,000-$500,000;
Funding Sources: Memberships; corporate sponsorships; grants
Staff: 3 staff member(s); 100 volunteer(s)
Membership: Represents both directly & indirectly the over 40,000 livestock & poultry producers & related agri-food businesses in Ontario; *Fees:* $35-$1,000
Activities: Consumer & producer displays; public speaking; agri-food spokespeople training; media relations; industry representation & services; referral & research; *Awareness Events:* Canadian National Exhibition Model Farm; *Speaker Service:* Yes; *Library:* Yes, open by appointment
Mission: To support & promote the responsible production & marketing of livestock & poultry by Ontario farmers & through a variety of initiatives, to better inform the public of the excellence of animal agriculture

Ontario Federation of Agriculture (OFA)
Parent: Canadian Federation of Agriculture
Ontario AgriCentre, #206, 100 Stone Rd. West, London ON N1G 5L3
Tel: 519-821-8883; Fax: 519-821-8810
Toll-Free: 800-668-3276
e-mail: info@ofa.on.ca
URL: www.ofa.on.ca
Overview: A large provincial organization founded in 1936
Finances: *Funding Sources:* Membership fees; Sponsorships
Staff: 21 staff member(s)
Fees: $195
Activities: Engaging in advocacy activities; Providing networking opportunities
Meetings/Conferences:
For more information see Trade Shows, Conferences and Seminars Chapter
Ontario Federation of Agriculture 2012 Convention Other Conferences in 2012 2012, ON
Publications: *Better Farming*
Type: Magazine Frequency: m. Price: Free with Ontario Federation of Agriculture membership
Profile: A business magazine about Ontario agriculture
Country Guide
Type: Magazine
Profile: Suggestions to improve farm profitability plus innovative technologies
Ag Buyer's Guide [a publication of the Ontario Federation of Agriculture]
Type: Guide
Profile: Information to assist Ontario farmers purchase equipment
Ontario Federation of Agriculture Policy Handbook
Type: Handbook Number of Pages: 42 Price: Free with Ontario Federation of Agriculture membership
Profile: Topics addressed include animal welfare & control; education, schools, & training; energy; environment; farm implements; finance; labour, employment, & human resources; land use planning; marketing & production; rural affairs; science & technology; telecommunications; & transportation
Mission: To represent farm families throughout Ontario; To champion the interests of Ontario farmers; To work towards a sustainable future for farmers; *Member of:* Canadian Federation of Agriculture

Ontario Federation of Anglers & Hunters (OFAH)
Parent: Canadian Wildlife Federation
PO Box 2800, 4601 Gutheir Drive, Peterborough ON K9J 8L5
Tel: 705-748-6324; Fax: 705-748-9577
e-mail: ofah@ofah.org
URL: www.ofah.org
Overview: A medium-sized provincial charitable organization founded in 1928
Finances: *Annual Operating Budget:* $3 Million-$5 Million;
Funding Sources: Membership fees; donations
Staff: 35 staff member(s); 400 volunteer(s)
Membership: 83,000 individuals + 655 affiliated clubs; *Fees:* $45.50 adult; $57.50 family; $33.00 youth; $1,000 life; *Member Profile:* Interest in fish & wildlife conservation; *Committees:* Land Access; Forestry; Fisheries; Hunter Education
Activities: Ontario Family Fishing Weekend, July; Project Purple Week, Aug.
Mission: To save & defend from waste the natural resources of Ontario, its soils, minerals, air, water, forests & wildlife

Ontario Field Ornithologists (OFO)
PO Box 455, Stn. R, Toronto ON M4G 4E1
e-mail: membership@ofo.ca
URL: www.ofo.ca
Overview: A medium-sized international charitable organization founded in 1982
Finances: *Funding Sources:* Membership fees; Donations
Fees: $35 Canada; $40 USA; $45 international; $700 Canadian life membership; $800 USA life membership; $900 international life membership; *Member Profile:* Field ornithologists from Ontario & abroad; *Committees:* Annual Convention; Distinguished Ornithologist Award Nomination; Ontario Bird Records; OFO Website & Photo Page; ONTBIRDS Listserv
Activities: Offering field trips to birding spots in Ontario; Publishing site guides to birding areas of Ontario; Facilitating the exchange of information
Awards: Distinguished Ornithologist Award; Certificates of Appreciation (Award)
Meetings/Conferences:
For more information see Trade Shows, Conferences and Seminars Chapter
Ontario Field Ornithologists 2011 Annual Convention September 2011 Point Pelee, ON
Ontario Field Ornithologists 2012 Annual Convention Other Conferences in 2012 2012, ON
Publications: *OFO [Ontario Field Ornithologists] News*
Type: Newsletter Frequency: 3 pa Editor: Seabrooke Leckie
Price: Free with Ontario Field Ornithologists membership
Profile: Announcements, field trip reports, site guides, & Ontario Bird Records Committe reports
Ontario Birds
Type: Journal Frequency: 3 pa Editor: R. James; G. Coady; D.V. Weseloh Price: Free with Ontario Field Ornithologists membership
Profile: New information about the status, distribution, identification, & behaviour of birds in Ontario
Field Checklist of Ontario Birds
Type: Booklet Price: $2
Ornithology in Ontario
Type: Book Number of Pages: 400 Editor: Martin McNicholl; John Cranmer-Byng
Profile: Historical overview, archaeology, early naturalists, biographies, zoology, museums, bird banding, species accounts, & studies
Mission: To study bird life in Ontario

Ontario Fire Buff Associates (OFBA)
PO Box 802, Stn. Q, Toronto ON M4T 2N7
e-mail: ontariofirebuffs@yahoo.ca
URL: www.ofba.ca
Overview: A small provincial organization founded in 1971
Chief Officer(s):
Rick Loiselle, President
Finances: *Annual Operating Budget:* Less than $50,000
Staff: 170 volunteer(s)
Membership: 100-499; *Fees:* $15-$28; *Member Profile:* Open to any eligible individual or organization upon required recommendation, payment of fees & approval of the Board of Directors
Mission: To bring together people who share a common interest - the fire service of Ontario; *Member of:* International Fire Buff Associates

Ontario Food Processors Association (OFPA)
7660 Mill Rd., RR#4, Guelph ON N1S 6J1

Associations/Organizations / Ontario Forest Industries Association

Tel: 519-767-5599; Fax: 519-763-4164
e-mail: ofpa@sentex.net
Overview: A medium-sized provincial organization founded in 1935
Finances: Annual Operating Budget: $100,000-$250,000
Staff: 2 staff member(s)
Membership: 40 organizations; Committees: Regulation; Environment; Labour; Research
Mission: Represents fruit and vegetable processors in Ontario

Ontario Forest Industries Association (OFIA) / l'Industrie forestière de l'Ontario
#950, 20 Toronto St., Toronto ON M5C 2B8
Tel: 416-368-6188; Fax: 416-368-5445
e-mail: info@ofia.com
URL: www.ofia.com
Overview: A medium-sized provincial organization founded in 1943
Membership: 13 member companies + 10 affiliate members; Member Profile: Companies, ranging from large multinational corporations to small businesses, that produce materials such as pulp, paper, paperboard, plywood, panelboard, veneer, & lumber
Activities: Liaising with government & other business sectors; Developinig partnerships, such as the Ontario Forestry Coalition; Raising awareness of the forest industry in Ontario; Providing opportunities for members to discuss industry issues
Publications: Canadian Forests: A Primer
Number of Pages: 50 Author: Dr. Ken Armson ISBN: 1-895540-17-8
Profile: Part of the Environmental Literacy Series, the contents address the ownership & governance of forests, forest management, the economy
Mission: To act as a unified voice on behalf of member companies to ensure industry positions are considered; To respond to industry issues, such as economic, environmental, & technological developments
Environmental Activity: Working towards sustainable development, by balancing economic & environmental interests; Ensuring that member companies adhere to a Code of Forest Practices & a Statement of Environmental Policy

Ontario Forestry Association (OFA) / Association forestière de l'Ontario
Parent: Canadian Forestry Association
#701, 200 Consumers Rd., Toronto ON M2J 4R4
Tel: 416-493-4565; Fax: 416-493-4608
Toll-Free: 800-387-0790
e-mail: forestry@oforest.on.ca
URL: www.oforest.on.ca
Overview: A medium-sized provincial charitable organization founded in 1949
Finances: Annual Operating Budget: $250,000-$500,000
Staff: 2 staff member(s); 100 volunteer(s)
Membership: 1000; Fees: $45 individual, $15 student, $750 life; Committees: Public Forestry Education; Speakers Bureau; Trees Ontario; Woodland Owners; Honour Roll of Ontario Trees
Activities: Trees Ontario - partnership between association & Ontario Ministry of Natural Resources to facilitate sponsorship of tree establishment projects by corporations & interested groups wishing to demonstrate their concern for the environment; Smokey Bear; Forest Fire Prevention Campaign; Ontario Envirothon; National Forest Week; Focus on Forests First; Managed Forest Tax Program; Speaker Service: Yes
Awards: White Pine Award (Scholarship)
Awarded for postgraduate study in: Science, Forestry, Resource Management, Earth Sciences, Environmental Studies, Conservation, Natural Science Award Amount: Up to $500
Mission: To promote sound land use & full development protection & utilization of Ontario's forest resources for maximum public advantage; to increase public awareness, school education & natural appreciation of forests; to bring about better understanding of forests to people of all ages & backgrounds

Ontario Fruit & Vegetable Growers' Association (OFVGA) / L'Association des fruiticulteurs et des maraîchers de l'Ontario
#105, 355 Elmira Rd. North, Guelph ON N1K 1S5
Tel: 519-763-6160; Fax: 519-763-6604
e-mail: info@ofvga.org
URL: www.ofvga.org
Overview: A medium-sized provincial organization founded in 1859
Finances: Annual Operating Budget: $500,000-$1.5 Million; Funding Sources: Membership fees; advertising revenue
Staff: 7 staff member(s)
Membership: 7,500; Fees: $30

Activities: Speaker Service: Yes
Mission: Dedicated to the advancement of horticulture, working proactively through effective lobbying for the betterment of the industry & producers as a whole through advocacy, research, education, communication & marketing; Member of: Canadian Horticultural Council

Ontario Good Roads Association (OGRA)
#2, 6355 Kennedy Rd., Mississauga ON L5T 2L5
Tel: 905-795-2555; Fax: 905-795-2660
e-mail: info@ogra.org
URL: www.ogra.org
Social Media: www.twitter.com/Ont_Good_Roads
Overview: A medium-sized provincial organization founded in 1894
Finances: Funding Sources: Membership fees; Sponsorships
Membership: 400+ municipalities; Member Profile: Ontario municipalities; First Nations communities; Corporations; Life & honourary members; Committees: Executive; Policy; Member Services; Nominating; Combined Conference; Companions Program
Activities: Advocating for the collective interests of municipal transportation & works departments; Analyzing policies; Reviewing legislation; Consulting with stakeholders & partners; Offering education & training opportunities
Meetings/Conferences:
For more information see Trade Shows, Conferences and Seminars Chapter
Ontario Good Roads Association Snow School 2011
September 2011 Alliston, ON
Ontario Good Roads Association Environmentally Friendly Road Salt Storage Workshop
October 2011 Mississauga, ON
Ontario Good Roads Association Introduction to Contract Law Training
November 2011, ON
Ontario Good Roads Association Advanced Contract Law Training
November 2011, ON
Ontario Good Roads Association Contract Dispute Resolution Training
November 2011, ON
Ontario Good Roads Association / Rural Ontario Municipal Association 2012 Combined Conference
February 2012, ON
Ontario Good Roads Association / Rural Ontario Municipal Association 2013 Combined Conference
February 2013, ON
Ontario Good Roads Association / Rural Ontario Municipal Association 2014 Combined Conference
February 2014, ON
Publications: Milestones [a publication of the Ontario Good Roads Association]
Type: Magazine Frequency: 4 pa Accepts Advertising : Yes Editor: Colette Caruso
Profile: Articles of interest to the municipal services sector, including a conference issue & a winter maintenance issue
Ontario Good Roads Association Annual Report
Type: Yearbook Frequency: a.
Mission: To represent the transportation & public works-related interests of Ontario's municipalities & First Nation communities; To deliver programs & services that meet the needs of members; To support municipalities in the provision of effective & efficient transportation systems throughout Ontario
Environmental Activity: Providing workshops about winter maintenance materials, such as salt

The Ontario Greenhouse Alliance (TOGA)
PO Box 175, #6, 76 Main St., Grimsby ON L3M 1S5
Fax: 905-945-5767
Toll-Free: 888-480-0659
e-mail: info@theontariogreenhousealliance.com
URL: www.theontariogreenhousealliance.com
Overview: A small provincial organization founded in 2002
Chief Officer(s):
Rejean Picard, Chair
Member Profile: Ontario's greenhouse vegetable, pepper & flower growers
Mission: To provide an infrastructure & approach that will integrate all the current resources & future potential of the Ontario greenhouse stakeholders into a community & international marketplace presence, with the synergy & standards to be a world leader in greenhouse operations

The Ontario Greens See The Green Party of Ontario

Ontario Ground Water Association (OGWA)
Parent: Canadian Ground Water Association
48 Front St. East, Strathroy ON N7G 1Y6
Tel: 519-245-7194; Fax: 519-245-7196
URL: www.ogwa.ca
Previous Name: Ontario Water Well Association
Overview: A medium-sized provincial organization founded in 1952
Chief Officer(s):
Greg Bullock, President
Rob MacKinnon, Secretary-Treasurer
Anne Gammage, Office Manager, 519-245-7194, Fax: 519-245-7196
Finances: Funding Sources: Membership dues
Member Profile: Ground water professionals
Activities: Disseminating information & providing education about ground water; Promoting technical skills of ground water professional
Meetings/Conferences:
For more information see Trade Shows, Conferences and Seminars Chapter
Ontario Ground Water Association 2012 60th Annual Convention & Trade Show
Other Conferences in 2012 2012, ON
Publications: The Source [a publication of the Ontario Ground Water Association]
Type: Newsletter Accepts Advertising : Yes Editor: Shannon Savory
Profile: Ontario Ground Water Association information, plus feature articles & industry news
Mission: To protect & promote Ontario's ground water; To provide guidance to members, government representatives, & the public
Environmental Activity: Working to ensure the delivery of safe & clean water supplies throughout Ontario

Ontario Healthy Communities Coalition (OHCC) / Coalition des communautés en santé de l'Ontario
#1810, 2 Carlton St., Toronto ON M5B 1J3
Tel: 416-408-4841; Fax: 416-408-4843
Toll-Free: 800-766-3418
e-mail: info@healthycommunities.on.ca
URL: www.healthycommunities.on.ca
Overview: A medium-sized provincial charitable organization
Chief Officer(s):
Anderson Rouse, Coordinator, Finance & Administration
Lorna Heidenheim, Executive Director
lorna@healthycommunities.on.ca
Finances: Annual Operating Budget: $250,000-$500,000; Funding Sources: Trillium Foundation; Ministry of Health & Long Term Care; Ministry of Environment
Staff: 10 staff member(s); 2 volunteer(s)
Membership: 94 organizations; Member Profile: Provincial associations; community; individuals; Committees: Diversity; Communication; Resource Develoment; Food Security
Activities: Speaker Service: Yes; Library: Yes, Open to public, open by appointment
Mission: To achieve social, environmental, economic & physical well-being for individuals, communities & local governments throughout Ontario

Ontario Heritage Trust (OHT) / Fiducie du patrimoine ontarien
10 Adelaide St. East, Toronto ON M5C 1J3
Tel: 416-325-5000; Fax: 416-325-5071
e-mail: marketing@heritagefdn.on.ca
URL: www.heritagefdn.on.ca
Overview: A medium-sized provincial charitable organization founded in 1967
Chief Officer(s):
Richard Moorhouse, Exec. Director
Activities: Enters into conservation easement agreements with the owners of heritage properties to ensure that the significant heritage features of these properties are protected; holds provincially significant heritage properties & collections "in trust" on behalf of the people of Ontario; provides technical assistance to individuals & groups involved in heritage preservation; protects significant natural areas & geological land formations through Natural Heritage & Niagara Escarpment Programs
Mission: Dedicated to the preservation, protection & promotion of Ontario's built, natural & cultural heritage for all of us to enjoy now & for others to experience in the future

Ontario Horticultural Association (OHA)
312 Simcoe St., Tilsonburg ON N4G 2J6

Tel: 519-842-9829; Fax: 519-648-9716
e-mail: president@gardenontario.org
URL: www.gardenontario.org
Overview: A medium-sized provincial charitable organization founded in 1906
Chief Officer(s):
Jim Mabee, President
president@gardenontario.org
Finances: Annual Operating Budget: Less than $50,000; Funding Sources: Membership dues; grants; fundraising
Staff: 1 staff member(s)
Membership: 278 societies; 40,000 members; Fees: $1; Member Profile: Gardener
Mission: To promote civic beautification, preservation of the environment, youth work & education of many aspects of horticulture

Ontario Hospital Association (OHA)
Parent: Canadian Healthcare Association
#2800, 200 Front St. West, Toronto ON M5V 3L1
Tel: 416-205-1300; Fax: 416-205-1301
Toll-Free: 800-598-8002
e-mail: info@oha.com
URL: www.oha.ca
Overview: A medium-sized provincial organization founded in 1924
Membership: 159 public hospitals; Member Profile: Public hospitals throughout Ontario; Affiliated associations & organizations
Activities: Engaging in advocacy activities to help shape health care policy in Ontario; Building partnerships; Providing opportunities for professional development;
Publications: OHA [Ontario Hospital Association] Executive Report
Type: Newsletter Frequency: w. Editor: Alessandra Nigro Price: Free with membership in the Ontario Hospital Association
Profile: Current health care news
Healthcare Governance Update
Type: Newsletter
Profile: Information from the Governance Centre of Excellence to maintain & increase trustees' knowledge of health care governance issues
Hospital Perspectives
Type: Newsletter Editor: Tamarah Harel ISSN: 1198-0192
Profile: Articles about innovations in health care
Ontario Hospital Association Annual Report
Type: Yearbook Frequency: a.
Mission: To build a strong, innovative, & sustainable health care system that meets patient care needs throughout Ontario; To promote an efficent & effective health care system
Environmental Activity: Hosting conferences on healthy work environments & sustainable hospital practices

Ontario Industrial Fire Protection Association (OIFPA)
193 James St. South, Hamilton ON L8P 3A8
Tel: 905-527-0700; Fax: 905-527-6254
e-mail: oifpa@interlynx.net
URL: www.oifpa.org
Overview: A medium-sized provincial organization founded in 1981
Finances: Funding Sources: Membership fees
Member Profile: Individuals from the chemical industry & the oil & gas industry; Consulting engineers; Emergency response personnel; Municipal fire departments & fire protection consultants; Government agencies; Industrial underwriters
Activities: Creating networking opportunities with members from organizations such as municipal fire departments & government agencies; Providing educational seminars, on topics such as Ontario Fire Code updates, explosion protection, & fire pump installation
Publications: Firewatch
Type: Newsletter
Profile: Information updates from the association
Mission: To unite individuals with a concern for fire protection within Ontario's industrial community

Ontario Institute of Agrologists (OIA)
Parent: Agricultural Institute of Canada
Ontario AgriCentre, #108, 100 Stone Rd. West, Guelph ON N1G 5L3
Tel: 519-826-4226; Fax: 519-826-4228
Toll-Free: 866-339-7619
e-mail: info@oia.on.ca
URL: www.oia.on.ca

Overview: A medium-sized provincial organization founded in 1960
Finances: Annual Operating Budget: $100,000-$250,000
Staff: 3 staff member(s)
Membership: 900 individual; Fees: Variable; Member Profile: B.Sc (Agriculture) from Canadian university or equivalent; Committees: Act to Regulate Agrologists; Articling Agrologist Committee; Board of Examiners; Internet; Membership; Professional Development; Professional Standards; Public Relations
Activities: Internships: Yes
Awards: Public Relations Award (Award)
Presented to a member who has made an outstanding contribution to promoting OIA
Branch Newsletter Award (Award)
Presented to the branch newsletter editor deemed by the Membership Committee to produce the most effective branch newsletter for their members
Cheryl Somerville Memorial Distinguished Young Agrologist Award (Award)
Presented annually to an individual under 40 years of age who has made significant contributions to the agriculture & food industry in this province, the profession of agrology &/or the OIA
Distinguished Agrologist (Award)
Member individuals who have rendered signal service to the agricultural industry of Ontario &/or the affairs of the OIA
Honourary Life Member (Award)
Individuals who have rendered signal service to the agricultural industry of Ontario
President's Honour Roll (Award)
Member individuals who have contributed greatly to branch effectiveness during the year
Mission: OIA regulates Ontario's Professional Agrologists & ensures that competencies meet a Standard of Practice within a specific scope of agrology; ensures that business is conducted within a Code of Ethics; protects the public interest; grows the agri-life science industry; contributes to the excellence of colleagues; pursues professional development to enhance knowledge, skills & experience so they can practise science of agrology with skill, integrity & transparency.; Affiliation(s): Certified Crop Advisor Program; Ontario Agricultural Hall of Fame Association; Ontario Agricultural Training Institute; Ontario Farm Animal Council; Western Fair Association

Ontario Lumber Manufacturers' Association (OLMA) / Association des manufacturiers de bois de sciage de l'Ontario
PO Box 97530, #1202, 55 York St., Toronto ON M1C 4Z1
Tel: 416-367-9717; Fax: 416-367-3415
e-mail: info@olma.ca
URL: www.olma.ca
Overview: A medium-sized provincial organization founded in 1966
Member Profile: Ontario sawmills, planing mills, lumber remanufacturers, & MSR & Fj manufacturers; Ontario companies engaged in equipment manufacturing, & lumber sales & distribution
Activities: Training persons to classify lumber; Supervising the grading of lumber; Authorizing manufacturing facilities to mark pieces of lumber with the OLMA facsimile stamp; Mediating disputes between sellers & buyers of lumber with the OLMA stamp; Promoting trade & diversification; Improving access to markets for Canadian softwood lumber; Reviewing forestry issues & policies; Liaising with government
Awards: Ontario Lumber Manufacturers' Association Lumberjack Award (Award)
To recognize the outstanding lumberjack of the year
Mission: To ensure a sound & renewable forest economy; To oversee lumber grading licenses & quality control at member sawmills in Ontario; To ensure market access within Northern America, Europe, & Japan; Affiliation(s): Canadian Lumber Standards Accreditation Board; American Lumber Standards Committee, Inc.
Environmental Activity: Ensuring the role of forests in the envionment is protected

Ontario Lung Association (OLA)
Parent: Canadian Lung Association
573 King St. East, Toronto ON M5A 4L3
Tel: 416-864-9911; Fax: 416-864-9916
Toll-Free: 888-344-5864
e-mail: olalung@on.lung.ca; airquality@on.lung.ca; tobacco@on.lung.ca
URL: www.on.lung.ca
Overview: A large provincial charitable organization founded in 1945

Finances: Funding Sources: Donations; Fundraising; Sponsorships
Activities: Supporting lung health research; Providing education about asthma (Asthma Action Helpline) & chronic obstructive pulmonary disease (BreathWorks Program); Offering smoking cessation information; Awareness Events: Lungs Are For Life Program; The Amazing Pace; Tulip Day
Publications: Oxygen
Type: Newsletter
Profile: Lung health information, donor & research profiles, & forthcoming events
Asthma Action
Type: Newsletter
Breathworks
Type: Newsletter
Mission: To provide lung health information & support to people affected by lung disease; To prevent & control chronic lung disease
Environmental Activity: Offering indoor & outdoor air quality information

Ontario Marine Operators Association (OMOA)
15 Laurier Rd., Penetanguishene ON L9M 1G8
Tel: 705-549-1667; Fax: 705-549-1670
Toll-Free: 888-547-6662
e-mail: omoa@marinasontario.com
URL: www.marinasontario.com
Overview: A medium-sized provincial organization founded in 1967
Membership: 460+ individual marinas + 160 trade members; Member Profile: Ontario marinas; Yacht clubs; Marine dealers; Associated companies
Activities: Lobbying on behalf of the industry; Providing information; Encouraging safe boating; Participating in boat shows; Offering workshops
Publications: Boating Ontario: Marinas & Destination Guide
Type: Directory Frequency: a.
Profile: A guide to more than 450 marina members of the Ontario Marine Operators Association, with information about their facilities & services
Enviro Boater
Type: Manual
Profile: Suggestions for environment-friendly boating, produced by the Ontario Marine Operators Association, the Canadian Power & Sail Squadrons, & other interested organizations
Marina News
Type: Newsletter Frequency: 8 pa Price: Free with membership in the Ontario Marine Operators Association
Profile: Business suggestions & industry news, for members of the Ontario Marine Operators Association
Mission: To promote recreational boating throughout Ontario
Environmental Activity: Employing a director of environmental services; Offering a guide to environment-friendly boating

Ontario Medical Association (OMA)
Parent: Canadian Medical Association
#900, 150 Bloor St. West, Toronto ON M5S 3C1
Tel: 416-599-2580; Fax: 416-340-2944
Toll-Free: 800-268-7215
e-mail: info@oma.org; membership@oma.org
URL: www.oma.org
Overview: A large provincial organization founded in 1880
Membership: 30,000+; Member Profile: Practicing physicians, residents, & students who are enrolled in one of Ontario's faculties of medicine
Activities: Advocating for the health of Ontarians; Promoting health care services throughout Ontario; Providing a continuing medical education program; Offering tools to manage an effective practice, such as legal advice & incorporation services
Meetings/Conferences:
For more information see Trade Shows, Conferences and Seminars Chapter
Ontario Medical Association, Sport Medicine Section 2012 Annual Symposium: Sport Med
Other Conferences in 2012 2012, ON
Ontario Medical Association, Sport Medicine Section 2013 Annual Symposium: Sport Med
Other Conferences in 2013 2013, ON
Publications: Ontario Medical Review
Type: Journal
Mission: To represent the clinical, political, & economic interests of Ontario physicians; To promote an accessible, quality health-care system

Ontario Mineral Exploration Federation (OMEF) See Ontario Prospectors Association

Associations/Organizations / Ontario Mining Association

Ontario Mining Association (OMA)
Parent: Mining Association of Canada
#520, 5775 Yonge St., Toronto ON M2M 4J1
Tel: 416-364-9301; *Fax:* 416-364-5986
e-mail: pmcbride@oma.on.ca
URL: www.oma.on.ca
Overview: A medium-sized provincial organization founded in 1920
Finances: *Annual Operating Budget:* $500,000-$1.5 Million; *Funding Sources:* Membership fees
Staff: 6 staff member(s)
Membership: 45; *Committees:* Environmental Steering Committee; Energy; Workers Health & Safety
Activities: *Awareness Events:* Ontario Mining Week, 1st week of May
Mission: To help improve the competitiveness of the Ontario mineral industry

Ontario Municipal Human Resources Association (OMHRA)
#307, 1235 Fairview St., Burlington ON L7S 2K9
Tel: 905-525-4000; *Fax:* 905-525-9833
e-mail: admin@omhra.ca
URL: www.omhra.ca
Previous Name: Ontario Municipal Personnel Association
Overview: A medium-sized provincial organization founded in 1963
Finances: *Funding Sources:* Membership fees; Sponsorships
Member Profile: Ontario human resources professionals who are employed by municipalities, commissions, & local public sector boards
Activities: Facilitating the exchange of information from the field of human resources; Promoting education
Meetings/Conferences:
For more information see Trade Shows, Conferences and Seminars Chapter
Ontario Municipal Human Resources Association 2011 Fall Conference
Other Conferences in 2011 2011, ON
Mission: To provide direction on issues of human resources management; To represent the interests of the association, related to legislation & policies

Ontario Municipal Management Development Board *See* Ontario Municipal Management Institute

Ontario Municipal Management Institute (OMMI)
618 Balmoral Dr., Oshawa ON L1J 3A7
Tel: 905-434-8885; *Fax:* 905-434-7381
URL: www.ommi.on.ca
Previous Name: Ontario Municipal Management Development Board
Overview: A small provincial organization founded in 1979
Membership: 350; *Member Profile:* Local governments, including cities, towns, regions, & municipalities
Activities: Providing educational workshops & seminars; Conducting training opportunities; Certifying qualified candidates with the Certified Municipal Manager designation (CMM); Liaising with other professional local government associations
Awards: Excellence in Training (Award)
Distinguished Service Award (Award)
Publications: *You & Your Local Government*
Type: Handbook
Councillor Development Resource Manual
Type: Manual
Mission: To enhance management skills, in order to strengthen local government administration

Ontario Municipal Personnel Association *See* Ontario Municipal Human Resources Association

Ontario Municipal Water Association (OMWA)
c/o Doug Parker, 43 Chelsea Cres., Belleville ON K8N 4Z5
Tel: 613-966-1100; *Fax:* 613-966-3024
Toll-Free: 888-231-1115
e-mail: dparker@omwa.org
URL: www.omwa.org
Overview: A medium-sized provincial organization
Membership: 180+ public drinking water authorities in Ontario; *Fees:* Schedule available, based upon population; *Member Profile:* Ontario's public water supply authorities
Activities: Reviewing policy, & legislative, & regulatory issues; Liaising with government, agencies, & associations to maintain safe & sustainable water sources; Lobbying to improve conditions; Promoting high standards of treatment, infrastructure, & operations; Offering technical training for operating authorities, operators, & owners of drinking water systems; Encouraging dissemination of information for public education
Meetings/Conferences:
For more information see Trade Shows, Conferences and Seminars Chapter
Ontario Water Works Association / Ontario Municipal Water Association 2012 Annual Joint Conference & Trade Show
May 2012, ON
Publications: *Ontario Municipal Water Association Members' Handbook*
Type: Handbook
Councillors Handbook: Stewardship Responsibilities Under the Safe Drinking Water Act
Type: Handbook
Mission: To act as the voice of municipal water supply in Ontario; To ensure the safety, quality, reliability, & sustainability of drinking water in Ontario; *Affiliation(s):* Ontario Water Works Association (a section of the American Water Works Association)

Ontario Nature
#201, 366 Adelaide St. West, Toronto ON M5V 1R9
Tel: 416-444-8419; *Fax:* 416-444-9866
Toll-Free: 800-440-2366
e-mail: info@ontarionature.org
URL: www.ontarionature.org
Previous Name: Federation of Ontario Naturalists
Overview: A large provincial charitable organization founded in 1931
Finances: *Annual Operating Budget:* $1.5 Million-$3 Million; *Funding Sources:* Private donations; membership dues; foundations
Staff: 12 staff member(s); 100 volunteer(s)
Membership: 30,000 individuals + 140 member groups; *Fees:* $45 individual; $50 family; $40 school/library; $38 senior; $38 student; $160 bronze; $325 silver; $750 gold
Activities: *Library:* Yes, open by appointment
Mission: To promote knowledge, understanding & respect for Ontario's natural heritage & commitment to its conservation & protection on the part of the FON membership, landowners, decision makers & the general public; to seek legislation, policies, practices & institutions which permanently protect Ontario's natural ecosystem & indigenous biodiversity, including the establishment of a comprehensive natural heritage system for Ontario with an enlarged system of parks & other protected areas linked by a network of existing & rehabilitated natural corridors.; *Affiliation(s):* Coalition on the Niagara Escarpment; Conservation Council of Ontario; Great Lakes United; International Union for Conservation of Nature & Natural Resources; International Committee for Bird Preservation

Ontario Occupational Health Nurses Association (OOHNA)
#605, 302 The East Mall, Toronto ON M9B 6C7
Tel: 416-239-6462; *Fax:* 416-239-5462
e-mail: administration@oohna.on.ca
URL: www.oohna.on.ca
Overview: A medium-sized provincial organization founded in 1973
Finances: *Annual Operating Budget:* $250,000-$500,000; *Funding Sources:* Membership fees
Staff: 3 staff member(s); 7 volunteer(s)
Membership: 1,200; *Fees:* $384 regular; $168 associate; *Member Profile:* RN's practising occupational health & safety
Activities: *Speaker Service:* Yes
Awards: Award of Excellence (Award)
Pat Ewen Bursary Award (Award)
Lifetime Achievement Award (Award)
Mission: To foster a climate of excellence, innovation & partnership enabling Ontario Occupational Health Nurses to achieve positive workplace health & safety objectives; *Member of:* Canadian Occupational Health Nurses Association

Ontario Parks Association (OPA)
7856 - 5th Line South, RR#4, Milton ON L9T 2X8
Tel: 905-864-6182; *Fax:* 905-864-6184
Toll-Free: 866-560-7783
e-mail: opa@ontarioparksassociation.ca
URL: www.ontarioparksassociation.ca
Overview: A medium-sized provincial charitable organization founded in 1936
Chief Officer(s):
Paul Ronan, Executive Director, 905-864-6182 Ext. 6730
paul@ontarioparksassociation.ca
Shelley May, Coordinator, Operations & Administration, 905-864-6182 Ext. 6710
opa@ontarioparksassociation.ca
Finances: *Funding Sources:* Donations
Fees: $70 students & seniors; $130 individuals; $500 associates
Activities: Offering education to park professionals
Meetings/Conferences:
For more information see Trade Shows, Conferences and Seminars Chapter
Ontario Parks Association 2011 Registered Playground Practitioner Program
September 2011 Milton, ON
Ontario Parks Association 2012 56th Annual Educational Forum
Other Conferences in 2012 2012, ON
Ontario Parks Association 2012 Congress & Trade Show
Other Conferences in 2012 2012, ON
Ontario Parks Association 2012 Parks & Landscaping Equipment Safety Operations Program
Other Conferences in 2012 2012, ON
Ontario Parks Association 2012 Playground Introductory Compliance & Hazard Analysis Workshop
Other Conferences in 2012 2012, ON
Ontario Parks Association 2012 Ball Diamond Maintenance & Best Practices Workshop
Other Conferences in 2012 2012, ON
Ontario Parks Association 2012 Parks Oriented Chainsaw Safety Awareness & Basic Chipper Operations & Handling Course
Other Conferences in 2012 2012, ON
Ontario Parks Association 2012 Trails Specialist Workshop
Other Conferences in 2012 2012, ON
Ontario Parks Association 2012 Supervisor Competency Program
Other Conferences in 2012 2012, ON
Ontario Parks Association 2012 Accident / Incident Investigation Program
Other Conferences in 2012 2012, ON
Ontario Parks Association 2012 Parks Equipment Safety Training & Train the Trainer Program
Other Conferences in 2012 2012, ON
Ontario Parks Association 2012 Parks Confined Spaces Program
Other Conferences in 2012 2012, ON
Ontario Parks Association 2012 Municipal Integrated Pest Management Accreditation Workshop
Other Conferences in 2012 2012, ON
Publications: *Urban Parks in Ontario*
Type: Book *Author:* Dr. J.R. Wright
Profile: The evolution of parks & open space development
OPA [Ontario Parks Association] Playability Tool Kit: Building Accessible Playspaces
Type: Kit
Profile: Creating playspaces that are accessible to persons with disabilities
Mission: To develop & protect parks & green spaces in Ontario
Environmental Activity: Advocating for the protection of parks & open spaces throughout Ontario; Conserving parks, open spaces, & the environment

Ontario Pest Control Association *See* Structural Pest Management Association of Ontario

Ontario Petroleum Institute Inc. (OPI)
#104, 555 Southdale Rd. East, London ON N6E 1A2
Tel: 519-680-1620; *Fax:* 519-680-1621
e-mail: opi@ontpet.com
URL: www.ontpet.com
Overview: A medium-sized provincial organization founded in 1963
Finances: *Funding Sources:* Sponsorships
Member Profile: Geologists in Ontario; Geophysicists; Explorationists; Producers; Contractors; Petroleum engineers; Companies involved in the oil & gas, hydrocarbon storage, & solution mining industries
Activities: Liaising with government agencies; Disseminating information to members; Increasing public awareness of the importance of the industry in Ontario
Publications: *OPI [Ontario Petroleum Institute Inc.] Newsletter*
Type: Newsletter *Accepts Advertising* : Yes *ISSN:* 14802201
Profile: Membership updates, reports, conferences, & legislation information

Ontario Petroleum Institute Annual Conference & Trade Show Proceedings
Type: Yearbook Frequency: a.
Mission: To promote responsible exploration & development by Ontario's oil, gas, hydrocarbon storage, & solution-mining industries

Ontario Pipe Trades Council
Confederation Square, #203, 45 Goderich Rd., Hamilton ON L8E 4W8
Tel: 905-573-3703; *Fax:* 905-573-0804
e-mail: info@optc.org
URL: www.optc.org
Overview: A medium-sized provincial organization
Chief Officer(s):
Neil McCormack, Business Manager
Membership: 16 local unions
Mission: To promote the many technical, commercial & environmental benefits of the Pipe Trades & maximize their use in the construction industry; to promote the interest of the plumbing, pipe fitting, sprinkler fitting & HVAC industry in the province of Ontario

Ontario Plumbing Inspectors Association (OPIA)
129 Dumble Ave., Peterborough ON K9H 5A9
Tel: 705-742-7777; *Fax:* 705-742-5218
e-mail: sgould@city.peterborough.on.ca
URL: www.opia.info
Overview: A medium-sized provincial organization founded in 1920
Finances: *Annual Operating Budget:* $50,000-$100,000; *Funding Sources:* Membership fees
Staff: 14 volunteer(s)
Membership: 800; *Fees:* $60; *Committees:* Advisory; Auditors; Awards; Bulletin; Certification Review; Code Technical; Conference; Education; Election; Executive; Finance; Future Conference; Membership; Memorial; Nominations; Public Relations; Reciprocal Licensing; Resolutions; Special; Zone Meetings
Activities: CMX Show; CIPH Ex; Annual conference; *Library:* Yes, Not open to the public
Mission: To promote uniform enforcement of plumbing regulations; close liaison & interchange of ideas & knowledge between members of the OPIA & members of other associations; provide education & training to members & the industry; *Member of:* World Plumbing Council; Affiliation(s): Ontario Ministry of Municipal Affairs, Building Branch

Ontario Pollution Control Equipment Association (OPCEA)
PO Box 137, Midhurst ON L0L 1X0
Tel: 705-725-0917; *Fax:* 705-725-1068
e-mail: opcea@opcea.com
URL: www.opcea.com
Previous Name: Ontario Sanitation Equipment Association
Overview: A small provincial organization founded in 1970
Finances: *Funding Sources:* Membership fees
Membership: 160+; *Fees:* $210 initiation fee; $262 / year; *Member Profile:* Ontario firms that manufacture or distribute environmental & related equipment for the air & water pollution control marketplace
Publications: *OPCEA [Ontario Pollution Control Equipment Association] Membership Directory & Buyers Guide*
Type: Directory Frequency: a. Accepts Advertising : Yes Editor: Steve Davey
Profile: Listings of member companies, with their products & services, distributed to the Ontario marketplace
Influents [a publication of the Ontario Pollution Control Equipment Association]
Type: Magazine Accepts Advertising : Yes Editor: Cole Kelman
Profile: A combined publication of the Ontario Pollution Control Equipment Association & the Water Environment Association of Ontario, featuring information about forthcoming trade shows & events
Mission: To assist members in the promotion of their services & equipment in Ontario; Affiliation(s): Water Environment Association of Ontario

Ontario Printing & Imaging Association (OPIA)
#14, 2601 Matheson Blvd. East, Mississauga ON L4W 5A8
Tel: 905-602-4441; *Fax:* 905-602-9798
e-mail: info@opia.on.ca
URL: www.opia.on.ca
Overview: A medium-sized provincial organization
Chief Officer(s):
Mike McInnes, Chair
Kim Stewart, Vice-Chair
Tracey Preston, President
Ryan Anderson, Treasurer
Committees: Events; Government Affairs; Environment, Health & Safety; Human Resource Services; Membership; Communications; Strategic Planning
Activities: Providing technical advice; Facilitating the exchange of ideas; Offering print referral services
Awards: Excellence in Print Awards (Award)
Mission: To provide leadership for a successful printing & imaging industry in Ontario; Affiliation(s): Canadian Printing Industries Association (CPIA); Printing Industries of America (PIA); Graphic Arts Technical Foundation (GATF)
Environmental Activity: Offering advice to businesses about environmental & safety concerns

Ontario Professional Fire Fighters Association (OPFFA) / Association des pompiers professionnels de l'Ontario (ind.)
292 Plains Rd. East, Burlington ON L7T 2C6
Tel: 905-681-7111; *Fax:* 905-681-1489
URL: www.opffa.org
Previous Name: Provincial Federation of Ontario Fire Fighters
Overview: A medium-sized provincial organization founded in 1997
Chief Officer(s):
Fred LeBlanc, President
Mark McKinnon, Executive Vice-President
Barry Quinn, Secretary-Treasurer
Jeff Braun-Jackson, Office Manager & Researcher
Member Profile: Full-time professional fire fighters throughout Ontario; *Committees:* Education; Health & Safety & Section 21; Finance; Workplace Safety & Insurance Board; Occupational Disease; Pension; Legislative; Human Relations
Activities: Educating members to negotiate & administer collective agreements
Awards: The Ed Hothersall Award (Award)
To recognize an individual who has displayed a dedication for service to their association & the community
The Patrick J DeFazio Award (Award)
To recognize an individual who has contributed in the area of improving fire fighter health & safety
The Joe Adamkowski Award (Award)
To recognize an individual who has demonstrated dedication & diligence within their own Local, the OPFFA, or the IAFF
Meetings/Conferences:
For more information see Trade Shows, Conferences and Seminars Chapter
Ontario Professional Fire Fighters Association 2011 Annual Legislative Conference
November 2011, ON
Ontario Professional Fire Fighters Association Annual Fall 2011 Dr. Eric Taylor Labour Educational Seminar
Other Conferences in 2011 2011, ON
Ontario Professional Fire Fighters Association 2012 Annual Legislative Conference
November 2012, ON
Ontario Professional Fire Fighters Association 2012 15th Annual Convention
Other Conferences in 2012 2012, ON
Ontario Professional Fire Fighters Association 2012 Annual Health & Safety Seminar
Other Conferences in 2012 2012, ON
Affiliation(s): International Association of Fire Fighters

Ontario Professional Foresters Association (OPFA)
PO Box 91523, #201, 5 Wesleyan St., Georgetown ON L7G 2E2
Tel: 905-877-3679; *Fax:* 905-877-6766
e-mail: opfa@opfa.ca
URL: www.opfa.ca
Overview: A medium-sized provincial organization founded in 1957
Membership: 1,000; *Fees:* Schedule available
Mission: To serve the public interest by actively contributing to the sustainability of Ontario's forests through the establishment of professional standards, encouraging the adoption & use of best practices, & ensuring the competency of those who practice professional forestry

Ontario Professional Planners Institute (OPPI) / Institut des planificateurs professionnels de l'Ontario
Parent: Canadian Institute of Planners
#201, 234 Eglinton Ave. East, Toronto ON M4P 1K5
Tel: 416-483-1873; *Fax:* 416-483-7830
Toll-Free: 800-668-1448
e-mail: info@ontarioplanners.on.ca
URL: www.ontarioplanners.on.ca
Overview: A medium-sized provincial organization founded in 1986
Finances: *Funding Sources:* Membership fees; Program & activity revenue
Membership: 3,000+ planners + 500 students; *Member Profile:* Practising planners throughout Ontario; Students; *Committees:* Discipline; Nominations; Membership Services; Membership Outreach; Professional Development; Policy Development; Recognition; Student Liaison
Activities: Offering professional development courses; Preparing position statements, policy papers, & other documents of interest to planners; Presenting awards for excellence in planning; *Awareness Events:* World Town Planning Day
Publications: *Planning by Design: A Healthy Communities Handbook*
Type: Handbook
Profile: Produced by the Ontario Professional Planners Institute in partnership with the Ministry of Municipal Affairs & Housing
Ontario Planning Journal
Type: Journal Frequency: bi-m. Accepts Advertising : Yes Editor: Glenn Miller Price: $55 / year Canada; $65 / year International
Profile: Ontario Professional Planners Institute activities & planning issues
OPPI [Ontario Professional Planners Institute] Members Update
Type: Newsletter Frequency: m. Price: Free with membership in the Ontario Professional Planners Institute
Profile: Recent news from the institute for members only
Consultants' Directory [a publication of the Ontario Professional Planners Institute]
Type: Directory
Profile: A source used by OPPI members & potential clients
Mission: To act as the voice of Ontario's planning profession; To provide leadership on policies related to planning & development; Affiliation(s): Canadian Institute of Planners (CIP)
Environmental Activity: Providing leadership on policy related to the environment

Ontario Prospectors Association
c/o Garry Clark, 1000 Alloy Dr., Thunder Bay ON P7B 6A5
Tel: 807-622-3284; *Fax:* 807-622-4156
e-mail: gjclark@ontarioprospectors.com
URL: www.ontarioprospectors.com
Previous Name: Ontario Mineral Exploration Federation (OMEF)
Overview: A small provincial organization founded in 1987
Chief Officer(s):
Garry Clark, Executive Director
Wally Rayner, President
Roger Poulin, Vice-President
John McCance, Secretary:
Membership: 3,000; *Committees:* Audit; Membership; Symposium; Education; Land Use / Access; Issue Resolution; Communications; Policy; Finance
Activities: Engaging in lobbying activities; Designing prospector development initiatives; Providing information; Developing awareness of the industry; Offering networking opportunities; Presenting awards
Publications: *The Explorationist [a publication of the Northern Prospectors Association & the Ontario Prospectors Association]*
Type: Newsletter Frequency: 10 pa
Profile: Information distributed to OPA members, associates, & government personnel about Ontario's mineral exploration scene
The Ontario Prospector
Type: Magazine Frequency: s-a. Accepts Advertising : Yes Editor: Cadence Hays
Profile: Conference reports, feature articles, & buyers' guide
Building a Dialogue with Aboriginal Communities: A Guide for Junior Exploration Companies & Prospectors
Type: Guide
Ontario Mining & Exploration Directory
Type: Directory
Mission: To advance the interests of prospectors & the mineral exploration industry; to promote ethical standards among prospectors in Ontario; to ensure adherence by members to the code of conduct

Ontario Public Health Association (OPHA) / Association pour la santé publique de l'Ontario
Parent: Canadian Public Health Association
Lawrence Square, #310, 700 Lawrence Ave. West, Toronto ON M6B 3B4
Tel: 416-367-3313; *Fax:* 416-367-2844
Toll-Free: 800-267-6817

Associations/Organizations / Ontario Public Interest Research Group

e-mail: info@opha.on.ca
URL: www.opha.on.ca
Overview: A medium-sized provincial organization founded in 1949
Chief Officer(s):
Carol Timmings, President
ctimmings@opha.on.ca
Liz Haugh, Vice-President
lhaugh@wechealthunit.org
Finances: *Funding Sources:* Membership fees; Sponsorships
Membership: 3,000; *Fees:* $50 students, retired persons, unemployed individuals; $85 individuals; *Member Profile:* Individuals & constituent societies interested in advancing public health
Activities: Providing education opportunities; Analyzing policy; Advocating for public health policies to improve the health of Ontarians; Liaising with governments; Partnering with other organizations to address broader elements of public health issues
Meetings/Conferences:
For more information see Trade Shows, Conferences and Seminars Chapter
Ontario Public Health Association 2012 Annual General Meeting
Other Conferences in 2012 2012, ON
Publications: *Ontario Public Health Association E-Bulletin*
Type: Newsletter *Frequency:* m.
Profile: Current topics in public health & information about the association's workgroups & partnerships
Public Health Today
Type: Magazine *Price:* Free with membership in the Ontario Public Health Association
Mission: To provide leadership on issues affecting public health in Ontario; To strengthen the influence of persons involved in public & community health across Ontario; Affiliation(s): Canadian Public Health Association
Environmental Activity: Offering information related to community & public health; Promoting public health issues

Ontario Public Interest Research Group (OPIRG) / Groupe de recherche d'intérêt public de l'Ontario
North Borden Building, #101, 563 Spadina Ave., Toronto ON M5S 2J7
Tel: 416-978-7770; *Fax:* 416-971-2292
e-mail: opirg.toronto@utoronto.ca
URL: www.opirguoft.org
Overview: A medium-sized provincial organization founded in 1973
Finances: *Annual Operating Budget:* $50,000-$100,000; *Funding Sources:* Student & community membership fees
Staff: 2 staff member(s); 50 volunteer(s)
Membership: 30,000; *Fees:* $1-$5; *Member Profile:* U of T students mostly; *Committees:* Environment; Anti-Racism; Education; Global
Activities: Activism; education; research; action; social & environmental justice; *Speaker Service:* Yes; *Library:* Yes, open by appointment
Mission: To make information available to the general public that enables them to make informed decisions on issues & understand & possibly influence decisions made by others on their behalf; to provide an alternative to the information provided by the academic community, government & business; to offer an analysis of environmental & social issues aimed at motivating change & placing issues in the broader social, economic & political perspective in which they need to be understood

Ontario Refrigeration & Air Conditioning Contractors Association (ORAC)
#43, 6770 Davand Dr., Mississauga ON L5T 2G3
Tel: 905-670-0010; *Fax:* 905-670-0474
e-mail: info@orac.ca
URL: www.orac.ca
Overview: A medium-sized provincial organization
Fees: $1,500 initiation fee & $350 membership dues for provincial members; $1,500 initiation fee & $1,500 membership dues for associate members; *Member Profile:* Individuals, partnerships, & corporations in Ontario, who are engaged in selling, installing, repairing, & maintaining refrigeration & air conditioning equipment; Individuals, partnerships or corporations in Ontario, who provide materials, equipment, or training to the heating, ventilation, refrigeration & air conditioning industry
Activities: Liaising with government & other organizations that represent trade local, provincial, & national bodies; Managing a state of the art training centre; Educating the public about the profession
Meetings/Conferences:
For more information see Trade Shows, Conferences and Seminars Chapter
Ontario Refrigeration & Air Conditioning Contractors Association 2011 44th Annual General Meeting & President's Dinner Celebration
Other Conferences in 2011 2011, ON
Mission: To represent Ontario's contractor practitioners in the refrigeration & air conditioning trade; To enhance quality & efficiency in the industry to benefit customers

Ontario Respiratory Care Society (ORCS)
#201, 573 King St. East, Toronto ON M5A 4L3
Tel: 416-864-9911; *Fax:* 416-864-9916
e-mail: orcs@on.lung.ca
URL: www.on.lung.ca
Overview: A medium-sized provincial charitable organization
Chief Officer(s):
Sheila Gordon-Dillane, MPA, CAE, Director, Administration
Finances: *Funding Sources:* Sponsorships
Member Profile: Persons involved in respiratory care, such as pulmonary function technologists, nurses, occupational therapists & physiotherapists, dietitians, & social workers; *Committees:* Provincial; Research & Fellowship; Editorial Board; Education; Membership & Program Promotion
Activities: Funding graduate education & research in respiratory care; Providing education & disseminating information for health care professionals; Offering professional expertise to the Ontario Lung Association & other interested groups;
Awards: ORCS Research Grants (Grant)
ORCS Fellowship Awards (Award)
Education Awards for Advanced Respiratory Practice (Award)
Meetings/Conferences:
For more information see Trade Shows, Conferences and Seminars Chapter
Ontario Respiratory Care Society 2012 Annual Better Breathing Conference
Other Conferences in 2012 2012, ON
Publications: *ORCS [Ontario Respiratory Care Society] Update*
Type: Newsletter *Frequency:* 3 pa *Price:* Free with membership in the Ontario Respiratory Care Society
Profile: ORCS activities & respiratory articles
Research Review [a joint publication of the Ontario Respiratory Care Society & the Ontario Thoracic Society]
Frequency: a. *Price:* Free with membership in the Ontario Respiratory Care Society
Profile: Highlights of researchers & their studies
RHEIG [Respiratory Health Educators Interest Group] Connections
Frequency: 3 pa *Price:* Free with membership in the Ontario Respiratory Care Society
Profile: Published by the Respiratory Health Educators Interest Group for members of the group
Mission: To improve lung health through the provision of excellent interdisciplinary respiratory care

Ontario Retail Farm Equipment Dealers' Association *See* Canada East Equipment Dealers' Association

Ontario Retail Lumber Dealers Association *See* Lumber & Building Materials Association of Ontario

Ontario Rock Garden Society
88 Cottonwood Drive, Toronto ON M3C 2B4
URL: www.onrockgarden.com
Overview: A small provincial organization founded in 1984
Chief Officer(s):
Merle Burston, Chair
Andrew Osyany, Secretary
Finances: *Annual Operating Budget:* Less than $50,000; *Funding Sources:* Membership fees; plant sales
Membership: 450; *Fees:* $25 individual; $30 family; $10 student
Activities: 10 meetings per year; spring & fall plant sales; seed exchange in Dec.; handbook listing members, gardens to visit, mail order & non-mail order services; *Speaker Service:* Yes
Mission: To promote the study & cultivation of alpine & related garden plants & the creation of rock gardens; *Member of:* North American Rock Garden Society

Ontario Safety League (OSL) / Ligue de sécurité de l'Ontario
Bldg. 11, #100, 5045 Orbitor Dr., Mississauga ON L4W 4Y4
Tel: 905-625-0556; *Fax:* 905-625-0677
e-mail: info@osl.org
URL: www.osl.org
Overview: A medium-sized provincial licensing charitable organization founded in 1913
Finances: *Annual Operating Budget:* $1.5 Million-$3 Million
Staff: 10 staff member(s)
Membership: 300; *Fees:* $30-$300
Activities: Video production sales; courses for instructors of all vehicle types & road safety professionals; safety services for commercial fleets; *Speaker Service:* Yes; *Library:* OSL Film & Video Library; Not open to the public
Mission: Safety through education with an emphasis on traffic & child safety; Affiliation(s): Canada Safety Council; Provincial Safety Leagues/Councils

Ontario Sanitation Equipment Association *See* Ontario Pollution Control Equipment Association

Ontario Sewer & Watermain Construction Association (OSWCA)
#300, 5045 Orbitor Dr., Unit 12, Mississauga ON L4W 4Y4
Tel: 905-629-7766; *Fax:* 905-629-0587
e-mail: info@oswca.org
URL: www.oswca.org
Previous Name: Metropolitan Toronto Sewer & Watermain Contractors Association
Overview: A small local organization
Fees: $100
Activities: *Speaker Service:* Yes

Ontario Shade Tree Council *See* Ontario Urban Forest Council

Ontario Small Urban Municipalities (OSUM)
c/o Association of Municipalities of Ontario, #801, 200 University Ave., Toronto ON M5H 3C6
Tel: 416-971-9856; *Fax:* 416-971-6191
Toll-Free: 877-426-6527
e-mail: amo@amo.on.ca
URL: www.amo.on.ca//AM/Template.cfm?Section=What_s_New7
Overview: A medium-sized provincial organization
Finances: *Funding Sources:* Sponsorships
Membership: 100-499; *Member Profile:* Small urban municipalities in Ontario
Activities: Providing a forum for both elected & appointed municipal officials of Ontario's small urban municipalities to exchange information;
Meetings/Conferences:
For more information see Trade Shows, Conferences and Seminars Chapter
Ontario Small Urban Municipalities 2012 59th Annual Conference & Trade Show
May 2012 Huntsville, ON
Ontario Small Urban Municipalities 2013 60th Annual Conference & Trade Show
Other Conferences in 2013 2013, ON
Mission: To take matters which affect Ontario's small urban communities to the attention of the provincial & federal governments; *Member of:* Association of Municipalities of Ontario

Ontario Society for Environmental Education
PO Box 587, Lakefield ON K0L 2H0
Tel: 705-652-0923
e-mail: liz.straszynski@utschools.ca
URL: www.osee.org
Overview: A small provincial organization
Chief Officer(s):
Emily Addison, Membership Coordinator
Finances: *Annual Operating Budget:* Less than $50,000
Staff: 2 staff member(s); 10 volunteer(s)
Fees: $40 individual; $20 student; $57 overseas; $300 corporate; *Member Profile:* Teachers & outdoor education leaders
Mission: To develop a population that is aware of, & concerned about, the environment & its associated problems, & which has the knowledge, skills, attitudes, motivations & commitment to work individually & collectively toward solutions of current problems & the prevention of new ones (from UNESCO)

Ontario Society for Environmental Management (OSEM)
87 Irondale Dr., Toronto ON M9L 2S6
Tel: 416-746-9076; *Fax:* 416-743-3737
Toll-Free: 800-305-6736
e-mail: osem@rogers.com
Overview: A small provincial organization founded in 1976
Chief Officer(s):
Sue Ruggero, Administrator

Finances: *Annual Operating Budget:* Less than $50,000
Staff: 1 staff member(s)
Membership: 120; *Fees:* $95 full; $20 student; *Member Profile:* Open to those professionally involved in environmental management; potential members must have appropriate academic &/or professional credentials; *Committees:* Membership; Events
Activities: Seminars; conferences
Mission: To encourage the exchange of information on matters of environmental management through seminars, meetings, position papers, newsletter, etc.; to develop an interdisciplinary forum for information exchange with other professions; to help persons & institutions responsible for decisions affecting the environment to make & implement policy consistent with the Society's environmental management ethic; to encourage high standards of competence & ethics among environmental management practitioners; to encourage education in the field of environmental management; to encourage individuals to become environmental management practitioners

Ontario Society of Nutrition Professionals in Public Health (OSNPPH) / La société ontarienne des professionelles et professionnels de la nutrition en santé publique
c/o Ontario Public Health Association, #310, 700 Lawrence Ave. West, Toronto ON M6A 3B4
e-mail: info@osnpph.on.ca
URL: www.osnpph.on.ca
Overview: A small provincial organization founded in 1977
Chief Officer(s):
Michael Hurd, Chair
Janice Stewart, Secretary
Bart Bartle, Chair
Finances: *Annual Operating Budget:* Less than $50,000
Staff: 36 volunteer(s)
Membership: 145; *Fees:* $100; *Member Profile:* Dietitians/nutritionists in public health departments/units
Activities: Annual Nutrition Exchange, 2-day conference
Mission: To provide an official organization that will give nutrition personnel in public health a strong voice within public health & for commenting on public health issues; *Member of:* Ontario Public Health Association

Ontario Society of Professional Engineers (OSPE)
#502, 4950 Yonge St., Toronto ON M2N 6K1
Tel: 416-223-9961; *Fax:* 416-223-9963
Toll-Free: 866-763-1654
e-mail: info@ospe.on.ca
URL: www.ospe.on.ca
Overview: A large provincial organization
Chief Officer(s):
John Schindler, M.Eng., P.Eng., President & Chair
Danny Young, P.Eng, CEO
dyoung@ospe.on.ca
Mission: Advances the interests of professional engineers in Ontario by advocating on behalf of engineers & the profession; providing members with a sense of belonging & mutual support; supplying valued & innovative services; offering quality professional training

Ontario Society of Safety Engineering *See* Canadian Society of Safety Engineering, Inc.

Ontario Soil & Crop Improvement Association (OSCIA) / Association pour l'amélioration des sols et des récoltes de l'Ontario
1 Stone Rd. West, Guelph ON N1G 4Y2
Tel: 519-826-4214; *Fax:* 519-826-4224
Toll-Free: 800-265-9751
e-mail: oscia@ontariosoilcrop.org
URL: www.ontariosoilcrop.org
Overview: A medium-sized provincial organization founded in 1939
Chief Officer(s):
Harold Rudy, Executive Director, 519-826-4217
Julie Henderson, Financial Administrator, 519-826-4221
Steven Nadeau, Administrator, Information Technology, 519-826-6059
Andrew Graham, Manager, Programs, 519-826-4216
Mike Terpstra, Program Manager, Farm Business Management, 519-826-4218
Member Profile: Farmers & persons involved in agriculture in Ontario; *Committees:* Nomination; Resolutions; Finance; Research; Membership; Constitution & Bylaws; Annual Meeting; Ontario Soil Management Research; Soil & Water Quality Sub-Committee; Waste Utilization Sub-Committee; Field Crops Sub-Committee; Ontario Corn; Ontario Weed; Ontario Cereal Crop; Ontario Forage Crops; Ontario Oil & Protein; Biosolids Utilization; Ontario Forage Council; Ontario Agri-Food Education; AGCare; Ontario Field Crops Research Coalition; Canada's Outdoor Farm Show; Ontario Agri-Food Technologies; Soil Conservation Council of Canada
Activities: Offering information about agricultural management practices; Networking with farmers
Meetings/Conferences:
For more information see Trade Shows, Conferences and Seminars Chapter
Canada - Ontario Environmental Farm Plan Program 2011 Bruce County Workshop
June 2011 Bruce County, ON
Growing Your Farm Profits 2011 Bruce County Workshop
June 2011 Bruce County, ON
Growing Your Farm Profits 2011 Durham Region & City of Kawartha Lakes Workshop
June 2011 Goodwood, ON
Growing Your Farm Profits 2011 Waterloo Region Workshop
June 2011 Linwood, ON
Canada - Ontario Environmental Farm Plan Program 2011 Grenville Area Workshop
June 2011 Kemptville, ON
Canada - Ontario Environmental Farm Plan Program 2011 Perth Area Workshop
June 2011 Milverton, ON
Growing Your Farm Profits 2011 Grey County Workshop
June 2011 Markdale, ON
Growing Your Farm Profits 2011 Lennox & Addington & Hastings County Workshop
June 2011, ON
Canada - Ontario Environmental Farm Plan Program 2011 Grey County Workshop
June 2011 Markdale, ON
Growing Your Farm Profits 2011 Wellington County Workshop
June 2011 Elora, ON
Growing Your Farm Profits 2011 Durham Region & City of Kawartha Lakes Workshop
June 2011 Sunderland, ON
Ontario Soil & Crop Improvement Association 2011 Soil & Water Management Workshop
June 2011 Simcoe County, ON
Canada - Ontario Environmental Farm Plan Program 2011 Prescott United Counties Workshop
July 2011 St Isidore, ON
Growing Your Farm Profits 2011 Kent & Lambton Areas Workshop
July 2011 Ridgetown, ON
Growing Your Farm Profits 2011 Middlesex County Workshop
July 2011, ON
Growing Your Farm Profits 2011 Huron County Workshop
July 2011 Clinton, ON
Ontario Soil & Crop Improvement Association 2011 Sprayer Clinic
July 2011 Lindsay, ON
Ontario Soil & Crop Improvement Association 2011 Ontario Forage Expo
July 2011 Elora, ON
Ontario Soil & Crop Improvement Association 2011 FarmSmart Expo
July 2011 Elora, ON
Canada - Ontario Environmental Farm Plan Program 2011 Huron County Workshop
July 2011 Clinton, ON
Ontario Soil & Crop Improvement Association 2011 Southwest Crop Diagnostic Day
July 2011 Ridgetown, ON
Growing Your Farm Profits 2011 Huron County Workshop
August 2011 Clinton, ON
Growing Your Farm Profits 2011 Bruce County Workshop
August 2011 Bruce County, ON
Canada - Ontario Environmental Farm Plan Program 2011 Carleton Area Workshop
August 2011 Richmond, ON
Canada - Ontario Environmental Farm Plan Program 2011 Huron County Workshop
August 2011 Clinton, ON
Growing Your Farm Profits 2011 Wellington County Workshop
September 2011 Elora, ON
Growing Your Farm Profits 2011 Ottawa Carleton, Dundas, Lanark, & Grenville Areas Workshop
September 2011 Kemptville, ON
Growing Your Farm Profits 2011 Leeds Area Workshop
September 2011 Kemptville, ON
Growing Your Farm Profits 2011 Renfrew County Workshop
September 2011 Kemptville, ON
Canada - Ontario Environmental Farm Plan Program 2011 Bruce County Workshop
September 2011 Bruce County, ON
Growing Your Farm Profits 2011 Huron County Workshop
September 2011 Clinton, ON
Growing Your Farm Profits 2011 Wellington County Workshop
November 2011 Elora, ON
Growing Your Farm Profits 2011 Lanark Area Workshop
November 2011, ON
Growing Your Farm Profits 2011 Waterloo Region Workshop
November 2011 Linwood, ON
Growing Your Farm Profits 2011 Dundas Area Workshop
November 2011, ON
Growing Your Farm Profits 2011 Renfrew County Workshop
November 2011, ON
Growing Your Farm Profits 2011 Leeds Area Workshop
December 2011 Athens, ON
Growing Your Farm Profits 2012 Grenville Area Workshop
January 2012, ON
Growing Your Farm Profits 2012 Ottawa Carleton Area Workshop
January 2012, ON
Ontario Soil & Crop Improvement Association 2012 Provincial Annual Meeting
February 2012 London, ON
Growing Your Farm Profits 2012 Cochrane Area Workshop
Other Conferences in 2012 2012, ON
Ontario Soil & Crop Improvement Association 2013 Provincial Annual Meeting
Other Conferences in 2013 2013, ON
Ontario Soil & Crop Improvement Association 2014 Provincial Annual Meeting
Other Conferences in 2014 2014, ON
Publications: *Ontario Soil & Crop Improvement Association Newsletter*
Type: Newsletter *Frequency:* q. *Price:* Free with Ontario Soil & Crop Improvement Association membership
New Crops, Old Challenges: Tips & Tricks for Managing New Crops!
Number of Pages: 76
Profile: Crop profiles
Crop Advances: Field Crop Reports
Type: Yearbook *Frequency:* a.
Profile: Projects of the field crop team from the Agriculture Development Branch of the Ontario Ministry of Agriculture, Food, & Rural Affairs, in partnership with the Ontario Soil & Crop Improvement Association, commodity groups, & industry
Mission: To communicate & facilitate the responsible management of soil, water, air, & crops
Environmental Activity: Providing information about Ontario stewardship programs

Ontario Soybean Growers
AgriCentre, #201, 100 Stone Rd. West, Guelph ON N1G 5L3
Tel: 519-767-1744; *Fax:* 519-767-2466
e-mail: cansoy@soybean.on.ca
URL: www.soybean.on.ca
Previous Name: Ontario Soybean Growers' Marketing Board
Overview: A medium-sized provincial organization founded in 1949
Chief Officer(s):
Crosby Devitt, Research Manager
Mary Wiley, Communications Coordinator
mwiley@soybean.on.ca
Dale Petrie, General Manager
Finances: *Annual Operating Budget:* $1.5 Million-$3 Million
Staff: 10 staff member(s)
Membership: 25,000; *Member Profile:* Soybean producers
Mission: To enhance the marketing of Ontario soybeans

Ontario Soybean Growers' Marketing Board *See* Ontario Soybean Growers

Ontario Streams
50 Bloomington Rd. West, Aurora ON L4G 3G8
Tel: 905-713-7399; *Fax:* 905-713-7361
URL: www.ontariostreams.on.ca
Overview: A medium-sized provincial organization
Chief Officer(s):
Doug Forder, M.Sc, Field Supervisor
doug.forder@ontariostreams.on.ca

Associations/Organizations / Ontario Sustainable Energy Association

Mission: To promote the conservation & rehabilitation of streams & wetlands, through education & community involvement

Ontario Sustainable Energy Association (OSEA)
#201, 156 Front St. West, Toronto ON M5J 2L6
Tel: 416-977-4441; *Fax:* 416-977-4441
Toll-Free: 888-840-3447
e-mail: info@ontario-sea.org; employment@ontario-sea.org
URL: www.ontario-sea.org
Social Media:
www.facebook.com/ontariosea?v=wall#!/ontariosea?sk=info
Overview: A small provincial organization founded in 2002
Chief Officer(s):
Kristopher Stevens, Executive Director
Kristopher@ontario-sea.org
Harry French, Director, Community Power Services Group
harry@ontario-sea.org
Kate Holloway, Director, Business Development
kate@ontario-sea.org
Roberto Garcia, Coordinator, Community Power Services Group
roberto@ontario-sea.org
Craig Jackson, Coordinator, Community Power Services Group
craig@ontario-sea.org
Ian Jackson, Coordinator, Web, Data, & Social Media
ian@ontario-sea.org
Nicole Risse, Coordinator, Tradeshow, Events, & Logistics
ian@ontario-sea.org
Finances: *Funding Sources:* Sponsorships
Fees: $56.50 students; $113 minimum donation, friends; $565 - $1,695 supporters; $2,260 champions; $5,650 enablers
Activities: Engaging in advocacy activities, capacity building, & non-partisan policy work; Providing public outreach services
Meetings/Conferences:
For more information see Trade Shows, Conferences and Seminars Chapter
Ontario Sustainable Energy Association 2011 3rd Annual Community Power Conference & Power Networking Centre Trade Show
November 2011 Toronto, ON
Ontario Sustainable Energy Association 2012 Annual General Meeting
Other Conferences in 2012 2012 Toronto, ON
Ontario Sustainable Energy Association 2012 4th Annual Community Power Conference & Power Networking Centre Trade Show
Other Conferences in 2012 2012, ON
Ontario Sustainable Energy Association 2013 Annual General Meeting
Other Conferences in 2013 2013, ON
Publications: *Ontario Sustainable Energy Association E-Bulletin*
Type: Newsletter *Price:* Free with Ontario Sustainable Energy Association membership
Profile: Updates about the association & upcoming events
OSEA [Ontario Sustainable Energy Association] Member Directory
Type: Directory
Profile: Contact information for members
Green Energy ACTion Kit
Type: Kit *Price:* $10 + $13.50 shipping & handling, members; $20 + $13.40 S&H, non-members
Profile: Suggestions to help citizens advocate for green energy in Ontario
Community Power Financing Guidebook
Type: Manual *Price:* $40 + $13.50 shipping & handling, members; $65 + $13.40 S&H, non-members
Profile: Contents include pre-development financing, land acquisition, legal contracting, permits & approvals, resource assessment, & community engagement
Solar Thermal Community Action Manual
Type: Manual
Profile: Information for Canadians about residential-scale or small-scale commercial solar thermal installations, as well as the establishment of a community based organization
Solar PV Community Action Manual
Type: Manual
Profile: Information for Canadian residents about residential-scale or small-scale commercial Solar PV installations, as well as related topics such as financing & home assessment
Permitting & Approvals Processes for CP Projects [a publication of the Ontario Sustainable Energy Association]
Type: Guide *Price:* $40 + $13.50 shipping & handling, members; $65 + $13.50 S&H, non-members

Profile: An overview of the policy environment for biogas & wind projects in Ontario, of interest to municipal planners, project proponents, & the general public
Ontario Landowner's Guide to Wind Energy
Type: Guide *Author:* Paul Gipe; James Murphy *Price:* $10 + $13.50 shipping & handling, members; $20 + $13.50 S&H, non-members
Profile: A comprehensive manual for rural landowners & farmers who are interested in wind power
The Community Power Guidebook
Type: Guide
Profile: A guide to the development of a community power project, from conception to commissioning
Arts Revision Report: Renewables Without Limits [a publication of the Ontario Sustainable Energy Association]
Type: Report *Price:* $1 + $13.50 shipping & handling, members; $10 + $13.50 S&H, non-members
Profile: A review of Ontario's Renewable Energy Standard Offer Program
Recommendations for Procuring Sustainable Energy: An Addendum to Renewables Without Limits
Profile: An update to recommendations from the Arts Revision Report: Renewable Without Limits
Proposal for a Green Energy Act for Ontario
Profile: A proposal for renewable energy sources to protect the environment & to manage climate change
Powering Ontario Communities: Proposed Policy for Projects up to 10mw
Type: Study
Profile: Options to encourage small or community-owned renewable energy generation in Ontario
Mission: To represent & serve municipalities, First Nations, institutions, businesses, cooperatives, farms, & households; To support the work of local sustainable energy organizations
Environmental Activity: Enabling people to produce clean, sustainable enery in their homes & communities

Ontario Tender Fruit Producers
c/o Faye Clack Communications Inc., 170 Robert Speck Pkwy., Mississauga ON L4Z 3G1
Tel: 905-206-0577; *Fax:* 905-206-0581
e-mail: tenderfruit@fayeclack.com
URL: www.ontariotenderfruit.com
Overview: A small provincial organization founded in 1979
Membership: 500 grower members

Ontario Tire Dealers Association
PO Box 516, 34 Edward St., Drayton ON N0G 1P0
Tel: 888-207-9059; *Fax:* 866-375-6832
URL: www.otda.com
Overview: A medium-sized national organization
Chief Officer(s):
Robert Bignell, Executive Director
bbignell@otda.com
Glenn Warnica, President
gwarnica@sympatico.ca
Ron Spiewak, Secretary-Treasurer
rons@bellnet.ca
Eric Gilbert, Chair, Ontario Tire Dealers Associaton Committee
ericwaytire@primus.ca
Finances: *Funding Sources:* Membership fees; Fundraising
Activities: Educating members; Promoting standards of ethics; Engaging in lobbying activities
Meetings/Conferences:
For more information see Trade Shows, Conferences and Seminars Chapter
Ontario Tire Dealers Association 2011 Annual General Meeting
June 2011 Gatineau, QC
Ontario Tire Dealers Association 2012 Annual General Meeting
Other Conferences in 2012 2012
Publications: *Trends [a publication of the Ontario Tire Dealers Association]*
Type: Newsletter *Frequency:* q. *Accepts Advertising*: Yes
Profile: Information for members about industry issues
Ontario Tire Dealers Association Membership Directory
Type: Directory
Profile: Contact information about Ontario's tire professionals
Mission: To represent & promote members; *Affiliation(s):* Tire Dealers Association of Canada; Tire Industry Association
Environmental Activity: Participating in the development of an environmentally friendly scrap tire management program

Ontario Traffic Conference (OTC)
#2, 6355 Kennedy Rd., Mississauga ON L5T 2L5
Tel: 647-346-4050; *Fax:* 647-346-4060
e-mail: info@otc.org

URL: www.otc.org
Social Media: twitter.com/ontariotraffic
Overview: A medium-sized provincial organization
Mission: To improve traffic conditions & traffic safety in municipalities of Ontario

Ontario Trails Council
#130, 556 O'Connor Dr., Kingston ON K7P 1N3
Tel: 613-389-7678; *Fax:* 613-389-6329
Toll-Free: 877-668-7245
e-mail: admin@ontariotrails.on.ca
URL: www.ontariotrails.on.ca
Overview: A medium-sized provincial organization founded in 1988
Finances: *Annual Operating Budget:* Less than $50,000; *Funding Sources:* Membership fees; corporate donations
Membership: 500,000 individuals + 21 groups; *Fees:* $26.50 individual; $106-$795 club/association + GST; *Member Profile:* Association or club with interest in recreational trail acquisition, maintenance & use; individuals concerned with environment & trail recreation; *Committees:* Government Relations; Public Affairs; Trails Development
Activities: *Library:* Yes
Mission: To promote the creation, development, preservation, management & use of an integrated, recreational, multi-seasonal trail network in Ontario; interested in all types of trails for non-motorized & motorized (where applicable) use in all seasons; acquisition & conversion of Ontario's abandoned railway rights-of-way to linear greenways for year-round recreational activities for the people of Ontario; *Affiliation(s):* Bruce Trail Association; Canadian Motorcycling Association; Guelph Trail Club; Hike Ontario; Kawartha Rail-Trail; Ontario Federation of Snowmobile Clubs; Ontario Cycling Association; Ontario Competitive Trail Riders Association; Ontario Working Dog Association; Parry Sound Rail Line Task Force; Rideau Trail Association; Northland Associates; Ontario Trail Riders Association; Rails to Trails Conservancy - USA; Credit Valley Conservation Authority; Georgian Cycle & Ski Trail Association; Grand Valley Trail Association; Southeastern Ontario Rails to Tracks

Ontario Trucking Association (OTA)
Parent: Canadian Trucking Alliance
555 Dixon Rd., Toronto ON M9W 1H8
Tel: 416-249-7401; *Fax:* 416-245-6152
e-mail: info@ontruck.org
URL: www.ontruck.org
Overview: A large provincial organization founded in 1926
Finances: *Funding Sources:* Membership fees
Membership: 1,700 member companies; *Committees:* Axle Weight; Credit; Education; Executive; Social/Labour; Tech./Ops; Convention; Dues; Membership; Insurance; Finance; Environmental Issues
Activities: Drug Testing Consortium; training courses & seminars; Trucking Industry Compensation & Benefits Report; *Speaker Service:* Yes; *Library:* Yes
Mission: Canada's largest trade association representing companies & industry suppliers; provides political advocacy, education & information services to North American freight transport companies with operations in Ontario.

Ontario Urban Forest Council (OUFC)
#23/25, 1523 Warden Ave., Toronto ON M1R 4Z8
Tel: 416-936-6735; *Fax:* 416-291-9584
e-mail: jradec@mountpleasantgroup.com
URL: www.oufc.org
Previous Name: Ontario Shade Tree Council
Overview: A medium-sized provincial organization founded in 1964
Finances: *Annual Operating Budget:* Less than $50,000
Staff: 11 volunteer(s)
Membership: 189 corporate + 9 senior/lifetime + 55 individual; *Fees:* Student: $25; Individual: $75; Group/Corporate: $150
Activities: *Speaker Service:* Yes
Mission: To promote & assist in the protection & preservation of shade trees; to cooperate with all associations, government agencies, industry & individuals with a mutual interest in preserving & developing Ontario's shade tree heritage & landscape; to promote management of urban forest in Ontario; *Affiliation(s):* Urban Forest Network

Ontario Urban Transit Association *See* Ontario Community Transit Association

Ontario Vegetation Management Association (OVMA)
4 Spruce Blvd., Acton ON L7J 2Y2
Tel: 905-805-2294; *Fax:* 519-853-0352
e-mail: info@ovma.ca
URL: www.ovma.on.ca
Overview: A small provincial organization founded in 1984
Chief Officer(s):
Tom McLean, President
Fees: $75 individual; $250 corporate gold; *Member Profile:* Promotes environmentally safe vegetation management

Ontario Waste Management Association (OWMA) / Société ontarienne de gestion des déchets
#3, 2005 Clark Blvd., Brampton ON L6T 5P8
Tel: 905-791-9500; *Fax:* 905-791-9514
e-mail: contact@owma.org
URL: www.owma.org
Overview: A medium-sized provincial organization founded in 1977
Membership: 300; *Member Profile:* Private sector independent companies in Ontario which provide waste & recycling services; Associate members include equipment manufacturers, suppliers, legal firms, & consultants; *Committees:* EFW & WDF; Environmental Affairs; Financial Business Analysis; Green Energy & Greenhouse Gas Task Group; Hazardous Waste; Membership; Organics Diversion & Composting; Programs; Public Affairs; Safety & Transportation; Soils Caucus; Standards & Accreditation; Waste Diversion & Recycling; Waste Transfer & Disposal
Activities: Monitoring & assessing regulatory & policy initiatives; Promoting new standards & regulatory policies to improve waste management services; Providing information to members about government initiatives, waste management, & business issues
Mission: To act as the voice of the private sector waste industry in Ontario; To protect the enviroment by properly managing waste & recyclable materials
Environmental Activity: Offering professional advice to members about environmental management issues; Providing educational materials to the public to increase awarement of waste management issues

Ontario Water Garden Society *See* Greater Toronto Water Garden & Horticultural Society

Ontario Water Well Association *See* Ontario Ground Water Association

Ontario Water Works Association (OWWA)
#00, 1092 Islington Ave., Toronto ON M8Z 4R9
Tel: 416-231-1555; *Fax:* 416-231-1556
Toll-Free: 866-975-0575
e-mail: waterinfo@owwa.ca
URL: www.owwa.com
Overview: A medium-sized provincial organization
Chief Officer(s):
Saad Jasim, President
jasims@windsor.ijc.org
Lee Anne E. Jones, Vice-President
ljones@toronto.ca
Bill Balfour, Executive Director, 905-642-5283
bbalfour@owwa.ca
Lesia Lachmaniuk, Manager, Marketing & Membership, 416-231-1555, Fax: 416-231-1556
llachmaniuk@owwa.ca
Glenn Powell, Director, Communications, 905-827-4508, Fax: 905-827-6483
gpowell@owwa.ca
Ray Miller, Secretary-Treasurer
rmiller@clowcanada.com
Membership: 1,100+; *Member Profile:* Drinking water professionals in Ontario, such as hydrogeologists, scientists, engineers, chemists, & managers & technicians employed by Ontario's municipal water systems; *Committees:* Climate Change; C-PAC; Conference Management; Continuing Education; Cross Connection Control; Distribution; Government Affairs; Groundwater; Joint OWWA / OMWA; Management; Membership; OWWA / WEAO Joint Asset Management; Publications; Small Systems; Source Water Protection; Training, Certification, & Safety; Treatment; University Forum; Water Efficiency; Water for People - Canada; Young Professionals; Youth Education
Activities: Improving technology, science & management; Influencing government policy; Providing education for members; *Library:* Ontario Water Works Association Library

Publications: *Ontario Pipeline*
Type: Magazine Frequency: 3 pa Accepts Advertising : Yes
Profile: A joint publication of the Ontario Water Works Association, the Ontario Municipal Water Association, & the Ontario Water Works Equipment Association
Consultants' Listing [a publication of the Ontario Water Works Association]
Frequency: 3 pa Accepts Advertising : Yes
Mission: To protect public health through the delivery of safe, sufficient, & sustainable drinking water in Ontario; *Member of:* American Water Works Association; Affiliation(s): Ontario Municipal Water Association; Ontario Water Works Equipment Association
Environmental Activity: Promoting water stewardship

Ontario Wheat Producers' Marketing Board (OWPMB)
#201, 100 Stone Rd. West, Guelph ON N1G 5L3
Tel: 519-767-6537; *Fax:* 519-767-9713
Toll-Free: 800-943-2809
e-mail: general.mail@ontariowheatboard.com
URL: www.ontariowheatboard.com
Overview: A medium-sized provincial organization founded in 1958
Chief Officer(s):
David Whaley, Chair
Larry Shapton, General Manager

Ontario Woodlot Association
c/o G. Howard Ferguson Forest Stn., RR#4, 275 County Rd. 44, Kemptville ON K0G 1J0
Tel: 613-258-0110; *Fax:* 613-258-0207
Toll-Free: 888-791-1103
e-mail: info@ont-woodlot-assoc.org
URL: www.ont-woodlot-assoc.org
Overview: A small provincial organization founded in 1992
Chief Officer(s):
Dolf Harmsen, President
Pieter Leenhouts, Vice-President
Membership: 1,300; *Fees:* $35
Mission: To promote the wise & profitable use of Ontario's private land forest resource

Ontario Workers' Compensation Institute *See* Institute for Work & Health

Ordre des agronomes du Québec (OAQ)
#810, 1001, rue Sherbrooke est, Montréal QC H2L 1L3
Tél: 514-596-3833; *Téléc:* 514-596-2974
Ligne sans frais: 800-361-3833
Courriel: agronome@oaq.qc.ca
URL: www.oaq.qc.ca
Nom précédent: Corporation des agronomes du Québec
Aperçu: *Dimension:* moyenne; *Envergure:* provinciale; *Organisme sans but lucratif;* fondée en 1937
Finances: *Budget de fonctionnement annuel:* $500,000-$1.5 Million
Personnel: 10 membre(s) du personnel; 100 bénévole(s)
Membre: 3 189; *Critères d'admissibilite:* Agronomes
Prix, Bouses: Prix Henri-C.Bois (Prix)
Souligne la valeur inestimable du travail bénévole d'un agronome au sein de différents comités de l'OAQ
Médaille de distinction agronomique (Prix)
Décernée à un agronome pour souligner ses réalisations professionnelles exceptionnelles et son rayonnement au sein de la profession et de la collectivité
Ordre du Mérite agronomique (Prix)
Décerné à un agronome qui a rendu des services exceptionnels dans le domaine de l'agriculture ou pour la cause agronomique
Mérite spécial Adélard-Godbout (Prix)
Reconnaît l'apport exceptionnel d'une entreprise, d'un organisme, d'un individu ou d'un groupe d'individus au développement de l'agriculture, de l'agronomie et/ou du secteur agroalimentaire québécois
Mission: Assure les utilisateurs de services agronomiques et les consommateurs de la compétence, du professionnalisme et de l'engagement des agronomes et ainsi favoriser le mieux-être de la société

Ordre des arpenteurs-géomètres du Québec (OAGQ) / Québec Land Surveyors Association
Parent: Canadian Council of Land Surveyors
#350, 2954, boul Laurier, Sainte-Foy QC G1V 4T2
Tél: 418-656-0730; *Téléc:* 418-656-2760
Courriel: oagq@oagq.qc.ca
URL: www.oagq.qc.ca

Aperçu: *Dimension:* moyenne; *Envergure:* provinciale; fondée en 1882
Finances: *Budget de fonctionnement annuel:* $500,000-$1.5 Million
Personnel: 7 membre(s) du personnel; 40 bénévole(s)
Membre: 1 000; *Montant de la cotisation:* 830$; *Critères d'admissibilité:* BAC en géomatique; stage d'un an; examens de l'Ordre; *Comités:* Arbitrage; Assurances et sinistres; Discipline; Examinateurs; Formation; Inspection; Réglementation; Révision; Stages; Syndic
Activités: Congrès annuel; ateliers divers; *Stagiaires:* Oui; *Listes de destinataires:* Oui
Mission: La protection du public et le contrôle de la profession; *Membre de:* Association de géomatique municipale; Affiliation(s): Fédération des arpenteurs-géomètres du Québec

Ordre des chimistes du Québec (OCQ)
#2199, 300 rue Léo-Pariseau, Montréal QC H2X 4B3
Tél: 514-844-3644; *Téléc:* 514-844-9601
Courriel: information@ocq.qc.ca
URL: www.ocq.qc.ca
Aperçu: *Dimension:* moyenne; *Envergure:* provinciale; *Organisme de réglementation;* fondée en 1926
Finances: *Budget de fonctionnement annuel:* $500,000-$1.5 Million
Personnel: 5 membre(s) du personnel; 120 bénévole(s)
Membre: 2 500; *Critères d'admissibilite:* Chimistes, biochimistes, *Comités:* Réglementaires prévus par le code des professions (L.R.Q., chapitre C-26)
Mission: L'Ordre est une corporation professionnelle dont la raison d'être est la protection du public

Ordre des ingénieurs du Québec (OIQ)
Parent: Canadian Council of Professional Engineers
#350, 1100, rue De La Gauchetière ouest, Montréal QC H3B 2S2
Tél: 514-845-6141; *Téléc:* 514-845-1833
Ligne sans frais: 800-461-6141
Courriel: dirgen@oiq.qc.ca
URL: www.oiq.qc.ca
Aperçu: *Dimension:* grande; *Envergure:* provinciale; fondée en 1920
Finances: *Budget de fonctionnement annuel:* Plus de $5 Million
Personnel: 80 membre(s) du personnel; 600 bénévole(s)
Membre: 40 000; *Montant de la cotisation:* 180$; *Comités:* Discipline; Inspection professionnelle; Examinateurs; Surveillance de FERIQUE; Environnement; Technologie; Santé et sécurité du travail; Femmes en ingénierie
Activités: Préparation d'avis, mémoires et de documents professionnels; organisation ou préparation à des conférences; groupes de travail sur: la gestion des déchets solides, l'eau de consommation, le bilan technologique, l'analyse technologique des secteurs d'activité économique du Québec, le transfert de technologie, le génie-conseil; *Événements de sensibilisation:* Journée de l'ingénieur(e); *Stagiaires:* Oui; *Service de conférenciers:* Oui; *Bibliothèque:* Oui, Not open to the public
Prix, Bouses: Bourse Krashinsky (Prix)
Grand prix d'excellence (Prix)
Prix du Président au bénévolat (Prix)
Prix d'encouragement aux études supérieures (Prix)
Mission: Faire la promotion et s'assurer de la qualité des services rendus à la société par les ingénieurs, individuellement et collectivement, en tant que membres d'un corps professionnel; favoriser leur épanouissement professionnel et personnel; contribuer au développement socio-économique de la sociétéAffiliation(s): Conseil Interprofessionnel du Québec

Ordre des ingénieurs forestiers du Québec (OIFQ)
#110, 2750, rue Einstein, Québec QC G1P 4R1
Tél: 418-650-2411; *Téléc:* 418-650-2168
Courriel: oifq@oifq.com
URL: www.oifq.com
Aperçu: *Dimension:* moyenne; *Envergure:* provinciale; *Organisme sans but lucratif; Organisme de réglementation;* fondée en 1921
Finances: *Budget de fonctionnement annuel:* $500,000-$1.5 Million
Membre: 2 260; *Montant de la cotisation:* 435$; *Critères d'admissibilite:* Diplôme universitaire de premier cycle en foresterie
Activités: *Service de conférenciers:* Oui
Mission: Assurer la protection du public; assurer la qualité des services rendus au public québécois; favoriser l'amélioration continue de l'expertise et de la compétence des ingénieurs forestiers; mettre en place des actions favorisant la durabilité de l'aménagement forestier pour le bénéfice de l'ensemble de la

Associations/Organizations / Ordre des technologues professionnels du Québec

sociétéMembre de: Conseil interprofessionnel du Québec; Affiliation(s): Fédération canadienne des associations d'ingénieurs forestiers

Ordre des technologues professionnels du Québec (OTPQ)
Parent: Canadian Council of Technicians & Technologists
#720, 1265, rue Berri, Montréal QC H2L 4X4
Tél: 514-845-3247; Téléc: 514-845-3643
Ligne sans frais: 800-561-3459
Courriel: info@otpq.qc.ca
URL: www.otpq.qc.ca
Nom précédent: Corporation professionnelle des technologues professionnelles du Québec
Aperçu: Dimension: moyenne; Envergure: provinciale; fondée en 1927
Finances: Budget de fonctionnement annuel: $500,000-$1.5 Million
Personnel: 9 membre(s) du personnel
Membre: 5 000; Comités: Admission; Discipline; Inspection professionnelle; Prix
Activités: Stagiaires: Oui; Listes de destinataires: Oui
Prix, Bouses: Technologue de l'année (Prix)
Prix Robert Daigneault (Bénévole de l'année) (Prix)
Bourse méritas (Brouse)
Mission: Promouvoir et assurer la compétence des technologues professionnels dans l'intérêt public; Membre de: Conseil canadiens des techniciens et technologues

Ordre des urbanistes du Québec (OUQ)
Parent: Canadian Institute of Planners
#410, 85, rue St-Paul ouest, Montréal QC H2Y 3V4
Tél: 514-849-1177; Téléc: 514-849-7176
Courriel: info@ouq.qc.ca
URL: www.ouq.qc.ca
Nom précédent: Ordre professionnel des urbanistes du Québec
Aperçu: Dimension: moyenne; Envergure: provinciale; fondée en 1963
Membre: 700; Montant de la cotisation: 360$; Comités: Admission; Déontologie; Discipline; Formation Continue; Inspection Professionnelle
Mission: Assurer la protection du public dans l'exercice de la profession par ses membres et la promotion de la pratique de l'urbanisme au Québec

Ordre professionnel des urbanistes du Québec Voir Ordre des urbanistes du Québec

Organic Crop Improvement Association - Alberta Chapter #1 See Alberta Organic Producers Association

Organic Crop Improvement Association - New Brunswick (OCIA-NB)
2002 Cedar Camp Rd., South Beach Kings NB E4E 5E7
Tel: 506-433-3935
e-mail: ocianb@nbnet.nb.ca
Overview: A small provincial organization founded in 1987
Chief Officer(s):
Susan Tyler, Administrator
Fees: $30; Member Profile: Growers both in New Brunswick & northern Maine
Mission: To provide organic certification & crop improvement for New Brunswick farmers; Member of: OCIA International; Affiliation(s): New Brunswick Federation of Agriculture

Organic Crop Improvement Association - Québec & Ontario
25 Bryden Ave., Cornwall ON K6H 5M4
Tel: 613-933-6093; Fax: 613-933-6093
e-mail: ahoude@ocia.org
Also Known As: OCIA Québec & Ontario
Overview: A small provincial organization
Chief Officer(s):
Annie Houde, Regional Office Manager
Mission: To work as a farmer-owned & operated organization to support farmers with technical knowledge, skill & organizational aids to develop ecologically sound crop management systems; To administer the OCIA International certification program at the chapter level; To promote the OCIA seal & the principles of organic agriculture; Member of: Organic Crop Improvement Association (International)

Organic Crop Improvement Association (International) (OCIA) / Association pour l'amélioration des cultures biologiques (international)
1340 North Cotner, Lincoln NE 68505 USA
Tel: 402-477-2323; Fax: 402-477-4325
e-mail: info@ocia.org
URL: www.ocia.org
Also Known As: OCIA International
Overview: A medium-sized international licensing organization founded in 1988
Chief Officer(s):
Jeff See, Executive Director
Finances: Annual Operating Budget: $1.5 Million-$3 Million; Funding Sources: Member-owned & funded
Staff: 30 staff member(s)
Membership: 3,000+; Fees: US$75 corporate & chapter level; individual chapter membership fees vary; Member Profile: Farmers, processors & merchants who are committed to seeking alternatives to conventional chemical & energy-intensive food system; Committees: By-Laws; Crop Improvement; Finance; Inspector Accreditation; Internal Review; Certification Analysis; International Certification; International Standards; Chapter Licensing; Promotions; AGMM; Canadian Organic Regulatory Committee; Research & Education
Activities: Speaker Service: Yes
Mission: To support all farmers with the technical knowledge, skills & organizational aids they need to develop workable crop management systems capable of supplying the growing market demand for organic foods; to provide third party certification of organic foods; Member of: Organic Trade Association; Affiliation(s): International Federation of Organic Agriculture Movements; Japan Agriculture Standards; US National Organic Program; Conseil des Appelations Agroalimentaires du Québec; Costa Rica Ministry of Agriculture & Livestock; ISO Guide 65

Organic Crop Producers & Processors Ontario Inc. (OCPP)
PO Box 74, 2311 Elm Tree Rd., Cambray ON K0M 1E0
Tel: 705-374-5602; Fax: 705-374-5604
e-mail: ocpp@lindsaycomp.on.ca
URL: www.ocpro.ca
Also Known As: OCPRO
Overview: A small provincial organization founded in 1991
Chief Officer(s):
Larry Lenhardt
Activities: Organic food & community certification; Speaker Service: Yes
Member of: International Federation of Organic Agriculture Movements; Affiliation(s): Pro-Cert Organic Systems

Organic Food Production Association of North America See Organic Trade Association

Organic Producers Association of Manitoba Co-operative Inc. (OPAM)
PO Box 940, Virden MB R0M 2C0
Tel: 204-748-1315; Fax: 204-748-6881
e-mail: info@opam.mb.ca
URL: www.opam.mb.ca
Overview: A medium-sized provincial organization founded in 1988
Chief Officer(s):
Trevor Tuttosi, General Manager
Janet Liefso, Certification Manager
Membership: 881; Fees: $25 individual
Activities: Marketing seminars; farm tours; production seminars; AGM
Mission: To provide organic certification inspection service to farmers & processors; to teach & promote standards, methods & techniques for growing, producing & processing organically grown products

Organic Trade Association (OTA)
PO Box 547, 60 Wells St., Greenfield MA 01302 USA
Tel: 413-774-7511; Fax: 413-774-6432
e-mail: info@ota.com
URL: www.ota.com
Previous Name: Organic Food Production Association of North America
Overview: A medium-sized international organization founded in 1985
Finances: Annual Operating Budget: $500,000-$1.5 Million; Funding Sources: Membership fees; merchandise sales; fundraising
Staff: 22 staff member(s); 20 volunteer(s)
Membership: 1,500; Fees: Based on revenues; Member Profile: Organic food processors; certifiers; distributors; organic farm organizations; consultants; farmers; retail outlets; restaurants; Committees: Legislative; Quality Assurance; Marketing; International Relations; Organic Certifiers Council; Organic Fiber Council; Organic Suppliers Advisory Council; Canadian Council
Activities: Organic Harvest Month; Awareness Events: Organic Harvest Month, Sept.; Speaker Service: Yes
Mission: To encourage global sustainability through promoting & protecting the growth of diverse organic trade; Member of: International Federation of Organic Agriculture Movements

Organic Verification Organization of North America (OVONO US)
PO Box 146, Hitterdal MN 56552 USA
Tel: 218-962-3264
e-mail: info@organicfood.com
Overview: A small international organization
Chief Officer(s):
Matthew Moe, Contact
Mission: To provide certification services

Organisation de coopération et de développement économique See Organization for Economic Cooperation & Development

Organisation internationale de normalisation See International Organization for Standardization

Organisation maritime internationale See International Maritime Organization

Organisation météorologique mondiale See World Meteorological Organization

Organisation mondiale de la santé See World Health Organization

L'Organisation pour les carrières en environnement du Canada See Environmental Careers Organization of Canada

Organization for Economic Cooperation & Development (OECD) / Organisation de coopération et de développement économique (OCDE)
2, rue André-Pascal, Paris F-75775 France
Tel: 33-1-45-24-82-00; Fax: 33-1-45-24-85-00
e-mail: webmaster@oecd.org
URL: www.oecd.org
Overview: A large international organization founded in 1961
Chief Officer(s):
Angel Gurría, Secretary General
Membership: 30 member countries
Activities: Provides a forum for monitoring economic trends & coordinating economic policies among its 30 member countries: the free-market democracies of North America, Western Europe & the Pacific; provides the largest source of comparative data on the industrial economies in the world; produces a wide range of publications, economic surveys, statistics, analyses & policy recommendations
Mission: To achieve the highest sustainable economic growth & employment; to promote economic & social welfare throughout the OECD area by coordinating the policies of its member countries; to stimulate & harmonize its members' efforts in favour of developing countries; Member of: International Organization of Securities Commissions - Canada; Affiliation(s): International Energy Agency (IEA); Nuclear Energy Agency

Organization of CANDU Industries (OCI) / Association des industries CANDU
#102, 345 Kingston Rd., Pickering ON L1V 1A1
Tel: 905-509-0073
e-mail: mrwash@eagle.ca
URL: www.oci-aic.org
Overview: A medium-sized national organization founded in 1979
Finances: Annual Operating Budget: Less than $50,000; Funding Sources: Membership dues
Staff: 3 staff member(s)
Membership: 105; Fees: Schedule available; Member Profile: Manufacturing & engineering companies engaged in supply of goods & services for CANDU nuclear steam plants
Mission: To represent companies in the Canadian private sector engaged in the supply of goods & services for CANDU power plants in export markets; to provide a focal point for industrial collaboration between the private sector of Canada's nuclear industry & foreign purchasers of a CANDU plant; functions separately from AECL, but participates with it in the design, manufacture, construction & commissioning of CANDU facilities in foreign countries; Affiliation(s): Atomic Energy of Canada

Oslo & Paris Commissions See OSPAR Commission

Associations/Organizations / OSPAR Commission

OSPAR Commission (OSPAR)
New Court, 48 Carey St., London WC2A 2JQ United Kingdom
Tel: 44-207-430-5200; *Fax:* 44-207-430-5225
e-mail: secretariat@ospar.org
URL: www.ospar.org
Previous Name: Oslo & Paris Commissions
Overview: A small international organization founded in 1998
Chief Officer(s):
David Johnson, Executive Secretary
Finances: *Annual Operating Budget:* $500,000-$1.5 Million; *Funding Sources:* Membership
Staff: 12 staff member(s)
Membership: 15 European countries & EU; *Fees:* Annual contribution; *Committees:* Assessment & Monitoring; Eutophication; Hazardous Substances; Radioactive Substances; Biodiversity; Offshore Industry
Activities: Protection of the marine environment NE Atlantic
Mission: To control pollution of marine environment of the Northeast Atlantic

Ottawa Duck Club (ODC)
841 Kinsgmere Ave., Ottawa ON K2A 3J8
URL: www.ottawaduckclub.com
Overview: A small local organization founded in 1966
Chief Officer(s):
Bill Bower, President, 613-824-9104
bigbuckbill@hotmail.com
Fees: $20 individual; $25 family
Mission: To actively improve the nesting habitat for waterfowl and other birds along the Ottawa River.

Ottawa Environmental Law Clinic
University of Ottawa, Faculty of Law, #107, 35 Copernicus St., Ottawa ON K1N 6N5
Tel: 613-562-5800; *Fax:* 613-562-5319
e-mail: svstiphout@ecojustice.ca
Overview: A small local organization

Ottawa Field-Naturalists' Club (OFNC)
PO Box 35069, RPO Westgate, Ottawa ON K1Z 1A2
Tel: 613-722-3050
e-mail: ofnc@ofnc.ca; membership@ofnc.ca
URL: www.ofnc.ca
Overview: A small local charitable organization founded in 1879
Chief Officer(s):
Ken Allison, President
Ann MacKenzie, Vice-President
Frank Pope, Treasurer
Fees: $33 individuals; $36 families; $50 sustaining memberships; $500 life memberships; *Member Profile:* Individuals who share an interest in nature; *Committees:* Birds; Conservation; Education & Publicity; Excursions & Lectures; Nominations; Finance; Fletcher Wildlife Garden; Membership; Publications; Awards; Macoun Club for Young Naturalists
Activities: Encouraging research in all fields of natural history
Publications: *Trail & Landscape*
Type: Newsletter *Frequency:* q. *Editor:* Karen McLachlan-Hamilton *Price:* Free for OFNC members
Profile: Club activities & articles on the natural history of the Ottawa Valley
Nature & Natural Areas in Canada's Capital
Price: $5
Autobiography of John Macoun, Canadian Explorer & Naturalist, 1831-1920
Price: $20
Lichens of the Ottawa Region
Price: $10
A Guide to the Geology of the Ottawa District
Price: $5
A Guide to the Geology of the Gatineau-Lièvre District
Price: $5
A Birder's Checklist of Ottawa
Price: $2
Checklist of the Butterflies of the Ottawa District
Price: $2
Mission: To promote the preservation & conservation of Canada's natural heritage

Ottawa Orchid Society
PO Box 38038, 1430 Prince of Wales Dr., Ottawa ON K2C 1N0
URL: www.ottawaorchidsociety.com
Overview: A small local organization founded in 1978
Fees: $25
Activities: Offering programs about the care of orchids; *Awareness Events:* Annual Orchid Show; *Library:* Ottawa Orchid Society Library
Publications: *Spike [a publication of the Ottawa Orchid Society]*
Type: Newsletter *Frequency:* m. *Editor:* Rick Sobkowicz
Mission: To promote knowledge, development, improvement, & conservation of orchids

Ottawa Safety Council (OCSC) / Conseil de sécurité d'Ottawa
#105, 68 Robertson Rd., Nepean ON K2H 5Y8
Tel: 613-238-1513; *Fax:* 613-238-8744
e-mail: info@ottawasafetycouncil.ca
URL: www.ottawasafetycouncil.ca
Previous Name: Ottawa-Carleton Safety Council
Overview: A small local charitable organization founded in 1957
Activities: Providing safety programs, such as the school guard crossing program, the motorcycle training program, the Children's Safety Village, & a safety education outreach program; Offering a children's summer camp
Publications: *Ottawa Safety Council Newsletter*
Type: Newsletter
Profile: Council reports & program updates
Mission: To assist the citizens of Ottawa to protect themselves & others from injury, property destruction due to accidents, & accidental death

Ottawa Valley Health Libraries Association (OVHLA) / Association des bibliothèques de santé de la Vallée d'Outaouais
Parent: Canadian Health Libraries Association
c/o Children's Hospital of Eastern Ontario, 401 Smyth Rd., Ottawa ON K1H 8L1
Tel: 613-737-7600
e-mail: msampson@cheo.on.ca
URL: www.chla-absc.ca/ovhla
Overview: A small local organization founded in 1978
Chief Officer(s):
Margaret Sampson, President, 613-737-7600 Ext. 2207
msampson@cheo.on.ca
Amanda Hodgson, Secretary, 613-226-2553
AmandaH@cadth.ca
Finances: *Funding Sources:* Membership fees; Grants
Staff: 4 staff member(s)
Membership: 54; *Fees:* $20; *Member Profile:* Librarians; Library Technicians; *Committees:* Web
Mission: The Ottawa Valley Health Libraries Association / l'Association des Bibliothèques de la Santé de la Vallée de l'Outaouais is an association of over twenty health-related libraries whose purpose is to promote the provision of quality library services in the health sciences throughout the Ottawa Valley and the Outaouais. It was formed in 1994 through the amalgamation of the Ottawa-Hull Health Libraries Association and the OHA Region 9 chapter of the Ontario Health Libraries Association and is a chapter of the Ontario Health Libraries Association (OHLA) and the Canadian Health Libraries Association (CHLA).; *Member of:* Ontario Health Libraries Association (OHLA) and the Canadian Health Libraries Association (CHLA).

Ottawa Valley Rock Garden & Horticultural Society
PO Box 9123, Stn. T, Ottawa ON K1G 3T8
e-mail: info@ovrghs.ca
URL: www.ovrghs.ca
Overview: A small local organization founded in 1992
Chief Officer(s):
Josie Pazdzior, President
josiepaz@rogers.com
Margaret Don, Membership Secretary
Fees: $20 individual, $25 family
Activities: Meetings held second Saturday of each month from Sept.-May at Woodroffe Campus of Algonquin College
Affiliation(s): North American Rock Garden Society, Ontario Horticultural Association

Ottawa-Carleton Safety Council *See* Ottawa Safety Council

Outdoor Writers of Canada
PO Box 934, Cochrane AB T4C 1B1
Tel: 403-932-3585; *Fax:* 403-851-0618
e-mail: info@outdoorwritersofcanada.com
URL: www.outdoorwritersofcanada.com
Overview: A small national organization
Chief Officer(s):
George Gruenefeld, President
T.J. Schwanky, Executive Director
Fees: $85; $35 student

Outdoors Unlittered *See* Pitch-In Canada

Outdoors Unlittered (Alberta) *See* Pitch-In Alberta

Outward Bound Canada
996 Chetwynd Rd., RR #2, Burks Falls ON P0A 1C0
Fax: 705-382-5959
Toll-Free: 888-688-9273
URL: www.outwardbound.ca
Also Known As: Canadian Outward Bound Wilderness School
Overview: A small provincial charitable organization founded in 1976
Chief Officer(s):
Dave Wolfenden, Executive Director
Finances: *Annual Operating Budget:* $1.5 Million-$3 Million
Staff: 11 staff member(s); 20 volunteer(s)
Activities: Youth - 21-day Adventure courses available for 15-16 yrs. old & 22-day Voyageur programs for 17+ yrs.; Adults - courses vary from 7 - 24 days, including canoeing, sea-kayaking, hiking or dog-sledding & skiing; special courses for 50+ yrs., for women only & courses for managers & educators; leadership courses; *Internships:* Yes; *Speaker Service:* Yes
Mission: To promote self-reliance, care & respect for others, responsibility to community & concern for the environment; *Member of:* Ontario Camping Association; Ontario Society for Training & Development; Association for Experiential Education; Council of Outdoor Educators of Ontario

Oxford County Geological Society
Parent: Central Canadian Federation of Mineralogical Societies
820 Devonshire Avenue, Woodstock ON N4S 7W2
e-mail: marion.eccleston@sympatico.ca
Overview: A small local organization founded in 1977
Chief Officer(s):
Marion Eccleston, President
Grace Poole, Treasurer
Peter Nielsen, Secretary
Finances: *Funding Sources:* Membership dues
Staff: 5 volunteer(s)
Membership: 18 families; *Fees:* $18 family; $15 single; *Committees:* Field Trippers
Activities: Workshops; seminars; monthly meetings meetings 2nd Friday of the month; guest speakers; *Speaker Service:* Yes; *Library:* Yes, open by appointment
Mission: To arouse interest & knowledge in all fields of earth sciences; to ensure that all age-group needs are considered; *Member of:* Canadian Central Federation Minerals Society

Pacific NorthWest Economic Region (PNWER)
World Trade Center West, #460, 2200 Alaskan Way, Seattle WA 98121 USA
Tel: 206-443-7723; *Fax:* 206-443-7703
URL: www.pnwer.org
Previous Name: Pacific Northwest Legislative Leadership
Overview: A medium-sized local organization founded in 1989
Chief Officer(s):
Matt Morrison, Executive Director
matt@pnwer.org
Finances: *Annual Operating Budget:* $100,000-$250,000
Staff: 3 staff member(s); 6 volunteer(s)
Membership: 1,000-4,999; *Fees:* $250 individual; $500 non-profit; $1000 corporate; *Member Profile:* Consists of the Pacific Northwestern states of Alaska, Idaho, Montana, Oregon & Washington & the provinces of Alberta, British Columbia & the Yukon Territory; includes Legislators, Governors/Premiers & private sector individuals
Activities: 9 Working Groups; *Internships:* Yes
Mission: To promote greater collaboration among the seven state & provincial members in order to enhance the economic competitiveness of the region in international & domestic markets

Pacific Northwest Legislative Leadership *See* Pacific NorthWest Economic Region

Pacific Peoples Partnership (PPP)
#407, 620 View St., Victoria BC V8W 1J6
Tel: 250-381-4131; *Fax:* 250-388-5258
e-mail: info@pacificpeoplespartnership.org
URL: www.pacificpeoplespartnership.org
Previous Name: South Pacific Peoples Foundation

Associations/Organizations / Pacific States/British Columbia Oil Spill Task Force

Overview: A small international organization founded in 1975
Finances: *Annual Operating Budget:* $100,000-$250,000; *Funding Sources:* Membership dues; donors; sales; Canadian International Development Agency; professional service fees
Staff: 5 staff member(s); 15 volunteer(s)
Membership: 160; *Fees:* $35 regular; $45 family; $20 student; *Member Profile:* Supporter of SPPF's aims & objectives, Canadian citizen or a current resident of Canada, annual donation required; *Committees:* Program; Finance; Fundraising; Journal; Public Relations
Activities: Pacific Networking Conference, every two years; *Speaker Service:* Yes; *Library:* Resource Centre; Open to public.
Mission: To promote increased understanding of social justice, environment, development, health & other issues of importance to the people of the Pacific Islands; to support equitable, environmentally sustainable development & social justice in the region; *Member of:* Canadian Council for International Cooperation; British Columbia Council for International Cooperation; *Affiliation(s):* Nuclear Free & Independent Pacific Movement

Pacific Space Centre Society *See* H.R. MacMillan Space Centre Society

Pacific States/British Columbia Oil Spill Task Force
Environmental Emergencies Branch, BC Ministry of Environment, PO Box 9377, Stn. Prov Govt, Victoria BC V8W 9M6
Tel: 250-356-8383; *Fax:* 250-387-9935
URL: www.oilspilltaskforce.org
Chief Officer(s):
Jean R. Cameron, Executive Coordinator, 503-392-5860
JeanRCameron@oregoncoast.com
Graham Know, Coordinating Committee Member, Provincial Representative
Mission: The Pacific States/British Columbia Oil Spill Task Force was authorized by a Memorandum of Cooperation signed in 1989 by the Governors of Alaska, Washington, Oregon, and California and the Premier of British Columbia following the Nestucca and Exxon Valdez oil spills. These events highlighted their common concerns regarding oil spill risks and the need for cooperation across shared borders. In June 2001 a revised Memorandum of Cooperation was adopted to include the State of Hawaii and expand our focus to spill preparedness and prevention needs of the 21st century. Now in our second decade, we provide a forum where Task Force Members can work with stakeholders from the Western US and Canada to implement regional initiatives that protect 56,660 miles of coastline from Alaska to California and the Hawaiian archipelago. The Task Force Members are senior executives from the environmental agencies with oil spill regulatory authority in the states of Alaska, Washington, Oregon, California and Hawaii and the Province of British Columbia. Oil spill program managers from each member agency comprise the Task Force's Coordinating Committee, which oversees activities and projects as authorized by the Members when they adopt a Five Year Strategic Plan and Annual Work Plans. The Coordinating Committee convenes four times a year. The Task Force Members hold their Annual Meetings each summer, rotating locations among member jurisdictions

Pacific Urchin Harvesters Association (PUHA)
902 - 4th Street, New Westminster BC V3L 2W6
Tel: 604-524-0322; *Fax:* 604-524-1023
e-mail: info@puha.org
URL: www.puha.org
Overview: A small local organization
Chief Officer(s):
Ross Morris, Sec.-Treas., 604-524-0322
Mike Featherstone, President

Packaging Association of Canada (PAC) / Association canadienne de l'emballage
#E420, 2255 Sheppard Ave. East, Toronto ON M2J 4Y1
Tel: 416-490-7860; *Fax:* 416-490-7844
e-mail: info@pac.ca
URL: www.pac.ca
Overview: A large national organization founded in 1949
Membership: 2,000
Mission: To represent both users & suppliers on the strength of environmental & economic policy

Paddle Canada (PC) / Pagaie Canada
PO Box 20069, Stn. RPO Taylor-Kidd, Kingston ON K7P 2T6
Tel: 613-547-3196; *Fax:* 613-547-4880
Toll-Free: 888-252-6292
e-mail: info@paddlingcanada.com
URL: www.paddlingcanada.com
Previous Name: Canadian Recreational Canoeing Association
Overview: A large national licensing charitable organization founded in 1971
Finances: *Annual Operating Budget:* $500,000-$1.5 Million; *Funding Sources:* Membership fees; donations; program delivery; sponsorships
Staff: 1 staff member(s); 80 volunteer(s)
Membership: 6,000 individual; *Fees:* $42 individual; *Committees:* Canoeing Program Development; Environment; Heritage; Inclusion for Disabled; River Kayaking Program Development; Sea Kayaking Program Development
Activities: Regional committees & task forces review park management plans, hydroelectric developments & timber management plans; Waterwalker Film Festival held yearly to promote waterway conservation; educational programs; environmental awareness; heritage
Awards: Bill Mason Memorial Scholarship Fund (Scholarship) Scholarship to a Canadian student enrolled in outdoor recreational or environmental studies at a Canadian college or university *Award Amount:* $1,000 awarded annually
Mission: To promote all forms of recreational paddling to Canadians of diverse abilities, culture or age; to advocate for a healthy natural environment; to develop an appreciation for the canoe & the kayak in our Canadian heritage; *Affiliation(s):* Active Living Alliance for Canadians with a Disability; Canadian Heritage Rivers System; Girl Guides of Canada

Pagaie Canada *See* Paddle Canada

Pan American Center for Sanitary Engineering & Environmental Sciences (CEPIS)
Urbanizacion Camacho, La Molina, PO Box 4337, Calle Los Pinos 259, Lima 12 Peru
Tel: 51-1-437-1077; *Fax:* 51-1-437-8289
e-mail: cepis@cepis.ops-oms.org
URL: www.cepis.ops-oms.org
Overview: A large international organization founded in 1968
Finances: *Funding Sources:* PAHO; WHO; Peruvian government; other
Staff: 90 staff member(s)
Membership: Governments of 44 countries & territories; *Committees:* Direction; Administration; Informatics; Advisors; Laboratory; Information; Citizen Participation; Special Projects
Activities: Carries out programs aimed at strengthening national capacities for protecting environmental health & the management of risks derived from man-made contamination; *Library:* Yes, Open to public
Mission: To cooperate with the countries of the Americas to evaluate & manage environmental risk factors that, directly or indirectly, affect the health of the population

Panos Canada
Liu Institute Bldg., 6476 NW Marine Dr., Vancouver BC V6T 1Z2
Tel: 604-822-1275; *Fax:* 604-822-6966
e-mail: info@panoscanada.org
URL: www.panoscanada.ca
Overview: A medium-sized national organization
Chief Officer(s):
Jon Tinker, Executive Director
jtinker@panoscanada.org
Margaret Catley-Carlson, Honorary President
Mission: To work in Canada & internationally towards more sustainable development, greater security & peacebuilding; to help strengthen plural media & civil society, & raise public understanding of critical global issues

Panos London
9 White Lion St., London N1 9PD United Kingdom
Tel: 44-20-7278-1111; *Fax:* 44-20-7278-0345
e-mail: info@panos.org.uk
URL: www.panos.org.uk
Overview: A small international charitable organization founded in 1986
Finances: *Annual Operating Budget:* $1.5 Million-$3 Million
Staff: 35 staff member(s); 5 volunteer(s)
Mission: To promote development which is socially, environmentally & economically sustainable; to combine research with dissemination of information on issues such as AIDS, environment & race, biotechnology, global warming, media pluralism, migrant communities, narcotics, gender, population & health; *Affiliation(s):* InterWorld Radio

Panos Washington
Webster House, #T6, 1718 P St. NW, Washington DC 20036 USA
Tel: 202-429-0730
e-mail: washington@panoscaribbean.org
Overview: A medium-sized international organization founded in 1986
Chief Officer(s):
Jan Voordouw, Executive Director
Finances: *Annual Operating Budget:* $250,000-$500,000; *Funding Sources:* Bilateral, multilateral & non-governmental organizations; private foundations
Staff: 4 staff member(s)
Activities: *Library:* Yes, Open to public
Mission: To provide information resources on sustainable development issues; *Member of:* Inter Action

Paper & Paperboard Packaging Environmental Council (PPEC)
#3, 1995 Clark Blvd., Brampton ON L6T 4W1
Tel: 905-458-0087; *Fax:* 905-458-2052
e-mail: ppec@ppec-paper.com
URL: www.ppec-paper.com
Overview: A medium-sized national organization
Member Profile: Packaging mills, and packaging converters
Mission: Represents member companies to various levels of government, as well as to environmental and consumer interest groups; networks with other players in the paper industry to establish common interests; promotes environmentally sound practices in manufacture and recovery.; *Affiliation(s):* American Forest & Paper Association; Fibre Box Association; Association of Independent Corrugated Converters (AICC)

Paper Packaging Canada
Parent: Paper & Paperboard Packaging Environmental Council
#3, 1995 Clark Blvd., Brampton ON L6T 4W1
Tel: 905-458-1247; *Fax:* 905-458-2052
e-mail: info@paperpackaging.ca
URL: www.paperpackaging.ca
Overview: A medium-sized national organization
Membership: 1-99
Activities: Networking & information sharing; seminars; annual golf tournament
Mission: The association represents containerboard mill sites, corrugator plants, sheet plants and related industries; works together with other players in the paper industry to develop an agenda of common concerns and issues.

Parcs et loisirs de l'Ontario *See* Parks & Recreation Ontario

Parks & Recreation Ontario (PRO) / Parcs et loisirs de l'Ontario
Parent: Canadian Parks & Recreation Association
#302, 1 Concorde Gate, Toronto ON M3C 3N6
Tel: 416-426-7142; *Fax:* 416-426-7371
e-mail: pro@prontario.org
URL: www.prontario.org
Overview: A large provincial organization founded in 1984
Finances: *Annual Operating Budget:* $500,000-$1.5 Million; *Funding Sources:* Self-funding through programs; provincial grants for special projects; membership dues
Staff: 14 staff member(s); 100 volunteer(s)
Membership: 1,000; *Fees:* Schedule available; *Member Profile:* Individual; student; corporate; *Committees:* Anti-Harassment Policies; Day Care Reform; Government Relations; Benefits of Recreation; Violence in Recreation Activities
Activities: Recreation - An Essential Service; *Library:* Yes
Awards: ProAwards Program (Award) Recognizes individuals & organizations who have contributed to the advancement of parks & recreation in Ontario, in 3 sections: member, community & special awards
Hugh Clydesdale Bursary (Award) Awarded to promising female parks & recreation students or practitioners in Ontario to further their education *Award Amount:* up to $2000
Student Paper Competition (Award) To recognize the capabilities of students in writing a research paper on parks & recreation *Award Amount:* $100
Mission: Strives to enhance the quality of life, health & well-being of people, their communities & their environments; to advocate provincially for parks & recreation issues; to provide networking as well as multi-discipline professional development opportunities

Partenaires des parcs canadiens *See* Canadian Parks Partnership

Partenariat pour des environnements intérieurs sains *See* Healthy Indoors Partnership

Parti Vert d'Ontario *See* The Green Party of Ontario

Parti vert du Canada *See* Green Party of Canada

Parti Vert du Québec (PVQ) / Green Party of Québec
Parent: Green Party of Canada
#220, 10000 rue Lajeunesse, Montréal QC H3L 2E1
Tél: 514-303-7750
Ligne sans frais: 888-998-8378
Courriel: info@partivertquebec.org
URL: www.partivertquebec.org
Aperçu: *Dimension:* moyenne; *Envergure:* provinciale
Membre(s) du bureau directeur:
Guy Rainville, Chef

Partners FOR the Saskatchewan River Basin (PFSRB)
402 - 3rd Ave. South, Saskatoon SK S7K 3G5
Tel: 306-665-6887; *Fax:* 306-665-6117
Toll-Free: 800-567-8007
e-mail: partners@saskriverbasin.ca
URL: www.saskriverbasin.ca
Overview: A small local charitable organization founded in 1993
Chief Officer(s):
Jennifer Nelson, Manager
Finances: *Annual Operating Budget:* $250,000-$500,000
Staff: 2 staff member(s); 50 volunteer(s)
Membership: 110; *Fees:* $25 individual/family; $50-$10,000 corporations/organizations based on budget; *Member Profile:* Individuals & organizations from all sectors of society & all the geographic areas of the basin - Alberta, Saskatchewan & Manitoba
Activities: Watershed monitoring; low water landscaping; storm drain marking; basin-wide stewardship program; aquatic restoration projects; integrated research; ecotourism development & marketing; watershed stewardship program for children
Mission: To promote watershed sustainability through awareness, linkages & stewardship

Passons à l'action Canada *See* Pitch-In Canada

Peace & Environment Resource Centre
PO Box 4075, Stn. E, 174 First Ave., Ottawa ON K1S 5B1
Tel: 613-230-4590; *Fax:* 613-230-3608
e-mail: info@perc.ca
URL: www.perc.ca
Overview: A small local organization
Activities: *Library:* Yes

Peace Parkland Naturalists
PO Box 1451, Grande Prairie AB T8V 4Z2
Tel: 780-539-6102
URL: www.peacenaturalists.fanweb.ca
Overview: A small local organization founded in 1990
Chief Officer(s):
Margot Hervieux, Contact
Finances: *Annual Operating Budget:* Less than $50,000
Membership: 40; *Fees:* $10 individual; $15 family
Mission: To promote awareness & appreciation of the natural history of the Peace Region of northwestern Alberta; *Member of:* Federation of Alberta Naturalists

Peace Valley Environment Association (PVEA)
PO Box 6062, Fort St John BC V1J 4H6
e-mail: pvea@shaw.ca
URL: www.peacevalley.ca
Overview: A small local organization
Fees: $10
Mission: To protect and defend the natural environment of the Peace Valley area of British Columbia

P.E.I. Cattlemen's Association *See* Prince Edward Island Cattle Producers

PEI Trout Growers Association *See* Prince Edward Island Finfish Growers Association

PEI Tuberculosis League *See* Prince Edward Island Lung Association

The Pembina Institute
219 - 19 St. NW, Calgary AB T2N 2H9
Tel: 403-269-3344; *Fax:* 403-269-3377
URL: www.pembina.org

Overview: A medium-sized provincial charitable organization founded in 1985
Chief Officer(s):
Ed Whittingham, Executive Director
Membership: 32
Activities: Major program areas include Environmental Education & Publishing (teacher professional development; national environmental education resource cataloguing service; curricular materials for schools; classroom presentations & student workshops; community adult environmental education courses); Research, Development & Promotion of Environmental Policy (analyzing & developing municipal, provincial & federal energy-related environmental policy, as well as policy related to other conservation & recycling issues; *Speaker Service:* Yes; *Library:* Yes, Open to public, open by appointment
Mission: To develop & promote public policy & educational programs which protect the environment & encourage environmentally sound resource management strategies; to implement a conserver society; *Member of:* Canadian Renewable Energy Alliance

Pembroke Area Field Naturalists (PAFN)
PO Box 1242, Pembroke ON K8A 6Y6
Tel: 613-625-2263; *Fax:* 613-625-2263
Overview: A small local charitable organization founded in 1983
Chief Officer(s):
Leo Boland, President
Finances: *Annual Operating Budget:* Less than $50,000; *Funding Sources:* Donations; fundraising
Membership: 50; *Fees:* $15 individual; $20 family; $10 student/senior
Activities: Field walks
Member of: Federation of Ontario Naturalists

Pender Island Field Naturalists
4547 Bedwell Harbour Rd., RR#1, Pender Island BC V0N 2M2
Tel: 250-629-3381; *Fax:* 250-629-9956
e-mail: jankirkby@gulfislands.com
Overview: A small local organization
Chief Officer(s):
Sylvia Pincott, Contact
pincott@paralynx.com
Jan Kirkby, Director
Membership: 1-99; *Fees:* $18/year; *Member Profile:* Birding & botany enthusiasts

Peninsula Field Naturalists (PFN)
PO Box 23031, Stn. Midtown Plaza, 124 Welland Ave., St Catharines ON L2R 7P6
Tel: 905-892-2566; *Fax:* 905-892-6401
e-mail: jmpotter@vaxxine.com
Overview: A small local charitable organization founded in 1954
Finances: *Annual Operating Budget:* Less than $50,000; *Funding Sources:* Membership fees
Staff: 12 volunteer(s)
Membership: 100; *Fees:* $10 student; $20 adult; $25 family; *Member Profile:* Interest in natural history
Activities: Outdoor natural history walks; annual park clean-up; annual bird & plant inventories
Mission: To promote the enjoyment of nature through environmental appreciation & conservation; to encourage wise use & conservation of natural resources; to promote environmental protection; *Member of:* Ontario Nature; *Affiliation(s):* Canadian Nature Federation

People for the Ethical Treatment of Animals (PETA)
501 Front St., Norfolk VA 23510 USA
Tel: 757-622-7382; *Fax:* 757-628-0786
e-mail: info@peta.org
URL: www.peta.org
Overview: A large international charitable organization founded in 1980
Chief Officer(s):
Ingrid E. Newkirk, President
Mary Beth Sweetland, Vice-President
Finances: *Annual Operating Budget:* Greater than $5 Million; *Funding Sources:* Contributions
Staff: 180 staff member(s); 40 volunteer(s)
Membership: 1,800,000; *Fees:* US$16; $25 Cdn.
Activities: International campaigns on vegetarianism, against animal testing, against fur & dissection; *Internships:* Yes; *Rents Mailing List:* Yes; *Library:* PETA Library; Open to public,
Mission: To protect animals from exploitation & cruelty; to bring positive changes in the ways humans regard other species; to expose animal abuse so it will not be perpetuated; to promote a world in which animals are respected & people are aware of & concerned with how their daily decisions affect the lives of other sentient beings

People's Law School
#150, 900 Howe St., Vancouver BC V6Z 2M4
Tel: 604-331-5400; *Fax:* 604-331-5401
e-mail: staff@publiclegaled.bc.ca
URL: www.publiclegaled.bc.ca
Overview: A small provincial organization
Mission: To make law & legal system understandable & accessible to people of British Columbia; *Member of:* Public Legal Education Association of Canada

Pest Management Association of Alberta (PMAA)
Box 9, Site 5, RR#2, Cochrane AB T0L 0W0
Tel: 403-273-3025; *Fax:* 403-932-4388
e-mail: pmaa@telus.net
Previous Name: Structural Pest Management Association of Alberta
Overview: A small provincial organization
Chief Officer(s):
Amin Poonja, President
Member of: Canadian Pest Management Association

Pesticide Action Network North America (PANNA)
#500, 49 Powell St., San Francisco CA 94102 USA
Tel: 415-981-1771; *Fax:* 415-981-1991
e-mail: panna@panna.org
URL: www.panna.org
Overview: A medium-sized international charitable organization founded in 1983
Chief Officer(s):
Steve Scholl-Buckwald, CFO & Managing Director
Monica Moore, Founding Director
Finances: *Annual Operating Budget:* $1.5 Million-$3 Million; *Funding Sources:* Grants & individual donors
Staff: 21 staff member(s); 5 volunteer(s)
Membership: 225 affiliate organizations; *Fees:* US$35 organizations with paid staff; US$20 all volunteer organizations
Activities: Campaign to stop pesticide drift; documenting pesticide body burden; campaign to ban Lindane; holding corporations accountable for the use & promotion of pesticides & genetically engineered crops; campaign to transform agricultural development through the International Assessment of Agricultural Science & Technology for Development; California pesticide use reduction; public education; farmworkers' rights campaign; promotion of alternatives to pesticides; *Internships:* Yes; *Library:* Yes, open by appointment
Mission: Works to replace pesticide use with ecologically sound & socially just alternatives; links local & international consumer, labor, health, environment & agriculture groups into an international citizens' action network; network challenges the global proliferation of pesticides, defends basic rights to health & environmental quality & works to insure the transition to a just & viable society

Pesticide Education Network
1369 Matheson Rd., Ottawa ON K1J 8B5
Tel: 613-748-0317
e-mail: john@sankey.ws
URL: sankey.ws/pen.html; sankey.ws/hduup.html
Overview: A small local organization
Chief Officer(s):
John Sankey, Contact
Finances: *Annual Operating Budget:* Less than $50,000
Staff: 20 volunteer(s)
Membership: 1-99
Activities: Reduction of pesticide use within urban areas; *Speaker Service:* Yes

Peterborough Field Naturalists (PFN)
Parent: Ontario Nature
PO Box 1532, Peterborough ON K9J 7H7
Tel: 705-742-1524
URL: www.peterboroughnature.org
Overview: A small local organization founded in 1940
Membership: 200; *Fees:* $25 single; $30 family; $15 student; *Committees:* Program, Project
Activities: Monthly meetings with guest speakers, nature walks, birding excursions
Mission: To promote the enjoyment of nature through environmental appreciation & conservation; to encourage wise use & conservation of natural resources & environmental protection

Associations/Organizations / Petroleum Human Resources Council of Canada

Petroleum Human Resources Council of Canada (PHRCC)
#1538, 25 Avenue NE, Calgary AB T2E 8Y3
Tel: 403-537-1230; *Fax:* 403-537-1232
e-mail: info@petrohrsc.ca
URL: www.petrohrsc.ca
Overview: A medium-sized national organization
Chief Officer(s):
Cheryl Knight, Executive Director & CEO
Mission: Collaborative forum that addresses human resources issues within the petroleum industry

Petroleum Industry Training Service *See* Enform: The Safety Association for the Upstream Oil & Gas Industry

Petroleum Research Atlantic Canada (PRAC)
1321 Edward St., Halifax NS B3H 3H5
Tel: 902-494-2960; *Fax:* 902-494-2489
e-mail: info@pr-ac.ca
URL: www.pr-ac.ca
Overview: A small local organization founded in 2002
Chief Officer(s):
David Finn, President
Membership: 39; *Committees:* Environmental Impacts & Effects; Hydrocarbon Evaluation; Operations & Technology; Policy & Socio-Economics
Mission: To build petroleum-related research & development capability & capacity throughout Atlantic Canada; to establish research priorities, coordinate research proposals, provide seed funding for research & development, identify opportunities & provide support in the administration of research programs

Petroleum Services Association of Canada (PSAC)
#1150, 800 - 6 Ave. SW, Calgary AB T2P 3G3
Tel: 403-264-4195; *Fax:* 403-263-7174
e-mail: info@psac.ca
URL: www.psac.ca
Overview: A large national organization founded in 1981
Chief Officer(s):
Mark Salkeld, President & Chief Executive Officer
msalkeld@psac.ca
Elizabeth Aquin, Senior Vice-President
eaquin@psac.ca
Patrick J. Delaney, Vice-President, Health & Safety
pdelaney@psac.ca
Kelly Morrison, Director, Communications & Stakeholder Relations
kmorrison@psac.ca
Heather Doyle, Manager, Meetings & Events
hdoyle@psac.ca
Holly Kerr, Manager, Communications & Member Relations
hkerr@psac.ca
Membership: 250+ companies; *Member Profile:* Petroleum services industry companies; *Committees:* Corporate Finance; Education Fund; Health & Safety; Human Resources; Special Events; Transportation Issues; Cathodic Protection; Drilling Fluids; Oilwell Perforators' Safety Training & Advisory; Snubbing Services; Well Testing
Activities: Engaging in lobbying activities; Providing educational opportunities
Meetings/Conferences:
For more information see Trade Shows, Conferences and Seminars Chapter
Petroleum Services Association of Canada 2011 Petroleum Services Investment Symposium
June 2011 Calgary, AB
Petroleum Services Association of Canada 2011 Annual General Meeting, Canadian Drilling Activity Forecast Session, & Industry Dinner
Other Conferences in 2011 2011
Petroleum Services Association of Canada 2012 Annual Spring Conference
April 2012 Red Deer, AB
Petroleum Services Association of Canada 2012 Annual Mid-Year Update
Other Conferences in 2012 2012
Petroleum Services Association of Canada 2012 Annual General Meeting, Canadian Drilling Activity Forecast Session, & Industry Dinner
Other Conferences in 2012 2012
Petroleum Services Association of Canada 2013 Annual Spring Conference
April 2013 Red Deer, AB

Petroleum Services Association of Canada 2013 Annual Mid-Year Update
Other Conferences in 2013 2013
Petroleum Services Association of Canada 2013 Annual General Meeting, Canadian Drilling Activity Forecast Session, & Industry Dinner
Other Conferences in 2013 2013
Petroleum Services Association of Canada 2014 Annual Spring Conference
April 2014 Red Deer, AB
Petroleum Services Association of Canada 2014 Annual Mid-Year Update
Other Conferences in 2014 2014
Petroleum Services Association of Canada 2014 Annual General Meeting, Canadian Drilling Activity Forecast Session, & Industry Dinner
Other Conferences in 2014 2014
Publications: *Petroleum Services Association of Canada Membership Directory*
Type: Directory
Profile: Contact information for association members
Petroleum Services Association of Canada Annual Report
Type: Yearbook *Frequency:* a.
Profile: A review of the association's activities, released at the end of each October in conjunction with the Canadian Drilling Activity Forecast & the Annual General Meeting
Petroleum Services News
Type: Magazine *Frequency:* q. *Accepts Advertising*: Yes
Profile: Covering issues of importance to the upstream oil & gas industry
FAST-Line [a publication of the Petroleum Services Association of Canada]
Type: Newsletter *Frequency:* bi-weekly
Profile: Association news & upcoming events
Canadian Drilling Activity Forecast
Type: Yearbook *Frequency:* a.
Profile: Five years of historical data, plus forecasts for the coming year across Canada
Well Cost Study
Type: Study
Profile: Geological, technical, & financial data on wells drilled across Canada
Total Compensation Survey [a publication of the Petroleum Services Association of Canada]
Type: Yearbook *Frequency:* a.
Profile: An analysis of current salary & benefits practices in the petroleum service, supply, & manufacturing industry
Mission: To represent the supply, manufacturing, & service sectors of the upstream petroleum industry
Environmental Activity: Developing a Community Partners program to address concerns related to oil & gas activity

Petroleum Society of CIM
#425, 500 - 5th Ave. SW, Calgary AB T2P 3L5
Tel: 403-237-5112; *Fax:* 403-262-4792
e-mail: info@petsoc.org
URL: www.petsoc.org
Overview: A medium-sized national organization founded in 1949
Chief Officer(s):
Anthony Au, Treasurer
anthonya@petsoc.org
Finances: *Annual Operating Budget:* $250,000-$500,000; *Funding Sources:* Membership fees; advertising
Staff: 7 staff member(s); 100 volunteer(s)
Membership: 2,780 individual; 48 corporate
Activities: Monographs; scholarships; courses; SIG meetings; Environmental SIG
Mission: To promote the advancement & sharing of technology in petroleum exploration, production, transportation & marketing through publications, meetings, courses, networking & the recognition of individuals who have contributed to the society & the petroleum industry; *Member of:* Canadian Institute of Mining, Metallurgy & Petroleum

Petroleum Tank Management Association of Alberta (PTMAA)
#980, 10303 Jasper Ave., Edmonton AB T5J 3N6
Tel: 780-425-8265; *Fax:* 780-425-4722
Toll-Free: 866-222-8265
e-mail: ptmaa@ptmaa.ab.ca
URL: www.ptmaa.ab.ca
Overview: A medium-sized provincial licensing charitable organization founded in 1994
Chief Officer(s):
Mark Tse, Chair

Randy Hall, Secretary
Sim Koopmans, Treasurer
Activities: Monitoring new storage tank installations; Inspecting existing storage tank installations; Investigating accidents & incidents
Mission: To offer programs to enhance the management of petroleum storage tank systems in Alberta
Environmental Activity: Ensuring storage tank systems are designed, installed, upgraded or operated in accordance with the Alberta Fire Code; Monitoring of storage tank closures

Petroleum Technology Alliance Canada (PTAC)
Chevron Plaza, #400, 500 - 5th Ave. SW, Calgary AB T2P 3L5
Tel: 403-218-7700; *Fax:* 403-920-0054
e-mail: info@ptac.org
URL: www.ptac.org
Overview: A medium-sized national organization
Chief Officer(s):
Soheil Asgarpour, President
Mission: To facilitate innovation, technology transfer & research & development in the upstream oil & gas industry

Pharmaceutical Manufacturers Association of Canada *See* Canada's Research-Based Pharmaceutical Companies (Rx&D)

Physicians for a Smoke-Free Canada / Médecins pour un Canada sans fumée
1226A Wellington St., Ottawa ON K1Y 3A1
Tel: 613-233-4878; *Fax:* 613-233-7797
e-mail: psc@smoke-free.ca
URL: www.smoke-free.ca
Overview: A medium-sized national organization founded in 1985
Finances: *Funding Sources:* Health Canada; Membership dues
Staff: 1 staff member(s)
Membership: 1,500

Pickering & Ajax Citizens Together for the Environment (PACT)
966 Timmins Garden, Pickering ON L1W 2L2
e-mail: dj.steele@sympatico.ca
Overview: A small local organization founded in 1987
Chief Officer(s):
Dave Steele, Chairperson, 905-837-0117
Finances: *Funding Sources:* Fundraising
Staff: 14 volunteer(s)
Membership: 2,000
Activities: *Speaker Service:* Yes
Awards: High School Awards (Award)
Eligibility: Eight top students moving on to environmental subjects
Mission: To protect the environment in the Pickering/Ajax area, especially with reference to waste management issues; *Member of:* Ontario Environmental Network

Pickering Naturalists
PO Box 304, Pickering ON L1V 2R6
Tel: 905-831-1639
e-mail: pnclub@pickeringnaturalists.org
URL: www.pickeringnaturalists.org
Overview: A small local organization
Finances: *Funding Sources:* Membership dues
Fees: $21 individual; $25 family; $250 life
Member of: Federation of Ontario Naturalists

Pigeon Lake Regional Chamber of Commerce (PLRCC)
#6B Village Dr., Westerose AB T0C 2V0
Tel: 780-586-6263; *Fax:* 780-586-3667
e-mail: plchambe@telusplanet.net
URL: www.pigeonlakechamber.ca
Overview: A small local charitable organization founded in 1988
Chief Officer(s):
Darlene Kobeluck, Manager
Sharon Will, President
Finances: *Annual Operating Budget:* Less than $50,000; *Funding Sources:* Fundraising; Membership fees
Staff: 1 staff member(s); 70 volunteer(s)
Membership: 106; *Fees:* $60 + GST
Activities: Organizing dinner meetings & forums; *Library:* Tourist Booth; Open to public
Mission: To build an economic base for permanent & seasonal residence that will provide services for tourists, while maintaining environmental characteristics & quality of life; To promote the commercial, industrial, social, & civic interests of the community;

Affiliation(s): Alberta Chambers of Commerce
Environmental Activity: Protecting the environment

Pipe Line Contractors Association of Canada (PLCAC)
#201, 1075 North Service Rd. West, Oakville ON L6M 2G2
Tel: 905-847-9383; Fax: 905-847-7824
e-mail: plcac@pipeline.ca
URL: www.pipeline.ca
Overview: A small national organization founded in 1954
Finances: Annual Operating Budget: $500,000-$1.5 Million;
Funding Sources: Membership dues
Staff: 3 staff member(s)
Membership: 34 regular + 66 associate + 17 honorary; Member Profile: Open to pipe line contractors or suppliers

Pitch-In Alberta (PIA)
PO Box 45011, RPO Ocean Park, White Rock BC V4A 9L1
Tel: 604-290-0498; Fax: 604-535-4653
Toll-Free: 877-474-8244
e-mail: pitch-in@pitch-in.ca
URL: www.pitch-in.ca
Previous Name: Outdoors Unlittered (Alberta)
Overview: A medium-sized provincial charitable organization founded in 1974
Finances: Annual Operating Budget: $50,000-$100,000;
Funding Sources: Local governments; foundations; industry; individuals
Staff: 2 staff member(s)
Activities: Awareness Events: Pitch-In Canada Week, May; Coastal Clean Up Campaign, Sept.; Speaker Service: Yes; Library: Yes, Open to public, open by appointment
Mission: To carry out promotional, educational & action programs aimed at reducing, reusing, recycling & properly managing & disposing of waste & solid wastes in particular; to initiate cleanup & beautification programs; to secure support of all levels of government, industry, media, other public sector organizations & the public for these objectives; Member of: Pitch-In Canada; Affiliation(s): Clean World International

Pitch-In Canada (PIC) / Passons à l'action Canada
PO Box 45011, Stn. Ocean Park RPO, White Rock BC V4A 9L1
Fax: 604-535-4653
Toll-Free: 877-474-8244
e-mail: pitch-in@pitch-in.ca
URL: www.pitch-in.ca
Previous Name: Outdoors Unlittered
Overview: A medium-sized national charitable organization founded in 1967
Chief Officer(s):
Misha Cook, BA, Executive Director, 877-474-8244 Ext. 1
misha@pitch-in.ca
Lisa Davis, Project Coordinator, 877-474-8244 Ext. 2
lisa@pitch-in.ca
Finances: Funding Sources: Donations; Sponsorships; Grants; Fees for service; Merchandising of materials
Activities: Working with all levels of government & other organizations; Awareness Events: National Pitch-In Week; Library: Pitch-In Canada Resource Centre
Mission: To improve communities & the envionment by providing programs to reduce, re-use, recycle, & properly manage & dispose waste; Affiliation(s): Clean World International; Clean up the World
Environmental Activity: Initiating recycling & composting programs; Cleaning up areas; Offering The National Cell Phone Collection Program & the Shoreline Clean Up Program

Le plan nord-américain de gestion de la sauvagine See North American Waterfowl Management Plan

Planetary Association for Clean Energy, Inc. (PACE) / Société planétaire pour l'assainissement de l'énergie
#1001, 100 Bronson Ave., Ottawa ON K1R 6G8
Tel: 613-236-6265; Fax: 613-235-5876
e-mail: pacenet@canada.com
URL: pacenet.homestead.com
Overview: A medium-sized international charitable organization founded in 1975
Finances: Annual Operating Budget: $100,000-$250,000;
Funding Sources: Membership fees; donations
Staff: 2 staff member(s); 10 volunteer(s)
Membership: 3,600 in 60 countries; Fees: $350
Activities: Electromagnetic bioaffect, analyses & abatement; monitors unclean developments; peer review of new technologies; books, databases & technical reports; Internships: Yes; Speaker Service: Yes; Library: Yes, open by appointment

Mission: To steward & facilitate the implementation of clean energy systems worldwide

The Planning Forum See Strategic Leadership Forum, The Toronto Society for Strategic Management

Planning Institute of British Columbia (PIBC)
Parent: Canadian Institute of Planners
#110, 355 Burrard St., Vancouver BC V6C 2G8
Tel: 604-696-5031; Fax: 604-696-5032
Toll-Free: 866-696-5031
e-mail: info@pibc.bc.ca
URL: www.pibc.bc.ca
Overview: A medium-sized provincial organization founded in 1958
Finances: Annual Operating Budget: $50,000-$100,000
Staff: 2 staff member(s)
Membership: 1,300; Fees: $56.50-$255
Mission: To promote orderly use of land, buildings & natural resources; to maintain high standard of professional competence; to protect rights & interests of those engaged in planning profession

Plant Biology Research Institute Voir Institut de recherche en biologie végétale

Plant Engineering & Maintenance Association of Canada (PEMAC)
#402, 6 - 2400 Dundas St. West, Mississauga ON L5K 2R8
Tel: 905-823-7255; Fax: 905-823-8001
e-mail: mail@pemac.org
URL: www.pemac.org
Overview: A medium-sized national licensing organization founded in 1989
Finances: Annual Operating Budget: $250,000-$500,000;
Funding Sources: Membership fees; website; colleges
Staff: 1 staff member(s); 11+ volunteer(s)
Membership: 2,000; Fees: Including GST: $50.85 student; $101.70 - full individual; $310.75 - allied; $621.50 - corporate; Member Profile: Maintenance professionals & practitioners; Committees: Strategic Planning; Communications; Bylaws & Constitution; Membership; Education & Research; Programming
Activities: Certification Program, MMP - Maintenance Management Professional; Speaker Service: Yes; Library: Yes, open by appointmentNot open to the public
Awards: Annual Sergio Guy Memorial Award (Award)
Mission: To be recognized as a nationwide centre of excellence in plant engineering & maintenance; to form positive & constructive links with industry & service sectors, in support of local & nationwide developments & productivity; to deliver strongly identifiable services & commitments across the range of disciplines embraced by the association; to educate & introduce new concepts; to provide representation at all government levels; to provide career enhancement & networking opportunities; to promote research in the field of plant engineering & maintenance

Plastic Bag Association; Plastic Bag Information Clearing House See Film & Bag Federation

Plastic Loose Fill Council (PLFC)
PO Box 21040, Oakland CA 94620 USA
Tel: 510-654-0756; Fax: 510-654-0196
Toll-Free: 800-828-2214
URL: www.loosefillpackaging.com
Overview: A small national organization
Chief Officer(s):
John D. Mellott
Membership: 4; Member Profile: Manufacturers of expanded polystyrene loose fill packaging
Activities: Operates the Peanut Hotline, the consumer reuse program in US for plastic packaging peanuts
Mission: Promoted the reuse of plastic packing peanuts through its national collection program the Peanut Hotline, with over 240 drop-off sites in California

Plumbing & Mechanical Contractors Association of New Brunswick See Mechanical Contractors Association of New Brunswick

Pollution Control Association of Ontario See Water Environment Association of Ontario

The Pollution Probe Foundation (PPF)
#402, 625 Church St., Toronto ON M4Y 2G1
Tel: 416-926-1907; Fax: 416-926-1601
e-mail: pprobe@pollutionprobe.org
URL: www.pollutionprobe.org
Also Known As: Pollution Probe
Overview: A medium-sized national charitable organization founded in 1969
Finances: Annual Operating Budget: $1.5 Million-$3 Million;
Funding Sources: Individual & corporate charitable donations; foundation grants; publication sales; government grants
Staff: 16 staff member(s); 20 volunteer(s)
Membership: 100 corporate donors + 50 institutional
Activities: Programme areas include: Air, Water, Energy, Climate Change, Environment & Child Health, Mercury, Environmental Policy Development; Awareness Events: Clean Air Campaign & Commute
Mission: A registered Canadian charity which seeks to define environmental problems through research; to promote understanding through education & to press for practical solutions through advocacy. The organization is non-partison & works collaboratively with government agencies, other non-profit organizations, & private business to engage key issues & find solutions. Offices in Toronto & Ottawa; Member of: Canadian Environmental Network; Canadian Renewable Energy Alliance; Affiliation(s): Clean Air Network; Ontario Clean Air Alliance

Polystyrene Packaging Council (PSPC)
1300 Wilson Blvd., 8th Fl., Arlington VA 22209 USA
Tel: 703-741-5649; Fax: 703-741-5651
e-mail: pspc@plastics.org
URL: www.polystyrene.org
Overview: A small international organization
Chief Officer(s):
Michael H. Levy, Director
Finances: Annual Operating Budget: $500,000-$1.5 Million
Staff: 2 staff member(s)
Membership: 9; Fees: Schedule available; Member Profile: Major suppliers & manufacturers of polystyrene products
Mission: To promote & defend the polystyrene industry by providing a forum for issues of importance to the polystyrene industry; keeping markets free by eliminating or amending anti-polystyrene legislation & regulation & avoiding future burdensome polystyrene legislation/regulation; & serving as the polystyrene industry communications voice to selected audiences & the general public

Pommes de terre Nouveau-Brunswick See Potatoes NB

Population Connection (PC)
#500, 2120 L St. NW, Washington DC 20037 USA
Tel: 202-332-2200; Fax: 202-332-2302
Toll-Free: 800-767-1956
e-mail: info@populationconnection.org
URL: www.populationconnection.org
Previous Name: Zero Population Growth
Overview: A large international organization founded in 1968
Chief Officer(s):
John Seager, President & CEO
Finances: Annual Operating Budget: $3 Million-$5 Million;
Funding Sources: Memberships; foundations; private donations
Staff: 40 staff member(s); 20 volunteer(s)
Membership: 65,000; Fees: $25
Activities: Encourages better media coverage of population issues; Teachers PETNet (Population Education Trainers Network); roving reporters; legislative alert; campus organizing
Mission: To advocate progressive action to stabilize world population at a level that can be sustained by Earth's resources

Potash & Phosphate Institute/Potash & Phosphate Institute of Canada See International Plant Nutrition Institute

Potatoes NB / Pommes de terre Nouveau-Brunswick
PO Box 7878, Grand Falls NB E3Z 3E8
Tel: 506-473-3036; Fax: 506-473-4647
e-mail: ctpotato@potatoesnb.com
URL: www.potatoesnb.com
Previous Name: New Brunswick Potato Agency
Overview: A medium-sized provincial organization founded in 1979
Chief Officer(s):
Jean-Marie Pelletier, Chair
Finances: Annual Operating Budget: $1.5 Million-$3 Million
Staff: 13 staff member(s)
Membership: 400 individual

Associations/Organizations / Prairie Agricultural Machinery Institute

Mission: Producer driven organization working in close collaboration with industry partners in advocating, coordinating, promoting, negotiating & leading growth & development of NB potato producers; *Member of:* Canadian Horticultural Council

Prairie Agricultural Machinery Institute (PAMI)
PO Box 1150, Hwy. 5 West, Humboldt SK S0K 2A0
Tel: 306-682-2555; *Fax:* 306-682-5080
Toll-Free: 800-567-7264
e-mail: humboldt@pami.ca
URL: www.pami.ca
Overview: A medium-sized local charitable organization founded in 1974
Finances: *Funding Sources:* Fee-for-service work; Government
Staff: 45 staff member(s)
Activities: *Library:* PAMI Research Library
Publications: *The Rancher's Guide to Elk & Bison Handling Facilities*
Type: Book *Number of Pages:* 35 *Price:* $20 Canada; $25 international
Direct Seeding Manual: A Farming System for the New Millennium
Price: $50 Manitoba, Saskatchewan, & Alberta; $55 elsewhere
The Stockman's Guide to Range Livestock Watering from Surface Sources
Type: Book *Number of Pages:* 36 *Price:* $10 Canada; $12 international
Profile: Includes a workbook
Mission: To serve manufacturers & farmers in Manitoba & Saskatchewan's agricultural sector through applied research, development, & testing; *Affiliation(s):* Manitoba Ministry of Agriculture, Food, & Rural Initiatives; Saskatchewan Ministry of Agricultue

Prairie Conservation Forum
c/o Southern Region, Alberta Environment, 200 - 5th Ave. South, 2nd Fl., Lethbridge AB T1J 4L1
Tel: 403-381-5562; *Fax:* 403-382-4428
e-mail: info@albertapcf.org
URL: www.albertapcf.org
Overview: A small local organization
Chief Officer(s):
Cheryl Dash, Secretary
cheryl.dash@gov.ab.ca
Activities: Alberta Prairie Conservation Action Plan
Mission: Conservation of native prairie & parkland environments in Alberta

Prairie Fruit Growers Association (PFGA)
PO Box 2430, Altona MB R0G 0B0
Tel: 204-324-5058; *Fax:* 204-324-5058
e-mail: pfga@xplornet.com
URL: www.pfga.com
Overview: A small local organization founded in 1974
Finances: *Annual Operating Budget:* $100,000-$250,000
Staff: 1 staff member(s)
Membership: 115; *Fees:* $195
Mission: To educate members, access quality planting stock, direct research & develop markets; *Member of:* North American Berry Association

Prairie Implement Manufacturers Association; PIMA - Agricultural Manufacturers of Canada *See* AMC - Agricultural Manufacturers of Canada

Prairie Provinces Forestry Association *See* Manitoba Forestry Association Inc.

Praticiens de la santé naturelle du Canada *See* Natural Health Practitioners of Canada

Préservation du bois Canada *See* Wood Preservation Canada

Préservation du bois Canada *See* Canadian Wood Preservers Bureau

Prince Albert Model Forest Association Inc. (PAMF)
PO Box 2406, Prince Albert SK S6V 7G3
Tel: 306-922-1944; *Fax:* 306-763-6456
e-mail: pamf@sasktel.net
URL: www.pamodelforest.sk.ca
Overview: A small provincial organization founded in 1993
Chief Officer(s):
Susan Carr, General Manager
Finances: *Annual Operating Budget:* $250,000-$500,000;
Funding Sources: Canadian Forest Service; partners; grants

Staff: 2 staff member(s)
Committees: Science & Technology; Communications & Outreach; Beyond our Boundaries; Planning & Operations
Activities: Applied research in sustainable forestry; technology transfer of research findings; *Library:* PAMF Reference Library; Open to public
Mission: To work towards sustainable forest management through development & testing of new forest management tools, sharing our successes, developing linkages & expanding the PAMF partnership; *Member of:* Saskatchewan Forestry Association; Canadian Model Forest Network; *Affiliation(s):* University of Saskatchewan; University of Regina

Prince Edward Island Aquaculture Alliance (PEIAA)
101 Longworth Ave., 2nd Fl., Charlottetown PE C1A 5A9
Tel: 902-368-2757; *Fax:* 902-626-3954
e-mail: peiaqua@aquaculturepei.com
URL: www.aquaculturepei.com
Overview: A small provincial organization founded in 1998
Chief Officer(s):
Linda Duncan, Executive Director
Finances: *Annual Operating Budget:* $100,000-$250,000;
Funding Sources: Government; industry
Staff: 3 staff member(s)
Membership: 130+; *Fees:* $1,070 supporting; $267.50 supplier; $53.50 associate; *Member Profile:* Mussel, Oyster, Clam & Finfish culturists in PEI & companies which supply goods & services to them
Activities: Co-Host of International PEI Shellfish Festival; Co-Host of Great Atlantic Shellfish Exchange
Mission: To provide focus for the Prince Edward Island aquaculture industry; to enhance industry prosperity through its development as an effective world competitor; *Member of:* Canadian Aquaculture Industry Alliance

Prince Edward Island Cattle Producers (PEICP)
420 University Ave., Charlottetown PE C1A 7Z5
Tel: 902-368-2229; *Fax:* 902-367-3082
e-mail: cattlemen@eastlink.ca
URL: www.peicattleproducers.com
Previous Name: P.E.I. Cattlemen's Association
Overview: A medium-sized provincial organization founded in 1976
Chief Officer(s):
Peter Verleun, Chair
Rinnie Bradley, Executive Director
Justin Lawless, Coordinator, Atlantic Verified Beef Program
Brian Morrison, Secretary-Treasurer
Finances: *Funding Sources:* Mandatory levies; Membership fees
Membership: 550+; *Fees:* Levies collected by processing facilities or a $5 membership fee; *Member Profile:* Prince Edward Island beef producers
Activities: Representing the beef industry in Prince Edward Island; Providing education
Publications: *Beef Newsletter*
Type: Newsletter
Profile: Timely information for Prince Edward Island's beef producers
PEI Cattle Producers Annual Report with Financial Statements
Type: Yearbook *Frequency:* a.
Mission: To support the beef industry in Prince Edward Island; To ensure a responsible production of safe, quality beef; To foster a profitable industry; *Member of:* Canadian Cattlemen's Association (CCA)
Environmental Activity: Fostering environmentally sustainable beef production through leadership, education, & cooperation; Promoting the ALUS program for PEI landowners & farmers to protect water, fish, & wildlife habitat

Prince Edward Island Cultured Mussel Growers Association (PEICMGA)
PO Box 148, Murray River PE C0A 1W0
Tel: 902-962-3092
Overview: A small local organization founded in 1981
Membership: 90+
Activities: Promoting the cultured mussel industry in PEI; Liaising with the provincial government
Mission: To advance the well-being of the cultured mussel industry in Prince Edward Island; to provide a forum for mussel growers to discuss concerns; *Member of:* PEI Aquaculture Alliance

Prince Edward Island Eco-Net (PEIEN)
Parent: Canadian Environmental Network
126 Richmond St., Charlottetown PE C1A 1H9

Tel: 902-566-4170; *Fax:* 902-566-4037
e-mail: peien@isn.net
URL: www.peieconet.org
Social Media: www.facebook.com/peieconet?ref=ts
Also Known As: Prince Edward Island Environmental Network
Overview: A medium-sized provincial organization founded in 1990
Chief Officer(s):
Susan Hawkins, Executive Director
Finances: *Annual Operating Budget:* Less than $50,000
Membership: 29; *Fees:* $25
Activities: *Speaker Service:* Yes; *Library:* Yes
Mission: To promote communication & cooperation among ENGO's (Environmental NGO's) & between ENGO's & governments; to provide referral services; to coordinate workshops & conferences; to provide consultations; to publish & distribute information

Prince Edward Island Federation of Agriculture (PEIFA)
Parent: Canadian Federation of Agriculture
420 University Ave., Charlottetown PE C1A 7Z5
Tel: 902-368-7289; *Fax:* 902-368-7204
e-mail: ianm@peifa.ca
URL: www.peifa.ca
Overview: A medium-sized provincial organization founded in 1941
Finances: *Annual Operating Budget:* $100,000-$250,000
Staff: 4 staff member(s)
Membership: 500-999
Mission: To provide a united voice for Island farmers

Prince Edward Island Finfish Growers Association
c/o Dover Fish Hatchery, RR#2, Murray River PE C0A 1W0
Tel: 902-962-3446
Also Known As: Island Finfish Association
Previous Name: PEI Trout Growers Association
Overview: A small provincial organization founded in 2000
Chief Officer(s):
Leon Moyaert, President
Membership: 7 companie; *Member Profile:* Prince Edward Island individuals & companies occupied in finfish farming
Mission: To support farmers in Prince Edward Island who are engaged in the production of finfish species, such as Rainbow Trout, Arctic Charr, & Atlantic Salmon; *Affiliation(s):* Prince Edward Island Aquaculture Alliance (PEIAA)

Prince Edward Island Fishermen's Association (PEIFA)
#102, 420 University Ave., Charlottetown PE C1A 7Z5
Tel: 902-566-4050; *Fax:* 902-368-3748
e-mail: adminpeifa@pei.eastlink.ca;
researchpeifa@pei.eastlink.ca
URL: www.peifa.org
Overview: A small provincial organization
Fees: $105; *Member Profile:* Prince Edward Island fishers from the following Locals: Central Northumberland Strait Fishermen's Association (CNSFA), Eastern Kings Fishermen's Association (EKFA), North Shore Fishermen's Association (NSFA), Prince County Fishermen's Association (PCFA), Southern Kings & Queens Fishermen's Association (SKQFA), & Western Gulf Fishermen's Association (WGFA)
Activities: Liaising with government; Facilitating networking opportunities; Collaborating with fisher organizations in other provinces;
Mission: To represent fishermen across Prince Edward Island; To act as a single, united voice on behalf of Island fishers on industry issues

Prince Edward Island Forest Improvement Association (PEIFIA)
Parent: Canadian Forestry Association
c/o Richard Gill, RR#5, Mount Stewart PE C0A 1T0
Tel: 902-651-2059
Previous Name: Prince Edward Island Silvicultural Contractors Association
Overview: A medium-sized provincial organization
Finances: *Annual Operating Budget:* Less than $50,000
Staff: 1 staff member(s); 17 volunteer(s)
Fees: $40 individual; $30 associate
Activities: Umbrella organization of PEI forest-related groups

Prince Edward Island Ground Water Association
Parent: Canadian Ground Water Association
PO Box 857, RR#2, Cornwall PE C0A 1H0
Tel: 902-675-2360; *Fax:* 902-675-2360
Overview: A small provincial organization

Activities: Encouraging education about ground water resources
Mission: To promote the protection of ground water in Prince Edward Island; Affiliation(s): Canadian Ground Water Association
Environmental Activity: Increasing public awareness of the management of ground water

Prince Edward Island Institute of Agrologists (PEIIA)
Parent: **Agricultural Institute of Canada**
PO Box 2712, Charlottetown PE C1A 8C3
Tel: 902-892-1943; *Fax:* 902-892-0443
e-mail: peiia@pei.sympatico.ca
URL: www.peiia.ca
Overview: A small provincial organization
Finances: *Annual Operating Budget:* Less than $50,000; *Funding Sources:* Membership fees
Staff: 7 staff member(s)
Membership: 81; *Fees:* $115 P.Ag.; $70 AIT; $75 Permit to Practice; *Committees:* Education; Honours & Awards; Program; Publicity
Activities: Professional development; *Internships:* Yes
Awards: Recognition Award (Award)
Outstanding Agrologist Award (Award)
NSAC Scholarship Awards (Award)
Science Fair & Heritage Awards (Award)
Mission: To safeguard the public by ensuring its members are qualified & competent to provide knowledge & advice on agriculture & related areas

Prince Edward Island Lung Association
Parent: **Canadian Lung Association**
#2, 1 Rochford St., Charlottetown PE C1A 9L2
Tel: 902-892-5957; *Fax:* 902-566-9901
Toll-Free: 888-566-5864
e-mail: info@pei.lung.ca
URL: www.pei.lung.ca
Previous Name: PEI Tuberculosis League
Overview: A small provincial charitable organization founded in 1936
Finances: *Funding Sources:* Donations; Fundraising; Sponsorships
Activities: Promoting lung health in Prince Edward Island; Helping people to stop smoking through the Provincial Cessation Program (QuitCare)
Mission: To improve the respiratory health of Islanders through education, advocacy & research; To raise funds to support medical research
Environmental Activity: Raising awareness of the health effects of indoor & outdoor air pollution; Advocating for clean air

Prince Edward Island Salmon Association (PEISA)
PO Box 3315, Charlottetown PE C1A 8W5
Tel: 902-892-3635
e-mail: david.olafson@pei.sympatico.ca
Overview: A small provincial organization
Chief Officer(s):
David Olafson, Contact
Affiliation(s): Atlantic Salmon Federation

Prince Edward Island Silvicultural Contractors Association *See* Prince Edward Island Forest Improvement Association

Prince Edward Island Society of Certified Engineering Technologists *See* Association of Certified Engineering Technicians & Technologists of Prince Edward Island

Prince Edward Island Wildlife Federation
Parent: **Canadian Wildlife Federation**
#103B, 420 University Ave., Charlottetown PE C1A 7Z5
Tel: 902-892-3332; *Fax:* 902-892-3334
e-mail: peiwfft@pei.aibn.com
Overview: A small provincial organization founded in 1906
Membership: 800
Activities: Assists with the Central Queens, O'Leary Wildlife & Souris Wildlife Federations
Mission: To foster sound management & wise use of the renewable resources of PEI; to assist & encourage the enforcement of those game laws which are in keeping with the objectives of the Federation & to strive for better management & game laws where & when necessary; to cooperate with government departments & related groups where interests are mutual; to educate membership & the public, with particular emphasis upon conservation & safety; to represent the interests & concerns of PEI sportsmen

Prince George & District Truck Loggers Association *See* Central Interior Logging Association

Prince George Backcountry Recreation Society (PGBRS)
PO Box 26, Stn. A, Prince George BC V2L 4R9
Tel: 250-564-5256
e-mail: info@pgbrs.com
URL: www.pgbrs.com
Overview: A small local organization founded in 1998
Membership: 1,700
Mission: The primary mandate of the PGBRS is to promote and encourage safe non-motorized backcountry recreation in the Prince George region.; *Member of:* Federation of BC Naturalists

Prince George Naturalists (PGNC) / Club de naturalistes de Prince George
PO Box 1092, Stn. A, Prince George BC V2L 4V2
Tel: 250-963-7709
e-mail: clive_keen@hotmail.com
Overview: A small local organization founded in 1969
Finances: *Annual Operating Budget:* Less than $50,000
Membership: 48; *Fees:* $25 individual/family; $15 student
Activities: Monthly guest speakers; weekly field trips; birding; annual bird counts
Mission: To promote the enjoyment of nature through environmental appreciation & conservation; to encourage wise use & conservation of natural resources & environmental protection.; *Member of:* Federation of BC Naturalists

Prince George Recycling & Environmental Action Planning Society (REAPS)
PO Box 444, 1950 Gorse Street, Prince George BC V2L 4S6
Tel: 250-561-7327; *Fax:* 250-561-7324
e-mail: garden@reaps.org
URL: www.reaps.org
Overview: A small local organization founded in 1989
Finances: *Annual Operating Budget:* $50,000-$100,000; *Funding Sources:* Regional District Fraser Fort George
Staff: 2 staff member(s); 20 volunteer(s)
Membership: 55; *Fees:* $25 institutional; $8 student; $8 individual; $15 family
Activities: Adopt-a-Worm Program, Dump the Overfed Landfill, workshops on gardening, composting, recycling, Earth Day Celebration; *Awareness Events:* Earth Day, April 22; Composting Week, May 5; Enviro Week, June 5; *Library:* Yes, open by appointment
Mission: To educate the public on where & what can be recycled, how to compost & vermicompost, organic gardening, environmentally friendly alternatives & promotion of the 5 R's (Rethink, Refuse, Reduce, Recycle & Reuse)

Prince George Regional Forest Exhibition Society
#204, 850 River Rd., Prince George BC V2L 5S8
Tel: 250-563-8833; *Fax:* 250-563-3697
e-mail: info@forestandresources.org
URL: www.forestexpo.bc.ca
Also Known As: Forest Expo
Overview: A small international charitable organization founded in 1984
Finances: *Annual Operating Budget:* $250,000-$500,000
Staff: 2-5 staff member(s); 100 volunteer(s)
Membership: 30; *Member Profile:* Forest sector
Activities: Trade Show, seminars, luncheons with guest speakers, social events, international logger sport competitions
Mission: To stage equipment trade show & increase public awareness of the forest industry

Private Motor Truck Council of Canada (PMTC) / Association canadienne du camionnage d'entreprise (ACCE)
#115, 1660 North Service Rd. East, Oakville ON L6H 7G3
Tel: 905-827-0587; *Fax:* 905-827-8212
Toll-Free: 877-501-7682
e-mail: info@pmtc.ca
URL: www.pmtc.ca
Overview: A medium-sized national organization founded in 1977
Finances: *Annual Operating Budget:* $250,000-$500,000; *Funding Sources:* Seminars; social events; membership fees
Staff: 4 staff member(s)
Membership: 400; *Member Profile:* Private truck fleets or suppliers to same; private truck fleets operated by companies whose principal business is other than transportation, but use their own truck fleets to further their business

Activities: Seminars; annual conference; benchmarking and best practices survey; National Vehicle Graphics Design Competition
Awards: Vehicle Graphics Awards (Award)
Driver Hall of Fame (Award)
Fleet Safety Awards (Award)
Publications: *The Counsellor [a publication of the Private Motor Truck Council of Canada]*
Type: Magazine *Frequency:* q.
NewsBriefs [a publication of the Private Motor Truck Council of Canada]
Type: Newsletter
Mission: Recognized as the leader of the private trucking community in Canada; represents the varied interests of private fleet operators with integrity & sound business practices.; *Member of:* North American Private Truck Council; Affiliation(s): National Private Truck Council

Probe International (PI)
225 Brunswick Ave., Toronto ON M5S 2M6
Tel: 416-964-9223; *Fax:* 416-964-8239
e-mail: probeinternational@nextcity.com
URL: www.probeinternational.org
Overview: A medium-sized international charitable organization founded in 1980
Finances: *Annual Operating Budget:* $50,000-$100,000; *Funding Sources:* Private donations
Staff: 2 staff member(s)
Activities: *Speaker Service:* Yes; *Library:* Yes, open by appointment
Mission: To educate Canadians about the environmental, social, & economic effects of Canada's aid & trade abroad; To monitor & expose the effects of projects financed by Canadian tax dollars (through international financial institutions, such as the World Bank & the Asian Development Bank, & through agencies such as CIDA & the Export Development Corp.) & by Canadian corporations; *Member of:* Energy Probe Research Foundation; Canadian Environmental Network; Affiliation(s): Environment Liaison Centre (International); International Organization of Consumers Unions; Energy Probe; Environment Probe; Consumer Policy Institute; Environmental Bureau of Investigation

Product Care Association
12337 82A Ave., Surrey BC V3W 0L5
Tel: 604-592-2972; *Fax:* 604-592-2982
e-mail: contact@productcare.org
URL: www.productcare.org
Overview: A medium-sized national organization
Publications: *The Circular*
Type: Newsletter
Mission: A national, not-for-profit industry association that manages product stewardship programs for household hazardous and special waste; the association's programs aim to divert leftover and end of life products from landfills, waterways and sewers, and to reuse or recycle collected products where possible. Product Care provides information and resources on responsible use, storage, recycling and disposal of products to conumers, retailers and local governments.

Produits alimentaires et de consommation du Canada *See* Food & Consumer Products of Canada

Professional Engineers & Geoscientists Newfoundland & Labrador (PEG-NL)
Parent: **Canadian Council of Professional Engineers**
PO Box 21207, St. John's NL A1A 5B2
Tel: 709-753-7714; *Fax:* 709-753-6131
e-mail: main@pegnl.ca
URL: www.pegnl.ca
Previous Name: Association of Professional Engineers & Geoscientists of Newfoundland
Overview: A medium-sized provincial licensing organization founded in 1952
Finances: *Annual Operating Budget:* $250,000-$500,000; *Funding Sources:* Membership dues
Staff: 6 staff member(s); 200+ volunteer(s)
Membership: 2,500 individual + 286 student + 31 licensee + 296 corporate; *Fees:* $224 individual; $564-1,031 corporate; $530 licensee; *Member Profile:* Bachelor's degree in engineering or geoscience; *Committees:* Discipline; Board of Examiners; Awards; Professional Development & Education; Code of Ethics; Complaints; Conference; Environmental; Geoscience Issues; National Engineering Week; Endowment Fund
Activities: Administers The Engineers & Geoscientists Act in Newfoundland; *Awareness Events:* National Engineering Week; Science & Technology Week

Associations/Organizations / Professional Engineers Ontario

Awards: Award for Merit (Award)
To recognize members who have made outstanding contributions to the profession &/or to the community
Award for Service (Award)
Awarded to members who have served their profession diligently for many years & who have made substantial contributions to the Association & to the advancement of the professions
Environmental Award (Award)
Recognizes the application of science, technology & engineering to human & resource environmental management in Newfoundland & Labrador
Early Accomplishment Award (Award)
Given to members in recognition of exceptional achievement in the early years of an engineer's or geoscientist's professional career
Community Service Award (Award)
Given to members in recognition of outstanding service & dedication to society
Teaching Award (Award)
Mission: To provide competent & ethical practice of engineering & geoscience in Newfoundland & Labrador; to ensure public confidence, sustainability, & stewardship of the professions; to provide leadership to enhance quality of life through the application & management of engineering & geoscience;
Member of: Canadian Council of Professional Geoscientists
Environmental Activity: Environmental Committee

Professional Engineers Ontario (PEO)
Parent: **Canadian Council of Professional Engineers**
#1000, 25 Sheppard Ave. West, Toronto ON M2N 6S9
Tel: 416-224-1100; *Fax:* 416-224-8168
Toll-Free: 800-339-3716
e-mail: webmaster@peo.on.ca
URL: www.peo.on.ca
Previous Name: Association of Professional Engineers of Ontario
Overview: A large provincial licensing organization founded in 1922
Finances: *Annual Operating Budget:* Greater than $5 Million; *Funding Sources:* Membership fees
Staff: 70 staff member(s); 700 volunteer(s)
Membership: 70,000; *Fees:* Schedule available; *Committees:* Advisory Committee on Volunteers; Audit; Complaints Review Councillor; Executive; Fees Mediation; HR & Compensation; Joint Relations; Nominating; Professional Engineers Awards; Regional Councillors; Regional Nominating; Enforcement Committee; Professional Standards; Academic Requirements; Complaints Committee
Activities: *Speaker Service:* Yes
Awards: The Engineering Medal (Award)
Established 1964; silver medal awarded to members of PEO who have made a substantial contribution to the technical side of the profession in any of its branches; awarded in the following categories: engineering, management, research & development; there is no limit to the number of medals that may be awarded each year
V.G. Smith Award (Award)
Established 1962; awarded annually to a member of PEO who has achieved registration during the year by examination, with the highest standing of the candidates who have completed their examinations in that year
S.E. Wolfe Thesis Award (Award)
Established 1965; awarded to a member who has passed at least one of the association examinations, & whose thesis has been awarded the highest mark of all those presented during the year
The Professional Engineers Gold Medal (Award)
Established 1947; awarded to a member of PEO who has spent some years working in the profession & has subsequently given outstanding public service to the country in the federal, provincial, educational, charitable, or other fields; winner receives a gold medal & a citation
The Professional Engineers Citizenship Award (Award)
Established 1970; awarded to members of PEO who have made a substantial contribution in such fields as education, the arts, medicine, law, & social service while maintaining their identity as professional engineers; there is no limit to the number of these awards made each year
Order of Honour (Award)
An honorary society of PEO, the purpose of which is to recognize & honour those professional engineers & others who have rendered conspicuous service to the engineering profession in varying degrees & normally through the association; awards are made in three classes: Member, Officer, & Companion

Mission: To meet the needs of Ontario society by licensing & regulating the entire practice of professional engineering in an open, transparent, inclusive manner
Environmental Activity: Sponsor: The Living Earth at the Ontario Science Centre

Professional Outfitters Association of Alberta *See* Alberta Professional Outfitters Society

Programme des nations unies pour l'environnement *See* United Nations Environment Programme

Projets pour une agriculture écologique *See* Ecological Agriculture Projects

Propane Gas Association of Canada Inc. (PGAC) / Association canadienne du gaz propane inc.
#800, 717 - 7th Ave. SW, Calgary AB T2P 3C4
Tel: 403-543-6500; *Fax:* 403-543-6508
Toll-Free: 877-784-4636
e-mail: info@propanegas.ca
URL: www.propanegas.ca
Overview: A medium-sized national licensing organization founded in 1967
Membership: 270+; *Member Profile:* Producers; Wholesalers; Retailers; Transporters; Manufacturers of appliances, cylinders, & equipment; Associates
Activities: Providing industry related training & emergency response; Promoting the interests of the industry; Engaging in regulatory relations
Publications: *1075news bytes* [a publication of the Propane Gas Association of Canada Inc.]
Type: Newsletter *Frequency:* m.
Profile: For members
1075news talk [a publication of the Propane Gas Association of Canada Inc.]
Type: Newsletter *Frequency:* bi-m.
Profile: Also published in every edition of Propane Canada magazine
Mission: To act as the national voice of the Canadian propane industry; To supports its members in the development of a safe, environmentally responsible Canadian propane industry;
Affiliation(s): Propane Training Institute, a division of the PGAC; Liquefied Petroleum Gas Emergency Response Corporation, a wholly owned subsidiary of the PGAC

Prospectors & Developers Association of Canada (PDAC) / Association canadienne des prospecteurs & entrepreneurs
135 King St. East, Toronto ON M5C 1G6
Tel: 416-362-1969; *Fax:* 416-362-0101
e-mail: info@pdac.ca
URL: www.pdac.ca
Overview: A medium-sized national organization founded in 1932
Finances: *Funding Sources:* Membership fees
Membership: 6,000 individuals + 950 corporate members; *Fees:* $19.05 seniors; $166.67 regular individual; $350 corporate; *Member Profile:* Individuals, such as professional geoscientists, mining executives, prospectors, developers; geological consultants, & those working in the drilling, financial, investment, legal, & other related fields; Students; Corporate members, such as producing companies, junior non-producing exploration companies, & non-mining companies; *Committees:* Aboriginal Affairs; Audit; Awards; Convention Planning; Corporate Social Responsibility; Education; Environment; Executive; Finance & Taxation; Geosciences; Health & Safety; Human Resources Development; International; Lands & Regulations; Membership; Nomination; Public Affairs; Securities
Activities: Encouraging high standards of technical, environmental, safety, & social practices domestically & internationally; Compiling statistics; Providing information; Offering continuing education; Engaging in advocacy activities; Providing networking opportunities; *Speaker Service:* Yes; *Library:* Yes, Not open to the public
Meetings/Conferences:
For more information see Trade Shows, Conferences and Seminars Chapter
Prospectors & Developers Association of Canada (PDAC) 2012 International Convention, Trade Show, & Investors Exchange Mining Investment Show
Other Conferences in 2012 2012
Publications: *News & Activities* [a publication of the Prospectors & Developers Association of Canada]
Type: Newsletter *Frequency:* m.
Profile: Association activities & events of interest to members

Communiqué [a publication of the Prospectors & Developers Association of Canada]
Frequency: irreg.
Profile: Each occasional publication deals with a particular topic related to exploration & development
PDAC [Prospectors & Developers Association of Canada] Activities
Type: Yearbook *Frequency:* a.
Profile: Summary of the association's work distributed to all members
Exploration & Development Highlights
Type: Yearbook *Frequency:* a.
Profile: Articles about exploration & development activities in each Canadian province & territory distributed to all members
PDAC [Prospectors & Developers Association of Canada] in Brief
Type: Newsletter *Frequency:* q. *Editor:* Saley E. Lawton
Profile: Information about the association's activities for members
Mission: To protect & promote the interests of the Canadian mineral exploration & development sector

Protected Areas Association of Newfoundland & Labrador (PAA)
PO Box 1027, Stn. C, St. John's NL A1C 5M5
Tel: 709-726-2603; *Fax:* 709-726-2764
e-mail: paa@nf.aibn.com
URL: www.paanl.org
Overview: A small provincial charitable organization founded in 1989
Chief Officer(s):
Laura Jackson, Executive Director
laura.jackson@nf.aibn.com
Finances: *Annual Operating Budget:* $100,000-$250,000
Staff: 4 staff member(s); 45+ volunteer(s)
Membership: 500; *Fees:* $20 individual; *Member Profile:* People interested in conservation of nature, wilderness; *Committees:* Lac Joseph-Atikonak; Main River
Activities: Issue-related public meetings; *Awareness Events:* Benefit Concert, Nov.
Mission: To promote the establishment of a provincial network of reserves that preserve representative portions of all eco-regions & protect biodiversity, & to promote sound ecological practices that support sustainable development;
Member of: Newfoundland & Labrador Environment Network;
Affiliation(s): World Wildlife Fund Canada; Canadian Parks & Wilderness Society

Provancher Society of Natural History of Canada *Voir* Société Provancher d'histoire naturelle du Canada

Provincial Association of Home Builders of Québec *Voir* Association provinciale des constructeurs d'habitations du Québec inc.

Provincial Federation of Ontario Fire Fighters *See* Ontario Professional Fire Fighters Association

The Public Affairs Association of Canada (PAAC) / Association des affaires publiques du Canada
#301, 250 Consumers Rd., Toronto ON M2J 4V6
Tel: 416-367-2223; *Fax:* 416-495-8723
e-mail: info@publicaffairs.ca
URL: www.publicaffairs.ca
Overview: A medium-sized national organization founded in 1984
Finances: *Funding Sources:* Membership fees
Membership: 300; *Fees:* $200
Activities: *Rents Mailing List:* Yes
Mission: To improve the professionalism of members to enhance the relations of members' organizations with their publics

Public Health Association of British Columbia (PHABC)
Parent: **Canadian Public Health Association**
#219, 2187 Oak Bay Ave., Vancouver BC V8R 1G1
Tel: 250-595-8422; *Fax:* 250-595-8622
e-mail: admin@phabc.org
URL: www.phabc.org
Overview: A medium-sized provincial organization
Chief Officer(s):
Shannon Turner, President
Finances: *Annual Operating Budget:* $100,000-$250,000; *Funding Sources:* Membership dues; project grants
Staff: 2 staff member(s); 25 volunteer(s)

Associations/Organizations / Public Health Association of Nova Scotia

Membership: 300; *Fees:* $25 individual; $15 student; $50 organization
Activities: BC Healthy Communities Network
Mission: To constitute a special resource in BC for the betterment & maintenance of the population's health at the community & personal level

Public Health Association of Nova Scotia (PHANS)
Parent: Canadian Public Health Association
PO Box 33074, Halifax NS B3L 4T6
Tel: 902-477-2960; *Fax:* 902-477-4584
e-mail: phans@cpha.ca
URL: www.phans.ca
Overview: A small provincial charitable organization
Chief Officer(s):
Marie McCully Collier, President
Finances: *Annual Operating Budget:* Less than $50,000
Membership: 1-99; *Fees:* $40; $20 student/senior
Activities: Monitors social, political, economic & environmental developments that may influence public health; advocates for policy change on issues that affect health; responds to community health issues & concerns; liaises with other voluntary agencies & government departments to improve the health of Nova Scotians

Public Legal Education Association of Saskatchewan, Inc. (PLEA Sask.)
#300, 201 - 21st East, Saskatoon SK S7K 0B8
Tel: 306-653-1868; *Fax:* 306-653-1869
e-mail: plea@plea.org
URL: www.plea.org
Overview: A medium-sized provincial organization founded in 1980
Finances: *Annual Operating Budget:* $500,000-$1.5 Million
Staff: 8 staff member(s)
Membership: 50 institutional + 50 individual; *Fees:* $10 organization; $5 individual
Activities: *Speaker Service:* Yes
Mission: To educate & inform the people of Saskatchewan about the law & the legal system; *Member of:* Public Legal Education Association of Canada

Public Legal Information Association of Newfoundland (PLIAN)
Tara Place, #227, 31 Peet St., St. John's NL A1B 3W8
Tel: 709-722-2643; *Fax:* 709-722-0054
Toll-Free: 888-660-7788
e-mail: info@publiclegalinfo.com
URL: www.publiclegalinfo.com
Overview: A small provincial organization founded in 1984
Finances: *Annual Operating Budget:* $100,000-$250,000; *Funding Sources:* Justice Canada; Newfoundland Dept. of Justice; Law Foundation of Newfoundland
Staff: 4 staff member(s); 3 volunteer(s)
Membership: 30
Activities: *Speaker Service:* Yes
Mission: To provide plain language legal information to the general public of Newfoundland, in both official languages, through a telephone enquiry line, public speaking engagements, publications, & a lawyer referral service; *Member of:* Public Legal Information Association of Canada

Public Petroleum Data Model Association (PPDM)
PO Box 22155, Banker's Hall, Calgary AB T2P 4J5
Tel: 403-660-7817; *Fax:* 403-660-0540
e-mail: info@ppdm.org
URL: www.ppdm.org
Also Known As: PPDM Association
Overview: A small national organization founded in 1990
Chief Officer(s):
David Hood, Chair
Finances: *Annual Operating Budget:* $500,000-$1.5 Million
Staff: 60 volunteer(s)
Membership: 100+; *Fees:* Based on annual revenue; *Member Profile:* Oil & gas companies; software vendors; consultants; government agencies; *Committees:* Data management, Taxonomy & metadata, Well operations, Biostrategy, Land, Reserves, Well logs
Activities: Development of industry standard data model, standards for data exchange; *Speaker Service:* Yes
Mission: To develop an open standard data model as the foundation for managing information as an essential asset in the global business of oil & gas exploration & production

Pulp & Paper Technical Association of Canada (PAPTAC) / Association technique des pâtes et papiers du Canada
#1070, 740, rue Notre-Dame ouest, Montréal QC H3C 3X6
Tel: 514-392-0265; *Fax:* 514-392-0369
e-mail: ccrotogino@paptac.ca
URL: www.paptac.ca
Previous Name: Canadian Pulp & Paper Association - Technical Section
Overview: A medium-sized national organization founded in 1915
Chief Officer(s):
Greg Hay, Executive Director
ghay@paptac.ca
André Bernier, Chair
Finances: *Funding Sources:* Membership fees; Events
Publications: *Journal of Pulp and Paper Science (JPPS)*
Type: Journal *Frequency:* q.
Mission: To provide means for the interchange of knowledge & expertise among its members; to improve the skill levels & effectiveness of present & future employees through training & education; to provide technical & practical information on pulp & paper manufacture & use

Purebred Swine Breeders' Association of Canada *See* Canadian Swine Breeders' Association

Québec 4-H
#224, 1040, av Belvédère, Sillery QC G1S 3G3
Tel: 418-529-4705; *Fax:* 418-529-3021
e-mail: 4h.bc@clubs4h.qc.ca
URL: www.clubs4h.qc.ca
Previous Name: Québec Young Farmers
Overview: A medium-sized provincial organization founded in 1969
Finances: *Annual Operating Budget:* $50,000-$100,000
Staff: 1 staff member(s); 10 volunteer(s)
Membership: 450; *Fees:* Schedule available; *Member Profile:* Must be 6-21 years of age & member of Québec 4-H; *Committees:* Lifestock Management Tour; Provincial Rally
Mission: To develop life skills, such as leadership, cooperation, responsibility, & independence, for the English speaking rural youth of Québec, through achievement & skill-development; *Member of:* Canadian 4-H Council; Québec Community Groups Network

Québec Association of Energy Managers *Voir* Association québécoise pour la maîtrise de l'énergie

Québec Association of Fire Chiefs *Voir* Association des chefs en sécurité incendie du Québec

Québec Association of International Cooperation *Voir* Association québécoise des organismes de coopération internationale

Québec Bio-Industries Business Network *Voir* BIOQuébec

Québec Council on Tobacco & Health *Voir* Conseil québécois sur le tabac et la santé

Québec Environment Foundation *Voir* Fondation québécoise en environnement

Québec Environmental Law Centre *Voir* Centre québécois du droit de l'environnement

Québec Farmers' Association (QFA)
#255, 555, boul Roland-Therrien, Longueuil QC J4H 4E7
Tel: 450-679-0540; *Fax:* 450-463-5291
e-mail: qfa@upa.qc.ca
URL: www.quebecfarmers.org
Overview: A medium-sized provincial organization founded in 1957
Membership: 3,000; *Fees:* $56.98; *Member Profile:* Québec's English-speaking farmers & rural citizens
Member of: Quebec Community Groups Network

Québec Fish Processor Association *Voir* Association québécoise de l'industrie de la pêche

Québec Forest Research Council *Voir* Conseil de la recherche forestière du Québec

Québec Forestry Industry Council *Voir* Conseil de l'industrie forestière du Québec

Québec Gardens Association *Voir* Association des jardins du Québec

Québec Land Surveyors Association *Voir* Ordre des arpenteurs-géomètres du Québec

Québec Lung Association (QLA) / Association pulmonaire du Québec (APQ)
Parent: Canadian Lung Association
5790, av Pierre-de-Coubertin, Montréal QC H1N 1R4
Tel: 514-287-7400; *Fax:* 514-287-1978
Toll-Free: 888-768-6669
e-mail: info@pq.lung.ca; info@pq.poumon.ca
URL: www.pq.poumon.ca
Overview: A medium-sized provincial charitable organization founded in 1938
Finances: *Funding Sources:* Donations; Fundraising; Sponsorships
Activities: Supporting respiratory health research; Providing education about respiratory illness; Offering support groups for persons affected by lung disease; Organizing events to raise funds; *Awareness Events:* Provincial Ragweed Extermination Campaign
Publications: *Le Bulletin de l'association pulmonaire du Québec*
Type: Newsletter *Editor:* Louis P. Brisson *ISSN:* 0843-381X
Profile: Respiratory health information, plus donation news
Le Rapport annuel de l'association pulmonaire du Québec
Type: Yearbook *Frequency:* a.
Mission: To provide resources in Québec about lung cancer, chronic obstructive pulmonary disease, sarcoidosis, tuberculosis, asthma, chronic bronchitis, sleep apnea, pneumonia, & emphysema; *Member of:* World Health Organization; International Union against Tuberculosis & Lung Disease
Environmental Activity: Offering information about air pollution

Québec Medical Association *See* Association médicale du Québec

Québec Mining Association *Voir* Association minière du Québec

Québec Public Health Association *Voir* Association pour la santé publique du Québec

Québec Public Interest Research Group - McGill / Groupe de recherche d'intérêt public du Québec - McGill
3647, rue Université, 3e étage, Montréal QC H3A 2B3
Tél: 514-398-7432; *Téléc:* 514-398-8976
Courriel: qpirg@ssmu.mcgill.ca
URL: ssmu.mcgill.ca/qpirg/
Aperçu: Dimension: petite; Envergure: nationale
Critères d'admissibilite: Students
Mission: To work on social justice & environmental issues

Québec Rose Society *Voir* Société des roses du Québec

Québec Society for the Protection of Plants *Voir* Société de protection des plantes du Québec

Québec Society for the Defense of Animals *Voir* Société québécoise pour la défense des animaux

Québec Trucking Association Inc. *Voir* Association du camionnage du Québec inc.

Québec Water Bottlers' Association *Voir* Association des embouteilleurs d'eau du Québec

Québec Young Farmers *See* Québec 4-H

Québec-Labrador Foundation (Canada) Inc. (QLF (Canada)) / Fondation Québec Labrador du (Canada) inc.
#901, 505, boul René Lévesque ouest, Montréal QC H2Z 1Y7
Tel: 514-395-6020; *Fax:* 514-395-4505
e-mail: montreal@qlf.org
URL: www.qlf.org
Overview: A small national charitable organization founded in 1969
Chief Officer(s):
Christine Diguer, Montréal Office Manager
Finances: *Annual Operating Budget:* $500,000-$1.5 Million
Staff: 17 staff member(s)
Membership: 4,000 individual; 50 institutional
Awards: Sounds Conservancy Grants Program (Award)
Caring for the Earth Award (Award)
Mission: To promote local leadership & assist in improvement of human conditions in northern New England, Eastern Québec, & Canadian Atlantic provinces; to conserve cultural heritage & natural resources of region; to conduct scientific research; to

Associations/Organizations / Quesnel Naturalists

enrich educational experience of Canadian & US students; Affiliation(s): Atlantic Centre for the Environment

Quesnel Naturalists
3084 RedBluff Rd., Quesnel BC V2J 6C6
e-mail: shofmeie@goldcity.net
URL: www.bcnature.ca/pages/local_clubs/quesnel_naturalists.html
Overview: A small local organization
Membership: 40; *Fees:* $15 single; 20$ family
Mission: To promote the enjoyment of nature through environmental appreciation & conservation; to encourage wise use & conservation of natural resources & environmental protection.; *Member of:* Federation of BC Naturalists

Quetico Foundation
#1260, 390 Bay St., Toronto ON M5E 1G6
Tel: 416-941-9388; *Fax:* 416-941-9236
e-mail: office@queticofoundation.org
URL: www.queticofoundation.org
Overview: A small provincial charitable organization founded in 1954
Chief Officer(s):
Glenda McLachlan, Executive Director
Finances: *Funding Sources:* Endowment & donations
Staff: 1 staff member(s); 27 volunteer(s)
Membership: 28 trustees; *Fees:* $40; *Committees:* Executive; Finance; Investment; Funding; Publications
Activities: *Library:* John B. Ridley Research Library; Open to public
Mission: To preserve wilderness areas of Ontario for recreation & scientific use

Quidi Vidi Rennie's River Development Foundation (QVRRDF)
Nagle's Place, PO Box 5, St. John's NL A1B 2Z2
Tel: 709-754-3474; *Fax:* 709-754-5947
e-mail: info@fluvarium.ca
URL: www.fluvarium.ca
Overview: A small local organization founded in 1985
Chief Officer(s):
Deborah Picco Garland, Executive Director
Finances: *Annual Operating Budget:* $250,000-$500,000; *Funding Sources:* Admission fees; building rentals; catering services; corporate & private donations; fundraising
Staff: 7 staff member(s); 100 volunteer(s)
Membership: 200; *Fees:* $30.00; *Member Profile:* Friends of Rennie's River; *Committees:* Development; Education; Facilities & Operations; Finance; Science & Exhibitions
Activities: Environmental education; tourism; restoration & habitat enhancement; *Awareness Events:* River Dance, March; Duck Race, Sept.; Fish Fry, August
Mission: To promote responsible environmental stewardship; to raise awareness of the nature of freshwater systems; to provide leadership in urban watershed management; to operate The Fluvarium as a public centre for environmental education; *Member of:* Hospitality Newfoundland & Labrador; St. John's Board of Trade; Newfoundland & Labrador Environmental Industry Association

Radiation Safety Institute of Canada / Institut de radioprotection du Canada
Head Office & National Education Centre, #300, 165 Avenue Rd., Toronto ON M5R 3S4
Tel: 416-650-9090; *Fax:* 416-650-9920
Toll-Free: 800-263-5803
e-mail: info@radiationsafety.ca
URL: www.radiationsafety.ca
Social Media: www.facebook.com/group.php?gid=143472245714096
Previous Name: Canadian Institute for Radiation Safety
Overview: A medium-sized national charitable organization founded in 1981
Chief Officer(s):
Fergal Nolan, MA, DPhil, President & Chief Executive Officer
Bruce Sylvester, Vice-President, Finance & Administration
Mike Haynes, Scientific Director
Natalia Mozayani, Program Manager
Tara Hargreaves, Scientist & Coordinator, Training
Activities: Providing information about radiation & radiation safety
Meetings/Conferences:
For more information see Trade Shows, Conferences and Seminars Chapter
Radiation Safety Institute of Canada 2011 Radiation Safety Officer Professional Certificate Course
September 2011 Toronto, ON
Radiation Safety Institute of Canada 2011 Radiation Safety Officer Professional Certificate Course
October 2011 Toronto, ON
Radiation Safety Institute of Canada 2011 X-Ray Safety Officer Professional Certificate Course
November 2011 Toronto, ON
Radiation Safety Institute of Canada 2011 Radiation Safety Officer Professional Certificate Course
November 2011 Toronto, ON
Radiation Safety Institute of Canada 2012 All About X-ray Safety Employee Training Course
Other Conferences in 2012 2012 Toronto, ON
Radiation Safety Institute of Canada 2012 All About Radiation Safety Employee Training Course
Other Conferences in 2012 2012 Toronto, ON
Radiation Safety Institute of Canada 2012 Radiation Safety Awareness Education
Other Conferences in 2012 2012
Radiation Safety Institute of Canada 2012 X-ray Safety Awareness Education
Other Conferences in 2012 2012
Mission: To be an independent source for knowledge about radiation safety in the environment, the community, & the workplace
Environmental Activity: Promoting radiation safety

Radios Rurales Internationales *See* Farm Radio International

Rainforest Action Network (RAN)
#500, 221 Pine St., San Francisco CA 94104 USA
Tel: 415-398-4404; *Fax:* 415-398-2732
Toll-Free: 800-989-7246
e-mail: rainforest@ran.org
URL: www.ran.org
Overview: A medium-sized international organization founded in 1985
Finances: *Annual Operating Budget:* $1.5 Million-$3 Million; *Funding Sources:* 45% membership; 55% grants & donations
Staff: 27 staff member(s); 21 volunteer(s)
Membership: 32,000; *Fees:* $35
Activities: Oil Exploration Campaign; Old Growth Wood Consumption Campaign; Traditional Forest Peoples Campaign; Education Campaign; Grass Roots Team; Zero Emissions Campaign; Global Finance Campaign; *Awareness Events:* World Rainforest Week; *Internships:* Yes; *Library:* Yes,
Mission: To protect the Earth's rainforests & support the rights of their inhabitants through campaigns that work to bring corporate & government policies into alignment with popular support for rainforest conservation; *Member of:* Friends of the Earth International; Affiliation(s): 150 Rainforest Action Groups (RAGs) in the US & Europe; the RAGs are informally affiliated with RAN, receiving support materials, but no funding; RAGs organize local community actions

Rainforest Alliance (RA)
#500, 665 Broadway, New York NY 10012 USA
Tel: 212-677-1900; *Fax:* 212-677-2187
Toll-Free: 888-693-2784
e-mail: info@ra.org
URL: www.rainforest-alliance.org
Overview: A medium-sized international charitable organization founded in 1987
Chief Officer(s):
Tensie Whelan, Executive Director
Finances: *Annual Operating Budget:* Greater than $5 Million
Staff: 100 staff member(s); 25 volunteer(s)
Membership: 31,000; *Fees:* $35+ donation
Activities: *Internships:* Yes; *Rents Mailing List:* Yes
Mission: To protect ecosystems & the people & wildlife that depend on them by transforming land-use practices, business practices & consumer behavior

Rare Breeds Canada (RBC)
#1, 341 Clarkson Rd., RR#1, Castleton ON K0K 1M0
Tel: 905-344-7768; *Fax:* 905-344-7768
e-mail: rbc@rarebreedscanada.ca
URL: www.rarebreedscanada.ca
Overview: A medium-sized national charitable organization founded in 1986
Chief Officer(s):
Jane Mullen, Office Manager
Finances: *Annual Operating Budget:* Less than $50,000; *Funding Sources:* Membership dues
Staff: 1 staff member(s); 20 volunteer(s)
Membership: 600; *Fees:* $35 individual; $50 family; $100 corporate
Activities: *Speaker Service:* Yes
Mission: To make Canadians more aware of their agricultural heritage; through education & niche marketing involve them in conserving endangered breeds of farm livestock & poultry; Affiliation(s): Canadian Coalition for Biodiversity

Recreation & Parks Association of New Brunswick Inc. *See* Recreation New Brunswick

Recreation New Brunswick
Parent: Canadian Parks & Recreation Association
#34, 55 Whiting Rd., Fredericton NB E3B 5Y5
Tel: 506-459-1929; *Fax:* 506-450-6066
e-mail: info@recreationnb.ca
URL: www.recreationnb.ca
Previous Name: Recreation & Parks Association of New Brunswick Inc.
Overview: A medium-sized provincial organization founded in 1987
Chief Officer(s):
Jamie Shanks, Executive Director
rnb@recreationnb.ca
Finances: *Annual Operating Budget:* $100,000-$250,000
Fees: $87 general; $265-$565 municipal; $132 associate; $295 corporate
Activities: Annual conference; awards; resource centre; membership directory; workshops; counsellors conference; Canoe School; career videos for high schools
Mission: To develop a professional organization for members; to enhance the image of recreation to government & the general public; to develop liaisons with other recreation groups; to affect legislation in the field of recreation & parks; to expand the NB Skills Program for Management Volunteers; to promote the need for education for leisure

Recreation Newfoundland & Labrador
Parent: Canadian Parks & Recreation Association
Bldg. 810, Pleasantville, PO Box 8700, Stn. A, St. John's NL A1B 4J6
Tel: 709-729-3892; *Fax:* 709-729-3814
URL: www.recreationnl.com
Previous Name: Newfoundland & Labrador Parks & Recreation Association
Overview: A medium-sized provincial organization founded in 1971
Chief Officer(s):
Wanda Wight, President
wwight@nf.aibn.com
Gary Milley, Executive Director
garymilley@recreationnl.com
Finances: *Annual Operating Budget:* $100,000-$250,000; *Funding Sources:* Membership fees; services; government grants; corporate
Staff: 4 staff member(s)
Membership: 300 individual; *Fees:* Schedule available; *Member Profile:* Municipalities, communities, individuals, non-profit groups, students or businesses interested or involved in recreation; *Committees:* Executive; Finance; Marketing/Membership; AGM & Conference; Constitution/Nominations; Recreation Practitioners/Facilities; Recreation Inclusion Commitee; Awards
Activities: Playground Training Workshops; *Awareness Events:* Annual General Meeting & Conference; Arena Operators Course; Recreation Month, June; *Library:* Yes, Not open to the public
Awards: Bridging the Gap (Award)
Presented annually to recognize efforts of volunteers who have made a significant contribution to the development of recreational opportunities for persons with a diability in an integrated setting
Ebert J. Broomfield Memorial Scholarship (Scholarship)
Established in 1989; presented annually on a rotation basis between Eastern, Central, Western & Northern regions to a student based on academic achievement, athletic participation & community involvement
Pitcher Plant Award (Award)
Presented annually to recognize outstanding efforts in the development of recreation & leisure services in Newfoundland & Labrador
Cy Hoskins Award (Award)
Presented annually to a full-time recreation practitioner who has made significant contributions to the growth & development of parks, recreation & leisure services
Mission: To promote, foster & develop recreation; to provide a full range of services to enrich the concept of leisure throughout Newfoundland & Labrador; to enable individual citizens to

improve their quality of life.; Affiliation(s): Provincial/Territorial parks & recreation associations

Recycling Council of Alberta (RCA)
PO Box 23, Bluffton AB T0C 0M0
Tel: 403-843-6563; Fax: 403-843-4156
e-mail: info@recycle.ab.ca
URL: www.recycle.ab.ca
Overview: A medium-sized provincial charitable organization founded in 1987
Chief Officer(s):
Philippa Wagner, President
Olena Juzkiw, Secretary
Paula Kuryk, Treasurer
Fees: Fee based upon sales for corporations & small businesses; Fee based upon population for municipalities & regional waste authorities; Member Profile: Corporations; Small Businesses; Institutions; Governments; Municipalities; Regional Waste Authorities; Not-for-Profit Organizations; Individuals; Committees: Leadership & Advocacy; Small & Rural Communities; Communications; Indstrial, Commercial, & Institutional Sector Issues
Activities: Facilitating the exchange of information between environmental groups, governments, industries, & consumers; Providing public education campaigns; Encouraging research in the recycling of waste materials; Awareness Events: Waste Reduction Week, October; Speaker Service: Yes
Meetings/Conferences:
For more information see Trade Shows, Conferences and Seminars Chapter
Recycling Council of Alberta 2011 Waste Reduction Conference September 2011 Edmonton, AB
Recycling Council of Alberta 2012 Waste Reduction Conference October 2012 Jasper, AB
Recycling Council of Alberta Waste Reduction 2013 Conference Other Conferences in 2013 2013, AB
Publications: Enviro Business Guide
Type: Directory
Profile: Contact information & descriptions of businesses
Connector [a publication of the Recycling Council of Alberta]
Type: Newsletter
Profile: RCA activities, member profiles, & success stories
Mission: To promote & facilitate waste reduction, recycling, & resource conservation in Alberta
Environmental Activity: Encouraging policies that facilitate waste reduction, recycling, & resource conservation; Promoting industrial, commercial, & institutional waste reduction & stewardship; Encouraging market development for recycled materials & products

Recycling Council of British Columbia (RCBC)
#10, 119 West Pender St., Vancouver BC V6B 1S5
Tel: 604-683-6009; Fax: 604-683-7255
Toll-Free: 800-667-4321
e-mail: rcbc@rcbc.bc.ca; hotline@rcbc.bc.ca
URL: www.rcbc.bc.ca
Social Media:
www.facebook.com/home.php?sk=group_10340005498
Overview: A medium-sized provincial charitable organization founded in 1974
Chief Officer(s):
Brock Macdonald, Executive Director, 604-683-6009 Ext. 307
brock@rcbc.bc.ca
Anna Rochelle, Director, Finance, 604-683-6009 Ext. 302
anna@rcbc.bc.ca
Harvinder Gill, Manager, Information Services, 604-683-6009 Ext. 313
harv@rcbc.bc.ca
Ben Ramos, Manager, Member & Technology Services, 604-683-6009 Ext. 314
ben@rcbc.bc.ca
Finances: Funding Sources: Sponsorships; Donations
Member Profile: Individuals & corporations that support environmental sustainability
Activities: Conducting research; Providing information services; Participating in community-based events & activities; Establishing public policy positions; Awareness Events: Waste Reduction Week
Meetings/Conferences:
For more information see Trade Shows, Conferences and Seminars Chapter
Recycling Council of British Columbia 2011 37th Annual General Meeting & Zero Waste Conference: The Green Economy - Ready, Set, Grow!
June 2011 Whistler, BC
Recycling Council of British Columbia 2012 38th Annual General Meeting & Conference
Other Conferences in 2012 2012, BC
Publications: Best Practices for Multi-Family Food Scraps Collection
Type: Report Number of Pages: 18 Author: Jordan Best
Profile: Topics include barriers in the multi-family sector, materials collected, collection details, containers & liners, education & outreach, & incentives & policies
Organics Working Group Report: Recommendations for Residential Collection
Type: Report Number of Pages: 16
Profile: Recommendations developed by the Organics Working Group to service single family homes
On the Road to Zero Waste: Priorities for Local Governments
Type: Report Number of Pages: 16
Profile: Guidance for municipal & regional governments across British Columbia
Examining the Waste-to-Energy Option
Type: Report Number of Pages: 24 Author: Jordan Best
Profile: A background paper examining environmental performance & compatibility with zero waste principles
RCBC [Recycling Council of British Columbia] Backgrounder: Degradable Plastic Bags
Type: Report
Recycling Council of British Columbia Annual Report
Type: Yearbook Frequency: a.
Profile: Featuring the executive director's report, the auditor's report, & organizational information
Mission: To promote the principles of zero waste; To decrease British Columbia's environmental footprint
Environmental Activity: Providing a recycling hotline with information on waste reduction; Operating the RCBC Materials Exchange program for the reuse & recycling of discarded products & materials

Recycling Council of Manitoba; Resource Conservation Manitoba Inc. See Green Action Centre

Recycling Council of Ontario (RCO) / Conseil du recyclage de l'Ontario
#225, 215 Spadina Ave., Toronto ON M5T 2C7
Tel: 416-657-2797
Toll-Free: 888-501-9637
e-mail: rco@rco.on.ca
URL: www.rco.on.ca
Social Media: www.twitter.com/#!/RCOntario
Overview: A medium-sized provincial charitable organization founded in 1978
Chief Officer(s):
Jo-Anne St. Godard, Executive Director, 416-657-2797 Ext. 3
joanne@rco.on.ca
Diane Blackburn, Manager, Events, 416-657-2797 Ext. 4
events@rco.on.ca; diane@rco.on.ca
David Hanson, Program Manager, Waste Diversion Certification Program, 416-657-2797 Ext. 8
david@rco.on.ca
Sarah Mills, Manager, Special Projects & Take Back the Light, 416-657-2797 Ext. 7
sarah@rco.on.ca
Lucy Robinson, Manager, Member Relations, 416-657-2797 Ext. 1
lucy@rco.on.ca; members@rco.on.ca
Catherine Leighton, Coordinator, Special Projects, 416-657-2797 Ext. 5
catherine@rco.on.ca
Andrew Reeves, Coordinator, Outreach & Communications, 416-657-2797 Ext. 10
andrew@rco.on.ca
Finances: Funding Sources: Donations; Sponsorships
Fees: Schedule available based upon annual gross sales for; Member Profile: Businesses; Municipalities; Communities; Educational organizations; Individuals; Students; Families; Committees: Executive / Finance; Membership / Communications; Policy / Advocacy; Program Development; Events
Activities: Liaising with all levels of government, environmental organizations, & industry; Awareness Events: Waste Reduction Week in Ontario; Waste Free Lunch Challenge
Awards: Visual Arts, Sculpture, & Arts Installation Award (Award)
Business Award (Award)
Communications Award (Award)
Festivals & Events Award (Award)
Municipal Awards (Award)
Sustainable Product or Service Award (Award)
Waste Diversion Program Operator Award (Award)
Waste Reduction Week in Canada Participation Award (Award)
Meetings/Conferences:
For more information see Trade Shows, Conferences and Seminars Chapter
Recycling Council of Ontario 2012 Annual General Meeting Other Conferences in 2012 2012
Publications: Recycling Council of Ontario Annual Report
Type: Yearbook Frequency: a.
Profile: Operational highlights of the council
RCO [Recycling Council of Ontario] Highlights the Headlines
Price: Free with Recycling Council of Ontario membership
Profile: Information about local, national, & international environmental, waste management, & diversion issues
Recycling Council of Ontario e-Newsletter
Type: Newsletter Price: Free with Recycling Council of Ontario membership
Recycling Council of Ontario Member Bulletin
Type: Newsletter Frequency: irregular Price: Free with Recycling Council of Ontario membership
Mission: To minimize impact on the environment by eliminating waste
Environmental Activity: Providing education about the efficient use of resources

Red Deer River Naturalists (RDRN)
PO Box 785, Red Deer AB T4N 5H2
Tel: 403-347-8200; Fax: 403-347-8200
e-mail: rd.rn@hotmail.com
URL: www.rdrn.fanweb.ca
Previous Name: Alberta Natural History Society
Overview: A small local charitable organization founded in 1906
Finances: Annual Operating Budget: Less than $50,000; Funding Sources: Membership fees; donations; grants
Staff: 300 volunteer(s)
Membership: 300 individual; Fees: $15 individual; $20 family; Committees: Habitat Preservation
Activities: Field trips; Habitat Steward Program; educational programs; species counts
Mission: To foster increased knowledge, understanding & appreciation of natural history; to support conservation measures dealing with environment, wildlife & natural resources; to cooperate with other clubs & organizations having similar views & objectives; Member of: Federation of Alberta Naturalists; Affiliation(s): Canadian Nature Federation

Refreshments Canada / Association canadienne de l'industrie des boissons gazeuses
20 Bay St., 12th Fl., Toronto ON M5J 2N8
Tel: 416-362-2424; Fax: 416-362-3229
e-mail: info@refreshments.ca
URL: www.refreshments.ca
Previous Name: Canadian Bottlers of Carbonated Beverages; Canadian Soft Drink Association
Overview: A medium-sized national organization founded in 1942
Finances: Annual Operating Budget: $500,000-$1.5 Million
Staff: 8 staff member(s)
Membership: 45 organizations; Member Profile: Manufacturers & distributors of carbonated soft drinks & their suppliers
Activities: Library: Yes, open by appointmentNot open to the public
Mission: To represent soft drink bottlers, distributors, franchise houses & industry suppliers on a variety of issues

Refrigeration & Air Conditioning Contractors Association of British Columbia (RACCA-BC)
26121 Fraser Hwy., Aldergrove BC V4X 2E3
Tel: 604-856-8644
e-mail: raccabc@hrai.ca
Overview: A medium-sized provincial organization
Finances: Annual Operating Budget: Less than $50,000
Staff: 1 staff member(s)
Membership: 15 corporate
Mission: To act on behalf of the members to promote positive & effective employee development & labour relations

Refrigeration & Air Conditioning Contractors Association of Manitoba
807 McLeod Ave., Winnipeg MB R2G 0Y4
Tel: 204-949-2788
Overview: A small provincial organization
Mission: To promote the welfare of air conditioning & refrigerating contractors in Manitoba; to promote recognition of the trade with the general public, other associations &

Associations/Organizations / Refrigeration Service Engineers Society (Canada)

government; *Member of:* Heating, Refrigerating & Air Conditioning Institute of Canada

Refrigeration Service Engineers Society (Canada) (RSES Canada)
PO Box 3, Stn. B, Toronto ON M9W 5K9
Tel: 905-842-9199
Toll-Free: 877-955-6255
URL: www.rsescanada.com
Overview: A medium-sized national organization founded in 1952
Finances: *Annual Operating Budget:* $50,000-$100,000; *Funding Sources:* Membership dues; educational seminars
Staff: 2 volunteer(s)
Membership: 2,200; *Fees:* $125
Activities: Education program
Mission: To lead all segments of the HVAC industry by providing superior educational & training programs; to create an environment that encourages maximum member participation in the development & decision process of the Society; *Member of:* Refrigeration Service Engineers Society - International

Regina & District Labour Council (RDLC)
Parent: Saskatchewan Federation of Labour
2709 - 12th Ave., #E, Regina SK S4T 1J3
Tel: 306-757-7076; *Fax:* 306-585-2874
e-mail: rdlc@sasktel.net
URL: www.rdlc.sasktelwebsite.net
Overview: A medium-sized local organization
Chief Officer(s):
Janice Bernier, President, 306-775-2333
jmbernier@sasktel.net
Laurie Temple, Secretary
Carol Mullaney, Treasurer
Membership: 25,560; *Member Profile:* Nineteen unions & forty locals from Regina & the surrounding region
Activities: Increasing the council's affiliate base; Promoting the interests of affiliates; Liaising with the city council to discuss issues of importance to affilitates; Hosting an annual Day of Mourning Ceremony to recognize workers killed on the job; Ensuring that occupational health & safety laws are enforced; Supporting local causes to make the community a better place to work & live; Establishing the Janice Bernier Endowment Fund for long-term food sustainability with the United Way; Coordinating lobbies in Regina ridings
Mission: To advance the economic & social welfare of workers in Regina & the surrounding region; To engage in political activity at the municipal level; *Affiliation(s):* Canadian Labour Congress (CLC)
Environmental Activity: Presenting issues of importance to workers & their families to the Regina City Council, such as a Green Agenda for Cities & Communities

Regina Wildlife Federation (RWF)
PO Box 594, Regina SK S4P 3A3
Tel: 306-359-7733
e-mail: rwf1@accesscomm.ca
URL: nonprofits.accesscomm.ca/rwf
Overview: A medium-sized local charitable organization founded in 1962
Finances: *Annual Operating Budget:* Less than $50,000
Membership: 1,200; *Fees:* $10 to $80
Activities: *Speaker Service:* Yes
Mission: The RWF is a non-profit wildlife conservation organization.; *Member of:* Saskatchewan Wildlife Federation

The Regional Health Authorities of Manitoba (RHAM)
Parent: Canadian Healthcare Association
#2, 203 Duffield St., Winnipeg MB R3J 0H6
Tel: 204-833-1721; *Fax:* 204-940-2042
e-mail: mebbitt@rham.mb.ca
URL: www.rham.mb.ca
Previous Name: Manitoba Health Organizations
Overview: A medium-sized provincial organization founded in 1998
Finances: *Annual Operating Budget:* $3 Million-$5 Million; *Funding Sources:* Membership fees; service fees
Staff: 12 staff member(s)
Membership: 11; *Fees:* Schedule available
Activities: *Rents Mailing List:* Yes

Registered Professional Foresters Association of Nova Scotia (RPFANS)
PO Box 1031, Truro NS B2N 5G9
Tel: 902-893-0099
e-mail: contact@rpfans.ca
URL: www.rpfans.ca

Overview: A medium-sized provincial organization founded in 1999
Chief Officer(s):
Roger Aggas, Registrar
Mike Brown, Treasurer
Member Profile: Professional foresters in Nova Scotia; Foresters-in-training & students
Activities: Disciplining members who fail to comply with the code of ethics; Ensuring that the public receives proper forest management advice; Encouraging further education
Meetings/Conferences:
For more information see Trade Shows, Conferences and Seminars Chapter
Registered Professional Foresters Association of Nova Scotia 2012 Annual General Meeting
Other Conferences in 2012 2012, NS
Publications: Forest Steward [a publication of the Registered Professional Foresters Association of Nova Scotia]
Type: Newsletter
Profile: Contents include the message from the president & news from the association & forestry sector
Mission: To improve the holistic management of forest resources in Nova Scotia

Regroupement des associations forestières régionales du Québec
Parent: Canadian Forestry Association
#100, 138, rue Wellington nord, Sherbrooke QC J1H 5C5
Tél: 819-562-3388; *Téléc:* 819-562-2433
Courriel: info@afce.qc.ca
URL: www.afvsm.qc.ca/region.htm
Aperçu: *Dimension:* moyenne; *Envergure:* provinciale
Membre(s) du bureau directeur:
Daniel Archambault

Regroupement pour la surveillance du nucléaire See Canadian Coalition for Nuclear Responsibility

Regroupement QuébecOiseaux
CP 1000, Succ. M, 4545, av Pierre-de Coubertin, Montréal QC H1V 3R2
Tél: 514-252-3190; *Téléc:* 514-251-8038
Ligne sans frais: 866-583-4846
Courriel: info@quebecoiseaux.org
URL: www.quebecoiseaux.org
Nom précédent: Association québécoise des groupes d'ornithologues
Aperçu: *Dimension:* moyenne; *Envergure:* provinciale; *Organisme sans but lucratif; fondée en* 1981
Membre(s) du bureau directeur:
Jean-Sébastien Guénette, Directeur général
Finances: *Budget de fonctionnement annuel:* $100,000-$250,000
Personnel: 4 membre(s) du personnel; 13 bénévole(s)
Membre: 6,000; *Montant de la cotisation:* 20$ non-membre d'un club; 15$ membre d'un club; 50$ Organismes sans but lucratif; 100$ autres membres associés; *Critères d'admissibilité:* Toute personne intéressée par l'observation des oiseaux
Activités: Banques de données; *Stagiaires:* Oui
Mission: Favoriser le développement du loisir ornithologique; promouvoir l'étude des oiseaux; veiller à leur protection et à celle de leurs habitats

Renewable Natural Resources Foundation (RNRF)
5430 Grosvenor Lane, Bethesda MD 20814-2142 USA
Tel: 301-493-9101; *Fax:* 301-493-6148
e-mail: info@rnrf.org
URL: www.rnrf.org
Overview: A small national charitable organization founded in 1972
Chief Officer(s):
Robert D. Day, Executive Director
Membership: 12; *Member Profile:* Professional & scientific societies with interest in natural resources
Activities: Public policy roundtables, national congresses, annual awards, quarterly journal, internship program; *Internships:* Yes
Awards: Outstanding Achievement Award (Award)
Excellence in Journalism Award (Award)
Mission: To advance sciences & public education in renewable natural resources; to promote the application of sound, scientific practices in managing & conserving renewable natural resources; to foster coordination & cooperation among professional, scientific & educational organizations having leadership responsibilities for renewable natural resources; to develop a Renewable Natural Resources Center

Research & Development Institute for the Agri-Environment (IRDA) / Institut de recherche et de développement en agroenvironnement (IRDA)
Head Office & Research Center, PO Box 480, 3300, rue Sicotte, Saint-Hyacinthe QC J2S 7B8
Tel: 450-778-6522; *Fax:* 450-778-6539
URL: www.irda.qc.c
Overview: A medium-sized national organization founded in 2998
Chief Officer(s):
Bob van Oyen, President, Board
Gisèle Grandbois, President & Chief Executive Officer
Marc R. Laverdière, Scientific Director
Robert Doré, Director, Research Services & Human Resources
Activities: Publishing fact sheets, research reports, scientific papers, & technology transfer papers
Publications: Research & Development Institute for the Agri-Environment Annual Report
Type: Yearbook *Frequency:* a.
Research & Development Institute for the Agri-Environment Scientific Activity Report
Type: Yearbook
Agro Solutions / Revue Agrosolutions [a publication of the Research & Development Institute for the Agri-Environment]
Editor: Marcel Giroux
Mission: To contribute to the sustainable development of agriculture, through research, knowledge acquisition, & transfer activities

Réseau canadien d'éducation et de communication relatives à l'environnement See The Canadian Network for Environmental Education & Communication

Réseau canadien de l'eau See Canadian Water Network

Réseau canadien de l'environnement See Canadian Environmental Network

Réseau canadien de pâtes et papiers pour l'innovation en éducation et en recherche See Canadian Pulp & Paper Network for Innovation in Education & Research

Réseau canadien des centres de toxicologie See Canadian Network of Toxicology Centres

Réseau canadien des subventionneurs en environnement See Canadian Environmental Grantmakers' Network

Le Réseau canadien pour la conservation de la flore See Canadian Botanical Conservation Network

Réseau canadien sur les maladies génétiques See Canadian Genetic Diseases Network

Réseau de cellules souches See Stem Cell Network

Réseau des aliments et des matériaux d'avant-garde See Advanced Foods & Materials Network

Réseau écologique du Manitoba inc. See Manitoba Eco-Network Inc.

Réseau environnement
#220, 911, rue Jean Talon est, Montréal QC H2R 1V5
Tél: 514-270-7110; *Téléc:* 514-270-7154
Courriel: info@reseau-environnement.com
URL: www.reseau-environnement.com
Nom précédent: Association québécoise des techniques de l'environnement
Aperçu: *Dimension:* moyenne; *Envergure:* provinciale; *Organisme sans but lucratif; fondée en* 1959
Membre(s) du bureau directeur:
Josée Méthot, Directrice générale
Membre: 364 corpratif
Mission: Regrouper des entreprises spécialisées dans la gestion des déchets commerciaux, industriels et des services municipaux reliés à l'environnement; assurer l'avancement des technologies et de la science, la promotion des expertises et le soutien des activités en environnement

Réseau environnemental du Nouveau-Brunswick See New Brunswick Environmental Network

Réseau québécois des groupes écologistes (RQGE)
Parent: Canadian Environmental Network
1557-A, avenue Papineau, Montréal QC H2K 4H7
Tél: 514-392-0096
Courriel: info@rqge.qc.ca
URL: www.rqge.qc.ca

Associations/Organizations / Resource Efficient Agricultural Production

Aperçu: Dimension: petite; *Envergure: provinciale; Organisme sans but lucratif; fondée en 1983*
Finances: *Budget de fonctionnement annuel:* $50,000-$100,000
Personnel: 7 membre(s) du personnel; 10 bénévole(s)
Membre: 80; *Montant de la cotisation:* 10$ individu; 35$ groupe local; 50$ groupe national
Activités: *Service de conférenciers:* Oui
Mission: Réseau de services et d'information pour les groupes écologiques du Québec; aider les groupes à communiquer entre eux

Réseau régional du l'industrie biologique du Canada atlantique *See* Atlantic Canadian Organic Regional Network

Resource Efficient Agricultural Production (REAP Canada)
Glenaladale House, PO Box 125, 21111, ch Lakeshore, Sainte-Anne-de-Bellevue QC H9X 3V9
Tel: 514-398-7743; *Fax:* 514-398-7972
e-mail: info@reap-canada.com
URL: www.reap-canada.com
Also Known As: Sustainable Farming
Overview: A medium-sized national charitable organization founded in 1988
Finances: *Annual Operating Budget:* $250,000-$500,000
Staff: 4 staff member(s); 10 volunteer(s)
Membership: 500; *Fees:* $25 individual; $100 organization
Activities: Sustainable farming research into biomass energy on farm sustainable agriculture research for carbon dioxide reduction; *Speaker Service:* Yes; *Library:* Yes, open by appointment
Mission: To improve farm profits & productivity while minimizing adverse health & environmental effects; *Affiliation(s):* Canadian Organic Growers; Ecological Farmers Association of Ontario

Resource Recycling Inc.
PO Box 42270, Portland OR 97242-0270 USA
Tel: 503-233-1305; *Fax:* 503-233-1356
e-mail: info@resource-recycling.com
URL: www.resource-recycling.com
Overview: A medium-sized international organization founded in 1982
Chief Officer(s):
Cara Bergeson, Publisher & Conference Manager
Finances: *Annual Operating Budget:* $500,000-$1.5 Million
Staff: 8 staff member(s)
Activities: *Rents Mailing List:* Yes
Publications: *Resource Recycling*
Editor: Jerry Powell *Price:* $52 annual subscription
Profile: Monthly magazine

Resources for Global Sustainability (RGS)
PO Box 3665, Cary NC 27519-3665 USA
Fax: 919-363-9841
Toll-Free: 800-724-1857
Previous Name: Environmental Data Research Institute
Overview: A medium-sized local organization founded in 1996
Chief Officer(s):
Corinne Szymko Thiele, President
Finances: *Annual Operating Budget:* $100,000-$250,000
Staff: 4 staff member(s)
Activities: Databases & information services; grants database contains information on environmental awards made by US grant makers since Jan. 1988; issues standard reports on funding patterns for the previous calendar year; prepares custom reports in specialized subject areas (on request)
Mission: To develop information about environmental funding; to compile, analyze & disseminate information on environmental funding; to broaden & deepen the knowledge base from which grant makers & others make decisions

Retail Council of Canada (RCC) / Conseil canadien du commerce de détail
#800, 1255 Bay St., Toronto ON M5R 2A9
Tel: 416-922-6678; *Fax:* 416-922-8011
Toll-Free: 888-373-8245
e-mail: mboydbonsu@retailcouncil.org
URL: www.retailcouncil.org
Overview: A large national organization founded in 1963
Finances: *Annual Operating Budget:* $3 Million-$5 Million
Staff: 24 staff member(s)
Membership: 8,500 companies; *Fees:* Schedule available; *Member Profile:* Retailers of all sizes across Canada; *Committees:* Technology Committee; Resources Protection; Government Relations; Committees of the Board of Directors; Education Committee

Activities: *Speaker Service:* Yes; *Library:* Yes, open by appointmentNot open to the public
Mission: To be the best at delivering the services our retail members value most; to serve, promote & represent the diverse needs of Canada's retailing industry to the highest standards of quality; *Affiliation(s):* Canadian Health Food Association; Footwear Council of Canada; Le Conseil quebeçois du commerce de rétail; Retail Merchants' Association of Alberta; Retail Merchants' Association of Manitoba

Rhododendron Society of Canada (RSC)
RR#2, St George Brant ON N0E 1N0
Tel: 519-448-1537
Overview: A small national charitable organization founded in 1971
Chief Officer(s):
H.G. Hedges, Contact
Finances: *Annual Operating Budget:* Less than $50,000; *Funding Sources:* Membership dues; plant sales
Staff: 50 volunteer(s)
Membership: 400; *Fees:* $35; *Member Profile:* Growers of rhododendrons
Activities: Bulletins; flower shows; plant sales
Mission: To share information on rhododendrons; *Member of:* American Rhododendron Society

Richard Ivey Foundation
#400, 11 Church St., Toronto ON M5E 1W1
Tel: 416-867-9229; *Fax:* 416-601-1689
e-mail: info@ivey.org
URL: www.ivey.org
Overview: A medium-sized local charitable organization founded in 1947
Chief Officer(s):
Rosamond Ivey, Chair
Richard W. Ivey, Secretary-Treasurer
Bruce Lourie, Executive Director & President
Activities: Participating in the Conserving Canada's Forests program, by providing support to national or provincial charitable environmental organizations
Mission: To pursue & support excellence by making grants that will improve the well-being of Canadians. Today, the Conserving Canada's Forests Program provides critical support for environmental sustainability across the country.

Richmond Agricultural Society
Parent: Ontario Association of Agricultural Societies
PO Box 1210, Richmond ON K0A 2Z0
Tel: 613-838-3420; *Fax:* 613-838-3933
e-mail: richfair@storm.ca
URL: www.richmondfair.ca
Overview: A small local charitable organization founded in 1841
Chief Officer(s):
Dale Greene, General Manager/Secretary
Finances: *Annual Operating Budget:* $250,000-$500,000; *Funding Sources:* Provincial & regional government; local businesses, individuals
Staff: 3 staff member(s); 450 volunteer(s)
Membership: 400 individual; *Fees:* $7 individual; *Member Profile:* To promote agricultural awareness to the community; *Committees:* Over 30, Livestock, Homecraft, Kiddyland, Entertainment, 4-H, Advertising, Consessions
Activities: Richmond Fair, Sept.; livestock shows; fundraising events
Mission: To promote agricultural awareness to the community by hosting a Fall Agricultural Fair; *Member of:* Society of Composers, Authors & Music Publishers of Canada; *Affiliation(s):* Canadian Association of Fairs & Exhibitions; Ontario Association of Agricultural Societies

Richmond Hill Naturalists (RHN)
PO Box 33217, Stn. Harding Post Outlet, Richmond Hill ON L4C 9S3
Tel: 905-883-3047
e-mail: membership@rhnaturalists.ca; trips@rhnaturalists.ca
URL: www.rhnaturalists.ca
Overview: A small local organization founded in 1955
Chief Officer(s):
Marianne Yake, President, 905-883-3047
president@rhnaturalists.ca
Gene Denzel, Treasurer
treasurer@rhnaturalists.ca
Fees: $25 students; $30 individuals; $35 families
Activities: Offering field trips; Arranging programs on nature topics
Publications: *The RHN [Richmond Hill Naturalists] Bulletin*
Type: Newsletter *Frequency:* 9 pa *Accepts Advertising* : Yes

Editor: Denise Potter *Price:* Free with Richmond Hill Naturalists membership
Profile: Organization activities, nature news, & forthcoming events
Mission: To encourage interest in natural history; To preserve natural areas; To discover & appreciate the natural world
Environmental Activity: Participating in the Christmas Bird Count & the Great Backyard Bird Count

Rideau Environmental Action League (REAL)
PO Box 1061, Smiths Falls ON K7A 5A5
Tel: 613-283-9500; *Fax:* 613-283-9500
e-mail: info@realaction.ca
URL: www.realaction.ca
Overview: A medium-sized local organization founded in 1989
Chief Officer(s):
Barb Hicks, President
dhicks11@cogeco.ca
Membership: 26 corporate; *Fees:* $15 individual; $20 family; $5 student; $25 associate; $50 corporate
Mission: To conduct community-wide environmental projects and promote environmental improvements within the Town of Smiths Falls and Lanark, Leeds and Grenville Counties.; *Affiliation(s):* Green Communities Canada; Ontario Environmental Network

Rideau Trail Association (RTA)
PO Box 15, Kingston ON K7L 4V6
Tel: 613-545-0823
e-mail: info@rideautrail.org
URL: www.rideautrail.org
Social Media: facebook.com/sharer.php?u=http%3A%2F%2Fwww.rideautrail.org&src=sp
Overview: A small local charitable organization founded in 1971
Finances: *Funding Sources:* Donations
Membership: 1200; *Fees:* $25 individual; $30 household; $500 life membership
Activities: Hiking, cross-country skiing, & snowshoeing
Awards: End-to-End (Award)
Award Amount: Certificate & badge for those completing the trail
Outstanding Service Award (Award)
Annually for each club
Winter End-to-End (Award)
Award Amount: Certificate & badge for those completing the trail
Publications: *The Rideau Trail Guidebook*
Number of Pages: 109 *Editor:* Ernie Trischuk *ISBN:* 0-9693759-7-2 *Price:* $25.50 members; $39.95 non-members
Profile: Maps & trail directions & descriptions
Rideau Trail Association Newsletter
Type: Newsletter *Frequency:* q. *Price:* Free with RTA membership
Profile: Hiking articles & club activities
Rideau Trail Association E-Letter
Type: Newsletter *Frequency:* bi-weekly *Price:* Free with RTA membership
Mission: The Association is a non-profit organization that preserves & maintains a hiking trail from Kingston to Ottawa. It is comprised of 3 clubs - Kingston, Central (Perth), & Ottawa - that organize events year-round. It is a registered charity, BN: 119119485RR0001.; *Member of:* Hike Ontario

Rideau Valley Conservation Authority (RVCA)
PO Box 599, 3889 Rideau Valley Dr., Manotick ON K4M 1A5
Tel: 613-692-3571; *Fax:* 613-692-0831
Toll-Free: 800-267-3504
e-mail: postmaster@rvca.ca
URL: www.rvca.ca
Overview: A large local organization
Chief Officer(s):
Mary A. Bryden, Chair
Charles Billington, Executive Director
Finances: *Annual Operating Budget:* Greater than $5 Million; *Funding Sources:* Province; Fundraising; Municipalities
Staff: 60 staff member(s)
Membership: 30 municipalities
Mission: To advocate for clean water, natural shorelines and sustainable land use throughout the Rideau Valley watershed.

Rideau Valley Field Naturalists (RVFN)
PO Box 474, Perth ON K7H 3G1
Tel: 613-326-0106
e-mail: goodlife@rideau.net
URL: www.rvfn.ca
Overview: A small local organization founded in 1983
Finances: *Annual Operating Budget:* Less than $50,000; *Funding Sources:* Membership fees

Associations/Organizations / Rimbey Fish & Game Association

Staff: 12 volunteer(s)
Membership: 96; *Fees:* $5 student; $20 individual; $30 family/institution; *Committees:* Flora & Fauna; Outings
Activities: Monthly meetings except July & August; mall displays; educational outings; bird identification; clinics; bird, mammal & amphibian monitoring; *Library:* Yes
Mission: To promote the enjoyment of nature through environmental appreciation & conservation; to encourage the wise use & conservation of natural resources; to promote environmental protection; *Member of:* Federation of Ontario Naturalists; World Wildlife Federation; Canadian Nature Federation

Rimbey Fish & Game Association
PO Box 634, Rimbey AB T0C 2J0
Tel: 403-843-6564; *Fax:* 403-843-3898
Overview: A small local organization
Finances: *Annual Operating Budget:* Less than $50,000
Membership: 104; *Fees:* $29 family; $19 regular; $18 associate; $12 youth under 18
Activities: Fish & Game annual awards & trophies
Member of: Alberta Fish & Game Association

Roads & Transportation Association of Canada *See* Transportation Association of Canada

Robert Sauvé Occupational Health & Safety Research Institute *Voir* Institut de recherche Robert-Sauvé en santé et en sécurité du travail

The Rocky Mountain Institute (RMI)
1739 Snowmass Creek Rd., Old Snowmass CO 81654-9199 USA
Tel: 970-927-3851; *Fax:* 970-927-3420
e-mail: orders@rmi.org
URL: www.rmi.org
Overview: A medium-sized national organization founded in 1982
Chief Officer(s):
Michael Potts, President & CEO
Marty Pickett, Executive Director
Finances: *Annual Operating Budget:* Greater than $5 Million; *Funding Sources:* Personal donations; grants
Staff: 45 staff member(s)
Membership: 23,000; *Fees:* $10
Activities: *Internships:* Yes; *Speaker Service:* Yes; *Library:* Yes, open by appointment
Mission: To foster the efficient & sustainable use of resources as a path to global security; focuses on five program areas - energy, water, agriculture, economic renewal, security; stresses understanding the interconnections between resource issues, honoring people's integrity, seeking ideas that transcend ideology & harnessing the problem-solving power of free-market economics

Rocky Mountain Naturalists
PO Box 791, Cranbrook BC V1C 4J5
e-mail: scoutfir@shaw.ca
URL: www.kootenaynaturalists.org/rocky/index.html
Overview: A small local charitable organization founded in 1985
Chief Officer(s):
Mildred White, Director
Membership: 40; *Fees:* $20 single; $25 family
Activities: Field trips; study nights; conservation projects;
Mission: To promote the enjoyment of nature through environmental appreciation & conservation; to encourage the wise use & conservation of natural resources & environmental protection; *Member of:* Federation of BC Naturalists

Rose Society of Ontario *See* Canadian Rose Society

Royal Agricultural Winter Fair Association (RAWF) / Foire agricole royale d'hiver
The Ricoh Coliseum, 100 Princes' Blvd., Toronto ON M6K 3C3
Tel: 416-263-3400; *Fax:* 416-263-3488
e-mail: info@royalfair.org
URL: www.royalfair.org
Also Known As: Royal Winter Fair
Overview: A medium-sized national charitable organization founded in 1922
Finances: *Annual Operating Budget:* Greater than $5 Million; *Funding Sources:* Sponsors; government; gate admissions; advertising
Staff: 12 staff member(s); 1000 volunteer(s)
Activities: *Internships:* Yes

Awards: Performance Horse Awards (Award)
35 divisions & classes offer prizes; Leading International Rider is the highest honour in the horse show
Breeding Horse Awards (Award)
17 sections award prizes in this category
Agricultural Awards (Award)
Grand Champion is the highest honour in the following categories: dairy, beef, sheep, goats, swine, market livestock, field crops, vegetables, honey & maple, poultry, jams/jellies/pickles, dairy products, square dancing, fiddling, fleece wool, rabbits, & eight youth activities
Mission: To promote excellence in agricultural & equestrian activities through world class competition, exhibitions & education; *Member of:* Canadian Association of Fairs & Exhibitions

Royal Botanical Gardens (RBG) / Les jardins botaniques royaux
680 Plains Rd. West, Hamilton ON L7T 4H4
Tel: 905-527-1158; *Fax:* 905-577-0375
Toll-Free: 800-694-4769
e-mail: info@rbg.ca
URL: www.rbg.ca
Overview: A medium-sized local organization founded in 1932
Chief Officer(s):
Mark C. Runciman, Executive Director
mrunciman@rbg.ca
Finances: *Annual Operating Budget:* Greater than $5 Million; *Funding Sources:* Ministry of Citizenship, Culture & Recreation
Staff: 37 staff member(s); 400 volunteer(s)
Membership: 7,500; *Fees:* $50 single; $70 dual; $25 youth; $750+ corporate
Activities: Over 150 programs a year for all ages including gardening, plant care, art, cooking, environmental awareness & wildlife; over 30 public festivals/events; RBG is open year-round & receives approx. 500,000 visitors annually; 5 garden areas: Arboretum, Laking Garden, Rock Garden, Hendrie Park, Mediterannean Greenhouse; *Speaker Service:* Yes
Mission: To be recognized in Canada & throughout the world for its unique contribution to the collection, research, exhibition, & interpretation of the plant world & for the development of public understanding & appreciation of the relationship between the plant world, humanity, & the rest of nature; *Member of:* American Association of Botanical Gardens; Archives Association of Ontario; Canadian Museum Association; Museum Trustee Association

The Royal Canadian Geographical Society (RCGS) / La Société géographique royale du Canada
39 McArthur Ave., Ottawa ON K1L 8L7
Tel: 613-745-4629; *Fax:* 613-744-0947
Toll-Free: 800-267-0824
e-mail: rcgs@rcgs.org
URL: www.rcgs.org
Overview: A large national organization founded in 1929
Finances: *Funding Sources:* Membership fees; Donations
Activities: Presenting education programs through the education committee, The Canadian Council for Geographic Education; Conducting research; *Speaker Service:* Yes
Awards: Camsell Medal (Award)
To recognize individuals who have given outstanding service to The Royal Canadian Geographical Society
Canadian Award for Environmental Innovation (Award)
Presented by The Royal Canadian Geographical Society & 3M Canada to recognize individuals who contribute to the restoration & protection of the environment *Deadline:* August 31
The Massey Medal (Award)
Awarded annually for outstanding achievement in the exploration, development, or description of the geography of Canada
The Gold Medal (Award)
To recognize an achievement of one or more individuals in the field of geography, or a significant national or international event
Geographic Literacy Award (Award)
To honour the contributions of a Canadian geography educator
Research Grants (Grant)
Award Amount: Up to $3000 for individuals; Up to $5000 for groups
Meetings/Conferences:
For more information see Trade Shows, Conferences and Seminars Chapter
The Royal Canadian Geographical Society 2011 Annual General Meeting & Annual Dinner of the College of Fellows
November 2011

The Royal Canadian Geographical Society 2012 Annual General Meeting & Annual Dinner of the College of Fellows
November 2012
Publications: *Canadian Geographic*
Type: Magazine *Frequency:* bi-m. *ISSN:* 1182-3895
Profile: Subscription includes 4 issues of Canadian Geographic Travel
Roayl Canadian Geographical Society Annual Report
Type: Yearbook *Frequency:* a.
Profile: Featuring the Society's audited financial statements
géographica
Type: Magazine *Language:* F
Profile: The Royal Canadian Geographical Society's French publication
Mission: To impart a broader knowledge of Canada, including its environmental, economic, & social challenges, as well as it natural & cultural heritage

Royal City Field Naturalists
#903, 1219 Harwood St., Vancouver BC V3M 2L2
Tel: 604-609-0679
e-mail: gllew@telus.net
Overview: A small local organization
Membership: 12; *Fees:* $25;
Mission: To promote the enjoyment of nature through environmental appreciation & conservation; to encourage wise use & conservation of natural resources & environmental protection; *Member of:* Federation of BC Naturalists

The Royal Society of Canada (RSC) / La Société royale du Canada
170 Waller St., Ottawa ON K1N 9B9
Tel: 613-991-6990; *Fax:* 613-991-6996
e-mail: theacademies@rsc.ca
URL: www.rsc.ca
Also Known As: Canadian Academy of the Sciences & Humanities
Overview: A medium-sized national charitable organization founded in 1882
Finances: *Funding Sources:* Membership dues; endowments; government; corporate
Staff: 5 staff member(s)
Membership: 2000 fellows; *Member Profile:* Fellows are elected by their peers on the basis of distinction in their field;
Committees: Promotion of Women in Scholarship; Freedom of Scholarship
Activities: *Library:* Yes, Open to public
Awards: Award in Gender Studies (Scholarship)
Miroslaw Romanowski Medal (Award)
Established in 1994; awarded every year in recognition of significant contributions to the resolution of scientific aspects of environmental problems or for important improvements to the quality of an eco-system in all aspects, terrestrial, atmospheric & aqueous brought about by scientific means. *Award Amount:* $3,000 & a medal Contact: Geneviève Gouin, Coordinator, 613/991-5760
Ecology Award (Scholarship)
John L. Synge Award (Award)
Established 1986; awarded at irregular intervals for outstanding research in any of the branches of mathematics *Award Amount:* $2,500 & a diploma
Alice Wilson Award (Award)
Awarded annually to a woman of outstanding academic qualifications who is entering a career in scholarship or research at the post-doctoral level *Award Amount:* $1,000 & a diploma
Eadie Medal (Award)
Established 1975; awarded annually in recognition of major contributions to any field in engineering or applied science with preference given to those having an impact on communications. *Award Amount:* $3,000 & a bronze medal Contact: Geneviève Gouin, Coordinator, 613/991-5760
Jason A. Hannah Medal (Award)
Established 1976; awarded annually for an important publication in the history of medicine *Award Amount:* $1,500 & a bronze medal
Centenary Medal (Award)
Established 1982; awarded at irregular intervals in recognition of outstanding contributions to the object of the society & to recognize links to international organizations
The McNeil Medal (Award)
Awarded to encourage communication of science to students & the public *Award Amount:* $1,500 bursary & a medal
The Henry Marshall Tory Medal (Award)
Established 1941; awarded every two years (since 1947) for outstanding research in a branch of astronomy, chemistry, mathematics, physics, or an allied science

Associations/Organizations / The Rubber Association of Canada

The J.B. Tyrrell Historical Medal (Award)
Established 1927; awarded at least every two years for outstanding work in the history of Canada
Bancroft Award (Award)
Established 1968; awarded every two years for publication, instruction & research in the earth sciences that have conspicuously contributed to public understanding & appreciation of the subject *Award Amount:* $2,500 & a presentation scroll Contact: Geneviève Gouin, Coordinator, 613/991-5760
Rutherford Memorial Medals: Chemistry & Physics (Award)
Established 1980; awarded annually for outstanding research, one in chemistry, one in physics *Award Amount:* Two medals & $2,500 each
Innis-Gérin Medal (Award)
Established 1966; awarded every two years for a distinguished & sustained contribution to the literature of the social sciences including human geography & social psychology
The McLaughlin Medal (Award)
Awarded annually for important research of sustained excellence in any branch of medical science *Award Amount:* $2,500 & a medal
Lorne Pierce Medal (Award)
Established 1926; awarded every two years for an achievement of special significance & conspicuous merit in imaginative or critical literature written in either English or French, preferably dealing with a Canadian subject
Willet G. Miller Medal (Award)
Established 1943; awarded every two years for outstanding research in any branch of the earth sciences Contact: Geneviève Gouin, Coordinator, 613/991-5760
Sir John William Dawson Medal (Award)
Established 1985; awarded for important & sustained contributions by one individual in at least two different fields in the general areas of interest of the Society or in a broad domain that transcends the usual disciplinary boundaries *Award Amount:* $2,500 & a silver medal
Pierre Chauveau Medal (Award)
Established 1951; awarded every two years (since 1966) for a distinguished contribution to knowledge in the humanities other than Canadian literature & Canadian history
The Flavelle Medal (Award)
Established 1924; awarded every two years (since 1966) for an outstanding contribution to biological science during the preceding 10 years or for significant additions to a previous outstanding contribution to biological science
Mission: To promote learning & research in the arts, humanities & sciences in Canada; in its role as a National Academy, to draw on the breadth of knowledge & expertise of its members to recognize & honour distinguished accomplishments; to advise on the state of scholarship & culture across Canada; to inform the public on noteworthy social, scientific & ethical questions of the day; it is organized into three academies covering the arts & humanities, the social sciences, & the natural & applied sciences
Environmental Activity: RSC established Canadian Global Change Program (CGCP) to ensure that global change research in Canada is cohesive, comprehensive & responsive to national needs & international initiatives; areas of attention include the Arctic, & critical zones

The Rubber Association of Canada (RAC) / Association canadienne de l'industrie du caoutchouc
Plaza 4, #250, 2000 Argentia Rd., Mississauga ON L5N 1W1
Tel: 905-814-1714; *Fax:* 905-814-1085
e-mail: info@rubberassociation.ca
URL: www.rubberassociation.ca
Overview: A large national organization founded in 1920
Finances: *Annual Operating Budget:* $250,000-$500,000; *Funding Sources:* Membership dues
Staff: 4 staff member(s)
Membership: 24 corporate; *Fees:* Based on volume of product; *Member Profile:* Manufacturers of products made from rubber; suppliers; importers; *Committees:* Customs & Tariffs; General Rubber Products; Human Resources; Occupational Health & Safety; Workers' Compensation; Environment; Tire Statistical; Tire Technical; Scrap Tire
Activities: *Speaker Service:* Yes
Mission: To upgrade & maintain good industry/government working relations; to explore ways of improving industry competitiveness & efficiency; to promote safety in members' products, in their use & in the workplace; to promote expansion & profitability of Canadian rubber industry manufacturing units; to enhance standing of Canadian rubber industry worldwide; to provide members with industry marketing statistics

Environmental Activity: Environment Committee to monitor provincial regulations, with particular emphasis on hazardous wastes

Rubber Manufacturers Association (RMA)
#900, 1400 K St. NW, Washington DC 20005 USA
Tel: 202-682-4800
e-mail: info@rma.org
URL: www.rma.org
Previous Name: The Scrap Tire Management Council
Overview: A small national organization founded in 1990
Chief Officer(s):
Charles A. Cannon, President/CEO
Member Profile: Tire group companies include tire manufacturers & retread & repair material suppliers; Elastomer Products Group companies include manufacturers of non-tire elastomer products & suppliers of raw materials & machinery
Activities: Producing publications on consumer tire information, the market, industry standards, government affairs, safety, scrap tire activities, & tire service professionals; *Awareness Events:* National Tire Safety Week, June
Meetings/Conferences:
For more information see Trade Shows, Conferences and Seminars Chapter
Rubber Recycling 2012 Biennial Symposium
Other Conferences in 2012 2012
Publications: *Rubber Manufacturers Association Member Directory*
Type: Directory
Profile: RMA member company contact & product information
Mission: To advocate on behalf of the rubber products industry
Environmental Activity: Supporting programs to clean up scrap tire stockpiles to eliminate environmental threats; Promoting training of fire service personnel to deal with scrap tire fires

Ruiter Valley Land Trust (RVLT) / Fiducie foncière Vallée de Ruiter
PO Box 462, Mansonville QC J0E 1X0
e-mail: info@ruitervalley.org
URL: www.ruitervalley.org
Overview: A small local charitable organization founded in 1987
Chief Officer(s):
Stansje Plantenga, President
Finances: *Annual Operating Budget:* $50,000-$100,000
Membership: 300; *Fees:* $25 individual; $40 family; $100 patron
Activities: *Speaker Service:* Yes
Mission: To acquire & protect forest land; Affiliation(s): Nature Conservancy of Canada

Rural Advancement Foundation International *See* ETC Group

Rural Municipal Administrators' Association of Saskatchewan (RMAA)
PO Box 130, Wilcox SK S0G 5E0
Tel: 306-732-2030; *Fax:* 306-732-4495
e-mail: rmaa@sasktel.net
URL: www.rmaa.ca
Previous Name: Rural Municipal Secretary-Treasurers' Association of Saskatchewan
Overview: A medium-sized provincial organization founded in 1955
Finances: *Funding Sources:* Membership fees; Sponsorships
Member Profile: Practising rural municipal administrators, assistant administrators, secretary-treasurers & assistant secretary-treasurers in Saskatchewan; Associate members include non-practising rural municipal administrators & secretary-treasurers; Honorary life members; *Committees:* Forms & Computer Programs; Curling; Salary Negotiations; Local Government Administration Program; Seminars / Workshops / Guest Speakers; Board of Examiners; Disciplinary; Municipal Employees' Pension Plan; Golfing; Executive & Finance; Wine & Cheese Reception; Convention Sponsors / Door Prizes; Rural Advisory to SAMA; Professional Development; Enhanced Benefits; Resolutions; Humanitarian Services; Board of Reference; Council Mediation; Career Promotion; RMAA Home Page; Workshop; Ex-Officio to S.A.R.M.
Activities: Coordinating the certification of rural municipal administrator in Saskatchewan; Providing professional development activities; Carrying out disciplinary measures regarding professional practice
Mission: To address the needs of rural administrators in Saskatchewan; Affiliation(s): Saskatchewan Association of Rural Municipalities

Rural Municipal Secretary-Treasurers' Association of Saskatchewan *See* Rural Municipal Administrators' Association of Saskatchewan

Ruth's Daughters of Canada
71 Elm Grove Ave., Toronto ON M6K 2J2
Tel: 416-599-7937
URL: www.ruthsdaughters.com
Also Known As: Daughters of Ruth
Overview: A small national organization
Member Profile: Women of faith attending mosque, synagogue, church or temple
Activities: Annual national gathering
Mission: The Association offers support to women who are victims of domestic violence. Its chapters center around prayer, friendship & outreach, & also develops action plans to prevent violence against women.

Safe Workplace Promotion Services Ontario (SWPSO)
Centre for Health & Safety Innovation, #300, 5110 Creekbank Rd., Mississauga ON L4W 0A1
Tel: 905-614-1400; *Fax:* 905-614-1414
Toll-Free: 877-494-9777
e-mail: customercare@wsps.ca
URL: www.wsps.ca
Merged from: Industrial Accident Prevention Association; Ontario Service Safety Alliance; Farm Safety Association
Overview: A large provincial organization founded in 2010
Finances: *Funding Sources:* Workplace Safety & Insurance Board
Membership: 50,000+ firms
Activities: *Library:* Information Centre; Open to public, open by appointment
Awards: Safety Award (Award)
J.V. Findlay Bursary (Scholarship)
Issued annually to assist an outstanding student with post-secondary education in occupational health & safety
President's Award (Award)
Achievement Award (Award)
Publications: *Accident Prevention*
Type: Magazine *Frequency:* bi-m. *Price:* Free to members; $22 Canadian; $29 U.S.A.; $40 Foreign
Profile: Insights & experience of IAPA field staff, member firms, & partner organizations
Mission: WSPS is a not-for-profit organization with a mandate to meet the health & safety needs of businesses in the agricultural, manufacturing & service industries. It provides programs, products, & services for the prevention of injury & illness.; Affiliation(s): Amalgamated Industry Groups - Ceramics & Stone Accident Prevention Association; Chemical Industries Accident Prevention Association; Food Products Accident Prevention Association; Grain, Feed & Fertilizer Accident Prevention Association; Leather, Rubber & Tanners Accident Prevention Association; Metal Trades Accident Prevention Association; Printing Trades Accident Prevention Association; Textile & Allied Industries Accident Prevention Association; Woodworkers' Accident Prevention Association; High Tech; Offices & Related Services

Safety Services Manitoba (SSM)
#3, 1680 Notre Dame Ave., Winnipeg MB R3H 1H6
Tel: 204-949-1085; *Fax:* 204-949-2897
Toll-Free: 800-661-3321
e-mail: registrar@safetyservicesmanitoba.ca
URL: www.safetyservicesmanitoba.ca
Previous Name: Manitoba Safety Council
Overview: A medium-sized provincial licensing charitable organization founded in 1920
Finances: *Funding Sources:* Membership & course fees; fundraising
Staff: 10 staff member(s)
Fees: $500 partner; $750 leader; *Committees:* Executive; Motorcycle; Seat Belt; Operation Lifesaver; Road Safety Conference; OHS Conference
Activities: *Awareness Events:* Conference & AGM; Annual Golf Classic; Operation Red Nose
Mission: To prevent accidental injury or occupational illness in Manitoba by providing effective safety & health programs.

Safety Services New Brunswick (SSNB) / Services de Sécurité Nouveau-Brunswick
#204, 440 Wilsey Rd., Fredericton NB E3B 7G5
Tel: 506-458-8034; *Fax:* 506-444-0177
Toll-Free: 877-762-7233

e-mail: info@safetyservicesnb.ca
URL: www.safetyservicesnb.ca
Previous Name: New Brunswick Safety Council Inc.
Overview: A small provincial charitable organization founded in 1967
Chief Officer(s):
Bill Walker, President & CEO, 506-444-0171
bill@safetyservicesnb.ca
Jim Arsenault, Director of OSH & Traffic Training, 506-444-0178
jim@safetyservicesnb.ca
Finances: *Annual Operating Budget:* $250,000-$500,000; *Funding Sources:* Safety training & workshop fees; membership fees; donations; grants
Staff: 8 staff member(s); 50 volunteer(s)
Membership: 200; *Fees:* Schedule available; *Committees:* Financial; Operation Lifesaver
Activities: *Speaker Service:* Yes
Mission: To promote traffic, occupational & public safety issues & practices through safety training courses & programs, educational material, public information, safety campaigns & conferences.; *Member of:* National Safety Council; *Affiliation(s):* Canada Safety Council

Saint John Animal Rescue League
134 Taylor Ave., Saint John NB E2K 3E6
Tel: 506-642-0920; *Fax:* 506-634-6101
e-mail: arladmin@nb.aibn.com
URL: www.saintjohnanimalrescue.com
Overview: A small local charitable organization founded in 1913
Finances: *Funding Sources:* Donations; Fundraising; Sponsorships; Membership fees; Services
Fees: $25
Activities: Finding homes for animals; Educating residents of Saint John about humane treatment of animals, including information sessions at local schools; Providing humane euthanasia at owners' request; Conducting a seniors' program; Offering public tours; *Awareness Events:* Pets in the Park, including the Annual Dog Jog, July; "No Fleas" Flea Market; Be Kind To Animals Week, May
Publications: *ARL [Animal Rescue League] Shelter Speak Type:* Newsletter *Frequency:* 3-4 pa *Price:* Free with League membership
Profile: Fundraising & donation updates & League information
Mission: To provide rescue, care, & temporary shelter to stray & unwanted animals in the Saint John area

Saint John Naturalists' Club
PO Box 2071, Saint John NB E2L 3T5
URL: saintjohnnaturalistsclub.org
Also Known As: sjnc
Overview: A small local organization founded in 1962
Chief Officer(s):
Jim Wilson, President
Paul Mansz, Vice-President
Mike Bamford, Secretary
Cheryl Gass, Treasurer
Fees: $20 individuals; $25 families; *Member Profile:* Individuals interested in the conservation, study, & enjoyment of nature in New Brunswick; *Committees:* Program; Social; PLBO (Point Lepreau Bird Observatory)
Activities: Hosting monthly meeting at the New Brunswick Museum; Planning field trips; Administering the Point Lepreau Bird Observatory project
Publications: *Saint John Naturalists' Club Bulletin Type:* Newsletter
Profile: Information assembled by a different editor for each issue
Affiliation(s): NatureNB (The New Brunswick Federation of Naturalists)

St. John's Clean & Beautiful (SJCAB)
PO Box 13674, Stn. A, 570 Newfoundland Dr., St. John's NL A1B 4G3
Tel: 709-570-0350; *Fax:* 709-754-3100
e-mail: sjcab@cleanandbeautiful.nf.ca
URL: www.cleanandbeautiful.nf.ca
Overview: A small local organization founded in 1992
Activities: Increasing public awareness in the city's cleanliness; Encouraging community involvment; Promoting partnerships; Coordinating efforts for litter reduction; Planning beautification projects; Publishing brochures, such as the Litter Free Event Guide, the Graffiti Removal Guide, Are You Running a Dirty Business? & Beautiful Gardens & A Healthy Environment
Mission: To inspire community pride & action in St. John's to lead to a clean community; *Affiliation(s):* Keep America Beautiful, Inc. (KAB)

St. John's Harbour ACAP *See* Northeast Avalon ACAP, Inc.

St. Lawrence Economic Development Council *Voir* Société de développement économique du Saint-Laurent

St Mary's River Association (SMRA)
PO Box 179, Sherbrooke NS B0J 3C0
Tel: 902-522-2099; *Fax:* 902-522-2241
e-mail: stmarysriver@ns.sympatico.ca
Overview: A small local charitable organization founded in 1979
Chief Officer(s):
Dale Archibald, President
Finances: *Annual Operating Budget:* $50,000-$100,000; *Funding Sources:* Private donations; industry donations; fundraising activities
Staff: 1 staff member(s)
Membership: 273; *Fees:* $20 regular; $50 contributing; $200 corporate; $5 junior; $500 gold; $300 silver; $100 bronze; *Member Profile:* Anglers; conservationists; business; *Committees:* Newsletter; Membership; River Projects; Fundraising; Interpretive Centre
Activities: River habitat improvement; operation of interpretive centre; fundraising; newsletter; community events; *Library:* Yes
Mission: To further in all ways possible the conservation, protection, propagation & perpetuation of the fishery in the St Mary's River & its tributaries in eastern Nova Scotia; to support & assist the efforts of the federal Department of Fisheries, provincial Department of Fisheries, other government bodies & voluntary associations in any program to conserve & improve the fishery; to impress upon all concerned that the fresh & salt water fishery must be developed, harvested & protected in a spirit of cooperation, with each being dependent on the other for survival & each recognizing the need for conservation measures in this area; to work with the federal, provincial & municipal governments & the private sector in undertaking capital works programs which will enhance the fishery in the St Mary's River & tributaries; *Member of:* Atlantic Salmon Federation; Nova Scotia Salmon Association

Salmon Arm Bay Nature Enhancement Society (SABNES)
PO Box 27, Salmon Arm BC V1E 4N2
Tel: 250-833-9717
URL: www.sabnes.org
Overview: A small local organization founded in 1986
Chief Officer(s):
Mike Saul, Treasurer
Finances: *Funding Sources:* corporate sponsorship
Fees: $10 individual; $20 family; $50 sustaining individual; $100 sustaining family; $500 life membership; $50-2500 corporate membership
Mission: To assist the Wildlife Branch of the provincial government with the development and operation of their management plan for the Salmon Arm foreshore as a Nature Conservancy and viewing area; to develop, operate and promote a system of walkways, viewing areas and interpretive facilities for scientific, educational, environmental protection and public viewing purposes; and to promote environmental awareness and assist in projects meeting that goal in the Salmon Arm area.

Salmon Preservation Association for the Waters of Newfoundland (SPAWN)
93 West St., Corner Brook NL A2H 2Y6
Tel: 709-634-3012; *Fax:* 709-634-4091
Toll-Free: 866-634-3012
e-mail: spawn@nf.aibn.com
URL: www.spawn1.ca
Overview: A small local charitable organization founded in 1979
Chief Officer(s):
John McCarthy, President
Finances: *Annual Operating Budget:* $50,000-$100,000; *Funding Sources:* Auctions
Staff: 1 staff member(s); 300 volunteer(s)
Membership: 300; *Fees:* $20 Canadian member; US$20 American member; US$25 outside North America; *Member Profile:* Conservationists; *Committees:* Enhancement; Enforcement; Habitat; Dinner/Auction; Magazine
Activities: Conservation projects; data collection; *Library:* Yes, open by appointment
Member of: Salmonid Council of Newfoundland & Labrador; *Affiliation(s):* Atlantic Salmon Federation

Salt Institute
Fairfax Plaza, #600, 700 North Fairfax St., Alexandria VA 22314-2040 USA
Tel: 703-549-4648; *Fax:* 703-548-2194
e-mail: info@saltinstitute.org
URL: www.saltinstitute.org
Overview: A medium-sized national organization founded in 1914
Finances: *Annual Operating Budget:* $500,000-$1.5 Million; *Funding Sources:* Membership dues
Staff: 4 staff member(s)
Membership: 6 regular + 31 associate; *Fees:* Based on salt sales by company; *Member Profile:* Manufacturers, producers & sellers of sodium chloride; *Committees:* Highway; Safety & Environment
Activities: *Speaker Service:* Yes; *Library:* Yes, Not open to the public
Awards: Excellence in Storage Award (Award)
Mission: The Institute advocates responsible salt use, enabling improved quality of water, healthy nutrition, & safe roadways.; *Affiliation(s):* Transportation Association of Canada

Saltcoats Agricultural Society
PO Box 126, Saltcoats SK S0A 3K0
Tel: 306-744-2998
e-mail: pjmcal@sasktel.net
Also Known As: Saltcoats Agricultural & Horticultural Society
Overview: A small local organization founded in 1888
Activities: *Awareness Events:* Saltcoats Annual Fair, Aug.
Mission: To promote general agriculture through an annual agricultural fair; To promote horticulture through competition & educational seminars; *Member of:* Saskatchewan Association of Agricultural Societies & Exhibitions

Sarnia-Lambton Environmental Association
#111, 265 Front St. North, Sarnia ON N7T 7X1
Tel: 519-332-2010; *Fax:* 519-332-2015
URL: www.sarniaenvironment.com
Previous Name: Lambton Industrial Society: An Environmental Co-operative
Overview: A small local organization founded in 1952
Finances: *Annual Operating Budget:* $500,000-$1.5 Million
Staff: 3 staff member(s); 50 volunteer(s)
Membership: 14 corporate + 2 associate; *Fees:* Variable; *Member Profile:* Industrial facilities operating in Lambton County; *Committees:* Technical; Air; Land; Water; Public Affairs
Activities: Environmental research; monitoring regional air & water quality; *Awareness Events:* EnviroFest, May; *Speaker Service:* Yes; *Library:* Yes, Open to public
Mission: To be recognized by members, regulatory agencies & the community for excellence in promoting & fostering a healthy environment consistent with sustainable development

Sarnia-Lambton Environmental Association (SLEA)
1489 London Rd., Sarnia ON N7S 1P6
Tel: 519-332-2010; *Fax:* 519-332-2015
URL: www.sarniaenvironment.com
Overview: A small local organization founded in 1952
Chief Officer(s):
Dean Edwardson, General Manager
Membership: 20
Mission: To monitor ambient environmental conditions to assess the impact of its members on the local environment's air, water and soil.

Saskatchewan Anti-Tuberculosis League *See* Saskatchewan Lung Association

Saskatchewan Applied Science Technologists & Technicians (SASTT)
Parent: **Canadian Council of Technicians & Technologists**
363 Park St., Regina SK S4N 5B2
Tel: 306-721-6633; *Fax:* 306-721-0112
e-mail: info@sastt.ca
URL: www.sastt.ca
Previous Name: Society of Engineering Technicians & Technologists of Saskatchewan (SETTS)
Overview: A medium-sized provincial licensing organization founded in 1965
Finances: *Funding Sources:* Membership fees
Member Profile: Individuals who have a recognized level of post-secondary academic & practical training in a specialized applied science or engineering technology field in Saskatchewan
Activities: Increasing the knowledge of applied science technologists & certified technicians; Raising awareness & understanding of applied science technologists & certified technicians; *Awareness Events:* Technology Week, November

Awards: ASET / SASTT Lloydminster Scholarship (Scholarship)
To recognize a graduating student from a high school in the attendance area of The Lloydminster Bi-Provincial Chapter of ASET / SASTT, who plans to continue his or her education in applied science technology, information technology, or engineering technology *Deadline:* August 20 *Award Amount:* $500
Outstanding Technical Achievement Award (Award)
To recognize excellence in professional life
Outstanding Employer Award (Award)
To recognize outstanding technical achievement by employers of applied science & engineering technologists & technicians in Saskatchewan
Merit Award (Award)
To recognize persons who have distinguished themselves in the service of the association
Applied Research Project Award (Award)
To recognize the outstanding achievement of a graduating student *Deadline:* June 30
SASTT Student Awards (Award)
To recognize students from recognized programs at Saskatoon's Kelsey Campus, Moose Jaw's Palliser Campus, & Regina's Wascana Campus *Award Amount:* $250
Publications: *Saskatchewan Applied Science Technologists & Technicians Salary Survey*
Type: Survey *Frequency:* a.
Profile: Information distributed to all Saskatchewan Applied Science Technologists & Technicians members
SASTT [Saskatchewan Applied Science Technologists & Technicians] Journal
Type: Journal *Frequency:* q. *Accepts Advertising* : Yes
Profile: Technical articles, association news, & upcoming events
Mission: To regulate the professional conduct of applied science technologists & certified technicians in Saskatchewan, in order to protect the public

Saskatchewan Association of Agricultural Societies & Exhibitions (SAASE)
PO Box 31025, Regina SK S4R 8R6
Tel: 306-565-2121; *Fax:* 306-565-2079
e-mail: gduck.saase@sasktel.net
URL: www.saase.ca
Overview: A medium-sized provincial organization founded in 1987
Finances: *Annual Operating Budget:* $250,000-$500,000
Staff: 1 staff member(s)
Membership: 74 organizations
Mission: To provide the forum for exchange of ideas among Association members; to provide educational opportunities for members; to address relevant issues affecting members; to provide for district, board & provincial meetings of members; to promote fair & agricultural industry; to help promote & form new societies; to provide a liaison with the extension program of University of Saskatchewan; to assist governments & universities to reach their agricultural & educational objectives; *Member of:* Foundation for Animal Care Saskatchewan; International Association of Fairs & Exhibitions; Agriculture in the Classroom; *Affiliation(s):* Canadian Association of Fairs & Exhibitions

Saskatchewan Association of Landscape Architects (SALA)
#200, 642 Broadway Ave., Saskatoon SK S7N 1A9
URL: www.sala.sk.ca
Overview: A small provincial organization founded in 1979
Member Profile: Landscape architects in Saskatchewan
Awards: SALA Academic Award (Award)
Design Excellence Awards (Award)
Mission: To promote, improve, & advance the profession of landscape architecture; to maintain standards of professional practice & conduct; *Member of:* Canadian Society of Landscape Architects

Saskatchewan Association of Rehabilitation Centres (SARC)
111 Cardinal Cres., Saskatoon SK S7L 6H5
Tel: 306-933-0616; *Fax:* 306-653-3932
Toll-Free: 800-667-3016
e-mail: contact@sarcan.sk.ca
URL: www.sarcan.sk.ca
Also Known As: SARCAN
Overview: A medium-sized provincial charitable organization founded in 1968
Membership: 79 SARC members; *Fees:* $350 affiliate; $550 regular & Associate
Activities: Network of organizations which provide vocational & residential services to persons with disabilites
Mission: To provide vision, leadership & support to agencies through advocacy, education, provision & development of employment opportunities
Environmental Activity: SARCAN recycling division collects, processes & markets over 160 million aluminum, plastic, glass & metal used beverage containers annually & ships these to market; cloth recycling; wood products; document shredding

Saskatchewan Association of Rural Municipalities (SARM)
2075 Hamilton St., Regina SK S4P 2E1
Tel: 306-757-3577; *Fax:* 306-565-2141
Toll-Free: 800-667-3604
e-mail: sarm@sarm.ca
URL: www.sarm.ca
Overview: A medium-sized provincial organization founded in 1905
Membership: 296; *Member Profile:* Rural municipalities in Saskatchewan
Activities: Researching policies; Reviewing legislation; Providing employee benefits, municipal insurance, & fuel supply programs;
Meetings/Conferences:
For more information see Trade Shows, Conferences and Seminars Chapter
Saskatchewan Association of Rural Municipalities 2011 Midterm Convention
November 2011 Regina, SK
Saskatchewan Association of Rural Municipalities 2012 Annual Convention
March 2012 Regina, SK
Saskatchewan Association of Rural Municipalities 2012 Midterm Convention
November 2012 Saskatoon, SK
Saskatchewan Association of Rural Municipalities 2013 Annual Convention
March 2013 Saskatoon, SK
Saskatchewan Association of Rural Municipalities 2013 Midterm Convention
November 2013 Regina, SK
Publications: *Rural Councillor*
Type: Magazine *Frequency:* bi-m. *Accepts Advertising* : Yes
Profile: Issues facing rural Saskatchewan
Mission: To represent & advocate for rural municipal government in Saskatchewan

Saskatchewan Camping Association (SCA)
Parent: Canadian Camping Association
3950 Castle Rd., Regina SK S4S 6A4
Tel: 306-586-4026; *Fax:* 306-790-8634
e-mail: info@saskcamping.ca
URL: www.saskcamping.ca
Overview: A medium-sized provincial organization founded in 1974
Chief Officer(s):
Donna Wilkinson, Executive Director, 306-586-4026
donnaw@sasktel.net
Finances: *Funding Sources:* Sask Lotteries Trust Fund
Member Profile: Camps in Saskatchewan
Activities: Engaging in advocacy activities; Facilitating the sharing of ideas among camp leaders; Providing education for camp leaders
Meetings/Conferences:
For more information see Trade Shows, Conferences and Seminars Chapter
Saskatchewan Camping Association 2012 Education Day
Other Conferences in 2012 2012, SK
Saskatchewan Camping Association 2012 Annual General Meeting
Other Conferences in 2012 2012, SK
Saskatchewan Camping Association 2013 Annual General Meeting
Other Conferences in 2013 2013, SK
Publications: *Saskatchewan Directory of Camps*
Type: Directory
Profile: Listings of camps that are members of the Saskatchewan Camping Association
SCAN: The Saskatchewan Camping Association Newsletter
Type: Newsletter *Accepts Advertising* : Yes *Price:* Free with Saskatchewan Camping Association membership
Profile: News, issues, & articles of interest to the camping community of Saskatchewan
Mission: To promote the development of quality organized camping in Saskatchewan; To act as the voice for leaders of organized camps throughout Saskatchewan
Environmental Activity: Partnering with the Canadian Camping Association & the Charitree foundation to provide trees for camps; Encouraging responsible use of the natural environment & its resources by campers

Saskatchewan Coalition for Tobacco Reduction (SCTR)
2110 Hamilton St., Regina SK S4P 2E3
Tel: 306-779-1216
e-mail: blauj@sasktel.net
URL: www.sctr.sk.ca
Previous Name: Saskatchewan Interagency Council on Smoking & Health
Overview: A small provincial organization founded in 1975
Chief Officer(s):
B. Giles, Secretary
J. Blau, President
Finances: *Annual Operating Budget:* Less than $50,000; *Funding Sources:* Grants
Membership: 23
Mission: To advocate, coordinate & educate to ensure a tobacco-free Saskatchewan for all its residents; *Member of:* Canadian Centre for Tobacco Control

Saskatchewan Construction Safety Association Inc. (SCSA)
498 Henderson Dr., Regina SK S4N 6E3
Tel: 306-525-0175; *Fax:* 306-525-1542
Toll-Free: 800-817-2079
e-mail: billj@scsaonline.ca
URL: www.scsaonline.ca
Overview: A medium-sized provincial organization founded in 1995
Fees: $750 Supporter member; *Member Profile:* Saskatchewan companies with an active Workers' Compensation Board account within the construction rate group; Supporter members with accounts outside the construction rate group
Publications: *Safety Advocate Newsletter*
Type: Newsletter
Mission: To provide safety programs & servies to construction employers & employees in order to reduce human & financial loss associated with injuries in the construction industry

Saskatchewan Eco-Network (SEN)
Parent: Canadian Environmental Network
#203, 115 - 2 Ave. North, Saskatoon SK S7K 2B1
Tel: 306-652-1275; *Fax:* 306-665-2128
e-mail: sen@link.ca
URL: www.econet.sk.ca
Overview: A small provincial organization founded in 1980
Member Profile: Non-profit, non-governmental organizations in Saskatchewan concerned with environmental issues;
Committees: Forests Working Group; Energy Working Group; Wilderness Protection Working Group; Biotechnology Working Group; Pesticides Working Group; Water Working Group
Activities: Promoting networking opportunities for members; Providing referrals for members, media, government personnel, & the public
Publications: *SEN [Saskatchewan Eco-Network] Bulletin*
Type: Newsletter *Frequency:* bi-weekly *Price:* Free
Profile: News & events from across Saskatchewan
Saskatchewan's Green Directory
Type: Directory
Profile: A project of the Saskatchewan Eco-Network, with assistance from the Saskatchewan Research Council & the Ministry of Environment, the directory presents information about green products for consumers.
Mission: To provide educational activities to develop an awareness of conservation & enhancement of the environment; *Affiliation(s):* Canadian Environmental Network
Environmental Activity: Offering news & information on topics such as pesticides, global warming, endangered species, mining, water, organic agriculture, & The Great Sand Hills

Saskatchewan Environmental Industry & Managers' Association (SEIMA)
#113, 2505 - 11th Ave., Regina SK S4P 0K6
Tel: 306-543-1567; *Fax:* 306-543-1568
e-mail: info@seima.sk.ca
URL: www.seima.sk.ca
Previous Name: Saskatchewan Environmental Managers Association
Overview: A medium-sized provincial organization founded in 1993
Chief Officer(s):

Associations/Organizations / Saskatchewan Environmental Society

Lloyd Saul, President, 306-789-5222, Fax: 306-789-9490
lsaul@sasktel.net
Greg Kuntz, Vice-President, 306-721-7611, Fax: 306-721-8128
greg_kuntz@clifton.ca
Kathleen Livingston, Executive Director & COO
klivingston@seima.sk.ca
Jackie Presnell, Secretary, 306-933-7368, Fax: 306-933-8200
jpresnell@innovationplace.ca
Fred Antunes, Treasurer, 306-546-4220, Fax: 306-546-4262
fantunes@mdhsolutions.com
Kevin Marpole, Manager, Environmental Innovations
kmarpole@seima.sk.ca
Robbi Humble, Coordinator, Green Team
rhumble@seima.sk.ca
Membership: 127; *Fees:* $25 students; Schedule, based upon number of employees for corporate & associate members; *Member Profile:* Environmental managers from various industries in Saskatchewan, such as agriculture, mining, & forestry; Companies in Saskatchewan's environmental industry; Suppliers to Saskatchewan's environmental industry; Students
Activities: Engaging in advocacy activities; Liaising with governments; Providing access to current industry intelligence, such as environmental legislation & regulations, & potential opportunities; Offering professional development activities for Saskatchewan's environmental businesses & managers, such as seminars & conferences; Facilitating networking opportunities with industry colleagues, for the exchange of information & ideas; Presenting an Aboriginal Youth Career Fair
Publications: *Saskatchewan Environmental Industry & Managers' Association Member Directory & Buyer's Guide*
Type: Directory *Frequency:* a. *Price:* Free with membership in Saskatchewan Environmental Industry & Managers' Association
Profile: Information about Saskatchewan Environmental Industry & Managers' Association member businesses & their areas of specialization, to provide marketing support for its users throughout North American & Europe
Saskatchewan Environmental Industry & Managers' Association Newsletter
Type: Nesletter
Mission: To act as the voice of practitioners in Saskatchewan's environmental industry on environmental matters; To promote responsible environmental management in the province; To develop the environmental industry in Saskatchewan

Saskatchewan Environmental Managers Association *See* Saskatchewan Environmental Industry & Managers' Association

Saskatchewan Environmental Society (SES)
PO Box 1372, #203, 115 - 2nd Ave. North, Saskatoon SK S7K 3N9
Tel: 306-665-1915; *Fax:* 306-665-2128
e-mail: info@environmentalsociety.ca
URL: www.environmentalsociety.ca
Overview: A medium-sized provincial charitable organization founded in 1970
Finances: *Funding Sources:* Membership fees; Donations; Fundraising; Sponsorships
Fees: $20 / year; *Member Profile:* Persons concerned about the environment
Activities: Advocacy; policy development; educational projects; reports & fact sheets; *Speaker Service:* Yes; *Library:* Saskatchewan Environmental Society Resource Centre
Publications: *Saskatchewan Environmental Society Newsletter*
Type: Newsletter *Frequency:* bi-m.
Profile: Information about the society's involvement in environmental issues, plus upcoming events, for society members
Mission: The Society works to maintain the integrity of Saskatchewan's forests, farmlands and natural prairie landscapes; protect the atmosphere, and promote energy conservation and the development of renewable energy resources; and build sustainable communities, responsible waste management, and enhanced water quality in the province's lakes and rivers.; *Member of:* Canadian Renewable Energy Alliance
Environmental Activity: Monitoring environmental issues; participating in multi-stakeholder task groups & environmental assessment processes; providing information services & educational material on environmental issues, such as books, videos, & teaching manuals

Saskatchewan Forestry Association (SFA)
Parent: Canadian Forestry Association
#139, 1061 Central Ave., Prince Albert SK S6V 4V4
Tel: 306-763-2189; *Fax:* 306-763-6456
e-mail: info@whitebirch.ca
URL: www.whitebirch.ca
Overview: A medium-sized provincial charitable organization founded in 1972
Finances: *Funding Sources:* Membership fees; Donations; Sponsorships; Fundraising
Fees: Schedule available for corporations, based upon size; *Member Profile:* Individuals, families, groups, & corporations who care about the future of Saskatchewan's forest resources
Activities: Delivering forest education materials & programming to schools & the public; Managing interpretive trails
Meetings/Conferences:
For more information see Trade Shows, Conferences and Seminars Chapter
Saskatchewan Forestry Association 2012 Annual General Meeting
Other Conferences in 2012 2012, SK
Publications: *TreeLines [a publication of the Saskatchewan Forestry Association]*
Type: Newsletter *Frequency:* q. *Editor:* Andrea Atkinson *Price:* Free with membership in the Saskatchewan Forestry Association
Profile: Information about association activities & forestry industry issues, as well as a "Teacher's Corner" for educators
Mission: To promote the wise use, protection, & management of forests, water, & wildlife in Saskatchewan; *Affiliation(s):* Canadian Forestry Association
Environmental Activity: Increasing public awareness of the management & protection of Saskatchewan's forests

Saskatchewan Ground Water Association (SGWA)
Parent: Canadian Ground Water Association
PO Box 9434, Saskatoon SK S7K 7E9
Tel: 306-244-7551; *Fax:* 306-343-0001
Previous Name: Saskatchewan Water Well Association
Overview: A small provincial organization
Activities: Providing education about ground water
Mission: To act as the voice of the ground water industry throughout Saskatchewan; To promote the management of ground water throughout the province

Saskatchewan Health Libraries Association (SHLA)
Parent: Canadian Health Libraries Association
c/o Regina-Qu'Appelle Health Region, Health Sciences Library, 1440 - 14th Ave., Regina SK S4P 0W5
Tel: 306-766-3833; *Fax:* 306-766-3839
e-mail: kelly.mcivor@usask.ca
URL: www.lib.sk.ca/shla/
Overview: A medium-sized provincial organization founded in 1988
Chief Officer(s):
Kelly McIvor, President
Finances: *Annual Operating Budget:* Less than $50,000
Membership: 33; *Fees:* $10
Mission: To promote access to health care literature for physicians & allied health care staff

Saskatchewan Herb & Spice Association
PO Box 18, Phippen SK S0K 3E0
Tel: 306-694-4622; *Fax:* 306-644-2182
e-mail: shsa@sasktel.net
URL: www.saskherbspice.org
Overview: A small provincial organization
Chief Officer(s):
Connie Kehler, Executive Director
Membership: 300; *Fees:* $65 regular; $220 corporate; $540 corporate sponsorship
Activities: Member networking; annual member directory; public awareness; ongoing research of production & market promotion
Mission: To support research, development & promotion of crops & products from yesterday & tomorrow for producers to processors to retails today

Saskatchewan Interagency Council on Smoking & Health *See* Saskatchewan Coalition for Tobacco Reduction

Saskatchewan Katahdin Sheep Association Inc. (SKSA)
Parent: Canadian Katahdin Sheep Association Inc.
PO Box 548, Quill Lake SK S0A 3E0
Tel: 306-383-2861
URL: www.saskkatahdinsheep.com
Overview: A small provincial organization founded in 1993
Chief Officer(s):
Jean L'Arrivee, President, 306-769-8981, Fax: 306-769-8916
landjlarrivee@sasktel.net
Janette Mish, Vice-President, 306-429-2221, Fax: 306-429-2221
jmish@sasktel.net
Donna Schryver, Secretary, 306-383-2861
schryvers@sasktel.net
Donna Bruynooghe, Treasurer, 306-937-2041
dbruynooghe@highways.gov.sk.ca
Membership: 1-99; *Fees:* $10 junior members, age 15 & under; $25 senior members; *Member Profile:* Owners of Canadian registered Katahdin sheep in Saskatchewan; *Committees:* Show & Sale; New Producer Liaison
Activities: Distributing breed information; Preparing displays for various shows throughout the province; Creating networking opportunities with other sheep producers; Providing education, such as on-farm seminars & hands-on-training sessions; Showing sheep at events such as the Canadian Western Agribition
Publications: *News for Ewes*
Type: Newsletter *Frequency:* q. *Accepts Advertising :* Yes *Editor:* Janette Mish
Saskatchewan Katahdin Sheep Association Membership Directory
Type: Directory *Price:* Free
Mission: To develop & advance the Katahdin sheep breed in Saskatchewan

Saskatchewan Land Surveyors' Association (SLSA)
Parent: Canadian Council of Land Surveyors
#230, 408 Broad St., Regina SK S4R 1X3
Tel: 306-352-8999; *Fax:* 306-352-8366
e-mail: info@slsa.sk.ca
URL: www.slsa.sk.ca
Overview: A small provincial licensing organization founded in 1910
Member Profile: Registered members of the association, who are licensed to practice as Saskatchewan land surveyors in Saskatchewan, in accordance with the provisions of the Land Surveyors & Professional Surveyors Act of Saskatchewan
Activities: Providing continuing education to licensed members; Investigating complaints from the public
Awards: I.W. Tweddell Memorial Award (Scholarship)
Eligibility: A student land surveyor from Saskatchewan enrolled in a program that will result in a Certificate of Completion from The Canadian Board of Examiners for Professional Surveyors
Deadline: May 31 *Award Amount:* $1,250
Publications: *SLSA [Saskatchewan Land Surveyors' Association] Corner Post*
Type: Newsletter *Frequency:* q. *Accepts Advertising :* Yes *Editor:* Doug A. Bouck, SLS
Profile: Articles about surveying, in addition to regular features, such as the president's message & council highlights
Mission: To uphold the stewardship & standards of the legal survey profession in Saskatchewan; To regulate & govern members in the practice of professional land surveying & professional surveying; To ensure the competency of members; To administer the profession to protect the public

Saskatchewan Livestock Association (SLA)
Canada Center Building, Evraz Place, PO Box 3771, Regina SK S4P 3N8
Tel: 306-757-6133; *Fax:* 306-525-5852
e-mail: sla@accesscomm.ca
URL: www.sasklivestock.com
Overview: A medium-sized provincial organization founded in 1075
Chief Officer(s):
Murray Andrew, Executive Director
Meetings/Conferences:
For more information see Trade Shows, Conferences and Seminars Chapter
Saskatchewan Beef Industry 2012 3rd Annual Conference
Other Conferences in 2012 2012, SK
Mission: To promote cooperation among the livestock organizations in Saskatchewan; To communicate opinions of livestock producers to government & other agencies; To encourage improvement in the production of livestock

Saskatchewan Lung Association
Parent: Canadian Lung Association
1231 - 8 St. East, Saskatoon SK S7H 0S5
Tel: 306-343-9511; *Fax:* 306-343-7007
Toll-Free: 888-566-5864
e-mail: info@sk.lung.ca
URL: www.sk.lung.ca
Previous Name: Saskatchewan Anti-Tuberculosis League

Overview: A medium-sized provincial charitable organization founded in 1911
Finances: *Funding Sources:* Donations; Sponsorships; Fundraising
Fees: $25
Activities: Supporting & conducting research into respiratory health & disease; Providing educational programs; Offering the most current lung health information; Organizing sleep apnea support groups; Promoting the prevention of lung disease; Raising public awareness of the impact of respiratory diseases; Collaborating with other organizations to work toward lung health; *Awareness Events:* Breath of Spring Tulip Campaign; Loonies for Lungs
Publications: *Lung Association of Saskatchewan Annual Report*
Type: Yearbook *Frequency:* a.
Breathworks: COPD Newsletter
Type: Newsletter
Profile: Educational articles plus notices of forthcoming support group meetings
Nightly Nezzz Newsletter
Type: Newsletter *Frequency:* q.
Profile: Information for persons with sleep apnea & their families
Mission: To improve respiratory health & overall quality of life; To advocate for support of education & research

Saskatchewan Medical Association (SMA)
Parent: Canadian Medical Association
#402, 321A - 21st St. East, Saskatoon SK S7K 0C1
Tel: 306-244-2196; *Fax:* 306-653-1631
Toll-Free: 800-667-3781
e-mail: sma@sma.sk.ca
URL: www.sma.sk.ca
Overview: A medium-sized provincial organization founded in 1906
Member Profile: Saskatchewan physicians; *Committees:* Rural & Regional Practice; Continuing Medical Education Fund Advisory; Specialist Recruitment & Retention Fund; Information Technology; Membership Services; Medical Benevolent Society; Sports
Activities: Engaging in advocacy activities; Promoting quality health care in Saskatchewan; Acting as the bargaining agent for fee-for-service physicians; Providing information about health care issues in Saskatchewan; Supporting continuing professional learning; Managing funds to offer programs such as bursaries & educational grants; Supporting physician health, through programs such as the Saskatchewan Physician Support Program
Publications: *SMA [Saskatchewan Medical Association] News*
Type: Newsletter
Profile: Association issues & events
Mission: To represent physicians in Saskatchewan; To advance the professional, educational, & economic welfare of physicians in the province

Saskatchewan Mining Association (SMA)
Parent: Mining Association of Canada
#1500, 2002 Victoria Ave., Regina SK S4P 0R7
Tel: 306-757-9505; *Fax:* 306-569-1085
e-mail: saskmining@sasktel.net
URL: www.saskmining.ca
Overview: A small provincial organization founded in 1965
Finances: *Funding Sources:* Membership fees
Committees: Safety; Public Awareness; Human Resources; Taxation; Environmental; Geotechnical
Activities: Liaising with both provincial & federal governments; Organizing research into matters such as industrial relations; Cooperating with similar organizations; *Awareness Events:* Saskatchewan Mining Week, May
Mission: To ensure the safe & profitable development of mineral resources in Saskatchewan; To act as the voice of the mining industry throughout the province; To promote understanding of the development of mineral resources in Saskatchewan
Environmental Activity: Coordinating programs on issues such as health, safety, & environmental impact; Promoting environmental stewardship & sustainability in Saskatchewan's mining industry

Saskatchewan Nursery Landscape Association (SNLA)
Parent: Canadian Nursery Landscape Association
c/o Landscape Alberta Nursery Trades Association, #200, 10331 - 178 St., Edmonton AB T5S 1R5
Tel: 780-489-1991; *Fax:* 780-444-2152
Toll-Free: 866-383-4711
e-mail: rebecca@canadanursery.com
URL: www.snla.ca
Previous Name: Saskatchewan Nursery Trades Association
Overview: A medium-sized provincial organization
Finances: *Annual Operating Budget:* Less than $50,000
Membership: 70; *Fees:* Schedule available;

Saskatchewan Nursery Trades Association *See*
Saskatchewan Nursery Landscape Association

Saskatchewan Outdoor & Environmental Education Association (SOEEA)
26 Corkery Bay, Regina SK S4T 7K6
e-mail: soeea.sk@gmail.com
URL: www.soeea.sk.ca
Overview: A small provincial organization founded in 1972
Chief Officer(s):
Jol Siemens, President
memyselfandjo@yahoo.ca
Kyle Lichtenwald, Vice-President
thekyleguy@gmail.com
Karen McIver, Director, Programs
karen.mciver@gmail.com
Mark Wilson, Treasurer
mark.wilson@rbe.sk.ca
Committees: Communications Working Goup; Decision Makers Working Group; Education Working Group; Partners Working Group; Public & Families Working Group
Activities: Developing & evaluating education activities; Providing professional development workshops; Partnering with related organizations; Facilitating networking opportunities
Awards: B.M. Melanson Award (Award)
To be presented periodically to an individual who has made an outstanding contribution to outdoor & environmental education in Saskatchewan; candidates shall be active participants in outdoor & environmental education in Saskatchewan; candidates need not be a member of SOEEA Contact: Yvette Crane
Publications: *Envisage [a publication of the Saskatchewan Outdoor & Environmental Education Association]*
Type: Newsletter *Frequency:* q.
Profile: Articles on topics such as educational strategies & instructional methods
Green Teacher
Mission: To encourage educators & people who participate in outdoor education to teach & practise environmental responsibility; Affiliation(s): North American Association for Environmental Education
Environmental Activity: Funding community or school groups to carry out environmental action projects for recreational or educational purposes; Supporting environmental education; Encouraging outdoor & environmental skills & practices

Saskatchewan Parks & Recreation Association (SPRA)
Parent: Canadian Parks & Recreation Association
#100, 1445 Park St., Regina SK S4N 4C5
Tel: 306-780-9231; *Fax:* 306-780-9257
Toll-Free: 800-563-2555
e-mail: office@spra.sk.ca
URL: www.spra.sk.ca
Overview: A medium-sized provincial charitable organization founded in 1962
Chief Officer(s):
Norm Campbell, CEO
ncampbell@spra.sk.ca
Randy Durovick, Manager, Corporate Services
rdurovick@spra.sk.ca
John Firnesz, Program Manager
jfirnesz@spra.sk.ca
Finances: *Annual Operating Budget:* $500,000-$1.5 Million; *Funding Sources:* Lottery ticket sales
Staff: 18 staff member(s); 200 volunteer(s)
Membership: 600 organizations; *Fees:* Schedule available
Activities: Resource Centre; leadership training; funding; advocacy; workshops; *Speaker Service:* Yes; *Library:* Resource Centre for Sport, Culture & Recreation; Open to public
Mission: To stimulate & advance parks, recreation & leisure activities, facilities & programs in Saskatchewan

Saskatchewan Public Health Association Inc.
Parent: Canadian Public Health Association
PO Box 845, Regina SK S4P 3B1
e-mail: terry.gibson@saskatoonhealthregion.ca
Overview: A small provincial organization
Chief Officer(s):
Saqib Shahab, President
saqib.shahab@shr.sk.ca
Membership: 4 institutional; 124 individual; 4 student
Mission: To constitute a resource in Saskatchewan for the improvement & maintenance of health

Saskatchewan Safety Council
445 Hoffer Dr., Regina SK S4N 6E2
Tel: 306-757-3197; *Fax:* 306-569-1907
e-mail: ssc@sasksafety.org
URL: sasksafety.org
Overview: A small provincial organization founded in 1955
Fees: Based on size of workplace

Saskatchewan Soil Conservation Association (SSCA)
PO Box 1360, Indian Head SK S0G 2K0
Tel: 306-695-4233; *Fax:* 306-695-4236
Toll-Free: 800-213-4287
e-mail: info@ssca.ca
URL: www.ssca.ca
Overview: A small provincial charitable organization founded in 1987
Chief Officer(s):
Blair McClinton, P.Ag., Executive Manager, 306-695-4235
bmcclinton@ssca.ca
Marilyn Martens, Office Manager, 306-695-4233
Finances: *Funding Sources:* Donations; Federal-Provincial sustainable agriculture programs
Membership: 800; *Member Profile:* Farmers in Saskatchewan
Activities: Sharing soil conservation information
Meetings/Conferences:
For more information see Trade Shows, Conferences and Seminars Chapter
Conservation Agriculture 2012 Annual Conference
Other Conferences in 2012 2012, SK
Saskatchewan Soil Conservation Association 2012 Annual Crop Advisor Workshop
Other Conferences in 2012 2012, SK
Publications: *Prairie Steward*
Type: Newsletter *Frequency:* 3 pa
Profile: Association news & technical articles for Saskatchewan Soil Conservation Association members
Prairie Soils & Crops eJournal
Type: Journal
Profile: Peer-reviewed information from the Saskatchewan Soil Conservation Association, Agriculture & Agri-Food Canada, & the University of Saskatchewan for prairie producers & agrologists
Direct Seeding Manual
Type: Manual
Profile: Developed & published with the Prairie Agricultural Machinery Institute for Saskatchewan growers
Mission: To improve the land & environment; To increase public awareness of soil conservation; To promote conservation production systems to Saskatchewan producers
Environmental Activity: Offering soil conservation education programs, such as Project SOILS, a joint project with Agriculture in the Classroom; Promoting the use of agriculture soil sinks as part of Canada's greenhouse gas management strategy

Saskatchewan Stock Growers Association (SSGA)
Main Floor, Canada Centre Building, Evraz Place, PO Box 4752, Regina SK S4P 3Y4
Tel: 306-757-8523; *Fax:* 306-569-8799
e-mail: ssga@sasktel.net; ssga.admin@sasktel.net
URL: www.skstockgrowers.com
Overview: A medium-sized provincial organization founded in 1913
Finances: *Funding Sources:* Membership fees
Fees: $105 / 1 year; $194.25 / 2 years; $262.50 / 3 years; $1050 / lifetime; *Member Profile:* Active members are individuals engaged in livestock production in Saskatchewan; Affiliate members are groups that are engaged in livestock marketing; Associate members have an interest in the industry
Activities: Providing education; Engaging in research; Advocating on behalf of the beef industry
Awards: Stewardship Award (Award)
To recognize excellence & environmental stewardship in the ranching industry
Publications: *Beef Business*
Type: Magazine *Frequency:* bi-m. *Accepts Advertising*: Yes
Editor: Jim Warren *Price:* Included with SSGA membership
Profile: Industry news, markets & trade, features, analysis & opinion, science & productions, association news & reports, & stewardship

Associations/Organizations / Saskatchewan Trade & Export Partnership Inc.

Mission: To serve, protect, & advance the interests of the beef industry in Saskatchewan; To represent the cattle industry in Saskatchewan on the legislative front; *Member of:* Canadian Cattlemen's Association; Affiliation(s): Saskatchewan Prairie Conservation Action Plan (SK PCAP) Partnership
Environmental Activity: Providing information about stewardship

Saskatchewan Trade & Export Partnership Inc. (STEP)
PO Box 1787, #320, 1801 Hamilton St., Regina SK S4P 3C6
Tel: 306-787-9210; *Fax:* 306-787-6666
Toll-Free: 877-313-7244
e-mail: inquire@sasktrade.com
URL: www.sasktrade.com
Overview: A medium-sized provincial organization founded in 1996
Chief Officer(s):
Lionel LaBelle, President & CEO, 306-787-1550
Nicole Grande, Administrative Coordinator, 306-787-7977
Heather Swan, Manager, Corporate Services, 306-787-6666
Janice Lawless, Membership Coordinator, 306-787-7919
Stephanie Pappas, Technology & Communications, 306-787-3223
Brad Michnik, Executive Director, Trade Development, 306-933-6555
Finances: *Annual Operating Budget:* $1.5 Million-$3 Million; *Funding Sources:* Private & public funding
Staff: 26 staff member(s)
Membership: 426; *Member Profile:* Saskatchewan exporters & companies providing services to exporters
Activities: Trade missions; Market intelligence; International finance solutions; Export education; Marketing services; *Library:* Yes, Not open to the public
Publications: *STEP Global Newsletter*
Type: Newsletter *Frequency:* q.
Mission: To work in partnership with Saskatchewan exporters & emerging exporters to maximize commercial success in global ventures; To deliver custom export solutions & market intelligence to member companies; To coordinate international development projects

Saskatchewan Trucking Association (STA)
Parent: Canadian Trucking Alliance
1335 Wallace St., Regina SK S4N 3Z5
Tel: 306-569-9696; *Fax:* 306-569-1008
Toll-Free: 800-563-7623
e-mail: ttoope@sasktrucking.com
URL: www.sasktrucking.com
Overview: A medium-sized provincial licensing organization founded in 1937
Finances: *Annual Operating Budget:* $250,000-$500,000; *Funding Sources:* Membership fees; sponsorship of programs
Staff: 5 staff member(s)
Membership: 300; *Fees:* Schedule available
Activities: Truck Driver Roadeos
Awards: Safe Driver Award Program (Award)
Mission: Helps the industry fight its battles in everything from deregulation to weights and measures. Represents the industry in discussions with government

Saskatchewan Urban Municipalities Association (SUMA)
#200, 2222 - 13th Ave., Regina SK S4P 3M7
Tel: 306-525-3727; *Fax:* 306-525-4373
e-mail: suma@suma.org
URL: www.suma.org
Overview: A medium-sized provincial organization founded in 1906
Finances: *Funding Sources:* Membership fees
Staff: 13 staff member(s)
Membership: 465 municipalities; *Fees:* $175+; *Committees:* Protective Services; Environment; Sustainable Communities; Convention Planning; Resolutions; Transportation; Bylaw Review; Corporate Services
Activities: Group Benefits; Group Purchasing; *Rents Mailing List:* Yes
Awards: Honourary, Meritorius, Life Awards (Award)
Mission: To work to enhance urban life in Saskatchewan, by providing administrative & consultative services to members, a forum for the discussion & resolution of current issues, & a negotiating vehicle for improvements in legislation, financing & programs. SUMA provides information & training for aldermen & mayors, and group benefits for its members; *Member of:* Federation of Canadian Municipalities

Saskatchewan Waste Reduction Council (SWRC)
203 Idylwyld Dr. South, Saskatoon SK S7M 1L6
Tel: 306-931-3242; *Fax:* 306-665-2128
e-mail: info@saskwastereduction.ca
URL: www.saskwastereduction.ca
Overview: A medium-sized provincial charitable organization founded in 1991
Fees: $25 individual; $50 non-profit organization & school; $100-$150 business & municipality; $200 association; $1,000 supporting member; *Member Profile:* Individuals; Non-profits or other organizations; Schools; Municipalities; Associations
Activities: *Awareness Events:* Waste Reduction Week in Saskatchewan
Awards: Waste Minimization Awards (Award)
Publications: *WasteWatch*
Frequency: q.
Mission: To help Saskatchewan & its people attain the environmental, economic & cultural benefits that come from reducing waste; to establish an information & education network for all groups interested in waste reduction; to provide accurate, balanced information on waste reduction, with particular emphasis on municipal solid waste & dangerous waste goods; to encourage all sectors to begin reducing waste in all areas of their lives; to encourage policy development, legislation & research on reducing waste in Saskatchewan; *Member of:* Saskatchewan Eco-Network; Saskatchewan Environmental Society

Saskatchewan Water Well Association *See* Saskatchewan Ground Water Association

Saskatchewan Wildlife Federation (SWF)
Parent: Canadian Wildlife Federation
9 Lancaster Rd., Moose Jaw SK S6J 1M8
Tel: 306-692-8812; *Fax:* 306-692-4370
Toll-Free: 877-793-9453
e-mail: sask.wildlife@sasktel.net
URL: www.swf.sk.ca
Social Media:
www.facebook.com/pages/Saskatchewan-Wildlife-Federation/178255362147
Overview: A medium-sized provincial charitable organization founded in 1929
Chief Officer(s):
Darrell Crabbe, Executive Director
dcrabbe.swf@sasktel.net
Marilee Herone, Manager, Office
mheron.swf@sasktel.net
Maureen Horrocks, Coordinator, Communications
maureenhorrocks@gmail.com
Jim Kroshus, Coordinator, Habitat Trust Land
jkroshus.swf@sasktel.net
Adam Matichuk, Coordinator, Fisheries Project
amatichuk.swf@sasktel.net
JeanAnne Prysliak, Coordinator, Education Program
jprysliak.swf@sasktel.net
Finances: *Funding Sources:* Membership fees; Donations; Fundraising
Membership: 30,000+
Activities: Advocating on behalf of members; *Awareness Events:* Great Canadian Shoreline Cleanup, September
Meetings/Conferences:
For more information see Trade Shows, Conferences and Seminars Chapter
Saskatchewan Wildlife Federation 2011 Plant Identification Workshop
June 2011 Candiac, SK
Saskatchewan Wildlife Federation 2012 83rd Annual Convention
Other Conferences in 2012 2012, SK
Publications: *Outdoor Edge [a publication of the Saskatchewan Wildlife Federation]*
Type: Magazine *Price:* Free with Saskatchewan Wildlife Federation membership
Mission: To promote the wise use & management of natural resources in Saskatchewan
Environmental Activity: Encouraging hunting, fishing, & trapping in a responsible manner, in accordance with regulations; Maintaining conservation policies; Providing conservation education; Working with governments on projects such as stream enhancement & fish stocking

Saskatoon Wildlife Federation
PO Box 32041, Saskatoon SK S7S 1N8
Tel: 306-242-1666; *Fax:* 306-933-0617
e-mail: claudia.m.swild@sasktel.net
URL: www.saskatoonwildlifefederation.com
Overview: A small local organization founded in 1931
Membership: 1,400; *Fees:* $50
Mission: Saskatoon Wildlife Federation is a non-profit organization committed to providing a clean welcoming enviroment for individuals who enjoy hunting, fishing and various other outdoor sports. The organization works closely with Ducks Unlimited and other groups to preserve wetlands and other wildspaces for habitat.; *Member of:* Saskatchewan Wildlife Federation

Sault Naturalists
PO Box 21035, 306 Northern Ave. East, Sault Ste Marie ON P6B 6H3
e-mail: carrie@ginou.ca
URL: soonats.pbwiki.com
Overview: A small local organization
Finances: *Annual Operating Budget:* Less than $50,000
Staff: 30 volunteer(s)
Fees: $20 individual; $25 family; $10 student
Mission: To promote the enjoyment of nature through environmental appreciation & conservation; to encourage wise use & conservation of natural resources; *Member of:* Federation of Ontario Naturalists; Affiliation(s): Canadian Nature Federation

SauveTerre *See* Earthsave Canada

Save Ontario Shipwrecks (SOS)
PO Box 2389, Blenheim ON N0P 1A0
Tel: 519-676-4110; *Fax:* 519-676-7058
e-mail: rjequip@on.aibn.com
URL: www.saveontarioshipwrecks.on.ca
Social Media: www.facebook.com/group.php?gid=68638569592
Overview: A small provincial organization founded in 1981
Chief Officer(s):
Michael Hill, President, 613-767-7446
Jonathan Ferguson, Secretary
jonathanferguson@hotmail.com
Finances: *Annual Operating Budget:* Less than $50,000
Membership: 350-400; *Fees:* $25 individual; $40 family/institution; $250 corporate; *Committees:* Data Base; Forum; Education; Membership; Promotion
Mission: To promote & preserve Ontario's marine heritage; *Member of:* Canadian Maritime Heritage Federation; Affiliation(s): Underwater Council

Science Alberta Foundation
#260, 3512 - 33 St. NW, Calgary AB T2L 2A6
Tel: 403-220-0077; *Fax:* 403-284-4132
e-mail: info@sciencealberta.org
URL: www.sciencealberta.org
Overview: A medium-sized provincial organization founded in 1990
Finances: *Funding Sources:* Provincial government; private donations
Activities: Science-in-a-Crate; science festivals
Mission: To increase science literacy by creating innovative programs for all Albertans

The Scrap Tire Management Council *See* Rubber Manufacturers Association

Sea Shepherd Conservation Society (SSCS)
PO Box 48446, Vancouver BC V7X 1A2
Tel: 604-688-7325
e-mail: canada@seashepherd.org
URL: www.seashepherd.org
Social Media:
www.facebook.com/seashepherdconservationsociety
Overview: A medium-sized national organization founded in 1977
Finances: *Annual Operating Budget:* $500,000-$1.5 Million
Membership: 30,000; *Fees:* $25
Activities: Volunteers work as crew members aboard our ships to investigate & document any violations of international laws, treaties or regulations against marine wildlife & then enforce those laws; *Speaker Service:* Yes
Mission: Investigates & documents violations of international laws, regulations & treaties protecting marine wildlife species; involved with the enforcement of these laws when there is no enforcement by national governments or international regulatory organizations

Sea Shepherd Conservation Society - USA (SSCS)
PO Box 2616, Friday Harbor WA 98250 USA

Associations/Organizations / Seagull Foundation

Tel: 360-370-5650; Fax: 360-370-5651
e-mail: info@seashepherd.org
URL: www.seashepherd.org
Overview: A large international charitable organization founded in 1977
Chief Officer(s):
Paul Watson, Founder & President
Carla Robinson, Administrative Director
Farley Mowat, Honorary Chair
Finances: *Annual Operating Budget:* $500,000-$1.5 Million; *Funding Sources:* Grants, public contributions
Staff: 5 staff member(s); 40 volunteer(s)
Membership: 30,000 worldwide; *Fees:* $25
Activities: Research, documentation & enforcement of international marine conservation law; *Rents Mailing List:* Yes; *Library:* Sea Shepherd Media Library
Mission: A direct action organization to protect dolphins, whales, seals & other marine life

Seagull Foundation
PO Box 108, Pugwash NS B0K 1L0
Tel: 902-243-2416
Overview: A small local charitable organization
Chief Officer(s):
Bonnie Bond, Chair
Finances: *Annual Operating Budget:* Less than $50,000
Staff: 1 staff member(s); 2 volunteer(s)
Mission: To protect significant wilderness areas; to support environmental education & conservation; to support Third World development projects; to support programs that create environmental awareness

SeCan Association / Association SeCan
#501, 300 March Rd., Kanata ON K2K 2E2
Tel: 613-592-8600; Fax: 613-592-9497
Toll-Free: 800-764-5487
e-mail: seed@secan.com
URL: www.secan.com
Overview: A small national organization founded in 1976
Finances: *Annual Operating Budget:* $1.5 Million-$3 Million
Staff: 10 staff member(s)
Membership: 1,000; *Fees:* $525; *Committees:* Cereals, Oilseeds & Special Crops; Forage; Promotion; Liaison
Activities: *Library:* Yes
Mission: As Canada's Seed Partner, SeCan actively seeks partnerships which promote profitability in Canadian agriculture. SeCan is the largest supplier of certified seed to Canadian farmers with more than 1,000 members from coast to coast engaged in seed production, processing and marketing. They are a private, not-for-profit, member corporation with the primary goal of accessing and promoting leading genetics.

Sechelt Marsh Protective Society *See* Sunshine Coast Natural History Society

Secrétariat des conférences intergouvernementales canadiennes *See* Canadian Intergovernmental Conference Secretariat

Sectorial Association - Transportation Equipment & Machinery Manufacturing *Voir* Association sectorielle - Fabrication d'équipement de transport et de machines

SEEDS Foundation
#400, 144 - 4th Ave. SW., Calgary AB T2P 3N4
Tel: 403-221-0835; Fax: 403-221-0876
Toll-Free: 800-661-8751
e-mail: seeds@telusplanet.net
URL: www.seedsfoundation.ca
Social Media:
www.facebook.com/pages/SEEDS-Foundation/117021191648133
Also Known As: Society, Environment & Energy Development Studies Foundation
Overview: A medium-sized national charitable organization founded in 1976
Finances: *Annual Operating Budget:* $250,000-$500,000; *Funding Sources:* Donations (industry, business); government (federal/provincial, less than 5%); private foundations
Staff: 6 staff member(s); 19 volunteer(s)
Membership: 19; *Committees:* Education; Environment; Industry
Activities: Green School Program, environmental action program for elementary school students; Challenge Programs; Water & Clean Air; Writing & Bird challenges for elementary & junior high school students; Creating a Climate of Change Multimedia Program; Energy Literacy Series; Taking Action on Climate Change; *Awareness Events:* Green School Celebrations; Annual Bird Challenge; *Speaker Service:* Yes
Mission: To provide educational support materials & professional assistance to teachers in the area of energy, environment & sustainable development; to work toward the development of a society which understands & is committed to actions leading to wise stewardship of resources, resource use & the environment
Environmental Activity: Climate Change Program; The Green School Program; The Heat Challenge; May Bird Count Challenge

Seeds of Diversity Canada (SoDC) / Semences du patrimoine Canada
PO Box 36, Stn. Q, Toronto ON M4T 2L7
Toll-Free: 866-509-7333
e-mail: mail@seeds.ca
URL: www.seeds.ca
Also Known As: Heritage Seed Program
Overview: A medium-sized national organization founded in 1984
Chief Officer(s):
Bob Wildfong, Executive Director
Judy Newman, Office Manager
Valérie Girard, Communication Coordinator
Finances: *Funding Sources:* Membership fees; grants
Staff: 2 staff member(s)
Membership: 1,700; *Fees:* $30 regular; $50 overseas; $25 fixed income
Activities: Canadian Tomato Project; Great Canadian Garlic Collection; Pollination Canada; *Awareness Events:* Seedy Saturdays & Seedy Sundays
Mission: To search out & preserve rare & endangered varieties of vegetables, fruits, flowers, herbs & grains; *Affiliation(s):* Rare Breeds Canada; Canadian Organic Growers

Semences du patrimoine Canada *See* Seeds of Diversity Canada

Seniors for Nature Canoe Club
PO Box 94051, Stn. Bedford Park, Toronto ON M4N 3R1
e-mail: info@sfncc.org
URL: www.sfncc.org
Overview: A small local organization founded in 1985
Finances: *Annual Operating Budget:* Less than $50,000; *Funding Sources:* Membership fees
Staff: 12 volunteer(s)
Membership: 135 senior; *Fees:* $35; *Member Profile:* Over 55 years of age; able to help transport & steer canoes & to swim; *Committees:* Program & Training; Purchasing & Inventory; Membership; Social; Publicity & Newsletter
Activities: Canoeing, hiking, skiing, biking, camping trips
Mission: To offer seniors the opportunity to canoe, camp, hike, ski & cycle; *Member of:* Federation of Ontario Naturalists

Sensibilisation au cancer du sein *See* Breast Cancer Action

Services de Sécurité Nouveau-Brunswick *See* Safety Services New Brunswick

Severn Sound Environmental Association (SSEA)
67 Fourth St., Midland ON L4R 3S9
Tel: 705-527-5166; Fax: 705-527-5167
URL: www.severnsound.ca
Overview: A small local organization
Chief Officer(s):
Keith Sherman, Executive Director
Membership: 9 municipalities
Mission: To forge cooperative initiatives to address environmental issues by planning, designing, arranging funding and implementing environmental projects and promoting a sustainable Severn Sound community.
Environmental Activity: environmental monitoring

SHAD Valley International
8 Young St. East, Waterloo ON N2J 2L3
Tel: 519-884-8844; Fax: 519-884-8191
e-mail: info@shad.ca
URL: www.shad.ca
Previous Name: Canadian Centre for Creative Technology
Overview: A medium-sized national charitable organization founded in 1981
Finances: *Annual Operating Budget:* $500,000-$1.5 Million
Staff: 7 staff member(s); 100 volunteer(s)
Membership: 6,000
Activities: Shad Valley program involves 500+ outstanding senior high school students, some 200 corporate partners, 9 Canadian universities & 1 international university (in Scotland) each summer in an academic/co-op experience; *Speaker Service:* Yes
Mission: To advance the scientific & technological capabilities of youth, integrated with the development of their entrepreneurial spirit; to collaborate with education, business & other communities, both domestic & international, to provide exceptional development opportunities

Sheet Metal & Air Conditioning Contractors' National Association (SMACNA)
4201 Lafayette Center Dr., Chantilly VA 20151-1209 USA
Tel: 703-803-2980; Fax: 703-803-3732
e-mail: info@smacna.org
URL: www.smacna.org
Overview: A large international organization founded in 1943
Finances: *Annual Operating Budget:* Greater than $5 Million; *Funding Sources:* Membership dues; industry fund
Staff: 42 staff member(s)
Membership: 2,100
Activities: *Library:* Yes, open by appointment
Mission: To develop technical standards & guidelines for use by the design community in specifying sheet metal installations & for use in the fabrication & installation of HVAC, architectural & specialty sheet metal systems

Sheet Metal Contractors Association of Alberta (SMCAA)
#203, 2725 - 12th St. NE, Calgary AB T2E 7J2
Tel: 403-250-7040; Fax: 403-735-5910
Toll-Free: 888-265-6665
e-mail: wilma@smcaa.ca
URL: www.albertasheetmetal.com
Previous Name: Edmonton Association of Sheet Metal & Air Conditioning Contractors
Overview: A small local organization
Activities: Providing educational programs; Preparing information about the profession for participation in career fairs
Member of: Sheet Metal & Air Conditioning Contractors' National Association

Shipbuilding Association of Canada / Association de la construction navale du Canada
#1502, 222 Queen St., Ottawa ON K1P 5V9
Tel: 613-232-7127; Fax: 613-238-5519
e-mail: pcairns@cfncon.com
URL: www.shipbuilding.ca
Previous Name: Canadian Maritime Industries Association
Overview: A medium-sized national organization founded in 1995
Finances: *Funding Sources:* Membership dues
Membership: 1-99; *Fees:* Schedule available; *Member Profile:* Canadian organizations engaged in provision of services, products &/or facilities related to ship design, shipbuilding & ship repair, must be 65% Canadian content/owned; *Committees:* Technical; Finance; Personnel; International Marketing; Procurement Outlook; SAC/Government Working Groups
Activities: *Rents Mailing List:* Yes
Mission: Represents the interests of the Canadian shipbuilding, ship repair & associated marine equipment & services industries

Shuswap Naturalists
PO Box 1076, Salmon Arm BC V0E 2T0
Tel: 250-833-1098
e-mail: info@shuswapnaturalists.org
URL: www.shuswapnaturalists.org
Overview: A small local charitable organization founded in 1971
Membership: 32; *Fees:* $20 single; $30 family
Mission: To promote the enjoyment of nature through environmental appreciation & conservation; to encourage wise use & conservation of natural resources & environmental protection.; *Member of:* Federation of BC Naturalists

Sierra Club
85 Second St., 2nd Fl., San Francisco CA 94105-3441 USA
Tel: 415-977-5500; Fax: 415-977-5799
e-mail: information@sierraclub.org
URL: www.sierraclub.org
Social Media: www.facebook.com/SierraClub;
www.twitter.com/sierra_club
Overview: A large international organization founded in 1892
Chief Officer(s):
Marilyn Wall, Secretary
Allison Chin, President
Finances: *Annual Operating Budget:* $3 Million-$5 Million
Membership: 1,300,000; *Fees:* US$39 regular; $25 student/senior/limited income

Associations/Organizations / Sierra Club of British Columbia

Activities: Conservation Programs (lobbying, expert testimony, grassroots activism, public education on major conservation campaigns); Sierra Book Clubs (nearly 600 titles published - 100 Bush St., 13th Fl., San Francisco, CA 94104 415/291-1600); Outings; *Library:* Yes, Not open to the public
Mission: To promote conservation of the natural environment by influencing public policy decisions - legislative, administrative, legal & electoral; to explore, enjoy & protect the wild places of the earth; to practise & promote the responsible use of the earth's ecosystems & resources; to educate & enlist humanity to protect & restore the quality of the natural & human environment; to use all lawful means to carry out these objectives at the federal, state & local levels

Sierra Club of British Columbia (SCBC)
#302, 733 Johnson St., Victoria BC V8W 3L7
Tel: 250-386-5255; *Fax:* 250-386-4453
e-mail: info@sierraclub.bc.ca
URL: www.sierraclub.bc.ca
Social Media: www.facebook.com/pages/Sierra-Club-BC/136350861428
Overview: A medium-sized provincial organization founded in 1969
Finances: *Annual Operating Budget:* $500,000-$1.5 Million
Staff: 20 staff member(s); 40 volunteer(s)
Membership: 2,500; *Fees:* Schedule available; *Committees:* Regional Conservation
Activities: *Internships:* Yes; *Speaker Service:* Yes
Mission: To explore, enjoy & protect the country's forests, waters, wildlife & wilderness; *Member of:* Wild Salmon Coalition

Sierra Club of Canada (SCC) / Sierre club du Canada
#412, 1 Nicholas St., Ottawa ON K1N 7B7
Tel: 613-241-4611; *Fax:* 613-241-2292
Toll-Free: 888-810-4204
e-mail: info@sierraclub.ca
URL: www.sierraclub.ca
Social Media: www.facebook.com/sierraclubcanada
Overview: A medium-sized national charitable organization founded in 1992
Chief Officer(s):
John Bennett, Executive Director
Anowara Baqi, CFO
Tania Beriau, Development Director
Daniel Spence, Director, Communications
Finances: *Annual Operating Budget:* $500,000-$1.5 Million; *Funding Sources:* Foundations; Governments; Individual donors
Staff: 20 staff member(s)
Activities: Program Areas: Atmosphere & Energy; Health & Environment; Environmental Education; Protecting Biodiversity; Transition to a Sustainable Economy; *Internships:* Yes; *Rents Mailing List:* Yes
Publications: The RIO Report [a publication of the Sierra Club of Canada]
Type: Annual Report *Frequency:* a.
SCAN - Sierra Club of Canada Activist News
Type: Newsletter
Mission: To develop a diverse, well-trained grassroots network, working to protect the integrity of our global ecosystems; To focus on five overriding threats: loss of animal & plant species, deterioration of the planet's oceans & atmosphere, the ever-growing presence of toxic chemicals in all living things, destruction of our remaining wilderness, spiralling population growth & overconsumption; *Member of:* CANET; Green Budget Coalition; Canadian Renewable Energy Alliance; *Affiliation(s):* Common Front on the World Trade Organization

Sierra Club of Canada - Ontario Chapter
#102, 24 Mercer St., Toronto ON M5V 1H3
Tel: 416-960-9606; *Fax:* 416-960-0020
e-mail: info@sierraclub.on.ca
URL: www.sierraclub.on.ca
Previous Name: Sierra Club of Eastern Canada
Overview: A medium-sized local organization founded in 1972
Finances: *Annual Operating Budget:* Less than $50,000; *Funding Sources:* Membership dues; donations; foundations; special events
Staff: 1 staff member(s)
Membership: 2,100; *Fees:* Donations of $20 or more; *Committees:* Conservation
Activities: Environmental advocacy; outings; *Internships:* Yes; *Speaker Service:* Yes
Affiliation(s): Sierra Club of Canada; Sierra Club - USA

Sierra Club of Canada - Prairie Chapter
6328 - 104 St., Edmonton AB T6H 2K9
Tel: 780-439-1160; *Fax:* 780-437-3932
e-mail: prairie.chapter@sierraclub.ca
URL: www.sierraclub.ca/prairie/
Overview: A medium-sized local organization
Chief Officer(s):
Lindsay Telfer, Chapter Director
Mission: Program areas: energy; health communities; protecting biodiversity; training & support

Sierra Club of Eastern Canada *See* Sierra Club of Canada - Ontario Chapter

Sierra Legal Defence Fund *See* Ecojustice Canada

Sierra Youth Coalition / Coalition Jeunesse Sierra
#406, 1 Nicholas St., Ottawa ON K1N 7B7
Tel: 613-241-1615; *Fax:* 613-241-2292
Toll-Free: 888-790-7393
e-mail: info@syc-cjs.org
URL: www.syc-cjs.org
Overview: A medium-sized local organization
Chief Officer(s):
Greg Boyle, National Director
director@syc-cjs.org
Member Profile: Sierra Club of Canada members 25 or under & students of any age
Mission: To empower young people to become active community leaders who contribute to making Canada a more sustainable society.

Sierre club du Canada *See* Sierra Club of Canada

Similkameen Naturalist Club
C5, Site 33, RR#1, Cawston BC V0X 1C0
Tel: 250-499-5404; *Fax:* 250-499-5379
e-mail: mariposaorgf@hotmail.com
Overview: A small local organization
Chief Officer(s):
Lee McFayden, Director

Similkameen Okanagan Organic Producers Association (SOOPA)
PO Box 577, Keremeos BC V0X 1N0
Tel: 250-499-5381; *Fax:* 250-499-5381
e-mail: soopa@nethop.net
URL: www.certifiedorganic.bc.ca
Overview: A small local organization founded in 1986
Chief Officer(s):
Yuri Zebroff, Administrator
Guy Villecourt, President
Finances: *Annual Operating Budget:* Less than $50,000
Staff: 1 staff member(s); 15 volunteer(s)
Membership: 41 certified + 5 transitional + 7 associate; *Fees:* $200 certified & transitional depending on size of farm; $50 associate
Mission: To set & maintain high standards of organic food production; to encourage growers to develop their horticultural skills; to educate consumers & encourage other farmers to begin to use sustainable farming methods; *Affiliation(s):* Certified Organic Associations of BC

Skeena Valley Naturalists
1677 Lupine St., Terrace BC V8G 0G1
Tel: 250-798-2535
e-mail: weena@telus.net
Overview: A small local organization
Chief Officer(s):
Judy Chrysler, Director
Membership: 21; *Fees:* $15
Activities: Birdwatching

Small Water Users Association of BC
4167 Highway 3A, Nelson BC V1L 6N1
Tel: 250-825-4308
e-mail: smallwaterusers@shaw.ca
URL: www.smallwaterusers.com
Overview: A medium-sized provincial organization founded in 2003
Chief Officer(s):
Denny Ross-Smith, Executive Director
Membership: 258; *Fees:* $35 basic fee (+$1 per connection); $90 affiliate
Mission: The Small Water Users Association of BC is a new non-profit society dedicated to serving the interests of small water systems (1 to 300 connections) throughout British Columbia.

Smart Commute
850 Coxwell Ave., 2nd Fl., Toronto ON M4C 5R1
Tel: 416-406-0489; *Fax:* 416-392-0071
Toll-Free: 866-658-9890
e-mail: info@smartcommute.ca
URL: www.smartcommute.ca
Overview: A small local organization
Chief Officer(s):
Ryan Canyon, Project Director
ryan@smartcommute.ca
Finances: *Annual Operating Budget:* $500,000-$1.5 Million; *Funding Sources:* Transport Canada; Greater Toronto Area Municipalities
Membership: 100-499
Mission: To reduce the stress on our lives, roads & environment; to reduce traffic congestion & to take action on climate change through transportation efficiency

Smoke-Free Nova Scotia
PO Box 822, Lower Sackville NS B4V 3V3
Tel: 902-864-9633; *Fax:* 902-864-6946
Toll-Free: 866-777-7374
e-mail: carivanlingen@smokefreens.ca
URL: www.smokefreens.ca
Previous Name: Nova Scotia Council on Smoking & Health
Overview: A small provincial organization
Finances: *Annual Operating Budget:* Less than $50,000; *Funding Sources:* Provincial government grants; membership fees
Staff: 1 staff member(s); 12 volunteer(s)
Membership: 12; *Fees:* $20-200; *Member Profile:* Health professionals; health agencies; individuals
Activities: *Awareness Events:* National Non-Smoking Week; World No Tobacco Day
Mission: Committed to the achievement of a tobacco-free Nova Scotia; *Member of:* Canadian Council on Smoking & Health

Smoking & Health Action Foundation
#221, 720 Spadina Ave., Toronto ON M5S 2T9
Tel: 416-928-2900; *Fax:* 416-928-1860
e-mail: toronto@nsra-adnf.ca
URL: www.nsra-adnf.ca
Overview: A small local organization founded in 1974
Chief Officer(s):
Garfield Mahood, Executive Director
Finances: *Funding Sources:* Federal government
Staff: 10 staff member(s); 50 volunteer(s)
Mission: To conduct public policy research & education designed to reduce tobacco-related disease & death

Social Ecology Research Group *Voir* Groupe de recherche en écologie sociale

Social Investment Organization (SIO)
184 Pearl St., 2nd Fl., Toronto ON M5H 1L5
Tel: 416-461-6042; *Fax:* 416-461-2481
e-mail: info@socialinvestment.ca
URL: www.socialinvestment.ca
Also Known As: Canadian Association for Socially Responsible Investment
Overview: A medium-sized national organization founded in 1989
Chief Officer(s):
Eugene Ellmen, Executive Director
Andrika Boshyk, Assistant Director
Finances: *Annual Operating Budget:* $250,000-$500,000
Staff: 2 staff member(s); 20 volunteer(s)
Membership: 450+; *Fees:* $5,000 associate; $1,500 supporting; $350 professional; *Member Profile:* Asset management companies; investment fund companies; financial advisors; investors
Activities: *Awareness Events:* SIO Conference; *Internships:* Yes; *Speaker Service:* Yes; *Rents Mailing List:* Yes
Mission: To take a leadership role in coordinating the SRI agenda in Canada; to raise public awareness of SRI in Canada; to reach out to other groups interested in SRI; to provide information on SRI to our members & the public

Societas Internationalis Limnologiae *See* International Society of Limnology

Société canadienne d'agroéconomie *See* Canadian Agricultural Economics Society

Société canadienne d'allergie et d'immunologie clinique *See* Canadian Society of Allergy & Clinical Immunology

Société canadienne de biochimie et de biologie moléculaire et cellulaire See The Canadian Society of Biochemistry, Molecular & Cellular Biology

Société canadienne de bioéthique See Canadian Bioethics Society

Société canadienne de génie agroalimentaire et de bioingénierie See Canadian Society for Bioengineering

Société canadienne de génie biomédical inc. See Canadian Medical & Biological Engineering Society

Société canadienne de génie civil See Canadian Society for Civil Engineering

Société canadienne de génie industriel See Canadian Society for Industrial Engineering

Société canadienne de génie mécanique See Canadian Society for Mechanical Engineering

Société canadienne de l'énergie du sol See Earth Energy Society of Canada

La société canadienne de l'espace See Canadian Space Society

Société canadienne de la santé et de la sécurité, inc. See Canadian Society of Safety Engineering, Inc.

Société canadienne de la santé internationale See Canadian Society for International Health

Société canadienne de la science du sol See Canadian Society of Soil Science

Société canadienne de météorologie et d'océanographie See Canadian Meteorological & Oceanographic Society

Société canadienne de Minéralogie See Canadian Mineral Society

Société canadienne de physiologie See Canadian Physiological Society

Société canadienne de physiologie végétale See Canadian Society of Plant Physiologists

Société Canadienne de Phytopathologie See Canadian Phytopathological Society

Société canadienne de science animale Voir Canadian Society of Animal Science

Société canadienne de science de laboratoire médical See Canadian Society for Medical Laboratory Science

Société canadienne de science horticole See Canadian Society for Horticultural Science

Société canadienne de télédétection See Canadian Remote Sensing Society

Société canadienne de zoologie See Canadian Society of Zoologists

Société canadienne des biologistes de l'environnement See Canadian Society of Environmental Biologists

Société canadienne des clinico-chimistes See Canadian Society of Clinical Chemists

La société canadienne des éleveurs de moutons See Canadian Sheep Breeders' Association

Société canadienne des microbiologistes See Canadian Society of Microbiologists

Société canadienne du cancer See Canadian Cancer Society

Société canadienne pour l'étude de l'éthique appliquée See Canadian Society for the Study of Practical Ethics

Société canadienne pour la conservation de la nature See The Nature Conservancy of Canada

Société Cousteau See The Cousteau Society

Société d'agriculture de Chicoutimi Voir Expo agricole de Chicoutimi

Société d'animation du Jardin et de l'Institut botanique Voir Les Amis du Jardin botanique de Montréal

Société d'entomologie du Québec (SEQ)
Insectarium de Montréal, 4581, rue Sherbrooke est, Montréal QC H1X 2B2
Courriel: secretariat@seq.qc.ca
URL: www.seq.qc.ca
Aperçu: Dimension: petite; Envergure: provinciale; Organisme sans but lucratif; fondée en 1873
Membre(s) du bureau directeur:
Geneviève Labrie, Secrétaire
Timothy Work, Président
Finances: Budget de fonctionnement annuel: Moins de $50,000
Personnel: 15 bénévole(s)
Membre: 230; Montant de la cotisation: 40$; Critères d'admissibilite: Entomologiste
Mission: Promouvoir et soutenir l'intérêt et le développement de l'entomologie en matière de recherche, d'éducation et de conservation; Affiliation(s): Société d'entomologie du Canada

Société d'études socialistes See Society for Socialist Studies

Société d'Horticulture et d'Écologie de Prévost
CP 611, Prévost QC J0R 1T0
Tél: 450-224-9252
Aperçu: Dimension: petite; Envergure: locale
Membre(s) du bureau directeur:
Florence Frigon, Présidente
Activités: Conférences; voyages horticoles; ateliers
Affiliation(s): Fédération des Sociétés d'horticulture et d'écologie du Québec

La société de biophysique du Canada See Biophysical Society of Canada

Société de conservation de la Baie de l'Isle-Verte
CP 151, 371, rte 132 Est, L'Isle-Verte QC G0L 1K0
Tél: 418-898-4075
Courriel: scobiv@icrdl.net
Aperçu: Dimension: petite; Envergure: locale; Organisme sans but lucratif; fondée en 1984
Membre(s) du bureau directeur:
Gerard Michaud
Finances: Budget de fonctionnement annuel: $100,000-$250,000; Fonds: Gouvernement fédéral
Personnel: 20 membre(s) du personnel; 3 bénévole(s)
Membre: 15 individu
Activités: Interprétation du marais salé, de la sauvagine et du baguage de la sauvagine; sentiers de randonnées pédestres
Mission: Mise en valeur de la réserve national de faune, patrimoine culturel, historique et naturel de l'Isle-Vertex; gestion de trois centres d'interprétation

Société de coopération pour le développement international (SOCODEVI)
#160, 850, av Ernest-Gagnon, Québec QC G1S 4S2
Tél: 418-683-7225; Téléc: 418-683-5229
Courriel: info@socodevi.org
URL: www.socodevi.org
Aperçu: Dimension: moyenne; Envergure: internationale; Organisme sans but lucratif; fondée en 1985
Finances: Budget de fonctionnement annuel: Plus de $5 Million
Personnel: 200 membre(s) du personnel
Membre: 20 entreprises coopératives et mutualistes; Critères d'admissibilite: Coopératives et mutuelles
Activités: Bibliothèque: Oui, Not open to the public
Mission: Avec l'engagement de ses institutions membres, et par la mise en valeur de la formule coopérative ou d'autres formes associatives; contribue au développement durable des pays òu elle intervient en ayant pour objectif que les populations se prennent en charge

Société de développement économique du Saint-Laurent (SODES) / St. Lawrence Economic Development Council
271, rue de l'Estuaire, Québec QC G1K 8S8
Tél: 418-648-4572; Téléc: 418-648-4627
Courriel: sodes@st-laurent.org
URL: www.st-laurent.org
Aperçu: Dimension: moyenne; Envergure: locale; Organisme sans but lucratif; fondée en 1985
Membre(s) du bureau directeur:
Robert Masson, Président
robert.masson@st-laurent.org
Finances: Budget de fonctionnement annuel: $100,000-$250,000
Personnel: 4 membre(s) du personnel
Membre: 100; Montant de la cotisation: Barème; Comités: Développement; Environnement; Réglementation; Tourisme; Assurances; Fiscalité municipale
Activités: Journée Saint-Laurent; Journée Martitime Québécoise; Service de conférenciers: Oui
Mission: Promouvoir le St-Laurent comme axe de développement; protéger les intérêts de la communauté maritime du St-Laurent et la représenter auprès des gouvernements; rassembler la communauté maritime du St-Laurent et mettre à sa disposition un forum d'échange et de concertation
Environmental Activity: Code d'éthique

Société de génétique du Canada See Genetics Society of Canada

Société de protection des plantes du Québec / Québec Society for the Protection of Plants
CP 3158, 801 Route 344, L'Assomption QC J5W 4M9
Courriel: g.richard@ciel-cvp.ca
Aperçu: Dimension: petite; Envergure: provinciale; fondée en 1908
Membre(s) du bureau directeur:
Valérie Gravel, Présidente
Geneviève Richard, Secrétaire
Membre: 150; Montant de la cotisation: 40$; 20$ étudiants/personnes retraitées;
Prix, Bouses: Bourse annuelle (Bourse d études)
Pour encourager les étudiants et les étudiants à poursuivre des études graduées dans le domaine de la protection des végétaux
Award Amount: 1 000$
Prix W.E. Sackston (Prix)
Pour la meilleure communication étudiante présentée lors de son congrès annuel
Mission: Vouée à la protection des plantes; regroupe des chercheurs universitaires et gouvernementaux, des agronomes, des biologistes, des ingénieurs forestiers, des technologistes, des étudiants, ainsi que toute personne intéressée à la protection des plantes.

Société de recherche sur le cancer See Cancer Research Society

Société de toxicologie du Canada See Society of Toxicology of Canada

Société des canadiennes dans la science et la technologie See Society for Canadian Women in Science & Technology

Société des éleveurs de bovins canadiens See Canadian Cattle Breeders' Association

Société des énergie solaire et durable du Canada Inc. See Solar & Sustainable Energy Society of Canada Inc.

Société des établissements de plein air du Québec (SEPAQ)
Place de la Cité, Tour Cominar, #250, 2640 boul Laurier, Québec QC G1V 5L2
Tél: 418-890-6527; Téléc: 418-528-6025
Ligne sans frais: 800-665-6527
Courriel: inforeservation@sepaq.com
URL: www.sepaq.com
Nom précédent: Société des parcs de sciences naturelles du Québec
Aperçu: Dimension: petite; Envergure: provinciale
Mission: La Sépaq est une société d'État qui a pour mandat d'administrer et de développer des territoires naturels et des équipements touristiques qui lui sont confiés en vertu de sa loi constitutive. Elle s'est donnée la mission d'assurer l'accessibilité, la mise en valeur et la protection de ces équipements publics pour le bénéfice de sa clientèle, des régions du Québec et des générations futures

Société des gens de ferme et des gens de ville See FarmFolk/CityFolk Society

Société des ingénieurs professionnels et associés See Society of Professional Engineers & Associates

Société des ornithologistes du Canada See Society of Canadian Ornithologists

Société des parcs de sciences naturelles du Québec Voir Société des établissements de plein air du Québec

Société des roses du Québec / Québec Rose Society
31, av Lorne, Saint-Lambert QC J4P 2G7

Associations/Organizations / Société Provancher d'histoire naturelle du Canada

Tél: 450-653-9590
Courriel: mor-pol@sympatico.ca
URL: www.rosesquebec.org
Aperçu: Dimension: petite; *Envergure:* provinciale
Membre(s) du bureau directeur:
Diane Vigneault, Présidente
Montant de la cotisation: $25 individuel; 30$ couple
Mission: Étudier, promouvoir et encourager la culture des roses

Société des techniciens et des technologues agréés du génie du Nouveau-Brunswick *See* New Brunswick Society of Certified Engineering Technicians & Technologists

Société du cancer du sein du Canada *See* Breast Cancer Society of Canada

La Société géographique royale du Canada *See* The Royal Canadian Geographical Society

Société internationale de biométéorolgy *See* International Society of Biometeorology

Société Internationale de Mécanique des Sols et de la Géotechnique *See* International Society for Soil Mechanics & Geotechnical Engineering

Société médicale du Nouveau-Brunswick *See* New Brunswick Medical Society

Société mondiale pour la protection des animaux *See* World Society for the Protection of Animals

Société nucléaire canadienne *See* Canadian Nuclear Society

Société ontarienne de gestion des déchets *See* Ontario Waste Management Association

La société ontarienne des professionelles et professionnels de la nutrition en santé publique *See* Ontario Society of Nutrition Professionals in Public Health

Société planétaire pour l'assainissement de l'énergie *See* Planetary Association for Clean Energy, Inc.

Société pour la nature et les parcs du Canada *See* Canadian Parks & Wilderness Society

Société pour la nature et les parcs du Canada, Section Québec *Voir* Canadian Parks & Wilderness Society

Société Provancher d'histoire naturelle du Canada (SPHNC) / Provancher Society of Natural History of Canada
1400 rue de l'Aéroport, Québec QC G2G 1G6
Tél: 418-831-4188; *Téléc:* 418-831-8744
Courriel: provancher@videotron.ca
URL: www.provancher.qc.ca
Aperçu: Dimension: petite; *Envergure:* provinciale; *Organisme sans but lucratif; fondée en* 1919
Membre(s) du bureau directeur:
Michel Lepage, Président
Finances: Budget de fonctionnement annuel: $100,000-$250,000
Personnel: 7 membre(s) du personnel; 25 bénévole(s)
Membre: 50 institutionnel; 1,500 individu; 30 associé*Montant de la cotisation:* 50$ corporatif; 25$ famille; 20$ individu; *Critères d'admissibilite:* Amant de la nature
Mission: Société visant la protection de milieux naturels et l'éducation en sciences naturelles; *Membre de:* Reseau de milieux naturels protégés du Québec

Société québécoise d'assainissement des eaux (SQAE)
CP 386, Succ. Tour de la Bourse, #310, 800 Square Victoria, Montréal QC H4Z 1J2
Tél: 514-873-7411; *Téléc:* 514-873-7879
Courriel: marc.pinsonnault@sqae.gouv.qc.ca
Aperçu: Dimension: grande; *Envergure:* provinciale; *fondée en* 1980
Finances: Budget de fonctionnement annuel: Plus de $5 Million
Personnel: 2 membre(s) du personnel
Membre: 1-99
Mission: Offrir aux municipalités des services-conseils, de l'aide technique et des services professionnels en matière de gestion afin de réaliser le volet municipal du Programme d'assainissement des eaux du Québec; agir à titre de conseillère en matière d'exploitation auprès des municipalités; agir à l'extérieur du Québec, en association avec les entreprises québécoises dans le domaine de l'eau; fournir des biens et services reliés à l'expérience que la société a acquise au Québec; faire la promotion de ces biens et services; favoriser le développement du potentiel technologique et industriel du Québec dans ce domaine; *Membre de:* Centre Grands Projets - Association qualité

Société québécoise de récupération et de recyclage
#200, 420, boul Charest est, Québec QC G1K 8M4
Tél: 418-643-0394; *Téléc:* 418-643-6507
Ligne sans frais: 800-807-0678
Courriel: info@recyc-quebec.gouv.qc.ca
URL: www.recyc-quebec.gouv.qc.ca
Également appelé: RECYC-QUÉBEC
Aperçu: Dimension: moyenne; *Envergure:* provinciale; *Organisme sans but lucratif; fondée en* 1990
Membre(s) du bureau directeur:
Ginette Bureau, Président-directeur général
Johanne Riverin, Vice-présidente, Communications, sensibilisation et éducation
Finances: Budget de fonctionnement annuel: Plus de $5 Million
Activités: Coordination des activités de mise en valeur; gestion intégrée des pneus hors d'usage; gestion de la consigne sur les contenants à remplissage unique de bière ou de boissons gazeuses; développement des marchés et technologies dans le domaine de la mise en valeur des matières résiduelles; R&D; information, sensibilisation et éducation; promotion des produits québécois à contenu recyclé*publication de répertoires, guides, études et fiches; campagne sur la récupération des contenants à remplissage unique consignés; *Evénements de sensibilisation:* Semaine québécoise de réduction des déchets; *Stagiaires:* Oui
Mission: Promouvoir, développer et de favoriser la réduction, le réemploi, la récupération et le recyclage des contenants, d'emballages, de matières ou de produits ainsi que leur valorisation dans une perspective de conservation des ressources

Société québécoise de spéléologie (SQS)
CP 1000, Succ. M, 4545, av Pierre-de Coubertin, Montréal QC H1V 3R2
Tél: 514-252-3006; *Téléc:* 514-252-3201
Ligne sans frais: 800-338-6636
Courriel: info-sqs@speleo.qc.ca
URL: www.speleo.qc.ca
Aperçu: Dimension: moyenne; *Envergure:* provinciale; *Organisme sans but lucratif; fondée en* 1970
Finances: Budget de fonctionnement annuel: $100,000-$250,000
Personnel: 4 membre(s) du personnel; 200 bénévole(s)
Membre: 4 000; *Montant de la cotisation:* 35$ 1 an, 60$ 2 ans; 500$ à vie
Activités: *Stagiaires:* Oui; *Bibliothèque:* Centre de documentation
Mission: La Société québécoise de spéléologie (SQS) a pour mission de favoriser le développement de la spéléologie ainsi que la préservation du milieu cavernicole et de son environnement. Organisme privé, sans but lucratif, la SQS est la fédération qui regroupe les spéléologues du Québec.; *Membre de:* Union internationale de spéléologie; Regroupement Loisir Québec

Société québécoise des hostas et des hémérocalles (SQHH)
4101 est, rue Sherbrooke, Montréal QC H1X 2B2
Tél: 514-868-3078
Courriel: sqhh-qhhs@live.ca
URL: sites.google.com/site/hostaquebec
Aperçu: Dimension: petite; *Envergure:* provinciale
Membre(s) du bureau directeur:
Réjean Millette, Président
info@millettephotomedia.com
Montant de la cotisation: 39$ individu 43$ famille

Société québécoise du dahlia
a/s Dépt. de Biologie, Cégep de Saint-Laurent, 625, av Sainte-Croix, Saint-Laurent QC H4L 3X7
Tél: 450-747-6521
Courriel: assjbinc@videotron.ca
URL: www.sqdahlia.qc.ca
Aperçu: Dimension: petite; *Envergure:* locale; *Organisme sans but lucratif; fondée en* 1992
Membre(s) du bureau directeur:
Jacques Bouchard, Président
Finances: Budget de fonctionnement annuel: Moins de $50,000
Personnel: 9 membre(s) du personnel
Membre: 250; *Montant de la cotisation:* $15; *Critères d'admissibilité:* Amateurs de dahlias et de beaux jardins
Activités: Expositions; conférences; salons annuels; *Service de conférenciers:* Oui

Mission: Regrouper les amateurs de dahlias et encourager la culture de cette plante; favoriser les échanges d'informations et de spécimens entre les membres; Affiliation(s): American Dahlia Society; Fédération des Sociétés d'horticulture et d'Écologie du Québec; Société Canadienne du Glaïeul

Société québécoise pour la défense des animaux (SQDA) / Québec Society for the Defense of Animals (QSDA)
Parent: Canadian Federation of Humane Societies
#102, 847, rue Cherrier, Montréal QC H2L 1H6
Tél: 514-524-1970
Courriel: info@sqda.org
URL: www.sqda.org
Aperçu: Dimension: moyenne; *Envergure:* provinciale; *Organisme sans but lucratif; fondée en* 1976
Finances: Budget de fonctionnement annuel: Moins de $50,000
Membre: 500; *Montant de la cotisation:* 20$/an; 250$ bienfaiteur
Activités: *Evénements de sensibilisation:* Campagne annuelle de déménagement
Mission: Faire connaître et respecter le monde animal par tous les moyens possibles; obtenir une législation modifiée pour la protection de toute espèce; combattre la destruction de notre faune; exposer l'aberration de l'élevage intensif; contrôler l'expérimentation animale; Affiliation(s): The World Society for the Protection of Animals - England; The Royal Society for the Prevention of Cruelty to Animals - England; The Canadian Federation of Humane Societies; Société nationale pour la défense des animaux - France

La Société royale du Canada *See* The Royal Society of Canada

Société zoologique de Montréal *See* Zoological Society of Montréal

Society for Canadian Women in Science & Technology (SCWIST) / Société des canadiennes dans la science et la technologie
#471, 411 Dunsmuir St., Vancouver BC V6B 1X4
Tel: 604-893-8657; *Fax:* 604-893-8692
e-mail: scwist@sfu.ca
URL: www.harbour.sfu.ca/scwist/
Overview: A small national charitable organization founded in 1981
Membership: 280; *Fees:* $60 professional; $20 student/retired/unemployed; *Member Profile:* Interest in promoting women in science & technology
Activities: 5-6 regular program meetings of various topics; collection of gender free science & mathematics examples of questions; Ms. Infinity & Hands On Math & Sciences held in May in community colleges & high schools throughout province; *Speaker Service:* Yes; *Library:* Resource Centre
Mission: To promote equal opportunities for women in scientific, technical & engineering careers; to educate public about careers in science & technology particularly to improve social attitudes on the stereotyping of careers in science; to assist educators by providing current information on careers & career training in sciences & scientific policies; Affiliation(s): BC Ministry of Advanced Education, Training & Technology; Industry, Science & Technology Canada; BC Ministry of Education; Canada Employment & Immigration Council; Secretary of State Canada, Women's Program; University of BC, Faculty of Science; Simon Fraser University; BC Institute of Technology; Capilano College; Vancouver School Board; Knowledge Network; Vancouver Foundation; Immigrant Women in Science Program; Douglas College

Society for Conservation Biology (SCB)
1017 O St. NW, Washington DC 20001-4229 USA
Tel: 202-234-4133; *Fax:* 703-995-4633
e-mail: information@conbio.org
URL: www.conbio.org
Overview: A medium-sized international organization founded in 1985
Chief Officer(s):
Colleen Cassady St. Clair, Canadian Board Member
cstclair@ualberta.ca
Pam Krannitz, Canadian Board Member
pam.krannitz@ec.gc.ca
Alan D. Thornhill, Executive Director
Membership: 10,000+; *Member Profile:* Persons from around the world, who are interested in the study & conservation of biological diversity, such as conservation workers, educators, government workers, resource managers, & students
Activities: Providing recommendations about policies to advance the conservation of biological diversity; Developing

educational programs; Providing mentorship opportunities in the field of conservation; Facilitating networking with the professional community
Publications: *Conservation Biology*
Type: Journal *Frequency:* bi-m. *Editor:* Erica Fleishman *ISSN:* 0888-8892
Profile: Information about conservation science for members of the Society for Conservation Biology
Conservation
Type: Magazine *Frequency:* q. *Accepts Advertising* : Yes *Editor:* Kathryn A. Kohm
Profile: Conservation articles for members of the Society for Conservation Biology
SCB [Society for Conservation Biology] Newsletter
Type: Newsletter *Frequency:* q. *Editor:* Sharon Collinge *Price:* Free with membership in the Society for Conservation Biology
Conservation Letters, A Journal of the Society for Conservation Biology
Type: Journal *Editor:* Corey Bradshaw
Profile: Empirical, theoretical, & interdisciplinary research about the conservation of biological diversity worldwide
Mission: To advance the scientific study of the phenomena that affect the maintenance, loss, & restoration of biological diversity; To promote the practice of conserving biological diversity
Environmental Activity: Disseminating scientific information & recommendations needed to conserve biological diversity

Society for Ecological Restoration International (SER)
#1, 285 West 18th St., Tucson AZ 85701 USA
Tel: 520-622-5485; *Fax:* 520-626-5485
URL: www.ser.org
Overview: A medium-sized international organization founded in 1988
Membership: 2,300 members from 37 countries; *Member Profile:* Individuals & organizations involved in ecologically-sensitive repair & the management of ecosystems, such as scientists, ecological consultants, planners, engineers, teachers, growers, & natural areas managers; *Committees:* Awards; Education & Training; Publications; Science & Policy
Activities: Raising public awareness of restoration; Facilitating communication among restorationists; Encouraging research; Providing input to discussions of public policy
Awards: John Rieger Award (Award)
Awarded to those that have dedicated their time & skills to the advancement of ecological restoration &/or to the devleopment of the Society
Model Project Award (Award)
Recognizes those restoration projects that have truly advanced with craft of ecosystem restoration & upon which future projects may well be modeled
Full Circle Award (Award)
Awarded to those indigenous people whose projects have brought ecosystems full circle, returning them to their condition prior to the impacts caused by non-indigenous peoples
Project Facilitation Award (Award)
Awarded in recognition of well-conceived & properly initiated ecosystem restoration projects that may require or significantly benefit from supplemental funding
Theodore M. Sperry Award (Award)
Recognizes achievement in those elements & approaches that improve restoration programs
Communication Award (Award)
Acknowledges the importance of all forms of communication that advance the goals of the Society
Meetings/Conferences:
For more information see Trade Shows, Conferences and Seminars Chapter
SER 4th International World Conference on Ecological Restoration: Re-establishing the Link between Nature & Culture
August 2011 Mérida, Yucatán
Publications: *Restoration Ecology*
Type: Journal *Frequency:* q.
Profile: Peer-reviewed scientific & technical research articles on topics of restoration & ecological principles
Ecological Restoration
Type: Journal *Frequency:* q. *Price:* Included with Society for Ecological Restoration International membership
Profile: Philosophical essays & summaries of current projects & techniques
Society for Ecological Restoration International Newsletter
Type: Newsletter *Frequency:* q.
Profile: Up-to-date information for members about the Society & it chapters

Restore [a publication of the Society for Ecological Restoration International]
Type: Newsletter *Frequency:* w.
Profile: Annotated links to news stories from around the globe
Mission: To promote ecological restoration as a means of sustaining the diversity of life; To reestablish an ecologically healthy relationship between nature & culture
Environmental Activity: Promoting ecological restoration around the world

Society for Environmental Graphic Design (SEGD)
#400, 1000 Vermont Ave., NW, Washington DC 20005 USA
Tel: 202-638-5555; *Fax:* 202-638-0891
e-mail: segd@segd.org
URL: www.segd.org
Overview: A medium-sized international organization
Chief Officer(s):
Leslie Gallery Dilworth, Chief Executive Officer, 202-638-5555
leslie@segd.org
Ann Makowski, Chief Operating Officer, 202-638-5555
Craig M. Berger, Director, Education & Professional Training, 202-638-5555
Membership: 1,600+; *Member Profile:* Individuals who work in the planning, design, fabrication, & implementation of communications in the built environment
Activities: Fostering research; Providing educational resources; Refining standards of practice; Collaborating across various design disciplines; Offering referrals to fabricators or designers; Providing networking opportunities
Meetings/Conferences:
For more information see Trade Shows, Conferences and Seminars Chapter
Society for Environmental Graphic Design 2011 Conference & Expo
June 2011 Montréal, QC
Publications: *segdDESIGN: The International Journal of Environmental Graphic Design*
Type: Journal *Frequency:* q. *Accepts Advertising* : Yes *Editor:* Pat Matson Knapp
Profile: Information about the people, research, technologies, materials, & resources that influence communications in the built environment
Society for Environmental Graphic Design Membership Directory
Type: Directory

Society for Organic Urban Land Care
PO Box 8548, Victoria BC V8P 1L4
Tel: 250-386-7685
e-mail: info@organiclandcare.org
URL: www.organiclandcare.org
Also Known As: SOUL
Overview: A small national organization
Chief Officer(s):
Lisa Atkins, President
Membership: 100; *Fees:* $30 public/professional; $250 supporting
Mission: SOUL was formed in response to the growing need for ecologically responsible land care practices. Our mission is to promote and support organic practices in our communities through education, certification and standardization.

Society for Research on Nicotine & Tobacco (SNRT)
#3800, 2810 Crossroads Dr., Madison WI 53718 USA
Tel: 608-443-2462; *Fax:* 608-443-2474
e-mail: info@srnt.org
URL: www.smt.org
Overview: A small international organization
Chief Officer(s):
Bruce Wheeler, Executive Director, 608-443-2462 Ext. 143
Dianne Benson, Financial Contact, 608-443-2462 Ext. 147
Member Profile: Full members possess training beyond the undergraduate level, plus at least one peer-reviewed publication on nicotine, tobacco-control, or a related topic; Affiliate members possess a documented interest in some aspect of research on nicotine or tobacco-control; Retired full members; Students
Activities: Encouraging scientific research on on public health efforts for the prevention & treatment of cigarette & tobacco use; Sponsoring publications & scientific meetings on the effects of nicotine; Engaging in advocacy activities
Publications: *SRNT [Society for Research on Nicotine & Tobacco] Newsletter*
Type: Newsletter *Editor:* Karen Cropsey
Profile: Current society information for members, featuring reviews, meetings, publications, position openings, & funding news

Nicotine & Tobacco Research: The Journal of SRNT [Society for Research on Nicotine & Tobacco]
Type: Journal *Frequency:* m. *ISSN:* 1462-2203
Profile: Peer reviewed articles about the study of nicotine & tobacco
Society for Research on Nicotine & Tobacco Annual Meeting Abstracts
Type: Yearbook *Frequency:* a.
SRNT [Society for Research on Nicotine & Tobacco] Membership Directory
Type: Directory
Mission: To generate new knowledge about nicotine

Society for Socialist Studies (SSS) / Société d'études socialistes (SÉS)
National Office, 172 Allwright Close, Red Deer AB T4R 3P1
Tel: 403-342-7989; *Fax:* 403-342-7989
e-mail: kcollier@shaw.ca
URL: www.socialiststudies.ca
Overview: A small national charitable organization founded in 1967
Chief Officer(s):
Ken Collier, President
June Madeley, Secretary
madelejm@hotmail.com
Debbie Dergousoff, Treasurer
manyad@uvic.ca
Finances: *Funding Sources:* Membership fees
Membership: 350; *Fees:* $75 regular; $40 low income, unemployed, student, retired; $100 Canadian institution; US$100 foreign institutions; *Member Profile:* Membership includesany person underwriting the Society's purpose.; *Committees:* Canadian Federation of Humanities and Social Sciences Congress Programme Committee; Journal Editorial Committee
Activities: Organizes conferences, seminars, & workshops; publishes educational material; advances public education
Publications: *Socialist Studies: Journal of the Society for Socialist Studies*
Type: Journal *Editor:* Sandra Rollings-Magnusson
Mission: The Society creates, fosters, & publishes, academic & scholarly research & analysis in Canada, with emphasis on socialist, feminist, anti-racist, & ecological points of view.;
Member of: Humanities & Social Science Federation of Canada

Society of Canadian Ornithologists (SCO) / Société des ornithologistes du Canada (SOC)
a/s Thérèse Beaudet, SCO Membership Secretary, 1281, ch des Lièges, St-Jean de l'Ile d'Orléans QC G0A 3W0
e-mail: beaudet.lamothe@sympatico.ca
URL: www.sco-soc.ca
Overview: A medium-sized national charitable organization founded in 1983
Finances: *Funding Sources:* Membership fees; Donations
Membership: 357; *Fees:* $10 students; $25 regular members; $35 international members; $50 sustaining members; $500 life members; *Member Profile:* Amateur & professional ornithologists
Activities: Connecting with other professional ornithological societies; Disseminating information about the birds of Canada; Offering grants to study birds
Awards: Jamie Smith Memorial Award (Award)
Taverner Awards (Award)
James L. Baillie Student Research Award (Award)
Fred Cooke Student Research Award (Award)
Doris Huestis Speirs Award (Award)
Meetings/Conferences:
For more information see Trade Shows, Conferences and Seminars Chapter
Society of Canadian Ornithologists / Société des ornithologistes du Canada 2012 30th Annual Meeting
Other Conferences in 2012 2012
Publications: *Picoïdes: Bulletin of the Society of Canadian Ornithologists / Bulletin de la Société des Ornithologistes du Canada*
Type: Newsletter *Language:* B *Editor:* Rob Warnock
Profile: President, committee, & meeting reports, announcements, award news, research articles, essays, book reviews, bird surveys, & conservation information
Avian Conservation & Ecology
Type: Journal
Profile: Published by the Society of Canadian Ornithologists / Société des ornithologistes du Canada & Bird Studies Canada
Biology & Conservation of Forest Birds
Editor: A.W, Diamond; D.N. Nettleship
Profile: A series of manuscripts from a Society of Canadian Ornithologists / Société des ornithologistes du Canada meeting

Associations/Organizations / Society of Chemical Industry - Canadian Section

Mission: To support research to understand & conserve Canadian birds; To represent Canadian ornithologists
Environmental Activity: Responding to requests for information about avian conservation issues; Encouraging the application of scientific bird studies to the field of conservation

Society of Chemical Industry - Canadian Section (SCI)
#550, 130 Slater St., Ottawa ON K1P 6E2
e-mail: scicanada@soci.org
URL: www.soci.org
Overview: A small international organization founded in 1881
Finances: *Annual Operating Budget:* Less than $50,000; *Funding Sources:* Membership fees; events
Staff: 12 volunteer(s)
Membership: 120 in Canada; *Fees:* $95
Activities: Sponsors Le Sueur Memorial Lectures & Purvis Memorial Lectures
Awards: Canada Medal Award (Award)
Established 1939; awarded every two years for outstanding services in the Canadian chemical industry; recipient delivers an address at a meeting of the society
Le Sueur Memorial Award (Award)
Established 1955 to commemorate Ernest A. Le Sueur; award is presented in recognition of outstanding innovation in the Canadian chemical industry
Purvis Memorial Lectures (Award)
Established 1947; award is presented every two years in honour of Arthur Blaikie Purvis; recipient delivers an address at a meeting of the society
Student Merit Awards (Scholarship)
Established 1961; presented annually to the top graduating students in chemical-related disciplines in Canadian universities; disciplines include chemistry, biochemistry, chemical engineering, engineering chemistry, fuels & materials engineering, & nutritional science *Award Amount:* Awards consist of an engraved gold plaque & a one-year subscription to "Chemistry & Industry"
International Award (Award)
Established 1976; award is presented in recognition of outstanding service in the chemical industry in the international sphere, preferably to Canadians or persons who have contributed measurably to the Canadian chemical scene
Mission: To encourage acquaintance & understanding among responsible individuals in the various fields of the industrial chemical process industries; to promote acquaintance & understanding between the chemical industry & the universities & governments; to encourage scientific education in universities by recognizing student achievements; to reward outstanding achievement in the Canadian chemical & allied industries & universities through awards & honorary lectureships; to promote communication between the members of the Canadian chemical & allied industries & those of other countries

Society of Engineering Technicians & Technologists of Saskatchewan (SETTS) *See* Saskatchewan Applied Science Technologists & Technicians

Society of Engineering Technologists of BC *See* Applied Science Technologists & Technicians of British Columbia

Society of Environmental Toxicology & Chemistry (SETAC)
SETAC Asia / Pacific, SETAC Latin America, & SETAC North America, 1010 - 12th Ave. North, Pensacola FL 32501-3370 USA
Tel: 850-469-1500; *Fax:* 850-469-9778
e-mail: setac@setac.org
URL: www.setac.org
Overview: A small international organization founded in 1979
Chief Officer(s):
Mike Mozur, Executive Director
mike.mozur@setac.org
Linda Fenner, Manager, Finance
linda.fenner@setac.org
Mimi Meredith, Manager, Publications
mimi.meredith@setac.org
Bruce Vigon, Manager, Scientific Affairs
bruce.vigon@setac.org
Member Profile: Individuals & institutions involved in environmental research, development, & education, as well as the management & regulation of natural resources; *Committees:* Awards & Fellowships; Development; Education; Endowment Fund; Finance; Long-range Planning; Meetings; Membership; Mentoring; Nominations; Regional Chapters; Short Courses; Student Activities; Student Council; Technical
Awards: SETAC/ABC Laboratories Environmental Education Award (Award)
Given to an individual, group, organization, or coporation for significant contributions to environmental education
SETAC Government Service Award (Award)
Recognizes exemplary dedication & service by a scientist or scientific organization toward promoting the collective application of environmental toxicology & chemistry to risk assessment in a governent function
Environmental Toxicology & Chemistry Best Student Paper Award (Award)
Recognizes the best paper published by a student in ET&C during the last year
SETAC/Battelle Best Student Platform & Poster Presentation Awards (Award)
Given to the best student platform & poster presentations at the SETAC annual meetings *Eligibility:* Must be a member of SETAC
Rachel Carson Award (Award)
Given to an individual who has substantially increased public awareness & understanding of an issue concerning contaminants in the environment *Eligibility:* Recipient's action must result in a redefinition of environmental policies & practices
Herb Ward Exceptional Service Award (Award)
Given to SETAC members who have performed long-term, exceptionally high-quality service for SETAC
SETAC Founders Awards (Award)
Given to a person with an outstanding career who has made clearly identifiable contributions in the environmental sciences that are consistent with the goals of SETAC
SETAC Student Travel Awards Program (Award)
Provides travel support assistance for graduate students to attend the SETAC annual meeting
SETAC Program for North American Minority Students & Mentors (Award)
Program introduces North American minority students &/or their faculty mentors to the Society & the professional opportunities offered in the fields of environmental toxicoloy, environmental chemistry & risk assessment *Award Amount:* Selected individuals receive 1 year membership to the Society & funds to support their travel
SETAC/Taylor & Francis Advanced Training Fellowship (Grant)
To provide pre-doctoral or post-doctoral scholars the opportunity to expand their research skills & grantsmanship through specialized training not available at their institution
SETAC/Roy F. Weston Environmental Chemistry Award (Award)
Given to a scientist under the age of 40 for contributions made to the field of environmental chemistry
SETAC/EA Engineering Jeff Black Award (Award)
Eligibility: SETAC members & masters students who have been accepted to or are participating in an environmental science or engineering award *Award Amount:* US$2,000 & certificate
Meetings/Conferences:
For more information see Trade Shows, Conferences and Seminars Chapter
Society of Environmental Toxicology & Chemistry North America 32nd Annual Meeting
November 2011 Boston, MA
Society of Environmental Toxicology & Chemistry North America 33rd Annual Meeting
November 2012 Long Beach, CA
Society of Environmental Toxicology & Chemistry North America 2013 34th Annual Meeting
Other Conferences in 2013 2013
Publications: *Environmental Toxicology & Chemistry*
Type: Journal *Editor:* C.H. Ward *ISSN:* 0730-7268
Integrated Environmental Assessment & Management
Type: Journal *Editor:* Richard J. Wenning *ISSN:* 1551-3777
Society of Environmental Toxicology & Chemistry Annual Report
Type: Yearbook *Frequency:* a.
Mission: To develop principles & practices for the protection, enhancement, & management of sustainable environmental quality
Environmental Activity: Researching stressors in the environment; Providing education in the environmental sciences

Society of Fire Protection Engineers (SFPE)
#620E, 7315 Wisconsin Ave., Bethesda MD 20814 USA
Tel: 301-718-2910; *Fax:* 301-718-2242
e-mail: sfpehqtrs@sfpe.org
URL: www.sfpe.org
Overview: A medium-sized international organization founded in 1950
Chief Officer(s):
David D. Evans, Executive Director
devans@sfpe.org
Finances: *Annual Operating Budget:* $500,000-$1.5 Million
Staff: 6 staff member(s)
Membership: 4,500; *Fees:* US$195
Activities: *Rents Mailing List:* Yes
Mission: To advance the practice & science of fire protection engineering & its allied fields; to maintain a high ethical standard among its members; to foster fire protection engineering education

Society of Petroleum Engineers (SPE)
PO Box 833836, Richardson TX 75083-3836 USA
Tel: 972-952-9393; *Fax:* 972-952-9435
Toll-Free: 800-456-6863
e-mail: spedal@spe.org
URL: www.spe.org
Overview: A large international organization founded in 1957
Chief Officer(s):
Mark A. Rubin, Executive Director
Finances: *Annual Operating Budget:* $3 Million-$5 Million
Staff: 87 staff member(s)
Membership: 79,000+ (active operations in some 50 countries); *Member Profile:* Managers, engineers, operating personnel & scientists engaged in the exploration, drilling & production sectors of the global oil & gas industry
Activities: *Internships:* Yes; *Speaker Service:* Yes; *Library:* Yes, Not open to the public
Mission: To collect, disseminate & exchange technical knowledge concerning the exploration, development & production of oil & gas resources & related technologies for the public benefit; provide opportunities for professionals to enhance their technical & professional competence

Society of Professional Engineers & Associates (SPEA) / Société des ingénieurs professionnels et associés
#2, 2275 Speakman Dr., Mississauga ON L5K 1B1
Tel: 905-823-3606; *Fax:* 905-823-9602
URL: www.spea.ca
Overview: A medium-sized national organization founded in 1974
Chief Officer(s):
Peter White, President
Val Aleyaseen, Chair, Membership
Vincent Tume, Secretary
Brian Girard, Treasurer
Membership: 900+ engineers & scientists + 300 technologists & tradespeople; *Member Profile:* Scientists, engineers, technologists, & tradespeople who work for Atomic Energy of Canada Limited (AECL) in Mississauga, Ontario & abroad
Mission: To represent scientists, engineers, technologists, & tradespeople who work for Atomic Energy of Canada Limited (AECL) in Mississauga, Ontario & abroad

Society of the Plastics Industry of Canada *See* Canadian Plastics Industry Association

Society of the Plastics Industry, Inc. (SPI)
#1000, 1667 K St. NW, Washington DC 20006 USA
Tel: 202-974-5200; *Fax:* 202-296-7005
e-mail: info@socplas.org
URL: www.plasticsindustry.org
Overview: A large international organization founded in 1937
Chief Officer(s):
William R. Carteaux, President
Finances: *Annual Operating Budget:* Greater than $5 Million
Staff: 65 staff member(s)
Membership: 1,100; *Member Profile:* Members represent the entire plastics supply chain
Activities: Operates 12 divisions: Epoxy Resin Systems Task Group, Film & Bag Federation, Food, Drug & Cosmetic Packaging Materials, Fluropolymers, Machinery, Molders, Moldmakers, Organic Peroxide Producers Safety, Sheet Producers, Structural Plastics, Thermoforming Institute, Vinyl Formulators; *Library:* Plastics Data Source
Mission: To be a world class trade association representing the entire plastics industry in a way that promotes the development of the plastics industry & enhances the public's understanding of its contributions while meeting the needs of society & providing value to its members

Society of Toxicology (SOT)
#300, 1821 Michael Faraday Dr., Reston VA 20190 USA

Associations/Organizations / Society of Toxicology of Canada

Tel: 703-438-3115; *Fax:* 703-438-3113
e-mail: sothq@toxicology.org
URL: www.toxicology.org
Overview: A large international organization
Chief Officer(s):
Cheryl Lyn Walker, President
Rosibel Alvarenga, Contact, Membership & Customer Service, 703-438-3115 Ext. 1432
rosibel@toxicology.org
Betty Eidemiller, Contact, Teacher & Student Inquiries, 703-438-3115 Ext. 1430
bettye@toxicology.org
Martha Lindauer, Contact, Press & Media Inquiries, 703-438-3115 Ext. 1640
martha@toxicology.org
Member Profile: Scientists from academic institutions, government, & industry who practice toxicology
Meetings/Conferences:
For more information see Trade Shows, Conferences and Seminars Chapter
Society of Toxicology 51st Annual Meeting & ToxExpo
March 2012 San Francisco, CA
Society of Toxicology 52nd Annual Meeting & ToxExpo
March 2013 San Antonio, TX
Society of Toxicology 53rd Annual Meeting & ToxExpo
March 2014 Boston, MA
Publications: *ToxSci Journal*
Type: Journal
Society of Toxicology Membership Directory
Accepts Advertising : Yes
Profile: Names, addresses, & e-mail addresses for more than 6,000 SOT members
Communiqué [a publication of the Society of Toxicology]
Type: Newsletter *Frequency:* q. *Accepts Advertising* : Yes
Profile: Society of Toxicology news; Member spotlight; Regional chapters, specialty sections, & special interest groups; Annual meeting; Science news
Preliminary Program [a publication of the Society of Toxicology]
Accepts Advertising : Yes
Profile: Information about the annual meeting program, a registration form, & housing information
ToxExpo Directory
Accepts Advertising : Yes
Mission: To advance the science of toxicology; To promote the acquisition & utilization of knowledge in toxicology; To protect public health

Society of Toxicology of Canada (STC) / Société de toxicologie du Canada
PO Box 55094, Montréal QC H3G 2W5
Tel: 514-697-9219; *Fax:* 514-697-9309
e-mail: stcsecretariat@mcgill.ca
URL: www.stcweb.ca
Overview: A medium-sized national organization founded in 1964
Finances: *Funding Sources:* Membership fees
Staff: 1 staff member(s); 20 volunteer(s)
Membership: 400; *Fees:* $30-$100; *Member Profile:* Ordinary - qualified individual who has continuing professional interest in field of toxicology; associate - individual who has not satisfied requirement for ordinary membership; student - graduate student enrolled in postgraduate degree program with major emphasis on toxicology; *Committees:* Awards; Editorial/Newsletter; Education; Finance; Membership; Nominating; Science Policy; Scientific Program; Symposium; Web Site
Mission: To promote acquisition, facilitate dissemination & encourage utilization of knowledge in the science of toxicology; *Affiliation(s):* Canadian Federation of Biological Societies; International Union of Toxicology

Society Promoting Environmental Conservation (SPEC)
2150 Maple St., Vancouver BC V6J 3T3
Tel: 604-736-7732; *Fax:* 604-736-7115
e-mail: admin@spec.bc.ca
URL: www.spec.bc.ca
Overview: A medium-sized provincial charitable organization founded in 1969
Finances: *Funding Sources:* Donations
Activities: Advocating for food safety & security; Providing public education programs; Reducing the use of hazardous pesticides
Publications: *SPECTRUM [a publication of the Society Promoting Environmental Conservation]*
Type: Newsletter

Profile: Society Promoting Environmental Conservation activities, news releases, upcoming events, & articles
Mission: To address environmental issues in British Columbia, with a focus on urban communities in the Lower Mainland & the Georgia Basin; To encourage policies that lead to urban sustainability
Environmental Activity: Protecting land & water resources; Raising public awareness about environmental issues; Promoting sustainable urban transportation; Encouraging waste reduction; Promoting the use of renewable energy; Encouraging energy conservation

Soil & Water Conservation Society (SWCS)
945 SW Ankeny Rd., Ankeny IA 50023-9723 USA
Tel: 515-289-2331; *Fax:* 515-289-1227
e-mail: swcs@swcs.org
URL: www.swcs.org
Overview: A large international organization founded in 1945
Chief Officer(s):
Jim Gulliford, Executive Director, 515-289-2331 Ext. 113, Fax: 515-289-1227
jim.gulliford@swcs.org
Jim Bruce, Representative, Canadian Policy, 613-731-5929
jpbruce@sympatico.ca
Dewayne Johnson, Director, Professional Development, 515-289-2331 Ext. 114, Fax: 515-289-1227
dewayne.johnson@swcs.org
Hockaday Robin, Specialist, Membership Services, 515-289-2331 Ext. 118, Fax: 515-289-1227
memberservices@swcs.org
Membership: 5,000-14,999; *Member Profile:* Researchers; Administrators; Educators; Planners; Technicians; Legislators; Farmers & ranchers; Local conservation officials; Consultants; Students
Awards: Donald A. Williams Soil Conservation Scholarship (Scholarship)
Offered to members wanting to improve their professional competency *Deadline:* 1-Apr *Award Amount:* $1,500
Kenneth E. Grant Research Scholarship (Scholarship)
For graduate level research *Deadline:* Spring of each year
Mission: To promote the conservation of soil, water, & related resources; To promote an ethic that recognizes the interdependence of people & the environment

Soil Conservation Council of Canada (SCCC)
PO Box 998, Indian Head SK S0G 2K0
Tel: 306-972-7293; *Fax:* 306-695-3442
e-mail: info@soilcc.ca
URL: www.soilcc.ca
Overview: A medium-sized national charitable organization founded in 1987
Chief Officer(s):
Glen Shaw, Executive Director, 306-972-7293, Fax: 306-695-3442
info@soilcc.ca
Don McCabe, President
Finances: *Funding Sources:* Corporations; Government
Fees: $35 individuals
Activities: Raising awareness about the causes of soil degradation; Presenting conservation issues to the government, private industry, producers, & the public; Delivering agriculture & environment programs for producers; Facilitating information exchange among researchers, government representatives, industry, & farmers; Partnering with similar organizations; *Awareness Events:* National Soil Conservation Week, April
Publications: *The Protector [a publication of the Soil Conservation Council of Canada]*
Type: Newsletter
Profile: Up-to-date information about the Council's activities
Mission: To act as the voice of soil conservation in Canada
Environmental Activity: Administering Canada's Agricultural Producers Addressing Environmental Issues (CAPAEI); Administering the Greenhouse Gas Mitigation Program for Canadian Agriculture (GHGMP), with three other national organizations

Solar & Sustainable Energy Society of Canada Inc. (SESCI) / Societé des énergie solaire et durable du Canada Inc.
c/o Frederic Pouyot, #173, 207 Bank St., Ottawa ON k2P 2N2
Tel: 613-686-4474; *Fax:* 613-533-6550
e-mail: bruce@techonfoot.com
URL: www.sesci.ca
Previous Name: Solar Energy Society of Canada Inc.
Overview: A medium-sized national charitable organization founded in 1974

Finances: *Annual Operating Budget:* $50,000-$100,000; *Funding Sources:* Membership fees; Donations
Fees: $20 students; $40 seniors; $100 regular members; $200 small organizations; $300 libraries; $500 medium organizations; $2000 large organizations
Activities: Presenting briefs & position papers to government departments in the environment, energy resource, & finance sectors; Liaising with other solar energy societies & environmental groups; Encouraging the exchange of information
Meetings/Conferences:
For more information see Trade Shows, Conferences and Seminars Chapter
Solar & Sustainable Energy Society of Canada Inc. 2012 Annual Conference
Other Conferences in 2012 2012
Photovoltaics Industry 2012 5th Annual Workshop
Other Conferences in 2012 2012
Photovoltaics Industry 2013 6th Annual Workshop
Other Conferences in 2013 2013
Publications: *SOL [a publication of the Solar & Sustainable Energy Society of Canada Inc.]*
Type: Newsletter *Frequency:* q. *Price:* Free with Solar & Sustainable Energy Society of Canada Inc. membership
Profile: Developments in Canada's renewable energy industry, topical articles, & Solar & Sustainable Energy Society of Canada's forthcoming events & activities
Canadian Renewable Energy Guide
Type: Guide
Profile: Comprehensive information about the use of renewables throughout Canada
Mission: To act as a voice for renewable energy in Canada; To increase the use of solar & sustainable energy in Canada; To support energy conservation; *Affiliation(s):* International Solar Energy Society (ISES)
Environmental Activity: Raising awareness of solar & sustainable energy in Canada; Encouraging improvements in solar energy applications

Solar Energy Society of Canada Inc. *See* Solar & Sustainable Energy Society of Canada Inc.

Solid Waste Association of North America (SWANA)
PO Box 7219, #700, 1100 Wayne Ave., Silver Spring MD 20907-7219 USA
Tel: 301-467-9262; *Fax:* 301-589-7068
e-mail: info@swana.org
URL: www.swana.org
Previous Name: Government Refuse Collection & Disposal Association
Overview: A medium-sized international organization founded in 1961
Finances: *Annual Operating Budget:* $3 Million-$5 Million; *Funding Sources:* Membership dues; publications
Staff: 25 staff member(s)
Membership: 7,000; *Fees:* $169 USD - Public Sector; $229 USD - Small Business; $329 USD - Private Sector; *Committees:* Collection; Recycling; Landfill; Landfill Gas; Management; Special Waste; Waste-to-Energy
Activities: Technical divisions: collection & transfer, waste-to-energy, landfill gas management, landfill management, planning & management, special waste management; waste reduction, recycling & composting, communication, education & marketing; publications; trade shows & conferences; *Internships:* Yes; *Library:* Yes, Open to public
Mission: To serve individuals & communities responsible for the operation & management of solid waste management systems; To advance professional standards in the field through training programs, technical assistance, & education; *Member of:* International Solid Waste Association; Federation of Canadian Municipalities

Solidarité européenne pour une égale participation des peuples *See* European Solidarity Towards Equal Participation of People

Somenos Marsh Wildlife Society
PO Box 711, Duncan BC V9L 3Y1
Tel: 250-746-7030
e-mail: info@somenosmarsh.com
URL: www.somenosmarsh.com
Overview: A small local organization
Chief Officer(s):
Paul Fletcher, President
Membership: 200; *Fees:* $20-$35
Mission: To preserve wetland habitat in Somenos Basin; to build wildlife viewing facilities; *Member of:* Cowichan Watershed

Council; BC Environmental Network; Canadian Nature Federation

South Lake Simcoe Naturalists
PO Box 1044, Sutton West ON L0E 1R0
Tel: 416-722-8021
e-mail: harpley@ils.net
Overview: A small local organization founded in 1980
Chief Officer(s):
Paul Harpley, President
Finances: *Annual Operating Budget:* Less than $50,000; *Funding Sources:* Federal & provincial governments; private
Staff: 3 staff member(s); 20+ volunteer(s)
Membership: 50-100; *Fees:* $16 individual; $20 family; *Committees:* Conservation; Forest Loss - York Region; Environmental Activism
Activities: Wildlife research; breeding bird census; South Lake Simcoe Wildlife Research Station (seasonal); lectures; outings; land use planning; *Internships:* Yes; *Speaker Service:* Yes
Mission: Conservation, education & recreation organization concerned with the study & experience of nature & the relationships between it & humans; *Member of:* Federation of Ontario Naturalists

South Pacific Peoples Foundation See Pacific Peoples Partnership

South Peel Naturalists' Club (SPNC)
PO Box 69629, 109 Thomas St., Oakville ON L6J 7R4
Tel: 905-279-8807
e-mail: mail@spnc.ca
URL: www.spnc.ca
Overview: A small local organization founded in 1952
Chief Officer(s):
Don Morrison, President
Finances: *Annual Operating Budget:* Less than $50,000; *Funding Sources:* Membership fees; donations
Staff: 35-4 volunteer(s)
Membership: 200; *Fees:* $25
Member of: Federation of Ontario Naturalists; *Affiliation(s):* Canadian Nature Federation

Southeast Environmental Association (SEA)
PO Box 1500, 41 Woods Islands Hill, Montague PE C0A 1R0
Tel: 902-838-3351; *Fax:* 902-838-0610
e-mail: sea@pei.aibn.com
URL: www.seapei.ca
Overview: A medium-sized provincial organization founded in 1992
Chief Officer(s):
Sarah Jane Bell, Coordinator
Edgar Dewar, Chair
Mission: To protect, maintain, and enhance the ecology of south eastern Prince Edward Island for the environmental, social, and economic well being of area residents.

Southern Alberta Health Libraries Association (SAHLA)
Parent: **Canadian Health Libraries Association**
c/o Health Sciences Library, University of Calgary, 3330 University Dr. NW, Calgary AB T2N 4N1
Tel: 403-220-6858; *Fax:* 403-282-7992
e-mail: sahla@sahla.org
URL: www.sahla.org
Overview: A small local organization
Chief Officer(s):
Taryn Lenders, President
taryn.lenders@calgaryhealthregion.ca
Finances: *Annual Operating Budget:* Less than $50,000
Membership: 1-99; *Fees:* $15

Southern Interior Local Government Association (SILGA)
1996 Sheffield Way, Kamloops BC V2E 2M2
Tel: 250-374-3678; *Fax:* 250-374-3678
URL: www.silga.ca
Previous Name: Okanagan Mainline Municipal Association; Okanagan Valley Municipal Association; Okanagan Valley Mayors & Reeves Association
Overview: A small local organization
Chief Officer(s):
Kevin Flynn, President
Noreen Guenther, First Vice-President
Harry Kroeker, Second Vice-President

Membership: 36 municipalities; *Member Profile:* Elected officials from cities, towns, villages, districts, & regional districts in south central British Columbia
Activities: Working on water treatment standards issues; Organizing workshops for members; Liaising with the provincial & federal governments
Mission: To represent the municipalities & regional districts of the Okanagan Mainline area

Southern Ontario Orchid Society
75 Ternhill Cres., North York ON M3C 2E4
Tel: 905-640-5643; *Fax:* 905-640-0696
e-mail: info@soos.ca
URL: www.soos.ca
Overview: A small local organization
Fees: $25

Southern Ontario Seismic Network (SOSN)
c/o University of Western Ontario, London ON N6A 5B7
Tel: 519-661-3605; *Fax:* 519-661-3198
URL: www.gp.uwo.ca
Overview: A small local organization
Chief Officer(s):
R.F. Mereu, Administrator
rmereu@uwo.ca
Mission: To obtain information on the seismicity and seismic hazards of a region of southern Ontario in which a number of nuclear power facilities are located.; *Member of:* POLARIS Network; Canadian National Seismograph Network

Southwestern Nova Scotia Fish Packers Association See Nova Scotia Fish Packers Association

Specification Writers Association of Canada See Construction Specifications Canada

Spectroscopy Society of Canada See Canadian Society for Analytical Sciences & Spectroscopy

Stanley Park Ecology Society (SPES)
PO Box 5167, Vancouver BC V6B 4B2
Tel: 604-257-6908; *Fax:* 604-257-8378
e-mail: info@stanleyparkecology.ca
URL: www.stanleyparkecology.ca
Overview: A small local organization founded in 1988
Chief Officer(s):
Patricia Thomson, Executive Director
Fees: $20 individual; $15 senior/junior/volunteer; $40 family
Mission: To encourage stewardship of our natural world through environmental education & action & by fostering awareness of the fragile balance that exists between urban populations & nature

Steel Recycling Institute (SRI)
680 Andersen Dr., Pittsburgh PA 15220 USA
Tel: 412-922-2772
URL: www.recycle-steel.org
Overview: A medium-sized international organization founded in 1988
Chief Officer(s):
James Woods, Director, Public & Education Relations, 412-922-2772 Ext. 215
Mission: To promote the recycling of steel products
Environmental Activity: Providing education about the benefits of recycling steel; Working with both the private & public sectors to increase the volume of steel diverted from landfills

Stem Cell Network (SCN) / Réseau de cellules souches
#501 Smyth Rd., Room CCW-6189, Ottawa ON K1H 8L6
Tel: 613-739-6675
e-mail: info@stemcellnetwork.ca
URL: www.stemcellnetwork.ca
Overview: A medium-sized national organization founded in 2001
Chief Officer(s):
Drew Lyall, Executive Director
Lisa Willemse, Director of Communications
Mission: To investigate the immense therapeutic potential of stem cells for the treatment of diseases currently incurable by conventional approaches; *Member of:* Networks of Centres of Excellence

Stockholm Environment Institute (SEI)
Kräftriket 2B, Stockholm SE-106 91 Sweden

Tel: 46-8-674-7200
e-mail: johan.rockstrom@sei.se
URL: www.sei.se
Overview: A medium-sized international organization founded in 1988
Chief Officer(s):
Johna Rockström, Executive Director
Finances: *Annual Operating Budget:* Greater than $5 Million; *Funding Sources:* Government; other sources in Sweden, UK, USA
Staff: 60 staff member(s); 2 volunteer(s)
Activities: *Internships:* Yes; *Speaker Service:* Yes; *Library:* Yes, open by appointment
Mission: International research institute focusing on local, regional & global environmental issues

Strategic Leadership Forum, The Toronto Society for Strategic Management (SLF)
75 Dunkirk Rd., Toronto ON M4C 2M5
Tel: 416-574-1832; *Fax:* 647-436-3599
e-mail: membership@slftoronto.com
URL: strategicleadershipforum.camp9.org
Previous Name: The Planning Forum
Overview: A medium-sized national organization founded in 1950
Finances: *Annual Operating Budget:* $100,000-$250,000; *Funding Sources:* Membership fees; program fees; sponsorship revenue
Staff: 1 staff member(s); 24 volunteer(s)
Membership: 500; *Fees:* $295 executive; $175 academic; $1,180 corporate; *Member Profile:* Managers, directors, vice-presidents
Activities: Meetings: breakfast, luncheon, half-day, full-day & evening
Mission: To provide our community of members with an independent & intellectually challenging forum that delivers practical insights & interactions on strategic management & leadership

Strathcona Park Lodge & Outdoor Education Centre
PO Box 2160, Campbell River BC V9W 5C5
Tel: 250-286-3122; *Fax:* 250-286-6010
e-mail: info@strathcona.bc.ca
URL: www.strathcona.bc.ca
Also Known As: Canadian Outdoor Leadership Training Centre Ltd.
Overview: A medium-sized local organization founded in 1959
Finances: *Annual Operating Budget:* $1.5 Million-$3 Million; *Funding Sources:* Private
Staff: 65 staff member(s)
Membership: 1-99
Activities: Kayaking; canoeing; sailing; ropes courses; rock climbing; mountaineering; hiking; backpacking; orienteering; wilderness ethics; survival; environmental education; *Library:* Yes, Open to public
Mission: To teach the wonder, spirit & worth of people & the natural world through outdoor pursuits; *Member of:* Outdoor Recreation Council of British Columbia; *Affiliation(s):* Sea Kayak Guides Alliance of BC; Tourism Association of Vancouver Island

Structural Pest Management Association of Alberta See Pest Management Association of Alberta

Structural Pest Management Association of British Columbia (SPMABC)
c/o Integrated Pest Supplies, #108, 360 Edworthy Way, New Westminster BC V3L 5T8
Tel: 604-520-9900; *Fax:* 604-522-5557
Toll-Free: 800-465-5511
e-mail: info@spmabc.com
URL: www.spmabc.com
Overview: A small provincial organization
Chief Officer(s):
Larry Cross, President
Membership: 54; *Fees:* $295-$420
Member of: Canadian Pest Management Association

Structural Pest Management Association of Ontario (SPMAO)
#100E, 3800 Steeles Ave. West, Woodbridge ON L4L 4G9
Toll-Free: 800-461-6722
e-mail: info@spmao.ca
URL: www.spmao.ca
Previous Name: Ontario Pest Control Association
Overview: A small provincial organization founded in 1950
Chief Officer(s):

Ted Berdowski, President, 905-680-1830
Finances: *Annual Operating Budget:* Less than $50,000
Staff: 1 staff member(s); 11 volunteer(s)
Membership: 100; *Fees:* $325 active; $275 allied; $215 associate
Activities: Monthly meetings; annual conference; satellite meetings; *Library:* Yes, Not open to the public
Member of: Canadian Pest Management Association; National Pest Management Association (U.S.); Urban Pest Management Council of Canada

Sudbury Rock & Lapidary Society (SRLS)
c/o 3171 Romeo St., Val Caron ON P3N 1G5
Tel: 705-897-6216
e-mail: mineral@isys.ca
URL: www.ccfms.ca/Clubs/Sudbury/
Overview: A small local organization founded in 1984
Chief Officer(s):
Roger Poulin, President
Ruth Debicki, Vice-President
Gil Benoit, Treasurer
Membership: 85; *Fees:* $10; *Member Profile:* Amateurs; Hobbyists; Professionals
Activities: Hosting monthly meetings at the Naughton Community Centre; Offering courses in lapidary arts & silver smithing; Organizing field trips; *Library:* Sudbury Rock & Lapidary Society Library
Publications: *Nickel Basin Rockhound*
Type: Newsletter *Frequency:* 10 pa *Number of Pages:* 10
Editor: Dick Adlington *Price:* Free with SRLS membership
Profile: Information for SRLS members
Mission: To promote rock, mineral, gem, & fossil collecting, & lapidary for both recreation & education; *Member of:* Central Canadian Federation of Mineralogical Societies

Sunshine Coast Natural History Society (SCNHS)
PO Box 543, Sechelt BC V0N 3A0
Tel: 604-885-5539; *Fax:* 604-885-2904
e-mail: greenfieldtony@hotmail.com
Previous Name: Sechelt Marsh Protective Society
Overview: A small local organization founded in 1978
Finances: *Annual Operating Budget:* Less than $50,000; *Funding Sources:* Membership fees; municipal grant
Staff: 20 volunteer(s)
Membership: 120; *Fees:* $25
Activities: Monthly meetings; field trips; *Awareness Events:* Christmas Bird Count
Member of: Federation of BC Naturalists

Sustainable Buildings Canada (SBC) / Bâtiments Durables Canada
#1801, 18 Eastern Ave., lower level, Toronto ON M5A 1H5
Tel: 416-364-0050; *Fax:* 416-364-0606
e-mail: sbc@sbcanada.org
URL: www.sbcanada.org
Overview: A small national organization
Chief Officer(s):
Constantine (Taki) Eladis, Chair
Michael Singleton, Executive Director
Mission: To showcase to the world the Canadian cooperation that exists between the private sector & government, working together to implement innovative solutions to mitigate climate change, while serving the buildings industry

Sustainable Development Technology Canada (SDTC)
#1850, 45 O'Connor St., Ottawa ON K1P 1A4
Tel: 613-234-6313; *Fax:* 613-234-0303
e-mail: info@sdtc.ca
URL: www.sdtc.ca
Overview: A medium-sized national organization founded in 2001
Chief Officer(s):
Vicky J. Sharpe, President & Chief Executive Officer
vj.sharpe@sdtc.ca
George Angus, Sr. Vice-President & Chief Operating Officer
g.angus@sdtc.ca
Rob Barkwell, Manager, Applications
r.barkwell@sdtc.ca
Patrice Breton, Director, Communications
p.breton@sdtc.ca
Finances: *Funding Sources:* Government of Canada
Staff: 41 staff member(s)
Committees: Corporate Governance; Human Resources; Project Review; Audit & Grant Investment

Publications: *Sustainable Development Technology Canada Annual Report*
Type: Yearbook *Frequency:* a.
Sustainable Development Technology Canada Corporate Plan
Mission: To create a healthy environment and a high quality of life for Canadians; To identify & fund technologies with strong competitive & environmental potential
Environmental Activity: Supporting clean technology projects

Sustainable Forestry Initiative
#700, 900 - 17th St. NW, Washington DC 20006 USA
Tel: 202-596-3451; *Fax:* 202-596-3451
e-mail: info@sfiprogram.org
URL: www.sfiprogram.org
Social Media: www.twitter.com/#!/sfiprogram
Overview: A large international charitable organization founded in 1994
Chief Officer(s):
Kathy Abusow, President & Chief Executive Officer, 613-722-8734
Kathy.abusow@sfiprogram.org
Rick Cantrell, Vice-President & Chief Operating Officer
Rick.Cantrell@sfiprogram.org
Danny Karch, Director, Green Building, 450-659-8733, Fax: 450-659-8763
danny.karch@sfiprogram.org
Allison Welde, Director, Conservation Partnerships & Communications
Allison.Welde@sfiprogram.org
Activities: Promoting research to improve forestry practices
Meetings/Conferences:
For more information see Trade Shows, Conferences and Seminars Chapter
Sustainable Forestry Initiative 2011 Annual Conference: The Bigger Picture - Conservation, Integrity, Community
September 2011 Burlington, VA
Sustainable Forestry Initiative 2012 Annual Conference
Other Conferences in 2012 2012
Publications: *Sustainable Forestry Initiative Newsletter*
Type: Newsletter *Frequency:* bi-m.
Profile: Recent information about the SFI program, including conservation grants updates, new certifications, & program statistics
Mission: To promote sustainable forest management; To maintain & improve the sustainable forestry certification program
Environmental Activity: Empowering consumers to make responsible environmental choices by purchasing products from a certified forest or sourcing; Protecting forests, including water quality & habitat; Offering training related to the practice of responsible forestry

Sustainable Urban Development Association (SUDA)
2637 Council Ring Rd., Mississauga ON L5L 1S6
Tel: 416-400-0553
e-mail: mail@suda.ca
URL: www.suda.ca
Overview: A medium-sized national organization
Mission: To foster a healthy natural environment by providing information about ways in which cities can become more efficient in the land, material, water and energy resources, and highly supportive of sustainable transportation.

Swift Current Agricultural & Exhibition Association
PO Box 146, Swift Current SK S9H 3V5
Tel: 306-773-2944; *Fax:* 306-773-7015
e-mail: swiftcurrentex@sasktel.net
URL: www.swiftcurrentex.com
Overview: A small provincial charitable organization founded in 1938
Finances: *Annual Operating Budget:* $500,000-$1.5 Million
Staff: 4 staff member(s); 500 volunteer(s)
Membership: 78; *Fees:* $5
Activities: Agricultural Fairs, Exhibitions, Livestock shows & sales, Trade shows;
Mission: To facilitate education, entertainment, exhibitions & agricultural programs for the cultural & economic benefits of the community; *Member of:* Saskatchewan Association of Agricultural Societies & Exhibitions

Swift Current Creek Watershed Stewards (SCCWS)
PO Box 1088, Swift Current SK S9H 3X3
Tel: 306-778-5007; *Fax:* 306-778-5020
e-mail: stewards@sccws.com
URL: www.sccws.com
Overview: A small local organization
Chief Officer(s):

Arlene Unvoas, Executive Director
Mission: To enhance water quality and stream health of the Swift Current Creek Watershed by promoting awareness and understanding among water users.

Sydenham Field Naturalists (SFN)
PO Box 22008, Wallaceburg ON N8A 5G4
Overview: A small local charitable organization founded in 1985
Chief Officer(s):
Brett Groves, President
Finances: *Funding Sources:* Bingo profits; private donations; grants
Membership: 35-40; *Fees:* $15 single; $25 family
Activities: Field trips; planting of native shrubs/wildflowers; indoor meetings; wood lot acquisition
Mission: To preserve wildlife, promote public interest, cooperate with others with similar interests, consider matters of environmental concern; *Member of:* Federation of Ontario Naturalists; Canadian Nature Federation; Carolinian Canada

Syndicat canadien des communications, de l'énergie et du papier *See* Communications, Energy & Paperworkers Union of Canada

Syndicat national des cultivateurs *See* National Farmers Union

TD Friends of the Environment Foundation / Fondation des amis de l'environnement TD
#1100, 45 O'Connor St., Ottawa ON K1P 1A4
Tel: 613-782-1196; *Fax:* 613-783-6319
Toll-Free: 800-361-5333
e-mail: tdfef@td.com
URL: www.td.com/fef/
Previous Name: Friends of the Environment Foundation
Overview: A medium-sized national charitable organization founded in 1990
Chief Officer(s):
Matthew Fortier, Regional Manager, ON North & East, National Programs
Finances: *Funding Sources:* TD Canada Trust & its customers
Membership: 1,000+
Activities: 110+ local chapters across Canada; *Speaker Service:* Yes
Mission: To protect & preserve the Canadian environment

The technical society of the Canadian Nuclear Association (CNA) *See* Canadian Nuclear Society

Technologies Industry Association of BC *See* British Columbia Technology Industries Association

TechNova
Parent: Canadian Council of Technicians & Technologists
#A308, Cambridge 1, 202 Brownlow Ave., Dartmouth NS B3B 1T5
Tel: 902-463-3236; *Fax:* 902-465-7567
Toll-Free: 866-723-8867
e-mail: info@technova.ca
URL: www.technova.ca
Also Known As: Society of Certified Engineering Technicians & Technologists of Nova Scotia
Overview: A medium-sized provincial licensing organization founded in 1967
Finances: *Annual Operating Budget:* $100,000-$250,000; *Funding Sources:* Memberships
Staff: 1 staff member(s); 9 volunteer(s)
Membership: 1,500+; *Fees:* $150
Mission: Certifying engineering & applied science technicians & technologists for the betterment of the public & the welfare of the environment

Tellus Institute
11 Arlington St., Boston MA 02116-3411 USA
Tel: 617-266-5400; *Fax:* 617-266-8303
e-mail: info@tellus.org
URL: www.tellus.org
Overview: A medium-sized international charitable organization founded in 1976
Chief Officer(s):
Paul Raskin, President & Director
Finances: *Annual Operating Budget:* Greater than $5 Million; *Funding Sources:* Government agencies; Foundations; Non-governmental organizations
Staff: 42 staff member(s); 2 volunteer(s)

Associations/Organizations / Temiskaming Environmental Action Committee

Activities: Conducts research, consulting & communication; addresses policy & planning issues in areas such as energy, water, waste, & land use; analyzes problems & evaluates options for technological & institutional change; develops & disseminates decision-support tools to strengthen capacity to develop effective resource & environmental strategies;
Mission: Conducts a diverse program of research, consulting & communications; addresses policy & planning issues in such areas as energy, water, waste & land use for a sustainable world for future generations; *Member of:* Stockholm Environment Institute

Temiskaming Environmental Action Committee (TEAC)
PO Box 541, New Liskeard ON P0J 1P0
Tel: 705-678-2404; *Fax:* 705-647-7511
Overview: A small local organization
Membership: 1-99
Activities: *Speaker Service:* Yes
Mission: To raise public awareness of environmental issues; Affiliation(s): Northwatch; Public Concern Temiskaming; Ontario Environmental Network

Thames Region Ecological Association (TREA)
1017 Western Rd., London ON N6G 1G5
Tel: 519-672-5991; *Fax:* 519-645-0981
e-mail: trea@wwdc.com
URL: www.trea.ca
Overview: A small local charitable organization founded in 1986
Finances: *Annual Operating Budget:* Less than $50,000;
Funding Sources: Government; membership fees; Compost Day
Staff: 1 staff member(s); 40 volunteer(s)
Membership: 60 individual; *Fees:* $20 individual
Activities: TREATop; waste group; home cocmposting program; TREATalk, tree planting; pesticide group; London Bicycle Festival; *Speaker Service:* Yes
Mission: Committed to educating ourselves & the community towards development of an ecologically responsible & sustainable future through awareness, reflection, caring & action; *Member of:* Grosvenor Lodge Resource Centre for Heritage & Environment; Affiliation(s): Urban League of London; London Composts

Thermal Environmental Comfort Association (TECA)
PO Box 73105, Stn. Evergreen RO, Surrey BC V3R 0J2
Tel: 604-594-5956; *Fax:* 604-594-5091
Toll-Free: 888-577-3818
e-mail: training@teca.ca
URL: www.teca.ca
Overview: A large provincial organization
Chief Officer(s):
Terry Regier, President
Membership: 298; *Fees:* $185-$350; $100 associate
Mission: To offer the residential heating, cooling and ventilation industry up-to-date training courses and a collective voice in local and provincial issues.

Thermal Insulation Association of Alberta
10215 - 176 St., Edmonton AB T5S 1M1
Tel: 780-457-9890; *Fax:* 780-457-9928
e-mail: thermal9@telus.net
URL: www.tiaa.cc
Overview: A small provincial organization
Mission: To improve & elevate the technical & general knowledge of the mechanical insulation industry in Alberta, promoting excellence in manufacture, application, & installation of all insulation products & materials; *Member of:* Thermal Insulation Association of Canada

Thunder Bay Field Naturalists (TBFN)
PO Box 10073, Thunder Bay ON P7B 6T6
Tel: 807-474-6007
e-mail: ertolaht@tbaytel.net
URL: www.tbfn.net
Overview: A small local charitable organization founded in 1933
Finances: *Annual Operating Budget:* $50,000-$100,000;
Funding Sources: Membership fees; donations; grants
Staff: 11 volunteer(s)
Membership: 200; *Fees:* $30 family; $25 single; $20 students/seniors; $350 life; *Member Profile:* Those interested in the study of nature & the environment; *Committees:* Nature Reserves; Bird Records; Peregrine Falcon Recovery; Bluebird Recovery
Activities: Adult & Junior Nature; oriented field trips; indoor lectures; *Speaker Service:* Yes
Mission: To promote the enjoyment of nature through environmental appreciation & conservation; to encourage wise use & conservation of natural resources; to promote environmental protection; *Member of:* Federation of Ontario Naturalists; Affiliation(s): Thunder Cape Bird Observatory

Timberline Trail & Nature Club
701 - 105th Ave., Dawson Creek BC V1G 2K5
Tel: 250-782-7680
Overview: A small local organization
Mission: To promote the enjoyment of nature through environmental appreciation & conservation; to encourage wise use & conservation of natural resources & environmental protection.; *Member of:* Federation of BC Naturalists

Tire Stewardship BC Association (TSBC)
PO Box 5366, Victoria BC V8R 6S4
Tel: 250-598-9112; *Fax:* 250-598-9119
Toll-Free: 866-759-0488
URL: www.tirestewardshipbc.ca
Overview: A small provincial organization founded in 2006
Chief Officer(s):
Don Blythe, Chair
Glenn Maidment, Secretary
Mission: The Tire Stewardship BC Association was founded by the Rubber Association of Canada, The Retail Council of Canada and the Western Canada Tire Dealers. In 2007 the New Car Dealers Association joined the Association. TSBC is governed by a Board that is made up of representatives from these four organizations

Toronto Biotechnology Initiative (TBI) / L'Initiative torontoise de biotechnologie
#120-C, 101 College Street, Toronto ON M5G 1L7
Tel: 416-673-6699; *Fax:* 866-218-4904
Toll-Free: 866-218-4904
e-mail: ali.ibrahimi@ontbi.org
URL: www.torontobiotech.org
Overview: A small local organization founded in 1989
Chief Officer(s):
Ali Ibrahimi, Manager, Communications & Membership
Finances: *Annual Operating Budget:* $50,000-$100,000;
Funding Sources: Membership fees
Membership: 300; *Fees:* $200 regular; $100 student;
Committees: Biofinance; Breakfast Meetings; Education; Membership; Public Interest Forum; Regulatory; Technology Transfer
Activities: Biofinance (events, awards dinner); Bioscan newsletter; community service award; education; entrepreunership program; international program; monthly meetings; public interest forum; regulatory affairs
Mission: To further biotechnology in the Greater Toronto Area; to further TBI as a leading Canadian biotechnology organization; to further the Greater Toronto Area as a major international centre for biotechnology; Affiliation(s): Biotechnology Industry Organization; Council of Biotechnology Centres; BIOTECanada

Toronto Entomologists Association (TEA)
1606 Crediton Pkwy., Mississauga ON L5G 3X3
Tel: 905-727-6993
e-mail: info@OntarioInsects.org
URL: www.ontarioinsects.org
Overview: A small local charitable organization founded in 1969
Finances: *Annual Operating Budget:* Less than $50,000;
Funding Sources: Membership fees; donations
Membership: 170; *Fees:* $15 student; $25 individual; $30 family; *Member Profile:* Amateur insect enthusiasts; professionals
Activities: Butterfly counts
Mission: To maintain an interest in the insects, particularly the butterflies & moths of Ontario; to record life histories, changes in distribution, unusual records, etc., of Ontario butterflies & moths; *Member of:* Federation of Ontario Naturalists

Toronto Environmental Alliance (TEA)
#201, 30 Duncan St., Toronto ON M5V 2C3
Tel: 416-596-0660; *Fax:* 416-596-0345
e-mail: tea@torontoenvironment.org
URL: www.torontoenvironment.org
Overview: A small local organization
Chief Officer(s):
Franz Hartmann, Executive Director
Finances: *Annual Operating Budget:* $250,000-$500,000
Staff: 7 staff member(s); 200 volunteer(s)
Membership: 8,000; *Fees:* $25; *Committees:* Water; Climate Change; Waste; Smog; Transit
Activities: *Library:* Yes, open by appointmentNot open to the public

Mission: To bring together groups & individuals who share the common goal of making the communities of Greater Toronto area operate in an ecologically sustainable manner; *Member of:* Ontario Environmental Network

Toronto Field Naturalists (TFN)
#1519, 2 Carlton St., Toronto ON M5B 1J3
Tel: 416-593-2656
e-mail: office@torontofieldnaturalists.org
URL: www.torontofieldnaturalists.org
Social Media: www.facebook.com/TorontoFieldNaturalists
Overview: A medium-sized local charitable organization founded in 1923
Chief Officer(s):
Bob Kortright, President
Walter Weary, Secretary-Treasurer
Finances: *Funding Sources:* Membership fees; Donations
Staff: 0 staff member(s)
Fees: $20 youth; $30 single seniors; $40 adults & senior families; $50 families
Activities: Partnering with organizations such as Ontario Nature, Toronto Green Community, Toronto Parks & Recreation, & the Toronto & Region Conservation Authority; Engaging in advocacy activities; Organizing monthly talks by experts on natural history topics
Meetings/Conferences:
For more information see Trade Shows, Conferences and Seminars Chapter
Toronto Field Naturalists 2011 Monthly Talk
September 2011 Toronto, ON
Toronto Field Naturalists 2011 Monthly Talk
October 2011 Toronto, ON
Toronto Field Naturalists 2011 Monthly Talk
November 2011 Toronto, ON
Toronto Field Naturalists 2011 Monthly Talk
December 2011 Toronto, ON
Toronto Field Naturalists 2012 Monthly Talk
January 2012 Toronto, ON
Toronto Field Naturalists 2012 Monthly Talk
February 2012 Toronto, ON
Toronto Field Naturalists 2012 Monthly Talk
March 2012 Toronto, ON
Toronto Field Naturalists 2012 Monthly Talk
April 2012 Toronto, ON
Toronto Field Naturalists 2012 Monthly Talk
May 2012 Toronto, ON
Publications: *Toronto Field Naturalist*
Type: Newsletter *Frequency:* 8 pa
Profile: Information about nature in Toronto, environmental issues, & the organization's upcoming activities
Mission: To promote the enjoyment & preservation of nature; To raise public interest in natural history
Environmental Activity: Organizing stewardship work parties to clear trails & remove invasive species; Protecting & enhancing ravines, parks, & the waterfront in Toronto; Educating the public about nature

Toronto Health Libraries Association (THLA)
Parent: Canadian Health Libraries Association
PO Box 94056, 3409 Yonge St., Toronto ON M4N 2L0
Tel: 416-485-0377; *Fax:* 416-485-6877
e-mail: president@thla.ca
URL: www.thla.ca
Overview: A small local organization founded in 1965
Chief Officer(s):
Weina Wang, President
Finances: *Annual Operating Budget:* Less than $50,000;
Funding Sources: Membership dues
Membership: 150; *Fees:* $25 individual; $15 student/retired/unemployed; *Member Profile:* Professional association for health librarians
Mission: To promote the provision of quality library service to the health community; to encourage communication & cooperation among members & to foster their professional development; to consult & collaborate with other professional, technical & scientific organizations in matters of mutual interest; Affiliation(s): Ontario Hospital Libraries Association

Toronto Institute of Medical Technology *See* The Michener Institute for Applied Health Sciences

Toronto Ornithological Club (TOC)
e-mail: info@torontobirding.ca
URL: www.torontobirding.ca
Overview: A small local organization founded in 1934
Finances: *Annual Operating Budget:* Less than $50,000

Membership: 150+; Fees: $25; Committees: Outings; Records; Editorial; Archives; Conservation
Activities: Bird outings; High Park hawk watch; fall field day
Mission: To afford opportunities for the meeting together of ornithologists at regular intervals for discussion; to facilitate cooperation in ornithological studies; to review & report on ornithological topics; to establish a liaison between members & visiting naturalists; Member of: Federation of Ontario Naturalists

Toronto Renewable Energy Co-operative (TREC)
#405, 401 Richmond St. W., Toronto ON M5V 3A8
Tel: 416-977-5093; Fax: 416-306-6476
Toll-Free: 866-560-9463
e-mail: info@trec.on.ca
URL: www.trec.on.ca
Social Media: twitter.com/TRECoop
Overview: A small local organization founded in 1998
Finances: Funding Sources: Donations
Activities: Community energy projects; interactive, hands-on education; Green City Bike Tours; Green Collar Career program; Our Power solar initiative; solar home tours; round table discussions; Bruce County wind energy co-operative project
Mission: A non-profit organization of citizens dedicated to renewable energy and energy conservation; Member of: Canadian Renewable Energy Alliance; Affiliation(s): Toronto District School Board; Ontario Trillium Foundation; Ontario Power Authority Conservation Fund; Toronto Atmospheric Fund; Community Power Fund; Ontario Sustainable Energy Ass'n

Toronto Sheet Metal & Air Handling Group; Environmental Sheet Metal Association Toronto See Toronto Sheet Metal Contractors Association

Toronto Sheet Metal Contractors Association (TSMCA)
#26, 30 Wertheim Ct., Richmond Hill ON L4B 1B9
Tel: 905-886-9627; Fax: 905-886-9959
e-mail: shtmetal@bellnet.ca
URL: www.tsmca.org
Previous Name: Toronto Sheet Metal & Air Handling Group; Environmental Sheet Metal Association Toronto
Overview: A medium-sized local organization
Chief Officer(s):
Gary Townshend, President
Finances: Annual Operating Budget: $250,000-$500,000; Funding Sources: Collective Agreement Assessment
Staff: 5 staff member(s)
Membership: 102 individual
Member of: Ontario Sheet Metal & Air Handling Group

Toronto Transportation Society (TTS)
PO Box 5187, Stn. A, Toronto ON M5W 1N5
e-mail: ttswebmaster@torontotransportationsociety.org
URL: www.torontotransportationsociety.org
Overview: A small local organization founded in 1973
Chief Officer(s):
Kevin Nichol, President
Finances: Funding Sources: Membership dues
Staff: 7 volunteer(s)
Membership: 131; Fees: $20; Committees: Executive; Trips & Excursions
Activities: Library: Yes
Mission: To afford persons interested in transportation by land, facilities for discussion & exchange of information
Environmental Activity: pro-transit suggestions to politicians & transit operating agencies; lobbies on pro-transit issues

Toronto Zoo
361A Old Finch Ave., Toronto ON M1B 5K7
Tel: 416-392-5900; Fax: 416-392-5863
e-mail: torontozoo@torontozoo.ca
URL: www.torontozoo.com
Previous Name: Zoological Society of Metropolitan Toronto
Overview: A small local organization founded in 1969
Finances: Annual Operating Budget: $500,000-$1.5 Million; Funding Sources: Grants; Events; Corporate; Memberships; Bequests
Staff: 5 staff member(s); 45 volunteer(s)
Membership: 20,000; Fees: Schedule available; Committees: Executive; Finance; Sponsorship
Activities: Rents Mailing List: Yes
Mission: To support the Toronto Zoo in its efforts to conserve species diversity through conservation, education, & research; Affiliation(s): Canadian Association of Zoos, Parks & Aquariums; American Association of Zoos, Parks & Aquariums; Canadian Centre for Philanthropy

The Township of Muskoka Lakes Ratepayers' Association (TMLRA)
PO Box 336, Port Carling ON P0B 1J0
Tel: 705-765-0022; Fax: 705-765-0023
e-mail: tmlra@muskoka.com
URL: www.tmlra.on.ca
Overview: A small local organization founded in 1976
Chief Officer(s):
J. Douglas Bryden, President
Mission: Preservation, fairness & enhancement for & with property owners in the Township of Muskoka Lakes & beyond

Toxics Watch Society of Alberta (TWS)
1-6328A - 104 St. NW, Edmonton AB T6H 2K9
Tel: 780-439-1912; Fax: 780-433-3792
e-mail: info@toxwatch.ca
URL: www.toxwatch.ca
Overview: A small provincial organization founded in 1986
Chief Officer(s):
Conrad Nobert, President
Finances: Annual Operating Budget: Less than $50,000
Staff: 2 staff member(s); 7 volunteer(s)
Membership: 100; Fees: $10; Committees: Clear Air Strategic Alliance; AEN Steering; Beverage Container Management Board: Tire Recycling Management Board
Activities: Public Information Service; Library: Resource Library; Open to public
Mission: To promote reduction in the common use of toxic substances & zero discharge of toxic wastes; to ensure clean air & water & safe food for Albertans; to facilitate sustainable communities & environmental citizenship; Member of: Alberta Environmental Network; Canadian Environmental Network; Affiliation(s): Environmental Resource Centre; Tomorrow Foundation for a Sustainable Future

Trans Canada Trail Foundation (TCTF) / Fondation du sentier transcanadian
43, av Westminster nord, Montréal QC H4X 1Y8
Tel: 514-485-3959; Fax: 514-485-4541
Toll-Free: 800-465-3636
e-mail: info@tctrail.ca
URL: www.tctrail.ca
Overview: A medium-sized national charitable organization founded in 1992
Chief Officer(s):
Deborah Apps, President & CEO
Finances: Annual Operating Budget: $250,000-$500,000; Funding Sources: Public donations
Staff: 11 staff member(s); 1 volunteer(s)
Membership: 2,500; Fees: $75-150
Activities: Trail-building; trail locators & signage; guidebooks & maps
Mission: To promote & coordinate the planning, designing & building of a continuous, shared-use recreation trail that winds its way through every Province & Territory

Trans Canada Yellowhead Highway Association (TCYHA)
#332, 10113 - 104 Street, Edmonton AB T5J 1A1
Tel: 780-429-0444; Fax: 780-426-5078
URL: www.yellowheadit.com
Previous Name: Yellowhead Highway Association
Overview: A small local organization founded in 1947
Chief Officer(s):
Irene Davidson-Fisher, CEO
Finances: Annual Operating Budget: $100,000-$250,000
Staff: 3 staff member(s); 1 volunteer(s)
Membership: 390; Member Profile: Municipal, commercial, & corporate organizations & individuals
Mission: To improve highway infrastructure & promote tourism along the TransCanada/Yellowhead highway corridor

Transport 2000 Canada See Transport Action Canada

Transport Action Canada
Bronson Centre, PO Box 858, Stn. B, #303, 211 Bronson Ave., Ottawa ON K1P 5P9
Tel: 613-594-3290; Fax: 613-594-3271
e-mail: info@transport-action.ca
URL: www.transport-action.ca
Previous Name: Transport 2000 Canada
Overview: A medium-sized national charitable organization founded in 1976
Chief Officer(s):
David Jeanes, President
Justin Bur, VP East
Peter Lacey, VP West
Tony Turrittin, Secretary
Klaus Beltzner, Treasurer
Bert Titcomb, Manager
Finances: Annual Operating Budget: $50,000-$100,000; Funding Sources: Donations
Staff: 15 volunteer(s)
Membership: 1,500; Fees: $35 regular; $30 senior; $50 family; $75 affiliate non-profit; $170corporate
Activities: Research, public education & advocacy, representation of the consumer interests before federal, provincial, municipal public hearings & regulatory bodies, direction of consumer complaints to public carriers; Speaker Service: Yes; Library: Yes, Open to public
Mission: National federation of environmental & consumer groups concerned about the importance of transportation on our environment & quality of life; to inform Canadians of the need for a coherent national transport policy which recognizes that conservation of resources must be a priority & that access to good public transportation is a right of all Canadians; to work for the improvement & greater use of bus & rail transportation in the interests of public safety, social equity & the protection of the environment; to press for the coordination of all transport services for the benefit of users; to demand more attention to the needs of pedestrians, cyclists & public transport users; to maximize the use of the energy-efficient rail & marine modes for the shipment of freight. PUBLICATIONS: National Transport Newsletter.; Affiliation(s): Transport 2000 International

Transportation Association of Canada (TAC) / Association des transports du Canada (ATC)
2323 St. Laurent Blvd., Ottawa ON K1G 4J8
Tel: 613-736-1350; Fax: 613-736-1395
e-mail: secretariat@tac-atc.ca
URL: www.tac-atc.ca
Previous Name: Roads & Transportation Association of Canada
Overview: A large national organization founded in 1970
Finances: Annual Operating Budget: Greater than $5 Million
Staff: 30 staff member(s); 500 volunteer(s)
Membership: 550 corporate; Fees: Schedule available; Committees: Technical & Research; Editing & Publications; Rules of the Road; Project; Technical Steering; Asphalts Advisory; Operations; Pavements; Structures; Aviation; Conference Technical Program; Geometric Design; Goods Movement; Soils & Materials; Traffic; Transit Planning; Technology
Activities: Library: Technical Information Centre; open by appointment
Mission: To promote the provision of safe, efficient, effective & environmentally sustainable transportation services in support of Canada's social & economic goals; to act as a neutral forum for the discussion of transportation issues & matters; to act as a technical focus in the highway transportation area. PUBLICATIONS: TAC News.

Tree Canada Foundation (TCF) / Fondation canadienne de l'arbre
#402, 222 Somerset St. West, Ottawa ON K2P 2G3
Tel: 613-567-5545; Fax: 613-567-5270
Toll-Free: 877-666-1444
e-mail: tcf@treecanada.ca
URL: www.treecanada.ca
Overview: A small national organization founded in 1992
Chief Officer(s):
Michael Rosen, President
Finances: Annual Operating Budget: $1.5 Million-$3 Million
Staff: 4 staff member(s); 1300 volunteer(s)
Activities: Speaker Service: Yes
Awards: Awards (Grant)
National tree-planting & tree-care program designed to offset the problem of global warming; provides technical advice & financial assistance to qualifying partners for certain planting costs & for buying trees; partners are expected to contribute cash &/or in-kind services Eligibility: Groups interested in tree-planting programs
Mission: To provide education, technical support, resources & financial support through working partnerships to encourage Canadians to plant & care for trees in our urban & rural environment in an effort to help reduce the harmful effects of carbon dioxide emissions

Trout Unlimited Canada (TUC)
PO Box 339, Stn. T, Calgary AB T2G 2H9
Tel: 403-221-8360; Fax: 403-221-8368
Toll-Free: 800-909-6040

Associations/Organizations / Truck Loggers Association

e-mail: tuc@tucanada.org
URL: www.tucanada.org
Overview: A small national charitable organization founded in 1972
Chief Officer(s):
Doug Cressman, CEO
Finances: Annual Operating Budget: $500,000-$1.5 Million
Staff: 10 staff member(s); 1000 volunteer(s)
Membership: 4,000; Fees: $30
Activities: Yellow Fish Road Program; Library: Yes, open by appointment
Mission: To promote the conservation & wise use of trout & other coldwater fisheries & their watersheds, through the undertaking of habitat restoration & enhancement, research, management, & public education
Environmental Activity: Restoring habitats

Truck Loggers Association (TLA)
#725, 815 Hastings St. West, Vancouver BC V6C 1B4
Tel: 604-684-4291; Fax: 604-684-7134
e-mail: contact@tla.ca
URL: www.tla.ca
Overview: A medium-sized provincial organization founded in 1942
Chief Officer(s):
Dave Lewis, Executive Director
contact@tla.ca
Finances: Annual Operating Budget: $500,000-$1.5 Million
Staff: 5 staff member(s); 17 volunteer(s)
Membership: 600 institutional
Affiliation(s): Pacific Logging Congress

Tunnelling Association of Canada (TAC) / Association canadienne des tunnels
c/o Earthtech, 105 Commerce Valley Dr. West, 7th Fl., Markham ON L3T 7W3
Tel: 905-886-7022
e-mail: info@tunnelcanada.ca
URL: www.tunnelcanada.ca
Overview: A medium-sized national organization
Chief Officer(s):
Derek Zoldy, Treasurer
Garry Stevenson, President
Membership: 350 individual, student & corporate members; Fees: $50 individual; $15 student; $250 corporate
Mission: To promote Canadian tunnelling & underground excavation technologies, & safe design, construction & maintenance; to facilitate information exchange; to represent the tunnelling community in matters of public & technical concern; to publish a Canadian registry of tunnels, underground excavations & similar works; Member of: Canadian Geotechnical Society

Underwater Archaeological Society of British Columbia (UASBC)
c/o Vancouver Maritime Museum, 1905 Ogden Ave., Vancouver BC V6J 1A3
Tel: 604-942-9908; Fax: 604-980-0358
e-mail: uasbc@uasbc.com
URL: www.uasbc.com
Overview: A small provincial charitable organization founded in 1975
Finances: Annual Operating Budget: $50,000-$100,000; Funding Sources: Membership dues; government; corporate
Staff: 1 staff member(s); 150 volunteer(s)
Membership: 175; Fees: $35 single; $88 corporate; $40 family; $26 senior; $18 student; Committees: Explorations; Education; Conservation
Activities: Archaeological site surveys, heritage awareness promotion; operates 4 chapters in Vancouver, Victoria, Kootenay & Okanagan; Speaker Service: Yes; Library: Archives; open by appointment
Mission: To promote the science of underwater archaeology; to conserve, preserve & protect the maritime heritage lying beneath our coastal & inland waters; Member of: Outdoor Recreation Council of British Columbia

UNEP - World Conservation Monitoring Centre (UNEP-WCMC)
219 Huntingdon Rd., Cambridge CB3 0DL United Kingdom
Tel: 44-1223-277-314; Fax: 44-1223-277-136
e-mail: info@unep-wcmc.org
URL: www.unep-wcmc.org/
Previous Name: World Conservation Monitoring Centre
Overview: A small international charitable organization founded in 1988
Chief Officer(s):
Jon Hutton, Director

Activities: Library: Yes, open by appointment
Mission: To provide information services on conservation & sustainable use of the world's living resources; to help others to develop information system on their own; Affiliation(s): United Nations Environment Programme

Unifarm See Wild Rose Agricultural Producers

Union des cultivateurs franco-ontariens (UCFO)
2474 rue Champlain, Clarence Creek ON K0A 1N0
Tél: 613-488-2929; Téléc: 613-488-2541
Ligne sans frais: 877-425-8366
Courriel: ucfo@lavoieagricole.ca
URL: www.ucfo.ca
Aperçu: Dimension: petite; Envergure: provinciale; Organisme sans but lucratif; fondée en 1929
Membre(s) du bureau directeur:
Pierre Bercier, Président
Simon Durand, Directeur général
sdurand@lavoieagricole.ca
Finances: Budget de fonctionnement annuel: $100,000-$250,000
Personnel: 7 membre(s) du personnel; 10 bénévole(s)
Membre: 300; Montant de la cotisation: 15$ membre régulier; 35$ membre auxiliaire; Critères d'admissibilite: Agriculteurs, agricultrices de l'Ontario
Activités: Programme de développement de leadership coopératif; formation agricole; travaux pour la création d'une coopérative de développement régional
Mission: Regrouper les franco-ontariens et les franco-ontariennes qui oeuvrent dans le secteur agricole; concerter pour la protection de nos droits; promouvoir nos intérêts; informer notre communautéappuyer les institutions et groupements qui favorisent notre développement; développer notre sentiment et fiertéstimuler le développement social et économique des régions agricoles et rurales

Union des municipalités du Québec (UMQ)
#680, 680, rue Sherbrooke ouest, Montréal QC H3A 2M7
Tél: 514-282-7700; Téléc: 514-282-8793
Courriel: info@umq.qc.ca
URL: www.umq.qc.ca
Aperçu: Dimension: grande; Envergure: provinciale; Organisme sans but lucratif; fondée en 1919
Membre(s) du bureau directeur:
Pierre Prévost, Directeur général par intérim
Robert Coulombe, Président
r.coulombe@ville.maniwaki.qc.ca
Finances: Budget de fonctionnement annuel: $3 Million-$5 Million
Personnel: 35 membre(s) du personnel
Membre: 300; Montant de la cotisation: 0,46$ per capita; Critères d'admissibilité: Toutes les municipalités du Québec
Activités: Formation des élus et des gestionnaires municipaux; Stagiaires: Oui; Service de conférenciers: Oui; Listes de destinataires: Oui; Bibliothèque: Oui, Not open to the public
Mission: Au bénéfice des citoyens, représenter les municipalités auprès du gouvernement et contribuer à l'efficience de gestion des municipalités.; Membre de: Fédération canadienne des municipalités; Affiliation(s): Conseil du patronat du Québec; Fédération canadienne des municipalités

Union des municipalités régionales de comté et des municipalités locales du Québec Voir Fédération Québécoise des Municipalités

Union des producteurs agricoles (UPA)
Parent: Canadian Federation of Agriculture
#100, 555, boul. Roland-Therrien, Longueuil QC J4H 3Y9
Tél: 450-679-0530
Courriel: upa@upa.qc.ca
URL: www.upa.qc.ca
Aperçu: Dimension: grande; Envergure: provinciale; fondée en 1924
Finances: Budget de fonctionnement annuel: $3 Million-$5 Million
Membre: 43 000
Mission: Promouvoir, défendre et développer les intérêts professionnels, économiques, sociaux et moraux des producteurs agricoles et forestiers, sans distinction de race, de nationalité, de sexe, de langue et de croyance; Membre de: Fédération canadienne des producteurs de lait

Union géodésique et géophysique internationale See International Union of Geodesy & Geophysics

Union géographique internationale See International Geographic Union

Union géophysique canadienne See Canadian Geophysical Union

Union internationale de la science du sol See International Union of Soil Sciences

Union internationale des architectes (UIA) / International Union of Architects
33, av du Maine, Paris F-75755 France
Tel: 33-1-45-24-36-88; Fax: 33-1-45-24-02-78
e-mail: uia@uia-architectes.org
URL: www.uia-architectes.org/
Overview: A medium-sized international organization founded in 1948
Finances: Annual Operating Budget: $500,000-$1.5 Million
Staff: 7 staff member(s)
Membership: 124 member countries; Member Profile: National associations of architects
Activities: Work groups; congresses; seminars; competitions, etc.; Rents Mailing List: Yes
Awards: UIA Gold Medal (Award)
Awarded to a living architect in recognition of his/her life's work & contribution to mankind, to society & to the promotion of the art of architecture; awarded every three years
Auguste Perret Prize (Award)
Awarded every three years for technology applied to architecture
Jean Tschumi Prize (Award)
Awarded every three years for architectural criticism &/or education
Sir Robert Matthew Prize (Award)
Awarded every three years for improvement in the quality of human settlements
Sir Patrick Abercrombie Prize (Award)
Awarded every three years for town Planning & territorial development
Mission: To create among architects, ties based on friendship, understanding & mutual esteem; to enable them to confront their ideas & concepts, share their experiences, broaden their knowledge & learn from their differences in order to better fulfill their role in the improvement of Man's living conditions & environment
Environmental Activity: Declaration of Interdependence for a Sustainable Future, adopted June 1993, commits UIA members to place environmental & social sustainability at the core of practices & professional responsibilities

Union internationale des instituts de recherches forestières See International Union of Forest Research Organizations

Union internationale des sciences biologiques See International Union of Biological Sciences

Union mondiale pour la nature - Bureau de Montréal (UICN)
#500, 555, boul René-Levesque ouest, Montréal QC H2Z 1B1
Tél: 514-287-9704; Téléc: 514-287-9687
Courriel: canada@iucn.org
URL: www.iucn.org/places/canada
Aperçu: Dimension: moyenne; Envergure: internationale; fondée en 1948
Membre(s) du bureau directeur:
John Herity, Director, Canada Office
Finances: Budget de fonctionnement annuel: $500,000-$1.5 Million
Personnel: 5 membre(s) du personnel
Membre: 35
Mission: Influer sur les sociétés du monde entier, de les encourager et de les aider pour qu'elles conservent l'intégrité et la diversité de la nature et veillent à ce que toute utilisation des ressources naturelles soit équitable et écologiquement durable; garantir que l'utilisation des ressources naturelles soit rationnelle, équitable et durable; orienter le développement des communautés humaines vers des modes de vie qui soient à la fois de qualité et en harmonie durable avec les autres éléments de la biosphère; Membre de: The World Conservation Union

Union of British Columbia Municipalities
#60, 10551 Shellbridge Way, Richmond BC V6X 2W9
Tel: 604-270-8226; Fax: 604-270-9116
e-mail: ubcm@civicnet.bc.ca
URL: www.civicnet.bc.ca
Overview: A medium-sized provincial organization founded in 1905
Chief Officer(s):
Richard Taylor, Executive Director

Brenda Binnie, President
Finances: *Annual Operating Budget:* $500,000-$1.5 Million
Staff: 12 staff member(s)
Membership: 156 municipalities + 28 regional districts;
Committees: Aboriginal Affairs; Community & Resources; Convention; Environment; Executive; Justice & Protective Services; Local Government Awareness; Member Services; New Directions in Health Task Force; Resolutions
Activities: *Awareness Events:* Local Government Awareness Month, April; *Speaker Service:* Yes; *Library:* Yes, Open to public
Meetings/Conferences:
For more information see Trade Shows, Conferences and Seminars Chapter
Union of British Columbia Municipalities 2011 Annual Convention
September 2011 Vancouver, BC
Union of British Columbia Municipalities 2012 Annual Convention
September 2012 Kelowna, BC
Union of British Columbia Municipalities 2013 Annual Convention
September 2013 Vancouver, BC
Union of British Columbia Municipalities 2014 Annual Convention
October 2014 Victoria, BC
Union of British Columbia Municipalities 2015 Annual Convention
September 2015 Vancouver, BC
Union of British Columbia Municipalities 2016 Annual Convention
September 2016 Penticton, BC
Union of British Columbia Municipalities 2017 Annual Convention
September 2017 Vancouver, BC
Union of British Columbia Municipalities 2019 Annual Convention
September 2019 Vancouver, BC
Mission: To provide a common voice for local government; *Member of:* Federation of Canadian Municipalities

Union of Energy, Mines & Resources Employees *See* Natural Resources Union

Union of Nova Scotia Municipalities (UNSM)
#1106, 1809 Barrington St., Halifax NS B3J 3K8
Tel: 902-423-8331; *Fax:* 902-425-5592
e-mail: mainunsm@eastlink.ca
URL: www.unsm.ca
Overview: A medium-sized provincial organization founded in 1905
Chief Officer(s):
Kenneth Simpson, Executive Director
Judy Webber, Event Planner/Financial Officer
Finances: *Annual Operating Budget:* $250,000-$500,000; *Funding Sources:* Membership dues
Staff: 3 staff member(s); 20 volunteer(s)
Membership: 455 individual; *Member Profile:* Elected to municipal office
Activities: *Library:* Yes, open by appointment
Mission: To research, promote & represent provincial interests of local government; *Member of:* Federation of Canadian Municipalities

Union québécoise pour la conservation de la nature *Voir* Nature Québec

Union Saint Laurent/Grands Lacs *See* Great Lakes United

United Nations Association in Canada (UNAC) / Association canadienne pour les Nations-Unies (ACNU)
#300, 309 Cooper St., Ottawa ON K2P 0G5
Tel: 613-232-5751; *Fax:* 613-563-2455
e-mail: info@unac.org
URL: www.unac.org
Also Known As: UNA - Canada
Overview: A medium-sized international charitable organization founded in 1946
Finances: *Annual Operating Budget:* $500,000-$1.5 Million; *Funding Sources:* Individual donations; corporate support; government grants
Staff: 12 staff member(s); 200 volunteer(s)
Membership: 100 corporate + 12,000 individual; *Fees:* Suggested minimum of $25
Activities: Projects include: Healthy Children, Healthy Communities; Model United Nations; United Nations Professional Placement Programme; *Awareness Events:* UN Day, Oct. 24; Canadian International Model United Nations Conference; *Library:* Resource Centre; Open to public
Awards: Pearson Peace Medal (Award)
Awarded to a Canadian who has contibuted significantly to humanitarian causes
Mission: To study international problems & Canada's relationship to them as a member of the UN & its related agencies; to foster mutual understanding, goodwill & cooperation between the people of Canada & those of other countries, with the object of promoting peace & justice; to study possible courses of action in the field of international affairs; to work for support by the government & the people of Canada for desirable policies; to furnish information about & stimulate public interest in the UN & its various agencies which have been established for direct or indirect promotion of international order, justice & security; to foster national commitment to principles of multilateralism & international cooperation; *Affiliation(s):* World Federation of United Nations Associations

United Nations Conference on Trade & Development (UNCTAD) / Conférence des Nations Unies sur le commerce et le développement (CNUCED)
Palais des Nations, 8-14, av de la Paix, Geneva 10 1211 Switzerland
Tel: 41-22-917-5634; *Fax:* 41-22-917-0042
e-mail: info@unctad.org
URL: www.unctad.org
Overview: A large international organization founded in 1964
Finances: *Annual Operating Budget:* Greater than $5 Million
Staff: 394 staff member(s)
Membership: 192 countries; *Committees:* Trade in Goods & Services, & Commodities; Investment, Technology & Related Financial Issues; Enterprise, Business Facilitation & Development
Activities: Promotes & examines the participation of developing countries in international trade & investment; monitors the implementation of the UN Programme of Action for the Least Developed Countries (LDCs); analyzes trends in foreign direct investment & their impact on development; strengthens the service sector capacity in developing countries; promotes the integration of trade, environment & development; reduces commodity dependence through diversification & risk management; faciliates trade; *Internships:* Yes; *Speaker Service:* Yes; *Library:* Yes, Not open to the public
Mission: Fostering sustainable growth & development in developing countries & countries in transition through analytical & operational activities in the areas of trade & related development issues, such as finance, technology, investment, enterprise development, & environment

United Nations Development Program (UNDP)
One United Nations Plaza, New York NY 10017 USA
Tel: 212-906-5000; *Fax:* 212-906-5364
e-mail: webmaster@undp.org
URL: www.undp.org
Overview: A medium-sized international organization
Chief Officer(s):
Kemal Dervis, Administrator
William Orme, Chief, External Communications
Mission: To help the United Nations become a powerful & cohesive force for sustainable human development; to focus its own resources on a series of objectives central to sustainable human development: democratic governance, poverty reduction, crisis prevention & recovery, energy & environment, information & communications technology & HIV/AIDS: helps developing countries attract & use aid effectively; to promote the protection of human rights & the empowerment of women

United Nations Environment Programme (UNEP) / Programme des nations unies pour l'environnement
Regional Office for North America, #506, 900 - 17th St. NW, Washington DC 20006 USA
Tel: 202-785-0465; *Fax:* 202-785-2096
e-mail: info@rona.unep.org
URL: www.rona.unep.org
Overview: A large international organization founded in 1972
Chief Officer(s):
Amy Fraenkel, Regional Director
Robin Burgess, Finance/Administration
Finances: *Annual Operating Budget:* Greater than $5 Million; *Funding Sources:* UN member countries; private sector
Staff: 20 staff member(s)
Activities: Development of environmental law; collection & dissemination of environmental data; assistance to developing countries; *Awareness Events:* World Environment Day, June 5; *Internships:* Yes; *Speaker Service:* Yes
Mission: To provide leadership & encourage partnership in caring for the environment by inspiring, informing & enabling nations & peoples to improve their quality of life without compromising that of future generations; *Affiliation(s):* Canadian Committee for UNEP

United Nations Industrial Development Organization (UNIDO)
Vienna International Centre, PO Box 300, Vienna A-1400 Austria
Tel: 43-1-26026-0; *Fax:* 43-1-269-2669
e-mail: unido@unido.org
URL: www.unido.org
Overview: A large international organization founded in 1966
Finances: *Annual Operating Budget:* Greater than $5 Million; *Funding Sources:* Regular & operational budgets; special contributions for technical cooperation activities
Staff: 630 staff member(s)
Membership: 173 countries; *Fees:* Regular & operational budgets; Special contributions for technical cooperation activities; *Member Profile:* States ratifying the UNIDO Constitution; *Committees:* Governing Bodies: Director-General, Member States, General Conference, Industrial Development Board; Program & Budget Committee
Activities: Business Plan is to strengthen industrial capacities; cleaner & sustainable industrial development; focused on least developed countries, in particular Africa, on agro-based & industries & small & medium enterprises; *Awareness Events:* Africa Industrialization Day; *Internships:* Yes
Mission: Specialized agency that focuses its efforts on relieving poverty by fostering productivity growth; helps developing countries & countries in transition in their fight against marginalization in today's globalized world; mobilizes knowledge, skills, information & technology to promote productive employment, a competitive economy & a sound environment; *Member of:* a

Upper Thames River Conservation Authority
1424 Clarke Rd., London ON N5V 5B9
Tel: 519-451-2800; *Fax:* 519-451-1188
e-mail: infoline@thamesriver.on.ca
URL: www.thamesriver.on.ca
Previous Name: Upper Thames River Conservation Foundation
Overview: A small local organization founded in 1947
Chief Officer(s):
Ian Wilcox, General Manager
wilcoxi@thamesriver.on.ca
Mission: To establish and undertake, in the area in which it has jurisdiction, a program designed to further the conservation, restoration, development and management of natural resources other than gas, oil, coal and minerals

Upper Thames River Conservation Foundation *See* Upper Thames River Conservation Authority

The Uranium Institute *See* World Nuclear Association

Urban & Regional Information Systems Association (URISA)
#305, 1460 Renaissance Dr., Park Ridge IL 60068 USA
Tel: 847-824-6300; *Fax:* 847-824-6363
e-mail: info@urisa.org
URL: www.urisa.org
Overview: A small international organization founded in 1963
Chief Officer(s):
Wendy Nelson, Executive Director
Finances: *Annual Operating Budget:* $1.5 Million-$3 Million
Staff: 9 staff member(s)
Membership: 3,500; *Fees:* US$132; *Member Profile:* IT professionals in all levels of government
Mission: To support the effective application of information technology; to provide a means for the exchange of information among members & others; to develop members' skills & knowledge relating to information management technology & systems; provides ongoing educational programs about Geographic Information Systems (GIS) & automated information management within all levels of government & a wide cross-section of the private sector (GIS - computer based technology that captures, stores, analyzes & displays information about places on the earth's surface; more than 80 percent of all information used by local governments is geographically referenced; with GIS any location, any point on

Associations/Organizations / Urban Development Institute of Canada

the map can become an index to cultural, economic, environmental, demographic & political information about that location)

Urban Development Institute of Canada (UDI) / Institut de développement urbain du Canada
200-602 West Hastings St., Vancouver BC V6B 1P2
Tel: 604-669-9585; Fax: 604-689-8691
e-mail: info@udi.org
URL: www.udi.bc.ca
Overview: A large national organization
Chief Officer(s):
Maureen Enser, Executive Director
menser@udi.org
Jeff Fisher, Deputy Executive Director
jfisher@udi.org
Finances: Annual Operating Budget: $500,000-$1.5 Million; Funding Sources: Membership dues
Staff: 10 staff member(s)
Membership: 1,500 corporations; Fees: Schedule available
Activities: Speaker Service: Yes; Library: Yes, open by appointment
Mission: To promote wise, efficient & productive urban growth; to be an effective voice of the land development & property management industry at all levels of government; to serve as a forum for the exchange of knowledge, experience & research on land use planning & development

Urban Municipal Administrators' Association of Saskatchewan (UMAAS)
PO Box 603, Hudson Bay SK S0E 0Y0
Tel: 306-865-2825; Fax: 306-865-2800
e-mail: umaas@sasktel.net
URL: www.umaas.ca
Overview: A medium-sized provincial organization founded in 1974
Chief Officer(s):
Richard Dolezsar, Executive Director
Finances: Annual Operating Budget: Less than $50,000; Funding Sources: Membership; convention; donations
Membership: 350+; Fees: Schedule available; Member Profile: Local government administration certificate; employment in urban municipal government in Saskatchewan; Committees: Education; Discipline; Advisory; Administration; Convention

Urban Pest Management Council of Canada / Conseil canadien de la lutte antiparasitaire en milieu urbain
#627, 21 Four Seasons Pl., Toronto ON M9B 6J8
Tel: 416-622-9771; Fax: 416-622-6764
e-mail: fixterk@croplife.ca
URL: www.urbanpestmanagement.ca
Overview: A medium-sized national organization
Chief Officer(s):
Kristina Fixter, Contact
fixterk@croplife.ca
Mission: The Urban Pest Management Council of Canada represents the manufacturers, formulators, distributors and allied associations of specialty pest management products, for the consumer or professional markets used in turf, ornamental, pest management, forestry, aquatic, vegetation management and other non-food/fibre applications

U.S. Green Building Council
#300, 1800 Massachusetts Avenue NW, Washington DC 20036 USA
Tel: 202-742-3792; Fax: 202-828-5110
e-mail: info@usgbc.org
URL: www.usgbc.org
Overview: A medium-sized national organization
Chief Officer(s):
S. Richard Fedrizzi, President & CEO
Mike Opitz, Vice-President LEED
Rob Watson, Director
Membership: 15,000+; Fees: Schedule available; Committees: Executive; Finance; Governance
Activities: Promotes LEED, Leadership in Energy & Environmental Design, green building rating system, a voluntary consensus-based national standard for developing high-performance, sustainable buildings
Mission: To promote buildings that are environmentally responsible, profitable & healthy places to live & work

Uxbridge Conservation Association (UCA)
RR#3, Kirkfield ON K0M 2B0
Tel: 905-852-3044
Overview: A small local organization founded in 1987

Chief Officer(s):
Maureen Reilly, Researcher
Finances: Annual Operating Budget: Less than $50,000
Staff: 6 volunteer(s)
Fees: $10 student; $15 individual
Affiliation(s): Ontario Environment Network; Durham Environment Network

Valhalla Wilderness Society (VWS)
PO Box 329, New Denver BC V0G 1S0
Tel: 250-358-2333; Fax: 250-358-7950
e-mail: info@vws.org
URL: www.vws.org
Overview: A small local charitable organization founded in 1975
Chief Officer(s):
Colleen McCrory, Executive Director
colleenm@vws.org
Finances: Funding Sources: Foundations; donations; merchandise sales
Staff: 2 staff member(s); 8 volunteer(s)
Membership: 100-499; Fees: $10
Activities: Protection of forest wilderness
Affiliation(s): Taiga Rescue Network; Canada's Future Forest Alliance

The Van Horne Institute for International Transportation & Regulatory Affairs
#620 Earth Sciences Bldg., 2500 University Dr. NW, Calgary AB T2N 1N4
Tel: 403-220-8455; Fax: 403-282-4663
e-mail: vanhorne@ucalgary.ca
URL: www.vanhorne.info/
Overview: A small international organization founded in 1991
Chief Officer(s):
Peter C. Wallis, President & CEO
Sarah Ingram, Programs Manager
ingrams@ucalgary.ca
Carla Frede, Webmaster
Mel Belich, Chairman
Finances: Annual Operating Budget: Less than $50,000; Funding Sources: Private sector
Staff: 4 staff member(s)
Membership: 60; Member Profile: Government; industry; education; Committees: Centre for Transportation; Centre for Regulatory Affairs; Centre for Innovation & Communication
Activities: Transporation research & education; programs to assist in improving the efficiency & equity of transportation & regulated industries; Speaker Service: Yes; Rents Mailing List: Yes; Library: Yes, Open to public
Mission: To contribute to public policy development & education in the areas of transportation & regulated industries.
PUBLICATIONS: On-Trac.; Affiliation(s): University of Calgary; University of Alberta; Southern Alberta Institute of Technology

Vancouver Botanical Gardens Association See VanDusen Botanical Garden Association

Vancouver Electric Vehicle Association (VEVA)
PO Box 3456, 349 West Georgia St., Vancouver BC V6B 3Y4
Tel: 604-878-9500; Fax: 604-327-8246
e-mail: info@veva.bc.ca
URL: www.veva.bc.ca
Overview: A small local organization founded in 1987
Chief Officer(s):
Don Chandler, President
vevapres@veva.dhs.org
Robert Shaw, Vice-President
vevapolicy@veva.dhs.org
Fees: $25; $10 students
Mission: To promote the development of clean alternative transportation with a focus on electric vehicles

Vancouver Natural History Society See Nature Vancouver

Vancouver Regional Construction Association (VRCA)
3636 - 4th Ave. East, Vancouver BC V5M 1M3
Tel: 604-294-3766; Fax: 604-298-9472
e-mail: vrca@vrca.bc.ca
URL: www.vrca.bc.ca
Previous Name: Amalgamated Construction Association of British Columbia
Overview: A medium-sized provincial organization founded in 1965

Finances: Annual Operating Budget: $500,000-$1.5 Million; Funding Sources: Membership dues; sale of documents
Staff: 9 staff member(s); 50 volunteer(s)
Membership: 650 organizations; Fees: Schedule available; Committees: Membership; Arbitration; Education; Special Events; Awards; Life Member; Standard Practices
Activities: Library: Yes, Not open to the public
Awards: Safety Award (Award)
General Contractor Award (Award)
Trade Contractor Award (Award)
Mechanical Contractor Award (Award)
Electrical Contractor Award (Award)
Outstanding Woman in Construction Award (Award)
Mission: To promote construction investment & efficiency in the BC construction industry; to represent all sectors of the industry to government & the public; Member of: British Columbia Construction Association; Affiliation(s): Canadian Construction Association

VanDusen Botanical Garden Association (VBGA)
5251 Oak St., Vancouver BC V6M 4H1
Tel: 604-257-8666
e-mail: volunteer@vandusen.org
URL: www.vandusengarden.org
Previous Name: Vancouver Botanical Gardens Association
Overview: A small local charitable organization founded in 1965
Chief Officer(s):
Judy Aird, Volunteer Director
Finances: Annual Operating Budget: $500,000-$1.5 Million; Funding Sources: Membership fees; private donations; special events
Staff: 10 staff member(s); 1200 volunteer(s)
Membership: 9,000; Fees: $10-65; Committees: Buildings & Grounds; Education; Finance; Fundraising; Library; Marketing; Membership; Nominating; Volunteers; Diversity
Activities: Library: VanDusen Library
Mission: To support & promote VanDusen Gardens as an outstanding botanical garden; to act as a source & focus of excellence in botanical/horticultural plant conservation & education; to enhance & perpetuate the Garden as a place of beauty, pleasure & inspiration for all; Affiliation(s): American Association of Botanical Gardens & Arboretums

Vanscoy & District Agricultural Society
PO Box 35, Vanscoy SK S0L 3J0
Tel: 306-978-4481
Overview: A small local organization founded in 1983
Finances: Funding Sources: Saskatchewan lotteries; fundraising
Staff: 100 volunteer(s)
Membership: 200; Fees: $1
Activities: Rodeo; Taste of RM; Perennial Exchange; fair
Mission: To improve agriculture & the quality of life in the community by educating members & the community; to provide a community forum for discussion of agricultural issues; to encourage the conservation of natural resources; Member of: Saskatchewan Association of Agricultural Societies & Exhibitions

Vegetable & Potato Producers' Association of Nova Scotia See Horticulture Nova Scotia

Vegetable Growers' Association of Manitoba (VGAM)
PO Box 984, Portage la Prairie MB R1N 3C3
Tel: 204-428-3188; Fax: 204-428-3245
e-mail: vgam@escape.ca
Overview: A small provincial organization founded in 1953
Finances: Funding Sources: Membership fees
Activities: Providing information to assist members
Mission: To support Manitoba's vegetable growers; Member of: Canadian Horticultural Council

Vermilion Forks Field Naturalists
PO Box 1298, Princeton BC V0X 1W0
Tel: 250-295-7078
e-mail: corache@persona.ca
Overview: A small local organization
Chief Officer(s):
M. Scouten, Vice-President

Vermilion River Naturalist Club
6510 - 53 Ave., Vermilion AB T9K 1X7
Tel: 403-853-4914
URL: www.vermilioninfo.com/vrnc/
Overview: A small local organization
Chief Officer(s):

Stuart Heard, President
Fees: $15 family; $10 individual; $5 student
Member of: Federation of Alberta Naturalists

Victoria Lapidary & Mineral Society (VLMS)
c/o Burnside Bowling Club, PO Box 5114, Stn. B, 274 Hampton St., Victoria BC V8R 6N3
e-mail: vlms@islandnet.com
URL: www.islandnet.com/~vlms
Overview: A small local organization
Chief Officer(s):
Magdalene Magon, President
Irene Phillips, Vice-President
Sandy Burns, Treasurer
Finances: *Funding Sources:* Annual auction
Membership: 100; *Fees:* $20 individual; $30 couple; $35 family;
Member Profile: Individuals with an interest in rocks, crystals, minerals, lapidary arts, or earth sciences
Activities: Providing classes for members; Hosting monthly meetings with guest speakers at the Burnside Bowling Clubhouse; Planning field trips; *Library:* Victoria Lapidary & Mineral Society Library
Publications: *Victoria Lapidary & Mineral Society Newsletter*
Type: Newsletter *Editor:* Barbara Smith
Profile: Information for VLMS members
Affiliation(s): British Columbia Lapidary Society; Gem & Mineral Federation of Canada

Victoria Natural History Society
PO Box 5220, Stn. B, Victoria BC V8R 6N4
Tel: 250-479-2054
URL: www.vicnhs.bc.ca/
Overview: A small local organization founded in 1944
Finances: *Annual Operating Budget:* Less than $50,000; *Funding Sources:* Membership fees
Staff: 200 volunteer(s)
Membership: 750; *Fees:* $30 Regular; $35 Family
Activities: Christmas Bird Count; *Speaker Service:* Yes; *Library:* Yes, Open to public
Mission: To stimulate active interest in natural history; to study & protect flora & fauna & their habitats; *Member of:* Federation of BC Naturalists; *Affiliation(s):* Canadian Nature Federation

Victoria Orchid Society
1199 Tattersall Dr., Victoria BC V8P 1Y8
e-mail: nmiklic3@telus.net
URL: www.victoriaorchidsociety.ca
Overview: A small local organization
Chief Officer(s):
Don Miklic, President
Membership: 153; *Fees:* $15 single; $20 family

The Vinyl Institute (VI)
1300 Wilson Blvd., Arlington VA 22209 USA
Tel: 703-741-5670; *Fax:* 703-741-5672
Toll-Free: 800-969-8469
URL: www.vinylinfo.org
Overview: A small local organization founded in 1982
Chief Officer(s):
Tim Burns, President
Mission: Clearinghouse for information about vinyl's environmental performance

Voyageur Trail Association
PO Box 20040, 150 Churchill Blvd., Sault Ste Marie ON P6A 6W3
Tel: 705-253-5353; *Fax:* 705-779-1111
Toll-Free: 877-393-4003
e-mail: info@voyageurtrail.ca
URL: www.voyageurtrail.ca
Overview: A small local charitable organization founded in 1974
Finances: *Annual Operating Budget:* Less than $50,000; *Funding Sources:* Membership fees & donations
Staff: 200+ volunteer(s)
Membership: 200; *Fees:* $30 family; $25 adult; $10 student
Activities: Trail follows the clear waters of North Channel to the cold granite coast of Lake Superior (640 km completed; 470+ km planned)
Mission: The Voyageur Trail Association remains today as a trail building and maintenance organization to a trail building-and-hiking organization with several public outings held throughout the year in various clubs; *Member of:* Hike Ontario; *Affiliation(s):* National Trail; Trans Canada Trail

Vulcan & District Fish & Game Club
PO Box 301, Vulcan AB T0L 2B0

Tel: 403-485-6744
e-mail: pmatlock@agt.net
Overview: A small local organization
Member of: Alberta Fish & Game Association

The W. Garfield Weston Foundation
c/o George Weston Ltd., #2001, 22 St. Clair Ave. East, Toronto ON M4T 2S3
Tel: 416-922-2500; *Fax:* 416-967-7949
e-mail: info@westonfoundation.org
URL: www.westonfoundation.org
Overview: A medium-sized national organization
Chief Officer(s):
Susan Cohen, Executive Director
Mission: Focuses on education (through a scholarship & bursary program), conservation (via habitat conservation projects through national organizations only), & trustee-initiated grants (for which applications are not accepted)

Warmer Bulletin - Residua Ltd.
Yellow Cottage, Draughton, Skipton, North Yorkshire BD23 6EA United Kingdom
Tel: 44-0-1756-711-363; *Fax:* 44-0-1756-711-360
e-mail: info@resourcesnotwaste.org
URL: www.resourcesnotwaste.org
Previous Name: Warmer Campaign (World Action for Recycling Materials & Energy from Rubbish)
Overview: A medium-sized international charitable organization founded in 1984
Chief Officer(s):
Kit Strange, Director
Membership: 2,000; *Fees:* Depends on location & status
Activities: *Library:* Yes, Open to public, open by appointment
Mission: To collect & disseminate information on household waste, its minimization, reuse, recycling & energy from waste

Warmer Campaign (World Action for Recycling Materials & Energy from Rubbish) *See* Warmer Bulletin - Residua Ltd.

Waswanipi Cree Model Forest
3 Rte 113, Waswanipi QC J0Y 3C0
Tel: 819-753-2900; *Fax:* 819-753-2904
e-mail: pgull@waswanipi.com
Overview: A small local organization
Chief Officer(s):
Rhonda Oblin, General Manager
Member of: Canadian Model Forest Network

Water Environment Association of Ontario (WEAO)
PO Box 176, Milton ON L9T 4N9
Tel: 416-410-6933; *Fax:* 416-410-1626
e-mail: julie.vincent@weao.org
URL: www.weao.org
Previous Name: Pollution Control Association of Ontario
Overview: A medium-sized provincial organization founded in 1971
Finances: *Funding Sources:* Membership fees; Sponsorships
Member Profile: Technical & professional individuals committed to the preservation & enhancement of Ontario's water environment, such as scientists, operators, engineers, & students; Employees of consulting firms, industries, equipment manufacturers, municipalities, colleges & universities, & provincial & federal government agencies; *Committees:* Asset Management; Communications; Conference; Environmental, Health, Safety & Security; Government Affairs; New Professionals; Operations Challenge; Promotions & Events Planning; Public Education; Residuals & Biosolids; Water for People - Canada; Wastewater Collection Systems; Wastewater Treatment & Technology
Activities: Delivering services to members; Providing a forum for members to interact for educational & professional advancement; Increasing public understanding; Promoting careers in the water environment industry
Awards: Exemplary Biosolids Management Award (Award)
To recognize biosolides practitioners who go beyond the normal requirements in the practice of managing biosolids
Geoffrey T. G. Scott Memorial Award (Award)
To honour outstanding leadership & inspiration in the water environment industry
Golden Manhole Award (Award), Water Environment Association of Ontario Golden Manhole Selection
Contact: John Himanen, Committee Chair *Contact Detail:* E-mail: john.himanen@genivar.com
Meetings/Conferences:
For more information see Trade Shows, Conferences and Seminars Chapter

Water Environment Association of Ontario 2011 Specialty Seminar: Whole WWTP Modeling - Overview, Tools, & Future Needs
June 2011 Milton, ON
Canadian Biosolids & Residuals 2011 6th Joint Conference & The 34th Québec Symposium on Wastewater: Biosolids Beneficial Use Trends - Here & There
September 2011 Québec, QC
Water Environment Association of Ontario 2012 41st Annual Technical Symposium & OPCEA Exhibition: One World . . . One Water Environment
April 2012 Ottawa, ON
Water Environment Association of Ontario 2013 42nd Annual Technical Symposium & Exhibition
Other Conferences in 2013 2013, ON
Publications: *INFLUENTS [a publication of the Water Environment Association of Ontario]*
Type: Magazine *Frequency:* q. *Accepts Advertising:* Yes
Profile: Features on current issues, educational articles, project profiles, people in the news, committee reports, events, & marketplace developments
Mission: To advance the water environment industry. To promote sound public policy; *Member of:* Water Environment Federation (WEF); *Affiliation(s):* Canadian Water & Wastewater Association
Environmental Activity: Promoting the water environment industry; Participating in environmental policy discussions

Water Environment Federation (WEF)
601 Wythe St., Alexandria VA 22314-1994 USA
Tel: 703-684-2400; *Fax:* 703-684-2492
Toll-Free: 800-666-0206
e-mail: csc@wef.org
URL: www.wef.org
Social Media: www.facebook.com/group.php?gid=26453073562; www.twitter.com/#!/WEForg
Previous Name: Federation of Sewage Works Associations; Federation of Sewage & Industrial Wastes Associations; Water Pollution Control Federation
Overview: A large international organization founded in 1928
Chief Officer(s):
Jeff Eger, Executive Director
jeger@wef.org
Linda Kelly, Director, Communications
lkelly@wef.org
Membership: 36,000 individuals + 75 affiliated associations;
Member Profile: Water quality professionals from around the globe
Activities: Providing water quality information; Offering networking opportunities
Meetings/Conferences:
For more information see Trade Shows, Conferences and Seminars Chapter
Water Environment Federation 2011 Collection Systems Conference: Rehab or Roulette? Is our Environment at Risk?
June 2011 Raleigh, NC
Water Environment Federation 2011 Energy & Water Conference: Efficiency, Generation, Management, & Climate Impacts
July 2011 Chicago, IL
Water Environment Federation WEFTEC 2011: 84th Annual Water Environment Federation Technical Exhibition & Conference
October 2011 Los Angeles, CA
Water Environment Federation 2012 Utility Management Conference
January 2012 Miami, FL
Water Environment Federation 2012 Residuals & Biosolids Conference: Advancing Residuals Management - Technologies & Applications
March 2012 Raleigh, NC
Water Environment Federation WEFTEC 2012: 85th Annual Water Environment Federation Technical Exhibition & Conference
September 2012 New Orleans, LA
Water Environment Federation WEFTEC 2013: 86th Annual Water Environment Federation Technical Exhibition & Conference
October 2013 Chicago, IL
Water Environment Federation WEFTEC 2014: 87th Annual Water Environment Federation Technical Exhibition & Conference
October 2014 New Orleans, LA
Water Environment Federation WEFTEC 2015: 88th Annual Water Environment Federation Technical Exhibition &

Associations/Organizations / The Waterbird Society

Conference
September 2015 Chicago, IL
Water Environment Federation WEFTEC 2016: 89th Annual Water Environment Federation Technical Exhibition & Conference
Other Conferences in 2016 2016 New Orleans, LA
Water Environment Federation WEFTEC 2017: 90th Annual Water Environment Federation Technical Exhibition & Conference
Other Conferences in 2017 2017
Publications: *Biosolids Technical Bulletin [a publication of the Water Environment Federation]*
Type: Newsletter *Editor:* Cathy Vidito (cvidito@wef.org)
Profile: For persons interested in residuals & biosolids management
Industrial Wastewater [a publication of the Water Environment Federation]
Type: Newsletter *Editor:* LaShell Stratton
Profile: A technical bulletin for persons who manage company wastes
Utility Executive [a publication of the Water Environment Federation]
Type: Newsletter *Editor:* LaShell Stratton
Profile: Issues of interest to executives & managers of water & wastewater treatment plants
Water Environment Research [a publication of the Water Environment Federation]
Type: Journal *Frequency:* m. *Editor:* Anthony Krizel (akrizel@wef.org) *Price:* $100 (print only) with Water Environment Federation membership
Profile: Peer-reviewed research papers related to pollution control, water quality, & management
Water Environment Laboratory Solutions [a publication of the Water Environment Federation]
Type: Newsletter *Editor:* Steve Spicer (sspicer@wef.org)
Profile: Contents include equipment use, sample tracking, quality control, analytical methods, & certification
Water Environment & Technology [a publication of the Water Environment Federation]
Type: Magazine *Accepts Advertising* : Yes *Editor:* Melissa Jackson
Profile: Information for water professionals such as regulatory & legislative impacts, technologies, solutions, & professional development activities
Water Practice [a publication of the Water Environment Federation]
Editor: Melissa Jackson (mjackson@wef.org)
WEF [Water Environment Federation] Highlights
Type: Newsletter *Editor:* Jennifer Fulcher (jfulcher&wef.org)
Profile: Water Environment Federation activities & information for members
World Water
Type: Magazine
Profile: An international magazine focussing on water issues, such as groundwater, wastewater, sludge, desalination, & treatment
Water Environment Regulation Watch
Type: Newsletter *Frequency:* m.
Profile: Reports of federal government actions related to water quality
Mission: To ensure clean water for the protection of public health; To advance the water profession
Environmental Activity: Working for a sustainable water environment

The Waterbird Society
c/o ONSA, #680, 5400 Bosque Blvd., Waco TX 76710-4446 USA
URL: www.waterbirds.org
Previous Name: Colonial Waterbird Society
Overview: A small international organization founded in 1976
Finances: *Funding Sources:* Membership dues
Fees: $40 students; $50 regular members; $55 families; $900 lifetimes members (Fees include copies of the paper journal); *Member Profile:* Persons interested in studying & monitoring aquatic birds; *Committees:* Archives; Membership; Nominations; Bylaws; International Awards; Finance & Investment; Resolutions; Student Awards; Research Grants; Distinguished Service Awards; Scientific Program; Conservation; Publications; Future Meetings
Activities: Facilitating communication among persons who study waterbirds
Publications: *Waterbirds*
Type: Journal *Frequency:* 3 pa *Editor:* Dr. Robert W. Elner
Profile: Papers about biology, conservation, & techniques for study of the world's waterbirds, such as wading birds, seabirds, waterfowl, & shorebirds
Mission: To study & conserve all aquatic birds; *Affiliation(s):* Ornithological Council; American Bird Conservancy
Environmental Activity: Protecting waterbird habitats; Contributing to the management of stressed populations of aquatic birds

WaterCan / Eau Vive
321 Chapel St., Ottawa ON K1N 7Z2
Tel: 613-230-5182; *Fax:* 613-230-0712
Toll-Free: 800-370-5658
e-mail: info@watercan.com
URL: www.watercan.com
Overview: A small international charitable organization founded in 1987
Finances: *Annual Operating Budget:* $500,000-$1.5 Million; *Funding Sources:* Direct mail; special events; corporate donations; private donations; government grants; foundations
Staff: 7 staff member(s); 200 volunteer(s)
Membership: 1-99
Activities: Partnerships with local/indigenous organizations; technical training; knowledge networks in the international water & sanitation sector; education activities to raise awareness on the health & development benefits of clean water in the developing world; *Awareness Events:* World Water Day, March 22; *Library:* Yes, Open to public, open by appointment
Mission: To support integrated water supply, sanitation, & hygiene promotion projects that assist rural communities & the urban poor in Africa; *Member of:* Canadian Water Resources Association; Canadian Water & Wastewater Association

Waterloo Regional Heritage Foundation (WRHF)
Regional Admin. Building, 150 Frederick St., 2nd Fl., Kitchener ON N2J 4J3
Tel: 519-575-4493; *Fax:* 519-575-4481
e-mail: gmike@region.waterloo.on.ca
URL: www.wrhf.org
Overview: A small local organization founded in 1973
Chief Officer(s):
Sandy Rung, Chair
Finances: *Annual Operating Budget:* $100,000-$250,000; *Funding Sources:* Regional Municipality of Waterloo
Staff: 2 staff member(s)
Membership: 18; *Committees:* Allocations & Finance; Awards; Communications
Activities: *Awareness Events:* Heritage Day
Awards: Regional Award for Heritage Research (Scholarship) For M.A. or Ph.D. student, resident of, or registered at a university in, the Waterloo region
Mission: To act as funding & support umbrella for organizations throughout the Region of Waterloo to preserve its heritage; *Member of:* Heritage Canada

Waterton Natural History Association (WNHA)
PO Box 145, Waterton Park AB T0K 2M0
Tel: 403-859-2624; *Fax:* 403-859-2624
e-mail: wnha@telusplanet.net
URL: www.wnha.ca
Overview: A small local charitable organization founded in 1983
Finances: *Annual Operating Budget:* $50,000-$100,000; *Funding Sources:* Fund-raising
Staff: 1 staff member(s); 20 volunteer(s)
Membership: 395; *Fees:* $20 individual lifetime; $25 family lifetime
Activities: Museum upgrade; *Awareness Events:* Heritage Ball, Sept.
Mission: To further the understanding & appropriate use of Waterton Lakes National Park; to provide & publish materials relevant to Waterton/Glacier International Peace Park; *Member of:* Canadian Parks Partnership; Alberta Museums Association; Alberta Historical Society; Canadian Booksellers Association

Weed Science Society of America (WSSA)
PO Box 7050, Lawrence KS 66044-8897 USA
Fax: 785-843-1274
Toll-Free: 800-627-0629
e-mail: wssa@allenpress.com
URL: www.wssa.net
Overview: A small national organization
Chief Officer(s):
Joyce Lancaster, Executive Secretary
Mission: To protect the environment through the use of safe & efficient weed control practices; to facilitate the exchange of information about weeds & their control; to enhance professionalism among scientists in teaching, extension & research

West Coast Environmental Law Research Foundation (WCEL)
200 - 2006 West 10th Ave., Vancouver BC V6J 2B3
Tel: 604-684-7378; *Fax:* 604-684-1312
Toll-Free: 800-330-9235
e-mail: admin@wcel.org
URL: www.wcel.org
Overview: A medium-sized local charitable organization founded in 1974
Chief Officer(s):
Patricia Chew, Executive Director
patricia_chew@wcel.org
Finances: *Funding Sources:* Core funding from the Law Foundation of BC; programmatic funding from foundation grants
Staff: 10 staff member(s)
Fees: $20; *Committees:* Board of Directors; Environmental Dispute Resolution Fund Management Committee
Activities: *Internships:* Yes; *Library:* Yes, Open to public
Awards: Dr. Andrew Thompson Award (Award)
Mission: To provide summary legal advice to anyone in British Columbia with environmental concerns; to protect & enhance the environment of British Columbia; to foster public participation in environmental decision making; to provide legal aid for citizens with environmental concerns; to undertake law review & law reform projects, legal research & education, community legal outreach; & to operate an archival & on-line law library; *Member of:* BC Environmental Network; *Affiliation(s):* West Coast Environmental Law Association; Law Foundation of British Columbia; Environmental Dispute Resolution Fund

West Elgin Nature Club
PO Box 7, West Lorne ON N0L 2P0
URL: www.naturallyelgin.org
Overview: A small local organization
Chief Officer(s):
Joan Neil, Contact
Fees: $6 individual; $10 family
Member of: Federation of Ontario Naturalists

West Kootenay Naturalists Association
1054 Bridgeview Cres., Castlegar BC V1N 4L1
Tel: 250-304-6840
e-mail: bhancock@shaw.ca
URL: www.columbiariver.ca/wkna
Overview: A small local organization founded in 1973
Finances: *Annual Operating Budget:* Less than $50,000; *Funding Sources:* Donations; membership fees
Membership: 65; *Fees:* $27 single; $42 family; *Committees:* Program; Banquet; Website; Area Reps; Water Use Planning; Conservation; Nominating; Bird Count
Activities: Botany & ornithology hikes; scenic hikes, skiing/snow shoeing; trail maintenance; bird counts; Violin Lake Conservation Project; educational presentations; Waldie Island Heron Project; *Awareness Events:* Rivers Day; National Wildlife Week; Mel DeAnna Trail Cleanup; Parks Day
Awards: Selkirk College Foundation Bursary (Scholarship)
Mission: To promote the enjoyment of nature through environmental appreciation & conservation; to encourage wise use & conservation of natural resources & environmental protection.; *Member of:* Federation of BC Naturalists; *Affiliation(s):* Creston Valley Wildlife Management Area

Western Canada Tire Dealers Association (WCTD)
948 Jim Common Dr. North, Sherwood Park AB T8H 1Y3
Tel: 780-449-1130; *Fax:* 780-449-1284
e-mail: wctd2@telus.net
URL: www.wctd.ca
Overview: A medium-sized local organization founded in 1962
Chief Officer(s):
Paul Newton, President, 306-244-9512, Fax: 306-244-9516
Paul_Newton@SWTire.com
Matt Matlock, Executive Director, 780-449-1130, Fax: 780-449-1284
wctd2@telus.net
Membership: 950+; *Fees:* $100; *Member Profile:* Independent tire dealers & retreaders from the Yukon, Northwest Territories, British Columbia, Alberta, Saskatchewan, Manitoba, & western Ontario; Manufacturers; Distributors; Exporters; Dealer support services
Activities: Maintaining standards of excellence for tire dealers; Providing a forum for members to discuss issues within the industry; Assisting members to develop beneficial business plans; Representing members on scrap tire boards across western Canada; Offering the Tire Certification Training Program to train employees, plus seminars on various subjects

Associations/Organizations / Western Canada Water

Awards: Western Canada Tire Dealers Academic Scholarship (Scholarship)
Award Amount: 5 scholarships of $2,000 each *Contact:* Dan Harper, Chair, WCTD Scholarship Committee *Contact Detail: Address:* 948 Jim Common Dr. North, Sherwood Park, AB, T8H 1Y3
WCTD Hall of Fame (Award)
To recognize individuals who have made outstanding contributions for the betterment of the industry
Publications: Tracker
Type: Newsletter *Frequency:* 5 pa *Accepts Advertising*: Yes
Profile: Informative stories, guest editorials from industry leaders, & special reports on issues, for small to medium-sized enterprises throughout western Canada
Mission: To establish standards of excellence for members; To promote a professional image in the industry; To act as a unified voice in dealings with government agencies & equipment distributors; To inform members of advancements in products & services

Western Canada Water (WCWWA)
PO Box 1708, 126 - 3rd Ave. West, Cochrane AB T4C 1B6
Tel: 403-709-0064; *Fax:* 403-709-0068
Toll-Free: 877-283-2003
e-mail: member@wcwwa.ca
URL: www.wcwwa.ca
Overview: A medium-sized regional organization founded in 1948
Chief Officer(s):
Audrey Arisman, Executive Director, 403-709-0064, Fax: 403-709-0068
aarisman@wcwwa.ca
Membership: 4,000; *Committees:* Alberta Provincial Council; Saskatchewan Provincial Council; Manitoba Provincial Council; Joint Operators; Conference Planning; Editorial
Activities: Offering education & training
Meetings/Conferences:
For more information see Trade Shows, Conferences and Seminars Chapter
Western Canada Water 2011 Young Professionals Networking Event
June 2011 Edmonton, AB
Western Canada Water 2011 63rd Annual Conference & Exhibition: Cycles - Challenges & Opportunities
September 2011 Saskatoon, SK
Western Canada Water 2012 64th Annual Conference & Exhibition
Winnipeg 2012 Winnipeg, MB
Western Canada Water 2013 65th Annual Conference & Exhibition
September 2013 Edmonton, AB
Western Canada Water 2014 66th Annual Conference & Exhibition
September 2014 Regina, SK
Western Canada Water 2015 67th Annual Conference & Exhibition
September 2015 Winnipeg, MB
Western Canada Water 2016 68th Annual Conference & Exhibition
Other Conferences in 2016 2016 Calgary, AB
Western Canada Water 2017 69th Annual Conference & Exhibition
Other Conferences in 2017 2017
Publications: Western Canada Water Member Newsletter
Type: Newsletter
Profile: Membership information & news about forthcoming events
Western Canada Water
Type: Magazine *Frequency:* q. *Accepts Advertising*: Yes *Editor:* Terry Ross (terry@kelman.ca) *ISSN:* 1483-7730 *Price:* Free with Western Canada Water membership
Profile: Theme issues, plus regular departments such as the president's message, the calendar of events, going green, news from the field, the minister's forum, & a new product showcase
Mission: To advance support for water professionals throughout western Canada; *Affiliation(s):* Alberta Water & Wastewater Operator Association (AWWOA); Manitoba Water & Wastewater Association (MWWA); Municipal Service & Suppliers Association (MSSA); Northern Territories Water & Waste Association (NTWWA); Saskatchewan Water & Wastewater Association (SWWA); Western Canada Water Environment Association (WCWEA)
Environmental Activity: Providing water conservation strategies

Western Canada Wilderness Committee (WCWC)
227 Abbott St., Vancouver BC V6B 2K7
Tel: 604-683-8220; *Fax:* 604-683-8229
Toll-Free: 800-661-9453
e-mail: info@wildernesscommittee.org
URL: www.wildernesscommittee.org
Also Known As: Wilderness Committee
Overview: A large international charitable organization founded in 1980
Finances: *Annual Operating Budget:* $1.5 Million-$3 Million; *Funding Sources:* Donations; membership dues; merchandise sales; grants
Staff: 22 staff member(s); 300 volunteer(s)
Membership: 26,000; *Fees:* $30
Activities: Research; education; slide shows; events; trailbuilding; speaking tours; conferences; media relations; *Speaker Service:* Yes; *Library:* Yes, open by appointment
Mission: To work for the protection of Canadian & the Earth's wilderness through research & education; to promote the principles which achieve ecologically sustainable communities

Western Canadian Shippers' Coalition (WCSC)
31 Centennial Pkwy., Delta BC V4L 2C3
Tel: 604-943-8984; *Fax:* 604-943-8936
Overview: A medium-sized provincial organization
Member Profile: Companies & associations involved in the transportation industry in western Canada

Western Employers Labour Relations Association
#203, 27126 Fraser Hwy., Langley BC V4W 3P6
Tel: 604-857-5540; *Fax:* 604-857-5547
e-mail: westernemployers@welra.com
URL: www.welra.com
Previous Name: Metal Industries Association
Overview: A medium-sized local organization

Western Fertilizer & Chemical Dealers Association See Canadian Association of Agri-Retailers

Western Newfoundland Model Forest See Model Forest of Newfoundland and Labrador

Western Red Cedar Lumber Association (WRCLA)
Pender Place 1, #1501, 700 West Pender St., Vancouver BC V6C 1G8
Tel: 604-684-0266; *Fax:* 604-687-4930
Toll-Free: 866-778-9096
e-mail: wrcla@wrcla.org
URL: www.wrcla.org
Overview: A small local organization founded in 1954
Chief Officer(s):
Peter Lang, General Manager
Membership: 22; *Fees:* Based on shipments; *Member Profile:* Producers of Western Red cedar
Mission: Trade association representing quality producers of Western Red Cedar lumber products in BC & the Pacific Northwest states; members are dedicated to producing quality siding, decking, paneling, outdoor & other specialty cedar products

Western Retail Lumber Association (WRLA)
Western Retail Lumber Association Inc., #1004, 213 Notre Dame Ave., Winnipeg MB R3B 1N3
Tel: 204-957-1077; *Fax:* 204-947-5195
Toll-Free: 800-661-0253
e-mail: wrla@wrla.org
URL: www.wrla.org
Overview: A medium-sized local organization founded in 1890
Fees: Schedule available
Meetings/Conferences:
For more information see Trade Shows, Conferences and Seminars Chapter
Western Retail Lumber Association 2012 Prairie Showcase Buying Show & Convention
January 2012 Saskatoon, SK
Western Retail Lumber Association 2014 Prairie Showcase Buying Show & Convention
January 2014 Saskatoon, SK
Publications: The YardStick [a publication of the Western Retail Lumber Association]
Type: Magazine *Frequency:* 6 pa
Mission: To serve & promote needs & common interests of lumber, building materials & hard goods industry on the Prairies

Western Silvicultural Contractors' Association (WSCA)
#720, 999 West Broadway, Vancouver BC V5Z 1K5
Tel: 604-736-8660; *Fax:* 604-738-4080
e-mail: info@wsca.ca
URL: www.wsca.ca
Overview: A medium-sized local organization founded in 1980
Finances: *Annual Operating Budget:* $50,000-$100,000
Staff: 2 staff member(s); 15 volunteer(s)
Membership: 75; *Fees:* Schedule available; *Member Profile:* Silvicultural contractors
Mission: Dedicated to improving working conditions, quality of life and safety for all silviculture workers.

Western Transportation Advisory Council (WESTAC)
#1140, 800 Pender St. West, Vancouver BC V6C 2V6
Tel: 604-687-8691; *Fax:* 604-687-8751
e-mail: infoservices@westac.com
URL: www.westac.com
Overview: A small local organization founded in 1973
Chief Officer(s):
Lisa Baratta, Director, Strategy
Ruth Sol, President
Marcella Szel, Chairman (Executive Committee)
Lois Jackson, Chairman of the Board
Finances: *Annual Operating Budget:* $500,000-$1.5 Million; *Funding Sources:* Membership fees; project fees; professional services fees
Staff: 4 staff member(s)
Membership: 52 corporate; *Fees:* Revenue-related scale; *Member Profile:* Carriers; shippers; ports & terminals; labour unions; government
Activities: *Library:* Yes, open by appointment
Mission: To advance Western Canadian economy through the improvement of the region's transportation system.

Weyburn Agricultural Society
PO Box 699, Weyburn SK S4H 2K8
Tel: 306-842-4052; *Fax:* 306-842-1469
e-mail: agsociety@accesscomm.ca
URL: www.weyburnagsociety.com
Overview: A small local charitable organization founded in 1908
Finances: *Annual Operating Budget:* $50,000-$100,000
Staff: 1 staff member(s); 250 volunteer(s)
Membership: 36 senior/lifetime; 120 individual; *Fees:* Schedule available; *Member Profile:* Interest in agriculture; *Committees:* Attractions; Commercial; Hospitality; Gates; Horse; Cattle; 4H Youth; 4H Calf; Publicity
Activities: *Awareness Events:* Weyburn Agricultural Society Fair, July; Weyburn Rodeo, Aug.; *Library:* Yes, Open to public
Mission: To promote agriculture; to act as a liaison between the rural & urban population; to promote education on agriculture-related subjects; *Member of:* Saskatchewan Association of Agricultural Societies & Exhibitions; *Affiliation(s):* Western Canada Fairs; Canadian Association of Exhibitions

Weyburn Wildlife Federation
415 - 3 Ave. NW, Weyburn SK S4H 1R2
Tel: 306-842-7658
Overview: A small local organization
Member of: Saskatchewan Wildlife Federation

Whitchurch-Stouffville Recycling Group
377 Elm Rd., Stouffville ON L4A 8A3
e-mail: recycling.group@sympatico.ca
Overview: A small local organization
Mission: Runs an exchange for those who have items they wish to give away

Whitecourt Fish & Game Association
PO Box 3, Whitecourt AB T7S 1N3
Tel: 780-778-3044; *Fax:* 780-706-3999
e-mail: btrigg@telusplanet.net
URL: www.wfga.ca
Overview: A small local licensing charitable organization
Finances: *Annual Operating Budget:* Less than $50,000
Membership: 100; *Fees:* $25 regular; $15 associate; $35 family; $25 range passes
Activities: Archery & gun ranges; hunter education; 3D archery shoots; birdhouse building
Member of: Alberta Fish & Game Association; *Affiliation(s):* Alberta Bow Hunting Association

Whole Village
20725 Shaws Creek Rd., Caledon ON L7K 1L7

Associations/Organizations / Wild Bird Care Centre

Tel: 519-941-1099
e-mail: info@wholevillage.org
URL: www.wholevillage.org
Overview: A small local organization founded in 1996
Finances: Annual Operating Budget: $100,000-$250,000; Funding Sources: Membership fees; member loans; grants
Staff: 55 volunteer(s)
Membership: 25; Fees: $10/month or $120/year; Committees: Legal/Financial; Communications; Education; Farm; Community Dynamics
Activities: Sustainable agriculture; green construction; community development; Internships: Yes; Speaker Service: Yes
Mission: To create an example of sustainable living; Member of: Ecovillage Network of Canada; Canadian Cohousing Network; Canadian Organic Growers; Affiliation(s): National Farmers Union; Ecological Farm Association of Ontario

Wild Bird Care Centre (WBCC)
PO Box 11159, Nepean ON K2H 7T9
Tel: 613-828-2849
e-mail: mojo@wildbirdcarecentre.org
URL: www.wildbirdcarecentre.org
Overview: A medium-sized national organization founded in 1981
Chief Officer(s):
Kathy Nihei, Founder
Fees: $25 single; $40 family; $15 student/senior; $50 school; $100 business; $1000+ corporate/patron
Mission: To assess, treat, and rehabilitate sick, orphaned, or injured wild birds before releasing them back to the wild.

Wild Rose Agricultural Producers
#102, 115 Portage Close, Sherwood Park AB T8H 2R5
Tel: 780-416-6530; Fax: 780-416-6531
Toll-Free: 888-616-6530
e-mail: info@wrap.ab.ca
URL: www.wrap.ab.ca
Previous Name: Unifarm
Overview: A medium-sized provincial organization founded in 1996
Finances: Annual Operating Budget: $100,000-$250,000
Membership: 1,000 individuals; Fees: $140 producer; $65 associate
Mission: To represent its members at the regional, provincial & national level for the benefit of agriculture; to create an atmosphere of cooperation & communication to ensure that areas of common concern among all producers are dealt with to the benefit of agriculture as a whole

Wilderness Canoe Association (WCA)
PO Box 91068, 2901 Bayview Ave., Toronto ON M2K 2Y6
Tel: 416-223-4646
e-mail: info@wildernesscanoe.ca
URL: www.wildernesscanoe.ca
Overview: A small local organization founded in 1973
Chief Officer(s):
Aleks Gusev, Chair
chair@wildernesscanoe.ca
Finances: Annual Operating Budget: Less than $50,000
Membership: 750; Fees: $35 single; $45 family
Activities: Awareness Events: Wine & Cheese, Nov.; Outdoor Adventure Show, Feb.
Mission: Organization of individuals interested in wilderness travel, mainly by canoe, kayak, and backpacking and, in winter, by skis and snowshoes; Member of: Federation of Ontario Naturalists

Wilderness Tourism Association (WTA)
PO Box 2160, Campbell River BC V9W 5C5
Tel: 250-286-4080; Fax: 250-286-6010
e-mail: admin@wilderness-tourism.bc.ca
URL: www.wilderness-tourism.bc.ca
Overview: A small local organization founded in 1999
Chief Officer(s):
Brian Gunn, President
Geoff Straight, Vice-President
Finances: Funding Sources: Membership fees; donations
Staff: 7 volunteer(s)
Membership: 103; Fees: Schedule available; Member Profile: Wilderness tourism operator
Mission: To protect a land base for the wilderness tourism industry

Wildlife Foundation of Manitoba; Fort Whyte Centre for Environmental Education See FortWhyte Alive

Wildlife Habitat Canada (WHC) / Habitat faunique Canada (HFC)
#310, 1740 Courtwood Cres., Ottawa ON K2C 2B5
Tel: 613-722-2090; Fax: 613-722-3318
Toll-Free: 800-669-7919
e-mail: reception@whc.org
URL: www.whc.org
Social Media: www.facebook.com/pages/Wildlife-Habitat-Canada/124492716000
Overview: A medium-sized national organization founded in 1984
Finances: Annual Operating Budget: $3 Million-$5 Million; Funding Sources: Canadian Wildlife Habitat Conservation Stamp; donations
Staff: 10 staff member(s)
Activities: Awareness Events: National Wildlife Week; Rents Mailing List: Yes
Mission: To promote the conservation, restoration & enhancement of wildlife habitat to retain diversity, distribution & abundance of wildlife; to provide a funding mechanism for the conservation, restoration & enhancement of wildlife habitat in Canada; to foster coordination & leadership in the conservation, restoration & enhancement of wildlife habitat in Canada

Wildlife Haven Rehabilitation Centre
PO Box 49, Glenlea MB R0G 0S0
Tel: 204-883-2122; Fax: 204-883-2582
e-mail: mwrocent@skyweb.ca
URL: www.mwro.mb.ca
Previous Name: Manitoba Wildlife Rehabilitation Organization
Overview: A small provincial charitable organization founded in 1984
Finances: Annual Operating Budget: $50,000-$100,000
Staff: 3 staff member(s); 40 volunteer(s)
Membership: 550; Fees: $50 family; $30 individual; Member Profile: Individuals with an appreciation for wildlife & nature; all ages; Committees: Education; Fundraising; Relocation
Activities: Education; rehabilitation; Internships: Yes; Speaker Service: Yes
Mission: To maintain & preserve the province's wildlife; to receive & professionally handle injured & orphaned native wildlife; to promote public education in wildlife conservation & appreciation; to establish & maintain a Wildlife Rehabilitation Centre; to stimulate & conduct applied noninvasive research; to record data & preserve materials pertaining to rehabilitation & captive breeding of endangered species; Member of: International Wildlife Rehabilitation Council

Wildlife Preservation Canada (WPC) / Conservation de la faune au Canada
RR#5, 5420 Hwy. 6 North, Guelph ON N1H 6J2
Tel: 519-836-9314; Fax: 519-836-8840
Toll-Free: 800-956-6608
e-mail: admin@wildlifepreservation.ca
URL: www.wildlifepreservation.ca
Social Media: www.facebook.com/group.php?gid=141989432535249
Previous Name: Wildlife Preservation Trust Canada
Overview: A medium-sized national charitable organization founded in 1985
Chief Officer(s):
Elaine Williams, Executive Director
H. Alec B. Monro, President
Jessica Steiner, Recovery Biologist
Ellen Reinhart, Contact, Member & Donor Relations
Activities: Providing training & outreach programs; Administering conservation grants
Meetings/Conferences:
For more information see Trade Shows, Conferences and Seminars Chapter
Wildlife Preservation Canada Stories from the Field
June 2011 Guelph, ON
Publications: On the Edge [a publication of Wildlife Preservation Canada]
Type: Newsletter Frequency: 3 pa
Profile: Information about recovery & conservation efforts of Wildlife Preservation Canada
Home on the Range [a publication of Wildlife Preservation Canada]
Type: Newsletter
Profile: Updates on the Eastern Loggerhead Shrike recovery program
Wildlife Preservation Canada Annual Report
Type: Yearbook Frequency: a.
Profile: Financial highlights & donation information
Mission: To save endangered animal species from extinction in Canada & internationally
Environmental Activity: Engaging in focused species conservation, such as the Burrowing Owl, the Eastern Loggerhead Shrike, the Spiny Softshell Turtle, the Swift Fox, & the Vancouver Island Marmot in Canada; Partnering with other conservation organizations

Wildlife Preservation Trust Canada See Wildlife Preservation Canada

Wildlife Rescue Association of British Columbia (WRA)
5216 Glencarin Dr., Burnaby BC V5B 3C1
Tel: 604-526-2747; Fax: 604-524-2890Crisis Hot-Line: 604-526-7275
e-mail: info@wildliferescue.ca
URL: www.wildliferescue.ca
Social Media: www.facebook.com/group.php?gid=335147280556
Previous Name: Lower Mainland Wildlife Rescue Association
Overview: A medium-sized provincial charitable organization founded in 1979
Chief Officer(s):
Glenn J. Boyle, PhD, Executive Director
glenn@wildliferescue.ca
Sheila Gardiner, BSc, RVT, Administrator
sheila@wildliferescue.ca
Linda Bakker, MA, Coordinator, Volunteers
linda@wildliferescue.ca
Krystal Brennan, Coordinator, Education
krystal@wildliferescue.ca
Yolanda Brooks, Coordinator, Communications
yolanda@wildliferescue.ca
Lani Sheldon, BSc, Team Leader, Wildlife Rehabilitation
lani@wildliferescue.ca
Crystal Simmons, Liaison, Care Centre
crystal@wildliferescue.ca
Fees: $15 students & seniors; $25 individuals; $35 families; $250 businesses & life memberships
Activities: Providing education & outreach services
Meetings/Conferences:
For more information see Trade Shows, Conferences and Seminars Chapter
Wildlife Rescue Association of British Columbia 2011 Annual General Meeting
June 2011 Burnaby, BC
Publications: To the Rescue [a publication of the Wildlife Rescue Association of British Columbia]
Type: Newsletter Frequency: 3 pa Accepts Advertising : Yes
Editor: Yolanda Brooks
Profile: Educational information, success stories, care centre news, forthcoming events, donation information, campaigns, & a volunteer update from the association
Mission: To rehabilitate wildlife; To promote the welfare of wild animals in the urban environment
Environmental Activity: Caring for injured, orphaned, & pollution-damaged wild animals; Creating a wildlife habitat garden

Williams Lake Field Naturalists
1305A Borland Rd., Williams Lake BC V2G 5K5
Tel: 250-392-7680
Overview: A small local charitable organization
Fees: $22 individual; $27 family
Activities: Library: Yes, Open to public
Mission: To promote the enjoyment of nature through environmental appreciation, education & conservation; to encourage wise use & conservation of natural resources & environmental protection; to administer the Scout Island Nature Centre in Williams Lake; Member of: Federation of BC Naturalists

Willow Beach Field Naturalists (WBFN)
PO Box 421, Port Hope ON L1A 3W4
Tel: 905-372-7407
e-mail: mbiggar.wbfn@gmail.com
Overview: A small local charitable organization founded in 1953
Chief Officer(s):
Michael Biggar, President
mbiggar.wbfn@gmail.com
Finances: Annual Operating Budget: Less than $50,000; Funding Sources: Membership fees; donations
Membership: 200; Fees: $20; Member Profile: Interest in all aspects of nature & conservation

Activities: Monthly meetings; outings; bird counts; breeding bird atlas
Mission: Protection & enhancement of the natural heritage of Northumberland County & surrounding areas; to develop knowledge of our natural heritage; to record & share this knowledge; to encourage the preservation, renewal & enhancement of our natural heritage; *Member of:* Ontario Nature

Windfall Ecology Centre
93A Industrial Parkway S., Aurora ON L4G 3V5
Toll-Free: 866-280-4431
e-mail: info@windfallcentre.ca
URL: www.windfallcentre.ca
Overview: A medium-sized provincial organization founded in 1998
Activities: Programs for youth; First Nations joint projects; Well Aware and other water protection programs; Safe Routes to School, and ecoDriver; projects in wind energy, solar energy, and geothermal energy; Windfall Home Energy Assessment program; *Awareness Events:* Windfall Ecology Festival, June; Annual Trash Fashion Show; *Internships:* Yes
Mission: Windfall Ecology Centre is a community-based, non-profit organization dedicated to education and advocacy in the areas of energy conservation, renewable energy production, water protection and leadership development.; *Member of:* Canadian Renewable Energy Alliance; Green Communities Canada; Ontario Sustainable Energy Association; Climate Action Network; Ontario Environment Network; *Affiliation(s):* David Suzuki Foundation; Halton Recycling; Katimavik; Kortright Centre for Conservation; Lake Simcoe and Region Conservation Authority

The Women & Environments Education & Development Foundation *See* Women's Healthy Environments Network

Women's Environment & Development Organization (WEDO)
355 Lexington Ave., 3rd Fl., New York NY 10017 USA
Tel: 212-973-0325; *Fax:* 212-973-0335
e-mail: wedo@wedo.org
URL: www.wedo.org
Overview: A medium-sized international organization founded in 1989
Chief Officer(s):
June Zeitlin, Executive Director
Activities: Monitor Implementation (focuses on specific recommendations for women); Outreach & Leadership (to help women become policy makers as well as policy monitors); Education & Communications; *Internships:* Yes
Mission: To empower women to be equal & active decision makers in environment & development matters

Women's Healthy Environments Network
#400, 215 Spadina Ave., Toronto ON M5T 2C7
Tel: 416-928-0880; *Fax:* 416-644-0116
e-mail: office@womenshealthyenvironments.ca
URL: www.womenshealthyenvironments.ca
Also Known As: WHEN Foundation
Previous Name: The Women & Environments Education & Development Foundation
Overview: A medium-sized national charitable organization founded in 1987
Finances: *Funding Sources:* Government; corporate; private foundations
Staff: 1 staff member(s)
Fees: $20 individual; $30 institution
Activities: *Speaker Service:* Yes; *Library:* WEED Resource Centre
Mission: To provide a forum for communication; to conduct research on issues relating to women in their environments of planning, health, ecology, workplace design, community development & urban & rural sociology & economy; *Affiliation(s):* National Action Committee on the Status of Women

Wood Buffalo Environmental Association (WBEA)
#100, 330 Thickwood Blvd., Fort McMurray AB T9K 1Y1
Tel: 780-799-4420
e-mail: info@wbea.org
URL: www.wbea.org
Overview: A small local organization
Chief Officer(s):
Carna MacEachern, Executive Director
Ann Dort-MacLean, President
Membership: 28 corporate

Mission: To provide state of the art air monitoring system that meets the needs of residents and stakeholders in the Wood Buffalo Region.

Wood Energy Technology Transfer Inc. (WETT)
#7, 296 Jarvis St., Toronto ON M5B 2C5
Tel: 416-968-7718; *Fax:* 416-968-6818
Toll-Free: 888-358-9388
e-mail: WETT@funnel.ca
URL: www.wettinc.ca
Overview: A medium-sized national organization founded in 1993
Chief Officer(s):
Anthony Laycock, Executive Director
Finances: *Annual Operating Budget:* $100,000-$250,000; *Funding Sources:* Membership dues; member services
Staff: 2 staff member(s)
Membership: 1,400; *Fees:* $40-$75
Activities: Administers Wood Energy Technical Training Program for providers, installers, inspectors & cleaners of wood heat services;
Mission: To promote the safe & effective use of wood burning systems, WETT maintains a training program designed to confirm & recognize the knowledge & skills of practising wood energy professionals; to provide training to new people entering the industry; to provide training to non-industry professionals such as inspectors; to provide training to specialty audiences such as volunteer firefighters & carpenters in remote communities

Wood Manufacturing Council (WMC) / Conseil des fabricants de bois (CFB)
#1016, 130 Albert St., Ottawa ON K1P 5G4
Tel: 613-567-5511; *Fax:* 613-567-5411
e-mail: wmc@wmc-cfb.ca
URL: www.wmc-cfb.ca
Overview: A medium-sized national organization
Chief Officer(s):
Richard Lipman, President
Finances: *Funding Sources:* Federal government
Mission: To plan, develop & implement human resources strategies that support the long-term growth & competitiveness of Canada's advanced wood products manufacturing industry & meet the developmental needs of its workforce

Wood Preservation Canada (WPC) / Préservation du bois Canada
#202, 2141 Thurston Dr., Ottawa ON K1G 6C9
Tel: 613-737-4337; *Fax:* 613-247-0540
e-mail: info@woodpreservation.ca
URL: www.woodpreservation.ca
Previous Name: Canadian Institute of Treated Wood
Overview: A medium-sized national organization founded in 1955
Mission: To represent, support & promote the treated wood industry in Canada
Environmental Activity: Producing safe, quality products in an environmentally sound manner; Promoting responsible stewardship of resources; Conserving forests through pressure treating

Woodstock Field Naturalists
PO Box 20037, RPO Woodstock Centre, Woodstock ON N4S 8X8
e-mail: rogeboyd@oxford.net
URL: www.execulink.com/~wfnc
Overview: A small local organization founded in 1934
Fees: $20 individual; $25 family
Mission: To promote the enjoyment of nature; to learn about natural history; to promote preservation of the environment through active participation in conservation projects; *Member of:* Federation of Ontario Naturalists

World Agroforestry Centre
PO Box 30677, United Nations Ave., Gigiri, Nairobi 00100 Kenya
Tel: 254 20 7224000; *Fax:* 254 20 7224001
e-mail: icraf@cgiar.org
URL: www.worldagroforestry.org
Previous Name: International Centre for Research in Agroforestry (ICRAF)
Overview: A large international organization founded in 1977
Finances: *Annual Operating Budget:* Greater than $5 Million; *Funding Sources:* Donations; foundations
Staff: 402 staff member(s)
Activities: *Awareness Events:* Field Days; *Rents Mailing List:* Yes; *Library:* ICRAF Library; open by appointment

Mission: To improve human welfare by alleviating poverty, increasing cash income, improving food & nutritional security, & enhancing environmental resilience in the tropics; to conduct strategic & applied research, in partnership with national agricultural systems, for more sustainable & productive land use. Programmes in Africa, India, Sri Lanka, Bangladesh, Indonesia, the Philippines, Viet Nam, Thailand, China, Brazil & Peru.; *Member of:* Consultative Group on International Agricultural Research

World Aquaculture Society (WAS)
143 J.M. Parker Coliseum, LSU, Baton Rouge LA 70806 USA
Tel: 225-578-3137; *Fax:* 225-578-3493
e-mail: carolm@was.org
URL: www.was.org
Previous Name: World Mariculture Society
Overview: A medium-sized international organization founded in 1970
Membership: 4,000+ direct & affiliated; *Fees:* $60 individual; $250 corporate; $40 student
Mission: To secure, evaluate, promote & distribute educational, scientific & technological advancement of aquaculture & mariculture throughout the world; *Affiliation(s):* Aquaculture Association of Canada; Caribbean Aquaculture Association; European Acquaculture Association

World Association for World Federation *See* World Federalist Movement

World Association of Industrial & Technological Research Organizations (WAITRO)
c/o SIRIM Berhad, 1 Persiaran Dato'Menteri, PO Box 7035, Section 2, Shah Alam 40911 Malaysia
Tel: 603-544-6635; *Fax:* 603-554- 673
e-mail: info@waitro.sirim.my
URL: www.waitro.org
Overview: A small international organization founded in 1970
Membership: 200; *Fees:* Based on country's GNI, according to the World Bank; *Member Profile:* Technical membership - laboratories & other organizations actively engaged in industrial & technological research & development; sustaining membership - bodies active in encouraging & promoting technological research & assisting the Association with financial support or by otherwise advancing its aims
Mission: To be the leading global network of research & technological organizations through collaboration & knowledge sharing for sustainable development; encourage & facilitate transfer of research results & technical know-how; promote exchange of experience in research & technology management; enhance capabilities in management of research & technological organizations; identify & promote fields of research suitable for international collaboration, new opportunities & markets; promote technological research & capability building in developing countries; *Affiliation(s):* Research & Productivity Council; Centre de recherche industrielle du Québec; International Development Research Centre; Canadian International Development Agency; BC Research

World Blue Chain for the Protection of Animals & Nature / La Chaine bleue mondiale
Avenue de Visé 39, Brussels B-1170 Belgium
Tel: 32-2-673-5230; *Fax:* 32-2-672-0947
e-mail: contact@bwk-cbm.be
URL: www.bwk-cbm.be
Also Known As: Blauwe Wereldketen
Overview: A medium-sized international organization founded in 1962
Finances: *Annual Operating Budget:* $250,000-$500,000
Staff: 9 staff member(s); 250 volunteer(s)
Membership: 35,000 individual; *Fees:* 7.50, 12.50, 30.00 euros
Activities: *Library:* Yes, Open to public, open by appointment
Mission: Protection of animals by inspections, propaganda & cultural education; *Member of:* World Society for Protection of Animals

World Business Council for Sustainable Development (WBCSD)
4, ch de Conches, Geneva 1231 Switzerland
Tel: 41-22-839-3100; *Fax:* 41-22-839-3131
e-mail: info@wbcsd.org
URL: www.wbcsd.ch
Overview: A small international organization
Chief Officer(s):
James E. Rogers, Chairman, President & CEO
Markus Akermann, CEO
Membership: 170 companies in 35 countries

Associations/Organizations / World Coal Institute

Mission: To provide business leadership as a catalyst for change toward sustainable development; to promote the role of eco-efficiency, innovation & corporate social responsibility; Affiliation(s): The EXCEL Partnership (Canada)

World Citizens Assembly See Association of World Citizens & World Citizens Foundation

World Coal Institute (WCI)
Cambridge House, 22 The Quadrant, 2nd Fl.,
Richmond-upon-Thames TW9 1BP United Kingdom
Tel: 44-20-8940-0477; *Fax:* 44-20-8940-9624
e-mail: info@worldcoal.org
URL: www.worldcoal.org
Overview: A small international organization founded in 1985
Chief Officer(s):
Milton Catelin, Chief Executive
Christine Copley, Senior Manager
Roger Wicks, Chair
Finances: *Annual Operating Budget:* $500,000-$1.5 Million
Staff: 4 staff member(s)
Membership: 20; *Committees:* Executive; Standing
Activities: *Library:* Yes
Mission: To promote the use of coal as an economic & environmentally sound energy source; to provide a voice for coal in international debates on energy & the environment; to improve public awareness of the merits & importance of coal as the single largest source of fuel for the generation of electricity; to ensure that decision makers, & public opinion generally, are fully informed on the advances in modern clean coal technology; to widen understanding of the vital role that metallurgical coal fulfills in the worldwide production of steel; to support other sectors of the worldwide coal industry

World Conservation Monitoring Centre See UNEP - World Conservation Monitoring Centre

The World Conservation Union; International Union for Conservation of Nature & Natural Resources See International Union for Conservation of Nature

World Energy Council (WEC) / Conseil Mondial de l'Energie (CME)
Regency House, 1-4 Warwick St., 5th Fl., London W1B 5LT United Kingdom
Tel: 44-20-7734-5996; *Fax:* 44-20-7734-5926
e-mail: info@worldenergy.org
URL: www.worldenergy.org
Overview: A small international organization founded in 1923
Chief Officer(s):
Pierre Gadonneix, Chair
Finances: *Annual Operating Budget:* $3 Million-$5 Million
Staff: 14 staff member(s)
Membership: 92 member countries; *Fees:* Variable; *Member Profile:* Commercial; government; non-government
Activities: Energy; energy conservation; *Library:* Information Services; open by appointment
Meetings/Conferences:
For more information see Trade Shows, Conferences and Seminars Chapter
World Energy 2013 22nd Congress
Other Conferences in 2013 2013 Daegu City
Mission: To promote the sustainable supply & use of energy for the greatest benefit of all

World Energy Council - Canadian Member Committee See Energy Council of Canada

World Federalist Movement (WFM) / Mouvement féderalist mondial
708 Third Ave., 24th Fl., New York NY 10017 USA
Tel: 212-599-1320; *Fax:* 212-599-1332
e-mail: info@wfm.org
URL: www.wfm.org
Previous Name: World Association for World Federation
Overview: A medium-sized international organization founded in 1947
Chief Officer(s):
William R. Pace, Executive Director
Finances: *Annual Operating Budget:* $100,000-$250,000
Membership: 39 affiliated organizations
Activities: Conferences; seminars; policy research; publishing of papers & monographs; lobbying; *Library:* Yes

Mission: An international citizens movement working for justice, peace & sustainable prosperity; calls for an end to the rule of force through a world governed by law, based on strengthened & democratized world institutions; Affiliation(s): World Federalists of Canada

World Federation of Ukrainian Engineering Societies (WFUES)
27 Newell Ct., Toronto ON M9A 4T9
Tel: 416-235-2610; *Fax:* 416-240-9095
e-mail: jgk@the-wire.com
Overview: A medium-sized international organization founded in 1973
Finances: *Annual Operating Budget:* Less than $50,000; *Funding Sources:* Membership fees
Staff: 6 volunteer(s)
Membership: 5,000 individuals; *Fees:* Schedule available; *Member Profile:* Licensed professional engineer in respective country; *Committees:* Environmental; Educational; Social Events
Activities: *Speaker Service:* Yes
Mission: To maintain Ukrainian engineering tradition & culture; to publish Ukrainian engineering news; to organize conferences & seminars on technical subjects; to exchange information on technology & facilitate technology transfer
Environmental Activity: Provides information on environmental matters

World Fuel Cell Council
Franfurter Strasse 10-14, Eschborn D-65760 Germany
e-mail: info@fuelcellworld.org
URL: www.fuelcellworld.org
Overview: A medium-sized international organization founded in 1991
Member Profile: Companies involved in the development & use of a variety of fuel cell technologies for both stationary & mobile applications
Mission: To promote the most rapid commercialization of this benign technology worldwide

World Future Society (WFS)
#450, 7910 Woodmont Ave., Bethesda MD 20814-3032 USA
Tel: 301-656-8274; *Fax:* 301-951-0394
Toll-Free: 800-989-8274
e-mail: info@wfs.org
URL: www.wfs.org
Overview: A medium-sized international organization founded in 1966
Finances: *Funding Sources:* Membership fees
Membership: 25,000 in over 80 countries; *Fees:* $49; *Member Profile:* Persons who would like to know more about what the future will hold, including sociologists, scientists, corporate planners, educators, students, & retirees
Activities: *Speaker Service:* Yes
Publications: *The Futurist*
Type: Magazine *Frequency:* bi-m. *Accepts Advertising*: Yes
Editor: Cindy Wagner *Price:* $49
Profile: Feature articles, news briefs, & book reviews
Future Times
Type: Newsletter *Frequency:* m. *Editor:* Cindy Wagner
Profile: News & previews from the Society
Future Survey
Frequency: m. *Editor:* Michael Marien *Price:* $109 individuals; $165 institutions
Profile: Abstract of books, articles, & reports about the future
Futures Research Quarterly
Type: Journal *Frequency:* q. *Editor:* Timothy Mack *Price:* $85 individuals; $110 institutions
Profile: Refereed journal with articles, news items, reprints of classic papers, & reviews of selected new books or reports for those professionals involved with the theory, methodology, practice, & use of futures research
Mission: The nonpartisan scientific & educational association serves as a clearinghouse for ideas about the future, including forecasts, recommendations, & alternative scenarios.

World Health Organization (WHO) / Organisation mondiale de la santé (OMS)
20, avenue Appia, 27, Geneva CH-1211 Switzerland
Tel: 41-22-791-21-11; *Fax:* 41-22-791-31-11
e-mail: inf@who.int
URL: www.who.int
Overview: A large international organization founded in 1948
Membership: 193
Activities: Global strategy to achieve optimal health for all peoples of the world is based on the primary health care approach, involving the following components: education concerning prevailing health problems, proper food supply & nutrition, safe water & sanitation, maternal & child health, immunization against major infectious diseases, prevention & control of local diseases, appropriate treatment of common diseases & injuries, provision of essential drugs; *Awareness Events:* World Health Day, April 7; World No-Tobacco Day, May 31; World AIDS Day, Dec. 1; World TB (Tuberculosis) Day, March
Mission: To attain for all peoples the highest possible level of health

World Mariculture Society See World Aquaculture Society

World Meteorological Organization (WMO) / Organisation météorologique mondiale (OMM)
Information & Public Affairs, PO Box 2300, 7 bis, av de la Paix, Geneva 2, Geneva CH-1211 Switzerland
Tel: 41-22-730-8111; *Fax:* 41-22-730-8181
e-mail: cpa@wmo.int
URL: www.wmo.int
Overview: A medium-sized international organization founded in 1950
Finances: *Annual Operating Budget:* Greater than $5 Million; *Funding Sources:* Member governments
Staff: 246 staff member(s)
Membership: 187 governments; *Fees:* Assessed contributions; *Committees:* WMO Congress; Executive Council; Regional Associations; Technical
Activities: World Weather Watch; World Climate; Atmospheric Research & Environment; Applications of Meteorology; Hydrology & Water Resources; Education & Training; Technical Cooperation; Regional; *Library:* WMO Technical Library; Open to public
Mission: Coordinates global scientific activity to allow prompt & accurate weather information & other services for public, private & commercial use; contributes to the safety of life & property, the socio-economic development of nations & the protection of the environment; disaster mitigation & reduction

World Nuclear Association (WNA)
Carlton House, 22A St. James's Sq., London SW1Y 4JH United Kingdom
Tel: 44-20-7451-1520; *Fax:* 44-20-7839-1501
e-mail: wna@world-nuclear.org
URL: www.world-nuclear.org
Previous Name: The Uranium Institute
Overview: A medium-sized international charitable organization founded in 1975
Finances: *Annual Operating Budget:* $1.5 Million-$3 Million
Staff: 17 staff member(s)
Membership: 120; *Fees:* Schedule available; *Member Profile:* Uranium producers, electrical utilities, fuel processing, handling & trading companies, government organizations
Activities: *Library:* Yes, open by appointment
Mission: To promote the use of nuclear energy for peaceful purposes; to provide a forum for research & debate on economic & political issues affecting the nuclear industry; to play a central role in the collection, analysis & communication of information on all aspects of the industry & related subjects

World Organization of Building Officials (WOBO)
155 Bearspaw Meadows, Calgary AB T3L 2M3
Tel: 403-239-2889; *Fax:* 403-547-4546
URL: www.nfpa.org/wobo/index.html
Overview: A medium-sized international organization founded in 1984
Finances: *Annual Operating Budget:* $50,000-$100,000; *Funding Sources:* Membership fees
Membership: 600; *Fees:* US$35 individuals; US$175 group
Activities: *Internships:* Yes; *Speaker Service:* Yes; *Rents Mailing List:* Yes
Mission: To improve the quality of life & resource optimization internationally, through the development, exchange & application of knowledge & experience, affecting the health, safety, welfare & usefulness of the built environment; to promote safeguards from potential hazards & to recommend solutions for preventing fire risks in existing buildings or buildings under construction; to promote the concept of standardizing construction training, materials, equipment & appliances; to promote the unification of legislation pertaining to the administration & enforcement of codes & standards; to update the development of technology; *Member of:* Habitat International Coalition; Affiliation(s): Special conservative status with Economic & Social Council of the United Nations & the United Nations Industrial Development Organization

World Packaging Organization (WPO)
c/o STFI-Packforsk, PO Box 5604, Stockholm S-11486 Sweden
Tel: 46-8-676-7000; Fax: 46-8-411-5518
e-mail: carl.olsmats@stfi.se
URL: www.worldpackaging.org
Overview: A medium-sized international organization founded in 1968
Chief Officer(s):
Carl Olsmats, General Secretary
carl.olsmats@stfi.se
Keith Pearson, President
glacier@tiscali.co.za
Fees: 300 Euros
Mission: The World Packaging Organisation is a non-profit, non-governmental, international federation of national packaging institutes, regional packaging federations and other interested parties including individuals, corporations and trade associations

World Petroleum Congress (WPC) / Congrès mondiaux du pétrole
#1, 1 Duchess St., 4th Fl., London W1W 6AN United Kingdom
Tel: 44-20-7637-4958; Fax: 44-20-7637-4965
e-mail: secretariat@world-petroleum.org
URL: www.world-petroleum.org
Overview: A medium-sized international organization founded in 1933
Chief Officer(s):
Pierce Riemer, Director General
pierce@world-petroleum.org
Ulrike von Lonski, Director of Communications
ulrike@world-petroleum.org
Finances: *Funding Sources:* Membership dues; royalties; levy on registration
Staff: 4 staff member(s)
Membership: 57 countries; *Fees:* Schedule available; *Member Profile:* Major oil producing & consuming nations of the world; each country has a National Committee made up of representatives of the oil industry, academic & research institutions, & government departments; *Committees:* Permanent Council; Executive Board; Scientific Program; Congress Arrangements; Environmental Affairs; Development
Mission: To help the oil industry in the development of petroleum resources & the use of petroleum products for the benefit of mankind; to promote petroleum science & technology; to encourage the application of scientific advances & the transfer of technology; *Affiliation(s):* IEA; OPEN; United Nations

World Resources Institute (WRI)
#800, 10 G St. NE, Washington DC 20002 USA
Tel: 202-729-7600; Fax: 202-729-7610
e-mail: rspeight@wri.org
URL: www.wri.org
Overview: A small international organization founded in 1982
Chief Officer(s):
Jonathan Lash, President
jlash@wri.org
Manish Bapna, Exec. Vice-President & Managing Dir
mbapna@wri.org
Steve Barker, CFO & Vice-President, Finance & Administration
sbarker@wri.org
Activities: Policy studies to present accurate infromation about global resources & environmental conditions, analysis of emerging issues & development of creative yet workable policy responses; in developing countries, provides field services & technical support for governments & nongovernmental organizations that are working to ensure the sustainability of natural resources; *Internships:* Yes; *Library:* Yes, Open to public, open by appointment
Mission: To generate accurate information about global resources & environmental conditions, analyze emerging issues & develop creative responses to both problems & opportunities; to bring the insights of scientific research, economic analysis & practical experience to political, business & other leaders around the world by publishing books, reports & papers

World Safety Organization (WSO)
WSO World Management Centre, PO Box 518, 106 West Young Ave., #F, Warrensburg MO 64093 USA
Tel: 660-747-3132; Fax: 660-747-2647
e-mail: info@worldsafety.org
URL: www.worldsafety.org
Overview: A medium-sized international organization founded in 1875
Finances: *Annual Operating Budget:* $250,000-$500,000
Staff: 4 staff member(s)
Membership: 12,000; *Fees:* $55 associate; $80 affiliate; $35 student; $185 institution; $1,000 corporate; *Member Profile:* Open to all individuals & entities involved in the safety & accident prevention field; *Committees:* Transportation Safety; Construction Safety; Environmental Safety & Health; Occupational Safety & Health; Conference Organizing; Awards; Ethics; Membership Development; Certification Board
Activities: World Safety & Accident Prevention Congress (every 2-6 years); World Safety & Accident Prevention Educational Conference (annually); professional development courses & seminars; *Library:* Yes
Awards: WSO Concerned Company/Corporation Honorable Mention Certificate (Award)
WSO Educational Award (Award)
WSO Concerned Organization Award (Award)
WSO Safety Person of the Year (Award)
WSO James K. Williams Award (Award)
WSO Concerned Citizen Award (Award)
WSO Concerned Professional Award (Award)
WSO Concerned Company/Corporation Award (Award)
Mission: To protect people, property, resources & the environment & to internationalize occupational & environmental safety through exchange of knowledge, programs, etc.; *Member of:* Consultative Status Category II (non-governmental) with Economic & Social Council of the United Nations

World Society for Ekistics (WSE)
24, Strat. Syndesmou St., Athens 106 73 Greece
Tel: 30-210-3623-216; Fax: 30-210-3629-337
e-mail: ekistics@otenet.gr
URL: www.ekistics.org
Overview: A small international organization founded in 1965
Finances: *Annual Operating Budget:* Less than $50,000; *Funding Sources:* Membership dues; grants
Staff: 5 volunteer(s)
Membership: 200; *Fees:* $40
Activities: Human settlements
Mission: To advance the science of ekistics (human settlements) by drawing on the research & experience of professionals in such fields as architecture, engineering, ekistics, regional & city planning & sociology

World Society for the Protection of Animals (WSPA) / Société mondiale pour la protection des animaux
#960, 90 Eglinton Ave. East, Toronto ON M4P 2Y3
Tel: 416-369-0044; Fax: 416-369-0147
Toll-Free: 800-363-9772
e-mail: wspa@wspa.ca
URL: www.wspa.ca
Social Media: www.facebook.com/group.php?gid=143249880633
Overview: A large international charitable organization founded in 1953
Chief Officer(s):
Michelle Cliffe, Communications Manager
Finances: *Annual Operating Budget:* $1.5 Million-$3 Million; *Funding Sources:* General public
Staff: 9 staff member(s); 20 volunteer(s)
Membership: 900 member organizations in 150 countries; *Fees:* $25;
Mission: To promote effective means for the prevention of cruelty to, & relief of suffering of animals in any part of the world; 15 offices worldwide

World Wildlife Fund - Canada (WWF-Canada) / Fonds mondial pour la nature
#410, 245 Eglinton Ave. East, Toronto ON M4P 3J1
Tel: 416-489-8800; Fax: 416-489-3611
Toll-Free: 800-267-2632
e-mail: ca-panda@wwfcanada.org
URL: www.wwf.ca
Social Media: www.facebook.com/WWFCanada
Overview: A large international charitable organization founded in 1967
Chief Officer(s):
Patricia Koval, Chair
Gerald Butts, President & CEO
Arlin Hackman, Vice-President, Conservation
Mary Deacon, Vice-President, Conservation Advancement
Grahame Cliff, Vice-President, Finance & Administration
Christina Topp, Vice-President, Marketing & Communications
Robert Rangeley, Vice-President, Atlantic Region
Finances: *Annual Operating Budget:* Greater than $5 Million; *Funding Sources:* Individuals; corporate donations; government; foundations
Staff: 80 staff member(s)
Membership: 64,000; *Fees:* Donation of $25 or more
Activities: Endangered Species Recovery Fund; Marine, Forests & Trade Biodiversity; Arctic; *Rents Mailing List:* Yes
Awards: Endangered Species Recovery Fund (Grant) Sponsors high-priority conservation projects to assist the recovery of endangered wildlife & their natural habitats. This program is under review *Eligibility:* Must be affiliated with a non-governmental organization or non-profit body with a mandate for conservation *Deadline:* Mid to late Jan.
Endangered Spaces Campaign Local Action Fund (Grant) Sponsors site-specific, public awareness activities to advance protection of terrestrial & marine areas across Canada *Eligibility:* Must be affiliated with a non-governmental organization or non-profit body with a mandate for conservation *Deadline:* Mid to late Nov. Contact: Project Manager, Jarmila Becka Lee
Mission: To conserve wild animals, plants & habitats for their own sake & the long-term benefit of people; to protect the diversity of life on earth; to stop, & eventually reverse, the accelerating degradation of our planet's natural environment, & to help build a future in which humans live in harmony with nature; *Affiliation(s):* World Wide Fund for Nature (International)
Environmental Activity: Protecting wildlife & wild places in Canada & Latin America

World Wildlife Fund - USA (WWF-USA) / Fonds mondial pour la nature
PO Box 97180, 1250 - 24 St. NW, Washington DC 20090-7180 USA
Tel: 202-293-4800; Fax: 202-293-9211
Toll-Free: 800-960-0993
e-mail: PlResponse@worldwildlife.org
URL: www.worldwildlife.org
Overview: A large international organization founded in 1961
Chief Officer(s):
Carter S. Roberts, President
Bruce Babbitt, Chairman
Finances: *Funding Sources:* Contributions from members; grants from foundations, corporations & government agencies
Membership: 1,000,000+
Activities: Golden Lion Tarmarin Project, Brazil; Hol Chan Marine Reserve, Belize; involved in over 50 projects involving protection of tropical rainforests; Osborn Center works to make the wise management & efficient use of renewable resources a more central element in the economic development plans of developing nations; conducts field work & policy research to promote sustainable & efficient approaches to community development in the US; *Library:* Yes, Open to public
Mission: The largest private US organization working worldwide to conserve nature; to preserve the diversity & abundance of life on Earth & the health of ecological systems by protecting natural areas & wild populations of plants & animals, including endangered species; to promote sustainable approaches to the use of renewable natural resources; to promote more efficient use of resources & energy & the maximum reduction of pollution; committed to reversing the degradation of natural environment & to building a future in which human needs are met in harmony with nature; strives to determine how best to manage individual species & habitats & to obtain critical data for setting conservation priorities; *Affiliation(s):* WWF has national organizations, national associates & representatives in nearly 40 countries across five continents; affiliation with international WWF network headquarters in Gland, Switzerland

World Wildlife Fund for Nature *See* WWF International

Worldwatch Institute
1776 Massachusetts Ave. NW, Washington DC 20036-1904 USA
Tel: 202-452-1999; Fax: 202-296-7365
e-mail: worldwatch@worldwatch.org
URL: www.worldwatch.org
Overview: A medium-sized international charitable organization founded in 1974
Chief Officer(s):
Christopher Flavin, President
Finances: *Annual Operating Budget:* $3 Million-$5 Million
Staff: 30 staff member(s)
Activities: *Internships:* Yes; *Rents Mailing List:* Yes; *Library:* Yes, Not open to the public
Mission: Research organization that works for an environmentally sustainable & socially just society; provides compelling, accessible fact-based analysis of critical global issues; informs people about the interaction between nature, people & economies; focuses on the underlying causes & practical solutions to the world's problems

WWF International (WWF)
Avenue du Mont-Blanc, Gland CH-1196 Switzerland
Tel: 41-22-364-9111; *Fax:* 41-22-364-8836
URL: www.panda.org
Also Known As: World Wide Fund for Nature
Previous Name: World Wildlife Fund for Nature
Overview: A large international charitable organization founded in 1961
Chief Officer(s):
Emeka Anyaoku, President
James P. Leape, Director General
Finances: *Annual Operating Budget:* Greater than $5 Million; *Funding Sources:* Individuals & general donations; legacies & bequests; corporate subscriptions & donations
Staff: 3800 staff member(s)
Membership: 4.7 million; *Fees:* Schedule available
Activities: Six international environmental issues: Climate Change, Endangered Seas, Forests, Fresh Water Programmes, Species, Toxics; sponsors educational & training programs for park & wildlife managers, ecologists & teachers
Mission: To stop the degradation of the planet's natural environment & to build a future in which humans live in harmony with nature by conserving the world's biological diversity, ensuring that the use of renewable & natural resources is sustainable, promoting the reduction of pollution & wasteful consumption; *Affiliation(s):* The World Conservation Union; International Council for Bird Protection; International Waterfowl Research Bureau; Charles Darwin Foundation

WWOOF Canada (WWOOF Canada)
4429 Carlson Rd., Nelson BC V1L 6X3
Tel: 250-354-4417
e-mail: wwoofcan@shaw.ca
URL: www.wwoof.ca
Also Known As: Willing Workers on Organic Farms, World Wide Opportunities on Organic Farms
Overview: A small national organization founded in 1985
Finances: *Annual Operating Budget:* Less than $50,000
Staff: 1 staff member(s); 2000 volunteer(s)
Membership: 20,000; *Fees:* $45
Activities: WWOOFing is a cultural exchange & a helping exchange; *Internships:* Yes
Mission: WWOOF Aims to get firsthand experience of organic farming & gardening and to lend a helping hand wherever needed; *Member of:* WWOOF International Federation

Yellowhead Highway Association *See* Trans Canada Yellowhead Highway Association

York Rose & Garden Society *See* Greater Toronto Rose & Garden Society

Youth Challenge International (YCI)
#305, 20 Maud St., Toronto ON M5V 2M5
Tel: 416-504-3370; *Fax:* 416-504-3376
e-mail: generalinfo@yci.net
URL: www.yci.com
Overview: A small international charitable organization founded in 1989
Chief Officer(s):
Marion Younan, Chair & President
Bryan Cox, Executive Director
Finances: *Annual Operating Budget:* $500,000-$1.5 Million; *Funding Sources:* Private sources; foundations; government
Staff: 13 staff member(s); 200 volunteer(s)
Membership: 100; *Fees:* $15; *Committees:* Social Justice; Global Development Education
Activities: Challenger Programme offers youth an opportunity for personal development through four challenges - selection, preparation, field project & returning home; a 10-week field programme followed by the transformation of skills into civic action in their home communities
Mission: To promote young people's active, responsible & continuing participation in the issues of local & global development; to promote & support the establishment of a YCI global network, with partners in developed & developing regions of the world; to foster increased international cooperation between individuals, communities, service organizations, governments & agencies by focusing expertise & materials upon locally identified problems in developing regions

Yukon Chamber of Mines (YCM)
3151B - 3rd Ave., Whitehorse YT Y1A 1G1
Tel: 867-667-2090; *Fax:* 867-668-7127
e-mail: info@ycmines.ca
URL: www.ycmines.ca
Overview: A medium-sized provincial organization founded in 1959
Finances: *Annual Operating Budget:* $100,000-$250,000; *Funding Sources:* Membership fees; government funding
Staff: 2 staff member(s)
Membership: 350; *Fees:* $50 individual; $120-$6000 other; *Member Profile:* Operating mines; service & supply; seasonal mines; individuals
Activities: *Awareness Events:* Geoscience Forum, 3rd week of Nov.; *Library:* Yes, Open to public
Mission: Provides services to members, with a focus on the mining industry; promotes responsible exploration and sustainable mining practices; *Affiliation(s):* Mining Association of Canada

Yukon Conservation Society (YCS)
302 Hawkins St., Whitehorse YT Y1A 1X6
Tel: 867-668-5678; *Fax:* 867-668-6637
e-mail: ycs@ycs.yk.ca
URL: www.yukonconservation.org
Overview: A small provincial charitable organization founded in 1968
Chief Officer(s):
Karen Baltgailis, Executive Director
Georgia Greetham, Coordinator, Office
Sue Kemmett, Coordinator, Forestry
Anne Middler, Coordinator, Energy
Lewis Rifkind, Coordinator, Mining
Finances: *Funding Sources:* Membership fees; Donations
Membership: 400; *Fees:* $10 students; $25 individuals & corporate or business memberships; $40 families; *Committees:* Personnel Standing Committee; Executive Standing Committee; Finance Standing Committee; Membership / Fundraising Standing Committee; Energy & Climate Change Working Group; Forestry Working Group; Habitat & Wildlife Working Group; Mining Working Group; Whitehorse Area Issues Working Group
Activities: Influencing environmental policy in the North; Providing environmental educational programs; Raising environmental awareness & the realization that human well-being is dependent upon fully functioning healthy ecosystems; *Library:* Yukon Conservation Society Library; Open to public, open by appointment
Meetings/Conferences:
For more information see Trade Shows, Conferences and Seminars Chapter
Yukon Conservation Society Interpretive Guided Nature Hikes (Canyon City historical nature hikes, special hikes with guest naturalists & family walks)
July 2011, YK
Ed-Ventures 2011 for Kids
July 2011 Whitehorse, YK
Yukon Conservation Society 2012 Annual Bird-a-thon
May 2012, YK
Yukon Conservation Society Interpretive Guided Nature Hikes (Canyon City historical nature hikes, special hikes with guest naturalists & family walks)
July 2012, YK
Yukon Conservation Society 2012 Ed-Ventures for Kids
July 2012 Whitehorse, YK
Yukon Conservation Society 2012 Annual General Meeting
Other Conferences in 2012 2012, YK
Publications: *Walk Softly*
Type: Newsletter *Frequency:* q. *Editor:* Georgia Greetham *Price:* Free with Yukon Conservation Society membership; $25 non-members
Profile: Information about current & upcoming issues & events
Mission: To pursue ecosystem well-being throughout the Yukon & beyond
Environmental Activity: Developing an educational website (climatechangenorth.ca), with partners in Yukon, the Northwest Territories, & Nunavut, for students from kindergarten to grade 12; Offering Leave No Trace Awareness workshops & trainer courses for outdoor enthusiasts

Yukon Environmental Network
Parent: Canadian Environmental Network
PO Box 30097, Whitehorse YT Y1A 5M2
Tel: 867-668-5678; *Fax:* 867-668-6637
e-mail: yukonenvironet@gmail.com
Previous Name: Nornet-Yukon
Overview: A small provincial organization
Chief Officer(s):
Susan Davis, Coordinator

Yukon Fish & Game Association (YFGA)
Parent: Canadian Wildlife Federation
509 Strickland St., Whitehorse YT Y1A 2K5
Tel: 867-667-4263; *Fax:* 867-667-4237
URL: www.yukonfga.ca
Overview: A medium-sized provincial organization founded in 1945
Chief Officer(s):
Gord Zealand, Executive Director
yfgaexdir@klondiker.com
Jillian Mclellan, Office Administrator
yfga@klondiker.com
Finances: *Funding Sources:* Membership fees; Donations; Sponsorships
Fees: $30 singles; $35 families; $500 corporate & lifetime membership
Activities: Providing hunter education & ethics development; Promoting proper catch & release; Meeting with government regarding fish & wildlife issues; Promoting sportsmanship; Managing the Whitehorse Rapids fish ladder & tourist facility; Overseeing the operation of a salmon hatchery
Meetings/Conferences:
For more information see Trade Shows, Conferences and Seminars Chapter
Yukon Fish & Game Association 2011 Outdoor Woman Program
June 2011 Whitehorse, YT
Yukon Fish & Game Association Outdoor Education Camp
July 2011 Whitehorse, YT
Yukon Fish & Game Association 2012 Annual Meeting, Banquet, & Awards
Other Conferences in 2012 2012, YT
Publications: *Outdoor Edge [a publication of the Yukon Fish & Game Association]*
Type: Newsletter *Frequency:* bi-m. *Accepts Advertising* : Yes
Price: Free with Yukon Fish & Game Association membership
Profile: A publication sent to more than 450 households in the Yukon & throughout Canada
Mission: To ensure the long-term management of fish, wildlife, & outdoor recreational resources in the Yukon; To improve wildlife habitat
Environmental Activity: Promoting conservation & habitat protection; Participating in the Wolf Creek salmon release, the fish stocking of Pothole Lakes, & the Turn In Poachers & Polluters (TIPS) program; Raising awareness of the dangers of air, water, & land pollution

Yukon Public Health Association (YPHA)
Parent: Canadian Public Health Association
Tel: 867-393-8784
Overview: A small provincial organization
Chief Officer(s):
Ron Pearson, Contact
Val Pike, President
val.pike@wgh.yk.ca
Mission: Established to strengthen the impact of people who are active in public and community health throughout the Yukon through education, awareness, public participation and building of partnerships and networks

Yukon Public Legal Education Association (YPLEA)
PO Box 2799, Yukon College, Whitehorse YT Y1A 5K4
Tel: 867-668-5297; *Fax:* 867-668-5541
Toll-Free: 866-667-4305
e-mail: yplea@yukoncollege.yk.ca
URL: www.yplea.com
Overview: A medium-sized provincial organization founded in 1984
Chief Officer(s):
Robert Pritchard, Contact
Finances: *Annual Operating Budget:* $50,000-$100,000
Staff: 2 staff member(s); 7 volunteer(s)
Fees: $10
Activities: *Speaker Service:* Yes; *Library:* Yes
Mission: To provide free legal information to Yukoners & promote greater accessibility to the legal system

Yukon Tourism Education Council (YTEC)
#C, 202 Strickland St., Whitehorse YT Y1A 2J8
Tel: 867-667-4733; *Fax:* 867-667-2688
e-mail: yukontec@internorth.com
URL: www.yukontec.ca
Overview: A small provincial organization
Chief Officer(s):
Darlene Doerksen, Chief Executive Officer
Activities: Providing education & training

Publications: *Yukon Tourism Education Council Newsletter* *Type:* Newsletter *Frequency:* m.
Mission: To foster industry led development of a professional tourism workforce

Zero Population Growth *See* Population Connection

ZOOCHECK Canada Inc.
788 1/2 O'Connor Dr., Toronto ON M4B 2S6
Tel: 416-285-1744; *Fax:* 416-285-4670
e-mail: zoocheck@zoocheck.com
URL: www.zoocheck.com
Overview: A small national organization founded in 1984
Finances: *Funding Sources:* Donations
Activities: *Speaker Service:* Yes; *Rents Mailing List:* Yes
Mission: Zoocheck works to improve wildlife protection in Canada and to end the abuse, neglect and exploitation of individual wild animals through: investigation & research; public education & awareness campaigns; capacity building initiatives; legal programs; legislative actions.

Zoological Society of Manitoba
54 Zoo Dr., Winnipeg MB R3P 2N8
Tel: 204-982-0660; *Fax:* 204-982-0673
e-mail: zooquestions@zoosociety.com
URL: www.zoosociety.com
Overview: A small provincial charitable organization founded in 1956
Chief Officer(s):
Julie Eccles, General Manager, 204-982-0662
Finances: *Annual Operating Budget:* $1.5 Million-$3 Million
Staff: 40 staff member(s); 100 volunteer(s)
Membership: 5,000; *Fees:* $52
Activities: Boo at the Zoo; Lights of the Wild; Animalia
Mission: The Zoological Society of Manitoba functions in three roles: 1. To promote the welfare and continuation of the Society; 2. To focus on the development of Assiniboine Park Zoo, making it a collection of merit and distinction; 3. To match concern with action for the preservation of earth's wildlife and their habitat; Affiliation(s): American Zoo & Aquarium Association

Zoological Society of Metropolitan Toronto *See* Toronto Zoo

Zoological Society of Montréal / Société zoologique de Montréal
#525, 117, rue Ste-Catherine ouest, Montréal QC H3B 1H9
Tel: 514-845-8317
e-mail: contact@zoologicalsocietymtl.org
URL: www.zoologicalsocietymtl.org
Overview: A small local organization founded in 1964
Membership: 500; *Fees:* $35 individual; $55 family
Activities: *Speaker Service:* Yes
Mission: To promote & develop interest in & knowledge of wildlife; to encourage the study of biology & nature sciences; to encourage the protection of wildlife

Educational Programs Index

A
Acadia University, 1033
Aurora College - Thebacha Campus, 1033

B
Bishop's University, 1034, 1035
Brandon University, 1033
British Columbia Institute of Technology (BCIT), 1029, 1030

C
Camosun College, 1030
Cape Breton University, 1033
Carleton University, 1034
College of the Rockies, 1030
Concordia University, 1035
Concordia University College of Alberta, 1029

D
Dalhousie University, 1033, 1034
Douglas College, 1030

F
First Nations University of Canada, 1035

I
Institute for Resources, Environment & Sustainability (IRES) at the University of British Columbia (UBC), 1030

K
The King's University College, 1029

L
Langara College, 1030

M
McGill University, 1035
Memorial University of Newfoundland, 1033
Mount Allison University, 1033

N
Nicola Valley Institute of Technology (NVIT), 1030
Nova Scotia Agricultural College, 1034

O
Okanagan College, 1030
Olds College, 1029

Q
Queen's University, 1034
Quest University Canada, 1030

R
Red Deer College, 1029
Redeemer University College, 1034
Royal Roads University, 1030, 1031

S
Saint Mary's University, 1034
St. Francis Xavier University, 1034
St Mary's University, 1029
Selkirk College, 1031
Simon Fraser University, 1031
Sir Wilfred Grenfell College, 1033

T
Thompson River University, 1031
Trent University, 1034
Trinity Western University, 1031

U
Université du Québec à Rimouski, 1035
Université du Québec à Trois-Rivières, 1035
University of Alberta, 1029
University of British Columbia (UBC), 1031, 1032
University of Calgary, 1029
University of Lethbridge, 1029
University of Manitoba, 1033
University of Northern British Columbia (UNBC) & University of British Columbia (UBC), 1032
University of Ottawa, 1034
University of Prince Edward Island, 1034
University of Regina, 1035
University of Saskatchewan, 1035
University of Victoria (UVic), 1032
University of Waterloo, 1034
The University of Winnipeg, 1033

V
Vancouver Island University, 1032, 1033

Y
York University, 1034
Yukon College, 1036
Yukon College Northern, 1036

Educational Programs

Alberta

Concordia University College of Alberta

Environmental Science
7128 Ada Blvd, Edmonton AB T5B 4E4 Canada
Tel: 780-479-8481; *Fax:* 780-474-1933
Toll-Free: 866-479-5200
URL: www.concordia.ab.ca
Description: Environmental Science is an exciting and relatively new field which explores environmental principles and the interaction of humans and the environment. As a student in the Environmental Science program, you will investigate the effect of human activities on the environment and ways by which we all can become environmentally responsible citizens.

The King's University College

Environmental Studies
9125-50 Street, Edmonton AB T6B 2H3 Canada
Tel: 780-465-3500; *Fax:* 780-465-3534
Toll-Free: 800-661-8582
e-mail: general-info@kingsu.ca
URL: www.kingsu.ca
Description: A study of the environment that involves many disciplines. Examines the relationship between human activities and the natural world, covers many traditional science subjects in the investigation of terrestrial (earth), aquatic (water), and atmospheric (air) systems and their interactions.

Olds College

Land & Water Resources Program
4500-50th Street, Olds AB T4H 1R6 Canada
Tel: 403-556-8281; *Fax:* 403-556-4711
Toll-Free: 800-661-6537
e-mail: info@oldscollege.ca
URL: www.oldscollege.ca
Description: Program offers training in environmentally sustainable management of rural land. It involves the study of soil, water, plants, ecosystems and environmental sciences with applications to the workplace.

Red Deer College

Environmental and Conservation Sciences Program
100 College Blvd, PO Box 5005, Red Deer AB T4N 5H5 Canada
Tel: 403-342-3300; *Fax:* 403-340-8940
URL: www.rdc.ab.ca
Description: This program is for students interested in the natural world, its management, conservation and ecological perspectives. The program emphasizes integrating natural science, management, and social science as related to environmental issues. It also offers students courses and team projects that integrate both biophysical and socioeconomic aspects of the environment in cooperation with practicing professionals and experts.

St Mary's University

Biological Conservation
14500 Bannister Rd SE, Calgary AB T2X 1Z4 Canada
Tel: 403-531-9130; *Fax:* 403-531-9136
URL: www.stmu.ab.ca
Description: The application of ecological theory and principles to the conservation and management of natural and modified exosystems, with emphasis on presercation of biodiversity and sustainable development. Topics include disturbance as an ecological process, ecological and evolutionary responsiveness of natural systems, ecology of resource harvesting, management of endangered habitats and populations, implications of human population growth, and global change.

University of Alberta

Environmental Science and Environmental Studies
Augustana Campus, 4901-46 Avenue, Camrose AB T4V 2R3 Canada
Tel: 780-679-1100; *Fax:* 780-679-1129
URL: www.augustana.ualberta.ca
Description: These interdisciplinary areas of study examine natural proccesses in the environment, the dependence of human society on nature, and our impact on nature through culture ans technology. Environmental Science emphasizes a natural science curriculum, while Environmental Studies integrates natural sciences, social sciences, and the humanities. Both Environmental Science and Environmental Studies explore issues related to out growing human population, use and overuse of resources, damage caused by pollution and disturbance, and the endangerment and extinction of species and natural ecosystems.

University of Alberta

Environmental Earth Sciences
Dept of Earth & Atmospheric Sciences, 1-26 Earth Sciences Building, Edmonton AB T6G 2E3 Canada
Tel: 780-492-3265; *Fax:* 780-492-2030
e-mail: eas.inquiries@ualberta.ca
URL: easweb.eas/ualberta.ca
Description: Environmental Earth science is the study of interactions between humans and Earth's natural environment. You will study the influence of human activities on the local and global environment as well as how human actions are shaped and controlled by the geologic and geomorphic processes occurring around us.

University of Calgary

Environmental Science Program
2500 University Drive NW, Calgary AB T2N 1N4 Canada
Tel: 403-220-8367; *Fax:* 403-210-8126
e-mail: ensc@ucalgary.ca
URL: www.ucalgary.ca
Description: Emphasizes a multi-disciplinary approach to understanding environmental issues facing society. It is a Collaborative Program administered jointly by the Faculties of Science and Social Sciences. It is designed to be a small program, with some 40 students a year, where hands-on experience is central. The program launched in 1996 and has more than 300 graduates.

University of Calgary

Earth Science Program
356 Earth Sciences Bldg, 2500 University Drive NW, Calgary AB T2N 1N4 Canada
Tel: 403-220-8929; *Fax:* 403-282-6561
e-mail: earthsci@ucalgary.ca
URL: www.ucalgary.ca
Description: Provides students with a mutli-disciplinary approach to studying the Earth. Students in this program are provided with a strong foundation in archaeology, geography, geology, and geophysics. Majors are exposed to extensive field and laboratory experiences. The program has a problem-solving focus with the following themes: climate and hydrology, biosphere interactions, global processes and change, earth science techniques.

University of Calgary

Geomatics Engineering
Dept of Geomatics Engineering, 2500 University Drive NW, Calgary AB T2N 1N4 Canada
Tel: 403-220-5834; *Fax:* 403-284-1980
e-mail: geomatics@geomatics.ucalgary.ca
URL: www.geomatics.ucalgary.ca
Description: Geomatics Engineering is an emerging information technology in the 21st Century. Geomatics deals with the acquisition, modeling, analysis and management of spatial data and includes exciting applications such as positioning by satellites, remote sensing, land surveying, and geospatial information management. Geomatics is one of the fastest growing information sciences in Canada and throughout the World.

University of Lethbridge

Environmental Science Program
4401 University Drive, Lethbridge AB T1K 3M4 Canada
Tel: 403-320-5700; *Fax:* 403-329-5159
e-mail: inquiries@uleth.ca
URL: www.uleth.ca
Description: A four-year program available to continuing students at the University of Lethbridge. This multidisciplinary major provides general science-based training which is completed by one semester of technical training at Lethbridge Community College in the third year of studies. The primary focus of this program is to enhance technical and practical skills in resource management with extensive theoretical knowledge in biology, geography, chemistry, physics and other related areas.

British Columbia

British Columbia Institute of Technology (BCIT)

Fish, Wildlife & Recreation (FWR)
3700 Willingdon Avenue, Burnaby BC V5G 3H2 Canada
Tel: 604-434-5734
Description: Part of the School of Construction and the Environment, FWR covers the management of fish, wildlife, and wild land recreation and includes habitat ecology, environmental inventory techniques, and environmental law with respect to these resources. Renewable Resources DIP

British Columbia Institute of Technology (BCIT)

Sustainable Resource Management (SRM)
3700 Willingdon Avenue, Burnaby BC V5G 3H2 Canada
Tel: 604-434-5734
Description: Provides a broad range of resource management skills for work in urban and rural settings, focusing on safety, field and academic training. There are 2 tracks in SRM: Forest Management and Environmental and Community Planning. SRM, FM or ECP, Part-time Diploma of Technology; Natural Resources Certificate (NRC)

British Columbia Institute of Technology (BCIT)

Environmental Engineering Technology
3700 Willingdon Avenue, Burnaby BC V5G 3H2 Canada
Tel: 604-434-5734
Description: Designed to provide the additional skills and knowledge that engineering and science graduates require to successfully work on environmental assignments such as site remediation, site audits, waste treatments facilities, wastewater management, hydrogeology, residuals management, solid waste management, industrial air pollution, and recycling projects. Full- or Part-time Bachelor of Technology.

British Columbia Institute of Technology (BCIT)

Ecological Restoration
3700 Willingdon Avenue, Burnaby BC V5G 3H2 Canada
Tel: 604-434-5734
Description: A scientific discipline that has emerged due to the increasing need to restore damaged ecosystems; graduates leave with a strong foundation in the methods available to restore a broad range of ecosystems that have been impacted by human influences. The program combines classroom and field activities for a more complete education. Full- or Part-time Bachelor of Technology.

British Columbia Institute of Technology (BCIT)

Environmental Health Technology
3700 Willingdon Avenue, Burnaby BC V5G 3H2 Canada
Tel: 604-434-5734
Description: The position of Public Health Inspector/Environmental Health Officer (PHI/EHO) is vital and this program aims to prepare students to enter the field as effective members of the multidisciplinary health team. Graduates will be able to recognize, evaluate and manage environmental factors that will impact that impact on human health, including long-range planning and environmental pollution situations, inspection and monitoring techniques. Full-time Bachelor of Technology

British Columbia Institute of Technology (BCIT)

Geographic Information Systems (GIS)
3700 Willingdon Avenue, Burnaby BC V5G 3H2 Canada
Tel: 604-434-5734
Description: Cirriculum combines theory and practice and covers GIS principles, training in software, technical issues,

Educational Programs / British Columbia Institute of Technology (BCIT)

remote sensing, digital mapping, and management issues, and includes a work experience requirements. Full- or Part-time Advanced Diploma

British Columbia Institute of Technology (BCIT)

Geomatics Engineering Technology
3700 Willingdon Avenue, Burnaby BC V5G 3H2 Canada
Tel: 604-434-5734
Description: This degree program offers two stream options: Surveying/Mapping, and GIS. The first will appeal to Geomatics Engineering technologists pursuing accreditation or otherwise developing their careers. The latter will teach professionals and students how to integrate GIS technology into their professions. Degrees: Bachelor of Technology (Surveying/Mapping); Geomatics DIP (Field Surveying or Digital Mapping).

Camosun College

Environmental Technology Program
Lansdowne Campus, Fisher Bldg #246, 3100 Foul Bay Road, Victoria BC V8P 5J2 Canada
Tel: 250-370-3000; *Fax:* 250-370-3551
URL: www.camosun.ca
Description: Gain academic expertise combined with hands-on laboratory and field skills to be ready to enter the work force as a Technologist. Students learn a range of skills and knowledge in such areas as: GIS map-reading, aquatic monitoring, soil classification, air quality, environmental impact assessments, sustainable resource and waste management, and horticulture and biodiversity. This program has a block transfer to the BSc in Environmental Science program at Royal Roads University. Paid work experience is also available with private and public sector employers: Institute of Ocean Science, Dept of National Defence, BC Hydro, First Nations organizations, numerous federal and provincial ministries and departments such as Forestry, Fisheries, Parks, and Water Management, and various municipalities and regional districts. Degree: DIP.

College of the Rockies

Natural Building Program
555 McKenzie Street, Kimberley BC V1A 2C1 Canada
Tel: 250-427-7116; *Fax:* 250-427-3034
Toll-Free: 877-489-2687
URL: www.cotr.ca/natural/cptr_web.asp?IDNumber=168
Description: Learn the fundamentals of construction, natural building design, post and beam, straw bale, natural building components, and natural plasters and finishes in this 7-week program. Includes seminar series involving specialized topics like yurts, rammed earth, earth ships and others.

Douglas College

Environmental Studies
NW Campus, 700 Royal Avenue, New Westminster BC Canada
Tel: 604-527-5400
URL: www.douglascollege.ca
Description: Associate of Arts Degree with an emphasis on Environmental Studies consists of a series of university transfer courses for the student interested in Earth functions and systems, the environment and global climate change, humans interaction with Earth, or the fields of park and urban planning, environmental consultation, and environmental education.

Douglas College

Earth Science
DL Campus, 1250 Pinetree Way, Coquitlam BC V3M 5Z5 Canada
Tel: 604-527-6500; *Fax:* 604-527-5095
URL: www.douglascollege.ca
Description: Study the materials, processes and history of our plant, including natural resources, natural hazards, rocks, minerals, fossils, and environmental issues, and learn how we explore for natural resources and about global clmiate change as a recurring phenomenon. 2-year Diploma.

Douglas College

Environmental Science
DL Campus, 1250 Pinetree Way, Coquitlam BC V3M 5Z5 Canada
Tel: 604-527-6500; *Fax:* 604-527-5095
URL: www.douglascollege.ca
Description: Study the interactions among Earth's fundamental systems: Lithosphere, Biosphere, Atmosphere, Hydrosphere; Explore the mechanisms of global change and the impact of human activites; Examine the nature of science. 2-year Diploma.

Douglas College

Environmental Studies
DL Campus, 1250 Pinetree Way, Coquitlam BC V3M 5Z5 Canada
Tel: 604-527-6500; *Fax:* 604-527-5095
URL: www.douglascollege.ca
Description: Learn about the Earth and how it functions, environmental citizenship, environmental law, global warming, and more, in preparation for careers such as park and urban planning, environmental consultation, and environmental education.AA

Institute for Resources, Environment & Sustainability (IRES) at the University of British Columbia (UBC)

Resource Management & Environmental Studies (RMES)
AERL, 429-2202 Main Hall, Vancouver BC V6T 1Z4 Canada
Tel: 604-822-7725; *Fax:* 604-822-9250
URL: www.ires.ubc.ca
Description: An interdisciplinary Graduate program tailored to the goals of the student, and focused on research across a wide range of environmental concerns including: land management, environmental assessment, fisheries management, water resource management, agroforestry, and science and policy. Degrees: MSc, MA; PhD; Certificate program in Watershed Management.

Langara College

Ecology
100 West 49th Avenue, Vancouver BC V5Y 2Z6 Canada
Tel: 604-323-5517
e-mail: erawling@langara.bc.ca
URL: www.langara.bc.ca/science-technology/ecology/index.html
Description: Studying Ecology at Langara you will be exposed to classroom theory, natural history, experimental methodology, and field work while learning how interactions with the environment affest the distribution and abundance of organzisms, where organisms occur, and their populations. Degree: ASc

Langara College

Environmental Studies
100 West 49th Avenue, Vancouver BC V5Y 2Z6 Canada
Tel: 604-323-5908
URL: www.langara.bc.ca/liberal-arts/environmental-studies/index.html
Description: Gain an awareness, knowledge, skills, experience, and environmental understanding in this interdisciplinary liberal arts program. The program draws from four critical areas of study - biology, chemistry, english, and georgaphy - as well as specific environmental courses. Degree: AA

Nicola Valley Institute of Technology (NVIT)

Natural Resource Technology
4155 Belshaw Street, Merritt BC V1K 1R1 Canada
Tel: 250-378-3300; *Fax:* 250-378-3332
Toll-Free: 877-682-3300
URL: www.nvit.ca
Description: The program provides training that reflects traditional native ethics of respect and care in the managment and protection of forests, grassland, range, fish, wildlife, and wilderness resources; creating graduates who are sensitive to, and understanding of, environmental issues. Degrees: NRT Certificate; NRT Diploma.

Okanagan College

Water Quality & Environmental Engineering - Environmental Monitoring & Water Quality
1000 KLO Road, Kelowna BC V1Y 4X8 Canada
Tel: 250-862-5468
URL: www.okanagan.bc.ca
Description: Provides training for technologists responsible for monitoring water in domestic, industrial, and environmental settings, in the public and private sectors. Students gain an understanding of techniques to assess chemical, biological, and physical aspects of water quality. 2-yr DIP.

Quest University Canada

Adventure Pursuits, Leadership and Sustainability of the Natural Environment
3200 University Boulevard, Squamish BC V8B 0N8 Canada
Tel: 604-898-8000; *Fax:* 604-815-0829
Toll-Free: 888-789-7808
e-mail: info@questu.ca
URL: www.questu.ca
Description: After completing the Foundation Program at Quest University Canada, students can choose to complete elective blocks in Adventure Pursuits, Leadership and Sustainability of the Natural Environment. The program is designed to questiona dn create personal and communal values, teach responsible stewardship, and to foster sustainable environmental practices. The courses available include the Wilderness Environment, Marine Ecology, and Climate Change and its Effect on Adventure Pursuits.

Quest University Canada

Life and the Natural Environment: The Life Sciences
3200 University Boulevard, Squamish BC V8B 0N8 Canada
Tel: 604-898-8000; *Fax:* 604-815-0829
Toll-Free: 888-789-7808
e-mail: info@questu.ca
URL: www.questu.ca
Description: After completing the Foundation Program at Quest University Canada, students can choose to complete their independent concentration program in the Life and the Natural Environment program. With a concentration in Ecology, students can take courses that include Forest Environments, Aquatic Ecosystems, and Environmental Chemistry.

Royal Roads University

Environmental Science
2005 Sooke Road, Victoria BC V9B 5Y2 Canada
Tel: 250-391-2511; *Fax:* 250-391-2500
Toll-Free: 800-788-8028
URL: www.royalroads.ca
Description: Learn about environmental management, economics, law, community relations, communication skills, and sustainable development, to gain problem solving skills for business and government. BSc

Royal Roads University

Environmental Practice
2005 Sooke Road, Victoria BC V9B 5Y2 Canada
Tel: 250-391-2511; *Fax:* 250-391-2500
Toll-Free: 800-788-8028
URL: www.royalroads.ca
Description: An innovative, distance-based program designed to help graduates gain neccessary academic credentials, and assist practitioners with ongoing skills and professional development. Certificate program.

Royal Roads University

Environmental Management
2005 Sooke Road, Victoria BC V9B 5Y2 Canada
Tel: 250-391-2511; *Fax:* 250-391-2500
Toll-Free: 800-788-8028
URL: www.royalroads.ca
Description: Acquire skills and knowledge in the field for use in planning and management in addressing environmental issues from a sustainability perspective. BSc

Royal Roads University

Environment and Management
2005 Sooke Road, Victoria BC V9B 5Y2 Canada
Tel: 250-391-2511; *Fax:* 250-391-2500
Toll-Free: 800-788-8028
URL: www.royalroads.ca
Description: The mission of the program is to produce graduates who are knowledgeable and effective professional and leaders in environmental sustainability. Master the assessment of environmental, social, cultural, political, legal, and economic elements of sustaining and enhancing environmental health and ecosystem well-being. Degrees: MA; MSc

Royal Roads University

Environmental Education & Communication
2005 Sooke Road, Victoria BC V9B 5Y2 Canada
Tel: 250-391-2511; *Fax:* 250-391-2500
Toll-Free: 800-788-8028
URL: www.royalroads.ca
Description: All programs in this Graduate degree have an online portion and short sessions, allowing the working professional to earn their advanced diploma or certificate. This is a leadership program focused on developing competency and skill in educators and communicators who have an interest in, or a responsibility for, presenting environmental information to audiences. Degrees: ENVEDCO-MA; ENVEDCO-CERT; ENVEDCO-DIP

Selkirk College

Forest Technology
301 Frank Beinder Way, Castlegar BC V1N 4L3 Canada
Tel: 250-365-7292; *Fax:* 250-365-6568
Toll-Free: 888-953-1133
URL: www.selkirk.ca/programs/rr
Description: Selkirk's Forestry program is known throughout the country for exellence in forest technology education, emphasizing an ecological approach to forest land management and achievement of proficeiency is advanced technology. Subjects of study include applied ecology, planning, regeneration, inventory, hydrology, habitat and forest protection, GIS and GPS technologies. 2-year Diploma.

Selkirk College

Renewable Energy
301 Frank Beinder Way, Castlegar BC V1N 4L3 Canada
Tel: 250-365-7292; *Fax:* 250-365-6568
Toll-Free: 888-953-1133
URL: www.selkirk.ca/programs/rr
Description: A new program of study designed to prepare students to enter the work force in with knowledge of some of the diverse technologies in the renweable energies field. 1-year Certificate.

Selkirk College

Integrated Environmental Planning
301 Frank Beinder Way, Castlegar BC V1N 4L3 Canada
Tel: 250-365-7292; *Fax:* 250-365-6568
Toll-Free: 888-953-1133
URL: www.selkirk.ca/programs/rr
Description: A nationally accredited program designed to prepare students to meet growing needs for technologists capable of assisting in all areas of environmental assessment and monitoring. Graduates are trained in GIS data entry and spacial analysis using Arc GIS and other software, environmental chemistry, ecology, hydrology, communication, economics and planning, in addition to a number of other areas of study pursued in the classroom, laboratory, and field. 2-year Diploma

Selkirk College

Recreation, Fish and Wildlife
301 Frank Beinder Way, Castlegar BC V1N 4L3 Canada
Tel: 250-365-7292; *Fax:* 250-365-6568
Toll-Free: 888-953-1133
URL: www.selkirk.ca/programs/rr
Description: A nationally accredited program, the focus of which is to provide relevant learning experience for individuals seeking careers in parks, forest recreation, fish and wildlife management, conservation or commercial recreation. The emphasis of the program is in the growing field of recreation and tourism, and fish and wildlife management i the working forest and protected areas. 2-year Diploma

Selkirk College

Geographic Information Systems (GIS)
301 Frank Beinder Way, Castlegar BC V1N 4L3 Canada
Tel: 250-365-7292; *Fax:* 250-365-6568
Toll-Free: 888-953-1133
URL: www.selkirk.ca/programs/rr
Description: GIS training at Selkirk prepares individuals to be trained geospatial experts int he environmental plannign, business, industry, and resource sectors. Real world projects enable students to gain expertise in GIS, GIS remote sensing, Internet mapping,technology, database management applications, GPS, 3D visualization and a variety of related software applications. Degrees: Adv. DIP; BGIS.

Simon Fraser University

Resource Management
TASC I #8405, 8888 University Drive, Burnaby BC V5A 1S6 Canada
Tel: 778-782-4659; *Fax:* 778-782-4968
e-mail: reminfo@sfu.ca
URL: www.rem.sfu.ca
Description: This Masters program is designed for recent graduates from a range of discplines and for individuals with experience in private or public organizations in dealing with natural resources and the environment. Provides understanding of the strategies and techniques of natural resource and environmental planning and management, biological, social, physical, economic and institutional implications of resouce decisions. REM Students have the option of completing the Resource and Environmental Planning Program, as well. Accredited and recognized by the CIP and PIBC, the advantages of this degree course include the option of membership in the CIP and the PIBC, improved employment prospects, participation in conferences and workshops, and access to professional development programs. Degrees: MSc MRM (Planning)

Simon Fraser University

Resource & Environmental Management
TASC I #8405, 8888 University Drive, Burnaby BC V5A 1S6 Canada
Tel: 778-782-4659; *Fax:* 778-782-4968
e-mail: reminfo@sfu.ca
URL: www.rem.sfu.ca
Description: This PhD program provides an opportunity for pursuing high-level research and interdisciplinary edutcation in natural resources and environmental management. Coursework and research supervision are available over a wide range of natural and social sciences.

Thompson River University

Environmental Science
Box 3010, 900 McGill Road, Kamloops BC V2C 5N3 Canada
Tel: 250-828-5000
URL: www.tru.ca
Description: The TRU MSc in Environmental Science is an interdisciplinary research program designed to produce graduates who have a broad range of skills and knowledge that they can apply in an integrative and innovative approach in the field. MSc.

Thompson River University

Environmental Sciences Seminar Series
Box 3010, 900 McGill Road, Kamloops BC V2C 5N3 Canada
Tel: 250-828-5000
URL: www.tru.ca/science/msces/mscseminar.html
Description: Environmental Sciences is a broad filed that attempts to understand and solve environmental problems, integrating the diversity of elements involved, including: biology, natural resources sciences, geography, politics, history, philosophy, geology, tourism, sociology, education, physics, chemistry, mathematics,and economics. Most seminars are Thursdays from 3:30 to 4:30 unless otherwise indicated.

Thompson River University

Natural Resource Sciences
Box 3010, 900 McGill Road, Kamloops BC V2C 5N3 Canada
Tel: 205-371-5530
e-mail: bheise@tru.ca
URL: www.tru.ca/science/nrs
Description: By understanding the scientific, economis, and social basis of natural resource issues, graduates will be able to effectively interface between diverse interest groups, all having a stake in how our terrestrial and aquatic resources are managed. Students will learn technical skills, social investment in the field, and economic factors, work in research settings, and have the option of applying to the Honours program. Degrees: BSc. Forestry Transfer program option also available with UNBC or UBC.

Trinity Western University

Environmental Studies
7600 Glover Road, Langley BC V2Y 1Y1 Canada
Tel: 604-888-7511
URL: www.twu.ca
Description: Students will gain practical environmental experience working at one of TWU's Eco-Study Areas, and real-world perspective through the multidisciplinary courses. Offers a number of ES streams, including: natural systems and resources; biochemical studies; physical and analytical studies; environmental management and planning Degrees: BA; BSc

Trinity Western University

Ecology
7600 Glover Road, Langley BC V2Y 1Y1 Canada
Tel: 604-888-7511
URL: www.twu.ca
Description: Through the Biology department at TWU, students work in research areas, developing occupational skills in Ecology. With off-campus field courses available in Washington State, Hawaii, Florida, India and Africa. Degree: BSc

University of British Columbia (UBC)

Atmospheric Science
Dept of EOS, 6399 Stores Road, Vancouver BC V6T 1Z4 Canada
Tel: 604-822-2713; *Fax:* 604-822-6088
e-mail: gradsec@eos.ubc.ca
URL: www.eos.ubc.ca
Description: UBC offers degrees in the study of Atmospheric Science, including the following research areas: micrometeorology, weather, air pollution and atmospheric chemistry, climate, biometeorology, and geophysical fluid dynamics. Degrees: PhD; MSc; BSc.

University of British Columbia (UBC)

Earth & Ocean Sciences
Dept of EOS, 6399 Stores Road, Vancouver BC V6T 1Z4 Canada
Tel: 604-822-2713; *Fax:* 604-822-6088
URL: www.eos.ubc.ca
Description: The Earth & Ocean Sciences Department (EOS) at UBC is one of the largest and most diverse of its kind in the world. This BSc with an Honours option is a flexible degree program that encompasses a broad spectrum of disciplines, with focus upon specializations such as geophysics, oceanography, environmental geology, or atmospheric sciences.

University of British Columbia (UBC)

Environmental Science
Dept of EOS, 6339 Stores Road, Vancouver BC V6T 1Z4 Canada
Tel: 604-822-2713; *Fax:* 604-822-6088
URL: www.eos.ubc.ca
Description: Designed to give students a broad perspective on the environment, the program concentrates on understanding the major environmental issues facing human societies with a cross-disciplinary approach. Degrees: BSc; BSc Honours.

University of British Columbia (UBC)

Geological Engineering
Dept of EOS, 6339 Stores Road, Vancouver BC V6T 1Z4 Canada
Tel: 604-822-2713; *Fax:* 604-822-6088
e-mail: gradsec@eos.ubc.ca
URL: www.eos.ubc.ca
Description: This program is intended for students interested in the applications of earth sciences principals to engineering problems, and allows the student to base their studies either in the EOS Departments or Applied Science such as Civil or Mining Engineering. The program is highly interdisciplinary and draws upon courses labs, and faculty members from the departments of EOS, Civil and Mining Engineering, Forestry, Geography, and others. Degrees: PhD; MASc; MA Eng.

University of British Columbia (UBC)

Environmental Design Program (ENDS)
Environmental Design Program, 370-2357 Main Mall, Vancouver BC V6T 1Z4 Canada
Tel: 604-822-9616; *Fax:* 604-822-2184
e-mail: larc@interchange.ubc.ca
URL: www.sala.ubc.ca
Description: The program focuses on themes emphasizing analysis and representation, history and theory, technology and practice, all anchored by a Core Studio Design

Educational Programs / University of British Columbia (UBC)

cusrriculum. At the heart of the ENDS program is the goal of developing students into a constituency aware of the real challenges and opportunities in forming space and designing with the land who finds common ground first as a community, considering its central focus issues relevant to contemporary society. Their designs will be critically engaged and imaginatively considered, engendering social and ecological rediscovery. Degree: BSc ENDS

University of British Columbia (UBC)

Forest Sciences
Forest Resources Management - 2045-2424 Main Mall, Vancouver BC V6T 1Z4 Canada
Tel: 604-822-3482; *Fax:* 604-822-9106
e-mail: frm.recept@ubc.ca
URL: www.forestry.ubc.ca
Description: The Bachelor of Science in Forestry program focuses on the specific principles related to the growth and development of forest organisms, and the ecology of plant and animal communities.

University of British Columbia (UBC)

Natural Resources Conservation
Forest Resources Management - 2045-2424 Main Mall, Vancouver BC V6T 1Z4 Canada
Tel: 604-822-3482; *Fax:* 604-822-9106
e-mail: frm.recept@ubc.ca
URL: www.forestry.ubc.ca
Description: The Bachelor of Science in Natural Resources Conservation program provides students with skills and knowledge to meet the challenges of maintaining healthy ecosystems and protecting natural environments in an era of changing climate.

University of British Columbia (UBC)

Forest Operations Program
Forest Resources Management - 2045-2424 Main Mall, Vancouver BC V6T 1Z4 Canada
Tel: 604-822-3482; *Fax:* 604-822-9106
e-mail: frm.recept@ubc.ca
URL: www.forestry.ubc.ca
Description: The Bachelor of Science in Forestry, Forest Operations program focuses on preparing students for plannig and implementing complex harvesting operations that maximize exonomic returns and minimize environmental impact. The program is based on biological, physical and social sciences.

University of British Columbia (UBC)

Forest Resources Management
Forest Resources Management - 2045-2424 Main Mall, Vancouver BC V6T 1Z4 Canada
Tel: 604-822-3482; *Fax:* 604-822-9106
e-mail: frm.recept@ubc.ca
URL: www.forestry.ubc.ca
Description: The Bachelor of Science in Forestry, Forest Resources Management program teaches students how to integrate the use of a wide variety of natural resources including range, recreation, timber, water and wildlife.

University of Northern British Columbia (UNBC)

Ecosystem Science & Management
3333 University Way, Prince George BC V2N 4Z9 Canada
Description: Houses faculty with interests in all aspects of ecosystem function, from cellular and molecular scale to the role of humans in modifying these ecosystems. The interdisciplinary nature of the ESM reflects the interwoven interests of faculty and the necessity of incorporating diverse perspectives in ecosystem management, from natural science to social science. Accredited by the Canadian Forestry Accreditation Board. Cooperative education options, and research opportunities abound. Degrees: BSc: Biology, NRM - Forest Ecology & Management, Wildlife and Fisheries, Environmental Studies; MA, MSc, MNRES or PhD in Natural Resources & Environmental Studies; additional masters and doctoral level interdisciplinary programs.

University of Northern British Columbia (UNBC)

Environmental Studies
3333 University Way, Prince George BC V2N 4Z9 Canada
URL: www.unbc.ca
Description: The program offers a selection of emphases from social science and humanities perspectives to Global Environmental Change. This is a BA program.

University of Northern British Columbia (UNBC)

Environmental Science & Engineering
3333 University Way, Prince George BC V2N 4Z9 Canada
Description: The Environmental Science focus is designed to train scientists who will understand how the environment functions, and how to mitigate effects on the environments when functions and processes are disrupted. The Engineering focus teaches students to be aware of the need to integrate environmental and economic factors in providing environmental analysis and engineering design across a range of disciplines. Degrees: BSc Environmental Science; BASc Environmental Engineering; MSc NRES Environmental Science; MNRES Natural Resources & Environmental Studies; PhD Natural Resources & Environmental Studies

University of Northern British Columbia (UNBC)

Natural Resource Management and Environmental Studies Graduate Program
3333 University Way, Prince George BC V2N 4Z9 Canada
Description: Primarily concerned with "People and The Environment", with streams in Geography, Environmental Studies, Tourism, Biology, Environmental Science, Forestry, and Recreational Resource Management. Working with research partners from the local to the international levels. Degrees: Phd NRES, MA NRES, MSc NRES

University of Northern British Columbia (UNBC) & University of British Columbia (UBC)

Environmental Engineering (Joint Program)
Environmental Engineering, 2360 East Mall, Vancouver BC V6T 1Z3 Canada
Tel: 604-827-3415; *Fax:* 604-822-6003
e-mail: info@enve.ubc.ca
URL: www.enve.ubc.ca
Description: A joint degree program offered by UBC and UNBC capitalizes on each university's strengths in sciences and engineering, and is the only Environmental Engineering program in the province. The first two-years are spent building the science foundation at UNBC, and the third and fourth will be spent building your engineering skills UBC. Then a final term at UNBC focusing on practical environmental engineering design problems. Degrees: BASc; upon graduation, eligible for registration as Professional Engineers (P.Eng.) with the Canadian Engineering Accreditation Board and the Association of P.Eng. & Geoscientists of BC.

University of Victoria (UVic)

Earth and Ocean Science Graduate Program
School of Earth and Ocean Science (SEOS), Petch 168, 3800 Finnerty Rd, Victoria BC V8P 5C2 Canada
Tel: 250-472-5133; *Fax:* 250-721-6200
e-mail: eosc@uvic.ca
URL: www.seos.uvic.ca
Description: Graduate Program at the School of Earth and Ocean Science (SEOS), research areas include a strong focus on earth system science with special studies in marine geology and geophysics, paleoceanography, tectonics, atmospheric modelling, air-sea interaction, biological oceanography, and various other areas. Degrees: PhD; MSc.

University of Victoria (UVic)

Environmental Studies
School of Environmental Studies, 2800 Finnerty Road, Victoria BC V8W 3R4 Canada
Tel: 250-721-7354; *Fax:* 250-721-8985
e-mail: ses@uvic.ca
URL: http://web.uvic.ca/enweb/
Description: Graduate Program at the School of Environmental Studies offers 3 core, interdisciplinary research areas in Ecological Restoration, Ethnoecology and Political Ecology. Degrees: MA; MSc in Environmental Studies.

University of Victoria (UVic)

Earth and Ocean Science Combined Major Programs - Undergraduate
School of Earth and Ocean Science (SEOS), Petch 168, 3800 Finnerty Rd, Victoria BC V8P 5C2 Canada
Tel: 250-472-5133; *Fax:* 250-721-6200
e-mail: eosc@uvic.ca
URL: www.seos.uvic.ca
Description: These Earth Science Programs require a core of Earth Science studies and corequisit studies in the partner science(s). BSc Degrees: Earth Sciences; Combined Major & Honours in Physics and Earth Sciences (Geophysics); Combined Major & Honours in Physics and Ocean Sciences (Ocean-Atmosphere Dynamics); Combined Major & Honours in Chemistry and Earth & Ocean Sciences; Combined Major & Honours in Physical Geograohy and Earth & Ocean Sciences; Combined Major & Honours in Biology and Earth & Ocean Sciences; Minor in Ocean Sciences.

Vancouver Island University

Forest Resources Technology
100 Fifth Street, Nanaimo BC V9R 5S5 Canada
Tel: 250-753-3245; *Fax:* 250-740-6556
URL: viu.ca/forestry/index.asp
Description: This program provides technical training required for starting a career in most fields of forest technology, with emphasis on the recognition and appreciation of all major values of the forest including timber, recreation, wildlife, range, fish, water, and aesthetics. Bridge programs to UBC Bachelor programs are available, as is the opportunity to take the first two years of the UBC program at VIU. 2-year Technology Diploma

Vancouver Island University

Green Building & Renewable Energy Technician
100 Fifth Street, Nanaimo BC V9R 5S5 Canada
Toll-Free: 888-920-2221
URL: viu.ca
Description: A 2-year diploma program that addresses energy efficiency and renewable energy applications in buildings. Graduates will be prepared to participate in the emerging green building industry or the renewable energy industry, providing technical communication, design, assessment, and evaluation services to engineers, contractors, architects, project and facilities managers.

Vancouver Island University

Resource Management Officer Technology
100 Fifth Street, Nanaimo BC V9R 5S5 Canada
Tel: 250-753-3245; *Fax:* 250-740-6482
e-mail: Marilyn.Funk@viu.ca
URL: viu.ca/rmot/index.asp
Description: This program is designed to prepare students for careers related to the protection and management of Canada's fisheries, wildlife, and parks resources. RMOT students work first-hand with natural resource law enforcement agencies and are supported by an Advisory Committee made up of members of Federal Dept of Fisheries & Oceans, Provincial Ministry of Environment, BC Parks, Parks Canada, Environment Canada, and from resource users groups. 2-year Diploma.

Vancouver Island University

Natural Resource Protection
100 Fifth Street, Nanaimo BC V9R 5S5 Canada
Tel: 250-753-3245; *Fax:* 250-740-6482
e-mail: Marilyn.Funk@viu.ca
URL: viu.ca/rmot/index.asp
Description: The program builds on the existing 2-year RMOT diploma for a BSc of Natural Resource Protection, for career opportunities in conservation and protection. In addition to advanced courses in natural resource management and law enforcement, there will be a four-month field practicum in the fall of the fourth yearduring which students will be able to choose an off-campus field placement in enforcement or resource management.

Vancouver Island University

Natural Resources Extension Program
100 Fifth Street, Nanaimo BC V9R 5S5 Canada
Tel: 250-740-6377
e-mail: nrep@viu.ca
URL: viu.ca/nrep/index.asp
Description: The NREP is one of Canada's leading providers of applied, community-based natural resources professional development training. A series of 1-3 or 15-25 day certification programs are available in these areas: Aquatic, Environemntal Monitoring, Erosion & Sediment Control, Riparian, Fisheries, Aboriginal Environmental Tech, Fisheries Field Tech, Essential Fisheries Field Skills, Environmental Professional; and a 2-year Diploma program in First Nation Fisheries Technologist (FNFTDP).

Vancouver Island University

Forest Resource Management-Transfer Program
100 Fifth Street, Nanaimo BC V9R 5S5 Canada
Tel: 250-753-3245; *Fax:* 250-740-6556
e-mail: wilkinsoj@viu.ca
URL: viu.ca/forestry/index.asp
Description: VIU offers the equivalent of the first two years of the UBC Science in Forestry (BSF) degree program with direct tranfer into the 3rd year at UBC. (See listing under Forestry Resource Management)

Vancouver Island University

Renewable Energy Technology
100 Fifth Street, Nanaimo BC V9R 5S5 Canada
Tel: 250-740-6160; *Fax:* 250-740-6452
e-mail: ccs@viu.ca
URL: viu.ca
Description: An online Certificate program focusing on renewable energy and various technologies of renewable energy, providing graduates with an understanding of the implications of our use of non-renewable energy and options for the production and use of renewable energy. The ultimate goal of the program is to deliver training which leads to promotion, adaptation and growth of renewable energy technology deployment across Canada.

Manitoba

Brandon University

Environmental Science Program
270-18th Street, Brandon MB R7A 6A9 Canada
Tel: 204-728-9520; *Fax:* 204-726-4573
URL: www.brandonu.ca
Description: Environmental Science is the interdisciplinary study of the environment, its functioning and its relationship to human activities. It encompasses many of the traditional science disciplines, but uses these in the study of terrestrial, aquatic and atmospheric systems and their interactions.

University of Manitoba

Department of Environment & Geography
440 Wallace Bulding, University of Manitoba, Winnipeg MB R3T 2N2 Canada
Tel: 204-474-7252
e-mail: faculty_environment@umanitoba.ca
URL: www.umanitoba.ca
Description: In order to properly explain human-environment interactions in ecological, geological, social and economic capacities, the Environment, Earth and Resources Faculty is interdisciplinary. Students have their choice of six degrees including a Bachelor of Environmental Science degree and a Bachelor of Environmental Studies degree.

The University of Winnipeg

Environmental Studies
515 Portage Avenue, Winnipeg MB R3B 2E9 Canada
Tel: 204-786-7811
e-mail: websuggest@uwinnipeg.ca
URL: www.uwinnipeg.ca
Description: Environmental Studies is an interdisciplinary program that takes an holistic approach to the environment. Following the general principles of sustainability, the BA programs offer an integrated understanding of the environment, acknowledging human impact, and providing a framework to develop future solutions to environmental problems within two distinct streams: Issues in Sustainability and Urban Policy and the Environment. The BSc programs provide four options to choose from: Forest Ecology, Forest Policy and Management, Chemistry, and Global Environmental Systems.

New Brunswick

Mount Allison University

Environmental Studies
Room 307 Avard Dixon, 144 Main Street, Sackville NB E4L 1A7 Canada
Description: The ES program brings together the various strands of environmental thinking that exist within different disciplines in geography, economics, philosophy, anthropology, etc. and encourages students to harvest the most relevant ideas and synthesize these in a manner that enables a comprehensive environmental literacy.

Newfoundland and Labrador

Memorial University of Newfoundland

Marine Environmental
PO Box PO Box 4920, St. John's NL A1C 5R3 Canada
Tel: 709-778-0454; *Fax:* 709-778-0346
Toll-Free: 800-563-5799
URL: www.mi.mun.ca
Description: With a Diploma of Technology in Marine Environmental Technology, you will be able to develop environmentally sound projects and work to prevent and create responses to marine pollution or degradation. You will go from lakes to rivers and coastal zones to the fragile offshore. You will be responsible for protecting the marine environment and developing solutions to manage marine resources.

Memorial University of Newfoundland

Integrated Coastal and Ocean Management
PO Box PO Box 4920, St. John's NL A1C 5R3 Canada
Tel: 709-778-0454; *Fax:* 709-778-0346
Toll-Free: 800-563-5799
URL: www.mi.mun.ca
Description: This advanced diploma program focuses on the bio-ecological, socio-economic, cultural and technological elements of coastal zone development and management. It will prepare students for a career related to planning and management of coastal and ocean activities or coastal zone development.

Sir Wilfred Grenfell College

Environmental Science
1 University Drive, Corner Brook NL A2H 6P9 Canada
Tel: 709-637-6200
URL: www.swgc.mun.ca
Description: The Bachelor of Science in Environmental Science degree is interdisciplinary, combining aspects of all of the natural sciences, specifically as they contribute to a greater awareness and understanding of the environment. The program provides a broad education and includes courses designed to enhance the student's appreciation of the scientific, social, cultural and political issues that impinge on the environment.

Sir Wilfred Grenfell College

Environmental Studies
1 University Drive, Corner Brook NL A2H 6P9 Canada
Tel: 709-637-6200
URL: www.swgc.mun.ca
Description: The aim of the Bachelor of Arts in Environmental Studies program is to encourage students to critically examine and develop a broad yet integrated understanding of environmental issues, problems, and possible solutions.

Sir Wilfred Grenfell College

Sustainable Resource Management
1 University Drive, Corner Brook NL A2H 6P9 Canada
Tel: 709-637-6200
URL: www.swgc.mun.ca
Description: The Sustainable Resource Management (SRM) Program is a new Bachelor of Resource Management degree (BRM) that bridges scientific concerns about natural resources with policy development and management. The program aims to produce a different type of resource manager, graduates who have an understanding of ethics, as well as the many ecological, sociological and economic factors. The program acknowledges the goals of sustainable development while simultaneously recognizing the move from the more traditional concept of resource management towards a broader management approach.

Nova Scotia

Acadia University

Environmental Geoscience
Dept of Earth & Environmental Science, PO Box 12 University Ave, Huggins Hall, 3rd Fl, Wolfville NS B4P 2R6 Canada
Tel: 902-585-1208; *Fax:* 902-585-1816
e-mail: ees@acadiau.ca
URL: ees.acadiau.ca/
Description: The program is designed to prepare graduates for the requirements needed for professional registration as a Professional or Environmental Geoscientist in Nova Scotia. The program is offered at the undergraduate and graduate levels.

Acadia University

Environmental Science
Dept of Earth & Environmental Science, PO Box 12 University Ave, KC Irving Centre LL, Wolfville NS B4P 2R6 Canada
Tel: 902-585-1208; *Fax:* 902-585-1816
e-mail: ees@acadiau.ca
URL: ees.acadiau.ca/
Description: A four-year program available at both a BSc and BSc (Honours) level. Focus areas include: land use management; natural resource management; sustainable development; environmental health; ecology; conservation biology; and environmental geology/terrain analysis.

Aurora College - Thebacha Campus

Environmental Monitoring Training
50 Conibear Crescent, PO Box 600, Fort Smith NT X0E 0P0 Canada
Tel: 867-872-7500; *Fax:* 867-872-4511
Toll-Free: 866-266-4966
URL: www.auroracollege.nt.ca
Description: The five-week Environmental Monitoring Training Program provides students with the foundation, knowledge and skills to participate in environmental monitoring activities. The program is concentrated on students who are interested in working in the environmental sector and require pre-technician level training on environmental concepts and measures.

Aurora College - Thebacha Campus

Environment and Natural Resources Technology Program
50 Conibear Crescent, PO Box 600, Fort Smith NT X0E 0P0 Canada
Tel: 867-872-7500; *Fax:* 867-872-4511
Toll-Free: 866-266-4966
URL: www.auroracollege.nt.ca
Description: The Aurora College Environment and Natural Resources Technology Program (ENRTP) can prepare you for a great career working as a resource officer, an environmental technician or as an environmental manager. Courses cover wildlife management, environmental assessment, applied technology such as Geographic Information Systems, resource conservation and much more. ENRTP includes field camps with plenty of hands-on learning opportunities.

Cape Breton University

Engineering Technology-Environmental Studies
1250 Grand Lake Road, PO Box 5300, Sydney NS B1P 6L2 Canada
Tel: 902-563-1113; *Fax:* 902-563-1813
e-mail: engineering@cbu.ca
URL: faculty.capebretonu.ca/engineering/index.html
Description: This Bachelor degree program combines theoretical principles with hand-on experience related to the understanding of biological, chemical, geological, and engineering principles applied to the environment. Emphasis is placed on assessment of air quality, water and soil, sustainable development, and management of waste products and pollutants.

Dalhousie University

Faculty of Science-Environmental Programs
Halifax NS B3H 4J1 Canada
Tel: 902-494-2791
URL: environmental.science.dal.ca/index.html
Description: The program choices available for studies in the environment include: BSc Honours/Major in Environmental Science; BSc Double Major (i.e. Environmental Science and Community Design; Environmental Science and International Development; or any subject in the Faculty of Arts & Social Sciences); Minor in Environmental Studies; or Double Major/Combined Honours with Concentration in Environmental Science.

Dalhousie University

School for Resource and Environmental Studies (SRES)
6100 University Ave, Ste 5010, PO Box Kenneth C. Rowe Mgmt Bldg, Halifax NS B3H 3J5 Canada

Tel: 902-494-3632; Fax: 902-494-3728
e-mail: sres@dal.ca
URL: sres.management.dal.ca
Description: The school offers two graduate programs in environmental management, science and policy. The first is a Master of Environmental Studies (MES), which is a two-year program that includes both course work and a thesis. The second is a Master of Resource and Environmental Management (MREM), which is a 16-month program that includes course work and an internship. Both programs emphasize interactions between social and natural sciences needed for resolving the complex environmental and resource management problems.

Dalhousie University

Marine & Environmental Law Programme (MELP)
6061 University Ave, PO Box Dalhousie Law School, Halifax NS B3H 4H9 Canada
Tel: 902-494-1988; Fax: 902-494-1316
e-mail: melp@dal.ca
URL: www.dal.ca/law/MELP
Description: This certificate programme provides LL.B. and post graduate students (LL.M. and Doctoral) with extensive academic course offerings in the fields of Marine Law and Enironmental Law, taught from domestic and international perspectives.

Nova Scotia Agricultural College

Environmental Sciences
PO Box 550, Truro NS B2N 5E3 Canada
Tel: 902-893-6600
e-mail: gwstratton@nsac.ca
URL: nsac.ca/envsci/
Description: The Environmental Science program allows students to pursue studies in the following range of specialty subject areas: Environmental Biology, Environmental Chemistry, Environmental Economics, Environmental Soil Science, Waste Management, and Pest Management. The Bio-Environmental Engineering Centre (BEEC) is frequently used as a research and demonstration facility.

Nova Scotia Agricultural College

Bio-Environmental Systems Management
Banta Building, PO Box 550, Truro NS B2N 5E3 Canada
Tel: 902-893-6710
e-mail: engineering@nsac.ca
URL: nsac.ca/eng/
Description: A four-year (B.Sc.) science program designed to provide a background in the management of technology associated with environmental and biological systems.

Nova Scotia Agricultural College

Graduate Studies
PO Box 550, Truro NS B2N 5E3 Canada
Tel: 902-893-6600
e-mail: gradstudies@nsac.ca
URL: nsac.ca/gradstudies
Description: Graduate students have the choice of concentrating their study and research towards a M.Sc. in Environmental Science, Animal Science, Plant Science, or Soil Science and Agricultural Chemistry.

Saint Mary's University

Environmental Studies
923 Robie Street, Halifax NS B3H 3C3 Canada
Tel: 902-420-5744
e-mail: gpiper@smu.ca
URL: www.smu.ca/academic/science/envstud/
Description: The program offers a concentration, major, Honours and minor. The program combines core sciences with management, social sciences and humanities and leads to a Bachelor of Science in Environmental Studies.

St. Francis Xavier University

Environmental Sciences
Physical Sciences Complex, 1 West St, PO Box Office 2052, Antigonish NS B2G 2W5 Canada
Tel: 902-867-5109; Fax: 902-867-2414
e-mail: lkellman@stfx.ca
URL: envsciences.stfx.ca
Description: The Environmental Sciences program offers Honours and advanced majors in four different concentrations-biology, chemistry, biochemistry, and climate/water. Each concentration offers an integrated approach to understanding the interaction of biological, chemical and physical systems and processes in the environment.

Ontario

Carleton University

Institute of Environmental Studies
2240 Herzberg Bldg, 1125 Colonel By Drive, Ottawa ON K1S 5B6
Tel: 613-520-4461; Fax: 613-520-3422
e-mail: environmentalscience@carleton.ca
URL: www.carleton.ca/envirosci
Description: Protection of the environment, its plants and wildlife, and the effects of pollution on human health are burning issues. They may be as local as the planning of a pipeline or as a broad-ranging as global climate change.

Carleton University

Department of Geology and Environmental Studies
B349 Loeb Bldg, 1125 Colonel By Drive, Ottawa ON K1S 5B6 Canada
Tel: 613-520-2561; Fax: 613-520-4301
URL: www.carleton.ca/envirstd
Description: A multidisciplinary program, based on the social sciences, humanities and sciences. It is designed to educate and prepare informed, skilled individuals to participate in the design of sustainable solutions to environmental conflicts and to shape the larger environmental debates critical to our future.

Carleton University

Technology, Society, Environmental Studies
2240 HP, 1125 Colonel By Drive, Ottawa ON K1S 5B6 Canada
Tel: 613-520-4461; Fax: 613-520-3422
URL: www.carleton.ca/tse
Description: Covers a wide range of topics from technology in ancient societies to contemporary issues in risk, innovation, forecasting, information technology, environmental sustainability, product life cycle analysis, energy use and the philosophy of technology.

Queen's University

Environmental Studies Program
School of Environmental Science, Biosciences Complex, Room 3134, Kingston ON K7L 3N6 Canada
Tel: 613-533-6602; Fax: 613-533-6090
e-mail: envst@queensu.ca
URL: www.queensu.ca
Description: An interdisciplinary undergraduate and graduate training that integrates the concepts of environmental toxicology and chemistry, ecosystems, human health, environmental policy and management, as well as the importance of social, cultural, and economic systems into the overarching theme of sustainability.

Redeemer University College

Environmental Studies Program
777 Garner Road E, Ancaster ON L9K 1J4 Canada
Tel: 905-648-2131; Fax: 905-648-2134
Toll-Free: 877-779-0913
URL: www.redeemer.ca
Description: Teaches about the impact of humans on the environment and how we can live in ways that reduce our negative impact. As an environmental studies student, you will develop a comprehensive approach to environmental issues, addressing Biblical, ethical, economic political social and scientific aspects.

Trent University

Environmental and Resource Studies Program
1600 W Bank Drive, Peterborough ON K9J 7B8 Canada
Tel: 705-748-1011; Fax: 705-748-1569
e-mail: ers@trentu.ca
URL: www.trenut.ca
Description: Whether the issue is water pollution, climate change, revegetation of industrial sites, environmental law and policy, modeling health effects of toxins, the challenge of global forces, community-level natural resource stewardship, or renewable energy alternatives, the ERS program and affiliated departments offer superb expertise and hands-on experience.

University of Ottawa

Environmental Sciences Program
Marion Hall, Room 201, Ottawa ON K1N 6N5 Canada
Tel: 613-562-5800; Fax: 613-562-5192
e-mail: evs@uottawa.ca
URL: www.environmental.uottawa.ca
Description: The EVS program is the study of natural systems, of resource use and development, of the migration of contaminants in the environment and of their impace on the ecosystem as a whole.

University of Waterloo

Department of Environment and Resource Studies
200 University Avenue W, Waterloo ON N2L 3G1 Canada
Tel: 519-888-4567
URL: www.environment.uwaterloo.ca
Description: The Department of Environment and Resource studies, located within the larger Faculty of Environment, offers programs which focus on sustainability and the ethics of solving environmental and resource problems, using techniques and ideas from many disciplines-ecology, environmental governance, energy, water, waste management, media and environmental assessment.

York University

Environmental and Health Studies Program
Glendon Campus, York Hall 162, 2275 Bayview Avenue, Toronto ON M4N 3M6 Canada
Tel: 416-487-6732; Fax: 416-487-6851
e-mail: mds@glendon.yorku.ca
URL: www.glendon.yorku.ca
Description: A focused yet comprehensive analysis of issues in the fields of environment and health. This program will give you the opportunity to obtain a solid grasp of the bio-medical and environmental sciences within the broader context of a liberal arts education. Provides a chance to explore a variety of health-related issues, and your degree will help you understand the historical roots of contemporary environmental and bio-medical controversies.

Prince Edward Island

University of Prince Edward Island

Environmental Studies
550 University Avenue, Charlottetown PE C1A 4P3 Canada
Tel: 902-620-5066
e-mail: enviro@upei.ca
URL: www.upei.ca
Description: The environmental studies program aims to equip students with the knowledge to understand the environmental connections across academic fields, to critically analyze complex environmental issues, and to propose sound options toward sustainable solutions.

University of Prince Edward Island

Department Of Biology
550 University Avenue, Charlottetown PE C1A 4P3 Canada
Tel: 902-566-0301; Fax: 902-566-0740
e-mail: biology@upei.ca
URL: www.upei.ca
Description: The Department of Biology offers exciting research opportunities in many different areas including Ecology & Wildlife Biology, Plant Science, Marine and Freshwater Biology and Animal Behavior.

Québec

Bishop's University

Department of Biology
2600 College Street, Sherbrooke QC J1M 1Z7 Canada
Tel: 819-822-9600; Fax: 819-822-9661
URL: www.ubishops.ca
Description: The biology programs at Bishop's University provide a broad foundation in the field of biology and prepares students for many opportunities. The options available include graduate studies in biological or life science, and professional studies in veterinary medicine, the allied health sciences, forestry, wildlife biology and many other areas. A degree in biology also prepares students for direct employment in the biotechnology sector, environmental biology, or the allied health fields.

Bishop's University

Department of Environmental Studies & Geography
2600 College Street, Sherbrooke QC J1M 1Z7 Canada
Tel: 819-822-9600; *Fax:* 819-822-9661
URL: www.ubishops.ca
Description: A degree in Environmental Studies and Geography has a major focus on human-environment interaction, and provides students with a broad discipline which analyzes the distribution and interrelationships of physical and human phenomena on the earth. It combines subject matter and methodologies from the natural and social sciences.

Concordia University

Department of Biology
7141 Sherbrooke Street West, Montreal QC H4B 1R6 Canada
Tel: 514-848-2424; *Fax:* 518-848-2881
URL: www.concordia.ca
Description: The Department of Biology offers a broad education in the fundamentals of the biological sciences. Programs available include Biochemistry, Aquatic Ecology, Plant Biology and Ecotoxicology. The programs also allow students to conduct original, independent research, where students can expand their horizons in the field of biology.

McGill University

Environment
Room MS2-O32, MacDonald-Stewart Bldg, 21111 Lakeshore Road, Ste Anne de Bellevue QC H9X 3V9 Canada
Tel: 514-398-7707; *Fax:* 514-398-7766
URL: www.mcgill.ca
Description: This major has two components: Core & Domain. The Core exposes students to a variety of approaches, perspectives and world views to give an understanding of the complexity and conflicts that underlie most environmental problems. The Domain is the area of specialization the student chooses and is immersed in cutting-edge interdisciplinary fields to provide expertise. Degrees: BA; BSc; BA&Sc.

McGill University

Environmental Biology
Room MS2-O32, MacDonald-Stewart Bldg, 21111 Lakeshore Road, Ste Anne de Bellevue QC H9X 3V9 Canada
Tel: 514-398-7707; *Fax:* 514-398-7766
URL: www.mcgill.ca
Description: A vibrant learning experience in the providing students extensive field training in the diversity, biology, convservations and ecology of a broad range of organisms, from plants and animals to microbes. Students will study ecosystems, species, and the adaptation, to name a few. BSc.

Université du Québec à Rimouski

Nordicity
300 allee des Ursulines, PO Box C.P. 3300, succ. A, Rimouski QC G5L 3A1 Canada
Tel: 418-723-1986; *Fax:* 418-724-1525
Toll-Free: 800-511-3382
URL: www.uqar.uquebec.ca
Description: The Nordicity program at The University of Quebec at Rimouski offers degrees in the following programs: Biology, Wildlife Management, Wildlife Management & Habitats, and Environmental Studies.

Université du Québec à Rimouski

Marine Science
300 allee des Ursulines, PO Box C.P. 3300, succ. A, Rimouski QC G5L 3A1 Canada
Tel: 418-723-1986; *Fax:* 418-724-1525
Toll-Free: 800-511-3382
URL: www.uqar.uquebec.ca
Description: The Marine Science program at The University of Quebec at Rimouski offers a Master's Degree in Oceanography which is aimed at training scientists to adopt a comprehensive, multidisciplinary approach to the study of ocean phenomena. The program also offers a PhD in Oceanography which focuses on training independent researchers on the cutting edge of their field.

Université du Québec à Trois-Rivières

Environmental Studies
3315 Bd Des Forges, Trois-Rivieres QC QC G87 Canada
Tel: 819-376-5011; *Fax:* 819-376-5012
Toll-Free: 800-365-0922
e-mail: crmultiservice@uqtr.ca
URL: www.uqtr.uquebec.ca
Description: This Masters Degree program is designed to train research students who can then go on to do a doctorate in biophysics or energy and materials science at Universite du Quebec a Trois-Rivieres.

Saskatchewan

First Nations University of Canada

Resource and Environmental Studies
1 First Nations Way, Regina SK S4S 7K2 Canada
Tel: 306-790-5950; *Fax:* 306-790-5993
e-mail: fgendron@firstnationsuniversity.ca
URL: www.firstnationsuniversity.ca
Description: The program is a collaborative degree program beginning with two years at SIAST Woodland Campus (Diploma in Resource and Environmental Law) and then a transfer for two more years at First Nations University of Canada. Students will learn indigenous perspectives in the areas of conservation, the environment, and natural resource issues.

First Nations University of Canada

Environmental Health and Science
1 First Nations Way, Regina SK S4S 7K2 Canada
Tel: 306-790-5950; *Fax:* 306-790-5993
e-mail: lstricker@firstnationsuniversity.ca
URL: www.firstnationsuniversity.ca
Description: This four year program leads to a BASc in Environmental Health and Science. It emphasizes First Nations traditions and culture while equipping graduates with the skills and knowledge necessary to address environmental health and science problem areas.

University of Regina

Department Of Biology
3737 Wascana Parkway, Regina SK S4S 0A2 Canada
Tel: 306-585-4145; *Fax:* 306-337-2410
URL: www.uregina.ca/biology
Description: The department offers regular and Honours degrees, and Masters and PhD programs. Specializations include: Ecology and Environmental Biology; Cellular and Molecular Biology. Small classes are combined with high quality lab time and hands on training.

University of Regina

Environmental Systems Engineering
Faculty of Engineering Bldg, Rm 409, Regina SK S4S 0A2 Canada
Tel: 306-585-4734; *Fax:* 306-585-4855
e-mail: engg@uregina.ca
URL: enggdynamic.uregina.ca
Description: A four-year program that teaches the application of Systems Engineering principles to environmental problems associated with water resources, transportation, industrial development and waste management. Students design and manage environmental/transportation systems and conduct environmental impact and remediation studies.

University of Saskatchewan

Environmental Engineering
57 Campus Dr, #1B95 College of Eng., Saskatoon SK S7N 5A9 Canada
Tel: 306-966-7827; *Fax:* 306-966-5407
e-mail: biomedical.engineering@usask.ca
URL: www.engr.usask.ca/departments/environmental/
Description: Offers a Bachelor of Engineering four-year degree. Multidisciplinary training includes a variety of engineering disciplines including: geological engineering, agriculture and bioresource engineering, chemical engineering, and civil engineering.

University of Saskatchewan

Land Use & Environmental Studies
9 Campus Drive, Room 265 Arts, PO Box College of Arts & Sciences, Saskatoon SK S7N 5A5 Canada
URL: www.arts.usask.ca/students/academics/programs/landuse
Description: Students can pursue a general major in Land Use & Environmental Studies (LUEST) or can major in LUEST with a specialization in Biology, Economics, Geography or Sociology. A five-year Co-operative Education Program is also available. A degree provides graduates with the academic background necessary for employment in various areas of environmental management.

University of Saskatchewan

Soil & Environmental Science
51 Campus Dr, Dept. of Soil Science, Saskatoon SK S7N 5A8 Canada
Tel: 306-966-6825; *Fax:* 306-966-6881
URL: agbio.usask.ca/index.php
Description: Majors in Soil Science or Environmental Science are provided through the Department of Soil Science. Completing a four-year undergraduate program will lead to a Bachelor of Science (B.S.A.). Envirnmental Science includes the study of emerging environmental issues including preservation of wetlands, ozone depletion, and disposal of toxic chemicals. Soil is an essential part of the environment, and the Soil Science program provides an in-depth study of the role soils playsin environmental management.

University of Saskatchewan

Renewable Resource Management
51 Campus Dr, Dept. of Soil Science, Saskatoon SK S7N 5A8 Canada
Tel: 306-966-4056; *Fax:* 306-966-8894
e-mail: ag.bio@usask.ca
URL: agbio.usask.ca/index.php
Description: The BSc in Renewable Resource Management is an applied science degree that focuses on the study of water and biological resources and the management of land. Careers in this sector will include helping to protect the environment and ecosystems from industrial damage, determining how to make some of our industries sustainable, or helping to produce food.

University of Saskatchewan

Plant Science
51 Campus Dr, Room 4D36 Ag Bldg, PO Box Dept of Plant Sciences, Saskatoon SK S7N 5A8 Canada
Tel: 306-966-5855; *Fax:* 306-966-5015
e-mail: bruce.coulman@usask.ca
URL: agbio.usask.ca
Description: The Plant Science program offers studies in agronomy, horticulture science, crop science, plant ecology, or rangeland studies. Plant science involves the study of improvement, production, and utilization of plants in agriculture and the role plants play in natural and managed environments. Students can earn a four-year B.S.A which can be a stepping stone into other areas such as health sciences, international studies, or environmental law. A Masters degree or Ph.D. is also available, leading into a career as a research scientist.

University of Saskatchewan

Graduate Programs at School of Environment & Sustainability
15 Campus Drive, Room 217, Law Bldg, Saskatoon SK S7N 5A6 Canada
Tel: 306-966-1985; *Fax:* 306-966-5900
e-mail: sens.info@usask.ca
URL: www.usask.ca
Description: Graduate programs offered by the School of Environment and Sustainability are designed to prepare a new generation of skilled professionals, researchers and academics to address the challenges facing the environment, both locally and globally. The Master of Sustainable Environmental Management, Master of Environment and Sustainability, and Doctor of Philosophy in Environment and Sustainability programs are interdisciplinary in nature and practical in their focus.

University of Saskatchewan

Indigenous Land Management Institute (ILMI)
51 Campus Drive, 2D06, Saskatoon SK S7N 5A8 Canada
Tel: 306-966-4045
e-mail: david.natcher@usask.ca
URL: www.usask.ca

Educational Programs / Yukon College

Description: The ILMI was established to respond to the need of Aboriginal Peoples to gain access to research-based information that can be used in making informed land management decisions. Aboriginal peoples are assuming a greater role in the management and administration of land and resources. The institute brings together teaching, research, outreach and engagement activities in the area of indigenous land and resource management under one unit. Themes include Environmental Sustainability and Governance of Land.

Yukon Territory

Yukon College

Renewable Resources Management
500 College Drive, PO Box 2799, Whitehorse YT Y1A 5K4
Canada

Tel: 867-668-8760; *Fax:* 867-668-5210
e-mail: stt@yukoncollege.yk.ca
URL: www.yukoncollege.yk.ca
Description: A two-year diploma program designed for those seeking immediate employment in the field of renewable resources or for those looking for practical training before moving on to a university.

Yukon College Northern

Northern Environmental Studies
500 College Drive, PO Box 2799, Whitehorse YT Y1A 5K4
Canada

Tel: 867-668-8770; *Fax:* 867-668-8805
e-mail: liberalarts@yukoncollege.yk.ca
URL: www.yukoncollege.yk.ca/arts_science/
Description: A two-year diploma program that examines a variety of environment issues of northern concern including: resource depletion, wilderness fragmentation, pollution and global climate changes, and loss of biodiversity. Students may transfer to degree programs at other Canadian and American institutions.

Foundations & Grants Index

A

The Aboriginal Funds for Species at Risk, 1045
ACAP Saint John, 1042
African Wildlife Foundation, 1040
Agricultural Institute of Canada Foundation, 1043
Alberta Conservation Association, 1039
Alberta Ecotrust Foundation, 1039
Alberta Lottery Fund, 1039
Alberta Real Estate Foundation, 1039
Alberta Sport, Recreation, Parks & Wildlife Foundation, 1039
Alpine Club Environment Fund, 1039
Animal Welfare Foundation of Canada, 1043
Atlantic Canada Sustainability Initiative, 1042
Ausable Bayfield Conservation Foundation, 1043
The Avian Preservation Foundation, 1040

B

Bay of Fundy Ecosystem Project, 1042
Bedeque Bay Environmental Management Association, 1045
Bluenose Coastal Action Foundation, 1042
British Columbia Agriculture Council, 1040
British Columbia Conservation Foundation, 1040
British Columbia Hydro Bridge Coastal Restoration Program, 1040

C

Calgary Foundation, 1039
Canada Foundation for Innovation, 1043
Canada-Alberta Municipal Rural Infrastructure Fund, 1039
Canadian Foundation for Climate and Atmospheric Sciences, 1043
Canadian Institutes of Health Research, 1043
Canadian Ornamental Plant Foundation, 1043
Canadian Shield Foundation, 1041
Canadian Wildlife Service, 1045
Carthy Foundation, 1039
Catherine Donnelly Foundation, 1043
Centre for Rural Sustainability, 1042
The ChariTREE Foundation, 1040
City of Edmonton, 1039
Clean Air Foundation, 1043
Clean Annapolis River Project, 1042
Clean Nova Scotia, 1043
Coastal Ecosystems Research Foundation, 1040
Commission for Environmental Cooperation, 1045
Communities of Tomorrow, 1046
Comox Valley Community Foundation, 1040
Conservation Council of New Brunswick, 1042
Conservation Foundation, 1043
Conservation Halton Foundation, 1043
Credit Valley Conservation Foundation, 1043

D

David Suzuki Foundation, 1040
Donner Canadian Foundation, 1043

E

Edmonton Space & Science Foundation, 1039
The EJLB Foundation, 1046
Endswell Foundation, 1040
Energy Probe Research Foundation, 1043
Environmental Coalition of Prince Edward Island, 1045
Environmental Health Foundation of Canada, 1040
Evergreen, 1043

F

Federation of Canadian Municipalities, 1044
Fish & Wildlife Compensation Program, 1040
Fondation Hydro-Québec pour l'environnement, 1046
Fonds d'action québécois pour le développement durable, 1046
Foundation for Environmental Conservation, 1039
Foundation for International Environmental Law & Development, 1039
Friends of the Greenbelt Foundation, 1044

G

George Cedric Metcalf Charitable Foundation, 1044
The GLOBE Foundation of Canada, 1040
Grand River Conservation Foundation, 1044
Greater Saint John Community Foundation, 1042

H

Harmony Foundation of Canada, 1040
Helen McCrea Peacock Foundation, 1044

I

Investment Agriculture Foundation of British Columbia, 1040
Island Nature Trust, 1045

J

Jack Miner Migratory Bird Foundation, Inc., 1044
Jour de la Terre Québec, 1046

K

The Kongsgaard-Goldman Foundation, 1046

L

Labrador Southeast Coastal Action Program Inc., 1042
Laidlaw Foundation, 1046
Lake Simcoe Region Conservation Foundation, 1044
Lethbridge Community Foundation, 1039
Lifeforce Foundation, 1040
Live Green Toronto, 1044

M

Manitoba Hydro, 1041
Marmot Recovery Foundation, 1040
Max Bell Foundation, 1039
The McLean Foundation, 1044
Miramichi River Environmental Assessment Committee, 1042
Mountain Equipment Co-op (Environment Fund Grants), 1040
The Murphy Foundation Incorporated, 1041

N

Nanaimo Community Foundation, 1041
Natural Resources Canada, 1044
Nature Trust of New Brunswick, 1042
The Neptis Foundation, 1044
New Brunswick Environmental Network, 1042
New Brunswick Environmental Trust Fund, 1042
New Brunswick Wildlife Trust Fund, 1042
Niagara Peninsula Conservation Foundation, 1044
Nova Forest Alliance, 1043
Nova Scotia. Dept. of Natural Resources, 1043
Nova Scotia Environmental Network, 1043

O

Oak Ridges Moraine Foundation, 1044
Okanagan Water Basin Board, 1041
Ontario. Ministry of Energy & Infrastructure, 1044
The Ontario Trillium Foundation, 1044

P

Pacific Salmon Foundation, 1041
The Pollution Probe Foundation, 1044
Prince Edward Island. Dept. of Environment, Energy & Forestry, 1045

Q

Québec-Labrador Foundation (Canada) Inc., 1046
Quetico Foundation, 1044
Quidi Vidi Rennie's River Development Foundation, 1042

R

Real Estate Foundation of British Columbia, 1041
Renewable Natural Resources Foundation, 1041
Richard Ivey Foundation, 1044

S

Sable Island Preservation Trust, 1043
The Salamander Foundation, 1044
Science Alberta Foundation, 1039
Seagull Foundation, 1043
SEEDS Foundation, 1039
Shell Environmental Fund, 1039
Suncor Energy Foundation, 1039
Sustainable Development Innovations Fund, 1041

T

T. Buck Suzuki Environmental Foundation, 1041
TD Friends of the Environment Foundation, 1044
Temagami Community Foundation, 1044
The Thomas Sill Foundation Inc., 1042
Tides Canada Foundation, 1041
Toronto Atmospheric Fund, 1044
Toronto Parks & Trees Foundation, 1045
T.R. Meighen Family Foundation, 1045
Transport Canada, 1045
Tree Canada Foundation, 1045
Trees Ontario, 1045
Turner Foundation, Inc., 1041

U

Unilever Canada Foundation, 1045

V

Vancouver City Savings Credit Union, 1041
Vancouver Foundation, 1041
Victoria Foundation, 1041

W

The W. Garfield Weston Foundation, 1045
Walter & Duncan Gordon Foundation, 1045
The Weeden Foundation, 1042
West Coast Environmental Law Research Foundation, 1041
The William and Flora Hewlett Foundation, 1041
Winnipeg Foundation, 1042

Foundations & Grants

International

Foundation for Environmental Conservation (FEC)
1148 Moiry, Switzerland
Fax: 41-21-8666-6616
e-mail: envcons@ncl.ac.uk
URL: www.ncl.ac.uk/icef
Description: To undertake, in cooperation with appropriate individuals, organizations & other groups, all possible activities to further environmental conservation global sustainability.

Foundation for International Environmental Law & Development (FIELD)
3 Endsleigh St., London WC1H 0DD United Kingdom
Tel: 44-20-7872-7200; Fax: 44-20-7388-2826
e-mail: field.org@field.org.uk
URL: www.field.org.uk
Description: FIELD is a group of public international lawyers committed to helping vulnerable countries, communities and campaigners negotiate for fairer international environmental laws.

Alberta

Alberta Conservation Association (ACA)
101 - 9 Chippewa Rd., Sherwood Park AB T8A 6J7 Canada
Tel: 780-410-1999; Fax: 780-464-0141
e-mail: info@ab-conservation.com
URL: www.ab-conservation.com
Description: Formed in 1997, Alberta Conservation Association (ACA) is a not-for-profit, registered charity largely funded by Alberta's hunters and anglers through licence levies, and a growing number of corporate partners. Annually, ACA directs more than $10 million towards conservation efforts, delivering a wide variety of projects, programs and services across the province. Key conservation programs include Wildlife, Fisheries, Land Management and Communications (Grants in Biodiversity Program, Grant Eligible Conservation Fund, ACA Chair in Fisheries and Wildlife at the University of Alberta).

Alberta Ecotrust Foundation
1020 - 1202 Centre St. SE, Calgary AB T2G 5A5 Canada
Tel: 403-209-2245; Fax: 403-209-2086
Toll-Free: 800-465-2147
URL: www.albertaecotrust.com
Description: Conceived in 1991, Alberta Ecotrust is a unique partnership between the corporate sector and the environmental community. Together, they invest in the people and projects that help to make Alberta a stronger, more sustainable place to live, work and play. They achieve this goal through three main programs: environmental grant making, capacity building, and community collaboration. Together, we fund non-profit environmental projects, strengthen the ability of the voluntary sector to affect positive environmental change, and promote the environment as the foundation of a healthy community.

Alberta Lottery Fund
50 Corriveau Ave., St. Albert AB T8N 3T5 Canada
Fax: 780-447-8903
Toll-Free: 800-642-3855
URL: http://albertalotteryfund.ca
Description: The Alberta Lottery Fund is made up of the government's share of net revenues from VLTs, slot machines and ticket lotteries. These revenues total more than $1.5 billion each year, and are used to support thousands of volunteer, public and community-based initiatives annually. Revenues from the Alberta Lottery Fund are allocated to 13 specific ministries, including the Ministry of Environment.

Alberta Real Estate Foundation
#301-1240 Kensington Rd. NW, Calgary AB T2N 3P7 Canada
Tel: 403-228-4786; Fax: 403-229-1572
Toll-Free: 800-520-2485
e-mail: questions@aref.ab.ca
URL: www.aref.ab.ca
Description: The Alberta Real Estate Foundation supports real estate initiatives which benefit the industry and the people of Alberta. The Land Stewardship & Environment area of interest is to enable Albertans to understand and respond to changing land use patterns, growth pressures, air and water management issues and to enhance the ecological quality of their communities.

Alberta Sport, Recreation, Parks & Wildlife Foundation (ASRPWF)
Standard Life Centre, #901, 10405 Jasper Ave., Edmonton AB T5J 4R7
Tel: 780-415-1167
URL: www.tpr.alberta.ca/asrpwf
Description: The Alberta Sport, Recreation, Parks & Wildlife Foundation works to enhance sport, recreation, park, wildlife & conservation opportunities in Alberta. Financial support to organizations, to work towards a healthy population, economy, & natural environment, is provided through grants. The Park & Wildlife Ventures program provides funds to promote conservation in Alberta & to purchase lands which are ecologically sensitive, important to wildlife, or bordering other conservation lands.

Alpine Club Environment Fund
PO Box 8040, Indian Flats Rd., Canmore AB T1W 2T8 Canada
Tel: 403-678-3200; Fax: 403-678-3224
e-mail: info@AlpineClubofCanada.ca
URL: www.alpineclubofcanada.ca/grants/environment.html
Description: The purpose of the Fund is to provide support that contributes to the protection and preservation of mountain and climbing environments, including the preservation of alpine flora and fauna in their natural habitat.

Calgary Foundation
#700, 999 - 8th St. SW, Calgary AB T2R 1J5
Tel: 403-802-7700; Fax: 403-802-7701
e-mail: grants@thecalgaryfoundation.org
URL: www.thecalgaryfoundation.org
Overview: A organization founded in 1955
Description: The Calgary Foundation provides grants to support organizations in the following areas: arts & heritage, education, environment, health, human Services, & neighbourhoods. Projects must be in Calgary, or benefit the residents of Calgary & area.

Canada-Alberta Municipal Rural Infrastructure Fund (CAMRIF)
Twin Atria 1, 4999 - 98th Ave., 2nd Fl., Edmonton AB T6B 2X3 Canada
Tel: 780-422-1151; Fax: 780-427-5505
Toll-Free: 800-396-0214
e-mail: camrif@gov.ab.ca
URL: www.camrif.ca
Description: The Fund supports projects that enhance & renew public infrastructure, improve the quality of the environment, protect health & safety, support long-term economic growth, & develop sustainable communities in the smaller urban centres & rural municipalities of Alberta.

Carthy Foundation
PO Box 2554, Stn. M, Calgary AB T2P 2M7 Canada
Tel: 403-231-7922; Fax: 403-231-7959
URL: www.carthyfoundation.org
Description: Carthy Foundation, based in Calgary, Alberta, is a private foundation established in 1965. Carthy Foundation has two granting programs: Youth: Initiatives will have a primary focus on youth development or youth problem prevention; Environment: Initiatives will focus on market-based mechanisms, or urban ecology and ecological design.

City of Edmonton
Energy Management Revolving Fund
Century Place, 9803 - 102A Ave., 2nd Fl., Edmonton AB T5J 3A3 Canada
Tel: 780-496-2791; Fax: 780-496-5657
e-mail: env@edmonton.ca
URL: www.edmonton.ca/environmental/programs/
Description: The fund, established in 1995, provides support to energy efficiency projects such as upgrades to lighting, heating, cooling & ventilation systems, & envelope upgrades. The amount borrowed against the fund is repaid over a period of up to 8 years.

Edmonton Space & Science Foundation (ESSF)
11211 - 142 St., Edmonton AB T5M 4A1 Canada
Tel: 780-452-9100; Fax: 780-455-5882
e-mail: info@telusworldofscienceedmonton.com
URL: www.telusworldofscience.com/edmonton
Description: To inspire & motivate people to learn about & contribute to science & technology advances that strengthen themselves, their family & community.

Lethbridge Community Foundation
Professional Bldg., 404 - 8th St. South, Lethbridge AB T1J 2J7
Tel: 403-328-5297; Fax: 403-328-6061
e-mail: office@lethbridgecommunityfoundation.ca
URL: www.lethbridgecommunityfoundation.org
Overview: A organization founded in 1966
Description: The Lethbridge Community Foundation provides grants, to local non-profit organizations, in the following fields of interest: arts & culture, community service, education, environment, health, history, & recreation.; Member of: Community Foundations of Canada

Max Bell Foundation
#380, 1201 - 5th St. S.W., Calgary AB T2R 0Y6 Canada
Tel: 403-215-7310; Fax: 403-215-7319
URL: www.maxbell.org
Description: Max Bell Foundation is a Canadian independent grantmaking foundation that pursues its mission and strategic priority by supporting Canadian registered charities with project grants and internship/fellowship grants. The Foundation seeks to support environment initiatives that align with our mission and granting guidelines. We are interested in supporting projects that understand and take account of the social and economic contexts in which environmental concerns emerge as public policy and practice.

Science Alberta Foundation
#260, 3512 - 33 St. NW, Calgary AB T2L 2A6 Canada
Tel: 403-220-0077; Fax: 403-284-4132
e-mail: info@sciencealberta.org
URL: www.sciencealberta.org
Description: Science Alberta Foundation is a non-profit organization committed to increasing science literacy and awareness. They develop engaging resources that bring science to life for Albertans of all ages, in every corner of the province. Science Alberta Foundation collaborates with educators, parents, community leaders and scientists to develop programs, such as Science-In-A-Crate and Festivals of Science that showcase the importance science plays in our everyday lives.

SEEDS Foundation
#400, 144 - 4th Ave. SW., Calgary AB T2P 3N4 Canada
Tel: 403-221-0831; Fax: 403-221-0888
Toll-Free: 800-661-8751
e-mail: seeds@telusplanet.net
URL: www.seedsfoundation.ca
Also Known As: Society, Environment & Energy Development Studies Foundation
Description: To provide educational support materials & professional assistance to teachers in the area of energy, environment & sustainable development; to work toward the development of a society which understands & is committed to actions leading to wise stewardship of resources, resource use & the environment.

Shell Environmental Fund
PO Box 100, Stn. M, Calgary AB T2P 2H5 Canada
Tel: 403-691-2071; Fax: 403-269-8031
e-mail: admin-sef@shell.com
URL: www.shell.ca
Description: The Shell Environmental Fund (SEF) provides financial support for grass roots, action-oriented projects that improve and protect the Canadian environment.

Suncor Energy Foundation
PO Box 38, 112 - 4 Ave. S.W., Calgary AB T2P 2V5 Canada
Tel: 403-269-8775
e-mail: sef@suncor.com
URL: aww.suncor.com/default.aspx?cid=239&lang=1
Description: The Suncor Energy Foundation is a private, non-profit, charitable foundation established by Suncor Energy Inc. in 1998 to receive Suncor's contributions and support registered Canadian charitable organizations. The Foundation complements other forms of community investments by Suncor, such as product or in-kind contributions, sponsorships, and

employee giving and volunteer efforts. Funded entirely by Suncor, the Foundation's funding priorities are educational, environmental and community-based initiatives that are aligned with Suncor's key operating communities. The Foundation seeks unique opportunities to enhance the quality of life in those communities and to add value through effective collaborations.

British Columbia

African Wildlife Foundation (AWF)
#120, 1400 Sixteenth St. NW, Washington DC 20036 USA
Tel: 202-939-3333; *Fax:* 202-939-3332
Toll-Free: 888-494-5354
e-mail: africanwildlife@awf.org
URL: www.awf.org
Description: To promote conservation of Africa's wildlife & natural resources; to promote belief that the survival of African wildlife lies in a working knowledge of the relationship between man, his economics & his environment; to promote, establish & support grassroots & institutional programs in conservation education, wildlife management & training, & management of threatened conservation areas; to manage projects aimed at saving endangered species (eg. the African Elephant, Mountain Gorilla, Rhinoceros).

The Avian Preservation Foundation (APF)
PO Box 123, Chemainus BC V0R 1K0 Canada
Tel: 250-246-4803; *Fax:* 250-246-4912
e-mail: exec@aacc.ca
URL: www.aacc.ca
Description: To support recognized expert aviculturists who are endeavouring to breed rare & endangered avian species; to establish a Canadian breeding centre for rare & endangered avian species; to establish a monitoring body for captive avian stocks in Canada through surveys & computer software; to create & maintain a breeding program throughout Canada for avian species currently listed as endangered; to create a captive preservation program for rare & endangered species within zoos, bird parks & sanctuaries where re-introduction into the natural habitat is not possible or practical.

British Columbia Agriculture Council (BCAC)
#140, 32160 South Fraser Way, Abbotsford BC V2T 1W5
URL: www.bcac.bc.ca
Overview: A organization founded in 1997
Description: The Agriculture Environment Initiatives, of the British Columbia Agriculture Council, feature assistance to resolve environmental & wildlife issues related to agriculture in the province.

British Columbia Agriculture Council (AEWF)
Agriculture Environment & Wildlife Fund
1473 Water St., Kelowna BC V1Y 1J6
Tel: 250-763-9790; *Fax:* 250-762-2997
URL: www.bcac.bc.ca
Description: In order to advance the environmental sustainability of the agricultural industry in British Columbia, the Agriculture Environment & Wildlife Fund assists the agricultural sector to resolve environmental issues.

British Columbia Agriculture Council (AESI)
Agriculture Environment Stewardship Initiative
1473 Water St., Kelowna BC V1Y 1J6
Tel: 250-763-9790
Overview: A organization founded in 2001
Description: The Agriculture Environment Stewardship Initiative funds projects to resolve environmental & wildlife issues within British Columbia's agricultural sector. Applications for this funding are submitted or supported by farming organizations.

British Columbia Agriculture Council (BC EFP)
Canada - British Columbia Environmental Farm Plan Program
c/o Agricultural Research & Development Corporation, #140, 32160 South Fraser Way, Abbotsford BC V2T 1W5
Toll-Free: 866-522-3447
e-mail: reg@ardcorp.ca
URL: www.bcac.bc.ca/EFP_pages/about_us/index.html
Overview: A organization founded in 2003
Description: The British Columbia Agriculture Council is the delivery agent of the Canada - British Columbia Environmental Farm Plan Program, in partnership with Agriculture & Agri-food Canada & the British Columbia Ministry of Agriculture & Lands. The Program is designed to provide funding to enhance the stewardship practices of British Columbia's farms & ranches.

British Columbia Conservation Foundation (BCCF)
#206, 17564 - 56A Ave., Surrey BC V3S 1G3 Canada
Tel: 604-576-1433; *Fax:* 604-576-1482
e-mail: bccfho@bccf.com
URL: www.bccf.com
Description: The British Columbia Conservation Foundation (BCCF) was founded and incorporated under the Society Act of British Columbia in 1969, by the Directors of the BC Wildlife Federation, to contribute significantly to the perpetuation and expansion of fish and wildlife populations through the efficient implementation of projects in the field. They are a federally registered charity dedicated to the conservation and stewardship of British Columbia's ecosystems and species.

British Columbia Hydro Bridge Coastal Restoration Program (BCRP)
#E16, 6911 Southpoint Dr., Burnaby BC V3N 4X8
Tel: 604-528-8136
e-mail: bcrp@bchydro.com
URL: www.bchydro.com/bcrp
Overview: A organization founded in 1999
Description: British Columbia Hydro's Bridge Coastal Restoration Program aims to restore fish & wildlife resources impacted by hydroelectric facilities in the Bridge Coastal Generation Area. Projects funded by the program must involve restoration, conseravation, or research.

The ChariTREE Foundation
PO Box CL-58, Bowen Island BC V0N 1G0 Canada
Tel: 604-947-6803
Toll-Free: 888-947-6803
e-mail: info@charitree.ca
URL: http://charitree.ca
Description: The ChariTREE Foundation (TCF) is Canada's kid's environmental learning charity. TCF is a registered Canadian environmental charity established to help the planet by creating and supporting tree planting projects that benefit kids.

Coastal Ecosystems Research Foundation
General Delivery, Dawson's Landing BC V0N 1M0 Canada
Tel: 44-0-7745-730873; *Fax:* 815-327-0173
e-mail: info@cerf.bc.ca
URL: www.cerf.bc.ca
Description: To fund ecological research through eco-tourism.

Comox Valley Community Foundation
PO Box 3126, #201J, 2435 Mansfield Dr., Courtenay BC V9N 5N4
Tel: 250-338-8444
e-mail: cvcf@shawcable.com
URL: www.cvcfoundation.org
Description: The Comox Valley Community Foundation Board provides grants for projects in the following fields: arts & culture, education & youth, environment, health & welfare, & seniors. Projects must benefit British Columbia's Comox Valley region. Recipients have included the Comox Valley Naturalists Society, the Comox Valley Project Watershed Society, & Conservancy Hornby Island.

David Suzuki Foundation (DSF)
#219, 2211 - 4th Ave. West, Vancouver BC V6K 4S2 Canada
Tel: 604-732-4228; *Fax:* 604-732-0752
Toll-Free: 800-453-1533
e-mail: contact@davidsuzuki.org
URL: www.davidsuzuki.org
Description: To seek out & commission the best, most up-to-date research to help reveal ways we can live in balance with nature; to support the implementation of ecologically sustainable models - from local projects, such as habitat restoration, to international initiatives, such as better frameworks for economic decisions; to ensure the solutions developed through research & application to reach the widest possible audience, & help mobilize broadly supported change; to urge decision makers to adopt policies which encourage & guide individuals & businesses, so their daily decisions reflect the need to act within nature's constraints.

Endswell Foundation
200-163 W. Hastings St., Vancouver BC V6B 1H5 Canada
Tel: 604-844-7448; *Fax:* 604-844-7441
e-mail: endswell@renewalpartners.com
URL: www.renewalpartners.com
Description: The Endswell Foundation is an independent registered charity, operating under the Renewal group of organizations. Endswell has played a role in many initiatives, large and small, that have helped to preserve BC's wildernesses. Over the past 15 years the Endswell Foundation made over 700 grants totalling over $20 million dollars.

Environmental Health Foundation of Canada (EHFC)
Stn. #720, 999 West Broadway Ave., Vancouver BC V5Z 1K5 Canada
URL: www.ehfc.ca
Description: The research & educational arm of the Canadian Institute of Public Health Inspectors; Dedicated to advancing environmental health in Canada through thedevelopment & implementation of education & research initiatives.

Fish & Wildlife Compensation Program (FWCP)
#103, 333 Victoria St., Nelson BC V1L 4K3
Tel: 250-352-6874; *Fax:* 250-352-6178
e-mail: info@fwcp.ca
URL: www.fwcp.ca
Overview: A organization founded in 1995
Description: The Fish & Wildlife Compensation Program's mission is to offset the impacts of hydro dams in the Columbia Basin. Funds are invested in fish & wildlife projects. Many of the funded projects focus upon species-at-risk. Examples of funding include lake restoration programs, habitat restoration, species monitoring, & land acquisition for conservation purposes.

The GLOBE Foundation of Canada
World Trade Centre, #578, 999 Canada Pl., Vancouver BC V6C 3E1 Canada
Tel: 604-775-7300; *Fax:* 604-666-8123
Toll-Free: 800-274-6097
e-mail: info@globe.ca
URL: www.globe.ca
Description: The not-for-profit organization strives to find practical business-oriented solutions to environmental problems. It helps companies & individuals realize the value of economically viable environmental business opportunities.

Harmony Foundation of Canada
PO Box 50022, #15, 1594 Fairfield Rd., Victoria BC V8S 1G1 Canada
Tel: 250-380-3001; *Fax:* 250-380-0887
e-mail: harmony@islandnet.com
URL: www.harmonyfdn.ca
Description: To encourage development which is socially & environmentally sustainable; To strive towards ecological stability, long-term prosperity, & social harmony.

Investment Agriculture Foundation of British Columbia
PO Box 8248, 808 Douglas St., 3rd Fl., Victoria BC V8W 3R9
Tel: 250-356-1662; *Fax:* 250-953-5162
e-mail: info@iafbc.ca; funding@iafbc.ca
URL: www.iafbc.ca
Description: The Investment Agriculture Foundation of British Columbia provides assistance to the agricultural & food processing industries of British Columbia. The following are areas which qualify for funding: plant industries; animal industries; processing industries; environmental issues; & other issues, such as the livestock waste tissue initiative, the agri-tourism initiative, & the aboriginal agriculture initiative. Examples of environmental funding programs are environmental farm planning & the agriculture, environment & wildlife fund.

Lifeforce Foundation
PO Box 3117, Vancouver BC V6B 3X6 Canada
Tel: 604-649-5258
e-mail: lifeforcesociety@hotmail.com
URL: www.lifeforcefoundation.org
Description: Dedicated to raising public awareness of the interrelationship of human, animal & environmental problems; to urge society to address & solve problems by taking into consideration the long-term effects on all parts of the ecosystem.

Marmot Recovery Foundation
PO Box 2332, Stn. A, Nanaimo BC V94 6X6 Canada
Tel: 250-753-8080; *Fax:* 250-753-8070
Toll-Free: 877-462-7668
e-mail: marmot@islandnet.com
URL: www.marmots.org
Description: To manage the recovery effort for one of North America's most endangered mammals: the Vancouver Island marmot (Marmota vancouverensis).

Mountain Equipment Co-op (Environment Fund Grants)
149 West 4th Ave., Vancouver BC V5Y 4A6 Canada
Toll-Free: 866-632-3863
e-mail: community@mec.ca
URL: www.mec.ca
Description: The Mountain Equipment Co-op (MEC) wants to ensure that the environments of those outdoor areas that have

important wilderness or recreational value are preserved. To this end, MEC has established a program to support the projects of Canadian-based environmental and conservation groups who deal with issues affecting the environment. MEC will financially support activities, projects, research, and education concerned with environmental conservation and wilderness protection. Categories of projects supported are environmental research projects; studentships (research or advocacy prooijects under the direction of a supervisor); advocacy and education projects that aadvance conservation and environmental causes; projects that facilitate public accesss to or recreational use of areas having significant recreational or wilderness value to MEC members; and land aquisitions for conservation.

Nanaimo Community Foundation (NCF)
#106, 619 Comox Rd., Nanaimo BC V9R 5V8
e-mail: administrator@nanaimocommunityfoundation.com
URL: www.nanaimocommunityfoundation.com
Overview: A organization founded in 1982
Description: The Nanaimo Community Foundation supports programs in the following categories: arts, culture & recreation; children & youth; community infrastructure & environment; education; health care; & seniors & housing. Grants are available to non-profit societies in British Columbia, which are also federally registered charities. Projects must take place in the County of Nanaimo.

Okanagan Water Basin Board (OBWB)
1450 KLO Rd., Kelowna BC V1W 3Z4 Canada
Tel: 250-469-6271; *Fax:* 250-762-7011
e-mail: info@obwb.ca
URL: www.obwb.ca
Description: The Okanagan Basin Water Board (OBWB) was instituted in 1970 through a collaboration of the three Okanagan regional districts to provide leadership on water issues that span the entire valley - recognizing the need to work together to protect our common resources. The purpose of the OBWB is to provide leadership to protect and enhance quality of life in the Okanagan Basin through sustainable water resource management.

Pacific Salmon Foundation
#300 - 1682 West 7th Ave., Vancouver BC V6J 4S6 Canada
Tel: 604-664-7664; *Fax:* 604-664-7665
e-mail: salmon@psf.ca
URL: www.psf.ca
Description: PSF continues to raise funds and direct funding to grassroots, volunteer and community driven projects focused on the conservation and recovery of Pacific salmon. PSF supports research and science, then integrates this knowledge into program plans at the community and watershed level. PSF works with First Nations, private companies, educational institutions, non-profit groups, all levels of government, and commercial and recreational anglers to bring salmon back to our streams.

Real Estate Foundation of British Columbia
Marine Bldg., #570, 355 Burrard St., 5th Fl., Vancouver BC V6C 2G8
Tel: 604-688-6800; *Fax:* 604-688-3669
Toll-Free: 866-912-6800
e-mail: askme@realestatefoundation.com
URL: www.realestatefoundation.com
Overview: A organization founded in 1985
Description: To benefit the people of British Columbia, the Real Estate Foundation of British Columbia supports sustainable real estate & land use practices. Non-profit organizations, such as the BC Ground Water Association, are recipients of project funding & endowment grants.

T. Buck Suzuki Environmental Foundation
#100 - 326 12th St., New Westminster BC V3M 4H6 Canada
Tel: 604-519-3635; *Fax:* 604-524-6944
e-mail: tbsef@bucksuzuki.org
URL: www.bucksuzuki.org
Description: The T. Buck Suzuki Foundation works to ensure that fish bearing marshes, streams, rivers, lakes are not polluted, dammed, diverted, wasted or degraded. The Foundation was set up in 1981 by the United Fishermen and Allied Workers' Union.

Tides Canada Foundation
400-163 Hastings St. West, Vancouver BC V6B 1H5 Canada
Tel: 604-647-6611; *Fax:* 866-780-6611
e-mail: info@tidescanada.org
URL: http://tidescanada.org
Description: Tides Canada provides innovative philanthropic, financial and project management services for change makers - philanthropists, foundations, activists, and civil organizations.

Turner Foundation, Inc.
133 Luckie St. NW, 2nd Fl., Atlanta GA 30303 USA
Tel: 404-681-9900; *Fax:* 404-681-0172
URL: www.turnerfoundation.org
Description: The objective for this grant program is the protection of rivers, lakes, wetlands, aquifers, oceans, and other water systems from contamination, degradation, and other abuses. The Turner Foundation invests in select national and priority state level efforts to conserve wildlife and habitat. Internationally, the Turner Foundation supports wildlife and habitat conservation in the Russian Far East (specifically salmon conservation) and along the central coast of British Columbia.

Vancouver City Savings Credit Union
The Vancity enviroFund
PO Box 2120, Stn. Terminal, Vancouver BC V6B 5R8 Canada
Toll-Free: 888-826-2489
URL: www.vancity.com/MyCommunity/;
www.vancity.com/grants/
Description: The Fund was established to support community initiatives that address local environmental concerns. The Fund has supported organizations such as The Bowen Island Conservancy, The Centre for Sustainable Food Systems at UBC Farm, & The Delta Farmland & Wildlife Trust. See the website for grant guidelines & criteria.

Vancouver City Savings Credit Union
Climate Change Solutions Program
PO Box 2120, Stn. Terminal, Vancouver BC V6B 5R8 Canada
Toll-Free: 888-826-2489
URL:
www.vancity.com/MyCommunity/OurVision/ActingOnClimate Change
Description: The Climate Change Solutions program is focused on curbing climate change by taking action as an organization "where we live", and supporting our members and community to do the same. They accomplish this by: reducing our organizational environmental impact by reducing our emissions from energy use, paper use, and employee travel; helping members to reduce their impact by offering unique products to our members; supporting community groups who are also taking action, by investing in community and industry leaders working towards solutions (e.g., Green Building Grants, investment in micro-hydro projects and green buildings); and advocating for development and advancement of public policy solutions to climate change.

Vancouver Foundation
Harbour Centre, PO Box 12132, #1200, 555 West Hastings St., Vancouver BC V6B 4N6
Tel: 604-688-2204; *Fax:* 604-688-4170
e-mail: info@vancouverfoundation.ca
URL: www.vancouverfoundation.bc.ca
Overview: A organization founded in 1943
Description: The Vancouver Foundation supports charities & innovative projects in British Columbia. The Foundation funds the following areas: animal welfare; arts & culture; children, youth, & families; education; environment; health & social development; health & medical research; youth homelessness; & youth philanthropy.; *Member of:* Community Foundations of Canada

Victoria Foundation
#109, 645 Fort St., Victoria BC V8W 1G2
Tel: 250-381-5532; *Fax:* 250-480-1129
e-mail: info@victoriafoundation.bc.ca
URL: www.victoriafoundation.bc.ca
Overview: A organization founded in 1936
Description: The Victoria Foundation's funds support local registered charities in the following fields: arts, culture, & heritage, community services, education, environment, & health & recreation. Examples of organizations which have received grants include the Federation of BC Naturalists & the SeaChange Marine Conservation Society.

West Coast Environmental Law Research Foundation (WCEL)
200 - 2006 West 10th Ave., Vancouver BC V6J 2B3 Canada
Tel: 604-684-7378; *Fax:* 604-684-1312
Toll-Free: 800-330-9235
e-mail: admin@wcel.org
URL: www.wcel.org
Description: To provide summary legal advice to anyone in British Columbia with environmental concerns; to protect & enhance the environment of British Columbia; to foster public participation in environmental decision making; to provide legal aid for citizens with environmental concerns; to undertake law review & law reform projects, legal research & education, community legal outreach; & to operate an archival & on-line law library.

The William and Flora Hewlett Foundation
2121 Sand Hill Rd., Menlo Park CA 94025 USA
Tel: 650-234-4500; *Fax:* 650-234-4501
URL: www.hewlett.org
Description: The William and Flora Hewlett Foundation provides assistance to organizations working on environmental issues primarily in the North American West, specifically Montana, Wyoming, Colorado, New Mexico, Arizona, Nevada, Utah, Idaho, Washington, Oregon, California, Alaska, and Hawaii, as well as the western provinces of Canada and the northern states of Mexico bordering the United States. The principle objectives of the Environment program are to assist communities and organizations throughout the West to manage the development of natural resources and to redirect or absorb increases in population growth in ways that are sustainable and that respect the special qualities of the western landscape.

Manitoba

Canadian Shield Foundation
#401, 250 Wellington Cres., Winnipeg MB R3M 0B3 Canada
Tel: 204-989-7580; *Fax:* 204-989-7581
e-mail: canadianshieldfoundation@shaw.ca
Description: The Foundation's stated purpose is to promote ecology in the Canadian Shield. Funding interests may include education, science, environment and conservation.

Manitoba Hydro
Forest Enhancement Program
PO Box 815, Stn. Main, Winnipeg MB R3C 2P4 Canada
Tel: 204-474-3311
e-mail: publicaffairs@hydro.mb.ca
URL: www.hydro.mb.ca
Description: The program funds projects that enhance & sustain the forest environment in Manitoba. Projects which address climate change impacts are of special interest. Project categories: tree planting, forest education projects, projects which are innovative in perspective & may deal with issues such as sustainability, forest protection, urban forestry, etc.

Manitoba Hydro
Environmental Partnership Fund
PO Box 815, Stn. Main, Winnipeg MB R3C 2P4 Canada
Tel: 204-474-3311
e-mail: publicaffairs@hydro.mb.ca
URL: www.hydro.mb.ca
Description: The fund provides support to education relating to sustainable development. Applicants open to educators, education institutions, NGOs, & not-for-profit community organizations.

The Murphy Foundation Incorporated
#919, 167 Lombard Ave., Winnipeg MB R3B 0V3 Canada
Tel: 204-942-5281; *Fax:* 204-957-5866
Description: Provides funds for projects in the areas of wildlife habitat, wildfowl habitat, & medical education & research.

Renewable Natural Resources Foundation (RNRF)
5430 Grosvenor Lane, Bethesda MD 20814-2142 USA
Tel: 301-493-9101; *Fax:* 301-493-6148
e-mail: info@rnrf.org
URL: www.rnrf.org
Description: To advance sciences & public education in renewable natural resources; to promote the application of sound, scientific practices in managing & conserving renewable natural resources; to foster coordination & cooperation among professional, scientific & educational organizations having leadership responsibilities for renewable natural resources; to develop a Renewable Natural Resources Center.

Sustainable Development Innovations Fund (SDIF)
160-123 Main St., Winnipeg MB R3C 1A5 Canada
Tel: 204-945-8443; *Fax:* 204-945-1211
Toll-Free: 800-282-8069
e-mail: pollupreve@gov.mb.ca
URL: www.gov.mb.ca/conservation/pollutionprevention/sdif

Description: The Sustainable Development Innovations Fund (SDIF) is a $3.4 million Fund, which was created in October 1989 to provide financial assistance towards development, implementation and promotion of environmental innovation and sustainable development projects. The SDIF provides support to research studies, demonstration of new technology, community enhancement and educational projects, which further the sustainability of Manitoba's economy, human health and social well-being, and help to protect Manitoba's environment. The Fund encourages the creation of sustainable communities and helps them meet their needs by providing grant funding to projects that demonstrate: Partnerships between groups and individuals; Pride in the community; Concern for the environment.

The Thomas Sill Foundation Inc.
115 Plymouth St., Winnipeg MB R2X 2T3 Canada
Tel: 204-947-3782; *Fax:* 204-956-4702
URL: www.thomassillfoundation.com
Description: The Thomas Sill Foundation exists to provide encouragement and financial assistance to qualifying organizations operating in Manitoba that are working to advance the quality of life in the province, including the Lake Winnipeg Project.

Winnipeg Foundation
#1350, One Lombard Pl., Winnipeg MB R3B 0X3
Tel: 204-944-9474; *Fax:* 204-942-2987
Toll-Free: 877-974-3631
e-mail: info@wpgfdn.org
URL: www.wpgfdn.org
Overview: A organization founded in 1921
Description: To benefit the community, The Winnipeg Foundation provides grants to local non-profit organizations in the following fields of interest: arts & culture, community service, education & employment, environment, health, heritage, & recreation. An example of a project supported by the Foundation is the Downtown Greenspaces Strategy in Winnipeg.; *Member of:* Community Foundations of Canada

New Brunswick

ACAP Saint John (ACAPSJ)
PO Box 6878, Stn. A, 76 Germain St., Saint John NB E2L 4S4 Canada
Tel: 506-652-2227; *Fax:* 506-633-2184
e-mail: acapsj@rogers.com
URL: www.acapsj.com
Overview: A organization founded in 1991
Description: ACAP Saint John is a community-based non-profit organization under Environment Canada's Atlantic Coastal Action Program, one of 16 such organizations. ACAP Saint John is decidated to promoting and funding local environmental projects. ACAP Saint John encourages local involvement from all areas of the Saint John community, from industry to academia to all levels of government.

Conservation Council of New Brunswick (CCNB)
180 St. John St., Fredericton NB E3B 4A9 Canada
Tel: 506-458-8747; *Fax:* 506-458-1047
URL: http://conservationcouncil.ca
Overview: A organization founded in 1969
Description: The Conservation Council of New Brunswick is a member-based organization dedicated to promoting environmental issues and solutions. The Council advocates solutions through education, research, and grassroots action.

Greater Saint John Community Foundation
Brunswick Square, PO Box 20061, 40 King St., Saint John NB E2L 5B2 Canada
Tel: 506-672-8880; *Fax:* 506-672-8881
e-mail: sjfoundation@nb.aibn.com
URL: www.saint-john-foundation.nb.ca
Description: Established in 1976, this is an independent charity serving as a trustee of gifts. Incorporated environmental groups, convservation authorities & universities within a radius of 50km of Saint John, NB, may apply. Projects which improve the quality of life for the community are considered.

Miramichi River Environmental Assessment Committee (MREAC)
PO Box 85, 21 Cove Rd., Miramichi NB E1V 3M2 Canada
Tel: 506-778-8591; *Fax:* 506-773-9755
e-mail: mreac@nb.aibn.com
URL: www.mreac.org
Overview: A organization founded in 1989

Description: The Miramichi River Environmental Assessment Committee (MREAC) is a community based organization dedicated to the environmental improvement of the Miramichi River ecosystem established in 1989. In 1993, the MREAC joined Environment Canada's Atlantic Coastal Action Program (ACAP). MREAC focuses on science based research and other environmental projects to protect and manage the Miramichi River watershed.

Nature Trust of New Brunswick / Fondation pour la protection des sites naturels du Nouveau-Brunswick
PO Box 603, Stn. A, 404 Queen St., 3rd Fl., Fredericton NB E3B 5A6 Canada
Tel: 506-457-2398; *Fax:* 506-450-2137
e-mail: ntnb@nbnet.nb.ca
URL: www.naturetrust.nb.ca
Description: The Nature Trust of New Brunswick is a charitable land trust dedicated to the preservation and conservation of New Brunswick's natural landscape. The goals of the trust are to identify, classify, protect, and preserve natural areas in New Brunswick, and to foster awareness and appreciation of natural heritage.

New Brunswick Environmental Network (NBEN) / Réseau environnemental du Nouveau-Brunswick (RENB)
#432, 236 St. George St., Moncton NB E1C 1W1 Canada
Tel: 506-855-4114; *Fax:* 506-433-6111
e-mail: nben@nben.ca
URL: www.nben.ca
Overview: A organization founded in 1991
Description: The New Brunswick Environmental Network (NBEN) is a network of over 70 non-profit environmental organizations. The goal of the Network is to facilitate communication and cooperation between these organizations and government and industry to promote growth of environmental activities and projects in New Brunswick.

New Brunswick Environmental Trust Fund
Marysville Place, PO Box 6000, Fredericton NB E3B 5H1 Canada
Tel: 506-444-2654; *Fax:* 506-444-2734
URL: www.gnb.ca/0009/index-e.asp
Description: The Fund provides assistance for action-oriented projects with tangible, measurable results, aimed at protecting, preserving and enhancing the Province's natural environment.

New Brunswick Wildlife Trust Fund
PO Box 30030, Fredericton NB E3B 0H8 Canada
Tel: 506-453-6655; *Fax:* 506-462-5054
e-mail: wildcoun@nbnet.nb.ca
URL: www.nbwtf.ca
Description: The New Brunswick Wildlife Trust Fund has been established to fund a range of programs for the enhancement of New Brunswick's wildlife, fish and their habitats. The main source of revenue is from a conservation fee on hunters, anglers, and fur harvesters licences. Other conservation-supporting New Brunswickers can contribute by purchasing the special Conservation licence plates or by becoming an "Supporter". Money was also received from Maritime Road Development Corporation to compensate for environmental impacts on watercourses.

Newfoundland and Labrador

Labrador Southeast Coastal Action Program Inc. (LSCAP)
PO Box 189, 3 Penney's Lane, Port Hope Simpson NL A0K 4E0 Canada
Tel: 709-960-1010; *Fax:* 709-960-1012
e-mail: lscap@nf.aibn.com
URL: www.lscap.ca
Description: The Labrador Southeast Coastal Action Program (LSCAP) was established in 2006, and is a part of Environment Canada's Atlantic Coastal Action Program. The LSCAP is a non-profit organization dedicated to conducting and supporting environmental efforts in the area.

Quidi Vidi Rennie's River Development Foundation (QVRRDF)
Nagle's Place, PO Box 5, St. John's NL A1B 2Z2 Canada
Tel: 709-754-3474; *Fax:* 709-754-5947
e-mail: info@fluvarium.ca
URL: www.fluvarium.ca
Description: To promote responsible environmental stewardship; to raise awareness of the nature of freshwater systems; to provide leadership in urban watershed management; to operate The Fluvarium as a public centre for environmental education.

Northwest Territories

The Weeden Foundation
747 Third Ave., 34th Fl., New York NY 10017 USA
Tel: 212-888-1672; *Fax:* 212-888-1354
e-mail: weedenfdn@weedenfdn.org
URL: www.weedenfdn.org
Description: The foundation embraces the protection of biodiversity as its main priority. The foundation is particularly interested in new and innovative efforts that help to develop sustainable models for conservation action. Projects that serve as catalysts inducing others to lend support receive priority consideration. Foundation habitat protection grants have concentrated on the Pacific Northwest, that is Northern California, Oregon, and Washington, and up into British Columbia and Southeast Alaska. This reflects a longstanding interest in coastal temperate forests, which also extends into the Southern Hemisphere of the Americas. In addition, some grants have been awarded to projects in the intermountain west, notably the northern Rockies.

Nova Scotia

Atlantic Canada Sustainability Initiative (ACSI)
c/o School of Recreation Management & Kinesiology, Acadia University, 550 Main St., Wolfville NS B4P 2R6 Canada
Tel: 902-585-1160; *Fax:* 902-585-1702
e-mail: coordinator@atlanticsustainability.ca
URL: www.atlanticsustainability.ca
Description: The Atlantic Canada Sustainability Initiative (ACSI) is a collaborative project designed to promote and encourage sustainability in Atlantic Canada. It was developed by a network of municipalities, businesses and NGOs in Atlantic Canada in order to better understand the challenges and opportunities of sustainability and to promote sustainability initiatives.

Bay of Fundy Ecosystem Project (BOFEP)
Acadia University, PO Box 115, 23 Westwood Ave., Wolfville NS B4P 2R6 Canada
Tel: 902-585-1113; *Fax:* 902-585-1054
e-mail: secretariat@bofep.org
URL: www.bofep.org
Overview: A organization founded in 1995
Description: The Bay of Fundy Ecosystem Partnership is a collaboration of individuals and groups that seek the well-being of the Bay of Fundy by promoting the integrity, vitality, biodiversity and productivity of the Bay of Fundy Ecosystem, and the social well-being and economic sustainability of its coastal communities and facilitating communication and co-operation among individuals and organizations interested in understanding, sustainably using and conserving the resources, habitats and ecological processes of the Bay of Fundy.

Bluenose Coastal Action Foundation (BCAF)
PO Box 10, 493 Main St., Mahone Nay NS B0J 2E0 Canada
URL: www.coastalaction.org
Overview: A organization founded in 1993
Description: The Bluenose Coastal Action Foundation (BCAF) was established in 1993 to develop action plans to restore human-impacted coastal environments in Lunenburg County Nova Scotia with sustainable use as the goal. The Foundation seeks to facilitate the necessary actions to protect and enhance coastal areas and watersheds through research, education and action.

Centre for Rural Sustainability (CRS)
c/o School of Kinesiology, Acadia University, 550 Main St., Wolfville NS B4P 2R6 Canada
Tel: 902-585-1123; *Fax:* 902-585-1702
e-mail: info@ruralsustainability.org
URL: www.ruralsustainability.org
Description: The Centre for Rural Sustainability is a non-profit organization that works with grassroots groups, educators, youth, and community leaders to promote the growth of sustainable communities and economies in rural Nova Scotia. Services provided include consultation and fundraising assistance.

Clean Annapolis River Project (CARP)
PO Box 395, 151 Victoria St., Annapolis Royal NS B0S 1A0 Canada
Tel: 902-532-7533; *Fax:* 902-532-3038
Toll-Free: 888-547-4344

e-mail: carp@annapolisriver.ca
URL: www.annapolisriver.ca
Overview: A organization founded in 1990
Description: The Clean Annapolis River Project (CARP) is a charitable, community-owned corporation created to work with the community and interested organizations to foster the conservation, restoration and sustainable use of the freshwater and marine ecosystems of Southwestern Nova Scotia's Annapolis River and its watershed. Since 1990 CARP has developed several projects that address pertinent environmental issues in the Annapolis River watershed. These projects range from environmental monitoring to public education to habitat restoration to home assessment.

Clean Nova Scotia
126 Portland St., Dartmouth NS B2Y 1H8 Canada
Tel: 902-420-3474; *Fax:* 902-424-5334
e-mail: cns@clean.ns.ca
URL: www.clean.ns.ca
Overview: A organization founded in 1988
Description: Clean Nova Scotia is a not-for-profit organization founded in 1988, with the mandate to work with individuals, government, business, and communities to improve the environment of Nova Scotia. Clean Nova Scotia is focused on achieving specific goals, such as reduction of fossil fuel use, education, waste reduction, resource conservation and protection, and clean air.

Nova Forest Alliance (NFA)
285 George St., Stewiacke NS B0N 2J0 Canada
Tel: 902-639-2921; *Fax:* 902-639-2981
e-mail: info@novaforestalliance.com
URL: www.novaforestalliance.com
Description: The Nova Forest Alliance (NFA) is a partnership of environmentalists, researcgers, academic institutions, industry, and government agencies committed to finding sustainable forest management solutions in Nova Scotia. The Alliance works on collaborative research and the promotion of sustainable resource management programs to help maintain the ecological integrity of the province.

Nova Scotia. Dept. of Natural Resources
Nova Scotia Habitat Conservation Fund
Wildlife Div., Nova Scotia Dept. of Natural Resources, 136 Exhibition St., Kentville NS B4N 4E5 Canada
Tel: 902-679-6091; *Fax:* 902-679-6176
e-mail: habfund@gov.ns.ca
URL: www.gov.ns.ca/natr/wildlife/habfund/
Description: The Fund assists with projects that protect & enhance wildlife habitats. Priority activities are delineated under the four key objectives of Enhancement, Acquisition, Research, & Education.

Nova Scotia Environmental Network (NSEN)
55 Willowbend Ct., Halifax NS B3M 3L3 Canada
Tel: 902-454-6846; *Fax:* 902-454-6841
e-mail: nsen@cen-rce.org
URL: www.nsen.ca
Overview: A organization founded in 1991
Description: The Nova Scotia Environmental Network (NSEN) is a non-profit organization dedicated to connecting environmental and health organizations to enhance environmental and sustainability projects in Nova Scotia. The NSEN's goal is to provide support for its members by facilitating information exchange and action plans.

Sable Island Preservation Trust (SIPT)
PO Box 622, #310, 1657 Barrington St., Halifax NS B3J 2R7 Canada
Tel: 902-425-7225; *Fax:* 902-425-4793
Toll-Free: 877-707-7225
URL: www.sabletrust.ns.ca
Description: Sable Island Preservation Trust is a non-profit organization established in 1997 to help preserve and protect the Sable Island ecosystem. The Trust's goal is to promote and conduct scientific research, monitoring, andconservation programs which will ensure the long-term stability and viability of Sable Island.

Seagull Foundation
PO Box 108, Pugwash NS B0K 1L0 Canada
Tel: 902-243-2416
Description: To protect significant wilderness areas; to support environmental education & conservation; to support Third World development projects; to support programs that create environmental awareness.

Ontario

Agricultural Institute of Canada Foundation (AICF)
#900, 280 Albert St., Ottawa ON K1P 5G8 Canada
Tel: 613-232-9459; *Fax:* 613-594-5190
Toll-Free: 888-277-7980
e-mail: office@aic.ca
URL: www.aic.ca
Description: Enhancing agriculture & the role it plays in providing Canadians with a safe, affordable, nutritious food supply; supporting activities by universities that improve students' knowledge and understanding of the agricultural industry and its importance to the economy and the environment.

Animal Welfare Foundation of Canada (AWF)
#343, 300 Earl Grey Dr., Ottawa ON K2T AC1 Canada
e-mail: info@awfc.ca
URL: www.awfc.ca
Description: The Animal Welfare Foundation of Canada is a registered charity, supported by donors and administered by a volunteer Board of Directors. The Foundation seeks to improve the quality of life for animals in this country. Since the 1960s the Foundation, an independent watchdog organization, has been at the forefront of issues of humane care of animals in Canada.

Ausable Bayfield Conservation Foundation
71108 Morrison Line, RR#3, Exeter ON N0M 1S5 Canada
Tel: 519-235-2610; *Fax:* 519-235-1963
Toll-Free: 888-286-2610
e-mail: info@abca.on.ca
URL: www.abca.on.ca
Description: Raising funds for conservation, preservation & protection of the natural landscapes of the Ausable River, Bayfield River & Packhill Creek watersheds.

Canada Foundation for Innovation
#450, 230 Queen St., Ottawa ON K1P 5E4 Canada
Tel: 613-947-6496; *Fax:* 613-943-0923
e-mail: info@innovation.ca
URL: www.innovation.ca
Description: The Foundation is an independent corporation, created by the Government of Canada, with a mandate to fund research infrastructure, with particular reference to the research efforts of Canadian universities & colleges, research hospitals, & non-profit research organizations.

Canadian Foundation for Climate and Atmospheric Sciences (CFCAS)
#901, 350 Sparks St., Ottawa ON K1R 7S8 Canada
Tel: 613-238-2223; *Fax:* 613-238-2227
e-mail: bellerive@cfcas.org
URL: www.cfcas.org
Description: The Canadian Foundation for Climate and Atmospheric Sciences provides focused support for excellent university-based research on weather and climate.

Canadian Institutes of Health Research (CIHR)
160 Elgin St., 9th Fl., 4809A, Ottawa ON K1A 0W9 Canada
Tel: 613-941-2672; *Fax:* 613-954-1800
Toll-Free: 888-603-4178
e-mail: info@cihr-irsc.gc.ca
URL: www.cihr-irsc.gc.ca
Description: Established in 2000, CIHR is the agency responsible for funding health research in Canada. Research focusing on environmental impacts on health is just one of many areas the Institute may consider for support.

Canadian Ornamental Plant Foundation (COPF)
5A - #218, 975 McKeown Ave., North Bay ON P1B 9P2 Canada
Tel: 705-495-2563; *Fax:* 705-495-1449
Toll-Free: 800-265-1629
e-mail: info@copf.org
URL: www.copf.org
Description: To encourage new plant development by strengthening relations between growers & breeders for the benefit of the horticulture industry.

Catherine Donnelly Foundation
10 Montcrest Blvd., Toronto ON M4K 1J7 Canada
Tel: 416-461-2996; *Fax:* 416-465-4193
e-mail: info@catherinedonnellyfoundation.org
URL: www.catherinedonnellyfoundation.org
Description: Environmental Enhancement Initiatives: The Foundation will consider applications that advance inter-religious/cultural cooperation on ecological issues; promote public engagement in environmental education and advocacy; advance community based environmental research; advocate ecologically sustainable communities that demonstrate ecological integrity. The Foundation will support groups, projects and initiatives that: Advance a religious/spiritual experience of the earth that leads to healing action for the earth; Promote environmental education that supports broad based public engagement and advocacy; Advocate, build and model sustainable communities that demonstrate ecological integrity; Advance practical and community based environmental research.

Clean Air Foundation
#201, 1216 Yonge St., Toronto ON M4T 1W1 Canada
Tel: 416-922-9038; *Fax:* 416-922-1028
URL: www.cleanairfoundation.org
Description: Dedicated to developing, implementing & managing public engagement programs & other strategic approaches that lead to measurable emission reductions, to improve air quality & protect the climate.

Conservation Foundation
5 Shoreham Dr., Toronto ON M3N 1S4 Canada
Tel: 416-667-6279; *Fax:* 416-667-6275
e-mail: fdn@trca.on.ca
URL: www.trca.on.ca
Description: A leader in the acquisition & management of 13,150 hectares of regional greenspace & watershed conservation lands through its support of watershed management, reforestation, wildlife habitats, public access & recreation, historic sites & environmental rehabilitation of natural spaces.

Conservation Halton Foundation
2596 Britannia Rd., RR#2, Milton ON L9T 2X6 Canada
Tel: 905-336-1158; *Fax:* 905-336-7014
e-mail: admin@hrca.on.ca
URL: www.conservationhalton.on.ca
Description: To raise funds for Conservation Halton projects & programs that protect & enhance the natural environment.

Credit Valley Conservation Foundation
1255 Old Derry Rd. West, Mississauga ON L5N 6R4 Canada
Tel: 905-670-1615; *Fax:* 905-670-2210
Toll-Free: 800-668-5557
e-mail: cvc@creditvalleycons.com
URL: www.creditvalleycons.com
Description: To raise funds & awareness in support of Credit Valley Conservation's goal of an environmentally healthy river for economically & socially healthy communities.

Donner Canadian Foundation
8 Prince Arthur Ave., 3rd Fl., Toronto ON M5R 1A9 Canada
Tel: 416-920-6400; *Fax:* 416-920-5577
e-mail: gosney@donner.ca
URL: www.donnerfoundation.org
Description: The Donner Canadian Foundation was established in 1950 by William H. Donner. In the mid-1960s, the Foundation began to focus on specific program interests, among these, research on public policy. The Donner family chose Canada's centennial year, 1967, to embark on a course of professional grantmaking that has contributed well over $100 million to more than 1,000 projects across Canada and around the world. In addition to ongoing funding of public policy research, the Foundation supports environmental, international development, and social service projects.

Energy Probe Research Foundation (EPRF)
225 Brunswick Ave., Toronto ON M5S 2M6 Canada
Tel: 416-964-9223; *Fax:* 416-964-8239
e-mail: webadmin@eprf.ca
URL: www.eprf.ca
Description: To educate Canadians about the benefits of conservation & renewable energy; to help Canada secure long-term energy self-sufficiency in the shortest possible time with the fewest disruptive effects & with the greatest societal, environmental & economic benefits; to provide business, government & the public with information on energy & energy-related issues; to help Canada contribute to global harmony & prosperity; recipient of the 1990 Lieutenant Governor's Conservation Award, the first time that an environmental organization has been so honoured; divisions include Energy Probe, Probe International, Environment Probe, Margaret Laurence Fund, Consumer Policy Institute, Environmental Bureau of Investigations, Urban Renaissance Institute.

Evergreen
Common Grounds
355 Adelaide St. West, 5th Fl., Toronto ON M5V 1S2 Canada

Foundations & Grants / Federation of Canadian Municipalities

Tel: 416-596-1495; Fax: 416-596-1443
e-mail: info@evergreen.ca
URL: www.evergreen.ca
Description: Common Grounds provides grants to community groups doing environmental stewardship work. This is a national service which helps to protect natural & cultural landscapes, protect spaces for recreation & education, & restore areas that have been damaged. Offices in Toronto, Montréal & Vancouver.

Federation of Canadian Municipalities (FCM)
Green Municipal Fund
24 Clarence St., Ottawa ON K1N 5P3 Canada
Tel: 613-907-6357; Fax: 613-244-1515
e-mail: gmf@fcm.ca
URL: www.sustainablecommunities.fcm.ca
Description: FCM's Green Municipal Fund provides financial resources (grants & loans) & services to Canadian municipal governments for the purpose of improving environmental performance & reducing greenhouse gas emissions.

Friends of the Greenbelt Foundation
#201, 68 Scollard St., Toronto ON M5R 1G2 Canada
Tel: 416-960-0001; Fax: 416-960-0030
e-mail: info@ourgreenbelt.ca
URL: www.greenbelt.ca
Description: The Friends of the Greenbelt Foundation is a not-for-profit organization. The Foundation was created to help foster our Greenbelt's living countryside by nurturing and supporting activities that preserve its environmental and agricultural integrity.

George Cedric Metcalf Charitable Foundation
174 Ave. Rd., Toronto ON M5R 2J1 Canada
Tel: 416-926-0366; Fax: 416-926-0370
e-mail: info@metcalffoundation.com
URL: www.metcalffoundation.com
Description: The Metcalf Environment Program seeks to strengthen and enhance the effectiveness of people and organizations working together to ensure the ecological health and integrity of Southern Ontario's natural and working lands.

Grand River Conservation Foundation
400 Clyde Rd., Cambridge ON N1R 5W6 Canada
Tel: 519-621-2761; Fax: 519-621-4844
Toll-Free: 877-294-7263
e-mail: foundation@grandriver.ca
URL: www.grandriver.ca
Description: To provide leadership & support within the community of the Valley of the Grand River for the protection, conservation, responsible use & management of its natural resources, in response to the needs & wishes & for the ongoing enjoyment of its residents, as well as of the broader community of our province & country.

Helen McCrea Peacock Foundation
#1603, 33 Bloor St. East, Toronto ON M4W 3H1 Canada
Tel: 416-921-2035
e-mail: ngodkewitsch@tcf.ca
URL: www.tcf.ca/Default.aspx?tabid=136
Description: The Helen McCrea Peacock Foundation supports environmental organizations whose work and initiatives have a positive impact on the environment with a focus on remediation. The Foundation will fund: Registered Canadian charitable organizations & Environmental initiatives carried out within the Province of Ontario.

Jack Miner Migratory Bird Foundation, Inc.
PO Box 39, Kingsville ON N9Y 2E8 Canada
Tel: 519-733-4034
Toll-Free: 877-289-8328
e-mail: info@jackminer.com
URL: www.jackminer.com
Description: The sanctuary provides food, shelter & protection to migratory water fowl, tags birds & tracks migration patterns.

Lake Simcoe Region Conservation Foundation
PO Box 282, 120 Bayview Pkwy., Newmarket ON L3Y 4X1 Canada
Tel: 905-967-0112; Fax: 905-964-1265
Toll-Free: 800-465-0437
e-mail: foundation@lsrca.on.ca
URL: www.lsrca.on.ca/Foundation/index.html
Description: The Lake Simcoe Conservation Foundation (LSCF) invests in projects designed to protect and restore Lake Simcoe. Working in partnership with the Lake Simcoe Region Conservation Authority (LSRCA), watershed municipalities and other partners, they enable vital work to be done that maintains the natural environment, and in many places return the land and the rivers and the streams to a natural state.

Live Green Toronto
Eco-Roof Incentive Program
Toronto Environment Office, City of Toronto, 100 Queen St. West, East Tower, 21st Fl., Toronto ON M5H 2N2 Canada
e-mail: mygreenquestion@toronto.ca; teo@toronto.ca
URL: www.toronto.ca/livegreen/; www.toronto.ca/teo/
Description: Established in 2009, the incentive program promotes the use of green & cool roofs on Toronto's commercial, industrial & institutional buildings. Downloadable application form available on the website. Rebates & refunds for other energy saving practices also available.

The McLean Foundation
#1008, 2 St. Clair Ave. West, Toronto ON M4V 1L5 Canada
Tel: 416-964-6802; Fax: 416-964-2804
e-mail: mcleanfoundation.ca
URL: http://mcleanfoundation.ca
Description: The foundation makes grants in a wide range of areas, including arts, conservation, education, health and welfare. It maintains a flexible policy, with particular emphasis on projects showing promise of general social benefit but which may initially lack broad public appeal. In the 63 years of its existence, The McLean Foundation has received net investment income of $36,097,636 and has paid out a total of $37,946,157.

Natural Resources Canada
EcoENERGY Retrofit Incentive
580 Booth St., Ottawa ON K1A 0E4 Canada
Tel: 613-944-4506; Fax: 613-992-3161
e-mail: Chantal.Brouillard@NRCan-RNCan.gc.ca
URL: www.ecoaction.gc.ca/ecoenergy-ecoenergie/index-eng.cfm
Description: The ecoENERGY Retrofit - Homes program will provide homeowners with grants of up to $5,000 to offset the cost of making energy-efficiency improvements. Grants apply to a range of measures that reduce energy consumption and provide for a cleaner environment, from increasing insulation to upgrading windows and doors. To qualify, homeowners must first have a pre-retrofit energy evaluation by a certified evaluator and a post evaluation following the renovations. Funds are available for a limited time (to March 31, 2011) and are subject to availability.

The Neptis Foundation
501 - 1240 Bay St., Toronto ON M5R 2A7 Canada
Tel: 416-972-9199; Fax: 416-972-9198
URL: www.neptis.org
Description: The Neptis Foundation conducts and publishes nonpartisan research on the past, present and future of urban regions. An independent, privately-capitalized, charitable foundation, Neptis contributes timely, reliable knowledge and analysis on regional urban development to support informed public decisions and foster understanding of regional issues.

Niagara Peninsula Conservation Foundation (NPCF)
250 Thorold Rd. West, 3rd Fl., Welland ON L3C 3W2 Canada
Tel: 905-788-3135; Fax: 905-788-1121
e-mail: mcdougal@conservation-niagara.on.ca
URL: www.conservation-niagara.on.ca
Description: To assist the Niagara Peninsula Conservation Authority in the cultivation & advancement of conservation by actively seeking support for conservation projects & programs through fundraising efforts & by serving as the custodian for these donations & gifts.

Oak Ridges Moraine Foundation (ORMF)
The Gate House, 13990 Dufferin St. North, King City ON L7B 1B3 Canada
Tel: 905-833-5733; Fax: 905-833-8379
e-mail: support@ormf.com
URL: www.moraineforlife.org
Description: To date the Foundation has distributed $11.5 million in grants. Working closely with ORM partners, they have leveraged $25.3 million in partner funding, resulting in nearly $37 million in 145 new conservation and protection projects on the Moraine.

Ontario. Ministry of Energy & Infrastructure (OSTHI)
Ontario Solar Thermal Heating Incentive Program
Hearst Block, 900 Bay St., 4th Flo., Toronto ON M7A 2E1 Canada
Toll-Free: 888-668-4636
Description: The program supports the installation of solar thermal heating equipment. Applicants must be an industrial, commerical or institutional entity to be considered. Application forms available on the Ministry website.

The Ontario Trillium Foundation
45 Charles St. East, 5th Fl., Toronto ON M4Y 1S2 Canada
Tel: 416-963-4927; Fax: 416-963-8781
Toll-Free: 800-263-2887
e-mail: trillium@trilliumfoundation.org
URL: www.trilliumfoundation.org
Description: The Ontario Trillium Foundation is an agency of the Government of Ontario. The Ontario Trillium Foundation distributes its funding to charities and not-for-profits through two granting programs: Community and Province-Wide. Within those programs, funding is allocated in four sectors: Arts and Culture, Environment, Sports and Recreation, and Human and Social Services.

The Pollution Probe Foundation (PPF)
#402, 625 Church St., Toronto ON M4Y 2G1 Canada
Tel: 416-926-1907; Fax: 416-926-1601
e-mail: pprobe@pollutionprobe.org
URL: www.pollutionprobe.org
Description: A registered Canadian charity which seeks to define environmental problems through research; to promote understanding through education & to press for practical solutions through advocacy. The organization is non-partison & works collaboratively with government agencies, other non-profit organizations, & private business to engage key issues & find solutions. Offices in Toronto & Ottawa.

Quetico Foundation
#1260, 390 Bay St., Toronto ON M5E 1G6 Canada
Tel: 416-941-9388; Fax: 416-941-9236
e-mail: office@queticofoundation.org
URL: www.queticofoundation.org
Description: To preserve wilderness areas of Ontario for recreation & scientific use.

Richard Ivey Foundation
#400, 11 Church St., Toronto ON M5E 1W1 Canada
Tel: 416-867-9229; Fax: 416-601-1689
e-mail: info@ivey.org
URL: www.ivey.org
Description: To pursue & support excellence by making grants that will improve the well-being of Canadians. Today, the Conserving Canada's Forests Program provides critical support for environmental sustainability across the country.

The Salamander Foundation
#1201, 180 Bloor St. West, Toronto ON M5S 2V6 Canada
Tel: 416-972-9200; Fax: 416-972-9203
e-mail: info@salamanderfoundation.org
URL: www.salamanderfoundation.org
Description: The Salamander Foundation currently has two areas of interest: Arts and Culture, and the Environment. The Foundation seeks to promote continuity and discovery in the arts and in culture, and to recognize the forms, functions and interactions of natural systems in the environment.

TD Friends of the Environment Foundation
#1100, 45 O'connor St., Ottawa ON K1P 1A4 Canada
Tel: 613-782-1196; Fax: 613-783-6319
Toll-Free: 800-361-5333
e-mail: tdfef@td.com
URL: www.td.com/fef
Description: The TD Friends of the Environment Foundation (TD FEF) is a national organization with a grassroots focus that funds local projects dedicated to preserving the environment. They work with Canadians who are committed to protecting the environment in their own community and across the country. Since 1990, the TD Friends of the Environment Foundation has provided more than $47 million to support over 17,500 grassroots environmental projects in communities across Canada. And every year TD Bank Financial Group contributes an additional $1 million to TD FEF.

Temagami Community Foundation
PO Box 338, Temagami ON P0H 2H0 Canada
Tel: 705-569-3737
e-mail: temafoun@onlink.net
URL: www.temagamifoundation.ca
Description: The Temagami Community Foundation is a public Canadian Charitable Foundation. Grants are available for sustainable development & environmental initiatives.

Toronto Atmospheric Fund
75 Elizabeth St., Toronto ON M5G 1P4 Canada

Tel: 416-392-0271; Fax: 416-338-0616
e-mail: taf@toronto.ca
URL: www.toronto.ca/taf
Description: Toronto City Council established the Toronto Atmospheric Fund (TAF) in 1991 to finance Toronto-based initiatives that combat global climate change and improve air quality. TAF provides grants and loans and undertakes special projects to advance its mandate. Working with all sectors of the community, and with city departments and agencies, TAF leverages its resources to develop innovative local actions that lead to significant emission reduction results. On an annual basis, TAF has approximately $1.2 million available for grants and special projects. Up to $8 million in financing is currently available for mandate-related loans.

Toronto Parks & Trees Foundation
#123, 157 Adelaide St. W., Toronto ON M5H 4E7 Canada
Tel: 416-397-5178; Fax: 416-392-3355
e-mail: parksandtrees@toronto.ca
URL: www.torontoparksandtrees.org
Description: The Foundation coordinates with City of Toronto Parks, Forestry & Recreation to indentify areas of need with regard to the city's parks & public spaces.It raises funds to support park beautification.

T.R. Meighen Family Foundation
#200, 12 Birch Ave., Toronto ON M4V 1C8 Canada
Tel: 416-413-1999; Fax: 416-413-0015
e-mail: info@meighen.ca
URL: www.meighen.ca
Description: The T.R. Meighen Family Foundation is a private charitable foundation that was established by letters patent in April 1969 with a gift from the founder, Mr. Theodore Roosevelt Meighen. Over the past 37 years the foundation has granted over 15 million dollars to various projects. Most of this support has been directed to community based activities in the fields of education, health, social welfare, cultural and environmental conservation.

Transport Canada
Moving on Sustainable Transportation Program
Place de Ville, Tower C, 18th Fl., 330 Sparks St., Ottawa ON K1A 0N5 Canada
Tel: 613-998-6607; Fax: 613-949-3874
e-mail: MOST-SRTD@tc.gc.ca
URL: www.tc.gc.ca/programs/environment/MOST/menu.htm
Description: Transport Canada has established the Moving On Sustainable Transportation (MOST) Program to support projects that produce the kinds of education, awareness and analytical tools we need if we are to make sustainable transportation a reality. The MOST Program will provide funding to help support projects that will: Stimulate the development of innovative tools, approaches and practices for increasing the sustainability of Canada's transportation system and the use of sustainable modes of transportation; Realize quantifiable environmental and sustainable development results on Transport Canada's sustainable development priorities; and Provide Canadians with practical information, tools and opportunities for better incorporating sustainable transportation options into their daily lives.

Tree Canada Foundation (TCF)
#402, 222 Somerset St. West, Ottawa ON K2P 2G3 Canada
Tel: 613-567-5545; Fax: 613-567-5270
Toll-Free: 877-666-1444
e-mail: tcf@treecanada.ca
URL: www.treecanada.ca
Description: To provide education, technical support, resources & financial support through working partnerships to encourage Canadians to plant & care for trees in our urban & rural environment in an effort to help reduce the harmful effects of carbon dioxide emissions.

Trees Ontario
50 Million Tree Program
#701, 200 Consumers Rd., Toronto ON M2J 4R4 Canada
Tel: 416-646-1193; Fax: 416-493-4608
Toll-Free: 877-646-1193
e-mail: info@treesontario.on.ca
URL: www.treesontario.ca
Description: A program introduced in 2007 by the Ontario Government to fund the planting of 50 million trees across the province by 2020, as part of its commitment to reduce greenhouse gas effects, fight climate change & "green" the province.

Unilever Canada Foundation
#1500, 160 Bloor St. East, Toronto ON M4W 3R2 Canada
Tel: 416-964-1857; Fax: 416-963-5197
URL: www.unilever.ca/ourvalues/environmentandsociety/UC_Foundation
Description: Founded as a registered charity in 1995 - The Unilever Canada Foundation donates approximately 1% of Unilever Canada's pre-tax profit towards its community initiatives. Unilever Canada's community vitality initiative focuses mainly on the two areas that we feel are most significant to Canada and its people; - helping the healthy development of children between the ages of 0-5 and the environment - by protecting rivers, lakes and wetlands.

The W. Garfield Weston Foundation
c/o George Weston Ltd., #2001, 22 St. Clair Ave. East, Toronto ON M4T 2S3 Canada
Tel: 416-922-2500; Fax: 416-967-7949
e-mail: info@westonfoundation.org
URL: www.westonfoundation.org
Description: Focuses on education (through a scholarship & bursary program), conservation (via habitat conservation projects through national organizations only), & trustee-initiated grants (for which applications are not accepted).

Walter & Duncan Gordon Foundation
#400, 11 Church St., Toronto ON M5E 1W1 Canada
Tel: 416-601-4776; Fax: 416-601-1689
e-mail: gordon@gordonfn.org
URL: www.gordonfn.org
Description: The Walter & Duncan Gordon Foundation is dedicated to the development of sound and innovative public policies, founded on those values fundamental to Canadians, and designed to foster the continuing evolution of a dynamic and independent Canada. They believe that human development needs must be met in a way that recognizes the imperative to protect the environment.

Prince Edward Island

Bedeque Bay Environmental Management Association (BBEMA)
PO Box 8310, Emerald PE C0B 1M0 Canada
Tel: 902-886-3211
URL: www.bbema.ca
Overview: A organization founded in 1992
Description: The Bedeque Bay Environmental Management Association (BBEMA) is a not-for-profit charitable organization originally established in 1992 as an Atlantic Coastal Action Program site under Environment Canada. The BBEMA's goal is to provide sustainable environmental opportunities to the citizens of the area through planning, education, partnerships, and projects. The BBEMA focuses on soil erosion, water quality, natural habitat conservation, climate change, and public awareness projects and actitivies.

Environmental Coalition of Prince Edward Island (ECO-PEI)
126 Richmond St., Charlottetown PE C1A 1H9 Canada
Tel: 902-566-4696; Fax: 902-566-4037
e-mail: energy@ecopei.ca
URL: www.ecopei.ca
Overview: A organization founded in 1988
Description: The Environmental Coalition of Prince Edward Island (ECO-PEI) is a community based action group formed in 1988. ECO-PEI's goal is to work in partnership to understand and improve the Island environment. Projects supported by ECO-PEI include research into renewable energy and energy efficiency and natural resource conservation.

Island Nature Trust
PO Box 265, Charlottetown PE C1A 7K4 Canada
Tel: 902-566-9150; Fax: 902-628-6331
e-mail: intrust@eastlink.ca
URL: www.islandnaturetrust.ca
Overview: A organization founded in 1979
Description: The Island Nature Trust is a non-government, not-for-profit organization dedicated to protection and management of Natural Areas on Prince Edward Island. The Trust conducts and supports projects including land aquisition and protection, habitat restoration and management, conservation, and education.

Prince Edward Island. Dept. of Environment, Energy & Forestry
Greening Spaces Program
J. Frank Gaudet Tree Nursery, PO Box 2000, Charlottetown PE C1A 7N8 Canada
Tel: 902-368-4800; Fax: 902-368-4806
e-mail: greeningspaces@gov.pe.ca
URL: www.gov.pe.ca
Description: Funds tree planting projects, provides quality native tree & shrub seedlings, education materials, & technical advice. Communities, schools & volunteer interest groups are invited to submit proposals for projects.

Prince Edward Island. Dept. of Environment, Energy & Forestry
Environment Futures Program
J. Frank Gaudet Tree Nursery, PO Box 2000, Charlottetown PE C1A 7N8 Canada
Tel: 902-368-5000; Fax: 902-368-5830
URL: www.gov.pe.ca
Description: A summer program that trains high school & university students to do environmental protection work in their regions. Organizations may apply to have student work teams provide labour for their environmental projects. Projects such as enhancement of fish & wildlife habitat, soil erosion control, protecting & enhancing natural areas, & solid waste management/clean-up are suggested, but other projects that provide demonstrable environmental benefit to the community, & offer educational & work experience to students will be considered for funding.

Québec

The Aboriginal Funds for Species at Risk
Gatineau QC K1A 0H3 Canada
URL: www.recovery.gc.ca/afsar-faep/
Description: Established in 2004, AFSR recognizes the role Aboriginal people play in wildlife conservation & is comprised of 2 funds: the Aboriginal Capacity Building Fund, & the Aboriginal Critical Habitat Protection Fund. The aim of the funds is to help Aboriginal communities & organizations build capacity to enable participation in the conservation & recovery of protected species & species at risk, & to protect & recover the critical habitat of species at risk on Aboriginal lands. Regional offices across Canada - please consult the website for complete contact details.

Canadian Wildlife Service
Habitat Stewardship Program
351 boul St-Joseph, Gatineau QC K1A 0H3 Canada
Tel: 819-997-1301; Fax: 819-953-7177
URL: www.cws-scf.ec.gc.ca/hsp-pih
Description: As part of Canada's national strategy for the protection of species at risk, the federal government established the Habitat Stewardship Program (HSP) for Species at Risk. The HSP became operational in 2000-2001 and allocates up to $10 million per year to projects that conserve and protect species at risk and their habitats. The overall goal of the HSP is to "contribute to the recovery of endangered, threatened, and other species at risk, and to prevent other species from becoming a conservation concern, by engaging Canadians from all walks of life in conservation actions to benefit wildlife."

Canadian Wildlife Service
Interdepartmental Recovery Fund
351 boul St-Joseph, 4e étage, Gatineau QC K1A 0H3 Canada
Tel: 819-997-4325; Fax: 819-956-5993
URL: www.sararegistry.gc.ca/involved/funding/irf_fir/default_e.cfm
Description: As part of the National Strategy for the Protection of Species at Risk, the federal government has established the Interdepartmental Recovery Fund (IRF) for federal departments and departmental corporations. The IRF became operational in the 2002-2003 fiscal year. The IRF provides funding to federal departments and departmental corporations for implementing recovery activities for species designated by the Committee on the Status of Endangered Wildlife in Canada (COSEWIC) as nationally extirpated, endangered or threatened that are on federal lands or under federal jurisdiction. IRF also supports surveys of endangered, threatened and extirpated species on federal lands. As such, it supports federal organizations in their efforts to meet the requirements of the Species At Risk Act. This program also fosters partnerships among federal organizations and with other organizations interested in the recovery of species at risk.

Commission for Environmental Cooperation (CEC)
393, rue St-Jacques Ouest, Montréal QC H2Y 1N9 Canada
Tel: 514-350-4300; Fax: 514-350-4314
e-mail: info@cec.org
URL: www.cec.org

Description: The Commission for Environmental Cooperation (CEC) is an international organization created by Canada, Mexico and the United States under the North American Agreement on Environmental Cooperation (NAAEC). The CEC was established to address regional environmental concerns, help prevent potential trade and environmental conflicts, and to promote the effective enforcement of environmental law. The Agreement complements the environmental provisions of the North American Free Trade Agreement (NAFTA).

The EJLB Foundation
#1050, 1350 rue Sherbrooke ouest, Montréal QC H3G 1J1 Canada
Tel: 514-843-4080
URL: www.ejlb.qc.ca
Description: The EJLB Foundation has two main areas of interest: Mental health and support to community organizations providing assistance to persons suffering from mental illness; Protection of the environment, mainly through the acquisition and preservation, throughout Canada, of natural areas of ecological significance or of importance to the urban landscape. The Foundation also provides support, on a case by case basis, for a variety of other concrete environmental endeavours.

Fondation Hydro-Québec pour l'environnement
740, rue Notre-Dame Ouest, 8e étage, Montréal QC H3C 3X6 Canada
Tel: 514-289-5384; *Fax:* 514-289-2079
e-mail: fondation-environnement@hydro.qc.ca
URL: www.hydroquebec.com/fondation-environnement
Description: The Fondation Hydro-Québec pour l'environnement is a nonprofit organization whose mission is to help Québec communities develop a sense of ownership of their environment, enjoy it responsibly and pass on their natural heritage to future generations. The Foundation funds tangible initiatives that have positive environmental and social impacts and that serve the interests of local communities throughout Québec. It partners with local organizations on projects designed to: protect, restore and enhance natural habitats, and educate target audiences about local environmental issues.

Fonds d'action québécois pour le développement durable (FAQDD)
#200, 840, rue Raoul-Jobin, Québec QC G1N 1S7 Canada
Tel: 418-692-5888; *Fax:* 418-692-1148
e-mail: infos@faqdd.qc.ca
URL: www.faqdd.qc.ca
Description: Sponsored by the Government of Québec, the fund provides assistance to projects that emphasize behavioural changes that lead to positive steps towards sustainable development improvement. Projects., which may focus on air, water, soil, biodiversity, health, etc., must be collaborative in nature (between non-profit & business partners, for example).

Fonds d'action québécois pour le développement durable (FAQDD)
#200 - 840, rue Raoul-Jobin, Québec QC G1N 1S7 Canada
Tel: 418-692-5888; *Fax:* 418-692-1148
e-mail: infos@faqdd.qc.ca
URL: www.faqdd.qc.ca
Description: Créé en mars 2000, le Fonds d'action québécois pour le développement durable (FAQDD) est un organisme à but non lucratif qui offre des programmes d'aide financière destinés à soutenir l'intégration du développement durable au cour des comportements des Québécoises et des Québécois. Pour la réalisation de sa mission, le FAQDD s'est vu confié une enveloppe budgétaire de 51 millions de dollars du gouvernement du Québec.

Jour de la Terre Québec
Fonds Écomunicipalité IGA
#504, 460, rue Sainte-Catherine Ouest, Montréal QC H3B 1A7 Canada
Tel: 514-728-0116
Toll-Free: 800-424-8758
e-mail: fonds@jourdelaterre.org
URL: www.jourdelaterre.org
Description: The fund, jointly sponsored by Jour de la Terre Québec & IGA, was established to provide Québec organizations & municipalities funding for sustainable development projects. Projects should focus on environmental conservation, protection, and reclamation, or recycling/reuse, & should outline practical strategies & solutions.

Québec-Labrador Foundation (Canada) Inc.
#901, 505 boul. René Lévesque Ouest, Montréal QC H2Z 1Y7 Canada
Tel: 514-395-6020; *Fax:* 514-395-4505
e-mail: montreal@qlf.org
URL: www.qlf.org
Description: To promote local leadership & assist in improvement of human conditions in northern New England, Eastern Québec, & Canadian Atlantic provinces; to conserve cultural heritage & natural resources of region; to conduct scientific research; to enrich educational experience of Canadian & US students.

Saskatchewan

Communities of Tomorrow
Innovation Place, #250, 10 Research Dr., Regina SK S4S 7J7 Canada
Tel: 306-522-6699; *Fax:* 306-522-6695
e-mail: info@communitiesoftomorrow.ca
URL: www.communitiesoftomorrow.ca
Description: Communities of Tomorrow brings together into a non-profit corporation The City of Regina, The University of Regina, The Saskatchewan Ministry of Enterprise & Innovation, Western Economic Diversification Canada, & the National Research Council. The role of the corporation is to build partnerships that create sustainable communities in Saskatchewan, with a view to addressing such areas as transportation, water, sewer, & waste systems, & developing innovative solutions to infrastructure challenges in municipalities.

The Kongsgaard-Goldman Foundation
#602, 1932 First Ave., Seattle WA 98101 USA
Tel: 206-448-1874; *Fax:* 206-448-1973
e-mail: kgf@kongsgaard-goldman.org
URL: www.kongsgaard-goldman.org
Description: The Kongsgaard-Goldman Foundation is a small, private foundation formed in 1988. The Foundation provides support to a wide range of nonprofit organizations in the Pacific Northwest (Washington, Oregon, Idaho, Alaska, Montana and British Columbia, Canada). Within the program areas of human rights, civic development, environmental protection, and arts and humanities, the Foundation favors projects reflecting a deep and broad level of citizen participation and leadership. Our priority is to help fund the building of grassroots organizations with the power to change their communities and improve their lives.

Yukon Territory

Laidlaw Foundation
#2000, 365 Bloor St. East, Toronto ON M4W 3L4 Canada
Tel: 416-964-3614; *Fax:* 416-975-1428
e-mail: mail@laidlawfdn.org
URL: www.laidlawfdn.org
Description: The Foundation's current work promotes positive youth development through inclusive youth engagement in the arts, environment and in community. It recognizes that all young people need the unconditional support of significant adults in their lives and need multiple opportunities to locate an individual talent and the resources necessary to develop that talent.

Law Firms Index

A

Ackroyd LLP Barristers & Solicitors, 1054
Aikins, MacAulay & Thorvaldson LLP, 1063
Aird & Berlis LLP, 1072
Alexander Holburn Beaudin & Lang, LLP, 1057
Anderson, Greg W., Barrister, Solicitor, Notary, 1071
Antymniuk & Antymniuk, 1063
Austring, Fendrick, Fairman & Parkkari, 1091

B

Baker & Baker, 1057
Baker & McKenzie LLP, 1072
Barbeau, Evans, Goldstein, 1057
Barry Spalding - Moncton Office, 1064
Barry Spalding - Saint John Office, 1065
Bartlet & Richardes LLP, 1081
Beament Green, 1070
Beaudry, Bertrand Avocats, 1082
Bélanger, Sauvé, 1082
Bennett Jones LLP - Calgary Office, 1049
Benson Myles, 1065
Bernard & Partners, 1057
Bérubé & Pion, SENCRL, 1089
Besnier, Dion & Rondeau, 1089
Birchall Northey, 1072
Bishop & McKenzie LLP, 1049, 1054
Blais, Roger avocat inc, 1082
Blake, Cassels & Graydon LLP - Calgary, 1049
Blake, Cassels & Graydon LLP - Toronto, 1072
Blake, Cassels & Graydon LLP - Vancouver, 1057
Blaney McMurtry LLP, 1073
Borden Ladner Gervais LLP - Calgary, 1049
Borden Ladner Gervais LLP - Montréal, 1082
Borden Ladner Gervais LLP - Ottawa, 1070
Borden Ladner Gervais LLP - Toronto, 1073
Borden Ladner Gervais LLP - Vancouver, 1058
Boughton Law Corporation, 1058
Boyne Clarke, 1067
Bratty & Partners LLP, 1081
Brazeau Seller LLP, 1070
Brodeur, Boileau, 1089
Brownlee LLP, 1054
Burchell Hayman Parish, 1067
Burchell, MacDougall, 1067, 1068
Burlew, Edward L., 1072
Burnet, Duckworth & Palmer LLP, 1050
Burns, Fitzpatrick, Rogers & Schwartz, 1058
Burton Ronald W. Lawyers, 1067

C

Cain Lamarre Casgrain Wells - Alma, 1082
Cain Lamarre Casgrain Wells - Amos, 1082
Cain Lamarre Casgrain Wells - Amqui, 1082
Cain Lamarre Casgrain Wells - Chicoutimi, 1082
Cain Lamarre Casgrain Wells - Drummondville, 1082
Cain Lamarre Casgrain Wells - Montréal, 1083
Cain Lamarre Casgrain Wells - Québec, 1087
Cain Lamarre Casgrain Wells - Rimouski, 1089
Cain Lamarre Casgrain Wells - Sept-Iles, 1089
Cain Lamarre Casgrain Wells - Val-d'Or, 1089
Campbell Lea, 1082
Campbell Marr, 1063
Carscallen Leitch LLP, 1050
Cassels Brock & Blackwell LLP, 1074
Cherkewich, Ron, 1089
Chown, Cairns LLP, 1071
Clark Drummie, 1065
Clark Wilson LLP, 1058
Cline, Backus, Nightingale & McArthur, LLP, 1071
Cohen Highley LLP, 1069
Conway Davis Gryski, 1074
Cook Roberts LLP, 1062
Cox and Palmer - Charlottetown, 1082
Cox and Palmer - Fredericton, 1064
Cox and Palmer - Halifax, 1067
Cox and Palmer - St. John's, 1065
Crease Harman & Company, 1062
Cunningham, Swan, Carty, Little & Bonham LLP, 1069

D

D'Arcy & Deacon LLP, 1063
Daigneault, avocats inc., 1083
Daniel & Partners LLP, 1072
Davies Howe Partners, 1074
Davies Ward Phillips & Vineberg LLP, 1074
Davies Ward Phillips & Vineberg S.E.N.C.R.L., s.r.l., 1083
Davis & Company LLP, 1091, 1066
Davis LLP - Calgary, 1050
Davis LLP - Edmonton, 1054
Davis LLP - Montréal, 1083
Davis LLP - Toronto, 1074
Davis LLP - Vancouver, 1058
Delorme, LeBel, Bureau, s.e.n.c., 1089
Donnelly & Murphy, 1068
Donovan & Company, 1059
Dufour Scott Phelps & Mason, 1090
DuMoulin, Boskovich, 1059
Duncan & Craig LLP, Lawyers & Mediators, 1055
Dunsford & Scott, 1056

E

Eccleston LLP, 1075
Edwards, Kenny & Bray LLP, 1059
Eggum, Abrametz, Eggum, 1090
Emery Jamieson LLP, 1055
Environmental Law Centre (Alberta) Society, 1055
Erickson & Partners, 1072

F

Farris, Vaughan, Wills & Murphy LLP, 1059
Fasken Martineau - Calgary, 1050
Fasken Martineau - Montréal, 1083
Fasken Martineau - Québec, 1087
Fasken Martineau - Toronto, 1075
Fasken Martineau - Vancouver, 1059
Ferland & Bélair, 1082
Field Law - Calgary, 1050
Field Law - Edmonton, 1055
Field Law - Yellowknife, 1066
Fleming LLP, Barristers & Solicitors, 1051
Fraser Milner Casgrain LLP - Calgary, 1051
Fraser Milner Casgrain LLP - Edmonton, 1055
Fraser Milner Casgrain LLP - Ottawa, 1070
Fraser Milner Casgrain LLP - Toronto, 1075
Fraser Milner Casgrain LLP - Vancouver, 1060
Fraser Milner Casgrain S.E.N.C.R.L./LLP, 1083
Fulton & Company LLP, Lawyers & Trade-Mark Agents, 1056

G

Ganapathi & Company, 1060
Gardiner, Roberts LLP, 1075
Gilbert McGloan Gillis, 1065
Gilchrist & Company, 1057
Glaholt LLP, 1075
Good, Donald R., 1070
Goodmans LLP, 1075
Gorman Nason, 1065
Gowling Lafleur Henderson LLP - Calgary, 1051
Gowling Lafleur Henderson LLP - Kanata, 1069
Gowling Lafleur Henderson LLP - Toronto, 1075
Gowling Lafleur Henderson LLP - Vancouver, 1060
Gowling Lafleur Henderson S.E.N.C.R.L./LLP, 1084
Graham Wilson & Green, Barristers & Solicitors, Notaries, Mediators, 1068
Grondin, Poudrier, Bernier, 1087

H

Heelis, Williams, Little & Almas LLP, Barristers & Solicitors, 1072
Heenan Blaikie LLP - Calgary, 1051
Heenan Blaikie LLP - Ottawa, 1070
Heenan Blaikie LLP - Toronto, 1075
Heenan Blaikie LLP - Vancouver, 1060
Heenan Blaikie LLP - Victoria, 1062
Heenan Blaikie S.E.N.C.R.L./SRL - Québec, 1087
Heenan Blaikie S.E.N.C.R.L/SRL, 1084
Heenan Blaikie S.E.N.C.R.L/SRL - Sherbrooke, 1089
Heenan Blaikie S.E.N.C.R.L/SRL - Trois-Rivières, 1089
Hénaire, Louis, 1089
Hicks Morley Hamilton Stewart Storie LLP, 1069, 1070, 1076
Hodgson Russ LLP, 1077
Hook & Smith, 1063
Howard Ryan Kelford Knott & Dixon, 1068
Howard Ryan Kelford Knott & Dixon, Barristers & Solicitors, 1071
Howell Fleming LLP, 1071
Hughes, Amys LLP, 1077
Hume, Forrest C., Law Corporation, 1060
Hunter Litigation Chambers, 1060
Hutchins Caron & Associates, 1060
Hutchins Caron & Associés, 1085

J

Joli-Cour Lacasse Avocats, 1088

K

Kahn Zack Ehrlich Lithwick, 1057
Kanuka Thuringer LLP, Barristers & Solicitors, 1090, 1091
Kay, McVey, Smith & Carlstrom LLP, 1056
Kirwin LLP, 1055

L

Lalonde Geraghty Riendeau Lapierre, 1089
Lamarre Perron Lambert Vincent, 1085
Lang Michener LLP - Ottawa, 1070
Lang Michener LLP - Toronto, 1077
Lang Michener LLP - Vancouver, 1060
Langlois Kronström Desjardins, 1085, 1088
Lapointe Rosenstein Marchand Melançon, 1085
Lavery, de Billy - Montréal, 1085
Lavery, de Billy - Ottawa, 1070
Lavery, de Billy - Québec, 1088
Lawrence, Lawrence, Stevenson, 1068
Lawson Lundell LLP - Calgary, 1051
Lawson Lundell LLP - Vancouver, 1060
Lawson Lundell LLP - Yellowknife, 1066
Lazier Hickey Langs O'Neal, 1068
Lee & Lee, 1063
Lesperance Mendes, 1061
Levy, Alan D., 1077
Linda Willcox Whetung Professional Corporation, 1071
Lindsay Kenney LLP, 1056, 1061
Loopstra Nixon LLP, 1077

M

Machida Mack Shewchuk Meagher LLP, 1052
MacInnis, Kenneth Associates, 1067
MacKenzie Fujisawa LLP, 1061
MacLachlan McNab Hembroff, 1056
Macleod Dixon LLP, 1052, 1077
MacPherson Leslie & Tyerman LLP - Calgary, 1052
MacPherson Leslie & Tyerman LLP - Regina, 1090
MacPherson Leslie & Tyerman LLP - Saskatoon, 1090
Madorin, Snyder LLP, 1069
Magwood, Van De Vyvere, Thompson, & Grove-McClement LLP, 1081
Marshall & Lamperson, 1057
Martin Sheppard Fraser LLP, 1070
Martin Whalen Hennebury Stamp, 1066
Matheson & Murray, 1082
Mattson, Mark O., 1077
McCaffery Mudry Pritchard LLP, Barristers & Solicitors, 1052
McCarthy Tétrault LLP - Calgary, 1052
McCarthy Tétrault LLP - Montréal, 1086
McCarthy Tétrault LLP - Ottawa, 1070
McCarthy Tétrault LLP - Québec, 1088
McCarthy Tétrault LLP - Toronto, 1077
McCarthy Tétrault LLP - Vancouver, 1061
McCullough O'Connor Irwin LLP, 1061
McDougall Gauley, 1089, 1090

Law Firms Index

McInnes Cooper, 1064, 1067, 1066
McKenzie Lake Lawyers LLP, 1069
McLennan Ross LLP, 1053, 1055, 1066
McMillan Binch Mendelsohn - Montréal, 1086
McMillan Binch Mendelsohn - Toronto, 1077
Merchant Law Group LLP - Calgary, 1053
Merchant Law Group LLP - Edmonton, 1055
Merchant Law Group LLP - Saskatoon, 1090
Merchant Law Group LLP - Victoria, 1062
Miles, Davison LLP, 1053
Miller Thomson LLP - Calgary, 1053
Miller Thomson LLP - Edmonton, 1055
Miller Thomson LLP - Markham, 1069
Miller Thomson LLP - Montréal, 1086
Miller Thomson LLP - Toronto, 1077
Miller Thomson LLP - Vancouver, 1061
Miller Thomson LLP - Waterloo, 1081
Monty, Coulombe, 1089
Moore-Stewart, Robert, 1062
Morelli Chertkow LLP, Lawyers, 1056
Morency Avocats, 1088
Muttart Tufts Dewolfe & Coyle, 1068

N

Nelligan O'Brien Payne, 1068, 1069, 1071, 1081
Nimegeers, Schuck, Wormsbecker & Bobbitt, 1091
Nixon Wenger, 1062

O

O'Connor MacLeod Hanna LLP, 1070
Ogilvy Renault LLP/S.E.N.C.R.L., s.r.l. - Toronto, 1053, 1086, 1071, 1088, 1078
Osler, Hoskin & Harcourt LLP - Calgary, 1053
Osler, Hoskin & Harcourt LLP - Toronto, 1079
Osler, Hoskin & Harcourt S.E.N.C.R.L./LLP, 1086
Ottenheimer Baker, 1066
Outerbridge Miller Sefton, 1079

P

Parlee McLaws LLP, 1053, 1055
Paterson, MacDougall LLP, Barristers, Solicitors, 1079
Patterson Law, 1067, 1068

Patton Cormier & Associates, 1069
Pearl & Associates, 1086
Perley-Robertson, Hill & McDougall LLP, 1071
Pink Larkin, 1064
Pitblado LLP, 1063
Poch, Harry Environmental Lawyer, 1079
Poole Althouse, Barristers & Solicitors, 1065
Pullan Kammerloch Frohlinger, 1064
Pushor Mitchell LLP, Lawyers & Trade-Mark Agents, 1056

R

Ramsay Lampman Rhodes, 1056
Ratcliff & Company LLP, 1057
Renick, Jim Law Office, 1068
Reynolds, Mirth, Richards & Farmer LLP, 1056
Richards Buell Sutton LLP, 1062
Rick & Associates, 1071
Riopelle Griener Professional Corporation, 1070, 1072
Rioux Bossé Massé Moreau, 1089
Ritch Durnford, Lawyers, 1067
Roach, Schwartz & Associates, Barristers & Solicitors, 1079
Robertson Stromberg Pedersen LLP, 1091
Robinson Sheppard Shapiro LLP, 1086
Rosenberg & Rosenberg, 1062
Rosenbloom & Aldridge, 1062
Ross & McBride LLP, 1069
Russell Christie LLP, 1070

S

Saxe, Dianne, 1079
Scarfone Hawkins LLP, 1069
Scott Venturo LLP, 1053
Shibley Righton LLP, 1079, 1081
Shook, Wickham, Bishop & Field, 1056
SimpsonWigle LAW LLP, 1068, 1069
Singleton Urquhart LLP, 1062
Siskind, Cromarty, Ivey & Dowler LLP, 1069
Smith, Kenneth W., Barrister & Solicitor, 1071
Soloway, Wright LLP, 1071
Stewart & Turner, 1067
Stewart McKelvey Stirling Scales - Fredericton, 1064
Stewart McKelvey Stirling Scales - Halifax, 1067
Stewart McKelvey Stirling Scales - Moncton, 1064

Stewart McKelvey Stirling Scales - Saint John, 1065
Stewart McKelvey Stirling Scales - St. John's, 1066
Stikeman Elliott LLP - Calgary, 1053
Stikeman Elliott LLP - Montréal, 1087
Stikeman Elliott LLP - Ottawa, 1071
Stikeman Elliott LLP - Toronto, 1079
Stikeman Elliott LLP - Vancouver, 1062
Stitt Feld Handy Group, 1080
Stones Carbert Waite Wells LLP, 1054
Stringer, Brisbin, Humphrey Management Lawyers, 1080
Sutts, Strosberg LLP, 1082
Sylvain, Parent, Gobeil, 1089

T

Templeman Menninga LLP, 1068
Thoman Soule LLP, Lawyers, 1069
Thompson Dorfman Sweatman LLP, 1064
Thomson, Rogers, 1080
Torys LLP, 1080
Tremblay, Bois, Mignault & Lemay, 1089
Turkstra Mazza Associates, 1069

W

Wallace Meschishnick Clackson Zawada, 1091
Walsh Wilkins Creighton LLP, 1054
Warren Tettensor Amantea LLP, 1054
Waterstone Law Group LLP, 1056
Weaver, Simmons LLP, 1072
Weiler, Maloney, Nelson, 1072
WeirFoulds LLP, 1081
Wickwire Holm, 1068
Wilbur & Wilbur, 1065
Willms & Shier Environmental Lawyers LLP, 1081
Wilson Laycraft, 1054
Wishart Law Firm LLP, 1071
Wolch, Hursh, deWit & Watts, 1054
Woodward & Company, 1063

Y

Young, Anderson, 1062

Law Firms

Alberta

Calgary

Bennett Jones LLP - Calgary Office
#4500, Bankers Hall East Tower 855 - 2nd St. SW, Calgary AB T2P 4K7
403-298-3100 403-265-7219 Telex: 038-24524
firmwatch@bennettjones.ca
www.bennettjones.ca
Profile: 6 Offices, 159 Lawyers, Founded in: 1922
Our energy & natural resources department is among the most comprehensive in Canada; part of the development of Canadian natural resources for almost 100 years, we have diverse & comprehensive experience in North America's energy & natural resource sectors; our environmental/regulatory department is comprised of lawyers who have experience in a broad range of practice areas
Environmental Lawyers:
Karen Beattie
   403-298-2076
   beattiek@bennettjones.ca
Marie H. Buchinski, Regulatory; Environmental
   403-298-8136
   buchinskim@bennettjones.ca
Michael W. Callihoo
   403-298-2074
   callihoom@bennettjones.ca
John N. Craig, Construction
   403-298-3463
   craigj@bennettjones.ca
John R. Gilmore, Occupational Health & Safety
   403-298-3297
   gilmorej@bennettjones.ca
Bradley S. Gilmour, Environmental; Regulatory
   403-298-3382
   gilmourb@bennettjones.ca
Donald E. Greenfield, Energy & Natural Resources; Oil & Gas
   403-298-3248
   greenfieldd@bennettjones.ca
Nicholas M. Gretener, Regulatory; Environmental; Electricity Generation; Oil & Gas; Utilities
   403-298-3405
   gretenern@bennettjones.ca
Loyola G. Keough, Regulatory; Environmental
   403-298-3429
   keoughl@bennettjones.ca
M. Kristen Lozynsky, Regulatory; Environmental
   403-298-3341
   lozynskyk@bennettjones.ca
John G. Martland, Q.C., Health
   403-298-3186
   martlandj@bennettjones.ca
Darcy D. Moch, Oil & Gas
   403-298-3390
   mochd@bennettjones.ca
Shawn M. Munro, Environmental; Regulatory
   403-298-3481
   munros@bennettjones.ca
Daron K. Naffin
   403-298-3668
   naffind@bennettjones.ca
Jean-Pierre Pham
   403-298-4462
   phamj@bennettjones.ca
Valerie R. Prather, Litigation; Regulatory
   403-298-3486
   pratherv@bennettjones.ca
Lawrence E. Smith, Q.C., Regulatory; Environmental; Electricity Generation; Oil & Gas; Utilities
   403-298-3315
   smithl@bennettjones.ca
John L. Townley, Health
   403-298-3458
   townleyj@bennettjones.ca

Bishop & McKenzie LLP
#1700, 530 - 8th Ave. SW, Calgary AB T2P 3S8
403-237-5550 403-263-3423
calgary@bishopmckenzie.com
www.bishopmckenzie.com
Profile: 8 Lawyers
Environmental Lawyers:
Armand J. Moss, Q.C., Environmental Law
   403-750-7975
   a.moss@bishopmckenzie.com

Blake, Cassels & Graydon LLP - Calgary
#3500, East Tower, Bankers Hall 855 - 2nd St. SW, Calgary AB T2P 4J8
403-260-9600 403-260-9700
calgary@blakes.com
www.blakes.com
Profile: 100 Lawyers, Founded in: 1856
Energy; Environmental; Litigation; Mining; Oil & Gas
Environmental Lawyers:
Ross A. Bentley, Energy; Oil & Gas; Infrastructure
   403-260-9720
   ross.bentley@blakes.com
Chris A. Christopher, Oil & Gas; Energy
   403-260-9662
   chr@blakes.com
Scott W.N. Clarke, Energy
   403-260-9712
   scott.clarke@blakes.com
Mitchell Cohen, Oil & Gas; Energy
   403-260-9650
   mitchell.cohen@blakes.com
Dallas L. Droppo, Q.C., Oil & Gas; Mining; Energy
   403-260-9612
   dallas.droppo@blakes.com
Pat C. Finnerty, Energy; Oil & Gas
   403-260-9608
   pcf@blakes.com
Dan P.E. Fournier, Q.C., Energy; Oil & Gas
   403-260-9636
   dan.fournier@blakes.com
Brock W. Gibson, Q.C., Chair, Oil & Gas; Energy
   403-260-9610
   brock.gibson@blakes.com
Mungo Hardwicke-Brown, Energy; Oil & Gas; Infrastructure
   403-260-9674
   MHB@blakes.com
Duff Harper, Environmental; Energy; CleanTech
   403-260-9710
   dufferin.harper@blakes.com
Michael Laffin, Oil & Gas; Energy
   403-260-9692
   michael.laffin@blakes.com
Webster Macdonald, Q.C., Energy; Oil & Gas; Construction
   403-260-9604
   web.macdonald@blakes.com
Michael McCachen, Oil & Gas; Energy
   403-260-9792
   michael.mccachen@blakes.com
Dalton W. McGrath, Q.C., Energy; Environmental
   403-260-9654
   dalton.mcgrath@blakes.com
Ken Mills, Managing Parnter, Litigation; Environmental; Energy; Construction
   403-260-9648
   ken.mills@blakes.com
Warren B. Nishimura, Oil & Gas
   403-260-9664
   warren.nishimura@blakes.com
Lars Olthafer, Energy; Environmental; Oil & Gas; Regulatory
   403-260-9633
   lars.olthafer@blakes.com
Darel Grant Samuelson, Oil & Gas
   403-260-9630
   darel.samuelson@blakes.com
Sabeen Sheikh, Energy; Oil & Gas; Infrastructure
   403-260-9707
   sabeen.sheikh@blakes.com
David V. Tupper, Oil & Gas; Construction; Environmental
   403-260-9722
   david.tupper@blakes.com
C. Kemm Yates, Q.C., Energy; Regulatory; Litigation & Dispute Resolution; Alternative Dispute Resolution
   403-260-9667
   kemm.yates@blakes.com

Borden Ladner Gervais LLP - Calgary
Centennial Place, East Tower #1900, 520 - 3rd Ave. SW, Calgary AB T2P 0R3
403-232-9500 403-266-1395
info@blg.com
www.blg.com
Profile: 111 Lawyers
Environmental Lawyers:
Sheila Acharya Van Horne, Health Law
   403-232-9626
   sacharyavanhorne@blg.com
Julio N. Arboleda Ramirez, Partner, Energy; Oil & Gas; Climate Change
   403-232-9601
   jarboleda@blg.com
Randall W. Block, Q.C., Partner, Energy; Oil & Gas
   403-232-9572
   rblock@blg.com
Bruce Churchill-Smith, Q.C., Partner, Oil & Gas Litigation
   403-232-9669
   bchurchillsmith@blg.com
Darryl Douglas, Oil & Gas
   403-232-9519
   ddouglas@blg.com
Donald B. Edwards, Partner, Natural Resources
   403-232-9635
   dedwards@blg.com
Jennifer Faircloth, Partner, Oil & Gas Litigation
   403-232-9643
   jfaircloth@blg.com
David Farmer, Natural Resources; Energy Law; Environment
   403-232-9656
   dfarmer@blg.com
Frank R. Foran, Q.C., Energy Law & Litigation; Energy Law; Regulatory & Compliance; Oil & Gas Industry; Electricity Industry; Construction Industry
   403-232-9443
   fforan@blg.com
R.J. Daniel Gilborn, Oil & Gas Litigation
   403-232-9690
   dgilborn@blg.com
William C. Guinan, Partner, Oil & Gas
   403-232-9458
   bguinan@blg.com
Patrick Heinsen, Partner, Construction
   403-232-9614
   pheinsen@blg.com
Kent D. Howie, Partner, Energy; Electricity
   403-232-9535
   khowie@blg.com
John L. Ircandia, Partner, Oil & Gas Litigation
   403-232-9406
   jircandia@blg.com
Joel B. Jones, Climate Change & Emissions Trading; Oil & Gas; Environment
   403-232-9658
   jjones@blg.com
Ryan R. Kary, Construction Litigation
   403-232-9516
   rkary@blg.com
Larwrence M. Kwinter, Partner, Health Law
   403-232-9554
   lkwinter@blg.com
Bruce A. Lawrence, Partner, Natural Resources; Oil & Gas
   403-232-9597
   blawrence@blg.com
Matti Lemmens, Oil & Gas Litigation
   403-232-9511
   mlemmens@blg.com
Matthew Lui, Oil & Gas
   403-232-9588
   mlui@blg.com
Travis Lysak, Oil & Gas Litigation
   403-232-9719
   tlysak@blg.com
David T. Madsen, Partner, Oil & Gas
   403-232-9612
   dmadsen@blg.com

Law Firms / Alberta

Michael A. Marion, Partner, Energy Litigation; Oil & Gas; Electricity; Environment
403-232-9464
mmarion@blg.com
Kirk Mason, Construction
403-232-9514
kmason@blg.com
Michael G. Massicotte, Partner, Environmental Law; Energy Litigation; Oil & Gas; Health Law
403-232-9602
mmassicotte@blg.com
Neil McCrank, Q.C., P.Eng, Counsel, Oil & Gas; Energy Litigation
403-232-9749
nmccrank@blg.com
Rob McCulloch, Oil & Gas
403-232-9638
rmcculloch@blg.com
Patricia L. Morrison, Partner, Environmental Law; Construction
403-232-9472
pmorrison@blg.com
Katherine Murphy, Oil & Gas Litigation
403-232-9701
kamurphy@blg.com
Allan D. Nielsen, Q.C., Partner, Oil & Gas Industry
403-232-9487
anielsen@blg.com
Evan Nuttall, Partner, Construction Litigation
403-232-9403
enuttall@blg.com
Thomas F. Pepevnak, Partner, Energy; Oil & Gas
403-232-9652
tpepevnak@blg.com
Michael J. Perkins, Partner, Natural Resources; Oil & Gas; Mining
403-232-9410
mperkins@blg.com
Ross A. Reaburn, Counsel, Electricity Industry; Climate Change; Oil & Gas Industry; Petrochemical Industry; Forestry Industry
403-232-9491
rreaburn@blg.com
Beth Reimer-Heck, Q.C., Counsel, Environmental Law; Oil & Gas
403-232-9654
breimerheck@blg.com
Brian E. Roberts, Partner, Oil & Gas
403-232-9512
broberts@blg.com
Laurie M. Robson, Partner, Occupational Health & Safety; Construction; Oil & Gas
403-232-9482
lrobson@blg.com
Alan L. Ross, Partner, Climate Change; Environmental Law; Oil & Gas; Electricity
403-232-9712
aross@blg.com
Karen A. Salmon, Partner, Energy; Oil, Gas & Electricity Litigation
403-232-9476
ksalmon@blg.com
Geoffrey Stenger, Construction
403-232-9542
gstenger@blg.com
James W. Surbey, Senior Partner, Oil & Gas
403-232-9537
jsurbey@blg.com
Edward W. Tapuska, Partner, Oil & Gas
403-232-9785
etapuska@blg.com
Chidinma Thompson, Climate Change; Environmental Law; Oil & Gas; Aboriginal Law
403-232-9666
cthompson@blg.com
Jeffrey D. Vallis, Q.C., Partner, Construction; Oil & Gas
403-232-9404
jvallis@blg.com
David C. Whelan, Managing Partner, Climate Change
403-232-9555
dwhelan@blg.com
Hugh D. Williamson, Q.C., Partner, Environmental Law; Regulatory & Compliance; Oil & Gas Industry; Petrochemical Industry
403-232-9541
hwilliamson@blg.com

Steve W. Wilson, Partner, Health Law
403-232-9456
swwilson@blg.com

Burnet, Duckworth & Palmer LLP
#1400, First Canadian Centre 350 - 7th Ave. SW, Calgary AB T2P 3N9
403-260-0100 403-260-0332
counsel@bdplaw.com
www.bdplaw.com
Profile: 1 Offices, 125 Lawyers, Founded in: 1915
Legal services in the commercial area relate to the following: oil & gas acquisitions & divestitures; public & private energy financing; major energy projects; exploration & development business structures; the formulation of energy policy; & legislation relating to federal & provincial petroleum & natural gas lands. Environmental lawyers offer clients comprehensive legal services encompassing virtually every aspect of regulatory environmental law & occupational health & safety issues.
Environmental Lawyers:
R. Bruce Allford, Energy
  403-260-0247
  rba@bdplaw.com
Brandon Barnes, Regulatory Energy
  403-260-0130
  jbb@bdplaw.com
Paul A. Beke, Occupational Health & Safety
R. Bruce Brander, Energy & Non-Energy Developments (Regulatory)
  403-260-0165
  rbb@bdplaw.com
Harry S. Campbell, Q.C., Energy
John H. Cuthbertson, Energy
John C. Goetz, Energy
David R. Haigh, Q.C., Occupational Health & Safety
Mark T. Houston, Energy
Cal Johnson, Q.C., Energy
  403-260-0202
  cdj@bdplaw.com
Jonathan M. Liteplo, Regulatory Energy; Water & Drainage Regulatory
  403-260-0310
  jml@bdplaw.com
John Lowe, Regulatory Energy & Telecommunications
  403-260-0257
  jel@bdplaw.com
Daniel J. McDonald, Q.C., Occupational Health & Safety
  403-260-5724
  djm@bdplaw.com
Keith F. Miller, Energy & Non-Energy Development (Regulatory)
  403-260-0153
  kfm@bdplaw.com
Douglas G. Mills, Occupational Health & Safety
J. Stuart Money, Energy
Melissa Moulton Tennison, Occupational Health & Safety
James D. Murphy, Occupational Health & Safety
Arnold Olyan, Energy
  403-260-0249
  aho@bdplaw.com
Patricia E. Olyslager, Occupational Health & Safety
Danielle M. Parrotta, Energy
Alan T. Pettie, Energy
Rory G. Polson, Energy
Kathy L. Pybus, Energy
  403-260-0196
  klp@bdplaw.com
Alicia K. Quesnel, Energy
Patricia Quinton-Campbell, Regulatory; Energy
  403-260-0308
  pqc@bdplaw.com
Jeff Sharpe, Occupational Health & Safety
Allan R. Twa, Q.C., Energy
  403-260-0221
  art@bdplaw.com
Jody Wivcharuk, Energy
Carolyn A. Wright, Energy

Carscallen Leitch LLP
#1500, 407 - 2 St. SW, Calgary AB T2P 2Y3
403-262-3775 403-262-2952
info@cllawyers.com
www.cllawyers.com
Profile: 1 Offices, 29 Lawyers
Environmental Lawyers:
Geoffrey D. Baker, Oil & Gas
Glenn C. Blackett, Oil & Gas

Stanley Carscallen, Q.C., Oil & Gas
Christina A. Dozzi, Oil & Gas
Donald C. Edie, Q.C., Oil & Gas
Michael B. Niven, Oil & Gas
Kendall W. Waiting, Oil & Gas

Davis LLP - Calgary
#1000, Livingston Place 250 - 2nd St. SW, Calgary AB T2P 0C1
403-296-4470 403-296-4474
www.davis.ca
Profile: 8 Offices, Founded in: 1892
The Environmental Law Group consists of a team of lawyers with extensive experience in advising clients in all aspects of environmental law. Experience ranges from providing clients with an understanding of the ever-changing regulatory landscape, to acting on civil litigation & in the defence of environmental prosecutions.
Environmental Lawyers:
Derrick K. Auch, Mining law; Energy & utilities
  403-698-8714
  dauch@davis.ca
James Bancroft, Q.C., Environmental law
  403-698-8764
  jbancroft@davis.ca
James G.M. Bell, Mining law; Energy & utilities; Mining law
  403-698-8707
  james.bell@davis.ca
Timothy P. Chick, Environmental law; Mining law
  403-698-8710
  tchick@davis.ca
Terence Dalgleish, Q.C., Energy & utilities
  403-698-8740
  tdalgleish@davis.ca
Roy H. Hudson, Climate change law; Mining law
  403-698-8708
  rhusdon@davis.ca
Daniel E. Kenney, Energy & utilities; Mining law
  403-698-8704
  dkenney@davis.ca
Robert Perrin, Environmental law; Energy & utilities
  403-698-8751
  rperrin@davis.ca
Dana Schindelka, Environmental law; Energy & utilities; Municipal law
  403-698-8705
  dschindelka@davis.ca
David J. Stratton, Q.C., Forestry law
  403-296-4470
  dstratton@davis.ca
Donald J. Wilson, Environmental law
  780-429-6817
  dwilson@davis.ca
Trevor Wong-Chor, Energy & utilities
  403-698-8711
  twong-chor@davis.ca
Brian Yaworski, Q.C., Energy & utilities; Mining law; Climate change law
  403-698-8746
  byaworski@davis.ca

Fasken Martineau - Calgary
#3400, First Canadian Centre 350 - 7th Ave. SW, Calgary AB T2P 3N9
403-261-5350 403-261-5351
calgary@fasken.com
www.fasken.com
Profile: 24 Lawyers, Founded in: 1863
Environmental; Energy; Natural Resource Law
Environmental Lawyers:
A.W. (Sandy) Carpenter, Energy, Environmental & Regulatory Law
  scarpenter@cgy.fasken.com
Peter Feldberg, Energy, Environmental and Regulatory Law
  pfeldberg@cgy.fasken.com
Alex Kotkas, Energy, Environmental and Regulatory Law
  akotkas@cgy.fasken.com
R. Greg Powers, Q.C., Oil & Gas
  gpowers@cgy.fasken.com

Field Law - Calgary
#400, The Lougheed Building 604 - 1st St. SW, Calgary AB T2P 1M7
403-260-8500 403-264-7084
ijvanderlee@fieldlaw.com; lmccambley@fieldlaw.com
www.fieldlaw.com
Profile: 40 Lawyers, Founded in: 1915

Law Firms / Alberta

Environmental Lawyers:
Michael F. Casey, Q.C., Construction
403-260-8505
mcasey@fieldlaw.com
Peter L. Collins, Environmental
403-260-8516
pcollins@fieldlaw.com
William T. Corbett, Q.C., Energy & Natural Resources
403-260-8504
bcorbett@fieldlaw.com
Jim Doyle, First Nations; Municipal
403-260-8578
jdoyle@fieldlaw.com
Todd W. Kathol, Construction
403-260-8581
tkathol@fieldlaw.com
Gabrielle C. Kaufmann, Energy & Natural Resources Law
403-260-8564
gkaufmann@fieldlaw.com
Jean C. van der Lee, Construction
403-260-8520
jvanderlee@fieldlaw.com

Fleming LLP, Barristers & Solicitors
#900, 926 - 5th Ave. SW, Calgary AB T2P 0N7
403-266-5550 403-265-6910 877-566-5550
www.flemingllp.com
Profile: 2 Offices, 10 Lawyers, Founded in: 1921
Environmental Lawyers:
Carmen Alger, Municipal law
Predrag Anic, Administrative law

Fraser Milner Casgrain LLP - Calgary
Bankers Court 850 - 2nd St. SW, 15th Fl., Calgary AB T2P 0R8
403-268-7000 403-268-3100
matt.lindsay@fmc-law.com
www.fmc-law.com
Profile: 115 Lawyers,
The firm offers expertise in Energy Law; Oil & Gas Industry Matters (including heavy oil, oil sands, liquefied natural gas, pipeline projects, project finance, ligitation, mergers & acquisitions; and restructuring & insolvency); & Environmental Law
Environmental Lawyers:
Douglas J. Black, Q.C., Energy & Natural Resources Law
doug.black@fmc-law.com
Tamela J. Coates, Environmental Law
403-268-6860
tamela.coates@fmc-law.com
Douglas E. Crowther, Energy & Natural Resources; Environmental Law; Power
403-268-6821
douglas.crowther@fmc-law.com
Laura K. Estep, Energy & Natural Resources
403-268-6308
laura.estep@fmc-law.com
William G. Gilliland, Energy & Natural Resources; Mining
william.gilliland@fmc-law.com
Michael A. Hurst, Energy & Natural Resources Law
michael.hurst@fmc-law.com
Matthew R. Lindsay, Managing Partner (Calgary), Energy Law; Oil & Gas Industry; Construction Industry
403-268-3037
matt.lindsay@fmc-law.com
Alexander G. MacWilliam, Environmental Law; Energy & Natural Resources; Transportation
403-268-7090
alex.macwilliam@fmc-law.com
Robert J. McKinnon, Energy & Natural Resources
403-268-7191
robert.mckinnon@fmc-law.com
Allan L. McLarty, Q.C., Energy & Natural Resources; Power; Mining
allan.mclarty@fmc-law.com
Richard A. Neufeld, Environmental Law; Energy & Natural Resources; Mining; Aboriginal Law
403-268-7023
richard.neufeld@fmc-law.com
Robert W. Poffenroth, Q.C., Energy & Natural Resources
robert.pottenroth@fmc-law.com
Bernie J. Roth, Environmental Law; Energy & Natural Resources
403-268-6888
bernard.roth@fmc-law.com
Scott W. Sangster, Energy & Natural Resources Law
403-268-7286
scott.sangster@fmc-law.com

Robert J. Simpson, Construction
robert.simpson@fmc-law.com
B.A.R. Smith, Q.C., Energy & Natural Resources
quincy.smith@fmc-law.com
Gordon L. Tarnowsky, Energy & Natural Resources
gordon.tarnowsky@fmc-law.com
E. David D. Tavender, Q.C., Energy & Natural Resources
403-268-7010
david.tavender@fmc-law.com
Heather L. Treacy, Aboriginal Law
Lowell A. Westersund, Q.C.
lowell.westersund@fmc-law.com
Laura J. Zurowski, Health
403-268-7048
laura.zurowski@fmc-law.com

Gowling Lafleur Henderson LLP - Calgary
#1400, Scotia Centre 700 - 2nd St. SW, Calgary AB T2P 4V5
403-298-1000 403-263-9193
kenneth.warren@gowlings.com
www.gowlings.com
Profile: 112 Lawyers, Founded in: 1972
Services include legal advice in the following areas: Corporate Transactions; Real Estate; Brownfields; Litigation & Advocacy; Environmental Assessments; Climate Change; Toxic Substances; Waste Management; First Nations/Aboriginal Rights; Water & Wastewater Treatement & Management; Transportation of Dangerous Goods; Emergency Response; International Development; & Environmental Law Training
Environmental Lawyers:
David J. Brett, Environmental Law; Energy; Aboriginal Law; Regulatory
403-298-1804
david.brett@gowlings.com
Patrick Burgess, Energy; Infrastructure
403-298-1980
patrick.burgess@gowlings.com
John R. Cusano, Environmental Law; Energy; Oil & Gas; Regulatory
403-298-1826
john.cusano@gowlings.com
Paul Edwards, Oil & Gas; Environmental Law
403-292-9815
paul.edwards@gowlings.com
Richard J.C. Grant, Energy; Aboriginal Law; Natural Resources; Infrastructure; Regulatory
403-298-1062
richard.grant@gowlings.com
Ron Hansford, Oil & Gas; Energy; Aboriginal Law; Regulatory
403-298-9862
ron.hansford@gowlings.com
Alan S. Hollingworth, Q.C., Energy; Environmental Law; Oil & Gas; Aboriginal Law; Infrastructure
403-298-1824
alan.hollingworth@gowlings.com
Geoffrey D. Holub, Energy; Oil & Gas; Construction Law
403-298-1089
geoffrey.holub@gowlings.com
John N. Iredale, Q.C., Natural Resources Law; Oil & Gas; Energy; Infrastructure
403-298-1850
john.iredale@gowlings.com
Patricia Leeson, Environmental Law; Energy; Climate Change
403-298-1821
patricia.leeson@gowlings.com
Forbes Newman, Q.C., Energy; Oil & Gas
403-292-9809
forbes.newman@gowlings.com
Garth E. Parker, Energy; Natural Resources Law; Construction Law; Infrastructure; Oil & Gas
403-298-1930
garth.parker@gowlings.com
James H. Smellie, Energy; Environmental Law; Regulatory
403-298-1816
james.smellie@gowlings.com

Heenan Blaikie LLP - Calgary
Fifth Avenue Place 425 - 1st St. SW, 12th Fl., Calgary AB T2P 3L8
403-232-8223 403-234-7987
www.heenanblaikie.com
Profile: 32 Lawyers
Environmental Lawyers:
Cynthia Amsterdam, Partner, Energy & Resources Litigation; Health; Construction Litigation
403-261-3469
camsterdam@heenan.ca
Robb D. Beeman, Partner, Energy & Resources Litigation
403-261-3452
rbeeman@heenan.ca
Brian Bidyk, Partner, Energy; Natural Resources; Climate, Cleantech & Sustainability
403-781-3389
bbidyk@heenan.ca
Michael J. Black, Energy & Natural Resources
403-261-3467
mblack@heenan.ca
David Elder, Energy
403-261-3464
delder@heenan.ca
Jillian Frank, Partner, Occupational Health & Safety
403-232-8223
jfrank@heenan.ca
Caireen E. Hanert, Partner, Energy & Resources Litigation; Construction Litigation
403-234-1262
chanert@heenan.ca
James R. Maclean, Energy; Natural Resources
403-261-3462
jmaclean@heenan.ca
Dawn Mains, Trade-mark Agent, Energy
403-261-3463
dmains@heenan.ca
Christopher B. Manderville, Partner, Natural Resources
403-234-1258
cmanderville@heenan.ca
Adrienne A. O'Reilly, Natural Resources
403-234-1259
aoreilly@heenan.ca
James Pasieka, Partner, Energy; Natural Resources
403-781-3382
jpasieka@heenan.ca
Christopher R. Peng, Partner, Energy
403-261-5232
cpeng@heenan.ca
Umesh (Mason) Shan, Energy
403-261-5514
mshan@heenan.ca
E. Mitchell Shier, Counsel, Energy; Environmental Law; Natural Resources
403-781-3394
mshier@heenan.ca
Edward A. Wooldridge, Partner, Energy
403-261-3454
ewooldridge@heena.ca

Lawson Lundell LLP - Calgary
#3700, Bow Valley Square 2 205 - 5th Ave. SW, Calgary AB T2P 2V7
403-269-6900 403-269-9494
genmail@lawsonlundell.com
www.lawsonlundell.com
Profile: 8 Lawyers, Founded in: 1997
Environmental Law expertise includes services to the energy sector: project development, acquisitions & divestitures, climate change & emission tracking, corporate transactions & environmental litigation, dispute resolution, regulatory defense matters, environmental assessments, toxic torts, permit appeals, administrative actions, & regulatory inspections & investigations
Environmental Lawyers:
Andrew P. Bedford, B.A., LL.B., Partner, Energy Law
403-218-7522
abedford@lawsonlundell.com
Clara C. Ferguson, B.A., M.P.A., LL.B., Associate, Aboriginal Law; Energy Law; Public Utility & Regulatory
403-218-7532
cferguson@lawsonlundell.com
Krista L. Hughes, B.A., LL.B., Associate, Aboriginal Law; Public Utility & Regulatory; Climate Change
403-781-9468
khughes@lawsonlundell.com
Lewis L. Manning, B.A., LL.B., LL.M., Partner, Energy Law; Public Utility & Regulatory Law
403-782-9458
lmanning@lawsonlundell.com
John M. Olynyk, B.Sc., M.Sc., LL.B., Administrative Partner, Aboriginal Law; Energy Law; Environmental Law; Climate Change
403-781-9472
jolynyk@lawsonlundell.com

Law Firms / Alberta

Machida Mack Shewchuk Meagher LLP
#1300 707 - 7th Ave. SW, Calgary AB T2P 3H6
403-221-8333 403-221-8339
nmachida@mmsmlawyers.com
Profile: 1 Offices, 6 Lawyers, Founded in: 1989
Environmental Lawyers:
N.K. Machida, Oil & Gas; Waste; Regulatory

Macleod Dixon LLP
#3700, Canterra Tower 400 Third Ave. SW, Calgary AB T2P 4H2
403-267-8222 403-264-5973
danielle.gill@macleoddixon.com
www.macleoddixon.com
Profile: 7 Offices, 250 Lawyers, Founded in: 1912
Environmental Lawyers:
Lori M. Bevan, Energy & Resources
  403-267-8349
  lori.bevan@macleoddixon.com
Rick P. Borden, Partner, Cleantech
  403-267-8362
  rick.borden@macleoddixon.com
Everett L. Bunnell, Q.C., Partner, Energy & Resources; Environmental
  403-267-9545
  everett.bunnell@macleoddixon.com
Fraser Bush, Energy & Resources; Environmental
  403-267-8361
  fraser.bush@macleoddixon.com
Ray Raymond Chartier, Partner, Energy & Resources; Aboriginal Law
  403-267-8172
  ray.chartier@macleoddixon.com
James H. Coleman, Partner, Energy & Resources; Mining
  403-267-8373
  jim.coleman@macleoddixon.com
Thomas Collopy, Energy & Resources
  403-267-9429
  thomas.collopy@macleoddixon.com
David Craddock, Partner, Energy & Resources; Health Infomatics; Construction
  403-267-9558
  david.craddock@macleoddixon.com
David Cuschieri, Energy & Resources
  403-267-8139
  david.cuschieri@macleoddixon.com
Don G. Davies, Partner, Environmental & Aboriginal Issues
  403-267-8183
  don.davies@macleoddixon.com
Paul P. Drager, Q.C., Partner, Energy & Resources; Mining
  403-267-8261
  paul.drager@macleoddixon.com
David A. Eeles, Partner, Renewable Energy Projects
  403-267-8232
  david.eeles@macleoddixon.com
Wayne W. Fedun, Partner, Energy & Resources; Aboriginal Law
  403-267-9414
  wayne.fedun@macleoddixon.com
Frances Ferguson, Energy & Resources
  403-267-8119
  frances.ferguson@macleoddixon.com
Joel S. Friley, Partner, Cleantech; Construction
  403-267-8202
  joel.friley@macleoddixon.com
Robert J. Froehlich, Energy & Resources
  403-267-9554
  robert.froehlich@macleoddixon.com
Crae Garrett, Partner, Energy & Resources; Mining
  403-267-8254
  crae.garrett@macleoddixon.com
Douglas A. Graham, Q.C., Partner, Environmental & Litigation Law; Construction
  403-267-8280
  doug.grahamd@macleoddixon.com
Glenda F. Graham, Q.C., Partner, Energy & Resources
  403-267-8284
  glenda.graham@macleoddixon.com
Tad Gruchalla-Wesierski, Partner, Mining
  403-267-8149
  tad.gruchalla-wesierski@macleoddixon.com
Dave. A. Guichon Jr., Partner, Energy & Resources
  403-267-9511
  dave.guichon@macleoddixon.com
Alan Harvie, Partner, Cleantech; Energy & Resources; Environmental; Aboriginal Law
  403-267-9411
  alan.harvie@macleoddixon.com
Bradley J. Hayden, Partner, Energy & Resources
  403-267-8360
  brad.hayden@macleoddixon.com
Thomas E. Hirst, Q.C., Partner, Energy & Resources
  403-267-8211
  tom.hirst@macleoddixon.com
R. Craig Hoskins, Partner, Cleantech
  403-267-8204
  craig.hoskins@macleoddixon.com
Darren B. Hribar, Partner, Cleantech
  403-267-9416
  darren.hribar@macleoddixon.com
Terrance M. Hughes, Partner, Energy & Resources
  403-267-8117
  terry.hughes@macleoddixon.com
Ryan W. Keays, Energy & Resources
  403-267-9523
  ryan.keays@macleoddixon.com
Allison G. Kuntz, Construction
  403-267-8323
  allison.kuntz@macleoddixon.com
Dennis P. Langen, Energy & Resources; Environmental
  403-267-8346
  dennis.langen@macleoddixon.com
E. Jung Lee, Partner, Natural Resources; Aboriginal Law
  403-267-8308
  jung.lee@macleoddixon.com
KayLynn G. Litton, Partner, Energy & Resources; Aboriginal Law
  403-267-8192
  kaylynn.litton@macleoddixon.com
Kerrie J. Logan, Partner, Energy & Resources
  403-267-8340
  kerrie.logan@macleoddixon.com
Harry J. Ludwig, Partner, Cleantech; Health Infomatics
  403-267-8235
  harry.ludwig@macleoddixon.com
Robert T. Malcolm, Q.C., Partner, Energy & Resources
  403-267-9401
  bob.malcolm@macleoddixon.com
John J. Marshall, Q.C., Partner, Resource Sector Dispute Resolution
  403-267-8282
  jack.marshall@macleoddixon.com
James F. Maxwell, Partner, Environmental
  403-267-8240
  jim.maxwel@macleoddixon.com
Trent J. Mercier, Energy & Resources
  403-267-9435
  trent.mercier@macleoddixon.com
Anthony (Tony) Morris, Partner, Health Infomatics
  403-267-8187
  tony.morris@macleoddixon.com
J. Jay Park, Q.C., Partner, Energy & Resources
  403-267-8354
  jay.park@macleoddixon.com
Rujuta Patel, Partner, Energy & Resources
  403-267-9422
  rujuta.patel@macleoddixon.com
Chrysten E. Perry, Partner, Energy & Resources
  403-267-8170
  chrysten.perry@macleoddixon.com
Robert A. Rakochey, Partner, Construction
  403-267-8234
  rob.rakochey@macleoddixon.com
Andrew R. Robertson, Partner, Health Infomatics
  403-267-8287
  andrew.robertson@macleoddixon.com
Roger F. Smith, Partner, Construction
  403-267-9409
  roger.smith@macleoddixon.com
Colleen T. Stevenson, Energy & Resources
  403-267-8158
  colleen.stevenson@macleoddixon.com
Thomas E. Valentine, Partner, Energy & Resources
  403-267-8154
  tom.valentine@macleoddixon.com
Judson E. Virtue, Partner, Environmental
  403-267-9541
  jud.virtue@macleoddixon.com
Brad J. Werenka, Environmental; Energy & Resources
  403-267-8371
  brad.werenka@macleoddixon.com
Elizabeth Williams, Health Infomatics
  403-267-8383
  elizabeth.williams@macleoddixon.com

MacPherson Leslie & Tyerman LLP - Calgary
#1600, Centennial Place 520 - 3rd Ave. SW, Calgary AB T2P 0R3
403-693-4300 403-508-4349
www.mlt.com
Profile: 20 Lawyers, Founded in: 1920
MLT provides advice on environmental compliance & successor liability, & environmental risks of mergers & acquisitions. It has developed environmental due diligence systems & policies, including environmental audit programs. Experience includes advising during the planning phases of major industrial & mining projects, site decommissioning, transferring assets between parties, & moving hazardous products.
Environmental Lawyers:
Scott A. Exner, Partner, Mining & Natural Resources
  403-693-4301
  exner@mlt.com
Sean Fairhurst, Counsel, Construction
  403-693-4307
  sfairhurst@mlt.com
A. Robson Garden, Q.C., Counsel, Mining & Natural Resources
  403-639-4304
  rgarden@mlt.com
Heather A. Sanderson, Counsel, Construction
  403-693-4311
  hsanderson@mlt.com
Scott Whitby, Partner, Energy; Mining & Natural Resources
  403-693-4341
  swhitby@mlt.com

McCaffery Mudry Pritchard LLP, Barristers & Solicitors
#2200, 736 - 6 Ave. SW, Calgary AB T2P 3T7
403-260-1400 403-260-1444
postmaster@mccafferylaw.ca
www.mccafferylaw.ca
Profile: 1 Offices, 7 Lawyers, Founded in: 1922
Areas of practice include administrative law & environmental litigation.
Environmental Lawyers:
David R. Black
Gordon M. Bradley
Katherine E. Lindeman
Sheila K. Mann
Shannon K. McGinty
T.T. (Tom) Mudry
J.P. (Scott) Pritchard

McCarthy Tétrault LLP - Calgary
#3300, 421 - 7th Ave. SW, Calgary AB T2P 4K9
403-260-3500 403-260-3501
calgary@mccarthy.ca; gturnbull@mccarthy.ca
www.mccarthy.ca
Profile: 7 Offices, 83 Lawyers,
Biotechnology; Energy; Environmental; Municipal
Environmental Lawyers:
Lisa M. Asbreuk, Environmental; Oil & Gas; Power
  403-260-3538
  lasbreuk@mccarthy.ca
Don Davies, Oil & Gas; Energy
  403-260-3681
  ddavies@mccarthy.ca
Robert N. DePoe, Oil & Gas; Energy
  403-260-3702
  rdepoe@mccarthy.ca
Derek S. Flaman, Natural Resources; Energy
  403-206-5559
  dflaman@mccarthy.ca
Michael Ford, Energy; Oil & Gas
  403-260-3619
  mford@mccarthy.ca
Terrance M. Hughes, Energy; Oil & Gas
  403-260-3663
  thughes@mccarthy.ca
Thomas F. Isaac, Aboriginal; Environmental; Mining; Oil & Gas
  403-260-3708
  tisaac@mccarthy.ca
Owen A. Johnson, Mining; Oil & Gas
  403-260-3655
  ojohnson@mccarthy.ca
Robert D. McCue, Energy; Oil & Gas
  403-260-3568
  rmccue@mccarthy.ca
Donald J. McLeod, Environmental
  403-260-3748
  dmcleod@mccarthy.ca

Debra Poon, Counsel, Mining; Oil & Gas
  403-260-3743
  dpoon@mccarthy.ca
William H. Smith, Q.C., Biotech/Life Sciences
  403-260-3653
  wsmith@mccarthy.ca
John B. Zaozirny, Q.C., Natural Resources & Energy
  403-260-3613
  jbzaozir@mccarthy.ca

McLennan Ross LLP
#1600, Stock Exchange Tower 300 - 5th Ave. SW, Calgary AB T2P 3C4
403-543-9120 403-543-9150 888-543-9120
info@mross.com
www.mross.com
Profile: 3 Offices, 21 Lawyers, Founded in: 1903
Energy, Environmental & Regulatory; Labour & Employment; Occupational Health & Safety; Construction; Health Law; Municipal
Environmental Lawyers:
Donald W. Dear, Energy; Environmental; Regulatory; Construction
  403-303-9107
  ddear@mross.com
Sean Fairhurst, Construction
  403-303-9101
  sfairhurst@mross.com
David J. Farmer, Energy, Environmental & Regulatory
  403-303-9118
  dfarmer@mross.com
Gavin S. Fitch, Energy; Environmental; Regulatory
  403-303-9120
  gfitch@mross.com
James P. Flanagan, Construction
  403-303-9102
  jflanagan@mross.com
Vanessa R. Pfaff, Energy; Environmental; Regulatory
  403-303-9103
  vpaff@mross.com

Merchant Law Group LLP - Calgary
#400 Deerfoot 17 Bldg. 2710 - 17th Ave. SE, Calgary AB T2A 0P6
403-225-7777 403-273-9411 866-225-7777
merchant@merchantlaw.com
www.merchantlaw.com
Profile: 14 Lawyers
Environmental Lawyers:
Ronald E. Kampitsch, Energy Conservation; Health

Miles, Davison LLP
#1600 Bow Valley Square II 205 - 5th Ave. SW, Calgary AB T2P 2V7
403-298-0333 403-263-6840
thefirm@milesdavison.com
www.milesdavison.com
Profile: 1 Offices, 24 Lawyers, Founded in: 2001
Environmental Lawyers:
Jason J. Irwin, Alternative Energy
  403-298-0336
  jirwin@milesdavison.com

Miller Thomson LLP - Calgary
#3000 700 - 9th Ave. SW, Calgary AB T2P 3V4
403-298-2400 403-262-0007 888-298-2400
calgary@millerthomson.com
www.millerthomson.com
Profile: 41 Lawyers,
Energy; Municipal & Planning; Oil & Gas; Construction; Forestry
Environmental Lawyers:
Gerald D. Chipeur, Q.C., Partner, Environmental Law; Aboriginal Law; Health Law
  403-298-2434
  gchipeur@millerthomson.com
Kathleen J. Kendrick, Associate, Environmental Law; Construction Law
  403-298-2455
  kkendrick@millerthomson.com
Jeffrey N. Thom, Q.C., Associate Counsel, Oil & Gas
  403-298-2436
  jthom@millerthomson.com

Ogilvy Renault LLP/S.E.N.C.R.L., s.r.l. - Calgary
#1000 110 - 9th Ave. SW, Calgary AB T2P 0T1
403-355-3550 403-355-3551
calgary@ogilvyrenault.com
www.ogilvyrenault.com
Profile: 11 Lawyers,
Environmental risk management, counsel, assistance in all forms of transactional matters, representation & litigation
Environmental Lawyers:
Chris Harris, Energy
  403-355-3837
  charris@ogilvyrenault.com
Nick J. Kangles, Senior Partner, Energy
  403-355-3835
  nkangles@ogilvyrenault.com
Scott Rusty Miller, Senior Partner, Energy; Environment
  403-355-3831
  smiller@ogilvyrenault.com
Miles F. Pittman, Partner, Cleantech; Energy
  403-355-3834
  mpittman@ogilvyrenault.com
R. Ben Rogers, Partner, Energy
  403-355-3833
  brogers@ogilvyrenault.com

Osler, Hoskin & Harcourt LLP - Calgary
#2500, TransCanada Tower 450 - 1st St. SW, Calgary AB T2P 5H1
403-260-7000 403-260-7024
counsel@osler.com
www.osler.com
Profile: 60 Lawyers
Environmental Lawyers:
Robert Ashcroft, Energy
  403-260-7087
  rashcroft@osler.com
Simon C. Baines, Partner, Energy
  403-260-7010
  sbaines@osler.com
Donald Boykiw, Partner, Energy
  403-260-7084
  dboykiw@osler.com
Janice Buckingham, Partner, Energy
  403-260-7006
  jbuckingham@osler.com
Lorne Carson, Partner, Energy
  403-260-7083
  lcarson@osler.com
Shawn Denstedt, Q.C., Partner, Climate Change & Emissions Trading; Energy; Environmental, Regulatory & Aboriginal
  403-260-7088
  sdenstedt@osler.com
Robert Desbarats, Q.C., Partner, Energy
  403-260-7015
  rdesbarats@osler.com
Neil Herle, Energy; Environmental Financing
  403-260-7072
  nherle@osler.com
Josef Hocher, Partner, Energy
  403-260-7066
  jhocher@osler.com
Matthew Keen, Climate Change & Emissions Trading; Environmental, Regulatory & Aboriginal; Litigation
  403-260-7005
  mkeen@osler.com
Cheryl Kelly, Energy; Environmental Financing
  403-260-7039
  ckelly@osler.com
Maureen Killoran, Partner, Energy; Environmental, Regulatory & Aboriginal; Litigation
  403-260-7003
  mkilloran@osler.com
Daina Kvisle, Energy
  403-260-7086
  dkvisle@osler.com
Gordon Nettleton, Partner, Climate Change & Emissions Trading; Energy; Environmental, Regulatory & Aboriginal; Litigation
  403-260-7047
  gnettleton@osler.com
Terri-Lee V. Oleniuk, Climate Change & Emissions Trading; Energy; Environmental, Regulatory & Aboriginal; Litigation
  403-260-7034
  toleniuk@osler.com
Paula Olexiuk, Partner, Construction; Energy
  403-260-7080
  polexiuk@osler.com
R.J. Jack Thrasher, Q.C., Partner, Energy
  403-260-7019
  jthrasher@osler.com
Frank Turner, Partner, Energy; Mining
  403-260-7017
  fturner@osler.com
Dylan Vandervecht, Energy
  403-260-7069
  dvandervecht@osler.com

Parlee McLaws LLP
#3400 Suncor Energy Centre 150 - 6th Ave. SW, Calgary AB T2P 3Y7
403-294-7000 403-265-8263
lawyers@parlee.com
www.parlee.com
Profile: 2 Offices, 82 Lawyers, Founded in: 1883
Aboriginal; Natural Resources
Environmental Lawyers:
Terry R. Davis, Partner, Environmental Law; Aboriginal Law
  403-294-7091
  tdavis@parlee.com
Shannon L. Kelley, Natural Resources
  403-294-3456
  skelley@parlee.com
Heidi L. Meldrum, Natural Resources
  403-294-7098
  hmeldrum@parlee.com
Nancy M. Penner, Counsel, Natural Resources
  403-294-7011
  npenner@parlee.com
Jayne R. Roberts, Occupational Health & Safety
  403-294-7053
  jroberts@parlee.com

Scott Venturo LLP
#203 Eau Claire Market 200 Barclay Parade SW, Calgary AB T2P 4R5
403-261-9043 403-265-4632 877-505-5651
www.scottventuro.com
Profile: 1 Offices, 22 Lawyers, Founded in: 1986
Environmental Lawyers:
Colin D. McKinnon, Construction Litigation
  403-231-8213
  c.mckinnon@scottventuro.com
Janet E. Russell, Partner, Environmental Law; Aboriginal Law
  403-231-8235
  j.russell@scottventuro.com
Richard C. Tanner, Construction Litigation
  403-231-8258
  r.tanner@scottventuro.com

Stikeman Elliott LLP - Calgary
#4300 Bankers Hall West 888 - 3rd St. SW, Calgary AB T2P 5C5
403-266-9000 403-266-9034
sstone@stikeman.com
www.stikeman.com
Profile: 41 Lawyers, Founded in: 1992
Energy law
Environmental Lawyers:
Harold K. Andersen, Partner, Emissions Trading & Climate Change; Energy
  403-266-9063
  handersen@stikeman.com
Glenn Cameron, Partner, Renewable Energy
  403-266-9011
  gcameron@stikeman.com
Mark A. Christensen, Environmental
  403-266-9087
  mchristensen@stikeman.com
Leland P. Corbett, Partner, Energy
  403-266-9046
  lcorbett@stikeman.com
Luigi A. Cusano, Partner, Environmental; Renewable Energy
  403-266-9097
  lcusano@stikeman.com
Evan Dickinson, Energy, Environmental & Regulatory Law
  403-266-9074
  edickinson@stikeman.com
Bradley B. Grant, Partner, Emissions Trading & Climate Change; Energy
  403-266-9008
  bgrant@stikeman.com

Law Firms / Alberta

Benjamin Hudson, Emissions Trading & Climate Change
  403-266-9049
  bhudson@stikeman.com
April Kosten, Energy
  403-266-9010
  akosten@stikeman.com
Lisa A. McDowell, Partner, Energy; Mining
  403-266-9099
  lmcdowell@stikeman.com
Lisa A. McDowell, Partner, Energy; Mining
  403-266-9099
  lmcdowell@stikeman.com
Michael Mestinsek, Partner, Construction Litigation; Environmental Litigation
  403-266-9078
  mmestinsek@stikeman.com
Stuart M. Olley, Partner, Energy; Mining
  403-266-9057
  solley@stikeman.com
L. Greg Plater, Partner, Construction Litigation; Environmental; Forestry & Forest Products
  403-266-9051
  gplater@stikeman.com
Douglas Richardson, Partner, Emissions Trading & Climate Change
  403-266-9048
  drichardson@stikeman.com
Chris S. Scherman, Energy
  403-781-9176
  cscherman@stikeman.com
Matthew Synnott, Emissions Trading & Climate Change; Environmental; Renewable Energy
  403-266-9028
  msynnott@stikeman.com
David M. Wood, Partner, Energy; Environmental
  403-266-9068
  dwood@stikeman.com

Stones Carbert Waite Wells LLP
#2000 Encor Place 645 - 7th Ave. SW, Calgary AB T2P 4G8
403-263-5656 403-263-5553
info@scwlawyers.com
www.scwlawyers.com
Profile: 1 Offices, 14 Lawyers
Environmental Lawyers:
Blair R. Carbert, Founding Partner, Health Law
  403-705-3304
  carbert@scwlawyers.com
Kelly P. Colborne, Health Law; Construction Litigation
  403-705-3337
  colborne@scwlawyers.com
Michelle L. Colley, Health
  403-705-3309
  colley@scwlawyers.com
Roxanne M. Davis, Construction Litigation; Health Law
  403-705-3335
  davis@scwlawyers.com
Bradley S. Dobbin, Construction Litigation
  403-705-3330
  dobbin@scwlawyers.com
Bryan L. Gallant, Health Law
  403-705-3310
  gallant@scwlawyers.com
Melissa A. Rico, Health Law
  403-705-3308
  rico@scwlawyers.com
Michael A. Waite, Partner, Health Law; Energy Litigation; Construction Litigation
  403-705-3307
  waite@scwlawyers.com
Gregory S. Wells, Q.C., Construction Litigation; Environmental Litigation
  403-705-3328
  wells@scwlawyers.com

Walsh Wilkins Creighton LLP
#2800 801 - 6 Ave. SW, Calgary AB T2P 4A3
403-267-8400 403-264-9400
mail@wwclawyers.com
www.wwclawyers.com
Profile: 3 Offices, 18 Lawyers
Environmental Lawyers:
Raymond G. Hunt, Construction Law
  403-267-8410
  rhunt@wwclawyers.com

Warren Tettensor Amantea LLP
1413 - 2nd St. SW, Calgary AB T2R 0W7
403-228-7007 403-244-1948
info@warren.ab.ca
www.warren.ab.ca
Profile: 1 Offices, 12 Lawyers, Founded in: 1969
Environmental Lawyers:
Joseph B. Amantea, Partner, Construction Law
  403-228-8374
  amantea@warren.ab.ca
Tara L. Petersen, Partner, Construction Litigation
  403-228-8383
  petersen@warren.ab.ca

Wilson Laycraft
#1601 333 - 11th Ave. SW, Calgary AB T2R 1L9
403-290-1601 403-290-0828
reception@wilcraft.com
www.wilcraft.com
Profile: 1 Offices, 10 Lawyers, Founded in: 1985
Environmental Lawyers:
Brian K. Dell, Construction Law
  403-441-2098
  bdell@wilcraft.com
Ronald S. Girvitz, Oil & Gas; Occupational Health & Safety
  403-441-2099
  ronsg@wilcraft.com
James B. Laycraft, Q.C., Founding Partner, Oil & Gas Litigation
  403-441-2095
  jamesbl@wilcraft.com

Wolch, Hursh, deWit & Watts
#1500, 633 - 6 Ave. SW, Calgary AB T2P 2Y5
403-265-6500 403-263-1111
hersh@wolch.com; lhursh@shawcable.com;
wtdewit@shawcable.com
Profile: 1 Offices, 4 Lawyers, Founded in: 1995
Defending against environmental prosecutions
Environmental Lawyers:
James J. Ogle, Q.C.
  jim.ogle@shawcable.ca
Earl C. Wilson, Q.C.
  ecw@shawcable.ca

Edmonton

Ackroyd LLP Barristers & Solicitors
#1500, First Edmonton Place 10665 Jasper Ave., Edmonton AB T5J 3S9
780-423-8905 780-423-8946
aprd@ackroydlaw.com
www.ackroydlaw.com
Profile: 2 Offices, 17 Lawyers, Founded in: 1950
Health; Environment; Oil & Gas
Environmental Lawyers:
Karin E. Buss, Environmental Law; First Nations and Aboriginal
  780-412-2704
  kbuss@ackryodlaw.com
William L. McElhanney, Oil and Gas; Forestry and Natural Resources; Metis and Indian Law
Todd Nahirnik, Environmental; Oil and Gas; Aboriginal
  780-412-2707
  tnahirnik@ackryodlaw.com
Dennis B. Roth, Oil & Gas; Native
Richard C. Secord, Environmental Law
  780-412-2717
  rsecond@ackroydlaw.com
Jerome N. Slavik, Native

Bishop & McKenzie LLP
#2500, 10104 - 103 Ave., Edmonton AB T5J 1V3
780-426-5550 780-426-1305
edmonton@bishopmckenzie.com
www.bishopmckenzie.com
Profile: 2 Offices, 29 Lawyers
Environmental Lawyers:
Donald G. Bishop, Q.C., Environmental Law
  d.bishop@bishopmckenzie.com
Robert A. Farmer, Environmental Law
  r.farmer@bishopmckenzie.com
John J. Kane, Q.C., Environmental Law
  j.kane@bishopmckenzie.com
Ross D. Kneteman, Environmental Law
  r.kneteman@bishopmckenzie.com
Armand J. Moss, Q.C.
  403-750-7975
  a.moss@bishopmckenzie.com
Carmen L. Plante, Environmental Law
  c.plante@bishopmckenzie.com
W. Benjamin Russell, Municipal Law
  b.russell@bishopmckenzie.com
J. Philip Warner, Q.C., Municipal Law
  p.warner@bishopmckenzie.com

Brownlee LLP
#2200, Commerce Place 10155 - 102 St., Edmonton AB T5J 4G8
780-497-4800 780-424-3254
e-mail@brownleelaw.com
www.brownleelaw.com
Profile: 2 Offices, 59 Lawyers,
Brownlee LLP is a full service law firm, with a broad background & depth in almost all legal disciplines. While the overall practice of the firm can be described as general, within its membership the individual lawyers are each engaged in a variety of particular areas including, but not limited to, civil litigation, municipal & administrative law, & corporate / commercial law.
Environmental Lawyers:
J. Robert Black, Q.C., Environmental liability; Municipal liability
  bblack@brownleelaw.com
Shari L. Boyd, Municipal law; Planning & development
  sboyd@brownleelaw.com
Shad A. Chapman, Oil & gas
  schapman@brownleelaw.com
Steven T. Connors, Municipal law
  sconnors@brownleelaw.com
Colin R. Fetter, Municipal law
  cfetter@brownleelaw.com
Jeneane S. Grundberg, Environmental law; Municipal law; Land use planning; Development & zoning; Administrative law; Public utilities law
  jgrundberg@brownleelaw.com
Michael S. Gunther, Municipal law
  mgunther@brownleelaw.com
Kirsten M.L. Hayne, Occupational health & safety
  khayne@brownleelaw.com
James A. Hea, Municipal litigation
  jhea@brownleelaw.com
Gary A. Holan, Municipal litigation
  gholan@brownleelaw.com
Kristjana E. Kellgren, Q.C., Municipal law; Utilities & regulatory law
  kkellgren@brownleelaw.com
Derek J. King, Environmental law; Municipal law; Land use planning
  dking@brownleelaw.com
Alvin R. Kosak, Environmental law; Municipal law
  akosak@brownleelaw.com
Peter K. Krysiak, Municipal law
  pkrysiak@brownleelaw.com
Thomas D. Marriott, Utility regulation; Municipal law
  tmarriott@brownleelaw.com
John C. McDonnell, Infrastructure; Utility services
  jmcdonnell@brownleelaw.com
Raymond G. Miki, Municipal law
  gmiki@brownleelaw.com
Ronald R. Nelson, Environmental law; Municipal law
  rnelson@brownleelaw.com
Daniel R. Peskett, Occupational health & saftey
  dpeskett@brownleelaw.com
Adina Preda, Municipal law
  apreda@brownleelaw.com
Raymond C. Purdy, Q.C., Managing Partner, Public utilities; Natural gas cooperatives (general counsel & regulation; Energy
  rpurdy@brownleelaw.com
Lorne I. Randa, Municipal law
  lranda@brownleelaw.com
Barry A. Sjolie, Q.C., Environmental law; Municipal law; Land use; Development & zoning; Public utilities
  bsjolie@brownleelaw.com
Rodd C. Thorkelsson, Municipal law; Public utilities; Natural gas cooperatives
  rthorkelsson@brownleelaw.com
Shannon L. Wyatt, Municipal law
  swyatt@brownleelaw.com

Davis LLP - Edmonton
#1201, Scotia Tower 2 10060 Jasper Ave., Edmonton AB T5J 4E5

780-426-5330 780-428-1066
www.davis.ca
Profile: 8 Offices, Founded in: 1892
Aboriginal; Municipal; Energy; Environment; Forestry; Mining
Environmental Lawyers:
Wendy-Anne Berkenbosch, Environmental Law
　780-409-6810
　wberkenbosch@davis.ca
Jennifer L. Cleall, Environmental law; Climate change law
　780-429-6838
　jcleall@davis.ca
Deborah L. Dresen, Environmental law
　780-429-6820
　ddresen@davis.ca
Rachel J. Hamilton, Climate change law; Energy & utilities
　780-429-6633
　rhamilton@davis.ca
Priscilla E.S.J. Kennedy, Environmental law
　780-429-6830
　pkennedy@davis.ca
Colin G.W. Lipsett, Energy & utilities; Environmental law; Municipal law
　780-429-6821
　clipsett@davis.ca
Craig D. Rose, R.P.F., Environmental law; Forestry law; Climate change law
　780-429-6807
　crose@davis.ca
Robert A. Seidel, Q.C., National Managing Partner, Environmental law; Forestry law; Climate change law; Municipal law; Energy & utilities; Projects, infrastructure, & P3
　780-429-6814
　rseidel@davis.ca
David J. Stratton, Q.C., Forestry Law; Projects, infrastructure, & P3
　780-429-6804
　dstratton@davis.ca
Robert B. White, Q.C., Environmental law
　780-429-6803
　rwhite@davis.ca
Donald J. Wilson, Environmental law
　780-429-6817
　dwilson@davis.ca

Duncan & Craig LLP, Lawyers & Mediators
#2800, Scotia Place 10060 Jasper Ave., Edmonton AB T5J 3V9
780-428-6036 780-428-9683 800-782-9409
edmonton@dcllp.com
www.dcllp.com
Profile: 5 Offices, 46 Lawyers, Founded in: 1894
Agribusiness; Natural Resource & Development
Environmental Lawyers:
John A. Kosolowski, Agribusiness
　780-441-4307
　jkoslowski@dcllp.com

Emery Jamieson LLP
#1700, Oxford Tower 10235 - 101st St., Edmonton AB T5J 3G1
780-426-5220 780-420-6277 866-212-5220
general@emeryjamieson.com
www.emeryjamieson.com
Profile: 1 Offices, 26 Lawyers, Founded in: 1893
Emery Jamieson's practice areas include administrative law & municipal law. The firm's work includes appearances before administrative tribunals, such as the Energy Resources Conservation Board, the Natural Resources Conservation Board, the Municipal Government Board, the Energy Utilities Board, & the Subdivision & Development Appeal Board.
Environmental Lawyers:
Richard B. Drewry, Q.C., Administrative law; Municipal law
Kember Handzic, Administrative law; Municipal law
Kate L. Hurlburt, Administrative law; Municipal law
Erin Raaen-Gossell, Administrative law; Municipal law
Phyllis A. Smith, Q.C., Administrative law; Municipal law

Environmental Law Centre (Alberta) Society
#800, 10025 - 106 St., Edmonton AB T5J 1G4
780-424-5099 780-424-5133 800-661-4238
elc@elc.ab.ca
www.elc.ab.ca
Profile: 1 Offices, 4 Lawyers, Founded in: 1982
Environmental Lawyers:
Laura Bowman, Staff Counsel, Environmental law
　lbowman@elc.ab.ca

Jason Unger, Staff counsel, Water law; Wildlife law; Administrative law
　junger@elc.ab.ca

Field Law - Edmonton
#2000, Oxford Tower 10235 - 101st St., Edmonton AB T5J 3G1
780-423-3003 780-428-9329 800-222-6479
wbrown@fieldlaw.com; lturner@fieldlaw.com
www.fieldlaw.com
Profile: 3 Offices, 59 Lawyers, Founded in: 1915
Energy & Natural Resource Law; Environmental Law; Municipal Law
Environmental Lawyers:
Daniel P. Carroll, First Nations
　780-423-7614
　dcarroll@fieldlaw.com
Derek A. Cranna, First Nations; Occupational Health & Safety
　780-423-7665
　dcranna@fieldlaw.com
Dale Cunningham, First Nations
　780-423-7610
　dcunningham@fieldlaw.com
Adrian R. Currie, Environmental
　780-423-7619
　acurrie@fieldlaw.com
Sandeep K. Dhir, Municipal Law
　780-423-9587
　sdhir@fieldlaw.com
P. Jon Faulds, Q.C., First Nations
　780-423-7625
　jfaulds@fieldlaw.com
Kevin S. Feth, First Nations
　780-423-7626
　kfeth@fieldlaw.com
J. David McInnes, Energy & Natural Resources; First Nations
　780-423-7651
　dmcinnes@fieldlaw.com
Donald K. Neeland, Energy & Natural Resources
　780-423-7660
　dneeland@fieldlaw.com
Rick Pabst, Municipal Law
　780-423-7664
　rpabst@fieldlaw.com
Robert H. Teskey, Q.C., Energy & Natural Resources
　780-423-7688
　rteskey@fieldlaw.com

Fraser Milner Casgrain LLP - Edmonton
#2900, Manulife Place 10180 - 101 St., Edmonton AB T5J 3V5
780-423-7100 780-423-7276
dennis.picco@fmc-law.com
www.fmc-law.com
Profile: 70 Lawyers
FMC Edmonton serves the energy, engineering, forest products, technology, & transportation industries in the city
Environmental Lawyers:
Shauna Finlay, Administrative; Environmental; Occupational Health & Safety
　780-423-7392
　shauna.finlay@fmc-law.com
Gordon A. Salembier, Q.C., Energy & Natural Resources
　780-423-7232
　gordon.salembien@fmc-law.com
Terry J. Williams, Aboriginal Law
　780-423-7366
　terry.williams@fmc-law.com
Barry Zalmanowitz, Q.C., Energy & Natural Resources; Competition Law
　780-423-7344
　barry.zalmanowitz@fmc-law.com

Kirwin LLP
#200, 10339 - 124 St. NW, Edmonton AB T5N 3W1
780-448-7401 780-453-3281
mail@kirwinllp.com
Profile: 1 Offices, 7 Lawyers, Founded in: 1987
Environmental Lawyers:
Mark M. Kirwin, BA, LLB, Environmental law

McLennan Ross LLP
#600, West Chambers 12220 Stony Plain Rd., Edmonton AB T5N 3Y4
780-482-9200 780-482-9100 800-567-9200
info@mross.com
www.mross.com
Profile: 3 Offices, 46 Lawyers, Founded in: 1903
The Energy, Environmental & Regulatory Practice Group has specific expertise in environmental licensing, regulatory affairs, effluent & air emission issues, contaminated sites, & oil & gas issues. Environmental law expertise covers the oil & gas, forestry, petrochemical, mining, transportation & waste management sectors. Clients include industries, landowners, & governments & their environmental regulatory bodies.
Environmental Lawyers:
Daniel R. Bokenfohr, Occupational Health & Safety
　780-482-9118
　dbokenfohr@mross.com
Chad J. Brown, Occupational Health & Safety
　780-482-9209
　cbrown@mross.com
Stuart W. Chambers, Energy; Environmental; Regulatory
　780-482-9113
　schambers@mross.com
Michelle G. Crighton, Occupational Health & Safety
　780-482-9228
　mcrighton@mross.com
M.J.(Pemme) Cunliffe, Occupational Health & Safety
　780-482-9217
　pcunliffe@mross.com
Frederick A. Day, Q.C., Occupational Health & Safety
　780-482-9208
　fday@mross.com
Corbin D. Devlin, Energy; Environmental; Regulatory; Construction
　780-482-9261
　cdevlin@mross.com
Doug I. Evanchuk, Energy; Environmental; Regulatory
　780-482-9106
　devanchuk@mross.com
Scott Hipfner, Energy; Environmental; Regulatory
　780-482-9112
　shipfner@mross.com
Ronald M. Kruhlak, Regulatory; Environmental; Energy; Litigation; Appeals & Approvals
　780-482-9226
　rkruhlak@mross.com
James Mallet, Energy; Environmental; Regulatory
　780-482-9211
　jmallet@mross.com
David Myrol, Occupational Health & Safety
　780-482-9290
　dmyrol@mross.com
Christopher W. Spasoff, Energy; Environmental & Regulatory
　780-482-9236
　cspasoff@mross.com
Peter P. Taschuk, Q.C., Energy; Environmental; Regulatory
　780-482-9203
　ptaschuk@mross.com

Merchant Law Group LLP - Edmonton
#310 Kingsway Garden Mall NW, Edmonton AB T5G 3A6
780-474-7777 780-474-4064 866-225-7777
merchant@merchantlaw.com; edmonton@merchantlaw.com
www.merchantlaw.com
Profile: 10 Lawyers
Environmental Lawyers:
Ronald E. Kampitsch, Energy Conservation; Health

Miller Thomson LLP - Edmonton
#2700 Commerce Place 10155 - 102nd St., Edmonton AB T5J 4G8
780-429-1751 780-424-5866 800-215-1016
edmonton@millerthomson.com
www.millerthomson.com
Profile: 48 Lawyers, Founded in: 1953
Aboriginal Law; Energy Law; Environmental Law; Municipal & Planning; Oil & Gas; Mining; Construction Law; Forestry
Environmental Lawyers:
Debra Curcio Lister, Partner
　780-429-9763
　dcurciolister@millerthomson.com

Parlee McLaws LLP
#1500 Manulife Place 10180 - 101 St., Edmonton AB T5J 4K1
780-423-8500 780-423-2870
lawyers@parlee.com
www.parlee.com
Profile: 52 Lawyers, Founded in: 1883
Aboriginal; Natural Resources
Environmental Lawyers:
Terrence A. Cockrall, Q.C., Counsel, Natural Resources
　780-423-8634
　tcockrall@parlee.com

Law Firms / British Columbia

Jeremy H.H. Hockin, Partner, Natural Resources
780-423-8532
jhockin@parlee.com
Robert P. James, Partner, Occupational Health & Safety
780-423-8554
rjames@parlee.com

Reynolds, Mirth, Richards & Farmer LLP
#3200, Manulife Place 10180 - 101 St., Edmonton AB T5J 3W8
780-425-9510 780-429-3044 800-661-7673
mail@rmrf.com
www.rmrf.com
Profile: 1 Offices, 36 Lawyers, Founded in: 1915
Environmental Lawyers:
William W. Barclay, Municipal
780-497-3379
wbarclay@rmrf.com
Doris. Bonora, Aboriginal; Municipal
780-497-3370
dbonora@rmrf.com
Shelly Chamaschuk, Health
780-497-3364
schamasc@rmrf.com
Paul Eastwood, Health
780-497-3302
peastwoo@rmrf.com
Rick Ewasiuk, Q.C., Health
780-497-3384
rewasiuk@rmrf.com
Allan Farmer, Q.C., Municipal
780-497-3360
afarmer@rmrf.com
R.A. Graesser, Q.C.
780-497-3352
William Hurlburt, Q.C., Counsel, Aboriginal; Health
780-425-9510
mail@rmrf.com
Cherisse Killick-Dzenick, Municipal
780-497-3372
ckillick@rmrf.com
Frederick Kozak, Health
780-497-3358
fkozak@rmrf.com
Albert Lavergne, Municipal
780-497-3310
alavergne@rmrf.com
Randall McCreary, Aboriginal; Municipal
780-497-3348
rmccreary@rmrf.com
Sheila McNaughtan, Municipal
780-497-3362
smcnaughtan@rmrf.com
Sonny Mirth, Q.C., Health
780-497-3346
Margaret Mrazek, Q.C., Health
780-497-3356
mmrazek@rmrf.com
Denis Noel, Aboriginal; Health
780-497-3366
dnoel@rmrf.com

Grande Prairie

Kay, McVey, Smith & Carlstrom LLP
#600, Windsor Ct. 9835 - 101st Ave., Grande Prairie AB T8V 5V4
780-532-7771 780-532-1158 888-531-7771
ksms@kayship.com
www.kayship.com
Profile: 4 Offices, 11 Lawyers, Founded in: 1923
Municipal Law
Environmental Lawyers:

Lethbridge

MacLachlan McNab Hembroff
1003 - 4th Ave. South, Lethbridge AB T1J 0P7
403-381-4966 403-329-9300
mmh@mmhlawyers.com
www.mmhlawyers.com
Profile: 1 Offices, 6 Lawyers, Founded in: 1996
Environmental Lawyers:
Thomas B. MacLachlan, Irrigation
maclachlan@mmhlawyers.com

Rocky Mountain House

Dunsford & Scott
P.O Box 370 5135 - 48 Ave., Rocky Mountain House AB T4T 1A3
403-845-7112 403-845-4670
reception@dunsfordandscott.com
Profile: 1 Offices, 3 Lawyers
Environmental Lawyers:
L.G. Dunsford
S.M. Scott, Estate, Real estate

British Columbia

Ashcroft

Morelli Chertkow LLP, Lawyers
P.O Box 106 401 Railway Ave., Ashcroft BC V0K 1A0
250-453-2320 250-453-2622
info@morellichertkow.com
www.morellichertkow.com
Profile: 3 Offices
Environmental Lawyers:

Campbell River

Shook, Wickham, Bishop & Field
906 Island Hwy., Campbell River BC V9W 2C3
250-287-8355 250-287-8112
info@crlawyers.ca
www.crlawyers.ca
Profile: 1 Offices, 9 Lawyers, Founded in: 1975
Environmental Lawyers:
Daniel A.J. Wickham, Partner, Forestry & Logging Law
250-287-8355
wickham@crlawyers.ca

Chilliwack

Waterstone Law Group LLP
#201, 45793 Luckakuck Way, Chilliwack BC V2R 5S3
604-824-7777 604-824-7770 800-677-8772
info@waterstonelaw.com
www.waterstonelaw.com
Profile: 2 Offices, 7 Lawyers, Founded in: 1994
An area of practice is municipal law.
Environmental Lawyers:
Lawrence Smith, Municipal law; Employment law
lsmith@waterstonelaw.com

Duncan

Ramsay Lampman Rhodes
130 Trans Canada Hwy., Duncan BC V9L 3P7
250-746-8800 800-263-3321
info@rlr-law.com
www.rlr-law.com
Environmental Lawyers:

Kamloops

Fulton & Company LLP, Lawyers & Trade-Mark Agents
#300, 350 Lansdowne St., Kamloops BC V2C 1Y1
250-372-5542 250-851-2300
law@fultonco.com
www.fultonco.com
Profile: 4 Offices, 21 Lawyers, Founded in: 1885
Environmental Lawyers:
Leah C. Card, Forestry law; Local government law
lcard@fultonco.com
Samuel S. Dabner, Local government law
sdabner@fultonco.com
John H. Grover, Local government law
jgrover@fultonco.com
J. Rick Heney, Local government law
rheney@fultonco.com
Dennis Hori, Local government law
dhori@fultonco.com
Alana K. Hughes, Municipal law
ahughes@fultonco.com
Jeffrey W. Locke, Local government law
jlocke@fultonco.com
Leonard S. Marchand, Local government law
lmarchand@fultonco.com
Denise E. McCabe, Local government law
dmccabe@fultonco.com
Brian D. Ross, Local government law
bross@fultonco.com
Frank R. Scordo, Local government law
fscordo@fultonco.com
Nick H.M. Weiser, Local government law
nweiser@fultonco.com

Morelli Chertkow LLP, Lawyers
#300 180 Seymour St., Kamloops BC V2C 2E3
250-374-3344 250-374-1144 888-374-3350
info@morellichertkow.com
www.morellichertkow.com
Profile: 3 Offices, 11 Lawyers, Founded in: 1911
Environmental Lawyers:
John M. Hogg, Q.C., Administrative law
jhogg@morellichertkow.com
Rachel R. Lammers, Administrative Law
rlammers@morellichertkow.com
Robert W. McDiarmid, Q.C., Administrative law; Construction law
rmcdiarmid@morellichertkow.com
Leigh Pedersen, Administrative law
lpedersen@morellichertkow.com

Kelowna

Pushor Mitchell LLP, Lawyers & Trade-Mark Agents
1665 Ellis St., 3rd Fl., Kelowna BC V1Y 2B3
250-762-2108 250-762-9115 800-558-1155
lawyers@pushormitchell.com
www.pushormitchell.com
Profile: 1 Offices, 31 Lawyers, Founded in: 1973
Environmental Lawyers:
Leona V. Baxter, Maritime law
baxter@pushormitchell.com

Langley

Lindsay Kenney LLP
#400, 20033 - 64th Ave., Langley BC V2Y 1M9
604-534-5114 604-534-5927 866-687-1323
info@lklaw.ca
www.lklaw.ca
Profile: 16 Lawyers
Environmental Lawyers:
Trevor S. Fowler, Partner, Construction Law & Litigation
tfowler@lklaw.ca

Waterstone Law Group LLP
#304, 20338 - 65th Ave., Langley BC V2Y 2K3
604-533-2300 604-533-2387 800-880-1667
info@waterstonelaw.com
www.waterstonelaw.com
Profile: 2 Offices, 4 Lawyers, Founded in: 1994
Environmental Lawyers:
Clint S. Harcourt, Partner, Municipal law
charcourt@waterstonelaw.com

Nanaimo

Ramsay Lampman Rhodes
111 Wallace St., Nanaimo BC V9R 5B2
250-754-3321 250-754-1148 800-263-3321
info@rlr-law.com
www.rlr-law.com
Profile: 2 Offices, 16 Lawyers
Environmental Lawyers:
Peter C.P Behie, Q.C., Partner, Construction Law; Aboriginal & First Nations Law
pbehie@rlr-law.com
Derek Jonson, Partner, Construction Law
djonson@rlr-law.com
Jonathan W. Lampman, Counsel, Forestry Law; Land Use & Regulation
jlampman@rlr-law.com
Jennifer Millbank, Construction Law
jmillbank@rlr-law.com

North Vancouver

Ratcliff & Company LLP
#500 East Tower 221 West Esplanade, North Vancouver BC V7M 3J3
604-988-5201 604-988-1452
admin@ratcliff.com
www.ratcliff.com
Profile: 1 Offices, 27 Lawyers, Founded in: 1950
Our firm has developed a broad & comprehensive practice that now includes general aboriginal litigation, aboriginal & treaty rights, land claims & treaty negotiations, reserve-related claims, aboriginal governance, employment issues, fisheries & forestry matters
Environmental Lawyers:
Kate Blomfield, Environmental Law; First Nations
Michelle M. Ellison, Environmental Law; Aboriginal Law
Lesley A. Giroday, Environmental Law; Forestry Land Use & Issues; First Nations
Stephanie A. Kearns, Environmental Law; Aboriginal Law
Matthew F. Kirchner, Partner, Environmental Law; Forestry Land Use & Issues; First Nations
Greg J. McDade, Q.C., Managing Partner, Environment; Forestry; First Nations
John R. Rich, Partner, Environment; Land & Resource Use; First Nations
Melinda J. Skeels, Environmental Law; Aboriginal Law
James P. Tate, Partner, Forestry Land Use & Issues; Aboriginal Law

Penticton

Gilchrist & Company
#101, 123 Martin St., Penticton BC V2A 7X6
250-492-3033 250-492-6162
info@gilchristlaw.com
www.gilchristlaw.com
Profile: 1 Offices, 4 Lawyers, Founded in: 1938
Environmental Lawyers:
Richard P. Thompson, Municipal law

Qualicum Beach

Marshall & Lamperson
CP 879 710 Memorial Ave., Qualicum Beach BC V9K 1T2
250-752-5615 250-752-2055
doug@qualicumlaw.ca
Profile: 1 Offices, 2 Lawyers, Founded in: 1996
Environmental Lawyers:
Douglas H. Marshall

Richmond

Kahn Zack Ehrlich Lithwick
#270, 10711 Cambie Rd., Richmond BC V6X 3G5
604-270-9571 604-270-8282 888-529-6368
general@kzellaw.com
www.kzellaw.com
Profile: 1 Offices, 10 Lawyers, Founded in: 1973
The firm offers full service, in areas including construction.
Environmental Lawyers:
Marvin Lithwick, Partner, Construction
  604-232-7204
  lithwick@kzellaw.com

Vancouver

Alexander Holburn Beaudin & Lang, LLP
#2700, P.O Box 10057 700 West Georgia St., Vancouver BC V7Y 1B8
604-484-1700 604-484-9700 877-688-1351
info@ahbl.ca
www.ahbl.ca
Profile: 1 Offices, 75 Lawyers, Founded in: 1973
Environmental Lawyers:
Greg J. Allen, Local government
  604-484-1775
Rebecca Beatch, Construction & engineering
  604-484-1737
  rbeatch@ahbl.ca
Gordon A. Buck, Construction & engineering
  604-484-1755
Megan Chorloton, Q.C., Local government
  604-484-1766
  mchorloton@ahbl.ca
Patrick S. Cleary, Construction & engineering
  604-484-1741
  pcleary@ahbl.ca
Todd R. Davies, Transportation law
  604-484-1799
Bruno De Vita, Local government
  604-484-1709
Michael A. Dery, Transportation law
  604-484-1742
James A. Dowler, Environmental law; Local government
  604-484-1706
  jdowler@ahbl.ca
Ahmad Erfan, Transportation law
  604-484-1778
  aerfan@ahbl.ca
Fritz C. Gaerdes, Transportation law
  604-484-1769
David A. Garner, Managing Partner, Environmental law; Health law; Construction & engineering
  604-484-1708
David A. Gooderham, Local government
  604-484-1788
  dgooderham@ahbl.ca
D. John Goundrey, Environmental law; Health law; Transportation law; Local government
  604-484-1710
  jgoundrey@ahbl.ca
Christopher E. Hirst, Construction & engineering; Environmental law; Local government
  604-484-1712
Dianna S. Hwang, Local government
  604-484-1744
F. Stuart Lang, Health law
  604-484-1770
  slang@ahbl.ca
Andrew S. MacKay, Health law
  604-484-1715
  amackay@ahbl.ca
David F. McEwen, Q.C., Transportation law
  604-484-1748
  dmcewen@ahbl.ca
David T. McKnight, Local government
  604-484-1716
  dmcknight@ahbl.ca
Gary M. Nijman, Environmental law; Transportation law
  604-484-1719
  gnijman@ahbl.ca
Robert W. Pakrul, Health law; Transportation law
  604-484-1720
  rpakrul@ahbl.ca
Darryl G. Pankratz, Transportation law
  604-484-1721
  dpankratz@ahbl.ca
Jeremy M. Poole, Local government
  604-484-1722
  jpoole@ahbl.ca
Renee D. Ritchot, Transportation law
  604-484-1703
Lawrence (Lanny) N. Robinson, Local government
  604-484-1752
Michael V. Roche, Environmental law; Health law; Transportation law
  604-484-1724
  mroche@ahbl.ca
Dana L. Romanick, Environmental law
  604-484-1753
  dromanick@ahbl.ca
R. Patrick Saul, Transportation law
  604-484-1728
  psaul@ahbl.ca
Douglas G. Schmitt, Environmental law; Transportation law
  604-484-1754
  dschmitt@ahbl.ca
Emily A. Stock, Construction & engineering
  604-484-1756
Sharon M. Urquhart, Environmental law; Transportation law
  604-484-1757
Eileen E. Vanderburgh, Health law; Local government
  604-484-1732
David B. Wende, Construction & engineering
  604-484-1795
  dwende@ahbl.ca

Baker & Baker
808 Nelson St., 17th Fl., Vancouver BC V6Z 2H2
604-642-0107 604-681-3504
info@bakerbaker.ca
www.bakerbaker.ca
Profile: 1 Offices, 3 Lawyers, Founded in: 1986
Environmental Lawyers:
Jonathan B. Baker

Barbeau, Evans, Goldstein
#280, 666 Burrard St., Vancouver BC V6C 2X8
604-688-4900 604-688-0649
info@beg-law.com
www.beg-law.com
Profile: 1 Offices, 4 Lawyers,
Expertise in all aspects of Construction Law to serve the full spectrum of clients; from contractors & engineers, to owners & their project managers
Environmental Lawyers:
Philip Walters, Occupational Health & Safety

Bernard & Partners
#1500, 570 Granville St., Vancouver BC V6C 3P1
604-681-1700 604-681-1788
tuytel@bernardpartners.com
www.bernardpartners.com
Profile: 1 Offices, 15 Lawyers, Founded in: 2002
Bernard & Partners is a Vancouver based law firm, which provides legal services in both a commercial & litigation context. The goal of the firm is to provide innovative & cost-effective solutions to each client's legal needs. Lawyers at Bernard & Partners focus their efforts in a number of practice areas, including the following: Environmental law; Fisheries; Occupational health & safety; Employment law; Admiralty & maritime; Corporate, commercial & real estate; Business relocation, including immigration; Insurance defence (personal injury, disability, medical malpractice, products liability); & Litigation, including mediation & arbitration. Bernard & Partners has a wide range of experience in commercial transactions in the marine & fisheries community, international shipping, transportation, & in a variety of leading British Columbia industries. The firm's maritime litigation practice includes representation of shipowners & charterers, both local & foreign, all the major P&I Clubs, as well as a broad range of domestic & international underwriters. Lawyers at the firm are actively involved as members & directors of a number of organizations, including the following: the Canadian Maritime Law Association; the Vancouver Maritime Arbitrators Association; the Vancouver Maritime Museum; the Chamber of Shipping of British Columbia; & the International Sailors' Society Canada.
Environmental Lawyers:
Neo J. Tuytel
  604-661-0614

Blake, Cassels & Graydon LLP - Vancouver
#2600, Three Bentall Centre P.O Box 49314 595 Burrard St., Vancouver BC V7X 1L3
604-631-3300 604-631-3309
vancouver@blakes.com
www.blakes.com
Profile: 90 Lawyers, Founded in: 1856
Energy; Environmental; First Nations & Aboriginal; Forestry; Mining; Oil & Gas
Environmental Lawyers:
Paul R. Cassidy, Environmental; Oil & Gas; Energy; CleanTech
  604-631-3390
  paul.cassidy@blakes.com
Caroline Findlay, Environmental; Forestry; Energy; CleanTech; Aboriginal Law
  604-631-3333
  caroline.findlay@blakes.com
Roy W. Millen, Aboriginal Law; Energy; Municipal & Planning
  604-631-4220
  roy.millen@blakes.com
James M. Sullivan, Environmental; Litigation & Dispute Resolution
  604-631-3358
  james.sullivan@blakes.com
Janice H. Walton, Environmental; Forestry; Oil & Gas; CleanTech
  604-631-3354
  janice.walton@blakes.com
David Zacks, Q.C., Energy
  604-631-3361
  david.zacks@blakes.com

Law Firms / British Columbia

Borden Ladner Gervais LLP - Vancouver
#1200 Waterfront Centre P.O Box 48600 200 Burrard St.,
Vancouver BC V7X 1T2
604-687-5744 604-687-1415
info@blg.com
www.blg.com
Profile: 134 Lawyers, Founded in: 1911
Energy; Forestry & Mining; Municipal; Oil & Gas; Environmental
Environmental Lawyers:
Jennifer Archer, Environmental Law; Electricity Markets
 604-640-4114
 jarcher@blg.com
David K. Camp, Partner, Environmental Law; Forestry Law; Mining; Aboriginal Law
 604-640-4104
 dcamp@blg.com
Daniel Cowper, Construction
 604-640-4080
 dcowper@blg.com
Amy Davison, Partner, Construction Litigation
 604-640-4210
 adavison@blg.com
S. Luke Dineley, Environmental Law
 604-640-4219
 ldineley@blg.com
Christopher W. Eagles, Partner, Construction
 604-640-4136
 ceagles@blg.com
Gerald W.J. Ghikas, Q.C., Senior Partner, Energy; Electricity Markets; Mining
 604-640-4112
 gghikas@blg.com
Angus M. Gunn Jr., Partner, Construction Law; Environmental Law
 604-640-4084
 agunn@blg.com
Larry R. Jackie, Q.C., Senior Partner, Environmental Law; Health Law
 604-640-4115
 ljackie@blg.com
M.Scott Kerwin, Partner, Environmental Law; Aboriginal Law
 604-640-4029
 skerwin@blg.com
Summer Lane, Health Law; Biotech & Pharmaceuticals
 604-640-1499
 sulane@blg.com
Dirk Laudan, Partner, Construction Litigation
 604-640-4154
 dlaudan@blg.com
Casey L. Leggett, Construction Law
 604-640-4229
 cleggett@blg.com
Mark Leung, Environmental Law; Oil & Gas
 604-632-3540
 mleung@blg.com
Andrew Loh, Partner, Health Law; Biotech & Pharmaceuticals
 604-640-4069
 aloh@blg.com
Paul J. Lowry, Partner, Energy; Oil & Gas; Electricity Markets; Construction Law
 604-640-4212
 plowry@blg.com
Stephanie P. Lysyk, Environmental Law; Aboriginal Law/Litigation; Mining
 604-640-4100
 slysyk@blg.com
P.D. (Don) MacDonald, Partner, Climate Change; Environmental Law
 604-640-4119
 pdmacdonald@blg.com
Graeme D. Martindale, Partner, Mining
 604-640-4179
 gmartindale@blg.com
Grant H. Mayovsky, Partner, Construction Litigation
 604-640-4165
 gmayovsky@blg.com
William K. McNaughton, National Leader, Environmental, Climate Change; Environmental Litigation; Environmental Law; Forestry Law; Mining
 604-640-4120
 wmcnaughton@blg.com
David L. Miachika, P.Eng, Partner, Construction Litigation; Environment
 604-640-4220
 dmiachika@blg.com

Sean A. Muggah, Partner, Energy; Electricity Markets
 604-640-4020
 smuggah@blg.com
Christopher J. O'Connor, Q.C., C.Arb., FCIArb, Partner, Construction Law & Litigation
 604-640-4125
 coconnor@blg.com
Vincent R. Orchard, Q.C., Senior Counsel, Health Law; Aboriginal Law
 604-640-4126
 vorchard@blg.com
Deborah H. Overholt, Managing Partner, Climate Change; Environmental Law; Mining; Forestry Law; Energy; Oil & Gas; Electricity Markets
 604-640-4164
 doverholt@blg.com
Robert G. Owen, Partner, Forestry Law
 604-640-4044
 rowen@blg.com
Ryan Parsons, Environmental Law
 604-640-4221
 rparsons@blg.com
Fred R. Pletcher, Partner, Mining; Biotech & Pharmaceuticals
 604-640-4245
 fpletcher@blg.com
Blair A. Rebane, Partner, Construction Law
 604-640-4130
 brebane@blg.com
Dionysios Rossi, Environmental Law; Oil & Gas; Maritime Law
 604-640-4110
 drossi@blg.com
Doug R. Sanders, P.Eng, Partner, Construction Law; Environmental Law; Biotech & Pharmaceuticals
 604-640-4128
 dsanders@blg.com
Maryam Sherkat, Maritime Law; Environmental Law
 604-640-4231
 msherkat@blg.com
Jay C.H. Shin, Partner, Oil & Gas; Mining
 604-640-4064
 jshin@blg.com
Robert R. Shouldice, Partner, Energy; Oil & Gas; Electricity Markets
 604-640-4145
 rshouldice@blg.com
Michael A. Skene, Partner, Construction Litigation
 604-640-4248
 mskene@blg.com
Matthew Swanson, Construction Law
 604-632-3474
 mswanson@blg.com
G. Ross Switzer, Partner, Climate Change; Environmental Law; Forestry Law; Mining
 604-640-4150
 rswitzer@blg.com
Kenneth J. Tyler, Partner, Environmental Litigation; Aboriginal Law
 604-640-4185
 ktyler@blg.com
Graham Walker, Partner, Climate Change; Maritime Law; Environmental Law; Construction; Forestry Law; Mining
 604-640-4045
 gwalker@blg.com
Kylie E. Walman, Environmental Law; Aboriginal Law
 604-632-3475
 kwalman@blg.com
Rick L. Williams, Partner, Climate Change; Oil & Gas; Environmental Law; Health Law; Maritime Law
 604-640-4074
 rwilliams@blg.com
Brad Woods, Energy; Environmental Law
 604-640-4201
 bwoods@blg.com

Boughton Law Corporation
#700, P.O Box 49290 595 Burrard St., Vancouver BC V7X 1S8
604-687-6789 604-683-5317
lawyers@boughton.ca
www.boughton.ca
Profile: 2 Offices, 50 Lawyers, Founded in: 1949
Environmental Lawyers:
John Mostowich
 604-647-4113
 jmostowich@boughton.ca

Burns, Fitzpatrick, Rogers & Schwartz
#1400, 510 Burrard St., Vancouver BC V6C 3A8
604-685-0121 604-685-2104
bfrs@bfrs.ca
www.bfrs.ca
Profile: 1 Offices, 8 Lawyers
Environmental Lawyers:
Stephen Z. Schwartz
 604-685-0121 ext. 317
 sschwartz@bfrs.ca

Clark Wilson LLP
#800, 885 Georgia St. West, Vancouver BC V6C 3H1
604-687-5700 604-687-6314
agb@cwilson.com
www.cwilson.com
Profile: 1 Offices, 80 Lawyers, Founded in: 1911
Environmental Lawyers:
Allyson L. Baker, Construction
 604-891-7732
 alb@cwilson.com
R. Glen Boswall, Construction
 604-643-3125
 rgb@cwilson.com
Nicole M. Byres, Energy; Municipal
 604-643-3173
 nmb@cwilson.com
Darren T. Donnelly, Municipal
 604-643-3115
 dtd@cwilson.com
Andrea M. East, Energy
 604-891-7752
 ame@cwilson.com
Tony Fogarassy, Energy; Environmental
 604-643-3130
 txf@cwilson.com
Keri T. Grenier, Construction
 ktg@cwilson.com
Jonathan L.S. Hodes, Environmental; Construction
 604-643-3168
 jlh@cwilson.com
William D. Holder, Municipal
 604-643-3169
 wdh@cwilson.com
Samantha Ip, Construction
 604-643-3172
 ssi@cwilson.com
R. Brock Johnston, Energy
 rbj@cwilson.com
William L. Macdonald, Energy
 604-643-3118
 wlm@cwilson.com
Amy A. Mortimore, Construction
 604-643-3177
 aam@cwilson.com
Derek J. Mullan, Q.C., Construction
 604-643-3162
 djm@cwilson.com
D. Lawrence Munn, Energy
 604-643-3160
 lm@cwilson.com
Roy A. Nieuwenburg, Environmental & Construction Law; Expropriation; Energy; Municipal
 604-643-3112
 ran@cwilson.com
Aaron B. Singer, Environmental Law
 604-643-3108
 abs@cwilson.com
Hannelie G. Stockenstrom, Construction; Energy; Environmental Law; Municipal
 604-643-3145
 hgs@cwilson.com
Peter M. Tolensky
 604-643-3164
 pmt@cwilson.com
Sean D. Vanderfluit, Construction
 604-643-3176
 sdv@cwilson.com
Adam I. Zasada, Construction
 604-891-7742
 aiz@cwilson.com

Davis LLP - Vancouver
#2800, Park Place 666 Burrard St., Vancouver BC V6C 2Z7
604-687-9444 604-687-1612
www.davis.ca

Profile: 8 Offices, Founded in: 1892
As a full-service law firm, Davis LLP provides a comprehensive range of legal services to clients around the world, through offices across Canada & in Japan. The firm has 88 partners worldwide, & 134 other lawyers around the world. Business can be conducted in English, French, Japanese, Spanish, Mandarin, Cantonese, Korean, German, Italian, Dutch, Estonian, & Polish. Established in Vancouver in 1892, the firm has more than 220 lawyers working in integrated practice groups that focus on client service & specialization. Davis strives to help clients achieve their business objectives & resolve business problems quickly & effectively. The firm is strong in all the traditional areas of legal practice, & also offers the knowledge base of a broad array of innovative practice groups & integrated specialties, such as projects, infrastructure & P3, & climate change / renewable energy. Across the firm, lawyers continuously cultivate commercial & government relationships to both facilitate the conduct of business & to identify new business opportunities for clients. Davis & its lawyers are recognized as leaders in numerous domestic & international ratings publications.
Environmental Lawyers:
Robert T. Banno, Mining law
 604-643-2903
 rbanno@davis.ca
Donald R.M. Bell, Mining law
 604-643-2949
 dbell@davis.ca
Frank S. Borowicz, QC, JP, CA (Hon), Counsel, Energy & utilities
 604-643-2906
 fsborowicz@davis.ca
Douglas B. Buchanan, Q.C., Energy & utilities
 604-643-2907
 dbuchanan@davis.ca
Andrew J.G. Burton, Energy & utilities
 604-643-2962
 aburton@davis.ca
D. Ross Clark, Q.C., Environmental law
 604-643-2911
 drclark@davis.ca
Donald R. Collie, Mining law
 604-643-6472
 dcollie@davis.ca
Dean L. Dalke, Energy & utilities; Municipal law
 604-643-6369
 ddalke@davis.ca
Warren H. Downs, Environmental law; Forestry law; Energy & utilities
 604-643-2916
 whdowns@davis.ca
W. Ross Ellison, Q.C., Municipal law
 604-643-2918
 rellison@davis.ca
Patrick J. Furlong, Energy & utilities; Mining law
 604-643-2923
 pjfurlong@davis.ca
Shawn Hatch, Forestry law
 604-643-2969
 shatch@davis.ca
Jason K. Herbert, Energy & utilities
 604-643-2928
 jherbert@davis.ca
Brian F. Hiebert, Managing Partner, Energy & utilities; Forestry law; Mining law; Environmental law; Climate change law
 604-643-2917
 bhiebert@davis.ca
Jeffrey D. Horswill, Climate change law
 604-643-6357
 jhorswill@davis.ca
Daniel R. Jarvis, Climate change law
 604-643-2950
 djarvis@davis.ca
Rolf N. Kaplun, Forestry law; Energy & utilities
 604-643-2933
 rkaplun@davis.ca
P. John Landry, Energy & utilities
 604-643-2935
 pjl@davis.ca
Garry E.P. Mancell, Forestry law; Environmental law; Energy & utilities
 604-643-2977
 garry_mancell@davis.ca
Robert E. Marriott, Forestry Law
 604-643-2944
 remarriott@davis.ca
Brent A. Meckling, Environmental Law; Forestry law; Construction law
 604-643-6405
 bmeckling@davis.ca
Alan L. Monk, Mining law
 604-643-2978
 amonk@davis.ca
Stuart B. Morrow, Mining law; Energy & utilities
 604-643-2948
 sbmorrow@davis.ca
Dale B. Pope, Q.C., Environmental law; Energy & utilities; Mining law
 604-643-6317
 dpope@davis.ca
David R. Reid, Mining law
 604-643-6428
 drreid@davis.ca
Lisa J. Robinson, Environmental law
 604-643-2987
 lrobinson@davis.ca
Dale G. Sanderson, Q.C., Energy & utilities
 604-643-6330
 dsanderson@davis.ca
Mark A. Schmidt, Forestry law
 604-643-6401
 mschmidt@davis.ca
Douglas G. Shields, Mining law
 604-643-2998
 dshields@davis.ca
Franco E. Trasolini, Municipal law
 604-643-2964
 ftrasolini@davis.ca
Simon R. Wells, Environmental law; Municipal law; Forestry law
 604-643-6460
 simon_wells@davis.ca
Rebecca R. von Rüti, Environmental law
 604-643-6493
 rvonruti@davis.ca

Donovan & Company
73 Water St., 6th Fl., Vancouver BC V6B 1A1
604-688-4272 604-688-4282
allan_donovan@aboriginal-law.com
www.aboriginal-law.com
Profile: 1 Offices, 9 Lawyers, Founded in: 1996
Donovan & Company is a law firm in Vancouver, British Columbia that practices exclusively in the area of aboriginal law.
Environmental Lawyers:
Myriam Brulot, Aboriginal Law
 myriam_brulot@aboriginal-law.com
Allan Donovan, Aboriginal Law
 allan_donovan@aboriginal-law.com
Nathalie Golay, Aboriginal Law
 nathalie_golay@aboriginal-law.com
Jennifer Griffith, Aboriginal Law
 jennifer_griffith@aboriginal-law.com
Courtney MacFarlane, Aboriginal Law
 courntey_macfarlane@aboriginal-law.com
Karim Ramji, Aboriginal Law
 karim_ramji@aboriginal-law.com
Bram Rogachevsky, Aboriginal Law
 bram_rogachevsky@aboriginal-law.com
Niki Sharma, Aboriginal Law
 niki_sharma@aboriginal-law.com
Merrill Shepard, Aboriginal Law
 merrill_shepard@aboriginal-law.com

DuMoulin, Boskovich
#1800, Manulife Place Box 52 1095 West Pender St., Vancouver BC V6E 2M6
604-669-5500 604-688-8491 800-288-9893
info@dubo.com
www.dubo.com
Profile: 2 Offices, 16 Lawyers, Founded in: 1972
The partnership of DuMoulin Boskovich is built upon the practice areas of fisheries law, real estate, corporate governance and litigation, all of which have been infused with environmental concerns, regulations and practices
Environmental Lawyers:
Joseph A. Boskovich, Fishing & Maritime
 604-669-5500 ext. 214
 joe@dubo.com
Joanne Lentsch, Fishing & Maritime
 604-669-5500 ext. 213
 joanne@dubo.com

Edwards, Kenny & Bray LLP
#1900, The Grosvenor Bldg. 1040 West Georgia St., Vancouver BC V6E 4H3
604-689-1811 604-689-5177
inquiry@ekb.com
www.ekb.com
Profile: 1 Offices, 23 Lawyers, Founded in: 1965
We are recognized as one of Canada's leading firms in environmental law; we provide advice & representation in relation to matters such as: waste management, contaminated lands, pollution control, assisting in formulating & implementing compliance strategies, environmental due diligence for corporate transactions, remediation projects, etc.
Environmental Lawyers:
A. Thomas Clarke, Hazardous Waste Management
Douglas K. Harrison, Environmental Audits; General Advice; Asbestos
Geoffrey M. Sherrott
Robert G. Ward, Toxic Tort Litigation

Farris, Vaughan, Wills & Murphy LLP
700 West Georgia St., 25th Floor, Vancouver BC V7Y 1B3
604-684-9151 604-661-9349 Telex: 04-507819
info@farris.com
www.farris.com
Profile: 3 Offices, 87 Lawyers, Founded in: 1903
Environmental Lawyers:
Robert S. Anderson
 604-661-9372
 randerson@farris.com
Brian R. Canfield
 604-661-9362
 bcanfield@farris.com
Ron A. Chin
 604-661-9333
 rchin@farris.com
Scott A. Dawson
 604-661-9354
 sdawson@farris.com
Robert J. McDonell
 604-661-9371
 rmcdonell@farris.com
J. Kenneth McEwan, Q.C.
 604-661-9356
 kmcewan@farris.com

Fasken Martineau - Vancouver
#2900, 550 Burrard St., Vancouver BC V6C 0A3
604-631-3131 604-631-3232 866-635-3131
vancouver@fasken.com
www.fasken.com
Profile: 8 Offices, 650 Lawyers, Founded in: 1889
Environmental Services: Environmental, Energy & Natural Resource Law
Environmental Lawyers:
Ron Ezekiel
 604-631-4708
 rezekiel@van.fasken.com
Heidi Granger
 604-631-4790
 hgranger@van.fasken.com
Robert M. Lonergan
 604-631-4718
 rlonergan@van.fasken.com
Larry J. Nelson
 604-631-4726
 lnelson@van.fasken.com
Kevin O'Callaghan
 604-631-4839
 kocallaghan@van.fasken.com
Michelle Pockey
 604-631-4825
 mpockey@van.fasken.com
Darrell W. Podowski
 604-631-3229
 dpodowski@van.fasken.com
Douglas G.S. Rae, Q.C, Forestry
Dennis Ryan
 604-631-4872
 dryan@van.fasken.com
Paul C. Wilson
 604-631-4728
 pwilson@van.fasken.com
Alan D. Winter, Occupational Health

Law Firms / British Columbia

Fraser Milner Casgrain LLP - Vancouver
250 Howe St., 20th Fl., Vancouver BC V6C 3R8
604-687-4460 604-683-5214 Telex: 04-55593
john.sandrelli@fmc-law.com
www.fmc-law.com
Profile: 50 Lawyers, Founded in: 1980
The firm provides legal services in the areas of Energy Law, & Mining Law
Environmental Lawyers:
Brian E. Abraham, Environmental; Securities & Mining Law
  604-443-7134
  brian.abraham@fmc-law.com
Waldemar Braul, Environmental Law, Aboriginal Law
  604-443-7148
  wally.braul@fmc-law.com
Colin J. McIver, Environmental Law; Energy & Natural Resources; Mining
  604-443-7128
  colin.mciver@fmc-law.com

Ganapathi & Company
#302, 1224 Hamilton St., Vancouver BC V6B 2S8
604-689-9222 604-689-4888 866-689-9222
nathan@ganapathico.com; info@ganapathico.com
www.ganapathico.com
Profile: 1 Offices, 2 Lawyers, Founded in: 1975
Ganapathi & Company practises environmental law & fisheries law. Environmental services include the integration of envionmental & ecological factors into planning & decision-making processes. Work related to the fisheries includes marine habitat protection, hatchery law, & fisheries offences.
Environmental Lawyers:
Michael Z. Galambos
  mgalambos@ganapathico.com
Nathan S. Ganapathi
  nathan@ganapathico.com

Gowling Lafleur Henderson LLP - Vancouver
#2300, Bentall V 550 Burrard St., Vancouver BC V6C 2B5
604-683-6498 604-683-3558
shayne.strukoff@gowlings.com
www.gowlings.com
Profile: 50 Lawyers
Environmental Lawyers:
K. Alan Blair, Environmental Law; Occupational Health & Safety; Regulatory & Compliance; Government Affairs; Mining Industry; Oil & Gas Industry; Chemical Industry; Manufacturing Industries
  604-891-2288
  alan.blair@gowlings.com
G. Henry Ellis, Energy Law; Infrastructure; Power Production & Distribution; Hydro Projects; Biomass Projects; Licensing; Regulatory & Compliance
  604-891-2250
  henry.ellis@gowlings.com
Martin L. Palleson, Environmental Law; Aboriginal Law; Natural Resources Law
  604-443-7622
  martin.palleson@gowlings.com
Donald J. Weaver, Energy Law; Infrastructure Industry; Mining Industry; Energy Distribution Industry; Forestry Industry
  604-891-2731
  don.weaver@gowlings.com

Heenan Blaikie LLP - Vancouver
#2200 1055 West Hastings St., Vancouver BC V6E 2E9
604-669-0011 604-669-5101
www.heenanblaikie.com
Profile: 43 Lawyers, Founded in: 1973
Environmental Lawyers:
Susan Arnold, Partner, Occupational Health & Safety
  604-891-1151
  sarnold@heenan.ca
Dean Crawford, Partner, Health
  604-891-1162
  dcrawford@heenan.ca
H. David Edinger, Partner, Construction Litigation
  604-891-1158
  hedinger@heenan.ca
Jillian Frank, Occupational Health & Safety
  604-891-1160
  jfrank@heenan.ca
Peter A. Gall, Q.C., Partner, Occupational Health & Safety
  604-891-1152
  pgall@heenan.ca
Jonathan D. Greenberg, Counsel, Energy
  604-891-1153
  jgreenberg@heenan.ca
Jay Hayden, Partner, Energy; Climate, Cleantech & Sustainability
  604-891-1167
  jhayden@heenan.ca
John A. Legge, Partner, Construction Litigation; Energy & Resources Litigation
  604-891-1187
  jlegge@heenan.ca
T. Murray Rankin, Q.C., Partner, Environmental Law; Aboriginal law; Natural Resources
  250-381-1010
  mrankin@heenan.ca
Tobin Robbins, Partner, Transportation
  604-891-1194
  trobbins@heenan.ca
Richard Shrieves, Partner, Natural Resources; Construction; Aboriginal Law
  604-891-1169
  rshrieves@heenan.ca
Catherine Wade, Partner, Mining
  604-891-1165
  cwade@heenan.ca

Hume, Forrest C., Law Corporation
#700, 1080 Howe St., Vancouver BC V6Z 2T1
604-488-1499 604-488-1489
fchume@humelawcorp.com
Profile: 1 Offices, 2 Lawyers, Founded in: 1999
Environmental Lawyers:
Ryan C. Gallagher, Transportation Law
Forrest Clyde Hume, Transportation Law

Hunter Litigation Chambers
#2100 1040 West Georgia St., Vancouver BC V6E 4H1
604-891-2400 604-647-4554
www.litigationchambers.com
Profile: 1 Offices, 19 Lawyers, Founded in: 2006
Environmental Lawyers:
Randy J. Kaardal, Senior Counsel, Natural Resources
  604-647-4559
  rkaardal@litigationchambers.com
Mark S. Oulton, Forestry
  604-891-2408
  moulton@litigationchambers.com
Martin Taylor, Q.C., Energy
  604-647-4566
  mtaylor@litigationchambers.com

Hutchins Caron & Associates
#400, 601 West Broadway, Office 5, Vancouver BC V5Z 4C2
604-871-4327 604-871-4336
admin@hutchinslegal.ca
www.hutchinslegal.ca
Profile:
The firm is engaged in the practice of Aboriginal law, including resource management & development & environmental protection.
Environmental Lawyers:

Lang Michener LLP - Vancouver
#1500, Royal Centre CP 11117 1055 West Georgia St., Vancouver BC V6E 4N7
604-689-9111 604-685-7084
swortley@lmls.com (Stephen Wortley, Chair, Western Division)
www.langmichener.ca
Profile: 3 Offices, 74 Lawyers, Founded in: 1926
Lang Michener established a multi-disciplinary practice group, known as the Environment, Energy & Emissions Trading Group. This practice group helps companies with business & legal issues related to environmental matters. Lawyers at Lang Michener also serve the forestry & paper products industry, the aviation, rail, & marine industries, as well as the Canadian & international mining & natural resource industry.
Environmental Lawyers:
Desmond Balakrishnan, Mining & natural resources
Cheri Bocking, Mining & natural resources
Peter Botz, Forestry; Mining & natural resources
Corin Bowman, Environmental law; Energy; Emissions; Power generation; Utilities
Casper Bych, Mining & natural resources
Damon Chisholm, Mining & natural resources
Keith E. Clark, Environmental law; Energy; Emissions; Power generation; Utilities; Forestry; Mining & natural resources
David J. Cowan, Mining & natural resources
Thomas J. Deutsch, Mining & natural resources
Daniel D. Dex, Mining & natural resources
Claire E. Ellett, Environmental litigation; Administrative law
G. Barry Finlayson, Mining & natural resources
Gary C. Floyd, Mining & natural resources
Karl E. Gustafson, Q.C., Environmental law; Energy; Power generation; Utilities; Emissions; Forestry; Mining & natural resources; Transportation & logistics (marine, aviation, & rail)
Linda J. Hogg, Mining & natural resources
Cory Kent, Mining & natural resources
Roderick Kirkham, Mining & natural resources
Anthony H.S. Knight, Mining & natural resources
Sandra M. Knowler, Forestry; Mining & natural resources; Transportation & logistics (marine, aviation, & rail)
Christine Man, Mining & natural resources
Christine Mingie, Forestry; Mining & natural resources
John D. Morrison, Mining & natural resources
  jmorrison@lmls.com
James R. Munro, Mining & natural resources
Mark Neighbor, Mining & natural resources
Sean O'Neill, Mining & natural resources
Siobhan O'Sullivan, Transportation & logistics (marine, aviation, & rail)
Herbert I. Ono, Mining & natural resources
Laurel M. Petryk, Mining & natural resources
Darrell W. Podowski, Mining & natural resources
John D. Reynolds, Mining & natural resources; Transportation & logistics (marine, aviation, & rail)
Nika Robinson, Mining & natural resources
David J. Ross, Forestry; Mining & natural resources
Amandeep Sandhu, Forestry
Jeremy Shelford, Forestry
Tom Theodorakis, Forestry; Transportation & logistics (marine, aviation, & rail)
François E.J. Tougas, Forestry; Mining & natural resources; Transportation & logistics (marine, aviation, & rail)
R. Michael Tourigny, Forestry; Mining & natural resources
Ningyan (Sandy) Wang, Forestry; Mining & natural resources
Stephen D. Wortley, Forestry; Mining & natural resources
Joan M. Young, Administrative law
Bernhard Zinkhofer, Mining & natural resources
Louis J. Zivot, Transportation & logistics (marine, aviation, & rail)

Lawson Lundell LLP - Vancouver
#1600, Cathedral Place 925 West Georgia St., Vancouver BC V6C 3L2
604-685-3456 604-669-1620
genmail@lawsonlundell.com
www.lawsonlundell.com
Profile: 3 Offices, 100 Lawyers, Founded in: 1886
Environmental Law Group is regularly involved in corporate transactions & environmental litigation, including dispute resolution, regulatory defense matters, environmental assessments, toxic torts, permit appeals, administrative actions & regulatory inspections & investigations; other environmental areas: energy law; forestry; mining; oil & gas; aboriginal law
Environmental Lawyers:
Khaled S. Abdel-Barr, B.Comm., J.D., LL.B., Partner, Mining & Natural Resources Law
  604-631-9233
  kabdel-barr@lawsonlundell.com
Brad Armstrong, QC, B.A.,M.Sc.,LL.B., Partner, Aboriginal Law; Climate Change; Environmental Law & Prosecutions; Project Permitting; Regulatory Compliance
  604-631-9126
  barmstrong@lawsonlundell.com
Chris G. Baldwin, B.A., J.D., Partner, Mining & Natural Resources Law; Aboriginal Law
  604-631-9151
  cbaldwin@lawsonlundell.com
Keith Bergner, B.A., LL.B., Partner, Aboriginal Law; Energy Law; Environmental Law; Project Permitting; Public Utility & Regulatory; Regulatory Compliance
  604-631-9119
  kbergner@lawsonlundell.com
Kinji C. Bourchier, B.A., LL.B., Partner, Environmental Law & Prosecutions
  604-631-9267
  kbourchier@lawsonlundell.com
Amy J. Carruthers, Partner, Climate Change; Energy
  604-631-6711
  acarruthers@lawsonlundell.com
Gordon R. Chambers, B.Comm., LL.B., Partner, Mining & Natural Resources Law
  604-631-9191
  grchambers@lawsonlundell.com

Law Firms / British Columbia

Gordon R. Chambers, B.Comm., LL.B., Partner, Mining &
Natural Resources Law
604-631-9191
grchambers@lawsonlundell.com
Randall C. Chatwin, Mining
604-631-6799
rchatwin@lawsonlundell.com
Jeff Christian, B.A.Sc., LL.B., Partner, Energy Law; Public Utility
& Regulatory
604-631-9115
jchristian@lawsonlundell.com
Lauren E. Cook, Environmental Prosecutions
604-631-9111
lcook@lawsonlundell.com
Gordon M. Craig, B.A., LL.B., Partner, Energy Law; Climate
Change; Public Utility & Regulatory
604-631-9155
gcraig@lawsonlundell.com
Laura E. Duke, Environment; Aboriginal Law
604-631-9129
lduke@lawsonlundell.com
William M. Everett, Q.C., B.A., LL.B., Partner, Environmental
Litigation
604-631-9171
wmeverett@lawsonlundell.com
Brian D. Fulton, B.A., LL.B., Partner, Energy Law
604-631-9185
bfulton@lawsonlundell.com
Christopher R.C. Funt, Energy Law; Envvironment; Aboriginal
Law
604-631-9272
cfunt@lawsonlundell.com
Sara J. Gregory, Environmental Prosecutions
604-631-6785
sgregory@lawsonlundell.com
Marianna Jasper, Energy; Environment; Aboriginal Law
604-631-9242
mjasper@lawsonlundell.com
Christine J. Kowbel, Climate Change; Environment; Aboriginal
Law
604-631-6762
ckowbel@lawsonlundell.com
Michael L. Lee, BSc.,B.A.,M.A.,LL.B., Partner, Mining & Natural
Resources Law
604-631-9139
mlee@lawsonlundell.com
Jennifer S. Nyland, Environment; Energy
604-631-9287
jnyland@lawsonlundell.com
Clifford G. Proudfoot, LL.B., LL.M., Partner, Aboriginal Law;
Environmental Law & Prosecutions; Regulatory Compliance
604-631-9217
cproudfoot@lawsonlundell.com
Chris W. Sanderson, Q.C., B.A., LL.B., Partner, Energy Law;
Public Utility & Regulatory
604-631-9183
csanderson@lawsonlundell.com
Jerrold W. Schramm, B.Comm., LL.B., Partner, Mining & Natural
Resources Law; Energy Law
604-631-9131
jschramm@lawsonlundell.com
Ron A. Skolrood, B.A., LL.B., LL.M., Partner, Aboriginal Law
604-631-9134
rskolrood@lawsonlundell.com
Ian D. Webb, B.Sc., LL.B., Partner, Energy Law; Public Utility &
Regulatory
604-631-9117
iwebb@lawsonlundell.com

Lesperance Mendes
#410, 900 Howe St., Vancouver BC V6Z 2M4
604-685-3567 604-685-7505
kmw@lmlaw.ca
www.lmlaw.ca
Profile: 1 Offices, 5 Lawyers, Founded in: 1997
Environmental Law
Environmental Lawyers:
Sat D. Harwood
604-685-3550
sdh@lmlaw.ca
Robert J. Lesperance, Civil & Criminal Liability; Environmental
Contamination; Environmental Management Systems; Due
Diligence
604-685-4822
rjl@lmlaw.ca

Lindsay Kenney LLP
#1800, 401 West Georgia St., Vancouver BC V6B 5A1
604-687-1323 604-687-2347 866-687-1323
info@lklaw.ca
www.lklaw.ca
Profile: 3 Offices, 55 Lawyers, Founded in: 1980
Environmental Lawyers:
Paul Backhouse, Construction Law & Litigation
604-484-3058
pbackhouse@lklaw.ca
Melissa Bryden, Construction Law & Litigation
604-484-3052
mbryden@lklaw.ca
Jesse Halperin, Construction Law & Litigation
604-484-3080
jhalperin@lklaw.ca
Richard B. Lindsay, Q.C., Founding Partner, Energy;
Construction Law & Litigation
604-484-3067
rlindsay@lklaw.ca
Christopher D. Martin, Construction Law & Litigation
604-484-3085
cmartin@lklaw.ca
Greg S. Miller, Partner, Construction Law & Litigation
604-484-3070
gmiller@lklaw.ca
Carmen Tham, Construction Law & Litigation
604-484-3056
ctham@lklaw.ca

MacKenzie Fujisawa LLP
#1600, 1095 West Pender St., Vancouver BC V6E 2M6
604-689-3281 604-685-6494
lawyers@maclaw.bc.ca
www.mackenziefujisawa.com
Profile: 1 Offices, 19 Lawyers, Founded in: 1963
Environment Issues; Real Property Transactions; Waste
Management Litigation; Environmental Criminal Defence
Environmental Lawyers:
William A. Ferguson, Aboriginal
604-443-1211
Christopher Harvey, Q.C., Marine; Aviation; Environmental;
National Resources
604-443-1202
charvey@maclaw.bc.ca
Kenneth V. Krohman, Environment Issues; Real Property
Transactions
604-443-1208
kkrohman@maclaw.bc.ca
Brian C. Poston, Maritime; Aviation
604-443-1213
Christopher J. Watson, Aboriginal; Fisheries
604-443-1225
cwatson@maclaw.bc.ca
Robert V. Wickett, Waste Management Litigation; Environmental
Criminal Defence
604-443-1242
rwickett@maclaw.bc.ca
Robert H. Wynick, Environmental Issues; Real Property
Transactions
604-443-1209
rwynick@maclaw.bc.ca

McCarthy Tétrault LLP - Vancouver
#1300, Pacific Centre CP 10424 777 Dunsmuir St., Vancouver
BC V7Y 1K2
604-643-7100 604-643-7900
vancouver@mccarthy.ca
www.mccarthy.ca
Profile: 7 Offices, 108 Lawyers, Founded in: 1960
Biotechnology; Energy; Environmental; Municipal
Environmental Lawyers:
Sam Adkins, Aboriginal; Mining
604-643-7984
sadkins@mccarthy.ca
Nicholas R. Hughes, Aboriginal; Environmental; Civil Litigation
604-643-7106
rhughes@mccarthy.ca
Thomas F. Isaac, Aboriginal; Environmental; Oil & Gas; Mining;
Power
604-643-5987
tisaac@mccarthy.ca
Peter H. Kenward, Municipal Planning; Land Development &
Planning; Envronmental
604-643-7962
pkenward@mccarthy.ca
D. Anthony Knox, Aboriginal Law; Mining Law
604-643-7916
tknox@mccarthy.ca
Robert J. Miller, Aboriginal; Energy; Environmental; Mining
604-643-5897
rmiller@mccarthy.ca
Warren B. Milman, Environmental
604-643-7104
wmilman@mccarthy.ca
Linda G. Parker, Municipal Planning; Environmental Law
604-643-7909
lparker@mccarthy.ca
Robin M. Sirett, Energy; Oil & Gas
604-643-7911
rsirett@mccarthy.ca
James A. Titerle, Natural Resources; Environmental
604-643-7949
jtiterle@mccarthy.ca

McCullough O'Connor Irwin LLP
#2610 Oceanic Plaza 1066 West Hastings St., Vancouver BC
V6E 3X1
604-687-7077 604-687-7099
moimail@moisolicitors.com
www.moisolicitors.com
Profile: 1 Offices, 14 Lawyers, Founded in: 1994
Environmental Lawyers:
Mia Bacic, Partner, Clean Energy; Mining; Construction
604-646-3319
mbacic@moisolicitors.com

Miller Thomson LLP - Vancouver
#1000 Robson Ct. 840 Howe St., Vancouver BC V6Z 2M1
604-687-2242 604-643-1200 800-794-6866
vancouver@millerthomson.com
www.millerthomson.com
Profile: 59 Lawyers, Founded in: 2000
Aboriginal; Energy; Municipal & Planning; Oil & Gas;
Construction; Forestry
Environmental Lawyers:
Wendy A. Baker, Q.C., Partner, Environmental Law;
Construction Litigation; Aboriginal Law
604-643-1285
wbaker@millerthomson.com
Charles W. Bois, Partner, CleanTech; Environmental Law;
Natural Resources; Renewable Energy; Aboriginal Law;
Construction
604-643-1224
cbois@millerthomson.com
Tony Crossman, Partner, Envirnomental Law; CleanTech;
Aboriginal Law; Energy
604-643-1244
tcrossman@millerthomson.com
Sarah D. Hansen, Partner, Energy; CleanTech; Forestry;
Environmental; Aboriginal Rights
604-643-1273
shansen@millerthomson.com
Oleh W. Ilnyckyj, Partner, Health
604-643-1247
oilnyckyj@millerthomson.ca
Daniel L. Kiselbach, Partner, Environment Law
604-643-1263
dkiselbach@millerthomson.com
Amyn F. Lalji, Partner, Environmental Law; Mining; Aboriginal
Law
604-643-1201
alalji@millerthomson.com
Peter J.G. McArthur, Partner, Mining; Natural Resources
604-643-1219
pmcarthur@millerthomson.ca
Paul A. McDonnell, Partner, Construction Litigation
604-643-1235
pmcdonnell@millerthomson.com
Ryan W. Morasiewicz, Health
604-643-1202
rmorasiewicz@millerthomson.com
Matthew M. Morawski, Construction Litigation
604-643-1213
mmorawski@millerthomson.com
Owen D. Pawson, Partner, Construction Litigation
604-643-1254
opawson@millerthomson.ca
Michael J. Percival, Partner, Construction Litigation
604-643-1230
mpercival@millerthomson.ca

Law Firms / British Columbia

David Rice, Counsel, Energy; Forestry
604-643-1209
drice@millerthomson.com
Darrell W. Roberts, Q.C., Counsel, Construction Litigation
604-643-1280
droberts@millerthomson.ca
Stephen R. Ross, Partner, Construction Litigation; Forestry
604-643-1205
sross@millerthomson.com
Gregory C. Smith, Partner, Mining
604-643-1258
gsmith@millerthomson.ca
Donald J. Sorochan, Q.C., Partner, Construction Litigation
604-643-1214
dsorodhan@millerthomson.com
Karen L. Weslowski, Partner, Construction Litigation
604-643-1290
kweslowski@millerthomson.com

Richards Buell Sutton LLP
#700 401 West Georgia St., Vancouver BC V6B 5A1
604-682-3664 604-688-3830
info@rbs.ca
www.rbs.ca
Profile: 1 Offices, 37 Lawyers, Founded in: 1871
Environmental Lawyers:
Michael P. Shane, Partner, Environmental Waste Management
604-661-9223
mshane@rbs.ca

Rosenberg & Rosenberg
671D Market Hill, Vancouver BC V5Z 4B5
604-879-4505 604-879-4934
rosenberg_law@telus.net
Profile: 1 Offices, 3 Lawyers, Founded in: 1980
Environmental Lawyers:
P.S. Rosenberg, Environmental Litigation
David M. Rosenberg, Environmental Litigation
Diane Somers

Rosenbloom & Aldridge
#440, 355 Burrard St., Vancouver BC V6C 2G8
604-605-5555 604-684-6402
rosenbloom_aldridge@telus.net
Profile: 1 Offices, 3 Lawyers
Environmental Lawyers:
Donald J. Rosenbloom

Singleton Urquhart LLP
#1200 925 Georgia St. West, Vancouver BC V6C 3L2
604-682-7474 604-682-1283
su@singleton.com
www.singleton.com
Profile: 1 Offices, 35 Lawyers, Founded in: 1986
Environmental Lawyers:
Daniel Barber, Construction
dbarber@singleton.com
Stephen J. Berezowskyj, Partner, Construction
604-682-7474
sjb@singleton.com
Scott Brearley, Construction
sbrearley@singleton.com
Derek A. Brindle, Q.C., Counsel, Construction
dbrindle@singleton.com
Barbara Cornish, Partner, Construction
bcornish@singleton.com
Mitch Dermer, Construction
mdermer@singleton.com
Jennifer Frahm, Construction; Environmental Law
jfrahm@singleton.com
Jeffrey A. Hand, Partner, Construction
jhand@singleton.com
Robert A. Hodgins, Partner, Construction
rhodgins@singleton.com
Roger E. Holland, Partner, Construction
rholland@singleton.com
Ian C. Jones, Environmental Law
ijones@singleton.com
Steven L. Lesiuk, Environmental Law
slesiuk@singleton.com
Melissa Nagelbach, Construction
mnagelbach@singleton.com
Cornel Peana, Construction
cpeana@singleton.com
Michael Peraya, Construction
mperaya@singleton.com

David G. Perry, Partner, Environmental Law
dperry@singleton.com
Elizabeth (Betsy) Segal, Construction
esegal@singleton.com
Michael D. Shirreff, Construction
asherriff@singleton.com
John R. Singleton, Q.C., Partner, Environmental Law; Construction
jsingleton@singleton.com
Mark C. Stacey, Partner, Construction
mstacey@singleton.com
Wei Kiat Sun, Construction
wsun@singleton.com
Mark S. Thompson, Partner, Construction
mthompson@singleton.com
Glenn A. Urquhart, Q.C., Counsel, Construction
gurquhart@singleton.com

Stikeman Elliott LLP - Vancouver
#1700, Park Place 666 Burrard St., Vancouver BC V6C 2X8
604-631-1300 604-681-1825 866-631-1300
info@stikeman.com
www.stikeman.com
Profile: 41 Lawyers, Founded in: 1988
Environmental Lawyers:
Amyn M. Abdula, Pharmaceuticals, Biotechnology & Life Sciences; Energy; Forestry & Forest Products
604-631-1322
aabdula@stikeman.com
Michael S. Allen, Partner, Renewable Energy; Forestry & Forest Products; Mining
604-631-1346
mallen@stikeman.com
John F. Anderson, Partner, Forestry & Forest Products; Mining
604-631-1307
janderson@stikeman.com
Jonathan S. Drance, Partner, Emissions Trading & Climate Change; Forestry & Forest Products
604-631-1361
jdrance@stikeman.com
Annette E.F. Dueck, Mining
604-631-1315
adueck@stikeman.com
Ross A. MacDonald, Managing Partner, Construction Litigation; Environmental Law
604-631-1367
rmacdonald@stikeman.com
Neville J. McClure, Partner, Mining
604-631-1324
nmcclure@stikeman.com
Jonathan M. McLean, Senior Counsel, Construction Litigation; Environmental Litigation
604-631-1347
jmclean@stikeman.com
John E. Stark, Partner, Pharmaceuticals, Biotechnology & Life Sciences; Construction Litigation; Forestry & Forest Products; Mining
604-631-1395
jstark@stikeman.com
Jamie Templeton, Energy; Emissions Trading & Climate Change
604-631-1441
jtempleton@stikeman.com

Young, Anderson
#1616, Nelson Square CP 12147 808 Nelson St., Vancouver BC V6Z 2H2
604-689-7400 604-689-3444 800-665-3540
reception@lya.bc.ca
www.lya.bc.ca
Profile: 2 Offices, 19 Lawyers, Founded in: 1982
Environmental Lawyers:
Bill Buholzer, Municipal
Reece Harding, Litigation
Sukhbir Manhas, Litigation
Barry Williamson, Litigation
Raymond E. Young, Municipal

Vernon

Nixon Wenger
3201 - 30 Ave., 4th Fl., Vernon BC V1T 2C6
250-542-5353 250-542-7273 800-243-5353
nw@nixonwenger.com
www.nixonwenger.com
Profile: 1 Offices, 19 Lawyers, Municipal Law & Land Development

Environmental Lawyers:
Kent G. Burnham, Partner, Civil Litigation; Personal Injury
Carolyn R. Christiansen, Associate, Family Law
Philip A. Dyck, Partner, Family Law
Leanne F. Rutley, Associate, Corporate; Commercial

Victoria

Cook Roberts LLP
1175 Douglas St., 7th Fl., Victoria BC V8W 2E1
250-385-1411 250-413-3300
lawmark@cookroberts.bc.ca
www.cookroberts.bc.ca
Profile: 1 Offices, 20 Lawyers, Founded in: 1970
Environmental Assessments & Review; Pollution & Contamination Claims & Defense; Environmental Prosecution & Defense; Aboriginal Law Issues
Environmental Lawyers:
Robert C. Freedman, Aboriginal Litigation & Treaty Rights
250-385-1411
rfreedman@cookroberts.bc.ca
Robert J.M. Janes, Aboriginal Litigation
250-385-1411
rjanes@cookroberts.bc.ca
Dominique A. Nouvet, Aboriginal Litigation & Treaty Rights
250-385-1411
dnouvet@cookroberts.bc.ca

Crease Harman & Company
#800, 1070 Douglas St., Victoria BC V8W 2S8
250-388-5421 250-388-4294
creaseharman@creaseharman.com
www.creaseharman.com
Profile: 1 Offices, 14 Lawyers, Founded in: 1879
Offers comprehensive advice in relation to all forms of municipal law; provides legal advice & representation in relation to all aspects of environmental law, including regulatory issues
Environmental Lawyers:
Bruce Hallsor, Municipal Law; Environmental Law
hallsor@creaseharman.com
Peter W. Klassen, Municipal Law
pwklassen@creaseharman.com

Heenan Blaikie LLP - Victoria
#514 737 Yates St., Victoria BC V8W 1L6
250-381-9321 250-381-7023
www.heenanblaikie.com
Profile: 14 Lawyers, Founded in: 1973
Environmental Lawyers:
Lawrence Alexander, Environmental Law; Natural Resources; Energy
250-220-4342
lalexander@heenan.ca
Susan P. Arnold, Partner, Occupational Health & Safety
250-381-9321
sarnold@heenan.ca
Peter A. Gall, Q.C., Partner, Occupational Health & Safety
250-381-9321
pgalld@heenan.ca
Jay Hayden, Partner, Energy; Climate, Cleantech & Sustainability
250-381-9321
jhayden@heenan.ca
T. Murray Rankin, Q.C., Partner, Environmental Law; Aboriginal Law; Natural Resources
250-381-9321
mrankin@heenan.ca
Richard Shrieves, Partner, Aboriginal Law; Natural Resources
250-381-9321
rshrieves@heenan.ca

Merchant Law Group LLP - Victoria
.531 Quadra St., Victoria BC V8V 3S4
250-385-7777 250-478-9943 866-765-7777
merchant@merchantlaw.com
Profile: 2 Lawyers
Environmental Lawyers:
Darren G. Williams, Energy

Moore-Stewart, Robert
#616, 620 View St., Victoria BC V8W 1J6
250-380-1887 250-380-9134
rmoorest@telus.net
Profile: 1 Offices, 1 Lawyers,
Defence lawyer for environmental activists & others involved in injunctions & related civil litigation

Environmental Lawyers:
Robert Moore-Stewart, Anti-Nuclear; Anti-Oldgrowth Logging
  rmoorest@direct.ca

Woodward & Company
844 Courtney St., 2nd Fl., Victoria BC V8W 1C4
250-383-2356 250-380-6560
reception@woodwardandcompany.com
www.woodwardandcompany.com
Profile: 1 Offices, 14 Lawyers, Founded in: 1980
Largest Aboriginal law specialty firm in Canada
Environmental Lawyers:
Murray Browne
Gary Campo
Pat Hutchings
Heather Mahony
David Robbins
E. Jack Woodward

Manitoba

Carman

Lee & Lee
5 Centre Ave. West, Carman MB R0G 0J0
204-745-6751 204-745-3481
Profile: 1 Offices, 2 Lawyers
Environmental Lawyers:
Brock G. Lee, Q.C.

Winnipeg

Aikins, MacAulay & Thorvaldson LLP
Commodity Exchange Tower 360 Main St., 30th Fl., Winnipeg MB R3C 4G1
204-957-0050 204-957-0840
amt@aikins.com
www.aikins.com
Profile: 1 Offices, 93 Lawyers, Founded in: 1879
Aboriginal; Environmental; Municipal
Environmental Lawyers:
Theodor E. Bock, Aboriginal Law
  204-957-4673
  reb@aikins.com
Aaron J. Bowler, Environmental Law; Aboriginal Law; Municipal
  204-957-4892
  ajb@aikins.com
John R. Braun, Aboriginal Law
  204-957-4672
  jrb@aikins.com
Charles L. Chappell, Environmental Law; Municipal
  204-957-4638
  clc@aikins.com
Thomas P. Dooley, Environmental Law
  204-957-4628
  tpd@aikins.com
James A. Ferguson, Aboriginal Law
  204-957-4696
  jaf@aikins.com
James E. Foran, Q.C., Transportation
  204-957-4613
  jef@aikins.com
Allan F. Foran, Environmental Law; Transportation
  204-957-4664
  aff@aikins.com
Robert T. Gabor, Q.C., Environmental Law; Transportation
  204-957-4642
  rtg@aikins.com
Betty A. Johnstone, Aboriginal Law
  204-957-4650
  baj@aikins.com
Adam L. Levene, Aboriginal Law
  204-957-4632
  all@aikins.com
Colin R. MacArthur, Q.C., Municipal Law
  204-957-4627
  crm@aikins.com
A.J. (Telly) Mercury, Q.C., Municipal Law
  204-957-4610
  ajm@aikins.com
Herbert J. Peters, Aboriginal Law
  204-957-4634
  hjp@aikins.com
Michelle R. Redekopp, Transportation
  204-957-4698
  mrr@aikins.com
Barbara M. Shields, Aboriginal Law
  204-957-4615
  bms@aikins.com
Rod E. Stephenson, Q.C., Environmental Law
  204-957-4635
  res@aikins.com
Lucia M. Stuhldreier, Transportation
  204-957-4676
  lms@aikins.com
G. Bruce Taylor, Environmental Law; Aboriginal Law
  204-957-4669
  gbt@aikins.com
Nigel J. Thompson, Environmental Law; Aboriginal Law
  204-957-4659
  njt@aikins.com
Robert L. Tyler, Environmental Law; Municipal
  204-957-4630
  rlt@aikins.com
Joel A. Weinstein, Q.C., Aboriginal Law
  204-957-4631
  jaw@aikins.com

Antymniuk & Antymniuk
#11, 1500 Dakota St., Winnipeg MB R2N 3Y7
204-254-3511 204-257-5139
Profile: 1 Offices, 3 Lawyers
Environmental Lawyers:
Gregory T. Jowett

Campbell Marr
10 Donald St., Winnipeg MB R3C 1L5
204-942-3311 204-943-7997
dimarr@campbellmarr.com
www.campbellmarr.com
Profile: 1 Offices, 13 Lawyers, Founded in: 1990
Environmental Lawyers:
Anders Bruun, Agricultural Law
  204-942-3311
  abruun@campbellmarr.com
Kenton Fast, Agricultural Law
  204-942-3311
  klfast@campbellmarr.com
Roger B. King, Q.C.
  204-942-3311
  rking@campbellmarr.com
Douglas J. MacKenzie, Aboriginal Law
  204-942-3311
  djmack@campbellmarr.com
Garth P. Reimer, Agricultural Law
  204-942-3311
  greimer@campbellmarr.com

D'Arcy & Deacon LLP
330 St. Mary Ave., 12th Fl., Winnipeg MB R3C 4E1
204-942-2271 204-943-4242
inquiries@darcydeacon.com
www.darcydeacon.com
Profile: 1 Offices, 34 Lawyers, Founded in: 1860
Our lawyers advise on & have represented corporations & individuals relating to environmental issues; we represent clients in civil litigation involving allegations of environmental damage; we offer advice with respect to potential environmental liability issues & environmental disclosure
Environmental Lawyers:
Harold Cochrane, Aboriginal
  204-925-5387
  hcochrane@darcydeacon.com
John E. Deacon, Q.C., Municipal
  204-925-5352
  jdeacon@darcydeacon.com
Michael G. Finlayson, Construction
  204-925-5363
  mfinlayson@darcydeacon.com
Jonathan L. Goldenberg, Agricultural; Pharmaceutical
  204-925-5371
  jgoldenberg@darcydeacon.com
Roger D. Gripp, Municipal
  204-925-5369
  rgripp@darcydeacon.com
Greg A. Johnson, Aboriginal
  204-925-5374
  gjohnson@darcydeacon.com
Brenda A. Johnston, Aboriginal
  204-925-5395
  bjohnson@darcydeacon.com
Brian J. Meronek, Q.C., Municipal
  204-925-5355
  bmeronek@darcydeacon.com
B. Patrick Metcalfe, Construction; Environmental
  204-925-5350
  pmetcalfe@darcydeacon.com
Bradley D. Regehr, Aboriginal; Environmental
  204-925-5388
  bregehr@darcydeacon.com
Richard M. Rice, Aboriginal; Pharmaceutical
  204-925-5358
  rrice@darcydeacon.com
Michael D. Richards, Construction; Pharmaceutical
  204-925-5373
  mrichards@darcydeacon.com
Grant A. Stefanson, Aboriginal; Pharmaceutical
  204-925-5376
  gstefanson@darcydeacon.com
John C. Stewart, Agricultural
  204-925-5368
  jstewart@darcydeacon.com
Michael D. Werier, Health
  204-925-5359
  mwerier@darcydeacon.com
Michael Willcock, Health; Municipal
  204-925-5361
  mwillcock@darcydeacon.com
Russell G. Wookey, Construction; Municipal
  204-925-5360
  rwookey@darcydeacon.com
Darcie C. Yale, Health
  204-925-5381
  dyale@darcydeacon.com

Hook & Smith
#201, 3111 Portage Ave., Winnipeg MB R3K 0W4
204-885-4520 204-837-9846
general@hookandsmith.com
Profile: 1 Offices, 4 Lawyers, Founded in: 1984
Environmental Lawyers:
Winston F. Smith, Q.C., Transporation
  wsmith@hookandsmith.com

Pitblado LLP
#2500, Commodity Exchange Tower 360 Main St., Winnipeg MB R3C 4H6
204-956-0560 204-957-0227
firm@pitblado.com
www.pitblado.com
Profile: 1 Offices, 57 Lawyers, Founded in: 1882
Environmental Lawyers:
Jeff A. Baigrie, Agriculture; Construction Law
  204-956-3558
Joseph D. Barnsley, Aviation; Transportation
  204-956-3522
Mark R. Beard, Environmental Due Diligence
  204-956-3510
  beard@pba-law.com
Tracey L. Epp, Health Law
  204-956-3557
William S. Gardner, Health & Medical
  204-956-3560
Richard J. Handlon, Recontamination & Damage; Medical Law; Construction Law
  204-956-3556
Bruce H. King, Agriculture
  204-956-3541
Jack R. London, Q.C., Counsel, Aboriginal Law; Construction law
  204-956-3500
Howard P. Nerman, Aboriginal Issues
  204-956-3530
  nerman@pba-law.com
David G. Newman, Aboriginal Law
  204-956-3521
David B.N. Ramsay, Construction Law
  204-956-3529
Bryan P. Schwartz, Associate Counsel, Aboriginal Law
  204-474-6142
Thomas W. Turner, Construction Law
  204-956-3516

Law Firms / New Brunswick

Pullan Kammerloch Frohlinger
#300, 240 Kennedy St., Winnipeg MB R3C 1T1
204-956-0490 204-947-3747
firm@pkf-law.com
www.pkflawyers.com
Profile: 2 Offices, 10 Lawyers
Environmental Lawyers:
Thomas Frohlinger, Mining; Quarrying; Northern Tourism Development
frohlinger@pkf-law.com

Thompson Dorfman Sweatman LLP
#2200, CanWest Global Place 201 Portage Ave., Winnipeg MB R3B 3L3
204-957-1930 204-934-0570
tds@tdslaw.com
www.tdslaw.com
Profile: 1 Offices, 68 Lawyers, Founded in: 1887
Natural Resource Management/Aboriginal Land Use; Land Claims; Urban Aboriginal Issues; Contaminated Sites; Environmental Issues in Commercial Acquisitions; Sustainable Development
Environmental Lawyers:
Richard H.G. Adams, Construction
  204-934-2439
  rhga@tdslaw.com
Robert J.M. Adkins, Aboriginal; Construction; Environmental & Sustainable Development; Municipal; Natural Resources & Energy
  204-934-2483
  rjma@tdslaw.com
Glen W. Agar, Natural Resources & Energy
  204-934-2590
  gwa@tdslaw.com
G.V. Brickman, Q.C., Natural Resources & Energy
  204-934-2428
  gvb@tdslaw.com
William J. Burnett, Q.C., Aboriginal; Construction; Natural Resources & Energy
  204-934-2487
  wjb@tdslaw.com
Karen L. Clearwater, Environmental & Sustainable Development
  204-934-2362
  klc@tdslaw.com
Kara L. Crawford, Aboriginal; Environmental & Sustainable Development; Municipal; Natural Resources & Energy
  204-934-2346
  kc@tdslaw.com
James G. Edmond, Construction; Environmental & Sustainable Development
  204-934-2450
  jge@tdslaw.com
Douglas J. Forbes, Environmental; Construction
  204-934-2426
  djf@tdslaw.com
Monina A.P. Glowacki, Construction
  204-934-2380
  mapg@tsdlaw.com
Maria L. Grande, Construction
  204-934-2573
  mlg@tdslaw.com
Antoine F. Hacault, Municipal
  204-934-2513
  afh@tdslaw.com
M. Lynne Harrison, Aboriginal; Construction; Natural Resources & Energy
  204-934-2506
  mlh@tdslaw.com
Jamie A. Kagan, Construction
  204-934-2309
  jk@tdslaw.com
Keith D. LaBossiere, Construction
  204-934-2587
  tdl@tdslaw.com
Sarantos Mattheos, Construction; Municipal
  204-964-2518
  sm@tdslaw.com
Ross A. McFayden, Municipal
  204-934-2378
  ram@tdslaw.com
Kathleen C. Murphy, Aboriginal; Environmental & Sustainable Development; Municipal; Natural Resources & Energy
  204-934-2567
  kcm@tdslaw.com

Ross A.L. Nugent, Q.C., Municipal
  204-934-2431
  raln@tdslaw.com
E. William Olson, Q.C., Construction
  204-934-2534
  ewo@tdslaw.com
Chrys Pappas, Q.C., Municipal
  204-934-2452
  cp@tdslaw.com
Sacha R. Paul, Aboriginal; Environmental & Sustainable Development; Natural Resources & Energy
  204-934-2571
  srp@tdslaw.com
Walter L. Ritchie, Q.C., Construction
  204-934-2422
  wlr@tdslaw.com
Sheryl A. Rosenberg, Environmental & Sustainable Development; Natural Resources & Energy
  204-934-2312
  sar@tdslaw.com
P. Michael Sinclair, Q.C., Managing Partner, Natural Resources & Energy
  204-934-2493
  pms@tdslaw.com
Arthur J. Stacey, Construction
  204-934-2537
  ajs@tdslaw.com
John D. Stefaniuk, Environmental & Sustainable Development; Municipal; Natural Resources & Energy
  204-934-2597
  jds@tdslaw.com
Lisa J. Stiver, Environmental & Sustainable Development; Municipal
  204-934-2375
  ljs@tdslaw.com
B. Douglas Tait, Municipal
  204-934-2440
  bdt@tdslaw.com
Gregory J. Tallon, Construction
  204-934-2478
  gjt@tdslaw.com
Andrew L. Thompson, Municipal
  204-934-2358
  alt@tdslaw.com
Lynda K. Troup, Municipal
  204-934-2337
  lkt@tdslaw.com
Cheryl A. Walker, Municipal
  204-934-2369
  caw@tdslaw.com
Jonathan M. Woolley, Construction; Environmental & Sustainable Development
  204-934-2367
  jmw@tdslaw.com

New Brunswick

Fredericton

Cox and Palmer - Fredericton
#400, Phoenix Square P.O Box 310 A371 Queen St., Fredericton NB E3B 4Y9
506-453-7771 506-453-9600
fredericton@coxandpalmer.com
www.coxandpalmer.com
Profile: 28 Lawyers
Environmental Lawyers:
David T. Hashey, Q.C., Fisheries & Marine; Natural Resources & Energy
  506-453-9672
  dhashey@coxandpalmer.com
Bruce D. Hatfield, Q.C., Municipal Law
  506-453-9674
  bhatfield@coxandpalmer.com
David M. Norman, Q.C., Natural Resources & Energy
  506-453-9678
  dnorman@coxandpalmer.com
Walter D. Vail, Q.C., Environmental Law
  506-453-9602
  wvail@coxandpalmer.com

McInnes Cooper
#600, Barker House P.O Box 610 A570 Queen St., Fredericton NB E3B 5A6

506-458-8572 506-458-9903
mcftn@mcinnescooper.com
www.mcinnescooper.com
Profile: 11 Lawyers
Environmental Lawyers:
Leonard T. Hoyt, Q.C., Energy; Renewable Energy
  506-458-1622
  len.hoyt@mcinnescooper.com
Alan T. Rockwell, Energy; Municipal & Land Use Planning
  506-458-1547
  alan.rockwell@mcinnescooper.com
Patrick V. Windle, Construction Industry
  506-458-1628
  patrick.windle@mcinnescooper.com
David Duncan Young, Construction Industry
  506-458-1623
  david.young@mcinnescooper.com

Pink Larkin
#210, 1133 Regent St., Fredericton NB E3B 3Z2
506-458-1989 506-458-1127
www.pinklarkin.com
Profile: 2 Offices, 4 Lawyers,
Firm services include occupational health & safety, municipal law, & environmental law.
Environmental Lawyers:
David Mombourquette, Labour & employment law, including occupational health & safety

Stewart McKelvey Stirling Scales - Fredericton
#600 Frederick Square P.O Box 730 77 Westmorland St., Fredericton NB E3B 5B4
506-458-1970 506-444-8974
fredericton@smss.com
www.smss.com
Profile: 15 Lawyers
Environmental Lawyers:
Clarence L. Bennett, Occupational Health & Safety; Construction Law
  506-444-8978
  cbennett@smss.com
Hugh J. Cameron, Partner, Construction Law
  506-443-0120
  hcameron@smss.com
J.E. Britt Dysart, Partner, Construction Law
  506-443-0153
  bdysart@smss.com
Gérard V. La Forest, C.C., Q.C., Counsel, Environmental Law
  506-443-0135
  glaforest@smss.com
J. Gordon Petrie, Q.C., Partner, Construction Law
  506-443-0150
  gpetrie@smss.com
Richard G. Petrie, Partner, Energy & Natural Resources; Environmental Law; Forestry; Occupational Health & Safety
  506-443-0155
  rpetrie@smss.com
Nicholas N. Russon, Construction Law
  506-443-0128
  nrusson@smss.com

Moncton

Barry Spalding - Moncton Office
#100, P.O Box 1066 Main1077 St. George Blvd., Moncton NB E1C 8P2
506-859-1244 506-859-1249
info@barryspalding.com
www.barryspalding.com
Profile: 7 Lawyers
Environmental Lawyers:
Richard E. DeBow, Construction Law
  red@law-bsr.com

Stewart McKelvey Stirling Scales - Moncton
#601 Blue Cross Centre P.O Box 28051 644 Main St., Moncton NB E1C 9N4
506-853-1970 506-858-8454
moncton@smss.com
www.smss.com
Profile: 15 Lawyers
Environmental Lawyers:
Levi E. Clain, Q.C., Environmental Law; Constuction
  506-383-2229
  lclain@smss.com

Robert M. Dysart, Construction
  506-383-2230
  rdysart@smss.com
Charles A. LeBlond, Q.C., Construction
  506-853-1976
  cleblond@smss.com
Sasha D. Morisset, Occupational health & safety
  506-853-1942
  smorisset@smss.com
Christopher J. Stewart, Energy & Natural Resources; Marine Law
  506-383-2224
  cstewart@smss.com

Riverview

Wilbur & Wilbur
706B Coverdale Rd., Riverview NB E1B 3L1
506-387-7715 506-387-5875
swilbur@wilburandwilbur.com
www.wilburandwilbur.com
Profile: 1 Offices, 2 Lawyers, Founded in: 1987
Environmental Lawyers:
Stephen P. Wilbur
  swilbur@wilburandwilbur.com

Saint John

Barry Spalding - Saint John Office
#710, Mercantine Centre P.O Box 6010 A55 Union Street, Saint John NB E2L 4R5
506-633-4226 506-633-4206 888-743-4226
info@barryspalding.com
www.barryspalding.com
Profile: 2 Offices, 20 Lawyers
Environmental Lawyers:
John P. Barry, Q.C., Environmental Law
David G. Barry, Q.C., Construction Law
  dgb@law-bsr.com
Andy W. Lodge, Construction Law
Howard A. Spalding, Q.C., Construction Law
Deirdre L. Wade, Construction Law; Environmental Law
Peter T. Zed, Q.C., Environmental Law
  ptz@law-bsr.com

Clark Drummie
P.O Box 6850 40 Wellington Row, Saint John NB E2L 4S3
506-633-3800 506-633-3811
cd@clarkdrummie.ca
www.clarkdrummie.ca
Profile: 2 Offices, 22 Lawyers
Environmental Lawyers:
M. Robert Jette, Q.C., Admiralty & Maritime

Gilbert McGloan Gillis
P.O Box 7174 22 King St., Saint John NB E2L 1G3
506-634-3600 506-634-3612 888-246-4529
gmg@gmglaw.com
www.gmglaw.com
Profile: 1 Offices, 15 Lawyers, Founded in: 1929
Environmental Lawyers:
David N. Rogers, Admiralty Law
  dnrogers@gmglaw.com

Gorman Nason
P.O Box 7286 A121 Germain St., Saint John NB E2L 4S6
506-634-8600 506-634-8685
info@GormanNason.com
www.gormannason.com
Profile: 1 Offices, 10 Lawyers,
Areas of practice include municipal planning & zoning, & enviromental law.
Environmental Lawyers:

Stewart McKelvey Stirling Scales - Saint John
#1000 Brunswick House P.O Box 7289 A44 Chipman Hill, Saint John NB E2L 4S6
506-632-1970 506-652-1989
saint-john@smss.com
www.smss.com
Profile: 30 Lawyers
Environmental Lawyers:
William B. Goss, Q.C., Partner, Occupational Health & Safety
  506-632-4515
  wgoss@smss.com

Gregory S. Harding, Partner, Energy & Natural Resources; Construction Law
  506-634-6417
  gharding@smss.com
J. Paul M. Harquail, Partner, Environmental Law; Marine Law; Occupational Health & Safety
  506-632-8313
  pharquail@smss.com
Catherine A. Lahey, Managing Partner, Environmental Law; Occupational Health & Safety
  506-632-8307
  clahey@smss.com
James F. LeMesurier, Partner, Occupational Health & Safety
  506-632-2776
  jlemesurier@smss.com
Neal L.D. Leard, Partner, Energy & Natural Resources; Construction Law
  506-634-6416
  nleard@smss.com
Kenneth B. McCullogh, Q.C., Partner, Construction Law; Marine Law
  506-632-2781
  kmccullogh@smss.com
E. Neil McKelvey, Q.C., Counsel, Construction Law; Marine Law
  506-632-2770
  nmckelvey@smss.com
Gerald S. McMackin, Q.C., Partner, Energy & Natural Resources; Health
  506-632-2768
  gmcmackin@smss.com
Darrell J. Stephenson, Partner, Energy & Natural Resources; Marine Law
  506-632-2790
  dstephenson@smss.com
Robert G. Vincent, Q.C., Partner, Environmental Law; Energy & Natural Resources; Occupational Health & Safety
  506-632-2780
  rvincent@smss.com
Misty R. Watson, Construction Law
  506-632-8317
  mwatson@smss.com

St Stephen

Clark Drummie
46 Milltown Blvd., St Stephen NB E3L 1G3
506-466-2338 506-466-0160
cdss@clarkdrummie.ca
www.clarkdrummie.ca
Profile: 3 Lawyers
Environmental Lawyers:
G. Fred Nicholson, Q.C., General Practice
  506-466-2338
  gfn@clarkdrummie.ca

Newfoundland & Labrador

Corner Brook

Poole Althouse, Barristers & Solicitors
Western Trust Bldg. P.O Box 812 49 - 51 Park St., Corner Brook NL A2H 6H7
709-634-3136 709-634-8247 877-634-3136
info@pa-law.ca
www.poolealthouse.ca
Profile: 1 Offices, 10 Lawyers, Founded in: 1956
Environmental Lawyers:
D. Paul Althouse, Q.C., Partner, Municipal law
  709-637-6424
  dpalthouse@pa-law.ca
Joseph S. Hutchings, Q.C., Partner, Administrative law; Public utilities
  709-637-6425
  jhutchings@pa-law.ca
George L. Murphy, Q.C., Partner, Municipal law
  709-637-6428
  gmurphy@pa-law.ca
Dean A. Porter, Administrative law; Municipal law
  709-634-3136
  dporter@pa-law.ca
Cillian D. Sheahan, Municipal law
  709-637-6426
  csheahan@pa-law.ca

Katrina E. Warren, Administrative law
  709-637-6442
  kwarren@pa-law.ca

St. John's

Benson Myles
#900, Atlantic Place P.O Box 1538 215 Water St., St. John's NL A1C 5N8
709-579-2081 709-579-2647
info@bensonmyles.com
www.bensonmyles.com
Profile: 1 Offices, 21 Lawyers
Environmental Lawyers:
Benjamin J. Kavanagh, Oil & Gas; Mining
  709-570-7252
  bkavanagh@bensonmyles.com
R. Wayne Myles, Q.C., Mining, Oil & Gas, Transportation
  709-570-7232
  wmyles@bensonmyles.com
Geoffrey L. Spencer, Transportation
  709-570-7263
  gspencer@bensonmyles.com

Cox and Palmer - St. John's
#1000, Scotia Centre 235 Water St., St. John's NL A1C 1B6
709-738-7800 709-738-7999
stjohns@coxandpalmer.com
www.coxandpalmer.com
Profile: 8 Offices, 43 Lawyers, Founded in: 1952
Assists municipalities, mining companies, manufacturers, land-owners, lenders and others in a wide range of environmental matters. Services include advising and representing clients throughout the environmental assessment process and in prosecutions under environmental protection legislation.
Environmental Lawyers:
Sandra R. Chaytor, Q.C., Environmental Law
  709-570-5329
  schaytor@coxandpalmer.com
John C. Crosbie, P.C., Q.C., O.C., Fisheries & Marine
  709-570-5501
  jcrosbie@coxandpalmer.com
Brenda B. Grimes, Health Law
  709-570-5542
  bgrimes@coxandpalmer.com
Christopher Hickey, Fisheries & Marine
  709-570-5522
  chickey@coxandpalmer.com
Stephanie S. Hickman, Natural Resources & Energy; Construction
  709-570-5536
  shickman@coxandpalmer.com
Shawn M. Kavanagh, Natural Resources & Energy
  709-570-5524
  skavanagh@coxandpalmer.com
Alexander MacDonald, Q.C., Construction; Natural Resources
  709-570-5512
  amacdonald@coxandpalmer.com
Kimberly J. Mackay, Municipal Law
  709-520-5521
  kmackay@coxandpalmer.com
M. John Mate, Fisheries & Marine
  709-570-5530
  jmate@coxandpalmer.com
Paul M. McDonald, Health Law
  709-570-5328
  pmcdonald@coxandpalmer.com
Jeffery W. Miller, Natural Resources & Energy
  709-570-5341
  jmiller@coxandpalmer.com
Tracey Pennell, Environmental Law; Natural Resources & Energy
  709-570-5514
  tpennell@coxandpalmer.com
D. Richard Robbins, Natural Resources & Energy
  709-570-5325
  rrobbins@coxandpalmer.com
Randall W. Smith, Environmental; Fisheries and Marine; Municipal
  709-570-5326
  rsmith@coxandpalmer.com
J. Alex Templeton, Fisheries & Marine Law
  709-570-5560
  atempleton@coxandpalmer.com

Law Firms / Northwest Territories

Mandy L. Woodland, Health Law; Maritime Law
709-570-5564
mwoodland@coxandpalmer.com
Douglas Wright, Fisheries & Marine
709-520-5544
dwright@coxandpalmer.com

Martin Whalen Hennebury Stamp
P.O Box 5910 15 Church Hill, St. John's NL A1C 5X4
709-754-1400 709-754-0915
info@mwhslaw.com
www.mwhslaw.com
Profile: 1 Offices, 11 Lawyers,
Fisheries & Marine; Oil & Gas
Environmental Lawyers:

McInnes Cooper
P.O Box 5939 10 Fort William Place, 5th Fl., St. John's NL A1C 5X4
709-722-8735 709-722-1763
mcsjs@mcinnescooper.com
www.mcinnescooper.com
Profile: 23 Lawyers, Founded in: 1859
Environmental Lawyers:
O. Noel Clarke, Q.C., Energy and Natural Resources
709-724-8232
noel.clarke@mcinnescooper.com
Dennis N. Clarke, Energy; Environmental Law; Waste Management
709-724-8282
dennis.clarke@mcinnescooper.com
Gregory J. Connors, Natural Resources
709-724-8264
greg.connors@mcinnescooper.com
Michael J. Crosbie, Construction Industry; Municipal
709-724-8242
michael.crosbie@mcinnescooper.com
J. David B. Eaton, Q.C., Construction Industry
709-724-8262
david.eaton@mcinnescooper.com
John M. Green, Q.C., Natural Resources
709-724-8238
john.green@mcinnescooper.com
Deborah L.J. Hutchings, Energy; Environmental Law; Maritime Law
709-724-8254
deborah.hutchings@mcinnescooper.com
John V. O'Dea, Construction Industry
709-724-8261
john.odea@mcinnescooper.com
Jacqueline A.M. Penney, Energy & Natural Resources
709-724-8239
jackie.penney@mcinnescooper.com
Douglas B. Skinner, Maritime Law
709-724-8249
doug.skinner@mcinnescooper.com
James L. Thistle, Q.C., Construction Industry; Energy; Environmental Law; Natural Resources
709-724-8247
jim.thistle@mcinnescooper.com
Caroline C. Watton, Natural Resources Law
709-724-8251
caroline.watton@mcinnescooper.com

Ottenheimer Baker
Baine Johnson Centre P.O Box 5457 10 Fort William Pl., St. John's NL A1C 5W4
709-722-7584 709-722-9210
info@ottenheimerbaker.com
www.ottenheimerbaker.com
Profile: 1 Offices, 22 Lawyers, Founded in: 1972
Environmental Lawyers:
Robert B. Andrews, Q.C., Partner, Construction Law
709-570-7331
randrews@ottenheimerbaker.com
Mark R. Andrews, Partner, Natural Resources; Oil & Gas Law; Mining Law
709-570-7341
mandrews@ottenheimerbaker.com
John A. Baker, Q.C., Founding Partner, Natural Resources; Oil & Gas Law; Mining Law
709-570-7305
jbaker@ottenheimerbaker.com
William C. Boyd, Managing Partner, Maritime Law; Fisheries
709-570-7306
wboyd@ottenheimerbaker.com
Gregory W. Dickie, Q.C., Partner, Oil & Gas Law
709-570-7307
gdickie@ottenheimerbaker.com
John W. Lavers, Partner, Maritime Law; Fisheries; Aboriginal Law
709-570-7324
jlavers@ottenheimerbaker.com
Raelene L. Lee, Partner, Construction; Occupational Health & Safety
709-570-7322
rlee@ottenheimerbaker.com
Rosalie E. McGrath, Partner, Natural Resources; Oil & Gas Law; Maritime & Fisheries
709-570-7344
rmcgrath@ottenheimerbaker.com
Beth M.W. McGrath, Natural Resources; Oil & Gas Law; Mining Law
709-570-7342
bmcgrath@ottenheimerbaker.com
Geoffrey K. Penney, Partner, Maritime & Fisheries
709-570-7312
gpenney@ottenheimerbaker.com
Neil F. Pittman, Partner, Natural Resources; Oil & Gas Law
709-570-7358
npittman@ottenheimerbaker.com
Daniel W. Simmons, Partner, Construction Law
709-570-7328
dsimmons@ottenheimerbaker.com
Wayne F. Spracklin, Q.C., Partner, Maritime Law; Fisheries
709-570-7321
wspracklin@ottenheimerbaker.com
Sheri H. Wicks, Partner, Construction Law; Aboriginal Law
709-570-7360
swicks@ottenheimerbaker.com

Stewart McKelvey Stirling Scales - St. John's
#1100 Cabot Place P.O Box 5038 100 New Gower St., St. John's NL A1C 5V3
709-722-4270 709-722-4565
st-johns@smss.com
www.smss.com
Profile: 33 Lawyers
Environmental Lawyers:
Daniel M. Boone, Managing Partner, Health
709-570-8879
dboone@smss.com
Geoffrey E.J. Brown, Q.C., Partner, Environmental Law; Construction Law
709-570-8845
gbrown@smss.com
Paul L. Coxworthy, Partner, Energy & Natural Resources; Health
709-570-8830
pcoxworthy@smss.com
Gerry R. Fleming, Partner, Construction Law
709-570-8836
gfleming@smss.com
Janet L. Grant, Health
709-570-5794
jgrant@smss.com
Bruce C. Grant, Q.C., Partner, Energy & Natural Resources; Construction Law
709-570-8882
bgrant@smss.com
Neil L. Jacobs, Partner, Health
709-570-8888
njacobs@smss.com
Jennifer E. Lundrigan, Environmental Law; Marine Law
709-570-8823
jlundrigan@smss.com
Gregory A.C. Moores, Partner, Environmental Law; Energy & Natural Resources; Construction Law
709-570-5797
gmoores@smss.com
Stephen F. Penney, Partner, Construction Law; Occupational Health & Safety
709-570-8881
spenney@smss.com
Twila E. Reid, Partner, Occupational Health & Safety
709-570-8828
treid@smss.com
Dennis J. Ryan, Partner, Energy & Natural Resources
709-570-8824
dryan@smss.com
Maureen E. Ryan, Partner, Energy & Natural Resources
709-570-8880
mryan@smss.com
Steven A. Scruton, Energy & Natural Resources; Marine Law; Aboriginal Law
709-570-8837
sscruton@smss.com
Colm St. Roch Seviour, Partner, Mining; Energy & Natural Resources; Environmental Law; Forestry; Construction Law
709-570-8847
cseviour@smss.com
Harold M. Smith, Q.C., Partner, Energy & Natural Resources; Occupational Health & Safety
709-570-8895
hsmith@smss.com
Tauna M. Staniland, Energy & Natural Resources
709-570-8842
tstaniland@smss.com
Cecily Y. Strickland, Partner, Environmental Law; Energy & Natural Resources; Occupational Health & Safety
709-570-8826
cstrickland@smss.com
Ruth E. Trask, Environmental Law
709-570-8893
rtrask@smss.com
Ian C. Wallace, Partner, Occupational Health & Safety
709-570-8839
iwallace@smss.com
Kimberley A. Walsh, Partner, Energy & Natural Resources; Marine Law
709-570-8834
kwalsh@smss.com
Rodney J. Zdebiak, Partner, Energy & Natural Resources
709-570-8841
rzdebiak@smss.com

Northwest Territories

Yellowknife

Davis & Company LLP
#802, Northwest Tower 5201 - 50th Ave., Yellowknife NT X1A 3S9
867-669-8400 867-669-8420
www.davis.ca
Profile: 8 Offices, Founded in: 1892
Aboriginal; Mining; Oil & Gas
Environmental Lawyers:

Field Law - Yellowknife
#201, 5120 - 49th St., Yellowknife NT X1A 1P8
867-920-4542 867-873-4790
pwilliams@fieldlaw.com
www.fieldlaw.com
Profile: 1 Lawyers, Founded in: 2000
Aboriginal Rights; Land Claim Implementation; Defense & Occasional Prosecution; Arbitrations under Forest Management Act
Environmental Lawyers:
Jack R. Williams, First Nations; Energy & Natural Resources
867-920-4542
jwilliams@fieldlaw.com

Lawson Lundell LLP - Yellowknife
#200, P.O Box 818 4915 - 48 St., Yellowknife NT X1A 2N6
867-669-5500 867-920-2206 888-465-7608
genmail@lawsonlundell.com
www.lawsonlundell.com
Profile: 3 Lawyers, Founded in: 1910
Environmental Lawyers:
Paul N.K. Smith, Partner, Environmental; Occupational Health & Safety; Mining; Energy; Natural Resources
867-669-5532
psmith@lawsonlundell.com

McLennan Ross LLP
#1001, Precambrian Bldg. 4920 - 52 St., Yellowknife NT X1A 3T1
867-766-7677 867-766-7678 888-836-6684
info@mross.com
www.mross.com
Profile: 3 Lawyers
Environmental Lawyers:
Edward Gullberg, Municipal
780-482-9112
egullberg@mross.com
Glenn D. Tait, Municipal
867-766-7676
gtait@mross.com

Nova Scotia

Berwick

Stewart & Turner
P.O Box 208 196 Cottage St., Berwick NS B0P 1E0
902-538-3123 902-538-7933
Profile: 1 Offices, 2 Lawyers
Environmental Lawyers:
Robert C. Stewart
Greg J. Turner

Dartmouth

Boyne Clarke
#700, Belmont House P.O Box 876 33 Alderney Dr., Dartmouth NS B2Y 3Z5
902-469-9500 902-463-7500 800-207-6589
info@boyneclarke.ns.ca
www.boyneclarke.ns.ca
Profile: 1 Offices, 39 Lawyers, Founded in: 1972
Administrative Law, Due Diligence, Management of Environmental Liability, Litigation
Environmental Lawyers:
James D. MacNeil
  902-460-3457
  jmacneil@boyneclarke.ns.ca
Robert Miedema
  902-460-3409
  rmiedema@boyneclarke.ns.ca
Gordon F. Proudfoot, Q.C.
  902-460-3418
  gproudfoot@boyneclarke.ns.ca
Kathryn A. Raymond, Health
Leah D. Rimmer, Health
  902-460-3459
  lrimmer@boyneclarke.ca
Cynthia M. Scott, Health
David A. Thompson, Oil & Gas
  902-460-3421
  dthompson@boyneclarke.ca
John A. Young, Q.C., Oil & Gas; Corporate & Commercial Law
  902-460-3406
  jyoung@boyneclarke.ns.ca

Burton Ronald W. Lawyers
169 Main St., Dartmouth NS B2X 1S1
902-434-4492 902-434-5485
burtonl@ns.sympatico.ca
Profile: 1 Lawyers
Environmental Lawyers:
Ronald W. Burton

Halifax

Burchell Hayman Parish
#1800, 1801 Hollis St., Halifax NS B3J 3N4
902-423-6361 902-420-9326
firm@burchells.ca
www.burchells.ca
Profile: 1 Offices, 23 Lawyers, Founded in: 1912
Environmental Lawyers:
D. Bruce Clarke, Aboriginal & Treaty Rights
  902-423-6361
  bclarke@burchells.ca
Stuart C.B. Gilby, Aboriginal; Environmental; Natural Resources Law
  902-423-6361
  sgilby@burchells.ca
David G. Hutt, Transportation Law
  902-442-8373
  dhutt@burchells.ca

Burchell, MacDougall
#210, Clayton Professional Centre 255 Lacewood Drive, Halifax NS B3M 4G2 Canada
902-445-5511 902-443-2600 800-552-1451
halifax@burchellmacdougall.com
www.burchellmacdougall.com
Profile: 4 Lawyers
Environmental Lawyers:
Michael Maddalena, Fisheries
  902-445-2588
  mmaddalena@burchellmacdougall.com

Cox and Palmer - Halifax
#1100, Purdy's Wharf, Tower One P.O Box 2380 Central1959 Water St., Halifax NS B3J 3E5
902-421-6262 902-421-3130
halifax@coxandpalmer.com
www.coxandpalmer.com
Profile: 50 Lawyers
Environmental Lawyers:
D. Kevin Burke, Transportation Law
  902-491-4202
  kburke@coxandpalmer.com
Robert W. Carmichael, Oil & Gas
  902-491-4102
  rcarmichael@coxandpalmer.com
Anthony L. Chapman, Q.C., Environmental Law
  902-491-4106
  achapman@coxandpalmer.com
Daniel F. Gallivan, Q.C., Oil & Gas
  902-491-4126
  dgallivan@coxandpalmer.com
John A. Keith, Municipal
  902-491-4217
  jkeith@coxandpalmer.com
Kevin Latimer, Q.C., Municipal and Planning Law
  902-491-4212
  klatimer@coxandpalmer.com
Andrew D. Taillon, Municipal Law
  902-491-4209
  ataillon@coxandpalmer.com

MacInnis, Kenneth Associates
#340, 1801 Hollis St., Halifax NS B3J 3N4
902-421-1817 902-423-8504
Profile: 1 Offices, 3 Lawyers
Environmental Lawyers:
Kenneth MacInnis, Environmental; Marine

McInnes Cooper
Purdy's Wharf Tower II P.O Box 730 1300-1969 Upper Water St., Halifax NS B3J 2V1
902-425-6500 902-425-6350
mchfx@mcinnescooper.com
www.mcinnescooper.com
Profile: 62 Lawyers,
Aboriginal Law; Energy Law; Environmental Law; Maritime Law; Municipal & Land Use Planning
Environmental Lawyers:
Michelle C. Awad, Energy; Construction
  902-444-8509
  michelle.awad@mcinnescooper.com
Robert G. Belliveau, Q.C., Environmental Law
  902-444-8513
  robert.belliveau@mcinnescooper.com
David Demirkan, Maritime Law; Municipal & Land Use Planning
  902-424-1388
  david.demirkan@mcinnescooper.com
Kevin D. Gibson, Construction
  902-444-8539
  kevin.gibson@mcinnescooper.com
David A. Graves, Construction
  902-424-1330
  david.graves@mcinnescooper.com
Thomas E. Hart, Aboriginal Law; Environmental Law; Maritime Law
  902-424-1329
  tom.hart@mcinnescooper.com
Sarah M. Kirby, Maritime Law
John Kulik, Construction
  902-424-1339
  john.kulik@mcinnescooper.com
Douglas Lutz, Energy
  902-424-1352
  doug.lutz@mcinnescooper.com
George W. MacDonald, Q.C., Construction
  902-424-1365
  george.macdonald@mcinnescooper.com
Aidan J. Meade, Construction; Energy
Harvey L. Morrison, Aboriginal Law; Construction; Environmental Law
Christopher C. Robinson, Q.C., Construction; Energy
  902-424-1325
  chris.robinson@mcinnescooper.com
Wylie Spicer, Q.C., Energy; Maritime Law
  902-424-1366
  wylie.spicer@mcinnescooper.com

Patterson Law
#510, 1718 Argyle St., Halifax NS B3J 3N6
902-405-8000 902-405-8001
contactus@pattersonlaw.ca
www.pattersonlaw.ca
Profile: 2 Offices
Environmental Lawyers:

Ritch Durnford, Lawyers
#1200, CIBC Bldg. 1809 Barrington St., Halifax NS B3J 3K8
902-429-3400 902-422-4713
info@ritchdurnford.com; library@ritchdurnford.com
www.ritchdurnford.com
Profile: 1 Offices, 16 Lawyers,
Areas of practice include municipal law & litigation of admiralty, environmental & marine claims.
Environmental Lawyers:
Philip M. Chapman, Marine; Environmental Law
  pmc@hrlaw.net
Peter D. Darling, Transportation; Fishing Industry
  pdd@hrlaw.net
Lisa Richards, Municipal Law
  lr@hrlaw.net
Roger T. Shepard, Municipal Law
  rts@hrlaw.net
Matthew G. Williams, Maritime Law
  mgw@hrlaw.net

Stewart McKelvey Stirling Scales - Halifax
#900 Purdy's Wharf Tower One P.O Box 997 Central1959 Upper Water St., Halifax NS B3J 2X2
902-420-3200 902-420-1417
halifax@smss.com
www.smss.com
Profile: 6 Offices, 220 Lawyers, Founded in: 1867
Environmental Lawyers:
T. Arthur Barry, Q.C., Construction
  902-420-3364
  abarry@smss.com
Daniela F. Bassan, Energy & Natural Resources; Environmental
  902-420-3354
  dbassan@smss.com
Lydia S. Bugden, Energy & Natural Resources
  902-420-3372
  lbugden@smss.com
Tyana R. Caplan, Health
  902-420-3356
  tcaplan@smss.com
Warren B. Chornoby, Energy & Natural Resources
  902-420-3339
  wchornoby@smss.com
James M. Dickson, Corporate/Commercial; Environmental Audits; Due Diligence; Environmental Assessments & Approvals; Site Remediation & Rec
  902-420-3308
  jmd@smss.com
Meinhard Doelle, Energy & Natural Resources; Environmental
  902-420-3352
  mdoelle@smss.com
David P.S. Farrar, Construction
  902-420-3362
  dfarrar@smss.com
Robert G. Grant, Q.C., Energy & Natural Resources; Environmental; Public Hearings; Defence of Prosecutions; Environmental Liability
  902-420-3328
  rgrant@smss.com
David G. Henley, Marine Law; Energy & Natural Resources; Environmental; Construction
  902-420-3381
  dhenley@smss.com
Mark E. MacDonald, Q.C., Litigation; Defence of Prosecutions; Marine
  902-420-3329
  mmacdonald@smss.com
D. Geoffrey Machum, Construction
  902-420-3330
  gmachum@smss.com
Carman G. McCormick, Q.C., Health
John S. McFarlane, Q.C., Environmental
  902-420-3315
  jmcfarlane@smss.com
David A. Miller, Q.C., Construction
  902-420-3319
  dmiller@smss.com

William Moreira, Marine Law; Energy; Natural Resources
902-420-3346
wmoreira@smss.com
Colin D. Piercey, Energy & Natural Resources; Environmental; Construction
902-420-3345
cpiercey@smss.com
Nancy G. Rubin, Energy & Natural Resources
902-420-3337
nrubin@smss.com
William L. Ryan, Q.C., Construction
Richard F. Southcott, Marine Law; Environmental; Energy & Natural Resources
902-420-3304
rsouthcott@smss.com

Wickwire Holm
#2100, P.O Box 1054 1801 Hollis St., Halifax NS B3J 2X6
902-429-4111 902-429-8215 866-429-4111
wh@wickwireholm.com
www.wickwireholm.com
Profile: 3 Offices, 22 Lawyers
Environmental Lawyers:
Sean Foreman, Partner
902-482-7020
sforeman@wickwireholm.com
Dufferin R. Harper, Partner
902-482-7010
dharper@wickwireholm.com

Kentville

Muttart Tufts Dewolfe & Coyle
P.O Box 515 20 Cornwallis St., Kentville NS B4N 3X3
902-678-2157 902-678-9455
mtdc_law@mtdc.ns.ca
www.mtdc.ns.ca
Profile: 1 Offices, 7 Lawyers, Founded in: 1968
Legal counsel to various local governments including the regional solid waste management authority; represents private individuals & corporations on environmental issues, especially those related to agri-business & land-use planning
Environmental Lawyers:
Geoffrey P. Muttart, Environmental law & land-use planning
gmuttart@mtdc.ns.ca

Truro

Burchell, MacDougall
P.O Box 1128 710 Prince St., Truro NS B2N 5H1
902-895-1561 902-895-7709 800-565-1200
truro@burchellmacdougall.com
www.burchellmacdougall.com
Profile: 3 Offices, 18 Lawyers
Environmental Lawyers:
John R.M. Akerman, Q.C., Municipal Law
902-895-1561 ext. 553
jakerman@burchellmacdougall.com
Cameron S. McKinnon, Environmental Law
902-895-1561 ext. 540
cmckinnon@burchellmacdougall.com
Brian W. Stilwell, Environmental Law
902-895-1561
bstilwell@burchellmacdougall.com
Michael Stokoe, Farm, Fisheries and Resources Group
902-896-7550
mstokoe@burchellmacdougall.com

Patterson Law
P.O Box 1068 10 Church St., Truro NS B2N 5G9
902-897-2000 902-893-3071
dshive@pattersonlaw.ca
www.pattersonlaw.ca
Profile: 2 Offices, 31 Lawyers
Environmental Lawyers:
Lloyd I. Berliner, Forestry
902-897-2000
lberliner@pattersonlaw.ca
Douglas A. Caldwell, Q.C., Administrative law
902-897-2000
dcaldwell@pattersonla.ca
J. Ronald Creighton, Q.C., Forestry
902-897-2000
rcreighton@pattersonlaw.ca

Jane M. Gourley-Davis, Agriculture
902-896-6189
jgourley-davis@pattersonlaw.ca
Jennifer J. Hamilton Upham, Agriculture
902-896-6192
jupham@pattersonlaw.ca
Dennis J. James, Administrative law; Municipal law
902-896-6149
djames@pattersonlaw.ca
Robert L. Mellish, Agriculture
902-444-8486
rmellish@pattersonlaw.ca
L. Martina Munden, Administrative law; Health law
902-896-6165
mmunden@pattersonlaw.ca
Robert H. Pineo, Administrative law; Agriculture
902-896-6177
rpineo@pattersonlaw.ca
George L. White, Q.C., TEP, Forestry; Agriculture
902-896-6163
gwhite@pattersonlaw.ca

Wolfville

Burchell, MacDougall
P.O Box 1330 29 Elm St., Wolfville NS B4P 2A1
902-542-4543 902-542-5474 800-329-0121
wolfville@burchellmacdougall.com
www.burchellmacdougall.com
Profile: 2 Lawyers
Environmental Lawyers:
Michael R. Brooker, Q.C., Environmental Litigation
902-542-4048
mbrooker@burchellmacdougall.com
Daniel L. Oulton, Agricultural Law
902-542-4071
doulton@burchellmacdougall.com

Ontario

Alexandria

Nelligan O'Brien Payne
139 Main St. South, Alexandria ON K0C 1A0
613-525-2396 613-525-2752 888-565-9912
info@nelligan.ca
www.nelligan.ca
Profile: 4 Offices, 46 Lawyers
Environmental Lawyers:

Barrie

Graham Wilson & Green, Barristers & Solicitors, Notaries, Mediators
#107, 190 Cundles Rd. East, Barrie ON L4M 4S5
705-737-1811 705-737-5390
gwg@gwg.on.ca
www.gwg.on.ca
Profile: 1 Offices, 12 Lawyers, Founded in: 1975
Environmental Lawyers:
George G. Cameron, Land development
ggc@gwg.on.ca
Shari D. Elliott, Environmental law; Municipal law
sde@gwg.on.ca
E. Marshall Green, Municipal law
emg@gwg.on.ca
Douglas L. MacLeod, Workplace safety; Occupational health & safety
dlm@gwg.on.ca
Paul A. Rabinovitch, Land development; Municipal law
par@gwg.on.ca
Tom C. Tsakopoulos, Municipal Law
tct@gwg.on.ca
Mary E. Vallee, Municipal litigation
mev@gwg.on.ca

Belleville

Templeman Menninga LLP
#200 P.O Box 234 205 Dundas St. East, Belleville ON K8N 5A2
613-966-2620 613-966-2866
info@tmlegal.com
www.templemanmenninga.com

Profile: 4 Offices, 23 Lawyers, Founded in: 1981
The firm also has offices in Kingston, Brockville & Whitby, Ontario.
Environmental Lawyers:
Stephen Ellsworth, Environmental Law
se@tmlegal.ca
Wayne Fairbrother, Partner, Municipal; Landfill Site Management; Environmental Assessment
dwf@tmlegal.ca
Jeff Paine, Water Resources; Environment
jp@tmlegal.ca
Jennifer G. Savini, Environmental Litigation
jag@tmlegal.ca

Brampton

Lawrence, Lawrence, Stevenson
43 Queen St. West, Brampton ON L6Y 1L9
905-451-3040 905-451-5058
lls@lawrences.com
www.lawrences.com
Profile: 1 Offices, 14 Lawyers, Founded in: 1924
Environmental Lawyers:
Heather M. Picken, General Environmental; Real Estate
905-452-6891
lls@lawrences.com

Burlington

SimpsonWigle LAW LLP
#501 Sims Square Bldg. 390 Brant St., Burlington ON L7R 4J4
905-639-1052 905-333-3960 800-434-4414
info@simpsonwigle.com
www.simpsonwigle.com
Profile: 2 Offices, 27 Lawyers, Founded in: 1990
Environmental Lawyers:
Serena Lee, Mining; Health
lees@simpsonwigle.com
Derek A. Schmuck, Partner, Construction Law ext. 353
schmuckd@simpsonwigle.com

Carelton Place

Howard Ryan Kelford Knott & Dixon
9 Emily St., Carelton Place ON K7C 1R9
613-253-9772 613-253-0772
Profile: 2 Offices, 5 Lawyers,
The firm is engaged in the practice of municipal law.
Environmental Lawyers:

Essex

Renick, Jim Law Office
14 Wilson Ave., Essex ON N8M 2L7
519-776-9020 519-776-9027
info@walstedtrenick.com
Profile: 1 Offices, 1 Lawyers,
Environmental law services to municipal & corporate business clients
Environmental Lawyers:
J. James Renick, Environmental; Municipal

Goderich

Donnelly & Murphy
18 Court House Square, Goderich ON N7A 3Y7
519-524-2154 519-524-8550
admin@dmlaw.on.ca
Profile: 1 Offices, 7 Lawyers
Environmental Lawyers:
D.J. Murphy, Q.C., Municipal Law; Environmental Law
519-524-2154
dmurphy@dmlaw.on.ca

Hamilton

Lazier Hickey Langs O'Neal
25 Main St. West, 15th Fl., Hamilton ON L8P 1H1
905-525-3652 905-525-6278
lawfirm@lazierhickey.com
www.lazierhickey.com
Profile: 1 Offices, 10 Lawyers, Founded in: 1863
Environmental Lawyers:
Thomas E. Lazier

Ross & McBride LLP
Commerce Place P.O Box 907 1 King Street West, 10th Fl., Hamilton ON L8N 3P6
905-526-9800 905-526-0732
contact@rossmcbride.com
www.rossmcbride.com
Profile: 1 Offices, 37 Lawyers, Founded in: 1890
Environmental Lawyers:
Paul D. Paradis, Partner, Environmental Law
905-572-5811
paul.paradis@rossmcbride.com
Rick D. Simmons, Occupational Health & Safety
905-572-5833
rsimmons@rossmcbride.com

Scarfone Hawkins LLP
P.O Box 926 Depot 11 James St. South, 14th Fl., Hamilton ON L8N 3P9
905-523-1333 905-523-5878
info@shlaw.ca
www.scarfonehawkinsllp.com
Profile: 1 Offices, 19 Lawyers, Founded in: 1975
Environmental Lawyers:
Donald B. Hawkins, Construction Law
dhawkins@shlaw.ca
Catherine Buntain Jeske, Construction Law
cjeske@shlaw.ca
James W. Mahler, Construction Law
jmahler@shlaw.ca
Matthew G. Moloci, Construction Law
moloci@shlaw.ca
Krystyn Ordyniec, Construction Law
kordyniec@shlaw.ca
Frank Pignoli, Environmental Torts; Construction Law
fpignoli@shlaw.ca
James A. Scarfone, Environmental Litigation
scarfone@shlaw.ca
Joseph G. Speranzini, Construction Law
speranzini@shlaw.ca
Michael Stanton, Construction Law
mstanton@shlaw.ca
Jeffrey C. Teal, Construction Law; Health Law
jteal@shlaw.ca
David Thompson, Construction Law
thompson@shlaw.ca
Michael J. Valente, Construction Law
mvalente@shlaw.ca
Colleen Yamashita, Construction Law
cyamashita@shlaw.ca

SimpsonWigle LAW LLP
#200 1 Hunter Street East, Hamilton ON L8N 3R1
905-528-8411 905-528-9008 800-464-4414
info@simpsonwigle.com
www.simpsonwigle.com
Profile: 18 Lawyers, Founded in: 1986
Environmental Lawyers:
Timothy Bullock, Managing Partner, Construction Law ext. 354
bullockt@simpsonwigle.com
Brian J. Decaire, Construction Law ext. 337
decaireb@simpsonwigle.com
Catherine A. Olsiak, Health Law ext. 362
olsiakc@simpsonwigle.com
Derek A. Schmuck, Partner, Construction Law ext. 353
schmuck@simpsonwigle.com

Thoman Soule LLP, Lawyers
P.O Box 187 LCD 146 Jackson St. East, Hamilton ON L8N 3C5
905-529-8195 905-529-7906
info@thomansoule.com
www.thomansoule.com
Profile: 1 Offices, 6 Lawyers, Founded in: 1930
Environmental Lawyers:
Frederick E. Leitch, Environmental assessment advocacy; Administrative law litigation; Municipal advocacy
fleitch@thomansoule.com

Turkstra Mazza Associates
15 Bold St., Hamilton ON L8P 1T3
905-529-3476 905-529-3663
Profile: 1 Offices, 6 Lawyers, Founded in: 1977
Environmental Lawyers:
Herman Turkstra, Partner, Environmental Law
hturkstra@tmalaw.ca

Kanata

Gowling Lafleur Henderson LLP - Kanata
#740 Tower B 555 Legget Dr., Kanata ON K2K 2X3 Canada
613-233-1781 613-591-0249
www.gowlings.com
Profile: 3 Lawyers
Environmental Lawyers:

Kingston

Cunningham, Swan, Carty, Little & Bonham LLP
#201, City Place II 1473 John Counter Blvd., Kingston ON K7M 8Z6
613-544-0211 613-542-9814
info@cswan.com
www.cswan.com
Profile: 1 Offices, 18 Lawyers, Founded in: 1988
Municipal Law; Land Use Planning; Health Law
Environmental Lawyers:
Roy B. Conacher, Q.C., Planning & Development
613-544-7030
rconacher@cswan.com
R.A. Little, Q.C., Municipal Law; Health Law
613-546-8070
rlittle@cswan.com
R.P. Tchegus, Planning & Development
613-546-8073
rtchegus@cswan.com
T.J. Wilkin, Planning & Development; Municipal Law
613-546-8074
twilkin@cswan.com

Hicks Morley Hamilton Stewart Storie LLP
#310, 366 King St. East, Kingston ON K7K 6Y3
613-549-6353 613-549-4068
www.hicksmorley.com
Profile: 5 Offices, 4 Lawyers, Founded in: 1972
Environmental practice areas include occupational health.
Environmental Lawyers:
Kees W. Kort, Municipal Law
kees-kort@hicksmorley.com
Vince M. Panetta, Municipal Law; Construction
vince-panetta@hicksmorley.com
D. Alan Whyte, Municipal Law
alan-whyte@hicksmorley.com

Nelligan O'Brien Payne
#202, The Woolen Mill 4 Cataraqui St., Kingston ON K7K 1Z7
613-531-7905 613-531-0857 888-565-9912
info@nelligan.ca
www.nelligan.ca
Profile: 4 Offices, 46 Lawyers
Environmental Lawyers:

Kitchener

Madorin, Snyder LLP
P.O Box 1234 C55 King St. West, Kitchener ON N2G 4G9
519-744-4491 519-741-8060
reception@kw-law.com
www.kw-law.com
Profile: 1 Offices, 18 Lawyers, Founded in: 1950
Environmental Lawyers:
W.H.P. Madorin, Q.C., Managing Partner, Environmental law
whpm@kw-law.com
Leanne E. Way, Municipal law
lew@kw-law.com

London

Cohen Highley LLP
One London Pl. 255 Queens Ave., 11th Fl., London ON N6A 5R8
519-672-9330 519-672-5960
hall@cohenhighley.com
www.cohenhighley.com
Profile: 3 Offices, 22 Lawyers, Founded in: 1974
Environmental; Energy; Native
Environmental Lawyers:
Paul G. Vogel
vogel@cohenhighley.com

Hicks Morley Hamilton Stewart Storie LLP
#1608, 148 Fullerton St., London ON N6A 5P3
519-433-7515 519-433-8827
www.hicksmorley.com
Profile: 5 Offices, 5 Lawyers,
Environmental areas of practice include workplace safety & insurance.
Environmental Lawyers:

McKenzie Lake Lawyers LLP
300 Dundas St., London ON N6B 1T6
519-672-5666 519-672-2674
info@mckenzielake.com
www.mckenzielake.com
Profile: 1 Offices, 35 Lawyers, Founded in: 1988
McKenzie Lake Lawyers LLP has expertise in the area of land development,.
Environmental Lawyers:
Cézanne M. Charlebois, Occupational health & safety; Administrative law
519-672-5666 ext. 391
Charlebois@mckenzielake.com
Diane Chick, Administrative law
519-672-5666 ext. 363
chick@mckenzielake.com
Kevin A. Egan, Administrative law; Workplace safety
519-672-5666 ext. 315
egan@mckenzielake.com
G. Mort Glanville, Q.C., Land development
519-672-5666 ext. 338
glanville@mckenzielake.com
Lisa Kwasek, Administrative law
519-672-5666 ext. 342
kwasek@mckenzielake.com
Stuart R. Mackay, Administrative law
519-672-5666 ext. 326
mackay@mckenzielake.com
David R. Nash, Administrative law
519-672-5666 ext. 347
nash@mckenzielake.com
Sandra E. Van Ymeren, Land development
519-672-5666 ext. 327
vanymeren@mckenzielake.com

Patton Cormier & Associates
#1512, 140 Fullarton St., London ON N6A 5P2
519-432-8282 519-432-7285
apatton@pattoncormier.ca
Profile: 1 Offices, 4 Lawyers
Environmental Lawyers:
Elizabeth Cormier, Municipal
Alan R. Patton, Municipal

Siskind, Cromarty, Ivey & Dowler LLP
P.O Box 2520 680 Waterloo St., London ON N6A 3V8
519-672-2121 519-672-6065 877-672-2121
info@siskinds.com
www.siskinds.com
Profile: 5 Offices, 65 Lawyers, Founded in: 1933
Defend, prosecute under the Environmental Protection Act; expertise in Building Code Act applications involving environmental issues, obtaining waste related approvals & providing advice on maintaining compliance & handling waste disposal issues for industrial & municipal clients
Environmental Lawyers:
Paula Lombardi
519-660-7850
paula.lombardi@siskinds.com
Andrew Wright
519-660-7751
andrew.wright@siskinds.com

Markham

Miller Thomson LLP - Markham
#600 60 Columbia Way, Markham ON L3R 0C9
905-415-6700 905-415-6777 866-348-2432
markham@millerthomson.com
www.millerthomson.com
Profile: 13 Lawyers, Founded in: 1957
Aboriginal Law; Energy Law; Municipal & Planning; Oil & Gas; Construction; Forestry
Environmental Lawyers:
Roderick M. McLeod, Q.C., Environmental Law; Policy
905-415-6707
rmcleod@millerthomson.com

Law Firms / Ontario

J. Bruce McMeekin, Municipal; Environmental Law; Regulations
905-415-6791
bmcmeekin@millerthomson.com
John R. Tidball, Environmental Law; Waste Management
905-415-6710
jtidball@millerthomson.com

Niagara Falls

Martin Sheppard Fraser LLP
P.O Box 900 4701 St. Clair Ave., 2nd Fl., Niagara Falls ON L2E 6V7
905-354-1611 905-354-5540 800-263-2502
lawyers@martinshep.com
www.martinshep.com
Profile: 2 Offices, 13 Lawyers, Founded in: 1887
Environmental Lawyers:
Andrew J. Larmand, Health
larmand@martinshep.com

Oakville

O'Connor MacLeod Hanna LLP
700 Kerr St., Oakville ON L6K 3W5
905-842-8030 905-842-2460
info@omh.ca
www.omh.ca
Profile: 1 Offices, 20 Lawyers, Founded in: 1991
Advises & represents both public & private sector clients on a full range of Municipal, Environmental & Administrative Law issues
Environmental Lawyers:
Andrew C. Knox, Q.C., Municipal & Land Development
905-849-5010
knox@omh.ca
James McAskill, Municipal & Land Use
905-842-8030 ext. 3304
mcaskill@omh.ca
Blair S. Taylor, Municipal; Administration
905-842-8030 ext. 3352
taylor@omh.ca
Harold R. Watson, Municipal; Land Use
905-849-5016
watson@omh.ca
Kenneth W. Watts, Construction
905-842-8030 ext. 3361
watts@omh.ca
Kelly G. Yerxa, Municipal Planning; Land Use
905-842-8030 ext. 3345
yerxa@omh.ca

Orillia

Russell Christie LLP
P.O Box 158 505 Memorial Ave., Orillia ON L3V 6J3
705-325-1326 705-327-1811
rcmkw@russellchristie.com
Profile: 1 Offices, 7 Lawyers, Founded in: 1960
Environmental Lawyers:
Douglas S. Christie
dchristie@russellchristie.com
William S. Koughan
bkoughan@russellchristie.com
Wharton D. Russell, Q.C.
wdrussell@russellchristie.com

Orléans

Riopelle Griener Professional Corporation
2888 St. Joseph Blvd., Orléans ON K1C 1G7
613-834-4800 613-834-4828 877-834-4855
www.rglaw.ca
Profile: 2 Offices, 2 Lawyers, Founded in: 2005
Environmental Lawyers:
Robert M. Riopelle, Municipal law; Administrative law
613-834-4800
robert@rglaw.ca

Ottawa

Beament Green
979 Wellington Ave., Ottawa ON K1Y 2X7
613-241-3400 613-241-8555
info@beament.com
www.beament.com

Profile: 1 Offices, 6 Lawyers,
Our litigators have created significant legal precedents affecting all parties in the evolving area of environmental law; our experience in all aspects of environmental law allows us to provide practical & effective representation for our clients dealing with environmental authorities or consultants; we provide unparalleled representation of our clients in the prosecution or defence of land contamination issues
Environmental Lawyers:
Michael S. Hebert
mhebert@beament.com

Borden Ladner Gervais LLP - Ottawa
#1100 World Exchange Plaza 100 Queen St., Ottawa ON K1P 1J9
613-237-5160 613-230-8842
info@blg.com
www.blg.com
Profile: 93 Lawyers
Environmental Lawyers:
Janet Bradley, Environmental Law; Municipal Law
613-787-3749
jbradley@blg.com
Fay K. Brunning, Health Law
613-787-3504
fbrunning@blg.com
J.Bruce Carr-Harris, Construction & Engineering
613-787-3505
bcarr-harris@blg.com
Peter K. Doody, Environmental Law; Aboriginal
613-787-3510
pdoody@blg.com
Marc Jolicoeur, Forestry Law
613-787-3515
mjolicoeur@blg.com
Timothy J. McCunn, Biotech & Pharmaceutical
613-787-3532
tmccunn@blg.com
Peter C.P. Thompson, Q.C., Electricity Markets; Oil & Gas
613-787-3528
pthompson@blg.com

Brazeau Seller LLP
#750, 55 Metcalfe St., Ottawa ON K1P 6L5
613-237-4000 613-237-4001
www.brazeauseller.com
Profile: 1 Offices, 17 Lawyers, Founded in: 1989
Environmental Lawyers:
Frederick Cogan, Q.C., Counsel, Municipal Law
613-237-4000 ext. 251
fcogan@brazeauseller.com

Fraser Milner Casgrain LLP - Ottawa
#1420, 99 Bank St., Ottawa ON K1P 1H4
613-783-9611 613-783-9690 Telex: 06-219825 FRASB
tom.houston@fmc-law.com
www.fmc-law.com
Profile: 25 Lawyers
Environmental Lawyers:
John F. Blakney, Environmental Law; Transportation; Health
613-783-9602
john.blakney@fmc-law.com
Susan H. Brown, Environmental Law
613-783-9658
susan.brown@fmc-law.com
Philip M. Rimer, Aboriginal Law; Infrastructure & Construction Matters; Property Development; Land Use Planning
613-783-9634
philip.rimer@fmc-law.com

Good, Donald R.
Merivale Depot P.O Box 5118, Ottawa ON K2C 3H4
613-228-9676 613-228-7404 800-661-8837
farmlaw@on.aibn.com
Profile: 2 Offices, 2 Lawyers, Founded in: 1981
Environmental Lawyers:
Donald R. Good, Agriculture; Emergency Response; Environmental Impact Assessment; Environmental Permits & Regulation Standards

Heenan Blaikie LLP - Ottawa
#300 55 Metcalfe St., Ottawa ON K1P 6L5
613-236-1668 613-236-9632
www.heenanblaikie.com
Profile: 36 Lawyers
Environmental Lawyers:

Justin Bertrand, Construction Litigation
613-236-1627
jbertrand@heenan.ca
Pierre Champagne, Partner, Construction Litigation
613-236-4859
pchampagne@heenan.ca
Benoit M. Duchesne, Partner, Construction Litigation; Aboriginal Law
613-236-1946
bduchesne@heenan.ca
Justin R. Fogarty, Counsel, Construction
613-236-1668
jfogarty@heenan.ca
Louis-Pierre Grégoire, Construction Litigation
613-236-1751
lpgregoire@heenan.ca
Kevin D. MacNeill, Partner, Occupational Health & Safety
613-236-1668
kmacneill@heenan.ca
Peter Mantas, Partner, Environmental Law
613-237-1733
pmantas@heenan.ca
Dan Palayew, Partner, Occupational Health & Safety
613-236-6970
dpalayew@heenan.ca
Jeff Saikaley, Construction Litigation
613-236-1629
jsaikaley@heenan.ca
Marc Sauvé, Construction Litigation
613-236-6945
msauve@heenan.ca
Julie Thibault, Occupational Health & Safety
613-236-2161
juthibault@heenan.ca
Ivan G. Whitehall, Q.C., Counsel, Construction Litigation; Aboriginal Law
613-236-1696
iwhitehall@heenan.ca

Hicks Morley Hamilton Stewart Storie LLP
#2000, 150 Metcalfe St., Ottawa ON K2P 1P1
613-234-0386 613-234-0418
www.hicksmorley.com
Profile: 5 Offices, 9 Lawyers,
Environmental practice areas include occupational health & workplace safety & insurance.
Environmental Lawyers:

Lang Michener LLP - Ottawa
#300, 50 O'Connor St., Ottawa ON K1P 6L2
613-232-7171 613-231-3191
mrankin@langmichener.ca (M. Rankin, Office Managing Partner)
www.langmichener.ca
Profile: 3 Offices, 30 Lawyers, Founded in: 1984
Lang Michener LLP assists organizations with legal issues related to the environment & energy, through its Environment, Energy & Emissions Trading Group. The lawyers at Lang Michener also provide legal advice to the aviation, rail, & marine industries, the Canadian & international mining & natural resource industry & to the forestry & paper products industry.
Environmental Lawyers:
David Debenham, Environmental law
C.J. Michael Flavell, Q.C., Forestry; Transportation & logistics (marine, aviation, & rail)
John G.M. Hooper, Q.C., Health care & life sciences
Marie-France Major, Mining & natural resources
Martin G. Masse, Forestry
Eugene Meehan, Q.C., Forestry; Transportation & logistics (marine, aviation, & rail)
Terry W. Peterman, Mining & natural resources

Lavery, de Billy - Ottawa
#1810, 360 Albert St., Ottawa ON K1R 7X7
613-594-4936 613-594-8783
www.laverydebilly.com
Profile: 5 Lawyers, Founded in: 1913
Environmental Lawyers:
Jacques Y. Desjardins, Partner, Construction & Surety Law
613-560-2522
jdesjardins@lavery.ca
Mélanie Vadeboncoeur, Construction & Surety Law
613-560-2528
mvadeboncoeur@lavery.ca

McCarthy Tétrault LLP - Ottawa
#1400, The Chambers 40 Elgin St., Ottawa ON K1P 5K6

Law Firms / Ontario

613-238-2000 613-563-9386
ottawa@mccarthy.ca
www.mccarthy.ca
Profile: 7 Offices, 14 Lawyers,
Municipal; Environmental; Biotechnology; Energy
Environmental Lawyers:
Robert D. Chapman, Biotechnology
   613-238-2111
   rchapman@mccarthy.ca
Anna M. Tosto, Energy
   613-238-2167
   atosto@mccarthy.ca

Nelligan O'Brien Payne
#1500, 50 O'Connor St., Ottawa ON K1P 6L2
613-238-8080 613-238-2098 888-565-9912
info@nelligan.ca
www.nelligan.ca
Profile: 4 Offices, 46 Lawyers
Environmental Lawyers:
Deborah A. Bellinger, Environmental Law
   debbie.bellinger@nelligan.ca
Geoffrey Cantello, Municipal law
   geoffrey.cantello@nelligan.ca
Colin Dubeau, Municipal law
   colin.dubeau@nelligan.ca
Suzanne M. Farag, Municipal law
   suzanne.farag@nelligan.ca
John Nelligan, Q.C., LSM, D.U., Municipal law
   john.nelligan@nelligan.ca
Allan R. O'Brien, Municipal law
   allan.obrien@nelligan.ca
David R. Shelly, Municipal law
   david.shelly@nelligan.ca

Ogilvy Renault LLP/S.E.N.C.R.L., s.r.l. - Ottawa
#1500 45 O'Connor St., Ottawa ON K1P 1A4
613-780-8661 613-230-5459
ottawa@ogilvyrenault.com
www.ogilvyrenault.com
Profile: 39 Lawyers
Environmental Lawyers:
Mary J. Gleason, Partner, Occupational Health & Safety
   613-780-8635
   mgleason@ogilvyrenault.com
Sally A. Gomery, Partner, Construction; Engineering
   613-780-8604
   sgomery@ogilvyrenault.com
Matthew J. Halpin, Partner, Environmental Litigation
   613-780-8654
   mhalpin@ogilvyrenault.com
Martha A. Healey, Partner, Life Sciences; Health
   613-780-8638
   mhealey@ogilvyrenault.com
Pierre-Paul Henrie, Partner, Cleantech
   613-780-3777
   phenrie@ogilvyrenault.com
Tina H. Hill, Construction; Engineering
   613-780-1550
   thill@ogilvyrenault.com
Charles E. Hurdon, Partner, Occupational Health & Safety
   613-780-8653
   churdon@ogilvyrenault.com
Grant A. Jameson, Senior Partner, Cleantech; Life Sciences
   613-780-1530
   gjameson@ogilvyrenault.com
Dan J. Leduc, Partner, Construction Law; Engineering
   613-230-5459
   djleduc@ogilvyrenault.com
Norman B. Lieff, Senior Partner, Cleantech; Mining & Resources
   613-780-8611
   nlieff@ogilvyrenault.com
D. John Naccarato, Senior Partner, Cleantech; Construction Law; Mining & Resources
   613-780-8608
   jnaccarato@ogilvyrenault.com
Andrew Pritchard, Senior Partner, Energy
   613-780-8607
   apritchard@ogilvyrenault.com
Ned A. Steinman, Partner, Mining & Resources
   613-780-8692
   nsteinman@ogilvyrenault.com
Todd Storms, Construction Law
   613-780-3766
   tstorms@ogilvyrenault.com

Perley-Robertson, Hill & McDougall LLP
#1400, 340 Albert St., Ottawa ON K1R 0A5
613-238-2022 613-238-8775 800-268-8292
lawyers@perlaw.ca
www.perlaw.ca
Profile: 1 Offices, 36 Lawyers, Founded in: 1971
Environmental Lawyers:
Lynda A. Bordeleau
   613-566-2847
   lbordeleau@perlaw.ca
Joshua P. Moon
   613-566-2801
   jmoon@perlaw.ca

Rick & Associates
#109 591 March Rd., Ottawa ON K2K 2M5
613-592-0088 613-592-3322
info@rickassociates.com
www.rickassociates.com
Profile: 2 Offices, 3 Lawyers, Founded in: 1993
A second office is located at 359 Ottawa St., Almonte, ON, 613-256-3480.
Environmental Lawyers:
W. John Rick, Managing Partner, Environmental Law
   jrick@rickassociates.com

Soloway, Wright LLP
#900, 427 Laurier Ave. West, Ottawa ON K1R 7Y2
613-236-0111 613-238-8507 800-207-5880
info@solowaywright.com
www.solowaywright.com
Profile: 2 Offices, 21 Lawyers, Founded in: 1946
Environmental Lawyers:
Alan K. Cohen, Municipal Law
   613-782-3217
   cohena@solowaywright.com
Donna M. Crabtree, Litigation Law
   613-782-3223
   dcrabtree@solowaywright.com
Douglas B. Kelly, Municipal Law
   613-782-3215
   kellyd@solowaywright.com
Paull N. Leamen, Litigation
   613-782-3233
   leamenp@solowaywright.com
Kenneth M. Wright, Litigation
   613-782-3231
   wrightk@solowaywright.com

Stikeman Elliott LLP - Ottawa
#1600, 50 O'Connor St., Ottawa ON K1P 6L2
613-234-4555 613-230-8877 877-776-2263
www.stikeman.com
Profile: 13 Lawyers, Founded in: 1981
Environmental Lawyers:
Susan M. Hutton, Partner, Pharmaceuticals, Biotechnology & Life Sciences; Construction Litigation; Energy; Forestry & Forest Products; Mining
   613-566-0530
   shutton@stikeman.com
T. Gregory Kane, Q.C., Partner, Renewable Energy
   613-566-0524
   gkane@stikeman.com
Stuart C. McCormack, Managing Partner, Pharmaceuticals, Biotechnology & Life Sciences
   613-566-0526
   smccormack@stikeman.com
Nicholas P. McHaffie, Partner, Environmental Litigation; Pharmaceuticals, Biotechnology & Life Sciences
   613-566-0546
   nmchaffie@stikeman.com

Perth

Anderson, Greg W.. Barrister, Solicitor, Notary
10 Market Sq., Perth ON K7H 1V7
613-267-9898 613-267-2741
greg@greganderson.ca
www.greganderson.ca
Profile: 1 Offices, 1 Lawyers
Environmental Lawyers:
Greg W. Anderson, B.A., J.D., Municipal law

Smith, Kenneth W., Barrister & Solicitor
P.O Box 157 27 Foster St., Perth ON K7H 3E3
613-267-5910 613-264-0789
kenwsmith@on.aibn.com
www.kennethwsmith.com
Profile: 1 Offices, 1 Lawyers, Founded in: 1979
Environmental Lawyers:

Peterborough

Howell Fleming LLP
P.O Box 148 415 Water St., Peterborough ON K9J 6Y5
705-745-1361 705-745-6220
lkulatungam@howellfleming.com
www.howellfleming.com
Profile: 1 Offices, 10 Lawyers, Founded in: 1881
The firm is engaged in the practice of municipal, planning, & environment law.
Environmental Lawyers:
M. John Ewart, Municipal
   jewart@howellfleming.com
Gavin R. Muir, Municipal
   gmuir@howellfleming.com
Robert E. Pakenham, Municipal
   rpakenham@howellfleming.com

Linda Willcox Whetung Professional Corporation
521 George St. North, Peterborough ON K9J 6Y5
705-743-6470 705-743-3128
linda@lindawhetung.com
www.lindawhetung.com
Profile: 1 Offices, 1 Lawyers, Founded in: 1936
Environmental Lawyers:
Linda Louise Willcox Whetung, Municipal law

Sault Ste Marie

Wishart Law Firm LLP
#500, 390 Bay St., Sault Ste Marie ON P6A 1X2
705-949-6700 705-949-2465
wishart@wishartlaw.com
www.wishartlaw.com
Profile: 2 Offices, 6 Lawyers, Founded in: 1975
Environmental Lawyers:
Gordon P. Acton
Orlando M. Rosa, Petroleum Outlets; Railways; Federal & Provincial Environmental Legislation
   orosa@wishartlaw.com

Simcoe

Cline, Backus, Nightingale & McArthur, LLP
P.O Box 528 Main39 Colborne St. North, Simcoe ON N3Y 4N5
519-426-6763 519-426-2055
cbnmlaw@kwic.com
www.clinebackus.com
Profile: 1 Offices, 8 Lawyers, Founded in: 1963
Environmental Lawyers:
Thomas A. Cline, Q.C., Municipal Law; Land Use Planning; Environmental municipal assessment
   cline@clinebackus.com

Smiths Falls

Howard Ryan Kelford Knott & Dixon, Barristers & Solicitors
2 Main St. East, Smiths Falls ON K7A 1A2
613-283-6772 613-283-8840 888-852-5175
lthompson@smithsfallslaw.ca
www.smithsfallslaw.ca
Profile: 2 Offices, 5 Lawyers, Founded in: 1976
The firm is engaged in the practice of municipal law.
Environmental Lawyers:
Paul T. Howard, Land development; Municipal law
Shane A. Kelford, Municipal law

St Catharines

Chown, Cairns LLP
P.O Box 760 80 King St., St Catharines ON L2R 6Y8
905-688-4500 905-688-0015
lawyers@chowlaw.com
www.chownlaw.com
Profile: 1 Offices, 17 Lawyers
Environmental Lawyers:
B.A. Banfield
D.M. Kerr, Offences

Law Firms / Ontario

G.G. Parker

Daniel & Partners LLP
Dominion Bldg. P.O Box 24022 39 Queen St., St Catharines ON L2R 7P7
905-688-9411 905-688-5747 800-263-3650
lawyers@niagaralaw.ca
Profile: 1 Offices, 9 Lawyers, Founded in: 1922
Environmental Lawyers:
Harry J. Daniel, Q.C.
 danielh@dwlaw.net

Heelis, Williams, Little & Almas LLP, Barristers & Solicitors
P.O Box 1056 14 Church St., St Catharines ON L2R 7A3
905-687-8200 905-684-4844
rwilliam@14churchstlawoffice.com
www.14churchstlawoffice.com
Profile: 1 Offices, 6 Lawyers, Founded in: 1976
Environmental Lawyers:
H.A. Patrick (Pat) Little, Administrative law; Municipal law
 plittle@14churchstlawoffice.com
Joseph C. McCallum, Administrative law
 jmccallum@14churchstlawoffice.com

Sudbury

Weaver, Simmons LLP
#400, 233 Brady Street, Sudbury ON P3B 4H5
705-674-6421 705-674-9948
thefirm@weaversimmons.com
www.weaversimmons.com
Profile: 34 Lawyers, Founded in: 1931
Environmental Lawyers:
Peter Archambault, Municipal Law
 705-671-3292
 pjarchambault@weaversimmons.com
R. Martin Bayer, Aboriginal Law
 705-671-3286
 rmbayer@weaversimmons.com
Harold P. Beaudry, Q.C., Counsel, Transportation
 705-671-3270
 hpbeaudry@weaversimmons.com
Jack Braithwaite, Counsel
 705-671-3288
 jbraithwaite@weaversimmons.com
Geoff Jeffery, Occupational Health & Safety
 705-671-3269
 gjeffery@weaversimmons.com
P. Berk Keaney
 705-671-3296
 pbkeaney@weaversimmons.com
Andrew M. Little, Natural Resources Law; Mining
 705-671-3291
 amlittle@weaversimmons.com
Steve S. Moutsatsos, Occupational Health & Safety; Aboriginal Law; Natural Resources Law; Mining
 705-671-3290
 ssmoutsatsos@weaversimmons.com
James C. Simmons, Q.C.
 705-671-3299
 jcsimmons@weaversimmons.com
Daniel C. Sirois, Occupational Health & Safety
 705-671-3287
 dcsirois@weaversimmons.com

Thornhill

Burlew, Edward L.
16 John St., Thornhill ON L3T 1X8
905-882-2422 905-882-2431 888-486-5677
Profile: 1 Offices, 1 Lawyers, Founded in: 1979
Environmental Lawyers:
Edward L. Burlew

Thunder Bay

Erickson & Partners
291 South Court St., Thunder Bay ON P7B 2Y1
807-345-1213 807-345-2526 800-465-3912
Profile: 1 Offices, 8 Lawyers
Environmental Lawyers:
John W. Erickson, Q.C.

Weiler, Maloney, Nelson
#201, 1001 William St., Thunder Bay ON P7B 6M1
807-623-1111 807-623-4947
weilers@wmnlaw.com
www.weilers.ca
Profile: 1 Offices, 11 Lawyers, Founded in: 1946
Environmental Lawyers:
Brian A. Babcock, Partner, Municipal law
 bbabcock@wmnlaw.com
Ross Judge, Counsel, Municipal law; Aboriginal law
 rjudge@wmnlaw.com
Bradley A. Smith, Partner, Aboriginal Law
 basmith@wmnlaw.com

Timmins

Riopelle Griener Professional Corporation
#202, 85 Pine St. South, Timmins ON P4N 2K1
705-264-9591 705-264-1393 866-624-1614
www.rglaw.ca
Profile: 2 Offices, 6 Lawyers, Founded in: 2005
Environmental Lawyers:
Joshua Bond, Municipal law; Administrative law
 705-264-9591
 josh@rglaw.ca
Gordon G. Conley, Municipal law; Administrative law
 705-264-9591
 gordon@rglaw.ca

Toronto

Aird & Berlis LLP
1800 Brookfield Place Box 754 181 Bay St., Toronto ON M5J 2T9 Canada
416-863-1500 416-863-1515
www.airdberlis.com
Profile: 130 Lawyers, Founded in: 1919
Legal services in the areas of Energy Law, Environmental Law, Municipal Law & Land Use Planning
Environmental Lawyers:
Fred D. Cass, Energy Law; Regulatory & Compliance; Electricity Industry; Oil & Gas Industry
 416-865-7742
 fcassl@airdberlis.com
Ron Clark, Energy Law; Electricity Industry
 416-865-7701
 rclark@airdberlis.com
Ken Clark, Energy Law
 416-865-4736
 kclark@airdberlis.com
Thomas A. Fenton, Energy Law; Natural Resources Law
 416-865-4631
 tfenton@airdberlis.com
Patricia A. Foran, Municipal & Land Use Planning
 416-865-3425
 pforan@airdberlis.com
Donald B. Johnston, Natural Resources Practice; Renewable Fuel Industry
 416-865-3072
 djohnston@airdberlis.com
Dennis M. O'Leary, Energy Law; Environmental Law; Transportation Law; Regulatory & Compliance; Electricity Industry; Landfills & Waste Facilities Matters; Environmental Assessment Matters; Transport of Dangerous Goods Matters
 416-865-4711
 doleary@airdberlis.com
Scott Stoll, Energy Law; Environmental Law; First Nations Practice; Infrastructure Practice; Electricity Industry; Natural Gas Industry; Regulatory & Compliance; Environmental Assessment Matters; Land Remediation Matters
 416-865-4703
 sstoll@airdberlis.com

Baker & McKenzie LLP
#2100, Brookfield Place P.O Box 874 181 Bay St., Toronto ON M5J 2T3
416-863-1221 416-863-6275
www.bakernet.com
Profile: 2 Offices, 51 Lawyers, Founded in: 1959
Advising on the restoration of contaminated properties; compliance with environmental laws; the development of training requirements & procedure when handling hazardous substances; officer & director liability; corporate/commercial transactions with environmental implications; environmental litigation matters; ISO 14001 registration & certification; branches in 30 foreign countries
Environmental Lawyers:
Jonathan Cocker
 416-865-6968
 jonathan.d.cocker@bakernet.com

Birchall Northey
533 College Street, Toronto ON M6G 1A8
416-860-1212 416-860-1827
admin@birchallnorthey.com
www.birchallnorthey.com
Profile: 2 Offices, 2 Lawyers, Founded in: 1997
Environmental Lawyers:
Rodney V. Northey
 416-860-1412
 bnrn@learned.com

Blake, Cassels & Graydon LLP - Toronto
#4000, Commerce Court West 199 Bay St., Toronto ON M5L 1A9
416-863-2400 416-863-2653 Telex: 06-219687
toronto@blakes.com
www.blakes.com
Profile: 12 Offices, 550 Lawyers, Founded in: 1856
Blake's environmental lawyers appear before all levels of Canadian courts & tribunals; they have been involved in the establishing of municipal landfill operations, the import, export & disposal of hazardous substances, mineral aggregate extraction, the redevelopment of old industrial lands, & major construction projects in the oil & gas, electrical power & telecommunications sectors; the group regularly defends corporations, municipalities & individuals charged with environmental offences; prosecutes & defends claims respecting the escape of dangerous substances, noise & odour nuisances, insurance coverage for environmental damage, & professional negligence concerning environmental & engineering consulting services
Environmental Lawyers:
Tim W. Bermingham, Municipal & Planning; Environmental; Litigation & Dispute Resolution; CleanTech; Land Use Law; Water Law
 416-863-2946
 tim.bermingham@blakes.com
Ted Betts, CleanTech
 416-863-4198
 ted.betts@blakes.com
Richard Corley, CleanTech; Energy
 416-863-2183
 richard.corley@blakes.com
Robert M. Fishlock, Environmental; Litigation & Dispute Resolution; CleanTech
 416-863-2904
 robert.fishlock@blakes.com
Ben A. Jetten, Litigation & Dispute Resolution; Aboriginal Law; Environmental; Communications; Municipal & Planning
 416-863-2938
 ben.jetten@blakes.com
Jonathan W. Kahn, Environmental; Municipal & Planning; Litigation & Dispute Resolution; CleanTech; Agribusiness & Food
 416-863-3868
 jonathan.kahn@blakes.com
Glenn F. Leslie, Partner & General Counsel, Energy
 416-863-2672
 glenn.leslie@blakes.com
Kate McGilvray, Energy
 416-863-2243
 kate.mcgilvray@blakes.com
Mario Nigro, Energy
 416-863-2537
 mario.nigro@blakes.com
David O'Brien, Environmental
 416-863-2917
 david.obrien@blakes.com
R. Kenneth S. Pearce, Energy
 416-863-3286
 kenneth.pearce@blakes.com
André B. Perey, CleanTech
 416-863-2291
 andre.perey@blakes.com
Bryson A. Stokes, Energy; Oil & Gas
 416-863-2179
 bryson.stokes@blakes.com
Gerald S. Swinkin, Municipal & Planning; Environmental; Real Estate

416-863-5845
 gerald.swinkin@blakes.com
Lauren Temple, CleanTech
 416-863-3179
 lauren.temple@blakes.com
Judy L. Wilson, Environmental
 416-863-5820
 judy.wilson@blakes.com
Sharon Wong, Energy; CleanTech; Regulatory
 416-863-4178
 sharon.wong@blakes.com
Leslie Wong, Energy
 416-863-4323
 leslie.wong@blakes.com

Blaney McMurtry LLP
#1500, 2 Queen St. East, Toronto ON M5C 3G5
416-593-1221 416-593-5437 Telex: 06-22326
info@blaney.com
www.blaney.com
Profile: 1 Offices, 108 Lawyers, Founded in: 1954
Environmental Lawyers:
Timothy P. Alexander, Construction; Engineering Services
 416-593-3900
 talexander@blaney.com
Geza R. Banfai, Construction; Engineering Services
 416-593-3904
 gbanfai@blaney.com
Joanna Carroll, Construction; Engineering Services
 416-593-3911
 jcarroll@blaney.com
Dominic T. Clarke, Aboriginal
 416-593-3968
 dclarke@blaney.com
Chris Ellis, Construction; Engineering Services
 416-593-3954
 cellis@blaney.com
Elizabeth J. Forster, Construction; Engineering Services
 416-593-3919
 eforster@blaney.com
Jeffery L. Freelan, Municipal; Environmental
 416-593-3921
 jfreelan@blaney.com
Louis-Pierre Gregoire, Construction; Engineering Services
 416-593-3941
 lgregoir@blaney.com
Andrew J. Heal, Construction; Engineering Services; Municipal; Environmental
 416-593-3934
 aheal@blaney.com
Michele A. Hecke, Construction; Engineering Services
 416-593-3935
 mhecke@blaney.com
Roger Horst, Aboriginal
 416-593-3938
 rhorst@blaney.com
Steven P. Jeffery, Municipal; Environmental
 416-593-3939
 sjeffery@blaney.com
Chad Kopach, Construction; Engineering Services
 416-593-2985
 ckopach@blaney.com
Tanya Litzenberger, Construction; Engineering Services
 416-593-2954
 tlitzenberger@blaney.com
William R. McMurtry, Q.C., Aboriginal
 416-593-3948
 bmcmurtry@blaney.com
Robert Muir, Construction; Engineering Services
 416-593-3951
 rmuir@blaney.com
Robert J. Potts, Aboriginal
 416-593-3952
 bpotts@blaney.com
Maria Scarfo
 mscarfo@blaney.com
Robert C. Taylor, Construction; Engineering Services
 416-593-2957
 rtaylor@blaney.com
Brett J. Tkatch, Municipal; Environmental
 416-593-3969
 btkatch@blaney.com
David S. Wilson, Construction; Engineering Services; Municipal; Environmental
 416-593-3970
 dwilson@blaney.com

Roderick S.W. Winsor
 rwinsor@blaney.com

Borden Ladner Gervais LLP - Toronto
Scotia Plaza 40 King St. West, 44th Fl., Toronto ON M5H 3Y4
416-367-6000 416-367-6749 Telex: 0622687 Betor
info@blg.com
www.blg.com
Profile: 6 Offices, 750 Lawyers, Founded in: 1936
Environmental Lawyers:
Matthew R. Alter, Partner, Construction Litigation
 416-367-6196
 malter@blg.com
Edward A. Ayers, Q.C., Partner, Construction Law
 416-367-6153
 eayers@blg.com
Denise L. Bambrough, Partner, Construction Law
 416-367-6008
 dbambrough@blg.com
Michel Beaumier, Environmental Law
 416-367-6265
 mbeaumier@blg.com
Keri E.D. Bedeau, Construction Law
 416-367-6001
 kbedeau@blg.com
Daniel A. Boan, Partner, Construction Law
 416-367-6665
 dboan@blg.com
Barry H. Bresner, Senior Partner, Environmental Litigation
 416-367-6167
 bbresner@blg.com
Daniel Brinza, Environment; Health Law; Renewable Energy; Biotechnology Issues
 416-367-6634
 dbrinza@blg.com
Katherine L. Byrick, Partner, Health Law
 416-367-6012
 kbyrick@blg.com
Lisa C. Cabel, Health & Safety
 416-367-6217
 lcabel@blg.com
William D.T. Carter, Senior Partner, Health Law Litigation
 416-367-6173
 wcarter@blg.com
Adam Chamberlain, Partner, Climate Change; Resources & Environmental Law; Forestry Law
 416-367-6172
 achamberlain@blg.com
Cynthia D. Clarke, Health Law
 416-367-6203
 cclarke@blg.com
Simon A. Clements, Partner, Health Law
 416-367-6130
 sclements@blg.com
Rick F. Coburn, Partner, Environmental Law; Land Planning
 416-367-6038
 rcoburn@blg.com
Bernadette Corpuz, Energy
 416-367-6747
 bcorpuz@blg.com
Kate Crawford, Health Law
 416-367-6729
 kcrawford@blg.com
Domenic Damiani, Partner, Energy
 416-367-6030
 ddamiani@blg.com
M. Jeffrey Dermer, Partner, Construction; Biotech & Pharmaceutical
 416-367-6182
 jdermer@blg.com
Dolores Di Felice, Partner, Mining
 416-367-6128
 ddifelice@blg.com
Heather Douglas, Partner, Health Services
 416-361-6177
 hdouglas@blg.com
Eric J. Dufour, Partner, Energy; Natural Resources; Forestry
 416-367-6101
 edufour@blg.com
Mark J. Fecenko, Partner, Health; Biotechnology; Life Sciences
 416-367-6711
 mfecenko@blg.com
Bonnie Freedman, Health; Biotechnology & Pharmaceuticals
 416-367-6239
 bofreedman@blg.com

Shane Freitag, Partner, Energy Markets; Electricity & Natural Gas
 416-367-6137
 sfreitag@blg.com
Barry L. Glaspell, Partner, Health Services
 416-367-6104
 bglaspell@blg.com
Mary Lynn Gleason, Partner, Health Law
 416-367-6112
 mgleason@blg.com
Tanya M. Goldberg, Partner, Health Law
 416-367-6002
 tgoldberg@blg.com
Robyn A. Grant, Partner, Health Law
 416-367-6716
 rgrant@blg.com
Jonathan Gutman, Health Law
 416-367-6209
 jgutman@blg.com
Patrick J. Hawkins, Partner, Health Law
 416-367-6065
 phawkins@blg.com
Ian J. Houston, Partner, Construction Law
 416-367-6111
 ijhouston@blg.com
Daphne G. Jarvis, Partner, Health Law
 416-367-6216
 djarvis@blg.com
Bruce Karn, Construction Litigation
 416-367-6377
 bkarn@blg.com
Karen Kiang, Construction Law
 416-367-6202
 kkiang@blg.com
David Klacko, Environment & Urban Planning
 416-367-6352
 dklacko@blg.com
Ewa Krajewska, Health Law
 416-367-6244
 ekrajewska@blg.com
Gabrielle K. Kramer, Partner, Environmental Law
 416-367-6113
 gkramer@blg.com
Norman G. Letalik, Partner, Maritime & Shipping Law
 416-367-6344
 nletalik@blg.com
James W. MacLellan, Partner, Construction Law
 416-367-6692
 jmaclellan@blg.com
Anna L. Marrison, Partner, Health Law
 416-367-6674
 amarrison@blg.com
Ian Mathany, Environmental Law
 416-367-6095
 imathany@blg.com
W. Paul McCarten, Partner, Energy; Environmental Law
 416-367-6230
 pmccarten@blg.com
Michael K. McKelvey, Partner, Health Litigation
 416-367-6170
 mmckelvey@blg.com
William R. McLean, Partner, Alternative & Renewable Energy
 416-367-6021
 wmclean@blg.com
Ladan Mehranvar, Environmental Law
 416-367-6540
 lmehranvar@blg.com
Jeffrey P. Mitchell, Partner, Occupational Health & Safety
 416-367-6226
 jmitchell@blg.com
John J. Morris, Partner, Health Law; Construction Litigation
 416-367-6241
 jmorris@blg.com
Laleh Moshiri, Health Law
 416-367-6133
 lmoshiri@blg.com
Ira G. Parghi, Partner, Health Law
 416-367-6228
 iparghi@blg.com
J. Pitman Patterson, Partner, Environmental Litigation
 416-367-6109
 ppatterson@blg.com
Heather Pessione, Health Law
 416-367-6589
 hpessione@blg.com

Law Firms / Ontario

R. Bruce Reynolds, Partner, Construction Litigation
416-367-6255
breynolds@blg.com

J. Mark Rodger, Senior Partner, Energy; Electricity, Natural Gas, Water
416-367-6190
mrodger@blg.com

Martin Sclisizzi, Partner, Environmental Litigation
416-367-6027
msclisizzi@blg.com

Richard H. Shaban, Senior Partner, Construction Law
416-367-6262
rshaban@blg.com

Colleen M. Shannon, P.Eng, Partner, Environmental Law
416-367-6154
cshannon@blg.com

James C. Sidlofsky, Partner, Energy; Electricity
416-367-6277
jsidlofsky@blg.com

Andrew Smith, Energy
416-367-6734
ansmith@blg.com

Douglas O. Smith, Partner, Health Law
416-367-6015
dsmith@blg.com

Frank J. Sperduti, Partner, Environmental Law
416-367-6243
fsperduti@blg.com

John A.D. Vellone, Energy Law
416-367-6730
jvellone@blg.com

Barbara J. Walker-Renshaw, Partner, Health Law
416-367-6744
bwalkerrenshaw@blg.com

Albert Wallrap, Construction; Environment
416-367-6081
awallrap@blg.com

Stephen F. Waqué, Senior Partner, Environmental Litigation; Municipal Law
416-367-6275
swaque@blg.com

Michele Warner, Health Law
416-367-6738
miwarner@blg.com

Mark Wheeler, Partner, Mining
416-350-3501
mwheeler@blg.com

Wendy Whelan, Health Law
416-367-6493
wwhelan@blg.com

Gillian Wilkins, Health Law
416-367-6593
gwilkins@blg.com

Saba Zadeh, Energy Law; Electricity
416-367-6582
szadeh@blg.com

Randy M. Zettle, Health Law
416-367-6146
rzettle@blg.com

Mélanie de Wit, Health Law
416-367-6180
mdewit@blg.com

Cassels Brock & Blackwell LLP
#2100, Scotia Plaza 40 King St. West, Toronto ON M5H 3C2
416-869-5386 416-350-6912 Telex: 06-23415
lsaltman@casselsbrock.com
www.casselsbrock.com
Profile: 1 Offices, 203 Lawyers, Founded in: 1888
Environmental Lawyers:
Donald R. Arthurs
 416-869-5494
 darthurs@casselsbrock.com
James Ayres, Municipal; Planning; Environmental
Ian A. Blue, Q.C.
 416-869-5352
 iblue@casselsbrock.com
John W.R. Day
 416-869-5364
 jday@casselsbrock.com
Stanley M. Makuch
 416-869-5977
 smakuch@casselsbrock.com
John P. McGowan
 416-869-5780
 jmcgowan@casselsbrock.com

Bruce A. Thomas, Q.C.
 416-869-5455
 eschaab@casselsbrock.com
Ann L. Watterworth, Business law
 416-869-5484
 awatterworth@casselsbrock.com

Conway Davis Gryski
#601, 130 Adelaide St. West, Toronto ON M5H 3P5
416-214-4554 416-214-9915 877-559-4554
contactus@cdglaw.net
www.conwaydavisgryski.com
Profile: 1 Offices, 5 Lawyers, Founded in: 1996
Conway Davis Gryski is one of the leading law firms practising in the area of municipal assessment and taxation. We act exclusively on behalf of assessing authorities and municipalities.
Environmental Lawyers:
Chester Gryski, Land assessment
 416-214-0988
 gryski@cdglaw.net
Donald G. Mitchell, Land assessment
 416-214-0976
 mitchell@cdglaw.net

Davies Howe Partners
99 Spadina Ave., 5th Fl., Toronto ON M5V 3P8
416-977-7088 416-977-8931
info@davieshowe.com
www.davieshowe.com
Profile: 1 Offices, 10 Lawyers, Founded in: 1995
Energy/Regulatory; Land Use & Development; Advocacy
Environmental Lawyers:
John Alati, Environmental Law; Energy; Land Use Planning
 johna@davieshowe.com
Kimberly L. Beckman, Land Use; Land Development
 kimb@davieshowe.com
Jeffrey L. Davies, Applications and appeals under the Planning Act
 jeffd@davieshowe.com
Mark Flowers, Municipal Law; Land Use Planning & Development Law
 markf@davieshowe.com
Michael Melling, Municipal Law; Land Use
 michaelm@davieshowe.com
Matthew Rea, Land Use Planning
 matthewr@davieshowe.com
Susan Rosenthal, Land Use Planning
 susanr@davieshowe.com

Davies Ward Phillips & Vineberg LLP
#4400, 1 First Canadian Place, Toronto ON M5X 1B1
416-863-0900 416-863-0871
info@dwpv.com
www.dwpv.com
Profile: 3 Offices, 240 Lawyers, Founded in: 1961
Environmental Lawyers:

Davies Ward Phillips & Vineberg LLP
First Canadian Place 100 King St. West, 44th Floor, Toronto ON M5X 1B1
416-863-0900 416-863-0871
mkoszegi@dwpv.com
www.dwpv.com
Profile: 3 Offices, 242 Lawyers, Founded in: 1961
With offices in Toronto, Montréal & New York, the firm's Environmental practice comprises a cross-disciplinary team with expertise in a number of areas including: Energy Law, including wind, solar & renewable energy projects, & oil & gas, nuclear, & hydroelectric projects; Environmental Law, including regulatory & compliance matters, climate change & emission trading, & contaminated sites
Environmental Lawyers:
William M. Ainley, Senior Partner, Energy Law; Mining Industry
 416-863-5509
 wainley@dwpv.com
Ian R. McBride, Energy Law; Mining Law
 416-863-5530
 imcbride@dwpv.com
D. Shawn McReynolds, B.A., LL.B., Managing Partner
 416-863-5538
 smcreynolds@dwpv.com
Alexandria J. Pike, Energy Law; Environmental Law; Mining Industry; Chemical Industry; Pulp & Paper Industry; Manufacturing Industry; Oil & Gas Industry; Hydroelectric Power Industry; Renewable Energy Industry; Nuclear Industry
 416-367-6989
 apike@dwpv.com

Alexandria J. Pike, Environmental Law; Energy Law; Environmental Assessments; Permitting; Mining Industry; Manufacturing Industry; Chemical Industry; Pulp & Paper Industry; Oil & Gas Industry; Nuclear Industry; Renewable Energy Industry
 416-367-6989
 apike@dwpv.com
Sarah V. Powell, Environmental Law; Energy Law; Environmental Assessments & Approvals; Class Actions
 416-367-6931
 spowell@dwpv.com
Sarah V. Powell, B.A., LL.B., Partner, Environmental Law; Energy Law; Environmental Assessments & Approvals; Class Actions; Contaminated Sites; Infrastructure; Natural Resource Projects
 416-367-6931
 spowell@dwpv.com
James R. Reid, Energy Law
 416-367-6974
 jreid@dwpv.com
Philippe C. Rousseau, Energy Law; Renewable Energy Industry; Solar Power Industry; Hydroelectric Power Industry; Nuclear Power Industry; Wind Power Industry; Oil & Gas Industry; Remediation Industry
 416-863-5589
 prousseau@dwpv.com

Davis LLP - Toronto
#5600, 1 First Canadian Place P.O Box 367 100 King St. West, Toronto ON M5X 1E2
416-365-3500 416-365-7886
www.davis.ca
Profile: 8 Offices, Founded in: 1892
Environmental Lawyers:
Alexis Alyea, Environmental law; Municipal law
 416-369-5262
 aalyea@davis.ca
Chris Barnett, Municipal law; Environmental law
 416-365-3502
 cbarnett@davis.ca
Donald R.M. Bell, Mining law; Projects, infrastructure, & P3
 416-369-5265
 dbell@davis.ca
Laura K. Bisset, Environmental law; Municipal law
 416-941-5400
 lbisset@davis.ca
Douglas Buchanan, Q.C., Energy & utilities; Projects, infrastructure, & P3
 416-365-3507
 dbuchanan@davis.ca
Andrew J.G. Burton, Energy & utilities; Projects, infrastructure, & P3
 416-365-3520
 aburton@davis.ca
Tudor Carsten, Environmental law
 416-365-3505
 tcarsten@davis.ca
Tobor Emakpor, Energy & Utilities; Projects, infrastructure, & P3
 416-365-3504
 temakpor@davis.ca
Lana J. Finney, Environmental law; Municipal law
 416-941-5409
 lfinney@davis.ca
Liliane E. Gingras, Environmental law
 416-941-5404
 lgingras@davis.ca
Celia Johnson, Mining law; Projects, infrastructure, & P3
 416-369-5266
 cjohnson@davis.ca
Andrew Lord, Climate change law; Energy & utilities
 416-369-5264
 alord@davis.ca
Mitchell Mostyn, Energy & utilities; Projects, infrastructure, & P3
 416-365-5254
 mmostyn@davis.ca
Richard R. Neville, Environmental law
 416-365-3526
 rneville@davis.ca
Amy Pressman, Environmental law
 416-369-5293
 apressman@davis.ca
Lisa J. Robinson, Environmental law
 416-941-5406
 lrobinson@davis.ca

Eccleston LLP
#3820, Toronto Dominion Centre Box 230 66 Wellington St. West, Toronto ON M5K 1J3
416-504-2722 416-504-2686
www.ecclestonllp.com
Profile: 1 Offices, 6 Lawyers, Founded in: 1994
Construction Law
Environmental Lawyers:
Kenneth P. Eccleston, B.A., LL.B., Partner, Construction Law
  ken@ecclestonllp.com
Janice L. Quigg, Associate, Construction Law
  jquigg@ecclestonllp.com

Fasken Martineau - Toronto
#4200, TD Centre P.O Box 20 66 Wellington St. West, Toronto ON M5K 1N6
416-366-8381 416-364-7813 800-268-8424
toronto@fasken.com
www.fasken.com
Profile: 8 Offices, 650 Lawyers, Founded in: 1863
Environmental Services: Environmental, Energy & Natural Resource Law
Environmental Lawyers:
Peter Ascherl, Partner, Environmental Law
  416-868-3499
  pascherl@fasken.com
Rosalind H. Cooper, Partner, Environmental Law
  416-865-5127
  rcooper@fasken.com
Charles L.K. Higgins, Environmental
  416-865-4392
  chiggins@tor.fasken.com
Charles Kazaz, Partner
  416-868-3517
  ckazaz@fasken.com
Daniel R. Law, Partner, Environmental Law
  416-868-3479
  dlaw@fasken.com
Douglas V. Tingey
  416-865-5126
  dtingey@tor.fasken.com

Fraser Milner Casgrain LLP - Toronto
400 Toronto-Dominion Centre 77 King St. West, Toronto ON M5K 0A1
416-863-4511 416-863-4592
www.fmc-law.com
Profile: 6 Offices, 500 Lawyers, Founded in: 1839
In the environmental law area, the firm provides services in Energy Law, including CleanTech, Climate Change, Electricity Industry, Oil & Gas Industry, Renewable Energy Industry; Environmental Law; Forest Products Industry; Natural Resources & Infrastructure; Mining Industry; and Land Use Planning/Property Development
Environmental Lawyers:
Abbas Ali Khan, Alternative Energy Industry; Mining Industry
  416-863-4398
  abbas.alikhan@fmc-law.com
Vivek Bakshi, Energy Law; Natural Resources Law & Project Finance; Infrastructure Industry; Oil & Gas Industry; Electricity Industry; CleanTech; Climate Change Matters; Renewable Energy Matters
  416-863-4658
  vivek.bakshi@fmc-law.com
Patrick J. Devine, Land Use Planning; Property Development
  416-863-4515
  patrick.devine@fmc-law.com
Jerry H. Farrell, Counsel, Energy Law; Regulatory & Compliance; Electricity Industry; Natural Gas Industry
  416-863-4384
  jerry.farrell@fmc-law.com
Don Macintosh, Energy Industry; Climate Change; CleanTech; Oil & Gas Industry; Renewable Energy Industry; Transportation Industry
  416-361-2330
  don.macintosh@fmc-law.com
David McCutcheon, Environmental Law; Aboriginal Law; Pulp & Paper Industry; Mining Industry
  416-863-4538
  david.mccutcheon@fmc-law.com
Helen Newland, Energy Law; Energy Project Development; Utilities Regulatory
  416-863-4471
  helen.newland@fmc-law.com
Jason Park, Land Use Planning; Property Development; Municipal Law
  416-863-4786
  jason.park@fmc-law.com
Andrew E. Salem, Land Use Planning; Property Development; Planning & Development Approvals; Municipal Law; Government Affairs; Energy Industry; Conservation Industry
  416-863-4728
  andrew.salem@fmc-law.com
Marina E. Sampson, Environmental Law & Litigation; Energy Law & Litigation; Renewable Energy Industry
  416-863-4783
  marina.sampson@fmc-law.com
Michael Schafler, Energy Law; Renewable Energy Industry; Oil & Gas Industry; Mining Industry; Forestry Industry; Litigation & Dispute Resolution; Class Actions
  416-863-4457
  michael.schafler@fmc-law.com
Paul D. Shantz, Counsel, Environmental Law; Land Use Planning; Property Development; Environmental Assessments
  416-863-4768
  paul.shantz@fmc-law.com

Gardiner, Roberts LLP
#3100, Scotia Plaza 40 King St. West, Toronto ON M5H 3Y2
416-865-6600 416-865-6636
www.gardiner-roberts.com
Profile: 1 Offices, 67 Lawyers
Environmental Lawyers:
Richard J. Hassard, Q.C., Counsel, Environmental
  416-865-6682
  rhassard@gardiner-roberts.com

Glaholt LLP
#800, 141 Adelaide St. West, Toronto ON M5H 3L5
416-368-8280 416-368-3467 866-452-4658
bb@glaholt.com
www.glaholt.com
Profile: 1 Offices, 9 Lawyers, Founded in: 1987
Construction law practice
Environmental Lawyers:
Brendan D. Bowles, Construction Litigation
  416-368-8280 ext. 121
  bb@glaholt.com
Duncan W. Glaholt, Construction Law
  416-368-8280 ext. 118
  dwg@glaholt.com

Goodmans LLP
#3400, Bay Adelaide Centre 333 Bay St., Toronto ON M5H 2S7
416-979-2211 416-979-1234
info@goodmans.ca
www.goodmans.ca
Profile: 2 Offices, 200 Lawyers, Founded in: 1917
The firm's environmental law practice is multidisciplinary in nature, with expertise in a diverse range of specialities including litigation, real estate law, municipal & planning matters, land development issues, regulatory & compliance requirements, and government affairs. Environmental law factors into all commercial transactions where environmental matters are a concern
Environmental Lawyers:
Joseph Cosentino, Energy Law; Construction Law; Electricity Industry
  416-597-4245
  jcosentino@goodmans.ca
Tom Friedland, Environmental Law; Municipal Law
  416-597-4218
  tfriedland@goodmans.ca
Daniel Gormley, Energy Law; Electricity Industry; Renewable Energy Industry; Solar Energy Industry
  416-597-4111
  dgormley@goodmans.ca
Catherine Lyons, Municipal Law; Environmental Law; Heritage Lands; Brownfield Development; Greenfield Development; Infrastructure
  416-597-4183
  clyons@goodmans.ca
Thomas Macdonald, Environmental Law; Contaminated Real Estate Matters
  416-597-4133
  tmacdonald@goodmans.ca
Peter Ruby, Energy Law; Electricity Industry; Government Affairs; Green Energy Industry
  416-597-4184
  pruby@goodmans.ca

Gowling Lafleur Henderson LLP - Toronto
#1600, 1 First Canadian Place 100 King St. West, Toronto ON M5X 1G5
416-862-7525 416-862-7661
www.gowlings.com
Profile: 10 Offices, 244 Lawyers, Founded in: 1887
Environmental law expertise in Climate Change, Energy, Infrastructure, Mining, & Technology
Environmental Lawyers:

Heenan Blaikie LLP - Toronto
#2900 Bay Adelaide Centre P.O Box 2900 333 Bay St., Toronto ON M5H 2T4
416-360-6336 416-360-8425
www.heenanblaikie.com
Profile: 150 Lawyers, Founded in: 1973
Environmental Lawyers:
Ahab Abdel-Aziz, Partner, Environmental Law; Regulatory & Public Law; Energy & Resources Litigation
  416-643-6929
  aabdelaziz@heenan.ca
Samantha Ambrozy, Construction Litigation
  416-360-3546
  sambrozy@heenan.ca
Samantha Ambrozy, Commercial Litigation
  416-360-3546
  sambrozy@heenan.ca
Cynthia Amsterdam, Partner, Energy & Resources Litigation; Health; Construction Litigation
  416-360-2880
  camsterdam@heenan.ca
Brett Baker, Counsel, Energy; Natural Resources; Environmental Law
  416-643-6939
  bbaker@heenan.ca
Geza Banfai, Partner, Construction; Infrastructure & Construction Litigation
  416-643-6968
  gbanfai@heenan.ca
Matthew Benson, Environmental Law; Energy & Resources Litigation
  416-643-6956
  mbenson@heenan.ca
Henry Bertossi, Partner, Health
  416-643-6862
  hbertossi@heenan.ca
Brian W. Burkett, Occupational Health & Safety
  416-360-3529
  bburkett@heenan.ca
David Carbonaro, Partner, Mining
  416-643-6836
  dcarbonaro@heenan.ca
Simon Chester, Partner, Environmental Law
  416-643-6905
  schester@heenan.ca
Michael Davies, Partner, Construction
  416-643-6807
  mdavies@heenan.ca
Henry Y. Dinsdale, Partner, Occupational Health & Safety
  416-360-3528
  hdinsdale@heenan.ca
Cheryl A. Edwards, Partner, Occupational Health & Safety
  416-360-2897
  cedwards@heenan.ca
Andrew Elbaz, Energy; Natural Resources
  416-643-6974
  aelbaz@heenan.ca
Julia Falevich, Construction Litigation
  416-643-6979
  jfalevich@heenan.ca
Joanna Fine, Health
  416-360-3599
  jfine@heenan.ca
Allen H. Garson, Partner, Climate, Cleantech & Sustainability; Infrastructure
  416-360-3533
  agarson@heenan.ca
Margaret Gavins, Partner, Occupational Health & Safety
  416-360-3557
  mgavins@heenan.ca
Ian Godfrey, Partner, Construction Litigation
  416-360-3551
  igodfrey@heenan.ca
Jeffrey Goodman, Partner, Occupational Health & Safety
  416-643-6824
  jgoodman@heenan.ca

Law Firms / Ontario

Jayashree Goswami, Construction Litigation; Condominium Law
416-643-6936
jgoswami@heenan.ca
Don Jack, Partner, Construction Litigation
416-643-6933
djack@heenan.ca
George J. Karayannides, Partner, Transportation
416-360-3521
georgek@heenan.ca
Adam Kardash, Partner, Health
416-360-3559
akardash@heenan.ca
Tony Kiru, Partner, Construction; Real Estate
416-360-3547
tkiru@heenan.ca
Kenneth David Kraft, Partner, Transportation
416-643-6822
kkraft@heenan.ca
Howard Krupat, Partner, Construction Litigation; Infrastructure
416-643-6969
hkrupat@heenan.ca
Tim Lawson, Partner, Occupational Health & Safety
416-360-3522
tlawson@heenan.ca
Corey MacKinnon, Natural Resources; Mining
416-643-6850
cmackinnon@heenan.ca
Kevin D. MacNeill, Partner, Occupational Health & Safety
416-360-2602
kmacneill@heenan.ca
Alejandro Manevich, Energy; Environmental Law
416-643-6944
amanevich@heenan.ca
Gregs T. McGinnis, Partner, Construction
416-643-6957
gmcginnis@heenan.ca
James McVicar, Partner, Mining
416-643-6903
jmcvicar@heenan.ca
Lynn Mitchell, Partner, Environmental Law; Energy & Resources Litigation
416-643-6931
lmitchell@heenan.ca
Maureen Quinlan, Partner, Occupational Health & Safety
416-643-6812
mquinlan@heenan.ca
Wendy S. Reed, Counsel, Climate, Cleantech & Sustainability
416-360-3542
wreed@heenan.ca
Katrina Reyes, Environmental Law; Energy & Resources Litigation
416-643-6990
kreyes@heenan.ca
Bonnie Roberts Jones, Construction Litigation; Condominium Law
416-360-3567
brobertsjones@heenan.ca
L. David Roebuck, Partner, Environmental Law
416-643-6887
droebuck@heenan.ca
Kevin Rooney, Partner, Natural Resources; Mining
416-643-6899
krooney@heenan.ca
Rhonda R. Shirreff, Occupational Health & Safety
416-643-6858
rshirreff@heenan.ca
Gavin Sinclair, Partner, Energy
416-643-6963
gsinclair@heenan.ca
Kara Smith, Energy & Resources Litigation
416-643-6925
ksmith@heenan.ca
Jon S. Smithen, Environment Law
416-643-6918
jsmithen@heenan.ca
Michael Smyth, Partner, Occupational Health & Safety
416-360-2887
msmyth@heenan.ca
Steven Sokalsky, Energy; Environmental Law
416-643-6941
ssokalsky@heenan.ca
Jonathan Stainsby, Partner, Construction Litigation
416-360-3568
jstainsby@heenan.ca

Stephanie J. Sykes, Partner, Mining
416-643-6906
ssykes@heenan.ca
Shane Todd, Occupational Health & Safety
416-643-6958
stodd@heenan.ca
Verki Tunteng, Energy
416-643-6898
vtunteng@heenan.ca
Claire Vachon, Partner, Occupational Health & Safety
416-643-6803
cvachon@heenan.ca
Jackie VanDerMeulen, Occupational Health & Safety
416-643-6987
jvandermeulen@heenan.ca
Steve Vaughan, Partner, Energy & Resources Litigation; Natural Resources; Mining
416-643-6924
svaughan@heenan.ca
Joel Watson, Partner, Construction Litigation; Real Estate
416-643-6955
jwatson@heenan.ca
Leslie Wittlin, Partner, Natural Resources
416-643-6961
lwittlin@heenan.ca
Julian Worsley, Partner, Health
416-643-6871
jworsley@heenan.ca

Hicks Morley Hamilton Stewart Storie LLP
TD Tower, TD Centre Box 371 P.O Box 371 TD Centre66 Wellington St., 30th Fl., Toronto ON M5K 1K8
416-362-1011 416-362-9680
www.hicksmorley.com
Profile: 5 Offices, 84 Lawyers,
Environmental practice areas include occupational health & workplace safety & insurance.
Environmental Lawyers:
Martin J. Addario, Partner, Healthcare; Mining/Resources; Petrochemical; Steel; Transportation/Automotive
416-864-7312
martin-addario@hicksmorley.com
Martin J. Addario, Partner, Healthcare; Mining/Resources; Petrochemical; Steel; Transportation/Automotive
416-864-7312
martin-addario@hicksmorley.com
John-Paul Alexandrowicz, Partner, Construction; Transportation/Automotive
416-864-7292
jpa@hicksmorley.com
Michelle A. Alton, Associate, Occupational Health
416-864-7238
michelle-alton@hicksmorley.com
Harvey A. Beresford, Q.C., Partner, Healthcare; Mining/Resources
416-864-7262
harvey-beresford@hicksmorley.com
Kathryn J. Bird, Associate, Healthcare; Occupational Health; Mining/Resources; Construction; Energy; Petrochemical; Transportation/Automotive
416-864-7353
kathryn-bird@hicksmorley.com
David W. Brady, Partner, Occupational Health; Healthcare; Mining/Resources; Steel; Transportation/Automotive
416-864-7310
david-brady@hicksmorley.com
John E. Brooks, Partner, Healthcare
416-864-7226
john-brooks@hicksmorley.com
John J. Bruce, Partner, Construction; Healthcare; Occupational Health; Mining/Resources; Petrochemical; Transportation/Automotive
416-864-7285
john-bruce@hicksmorley.com
Donna M. D'Andrea, Partner, Occupational Health; Steel; Mining/Resources; Transportation/Automotive
416-864-7275
donna-dandrea@hicksmorley.com
John C. Field, Partner, Occupational Health; Mining/Resources; Steel; Petrochemical; Transportation/Automotive
416-864-7301
john-field@hicksmorley.com
Allyson M. Fischer, Partner, Mining/Resources; Petrochemical; Transportation/Automotive
416-864-7216
allyson-fischer@hicksmorley.com

Daniel B. Fogel, Partner, Construction; Steel; Transportation/Automotive
416-864-7349
daniel-fogel@hicksmorley.com
Stephen F. Gleave, Partner, Mining/Resources; Petrochemical; Transportation/Automotive
416-864-7208
stephen-gleave@hicksmorley.com
Michael A. Hines, Partner, Steel
416-864-7248
michael-hines@hicksmorley.com
Amanda J. Hunter, Partner, Transportation/Automotive
416-864-7265
amanda-hunter@hicksmorley.com
Elisha C. Jamieson, Associate, Transportation/Automotive
416-864-7344
elisha-jamieson@hicksmorley.com
Wallace M. Kenny, Partner, Mining/Resources; Steel; Transportation/Automotive
416-864-7306
wallace-kenny@hicksmorley.com
Mireille Khoraych, Associate, Occupational Health; Steel; Transportation/Automotive
416-864-7356
mireille-khoraych@hicksmorley.com
Elizabeth Kosmidis, Associate, Construction; Occupational Health
416-864-7246
elizabeth-kosmidis@hicksmorley.com
William L. LeMay, Partner, Construction; Mining/Resources; Transportation/Automotive
416-864-7276
william-lemay@hicksmorley.com
Robert W. Little, Partner, Occupational Health; Transportation/Automotive; Mining/Resources; Petrochemical; Steel
416-864-7332
robert-little@hicksmorley.com
Jason E. Mandlowitz, VP, Consulting Services, Occupational Health
416-864-7278
jason-mandlowitz@hicksmorley.com
M. Patrick Moran, Partner, Construction; Transportation/Automotive; Mining/Resources; Petrochemical; Steel; Occupational Health
416-864-7308
patrick-moran@hicksmorley.com
Simon E. Mortimer, Partner, Transportation/Automotive; Mining/Resources; Steel
416-864-7311
simon-mortimer@hicksmorley.com
Tom Moutsatsos, Partner, Energy
416-864-7293
tom-moutsatsos@hicksmorley.com
Patty G. Murray, Partner, Transportation/Automotive; Steel; Healthcare
416-864-7307
patty-murray@hicksmorley.com
Susan L. Nickerson, Partner, Transportation/Automotive; Mining/Resources
416-864-7257
susan-nickerson@hicksmorley.com
Leola W. Pon, Associate, Occupational Health
416-864-7294
leola-pon@hicksmorley.com
Gregory J. Power, Associate, Construction
416-864-7240
gregory-power@hicksmorley.com
Lauri A. Reesor, Associate, Mining/Resources
416-864-7288
lauri-reesor@hicksmorley.com
Christopher G. Riggs, Q.C., Partner, Steel
416-864-7322
christopher-riggs@hicksmorley.com
M. David Ross, Associate, Construction; Occupational Health; Transportation/Automotive; Mining/Resources; Petrochemical; Steel; Energy
416-864-7438
david-ross@hicksmorley.com
John W. Saunders, Partner, Transportation/Automotive; Mining/Resources; Steel; Occupational Health
416-864-7247
john-saunders@hicksmorley.com
Stephen J. Shamie, Managing Partner, Steel
416-864-7304
stephen-shamie@hicksmorley.com

Scott G. Thompson, Partner, Construction;
  Transportation/Automotive; Mining/Resources; Petrochemical;
  Steel; Occupational Health
  416-864-7283
  scott-thompson@hicksmorley.com
Andrew N. Zabrovsky, Associate, Transportation/Automotive;
  Occupational Health
  416-864-7536
  andrew-zabrovsky@hicksmorley.com
Nadine S. Zacks, Associate, Occupational Health; Construction;
  Transportation/Automotive
  416-864-7484
  nadine-zacks@hicksmorley.com

Hodgson Russ LLP
#2309, P.O Box 30 150 King St. West, Toronto ON M5H 1J9
416-595-5100 416-595-5021
info@hodgsonruss.com
www.hodgsonruss.com
Profile: 6 Offices, 3 Lawyers
Environmental Lawyers:
George J. Eydt, Partner, Life Sciences
  416-595-2671
  geydt@hodgsonruss.com
Richard B. Raymer, Partner, Life Sciences
  416-595-2681
  rraymer@hodgsonruss.com

Hughes, Amys LLP
#200, 48 Yonge St., Toronto ON M5E 1G6
416-367-1608 416-367-8821 800-565-1713
info@hughesamys.com
www.hughesamys.com
Profile: 2 Offices, 28 Lawyers, Founded in: 1918
Environmental Lawyers:
Michael S. Teitelbaum, Partner, Environmental Law
  416-367-1608 ext. 257
  mteitelbaum@hughesamys.com
Wendell S. Wigle, Q.C., Senior Partner, Environmental Litigation
  416-367-1608 ext. 235
  wwigle@hughesamys.com

Lang Michener LLP - Toronto
#2500, Brookfield Place 181 Bay St., Toronto ON M5J 2T7
416-360-8600 416-365-1719
rrcranston@langmichener.ca (Office Managing Partner)
www.langmichener.ca
Profile: 3 Offices, 90 Lawyers, Founded in: 1927
The Environment, Energy & Emissions Trading Group of Lang
Michener LLP helps organizations with legal & business issues
related to environmental projects & matters. Lang Michener's
lawyers also serve clients in the forestry & paper products
industry, the aviation, rail, & marine industries, & the Canadian &
international mining & natural resource industry.
Environmental Lawyers:
Denno Chen, Mining & natural resources
Paul Collins, Mining & natural resources
John S. Contini, Mining & natural resources; Transportation &
  logistics (marine, aviation, & rail)
Robert R. Cranston, Mining & natural resources
Joseph C. D'Angelo, Transportation & logistics (marine, aviation,
  & rail)
Matthew L. Dewar, Transportation & logistics (marine, aviation,
  & rail)
Howard M. Drabinsky, Forestry
Peter Giddens, Environmental law; Energy; Emissions
Glenn Grenier, Transportation & logistics (marine, aviation, &
  rail)
David Hager, Transportation & logistics (marine, aviation, & rail)
Henry Krupa, Environmental law; Energy; Power generation;
  Utilities; Emissions
Hartley Lefton, Mining & natural resources
Howard A. Levitt, Forestry; Mining & natural resources;
  Transportation & logistics (marine, aviation, & rail)
Greg McIlwain, Mining & natural resources; Transportation &
  logistics (marine, aviation, & rail)
Bruce A. McKenna, Mining & natural resources
Brent McPherson, Mining & natural resources
Mark S. Mitchell, Forestry; Mining & natural resources
J. Michael Mulroy, Transportation & logistics (marine, aviation, &
  rail)
James B. Musgrove, Forestry; Mining & natural resources
Contance C. Olsheski, Transportation & logistics (aviation,
  marine, & rail)
Frank Palmay, P.Eng, Mining & natural resources

J. Mark Richardson, Transportation & logistics (marine, aviation,
  & rail)
William A. Rowlands, Mining & natural resources
William J.V. Sheridan, Mining & natural resources
Hellen L. Siwanowicz, Mining & natural resources;
  Transportation & logistics (marine, aviation, & rail)
Andrew W.H. Tam, Mining & natural resources
David E. Thring, Environmental law; Energy; Power generation;
  Utilities; Emissions
Cyndee Todgham Cherniak, Environmental law; Energy; Power
  generation; Utilities; Emissions; Transportation & logistics
  (marine, aviation, & rail)
George Waggott, Forestry; Mining & natural resources;
  Transportation & logistics (marine, aviation, & rail)
R. Nairn Waterman, Mining & natural resources
Peter E.J. Wells, Environmental litigation
Stephen White, Mining & natural resources
David N.W. Young, Environmental law; Energy; Emissions;
  Power generation; Utilities

Levy, Alan D.
75 Robert St., Toronto ON M5S 2K4
416-929-8282 416-929-9895
alan@alanlevy.ca
www.alanlevy.ca
Profile: 1 Offices, 1 Lawyers
Environmental Lawyers:
Alan D. Levy, B.A., LL.B., Environmental & Municipal Law

Loopstra Nixon LLP
#600, Woodbine Place 135 Queens Plate Dr., Toronto ON M9W
6V7
416-746-4710 416-746-8319
TheStraightAnswer@loonix.com
www.loopstranixon.com
Profile: 1 Offices, 18 Lawyers,
Regulatory
Environmental Lawyers:
C.M. Loopstra, Q.C., Municipal; Aggregate; Environmental
  Assessments; Transportation
  cloopstra@loonix.com

Macleod Dixon LLP
#2300 TD Waterhouse Tower P.O Box 128 79 Wellington St.
West, Toronto ON M5K 1H1
416-360-8511 416-360-8277
www.macleoddixon.com
Profile: 41 Lawyers, Founded in: 1912
Environmental Lawyers:
Avril Cole, Mining; Energy & Resources
  416-202-6744
  avril.cole@macleoddixon.com
James H. Coleman, Q.C., Partner, Mining; Energy & Resources
  416-267-8373
  jim.coleman@macleoddixon.com
Elisabeth (Lisa) DeMarco, Partner, Cleantech; Energy &
  Resources; Environmental
  416-203-4431
  elisabeth.demarco@macleoddixon.com
Madeleine Donahue, Partner, Cleantech; Environmental; Health
  Infomatics; Aboriginal Law; Mining
  416-202-6745
  madeleine.donahue@macleoddixon.com
Janne Duncan, Partner, Cleantech; Mining
  416-202-6715
  janne.duncan@macleoddixon.com
Robert W. Eberschlag, Partner, Cleantech; Mining
  416-202-6710
  robert.eberschlag@macleoddixon.com
Robert I. Frank, Partner, Cleantech; Energy & Resources
  416-202-6741
  robert.frank@macleoddixon.com
Ryan Hauk, Construction
  416-203-4468
  ryan.hauk@macleoddixon.com
Edward A. Heakes, Partner, Cleantech
  416-202-6707
  ed.heakes@macleoddixon.com
Pamela Horton, Partner, Construction
  416-203-4432
  pamela.horton@macleoddixon.com
David Knight, Partner, Cleantech; Mining
  416-203-4460
  david.knight@macleoddixon.com

Richard Lachcik, Partner, Cleantech; Mining
  416-202-6711
  richard.lachcik@macleoddixon.com
Darryl Levitt, Counsel, Mining
  416-202-6713
  darryl.levitt@macleoddixon.com
Alexander Liszka, Mining; Energy & Resources; Construction
  416-202-6740
  alexander.liszka@macleoddixon.com
Byron Loeppky, Partner, Cleantech
  416-202-6709
  byron.loeppky@macleoddixon.com
Cathy Ma, Energy & Resources
  416-203-4456
  cathy.ma@macleoddixon.com
Michael R. Moher, Partner, Cleantech; Energy & Resources
  416-202-6701
  mike.moher@macleoddixon.com
Richard Oliver, Construction
  416-202-6735
  richard.oliver@macleoddixon.com
Michael Sabusco, Partner, Mining
  416-202-6731
  michael.sabusco@macleoddixon.com
Marvin Singer, Partner, Mining; Cleantech
  416-203-4426
  marvin.singer@macleoddixon.com
Vera Vynohrad, Partner, Cleantech
  416-203-4458
  vera.vynohrad@macleoddixon.com
Roger Watkiss, Partner, Cleantech; Construction; Health
  Infomatics
  416-202-6716
  roger.watkiss@macleoddixon.com

Mattson, Mark O.
17 Fenwood Heights, Toronto ON M1M 2V6
416-265-6548
Profile: 1 Offices, 1 Lawyers
Environmental Lawyers:
Mark O. Mattson, Environmental Law; Regulatory Law
  mark@waterkeeper.ca

McCarthy Tétrault LLP - Toronto
#5300, Toronto-Dominion Bank Tower, Toronto ON M5K 1E6
416-362-1812 416-868-0673
toronto@mccarthy.ca
www.mccarthy.ca
Profile: 7 Offices, 319 Lawyers, Founded in: 1855
Biotechnology; Energy; Environmental; Municipal
Environmental Lawyers:
Peter Brady
John Dawson
Stephen Diamond
Douglas Hamilton
John Inglis
Peter Quinn
Marcia Taggart
Douglas Thomson
Gordon Willcocks

McMillan Binch Mendelsohn - Toronto
#4400, BCE Place, Bay Wellington Tower 181 Bay St., Toronto
ON M5J 2T3
416-865-7000 416-865-7048 888-622-4624
info@mcmillan.ca
www.mcmillan.ca
Profile: 2 Offices, 145 Lawyers, Founded in: 1903
Environmental Lawyers:
Carmen Diges, Natural Resources
  416-865-7925
  carmen.diges@mcmbm.com
W. Brad Hanna, Litigation
  416-865-7276
  bhanna@mcmbm.com
Michael M. Peterson, Environmental
  416-865-7839
  michael.peterson@mcmbm.com
Leonard Ricchetti, Litigation
  416-865-7159
  lricchetti@mcmbm.com

Miller Thomson LLP - Toronto
#5800 Scotia Plaza P.O Box 1011 40 King St. West, Toronto ON
M5H 3S1

Law Firms / Ontario

416-595-8500 416-595-8695 888-762-5559
toronto@millerthomson.com
www.millerthomson.com
Profile: 11 Offices, 470 Lawyers, Founded in: 1957
Miller Thomson's Environmental Law Group lawyers are legal planners, negotiators and advocates. Many have experience as professional engineers, regulators, prosecutors and policy makers. Our lawyers have cultivated a thorough knowledge of government processes and regulators and continue to maintain excellent relationships with existing personnel. Owing to the size and expertise of our Group and the relationships our lawyers havewith a wide variety of environmental consultants, our partners delegate internally and out-source to consultants and paralegals to the client's advantage. Thus, we are always able to offer cost-effective and timely legal advice.

Environmental Lawyers:

Aaron E. Atcheson, Partner
  519-931-3526
  aatcheson@millerthomson.com
Robin Bajer, Associate
  604-643-1295
  rbajer@millerthomson.com
Bryan J. Buttigieg, Partner
  416-595-8172
  bbuttigieg@millerthomson.com
Gerald D. Chipeur, Partner
  403-298-2434
  gchipeur@millerthomson.com
Louis Coallier, Partner
  514-871-5488
  lcoallier@millerthomsonpouliot.com
Eric Couture, Partner
  519-871-5489
  ecouture@millerthomsonpouliot.com
Tony Crossman, Partner
  604-643-1244
  tcrossman@millerthomson.com
Debra Curcio Lister, Partner
  780-429-9763
  dcurciolister@millerthomson.com
Tamara Farber, Partner
  416-595-8520
  tfarber@millerthomson.com
Sandra A. Gogal, Partner
  416-595-8574
  sgogal@millerthomson.com
Luc Gratton, Partner
  514-871-5482
  lgratton@millerthomsonpouliot.com
Sarah D. Hansen, Associate
  604-643-1273
  shansen@millerthomson.com
Kathleen J. Kendrick, Associate
  403-298-2455
  kkendrick@millerthomson.com
Daniel L. Kiselbach, Partner
  604-643-1263
  dkiselbach@millerthomson.com
Rosanne M. Kyle, Partner
  604-643-1235
  rkyle@millerthomson.com
Grace Mackintosh, Associate
  403-298-2466
  gmackintosh@millerthomson.com
Roderick M.. McLeod, Counsel
  905-415-6707
  rmcleod@millerthomson.com
Bruce J. McMeekin, Partner
  905-415-6791
  bmcmeekin@millerthomson.com
Teresa Meadows, Associate
  780-429-9706
  tmeadows@millerthomson.com
Brent J. Muir, Partner
  514-871-5478
  bmuir@millerthomsonpouliot.com
Robin-Lee A. Norris, Partner
  519-780-4638
  morris@millerthomson.com
Steven J. O'Melia, Associate Counsel
  519-593-3289
  somelia@millerthomson.com
Pierre Paquet, Partner
  514-871-5427
  ppaquet@millerthomsonpouliot.com

Angela Rinaldis, Associate
  604-643-1294
  arinaldis@millerthomson.com
John R. Tidball, Partner
  905-415-6710
  jtidball@millerthomson.com
Louise Tremblay, Partner
  514-871-5476
  ltremblay@millerthomsonpouliot.com
Alexandra L. White, Associate
  416-595-8667
  awhite@millerthomson.com

Ogilvy Renault LLP/S.E.N.C.R.L., s.r.l. - Toronto
#3800 Royal Bank Plaza South Tower P.O Box 84 200 Bay St., Toronto ON M5J 2Z4
416-216-4000 416-216-3930
toronto@ogilvyrenault.com
www.ogilvyrenault.com
Profile: 139 Lawyers,
Environmental risk management, counsel, assistance in all forms of transactional matters, representation & litigation

Environmental Lawyers:

Leeora Avrahami, Occupational Health & Safety
  416-216-4843
  lavrahami@ogilvyrenault.com
David Badurina, Life Sciences; Microbiology
  416-216-1904
  dbadurina@ogilvyrenault.com
David J. Bannon, Partner, Occupational Health & Safety
  416-216-3907
  dbannon@ogilvyrenault.com
John Beauchamp, Environment; Energy
  416-216-1927
  jbeauchamp@ogilvyrenault.com
Penny S. Bonner, Senior Partner, Life Sciences; Bioethics; Natural Health Products; Biotechnology
  416-216-6629
  pbonner@ogilvyrenault.com
Andrea Brewer, Mining & Resources
  416-216-1917
  abrewer@ogilvyrenault.com
James R. Cade, Senior Partner, Cleantech; Life Sciences
  416-216-4840
  jcade@ogilvyrenault.com
Richard J. Charney, Senior Partner, Occupational Health & Safety; Mining & Resources
  416-216-1867
  rcharney@ogilvyrenault.com
Jung-Kay Chiu, Partner, Cleantech; Life Sciences; Genetics; Molecular Biology; Biotechnology
  416-216-2994
  jchiu@ogilvyrenault.com
Mark A. Convery, Senior Partner, Cleantech
  416-216-4803
  mconvery@ogilvyrenault.com
Rebecca Crane, Cleantech; Life Sciences; Pharmaceutical Industry
  416-216-1886
  rcrane@ogilvyrenault.com
Pierre R. Dagenais, Partner, Mining & Resources
  416-216-1857
  pdagenais@ogilvyrenault.com
Jill Daley, Life Sciences; Natural Healthcare
  416-216-1930
  jdaley@ogilvyrenault.com
Jeremy J. Devereux, Partner, Mining Law; Natural Resources
  416-216-4073
  jdevereux@ogilvyrenault.com
Paul J. Field, Partner, Cleantech; Mining & Resources
  416-216-3903
  pfield@ogilvyrenault.com
Paul Fitzgerald, Partner, Mining & Resources
  416-216-3941
  pfitzgerald@ogilvyrenault.com
Andrew Fleming, Senior Partner, Mining & Resources
  416-216-4007
  afleming@ogilvyrenault.com
Brian W. Gray, Senior Partner, Cleantech; Life Sciences
  416-216-1905
  bgray@ogilvyrenault.com
Andrew Grossman, Partner, Cleantech; Energy; Mining & Resources
  416-216-2312
  agrossman@ogilvyrenault.com

Jeremy Grushcow, Partner, Cleantech; Life Sciences
  416-216-2301
  jgrushcow@ogilvyrenault.com
James A. Hodgson, Senior Partner, Construction Litigation
  416-216-2989
  jhodgson@ogilvyrenault.com
Sanjay Joshi, Partner, Energy; Mining & Resources
  416-216-3984
  sjoshi@ogilvyrenault.com
Richard J. King, Partner, Environmental Law; Energy Law; Aboriginal Law; Cleantech
  416-216-2311
  rking@ogilvyrenault.com
Jay A. Lefton, Senior Partner, Cleantech; Life Sciences
  416-216-4018
  jlefton@ogilvyrenault.com
Suzana A. Lobo, Cleantech
  416-216-2990
  slobo@ogilvyrenault.com
Madeleine L.S. Loewenberg, Occupational Health & Safety
  416-216-3932
  mloewenberg@ogilvyrenault.com
Alan Mark, Senior Partner, Energy
  416-216-4865
  amark@ogilvyrenault.com
Jason C. Markwell, Partner, Life Sciences
  416-216-2977
  jmarkwell@ogilvyrenault.com
Michael G. McFadden, Partner, Occupational Health & Safety
  416-216-3973
  mmcfadden@ogilvyrenault.com
Peter S. Newell, Senior Partner, Cleantech; Mining & Resources
  416-216-2963
  pnewell@ogilvyrenault.com
Sandra Nissan, Partner, Cleantech; Mining & Resources
  416-216-3965
  snissan@ogilvyrenault.com
James Padwick, Cleantech; Energy; Environmental Law
  416-216-1912
  jpadwick@ogilvyrenault.com
Robert L. Percival, Partner, Cleantech
  416-216-4075
  rpercival@ogilvyrenault.com
Aditya Rebbapragada, Mining & Resources
  416-216-2975
  arebbapragada@ogilvyrenault.com
Heidi Reinhart, Mining & Resources
  416-216-2979
  hreinhart@ogilvyrenault.com
Mark Sajewycz, Partner, Mining & Resources
  416-216-1924
  msajewycz@ogilvyrenault.com
Yursa Siddiquee, Partner, Mining & Resources; Health Sciences; Energy
  416-216-4062
  ysiddiquee@ogilvyrenault.com
C. Nicole Sigouin, Partner, Cleantech; Mining & Resources
  416-216-3929
  nsigouin@ogilvyrenault.com
Cathy Singer, Partner, Mining & Resources
  416-216-4053
  csinger@ogilvyrenault.com
Walied Soliman, Partner, Cleantech; Mining & Resources
  416-216-4820
  wsoliman@ogilvyrenault.com
Pierre L. Soulard, Partner, Mining & Resources
  416-216-4806
  psoulard@ogilvyrenault.com
Ned A. Steinman, Partner, Construction; Mining & Resources; Real Estate
  416-216-3915
  nsteinman@ogilvyrenault.com
Richard S. Sutin, Senior Partner, Cleantech; Life Sciences; Mining & Resources
  416-216-4821
  rsutin@ogilvyrenault.com
Derrick C. Tay, Senior Partner, Environmental Law
  416-216-4832
  tday@ogilvyrenault.com
Michael Torrance, Mining & Resources; Health
  416-216-1908
  mtorrance@ogilvyrenault.com
John B. West, Senior Partner, Occupational Health & Safety
  416-216-3976
  jwest@ogilvyrenault.com

Anna Wilkinson, Cleantech; Life Sciences
  416-216-3975
    awilkinson@ogilvyrenault.com
Jordan D. Winch, Partner, Occupational Health & Safety
  416-216-4788
    jwinch@ogilvyrenault.com

Osler, Hoskin & Harcourt LLP - Toronto
#6100, P.O Box 50 One First Canadian Place, Toronto ON M5X 1B8
416-362-2111 416-862-6666
counsel@osler.com
www.osler.com
Profile: 5 Offices, 450 Lawyers
Environmental Lawyers:
Mark Austin, Partner, Health; Life Sciences
  416-862-6524
    maustin@osler.com
Jason Ball, Health
  416-862-5963
    jball@osler.com
Chad Bayne, Partner, Mining
  416-862-4708
    cbayne@osler.com
D. Robert Beaumont, Partner, Construction
  416-862-5861
    rbeaumont@osler.com
Michael H.D. Bowman, Partner, Environmental, Regulatory & Aboriginal; Litigation
  416-862-6834
    mbowman@osler.com
James R. Brown, Mining
  416-862-6647
    jbrown@osler.com
John B. (Jack) Cook, Partner, Climate Change & Emissions Trading; Environmental, Regulatory & Aboriginal; Litigation
  416-862-4896
    jcook@osler.com
Raj Dhaliwal, Construction; Energy; Renewable Energy & Environmental Financing
  416-862-6816
    rdhaliwal@osler.com
Tobor Emakpor, Partner, Construction
  416-862-4268
    temakpor@osler.com
Jennifer Fairfax, Construction; Environmental, Regulatory & Aboriginal; Litigation
  416-862-5998
    jfairfax@osler.com
Jeremy Fraiberg, Partner, Mining
  416-862-6505
    jfraiberg@osler.com
Roger Gillott, Partner, Construction
  416-862-6818
    rgillott@osler.com
Brian Gray, Mining
  416-862-4862
    bgray@osler.com
David Hanick, Partner, Mining
  416-862-5979
    dhanick@osler.com
Sarah Harrison, Health
  416-862-4925
    sharrison@osler.com
Simon Hodgett, Partner, Health
  416-862-6819
    shodgett@osler.com
Paul Ivanoff, Partner, Construction
  416-862-4223
    pivanoff@osler.com
Ken Jennings, Energy; Construction
  416-862-4935
    kjennings@osler.com
Jennifer Kelly, Construction
  416-862-4720
    jkelly@osler.com
C.W. Daniel Kirby, Partner, Climate Change & Emissions Trading; Environmental, Regulatory & Aboriginal; Litigation
  416-862-6661
    dkirby@osler.com
Harvey Kirsh, Senior Partner, Construction
  416-862-6844
    hkirsh@osler.com
Paul J. Morassutti, Partner, Environmental, Regulatory & Aboriginal
  416-862-6806
    pmorassutti@osler.com
Jeffrey Murray, Energy
  416-862-4250
    jmurray@osler.com
Jay Nathwani, Construction
  416-862-5885
    jnathwani@osler.com
Christopher Portner, Partner, Energy
  416-862-6412
    cportner@osler.com
Andrew Powers, Mining
  416-862-6847
    apowers@osler.com
Jacob A. Sadikman, Climate Change & Emissions Trading; Renewable Energy & Environmental Financing
  416-862-4931
    jsadikman@osler.com
Rocco M. Sebastiano, Partner, Energy
  416-862-5859
    rsebastiano@osler.com
Elliot A. Smith, Construction; Energy
  416-862-6435
    esmith@osler.com
Steve Suarez, Partner, Mining
  416-862-5905
    ssuarez@osler.com
Paula Trattner, Partner, Health
  416-862-6495
    ptrattner@osler.com
David Vernon, Mining
  416-862-5966
    dvernon@osler.com
Michael Watts, Partner, Health
  416-862-6605
    mwatts@osler.com
Andrew Wong, Partner, Construction; Energy
  416-862-6564
    anwong@osler.com
Richard Wong, Partner, Construction; Energy
  416-862-6467
    rwong@osler.com

Outerbridge Miller Sefton
#920, 4 King St. West, Toronto ON M5H 1B6
416-360-6182 416-360-7729
info@omslaw.com
www.omslaw.com
Profile: 1 Offices, 3 Lawyers,
Occupational Health & Safety; Environmental Issues; Municipal & Land Use Planning
Environmental Lawyers:
Cynthia R.C. Sefton, Environmental Liability

Paterson, MacDougall LLP, Barristers, Solicitors
#900, P.O Box 100 1 Queen St. East, Toronto ON M5C 2W5
416-366-9607 416-366-3743
bmacdoug@pmlaw.com
www.pmlaw.com
Profile: 1 Offices, 13 Lawyers,
The law firm provides representation in commercial, litigation & environmental marine matters. Clients include the following: ship owners, stevedores, agents, marina operators, & protection & indemnity associations.
Environmental Lawyers:
Matthew A. Biderman, Marine law
    mbiderman@pmlaw.com
Clay Hunter, Marine law
    chunter@pmlaw.com
Peter F.M. Jones, Marine law
    pfmjones@pmlaw.com
Carol E. McCall, Marine law
    cmccall@pmlaw.com

Poch, Harry Environmental Lawyer
20 Beaverhall Dr., Toronto ON M2L 2C7
416-444-7971 416-444-8971
harrypoch@rogers.com
Profile: 1 Offices, 1 Lawyers, Founded in: 1979
Environmental Lawyers:
Harry Poch, Environmental Litigation & Hearings

Roach, Schwartz & Associates, Barristers & Solicitors
688 St. Clair Ave. West, Toronto ON M6C 1B1
416-657-1465 416-657-1511
www.roachschwartz.com
Profile: 1 Offices, 7 Lawyers, Founded in: 1968
Environmental Lawyers:
V. (Bala) Balasubramanian, Administrative law
    bala@roachschwartz.com
Michael A. Leitold, Administrative law
    mleitold@roachschwartz.com
Charles C. Roach, Administrative law
    croach@roachschwartz.com
Kikélola Roach, Administrative law
    kroach@roachschwartz.com
Peter M. Rosenthal, Administrative law
    peterr@roachschwartz.com
Sarah Shartal Levinthal, Administrative law
    sshartal@roachschwartz.com

Saxe, Dianne
#1506, 355 St. Clair Ave. West, Toronto ON M5P 1N5
416-962-5882 416-962-8817
admin@envirolaw.com
www.envirolaw.com
Profile: 1 Offices, 2 Lawyers, Founded in: 1991
Environmental Lawyers:
David Bell, Litigation
    dbell@envirolaw.com
Jackie Campbell
    jcampbell@envirolaw.com
Dianne Saxe, Environmental; Arbitration & Mediation; Pro-active Due Diligence; Waste Management; Commercial; Real Estate; Environment
    dsaxe@envirolaw.com

Shibley Righton LLP
#700, 250 University Ave., Toronto ON M5H 3E5
416-214-5200 416-214-5400 877-214-5200
torontoinfo@shibleyrighton.com
www.shibleyrighton.com
Profile: 2 Offices, 32 Lawyers, Founded in: 1964
Areas of practice at Shibley Righton LLP, Barristers & Solicitors include municipal & planning law & energy law.
Environmental Lawyers:
John Bell, Municipal & planning law
  416-214-5212
    john.bell@shibleyrighton.com

Stikeman Elliott LLP - Toronto
#5300, Commerce Court West 199 Bay St., Toronto ON M5L 1B9
416-869-5500 416-947-0866 877-973-5500 Telex: 06-22536
info@stikeman.com
www.stikeman.com
Profile: 8 Offices, 216 Lawyers, Founded in: 1952
In 2008, the firm launched a national "GoingGreen" program to formalize their commitment to environmental stewardship, with programs including comprehensive recycling, and energy & resource conservation initiatives.
Environmental Lawyers:
Rhoda Aylward, Mining
  416-869-5292
    raylward@stikeman.com
Roderick F. Barrett, Managing Partner, Construction Litigation
  416-869-5524
    rbarrett@stikeman.com
Nili Birshtein, Environmental; Real Estate
  416-869-5298
    nbirshtein@stikeman.com
Andrew Bozzato, Energy; Mining
  416-869-6801
    abozzato@stikeman.com
William J. Braithwaite, Senior Partner, Energy
  416-869-5654
    wbraithwaite@stikeman.com
Elizabeth Breen, Partner, Mining
  416-869-5267
    ebreen@stikeman.com
Eric H. Bremermann, Partner, Renewable Energy
  416-869-6821
    ebremermann@stikeman.com
Eric H. Bremermann, Partner, Renewable Energy
  416-869-6821
    ebremermann@stikeman.com
Matthew Cameron, Renewable Energy
  416-869-6841
    mcameron@stikeman.com

Law Firms / Ontario

Kathryn I. Chalmers, Senior Partner, Environmental
416-869-5544
kchalmers@stikeman.com
Timothy Chubb, Partner
416-869-5206
tchubb@stikeman.com
Richard E. Clark, Senior Partner, Pharmaceuticals, Biotechnology & Life Sciences
416-869-5546
rclark@stikeman.com
Larry Cobb, Partner, Environmental
416-869-5618
lcobb@stikeman.com
Larry Cobb, Partner, Environmental
416-869-5618
lcobb@stikeman.com
Curtis A. Cusinato, Partner, Pharmaceuticals, Biotechnology & Life Sciences
416-869-5221
ccusinato@stikeman.com
Alan D'Silva, Partner, Environmental Litigation; Pharmaceuticals, Biotechnology & Life Sciences
416-869-5204
adsilva@stikeman.com
James C. Davis, Senior Partner, Forestry & Forest Products; Construction Litigation; Pharmaceuticals, Biotechnology & Life Sciences
416-869-5539
jdavis@stikeman.com
John R. Dow, Partner, Construction Litigation
416-869-5615
jdow@stikeman.com
Patrick Duffy, Energy; Envirnomental
416-869-5257
pduffy@stikeman.com
Jeffrey Elliot, Partner, Emissions Trading & Climate Change; Renewable Energy
416-869-5655
jelliot@stikeman.com
Ruth Elnekave, Emissions Trading & Climate Change; Energy
416-869-5563
relnekave@stikeman.com
David N. Finkelstein, Partner, Construction Litigation
416-869-5536
dfinkelstein@stikeman.com
Alison Forbes, Energy
416-869-5268
aforbes@stikeman.com
Ivan Grbesic, Partner, Mining
416-869-5229
igrbesic@stikeman.com
Peter E. Hamilton, Partner, Mining
416-869-5564
phamilton@stikeman.com
James W. Harbell, Partner, Construction Litigation; Renewable Energy; Environmental; Oil & Gas
416-869-5690
jharbell@stikeman.com
Douglas Harrison, Partner, Environmental Litigation
416-869-5693
dharrison@stikeman.com
Brenda Hebert, Senior Partner, Construction Litigation; Renewable Energy
416-869-5578
bhebert@stikeman.com
Phil J. Henderson, Partner, Energy
416-869-5691
phenderson@stikeman.com
Jeff Hershenfield, Energy
416-869-5205
jhershenfield@stikeman.com
Melissa Hogg, Energy; Litigation
416-869-6826
hhogg@stikeman.com
Samantha G. Horn, Partner, Pharmaceuticals, Biotechnology & Life Sciences
416-869-5636
shorn@stikeman.com
Katherine Kay, Partner, Pharmaceuticals, Biotechnology & Life Sciences
416-869-5507
kkay@stikeman.com
Jay C. Kellerman, Partner, Pharmaceuticals, Biotechnology & Life Sciences; Mining
416-869-5201
jkellerman@stikeman.com
James Klein, Energy
416-869-5651
jklein@stikeman.com
P. Jason Kroft, Partner, Emissions Trading & Climate Change; Renewable Energy
416-869-5534
jkroft@stikeman.com
Elise Lenser, Mining
416-869-6802
elenser@stikeman.com
Amanda Linett, Partner, Mining
416-869-5217
alinett@stikeman.com
Rosemarie Lipman, Energy
416-869-5540
rlipman@stikeman.com
Daphne J. MacKenzie, Partner, Forestry & Forest Products; Mining
416-869-5695
dmackenzie@stikeman.com
Quentin Markin, Partner, Mining
416-869-5213
gmarkin@stikeman.com
Raymond A. McDougall, Partner, Mining
416-869-5227
rmcdougall@stikeman.com
D'Arcy Nordick, Partner, Mining
416-869-5508
dnordick@stikeman.com
Richard C. Owen, Counsel, Pharmaceuticals, Biotechnology & Life Sciences
416-869-6878
rowen@stikeman.com
C. Mario Paura, Partner, Mining
416-869-5638
mpaura@stikeman.com
Bruce Pollock, Partner, Environmental
416-869-5566
bpollock@stikeman.com
Ian G. Putnam, Partner, Energy; Forestry & Forest Products; Mining
416-869-5506
iputnam@stikeman.com
Dee Rajpal, Partner, Pharmaceuticals, Biotechnology & Life Sciences; Mining
416-869-5576
drajpal@stikeman.com
Sarah Rancier, Mining
416-869-5558
srancier@stikeman.com
Darin R. Renton, Partner, Mining
416-869-5685
drenton@stikeman.com
Danielle Royal, Partner, Construction Litigation
416-869-5254
droyal@stikeman.com
Melissa Schyven, Renewable Energy
416-869-5232
mschyven@stikeman.com
Lewis T. Smith, Partner, Renewable Energy
416-869-5210
ltsmith@stikeman.com
Lanette Wildinson, Energy
416-869-6846
lwilkinson@stikeman.com
Colin Yao, Mining
416-869-6827
cyao@stikeman.com
Glenn Zacher, Partner, Emissions Trading & Climate Change; Energy
416-869-5688
gzacher@stikeman.com

Stitt Feld Handy Group
112 Adelaide St. East, Toronto ON M5C 1K9
416-307-0000 416-307-0011 800-318-9741
contact@adr.ca
www.sfhgroup.com
Profile: 1 Offices, 6 Lawyers, Founded in: 1994
The Stitt Feld Handy Group is a Canadian based Alternative Dispute Resolution firm specializing in professional development training and dispute resolution services.
Environmental Lawyers:
Frank Handy, Land Use Planning; Development Impact
frank@adr.ca

Stringer, Brisbin, Humphrey Management Lawyers
#1100, 110 Yonge St., Toronto ON M5C 1T4
416-862-1616 416-363-7358 866-821-7306
chumphrey@sbhlawyers.com
www.sbhlawyers.com
Profile: 2 Offices, 11 Lawyers,
Firm members are recognized by the business community & the profession as being among the leading health & safety practitioners in Ontario
Environmental Lawyers:
Cheryl A. Edwards, Occupational Health & Safety
cedwards@sbhlawyers.com
Nadia Pazzano, Occupational Health & Safety
npazzano@sbhlawyers.com

Thomson, Rogers
#3100, 390 Bay St., Toronto ON M5H 1W2
416-868-3100 416-868-3134 888-223-0448
info@thomsonrogers.com
www.thomsonrogers.com
Profile: 1 Offices, 33 Lawyers, Founded in: 1936
The firm provides legal services in the areas of Environmental Law, and Expropriations Law
Environmental Lawyers:
Roger T. Beaman, Municipal & Environmental Law Practice; Municipal Law; Environmental Law; Planning Law; Expropriations Law
416-868-3157
rbeaman@thomsonrogers.com
Alstair H. A. Burton, Environmental Law; Environmental Approvals; Municipal Law; Land Use Planning; Expropriations Law
416-868-3113
aburton@thomsonrogers.com
Stephen J. D'Agostino, Environmental Law; Environmental Assessments & Approvals; Municipal Law; Planning Law; Landfill Matters; Expropriations Law; Telecommunications Networks Matters; Electric Generating Facilities Permitting
416-868-3126
sdagostino@thomsonrogers.com
Jeffrey J. Wilker, Environmental Law; Municipal Law; Land Use Litigation; Planning Law; Expropriations Law
416-868-3118
jwilker@thomsonrogers.com

Torys LLP
#3000, Toronto-Dominion Centre P.O Box 270 79 Wellington St. West, Toronto ON M5K 1N2
416-865-0040 416-865-7380
info@torys.com
www.torys.com
Profile: 3 Offices, 276 Lawyers, Founded in: 1941
Torys' Environmental, Health & Safety practice group is international in reach. It has acted as lead counsel in civil cases & defence of prosecutions, & has expertise in: infrastructure projects; the regulatory framework & required approvals; preparation & management of approval applications & environmental assessments; drafting of contractual provisions to address environmental risks; & project diligence & oversight regarding compliance. The practice group's members have served as chairs of the CBA's Environmental Law Section, & continue to participate in a number of national environmental associations
Environmental Lawyers:
Mark W. S. Bain, Infrastructure & Energy; Project Finance; Water & Wastewaster Industry; Urban Redevelopment Matters; Aboriginal Law
416-865-7349
mbain@torys.com
David P. Chernos, Environmental Law & Litigation
416-865-8246
dchernos@torys.com
David A. Dell, Infrastructure & Energy; Power Project Development & Finance; Construction Law
416-865-8100
ddell@torys.com
Aaron S. Emes, Infrastructure & Energy; Nuclear Industry; Power Generation Industry
416-865-7669
aemes@torys.com
Daniel A. Ford, Infrastructure & Energy; Wind Energy Industry
416-865-7372
dford@torys.com
Michael J. Fortier, Environmental Law; Aboriginal Law; Climate Change & Emissions Trading; Chemical Industry; Energy Industry; Manufacturing Industry; Mining Industry; Water &

Wastewaster Industry; Regulatory & Compliance
416-865-8147
mfortier@torys.com
Sabrina A. Gherbaz, Infrastructure & Energy; Climate Change & Emissions Trading; Energy Project Development & Finance
416-865-8179
sgherbaz@torys.com
Valerie Helbronner, Infrastructure & Energy; Renewable Energy Project Development & Finance; Wind Energy Projects; Solar Energy Projects; Biomass Energy Projects; Hydro Project Development; Aboriginal Law; Regulatory & Compliance
416-865-7516
vhelbronner@torys.com
Krista F. Hill, Infrastructure & Energy; Energy Law; Natural Resources Law
416-865-7953
khill@torys.com
Patricia D. S. (Trisha) Jackson, Environmental Law & Litigation; Energy Law & Litigation
416-865-7323
tjackson@torys.com
Charles Keizer, Infrastructure & Energy; Energy Law; Regulatory & Compliance; Project Development & Finance; Power Generation Industry; Renewable Energy Industry
416-865-7512
ckeizer@torys.com
Scott Kraag, Renewable Energy Project Development & Finance; Infrastructure Development & Finance; Mining Industry
416-865-7980
skraag@torys.com
Alison Lacy, Energy Project Development & Finance; Electricity Industry; Mining Industry; Natural Resources Industry
416-865-7503
alacy@torys.com
Tara A. Mackay, Infrastructure & Energy; Public Infrastructure Projects; Project Development & Finance
416-865-7528
tmackay@torys.com
Dennis E. Mahony, Environmental Law; Climate Change & Emissions Trading; Infrastructure & Energy; Pulp & Paper Industry; Mining Industry; Chemical Industry; Water & Wastewater Industry; Manufacturing Industry; Regulatory & Compliance
416-865-8214
dmahony@torys.com
Michael T. Pickersgill, Climate Change & Emissions Trading; Mining & Metals Industry
416-865-8180
mpickersgill@torys.com
Philip D. A. Symmonds, Energy & Infrastructure; Energy Project Development & Finance; Solar Energy Industry; Nuclear Energy Industry; Hydroelectric Power Industry; Mining & Metals Industry
416-865-8219
psymmonds@torys.com
John J. Tobin, Energy Project Development & Finance; Climate Change Matters; Wind Energy Industry; Solar Energy Industry; Hydroelectric Power Industry
416-865-7999
jtobin@torys.com
Jonathan B. Weisz, Energy & Infrastructure; Mining Industry; Energy Project Development & Finance; Climate Change & Emissions Trading
416-865-8157
jweisz@torys.com

WeirFoulds LLP
#1600, Exchange Tower P.O Box 480 130 King St. West, Toronto ON M5X 1J5
416-365-1110 416-365-1876
firm@weirfoulds.com
www.weirfoulds.com
Profile: 1 Offices, 78 Lawyers, Founded in: 1860
Environmental Lawyers:
J.M. Buhlman
 416-947-5070
 jbuhlman@weirfoulds.com
J.G. Cowan
 416-947-5007
 jcowan@weirfoulds.com
S.G. Foran
 416-947-5019
 sforan@weirfoulds.com
S.A. Metcalfe
 416-947-5084
 smetcalfe@weirfoulds.com
W.A.D. Millar
 416-947-5021
 dmillar@weirfoulds.com
R.B. Warren
 416-947-5075
 rwarren@weirfoulds.com

Willms & Shier Environmental Lawyers LLP
#900. 4 King St. West, Toronto ON M5H 1B6
416-863-0711 416-863-1938
info@willmsshier.com
www.willmsshier.com
Profile: 1 Offices, 11 Lawyers, Founded in: 1975
Willms & Shier Environmental Lawyers LLP guides companies & municipalities to environmental due diligence in managing industrial operations, contaminated land clean-up, transactions, & lawsuits. Clients are represented in civil litigation trials & at regulatory tribunal hearings. The firm defends clients from prosecutions, & helps them to obtain apporvals for air emissions, water discharges, & waste management & disposal. The following are the firm's practice areas: Aboriginal law; Clean technology; Energy law; Environmental litigation; Government policy & law; Natural resource law; Approvals & compliance; Contaminated land & Brownfields; Environmental law for municipalities; Environmental management; Land use planning & development; & Regulatory orders & prosecutions. Approvals & compliance work by the firm is as follows: Air, noise & vibration emissions; Drinking water & source protection; Environmental assessment; Industrial pollution control; Pesticides & new substances notification; Waste management; & wastewater treatment.
Environmental Lawyers:
Juli Abouchar, Environmental law for municipalities; Regulatory orders & prosecutions; Government policy & law; Land use planning & development; Aboriginal law; Energy law; Natural resource law; & Clean technology
 416-862-4836
 jabouchar@willmsshier.com
Jennifer Agnolin, Environmental law for municipalities; Approvals & compliance; Aboriginal law; Energy law; Clean technology
 416-862-4830
 jagnolin@willmsshier.com
Vivienne M. Ball, Contaminated land & Brownfields; Environmental litigation; Regulatory orders & prosecutions; Natural resources law
 416-862-4824
 vball@willmsshier.com
Raj Bharati, Contaminated land & Brownfields; Environmental litigation; Regulatory orders & prosecutions; Environmental law for municipalities; Approvals & compliance
 416-862-4825
 rbharati@williamshier.com
John Georgakopoulos, Compliance with federal & provincial laws; Litigation of environmental claims
 416-862-4826
 jgeorgakopoulos@willmsshier.com
Paul M. Manning, Environmental management; Land use planning & development; Energy law
 416-862-4843
 pmanning@willmsshier.com
Marc McAree, Environmental litigation; Contaminated land & Brownfields; Regulatory orders & prosecutions; Environmental law for municipalitites; Environmental management
 416-862-4820
 mmcaree@willmsshier.com
P. Douglas Petrie, Environmental law for municipalities; Environmental management; Land use planning & development; Regulatory orders & prosecutions; Approvals & compliance; Government policy & law
 416-862-4835
 dpetrie@willmsshier.com
Donna S.K. Shier, All aspects of environmental law
 416-862-4822
 dshier@willmsshier.com
Jacquelyn Stevens, Environmental litigation; Contaminated land & Brownfields; Aboriginal law; Natural resources law
 416-862-4828
 jstevens@willmsshier.com
John R. Willms, Environmental law for municipalities; Environmental management; Land use planning & development; Natural resources law; Energy law
 416-862-4821
 jwillms@willmsshier.com

Vankleek Hill

Nelligan O'Brien Payne
P.O Box 190 86 High St., Vankleek Hill ON K0B 1R0
613-678-2490 613-678-3762 888-565-9912
info@nelligan.ca
www.nelligan.ca
Profile: 4 Offices, 46 Lawyers
Environmental Lawyers:

Vaughan

Bratty & Partners LLP
#200, 7501 Keele St., Vaughan ON L4K 1Y2
905-760-2600 905-760-2900
info@bratty.com
www.bratty.com
Profile: 1 Offices, 14 Lawyers,
Our lawyers & their staff are experienced in all aspects of greenfields & brownfields development, including: land acquisition, subdivision & planning matters
Environmental Lawyers:
Daniel Botelho
Michael N. Durisin
Brian B. Finer
Barry A. Horosko
Helen A. Mihailidi
Larry Trifon

Walkerton

Magwood, Van De Vyvere, Thompson, & Grove-McClement LLP
#8280, P.O Box 880 215 Durham St., Walkerton ON N0G 2V0
519-881-3230 519-881-3595
wmvt@bmts.com
Profile: 1 Offices, 4 Lawyers, Founded in: 1957
Environmental Lawyers:
Tammy W. Grove-McClement, Municipal law
George C. Magwood, Municipal law

Waterloo

Miller Thomson LLP - Waterloo
#300 Accelerator Bldg. 295 Hagey Blvd., Waterloo ON N2L 6R5
519-579-3660 519-743-2540 866-658-0091
waterloo@millerthomson.com
www.millerthomson.com
Profile: 28 Lawyers,
Aboriginal Law; Energy Law; Municipal & Planning; Oil & Gas; Construction; Forestry
Environmental Lawyers:
F. Stephen Finch, Q.C.
 519-593-3210
 sfinch@millerthomson.com
Gregory P. Hanmer, Environmental; Health
 519-593-3233
 ghanmer@millerthomson.com
Robin-Lee Norris
 519-780-4638
 rnorris@millerthomson.com
Richard J. Trafford
 519- -
 rtrafford@millerthomson.com

Windsor

Bartlet & Richardes LLP
#1000, Canada Bldg. 374 Ouellette Ave., Windsor ON N9A 1A9
519-253-7461 519-253-2321
mail@bartlet.com
www.bartlet.com
Profile: 1 Offices, 13 Lawyers, Founded in: 1887
Environmental Lawyers:
D. Stephen Jovanovic, Construction Law

Shibley Righton LLP
#301, 2510 Ouellette Ave., Windsor ON N8X 1L4
519-969-9844 519-969-8045 866-422-7988
Profile: 2 Offices
Environmental Lawyers:

Law Firms / Prince Edward Island

Sutts, Strosberg LLP
#600, Westcourt Place 251 Goyeau St., Windsor ON N9A 6V4
519-258-9333 519-186-6613
www.strosbergco.com
Profile: 1 Offices, 20 Lawyers, Founded in: 1958
Environmental Law: Counseling & Audits, Crisis Management, Pollution & Contamination, Transactions, Land Development
Environmental Lawyers:
James K. Ball, Construction & Development; Environmental; Land Development
Werner H. Keller, Environmental
 519-561-6233
 werner_h_keller@strosbergco.com
David L. Robins, Environmental
Clifford N. Sutts, Q.C., Construction & Development; Environmental; Land Development
 519-561-6229
 cnsutts@strosbergco.com

Prince Edward Island
Charlottetown

Campbell Lea
P.O Box 429 15 Queen St., Charlottetown PE C1A 7K7
902-566-3400 902-566-9266
office@campbelllea.com
www.campbelllea.com
Profile: 1 Offices, 9 Lawyers
Environmental Lawyers:
William G. Lea, Q.C.
 bill.lea@mac.com

Cox and Palmer - Charlottetown
Landing Place 20 Great George St., Charlottetown PE C1A 4J6
902-628-1033 902-566-2639
charlottetown@coxandpalmer.com
www.coxandpalmer.com
Profile: 11 Lawyers,
Aboriginal; Energy, Oil & Gas; Marine
Environmental Lawyers:
Karen A. Campbell, Q.C., Municipal Law
 902-629-3911
 kcampbell@coxandpalmer.com
David W. Hooley, Q.C., Environmental; Municipal Law
 902-629-3903
 dhooley@coxandpalmer.com
Patricia McPhail, Municipal Law
 902-629-3936
 pmcphail@coxandpalmer.com
Wendy E. Reid, Q.C., Municipal Law
 902-629-3907
 wreid@coxandpalmer.com
P. Alanna Taylor, Municipal Law
 902-629-3921
 ataylor@coxandpalmer.com

Matheson & Murray
#202, Queen Square 119 Queen St., Charlottetown PE C1A 4B3 Canada
902-894-7051 902-368-3762
info@mathesonandmurray.com
www.mathesonandmurray.com
Profile: 1 Offices, 8 Lawyers, Founded in: 1981
Environmental Lawyers:
M. Lynn Murray, Q.C., Environmental Law
 902-368-7821
 lmurray@mathesonandmurray.com
Kerri Lynn Seward Carpenter, Environmental Law
 902-368-7826
 kseward@mathesonandmurray.com

Québec
Alma

Cain Lamarre Casgrain Wells - Alma
#03 Complexe Jacques-Gagnon 100, rue St-Joseph sud, Alma QC G8B 7A6
418-669-4580 418-669-0088
info@clcw.ca
www.clcw.qc.ca
Profile: 4 Lawyers
Environmental Lawyers:
Denis Bonneville, Santé
 denis.bonneville@clcw.ca
Martine Tremblay, Droit de l'environnement
 martine.tremblay@clcw.ca

Amos

Cain Lamarre Casgrain Wells - Amos
#201 101, 1re av est, Amos QC J9T 1H4
819-727-4153 819-727-9769
info@clcw.ca
www.clcw.ca
Profile: 2 Lawyers
Environmental Lawyers:
Marianne Gagnon-Bourget, Santé
 marianne.gagnon.bourget@clcw.ca

Amqui

Cain Lamarre Casgrain Wells - Amqui
20, rue Desbiens, Amqui QC G5J 3P1
418-629-3302 418-629-3333
info@clcw.ca
www.clcw.qc.ca
Profile: 2 Lawyers
Environmental Lawyers:
François Bérubé, Associé, Droit de la construction
 francois.berube@clcw.ca

Chicoutimi

Cain Lamarre Casgrain Wells - Chicoutimi
#600 CP 5420 255, rue Racine est, Chicoutimi QC G7H 6J6
418-545-4580 418-549-9590
info@clcw.ca
www.clcw.qc.ca
Profile: 31 Lawyers
Environmental Lawyers:
Jean-Sébastien Bergeron, Droit de l'environnement
 jean.sebastien.bergeron@clcw.ca
Richard Bergeron, Associé, Droit de la construction
 richard.bergeron@clcw.ca
Karine Boies, Droit de l'environnement
 karine.boies@clcw.ca
François Bouchard, Associé, Droit de l'environnement
 francois.bouchard@clcw.ca
Raynald Brassard, Santé
 raynald.brassard@clcw.ca
Louis Coulombe, Associé, Droit de la construction
 louis.coulombe@clcw.ca
Jean-François Delisle, Droit de l'environnement
 jean.francois.delisle@clcw.ca
Chantal Lavallée, Associée, Santé
 chantal.lavallee@clcw.ca
Marie-Claude Néron, Santé
 marie.claude.neron@clcw.ca
Annie Tremblay, Santé; Droit de la construction
 annie.tremblay@clcw.ca
Dominic Tremblay, Droit de l'environnement
 dominic.tremblay@clcw.ca
Guy Wells, Associé, Santé
 guy.wells@clcw.ca

Drummondville

Blais, Roger avocat inc
215, rue Lindsay, Drummondville QC J2C 1N8
819-477-2235 819-477-8674
blaisavocats@bellnet.ca
Profile: 1 Offices, 2 Lawyers, Founded in: 1970
Environmental Lawyers:
Roger Blais

Cain Lamarre Casgrain Wells - Drummondville
#201 330, rue Cormier, Drummondville QC J2C 8B3
819-477-2544 819-477-4343
info@clcw.ca
www.clcw.qc.ca
Profile: 12 Lawyers
Environmental Lawyers:
Marc Boisselle, Associé directeur régional, Droit de la construction
 marc.boisselle@clcw.ca
Jean-François Brouillard, Associé, Litige de la construction
 jean.francois.brouillard@clcw.ca

Maurice Laplante, Environnement
 maurice.laplante@clcw.ca

Gatineau

Beaudry, Bertrand Avocats
Maison du Citoyen 25, rue Laurier, 4e étage, Gatineau QC J8X 4C8
819-770-4880 819-595-4979
avocats@beaudry-bertrand.com
Profile: 1 Offices, 10 Lawyers, Founded in: 1929
Environmental Lawyers:
Pierre Dallaire, Municipal Law
Darquise Jolicoeur, Environmental Law
 djolicoeur@beaudry-bertrand.com
Pierre McMartin, Construction Law

Joliette

Bélanger, Sauvé
#101, 574, rue Saint-Viateur, Joliette QC J6E 3B6
450-755-3081 450-755-6721
info@belangersauve.com
www.belangersauve.com
Profile: 4 Offices, 73 Lawyers, Founded in: 1967
Environmental Lawyers:
Denis Beaupré, Environmental Law; Land Use and Development
 450-755-3011
 dbeaupre@belangersauve.com
Yves Chaîné, Environmental Law
 450-755-3011
 ychaine@belangersuave.com

Ferland & Bélair
#150, 430, rue de Lanaudière, Joliette QC J6E 7X1
450-759-7412 450-759-5366 888-759-7412
avocats@ferlandbelair.ca
Profile: 1 Offices, 3 Lawyers, Founded in: 1981
Environmental Lawyers:
Michel Ferland, Municipal & Construction

Montréal

Bélanger, Sauvé
#1700, 1, Place Ville Marie, Montréal QC H3B 2C1
514-878-3081 514-878-3053
info@belangersauve.com
www.belangersauve.com
Profile: 4 Offices, 73 Lawyers, Founded in: 1967
Environmental Lawyers:
Sylvain Bélair
 sbelair@belangersauve.com
Michel Cantin
 514-878-3089
 mcantin@belangersauve.com
Yvon Denault
 514-878-3089
 ydenault@belangersauve.com
Alain-Claude Desforges
 acdesforges@belangersauve.com
Marc Lalonde
 514-878-3089
 mlalonde@belangersauve.com
Marc Lapierrière
 514-878-3089
Diane Larose
 514-878-3089
 dlarose@belangersauve.com
Pierre LePage
 514-878-3089
 plepage@belangersauve.com
Pierre B. Paquin
 514-878-3089
 pbpaquin@belangersauve.com

Borden Ladner Gervais LLP - Montréal
#900 1000, rue de La Gauchetière ouest, Montréal QC H3B 5H4
514-879-1212 514-954-1905
info@blg.com
www.blg.com
Profile: 131 Lawyers
Environmental Lawyers:
Daniel Ayotte, Partner, Construction Law
 514-954-3138
 dayotte@blg.com

Marc A. Babinski, Partner, Climate Change; Biotech & PharmaceuticalS
514-954-2566
mbabinski@blg.com
P.Jeremy Bolger, Partner, Maritime Law
514-954-3119
jbolger@blg.com
Sylvie Bouvette, Partner, Oil & Gas; Electricity Markets
514-954-2507
sbouvette@blg.com
Timothy R. Carsley, Partner, Biosciences; Biotech & Pharmaceuticals
514-954-3127
tcarsley@blg.com
Mélanie Champagne, Health Law
514-954-3116
mchampagne@blg.com
Lynne Chlala, Health Law
514-954-3101
lchlala@blg.com
Louis Clément, Partner, Health Law; Forestry Law; Biotech & Pharmaceuticals; Mining
514-954-2524
lclement@blg.com
Saverio (Sam) Coppola, Partner, Climate Change
514-954-3110
scoppola@blg.com
Nicola Corbo, Construction Law
514-954-3163
ncorbo@blg.com
Suzanne Courchesne, Partner, Health Law; Biotech & Pharmaceuticals
514-954-3112
scourchesne@blg.com
Giovanni De Sua, Maritime Law; Mining
514-954-3140
gdesua@blg.com
Yves A. Dubois, Partner, Environmental Law; Electricity Markets
514-954-3130
ydubois@blg.com
Jean-Marie Fontaine, Partner, Maritime Law
514-954-3196
jfontaine@blg.com
Daniel Grodinsky, Maritime Law
514-954-2503
dgrodinsky@blg.com
François Grondin, Partner, Environmental Law
514-954-3153
fgrondin@blg.com
Simon Grégoire, Partner, Construction Litigation
514-954-3151
sgregoire@blg.com
Catherine Guertin, Partner, Mining Law
514-954-3179
cguertin@blg.com
Yvan Houle, Partner, Construction Law; Maritime Law; Aboriginal Law
514-954-3146
yhoule@blg.com
Jacques Laurent, Partner, Climate Change; Electricity Markets
514-954-3193
jlaurent@blg.com
Gabriel Lefebvre, Construction Law
514-954-2580
glefebvre@blg.com
Marie-Eve Leveillé, Construction Law & Litigation
514-954-2506
mleveille@blg.com
François Longpré, Partner, Occupational Health & Safety
514-954-2543
flongpre@blg.com
Catherine Lussier, Construction Law
514-954-2550
clussier@blg.com
Caroline Matte, Partner, Health Law; Environmental Law; Biotech & Pharmaceuticals
514-954-2519
cmatte@blg.com
Darren McGuire, Partner, Maritime Law
514-954-3105
dmcguire@blg.com
Patrice Morin, Partner, Construction Law
514-954-3104
pmorin@blg.com

John G. Murphy, Partner, Construction Law
514-954-3155
jmurphy@blg.com
Peter G. Pamel, Partner, Maritime Law; climate Change; Mining
514-954-3169
ppamel@blg.com
Stéphane Pitre, Partner, Construction Law
514-954-3147
spitre@blg.com
Katherine Poirier, Partner, Health Law; Occupational Safety
514-954-3175
kpoirier@blg.com
Julia Pomeroy, Health Law
514-954-3152
jpomeroy@blg.com
Guy J. Pratte, Partner, Environmental Law
514-954-2545
gpratte@blg.com
Emmanuelle Rolland, Partner, Health Law
514-954-3145
erolland@blg.com
Marie-Claude Sarrazin, Construction Law
514-954-3167
msarrazin@blg.com
Tammy Shulman, Partner, Energy; Oil & Gas; Electricity Markets
514-954-3183
tshulman@blg.com
Pierrette Sinclair, Counsel, Environmental Law; Climate Change; Energy; Oil & Gas; Electricity Markets; Natural Resources; Forestry; Mining
514-954-2527
psinclair@blg.com
Marc Unger, Environmental Law; Climate Change
514-954-2515
munger@blg.com
Robert Wilkins, Maritime Law
514-954-3184
rwilkins@blg.com

Cain Lamarre Casgrain Wells - Montréal
#2780 630, boul René-Lévesque ouest, Montréal QC H3B 1S6
514-393-4580 514-393-9590
info@clcw.ca
www.clcw.qc.ca
Profile: 36 Lawyers
Environmental Lawyers:
François Lamarre, Droit de la construction
 francois.lamarre@clcw.ca
Mario Proulx, Droit de la construction
 mario.proulx@clcw.ca
Sylvain Toupin, Santé et sécurité du travail
 sylvain.toupin@clcw.ca
André Tremblay, Droit de la santé
 andre.tremblay@clcw.ca
Marie-Josée Trudeau, Environnement; Agroalimentaire
 marie.josee.trudeau@clcw.ca

Daigneault, avocats inc.
#400, Place D'Youville 353, rue Saint-Nicolas, Montréal QC H2Y 2P1
514-985-2929 514-985-0595 888-228-5834
enviro@rdaigneaultinc.com
www.daigneaultinc.com
Profile: 1 Offices, 5 Lawyers, Founded in: 2001
The firm specializes in environmental, resource, & land-use law.
Environmental Lawyers:
Robert Daigneault
Lucie Gosselin
Marie-Andrée Lévesque
Hervé Pageot
Roger Paiement

Davies Ward Phillips & Vineberg S.E.N.C.R.L., s.r.l.
1501, av McGill College, 26e étage, Montréal QC H3A 3N9
514-841-6400 514-841-6499 888-841-6400
jfournier@dwpv.com
www.dwpv.com
Profile: 3 Offices, 242 Lawyers, Founded in: 1895
Environmental Law; Environmental Transactions; Energy Law; Energy Transactions; Regulatory & Compliance; Climate Change & Emission Trading; Contaminated Sites; Natural Resources Projects; Renewable Energy Industry; Oil & Gas Industry; Hydroelectric Industry; Nuclear Industry
Environmental Lawyers:
Marc-André Boutin, Environmental Law & Litigation
514-841-6527
maboutin@dwpv.com
Nicolas X. Cloutier, Land Use Planning & Development; Zoning, Subdivision & Site Planning; Land Expropriation; Farmland Protection
514-841-6535
ncloutier@dwpv.com
Laurence Detière, Environmental Law
514-841-6528
ldetiere@dwpv.com
Alain Gaul, Environmental Law
514-841-6577
agaul@dwpv.com
Michel Pelletier, Environmental Law; Brownfield Redevelopment
514-841-6455
mpelletier@dwpv.com
Hillel W. Rosen, Renewable Energy Projects; Forest Products Industry
514-841-6443
hrosen@dwpv.com

Davis LLP - Montréal
#1400, 1501, av McGill College, Montréal QC H3A 3M8
514-392-1991 514-392-1999
www.davis.ca
Profile: 8 Offices, Founded in: 1892
Environmental Lawyers:
David W. Rothschild, Environmental law
514-392-8401
drothschild@davis.ca
Stephan Scott Trudeau, Environmental law; Climate change law; Projects, infrastructure, & P3; Energy & utilities; Mining law
514-392-8426
strudeau@davis.ca

Fasken Martineau - Montréal
#3700, Tour de la Bourse CP 242 800, Place Victoria, Montréal QC H4Z 1E9
514-397-7400 514-397-7600 800-361-6266
montreal@fasken.com
www.fasken.com
Profile: 8 Offices, 650 Lawyers, Founded in: 1907
Environmental Lawyers:
Marie-Claude Bellemare
514-397-7571
mbellemare@mtl.fasken.com
Luc Bourbonnais, Energy, Environmental and Regulatory
514-397-4356
lbourbonnais@mtl.fasken.com
Louise Bélanger, Municipal Law
514-397-7567
lbelanger@mtl.fasken.com
Florence Dagicour, Environmental Law; Climate change; Nuclear Law
514-397-5236
fdagicour@mtl.fasken.com
André Durocher, Partner, Environmental Law; Municipal Law; Pharmaceutical Law; Aboriginal Law
514-397-7495
adurocher@mtl.fasken.com
Marc-André Fabien, Administrative & Quasi Criminal Litigation
514-397-7557
mfabien@mtl.fasken.com
Gaël C. Gravenor, Energy, Environmental & Regulatory
514-397-7524
ggravenor@mtl.fasken.com
Shelley L. Kath
514-397-5236
skath@mtl.fasken.com
Charles Kazaz, Environmental Law; Waste Management; Mining
514-397-4348
ckazaz@tor.fasken.com
Pierre B. Meunier, Environmental Law; Energy Regulatory Law
514-397-4380
pmeunier@mtl.fasken.com
André Turmel, Energy and Climate Change Law
514-397-5141
aturmel@mtl.fasken.com

Fraser Milner Casgrain S.E.N.C.R.L./LLP
#3900, 1, Place Ville-Marie, Montréal QC H3B 4M7
514-878-8800 514-866-2241 Telex: 05-24195
claude.morency@fmc-law.com
www.fmc-law.com

Law Firms / Québec

Profile: 100 Lawyers,
The firm provides legal services in the areas of Construction & Infrastructure Law; Forest Products; Hydroelectric Energy; Mining Law; & Natural Resources Law

Environmental Lawyers:
Jean Bazin, Q.C., Environmental & Natural Resources; Aboriginal Law; Energy; Business Strategies
 514-878-8804
 jean.bazin@fmc-law.com
Alexandre Boileau, Construction
 514-878-5836
 alexandre.boileau@fmc-law.com
Michel A. Brunet, Construction
 514-878-8832
 michel.brunet@fmc-law.com
Mathilde Carrière, Energy; Construction
 514-878-5823
 mathilde.carriere@fmc-law.com
Marie-Hélène Dufour, Construction
 514-878-5876
 m-h.dufour@fmc-law.com
Jean-Pierre Dépelteau, Energy, Construction
 514-878-8814
 j-p.depelteau@fmc-law.com
Pierre Grenier, Construction
 514-878-8851
 pierre.grenier@fmc-law.com
Jean Groleau, Construction
 514-878-8851
 jean.groleau@fmc-law.com
Mélanie Jacques, Construction
 514-878-5869
 melanie.jacques@fmc-law.com
Gentiane Joyal, Environment & Natural Resources
 514-878-5826
 gentiane.joyal@fmc-law.com
Serge Lalonde, Energy; Litigation; Construction
 514-878-5815
 serge.lalonde@fmc-law.com
John F. Lemieux, Aboriginal Law
 514-878-8811
 john.lemieux@fmc-law.com
Stephen Lloyd, Aboriginal Law
 514-878-5831
 stephen.lloyd@fmc-law.com
Denis Manzo, Transportation
Nicolas Roy, Energy
 514-878-5861
 nicolas.roy@fmc-law.com
Gil Rémillard, Counsel, Environment & Natural Resources; Litigation
 514-878-8864
 gil.remillard@fmc-law.com
Charles R. Spector, Energy, Municipal
 514-878-8847
 charles.spector@fmc-law.com
Jean-François Vézina, Construction
 514-878-8885
 j-f.vezina@fmc-law.com
Margaret Weltrowska, Construction
 514-878-5841
 margaret.weltrowska@fmc-law.com

Gowling Lafleur Henderson S.E.N.C.R.L./LLP
1, Place Ville Marie, 37e étage, Montréal QC H3B 3P4
514-878-9641 514-878-1450
robert.dorion@gowlings.com
www.gowlings.com
Profile: 100 Lawyers,
Environmental Law; Energy Law; Aboriginal Law; Climate Change; Infrastructure; Regulatory & Compliance

Environmental Lawyers:
Denis Blanchette, Aboriginal Law; Environmental Law
 514-392-9445
 denis.blanchette@gowlings.com
Douglas W. Clarke, Climate Change; Greenhouse Gas Emissions Regulatory; Carbon Finance; Technology Industry & CleanTech; Wind Farm Project Finance
 514-392-9518
 douglas.clarke@gowlings.com
Jean-Sébastien Clément, Aboriginal Law; Natural Resources Law; Forestry related Legal Matters; Environmental Law; Class Actions; Government Affairs
 514-392-9567
 jean-sebastien.clement@gowlings.com
François Dandonneau, Aboriginal Law; First Nations & Hydro-Québec Matters
 514-392-9503
 francois.dandonneau@gowlings.com
Paul R. Granda, Environmental Law; Regulatory & Compliance; Brownfield Redevelopment; Environmental Management Systems; Waste Management Industry; Oil Industry; Mining Industry; Chemical Industry; Forestry Industry; Professional Liability
 514-392-9598
 paul.granda@gowlings.com
John Hurley, Aboriginal Law; Environmental Law; Energy Law; Infrastructure; Regulatory; Government Affairs; Natural Resources Law; Power Project Matters
 514-392-9431
 john.hurley@gowlings.com
Pierre Legault, Energy Law; Electricity & Power Generation Matters; Power Transmission Agreements; Regulatory
 514-392-9599
 pierre.legault@gowlings.com
Emmanuel Manolakis, Biomass Conversion; Biotechnology; Alternative Fuels
 514-392-9592
 emmanuel.manolakis@gowlings.com
Charles-Antoine Robitaille, Infrastructure; Energy Law; Energy Projects; Construction Law; Natural Resources Industry
 514-392-9584
 charlesantoine.robitaille@gowlings.com

Heenan Blaikie S.E.N.C.R.L/SRL
#2500 1250, boul René-Lévesque ouest, Montréal QC H3B 4Y1
514-846-1212 514-846-3427
www.heenanblaikie.com
Profile: 9 Offices, 550 Lawyers, Founded in: 1973

Environmental Lawyers:
Marcel Aubut, Partner, Construction; Energy
 514-846-2326
 maubut@heenan.ca
Poupak Bahamin, Partner, Natural Resources; Mining
 514-846-2377
 pbahamin@heenan.ca
Geneviève Beaudin, Occupational Health & Safety
 514-846-2393
 gbeaudin@heenan.ca
Marie-Claude Bellemare, Partner, Environmental Law; Energy; Natural Resources
 514-846-7224
 mcbellemare@heenan.ca
Max R. Bernard, Partner, Construction; Real estate
 514-846-2216
 mbernard@heenan.ca
Peter M. Blaikie, Founding Partner, Construction
 514-846-2328
 pblaikie@heenan.ca
Robert Bonhomme, Partner, Occupational Health & Safety
 514-846-2260
 rbonhomme@heenan.ca
Jacques Bouchard Jr., Partner, Mining
 514-846-2252
 jbouchard@heenan.ca
Amélie Bélisle, Occupational Health & Safety
 514-846-2224
 abelisle@heenan.ca
Jean E. Clerk, Partner, Transportation
 514-846-2262
 jclerk@heenan.ca
Magali Cournoyer-Proulx, Partner, Health
 514-846-2292
 mproulx@heenan.ca
Marie Cousineau, Occupational Health & Safety
 514-846-2346
 mcousineau@heenan.ca
Christophe De Koster, Partner, Energy; Not-For-Profit Organizations
 514-846-4760
 cdekoster@heenan.ca
Ilan Dunsky, Partner, Energy; Natural Resources; Transportation
 514-846-4763
 idunsky@heenan.ca
Marie-Christine Frenette, Energy
 514-846-2334
 mcfrenette@heenan.ca
Simon Gagné, Partner, Health
 514-846-2277
 simon@heenan.ca
Eva Gazurek, Natural Resources; Mining
 514-846-2322
 egazurek@heenan.ca
Joel Goldberg, Partner, Environmental Law; Construction
 514-846-2310
 jgoldberg@heenan.ca
Lucie Guimond, Partner, Occupational Health & Safety
 514-846-2304
 lguimond@heenan.ca
Marie-Josée Hogue, Partner, Health
 514-846-2201
 mhogue@heenan.ca
Tibor Holländer, Partner, Health
 514-846-2384
 thollander@heenan.ca
Véronique Iezzoni, Partner, Health
 514-846-2230
 viezzoni@heenan.ca
David Joanisse, Partner, Construction Litigation
 514-846-2261
 djoanisse@heenan.ca
Pierre-Marc Johnson, Counsel, Environmental Issues; Health
 514-846-2200
 pjohnson@heenan.ca
Manon Jolicoeur, Partner, Construction
 514-846-2220
 mjolicoeur@heenan.ca
Kosta Kostic, Partner, Mining
 514-846-2395
 kkostic@heenan.ca
Simon Labarge, Occupational Health & Safety
 514-846-7248
 slaberge@heenan.ca
Pierre Langlois, Partner, Environmental Law; Natural Resources; Mining
 514-846-7234
 planglois@heenan.ca
Marie-Christine Lauzone, Occupational Health & Safety
 514-846-2290
 mlauzon@heenan.ca
Francine Legault, Partner, Occupational Health & Safety
 514-846-2348
 flegault@heenan.ca
Eric M. Levy, Partner, Mining
 514-846-2256
 elevy@heenan.ca
Eric Maldoff, Partner, Health; Aboriginal Law
 514-846-2249
 emaldoff@heenan.ca
Bruce McNiven, Partner, Health
 514-846-2244
 bmcniven@heenan.ca
Patrick A. Molinari, Health
 514-846-2343
 pmolinari@heenan.ca
Gary D.D. Morrison, Partner, Construction
 514-846-2268
 gmorrison@heenan.ca
Dominique Ménard, Partner, Construction Litigation
 514-846-2238
 domenard@heenan.ca
Alexandre Panneton, Construction Litigation
 514-846-2246
 apanneton@heenan.ca
Claude Paquet, Partner, Environmental Law
 514-846-2378
 cpaquet@heenan.ca
Rhéaume Perreault, Partner, Health; Occupational Health & Safety
 514-846-2306
 rperreaul@heenan.ca
Sylvain Poirier, Partner, Health
 514-846-2273
 spoirier@heenan.ca
Michel Poirier, Partner, Land Use; Environmental Law; Municipal Law
 514-846-2295
 mpoirier@heenan.ca
Normand Quesnel, Partner, Construction
 514-846-2217
 nquesnel@heenan.ca
Karen M. Rogers, Partner, Construction Litigation; Real Estate
 514-846-2210
 krogers@heenan.ca.ca
Mélanie Sauriol, Occupational Health & Safety
 514-846-2281
 msauriol@heenan.ca

Law Firms / Québec

Sarah-Anne Savoie, Health
514-846-7055
sasavoie@heenan.ca
Lampros Stougiannos, Energy
514-846-6882
lstougiannos@heenan.ca
Chantal Sylvestre, Partner, Energy; Real Estate
514-846-2344
csylvestr@heenan.ca
Charles Olivier Thibault, Health
514-846-2276
cothibeault@heenan.ca
Philippe Tremblay, Partner, Construction Litigation
514-846-2237
ptremblay@heenan.ca
Stephan H. Trihey, Partner, Construction Litigation
514-846-7228
strihey@heenan.ca
Yves Turgeon, Partner, Natural Resources; Construction
514-846-2818
yturgeon@heenan.ca
Virginie Vigeant, Occupational Health & Safety
514-846-2285
vvigeant@heenan.ca
Neil Wiener, Partner, Mining
514-846-2208
nwiener@heenan.ca
Jeremy Wisniewski, Construction Litigation
514-846-2274
jwisniewski@heenan.ca

Hutchins Caron & Associés
#700, 485 rue McGill, Montréal QC H2Y 2H4
514-849-2403 514-849-4907 877-849-2403
admin@hutchinslegal.ca
www.hutchinslegal.ca
Profile: 2 Offices, 5 Lawyers,
Le cabinet possède près de trente années d'expérience, notamment dans les domaines du droit autochtone et du droit de l'environnement.
Environmental Lawyers:
Monique Caron, Droit autochtone; Droit de l'environnement
mcaron@hutchinslegal.ca
Julie Corry, Droit autochtone; Droit de l'environnement
jcorry@hutchinslegal.ca
Lysane Cree, Droit autochtone; Droit de l'environnement
lcree@hutchinslegal.ca
Peter W. Hutchins, Associé, Droit de l'environnement; Droit autochtone
phutchins@hutchinslegal.ca
David Kalmakoff, Droit autochtone; Droit de l'environnement
dkalmakoff@hutchinslegal.ca

Lamarre Perron Lambert Vincent
#200, 480, boul St-Laurent, Montréal QC H2Y 3Y7
514-798-1515 514-798-5599
Profile: 1 Offices, 6 Lawyers, Founded in: 1957
Environmental Lawyers:
Paul Lamarre
450-674-7574
p.lamarre@lplv.com

Langlois Kronström Desjardins
1002, rue Sherbrooke ouest, 28e étage, Montréal QC H3A 3L6
514-842-9512 514-845-6573 888-650-7001
info@lkd.ca
www.langloiskronstromdesjardins.com
Profile: 33 Lawyers
Environmental Lawyers:
Serge Amar, Associé, Droit de la construction; Santé
514-282-7828
serge.amar@lkd.ca
Gerry Apostolatos, Associé, Droit de la construction
514-282-7831
gerry.apostolatos@lkd.ca
Martine Bergeron, Santé
514-282-7836
martine.bergeron@lkd.ca
Yann Bernard, Associé, Santé & sécurité au travail
514-282-7838
yann.bernard@lkd.ca
Annie Bourgeois, Santé & sécurité au travail
514-282-7834
annie.bourgeois@lkd.ca

Louise Boutin, Associée, Santé; Droit de la construction
514-282-7833
louise.boutin@lkd.ca
Stefan Chripounoff, Énergie & ressources naturelles
514-282-7807
stefan.chripounoff@lkd.ca
Catherine Galardo, Santé
514-282-7810
catherine.galardo@lkd.ca
Pierre Galardo, Associé, Santé; Urbanisme
514-282-7819
pierre.galardo@lkd.ca
Céline Garneau, Associée, Droit de la construction
514-282-7818
celine.garneau@lkd.ca
Alexander Herman, Santé
514-282-7801
alexander.herman@lkd.ca
Tina Hobday, Associée, Énergie & ressources naturelles
514-282-7816
tina.hobday@lkd.ca
Michel Huart, Énergie & ressources naturelles; Environment
514-282-7829
michel.huart@lkd.ca
Dimitri Maniatis, Associé, Énergie & ressources naturelles
514-282-7832
dimitri.maniatis@lkd.ca
Marie-Geneviève Masson, Associée, Santé
514-282-7821
marie-genevieve.masson@lkd.ca
René Paquette, Associé, Santé & sécurité au travail
514-282-7826
rene.paquette@lkd.ca
Marc-André Sansregret, Associé, Droit de la construction
514-282-7839
marc-andre.sansregret@lkd.ca
Rébecca St-Pierre, Santé
514-282-7824
rebecca.st-pierre@lkd.ca

Lapointe Rosenstein Marchand Melançon
#1400, 1250, boul René-Lévesque ouest, Montréal QC H3B 5E9
514-925-6300 514-925-9001 800-728-6228
www.lrmm.com
Profile: 1 Offices, 70 Lawyers, Founded in: 1966
Environmental Lawyers:
Frédéric Blanchette, Associé, Droit de la construction
514-925-6375
frederic.blanchette@lrmm.com
Louis P. Brien, Associé, Droit de la construction
514-925-6348
louis.brien@lrmm.com
Jeanne Fortin, Associée, Droit de l'énergie
514-925-6311
jeanne.fortin@lrmm.com
Guillaume Hébert, Associé, Droit de la construction
514-925-6378
guillaume.hebert@lrmm.com
Paul A. Melançon, Associé, Droit de la construction
514-925-6308
paul.melancon@lrmm.com
Michel G. Ménard, Associé, Droit de la construction
514-925-6328
michel.menard@lrmm.com
Bertrand Paiement, Associé, Droit de la construction
514-925-6309
bertrand.paiement@lrmm.com
Mark M. Rosenstein, Associé, Droit de l'énergie
514-925-6335
mark.rosenstein@lrmm.com
André Rousseau, Associé, Droit de la construction
514-925-6389
andre.rousseau@lrmm.com
Stéphane Roy, Associé, Droit de la construction; Droit de l'énergie
514-925-6349
stephane.roy@lrmm.com
Michel Tourangeau, Associé, Droit de la construction
514-925-6317
michel.tourangeau@lrmm.com
Ruth Veilleux, Associée, Droit de la construction
514-925-6329
ruth.veilleux@lrmm.com

Lavery, de Billy - Montréal
#4000, 1, Place Ville-Marie, Montréal QC H3B 4M4

514-871-1522 514-871-8977
info@lavery.qc.ca
www.laverydebilly.com
Profile: 3 Offices, 146 Lawyers, Founded in: 1913
Environmental Lawyers:
Pierre-L. Baribeau, Health Law
514-877-2965
pbaribeau@lavery.ca
Loïc Berdnikoff, Health Law
514-877-2981
lberdnikoff@lavery.ca
Yvan Biron, Environmental, Energy & Natural Resources Law
514-877-2910
ybiron@lavery.ca
Michel Blouin, Mining Law
514-877-3041
mblouin@lavery.ca
Monique Brassard, Health Law
514-877-2942
mbrassard@lavery.ca
Anne Bélanger, Health Law
514-877-3091
abelanger@lavery.ca
Marie-Claude Cantin, Partner, Construction & Surety Law
514-877-3006
mccantin@lavery.ca
Louis Charette, Partner, Transportation Law
514-877-2946
lcharette@lavery.ca
Melanie Chartrand, Mining Law
514-878-5663
mchartrand@lavery.ca
Daniel Alain Dagenais, Partner, Construction & Surety Law; Mining
514-877-2924
dadagenais@lavery.ca
Marc Dagenais, Partner, Environmental, Energy & Natural Resources Law; Mining Law
514-877-2995
mdagenais@lavery.ca
Pierre Denis, Partner, Mining Law
514-877-2908
pdenis@lavery.ca
Raymond Doray, Partner, Health Law
514-877-2913
rdoray@lavery.ca
Geneviève Fournier, Mining Law
514-877-3055
gfournier@lavery.ca
Philippe Frère, Partner, Aboriginal Law
514-877-2978
pfrere@lavery.ca
Marie-Andrée Gagnon, Health Law
514-877-3011
magagnon@lavery.ca
Nicolas Gagnon, Partner, Construction & Surety Law
514-877-3046
ngagnon@lavery.ca
Jocelyne Gagné, Partner, Construction & Surety Law
514-878-5542
jgagne@lavery.ca
Julie Grondin, Construction & Surety Law
514-877-2957
jgrondin@lavery.ca
Benjamin David Gross, Partner, Mining Law
514-877-2983
bgross@lavery.ca
Jean Hébert, Partner, Construction & Surety Law
514-877-2926
jhebert@lavery.ca
Maude Lafortune-Bélair, Health Law
514-877-3077
mlafortunebelair@lavery.ca
Jean-François Lepage, Partner, Health Law
514-877-2970
jflepage@lavery.ca
Jean-Philippe Lincourt, Transportation Law; Environmental Law
514-877-2922
jplincourt@lavery.ca
Anne-Marie Lévesque, Health Law
514-877-2944
amlevesque@lavery.ca
Zeïneb Mellouli, Environmental, Energy & Natural Resources Law
514-877-3056
zmellouli@lavery.ca

Law Firms / Québec

Véronique Morin, Health Law
  514-877-3082
  vmorin@lavery.ca
Philip Nolan, Partner, Mining Law
  514-877-2914
  pnolan@lavery.ca
Jacques Nols, Partner, Health Law
  514-877-2932
  jnols@lavery.ca
Frédéric Pagé, Environmental, Energy & Natural Resources Law; Mining Law; Aboriginal Law
  514-877-3095
  fpage@lavery.ca
Jacques Perron, Partner, Transportation Law
  514-877-2905
  jperron@lavery.ca
Martin Pichette, Partner, Construction & Surety Law; Transportation Law
  514-877-3032
  mpichette@lavery.ca
Sophie Prégent, Environmental, Energy & Natural Resources Law; Aboriginal Law
  514-877-2948
  spregent@lavery.ca
Mathieu Quenneville, Environmental, Energy & Natural Resources Law; Aboriginal Law
  514-877-3087
  mquenneville@lavery.ca
Patrice Racicot, Partner, Construction & Surety Law
  514-878-5567
  pracicot@lavery.ca
Dina Raphaël, Partner, Construction & Surety Law
  514-877-3013
  draphael@lavery.ca
Carl M. Ravinsky, Partner, Mining Law
  514-878-5594
  cravinsky@lavery.ca
Michel Servant, Partner, Mining Law
  514-877-2915
  mservant@lavery.ca
Virginie Simard, Health Law
  514-877-2931
  vsimard@lavery.ca
Dominique Vallières, Construction & Surety Law
  514-877-2917
  dvallieres@lavery.ca
Emil Vidrascu, Partner, Construction & Surety Law
  514-877-3007
  evidrascu@lavery.ca
Luc Villiard, Partner, Construction & Surety Law
  514-877-2951
  lvilliard@lavery.ca
Sébastien Vézina, Partner, Mining Law
  514-877-2964
  svezina@lavery.ca
Michel Yergeau, Partner, Environmental, Energy & Natural Resources Law; Aboriginal Law
  514-877-2911
  myergeau@lavery.ca
Philippe d'Etcheverry, Construction & Surety Law
  514-877-2996
  pdetcheverry@lavery.ca

McCarthy Tétrault LLP - Montréal
#2500, 1000, rue de la Gauchetière ouest, Montréal QC H3B 0A2
514-397-4100 514-875-6246 877-397-4100
www.mccarthy.ca
Profile: 7 Offices, 164 Lawyers, Founded in: 1855
Biotechnology; Energy; Environmental; Municipal
Environmental Lawyers:
Julie Belley Perron, Environmental Law
  514-397-5451
  jbperron@mccarthy.ca
Ann M. Bigué, Energy; Aboriginal Rights; Environmental Assessment
  514-397-4127
  abigue@mccarthy.ca
Martin Boodman, Environmental Litigation
  514-397-4117
  mboodman@mccarthy.ca
Andrée-Claude Bérubé, Environmental Law; Environmental Aspects of Financial Transactions; Energy
  514-397-5476
  acberube@mccarthy.ca
Michel Gagné, General Counsel; Litigation
  514-397-4204
  mgagne@mccarthy.ca
Mira Gauvin, Environmental Law
  514-397-4134
  mgauvin@mccarthy.ca
Mira Gauvin, Environmental Law
  514-397-4134
  mgauvin@mccarthy.ca
François Grondin, Litigation; Business Transactions; Environmental Litigation
  514-397-4283
  fgrondin@mccarthy.ca
Jérémie-Nicolas Moisan, Environmental Litigation
  514-397-7854
  jnmoisan@mccarthy.ca
Ann-Marie Sheahan, Environmental Law; Climate Change; Mining; Oil & Gas
  514-397-4212
  amsheahan@mccarthy.ca
Chantal C. Tremblay, Environmental Litigation
  514-397-4231
  cctremblay@mccarthy.ca
Cindy Vaillancourt, Environmental Law
  514-397-4177
  cvaillancourt@mccarthy.ca

McMillan Binch Mendelsohn - Montréal
#2700, 1000, rue Sherbrooke ouest, Montréal QC H3A 3G4
514-987-5000 514-987-1213
info@mcmillan.ca
www.mcmillan.ca
Profile: 47 Lawyers, Founded in: 1951
Environmental Lawyers:
Alain Breault, Litigation; Environmental Law
  514-987-5037
  alain.breault@mcmbm.com
Earl S. Cohen, Real Estate; Environmental Law
  514-987-5045
  earl.cohen@mcmbm.com
Céline Tessier
  514-987-5032
  celine.tessier@mcmbm.com

Miller Thomson LLP - Montréal
Tour CIBC 1155, boul René-Lévesque ouest, 31e étage, Montréal QC H3B 3S6
514-875-5210 514-875-4308 888-875-5210
info@millerthomsonpouliot.com
www.millerthomson.com
Profile: 62 Lawyers, Founded in: 1952
Environmental Lawyers:
Lonnie Brodkin-Schneider, Associée, Santé
  514-871-5449
  lbschneider@millerthomsonpouliot.com
Christian J. Brossard, Associé, Litige construction
  514-871-5407
  cjbrossard@millerthomsonpouliot.com
Normand D'Amour, Associé, Litige construction
  514-871-5487
  ndamour@millerthomsonpouliot.com
Benoît Gascon, Associé, Industrie minière
  514-871-5490
  bgascon@millerthomsonpouliot.com
Adina-Cristina Georgescu, Environnement; Technologies vertes; Santé; Énergie et ressources naturelles
  514-871-5494
  acgeorgescu@millerthomsonpouliot.com
Luc Gratton, Associé, Technologies vertes; Production d'énergie
  514-871-5482
  lgratton@millerthomsonpouliot.com
Antonio Iacovelli, Litige construction
  514-841-5483
  aiacovelli@millerthomsonpouliot.com
Frank Mariage, Associé, Industrie minière
  514-871-5446
  mariage@millerthomsonpouliot.com
J. Brent Muir, Associé, Industrie minière
  514-871-5478
  bmuir@millerthomsonpouliot.com
Marc Pothier, Associé, Industrie minière
  514-871-5442
  mpothier@millerthomsonpouliot.com
Louis-Michel Tremblay, Associé, Litige construction
  514-871-5421
  lmtremblay@millerthomsonpouliot.com
Mathieu Turcotte, Associé, Litige construction
  514-871-5492
  mturcotte@millerthomsonpouliot.com

Ogilvy Renault LLP/S.E.N.C.R.L., s.r.l. - Montréal
#1100, 1981, av McGill College, Montréal QC H3A 3C1
514-847-4747 514-286-5474
montreal@ogilvyrenault.com
www.ogilvyrenault.com
Profile: 6 Offices, 420 Lawyers, Founded in: 1879
Environmental risk management, counsel, assistance in all forms of transactional matters, representation & litigation
Environmental Lawyers:
Jean G. Bertrand, Transportation, Civil & Penal Litigation
  514-847-4401
  jbertrand@ogilvyrenault.com
Louis-Paul Cullen, Civil & Penal Litigation; Transactional Matters
  514-847-4504
  lcullen@ogilvyrenault.com
Richard L. Desgagnés, Civil Litigation with emphasis on Marine Pollution
  514-847-4431
  rdesgagnes@ogilvyrenault.com
Éric Dunberry, Civil & Penal Litigation
  514-847-4492
  edunberry@ogilvyrenault.com
François Fontaine, Civil & Penal Litigation
  514-847-4413
  ffontaine@ogilvyrenault.com
Anne-Louise Lamarre, Transactional Matters
  514-847-4482
  alamarre@ogilvyrenault.com
Sophie Perreault, Civil & Penal Litigation; Transactional Matters
  514-847-4810
  sperreault@ogilvyrenault.com
Jean Piette, Transactional, Administrative & Constitutional Matters
  514-847-4584
  jpiette@ogilvyrenault.com
Paul Prosterman, Insurance Aspects; Civil Litigation
  514-847-4481
  pprosterman@ogilvyrenault.com
Michel G. Sylvestre, Civil, Administrative & Penal Litigation
  514-847-4460
  msylvestre@ogilvyrenault.com

Osler, Hoskin & Harcourt S.E.N.C.R.L./LLP
#2100, 1000, rue de la Gauchetière ouest, Montréal QC H3B 4W5
514-904-8100 514-904-8101
counsel@osler.com
www.osler.com
Profile: 70 Lawyers
Environmental Lawyers:
Nathalie Beauregard, Partner, Renewable Energy & Environmental Financing; Life Sciences
  514-904-8121
  nbeauregard@osler.com
Guy Lord, Partner, Life Sciences
  514-904-8124
  glord@osler.com
Karen Shaw, Life Sciences
  514-904-5391
  kshaw@osler.com

Pearl & Associates
1170, Place du Frère André, 4e étage, Montréal QC H3B 3C6
514-861-1170 514-861-0850 866-710-1170
lawyers@pearlandassociates.com
Profile: 1 Offices, 3 Lawyers
Environmental Lawyers:
Reevin Pearl

Robinson Sheppard Shapiro LLP
#4600 800, Place Victoria, Montréal QC H4Z 1H6
514-878-2631 514-878-1865 Telex: 05-27343
info@rsslex.com
www.rsslex.com
Profile: 2 Offices, 71 Lawyers, Founded in: 1921
Bureau de Quebec: #209, 686 Grande-Allée est, Québec, QC, G1R 2K5, 418-907-9445
Environmental Lawyers:
Jean Denis Boucher, Associé, Santé et sécurité au travail
  514-393-4047
  jdboucher@rsslex.com

Law Firms / Québec

Jacques Bélanger, Santé et sécurité au travail
514-393-4018
jbelanger@rsslex.com
France Dulude, Associée, Droit de la construction
514-393-4029
fdulude@rsslex.com
Jean-Marc Fortier, Associé, Ressources naturelles (minier)
514-393-7400
jmfortier@rsslex.com
Theodore Goloff, Associé, Santé et sécurité au travail
514-393-4007
tgoloff@rsslex.com
Marc Prévost, Associé, Droit de la construction
514-393-7453
mprevost@rsslex.com
Philippe-André Tessier, Associé, Santé et sécurité au travail
514-393-7454
patessier@rsslex.com

Stikeman Elliott LLP - Montréal
#4000, 1155, boul René-Lévesque ouest, Montréal QC H3B 3V2
514-397-3000 514-397-3222 Telex: 05-267316
www.stikeman.com
Profile: 153 Lawyers, Founded in: 1952
Environmental Lawyers:
Lev Alexeev, Droit minier; Énergie
514-397-2416
lalexeev@stikeman.com
Marc B. Barbeau, Associé, Foresterie et produits forestiers
514-397-3212
mbarbeau@stikeman.com
Bruno Barrette, Associé, Pharmaceutiques, biotechnologie et sciences de la vie
514-397-3297
bbarrette@stikeman.com
Marie-Andrée Beaudry, Associée, Énergie
514-397-3663
mabeaudry@stikeman.com
Olivier Boulva, Énergie
514-397-6488
oboulva@stikeman.com
Louis P. Bélanger, Associé, Litige en environnement
514-397-3078
lbelanger@stikeman.com
Jean Carrier, Associé, Droit de l'environnement; Droit minier; Énergie; Foresterie et produits forestiers
514-397-3101
jcarrier@stikeman.com
Edward B. Claxton, Associé, Pharmaceutiques, biotechnologie et sciences de la vie
514-397-3364
eclaxton@stikeman.com
Peter J. Cullen, Associé, Énergie
514-397-3135
pcullen@stikeman.com
Pierre-Paul Daunais, Litige en construction
514-397-2428
ppdaunais@stikeman.com
Marie-Claude David, Droit de l'environnement
514-397-3298
mcdavid@stikeman.com
Michel Décary, c.r., Associé, Litige en construction
514-397-3099
mdecary@stikeman.com
Myriam Fortin, Droit de l'environnement; Énergie; Droit minier
514-397-3270
mfortin@stikeman.com
Patrick Girard, Associé, Énergie; Litige en construction; Litige en environnement
514-397-3657
pgirard@stikeman.com
Kevin Kyte, Associé, Foresterie et produits forestiers; Pharmaceutiques, biotechnologie et sciences de la vie
514-397-3346
kkyte@stikeman.com
Pierre-Yves Leduc, Associé, Pharmaceutiques, biotechnologie et sciences de la vie
514-397-3696
pyleduc@stikeman.com
Christine Legé, Énergie
514-397-6465
clege@stikeman.com
Valérie Mac-Seing, Associée, Droit de la construction
514-397-2425
vmacseing@stikeman.com

Yves Martineau, Associé, Litige en construction
514-397-3380
ymartineau@stikeman.com
David Massé, Droit minier
514-397-3685
dmasse@stikeman.com
Nathalie Mercier-Filteau, Litige en construction
514-397-3691
nmercierfilteau@stikeman.com
Éric Mongeau, Associé, Droit de la construction; Énergie
514-397-3043
emongeau@stikeman.com
Bertrand P. Ménard, Associé, Droit de la construction; Énergie
514-397-3147
bmenard@stikeman.com
Charles Nadeau, Associé, Litige en construction
514-397-3388
cnadeau@stikeman.com
François H. Ouimet, Associé, Droit de la construction
514-397-3057
fouimet@stikeman.com
Frédéric Paré, Litige en construction; Litige en environnement
514-397-3690
fpare@stikeman
Frédéric Pierrestiger, Associé, Litige en construction
514-397-3278
fpierrestiger@stikeman.com
Erik Richer La Flèche, Associé, Énergie renouvelable; Droit de la construction; Droit minier
514-397-3109
ericherlafleche@stikeman.com
Steeve Robitaille, Associé, Foresterie et produits forestiers
514-397-3024
srobitaille@stikeman.com
Richard J. Rusk, Associé, Litige en environnement
514-397-3268
rrusk@stikeman.com
Sébastien Thomas, Droit de la construction
514-397-3336
sthomas@stikeman.com
claire Zikovsky, Associée, Énergie
514-397-3340
czikovsky@stikeman.com
Alix d'Anglejan-Chatillon, Associée, Échange de droits d'émission et changements climatiques
514-397-3240
adanglejan@stikeman.com

Québec

Cain Lamarre Casgrain Wells - Québec
#440 580, Grande Allée est, Québec QC G1R 2K2
418-522-4580 418-529-9590
info@clcw.ca
www.clcw.qc.ca
Profile: 32 Lawyers
Environmental Lawyers:
Mélanie Boivin, Droit de la santé
melanie.boivin@clcw.ca
Anne-Marie Béchard, Santé et sécurité du travail
anne.marie.bechard@clcw.ca
Pierre Caouette, Santé et sécurité du travail
pierre.caouette@clcw.ca
Hélène Carrier, Droit de la santé
helene.carrier@clcw.ca
Geneviève Carrier, Santé et sécurité du travail
genevieve.carrier@clcw.ca
Hubert Crépault, Droit minier
hubert.crepault@clcw.ca
Normand Drolet, Associé, Santé et sécurité du travail
normand.drolet@clcw.ca
Raymond Gouge, Santé et sécurité au travail
raymond.gouge@clcw.ca
Marie-Douce Huard, Droit de la construction
marie.douce.huard@clcw.ca
Karl Jessop, Associé, Santé et sécurité du travail
karl.jessop@clcw.ca
Sylvain Lepage, Associé, Litige de la construction
sylvain.lepage@clcw.ca
Pierre Martin, Droit de la construction; Droit de la santé
pierre.martin@clcw.ca
Dominique Pelletier-Giroux, Droit de la santé
dominique.pelletier.giroux@clcw.ca
Simon Rainville, Droit de la construction
simon.rainville@clcw.ca

Fasken Martineau - Québec
#800, 140, Grande Allée est, Québec QC G1R 5M8
418-640-2000 418-647-2455 800-463-2827
quebec@fasken.com
www.fasken.com
Profile: 8 Offices, 650 Lawyers, Founded in: 1983
Environmental Services: Environmental, Energy & Natural Resource Law
Environmental Lawyers:
Jean M. Gagné, Mining; Forestry
418-640-2010
jgagne@qc.fasken.com
Martin R. Gagné, Mining; Forestry
418-640-2001
mrgagne@qc.fasken.com
Annick Gilbert, Municipal Law
agilbert@qc.fasken.com
Ianny Xénopoulos, Mining; Forestry
418-640-2020
ixenopoulos@qc.fasken.com

Grondin, Poudrier, Bernier
#900, 500, Grande Allée est, Québec QC G1R 2J7
418-683-3000 418-683-8784 800-463-5172
gpb@grondinpoudrier.com
www.grondinpoudrier.com
Profile: 2 Offices, 36 Lawyers, Founded in: 1948
Environmental Lawyers:
Denis Bradet, Droit de la santé et de la sécurité du travail
dbradet@grondinpoudrier.com
Marie-José Côté, Droit de la construction
mjcote@grondinpoudrier.com
Marc Delâge, Environnement, Droit du transport
mdelage@grondinpoudrier.com
Marie-Christine Dufour, Droit de la santé et de la sécurité du travail
mcdufour@grondinpoudrier.com
Marc Hurtubise, Droit de la santé et de la sécurité du travail
mhurtubise@grondinpoudrier.com
Jean Morin, Construction
jmorin@grondinpoudier.com
Bruno Néron, Droit de la santé et de la sécurité du travail
bneron@grondinpoudrier.com
Pierre Ouellet, Construction
pouellet@grondinpoudrier.com
Gilles Reny, Droit minier
greny@grondinpoudrier.com
John White, Droit de la construction
jwhite@grondinpoudrier.com

Heenan Blaikie S.E.N.C.R.L./SRL - Québec
#600 900, boul René-Lévesque est, Québec QC G1R 2B5
418-524-5131 418-524-1717
www.heenanblaikie.com
Profile: 44 Lawyers, Founded in: 1973
Environmental Lawyers:
Marcel Aubut, Q.C., Partner, Energy; Construction; Aboriginal Law
418-529-4254
maubut@heenan.ca
Pierre Beaulieu, Partner, Construction
418-649-5464
pbeaulieu@heenan.ca
Pierre C. Bellavance, Partner, Environmental Law; Health
418-649-5476
pbellavance@heenan.ca
Anik Bernatchez, Construction
418-649-5467
abernatchez@heenan.ca
David F. Blair, Partner, Transportation
418-649-5483
dblair@heenan.ca
Louis Carrière, Partner, Construction Litigation
418-649-5465
lcarriere@heenan.ca
Nicolas Croteau, Construction
418-649-5477
ncroteau@heenan.ca
Louis-Antoine Côté, Occupational Health & Safety
418-649-5067
lcote@heenan.ca
Jean-François Dolbec, Partner, Occupational Health & Safety
418-649-5645
jfdolbec@heenan.ca

Christian Drolet, Partner, Occupational Health & Safety
418-649-5480
cdrolet@heenan.ca
Olivier Hébert, Construction Litigation; Health
418-649-5026
ohebert@heenan.ca
Isabelle L'Écuyer, Health
418-649-5080
ilecuyer@heenan.ca
Annie-Claude Labrecque, Construction Litigation
418-649-5472
alabrecque@heenan.ca
Isabelle Landry, Environmental Law; Energy
418-649-5479
ilandry@heenan.ca
Pierre Larrivée, Partner, Construction Litigation; Health
418-649-5532
plarrivee@heenan.ca
André Lepage, Partner, Occupational Health & Safety
418-649-5487
alepage@heenan.ca
Samuel Massicotte, Construction Litigation
418-649-5474
smassicotte@heenan.ca
Pierre-Étienne Morand, Occupational Health & Safety
418-649-5339
pemorand@heenan.ca
Pierre-Olivier Ménard Dumas, Transportation
418-649-5073
podumas@heenan.ca
Pierre Picard, Construction
418-649-5466
ppicard@heenan.ca
Gilles Rancourt, Occupational Health & Safety
418-649-5493
grancourt@heenan.ca
Simon Ruel, Health
418-649-5131
sruel@heenan.ca
Mario Welsh, Partner, Construction Litigation
418-649-5473
mwelsh@heenan.ca

Joli-Cour Lacasse Avocats
#600, 1134, Grande Allée Ouest, Québec QC G1S 1E5
418-681-7007 418-681-7100
communications@jolicoeurlacasse.com
www.jolicoeurlacasse.com
Profile: 3 Offices, 26 Lawyers, Founded in: 1963
Environmental Lawyers:
Vincent Gingras, Municipal
Guy Godreau
Raymond Mainguy, Municipal

Langlois Kronström Desjardins
#300, 801, Grande Allée ouest, Québec QC G1S 1C1
418-650-7000 418-650-7075 888-650-7001
info@lkd.ca
www.langloiskronstromdesjardins.com
Profile: 2 Offices, 81 Lawyers
Environmental Lawyers:
Hans Bois, Associé, Santé
418-650-7075
hans.bois@lkd.ca
François Bouchard, Associé, Santé et sécurité au travail
418-650-7903
francois.bouchard@lkd.ca
Marie-Claude Carrier, Associé, Droit de la construction
418-650-7906
marie-claude.carrier@lkd.ca
Bernard Cliche, Associé, Santé et sécurité au travail
418-650-7028
bernard.cliche@lkd.ca
Jean Patrick Dallaire, Droit de la construction
418-650-7075
jean-patrick.dallaire@lkd.ca
Henri Grondin, c.r., c.q., Avocat, Santé et sécurité au travail; Droit autochtone
418-650-7075
henri.grondin@lkd.ca
Michel Jolin, Associé, Énergie & ressources naturelles; Environnement; Santé et sécurité au travail
418-650-7019
michel.jolin@lkd.ca

Simon Kearney, Santé et sécurité au travail
418-650-7011
simon.kearney@lkd.ca
Conrad Laflamme, Droit de la construction
418-650-7003
conrad.laflamme@lkd.ca
Sébastien Laprise, Associé, Environnement; Expropriation; Droit de la construction; Urbanisme
418-650-7915
sebastien.laprise@lkd.ca
Éric Latulippe, Associé, Santé et sécurité au travail
418-650-7904
eric.latulippe@lkd.ca
Pierre-Olivier Lessard, Santé et sécurité au travail
418-650-7064
pierre-olivier.lessard@lkd.ca
John O'Connor, Associé, Responsabilité environnementale; Accidents maritimes; Sauvetage
418-650-7002
john.oconnor@lkd.ca
Yan Paquette, Droit de la construction; Santé
418-640-7041
yan.paquette@lkd.ca
Jean-François Pichette, Associé, Droit de la construction
418-650-7907
jean-francois.pichette@lkd.ca
Richard Ramsay, Associé, Environnement
418-650-7905
richard.ramsay@lkd.ca
Alain Robitaille, Associé, Droit de la construction
418-650-7026
alain.robitaille@lkd.ca
Julie Samson, Santé & sécurité au travail
418-650-7075
julie.samson@lkd.ca
Bruno Sylvestre, Environnement; Urbanisme
418-650-7911
bruno.sylvestre@lkd.ca
Paule Veilleux, Associé, Santé
418-650-7008
paule.veilleux@lkd.ca

Lavery, de Billy - Québec
#500, 925, Grande Allée ouest, Québec QC G1S 1C1
418-688-5000 418-688-3458 800-463-4002
info@lavery.qc.ca
www.laverydebilly.com
Profile: 21 Lawyers, Founded in: 1913
Environmental Lawyers:
Pierre Beaudoin, Partner, Health Law; Transportation Law
418-266-3068
pbeaudoin@lavery.ca
Daniel Bouchard, Partner, Environmental, Energy & Natural Resources Law
418-266-3055
dbouchard@lavery.ca
Jules Brière, Partner, Health Law; Aboriginal Law
418-266-3093
jbriere@lavery.ca
Marie-Eve Clavet, Health Law
418-266-3067
meclavet@lavery.ca
Olga Farman, Health Law
418-266-3052
ofarman@lavery.ca
Hélène Gauvin, Health Law
418-266-3053
hgauvin@lavery.ca
Claude Lacroix, Partner, Construction & Surety Law
418-266-3063
clacroix@lavery.ca
Denis Michaud, Environmental, Energy & Natural Resources Law
418-266-3058
dmichaud@lavery.ca
Louis Rochette, Partner, Health Law; Life Sciences
418-266-3077
lrochette@lavery.ca

McCarthy Tétrault LLP - Québec
Le Complexe St-Amable 1150, rue de Claire-Fontaine, 7e étage, Québec QC G1R 5G4
418-521-3000 418-521-3099
quebec@mccarthy.ca
www.mccarthy.ca
Profile: 7 Offices, 32 Lawyers

Environmental Lawyers:
Pierre Boivin, Mining; Energy
418-521-3012
pboivin@mccarthy.ca
Philippe Boivin, Biotech/Life Sciences
418-521-3014
pboivin@mccarthy.ca
Anastassia Chtaneva, Energy & Infrastructure financing
418-521-3054
achtaneva@mccarthy.ca
Marc N. Dorion, Q.C., Energy
418-521-3007
mdorion@mccarthy.ca
Pauline Motard, Energy Law
418-521-3055
pmotard@mccarthy.ca

Morency Avocats
#400, 3075, ch des Quatre-Bourgeois, Québec QC G1W 4X5
418-651-9900 418-651-5184
avocats@morencyavocats.com
www.morencyavocats.com
Profile: 4 Offices, 31 Lawyers, Founded in: 1969
Environmental Lawyers:
Philippe Asselin, Municipal Law
passelin@morencyavocats.com
Sandra Bilodeau, Municipal; Environmental Law
sbilodeau@morencyavocats.com
Martin Bouffard, Municipal Law
mbouffard@morencyavocats.com
Jean-Claude Girard, Municipal Law
jcgirard@morencyavocats.com
Bertrand Gobeil, Municipal
bgobeil@morencyavocats.com
Dennis Pakenham, Municipal Law
dpakenham@morencyavocats.com
Jacques Tremblay, Land Use Management; Municipal Law
jtremblay@morencyavocats.com
Charles A. Veilleux, Municipal
cveilleux@morencyavocats.com

Ogilvy Renault LLP/S.E.N.C.R.L., s.r.l. - Québec
#1500 Complexe Jules-Dallaire/Tour Ogilvy Renault 2828, boul Laurier, Québec QC G1V 0B9
418-640-5000 418-640-1500
quebec@ogilvyrenault.com
www.ogilvyrenault.com
Profile: 49 Lawyers, Founded in: 1879
Environmental Lawyers:
Geneviève Baillargeon Bouchard, Santé et sécurité au travail
418-640-5169
gbaillargeon@ogilvyrenault.com
Maxime Cantin, Associé, Droit de la construction
418-640-5961
mcantin@ogilvyrenault.com
Sylvain Chabot, Associé, Santé et sécurité au travail
418-640-5071
schabot@ogilvyrenault.com
Pierre Cimon, Associé principal, Droit de la construction
418-640-5004
pcimon@ogilvyrenault.com
Jean-Sébastien Cloutier, Santé et sécurité au travail
418-640-5046
jcloutier@ogilvyrenault.com
Mylaine Desrosiers-Harvey, Droit de la construction
418-640-5241
myharvey@ogilvyrenault.com
Marie-Jeanne Duval, Droit de la construction
418-640-5061
mduval@ogilvyrenault.com
Julie Falardeau, Santé et sécurité au travail
418-640-5852
jfalardeau@ogilvyrenault.com
Ian Gosselin, Associé, Droit de la construction; Énergie
418-640-5029
igosselin@ogilvyrenault.com
Kateri-Anne Grenier, Associée, Droit de la construction; Litige en construction
418-640-5932
kgrenier@ogilvyrenault.com
Jean Houle, Associé principal, Santé et sécurité au travail
418-640-5036
jhoule@ogilvyrenault.com
Pierre-Christian Labeau, Mines et ressources naturelles; Droit autochtone

418-640-5008
plabeau@ogilvyrenault.com
Lucie Pariseau, Associée, Droit de la construction
418-640-5017
lpariseau@ogilvyrenault.com
Jean Piette, Associé principal, Droit de l'environnement; Énergie; Mines et ressources naturelles
418-640-5002
jpiette@ogilvyrenault.com
Jocelyn F. Rancourt, Associé, Santé et sécurité au travail
418-640-5003
jrancourt@ogilvyrenault.com
Joanie Simard, Santé et sécurité au travail
418-640-5067
jsimard@ogilvyrenault.com
Vincent St-Pierre, Droit de la construction
418-640-5038
vstpierre@ogilvyrenault.com
Louis Ste-Marie, Associé, Santé et sécurité au travail
418-640-5060
lste-marie@ogilvyrenault.com
Charles Taschereau, Associé, Droit de la construction
418-640-5948
ctaschereau@ogilvyrenault.com

Tremblay, Bois, Mignault & Lemay
#200, 1195, av Lavigerie, Québec QC G1V 4N3
418-658-9966 418-658-6100 800-807-9966 Telex: 051-3786QBC
avocats@tremblaybois.qc.ca
www.tremblaybois.qc.ca
Profile: 1 Offices, 34 Lawyers, Founded in: 1953
Environmental Lawyers:
Yves Boudreault, Evaluation; Legislation
André Lemay, Gestion

Rimouski

Cain Lamarre Casgrain Wells - Rimouski
#400 Edifice Trust General CP 580 2, boul St-Germain est, Rimouski QC G5L 7C6
418-723-3302 418-722-6939
info@clcw.ca
www.clcw.qc.ca
Profile: 9 Lawyers
Environmental Lawyers:
Yvan Bujold, Associé, Droit de la santé
yvan.bujold@clcw.ca

Rivière-du-Loup

Rioux Bossé Massé Moreau
CP 487 12, rue de la Cour, Rivière-du-Loup QC G5R 3Z1
418-862-3565 418-862-4408
rbmm@qc.aira.com
www.rbmm.qc.ca
Profile: 1 Offices, 6 Lawyers, Founded in: 1969
Environmental Lawyers:
Gilles Moreau

Saint-Hyacinthe

Brodeur, Boileau
1700, rue Girouard ouest, Saint-Hyacinthe QC J2S 3A1
450-773-8566 450-778-3749
Profile: 1 Offices, 3 Lawyers
Environmental Lawyers:
Lindor Brodeur, Municipal Liability

Saint-Jean-sur-Richelieu

Bérubé & Pion, SENCRL
#225, 145, boul St-Joseph, Saint-Jean-sur-Richelieu QC J3B 1W5
450-359-7171 450-359-9957
Profile: 1 Offices, 3 Lawyers, Founded in: 2006
Environmental Lawyers:
Paul C. Bérubé

Saint-Jérôme

Lalonde Geraghty Riendeau Lapierre
44, rue De Martigny ouest, Saint-Jérôme QC J7Z 2E9
450-436-8022 450-436-5185
lalondegeraghty@lgrl.ca
www.lgrl.ca
Profile: 2 Offices, 8 Lawyers, Founded in: 2002
Droit de la construction; droit d'urbanisme; droit municipal
Environmental Lawyers:
D. Geraghty

Sainte-Marie

Sylvain, Parent, Gobeil
CP 40 225, rue du College, Sainte-Marie QC G6E 3B4
418-387-2727 418-387-7070
spgs@globetrotter.net
Profile: 1 Offices, 4 Lawyers, Founded in: 1970
Environmental Lawyers:
Jean-Guy Parent, Agriculture; Commercial; Industries
Patrice Simard, Agriculture; Municipal

Sept-Iles

Besnier, Dion & Rondeau
865, boul Laure, Sept-Iles QC G4R 1Y6
418-962-9775 418-968-6806
besnier.avocats@cgocable.ca
Profile: 1 Offices, 6 Lawyers, Founded in: 1971
Environmental Lawyers:
Hubert Besnier

Cain Lamarre Casgrain Wells - Sept-Iles
1, rue de Mingan, Sept-Iles QC G4R 4L8
418-962-6572 418-968-8576
info@clcw.ca
www.clcw.qc.ca
Profile: 6 Lawyers
Environmental Lawyers:
Marc Brouillette, Associé, Droit de la santé
marc.brouillette@clcw.ca
Julie Lapointe, Droit de la santé
julie.lapointe@clcw.ca
Mélanie Trudeau, Droit de la santé; Affaires autochtones
melanie.trudeau@clcw.ca

Sherbrooke

Delorme, LeBel, Bureau, s.e.n.c.
#100, 2355, rue King ouest, Sherbrooke QC J1J 2G6
819-566-6222 819-566-4221
dlb@dlbavocats.com
Profile: 1 Offices, 7 Lawyers, Founded in: 1979
Environmental Lawyers:
Paul Bureau, Waterworks & Sewer Systems; Waste Management Systems; Pulp & Paper Regulations
819-566-6222
pbureau@dlbavocats.com

Heenan Blaikie S.E.N.C.R.L/SRL - Sherbrooke
#210 455, rue King ouest, Sherbrooke QC J1H 6E9
819-346-5058 819-346-5007
www.heenanblaikie.com
Profile: 31 Lawyers, Founded in: 1973
Environmental Lawyers:
Geneviève Chamberland, Health
819-346-2562
gchamberland@heenan.ca
Simon Delisle-Beaulieu, Occupational Health & Safety
819-346-2103
sdelisle@heenan.ca
Danielle Gauthier, Partner, Occupational Health & Safety
819-346-8073
dgauthier@heenan.ca
Cheryl Gilbert, Health
819-346-2207
cgilbert@heenan.ca
Jean-François Pagé, Partner, Occupational Health & Safety
819-346-7999
jfpage@heenan.ca
Sébastien Pierre-Roy, Construction Litigation; Health
819-346-7928
spierreroy@heenan.ca
Hubert Pépin, Partner, Construction
819-346-0638
hpepin@heenan.ca
Claude Villeneuve, Partner, Occupational Health & Safety
819-346-4117
cvilleneuve@heenan.ca
Yanick Vlasak, Partner, Construction Litigation
819-346-3720
yvlasak@heenan.ca

Monty, Coulombe
#200, 234, rue Dufferin, Sherbrooke QC J1H 4M2
819-566-4466 819-565-2891
legal@montycoulombe.com
Profile: 20 Lawyers, Founded in: 1978
Environmental Lawyers:

Trois-Rivières

Heenan Blaikie S.E.N.C.R.L/SRL - Trois-Rivières
#360 1500, rue Royale, Trois-Rivières QC G9A 6E6
819-373-7000 819-373-0943
www.heenanblaikie.com
Profile: 8 Lawyers, Founded in: 1973
Environmental Lawyers:
Jean Boulet, Partner, Occupational Health & Safety
819-373-4370
jboulet@heenan.ca
Marc-André Germain, Occupational Health & Safety
819-373-5543
magermain@heenan.ca
Marie-Josée Hétu, Partner, Occupational Health & Safety
819-373-4274
mhetu@heenan.ca
Myriam Lavallée, Occupational Health & Safety
819-373-0339
mlavallee@heenan.ca

Hénaire, Louis
CP 1745 983, rue Hart, Trois-Rivières QC G9A 5M4
819-379-3355 819-379-1227
Profile: 1 Offices, 1 Lawyers
Environmental Lawyers:
Louis Hénaire

Val-d'Or

Cain Lamarre Casgrain Wells - Val-d'Or
#202 855, 3e av, Val-d'Or QC J9P 1T2
819-825-4153 819-825-9769
info@clcw.ca
www.clcw.qc.ca
Profile: 16 Offices, 160 Lawyers, Founded in: 1999
Environmental Lawyers:
Robert-André Adam, Associé, Santé
robert.andre.adam@clcw.ca
Alexandre Cimon, Santé et Sécurité
alexandre.cimon@clcw.ca
Stéphanie Lachance, Santé; Affaires autochtones
stephanie.lachance@clcw.ca
Pascal Porlier, Droit de la construction; Affaires autochtones
pascal.porlier@clcw.ca

Saskatchewan

Estevan

McDougall Gauley
#300, Wicklow Centre 1133 - 4th St., Estevan SK S4A 0W6
306-634-6334 306-634-3852
bbridges@mcdougallgauley.com
www.mcdougallgauley.com
Profile: 2 Lawyers
Environmental Lawyers:
Barry D. Bridges, Oil & Gas, Natural Resources & Energy Law
bbridges@mcdougallgauley.com
Chad W. Jesse, Oil & Gas, Natural Resources & Energy Law
cjesse@mcdougallgauley.com

Prince Albert

Cherkewich, Ron
#3, 27 - 11 St. West, Prince Albert SK S6V 3A8
306-764-1537 306-763-0505
ron.cya@sasktel.net
Profile: 1 Offices, 1 Lawyers, Founded in: 1969
Indian Reserve Governance; Forestry & Northern Development Issues in Northern Saskatchewan

Law Firms / Saskatchewan

Environmental Lawyers:

Eggum, Abrametz, Eggum
#101, 88 - 13th St. East, Prince Albert SK S6V 1C6
306-763-7441 306-764-2882
klleggum@inet2000.com; petervabrametz@inet2000.com
Profile: 1 Offices, 4 Lawyers
Environmental Lawyers:
Krista L.L. Eggum

Regina

Kanuka Thuringer LLP, Barristers & Solicitors
#1400, 2500 Victoria Ave., Regina SK S4P 3X2
306-525-7200 306-359-0590
firm@kanukathuringer.com
www.kanukathuringer.com
Profile: 2 Offices, 28 Lawyers, Founded in: 1952
Kanuka Thuringer LLP is an established Saskatchewan law firm. It is based in Regina & Swift Current, but the firm regularly provides services to clients throughout the province. The cliente is varied, including local, national, international corporations, individuals, non-profit organizations, entrepreneurs, & small businesses. Kanuka Thuringer LLP has a diverse practice, but it is likely best known for providing business advice & dispute resolution in its signature practice areas of business law, energy & natural resources, financial services, construction, family law, & transportation.
Environmental Lawyers:
Keith D. Boyd, Q.C., Oil & Gas; Land & natural resources; Surface rights
 306-525-7203
 kboyd@kanukathuringer.com
Murray W. Douglas, Commercial litigation (energy industry)
 306-525-7227
 mdouglas@kanukathuringer.com
James S. Ehmann, Q.C., Oil & gas litigation
 306-525-7225
 jehmann@kanukathuringer.com
Azure-Dee A. Farago, Environmental & natural resouces law
 306-525-7235
 afarago@kanukathuringer.com
Paul J. Harasen, Employment & labour law; Construction law
 306-525-7230
 pharasen@kanukathuringer.com
Carrie G. Ho, Natural resources; Environmental law
 306-525-7237
 cho@kanukathuringer.com
Keith D. Kilback, Managing Partner, Transportation; Commercial litigation (Oil & gas, construction)
 306-525-7229
 kkilback@kanukathuringer.com
T. Micheal McDougall, Oil & Gas; Water regulation; Environmental law
 306-525-7211
 mmcdougall@kanukathuringer.com
Matthew A. Park, Environmental law; Oil & gas; Energy; Natural resources law
 306-525-7223
 mpark@kanukathuringer.com
Ronald M. Warsaba, Oil & gas
 306-525-7207
 rwarsaba@kanukathuringer.com

MacPherson Leslie & Tyerman LLP - Regina
#1500, Hill Centre I 1874 Scarth St., Regina SK S4P 4E9
306-347-8000 306-352-5250
www.mlt.com
Profile: 4 Offices, 40 Lawyers, Founded in: 1920
Agribusiness; Aboriginal Law; Natural Resources Law
Environmental Lawyers:
Leonard D. Andrychuk, Q.C., Partner, Construction; Environmental; First Nations
 306-347-8440
 landrychuk@mlt.com
Randy U. Brunet, Partner, Health Care
 306-347-8415
 rbrunet@mlt.com
Brianna Demofsky, Health
 306-347-8459
 bdemofsky@mlt.com
John A. Dipple, Partner, Energy; Construction
 306-347-8414
 jdipple@mlt.com

Deron A. Kuski, Partner, Construction
 306-347-8404
 dkuski@mlt.com
Harold H. MacKay, Q.C., O.C., Counsel, Natural Resources Law
 306-347-8417
 hmackay@mlt.com
Robert B. Pletch, Q.C., Chairman, Mining & Natural Resources
 306-347-8416
 rpletch@mlt.com
Hilary Stedwill, Construction; Environment
 306-347-8486
 hstedwill@mlt.com
Bradley N. Vance, Counsel, Health
 306-347-8604
 bvance@mlt.com
Donald K. Wilson, Q.C., Managing Partner, Mining & Natural Resources
 306-347-8437
 dwilson@mlt.com
Erin Wolff, Health
 306-347-8449
 ewolff@mlt.com

McDougall Gauley
1500 - 1881 Scarth St., Regina SK S4P 4K9
306-757-1641 306-359-0785
mramsay@mcdougallgauley.com
www.mcdougallgauley.com
Profile: 4 Offices, 33 Lawyers, Founded in: 2001
Environmental Lawyers:
Darren W. Carlson, Oil & Gas, Natural Resources & Energy Law
 306-565-5194
 dcarlson@mcdougallgauley.com
Terence G. Graf, Q.C., Healthcare Law
 306-565-5106
 tgraf@mcdougallgauley.com
Neil N. Karkut, Oil & Gas, Natural Resources & Energy Law
 306-565-5193
 nkarkut@mcdougallgauley.com
G. Brett Ledingham, Oil & Gas, Natural Resources & Energy Law
 306-565-5151
 bledingham@mcdougallgauley.com
Michael W. Milani, Q.C., Oil & Gas, Natural Resources & Energy Law
 306-565-5117
 mmilani@mcdougallgauley.com
Dan G. Morris, Oil & Gas, Natural Resources & Energy Law
 306-565-5181
 dmorris@mcdougallgauley.com
Kenneth A. Ready, Q.C., Healthcare Law
 306-565-5125
 kready@mcdougallgauley.com
Murray R. Sawatzky, Q.C., Construction Law; Environmental Law
 306-565-5141
 msawatzky@mcdougallgauley.com
Angela Stolz, Environmental Law
 306-565-5113
 astolz@mcdougallgauley.com

Saskatoon

Dufour Scott Phelps & Mason
#400, 135 - 21st St. East, Saskatoon SK S7K 0B4
306-244-2201 306-244-2420
www.dufourlaw.com
Profile: 1 Offices, 5 Lawyers
Environmental Lawyers:
Geoff Dufour, Environmental Law
 g.dufour@dufourlaw.com

MacPherson Leslie & Tyerman LLP - Saskatoon
#1500, 410 - 22nd St. East, Saskatoon SK S7K 5T6
306-975-7100 306-975-7145
www.mlt.com
Profile: 37 Lawyers
Environmental Lawyers:
John Agioritis, Environment
 306-975-7143
 jagioritis@mlt.com
Danny R. Anderson, Partner, Energy; Mining & Natural Resources
 306-975-7133
 danderson@mlt.com

Naheed Bardai, Partner, Construction
 306-975-7115
 nbardai@mlt.com
Kelly Caruk, Mining & Natural Resources
 306-975-7129
 kcaruk@mlt.com
Lynn E. Hnatick, Partner, Mining & Natural Resources
 306-975-7104
 lhnatick@mlt.com
Rangi G. Jeerakathil, Partner, Energy; Environment; First Nations
 306-975-7107
 rjeerakathil@mlt.com
Josh Lommer, Mining & Natural Resources
 306-975-7139
 jlommer@mlt.com
R. Neil MacKay, Q.C., Partner, Mining & Natural Resources
 306-975-7124
 nmackay@mlt.com
Brent Robinson, Mining & Natural Resources
 306-956-6965
 brobinson@mlt.com
Ryan Rodier, Energy; Environment; First Nations
 306-975-7113
 rrodier@mlt.com
Leah A. Schatz, Partner, Health
 306-975-7144
 lschatz@mlt.com
Tyler Wake, Mining & Natural Resources
 306-975-7134
 twake@mlt.com
Chris A. Woodland, Partner, Construction
 306-975-7128
 cwoodland@mlt.com
Penny L. Yeager, Energy; Mining & Natural Resources
 306-975-7131
 pyeager@mlt.com

McDougall Gauley
P.O Box 638 701 Broadway Ave., Saskatoon SK S7K 3L7
306-653-1212 306-652-1323
lvanin@mcdougallgauley.com
www.mcdougallgauley.com
Profile: 37 Lawyers
Environmental Lawyers:
Christopher C. Boychuk, Q.C., Construction Law; Health Law
 306-665-5456
 cboychuk@mcdougallgauley.com
Chantelle C. Eisner, Healthcare Law
 306-665-5424
 ceisner@mcdougallgauley.com
David (Tom) E. Gauley, Q.C., Healthcare Law
 306-665-5422
 tgauley@mcdougallgauley.com
Chad M. Haaf, Oil & Gas, Natural Resources & Energy Law
 306-665-5494
 chaaf@mcdougallgauley.com
Derek D. Hoffman, Oil & Gas, Natural Resources & Energy Law
 306-665-5477
 dhoffman@mcdougallgauley.com
Lindsay M. Jones, Environmental Law
 306-665-5436
 ljones@mcdougallgauley.com
Brad S. Mitchell, Natural Resource Law; Environmental Law
 306-665-5449
 bmitchell@mcdougallgauley.com
William A. Nickel, Oil & Gas, Natural Resources & Energy Law
 306-665-5448
 bnickel@mcdougallgauley.com
Dusty L. Robinson, Oil & Gas, Natural Resources & Energy Law
 306-665-5446
 drobinson@mcdougallgauley.com
William J. Shaw, Oil & Gas, Natural Resources & Energy Law
 306-665-5426
 bshaw@mcdougallgauley.com

Merchant Law Group LLP - Saskatoon
#501 224 - 4th Ave. South, Saskatoon SK S7K 5M5
306-653-7777 306-975-1983 866-567-7777
merchant@merchantlaw.com
www.merchantlaw.com
Profile: 7 Lawyers
Environmental Lawyers:

Robertson Stromberg Pedersen LLP
#600 Canada Building 105 - 21st St. East, Saskatoon SK S7K 0B3
306-652-7575 306-652-2445 800-667-0070
www.thinkrsplaw.com
Profile: 2 Offices, 21 Lawyers, Founded in: 1918
Environmental Lawyers:
Misty Alexandre, Construction Law
 306-933-1352
 m.alexandre@thinkrsplaw.com
Melvin Gerspacher, Managing Partner, Natural Resources
 306-933-1324
 m.gerspacher@thinkrsplaw.com
Bill D. Preston, Q.C., Construction Law
 306-933-1388
 b.preston@thinkrsplaw.com
Leslie W. Prosser, Q.C., Managing Partner, Natural Resources
 306-933-1302
 l.prosser@thinkrsplaw.com
Reynold A. Robertson, Q.C., Construction Law
 306-933-1348
 r.robertson@thinkrsplaw.com
Kenneth K.E. Ziegler, Forestry; Aboriginal Law
 306-933-1314
 k.ziegler@thinkrsplaw.com

Wallace Meschishnick Clackson Zawada
#901, 119 - 4th Ave. South, Saskatoon SK S7K 5X2
306-933-0004 306-933-2006
info@wmcz.com
www.wmcz.com
Profile: 1 Offices, 16 Lawyers
Environmental Lawyers:
Colin D. Clackson, Environmental Litigation
 colin.clackson@wmcz.com
David B. Jahnke, Agribusiness
 david.jahnke@wmcz.com
Gary A. Meschishnick, Aboriginal Law; Environmental & Water Law
 gary.meschishnick@wmc3.com
Craig A. Zawada, Environmental Law; Agricultural Law; Agricultural biotechnology
 craig.zawada@wmcz.com

Swift Current

Kanuka Thuringer LLP, Barristers & Solicitors
El Wood Bldg. 350 Cheadle St. West, Swift Current SK S9H 4G3
306-773-4800 306-773-0040
firm@kanukathuringer.com
www.kanukathuringer.com
Profile: 2 Offices, 4 Lawyers,
Kanuka Thuringer LLP is an established Saskatchewan law firm. It is based in Regina & Swift Current, but the firm regularly provides services to clients throughout the province. The cliente is varied, including local, national, international corporations, individuals, non-profit organizations, entrepreneurs, & small businesses. Kanuka Thuringer LLP has a diverse practice, but it is likely best known for providing business advice & dispute resolution in its signature practice areas of business law, energy & natural resources, financial services, construction, family law, & transportation.
Environmental Lawyers:
Andrea V. Argue, Agriculture
 aargue@kanukathuringer.com
Lindsay A. Melhoff, Natural resource law
 306-773-4806
 lmelhoff@kanukathuringer.com

Weyburn

Nimegeers, Schuck, Wormsbecker & Bobbitt
P.O Box 8 319 Souris Ave. NE, Weyburn SK S4H 2J8
306-842-4654 306-842-0522
law@nswb.com
www.nswb.com
Profile: 1 Offices, 7 Lawyers, Founded in: 1967
Environmental Lawyers:

Yukon Territory

Whitehorse

Austring, Fendrick, Fairman & Parkkari
The Drury Bldg. 3081 - 3rd Ave., Whitehorse YT Y1A 4Z7
867-668-4405 867-668-3710 800-661-0533
info@lawyukon.com
www.lawyukon.com
Profile: 1 Offices, 8 Lawyers, Founded in: 1961
Environmental Lawyers:
H. Shayne Fairman

Davis & Company LLP
#201, 4109 - 4th Ave., Whitehorse YT Y1A 1H6
867-393-5100 867-667-2669
www.davis.ca
Profile: 8 Offices, Founded in: 1892
Environmental Lawyers:

Libraries & Resource Centres Index

A

A.D. Allen Chemistry Library, 1156
Abbotsford Campus Library, 1110
Abbott Laboratories Limited, 1184
Acadia University, 1137
Acuren Inc., 1104
ADI Group, 1127
Aerospace Engineering Test Establishment, 1103
Aerospace Technology Campus, 1115
Ag-WestBio Inc., 1189
Agra Earth & Environmental Limited, 1104
Agriculture & Agri-Food Canada, 1147
Agriculture Producers Association of New Brunswick, 1127
Agrium Inc., 1099
Aircraft Certification, 1147
Aircraft Services Directorate, 1147
Aker Kvaerner Chemetics Inc., 1117
Akerley Campus, 1135
Alberta Children's Hospital Library, 1099
Alberta Community Development, 1110
Alberta Dept. of Energy, 1099
Alberta Government Library, 1104
Alberta Hospital Edmonton, 1104
Alberta Justice, Office of the Chief Medical Examiner, 1104
Alberta Land Surveyors' Association, 1104
Alberta Research Council, 1104
Alberta Speleological Society, 1099
Alberta Wilderness Resource Centre, 1099
Alcan International Ltée., 1168
Algoma University College, 1154
Algonquin College of Applied Arts & Technology, 1147
Allergy/Asthma Information Association, 1164
Allyn & Betty Taylor Library, 1143
AMEC Inc., 1099
Anadarko Canada Corp., 1099
ARC Vegreville Library & Information Centre, 1109
Architecture & Fine Arts Library, 1122
Assiniboine Community College, 1121
Association for Mineral Exploration British Columbia, 1117
Association of Municipalities of Ontario, 1156
Athabasca University, 1099
Atlantic Region, 1135
Atlantic Regional Library, 1135
Atlantic Salmon Federation, 1126
Atlin Campus, 1110
Atomic Energy of Canada Ltd., 1139
Augustana Faculty, 1103
Aurora College, 1133
Aurora College. Aurora Research Institute, 1133

B

Bathurst Campus, 1126
Bay St George Campus, Stephenville Crossing Building, 1133
Beaton Institute, 1134
Bedford Institute of Oceanography, 1135
Bell Canada, 1170
Bell Helicopter Textron, 1169
Belzberg Library, 1117
Bibliothèque canadienne de l'agriculture - Sainte-Foy, 1184, 1177
Bibliothèque centrale, 1170
Bibliothèque d'aménagement, 1170
Bibliothèque de botanique - L'Institut de recherche en biologie végétale, 1170
Bibliothèque de chimie, 1170
Bibliothèque de didacthèque, 1170
Bibliothèque de droit, 1170
Bibliothèque de droit Brian-Dickson, 1147
Bibliothèque de droit et publications gouvernementales, 1184
Bibliothèque de géographie, 1177
Bibliothèque de musique, 1185
Bibliothèque de physique, 1170
Bibliothèque des sciences, 1171
Bibliothèque des sciences de la santé, 1171, 1147, 1185
Bibliothèque des sciences et de génie, 1185
Bibliothèque des sciences humaines et sociales, 1177
Bibliothèque des sciences juridiques, 1171
Bibliothèque paramédicale, 1171
Bibliothèque scientifique Charles-Auguste-Gauthier, 1177
Biomedical Branch Library, 1117
Bishop's University, 1185
Blind River Refinery, 1139
Boehringer Ingelheim (Canada) Ltd., 1167
Bombardier Inc./Canadair Aerospace & Defence Groups, 1171
Bonavista Campus Learning Resource Centre, 1130
Bora Laskin Law Library, 1156
Bracken Health Sciences Library, 1142
Branch Library, 1147
Brandon Regional Health Centre, 1121
Brandon Research Centre, 1122
Brandon University, 1122
Brantford Campus, 1139
British Columbia Ferry Services, 1120
British Columbia Health & Human Services, 1120
British Columbia Housing, 1110
British Columbia Hydro, 1110
British Columbia Institute of Technology, 1110
British Columbia Ministry of Economic Development, 1120
British Columbia Ministry of Energy & Mines, 1120
British Columbia Ministry of Environment, 1120
British Columbia Utilities Commission, 1117
Broadway Campus Library, 1117
Brock University, 1153
Brockville Campus, 1139
Brooks Campus, 1099
Buffalo Lake Naturalists Club, 1109
Burin Campus Library, 1130
Burnaby Hospital, 1110

C

C.D. Howe Institute, 1157
CAE Electronics Ltd., 1184
Calgary Engineering & Environmental Services, 1099
Calgary Health Region, 1099
Calgary Library, 1100
Calgary Library & Information Centre, 1100
Calgary Utilities & Environmental Protection, 1100
Calgary Zoological Society, 1100
Cambrian College, 1155
Cameco Corporation, 1189
Cameron Science & Technology Library, 1104
Camosun College, 1120
Campbell River Campus Library, 1111
Campus d'Edmundston, 1126
Campus de Bathurst, Bibliothèque, 1126
Campus de Campbellton, Bibliothèque, 1126
Campus de Charlesbourg, 1177
Campus de Dieppe, Bibliothèque, 1126
Campus de Shippagan, 1130
Campus Notre-Dame-de-Foy, 1182
Canada Centre for Inland Waters, 1139
Canada Dept. of National Defence & the Canadian Forces, 1148
Canada Institute for Scientific & Technical Information (CISTI), 1148
Canada Mortgage & Housing Corporation, 1148
Canada Revenue Agency, 1148
Canada Science & Technology Museum, 1148
Canada-Newfoundland Offshore Petroleum Board, 1131
Canadian Agriculture Library (Summerland), 1116
Canadian Agriculture Library - Kentville, 1137
Canadian Agriculture Library - Lethbridge, 1108
Canadian Agriculture Library - Saskatoon, 1189
Canadian Association of Oilwell Drilling Contractors, 1100
Canadian Bottled Water Association, 1153
Canadian Centre For Energy Information, 1100
Canadian Centre for Pollution Prevention, 1156
Canadian Circumpolar Library, 1104
Canadian Energy Research Institute, 1100
Canadian Forces Medical Group Headquarters, 1148
Canadian Forces Northern Area Headquarters, 1133
Canadian Grain Commission, 1122
Canadian Heritage, 1167
Canadian Institute for NDE, 1140
Canadian Institute of Biotechnology, 1148
Canadian Institute of Geomatics, 1149
Canadian Institute of Resources Law, 1100
Canadian Meteorological Centre, 1167
Canadian Museum of Nature, 1149
Canadian Nuclear Safety Commission, 1149
Canadian Organic Growers Inc., 1149
Canadian Pacific Railway, 1100
Canadian Sugar Institute, 1156
Canadian Transportation Agency, 1167
Canadian University College, 1108
Canadian Urban Transit Association, 1156
Canadian Water Quality Association, 1156
Canadian Wheat Board, 1123
Canadian Wildlife Federation, 1149
Canadian Wildlife Service, 1129
CANMET Information Centre, 1149
CanTox Health Sciences International, 1144
Cape Breton District Health Authority, 1137
Cape Breton University, 1137
Capilano College, 1114
Capital Health, 1135
Carbonear Campus Library, 1130
Caritas Health Group, 1104
Carleton University, 1149
Cartothèque, 1185
Casa Loma Campus, 1156
Casa Loma ESL Resource Centre, 1157
CÉGEP d'André-Laurendeau, 1169
CÉGEP de Baie-Comeau, 1166
CÉGEP de Beauce-Appalaches, 1183
CÉGEP de Chicoutimi, 1166
CÉGEP de Drummondville, 1167
CÉGEP de Granby, 1168
CÉGEP de Jonquière, 1168
CÉGEP de l'Abitibi-Témiscamingue, 1182
CÉGEP de la Pocatière, 1177
CÉGEP de Lévis-Lauzon, 1169
CÉGEP de Marie-Victorin, 1171
CÉGEP de Matane, 1169
CÉGEP de Rimouski, 1181
CÉGEP de Rivière-du-Loup, 1181
CÉGEP de Saint-Hyacinthe, 1183
CÉGEP de Saint-Laurent, 1184
CÉGEP de Sainte-Foy, 1178
CÉGEP de Sept-Iles, 1184
CÉGEP de Sherbrooke, 1185
CÉGEP de Sorel-Tracy, 1186
CÉGEP de St-Jérôme, 1184
CÉGEP de Trois-Rivières, 1186
CÉGEP de Victoriaville, 1187
CÉGEP du Vieux-Montréal, 1171
CÉGEP Limoilou, 1178
CÉGEP Régional de Lanaudière à Joliette, 1168
CÉGEP St-Jean-sur-Richelieu, 1183
Centennial College of Applied Arts & Technology, 1157
Central Newfoundland Regional Health Centre, 1131
Centre d'excellence en sciences agricoles et biotechnologiques, 1128
Centre de documentation, 1171
Centre de documentation (Génie), 1178
Centre de recherche et de développement sur les aliments, 1183
Centre de recherche industrielle du Québec, 1178
Centre de santé et de services sociaux de Laval, 1169
Centre de santé et de services sociaux Richelieu-Yamaska, 1183
Centre des études collégiales - Carleton, 1166
Centre des Iles, 1167
Centre for Developing Area Studies, 1171
Centre for Newfoundland Studies, 1131
Centre hospitalier de l'Université de Montréal Hôtel-Dieu, 1171, 1172

Libraries & Resource Centres Index

Centre hospitalier des Vallées de l'Outaouais Hôpital de Hull, 1167
Centre hospitalier régional du Grand-Portage, 1182
Centre hospitalier universitaire de Sherbrooke Hôtel-Dieu, 1185
Centre québécois de formation aéronautique, 1183
Centre régional de santé et de services sociaux Rimouski, 1181
Centre spécialisé des Pêches - Grande-Rivière, 1168
CH2M Hill Canada Limited, 1157
Chamber of Mines of Eastern British Columbia, 1113
Champlain-Saint Lambert, 1184
Chatham-Kent Health Alliance, 1139
Chetwynd Campus, 1111
Chevron Canada Resources, 1100
Chilliwack Campus, Library, 1111
CHUQ-CHUL, 1178
Churchill Northern Studies Centre, 1122
CHUS Hôtel-Dieu, 1185
City Hospital, Saskatoon, 1189
Civil Aviation Technical Reference Centre, 1128
Clarenville Campus Learning Resource Centre, 1130
Clean North, 1154
Clean Nova Scotia, 1135
CMC Electronics Inc., 1184
Coady International Institute, 1134
Collège André-Grasset, 1172
Collège Bourget, 1181
Collège d'Ahuntsic, 1172
Collège d'Alma, 1166
Collège de Maisonneuve, 1172
Collège de Rosemont, 1172
Collège de Saint-Félicien, 1182
Collège Édouard-Montpetit, 1169
Collège Français, 1172
Collège Jean-de-Brébeuf, 1172
Collège Laflèche, 1186
Collège Lasalle, 1172
Collège Lionel-Groulx, 1182
Collège Mérici, 1178
Collège Montmorency, 1169
Collège O'Sullivan, 1172
College of New Caledonia, 1115
College of the North Atlantic, 1133
College of the North Atlantic, Corner Brook Campus, 1130
College of the Rockies, 1111
Collège Shawinigan, 1184
Collège St-Jean-Vianney, 1173
Collège Stanislas inc, 1177
Collège universitaire de St-Boniface, 1123
Commerce Court Educational Resources, 1146
Commission de la santé et de la sécurité du travail, 1173
Commission de toponymie du Québec, Bibliothèque (Library), 1178
Concordia Hospital, 1123
Concordia University College of Alberta, 1104
Concordia University Libraries, 1173
Conestoga College Institute of Technology & Advanced Learning, 1143
Confederation College, 1155
Connexions Information Sharing Services, 1157
Conservation & Environment Library, 1123
Conservation Council of New Brunswick, 1127
Cornwall Campus, 1140
Cottonwood Consultants Ltd, 1100
Cowichan Campus, 1112
Credit Valley Hospital, 1145
Creston Campus, 1111
Crompton Co./Cie, 1140
CSA International, 1157
Cypress Hills Regional College, 1191

D

Dalhousie University Libraries, 1135
Dana Porter Library, 1164
David Winton Bell Memorial Library, 1153
Davis Campus, 1139
Davis Centre Library, 1164
Dawson College, 1173
DBM6/LSTL Building, 1149
Defence R & D Canada - Atlantic, 1135
Defence R & D Canada - Ottawa, 1149
Defence R & D Canada - Suffield, 1109

Devon Canada Corporation, 1100
Devon Library & Information Centre, 1103
DeVry Institute of Technology, 1101
Diana M. Priestly Law Library, 1120
District Health Authorities 1, 2 & 3 (Western Nova Scotia), 1138
Dofasco Inc., 1140
Donald W. Craik Engineering Library, 1123
Donald-Petzel Memorial Library, 1178
Doucette Library of Teaching Resources, 1101
Douglas College, 1114
Downtown Campus Library, 1117
Dr. D.A. Thompson Memorial Library, 1126
Dr. Everett Chalmers Regional Hospital, 1127
DRDC Valcartier, R&D pour La defense Canada, Valcartier, 1186
Ducks Unlimited Canada, 1122
Durham College of Applied Arts & Technology, 1147

E

E.I. duPont Canada Company, 1145
E.K. Williams Law Library, 1123
EarthSave Canada, 1117
Eastern Cereal & Oilseed Research Centre Library, 1149
Eastern Division Library/Bibliothèque de la division de l'est, 1178
Ecojustice Canada, 1117
École nationale d'aérotechnique, 1183
École polytechnique de Montréal, 1173
Ecologistics Research Services, 1155
Econotech Services Ltd., 1112
ECORC Plant Research Library, 1150
Edmonton Planning & Development Dept. Library, 1105
Edmonton Transportation & Streets Dept., 1105
Elizabeth Dafoe Library, 1123
EnCana Corporation, 1101
Energy Diversification Research Laboratory, 1186
Energy Probe Research Foundation, 1157
Energy Resources Conservation Board (ERCB), 1101
Energy, Minerals & Metals Information Centre, 1150
Engineering & Computer Science Library, 1157
Engineering & Science Library, 1142
Engineering Branch, 1150
Engineering Library, 1127, 1189
Entomological Society of British Columbia, 1112
Entomological Society of Ontario, 1140
Environment Canada, 1167
Environment Canada Library, Downsview, 1157
Environmental Commissioner of Ontario, 1157
Environmental Law Centre, 1105
EPCOR, 1105
Eric Marshall Aquatic Research Library (Central and Artic Library), 1123
EVS Environment Consultants Ltd., 1114

F

Falconbridge Limited, 1140
Fanshawe College of Applied Arts & Technology, 1143
Farm Safety Association Inc., 1140
Federation of Ontario Naturalists, 1157
First Nations University of Canada, 1187
Fisheries & Marine Institute, 1132
Fisheries & Oceans Canada, 1150
Five Hills Health Region, 1187
Food Development Centre, 1122
Fort Nelson Campus, 1112
Fort St. John Campus, 1112
FP Innovations - Paprican Division, Vancouver, 1117
FP Innovations Forintek Division, 1117
FPInnovations, 1177
Frost Campus, School of Environmental & Natural Resources Sciences, 1143

G

G.P. Lewis Library, 1145
Gabriel Dumont Institute of Native Studies & Applied Research, 1188
Gallagher Library of Geology & Geophysics, 1101
Gander Campus Library & Career Exploration Centre, 1131
Gazoduc Trans Québec & Maritimes Inc., 1166
Genaire Limited, 1146

General Medical Library, 1141
Geographic, Statistical and Government Information Centre, 1150
George Brown College of Applied Arts & Technology, 1157
Georges P. Vanier Library, 1173
Georgian College of Applied Arts & Technology, 1138
Gerard V. La Forest Law Library, 1127
Gerstein Science Information Centre, 1158
Golder Associates Ltd., 1145
Grand Falls-Windsor Campus Library, 1131
Grande Prairie Regional College, 1107
Grant MacEwan University, 1105
Great Lakes Forestry Centre, 1154
Greenhouse & Processing Crops, 1141
GSC - Quebec Library, 1179

H

H.H. Angus & Associates, 1158
Haileybury Campus, 1140
Hamilton Health Sciences, 1141
Hamiota District Health Centre, 1122
Hatch, 1145
Hatch Energy, 1146
Health Canada, 1150
Health Canada, Health Products & Food Branch, 1150
Health Sciences Library, 1101, 1141, 1189, 1132
HEC Montréal, 1173
HECS Library, 1150
Hemisphere Engineering Inc, 1105
Henderson Medical Library, 1141
Heritage College, 1168
Héritage Montréal, 1173
Holland College, 1165
Homewood Health Centre, 1140
Horticultural Research Institute of Ontario, 1164
Hospital for Sick Children, 1158
Humber College Institute of Technology & Advanced Learning, 1158
Husky Oil Operations Ltd., 1101
Hycal Environmental Sciences, 1101
Hydro-Québec, 1173

I

IBI Group, 1158
IBM Canada Ltd., 1144
Imperial Oil Limited, 1158
Imperial Oil Resources Limited, 1101
Inco Technical Services Limited, 1145
Indian Head Research Farm, 1187
Industrial Accident Prevention Association, 1145
Industrial Technology Centre, 1123
Information Centre (Calgary), 1101
INRS - Université du Québec, CGC - Québec, 1179
Institut de l'Énergie et de l'environnement de la francophonie, 1179
Institut de technologie agro-alimentaire de Saint-Hyacinthe, 1177, 1183
Institut maritime du Québec, 1181
Institut Maurice-Lamontagne, 1170
Institut Teccart Inc., 1174
Institute for Research in Construction, 1150
Institute of Ocean Sciences, 1116
Institute of Technology Campus, 1135
Institute of Urban Studies, 1124
Intergovernmental Committee on Urban & Regional Research (ICURR), 1158
International Civil Aviation Organization, 1174
International Institute for Sustainable Development, 1124
International Joint Commission, 1150
Interurban Campus, 1120
Ispat Sidbec inc., 1167

J

Jacobs Canada Inc., 1101
James N. Allan Campus, 1155
Jardin Botanique de Montréal, 1174
John & Dotsa Bitove Family Law Library, 1144
John Alexander Weir Memorial Law Library, 1105
John B. Ridley Research Library, 1138

Libraries & Resource Centres Index

John H. Daniels Faculty of Architecture, Lanscape & Design, 1158
John W. Scott Health Sciences Library, 1105
Justice Institute of British Columbia, 1114

K

Kamloops Range Research Unit, 1112
Kawartha World Issues Centre, 1152
Keyano College, 1107
King Campus, 1142
Kingstec Campus, 1137
Kingston General Hospital, 1142
Kingston R & D Centre, 1142
Kirkland Lake Campus, 1143
Klohn Crippen Berger Ltd., 1118
KSH Solutions Inc. (KSH), 1174
Kwantlen University College, 1112

L

La Cité Collégiale, 1151
Labatt Breweries Canada, 1144
Laboratory & Scientific Services Directorate, 1151
Labrador West Campus, 1131
Lacombe Research Centre, 1108
Lady Davis Institute for Medical Research of the Sir Mortimer B. Davis - Jewish General Hospital, 1174
Lafarge Canada Inc., 1174
Lakehead University, 1146, 1156
Lakeland College, 1109
Lakeshore Campus, 1159
Lambton College of Applied Arts & Technology, 1154
LandOwner Resource Centre, 1144
Langara College, 1118
Langley Campus, 1113
Lanxess Inc. - Sarnia, 1154
Laurentian Forestry Centre, 1179
Laurentian University, 1155
Law Library, 1102, 1189
Legal Information Society of Nova Scotia, 1135
Lester B. Pearson College of the Pacific, 1121
Lethbridge Community College, 1108
Libraries of Niagara College, 1165
Library (Burnaby), 1110
Library (Edmonton), 1105
Library (Vancouver), 1118
Life Sciences Library, 1174
London Health Sciences Centre, 1144
Loyalist College of Applied Arts & Technology, 1138

M

Macdonald Campus Library, 1182
MacDonald Dettwiler & Associates Ltd., 1115
Malaspina University-College, 1113
Manitoba Dept. of Conservation, Environment Canada & Canadian Council of Ministers of the Environment, 1124
Manitoba Dept. of Science, Technology, Energy & Mines, 1124
Manitoba Eco-Network Inc., 1124
Manitoba Hydro, 1124
Manitoba Museum, 1124
Manitoba Naturalists Society, 1124
Map and Data Library, 1159
Map Library, 1159, 1121
Maps, Data & Government Information Centre (MADGIC), 1142
Marianopolis College, 1174
Marine Campus, 1114
Maritime College of Forest Technology, 1127
Markham Campus, 1144
Matériauthèque, 1186
McGill University, 1174
McMaster University, 1141
MDA Space, 1182
Medical Reform Group of Ontario, 1159
Medicine Hat College, 1109
Memorial University of Newfoundland, 1132
Merck Frosst Canada Inc., 1168
Metro Vancouver (formerly Greater Vancouver Regional District), 1110
MFL Occupational Health Centre, 1124
Millard Health, 1105

Mines & Aggregates Safety & Health Association, 1146
Miramichi Campus Library, 1128
Misericordia Community Hospital, 1106
Misericordia Health Centre, 1124
Mission Campus at Heritage Park Centre Library, 1113
Mohawk College of Applied Arts & Technology, 1141
Mohawk-McMaster Institute for Applied Health Sciences, 1141
Moncton Campus, Library, 1128
Montréal General Hospital, 1174
Mount Allison University, 1129
Mount Royal College, 1102
Mount Sinai Hospital, 1159

N

Nahum Gelber Law Library, 1174
National Air Photo Library, 1151
National Capital Commission, 1151
National Capital Region, 1151
National Energy Board, 1102
National Energy Conservation Association, 1125
National Hydrology Research Centre, National Water Research Institute, 1189
Natural Resources Canada, 1151
Natural Resources Canada Library - Earth Sciences (Vancouver), 1118
Natural Resources Canada, Canadian Forest Service, 1127
Natural Sciences Library, 1189
Nature Canada, 1151
Neil John Maclean Health Sciences Library, 1125
New Brunswick Community College, 1127
New Brunswick Dept. of Environment, 1128
New Brunswick Dept. of Wellness, Culture & Sport, 1129
New Brunswick Museum, 1129
Newfoundland & Labrador Dept. of Forest Resources & Agrifood, 1130
Newfoundland & Labrador Dept. of Government Services, 1131
Newfoundland & Labrador Dept. of Health & Community Services, 1132
Newfoundland & Labrador Dept. of Innovation, Trade & Rural Development, 1132
Newfoundland & Labrador Dept. of Natural Resources, 1132
Newfoundland & Labrador Housing Corp., 1132
Newfoundland & Labrador Hydro, 1132
Newfoundland Ocean Industries Association, 1132
Nexen Inc., 1102
Niagara Parks Botanical Gardens School of Horticulture, 1146
Nickel Institute, 1159
Nicola Valley Institute of Technology, 1113
Nippissing University/Canadore College, 1146
Noranda Earth Sciences Library, 1159
NorQuest College, 1106
North Island College Library, 1111
Northern Alberta Institute of Technology, 1106
Northern College of Applied Arts & Technology, 1156
Northern Forestry Centre, 1106
Northern Lakes College - Grouard Campus, 1108
Northern Lakes College - Slave Lake, 1109
Northern Lights College, 1111
Northern Lights Regional Health Centre, 1107
Northwest Atlantic Fisheries Centre, 1132
Northwest Community College Library, 1116
Northwest Territories Legislative Assembly, 1134
Northwest Territories Public Works & Services, 1134
Northwest Territories Resources, Wildlife & Economic Development, 1134
Notre Dame Bay Memorial Health Centre, 1133
NOVA Chemicals Ltd., 1102
Nova Scotia Agricultural College, 1137
Nova Scotia Community College, 1136
Nova Scotia Dept. of Natural Resources, 1136
Nova Scotia Dept. of Transportation & Public Works, 1136
Nova Scotia Environment & Labour, 1136
NPS Pharmaceuticals, 1159
NRC Information Centre, 1166
NRC Information Centre - Halifax, 1136
NRC Information Centre - St John's, 1133
NRC Information Centre - Saskatoon, 1189
NRC Information Centre Montréal, 1174
Nuclear Awareness Project, 1164
Nunavut Arctic College, 1138

Nunavut Dept. of Environment, 1138
Nunavut Research Institute, 1138

O

Office of the Fire Marshal, 1159
Oil Museum of Canada, 1146
Okanagan College, 1112
Olds College, 1109
Ontario Energy Board, 1159
Ontario Farm Animal Council, 1140
Ontario Federation of Anglers & Hunters, 1153
Ontario Forestry Safe Workplace Association, 1146
Ontario Ministry of Economic Development & Trade, 1159
Ontario Ministry of Environment, 1160
Ontario Ministry of Health & Long-Term Care, 1160
Ontario Ministry of Municipal Affairs & Housing, 1160
Ontario Ministry of Natural Resources, 1153
Ontario Ministry of Northern Development & Mines, 1155
Ontario Ministry of Transportation, 1154
Ontario Petroleum Institute Inc., 1144
Ontario Power Generation, 1160
Ontario Public Interest Research Group - Toronto/Downtown Women's Centre, 1160
Ontario Regional Library, 1160
Ontario Safety League, 1145
Ontario Science Centre, 1160
Ontario Trails Council, 1153
Orillia Campus, 1147
Osgoode Hall Law School, 1160
Ottawa Hospital, 1151
Ottawa Hospital - Civic Campus, 1151
Ottawa Hospital-Riverside Campus, 1151
Owen Sound Campus, 1152
Oxford County Geological Society, 1156

P

Pacific & Yukon Region - Vancouver, 1118
Pacific & Yukon Region - Whitehorse, 1191
Pacific Biological Station, 1113
Pacific Forestry Centre, 1121
Pacific Region, 1110, 1118
Pacific Regional Library, 1118
Pacific Salmon Commission, 1118
Parc Aquarium du Québec, 1179
Paul Martin Law Library, 1165
Pavillon Félix-Leclerc, 1168
Peace & Environment Resource Centre, 1151
Pêches et aquaculture commerciales, 1167
Pembrook Campus, 1152
Penticton Campus, 1114
Perkin Elmer Optoelectronics, 1187
Perth Campus, 1152
Peter Lougheed Centre Library, 1102
Petroleum Industry Training Service, 1102
Pfizer Canada, Inc., 1169
Physics Library, 1160
Placentia Campus Learning Resource Centre, 1131
Point Pelee National Park, 1143
Pollutech Environmental Ltd., 1146
Port Alberni Regional Campus Library, 1114
Port aux Basques Campus Library, 1131
Port Hardy Centre, 1115
Portage College, 1108
POS Bio-sciences, 1190
Potash Corporation of Saskatchewan Inc., 1190
Potato Research Centre, 1128
Powell River Campus, 1115
Powertech Labs Inc., 1116
Prairie & Northern Region - Edmonton, 1106
Prairie & Northern Region - Yellowknife, 1134
Prairie Agricultural Machinery Institute, 1187
Prairie Association for Water Management, 1108
Prairie Farm Rehabilitation Administration, 1188
Prairie Northern Wildlife Research Centre, 1190
Prairie Region, 1190
Pratt & Whitney Canada Inc., 1169
Prince Albert Model Forest Association Inc., 1187
Prince Edward Island Dept. of Provincial Treasury, 1165
Prince Edward Island Food Technology Centre, 1165

Libraries & Resource Centres Index

Prince Philip Drive Campus Library, 1133
Prospectors & Developers Association of Canada, 1160
Public Health Library, 1152
Public Health Services, 1190
Public Works & Government Services Canada, 1168
Pulp & Paper Research Institute of Canada (PAPRICAN), 1177

Q

QIT-Fer et Titane inc, 1186
Québec Conseil de la science et de la technologie, 1179
Québec Ministère de l'agriculture, des pêcheries et de l'alimentation, 1179
Québec Ministère de la santé et des services sociaux, 1179
Québec Ministère de la Sécurité Publique - Direction des Communications, 1175
Québec Ministère des affaires municipales et des Régions, 1179
Québec Ministère des Ressources naturelles et de la Faune, 1179
Québec Ministère des transports, 1180
Québec Ministère du Développement durable, de l'Environnement et des Parcs, 1180
Québec Ministère du Développement économique, de l'Innovation et de l'Exportation, 1180
Québec Office des personnes handicapées, 1175
Québec Régie de l'assurance-maladie, 1180
Quebec Regional Library, 1169
Quebec Young Farmers' Provincial Federation, 1182
Queen Elizabeth II Hospital, 1108
Queen's University, 1142

R

R. Howard Webster Library, 1175
R.V. Anderson Associates Limited, 1161
Radiation Safety Institute of Canada, 1160
Red Deer College, 1109
Red River Apiarists' Association, 1122
Red River College, 1125
Reference Resource Centre, 1165
Regina Qu'Appelle Health Region - Wascana Rehabilitation Centre, 1188
Regina Qu'Appelle Health Region Library Services - Regina General Hospital, 1188
Région du Québec, 1180
René Gervais Inc., Consultants, 1166
Research & Business Development Library, 1142
Research Department Information Resources, 1154
Resource Conservation Manitoba, 1125
Rheinmetall Canada Inc., 1183
Richmond Campus, 1115
Rideau Valley Field Naturalists, 1152
Riverview Hospital, 1115
Rockyview Hospital Library, 1102
Royal Botanical Gardens, 1139
Royal Columbian Hospital - Simon Fraser Health Authority, 1114
Royal Military College of Canada, 1142
Royal Ontario Museum Libraries, 1161
Royal Roads University, 1121
Royal Tyrrell Museum of Palaeontology, 1104
Royal Victoria Hospital, 1175
Ryerson University, 1161

S

S.L. Ross Environmental Research Ltd., 1152
Saint John Campus Library, 1129
St. Andrews Biological Station, 1129
St. Andrews Campus, 1129
St Anthony Campus Library, 1131
St Boniface General Hospital, 1125
St Clair College of Applied Arts & Technology, 1165
St Francis-Xavier University, 1134
St James Library/Learning Commons, 1161
St John's Department of Planning, 1133
St Joseph's Health Care, London, 1144
St Joseph's Hospital (Hamilton), 1141
St Joseph's Hospital (Saint John), 1129
St Lawrence College, 1143
St Mary's University, 1136
St Michael's Hospital, 1161
St Paul's Health Sciences Library, 1118

St Paul's Hospital (Grey Nuns) of Saskatoon, 1190
Salmon Arm Campus, 1116
Sanofi Pasteur Limited, 1161
Sarnia-Lambton Environmental Association, 1154
Saskatchewan Environment, 1187
Saskatchewan Environmental Society, 1190
Saskatchewan Forest Centre, 1187
Saskatchewan Health, 1188
Saskatchewan Highways & Transportation, 1188
Saskatchewan Institute of Applied Science & Technology, 1188
Saskatchewan Research Council, 1190
Saskatchewan Watershed Authority, 1187
Saskatoon Campus Library, 1190
SaskPower Corporation, 1188
SaskTel, 1188
Sault Area Hospital, 1154
Sault College of Applied Arts & Technology, 1154
School of Architecture, 1139
Schulich Library of Science & Engineering, 1175
Science & Engineering Division, 1118
Science & Forestry Library, 1128
Science Library, 1111
Science/Engineering Library, 1143
Sciences & Technology Library, 1125
Sea Lamprey Control Centre, 1155
Seal Cove Campus Library, 1130
Semi-Arid Prairie Agricultural Research Centre, 1191
Seneca College of Applied Arts & Technology, 1161
Seneca@York Campus, 1161
Service de l'urbanisme, 1175
Seven Oaks General Hospital, 1125
Sexton Design & Technology Library, 1136
Shell Canada Limited, 1102
Sheridan Institute of Technology and Advanced Learning, 1146
Sheridan Park Site, 1145
SIAST Kelsey Campus, 1190
SIAST Palliser Campus, 1187
SIAST Wascana Campus, 1188
Silver King Campus, 1114
Simon Fraser University, 1111
Sir F.G. Banting Research Centre, 1152
Sir Mortimer B. Davis Jewish General Hospital, 1175
Sir Sandford Fleming College of Applied Arts & Technology, 1153
Sir Wilfred Grenfell College, 1131
SNC-Lavalin Engineers & Constructors Inc., 1161
SNC-Lavalin inc., 1175
Société générale de financement du Québec (SGF), 1175
Société habitation du Québec, 1175
Société québécoise de spéléologie, 1176
SOQUEM INC., 1180
South Campus, 1106
South-East Regional Health Authority, 1128
Southern Alberta Institute of Technology, 1103
Southern Crop Protection & Food Research Centre, 1164
Sproule Associates Limited, 1103
Steacie Science and Engineering Library, 1161
Stoney Creek Campus, 1155
Strait Area Campus, 1137
Strathcona County, 1109
Strathcona Park Lodge & Outdoor Education Centre, 1111
Succursale de Québec, 1180
Sudbury Rock & Lapidary Society, 1155
Suncor Inc., 1103
Sunnybrook Health Sciences Centre - Sunnybrook Campus, 1162
Surrey Campus, 1116
Surrey Library, 1116
Surrey Memorial Hospital, 1116
Syncrude Canada Ltd., 1106

T

Talisman Energy Inc., 1103
Technical Library, 1188
Technical Reference Centre, 1162
Technical Services Library, 1135
Teck Cominco Metals Ltd., 1116
Teck Resources, 1118
TECSULT inc, 1176
Télé-Université, 1180

Teshmont Consultants LP, 1125
Thames Campus Resource Centre, 1139
The King's University College, 1106
The Michener Institute for Applied Health Sciences, 1162
The Pembina Institute for Appropriate Development, 1103
The Resource Library for the Environment and the Law, 1162
The Scarborough Hospital - General Campus, 1162
The Scarborough Hospital - Grace Campus, 1162
Thompson Rivers University, 1112
Thompson, Cariboo, Shuswap Health Sciences Library, 1112
3M Canada Company, 1144
Thurber Group, 1121
Toronto Botanical Garden, 1162
Toronto East General Hospital, 1162
Toronto Public Health, 1162
Toronto Rehab, 1162
Toronto Urban Development Services City Planning, 1162
Toronto Western Hospital, 1162
Toronto Zoo, 1163
Trafalgar Campus Library, 1146
TransAlta Utilities Corporation, 1103
TransCanada PipeLines Limited, 1103
Transport Canada, 1152
Transportation Association of Canada, 1152
Transportation Health & Safety Association of Ontario, 1163
Trent University, 1153
Trillium Health Centre-Mississauga Site, 1145
Trinity Western University, 1113
Triton Environmental Consultants Ltd., 1116
Truro Campus, 1137

U

U.S. Steel Canada, 1141
UMA Engineering Ltd., 1106
Union Carbide/Pétromont, 1176
Union Gas Ltd., a Duke Energy Company, 1140
Union of British Columbia Municipalities, 1116
Union québécoise pour la conservation de la nature, 1180
United Nations Environment Programme - Convention on Biological Diversity, 1176
Université d'Ottawa, 1152
Université de Hearst, 1141
Université de l'Alberta Bibliothèque Saint-Jean, 1107
Université de Moncton, 1129
Université de Montréal, 1176
Université de Sherbrooke, 1185
Université du Québec à Chicoutimi, 1166
Université du Québec à Montréal, 1176
Université du Québec à Rimouski, 1181
Université du Québec à Trois-Rivières, 1186
Université du Québec École de technologie supérieure, 1176
Université du Québec en Abitibi-Témiscamingue, 1182
Université du Québec INRS - Institut Armand-Frappier, 1169
Université du Québec Institut national de la recherche scientifique, INRS-Urbanisation, Culture et Societé, 1180, 1176
Université Laval, 1181
Université Sainte-Anne, 1134
University College of the Fraser Valley, 1110
University College of the North, 1122
University Health Network, 1163
University Map Library, 1154, 1164
University of Alberta, 1107
University of Alberta Dept. of Physiology, 1107
University of Alberta Dept. of Rural Economy, 1107
University of Alberta J.P. Das Developmental Disabilities Centre, 1107
University of Alberta School of Native Studies, 1107
University of British Columbia, 1119
University of Calgary, 1103
University of Guelph, 1140
University of Guelph Collège d'Alfred, 1138
University of Guelph Kemptville College, 1142
University of Guelph Ridgetown Campus, 1153
University of Lethbridge, 1108
University of Manitoba Libraries, 1125
University of New Brunswick, 1128
University of Northern British Columbia, 1115
University of Prince Edward Island, 1166
University of Regina Library, 1189
University of Saskatchewan, 1191

Libraries & Resource Centres Index

University of Sudbury, 1155
University of Toronto at Mississauga, 1145
University of Toronto Innis College, 1163
University of Toronto Libraries, 1163
University of Toronto Massey College, 1163
University of Toronto Scarborough Library, 1163
University of Victoria Libraries, 1121
University of Victoria School of Health Information Science, 1121
University of Waterloo, 1164
University of Western Ontario Dept. of Geography, 1144
University of Western Ontario Libraries, 1144
University of Windsor, 1165
University of Winnipeg, 1125

V

Vale Inco, 1163
Vancouver Aquarium Marine Science Centre, 1119
Vancouver Coastal Health Authority, 1119
Vancouver Community College, 1119
Vancouver Community Services Group, 1119
Vancouver Museum, 1119
VanDusen Gardens Library, 1119

Vernon Campus, 1120
Victoria General Hospital (Winnipeg), 1126

W

W.K. Kellogg Health Sciences Library, 1137
Walker, Nott, Dragicevic Associates Limited, 1163
Walter Hitschfeld Geographic Information Centre, 1177
Ward Chipman Library, 1129
Waterfront Regeneration Trust, 1163
Watts, Griffis & McOuat Limited, 1163
West Coast Environmental Law Research Foundation, 1119
Western Development Museum, 1191
Western Health Care Corporation, 1131
Westmount Campus, 1107
Wilfrid Laurier University, 1165
William C. Wonders Map Collection, 1107
William R. Lederman Law Library, 1143
William R. Newman Library, 1126
Williams Lake Campus, 1121
Windsor Regional Hospital - Metropolitan Campus, 1165
Winnipeg Research Centre, 1126
Winnipeg Water & Waste Dept., 1126

Women's College Hospital, 1163
Woodstock Campus, 1165
Woodstock Campus, Library, 1130
Woodward Biomedical Library, 1119
Workers' Compensation Board Northwest Territories, 1134
Workers' Compensation Board of Alberta, 1107

X

Xerox Research Centre of Canada, 1146

Y

Yellowquill College, 1126
York University Glendon College Campus, 1163
York University Libraries, 1164
Yukon Chamber of Mines, 1191
Yukon College, 1191
Yukon Conservation Society, 1191
Yukon Dept. of Energy, Mines & Resources, 1191
Yukon Dept. of Environment, 1191
Yukon Energy Solutions Centre, 1191
Yukon Workers' Compensation Health & Safety Board, 1192

Libraries & Resource Centres

Alberta

Athabasca: **Athabasca University Library**
1 University Dr.
Athabasca, AB T9S 3A3
800-788-9041 ext: 6254
Fax: 780-675-6477
e-mail: library@athabascau.ca
URL: library.athabascau.ca
National Library Symbol: AEAU
Consortia Membership: The Alberta Library; Canadian Research Knowledge Network (CRKN); Council of Prairie and Pacific University Libraries (COPPUL); Health Knowledge Network (HKN)
Founded in: 1970
Hours: M-F 8:30-4:30
Acquisitions Budget: $250,000 - $499,999
For Print: $50,000 - $99,999
For Electronic: $250,000 - $499,999
Special Collections: Byrne Collection; The Reverend Edward Checkland Collection (Distance Education); University archives
Subjects covered: Distance Education, Women's Studies
Services:
Internet Access
Inter-Library Loan (ILL)
Digital Reference Centre for distance learners
Microform Equipment: Reader
Personnel:
Steve Schafer, Director, Library Services
steves@athabascau.ca
Kay Johnson, Head, Reference & Circulation Services
Douglas Kariel, Head, Technical Services & Systems
Judy Stady, Supervisor, Interlibrary Loan
Elaine Magusin, Reference Services Librarian
Tony Tin, Electronic Resources Librarian
Lorraine Hirning, Serials Technician
Keith Walker, Chief Librarian
kwalker@mhc.ab.ca
Kimara White, Library Technician

Brooks: **Brooks Campus Library**
200 Horticultural Station Rd. East
Brooks, AB T1A 3Y6
Mailing Address: 299 College Dr. SE
Medicine Hat, AB T1A 3Y6
403-362-1690
Fax: 403-362-8926
866-282-8394
e-mail: info@brookscampus.ca
illo@mhc.ab.ca
Founded in: 1979
Hours: M-Th 8:00-8:00; F 8:00-4:00
Note: Address all correspondence to main library
Services:
Internet Access
Inter-Library Loan (ILL)
Personnel: Summary: 3 Total; 3 Technical(s)

Calgary: **Agrium Inc. Library**
13131 Lake Fraser Dr. SE
Calgary, AB T2J 7E8
403-225-7000
Fax: 403-225-7609
e-mail: avirgini@agrium.com
URL: www.agrium.com
National Library Symbol: AEEC
No public access
Founded in: 1980
Hours: M-F
Acquisitions Budget: $25,000 - $49,999
Note: For research materials at Redwater Technical Library, contact main library.
Subjects covered: Engineering, Environment, Business, Agriculture, Chemistry
Services:
Inter-Library Loan (ILL)
Personnel: Summary: 1 Total; 1 Technical(s)

Alexis Virginillo, Business Research Librarian
avirgini@agrium.com
Spencer Stevens, Library Technician
spencer.stevens@calgaryhealthregion.ca
Nancy Carlin, Library Technician
nancy.carlin@calgaryhealthregion.ca

Calgary: **Alberta Children's Hospital Library**
1820 Richmond Rd. SW
Calgary, AB T2T 5C7
403-943-7077
Fax: 403-543-9108
e-mail: ach.library@calgaryhealthregion.ca
National Library Symbol: ACACH
No public access
Hours: M-F 8:00-4:15
Acquisitions Budget: $25,000 - $49,999
Subjects covered: Child Health Care
Services:
Inter-Library Loan (ILL) for a fee of $5
Personnel: Summary: 2 Total; 2 Technical(s); 5 Volunteer(s)

Calgary: **Alberta Dept. of Energy Calgary Reference Centre**
#300, 801 - 6th Ave. SW
Calgary, AB T2P 3W2
403-297-5483
Fax: 403-297-8954
e-mail: calgarylibrary@enr.gov.ab.ca
URL: www.energy.gov.ab.ca/About_us/998.asp
National Library Symbol: ACPMC
Hours: M-F
Subjects covered: Energy, Mineral Resources, Energy Prices
Services:
Inter-Library Loan (ILL)
Personnel: Summary: 2 Total; 1 Professional(s); 1 Technical(s)
Nancy Stasiuk, Library Technician

Calgary: **Alberta Speleological Society Library**
c/o #904, 836 - 15th Ave. SW
Calgary, AB T2R 1S2
URL: www.caving.ab.ca
Founded in: 1968
Hours: by appointment only
Special Collections: Reports, books, & periodicals pertaining to cave & karst explorations, science, conservation & related items
Subjects covered: Reports, books, & periodicals pertaining to cave & karst explorations, science, conservation & related items
Services:

Calgary: **Alberta Wilderness Resource Centre Library**
455 - 12th St., NW
Calgary, AB T2P 2E1
Mailing Address: PO Box 6398, Stn D
Calgary, AB T2P 2E1
403-283-2025
Fax: 403-270-2743
866-313-0713
e-mail: awa.wrc@shaw.ca
awa.info@shawcable.com
URL: www.albertawilderness.ca
Hours: by appointment only
Acquisitions Budget: $25,000 - $49,999
Subjects covered: Wilderness, Land Use, Forestry, Wildlife, Natural Resources, Conservation, National Parks, Environment, Protected Areas, Rivers
Services:
Internet Access
Personnel: Summary: 1 Total; 1 Professional(s)
Shirley Bray, Director

Calgary: **AMEC Inc. Information Resource Centre**
#900, 801 - 6th Ave. SW
Calgary, AB T2P 3W3
403-298-4170
Fax: 403-298-4125
e-mail: tim.elliott@amec.com
URL: www.amec.com

National Library Symbol: ACME
Hours: 7:30-5:00 by appointment only
Acquisitions Budget: $25,000 - $49,999
Subjects covered: Energy, Environment, Physical Science, Engineering, Technology, Natural Resources
Services:
Inter-Library Loan (ILL)
Personnel: Summary: 1 Total; 1 Professional(s); 1 Technical(s)
Tim Elliott, Librarian
tim.elliott@amec.com
Joanna Becker, Head, Technical Services
Carol Ann Ruaro, Document Control/Library
carolann.ruaro@amec.com

Calgary: **Anadarko Canada Corp. Library**
425 - 1st St. SW
Calgary, AB T2P 4V4
Mailing Address: PO Box 2595, Stn M
Calgary, AB T2P 4V4
403-231-0245
e-mail: robert_mclauchlin@anadarko.com
National Library Symbol: ACNER
No public access
Hours: M-F 7:00-4:00
Subjects covered: Oil & Gas, Geology, Geophysics
Services:
Inter-Library Loan (ILL)
Personnel: Summary: 2 Total; 1 Professional(s); 1 Technical(s)
Robert McLauchlin, Supervisor
Jean Pearson, Contact
jean_pearson@anadarko.com

Calgary: **Calgary Engineering & Environmental Services**
Utilities & Environmental Protection, Library
800 Macleod Trail SE
Calgary, AB T2P 2M5
Mailing Address: PO Box 2100, Stn M
Calgary, AB T2P 2M5
403-268-3783
Fax: 403-268-8260
e-mail: lorette.linde@calgary.ca
National Library Symbol: ACE
Founded in: 1985
Hours: M-F 7:30-12:00, 1:30-4:00 by appointment only
Acquisitions Budget: $50,000 - $99,999
Special Collections: Municipal & Environmental Engineering, Soil Reports, Environmental Assessments
Subjects covered: Engineering, Technology, Housing, Municipal Engineering, Physical Sciences
Services:
Inter-Library Loan (ILL)
Personnel: Summary: 2 Total; 1 Technical(s)
Lorette Linde, Librarian/Records Administrator
lorette.linde@calgary.ca
403-268-3783

Calgary: **Calgary Health Region Library Services**
1403 - 29th St. NW
Calgary, AB T2N 2T9
403-944-4849
Fax: 403-944-1174
e-mail: fhh.library@calgaryhealthregion.ca
URL: hinc.ucalgary.ca
National Library Symbol: ACFH
Consortia Membership: Health Knowledge Network (HKN)
Hours: M-F 8:00-4:15
Subjects covered: Nursing, Physical Therapy, Psychiatry, Psychology, Occupational Therapy, Patient Education, Consumer Health, Social Work, Pastoral Care & Health Care Administration
Services:
Internet Access
Inter-Library Loan (ILL)
Personnel: Summary: 2 Total; 2 Technical(s)
Elizabeth Aitken, Acting Regional Manager
elizabeth.aitken@calgaryhealthregion.ca
403-943-0192

Judith Meyers, Librarian
jmeyers@hatchenergy.com

Calgary: Calgary Library
#700, 840 - 7th Ave. SW
Calgary, AB T2P 3G2
403-920-3101
Fax: 403-266-5736
e-mail: jmeyers@hatchenergy.com
No public access
Hours: Tu-Th 8:30-4:00
Acquisitions Budget: 0-$9,999
For Print: 0-$9,999
For Electronic: 0-$9,999
Population Served: 360
Subjects covered: Power engineering, Water resouces engineering, Hydrocarbon engineering, Tranportation engineering
Services:
Personnel: *Summary:* 1 Professional(s)
Florrie Cook, Head Librarian
fcook@nrcan.gc.ca
Edward Hau, Bibliographic & Computing Services Librarian
Joanne McCloskey, Head of Acquistions

Calgary: Calgary Library
3303 - 33rd St. NW, 2nd Fl.
Calgary, AB T2L 2A7
403-292-7165
Fax: 403-292-5377
e-mail: calgary.ref@nrcan.gc.ca
URL: ess.nrcan.gc.ca
National Library Symbol: ACSP
Founded in: 1967
Hours: M-Th 8:00-12:00, 12:45-4:00; F 8:00-12:00, 12:45-3:15
Acquisitions Budget: $100,000 - $249,999
For Print: $50,000 - $99,999
For Electronic: 0-$9,999
Note: Limited online searching. Formerly the Institute of Sedimentary & Petroleum Geology. Photocopying: .25/pg, .10/pg for students. Memberships: $50/yr.
Special Collections: Geology, Petroleum, Coal, Paleontology, Regional Geology (Western Canada, Sedimentary Basin & Arctic)
Subjects covered: Earth Sciences, Maps
Services:
Inter-Library Loan (ILL)
Memberships
Microform Equipment: Reader
Personnel: *Summary:* 3 Total; 2 Professional(s); 1 Technical(s)
Guy Trott, Library Manager
trott@albertainnovates.ca

Calgary: Calgary Library & Information Centre
3608 - 33rd St. NW
Calgary, AB T2L 2A6
403-210-5292
Fax: 403-210-5380
e-mail: calgary_library@arc.ab.ca
National Library Symbol: ACRS
Consortia Membership: NEOS Library Consortium
Hours: M-F 8:15-12:00, 1:00-4:30 by appointment only
Special Collections: Heavy Oil Recovery
Subjects covered: Artificial Intelligence, Industrial Engineering, Advanced Manufacturing Technologies
Services:
Inter-Library Loan (ILL)
Personnel: *Summary:* 1 Total; 1 Professional(s)

Calgary: Calgary Utilities & Environmental Protection
Land Information & Mapping Library
#G8, 800 Macleod Trail SE, 8th Fl.
Calgary, AB T2P 2M5
Mailing Address: PO Box 2100, Stn. M
Calgary, AB T2P 2M5
403-268-3783
Fax: 403-268-8260
e-mail: lorette.linde@calgary.ca
URL: www.calgary.ca
Founded in: 1972
Hours: M-F 8:00-4:00
Special Collections: City of Calgary internal documents; Standards; Dictionaries; Directories; Regulations; Audio-visual materials; Consultants' reports; Journals; Newspapers; Newsletters

Subjects covered: Engineering; Computers; Environment; Utilities
Services:
Personnel: *Summary:* 1 Technical(s)
Lorette Linde, Librarian/Records Administrator

Calgary: Calgary Zoological Society Library
1300 Zoo Rd. NE
Calgary, AB T2E 7V6
403-232-9327
Fax: 403-237-7582
URL: www.calgaryzoo.org
Hours: M-F 8:00-12:00, 1:00-4:00 by appointment only
Acquisitions Budget: 0-$9,999
Subjects covered: Zoology, Horticulture, Animal Husbandry
Services:
Personnel:
Deanna Snell, Registrar
deannas@calgaryzoo.ab.ca
403-232-9327

Calgary: Canadian Association of Oilwell Drilling Contractors Library
#800, 540 - 5 Ave. SW
Calgary, AB T2P 0M2
403-264-4311
Fax: 403-263-3796
e-mail: info@caodc.ca
URL: www.caodc.ca/
Founded in: 1949
Hours: M-F 8:00-4:30 by appointment only
Subjects covered: Oilwells, Drilling
Services:
Personnel: *Summary:* 1 Other employees
Leslie A. Diegel, Manager, Administration

Calgary: Canadian Centre For Energy Information Library
#1600, 800 - 6th Ave. SW
Calgary, AB T2P 3G3
403-263-7722
Fax: 403-237-6286
877-606-4636
e-mail: info@centreforenergy.com
URL: www.centreforenergy.com
No public access
Founded in: 1975
Subjects covered: Petroleum, Natural Gas, Sour Gas, Crude Oil, Canadian Energy
Services:
Personnel: *Summary:* 1 Total; 4 Professional(s); 1 Technical(s)
Colleen Killingsworth, President

Calgary: Canadian Energy Research Institute
I.N. McKinnon Memorial Library
#125, 3512 - 33rd St. NW
Calgary, AB T2L 2A6
403-220-2394
Fax: 403-284-4181
e-mail: library@ceri.ca
National Library Symbol: ACINM
Founded in: 1979
Hours: M-Th 8:30-5:00; F 8:30-4:30 by appointment only
Acquisitions Budget: $25,000 - $49,999
For Print: 0-$9,999
For Electronic: $25,000 - $49,999
Population Served: 30
Subjects covered: Energy, Energy Economics/Environment
Services:
Remote Access
Inter-Library Loan (ILL)
Personnel: *Summary:* 1 Total; 1 Technical(s)
Lucinda Kulawik, Librarian
lkulawik@ceri.ca
403-220-2394

Calgary: Canadian Institute of Resources Law Library
#3353, Murray Fraser Hall, University of Calgary
2500 University Dr. NW
Calgary, AB T2N 1N4
403-220-3200
Fax: 403-282-6182

e-mail: cirl@ucalgary.ca
URL: www.cirl.ca
Profile: A leading, national centre of expertise on legal & policy issues relating to Canada's natural resources. Since its establishment, it has pursued a 3-fold mandate of research, education & publication; it initiates projects & responds to requests from the public & private sectors, & from non-governmental organizations
Founded in: 1979
Hours: M-F by appointment only
Acquisitions Budget: For Print: 0-$9,999
For Electronic: 0-$9,999
Note: The Canadian Institute of Resources Law (CIRL) is a leading national centre of expertise on legal & policy issues relating to Canada's natural resources, with a mandate to undertake research, publication & educational programmes. A non-profit organization, CIRL maintains a small library serving lawyers, government & industry personnel & law students
Subjects covered: Energy Regulation & Policy; Environmental Law & Policy; Aboriginal Law, Water Law & Policy; Forestry Law & Policy; Mining Law & Policy
Services:
Personnel: *Summary:* 6 Professional(s)
J. Owen Saunders, Executive Director
josaunde@ucalgary.ca
Sue Parsons, Information Resources Officer
sue.parsons@ucalgary.ca

Calgary: Canadian Pacific Railway
Business Information Services/Centre d'info-affaires
#2000, 401 - 9th Ave. SW
Calgary, AB T2P 4Z4
403-319-6191
Fax: 403-319-6257
e-mail: business_info_services@cpr.ca
URL: www.cpr.ca
National Library Symbol: ACCPR
Founded in: 1972
Hours: by appointment only
Subjects covered: Transportation, Industry, Business
Services:
Inter-Library Loan (ILL)
Personnel: *Summary:* 5 Total; 3 Professional(s)
Carole Lacourte, Senior Manager
Gail Fraser, Analyst
403-319-6193
Jennifer St. John, Analyst
403-319-6189

Calgary: Chevron Canada Resources Library
500 - 5th Ave. SW
Calgary, AB T2P 0L7
403-234-5200
URL: www.chevron.com
www.chevron.ca
No public access
Founded in: 1954
Subjects covered: Physical Sciences, Engineering, Technology, Natural Resources, Earth Sciences
Services:

Calgary: Cottonwood Consultants Ltd Library
615 Deercroft Way SE
Calgary, AB T2J 5V4
403-271-1408
Subjects covered: Environment
Services:
Personnel:
Cliff Wallis, Environmental Researcher

Calgary: Devon Canada Corporation Corporate Library
#2000, 400 - 3rd Ave. SW
Calgary, AB T2P 4H2
403-232-5581
Fax: 403-213-8099
National Library Symbol: ACH
No public access
Hours: M-F 8:00-12:00, 1:00-5:00
Acquisitions Budget: $250,000 - $499,999
For Print: $100,000 - $249,999
For Electronic: $250,000 - $499,999
Population Served: 1500
Special Collections: GSC Publications

Subjects covered: Energy, Mineral Resources, Oil & Gas, Engineering.
Services:
Remote Access
Internet Access
Access to Subscription Databases
Inter-Library Loan (ILL)
Personnel: *Summary:* 3 Total; 1 Professional(s); 2 Other employees;
Mariela Parra, Corporate Librarian
mariela.parra@devoncanada.com
403-232-5581

Calgary: **DeVry Institute of Technology**
Calgary Library
2700 - 3rd Ave. SE
Calgary, AB T2A 7W4
403-235-3450
Fax: 403-207-6227
800-363-5558
e-mail: scampbell@devry.edu
URL: www.devry.ca/student_library.html
No public access
Hours: M, W, F 8:00-6:00; Tu-Th 8:00-5:00
Acquisitions Budget: $10,000 - $24,999
Subjects covered: Business, Electronics, Computer, General Education
Services:
Remote Access
Internet Access
Access to Subscription Databases
Inter-Library Loan (ILL)
Personnel:
Suzzette Campbell, Library Assistant
406-207-3100
Barbara Brydges, Director
brydges@ucalgary.ca
403-220-6295

Calgary: **Doucette Library of Teaching Resources**
370 Education Block, 2500 University Dr. NW
Calgary, AB T2N 1N4
403-220-5637
Fax: 403-220-8211
URL: www.educ1.ucalgary.ca/doucette/index.shtml
Profile: Education
Hours: M-Su
Special Collections: Alberta curriculum documents, curriculum resource materials, professional support materials, children's literature, French language materials, audiovisual resources, historical collection, thesis collection.
Subjects covered: Education
Personnel:

Calgary: **EnCana Corporation**
Information Centre
150 - 9 Ave., SW
Calgary, AB T2P 2S5
403-645-7645
Fax: 403-645-7649
National Library Symbol: ACPP
No public access
Hours: M-F 7:30-5:00
Acquisitions Budget: $250,000 - $499,999
Subjects covered: Energy; Oil & Gas
Services:
Access to Subscription Databases
Personnel: *Summary:* 4 Total; 4 Technical(s)
Jeanne Kimber, Group Leader, Information Centre
Alicia Hawkings, Information Analyst
alicia.hawkings@encana.com
403-645-3085
Pat Bolander, Information Technician
pat.bolander@encana.com
403-645-7641
Barb Miller, Information Technician
barb.miller@encana.com
403-645-6642

Calgary: **Energy Resources Conservation Board (ERCB)**
Library
640 - 5th Ave. SW
Calgary, AB T2P 3G4
403-297-8242
Fax: 403-297-3517

e-mail: angela.burns@ercb.ca
URL: www.ercb.ca
National Library Symbol: ACER
Founded in: 1956
Hours: M-F 12:00-4:00
Acquisitions Budget: $50,000 - $99,999
Special Collections: EUB publications & decisions
Subjects covered: Energy, Natural Resources, Conservation
Services:
Internet Access for a fee
Inter-Library Loan (ILL)
Microform Equipment: Reader
Personnel: *Summary:* 3 Total; 1 Professional(s); 3 Technical(s); 1 Other employees
Angela Burns, Librarian
angela.burns@ercb.ca
403-297-3515
Claudette Cloutier, Manager
ccloutie@ucalgary.ca
403-220-3447
Regina Shedd, Reference Specialist
Patricia Johnson, Reference Specialist
Sandy Blazina, Document Delivery Specialist

Calgary: **Gallagher Library of Geology & Geophysics**
#180, Earth Science Bldg., 2500 University Dr. NW
Calgary, AB T2N 1N4
403-220-5953
Fax: 403-282-6075
e-mail: gallagher.library@ucalgary.ca
URL: library.ucalary.ca/branches/gallagherlibrary
National Library Symbol: ACU
Founded in: 1974
Hours: M-Th 8:30am-9:00pm; F 8:30-4:30; Sa 12:00-4:00
Acquisitions Budget: $50,000 - $99,999
Subjects covered: Energy, Natural Resources, Physical Sciences, Earth Sciences, Mineral Resources, Sedimentary & Petroleum Geology, Geophysics
Services:
Internet Access
Access to Subscription Databases
Inter-Library Loan (ILL)
Personnel: *Summary:* 3 Total; 1 Professional(s); 2 Other employees
Christine Hayward, Interim Director
hayward@ucalgary.ca
403-220-6858
Lorraine Toews, Head, Public Services
ltoews@ucalgary.ca
403-220-3750
Helen Lee Robertson, Liaison/Document Delivery
roberthl@ucalgary.ca
403-220-3736
Lorraine Baker, ILL Assistant

Calgary: **Health Sciences Library**
Health Sciences Centre, 3330 Hospital Dr. NW
Calgary, AB T2N 4N1
403-220-6857
Fax: 403-282-7992
e-mail: medlibr@ucalgary.ca
meddoc@ucalgary.ca
URL: library.ucalgary.ca/branches/healthscienceslibrary
National Library Symbol: ACUM
Founded in: 1972
Hours: M-Th 8:15am-10:00pm; F 8:15-6:00; Sa 10:00-18:00; Su 12:00-8:00
Acquisitions Budget: $1,000,000 plus
Special Collections: Family Medicine, History of Medicine
Subjects covered: Medicine, Health Sciences, Nursing
Services:
Internet Access
Access to Subscription Databases
Inter-Library Loan (ILL) for a fee
Microform Equipment: Computer; Reader
Personnel: *Summary:* 16 Total; 4 Professional(s); 11 Technical(s)

Calgary: **Husky Oil Operations Ltd.**
Corporate Library
#1900, 707 - 8th Ave. SW
Calgary, AB T2P 3G7
403-298-7057
Fax: 403-298-6263
e-mail: wanda.oleszkiewicz@huskyenergy.ca

No public access
Founded in: 1975
Hours: 8:00-5:00
Subjects covered: Earth Sciences, Petroleum, Engineering, Technology, Business, Management
Services:
Inter-Library Loan (ILL)
Personnel: *Summary:* 3 Total; 1 Professional(s); 1 Technical(s)
Wanda Oleszkiewicz, Librarian
wanda.oleszkiewicz@huskyenergy.ca

Calgary: **Hycal Environmental Sciences**
Library
1338A - 36th Ave. NE
Calgary, AB T2E 6T6
403-250-5800
Fax: 403-291-2395
e-mail: hycal@ibm.net
URL: www.hycal.com
Subjects covered: Environment
Services:
Barb Landes, Contact

Calgary: **Imperial Oil Resources Limited**
Research Library
3535 Research Rd. NW
Calgary, AB T2L 2K8
403-284-7417
Fax: 403-284-7589
e-mail: iol.calgary.library@esso.ca
National Library Symbol: ACIPRD
No public access
Acquisitions Budget: $25,000 - $49,999
Subjects covered: Petroleum Engineering, Ice Engineering, Soil Mechanics, Oil Spill, Corrosion
Services:
Personnel: *Summary:* 1 Total; 1 Professional(s)

Calgary: **Imperial Oil Resources Limited**
Information Centre - 12050 FAP
237 - 4th Ave. SW, 12050 FAP
Calgary, AB T2P 0H6
403-237-4520
Fax: 403-237-3728
e-mail: iol.calgary.library@esso.ca
National Library Symbol: ACI
No public access
Subjects covered: Energy
Services:
Inter-Library Loan (ILL)
Personnel: *Summary:* 4 Total; 3 Professional(s); 1 Technical(s)
Karen McManus, Librarian
karen.mcmanus@gov.ab.ca

Calgary: **Information Centre (Calgary)**
Government of Alberta, Justice, Office of the Chief Medical Examiner
4070 Bowness Rd. NW
Calgary, AB T3B 3R7
Mailing Address: 4070 Bowness Rd. NW
Calgary, AB T3B 3R7
403-297-8123
Fax: 403-297-3429
e-mail: karen.mcmanus@gov.ab.ca
National Library Symbol: ACCME
No public access
Hours: Staff available W 8:30-3:30 only
Acquisitions Budget: 0-$9,999
For Print: 0-$9,999
For Electronic: 0-$9,999
Subjects covered: Forensic Medicine, Toxicology, Bereavement, Death Investigation
Services:
Inter-Library Loan (ILL)
Personnel: *Summary:* 1 Professional(s);

Calgary: **Jacobs Canada Inc.**
Library
PO Box 5244, Stn A
Calgary, AB T2H 2N7
403-258-6527
e-mail: carol.seebruch@jacobs.com
No public access
Founded in: 1978
Hours: M-F

Acquisitions Budget: $50,000 - $99,999
Subjects covered: Physical Sciences, Engineering, Technology
Services:
Inter-Library Loan (ILL)
Microform Equipment: Reader
Personnel: Summary: 1 Total; 1 Professional(s)
Carol A. Seebruch, Information Resources Coordinator
carol.seebruch@jacobs.com

Calgary: Law Library
2500 University Dr. NW
Calgary, AB T2N 1N4
403-220-7274
Fax: 403-282-3000
e-mail: lawlib@ucalgary.ca
lawill@ucalgary.ca
URL: library.ucalgary.ca/branches/lawlibrary
National Library Symbol: ACUL
Founded in: 1976
Hours: M-Th 8:00am-10:00pm; F 8:00-6:00; Sa 10:00-6:00; Su 10:00-8:00
Subjects covered: Law
Services:
Inter-Library Loan (ILL)
Microform Equipment: Reader
Personnel: Summary: 2 Professional(s); 5 Technical(s)

Calgary: Mount Royal College Library
4825 Mount Royal Gate SW
Calgary, AB T3E 6K6
403-440-6140
Fax: 403-440-6758
e-mail: rthrasher@mtroyal.ca
URL: library.mtroyal.ca
National Library Symbol: ACMR
Consortia Membership: The Alberta Library
Founded in: 1911
Hours: M-Th 7:45am-10:00pm; F 7:45M-8:00pm; Sa-Su 10:00-8:00
Acquisitions Budget: $500,000 - $999,999
For Print: $500,000 - $999,999
For Electronic: $100,000 - $249,999
Note: The library is an affiliate member of the Council of Prairie and Pacific University Libraries (COPPUL).
Special Collections: Canadian Public Relations Society
Subjects covered: Applied Degrees
Services:
Internet Access
Inter-Library Loan (ILL)
Microform Equipment: Reader
Personnel: Summary: 41 Total; 9 Professional(s); 36 Technical(s)
Ross Thrasher, Director of Library Services
rthrasher@mtroyal.ca
403-440-6134
Margot Millard, Instructional Services Librarian
Ross Sherwin, Instructional Services Librarian
rsherwin@mtroyal.ca
403-240-6086
Carol Sinanan, Instructional Services Librarian
csinanan@mtroyal.ab.ca
403-240-6128
Meagan Weber, Collections Librarian
mweber@mtroyal.ca
Pearl Herscovitch, Coordinator, Access Services
pherscovitch@mt.royal.ca
Margy Macmillan, Coordinator, Information Services
mmacmillan@myroyal.ca
Janet Monteith, Coordinator, Technical Services
jmonteith@mtroyal.ca
Geoff Owens, Coordinator, Access Services
gowens@mtroyal.ca
Alan Waugh, Library Systems User Analyst

Calgary: National Energy Board / L'Office national de l'energie Library
444 - 7th Ave. SW
Calgary, AB T2P 0X8
403-299-3561
Fax: 403-292-5576
800-899-1265
e-mail: library@neb-one.gc.ca
bibliotheque@neb-one.gc.ca
URL: www.neb-one.gc.ca

Profile: Provides a range of services including consultation of regulatory documents, copies of NEB publications, referrals to other sources of information
National Library Symbol: ACNEB
Consortia Membership: Council of Federal Libraries (CFL) Consortium
Founded in: 1959
Hours: M-F 9:00-4:00
Acquisitions Budget: $250,000 - $499,999
Population Served: 1748
Note: Public cannot borrow materials directly, but can order them through inter-library loans
Special Collections: Statutes, federal regulations, books, annual reports; directories, encyclopediae, industry-related indexes; journals, newspapers; half of collection is directly related to NEB hearings
Subjects covered: Energy, Natural Resources
Services:
Internet Access
Inter-Library Loan (ILL)
Photocopies at no charge
Personnel: Summary: 5 Total; 1 Professional(s); 3 Technical(s); 1 Other employees;
Shelley Watt, Group Leader
403—29-9-35

Calgary: Nexen Inc. Library
801 - 7th Ave. SW
Calgary, AB T2P 3P7
403-699-5425
Fax: 403-232-1826
e-mail: marlene_robertson@nexeninc.com
National Library Symbol: ACCO
No public access
Founded in: 1978
Hours: M-F
Acquisitions Budget: $50,000 - $99,999
Subjects covered: Oil & Gas, Business
Services:
Inter-Library Loan (ILL)
Personnel: Summary: 3 Total; 1 Professional(s); 2 Technical(s)
Marlene Robertson, Librarian
marlene_robertson@nexeninc.com
Louise Dickson, Library Technician
403-699-5130
Linda North, Library Clerk

Calgary: NOVA Chemicals Ltd. Library
1000 - 7th Ave. SW
Calgary, AB T2P 5C6
403-750-3600
Fax: 403-291-3208
e-mail: library@novachem.com
URL: www.novachem.com
National Library Symbol: ACNH
No public access
Hours: M-F 8:00-5:00
Subjects covered: Plastics, Petrochemicals, Polymers, Fluid Dynamics
Services:
Inter-Library Loan (ILL)
Microform Equipment: Reader
Personnel: Summary: 9 Total; 6 Professional(s); 2 Technical(s)
Pesh Patel, Team Leader
patelpg@novachem.com
403-250-0659
Tuyet Lam, Medical Library Technician
Kathie Gaudes, Library Technician

Calgary: Peter Lougheed Centre Library
3500 - 26 Ave. NE
Calgary, AB T1Y 6J4
403-943-4737
Fax: 403-219-3559
e-mail: tlam@ucalgary.ca
National Library Symbol: ACPLC
Hours: M-F 8:00-4:00
Note: Health Connection (Consumer Health Library)
Subjects covered: Medicine, Nursing, Health Sciences
Services:
Inter-Library Loan (ILL)
Personnel:

Calgary: Petroleum Industry Training Service Library
1538-25th Ave. NE
Calgary, AB T2E 8Y3
403-250-0883
Fax: 403-291-9408
e-mail: tickell@pits.ca
URL: www.pits.ca
Subjects covered: Energy, Petroleum
Services:
Personnel:
Brad Tickell, Library Technician
tickell@pits.ca
Kathryn McKenzie, Medical Library Technician
kathryn.mckenzie@crha-health.ab.ca
403-541-3483
Kathryn McKenzie, Medical Library Technician
kathryn.mckenzie@crha-health.ab.ca
403-541-3483

Calgary: Rockyview Hospital Library
7007 - 14 St. SW
Calgary, AB T2V 1P9
403-943-3000
National Library Symbol: KCRVH
Hours: M-F 8:00-4:15
Acquisitions Budget: $50,000 - $99,999
Note: Health Connection (Consumer Health Library)
Special Collections: Health Connection (Consumer Health)
Subjects covered: Medicine, Nursing, Allied Health, Consumer Health
Services:
Internet Access
Inter-Library Loan (ILL) for a fee of 3$/ per article
Personnel: Summary: 1 Professional(s); 9 Technical(s); 5 Volunteer(s)

Calgary: Shell Canada Limited Corporate Library
400 - 4th Ave. SW
Calgary, AB T2P 2H5
Mailing Address: PO Box 100
Calgary, AB T2P 2H5
403-691-2227
e-mail: sharon.craik@shell.com
National Library Symbol: ACSC
No public access
Founded in: 1958
Hours: M-F 7:00-4:00
Acquisitions Budget: $25,000 - $49,999
Special Collections: Earth Sciences, Business, Petroleum Engineering
Subjects covered: Business Management, Energy & Mineral Resources, Physical Sciences, Engineering, Technology
Services:
Electronic Document management; Web site maintenance
Personnel: Summary: 4 Total; 1 Technical(s)
Sharon Craik, Information Agent
sharon.craik@shell.com

Calgary: Shell Canada Limited Calgary Research Centre Library
3655 - 36th St. NW
Calgary, AB T2P 1Y8
403-284-6610
Fax: 403-284-6662
800-661-1600
e-mail: questions@Shell.com
URL: www.shell.ca
National Library Symbol: ACSCL
No public access
Founded in: 1982
Hours: M-F
Acquisitions Budget: For Print: 0-$9,999
Subjects covered: Engineering, Analytical Chemistry, Oil Sands, Refining
Services:
Inter-Library Loan (ILL)
Personnel: Summary: 1 Professional(s)
Mila Carozzi, Senior Information Agent
mila.carozzi@shell.ca
403-284-6610

Libraries & Resource Centres / Alberta

Calgary: **Southern Alberta Institute of Technology Library**
1301 - 16th Ave. NW
Calgary, AB T2M 0L4
403-284-8616
Fax: 403-284-8619
e-mail: library@sait.ca
library.dds@sait.ca
URL: www.sait.ca/library
National Library Symbol: ACSA
Consortia Membership: The Alberta Library
Founded in: 1916
Hours: Sept.-May: M-Th 7:30am-11:00pm; F 7:30-5:00; Sa, Su 10:00-5:00. June-Aug.: M-Th 8:00-6:30; F 8:00-5:00
Acquisitions Budget: $250,000 - $499,999
For Print: $100,000 - $249,999
For Electronic: $100,000 - $249,999
Note: The library is an affiliate member of the Council of Prairie and Pacific University Libraries (COPPUL).
Special Collections: Standards, Statistics Canada, SAIT Archives
Subjects covered: Communications, Technology, Physical Sciences, Engineering, Economics, Medicine, Nursing, Health Sciences, Business, Media, Allied Health
Services:
Internet Access
Access to Subscription Databases
Inter-Library Loan (ILL) for a fee
Fee Based Research
Microform Equipment: Computer; Reader
Personnel: *Summary:* 22 Total; 5 Professional(s); 10 Technical(s); 7 Other employees
Susan Brayford, Manager, Library Operations
susan.brayford@sait.ca
403-210-4477
Dave Weber, Supervisor, Customer Relations
dave.weber@sait.ca
403-284-8476
Anne Marie DeGroot, Systems Administrator
annemarie.degroot@sait.ca
403-284-8648

Calgary: **Sproule Associates Limited Library**
#900, North Tower, Sunlife Plaza, 140-4th Ave. SW
Calgary, AB T2P 3N3
403-294-5514
Fax: 403-294-5590
877-777-6135
e-mail: library@sproule.com
URL: www.sproule.com
No public access
Hours: M-F 8:00-4:30
Subjects covered: Physical Sciences, Engineering, Technology
Services:
Personnel:
Rita Loughlin, Records/Information Manager

Calgary: **Suncor Inc. Library**
112 - 4 Ave. SW
Calgary, AB T2P 2V5
Mailing Address: PO Box 38
Calgary, AB T2P 2V5
403-269-8128
Fax: 403-269-6200
e-mail: bzinter@suncor.com
No public access
Hours: M-F
Subjects covered: Oil & Gas, Petroleum, Geology, Petroleum Engineering, Business
Services:
Inter-Library Loan (ILL)
Personnel: *Summary:* 1 Total; 1 Professional(s)
Barbara Zinter, Communications Researcher
bzinter@suncor.com
403-269-8128

Calgary: **Talisman Energy Inc. Information Resource Centre**
#2000, 888 - 3rd St. SW
Calgary, AB T2P 5C5
403-237-1429
Fax: 403-231-2823
e-mail: irc@talisman-energy.com
National Library Symbol: ACBPE
No public access
Subjects covered: Physical Sciences, Engineering, Technology, Energy, Natural Resources
Services:
Personnel: *Summary:* 5 Total; 2 Professional(s); 3 Technical(s)
Cathy Ross, Coordinator, Information Resources
cross@talisman-energy.com
403-237-1040

Calgary: **TransAlta Utilities Corporation Regulatory Library**
Tower 2-4E, 110 - 12th Ave. SW
Calgary, AB T2P 2M1
406-267-7526
Fax: 403-267-2575
Hours: M-F by appointment only
Services:
Inter-Library Loan (ILL)
Personnel:
Susan Wusatz, Librarian

Calgary: **TransCanada PipeLines Limited Library & Research Centre**
TransCanada Tower, 450 - 1st St. SW
Calgary, AB T2P 4K5
Mailing Address: PO Box 1000, Stn M
Calgary, AB T2P 4K5
403-920-7818
Fax: 403-920-2342
e-mail: corporate_library@transcanada.com
URL: www.transcanada.com
National Library Symbol: ACTRPL
Founded in: 1957
Hours: M-F 7:30-5:00 by appointment only
Acquisitions Budget: $100,000 - $249,999
For Print: $50,000 - $99,999
For Electronic: $100,000 - $249,999
Subjects covered: Energy, Engineering, Technology, Natural Gas Transportation
Personnel: *Summary:* 2 Total; 1 Technical(s)
Virginia Guzzardi, Research Analyst

Calgary: **University of Calgary University Library**
2500 University Dr. NW
Calgary, AB T2N 1N4
403-220-5953
Fax: 403-282-1218
e-mail: libinfo@ucalgary.ca
illacu@isis.lib.ucalgary.ca
URL: library.ucalgary.ca
National Library Symbol: ACU
Consortia Membership: The Alberta Library; Canadian Research Knowledge Network (CRKN); Council of Prairie and Pacific University Libraries (COPPUL); Health Knowledge Network (HKN); Health Information Network
Founded in: 1966
Hours: M-Th 7:30am-10:45pm; F 7:30am-7:45pm; Sa 10:00-5:45; Su 10:00-10:45
Acquisitions Budget: $1,000,000 plus
For Print: $1,000,000 plus
For Electronic: $1,000,000 plus
Population Served: 28622
Services:
Remote Access
Internet Access
Access to Subscription Databases
Inter-Library Loan (ILL)
Fee Based Research
Microform Equipment: Computer; Reader
Personnel: *Summary:* 221 Total; 43 Professional(s); 5 Technical(s); 173 Other employees
H. Thomas Hickerson, University Librarian
Peggy White, Interim Associate University Librarian, Client Services
pwhite@ucalgary.ca
403-220-3611
Helen Clarke, Associate Vice Provost, Collections & Technical Services
hclarke@ucalgary.ca
403-220-3755
Terry Reilly, Director, Archives & Special Collections
reilly@ucalgary.ca
Mary Westell, Assoc. University Librarian, Info. Technology & Scholarly Publishing
westell@ucalgary.ca
403-220-3764
Mary McConnell, Associate University Librarian, Planning & Administration
mmconne@ucalgary.ca
403-220-3725
Nancy Goebel, Head Librarian
nancy.goebel@ualberta.ca
Paul Neff, Reference Librarian
paul.neff@ualberta.ca

Camrose: **Augustana Faculty Library**
Classroom Bldg.
4901 - 46th Ave.
Camrose, AB T4V 2R3
780-679-1156
Fax: 780-679-1594
Other contact info: Phone, ILL: 780-679-1593
e-mail: library@augustana.ca
libill@augustana.ca
National Library Symbol: ACAL
Consortia Membership: NEOS Library Consortium
Founded in: 1911
Hours: Winter: M-Th 8:30am-10:00pm; F 8:30-4:00; Sa 1:00-5:00; Su 2:00-10:00. Summer: M-F 8:30-12:00 by appointment only
Note: Augustana Faculty was formerly known as Augustana University College.
Services:
Inter-Library Loan (ILL)
Microform Equipment: Reader
Personnel: *Summary:* 10 Total; 3 Professional(s); 1 Technical(s); 5 Other employees;
Diane Shaver, Head
613-997-9573
S. Nelson, Head, Reference
819-667-9145
Keri St. Louis, Head, Acquisitions
S. Massicotte, Head, Systems

Cold Lake: **Aerospace Engineering Test Establishment Technical Reference Library/Bibliothèque de référence technique**
Canadian Forces Base, Cold Lake, PO Box 6550, Stn Forces
Cold Lake, AB T9M 2C6
780-840-8000 ext: 8062
Fax: 780-840-7381
URL: www.forces.gc.ca/aete
National Library Symbol: AMECFA
Hours: M-F 7:30-4:00 by appointment only
Note: Physical location: Louis St Laurent Bldg., 555, boul de la Carrière, 1e étage, Gatineau QC
Subjects covered: Materials from former Maritime & Land Technical libraries & Ammunition library
Services:
Microform Equipment: Computer; Reader
Personnel:

Devon: **Devon Library & Information Centre**
#A129, 1 Oil Patch Dr.
Devon, AB T9G 1A8
780-987-8773
Fax: 780-987-8778
e-mail: devon_library@arc.ab.ca
URL: www.arc.ab.ca
National Library Symbol: ADCR
Consortia Membership: NEOS Library Consortium
Hours: M-F 8:15-12:00
Note: Library holdings may be accessed through the NEOS Library Consortium Catalogue
Subjects covered: Coal & Hydrocarbon Processing, Chemistry & Chemical Engineering, Oil Sands/Heavy Oil Upgrading, Catalysis
Services:
Internet Access
Microform Equipment: Reader

Drayton Valley: **The Pembina Institute for Appropriate Development Library**
PO Box 7558
Drayton Valley, AB T7A 1S7
780-542-6272
Fax: 780-542-6464

Libraries & Resource Centres / Alberta

e-mail: info@pembina.org
URL: www.pembina.org
Subjects covered: Environment
Services:

Drumheller: **Royal Tyrrell Museum of Palaeontology Library**
Hwy. 838, Midland Provincial Park, PO Box 7500
Drumheller, AB T0J 0Y0
403-823-7707 ext: 6213
Fax: 403-823-7131
888-440-4240
Other contact info: 1-888-310-0000 & ask for 823-7707 (in Alberta)
e-mail: tyrrell.library@gov.ab.ca
URL: www.tyrrellmuseum.com
National Library Symbol: ADTMP
Founded in: 1982
Hours: M-F 8:15-4:30 by appointment only
Acquisitions Budget: $50,000 - $99,999
Special Collections: Tyrrell Museum Archives, 20,000 slides & photographs, field notes
Subjects covered: Life Sciences, Palaeontology, Geology, Natural History
Services:
Inter-Library Loan (ILL)
Fee Based Research
Microform Equipment: Computer; Reader
Personnel: *Summary:* 1 Total; 1 Professional(s)
Elizabeth Davis, Library Technician

Edmonton: **Acuren Inc. Library**
7450 - 18th St.
Edmonton, AB T6P 1N8
780-440-2131
Fax: 780-440-1167
800-663-9729
e-mail: info-ab@acuren.com
URL: www.acuren.com
Hours: M-F 8:00-5:00 by appointment only
Acquisitions Budget: $25,000 - $49,999
Subjects covered: Physical Sciences, Engineering, Technology
Services:
Inter-Library Loan (ILL)
Personnel:
Susan Lim, Library Clerk
780-440-2920 ext. 134

Edmonton: **Agra Earth & Environmental Limited Library**
4810 - 93rd St.
Edmonton, AB T6E 5M4
780-436-2152
Fax: 780-435-8425
No public access
Founded in: 1952
Acquisitions Budget: $25,000 - $49,999
Subjects covered: Environment, Physical Sciences, Engineering, Technology
Services:
Personnel:
Angela Kupper, Contact

Edmonton: **Alberta Government Library (Administration), Alberta Restructuring & Government Efficiency**
South Tower, Capital Health Centre, South Tower
10030 - 107 St., 11th Fl.
Edmonton, AB T5J 3E4
780-415-8344
Fax: 780-415-6091
e-mail: robert.a.bateman@gov.ab.ca
Consortia Membership: NEOS Library Consortium
Founded in: 2000
Hours: M-F 8:15-4:30
Acquisitions Budget: For Print: $250,000 - $499,999
Population Served: 23000
Subjects covered: Government
Services:
Personnel:
Robert Bateman, Director
robert.a.bateman@gov.ab.ca
780-415-6091
Eileen Candy, Library Technician
eileencandy@cha.ab.ca

Edmonton: **Alberta Hospital Edmonton Library**
17480 Fort Rd. SW
Edmonton, AB T5J 2J7
Mailing Address: PO Box 307
Edmonton, AB T5J 2J7
780-472-5268
Fax: 780-472-5608
e-mail: AHELibrary@capitalhealth.ca
National Library Symbol: AEAH
Consortia Membership: NEOS Library Consortium
Founded in: 1955
Hours: M-F 8:00-4:15
Acquisitions Budget: $25,000 - $49,999
Population Served: Serves mental health staff & patients.
Subjects covered: Mental health
Services:
Inter-Library Loan (ILL)
Personnel: *Summary:* 1 Technical(s)

Edmonton: **Alberta Justice, Office of the Chief Medical Examiner Information Centre (Edmonton)**
7007 - 116th St.
Edmonton, AB T6H 5R8
780-427-4987
Fax: 780-422-1265
National Library Symbol: AEOCME
No public access
Founded in: 1981
Hours: W 8:00-4:00
Acquisitions Budget: 0-$9,999
Subjects covered: Pathology, Forensic Medicine, Toxicology, Bereavement, Death Investigation
Services:
Inter-Library Loan (ILL)
Personnel: *Summary:* 1 Total; 1 Professional(s)
Natalie LaFleur, Librarian
natalie.lafleur@gov.ab.ca

Edmonton: **Alberta Land Surveyors' Association ALSA Library**
#1000, 10020 - 101 A Ave.
Edmonton, AB T5J 3G2
780-429-8805
Fax: 780-429-3374
800-665-2572
e-mail: info@alsa.ab.ca
URL: www.alsa.ab.ca
Founded in: 1910
Special Collections: Technical reports
Subjects covered: Surveying; Mapping; Geomatics
Services:
Personnel:
Brian Munday, Executive Director
Sharon Stecyk, Executive Assistant
Dawn Phelan, Information Services Administrator

Edmonton: **Alberta Research Council Library & Information Centre**
250 Karl Clark Rd.
Edmonton, AB T6N 1E4
780-450-5229
Fax: 780-450-8996
e-mail: Millwoods_library@arc.ab.ca
URL: www.arc.ab.ca
National Library Symbol: AER
Consortia Membership: NEOS Library Consortium
Hours: M-F: 8:15-12:00, 1:00-4:30
Subjects covered: Advanced Materials & Processes, Biotechnology, Environmental Research & Engineering, Forestry Research, Industrial Engineering, Manufacturing Technologies, Pharmaceuticals, Pulp & Paper, Heavy Oil / Oil Sands
Services:
Inter-Library Loan (ILL)
Personnel: *Summary:* 7 Total; 1 Professional(s); 2 Technical(s)
Margaret Law, Associate Director Libraries
margaret.law@ualberta.ca
Susan Moysa, Reference Coordinator
susan.moysa@ualberta.ca
780-492-7907
Sandy Campbell, Collection Coordinator
sandy.campbell@ualberta.ca
780-492-7915

Edmonton: **Cameron Science & Technology Library**
1-20 Cameron Library, University of Alberta
Edmonton, AB T6G 2J8
780-492-7912
Fax: 780-492-2721
e-mail: sciref@library.ualberta.ca
National Library Symbol: AEU
Consortia Membership: NEOS Library Consortium
Founded in: 1964
Hours: M-Th 8:00-8:00; F 8:00-5:00; Sa, Su 11:00-5:00
Acquisitions Budget: $500,000 - $999,999
Note: Comprises the main Science & Technology Library, the Canadian Circumpolar Library, the Mathematics Library, the Physical Sciences Library, & the William C. Wonders Map Collection. Member of NEOS, COPPUL & TAL
Subjects covered: Science, Engineering, Home Economics, Agriculture, Forestry, Northern
Services:
Internet Access
Inter-Library Loan (ILL)
Microform Equipment: Computer; Reader
Personnel: *Summary:* 41 Total; 9 Professional(s); 32 Technical(s); 3 Volunteer(s)

Edmonton: **Canadian Circumpolar Library**
Cameron Library, University of Alberta
Edmonton, AB T6G 2E9
780-492-7915
Fax: 780-492-2721
e-mail: elaine.simpson@ualberta.ca
National Library Symbol: AEUB
Founded in: 1961
Hours: M-Th 8:00-8:00; F 8:00-5:00; Sa, Su 11:00-5:00
Note: Formerly: Boreal Institute for Northern Studies Library. Member of NEOS, COPPUL & The Alberta Library
Special Collections: Theses, Expeditions
Subjects covered: Area oriented - all subjects Arctic, Canadian North, other cold regions; Canadian native materials
Services:
Inter-Library Loan (ILL)

Edmonton: **Caritas Health Group Library**
1100 Youville Dr. West
Edmonton, AB T6L 5X6
780-735-7300
Fax: 780-735-7202
e-mail: caritas-lbr@cha.ab.ca
National Library Symbol: AEGNH
Consortia Membership: NEOS Library Consortium
Hours: M-F 8:00-4:15
Acquisitions Budget: $250,000 - $499,999
Subjects covered: Medicine, Health Sciences
Services:
Inter-Library Loan (ILL) for a fee of $6
Personnel: *Summary:* 6 Total; 1 Professional(s); 2 Technical(s); 2 Other employees
Connie Clifford, Manager, Learning Resources

Edmonton: **Concordia University College of Alberta Arnold Guebert Memorial Library**
7128 Ada Blvd.
Edmonton, AB T5B 4E4
780-479-9338
Fax: 780-471-6796
866-479-5200
e-mail: library@concordia.ab.ca
circle@concordia.ab.ca
URL: library.concordia.ab.ca
National Library Symbol: AEC
Consortia Membership: Canadian Research Knowledge Network (CRKN); Council of Prairie and Pacific University Libraries (COPPUL); NEOS Library Consortium
Founded in: 1926
Hours: Sept-Apr: M-Th 8:00-9:00; F 8:00-5:00; Sa 11:00-5:00; Su 1:00-9:00. May-Aug: M-F 8:00-5:00.
Acquisitions Budget: $250,000 - $499,999
Population Served: 1400
Subjects covered: Undergraduate, Religion, Math, Philosophy, Psychology, Chemistry, English, Biology, Environmental Sciences, History, After-Degree in Education, After-Degree in Environmental Health, Information Systems Security, Career Development, Music
Services:
Remote Access
Internet Access

Access to Subscription Databases
Inter-Library Loan (ILL)
Microform Equipment: Computer; Reader
Personnel: *Summary:* 12 Total; 3 Professional(s); 7 Technical(s); 2 Other employees
Dan Mirau, Library Director
dan.mirau@concordia.ab.ca
780-479-9334
Eileen Goodfellow, Head of Technical Services
eileen.goodfellow@concordia.ab.ca
780-479-9326
Anna Spencer, Head of Acquisitions
anna.spencer@concordia.ab.ca
780-479-9333
Karen Hildebrandt, Library Systems Coordinator
khildebrandt@concordia.ab.ca
780-479-9336
Lynette Toews-Neufeldt, Reference Services Coordinator
ltoews-neufeldt@concordia.ab.ca
780-479-9339
Karen Visser, Access Services Coordinator
karen.visser@concordia.ab.ca
780-479-9327
Erica Hebert, Associate Reference Librarian
erica.hebert@concordia.ab.ca
780-479-9293

Edmonton: Edmonton Planning & Development Dept. Library
10250 - 101 St., 6th Fl.
Edmonton, AB T5J 3P4
780-496-6165
Fax: 780-401-7069
e-mail: katherina.hui@edmonton.ca
Founded in: 1970
Hours: M-F 8:30-12:00, 1:00-4:30 by appointment only
Acquisitions Budget: $25,000 - $49,999
For Print: $25,000 - $49,999
For Electronic: 0-$9,999
Special Collections: Land Use Planning, Urban Design
Subjects covered: Housing, Planning & Public Works, Local Government, City Planning, Transportation Planning, Historic Preservation, Downtown & Neighbourhood Planning
Services:
Inter-Library Loan (ILL)
Fee Based Research
Personnel: *Summary:* 2 Total; 2 Professional(s)
Bonny Bellward, Library Assistant
bonny.bellward@edmonton.ca
780-496-6165
Katherina Hui, Librarian

Edmonton: Edmonton Transportation & Streets Dept.
Engineering Services Library
9803 - 102A Ave., 15th Fl.
Edmonton, AB T5J 3A3
780-496-6771
Fax: 780-944-7653
e-mail: debbie.denolf@edmonton.ca
Founded in: 1986
Hours: M-F 8:00-4:30
Subjects covered: Transportation, Engineering, Testing
Services:
Personnel:
Debbie Denolf, Administrative Assistant

Edmonton: Environmental Law Centre Library
#800, 10025 - 106 St.
Edmonton, AB T5J 1G4
780-424-5099
Fax: 780-424-5133
800-661-4238
URL: www.elc.ab.ca
National Library Symbol: AEELC
Founded in: 1982
Hours: M-F 8:30-12:00, 1:00-4:30
Special Collections: Cases-reported & unreported; Decisions of administrative boards
Subjects covered: Environmental law & policy; Natural resources law
Services:
Internet Access
Inter-Library Loan (ILL)
Personnel: *Summary:* 1 Total; 1 Professional(s)

Iris Djurfors, Librarian
ldjurfors@elc.ab.ca
780-424-5099

Edmonton: EPCOR
Research Services
10065 Jasper Ave., Lower Main Fl.
Edmonton, AB T5J 3B1
780-412-3374
Fax: 780-412-7799
e-mail: librarytechnician@epcor.ca
afung@epcor.ca
URL: www.epcor.ca
National Library Symbol: AEEP
No public access
Subjects covered: Engineering, Technology, Physical Sciences, Electronics, Computer Data
Services:
Inter-Library Loan (ILL)
Personnel: *Summary:* 1 Technical(s)
Aileen Fung, Research Services Assistant
afung@epcor.ca

Edmonton: Grant MacEwan University
Learning Resources Centre
10700 - 104 Ave.
Edmonton, AB T5J 2P2
Mailing Address: PO Box 1796
Edmonton, AB T5J 2P2
780-497-5850
Fax: 780-497-5895
e-mail: bezenar@yeats.gmcc.ab.ca
URL: www.lrc.macewan.ca
National Library Symbol: AEGMCT
Consortia Membership: The Alberta Library; Health Knowledge Network (HKN); NEOS Library Consortium
Founded in: 1971
Hours: Winter: M-Th 7:30-11:00; F 7:30-9:00; Sa, Su 10:00-6:00
Acquisitions Budget: $500,000 - $999,999
Note: The library is an affiliate member of the Council of Prairie and Pacific University Libraries (COPPUL).
Subjects covered: Arts, Fine Arts, Business, Science, Nursing, Social Services
Services:
Internet Access
Inter-Library Loan (ILL)
Access to online catalogue & databases
Microform Equipment: Computer; Reader
Personnel: *Summary:* 43 Total; 9 Professional(s); 35 Other employees
Joanne Kemp, Director, Learning Resource Centre
kempj@macewan.ca
780-497-5892
Debbie McGugan, Head, Reference Services
mcgugand@macewan.ca
780-497-5894
Jill Day, Supervisor, Technical Services
dayj@macewan.ca
780-497-5867
John McGrath, Information Technology Services Coordinator
mcgrathj@macewan.ca
780-497-5890

Edmonton: Hemisphere Engineering Inc Library
10950 - 119th St.
Edmonton, AB T5H 3P5
780-452-1800
Fax: 780-453-5205
URL: hemisphere-eng.com
No public access
Founded in: 1958
Acquisitions Budget: $25,000 - $49,999
Subjects covered: Physical Sciences, Engineering, Technology
Services:
Kathryn Arbuckle, Head
kathryn.arbuckle@ualberta.ca
780-492-3717
Wanda Quoika-Stanka, Reference Services Coordinator
wanda.quoika-stanka@ualberta.ca
780-492-1448
Barbara Burrows, Collections Coordinator
barbara.burrows@ualberta.ca
780-492-5562

Edmonton: John Alexander Weir Memorial Law Library
2nd Floor, Law Centre, University of Alberta
Edmonton, AB T6G 2H5
780-492-3371
Fax: 780-492-7546
e-mail: lawref@library.ualberta.ca
URL: www.library.ualberta.ca/aboutus/law/index.cfm
National Library Symbol: AEUL
Consortia Membership: NEOS Library Consortium
Hours: M-Th 8:00am-10:00pm; F 8:00-6:00; Sa 11:00-6:00; Su 11:00-10:00
Acquisitions Budget: $500,000 - $999,999
Subjects covered: Anglo-American Law (mainly coverage strong in countries that use the common law system); Constitutional Law; Environment Law; Health Law; Human Rights; Aboriginal Law
Services:
Microform Equipment: Computer; Reader
Personnel: *Summary:* 10 Total; 3 Professional(s); 7 Other employees
Margaret Law, Assoc. Dir., Science/Technology & Health Sciences Libraries
margaret.law@ualberta.ca
780-492-7918
Denise Koufogiannakis, Head, Reference
Linda Seale, Site Manager
Liza Chan, Research Librarian

Edmonton: John W. Scott Health Sciences Library
#2K3.28 Walter C. Mackenzie Health Sciences Centre, University of Alberta
Edmonton, AB T6G 2R7
780-492-7947
Fax: 780-492-6960
e-mail: jwsinfo@library.ualberta.ca
URL: www.library.ualberta.ca/subject/healthsciences/index.cfm
National Library Symbol: AEU
Consortia Membership: NEOS Library Consortium
Hours: M-F 8:00-8:00; Sa, Su 11:00-8:00
Acquisitions Budget: $500,000 - $999,999
Note: Research Librarian a joint appointment with Alberta Heritage Foundation for Medical Research
Subjects covered: Medicine, Health Sciences
Services:
Internet Access
Inter-Library Loan (ILL)
Document delivery
Microform Equipment: Computer; Reader
Personnel: *Summary:* 16 Total; 8 Professional(s); 12 Technical(s)
Maggie Scott, Librarian
mscott@thurber.ca

Edmonton: Library (Edmonton)
#200, 9636 - 51st Ave.
Edmonton, AB T6E 6A5
780-438-1460
Fax: 780-437-7125
e-mail: mscott@thurber.ca
URL: www.thurber.ca
No public access
Subjects covered: Environmental & Geotechnical Engineering
Services:
Personnel: *Summary:* 1 Total; 1 Professional(s)
Roger Salus, Library Technician
roger.salus@millardhealth.com

Edmonton: Millard Health
Clinical Library
131 Airport Rd.
Edmonton, AB T5G 0W6
780-498-3221
Fax: 780-498-7858
888-498-9902
URL: www.millardhealth.com
Consortia Membership: Health Knowledge Network (HKN)
No public access
Founded in: 1995
Hours: M-Th 7:00-5:00, F 7:00-4:30
Acquisitions Budget: $25,000 - $49,999
Subjects covered: Rehabilitation, Disability, Psychosocial & Medical Issues
Services:
Internet Access

Libraries & Resource Centres / Alberta

Personnel: *Summary:* 4 Total; 1 Technical(s); 3 Other employees
Connie Clifford, Librarian

Edmonton: Misericordia Community Hospital
Dr. Morris Weinlos Library
#INW-32, 16940 - 87th Ave.
Edmonton, AB T5R 4H5
780-930-5708
Fax: 780-930-5509
e-mail: ccliffor@cha.ab.ca
mis-lbr@cha.ab.ca
National Library Symbol: AEMH
Consortia Membership: NEOS Library Consortium
Founded in: 1971
Hours: M-F 8:15-4:30
Acquisitions Budget: $50,000 - $99,999
Subjects covered: Medicine, Nursing, Health Sciences
Services:
Remote Access
Inter-Library Loan (ILL)
Personnel: *Summary:* 3 Total; 1 Professional(s); 1 Technical(s); 1 Other employees;

Edmonton: NorQuest College
Library & Information Services
10215 - 108th St., 5th Fl.
Edmonton, AB T5J 1L6
780-644-6070
Fax: 780-644-6082
e-mail: library@norquest.ca
URL: library.norquest.ca
National Library Symbol: AECV
Consortia Membership: The Alberta Library
Founded in: 1970
Hours: M-Th 7:30am-8:00pm; F 7:30-5:00; Sa 12:00-4:00
Acquisitions Budget: $50,000 - $99,999
Subjects covered: Education, English as a Second Language, Literacy, Vocational Training, Skills Training
Services:
Internet Access
Access to Subscription Databases
Inter-Library Loan (ILL)
Personnel: *Summary:* 11 Total; 1 Professional(s); 6 Technical(s); 4 Other employees
Joan Morrison, Instructional Librarian
joan.morrison@norquest.ca

Edmonton: Northern Alberta Institute of Technology
McNally Library
#3000, 11762 - 106 St. NW
Edmonton, AB T5G 3H3
780-471-8844
Fax: 780-471-8813
877-222-1722
e-mail: illo@nait.ab.ca
URL: www.nait.ab.ca/tci/search/libmap.asp
National Library Symbol: AENA
Consortia Membership: The Alberta Library; Health Knowledge Network (HKN)
Founded in: 1963
Hours: M-Su
Acquisitions Budget: $250,000 - $499,999
Subjects covered: Business, Physical & Health Sciences, Engineering, Trades, Computers, Technology
Services:
Remote Access
Internet Access
Inter-Library Loan (ILL)
Microform Equipment: Computer; Reader
Personnel:
Helga Kinnaird, Manager, Technology & Curriculum Innovation Operations
helgak@nait.ab.ca
780-471-8712
Harriet Arnold, Coordinator, Information Research & Instruction
harrieta@nait.ab.ca
780-471-8796
Liz Pegoraro, Coordinator, Information Support
lizp@nait.ca
Wayne Hofman, Coordinator, LR Computer Services
whofman@nait.ab.ca
Denise Leroy, Acting Head, Library Services
dleroy@nrcan.gc.ca
780-435-7324
Debbie Oranchuk, Library Assistant

Edmonton: Northern Forestry Centre
Library
5320 - 122nd St.
Edmonton, AB T6H 3S5
780-435-7310
Fax: 780-435-7359
e-mail: ill@nofc.forestry.ca
URL: cfs.nrcan.gc.ca/regions/nofc
National Library Symbol: AEF
Founded in: 1948
Hours: M-F 8:00-4:00
Acquisitions Budget: $50,000 - $99,999
Special Collections: Trees, Insects, Diseases of Trees, Hydrology, Forest Influences, Biomass, Depository for all Canadian Forest Service publications, selection of U.S. & foreign forestry-related publications, Woodlot Extension Library, ENFOR Publications
Subjects covered: Natural Resources, Conservation, Environment, Forest Entomology, Plant Pathology, Forest Influences, Climate Change, Hydrology, Silviculture, Economics, Forest Fire Research, Socio-Economic Research
Services:
Inter-Library Loan (ILL)
Microform Equipment: Computer; Reader
Personnel: *Summary:* 2 Total; 1 Professional(s); 1 Technical(s)
Terri Fraser, Head, Regional Library & Records Services
terri.fraser@ec.gc.ca

Edmonton: Prairie & Northern Region - Edmonton
Library - Environment Canada
#200, 4999 - 98th Ave.
Edmonton, AB T6B 2X3
780-951-8817
Fax: 780-951-8819
e-mail: Library.Edm@ec.gc.ca
URL: www.ec.gc.ca/library
National Library Symbol: AEECW
Hours: M-F 1:00-4:00
Acquisitions Budget: $25,000 - $49,999
Subjects covered: Environment
Services:
Inter-Library Loan (ILL)
Personnel: *Summary:* 2 Total; 1 Professional(s); 1 Technical(s)
Katherine Koch, Librarian
kochk@macewan.ca
780-497-4055
Marge Gray, Reference Library Technician
graym@macewan.ca
780-497-4052
Janet Day, Library Technician
dayj@macewan.ca
780-497-4054
Sandra Plouffe, Circulation Assistant
plouffes@macewan.ca
780-497-4054

Edmonton: South Campus
Learning Resources Centre
7319 - 29 Ave.
Edmonton, AB T6K 2P1
780-497-4054
Fax: 780-497-4184
URL: www.lrc.macewan.ca
National Library Symbol: AEGMMW
Consortia Membership: NEOS Library Consortium
Founded in: 1971
Hours: Winter: M-Th 7:45am-8:00pm; F 7:45-5:30; Sa 11:00-4:00
Acquisitions Budget: $50,000 - $99,999
For Print: $50,000 - $99,999
For Electronic: $10,000 - $24,999
Population Served: 1300
Subjects covered: Massage Therapy, Social Work, Child & Youth Care, Rehabilitation Practitioner, Police & Security Corrections, Mental Health, Management, Accounting
Services:
Remote Access
Internet Access
Inter-Library Loan (ILL)
Laser printing
Microform Equipment: Computer; Reader
Personnel: *Summary:* 5 Total; 1 Professional(s); 4 Technical(s)

Edmonton: Syncrude Canada Ltd.
Research Library
9421 - 17th Ave. SW
Edmonton, AB T6N 1H4
780-970-6800
Fax: 780-970-6805
e-mail: macgillivray.paula@syncrude.com
National Library Symbol: AESC
No public access
Founded in: 1964
Acquisitions Budget: $50,000 - $99,999
For Print: $50,000 - $99,999
For Electronic: 0-$9,999
Subjects covered: Oil Sands, Engineering, Chemistry, Chemical Engineering, Metallurgy, Petroleum Refining, Reclamation, Tailings, Engineering Mechanics & Materials, Geology, Fluid Mechanics, Physical & Analytical Chemistry
Services:
Microform Equipment: Reader
Personnel: *Summary:* 1 Technical(s)
Paula MacGillivray, Library Resource Manager
macgillivray.paula@syncrude.com

Edmonton: The King's University College
Simona Maaskant Library
9125 - 50 St.
Edmonton, AB T6B 2H3
780-465-8304
Fax: 780-465-3534
e-mail: library@kingsu.ca
URL: www.kingsu.ca
National Library Symbol: AEKC
Consortia Membership: Canadian Research Knowledge Network (CRKN); Council of Prairie and Pacific University Libraries (COPPUL); Health Knowledge Network (HKN); NEOS Library Consortium
Founded in: 1979
Hours: Sept.-Apr.: M-Th 7:45am-9:00pm; F 7:45-5:00; Sa 10:00-5:00. May-Aug.: M-F 8:00-4:00
Acquisitions Budget: $100,000 - $249,999
For Print: $100,000 - $249,999
For Electronic: $25,000 - $49,999
Special Collections: Dutch language collection
Services:
Remote Access
Internet Access
Access to Subscription Databases
Inter-Library Loan (ILL)
Selected internet resources available from an Internet Resources page
Microform Equipment: Computer; Reader
Personnel: *Summary:* 7 Total; 2 Professional(s); 2 Technical(s); 3 Other employees
G. Marcille Frederick, Director of Library Services
marcille.frederick@kingsu.ca
780-465-3500 ext. 8053
Karna Antoniw, Reference Librarian
karna.antoniw@kingsu.ca
780-465-3500 ext. 8052
Katherine Jenkins, Contact, Technical Services/Acquisitions & Cataloguing
katherine.jenkins@kingsu.ca
780-465-3500 ext. 8051
Merlene Staatz, Contact, Technical Services, Serials, Interlibrary Loans
merlene.staatz@kingsu.ca
780-564-3500 ext. 8054
Hyacinth Barrett, Contact, Circulation Services
hyacinth.barrett@kingsu.ca
780-465-3500 ext. 8016

Edmonton: UMA Engineering Ltd.
Information Management
17007 - 107th Ave.
Edmonton, AB T5S 1G3
780-486-7000
Fax: 780-486-7070
No public access
Acquisitions Budget: $25,000 - $49,999
Subjects covered: Physical Sciences, Engineering, Technology
Services:
Inter-Library Loan (ILL)
Personnel:
Karen Olson, Information Management
780-486-7000

Edmonton: **Université de l'Alberta Bibliothèque Saint-Jean**
8406, rue Marie-Anne Gaboury
Edmonton, AB T6C 4G9
780-465-8711
Fax: 780-468-2550
e-mail: diane.delongchamp@ualberta.ca
URL: www.library.ualberta.ca/francais
National Library Symbol: AEUSJ
Consortia Membership: NEOS Library Consortium
Founded in: 1910
Hours: L-J 8h30-21h30; V 8h30-16h30; S-D 12h-17h
Acquisitions Budget: For Print: $100,000 - $249,999
For Electronic: $10,000 - $24,999
Note: Part of NEOS
Subjects covered: Éducation, pédagogie, sciences sociales, sciences humaines et sciences pures, littérature francophone de l'Ouest canadien
Services:
Remote Access
Internet Access
Access to Subscription Databases
Inter-Library Loan (ILL)
Microform Equipment: Computer; Reader
Personnel: *Summary:* 9 Total; 3 Professional(s); 1 Technical(s); 5 Other employees;
Tatiana Usova, Directrice
usova@ualberta.ca
780-465-8710
Kim Frail, Bibliothécaire/Services publics
780-465-8712
Diane Delongchamp, Aide bibliothécaire/Collections
David Martin, Responsable, acquisitions
david.martin@ualberta.ca
780-465-8709

Edmonton: **University of Alberta Cameron Library - Library Administration Department**
#5-02 Cameron Library, University of Alberta
Edmonton, AB T6G 2J8
780-492-6491
URL: www.library.ualberta.ca/
National Library Symbol: AEU
Consortia Membership: The Alberta Library; Canadian Research Knowledge Network (CRKN); Council of Prairie and Pacific University Libraries (COPPUL); Health Knowledge Network (HKN); NEOS Library Consortium
Founded in: 1909
Hours: M-F 8:30-4:30
Services:
Inter-Library Loan (ILL) for a fee
Fee Based Research
Microform Equipment: Computer; Reader
Personnel: *Summary:* 1 Total; 1 Professional(s)
Karen Adams, Director, Library Services & Information Resources
karen.adams@ualberta.ca
780-492-6491
Tina James, Associate Director, Facilities & Administration
Kathleen DeLong, Associate Director, Finance & Human Resources

Edmonton: **University of Alberta Dept. of Physiology Reading Room**
755 Medical Sciences Bldg., University of Alberta
Edmonton, AB T6G 2H7
780-492-3359
Fax: 780-492-8915
URL: www.physiology.ualberta.ca
No public access
Founded in: 1965
Services:
Personnel:
Donna Simpson, Office Clerk
des@ualberta.ca
780-492-1238

Edmonton: **University of Alberta Dept. of Rural Economy Library**
#504, General Services Bldg.
Edmonton, AB T6G 2H1
780-492-0815
Fax: 780-492-0268
URL: www.re.ualberta.ca

Founded in: 1976
Hours: M-F 9:30-12:00, 12:30-4:00
Acquisitions Budget: $10,000 - $24,999
For Print: $10,000 - $24,999
For Electronic: 0-$9,999
Subjects covered: Agricultural Economics, Forest Economics, Rural Sociology, Agribusiness, Environmental Economics, Environmental Sociology
Services:
Personnel: *Summary:* 1 Total; 1 Technical(s)
Dawn Zrobok, Library Assistant

Edmonton: **University of Alberta J.P. Das Developmental Disabilities Centre Library**
#6-123D, Education Bldg. North
Edmonton, AB T6G 2G5
780-492-4505
Fax: 780-492-1318
e-mail: j.p.das@ualberta.ca
URL: www.ualberta.ca/~jpdasddc/INDEX.html
No public access
Services:
Personnel:
Richard Sobsey, Contact
dick.sobsey@ualberta.ca
780-492-3755

Edmonton: **University of Alberta School of Native Studies Resource Reading Room**
#5, 182 Education North
Edmonton, AB T6G 2G5
780-492-2991
Fax: 780-492-0527
e-mail: nativest@ualberta.ca
URL: www.ualberta.ca/nativestudies
Hours: Sept-May: M-F 8:30-12:00, 1:00-4:30. May-Aug: M-F 8:00-12:00, 1:00-4:00
Subjects covered: Native Studies
Services:
Personnel: *Summary:* 1 Total; 1 Other employees
Connie Vogler, Library Technician

Edmonton: **Westmount Campus Branch Library**
#218, 11140 - 131 St.
Edmonton, AB T5M 1C1
780-644-6709
Hours: M-F 8:00-3:45
Special Collections: English as a Second Language collection
Services:
Internet Access
Personnel:
David Jones, Map Librarian
david.jones@ualberta.ca

Edmonton: **William C. Wonders Map Collection**
University of Alberta, Cameron Library, Main Fl.
Edmonton, AB T6G 2J8
780-492-2728
Fax: 780-492-2721
e-mail: david.jones@ualberta.ca
National Library Symbol: AEUM
Founded in: 1966
Hours: M-Th 8:00-8:00; F 8:00-5:00; Sa, Su 11:00-5:00
Acquisitions Budget: $10,000 - $24,999
Note: Member of NEOS Consortium
Special Collections: Western & Northern Canada; Austro-Hungary & Central Europe; UK
Subjects covered: Worldwide Topographic & Thematic Maps
Services:
Internet Access
Inter-Library Loan (ILL)
Microform Equipment: Reader
Personnel: *Summary:* 2 Total; 1 Professional(s); 1 Technical(s)

Edmonton: **Workers' Compensation Board of Alberta Medical Services, Medical Library**
9912 - 107 St.
Edmonton, AB T5J 2S5
Mailing Address: PO Box 2415
Edmonton, AB T5J 2S5
780-498-4000
Fax: 780-498-7807

No public access
Subjects covered: Medical, Rehabilitation, Occupational Health & Safety, Sports Medicine
Services:

Fort McMurray: **Keyano College Library & Media Services**
8115 Franklin Ave.
Fort McMurray, AB T9H 2H7
780-791-4917
Fax: 780-791-4935
800-251-1408
Other contact info: ext 4917
e-mail: interlibrary.loans@keyano.ca
URL: www.keyano.ca/library/index.htm
National Library Symbol: AFMK
Consortia Membership: The Alberta Library
Founded in: 1965
Hours: M-T 8:30am-9:00 pm; F 8:30-4:30; Sa-Su 12:00-4:00
Acquisitions Budget: $50,000 - $99,999
For Print: $50,000 - $99,999
For Electronic: $25,000 - $49,999
Services:
Internet Access
Access to Subscription Databases
Personnel: *Summary:* 9 Total; 2 Professional(s); 2 Technical(s); 5 Other employees
John Burgess, Director, Library & Educational Resources
Wanda Philipow, Coordinator, Technical Services
wanda.philipow@keyano.ca
780-791-8976
Evelyn Graham, Serials Technician
evelyn.graham@keyano.ca
780-791-4916
Laura Zinck, Information Librarian
laura.zinck@keyano.ca
780-791-7911
Heidi Schellenberg, Circulation Clerk
heidi.schellenberg@keyano.ca
780-791-4917

Fort McMurray: **Northern Lights Regional Health Centre Dr. John Rempel Learning Resource Centre**
7 Hospital St.
Fort McMurray, AB T9H 1P2
780-791-6084
Fax: 780-791-3029
e-mail: jweigelt@nlhr.ca
National Library Symbol: AFMH
No public access
Founded in: 1981
Acquisitions Budget: $25,000 - $49,999
Subjects covered: Health Sciences, Medicine, Hospital Administration, Nursing
Services:
Inter-Library Loan (ILL)
Personnel: *Summary:* 1 Professional(s)
Barb Di Persio, Director HR
hdipersio@nlhr.ca
780-791-6176
JoAnne Weigelt, Clerk
jweigelt@nlhr.ca

Grande Prairie: **Grande Prairie Regional College Library & Media Services**
10726 - 106th Ave.
Grande Prairie, AB T8V 4C4
780-539-2939
Fax: 780-539-2832
888-539-4772
e-mail: library@gprc.ab.ca
URL: www.gprc.ab.ca/departments/library/
National Library Symbol: AGPC
Consortia Membership: The Alberta Library; Health Knowledge Network (HKN); NEOS Library Consortium
Founded in: 1966
Hours: Fall & Winter: M-Th 8:00am-9:00pm; F 8:00-6:00; Sa, Su 12:00-6:00; Spring & Summer: M-F 8:30-4:30
Acquisitions Budget: For Print: $100,000 - $249,999
Population Served: 2500
Subjects covered: Arts, Humanities, Science & Technology, Technical
Services:
Remote Access
Internet Access

Libraries & Resource Centres / Alberta

Access to Subscription Databases
Inter-Library Loan (ILL)
Microform Equipment: Computer; Reader
Personnel: *Summary:* 17 Total; 2 Professional(s); 15 Technical(s)
Jennifer Thomas, Chair
jthomas@gprc.ab.ca
780-539-2772
Ann Gish, Librarian
agish@gprc.ab.ca
780-539-2940

Grande Prairie: **Queen Elizabeth II Hospital Regional Library**
10409 - 98th St.
Grande Prairie, AB T8V 2E8
Mailing Address: Bag 2600
Grande Prairie, AB T8V 2E8
780-538-7124
Fax: 780-538-7507
e-mail: kana.lizotte@pcha.ca
Founded in: 1984
Hours: M-F 8:00-4:15
Acquisitions Budget: $25,000 - $49,999
Note: Library Databases: Microcat & Ultraplus
Subjects covered: Health Science, Medicine, Nursing
Services:
Inter-Library Loan (ILL)
Personnel: *Summary:* 2 Total; 1 Technical(s); 1 Other employees; 1 Volunteer(s)

Grouard: **Northern Lakes College - Grouard Campus Library**
PO Bag 3000
Grouard, AB T0G 1C0
e80-751-3275
Fax: 780-751-3386
e-mail: prosserh@northernlakescollege.ca
URL: www.northerncollege.ca
National Library Symbol: AGVC
Founded in: 1975
Hours: M-F 8:15-4:30
Acquisitions Budget: $100,000 - $249,999
For Print: $100,000 - $249,999
For Electronic: $50,000 - $99,999
Special Collections: First Nations Collection
Subjects covered: Vocational Training, Education
Services:
Remote Access
Internet Access
Access to Subscription Databases
Inter-Library Loan (ILL)
Microform Equipment: Computer; Reader
Personnel: *Summary:* 1 Professional(s); 4 Technical(s)
Helen Prosser, Coordinator, Library Services
780-849-8671

Hanna: **Prairie Association for Water Management Library**
PO Box 1949
Hanna, AB T0J 1P0
403-854-2509
Subjects covered: Environment
Services:

Lac La Biche: **Portage College Library**
9531 - 94 Ave.
Lac La Biche, AB T0A 2C0
Mailing Address: PO Box 417
Lac La Biche, AB T0A 2C0
780-623-5650
Fax: 780-623-5656
866-623-5551
e-mail: barbara.g.palmer@portagecollege.ca
library@portagecollege.ca
URL: www.portagecollege.ca
National Library Symbol: ALLBVC
Consortia Membership: The Alberta Library
Founded in: 1987
Hours: M-Th 8:00am-9:00pm; F 8:00-4:30; Sa 1:00-4:00; Su 1:00-7:00; Summer: M-F 8:00am-4:30
Acquisitions Budget: $50,000 - $99,999
For Print: $50,000 - $99,999
For Electronic: 0-$9,999
Population Served: 920

Subjects covered: Upgrading, Vocational Training, Native Studies, Community Social Work, Emergency Medical Technician, University Studies
Services:
Remote Access
Internet Access for a fee
Inter-Library Loan (ILL)
Personnel: *Summary:* 7 Total; 2 Professional(s); 1 Technical(s); 4 Other employees
Vacant, Manager, Library Services
780-623-5653
Terry Donovan, Public Services Librarian
terry.donovan@portagecollege.ca
780-623-5755
Marcia Holmes, Technical Services Technician
marcia.holmes@portagecollege.ca
780-623-5632
Janice Bryks, Acquisitions Assistant
janice.bryks@portagecollege.ca
780-623-5654
Reno Larocque, Serials Assistant
reno.larocque@portagecollege.ca
780-623-3501
Michele Norton, Circulation Assistant
michele.norton@portagecollege.ca
780-623-5655

Lacombe: **Canadian University College Library**
5410 Ramona Ave.
Lacombe, AB T4L 2B7
403-782-3381
Fax: 403-782-3977
e-mail: library@cauc.ca
URL: www.cauc.ca/MainPages/Library/Library_Index.htm
National Library Symbol: ACHCU
Consortia Membership: NEOS Library Consortium
Founded in: 1907
Hours: Fall/Winter: M-Th 8:00am-10:30pm; F 8:00-3:00; Su 1:00-10:30; Summer: M-Th 1:00-10:00; F 1:00-3:00; Su 1:00-4:00; 6:00-10:30; Breaks M-Th 1:00-3:00
Acquisitions Budget: $50,000 - $99,999
For Print: $50,000 - $99,999
For Electronic: $10,000 - $24,999
Note: Database access available.
Special Collections: Seventh-Day Adventist Church
Subjects covered: Humanities, Social Science, Science, Religion
Services:
Remote Access
Internet Access
Access to Subscription Databases
Microform Equipment: Reader
Personnel: *Summary:* 15 Total; 2 Professional(s); 1 Technical(s); 12 Other employees
Joyce Van Scheik, Librarian
jvansche@cauc.ca
403-782-3381
Carol Nickes, Assistant Librarian
403-782-3381
Bernice Leavitt, Supervisor, Technical Services
Kathryn Moore, Librarian
MooreKE@agr.gc.ca

Lacombe: **Lacombe Research Centre**
6000 C&E Trail
Lacombe, AB T4L 1W1
403-782-8136
Fax: 403-782-6120
e-mail: MooreKE@agr.gc.ca
URL: res2.agr.ca/lacombe/
National Library Symbol: ALAAG
Founded in: 1984
Hours: Tu-Th 9:00-4:00
Acquisitions Budget: $25,000 - $49,999
Subjects covered: Agriculture, Food, Food Safety, Meat Research
Services:
Inter-Library Loan (ILL)
Personnel: *Summary:* 1 Total; 1 Professional(s)
Cheryl Ronning Mains, Librarian Chief, Information Services, Western Region

Lethbridge: **Canadian Agriculture Library - Lethbridge**
5403 - 1st Ave. South
Lethbridge, AB T1J 4B1
Mailing Address: PO Box 3000
Lethbridge, AB T1J 4B1
403-317-3310
Fax: 403-382-3156
e-mail: ronningmainc@agr.gc.ca
National Library Symbol: ALAG
Founded in: 1950
Hours: M-F 8:00am-12:00pm, 1:00-4:00 by appointment only
Subjects covered: Agriculture, Crop Entomology, Animal & Crop Science, Soils
Services:
Inter-Library Loan (ILL) for a fee
Personnel: *Summary:* 2 Total; 1 Professional(s); 1 Technical(s)

Lethbridge: **Lethbridge Community College Buchanan Library**
3000 College Dr. South
Lethbridge, AB T1K 1L6
403-320-3352
Fax: 403-320-1461
800-572-0103
e-mail: kathy.lea@lethbridgecollege.ab.ca
URL: peregrine.lethbridgecollege.ab.ca
National Library Symbol: ALC
Consortia Membership: The Alberta Library
Founded in: 1957
Hours: M-Th 7:30am-9:45pm; F 7:30-4:45; Sa 11:30-6:30; Su 1:00-8:30
Subjects covered: Agriculture, Criminal Justice, Physical Sciences, Engineering Technologies, Environmental Sciences, Health & Human Services
Services:
Internet Access
Inter-Library Loan (ILL)
Email for LCC students, CD products
Microform Equipment: Computer; Reader
Personnel: *Summary:* 2 Professional(s); 25 Other employees
Fiona Dyer, Manager, Library Services
fiona.dyer@lethbridgecollege.ab.ca

Lethbridge: **University of Lethbridge Library**
4401 University Dr.
Lethbridge, AB T1K 3M4
403-329-2265
Fax: 403-329-2234
e-mail: libadmin@uleth.ca
URL: www.uleth.ca/lib/
National Library Symbol: ALU
Consortia Membership: The Alberta Libary; Canadian Research Knowledge Network (CRKN); Council of Prairie and Pacific University Libraries (COPPUL); Health Knowledge Network (HKN)
Founded in: 1967
Hours: M-Su
Acquisitions Budget: $1,000,000 plus
For Print: $500,000 - $999,999
For Electronic: $500,000 - $999,999
Population Served: 10000
Special Collections: Canadiana (Woodworth) Collection
Services:
Remote Access
Internet Access
Access to Subscription Databases
Inter-Library Loan (ILL)
Microform Equipment: Computer; Reader
Personnel: *Summary:* 53 Total; 15 Professional(s); 32 Technical(s); 6 Other employees
Marinus Swanepoel, University Librarian
librarian@uleth.ca
Donna Seyed Mahmoud, Associate University Librarian
libadmin@uleth.ca
403-329-2031
Bill Glaister, Coordinator of Faculty of Education Curriculum Lab
bill.glaister@uleth.ca
403-329-2715
Bev Mew, Head, Information Services
bev.mew@drdc-rddc.gc.ca
409-544-3388

Libraries & Resource Centres / Alberta

Medicine Hat: **Defence R & D Canada - Suffield Library**
PO Box 4000, Stn Main
Medicine Hat, AB T1A 8K6
403-544-4820
Fax: 403-544-3388
e-mail: bev.mew@drdc-rddc.gc.ca
National Library Symbol: ARS
No public access
Founded in: 1941
Hours: M-F
Acquisitions Budget: $100,000 - $249,999
Subjects covered: Technology, Engineering, Physical Sciences, Chemical & Biological Sciences
Services:
Personnel: *Summary:* 2 Total; 1 Professional(s); 1 Technical(s)

Medicine Hat: **Medicine Hat College Library**
299 College Dr. SE
Medicine Hat, AB T1A 3Y6
403-529-3867
Fax: 403-504-3517
866-282-8394
e-mail: info@mhc.ab.ca
illo@mhc.ab.ca
URL: www.mhc.ab.ca
National Library Symbol: AMMC
Consortia Membership: The Alberta Library
Founded in: 1965
Hours: M-Th 7:30-10:00; F 7:30-6:00; Sa 9:00-5:00; Su 1:00-8:00
Acquisitions Budget: $250,000 - $499,999
For Print: $100,000 - $249,999
For Electronic: $50,000 - $99,999
Note: Ariel: 192.139.34.241
Subjects covered: Undergraduate College Prep
Services:
Internet Access
Inter-Library Loan (ILL)
Microform Equipment: Computer; Reader
Personnel: *Summary:* 8 Total; 3 Professional(s); 15 Technical(s)
Keith Walker, Chief Librarian
kwalker@mhc.ab.ca
Lilian Li, Information/Technology Librarian
lli@mhc.ab.ca
403-529-3869
Barb Banasch, Circulation Supervisor
Terry Lagran, Acquisitions Technician
403-529-3871
Sheila Drummond, Reference Librarian

Olds: **Olds College Library**
4500 - 50th St.
Olds, AB T4H 1R6
403-556-4600
Fax: 403-556-4705
e-mail: library@oldscollege.ca
libraryill@oldscollege.ca
URL: www.oldscollege.ca/library
National Library Symbol: AOAC
Consortia Membership: The Alberta Library; NEOS Library Consortium
Founded in: 1913
Hours: School Term: M-Th 7:45am-10:00pm; Sa 11:00-5:00; Su 10:00-10:00. Summer: hours vary
Acquisitions Budget: $100,000 - $249,999
Subjects covered: Agriculture, Horticulture, Animal Science, Land Science, Business, Agricultural Mechanics
Services:
Internet Access
Inter-Library Loan (ILL)
Microform Equipment: Computer; Reader
Personnel: *Summary:* 7 Total; 1 Professional(s); 6 Technical(s)
Robin Minion, Manager, Library Services
rminion@oldscollege.ca
403-556-4602
Scott Mckay, Head of Technical Services
smckay@oldscollge.ca
403-556-4604
Kathleen Johnston, Head of Acquisitions
kjohnston@oldscollege.ca
403-556-4603

Red Deer: **Red Deer College Library**
100 College Blvd.
Red Deer, AB T4N 5H5
Mailing Address: PO Box 5005
Red Deer, AB T4N 5H5
403-342-3344
Fax: 403-346-8500
e-mail: ill@rdc.ab.ca
URL: library.rdc.ab.ca
National Library Symbol: ARDC
Consortia Membership: The Alberta Library; Health Knowledge Network (HKN); NEOS Library Consortium
Founded in: 1965
Hours: M-Su
Acquisitions Budget: $250,000 - $499,999
Note: The library is an affiliate member of the Council of Prairie and Pacific University Libraries (COPPUL).
Special Collections: Alberta K-12 curriculum
Subjects covered: University transfer, Degree completion, Certificate/Diploma, Apprenticeship/Trades
Services:
Remote Access
Internet Access
Inter-Library Loan (ILL)
Microform Equipment: Reader
Personnel: *Summary:* 7 Total; 3 Professional(s); 3 Technical(s)
Alice McNair, Chair
alice.mcnair@rdc.ab.ca
403-342-3306
Maureen Toews, Librarian
maureen.toews@rdc.ab.ca
403-342-3351
Kristine Plastow, Librarian
kristine.plastow@rdc.ab.ca
403-342-3578
Leslie Beattie, Librarian
leslie.beattie@rdc.ab.ca
403-342-3352
Charlene Jones, Program & Service Manager
charlene.jones@rdc.ab.ca
403-342-3547

Sherwood Park: **Strathcona County Learning Centre**
#172, 2257 Premier Way
Sherwood Park, AB T8H 2M8
780-416-8844
Fax: 780-416-8857
e-mail: library@lakelandc.ab.ca
URL: www.lakelandc.ab.ca
National Library Symbol: ALLC
Founded in: 1989
Hours: M-Th 8:15-10:00; F 8:15-4:30; Sa, Su 1:00-5:00
Services:
Internet Access
Access to Subscription Databases
Inter-Library Loan (ILL)
Personnel: *Summary:* 6 Total; 3 Technical(s); 3 Other employees

Slave Lake: **Northern Lakes College - Slave Lake Library**
1201 Main St. SE
Slave Lake, AB T0G 2A3
780-849-8670
Fax: 780-849-2570
533-652-3456
e-mail: library@northernlakescollege.ca
URL: www.northernlakescollege.ca
National Library Symbol: ASAV
Consortia Membership: The Alberta Library
Founded in: 1990
Hours: M-W 8:15-4:30, 6:00-9:00; T-F 8:15-4:30. Evening hours take place from Oct.-June only.
Acquisitions Budget: $100,000 - $249,999
For Print: $100,000 - $249,999
For Electronic: $25,000 - $49,999
Population Served: 1000
Special Collections: Native Peoples
Subjects covered: Education, Upgrading, Social Work
Services:
Remote Access
Internet Access
Access to Subscription Databases
Inter-Library Loan (ILL)
Microform Equipment: Reader
Personnel: *Summary:* 6 Total; 1 Professional(s); 1 Technical(s); 4 Other employees
Helen Prosser, Coordinator, Library Services
prosserh@northernlakescollege.ca
780-849-8671

Stettler: **Buffalo Lake Naturalists Club Library**
PO Box 1802
Stettler, AB T0C 2L0
403-742-4800
No public access
Subjects covered: Conservation
Services:
Personnel:
Marion McCarty, Librarian
Wilma Zurfluh, Staff
Audrey Lyons, Acquisitions/Cataloguing
audrey@arc.ab.ca
780-632-8417
Melanie Thibault, ILL Technician
melanie@arc.ab.ca
780-632-8419

Vegreville: **ARC Vegreville Library & Information Centre**
Alberta Research Council
Hwy. 16A, 75th St., PO Bag 4000
Vegreville, AB T9C 1T4
780-632-8417
Fax: 780-632-8300
-310-0000
e-mail: library@arc.ab.ca
veg_library@arc.ab.ca
URL: www.arc.ab.ca/corp/Library/ARC_library2.htm
National Library Symbol: AVEE
Consortia Membership: NEOS Library Consortium
Founded in: 1979
Hours: M-F 8:15-4:30
Acquisitions Budget: $50,000 - $99,999
For Print: 0-$9,999
For Electronic: $50,000 - $99,999
Subjects covered: Veterinary Sciences, Plant Science, Environmental Chemistry, Air, Water & Waste Management, Environmental Toxicology & Enhancement, Wildlife Ecology, Aquatic Biology, Forestry & Soils
Services:
Internet Access
Access to Subscription Databases
Inter-Library Loan (ILL)
Fee Based Research
Microform Equipment: Computer; Reader
Personnel: *Summary:* 2 Total; 1 Technical(s); 1 Other employees

Vermilion: **Lakeland College Vermillion Campus**
5707 - 47th Ave. West
Vermilion, AB T9X 1K5
780-853-8460
Fax: 780-853-8662
e-mail: library@lakelandc.ab.ca
ariel@lakelandc.ab.ca
URL: www.lakelandc.ab.ca
National Library Symbol: AUC
Consortia Membership: The Alberta Library; NEOS Library Consortium
Founded in: 1913
Hours: M-Th 8:15am-10:00pm; F 8:15-4:30; Sa, Su 1:00-5:00
Acquisitions Budget: $50,000 - $99,999
Subjects covered: Agriculture, Environment, Interior Design, Early Childhood Education, Trades, Business
Services:
Remote Access
Internet Access
Access to Subscription Databases
Inter-Library Loan (ILL)
Personnel: *Summary:* 8 Total; 2 Professional(s); 2 Technical(s); 4 Other employees
Wanjiku Kaai, Librarian, Public Services
wanjiku.kaai@lakelandcollege.ca
780-853-8731

Libraries & Resource Centres / British Columbia

Wetaskiwin: **Alberta Community Development Reynolds-Alberta Museum Library**
PO Box 6360
Wetaskiwin, AB T9A 2G1
780-361-1351
Fax: 780-361-1239
800-661-4726
e-mail: refctr.ram@gov.ab.ca
ram@gov.ab.ca
URL: www.reynoldsalbertamuseum.com
National Library Symbol: AWRAM
Founded in: 1992
Hours: Sept-May: T-Su 10:00-5:00; May-July: M-Su 10:00-5:00; July-Sept M-Su 10:00-6:00
Acquisitions Budget: 0-$9,999
Note: Located 2 kms west of Wetaskiwin on Hwy. 13.
Special Collections: Library collection of Canada's Aviation Hall of Fame availabe through request of Hall of Fame curator.
Subjects covered: Transportation, Agriculture, Industry, Technology, Aviation
Services:
Inter-Library Loan (ILL)
Microform Equipment: Reader
Personnel: *Summary:* 2 Total; 1 Professional(s); 1 Other employees; 3 Volunteer(s)
Randy Kvill, Curator, Agriculture & Documentary Collections
randy.kvill@gov.ab.ca
780-361-1351 ext. 254/2

British Columbia

Abbotsford: **Abbotsford Campus Library**
33844 King Rd.
Abbotsford, BC V2S 7M8
604-854-4545
Fax: 604-853-8055
Hours: M-Th 8:00am-10:00pm; F 8:00-4:30; Sa 10:00-4:00
Services:
Internet Access
Access to Subscription Databases
Inter-Library Loan (ILL)
Microform Equipment: Computer; Reader
Jennifer Joslin, Library Technician
joslinjm@csc-scc.gc.ca

Abbotsford: **Pacific Region Regional Health Centre Library**
33844 King Rd.
Abbotsford, BC V2S 4P4
Mailing Address: PO Box 3000
Abbotsford, BC V2S 4P4
604-870-7700 ext: 3259
National Library Symbol: BARP
No public access
Hours: M-W 9:00-4:30; Th, F 1:00-6:00
Acquisitions Budget: $25,000 - $49,999
Subjects covered: Psychology, Psychiatry, Health
Services:
Inter-Library Loan (ILL)
Personnel: *Summary:* 1 Total; 1 Technical(s)

Abbotsford: **University College of the Fraser Valley**
33844 King Rd.
Abbotsford, BC V2S 7M8
604-854-4545
Fax: 604-853-8055
URL: www.ucfv.ca/library
National Library Symbol: BCLF
Consortia Membership: British Columbia Electronic Network (BC ELN); Canadian Research Knowledge Network (CRKN); Council of Prairie and Pacific University Libraries (COPPUL)
Founded in: 1974
Acquisitions Budget: $500,000 - $999,999
Special Collections: Fraser Valley Heritage Collection
Subjects covered: University & Community College Level Subject Areas
Services:
Personnel:
Kim Isaac, Director of Library Services
604-864-4696
Patti Wilson, Public Services Coordinator
604-504-7441 ext. 4277
Corinne McConchie, Systems & Technical Services Librarian
604-504-7441 ext. 4268
Barbara Ancheta, Contact
banchetta@nlc.bc.ca

Atlin: **Atlin Campus Library**
3rd St. & Pearl Ave.
Atlin, BC V0W 1A0
250-651-7762
Fax: 250-651-7730
National Library Symbol: BDCNL
Hours: Tu, Th 12:00-5:00
Acquisitions Budget: $25,000 - $49,999
Services:
Remote Access
Internet Access
Access to Subscription Databases
Inter-Library Loan (ILL) for a fee
Microform Equipment: Reader
Personnel: *Summary:* 3 Total; 1 Professional(s); 2 Technical(s)

Burnaby: **British Columbia Housing Records & Information Centre**
#1700, 4555 Kingsway
Burnaby, BC V5H 4V8
604-433-1711
Fax: 604-439-4722
e-mail: webeditor@bchousing.org
URL: www.bchousing.org
National Library Symbol: NFCBF
No public access
Founded in: 1985
Acquisitions Budget: $25,000 - $49,999
Subjects covered: Social Housing, Urban Planning, Social Policy, Statistics, Construction, Property Management
Services:
Personnel: *Summary:* 55 Total
Lorna Balderstone, Library/Records Clerk
lbalders@bchmc.bc.ca
604-439-4750 ext. 369

Burnaby: **British Columbia Hydro Corporate Research & Information Services**
6911 Southpoint Dr.
Burnaby, BC V3N 4X8
604-528-3008
Fax: 604-528-3137
URL: www7.bchydro.com
National Library Symbol: BVAH
No public access
Hours: M-F 8:00-4:30
Special Collections: A/V Collection
Subjects covered: Physical Sciences, Electric Utilities, Energy & Mineral Resources, Standards & Specifications, Engineering
Services:
Personnel: *Summary:* 6 Total; 1 Professional(s); 3 Technical(s)
Patricia Crawford, Head of Library

Burnaby: **British Columbia Institute of Technology Library Services**
3700 Willingdon Ave.
Burnaby, BC V5G 3H2
604-432-8371
Fax: 604-430-5443
e-mail: interilb@bcit.ca
URL: www.lib.bcit.ca
National Library Symbol: BBIT
Consortia Membership: British Columbia Electronic Network (BC ELN)
Founded in: 1965
Hours: M-Th 7:30am-10:30pm; F 7:30-5:00; Sa, Su 9:00-5:00
Acquisitions Budget: $500,000 - $999,999
For Print: $250,000 - $499,999
For Electronic: $250,000 - $499,999
Note: The library is an affiliate member of the Council of Prairie and Pacific University Libraries (COPPUL).
Special Collections: International Maritime Organ1zation, Standards, Aircraft Technical Reports, BCIT Archives
Subjects covered: Health Sciences, Business, Transportation, Aviation, Marine Engineering, Computer Studies
Services:
Remote Access
Inter-Library Loan (ILL)
Microform Equipment: Reader
Personnel: *Summary:* 34 Total; 10 Professional(s); 1 Technical(s); 23 Other employees
David Pepper, Director, Library Services
david_pepper@bcit.ca
604-432-8360

Bill Nadiger, Librarian, Transportation
bill_nadiger@bcit.ca
604-453-4042
Patricia Cumming, Librarian, Electronics; Marketing Coordinator
patricia_cumming@bcit.ca
604-453-4064
Merilee MacKinnon, Librarian, Construction Trades & Technologies; Reference Coordinator
merilee_mackinnon@bcit.ca
604-432-8647
Kathleen Dutchak, Services & Systems Librarian
kathleen_dutchak@bcit.ca
604-453-4041

Burnaby: **Burnaby Hospital H.H.W. Brooke Memorial Library**
3935 Kincaid St.
Burnaby, BC V5G 2X6
604-412-6255
Fax: 604-412-6177
e-mail: hoong.lim@fraserhealth.ca
Hours: M-F 8:00-4:00 by appointment only
Acquisitions Budget: $25,000 - $49,999
Note: Part of Fraser Health Authority
Subjects covered: Medicine; Nursing
Services:
Internet Access
Access to Subscription Databases
Inter-Library Loan (ILL)
Personnel: *Summary:* 1 Professional(s)
Hoong Lim, Librarian
Hoong.Lim@fraserhealth.ca
Tomi Inkinen, Library Technician
tinkinen@golder.com

Burnaby: **Library (Burnaby)**
#500, 4260 Still Creek Dr.
Burnaby, BC V5C 6C6
604-296-4200
Fax: 604-298-5253
e-mail: tinkinen@golder.com
No public access
Hours: M-F
Acquisitions Budget: $25,000 - $49,999
Special Collections: Environmental Waste Management, Mining, Rock Mechanics, Hydrogeology
Subjects covered: Engineering, Environment, Mining, Geotechnical
Services:
Inter-Library Loan (ILL)
Personnel: *Summary:* 1 Total; 1 Professional(s)

Burnaby: **Metro Vancouver (formerly Greater Vancouver Regional District) Harry Lash Library**
4330 Kingsway
Burnaby, BC V5H 4G8
604-432-6335
Fax: 604-432-6445
e-mail: library@metrovancouver.org
URL: www.metrovancouver.org/about/catalogue/Pages/default.aspx
National Library Symbol: BBGV
Founded in: 1970
Hours: M-F 8:00-4:30
Acquisitions Budget: $25,000 - $49,999
Note: Annette Dignan & Thora Gislason jobshare position of Librarian.
Special Collections: Collection of GVRD reports; publications relevant to GVRD & municipal functions & operations
Subjects covered: Regional & Urban Development, Planning & Public Policy, Housing, Parks & Outdoor Recreation, Sewage & Solid Waste Disposal, Drinking Water Supply, Air Quality & Source Control, Urban Transit
Services:
Remote Access
Inter-Library Loan (ILL)
Personnel: *Summary:* 3 Total; 2 Professional(s); 1 Technical(s);

Annette Dignan, Librarian
annette.dignan@metrovancouver.org
Thora Gislason, Librarian
Janice Dudas, Library Technician
Elizabeth Hardacre, Librarian
elizabeth_hardacre@hc-sc.gc.ca

Libraries & Resource Centres / British Columbia

Burnaby: **Science Library**
#400, 4595 Canada Way
Burnaby, BC V5G 4P2
Mailing Address: 3155 Willingdon Green
Burnaby, BC V5G 4P2
604-666-3147
Fax: 604-666-3149
e-mail: elizabeth_hardacre@hc-sc.gc.ca
National Library Symbol: BVANH
No public access
Hours: M-F 8:00-4:00
Acquisitions Budget: $25,000 - $49,999
Subjects covered: Microbiology, Analytical Chemistry, Food Science & Technology, Analysis & Regulation, Drug Manufacturing, Cosmetics Regulation
Services:
Personnel:

Burnaby: **Simon Fraser University**
W.A.C. Bennett Library
8888 University Dr.
Burnaby, BC V5A 1S6
604-291-4084
Fax: 604-291-3023
e-mail: lib-plc@sfu.ca
libloan@sfu.ca
URL: www.lib.sfu.ca/
National Library Symbol: BVAS
Consortia Membership: British Columbia Electronic Network (BC ELN); Canadian Research Knowledge Network (CRKN); Council of Prairie and Pacific University Libraries (COPPUL)
Founded in: 1965
Hours: M-Th 8:00am-11:45pm; F 8:00-8:00; Sa, Su 10:00-10:00
Acquisitions Budget: $1,000,000 plus
Special Collections: Contemporary Literature, Post-War Avant-Garde Poetry, Wordsworth Collection, Editorial Cartoons
Subjects covered: Humanities, Sciences, Social Sciences, Business, Education
Services:
Remote Access
Internet Access
Access to Subscription Databases
Inter-Library Loan (ILL)
Microform Equipment: Reader
Personnel: *Summary:* 147 Total; 43 Professional(s); 5 Technical(s); 100 Other employees
Lynn Copeland, Dean of Library Services
copeland@sfu.ca
604-291-3265
Todd Mundle, Associate University Librarian
tmundle@sfu.ca
604-291-3266
Elaine Fairey, Associate University Librarian
efairey@sfu.ca
604-291-3252
Brian Owen, Associate University Librarian
brian_owen@sfu.ca
604-268-7095
Gwen Bird, Associate University Librarian, Collection Services
604-291-3263
Jana Allingham, Library Assistant
jana.allingham@nic.bc.ca
Kerry Strain, Library Assistant
kerry.strain@nic.bc.ca
250-923-9785

Campbell River: **Campbell River Campus Library**
1685 South Dogwood St.
Campbell River, BC V9W 8C1
250-923-9785
Fax: 250-923-9786
e-mail: diane.newman@nic.bc.ca
URL: library.nic.bc.ca
National Library Symbol: BCOMN
No public access
Hours: M-Th 8:00-7:30; F 8:00-4:00
Acquisitions Budget: For Print: $25,000 - $49,999
Population Served: Students & staff
Services:
Remote Access
Inter-Library Loan (ILL)
Microform Equipment: Reader
Personnel: *Summary:* 2 Technical(s)

Campbell River: **Strathcona Park Lodge & Outdoor Education Centre**
Library
PO Box 2160
Campbell River, BC V9W 5C5
250-286-3122
Fax: 250-286-6010
e-mail: info@strathcona.bc.ca
URL: www.strathcona.bc.ca
No public access
Founded in: 1959
Hours: Winter: Su-Su 8:00-5:00. Summer: Su-Su 8:00-8:00
Note: Library is for use by residents & guests of lodge & by students of Canadian Outdoor Leadership Training (C.O.L.T.)
Subjects covered: Outdoor education; Wilderness leadership; Survival skills
Services:
Personnel:
Jim Miller, C.O.L.T. Director

Castlegar: **Selkirk College**
Library
301 Frank Beinder Way
Castlegar, BC V1N 4L3
250-365-1229
Fax: 250-365-7259
888-953-1133
e-mail: bcs@selkirk.ca
URL: library.selkirk.bc.ca
National Library Symbol: BCS
Consortia Membership: British Columbia Electronic Network (BC ELN)
Founded in: 1966
Hours: M, F 8:30-5:00; Tu-Th 7:30-7:00; Sa, Su 12:00-4:00
Acquisitions Budget: $50,000 - $99,999
For Print: $50,000 - $99,999
For Electronic: $10,000 - $24,999
Special Collections: West Kootenay Collection; Doukhobor Collection
Services:
Remote Access
Internet Access
Access to Subscription Databases
Inter-Library Loan (ILL)
Microform Equipment: Computer; Reader
Personnel: *Summary:* 9 Total; 2 Professional(s); 1 Technical(s); 6 Other employees
Gregg Currie, College Librarian
250—36-5-12
Danielle Cossarini, Librarian
Sian Landis, Librarian
Kathy Hecker, Library Contact
khecker@nlc.bc.ca

Chetwynd: **Chetwynd Campus**
Library
5132 - 50th St.
Chetwynd, BC V0C 1J0
Mailing Address: PO Box 1180
Chetwynd, BC V0C 1J0
250-788-2248
Fax: 250-788-9706
Hours: M-Th 8:00-7:00; F 8:00-4:00
Acquisitions Budget: $25,000 - $49,999
Services:
Personnel:

Chilliwack: **Chilliwack Campus, Library**
45635 Yale Rd.
Chilliwack, BC V2P 6T4
604-795-2824
Fax: 604-792-8550
National Library Symbol: BCLF
Founded in: 1974
Hours: M-Th 8:00am-9:00pm; F 8:00-4:30; Sa 10:00-4:00
Services:
Internet Access
Access to Subscription Databases
Microform Equipment: Computer; Reader
Personnel: *Summary:* 3 Technical(s)

Courtenay: **North Island College Library**
Comox Valley Campus
2300 Ryan Rd.
Courtenay, BC V9N 8N6

250-334-5037
Fax: 250-334-5291
e-mail: guenther@nic.bc.ca
URL: library.nic.bc.ca
National Library Symbol: BCOMN
Consortia Membership: British Columbia Electronic Network (BC ELN)
Founded in: 1991
Hours: M-Th 8:00-7:30; F 8:00-4:00
Acquisitions Budget: $25,000 - $49,999
Subjects covered: Social & General Sciences, Humanities, Art
Services:
Internet Access
Access to Subscription Databases
Inter-Library Loan (ILL)
Personnel: *Summary:* 4 Total; 2 Professional(s); 2 Technical(s)
Mary Ann Guenther, Coordinator, Library Services
guenther@nic.bc.ca
250-334-5001
Amanda Pitchford, Collections/Reference Librarian
amanda.pitchford@nic.bc.ca
250-334-5097
Hélène Wickins, Library Assistant
wickins@nic.bc.ca

Cranbrook: **College of the Rockies**
Learning Resources Centre
2700 College Way
Cranbrook, BC V1C 5L7
Mailing Address: PO Box 8500
Cranbrook, BC V1C 5L7
250-489-8291
Fax: 250-489-8256
e-mail: library@cotr.bc.ca
fleming@cotr.bc.ca
URL: www.cotr.bc.ca
National Library Symbol: BCREK
Consortia Membership: British Columbia Electronic Network (BC ELN)
Founded in: 1975
Hours: M-Th 7:45-9:30; Fr 7:45-5:00; Sa 10:00-4:00; Su 12:00-4:00
Acquisitions Budget: For Print: $25,000 - $49,999
Population Served: 83000
Services:
Internet Access
Access to Subscription Databases
Inter-Library Loan (ILL)
Microform Equipment: Reader
Personnel: *Summary:* 6 Total; 1 Professional(s); 5 Technical(s)
Barbara Janzen, Library Coordinator & Public Services Librarian
janzen@cotr.bc.ca
250-489-8293
Susan Fleming, Library Technician
fleming@cotr.bc.ca
250-489-8291 ext. 3291
Lynn Hughes, Library Technician (Copyright)
hughes@cotr.bc.ca
250-489-2751 ext. 3407
Maureen Davidson, Library Technician (Cataloguing)
davidson@cotr.bc.ca
250-489-2751

Creston: **Creston Campus**
Library
301 - 16th Ave.
Creston, BC V0B 1G0
Mailing Address: PO Box 1978
Creston, BC V0B 1G0
250-428-5332
Fax: 250-428-4314
URL: www.cotr.bc.ca
Services:

Dawson Creek: **Northern Lights College**
Dawson Creek Library
11401 - 8th St.
Dawson Creek, BC V1G 4G2
250-784-7533
Fax: 250-784-7567
e-mail: dc-lib@nlc.bc.ca
URL: www.nlc.bc.ca/library/
National Library Symbol: BDCNL
Consortia Membership: British Columbia Electronic Network (BC ELN)
Hours: M-Th 8:30-8:00; F 8:30-4:30; Sa 1:00-5:00

Libraries & Resource Centres / British Columbia

Services:
Remote Access
Internet Access
Inter-Library Loan (ILL)
Bibliographic instruction; Group study room; TV/VCR room; TeleSensory magnifier unit; Computer lab
Personnel:
Janet Beavers, Librarian
Gloria Rounds, Library Contact

Delta: Econotech Services Ltd. Library
852 Derwent Way
Delta, BC V3M 5R1
604-526-4221
Fax: 604-526-1898
800-463-5700
e-mail: info@econotech.com
URL: www.econotech.com
Founded in: 1972
Hours: M-F 8:00-4:30 by appointment only
Subjects covered: Industry, Pulp & Paper
Services:
Personnel:
Norma Becker, Librarian
Eileen Edmunds, Librarian
edmundse@mala.bc.ca
250-746-3517
Eileen Edmunds, Regional Campus Librarian
edmundse@mala.bc.ca
Eileen Edmunds, Regional Campus Librarian
edmundse@mala.bc.ca

Duncan: Cowichan Campus Library
222 Cowichan Way
Duncan, BC V9L 6P4
250-746-3517
Fax: 250-746-3531
e-mail: edmundse@mala.bc.ca
illbnm@mala.bc.ca
URL: www.mala.bc.ca/library
National Library Symbol: BNM
Founded in: 1989
Hours: M-Th 8:00am-9:00pm; F 8:00-4:00; Sa 12:00-4:00
Acquisitions Budget: $25,000 - $49,999
Services:
Internet Access
Access to Subscription Databases
Inter-Library Loan (ILL)
Microform Equipment: Reader
Personnel: *Summary:* 7 Total; 1 Professional(s); 3 Technical(s); 2 Other employees
Erin Nagy, Library Clerk
enagy@nlc.bc.ca
250-774-2741 ext. 4640

Fort Nelson: Fort Nelson Campus Library
5201 Simpson Trail
Fort Nelson, BC V0C 1R0
250-774-2741
Fax: 250-774-2750
e-mail: enagy@nlc.bc.ca
National Library Symbol: BDCNL
Hours: M-Th 7:30-6:00; F 8:30-4:30
Acquisitions Budget: For Print: 0-$9,999
For Electronic: 0-$9,999
Population Served: 6000
Subjects covered: History, Computer, Psychology
Services:
Remote Access
Internet Access
Inter-Library Loan (ILL)
Personnel:
Dawna Turcotte, Campus Librarian
dturcotte@nlc.bc.ca
250-787-6213
Tricia Hotchkiss, Library Services Assistant

Fort St. John: Fort St. John Campus Library
9820 - 120 St.
Fort St. John, BC V1J 6K1
Mailing Address: PO Box 1000
Fort St. John, BC V1J 6K1

250-787-6213
Fax: 250-785-1294
866-463-6652
e-mail: fsj-lib@nlc.bc.ca
URL: library.nlc.bc.ca
National Library Symbol: BDCNL
Founded in: 1977
Hours: M-Th 8:30-8:00; F 8:30-4:30; Sa 12:00-4:00
Acquisitions Budget: $25,000 - $49,999
Services:
Remote Access
Internet Access
Access to Subscription Databases
Inter-Library Loan (ILL) for a fee of Free to students; $5.50 for community users
Microform Equipment: Reader
Personnel: *Summary:* 3 Total; 1 Professional(s); 2 Technical(s)

Kamloops: Entomological Society of British Columbia Library
c/o BC Ministry of Forests and Range, 515 Columbia St.
Kamloops, BC V2C 2T7
250-828-4179
Fax: 250-828-4154
e-mail: Lorraine.Maclauchlan@gov.bc.ca
URL: esbc.harbour.com/
Founded in: 1902
Hours: by appointment only
Subjects covered: Entomological serials from around the world
Services:
Personnel:
R. Bennett, Contact
Carol Fagan, Office Manager
250-554-5201
Lorelei Sterling, Administrative Assistant
250-554-5216

Kamloops: Kamloops Range Research Unit Library
3015 Ord Rd.
Kamloops, BC V2B 8A9
250-554-5203
Fax: 250-554-5229
Hours: M-F 8:00-12:00, 1:00-4:30
Acquisitions Budget: $25,000 - $49,999
Subjects covered: Agriculture, Soils, Range Management, Forage Agronomy
Services:
Inter-Library Loan (ILL)
Personnel:

Kamloops: Thompson Rivers University Kamloops Campus Library
PO Box 3010
Kamloops, BC V2C 5N3
250-828-5300
Fax: 250-828-5313
URL: www.tru.ca/library/
National Library Symbol: BKCC
Consortia Membership: British Columbia Electronic Network (BC ELN); Canadian Research Knowledge Network (CRKN); Council of Prairie and Pacific University Libraries (COPPUL)
Founded in: 1970
Hours: M-Su
Note: British Columbia Open University & University College of the Cariboo have merged to create Thompson Rivers University
Services:
Inter-Library Loan (ILL)
Microform Equipment: Reader
Personnel: *Summary:* 23 Total
Nancy Levesque, Director
levesque@tru.ca
250-828-5305
Peter Peller, Public Services Librarian
ppeller@tru.ca
250-828-5304
Kathy Gaynor, Information Services Librarian
kgaynor@tru.ca
250-377-6055
Penny Haggarty, Collections Librarian
phaggarty@tru.ca
250-828-5303
Michael Coyne, Systems Librarian
mcoyne@tru.ca
250-828-5021

Daniel Brendle-Moczuk, Instruction Librarian
dmoczuk@tru.ca
250-371-5775
Brenda Smith, Access Services Librarian
brsmith@tru.ca
250-828-5098

Kamloops: Thompson, Cariboo, Shuswap Health Sciences Library
Royal Inland Hospital
311 Columbia St.
Kamloops, BC V2C 2T1
Mailing Address: 311 Columbia St.
Kamloops, BC V2C 2T1
250-314-2234
Fax: 250-314-2189
e-mail: tcslibrary@interiorhealth.ca
National Library Symbol: BCCRAL
Consortia Membership: Interior Health Libraries
No public access
Acquisitions Budget: $100,000 - $249,999
For Print: $10,000 - $24,999
For Electronic: $50,000 - $99,999
Population Served: 4000
Note: Library provides resources & information services to Hospital personnel
Subjects covered: Medicine, Nursing, Health Science
Services:
Remote Access
Inter-Library Loan (ILL)
Personnel: *Summary:* 2 Total; 1 Professional(s); 1 Technical(s)
Lisa Gysel, Librarian
lisa.gysel@interiorhealth.ca
Paula Hardy, Library Technician

Kelowna: Okanagan College Library
1000 KLO Rd.
Kelowna, BC V1Y 4X8
250-862-5445
Fax: 250-862-5609
URL: www.okanagan.bc.ca
National Library Symbol: BKOC
Consortia Membership: British Columbia Electronic Network (BC ELN)
Hours: M-Th 8:00am-10:00pm; F 8:00-6:00; Sa 9:00-5:00; Su 9:00-5:00
Acquisitions Budget: $500,000 - $999,999
Note: The library is an affiliate member of the Council of Prairie and Pacific University Libraries (COPPUL).
Services:
Personnel: *Summary:* 76 Total; 10 Professional(s); 28 Technical(s); 38 Other employees
Ross Tyner, Director, Library Services
rhtyner@okanagan.bc.ca
250-762-5445 ext. 4665
Gilbert Bede, Librarian, Systems & Acquisitions
gbede@okanagan.bc.ca
250-762-5445 ext. 4751
Eva Engman, Librarian, Collections & Cataloguing
eengman@okanagan.bc.ca
250-762-5445 ext. 4490

Langley: Kwantlen University College Library Administration
20901 Langley By-Pass
Langley, BC V3W 2M8
Mailing Address: 12666 - 72nd Ave.
Surrey, BC V3W 2M8
604-599-3204
Fax: 604-599-3202
e-mail: cathy.macdonald@kwantlen.ca
URL: www.kwantlen.ca/library
National Library Symbol: BSKC
Consortia Membership: British Columbia Electronic Network (BC ELN)
Founded in: 1981
Hours: M-Th 7:45am-9:00pm; F 7:45-5:00; Sa 10:00-4:00
Acquisitions Budget: $500,000 - $999,999
Population Served: 18000; students + faculty & staff
Note: The library is an affiliate member of the Council of Prairie and Pacific University Libraries (COPPUL).
Subjects covered: Music, Horticulture, Fashion Design, Interior Design, Nursing, Business, University Transfer Courses, Trades, Applied Skills BA Degree Programs

Libraries & Resource Centres / British Columbia

Services:
Internet Access
Access to Subscription Databases
Inter-Library Loan (ILL)
Audiovisual services
Microform Equipment: Computer; Reader
Personnel: *Summary:* 40 Total; 15 Professional(s); 3 Technical(s); 27 Other employees
Cathy MacDonald, Dean of Learner Resources
cathy.macdonald@kwantlen.ca
604-599-3400
Susan Bruchet, Public Services & Electronic Resources Librarian
susan.bruchet@kwantlen.ca
604-599-3404
Phyllis Liu, Technical Services Librarian
phyllis.liu@kwantlen.ca
604-599-2591
Robert Gore, Collections Librarian
robert.gore@kwantlen.ca
604-599-2680
Caroline Daniels, Systems & Web Librarian
caroline.daniels@kwantlen.ca
604-599-2701
Colleen Van de Voort, Borrower Services Librarian
colleen.vandevoort@kwantlen.ca
604-599-2090
Jan Penhorwood, Chair & Public Services Librarian
jan.penhorwood@kwantlen.ca
604-599-3236
Margaret Brown, Serials & Government Publications Librarian
margaret.brown@kwantlen.ca
604-599-2087
Linda Rogers, Collections Librarian
604-599-2540
Sigrid Kargut, Public Services Librarian
604-599-2088
Denise Dale, Public Services Librarian & Archives
604-599-3486
Lin Brander, Public Services Librarian
604-599-3235
Mirela Djokic, Public Services Librarian
604-599-3199
Chris Burns, Public Services Librarian - Degrees & Research
604-599-3198
Lisa Hubick, Public Services Librarian & Public Relations
Ulrike Kestler, Public Services Librarian
604-599-3199
Cathy MacDonald, Dean of Learner Resources
cathy.macdonald@kwantlen.ca
604-599-2591

Langley: Langley Campus Library
20901 Langley By-Pass
Langley, BC V3A 2M8
Mailing Address: 12666 - 72nd Ave.
Surrey, BC V3A 2M8
604-599-3212
URL: www.kwantlen.ca/library
National Library Symbol: BSKC
Hours: M-Th 7:45am-9:00pm; F 7:45-5:00; Sa 10:00-4:00
Subjects covered: Horticulture, Music
Services:
Internet Access
Inter-Library Loan (ILL)
Microform Equipment: Computer; Reader
Personnel: *Summary:* 9 Total; 3 Professional(s); 6 Other employees

Langley: Trinity Western University Norma Marion Alloway Library
7600 Glover Rd.
Langley, BC V2Y 1Y1
604-513-2023
Fax: 604-513-2063
e-mail: library@twu.ca
ill@twu.ca
URL: www.twu.ca/library
National Library Symbol: BLTW
Consortia Membership: British Columbia Electronic Network (BC ELN); Canadian Research Knowledge Network (CRKN); Council of Prairie and Pacific University Libraries (COPPUL)
Founded in: 1962
Hours: M-Th 7:45am-11:00pm; F 7:45-6:00; Sa 10:00-6:00; Su 1:30-5:00

Acquisitions Budget: $50,000 - $99,999
For Print: $50,000 - $99,999
For Electronic: $50,000 - $99,999
Note: Associated Canadian Theological Schools library has integrated with Trinity Western University
Special Collections: Robert N. Thompson Collection, University Archives, Mel Smith Papers
Subjects covered: Arts, Liberal Arts, Sciences, Nursing, Business, Religious Studies
Services:
Remote Access
Internet Access for a fee of $60/yr
Inter-Library Loan (ILL)
Microform Equipment: Computer; Reader
Personnel: *Summary:* 15 Total; 7 Professional(s); 10 Technical(s)
Ted Goshulak, University Librarian
Ron Braid, Head, Reference
Suzana Maunaga, Head, Cataloguing
Stan Olson, Head, Acquisitions & Systems
Bill Badke, Head, Theology
Sylvia Stopforth, Head, Archives
stopfort@twu.ca

Merritt: Nicola Valley Institute of Technology Library
4155 Belshaw St.
Merritt, BC V1K 1R1
250-378-3302
Fax: 250-378-3332
877-682-3300
e-mail: info@nvit.bc.ca
sgarcia@nvit.bc.ca
URL: www.nvit.bc.ca/library/index.htm
National Library Symbol: BMNVI
Consortia Membership: British Columbia Electronic Network (BC ELN)
Founded in: 1979
Hours: Sept.-Apr.: M-Th 8:30-8:30; F 8:30-4:30; Sa 12:00-6:00; Su 12:00-4:00. May-Aug.: M-F 8:30-4:30.
Acquisitions Budget: $25,000 - $49,999
For Print: $25,000 - $49,999
For Electronic: $10,000 - $24,999
Population Served: 500
Note: Member of BC Electronic Library Network
Subjects covered: First Nations; Social Work; Forestry; Natural Resource Technologies; Academic & Indigenous Studies; Aboriginal Community Economic Development
Services:
Remote Access
Internet Access
Inter-Library Loan (ILL) for a fee
Current awareness service; Computer lab; Instructional equipment & mobile computer loans
Personnel: *Summary:* 112 Total; 33 Professional(s); 20 Technical(s); 59 Other employees
Jim Bruce, College Librarian
jbruce@nvit.bc.ca
250-378-3303
Sherry Garcia, Library Coordinator
250-378-3302

Mission: Mission Campus at Heritage Park Centre Library
33700 Prentis Ave.
Mission, BC V2V 7B1
Mailing Address: PO Box 1000
Mission, BC V2V 7B1
604-820-6009
Fax: 604-826-0681
National Library Symbol: BCLF
Hours: M-Th 8:30-7:00
Services:
Internet Access
Access to Subscription Databases
Microform Equipment: Computer; Reader
Personnel: *Summary:* 1 Technical(s)

Nanaimo: Malaspina University-College Library
900 - 5th St.
Nanaimo, BC V9R 5S5
250-740-6330
Fax: 250-740-6473
e-mail: library@mala.bc.ca

illbnm@mala.bc.ca
URL: www.mala.ca/library
National Library Symbol: BNM
Consortia Membership: British Columbia Electronic Network (BC ELN); Canadian Research Knowledge Network (CRKN); Council of Prairie and Pacific University Libraries (COPPUL)
Founded in: 1969
Hours: M-Th 7:00am-11:00pm; F 7:00-6:00; Sa, Su 10:00-6:00
Acquisitions Budget: $500,000 - $999,999
Note: Formerly known as Malaspina College
Subjects covered: Physical Sciences, Health & Human Sciences, History, Canadian History, First Nations, Business, Arts, Education
Services:
Remote Access
Internet Access
Access to Subscription Databases
Inter-Library Loan (ILL)
Microform Equipment: Computer; Reader
Personnel: *Summary:* 33 Total; 9 Professional(s); 26 Technical(s)
Bob Foley, Director of Library Services
foleyb@mala.bc.ca
250-740-6331
Jennifer Brownlow, Reference Librarian
brownlow@mala.bc.ca
250-740-6330 ext. 6335
Hans Fadum, Coordinator, Technical Services
fadum@mala.bc.ca
250-740-6330 ext. 2270
Gwen Bailey, Coordinator, Library Systems
baileyg@mala.bc.ca
250-740-6330 ext. 2444
Linda Leger, Collections Librarian
legerl@mala.bc.ca
250-753-3245 ext. 2347
Gordon Miller, Head, Library Services & Scientific Archives
millergo@pac.dfo-mpo.gc.ca
George Pattern, Head, Technical Services

Nanaimo: Pacific Biological Station Library
3190 Hammond Bay Rd.
Nanaimo, BC V9R 5K6
250-756-7071
Fax: 250-756-7053
e-mail: paclibrarypbs@dfo-mpo.gc.ca
www.pac.dfo-mpo.gc.ca
National Library Symbol: BNP
Founded in: 1913
Hours: M-F 8:30-4:30 by appointment only
Acquisitions Budget: $50,000 - $99,999
Special Collections: INPFC Documents
Subjects covered: Fisheries, Marine Sciences, Marine & Freshwater Ecology
Services:
Inter-Library Loan (ILL)
Microform Equipment: Computer; Reader
Personnel: *Summary:* 2 Total; 2 Professional(s);

Nelson: Chamber of Mines of Eastern British Columbia Library of Government Geological Reports
215 Hall St.
Nelson, BC V1L 5X4
250-352-5242
e-mail: chamberofmines@netidea.com
URL: www.cmebc.com
Founded in: 1925
Hours: M-F 10:00-4:00
Acquisitions Budget: $25,000 - $49,999
Subjects covered: Historical data on mines of BC; technical data on mining operations; area maps; geological & geochemical data
Services:
Internet Access for a fee of $2/15 minutes min.
Judy Deon, Library Director
jdeon@selkirk.ca
250-365-1382
Elizabeth Ball, Librarian
lball@selkirk.ca
250-365-1263
Kate Enewold, Library Systems Administrator
kenewold@selkirk.ca
250-365-1339

CANADIAN ENVIRONMENTAL RESOURCE GUIDE 2011-2012
1113

Libraries & Resource Centres / British Columbia

Kate Enewold, Library Systems Administrator
kenewold@selkirk.ca
250-365-1339

Nelson: Silver King Campus Library
2001 Silver King Rd.
Nelson, BC V1L 1C8
250-354-3249
Fax: 250-352-3180
e-mail: bcs@selkirk.ca
URL: library.selkirk.bc.ca
National Library Symbol: BCS
Founded in: 1966
Hours: M, W, Th, 8:20-12:30; Tu 8:20-4:00
Acquisitions Budget: $50,000 - $99,999
Services:
Personnel: *Summary:* 9 Total; 1 Technical(s)

New Westminster: Douglas College Library
700 Royal Ave.
New Westminster, BC V3L 5B2
Mailing Address: PO Box 2503
New Westminster, BC V3L 5B2
604-527-5478
Other contact info: 604-527-5176
e-mail: ill_bnwd@douglas.bc.ca
infodesk@douglas.bc.ca
URL: www.douglas.bc.ca
National Library Symbol: BNWD
Consortia Membership: British Columbia Electronic Network (BC ELN)
Founded in: 1969
Hours: Winter: M-Th 7:45am-10:00pm; F 7:45-5:30; Sa 9:00-5:00. Summer: M, F 7:45-4:30; Tu-Th 7:45am-9:00pm
Acquisitions Budget: $250,000 - $499,999
Note: The library is an affiliate member of the Council of Prairie and Pacific University Libraries (COPPUL).
Subjects covered: Arts, Sciences, Business, Nursing, Community, Social, Family, Environmental Science, Theatre
Services:
Access to Subscription Databases
Inter-Library Loan (ILL)
Personnel: *Summary:* 45 Total; 16 Professional(s); 27 Technical(s); 2 Other employees
Carole Compton-Smith, Director
compton-smithc@douglas.bc.ca
604-527-5182
Mary Matthews, Reference Services Librarian
matthewsm@douglas.bc.ca
604-777-6137
Debra Flewelling, Information Technology Librarian
flewellingd@douglas.bc.ca
604-527-5190
Gretchen Goertz, Technical Services Librarian
goertzg@douglas.bc.ca
604-527-5259
Dianne Hewitt, Web Development Librarian
hewittd@douglas.bc.ca
604-527-5181
Susan Ashcroft, Collections Librarian
ashcrofts@douglas.bc.ca
604-527-5189
Patti Romanko, Instructional Services Librarian
romankop@douglas.bc.ca
604-527-5183
Jean Cockburn, Electronic Resources Librarian
cockburnj@douglas.bc.ca
604-527-5184
Sandra Hochstein, Information Literacy Librarian
hochsteins@douglas.bc.ca
604-527-5181
Christian Guillou, Computer Services
guillouc@douglas.bc.ca
604-527-5184

New Westminster: Justice Institute of British Columbia Library
715 McBride Blvd.
New Westminster, BC V3L 5T4
604-528-5599
Fax: 604-528-5593
TDD: 6045285656
e-mail: library@jibc.ca
URL: www.jibc.ca
Social Media: www.facebook.com/justiceinstitute
Profile: Provides services to faculty & students enrolled incertificate, diploma & degree programs
National Library Symbol: BVAJI
Consortia Membership: British Columbia Electronic Network (BC ELN)
Founded in: 1978
Hours: M-F 8:00-5:00; Sa (Sept-June) 9:00-4:00
Acquisitions Budget: $50,000 - $99,999
For Print: $25,000 - $49,999
For Electronic: $25,000 - $49,999
Population Served: 42000
Note: Service to police officers, fire fighters, Court Services Branch personnel, Corrections Branch employees, paramedics, search & rescue volunteers, emergency management volunteers, emergency social services volunteers, family justice counsellors, & MCFD Youth Justice personnel
Special Collections: Justice & public safety topics; search & rescue; emergency management; criminology; corrections; forensic science; family violence; conflict resolution; policing
Subjects covered: Police Science, Fire Science, Emergency Medicine, Criminology, Penology, Corrections, Management, Adult Education, Disaster Planning, Search & Rescue
Services:
Remote Access
Internet Access
Inter-Library Loan (ILL)
Personnel: *Summary:* 6 Total; 4 Professional(s); 2 Technical(s)
April Haddad, Institute Librarian
ahaddad@jibc.ca
604-528-5594
Christine Babec, Reference Librarian
cbabec@jibc.ca
604-528-5595
Christine-Louise Dujmovich, Librarian, Reference & Electronic Resources
cdujmovich@jibc.ca
604-528-5597
Marjory Jardine, Librarian, Reference & Instruction
mjardine@jibc.ca
604-528-5592

New Westminster: Royal Columbian Hospital - Simon Fraser Health Authority Medical Library
330 East Columbia St.
New Westminster, BC V3L 3W7
604-520-4281
Fax: 604-520-4804
National Library Symbol: BNWRC
No public access
Hours: M-F
Acquisitions Budget: $50,000 - $99,999
Note: Part of Fraser Health Authority
Subjects covered: Medicine, Hospital Administration, Health Sciences, Nursing
Services:
Inter-Library Loan (ILL)
Personnel: *Summary:* 3 Total; 1 Professional(s); 2 Technical(s)
Sue Abzinger, Manager, Medical Library
604-520-4755

North Vancouver: Capilano College Library
2055 Purcell Way
North Vancouver, BC V7J 3H5
604-984-4944
Fax: 604-984-1728
e-mail: library@capcollege.bc.ca
URL: www.capcollege.bc.ca/services/learning-support/library/
National Library Symbol: BVAC
Consortia Membership: British Columbia Electronic Network (BC ELN)
Founded in: 1968
Hours: M-Th 8:00am-9:30pm; F 8:00-4:30; Sa, Su 1:00-5:00
Acquisitions Budget: $100,000 - $249,999
For Print: $100,000 - $249,999
For Electronic: $50,000 - $99,999
Special Collections: Records of the College, Jazz Music, Music Therapy, Tourism
Subjects covered: Arts, Sciences, Career, Vocational, Technical, Asian Pacific Business, Environmental, Paralegal Materials, Music, Film Studies, theatre
Services:
Remote Access
Internet Access
Access to Subscription Databases
Inter-Library Loan (ILL)
Microform Equipment: Computer; Reader
Personnel: *Summary:* 25 Total; 6 Professional(s); 19 Technical(s)
Maureen Witney, Librarian Coordinator
George Modenesi, Coordinator, Reference
gmodenes@capcollege.bc.ca
604-984-4944 ext. 2111
Sidney Myers, Technical Services Librarian
smyers@capcollege.bc.ca
604-984-4944 ext. 2129
Karin Hall, Collections Librarian
604-984-4944 ext. 2169
David Lambert, Circulation Librarian
dlambert@capcolleg.bc.ca
604-984-4944 ext. 2108
Annette Lorek, AV Librarian
alorek@capcollege.bc.ca
604-984-4944 ext. 2143

North Vancouver: EVS Environment Consultants Ltd. Library
195 Pemberton Ave.
North Vancouver, BC V7P 2R4
604-986-4331
Fax: 604-662-8548
877-986-4331
e-mail: info@evsenvironment.com
URL: www.evsenvironment.com
Hours: M-F 9:00-1:00 by appointment only
Subjects covered: Environment
Services:
Personnel:
Rhona Karbusicky, Librarian
Bill Nadiger, Marine Engineer Reference Librarian
bill_nadiger@bcit.ca
604-453-4042
Jennifer Hunter, Assistant
jennifer_hunter@bcit.ca

North Vancouver: Marine Campus Library
265 West Esplanade
North Vancouver, BC V7M 1A5
604-453-4107
Fax: 604-980-0827
URL: www.lib.bcit.ca
Hours: M-F 8:00-12:00, 1:00-4:00; Sa, Su 1:00-2:00
Subjects covered: Marine Engineering, Nautical Subjects, Safety, Shipping, Care & Transportation of Hazardous Materials (Hazmat), Seamanship
Services:
Access to Subscription Databases
Personnel: *Summary:* 2 Total; 1 Professional(s); 1 Technical(s)

Penticton: Penticton Campus Library
583 Duncan Ave.
Penticton, BC V2A 8E1
250-490-3951
Fax: 250-490-3954
Hours: M-Th 7:45am-9:00pm; F 7:45-5:00; Sa 8:30-4:30; Su 12:00-4:00
Services:
Inter-Library Loan (ILL)
Personnel:
Mary Anne Guenther, Coordinator, Library Services
250-334-5001
Sherry Kropninski, Library Technician
sherry.kropninski@nic.bc.ca
250-724-8733
Hannah Leprette, Library Assistant
hannah.leprette@nic.bc.ca
250-724-8760

Port Alberni: Port Alberni Regional Campus Library
3699 Roger St.
Port Alberni, BC V9Y 8E3
250-724-8733
Fax: 250-724-8780
e-mail: sherry.kropninski@nic.bc.ca
URL: library.nic.bc.ca

National Library Symbol: BCPNI
Founded in: 1992
Hours: Sept.-April: M-Th 8:30-8:00; F 8:30-4:30. May-June: M-F 8:30-4:30
Acquisitions Budget: For Print: $25,000 - $49,999
For Electronic: $10,000 - $24,999
Note: Public access limited to use of books & materials in library, OPAC station but not the student computers.
Services:
Remote Access
Internet Access
Access to Subscription Databases
Inter-Library Loan (ILL)
Personnel: Summary: 4 Total; 2 Technical(s); 2 Other employees

Port Coquitlam: **Riverview Hospital Library Services**
HEY Bldg., 2601 Lougheed Hwy.
Port Coquitlam, BC V3C 4J2
604-524-7386
Fax: 604-524-7021
e-mail: library@bcmhs.bc.ca
URL: www.bcmhs.bc.ca/library
National Library Symbol: BEC
Founded in: 1945
Hours: M-F 8:00-4:00
Special Collections: Rating Scales; Practice Guidelines
Subjects covered: Health Sciences, Psychiatry, All Aspects of Mental Health/Illness Rehabilitation, Medicine, Psychiatric Nursing
Services:
Internet Access
Access to Subscription Databases
Inter-Library Loan (ILL)
Instruction & end user databases. In library use only.
Personnel: Summary: 4 Total; 1 Professional(s); 2 Technical(s)
Greg Rowell, Manager, Library Services
growell@bcmhs.bc.ca
604-524-7018
Tracy Walsh, Library Technician
twalsh@bcmhc.bc.ca
604-524-7267

Port Hardy: **Port Hardy Centre**
9300 Trustee Rd.
Port Hardy, BC V0N 2P0
Mailing Address: PO Box 901
Port Hardy, BC V0N 2P0
250-949-2863
Fax: 250-949-2617
866-332-1113
e-mail: reference@nic.bc.ca
URL: library.nic.bc.ca
Hours: Sept.-June: M-Tu 8:30am-12:30pm; Tu 1:00-4:30; W 8:30-2:00; Th 6:00pm-9:00pm
Services:
Internet Access
Inter-Library Loan (ILL)
Personnel: Summary: 1 Total; 1 Other employees
Eileen Edmunds, Librarian
edmundse@mala.bc.ca
250-746-3517
Eileen Edmunds, Regional Campus Librarian
edmundse@mala.bc.ca
Eileen Edmunds, Regional Campus Librarian
edmundse@mala.bc.ca

Powell River: **Powell River Campus Library**
3960 Selkirk Ave.
Powell River, BC V8A 3C6
604-485-8044
Fax: 604-485-2868
e-mail: edmundse@mala.bc.ca
illbnm@mala.bc.ca
URL: www.mala.bc.ca/library
National Library Symbol: BNM
Founded in: 1978
Hours: M-Th 10:00-4:00; F 10:00-1:00
Acquisitions Budget: $25,000 - $49,999
Subjects covered: Academic Vocational Reference
Services:
Internet Access
Inter-Library Loan (ILL)

Personnel: Summary: 3 Total; 1 Professional(s); 2 Technical(s); 2 Other employees

Prince George: **College of New Caledonia Resource Centre**
3330 - 22nd Ave.
Prince George, BC V2N 1P8
250-561-5811
Fax: 250-561-5845
800-371-8111
TDD: 2505615952
e-mail: cnclibrary@cnc.bc.ca
URL: www.cnc.bc.ca
National Library Symbol: BPGC
Consortia Membership: British Columbia Electronic Network (BC ELN)
Founded in: 1969
Hours: M-W 8:00am-10:00pm; Th-F 8:00am-8:00pm; Sa-Su 12:00-5:00
Acquisitions Budget: $50,000 - $99,999
For Print: $25,000 - $49,999
For Electronic: $25,000 - $49,999
Subjects covered: Arts, Humanities, Science, Technologies
Services:
Remote Access
Internet Access
Inter-Library Loan (ILL)
Personnel: Summary: 16 Total; 5 Professional(s); 11 Technical(s)
Kathy Plett, Associate Director
plett@cnc.bc.ca
Jennifer Sauvé, Public Services Librarian
sauvej@cnc.bc.ca
250-562-2131 ext. 5297
Brenda Yee, Head, Technical Services
yee@cnc.bc.ca

Prince George: **University of Northern British Columbia Geoffrey R. Weller Library**
3333 University Way
Prince George, BC V2N 4Z9
250-960-6613
Fax: 250-960-6610
888-440-3440
Other contact info: Reference: 250-960-6475; ILL: 250-960-6460
e-mail: libcirc@unbc.ca
interlib@unbc.ca
URL: library.unbc.ca
National Library Symbol: BPGVB
Consortia Membership: British Columbia Electronic Network (BC ELN); Canadian Research Knowledge Network (CRKN); Council of Prairie and Pacific University Libraries (COPPUL)
Hours: M-Th 8:00am-11:00pm; F 8:00am-9:00pm; Sa 10:00-6:00; Su 10:00-9:00
Acquisitions Budget: $1,000,000 plus
For Print: $250,000 - $499,999
For Electronic: $500,000 - $999,999
Special Collections: Northern British Columbia Archives & Special Collections: focus is historical exploration, early surveying, travel literature, First Nations, ethnology, culture, industry & resource management; Rare book collection; Education resources relevant to the B.C. curriculum; Maps; Information repository on oil & gas exploration
Subjects covered: Natural Resource Management, First Nations Studies, Environmental Studies, Resource Recreation & Tourism
Services:
Remote Access
Internet Access
Inter-Library Loan (ILL) for a fee of free (students, faculty, staff); $2/request (alumni); $10/request (comm
Curriculum lab; Special equipment for patrons with disabilities; Audio/visual equipment
Microform Equipment: Computer; Reader
Personnel: Summary: 34 Total; 9 Professional(s); 25 Technical(s)
Gohar Ashoughian, University Librarian
libadmin@unbc.ca
250-960-6612
Joanne Matthews, Collections & Acquisitions Librarian
matthews@unbc.ca
250-960-6615
Ramona Rose, Head, Archives/Special Collections
roserm@unbc.ca
250-960-6603

Eleanor Annis, Catalogue Librarian
eleanora@unbc.ca
250-960-6617
Joann Murphy, Associate University Librarian
murphyj1@unbc.ca
250-960-6654
Gail Curry, Instruction/Data Librarian
curryg@unbc.ca
250-960-6607
Nancy E. Black, Distance & Document Delivery Librarian
blackn@unbc.ca
250-960-6473
Trina Fyfe, Northern Health Sciences Librarian
fyfet@unbc.ca
250-960-5195
Michael Purcell, Systems Librarian
purcell@unbc.ca
250-960-6601
Heather Empey, Educations Services Librarian
empeyh@unbc.ca
250-960-6468
Brigitte Peter-Cherneff, Institute Librarian
Brigitte_Peter-Cherneff@bcit.ca
604-453-4093
Bill Nadiger, Librarian
Bill_Nadiger@bcit.ca
Lori Pederson, Library Assistant
Lori_Pederson@bcit.ca
604-419-3708

Richmond: **Aerospace Technology Campus Library**
3800 Cessna Dr.
Richmond, BC V7B 0A1
604-419-3708
Fax: 604-207-8437
e-mail: LPederso@bcit.ca
URL: www.bcit.ca/library
Hours: M-F 7:30-7:00
Population Served: 400
Note: Card must be purchased to borrow material, $50/year
Special Collections: Aircraft Maintenance; Aviation; Avionics
Services:
Internet Access
Personnel:

Richmond: **MacDonald Dettwiler & Associates Ltd. Library**
13800 Commerce Pkwy.
Richmond, BC V6V 2J3
604-278-3411
Fax: 604-231-1837
888-780-6444
e-mail: info@mdacorporation.com
URL: www.mda.ca
No public access
Founded in: 1980
Special Collections: Remote Sensing Collection
Subjects covered: Science, Technology, High Technology, Electronics Engineering
Services:
Microform Equipment: Reader
Personnel: Summary: 1 Professional(s)
Julie Jarvis, Librarian
Cathy MacDonald, Dean of Learner Resources
cathy.macdonald@kwantlen.ca
604-599-2591

Richmond: **Richmond Campus Library**
8771 Lansdowne Rd.
Richmond, BC V3W 2M8
Mailing Address: 12666 - 72nd Ave.
Surrey, BC V3W 2M8
604-599-2638
Fax: 604-599-2644
National Library Symbol: BSKC
Founded in: 1981
Hours: M-Th 7:45am-9:00pm; F 7:45-5:00; Sa 10:00-4:00
Special Collections: Videos
Subjects covered: Fashion Design, Environmental Protection Technology, Journalism, Public Relations, University transfer courses, applied BA degree courses
Services:
Internet Access

Libraries & Resource Centres / British Columbia

Inter-Library Loan (ILL)
Microform Equipment: Computer; Reader
Personnel: *Summary:* 17 Total; 5 Professional(s); 12 Other employees

Richmond: **Triton Environmental Consultants Ltd. Library**
8971 Beckwith Rd.
Richmond, BC V6X 1V4
604-279-2093
Fax: 604-279-2047
e-mail: ameeder@triton-env.com
info@triton-env.com
URL: www.triton-env.com
National Library Symbol: BVAEN
No public access
Founded in: 1980
Subjects covered: Environment, Fisheries, Engineering, Hydrology
Services:
Inter-Library Loan (ILL)
Personnel: *Summary:* 1 Professional(s)
Anneli Meeder, Librarian
ameeder@triton-env.com

Richmond: **Union of British Columbia Municipalities Library**
#60, 10551 Shellbridge Way
Richmond, BC V6X 2W9
604-270-8226
Fax: 604-270-9116
e-mail: uncm@civicnet.bc.ca
URL: www.civicnet.bc.ca
Founded in: 1905
Hours: M-F 8:30-4:30 by appointment only
Acquisitions Budget: 0-$9,999
For Print: 0-$9,999
For Electronic: 0-$9,999
Population Served: BC local governments
Special Collections: Extensive, unorganized (as yet) archives of BC local government history
Subjects covered: Local Government, Legislation, Statistcs, History
Services:
Inter-Library Loan (ILL)
Personnel: *Summary:* 1 Total; 1 Professional(s)
Reiko Tagami, Information & Resolutions Coordinator
ubcm@civicnet.bc.ca
604-270-8226 ext. 115
Taryn Schmid, Librarian, Reference & Instruction
tschmid@okanagan.bc.ca

Salmon Arm: **Salmon Arm Campus Library**
2552 Trans Canada Hwy. NE
Salmon Arm, BC V1E 4N3
Mailing Address: PO Box 189
Salmon Arm, BC V1E 4N3
250-804-8851
Fax: 250-804-8852
Hours: M-Th 8:00am-9:00pm; F 8:00-4:30; Sa 8:30-4:00; Su 12:00-4:00
Personnel: *Summary:* 7 Total
Pamela Olson, Librarian
olsonp@pac.dfo-mpo.gc.ca

Sidney: **Institute of Ocean Sciences Library**
9860 West Saanich Rd.
Sidney, BC V8L 4B2
Mailing Address: PO Box 6000
Sidney, BC V8L 4B2
250-363-6392
Fax: 250-363-6749
e-mail: paclibraryios@pac.dfo-mpo.gc.ca
URL: www.pac.dfo-mpo.gc.ca/pages/libraries-bibliotheques/ios_e.html
National Library Symbol: BVIEM
Founded in: 1970
Hours: M-F 8:30-4:30 by appointment only
Special Collections: Published & unpublished books, journals & literature to support the research of the Institue & Natural Resources Canada's Pacific Geoscience Centre; Collections focus on oceanography, hydrography, ocean research, environmental science, geology, geophysics, seismology & earthquake studies
Subjects covered: Ocean Studies, Life Sciences, Earth Sciences, Geology
Services:
Inter-Library Loan (ILL)
Personnel: *Summary:* 1 Total
Lynne Boyd, Librarian
boydl@agr.gc.ca

Summerland: **Canadian Agriculture Library (Summerland)**
4200 Hwy. 97
Summerland, BC V0H 1Z0
250-494-2100
Fax: 250-494-0755
e-mail: parc@agr.gc.ca
National Library Symbol: BSUAG
Founded in: 1951
Hours: 8:30-4:00 by appointment only
Acquisitions Budget: For Print: 0-$9,999
Population Served: Dept. of Agriculture & Agri-Food staff
Note: Restricted service to the public because of staffing limits. On-site use of the collection. For ILL contact the Canadian Agriculture Library-Ottawa. See listing.
Subjects covered: Food Processing, Orchard Diseases & Pests, Biotechnology, Tree Fruit, Biological Control, Viticulture
Services:
Personnel: *Summary:* 1 Total; 1 Professional(s)
Elizabeth Irwin, Library Assistant
elizabeth.irwin@powertechlabs.com

Surrey: **Powertech Labs Inc. Library**
12388 - 88th Ave.
Surrey, BC V3W 7R7
604-590-7500
Fax: 604-590-7424
TDD: 6045906618
e-mail: elizabeth.irwin@powertechlabs.com
infor@powertechlabs.com
URL: www.powertechlabs.com
National Library Symbol: PLI
No public access
Founded in: 1980
Hours: Tu-Th 8:30-4:30
Acquisitions Budget: 0-$9,999
For Print: 0-$9,999
For Electronic: 0-$9,999
Population Served: 80
Note: TTY only; for hearing people please contact operator to find out how to contact Library Assistant through TTY
Special Collections: Canadian Electrical Association reports; EPRI reports
Subjects covered: Energy, Technology, Electrical & Chemical Research, Power Engineering Materials, Engineering & Applied Chemistry
Services:
Inter-Library Loan (ILL)
Personnel: *Summary:* 1 Total; 1 Technical(s)
Cathy MacDonald, Dean of Learner Resources
cathy.macdonald@kwantlen.ca
604-599-2591

Surrey: **Surrey Campus Library**
12666 - 72nd Ave.
Surrey, BC V3W 2M8
604-599-2105
Fax: 604-599-2106
National Library Symbol: BSKC
Founded in: 1981
Hours: M-Th 7:45am-9:00pm; F 7:45-5:00; Sa 10:00-4:00
Special Collections: College's video collection
Subjects covered: Nursing, Fine Arts, Academic transfer courses, University transfer courses, BA degree courses
Services:
Internet Access
Inter-Library Loan (ILL)
Microform Equipment: Reader
Personnel: *Summary:* 11 Total; 4 Professional(s); 8 Other employees;
Natialie Gick, Campus Librarian
ngick@sfu.ca
778-782-7417

Surrey: **Surrey Library**
250-13450 102nd Ave.
Surrey, BC V3T 0A3
778-782-7411
e-mail: lib-surrey@sfu.ca
Hours: M, T, Th 9:00-6:00; W 9:00-9:00; F 9:00-6:00
Personnel:

Surrey: **Surrey Memorial Hospital Bodhan Lesack Memorial Library**
13750 - 96th Ave.
Surrey, BC V3V 1Z2
604-585-5666 ext: 2467
Fax: 604-585-5540
e-mail: linda.howard@fraserhealth.ca
Allison.Lambert@fraserhealth.ca
URL: fhls.andornot.com
Regional System: Fraser Health Library Services
Consortia Membership: Health Libraries Association of BC, Electronic Health Library of BC
Founded in: 1987
Hours: M-F 9:00-5:00 by appointment only
Acquisitions Budget: $25,000 - $49,999
For Print: $10,000 - $24,999
For Electronic: $25,000 - $49,999
Population Served: Hospital staff, affiliated physicians, students
Note: Part of Fraser Health Authority; Member of Health Libraries Association of B.C.; Docline for ILL
Subjects covered: Clinical Medicine, Nursing, Allied Health Management
Services:
Inter-Library Loan (ILL)
Personnel: *Summary:* 5 Total; 1 Professional(s); 4 Technical(s); 2 Volunteer(s)
Linda Howard, Librarian
linda.howard@fraserhealth.ca
604-585-5666 ext. 2467

Terrace: **Northwest Community College Library**
5331 McConnell Ave.
Terrace, BC V8G 4X2
250-638-5407
Fax: 250-635-1594
e-mail: kwestby@nwcc.bc.ca
ill@nwcc.bc.ca
URL: www.nwcc.bc.ca
National Library Symbol: BTENW
Consortia Membership: British Columbia Electronic Network (BC ELN)
Founded in: 1977
Hours: M-Th 8:00am-9:00pm; F 8:00-5:00; Sa, Su 1:00-5:00
Acquisitions Budget: $50,000 - $99,999
For Print: $50,000 - $99,999
For Electronic: $10,000 - $24,999
Population Served: 2500
Special Collections: BC Northwest Archives, Children's Books, Literacy Collection, Government Documents, Forestry
Subjects covered: Trades, Social Services, Natural Resources, University 1st & 2nd year Arts & Science, Cook Training, Business Administration, Adult Upgrading, Early Childhood Education, Wilderness Guiding, Eco-Tourism, Applied Computers
Services:
Internet Access
Access to Subscription Databases
Inter-Library Loan (ILL) for a fee of Free to staff & students; $10 community
Microform Equipment: Reader
Personnel: *Summary:* 7 Total; 2 Professional(s); 3 Technical(s); 2 Other employees
Tim MacDonald, College Librarian
tmacdonald@nwcc.bc.ca
250-638-5407
Michele Cook, Eastern Region Librarian
mcook@nwcc.bc.ca
250-847-4461 ext. 5836

Trail: **Teck Cominco Metals Ltd. Information Resources**
PO Box 2000
Trail, BC V1R 4S4
250-364-4408
Fax: 250-364-4456
URL: www.teckcominco.com

National Library Symbol: BTC
No public access
Founded in: 1925
Hours: M-F
Acquisitions Budget: $50,000 - $99,999
Special Collections: Chemical & Metallurgical Abstracts, Metals Abstracts, Engineering Index, U.S. Patent Office Gazette
Subjects covered: Physical Sciences, Engineering, Technology, Chemicals, Metallurgy
Services:
Personnel: *Summary:* 1 Professional(s); 1 Technical(s)
Fran Noone, Information Specialist
fran.noone@teckcominco.com
250-364-4405

Vancouver: Aker Kvaerner Chemetics Inc. Research & Development
1818 Cornwall Ave.
Vancouver, BC V6J 1C7
604-734-1200
Fax: 604-734-0340
URL: www.akerkvaerner.com
National Library Symbol: BVACI
No public access
Special Collections: Chemical, Technical & Business Journals
Subjects covered: Chemicals, Engineering, Environment, Business, Technology
Services:
Inter-Library Loan (ILL)
Personnel:
Claudia Chandler, Chemical Info Specialist

Vancouver: Association for Mineral Exploration British Columbia
Charles S. Ney Library
#800, 889 West Pender St.
Vancouver, BC V6C 3B2
604-689-5271
Fax: 604-681-2363
URL: www.amebc.ca
Founded in: 1912
Hours: M-F 8:30-4:00
Acquisitions Budget: 0-$9,999
For Print: 0-$9,999
For Electronic: 0-$9,999
Population Served: 5000; Members & general public
Subjects covered: Mineral Exploration, Mining
Services:
Internet Access
Personnel:
Cassandra Hall, Director, Communications & External Relations
Karen Marotz, Head Librarian

Vancouver: Belzberg Library
Harbour Centre, 515 West Hastings St.
Vancouver, BC V6B 5K3
604-291-5050
Fax: 604-291-5052
URL: www.harbour.sfu.ca/belzberg/
Hours: M-Th 10:00-9:00; F 10:00-7:00; Sa 10:00-5:00
Subjects covered: Economics, Industry, Business, Finance, Banking Industry, Gerontology
Services:
Personnel:
Rita Dahlie, Interim Head
rita.dahlie@ubc.ca
604-822-4970

Vancouver: Biomedical Branch Library
Gordon and Leslie Diamond Health Centre
2775 Laurel St., Floor 2
Vancouver, BC V5Z 1M9
Mailing Address: 2775 Laurel St., Floor 2
Vancouver, BC V5Z 1M9
604-875-4505
Fax: 604-875-4689
Note: Off-campus branch
Subjects covered: Health Sciences, Clinical Medicine
Services:
Personnel: *Summary:* 5 Total; 1 Professional(s); 4 Technical(s)

Vancouver: British Columbia Utilities Commission Library
900 Howe St., 6th Fl.
Vancouver, BC V6Z 2N3
Mailing Address: PO Box 250
Vancouver, BC V6Z 2N3
604-660-4700
Fax: 604-660-1102
800-663-1385
e-mail: commission.secretary@bcuc.com
URL: www.bcuc.com
Founded in: 1973
Hours: M-F
Acquisitions Budget: $25,000 - $49,999
Special Collections: BCUC Hearings (transcripts & exhibits)
Subjects covered: Economics, Regulation, Housing, Planning & Public Works, Government, Architecture, Law, Law Enforcement, Public Utilities, Income Tax, Municipal Government, Provincial Statutes & Legislation, Canadian Statutes
Services:
Personnel:
Alison Cormack, Information Services Officer
Lila Heilbrunn, Director, Library & Learning Resources

Vancouver: Broadway Campus Library
1155 East Broadway
Vancouver, BC V5T 4V5
604-871-7326
Fax: 604-871-7446
TDD: 6048717325
e-mail: libraryhelp@vcc.ca
URL: library.vcc.ca
National Library Symbol: BVAVCC
Founded in: 1965
Hours: M-Th 8:00-8:00; F 8:00-4:00. Hours vary during the academic year - consult the libary website under 'Hours & Locations'
Acquisitions Budget: $100,000 - $249,999
For Print: $100,000 - $249,999
For Electronic: $50,000 - $99,999
Note: Computer loans & Internet access for students, faculty & staff only
Special Collections: Special Education, Braille Collection, Talking Books, Literacy, English as a Second Language, Career Resources
Subjects covered: Adult Basic Education, Automotive Trades, Business, Culinary Arts, Education, Health & Dental, Hospitality, Humanities, Music, Sciences, Technology
Services:
Remote Access
Internet Access
Access to Subscription Databases
Inter-Library Loan (ILL)
Group & quiet study facilities; audiovisual materials & equipment; scanning, printing & photocopying; library tours & research classes; homework help & tutoring; services & adaptive technologies for users who are deaf or hard of hearing, or with print disabilities; services for distance learners
Microform Equipment: Computer; Reader
Personnel: *Summary:* 30 Total; 11 Professional(s); 19 Technical(s)
Lila Heilbrunn, Director, Library & Learning Resources

Vancouver: Downtown Campus Library
250 West Pender St.
Vancouver, BC V6B 1S9
604-433-8339
Fax: 604-443-8329
TDD: 6044438549
e-mail: libraryhelp@vcc.ca
URL: library.vcc.ca
National Library Symbol: BVACC
Founded in: 1974
Hours: M-Th 7:30-8:00 p.m.; F 7:30-4:00. Hours may vary during the academic year
Acquisitions Budget: $50,000 - $99,999
Note: Internet access is provided to students, faculty & staff only
Subjects covered: Education, Vocational Education, Hospitality, Tourism, Culinary Arts, Health
Services:
Remote Access
Internet Access
Access to Subscription Databases
Inter-Library Loan (ILL)
Microform Equipment: Computer
Personnel: *Summary:* 10 Total; 3 Professional(s); 7 Technical(s)

Vancouver: EarthSave Canada
Library
S.P.E.C. Bldg., 2150 Maple St.
Vancouver, BC V6J 3T3
604-731-5885
Fax: 604-731-5805
e-mail: office@earthsave.bc.ca
URL: www.earthsave.bc.ca
Hours: Tu-Sa 12:00-4:00
Acquisitions Budget: 0-$9,999
For Print: 0-$9,999
For Electronic: 0-$9,999
Population Served: 600
Note: Lending for Earthsave members
Special Collections: Library carries over 500 boosk; magazines; videos; dvds; and audio cassettes covering health; nutrition; animal ethics; environmentalism; and vegetarian cooking.
Subjects covered: Health, Ecology, Ethics
Services:
Provides education on how your diet affects your health & the planet
Personnel: *Summary:* 2 Total; 2 Professional(s); 1 Volunteer(s)
Alison Cole, Office Manager
office@earthsave.bc.ca
604-222-8103

Vancouver: Ecojustice Canada
Library
#214, 131 Water St.
Vancouver
604-685-5618
Fax: 604-685-7813
800-926-7744
e-mail: info@ecojustice.ca
URL: www.ecojustice.ca
Social Media: www.facebook.com/ecojustice
Profile: Dedicated to using law to protect & restore Canada's environment; part of the environment protection movement; provides free legal expertise; offices in Vancouver, Toronto, Ottawa & Alberta
Founded in: 1990
Hours: by appointment only
Acquisitions Budget: 0-$9,999
For Print: 0-$9,999
For Electronic: 0-$9,999
Note: A non-profit environmental law organization
Subjects covered: Law, Environment
Services:
Personnel:
Devon Page, Executive Director
dpage@ecojustice.ca
Carol McDonald, Director of Admin. & Human Resources
cmcdonald@ecojustice.ca
Judy Mackenzie, Librarian
jmackenzie@paprican.ca

Vancouver: FP Innovations - Paprican Division, Vancouver
Research Library
3800 Wesbrook Mall
Vancouver, BC V6S 2L9
604-222-3261
Fax: 604-222-3262
e-mail: library@paprican.ca
URL: www.fpinnovations.ca
National Library Symbol: BVAPPR
No public access
Founded in: 1986
Hours: M-F 8:30-4:30
Subjects covered: Pulp & Paper Science & Technology, Forest Products
Services:
Inter-Library Loan (ILL)
Personnel: *Summary:* 1 Total; 1 Professional(s)

Vancouver: FP Innovations Forintek Division
Vancouver Library
2665 East Mall
Vancouver, BC V6T 1W5
604-224-3221 ext: 668
Fax: 604-222-5690
e-mail: holder@van.forintek.ca
URL: www.fpinnovations.ca
National Library Symbol: BVAFP
No public access

Libraries & Resource Centres / British Columbia

Founded in: 1927
Hours: M-F
Subjects covered: Forest Products Research, Sawmilling, Timber Engineering, Wood Preservation, Wood Chemistry, Wood Science, Secondary/Value Wood Processing
Services:
Inter-Library Loan (ILL)
Personnel: Summary: 2 Total; 1 Professional(s); 1 Technical(s)
Barbara Holder, Librarian
holder@van.forintek.ca
Amanda Gay, Library Technologist

Vancouver: Klohn Crippen Berger Ltd. Library
2955 Virtual Way, 5th Fl.
Vancouver, BC V5M 4X6
604-251-8435
Fax: 604-669-3835
e-mail: library@klohn.com
URL: www.klohn.com
National Library Symbol: BRKL
Hours: M-F by appointment only
Acquisitions Budget: $10,000 - $24,999
For Print: $10,000 - $24,999
For Electronic: 0-$9,999
Population Served: 230
Subjects covered: Soil Mechanics, Civil & Environmental Engineering, Community Development
Services:
Inter-Library Loan (ILL) for a fee of shipping
Personnel: Summary: 2 Total; 1 Professional(s); 1 Other employees
Kim Feltham, Library & Records Coordinator
kfeltham@klohn.com
604-251-8435

Vancouver: Langara College Library
100 West 49th Ave.
Vancouver, BC V5Y 2Z6
604-323-5384
Fax: 604-323-5512
e-mail: ill@langara.bc.ca
URL: www.langara.bc.ca/library
National Library Symbol: BVAVCL
Consortia Membership: British Columbia Electronic Network (BC ELN)
Founded in: 1970
Hours: M-Th 8:00am-9:00pm; F 8:00-6:00; Sa-Su 10:00-5:00; Summer Term: M-Th 8:00am-7:30pm; F 8:00-5:00
Acquisitions Budget: $100,000 - $249,999
For Print: $50,000 - $99,999
For Electronic: $50,000 - $99,999
Special Collections: BC History
Subjects covered: Academic & careers program
Services:
Remote Access
Internet Access
Access to Subscription Databases
Inter-Library Loan (ILL) for a fee of $5
Microform Equipment: Reader
Personnel: Summary: 27 Total; 9 Professional(s); 18 Technical(s)
Grace Makarewicz, Director, Library Services
gmakarewicz@langara.bc.ca
604-323-5460
Vivian Feng, Coordinator, Reference & Instructional Services
vfeng@langara.bc.ca
604-323-5346
Patricia Cia, Coordinator, Technical Services & Library Systems
pcia@langara.bc.ca
604-323-5243
Joyce Wong, Department Chair
joyce.wong@langara.bc.ca
604-323-5047
Alison Curtis, Coordinator, Collection Development
acurtis@langara.bc.ca
604-323-5465
Guy Robertson, Librarian
guy_robertson@telus.net
604-224-3143

Vancouver: Library (Vancouver)
#200, 1445 West Georgia St.
Vancouver, BC V8G 2T3
604-684-4384
Fax: 604-684-5124
e-mail: guy-robertson@telus.net
No public access
Founded in: 1957
Subjects covered: Physical Sciences, Maps, Geology, Soil Mechanics, Rock Mechanics. Comprehensive collections on geological hazards, including landslides, avalanches, earthquakes, ground subsidence & erosion. Other collections on BC soils, highways, harbours & terrain.
Services:
Personnel: Summary: 1 Total; 1 Professional(s); 2 Volunteer(s)
Elena Kuzmina, Head Librarian
Fontaine Hwang, Library Technician
fhwang@nrcan-rncan.gc.ca
604-666-3812

Vancouver: Natural Resources Canada Library - Earth Sciences (Vancouver)
625 Robson St., 15th Fl.
Vancouver, BC V6B 5J3
604-666-1147
Fax: 604-666-7186
e-mail: libvan@nrcan.gc.ca
URL: cgc.rncan.gc.ca/org/vancouver/library/index_e.php
National Library Symbol: BVAG
Founded in: 1973
Hours: M-F 8:30-4:30
Acquisitions Budget: $100,000 - $249,999
For Print: $100,000 - $249,999
For Electronic: $50,000 - $99,999
Special Collections: British Columbia Energy, Mines & Petroleum Resources publications, US Bureau of Mines publications, Energy Mines & Resources Canada publications, theses on the Canadian Cordillera, Natural Resources Canada publications, Environment Canada, USGS, Geological Survey of Canada
Subjects covered: Earth Sciences, Geoscience with special emphasis on North American Cordillera & Pacific margin, Micropaleontology, World wide earth sciences journals
Services:
Remote Access
Internet Access
Access to Subscription Databases
Inter-Library Loan (ILL)
Personnel: Summary: 2 Total; 1 Professional(s); 1 Technical(s); 1 Volunteer(s)
Andrew Fabro, Chief Librarian
andrew.fabro@ec.gc.ca

Vancouver: Pacific & Yukon Region - Vancouver Library - Environment Canada
#201, 401 Burrard St.
Vancouver, BC V6C 3S5
604-666-5914
Fax: 604-666-1788
Other contact info: 604-666-1794
e-mail: nvan.library@ec.gc.ca
URL: www.ec.gc.ca/default.asp?lang=en&n=b047b5b1-1
National Library Symbol: BVAEP
Founded in: 1973
Hours: M-F by appointment only
Services:
Inter-Library Loan (ILL)
Microform Equipment: Computer; Reader
Personnel: Summary: 1 Total; 1 Professional(s)
Marcia Croy Vanwely, Head, Library Services
croycanwelym@pac.dfo-mpo.gc.ca
604-666-6371
Louise Archibald, Senior Library Technician
604-666-3851

Vancouver: Pacific Region Library
401 Burrard St., 16th Fl.
Vancouver, BC V6C 3S4
604-666-3851
Fax: 604-666-3145
e-mail: paclibrary@dfo-mpo.gc.ca
croyvanwelym@pac.dfo-mpo.gc.ca
URL: www.pac.dfo-mpo.gc.ca/index-eng.htm
Social Media: twitter.com/#!/DFO_Pacific
National Library Symbol: BVAFI
Founded in: 1969
Hours: M-F 8:00-4:00 by appointment only
Acquisitions Budget: $25,000 - $49,999
Subjects covered: Fisheries Management, Aquatic Sciences, Economics, Aquaculture
Services:
Inter-Library Loan (ILL)
Microform Equipment: Computer; Reader
Personnel: Summary: 2 Total; 1 Professional(s); 1 Technical(s)
Jill Rowland, Librarian
rowlanj@tc.gc.ca

Vancouver: Pacific Regional Library
#620, 800 Burrard St.
Vancouver, BC V6Z 2J8
604-666-0578
National Library Symbol: BVATCA
Founded in: 1982
Hours: M-F 9:00-4:00 by appointment only
Acquisitions Budget: $25,000 - $49,999
Subjects covered: Transportation
Services:
Inter-Library Loan (ILL)
Microform Equipment: Computer; Reader
Personnel: Summary: 1 Total; 1 Professional(s);

Vancouver: Pacific Salmon Commission Library
#600, 1155 Robson St.
Vancouver, BC V6E 1B5
604-684-8081
Fax: 604-666-8707
e-mail: tarita@psc.org
library@psc.org
URL: www.psc.org
National Library Symbol: BVAPSC
Hours: M-F 8:00-4:00 by appointment only
Acquisitions Budget: 0-$9,999
For Print: 0-$9,999
For Electronic: 0-$9,999
Subjects covered: Fishery Management, Ichthyology, Salmon Biology
Personnel: Summary: 1 Professional(s)
Teri Tarita, Librarian
tarita@psc.org
Barbara Saint, Head
bsaint@interchange.ubc.ca

Vancouver: St Paul's Health Sciences Library
1081 Burrard St.
Vancouver, BC V6Z 1Y6
604-806-8425
Fax: 604-806-8013
e-mail: sphlib@interchange.ubc.ca
URL: www.library.ubc.ca/stpauls/
Founded in: 1950
Hours: M-Th 8:00am-9:00pm; F 8:00-5:00; Sa 12:00-5:00
Acquisitions Budget: $50,000 - $99,999
Note: Off-campus branch
Subjects covered: Health Sciences, Clinical Medicine
Services:
Remote Access
Internet Access
Access to Subscription Databases
Inter-Library Loan (ILL)
Personnel: Summary: 5 Total; 1 Professional(s); 3 Technical(s); 1 Other employees
Aleteia Greenwood, Head
aleteia.greenwood@ubc.ca
604-822-0689

Vancouver: Science & Engineering Division
1961 East Mall
Vancouver, BC V6T 1Z1
604-822-3295
Fax: 604-822-5366
e-mail: sciref@interchange.ubc.ca
URL: www.library.ubc.ca/scieng/
Hours: M-Su
Subjects covered: Physical Sciences, Technology, Engineering, Patents
Services:
Inter-Library Loan (ILL)
Microform Equipment: Computer; Reader
Personnel: Summary: 8 Total

Vancouver: Teck Resources Corporate Library
#3300, 550 Burrard St.
Vancouver, BC V6C 0B3

604-699-4000
Fax: 604-699-4711
e-mail: keith.low@teck.com
URL: www.teck.com
National Library Symbol: BVATE
Hours: M-F by appointment only
Special Collections: Company annual reports; government publications; geology materials; mining engineering
Subjects covered: Geology, Mining & Exploration, Environment, Economics
Services:
Inter-Library Loan (ILL)
Personnel: *Summary:* 4 Total; 2 Professional(s); 1 Technical(s)
Keith Low, Coordinator
604—69-9-40
Suzanne McBeath, Librarian
Susan Doricic, Library Technician

Vancouver: **University of British Columbia Library**
1961 East Mall
Vancouver, BC V6T 1Z1
604-822-6375
Fax: 604-822-3893
URL: www.library.ubc.ca
National Library Symbol: BVAU
Consortia Membership: British Columbia Electronic Network (BC ELN); Canadian Research Knowledge Network (CRKN); Council of Prairie and Pacific University Libraries (COPPUL)
Founded in: 1915
Hours: M-Su
Acquisitions Budget: $1,000,000 plus
For Print: $1,000,000 plus
For Electronic: $1,000,000 plus
Population Served: 45,000 students
Special Collections: Pacific Northwest History, Canadiana, English 19th Century Literature (Colbeck), History of Cartography, Cartographic Archives, Early Japanese Maps (Bean), English & American Children's Literature from 18th Century to 1930's, University Archives, UBC Theses, History of Medicine & Science, Oriental Collection including The P'u-pan Collection, Harry Hawthorne Angling Collection, Literature (Colbeck), Canadiana Maps (Rogers-Tucker), The Chung Collection, The H.C.S. Stravinsky Collection
Services:
Remote Access
Internet Access
Access to Subscription Databases
Inter-Library Loan (ILL)
Microform Equipment: Computer; Reader
Personnel: *Summary:* 310 Total; 73 Professional(s); 201 Technical(s); 36 Other employees
W. Peter Ward, University Librarian
peter.ward@ubc.ca
Jo Anne Newyear-Ramirez, Assist. University Librarian, Collections & Scholarly Communication
joanne.newyear-ramirez@ubc.ca
604-822-2740
Lea Starr, Associate University Librarian, Public Services
lea.starr@ubc.ca
604-822-2826
Tim Atkinson, Librarian, Technical Services
tim.atkinson@ubc.ca
604-822-6723

Vancouver: **Vancouver Aquarium Marine Science Centre**
Robin Best Library
845 Avison Way
Vancouver, BC V6B 3X8
Mailing Address: PO Box 3232
Vancouver, BC V6B 3X8
604-659-3474
Fax: 604-659-3515
e-mail: library@vanaqua.org
URL: www.vanaqua.org
No public access
Hours: Library is not open to the public, but will answer questions via e-mail.
Special Collections: Archives, Photographs
Subjects covered: Contains over 5,000 books & periodicals on the following topics: Tropical Fish; Freshwater & Marine Fish; Marine Mammals; Reptiles; Amphibians; Birds
Services:
Inter-Library Loan (ILL)
Personnel: *Summary:* 1 Professional(s); 1 Volunteer(s)

Dawn Bassett, Manager, Content & Information Resources
dawn.bassett@vanaqua.org
604-659-3404

Vancouver: **Vancouver Coastal Health Authority Library**
#200, 520 West 6th Ave.
Vancouver, BC V5Z 4H5
604-730-7656
Fax: 604-730-7660
e-mail: VCHLibraryServices@vch.ca
URL: www.vch.ca/libraryservices/index.htm
No public access
Founded in: 1979
Hours: M, W, Th, 8:30-4:30
Note: Public use of library on-site only. Library supports & trains volunteers to staff community health centre-based health information centres. Volunteer health finders provide access to health information using electronic & print resources, provides referral services to health agencies & health care providers.
Subjects covered: Long Term Care, Health Education, Community Health Services, Public Health
Services:
Inter-Library Loan (ILL) for a fee of reciprocal
Personnel: *Summary:* 2 Total; 1 Professional(s); 1 Technical(s)
Patricia Young, Librarian
Pat.Young@vch.ca
604-730-7653
Marjory Jardine, Librarian
Marjory.Jardine@vch.ca
604-730-7652
Paula Ludwig, Library Technician
Paula.Ludwig@vch.ca
604-730-7656

Vancouver: **Vancouver Community College Library & Media Services**
1155 East Broadway
Vancouver, BC V5T 4V5
604-443-3566
Fax: 604-443-8588
e-mail: lheilbrunn@vcc.ca
URL: www.vcc.ca/library
National Library Symbol: BVAVCC
Consortia Membership: British Columbia Electronic Network (BC ELN)
Founded in: 1965
Acquisitions Budget: $100,000 - $249,999
For Print: $50,000 - $99,999
For Electronic: $50,000 - $99,999
Population Served: Students
Special Collections: Collections in support of all VCC programs
Subjects covered: Humanities, Social Sciences, Applied Sciences, English as a Second Language, Tourism, Business, Hospitality, Pacific Rim, Food, Culinary Arts, Education, Health (including Nursing, Dental Technology, Dental Hygiene, Denturists, Lab Assistants), Trades training & Computer Technologists
Services:
Inter-Library Loan (ILL)
Public Services, Reference Services & Information Literacy, Technical Services, Library Systems, Circulation & ILL, Acquisitions, Collections, Cataloguing
Personnel: *Summary:* 33 Total; 9 Professional(s); 24 Technical(s)
Lila Heilbrunn, Director, Library & Learning Resources
lheilbrunn@vcc.ca
604-443-8566
Virginia Adams, Dept Head, Library Public Services
vadams@vcc.ca
604-871-7319
Ella-Fay Zalezsak, Coordinator, Technical Services
efzalezsak@vcc.ca
604-871-7385
Shirley Lew, Coordinator, Library Systems
slew@vcc.ca
604-871-7157

Vancouver: **Vancouver Community Services Group Community Services Library**
453 West 12th Ave.
Vancouver, BC V5Y 1V4
604-871-6088
Fax: 604-871-6408
e-mail: devon.rowcliffe@vancouver.ca
URL: vancouver.ca

Hours: M-F 8:30-4:30 by appointment only
Acquisitions Budget: $25,000 - $49,999
For Print: $25,000 - $49,999
Note: Publication sales.
Subjects covered: Housing, Planning & Public Works, Local Government, Architecture, Urban Planning, Heritage, Landscaping
Services:
Personnel: *Summary:* 1 Total; 1 Professional(s)
Devon Rowcliffe, Librarian
devon.rowcliffe@vancouver.ca
604-871-6088

Vancouver: **Vancouver Museum Library & Resource Centre**
1100 Chestnut St.
Vancouver, BC V6J 3J9
604-736-4431
Fax: 604-736-5417
URL: www.vanmuseum.bc.ca
No public access
Founded in: 1968
Subjects covered: Ethnology, Museology, Art, Culture, History, Asian Studies, Natural History, Anthropology, Archaeology, Museum Conservation
Services:
Personnel: *Summary:* 1 Other employees
Lynn Maranda, Curator of Anthropology
lmaranda@vanmuseum.bc.ca
604-730-5318

Vancouver: **VanDusen Gardens Library**
5251 Oak St.
Vancouver, BC V6M 4H1
604-257-8668
Fax: 604-266-4236
e-mail: library@vandusen.org
URL: www.city.vancouver.bc.ca
Founded in: 1977
Hours: Sept-June: T-F 10:00-3:00, W evenings 7:00-9:00, Su 1:00-4:00, July-Aug T-F 10:00-3:00
Acquisitions Budget: For Print: 0-$9,999
Services:
Personnel: *Summary:* 1 Total; 1 Professional(s); 12 Volunteer(s)
Marina Princz, Librarian

Vancouver: **West Coast Environmental Law Research Foundation**
Environmental Law Library
#1001, 207 West Hastings St.
Vancouver, BC V6B 1H7
604-684-7378
Fax: 604-684-1312
800-330-9235
e-mail: admin@wcel.org
URL: www.wcel.org
Hours: M-F 8:30-5:00
Acquisitions Budget: $25,000 - $49,999
Services:
Personnel:
Chris Heald, Systems Administrator
cheald@wcel.org
604-601-2514
Rita Dahlie, Head
rita.dahlie@ubc.ca
604-822-4970

Vancouver: **Woodward Biomedical Library**
2198 Health Sciences Mall
Vancouver, BC V6T 1Z3
604-822-4440
Fax: 604-822-5596
URL: www.library.ubc.ca/woodward/
National Library Symbol: BVAUW
Founded in: 1950
Hours: M-Th 8:00am-11:00pm; F 8:00-6:00; Sa 10:00-6:00; Su 12:00-6:00
Special Collections: History of Life Sciences collection; Various records relating to Canadian, British & European scientists
Subjects covered: Health Sciences, Clinical Medicine, Biology
Services:
Inter-Library Loan (ILL)
Personnel:
Jennifer Sigalet, Director, Library Services
jsigalet@okanagan.bc.ca

Libraries & Resource Centres / British Columbia

Vernon: **Vernon Campus Library**
7000 College Way
Vernon, BC V1B 2N5
250-503-2654
Fax: 250-558-4963
Hours: M-Th 7:30am-9:00pm; F 7:30-4:30; Sa 8:30-4:00, Su 12:00-4:00
Services:
Personnel:

Victoria: **British Columbia Ferry Services Library**
1112 Fort St.
Victoria, BC V8V 4V2
250-978-1241
Fax: 250-389-6127
e-mail: bcferries.library@bcferries.com
URL: www.bcferries.com
National Library Symbol: BVIFC
Hours: M-F 8:30-4:00
Special Collections: Clippings, Archive
Subjects covered: Marine Engineering, Shipping
Services:
Inter-Library Loan (ILL)
Personnel: *Summary:* 1 Total; 1 Professional(s)
Terrell Les Strange, Librarian
terrell.lesstrange@bcferries.com

Victoria: **British Columbia Health & Human Services Library**
1515 Blanshard St., 1st Fl.
Victoria, BC V8W 3C8
250-952-2196
Fax: 250-952-2180
e-mail: hlth.library@gov.bc.ca
URL: www.healthservices.gov.bc.ca/library
National Library Symbol: BVIHE
Founded in: 1978
Hours: M-F 8:30-4:30 by appointment only
Note: Provides library services to Ministry of Health Services & Ministry of Children & Family Development
Subjects covered: Public Health, Medicine, Nursing, Health Sciences, Community Mental Health Services, Family Health, Communicable Disease Control, Epidemiology, Health Administration, Dentistry, Nutrition, Resource Allocation, Health Economics, Child Welfare, Child Abuse & Neglect, Child Protection, Adoption, Family Issues, Social Work, Counselling, Employment Research, Labour, Market, Poverty, Public Welfare, Social Policy, Welfare Reform, Training
Services:
Inter-Library Loan (ILL)
Personnel: *Summary:* 8 Total; 3 Professional(s); 3 Technical(s); 2 Other employees;
Antje Helmuth, Head Librarian
Antje.Helmuth@gov.bc.ca

Victoria: **British Columbia Ministry of Economic Development Library, Jack Davis Building**
1810 Blanshard St., Main Fl.
Victoria, BC V8W 9N3
Mailing Address: PO Box 9321, Stn Prov Govt
Victoria, BC V8W 9N3
250-952-0583
Fax: 250-952-0581
e-mail: jennifer.lu@gov.bc.ca
National Library Symbol: ECONDEV
Founded in: 1910
Hours: Tu-F 10:30-4:30
Acquisitions Budget: $25,000 - $49,999
Note: The Competition, Science & Enterprise Ministry split into two ministries in February 1998 but the library is physically integrated while serving also the Ministry of Energy & Mines.
Special Collections: Geological Survey of Canada; US Geological Survey; TIDSA-Tourism; BC Company Reports; BC Mines Bulletins, Assessment Files/Reports
Subjects covered: Economics; Business; Energy; Mining; Petroleum
Services:
Internet Access
Inter-Library Loan (ILL)
Microform Equipment: Reader
Personnel: *Summary:* 2 Total; 1 Technical(s); 1 Other employees
Jennifer Lu, Library Technician
Jennifer.Lu@gov.bc.ca
250-952-0660
Rowena Wake, Library Assistant
250-952-0583

Victoria: **British Columbia Ministry of Energy & Mines Library**
1810 Blanshard St.
Victoria, BC V8W 9N3
Mailing Address: PO Box 9321
Victoria, BC V8W 9N3
250-952-0660
Fax: 250-952-0581
e-mail: jennifer.lu@gov.bc.ca
URL: www.em.gov.bc.ca/publicinfo/library/default.htm
National Library Symbol: BVIM
Founded in: 1896
Hours: Tu-F 10:30-4:30
Acquisitions Budget: $25,000 - $49,999
Note: The Ministry of Competition Science & Enterprise split into two ministries in February 1998 but the library is physically integrated while serving also the Ministry of Energy & Mines.
Special Collections: Tourism BC Reports, BC Mines Bulletins; Assessment Reports; Property Geological Survey of Canada Collection Files; US Geological Survey; BC & Canadian Company Annual Reports.
Subjects covered: Economics, Mining, Geology, Business
Services:
Internet Access
Inter-Library Loan (ILL)
Microform Equipment: Reader
Personnel: *Summary:* 2 Total; 1 Technical(s); 1 Other employees
Jennifer Lu, Library Technician
jennifer.lu@gov.bc.ca
250-952-0660
Janice Brisson, Library Assistant
Janice.M.Brisson@gov.bc.ca
250-952-0583

Victoria: **British Columbia Ministry of Environment Library**
851 Yates St.
Victoria, BC V8W 9C2
Mailing Address: PO Box 9523, Stn Prov Gov
Victoria, BC V8W 9C2
250-387-3628
Fax: 250-953-3079
e-mail: Forests.Library@gov.bc.ca
URL: www.for.gov.bc.ca/hfd/library/
National Library Symbol: BVIFO
Hours: M-F 8:00-4:30
Population Served: 5000
Note: Provides resources & services to Ministry of Forests & Range, Ministry of Sustainable Resource Management & Ministry of Water, Land & Air Protection. This is a technical library for the use of Ministry staff members. All others may use materials onsite or through interlibrary loans from their own institution's library. Article databases, online journals (except Open Access), & Table of Contents Service are restricted access.
Subjects covered: Botany, Computer Science, Ecology, Economics, Forest Engineering, Forest Recreation, GIS/GPS/Remote Sensing, Hydrology, Management, Range Management, Resource Management, Silverculture, Soils, Wildlife, Waste, Water & Wildlife Management, Habitat, Environmental Policy, Parks, Ecological Reserves
Services:
Remote Access
Internet Access
Inter-Library Loan (ILL)
Personnel: *Summary:* 4 Total; 1 Professional(s); 1 Technical(s); 2 Other employees
Pamela Wilkins, Ministry Librarian
Pamela.Wilkins@gov.bc.ca

Victoria: **Camosun College Lansdowne Library**
Alan Batey Library Media Centre
3100 Foul Bay Rd.
Victoria, BC V8P 5J2
Mailing Address: 3100 Foul Bay Rd.
Victoria, BC V8P 5J2

250-370-3619
Fax: 250-370-3624
e-mail: library@camosun.bc.ca
URL: camosun.bc.ca/services/library
National Library Symbol: BVIC
Consortia Membership: British Columbia Electronic Network (BC ELN)
Founded in: 1971
Hours: M-Th 9:00-9:00; F 9:00-5:00; Sa 10:00-6:00; Su 2:00-6:00
Acquisitions Budget: $100,000 - $249,999
For Print: $100,000 - $249,999
For Electronic: $25,000 - $49,999
Population Served: 10000
Note: Library hours are subject to change in spring and summer sessions.
Special Collections: Native studies, Criminology
Services:
Remote Access
Internet Access
Inter-Library Loan (ILL)
Microform Equipment: Reader
Personnel: *Summary:* 18 Total; 5 Professional(s); 2 Technical(s); 11 Other employees
Richard Baer, Chair, Library Services
baer@camosun.bc.ca
Neil A. Campbell, Law Librarian & Associate Professor
neilcam@uvic.ca
Caron Rollins, Associate Law Librarian
crollins@uvic.ca
250-721-8566
Serena Ableson, Assistant Law Librarian, Akitsiraq Law School
sableson@uvic.ca
250-721-8564
Irene Godfrey, Supervisor
irenegod@uvic.ca
250-721-8568
Richard McCue, Systems Administrator
rmccue@uvic.ca
250-472-4716

Victoria: **Diana M. Priestly Law Library**
McGill Rd.
Victoria, BC V8W 3B1
Mailing Address: PO Box 2300, Stn CSC
Victoria, BC V8W 3B1
250-721-8562
Fax: 250-472-4174
e-mail: lawill@uvic.ca
URL: library.law.uvic.ca
National Library Symbol: BVIVL
Founded in: 1974
Hours: M-Su
Acquisitions Budget: $500,000 - $999,999
Subjects covered: Law
Services:
Internet Access
Inter-Library Loan (ILL)
Microform Equipment: Computer; Reader
Personnel: *Summary:* 13 Total; 4 Professional(s); 9 Technical(s)
Devon King, Library Branch Supervisor
kingd@camosun.bc.ca
250-370-4531
Sheila Howard, Librarian
howard@camosun.bc.ca
250-370-4533

Victoria: **Interurban Campus Library**
Campus Centre
4461 Interurban Rd., 3rd Fl.
Victoria, BC V9E 2C1
250-370-3828
Fax: 250-370-4640
Other contact info: Information desk/Research assistance: 250-370-4630
e-mail: library@camosun.bc.ca
ill@camosun.bc.ca
URL: www.camosun.bc.ca/library/
Hours: M-W 8:00-8:00; Th 8:00-6:00; F 8:00-4:00
Note: Library hours are subject to change in spring and summer sessions.
Services:
Inter-Library Loan (ILL)

Library research classes
Microform Equipment: Reader
Personnel: *Summary:* 5 Total; 1 Professional(s); 1 Technical(s); 3 Other employees

Victoria: Lester B. Pearson College of the Pacific Norman McKee Lang Library
650 Pearson College Dr.
Victoria, BC V9C 4H7
250-391-2411
Fax: 250-391-2412
e-mail: scrowther@pearsoncollege.ca
URL: www.pearsoncollege.ca
National Library Symbol: BVILBP
Consortia Membership: British Columbia Electronic Network (BC ELN)
Founded in: 1974
Hours: M-Su 8:00am-11:00pm by appointment only
Acquisitions Budget: $25,000 - $49,999
Note: Services made available to the public by special arrangement
Special Collections: Collection of personal books of Lester B. Pearson, donated by his family; videotape collection of lectures of Dr. Giovanni Costigan; Race Rocks Collection
Services:
Internet Access
Inter-Library Loan (ILL)
Personnel: *Summary:* 18 Total; 1 Professional(s); 1 Technical(s); 16 Other employees
Sherry Crowther, Librarian
scrowther@pearsoncollege.ca
Lori Sugden, Map Curator
lsugden@uvic.ca
250-721-7356

Victoria: Map Library
McPherson Library, PO Box 1800, Stn CSC
Victoria, BC V8W 3H5
Mailing Address: PO Box 1800, Stn CSC
Victoria, BC V8W 3H5
250-721-7356
Fax: 250-721-8235
e-mail: maps@uvic.ca
URL: dirserv.uvic.ca
National Library Symbol: BVIV
Hours: Winter: M-Th 9:00-9:00; F 9:00-5:00; Sa, Su 1:00-5:00. Summer: M-F 9:00-5:00
Acquisitions Budget: $25,000 - $49,999
Special Collections: Maps & Air Photos of Southern Vancouver Island
Subjects covered: Maps, Air Photos, Geography, Earth Sciences
Services:
Remote Access
Internet Access
Microform Equipment: Reader
Personnel: *Summary:* 1 Total; 2 Technical(s)
Alice Solyma, Head, Library Services
asolyma@pfc.cfs.nrcan.gc.ca
250-363-0680

Victoria: Pacific Forestry Centre Library
506 West Burnside Rd.
Victoria, BC V8Z 1M5
250-363-0600
Fax: 250-363-0775
e-mail: webmaster@pfc.cfs.nrcan.gc.ca
interlibraryloans@pfc.forestry.ca
URL: cfs.nrcan.gc.ca/regions/pfc
National Library Symbol: BVIF
Founded in: 1960
Hours: M-F 9:00-4:00 by appointment only
Note: Member of Council of Canadian Forest Services Network
Special Collections: Depository for all Canadian Forestry Service publications, selection of other foreign forestry publications; Entomological Society of British Columbia Library Collection
Subjects covered: Natural Resources, Conservation, Environment, Forest Entomology, Plant Pathology, Silviculture, Forest Research, Remote Sensing
Services:
Inter-Library Loan (ILL)
Personnel: *Summary:* 2 Total; 1 Professional(s); 1 Technical(s); 2 Volunteer(s)

Victoria: Royal Roads University Library
2005 Sooke Rd.
Victoria, BC V9B 5Y2
250-391-2575
Fax: 250-391-2594
e-mail: rrulibrary@royalroads.ca
rruill@royalroads.ca
URL: www.royalroads.ca
National Library Symbol: BRC
Consortia Membership: British Columbia Electronic Network (BC ELN); Canadian Research Knowledge Network (CRKN); Council of Prairie and Pacific University Libraries (COPPUL)
Founded in: 1995
Hours: M-Th 8:30am-10:00pm; F 8:30-6:00; Sa 10:00-6:00; Su 10:00-8:00
Acquisitions Budget: $250,000 - $499,999
Note: Member of ELN; COPPUL.
Subjects covered: Environment, Business, Management, Leadership, Conflict Analysis
Services:
Internet Access
Inter-Library Loan (ILL) for a fee
Information literacy instruction, Reference, Reserve
Microform Equipment: Computer; Reader
Personnel: *Summary:* 13 Total; 5 Professional(s); 4 Technical(s); 4 Other employees;
Dana McFarland, University Librarian
dana.mcfarland@royalroads.ca
250-391-2575
Naomi Eichenlaub, Librarian, Technical Services

Victoria: Thurber Group Library
#100, 436 West Saanich Rd.
Victoria, BC V8Z 3E9
250-727-2201
Fax: 250-727-3710
e-mail: rormerod@thurber.ca
URL: www.thurber.ca
National Library Symbol: BVIT
No public access
Hours: M-F
Acquisitions Budget: 0-$9,999
For Print: 0-$9,999
For Electronic: 0-$9,999
Population Served: 120
Special Collections: Aerial Photographs, Maps, Standards & Test Procedures
Subjects covered: Physical Sciences, Maps, Geology, Geotechnical & Environmental Engineering
Services:
Internet Access
Inter-Library Loan (ILL)
Fee Based Research
Personnel: *Summary:* 1 Technical(s)
Rose Mary Ormerod, Library Head

Victoria: University of Victoria Libraries
University Librarian's Office
PO Box 1800
Victoria, BC V8W 3H5
250-721-8211
Fax: 250-721-8215
URL: gateway.uvic.ca
National Library Symbol: CABVIV
Consortia Membership: British Columbia Electronic Network (BC ELN); Canadian Research Knowledge Network (CRKN); Council of Prairie and Pacific University Libraries (COPPUL)
Founded in: 1963
Acquisitions Budget: For Print: $1,000,000 plus
For Electronic: $1,000,000 plus
Population Served: 30000
Services:
Internet Access
Inter-Library Loan (ILL)
Microform Equipment: Computer; Reader
Personnel: *Summary:* 141 Total; 41 Professional(s); 64 Technical(s); 36 Other employees
Marnie Swanson, University Librarian
mswanson@uvic.ca
250-721-8211
Joanne Henning, Associate University Librarian, Reference & Collections
jhenning@uvic.ca
250-721-8268

Ken Cooley, Associate University Librarian, IT & Technical Services
kcooley@uvic.ca
250-721-6088
Neil Campbell, Associate University Librarian, Law
saquila@uvic.ca
250-721-8238
Shailoo Bedi, Head, Access Services
sbedi@uvic.ca
250-721-8226

Victoria: University of Victoria School of Health Information Science Library
#A202, Human & Social Development Bldg.,
University of Victoria
Victoria, BC V8W 3P5
Mailing Address: PO Box 3050, Stn CSC
Victoria, BC V8W 3P5
250-721-8575
Fax: 250-472-4751
e-mail: his@uvic.ca
URL: hinf.uvic.ca
Hours: M-F 8:30-4:30
Services:
Personnel:
Leslie Wood, Department Secretary
lwood@uvic.ca
250-721-8576
Elizabeth Rennie, Williams Lake Campus Librarian
erennie@tru.ca
250-392-8031

Williams Lake: Williams Lake Campus Library
1250 Western Ave.
Williams Lake, BC V2G 1J6
250-392-8030
Fax: 250-392-8032
National Library Symbol: BWLCC
Services:
Personnel:

Manitoba

Brandon: Assiniboine Community College Library
1430 Victoria Ave. East
Brandon, MB R7A 2A9
204-725-8727
Fax: 204-725-8740
800-862-6307
e-mail: library@assiniboine.net
URL: public.assiniboine.net
National Library Symbol: MBAC
Consortia Membership: Manitoba Library Consortium Inc.
Founded in: 1965
Hours: M-Th 8:00-9:00; F 8:00-4:30; Sa 12:00-4:00
Acquisitions Budget: $50,000 - $99,999
Note: Students & Alumni have access to internet, general public does not
Subjects covered: Trades, Business, Agriculture, Nursing, Technology
Services:
Remote Access
Internet Access
Inter-Library Loan (ILL)
Microform Equipment: Reader
Personnel: *Summary:* 7 Total; 1 Professional(s); 2 Technical(s); 4 Other employees
Sandra Armstrong, Librarian
armstrong@assiniboine.net
204-725-8700 ext. 6635

Brandon: Brandon Regional Health Centre Health Resource Centre
150 McTavish Ave. East
Brandon, MB R7A 2B3
204-578-4080
Fax: 204-578-4984
e-mail: brhalib@brandonrha.mb.ca
library@brandonrha.mb.ca
URL: www.brandonrha.mb.ca/en/Health_Resource_Centre/
National Library Symbol: MBGH
Founded in: 1950
Hours: M-F 8:00-4:30

Libraries & Resource Centres / Manitoba

Acquisitions Budget: $50,000 - $99,999
Note: Member of Manitoba Health Libraries Association
Subjects covered: Medical, Nursing, Allied Health, Consumer Health, Hospital Administration
Services:
Internet Access
Access to Subscription Databases
Inter-Library Loan (ILL)
Personnel: *Summary:* 4 Total; 2 Technical(s); 2 Other employees
Wendy Wareham, Coordinator, Health Resource Centre
brhalib@brandonrha.mb.ca
204-578-4080
Carol Enns, Librarian
cenns@agr.gc.ca

Brandon: Brandon Research Centre Library & Information Centre

RR#3
Brandon, MB R7A 5Y3
Mailing Address: PO Box 1000A
Brandon, MB R7A 5Y3
204-726-7650 ext: 247
Fax: 204-728-3858
e-mail: cenns@agr.gc.ca
National Library Symbol: MBAG
Founded in: 1884
Hours: M-F 8:00-4:30
Special Collections: Station Scientists Reprints
Subjects covered: Land Resource Management, Beef Cattle Production & Barley Breeding
Services:
Inter-Library Loan (ILL) for a fee
Personnel: *Summary:* 2 Total; 1 Professional(s); 1 Technical(s)

Brandon: Brandon University John E. Robbins Library

270 - 18th St.
Brandon, MB R7A 6A9
204-727-9646
Fax: 204-726-1072
e-mail: interlend@brandonu.ca
URL: www.brandonu.ca/library
National Library Symbol: MBC
Consortia Membership: Canadian Research Knowledge Network (CRKN); Council of Prairie and Pacific University Libraries (COPPUL); Manitoba Library Consortium Inc.
Founded in: 1899
Hours: M-Th 8:30am-10:00pm; F 8:30-5:00; Sa 1:00-6:00; Su 1:00-8:00
Acquisitions Budget: $500,000 - $999,999
For Print: $500,000 - $999,999
For Electronic: $100,000 - $249,999
Note: University Archives is part of the library. Archives Fax: 204-726-1072
Special Collections: Great Plains Collection; 20th Century Literature by Native North American Authors; Music Scores, Audiotapes, CDs, Videos; Historical Collection of Jazz Recordings; Manitoba Pool Elevators Collection; Photo Collection of the Manitoba Provincial Exhibition (Royal Winter Fair); Brandon Sun Collection
Services:
Internet Access
Inter-Library Loan (ILL) for a fee
Microform Equipment: Computer; Reader
Personnel: *Summary:* 21 Total; 5 Professional(s); 16 Technical(s)
Linda Burridge, University Librarian
Burridge@brandonu.ca
204-727-9688
Rainer Schira, Reference Librarian
Schirar@brandonu.ca
204-727-7463
Tom Mitchell, Archivist
archives@brandonu.ca
204-727-9634
Chris Hurst, Head, Systems
hurst@brandonu.ca
204-727-9687
Carmen Kazakoff-Lane, Contact, ILL/OCLS
kazakoff@brandonu.ca
204-727-7483

Churchill: Churchill Northern Studies Centre Library

PO Box 610
Churchill, MB R0B 0E0
204-675-2307
Fax: 204-675-2139
e-mail: cnsc@churchillscience.ca
URL: www.churchillscience.ca
Founded in: 1976
Hours: M-F 9:00-5:00 by appointment only
Acquisitions Budget: $25,000 - $49,999
Subjects covered: Native Peoples & Northern Affairs, Physical Sciences, Maps
Services:
Internet Access
Personnel:
Michael Goodyear, Executive Director

Hamiota: Hamiota District Health Centre Library

177 Birch Ave. East
Hamiota, MB R0M 0T0
204-764-2412 ext: 327
Fax: 204-764-2049
Founded in: 1974
Hours: M-Su
Acquisitions Budget: $25,000 - $49,999
Subjects covered: Medical, Nursing, Allied Consumer Health
Services:
Inter-Library Loan (ILL)
Personnel: *Summary:* 1 Professional(s)
Jean Furgason, Library Clerk

The Pas: University College of the North Library

436 - 7th St. East
The Pas, MB R9A 1M7
Mailing Address: PO Box 3000
The Pas, MB R9A 1M7
204-627-8561
Fax: 204-623-4597
e-mail: library@ucn.ca
URL: www.keewatincc.mb.ca
National Library Symbol: MTPK
Consortia Membership: Manitoba Library Consortium Inc.
Founded in: 1966
Hours: M-Th 8:00am-9:00pm; F 8:00-4:00; Sun 1:00-5:00
Acquisitions Budget: $50,000 - $99,999
Note: The library is an affiliate member of the Council of Prairie and Pacific University Libraries (COPPUL).
Special Collections: Books, periodicals & newspapers, government publications, pamphlets, films, videotapes, audiotapes, kits, slides, filmstrips, microfilm, microfiche, microcomputer software, technical reports
Subjects covered: Education, Nursing, Natural Resources, Technology, Economics, Social Affairs, Dental Assistant, Trades, Psychology, Business, Child Care, Native Studies
Services:
Inter-Library Loan (ILL)
Microform Equipment: Computer; Reader
Personnel: *Summary:* 4 Total; 1 Professional(s); 3 Technical(s)
David Young, Librarian
dmyoung@ucn.ca
204-627-8604
Laura Afatsawo, Library Technician
lafatsawo@ucn.ca
Sharyl Latta, Library Techinician
slatta@ucn.ca

Portage la Prairie: Food Development Centre Library

810 Phillips St.
Portage la Prairie, MB R1N 3J9
Mailing Address: PO Box 1240
Portage la Prairie, MB R1N 3J9
204-239-3465
Fax: 204-239-3180
800-870-1044
URL: www.gov.mb.ca/agriculture/fdc/services/library/fdc10s00.html
National Library Symbol: MPCFP
Founded in: 1978
Hours: M-F 8:30-4:30 by appointment only
Acquisitions Budget: $25,000 - $49,999
For Print: $25,000 - $49,999
Population Served: 1000000
Note: Special operating agency of Manitoba Agriculture, Food & Rural Initiatives
Subjects covered: Agriculture, Food Science, Analytical Chemistry, Food Microbiology, Food Product Development, HACCP, Nutritional Information, Canadian & American Food Legislation, Nutraceuticals & Functional Foods, Economic Development, Government Information
Services:
Internet Access
Inter-Library Loan (ILL) for a fee of $5
Fee Based Research
Personnel: *Summary:* 1 Total; 1 Technical(s)

Steinbach: Red River Apiarists' Association Library

PO Box 1448
Steinbach, MB R0A 2A0
204-326-3763
e-mail: manbeekr@mts.net
No public access
Founded in: 1963
Subjects covered: Honey Production, Entomology (Bees), Pollination
Services:
Personnel:
Ron Rudiak, Secretary

Stonewall: Ducks Unlimited Canada Library

1 Mallard Bay, Hwy. 220
Stonewall, MB R0C 2Z0
Mailing Address: PO Box 1160
Stonewall, MB R0C 2Z0
204-467-3276
Fax: 204-467-9028
e-mail: i_glass@ducks.ca
URL: www.ducks.ca/conserve/research/library/index.html
National Library Symbol: MWDU
Founded in: 1998
Hours: M-F 8:30-4:30, by appointment only by appointment only
Acquisitions Budget: 0-$9,999
For Print: 0-$9,999
For Electronic: 0-$9,999
Subjects covered: Wetland Ecology & Management, Land Use, Environment, Waterfowl Ecology
Services:
Inter-Library Loan (ILL)
Personnel: *Summary:* 1 Total; 1 Professional(s)
Ian Glass, Librarian
Mary Lochhead, Head Librarian
mary_lochhead@umanitoba.ca
204-474-9217
Liv Valmstead, Reference Librarian
liv_valmstead@umanitoba.ca
204-474-8447

Winnipeg: Architecture & Fine Arts Library

#206, Russell Bldg.
Winnipeg, MB R3T 2N2
204-474-9216
Fax: 204-474-7539
URL: www.umanitoba.ca/libraries/units/archfa/
Profile: Supporting the research & teaching needs of the Faculty of Architecture, the Library contains the largest collection of resources on art, design & planning in Manitoba
National Library Symbol: MWUAF
Founded in: 1916
Hours: M-F 8:30-4:30
Acquisitions Budget: $50,000 - $99,999
Special Collections: Monographs, serials, videos & DVDs, CDROMs; Slide Collection; Architectural Drawings; Maps; Building File; Vertical Files
Subjects covered: Fine Arts, Architecture, City Planning, Interior Design, Landscape Architecture
Services:
Remote Access
Internet Access
Access to Subscription Databases
Inter-Library Loan (ILL)
Personnel: *Summary:* 9 Total; 2 Professional(s); 7 Technical(s)

Winnipeg: Canadian Grain Commission / Commission canadienne des grains Library

#600, 303 Main St.
Winnipeg, MB R3C 3G8

204-983-0878
Fax: 204-983-6098
e-mail: library@grainscanada.gc.ca
URL: www.grainscanada.gc.ca
National Library Symbol: MWGR
Founded in: 1913
Hours: M-F 8:00-4:30 by appointment only
Acquisitions Budget: $50,000 - $99,999
For Print: $50,000 - $99,999
For Electronic: $10,000 - $24,999
Special Collections: Canadian International Grains Institute: Lecture series 1973-2002.
Subjects covered: Grain Handling & Transportation; Grain Quality; Cereal Science; Oilseed Science
Services:
Internet Access
Inter-Library Loan (ILL) for a fee of Federal libraries: Free. Other libraries: $10/articles; $15/books
Personnel: *Summary:* 2 Total; 1 Professional(s); 1 Technical(s)
Dawn Bassett, Librarian
204-983-0878
Christine Wallmann, Library Technician
cwallmann@grainscanada.gc.ca
204-984-6336

Winnipeg: **Canadian Wheat Board / Commission canadienne du blé**
Library
423 Main St.
Winnipeg, MB R3C 2P5
Mailing Address: PO Box 816, Stn Main
Winnipeg, MB R3C 2P5
204-983-0239
Fax: 204-983-3841
800-275-4292
e-mail: library@cwb.ca
questions@cwb.ca
URL: www.cwb.ca
National Library Symbol: MWCWB
Founded in: 1973
Hours: M-F 8:30-4:15
Subjects covered: Grain Trade
Services:
Inter-Library Loan (ILL) for a fee of may apply
Personnel: *Summary:* 1 Professional(s); 2 Technical(s)

Winnipeg: **Collège universitaire de St-Boniface Bibliothèque Alfred-Monnin**
200, av de la Cathédrale
Winnipeg, MB R2H 0H7
204-235-4403
Téléc: 204-233-9472
Courriel: biblio@ustboniface.mb.ca
URL: www.ustboniface.mb.ca/cusb/biblio/
Sigle: MSC
Membre d'un consortium: Manitoba Library Consortium Inc.
Fondée en: 1818
Heures: L-J 8h-21h30; V 8h-16h30; S 10h-17h; D 13h-17h avec rendez-vous seulement
Budget d'acquisitions: $100,000 - $249,999
Population desservie: 1500
Collections spécialisées: Maurice Constantin-Weyer, études canadiennes, études féminines, histoire des francophones de l'Ouest, auteurs francophones de l'Ouest
Sujets: Administration, anglais, allemand, anthropologie, biologie, chimie, comptabilité, économie, éducation, espagnol, français, géographie, histoire, informatique, marketing, mathématiques, philosophie, physique, politique, psychologie, religion, sociologie, soins de santé, statistiques, traduction
Services:
Accès public à l'internet
Prêts entre bibliothèques(PEB) frais
Lecteur/reproduction de microformes: Ordinateur; Lecteurs
Personnel: *Sommaire:* 12 Total; 2 Professionnel(s); 3 Technicien(s); 7 Autre(s) employé(s)
Marcel Boulet, Directeur
mboulet@ustboniface.mb.ca
204-233-0210 ext. 331
Daniel Beaulieu, Bibliothécaire de référence
dbeaulie@ustboniface.mb.ca
204-233-0210 ext. 308
Carole Pelchat, Archiviste, Gestionnaire de documents
cbarnabe@ustboniface.mb.ca
204-237-1818 ext. 398

Alice Gilbert-Collet, Bibliotechnicienne, Acquisitions
acollet@ustboniface.mb.ca
204-237-1818 ext. 362
Diane Johnson, Bibliotechnicienne, Traitement, catalogage, sys. info.
djohnson@ustboniface.mb.ca
204-237-1818 ext. 340
Brigitte L'Heureux, Bibliotechnicienne, Référence et service du prêt
blheureu@ustboniface.mb.ca
204-237-1818 ext. 213
Joanne Pelletier, Bibliotechnicienne, Service du prêt entre bibliothèques
jpelletier@ustboniface.mb.ca
204-237-1818 ext. 213
Thérèse Tinguely, Aide-bibliothécaire
ttinguel@ustboniface.mb.ca
204-235-4403

Winnipeg: **Concordia Hospital**
Library
1095 Concordia Ave.
Winnipeg, MB R2K 3S8
204-661-7163
Fax: 204-661-7282
e-mail: chlibrary@umanitoba.ca
URL: www.umanitoba.ca/libraries/health/concordia
National Library Symbol: MWCH
Founded in: 1975
Hours: M-F 8:30-4:30
Note: A branch of the University of Manitoba Neil John Maclean Health Sciences library
Subjects covered: Medicine, Nursing, Allied Health, Patient Care
Services:
Personnel: *Summary:* 2 Total; 1 Professional(s); 1 Technical(s)
Melissa Raynard, Hospital Librarian
melissa_raynard@umanitoba.ca
Joan Backer, Librarian
902-426-9278

Winnipeg: **Conservation & Environment Library**
#160, 123 Main St.
Winnipeg, MB R3C 1A5
204-945-7125
Fax: 204-948-2357
Other contact info: 204-945-7126
e-mail: shelley.penziwol.ec.gc.ca
URL: www.ec.gc.ca/library
National Library Symbol: MWECW
MWEEP
MWEAE
Hours: M-F 8:00-4:30
Special Collections: Climatology, Weather Services
Subjects covered: Climatology, Weather Services
Services:
Personnel: *Summary:* 2 Total; 2 Professional(s)
Norma Godavari, Head
norma_godavari@umanitoba.ca
204-474-9445

Winnipeg: **Donald W. Craik Engineering Library**
#351 Engineering Bldg.
Winnipeg, MB R3T 2N2
204-474-6360
Fax: 204-474-7520
URL: www.umanitoba.ca/libraries/units/engineering
Hours: M-F 8:30-4:30
Subjects covered: Physical Sciences, Engineering, Technology
Services:
Inter-Library Loan (ILL)
Microform Equipment: Computer; Reader
Personnel: *Summary:* 7 Total; 2 Professional(s); 4 Technical(s); 1 Other employees
John Eaton, Head Librarian
john_eaton@umanitoba.ca
204-474-9996
Muriel St. John, Reference Librarian
muriel_stjohn@umanitoba.ca
204-474-6372
Ariana Sirko, Technical Services Librarian
ariana_sirko@umanitoba.ca
204-474-6371

Winnipeg: **E.K. Williams Law Library**
#401, Robson Hall, 224 Dysart Rd.
Winnipeg, MB R3T 2N2

204-474-9995
Fax: 204-474-7582
e-mail: lawill@cc.umanitoba.ca
URL: www.umanitoba.ca/libraries/units/law/
National Library Symbol: MWUL
Founded in: 1922
Hours: M-Th 8:30-10:00; F 8:30-6:00; Sa, Su 1:00-5:00
Acquisitions Budget: $100,000 - $249,999
Special Collections: Aboriginal Justice, International Trade, Manitoba Legislation
Subjects covered: Law
Services:
Inter-Library Loan (ILL)
Microform Equipment: Computer; Reader
Personnel: *Summary:* 11 Total; 3 Professional(s); 8 Technical(s)
Nicole Michaud-Oystryk, Head
nicole_michaud-oystryk@umanitoba.ca
204-474-9211
Jim Blanchard, Head, Reference Service
blanchd@ms.umanitoba.ca
204-474-6846

Winnipeg: **Elizabeth Dafoe Library**
University of Manitoba, 25 Chancellors Circle
Winnipeg, MB R3T 2N2
204-474-9544
Fax: 792-174-7577
e-mail: daref@umanitoba.ca
URL: umanitoba.ca/libraries/units/dafoe/
National Library Symbol: MWU
Founded in: 1876
Hours: M-Su
Acquisitions Budget: $500,000 - $999,999
For Print: $500,000 - $999,999
Special Collections: Icelandic Collection, Slavic Collection, Archives & Special Collections
Subjects covered: Arts, Humanities, Culture, Nursing, Social Work, Human Ecology, Social Sciences, Education, Physical Education, Recreation Studies, Environment
Services:
Internet Access
Inter-Library Loan (ILL)
Microform Equipment: Computer; Reader
Personnel: *Summary:* 38 Total; 13 Professional(s); 25 Technical(s);
Elva Simundsson, Regional Librarian
simundssone@dfo-mpo.gc.ca
204-983-5170

Winnipeg: **Eric Marshall Aquatic Research Library (Central and Artic Library)**
Regional Library
501 University Cres.
Winnipeg, MB R3T 2N6
204-983-5170
Fax: 204-984-4668
e-mail: library-fwi@dfo-mpo.gc.ca
URL: www.dfo-mpo.gc.ca
National Library Symbol: MWFW
Founded in: 1966
Hours: M-F 8:30-4:00
Acquisitions Budget: $100,000 - $249,999
Special Collections: Fritsch collection of Freshwater Algae illustrations; Arctic Petroleum Operators Association reports
Subjects covered: Fisheries; Arctic marine studies; Environmental protection
Services:
Internet Access
Inter-Library Loan (ILL)
Microform Equipment: Computer; Reader
Personnel: *Summary:* 3 Total; 1 Professional(s); 1 Technical(s); 1 Other employees

Winnipeg: **Industrial Technology Centre Library & Technical Information**
#200, 78 Innovation Dr.
Winnipeg, MB R3T 6C2
204-480-0336
Fax: 204-480-0345
e-mail: library@itc.mb.ca
URL: www.itc.mb.ca
National Library Symbol: MWMRC
Consortia Membership: Manitoba Library Consortium Inc.
Founded in: 1981
Hours: M-F 8:30-4:30

Libraries & Resource Centres / Manitoba

Subjects covered: Engineering, Technology, Industry, Manufacturing, Industry Standards
Services:
Internet Access
Inter-Library Loan (ILL) for a fee of reciprocal
Fee Based Research
Personnel: *Summary:* 1 Total; 1 Professional(s)
Betty Dearth, Librarian
bdearth@itc.mb.ca
Michael Dudley, Research Associate
m.dudley@uwinnipeg.ca
204-982-1145

Winnipeg: **Institute of Urban Studies**
Library
#103, 520 Portage Ave.
Winnipeg, MB R3C 0G2
204-982-1145
Fax: 204-943-4695
e-mail: ius@uwinnipeg.ca
URL: ius.uwinnipeg.ca/library
Founded in: 1985
Hours: M-F 8:30-4:30
Acquisitions Budget: $25,000 - $49,999
Note: Loans to students, faculty & alumni of the Universities of Winnipeg & Manitoba, Red River College & Canadian Mennonite University
Special Collections: Winnipeg Core Area Initiative Partial Collection, Children & Youth in the Urban Environment, City of Winnipeg ACT Review
Subjects covered: Housing, Urban Ecology, Architecture, Urban Geography, Urban Sociology, Native Peoples, Public Administration, Urban History, Sustainable Development, Revitalization, Community Development, Urban Planning
Services:
Remote Access
Inter-Library Loan (ILL)
Personnel:

Winnipeg: **International Institute for Sustainable Development / Institut international du développement durable**
Library
161 Portage Ave. East, 6th Fl.
Winnipeg, MB R3B 0Y4
204-958-7724
Fax: 204-958-7710
e-mail: mroy@iisd.ca
smatwick@iisd.ca
URL: www.iisd.org
Founded in: 1993
Hours: M-F 8:30-4:30 by appointment only
Acquisitions Budget: $50,000 - $99,999
Subjects covered: Journals; Monographs; Documents relating to sustainable development, trade, UN negotiations, sustainable livelihoods, ecological economics, Agenda 21, environmental policy, agriculture, climate change
Services:
Remote Access
Internet Access
Personnel: *Summary:* 2 Total; 1 Professional(s); 1 Technical(s)
Marlene Roy, Information Resources Coordinator
mroy@iisd.ca

Winnipeg: **Manitoba Dept. of Conservation, Environment Canada & Canadian Council of Ministers of the Environment**
Conservation & Environment Library
#160, 123 Main St.
Winnipeg, MB R3C 1A5
204-945-7126
Fax: 204-948-2357
e-mail: wendy.barber@gov.mb.ca
wendy.barber@ec.gc.ca
URL: www.gov.mb.ca/conservation/library
National Library Symbol: MWEM
Consortia Membership: Manitoba Library Consortium Inc.
Founded in: 1972
Hours: M-F 8:00-4:00
Acquisitions Budget: $25,000 - $49,999
For Print: $25,000 - $49,999
For Electronic: 0-$9,999
Special Collections: Manitoba Environment Public Registry Files
Subjects covered: Air & Water Quality, Environmental Law & Legislation, Environmental Engineering, Pollution Prevention, Wildlife Management, Climatology, Meteorology, Hydrology, Fisheries, Forestry, Energy
Services:
Remote Access
Internet Access
Inter-Library Loan (ILL)
Personnel: *Summary:* 3 Total; 1 Professional(s); 2 Technical(s)
Wendy Barber, Coordinator, Library Services
Marvyl Ginter, Library Technician
marvyl.ginter@gov.mb.ca
204-945-7125

Winnipeg: **Manitoba Dept. of Science, Technology, Energy & Mines**
Mineral Resources Library
#360, 1395 Ellice Ave.
Winnipeg, MB R3G 3P2
204-945-6569
Fax: 204-945-8427
800-223-5215
e-mail: minesinfo@gov.mb.ca
URL: www.gov.mb.ca/stem/mrd/info/library/index.html
National Library Symbol: MWEMM
Consortia Membership: Manitoba Library Consortium Inc.
Founded in: 1975
Hours: M-F 8:30-4:30
Acquisitions Budget: For Print: 0-$9,999
For Electronic: 0-$9,999
Note: Resources may be used in-house, or through another library via interlibrary loan
Special Collections: Manitoba Geological Survey Reports & Maps, Geological Survey of Canada Publications; Government Publications, Journals, Video/Audio
Subjects covered: Geology, Mining, Petroleum
Services:
Remote Access
Internet Access
Inter-Library Loan (ILL)
GEOREF, Canadian MineSCAN and access to other databases; fact sheets; Bibliography of Rockhounding; photocopying
Personnel: *Summary:* 2 Total; 1 Professional(s); 1 Technical(s)
Lori Janower, Library Services Coordinator
Lori.Janower@gov.mb.ca

Winnipeg: **Manitoba Eco-Network Inc. / Réseau écologique du Manitoba**
Alice Chambers Memorial Library
#3, 303 Portage Ave.
Winnipeg, MB R3B 1E7
204-947-6511
Fax: 204-989-8476
e-mail: library@mbeconetwork.org
URL: www.mbeconetwork.org/library.asp
Hours: M-F 9:00-4:00
Acquisitions Budget: 0-$9,999
For Print: 0-$9,999
For Electronic: 0-$9,999
Special Collections: Public Registry items.
Subjects covered: Environment, Sustainable Development, Climate Change.
Services:
Inter-Library Loan (ILL) for a fee of at cost for non-members
Personnel: *Summary:* 1 Professional(s)
Tara Kenny, Library Technician

Winnipeg: **Manitoba Hydro**
Library
360 Portage Ave.
Winnipeg, MB R3C 2P4
Mailing Address: PO Box 815
Winnipeg, MB R3C 2P4
204-474-3614
Fax: 204-453-1838
e-mail: rlapierre@hydro.mb.ca
docdel@hydro.mb.ca
URL: www.hydro.mb.ca
National Library Symbol: MWH
Hours: M-F 8:00-4:30 by appointment only
Acquisitions Budget: $250,000 - $499,999
Subjects covered: Engineering, Electrical, Public Utilities
Services:
Inter-Library Loan (ILL)
Personnel: *Summary:* 6 Total; 2 Professional(s); 4 Technical(s)
Rhona Lapierre, Corporate Librarian
rlapierre@hydro.mb.ca
Angie Vaccaro, Reference Librarian
avaccaro@hydro.mb.ca
204-360-3945
Paulette Mazur, Cataloguing Technician
pmazur@hydro.mb.ca
204-474-3019

Winnipeg: **Manitoba Museum**
Library & Archives
190 Rupert Ave.
Winnipeg, MB R3B 0N2
204-988-0662
Fax: 204-942-3679
e-mail: csteffan@manitobamuseum.ca
URL: www.manitobamuseum.ca
National Library Symbol: MWMM
Consortia Membership: Manitoba Library Consortium Inc.
Founded in: 1970
Hours: M-F 8:30-4:30 by appointment only
Acquisitions Budget: $25,000 - $49,999
Special Collections: Oral history tapes collection
Subjects covered: Canadian, Natural, Human History, Physical Science, Ethnology, Applied Art, Astronomy, Museology
Services:
Inter-Library Loan (ILL)
Microform Equipment: Reader
Personnel: *Summary:* 2 Total; 1 Professional(s)
Patricia Henry, Library Technician

Winnipeg: **Manitoba Naturalists Society**
Library
#401, 63 Albert St.
Winnipeg, MB R3B 1G4
204-943-9029
Fax: 204-943-9029
e-mail: mns1@mts.net
URL: www.manitobanature.ca
Subjects covered: Wildlife, Environment, Natural History, Conservation
Services:
Personnel:
Susan Bellhouse, Office Administrator
Jenny Gates, Editor, The Bulletin

Winnipeg: **MFL Occupational Health Centre**
Library
#102, 275 Broadway
Winnipeg, MB R3C 4M6
204-949-0811
Fax: 204-956-0848
888-843-1229
e-mail: mflohc@mflohc.mb.ca
URL:
www.mflohc.mb.ca/mflohc_folder/information_&_resources.html
National Library Symbol: MWMFL
Founded in: 1983
Hours: M-F 9:00-5:00
Note: Internat access to OPAC. Library holdings are for use on site only. Library does not lend out.
Special Collections: Niosh
Subjects covered: Occupational Health, Labour, Social Affairs
Services:
Internet Access
Inter-Library Loan (ILL)
Personnel: *Summary:* 1 Total; 1 Technical(s)
Tiffany Pau, Library Coordinator
204-949-7909

Winnipeg: **Misericordia Health Centre**
Library
99 Cornish Ave.
Winnipeg, MB R3C 1A2
204-788-8109
Fax: 204-889-4174
888-315-9257
e-mail: library@miseri.winnipeg.mb.ca
mhclibrary@umanitoba.ca
URL: www.misericordia.mb.ca
umanitoba.ca/libraries/units/health/misericordia/
National Library Symbol: MWMG
Founded in: 1974
Hours: M-F 8:30-4:30
Acquisitions Budget: $25,000 - $49,999
Subjects covered: Medicine, Nursing, Health Sciences, Opthamology

Services:
Access to Subscription Databases
Inter-Library Loan (ILL)
Personnel: *Summary:* 1 Professional(s); 2 Volunteer(s)
Kathy Scheiffert, Library Technician

Winnipeg: National Energy Conservation Association Library
PO Box 2747, Stn Main
Winnipeg, MB R3C 4E7
204-956-5888
Fax: 204-956-5819
866-268-6322
e-mail: neca@neca.ca
URL: www.neca.ca
Subjects covered: Energy Conservation, Construction, Quality Assurance
Services:
Personnel:
Ryan Dalgleish, Manager
Laverne Dalgleish, CEO
Ada Ducas, Head Librarian
ada_ducas@umanitoba.ca
204-789-3821

Winnipeg: Neil John Maclean Health Sciences Library
727 McDermot Ave.
Winnipeg, MB R3E 0W3
Mailing Address: 770 Bannatyne Ave.
Winnipeg, MB R3E 0W3
204-789-3464
Fax: 204-789-3923
e-mail: njm_ref@umanitoba.ca
URL: www.umanitoba.ca/libraries/health
National Library Symbol: MWM
Founded in: 1928
Hours: M-F 8:00am-11:00pm; Sa 9:00am-11:00pm; Su 10:00-9:00. Reference Services: M-Th 9:00-9:00; Sa 9:00-5:00; Su 1:00-5:00. Reference hours may vary.
Acquisitions Budget: $500,000 - $999,999
Note: The Medical Library, Neilson Dental Library & Health Sciences Centre Library merged to form the Neil John Maclean Health Sciences Library
Special Collections: History of Medicine, Aboriginal Health, Archives of the Faculty of Medicine
Subjects covered: Medical Instruction, Consumer Health Information, Outreach, Aboriginal Health, Nursing, Allied Health, Dentistry, Dental Hygiene, Medical Rehabilitation, Hospital Administration, Medicine
Services:
Internet Access
Access to Subscription Databases
Inter-Library Loan (ILL)
e-journal Access
Personnel: *Summary:* 31 Total; 11 Professional(s); 20 Other employees

Winnipeg: Red River College Library
2055 Notre Dame Ave.
Winnipeg, MB R3H 0J9
204-632-2322
Fax: 204-697-4791
e-mail: library@rrc.mb.ca
URL: www.rrc.mb.ca/library/
National Library Symbol: MWRR
Consortia Membership: Manitoba Library Consortium Inc.
Founded in: 1963
Hours: M-Th 7:45-9:00; F 7:45-4:40; Sa 8:30-4:00
Acquisitions Budget: $250,000 - $499,999
Subjects covered: Business, Health Sciences, Engineering Technologies, Education, Child Care, Hospitality, Multimedia Technology, Graphic Arts
Services:
Remote Access
Internet Access
Access to Subscription Databases
Inter-Library Loan (ILL)
Microform Equipment: Reader
Personnel: *Summary:* 33 Total; 4 Professional(s); 19 Technical(s); 10 Other employees
Patricia Burt, Head Librarian
pburt@rrc.mb.ca
204-632-2882

Norman Beattie, Coordinator, Reference
mbeattie@rrcc.mb.ca
204-632-2470
Martin Beckwith, Coordinator, Technical Services & Systems
mbeckwit@rrc.mb.ca
204-632-2417
Phyllis Barich, Coordinator, Off Campus & Media Services
pbarich@ppc.mb.ca
204-632-3761

Winnipeg: Resource Conservation Manitoba Resource Library
303 Portage Ave., 3rd Fl.
Winnipeg, MB R3B 2B4
204-925-3777
Fax: 204-942-4207
e-mail: rcm@mb.sympatico.ca
info@resourceconservation.mb.ca
URL: www.resourceconservation.mb.ca
Founded in: 1985
Hours: M-F 9:00-5:00
Note: A non-profit, non-governmental environmental education group; Resource library is operated jointly with the Manitoba Eco-Network
Subjects covered: Environment
Services:

Winnipeg: St Boniface General Hospital Carolyn Sifton-Helene Fuld Library/Bibliothèque Carolyn Sifton-Helene Fuld
409 Tache Ave.
Winnipeg, MB R2H 2A6
204-237-2807
Fax: 204-235-3339
e-mail: sbghlibrary@umanitoba.ca
URL: www.umanitoba.ca/libraries/health/sbgh
National Library Symbol: MWSBM
Founded in: 1994
Hours: M-F 8:30-4:30
Acquisitions Budget: $50,000 - $99,999
Note: Satellite operation of the Neil John MacLean Health Sciences Library, University of Manitoba
Subjects covered: Medicine, Nursing
Services:
Inter-Library Loan (ILL)
DOCLINE
Personnel: *Summary:* 26 Total; 1 Professional(s); 3 Technical(s); 1 Volunteer(s)
Mark Rabnett, Hospital Librarian
mark_rabnett@umanitoba.ca
204-237-2808
Judy Harper, Head
judy_harper@umanitoba.ca
204-474-8302

Winnipeg: Sciences & Technology Library
#211, Machray Hall
Winnipeg, MB R3T 2N2
204-474-8171
Fax: 204-474-7627
e-mail: judy_harper@cc.umanitoba.ca
URL: www.umanitoba.ca/libraries/units/science/
Hours: M-Su
Acquisitions Budget: $500,000 - $999,999
Note: Most of the Agriculture & Engineering circulating collections are now located in the Sciences & Technology Library
Subjects covered: Life Sciences, Physical Sciences, Technology, Mathematics, Computer Science, Statistics, Science, Pharmacy, Agriculture, Food Sciences, Engineering
Services:
Inter-Library Loan (ILL)
Personnel: *Summary:* 5 Total; 5 Professional(s)

Winnipeg: Seven Oaks General Hospital Library
2300 McPhillips St.
Winnipeg, MB R2V 3M3
204-632-3124
Fax: 204-694-8240
e-mail: soghlibrarya@umanitoba.ca
National Library Symbol: MWSOGH
Founded in: 1981
Hours: M-F 8:30-4:30
Acquisitions Budget: $25,000 - $49,999
Note: Satellite operation of Neil John MacLean Health Sciences

Library, University of Manitoba
Subjects covered: Health, Nursing, Medicine
Services:
Internet Access
Inter-Library Loan (ILL)
Document Delivery
Personnel: *Summary:* 2 Total; 1 Professional(s); 1 Technical(s)
Analyn Baker, Librarian
204-632-3107
Stefania Zimarino, Library Technician
zimarino@cc.umanitoba.ca
204-632-3124

Winnipeg: Teshmont Consultants LP Library
1190 Waverley St.
Winnipeg, MB R3T 0P4
204-284-8100
Fax: 204-475-4601
866-333-8100
e-mail: teshmont@teshmont.com
URL: www.teshmont.com
Founded in: 1966
Subjects covered: Physical Sciences, Engineering, Technology, EHV-AC & HV-DC Transmission Systems
Services:
Personnel:
Susan Garvin, Librarian

Winnipeg: University of Manitoba Libraries Director's Office
Elizabeth Dafoe Library, University of Manitoba,
#156, 25 Chancellor's Circle
Winnipeg, MB R3T 2N2
204-474-9881
Fax: 204-474-7583
e-mail: illdaf@cc.umanitoba.ca
URL: www.umanitoba.ca/libraries/
National Library Symbol: MWU
Consortia Membership: Canadian Research Knowledge Network (CRKN); Council of Prairie and Pacific University Libraries (COPPUL); Manitoba Library Consortium Inc.
Founded in: 1885
Acquisitions Budget: $1,000,000 plus
For Print: $1,000,000 plus
Services:
Internet Access
Inter-Library Loan (ILL)
Microform Equipment: Computer; Reader
Personnel: *Summary:* 55 Professional(s); 150 Other employees
Karen Adams, Director of Libraries
Donna Breyfogle, Associate Director, Collections
Vacant, Head, Technical Services
Lynne Partington, Head, Bibliographic Control
Pat Nicholls, Head, Systems

Winnipeg: University of Winnipeg Library
515 Portage Ave.
Winnipeg, MB R3B 2E9
204-786-9808
Fax: 204-783-8910
888-393-1830
e-mail: infoedge@uwinnipeg.ca
ill@uwinnipeg.ca
URL: library.uwinnipeg.ca
National Library Symbol: MWUC
Consortia Membership: Canadian Research Knowledge Network (CRKN); Council of Prairie and Pacific University Libraries (COPPUL); Manitoba Library Consortium Inc.
Founded in: 1871
Hours: M-F 8:00am-10:45pm; Sa, Su 11:00-5:45
Acquisitions Budget: $1,000,000 plus
For Print: $500,000 - $999,999
For Electronic: $500,000 - $999,999
Population Served: 6748; Full-time students
Special Collections: University of Winnipeg Archives; United Church Conference of Manitoba & Northwestern Ontario Archives; William Wanka Collection; Drache Law Library; East European Genealogical Society Inc. Collection; Edith & Margaret Graham Picture Book Collection; George H. Reavis Reading Collection
Subjects covered: Liberal Arts
Services:
Remote Access
Internet Access

Access to Subscription Databases
Inter-Library Loan (ILL)
Fee Based Research
Personnel: *Summary:* 55 Total; 8 Professional(s); 33 Technical(s); 4 Other employees
Linda Dietrick, Acting University Librarian
l.dietrick@uwinnipeg.ca
Linwood DeLong, Collections Coordinator
linwood.delong@uwinnipeg.ca
204-786-9124
Christine Hoeppner, Digital Resources & Aquisitions Coordinator
c.hoeppner@uwinnipeg.ca
204-786-9813
Gabrielle Prefontaine, University Archivist/FIPPA Coordinator
g.prefontaine@uwinnipeg.ca
204-786-9914
Pat Duguay, Library Administration/Admin. Assistant
p.duguay@uwinnipeg.ca
204-786-9801

Winnipeg: Victoria General Hospital (Winnipeg) Library
2340 Pembina Hwy.
Winnipeg, MB R3T 2E8
204-477-3307
Fax: 204-269-7936
e-mail: vghlibrary@umanitoba.ca
URL: www.umanitoba.ca/libraries/units/health/vic/index.html
Hours: M-F 9:00-5:00 by appointment only
Services:
Internet Access
Access to Subscription Databases
Inter-Library Loan (ILL) for a fee of $10
Personnel: *Summary:* 1 Professional(s); 1 Technical(s)
Christine Shaw-Daigle, Head of Library
Christine_Shaw-Daigle@umanitoba.ca
204-477-3284
Mora Gregg, Head of Library
mora_gregg@umanitoba.ca
204-474-6334

Winnipeg: William R. Newman Library
#236 Agriculture Bldg., University of Manitoba
Winnipeg, MB R3T 2N2
204-474-8382
Fax: 204-474-7527
e-mail: agrref@ms.umanitoba.ca
URL: umanitoba.ca/libraries/units/agriculture
Founded in: 1997
Hours: M-Th 8:30-6:30; F 8:30-4:30. Summer: M-F 8:30-4:30
Subjects covered: Agriculture
Services:
Remote Access
Internet Access
Personnel: *Summary:* 2 Total; 1 Professional(s); 1 Technical(s)
Mike Malyk, Librarian
mmalyk@agr.gc.ca
Tim Verry, Library Assistant

Winnipeg: Winnipeg Research Centre Library
195 Dafoe Rd.
Winnipeg, MB R3T 2M9
204-983-0721
Fax: 204-983-4604
e-mail: mmalyk@agr.gc.ca
Library-wpg@agr.gc.ca
National Library Symbol: MWAG
Founded in: 1926
Hours: M-F 8:30-5:30 by appointment only
Acquisitions Budget: $25,000 - $49,999
For Print: 0-$9,999
For Electronic: $10,000 - $24,999
Note: Includes Morden Research Centre, Library Morden programs-Flax, Oilseeds, Peas, Beans, Agronomy
Special Collections: Buller Memorial Library Collection
Subjects covered: Agriculture, Grain Breeding, Plant Pathology, Physical Sciences, Chemistry, Stored Products, Entomology, Cereal Biotech, Cereal Quality, Flax, Peas/Beans, Oilseeds, Aronomy
Services:
Inter-Library Loan (ILL)
Personnel: *Summary:* 2 Total; 1 Professional(s); 1 Technical(s);

Winnipeg: Winnipeg Water & Waste Dept. Resource Centre
#109, 1100 Pacific Ave.
Winnipeg, MB R3E 3S8
204-986-5858
Fax: 204-986-6515
URL: www.winnipeg.ca/waterandwaste/library/default.stm
National Library Symbol: MWWW
Founded in: 1985
Hours: M-F 8:30-12:00, 1:00-4:00 by appointment only
Acquisitions Budget: For Print: 0-$9,999
For Electronic: 0-$9,999
Subjects covered: Municipal government utilities, Drinking water, Sewage treatment, Solid waste, Public administration
Services:
Personnel: *Summary:* 3 Total; 3 Technical(s)
Joann da Silva, Library Technician
jdasilva@winnipeg.ca
Glen Ellis, Library Technician
gellis@winnipeg.ca
204-986-4475
Doug Bogaski, Library Service Assistant
dbogaski@winnipeg.ca
204-986-3880

Winnipeg: Yellowquill College Library
340 Assiniboine Ave.
Winnipeg, MB R3C 0Y1
204-953-2800
Fax: 204-953-2810
e-mail: administration@yellowquillcollege.mb.ca
URL: www.yellowquillcollege.mb.ca
Hours: M-F 8:30-4:30
Services:
Personnel:
Mary Fagnan, Contact

New Brunswick

Claude Chiasson, Associate Director
cchiasson@mcft.ca

Bathurst: Bathurst Campus / Campus de Bathurst Library/Bibliothèque
725 College St.
Bathurst, NB E2A 3Z2
Mailing Address: PO Box 266
Bathurst, NB E2A 3Z2
506-546-4176
Fax: 506-546-2829
e-mail: info@mcft.ca
URL: www.mcft.ca
No public access
Founded in: 1980
Hours: 8:30am-10:00pm
Acquisitions Budget: For Print: 0-$9,999
Population Served: 20
Subjects covered: Forestry, Natural Resources, Environment, Conservation
Services:
Personnel: *Summary:* 3 Total; 1 Professional(s); 2 Technical(s)

Bathurst: Campus de Bathurst, Bibliothèque
CP 266
Bathurst, NB E2A 3Z2
506-547-7495
Téléc: 506-547-2174
Couriel: bibliotheque.ccnbbath.gnb.ca
Sigle: NBBCC
Fondée en: 1966
Heures: L-J 8h15-22h; V 8h15-16h
Budget d'acquisitions: $25,000 - $49,999
Services:
Personnel: *Sommaire:* 1 Professionnel(s); 1 Autre(s) employé(s)

Bathurst: Dr. D.A. Thompson Memorial Library
1750 Sunset Dr.
Bathurst, NB E2A 4L7
506-544-2446
Fax: 506-544-2017
e-mail: sdoucet@health.nb.ca
National Library Symbol: NBBC
No public access
Subjects covered: Health Sciences, Medicine, Hospital Administration
Services:
Inter-Library Loan (ILL)
Personnel:
Suzanne Doucet, Librarian
sdoucet@health.nb.ca
Denise Savoie, Bibliothécaire
ccnb.bibliocamp@gnb.ca
506-789-2383

Campbellton: Campus de Campbellton, Bibliothèque
rue Village, CP 309
Campbellton, NB E3N 3G7
506-789-2383
Téléc: 506-753-3523
Couriel: ccnb.bibliocamp@gnb.ca
Sigle: NBNBC
Fondée en: 1987
Heures: L-J 8h-20h; V 8h-16h
Budget d'acquisitions: $10,000 - $24,999
Matériel imprimé: $10,000 - $24,999
Matériel électronique: $10,000 - $24,999
Sujets: Sciences sociales, techniques de garde, sciences de la santé, techniques bois oeuvré
Services:
Accès public à l'internet frais de 10 $
Réseau en ligne
Prêts entre bibliothèques(PEB)
Personnel: *Sommaire:* 1 Total; 1 Professionnel(s); 1 Autre(s) employé(s);

Chamrock: Atlantic Salmon Federation / Fédération du saumon atlantique Library
15 Rankine Mill Rd.
Chamrock, NB E5B 2S8
Mailing Address: PO Box 5200
St Andrews, NB E5B 2S8
506-529-1033
Fax: 506-529-4438
e-mail: asfweb@nbnet.nb.ca
savesalmon@asf.ca
URL: www.asf.ca
Founded in: 1945
Hours: M-F 9:00-4:30
Acquisitions Budget: $25,000 - $49,999
Subjects covered: Salmon; Salmon Conservation; Salmon Aquaculture; Salmon Management
Services:
Personnel:
John Anderson, Head of Library
atlsal@nbnet.nb.ca
506-529-1023
Robert Turcotte, Bibliothécaire
robert.turcotte@gnb.ca

Dieppe: Campus de Dieppe, Bibliothèque
505, rue College Dieppe
Dieppe, NB E1A 6X2
506-856-2137
Couriel: robert.turcotte@gnb.ca
Fondée en: 1987
Heures: L-V 8h15-16h30
Services:
Personnel:
Guy Lefrançois, Bibliothécaire/Directeur
glefranc@umce.ca
506—73-7-52
Claire Charest Knoetze, Technicienne en documentation
cknoetze@umce.ca
506—73-7-52
Dany Marquis, Technicienne en documentation
dmarquis@umce.ca
506—73-7-52
Johanne Albert, Secrétaire
jalbert@umce.ca
506—73-7-50

Edmundston: Campus d'Edmundston Bibliothèque Rhéa-Larose
165, boul. Hébert
Edmundston, NB E3V 2S8
506-737-5058
Téléc: 506-737-5373
glefranc@umce.ca
URL: www.umoncton.ca/umce-bibliotheque

Libraries & Resource Centres / New Brunswick

Sigle: NBESLM
Fondée en: 1970
Heures: L-J 8h30-21h; V 8h30-17h; S, D 12h-17h3
Budget d'acquisitions: $50,000 - $99,999
Collections spécialisées: Plus de 75,000 volumes; livres rares; archives locales; publications gouvernementales
Sujets: Sylviculture, sciences humaines, administration, sciences infirmières; littérature, histoire, sciences
Services:
Accès public à l'internet
Prêts entre bibliothèques(PEB)
Aide à la recherche; locaux; ordinateurs, portables, imprimantes; réserve académique; Centre de documentation & d'études madawaskayennes
Personnel: *Sommaire:* 8 Total; 1 Professionnel(s); 2 Technicien(s); 5 Autre(s) employé(s)

Edmundston: **New Brunswick Community College / Collège Communautaire du Nouveau-Brunswick Campus d'Edmundston, Bibliothèque**
225, rue du Pouvoir
Edmundston, NB E3V 3K7
Adresse postale: CP 70
Edmundston, NB E3V 3K7
506-735-2557
Téléc: 506-735-2717
888-695-2262
Courriel: france.smyth@gnb.ca
Sigle: NBECC
Fondée en: 1987
Heures: L-V 8h15-16h30
Budget d'acquisitions: 0-$9,999
Matériel imprimé: 0-$9,999
Matériel électronique: 0-$9,999
Population desservie: 300
Collections spécialisées: Génie civil; hôtellerie; techniques de bureau
Sujets: Arts, sciences humaines, culture, alimentation, génie, technologie, cuisine avancée, construction, hôtellerie, restauration, télécommunications, informatique, tourisme, santé, techniques de bureau
Services:
Accès public à l'internet
Prêts entre bibliothèques(PEB)
Lecteur/reproduction de microformes: Lecteurs
Personnel: *Sommaire:* 2 Total; 1 Professionnel(s); 1 Autre(s) employé(s)
France Smyth, Bibliothécaire
france.smyth@gnb.ca
Pierrette Pelkey, Aide-bibliothécaire
506-473-7733
Pierrette Pelkey, Aide-bibliothécaire
506-473-7733

Fredericton: **ADI Group Library**
#300, 1133 Regent St.
Fredericton, NB E3B 3Z2
506-452-9000
Fax: 506-451-7451
e-mail: adigroup@adi.ca
dee@adi.ca
Hours: M-F by appointment only
Special Collections: CSA Standards; NFPA Codes; Statutes of New Brunswick
Subjects covered: Physical Sciences, Engineering, Technology, Housing, Planning, Public Works, Local Government, Architecture, Geography
Services:
Personnel: *Summary:* 1 Total; 1 Technical(s);
Debra E. Edmondson, Librarian
dee@adi.ca

Fredericton: **Agriculture Producers Association of New Brunswick / L'Association des producteurs agricoles du Nouveau-Brunswick Library**
#303, 259 Brunswick St.
Fredericton, NB E3B 1G8
506-452-8101
Fax: 506-452-1085
e-mail: alliance@fermeNBfarm.ca
URL: www.fermeNBfarm.ca
Hours: M-F
Subjects covered: Agriculture
Services:

Fredericton: **Conservation Council of New Brunswick Environmental Resource Centre**
180 St. John St.
Fredericton, NB E3B 4A9
506-458-8747
Fax: 506-458-1047
e-mail: info@conservationcouncil.ca
URL: www.conservationcouncil.ca
Hours: M-F 9:00-5:00
Subjects covered: Environment, Energy
Services:
Personnel:
Krista Morrissey, Executive Director

Fredericton: **Dr. Everett Chalmers Regional Hospital Health Sciences Library**
700 Priestman St.
Fredericton, NB E3B 5N5
Mailing Address: PO Box 9000
Fredericton, NB E3B 5N5
506-452-5432
Fax: 506-452-5585
e-mail: library.services@rvh.nb.ca
URL: www.rhvlibrary.nb.ca
National Library Symbol: NBFDEC
Founded in: 1976
Hours: Sept.-May: M-F 8:00-6:00; June-Aug.: M-F 8:00-4:30
Note: Member of Maritime Health Libraries Association/Canadian Health Libraries Association. Public may access Patient Library collection.
Special Collections: Classics of Medicine Series
Subjects covered: Medicine, Nursing, Health Sciences, Consumer Health
Services:
Internet Access
Inter-Library Loan (ILL)
Fee Based Research
Personnel: *Summary:* 2 Total; 1 Professional(s); 1 Technical(s); 1 Volunteer(s)
Paul Clark, Librarian
Paul.Clark@rvh.nb.ca
506-450-7308
Steve Lelievre, Head Librarian
lelievre@unb.ca
506-452-6039

Fredericton: **Engineering Library**
15 Dineen Dr.
Fredericton, NB E3B 5H5
Mailing Address: PO Box 7500
Fredericton, NB E3B 5H5
506-453-4747
Fax: 506-453-4829
e-mail: englib@unb.ca
URL: www.lib.unb.ca/engineering/
National Library Symbol: NBFU
Founded in: 1968
Hours: M-Su. Hours vary throughout the academic year
Acquisitions Budget: $50,000 - $99,999
Note: ILL supplemented by cooperative Document Delivery process, providing 7 day access for books & periodicals from other libraries
Special Collections: Engineering (all branches); Computer Science; Technical Reports; Standards; Engineering & Computer Science Theses
Subjects covered: Engineering, Technology, Computer Science
Services:
Remote Access
Internet Access
Access to Subscription Databases
Inter-Library Loan (ILL)
Quiet study space & group meeting rooms; laptop loans
Microform Equipment: Reader
Personnel: *Summary:* 8 Total; 1 Professional(s); 7 Technical(s)
Janet Moss, Head Law Librarian
jmoss@unb.ca
506-447-3266
Catherine Cotter, Reference & Instruction Librarian
cacotter@unb.ca
506-447-3265
Yolande Gagnon, Senior Library Assistant, Circulation & Serials Management
gagnon@unb.ca
506-458-7979

Fredericton: **Gerard V. La Forest Law Library**
41 Dineen Dr., University of New Brunswick
Fredericton, NB E3B 6C9
Mailing Address: Bag Sevice 44999
Fredericton, NB E3B 6C9
506-453-4734
Fax: 506-451-6948
e-mail: lawlib@unb.ca
URL: www.unbf.ca/law/library
National Library Symbol: NBFUL
Founded in: 1892
Hours: M-Th 8:00am-11:00pm; F 8:00-5:00; Sa 10:00-6:00; Su 12:00-11:00. Hours may vary throughout the academic year
Acquisitions Budget: $250,000 - $499,999
For Print: $100,000 - $249,999
For Electronic: $50,000 - $99,999
Note: Public access to internet where licences permit, for law related use only
Special Collections: Beaverbrook Law Collection; Gordon Fairweather Collection in Human Rights; Immigration & Refugee Law; digital collections include the Allan Legere Digital Archive; texts & treatises; Canadian and international law reports; government documents; statutes & regulations; periodicals; dissertations; law exams
Subjects covered: Law, Law Enforcement, Administration of Justice
Services:
Remote Access
Internet Access
Access to Subscription Databases
Inter-Library Loan (ILL)
Study rooms & equipment for persons with special needs; laptop loans; wireless access; public access computers; quiet study space & group meeting areas
Microform Equipment: Computer; Reader
Personnel: *Summary:* 10 Total; 3 Professional(s); 4 Technical(s); 3 Other employees;

Fredericton: **Maritime College of Forest Technology / Collège de technologie forestière des Maritimes Library**
1350 Regent St.
Fredericton, NB E3C 2G6
506-458-0199
Fax: 506-458-0652
e-mail: info@mcft.ca
URL: www.mcft.ca
Founded in: 1950
Hours: Tu, Th 6:00-9:00 by appointment only
Acquisitions Budget: 0-$9,999
Subjects covered: Forestry, Wildlife, Environment, Conservation
Services:
Personnel: *Summary:* 1 Total; 1 Professional(s)
Philip Hughes, Instructor/Librarian
phughes@mcft.ca
506-485-0199

Fredericton: **Natural Resources Canada, Canadian Forest Service / Ressources naturelles Canada. Service canadien des forêts Atlantic Forestry Centre**
1350 Regent St. South,
Fredericton, NB E3B 5P7
Mailing Address: PO Box 4000
Fredericton, NB E3B 5P7
506-452-3541
Fax: 506-452-3525
kdickson@nrcan.gc.ca
URL: www.nrcan.gc.ca/library/forestry-foresterie.htm
National Library Symbol: NBFE
Founded in: 1911
Hours: M-F 8:30-4:30 by appointment only
Note: Member of Council of Canadian Forest Service Libraries. Library serves the Atlantic Region; branch library located in Corner Brook, NL & reports to this main library
Special Collections: Canadian Forestry Service, USFS & Atlantic Provinces Government Publications
Subjects covered: Forestry, Genetics, Biodiversity, Botany, Entomology, Agriculture, Ecology, Sustainable Development
Services:
Inter-Library Loan (ILL)
Microform Equipment: Reader
Personnel: *Summary:* 2 Total; 1 Professional(s); 1 Technical(s)
Sandra Lowman, Regional Librarian

Libraries & Resource Centres / New Brunswick

Kelly Dickson, Library Technician
kdickson@nrcan-rncan.gc.ca
Kelly Dickson, Library Technician

Fredericton: **New Brunswick Dept. of Environment / Ministère de l'Environnement**
Library
20 McGloin St.
Fredericton, NB E3B 5H1
Mailing Address: PO Box 6000
Fredericton, NB E3B 5H1
506-453-2566
Fax: 506-453-3676
e-mail: gail.darby@gnb.ca
URL: www.gnb.ca/0009/index-e.asp
National Library Symbol: NBFME
Founded in: 1970
Hours: M-F by appointment only
Note: Please call for an appointment
Special Collections: Technical reports of the Department
Subjects covered: Environment, Conservation, Pesticides, Environmental Impact Assessment, Water Quality, Pollution, Local Government
Services:
Personnel:
Gail Darby, Librarian
gail.darby@gnb.ca
André Gionet, Head
gioneta@agr.gc.ca
506-452-4810

Fredericton: **Potato Research Centre / Centre de recherches sur la pomme de terre**
Canadian Agriculture Library - Fredericton/Bibliothèque canadienne de l'agriculture - Fredericto
850 Lincoln Rd.
Fredericton, NB E3B 4Z7
Mailing Address: PO Box 20280
Fredericton, NB E3B 4Z7
506-452-4810
Fax: 506-452-3316
e-mail: library-fredericton@agr.gc.ca
URL: res2.agr.gc.ca/fredericton/
National Library Symbol: NBFAG
Founded in: 1952
Hours: M-F 8:30-5:00 by appointment only
Acquisitions Budget: For Print: $25,000 - $49,999
Special Collections: Potatoes; Agriculture Canada publications
Subjects covered: Agriculture, Food, Potatoes, Soil Science
Services:
Inter-Library Loan (ILL) for a fee
Personnel: *Summary:* 1 Total; 1 Professional(s)
Francesca Holyoke, Head Librarian
holyoke@unb.ca
506-453-4965

Fredericton: **Science & Forestry Library**
4 Bailey Dr.
Fredericton, NB E3B 5H5
Mailing Address: PO Box 7500
Fredericton, NB E3B 5H5
506-453-4601
Fax: 506-453-3518
e-mail: scilib@unb.ca
URL: www.lib.unb.ca/science/
Founded in: 1976
Hours: M-Su. Hours vary throughout the academic year by appointment only
Special Collections: FORF (Forestry related pamphlet/report collection); GEOSCAN (NB Mineral Exploration Assessment Reports on microfiche)
Subjects covered: Physical Sciences, Engineering, Technology, Maps, Environment, Life Sciences, Medicine, Chemistry, Forestry, Earth Sciences
Services:
Remote Access
Internet Access
Inter-Library Loan (ILL)
Microform Equipment: Computer; Reader
Personnel: *Summary:* 8 Total; 2 Professional(s); 6 Technical(s);

Fredericton: **University of New Brunswick**
Harriet Irving Library
5 Macaulay Lane
Fredericton, NB E3B 5H5
Mailing Address: PO Box 7500
Fredericton, NB E3B 5H5
506-453-4740
Fax: 506-453-4595
e-mail: library@unb.ca
URL: www.lib.unb.ca
National Library Symbol: NBFU
Consortia Membership: Canadian Research Knowledge Network (CRKN); Council of Atlantic University Libraries (CAUL)
Founded in: 1967
Hours: M-Su. Hours vary throughout the academic year
Acquisitions Budget: $1,000,000 plus
For Print: $1,000,000 plus
For Electronic: $1,000,000 plus
Population Served: 14000
Note: The library is an affiliate member of the Council of Prairie and Pacific University Libraries (COPPUL).
Special Collections: Canadian Literature; Eileen Wallace Children's Literature Collection; Loyalist Collection
Subjects covered: Arts, Humanities, Physical Sciences, Engineering, Technology, Forestry, Tourism, Social Sciences
Services:
Remote Access
Internet Access
Access to Subscription Databases
Inter-Library Loan (ILL)
Fee Based Research
Electronic Text Centre; Digitization; Scanning; Photocopying & Printing; Access for persons with disabilities; Document Delivery; Wireless Computing
Microform Equipment: Computer; Reader
Personnel: *Summary:* 20 Professional(s)
John Teskey, Director of Libraries
jteskey@unb.ca
506-458-7582
Jocelyne Thompson, Associate Director, Collections Services
jlt@unb.ca
506-458-7053
Lesley Balcom, Associate Director, Learning & Research Services
lbalcom@unb.ca
506-458-7056
France Smyth, Bibliothécaire
France.Smyth@gnb.ca
506-735-2557
Pierrette Pelkey, Aide-bibliothécaire
pierrette.pelkey@gnb.ca
Pierrette Pelkey, Aide-bibliothécaire
pierrette.pelkey@gnb.ca

Grand-Sault: **Centre d'excellence en sciences agricoles et biotechnologiques**
Service d'information Bédard
160, rue Réservoir
Grand-Sault, NB E3Y 3W3
506-473-7764
Téléc: 506-473-7769
888-875-2322
Courriel: sib@gnb.ca
cesab@gnb.ca
Fondée en: 1995
Heures: L-V 8h15-16h15avec rendez-vous seulement
Budget d'acquisitions: 0-$9,999
Matériel imprimé: 0-$9,999
Matériel électronique: 0-$9,999
Population desservie: 300
Sujets: Agriculture, biotechnologie, agroforestrie
Services:
Accès public à l'internet
Prêts entre bibliothèques(PEB)
Personnel: *Sommaire:* 2 Total; 1 Professionnel(s); 1 Autre(s) employé(s)
Sam Inch, Librarian
sam.inch@gnb.ca

Miramichi: **Miramichi Campus Library**
80 University Ave.
Miramichi, NB E1N 3W4
Mailing Address: PO Box 1053
Miramichi, NB E1N 3W4

506-778-6000
Fax: 506-778-6001
e-mail: sam.inch@gnb.ca
National Library Symbol: NBCCC
Founded in: 1985
Hours: M-F
Acquisitions Budget: $50,000 - $99,999
Subjects covered: Computers, Social Sciences, Law, Environment, Educational Technology
Services:
Inter-Library Loan (ILL)
Microform Equipment: Reader
Personnel: *Summary:* 1 Total; 1 Professional(s)
Darla Davidson, Librarian
davidsd@tc.gc.ca
John Price, Assistant
pricej@tc.gc.ca
506-851-7329

Moncton: **Civil Aviation Technical Reference Centre / Centre de documentation technique de la navigabilité aérienne**
Heritage Court, 95 Foundry St.
Moncton, NB E1C 8K6
Mailing Address: PO Box 42
Moncton, NB E1C 8K6
506-851-7398
Fax: 506-851-7329
e-mail: trc-atl@tc.gc.ca
National Library Symbol: TRC
Hours: M-F by appointment only
Acquisitions Budget: $10,000 - $24,999
Special Collections: Periodicals, Archival Regulatory Materials
Subjects covered: Aviation, Government Regulations, Technical Documentation
Services:
Internet Access
Inter-Library Loan (ILL)
Microform Equipment: Computer; Reader
Personnel: *Summary:* 2 Total; 1 Technical(s); 1 Other employees;
Judy Chambers, Coordinator
judy.chanbers@gnb.ca
506-856-2226
Elizabeth J. Crawford, Coordinator
elizabeth.crawford@gnb.ca
506-856-2226
Marjorie Lutzac, Coordinator
marjorie.lutzac@gnb.ca
506-856-2226

Moncton: **Moncton Campus, Library**
1234 Mountain Rd.
Moncton, NB E1C 8H9
506-856-2226
Fax: 506-856-3288
URL: www.moncton.nbcc.nb.ca
National Library Symbol: NBMOCC
Hours: M-Th 8:00am-9:30pm; F 8:00-3:30
Acquisitions Budget: 0-$9,999
For Print: 0-$9,999
For Electronic: 0-$9,999
Population Served: 1200
Note: OPAC available on web.
Subjects covered: Physical Sciences, Engineering, Technology, Economics, Business, Electronics
Services:
Remote Access
Internet Access
Access to Subscription Databases
Inter-Library Loan (ILL)
Personnel: *Summary:* 2 Total; 1 Professional(s); 1 Technical(s)

Moncton: **South-East Regional Health Authority / Régie régionale de la santé Sud-Est**
Health Sciences Library
135 MacBeath Ave.
Moncton, NB E1C 6Z8
506-857-5447
Fax: 506-857-5785
e-mail: loleger@serha.ca
National Library Symbol: NBMMH
Founded in: 1963
Hours: M-F 9:00-4:00 by appointment only
Acquisitions Budget: $50,000 - $99,999
For Print: $50,000 - $99,999

For Electronic: $50,000 - $99,999
Population Served: 2700
Subjects covered: Health Sciences
Services:
Remote Access
Internet Access
Inter-Library Loan (ILL)
Personnel: *Summary:* 1 Professional(s); 3 Technical(s)
Lori W. Léger, M.Sc., MLIS, Manager of Library Services

Moncton: Université de Moncton
Bibliothèque Champlain
18, av. Antonine-Maillet
Moncton, NB E1A 3E9
506-858-4012
Téléc: 506-858-4086
Courriel: bichamp@umoncton.ca
URL: www.umoncton.ca/umcm-bibliotheque-champlain\
Profile: Adresse civique: 415, av. de l'Université
Sigle: NBMOU
Membre d'un consortium: Canadian Research Knowledge Network (CRKN); Council of Atlantic University Libraries (CAUL)
Fondée en: 1965
Heures: L-J 8h30-22h30; V 8h30-20h; S 12h-18h; D 13h-22h30
Budget d'acquisitions: $1,000,000 plus
Matériel imprimé: $500,000 - $999,999
Matériel électronique: $250,000 - $499,999
Collections spécialisées: Acadiana; collection du centres d'études acadiennes
Sujets: Génie; musique; nutrition; arts; humanités; sciences physiques
Services:
Accèss distance aux bases de donn
Accès public à l'internet
Réseau en ligne
Prêts entre bibliothèques(PEB)
Aide à la recherche; aide à la rédaction; locaux & casiers; réserve académique; services pour personnes ayant un handicap visuel
Lecteur/reproduction de microformes: Lecteurs
Personnel: *Sommaire:* 35 Total; 8 Professionnel(s); 7 Technicien(s); 20 Autre(s) employé(s)
Alain Roberge, Bibliothécaire en chef
alain.roberge@umoncton.ca
506—85-8-40
Héctor Alvarez, Chef des services publics
hector.alvarez@umoncton.ca
506—85-8-49
Victoria Volkanova, Chef du service des systèmes informatisés
victoria.volkanova@umoncton.ca
506—85-8-44
Andrew Fabro, Head Librarian
andrew.fabro@ec.gc.ca
Adele Cohen, Librarian
adele.cohen@ec.gc.ca
604-666-1794

Sackville: Canadian Wildlife Service
Atlantic Region Library
17 Waterfowl Lane
Sackville, NB E4L 1G6
506-364-5019
Fax: 506-364-5062
e-mail: jean.sealy@ec.gc.ca
URL: www.ec.gc.ca
National Library Symbol: NBSACW
Hours: M-F 8:30-12:00, 1:00-4:30
Acquisitions Budget: 0-$9,999
For Print: 0-$9,999
For Electronic: 0-$9,999
Note: Library is staffed from 8:30 to noon.
Subjects covered: Environment, Air/Water Pollution, Hazardous Substances, Climate
Services:
Internet Access
Access to Subscription Databases
Inter-Library Loan (ILL)
Microform Equipment: Reader
Personnel: *Summary:* 1 Total; 1 Professional(s);

Sackville: Mount Allison University
Ralph Pickard Bell Library
49 York St.
Sackville, NB E4L 1C6
506-364-2567
Fax: 506-364-2617
e-mail: circ@mta.ca
infodesk@mta.ca
URL: www.mta.ca/library
National Library Symbol: NBSAM
Consortia Membership: Canadian Research Knowledge Network (CRKN); Council of Atlantic University Libraries (CAUL)
Founded in: 1862
Hours: M-Su
Acquisitions Budget: $500,000 - $999,999
Special Collections: Winthrop Pickard Bell Collection of Acadiana
Subjects covered: Liberal Arts
Services:
Inter-Library Loan (ILL)
Microform Equipment: Computer; Reader
Personnel: *Summary:* 29 Total; 8 Professional(s); 21 Technical(s)
Bruno Gnassi, University Librarian

Saint John: New Brunswick Dept. of Wellness, Culture & Sport / Ministère du Mieux-être, Culture et Sport
Library & Archives
277 Douglas Ave.
Saint John, NB E2K 1E5
506-643-2300
Fax: 506-643-2360
National Library Symbol: NBFH
Hours: M-F 8:15-5:00 by appointment only
Special Collections: Department of Health Annual Reports 1887-present, Alcoholism & Drug Dependency, Premiers Council on Health Strategy Material, Mental Health collection - books S
Subjects covered: Medicine, Health Sciences, Social Affairs, Social Welfare, Public Health
Services:
Inter-Library Loan (ILL)
Personnel:
Felicity Osepchook, Manager
Felicity.Osepchook@nbm-mnb.ca
506-643-2324
Janet Bishop, Assistant
Jennifer Longon

Saint John: New Brunswick Museum
Archives & Research Library
277 Douglas Ave.
Saint John, NB E2K 1E5
506-643-2322
Fax: 506-643-2360
e-mail: archives@nmb-mnb.ca
URL: www.nbm-mnb.ca
National Library Symbol: NBSM
Hours: Sept-June: Tu-Sa 10:00-4:30. Jul-Aug: Tu-F 10:00-4:30
Acquisitions Budget: $25,000 - $49,999
Note: No access to subscription database through website.
Special Collections: Records and papers dealing with the economic, social, legal, military, relgious and political areas of life in New Brunswick, with a particular focus on the 19th century.
Subjects covered: Natural Sciences, Fine & Decorative Arts, New Brunswick History, Shipping, Archives
Services:
Remote Access
Internet Access
Access to Subscription Databases
Inter-Library Loan (ILL)
Personnel: *Summary:* 4 Total; 1 Professional(s); 3 Technical(s); 4 Volunteer(s)
Felicity Osepchook, Head
506-643-2324
Beverley Lyons, Librarian
beverley.lyons@gnb.ca

Saint John: Saint John Campus Library
L.R. Fulton Library & Audiovisual Centre
950 Grandview Ave.
Saint John, NB E2L 3V1
Mailing Address: PO Box 2270
Saint John, NB E2L 3V1
506-658-6727
Fax: 506-643-2853
Founded in: 1962
Hours: M-F 8:15-4:30
Acquisitions Budget: $25,000 - $49,999
Subjects covered: Trades & Technology
Services:
Inter-Library Loan (ILL)
Personnel: *Summary:* 3 Total; 1 Professional(s); 2 Other employees

Saint John: St Joseph's Hospital (Saint John)
Health Sciences Library
130 Bayard Dr.
Saint John, NB E2L 3L6
506-632-5555 ext: 5423
Fax: 506-632-5570
Founded in: 1914
Hours: M-F 8:00-3:30 by appointment only
Note: Part of Atlantic Health Sciences Corporation
Subjects covered: Medicine, Nursing.
Services:
Inter-Library Loan (ILL)
Personnel: *Summary:* 1 Total; 1 Professional(s)
Zetta G. Whelly, Librarian
Andrea Cunningham, Head, Reference
Terry Nikkel, Director, Information Services & Systems
tnikkel@unb.ca
506-648-5700
Linda Hansen, Electronic Services Librarian
lhansen@unb.ca
Janet Fraser, Bibliographic & Collection Services Librarian
jdfraser@unb.ca
506-648-5996

Saint John: Ward Chipman Library
Saint John Campus
100 Tucker Park Rd.
Saint John, NB E2L 4L5
Mailing Address: PO Box 5050
Saint John, NB E2L 4L5
506-648-5700
Fax: 506-648-5701
e-mail: wcl@unb.ca
URL: www.lib.unb.ca/wcl
National Library Symbol: NBSU
Founded in: 1965
Hours: M-Su. Hours may vary throughout the academic year
Acquisitions Budget: $250,000 - $499,999
Special Collections: Science Fiction & Fantasy Collection, Governors-General of Canada Collection, Beat Generation, Marine Biology
Services:
Remote Access
Internet Access
Inter-Library Loan (ILL)
Microform Equipment: Reader
Personnel: *Summary:* 19 Total; 8 Professional(s); 11 Technical(s)
Charlotte McAdam, Librarian
McAdamCJ@mar.dfo-mpo.gc.ca
506-529-5748

St Andrews: St. Andrews Biological Station Library
531 Brandy Cove Rd.
St Andrews, NB E5B 2L9
506-529-5909
Fax: 506-529-5862
e-mail: sta-library@mar.dfo-mpo.gc.ca
URL: www.dfo-mpo.gc.ca
National Library Symbol: NBAB
Founded in: 1908
Hours: M-F 8:00-4:30
Subjects covered: Aquaculture, Marine Biology, Oceanography
Services:
Remote Access
Internet Access
Access to Subscription Databases
Inter-Library Loan (ILL)
Microform Equipment: Reader
Personnel: *Summary:* 2 Total; 1 Professional(s); 1 Technical(s)
Mary Doon, Librarian
mary.doon@nbcc.ca

St. Andrews: St. Andrews Campus
99 Augustus St.
St. Andrews
506-529-5070
Fax: 506-529-5009
URL: www.nbcc.ca

National Library Symbol: NBSTAC
Founded in: 1987
Hours: M-Th 8:15am-9:00pm; F 8:15-4:30
Acquisitions Budget: $25,000 - $49,999
Subjects covered: Tourism & Travel, Economics, Boat Building, Business Education, Heating, Air Conditioning & Refrigeration, Hospitality, Hotel Management
Services:
Inter-Library Loan (ILL)
Personnel: *Summary:* 4 Total; 1 Professional(s); 1 Technical(s); 2 Other employees
Hélène McLaughlin, Directrice de la bibliothèque
mchelene@umcs.ca
506-33-6-34
Cédric Landry, Conseiller en documentation
cedric.landry@umcs.ca
506-33-6-34
Marie-Josée Diotte, Responsable, Service du prêt
mjdiotte@umcs.ca
506-33-6-34

Shippagan: **Campus de Shippagan Bibliothèque**
218, boul. J.-D.-Gauthier
Shippagan, NB E8S 1P6
506-336-3420
Téléc: 506-336-3434
800-363-8336
Couriel: biblioweb@umcs.ca
URL: www.umoncton.ca/umcs-bibliotheque
Sigle: NBSCU
Heures: L-J 8h30-22h45; V 8h30-19h45; S 10h-17h; D 13h-21h
Budget d'acquisitions: $50,000 - $99,999
Collections spécialisées: Près de 40,000 volumes; 325 titres de périodiques; 3,000 publications gouvernementales; livres rares; collections spécialisées en gestion de l'information & en pêche; collection de la Bibliothèque du CCNB de Bathurst; publications officielles
Services:
Accèss distance aux bases de donn
Accès public à l'internet
Réseau en ligne
Prêts entre bibliothèques (PEB)
Formation documentaire; réserve; salles de séminaire; laboratoire informatique; salle multimédia
Lecteur/reproduction de microformes: Ordinateur; Lecteurs
Personnel: *Sommaire:* 14 Total; 1 Professionnel(s); 3 Technicien(s); 10 Autre(s) employé(s)
Sara Martin, Library Services Coordinator
sara.martin@gnb.ca
506-325-4878

Woodstock: **Woodstock Campus, Library**
100 Broadway
Woodstock, NB E7M 5C5
506-325-4400 ext: 4878
Fax: 506-328-8426
e-mail: sara.martin@gnb.ca
National Library Symbol: NBWC
Founded in: 1984
Acquisitions Budget: 0-$9,999
Subjects covered: Agriculture, Arts, Economics, Communications, Mass Media, Business, Journalism, Photography, Carpentry, Secretarial Studies, Graphic Arts, Technology, Video Production
Services:
Internet Access
Inter-Library Loan (ILL)
Personnel: *Summary:* 1 Technical(s);

Newfoundland & Labrador

Tracy Mouland, Library Technician

Bonavista: **Bonavista Campus Learning Resource Centre**
301 Confederation Dr.
Bonavista, NL A0C 1B0
Mailing Address: PO Box 670
Bonavista, NL A0C 1B0
709-468-1716
Fax: 709-468-2004
e-mail: tracy.mouland@cna.nl.ca
URL: www.cna.nl.ca
Founded in: 1994
Hours: M-F 8:30-11:45, 12:15-4:00. Hours may vary during the academic year
Subjects covered: Adult Basic Education, Trades/Occupations, Natural Resources, Office Administration
Services:
Remote Access
Internet Access
Inter-Library Loan (ILL)
Personnel: *Summary:* 1 Technical(s)
Sandra Shallow, Library Technician
sandra.shallow@cna.nl.ca
709-891-5621

Burin Bay Arm: **Burin Campus Library**
105 Main St.
Burin Bay Arm, NL A0E 1G0
Mailing Address: PO Box 370
Burin Bay Arm, NL A0E 1G0
709-891-5622
Fax: 709-891-2256
Other contact info: Alternate phone: 709-891-5621
e-mail: sandra.shallow@cna.nl.ca
URL: www.cna.nl.ca
Hours: M-F 8:30-4:00
Special Collections: Social Justice Special Edition (Fredette/Matthews); The Days Special Collection (Labrador Reflections); French Language course materials; Maps
Subjects covered: Social Sciences, Business, Applied Arts, Technology
Services:
Remote Access
Internet Access
Access to Subscription Databases
Inter-Library Loan (ILL)
Orientation sessions; individual and group study facilities; computers; audiovisual equipment; scanner
Personnel: *Summary:* 1 Total; 1 Other employees
Stephen Nolan, Librarian
Brenda Peach, Library Technician
brenda.peach@cna.nl.ca
709-596-8940

Carbonear: **Carbonear Campus Library**
4 Pike's Lane
Carbonear, NL A1Y 1B5
Mailing Address: PO Box 60
Carbonear, NL A1Y 1B5
709-596-8925
Fax: 709-596-2688
e-mail: stephen.nolan@cna.nl.ca
URL: www.cna.nl.ca
Hours: M-F 8:30-5:00
Acquisitions Budget: 0-$9,999
For Print: 0-$9,999
For Electronic: 0-$9,999
Special Collections: Newfoundland Literature Collection
Subjects covered: Adult Education, Carpentry, Engineering Technology
Services:
Remote Access
Internet Access
Inter-Library Loan (ILL)
Quiet study space; personal computers
Personnel: *Summary:* 1 Professional(s); 1 Technical(s)
Joanne Deluney, Librarian
joanne.deluney@cna.nl.ca

Clarenville: **Clarenville Campus Learning Resource Centre**
#229, 69 Pleasant St.
Clarenville, NL A5A 1V9
709-466-6940
Fax: 709-466-2771
e-mail: joanne.deluney@cna.nl.ca
URL: www.cna.nl.ca
Hours: M-F 8:30-4:00
Subjects covered: Business, Trades/Occupations, Engineering Technology
Services:
Remote Access
Internet Access
Inter-Library Loan (ILL)
Personnel: *Summary:* 1 Professional(s)
Andrea Hyde, Librarian
andrea.hyde@cna.nl.ca
Theresa MacLean, Library Clerk
theresa.maclean@cna.nl.ca

Conception Bay South: **Seal Cove Campus Library**
1670 Conception Bay Hwy.
Conception Bay South, NL A1X 5C7
Mailing Address: PO Box 19003, Stn Seal Cove
Conception Bay South, NL A1X 5C7
709-744-6829
Fax: 709-744-3929
e-mail: libs@cna.nl.ca
URL: www.cna.nl.ca
National Library Symbol: NFSCS
Founded in: 1992
Hours: M-F 8:30-4:30
Acquisitions Budget: 0-$9,999
For Print: 0-$9,999
For Electronic: 0-$9,999
Population Served: 450
Special Collections: Newfoundland Collection
Subjects covered: Electrical, Oil Burner Mechanic, Commercial Cooking, Power Line Technician, Industrial Instrumentation, Petroleum Industry Training, Construction Technician, Adult Basic Education
Services:
Internet Access
Access to Subscription Databases
Inter-Library Loan (ILL)
Orientation sessions & tours; computers for research; office productivity tools; printing; audiovisual resource room; facilities for quiet individual & group study
Personnel: *Summary:* 2 Total; 1 Professional(s); 1 Other employees;
Marian Burnett, Librarian
marian.burnett@cna.nl.ca
709-637-8587

Corner Brook: **College of the North Atlantic, Corner Brook Campus Library**
141 O'Connell Dr.
Corner Brook, NL A2H 6H6
Mailing Address: PO Box 822
Corner Brook, NL A2H 6H6
709-637-8528
Fax: 709-634-2126
e-mail: libcb@cna.nl.ca
URL: www.cna.nl.ca/libraryservices/
National Library Symbol: NFCBFT
Hours: M-W 8:00-5:00, 6:00-9:00; Th, F 8:00-4:30; Su 1:00-5:00, 6:00-9:00. Hours may vary during the academic year
Acquisitions Budget: $25,000 - $49,999
Population Served: 1000
Subjects covered: Adult Basic Education, Adventure Tourism & Outdoor Recreation, Business, Industrial Technologies & Trades, Early Childhood Education, English as a Second Language, Fish & Wildlife, Forestry, Office Administration
Services:
Remote Access
Inter-Library Loan (ILL)
Group & individual study facilities; audiovisual room; computer access; photocopying
Personnel: *Summary:* 3 Total; 1 Professional(s); 2 Technical(s)

Corner Brook: **Newfoundland & Labrador Dept. of Forest Resources & Agrifood Forestry Library**
4 Herald Ave.
Corner Brook, NL A2H 6J8
Mailing Address: PO Box 2006
Corner Brook, NL A2H 6J8
709-637-2307
Fax: 709-637-2403
URL: www.nr.gov.nl.ca/agric/
National Library Symbol: NFCBF
Founded in: 1984
Hours: M-F by appointment only
Acquisitions Budget: $25,000 - $49,999
Special Collections: Newfoundland Forestry
Subjects covered: Natural Resources, Land Use, Environment
Services:
Inter-Library Loan (ILL)
Personnel: *Summary:* 1 Total; 1 Professional(s)
Bruce Boland, Librarian
bboland@gov.nl.ca
Elizabeth Behrens, Associate University Librarian
ebehrens@swgc.mun.ca
709-637-6236 ext. 6120

Corner Brook: **Sir Wilfred Grenfell College Ferriss Hodgett Library**
University Dr.
Corner Brook, NL A2H 6P9
709-637-6267
Fax: 709-637-6273
e-mail: library@swgc.mun.ca
URL: www.library.mun.ca/swgc
National Library Symbol: NFSCF
Founded in: 1964
Hours: M-Th 8:30-9:00; F 8:30-5:00; Sa, Su 10:00-5:00
Acquisitions Budget: $50,000 - $99,999
Services:
Internet Access
Access to Subscription Databases
Inter-Library Loan (ILL)
Microform Equipment: Reader
Personnel: *Summary:* 6 Total; 1 Professional(s); 5 Technical(s)

Corner Brook: **Western Health Care Corporation Health Sciences Library**
PO Box 2005
Corner Brook, NL A2H 6J7
709-637-5000 ext: 5218
Fax: 709-637-5453
library@healthwest.nf.ca
URL: www.healthwest.nf.ca
National Library Symbol: NFCBW
Services:
Internet Access
Inter-Library Loan (ILL) for a fee of $5
Personnel: *Summary:* 4 Total; 2 Professional(s); 1 Technical(s)
Kimberly Hancock, Director, Library Services
khanco@healthwest.nf.ca
709-637-5395
Karen Pätzold, Librarian

Gander: **Gander Campus Library & Career Exploration Centre**
1 Magee Rd.
Gander, NL A1V 1W8
Mailing Address: PO Box 395
Gander, NL A1V 1W8
709-651-4815
Fax: 709-651-4854
e-mail: karen.patzold.cna.nl.ca
libga@cna.nl.ca
URL: www.cna.nl.ca
Founded in: 1993
Hours: M-Th 8:00-12:00, 12:30-4:00; F 8:00-1:00
Note: Career Exploration Centre provides job search resources & a job board
Special Collections: Adult Basic Education textbook collection; literature & literary biographies; history; sociology; videos
Subjects covered: Industrial Trades, Automotive, Aircraft Technology, Hairstyling
Services:
Remote Access
Internet Access
Access to Subscription Databases
Inter-Library Loan (ILL)
Photocopying; laminating
Personnel: *Summary:* 1 Professional(s)

Grand Falls-Windsor: **Central Newfoundland Regional Health Centre Regional Resource Centre**
50 Union St.
Grand Falls-Windsor, NL A2A 2E1
709-292-2228
Fax: 709-292-2148
e-mail: efewer@cnhc.nf.ca
efewer@cwhbrc.ca
URL: www.cwhc.nf.ca/cnrhc.htm
Hours: M-F by appointment only
Acquisitions Budget: $25,000 - $49,999
Note: Member of Central West Health Care Board Library Services
Subjects covered: Medical, Para-Medical, Allied Health
Services:
Inter-Library Loan (ILL)
Personnel: *Summary:* 1 Total; 1 Technical(s)
Ellen C. Fewer, Library Technician
efewer@cnhc.nf.ca
James Hornell, Regional Director, Performance & Accountablity
709-292-2490

John Whelan, Librarian
john.whelan@cna.nl.ca

Grand Falls-Windsor: **Grand Falls-Windsor Campus Library**
5 Cromer Ave.
Grand Falls-Windsor, NL A2A 2J8
Mailing Address: PO Box 413
Grand Falls-Windsor, NL A2A 2J8
709-292-5637
Fax: 709-489-5765
e-mail: libgf@cna.nl.ca
Hours: M, F 8:30-5:00; Tu-Th 8:30am-9:30pm; Sa 9:00-4:00. Hours may vary during the academic year
Subjects covered: Business, Office Administration
Services:
Remote Access
Internet Access
Inter-Library Loan (ILL)
Library is wheelchair accessible; orientation sessions; photocopying
Personnel: *Summary:* 3 Total; 1 Professional(s); 2 Technical(s)
Roxanne Sutton, Librarian
roxanne.sutton@cna.nl.ca
Karen Pottle-Fewer, Library Technician
karen.pottle-fewer@cna.nl.ca

Labrador City: **Labrador West Campus Raymond J. Condon Memorial Library & Learning Resource Centre**
1 Campbell Dr.
Labrador City, NL A2V 2Y1
709-944-6862
Fax: 709-944-6581
e-mail: LibLW@cna.nl.ca
URL: www.cna.nl.ca
Founded in: 1990
Hours: M-Th 8:00-8:00; F 8:00-4:30. Spring & Summer: M-F 8:30-4:30
Acquisitions Budget: $10,000 - $24,999
Special Collections: Newfoundland Collection; maps; videos; material supporting courses, particularly in technology, science, mining
Subjects covered: Engineering Technology, Industrial Trades, Mining Technology
Services:
Remote Access
Internet Access for a fee
Access to Subscription Databases
Inter-Library Loan (ILL)
Personnel: *Summary:* 3 Total; 1 Professional(s); 2 Technical(s)

Mount Pearl: **Newfoundland & Labrador Dept. of Government Services Occupational Health & Safety Branch - Library & Information Services**
15 Dundee Ave.
Mount Pearl, NL A1B 4J6
Mailing Address: PO Box 8700
St. John's, NL A1B 4J6
709-729-5264
Fax: 709-729-3445
e-mail: mvarghese@mail.gov.nl.ca
URL: www.gs.gov.nl.ca/ohs/
National Library Symbol: NFSEL
Founded in: 1992
Hours: M-F 8:30-4:00 by appointment only
Subjects covered: Workplace Health & Safety, Labour
Services:
Inter-Library Loan (ILL)
Personnel: *Summary:* 1 Total; 1 Professional(s)
Mary Varghese, OHS Resource Librarian
mvarghese@gov.nl.ca
709-729-5264
Linda Reddigan, Librarian

Placentia: **Placentia Campus Learning Resource Centre**
1 Roosevelt Ave.
Placentia, NL A0B 2Y0
Mailing Address: PO Box 190
Placentia, NL A0B 2Y0
709-227-2037
Fax: 709-227-7185
e-mail: linda.reddigan@cna.nl.ca
URL: www.cna.nl.ca

Founded in: 1993
Hours: M, W 8:00-4:00, 6:00-9:00; Tu, Th 8:00-7:00; F 8:00-4:00. Hours may vary during the academic year
Subjects covered: Adult Basic Education; Heavy Equipment Operator, Machinist, Millwright, Welder programs
Services:
Internet Access
Inter-Library Loan (ILL)
Personnel: *Summary:* 1 Total
Barbara Devereaux, Library Technician

Port aux Basques: **Port aux Basques Campus Library**
59 Grand Bay Rd.
Port aux Basques, NL A0M 1C0
Mailing Address: PO Box 760
Port aux Basques, NL A0M 1C0
709-695-3343
Fax: 709-695-2963
e-mail: barbara.devereaux@cna.nl.ca
libpab@cna.nl.ca
Founded in: 1963
Hours: M-F 8:30-4:30
Subjects covered: Non-Destructive Testing, Cabinet Making, Business, Office Administration
Services:
Remote Access
Internet Access
Inter-Library Loan (ILL)
Personnel: *Summary:* 1 Technical(s)
Susan Prior, Librarian III
susan.prior@cna.nl.ca
709-758-7448

St Anthony: **St Anthony Campus Library**
PO Box 550
St Anthony, NL A0K 4S0
709-454-3559
Fax: 709-454-8808
e-mail: nina.woodward@cna.nl.ca
URL: www.cna.nl.ca
Hours: M, W 9:30-3:30; Tu 12:30-3:30; Th 9:30-3:00
Services:
Internet Access
Inter-Library Loan (ILL)
Personnel: *Summary:* 1 Total; 1 Other employees;

St. John's: **Canada-Newfoundland Offshore Petroleum Board Library**
TD Place, #500, 140 Water St.
St. John's, NL A1C 6H6
709-778-1400
Fax: 709-778-1473
e-mail: information@cnlopb.nl.ca
URL: www.cnlopb.nl.ca
Founded in: 1986
Hours: M-F
Acquisitions Budget: $25,000 - $49,999
Subjects covered: Offshore Petroleum Engineering
Services:
Microform Equipment: Reader
Personnel:
Debra Downing, Contact
Sheila Duff, Technical Files Clerk
709-778-1423
Joan Ritcey, Head
jritcey@mun.ca
Colleen Field, Assistant Head
Bert Riggs, Archivist

St. John's: **Centre for Newfoundland Studies Library**
Queen Elizabeth II Library, Memorial University
St. John's, NL A1B 3Y1
709-737-7475
Fax: 709-737-2153
e-mail: cnsqeii@mun.ca
URL: www.library.mun.ca/qeii/cns/cns_main.php
National Library Symbol: NFSM
Founded in: 1965
Hours: M-Th 8:30am-11:00pm; F 8:30-6:00; Sa 10:00-6:00; Su 1:30-10:00
Acquisitions Budget: $50,000 - $99,999
Note: Member of Atlantic Scholarly Information Network

Libraries & Resource Centres / Newfoundland & Labrador

Subjects covered: Newfoundland, Labrador, Social Sciences, Sciences, Humanities, Arts
Services:
Remote Access
Internet Access
Access to Subscription Databases
Inter-Library Loan (ILL)
Microform Equipment: Computer; Reader
Personnel: *Summary:* 15 Total; 3 Professional(s); 12 Technical(s)
Catherine Lawton, Librarian
catherine.lawton@mi.mun.ca
709-778-0662

St. John's: Fisheries & Marine Institute
Dr. C.R. Barrett Library
155 Ridge Rd.
St. John's, NL A1C 5R3
Mailing Address: PO Box 4920
St. John's, NL A1C 5R3
709-778-0662
Fax: 709-778-0316
e-mail: barrett@mi.mun.ca
URL: www.library.mun.ca/mi/
National Library Symbol: NFSCF
Founded in: 1964
Hours: M-Th 8:30-9:00; F 8:30-5:00; Sa, Su 10:00-5:00
Acquisitions Budget: $50,000 - $99,999
Note: Publications accessible through internet: info.library.mun.ca/marine.htm. The C.R. Barrett Library shares a joint-service library with the Ridge Road Campus of the College of the North Atlantic
Special Collections: Collection includes audio visual materials, ship drawings
Subjects covered: Engineering, Technology, Fisheries, Naval Architecture, Marine Engineering, Food Technology, Marine Emergency Duties, Nautical Science, Electronics, Marine Environment
Services:
Internet Access
Access to Subscription Databases
Inter-Library Loan (ILL)
Microform Equipment: Reader
Personnel: *Summary:* 6 Total; 1 Professional(s); 5 Technical(s)
George Beckett, Associate University Librarian, Health Sciences
georger@mun.ca
709-777-6670
Linda Barnett, Head of Public Services
lbarnett@mun.ca
709-777-6676

St. John's: Health Sciences Library
300 Prince Philip Dr., Memorial University of Newfoundland
St. John's, NL A1B 3V6
709-777-6672
Fax: 709-777-6866
e-mail: hslinfo@mun.ca
URL: www.library.mun.ca/hsl
National Library Symbol: NFSMM
Founded in: 1969
Hours: M-Th 8:00am-11:30pm; F 8:00-6:00; Sa 10:00-5:30; Su 12:00-8:30
Acquisitions Budget: $1,000,000 plus
For Print: $250,000 - $499,999
For Electronic: $500,000 - $999,999
Special Collections: History of Medicine Collection
Subjects covered: Medicine, Health Sciences, Pharmacy, Nursing
Services:
Remote Access
Internet Access
Access to Subscription Databases
Inter-Library Loan (ILL) for a fee of $2.50/article
Microform Equipment: Computer; Reader
Personnel: *Summary:* 24 Total; 7 Professional(s); 17 Technical(s)

St. John's: Memorial University of Newfoundland
Queen Elizabeth II Library
234 Elizabeth Ave.
St. John's, NL A1B 3Y1
709-737-7428
Fax: 709-737-2153
e-mail: qe2ill@mun.ca
URL: www.library.mun.ca

National Library Symbol: NFSM
Consortia Membership: Canadian Research Knowledge Network (CRKN); Council of Atlantic University Libraries (CAUL)
Founded in: 1925
Hours: M-Th 8:00am-11:45pm; F 8:00-5:45; Sa 10:00-5:45; Su 1:30-9:45
Acquisitions Budget: $500,000 - $999,999
Note: The library is an affiliate member of the Council of Prairie and Pacific University Libraries (COPPUL). Archive holdings are held at the Queen Elizabeth II library.
Special Collections: Centre for Newfoundland Studies
Services:
Internet Access
Access to Subscription Databases
Inter-Library Loan (ILL)
Microform Equipment: Computer; Reader
Personnel: *Summary:* 127 Total; 28 Professional(s); 99 Other employees
Richard H. Ellis, University Librarian
rhellis@mun.ca
709-737-7428
Karen Lippold, Head of Information Services
klippold@mun.ca
709-737-7428
Slavko Manojlovich, Assistant to Librarian, Systems & Planning
slavko@mun.ca
Patrick Warner, Head, Lending Services Division
pwarner@mun.ca
709-737-3189

St. John's: Newfoundland & Labrador Dept. of Health & Community Services
Library & Resource Centre
Confederation Bldg., West Block, 1st Fl., PO Box 8700
St. John's, NL A1B 4J6
709-729-2264
Fax: 709-729-5824
e-mail: hroberts@.gov.nl.ca
National Library Symbol: NFSHCS
Founded in: 1995
Hours: Winter: M-F 8:45-4:30. Summer: 8:45-4:00 by appointment only
Subjects covered: Social Work, Income Support, Health Policy
Services:
Internet Access
Inter-Library Loan (ILL)
Personnel:
Heather Roberts, Librarian
HRoberts@gov.nl.ca
709-729-2264

St. John's: Newfoundland & Labrador Dept. of Innovation, Trade & Rural Development
Information
Confederation Bldg., PO Box 8700
St. John's, NL A1B 4J6
709-729-7000
Fax: 709-729-0654
e-mail: ITRDinfo@gov.nl.ca
URL: www.intrd.gov.nl.ca/intrd/
Hours: M-F 8:30-4:30
Subjects covered: Industry, Trade, Technology
Services:
Microform Equipment: Reader

St. John's: Newfoundland & Labrador Dept. of Natural Resources
Geological Survey Library
50 Elizabeth Ave.
St. John's, NL A1B 4J6
Mailing Address: PO Box 8700
St. John's, NL A1B 4J6
709-729-1311
Fax: 709-729-4491
e-mail: paulabowdridge@gov.nl.ca
National Library Symbol: NFSMEM
Hours: M-F
Acquisitions Budget: $25,000 - $49,999
Special Collections: Company Reports, Geoscience of Newfoundland, Labrador & Offshore East
Subjects covered: Minerals, Mineral Industry, Earth Sciences
Services:
Internet Access
Access to Subscription Databases
Inter-Library Loan (ILL)
Microform Equipment: Reader

Personnel: *Summary:* 2 Total; 1 Professional(s); 2 Technical(s)
Catherine Patey, Geologist
catherinepatey@gov.nl.ca
709-729-6441

St. John's: Newfoundland & Labrador Housing Corp.
Resource Centre
2 Canada Dr.
St. John's, NL A1C 5J2
Mailing Address: PO Box 220
St. John's, NL A1C 5J2
709-724-3005
Fax: 709-724-3250
URL: www.nlhc.nf.ca
National Library Symbol: NFSHC
Founded in: 1988
Hours: M-F 8:30-4:30 by appointment only
Acquisitions Budget: For Print: $10,000 - $24,999
Subjects covered: Housing, Social Housing, Building & Construction, Land & Community Development
Services:
Inter-Library Loan (ILL)
Personnel: *Summary:* 2 Total; 1 Professional(s); 1 Other employees

St. John's: Newfoundland & Labrador Hydro
Records Management Library
Hydro Place, PO Box 12400
St. John's, NL A1B 4K7
709-737-1287
Fax: 709-737-1902
e-mail: vstandford@nlh.nf.ca
No public access
Hours: M-F
Subjects covered: Legal, Energy, Engineering, Environment
Services:
Inter-Library Loan (ILL)
Personnel: *Summary:* 3 Total; 3 Other employees
Victoria Standford, Librarian
vstandford@nlh.nf.ca
709-737-1287

St. John's: Newfoundland Ocean Industries Association
Library
#602, Atlantic Pl., 215 Water St.
St. John's, NL A1C 6C9
Mailing Address: PO Box 44
St. John's, NL A1C 6C9
709-758-6610
Fax: 709-758-6611
e-mail: noia@noianet.com
dfeltham@noianet.com
URL: www.noianet.com
National Library Symbol: NFSOI
Founded in: 1977
Hours: M-F 9:00-5:00 by appointment only
Acquisitions Budget: $25,000 - $49,999
Subjects covered: Natural Resources, Environment, Life Sciences, Ocean Industries, Marine, Fisheries, Oil & Gas
Services:
Inter-Library Loan (ILL)
Personnel: *Summary:* 12 Total; 9 Professional(s); 1 Technical(s); 2 Other employees
Joan Coote, Communications Support Coordinator
jcoote@noianet.com
709-758-6619
Dana Feltham, Head, Reference
dfeltham@noianet.com
709-758-6619
Peter Norman, Head, Systems
Annette Anthony, Librarian
Annette.Anthony@dfo-mpo.gc.ca
709-772-2022
Maria Belanger, Library Technician
Maria.Belanger@dfo-mpo.gc.ca
709-772-2020

St. John's: Northwest Atlantic Fisheries Centre
Library
80 East White Hills Rd., PO Box 5667
St. John's, NL A1C 5X1
Mailing Address: PO Box 5667
St. John's, NL A1C 5X1

709-772-2020
Fax: 709-772-2575
e-mail: NAFClibrary@dfo-mpo.gc.ca
National Library Symbol: NFSF
Founded in: 1930
Hours: M-F 8:00-4:00
Acquisitions Budget: $250,000 - $499,999
Subjects covered: Fisheries, Oceanography, Aquatic Pollution
Services:
Internet Access
Access to Subscription Databases
Inter-Library Loan (ILL)
Microform Equipment: Computer; Reader
Personnel: *Summary:* 3 Total; 1 Professional(s); 1 Technical(s)
Jennifer Mersereau, Client Services Officer
jennifer.mersereau@nrc-cnrc.gc.ca
709-772-2468

St. John's: **NRC Information Centre - St John's / Centre d'information CNRC, St John's Institute for Ocean Technology**
1 Kerwin Pl.
St. John's, NL A1B 3T5
Mailing Address: PO Box 12093
St. John's, NL A1B 3T5
709-772-2468
Fax: 709-772-3670
e-mail: nic.stjohns@nrc-cnrc.gc.ca
URL: cisti-icist.nrc-cnrc.gc.ca/eng/locations/cisti/stjohns.html
National Library Symbol: NFSNM
Founded in: 1985
Hours: M-F 8:30-4:30
Acquisitions Budget: $25,000 - $49,999
Note: ILL done via OON.
Special Collections: Reports of the Institute for Marine Dynamics
Subjects covered: Naval Architecture, Offshore Structures, Ice, Computational Hydrodynamics
Services:
Internet Access
Inter-Library Loan (ILL)
Fee Based Research
Personnel: *Summary:* 3 Total; 2 Professional(s); 1 Technical(s)
Susan Prior, Librarian
susan.prior@cna.nl.ca

St. John's: **Prince Philip Drive Campus Library**
1 Prince Philip Dr.
St. John's, NL A1C 5P7
Mailing Address: PO Box 1693
St. John's, NL A1C 5P7
709-758-7274
Fax: 709-758-7231
Other contact info: Reference Service: 709-758-7448
e-mail: susan.prior@cna.nl.ca
URL: www.cna.nl.ca
Founded in: 1965
Hours: M-W 8:00-5:00, 6:00-9:00; Th, F 8:00-4:30. Hours may vary during the acadmic year
Acquisitions Budget: $50,000 - $99,999
Subjects covered: Adult Basic Education, Automotive, Business, Diagnostic Ultrasonograhy, Early Childhood Education, English as a Second Language, Food Service & Nutrition, Hospitality, Graphic Design, Medical & paramedical sciences, Office Administration, Textile Studies
Services:
Remote Access
Internet Access
Access to Subscription Databases
Inter-Library Loan (ILL)
Audio Visual Centre; Career Centre; group & individual study facilities; computers, printers, transparency maker
Personnel: *Summary:* 5 Total; 1 Professional(s); 3 Technical(s); 1 Other employees

St. John's: **St John's Department of Planning Department of Planning**
10 New Gower St.
St. John's, NL A1C 5M2
Mailing Address: PO Box 908
St. John's, NL A1C 5M2
709-576-8285
Fax: 709-576-8625
e-mail: dsquires@stjohns.ca
planning@stjohns.ca
URL: www.stjohns.ca

Founded in: 1980
Hours: M-F 9:00-4:30 by appointment only
Subjects covered: Housing; Planning & Public Works; Local Government; Population Statistics; Land Use; Zoning
Services:
Fee Based Research
Personnel:
Lynn Cuff, Librarian III
lynn.cuff@cna.nl.ca
709-643-7752

Stephenville: **Bay St George Campus, Stephenville Crossing Building Learning Resource Centre**
L.A. Bown Bldg.
15 Washington Dr.
Stephenville, NL A2N 2Z6
Mailing Address: PO Box 5400
Stephenville, NL A2N 2Z6
709-464-5704
Fax: 709-646-5717
e-mail: Michelle.Fry@cna.nl.ca
URL: www.cna.nl.ca
Hours: M-Th 8:00-8:00; F 8:00-4:00; Sa 2:00-5:00; Su 6:00-9:00
Special Collections: Newfoundland collection
Services:
Internet Access
Inter-Library Loan (ILL)
Personnel: *Summary:* 1 Total; 1 Other employees

Stephenville: **College of the North Atlantic Bay St. George Campus Learning Resource Centres**
432 Massachusetts Dr.
Stephenville, NL A2N 2Z6
Mailing Address: PO Box 5400
Stephenville, NL A2N 2Z6
709-643-7762
Fax: 709-643-7786
e-mail: lynn.cuff@cna.nl.ca
URL: www.cna.nl.ca
Founded in: 1977
Hours: D.S.B Flowlow Bldg LRC: M-Th 8:00-8:00; F 8:00-4:00; Sa 2:00-6:00; Su 6:00-9:00. Other LRC's: M-F 8:00-4:00. Hours may vary during the academic year
Acquisitions Budget: $25,000 - $49,999
Note: Westviking College, Eastern College, Cabot College of Applied Arts, Technology & Continuing Education, & Central Newfoundland Regional College merged to create the College of the North Atlantic. The Bay St. George Campus includes the D.S.B. Fowlow Bldg Learning Resource Centre and the L.A. Bown LRC, located at 423 Massachusetts Dr. in Stephenville, and the Martin Gallant Bldg LRC located at 15 Washington Dr. in Stephenville Crossing. For information on Library Services available to the Ridge Road Campus, please see the entry for the Dr. C.R. Barrett Library, listed under Memorial University of Newfoundland
Special Collections: College of the North Atlantic Folklore & Language Archives; Newfoundland Collection
Subjects covered: Hospitality, Visual Arts, Film & Video Production, Music Industry/Production, Recording Arts, Journalism, Business Administration, Industrial Trades, Multimedia
Services:
Remote Access
Internet Access
Access to Subscription Databases
Inter-Library Loan (ILL)
Computer lab with networked computers, scanners, laser printers; photocopiers
Microform Equipment: Reader
Personnel: *Summary:* 4 Total; 1 Professional(s); 3 Technical(s);

Lynn Cuff, College Librarian, D.S.B. Fowlow Bldg LRC
lynn.cuff@cna.nl.ca
709-643-7762
Barbara King, Library Technician, D.S.B. Fowlow Bldg LRC
barb.king@cna.nl.ca
709-643-7752
Theresa Hynes, Library Technician, Martin Gallant Bldg LRC
theresa.hynes@cna.nl.ca
709-643-5704
Cathy Ash, Library Technician, L.A. Bown Bldg LRC
cathy.ash@cna.nl.ca
709-643-7787

Twillingate: **Notre Dame Bay Memorial Health Centre Library**
Twillingate, NL A0G 4M0
709-884-2131
Fax: 709-884-2586
e-mail: bhamlyn@cehcib.nf.ca
URL: www.cehcib.nf.ca
Founded in: 1924
Hours: M, F 8:00-11:45 by appointment only
Subjects covered: Health Sciences, Medicine, Nursing
Services:
Internet Access
Inter-Library Loan (ILL)
Personnel: *Summary:* 1 Technical(s)
Barbara Hamlyn, Librarian
bhamlyn@cehcib.nf.ca

Northwest Territories

Fort Smith: **Aurora College Thebacha Campus Library**
50 Conibear St.
Fort Smith, NT X0E 0P0
Mailing Address: PO Bag Service 2
Fort Smith, NT X0E 0P0
867-872-7544
Fax: 867-872-4511
e-mail: ahook@auroracollege.nt.ca
mharney@auroracollege.nt.ca
URL: www.auroracollege.nt.ca
National Library Symbol: NWFST
Founded in: 1983
Hours: M-F 8:30am-9:00pm; Sa 1:00-5:00; Su 1:00-9:00
Acquisitions Budget: $250,000 - $499,999
Subjects covered: All subjects with emphasis on Native Peoples & Northern Affairs
Services:
Remote Access
Internet Access
Access to Subscription Databases
Inter-Library Loan (ILL)
Microform Equipment: Reader
Personnel: *Summary:* 3 Total; 1 Professional(s); 1 Technical(s); 1 Other employees
Alexandra Hook, Librarian
ahook@auroracollege.nt.ca
867-872-7544
Margo Harney, Library Technicien
867-872-7549

Inuvik: **Aurora College. Aurora Research Institute Inuvik Research Centre Library**
191 Mackenzie Rd.
Inuvik, NT X0E 0T0
Mailing Address: PO Box 1450
Inuvik, NT X0E 0T0
867-777-3298 ext: 28
Fax: 867-777-4264
e-mail: library@nwtresearch.com
irc_library@gov.nt.ca
URL: www.nwtresearch.com
Consortia Membership: NWT Libraries
Hours: M-F 8:30-12:00, 1:00-5:00
Acquisitions Budget: 0-$9,999
For Print: 0-$9,999
For Electronic: 0-$9,999
Population Served: 3000
Special Collections: Northern rare books, maps, airphotos
Subjects covered: Arctic Research, Arctic Life Sciences, Arctic Earth Sciences, Arctic Social Sciences
Services:
Internet Access
Access to Subscription Databases
Inter-Library Loan (ILL)
Microform Equipment: Reader
Personnel:
Andrew Applejohn, Institute Director
867-777-3298
Kevin Rowe, Librarian

Yellowknife: **Canadian Forces Northern Area Headquarters Library**
PO Box 6666, Stn Main
Yellowknife, NT X1A 2R3

Libraries & Resource Centres / Nova Scotia

867-873-0700 ext: 805
Fax: 867-873-0708
e-mail: labonte.jk@forces.gc.ca
National Library Symbol: NWYND
Founded in: 1972
Hours: M-F 9:00-12:00, 1:00-4:00 by appointment only
Acquisitions Budget: $25,000 - $49,999
Subjects covered: Physical Sciences, Engineering, Technology, Northern Culture & History, Communications - subjects as applicable to military operations in the Canadian North
Services:
Internet Access
Personnel: *Summary:* 1 Total; 1 Technical(s)

Yellowknife: Northwest Territories Legislative Assembly
Legislative Library of the Northwest Territories
Legislative Assembly Bldg., PO Box 1320
Yellowknife, NT X1A 2L9
867-669-2202
Fax: 867-873-0207
e-mail: leglib@gov.nt.ca
URL: www.assembly.gov.nt.ca/library
National Library Symbol: NWYGI
Hours: M-F 8:30-5:00
Acquisitions Budget: $25,000 - $49,999
Special Collections: NWT Government Documents
Subjects covered: Native Peoples & Northern Affairs, Natural Resources, Environment, Politics, Public Administration
Services:
Inter-Library Loan (ILL)
Microform Equipment: Computer; Reader
Personnel: *Summary:* 4 Total; 2 Professional(s); 2 Technical(s);

Vera Raschke, Legislative Librarian
867-669-2203

Yellowknife: Northwest Territories Public Works & Services
Technical Services Library
Stuart M. Hodgson Bldg., 5009 - 49th St., 3rd Fl.
Yellowknife, NT X1A 2L9
Mailing Address: PO Box 1320
Yellowknife, NT X1A 2L9
867-920-6451
Fax: 867-873-0226
e-mail: janet_diveky@gov.nt.ca
Founded in: 1985
Hours: Tu-Th 9:00-2:00
Acquisitions Budget: 0-$9,999
Special Collections: Government of NWT building drawings (mylar, microfiche, whiteprint copies), O & M manuals for buildings, aerial photographs of communites, video (VHS & video 8) collection of building assessments
Subjects covered: Engineering, Contracting & Contract Law, Electrical Maintenance, Water/Sanitation, Construction, Product Information, Geotechnical/Granular, Architecture/Construction
Services:
Internet Access
Inter-Library Loan (ILL)
Microform Equipment: Computer; Reader
Personnel: *Summary:* 1 Total; 1 Technical(s)
Janet Diveky, Library Technician
janet_diveky@gov.nt.ca
867-920-6451

Yellowknife: Northwest Territories Resources, Wildlife & Economic Development
Library
#600, 5102 - 50th Ave.
Yellowknife, NT X1A 3S8
867-920-8606
Fax: 867-873-0293
e-mail: enriti_library@gov.nt.ca
URL: www.enr.gov.nt.ca/library/index.htm
National Library Symbol: NWYRR
Founded in: 1980
Hours: M-F 8:30-12:00, 1:00-5:00 by appointment only
Acquisitions Budget: $25,000 - $49,999
Subjects covered: Environment, Natural Resources, Wildlife, Minerals, Parks, Tourism, Oil & Gas, Economic Development
Services:
Inter-Library Loan (ILL)
Microform Equipment: Reader
Personnel: *Summary:* 2 Total; 1 Professional(s); 1 Technical(s); 1 Other employees

Kim Ullyot, Manager, Library & Info Services

Yellowknife: Prairie & Northern Region - Yellowknife Library - Environment Canada
#301, 5204 - 50th Ave.
Yellowknife, NT X1A 1E2
867-669-4717
Fax: 867-873-8185
e-mail: yel.library@ec.gc.ca
National Library Symbol: NWYECW
Hours: M-F 8:30-3:00 by appointment only
Acquisitions Budget: 0-$9,999
Subjects covered: Conservation, Natural Resources, Environmental Impact Analysis, Land Use, Pollution, Meteorology, Climatology, Hydrology, Water Management & Resources, Environmental Protection, Air Quality, Severe Weather & Environmental Emergencies
Services:
Inter-Library Loan (ILL)
Microform Equipment: Reader
Personnel: *Summary:* 1 Total; 1 Professional(s)

Yellowknife: Workers' Compensation Board Northwest Territories
Kathy Mackay Memorial Library
5022 - 49th St.
Yellowknife, NT X1A 2R3
Mailing Address: PO Box 8888
Yellowknife, NT X1A 2R3
867-920-3888
Fax: 867-873-4596
800-661-0792
URL: www.wcb.nt.ca
Founded in: 1986
Hours: M-F 8:30-5:00
Acquisitions Budget: $25,000 - $49,999
Services:
Inter-Library Loan (ILL)
Personnel: *Summary:* 2 Total; 1 Professional(s); 1 Other employees
Rita Denneron, Resource Library Technician
ritad@wcb.nt.ca
867-920-3835

Nova Scotia

Sheldon MacInnes, Celtic Music Researcher
sheldon_macinnes@uccb.ca
902-563-1308
Anne Connell, Archival Clerk
anne_connell@uccb.ca
902-563-1425
Gerardette Brown, Secretary
gerardette_brown@cbu.ca
902-563-1327

Sydney: Beaton Institute
1250 Grand Lake Rd.
Sydney, NS B1P 6L2
Mailing Address: PO Box 5300
Sydney, NS B1P 6L2
902-563-1329
Fax: 902-562-8899
e-mail: beaton@cbu.ca
URL: beaton.capebretonu.ca
Founded in: 1954
Hours: Tu, Th, F 9:00-4:00; W 9:00-7:00; Sa 9:00-12:00 once/month
Acquisitions Budget: $10,000 - $24,999
For Print: 0-$9,999
For Electronic: 0-$9,999
Population Served: 3204
Special Collections: Manuscripts, maps, tapes, photos, books, newspapers & pamphlets pertaining to culture & history of Cape Breton Island
Subjects covered: History, Culture, Maps, Genealogy
Services:
Internet Access
Fee Based Research
Microform Equipment: Reader
Personnel: *Summary:* 5 Total; 2 Professional(s); 3 Technical(s);

Catherine Irving, Librarian
Cathy Sears, Library Assistant

Antigonish: Coady International Institute
Marie Michael Library
St. Francis-Xavier University, PO Box 5000
Antigonish, NS B2G 2W5
902-867-3964
Fax: 902-867-3907
e-mail: cirving@stfx.ca
URL: www.stfx.ca/coady-library
National Library Symbol: NSASF
Founded in: 1959
Hours: M-F 9:00-5:00
Acquisitions Budget: $10,000 - $24,999
For Print: $10,000 - $24,999
For Electronic: 0-$9,999
Special Collections: Antigonish Movement, St Francis Xavier University Extension
Subjects covered: Cooperatives, International Development, Adult Education, Women in Development, Environment, Peacebuilding, Advocacy, Health
Services:
Remote Access
Internet Access
Inter-Library Loan (ILL)
Personnel: *Summary:* 2 Total; 1 Professional(s); 1 Technical(s)

Antigonish: St Francis-Xavier University
Angus L. Macdonald Library
PO Box 5000
Antigonish, NS B2G 2W5
902-867-2267
Fax: 902-867-5153
e-mail: illoan@stfx.ca
URL: library.stfx.ca
National Library Symbol: NSAS
Consortia Membership: Canadian Research Knowledge Network (CRKN); Council of Atlantic University Libraries (CAUL); Novanet
Founded in: 1853
Hours: M-Su
Acquisitions Budget: $50,000 - $99,999
Note: Member of CAUL, Council of Atlantic University Librarians, Atlantic Provinces Library Association
Special Collections: Celtic collections
Services:
Inter-Library Loan (ILL)
Microform Equipment: Computer; Reader
Personnel: *Summary:* 39 Total; 9 Professional(s); 23 Technical(s); 7 Other employees
Lynne Murphy, University Librarian
lmurphy@stfx.ca
902-867-2267
Barbara Phillips, Head, Information Services
bphillip@stfx.ca
902-867-3866
Elaine MacLean, Head, Technical Services
emaclean@stfx.ca
902-867-2221
Glenna Quinn, Head, Collection Development
gquinn@stfx.ca
902-867-2168
Gordon Bertrand, Head, Systems & Support Services
gbertran@stfx.ca
902-867-2334
Susan Cameron, Head, User Services
Rita Campbell, Librarian
rcampbel@stfx.ca
902-867-5218

Church Point: Université Sainte-Anne
Bibliothèque Louis-R.-Comeau
1695, rte 1
Church Point, NS B0W 1M0
Adresse postale: CP 40
Church Point, NS B0W 1M0
902-769-2114
Téléc: 902-769-0137
Courriel: corinne.arsenault@usainteanne.ca
URL: www.usainteanne.ca/biblio/
Sigle: NSCS
Membre d'un consortium: Canadian Research Knowledge Network (CRKN); Council of Atlantic University Libraries (CAUL)
Fondée en: 1890
Heures: D'automne-Hiver: L-J 9h-22h; V 9h-16h30, 18h-21h; S 13h-16h30; D 13h-16h30, 18h-22h30; Printemps L-J 9h-16h30, 18h-21h; V 9h-16h30, Sa-V Fermé
Budget d'acquisitions $100,000 - $249,999

Matériel imprimé: $50,000 - $99,999
Matériel électronique: $25,000 - $49,999
Population desservie: 700
Collections spécialisées: Collection Centre acadien
Services:
Accèss distance aux bases de donn
Accès public à l'internet
Réseau en ligne
Prêts entre bibliothèques(PEB)
Lecteur/reproduction de microformes: Ordinateur; Lecteurs
Personnel: *Sommaire:* 5 Total; 2 Professionnel(s); 3 Autre(s) employé(s)
Janice Boudreau, Directrice
janice.boudreau@usainteanne.ca
902-769-2114 ext. 161
Cécile Pothier-Comeau, Bibliothécaire
cecile.pothiercomeau@usainteanne.ca
902-769-2114 ext. 162
Corinne Arsenault, PEB
corinne.arsenault@usainteanne.ca
902-769-2114 ext. 163
Réjeanne LeBlanc-Comeau, Acquisitions
rejeanne.leblanccomeau@usainteanne.ca
902-769-2114 ext. 170
Claire Robicheau, Comptoir de prêt
claire.robicheau@usainteanne.ca
902-769-2114 ext. 158
Ann Roman, Librarian
ann.roman@nscc.ca

Dartmouth: Akerley Campus Library
21 Woodlawn Rd.
Dartmouth, NS B2W 2R7
902-491-4968
Fax: 902-491-4903
e-mail: library.akerley@nscc.ca
URL: www.library.nscc.ca
National Library Symbol: NSDRV
Consortia Membership: Novanet
Founded in: 1989
Hours: M-F 8:00-4:00
Services:
Personnel: *Summary:* 3 Total; 1 Professional(s); 2 Technical(s)
Kirk Johnstone, In charge

Dartmouth: Atlantic Region Library
Queen Square, 45 Alderney Dr., 5th Fl.
Dartmouth, NS B2Y 2N6
902-426-7219
Fax: 902-426-6143
Other contact info: 902-426-7232
e-mail: dawn.taylor-prime@ec.gc.ca
library@ec.gc.ca
National Library Symbol: NSDE
Founded in: 1981
Hours: M-F 7:00-3:30 by appointment only
Acquisitions Budget: $50,000 - $99,999
Subjects covered: Environment
Services:
Inter-Library Loan (ILL)
Microform Equipment: Reader
Personnel: *Summary:* 1 Professional(s); 1 Technical(s)

Dartmouth: Atlantic Regional Library
#1625, 1505 Barrington St.
Dartmouth, NS B3J 3Y6
902-426-6694
Fax: 902-426-6676
National Library Symbol: NSHHW
Hours: M-F 8:00-4:00
Special Collections: Food Science
Subjects covered: Health Sciences
Services:
Anna Fiander, Regional Librarian
902-426-3675 ext. 902-4
Lori Collins, Head of Reference
Maureen Martin, Head of Technical Services

Dartmouth: Bedford Institute of Oceanography / Institut océanographique de Bedford Library
Holland Bldg.
1 Challenger Dr., 4th Fl.
Dartmouth, NS B2Y 4A2
Mailing Address: PO Box 1006
Dartmouth, NS B2Y 4A2
902-426-6224
Fax: 902-496-1544
e-mail: BIOLibrary@mar.dfo-mpo.gc.ca
URL: www.mar.dfo-mpo.gc.ca/e/library/bio-e.html
National Library Symbol: NSDB
Founded in: 1962
Hours: M-F 9:00-4:30
Acquisitions Budget: $250,000 - $499,999
Subjects covered: Environmental Assessment, Oceanography, Marine Sciences
Services:
Internet Access
Inter-Library Loan (ILL)
Microform Equipment: Computer; Reader
Personnel: *Summary:* 10 Total; 4 Professional(s); 6 Technical(s)

Dartmouth: Clean Nova Scotia Resource Centre
126 Portland St.
Dartmouth, NS B2Y 1H8
902-420-3474
Fax: 902-424-5334
800-665-5377
e-mail: cns@clean.ns.ca
URL: www.clean.ns.ca
Founded in: 1987
Special Collections: Information on topics including climate change & energy, solid waste, health & the environment & water
Subjects covered: Magazines, journals & publications on environmental topics including litter, marine debris, recycling & waste reduction, climate change
Services:
Iris Ouellett, Library Manager
iris.ouellette@drdc-rddc.gc.ca
902-426-3100 ext. 135
Mary Gillis, Circulation Clerk
mary.gillis@drdc-rddc.gc.ca
902-426-3100 ext. 108

Dartmouth: Defence R & D Canada - Atlantic Library
9 Grove St.
Dartmouth, NS B2Y 3Z7
Mailing Address: PO Box 1012
Dartmouth, NS B2Y 3Z7
902-426-3100 ext: 135
Fax: 902-426-9654
e-mail: iris.ouellette@drdc-rddc.gc.ca
atl.library@drdc-rddc.gc.ca
National Library Symbol: NSHN
No public access
Hours: M-F 8:00-4:00
Acquisitions Budget: $100,000 - $249,999
For Print: $25,000 - $49,999
For Electronic: $50,000 - $99,999
Population Served: 250
Subjects covered: Engineering, Physical Sciences, Acoustics
Services:
Inter-Library Loan (ILL)
Microform Equipment: Reader
Personnel: *Summary:* 2 Total; 1 Technical(s); 1 Other employees;
Margaret E. Reid, Librarian

Fall River: Technical Services Library
107 Perrin Dr.
Fall River, NS B2T 1J6
902-860-2999
Fax: 902-861-4828
Founded in: 1978
Hours: M-F, by appointment only. by appointment only
Subjects covered: Transportation, Engineering, Technology, Materials & Construction
Services:
Inter-Library Loan (ILL)
Personnel: *Summary:* 1 Total; 1 Professional(s)

Halifax: Capital Health
Health Sciences Library, Halifax Infirmary Site
#2201, 1796 Summer St.
Halifax, NS B3H 3A7
Mailing Address: 1796 Summer St.
Halifax, NS B3H 3A7
902-473-4287
Fax: 902-473-7168
e-mail: cdhalib@cdha.nshealth.ca
URL: www.cdha.nshealth.ca
National Library Symbol: NSHQ
Founded in: 1996
Hours: M-F 8:30-4:30
Acquisitions Budget: $500,000 - $999,999
For Print: $50,000 - $99,999
For Electronic: $250,000 - $499,999
Population Served: 10000
Subjects covered: Health Sciences
Services:
Remote Access
Internet Access
Inter-Library Loan (ILL)
Personnel: *Summary:* 5 Total; 1 Professional(s); 3 Technical(s); 1 Other employees; 1 Volunteer(s)
Penny Logan, Manager, Library Services
penny.logan@cdha.nshealth.ca
902-473-4383

Halifax: Dalhousie University Libraries
Killam Memorial Library
6225 University Ave.
Halifax, NS B3H 4H8
902-494-3601
Fax: 902-494-2062
e-mail: dalhousie.libraries@dal.ca
killamcirc@dal.ca
URL: www.library.dal.ca
National Library Symbol: NSHD
Consortia Membership: Canadian Research Knowledge Network (CRKN); Council of Atlantic University Libraries (CAUL); Novanet
Founded in: 1968
Hours: M-F 8:00am-12:00am; Sa 10:00-6:00; Su 10:00am-12:00am
Acquisitions Budget: $1,000,000 plus
For Print: $500,000 - $999,999
For Electronic: $1,000,000 plus
Note: The library is an affiliate member of the Council of Prairie and Pacific University Libraries (COPPUL).
Special Collections: Kipling Collection, Morse Collection, J.J. Stewart Collection, Canadian Small Press Collection, Bacon Collection, Cockerell Collection, Canadiana
Subjects covered: Science, Social Sciences & Humanities
Services:
Internet Access
Inter-Library Loan (ILL)
Microform Equipment: Computer; Reader
Personnel: *Summary:* 75 Total; 20 Professional(s); 55 Technical(s)
William R. Maes, University Librarian
william.maes@dal.ca
902-494-3601
Sharon Longard, Reference
902-494-3611
Jane Archibald, Head, Technical Services
902-494-6688
Nola Brennan, Librarian
nola.brennan@nscc.ca

Halifax: Institute of Technology Campus Library
5685 Leeds St.
Halifax, NS B3J 3C4
Mailing Address: PO Box 2210
Halifax, NS B3J 3C4
902-491-4694
Fax: 902-491-4800
e-mail: library.institute@nscc.ca
URL: www.library.nscc.ca
National Library Symbol: NSHTI
Consortia Membership: Novanet
Founded in: 1972
Hours: M-Th 8:00-5:00; F 8:00-4:00
Services:
Personnel: *Summary:* 2 Total; 1 Professional(s); 1 Technical(s)

Halifax: Legal Information Society of Nova Scotia
5523B Young St.
Halifax, NS B3K 1Z7
902-454-2198
Fax: 902-455-3105

Libraries & Resource Centres / Nova Scotia

e-mail: lisns@legalinfo.org
URL: www.legalinfo.org
No public access
Founded in: 1982
Acquisitions Budget: 0-$9,999
For Print: 0-$9,999
Subjects covered: Law
Services:
Personnel:
Maria Franks, Executive Director
Wendy Turner, Manager, Legal Information Line & Lawyer Referral Service

Halifax: Nova Scotia Community College Library Services - Administration
5685 Leeds St.
Halifax, NS B3J 2X1
Mailing Address: PO Box 1153
Halifax, NS B3J 2X1
902-491-6772
Fax: 902-491-2178
e-mail: marie.deyoung@nscc.ca
URL: www.library.nscc.ca
Consortia Membership: Council of Atlantic University Libraries (CAUL); Novanet
Acquisitions Budget: $250,000 - $499,999
Services:
Personnel: *Summary:* 5 Total; 3 Professional(s); 2 Technical(s)
Andrea Stewart, Director, Library Services
andrea.stewart@nscc.ca
902-491-6772
Debbie Costelo, Public Services Librarian
debbie.costelo@nscc.ca
902-491-1031
Denise Parrott, Technical Services Librarian
denise.parrott@nscc.ca
902-893-5306

Halifax: Nova Scotia Dept. of Natural Resources Library
1701 Hollis, 3rd Fl.
Halifax, NS B3J 2T9
Mailing Address: PO Box 698
Halifax, NS B3J 2T9
902-424-8633
Fax: 902-424-7735
e-mail: nsdnrlib@gov.ns.ca
URL: www.gov.ns.ca/natr/library/library.htm
National Library Symbol: NSHDOM
Founded in: 1962
Hours: M-F 8:30-4:00
Acquisitions Budget: 0-$9,999
For Print: 0-$9,999
For Electronic: 0-$9,999
Special Collections: Nova Scotia Department of Mines Reports, Geological Survey of Canada Publications, Historical Aerial Photography (1931-1955), Historical Maps (A.F. Church), Crown Land Grants
Subjects covered: Mineral Resources, Mines, Mineral Development, Forestry, Parks & Recreation, Wildlife, GIS, Integrated Resource Management, Land Use
Services:
Remote Access
Internet Access
Access to Subscription Databases
Inter-Library Loan (ILL)
Online catalogue with other NS government libraries on Multilis; Web version available via web page
Microform Equipment: Computer; Reader
Personnel: *Summary:* 3 Total; 1 Professional(s); 1 Technical(s)
Tracy Lenfesty, Head librarian
lenfestl@gov.ns.ca
902-424-1290
Carol Payne, Library Staff
paynecz@gov.ns.ca

Halifax: Nova Scotia Dept. of Transportation & Public Works Library
1572 Granville St
Halifax, NS B3J 2N2
Mailing Address: PO Box 186
Halifax, NS B3J 2N2
902-424-6720
Fax: 902-424-0532

e-mail: tpwpaff@gov.ns.ca
URL: www.gov.ns.ca/tran
Hours: Open to public by appointment only by appointment only
Acquisitions Budget: $25,000 - $49,999
Subjects covered: Transportation, Engineering, Public Works
Services:
Inter-Library Loan (ILL)
Personnel: *Summary:* 1 Total; 1 Professional(s)
Margaret E. Reid, Librarian

Halifax: Nova Scotia Environment & Labour Library
5151 Terminal Rd., 5th Fl.
Halifax, NS B3J 2T8
Mailing Address: PO Box 697
Halifax, NS B3J 2T8
902-424-8474
Fax: 902-424-6925
e-mail: enlalibr@gov.ns.ca
National Library Symbol: NSDEL
Founded in: 1977
Hours: M-F 2:00-4:00 by appointment only
Acquisitions Budget: $50,000 - $99,999
Note: Participate in Provincial Interdepartmental
Special Collections: Occupational Health & Safety Video Collection; Uranium Exploration & Mining Collection; Environmental Impact & Assessment Collection; Nova Scotia Reports; Collective Agreements; Grievance Arbitrations; Workers' Compensation Appeals Tribunal/Workers' Compensation Board-Internal Appeals Decisions; Labour Standards Tribunal Decisions; Labour Relations Board/Construction Industry Panel Decisions; Industry Standards (ie. CSA, ASME, ANSI)
Subjects covered: Environment, Pollution Prevention, Air & Water Pollution, Solid Waste Management, Labour Law, Occupational Health & Safety
Services:
Internet Access
Access to Subscription Databases
Inter-Library Loan (ILL)
Fee Based Research
Microform Equipment: Computer; Reader
Personnel: *Summary:* 3 Total; 1 Professional(s); 1 Technical(s)
Natalie MacPherson, Information Resources Manager
enlalibr@gov.ns.ca
902-424-8474
Joanne Babin, Library Assistant
enlalibr@gov.ns.ca
Donna Curtis, Head
Anna Backman, Client Services Officer

Halifax: NRC Information Centre - Halifax Institute for Marine Biosciences
1411 Oxford St.
Halifax, NS B3H 3Z1
902-426-8250
Fax: 902-426-4900
e-mail: nic.halifax@nrc-cnrc.gc.ca
Bernadette.Kennedy@nrc.gc.ca
URL: cisti-icist.nrc-cnrc.gc.ca
Hours: M-F 8:30-5:00
Acquisitions Budget: $50,000 - $99,999
Note: Fee for services
Subjects covered: Aquaculture Production/Aquaculture Nutrition; Natural Toxins; Shellfish; Aquatic Animal Health; Mass Spectrometry Techologies; Natural Products; Proteomics; Biochemistry & Functional Genomics
Services:
Internet Access
Access to Subscription Databases
Inter-Library Loan (ILL)
Personnel: *Summary:* 2 Total; 1 Professional(s); 1 Technical(s)

Halifax: St Mary's University Patrick Power Library
5946 Inglis St.
Halifax, NS B3H 3C3
Mailing Address: 923 Robie St.
Halifax, NS B3H 3C3
902-420-5534
Fax: 902-491-8698
TDD: 9024205144
URL: www.smu.ca/library
National Library Symbol: NSHS
Consortia Membership: Canadian Research Knowledge Network (CRKN); Council of Atlantic University Libraries (CAUL); Novanet
Founded in: 1802
Hours: M-F 8:15am-11:00pm; Sa 11:00-2:00; Su 1:00-11:00
Acquisitions Budget: $500,000 - $999,999
Special Collections: Irish Studies
Subjects covered: Education, Business, Arts, Science
Services:
Remote Access
Internet Access
Inter-Library Loan (ILL)
Microform Equipment: Computer; Reader
Personnel: *Summary:* 45 Total; 9 Professional(s); 1 Technical(s); 35 Other employees
Madeleine Lefebvre, University Librarian
madeleine.lefebvre@stmarys.ca
902-420-5532
Douglas Vaisey, Librarian, Reference & Research
902-420-5540
David Manning, Head of Acquisitions
902-420-5535
Peter Webster, Librarian, Information Services
902-420-5507
Joyce Thomson, Librarian, Collections Development
902-420-6287
Heather Sanderson, Librarian, Information Literacy
902-420-5541
Donna Richardson, Associate University Librarian
donna.richardson@dal.ca
902-494-3979
Sarah Jane Dooley, Reference & Liaison Librarian
sdooley@dal.ca
902-494-3428
Allison Fulford, Head, Technical Services
allison.fulford@dal.ca
902-494-3255
Helen Powell, Head, Public Services
helen.powell@dal.ca
902-494-3285
Pamela Chase-Mobus, Acting Head, Circulation
pamela.chase@dal.ca
902-494-6095

Halifax: Sexton Design & Technology Library
1360 Barrington St.
Halifax, NS B3J 2X4
Mailing Address: PO Box 1000
Halifax, NS B3J 2X4
902-494-3249
Fax: 902-494-6089
Other contact info: Reference: 902/494-3965
e-mail: sexton.library@dal.ca
URL: sexton.library.dal.ca
National Library Symbol: NSHT
Consortia Membership: Novanet
Hours: M-Th 8:00am-12:00am; F 8:00am-9:00pm; Sa 9:00am-9:00pm; Su 10:00am-12:00am
Note: Part of Novanet.
Special Collections: Electronic Books; Journals, Images; Patents; Standards; Technical Reports; Theses
Subjects covered: Engineering (civil, electrical, computer, mathematical, industrial, biological, environmental, chemical, oil & gas, mechanical, materials, mining); Technology; Planning; Architecture
Services:
Internet Access
Inter-Library Loan (ILL)
Fee Based Research
Document delivery, Electronic reading room, Research service & instruction
Personnel:
Patrick Ellis, Acting Associate University Librarian, Health Sciences
patrick.ellis@dal.ca
902-494-1669
Judith Coughlan-Lambly, Head of Technical Services
judith.clambly@dal.ca
902-494-1670
Gail Fraser, Head of Acquisitions
gail.fraser@dal.ca
902-494-3741
Ann Barrett, Coordinator, Electronic Services
ann.barrett@dal.ca
902-494-1649

Halifax: **W.K. Kellogg Health Sciences Library**
Sir Charles Tupper Bldg., Dalhousie University
5850 College St.
Halifax, NS B3H 1X5
902-494-2458
Fax: 902-494-3750
e-mail: kellogg.library@dal.ca
kellogg.library@dal.ca
URL: www.library.dal.ca/kellogg/
National Library Symbol: NSHDM
Consortia Membership: Novanet
Founded in: 1879
Hours: M-Th 8:00am-11:00pm; F 8:00-7:00; Sa 10:00-6:00; Su 11:00-11:00
Acquisitions Budget: $100,000 - $249,999
Note: Member of Novanet
Subjects covered: Medicine, Dentistry, Health Services Administration, Human Communication Disorders, Nursing, Occupational Therapy, Pharmacy, Physiotherapy, Kinesiology
Services:
Remote Access
Internet Access
Access to Subscription Databases
Inter-Library Loan (ILL)
Personnel: *Summary:* 24 Total; 6 Professional(s); 18 Technical(s)
Jerry Miner, Manager, Library & Information Services
minerj@agr.gc.ca
Pat Melanson, Library Clerk
melansonpa@agr.gc.ca
902-679-5343

Kentville: **Canadian Agriculture Library - Kentville / Bibliothèque canadienne de l'agriculture - Kentville**
32 Main St.
Kentville, NS B4N 1J5
902-679-5508
Fax: 902-679-5784
e-mail: minerj@agr.gc.ca
melansonpa@agr.gc.ca
URL: res2.agr.ca/kentville/services/library-bibliotheque_e.html
National Library Symbol: NSKR
Founded in: 1952
Hours: M-F
Acquisitions Budget: $50,000 - $99,999
Subjects covered: Agriculture, Food
Services:
Inter-Library Loan (ILL)
Microform Equipment: Reader
Personnel: *Summary:* 2 Total; 1 Professional(s); 1 Technical(s)
Lana Kamennof-Sine, Librarian
lana.kamennof-sine@nscc.ca

Kentville: **Kingstec Campus Library**
236 Belcher St.
Kentville, NS B4N 3X3
902-679-7380
Fax: 902-679-5187
e-mail: library.kinstec@nscc.ca
URL: www.library.nscc.ca
National Library Symbol: NSKKR
Consortia Membership: Novanet
Founded in: 1965
Hours: M-F 8:00-5:00
Services:
Personnel: *Summary:* 2 Total; 1 Professional(s); 1 Technical(s)
Lana MacLean, Librarian
lana.maclean@nscc.ca

Port Hawkesbury: **Strait Area Campus Library**
226 Reeves St.
Port Hawkesbury, NS B9A 2A2
902-625-4364
Fax: 902-625-0193
e-mail: library.straitarea@nscc.ca
URL: www.library.nscc.ca
National Library Symbol: NSPHS
Consortia Membership: Novanet
Hours: M-F 8:00-4:00
Services:
Personnel: *Summary:* 2 Total; 1 Professional(s); 1 Technical(s)

Sydney: **Cape Breton District Health Authority Health Sciences Library**
1482 George St.
Sydney, NS B1P 1P3
902-567-8000 ext: 2738
Fax: 902-567-7878
URL: www.cbdha.nshealth.ca/library/
National Library Symbol: NSSCBH
Consortia Membership: Atlantic Health Knowledge Partnership
Hours: M-F 8:30-4:30 by appointment only
Acquisitions Budget: For Print: $25,000 - $49,999
For Electronic: $10,000 - $24,999
Note: Sydney Community Hospital, Sydney City Hospital & Cape Breton Mental Health Hospital have closed & have merged into one facility, Cape Breton Healthcare Complex
Subjects covered: Medical, Psychiatry, Pediatrics, Obstetrics & Gynecology, Nursing, Allied Health, Oncology, Mental Health
Services:
Remote Access
Inter-Library Loan (ILL)
Personnel: *Summary:* 2 Total; 1 Professional(s); 1 Technical(s); 1 Other employees
Patricia Foley, Health Sciences Librarian
foleyp@cbdha.nshealth.ca
902-567-8000 ext. 2738

Sydney: **Cape Breton University Library**
1250 Grand Lake Rd.
Sydney, NS B1P 6L2
Mailing Address: PO Box 5300
Sydney, NS B1P 6L2
902-563-1320
Fax: 902-563-1177
888-959-9995
Other contact info: Reference Desk: 902/563-1387
e-mail: library_circulation@cbu.ca
library_information_services@cbu.ca
library_interlibrary_loans@cbu.ca
URL: www.capebretonu.ca/library
National Library Symbol: NSSX
Consortia Membership: Canadian Research Knowledge Network (CRKN); Council of Atlantic University Libraries (CAUL); Novanet
Founded in: 1951
Hours: M-Th 8:30-10:00; F 8:30-5:00; Sa 11:00-4:00; Su 12:00-9:00
Acquisitions Budget: $50,000 - $99,999
For Print: $50,000 - $99,999
For Electronic: $50,000 - $99,999
Population Served: 3500
Note: Hours may vary depending upon time of year.
Special Collections: National Film Board Collection; Audio Collection; Bras d'or Institute Resource Center; Dr. Thomas Joseph Khattar Collection; Scottish Collection; Centre for International Studies
Services:
Remote Access
Internet Access
Inter-Library Loan (ILL)
Services include library instruction, reserve service & information & alerting services for faculty
Microform Equipment: Computer; Reader
Personnel: *Summary:* 17 Total; 6 Professional(s); 11 Technical(s)
Robert Campbell, Director, Library Services
Robert_Campbell@cbu.ca
Lou Duggan, Systems Librarian
Lou_Duggan@cbu.ca
902-563-1997
Cathy Chisholm, Information Services Librarian
Cathy_Chisholm@cbu.ca
902-563-1993
Mary Dobson, Information Services Librarian
Mary_Dobson@cbu.ca
902-563-1231
Anne Fisher, Information Services Librarian
Anne_Fisher@cbu.ca
902-563-1996
Laura Syms, Information Services Librarian
Laura_Syms@cbu.ca
902-563-1994
Debbie MacInnis, Paralibrarian/Head of Circulation
Debbie_MacInnis@cbu.ca
902-563-1674

Janine Mills, Paralibrarian (Cataloguing)
Janine_Mills@cbu.ca
902-563-1619
Nick Sobol, Paralibrarian (Serials)
Nick_Sobol@cbu.ca
902-563-1675

Truro: **Nova Scotia Agricultural College MacRae Library**
135 College Rd.
Truro, NS B2N 5E3
Mailing Address: PO Box 550
Truro, NS B2N 5E3
902-893-6669
Fax: 902-895-0934
e-mail: library@nsac.ca
URL: www.nsac.ca/library
National Library Symbol: NSTA
Consortia Membership: Canadian Research Knowledge Network (CRKN); Council of Atlantic University Libraries (CAUL); Novanet
Founded in: 1905
Hours: Academic Term: M-Th 8:30am-10:30pm; F 8:30-5:00; Sa 10:00-5:00; Su 10:00am-10:30pm; Summer: M-F 8:30-4:30
Acquisitions Budget: $250,000 - $499,999
For Print: $100,000 - $249,999
For Electronic: $100,000 - $249,999
Population Served: 1000
Special Collections: Agricola Collection
Subjects covered: Agriculture & Food, Agricultural Chemistry, Environmental Sciences, Agricultural Engineering, Aquaculture, Plant & Animal Sciences
Services:
Remote Access
Internet Access
Access to Subscription Databases
Inter-Library Loan (ILL)
Document delivery, Information Commons (42 PCs)
Microform Equipment: Reader
Personnel: *Summary:* 6 Total; 1 Professional(s); 2 Technical(s); 3 Other employees
Bonnie R. Waddell, Chief Librarian
902-893-6670
Janelle Brenton, Cataloguer
jbrenton@nsac.ca
902-893-4593
Verna Mingo, Head, Acquisitions/Serials
vmingo@nsac.ca
902-893-4581
Sherree Miller, Circulation Assistant
smiller@nsac.ca
902-893-4576
Cindy Stevens, Tech Services Assistant
cstevens@nsac.ca
902-893-4583
Charmaine Borden, Librarian
charmaine.borden@nscc.ca

Truro: **Truro Campus Library**
36 Arthur St.
Truro, NS B2N 1X5
902-893-5326
Fax: 902-895-5322
e-mail: library.truro@nscc.ca
URL: www.library.nscc.ca
National Library Symbol: NSTT
Consortia Membership: Novanet
Hours: M-F 8:00-4:30
Services:
Personnel: *Summary:* 2 Total; 1 Professional(s); 1 Technical(s)

Wolfville: **Acadia University Vaughan Memorial Library**
50 Acadia St.
Wolfville, NS B4P 2R6
Mailing Address: PO Box 4
Wolfville, NS B4P 2R6
902-585-1249
Fax: 902-585-1748
e-mail: reference.desk@acadiau.ca
ill@acadiau.ca
libweb@acadiau.ca
URL: library.acadiau.ca
Social Media:
www.facebook.com/group.php?gid=103755202996517

Libraries & Resource Centres / Nunavut

National Library Symbol: NSWA
Consortia Membership: Canadian Research Knowledge Network (CRKN); Council of Atlantic University Libraries (CAUL)
Founded in: 1838
Hours: M-Su
Special Collections: George Nowlan Collection; J.D. Logan Collection; Marshall Saunders Collection; Zeman Collection; Kirkconnell Collection; William Inglis Morse Collection; Eric R. Dennis Collection of Canadiana; Atlantic Baptist Historical Collection; Hannah Maria Norris Armstrong Fonds
Subjects covered: Liberal Arts, Humanities, Pure & Applied Sciences, Theology
Services:
Internet Access
Inter-Library Loan (ILL)
Microform Equipment: Reader
Personnel: *Summary:* 37 Total; 8 Professional(s); 29 Other employees;
Mike Beazley, Academic Librarian
mike.beazley@acadiau.ca
902-585-1523
Patricia Gallant, Academic Librarian
patricia.gallant@acadiau.ca
902-585-1403
Jennifer Richard, Head, Research Services
jennifer.richard@acadiau.ca
902-585-1528

Yarmouth: District Health Authorities 1, 2 & 3 (Western Nova Scotia)
Information Resources & Library Services
60 Vancouver St.
Yarmouth, NS B5A 2P5
902-742-3542 ext: 306
Fax: 902-742-1698
e-mail: jmacdonald@swndha.nshealth.ca
library@swndha.nshealth.ca
National Library Symbol: NSYR
Founded in: 1998
Note: Self services, may borrow with local public library borrowers card through agreement with public library. No service to public, no access to networks but public may borrow with public library card. Provides library services to the following hospitals: Annapolis Community Health Centre (Annapolis); Western Kings Memorial Hospital (Berwick); Digby General Hospital (Digby); Soldiers Memorial Hospital (Middleton); South Shore Regional Hospital (Bridgewater); Queens General Hospital (Liverpool); Fishermens Memorial Hospital (Lunenburg); Roseway Hospital (Shelburne); Valley Regional Hospital (Kentville); Eastern Kings Hospital (Wolfville); Yarmouth Regional Regional Hospital (Yarmouth)
Subjects covered: Health Sciences, Nursing, Medicine
Services:
Internet Access
Document Delivery, information retrieval, user education & acquisition
Personnel: *Summary:* 3 Total; 1 Professional(s); 2 Technical(s); 6 Volunteer(s)
Jackie MacDonald, Regional Librarian
jmacdonald@swndha.nshealth.ca
902-742-3542
Rose Clements, Interlending & Acquisitions
rclements@swdha.nshealth.ca

Nunavut

Igloolik: Nunavut Research Institute
Igloolik Research Centre Library
PO Box 210
Igloolik, NU X0A 0L0
867-934-2069
URL: www.nri.nu.ca
Founded in: 1975
Hours: by appointment only
Acquisitions Budget: $25,000 - $49,999
Special Collections: Inuit oral history & traditional knowledge
Subjects covered: Northern science & technology
Services:

Iqaluit: Nunavut Arctic College
Nunatta Campus Library
PO Box 600
Iqaluit, NU X0A 0H0
867-979-7220
Fax: 867-979-7102
e-mail: librarian@nac.nu.ca
URL: ww.nac.nu.ca
National Library Symbol: NUINAC
Founded in: 1988
Hours: M, W, F 8:45-12:00, 1:00-4:45; Tu, Th 8:45-12:00, 1:00-4:45, 6:00-8:00; Sa 1:00-5:00
Note: The College also maintains the Kivalliq Campus Library (Rankin Inlet), and the Kitikkmeot Campus Library (Cambridge Bay), each staffed by a library assistant on a part-time basis throughout the school year
Special Collections: Inuktitut materials collection, Northern resources collection, Rare books, the Taylor and Pilot collections on archaeology and Arctic exploration
Subjects covered: Adult Basic Education, Carpentry, Environmental Technology, Language & Culture, Jewellery & Metalwork, Management Studies, Office Administration, Teacher Education, Industrial Trades, Early Childhood Education, Nursing
Services:
Internet Access
Inter-Library Loan (ILL) for a fee
Table of Contents service; library tours & orientation sessions; public access computers; printing; photocopying
Personnel: *Summary:* 1 Professional(s); 1 Technical(s)
Rae-Lynne Patterson, Manager, Library Services

Iqaluit: Nunavut Dept. of Environment
Resource Centre
PO Box 1000, Stn 1310
Iqaluit, NU X0A 0H0
867-975-7722
Fax: 867-975-7742
e-mail: nuisd@gov.nu.ca
librarian@nwmb.com
URL: www.nwrcc.ca
National Library Symbol: NUISD
Founded in: 1999
Hours: M-F 8:30-5:00
Acquisitions Budget: 0-$9,999
For Print: 0-$9,999
For Electronic: 0-$9,999
Subjects covered: Wildlife; Environmental Protection; Economic Development; Resource Management
Services:
Inter-Library Loan (ILL)
Personnel:
Carolyn Mallory, Resource Centre Coordinator
867-975-7722

Ontario

Alfred: University of Guelph Collège d'Alfred
Bibliothèque
31, rue St-Paul
Alfred, ON K0B 1A0
Mailing Address: CP 580
Alfred, ON K0B 1A0
613-679-2218
Fax: 613-679-2423
URL: www.collegedalfred.ca
grpwse.alfredc.uoguelph.ca/bibliotheque/index.htm
National Library Symbol: OAMAC
Founded in: 1981
Hours: Sept.-Avr.: L-V 8h30-16h30, 17h30-20h30; Mai-Août: L-V 8h30-12h, 13h-16h.
Acquisitions Budget: $10,000 - $24,999
Note: Bilingue
Subjects covered: Agriculture, physiologie, alimentation, éducation, développement international, Francophonie, soins vétérinaires, environnement, ariculture biologique
Services:
Remote Access
Internet Access
Inter-Library Loan (ILL)
Fee Based Research
Microform Equipment: Computer; Reader
Personnel: *Summary:* 1 Professional(s); 1 Technical(s);
Robert St-Amant, Chef de section
Lyne Gagne-Lalonde, Technicienne en documentation

Atikokan: John B. Ridley Research Library
Quetico Park
Atikokan, ON P0T 1C0
807-929-2571 ext: 224
Fax: 807-929-2123
e-mail: andrea.allison@ontario.ca
URL: catalogue.legacyforest.ca
National Library Symbol: OATR
Founded in: 1986
Hours: Mid May-mid Sept.: 8:00-4:15, book appointment during off season
Acquisitions Budget: 0-$9,999
Special Collections: Wilderness Management, Quetico Park Archives, Oral History, Slide & Photograph Collection
Subjects covered: Natural History, Wilderness, Quetico-Superior Area
Services:
Inter-Library Loan (ILL)
Personnel: *Summary:* 1 Total; 1 Professional(s)
Andrea Allison, Librarian
807-929-2571 ext. 224

Barrie: Georgian College of Applied Arts & Technology
Library Commons
1 Georgian Dr.
Barrie, ON L4M 3X9
705-722-5139
Fax: 705-722-1508
877-890-8477
e-mail: ill@georgianc.on.ca
URL: library.georgianc.on.ca
National Library Symbol: OBAGC
Consortia Membership: Ontario Colleges Library Service
Founded in: 1967
Hours: M-Th 7:45am-11:00pm; F 7:45-5:00; Sa 10:00-5:00; Su 1:00-8:00
Acquisitions Budget: $50,000 - $99,999
For Electronic: $50,000 - $99,999
Special Collections: ies, Culture, Economics, Health Sciences, Engineering, Technology, Hospitality & Tourism
Subjects covered: Arts, Humanities, Culture, Economics, Health Sciences, Engineering, Technology, Hospitality & Tourism
Services:
Remote Access
Internet Access
Access to Subscription Databases
Inter-Library Loan (ILL)
Microform Equipment: Computer; Reader
Personnel: *Summary:* 25 Total; 8 Professional(s); 3 Technical(s); 14 Other employees
Katherine Wallis, Director, Learning Resource Centres
kwallis@georgianc.on.ca
705-728-1968 ext. 1684
Vicki MacMillan, Liberal Arts/University Studies Librarian
vmacmillan@georgianc.on.ca
705-728-1968 ext. 1807
Karen Halliday, Health Sciences Librarian
khalliday@georgianc.on.ca
705-728-1968 ext. 1753
Joanne Fowlie, Business Librarian
jfowlie@georgianc.on.ca
705-728-1968 ext. 1305
Kimberly Thomas, Technology Librarian
kthomas@georgianc.on.ca
705-728-1968 ext. 1847
Carol McNabb, Head, Technical Services
cmcnabb@georgianc.on.ca
708-728-1968 ext. 1679

Belleville: Loyalist College of Applied Arts & Technology
The Parrott Centre
376 Wallbridge-Loyalist Rd.
Belleville, ON K8N 5B9
Mailing Address: PO Box 4200
Belleville, ON K8N 5B9
613-969-1913 ext: 2249
Fax: 613-969-5183
888-569-2547
e-mail: library@loyalistc.ca
URL: www.loyalistlibrary.com
National Library Symbol: OBEL
Consortia Membership: Ontario Colleges Library Service
Founded in: 1968
Hours: M-Th 8:00am-9:00pm; F 8:00-4:30; Sa 9:00-4:00; Su 12:00-4:00. Summer: M-Th 8:00-4:30; F 8:00-12:00
Acquisitions Budget: $50,000 - $99,999
For Print: $50,000 - $99,999
For Electronic: $25,000 - $49,999
Population Served: 2700

Libraries & Resource Centres / Ontario

Note: Remote access to online databases for staff & students only
Special Collections: Lorraine Monk Photography Collection; John Peterson Photography Collection
Subjects covered: Law & Security, Nursing, Media, Human Studies, Business, Technology
Services:
Remote Access
Internet Access
Access to Subscription Databases
Inter-Library Loan (ILL)
Microform Equipment: Computer; Reader
Personnel: *Summary:* 10 Total; 1 Professional(s); 7 Technical(s); 2 Other employees
Ross Danaher, Director, Educational Resources
rdanaher@loyalistc.on.ca
613-969-1913 ext. 2339
Connie McDonald, Library Technician, Information
cmcdonal@loyalistc.on.ca
613-969-1913 ext. 2317
Lynn McCracken, Library Technician, Information/ILL
lmccrack@loyalistc.on.ca
613-969-1913 ext. 2175
Danielle Emon, Library Technician, Technical Services
emon@loyalistc.on.ca
613-969-1913 ext. 2183
Dayle Gorsline, Library Technician, Acquisitions & Electronic Resources
dgorsline@loyalistc.on.ca
613-969-1913 ext. 2216
Charles Martens, Superintendent

Blind River: Blind River Refinery
Information Centre
PO Box 1539
Blind River, ON P0R 1B0
705-356-1496 ext: 3266
Fax: 705-356-7772
e-mail: charlesmartens@cameco.com
No public access
Founded in: 1984
Acquisitions Budget: $25,000 - $49,999
Note: Internal use only for technical references for Health, Safety, Environment, Process Operations & Analytical Services; One Cameco Administrative Professional has responsibility to maintain basic service (ie Marianne Cleary)
Subjects covered: Physical Sciences, Engineering
Services:
Inter-Library Loan (ILL)
Personnel: *Summary:* 1 Total; 1 Other employees
Elaine De Bonis, Operations Manager
elaine.debonis@sheridanc.on.ca
905-459-7533 ext. 5283

Brampton: Davis Campus
Library Services
7899 McLaughlin Rd., Rm. B212
Brampton, ON L6V 1G6
Mailing Address: PO Box 7500
Brampton, ON L6V 1G6
905-845-9430 ext: 4338
Fax: 905-874-4346
e-mail: shahida.rashid@sheridanc.on.ca
URL: www1.sheridaninstitute.ca/services/library/
National Library Symbol: OBRASC
Hours: Sept.-June: M-Th 8:30am-10:00pm; F 8:30-4:30; Sa-Su 11:00-4:00. July-Aug.: M-F 8:30-4:30; Sa-Su 11:00-4:00
Acquisitions Budget: $50,000 - $99,999
Services:
Internet Access
Access to Subscription Databases
Inter-Library Loan (ILL) for a fee of as charged
Research
Microform Equipment: Computer; Reader
Personnel: *Summary:* 4 Total; 1 Professional(s); 2 Technical(s); 1 Other employees

Brantford: Brantford Campus
Library Resource Centre
411 Elgin St.
Brantford, ON N3T 5V2
519-758-6019
Fax: 519-758-6043
Hours: M-Th 8:30-7:00; F, Sa 8:30-4:30
Services:
Personnel: *Summary:* 6 Total; 1 Professional(s); 4 Technical(s)

Helen Pottinger, Library Technician
hpottinger@sl.on.ca
613-345-0660 ext. 3104

Brockville: Brockville Campus
Library
2288 Parkdale Ave.
Brockville, ON K6V 5X3
613-345-0556
e-mail: hpottinger@sl.on.ca
illbrock@sl.on.ca
URL: www.sl.on.ca/library
National Library Symbol: OBSL
Founded in: 1972
Hours: M-F 8:00-4:00
Acquisitions Budget: 0-$9,999
Note: Member of Ontario College & University Libraries Association
Subjects covered: Business, Law & Security, Nursing, Music Theatre, Pre-service Firefighter
Services:
Internet Access
Access to Subscription Databases
Inter-Library Loan (ILL) for a fee of Shipping cost
Fee Based Research
Microform Equipment: Computer; Reader
Personnel: *Summary:* 1 Total; 1 Technical(s)

Burlington: Canada Centre for Inland Waters
Library
867 Lakeshore Rd.
Burlington, ON L7R 4A6
Mailing Address: PO Box 5050
Burlington, ON L7R 4A6
905-336-4982
Fax: 905-338-4428
e-mail: librarybiblio.burlington@ec.gc.ca
National Library Symbol: OBUC
Founded in: 1968
Hours: by appointment only
Special Collections: AES Training Branch Archives; MSC Archives; WMO publications; Audio-visual materials; Journal collection; Microfiche reports; Observational weather data; Weather resources for children; Maps & atlases; Pamphlets; Great Lakes Remedial Action Plan reports; Ontario Region Canadian Wildlife Service reports
Subjects covered: Meteorology, Climatology, Atmospheric Research
Services:
Inter-Library Loan (ILL)
Personnel: *Summary:* 1 Professional(s); 2 Technical(s)

Burlington: Royal Botanical Gardens
Library
680 Plains Rd. West
Burlington, ON L8N 3H8
Mailing Address: PO Box 399
Hamilton, ON L8N 3H8
905-527-1158 ext: 531
Fax: 905-577-0375
URL: www.rbg.ca
Social Media: twitter.com/#!/RBGCanada
National Library Symbol: OHRB
No public access
Founded in: 1947
Acquisitions Budget: 0-$9,999
Note: Please email or phone in advance to make an appointment for reference service.
Special Collections: Nursery & seed trade catalogue collection; information on cultivar breeding & selection & introductions of Canadian origin
Subjects covered: Botany, Floristics, Ornamental Horticulture, Gardening, Landscape Design
Services:
Personnel: *Summary:* 8 Volunteer(s)
Mark Runciman, CEO, Royal Botanical Gardens
David Galbraith, Head, Scientific Development
Michele Laing, Branch Head
mlaing@library.uwaterloo.ca
519-888-4567 ext. 7620

Cambridge: School of Architecture
Musagetes Architecture Library
7 Melville St. South
Cambridge, ON N1S 2H4

519-888-4567 ext: 7607
Fax: 519-622-3525
e-mail: mlaing@library.uwaterloo.ca
URL: www.lib.uwaterloo.ca/musagetes/index.html
National Library Symbol: OWTU
Founded in: 2004
Hours: M-Th 8:30-8:30; F 8:30-6:00; Sa, Su 1:00-5:00
Subjects covered: Architecture Books, Journals; Rare Books; Product Catalogues
Services:
Inter-Library Loan (ILL)
Circulation, course reserves, reference & library instruction
Personnel:

Chalk River: Atomic Energy of Canada Ltd.
Chalk River Laboratories, Business Services
Chalk River Nuclear Laboratories
Chalk River, N K0J 1J0
613-584-3311 ext: 43900
e-mail: librarycr@aecl.ca
URL: www.aecl.ca/
National Library Symbol: OCKA
Consortia Membership: Council of Federal Libraries (CFL) Consortium
Founded in: 1945
Hours: M-F by appointment only
Special Collections: National depository for literature on Nuclear Science & Technology, Extensive collection on all aspects of peaceful uses of nuclear science & atomic energy
Subjects covered: Nuclear Energy, Nuclear Engineering, Environmental Protection, Metallurgy, Material Sciences
Services:
Inter-Library Loan (ILL)
Microform Equipment: Computer; Reader
Personnel: *Summary:* 5 Total; 1 Professional(s); 8 Technical(s)
Monica Lim, Section Head, AECL Library Services
limm@aecl.ca
613-584-3311 ext. 4626
Linda Crawford, Supervisor, CRL Library
crawfordl@aecl.ca
613-484-3311 ext. 4632

Chatham: Chatham-Kent Health Alliance
Medical Library
80 Grand Ave. West
Chatham, ON N7M 5L9
Mailing Address: PO Box 2030
Chatham, ON N7M 5L9
519-352-6401 ext: 6420
Fax: 519-436-2524
e-mail: library@ckha.on.ca
National Library Symbol: OCHAH
Consortia Membership: Ontario Health Libraries Association
Founded in: 1980
Hours: M-F 8:00-4:00 by appointment only
Note: The library is a member of SOHLIN & OHLA. Open to the public by appointment only
Subjects covered: Medicine, Nursing, Health Sciences
Services:
Inter-Library Loan (ILL)
Personnel: *Summary:* 1 Total; 1 Volunteer(s)
Margaret Campbell, Librarian
mcampbell@ckha.on.ca
Barry Vanbiesbrouck, Manager
bvanbies@stclairc.on.ca
Linda Grineage, Library Technician
lgrineage@stclaircollege.ca
Jeanette Giroux, Library Technician
jgiroux@stclaircollege.ca

Chatham: Thames Campus Resource Centre
1001 Grand Ave. West
Chatham, ON N7M 5W4
519-354-9100 ext: 3287
Fax: 519-354-5496
e-mail: jgiroux@stclaircollege.ca
Hours: M-F
Acquisitions Budget: $25,000 - $49,999
Subjects covered: Business, Social Service Nursing, Technical
Services:
Personnel: *Summary:* 6 Total; 2 Technical(s); 4 Other employees

CANADIAN ENVIRONMENTAL RESOURCE GUIDE 2011-2012
1139

Libraries & Resource Centres / Ontario

Chatham: Union Gas Ltd., a Duke Energy Company
Library Services
50 Keil Dr. North
Chatham, ON N7M 5M1
Mailing Address: PO Box 2001
Chatham, ON N7M 5M1
519-352-3100 ext: 2595
Fax: 519-436-5320
800-265-5230
URL: www.uniongas.com
No public access
Hours: 8:00-4:30
Subjects covered: Energy
Services:
Personnel:
Jane Perry, Librarian
Yollande Laperle, Director, Student Services
Jessie Robertson, Library Technician
JeRobertson@sl.on.ca
613-933-6080 ext. 2504

Cornwall: Cornwall Campus
Library
2 Belmont St.
Cornwall, ON K6H 4Z1
613-933-6080 ext: 2701
Fax: 613-937-1515
URL: www.sl.on.ca/library
National Library Symbol: OCSL
Founded in: 1967
Hours: M, W 8:30-2:00; Tu, Th 8:30-5:00
Acquisitions Budget: $10,000 - $24,999
Subjects covered: Business, Technology, Literature, Applied Arts, Science, Social Sciences
Services:
Inter-Library Loan (ILL)
Personnel: *Summary:* 3 Total; 1 Professional(s); 1 Technical(s)

Falconbridge: Falconbridge Limited
Falconbridge Technology Centre
Falconbridge, ON P0M 1S0
705-693-2761 ext: 3419
Fax: 705-699-3431
e-mail: kmunn@sudbury.falconbridge.com
No public access
Subjects covered: Mining, Metallury, Minierial Processing, Chemistry
Services:
Personnel: *Summary:* 1 Professional(s)
Karen Munn, Librarian
kmunn@sudbury.falconbridge.com

Guelph: Crompton Co./Cie
Research Library
120 Huron St.
Guelph, ON N1H 6N3
Mailing Address: PO Box 1120
Guelph, ON N1H 6N3
519-822-3790 ext: 425
Fax: 519-822-0809
wilma.dunnill@chemtura.com
National Library Symbol: OGDR
No public access
Founded in: 1943
Hours: M-F 8:00-4:00
Acquisitions Budget: $25,000 - $49,999
For Print: $25,000 - $49,999
For Electronic: 0-$9,999
Subjects covered: Physical Sciences, Technology, Chemistry
Services:
Remote Access
Inter-Library Loan (ILL)
Microform Equipment: Reader
Personnel: *Summary:* 5 Total; 1 Professional(s); 1 Technical(s)
Patrica Anne Harmon, Library Manager
ann.harmon@chmtura.com
203-573-2000
Wilma Dunnill, Library/Data Technician
wilma.dunnill@chemtura.com
519-822-3790 ext. 442

Guelph: Entomological Society of Ontario
Library
University of Guelph Library
Guelph, ON N1G 2W1
519-824-4120 ext: 54214
e-mail: jimbrett@uoguelph.ca
URL: www.entsocont.com
Note: An integral part of the University of Guelph Library
Subjects covered: Insects
Services:
Personnel:
Jim Brett, Contact
jimbrett@uoguelph.ca

Guelph: Farm Safety Association Inc.
Library
#101, 75 Farquhar St.
Guelph, ON N1H 3N4
Fax: 519-823-8880
800-361-8855
e-mail: info@farmsafety.ca
URL: www.fsai.on.ca
Special Collections: Farm health & safety educational videos
Subjects covered: Agriculture
Services:

Guelph: Homewood Health Centre
Library
150 Delhi St.
Guelph, ON N1E 6K9
519-824-1010
Fax: 519-824-8751
e-mail: pharjoyc@homewood.org
URL: www.homewood.org
Consortia Membership: WWD Health Library Netowrk, CHLA, OHLA, OLA
Founded in: 1975
Hours: Su-Th 9:00am-9:00pm; F 9:00-7:00; Sa 9:00-4:00 by appointment only
Acquisitions Budget: 0-$9,999
For Print: 0-$9,999
For Electronic: 0-$9,999
Population Served: Staff: 1,000
Special Collections: Collection includes pamphlets, consumer health information, fiction, magazines, newspaper, reference material, large-print books; talking books; music. The staff library includes clinical text books; professional journals; e-journals; college/university catalogues; hospital archives; quick reference; EbscoHost full text databases.
Subjects covered: Substance abuse; Psychiatry; Consumer health; Eating disorders
Services:
Remote Access
Internet Access
Access to Subscription Databases
Inter-Library Loan (ILL)
Personnel: *Summary:* 2 Total; 1 Professional(s); 1 Other employees; 52 Volunteer(s)
Joyce Pharoah, Coordinator of Library
pharjoyc@homewood.org
Jayne Harley, Library Clerk
harljay@homewood.org

Guelph: Ontario Farm Animal Council
Library
Ontario AgriCentre, #106, 100 Stone Rd. West
Guelph, ON N1G 5L3
519-837-1326
Fax: 519-837-3209
URL: www.ofac.org
Founded in: 1988
Hours: M-F 9:00-5:00 by appointment only
Note: Teacher kits, resources (videos) & lesson plans free to Ontario teachers-priced accordingly for out-of-province; student information packages-no charge; some material available on web site
Subjects covered: Farm Animals
Services:

Guelph: University of Guelph
McLaughlin Library
50 Stone Rd. East
Guelph, ON N1G 2W1
519-824-4120 ext: 2075
Fax: 519-824-6931
e-mail: mridley@uoguelph.ca
URL: www.lib.uoguelph.ca
National Library Symbol: OGU
Consortia Membership: Canadian Research Knowledge Network (CRKN); Ontario Council of University Libraries (OCUL); TriUniversity Group of Libraries (TUG)
Founded in: 1964
Hours: M-Su 7:00-10:00
Acquisitions Budget: $500,000 - $999,999
Special Collections: Theatre Archives, George Bernard Shaw Collection, Scottish Collection, L.M. Montgomery Collection, Apiculture, Ontario History, Travel in Ontario
Subjects covered: Arts, Humanities, Social Sciences, Sciences including Agribusiness, Agriculture, Family Studies, Hotel & Food Administration, Landscape Architecture, Regional History, Travel, Veterinary Medicine
Services:
Inter-Library Loan (ILL)
Microform Equipment: Computer; Reader
Personnel: *Summary:* 137 Total
Michael Ridley, Chief Librarian
mridley@uoguelph.ca
Brenda Morissette, Library Technician
morissetteb@northern.on.ca
705-672-3376 ext. 8806

Haileybury: Haileybury Campus
Library Resource Centre
640 Latchford St.
Haileybury, ON P0J 1K0
Mailing Address: PO Box 2060
Haileybury, ON P0J 1K0
705-672-3376 ext. 8806
Fax: 705-672-5404
e-mail: libraryh@northern.on.ca
morissetteb@northern.on.ca
National Library Symbol: OHAINC
Founded in: 1912
Hours: M, F 8:00-4:00; Tu-Th 8:00-7:00. Summer M-F 8:00-1:00, 2:00-4:00
Acquisitions Budget: $10,000 - $24,999
For Print: $10,000 - $24,999
For Electronic: 0-$9,999
Population Served: 300
Special Collections: Maps
Subjects covered: Mining, Geology, Natural Resources, Veterinary Sciences & Applied Arts, Social Work, Business, Instrumental, Social Sciences
Services:
Remote Access
Internet Access
Inter-Library Loan (ILL)
Personnel: *Summary:* 1 Total; 1 Professional(s)

Hamilton: Canadian Institute for NDE
Library
135 Fennell Ave. West
Hamilton, ON L8N 3T2
905-387-1655
Fax: 905-574-6080
800-964-9488
e-mail: info@cinde.ca
URL: www.csndt.org
Subjects covered: Educational & employment resources for NDT personnel; Technical information; Resources relating to nondestructive testing
Services:

Hamilton: Dofasco Inc.
Library Resource Centre
PO Box 2460
Hamilton, ON L8N 3J5
905-548-7200 ext: 6223
Fax: 905-548-4630
e-mail: linda_pauloski@dofasco.ca
URL: www.dofasco.ca
No public access
Founded in: 1961
Subjects covered: Steel Industry, Management, Ironmaking, Steelmaking, Coal, Coke, Finishing Processes
Services:
Personnel:
Linda Pauloski, Manager
Lois Wyndham, Team Leader, Library Services & Patient/Family Resource Ctrs
wyndham@hhsc.ca
905-527-4322 ext. 44247
Karen Murphy, Library Technician

Hamilton: General Medical Library
286 Victoria Ave. North
Hamilton, ON L8L 5G4
905-527-4322 ext: 44287
Fax: 905-577-1453
e-mail: libraryg@hhsc.ca
URL: www.hamiltonhealthsciences.ca/library
Founded in: 1931
Hours: by appointment only
Acquisitions Budget: $250,000 - $499,999
For Print: $100,000 - $249,999
For Electronic: $100,000 - $249,999
Subjects covered: Medicine, Health Sciences
Services:
Personnel: *Summary:* 4 Total; 1 Professional(s); 3 Technical(s)

Hamilton: Hamilton Health Sciences
Chedoke Library
PO Box 2000, Stn LCD 1
Hamilton, ON L8N 3Z5
905-521-2100 ext: 77741
Fax: 905-521-7925
e-mail: librarych@hhsc.ca
URL: www.hamiltonhealthsciences.ca/library
Hours: Tu, Th 8:30-4:30 by appointment only
Acquisitions Budget: $50,000 - $99,999
Note: The URL was not working and therefore the file could not be up-dated eh07*
Subjects covered: Child Development, Gerontology/Geriatrics, Rehabilitation
Services:
Inter-Library Loan (ILL)
Microform Equipment: Reader
Personnel: *Summary:* 2 Total; 1 Professional(s); 1 Technical(s);

Lois Wyndham, Librarian
Karen Murray, Library Technician
Dorothy Fitzgerald, Director
fitz@mcmaster.ca
Tom Flemming, Head of Public Services
tomflem@mcmaster.ca
Andrea McLelland, Information Resources Librarian
mclell@mcmaster.ca

Hamilton: Health Sciences Library
1200 Main St. West
Hamilton, ON L8N 3Z5
905-525-9140 ext: 22320
Fax: 905-528-3733
e-mail: hslib@mcmaster.ca
URL: hsl.mcmaster.ca
National Library Symbol: OHMB
Founded in: 1969
Hours: M-Th 8:00-11:30; F 8:00-10:00; Sa 10:00-7:00; Su 10:00-11:00
Acquisitions Budget: $500,000 - $999,999
Note: Also part of Hamilton Health Sciences Corp. Member of Hamilton & District Health Library Network.
Special Collections: History of Medicine (Canadian, World Wars), Archives
Subjects covered: Biomedical Sciences, Clinical Health Sciences, Medicine & Medical Specialities, Nursing, Occupational Therapy & Physiotherapy, Midwifery
Services:
Inter-Library Loan (ILL)
Personnel: *Summary:* 33 Total; 7 Professional(s); 5 Technical(s); 21 Other employees
Lois Wyndham, Team Leader, Library Services
Sandy Culley, Library Technician

Hamilton: Henderson Medical Library
711 Concession St.
Hamilton, ON L8V 1B3
905-527-0271 ext: 42099
Fax: 905-389-5247
e-mail: libraryh@hhsc.ca
URL: www.hamiltonhealthsciences.ca/library
Subjects covered: Medicine, Health Sciences
Services:
Personnel:

Hamilton: McMaster University
McMaster University Library
1280 Main St. West
Hamilton, ON L8S 4L6

905-525-9140 ext: 24359
Fax: 905-524-9850
e-mail: ilds@mcmaster.ca
URL: www.mcmaster.ca/library/
National Library Symbol: OHM
Consortia Membership: Canadian Research Knowledge Network (CRKN); Ontario Council of University Libraries (OCUL)
Founded in: 1887
Acquisitions Budget: $1,000,000 plus
For Print: $1,000,000 plus
For Electronic: $1,000,000 plus
Population Served: 28311
Special Collections: Bertrand Russell Archives, Eighteenth Century British & European Imprints, Canadian Archives (Social History, Labour Studies), Pacifism, Maps
Subjects covered: Business, Engineering, Humanities, Sciences, Social Sciences
Services:
Inter-Library Loan (ILL)
Microform Equipment: Computer
Personnel: *Summary:* 115 Total; 27 Professional(s); 88 Other employees
Jeffrey Trzeciak, University Librarian
905-525-9140 ext. 24359
Vivian Lewis, Associate University Librarian, Services
lewisvm@mcmaster.ca
905-525-9140 ext. 23883
Anne Pottier, Associate University Librarian, Collection Resources
pottier@mcmaster.ca
905-525-9140 ext. 22410
Paul Otto, Associate University Librarian, Information Technology
ottop@mcmaster.ca
905-525-9140 ext. 23995
Mary Ruth Linkert, Administrator
linkert@mcmaster.ca
905-525-9140 ext. 24355

Hamilton: Mohawk College of Applied Arts & Technology
Library Resource Centre
135 Fennell Ave. West
Hamilton, ON L8N 3T2
Mailing Address: PO Box 2034
Hamilton, ON L8N 3T2
905-575-2077
Fax: 905-575-2011
e-mail: braintogo@mohawkc.on.ca
URL: www.mohawkc.on.ca
National Library Symbol: OHMC
Consortia Membership: Ontario Colleges Library Service
Founded in: 1966
Hours: M-Th 8:30-10:00; F 8:30-4:30; Sa 11:00-3:00
Subjects covered: Industry, Nursing, Health Technology, Apprentice Trades, Physical Sciences, Technology
Services:
Internet Access
Access to Subscription Databases
Inter-Library Loan (ILL)
Microform Equipment: Reader
Personnel: *Summary:* 31 Total; 5 Professional(s); 18 Technical(s); 8 Other employees
Jo-Anne Westerby, Director, Library Resource Centre
joanne.westerby@mohawkcollege.ca
905-575-2079
Marilyn Mcdermott, Information Services Coordinator
marilyn.mcdermott@mohawkcollege.ca
905-575-2078
Maureen Price, Campus Librarian
maureen.price@mohawkcollege.ca
905-575-1212 ext. 4024

Hamilton: Mohawk-McMaster Institute for Applied Health Sciences
Library Resource Centre/Learning Commons
1400 Main St. West
Hamilton, ON L8N 3T2
Mailing Address: PO Box 2034
Hamilton, ON L8N 3T2
905-540-4247 ext: 26835
Fax: 905-528-5307
National Library Symbol: OHMCHC
Founded in: 1978
Hours: M-Th 8:30am-9:00pm; F 8:30-4:30; Sa 10:00-3:00
Acquisitions Budget: $25,000 - $49,999

Special Collections: Nursing, Radiography, Ultrasound, Occupational Therapy, Physical Therapy, Pharmacy, Medical Laboratory Technology
Subjects covered: Nursing & Allied Health
Services:
Internet Access
Inter-Library Loan (ILL) for a fee
Personnel: *Summary:* 5 Total; 1 Professional(s); 3 Technical(s); 1 Other employees

Hamilton: St Joseph's Hospital (Hamilton)
Library Services
50 Charlton Ave. East
Hamilton, ON L8N 4A6
905-522-1155 ext: 3410
Fax: 905-540-6504
e-mail: library@stjosham.on.ca
URL: www.stjosham.on.ca
Founded in: 1964
Hours: M, W, F 8:00-6:00; T, Th 8:00am-8:00pm; Sa 1:00-4:00 (Open on Saturdays Sept.-Apr. only). by appointment only
Acquisitions Budget: $25,000 - $49,999
Note: Member of Hamilton Health Library Network.
Subjects covered: Medicine, Health Sciences
Services:
Inter-Library Loan (ILL)
Microform Equipment: Reader
Personnel: *Summary:* 4 Total; 1 Professional(s); 1 Technical(s); 2 Other employees
Jean Maragno, Manager, Library Services
marag@mcmaster.ca
Lois Cottrell, Library Technician

Hamilton: U.S. Steel Canada
Corporate R & D Information Centre
386 Wilcox St.
Hamilton, ON L8N 3T1
Mailing Address: PO Box 2030
Hamilton, ON L8N 3T1
905-528-2511 ext: 2076
Fax: 905-777-7614
800-263-9305
e-mail: carol.cernile@stelco.ca
National Library Symbol: OHSCC
Hours: M-F by appointment only
Subjects covered: Steel Industry Research & Development
Services:
Inter-Library Loan (ILL)
Microform Equipment: Computer; Reader
Personnel: *Summary:* 1 Total; 1 Technical(s)
Carol Cernile, Research Library Technician
Lorraine Smith, Manager, Library & Information Services
smithlf@agr.gc.ca
519-738-2251 ext. 417

Harrow: Greenhouse & Processing Crops Research Centre
2585 County Rd. 20
Harrow, ON N0R 1G0
519-738-2251 ext: 417
Fax: 519-738-2929
e-mail: harrlib@agr.gc.ca
whitfieldg@agr.gc.ca
URL: res2.agr.ca/harrow
National Library Symbol: OHARAG
Hours: M-F 8:00-4:30
Acquisitions Budget: $50,000 - $99,999
Special Collections: Soil, Crop & Water Management
Subjects covered: Agriculture, Food, Greenhouse Vegetables, Field Vegetables, Clonal Genebank
Services:
Internet Access
Access to Subscription Databases
Inter-Library Loan (ILL)
Personnel: *Summary:* 1 Total; 1 Professional(s);

Hearst: Université de Hearst
Bibliothèque Maurice Saulnier
60, 9e rue
Hearst, ON P0L 1N0
Adresse postale: CP 580
Hearst, ON P0L 1N0
705-372-1781 ext: 235
Téléc: 705-362-7518
Couriel: johanne_morin@univhearst.edu
URL: www.uhearst.ca

Libraries & Resource Centres / Ontario

Sigle: OHCU
Fondée en: 1953
Heures: L-J 8h30-16h30, 18h30-21h; V 8h30-16h
Budget d'acquisitions: $25,000 - $49,999
Annotation: Affilié à l'Université Laurentienne
Services:
Personnel:
Johanne Morin-Corbeil, Bibliothécaire responsable
johanne_morin@univhearst.edu
Diane Gaulin, Responsable, Services techniques

Kemptville: University of Guelph Kemptville College
Purvis Library
830 Prescott St.
Kemptville, ON K0G 1J0
Mailing Address: PO Bag 2003
Kemptville, ON K0G 1J0
613-258-8336 ext: 634
Fax: 613-258-8294
URL: www.kemptvillec.uoguelph.ca/library2/mission.htm
National Library Symbol: OKEMC
Founded in: 1969
Hours: M-F, Su
Subjects covered: Food Service, Agriculture, Equine, Horticulture & Related Areas
Services:
Inter-Library Loan (ILL)
Personnel:
Debra Simpson, Library Associate
Tanis Fink, Chief Librarian and Director
tanis.fink@senecac.on.ca
416-491-5050 ext. 5161
Cynthia McKeich, Campus Librarian
cynthia.mckeich@seneca.on.ca
416-491-5050 ext. 5105

King City: King Campus
13990 Dufferin St.
King City, ON L7B 1B3
905-833-3333 ext: 5108
Hours: M-Th 7:30-7:30; F 7:30-5:00
Services:
Personnel:
Suzanne Maranda, Head
marandas@post.queensu.ca
613-533-6000 ext. 74522
Brett Waytuck, Head, Public Services & Education
brett.waytuck@queensu.ca
613-533-6000 ext. 77694
Anne Smithers, Head, Technical & Document Services
smithers@post.queensu.ca
613-533-6000 ext. 74530
Sandra Halliday, Librarian, Public Services/Circulation Supervisor
halliday@post.queensu.ca
613-533-6000 ext. 77568
Paola Durando, Librarian, Public Services
paola.durando@queensu.ca
613-533-6000 ext. 74733
Gillian Griffith, Librarian, Outreach Services
gillian.griffith@queensu.ca
613-533-6000 ext. 78136
Elizabeth MacDonald-Pratt, Co-ordinator, Circulation & Reserve
pratte@post.queensu.ca
613-533-2510
Darlene Lake, Co-ordinator, Document Services
ddl@post.queensu.ca
613-533-3039
Trish Morgan, Library Systems Support
morgant@post.queensu.ca
613-533-6000 ext. 74527
Amanda Ross, Librarian, Outreach Services
amanda.ross-white@queensu.ca
613-533-6000 ext. 78136
Sarah Wickett, Health Informatics Librarian
wickets@post.queens.ca
613-533-6000 ext. 77078

Kingston: Bracken Health Sciences Library
Botterell Hall, Queen's University, Ground Fl.
Kingston, ON K7L 3N6
613-533-3176
Fax: 613-533-6892
877-209-5641
e-mail: bracken.library@queensu.ca

okqh@post.queensu.ca
URL: library.queensu.ca/webmed
National Library Symbol: OKQH
Consortia Membership: Ontario Council of University Libraries (OCUL)
Founded in: 1854
Hours: M-F 8:00am-11:00pm; Sa 10:00-8:00; Su 10:00-10:00
Acquisitions Budget: $1,000,000 plus
For Print: $250,000 - $499,999
For Electronic: $1,000,000 plus
Subjects covered: Medicine, Nursing, Health Sciences, Life Sciences, Rehab Therapy
Services:
Internet Access
Inter-Library Loan (ILL) for a fee
Remote access to online databases & full-text resources-restricted to Queen's users
Microform Equipment: Reader
Personnel: Summary: 16 Total; 8 Professional(s); 11 Technical(s)
Sharon Murphy, Head, Engineering & Science Library
murphys@post.queensu.ca
613-533-2836

Kingston: Engineering & Science Library
Douglas Library, 93 University Ave., Queen's University
Kingston, ON K7L 5C4
613-533-6981
Fax: 613-533-2584
866-267-7407
e-mail: webeng@library.queensu.ca
engsci@post.queensu.ca
racerd@post.queensu.ca
URL: library.queensu.ca/webeng
National Library Symbol: OKQENG
Founded in: 1997
Hours: M-Su
Acquisitions Budget: $500,000 - $999,999
Note: Geological Sciences Reading Room, Miller Hall
613/533-6000 ext. 7822
Subjects covered: Pure & Applied Science
Services:
Remote Access
Internet Access
Access to Subscription Databases
Inter-Library Loan (ILL)
Microform Equipment: Computer; Reader
Personnel: Summary: 18 Total; 5 Professional(s); 10 Technical(s); 3 Other employees

Kingston: Kingston General Hospital
Medical Library
76 Stuart St.
Kingston, ON K7L 2V7
613-549-6666 ext: 4211
e-mail: kghlibr@kgh.kari.net
National Library Symbol: OKGH
Founded in: 1961
Hours: by appointment only
Subjects covered: Medicine, Nursing, Health Sciences
Services:
Personnel: Summary: 2 Total; 1 Professional(s); 1 Technical(s)
Margaret Darling, Library Manager
Brian Chenoweth, Information Specialist
brian.chenoweth@alcan.com
Cynthia Cain-Lough, Technician

Kingston: Kingston R & D Centre
Technical Information Centre
945 Princess St.
Kingston, ON K7L 5L9
Mailing Address: PO Box 8400
Kingston, ON K7L 5L9
613-541-2065
Fax: 613-541-2134
e-mail: brian.chenoweth@alcan.com
National Library Symbol: OKA
Founded in: 1946
Hours: by appointment only
Acquisitions Budget: $50,000 - $99,999
Special Collections: Patents
Subjects covered: Aluminum production, Fabrication, Alloys
Services:
Remote Access
Internet Access
Access to Subscription Databases

Personnel: Summary: 3 Total; 1 Professional(s); 2 Technical(s)
Jeffrey Moon, Head, Maps, Data & Government Information Centre
moonj@queensu.ca
Sheila Johnson, Public Services Librarian
johnsons@queensu.ca
Susan Greaves, GIS/Map Librarian
greaves@post.queensu.ca

Kingston: Maps, Data & Government Information Centre (MADGIC)
Joseph S. Stauffer Library, Lower Level
Kingston, ON K7L 5C4
Mailing Address: Documents Unit, Queen's University Library
Kingston, ON K7L 5C4
613-533-6314
Fax: 613-533-6401
e-mail: madgic@queensu.ca
URL: library.queensu.ca/webcdoc/
National Library Symbol: OKQ
Founded in: 1847
Hours: M-Su
Acquisitions Budget: $100,000 - $249,999
For Print: $100,000 - $249,999
Note: Unit includes Government Documents, Map & Air Photos Collection & Social Science Data Centre
Special Collections: Pre-Confederation & League of Nations material, Survey Data, Historical Cartography
Subjects covered: Economics, Statistics, Politics, History, Geography
Services:
Internet Access
Personnel: Summary: 6 Total; 3 Professional(s); 3 Technical(s);

Kingston: Queen's University
Joseph S. Stauffer Library
101 Union St., Queen's University
Kingston, ON K7L 5C4
613-533-2519
Fax: 613-533-6362
URL: library.queensu.ca/stauffer
National Library Symbol: OKQ
Consortia Membership: Canadian Research Knowledge Network (CRKN); Ontario Council of University Libraries (OCUL)
Hours: M-Th 8:00am-11:00pm; F 8:00-8:00; Sa 10:00-8:00; Su 10:00am-11:00pm
Special Collections: Edith & Lorne Pierce Collection of Canadiana; Buchan Collection; McNicol Collection; Dated Collection; Rare Books; 18th Century British Pamphlets
Services:
Internet Access
Inter-Library Loan (ILL)
Microform Equipment: Computer; Reader
Personnel: Summary: 180 Total; 180 Other employees
Paul Wiens, University Librarian
Cory Laverty, Acting Head, Reference
Wayne Jones, Head, Technical Services
Dianne Cook, Collection Development Librarian
cookdc@post.queensu.ca
613-533-2523
Mary Mason, Associate Librarian
masonm@post.queensu.ca
613-533-2516
Barbara Teatero, Associate Librarian
teaterob@post.queensu.ca

Kingston: Research & Business Development Library
461 Front Rd.
Kingston, ON K7L 5A5
Mailing Address: PO Box 5000
Kingston, ON K7L 5A5
613-548-5000
No public access
Founded in: 1955
Subjects covered: Engineering, Physical Sciences, Technology, Polymers
Services:

Kingston: Royal Military College of Canada / Collège militaire royal du Canada
Massey Library
PO Box 17000, Stn Forces
Kingston, ON K7K 7B4

Libraries & Resource Centres / Ontario

613-541-6000 ext: 6330
Fax: 613-542-5055
e-mail: library@rmc.ca
okr@rmc.ca
URL: www.rmc.ca/academic/library/
National Library Symbol: OKR
Consortia Membership: Canadian Research Knowledge Network (CRKN); Ontario Council of University Libraries (OCUL)
Founded in: 1876
Hours: M-Th 8:30-9:00; F 8:30-5:00; Sa 1:00-5:00; Su 1:00-8:00
Acquisitions Budget: $500,000 - $999,999
Special Collections: Military Studies
Subjects covered: Science, Engineering, Humanities, Social Science, Military Studies
Services:
Inter-Library Loan (ILL)
Microform Equipment: Reader
Personnel: *Summary:* 15 Total; 5 Professional(s); 3 Technical(s); 6 Other employees
Sarah Toomey, Acting Chief Librarian
toomey-s@rmc.ca
613-541-6000 ext. 6229

Kingston: **St Lawrence College Library**
100 Portsmouth Ave.
Kingston, ON K7L 5A6
613-544-5400 ext: 1705
Fax: 613-545-3914
e-mail: jillbaker@sl.on.ca
URL: www.sl.on.ca/library
National Library Symbol: OKSL
Consortia Membership: Ontario Colleges Library Service
Founded in: 1967
Hours: M-Th 8:00-8:00; F 8:00-4:00; Sa 12:00-4:00
Acquisitions Budget: $50,000 - $99,999
Subjects covered: Business, Technology, Health Sciences
Services:
Internet Access
Inter-Library Loan (ILL)
Microform Equipment: Computer; Reader
Personnel: *Summary:* 5 Total; 1 Professional(s); 4 Technical(s)
Leah Wales, Director of Business Operations & Special Events
Jill Baker, Librarian
Clarinda Olsen, Head, Science/Engineering Library, ILL & Reference
clarinda.olsen@rmc.ca
613-541-6000 ext. 6079
Carroll Balkham, Contact, Circulation & Journals
carroll.balkham@rmc.ca
613-541-6000 ext. 6312

Kingston: **Science/Engineering Library / Bibliothèque des sciences et du génie**
c/o Sawyer Bldg., #3083, 11 General Crerar Cres.
Kingston, ON K7K 7B4
Mailing Address: c/o PO Box 17000, Stn Forces
Kingston, ON K7K 7B4
613-541-6000 ext: 6312
Fax: 613-541-6636
e-mail: okrs@rmc.ca
URL: www.rmc.ca/academic/library/
National Library Symbol: OKRS
Founded in: 1977
Hours: M-Th 8:30-9:00; F 8:30-5:00; Sa 1:00-5:00; Su 1:00-8:00
Acquisitions Budget: $500,000 - $999,999
Subjects covered: Engineering; Mathematics; Computer Science; Physics; Chemistry; Environmental Science; Military Science & Technology; Nuclear Science; Oceanography; Space Science
Services:
Internet Access
Access to Subscription Databases
Inter-Library Loan (ILL)
Personnel: *Summary:* 1 Professional(s); 1 Technical(s); 2 Other employees
Nancy McCormack, Head, Law Library
nm4@post.queensu.ca
613-533-2465
Chris Lesarge, Assistant to Head
lesarge@post.queensu.ca
613-533-3179

Kingston: **William R. Lederman Law Library**
Macdonald Hall, 128 Union St., Queen's University
Kingston, ON K7L 3N6
613-533-2842
Fax: 613-533-2594
URL: library.queensu.ca/law/
Hours: M-Th 8:30-10:00; F 8:30-5:00; Sa 10:00-5:00; Su 10:00-10:00
Subjects covered: Canadian Law, Quebec Civil Law, International Law
Services:
Inter-Library Loan (ILL)
Personnel: *Summary:* 3 Professional(s); 7 Technical(s)
Serge Moreau, Administration
Elizabeth Rose, Library Technician
rosee@northern.on.ca
705-567-9291 ext. 700
Karen Barber, Library Technician
barberk@northern.on.ca
705-567-9291 ext. 700

Kirkland Lake: **Kirkland Lake Campus Library**
140 Government Rd. East
Kirkland Lake, ON P2N 3L8
705-567-9291 ext: 700
Fax: 705-567-3350
e-mail: libraryk@northern.on.ca
National Library Symbol: OKLNC
Hours: M-F
Acquisitions Budget: $25,000 - $49,999
Subjects covered: Business, Technology, Social Science
Services:
Inter-Library Loan (ILL)
Personnel: *Summary:* 2 Total; 1 Technical(s)

Kitchener: **Conestoga College Institute of Technology & Advanced Learning Learning Resource Centre**
299 Doon Valley Dr.
B Wing, Rm. #2B18
Kitchener, ON N2G 4M4
519-748-5220 ext: 3361
Fax: 519-748-3538
e-mail: lrcinfo@conestogac.on.ca
lschneider@conestogac.on.ca
URL: www.conestogac.on.ca/lrc/
National Library Symbol: OKITC
Consortia Membership: Ontario Colleges Library Service
Founded in: 1967
Hours: M-Th 7:30am-7:30pm; F 7:30-5:00; Sa-Su 1:00-4:00
Subjects covered: Engineering Technology, Health Sciences, Business, Genereal & Applied Arts
Services:
Remote Access
Inter-Library Loan (ILL) for a fee
Microform Equipment: Computer; Reader
Personnel: *Summary:* 17 Total; 2 Professional(s); 12 Technical(s); 3 Other employees
Linda Schneider, Manager
Manager

Leamington: **Point Pelee National Park Library**
RR#1, 407 Monarch Lane
Leamington, ON N8H 3V4
519-322-5700
Fax: 519-322-1678
e-mail: pelee.info@pc.bc.ca
Founded in: 1918
Hours: by appointment only
Special Collections: Mammal/bird study skins, Insect collections, Archaeological collection
Subjects covered: Ecosystem related, Park history
Services:

Lindsay: **Frost Campus, School of Environmental & Natural Resources Sciences Learning Resources & Support Services**
200 Albert St. South
Lindsay, ON K9V 5E6
Mailing Address: PO Box 8000
Lindsay, ON K9V 5E6
705-878-9319
Fax: 705-878-9313
e-mail: glavende@flemingc.on.ca
pajohnst@flemingc.on.ca
National Library Symbol: OLISF
Founded in: 1967
Hours: M-Th 7:45-4:30; F 7:45-4:00
Special Collections: Natural Resources, Maps, Terrain & Water, Fish & Wildlife, Cartography, Geographic Information Systems Technology, Geology, Forestry, Ecosystem Management, Drilling & Blasting, Heavy Equipment
Services:
Inter-Library Loan (ILL)
Personnel: *Summary:* 4 Total; 4 Technical(s)
Eeva Munoz, Assistant University Librarian, Allyn & Betty Taylor Library
ekmunoz@uwo.ca
519-679-2111 ext. 86362
Harriet Rykse, Research & Instructional Services
hrykse@uwo.ca
Joan Kammerer, Resource Support Services
kammerer@uwo.ca

London: **Allyn & Betty Taylor Library**
Natural Sciences Centre, University of Western Ontario
#1, 1151 Richmond St.
London, ON N6A 5B7
519-661-3167
Fax: 519-661-3435
e-mail: taylib@uwo.ca
URL: www.lib.uwo.ca/taylor/
National Library Symbol: OLUM
Founded in: 1878
Note: Houses all materials from the old Engineering Library
Subjects covered: Medicine, Health Sciences, Life Sciences, Technology, Dentistry, Nursing, Pure Sciences, Engineering-Civil, Chemical, Electrical, Material, Mechanical, Computer
Services:
Inter-Library Loan (ILL)
Computer printing
Microform Equipment: Reader
Personnel: *Summary:* 27 Total; 11 Professional(s); 17 Other employees

London: **Fanshawe College of Applied Arts & Technology Library & Media Services**
1003L, 1001 Fanshawe College Blvd.
P.O. Box 7005
London, ON N5Y 5R6
Mailing Address: PO Box 7005
London, ON N5Y 5R6
519-452-4240
Fax: 519-452-4473
e-mail: mgrof-iannelli@fanshawec.on.ca
eguthrie@fanshawec.on.ca
URL: www.fanshawec.ca/library/default.asp
National Library Symbol: OLFC
Consortia Membership: Ontario Colleges Library Service
Hours: Su 1:00-5:00; M-Th 8:00-10:00; Fr 8:00-4:30 (mid-Sept to end of April)
Acquisitions Budget: $50,000 - $99,999
Special Collections: Statistics Canada Collection
Subjects covered: Economics, Health Sciences, Engineering, Technology, Health Technology, Business
Services:
Internet Access
Access to Subscription Databases
Inter-Library Loan (ILL)
Microform Equipment: Reader
Personnel: *Summary:* 16 Total; 4 Professional(s); 13 Technical(s)
Martie Grof-Iannelli, Manager, Library & Media Services
mgrof-iannelli@fanshawec.on.ca
519-452-4240 ext. 4351
Suzanne O'Neill, Head, Reference & Public Services
soneill@fanshawec.on.ca
519-452-4240 ext. 4346
Vicky Mok, Head, Technical Services, Acquisitions & Systems
vmok@fanshawec.on.ca
519-452-4142
Martha Joyce, Head, Media Services
mjoyce@fanshawec.ca
519-452-4430 ext. 4556
John Sadler, Director
jsadler@uwo.ca
519-661-2111 ext. 88271
Marianne Welch, Reference/Collections Librarian
mwelch@uwo.ca
Elizabeth Bruton, Reference/Electronic Services Librarian
ebruton@uwo.ca

Libraries & Resource Centres / Ontario

Deb Grey, Reference Librarian
djgrey@uwo.ca

London: John & Dotsa Bitove Family Law Library
Josephine Spencer Niblett Bldg., University of Western Ontario
1151 Richmond St.
London, ON N6A 3K7
519-661-2111 ext: 88273
Fax: 519-661-2012
Other contact info: 519-661-2111, ext 88274
e-mail: lawlib@uwo.ca
URL: www.lib.uwo.ca/law/
National Library Symbol: OLUL
Founded in: 1959
Hours: M-Su
Special Collections: Law; Canadian legislation and law reports, the principal British and American legal sources, European and international materials
Subjects covered: Law
Services:
Personnel: *Summary:* 7 Total; 4 Professional(s); 3 Other employees

London: Labatt Breweries Canada
Library Services
150 Simcoe St.
London, ON N6A 4M3
519-667-7242
Fax: 519-667-7473
National Library Symbol: OLLCR
Founded in: 1963
Subjects covered: Food, Physical Sciences, Technology
Services:

London: London Health Sciences Centre
Library & Student Affairs
800 Commissioners Rd. East
London, ON N6A 4G5
519-685-8300 ext: 52042
National Library Symbol: OLWT
Hours: M-F 8:30-4:30
Acquisitions Budget: $100,000 - $249,999
Note: Site libraries located at University Campus, South Street Site, Victoria Campus, & London Regional Cancer Program
Subjects covered: Medicine, Nursing, Health Sciences
Services:
Inter-Library Loan (ILL) for a fee
Personnel: *Summary:* 9 Total; 2 Professional(s); 7 Technical(s)
Peggy O'Neil, Manager
peggy.o'neil@lhsc.on.ca
519-685-8500 ext. 75934

London: Ontario Petroleum Institute Inc.
Ontario Oil, Gas & Salt Resources Library
669 Exeter Rd.
London, ON N6E 1L3
519-686-2772
Fax: 519-686-7225
e-mail: info@osrlibrary.com
URL: www.ogsrlibrary.com
Founded in: 1998
Hours: M-F 8:00-4:30
Note: Service fees based on labour time, reproduction cost & a Member/Non-member structure
Special Collections: Information on over 20,000 wells
Subjects covered: Subsurface geology; Petroleum; Salt; Underground hydrocarbon storage resources of Ontario
Services:
On-site use of microscopes; Roller tables; Client workroom for viewing samples
Personnel:
Richard Ostrowski, Facilities & Program Administrator
richard@ogsrlibrary.com
Shelley Kilby, Operations
Joe Van Overberghe, Trustee

London: St Joseph's Health Care, London
Library Services
268 Grosvenor St.
London, ON N6A 4V2
Mailing Address: PO Box 5777
London, ON N6A 4V2
519-646-6000 ext: 64439
Fax: 519-646-6228
e-mail: stjoseph_library@sjhc.london.on.ca
URL: www.sjhc.london.on.ca

National Library Symbol: JEP
Consortia Membership: WOHKN
Founded in: 1966
Hours: M-F 8:30-5:00 by appointment only
Acquisitions Budget: $50,000 - $99,999
Note: Member of London Area Health Libraries Association
Subjects covered: Medicine, Health Sciences
Services:
Inter-Library Loan (ILL)
Personnel: *Summary:* 2 Total; 1 Professional(s); 1 Technical(s); 1 Volunteer(s)
Brad Dishan, Librarian
brad.dishan@sjhc.london.on.ca
519-646-6100 ext. 65727

London: 3M Canada Company
Corporate Library & Information Services
1840 Oxford St. East
London, ON N6A 4T1
Mailing Address: PO Box 5757
London, ON N6A 4T1
519-451-2500 ext: 2486
Fax: 519-452-6142
e-mail: cstephenson@mmm.com
National Library Symbol: OLTMC
No public access
Founded in: 1979
Hours: M-F, 7:00-4:30
Acquisitions Budget: $25,000 - $49,999
Subjects covered: Adhesives, Polymers, Plastics
Services:
Inter-Library Loan (ILL)
Microform Equipment: Computer; Reader
Personnel: *Summary:* 2 Professional(s); 1 Technical(s)
Cheryl Stephenson, Librarian
cstephenson@mmm.com

London: University of Western Ontario Dept. of Geography
Serge Sauer Map Library
1151 Richmond St. North
London, ON N6A 5C2
519-661-3424
Fax: 519-661-3750
e-mail: mapref@uwo.ca
URL: geography.uwo.ca/maplibrary/
National Library Symbol: OLUG
Founded in: 1966
Hours: Sept.-April: M-F 8:30-4:30; May-Aug.: M-F 9:30-4:30.
Acquisitions Budget: 0-$9,999
For Print: 0-$9,999
For Electronic: 0-$9,999
Special Collections: Canadiana, Great Lakes, Fire Insurance Plans
Subjects covered: Maps, Geography, Transportation, Cartography, Hydrology, Topography, Urban Studies
Services:
Remote Access
Internet Access
Inter-Library Loan (ILL)
Scanner, GIS workstation
Personnel: *Summary:* 6 Total; 1 Professional(s); 1 Technical(s); 4 Other employees; 1 Volunteer(s)
Cheryl Woods, Map Curator
cawoods@uwo.ca
519-661-3424

London: University of Western Ontario Libraries
University of Western Ontario
London, ON N6A 3K7
519-661-2111 ext: 84796
Fax: 519-661-2005
URL: www.lib.uwo.ca
National Library Symbol: OLU
Consortia Membership: Canadian Research Knowledge Network (CRKN); Ontario Council of University Libraries (OCUL)
Founded in: 1882
Acquisitions Budget: $500,000 - $999,999
Services:
Personnel: *Summary:* 176 Total; 75 Professional(s); 101 Other employees
Joyce C. Garnett, University Librarian
jgarnett@uwo.ca
Karen Marshall, Director, Library
karen.marshall@uwo.ca

Lorraine Busby, Associate University Librarian, Information Resources
lbusby@uwo.ca
Penny Westmacott, Director, Library Information Technology Services
pwestmac@uwo.ca
Wendy Kennedy, Associate University Librarian, Information Services
wkennedy@uwo.ca
Joe Vandeloo, Assistant University Librarian, Administrative Services
vandeloo@uwo.ca
Robin Keirstead, University Archivist
rkeirste@uwo.ca

Manotick: LandOwner Resource Centre
5524 Dickinson St.
Manotick, ON K4M 1A5
Mailing Address: PO Box 599
Manotick, ON K4M 1A5
613-692-2390
Fax: 613-692-2806
800-387-5304
e-mail: info@lrconline.com
URL: www.lrconline.com
Founded in: 1993
Hours: M-F 8:30-4:30
Acquisitions Budget: $25,000 - $49,999
Subjects covered: Agriculture, Forestry, Wildlife, Water, Soil, Land Management
Services:
Personnel: *Summary:* 2 Professional(s)

Markham: IBM Canada Ltd.
Research Information Centre
3600 Steeles Ave., #E-F2/270
Markham, ON L3R 9Z7
905-316-2507
Fax: 905-316-2535
e-mail: wharton@ca.ibm.com
URL: www.ibm.com/ca
No public access
Founded in: 1983
Hours: M-F
Subjects covered: Information Technology, Market Analysis, Sales, Canadian Business
Services:
Internet Access
Personnel: *Summary:* 1 Total; 1 Professional(s)
Anne Wharton, Coordinator
Joy Muller, Manager
joy.muller@seneca.on.ca
416-491-5050 ext. 7524
Patricia Presti, Campus Librarian
patricia.presti@seneca.on.ca
416-491-5050 ext. 7526

Markham: Markham Campus
10 Allstate Pkwy.
Markham, ON L3R 5P8
416-491-5050 ext: 7521
Hours: M-Th 8:00-8:00; F 8:00-5:00
Personnel:

Mississauga: CanTox Health Sciences International Library
#308, 2233 Argentia Rd.
Mississauga, ON L5N 2X7
905-542-2900
Fax: 905-542-1011
e-mail: info@cantox.com
URL: www.cantox.com
National Library Symbol: OOAKC
No public access
Founded in: 1989
Acquisitions Budget: $10,000 - $24,999
For Print: 0-$9,999
For Electronic: 0-$9,999
Population Served: 50
Subjects covered: Toxicology
Services:
Inter-Library Loan (ILL)
Personnel: *Summary:* 4 Total; 1 Professional(s); 3 Technical(s)
Sandra Stewart, Information Manager
Judy Hill, Senior Assistant
Noghat Shafaat, Assistant

Mississauga: Credit Valley Hospital
Dr. Keith G. MacDonald Health Sciences Library
2200 Eglinton Ave. West
Mississauga, ON L5M 2N1
905-813-2411
Fax: 905-813-4294
e-mail: pstoyanova@cvh.on.ca
URL: www.cvh.on.ca/library/index.php
National Library Symbol: OMCVH
Consortia Membership: Health Science Information Consortium of Toronto
Founded in: 1985
Hours: M-F 9:00-5:00
Acquisitions Budget: $50,000 - $99,999
For Print: $50,000 - $99,999
For Electronic: $25,000 - $49,999
Population Served: 4000
Note: Open to public for reference only
Special Collections: Consumer health collection
Subjects covered: Medicine; Nursing; Health Sciences; Allied Health; Public Health
Services:
Remote Access
Internet Access
Personnel: *Summary:* 2 Professional(s); 3 Volunteer(s)
Penka Stoyanova, Health Sciences Librarian
pstoyanova@cvh.on.ca
Melissa Paladines, Staff
mpaladines@cvh.on.ca
905-813-1100 ext. 6871

Mississauga: E.I. duPont Canada Company
Central Library
7070 Mississauga Rd.
Mississauga, ON L5M 2H3
Mailing Address: PO Box 2200
Mississauga, ON L5M 2H3
905-821-5782
Fax: 905-821-5519
e-mail: caren.a.larner@can.dupont.com
National Library Symbol: OMDC
No public access
Founded in: 1954
Hours: M-F
Acquisitions Budget: $50,000 - $99,999
Subjects covered: Business, Finance, Industry, Physical Sciences, Engineering, Technology, Intellectual Property, Corporate Law, Management
Services:
Inter-Library Loan (ILL)
Personnel: *Summary:* 1 Technical(s)
Caren Larner, Librarian

Mississauga: Golder Associates Ltd.
Library (Mississauga)
2390 Argentia Rd.
Mississauga, ON L5N 5Z7
905-567-4444
Fax: 905-567-6561
e-mail: mwrezel@golder.com
smcfarland@golder.com
URL: www.golder.com
No public access
Founded in: 1960
Acquisitions Budget: $25,000 - $49,999
Subjects covered: Physical Sciences, Engineering, Technology, Geology, Hydrogeology, Rock & Soil Mechanics
Services:
Personnel: *Summary:* 1 Total; 1 Professional(s)
Mira Wrezel, Librarian
mwrezel@golder.com
Vera Rodic, Information Specialist
vera.rodic@teckcominco.com

Mississauga: G.P. Lewis Library
2380 Speakman Dr.
Mississauga, ON L5K 1B4
905-822-2022 ext: 276
Fax: 905-822-2882
e-mail: technology.sales@teckcominco.com
URL: www.teckcominco.com
National Library Symbol: OMCS
Founded in: 1964
Hours: Tu-Th by appointment only
Acquisitions Budget: 0-$9,999
For Print: 0-$9,999

For Electronic: 0-$9,999
Subjects covered: Lead, Zinc Alloys, Metallurgy, Battery Equipment
Services:
Internet Access
Inter-Library Loan (ILL)
Personnel: *Summary:* 1 Total; 1 Technical(s)

Mississauga: Hatch
Information Research Centre
2800 Speakman Dr.
Mississauga, ON L5K 2R7
905-855-7600
Fax: 905-855-8270
e-mail: infocentre@hatch.ca
URL: www.hatch.ca
Profile: Hatch supplies engineering, project & construction management services, process & business consulting services to the mining, metallurgical & infrastructure industries
National Library Symbol: OTHA
Founded in: 1955
Hours: by appointment only
Acquisitions Budget: $50,000 - $99,999
Subjects covered: Physical Sciences, Engineering, Technology, Metallurgy
Services:
Internet Access
Access to Subscription Databases
Inter-Library Loan (ILL)
Fee Based Research
Microform Equipment: Reader
Personnel: *Summary:* 2 Total; 1 Professional(s); 1 Other employees
Carolyn Warnica, Information Specialist
Ljiljana Radman, Library Technician

Mississauga: Inco Technical Services Limited
Information Services
2060 Flavelle Blvd.
Mississauga, ON L5K 1Z9
905-403-2448
Fax: 905-403-2401
e-mail: jmaclachlan@inco.com
National Library Symbol: OMIN
No public access
Founded in: 1966
Hours: M-F 8:30-5:00
Acquisitions Budget: $25,000 - $49,999
Subjects covered: Metallurgy, Research & Development
Services:
Inter-Library Loan (ILL)
Personnel: *Summary:* 4 Total; 2 Professional(s); 1 Technical(s)
Janet MacLachlans, Supervisor, Information & Office Services
jmaclachlan@inco.com
905-403-2449
Janet MacLachlan, Research Librarian
905-403-2487
Diane Baksa, Information Technologist
905-403-2448

Mississauga: Industrial Accident Prevention Association
Information Centre
#300, 5110 Creekbank Rd.
Mississauga, ON L4W 0A1
905-614-4272 ext: 2298
Fax: 905-614-1414
800-406-4272
e-mail: infocentre@iapa.ca
URL: www.iapa.ca/resources/information_centre.asp
National Library Symbol: OTIAP
Founded in: 1977
Hours: M-F 9:00-4:00 by appointment only
Subjects covered: Industrial Hygiene, Occupational Safety & Health, Ergonomics
Services:
Internet Access
Personnel: *Summary:* 2 Total; 1 Professional(s); 1 Technical(s)
Zuzka Hora, Manager, Information Centre Team
zhora@iapa.on.ca

Mississauga: Ontario Safety League / Ligue de sécurité du Ontario
Video Library
#100, 5045 Orbitor Dr., Bldg. 11
Mississauga, ON L4W 4Y4

905-625-0556 ext: 21
Fax: 905-625-0677
e-mail: info@osl.org
URL: www.osl.org
No public access
Founded in: 1913
Hours: M-F 8:30-4:30
Subjects covered: Videos on road safety subjects
Services:
Personnel: *Summary:* 1 Professional(s)
Adele Ross, Video Librarian
staff@osl.org
Susan Salhia, Supervisor, SP Library
salhias@aecl.ca
905-823-9040 ext. 5249

Mississauga: Sheridan Park Site
Library
2251 Speakman Dr.
Mississauga, ON L5K 1B2
905-823-9060
Fax: 905-823-8229
National Library Symbol: OTAE
Founded in: 1958
Hours: M-F by appointment only
Subjects covered: Nuclear Energy, Nuclear Engineering, Environmental Protection, Metallurgy, Material Sciences
Services:
Inter-Library Loan (ILL)
Personnel: *Summary:* 4 Total; 4 Technical(s)

Mississauga: Trillium Health Centre-Mississauga Site
L.G. Brayley Health Sciences Library
100 Queensway West
Mississauga, ON L5B 1B8
905-848-7394
Founded in: 1981
Hours: M-F
Acquisitions Budget: $25,000 - $49,999
Note: Mississauga Hospital & Queensway Hospital amalgamated to create Trillium Health Centre
Subjects covered: Medicine, Health Sciences, Nursing
Services:
Inter-Library Loan (ILL)
Personnel: *Summary:* 1 Total; 1 Professional(s); 6 Volunteer(s)
Christina Woodward, Manager

Mississauga: University of Toronto at Mississauga
Library
#2109A South Bldg., 3359 Mississauga Rd. North
Mississauga, ON L5L 1C6
905-828-5236
Fax: 905-569-4320
e-mail: mavrinac@utm.utoronto.co
erinrs@credit.erin.utoronto.ca
URL: www.erin.utoronto.ca/library/
Founded in: 1967
Hours: M-Th open 24 hours; F 8:00am-11:00pm; Sa 10:00-9:00; Su 1:00pm onwards Hours vary depending on the time of year.
Acquisitions Budget: $1,000,000 plus
Special Collections: Forensic Science, Infant Studies, Government Documents (partial depository), Biotechnology
Subjects covered: Arts & Science
Services:
Internet Access
Access to Subscription Databases
Inter-Library Loan (ILL)
Microform Equipment: Computer; Reader
Personnel: *Summary:* 38 Total; 13 Professional(s); 25 Technical(s)
Mary Ann Mavrinac, Chief Librarian
mavrinac@utm.utoronto.ca
905-828-5235
Ian Whyte, Coordinator of Public Services
iwhyte@utm.utoronto.ca
905-828-5332
Shelley Hawrychuk, Coordinator of Collection Services
shawrych@utm.utoronto.ca
905-569-4365
June Seel, Manager, Library Systems
jseel@utm.utoronto.ca
905-569-4375
Sheril Hook, Coordinator of Instructional Services
shook@utm.utoronto.ca
905-828-3885

Libraries & Resource Centres / Ontario

Mississauga: Xerox Research Centre of Canada
XRCC Library
2660 Speakman Dr.
Mississauga, ON L5K 2L1
905-823-7091 ext: 302
Fax: 905-822-7022
e-mail: xrcc.library@xrcc.xeroxlabs.com
National Library Symbol: OMX
Founded in: 1974
Hours: M-F 8:30-5:00 by appointment only
Services:
Inter-Library Loan (ILL)
Personnel: *Summary:* 2 Total; 1 Professional(s); 1 Technical(s)
Carolyne Sidey, Manager
carolyne.sidey@xrcc.xeroxlabs.com

Niagara Falls: Hatch Energy
H.G. Acres Library
4342 Queen St.
Niagara Falls, ON L2E 6W1
Mailing Address: PO Box 1001
Niagara Falls, ON L2E 6W1
905-374-5200 ext: 5247
Fax: 905-374-1157
e-mail: mdamboise@hatchacres.com
National Library Symbol: ONFA
No public access
Founded in: 1959
Acquisitions Budget: $50,000 - $99,999
Subjects covered: Engineering, Technology
Services:
Personnel: *Summary:* 1 Total; 1 Professional(s)
Marion D'Amboise, Librarian

Niagara Falls: Niagara Parks Botanical Gardens School of Horticulture
C.H. Henning Library
2565 Niagara Pkwy. North
Niagara Falls, ON L2E 6T2
Mailing Address: PO Box 150
Niagara Falls, ON L2E 6T2
905-356-8554 ext: 226
Fax: 905-356-5488
e-mail: sohlib@niagaraparks.com
schoolofhorticulture@niagaraparks.com
National Library Symbol: ONFNP
Founded in: 1965
Hours: M-F by appointment only
Note: Public access reference only
Special Collections: Archives
Subjects covered: Horticulture, Botany, Landscape Architecture, Soil Science, Entomology, Plant Pathology
Services:
Personnel: *Summary:* 1 Total; 1 Technical(s)
Ruth Stoner, Librarian

Niagara on the Lake: Genaire Limited
Library
Hwy. 55, Niagara District Airport
Niagara on the Lake, ON L2R 6Z4
Mailing Address: PO Box 966
St Catharines, ON L2R 6Z4
905-684-1165
Fax: 905-684-2412
e-mail: genaireltd@aol.com
Information@genaireltd.com
URL: www.genaireltd.com
National Library Symbol: OSTCGL
No public access
Founded in: 1951
Acquisitions Budget: 0-$9,999
For Print: 0-$9,999
For Electronic: 0-$9,999
Special Collections: Technical data/publications
Subjects covered: National Defence
Services:
Personnel: *Summary:* 1 Total; 1 Technical(s)
Gloria Furtney, Librarian
gfurntney@genaireltd.com
Cherry Miller, Technician
cherrym@nipissingu.ca
705-474-3450 ext. 4221

North Bay: Commerce Court Educational Resources
60 Commerce Ct.
North Bay, ON P1B 8K9
Mailing Address: PO Box 5001
North Bay, ON P1B 8K9
705-474-7600 ext: 5614
Services:
Personnel:

North Bay: Mines & Aggregates Safety & Health Association
Library
690 McKeown Ave.
North Bay, ON P1B 9P1
Mailing Address: PO Box 2050, Stn Main
North Bay, ON P1B 9P1
705-474-7233 ext: 289
Fax: 705-472-5800
e-mail: info@masha.on.ca
URL: www.masha.on.ca
National Library Symbol: ONBMA
No public access
Hours: M-F 8:30-4:30
Note: Library for use by member firms
Special Collections: Mining, educational materials, newsletters, accident statistics, technical reports, videos & meeting products related to industrial & safety
Subjects covered: Mining, health, safety
Services:
Personnel: *Summary:* 1 Professional(s)
Bonnie Brownstein, Librarian
bonniebrownstein@mash.on.ca
705-479-7233 ext. 289

North Bay: Nippissing University/Canadore College Education Centre Library
100 College Dr.
North Bay, ON P1B 8L7
Mailing Address: PO Box 5002
North Bay, ON P1B 8L7
705-474-3450 ext: 4223
Fax: 705-497-1455
e-mail: info@eclibrary.ca
URL: www.eclibrary.ca
National Library Symbol: ONBEC
Consortia Membership: Ontario Colleges Library Service
Founded in: 1972
Hours: M-Su
Acquisitions Budget: $500,000 - $999,999
For Print: $100,000 - $249,999
For Electronic: $250,000 - $499,999
Population Served: 7819
Note: Serves Nipissing University & Canadore College
Special Collections: Statistics Canada depository
Services:
Internet Access
Access to Subscription Databases
Personnel: *Summary:* 21 Total; 5 Professional(s); 16 Technical(s)
Brian Nettlefold, Executive Director
briann@nipissingu.ca
705-474-3450 ext. 4220

North Bay: Ontario Forestry Safe Workplace Association
Library
690 McKeown Ave.
North Bay, ON P1B 9P1
Mailing Address: PO Box 2050, Stn Main
North Bay, ON P1B 9P1
705-474-7233
Fax: 705-474-4530
e-mail: info@ofswa.on.ca
URL: www.ofswa.on.ca
No public access
Hours: M-F 8:00-4:00
Note: Library for use by member firms
Subjects covered: General information, videos & technical reports about forestry occupational health & safety
Services:
Personnel:
Gaetane Dubois, Administrative Assistant

Oakville: Pollutech Environmental Ltd.
Library
#5, 768 Westgate Rd.
Oakville, ON L6L 5N2
905-847-0065
Fax: 905-847-3840
e-mail: gbrown@pollutechgroup.com
URL: www.pollutechgroup.com
Subjects covered: Environment
Services:
Personnel: *Summary:* 9 Total; 9 Professional(s)
Belinda Dixon, Administrative Assistant

Oakville: Sheridan Institute of Technology and Advanced Learning
Library Services
1430 Trafalgar Rd.
Oakville, ON L6H 2L1
905-845-9430 ext: 2480
Fax: 905-815-4123
e-mail: shahida.rashid@sheridanc.on.ca
janet.fear@sheridanc.on.ca
URL: www.sheridaninstitute.ca/services/library/library.htm
National Library Symbol: OOAKSC
Consortia Membership: Ontario Colleges Library Service
Founded in: 1967
Hours: M-Th 8:30am-9:00pm; F 8:30-4:30; Sa, Su 11:00-3:00
Acquisitions Budget: $50,000 - $99,999
Services:
Access to Subscription Databases
Inter-Library Loan (ILL)
Microform Equipment: Reader
Personnel: *Summary:* 4 Total; 1 Professional(s); 2 Technical(s); 1 Other employees
Joan Sweeney Marsh, Manager, Library Services
joan.sweeneymarsh@sheridanc.on.ca
Janet Fear, Reference
janet.fear@sheridanc.on.ca
905-845-9430 ext. 2484

Oakville: Trafalgar Campus Library
1430 Trafalgar Rd.
Oakville, ON L6H 2L1
905-845-9430 ext: 2480
Fax: 905-815-4123
National Library Symbol: OOAKSC
Founded in: 1967
Hours: M-Th 8:30am-9:00pm; F 8:30-4:30; Sa-Su 11:00-3:00
Acquisitions Budget: $50,000 - $99,999
Subjects covered: Arts, Animation, Ceramics, Glass, Photography, Textiles, Wood, Sculpture, Illustration, Business, Early Childhood Education, Corrections
Services:
Remote Access
Inter-Library Loan (ILL)
Microform Equipment: Computer; Reader
Personnel: *Summary:* 6 Total; 1 Professional(s); 3 Technical(s); 2 Other employees

Oil Springs: Oil Museum of Canada
2324 Kelly Rd.
Oil Springs, ON N0N 1P0
Mailing Address: PO Box 16
Oil Springs, ON N0N 1P0
519-834-2840
Fax: 519-834-2840
e-mail: omcchin@ebtech.net
oil.museum@county-lambton.on.ca
Hours: May-Oct.: M-Su 10:00-5:00. Nov.-April: M-F 10:00-5:00
Subjects covered: Materials relating to petroleum & the petroleum industry in Canada
Services:
Personnel: *Summary:* 1 Total; 1 Professional(s)
Connie Bell, Manager
connie.bell@county-lambton.on.ca
Chris Tomasini, Librarian, Orillia Campus
ctomasin@lakeheadu.ca
705-330-4008 ext. 2260
Kim Vallée, Senior Library Technician
kavallee@lakeheadu.ca
705-330-4008 ext. 2261

Orillia: Lakehead University
Orillia Library
500 University Ave.
Orillia, ON L3V 0B9
705-330-4008 ext: 2250
e-mail: orlibrary@lakeheadu.ca
URL: library.lakeheadu.ca/orillia
National Library Symbol: OPAL
Founded in: 2006
Acquisitions Budget: $25,000 - $49,999

Population Served: 1000
Subjects covered: Humanities; Social Sciences; Sciences
Services:
Remote Access
Internet Access
Access to Subscription Databases
Inter-Library Loan (ILL)
Reference workshops; Labtops; Headphones; White board markets; Group study rooms; Printing
Personnel: *Summary:* 4 Total; 1 Professional(s); 3 Technical(s); 1 Other employees
Phil Hull, Campus Librarian
phull@georgianc.on.ca
705-325-2740 ext. 3051
Jana Bickell, Library Technician
705-325-2740 ext. 3052
Rick Brown, Services Technician
705-325-2740 ext. 3055
Katrina Montgomery, Library Technician
705-325-2740 ext. 3053

Orillia: **Orillia Campus**
Learning Resource Centre
#1142, 825 Memorial Ave.
Orillia, ON L3V 6S2
Mailing Address: PO Box 2316
Orillia, ON L3V 6S2
705-325-2740 ext. 3050
Fax: 705-329-3107
e-mail: phull@georgianc.on.ca
URL: library.georgianc.on.ca
National Library Symbol: OORIGC
Founded in: 1967
Hours: Winter: M-Th 7:45am-8:00pm; F 7:45-4:30; Sa 12:00-4:00. Summer: M-F 8:30-4:30
Services:
Internet Access
Access to Subscription Databases
Inter-Library Loan (ILL)
Laser printing; Tours; Orientations; Video bookings; Student learning centres
Microform Equipment: Computer; Reader
Personnel: *Summary:* 5 Total; 1 Professional(s); 3 Technical(s); 1 Other employees

Oshawa: **Durham College of Applied Arts & Technology**
Library Resource Centre
2000 Simcoe St. North
Oshawa, ON L1H 7L7
Mailing Address: PO Box 385
Oshawa, ON L1H 7L7
905-721-2000 ext. 2214
Fax: 905-721-3029
e-mail: library@dc-uoit.ca
URL: www.durhamcollege.ca/EN/library/library.php
National Library Symbol: OOSHD
Consortia Membership: Ontario Colleges Library Service
Founded in: 1968
Hours: M-Th 8:00am-12:00am; F 8:00am-9:00pm; Sa, Su 10:00-6:00
Acquisitions Budget: $100,000 - $249,999
Note: Member of Durham Region Information Network (DRIN). Staff & student access for internet, Cd-roms & databases on & off campus. Public access on campus only.
Subjects covered: Health Sciences, Science & Technology, Design & Communication Arts, Business, Justice Studies, Manufacturing, Computers
Services:
Remote Access
Access to Subscription Databases
Inter-Library Loan (ILL)
Microform Equipment: Reader
Personnel: *Summary:* 20 Total; 9 Professional(s); 9 Technical(s); 2 Other employees
Carol Mittlestead, Acting Dean & Associate Librarian
carol.mittlestead@dc-uoit.ca
905-723-3111 ext. 2005
Faye Schofield, Technical Services Technician
Karin Downie, Access Service Manager
karin.downie@dc-uoit.ca
905-721-3111 ext. 2967
Gabor Feuer, Library IT Manager
gabor.feuer@dc-uoit.ca
905-721-3111 ext. 2974

Ottawa: **Agriculture & Agri-Food Canada / Agriculture et Agroalimentaire Canada**
Canadian Agriculture Library/Bibliothèque canadienne de l'agriculture
Sir John Carling Bldg.
#255, 930 Carling Ave.
Ottawa, ON K1A 0C5
613-759-7068
Fax: 613-759-6627
TDD: 6137597470
e-mail: calref@agr.ca
jacquesd@agr.gc.ca
URL: res2.agr.gc.ca/london/index_e.htm
National Library Symbol: OOAG
Consortia Membership: Council of Federal Libraries (CFL) Consortium
Founded in: 1910
Hours: M-F 8:30-4:30
Acquisitions Budget: $1,000,000 plus
Special Collections: FAO; Statistics Canada
Subjects covered: Agriculture; Horticulture; Dairying; Entomology; Pesticides; Plant Diseases; Soil Science; Veterinary Medicine
Services:
Remote Access
Internet Access
Access to Subscription Databases
Inter-Library Loan (ILL)
Microform Equipment: Reader
Personnel: *Summary:* 30 Professional(s); 6 Technical(s); 27 Other employees
Danielle Jacques, Acting Director
613-759-7083
Dena Speevak, Chief, Information Services
613-759-7071
Ingrit Monasterios, Chief, Information Resource Management
613-759-7093
Diane Rudzevicius, Acting Chief, Library Systems
613-579-6615
Jeff White, Head Librarian

Ottawa: **Aircraft Certification**
Technical Reference Centre
Place de Ville, Tower C
#465, 330 Sparks St.
Ottawa, ON K1A 0N8
613-952-4401
Fax: 613-990-5738
e-mail: whitejp@tc.gc.ca
National Library Symbol: OOTA
No public access
Hours: M-F 7:30-4:30
Special Collections: Aircraft technical manuals, regulatory documents, historic aviation regulations
Subjects covered: Transportation, Aircraft Manuals
Services:
Access to Subscription Databases
Microform Equipment: Computer; Reader
Personnel: *Summary:* 6 Total; 1 Professional(s); 5 Technical(s)
Janice White, Technical Librarian
613-998-8299
Tammy Charette, Staff

Ottawa: **Aircraft Services Directorate**
Technical Library, AAFBAA
200 Comet Pvt.
Ottawa, ON K1V 9B2
613-998-8299
Fax: 613-998-8326
e-mail: nichofr@tc.gc.ca
janice.white@tc.gc.ca
No public access
Hours: M-F
Acquisitions Budget: $50,000 - $99,999
Subjects covered: Transportation - Aviation
Services:
Personnel: *Summary:* 2 Total; 2 Professional(s); 1 Technical(s)

Ottawa: **Algonquin College of Applied Arts & Technology / Collège Algonquin des Arts appliqués et de la Technologie**
Woodroffe Campus, Learning Resource Centre
#C205, 1385 Woodroffe Ave.
Ottawa, ON K2G 1V8
613-727-4723 ext: 5834
Fax: 613-727-7642
e-mail: lrc@algonquincollege.com
URL: www.algonquincollege.com/lrc/
National Library Symbol: OOAC
Consortia Membership: Ontario Colleges Library Service
Founded in: 1967
Hours: Winter: M-Th 7:45am-9:00pm; F 7:45-5:00; Sa 11:00-5:00
Acquisitions Budget: $100,000 - $249,999
For Print: $100,000 - $249,999
For Electronic: $100,000 - $249,999
Note: Hours vary throughout year
Special Collections: Statistics Canada publications; Selective depository for government publications
Subjects covered: Business; Technology; Trades; Health Sciences; Applied Arts
Services:
Remote Access
Internet Access
Inter-Library Loan (ILL)
Personnel: *Summary:* 15 Total; 2 Professional(s); 12 Technical(s); 1 Other employees
Brenda Mahoney, Reference & Electronic Resources Librarian
mahoneb@algonquincollege.com
Maureen Sheppard, Technical Services & Systems Librarian
sheppam@algonquincollege.com
Glenn Macdougall, Director, Learning and Teaching Services
macdoug@algonquincollege.com
613-727-4723 ext. 7071
Sonia Poulin, Directrice
sonia.poulin@uottawa.ca
613-562-5845

Ottawa: **Bibliothèque de droit Brian-Dickson / Brian Dickson Law Library**
57 Louis-Pasteur Pvt.
Ottawa, ON K1N 6N5
613-562-5812
Téléc: 613-562-5279
URL: www.biblio.uottawa.ca/droit-law
Fondée en: 1973
Heures: L-D
Budget d'acquisitions: $1,000,000 plus
Sujets: Droit
Services:
Prêts entre bibliothèques(PEB)
Lecteur/reproduction de microformes: Lecteurs
Personnel: *Sommaire:* 4 Professionnel(s); 2 Technicien(s); 14 Autre(s) employé(s);
Dianne Kharouba, Director
kharouba@uottawa.ca
613-562-5418
Karine Fournier, Head, Reference
613-562-5800 ext. 8517

Ottawa: **Bibliothèque des sciences de la santé**
#1020, 451 Smyth Rd.
Ottawa, ON K1H 8M5
613-562-5407
Fax: 613-562-5401
e-mail: refrgn@uottawa.ca
illpebhs@uottawa.ca
URL: www.biblio.uottawa.ca/health
National Library Symbol: OOUH
Founded in: 1984
Hours: M-Th 8:15am-10:30pm; F 8:15-8:00; Sept.-May: Sa, Su 9:00-7:00
Acquisitions Budget: $500,000 - $999,999
Note: Bibliothèque bilingue.
Subjects covered: Physiotherapy, Medicine, Nursing, Occupational Therapy, Audiology, Speech Pathology
Services:
Internet Access
Inter-Library Loan (ILL) for a fee
SDI (fee)
Personnel: *Summary:* 9 Total; 3 Professional(s); 1 Technical(s); 5 Other employees

Ottawa: **Branch Library**
415 Legget Dr.
Ottawa, ON K2K 2B2
Mailing Address: PO Box 13330
Ottawa, ON K2K 2B2
613-592-6500
Fax: 613-592-7427

Libraries & Resource Centres / Ontario

National Library Symbol: OKCM
No public access
Founded in: 1984
Subjects covered: Engineering
Services:

Ottawa: **Canada Dept. of National Defence & the Canadian Forces / Ministère de la défense nationale et des forces canadiennes**
NDHQ Library
Major General George R. Pearkes Bldg., National Defence Headquarters
101 Colonel By Dr.
Ottawa, ON K1A 0K2
Mailing Address: National Defence Headquarters, 101 Colonel By Dr.
Ottawa, ON K1A 0K2
613-996-0831
Fax: 613-995-8176
National Library Symbol: OOND
Consortia Membership: Council of Federal Libraries (CFL) Consortium
Founded in: 1903
Hours: Public (need-to-know): M-F 9:00-3:00. Dept: 7:45-4:00 by appointment only
Acquisitions Budget: $100,000 - $249,999
For Print: $50,000 - $99,999
For Electronic: $50,000 - $99,999
Subjects covered: Defence, Military Administration, History especially Canadian Military History
Services:
Inter-Library Loan (ILL)
Personnel: *Summary:* 1 Professional(s); 5 Technical(s)
Paul Sawa, Library Manager
sawa.pr@forces.gc.ca
613-995-8837
Larry Monuk, Reference Clerk
monuk.lj@forces.gc.ca
613-996-0832
Nancy Stroud, Reference Clerk
stroud.nl@forces.gc.ca
613-996-0843
Brian Grier, Acquisitions Clerk
grier.jb@forces.gc.ca
613-995-2213
Heather Campbell, ILL Clerk
campbell.hl@forces.gc.ca
613-996-0833

Ottawa: **Canada Institute for Scientific & Technical Information (CISTI) / Institut canadien de l'information scientifique et technique (ICIST)**
Bldg. M-55, National Research Council
1200 Montreal Rd.
Ottawa, ON K1A 0S2
613-993-1600
Fax: 613-952-9112
800-668-1222
e-mail: info.cisti@nrc-cnrc.gc.ca
URL: cisti-icist.nrc-cnrc.gc.ca
National Library Symbol: ON
Consortia Membership: Council of Federal Libraries (CFL) Consortium
No public access
Founded in: 1924
Hours: M-F 8:30-4:30
Acquisitions Budget: $1,000,000 plus
For Print: $500,000 - $999,999
For Electronic: $500,000 - $999,999
Population Served: Serves BRI employees.
Note: Library staff is available during regular hours. Library is open to BRI employees 24 hours.
Subjects covered: Science, Technology, Engineering, Medicine
Services:
Remote Access
Internet Access
Access to Subscription Databases
Document delivery, Online catalogue, Tables of contents, Reference
Personnel: *Summary:* 250 Total; 132 Professional(s); 118 Other employees
Bernard Dumouchel, Director General
bernard.dumouchel@nrc-CNRC.GC.CA
613-993-2341
François Dubé, Director, Technology & Research Services
613-993-3234

Suzanne Bureau, Director, Collection & Metadata Services
613-993-9029
Michael Ireland, Acting Director, Information Access & Delivery
Cameron Macdonald, Director, Publishing (NRC Research Press)
613-993-1931
Michel Gauthieu, Director, NRC Information Services
613-993-3969
Pam Bjornson, Director, Business Affairs
613-993-9637
Lucie Molgat, Director, Csi Project Managment Office
613-991-2462

Ottawa: **Canada Mortgage & Housing Corporation / Société canadienne d'hypothèques et de logement**
Canadian Housing Information Centre
Library/Centre canadien de documentation sur l'habitation
#C1-200, 700 Montreal Rd.
Ottawa, ON K1A 0P7
613-748-2367
Fax: 613-748-4069
800-668-2642
TDD: 8003093388
e-mail: chic@cmhc-schl.gc.ca
URL: www.cmhc-schl.gc.ca/en/corp/li
National Library Symbol: OOCM
Consortia Membership: Council of Federal Libraries (CFL) Consortium
Founded in: 1979
Hours: M-F 9:00-4:00
Note: CMHC Library serves consumers, builders, developers, academics & industry decision-makers
Special Collections: Historical material; Corporation research reports; Images; Audiovisual materials
Subjects covered: Community development & planning; Housing; Management; Finance & economics; Public policy; Public administration
Services:
Inter-Library Loan (ILL)
Microform Equipment: Computer; Reader

Ottawa: **Canada Revenue Agency / Agence du revenu du Canada**
Headquarters Library/Bibliothèque de l'administration centrale
Place de Ville, Tower A, Concourse Level, 320 Queen St.
Ottawa, ON K1A 0L5
613-957-2278
Fax: 613-957-9514
e-mail: ottawa.OR-KRC@cra-arc.gc.ca
National Library Symbol: OONR
Consortia Membership: Council of Federal Libraries (CFL) Consortium
Founded in: 1942
Hours: M-F 8:00-4:00 by appointment only
Acquisitions Budget: $100,000 - $249,999
For Print: $100,000 - $249,999
For Electronic: $10,000 - $24,999
Special Collections: Taxation, Customs, Excise, Law Reports & Statutes
Subjects covered: Taxation, Law, Accounting, Government, Management
Services:
Access to Subscription Databases
Inter-Library Loan (ILL)
Fee Based Research
Microform Equipment: Reader
Personnel: *Summary:* 12 Total; 3 Professional(s); 3 Technical(s); 6 Other employees
Hillary Carr, Manager
Hiley.Carr@cra-arc.gc.ca
613-957-2275
Althea Sproule, Librarian
Althca.Sproule@cra-arc.gc.ca
613-941-3978
Rolla Haddad, Librarian
Rolla.Haddad@cra-arc.gc.ca
613-941-8553

Ottawa: **Canada Science & Technology Museum / Musée des sciences et de la technologie du Canada**
Library & Information Services
2380 Lancaster Rd.
Ottawa, ON K1G 5A3
Mailing Address: PO Box 9724, Stn T
Ottawa, ON K1G 5A3
613-991-2982
Fax: 613-990-3636
e-mail: library@technomuses.ca
URL: www.sciencetech.technomuses.ca
Social Media: www.flickr.com/photos/cstmweb
facebook: www.facebook.com/group.php?gid=53267368995
LInkin: www.linkedin.com/company/canada-science-and-technology-museum
tweeter: http://twitter.com/#!/SciTechMuseum
National Library Symbol: OONMS
Founded in: 1967
Hours: M-F 8:30-12:00, 1:00-4:00. Appointments are recommended but not necessary by appointment only
Acquisitions Budget: $25,000 - $49,999
Note: Also listing for Canada Aviation Museum. Horizon Library System (Dynix inc.) Youtube: www.youtube.com/user/cstmweb
Special Collections: Bicycling; Trade Literature; Railway Photographs & Railway Engineering Drawings; CN (Canadian National) Photo Collection; Archives
Subjects covered: Agricultural, Industrial & Space Technology; Graphic Arts; Communications; Energy; Physical Sciences; Transportation
Services:
Internet Access
Inter-Library Loan (ILL)
Photograph & engineering drawing reproduction
Microform Equipment: Computer; Reader
Personnel: *Summary:* 6 Total; 1 Professional(s); 4 Technical(s)
David McGee, Manager
dmcgee@technomuses.ca
613-991-4975
Sylvie Bertrand, Reader's Services Assistant
library@technomuses.ca
613-991-2982
Joyce Hay, Acquisitions Coordinator
jhay@technomuses.ca
613-991-5701

Ottawa: **Canadian Forces Medical Group Headquarters**
Medical Library
1745 Alta Vista Dr.
Ottawa, ON K1A 0K6
613-945-6517
Fax: 613-998-8093
National Library Symbol: OONDM
Founded in: 1961
Hours: M-F 8:30-4:30 by appointment only
Acquisitions Budget: $25,000 - $49,999
Subjects covered: Medicine, Health Sciences
Services:
Inter-Library Loan (ILL)
Personnel: *Summary:* 1 Professional(s); 1 Volunteer(s)
Philip B. Allan, Director, Library Services
p.allen@debbs.ndhq.dnd.ca

Ottawa: **Canadian Institute of Biotechnology**
Library
#420, 130 Albert St.
Ottawa, ON K1P 5G4
613-230-5585
Fax: 613-563-8850
e-mail: info@biotech.ca
URL: www.biotech.ca
Founded in: 1998
Note: Information packages available to the public.
Subjects covered: Biotechnology with various Canadian & international resources & newsletters
Services:
Personnel:
Dana Alexander, Manager, Public Affairs
613-230-5585 ext. 222

Ottawa: Canadian Institute of Geomatics / Association canadienne des sciences géomatiques
Archives
#400, 1390 Prince of Wales Dr.
Ottawa, ON K2C 3N6
613-224-9851
Fax: 613-224-9577
e-mail: editgeo@magma.ca
URL: www.cig-acsg.ca
Founded in: 1922
Hours: M-F 9:00-5:00
Acquisitions Budget: 0-$9,999
For Print: 0-$9,999
For Electronic: 0-$9,999
Special Collections: CIG archives of 116 years including technical writing & photos on surveying & mapping subjects
Subjects covered: Surveying, Photogeomatry, Remote Sensing, GIS GPS
Services:
Personnel:
Carol Railer, Production & Advertising Manager
Harold Jones, Staff

Ottawa: Canadian Museum of Nature / Musée canadien de la nature
Library & Archives
PO Box 3443, Stn D
Ottawa, ON K1P 6P4
613-364-4042
Fax: 613-364-4026
e-mail: cmnlib@mus-nature.ca
URL: www.nature.ca
National Library Symbol: OONMNS
Consortia Membership: Council of Federal Libraries (CFL) Consortium
Founded in: 1842
Hours: M-F 8:30-4:30
Acquisitions Budget: $50,000 - $99,999
For Print: $50,000 - $99,999
For Electronic: 0-$9,999
Note: Library located at 1740 Pink Rd., Aylmer QC J9J 3N7
Special Collections: Rare Books; Photo Collection; Nature Art Collection, Archives
Subjects covered: Natural Sciences, Botany, Invertebrate & Vertebrate Zoology, Mineral Sciences, Paleobiology, Natural History, Biodiversity
Services:
Inter-Library Loan (ILL)
Microform Equipment: Reader
Personnel: *Summary:* 4 Total; 2 Professional(s); 2 Technical(s); 1 Volunteer(s)
Patrice Stevenson, Librarian
pstevenson@mus-nature.ca
613-364-4045
Ted Sypniewski, Serials & Acquisitions Officer
613-566-4734
Chantal Dussault, Archivist
cdussault@mus-nature.ca
613-364-4047
Mike Wayne, Circulation & ILL
613-364-4042

Ottawa: Canadian Nuclear Safety Commission
Library
280 Slater St., 2nd Floor
Ottawa, ON K1P 1C2
Mailing Address: PO Box 1046, Stn B
Ottawa, ON K1P 1C2
613-943-1538
Fax: 613-995-5086
e-mail: library-bibliotheque@cnsc-ccsn.gc.ca
illpeb@cnsc-ccsn.gc.ca
URL: www.nuclearsafety.gc.ca
National Library Symbol: OOAECB
Consortia Membership: Council of Federal Libraries (CFL) Consortium
Hours: M-F 8:00-5:00
Acquisitions Budget: $100,000 - $249,999
Subjects covered: Nuclear Science & Technology, Radiation Protection, Radioactive Waste Management, Nonproliferation
Services:
Inter-Library Loan (ILL)
Personnel: *Summary:* 4 Total; 2 Professional(s); 2 Technical(s)
Frank Rautenkranz, Librarian
frank.rautenkranz@cnsc-ccsn.gc.ca
613-996-2060

Ottawa: Canadian Organic Growers Inc.
Mail-Lending Library
#B-1, 323 Chapel St.
Ottawa, ON K1N 7Z2
613-216-0741
Fax: 613-236-0743
888-375-7383
e-mail: library@cog.ca
URL: www.cog.ca
No public access
Acquisitions Budget: 0-$9,999
For Print: 0-$9,999
For Electronic: 0-$9,999
Population Served: 2200
Subjects covered: Organic Farming, Organic Gardening, Sustainable Horticulture
Services:
Access to Subscription Databases
Personnel: *Summary:* 1 Volunteer(s)
Kristine Swaren, Librarian

Ottawa: Canadian Wildlife Federation
Resource Centre
350 Michael Cowpland Dr.
Ottawa, ON K2M 2W1
613-599-9594
Fax: 613-599-4428
800-563-9453
e-mail: info@cwf-fcf.org
URL: www.cwf-fcf.org
Subjects covered: Educational materials about wildlife & habitat conservation, research & advocacy
Services:
Margaret Ahearn, Chief, CANMET Information Centre
mahearn@nrcan.gc.ca
613-995-4157
Lidia Taylor, Collection Development Librarian
613-943-8770
Lawrence Wardroper, Head, Systems
613-973-8772

Ottawa: CANMET Information Centre / Centre d'information CANMET
555 Booth St.
Ottawa, ON K1A 0G1
613-995-4157
Fax: 613-995-8730
e-mail: canlib@nrcan.gc.ca
National Library Symbol: OOM
Founded in: 1907
Hours: M-F
Acquisitions Budget: $50,000 - $99,999
Note: Director, Management Services Division: Jennifer Hollington
Subjects covered: Metallurgy, Energy Technology, Materials Science Mining
Services:
Inter-Library Loan (ILL)
Microform Equipment: Computer; Reader
Personnel: *Summary:* 11 Total; 5 Professional(s); 3 Technical(s); 3 Other employees

Ottawa: Carleton University
Maxwell MacOdrum Library
1125 Colonel By Dr.
Ottawa, ON K1S 5B6
613-520-2735
Fax: 613-520-2750
e-mail: university_librarian@carleton.ca
raceradm@library.carleton.ca
URL: www.library.carleton.ca
National Library Symbol: OOCC
Consortia Membership: Canadian Research Knowledge Network (CRKN); Ontario Council of University Libraries (OCUL)
Founded in: 1942
Hours: M-F 8:00am-2:00am; Sa-Su 10:00am-2:00am
Acquisitions Budget: $1,000,000 plus
For Print: $1,000,000 plus
For Electronic: $1,000,000 plus
Note: Limited access to walk-in users for internet & database access. Print copies from microfilm available. There is a $5 fee for photocopying (ILL). Remote access to online databases to members of the University only.
Special Collections: Batchinsky Collection (Ukrainian politics, 19th-20th century) Canadian, British & American small-press poetry, Canadian Institute of Historical Microreproductions (CIHM), French Revolution, Novosti Press Agency Photograph Files, William Blake (Trianon Press), Archival Materials-records of the library & other material relating to the University; The CBC Newsworld Collection; Extensive collection of maps, atlases, cartographic references & data. Carleton University Library has Canadian dissemination rights for the following data collections: Canadian Gallup polls, POLLARA polls, & the International Social Survey Project, I.C.A. Barbara Petchenik Children's Map Competition Archive.
Subjects covered: Humanities, Social Sciences, Architecture, Industrial Design, Journalism & Mass Communication, Public Administration, Science & Engineering, Canadian Federal & Provincial Government Documents & Publications of International Agencies, International Affairs
Services:
Remote Access
Inter-Library Loan (ILL) for a fee of $5 for photocopying articles.
Microform Equipment: Computer; Reader
Personnel: *Summary:* 104 Total; 25 Professional(s); 74 Technical(s); 6 Other employees
Margaret Haines, University Librarian
margaret_haines@carleton.ca
613-520-2725
Elizabeth Knight, Head, Reference Services
elizabeth_knight@carleton.ca
613-520-2600 ext. 8185
Colleen Neely, Head, Technical Services
colleen_neely@carleton.ca
613-520-2600 ext. 8140
Leslie Firth, Assistant Librarian, Systems
leslie_firth@carleton.ca
613-520-2600 ext. 2745
Susan Jackson, Head, Maps, Data & Government Information Centre
susan_jackson@carleton.ca
613-520-2600 ext. 8946

Ottawa: DBM6/LSTL Building
Material Group Technical Resource Centre
101 Colonel By Dr.
Ottawa, ON K1A 0K2
613-997-9574
Fax: 819-997-7135
National Library Symbol: OOLSTL
No public access
Hours: M-F
Subjects covered: Law, Law Enforcement
Services:
Inter-Library Loan (ILL)
Susan Hurst, Librarian
susan_hurst@drdc-rddc.gc.ca
Rachel Apps, Library Technician & Publications Officer
rachel.apps@drdc-rddc.gc.ca
613-998-2331
Elizabeth McGoldrick, Library Assistant
elizabeth.mcgoldrick@drdc-rddc.gc.ca
613-998-2371

Ottawa: Defence R & D Canada - Ottawa / R & D pour la défense Canada - Ottawa
Library
101 Colonel By Dr.
Ottawa, ON K1A 0Z4
613-998-2657
Fax: 613-998-2675
e-mail: susan.hurst@drdc-rddc.gc.ca
National Library Symbol: OODRC
Consortia Membership: Council of Federal Libraries (CFL) Consortium
No public access
Subjects covered: Engineering, Technology, Electronics, Radar, Networks, Communications, Navigation
Services:
Personnel: *Summary:* 1 Professional(s); 2 Technical(s)
Patricia Madaire, Librarian

Ottawa: Eastern Cereal & Oilseed Research Centre
Library
KW Neatby Bldg., Central Experimental Farm
960 Carling Ave.
Ottawa, ON K1A 0C6
613-759-1807
Fax: 613-759-1924
e-mail: madairep@agr.gc.ca
URL: res2.agr.ca/ecorc/

Libraries & Resource Centres / Ontario

National Library Symbol: OOAGE
Hours: by appointment only
Acquisitions Budget: $50,000 - $99,999
Subjects covered: Life Sciences, Entomology, Taxonomy, Botany, Crop Sciences, Soil Sciences
Services:
Microform Equipment: Reader
Personnel: *Summary:* 2 Total; 1 Professional(s); 1 Technical(s)
Lise Robillard, Library Assistant

Ottawa: **ECORC Plant Research Library**
Plant Research Library
William M. Saunders Bldg., Canadian Experimental Farm
Ottawa, ON K1A 0C6
613-759-1368
Fax: 613-759-1599
e-mail: ooagb@agr.gc.ca
National Library Symbol: OOAGB
Hours: M-F 8:30-4:30 by appointment only
Subjects covered: Agriculture; Horticulture
Services:
Personnel: *Summary:* 1 Total
Margaret Ahearn, Head of Library
613-995-4157

Ottawa: **Energy, Minerals & Metals Information Centre / Centre d'information sur les minéraux, métaux et l'énergie**
580 Booth St.
Ottawa, ON K1A 0E4
613-996-8282
Fax: 613-992-7211
e-mail: peb580@rncan.gc.ca
URL: www.nrcan-rncan.gc.ca/es/msd/emmic/web
National Library Symbol: OOMR
OOM
Founded in: 1958
Hours: M-F 8:30-4:30
Acquisitions Budget: $50,000 - $99,999
Subjects covered: Legislation, Policies, Management, Human Resources & Career Development, Energy, Minerals
Services:
Internet Access
Access to Subscription Databases
Inter-Library Loan (ILL) for a fee
Microform Equipment: Computer; Reader
Personnel: *Summary:* 14 Total; 6 Professional(s); 5 Technical(s); 3 Other employees
Rita Pascolo, Library Technician
rita.pascolo@tsb.gc.ca

Ottawa: **Engineering Branch Library**
1901 Research Rd.
Ottawa, ON K1A 1K8
613-990-0884
Fax: 613-998-5572
e-mail: rita.pascolo@tsb.gc.ca
National Library Symbol: OOTSE
Hours: Tu, Th 8:00-4:30, appointment required. by appointment only
Acquisitions Budget: 0-$9,999
For Print: 0-$9,999
For Electronic: 0-$9,999
Subjects covered: Engineering
Services:
Inter-Library Loan (ILL)
Personnel: *Summary:* 1 Total; 1 Technical(s)

Ottawa: **Fisheries & Oceans Canada / Pêches et océans Canada**
Library Policy & Services/Services et politiques de bibliothèque
200 Kent St., 7th Fl.
Ottawa, ON K1A 0E6
613-993-2950
Fax: 613-990-4901
e-mail: oofi@dfo-mpo.gc.ca
oofiillpeb@dfo-mpo.gc.ca
URL: www.dfo-mpo.gc.ca
National Library Symbol: OOFI
Consortia Membership: Council of Federal Libraries (CFL) Consortium
Founded in: 1979
Hours: M-F 8:00-5:00
Acquisitions Budget: $250,000 - $499,999
For Print: $50,000 - $99,999
For Electronic: $250,000 - $499,999
Subjects covered: Fisheries; Aquatic Sciences; Nautical Sciences
Services:
Inter-Library Loan (ILL)
Microform Equipment: Computer; Reader
Personnel: *Summary:* 7 Total; 3 Professional(s); 3 Technical(s); 1 Other employees
Emil Daniel, Manager
daniele@dfo-mpo.gc.ca
Darlene Tan, Reference Librarian
oofi@dfo-mpo.gc.ca
613-993-2950
Ginette Dion, Information Specialist
diog@dfo-mpo.gc.ca
613-998-1801
Jacquline Lalande, Systems Librarian
lanadej@dfo-mpo.gc.ca
616-993-6993
Christine Desgagnes, Library Assistant
613-993-6925
Cameron Metcalf, Head
cmetcalf@uottawa.ca

Ottawa: **Geographic, Statistical and Government Information Centre**
65, Université Privée
Ottawa, ON K1N 6N5
613-562-5211
Fax: 613-562-5133
e-mail: globe@uottawa.ca
URL: www.uottawa.ca/library/map
Hours: L-D
Acquisitions Budget: $25,000 - $49,999
Special Collections: Canadian air photos, Permafrost maps, Ottawa Hull local maps, Geomorphology
Subjects covered: Cartes geógraphiques, cartographie, géomorphologie, cartes topographiques, Canada
Services:
Internet Access
Inter-Library Loan (ILL)
GIS data support
Microform Equipment: Computer; Reader
Personnel: *Summary:* 3 Total; 1 Professional(s); 2 Technical(s)

Ottawa: **Health Canada / Santé Canada**
Departmental Library/Bibliothèque ministérielle
Jeanne Mance Bldg., 2nd Fl.
Ottawa, ON K1A 0K9
Mailing Address: A.L. 1902B
Ottawa, ON K1A 0K9
613-957-1545
e-mail: HCLibrary_BibliothequeSC@hc-sc.gc.ca
URL: www.sydneyplus.com/hc
National Library Symbol: OONHHS
Consortia Membership: Council of Federal Libraries (CFL) Consortium
Founded in: 1992
Hours: M-F 8:30-4:30 by appointment only
Acquisitions Budget: $50,000 - $99,999
Special Collections: WHO Depository
Subjects covered: Health, Health Policy, Health Services, Health Promotion, Health Economics, Mental Health, Native Health, Population Health
Services:
Internet Access
Inter-Library Loan (ILL)
Microform Equipment: Computer; Reader
Personnel: *Summary:* 13 Total; 2 Professional(s); 9 Technical(s);
Marty Lovelock, Chief Librarian
Marty_Lovelock@hc-sc.gc.ca
613-957-1547
Robin Nagy, Manager, Client Services
Robin_Nagy@hc-sc.gc.ca
613-954-8593
Jean King, Head, Acquisitions
Jean_King@hc-sc.gc.ca
613-957-1548

Ottawa: **Health Canada, Health Products & Food Branch**
Science Library Network/Réseau des bibliothèques scientifiques
Banting Research Centre, Tunney's Pasture
120 Parkdale Ave.
Ottawa, ON K1A 0L2
613-957-1026
Fax: 613-941-6958
e-mail: merle_mcconnell@hc-sc.gc.ca
National Library Symbol: OONHBR
Subjects covered: Health Sciences, Medicine, Pharmacology
Services:
Personnel:
Merle McConnell, Chief
Elizabeth Geehan, Head, Technical Services
Lyn Gamble, Head, Systems
Kathryn Jackson, Manager

Ottawa: **HECS Library / Bibliothèque DSESC**
269 Laurier Ave. West, 4th Fl.
Ottawa, ON K1A 0K9
613-957-1725
Fax: 613-941-8583
e-mail: hecs_library@hc-sc.gc.ca
Profile: The HECS (Healthy Environments and Consumer Safety) Branch helps Canadians maintain & improve their health by promoting healthy & safe living, working & recreational environments, by reducing the harm caused by tobacco, alcohol & other substances, environmental contaminants & unsafe consumer & industrial products
National Library Symbol: OONHH
Founded in: 1973
Hours: M-F 8:30-4:00
Note: Part of the Health Canada Science Library Network. Clients served: Healthy Environments & Consumer Safety Branch. Resources & services in English & French
Special Collections: Radiation Protection Library, Product Safety Library
Subjects covered: Exposure Levels, Environmental Health, Industrial Toxicology, Radiation Protection, Chemical Toxicology, Pesticides, Occupational Health, Hazardous Substances, Drinking Water Quality, Product Safety, Tobacco Control, Controlled Substances, Air Quality
Services:
Internet Access
Inter-Library Loan (ILL)
Microform Equipment: Reader
Personnel: *Summary:* 2 Professional(s); 1 Technical(s);
Mike Culhane, Head, Library & Internet Services
mike.culhane@nrc-cnrc.gc.ca
613-993-3774

Ottawa: **Institute for Research in Construction / Institut de recherche en construction**
Information Service Library/Internet Services
National Research Council
1200 Montreal Rd.
Ottawa, ON K1A 0R6
613-993-2466
Fax: 613-952-7671
e-mail: irc.library@nrc-cnrc.gc.ca
URL: irc.nrc-cnrc.gc.ca
National Library Symbol: OONBR
Founded in: 1952
Hours: M-F 8:15-4:30
Acquisitions Budget: $50,000 - $99,999
Subjects covered: Physical Sciences, Engineering, Technology, Construction, Construction Science & Technology, Fire Science, Construction Materials & Structures, Building Performance
Services:
Inter-Library Loan (ILL)
Personnel: *Summary:* 3 Total; 2 Professional(s); 1 Technical(s)

Ottawa: **International Joint Commission**
Resource Centre
234 Laurier Ave. West, 22nd Fl.
Ottawa, ON K1P 6K6
613-995-2984
Fax: 613-993-5583
e-mail: lalondem@ottawa.ijc.org
URL: www.ijc.org
Hours: M-F 8:30-5:00 by appointment only
Acquisitions Budget: $25,000 - $49,999
Subjects covered: Water documents/Great Lakes, Canada-US Transboundary Waters, Air Quality, Water Quality

Services:
Inter-Library Loan (ILL)
Personnel:
Marie Lalonde, Administrative Assistant
lalondem@ottawa.ijc.org
613-995-0184

Ottawa: **La Cité Collégiale**
Centre de documentation
801, promenade de l'Aviation
Ottawa, ON K1K 4R3
613-742-2493 ext: 2077
Téléc: 613-742-2498
Couriel: bibliotheque@lacitec.on.ca
pebill@lacitec.on.ca
URL: www.lacitec.on.ca/webdoc
Sigle: OOCCO
Membre d'un consortium: Ontario Colleges Library Service
Fondée en: 1990
Heures: Hiver: L-J 7h45-20h; V 7h45-17h; D 12h-16h. Été: L-V 7h45-16h
Budget d'acquisitions: $50,000 - $99,999
Sujets: Sciences humaines et santé, communication et média, technologie, commerce
Services:
Accèss distance aux bases de donn
Accès public à l'internet
Réseau en ligne
Prêts entre bibliothèques(PEB)
Personnel: *Sommaire:* 5 Total; 1 Professionnel(s); 4 Technicien(s); 2 Autre(s) employé(s)
Marie Robertson, Directrice
marober@lacitec.on.ca
613-742-2493 ext. 2168
Michael Rouzier, Bibliothécaire
mrouzi@lacitec.on.ca
613-742-2493 ext. 2563
Hélène Ratté, Bibliotechnicienne
hratte@lacitec.on.ca
613-742-2493 ext. 2082
Lyne Charron, Responsable, PEB
lcharr@lacitec.on.ca
613-742-2493 ext. 2078
Jocelyne Agnew, Bibliotechnicienne
jagnew@lacitec.on.ca
613-742-2493 ext. 2838
Fernande Renaud, Responsable, Périodiques
frenau@lacitec.on.ca
613-742-2493 ext. 2844
Ted J. Racine, Head
ted.racine@cbsa-asfc.gc.ca

Ottawa: **Laboratory & Scientific Services Directorate**
STI Centre
79 Bentley Ave.
Ottawa, ON K1A 0L8
613-954-6476
Fax: 613-952-7825
e-mail: ted.racine@cbsa-asfc.gc.ca
National Library Symbol: OOSTI
No public access
Founded in: 1974
Hours: M-F 8:00-4:00
Acquisitions Budget: $25,000 - $49,999
For Print: $25,000 - $49,999
For Electronic: $25,000 - $49,999
Special Collections: Sadtler Spectra, IR, C13 Proton NMR, World Customs Organization documents
Subjects covered: Physical Sciences, Engineering, Technology
Services:
Inter-Library Loan (ILL)
Microform Equipment: Computer; Reader
Personnel: *Summary:* 1 Total; 1 Professional(s)
William Voller, Manager
613-995-4288
Lenore Horton, Photo Technician
Tina Konopelky, Client Services Technician
Phillipe Bisson, Archives Technician
613-957-4547

Ottawa: **National Air Photo Library / Photothèque nationale de l'air**
#180, 615 Booth St.
Ottawa, ON K1A 0E9
613-995-4560
Fax: 613-995-4568

e-mail: napl@nrcan.gc.ca
URL: airphotos.nrcan.gc.ca
National Library Symbol: OOMNA
Founded in: 1925
Hours: M-Th 1:00-4:30
Acquisitions Budget: $25,000 - $49,999
Note: This library is a division of Geomatics Canada, which is also a branch of Natural Resources Canada
Special Collections: Air photos dating back to the 1920s
Subjects covered: Physical Sciences, Maps
Services:
Remote Access
Internet Access
Personnel: *Summary:* 3 Technical(s)

Ottawa: **National Capital Commission / Commission de la Capitale nationale**
Library
#202, 40 Elgin St.
Ottawa, ON K1P 1C7
613-239-5123
Fax: 613-239-5179
e-mail: rbouse@ncc-ccn.ca
URL: www.ncc-ccn.ca
National Library Symbol: OONCC
Hours: Tu-F 8:30-12:00, 12:30-4:30
Acquisitions Budget: $25,000 - $49,999
Subjects covered: Heritage, Housing, Planning, Public Works, Local Government, Architecture, Geography
Services:
Inter-Library Loan (ILL)
Personnel:
Rota Bouse, Manager
rbouse@ncc-ccn.ca
613-239-5123

Ottawa: **National Capital Region**
Ottawa Forestry Centre
580 Booth St.
Ottawa, ON K1A 0E4
613-947-7341
Fax: 613-947-7396
e-mail: cfs-scf@nrcan.gc.ca
URL: cfs.nrcan.gc.ca/regions/ncr
Founded in: 1911
Hours: M-F by appointment only
Services:
Inter-Library Loan (ILL)
Microform Equipment: Reader
Personnel: *Summary:* 2 Total; 1 Professional(s); 1 Technical(s)

Ottawa: **Natural Resources Canada / Ressources naturelles Canada**
Library/Bibliothèque
580 Booth St.
Ottawa, ON K1A 0E4
613-996-3919
Fax: 613-943-8742
e-mail: nrcanlibrary@nrcan.gc.ca
URL: www.nrcan.gc.ca/library/index.htm
Profile: Specialized libraries for forestry, energy, earth sciences, minerals & metals, management & economics. 13 locations across Canada
National Library Symbol: OOG
Consortia Membership: Council of Federal Libraries (CFL) Consortium
Founded in: 1846
Hours: M-F 8:30-4:00
Acquisitions Budget: $250,000 - $499,999
Special Collections: Sir William Logan Collection; Early Exploration Collection; Science of Geology Collection, Map Archival Collection; Photo collection (1842-present); Polunin Arctic exploration/history collection; Minproc, Mintec
Subjects covered: Earth Sciences, Geology, Geomatics, Biotechnology, renewable energy, climate change, hydrology, forestry, botany, entomology, physics, chemisty
Services:
Inter-Library Loan (ILL)
Microform Equipment: Reader
Personnel: *Summary:* 21 Total; 9 Professional(s); 10 Technical(s); 2 Other employees
Margaret Ahearn, Head Librarian
Lesley Hoermann, Head, Reference
Alison Whiddon, Collections Management
George Duimovich, Database Management

Ottawa: **Nature Canada**
Library
#300, 75 Albert St.
Ottawa, ON K1P 6A4
613-562-3447
Fax: 613-562-3371
800-267-4088
e-mail: info@naturecanada.ca
URL: www.naturecanada.ca
Founded in: 1939
Special Collections: Back issues of Nature Canada, published by CNF
Subjects covered: Educational materials about Canadian wild species & natural habitats
Services:

Ottawa: **Ottawa Hospital / Hôpital d'Ottawa**
Library
501 Smyth Rd.
Ottawa, ON K1H 8L6
613-737-8899 ext: 78530
Fax: 613-737-8521
e-mail: libraryservices@ottawahospital.on.ca
National Library Symbol: OOHG
No public access
Founded in: 1946
Hours: M-F 8:00-5:00
Acquisitions Budget: $250,000 - $499,999
Note: Amalgamation of the Civic Hospital, the General Hospital & the Ottawa Regional Cancer Centre Libraries
Special Collections: Sexual abuse; Special cancer collection
Subjects covered: Medicine, Nursing, Allied Health
Services:
Internet Access
Inter-Library Loan (ILL)
Personnel: *Summary:* 3 Total; 4 Professional(s); 6 Technical(s);

Margaret Quirie, Director
mquirie@ottawahospital.on.ca
613-798-5555 ext. 16910

Ottawa: **Ottawa Hospital - Civic Campus**
Dr. George Williamson Health Sciences Library
1053 Carling Ave.
Ottawa, ON K1Y 4E9
613-761-4450
Fax: 613-761-5292
URL: www.ottawahospital.on.ca/library
National Library Symbol: OOOCH
No public access
Founded in: 1960
Hours: M-F
Special Collections: Consumer Health Information
Subjects covered: Medicine, Nursing, Health Sciences, Allied Health Sciences
Services:
Internet Access
Inter-Library Loan (ILL)
Microform Equipment: Reader
Personnel: *Summary:* 6 Total; 2 Professional(s); 2 Technical(s)

Ottawa: **Ottawa Hospital-Riverside Campus**
Scobie Health Sciences Library
1967 Riverside Dr.
Ottawa, ON K1H 7W9
613-738-8230
Fax: 613-738-8532
e-mail: libraryservices@ottawahospital.on.ca
URL: www.ottawahospital.on.ca/library
National Library Symbol: OORH
No public access
Founded in: 1967
Hours: M-F 9:90-4:00
Acquisitions Budget: $25,000 - $49,999
Note: Member of Ottawa Valley Health Libraries Association (OVHLA)
Subjects covered: Medicine, Health Sciences, Nursing
Services:
Inter-Library Loan (ILL) for a fee
Personnel: *Summary:* 1 Total; 1 Professional(s); 2 Volunteer(s)
Kaitryn Campbell, Librarian

Ottawa: **Peace & Environment Resource Centre**
Library
174 First Ave.
Ottawa, ON K1S 5B1

Libraries & Resource Centres / Ontario

Mailing Address: PO Box 4075, Stn E
Ottawa, ON K1S 5B1
613-230-4590
e-mail: info@perc.org
URL: www.perc.ca/library/
Hours: W-F 12:00-6:00; Sa 10:00-4:00
Special Collections: Video, audiotape & CD collection; News clippings
Subjects covered: Environment
Services:

Ottawa: Public Health Library / Bibliothèque de la santé publique
100 Promenade Eglantine Driveway
Ottawa, ON K1A 0L2
613-957-1362
Fax: 613-957-4233
e-mail: ph_library@hc-sc.gc.ca
National Library Symbol: OONHL
Hours: M-F by appointment only
Acquisitions Budget: $50,000 - $99,999
Note: Part of Science Library Network.
Subjects covered: Infection Control, Epidemiology, Sexually Transmitted Diseases, Virology
Services:
Inter-Library Loan (ILL)
Personnel: Summary: 3 Total; 2 Professional(s); 1 Technical(s)
Terry Chernis, Manager
terry_chernis@hc-sc.gc.ca
613-957-1025

Ottawa: Sir F.G. Banting Research Centre / Centre de recherches Sir F.G. Banting Library/Bibliothèque
120 Parkdale Ave.
Ottawa, ON K1A 0L2
613-957-1022
Fax: 613-941-6957
e-mail: banting_library@hc-sc.gc.ca
National Library Symbol: OONHBR
Hours: M-F 8:30-4:30 by appointment only
Note: Inter-library loan & photocopying are limited/restricted; Part of the Science Library Network.
Subjects covered: Medical Devices, Nutrition, Pharmacology, Toxicology, Natural Health Products
Services:
Inter-Library Loan (ILL)
Personnel: Summary: 7 Total; 2 Professional(s); 4 Technical(s)

Ottawa: S.L. Ross Environmental Research Ltd. Library
#200, 717 Belfast Rd.
Ottawa, ON K1G 0Z4
613-232-1564
Fax: 613-232-6660
e-mail: info@slross.com
URL: www.slross.com
No public access
Founded in: 1981
Acquisitions Budget: $25,000 - $49,999
Subjects covered: Oil Spill Research, Spill Risk Assessment, Environmental Impact
Services:

Ottawa: Transport Canada / Transports Canada Central Library
275 Slater St., 6th Fl.
Ottawa, ON K1A 0N5
613-998-5128
Fax: 613-954-4731
e-mail: librreq@tc.gc.ca
National Library Symbol: OOT
Consortia Membership: Council of Federal Libraries (CFL) Consortium
Founded in: 1936
Hours: M-F 8:30-4:30
Acquisitions Budget: $250,000 - $499,999
For Print: $50,000 - $99,999
For Electronic: $100,000 - $249,999
Special Collections: Transport Canada publications; International Maritime Org committee papers; International Civil Aviation Org selected publications
Subjects covered: Transportation, Transportation Safety, Policy, Road Safety, Marine, Air & Intermodal
Services:
Internet Access

Inter-Library Loan (ILL)
Microform Equipment: Reader
Personnel: Summary: 8 Total; 3 Professional(s); 5 Technical(s)
Irene Vokac, Manager
vokaci@tc.gc.ca
613-990-1606
Maureen Boulianne, Team Leader, Library Client Services
boulim@tc.gc.ca
613-998-5139
John G. Germundson, System Administrator
germunj@tc.gc.ca
613-998-5151

Ottawa: Transportation Association of Canada / Association des transports du Canada Transportation Information Service
2323 St-Laurent Blvd.
Ottawa, ON K1G 4J8
613-736-1350
Fax: 613-736-1395
e-mail: TIS@tac-atc.ca
URL: www.tac-atc.ca
National Library Symbol: OORTA
Acquisitions Budget: $25,000 - $49,999
Note: Canadian Surface Transportation Research (online database); Library catalogue accessible on web site
Special Collections: Deposit Collections of Exchange Agreements with the American Association of State Highway & Transportation Officials, Australian Road Research Board, & the US Transportation Research Board
Subjects covered: Ground Transportation; Roads
Services:
Inter-Library Loan (ILL) for a fee of $25
Fee Based Research
Personnel: Summary: 3 Total; 1 Professional(s)
Glenn Cole, Manager, Technical Information Programs

Ottawa: Université d'Ottawa / University of Ottawa Bibliothèque Morisset/Morisset Library
65, rue Université
Ottawa, ON K1N 6N5
613-562-5213
Fax: 613-562-5133
TDD: 6135625800
e-mail: gblais@uottawa.ca
URL: www.uottawa.ca/library
National Library Symbol: OOU
Consortia Membership: Canadian Research Knowledge Network (CRKN); Ontario Council of University Libraries (OCUL)
Founded in: 1848
Hours: L-D
Acquisitions Budget: $500,000 - $999,999
Note: La Bibliothèque Vanier n'existe plus; elle est maintenant intégrée à la Bibliothèque Morisset.
Special Collections: Archives canadiennes du mouvement des femmes
Subjects covered: Arts et sciences
Services:
Internet Access
Access to Subscription Databases
Inter-Library Loan (ILL)
Data services
Microform Equipment: Reader
Personnel: Summary: 67 Total; 19 Professional(s); 14 Technical(s); 34 Other employees
Leslie Weiru, University Chief Librarian
lweir@uottawa.ca
613-562-5880
Hélène Carrier, Directrice
helene.carrier@uottawa.ca
613-562-5690
Sherri Pringle, Library Technician
springle@georgianc.on.ca
519-376-0840 ext. 2035
Cindy Watson, Library Technician
519-376-0840 ext. 2034

Owen Sound: Owen Sound Campus Learning Resource Centre
1450 - 8th St. East
Owen Sound, ON N4K 5R4
519-376-0840 ext: 2034
Fax: 519-376-5395
e-mail: springle@georgianc.on.ca
URL: library.georgianc.on.ca

National Library Symbol: OOWGC
Founded in: 1971
Hours: M-Th 8:00-8:00; F 8:00-4:00
Acquisitions Budget: $25,000 - $49,999
Special Collections: Marine Engineering & Navigation
Services:
Internet Access
Inter-Library Loan (ILL)
Microform Equipment: Reader
Personnel: Summary: 3 Technical(s)
Jennifer Bromley, Librarian
bromlej@algonquincollege.com
613-735-4707

Pembrook: Pembrook Campus Learning Resource Centre
#335, 315 Pembroke St. East
Pembroke, ON K8A 3K2
613-735-4700 ext: 2707
Fax: 613-735-8801
e-mail: bromlej@algonquincollege.com
illpemb@algonquincollege.com
URL: www.algonquincollege.com/lrc
National Library Symbol: OPEMAC
Founded in: 1967
Hours: M-Th 8:00-8:00; F 8:00-4:30
Acquisitions Budget: 0-$9,999
Subjects covered: Health Sciences, Forestry, Office Administration, Early Childhood Education, Outdoor Adventure
Services:
Microform Equipment: Reader
Personnel: Summary: 4 Total; 1 Professional(s); 2 Technical(s)
Ann MacPhail, Head, Resource Centre
macphaa@algonquincollege.com
613-267-2859 ext. 5638

Perth: Perth Campus Learning Resource Centre
#1, 7 Craig St.
Perth, ON K7H 1X7
613-267-2859 ext: 5607
Fax: 613-267-3950
e-mail: macphaa@algonquincollege.com
illpert@algonquincollege.com
National Library Symbol: OPAC
Hours: M-F
Acquisitions Budget: $25,000 - $49,999
For Print: 0-$9,999
For Electronic: $25,000 - $49,999
Population Served: 350; College community + public
Special Collections: Lanark County Historical Collection, Heritage
Subjects covered: Carpentry, Architecture, Trades, Health Sciences
Services:
Remote Access
Inter-Library Loan (ILL)
Fee Based Research
Microform Equipment: Computer; Reader
Personnel:

Perth: Rideau Valley Field Naturalists Library
PO Box 474
Perth, ON K7H 3G1
613-264-8295
Services:
Personnel:
Marianne Trickey, Historian

Peterborough: Kawartha World Issues Centre Resource Library
#B101, Environmental Sciences Bldg., East Bank,
Trent University
Peterborough, ON K9J 7A2
Mailing Address: PO Box 895
Peterborough, ON K9J 7A2
705-748-1680
Fax: 705-748-1681
e-mail: kwic@trentu.ca
URL: www.trentu.ca/org/kwic/main.html
Subjects covered: Environment, ecology, militarism, community development, Indigenous peoples, women's issues, foreign aid, Africa, Asia, Latin America, Middle East, media
Services:

Peterborough: Ontario Federation of Anglers & Hunters
Eaton Conservation Resource Library
4601 Guthrie Dr.
Peterborough, ON K9J 8L5
Mailing Address: PO Box 2800
Peterborough, ON K9J 8L5
705-748-6324
Fax: 705-748-9577
e-mail: ofah@ofah.org
URL: www.ofah.org
Hours: by appointment only
Subjects covered: Fishing, Hunting, Natural Resources
Services:
Personnel: *Summary:* 1 Total; 1 Other employees
Rhonda Sowers, Contact

Peterborough: Ontario Ministry of Natural Resources / Ontario. Ministère des richesses naturelles
Library Services
300 Water St.
Peterborough, ON K9J 8M5
Mailing Address: PO Box 7000
Peterborough, ON K9J 8M5
705-755-1888
Fax: 705-755-1882
e-mail: library.information@mnr.gov.on.ca
National Library Symbol: OTLF
Founded in: 1972
Hours: M-F by appointment only
Acquisitions Budget: $50,000 - $99,999
Special Collections: USDA Forestry Service publications, MNR publications
Subjects covered: Natural Resources, Conservation, Forestry, Fisheries, Wildlife, Water, Parks, Ecology, Land, Sustainable Development, GIS
Services:
Inter-Library Loan (ILL)
Research
Personnel: *Summary:* 5 Total; 2 Professional(s); 2 Technical(s); 1 Other employees
Heath Finaley, Senior Librarian
heath.finley@ontario.ca
705-755-1879
Deborah Palmer, Technical Services Librarian
deborah.palmer@ontario.ca
705-755-1881

Peterborough: Ontario Trails Council
Library
Trail Studies Unit, Environmental Science Bldg., Rm. A102
Trent University, PO Box 4800
Peterborough, ON K9J 7B8
705-748-1419
Fax: 705-748-1205
e-mail: jmarsh@trentu.ca
URL: www.trentu.ca/academic/trailstudies
Founded in: 1992
Hours: Sept.-April: M-Th
Note: Website describes research unit which maintains the library of 3,000+ documents on trails.
Subjects covered: Trails, trail plans, design manuals, user studies, impact studies, guidebooks, interpretive brochures & trail magazines
Services:
Personnel: *Summary:* 2 Volunteer(s)
John Marsh, Head
jmarsh@trentu.ca

Peterborough: Sir Sandford Fleming College of Applied Arts & Technology
Sutherland Campus, Learning Resource Centre
599 Brealey Dr.
Peterborough, ON K9J 7B1
705-749-5516
Fax: 705-749-5536
e-mail: ill-bra@flemingc.on.ca
URL: www.flemingc.on.ca
National Library Symbol: OPETSF
Consortia Membership: Ontario Colleges Library Service
Founded in: 1967
Hours: M-Th 8:00-8:00; F 8:00-4:00; Sa, Su 12:00-4:00
Subjects covered: Art, Psychology, Marketing, Sociology, Recreation, Nursing, Manufacturing, Law Enforcement, Electronics, Merchandising, Business
Services:
Inter-Library Loan (ILL)
Microform Equipment: Computer; Reader

Peterborough: Trent University
Thomas J. Bata Library
1600 Westbank Dr.
Peterborough, ON K9J 7B8
705-748-1011 ext. 1539
Fax: 705-748-1126
e-mail: robertclarke@trentu.ca
URL: www.trentu.ca/library/
National Library Symbol: OPET
Consortia Membership: Canadian Research Knowledge Network (CRKN); Ontario Council of University Libraries (OCUL)
Founded in: 1963
Hours: M-Th 8:00am-11:00pm; F 8:00-8:00; Sa 11:00-8:00; Su 11:00-11:00
Acquisitions Budget: $1,000,000 plus
For Print: $250,000 - $499,999
For Electronic: $500,000 - $999,999
Special Collections: Trent Collection, A.J.M. Smith Collection of Canadian Poetry, Floyd Chalmers Collection, G.M. Douglas Arctic Collection
Subjects covered: History, Native Studies, Canadiana
Services:
Remote Access
Internet Access
Access to Subscription Databases
Inter-Library Loan (ILL)
Microform Equipment: Computer; Reader
Personnel: *Summary:* 40 Total; 10 Professional(s); 30 Other employees;
Robert Clarke, University Librarian
robertclarke@trentu.ca
705-748-1011 ext. 1324
Jean Luyben, Library Instruction
jluyben@trentu.ca
705-748-1011 ext. 1528
Marisa Scigliano, Technical Services Librarian
mscigliano@trentu.ca
705-748-1101 ext. 1390
Barbara Znamirowski, Government Publications, Maps & Lab
bznamirowski@trentu.ca
Ken Field, Access Services Librarian
kfield@trentu.ca
Goro Ripley, Systems Librarian
gripley@trentu.ca
705-748-1011

Port Rowan: David Winton Bell Memorial Library
PO Box 160, 115 Front St.
Port Rowan, ON N0E 1M0
Fax: 519-586-3532
888-448-2473
e-mail: generalinfo@bsc-eoc.org
URL: www.bsc-eoc.org/research/lpwwrf/index.jsp
National Library Symbol: MDW
Founded in: 1952
Hours: M-F by appointment only
Special Collections: Rare book collection on waterfowl
Subjects covered: Conservation, Natural resources, Environment, Ornithology
Services:
Inter-Library Loan (ILL)
Personnel:
Wanda Gorsuch, Head

Richmond Hill: Canadian Bottled Water Association / Fédération canadienne des embouteilleurs d'eau
Library
#203-1, 70 East Beaver Creek Rd.
Richmond Hill, ON L4B 3B2
905-886-6928
Fax: 905-886-9531
e-mail: srbergmann1@aol.com
info@cbwa-bottledwater.org
URL: www.cbwa-bottledwater.org
Founded in: 1992
Hours: M-F 9:00-5:00 by appointment only
Subjects covered: Tap, Well & Bottled Water, Technology, Environment
Services:
Personnel:
S. Bergmann, Head
srbergmann1@aol.com
905-886-6928

Ridgetown: University of Guelph Ridgetown Campus
Library
120 Main St. East
Ridgetown, ON N0P 2C0
519-674-1540
Fax: 519-674-1539
e-mail: library@ridgetownc.uoguelph.ca
URL: www.ridgetownc.on.ca
National Library Symbol: ORRCAT
Regional System: Tri Universities Group (TUG)
Consortia Membership: University of Guelph
Founded in: 1952
Hours: Academic year: M-Th 8:30am-9pm; F 8:30-4:30; Sa 1:00-4:00
Population Served: Students + Staff
Note: Library serves the university community & certificate & diploma students
Special Collections: Soil Maps, Agricultural Statistics, Archives of Ridgetown College
Subjects covered: Agriculture, Horticulture, Veterinary Technology, Crop Science, Soil Science, Farm Business, Management, Livestock Production, Landscaping, Ornamental Horticulture
Services:
Remote Access
Internet Access
Inter-Library Loan (ILL)
Microform Equipment: Reader
Personnel: *Summary:* 1 Professional(s); 1 Technical(s)
Chantal Phillips, Head Librarian
cphillip@ridgetownc.uoguelph.ca
519-674-1521
Becky Clark, Library Assistant
library@ridgetown.uoguelph.ca
519-674-1540

St Catharines: Brock University
James A. Gibson Library
500 Glenridge Ave.
St Catharines, ON L2S 3A1
905-688-5550
Fax: 905-988-5490
e-mail: mgrove@brocku.ca
ostcb@brocku.ca
URL: www.brocku.ca/library/
National Library Symbol: OSTCB
Consortia Membership: Canadian Research Knowledge Network (CRKN)
Founded in: 1964
Hours: Reference M-Th 8:30-7:00; Fr 8:30-5:00; Sa&Sun closed.
Acquisitions Budget: $1,000,000 plus
For Print: $500,000 - $999,999
For Electronic: $1,000,000 plus
Special Collections: Niagara Regional Collection
Subjects covered: Humanities, Social Sciences, Science, Business, Education, Applied Health Sciences
Services:
Inter-Library Loan (ILL)
Reference, Copying, Instruction
Microform Equipment: Computer; Reader
Personnel: *Summary:* 73 Total; 19 Professional(s); 54 Technical(s)
Margaret Grove, University Librarian
mgrove@brocku.ca
905-688-5550 ext. 3226
Debbie Kalvee, Associate University Librarian, Services
dkalvee@brocku.ca
905-688-5550 ext. 3198
Pamela Jacobs, Associate University Librarian, Collection Resources
pjacobs@brocku.ca
905-688-5550 ext. 3961
Linda Lowry, Head, Reference
llowry@brocku.ca
905-688-5550 ext. 4650
Pat Longo, Head, Cataloguing Services
plongo@brocku.ca
905-688-5550 ext. 4488

Jonathan Yonker, Library Systems & Technologies
jyounker@brocku.ca
905-688-5550 ext. 4899
Robert Rossini, Head of Circulation
rossini@brock.ca
905-688-5550 ext. 3727

St Catharines: Ontario Ministry of Transportation Library
301 St Paul St.
St Catharines, ON L2R 7R4
905-704-2065
Fax: 905-704-2005
e-mail: library@mto.gov.on.ca
URL: www.mto.gov.on.ca/english/transrd/index.html
National Library Symbol: OTDT
No public access
Founded in: 1960
Hours: M-F 8:00-4:00
Acquisitions Budget: For Print: 0-$9,999
Note: ILL service only
Special Collections: TRB publications, Ontario roads studies
Subjects covered: Engineering, Technology, Transportation, Highway Engineering Material published by the Ministry
Services:
Personnel: Summary: 2 Total; 1 Professional(s); 1 Technical(s)
June E. Wilson, Information Broker
june.wilson@mto.gov.on.ca
A. Julia Manning, Reference
julia.manning@mto.gov.on.ca
Patricia Bartel, Library Staff
patricia.bartel@mto.gov.on.ca
Colleen Beard, Map Librarian
cbeard@brocku.ca

St Catharines: University Map Library
Mackenzie Chown Complex
#C306, 500 Glenridge Ave.
St Catharines, ON L2S 3A1
Mailing Address: 500 Glenridge Ave.
St Catharines, ON L2S 3A1
905-688-5550 ext: 3468
Fax: 905-682-9020
e-mail: cbeard@brocku.ca
URL: www.brocku.ca/maplibrary/
National Library Symbol: OSTCBG
Hours: (Mid-Sept to April) M-Th 8:30-7:00; Fr 8:30-4:30; Sa&Su closed. (April-Sept) M-F 8:30-4:30; Sa&Su closed.
Acquisitions Budget: $25,000 - $49,999
Special Collections: Historical Niagara Region, Welland Canals
Subjects covered: Geology, Airphotos, Digital Geographic Data, Topography
Services:
Personnel: Summary: 2 Total; 1 Professional(s); 1 Other employees

Sarnia: Lambton College of Applied Arts & Technology
Library Resource Centre
1457 London Rd.
Sarnia, ON N7S 6K4
519-542-7751 ext: 2441
e-mail: diane@lambton.on.ca/
URL: platinum.lambton.on.ca/lrc/
National Library Symbol: OSLC
Consortia Membership: Ontario Colleges Library Service
Founded in: 1967
Hours: M-F, 8:30-4:30
Services:
Remote Access
Internet Access
Inter-Library Loan (ILL)
Personnel: Summary: 6 Total; 7 Professional(s); 5 Technical(s)
Craig Reed, Director

Sarnia: Lanxess Inc. - Sarnia Information Center
1265 Vidal St.
Sarnia, ON N7T 7M2
Mailing Address: PO Box 3001
Sarnia, ON N7T 7M2
519-337-8251 ext: 5711
Fax: 519-339-7748
e-mail: rosemary.o'donnell@lanxess.com
National Library Symbol: OSP
Founded in: 1942
Hours: M-F by appointment only
Subjects covered: Rubber, Polymer Science, Chemistry, Chemical Engineering
Services:
Inter-Library Loan (ILL)
Microform Equipment: Reader
Personnel: Summary: 4 Total; 2 Professional(s); 1 Technical(s)
Rosemary F. O'Donnell, Manager
Tina Demars, Information Specialist
Nancy Bourque, Information Specialist

Sarnia: Research Department Information Resources
453 Christina St.
Sarnia, ON N7T 8C8
Mailing Address: PO Box 3022
Sarnia, ON N7T 8C8
519-339-2617
Fax: 519-339-4436
National Library Symbol: OSI
No public access
Founded in: 1928
Hours: M-F 8:00-4:30
Special Collections: Chemical Abstracts, API Abstracts, US Chemical Patents, Canadian Patents
Subjects covered: Chemistry, Petrochemicals
Services:
Internet Access
Inter-Library Loan (ILL)
Microform Equipment: Computer; Reader
Personnel: Summary: 2 Total; 1 Professional(s)

Sarnia: Sarnia-Lambton Environmental Association Resource Centre
#111, 265 North Front St.
Sarnia, ON N7T 7X1
519-332-2010
Fax: 519-332-2015
e-mail: admin@sarniaenvironment.com
URL: www.sarniaenvironment.com
Hours: M-F 8:30-4:30
Special Collections: Enviroscan newsletter, with environmental initiatives of member companies
Subjects covered: Study reports, government materials & reference texts related to timely local environmental issues, community involvement & industrial environmental management practices
Services:

Sault Ste Marie: Algoma University College Arthur A. Wishart Library
1520 Queen St. East
Sault Ste Marie, ON P6A 2G4
705-949-2101
Fax: 705-949-6583
e-mail: library@auc.ca
ill@tbird.auc.on.ca
URL: www.auc.ca
National Library Symbol: OSTMA
Founded in: 1967
Hours: Fall/Winter: M-Th 8:30am-10:30pm; F 8:30-4:30; Sa-Su 12:00-5:00; Spring: M-Th 8:30-8:00; F 8:30-4:30; Su 12:00-5:00; Summer: M-F 8:30-4:30; Sa-Su Closed
Acquisitions Budget: $100,000 - $249,999
For Print: $50,000 - $99,999
For Electronic: $50,000 - $99,999
Population Served: Students & community users
Note: Affiliated with Laurentian University
Special Collections: Government Publications (partial depository), Archival material
Subjects covered: Social Sciences, Humanities, Sciences
Services:
Internet Access
Access to Subscription Databases
Inter-Library Loan (ILL)
Microform Equipment: Reader
Personnel: Summary: 12 Total; 1 Professional(s); 5 Technical(s); 6 Other employees
Arthur Perlini, Academic Dean & Library Director

Sault Ste Marie: Clean North Environmental Resource Room
736A Queen St. East
Sault Ste Marie, ON P6A 2A9
705-945-1573
Fax: 705-945-0595
e-mail: info@cleannorth.org
URL: www.cleannorth.org
Hours: by appointment only
Subjects covered: Government documents, scientific papers, magazines, A/V media, curriculum materials & books on environmental issues
Services:
Personnel:
Kathleen Brosemer, Chair
Nancy Dukes, Contact

Sault Ste Marie: Great Lakes Forestry Centre Ontario Region Library
1219 Queen St. East
Sault Ste Marie, ON P6A 2E5
705-949-9461
Fax: 705-541-5700
e-mail: GLFCWeb@nrcan.gc.ca
URL: cfs.nrcan.gc.ca/regions/glfc
National Library Symbol: OSTMF
Founded in: 1949
Hours: M-F by appointment only
Acquisitions Budget: $50,000 - $99,999
Subjects covered: Natural Resources, Conservation, Environment, Forestry, Entomology
Services:
Inter-Library Loan (ILL)
Personnel: Summary: 1 Professional(s); 1 Technical(s)

Sault Ste Marie: Sault Area Hospital Health Sciences Library
969 Queen St. East
Sault Ste Marie, ON P6A 2C4
705-759-3434 ext: 4368
Fax: 705-759-3847
e-mail: youk@sah.on.ca
aslettk@sah.on.ca
URL: www.sah.on.ca/sahlibrary/index.html
National Library Symbol: OSTMPH
Founded in: 1979
Hours: M-F 9:00-4:00 by appointment only
Acquisitions Budget: $25,000 - $49,999
Population Served: Staff, public
Subjects covered: Medicine, Nursing, Allied Health, Health Administration
Services:
Remote Access
Internet Access
Access to Subscription Databases
Inter-Library Loan (ILL) for a fee of Free to staff; $5 for public
Database training
Personnel: Summary: 2 Total; 1 Professional(s); 1 Technical(s)
Kimberley Aslett, Head, Library
aslettk@sah.on.ca

Sault Ste Marie: Sault College of Applied Arts & Technology Library
443 Northern Ave.
Sault Ste Marie, ON P6A 5L3
Mailing Address: PO Box 60
Sault Ste Marie, ON P6A 5L3
705-759-2554 ext: 2711
Fax: 705-759-1319
e-mail: library@saultcollege.ca
URL: www.saultcollege.ca/library
National Library Symbol: OSTMSC
Consortia Membership: Ontario Colleges Library Service
Hours: Academic year: M-Th 8:00-8:00; F 8:00-4:30; Sa 12:00-5:00; Su 11:00-9:00. Spring & Summer hours: M-F, 8:30-4:00/4:30, depending on the time of year.
Acquisitions Budget: $50,000 - $99,999
For Print: $25,000 - $49,999
For Electronic: $25,000 - $49,999
Population Served: 3000
Subjects covered: Health Sciences, Technology, Business, Natural Resources, Native
Services:
Remote Access
Internet Access for a fee of $5
Inter-Library Loan (ILL)
Microform Equipment: Reader
Personnel: Summary: 6 Total; 1 Professional(s); 5 Technical(s)
Karen Barratt, Manager, Library Services
karen.barratt@saultcollege.ca

Robert Young, Contact
705-941-3002

Sault Ste Marie: Sea Lamprey Control Centre
Library
1 Canal Dr.
Sault Ste Marie, ON P6A 6W4
705-941-3002
URL: www.dfo-mpo.gc.ca/regions/central/science/sea-mer/index_e.htm
National Library Symbol: OSTMEF
No public access
Acquisitions Budget: $25,000 - $49,999
Note: Literature on hand is for staff only
Subjects covered: Sea lamprey control, Fisheries, Environment, Hydrology
Services:
Inter-Library Loan (ILL)
Personnel:
Donna Gates, Principal

Simcoe: James N. Allan Campus
Library & Media Services Branch
634 Ireland Rd.
Simcoe, ON N3Y 4K8
Mailing Address: PO Box 10
Simcoe, ON N3Y 4K8
519-426-8260
Fax: 519-428-3112
URL: www.fanshawec.on.ca/library/
Founded in: 1978
Services:
Internet Access
Inter-Library Loan (ILL)
Personnel:
Sandra Arklie, Library Supervisor
sandra.arklie@MohawkCollege.ca
905-575-1212 ext. 5038

Stoney Creek: Stoney Creek Campus
Library Resource Centre
481 Barton St. East
Stoney Creek, ON L8E 2L7
905-575-2504
Fax: 905-575-2549
e-mail: sandra.arklie@MohawkCollege.ca
Founded in: 1971
Hours: M-Th 8:30-7:00; F 8:30-4:00
Acquisitions Budget: $25,000 - $49,999
Subjects covered: Apprenticeship/Trades
Services:
Inter-Library Loan (ILL)
Personnel: *Summary:* 3 Professional(s)

Sudbury: Cambrian College
Library
1400 Barrydowne Rd.
3rd Fl., Rm. #3021
Sudbury, ON P3A 3V8
705-524-7333
Fax: 705-566-6163
e-mail: library@cambriancollege.ca
URL: www.cambriancollege.ca/departments/library
Social Media:
www.facebook.com/cambriancollege?sk=app_10442206389
tweeter: twitter.com/#!/CambrianCollege
National Library Symbol: OSUC
Consortia Membership: Ontario Colleges Library Service
Founded in: 1968
Hours: M-Th 8:00-8:00; F 8:00-5:00; Sa-Su 11:00-4:00
Acquisitions Budget: $50,000 - $99,999
Special Collections: College Art Collection
Subjects covered: Technology, Health Sciences, Social Sciences, Native Studies
Services:
Remote Access
Inter-Library Loan (ILL)
Personnel: *Summary:* 6 Total; 6 Technical(s)
France Quirion, Registrar/Director, Student Affairs
france.quirion@cambriancollege.ca
705-566-8101 ext. 7542

Sudbury: Laurentian University / Université Laurentienne
J.N. Desmarais Library/Bibliothèque J.N. Desmarais
935 Ramsey Lake Rd.
Sudbury, ON P3E 2C6
705-675-4800
Fax: 705-675-4877
800-461-4030
e-mail: library@laurentian.ca
Boojum@Laurentian
URL: www.laurentian.ca/library
National Library Symbol: OSUL
Consortia Membership: Canadian Research Knowledge Network (CRKN); Ontario Council of University Libraries (OCUL)
Founded in: 1960
Hours: Sept.-April: M-Th 8:00am-11:00pm; F 8:00-8:00; Sa-Su 10:00-8:00
Acquisitions Budget: $1,000,000 plus
For Print: $250,000 - $499,999
For Electronic: $1,000,000 plus
Special Collections: Collection Franco-Ontarienne, Northeastern Ontario Collection, Mining Environment
Subjects covered: Humanities, Professional School, Sciences, Social Sciences
Services:
Remote Access
Internet Access for a fee of $.07 if printing/copy
Access to Subscription Databases
Inter-Library Loan (ILL) for a fee
Microform Equipment: Computer; Reader
Personnel: *Summary:* 47 Total; 11 Professional(s); 6 Technical(s); 30 Other employees
Lionel Bonin, Director of Library
lbonin@laurentian.ca
705-675-4841
Ron Slater, Chair, Information & Instruction
rslater@laurentian.ca
705-675-1151 ext. 3329
Hélène Anselmo, Supervisor of Processing
hanselmo@laurentian.ca
705-675-1151 ext. 3311
Lise Séguin, Supervisor of Circulation
lseguin@laurentian.ca
705-675-1151 ext. 3336
Dan Scott, Systems Librarian
dscott@laurentian.ca
705-675-1151 ext. 3315
Sylvie Lafortune, Coordinator of ILL & Cataloguing
slafortune@laurentian.ca
705-675-1151 ext. 3318

Sudbury: Ontario Ministry of Northern Development & Mines
John B. Gammon Geoscience Library
Willet Green Miller Centre, 933 Ramsey Lake Rd.
Sudbury, ON P3E 6B5
705-670-5615
Fax: 705-670-5770
888-415-9845
e-mail: mines.library.ndm@ontaio.ca
URL: www.mndm.gov.on.ca/mndm/mines/ims/library/default_e.asp
National Library Symbol: OTDM
Hours: 8:30-5:00
Note: Library of the Ontario Geological Survey
Special Collections: Theses on Geology & Mining of Ontario, Geological & Geophysical Maps
Subjects covered: Geology, Mineral Resources, Mining, Mineral Economics
Services:
Inter-Library Loan (ILL)
Microform Equipment: Reader
Personnel: *Summary:* 2 Total; 1 Professional(s); 1 Other employees
Johanne Roux-Guindon, Library Technician
johanne.roux-guindon@ontario.ca

Sudbury: Sudbury Rock & Lapidary Society
Library
456 Kaireen St.
Sudbury, ON P3E 5R9
705-522-5140
e-mail: ruth.debicki@ontario.ca
URL: www.ccfms.ca/Clubs/Sudbury/
No public access
Founded in: 1987

Acquisitions Budget: 0-$9,999
For Print: 0-$9,999
For Electronic: 0-$9,999
Population Served: 100
Note: Library available only to members of the Sudbury Rock & Lapidary Society; Library housed at Naughton Community Centre
Special Collections: Mineralogical Record; Back issues of Lapidary Journal
Subjects covered: Rocks, Minerals, Gems, Fossils, Lapidary Arts
Services:
Personnel: *Summary:* 1 Volunteer(s)
Ruth Debicki, Librarian

Sudbury: University of Sudbury / Université de Sudbury
Library
935 Ramsey Lake Rd.
Sudbury, ON P3E 2C6
705-673-5661 ext. 216
Fax: 705-673-4912
e-mail: plaverdure@usudbury.ca
ill@usudbury.ca
URL: www.usudbury.com
National Library Symbol: OSUU
Founded in: 1963
Hours: M-Th 9:00am-9:00pm; F 9:00-4:30; Su 1:00-4:00. May-Aug.: M-F 8:30-4:00
Acquisitions Budget: $25,000 - $49,999
Note: Federated with Laurentian University
Special Collections: Luc Lacourciere, Fr. Chester Warenda, Rare Books
Subjects covered: Religion, Philosophy, Native People & Northern Affairs, History, Folklore
Services:
Remote Access
Internet Access
Inter-Library Loan (ILL)
Personnel:
Paul Laverdure, Library Director
plaverdure@usudbury.ca
705-673-5661 ext. 208
Jacques Trottier, Head of Circulation
705-673-5661 ext. 216
Rachel Pharand, Secretary
rpharand@usudbury.ca
705-673-5661 ext. 207
Daniel Moncion, IT Technician
706-673-5661 ext. 210

Thorndale: Ecologistics Research Services
Library
21599 Cherry Hill Rd.
Thorndale, ON N0M 2P0
519-461-1167
Fax: 519-461-1151
e-mail: info@ecologistics.com
URL: www.ecologistics.com
No public access
Services:
Personnel:
Brenda Fansher, Library Manager

Thunder Bay: Confederation College
Paterson Library Commons
1450 Nakina Dr.
Thunder Bay, ON P7C 4W1
Mailing Address: PO Box 398
Thunder Bay, ON P7C 4W1
807-475-6219
Fax: 807-622-3258
e-mail: library@confederationc.ca
URL: www.confederationc.on.ca/library
National Library Symbol: OTBCC
Consortia Membership: Ontario Colleges Library Service
Founded in: 1967
Hours: Fall & Winter: M-Th 8:00am-9:00pm; F 8:00-4:30; Sa 12:00-5:00; Su 2:00-9:00. Summer: M-F 8:30-4:30
Acquisitions Budget: $100,000 - $249,999
For Print: $100,000 - $249,999
For Electronic: $25,000 - $49,999
Special Collections: Womens' Issues, Learning Disabilities, International Business, Entrepreneurship, Print, A/V & CD-ROM circulating resources, foreign films

Libraries & Resource Centres / Ontario

Subjects covered: Aboriginal Studies, Applied Arts, Health Sciences, Business, Technology
Services:
Remote Access
Internet Access
Access to Subscription Databases
Inter-Library Loan (ILL) for a fee of $5
Microform Equipment: Computer; Reader
Personnel: *Summary:* 7 Total; 1 Professional(s); 5 Technical(s); 1 Other employees
Laraine Tapak, Director, Learning Resources
tapak@confederationc.on.ca
807-475-6241

Thunder Bay: Lakehead University Chancellor Paterson Library
955 Oliver Rd.
Thunder Bay, ON P7B 5E1
807-343-8205
Fax: 807-343-8007
URL: library.lakeheadu.ca
National Library Symbol: OPAL
Consortia Membership: Canadian Research Knowledge Network (CRKN); Ontario Council of University Libraries (OCUL)
Founded in: 1965
Hours: M-Th 8:00-11:30; Sa 10:00-9:00; Su 11:00-9:00
Acquisitions Budget: $1,000,000 plus
Population Served: 10000
Services:
Remote Access
Internet Access
Inter-Library Loan (ILL)
Microform Equipment: Computer; Reader
Personnel: *Summary:* 22 Total; 10 Professional(s); 12 Technical(s)
Anne Deighton, Chief Librarian
anne.deighton@lakeheadu.ca
807-343-8205

Tillsonburg: Oxford County Geological Society Library
24 Trottier Dr.
Tillsonburg, ON N4G 4P9
519-539-8890
Founded in: 1977
Acquisitions Budget: $25,000 - $49,999
Subjects covered: Earth Sciences, Lapidary, Minerals, Rock, Fossils
Services:
Personnel: *Summary:* 2 Volunteer(s)
Graham Stead, Contact
Marion Eccleston, President

Timmins: Northern College of Applied Arts & Technology Porcupine Campus, Library Resource Centre
PO Box 3211
Timmins, ON P4N 8R6
705-235-7150
Fax: 705-235-7279
e-mail: libraryp@northern.on.ca
URL: www.northernc.on.ca
National Library Symbol: OSPNC
Consortia Membership: Ontario Colleges Library Service
Hours: M-Th 8:00-8:00; F 8:00-7:00; Sa, Su 10:00-3:00
Acquisitions Budget: $25,000 - $49,999
Special Collections: Maps, Toy Library
Subjects covered: Technology, Applied Arts, Fine Arts, Business Administration, Health
Services:
Internet Access
Access to Subscription Databases
Inter-Library Loan (ILL)
Personnel: *Summary:* 6 Total; 2 Technical(s); 4 Other employees
Marie Leigh Sheppard, Library Technician
sheppardm@northern.on.ca
Christine Dorval, Library Technician
Patricia Meindl, Librarian
pmeindl@chem.utoronto.ca

Toronto: A.D. Allen Chemistry Library
80 St George St., Rm. 480
Toronto, ON M5S 3H6
416-978-3587
Fax: 416-946-8059
URL: www.chem.utoronto.ca
National Library Symbol: OTUC
Hours: M-F 9:00-5:00; hours may vary throughout the year
Subjects covered: Chemistry
Services:
Inter-Library Loan (ILL) for a fee
Personnel: *Summary:* 2 Professional(s); 1 Technical(s)

Toronto: Association of Municipalities of Ontario Resource Centre
#801, 200 University Ave.
Toronto, ON M5H 3C6
416-971-9856
Fax: 416-971-6191
e-mail: amo@amo.on.ca
URL: www.amo.on.ca
Founded in: 1991
Hours: M-F 10:00-4:00 by appointment only
Acquisitions Budget: $25,000 - $49,999
Subjects covered: Municipal government
Services:
Internet Access for a fee
Access to Subscription Databases
Fee Based Research
Personnel: *Summary:* 2 Total; 2 Professional(s);
Snezana Vukelic, Manager, Information Services
svukelic@amo.on.ca
416-971-9856 ext. 322
Julia Shiu, Information Analyst/Researcher
jshiu@amo.on.ca
416-971-9856 ext. 321
Gian Medves, Acting Chief Librarian
gian.medves@utoronto.ca
416—97-8-55
Susan Barker, Digital Services & Reference Librarian
susan.barker@utoronto.ca
416—97-8-57
Kathryn Roberts, Coordinator, Collection Services
k.roberts@utoronto.ca
416—97-8-61
Humayun Rashid, Reference Librarian & Cataloguer
humayn.rashid@utoronto.ca
416—97-8-42
Sooin Kim, Faculty Services Librarian
sooin.kim@utoronto.ca
416—94-6-59
Anna Szot-Sacawa, Circulation Coordinator
anna.szot.sacawa@utoronto.ca
416—97-8-59

Toronto: Bora Laskin Law Library
Flavelle House
78 Queen's Park Cres.
Toronto, ON M5S 2C5
416-978-1073
Fax: 416-978-8396
URL: www.law-lib.utoronto.ca
National Library Symbol: KLW
Founded in: 1956
Hours: M-Th 8:30 a.m.-11:00 p.m.; F 8:30-8:00; Sa, Su 10:00-8:00; hours vary in Summer
Acquisitions Budget: $500,000 - $999,999
Note: Library is wheelchair accessible
Special Collections: 285,000 volumes of primary legal material; 650 scholarly legal periodicals; online resources including Quicklaw, Westlaw, Lexis-Nexis, Westlaw; collection supports the Faculty of Law curriculum and faculty research interests
Subjects covered: Law, Law Enforcement
Services:
Remote Access
Internet Access
Inter-Library Loan (ILL) for a fee
Fee Based Research
Reference service; reading areas & group study rooms; computer laboratory
Microform Equipment: Computer; Reader
Personnel: *Summary:* 11 Total; 5 Professional(s); 4 Technical(s); 2 Other employees

Toronto: Canadian Centre for Pollution Prevention / Centre canadien pour la prévention de la pollution Pollution Prevention Library
#134, 215 Spadina Ave.
Toronto, ON M5T 2C7
416-979-3534
Fax: 519-979-3936
800-667-9790
e-mail: info@c2p2online.com
URL: www.c2p2online.com
Hours: M-F 8:30-5:00
Subjects covered: Manuals, subject files, videos, periodicals, clearinghouse items relating to pollution prevention.
Services:
Fee Based Research

Toronto: Canadian Sugar Institute Nutrition Information Service, Scientific Library
WaterPark Pl., #620, 10 Bay St.
Toronto, ON M5J 2R8
416-368-8091
Fax: 416-368-8426
e-mail: info@sugar.ca
URL: www.sugar.ca
No public access
Founded in: 1980
Special Collections: Consumer & professional research & resources
Subjects covered: Sugar; Carbohydrates & health; Nutrition
Services:

Toronto: Canadian Urban Transit Association Library
#1401, 55 York St.
Toronto, ON M5J 1R7
416-365-9800
Fax: 416-365-1295
e-mail: techservices@cutaactu.ca
URL: www.cutaactu.ca
No public access
Founded in: 1978
Acquisitions Budget: 0-$9,999
Note: Services restricted to members only
Subjects covered: Urban Transit Policy, Operations, Planning, Marketing, & Technology
Services:
Access to Subscription Databases
Personnel: *Summary:* 20 Professional(s)
Christopher Norris, Manager of Technical Services
norris@cutaactu.ca
416-365-9800 ext. 109
Ilja Green, Technical Services Assistant
techservices@cutaactu.ca
416-365-9800 ext. 113

Toronto: Canadian Water Quality Association / Association canadienne pour la qualité de l'eau Library
#330, 295 The West Mall
Toronto, ON M9C 4Z4
416-695-3068
Fax: 416-695-2945
866-383-7617
e-mail: info@cwqa.com
URL: www.cwqa.com
Subjects covered: Statistical information & other educational materials related to the water quality industry
Services:

Ita Ferdinand-Grant, Librarian
igrant@georgebrown.ca
416-415-5000 ext. 4635

Toronto: Casa Loma Campus Library
#330C, 160 Kendal Ave.
Toronto, ON M5T 2T8
Mailing Address: PO Box 1015, Stn B
Toronto, ON M5T 2T8
416-415-5000 ext: 4634
Fax: 416-415-4765
e-mail: igrant@georgebrown.ca
URL: llc.georgebrown.ca/llc/
National Library Symbol: OTGBC
Founded in: 1968
Hours: M-F 7:30am-10:00pm; Sa 10:00-6:00; Su 10:00-5:00
Acquisitions Budget: $100,000 - $249,999
Special Collections: Jewellery, Ontario Instititue of Quantity Surveyors
Subjects covered: Dental Assisting, Hygiene & Technology; Electrical & Electronics Engineering Technology; Information

Technology; Fitness Management; Theatre Arts, Jewellery Arts & Gemmology; Fashion Management & Arts; Building Technology; Micro-Electronics; English as a Second Language; Mechanical & Manufacturing Technology; Architectural Technology
Services:
Remote Access
Inter-Library Loan (ILL)
Personnel: *Summary:* 8 Total; 4 Professional(s); 4 Technical(s)
Marcia Pulleyblank, Librarian
416-415-5000 ext. 3057

Toronto: Casa Loma ESL Resource Centre
#315, 1 Dartnell Ave.
Toronto, ON M5R 3A3
416-415-5000 ext: 4950
URL: llc.georgebrown.ca/llc
Hours: M-Th 11:00-4:00; F 12:00-4:00

Toronto: C.D. Howe Institute
Library
#300, 67 Yonge St.
Toronto, ON M5E 1J8
416-865-1904
Fax: 416-865-1866
e-mail: cdhowe@cdhowe.org
library@cdhowe.org
URL: www.cdhowe.org
National Library Symbol: OTCDH
Founded in: 1973
Hours: M-W 8:00-5:00 by appointment only
Acquisitions Budget: $10,000 - $24,999
For Print: $10,000 - $24,999
Population Served: 20
Special Collections: Federal & provincial government documents, especially budget material
Subjects covered: Economics, Energy, Industry, Labour, International Trade, Industrial Relations, Public Policy
Services:
Inter-Library Loan (ILL)
Personnel: *Summary:* 1 Total; 1 Professional(s)
Jan Moffatt, Library & Information Services Coordinator

Toronto: Centennial College of Applied Arts & Technology
Learning & Resource Centres
PO Box 631, Stn A
Toronto, ON M1K 5E9
416-289-5000 ext: 2601
Fax: 416-289-5228
e-mail: illocen@centennialcollege.ca
URL: www.lrc.centennialcollege.ca
National Library Symbol: OTARC
Consortia Membership: Ontario Colleges Library Service
Founded in: 1966
Hours: M-Th 8:00am-7:00pm; F 8:00-4:00; Sa 11:00-3:00 (hours may vary according to campus & time of year)
Acquisitions Budget: $250,000 - $499,999
For Print: $250,000 - $499,999
For Electronic: $100,000 - $249,999
Population Served: Students, faculty & public
Note: Branches: Ashtonbee, Centre for Creative Communications, Progress, HP Science & Technology Centre, mailing address for all as above
Special Collections: John & Molly Pollock Holocaust Collection
Subjects covered: Business, Physical Sciences, Automotive, Health Sciences, Applied Arts, Humanities, Engineering, Technology, Economics, Aviation, Transportation
Services:
Remote Access
Internet Access
Inter-Library Loan (ILL)
Microform Equipment: Reader
Personnel: *Summary:* 30 Total; 5 Professional(s); 23 Technical(s); 2 Other employees
Gladys Watson, Director, Learning & Resource Centres
gwatson@centennialcollege.ca
416-289-5000 ext. 2601
Jan Tallon, Manager, Learning Centres & LRC Operations
jtallon@centennialcollege.ca
416-289-5000 ext. 2602
Dmitry Nikiforov, Acting Manager, Systems & Media
dnikiforov@centennialcollege.ca
416-289-5000 ext. 2612

Toronto: CH2M Hill Canada Limited
Library
255 Consumers Rd.
Toronto, ON M2J 5B6
416-499-9000 ext: 305
Fax: 416-499-4687
e-mail: dsawh@ch2m.com
National Library Symbol: OTGS
No public access
Founded in: 1984
Hours: M-F 8:00-4:00
Acquisitions Budget: $25,000 - $49,999
Subjects covered: Physical Sciences, Engineering, Technology
Services:
Inter-Library Loan (ILL)
Microform Equipment: Computer; Reader
Personnel: *Summary:* 1 Professional(s)
Dianne Sawh, Librarian
dsawh@ch2m.com

Toronto: Connexions Information Sharing Services
Library
#305, 489 College St.
Toronto, ON M6G 1A5
416-964-1511
e-mail: connexions@connexions.org
URL: www.connexions.org
Founded in: 1976
Hours: by appointment only
Acquisitions Budget: $25,000 - $49,999
Special Collections: Alternative Press
Subjects covered: Social Criticism, Activism, Environment
Services:
Personnel: *Summary:* 2 Total; 1 Professional(s); 1 Technical(s); 6 Volunteer(s)
Ulli Diemer, Head
Chris Defreltas, Head of Technical Services

Toronto: CSA International
Information Centre
178 Rexdale Blvd.
Toronto, ON M9W 1R3
416-747-4058
Fax: 416-747-4149
866-797-4272
e-mail: info@csa-international.org
URL: www.csa-international.org
National Library Symbol: OTCSA
Founded in: 1970
Hours: M-F 9:00-4:00
Population Served: 700
Special Collections: Standards Collections; Some collections are comprehensive
Subjects covered: Product testing & certification
Services:
Personnel: *Summary:* 4 Total
Susan Morley, Manager

Toronto: Energy Probe Research Foundation
Library
225 Brunswick Ave.
Toronto, ON M5S 2M6
416-964-9223
Fax: 416-964-8239
e-mail: webadmin@eprf.ca
URL: www.eprf.ca/eprf/index.html
Founded in: 1980
Subjects covered: Energy
Services:
Personnel:
Tom Adams, Executive Director
tomadams@nextcity.com
Patricia Adams, President
patriciaadams@nextcity.com
Lawrence Solomon, Managing Director
lawrencesolomon@nextcity.com
Jiabin Wang, Head of Library
jiabin.wang@utoronto.ca
416-946-5966
Neil Allen, Ciculation Supervisor
neil.allen@utoronto.ca
416-978-7681
Cris Sewerin, Librarian
cris.sewerin@utoronto.ca
416-946-4020

Gail Nichol, Librarian
gail.nichol@utoronto.ca
416-946-0389

Toronto: Engineering & Computer Science Library
University of Toronto
#2402, 10 King's College Rd.
Toronto, ON M5S 1A5
416-978-6494
Fax: 416-971-2091
e-mail: engincs.lib@utoronto.ca
URL: www.library.utoronto.ca/engineering-computer-science/
Founded in: 1974
Hours: M-Th 8:30am-10:30pm; F 8:30-6:00; Sa 9:00-5:00; Su 1:00-6:00
Subjects covered: Engineering, Applied Science, Computer Science
Services:
Remote Access
Internet Access
Access to Subscription Databases
Inter-Library Loan (ILL) for a fee
Personnel: *Summary:* 10 Total; 3 Professional(s); 6 Technical(s)
Dawn Taylor-Prime, Regional Librarian
dawn.taylor-prime@ec.gc.ca

Toronto: Environment Canada Library, Downsview / Environnement Canada bibliothèque, Downsview
4905 Dufferin St.
Toronto, ON M3H 5T4
416-739-5702
Fax: 416-739-4212
e-mail: downsview.library@ec.gc.ca
URL: www.msc-smc.ec.gc.ca/library
National Library Symbol: OTM
Founded in: 1871
Hours: M-F 8:30-4:30
Subjects covered: Environment, Natural Resources, Conservation
Services:
Inter-Library Loan (ILL)
Microform Equipment: Computer; Reader
Personnel:

Toronto: Environmental Commissioner of Ontario
Resource Centre
#605, 1075 Bay St.
Toronto, ON M5S 2B1
416-325-0363
Fax: 416-325-3370
e-mail: carrie.hackett@eco.on.ca
URL: www.eco.on.ca/
National Library Symbol: OTECO
Founded in: 1995
Hours: M-F 9:30-5:00
Acquisitions Budget: $10,000 - $24,999
Subjects covered: Environmental policy & law; Environmental Bill of Rights information; Environmental reports by Ontario ministries
Services:
Internet Access
Personnel: *Summary:* 1 Total; 1 Professional(s)
Carrie Hackett, Resource Centre Librarian
carrie.hackett@eco.on.ca
416-325-0363

Toronto: Federation of Ontario Naturalists
Ontario Nature Resources
#201, 366 Adelaide St. W
Toronto, ON M5V 1R9
416-444-8419
Fax: 416-444-9866
800-440-2366
e-mail: info@ontarionature.org
URL: www.ontarionature.org
Subjects covered: Natural History (focus on Ontario), Environmental Education, Conservation
Services:
'Teaching Naturally' resources in English & some in French

Toronto: George Brown College of Applied Arts & Technology
Educational Resources
PO Box 1015, Stn B
Toronto, ON M5T 2T9

Libraries & Resource Centres / Ontario

416-415-5000 ext: 2676
Fax: 416-415-2698
e-mail: ill@gbrownc.on.ca
URL: llc.georgebrown.ca/llc/
National Library Symbol: OTGBC
Consortia Membership: Ontario Colleges Library Service
Founded in: 1968
Acquisitions Budget: $50,000 - $99,999
Special Collections: Sommelier Wine Collection-St. James, OIQS-Ontario Institute of Quantity Surveyors-Casa Loma, Jewellery Arts-Casa Loma
Subjects covered: Arts, Medicine, Nursing, Health Sciences, Economics, Industry, Physical Sciences, Engineering, Applied Arts, Technology, Hospitality Services, Fashion, Social Sciences
Services:
Internet Access
Access to Subscription Databases
Inter-Library Loan (ILL)
Personnel: *Summary:* 22 Total; 4 Professional(s); 10 Technical(s); 10 Other employees
John L. Hardy, Director, Educational Resources
jhardy@gbrownc.on.ca
416-415-5000 ext. 2676
Joan Leishman, Director
j.leishman@utoronto.ca
Sandra Langlands, Reference/Research Unit Coordinator
s.langlands.melvin@utoronto.ca
416-978-6370
Bonnie Horne, Coordinator, Access & Information
b.horne@utoronto.ca
Helen Michael, Coordinator, Resource Sharing
helen.michael@utoronto.ca

Toronto: **Gerstein Science Information Centre**
7 & 9 King's College Circle
Toronto, ON M5S 1A5
Mailing Address: 7 King's College Circle
Toronto, ON M5S 1A5
416-978-2280
Fax: 416-971-2848
URL: www.library.utoronto.ca/gerstein/
National Library Symbol: OTUH
Hours: M-Su
Note: Pharmacy Library has closed & the collection integrated with Gerstein.
Special Collections: Technical reports, Microfiche, Landmarks of Science
Subjects covered: Health Sciences, Physical & Applied Sciences, Biological Sciences
Services:
Internet Access
Inter-Library Loan (ILL)
Microform Equipment: Computer; Reader
Personnel: *Summary:* 45 Total; 10 Professional(s); 35 Technical(s)

Toronto: **H.H. Angus & Associates Library**
1127 Leslie St.
Toronto, ON M3C 2J6
416-443-8200
Fax: 416-443-8290
e-mail: scottw@hhangus.com
URL: www.hhangus.com
National Library Symbol: OTHHA
No public access
Subjects covered: Mechanical & Electrical Engineering Consulting
Services:
Remote Access
Internet Access
Access to Subscription Databases
Personnel: *Summary:* 3 Total; 1 Professional(s); 2 Technical(s)
Wendy Scott, Librarian

Toronto: **Hospital for Sick Children Hospital Library**
555 University Ave.
Toronto, ON M5G 1X8
416-813-6693
Fax: 416-813-7523
e-mail: elizabeth.uleryk@sickkids.ca
hsclink@sickkids.ca
URL: www.sickkids.ca
National Library Symbol: OTHSC
Founded in: 1919
Hours: M-Th 8:00-8:00; F 8:00-6:00; Su 11:00-6:00 by appointment only
Acquisitions Budget: $50,000 - $99,999
Subjects covered: Pediatrics
Services:
Access to Subscription Databases
Inter-Library Loan (ILL) for a fee of $5/non-profit; $10/profit
Personnel: *Summary:* 8 Total; 3 Professional(s); 6 Technical(s)
Elizabeth Uleryk, Director
elizabeth.uleryk@sickkids.ca
416-813-6695
Tyla Holmes, Reference & Instruction Services Librarian
Thomasin Adams-Webber, Systems & Clinical Services Librarian

Toronto: **Humber College Institute of Technology & Advanced Learning**
North Campus Library
205 Humber College Blvd.
Toronto, ON M9W 5L7
416-675-5079
Fax: 416-675-7439
Other contact info: Reference: 416-675-6622, ext.4421
URL: www.library.humber.ca
Consortia Membership: Ontario Colleges Library Service
Founded in: 1967
Hours: Sept.-April: M-Th 7:45am-9:00pm; F 7:45-6:00; Sa 8:45-3:00; Su 12:00-5:00. May-June: M-Th 8:30-7:30; F 8:30-4:30; Sa 8:45-3:00. July-Aug.: M-Th 8:30-6
Special Collections: AV equipment & software; Record & CD collection
Subjects covered: Arts & Science; Business; Technology; Health Sciences; Media Studies
Services:
Internet Access
Microform Equipment: Computer; Reader
Personnel: *Summary:* 6 Total; 6 Professional(s)
Lynne Bentley, Director
lynne.bentley@humber.ca
416-675-6622 ext. 4574
Mark Bryant, Reference & Information Literacy Librarian
mark.bryant@humber.ca
416-675-6222 ext. 4170
Maureen Hyland, Collections Development & Technical Services Librarian
maureen.hyland@humber.ca
416-675-6622 ext. 4501
Nancy Pierobon, Health Sciences Librarian
Dawne Hoogkamer, Library Technician, Government Documents/Statistics Canada
Marlene Beck, Library Technician, Interlibrary Loans & Special Needs
marlene.beck@humber.ca
Jennifer Rayment, Library Technician, Periodicals
Lisa DiBarbora, Virtual Services Librarian
lisa.dibarbora@humer.ca
416-675-6622 ext. 4170
Gina Matesic, Guelph-Humber Librarian
gina.matesic@humber.ca
416-675-6622 ext. 6090

Toronto: **IBI Group Library**
230 Richmond St., 5th Fl.
Toronto, ON M5V 1V6
416-596-1930 ext: 817
Fax: 416-596-0644
e-mail: josther@ibigroup.com
toronto@ibigroup.com
URL: www.ibigroup.com
National Library Symbol: OTIBI
No public access
Founded in: 1974
Hours: M-F 9:00-5:00
Special Collections: IBI Group Reports
Subjects covered: Management & Computer Sciences, Health Care Planning, Facilities Design, Land Planning, Urban Regional Development Planning, Transportation Planning, Civil Engineering, Environmental Planning, Architecture, Interior Design
Services:
Inter-Library Loan (ILL)
Personnel: *Summary:* 2 Total; 1 Professional(s); 1 Technical(s)
Jennifer Osther, Librarian
josther@ibigroup.com
416-596-1930 ext. 1300
Cindy Wong, Library Techician
cindy.wong@ibigroup.com
416-596-1930 ext. 1301

Toronto: **Imperial Oil Limited**
Products Division, Engineering & Petroleum Information Centre
#4118, 90 Wynford Dr.
Toronto, ON M3C 1K5
416-441-7858
Fax: 416-441-7926
No public access
Founded in: 1982
Hours: M-W 8:00-4:30
Acquisitions Budget: $25,000 - $49,999
Subjects covered: Physical Sciences, Engineering, Technology, Natural Resources
Services:
Personnel: *Summary:* 1 Total; 1 Professional(s);
Ann Lum, Information Specialist

Toronto: **Intergovernmental Committee on Urban & Regional Research (ICURR) / Comité intergouvernemental de recherches urbaines et régionales (CIRUR)**
Library
#206, 40 Wynford Dr.
Toronto, ON M3C 1J5
416-952-1437
Fax: 416-973-1375
e-mail: icurrlib@icurr.org
URL: www.icurr.ca
Founded in: 1967
Hours: M-F 8:30-5:00 by appointment only
Acquisitions Budget: $25,000 - $49,999
Note: Online catalogue access
Special Collections: Municipal Bylaws
Subjects covered: Local Government; Urban Regional Planning; Environment; Municipal Issues
Services:
Internet Access
Fee Based Research
Also called Muniscope Information & Networking
Personnel: *Summary:* 3 Total; 2 Professional(s); 1 Other employees
Mark Rose, Librarian
mrose@icurr.org
Catherine Marchand, Executive Director
execdir@icurr.org
416-973-5645
Irene Puchalski, Librarian
irene.puchalski@utoronto.ca
416-978-6787

Toronto: **John H. Daniels Faculty of Architecture, Lanscape & Design**
Shore & Moffat Library
230 College St., 2nd Fl.
Toronto, ON M5T 1R2
416-978-2649
Fax: 416-971-2094
e-mail: library@daniels.utoronto.ca
URL: www.daniels.utoronto.ca/library
National Library Symbol: OTUSA
Founded in: 1998
Hours: M-Th 9:00-9:00; F 9:00-7:00; Sa 12:00-5:00. Hours may vary throughout the academic year
Acquisitions Budget: $25,000 - $49,999
Note: Loans are restricted to users with University of Toronto library cards.
Subjects covered: Architecture, Landscape Architecture, Design, Urban Studies
Services:
Remote Access
Internet Access
Access to Subscription Databases
Inter-Library Loan (ILL)
Personnel: *Summary:* 4 Total; 1 Professional(s); 2 Technical(s); 1 Other employees
Rita Howell, Librarian
rita.howell@humber.ca
416-675-6622 ext. 3351
Evelyn Hansen, Library Technician, Class Bookings, ILL & Special Needs

Libraries & Resource Centres / Ontario

evelyn.hansen@humber.ca
416-675-6622 ext. 3222
Lynda MacLeod, Library Technician, Periodicals, Government Documents
lynda.macleod@humber.ca
416-675-6622 ext. 3351
Karen Reece, Library Technician, Acquisitions
karen.reece@humber.ca
416-675-6622 ext. 3208
Liz Crum, Library Clerk, Reserves, AV Resources, Overdues
liz.crum@humber.ca
416-675-6622 ext. 3247

Toronto: Lakeshore Campus
Library
3199 Lakeshore Blvd. West
Toronto, ON M8V 1K8
416-675-6622 ext: 3247
Fax: 416-252-0918
Other contact info: Reference: 416-675-6622 ext.3351
URL: www.library.humber.ca
Founded in: 1975
Hours: Sept.-April: M-Th 7:45am-9:00pm; F 7:45-4:30; Sa 10:00-3:00; Su 12:00-5:00. May-June: M-Th 8:30-6:30; F 8:30-4:30. July-Aug.: M-F 8:30-4:30
Special Collections: Statistics Canada, Company report collections
Subjects covered: Child Care, Business, Microcomputer Training, Law Enforcement, Theatre, Music, Social Services
Services:
Internet Access
Inter-Library Loan (ILL)
Media Centre (audiovisual equipment, records, screening room)
Microform Equipment: Computer; Reader
Personnel: *Summary:* 7 Total; 2 Professional(s); 3 Technical(s); 2 Other employees
Berenica Vejvoda, Data Librarian
berenica.vejvoda.utoronto.ca
Marcel Fortin, GIS & Map Librarian
marcel.fortin@utoronto.ca

Toronto: Map and Data Library
Robarts Library
130 St. George St., 5th Fl.
Toronto, ON M5S 1A5
Mailing Address: 130 St George St., 5th Fl.
Toronto, ON M5S 1A5
416-978-5589
URL: mdl.library.utoronto.ca
National Library Symbol: OTUM
Founded in: 1996
Hours: M-F 8:30am-11:00pm; Sa 9:00am-10:00pm; Su 1:00-10:00
Acquisitions Budget: $50,000 - $99,999
Special Collections: Atlases; Toronto maps & aerial photos; Canada maps; rare maps; general topography; thematic world maps; GIS data
Subjects covered: Data Library Service Collection: Computer-readable numeric & textual research files, primarily in the social sciences & humanities; Map Library Collection: includes maps & atlases providing world wide coverage on a large range of subjects
Services:
Internet Access
Inter-Library Loan (ILL) for a fee
Microform Equipment: Reader
Personnel: *Summary:* 10 Total; 5 Professional(s); 6 Technical(s);
Trudy Bodak, Map Librarian
ybodak@yorku.ca
Mary McDowell, Map Library Assistant
marymc@yorku.ca
Dana Craig, Map Library Assistant
dcraig@yorku.ca

Toronto: Map Library
#102, Scott Library, 4700 Keele St.
Toronto, ON M3J 1P3
416-736-2100 ext: 33353
Fax: 416-736-5838
e-mail: tbodak@yorku.ca
Founded in: 1970
Hours: M-Th 10:00-9:00; F 10:00-5:00; Sa, Su 12:00-5:00
Acquisitions Budget: $25,000 - $49,999
Subjects covered: Maps of Toronto, Southern Ontario, Canada, United States, West Indies

Services:
Personnel: *Summary:* 3 Total; 1 Professional(s); 2 Technical(s)

Toronto: Medical Reform Group of Ontario
Resource Centre
PO Box 40074, RPO Marlee
Toronto, ON M6B 4K4
416-787-5246
Fax: 416-352-1154
e-mail: medicalreform@sympatico.ca
URL: www.hwcn.org/link/mrg/
Founded in: 1979
Hours: by appointment only
Acquisitions Budget: $25,000 - $49,999
Note: Resource Centre consists of association archives
Subjects covered: Health Reform
Services:
Personnel:
Janet Maher, Administrator

Toronto: Mount Sinai Hospital
Sidney Liswood Library
#18-234, 600 University Ave.
Toronto, ON M5G 1X5
416-586-4800 ext: 4614
Fax: 416-586-4998
e-mail: library@mtsinai.on.ca
National Library Symbol: OTMS
Founded in: 1990
Hours: M-F 8:30-8:00 by appointment only
Acquisitions Budget: $250,000 - $499,999
Subjects covered: Medicine, Nursing, Health Sciences
Services:
Internet Access
Inter-Library Loan (ILL)
Personnel: *Summary:* 5 Total; 2 Professional(s); 3 Technical(s)
Sandra Kendall, Director, Library Services
416-586-4800 ext. 4614

Toronto: Nickel Institute
Library
#1801, 55 University Ave.
Toronto, ON M5J 2H7
416-591-7999
Fax: 416-591-7987
e-mail: ni_toronto@nickelinstitute.org
URL: www.nickelinstitute.org
No public access
Services:
Personnel:
Barbara Fell, Publications Manager
Bruce Garrod, Head Librarian
bruce.garrod@utoronto.ca
416-978-3538
Eric James, Technician
eric.james@utoronto.ca
416-978-3024
Lynn Barrett, Technician
lynn.barrett@utoronto.ca
416-978-3024

Toronto: Noranda Earth Sciences Library
5 Bancroft Ave., 2nd Floor
Toronto, ON M5S 1A5
416-978-3024
Fax: 416-971-2101
e-mail: earth.sciences@utoronto.ca
URL: www.library.utoronto.ca/earth/
Hours: M-Th 9:00-9:00; F 9:00-5:00; Sa 9:00-5:00
Special Collections: University of Toronto Dissertations in Botany, Geology, Forestry; Environmental Grey Literature Collection
Subjects covered: Botany, Forestry, Geology
Services:
Remote Access
Internet Access
Access to Subscription Databases
Personnel: *Summary:* 10 Total; 1 Professional(s); 2 Technical(s); 6 Other employees;

Toronto: NPS Pharmaceuticals
Information Centre
South Tower, #800, 101 College St.
Toronto, ON M5G 1L8

416-849-5648
Fax: 416-849-5589
e-mail: pcasey@npsp.com
National Library Symbol: OMAI
No public access
Founded in: 1982
Hours: M-F
Subjects covered: Biotechnology, Microbiology, Biopharmaceuticals, Chemistry
Services:
Access to Subscription Databases
Inter-Library Loan (ILL)
Personnel: *Summary:* 1 Total; 1 Professional(s)
Pam Casey, Research Information Specialist
416-849-5648

Toronto: Office of the Fire Marshal
Fire Sciences Library & Audio-Visual Resource Centre
5775 Yonge St., 7th Fl.
Toronto, ON M2M 4J1
416-325-3235
Fax: 416-325-3213
e-mail: martha.murphy@ontario.ca
URL: www.ofm.gov.on.ca/english/Resources/default.asp
National Library Symbol: OTFM
Consortia Membership: Ontario Government Libraries Council (OGLC)
Founded in: 1962
Hours: M-F 8:30-4:15
Acquisitions Budget: $25,000 - $49,999
Note: Under the auspices of Ontario. Ministry of Community Safety & Correctional Services
Special Collections: Collection of ULC standards, CSA standards, NFPA codes, Building & fire codes
Subjects covered: Physical Sciences, Engineering, Technology, Fire Prevention, Fighting, Investigation, & Management, Hazardous Materials, Health & Safety, Building Construction, Arson, Fire Codes, Risk Management, Emergency Response, Juvenile Fire Setters
Services:
Internet Access
Inter-Library Loan (ILL)
Microform Equipment: Reader
Personnel: *Summary:* 3 Total; 1 Professional(s); 2 Technical(s)
Martha Murphy, Librarian
martha.murphy@jus.gov.on.ca
416-325-3235

Toronto: Ontario Energy Board / Commission d'énergie de l'Ontario
Information Resource Centre
#2601, 2300 Yonge St.
Toronto, ON M4P 1E4
Mailing Address: PO Box 2319
Toronto, ON M4P 1E4
416-440-7655
Fax: 416-440-7656
e-mail: lina.buccilli@oeb.gov.on.ca
URL: www.oeb.gov.on.ca
National Library Symbol: OTOEB
Founded in: 1982
Hours: M-F by appointment only
Acquisitions Budget: $25,000 - $49,999
Note: Under auspices of Ministry of Energy, Science & Technology
Special Collections: OEB & NEB transcripts & decisions (selected), Provincial & State boards/commissions (selected), Environmental materials, Annual Reports, Public Utilities Reports Digests 1934-, Public Utilities Fortnightly 1960-
Subjects covered: Utilities, Energy Resources & Regulation
Services:
Inter-Library Loan (ILL)
Personnel:
Lina Buccilli, Librarian
lina.buccilli@oeb.gov.on.ca

Toronto: Ontario Ministry of Economic Development & Trade
InfoSource
Hearst Block, 900 Bay St., 6th Fl.
Toronto, ON M7A 2E1
416-325-6148
Fax: 416-325-6825
e-mail: janice.somers@ontario.ca
URL: www.ontariocanada.com

Libraries & Resource Centres / Ontario

No public access
Founded in: 1994
Hours: M-F 8:30-4:30
Acquisitions Budget: For Print: 0-$9,999
For Electronic: $10,000 - $24,999
Population Served: 300
Subjects covered: Business, Economic Development, Industry, Enterprise, Trade, Investment
Services:
Personnel: *Summary:* 1 Total; 1 Professional(s)
Janice Somers, Information Specialist
janice.somers@ontario.ca
416-325-6148

Toronto: **Ontario Ministry of Environment**
Standards Development Branch Library
40 St Clair Ave. West, 7th Fl.
Toronto, ON M4V 1M2
416-327-4702
Fax: 416-327-2936
e-mail: denise.angeloni@ene.gov.on.ca
National Library Symbol: OTMEH
Hours: M-F 8:00-4:00 by appointment only
Acquisitions Budget: For Print: $25,000 - $49,999
For Electronic: 0-$9,999
Note: Science & Technology Branch library has merged with Standards Development Branch library
Special Collections: Eco-toxicity, Toxicology
Subjects covered: Environment, Health & Environmental Effects, Pesticides, Toxic Substances, Biotechnology, Phytotoxicology, Waste Management, Risk Management, Air Pollution, Toxicology, Aquatic Sciences, Environmental Sciences, Standards & Policy
Services:
Inter-Library Loan (ILL)
Personnel: *Summary:* 1 Total; 1 Professional(s)
Denise Angeloni, Scientific Information Specialist
denise.angeloni@ene.gov.on.ca
416-327-4702

Toronto: **Ontario Ministry of Environment**
Information Resource Centre
40 St Clair Ave. West, 11th Fl.
Toronto, ON M4V 1M2
416-327-1247
Fax: 416-327-1510
e-mail: irc.irc.moe@ontario.ca
National Library Symbol: OTME
Founded in: 1974
Hours: M-F (by appointment only) by appointment only
Note: Provides information research services to the Ministry of Energy & Infrastructure & to the Ministery of Environment.
Subjects covered: Sustainable Development; Environment; Conventional & Renewable Energy; Energy Policy; Conservation & Technology
Services:
Inter-Library Loan (ILL)
Personnel: *Summary:* 3 Total; 2 Professional(s); 1 Technical(s)
Marusia Borodacz, Team Leader
marusia.borodacz@ontario.ca
Simone O'Byrne, Information Specialist
Tana Chirita, Information Technician

Toronto: **Ontario Ministry of Environment**
Laboratory Library
125 Resources Rd.
Toronto, ON M9P 3V6
416-235-5751
Fax: 416-235-0189
e-mail: traceyann.crawford@ene.gov.on.ca
National Library Symbol: OTENL
Founded in: 1964
Hours: by appointment only
Subjects covered: Analytical Chemistry, Limnology, Fish Research, Environmental Studies, Water & Waste Treatment
Services:
Microform Equipment: Computer; Reader
Personnel:
Traceyann Crawford, Contact

Toronto: **Ontario Ministry of Health & Long-Term Care**
Laboratories Library
81 Resources Rd.
Toronto, ON M9P 3T1
416-235-5935
Fax: 416-235-6196
e-mail: phl_torontolibrary.moh@ontario.ca
National Library Symbol: OTDHL
Consortia Membership: HSICT
No public access
Founded in: 1963
Hours: M-F 8:00-4:00
Acquisitions Budget: $50,000 - $99,999
For Print: $25,000 - $49,999
For Electronic: 0-$9,999
Population Served: 650
Special Collections: CLSI Standards
Subjects covered: Microbiology, Laboratory Safety, Infectious Diseases
Services:
Internet Access
Personnel: *Summary:* 1 Total; 1 Technical(s)
Gabrielle Gaedecke, Library Technician

Toronto: **Ontario Ministry of Municipal Affairs & Housing**
InfoLink - Library & Information Centre
777 Bay St., 3rd Fl.
Toronto, ON M5G 2E5
416-585-7333
Fax: 416-585-7122
e-mail: infolink@mah.gov.on.ca
National Library Symbol: OTOH
No public access
Founded in: 1968
Hours: M-F 9:00-5:00
Subjects covered: Housing, Public Works, Local Government, Architecture, Planning, Geography, Low Income Housing, Housing Management, Conservation, Municipal Finance
Services:
Inter-Library Loan (ILL)
Fee Based Research
Personnel: *Summary:* 2 Total; 2 Professional(s)
Florence Lam, Information Specialist
Sarah Nichols, Information Specialist

Toronto: **Ontario Power Generation**
Business Information Centre
#H17 G10, 700 University Ave.
Toronto, ON M5G 1X6
416-592-2715
Fax: 416-592-7532
e-mail: library@opg.com
No public access
Hours: M-F 8:00-4:00
Acquisitions Budget: $500,000 - $999,999
Subjects covered: Energy
Services:
Personnel: *Summary:* 13 Total; 5 Professional(s); 3 Technical(s)
Nancy Fish, Manager, Library

Toronto: **Ontario Public Interest Research Group - Toronto/Downtown Women's Centre**
Dr. Chun Resource Library
#101, 563 Spadina Ave.
Toronto, ON M5S 2J7
416-978-7770
Fax: 416-971-2292
e-mail: drchunlibrary@hotmail.com
URL: www.drchunlibrary.com
Hours: M-Th 11:00-5:30
Note: Downtown Women's Centre resources is at this location
Subjects covered: Environmental & social justice information & research, educational materials
Services:
Personnel: *Summary:* 2 Professional(s)
Vashti Persad, Administrative Coordinaor
Eng K. Ching, Regional Librarian
chinge@tc.gc.ca

Toronto: **Ontario Regional Library**
4900 Yonge St., 3rd Fl.
Toronto, ON M2N 6A5
416-952-0441
Fax: 416-952-0417
e-mail: chinge@tc.gc.ca
National Library Symbol: OTTOA
Founded in: 1977
Hours: M-F 8:30-4:30
Acquisitions Budget: $25,000 - $49,999
Subjects covered: Transportation
Services:
Inter-Library Loan (ILL)
Personnel:

Toronto: **Ontario Science Centre**
Library
770 Don Mills Rd.
Toronto, ON M3C 1T3
416-696-3149
Fax: 416-696-3157
e-mail: vhatten@osc.on.ca
URL: www.ontariosciencecentre.ca
National Library Symbol: OTST
Founded in: 1966
Hours: M-F 8:45-5:00 by appointment only
Acquisitions Budget: $25,000 - $49,999
Special Collections: Exhibit slides, Audio-Visual
Subjects covered: General Sciences, Technology, Museum & Exhibit Design, Applied Arts, Museology
Services:
Inter-Library Loan (ILL)
Personnel: *Summary:* 1 Total; 1 Professional(s)
Valerie Hatten, Librarian

Toronto: **Osgoode Hall Law School**
Law Library
4700 Keele St.
Toronto, ON M3J 1P3
416-736-5206
Fax: 416-736-5298
e-mail: lawref@osgoode.yorku.ca
National Library Symbol: OTYL
Hours: M-Su
Special Collections: Canadian legal material published through 1900; U.K. material published through 1860 plus early trials published through 1900; Canadian & U.K. manuscripts; broadsides mainly from England; Osgoodiana Law
Subjects covered: Law
Services:
Inter-Library Loan (ILL)
Microform Equipment: Computer; Reader
Barbara Chu, Librarian
bchu@physics.utoronto.ca

Toronto: **Physics Library**
#211C, 60 St. George St.
Toronto, ON M5S 1A7
416-978-5188
Fax: 416-978-5919
URL: www.physics.utoronto.ca/library
discover.library.utoronto.ca
National Library Symbol: OTUP
No public access
Hours: M-F 9:00-5:00
Special Collections: Physics abstracts, 1969 to present online, pre-1969 paper copy; U of T Physics theses/dissertations
Subjects covered: Math, Physics, Atmospheric Sciences, Geophysics
Services:
Inter-Library Loan (ILL)
Personnel: *Summary:* 2 Total; 1 Professional(s); 1 Technical(s)

Toronto: **Prospectors & Developers Association of Canada**
Library
#900, 34 King St. East
Toronto, ON M5C 2X8
416-362-1969
Fax: 416-362-0101
e-mail: info@pdac.ca
Subjects covered: Mines, Minerals, Industry
Services:

Toronto: **Radiation Safety Institute of Canada**
Resource Library
#607, 1120 Finch Ave. West
Toronto, ON M3J 3H7
416-650-9090
Fax: 416-650-9920
800-263-5803
e-mail: info@radiationsafety.ca
URL: www.radiationsafety.ca
Founded in: 1980
Hours: M-F 9:00-4:00

Acquisitions Budget: 0-$9,999
Subjects covered: Radiation
Services:

Toronto: **Royal Ontario Museum Libraries**
100 Queen's Park Cres.
Toronto, ON M5S 2C6
416-586-5595
Fax: 416-586-5519
e-mail: info@rom.on.ca
library@rom.on.ca
URL: www.rom.on.ca
National Library Symbol: OTRM
Consortia Membership: University of Toronto Libraries
Founded in: 1961
Hours: M, W-F 12:00-4:30; Tu 12:00-5:30
Acquisitions Budget: $100,000 - $249,999
For Print: $100,000 - $249,999
Population Served: 2688
Note: Under the auspices of the Ministry of Culture. Closed stacks. Collection is non-circulating, however materials may be borrowed by ROM staff, University of Toronto faculty, and University of Toronto students enrolled in the Museum Studies Program. Consult the University of Toronto catalogue for holdings. Public may access the Library & Archives for reference use only
Special Collections: Main Library & Archives houses the Archives of the Royal Ontario Museum, as well as the J.H. Fleming Collection of books relating to ornithology; Rare Book Collection; H.H. Mu Far Eastern Library, the premier library in Canada devoted to the arts of the Orient
Subjects covered: Archaeology, Botany, Canadiana, Decorative Arts, Geology, Minerology, Museology, Ethnology, Palaeontology, Zoology, Textiles & Costume, Asian Art & Archaeology, Egyptology
Services:
Remote Access
Internet Access
Access to Subscription Databases
Inter-Library Loan (ILL) for a fee of $20
Scanning
Microform Equipment: Reader
Personnel: Summary: 5 Total; 2 Professional(s); 3 Technical(s); 2 Volunteer(s)
Arthur Smith, Head, Library & Archives
arthurs@rom.on.ca
Jack Howard, Far Eastern Librarian
jackh@rom.on.ca
416-586-5418

Toronto: **R.V. Anderson Associates Limited Library**
#400, 2001 Sheppard Ave. East
Toronto, ON M2J 4Z8
416-497-8600 ext: 212
Fax: 416-497-0342
e-mail: tzimmer@rvanderson.com
toronto@rvanderson.com
URL: www.rvanderson.com
National Library Symbol: OWAA
No public access
Founded in: 1948
Hours: M-F 9:00-5:00
Population Served: 200
Note: Extensive engineering journals collection
Subjects covered: Environmental & Civil Engineering, Telecommunications Engineering, Architecture
Services:
Inter-Library Loan (ILL)
Personnel: Summary: 3 Total; 2 Professional(s); 1 Technical(s)
Terri Zimmer, Librarian
tzimmer@randerson.com
416-497-8600 ext. 212
Leah Swift, Researcher
lswift@randerson.com
416-497-8600 ext. 212
Liane Wilson, Content Administrator
lwilson@randerson.com
416-497-8600 ext. 212

Toronto: **Ryerson University Library**
350 Victoria St., Rm. L387
Toronto, ON M5B 2K3
416-979-5000 ext: 7027
Fax: 416-979-5215

e-mail: archives@ryerson.ca
URL: www.ryerson.ca/archives/index.html
National Library Symbol: OTR
Consortia Membership: Canadian Research Knowledge Network (CRKN); Ontario Council of University Libraries (OCUL)
Founded in: 1947
Hours: M-F 8:00am-12:00am; Sa, Su 10:00am-12:00am
Acquisitions Budget: $1,000,000 plus
For Print: $1,000,000 plus
For Electronic: $1,000,000 plus
Special Collections: Collection dates from 1783 to present day and focuses on Ryerson University and its predecessor institutions, including items such as year books, photographs, film, sound recordings, manuals, newspapers, etc.
Subjects covered: Applied Arts, Engineering, Business, Community Services, Social Science, Communication & Design
Services:
Remote Access
Internet Access
Access to Subscription Databases
Inter-Library Loan (ILL)
Microform Equipment: Computer; Reader
Personnel: Summary: 81 Total; 23 Professional(s); 58 Other employees
Liz Bishop, Acting Chief Librarian
lbishop@ryerson.ca
416-979-5025
Daniel Phelan, Manager, Collection Services
dphelan@ryerson.ca
416-979-5146
Bob Jackson, Manager, Besse Information & Learning Commons
bjackson@ryerson.ca
416-979-5000 ext. 6890

Toronto: **St James Library/Learning Commons**
#121, 200 King St. East
Toronto, ON M5A 3W8
Mailing Address: 200 King St. East
Toronto, ON M5A 3W8
416-415-5000 ext: 2173
Founded in: 1976
Hours: M-F 7:30-10:00; Sa 10:00-6:00; Su 10:00-5:00 by appointment only
Special Collections: Canadian Guild of Sommeliers, Ontario Hostelry
Subjects covered: Hospitality, Nursing, Business, Graphic Arts, Community Services
Services:
Inter-Library Loan (ILL)
Personnel: Summary: 6 Total; 1 Professional(s); 5 Technical(s)

Toronto: **St Michael's Hospital Health Sciences Library**
#1-008, Queen Wing, 30 Bond St.
Toronto, ON M5B 1W8
416-864-5059
Fax: 416-864-5296
e-mail: hslibrary@smh.toronto.on.ca
URL: www.stmichaelshospital.com/learn/library.php
National Library Symbol: OTSM
No public access
Hours: M-F 8:00-8:00; Sa, Su 11:00-5:00. Patients only.
Subjects covered: Health Sciences, Medicine
Services:
Personnel: Summary: 6 Professional(s); 3 Technical(s)
Pam Richards, Manager
richardsp@smh.ca
416-864-6060 ext. 2924

Toronto: **Sanofi Pasteur Limited Balmer Neilly Library & Archives**
1755 Steeles Ave. West
Toronto, ON M2R 3T4
416-667-2662
Fax: 416-667-2850
e-mail: library.servicesca@sanofipasteur.com
URL: www.sanofipasteur.com
National Library Symbol: OTCL
Founded in: 1921
Hours: M-F 8:00-4:00 by appointment only
Subjects covered: Immunology, Virology, Bacteriology, Biotechnology
Services:
Inter-Library Loan (ILL)
Personnel: Summary: 3 Total; 2 Professional(s); 1 Technical(s)

Hugh McNaught, Information & Library Services Manager
hugh.mcnaught@sanofipasteur.com

Toronto: **Seneca College of Applied Arts & Technology Newnham Campus**
1750 Finch Ave. East
Toronto, ON M2J 2X5
416-491-5050 ext: 2099
URL: library.senecacollege.ca
National Library Symbol: OTSC
Consortia Membership: Ontario Colleges Library Service
Founded in: 1967
Hours: M-Th 8:00am-11:00pm; F 8:00-10:00; Sa 8:30-5:00; Su 9:00-5:00
Acquisitions Budget: $500,000 - $999,999
Note: Newnham Campus Learning Commons located here
Subjects covered: Applied Arts, Technology, Business, General Education
Services:
Internet Access
Access to Subscription Databases
Inter-Library Loan (ILL)
Personnel: Summary: 71 Total; 15 Professional(s); 32 Technical(s); 24 Other employees
Carolyn Lam, Associate Director
carolyn.lam@senecac.on.ca
416-491-5050 ext. 2097
Joy Muller, Manager
joy.muller@seneca.on.ca
416-491-5050 ext. 3042
James Buczynski, Campus Librarian
james.buczynski@seneca.on.ca
416-491-5050 ext. 3159

Toronto: **Seneca@York Campus**
70 The Pond Rd.
Toronto, ON M3J 3M6
416-491-5050 ext: 3055
Hours: M-F 8:00-10:30; Sa, Su 9:00-5:00
Personnel:
Aarash Kalra, Librarian
kalra@snc-lavalin.com
416-252-5311

Toronto: **SNC-Lavalin Engineers & Constructors Inc. Library**
2200 Lake Shore Blvd. West
Toronto, ON M8V 1A4
416-252-5311
Fax: 416-252-2058
URL: www.snclavalin.com
National Library Symbol: OWSNC
No public access
Founded in: 1950
Hours: M-F 9:00-5:00
Acquisitions Budget: $25,000 - $49,999
Special Collections: Company archives of reports & project related materials, CSA standards, International company standards
Subjects covered: Wastewater Treatment, Urban Planning, Environmental Assessment, Engineering, Mining
Services:
Inter-Library Loan (ILL)
Personnel: Summary: 1 Total
Leila Fernadez, Science Librarian
leilaf@yorku.ca

Toronto: **Steacie Science and Engineering Library**
4700 Keele St.
Toronto, ON M3J 1P3
416-736-5639
Fax: 416-736-5452
Founded in: 1970
Hours: M-Su
Acquisitions Budget: $500,000 - $999,999
Subjects covered: Life Sciences, Physical Sciences, Technology, Biological Sciences, Chemistry, Physics, Terrestrial & Space Sciences, Mathematics, Applied Computational Mathematics, Computer Science, Engineering
Services:
Internet Access
Inter-Library Loan (ILL)
Microform Equipment: Reader
Personnel: Summary: 9 Total; 3 Professional(s); 7 Technical(s)

Libraries & Resource Centres / Ontario

Toronto: Sunnybrook Health Sciences Centre - Sunnybrook Campus
MacDonald Library
2075 Bayview Ave.
Toronto, ON M4N 3M5
416-480-6100 ext: 4562
Fax: 416-480-6848
e-mail: farid.miah@sunnybrook.ca
URL: www.sunnybrook.ca
National Library Symbol: OTSMC
Founded in: 1968
Hours: M-F 9:00-5:00; Sa 1:00-5:00
Acquisitions Budget: $50,000 - $99,999
Population Served: 10000
Subjects covered: Medicine, Nursing, Health Sciences
Services:
Remote Access
Internet Access
Access to Subscription Databases
Personnel: *Summary:* 7 Total; 2 Professional(s); 3 Technical(s); 2 Other employees
Farid Miah, Manager
farid.miah@sb.ca
416-480-6100 ext. 2560
Henry Lam, Information Specialist
henry.lam@sw.ca
416-480-6100 ext. 2562
Linda Boyd, Library Technician
linda.boyd@sw.ca
416-480-6100 ext. 2561
Jane Sauder, Library Technician
jane.sauder@sw.ca
416-480-6100 ext. 2519
Teresa Cuke, Technical Reference Centre Librarian
cuket@tc.gc.ca
416-952-0351

Toronto: Technical Reference Centre
4900 Yonge St.
Toronto, ON M2N 6A5
416-952-0351
Fax: 416-952-0370
e-mail: cuket@tc.gc.ca
Hours: M-F 8:00-4:00 by appointment only
Acquisitions Budget: $25,000 - $49,999
For Print: $25,000 - $49,999
Subjects covered: Transportation, Aviation Regulations, Aircraft Data
Services:
Personnel: *Summary:* 1 Total; 1 Professional(s)

Toronto: The Michener Institute for Applied Health Sciences
Learning Resource Centre
222 St Patrick St., 2nd Floor
Toronto, ON M5T 1V4
416-596-3123
Fax: 416-596-3137
800-387-9066
e-mail: lrc@michener.ca
URL: www.michener.ca/lrc
National Library Symbol: OTTIM
No public access
Founded in: 1972
Hours: M-Th 8:00am-9:00pm; F 8:00-5:00; Sa-Su 9:00-5:00
Acquisitions Budget: $50,000 - $99,999
For Print: $50,000 - $99,999
For Electronic: $10,000 - $24,999
Services:
Inter-Library Loan (ILL)
Personnel: *Summary:* 3 Total; 1 Professional(s); 2 Technical(s)
Terry Sulymko, Director, Learning Resource Centre
tsulymko@michener.ca
416-596-3101 ext. 3454

Toronto: The Resource Library for the Environment and the Law / L'Association canadienne du droit de l'environnement
Library
#301, 130 Spadina Ave.
Toronto, ON M5V 2L4
416-960-2284
Fax: 416-960-9392
e-mail: millers@lao.on.ca

URL: www.cela.ca
www.ecolawinfo.org
Founded in: 1974
Hours: M-F 9:00-5:00
Acquisitions Budget: $10,000 - $24,999
For Print: $10,000 - $24,999
Note: Phone for current public access hours
Subjects covered: Environmental Law, Pollution, Pollution Control, Resource Management, Environmental Health, Land Use Planning, Trade, Water
Services:
Internet Access
Personnel: *Summary:* 7 Total; 1 Professional(s); 2 Volunteer(s)
Sarah Miller, Coordinator and Researcher
millers@lao.on.ca

Toronto: The Scarborough Hospital - General Campus
Health Sciences Library
3050 Lawrence Ave. East
Toronto, ON M1P 2V5
416-431-8114
Fax: 416-431-8232
e-mail: dlambert@tsh.to
fahmed@tsh.to
URL: www.library.tsh.to
No public access
Hours: M-F 8:00-4:30
Subjects covered: Medicine & Allied Health
Services:
Inter-Library Loan (ILL) for a fee of $12
Personnel: *Summary:* 2 Total; 1 Professional(s); 1 Technical(s); 3 Volunteer(s)
Deborah Lambert, Library Manager
dlambert@tsh.to
Fatimah Ahmed, Librarian
fahmed@tsh.to
Judy Ng, Library Technician
416-431-8200 ext. 6593

Toronto: The Scarborough Hospital - Grace Campus
Library
3030 Birchmount Rd.
Toronto, ON M1W 3W3
416-495-2437
Fax: 416-495-2562
e-mail: fahmed@tsh.to
URL: www.library.tsh.to
Hours: M-F 8:30-4:30
Subjects covered: Health Sciences, Medicine, Hospital Administration
Services:
Personnel:
Fatimah Ahmed, Librarian
fahmed@tsh.to

Toronto: Toronto Botanical Garden
Weston Family Library
777 Lawrence Ave. East
Toronto, ON M3C 1P2
416-397-1343
Fax: 416-397-1354
e-mail: library@torontobotanicalgarden.ca
URL: www.torontobotanicalgarden.ca
Founded in: 1959
Hours: M-Sa 10:00-5:00; Su 12:00-4:00
Acquisitions Budget: $10,000 - $24,999
For Print: $10,000 - $24,999
For Electronic: 0-$9,999
Population Served: 2227
Special Collections: Historical Collection, Children's Collection, Orchid Collection, Multimedia Collection, Herb Collection
Subjects covered: Horticulture, Floral Arts, Landscape Architecure, Botany
Services:
Internet Access
Public computer workstation for free internet access
Personnel: *Summary:* 1 Total; 1 Professional(s); 25 Volunteer(s)
Rob Caldwell, Manager, Information Services
416-397-1375

Toronto: Toronto East General Hospital
Health Sciences Library
825 Coxwell Ave.
Toronto, ON M4C 3E7

416-469-6010
Fax: 416-469-6106
National Library Symbol: OTEG
Founded in: 1960
Hours: M-F by appointment only
Services:
Personnel: *Summary:* 2 Total; 1 Professional(s)
Carole Tullis, Manager, Health Sciences Library

Toronto: Toronto Public Health
Library
277 Victoria St., 6th Fl.
Toronto, ON M5B 1W2
416-338-7865
Fax: 416-392-1483
e-mail: hlibrary@toronto.ca
Consortia Membership: Health Sciences Information Consortium of Toronto (HSICT)
Hours: M-F 8:30-4:30 by appointment only
Acquisitions Budget: $50,000 - $99,999
For Print: $10,000 - $24,999
For Electronic: $50,000 - $99,999
Population Served: 2000
Subjects covered: Public Health, Nursing, Medicine, Health Sciences, Public Health Policy
Services:
Personnel: *Summary:* 4 Total; 3 Professional(s); 1 Other employees
Bruce Gardham, Senior Librarian
416-338-8284

Toronto: Toronto Rehab
Library Services
550 University Ave.
Toronto, ON M5G 2A2
416-597-3422 ext: 3050
Fax: 416-591-6515
e-mail: libraryall@torontorehab.on.ca
URL: www.torontorehab.com
Hours: M-F 9:00-5:00
Acquisitions Budget: $50,000 - $99,999
Services:
Inter-Library Loan (ILL) for a fee of $10
Personnel: *Summary:* 7 Total; 3 Professional(s); 3 Technical(s)
Doreen Millman-Wilson, Manager, Library Services
millman-wilson.doreen@torontorehab.on.ca
Marcia Winterbottom, Electronic Resources-Systems Librarian
Joy Shanfield, Information Resources Specialist
Holly Phillips, Library Technician
Elizabeth Johnston, Library Assistant
Doris Extavour, Library Assistant

Toronto: Toronto Urban Development Services City Planning
Information Resource Centre
Metro Hall, 55 John St., 22nd Fl.
Toronto, ON M5V 3C6
416-392-1526
Fax: 416-392-3821
e-mail: dfowler@city.toronto.on.ca
Hours: by appointment only
Subjects covered: Building, Construction & Design, Codes & Standards, Urban Planning with emphasis on Toronto
Services:
Inter-Library Loan (ILL)
Personnel: *Summary:* 2 Total; 1 Professional(s)
Deborah Fowler, Librarian
dfowler@city.toronto.on.ca

Toronto: Toronto Western Hospital
R.C. Laird Health Sciences Library
Fell Pavilion, 399 Bathurst St., 3rd Fl.
Toronto, ON M5T 2S8
416-603-5750
Fax: 416-603-5326
No public access
Founded in: 1961
Hours: M-F
Subjects covered: Medicine, Nursing, Health Sciences
Services:
Inter-Library Loan (ILL)

Toronto: Toronto Zoo
Library
361A Old Finch Ave.
Toronto, ON M1B 5K7
416-392-5960
Fax: 416-392-4979
e-mail: echristens@torontozoo.ca
URL: www.torontozoo.com
Founded in: 1994
Hours: M-F 8:30-4:00 by appointment only
Acquisitions Budget: 0-$9,999
For Print: 0-$9,999
For Electronic: 0-$9,999
Services:
Access to Subscription Databases
Personnel: *Summary:* 1 Total; 1 Professional(s)
Elaine Christens, Curatorial Assistant
echristens@torontozoo.ca
416-392-5960

Toronto: Transportation Health & Safety Association of Ontario
Video Library
#101, 555 Dixon Rd.
Toronto, ON M9W 1H8
416-242-4771
Fax: 416-242-4714
800-263-5016
e-mail: info@thsao.on.ca
URL: www.thsao.on.ca
Subjects covered: Transportation, Health & Safety
Services:

Toronto: University Health Network
Toronto General Hospital Health Sciences Library
Eaton North Wing, #1-418, 200 Elizabeth St.
Toronto, ON M5G 2C4
416-340-3429
Fax: 416-340-4384
e-mail: uhnlibraries@uhn.on.ca
URL: www.uhn.on.ca
Founded in: 1964
Hours: M-Su by appointment only
Acquisitions Budget: $500,000 - $999,999
Services:
Internet Access
Inter-Library Loan (ILL) for a fee
Personnel: *Summary:* 20 Total; 9 Professional(s); 11 Technical(s); 3 Volunteer(s)

Toronto: University of Toronto Innis College
Innis Library
2 Sussex Ave., 2nd Fl.
Toronto, ON M5S 1J5
416-978-4497
Fax: 416-946-0168
e-mail: l.ferstman@utoronto.ca
URL: www.utoronto.ca/innis/library
Founded in: 1974
Hours: M-Th 9:30-6:00; F 9:30-5:00
Acquisitions Budget: $25,000 - $49,999
Special Collections: Cinema Collection
Subjects covered: Cinema Studies, Environmental Studies, Urban Studies
Services:
Internet Access
Inter-Library Loan (ILL)
Personnel: *Summary:* 1 Technical(s); 6 Other employees
Leonard Ferstman, Librarian

Toronto: University of Toronto Libraries
130 St George St.
Toronto, ON M5S 1A5
416-978-8450
Fax: 416-978-7653
e-mail: utweb@library.utoronto.ca
URL: www.library.utoronto.ca
National Library Symbol: UTL
Consortia Membership: Canadian Research Knowledge Network (CRKN); Ontario Council of University Libraries (OCUL)
Founded in: 1892
Hours: M-F 8:30am-12:00am; Sa 9:00am-10:00pm; Su 1:00-10:00pm
Acquisitions Budget: $500,000 - $999,999
Services:
Internet Access
Access to Subscription Databases
Inter-Library Loan (ILL)
Fee Based Research
Microform Equipment: Reader
Personnel:
Carole Moore, Chief Librarian
416-978-2292
Carol Jaffray, Head, Cataloguing
jaffray@library.utoronto.ca
416-978-8806
Graham Bradshaw, Head, Collection Development
graham.bradshaw@utoronto.ca
416-978-2289
Peter Clinton, Head, Systems
m.clinton@utoronto.ca

Toronto: University of Toronto Massey College
Robertson Davies Library
4 Devonshire Pl.
Toronto, ON M5S 2E1
416-978-2893
Fax: 416-978-1759
e-mail: massey.library@utoronto.ca
URL: www.utoronto.ca/massey/library.html
National Library Symbol: OTMC
Consortia Membership: University of Toronto campus library system
Founded in: 1963
Hours: M-F 9:00-12:30, 1:30-5:00; appointment advised
Acquisitions Budget: For Print: $25,000 - $49,999
Population Served: 750
Subjects covered: History of the Book, printing, papermaking, bookbinding, palaeography, calligraphy, type design, book collecting, bibliography; papers of Carl Dair; editions and translations of Robertson Davies
Services:
Internet Access
Personnel: *Summary:* 2 Total; 2 Professional(s)
Marie Korey, Librarian
P.J. MacDougall, Head, Reference

Toronto: University of Toronto Scarborough Library
1265 Military Trail
Toronto, ON M1C 1A4
416-287-7508
Fax: 416-287-7507
URL: content.library.utoronto.ca/utsc
Founded in: 1964
Hours: M-Su, library hours vary throughout the year; please check website
Acquisitions Budget: $100,000 - $249,999
Population Served: 10000
Note: Public access to resources is limited. Extensive electronic & print collections
Special Collections: Maps; Slides; CDs; DVDs; Videos; Digital Images
Services:
Remote Access
Internet Access
Access to Subscription Databases
Inter-Library Loan (ILL)
Microform Equipment: Computer; Reader
Personnel: *Summary:* 20 Total; 7 Professional(s); 13 Technical(s)
Victoria Owen, Head Librarian
owen@utsc.utoronto.ca
416-287-7519
Chad Crichton, Coordinator, Reference, Research & Instruction
ccrichton@utsc.utoronto.ca
416-287-7492
Catherine Devion, Coordinator, Circulation & Access
devion@utsc.utoronto.ca
416-287-7485
Patricia LaCivita, Coordinator, Collections & Information Management
lacivita@utsc.utoronto.ca
416-287-7484
Sarah Fedko, Coordinator, Campus Information Literacy
sfedko@utsc.utoronto.ca
416-208-2708

Toronto: Vale Inco
Records & Information Management
#1500, 145 King St. West
Toronto, ON M5H 4B7
416-361-7741
Fax: 416-361-7781
e-mail: valeinco@valeinco.com
No public access
Acquisitions Budget: $50,000 - $99,999
Special Collections: Annual Reports, Maps
Subjects covered: Economics, Industry, Energy, Natural Resources, Business, Banking, Taxation, Finance, Investment, Mining & Mining Processes, Geology, Mineral Economics
Services:
Inter-Library Loan (ILL)
Personnel: *Summary:* 4 Total; 1 Professional(s); 1 Technical(s)
Christina Wu, Librarian
416-361-7518

Toronto: Walker, Nott, Dragicevic Associates Limited
Library
172 St George St.
Toronto, ON M5R 2M7
416-968-3511
Fax: 416-960-0172
e-mail: admin@wndplan.com
URL: www.wndplan.com
No public access
Founded in: 1988
Acquisitions Budget: $25,000 - $49,999
Services:
Remote Access
Access to Subscription Databases
Personnel: *Summary:* 2 Total; 1 Professional(s); 1 Other employees
Jutta Szep, Librarian

Toronto: Waterfront Regeneration Trust
Library
#308, 372 Richmond St. West
Toronto, ON M5V 1X6
416-943-8080
Fax: 416-943-8068
e-mail: info@wrtrust.com
URL: www.waterfronttrail.org/library.html
Hours: by appointment only
Subjects covered: Waterfront planning & development; Shoreline management; Transportation; Environment; Tourism; Recreation
Services:
Personnel:
Marlaine Koehler, Contact

Toronto: Watts, Griffis & McOuat Limited
Library
#400, 8 King St. East
Toronto, ON M5C 1B5
416-364-6244
Fax: 416-864-1675
e-mail: wgm@wgm.on.ca
URL: www.wgm.on.ca
Founded in: 1971
Hours: by appointment only
Acquisitions Budget: $25,000 - $49,999
Subjects covered: Energy, Mineral Resources, Mining, Geology
Services:
Personnel: *Summary:* 1 Total; 1 Professional(s)

Toronto: Women's College Hospital
Medical Library
76 Grenville St.
Toronto, ON M5S 1B2
416-323-6078
Fax: 416-323-6322
No public access
Founded in: 1955
Hours: M-F 9:00-5:00
Special Collections: Hospital Archives
Subjects covered: Obstetrics, Gynecology, High Risk Pregnancy, Dermatology, Diabetes, Internal Medicine, Nursing
Services:
Inter-Library Loan (ILL)
Personnel: *Summary:* 4 Total;
Grazyna Wiercinska, Library Technician
Jane Sauder, Library Technician

Toronto: York University Glendon College Campus
Leslie Frost Library/Bibliothèque Leslie Frost
2275 Bayview Ave.
Toronto, ON M4N 3M6

416-487-6726
Fax: 416-487-6705
URL: www.library.yorku.ca
National Library Symbol: OTY
Founded in: 1960
Hours: M-Th 8:30-11:00; F 10:00-8:00; Sa 10:00-6:00; Su 12:00-8:00
Acquisitions Budget: $100,000 - $249,999
For Print: $50,000 - $99,999
For Electronic: $100,000 - $249,999
Note: Part of York University Libraries
Special Collections: 30% of collection in French, emphasis on dictionaries for translation
Subjects covered: Humanities, Social Sciences, Natural Science, Liberal Arts, International Relations, Translation
Services:
Inter-Library Loan (ILL)
Microform Equipment: Computer; Reader
Personnel: *Summary:* 6 Total; 3 Professional(s); 3 Technical(s)
Julianna Drexler, Head Librarian
drexler@yorku.ca
416-487-6729
Vivienne Monty, Reference Librarian
vmonty@yorku.ca
416-487-6729
Anne McGaughey, Reference Librarian
mcgaughe@yorku.ca
416-487-6729

Toronto: **York University Libraries**
Scott Library
4700 Keele St.
Toronto, ON M3J 1P3
416-736-5601
Fax: 416-736-5451
URL: www.library.yorku.ca
National Library Symbol: OTY
Consortia Membership: Canadian Research Knowledge Network (CRKN); Ontario Council of University Libraries (OCUL)
Founded in: 1971
Hours: M-Su
Acquisitions Budget: $500,000 - $999,999
Special Collections: Archives & Special Collections
Services:
Internet Access
Access to Subscription Databases
Inter-Library Loan (ILL)
Microform Equipment: Computer; Reader
Personnel: *Summary:* 175 Total; 53 Professional(s); 121 Technical(s)
Cynthia Archer, University Librarian
carcher@yorku.ca
Brent Roe, Associate University Librarian
broe@yorku.ca
Robert Thompson, Director, Library Computing Services
rthompson@yorku.ca
Karen Cassel, Head, Serials & Electronic Acquistions
cassel@yorku.ca
Nancy Hall, Head, Monograph Acquisitions
nhall@yorku.ca
Catherine Davidson, Associate University Librarian, Collections
cdavidson@yorku.ca

Uxbridge: **Nuclear Awareness Project**
Library
34 Church St.
Uxbridge, ON L9P 1M6
Mailing Address: PO Box 104
Uxbridge, ON L9P 1M6
905-852-0571
Fax: 905-852-0571
e-mail: nucaware@web.ca
Founded in: 1980
Hours: by appointment only
Acquisitions Budget: $25,000 - $49,999
Note: Hours vary, call for appointment
Subjects covered: Energy Issues, Nuclear Issues
Services:
Personnel: *Summary:* 2 Volunteer(s)
David H. Martin, Research Director

Vaughan: **Allergy/Asthma Information Association**
Information & Resource Centre
#1, 111 Zenway Blvd.
Vaughan, ON L4H 3H9
905-265-3322
Fax: 905-850-2070
800-611-7011
e-mail: admin@aaia.ca
URL: www.aaia.ca
Founded in: 1964
Hours: M-F 9:00-4:30
Note: Anaphylaxis reference kit
Special Collections: Wide range of allergy-related information letters, newsletter with information & tips; restaurant warning cards, allergy alert buttons, anaphylaxis education package.
Subjects covered: Allergy, Asthma, Anaphylaxis
Services:
Internet Access
Dorothy Drew, Librarian

Vineland: **Southern Crop Protection & Food Research Centre**
4902 Victoria Ave. North
Vineland, ON N5V 4T3
Mailing Address: PO Box 6000
London, ON N5V 4T3
905-568-4113 ext: 212
Fax: 905-562-4335
e-mail: lib-scpfrc@agr.gc.ca
URL: res2.agr.ca/london/index_e.htm
National Library Symbol: OLAG
Founded in: 1951
Subjects covered: Biochemistry, Entomology, Plant Diseases, Crop Pests, Pesticides
Services:
Inter-Library Loan (ILL)
Microform Equipment: Reader
Personnel:

Vineland Station: **Horticultural Research Institute of Ontario**
Library
Vineland Campus, University of Guelph, 4890 Victoria Ave. North
Vineland Station, ON L0R 2E0
Mailing Address: PO Box 7000
Vineland Station, ON L0R 2E0
905-562-4141
Fax: 905-562-3413
Founded in: 1970
Note: HRIO is part of the University of Guelph's Dept. of Plant Agriculture
Subjects covered: Horticulture; Floriculture; Viticulture; Mushroom Culture; Fruit & vegetable processing
Sheridan L. Alder, Librarian
alders@agr.gc.ca

Vineland Station: **Southern Crop Protection & Food Research Centre**
Canadian Agriculture Library
4902 Victoria Ave. North
Vineland Station, ON L0R 2E0
Mailing Address: PO Box 6000
Vineland Station, ON L0R 2E0
905-562-4113 ext: 212
Fax: 905-562-4335
e-mail: alders@agr.gc.ca
National Library Symbol: OVAGR
Hours: M-Th by appointment only
Acquisitions Budget: $25,000 - $49,999
Subjects covered: Plant Protection & Pathology, Entomology, Nematology
Services:
Inter-Library Loan (ILL)
Personnel: *Summary:* 1 Professional(s)
Mark Haslett, University Librarian
mhaslett@library.uwaterloo.ca

Waterloo: **Dana Porter Library**
200 University Ave. West
Waterloo, ON N2L 3G1
519-888-4567 ext: 32282
Fax: 519-888-4320
URL: www.lib.uwaterloo.ca
Hours: M-F 8:00am-11:00pm; Sa, Su 11:00-11:00
Subjects covered: Arts & Humanities, Social Sciences, Environmental Studies
Services:
Internet Access
Access to Subscription Databases
Inter-Library Loan (ILL)
Microform Equipment: Computer; Reader
Personnel:
Jennifer Haas, Department Head, Information Services & Resources, Davis Library
j2haas@library.uwaterloo.ca

Waterloo: **Davis Centre Library**
200 University Ave. West
Waterloo, ON N2L 3G1
519-888-4567 ext: 37469
Fax: 519-888-4311
URL: www.lib.uwaterloo.ca
Hours: M-F 8:00am-12:00am; Sa, Su 11:00am-12:00am
Subjects covered: Engineering, Mathematics, Applied Health Sciences, Sciences
Services:
Internet Access
Access to Subscription Databases
Inter-Library Loan (ILL)
Microform Equipment: Computer; Reader
Personnel:
Richard Hugh Pinnell, Manager, University Map Library & Branch Library Services
rhpinnell@library.uwaterloo.ca
519-888-4567 ext. 33412

Waterloo: **University Map Library**
Environmental Studies
#246, 200 University Ave. West
Waterloo, ON N2L 3G1
519-888-4311 ext: 32795
Fax: 519-888-4320
e-mail: rhpinnell@library.uwaterloo.ca
URL: www.lib.uwaterloo.ca/locations/umd/index.html
National Library Symbol: OWTU
Founded in: 1966
Hours: M-Th 8:30-7:00; F 8:30-4:30; Sa, Su 1:00-5:00
Subjects covered: Maps, Atlases, Aerial Photographs, Geospatial Data
Services:
Photocopying, Scanning, CD/DVD burning, Geospatial Data Service (Data Delivery & Instruction); Cartographic Reference; Circulation & Course Reserves; Library Instruction; ILL for maps
Personnel:

Waterloo: **University of Waterloo**
Administrative Offices
200 University Ave. West
Waterloo, ON N2L 3G1
519-888-4567 ext: 2282
Fax: 519-888-4320
Other contact info: ILL Fax: 519/888-4323
URL: www.lib.uwaterloo.ca/
National Library Symbol: OWTU
Consortia Membership: Canadian Research Knowledge Network (CRKN); Ontario Council of University Libraries (OCUL); TriUniversity Group of Libraries (TUG)
Founded in: 1957
Acquisitions Budget: $100,000 - $249,999
For Print: $100,000 - $249,999
For Electronic: $250,000 - $499,999
Population Served: 31000; Faculty, students + staff
Note: The University of Waterloo Library is in five locations: Dana Porter Library, Davis Centre Library, University Map Library, Musagetes Architecture Library & Optometry Learning Resource Centre. Online catalogue: Endeavor Voyager System
Services:
Remote Access
Internet Access
Access to Subscription Databases
Inter-Library Loan (ILL)
Microform Equipment: Computer; Reader
Personnel: *Summary:* 136 Total; 37 Professional(s); 2 Technical(s); 97 Other employees
Mark Haslett, University Librarian
mhaslett@library.uwaterloo.ca
519-888-4567 ext. 3568
Sharon Lamont, Director, Organizational Services
sljlamon@library.uwaterloo.ca
519-888-4567 ext. 33519
Allan Bell, Associate University Librarian, Information Technology Services
abell@library.uwaterloo.ca
519-888-4567 ext. 38215

Wish Leonard, Manager, Circulation Services, Resource Sharing
aleonard@library.uwaterloo.ca
519-888-4567 ext. 35430

Waterloo: Wilfrid Laurier University
Library
75 University Ave. West
Waterloo, ON N2L 3C5
519-884-0710 ext: 3246
Fax: 519-884-3209
e-mail: rmacneil@wlu.ca
URL: www.info.wlu.ca/academic/library.shtml
National Library Symbol: OWTL
Consortia Membership: Canadian Research Knowledge Network (CRKN); Ontario Council of University Libraries (OCUL); TriUniversity Group of Libraries (TUG)
Founded in: 1960
Hours: M-F 8:30am-10:00pm; Sa, Su 11:00-10:00
Acquisitions Budget: $1,000,000 plus
For Print: $1,000,000 plus
For Electronic: $1,000,000 plus
Population Served: 14000
Services:
Internet Access
Access to Subscription Databases
Inter-Library Loan (ILL)
Microform Equipment: Reader
Personnel: *Summary:* 54 Total; 15 Professional(s); 2 Technical(s); 37 Other employees
Sharon Brown, University Librarian
519-884-0710 ext. 3380
Diane Peters, Acting Head of Reference
dpeters@wlu.ca
519-884-0710 ext. 3419
Brooke Skelton, Head of Cataloguing
Joanne Oud, Collections & Acquisitions Dept. Head
joud@wlu.ca
519-884-0710 ext. 2073
Vera Fesnak, Head of Access Services
Linda Cracknell, Head, Acquisitions & Serials
Don Hamilton, Information Technology Manager
Joan Mitchell, Archives Librarian

Welland: Libraries of Niagara College
Learning Resource Centre
300 Woodlawn Rd.
Welland, ON L3C 7L3
905-735-2211
Fax: 905-736-6021
e-mail: skerr@niagaracollege.ca
URL: www.niagarac.on.ca
National Library Symbol: OWEN
Consortia Membership: Ontario Colleges Library Service
Founded in: 1967
Hours: M-F
Acquisitions Budget: $100,000 - $249,999
For Print: $50,000 - $99,999
For Electronic: $50,000 - $99,999
Population Served: 1050
Subjects covered: Health Studies, Applied Arts, Technology, Business, Community Services
Services:
Internet Access
Access to Subscription Databases
Inter-Library Loan (ILL)
Microform Equipment: Reader
Personnel: *Summary:* 10 Total; 2 Professional(s); 8 Technical(s)
Karen McGrath, Manager, Library Services
kmcgrath@niagaracollege.ca
905-735-2211 ext. 7799
Paul Murphy, Director
murphy6@uwindsor.ca
519-253-3000 ext. 2972
Annette Demers, Reference Librarian
ademers@uwindsor.ca
519-253-3000 ext. 2976

Windsor: Paul Martin Law Library
401 Sunset Ave.
Windsor, ON N9B 3P4
519-253-4232 ext: 2977
e-mail: lawill@uwindsor.ca
URL: www.uwindsor.ca/lawlibrary/
National Library Symbol: OWAL
Hours: M-Th 8:30am-11:50pm; F 8:30am-8:50pm; Sa 9:00-4:50; Su 1:00-11:50
Acquisitions Budget: $500,000 - $999,999
Subjects covered: Law
Services:
Inter-Library Loan (ILL)
Microform Equipment: Reader
Personnel: *Summary:* 11 Total; 2 Professional(s); 9 Technical(s)
Mae Carter, Reference Resource Clerk
carterm@windsor.ijc.org
519-257-6702

Windsor: Reference Resource Centre
100 Ouellette Ave., 8th Fl.
Windsor, ON N9A 6T3
519-257-6700
Fax: 519-257-6740
National Library Symbol: OWIJC
Hours: M-F 8:00-4:30
Subjects covered: Great Lakes environment
Services:
Personnel:

Windsor: St Clair College of Applied Arts & Technology
Library Resource Centre
2000 Talbot Rd. West
Windsor, ON N9A 6S4
519-972-2739
Fax: 519-972-2757
e-mail: library@stclaircollege.ca
gturnbull@stclaircollege.ca
URL: www.stclaircollege.ca
National Library Symbol: OWSC
Consortia Membership: Ontario Colleges Library Service
Founded in: 1967
Hours: Sept-April: M-Th 7:45am-10:00pm; F 7:45-6:00; Sa 9:00-5:00. May-Aug: M-Th 7:45am-9:00pm; F 7:45-4:30
Acquisitions Budget: $50,000 - $99,999
Services:
Internet Access
Access to Subscription Databases
Inter-Library Loan (ILL)
Personnel: *Summary:* 8 Total; 8 Technical(s)
Joan Oliver, Library Technician
joliver@stclairecollege.ca
519-972-2727 ext. 4692

Windsor: University of Windsor
Leddy Library
401 Sunset Ave.
Windsor
519-253-3000 ext: 3161
Fax: 519-971-3638
e-mail: gebbett@uwindsor.ca
URL: www.uwindsor.ca/library
Social Media: www.facebook.com/Leddy.Library
National Library Symbol: OWA
Consortia Membership: Canadian Research Knowledge Network (CRKN); Ontario Council of University Libraries (OCUL)
Founded in: 1960
Hours: M-Th 8:00am-2:00am, F 8:00am-11:00pm; Sa 10:00am-11:00pm; Su 10:00am-2:00am
Acquisitions Budget: $500,000 - $999,999
Population Served: Serves the university community & general public
Note: Systems Information: Endeavor; ILS: Voyager, ScholarsPortal; Member of Ontario Council of University Libraries Consortia (OCUL)
Special Collections: Material on Essex, Kent & Lambton County, Great Lakes
Subjects covered: Arts, Social Science, Humanities, Science, Engineering, Business, Education, Law
Services:
Remote Access
Internet Access
Access to Subscription Databases
Inter-Library Loan (ILL)
Microform Equipment: Reader
Personnel: *Summary:* 25 Professional(s); 52 Technical(s)
Gwendolyn Ebbett, University Librarian
gebbett@uwindsor.ca
519-253-3000 ext. 3161
Joan Dalton, Associate University Librarian
jdalton@uwindsor.ca
519-253-3000 ext. 3212
Cathy Maskell, Associate University Librarian
cmaskel@uwindsor.ca
519-253-3000 ext. 3206
Art Rhyno, Head, Systems Department
arhyno@uwindsor.ca
519-253-3000 ext. 3163
Peter Zimmerman, Head, Information Services Department
pzimmerman@uwindsor.ca
519-253-3000 ext. 3178

Windsor: Windsor Regional Hospital - Metropolitan Campus
Health Sciences Library
1995 Lens Ave.
Windsor, ON N8W 1L9
519-254-5577 ext: 52329
Fax: 519-985-2640
e-mail: library@wrh.on.ca
URL: www.wrh.on.ca
No public access
Hours: M-F 8:00-4:00
Services:
Personnel: *Summary:* 2 Total; 1 Professional(s)
Mary Ellen Bechard, Coordinator
Connie Tiltman, Library Technician
ctiltman@fanshawec.on.ca

Woodstock: Woodstock Campus
Resource Centre
369 Finkle St.
Woodstock, ON N4V 1A3
519-421-0144
Fax: 519-539-3870
e-mail: ctiltman@fanshawec.on.ca
Hours: M-F 8:30-4:30
Acquisitions Budget: $25,000 - $49,999
Subjects covered: Business, Computer, Nursing, Social Sciences
Services:
Inter-Library Loan (ILL)
Personnel: *Summary:* 1 Total; 1 Technical(s)

Prince Edward Island

Charlottetown: Holland College
Charlottetown Centre Library
140 Weymouth St.
Charlottetown, PE C1A 4Z1
902-566-9558
Fax: 902-566-9522
e-mail: library@hollandc.pe.ca
ill@hollandc.pe.ca
URL: www.hollandcollege.com/library
National Library Symbol: PCHC
Founded in: 1969
Hours: M,Tu,Th 8:30-7:00; W 8:30-9:00; F 8:30-5:00; Su 1:00-4:00
Acquisitions Budget: $25,000 - $49,999
Services:
Inter-Library Loan (ILL)
Microform Equipment: Reader
Personnel: *Summary:* 7 Total; 3 Professional(s); 4 Technical(s)
Patricia Doucette, Manager, Library Services
pmdoucette@hollandcollege.com
902-566-9558

Charlottetown: Prince Edward Island Dept. of Provincial Treasury
Provincial Map Library
11 Kent St.
Charlottetown, PE C1A 7N8
902-368-5133
Fax: 902-368-4399
Hours: M-F 8:30-5:00. Summer: M-F 8:00-4:00
Special Collections: Orthophotos
Subjects covered: Property mapping
Services:
Personnel:
Bill Burden, Librarian

Charlottetown: Prince Edward Island Food Technology Centre
Information Services
101 Belvedere Ave.
Charlottetown, PE C1A 7N8

Libraries & Resource Centres / Québec

Mailing Address: PO Box 2000
Charlottetown, PE C1A 7N8
902-368-5548
Fax: 902-368-5549
877-368-5548
e-mail: peiftc@gov.pe.ca
ftcweb@gov.pe.ca
URL: www.gov.pe.ca/ftc/
Founded in: 1987
Hours: M-F 8:30-4:00
Acquisitions Budget: $25,000 - $49,999
Subjects covered: Agriculture, Food, Technology, Food Research
Services:
Personnel: Summary: 2 Total; 2 Professional(s)
Kathy MacEwen, Information & Promotion Assistant
Jim Smith, Division Head, Technical Services/Research

Charlottetown: University of Prince Edward Island Robertson Library
550 University Ave.
Charlottetown, PE C1A 4P3
902-566-0343
Fax: 902-628-4305
e-mail: ill@upei.ca
URL: www.upei.ca/library/
National Library Symbol: PCU
Consortia Membership: Canadian Research Knowledge Network (CRKN); Council of Atlantic University Libraries (CAUL)
Founded in: 1969
Hours: M-Th 8:00am-11:00pm; F 8:00-6:00; Sa 9:00-10:00; Su 9:00-10:00
Acquisitions Budget: $500,000 - $999,999
Note: Provides all library services for the Atlantic Veterinary College.
Special Collections: Prince Edward Island Collection
Subjects covered: Humanities, Social Sciences, Science, Veterinary Medicine, Nursing, Education
Services:
Remote Access
Internet Access
Inter-Library Loan (ILL) for a fee of varies
Microform Equipment: Computer; Reader
Personnel: Summary: 26 Total; 7 Professional(s); 17 Technical(s); 2 Other employees
Mark Leggott, University Librarian
902-566-0460
Cathy Callaghan, Information Services Librarian
ccallaghan@upei.ca
506-566-0681

Québec

Alma: Collège d'Alma Bibliothèque
675, boul Auger ouest
Alma, QC G8B 2B7
418-668-2387 ext: 225
Téléc: 418-668-3806
Courriel: jtrepanier@calma.qc.ca
cpret@calma.qc.ca
URL: www.calma.qc.ca
Sigle: QALC
Membre d'un consortium: Réseau des services documentaires collégiaux (Resdoc)
Fondée en: 1971
Heures: L-J, 8h15-21h30; V 8h30-16h15; Été: L-J, 8h30-12h00, 13h00-16h00; V 8h30-12h00
Budget d'acquisitions: $25,000 - $49,999
Sujets: Sciences humaines, musique, art et lettres, agriculture
Services:
Accès public à l'internet
Prêts entre bibliothèques(PEB)
Lecteur/reproduction de microformes: Ordinateur; Lecteurs
Personnel: Sommaire: 3 Total; 1 Professionnel(s); 2 Technicien(s); 2 Autre(s) employé(s);
Janic Trépanier, SMTE - Responsable
jtrepanier@calma.qc.ca
418-668-2387 ext. 225
Nicole DuPerré, Technicienne en documentation

Baie-Comeau: CÉGEP de Baie-Comeau Centre des ressources éducatives
537, boul Blanche
Baie-Comeau, QC G5C 2B2
418-589-5707 ext: 325
Téléc: 418-589-9842
800-463-2030
Courriel: biblio@cegep-baie-comeau.qc.ca
URL: www.cegep-baie-comeau.qc.ca/services-offerts.html
Sigle: QHAC
Membre d'un consortium: Réseau des services documentaires collégiaux (Resdoc)
Fondée en: 1959
Heures: L-J 8h15-18h; V 8h15-16h
Budget d'acquisitions: $10,000 - $24,999
Collections spécialisées: Faune et flore, éducation specialisée
Services:
Accès public à l'internet
Réseau en ligne
Prêts entre bibliothèques(PEB)
Lecteur/reproduction de microformes: Ordinateur; Lecteurs
Personnel: Sommaire: 2 Total; 2 Technicien(s); 3 Autre(s) employé(s)
Danielle Boudreault, Technicienne en documentation
Mélanie C. Foster, Technicienne en documentation
Patrice Dupont, Information Specialist
Brigitte Paradis, Client Services Officer

Boucherville: NRC Information Centre / Centre d'information du CNRC
75, boul de Mortagne
Boucherville, QC J4B 6Y4
450-641-5132
Fax: 450-641-5133
e-mail: brigitte.paradis@nrc-cnrc.gc.ca
lynn_belanger@nrc-cnrc.gc.ca
URL: cisti-icist.nrc-cnrc.gc.ca/nis/boucherville_e.html
National Library Symbol: QBOG
Founded in: 1979
Hours: M-F 8:00-4:00 (only with appointments) by appointment only
Acquisitions Budget: $50,000 - $99,999
For Print: $10,000 - $24,999
For Electronic: $50,000 - $99,999
Population Served: 280
Subjects covered: Plastics, Metals, Ceramics, Instrumentation
Services:
Internet Access
Personnel: Summary: 6 Total; 5 Professional(s); 1 Technical(s); 1 Volunteer(s)

Brossard: Gazoduc Trans Québec & Maritimes Inc. Centre de documentation
525, 6300, av Auteuil
Brossard, QC J4Z 3P2
450-462-5300
Téléc: 450-462-5388
888-810-8800
Courriel: cdion@gazoductqm.com
Sigle: QMTQM
Fondée en: 1980
Heures: avec rendez-vous seulement
Budget d'acquisitions: $25,000 - $49,999
Sujets: Gaz naturel, énergie, environnement
Services:
Prêts entre bibliothèques(PEB)
Lecteur/reproduction de microformes: Lecteurs
Personnel:
Chantale Dion, Documentaliste
cdion@gazoductqm.com
450-462-5335

Cap-de-la-Madeleine: René Gervais Inc., Consultants Library
303, rue Dessureault
Cap-de-la-Madeleine, QC G8T 2L8
819-371-3313
Téléc: 819-371-2288
Sujets: Ingénierie
Services:
Personnel:
Réjean Blais, Technical Director
Madeleine Tremblay, Documentaliste
mtremblay@cgaspesie.qc.ca
Diane Leblanc, Agente de bureau
dleblanc@cgaspesie.qc.ca

Carleton: Centre des études collégiales - Carleton
776, boul Perron
Carleton, QC G0C 1J0
418-364-3341 ext: 228
Téléc: 418-364-7938
Courriel: mtremblay@cgaspesie.qc.ca
Membre d'un consortium: Réseau des services documentaires collégiaux (Resdoc)
Fondée en: 1989
Heures: L-V 8h-16h45
Budget d'acquisitions: Matériel imprimé: $10,000 - $24,999
Matériel électronique: $100,000 - $249,999
Population desservie: 350
Sujets: Éducation collégiale
Services:
Accès distance aux bases de donn
Accès public à l'internet
Réseau en ligne
Prêts entre bibliothèques(PEB) frais de 2$
Frais de recherche
Lecteur/reproduction de microformes: Lecteurs
Personnel: Sommaire: 3 Total; 1 Technicien(s); 2 Autre(s) employé(s);

Chicoutimi: CÉGEP de Chicoutimi Centre des médias
534, rue Jacques-Cartier est
Chicoutimi, QC G7H 1Z6
418-549-9520 ext: 337
Téléc: 418-549-1315
Courriel: gcusson@cegep-chicoutimi.qc.ca
lgaudrea@cegep-chicoutimi.qc.ca
Membre d'un consortium: Réseau des services documentaires collégiaux (Resdoc)
Fondée en: 1968
Heures: L-J 8h-21h; V 8h-16h
Budget d'acquisitions: $50,000 - $99,999
Sujets: Arts, humanités, pilotage, techniques de la santé
Services:
Accès distance aux bases de donn
Accès public à l'internet
Prêts entre bibliothèques(PEB) frais
Lecteur/reproduction de microformes: Lecteurs
Personnel: Sommaire: 13 Total; 2 Professionnel(s); 3 Technicien(s); 5 Autre(s) employé(s)
Gilles Cusson, Coordonnateur
Louis Gaudreau, Responsable, Référence
418-549-9520 ext. 345
Céline Roussel, Responsable, Services techniques
croussel@cegep-chicoutimi.qc.ca
Clothilde Brillant, Responsable, Acquisitions
418-549-9520 ext. 342

Chicoutimi: Université du Québec à Chicoutimi Bibliothèque Paul-Emile Boulet
555, boul de l'Université
Chicoutimi, QC G7H 2B1
418-545-5011 ext: 5630
Téléc: 418-693-5896
Courriel: gilles_carron@uqac.ca
peb.uqac@uqac.ca
URL: bibliotheque.uqac.ca
Sigle: QCU
Membre d'un consortium: Canadian Research Knowledge Network (CRKN); Conférence des recteurs et des principaux des universités du Québec (CREPUQ)
Fondée en: 1969
Heures: L-J 8h-22h30; V 8h-21h; Sa 9h-17h; D 12h-17h
Budget d'acquisitions: $500,000 - $999,999
Collections spécialisées: Génétique des populations; études régionales et moyen-nord
Sujets: Éducation, arts, sciences humaines, histoire, économie, sciences physiques, littérature, sciences sociales, sciences économiques, administration, sciences pures
Services:
Accès public à l'internet
Prêts entre bibliothèques(PEB)
Lecteur/reproduction de microformes: Ordinateur; Lecteurs
Personnel: Sommaire: 37 Total; 9 Professionnel(s); 12 Technicien(s); 16 Autre(s) employé(s)
Gilles Caron, Directeur
gcaron@uqac.ca
418-545-5011 ext. 5631
Laïla Ferris, Responsable, Information et gestion documentaire
Guy Tremblay, Responsable, Informatique
418-454-5011 ext. 2302

Chomedey: Boehringer Ingelheim (Canada) Ltd.
Library
2100, rue Cunard
Chomedey, QC H7S 2G5
450-682-4640 ext: 210
Fax: 450-682-4939
e-mail: shonsinger@lav.boehringer-ingelheim.com
info@lav.boehringer-ingelheim.com
National Library Symbol: QMBIM
No public access
Founded in: 1984
Acquisitions Budget: $25,000 - $49,999
For Print: $25,000 - $49,999
Subjects covered: Virologie
Services:
Inter-Library Loan (ILL)
Personnel: *Summary:* 3 Total; 2 Professional(s); 1 Technical(s)
Sandra Honsinger, Library Technician
Hélène Gagnon, Specialist, Scientific Information
Christine Martens, Specialist, Scientific Information

Contrecoeur: Ispat Sidbec inc.
Centre de documentation
4000, route des Aciéries
Contrecoeur, QC J0L 1C0
Adresse postale: 3900, route des Aciéries
Contrecoeur, QC J0L 1C0
450-392-3258
Téléc: 450-392-3222
Fermée au public
Heures: L-V 8h15-16h30
Sujets: Environnement
Services:
Personnel:
Sylvie Duhamel, Secrétaire du service
514-392-3258

Dorval: Canadian Meteorological Centre
Library
#500, 2121, rte Transcanadienne
Dorval, QC H9P 1J3
514-421-4754
Fax: 514-421-2106
Other contact info: 514-421-4758
e-mail: maryse.ferland@ec.gc.ca
URL: www.ec.gc.ca/library
National Library Symbol: QMEA
No public access
Services:
Fee Based Research

Drummondville: CÉGEP de Drummondville
Bibliothèque
960, rue St-Georges
Drummondville, QC J2C 6A2
819-478-4671
Téléc: 819-474-6859
Couriel: dionh@cdrummond.qc.ca
URL: www.cdrummond.qc.ca
Sigle: QDCE
Membre d'un consortium: Réseau des services documentaires collégiaux (Resdoc)
Fondée en: 1969
Heures: L-Me 8h-21h; J 8h-19h; V 1h-17h; Sa 12h-16h
Budget d'acquisitions: $25,000 - $49,999
Sujets: Arts, lettres et langues, sciences humaines, éducation physique, mathématiques, philosophie, sciences de la nature, techniques professionnelles: technologie de l'estimation et de l'évaluation immobilière, techniques administratives, musique, technologie musicale, techniques de bureau, électrotechnique, techniques de l'informatique, soins infirmiers, génie mécanique
Services:
Accès public à l'internet
Prêts entre bibliothèques(PEB)
Personnel: *Sommaire:* 13 Total; 1 Professionnel(s); 4 Technicien(s); 4 Autre(s) employé(s)
Mylène Lavoie, Conseillère pédagogique en bibliothéconomie
lavoiem@cdrummond.qc.ca
819-478-4671 ext. 278
Johanne Boisvert, Acquisitions
boisverj@cdrummond.qc.ca
819-478-4671 ext. 279
Nicole Landry, Responsable, Services techniques et de consultation
landryn@cdrummond.qc.ca
819-478-4671 ext. 281

Lucille Gagnon, Ateliers de production
gagnonl@cdrummond.qc.ca
819-478-4671 ext. 329
Françoise Desrosiers, Périodiques et service de consultation
desrosif@cdrummond.qc.ca
819-478-4671 ext. 280
Denise Boulay, Resp., Prêt et des équipements audiovisuels
boulayd@cdrummond.qc.ca
819-478-4671 ext. 277
Rachelle Leblanc, Responsable, Audiovidéothèque
leblancr@cdrummond.qc.ca
819-478-4671 ext. 276
Pauline Bonin, Secrétaire
boninp@cdrummond.qc.ca
819-478-4671 ext. 276
Lionel Boudreau, Responsable, bibliothèque
lboudreau@cgaspesie.qc.ca
418-986-5187 ext. 6233
Isabelle Vigneau, Agente de bureau
ivigneau@cgaspesie.qc.ca
418-986-5187

L'Étang-du-Nord: Centre des Iles
Bibliothèque
15, ch de la Piscine
L'Étang-du-Nord, QC G4T 3X4
418-986-5187
Téléc: 418-986-6788
Couriel: lboudreau@cgaspesie.qc.ca
Sigle: QIMC
Membre d'un consortium: Réseau des services documentaires collégiaux (Resdoc)
Heures: L-V 8h-17h
Budget d'acquisitions: $10,000 - $24,999
Matériel imprimé: $10,000 - $24,999
Matériel électronique: 0-$9,999
Population desservie: 2000
Services:
Accès public à l'internet
Réseau en ligne
Prêts entre bibliothèques(PEB)
Personnel: *Sommaire:* 2 Total; 1 Technicien(s); 1 Autre(s) employé(s)
Paul Carrier, Responsable, Référence
418-368-7615
Jocelyne Fournier, Prêt et acquisitions
Ghislain Chapados, Responsable, Prêt et Photocopie

Gaspé: Pêches et aquaculture commerciales
Centre de documentation
#205, 96, montée Sandy Beach
Gaspé, QC G0C 1R0
Adresse postale: CP 1070
Gaspé, QC G0C 1R0
418-368-7618
Téléc: 418-360-8211
Couriel: gaspedoc@mapaq.gouv.qc.ca
Sigle: QGAP
Fondée en: 1951
Heures: L-V 8h30-12h, 13h-16h30
Budget d'acquisitions: $25,000 - $49,999
Sujets: Pêche commerciale, biologie poisson, transformation et mise en marché, développement de nouveau produits, aquaculture
Services:
Accès public à l'internet
Prêts entre bibliothèques(PEB)
Lecteur/reproduction de microformes: Ordinateur; Lecteurs
Personnel: *Sommaire:* 3 Total; 1 Professionnel(s); 1 Technicien(s); 5 Autre(s) employé(s)

Gatineau: Canadian Heritage / Patrimoine Canadien
Research Services Knowledge Centre
#15-2-B, 15 Eddy St., 2nd Fl.
Gatineau, QC K1A 0M5
819-953-0527
Fax: 819-953-7988
e-mail: lib-bib@pch.gc.ca
URL: www.pch.gc.ca
National Library Symbol: OOSS
Consortia Membership: Council of Federal Libraries (CFL) Consortium
Founded in: 1993
Hours: M-F 8:00-4:30 by appointment only
Acquisitions Budget: $100,000 - $249,999
Subjects covered: Cultural industries & institutions; Arts;

Multiculturalism; Active citizenship & civic participation; Canadian identity; Official languages; Amateur sport; National parks; Canadian history & historical sites; Canadian content; Culture online
Services:
Internet Access
Access to Subscription Databases
Inter-Library Loan (ILL)
Reference; Research; Borrowing; Accessible technology for the disabled; Multimedia services; Training & conference facilities
Microform Equipment: Computer; Reader
Personnel: *Summary:* 8 Total; 7 Professional(s); 1 Technical(s)
Eric Wees, Acting Director
eric.wees@pch.gc.ca
819-994-6007
Finbarr Healy, Reference Librarian
finbarr.healy@pch.gc.ca
819-953-6978
Nathalie Côté, Client Service and Circulation Representative
819-995-3495
André Lalonde, Interlibrary Loans Technician
andre.lalonde@pch.gc.ca
819-997-5467
Jacques Brodeur, Team Lead, Cataloguing and Library System Administration
jacques_brodeur@pch.gc.ca
819-994-5915
Sue-Ann Woo, Cataloguer & Library System Administrator
sue-ann_woo@pch.gc.ca
819-994-3702
Michelle Ryan, Team Lead, Library Client Services
michelle.ryan@pch.gc.ca
819-953-7738

Gatineau: Canadian Transportation Agency / Office des transports du Canada
Library
15 Eddy St.
Gatineau, QC K1A 0N9
819-997-7160
Fax: 819-953-9815
888-222-2592
e-mail: cta.library@cta-otc.gc.ca
National Library Symbol: OOTT
Hours: M-F 9:00-4:00 by appointment only
Acquisitions Budget: $50,000 - $99,999
Subjects covered: Transportation, Legal
Services:
Inter-Library Loan (ILL)
Personnel: *Summary:* 2 Total; 1 Professional(s); 1 Technical(s)
Alison Hale, Librarian, Library Services
819-953-0482

Gatineau: Centre hospitalier des Vallées de l'Outaouais Hôpital de Hull
Bibliothèque
116, boul Lionel-Emond
Gatineau, QC J8Y 1W7
819-595-6050
Téléc: 819-595-6098
Couriel: Dianne_Couture@ssss.gouv.qc.ca
Sigle: QHSC
Heures: L-V 8h-16h
Sujets: Médecine
Services:
Prêts entre bibliothèques(PEB)
Personnel: *Sommaire:* 1 Technicien(s)
Dianne Couture, Bibliotechnicienne
Diane_Couture@ssss.gouv.qc.ca

Gatineau: Environment Canada / Environnement Canada
Departmental Library/Bibliothèque du ministère
Place Vincent Massey
351 St Joseph Blvd., 2nd Fl.
Gatineau, QC K1A 0H3
Mailing Address: 351 St Joseph Blvd., 2nd Fl.
Gatineau, QC K1A 0H3
819-997-1767
Fax: 819-997-5349
e-mail: biblio@ec.gc.ca
librarypvm@ec.gc.ca
URL: www.ec.gc.ca/library
National Library Symbol: OOFF
Consortia Membership: Council of Federal Libraries (CFL) Consortium

Libraries & Resource Centres / Québec

Founded in: 1973
Hours: M-F 8:30-4:30
Note: Microform facilites
Subjects covered: Global Warming, Biodiversity, Chemicals of Environmental Concern, Conservation, Sustainable Development, Pollution, Ozone Depletion, Water Resources, Pollution Prevention, Wildlife Management, Environmental Impact Analysis, Climatology & Meteorology
Services:
Internet Access
Inter-Library Loan (ILL)
Personnel: *Summary:* 11 Total; 4 Professional(s); 3 Technical(s); 2 Other employees
Julia McIntosh, Chief, Departmental Library
julia.mcintosh@ec.gc.ca
819-953-1373

Gatineau: **Heritage College / Collège Héritage Library**
325, boul Cité des Jeunes
Gatineau, QC J8Y 6T3
819-778-2270 ext: 1470
Fax: 819-778-7364
e-mail: libraryservices@cegep-heritage.qc.ca
URL: www.cegep-heritage.qc.ca
National Library Symbol: QHCH
Founded in: 1972
Hours: M-Th 7:45-5:00; F 7:45-4:30
Acquisitions Budget: $25,000 - $49,999
For Print: $25,000 - $49,999
For Electronic: $10,000 - $24,999
Population Served: 1000
Subjects covered: General Academic, Nursing, Computer Science, Early Childhood
Services:
Remote Access
Internet Access
Access to Subscription Databases
Inter-Library Loan (ILL)
Microform Equipment: Computer; Reader
Personnel: *Summary:* 4 Total; 1 Professional(s); 2 Technical(s); 2 Other employees
Natalie Meggison, Librarian
nmeggison@cegep-heritage.qc.ca
819-778-2270 ext. 1570
Marthe Francoeur, Bibliothécaire
mfrancoeur@cegepoutaouais.qc.ca

Gatineau: **Pavillon Félix-Leclerc**
820, boul La Gappe
Gatineau, QC J8T 7T7
819-770-4012
Téléc: 819-243-9007
Fermée au public
Budget d'acquisitions: Matériel imprimé: $100,000 - $249,999
Services:
Personnel: *Sommaire:* 1 Professionnel(s); 1 Technicien(s); 1 Autre(s) employé(s)

Gatineau: **Public Works & Government Services Canada / Travaux Publics et Services Gouvernmentaux Canada**
Departmental Library/Bibliothèque du ministère
#1B2, Place du Portage, Phase 3, 11 Laurier St.
Gatineau, QC K1A 0S5
819-956-3460
Fax: 819-997-8909
e-mail: biblio@tpsgc-pwgsc.gc.ca
National Library Symbol: OODP
Consortia Membership: Federal Libraries (CFL) Consortium
Founded in: 1962
Hours: M-F 8:00-4:00
Acquisitions Budget: For Print: $50,000 - $99,999
For Electronic: $25,000 - $49,999
Population Served: 14000
Note: Tupper branch library (OOPN) is now merged with this library (OODP).
Special Collections: Statistics Canada publications
Subjects covered: Economics; Industry; Business; Finance; Banking Industry; Accounting; Data Processing Procurement; Management Finance; Public Administration; Civil, Mechanical & Electrical Engineering; Architecture & Design; Real & Property Management; Urban Planning & Design, Computer Science
Services:
Remote Access
Inter-Library Loan (ILL)
Personnel: *Summary:* 9 Total; 3 Professional(s); 6 Technical(s)
Henne Kahwa, Manager, Library Services
henne.kahwa@pwgsc.gc.ca
819-956-3461
Minda Bojin, Chief, Metadata & Cataloguing Services
minda.bojin@pwgsc.gc.ca
819-956-7774
Eileen Lim, Chief, Client Services
eileen.lim@pwgsc.gc.ca
819-956-3464
Sylvette Seguin-Forget, Chief, Purchasing, Administration & Systems
sylvette.seguin-forget@pwgsc.gc.ca
819-956-3462

Granby: **CÉGEP de Granby**
Bibliothèque
235, rue Saint-Jacques
Granby, QC J2G 9H7
Adresse postale: CP 7000
Granby, QC J2G 9H7
450-372-6614 ext: 1205
Téléc: 450-372-6565
Courriel: dmarquis@cegepgranby.qc.ca
URL: www.cegepgranby.qc.ca/biblio/index.html
Membre d'un consortium: Réseau des services documentaires collégiaux (Resdoc)
Fondée en: 1966
Heures: L-J 7h45-17h30; V 7h45-16h15. Salle McLuhan: L-V 7h45-22h; S, D 8h-16h
Sujets: Arts et lettres, sciences humaines, culture, médecine, soins infirmiers, sciences de la santé, sciences pures, tourisme, production manufacturière, électronique industrielle, tech. administratives, bureautique, informatique
Services:
Accès public à l'internet
Prêts entre bibliothèques(PEB)
Lecteur/reproduction de microformes: Ordinateur; Lecteurs
Personnel:
Daniel Marquis, Bibliothécaire professionnel
Joanne Deschamps, Technicienne en documentation
Gilles Bernatchez, Technicien en documentation
gbernatchez@cgaspesie.qc.ca
418-385-2241 ext. 111

Grande-Rivière: **Centre spécialisé des Pêches - Grande-Rivière**
Bibliothèque
167, Grande Allée ouest
Grande-Rivière, QC G0C 1V0
Adresse postale: CP 220
Grande-Rivière, QC G0C 1V0
418-385-2241
Téléc: 418-385-2888
Courriel: gbernatchez@cgaspesie.qc.ca
URL: doc.cspeches.qc.ca/regard
Sigle: QGCSP
Membre d'un consortium: Réseau des services documentaires collégiaux (Resdoc)
Heures: L-V 8h15-16h30
Budget d'acquisitions: $25,000 - $49,999
Sujets: Pêche maritime, aquaculture, transformation produits marins, navigation maritime
Services:
Accès public à l'internet
Prêts entre bibliothèques(PEB)
Frais de recherche
Lecteur/reproduction de microformes: Lecteurs
Personnel:

Joliette: **CÉGEP Régional de Lanaudière à Joliette**
Bibliothèque
20, rue St-Charles
Joliette, QC J6E 4T1
450-759-1661
Téléc: 450-759-7120
Courriel: biblio@collanaud.qc.ca
URL: www.collanaud.qc.ca/Bibliotheque/
Membre d'un consortium: Réseau des services documentaires collégiaux (Resdoc)
Heures: L-V
Budget d'acquisitions: $50,000 - $99,999
Services:
Accès public à l'internet frais de 30$/an
Réseau en ligne
Prêts entre bibliothèques(PEB)
Personnel: *Sommaire:* 4 Total; 1 Professionnel(s); 3 Autre(s) employé(s)
Pierre-Marcel Brûlé, Coordonnateur

Jonquière: **Alcan International Ltée. / Alcan International Ltd**
Centre d'information technique
1955, boul Mellon
Jonquière, QC G7S 4K8
Adresse postale: CP 1250
Jonquière, QC G7S 4K8
418-699-6585 ext: 3800
Courriel: diane.mongrain@alcan.com
Sigle: QAA
Fermée au public
Fondée en: 1946
Budget d'acquisitions: $50,000 - $99,999
Sujets: Industrie de l'aluminium
Services:
Accès public à l'internet
Prêts entre bibliothèques(PEB)
Personnel: *Sommaire:* 3 Total; 1 Professionnel(s); 2 Technicien(s)
Diane Mongrain, Responsable du centre d'information
diane.mongrain@alcan.com

Jonquière: **CÉGEP de Jonquière**
Centre des ressources éducatives (diffusion)
2505, rue St-Hubert
Jonquière, QC G7X 7W2
418-547-2191 ext: 266
Téléc: 418-547-0917
Courriel: biblio@cjonquiere.qc.ca
URL: www.cjonquiere.qc.ca/cegep_jonquiere/
Membre d'un consortium: Réseau des services documentaires collégiaux (Resdoc)
Fondée en: 1967
Heures: L-J 8h-21h; V 8h-17h; S 13h-17h
Budget d'acquisitions: $100,000 - $249,999
Matériel imprimé: $100,000 - $249,999
Matériel électronique: $10,000 - $24,999
Collections spécialisées: Bibliothèque de la Pléiade, livres anciens
Sujets: Arts et lettres, sciences humaines, sciences administratives, sciences
Services:
Accès public à l'internet
Prêts entre bibliothèques(PEB)
Lecteur/reproduction de microformes: Ordinateur; Lecteurs
Personnel: *Sommaire:* 14 Total; 1 Professionnel(s); 5 Technicien(s); 7 Autre(s) employé(s)
Jean-Pierre Dufour, Adjoint à la direction des études
Hélène Jeannotte, Conseillère pédagogique et bibiothécaire
Line Kenny, Technicienne en documentation, prêt
Armande Dery, Technicienne en documentation, documents audio-visuals
Fabienne Simard, Technicienne en documentation, publications sériées
Nancy Compartino, Technicienne en documentation, traitement documentaire
Gervaise Aubin, Technicienne en documentation, prêt, référence, traitement documenta

Kirkland: **Merck Frosst Canada Inc.**
Research Library
16711 Transcanada Hwy.
Kirkland, QC H9H 3L1
514-428-3323
Fax: 514-428-8535
URL: www.merckfrosst.ca
National Library Symbol: QMCF
Founded in: 1937
Hours: by appointment only
Acquisitions Budget: $500,000 - $999,999
Note: Access by appointment based on need to access.
Subjects covered: Medicine, Pharmacy, Pharmacology, Biology, Genetics, Chemistry, Molecular Biology, Biochemistry, Microbiology
Services:
Inter-Library Loan (ILL)
Document delivery, Reference
Microform Equipment: Computer; Reader
Personnel: *Summary:* 7 Total; 7 Other employees
Josée Schepper, Manager
Mary-Lynn Gaal, Head, Reference
Susan Bowen, Head, Technical Services

Kirkland: **Pfizer Canada, Inc.**
Library & Information Services
17300 Transcanada Hwy.
Kirkland, QC H9J 2M5
514-693-4159
Fax: 514-426-7558
e-mail: sharon.pipon@pfizer.com
URL: www.pfizer.ca
National Library Symbol: QKPC
No public access
Founded in: 1980
Hours: M-F 8:00-5:00
Acquisitions Budget: $50,000 - $99,999
Subjects covered: Medicine, Nursing, Health Sciences, Pharmacology, Biomedicine
Services:
Personnel: *Summary:* 2 Professional(s); 1 Technical(s)
Sharon Pipon, Manager
sharon.pipon@pfizer.com
514-693-4159

Lasalle: **CÉGEP d'André-Laurendeau**
Bibliothèque
1111, rue Lapierre
Lasalle, QC H8N 2J4
514-364-3320 ext. 147
Téléc: 514-364-2627
Courriel: bibliotheque@claurendeau.qc.ca
lcorby@claurendeau.qc.ca
URL: www.claurendeau.qc.ca
Sigle: QLSC
Membre d'un consortium: Réseau des services documentaires collégiaux (Resdoc)
Heures: L-J 7h30-20h; V 7h30-17h
Budget d'acquisitions: $50,000 - $99,999
Services:
Accès public à l'internet
Prêts entre bibliothèques(PEB)
Personnel: *Sommaire:* 7 Total; 1 Professionnel(s); 3 Technicien(s); 3 Autre(s) employé(s)
Dianne Rochon, Responsable
dronchon@claurendeau.qc.ca
514-364-3320 ext. 158
Yves Juillet, Technicien en documentation
514-364-3320 ext. 147
Lisette Julien, Technicienne en documentation
ljuilen@claurendeau.qc.ca
514-364-3320 ext. 144
Danielle Messicotte, Technicienne en documentation
dmessicotte@claurendeau.qc.ca
514-364-3320 ext. 147
Robert Gauthier, Analyste
rgauthier@claurendeau.qc.ca
514-364-3320 ext. 122

Laval: **Centre de santé et de services sociaux de Laval**
Centre de documentation
1755, boul René-Laënnec
Laval, QC H7M 3L9
450-975-5493
Téléc: 450-975-5572
Courriel: llabelle.csssl@ssss.gouv.qc.ca
URL: www.cssslaval.qc.ca
Sigle: QLACS
Fondée en: 1979
Heures: L-V
Budget d'acquisitions: $25,000 - $49,999
Annotation: Membre de l'Association des Bibliothèques de la Santé affiliées à l'Université de Montréal (ABSAUM)
Sujets: Sciences de la santé
Services:
Prêts entre bibliothèques(PEB)
Personnel: *Sommaire:* 2 Total; 1 Professionnel(s); 1 Technicien(s)
France Pontbriand, Bibliothécaire
france_pontbriand@ssss.gouv.qc.ca
450-668-1010 ext. 2223

Laval: **Collège Montmorency**
Centre des ressources didactiques
475, boul de l'Avenir
Laval, QC H7N 5H9
450-975-6100
Téléc: 450-975-6496
Courriel: plavigueur@cmontmorency.qc.ca
jchoquette@cmontmorency.qc.ca
URL: biblio.cmontmorency.qc.ca
Membre d'un consortium: Réseau des services documentaires collégiaux (Resdoc)
Fondée en: 1969
Heures: L-J 8h-21h; V 8h-18h
Budget d'acquisitions: $100,000 - $249,999
Collections spécialisées: Informatique, électronique
Sujets: Éducation, architecture, soins infirmiers, réadaptation, muséologie, tourisme
Services:
Accèss distance aux bases de donn
Prêts entre bibliothèques(PEB) frais
Lecteur/reproduction de microformes: Lecteurs
Personnel: *Sommaire:* 8 Total; 1 Professionnel(s); 6 Technicien(s); 1 Autre(s) employé(s)
Philippe Lavigueur, Responsable, Référence
plavigueur@cmontmorency.qc.ca

Laval: **Université du Québec INRS - Institut Armand-Frappier**
Bibliothèque
531, boul des Prairies Laval-des-Rapides
Laval, QC H7V 1B7
450-687-5010 ext: 4265
Téléc: 450-686-5501
Courriel: prets-entre-biblio@inrs-iaf.uquebec.ca
Sigle: QMIM
Heures: L-V 9h-17havec rendez-vous seulement
Budget d'acquisitions: $250,000 - $499,999
Sujets: Microbiologie, virologie, epidémiologie, immunologie, médecine comparée, sciences alimentaires
Services:
Accès public à l'internet
Réseau en ligne
Prêts entre bibliothèques(PEB) frais
Frais de recherche
Personnel: *Sommaire:* 3 Total; 1 Professionnel(s); 1 Technicien(s); 1 Autre(s) employé(s)
Sophie Renaud, Directrice
Diane Sauvé, Bibliothécaire

Lévis: **CÉGEP de Lévis-Lauzon**
Services des ressources didactiques
205, rue Mgr Bourget
Lévis, QC G6V 6Z9
418-833-5110
Téléc: 418-833-7323
Courriel: paule.drouin@clevislauzon.qc.ca
sylvie.dube@clevislauzon.qc.ca
URL: www.clevislauzon.qc.ca/biblio/bibliotheque.php
Membre d'un consortium: Réseau des services documentaires collégiaux (Resdoc)
Fondée en: 1969
Heures: L-J 7h45-21h; V 7h45-18h; Sa 10h-16havec rendez-vous seulement
Budget d'acquisitions: Matériel imprimé: $100,000 - $249,999
Matériel électronique: 0-$9,999
Population desservie: 3500
Sujets: Sciences, électronique, biotechnologie, technologie, soins infirmiers, arts
Services:
Accès public à l'internet
Prêts entre bibliothèques(PEB) frais
Lecteur/reproduction de microformes: Lecteurs
Personnel: *Sommaire:* 9 Total; 1 Professionnel(s); 5 Technicien(s); 3 Autre(s) employé(s)
Paule Drouin, SMTE-Bibliothécaire
paule.drouin@clevislauzon.qc.ca
418-833-5110 ext. 3404
Sylvie Dubé, Référence-PEB
sylvie.dube@clevislauzon.qc.ca
418-833-5110 ext. 3409

Longueuil: **Collège Édouard-Montpetit**
Centre des ressources documentaires
945, ch de Chambly
Longueuil, QC J4H 3M6
450-679-2631 ext: 466
Téléc: 450-677-2945
louis-marie.dussault@college.em.qc.ca
URL: www2.college-em.qc.ca/biblio/
Fondée en: 1967
Heures: L-J 8h-20h; V 8h-16h30; S 9h-13h. Modification de cet horaire entre les sessions
Budget d'acquisitions: $50,000 - $99,999
Matériel imprimé: $50,000 - $99,999
Matériel électronique: $10,000 - $24,999
Population desservie: 13000
Collections spécialisées: Dentisterie, électrotechnique, optique, aérotechnique
Sujets: Santé, sciences sociales, techniques physiques, aérotechnique, sciences humaines, cinéma
Services:
Accès public à l'internet
Réseau en ligne
Prêts entre bibliothèques(PEB) frais de 10$
Lecteur/reproduction de microformes: Lecteurs
Personnel: *Sommaire:* 17 Total; 2 Professionnel(s); 6 Technicien(s); 9 Autre(s) employé(s)
Louis-Marie Dussault, Adjoint à la directrice
louis-marie.dussault@college-em.qc.ca
450-679-2631
Michelle Chartier, Responsable, services techniques
michelle.chartier@college-em.qc.ca
450-679-2631 ext. 609

Longueuil: **Pratt & Whitney Canada Inc.**
Engineering Information Services
1000, boul Marie Victorin
Longueuil, QC J4G 1A1
450-677-9411 ext: 2607
Fax: 450-647-9469
e-mail: lysane.st-amour@pwc.ca
URL: www.pwc.ca
National Library Symbol: QLOU
No public access
Founded in: 1958
Hours: M-F 8:00-4:30
Subjects covered: Technology, Engineering, Aeronautics, Metals
Services:
Personnel: *Summary:* 1 Total; 1 Professional(s)
Lysane St-Amour, Information Specialist
lysane.st-amour@pwc.ca
450-677-9411 ext. 2607
Chantal Boileau, Librarian
chantal_boileau@hc-sc.gc.ca
450-646-1353 ext. 369

Longueuil: **Quebec Regional Library**
1001, boul St-Laurent ouest
Longueuil, QC J4K 1C7
450-646-1353 ext: 222
Fax: 450-928-4102
National Library Symbol: QMNHH
Hours: M-F by appointment only
Acquisitions Budget: $25,000 - $49,999
Special Collections: Food Technology, Analytical Chemistry, Analysis & Regulation, Drug Manufacturing, Cosmetics Regulation, Microbiology
Services:
Personnel: *Summary:* 1 Total; 1 Technical(s)

Matane: **CÉGEP de Matane**
Bibliothèque
616, av St-Rédempteur
Matane, QC G4W 1L1
418-562-1240
Téléc: 418-566-2115
Courriel: cote@cgmatane.qc.ca
URL: www.cgmatane.qc.ca
Sigle: PMATC
Membre d'un consortium: Réseau des services documentaires collégiaux (Resdoc)
Heures: L-J 8h-17h, 19h-21h
Budget d'acquisitions: $25,000 - $49,999
Sujets: Tourisme, agriculture, aménagement, photographie
Services:
Prêts entre bibliothèques(PEB)
Personnel: *Sommaire:* 4 Total; 1 Professionnel(s); 1 Technicien(s); 3 Autre(s) employé(s)
Bobby Marmen, Conseiller pédagogique
marmen.bobby@cgmatane.qc.ca
418-562-1240 ext. 2101

Mirabel: **Bell Helicopter Textron**
Engineering Library
12800, rue de l'Avenir
Mirabel, QC J7J 1R4

450-971-6500 ext: 6638
Fax: 450-437-6382
e-mail: mlapalme@bellhelicopter.textron.com
National Library Symbol: QSTTB
No public access
Founded in: 1986
Acquisitions Budget: $25,000 - $49,999
Special Collections: BHTC Technical Reports & Manuals, Helicopter History
Subjects covered: Engineering, Technology, Transportation, Aerodynamics, Fluid Mechanics, Applied Mechanics, Aircraft (design, component fatigue, structures, weight control), Avionics, Dynamics, Electrical Engineering, Helicopter Flight Technology, Metallurgy, Metals, Plastics, Powerplant Design, Airworthiness, Safety, Vehicle Design, Helicopter Flight Technology
Services:
Internet Access
Inter-Library Loan (ILL)
Personnel: *Summary:* 1 Technical(s);
Monique Lapalme, Documentation Librarian II
mlapalme@bellhelicopter.textron.com
450-971-6500 ext. 6638
Christine Lemay, Bibliothécaire

Mont-Joli: **Institut Maurice-Lamontagne Bibliothèque**
850, rte de la Mer
Mont-Joli, QC G5H 3Z4
Adresse postale: CP 1000
Mont-Joli, QC G5H 3Z4
418-775-0552
Téléc: 418-775-0538
Couriel: LemayC@dfo-mpo.gc.ca
biblioIML@dfo-mpo.gc.ca
URL: www.qc.dfo-mpo.gc.ca/iml/en/gen/biblio.html
Sigle: QQPSM
Fondée en: 1987
Heures: L-V 8h30-16h30
Sujets: Océanographie, parasitologie, écotoxicologie, pêches, hydrographie
Services:
Lecteur/reproduction de microformes: Ordinateur
Personnel: *Sommaire:* 1 Total; 1 Professionnel(s)

Montréal: **Bell Canada Information Resource Centre/Centre d'information spécialisée**
87, rue Ontario ouest, 7e annex
Montréal, QC H2X 1Y8
514-870-8922
Fax: 514-870-9564
National Library Symbol: QMB
No public access
Founded in: 1927
Note: Electronic library with intranet site
Subjects covered: Telecommunications
Services:
Personnel: *Summary:* 6 Total; 6 Professional(s)
Stephanie Boyd, Associate Director
stephanie.boyd@bell.ca
514-870-8922
Rénald Beaumier, Directeur
beaumier.renald@uqam.ca
514-987-3000 ext. 4353
Anne Bourgeois, Bibliothécaire
bourgeois.anne@uqam.ca
514-987-3000 ext. 4343
Hélène Bussière, Bibliothécaire
bussiere.helene@uqam.ca
514-987-3000 ext. 6648
Gisèle Faubert, Bibliothécaire
faubert.gisele@uqam.ca
514-987-3000 ext. 4363
Madeleine Hébert-Erban, Bibliothécaire
hebert-erban.madeleine@uqam.ca
514-987-3000 ext. 4323
Gilles Janson, Bibliothécaire
janson.gilles@uqam.ca
514-987-3000 ext. 3813
Louis Le Borgne, Bibliothécaire
le_borgne.louis@uqam.ca
514-987-3000 ext. 7724
Catherine Passerieux, Bibliothécaire
passerieux.catherine@uqam.ca
514-987-3000 ext. 4609

Nicole Perron, Bibliothécaire
perron.nicole@uqam.ca
514-987-3000 ext. 7866
Ngoc Thanh Phan Nguyen, Bibliothécaire
phan-nguyen.thanh@uqam.ca
514-987-3000 ext. 4342
Pierrette Richer, Bibliothécaire
richer.pierrette@uqam.ca
514-987-3000 ext. 1073
Huguette Tanguay, Bibliothécaire
tanguay.huguette@uqam.ca
514-987-3000 ext. 4332

Montréal: **Bibliothèque centrale**
Pavillon Hubert-Aquin, local A-M100
400, rue St-Catherine Est
Montréal, QC H3C 3P3
514-987-6114
Téléc: 514-987-4213
Couriel: polnicky.diane@uqam.ca
URL: www.bibliotheques.uqam.ca.bibliotheques/centrale/
Heures: L-V 9h-22h; S, D 12h-17h
Budget d'acquisitions: $500,000 - $999,999
Sujets: Sciences humaines, lettres, langues et communications, sciences de la gestion
Services:
Accès public à l'internet
Réseau en ligne
Prêts entre bibliothèques(PEB)
Lecteur/reproduction de microformes: Lecteurs
Personnel: *Sommaire:* 50 Total; 13 Professionnel(s); 10 Technicien(s); 25 Autre(s) employé(s);
Monique St-Jean, Chef de bibliothèque
monique.st-jean@umontreal.ca
Ginette-Denyse Melançon-Bolduc, Responsable, Référence
ginette-denyse.melancon.bolduc@umontreal.ca

Montréal: **Bibliothèque d'aménagement**
#1162, 2940, ch de la Côte-Ste-Catherine
Montréal, QC H3C 3J7
Adresse postale: CP 6128, Succ Centre-ville
Montréal, QC H3C 3J7
514-343-7177
Téléc: 514-343-2183
Couriel: biblios@bib.umontreal.ca
pebqmu@bib.umontreal.ca
URL: www.bib.umontreal.ca
Heures: L-J 9h-22h; V 9h-17H; S, D 11h-17h
Budget d'acquisitions: $100,000 - $249,999
Sujets: Architecture, architecture de paysage, urbanisme, design industriel, histoire des jardins
Services:
Personnel: *Sommaire:* 10 Total; 2 Professionnel(s); 3 Technicien(s); 5 Autre(s) employé(s)
Georges Clonda, Chef de bibliothèque
georges.clonda@umontreal.ca
Denis Harpin, Responsable, Référence
denis.harpin@umontreal.ca

Montréal: **Bibliothèque de botanique - L'Institut de recherche en biologie végétale**
#E-328, 4101, rue Sherbrooke est
Montréal, QC H1X 2B2
514-872-8495
Téléc: 514-872-9406
Couriel: biblios@bib.umontreal.ca
pebqmu@bib.umontreal.ca
URL: www.bib.umontreal.ca
Heures: L-V 9h-17h
Budget d'acquisitions: $25,000 - $49,999
Collections spécialisées: Fonds Marie-Victorin (Herbier)
Sujets: Botanique, biologie végétale, biotechnologie des plantes, floristique, génétique, morphologie végétale, biologie moléculaire
Services:
Prêts entre bibliothèques(PEB)
Personnel: *Sommaire:* 2 Total; 1 Technicien(s)
Claire Dubois, Chef de bibliothèque
claire.dubois@umontreal.ca
Malivanh Sananikone, Responsable, Référence
malivanh.sananikone@umontreal.ca
514-343-6111 ext. 3571

Montréal: **Bibliothèque de chimie**
#H-715, Pavillon Roger-Gaudry, 2900, boul Édouard-Montpetit
Montréal, QC H3C 3J7

Adresse postale: CP 6128, Succ Centre-ville
Montréal, QC H3C 3J7
514-343-6459
Téléc: 514-343-5698
Couriel: biblios@bib.umontreal.ca
pebqmu@bib.umontreal.ca
URL: www.bib.umontreal.ca
Heures: L-J 8h30-21h; V 8h30-17h; 11h-17h
Budget d'acquisitions: $250,000 - $499,999
Sujets: Chimie analytique, chimie organique et inorganique, chimie physique, chimie théorique, biochimie, chimie des protéines, spectrométrie, polymères
Services:
Personnel: *Sommaire:* 5 Total; 1 Professionnel(s); 1 Technicien(s); 3 Autre(s) employé(s)

Montréal: **Bibliothèque de didacthèque**
Pavillion Marie-Victorin, 90, av. Vincent d'Indy, #A-128
Montréal, QC H3C 3J7
514-343-6195
Téléc: 514-343-2349
URL: www.bib.umontreal.ca/DI/
Fondée en: 1976
Heures: L, Me 8h30-20h; Ma, J, V 8h30-17h; S 11h-17h
Collections spécialisées: Matériel didactique, publications officielles, ouvrages de pédagogie, littérature jeunesse, accessoires didactiques, jeux éducatifs, audiovisuel, périodiques, logiciels éducatifs, matériel d'évaluation, dossiers de press,club vidéo.
Sujets: Ressources didactiques regroupant tous les documents disponibles en milieu scolaire pour les ordres d'enseignement préscolaire, primaire et secondaire.
Céline Amnotte, Directrice
celine.amnotte@umontreal.ca
Linda Patry, Chef, Services dév des collections et référence
linda.patry@umontreal.ca

Montréal: **Bibliothèque de droit**
Pavillon Maximilien-Caron, #4433, 3101, ch de la Tour
Montréal, QC H3C 3J7
Adresse postale: CP 6128, Succ Centre-ville
Montréal, QC H3C 3J7
514-343-7095
Téléc: 514-343-5928
Couriel: biblios@bib.umontreal.ca
pebqmu@bib.umontreal.ca
URL: www.bib.umontreal.ca
Heures: L-J 8h30-23h; V 8h30-21h; S, D 10h-19h
Budget d'acquisitions: $500,000 - $999,999
Sujets: Droit, justice
Services:
Personnel: *Sommaire:* 18 Total; 5 Professionnel(s); 4 Technicien(s); 9 Autre(s) employé(s);
Claire Dubois, Chef de bibliothèque
claire.dubois@umontreal.ca
Luce Brazeau, Responsable, Référence
luce.brazeau@umontreal.ca
514-343-6111 ext. 3570

Montréal: **Bibliothèque de physique**
#H-825, Pavillon Roger-Gaudry, 2900, boul Édouard-Montpetit
Montréal, QC H3C 3J7
Adresse postale: CP 6128, Succ Centre-ville
Montréal, QC H3C 3J7
514-343-6613
Téléc: 514-343-5698
Couriel: biblios@bib.umontreal.ca
pebqmu@bib.umontreal.ca
URL: www.bib.umontreal.ca
Heures: L-J 8h30-21h; V 8:30-17h; S 11h-17h
Budget d'acquisitions: $250,000 - $499,999
Sujets: Physique, astronomie, astrophysique, biophysique
Services:
Personnel: *Sommaire:* 3 Total; 1 Professionnel(s); 1 Technicien(s); 2 Autre(s) employé(s)
Marcel Simoneau, Directeur
simoneau.marcel@uqam.ca
514-987-3000 ext. 3570
Mychelle Boulet, Bibliothécaire
boulet.mychelle@uqam.ca
514-987-3000 ext. 3247
Karim Debbah, Bibliothécaire
karim.debbah@uqam.ca
514-987-3000 ext. 3403

Sylvie Goulet, Bibliothécaire
goulet.sylvie@uqam.ca
514-987-3000 ext. 3401
Camil David, Technicien en documentation
david.camil@uqam.ca
514-987-3000 ext. 7924
Denise Fortin-Carrière, Technicienne en documentation
fortin-carriere.denis@uqam.ca
514-987-3000 ext. 3402

Montréal: Bibliothèque des sciences
Pavillon Coeur des sciences, local KI-RR125
145, ave. du Président-Kennedy
Montréal, QC H3C 3P3
Adresse postale: CP 8889, Succ Centre-Ville
Montréal, QC H3C 3P3
514-987-6164
Téléc: 514-987-6821
Courriel: peb-sciences@uqam.ca
Sigle: QHUDS
Fondée en: 1974
Heures: L, Ma 8h30-22h; Me-V 8h30-20h; S 10h-17havec rendez-vous seulement
Budget d'acquisitions: $500,000 - $999,999
Sujets: Sciences pures et appliquées
Services:
Prêts entre bibliothèques(PEB)
Lecteur/reproduction de microformes: Ordinateur; Lecteurs
Personnel:
Diane Raymond, Directrice
diane.raymond@umontreal.ca
Danielle Tardif, Chef, Dév. collections/référence
danielle.tardif@umontreal.ca
514-343-6111 ext. 3583
Marie-Josée Leboeuf, Chef de service, Prêt et traitement des collections
514-343-7664

Montréal: Bibliothèque des sciences de la santé
#L-623, Pavillon Roger-Gaudry, 2900, boul Édouard-Montpetit
Montréal, QC H3C 3J7
Adresse postale: CP 6128, Succ Centre-ville
Montréal, QC H3C 3J7
514-343-6826
Téléc: 514-343-2350
Courriel: biblios@bib.umontreal.ca
pebqmum@bib.umontreal.ca
URL: www.bib.umontreal.ca
Sigle: QMUM
Fondée en: 1975
Heures: L-V 8h-21h; S, D 10h-18h
Budget d'acquisitions: $500,000 - $999,999
Sujets: Médecine, pharmacologie, médecine dentaire
Services:
Accès public à l'internet
Prêts entre bibliothèques(PEB)
Personnel: *Sommaire:* 25 Total; 6 Professionnel(s); 8 Technicien(s); 13 Autre(s) employé(s)
Micheline Drapeau, Directrice
drapeau.micheline@uqam.ca
514-987-3000 ext. 4301
Lynda Gadoury, Bibliothécaire
gadoury.lynda@uqam.ca
514-987-3000 ext. 4300
Liette Moreault, Bibliothécaire
moreault.liette@uqam.ca
514-987-3000 ext. 3681
Johanne Pellerin, Technicienne en documentation
pellerin.johanne@uqam.ca
514-987-3000 ext. 4302

Montréal: Bibliothèque des sciences juridiques
Pavillion Hubert-Aquin, local A-2190
400, rue St-Catherine Est
Montréal, QC H3C 3P3
Adresse postale: CP 8889, Succ Centre-ville
Montréal, QC H3C 3P3
514-987-6184
Téléc: 514-987-3494
Sigle: MUQ
Heures: L, Ma 8h30-22h; Me-V 8h30-20h; S 10h-17h
Budget d'acquisitions: $50,000 - $99,999
Sujets: Traités, recueils de lois, monographies, périodiques, ouvrages de référence sur le droit
Services:

Personnel: *Sommaire:* 3 Professionnel(s); 1 Technicien(s); 5 Autre(s) employé(s)
Johanne Rasmussen, Chef de bibliothèque
johanne.rasmussen@umontreal.ca
514-343-6111 ext. 1848
Viviane Angers, Bibliothécaire
viviane.angers@umontreal.ca
514-343-6111 ext. 1846
Denise Diamond, Bibliothécaire
denise.diamond@umontreal.ca
514-343-6111 ext. 2515
Louise Paradis, Bibliothécaire
514-343-6111 ext. 1845

Montréal: Bibliothèque paramédicale
#2120, 2375, ch Côte Ste Catherine
Montréal, QC H3C 3J7
Adresse postale: CP 6128, Succ Centre-ville
Montréal, QC H3C 3J7
514-343-6180
Téléc: 514-343-2306
Courriel: biblios@bib.umontreal.ca
pebqmu@bib.umontreal.ca
URL: www.bib.umontreal.ca
Sigle: QMUP
Fondée en: 1967
Heures: L-J 8h-22h30; V 8h-20h; S 10h-22h; D 11h-20
Budget d'acquisitions: $250,000 - $499,999
Sujets: Nutrition, réadaptation, sciences infirmières, ortho-audio, administration de la santé, médecine sociale et préventive, médecine du travail, diététique, technologies alimentaires, santé et sécurité au travail, toxicologie
Services:
Accès public à l'internet
Prêts entre bibliothèques(PEB)
Frais de recherche
Lecteur/reproduction de microformes: Ordinateur; Lecteurs
Personnel: *Sommaire:* 9 Total; 4 Professionnel(s); 3 Technicien(s); 8 Autre(s) employé(s)

Montréal: Bombardier Inc./Canadair Aerospace & Defence Groups
Technical Information Centre
PO Box 8087
Montréal, QC H3C 3G9
514-855-7281
Fax: 514-855-7203
e-mail: brenda.price@notes.canadair.ca
No public access
Founded in: 1947
Hours: M-F
Special Collections: NASA Reports; NACA Reports; ESDU's; AIAA; SAE; IEEE
Subjects covered: Aerospace Engineering; Electrical & Mechanical Engineering; Chemistry; Physics; Materials Science; Management; Computer Science; Finance & Customer Support; Human Resources & Legal
Services:
Microform Equipment: Computer; Reader
Personnel: *Summary:* 9 Total; 2 Professional(s); 6 Technical(s); 1 Other employees
Cecilia Dee, Supervisor
Caroline Fortin, Head, Systems & Technical Services
Gisèle Tellier, Head, Acquisitions
Brenda Price, Cataloguer & Head, ILL

Montréal: CÉGEP de Marie-Victorin
Bibliothèque
7000, rue Marie Victorin
Montréal, QC H1G 2J6
514-325-0150 ext: 2311
Téléc: 514-328-3830
Courriel: alain.vezina@collegemv.qc.ca
promotion@collegemv.qc.ca
URL: www.collegemv.qc.ca/fr/services/centres_de_ressources
Membre d'un consortium: Réseau des services documentaires collégiaux (Resdoc)
Fermée au public
Fondée en: 1962
Heures: L-J 8h-20h15; V 8h-15h
Annotation: Matériathèque (centre documentation des techniques en services de garde); Salles de travail de groupe; Appareils audiovisuels
Services:
Accès public à l'internet

Prêts entre bibliothèques(PEB)
Lecteur/reproduction de microformes: Lecteurs
Personnel: *Sommaire:* 4 Total; 3 Professionnel(s); 1 Technicien(s)
Alain Vézina, Bibliothécaire
alain.vezina@collegemv.qc.ca
514-325-0150 ext. 2311
Sylvie Gagnon-Goupil, Responsable, périodiques
Pierre Bélanger, Technicien en documentation
Nicole Bélanger-Cadieux, Responsable, acquisitions

Montréal: CÉGEP du Vieux-Montréal
Bibliothèque
255, rue Ontario est
Montréal, QC H2X 1X6
514-982-3437 ext: 2221
Téléc: 514-982-3448
Courriel: gestionnairew3@cvm.qc.ca
cjolicoeur@cvm.qc.ca
URL: www.cvm.qc.ca/biblio/
Membre d'un consortium: Réseau des services documentaires collégiaux (Resdoc)
Heures: L-J 8h-21h; V 8h-17havec rendez-vous seulement
Budget d'acquisitions:
Matériel imprimé: $50,000 - $99,999
Matériel électronique: $10,000 - $24,999
Population desservie: 6000
Collections spécialisées: Métiers d'art
Sujets: Sciences humaines et techniques
Services:
Personnel: *Sommaire:* 6 Total; 1 Professionnel(s); 5 Technicien(s); 5 Bénévole(s)
Catherine Jolicoeur, SMTE
cjolicoeur@cvm.qc.ca
Vy-Khanh Nguyen, Bibliothécaire
vy-khanh.nguyen@mtq.gouv.qc.ca
514-864-1666 ext. 5151

Montréal: Centre de documentation
35, rue de Port-Royal est, 4e étage
Montréal, QC H3L 3T1
514-864-1666 ext: 5150
Téléc: 514-864-3332
Courriel: doc-qmtra@mtq.gouv.qc.ca
URL: www.mtq.gouv.qc.ca
Sigle: QMTRA
Fondée en: 1978
Heures: L-V 8h30-12h, 13h-16h30
Budget d'acquisitions: $10,000 - $24,999
Matériel imprimé: 0-$9,999
Matériel électronique: 0-$9,999
Population desservie: 2000
Collections spécialisées: Transports Québec, Transports Canada, Transportation Research Board
Sujets: Transports urbains et publiques, urbanisme, environnement
Services:
Accès public à l'internet
Prêts entre bibliothèques(PEB)
Lecteur/reproduction de microformes: Lecteurs
Personnel: *Sommaire:* 3 Total; 1 Professionnel(s); 2 Technicien(s)
Iain Blair, Documentalist

Montréal: Centre for Developing Area Studies / Centre d'études sur les régions en développement
3715, rue Peel
Montréal, QC H3A 1X1
514-398-3507
Fax: 514-398-8432
e-mail: doc.cdas@mcgill.ca
URL: www.mcgill.ca/cdas
Hours: M-F 9:30-5:00
Acquisitions Budget: 0-$9,999
Special Collections: International development materials
Subjects covered: Politics, Environment
Services:
Inter-Library Loan (ILL)
Personnel: *Summary:* 1 Professional(s)

Montréal: Centre hospitalier de l'Université de Montréal Hôpital Notre-Dame
Bibliothèque médicale
1560, rue Sherbrooke est
Montréal, QC H2L 4M1
514-890-8000 ext: 27217
Téléc: 514-412-7569

Libraries & Resource Centres / Québec

Couriel: allarda@magellan.umontreal.ca
burker@magellan.umontreal.ca
06_chum_biblio_notre-dame@ssss.gouv.qc.
Sigle: QMHND
Heures: L-V 8h-17h
Budget d'acquisitions: $250,000 - $499,999
Annotation: Affiliée à L'Association des bibliothèques de la santé affiliées à l'Université de Montréal (ABSAUM).
Sujets: Sciences de la santé
Services:
Prêts entre bibliothèques(PEB) frais
Personnel: *Sommaire:* 1 Professionnel(s); 3 Technicien(s); 2 Autre(s) employé(s)
André Allard, Responsable
Louise Deschamps, Bibliotechnicienne

Montréal: **Centre hospitalier de l'Université de Montréal Hôpital Saint-Luc**
Bibliothèque
1058, rue St-Denis
Montréal, QC H2X 3J4
514-890-8000 ext: 35867
Fax: 514-412-7317
e-mail: maheud@ere.umontreal.ca
National Library Symbol: QMHSL
Founded in: 1945
Hours: L-V 8h-18h. A partir du 2 mai: L-V 8h-17h; S 9h-12h, 13h-17h; D 11h-17
Note: Membre de l'Association des bibliothèques de la santé affiliées à l'Université de Montréal (ABSAUM)
Special Collections: Hépatologie, médecine interne
Subjects covered: Sciences de la santé, médecine
Services:
Inter-Library Loan (ILL)
Personnel: *Summary:* 3 Total; 1 Professional(s); 2 Technical(s); 1 Volunteer(s)
André Allard, Responsable

Montréal: **Centre hospitalier de l'Université de Montréal Hôtel-Dieu**
Centre de documentation, Audiovidéothèque
3840, rue St-Urbain
Montréal, QC H2W 1T8
514-890-8000 ext. 14355
Téléc: 514-412-7194
Couriel: Andre.Allard.Chum@ssss.gouv.qc.ca
06_CHUM_biblio_hotel-dieu@ssss.gouv.qc.ca
Sigle: QMHD
Fondée en: 1947
Heures: L-V 8h-16h30
Budget d'acquisitions: $50,000 - $99,999
Annotation: Affilié à l'Association des bibliothèques de la santé affiliées à l'Université de Montréal (ABSAUM)
Sujets: Médecine, soins infirmiers, sciences de la santé
Services:
Accès public à l'internet
Prêts entre bibliothèques(PEB) frais de 7$
Personnel: *Sommaire:* 4 Total; 1 Professionnel(s); 3 Technicien(s);
André Allard, Responsable
Andre.Allard.Chum@ssss.gouv.qc.ca
514-890-8000 ext. 14355
Johanne Chaperon, Bibliotechnicienne
Johanne.Chaperon.Chum@SSSS.gouv.qc.ca
514-890-8000 ext. 14781

Montréal: **Collège André-Grasset**
Bibliothèque
1001, boul Crémazie est
Montréal, QC H2M 1M3
514-381-4293
Téléc: 514-381-7421
Couriel: ldelasabionniere@grasset.qc.ca
URL: www.grasset.qc.ca
Membre d'un consortium: Réseau des services documentaires collégiaux (Resdoc)
Heures: avec rendez-vous seulement
Budget d'acquisitions: Matériel imprimé: $10,000 - $24,999
Matériel électronique: 0-$9,999
Sujets: Enseignement
Services:
Réseau en ligne
Prêts entre bibliothèques(PEB) frais de 10$
Personnel: *Sommaire:* 6 Total; 1 Professionnel(s); 3 Technicien(s); 2 Autre(s) employé(s)

Céline Pelletier, Adjointe au Directeur des études
cpelletier@grasset.qc.ca
514-381-4293 ext. 272
Lucie de la Sablonniere, Spécialiste en moyen techniques d'enseignement
ldelasablonniere@grasset.qc.ca
514-381-4293 ext. 336

Montréal: **Collège d'Ahuntsic**
Centre de diffusion
9155, rue Saint-Hubert
Montréal, QC H2M 1Y8
514-389-5921
Téléc: 514-389-1422
Couriel: louise.landry@collegeahuntsic.qc.ca
URL: www.collegeahuntsic.qc.ca
Sigle: QMDCA
Membre d'un consortium: Réseau des services documentaires collégiaux (Resdoc)
Heures: L-J 8h-19h30; V 8h-17h; S 12h30-16h30
Services:
Accès public à l'internet
Réseau en ligne
Prêts entre bibliothèques(PEB)
Personnel: *Sommaire:* 12 Total; 1 Professionnel(s); 4 Technicien(s); 7 Autre(s) employé(s)
Isabelle Lamarre, Coordonnatrice, Service de soutien à l'apprentissage
isabelle.lamarre@collgeahuntsic.qc.ca
514-389-5921 ext. 2240

Montréal: **Collège de Maisonneuve**
Bibliothèque
3800, rue Sherbrooke est
Montréal, QC H1X 2A2
514-254-7131
Téléc: 514-254-9741
Couriel: biblio@cmaisonneuve.qc.ca
lulrich@cmaisonneuve.qc.ca
URL: www.cmaisonneuve.qc.ca/
Membre d'un consortium: Réseau des services documentaires collégiaux (Resdoc)
Heures: L-J 8h-21h; V 8h-16h30
Budget d'acquisitions: $100,000 - $249,999
Sujets: Bibliothèque académique de niveau collégial
Services:
Accès public à l'internet
Réseau en ligne
Prêts entre bibliothèques(PEB)
Lecteur/reproduction de microformes: Ordinateur; Lecteurs
Personnel: *Sommaire:* 17 Total; 2 Professionnel(s); 2 Technicien(s); 13 Autre(s) employé(s)
Monique Devost-Rivard, Coordonnatrice
mdevost@cmaisonneuve.qc.ca
Nathalie Ouellet, SMTE
nouellet@cmaisonneuve.qc.ca
Denise Bélanger, Responsable, Périodiques
dbelanger@cmaisonneuve.qc.ca
Lise Ulrich, Agente de bureau, Acquisitions
lulrich@cmaisonneuve.qc.ca
Denis Pichette, Technicien
dpichette@cmaisonneuve.qc.ca
Huguette Miron, Technicienne
mmiron@cmaisonneuve.qc.ca
Mario Paillé, SMTE
mpaille@cmaisonneuve.qc.ca
Viviane Brisette, Agente de bureau
vbrisette@cmaisonneuve.qc.ca

Montréal: **Collège de Rosemont**
Bibliothèque
6400, 16e av
Montréal, QC H1X 2S9
514-376-1620 ext: 265
Téléc: 514-376-1440
Couriel: jcorriveau@crosemont.qc.ca
URL: www.crosemont.qc.ca/400/bib.asp
www.biblioweb.info/crosemont/index.html
Membre d'un consortium: Réseau des services documentaires collégiaux (Resdoc)
Fondée en: 1968
Heures: L-Me 8h-21h; J 8h-18h; V 8h-16h30
Budget d'acquisitions: $25,000 - $49,999
Collections spécialisées: Acupuncture, laboratoire médical, thanatologie

Services:
Prêts entre bibliothèques(PEB)
Personnel: *Sommaire:* 1 Professionnel(s); 3 Technicien(s); 3 Autre(s) employé(s)
Josée Corriveau, Responsable
jcorriveau@crosemont.qc.ca

Montréal: **Collège Français**
Bibliothèque
185, rue Fairmount ouest
Montréal, QC H2T 2M6
514-495-2581
Téléc: 514-271-2823
Heures: L-V 8h30-17h30avec rendez-vous seulement
Services:
Personnel: *Sommaire:* 2 Total; 1 Professionnel(s); 1 Autre(s) employé(s)
Suzanne Howison, Bibliothécaire
514-495-2581 ext. 141

Montréal: **Collège Jean-de-Brébeuf**
Bibliothèque du cours collégial
5625, av Decelles
Montréal, QC H3T 1W4
514-342-9342 ext: 5346
Téléc: 514-342-1558
Couriel: bibliocol@brebeuf.qc.ca
URL: www.brebeuf.qc.ca
Membre d'un consortium: Réseau des services documentaires collégiaux (Resdoc)
Fondée en: 1957
Heures: L-J 8h-17h45; V 8h-16h
Budget d'acquisitions: $50,000 - $99,999
Services:
Réseau en ligne
Prêts entre bibliothèques(PEB)
Lecteur/reproduction de microformes: Lecteurs
Personnel: *Sommaire:* 2 Professionnel(s); 2 Technicien(s); 3 Autre(s) employé(s)
Violaine Fortier, Responsable
violaine.fortier@brebeuf.qc.ca
514-342-9342 ext. 5374
Lyne St-Hilaire, Bibliothécaire - Archiviste
lyne.st-hilaire@brebeuf.qc.ca
514-342-9342 ext. 5133
Noëlline Charron, Technicienne en documentation
noelline.charron@brebeuf.qc.ca
514-342-9342 ext. 5346

Montréal: **Collège Lasalle**
Centre de documentation
#4100, 2000, rue Sainte-Catherine ouest
Montréal, QC H3H 2T2
514-939-2006 ext: 4503
Fax: 514-939-7292
800-363-3541
e-mail: elebel@clasalle.com
URL: www.clasalle.com/centre_de_documentation
Founded in: 1959
Hours: L-J 7h30-20h; V 7h30-18h
Acquisitions Budget: $50,000 - $99,999
Subjects covered: Mode; tourisme; hôtellerie; gestion
Services:
Internet Access
Access to Subscription Databases
Personnel: *Summary:* 5 Total; 1 Professional(s); 2 Technical(s); 1 Other employees
Elisabeth Lebel, Chef, Centre de documentation
elebel@clasalle.com
Sylvie Auger, Technicienne en documentation
sauger@clasalle.com

Montréal: **Collège O'Sullivan / O'Sullivan College**
Bibliothèque
1191, rue de la Montagne
Montréal, QC H3G 1Z2
514-866-4622 ext: 115
Fax: 514-866-0668
No public access
Hours: 8:30-6:00
Acquisitions Budget: $25,000 - $49,999
Subjects covered: Business Administration, Paralegal, Computer Science, Office Systems Technology
Services:
Internet Access
Personnel: *Summary:* 1 Total; 1 Professional(s); 2 Volunteer(s)

Josée Descheneaux, Responsable

Montréal: Collège St-Jean-Vianney
Bibliothèque
12630, boul Gouin est
Montréal, QC H1C 1B9
514-648-3821
Téléc: 514-648-8401
Courriel: legaultc@st-jean-vianney.qc.ca
URL: www.st-jean-vianney.qc.ca
Membre d'un consortium: Réseau des services documentaires collégiaux (Resdoc)
Heures: L-V 7h30-16h
Services:
Personnel: *Sommaire:* 1 Professionnel(s); 1 Autre(s) employé(s);
Claudine Legault, Bibliothécaire
legaultc@st-jean-vianney.qc.ca
514-648-3821

Montréal: Commission de la santé et de la sécurité du travail
Centre de documentation (Montréal)
1199, rue de Bleury, 4e étage
Montréal, QC H3C 4E2
Adresse postale: CP 6067, Succ Centre-ville
Montréal, QC H3C 4E2
514-906-3760
Téléc: 514-906-3820
888-873-3160
Courriel: documentation@csst.qc.ca
anne.rondeau@csst.qc.ca
URL: centredoc.csst.qc.ca
Sigle: QMCSST
Fondée en: 1980
Heures: L-V 8h30-16h30
Collections spécialisées: Cis/Bit Sur CD-ROM, Rapports d'enquête d'accident accessibles en ligne
Sujets: Travail, droit, médecine, sciences de la santé, médecine du travail, hygiène industrielle, toxicologie, droit du travail, droit de la santé et de la sécurité au travail
Services:
Accès public à l'internet
Personnel: *Sommaire:* 15 Total; 8 Professionnel(s); 3 Technicien(s); 4 Autre(s) employé(s)
Carole Bergeron, Chef de service
514-906-3760

Montréal: Concordia University Libraries / Bibliothèques de l'Université Concordia
1400, boul de Maisonneuve ouest
Montréal, QC H3G 1M8
Mailing Address: 1455, boul de Maisonneuve ouest
Montréal, QC H3G 1M8
514-848-2424 ext: 7708
Fax: 514-848-2882
e-mail: ill@alcor.concordia.ca
URL: www.library.concordia.ca
National Library Symbol: CAQMG
Consortia Membership: Canadian Research Knowledge Network (CRKN); Conférence des recteurs et des principaux des universités du Québec (CREPUQ)
Founded in: 1974
Hours: Vanier: M-Th 8:30am-1:00am; Webster: open 24 hours: Summer M-Th 8:30am-10:00pm, Fr 8:30-5:00 pm, Sa-Su 10:00am-6:00 pm
Acquisitions Budget: $1,000,000 plus
Special Collections: Held at Vanier Library: Irving Layton Collection; Azrieli Collection; Masonic Collection; Rudnyckyj Collection; Gay & Lesbian Literature Collection; James Card Cinema Collection; Belloc Collection; McGee Collection; Peter Desbarats Collection; Antique Maps
Subjects covered: Arts, Humanities, Physical Sciences, Life Sciences, Economics, Commerce, Administration, Social Sciences, Visual Arts, Culture, Engineering, Biological Sciences, Performing Arts, Recreation, Exercise Science, Leisure Studies, Communication Studies
Services:
Remote Access
Internet Access
Access to Subscription Databases
Inter-Library Loan (ILL)
Microform Equipment: Computer; Reader
Personnel: *Summary:* 143 Total; 41 Professional(s); 102 Other employees

Gerald Beasley, University Librarian
Gerald.Beasley@concordia.ca
514-848-2424 ext. 7695
Jocelyn Godolphin, Associate University Librarian, Collection Services
Jocelyn.Godolphin@concordia.ca
514-848-2424 ext. 5255
Jean Marc Edwards, Associate University Librarian, Information Systems/Technology
Jean-Marc.Edwards@concordia.ca
514-848-2424 ext. 7732
David Thirlwall, Associate University Librarian, Personnel & Communication
David.Thirlwall@concordia.ca
514-848-2424 ext. 7693

Montréal: Dawson College
Library
3040, rue Sherbrooke ouest
Montréal, QC H3Z 1A4
514-931-8731
URL: dolls.dawsoncollege.qc.ca
Founded in: 1988
Hours: Winter: M-Th 8:00-7:30; F 8:00-5:00. Summer: M-Th 12:00-7:00
Special Collections: Audio & video tapes; CD-Roms; Audio CDs
Subjects covered: Social, political & physical science; Mathematics; Fine Arts & Music; Medicine; Agriculture; Technology; Law; Education; History; Geography; Philosophy
Services:
Internet Access
Access to Subscription Databases
Inter-Library Loan (ILL)
Group study rooms
Microform Equipment: Computer; Reader
Personnel:
Carolyn Gilmore, Coordinator
imcgilmore@dawsoncollege.qc.ca
Anne Scott, Technical Services Librarian
ascott@dawsoncollege.qc.ca
Donna Harris, Acquisitions Librarian
Andrew Milne, Cataloguing Librarian

Montréal: École polytechnique de Montréal
Bibliothèque
2500, ch de Polytechnique
Montréal, QC H3C 3A7
Adresse postale: CP 6079, Succ Centre-ville
Montréal, QC H3C 3A7
514-340-4666
Téléc: 514-340-4026
Courriel: biblio@polymtl.ca
biblio.peb@polymtl.ca
URL: www.polymtl.ca/biblio
Sigle: QMEP
Membre d'un consortium: Canadian Research Knowledge Network (CRKN); Conférence des recteurs et des principaux des universités du Québec (CREPUQ)
Fondée en: 1873
Heures: L-S
Budget d'acquisitions: $500,000 - $999,999
Annotation: Membre de CREPUQ (Conférence des recteurs et des principaux des universités du Québec).
Collections spécialisées: Normes techniques
Sujets: Génie, science et technologie
Services:
Accès public à l'internet
Réseau en ligne
Prêts entre bibliothèques(PEB)
Lecteur/reproduction de microformes: Ordinateur; Lecteurs
Personnel: *Sommaire:* 26 Total; 11 Professionnel(s); 14 Technicien(s); 9 Autre(s) employé(s)
Marc Hiller, Directeur par intérim de la bibliothèque
514-340-4711 ext. 4652
Marie-Hélène Dupuis, Responsable, Services d'accès à l'information
Minh-Thu Nguyen, Responsable, Services techniques
Marc Hiller, Responsable, Développement des collections
Greg Whitney, Responsable, Systèmes informatisés
Dubravka Kapa, Director
Dubravka.Kapa@concordia.ca
514-848-2424 ext. 7721

Montréal: Georges P. Vanier Library
Loyola Campus, 7141, rue Sherbrooke ouest
Montréal, QC H4B 1R6
514-848-2424 ext: 7766
Fax: 514-848-2804
e-mail: ill@alcor.concordia.ca
URL: www.library.concordia.ca
National Library Symbol: QML
Founded in: 1916
Hours: M-Th 8:30am-1:00am
Services:
Internet Access
Inter-Library Loan (ILL)
Microform Equipment: Computer; Reader
Personnel: *Summary:* 32 Total

Montréal: HEC Montréal
Bibliothèque Myrian et J.-Robert Ouimet
3000, ch Côte-Sainte-Catherine
Montréal, QC H3T 2A7
514-340-6220
Téléc: 514-340-5639
Courriel: biblio.info@hec.ca
peb.qmbe@hec.ca
URL: www.hec.ca/biblio/
Membre d'un consortium: Canadian Research Knowledge Network (CRKN); Conférence des recteurs et des principaux des universités du Québec (CREPUQ)
Fondée en: 1907
Heures: L-J 8h-22h30; V 8h-21h; S 10h-17h; D 12h-17h.
Budget d'acquisitions: $500,000 - $999,999
Annotation: Auparavant l'École des hautes études commerciales de Montréal
Collections spécialisées: Banques de données; périodiques électroniques; livres électroniques; ressources dans toutes les disciplines de la gestion
Sujets: Économie, industrie, administration
Services:
Prêts entre bibliothèques(PEB)
Personnel:
Maureen Clapperton, Directrice
maureen.clapperton@hec.ca
Sylvain Champagne, Directeur, Services à la clientèle
Bernard Bizimana, Directeur, Services techniques & informatisés

Montréal: Héritage Montréal
Bibliothèque
#0500, 100, rue Sherbrooke est
Montréal, QC H2X 1C3
514-286-2662
Fax: 514-286-1661
e-mail: contact@heritagemontreal.qc.ca
URL: www.heritagemontreal.qc.ca
Hours: Ma-V 14h-17h
Subjects covered: Livres; rapports d'études, monographies inédites; périodiques et dossiers internes de documentation sur l'histoire de l'architecture de la ville de Montréal et de l'Amérique du Nord, sur la renovation, sur l'urbanisme (conservation)
Services:

Montréal: Hydro-Québec
Bibliothèque
800, boul de Maisonneuve est
Montréal, QC H2L 4P5
Adresse postale: 855, rue Ste-Catherine
Montréal, QC H2L 4P5
514-840-5939
Téléc: 514-840-5044
Courriel: bibliotheque@hydro.qc.ca
URL: www.hydroquebec.com
Sigle: QMH
Fermée au public
Fondée en: 1962
Heures: L-V
Sujets: Énergie, génie civil, génie électrique, information et documentation, normes, télécommunications
Services:
Prêts entre bibliothèques(PEB) frais de 10$
Lecteur/reproduction de microformes: Ordinateur; Lecteurs
Personnel: *Sommaire:* 6 Total; 4 Professionnel(s); 2 Autre(s) employé(s)
Marc Archambault, Chef entreposage et exploitation des fonds documentaires
archambault.marc@hydro.qc.ca
514-289-5551 ext. 4472

Libraries & Resource Centres / Québec

Montréal: Institut Teccart Inc.
Bibliothèque
3030, rue Hochelaga
Montréal, QC H1W 1G2
514-526-2501
Téléc: 514-526-9192
866-832-2278
URL: www.teccart.qc.ca
Fondée en: 1945
Heures: L-S
Budget d'acquisitions: $25,000 - $49,999
Sujets: Sciences physiques, génie, technologie, électronique
Services:
Personnel: Sommaire: 1 Total; 1 Professionnel(s)
Carole Julien, Responsable
cjulien@teccart.qc.ca

Montréal: International Civil Aviation Organization / Organisation de l'aviation civile internationale
Web, Library & Archives Section
999, rue Université
Montréal, QC H3C 5H7
514-954-8207
Fax: 514-954-6077
e-mail: library@icao.int
URL: www.icao.int
National Library Symbol: QMIC
Founded in: 1946
Hours: M-F: 9:00-5:00 by appointment only
Special Collections: International Civil Aviation Organization, United Nations, & specialized agencies publications, serials, & monographs
Subjects covered: Air transportation; Civil aviation; Air law; Aviation medicine; Meteorology; Communications
Services:
Inter-Library Loan (ILL)
Microform Equipment: Computer; Reader
Personnel:
Ghislaine Giroux, Web & Library Assistant
ggiroux@icao.int

Montréal: Jardin Botanique de Montréal
Bibliothèque
4101, rue Sherbrooke est
Montréal, QC H1X 2B2
514-872-1824
Fax: 514-872-3765
URL: www2.ville.montreal.qc.ca/jardin/en/biblio/biblio.htm
National Library Symbol: QMJB
Founded in: 1950
Hours: L-V 9h-16h30; S 9h12h; 13h-16h30
Note: Ouverte au public, sans rendez-vous, pour consultation sur place
Special Collections: Phytopathologie, écologie végétale; botanique économique, entomologie
Subjects covered: Botanique, horticulture, aménagement paysagé
Services:
Inter-Library Loan (ILL)
Personnel: Summary: 6 Total; 1 Professionnel(s); 2 Technical(s); 3 Other employees
Céline Arseneault, Botaniste/bibliothécaire
Guy Frenette, Bibliotechnicien
guy-frenette@ville.montreal.qc.ca

Montréal: KSH Solutions Inc. (KSH)
Library
#1600, 3400, de Maisonneuve ouest
Montréal, QC H3Z 3B8
514-932-5337
Fax: 514-932-9700
National Library Symbol: QMSHE
No public access
Founded in: 1976
Hours: M-F
Acquisitions Budget: 0-$9,999
Note: Library is open part-time.
Subjects covered: Engineering; Forestry; Energy
Services:
Inter-Library Loan (ILL)
Personnel: Summary: 1 Total; 1 Professional(s)
Dorothy Ozolins, Librarian
514-932-4611
Arlene Greenberg, Chief Medical Librarian
514-340-8222 ext. 5930
Marek Pukteris, Library Technician

Montréal: Lady Davis Institute for Medical Research of the Sir Mortimer B. Davis - Jewish General Hospital
Medical Research Library
c/o 3755, côte Ste-Catherine
Montréal, QC H3T 1E2
514-340-8260 ext: 3795
Fax: 514-340-7502
e-mail: bcaplan@mail.mcgill.ca
URL: www.jgh.ca/research/ldi/index.html
No public access
Founded in: 1969
Hours: M-F
Acquisitions Budget: $50,000 - $99,999
Note: Member of McGill Affiliated Health Sciences Library Consortium & McGill Medical & Health Libraries Association. ILL phone: 514/340-8260
Subjects covered: Medical Research
Services:
Inter-Library Loan (ILL)
Personnel: Summary: 2 Total; 1 Professional(s); 1 Technical(s)

Montréal: Lafarge Canada Inc.
Technical Library
6150, av Royalmount
Montréal, QC H4P 2R3
Mailing Address: 6150 av Royalmount
Montréal, QC H4P 2R3
514-738-1202 ext: 2274
Fax: 514-738-1124
URL: www.lafarge-na.com
National Library Symbol: QLMC
No public access
Founded in: 1988
Subjects covered: Cement, Concrete, Engineering, Physical Sciences
Services:
Personnel: Summary: 2 Total; 1 Professional(s); 1 Technical(s);

Irene M. Paulmier, Head Librarian
Jim Henderson, Life Sciences Librarian
jim.henderson@mcgill.ca
514-398-4475 ext. 9115
Deanna Cowan, Head of Reference
deanna.cowan@mcgill.ca
514-398-4475 ext. 9669
Valerie Fortin, Collections Librarian
valerie.fortin@mcgill.ca
514-398-4475 ext. 9880
Eleanor MacLean, Biology Librarian
eleanor.maclean@mcgill.ca
514-398-4744
Angella Lambrou, Computer Services Librarian
angella.lambrou@mcgill.ca
514-398-4475 ext. 9184

Montréal: Life Sciences Library
3655, Promenade Sir William Osler
Montréal, QC H3G 1Y6
514-398-4475
Fax: 514-398-3890
e-mail: health.library@mcgill.ca
illqmmm@library.mcgill.ca
URL: www.health.library.mcgill.ca
National Library Symbol: QMMM
Founded in: 1823
Hours: M-F 8:30-6:45; Sa, Su 12:00-5:45
Acquisitions Budget: $500,000 - $999,999
Subjects covered: Medicine, Health Sciences, Surgery, Dentistry, Physical & Occupational Therapy, Nursing, Communication Disorders
Services:
Access to Subscription Databases
Inter-Library Loan (ILL)
Microform Equipment: Computer; Reader
Personnel: Summary: 20 Total; 6 Professional(s); 1 Technical(s); 14 Other employees

Montréal: Marianopolis College
Library
4873 Westmount Ave.
Montréal, QC H3Y 1X9
514-931-8792
Fax: 514-931-8790
800-332-1077
URL: www.marianopolis.edu
www.marianopolis.edu/Sites/Library/
Founded in: 1908
Hours: M-F 7:30-6:00
Services:
Personnel:
Judith Stonehewer, Chief Librarian
j.stonehewer@marianopolis.edu

Montréal: McGill University
3459, rue McTavish
Montréal, QC H3A 1Y1
514-398-4677
Fax: 514-398-3561
URL: www.mcgill.ca/library/
Consortia Membership: Canadian Research Knowledge Network (CRKN); Conférence des recteurs et des principaux des universités du Québec (CREPUQ)
Acquisitions Budget: $500,000 - $999,999
Services:
Personnel:
Janine Schmidt, Trenholme Director of Libraries
director.libraries@mcgill.ca

Montréal: Montréal General Hospital / L'Hôpital général de Montréal
Medical Library
#E6-157, 1650, av Cedar
Montréal, QC H3G 1A4
514-934-1934 ext: 43056
Fax: 514-934-8250
e-mail: library.mgh@muhc.mcgill.ca
URL: www.mghlib.mcgill.ca
National Library Symbol: QMGH
Founded in: 1955
Hours: M-Th 8:00-5:30; F 8:00-5:00
Acquisitions Budget: $50,000 - $99,999
Subjects covered: Medicine, Health Sciences
Services:
Inter-Library Loan (ILL)
Personnel: Summary: 4 Total; 1 Professional(s); 2 Technical(s)
Gary Lee Kober, Chief Librarian
gary.kober@muhc.mcgill.ca
John Hobbins, Law Librarian
john.hobbins@mcgill.ca
514-398-4715 ext. 168
Daniel Boyer, Wainwright Librarian
daniel.boyer@mcgill.ca
514-398-4715 ext. 156

Montréal: Nahum Gelber Law Library / Nahum Gelber Bibliothèque de droit
3660, rue Peel
Montréal, QC H3A 1W9
514-398-4715
Fax: 514-398-3585
e-mail: reference.law@mcgill.ca
lawill.library@mcgill.ca
URL: www.law.library.mcgill.ca
National Library Symbol: QMML
Founded in: 1890
Hours: M-T 9:00-9:45; F 9:00-7:45; Sa, Su 10:00-7:45
Acquisitions Budget: $500,000 - $999,999
Special Collections: Wainwright Antiquarian French Law collection; John Peters Humphrey United Nations collection
Subjects covered: Law
Services:
Inter-Library Loan (ILL)
Microform Equipment: Computer; Reader
Personnel: Summary: 17 Total; 5 Professional(s); 9 Technical(s);
Eveline Landa, Head
eveline.landa@cnrc-nrc.gc.ca
514-496-4254

Montréal: NRC Information Centre Montréal / Centre d'information du CNRC Montréal
6100, av Royalmount
Montréal, QC H4P 2R2
514-496-6117
Fax: 514-496-7885
e-mail: nic.montreal@cnrc-nrc.gc.ca
URL: cisti-icist.nrc-cnrc.gc.ca/nis/montreal_e.shtml
National Library Symbol: QMNB
Founded in: 1985
Hours: M-F 8:30-12:00, 1:00-4:30 by appointment only

Acquisitions Budget: $50,000 - $99,999
For Print: $25,000 - $49,999
For Electronic: $25,000 - $49,999
Subjects covered: Biotechnology, Bioengineering, Genetic Engineering, Environment, Bioprocess
Services:
Personnel: Summary: 3 Total; 2 Professional(s); 1 Technical(s)

Montréal: Québec Ministère de la Sécurité Publique - Direction des Communications
Laboratoire de sciences judiciaires et de médecine légale, Centre de documentation
Édifice Wilfrid Derome, 1701, rue Parthenais
Montréal, QC H2K 3S7
514-873-2704 ext: 446
Téléc: 514-873-4847
Courriel: lsjml-bib@msp.gouv.qc.ca
URL: www.msp.gouv.qc.ca/labo/index.asp
Sigle: QMJLP
Fondée en: 1968
Heures: L-V 8h30-12h, 13h-16h30avec rendez-vous seulement
Budget d'acquisitions: $10,000 - $24,999
Matériel imprimé: $10,000 - $24,999
Matériel électronique: 0-$9,999
Annotation: Collection: environ 6 000 monographies et environ 310 périodiques.
Collections spécialisées: Collection du Dr. Wilfrid Derome
Sujets: Médecine légale, chimie judiciaire, balistique, expertise de documents, toxicologie, explosifs, génétique légale, imagerie, biologie légale, anthropologie légale
Services:
Prêts entre bibliothèques(PEB) frais de 5$/demande
Consultation sur rendez-vous
Personnel: Sommaire: 2 Total; 1 Professionnel(s); 1 Autre(s) employé(s)
Guylaine Marion, Bibliothécaire
guylaine.marion@msp.gouv.qc.ca
514-873-3301 ext. 446
Suzie Savard, Autre personnel
suzie.savard@msp.gouv.qc.ca
514-873-3301 ext. 521

Montréal: Québec Office des personnes handicapées
Centre de documentation
#15.600, 500, boul René-Lévesque ouest,
15e étage
Montréal, QC H2Z 1W7
514-873-3574
Fax: 514-873-9706
888-264-2362
TDD: 5148733574
e-mail: documentation@ophq.gouv.qc.ca
URL: www.ophq.gouv.qc.ca
National Library Symbol: QDOPH
Founded in: 1979
Hours: L-V 8h30-12h, 13h-16h30
Acquisitions Budget: $25,000 - $49,999
Subjects covered: Sciences de la santé, affaires sociales, personnes handicapées, intégration sociale, déficience, adaptation/réadaptation, santé publique, promotion des droits, travail, éducation
Services:
Inter-Library Loan (ILL)
Personnel: Summary: 2 Total; 2 Professional(s); 1 Technical(s)
Sophie Janik, Responsable
514-873-3574
Myriam Thibault, Bibliothécaire
Carmen Dessureault, Bibliotechnicienne
Guylaine Beaudry, Director
Guylaine.Beaudry@concordia.ca
514-848-2424 ext. 7699

Montréal: R. Howard Webster Library
1400, boul de Maisonneuve ouest
Montréal, QC H3G 1M8
Mailing Address: 1455, boul de Maisonneuve ouest
Montréal, QC H3G 1M8
514-848-2424 ext: 7777
Fax: 514-848-2882
e-mail: ill@alcor.concordia.ca
URL: www.library.concordia.ca
National Library Symbol: QMG
Founded in: 1926
Hours: Academic year open 24 hours: Summer M-Th 8:30am-10:00pm, Fr 8:30-5:00 pm, Sa-Su 10:00am-6:00 pm

Services:
Internet Access
Inter-Library Loan (ILL)
Microform Equipment: Computer; Reader
Personnel:

Montréal: Royal Victoria Hospital
Medical Library
Rm H4.01, 687, av des Pins ouest
Montréal, QC H3A 1A1
Mailing Address: 687, av des Pins ouest
Montréal, QC H3A 1A1
514-934-1934 ext: 35290
Fax: 514-843-1483
e-mail: rvh.library@muhc.mcgill.ca
URL: muhclibraries.mcgill.ca
National Library Symbol: QMRV
Founded in: 1924
Hours: M-F 9:00-6:00
Subjects covered: Medicine, Nursing, Cardiology, Surgery, Emergency Medicine, Transplantation
Services:
Inter-Library Loan (ILL)
Personnel: Summary: 3 Total; 2 Professional(s); 2 Technical(s)
Elizabeth Lamont, Chief Librarian
elizabeth.lamont@muhc.mcgill.ca
514-934-1934 ext. 35293
Giovanna Badia, Librarian
giovanna.badia@muhc.mcgill.ca
514-934-1934 ext. 35292
Susan Morgan, Library Technician
susan.morgan@muhc.mcgill.ca
514-934-1934 ext. 35290
Myra Davies, Library Technician
myra.davies@muhc.mcgill.ca
514-934-1934 ext. 35291
Anne-Marie Hince, Library Assisntant
ami.library@muhc.mcgill.ca
514-934-1964 ext. 34528
Louis Houle, Librarian
louis.houle@mcgill.ca
514-398-4763
Marika Asimakopulos, Reference Librarian
marika.asimakopulos@mcgill.ca
514-398-7340
Darlene Canning, Computer Services Librarian
darlene.canning@mcgill.ca
514-398-4765
Natalie Waters, Computer & Instructional Services Librarian
natalie.waters@mcgill.ca
514-398-7125

Montréal: Schulich Library of Science & Engineering
809, rue Sherbrooke ouest
Montréal, QC H3A 2K6
514-398-4769
Fax: 514-398-3903
e-mail: schulich.library@mcgill.ca
illqmme.library@mcgill.ca
URL: www.library.mcgill.ca/schulich
National Library Symbol: QMME
Founded in: 1982
Hours: M-Th 8:30-10:45; F 8:30-6:45; Sa, Su 12:00-7:45
Acquisitions Budget: $1,000,000 plus
Special Collections: Mossman Collection on the History of Science & Ideas
Subjects covered: Physical Sciences, Engineering, Technology, Mathematics, Computer Science
Services:
Remote Access
Inter-Library Loan (ILL)
Microform Equipment: Computer; Reader
Personnel: Summary: 17 Total; 5 Professional(s); 11 Technical(s)

Montréal: Service de l'urbanisme
Centre de documentation Marie-Morin
#5.100, 303, rue Notre-Dame est
Montréal, QC H2Y 3Y8
Adresse postale: 5.100, 303, rue Notre-Dame est
Montréal, QC H2Y 3Y8
514-872-4119
Téléc: 514-872-7726
Courriel: ginettedugas@ville.montreal.qc.ca
Sigle: QMURB
Fermée au public

Fondée en: 1988
Heures: L-V 8h45-16h45
Budget d'acquisitions: $25,000 - $49,999
Sujets: Urbanisme, aménagement, patrimoine, architecture, gestion municipale
Services:
Prêts entre bibliothèques(PEB)
Personnel: Sommaire: 1 Total; 1 Professionnel(s)
Ginette Dugas, Conseillère en ressources documentaires
ginettedugas@ville.montreal.qc.ca
514-872-4119

Montréal: Sir Mortimer B. Davis Jewish General Hospital / Hôpital général juif
Health Sciences Library
#A-200, 3755, côte Ste-Catherine
Montréal
514-340-8222 ext: 5927
Fax: 514-340-7552
e-mail: library.jgh@mail.mcgill.ca
URL: www.jgh.ca/hsl
National Library Symbol: QMJG
Founded in: 1950
Hours: M-Th 8:30-7:30; F 8:30-4:30
Acquisitions Budget: $250,000 - $499,999
Note: Member of McGill Affiliated Health Sciences Library Consortium & McGill Medical & Health Libraries Association
Special Collections: General medical; Judaica & Medical Ethics
Subjects covered: Medicine, Nursing, Health Sciences, Allied Health, Patient Care
Services:
Inter-Library Loan (ILL) for a fee of $3 +
Personnel: Summary: 4 Total; 1 Professional(s); 4 Technical(s)
Arlene Greenberg, Chief Medical Librarian
arlene.greenberg@mail.mcgill.ca
514-340-8222 ext. 5930
Liz Breier, Library Technician
liz.breier@mail.mcgill.ca
514-340-8222

Montréal: SNC-Lavalin inc.
Bibliothèque principale
455, boul René-Lévesque ouest
Montréal, QC H2Z 1Z3
514-393-1000
Téléc: 514-866-0795
URL: www.snclavalin.com
Sigle: QMSNC
Fermée au public
Fondée en: 1911
Heures: L-V
Sujets: Génie, technologie, énergie, affaires, environnement, mines et métallurgie
Services:
Prêts entre bibliothèques(PEB)
Personnel: Sommaire: 3 Total; 1 Professionnel(s); 2 Technicien(s)
Lynda Thivierge, Bibliothécaire
Caroline Littlejohns, Bibliothécaire
Françoise Soubeyrand, Technicienne

Montréal: Société générale de financement du Québec (SGF)
Centre de documentation
#1500, 600, rue de la Gauchetière ouest
Montréal, QC H3B 4L8
514-876-9290 ext: 2213
Téléc: 514-395-8055
Courriel: mtanguay@sgfqc.com
URL: www.sgfqc.com
Fermée au public
Fondée en: 1978
Sujets: Capital de développement aux entreprises dans les secteurs de chimie, pétrochimie, mines, métaux, industries, foresterie, énergie, environnement, santé, technologie, agroalimentaire
Services:
Personnel: Sommaire: 2 Total; 1 Professionnel(s)
Marlene Tanguay, Documentaliste

Montréal: Société habitation du Québec
Succursale Montréal Centre de documentation
500, boul René-Lévesque ouest, 5e étage
Montréal, QC H2Z 1W7

Libraries & Resource Centres / Québec

514-873-9611
Téléc: 514-873-8340
800-463-4315
Courriel: sdih@shq.gouv.qc.ca
URL: www.habitation.gouv.qc.ca
Sigle: QMSHQ
Fondée en: 1987
Heures: L-V 8h30-12h, 13h-16h30
Budget d'acquisitions: $10,000 - $24,999
Sujets: Logement, construction, architecture, urbanisme
Services:
Accès public à l'internet
Prêts entre bibliothèques(PEB)
Personnel: *Sommaire:* 2 Total; 1 Professionnel(s); 1 Technicien(s)
Barbara Maass, Bibliothécaire responsable
barbara.maass@shq.gouv.qc.ca
514-873-9611

Montréal: **Société québécoise de spéléologie**
Centre de documentation
4545, av Pierre-de-Coubertin
Montréal, QC H1V 3R2
Adresse postale: CP 1000, Succ M
Montréal, QC H1V 3R2
514-252-3006
Téléc: 514-252-3201
800-338-6636
Courriel: info-sqs@speleo.qc.ca
URL: www.speleo.qc.ca
Fermée au public
Fondée en: 1970
Sujets: Spéléologie
Services:
Personnel: *Sommaire:* 1 Professionnel(s); 3 Technicien(s); 200 Bénévole(s)

Montréal: **TECSULT inc**
Bibliothèque
85, rue Ste-Catherine ouest
Montréal, QC H2X 3P4
514-287-8500 ext: 8546
Téléc: 514-287-8643
Courriel: biblitec@tecsult.com
Sigle: QMABB
Fondée en: 1978
Heures: L-V 8h-16h avec rendez-vous seulement
Budget d'acquisitions: $50,000 - $99,999
Sujets: Environnement, génie civil, gestion
Services:
Prêts entre bibliothèques(PEB)
Personnel: *Sommaire:* 1 Technicien(s)
Véronique Pepin, Responsable de la bibliothèque
514-287-8500 ext. 8546

Montréal: **Union Carbide/Pétromont**
Documentation Centre
10455, boul Metropolitain est
Montréal, QC H1B 1A1
Mailing Address: 10555, boul Metropolitain est
Montréal, QC H1B 1A1
514-640-6400 ext: 1634
Fax: 514-645-8149
800-267-6401
National Library Symbol: QMUC
No public access
Founded in: 1963
Acquisitions Budget: $25,000 - $49,999
Services:
Personnel:
Marie-C. Demers, Librarian

Montréal: **United Nations Environment Programme - Convention on Biological Diversity Information Centre**
#800, 413, rue St-Jacques
Montréal, QC H2Y 1N9
514-288-2220
Fax: 514-288-6588
e-mail: secretariat@cbd.int
URL: www.cbd.int
Hours: M-F 10:00-4:00
Services:

Montréal: **Université de Montréal**
Direction générale des bibliothèques
#3, 2910, boul Édouard-Montpetit
Montréal, QC H3C 3J7
Adresse postale: CP 6128, Succ Centre-ville
Montréal, QC H3C 3J7
514-343-6905
Téléc: 514-343-6457
Courriel: biblios@bib.umontreal.ca
pebqmu@bib.umontreal.ca
URL: www.bib.umontreal.ca
Sigle: QMU
Membre d'un consortium: Canadian Research Knowledge Network (CRKN); Conférence des recteurs et des principaux des universités du Québec (CREPUQ)
Fermée au public
Budget d'acquisitions: $1,000,000 plus
Services:
Numérisation de documents originaux individuels
Personnel: *Sommaire:* 22 Total; 2 Professionnel(s); 6 Technicien(s); 7 Autre(s) employé(s)
Jean-Pierre Côté, Directeur général
Ginette Grégoire, Directrice, Traitement et accès aux documents
ginette.gregoire@umontreal.ca
514-343-6111 ext. 5151
Michel Gaudreault, Directeur administratif
michel.gaudreault@umontreal.ca
514-343-6111 ext. 8733
Mireille Janeau, Directrice, Développement collections et acquisitions
mireille.janeau@umontreal.ca
Paul-Emil Provost, Directeur, Bureau systèmes
paul.emil.provost@umontreal.ca

Montréal: **Université du Québec à Montréal**
Direction des bibliothèques
455, boul René-Lévesque
Montréal, QC H3C 3P8
Adresse postale: CP 8889, Succ Centre-ville
Montréal, QC H3C 3P8
514-987-3000 ext: 3824
Téléc: 514-987-3542
Courriel: polnicky.diane@uqam.ca
peb-qmuq@uquebec.ca
URL: www.bibliotheques.uqam.ca
Sigle: QMUQ
Membre d'un consortium: Canadian Research Knowledge Network (CRKN); Conférence des recteurs et des principaux des universités du Québec (CREPUQ)
Fondée en: 1969
Heures: Sept.-mai: L-V 8h30-22h; S 11h-17h; D 12h-17h.
Mai-juin: L-M 8h30-22h; M, J, V 8h30-18h; S 12h-17h.
Juillet-août: L-J 9h-17h
Budget d'acquisitions: $1,000,000 plus
Matériel imprimé: $1,000,000 plus
Matériel électronique: $1,000,000 plus
Collections spécialisées: Audiovidéothèque, cartothèque, livres rares, testothèque, didactèque, microthèque, diapothèque
Sujets: Sciences sociales et humaines, droit, arts, technologies, musique, lettres, éducation, sciences, lettres, communication
Services:
Accèss distance aux bases de donn
Accès public à l'internet
Réseau en ligne
Prêts entre bibliothèques(PEB)
Lecteur/reproduction de microformes: Ordinateur; Lecteurs
Personnel: *Sommaire:* 45 Professionnel(s); 122 Technicien(s); 1 Autre(s) employé(s)
Lucie Gardner, Directrice générale
514-987-3824
Rénald Beaumier, Directeur, Bibliothèque centrale
beaumier.renald@uqam.ca
514-987-3000 ext. 4353
Claire Boisvert, Directrice, Services techniques
boisvert.claire@uqam.ca
514-987-8351
André Champagne, Directeur, Services informatiques
champagne.andre@uqam.ca
514-987-3000 ext. 3163
Lucie Verreault, Directrice, Bibliothèque sciences de l'éducation
verreault.lucie@uqam.ca
514-987-3000 ext. 3884
Patricia Black, Directrice, Bibliothèque des arts et musique
514-987-3000 ext. 3160
Stephen Park, Directeur, Bibliothèque sciences juridiques
514-987-3000 ext. 4301

Marcel Simoneau, Directrice, Bibliothèque des sciences
simoneau.marcel@uqam.ca
514-987-3000 ext. 3570

Montréal: **Université du Québec École de technologie supérieure**
Service de la bibliothèque
1100, rue Notre-Dame ouest
Montréal, QC H3C 1K3
514-396-8960
Téléc: 514-396-8633
Courriel: biblio@etsmtl.ca
bibref@etsmtl.ca
URL: www.etsmtl.ca/biblio
Sigle: QMUQET
Membre d'un consortium: Canadian Research Knowledge Network (CRKN); Conférence des recteurs et des principaux des universités du Québec (CREPUQ)
Fondée en: 1974
Heures: L-V 8h30-22h; S, D 11h-18h
Budget d'acquisitions: $500,000 - $999,999
Collections spécialisées: G
Sujets: Génie, technologie, construction, génie mécanique, génie électrique, génie civil, production automatisée, génie logiciel
Services:
Accèss distance aux bases de donn
Accès public à l'internet
Réseau en ligne
Prêts entre bibliothèques(PEB) frais de $3 ou plus
Lecteur/reproduction de microformes: Ordinateur; Lecteurs
Personnel: *Sommaire:* 19 Total; 7 Professionnel(s); 6 Technicien(s); 5 Autre(s) employé(s)
Louise Thibaudeau, Directrice
louise.thibaudeau@etsmtl.ca
514-396-8946
Guy Gosselin, Adjoint à la direction - Gestion des collections
guy.gosselin@etsmtl.ca
514-396-8882
Edith Healy, Responsable, référence
edith.healy@etsmtl.ca
514-396-8800 ext. 7583
Gaston Fournier, Responsable, Services techniques
gaston.fournier@etsmtl.ca
514-396-8800 ext. 7526
Denis Levasseur, Responsable, Web
514-396-8800 ext. 8881

Montréal: **Université du Québec Institut national de la recherche scientifique, INRS-Urbanisation, Culture et Societé**
385, rue Sherbrooke Est
Montréal, QC H2X 1E3
Adresse postale: 387, rue Sherbrooke Est
Montréal, QC H2X 1E3
514-499-4000
Téléc: 514-499-4065
Courriel: helene_houde@ucs.inrs.ca
peb.qmuqiu@uquebec.ca
sdis@adm.inrs.ca
URL: www.inrs-ucs.uquebec.ca
Fondée en: 1970
Heures: L-V 8h-18h
Sujets: Espace régional, espace urbain/métropolitain, espace micro-urbain, science et technologie
Services:
Prêts entre bibliothèques(PEB)
Personnel: *Sommaire:* 2 Total; 1 Professionnel(s); 1 Technicien(s)
Hélène Houde, Bibliothécaire
helene_houde@ucs.inrs.ca
514-499-4018
Ginette Casavant, Technicienne
ginette_casavant@ucs.inrs.ca
514-499-4017
Linda Joly, Commis bibliothèque
linda_joly@ucs.inrs.ca
514-499-8265
Anastassia Khouri, Coordinator
anastassia.khouri@mcgill.ca
514-398-4702
Rosa Orlandini, Manager
rosa.orlandini@mcgill.ca
514-398-8095

Montréal: **Walter Hitschfeld Geographic Information Centre**
#524, Burnside Hall, 805, rue Sherbrooke ouest
Montréal, QC H3A 2K6
514-398-8095
Fax: 514-398-4083
e-mail: gic.library@mcgill.ca
URL: www.library.mcgill.ca/gic/
National Library Symbol: QMMG
Founded in: 1945
Hours: M-Th 10:00-9:00; F 10:00-5:00; Sa, Su 12:00-5:00
Acquisitions Budget: $50,000 - $99,999
Special Collections: Maps, Atlases, Fire Insurance Plans, Soil Reports, Digital Data & Air Photos
Subjects covered: Cartography, Geographic Information Systems, Maps
Services:
Inter-Library Loan (ILL) for a fee
Personnel: *Summary:* 1 Total; 1 Professional(s); 2 Technical(s)
Carole Urbain, Directrice
carole.urbain@umontreal.ca
514-343-7424
Sophie Labelle, Technicienne en documentation
sophie.labelle@umontreal.ca
514-343-6111 ext. 8063
Maryna Beaulieu, Bibliothécaire
maryna.beaulieu@umontreal.ca
514-343-6111 ext. 994
Lucy Caetano, Commis
lucy.caetano@umontreal.ca
514-343-6111 ext. 8063

Outremont: **Bibliothèque de géographie**
520, ch Côte Ste-Catherine
Outremont, QC H3C 3J7
Adresse postale: CP 6128, Succ Centre-ville
Montréal, QC H3C 3J7
514-343-8063
Téléc: 514-343-8008
Courriel: biblios@bib.umontreal.ca
pebqmu@bib.umontreal.ca
URL: www.bib.umontreal.ca
Heures: L-J 9h-20h; V 9h-16h30; S 12h-17h
Budget d'acquisitions: $25,000 - $49,999
Population desservie: 1,500 étudiants, professeurs, chercheurs
Annotation: Service de formation documentaire
Sujets: Géographie physique, géographie humaine, cartographie et télédétection, géographie économique, géographie sociale, géographie des populations, géographie urbaine, géographie médicale
Services:
Accèss distance aux bases de donn
Accès public à l'internet
Réseau en ligne
Prêts entre bibliothèques(PEB)
Personnel: *Sommaire:* 3 Total; 1 Professionnel(s); 1 Technicien(s); 1 Autre(s) employé(s)

Outremont: **Collège Stanislas inc Bibliothèque**
780, boul Dollard
Outremont, QC H2V 3G5
514-273-9521
Téléc: 514-273-3409
Courriel: cdi@stanislas.qc.ca
URL: www.stanislas.qc.ca
Fermée au public
Services:
Personnel: *Sommaire:* 1 Professionnel(s); 2 Technicien(s)
Marie Olivier, Responsable

La Pocatière: **CÉGEP de la Pocatière Bibliothèque François-Hertel**
140, 4e av
La Pocatière, QC G0R 1Z0
418-856-1525
Téléc: 418-856-4589
Courriel: jldemers@cglapocatiere.qc.ca
URL: www.cglapocatiere.qc.ca
Membre d'un consortium: Réseau des services documentaires collégiaux (Resdoc)
Fondée en: 1978
Heures: L-Me 7h50-21h; J 7h50-18h; V 7h50-16h30
Budget d'acquisitions: $25,000 - $49,999
Collections spécialisées: Collection complète des oeuvres de François Hertel.
Services:
Accès public à l'internet
Prêts entre bibliothèques(PEB)
Personnel: *Sommaire:* 1 Professionnel(s); 2 Technicien(s); 4 Autre(s) employé(s)
Jean-Louis Demers, Bibliothécaire en chef
jldemers@cglapocatiere.qc.ca
418-856-1525 ext. 2228
Marthe Bergeron, Responsable, Référence et periodiques
Jocelyne Mignault, Responsable, Services techniques

La Pocatière: **Institut de technologie agro-alimentaire de la Pocatière Centre de documentation**
401, rue Poiré
La Pocatière, QC G0R 1Z0
418-856-1110 ext. 258
Téléc: 418-856-1719
Courriel: cditalp@agr.gouv.qc.ca
pduncan@agr.gouv.qc.ca
Sigle: QPES
Fondée en: 1859
Heures: L-V 7h30-17h; L-J 18h-21h
Budget d'acquisitions: $25,000 - $49,999
Sujets: Agriculture, alimentation, environnement, biologie, économie, entomologie, faune, sylviculture, ornithologie, zootechnie, pédologie, génie rural
Services:
Prêts entre bibliothèques(PEB)
Lecteur/reproduction de microformes: Lecteurs
Personnel: *Sommaire:* 2 Total; 1 Professionnel(s); 2 Technicien(s); 1 Autre(s) employé(s)
Pierre Duncan, Professionnel
pduncan@agr.gouv.qc.ca
418-856-1110 ext. 258
Dominique Therriault, Technicienne agricole
dominique.therriault@agr.gouv.qc.ca
418-856-1110 ext. 279
Agathe Plante, Agente de secrétariat
agathe.plante@agr.gouv.qc.ca
418-856-1110 ext. 257

Pointe-Claire: **FPInnovations Information Resources**
580, boul Saint-Jean
Pointe-Claire, QC H9R 3J9
514-694-1140
Fax: 514-694-4351
e-mail: stephanie-s@mtl.feric.ca
margaret-j@mtl.feric.ca
URL: www.feric.ca
National Library Symbol: QMFER
Founded in: 1976
Hours: M-F 9:00-5:00 by appointment only
Special Collections: Canadian & US patent collection on mechanization of wood harvesting & silviculture (last 10 years)
Subjects covered: Forestry, Forest Engineering, Wood Transportation, Natural Resources
Services:
Internet Access
Inter-Library Loan (ILL)
Personnel: *Summary:* 3 Total; 1 Professional(s); 1 Technical(s); 1 Other employees
Martine Brebeau, Head, Information Resources
Margaret Jeanvoine, Library Clerk
margaret-j@mtl.feric.ca

Pointe-Claire: **Pulp & Paper Research Institute of Canada (PAPRICAN) / Institut canadien de recherches sur les pâtes et papiers Library**
570, boul St-Jean
Pointe-Claire, QC H9R 3J9
514-630-4101 ext. 2313
Fax: 514-630-4134
e-mail: library@paprican.ca
National Library Symbol: QMPP
Founded in: 1929
Subjects covered: Engineering, Technology, Environment, Pulp and Paper, Chemistry, Physics, Environmental & Physical Sciences, Measurements & Standards
Services:
Personnel: *Summary:* 5 Total; 2 Professional(s); 2 Technical(s)
Linda Everett, Group Leader
leverett@paprican.ca
Francine Bernard, Bibliothécaire
bernardf@agr.gc.ca
418-657-7985 ext. 211

Québec: **Bibliothèque canadienne de l'agriculture - Sainte-Foy / Canadian Agriculture Library - Sainte-Foy**
2560, boul Hochelaga
Québec, QC G1V 2J3
418-657-7980 ext: 211
Téléc: 418-648-2402
Courriel: lussierc@agr.gc.ca
URL: www.agr.gc.ca
Sigle: QSFAG
Fondée en: 1970
Heures: 9h-13h, 13h30-16havec rendez-vous seulement
Sujets: Agriculture, Céréales, Plantes Fourragères, Biologie Moléculaire, Sols
Services:
Prêts entre bibliothèques(PEB)
Personnel:
Alain Bourque, Chef, Bibliothèque des sciences humaines et sociales
alain.bourque@bibl.ulaval.ca
418-656-2131 ext. 5196
Chantal St-Louis, Secteur de l'aide à la recherche
chantal.st-louis@bibl.ulaval.ca
418-656-2131 ext. 7965
Alain Gendron, Secteur de la circulation
alain.gendron@bibl.ulaval.ca
418-656-2131 ext. 7934
Françoise Sorieul, Secteur des collections spéciales
francoise.sorieul@bibl.ulaval.ca
418-656-2131 ext. 3227
Isabelle Archambault, Secteur de la consultation
isabelle.archambault@bibl.ulaval.ca
418-656-2131 ext. 3224

Québec: **Bibliothèque des sciences humaines et sociales**
Pavillon Jean-Charles-Bonenfant
Québec, QC G1K 7P4
418-656-3344
Courriel: peb_qqla@bibl.ulaval.ca
URL: www.bibl.ulaval.ca
Sigle: QQLA
Heures: L-V 8h30-23h; S, D 10h-17h30
Budget d'acquisitions: $1,000,000 plus
Sujets: Droit, arts, sciences humaines, sciences sociales
Services:
Accèss distance aux bases de donn
Accès public à l'internet
Réseau en ligne
Prêts entre bibliothèques(PEB)
Lecteur/reproduction de microformes: Ordinateur; Lecteurs
Personnel: *Sommaire:* 93 Total; 24 Professionnel(s); 16 Technicien(s); 47 Autre(s) employé(s)

Québec: **Bibliothèque scientifique Charles-Auguste-Gauthier**
1401, 18e rue
Québec, QC G1J 1Z4
418-649-5686
Téléc: 418-649-5627
Sigle: QQHEJ
Fondée en: 1963
Heures: L-V 8h30-16h30
Annotation: Affiliée aux Bibliothèques de Santé de la Région de Québec.
Collections spécialisées: Sciences neurologiques
Sujets: Médecine
Services:
Accès public à l'internet
Lecteur/reproduction de microformes: Lecteurs
Personnel:
Diane St-Pierre, Responsable
Marcelle Lauzon, Technicienne en documentation
mlauzon@climoilou.qc.ca

Québec: **Campus de Charlesbourg Centre des médias**
7600, 3e av est
Québec, QC G1H 7L4

Libraries & Resource Centres / Québec

418-647-6600 ext: 3653
Téléc: 418-624-3698
Courriel: mlauzon@climoilou.qc.ca
URL: www.climoilou.qc.ca
Fondée en: 1991
Heures: L-V 8h-17h
Budget d'acquisitions: $25,000 - $49,999
Services:
Prêts entre bibliothèques(PEB)
Lecteur/reproduction de microformes: Ordinateur; Lecteurs
Personnel: *Sommaire:* 2 Total; 1 Technicien(s); 3 Autre(s) employé(s)

Québec: **CÉGEP de Sainte-Foy**
Centre des médias
2410, ch Ste-Foy
Québec, QC G1V 1T3
418-659-6600 ext: 3603
Téléc: 418-659-4563
URL: biblio.cegep-ste-foy.qc.ca
Membre d'un consortium: Réseau des services documentaires collégiaux (Resdoc)
Fondée en: 1980
Heures: Sessions régulières: L-J 8h30-21h; V 7h30-18h30; Sa-D 12h-16h.
Budget d'acquisitions: $50,000 - $99,999
Annotation: Services: Salles de lecture et de travail
Services:
Accès distance aux bases de donn
Accès public à l'internet
Réseau en ligne
Prêts entre bibliothèques(PEB)
Personnel: *Sommaire:* 1 Professionnel(s); 5 Technicien(s); 7 Autre(s) employé(s)
Francine Piché, Coordonnatrice, service des ressources documentaires
francine.piche@cegep-ste-foy.qc.ca
418-659-6600 ext. 3603
Michelle Ribière, Bibliothécaire
michelle.ribiere@cegep-ste-foy.qc.ca
418-659-6600 ext. 3864

Québec: **CÉGEP Limoilou**
Bibliothèque
1300, 8e av
Québec, QC G1J 5L5
718-647-6600
Téléc: 418-647-6793
Courriel: daniel.vezina@climoilou.qc.ca
URL: www.climoilou.qc.ca
Membre d'un consortium: Réseau des services documentaires collégiaux (Resdoc)
Fondée en: 1967
Heures: L-J 7h50-21h30; V 7h50-17h
Budget d'acquisitions: $50,000 - $99,999
Collections spécialisées: Collection Pierre George Roy, Collection Gabriel Garcia Marquez
Services:
Accès public à l'internet
Réseau en ligne
Prêts entre bibliothèques(PEB)
Personnel: *Sommaire:* 5 Total; 1 Professionnel(s); 4 Technicien(s)
Alexandra Lavallée, Responsable
alexandra.lavallee@climoilou.qc.ca
418-647-6600 ext. 6884
Marie-Claude Beaudry, Technicienne en documentation
marie-claude.beaudry@climoilou.ca
418-647-6600 ext. 3653
Monique Morency, Personnel
mmorency@mtq.gouv.qc.ca

Québec: **Centre de documentation (Génie)**
930, ch Sainte-Foy, 6e étage
Québec, QC G1S 4X9
418-643-2156
Téléc: 418-646-6195
Courriel: doc-qtrd@mtq.gouv.qc.ca
URL: www.mtq.gouv.qc.ca
Sigle: QQTRD
Heures: L-V 8h30-12h, 13h-16h30
Collections spécialisées: Publications du Transportation Research Board
Sujets: Construction et entretien des routes, ponts, viaducs; transport; environnement
Services:
Accès public à l'internet
Prêts entre bibliothèques(PEB)
Personnel: *Sommaire:* 3 Total; 1 Technicien(s)

Québec: **Centre de recherche industriel du Québec**
Centre de documentation (Sainte-Foy)
333, rue Franquet
Québec, QC G1P 4C7
418-659-1550 ext: 2426
Téléc: 418-652-2225
800-667-2386
Courriel: infocriq@criq.qc.ca
huguette.beaumont@criq.qc.ca
URL: www.criq.qc.ca
Sigle: QSFCR
Fermée au public
Fondée en: 1971
Budget d'acquisitions: $50,000 - $99,999
Collections spécialisées: Normes: CSA, ASTM, ULC, CGA, BNQ, ONGC, AFNOR, ISO
Sujets: Normes, sciences et technologie, industrie, information et documentation, métallurgie, biotechnologie, R8D
Services:
Personnel: *Sommaire:* 1 Total; 1 Technicien(s)
Huguette Beaumont, Technicienne en documentation

Québec: **CHUQ-CHUL**
Bibliothèque Astrazeneca des sciences de la santé
#RC-315, 2705, boul Laurier
Québec, QC G1V 4G2
418-525-4444 ext: 17157
Téléc: 418-654-2143
Courriel: biblio.chul@dechuq.ulaval.ca
Sigle: QQLACH
Fondée en: 1968
Heures: L-V 8h30-16h30
Budget d'acquisitions: $50,000 - $99,999
Annotation: Groupe Biblio-Santé de la Région du Québec. Fax, Lizette Germain: 416/525-4170
Sujets: Santé, pédiatrie, opthalmologie, psychiatrie, rhumatologie
Services:
Accès public à l'internet
Prêts entre bibliothèques(PEB)
Personnel: *Sommaire:* 3 Total; 1 Professionnel(s); 2 Technicien(s)
Lizette Germain, Bibliothécaire
418-525-4444 ext. 52414
Denise Morin, Bibliotechnicienne
Patricia Chamberland, Bibliotechnicienne

Québec: **Collège Mérici**
Bibliothèque
755, Grande Allée ouest
Québec, QC G1S 1C1
418-683-2104 ext: 2213
Téléc: 418-682-8938
800-208-1463
URL: www.college-merici.qc.ca/index.php?id=33
Profile: Merici College is a private co-educational college-level institution dispensing a variety of pre-university & professional programs with an annual student enrolment of about 1 200. Founded by the sisters of the Ursuline Order, Merici College has remained faithful to a long tradition of excellence while constantly adjusting to the changing educational needs of its students
Sigle: QQCM
Membre d'un consortium: Réseau des services documentaires collégiaux (Resdoc)
Fondée en: 1930
Heures: L-J 8h-20h; V 8h-17h
Budget d'acquisitions: $25,000 - $49,999
Collections spécialisées: Natural Science, Social Science, Multimedia Design, Creative Advertising, Orthotics and Prosthetics, Special Education, Tourism, Hotel Management, Restaurant Management
Sujets: Sciences, sciences humaines, arts et lettres, communication visuelle, multimédia, dessin animé, orthèses et prothèses orthopédiques, administration, tourisme, hôtellerie, services alimentaires et restauration, loisirs, enseignement, recherche sociale, enquête, sondage, éducation spécialisée
Services:
Accès public à l'internet
Réseau en ligne
Prêts entre bibliothèques(PEB)
Personnel: *Sommaire:* 6 Total; 1 Professionnel(s); 1 Technicien(s); 4 Autre(s) employé(s)
Maryse Messely, Responsable, Bibliothèque
mmessely@college-merici.qc.ca
418-683-1591 ext. 2213
France Simard-Pageau, Technicienne, documentation
fpageau@college-merici.qc.ca
418-683-1591 ext. 2251

Québec: **Commission de toponymie du Québec, Bibliothèque (Library)**
Bibliothèque
750, boul Charest est
Québec, QC G1K 9K4
418-643-4575
Téléc: 418-528-1373
Courriel: qqolf@oqlf.gouv.qc.ca
URL: www.toponymie.gouv.qc.ca
Sigle: QQCT
Fondée en: 1977
Heures: L-V 8h30-12h, 13h-16h30avec rendez-vous seulement
Budget d'acquisitions: 0-$9,999
Matériel imprimé: 0-$9,999
Matériel électronique: 0-$9,999
Collections spécialisées: Monographies paroissiales; répertoires géographiques; rapports géologiques
Sujets: Toponymie, linguistique, géographie, histoire
Services:
Prêts entre bibliothèques(PEB)
Personnel: *Sommaire:* 1 Technicien(s)
Frederic Gagnon, Bibliothécaire
frederic.gagnon@oqlf.gouv.qc.ca
Ann Murchison, Librarian
amurchison@slc.qc.ca
416-656-6921 ext. 231
Joanne Kyvetos, Technician

Québec: **Donald-Petzel Memorial Library**
790, av Nérée-Tremblay
Québec, QC G1V 4K2
418-656-6921 ext: 230
Fax: 418-656-6925
e-mail: circulation@slc.qc.ca
URL: www.slc.qc.ca/library
National Library Symbol: QSTFCR
Founded in: 1958
Hours: M-Th 8:00-7:00; F 8:00-4:00
Acquisitions Budget: $25,000 - $49,999
For Print: $10,000 - $24,999
For Electronic: 0-$9,999
Subjects covered: Pre-University, Business
Services:
Remote Access
Internet Access
Access to Subscription Databases
Inter-Library Loan (ILL)
Microform Equipment: Computer; Reader
Personnel: *Summary:* 3 Total; 1 Professional(s); 1 Technical(s); 1 Other employees
Deirdre Moore, Librarian
Odile Fleury, Library Technologist

Québec: **Eastern Division Library/Bibliothèque de la division de l'est**
319, rue Franquet
Québec, QC G1P 4R4
418-659-2647
Fax: 418-659-2922
e-mail: deirdre.moore@qc.forintek.ca
odile.fleury@qc.forintek.ca
National Library Symbol: QSFF
No public access
Founded in: 1912
Hours: M-F
Acquisitions Budget: $50,000 - $99,999
Special Collections: Standards
Subjects covered: Solid wood products technology, Forest products, Value-Added wood products, Building systems, Composite products technology
Services:
Inter-Library Loan (ILL)
Personnel: *Summary:* 2 Total; 1 Professional(s); 1 Technical(s)

Libraries & Resource Centres / Québec

Québec: GSC - Quebec Library / Bibliothèque de la CGC - Québec
490, rue de la Couronne
Québec, QC G1K 9A9
418-654-2677
Téléc: 418-654-2660
Couriel: sdis@adm.inrs.ca
URL: gsc.nrcan.gc.ca/org/quebec/lib_e.php
Annotation: SEE INRS - Université du Québec, CGC Québec
Services:

Québec: INRS - Université du Québec, CGC - Québec
Bibliothèque
#1400, 490, de la Couronne
Québec, QC G1K 9A9
418-654-2577
Fax: 418-654-2660
e-mail: sdis@adm.inrs.ca
peb-qsfig@uquebec.ca
URL: sdis.inrs.ca
National Library Symbol: QSFIG
Consortia Membership: CREPUQ; SDIS; NRCanLibrary
Founded in: 1970
Hours: M-F 8:00-12:00, 1:00-4:00
Acquisitions Budget: $50,000 - $99,999
For Print: $25,000 - $49,999
For Electronic: $50,000 - $99,999
Population Served: 500
Subjects covered: Earth Sciences, Water Sciences, Environmental Sciences
Services:
Remote Access
Internet Access
Access to Subscription Databases
Inter-Library Loan (ILL)
Reference
Microform Equipment: Reader
Personnel: Summary: 6 Total; 1 Professional(s); 2 Technical(s); 3 Other employees
Jean-Daniel Bourgault, Head Librarian
jean-daniel.bourgault@ete.inrs.ca
418-654-2667
Anne Robitaille, Technician
418-654-2588
Chantal Paquin, Technician
418-654-3727

Québec: Institut de l'Énergie et de l'environnement de la francophonie
Bibliothèque
56, rue St-Pierre, 3e étage
Québec, QC G1K 4A1
418-692-5727
Téléc: 418-692-5644
Couriel: iepf@iepf.org
URL: www.iepf.org
Heures: L-V 9h-17h
Budget d'acquisitions: Matériel imprimé: 0-$9,999
Sujets: Énergie, Environnement
Services:
Personnel: Sommaire: 1 Total; 1 Professionnel(s)
Louis-Noël Jail, Chef du service, Information et documentation
Pauline Malenfant, Assistante
p.malenfant@iepf.org
418-692-5727 ext. 247
Jacinthe Potvin, Assistante
j.potvin@iepf.org
418-692-5727 ext. 227
Gilles Bizier, Bibliothécaire
gbizier@rncan.gc.ca
Eve Montminy, Technicienne en documentation
eve.montminy@rncan.gc.ca
418-648-4428

Québec: Laurentian Forestry Centre / Centre de foresterie des Laurentides
1055, rue du P.E.P.S.
Québec, QC G1V 4C7
Adresse postale: CP 10380, Succ. Ste-Foy
Québec, QC G1V 4C7
418-648-3335
Téléc: 418-648-5849
Couriel: webcfl@rncan.gc.ca
URL: www.cfs.nrcan.gc.ca/regions/lfc

Sigle: QQMF
Fondée en: 1954
Heures: L-V 8h-12h, 13h-16h
Budget d'acquisitions: $50,000 - $99,999
Matériel imprimé: $50,000 - $99,999
Matériel électronique: $25,000 - $49,999
Sujets: Foresterie, entomologie, biologie, mycologie, biotechnologie, génétique des plantes
Services:
Accès distance aux bases de donn
Accès public à l'internet
Prêts entre bibliothèques(PEB)
Personnel: Sommaire: 2 Total; 1 Professionnel(s); 1 Technicien(s)

Québec: Parc Aquarium du Québec
Centre de documentation
1675, av des Hôtels
Québec, QC G1W 4S3
418-659-5264
Téléc: 418-646-9238
866-659-5264
Couriel: masson.stephane@sepaq.com
URL: www.sepaq.com/aquarium
Sigle: QQZ
Fermée au public
Fondée en: 1972
Heures: L-V 9h-16h
Budget d'acquisitions: 0-$9,999
Population desservie: 90
Annotation: Formerly known as Société des parcs de sciences naturelles du Québec.
Sujets: Biologie
Services:
Prêts entre bibliothèques(PEB)
Personnel:
Stéphane Masson, Coordonateur scientifique
418-659-5264 ext. 251

Québec: Québec Conseil de la science et de la technologie
Centre de documentation
#3.45, 1200, rte de l'Église
Québec, QC G1V 4Z2
418-644-4187
Téléc: 418-646-0920
Couriel: monique.blouin@cst.gouv.qc.ca
URL: www.cst.gouv.qc.ca/-Centre-de-documentation-
Sigle: QQST
Fondée en: 1979
Heures: L-V 8h30-12h, 13h30-16h30avec rendez-vous seulement
Budget d'acquisitions: 0-$9,999
Matériel imprimé: 0-$9,999
Sujets: Politique scientifique et technologique, recherche et développement, nouvelles technologies
Services:
Prêts entre bibliothèques(PEB)
Personnel: Sommaire: 2 Total; 1 Professionnel(s); 1 Technicien(s)
José Vinals, Bibliothécaire
jose.vinals@cst.gouv.qc.ca
418-643-2378
Monique Blouin, Technicienne en documentation
monique.blouin@cst.gouv.qc.ca
418-644-4187

Québec: Québec Ministère de l'agriculture, des pêcheries et de l'alimentation
Bibliothèque
200, ch Ste-Foy
Québec, QC G1R 4X6
418-380-2100 ext: 3516
Téléc: 418-380-2175
Couriel: bibli200@mapaq.gouv.qc.ca
bib_peb@mapaq.gouv.qc.ca
Sigle: QQAG
Fondée en: 1943
Heures: L-V 8h30-12h, 13h-16h30
Budget d'acquisitions: $25,000 - $49,999
Annotation: Téléréférence réservé aux employés(es) du ministère.
Collections spécialisées: Publications du Mapaq
Sujets: Agriculture, alimentation
Services:
Prêts entre bibliothèques(PEB)

Personnel: Sommaire: 6 Total; 1 Professionnel(s); 4 Technicien(s); 1 Autre(s) employé(s)
Michel Lévesque, Chef de service
Anne Lafond, Technicienne en documentation
418-380-2100 ext. 3516
Line Gauvin, Technicienne en documentation
418-380-2100 ext. 3509
Guylaine Hazen, Technicienne en documentation
Suzy LaForest, Technicienne en documentation

Québec: Québec Ministère de la santé et des services sociaux
Centre de documentation
1075, ch Sainte-Foy, 5e étage
Québec, QC G1S 2M1
418-266-7007
Téléc: 418-266-7024
Couriel: peb.servdoc@msss.gouv.qc.ca
URL: www.msss.gouv.qc.ca/documentation/centrededoc.php
Sigle: QQIAS
Fondée en: 1983
Heures: L-V 8h30-12h, 13h-16h30
Budget d'acquisitions: $50,000 - $99,999
Sujets: Services sociaux, santé, santé mentale, personnes agées, la famille, jeunes, personnes handicapées, toxicomanie
Services:
Accès public à l'internet
Prêts entre bibliothèques(PEB) frais de Réciprocité
Lecteur/reproduction de microformes: Lecteurs
Personnel:
Claude Lamarre, Chef du service des ressources documentaires
claude.lamarre@msss.gouv.qc.ca
418-266-7005
Eugène Lakinsky, Responsable, Division recherche et diffusion
eugene.lakinsky@msss.gouv.qc.ca
418-266-7008
Denis Perreault, Responsable, Division catalogage et gestion des documents
denis.perreault@msss.gouv.qc.ca
418-266-7015
Joëlle Bédard, Acquisitions
joelle.bedard@msss.gouv.qc.ca
418-266-7012
Manon LaFontaine, Technicienne en documentation
peb.servdoc@msss.gouv.qc.ca
418-266-7020
Annick Lamontagne, Technicienne en documentation
peb.servdoc@msss.gouv.qc.ca
418-266-7020

Québec: Québec Ministère des affaires municipales et des Régions
Centre de documentation
10, rue Pierre-Olivier-Chauveau, Sous-sol, aile Chauveau
Québec, QC G1R 4J3
418-691-2018
Couriel: centre.doc@mamr.gouv.qc.ca
Sigle: QQAM
Fondée en: 1979
Heures: 8h30-12h, 13h-16h30
Budget d'acquisitions: $25,000 - $49,999
Matériel imprimé: $10,000 - $24,999
Matériel électronique: 0-$9,999
Population desservie: 500
Sujets: Affaires municipales; Administration municipale; Aménagement; Cartographie; Démographie; Droit et législation municipale; Finances municipales; Urbanisme
Services:
Prêts entre bibliothèques(PEB)
Personnel: Sommaire: 1 Total; 1 Technicien(s)
Julie Limoges, Technicienne de la documention

Québec: Québec Ministère des Ressources naturelles et de la Faune
Bibliothèque
D-316, 5700, 4e av ouest
Québec, QC G1H 6R1
418-627-8686
Téléc: 418-644-1124
Couriel: bibliotheque@mrnf.gouv.qc.ca
sylvie.laleberte@mrnf.gouv.qc.ca
Sigle: QQFO
Membre d'un consortium: Réseau informatisé des bibliothèques gouvernementales
Fondée en: 1994

Libraries & Resource Centres / Québec

Heures: L-V 8h30-12h, 13h-16h30
Budget d'acquisitions: $100,000 - $249,999
Matériel imprimé: $25,000 - $49,999
Matériel électronique: $100,000 - $249,999
Population desservie: 4600
Collections spécialisées: US Geology Survey; Commission géologique du Canada; Service géologique du Québec; The US Bureau of Mines; Documents des Services canadiens des forêts; US Department of Agriculture; Forestry Commission United Kingdom; Rapports annuels depuis le 19e siècle; DP, DPV, MB; US Bureau of Mines; Service canadien des forêts; Forestry Commission UK, DP, DPV, MS
Sujets: Forêts, sylviculture, énergie, mines, terres, géologie, faune, information foncière
Services:
Accès public à l'internet
Prêts entre bibliothèques(PEB)
Lecteur/reproduction de microformes: Ordinateur; Lecteurs
Personnel: *Sommaire:* 13 Total; 2 Professionnel(s); 8 Technicien(s); 3 Autre(s) employé(s)
Annie Turner, Bibliothécaire
annie.turner@mrnf.gouv.qc.ca
418-627-8686 ext. 3557
Pierrette Labbé, Technicienne en documentation
pierrette.labbe@mrnf.gouv.qc.ca
418-627-8686 ext. 3594
Lynda Racine, Technicienne en documentation
Lynda.Racine@mrnf.gouv.qc.ca
418-627-8686 ext. 3597
Carmel Blanchard, Technicienne en administration
Carmel.Blanchard@mrnf.gouv.qc.ca
418-627-8686 ext. 3457
Sylvie Laliberté, Technicienne en documentation
sylvie.laliberte@mrnf.gouv.qc.ca
418-627-8686 ext. 3664

Québec: Québec Ministère des transports
Centre de documentation (Bibliothèque centrale)
700, boul René-Lévesque est
Québec, QC G1R 5H1
418-643-3578
Téléc: 418-646-2343
Couriel: doc-qtr@mtq.gouv.qc.ca
URL: www.mtq.gouv.qc.ca
Sigle: QQTR
Fondée en: 1978
Heures: L-V 8h30-12h, 13h-16h30
Collections spécialisées: Transport Québec, Transports Canada, Transportation Research Board (E-U), Conférence européenne des ministres des transports, Institut national de recherche sur les transports et leur sécurité (France)
Sujets: Transports, énergie, environnement, génie, technologie, aménagement de territoire, urbanisme
Services:
Accès public à l'internet
Prêts entre bibliothèques(PEB)
Personnel: *Sommaire:* 15 Total; 4 Professionnel(s); 10 Technicien(s); 3 Autre(s) employé(s)
Donald Blais, Directeur

Québec: Québec Ministère du Développement durable, de l'Environnement et des Parcs
Centre de documentation
675, boul René-Lévesque est, 29e etage
Québec, QC G1R 5V7
418-521-3830
Téléc: 418-646-5974
800-561-1616
Couriel: biblio@mddep.gouv.qc.ca
pretbiblio@mddep.gouv.qc.ca
info@mddep.gouv.qc.ca
URL: www.menv.gouv.qc.ca
Sigle: QQEN
Fondée en: 1979
Heures: L, M, J, V 8h30-12h, 13h-16h30, Me 10h-12h, 1h-16h30
Budget d'acquisitions: $50,000 - $99,999
Collections spécialisées: Envirodoq
Sujets: Environnement, biologie, sciences physiques, technologie, chimie, faune, pollution, précipitations acides, aménagement, gestion de la faune
Services:
Accès public à l'internet
Réseau en ligne
Prêts entre bibliothèques(PEB)
Lecteur/reproduction de microformes: Lecteurs

Personnel: *Sommaire:* 9 Total; 2 Professionnel(s); 2 Technicien(s); 3 Autre(s) employé(s)
Gérard Nobréga, Responsable du centre de documentation
gerard.nobrega@mddep.gouv.qc.ca
418-521-3821 ext. 4136
Sylvain Blanchet, Bibliothécaire
sylvain.blanchet@mddep.gouv.qc.ca
418-521-3821 ext. 4138
Alain Aubin, Bibliothécaire
alain.aubin@mddep.gouv.qc.ca
418-521-3821 ext. 4129
Roland Turmel, Technicien, PEB

Québec: Québec Ministère du Développement économique, de l'Innovation et de l'Exportation
Bibliothèque
710, Place d'Youville, 2e étage
Québec, QC G1R 4Y4
418-691-5972
Téléc: 418-643-8936
Couriel: biblio@mderr.gouv.qc.ca
Sigle: QQIC
Fondée en: 1957
Heures: L-V 8h30-12h, 13h-16h30avec rendez-vous seulement
Budget d'acquisitions: $50,000 - $99,999
Matériel imprimé: $25,000 - $49,999
Matériel électronique: $25,000 - $49,999
Annotation: Accès à Internet, aux cédéroms et bases de données pour employés du ministère; Membre du Réseau Informatisé des Bibliothèques Gouvernementales
Sujets: Économie, industrie, commerce, coopération, relations industrielles, technologie, PME, commerce international
Services:
Prêts entre bibliothèques(PEB)
Personnel: *Sommaire:* 5 Total; 1 Professionnel(s); 1 Technicien(s); 1 Autre(s) employé(s)
Nicole Nadeau, Responsable
nicole.nadeau@mdeie.gouv.qc.ca
418-691-5698 ext. 4181
Aline Labreque, Bibliotechnicienne
aline.labrecque@mdeie.gouv.qc.ca
418-691-5698 ext. 4145

Québec: Québec Régie de l'assurance-maladie
Bibliothèque
1125, Grande Allée ouest
Québec, QC G1K 7T3
Adresse postale: CP 6600
Québec, QC G1K 7T3
418-682-5118
Téléc: 418-528-6864
Couriel: bibliotheque@ramq.gouv.qc.ca
Sigle: QQRAMQ
Fondée en: 1970
Heures: L-V 8h30-12h, 13h-16h30avec rendez-vous seulement
Budget d'acquisitions: Matériel imprimé: 0-$9,999
Collections spécialisées: Collection de la RAMQ
Sujets: Sciences de la santé, affaires sociales, administration publique, gestion, informatique, santé, services sociaux
Services:
Prêts entre bibliothèques(PEB)
Personnel: *Sommaire:* 1 Total; 1 Technicien(s)
Louise Guy, Bibliotechnicienne

Québec: Région du Québec
Main Library
1141, rte de l'Église, 1e étage
Québec, QC G1V 4H5
Mailing Address: CP 10100
Québec, QC G1V 4H5
418-648-4768
Fax: 418-648-7166
Other contact info: 418-649-6546
e-mail: Quebec.Biblio@ec.gc.ca
URL: www.ec.gc.ca/library
National Library Symbol: QQE
Acquisitions Budget: $25,000 - $49,999
Services:
Inter-Library Loan (ILL)
Microform Equipment: Computer; Reader
Personnel: *Summary:* 2 Total; 1 Professional(s); 1 Technical(s)

Québec: SOQUEM INC.
SOQUEM documentation
#500, 1000, rte de l'Église
Québec, QC G1V 3V9

418-658-5400 ext: 21
Téléc: 418-658-5459
Couriel: daniel.sauser@soquem.qc.ca
Sigle: SOQUEM
Fondée en: 1965
Heures: Meavec rendez-vous seulement
Budget d'acquisitions: 0-$9,999
Sujets: Géologie, ressources naturelles, cartes géographiques, sciences terrestres
Services:
Prêts entre bibliothèques(PEB)
Personnel: *Sommaire:* 1 Total; 1 Technicien(s)
Daniel Sauser, Technicien
daniel.sauser@soquem.qc.ca
418-650-5400
Barbara Maass, Bibliothécaire

Québec: Succursale de Québec
Centre de documentation
1054, rue Louis-Alexandre Taschereau, Aile Saint-Amable, 3e étage
Québec, QC G1R 5E7
418-646-7915
Téléc: 418-528-0403
Couriel: centredoc@shq.gouv.qc.ca
URL: www.habitation.gouv.qc.ca/
Sigle: QQSHQ
Fondée en: 1988
Heures: avec rendez-vous seulement
Sujets: Logement, construction, architecture, urbanisme
Services:
Accès public à l'internet
Prêts entre bibliothèques(PEB)
Personnel: *Sommaire:* 1 Total; 1 Professionnel(s)

Québec: Télé-Université
Service de la Bibliotech à distance
455, rue du Parvis
Québec, QC G1K 9H6
418-657-2747 ext: 5397
Téléc: 418-657-2094
800-463-4728
Couriel: rcroteau@teluq.ca
URL: www.bilio.teluq.ca
Sigle: QQUQT
Membre d'un consortium: Canadian Research Knowledge Network (CRKN); Conférence des recteurs et des principaux des universités du Québec (CREPUQ)
Fondée en: 1978
Heures: L-V 8h30-12h, 13h-16h30avec rendez-vous seulement
Budget d'acquisitions: $50,000 - $99,999
Collections spécialisées: Enseignement supérieurl; communication organisationnelle
Sujets: Éducation enseignement à distance; Technologie éducative; Éducation des adultes
Services:
Accès distance aux bases de donn
Accès public à l'internet
Réseau en ligne
Prêts entre bibliothèques(PEB) frais de selon réciprocité
Frais de recherche
Lecteur/reproduction de microformes: Ordinateur; Lecteurs
Personnel: *Sommaire:* 5 Total
Jean-Pierre Roy, Coodonnateur

Québec: Union québécoise pour la conservation de la nature / Québec Union for Nature Conservation
Bibliothèque
#207, 870, av De Salaberry
Québec, QC G1R 2T9
418-648-2104
Téléc: 418-648-0991
Couriel: conservons@naturequebec.org
URL: www.naturequebec.org
Heures: avec rendez-vous seulement
Sujets: Conservation
Services:
Personnel:
Andréanne Hamel, Responsable

Québec: Université du Québec Institut national de la recherche scientifique, INRS-ETE
Service de documentation et d'information spécialisées
2800, rue Einstein
Québec, QC G1V 4C7

Adresse postale: CP 7500
Québec, QC G1V 4C7
418-654-2577
Téléc: 418-654-2600
Courriel: sophie_renaud@inrs-ete.uquebec.ca
peb_qquie@uquebec.ca
URL:
www.inrs-ete.uquebec.ca/unites/documentation/documentation.htm
Sigle: QQUIE
Membre d'un consortium: Canadian Research Knowledge Network (CRKN); Conférence des recteurs et des principaux des universités du Québec (CREPUQ)
Fondée en: 1970
Heures: L-V
Budget d'acquisitions: $25,000 - $49,999
Sujets: Environnement, biologie, environnement aquatique, hydrologie, assainissement, gestion et administration de l'eau
Services:
Accès public à l'internet
Prêts entre bibliothèques(PEB)
Lecteur/reproduction de microformes: Lecteurs
Personnel: *Sommaire:* 3 Total; 2 Professionnel(s); 2 Technicien(s);
Sophie Renaud, Responsable
sophie_renaud@inrs-ete.uquebec.ca
418-654-2649
Jean-Daniel Bourgault, Bibliothécaire
bourgajd@inrs-ete.uquebec.ca
418-654-2663
Chantal Paquin, Technicienne
paquinch@inrs-ete.uquebec.ca
418-654-2577
Anne Robitaille, Responsable des acquisitions
anne.robitaille@inrs-ete.uquebec.ca
418-654-3724

Québec: Université Laval
Bibliothèque
Pavillon Jean-Charles-Bonenfant
Québec, QC G1K 7P4
418-656-2131 ext: 2008
Téléc: 418-656-7897
Courriel: bibl@bibl.ulaval.ca
qqla@bibl.ulaval.ca
qqlas@bibl.ulaval.ca
URL: www.bibl.ulaval.ca
Sigle: QQLA
Membre d'un consortium: Canadian Research Knowledge Network (CRKN); Conférence des recteurs et des principaux des universités du Québec (CREPUQ)
Fondée en: 1852
Heures: L-D
Budget d'acquisitions: $1,000,000 plus
Sujets: Sciences humaines et sociales, sciences pures et appliquées, sciences de la santé, droit
Services:
Accès distance aux bases de donn
Accès public à l'internet
Réseau en ligne
Prêts entre bibliothèques(PEB)
Lecteur/reproduction de microformes: Ordinateur; Lecteurs
Personnel: *Sommaire:* 213 Total; 60 Professionnel(s); 59 Technicien(s); 100 Autre(s) employé(s)
Silvie Delorme, Directrice
silvie.delorme@bibl.ulaval.ca
418-656-2131 ext. 3451
Louise Allard, Chef, Division du Traitement des fonds documentaires
louise.allard@bibl.ulaval.ca
418-656-2131 ext. 2888
Véronique Paré, Secteur des acquisitions
veronique.pare@bibl.ulaval.ca
418-656-2131 ext. 5991
Marcel Plourde, Secteur du catalogage
marcel.plourde@bibl.ulaval.ca
418-656-2131 ext. 6313
Jo-Anne Bélair, Secteur du répertoire de vedettes-matière
jo-anne.belair@bibl.ulaval.ca
418-656-2131 ext. 2871
Louise Pelletier, Pilote du système Unicorn
louise.pelletier@bibl.ulaval.ca
418-656-3131 ext. 13997
Guy Teasdale, Chef, Division Services soutien et développement

guy.teasdale@bibl.ulaval.ca
418-656-2131 ext. 3918
Martine Lemieux, Secteur du soutien informatique et administratif
martine.lemieux@bibl.ulaval.ca
418-656-2131 ext. 4672
Rida Benjelloun, Secteur recherche et développements numériques
rida.benjelloun@bibl.ulaval.ca
418-656-2131 ext. 2090
Daniel Bérubé, Communications
daniel.berube@bibl.ulaval.ca
418-656-2131 ext. 8600

Rigaud: Collège Bourget / Bourget College
Bibliothèque
65, rue Saint-Pierre
Rigaud, QC J0P 1P0
450-451-0815
Téléc: 450-451-4171
Courriel: biblio@collegebourget.qc.ca
URL: www.collegebourget.qc.ca
Sigle: QRCB
Fondée en: 1850
Heures: 8h15-16h15avec rendez-vous seulement
Budget d'acquisitions: $25,000 - $49,999
Sujets: Culture générale, sciences, langues
Services:
Réseau en ligne
Personnel: *Sommaire:* 3 Total

Rimouski: CÉGEP de Rimouski
Bibliothèque Gilles-Vigneault
60, rue de l'Évêché ouest
Rimouski, QC G5L 4H6
418-723-1880
Téléc: 418-724-4961
Courriel: didac@cegep-rimouski.qc.ca
reference@cegep-rimouski.qc.ca
URL: www.cegep-rimouski.qc.ca/biblio/
Sigle: ORIC
Membre d'un consortium: Réseau des services documentaires collégiaux (Resdoc)
Heures: L-J 8h-19h; V 8h-17h
Budget d'acquisitions: $50,000 - $99,999
Collections spécialisées: Laurentiana du Séminaire de Rimouski
Services:
Accès public à l'internet
Réseau en ligne
Prêts entre bibliothèques(PEB)
Lecteur/reproduction de microformes: Lecteurs
Personnel: *Sommaire:* 9 Total; 2 Professionnel(s); 5 Technicien(s); 3 Autre(s) employé(s);
Vacant, Responsable, Services aux usagers
Mario Côté, Coordonnateur
coorinf@cegep-rimouski.qc.ca
418-723-1880 ext. 2145
Ginette Michaud, Responsable, Services techniques
418-723-1880 ext. 2194

Rimouski: Centre régional de santé et de services sociaux Rimouski
Centre de documentation
150, av Rouleau
Rimouski, QC G5L 5T1
418-724-8394
Téléc: 418-724-8139
Courriel: nicole.belanger.crsssr@ssss.gouv.qc.ca
URL: www.chrr.qc.ca/
Sigle: QRCH
Heures: L-V 8h-16h
Budget d'acquisitions: $50,000 - $99,999
Sujets: Médecine, soins infirmiers
Services:
Accès public à l'internet
Personnel: *Sommaire:* 1 Technicien(s)
Nicole Bélanger, Bibliotechnicienne
Lise Gagné, Technicienne en documentation
lgagne@imq.qc.ca
418-724-2822 ext. 2012
Rena Deroy, Agente de bureau
418-724-2822 ext. 2040

Rimouski: Institut maritime du Québec
Bibliothèque
53, rue St-Germain ouest
Rimouski, QC G5L 4B4
418-724-2822 ext: 2019
Téléc: 418-724-0606
Courriel: lgagne@imq.qc.ca
URL: www.imq.qc.ca/bibliotheque/index.htm
Fondée en: 1976
Heures: L-V 8h-17h
Budget d'acquisitions: $25,000 - $49,999
Sujets: Architecture navale, navigation, mécanique de marine, plongée professionnelle, logistique du transport, droit maritime, électronique du maritime
Services:
Accès public à l'internet
Prêts entre bibliothèques(PEB)
Personnel: *Sommaire:* 2 Total; 1 Technicien(s); 1 Autre(s) employé(s)

Rimouski: Université du Québec à Rimouski
Bibliothèque
#J200, 300, Allée des Ursulines
Rimouski, QC G5L 3A1
418-723-1986 ext: 1470
Téléc: 418-724-1621
Courriel: peb_qru@uquebec.ca
URL: biblio.uqar.qc.ca
Sigle: QRU
Membre d'un consortium: Canadian Research Knowledge Network (CRKN); Conférence des recteurs et des principaux des universités du Québec (CREPUQ)
Fondée en: 1969
Heures: L-J 8h30-22h30; V 8h30-20h; S, D 12h-17h
Budget d'acquisitions: $250,000 - $499,999
Collections spécialisées: Développement régional, Est du Québec
Sujets: Biologie, environnement, océanographie, développement régional, pêcherie
Services:
Accès public à l'internet
Réseau en ligne
Prêts entre bibliothèques(PEB)
Lecteur/reproduction de microformes: Ordinateur; Lecteurs
Personnel: *Sommaire:* 23 Total; 7 Professionnel(s); 5 Technicien(s); 11 Autre(s) employé(s)
Denis Boisvert, Directeur
denis_boisvert@uqar.qc.ca
418-723-1986 ext. 1470
Claude Durocher, Coordonnateur, Services gestion documentaire
claude_durocher@uqar.qc.ca
418-723-1986 ext. 1474
Jacques St-Laurent, Commis specialisé en approvisionnements
jacques_st-laurent@uqar.qc.ca
418-723-1986 ext. 1500
Bruno Langlois, Responsable, Analyste information
burno_langlois@uqar.qc.ca
418-723-1986 ext. 1479

Rivière-du-Loup: CÉGEP de Rivière-du-Loup
Centre des ressources didactiques
80, rue Frontenac
Rivière-du-Loup, QC G5R 1R1
418-862-6903 ext: 238
Téléc: 418-862-4959
Courriel: martet@cegep-rdl.qc.ca
diaoue@cegep-rdl.qc.ca
URL: www.cegep-rdl.qc.ca
Sigle: QRLC
Membre d'un consortium: Réseau des services documentaires collégiaux (Resdoc)
Fondée en: 1969
Heures: L, Me 8h30-21h; Ma, J 8h30-18h; V 8h30-15h30
Budget d'acquisitions: $25,000 - $49,999
Collections spécialisées: Arts, loisirs, techniques en services de garde
Services:
Accès public à l'internet
Prêts entre bibliothèques(PEB)
Personnel: *Sommaire:* 6 Total; 1 Professionnel(s); 2 Technicien(s); 2 Autre(s) employé(s)
Joanne Laforest, Bibliothécaire
joalaf@cegep-rdl.qc.ca
418-862-6903 ext. 238

Chantal Leclerc, Bibliotechnicienne
chalec@cegep-rdl.qc.ca
Diane Ouellet, Bibliotechnicienne
diaoue@cegep-rdl.qc.ca

Rivière-du-Loup: **Centre hospitalier régional du Grand-Portage**
Bibliothèque médicale
75, rue St-Henri
Rivière-du-Loup, QC G5R 2A4
418-868-1010 ext: 2533
Téléc: 418-868-1035
URL: www.csssrivieredulopup.qc.ca
Heures: L-J 8h-16h
Sujets: Médecine, chirurgie
Services:
Personnel:
Suzanne Drapeau, Responsable

Rouyn-Noranda: **CÉGEP de l'Abitibi-Témiscamingue**
Bibliothèque
425, boul du Collège
Rouyn-Noranda, QC J9X 5M5
Adresse postale: CP 8000
Rouyn-Noranda, QC J9X 5M5
819-762-0931 ext: 1339
Téléc: 819-762-3815
866-234-3728
Couriel: aide.bibliotheque@uqat.ca
URL: cegepat.qc.ca/bibliotheque
Sigle: QRCN
Membre d'un consortium: Réseau des services documentaires collégiaux (Resdoc)
Fondée en: 1951
Heures: L-J 8h-21h45; V 8h-20h45; Sa-D 12h-16h15. Library hours vary depending on the campus.
Budget d'acquisitions: $50,000 - $99,999
Matériel imprimé: $50,000 - $99,999
Matériel électronique: 0-$9,999
Population desservie: 3 300 CÉGEP; 1 243 Université
Collections spécialisées: Collection de Louis-Edmond Hamelin, Collection de la Baie James, Collection Marcel de Grandpré, Collection en éducation nordique, centre de documentation régionale
Sujets: Éducation, administration, profession d'infirmier, psychologie, génie, foresterie, mines, sociologie
Services:
Accèss distance aux bases de donn
Accès public à l'internet
Réseau en ligne
Prêts entre bibliothèques(PEB)
Lecteur/reproduction de microformes: Lecteurs
Personnel: *Sommaire:* 14 Total; 1 Professionnel(s); 4 Technicien(s); 9 Autre(s) employé(s)
Luc Sigouin, Directeur
David Fournier-Viger, Bibliothécaire et référence
Lucie Laprise, Responsable, acquisitions/périodique

Rouyn-Noranda: **Université du Québec en Abitibi-Témiscamingue**
Bibliothèque
425, boul de l'Université
Rouyn-Noranda, QC J9X 5E5
Adresse postale: C.P. 800
Rouyn-Noranda, QC J9X 5E5
819-762-0931 ext: 1339
Téléc: 819-762-3815
Couriel: 1234@uqat.ca
aide.bibliotheque@uqat.ca
URL: www.uqat.ca/bibliotheque/
Sigle: QRUQR
Membre d'un consortium: Canadian Research Knowledge Network (CRKN); Conférence des recteurs et des principaux des universités du Québec (CREPUQ)
Fondée en: 1970
Heures: L-J 8h-21h45; V 8h-20h45; Sa-D 12h-16h15avec rendez-vous seulement
Budget d'acquisitions: $100,000 - $249,999
Matériel imprimé: $50,000 - $99,999
Matériel électronique: $50,000 - $99,999
Population desservie: 1243
Collections spécialisées: Collection en éducation nordique; centre de documention régionale
Sujets: Administration, sciences infirmières, génie, psychologie, mines, foresterie, gestion, sciences appliquées, sciences sociales, éducation, santé

Services:
Accèss distance aux bases de donn
Accès public à l'internet
Réseau en ligne
Prêts entre bibliothèques(PEB)
Lecteur/reproduction de microformes: Lecteurs
Personnel: *Sommaire:* 9 Total; 1 Professionnel(s); 8 Technicien(s)
Luc Sigouin, Directeur
Luc.Sigouin@uqat.ca
Thérèse Cyr, Responsable, Didacthèque
Therese.Cyr@uqat.ca
Liette Leclerc, Responsable, Traitement documentaire
liette.leclerc@uqat.ca
Manon Lapointe, Service du prêt
Manon.Lapointe@uqat.ca
Suzanne Daigle, Responsable, Publications gouvernementales
Suzanne.Daigle@uqat.ca
Lucie Laprise, Responsable, Acquisition et périodique
Lucie.Laprise@uqat.ca
Gisèle Neas, Responsable, Audiovidéothèque
Gisele.Neas@uqat.ca
David Fournier-Viger, Conseiller en documentation
david.fournier-viger@uqat.ca

Saint-Augustin-de-Desmaures: **Campus Notre-Dame-de-Foy**
Bibliothèque Jean-Paul-Desbiens
5000, rue Clément-Lockquell
Saint-Augustin-de-Desmaures, QC G3A 1B3
418-872-8242
Téléc: 418-872-3448
800-463-8041
Couriel: medias@cndf.qc.ca
biblio@cndf.qc.ca
URL: www.cndf.qc.ca/
Membre d'un consortium: Réseau des services documentaires collégiaux (Resdoc)
Fermée au public
Fondée en: 1965
Heures: L-V 8h-21h; Sa 10h-16h
Budget d'acquisitions: $25,000 - $49,999
Matériel imprimé: $25,000 - $49,999
Matériel électronique: $10,000 - $24,999
Sujets: Éducation, enseignement
Services:
Accès public à l'internet
Réseau en ligne
Prêts entre bibliothèques(PEB)
Personnel: *Sommaire:* 5 Total; 3 Technicien(s); 2 Autre(s) employé(s)
François Casabon, Coordonnateur Services des technologies de l'information
casabonf@cndf.qc.ca
418-872-8242 ext. 243
Andrée Lajoie, Technicienne en documentation
lajoiea@cndf.qc.ca
418-872-8242 ext. 293
Claude Roy, Directeur, Études
roy.claude@cndf.qc.ca
418-872-8242 ext. 109
Josée Gaudreau, Technicienne en documentation
gaudreauj@cndf.qc.ca
418-872-8242 ext. 229
Serge Gingras, Technicien en audiovisuel
gingrass@cndf.qc.ca
418-872-8242 ext. 368
Erica Burnham, Head of Library Services
erica.burnham@mcgill.ca
514-398-7876
Anna Stoute, Reference Librarian
anna.stoute@mcgill.ca
514-398-7881

Sainte-Anne-de-Bellevue: **Macdonald Campus Library**
21,111 Lakeshore Rd.
Sainte-Anne-de-Bellevue, QC H9X 3V9
514-398-7881
Fax: 514-398-7960
e-mail: macdonald.library@mcgill.ca
illmac.library@mcgill.ca
URL: www.mcgill.ca/macdonald-library/
National Library Symbol: QMAC
Founded in: 1907
Hours: M-Th 8:30-10:00; F 8:30-6:00; Sa 10:00-6:00; Su 2:00-10:00
Acquisitions Budget: $250,000 - $499,999
Special Collections: Lyman Entomology Collection
Subjects covered: Agriculture, Human Nutrition & Dietetics, Environment, Animal Science, Bioresource Engineering, Environmental Science, Biotechnology, Food Science, Plant Science, Soil Science, Parasitology
Services:
Internet Access
Inter-Library Loan (ILL)
Microform Equipment: Computer; Reader
Personnel: *Summary:* 8 Total; 2 Professional(s); 6 Other employees

Sainte-Anne-de-Bellevue: **MDA Space Library/Information Resource Centre/Bibliothèque/Centre de ressources d'information**
21025, rte Trans Canada
Sainte-Anne-de-Bellevue, QC H9X 3R2
514-457-2150 ext: 3259
Fax: 514-425-3048
e-mail: margaret.gross@mdacorporation.com
National Library Symbol: QSTAS
No public access
Hours: M-F
Subjects covered: Space, Electronics, Materials, Business
Services:
Inter-Library Loan (ILL)
Personnel: *Summary:* 1 Total; 1 Professional(s)
Margaret Gross, Manager
margaret.gross@mdacorporation.com

Sainte-Anne-de-Bellevue: **Quebec Young Farmers' Provincial Federation / Fédération des jeunes agriculteurs du Québec**
Library
PO Box 80
Sainte-Anne-de-Bellevue, QC H9X 3L4
514-398-7844
Fax: 514-398-7972
e-mail: tammy@qfaqyf.org
Founded in: 1969
Hours: 9:00-12:00, 1:00-5:00
Subjects covered: Agriculture, Food, Life Sciences
Services:
Personnel:
Tammy Oswick-Kearney, Provincial Coordinator
tammy@qfaqyf.org

Sainte-Thérèse: **Collège Lionel-Groulx**
Bibliothèque
100, rue Duquet
Sainte-Thérèse, QC J7E 3G6
450-430-3120 ext: 284
Téléc: 450-971-7883
Couriel: fmenard@clg.qc.ca
jgouin@clg.qc.ca
URL: www.clg.qc.ca
Membre d'un consortium: Réseau des services documentaires collégiaux (Resdoc)
Heures: L-J 8h-22h; V 8h-18h
Budget d'acquisitions: $50,000 - $99,999
Collections spécialisées: Partitions musicales, collections patrimoniales
Services:
Accès public à l'internet
Prêts entre bibliothèques(PEB)
Lecteur/reproduction de microformes: Lecteurs
Personnel: *Sommaire:* 12 Total; 1 Professionnel(s); 3 Technicien(s); 8 Autre(s) employé(s)
Françoise Ménard, Bibliothécaire professionnelle
rmenard@clg.qc.ca
450-480-3120 ext. 284
Chantal Lajambe, Technicienne, documentation
clajambe@clg.qc.ca

Saint-Félicien: **Collège de Saint-Félicien**
Centre de documentation
1105, boul Hamel
Saint-Félicien, QC G8K 2R8
Adresse postale: CP 7300
Saint-Félicien, QC G8K 2R8
418-679-5412 ext: 284
Téléc: 418-679-1040

Couriel: biblio@cstfelicien.qc.ca
URL: www.cstfelicien.qc.ca
Membre d'un consortium: Réseau des services documentaires collégiaux (Resdoc)
Fondée en: 1971
Heures: L-J 8h-20h; V 8h-17h
Budget d'acquisitions: $10,000 - $24,999
Services:
Prêts entre bibliothèques(PEB)
Personnel: *Sommaire:* 3 Total; 1 Professionnel(s); 2 Technicien(s)
Serge Bérubé, Conseiller pédagogique
Rodrigue Bouchard, Technicien en documentation
Lise Goulet, Secrétaire

Saint-Georges: CÉGEP de Beauce-Appalaches
Bibliothèque
1055, 116ième Rue
Saint-Georges, QC G5Y 3G1
418-228-8896 ext: 220
Téléc: 418-228-0562
Couriel: bibli@cegepba.qc.ca
URL: www.cegepba.qc.ca
Membre d'un consortium: Réseau des services documentaires collégiaux (Resdoc)
Heures: L-V 8h-17h30, 18h30-21h30avec rendez-vous seulement
Collections spécialisées: Collection Que sais-je?, dépôts de publications gouvernementales provinciales et fédérales
Sujets: Sciences humaines; soins infirmiers; sciences de la nature; mathématiques; informatique, génie-civil et techniques de production manufacturiers; techniques administratives; techniques de l'imprimerie et services de garde; arts et lettres; langues; éducation spécialisée
Services:
Prêts entre bibliothèques(PEB)
Lecteur/reproduction de microformes: Lecteurs
Personnel: *Sommaire:* 1 Professionnel(s); 2 Technicien(s); 2 Autre(s) employé(s)
Roger Charland, SMTE
rcharland@cegepba.qc.ca
Pierre Laberge, Bibliothécaire

Saint-Honoré-de-Chicoutimi: Centre québécois de formation aéronautique
Bibliothèque
1, rue de l'Aéroport
Saint-Honoré-de-Chicoutimi, QC G0V 1L0
418-673-3421 ext: 314
Téléc: 418-673-3950
Couriel: plaberge@cegep-chicoutimi.qc.ca
Heures: avec rendez-vous seulement
Annotation: Bilingue
Sujets: L'aéronautique
Services:
Personnel:
Lise Chaillez, Bibliothécaire
450-678-3561 ext. 4254
Lise De Courval, Technicienne en documentation

Saint-Hubert: École nationale d'aérotechnique
Bibliothèque
5555, Place de la Savane
Saint-Hubert, QC J3Y 8Y9
450-678-3561
Téléc: 450-678-3240
Couriel: ena.biblio@college-em.qc.ca
URL: www.college-em.qc.ca/
Sigle: QSTHUC
Fondée en: 1964
Heures: L-V 8h-17h30
Budget d'acquisitions: $50,000 - $99,999
Collections spécialisées: Périodiques en aérospatial
Sujets: Aérotechnique; Aéronautique; Aérospatiale
Services:
Accès public à l'internet
Prêts entre bibliothèques(PEB)
Personnel: *Sommaire:* 5 Total; 1 Professionnel(s); 1 Technicien(s); 3 Autre(s) employé(s);

Saint-Hyacinthe: CÉGEP de Saint-Hyacinthe
Centre des ressources didactiques
3000, av Boullé
Saint-Hyacinthe, QC J2S 1H9
450-773-6800
Téléc: 450-773-9971

Couriel: biblio@cegepssth.qc.ca
info@mediatheque.qc.ca
URL: www.biblios.saint-hyacinthe.qc.ca
Membre d'un consortium: Réseau des services documentaires collégiaux (Resdoc)
Fondée en: 1968
Heures: L-V
Budget d'acquisitions: $25,000 - $49,999
Sujets: Arts, sciences humaines, culture
Services:
Prêts entre bibliothèques(PEB)
Lecteur/reproduction de microformes: Lecteurs
Personnel: *Sommaire:* 1 Professionnel(s); 1 Technicien(s); 4 Autre(s) employé(s)
Marc Leclerc, Coordonnateur
Sylviane Houle, Bibliothécaire
Karen Wilton, Manager, Information Centre

Saint-Hyacinthe: Centre de recherche et de développement sur les aliments
3600, boul Casavant ouest
Saint-Hyacinthe, QC J2S 8E3
450-773-1105
Téléc: 450-773-8461
Couriel: dicampop@agr.gc.ca
frdclibrary@agr.gc.ca
Sigle: QSHAG
Heures: L-V 8h30-17h
Budget d'acquisitions: $50,000 - $99,999
Collections spécialisées: Agriculture, Engineering, Resource Conservation
Services:
Prêts entre bibliothèques(PEB) frais de 12$
Lecteur/reproduction de microformes: Lecteurs
Personnel: *Sommaire:* 2 Professionnel(s); 3 Technicien(s); 1 Autre(s) employé(s)

Saint-Hyacinthe: Centre de santé et de services sociaux Richelieu-Yamaska
Bibliothèque Roméo-Germain
2750, boul Laframboise
Saint-Hyacinthe, QC J2S 4Y8
450-771-3333 ext: 3242
Téléc: 450-771-3552
Couriel: alain.dery@rrsss16.gouv.qc.ca
peb.rsry@rrsss16.gouv.qc.ca
URL: www.rsry.qc.ca/francais/bibliotheques.htm
Sigle: QSTHC
Heures: L-V 8h30-16h30 (vendredi fermée de 11h30 à 12h30)avec rendez-vous seulement
Budget d'acquisitions: $50,000 - $99,999
Sujets: Sciences médicales, administration hospitalière
Services:
Prêts entre bibliothèques(PEB) frais de 5$ ou Gratuité réciproque
Frais de recherche
Personnel: *Sommaire:* 1 Technicien(s)
Alain Déry, Technicien en documentation
alain.dery@rrsss16.gouv.qc.ca

Saint-Hyacinthe: Institut de technologie agro-alimentaire de Saint-Hyacinthe
Centre de documentation
3230, rue Sicotte
Saint-Hyacinthe, QC J2S 7B3
Adresse postale: CP 70
Saint-Hyacinthe, QC J2S 7B3
450-778-6504
Téléc: 450-778-6536
Couriel: karine.levesque@mapaq.gouv.qc.ca
Sigle: QSTHTA
Fondée en: 1963
Heures: L-V
Sujets: Agriculture, Botanique, Alimentation
Services:
Prêts entre bibliothèques(PEB)
Lecteur/reproduction de microformes: Lecteurs
Personnel: *Sommaire:* 1 Professionnel(s); 3 Autre(s) employé(s)
Karine Lévesque, Bibliothécaire
450-778-6504 ext. 6279

Saint-Jean-sur-Richelieu: CÉGEP St-Jean-sur-Richelieu
Bibliothèque
30 boul de Séminaire
Saint-Jean-sur-Richelieu, QC J3B 7B1
Adresse postale: CP 1018
Saint-Jean-sur-Richelieu, QC J3B 7B1
450-347-5301
Téléc: 450-347-3329
Biblio@cstjean.qc.ca
URL: www.cstjean.qc.ca/webbiblio
Membre d'un consortium: Réseau des services documentaires collégiaux (Resdoc)
Fondée en: 1962
Heures: L-J 8h-20h30; V 8h-16h; S, D 12h-16h
Budget d'acquisitions: Matériel imprimé: $50,000 - $99,999
Annotation: Catalogue disponible sur Internet: regard.cstjean.qc.ca; Heures d'ouverture prolongées suite à un protocole d'entente avec la ville de St-Jean-sur-Richelieu; Abonnement gratuit pour les citoyens de St-Jean-sur-Richelieu
Sujets: Histoire québécoise, littérature québécoise, arts
Services:
Accès public à l'internet frais
Réseau en ligne
Prêts entre bibliothèques(PEB) frais
Personnel: *Sommaire:* 1 Professionnel(s); 2 Technicien(s); 3 Autre(s) employé(s)
Jean-Louis Demers, Responsable
450-347-5301 ext. 2161
Christine Bergeron, Technicienne en documentation
christine.bergeron@cstjean.qc.ca
450-347-5301 ext. 2680
Lucie Bouret, Technicienne en documentation
lucie.bouret@cstjean.qc.ca
450-347-5301 ext. 2280
Johanne Lorion, Technicienne en documentation
450-347-5301 ext. 2284
Danielle Gauthier, Secrétaire & acquisitions
450-347-5301 ext. 2333
Manon Benoit, Agente de bureau, Comptoir de prêt
450-347-5301 ext. 2552
Carole Leblanc, Agente de bureau, Comptoir de prêt
450-347-5301 ext. 2552
Pierre Di Campo, Bibliothécaire
Lise Lavallée, Assistante en bibliothèque
lavalleel@agr.gc.ca
450-346-4454 ext. 136

Saint-Jean-sur-Richelieu: Centre de recherche et de développement en horticulture
Bibliothèque St-Jean-sur-Richelieu
430, boul Gouin
Saint-Jean-sur-Richelieu, QC J3B 6Z8
450-346-4494 ext: 136
Téléc: 450-346-7740
Couriel: lavalleel@agr.gc.ca
URL: www.agr.gc.ca
Sigle: QSTJAG
Heures: L-V 8h-16havec rendez-vous seulement
Budget d'acquisitions: $25,000 - $49,999
Collections spécialisées: Horticulture ornementale, culture tropicale
Sujets: Cultures fruitières, génie et sol, cultures maraîchères, protection des plantes, agriculture
Services:
Prêts entre bibliothèques(PEB) frais
Lecteur/reproduction de microformes: Ordinateur
Personnel: *Sommaire:* 2 Total; 1 Professionnel(s)

Saint-Jean-sur-Richelieu: Rheinmetall Canada Inc.
Information Centre/Centre d'information
225, boul du Seminaire sud
Saint-Jean-sur-Richelieu, QC J3B 8E9
450-358-2000 ext: 2446
Fax: 450-358-1744
URL: www.rheinmetall.ca
No public access
Founded in: 1987
Acquisitions Budget: $50,000 - $99,999
Subjects covered: Engineering
Services:
Personnel: *Summary:* 1 Total; 1 Professional(s)
Diane Roy, Librarian

Libraries & Resource Centres / Québec

Saint-Jérôme: CÉGEP de St-Jérôme
Bibliothèque
455, rue Fournier
Saint-Jérôme, QC J7Z 4V2
450-436-1580 ext: 150
Téléc: 450-436-1756
URL: ww3.cstj.qc.ca/bibliotheque/
Sigle: QSTJEC
Membre d'un consortium: Réseau des services documentaires collégiaux (Resdoc)
Fondée en: 1970
Heures: L-J 8h-20h; V 8h-17h
Budget d'acquisitions: $50,000 - $99,999
Matériel imprimé: $25,000 - $49,999
Matériel électronique: 0-$9,999
Population desservie: 3,000 régulier; 4,000 formation continue
Annotation: Fédération des CEGEPS-RESDOC
Collections spécialisées: Dépositaire des publications du gouvernement du Canada
Sujets: Éducation
Services:
Accès public à l'internet
Réseau en ligne
Prêts entre bibliothèques(PEB)
Lecteur/reproduction de microformes: Ordinateur; Lecteurs
Personnel: *Sommaire:* 10 Total; 2 Professionnel(s); 4 Technicien(s); 4 Autre(s) employé(s)
Raymonde Trudel, Bibliothécaire responsable
rtrudel@cstj.qc.ca
450-436-1580 ext. 151
Monique Petit, Technicienne
mpetit@cstj.qc.ca
450-436-1580 ext. 148
Richard Laforge, Technicien
rlaforge@cstj.qc.ca
450-436-1580 ext. 153
Lorraine Lamoureux, Technicienne
llamoure@cstj.qc.ca
450-436-1580 ext. 227
Jocelyne Marchand, Commis
jmarchan@cstj.qc.ca
450-436-1580 ext. 159
Denise Lebel, Technicienne
dlebel@cstj.qc.ca
450-436-1580

Saint-Lambert: Champlain-Saint Lambert
Library
900 Riverside Dr.
Saint-Lambert, QC J4P 3P2
450-672-7360
Fax: 450-672-2152
URL: www.champlainonline.com
National Library Symbol: QSLCR
Founded in: 1975
Hours: M-Th 8:00-5:00; F 8:00-4:00
Acquisitions Budget: $25,000 - $49,999
For Print: $10,000 - $24,999
For Electronic: $10,000 - $24,999
Population Served: 2500
Services:
Remote Access
Internet Access
Access to Subscription Databases
Inter-Library Loan (ILL)
Microform Equipment: Computer; Reader
Personnel: *Summary:* 7 Total; 2 Professional(s); 4 Technical(s); 1 Other employees
Dale Huston, Reference Librarian
Sabrina Burke, Cataloguer
sburke@champlaincollege.qc.ca
450-672-7360
Kathy Mosher, Head Librarian
kmosher@champlaincollege.qc.ca
450-672-7360 ext. 200

Saint-Laurent: Abbott Laboratories Limited
Library
8401 Trans Canada Hwy.
Saint-Laurent, QC H3C 3K6
Mailing Address: CP 6150
Montréal, QC H3C 3K6
514-832-7000
Fax: 514-832-7857
URL: www.abbot.ca

National Library Symbol: QMALL
No public access
Founded in: 1944
Hours: Tu-Th 8:30-4:30
Acquisitions Budget: $50,000 - $99,999
Special Collections: Business, Management
Subjects covered: Medicine, Pharmacology, Toxicology, Nutrition
Services:
Inter-Library Loan (ILL)
Personnel: *Summary:* 1 Professional(s)
Georgette Vincze, Librarian
514-832-7734

Saint-Laurent: CAE Electronics Ltd.
Reference Library
CP 1800
Saint-Laurent, QC H4L 4X4
514-341-6780 ext: 2113
Fax: 514-341-7699
866-999-6223
e-mail: barbara@cae.ca
National Library Symbol: QMCAE
No public access
Founded in: 1950
Subjects covered: Computer Programming, Aviation, Aerospace & Nuclear Engineering, Flight Simulation
Services:
Personnel: *Summary:* 2 Total; 2 Technical(s)

Saint-Laurent: CÉGEP de Saint-Laurent
Centre des ressources didactiques
625, boul St-Croix
Saint-Laurent, QC H4L 3X7
514-747-6521 ext: 7424
Téléc: 514-748-1249
URL: www.cegep-st-laurent.qc.ca
Membre d'un consortium: Réseau des services documentaires collégiaux (Resdoc)
Heures: L-J 8h-18h15; V 8h-16h15
Budget d'acquisitions: $50,000 - $99,999
Services:
Prêts entre bibliothèques(PEB)
Lecteur/reproduction de microformes: Lecteurs
Personnel: *Sommaire:* 7 Total; 2 Professionnel(s); 2 Technicien(s); 3 Autre(s) employé(s)
Guy Gibeau, Adjoint au directeur des études
ggibeau@cegep-st-laurent.qc.ca
514-747-6521 ext. 7277
Mathieu Cormier, Adjoint au directeur des études
mcormier@cegep-st-laurent.qc.ca
514-747-6521 ext. 7218
Grant Forrest, Responsable, Référence
gforrest@cegep-st-laurent.qc.ca
514-747-6521 ext. 7212
Yolande Felx, SMTE
yfelx@cegep-st-laurent.qc.ca
514-747-6521 ext. 7211
Johanne Desjardins, Technicienne en documentation
jdesjardins@cegep-st-laurent.qc.ca
514-747-6521 ext. 7209

Saint-Laurent: CMC Electronics Inc.
Library
600, boul Dr Frederik Philips
Saint-Laurent, QC H4M 2S9
514-748-3148
Fax: 514-748-3100
e-mail: mary.thomson@cmcelectronics.ca
URL: www.cmcelectronics.ca
National Library Symbol: QMCM
No public access
Founded in: 1952
Hours: M-F 8:00-4:00
Acquisitions Budget: $25,000 - $49,999
Subjects covered: Electronics, Aeronautics, Communications
Services:
Internet Access
Inter-Library Loan (ILL)
Personnel: *Summary:* 1 Professional(s)
Mary Thomson, Librarian
mary.thomson@cmcelectronics.ca

Sept-Iles: CÉGEP de Sept-Iles
Bibliothèque
175, de la Vérendrye
Sept-Iles, QC G4R 5B7
418-962-9848
Téléc: 418-962-2458
Couriel: ksundara@cegep-sept-iles.qc.ca
Membre d'un consortium: Réseau des services documentaires collégiaux (Resdoc)
Fondée en: 1980
Heures: L-V 8h-17h; L, Me 19h-22h. Hors session: L-V 8h-17h
Budget d'acquisitions: $25,000 - $49,999
Collections spécialisées: Documentation pour l'histoire et l'économie de la Côte-Nord
Sujets: Économie, industrie, médecine, sciences de la santé, technologie, technique de bureau, électronique, informatique
Services:
Accès public à l'internet
Réseau en ligne
Prêts entre bibliothèques(PEB)
Lecteur/reproduction de microformes: Lecteurs
Personnel: *Sommaire:* 2 Total; 1 Professionnel(s); 1 Technicien(s)
Khamsing Sundara, Directeur
Suzanne Pinard, Technicienne en documentation

Shawinigan: Collège Shawinigan
Bibliothèque
2263, av du Collège
Shawinigan, QC G9N 6V8
Adresse postale: C.P. 610
Shawinigan, QC G9N 6V8
819-539-6401 ext: 2287
Téléc: 819-539-8819
Couriel: comptoir@collegeshawinigan.qc.ca
URL: www.collegeshawinigan.qc.ca
Sigle: QSHC
Membre d'un consortium: Réseau des services documentaires collégiaux (Resdoc)
Fondée en: 1969
Heures: L-J 8h-19h30; V 8h15-16h30
Budget d'acquisitions: $50,000 - $99,999
Services:
Prêts entre bibliothèques(PEB)
Lecteur/reproduction de microformes: Lecteurs
Personnel: *Sommaire:* 6 Total; 1 Professionnel(s); 2 Technicien(s); 3 Autre(s) employé(s)
Caroline Lessard, Coordonnatrice
clessard@collegeshawinigan.qc.ca
819-539-6401 ext. 2421
Renée Pouliot, Technicienne en documentation
rpouliot@collegeshawinigan.qc.ca
819-539-6401 ext. 2218
Céline Bourque, Technicienne en documentation
cbourque@collegeshawinigan.qc.ca
819-539-6401 ext. 2288
Josiane Sauvé, Spécialiste, Moyen et techniques d'enseignement
819-593-6401 ext. 2219
Suzanne Gagné-Giguère, Library Team Leader-Eastern Network
gagnegigueres@agr.gc.ca

Sherbrooke: Bibliothèque canadienne de l'agriculture - Lennoxville / Canadian Agriculture Library - Lennoxville
2000, rue College
Sherbrooke, QC J1M 1Z3
Mailing Address: CP 90
Lennoxville, QC J1M 1Z3
819-565-9171 ext: 202
Fax: 819-564-5507
e-mail: gagnegigueres@agr.gc.ca
National Library Symbol: QLAG
Hours: M-F 9:00-12:00, 1:30-4:00 by appointment only
Subjects covered: Agriculture, bovins laitiers, porcs
Services:
Personnel: *Summary:* 2 Total; 1 Professional(s); 1 Technical(s)
Karine Couture, Bibliothécaire responsable
karine.couture@usherbrooke.ca
819-821-8000 ext. 1096

Sherbrooke: Bibliothèque de droit et publications gouvernementales
boul Université
Sherbrooke, QC J1K 2R1

819-821-7519
Téléc: 819-821-7551
866-506-2433
Courriel: pretdr@usherbrooke.ca
URL: www.usherbrooke.ca/biblio/
Sigle: QSHERUD
Fondée en: 1961
Heures: L-J 8h15-23h; V 8h15-17h; Sa 9h-17h; D 11h-17h
Budget d'acquisitions: $250,000 - $499,999
Collections spécialisées: Droit; publications gouvernementales
Sujets: Droit, droit de la santé, droit fiscal
Services:
Accès public à l'internet
Réseau en ligne
Prêts entre bibliothèques(PEB) frais de 12$
Lecteur/reproduction de microformes: Ordinateur; Lecteurs
Personnel: *Sommaire:* 9 Total; 4 Professionnel(s); 4 Technicien(s); 1 Autre(s) employé(s)
Martin Poirier, Responsable
martin.poirier@usherbrooke.ca
819-821-8000 ext. 63558

Sherbrooke: **Bibliothèque de musique**
2500 boul. Université
Sherbrooke, QC J1K 2R1
819-821-8201
Téléc: 819-821-7635
Courriel: comptoir.musique@usherbrooke.ca
Heures: L-J 8h30-19h; V 8h30-16h30
Personnel:
Marthe Brideau, Responsable
marthe.brideau@usherbrooke.ca
819-564-5297
Mireille Lapierre, Assistance à l'usager
mireille.lapierre@usherbrooke.ca
819-564-5298

Sherbrooke: **Bibliothèque des sciences de la santé**
3001, 12e av nord
Sherbrooke, QC J1H 5N4
819-564-5296
Téléc: 819-820-6810
Courriel: bsante@courrier.usherb.ca
qsherc@biblio.usherb.ca
URL: www.usherbrooke.ca/biblio/
Sigle: QSHERC
Heures: L-J 8h30-23h; V 8h30-21h; Sa 9h-18h; D 13h-18h
Budget d'acquisitions: $500,000 - $999,999
Annotation: Ariel: 132.210.164.21
Sujets: Sciences de la santé, sciences infirmières
Services:
Prêts entre bibliothèques(PEB)
Personnel: *Sommaire:* 7 Total; 2 Professionnel(s); 3 Technicien(s); 3 Autre(s) employé(s)
Pierre Adant, Responsable
pierre.adant@usherbrooke.ca
819-821-8000 ext. 63598
Hélène Bernier, Bibliothécaire
helene.bernier@usherbrooke.ca
819-821-8000 ext. 62584

Sherbrooke: **Bibliothèque des sciences et de génie**
Université de Sherbrooke
Sherbrooke, QC J1K 2R1
819-821-7099
Téléc: 819-821-7245
866-506-2433
Courriel: pretsci@usherbrooke.ca
URL: www.usherbrooke.ca/biblio/
Sigle: QSHERUS
Fondée en: 1960
Heures: L-J 8h30-23h; V 8h30-21h; Sa, D 9h-17h;
Budget d'acquisitions: $500,000 - $999,999
Sujets: Biologie, chimie, mathématiques, informatique, sciences physiques, génie civil, génie chimique, génie électronique, génie mécanique, génie informatique
Services:
Accès public à l'internet
Réseau en ligne
Prêts entre bibliothèques(PEB)
Lecteur/reproduction de microformes: Lecteurs
Personnel: *Sommaire:* 10 Total; 2 Professionnel(s); 2 Technicien(s); 5 Autre(s) employé(s)

Sherbrooke: **Bishop's University**
John Bassett Memorial Library
2600 College St.
Sherbrooke, QC J1M 0C8
819-822-9600 ext. 2605
Fax: 819-822-9644
e-mail: ill@ubishops.ca
URL: www.ubishops.ca/library_info/
National Library Symbol: QLB
Consortia Membership: Canadian Research Knowledge Network (CRKN); Conférence des recteurs et des principaux des universités du Québec (CREPUQ)
Founded in: 1843
Hours: Academic year: M-F 8:00am-12:00am; Sa, Su 11:00am-12:00am
Acquisitions Budget: $500,000 - $999,999
For Print: $500,000 - $999,999
For Electronic: $250,000 - $499,999
Population Served: 3700
Special Collections: Archives of Bishop's University; Eastern Twp Archives; Archives of Church of England in Diocese of Quebec from year 1759 to the present
Subjects covered: Humanities, Business, Social Sciences, Sciences
Services:
Remote Access
Internet Access
Access to Subscription Databases
Inter-Library Loan (ILL)
Microform Equipment: Computer; Reader
Personnel: *Summary:* 21 Total; 7 Professional(s); 7 Technical(s); 15 Other employees
Sylvia Teasdale, University Librarian
steasdale@ubishops.ca
819-822-9600 ext. 2606
Gary McCormick, Reference Librarian
gmccormi@ubishops.ca
819-822-9600 ext. 2608
Lorraine Smith, Acquisitions/Cataloguing Librarian
lsmith@ubishops.ca
819-822-9600 ext. 2604
Ruth Sheeran, Assistant University Librarian
rsheeran@ubishops.ca
819-822-9600 ext. 2483
Karen Thorneloe, Reference Librarian
Daniel Bromby, Reference Librarian
Lucie Gendron, Responsable
lucie.gendron@usherbrooke.ca
819-821-8000 ext. 3870

Sherbrooke: **Cartothèque**
A8-122, Pavillon Albert Leblanc, Université de Sherbrooke
Sherbrooke, QC J1K 2R1
Adresse postale: Université de Sherbrooke
Sherbrooke, QC J1K 2R1
819-821-7560
Courriel: lucie.gendron@usherbrooke.ca
URL: www.usherbrooke.ca/biblio/bib/cartes/index.htm
Membre d'un consortium: Conférence des recteurs et des principaux des universités du Québec
Heures: L, V 8h15-17h; Ma-J 8h15-20h30; S 13h-17h
Budget d'acquisitions: $25,000 - $49,999
Matériel imprimé: $25,000 - $49,999
Collections spécialisées: 80 000 photographie aériennes, orthophotographies, images satellitaires, données géospaciales, cartes, atlas
Sujets: Géographie physique, géomatique, cartographie, environnement, télédétection
Services:
Prêts entre bibliothèques(PEB)
Référence; accès électronique réservé à la communauté universitaire
Personnel: *Sommaire:* 3 Total; 1 Professionnel(s); 2 Technicien(s);

Sherbrooke: **CÉGEP de Sherbrooke**
Centre des médias
475, rue du Cégep
Sherbrooke, QC J1E 4K1
819-564-6350 ext: 233
Téléc: 819-564-4025
Courriel: francine.pelletier@cegepsherbrooke.qc.ca
louise.marceau@cegepsherbrooke.qc.ca
URL: www.cegepsherbrooke.qc.ca/

Sigle: QSHERE
Membre d'un consortium: Réseau des services documentaires collégiaux (Resdoc)
Fondée en: 1967
Heures: L-J 8h-21h45; V 8h-16h45
Budget d'acquisitions: $50,000 - $99,999
Matériel imprimé: $10,000 - $24,999
Matériel électronique: $50,000 - $99,999
Services:
Accès distance aux bases de donn
Accès public à l'internet
Réseau en ligne
Prêts entre bibliothèques(PEB)
Lecteur/reproduction de microformes: Lecteurs
Personnel: *Sommaire:* 11 Total; 1 Professionnel(s); 3 Technicien(s); 7 Autre(s) employé(s)
Francine Pelletier, Bibliothécaire
819-564-6350 ext. 233
Louise Marceau, Technicienne en documentation
819-564-6350 ext. 238
Gilberte Poirier, Responsable

Sherbrooke: **Centre hospitalier universitaire de Sherbrooke Hôtel-Dieu**
Bibliothèque
#1110, 580, rue Bowen sud
Sherbrooke, QC J1G 2E8
819-346-1110 ext: 21126
Téléc: 819-822-6745
Courriel: g.poirier@abacom.com
URL: pole.usherbrooke.ca/fr/biblio/chus.html
Sigle: QSHERHD
Fermée au public
Heures: L-V 8h00-16h00
Budget d'acquisitions: $50,000 - $99,999
Sujets: Médecine
Services:
Prêts entre bibliothèques(PEB)
Personnel:

Sherbrooke: **CHUS Hôtel-Dieu**
Bibliothèque
580, rue Bowen sud
Sherbrooke, QC J1G 2E8
819-346-1110
Téléc: 819-822-6745
Courriel: cuse@abacom.com
Heures: L-Vavec rendez-vous seulement
Budget d'acquisitions: $50,000 - $99,999
Annotation: Association des services de documentation en santé de l'Estrie
Sujets: Médecine, soins infirmiers, tech médicale, administration
Services:
Prêts entre bibliothèques(PEB)
Personnel: *Sommaire:* 2 Total; 1 Professionnel(s); 1 Technicien(s)
Gilberte Poirier, Responsable

Sherbrooke: **Université de Sherbrooke**
Services des bibliothèques
Cité Universitaire
Sherbrooke, QC J1K 2R1
819-821-7550
Téléc: 819-821-7935
866-506-2433
Courriel: psheru@courrier.usherb.ca
URL: www.usherbrooke.ca/biblio/
Sigle: QSHERU
Membre d'un consortium: Canadian Research Knowledge Network (CRKN); Conférence des recteurs et des principaux des universités du Québec (CREPUQ)
Fondée en: 1964
Heures: L-J 8h30-23h; V 8h30-21h; S 9h-17h; D 11h- 17h
Budget d'acquisitions: $1,000,000 plus
Matériel imprimé: $1,000,000 plus
Matériel électronique: $1,000,000 plus
Annotation: Accès à distance aux bases de données en ligne uniquement pour l'univ. de Sherbrooke
Services:
Accès distance aux bases de donn
Accès public à l'internet
Réseau en ligne
Prêts entre bibliothèques(PEB) frais de 2 $
Lecteur/reproduction de microformes: Ordinateur; Lecteurs
Personnel: *Sommaire:* 75 Total; 23 Professionnel(s); 36 Technicien(s); 17 Autre(s) employé(s)

Sylvie Belzile, Directrice
sylvie.belzile@usherbrooke.ca
819-821-7550
France Paul, Responsable, Services techniques
france.paul@usherbrooke.ca
Pierre Adant, Responsable, Bibliothèque sciences et génie
pierre.adant@usherbrooke.ca
819-821-8000 ext. 3598
Diane Quirion, Responsable, Bibliothèque sciences humaines
diane.quirion@usherbrooke.ca
819-821-8000 ext. 3553
Karine Couture, Responsable, Bibliothèque droit et publications gouvernementales
karine.couture@usherbrooke.ca
819-821-8000 ext. 1096
Marthe Brideau, Responsable, Bibliothèque sciences de la santé
marthe.brideau@usherbooke.ca
819-564-5297

Sorel-Tracy: **CÉGEP de Sorel-Tracy**
Bibliothèque Roland-Gaudreau
3000, boul de Tracy
Sorel-Tracy, QC J3R 5B9
450-742-6651
Téléc: 450-742-1136
Couriel: jmrio@cegep-sorel-tracy.qc.ca
URL: www.cegep-sorel-tracy.qc.ca
www.cegep-sorel-tracy.qc.ca/jeanmarie_riopel/
Membre d'un consortium: Réseau des services documentaires collégiaux (Resdoc)
Fondée en: 1969
Heures: 15 août-31 mai: L-J 7h45-17h; V 7h45-16h. 1er juin-12 août: L-V 8h-16h
Budget d'acquisitions: $25,000 - $49,999
Services:
Accès public à l'internet
Réseau en ligne
Prêts entre bibliothèques(PEB)
Lecteur/reproduction de microformes: Ordinateur; Lecteurs
Personnel: *Sommaire:* 3 Total; 1 Professionnel(s); 2 Technicien(s); 3 Autre(s) employé(s)
Jean-Marie Riopel, Responsable SMTE
jmrio@cegep-sorel-tracy.qc.ca

Sorel-Tracy: **QIT-Fer et Titane inc**
Bibliothèque
1625, rte Marie-Victorin
Sorel-Tracy, QC J3R 1M6
450-746-3000 ext: 2065
Téléc: 450-746-4438
Couriel: info@qit.com
URL: www.qit.com
Sigle: QSOCS
Fermée au public
Fondée en: 1950
Heures: J-V
Budget d'acquisitions: $25,000 - $49,999
Collections spécialisées: Brevets
Sujets: Sciences physiques, génie, technologie
Services:
Personnel: *Sommaire:* 1 Total; 1 Professionnel(s)
Marc Duval, Bibliothécaire consultant
marc.duval@rtit.com
450-746-3000

Trois-Rivières: **CÉGEP de Trois-Rivières**
Centre documentaire Louis-Martel
3500, rue de Courval
Trois-Rivières, QC G9A 5E6
Adresse postale: CP 97
Trois-Rivières, QC G9A 5E6
819-376-1721
Téléc: 819-693-3844
Couriel: bibliotheque@cegeptr.qc.ca
URL: bilbio.cegeptr.qc.ca/
Sigle: QTCE
Membre d'un consortium: Réseau des services documentaires collégiaux (Resdoc)
Fondée en: 1968
Heures: L-J 8h-20h; V 8h-17h
Budget d'acquisitions: $50,000 - $99,999
Matériel imprimé: $25,000 - $49,999
Matériel électronique: $25,000 - $49,999
Annotation: Membre de l'Association pour l'avancement des sciences et des techniques de la documentation; Fédération des CEGEPS

Sujets: Éducation, enseignement général, sciences humaines pures et appliquées, littérature, philosophie, pédagogie
Services:
Accès public à l'internet
Réseau en ligne
Prêts entre bibliothèques(PEB)
Recherche
Lecteur/reproduction de microformes: Lecteurs
Personnel: *Sommaire:* 14 Total; 3 Professionnel(s); 4 Technicien(s); 7 Autre(s) employé(s)
Danièle Baillargeon, Bibliothécaire professionnelle
daniele.baillargeon@cegeptr.qc.ca
819-376-1721 ext. 2609
Monique Paradis, Bibliothécaire professionnelle
monique.paradis@cegeptr.qc.ca
819-376-1721 ext. 2603
Dominique Papin, Bibliothécaire professionnelle
dominique.papin@cegeptr.qc.ca
819-376-1721 ext. 2607
Solange Coulombe, Technicienne en documentation
solange.coulombe@cegeptr.qc.ca
819-376-1721 ext. 2605
Solange Thibeault, Technicienne en documentation
solange.thibeault@cegeptr.qc.ca
819-376-1721 ext. 2616

Trois-Rivières: **Collège Laflêche**
Centre des ressources didactiques
1687, boul du Carmel
Trois-Rivières, QC G8Z 3R8
819-375-7346
Téléc: 819-375-7347
Couriel: cecile.baril@clafleche.qc.ca
URL: www.clafleche.qc.ca
intranet.clafleche.qc.ca
Sigle: QTCLI
Fondée en: 1969
Heures: L-Me 7h45-18h; J, V 7h45-17havec rendez-vous seulement
Budget d'acquisitions: $25,000 - $49,999
Matériel imprimé: $10,000 - $24,999
Matériel électronique: $10,000 - $24,999
Services:
Accès public à l'internet
Prêts entre bibliothèques(PEB)
Personnel: *Sommaire:* 3 Total; 2 Technicien(s); 1 Autre(s) employé(s)
Lucie Hamel, Coordonnatrice
lucie.hamel@clafleche.qc.ca
Johanne Roberge, Technicienne
johanne.roberge@clafleche.qc.ca
Josée Aylwin, Technicienne
josee.aylwin@clafleche.qc.ca
Geneviève Lehoux, Technicienne
genevieve.lehoux@clafleche.qc.ca
Cécile Baril, Agente de bureau
cecile.baril@clafleche.qc.ca
Carmen Bournival, Technicienne en documentation
Lorraine Veronneau, Agente de bureau

Trois-Rivières: **Matériauthèque**
3500, rue de Courval
Trois-Rivières, QC G9A 5E6
Adresse postale: CP 97
Trois-Rivières, QC G9A 5E6
819-376-1721 ext: 2134
Téléc: 819-693-8023
Couriel: materiautheque@cegeptr.qc.ca
URL: www.cegeptr.qc.ca
Membre d'un consortium: Réseau des services documentaires collégiaux (Resdoc)
Fondée en: 1978
Heures: L-J 8h-18h, V 8h-17havec rendez-vous seulement
Budget d'acquisitions: 0-$9,999
Matériel imprimé: 0-$9,999
Matériel électronique: 0-$9,999
Sujets: Architecture, design d'intérieur, électrotechnique, méchanique du bâtiment
Services:
Accès public à l'internet
Personnel: *Sommaire:* 2 Total; 2 Technicien(s)

Trois-Rivières: **Université du Québec à Trois-Rivières**
Service de la bibliothèque
3351, boul des Forges
Trois-Rivières, QC G9A 5H7
Adresse postale: CP 500
Trois-Rivières, QC G9A 5H7
819-376-5005
Téléc: 819-376-5144
Couriel: peb_qtu@uqtr.ca
URL: www.uqtr.ca/biblio/
Sigle: QTU
Membre d'un consortium: Canadian Research Knowledge Network (CRKN); Conférence des recteurs et des principaux des universités du Québec (CREPUQ)
Fondée en: 1969
Heures: L-J 8h-22h45; V 8h-21h15; S, D 9h30-16h45
Budget d'acquisitions: $500,000 - $999,999
Collections spécialisées: Biophysique, pâtes et papiers, études québécoises, psychologie
Sujets: Arts, sciences humaines, économie, sciences, génie, technologie, biologie, administration, chimie, éducation, arts et lettres, sciences pures, sciences appliquées
Services:
Accès public à l'internet
Réseau en ligne
Prêts entre bibliothèques(PEB)
Lecteur/reproduction de microformes: Ordinateur; Lecteurs
Personnel: *Sommaire:* 22 Total
Lucien Forget, Directeur, Services à la clientèle, administration, gestion des coll
Benoit Séguin, Directeur, Développement, svs techniques et informatiques
Benoit Séguin, Responsable, systèmes
benoit_seguin@uqtr.uquebec.ca
Carol Lefrançois, Bibliothécaire
carol.lefrancois@drdc-rddc.gc.ca
418-844-4000 ext. 4244
Christiane Potvin, Technicienne en documentation
christiane.potvin@drdc-rddc.gc.ca
418-844-4000 ext. 4262

Val-Bélair: **DRDC Valcartier, R&D pour La defense Canada, Valcartier / DRDC Valcatier, Defence R&D Canada, Valcartier**
Bibliothèque/Library
2459, boul Pie-XI Nord
Val-Bélair, QC G3J 1X5
418-844-4000 ext: 4244
Téléc: 418-844-4624
Couriel: biblio@drdc-rddc.gc.ca
carol.lefrancois@drdc-rddc.gc.ca
Sigle: QQC
Fondée en: 1945
Heures: L-V 8h-16h30avec rendez-vous seulement
Budget d'acquisitions: $250,000 - $499,999
Collections spécialisées: Jane's Military Specifications
Sujets: Technologie, génie, sciences physiques, armement, électro-optique, chimie
Services:
Prêts entre bibliothèques(PEB)
Personnel: *Sommaire:* 3 Total; 1 Professionnel(s); 1 Technicien(s); 1 Autre(s) employé(s)
Marie-Josée Neveu, Library Services
marie-josee.neveu@nrcan.gc.ca
450-652-3210

Varennes: **Energy Diversification Research Laboratory**
Library Services
1615, boul Lionel-Boulet
Varennes, QC J3X 1S6
Mailing Address: CP 4800
Varennes, QC J3X 1S6
450-652-3210
Fax: 450-652-5177
URL: www.nrcan.gc.ca/libraries/
Founded in: 1992
Hours: M-F 8:30-4:30 by appointment only
Acquisitions Budget: $25,000 - $49,999
Subjects covered: Energy & Environment, Wastewater, Natural Gas, Photovoltaics
Services:
Internet Access
Inter-Library Loan (ILL)

Personnel: *Summary:* 1 Technical(s);

Vaudreuil-Dorion: Perkin Elmer Optoelectronics Library
22001, ch Dumberry
Vaudreuil-Dorion, QC J7V 8P7
450-424-2510 ext: 3370
Fax: 450-424-3413
e-mail: ann.walker@perkinelmer.com
National Library Symbol: QVGEC
No public access
Founded in: 1989
Hours: M-F 8:10-4:20
Acquisitions Budget: $25,000 - $49,999
Special Collections: RCA Review, Company Documents, Engineering Lab Notebooks
Subjects covered: Physical Sciences, Engineering, Technology, Electronics, Marketing, Metallurgy, Metals, Optics, Physics
Services:
Inter-Library Loan (ILL)
Current awareness, CISTI Source
Microform Equipment: Computer
Personnel: *Summary:* 1 Total; 1 Technical(s)
Ann Walker, Library/Technical Assistant
ann.walker@perkinelmer.com
450-424-3327

Victoriaville: CÉGEP de Victoriaville Centre de documentation
475, rue Notre Dame est
Victoriaville, QC G6P 4B3
819-758-6401 ext: 2485
Téléc: 819-758-2729
Courriel: mbechard@cgpvicto.qc.ca
URL: www.cgpvicto.qc.ca
Sigle: QVC
Membre d'un consortium: Réseau des services documentaires collégiaux (Resdoc)
Fondée en: 1968
Heures: L-V
Budget d'acquisitions: $25,000 - $49,999
Collections spécialisées: École du meuble et du bois ouvré
Services:
Accès public à l'internet
Réseau en ligne
Prêts entre bibliothèques(PEB)
Personnel: *Sommaire:* 4 Total; 1 Technicien(s); 3 Autre(s) employé(s)
Jules Chagnon, Coordonnateur
jchagnon@cgpvicto.qc.ca
819-758-6401 ext. 2484
Pierre Fortin, Technicien
fortin.pierre@cgvicto.qc.ca
819-758-6401 ext. 2489
Marjolaine Bechard, Services Publics
mbechard@cgpvicto.qc.ca
819-758-6401 ext. 2486

Saskatchewan

Humboldt: Prairie Agricultural Machinery Institute Library
Hwy. 5, West, PO Box 1150
Humboldt, SK S0K 2A0
306-682-2555 ext: 243
Fax: 306-682-5080
800-567-7264
e-mail: pami@sasktel.net
humboldt@pami.ca
URL: www.pami.ca
National Library Symbol: SHPA
Consortia Membership: Saskatchewan Libraries Multitype Database Licensing Program (MDLP)
Founded in: 1974
Hours: M-F 9:00-12:00, 1:00-5:00
Special Collections: Farm equipment testing collection, Standards, OECD/Nebraska tractor tests
Subjects covered: Agricultural Machinery, Engineering, Agriculture
Services:
Inter-Library Loan (ILL)
Personnel:
Sharon Doepker, Librarian

Indian Head: Indian Head Research Farm Library
RR#1, Government Rd., PO Box 760
Indian Head, SK S0G 2K0
306-695-2274
Fax: 306-695-3445
e-mail: clarkbe@agr.gc.ca
No public access
Hours: M-F 8:00-5:00
Acquisitions Budget: For Print: 0-$9,999
Services:
Remote Access

Moose Jaw: Five Hills Health Region Resource Centre
455 Fairford St. East
Moose Jaw, SK S6H 1H3
306-694-0374
Fax: 306-694-0270
e-mail: medlib@fhhr.ca
URL: www.fhhr.ca
Founded in: 1963
Hours: M, Tu, Th 8:00-12:00 by appointment only
Subjects covered: Medicine, Health Sciences, Nursing
Personnel: *Summary:* 2 Volunteer(s)
Judy Boyle, Director
judy@fhhr.ca
306-694-0246
Lucille Davie, Volunteer
306-694-0374
Vivian Fortin, Volunteer
306-694-0374

Moose Jaw: Saskatchewan Watershed Authority Library
111 Fairford St. East
Moose Jaw, SK S6H 7X9
306-694-3900
Fax: 306-694-3944
e-mail: comm@swa.ca
URL: www.swa.ca
National Library Symbol: AERIS
Founded in: 1986
Hours: M-F by appointment only
Acquisitions Budget: $25,000 - $49,999
Subjects covered: Water Resources, Water Management
Services:
Inter-Library Loan (ILL)
Personnel:
Arlene Adam, Librarian
306-694-3989
Beverley Brooks, Manager
306-691-8228

Moose Jaw: SIAST Palliser Campus Library
600 Saskatchewan St. West
Moose Jaw, SK S6H 4R4
Mailing Address: PO Box 1420
Moose Jaw, SK S6H 4R4
306-691-8228
Fax: 306-694-3427
866-460-4480
e-mail: palliserlibrary@siast.sk.ca
URL: www.siast.sk.ca/libraries
National Library Symbol: SMJT
Founded in: 1960
Hours: M-Th 8:00am-9:00pm; F 8:00-5:00; Sa, Su 1:00-5:00
Acquisitions Budget: $50,000 - $99,999
Subjects covered: Economics, Engineering, Technology, Industrial Arts, Business
Services:
Internet Access
Access to Subscription Databases
Inter-Library Loan (ILL)
Microform Equipment: Computer; Reader
Personnel: *Summary:* 4 Total; 2 Professional(s); 2 Technical(s); 2 Other employees

Prince Albert: Prince Albert Model Forest Association Inc. Library
#139, 1061 Central Ave.
Prince Albert, SK S6V 7G3
306-922-1944
Fax: 306-763-6456
e-mail: pamf@pamodelforest.sk.ca
URL: www.pamodelforest.sk.ca
Founded in: 1992
Hours: M-F 8:00-5:00
Note: Some publications available on website.
Subjects covered: Forest ecosystem, silviculture & biodiversity research reports
Services:

Prince Albert: Saskatchewan Environment Forest Information Centre
800 Central Ave.
Prince Albert, SK S6V 6G1
Mailing Address: PO Box 3003
Prince Albert, SK S6V 6G1
306-953-2444
Fax: 306-953-2360
e-mail: abattiste@serm.gov.sk.ca
National Library Symbol: SPAE
Founded in: 1974
Hours: M-F 8:00-12:00, 1:00-5:00
Acquisitions Budget: For Print: $10,000 - $24,999
Special Collections: Department Annual Reports, Department Technical Reports, Saskatchewan Aerial Photos
Subjects covered: Forestry, Agroforestry, Ecology
Services:
Internet Access
Access to Subscription Databases
Inter-Library Loan (ILL) for a fee
Personnel: *Summary:* 1 Professional(s); 1 Technical(s)
Angela Battiste, Information Specialist
abattiste@serm.gov.sk.ca
Jenny Rang Zhou, Library Technician
jrangzhou@saskforestcentre.ca
360-765-2864

Prince Albert: Saskatchewan Forest Centre Forest Information Centre (FIC)
#101, 1061 Cental Ave.
Prince Albert, SK S6V 4V4
306-765-2840
Fax: 306-765-2844
e-mail: info@saskforestcentre.ca
URL: www.saskforestcentre.ca
Consortia Membership: Saskatchewan Libraries Multitype Database Licensing Program (MDLP)
Hours: M-F 8:00-4:00
Note: The Centre is a partnership between the Saskatchewan Forest Centre & Saskatchewan Environment Forest Service.
Special Collections: Books; Journals; Maps; Aerial photographs
Subjects covered: Forestry
Services:
Inter-Library Loan (ILL)
Personnel:
Jenny Rhong Zhou, Library Technician

Regina: First Nations University of Canada Library
1 First Nations Way
Regina, SK S4S 7K2
306-790-5950 ext: 3429
Fax: 306-790-5990
URL: www.firstnationsuniversity.ca
Founded in: 1977
Hours: Fall & Winter: M-Th 8:00-8:10; F 8:00-4:10; Sa, Su 11:30-4:30. Summer M-F 8:00-4:10
Acquisitions Budget: $50,000 - $99,999
For Print: $50,000 - $99,999
For Electronic: $10,000 - $24,999
Population Served: 13000
Note: Affiliated with University of Regina; interlibrary loan available through the University
Special Collections: SIFC Archives
Subjects covered: Arts, Culture, Education, Humanities, Communications, Indigenous Studies, Indian Art, Indian Education, First Nations History, Indian Languages, Linguistics & Literature, Social Work, Administration & Management
Services:
Remote Access
Internet Access
Inter-Library Loan (ILL)
Microform Equipment: Computer; Reader
Personnel: *Summary:* 15 Total; 3 Professional(s); 5 Technical(s); 7 Other employees

Libraries & Resource Centres / Saskatchewan

Phyllis G. Lerat, University Librarian
plerat@firstnationsuniversity.ca
306-790-5950 ext. 3425
Rob Nestor, Librarian
rnestor@firstnationsuniversity.ca
306-790-5950 ext. 3426
Rob Nestor, Librarian
rnestor@firstnationsuniversity.ca
306-790-5950 ext. 3426

Regina: Gabriel Dumont Institute of Native Studies & Applied Research Library
College West, University of Regina
#218, 3717 Wascana Pkwy.
Regina, SK S4S 0A2
306-347-4124
Fax: 306-565-0809
e-mail: marilyn.belhumeur@uregina.ca
URL: www.gdins.org
Consortia Membership: Saskatchewan Libraries Multitype Database Licensing Program (MDLP)
Founded in: 1980
Special Collections: Rare history collection; Native studies; Archives
Subjects covered: Métis history & culture
Services:
Internet Access
Computer lab; Computer lab
Personnel: *Summary:* 2 Total; 1 Professional(s); 1 Technical(s)
Marilyn Belhumeur, Librarian
marilyn.belhumeur@uregina.ca
Pat Kelly, Library Technician

Regina: Prairie Farm Rehabilitation Administration Information Centre
#408, 1800 Hamilton St.
Regina, SK S4P 4L2
306-780-5100
Fax: 306-780-5018
e-mail: pfrinfo@em.agr.ca
URL: www.agr.gc.ca/pfra/
National Library Symbol: SRRE
Founded in: 1969
Hours: M-F 8:00-4:00
Services:
Personnel: *Summary:* 3 Total; 1 Professional(s); 1 Technical(s); 1 Other employees

Regina: Regina Qu'Appelle Health Region - Wascana Rehabilitation Centre
Health Sciences Library
2180 - 23rd Ave.
Regina, SK S4S 0A5
306-766-5441
Fax: 306-766-5460
e-mail: joan.harmsworthdow@rqhealth.ca
Profile: Provides reference & research services, and extends borrowing privileges to RQHR staff & physicians, and students of medicine. Public may use the library during specified hours
National Library Symbol: SRSH
Hours: M-F 8:30-4:30. Open but unstaffed on Fridays
Acquisitions Budget: $25,000 - $49,999
Note: Online resources restricted to RQHR staff & physicians
Subjects covered: Rehabilitation
Services:
Remote Access
Internet Access
Inter-Library Loan (ILL) for a fee of $5
Current awareness, document delivery, photocopying
Microform Equipment: Reader
Personnel: *Summary:* 1 Total; 1 Technical(s)
Joan Harmsworth Dow, Library Technician
library@rqhealth.ca
306-766-5441

Regina: Regina Qu'Appelle Health Region Library Services - Regina General Hospital
Health Sciences Library
1440 - 14th Ave.
Regina, SK S4P 0W5
306-766-4142
Fax: 306-766-3839
e-mail: library@rqhealth.ca
URL: www.rqhealth.ca
Profile: Provides reference & research services, and extends borrowing privileges to RQHR staff & physicians, and students of medicine. Public may use the library during specified hours
National Library Symbol: SRG
Consortia Membership: Saskatchewan Libraries Multitype Database Licensing Program (MDLP)
Hours: M-F 8:00-4:30
Note: Online resources restricted to RQHR staff & physicians
Special Collections: RQHR Archives houses student records from Regina General Hospital School of Nursing
Subjects covered: Medicine, Nursing, Health Sciences
Services:
Remote Access
Internet Access
Inter-Library Loan (ILL)
Current awareness, document delivery, photocopying; library orientation & instruction
Microform Equipment: Computer; Reader
Personnel: *Summary:* 9 Total; 4 Professional(s); 4 Technical(s); 1 Other employees
Susan Powelson, Director
library@rqhealth.ca
306-766-3830

Regina: Saskatchewan Health Policy & Planning Library
T.C. Douglas Building, 3475 Albert St., 3rd Fl.
Regina, SK S4S 6X6
306-787-3050
Fax: 306-787-2974
e-mail: info@health.gov.sk.ca
URL: www.health.gov.sk.ca/ph_br_policy_and_planning.html
Consortia Membership: Saskatchewan Libraries Multitype Database Licensing Program (MDLP)
Founded in: 1946
Subjects covered: Health services in Saskatchewan; Policy Issues
Services:
Internet Access
Inter-Library Loan (ILL)
Personnel:
Greg Rubin, Librarian
grubin@health.gov.sk.ca

Regina: Saskatchewan Highways & Transportation Resource Centre
1855 Victoria Ave., 11th Fl.
Regina, SK S4P 3T2
306-787-2099
Fax: 306-787-8700
e-mail: sspencer@highways.gov.sk.ca
National Library Symbol: SRHP
Consortia Membership: Saskatchewan Libraries Multitype Database Licensing Program (MDLP)
Founded in: 1973
Hours: M-F 8:00-4:30
Subjects covered: Transportation, Civil Engineering, Intellectual Capital, Knowledge Management
Services:
Internet Access
Inter-Library Loan (ILL)
Personnel: *Summary:* 1 Total; 1 Professional(s);
Shirley Spencer, Manager
shirley.spencer.hi0@govmail.gov.sk.ca
306-787-2099

Regina: Saskatchewan Institute of Applied Science & Technology Library
c/o Wascana Campus, 4500 Wascana Pkwy.
Regina, SK S4S 5X1
Mailing Address: PO Box 556, Wascana Campus
Regina, SK S4S 5X1
306-798-4321
Fax: 306-798-0560
e-mail: west@siast.sk.ca
URL: www.siast.sk.ca/libraries
Consortia Membership: Saskatchewan Libraries Multitype Database Licensing Program (MDLP)
No public access
Note: The library is an affiliate member of the Council of Prairie and Pacific University Libraries (COPPUL).
Services:
Personnel:
Heather West, Acting Director of Library Services

Regina: SaskPower Corporation Operations Support Library
2901 Powerhouse Dr.
Regina, SK S4N 0A1
306-566-3333
Fax: 306-566-3348
e-mail: twrighteastley@saskpower.com
National Library Symbol: SRPCRD
Hours: M-F 8:00-4:30 by appointment only
Acquisitions Budget: $50,000 - $99,999
Special Collections: Periodicals, Research Reports, Standards
Subjects covered: Electricity, Energy
Services:
Inter-Library Loan (ILL)
Personnel:
Teresa Wright Eastley, Librarian
twrighteastley@saskpower.com

Regina: SaskTel Corporate Resource Centre
2121 Saskatchewan Dr., 12th Fl.
Regina, SK S4P 3Y2
306-777-2899
Fax: 306-359-9022
e-mail: bev.fletcher@sasktel.sk.ca
National Library Symbol: SRST
No public access
Founded in: 1980
Hours: M-F 8:00-4:00
Acquisitions Budget: $50,000 - $99,999
Subjects covered: Telecommunications, Business, Management, Computing, Engineering
Services:
Inter-Library Loan (ILL)
Personnel: *Summary:* 2 Total; 1 Professional(s); 1 Other employees
Colleen McMahon, Manager, Competitive Intelligence
306-777-1333
Bev Fletcher, Library Technician
bev.fletcher@sasktel.sk.ca

Regina: SIAST Wascana Campus Library Services/Learning Centre
4500 Wascana Pkwy.
Regina, SK S4P 3S7
Mailing Address: PO Box 7150
Regina, SK S4P 3S7
306-798-0452
Fax: 306-798-0560
e-mail: wascanalibrary@siast.sk.ca
wasill@siast.sk.ca
URL: www.siast.sk.ca/libraries
National Library Symbol: SRRI
Consortia Membership: Health Knowledge Network (HKN)
Founded in: 1972
Hours: M-Th 7:30am-10:00pm; F 7:30-5:00; Sa 9:00-5:00; Su 11:00-5:00
Acquisitions Budget: $50,000 - $99,999
Note: Member of PLEIS.
Subjects covered: Agriculture, Health Sciences, Technology, Dental Assisting & Hygiene, Office/Industrial Education, Native Studies, Adult Education, Nursing, Early Childhood Education
Services:
Internet Access
Access to Subscription Databases
Inter-Library Loan (ILL)
Personnel: *Summary:* 13 Total; 3 Professional(s); 7 Technical(s); 3 Other employees
Nadine Zerr, Library Officer

Regina: Technical Library
6 Research Dr.
Regina, SK S4S 7J1
306-787-1881
Fax: 306-787-8811
e-mail: zerr@src.sk.ca
National Library Symbol: SSR
Founded in: 1981
Hours: M-F 8:00-12:00, 1:00-4:30
Note: Photocopying Fee: $8/item; Microform copy Fee: $8/item
Special Collections: SPE (Society of Petroleum Engineers) microfilm collections
Subjects covered: Petroleum Engineering, Enhanced Recovery, Reservoir & Chemical Engineering, Analytical Chemistry

Services:
Access to Subscription Databases
Inter-Library Loan (ILL) for a fee of $10
Microform Equipment: Computer; Reader
Personnel: *Summary:* 1 Professional(s)

Regina: University of Regina Library
Dr. John Archer Library
3737 Wascana Pkwy.
Regina, SK S4S 0A2
306-585-4133
Fax: 306-585-4878
e-mail: carol.hixson@uregina.ca
illsru@uregina.ca
URL: www.uregina.ca/library/
National Library Symbol: SRU
Consortia Membership: Canadian Research Knowledge Network (CRKN); Council of Prairie and Pacific University Libraries (COPPUL); Saskatchewan Libraries Multitype Database Licensing Program (MDLP)
Founded in: 1934
Hours: M-Th 8:00am-11:00pm; F 8:00-7:00; Sa 11:00-5:00; Su 1:00-11:00
Acquisitions Budget: $1,000,000 plus
For Print: $1,000,000 plus
For Electronic: $1,000,000 plus
Special Collections: Canadian Plains, Local History, Aboriginal Peoples
Subjects covered: Arts, Humanities, Culture, Education, Science, Engineering, Social Work, Social Sciences
Services:
Remote Access
Access to Subscription Databases
Inter-Library Loan (ILL)
Microform Equipment: Computer; Reader
Personnel: *Summary:* 75 Total; 19 Professional(s); 3 Technical(s); 53 Other employees
Carol Hixson, University Librarian
carol.hixson@uregina.ca
306-585-4132
Peter Resch, Assessment Librarian
peter.resch@uregina.ca
306-585-5107
Carol MacDonald, Head, Access Services
carol.macdonald@uregina.ca
306-585-4015
Edwin Perry, Head, Research Services
edwin.perry@uregina.ca
306-585-5109

Saskatoon: Ag-WestBio Inc.
Library
#101, 111 Research Dr.
Saskatoon, SK S7N 3R2
306-975-1939
Fax: 306-975-1966
e-mail: agwest@agwest.sk.ca
URL: www.agwest.sk.ca
Founded in: 1989
Hours: M-F 8:00-12:00, 1:00-4:30 by appointment only
Acquisitions Budget: 0-$9,999
Subjects covered: Science & Technology, Bio Product & Bio Processes, Health & Nutrition, Biotechnology
Services:
Personnel: *Summary:* 1 Total; 1 Other employees
Jackie Robin, Director, Communications
jackie.robin@agwest.sk.ca
306-975-1939

Saskatoon: Cameco Corporation
Library
2121 - 11th St. West
Saskatoon, SK S7M 1J3
306-956-6399
Fax: 306-956-6201
e-mail: phyllis_moen_nijssen@cameco.com
URL: www.cameco.com
National Library Symbol: SSMD
Founded in: 1962
Hours: by appointment only
Acquisitions Budget: $25,000 - $49,999
Subjects covered: Earth Sciences, Engineering, Mining, Environment, Nuclear Sciences
Services:
Personnel: *Summary:* 1 Professional(s); 1 Technical(s)

Phyllis Moen-Nijssen, Library Technician
phyllis_moen_nijssen@cameco.com
Joan Martin, Librarian
martinj@agr.gc.ca
306-956-7222
Gail Charabin, Library Assistant
306-956-7223

Saskatoon: Canadian Agriculture Library - Saskatoon
Library
107 Science Pl.
Saskatoon, SK S7N 0X2
306-956-7222
Fax: 306-956-7247
Other contact info: Alternate phone: 306/956-7223
e-mail: library-saskatoon@agr.gc.ca
URL: www.agr.gc.ca
National Library Symbol: SSAGR
Founded in: 1957
Hours: M-F 8:00-4:30 by appointment only
Acquisitions Budget: 0-$9,999
For Print: 0-$9,999
For Electronic: 0-$9,999
Subjects covered: Agriculture, Physical Sciences, Agronomy, Entomology, Crop Breeding & Protection, Biotechnology
Services:
Inter-Library Loan (ILL)
Personnel: *Summary:* 1 Professional(s); 1 Technical(s)

Saskatoon: City Hospital, Saskatoon
Medical Library
701 Queen St.
Saskatoon, SK S7K 0M7
306-655-8228
Fax: 306-655-8614
e-mail: blanchettes@sdh.sk.ca
library@saskatoonhealthregion.ca
URL: www.saskatoonhealthregion.ca
National Library Symbol: SSCH
No public access
Hours: M-F 7:30-3:30
Subjects covered: Medicine, Nursing, Health Sciences
Services:
Inter-Library Loan (ILL)
Personnel: *Summary:* 1 Technical(s)
Shirley Blanchette, Library Technician
blanchettes@sdh.sk.ca
Victor G. Wiebe, Engineering Librarian
victor.wiebe@usask.ca
306-966-5978

Saskatoon: Engineering Library
#1B08, Engineering Bldg., 57 Campus Dr.
Saskatoon, SK S7N 5A9
306-966-5976
e-mail: victor.wiebe@usask.ca
URL: library.usask.ca/engin/
Hours: M-Th 8:00am-10:00pm; F 8:00-6:00; Sa, Su 12:00-5:00
Subjects covered: Engineering, Computer Science
Services:
Internet Access
Personnel: *Summary:* 1 Professional(s); 5 Technical(s);
Janet Bangma, Head Librarian
janet.bangma@usask.ca

Saskatoon: Health Sciences Library
#B205 Health Sciences Bldg., 107 Wiggins Rd.
Saskatoon, SK S7N 5E5
306-966-5991
Fax: 306-966-5918
e-mail: uaskhsl@library.usask.ca
URL: library.usask.ca/hsl
National Library Symbol: SSUM
Hours: M-Th 8:00am-11:00pm; F 8:00-6:00; Sa 10:00-6:00; Su 10:00-9:00
Acquisitions Budget: $500,000 - $999,999
Special Collections: Baltzan Medical Canadiana, Brodie History of Medicine
Subjects covered: Medicine, Dentistry, Nursing, Physiotherapy, Biochemistry, Microbiology, Pharmacology, Physiology, Pharmacy, Nutrition
Services:
Internet Access
Access to Subscription Databases

Inter-Library Loan (ILL) for a fee of varies
Fee Based Research
Personnel: *Summary:* 14 Total; 4 Professional(s); 7 Technical(s); 3 Other employees
Kenneth Whiteway, Law Librarian
Ken.Whiteway@usask.ca
306-966-6032
Mary Tastad, Reference Librarian
tastad@duke.usask.ca
306-966-6020
Greg Wurzer, Reference Librarian
Bryan Fredrickson, Head, Acquisitions
fredrickson@sklib.usask.ca

Saskatoon: Law Library
15 Campus Dr.
Saskatoon, SK S7N 5A6
306-966-5927
Fax: 306-966-5932
e-mail: Ken.Whiteway@usask.ca
lawill@sklib.usask.ca
URL: library.usask.ca/law/
National Library Symbol: SSUL
Founded in: 1912
Hours: by appointment only
Subjects covered: Law
Services:
Inter-Library Loan (ILL)
Microform Equipment: Reader
Personnel: *Summary:* 3 Professional(s)

Saskatoon: National Hydrology Research Centre, National Water Research Institute / Institut national de recherche en hydrologie
Library- Environment Canada
11 Innovation Blvd.
Saskatoon, SK S7N 3H5
306-975-5559
Fax: 306-975-5513
e-mail: librarybiblio.saskatoonhrc@ec.gc.ca
librarynhrc@ec.gc.ca
URL: www.ec.gc.ca/scitech/default.asp?lang=En&n=44EEFEB3-1#nhrc
National Library Symbol: SSEH
Founded in: 1986
Hours: M-F by appointment only
Acquisitions Budget: $50,000 - $99,999
Note: The National Hydrology Research Centre (NHRC) in Saskatoon, Saskatchewan was established in 1986 to oversee the monitoring of stream and river levels at sites across Canada. Although based in Saskatchewan, the administrative headquarters for the NHRC is the NWRI laboratories in Burlington, Ontario, www.cciw.ca/nwri
Services:
Inter-Library Loan (ILL)
Microform Equipment: Reader
Personnel: *Summary:* 1 Total; 1 Professional(s)
Jane Lamothe, Head, Natural Sciences Library
jane.lamothe@usask.ca
306-966-6049

Saskatoon: Natural Sciences Library
#180 Geology Bldg., 114 Science Pl.
Saskatoon, SK S7N 5E2
306-966-6047
Fax: 306-966-1911
e-mail: nsmail@library.usask.ca
URL: library.usask.ca/nsl/
Hours: M-Th 8:00am-10:00pm; F 8:00-5:00; Sa, Su 12:00-5:00
Subjects covered: Physics, Chemistry, Biology, Computer Science, Maps
Services:
Inter-Library Loan (ILL)
Microform Equipment: Reader
Personnel: *Summary:* 7 Total; 2 Professional(s); 5 Technical(s)
Dianne Pammett, Information Specialist/Head
dianne.pammett@nrc-cnrc.gc.ca
Henry Chou, Client Services Officer
henry.chou@nrc-cnrc.gc.ca
306-975-5602

Saskatoon: NRC Information Centre - Saskatoon
110 Gymnasium Pl.
Saskatoon, SK S7N 0W9

Libraries & Resource Centres / Saskatchewan

306-975-5256
Fax: 306-975-6144
Other contact info: 306-975-5602
e-mail: nic.saskatoon@nrc-cnrc.gc.ca
URL: cisti-icist.nrc-cnrc.gc.ca/eng/locations/cisti/saskatoon.html
Founded in: 1948
Hours: M-F 8:30-4:30 by appointment only
Acquisitions Budget: $25,000 - $49,999
Subjects covered: Plant Biotechnology, Plant Molecular Biology, Plant Genetics
Services:
Internet Access
Inter-Library Loan (ILL) for a fee
Microform Equipment: Reader
Personnel: *Summary:* 2 Total; 1 Professional(s); 1 Technical(s);

Saskatoon: **POS Bio-sciences**
Information Services
118 Veterinary Rd.
Saskatoon, SK S7N 2R4
306-978-2811
Fax: 306-975-3766
800-230-2751
e-mail: ahankey@pos.ca
URL: www.pos.ca
Profile: The organization is involved in confidential contract research, toll processing & analytical services, and specializes in the extraction and purification of bio-based materials
National Library Symbol: SSPP
Consortia Membership: Saskatchewan Libraries Multitype Database Licensing Program (MDLP)
Founded in: 1977
Hours: M-F 8:00-4:00, by appointment by appointment only
Acquisitions Budget: $10,000 - $24,999
Note: Information services in support of the corporation's research and other activities
Subjects covered: Agriculture & food
Services:
Inter-Library Loan (ILL)
Fee Based Research
Personnel: *Summary:* 2 Total; 1 Professional(s); 1 Technical(s)
Aleksandra Hankey, Librarian
ahankey@pos.ca
306—97-8-28

Saskatoon: **Potash Corporation of Saskatchewan Inc.**
Library Services
#500, 122 - 1st Ave. South
Saskatoon, SK S7K 7G3
306-933-8501
Fax: 306-652-2699
800-667-0403
e-mail: marybelle.white@potashcorp.com
URL: www.potashcorp.com
National Library Symbol: SSPCT
Founded in: 1979
Hours: M-F by appointment only
Special Collections: PCS Historical File
Subjects covered: Agriculture, Mining, Process Engineering, Environment, Marketing, Fertilizer, Business
Services:
Inter-Library Loan (ILL)
Microform Equipment: Reader
Personnel: *Summary:* 1 Total
Marybelle White, Library Coordinator
marybelle.white@potashcorp.com

Saskatoon: **Prairie Northern Wildlife Research Centre**
Library
115 Perimeter Rd.
Saskatoon, SK S7N 0X4
306-975-4096
Fax: 306-975-4089
e-mail: CWS.library@ec.gc.ca
URL: www.ec.gc.ca/library
National Library Symbol: SSECW
Consortia Membership: Saskatchewan Libraries Multitype Database Licensing Program (MDLP)
Founded in: 1965
Hours: M-F 8:00-3:30 by appointment only
Services:
Inter-Library Loan (ILL)
Microform Equipment: Reader

Personnel: *Summary:* 1 Total; 1 Technical(s)
Adrian Johnson, Librarian
johnsonaa@csc-scc.gc.ca
306-975-5442

Saskatoon: **Prairie Region**
Regional Psychiatric Centre, Library
2520 Central Ave.
Saskatoon, SK S7K 3X5
Mailing Address: PO Box 9243
Saskatoon, SK S7K 3X5
306-975-5442
Fax: 306-975-6784
e-mail: johnsonaa@csc-scc.gc.ca
National Library Symbol: SSRP
No public access
Founded in: 1978
Hours: M-F 8:00-4:00
Acquisitions Budget: $25,000 - $49,999
Note: Combined patient/staff library
Subjects covered: Forensic Psychiatry, Health Sciences, Medicine, Nursing, Psychiatry, Psychology, Psychiatric Nursing
Services:
Personnel:

Saskatoon: **Public Health Services**
Resource Centre
#101, 310 Idylwyld Dr. North
Saskatoon, SK S7L 0Z2
306-655-4600
e-mail: lynne.warren@saskatoonhealthregion.ca
URL: www.saskatoonhealthregion.ca
National Library Symbol: SSCHE
Founded in: 1989
Hours: M-F 8:00-12:00, 12:30-4:30
Acquisitions Budget: $25,000 - $49,999
Subjects covered: Medicine, Health Sciences, Public Health
Services:
Inter-Library Loan (ILL)
Personnel: *Summary:* 1 Total; 1 Technical(s)
Lynne Warren, Library Technician
lynne.warren@saskatoonhealthregion.ca
306-655-4600

Saskatoon: **St Paul's Hospital (Grey Nuns) of Saskatoon**
Medical Library
1702 - 20th St. West
Saskatoon, SK S7M 0Z9
306-655-5224 ext: 5224
Fax: 306-655-5209
e-mail: library@saskatoonhealthregion.ca
URL: www.saskatoonhealthregion.ca
National Library Symbol: CABVAU
SK CPLS
Hours: M-F 8:00-4:30
Acquisitions Budget: 0-$9,999
For Print: 0-$9,999
For Electronic: 0-$9,999
Note: Services are available to staff, residents, students working at any Saskatoon Health facility, and patients and their families
Subjects covered: Medicine, Nursing, Health Sciences
Services:
Remote Access
Internet Access
Inter-Library Loan (ILL)
Personnel: *Summary:* 1 Technical(s)
Colleen Haichert, Library Technician
colleen.haichert@saskatoonhealthregion.com

Saskatoon: **Saskatchewan Environmental Society**
Library
#203, 115 - 2nd Ave. North
Saskatoon, SK S7K 2B1
306-665-1915
Fax: 306-665-2128
e-mail: info@environmentalsociety.ca
URL: www.environmentalsociety.ca
Founded in: 1988
Hours: M-F 9:00-5:00
Acquisitions Budget: 0-$9,999
For Print: 0-$9,999
For Electronic: 0-$9,999
Subjects covered: Nuclear energy, water pollution, energy efficient housing, sustainable development, community action,

world watch papers & magazines, alternatives journal, environmental issues
Services:
Personnel: *Summary:* 1 Total; 1 Professional(s); 40 Volunteer(s)

Saskatoon: **Saskatchewan Research Council**
Information Services
#125, 15 Innovation Blvd.
Saskatoon, SK S7N 2X8
306-933-5489
Fax: 306-933-7446
e-mail: library@src.sk.ca
URL: www.src.sk.ca/index.cfm
National Library Symbol: SSR
Consortia Membership: Saskatchewan Libraries Multitype Database Licensing Program (MDLP)
No public access
Founded in: 1947
Acquisitions Budget: $25,000 - $49,999
Special Collections: SRC publications in the fields of agriculture, biotechnology, alternative energy, environment, mining
Subjects covered: Engineering, Technology, Physical Sciences, Business, Agriculture, Geology
Services:
Internet Access
Inter-Library Loan (ILL) for a fee
Personnel: *Summary:* 1 Total; 1 Professional(s)
Laurier L. Schramm, President & CEO
Phyllis G. Lerat, Head, Library
plerat@firstnationsuniversity.ca
306-790-5950 ext. 3425
Sophie Bradley, Library Technician
sbradley@firstnationsuniversity.ca
306-931-1825
Dorothy Richard, Library Technician
drichard@firstnationsuniversity.ca
306-931-1824

Saskatoon: **Saskatoon Campus Library**
710 Duke St.
Saskatoon, SK S7K 0P8
306-931-1800 ext: 5425
Fax: 306-931-1847
e-mail: sbradley@firstnationsuniversity.ca
URL: www.firstnationsuniversity.ca/default.aspx?page=38
Founded in: 1985
Hours: M-Th 8:30-7:00; F 8:30-4:30
Acquisitions Budget: $50,000 - $99,999
Note: Affiliated with the University of Regina; address correspondence c/o 1 First Nations Way, Regina S4S 7K2. Direct phone: 306/931-1825
Special Collections: Office of the Treaty Commissioner Collection
Subjects covered: Aboriginal Social Work, Indigenous Studies, Business Administration
Services:
Internet Access
Access to Subscription Databases
Inter-Library Loan (ILL)
Research
Microform Equipment: Computer; Reader
Personnel: *Summary:* 8 Total; 2 Professional(s); 2 Technical(s); 4 Other employees
Tej Harrison, Librarian
Fabian Harrison, Librarian

Saskatoon: **SIAST Kelsey Campus**
Learning Resources Centre
Idylwyld & 33rd St. West, PO Box 1520
Saskatoon, SK S7K 3R5
306-933-6417
Fax: 306-964-1222
e-mail: kelseylibrary@siast.sk.ca
URL: www.siast.sk.ca/libraries
National Library Symbol: SSSI
Founded in: 1963
Hours: M-Th 7:30-9:00; F 7:30-5:00; Sa, Su 10:00-5:00
Acquisitions Budget: $50,000 - $99,999
Subjects covered: Health Sciences, Nursing, Trades & Technologies, Personal & Community Services, Adult Basic Education, Extension Services
Services:
Remote Access
Inter-Library Loan (ILL)

Testing
Microform Equipment: Reader
Personnel: *Summary:* 12 Total; 2 Professional(s); 5 Technical(s); 5 Other employees

Saskatoon: **University of Saskatchewan Murray Library**
Main Library, Murray Bldg., 3 Campus Dr.
Saskatoon, SK S7N 5A4
306-966-5927
Fax: 306-966-5932
TDD: 3069665921
e-mail: frank.winter@usask.ca
URL: library.usask.ca
National Library Symbol: SSU
Consortia Membership: Canadian Research Knowledge Network (CRKN); Council of Prairie and Pacific University Libraries (COPPUL); Health Knowledge Network (HKN); Saskatchewan Libraries Multitype Database Licensing Program (MDLP)
Founded in: 1912
Hours: M-Su
Acquisitions Budget: $1,000,000 plus
For Print: $1,000,000 plus
For Electronic: $1,000,000 plus
Special Collections: Adam Shortt Library of Western Canadiana
Services:
Internet Access
Inter-Library Loan (ILL)
Personnel: *Summary:* 147 Total; 41 Professional(s); 94 Technical(s); 12 Other employees
Vicki Williamson, Dean
vicki.williamson@usask.ca
306-966-5927
Ken Ladd, Associate Dean
ken.ladd@usask.ca
306-966-5946
David Fox, Head, Information Technology Services & Technical Services
david.fox@usask.ca
306-966-6031
Linda Fritz, Head, Research Services
linda.fritz@usask.ca
306-966-6003
Carol Shepstone, Head, Access Services
carol.shepstone@usask.ca
306-966-5960

Saskatoon: **Western Development Museum George Shepherd Library**
2935 Melville St
Saskatoon, SK S7J 5A6
306-934-1400
Fax: 306-934-4467
800-363-6345
e-mail: info@wdm.ca
URL: www.wdm.ca
Founded in: 1972
Hours: M-F 8:30-4:30
Acquisitions Budget: 0-$9,999
Personnel: *Summary:* 2 Total; 1 Professional(s); 1 Technical(s); 1 Volunteer(s)
Warren Clubb, Exhibits Curator
wclubb@wdm.ca
306-934-1400

Swift Current: **Cypress Hills Regional College Resource Centre**
129 - 2nd Ave. NE
Swift Current, SK S9H 4G3
306-773-1531
Fax: 306-773-2384
URL: www.cypresshillscollege.sk.ca
Hours: M-F 8:00-5:00
Subjects covered: Arts, Humanities, Life Skills, Technical
Services:
Personnel:
Joan Foster, University Coordinator/Career Counsellor
306-778-4571
Aidan Beaubier, Librarian
beaubiera@agr.gc.ca

Swift Current: **Semi-Arid Prairie Agricultural Research Centre Canadian Agriculture Library, Information Centre, Swift Current**
Airport Rd., PO Box 1030
Swift Current, SK S9H 3X2
306-778-7260
Fax: 306-778-3188
e-mail: sscag@agr.gc.ca
National Library Symbol: SSCAg
Founded in: 1921
Hours: M-F 8:00-4:30 by appointment only
Subjects covered: Cereal & Forage Production, Agrometeorology, Soil Science
Services:
Inter-Library Loan (ILL)
Microform Equipment: Computer; Reader
Personnel: *Summary:* 1 Professional(s); 1 Other employees

Yukon Territory

Whitehorse: **Pacific & Yukon Region - Whitehorse Library - Environment Canada**
91782 Alaska Hwy.
Whitehorse, YT Y1A 5B7
867-667-3407
Fax: 867-667-7962
e-mail: mary.martin@ec.gc.ca
URL: www.ec.gc.ca/library
National Library Symbol: YWEEP
Founded in: 1978
Hours: Tu 8:30-2:30 by appointment only
Services:
Inter-Library Loan (ILL)
Microform Equipment: Reader

Whitehorse: **Yukon Chamber of Mines Library**
3151B Third Ave.
Whitehorse, YT Y1A 1G1
867-667-2090
Fax: 867-668-7127
e-mail: info@ycmines.ca
URL: www.ycmines.ca
Hours: M-F 8:30-5:00 by appointment only
Acquisitions Budget: $25,000 - $49,999
Subjects covered: Mining, Minerals, Mining History
Services:
Internet Access
Personnel: *Summary:* 1 Total; 1 Other employees
Joanne Hainer, Executive Officer

Whitehorse: **Yukon College Library**
500 College Dr.
Whitehorse, YT Y1A 5K4
Mailing Address: PO Box 2799
Whitehorse, YT Y1A 5K4
867-668-8870
Fax: 867-668-8808
e-mail: rsuther@yukoncollege.yk.ca
library@yukoncollege.yk.ca
URL: www.yukoncollege.yk.ca/yclibrary
National Library Symbol: YWC
Consortia Membership: British Columbia Electronic Network (BC ELN)
Founded in: 1983
Hours: M-Th 10:00-9:00; F-Sa 11:00-5:00; Su 10:00-9:00
Acquisitions Budget: $50,000 - $99,999
Subjects covered: Native Peoples & Northern Affairs
Services:
Internet Access
Access to Subscription Databases
Inter-Library Loan (ILL)
Microform Equipment: Computer; Reader
Personnel: *Summary:* 11 Total; 3 Professional(s); 3 Technical(s); 5 Other employees
Robert Sutherland, Manager
rsuther@yukoncollege.yk.ca
867-668-8888
Krista Strombert, Reference Librarian
kstrombe@yukoncollege.yk.ca
867-668-8727
Laurie Prange, Cataloguing Librarian
lprange@yukoncollege.yk.ca
867-668-8769

Whitehorse: **Yukon Conservation Society Library**
302 Hawkins St.
Whitehorse, YT Y1A 1X6
867-668-5678
Fax: 867-668-6637
e-mail: ycsoffice@ycs.yk.ca
URL: www.yukonconservation.org/library/library.html
Founded in: 1968
Hours: M-F 10:00-2:00
Acquisitions Budget: $25,000 - $49,999
Services:
Personnel: *Summary:* 2 Professional(s); 1 Technical(s)

Whitehorse: **Yukon Dept. of Energy, Mines & Resources Library**
#335, 300 Main St.
Whitehorse, YT Y1A 2C6
Mailing Address: PO Box 2703 (K-335)
Whitehorse, YT Y1A 2C6
867-667-3111
Fax: 867-456-3888
e-mail: emrlibrary@gov.yk.ca
URL: www.emr.gov.yk.ca/library/
National Library Symbol: YWED
Founded in: 1978
Hours: M-F 8:30-4:30
Acquisitions Budget: $25,000 - $49,999
Services:
Internet Access for a fee
Inter-Library Loan (ILL)
Personnel: *Summary:* 4 Total
Aimee Ellis, Head, Library Services
Jeanette Van Esbroeck, Research & Cataloguing Librarian
Margaret Donnelly, Research & Cataloguing Librarian
Brenda Butler, Library Technician

Whitehorse: **Yukon Dept. of Environment Environment Yukon Library**
PO Box 2703
Whitehorse, YT Y1A 2C6
867-667-3029
Fax: 867-393-6219
800-661-0408
e-mail: Vicki.McCollum@gov.yk.ca
URL: www.environmentyukon.gov.yk.ca/lib.html
National Library Symbol: YWRR
Founded in: 1983
Hours: M-Th 8:30-12:00, 1:00-5:00 by appointment only
Acquisitions Budget: $10,000 - $24,999
For Print: $10,000 - $24,999
For Electronic: 0-$9,999
Subjects covered: Natural History, Biology, Zoology, Wildlife Conservation & Management & Environmental Issues
Services:
Internet Access
Inter-Library Loan (ILL) for a fee
Personnel: *Summary:* 1 Technical(s)
Vicki McCollum, Librarian
Vicki.McCollum@gov.yk.ca
867-667-3029

Whitehorse: **Yukon Energy Solutions Centre Library**
206A Lowe St.
Whitehorse, YT Y1A 1W6
867-393-7063
Fax: 867-393-7061
e-mail: esc@gov.yk.ca
URL: www.nrgsc.yk.ca
Founded in: 2001
Hours: M-F 8:00-5:00
Special Collections: Energy related publications
Subjects covered: Energy, Climate Change, Renewable Resources
Services:
Personnel:
Cathy Cottrell, Sr. Energy Efficiency Advisor
cathy.cottrell@nrgsc.yk.ca
867-393-7148

Libraries & Resource Centres / Yukon Territory

Whitehorse: **Yukon Workers' Compensation Health & Safety Board Library**
401 Strickland St.
Whitehorse, YT Y1A 5N8

867-667-8837
Fax: 867-393-6279
e-mail: linda.powers@gov.yk.ca
Hours: 9:00-4:30
Acquisitions Budget: $500,000 - $999,999

Services:
Internet Access
Access to Subscription Databases
Personnel:
Linda Powers, Contact
linda.powers@gov.yk.ca

Non-government Publications

Alternatives Journal: Canadian Environmental Ideas & Action
c/o Faculty of Environmental Studies, University of Waterloo, 200 University Ave. West, Waterloo, ON N2L 3G1
519-888-4442, Fax: 519-746-0292, 866-437-2587
infoalternativesjournal.ca
www.alternativesjournal.ca
Circulation: 4,500 Frequency: 6 times a year; ISSN: 1205-7398
A theme-based publication dedicated to illustrating the relationships between the environment and social justice, politics and the economy. It looks at the challenges and issues related to the interaction of humanity and the environment, and the responses to those issues.
Tara Flynn, Executive Editor

Canadian Environmental Protection
#201, 2323 Boundary Rd., Vancouver, BC V5M 4V8
604-291-9900, Fax: 604-291-1906
ebaum@baumpub.com
www.baumpub.com
Circulation: 20,000 Frequency: 8 times a year
This publication is one of Canada's most popular environmental trade publications, with four marketplace issues, an internet version and industry supplements. Some issues this magazine covers are bio-fuels, specialty gasses and air pollution.

Canadian Geographic
c/o Royal Canadian Geographical Society, 39 McArthur Ave., Ottawa, ON K1L 8L7
613-745-4629, Fax: 613-744-0947
editorial@canadiangeographic.ca
www.canadiangeographic.ca
Circulation: 222,000 Frequency: 6 times a year; ISSN: 0706-2168
Publication aims to promote Canada both to Canadians and around the world. It looks at issues relating to the nature and wildlife within Canada, and what can be done to preserve the natural Canadian landscape.
John L. Thomson, CEO & Publisher
Rick Boychuk, Editor

Canadian Wildlife
350 Michael Cowpland Dr., Kanata, ON K2M 2W1
613-599-9594, Fax: 613-599-4428, 800-563-9453
info@cwf-fcf.org
www.cwf-fcf.org
Frequency: 6 times a year
Aimed at both teenagers and adults, this magazine covers issues relating to Canadian and international wildlife, and reports on the work of the Canadian Wildlife Federation.

Eco Week.ca
#800, 12 Concorde Pl., Toronto, ON M3C 4J2
416-442-5600, Fax: 416-510-5133
dorchard@ecolog.com
www.ecoweek.ca
Frequency: weekly
Formally EcoLog Week, this publication aims to show its readers how to live a green lifestyle, as well keeping the public up-to-date on environmental issues of the day, including the environmental regulatory programs, new developments in waste-treatment, and how to get involved with local environmentalist organizations.
Lidia Lubka, Editor

EcoCompliance.ca
#800, 12 Concorde Place, Toronto, ON M3C 4J2
416-422-5600, Fax: 416-510-5148, 888-702-1111
llubka@ecolog.com
www.ecocompliance.ca
Frequency: Monthly
A monthly national newsletter that examines the developments and amendments in Canadian environmental law. It gives its readers commentary on new legislation, proposed environmental bills, changing environmental legislation, and all other issues affecting enviromental law policies in Canada.
Lidia Lubka, Associate Publisher

Ecoforestry
Ecoforestry Institute Society, PO Box 5070 B, Victoria, BC V8R 6N3
250-595-0655, Fax: 250- -
journal@ecoforestry.ca
ecoforestry.ca
Frequency: quarterly
Journal looks at issues relating to the forestry industry using a low-impact approach to forest management. Its goal is to increase public awareness of ecoforestry by working with community organizations, offering workshops to the public and providing information.

EnviroLine
PO Box 77042 Chinatown, 4905 - 23 Ave. NW, Calgary, AB T2G 5J8
403-263-3272, Fax: 403-263-3280
enviroline@shaw.ca; enviroca@cadvision.com
Circulation: 500 Frequency: 20 times a year
Provides Western Canadian resource industries with reviews of important and up-to-date environmental issues.
Mark Lowey, Publisher & Editor

EnviroZine
70 Crémazie St., 7th Fl., Gatineau, QC K1A 0H3
819-997-2800, Fax: 819-994-1412, 800-668-6767
enviroinfo@ec.gc.ca
www.ec.gc.ca/envirozine
Circulation: available online only Frequency: monthly ISSN: English ed. ISSN 1499-1411; French ed. 1499-142X
This webzine covers a wide range of environmental issues that are of importance to Canadians. It provides information in several categories, such as Air, Climate Change, Environmental Action, Nature and Wildlife, Pollution, Science & Technology, Water, and Weather, and attracts readers from 58 countries.

Environmental Reviews
M-55, 1200 Montreal Rd., Ottawa, ON K1A 0R6
613-993-9101, Fax: 613-952-9907, 877-672-2672
pubs@nrc-cnrc.gc.ca; info@nrc-cnrc.gc.ca
pubs.nrc-cnrc.gc.ca
Circulation: 300 Frequency: Annually ISSN: 1208-6053
Publication presents reviews on a range of environmental issues and topics, emphasizing the effects humans have on natural and manmade ecosystems. Topics investigated in this publication include climate change, air and marine pollution, erosion and agroforestry.
Bruce P. Dancik, Editor
Bushra Waheed, Managing Editor
Cameron Macdonald, Director

Environmental Science & Engineering Magazine
#30, 220 Industrial Parkway South, Aurora, ON L4G 3V6
905-727-4666, Fax: 905-841-7271
sandra@esemag.com
www.esemag.com
Circulation: 19,000 Frequency: 6 times a year
This publicationis the largest documentary magazine in Canada and has articles on various environmental issues, including air pollution, water filtration, hazardous waste, alternative energy, greenhouse gasses, among others.

Green Living Magazine
Green Living Enterprises, 66 the Esplanade, Toronto, ON M5E 1A6
416-360-0044, 416-362-2387
info@green-living.ca
www.greenlivingmagazine.ca
Circulation: 150,000 Frequency: quarterly
Green Living Magazine attempts to promote living a green lifestyle to its readers by providing information about organics, health, the environment and eco-consumer products. They support sustainable and healthy living and publicizing the green message.
Laurie Simmonds, Publisher

Journal of Environmental Engineering and Science
M-55, 1200 Montreal Rd., Ottawa, ON K1A 0R6
613-993-9084, Fax: 613-952-7656, 800-668-1222
pubs@nrc-cnrc.gc.ca
pubs.nrc-cnrc.gc.ca
Frequency: 6 times a year ISSN: 1496-256X
This publication provides a forum for the discussion of environmental engineering and science research. Topics this journal explores include environmental engineering, physical and analytical sciences, life sciences related to environmental issues, health sciences, and oceanography.

La Maison du 21e siècle
2955, lac Lucerne, Sainte-Adèle, QC J8B 3K9
450-228-1555, Fax: 450-228-1555
info@21esiecle.qc.ca
www.21esiecle.qc.ca
Frequency: 4 fois par an
André Fauteux, Éditeur

Natural Life
Life Media, #508, 264 Queens Quay West, Toronto, ON M5J 1B5
416-260-0303, 800-215-9574
natural@life.ca
www.life.ca
Circulation: 35,000 Frequency: 6 times a year; ISSN 0701-8002
This independently owned magazine has an international focus on providing intelligent and in-depth practical information on issues such as healthy cooking, organic gardening, sustainable homes, natural parenting, wellness and natural healing, eco-leisure and eco-travel and sustainable business.
Wendy Priesnitz, Editor
Rolf Priesnitz, Publisher

Nature Canada
c/o Nature Canada, #900, 84 Albert St., Ottawa, ON K1P 6A4
613-562-3447, Fax: 613-562-3371, 800-267-4088
info@naturecanada.ca
naturecanada.ca
Circulation: 26,400 Frequency: 4 times a year; ISSN: 0374-9894
The mission of this magazine is to protect nature, its diversity and the processes that sustain it, and does this by providing information regarding several environmental topics including bird conservation, wilderness protection, endangered species and national parks. The publication supports community-based efforts to protect wildlife; encourages the development of an effective network of parks and protected areas across Canada; and promoting biodiversity in Canada and abroad.

ON Nature
Federation of Ontario Naturalists, #201, 366 Adelaide St. West, Toronto, ON M5V 1R9
416-444-8419, Fax: 416-444-9866, 800-440-2366
onnature@ontarionature.org
www.ontarionature.org
Circulation: 14,500 Frequency: 4 times a year; ISSN: 0227-793X
ON Nature attempts to bring its readers closer to nature by providing information about Ontario's natural areas and wildlife, and by providing insight into current environmental issues. Magazine features articles by nature specialists, colour photography, information regarding wilderness travel and up-to-date news on conservation battles.
Caroline Schultz, Executive Director
Victoria Foote, Editor

Québec Oiseaux
1251, rue Rachel est, Montréal, QC H2S 2J9
514-521-8356, Fax: 514-521-5711
quebecoiseaux@aqgo.qc.ca
www.quebecoiseaux.qc.ca
Circulation: 7 928 Frequency: 4 fois par an
Michel Préville, Rédacteur-en-chef

Recycling Canada
PO Box 378, Campbellford, ON K0L 1L0
705-653-1112, Fax: 705-653-1113
dbp@personainternet.com
Mark Sabourin, Publisher & Editor

Recycling Product News
#201, 2323 Boundary Rd., Vancouver, BC V5M 4V8
604-291-9900, Fax: 604-291-1906
ebaum@baumpub.com
www.baumpub.com
Circulation: 18,000 Frequency: 8 times a year
Publication focuses on products, technologies services and industry news in recycling and waste management, ranging from composting to scrap metal.
Engelbert J. Baum, Publisher
Keith Barker, Editor

Non-government Publications

Shared Vision
#301, 873 Beatty St., Vancouver, BC V6B 2M6
604-733-5062, Fax: 604-731-1050
publisher@shared-vision.com
www.shared-vision.com
Circulation: 42,000 Frequency: 12 times a year
This publication attempts to help its readers live healthy, happy lives while creating and maintaining a sustainable society. The magazine features information on topics including green living, natural wellness, and organic food.
Rebecca Edhraim, Publisher

Solid Waste & Recycling
#800, 12 Concorde Place, Toronto, ON M3C 4J2
416-510-6798, Fax: 416-510-5133, 800-268-7742
bobrien@solidwastemag.com
www.solidwastemag.com
Circulation: 9,426 Frequency: 6 times a year
This publication dicusses all issues and topics pertaining to recycling and waste management.

The Atlantic Salmon Journal
Atlantic Salmon Federation, PO Box 5200, St Andrews, NB E5B 3S8
506-529-1033, Fax: 506-529-4438
tiffinic@nb.aibn.com
www.asf.ca
Circulation: 11,000 Frequency: 4 times a year
This magazine is the world's oldest publication regarding conservation-minded salmon angling, covering issues related to fly-fishing for Atlantic salmon and the over-all protection of the species.
Martin Silverstone, Editor

The Sustainable Times
1225 Prospect Bay Rd., Prospect Village, NS B3T 2A6
902-850-2510
times@chebucto.ns.ca
www.sustainabletimes.ca
Circulation: online only
A webzine that discusses and publicizes global issues including environmetalism, the Third World, and Fair Trade. The webzine is published by CUSO, which works for sustainable developtment in places such as Africa, Asia, Latin America and the Caribbean.
Sean Kelly, Editor

Vecteur Environnement
#220, 911, rue Jean-Talon est, Montréal, QC H2R 1V5
514-270-7110, Fax: 514-270-7154
info@reseau-environnement.com
www.reseau-environnement.co m
Circulation: 4 000 Frequency: 5 fois par an; français
Revue de l'industrie, des sciences et techniques de l'environnement du Québec; publiée par RÉSEAU environnement
Martine Boivin, Rédactrice-en-chef

Watershed Sentinel
c/o Watershed Sentinel Educational Society, PO Box 39, Whaletown, BC V0P 1Z0
250-935-6992, Fax: 250-935-6992
editor@watershedsentinel.ca
www.watershedsentinel.ca
Circulation: 5,000 Frequency: 6 times a year
This West Coast based publication focuses on how humanity affect the environment around them, by looking at issues such as logging and fishing practices and air and water pollution. It covers both bioregional and global perspectives on topics such as the environment, health and sustainability.
Delores Broten, Publisher & Editor

Women & Environments International Magazine
HNES Building, room 234, York University, 4700 Keele St., Toronto, ON M3J 1P3
416-736-2100, Fax: 416-736-5679
weimag@yorku.ca
www.weimag.com
Circulation: 2,000 Frequency: 2 times a year
Publication examines the relationships between women and the environment from a feminist perspective. It provides a forum for academic research and theory, professional practice and community experience and covers topics such as ecology and environmental activism, community development, childcare, and urban and rural agriculture.
Prabha Khosla
Reggie Modlich

Government Distribution Centres

The following offices may be contacted for copies of federal/provincial legislation.

Canada

Communications Canada (7352)
The documents comprising the Consolidated Statutes & Regulations are reproduced in HTML only & are not available in PDF. Documents can be reproduced in accordance with the Reproduction of Federal Law Order.
For federal statutes & regulations see: laws-lois.justice.gc.ca/

Alberta

Queen's Printer (7355)
Edmonton Bookstore
Fifth Floor, Park Plaza
10611 - 98 Avenue
Edmonton AB T5K 2P7
780/427-4952; Fax: 780/452-0668
Toll Free: 1-800-310-0000
Email: qp@gov.ab.ca
URL: www.qp.gov.ab.ca/
For provincial statutes & regulations see: www.qp.gov.ab.ca/catalogue/display/cfm?page_id=40
The monthly e-Bookmark newsletter is produced by the Alberta Queen's Printer to keep customers informed of changes to Alberta's laws, as well as new and updated products and services via email. To subscribe, send an email or fax as listed above, including your email address.

British Columbia

British Columbia (7356)
Crown Publications, Inc.
106 Ontario St.
Victoria, BC, V8V 1M9
250/386-4636; Fax: 250/386-0221
Email: crown@crownpub.bc.ca
URL: www.crownpub.bc.ca
Crown Bookstore
514 Government St.
Victoria BC V8L 2L7
250/356-6778
Fax: 250/356-0404
URL: crownpub.bc.ca/
For provincial statutes & regulations see: www.leg.bc.ca

Manitoba

Statutory Publications (7357)
20-200 Vaughan St.
Winnipeg MB R3C 1T5
204/945-3101
Toll free Manitoba only: 1-800-321-1203
Fax: 204/945-7172
Email: statpub@gov.mb.ca
URL: www.gov.mb.ca/queensprinter
For provincial statutes & regulations see URL above.

New Brunswick

Queen's Printer (7358)
#117, 670 King St.
Fredericton NB E3B 5H1
506/453-2520; Fax: 506/457-7899
Email: queens.printer@gnb.ca
URL: www.gnb.ca/0062/acts/index-e.asp
For provincial statutes see URL above.

Newfoundland & Labrador

Queen's Printer (7359)
Office of the Queen's Printer
Dept. of Government Services
Ground Floor, Confederation Building, East Block
PO Box 8700
St. John's NF A1B 4J6
709/729-3649
URL: www.gs.gov.nl.ca/printer/index.html
For provincial statutes & regulations see: www.assembly.nl.ca

Northwest Territories

Northwest Territories (7360)
Consolidations of statutes & regulations can be viewed in either PDF or WordPerfect.
See: www.justice.gov.nt.ca/legislation/searchleg&reg.shtml

Nova Scotia

Government Publications (7361)
PO Box 637
Halifax NS, B3J 2T3
902/424-5200
Toll free within Nova Scotia: 1-800-670-4357
Fax: 902/424-0516
URL: www.gov.ns.ca/snsmr/publications/
For provincial statutes & regulations see:
www.gov.ns.ca/legislature/legc//index.htm

Nunavut

Law Library (7362)
Nunavut Justice Centre, Building 510
PO Box 297
Iqaluit NU X0A 0H0
867/975-6134; Fax: 867/975-6380
Email: courtlibrary@gov.nu.ca
URL: www.nucj.ca/library/library..htm
For territorial statutes & regulations see URL above.

Ontario

Publications Ontario (7363)
50 Grosvenor St.
Toronto ON M7A 1N8
416/326-5300
Toll free in Ontario: 1-800-668-9938
Fax: 613/566-2234
TTY Toll free in Ontario: 1-800-268-7095
URL: www.publications.serviceontario.ca/ecom
For provincial statutes & regulations see: www.e-laws.gov.on.ca/

Prince Edward Island

Queen's Printer & Document Publishing Centre (7364)
Island Information Service
PO Box 2000
Charlottetown PE C1A 7N8
902/368-4000
Email: island@gov.pe.ca
URL: www.gov.pe.ca/publications/index.php3
For provincial statutes & regulations see: www.gov.pe.ca/law/index.php3

Québec

Les Publications du Québec (7365)
1000, route de l'Église, 5e étage
Québec, QC G1V 3V9
418/643-5150
Toll free in Québec: 1-800-463-2100
Email: publicationsduquebec@spq.gouv.qc.ca
URL: www.publicationsduquebec.gouv.qc.ca
For provincial statutes & regulations see URL above.

Saskatchewan

Queen's Printer (7366)
#B19, 3085 Albert St.
Regina SK S4S 0B1
306/787-6894
Toll Free in Saskatchewan: 1-800-226-7302
Fax: 306/798-0835
Email: qprinter@gov.sk.ca
URL: www.qp.gov.sk.ca/
For provincial statutes & regulations see URL above.

Yukon

Queen's Printer Subscriptions (7367)
Box 2703
Whitehorse YK Y1A 2C6
867/667-8573
Fax: 867/393-6210
Email: queens.printer@gov.yk.ca
URL: www.hpw.gov.yk.ca/selling/legissubs.html
For territorial statutes & regulations see: www.justice.gov.yk.ca/legislation/index.html

Research Centres Index

A

Acadia University, 1205
Alberta Biodiversity Monitoring Institute, 1199
Alberta Centre for Surface Engineering & Science, 1199
Alberta Ingenuity Centre for In Situ Energy, 1199
Alberta Sulphur Research Ltd., 1199
Alberta Water Research Institute, 1199
Alex Fraser Research Forest, 1200
Aleza Lake Research Forest Society, 1200
Aquaculture Collaborative Research and Development Program, 1203
Aquatic Ecosystems Research Laboratory, 1200
Arctic Institute of North America, 1199
Atlantic Coastal Action Program, 1206
Atlantic Cooperative Wildlife Ecology Research Network, 1206
Atlantic Environmental Prediction Research Initiative, 1206
Atlantic Forestry Centre, 1203
Atlantic Laboratory for Environmental Testing, 1203

B

Bamfield Marine Sciences Centre, 1201
Bedford Institute of Oceanography, 1206
Biodiversity Research Centre, 1201
Biogeoscience Institute, 1199
Biometeorology & Soil Physics Group of The University of British Columbia, 1201
British Columbia Environmental & Occupational Health Research Network, 1201

C

C-Core Innovative Engineering Solutions, 1204
Canada. Fisheries & Oceans Canada, 1211, 1207
Canadian Building Energy End-Use Data & Analysis Centre, 1199
Canadian Centre for Climate Modelling & Analysis, 1201
Canadian Centre for Health & Safety in Agriculture, 1212
Canadian Circumpolar Institute, 1199
Canadian Cooperative Wildlife Health Centre, 1211, 1212
Canadian Energy Research Institute, 1199
Canadian Network of Toxicology Centres, 1207
Canadian Plains Research Center, 1212
Canadian Water Network, 1207
Canmet Energy Technology Centre, 1199, 1207, 1211
Cape Breton University, 1206
Center for Earth Observation Sciences, 1199
Center for Metallurgical Process Engineering, 1201
Centre de recherche industrielle du Québec, 1211
Centre for Applied Business Research in Energy & the Environment, 1199
Centre for Applied Petroleum Sciences, 1206
Centre for Aquaculture & Environmental Research, 1201
Centre for Enhanced Forest Management, 1199
Centre for Environmental Engineering Research & Education, 1199
Centre for Environmental Research in Minerals, Metals, & Materials, 1201
Centre for Forest Biology, 1201
Centre for Forest Interdisciplinary Research, 1203
Centre for Global Studies, 1201
Centre for Health & Environment Research, 1201
Centre for Intelligent Mining Systems, 1199
Centre for Marine Environmental Prediction, 1206
Centre for Natural Hazard Research, 1201
Centre for Northern Agroforestry & Afforestation, 1212
Centre for Ocean Model Development for Applications, 1206
Centre for Offshore Oil and Gas Environmental Research, 1206
Centre for Sustainable Community Development, 1201
Centre for Sustainable Infrastructure Research, 1212
Centre for Wildlife Ecology, 1201
Centre géoscientifique de Québec, 1211
Centre of Environmental Excellence, 1204
Centre of Excellence for Earth and Environmental Technologies, 1207
Chemical Ecology Research Group, 1201
Clean Energy Research Centre, 1201
Co-operative Resource Management Institute in Resource & Environmental Management, 1201
Coastal CURA, 1206
Coastal Zones Research Institute Inc., 1203
Community - University Research for Recovery Alliance, 1204
Cooperative Resource Management Institute, 1201
Cultus Lake Salmon Research Laboratory, 1201

D

Dalhousie University, 1206

E

East Coast Ecosystems Research Organization, 1206
Eastern Canada Soil and Water Conservation Centre, 1203
Eastern Scotian Shelf Integrated Management Initiative, 1206
ecoNova Scotia for Clean Air and Climate Change, 1206
Edmonton Waste Management Centre of Excellence, 1199, 1200
Environment Canada, 1211, 1208, 1207, 1203
Environmental Health Research Network, 1211
Environmental Research & Studies Centre, 1200
Environmental Sciences Research Centre, 1206
Evolutionary & Behavioural Ecology Research Group, 1202

F

Fishermen & Scientists Research Society, 1206
Food & Resource Economics Group of The University of British Columbia, 1202
Freshwater Institute Science Laboratory, 1203

G

Geological Survey of Canada, 1207, 1208
GPI Atlantic, 1207
Great Lakes Environmental Research Laboratory, 1203
Great Lakes Research Consortium, 1205
Guelph Turfgrass Institute & Environmental Research Centre, 1208
Gulf Fisheries Centre, 1203

H

Habitat Conservation Trust Foundation, 1202
The Halifax STAR Project, 1207
Health Canada, 1208
Huntsman Marine Science Centre, 1203, 1204

I

I.K Barber Enhanced Forestry Laboratory, 1202
Imperial Oil - Alberta Ingenuity Centre for Oil Sands Innovation, 1200
Institute for Coastal & Oceans Research, 1202
Institute for Environmental Monitoring and Research, 1204
Institute for Integrated Energy Systems, 1202
Institute for Resources, Environment & Sustainability, 1202
Institute for Sustainable Energy, Environment, & Economy, 1200
Institute of Ocean Sciences, 1202
International Resource Industries & Sustainability Centre, 1200

J

The Jane Goodall Institute of Canada, 1208
John Prince Research Forest, 1202

K

Kahiltna Research Group, 1202

L

Lakehead University, 1208
Laurentian University, 1208, 1209
Liu Institute for Global Issues, 1202

M

Macleod Institute, 1200
Maritime College of Forest Technology, 1204
McGill University, 1211
McMaster University, 1209
Memorial University of Newfoundland, 1205, 1204
Miistakis Institute for the Rockies, 1200
Mount Allison University, 1204
Mushkegowuk Environmental Research Centre, 1209

N

National Hydrology Research Centre, 1212
National Research Council Institute for Marine Biosciences, 1207
National Water Research Institute, 1209
Natural Resources & Environmental Studies Institute, 1202
Norman B. Keevil Institute of Mining Engineering, 1202
North Pacific Marine Science Organization, 1202
Northern Forestry Centre, 1200
Northwest Atlantic Fisheries Centre, 1205
Nova Scotia Department of Natural Resources, 1207

O

Offshore Energy Research, 1207
Oil Sands Tailing Research Facility, 1200
Ontario Centre for Environmental Technology Advancement, 1209
Ouranos, 1211

P

Pacific Biological Station, 1202
Pacific Environmental Science Centre, 1202
Pacific Forestry Centre, 1202
Pacific Geoscience Centre, 1203
Pacific Wildlife Research Centre, 1203
Petroleum Research Atlantic Canada, 1205
Pipeline Engineering Center, 1200
Prairie & Northern Laboratory for Environmental Testing, 1200
Prairie Northern Wildlife Research Centre, 1200, 1205, 1212, 1203, 1207
Pulp & Paper Centre, 1203

Q

Québec. Ministère du Développement durable, de l'Environnement et des Parcs, 1211
Queen's University, 1209
Quesnel River Research Centre, 1203

R

Rural Development Institute, 1203

S

St. Andrews Biological Station, 1204
St. Francis Xavier University, 1207
St. Georges Bay Ecosystem Project, 1207
St. Mary's University, 1207
Soil - Water Environmental Group of The University of British Columbia, 1203
Soil - Water Environmental Laboratory of The University of British Columbia, 1203
Southern Gulf of St. Lawrence Coalition on Sustainability, 1204
Sustainable Forest Management Network, 1200

T

Tree Ring Lab, 1203

U

Université du Québec, 1211, 1212
Université du Québec à Montréal, 1212
University of Guelph, 1209
University of New Brunswick, 1204
University of Ottawa, 1209, 1210
University of Prince Edward Island, 1211
University of Regina, 1212
University of Toronto, 1210
University of Waterloo, 1210
University of Windsor, 1210
Upper Lakes Environmental Research Network, 1210

W

Water & Climate Impacts Research Centre, 1203
Wilfrid Laurier University, 1210, 1211

Y

York University, 1211
Yukon College, 1212

Research Centres

Alberta

Alberta Biodiversity Monitoring Institute (ABMI)
University of Alberta, #405CW, Biological Sciences Building, Edmonton AB T6G 2E9
Tel: 780-492-5766; *Fax:* 780-492-7635
e-mail: abmiinfo@ualberta.ca
URL: www.abmi.ca
Description: The Alberta Biodiversity Monitoring Institute facilitates environmental management, by monitoring ecosystems, species, & habitats in Alberta. The Institute's research on the state of Alberta's biodiversity is used to support decision-making related to natural resources.

Alberta Biodiversity Monitoring Institute
Vegreville
ABMI Monitoring Centre, Alberta Research Council, PO Box 4000, Vegreville AB T9C 1T4
Tel: 780-632-8356; *Fax:* 780-632-8379

Alberta Centre for Surface Engineering & Science (ACSES)
University of Alberta, #607, Chemical & Materials Engineering Bldg., Edmonton AB T6G 2G6
Tel: 780-492-1246; *Fax:* 780-492-1250
URL: www.ualberta.ca/ACSES/ACSES3/index.htm
Description: The Alberta Centre for Surface Engineering & Science of the University of Alberta is involved in research related to corrosion & wear, natural resource extraction, & microfabrication. An application of research is the development of methods to reduce waste produced in oil sands extraction.

Alberta Ingenuity Centre for In Situ Energy
Calgary Centre for Innovative Technology Bldg., University of Calgary, #018, 2500 University Dr. NW, Calgary AB T2N 1N4
Tel: 403-210-9610; *Fax:* 403-210-3973
e-mail: sdooley@ucalgary.ca
URL: www.aicise.ca
Overview: A organization founded in 2004
Description: An initiative of the Institute for Sustainable Energy, Environment, & Economy (ISEEE) & the Alberta Ingenuity Centre Program, the Alberta Ingenuity Centre for In Situ Energy strives to develop environmentally sustainable, efficient, & cost-effective practices & processes for in situ recovery & upgrading of the oil sands in Alberta. The energy research & innovation centre works to significantly reduce environmental impacts of Alberta's oil sands resources. The following are examples of the Centre's areas of research: Catalysts & catalytic process design for in situ upgrading; Integrated recovery & upgrading in in situ conditions; Integrated dynamic reservoir characterization; Chemical monitoring, bitumen characterization & petroleum informatics; & Advanced reactive reservoir simulation.

Alberta Sulphur Research Ltd. (ASRL)
Center for Applied Catalysis & Industrial Sulfur Chemistry, #6, 3535 Research Rd. NW, University Research Centre, Calgary AB T2L 2K8
Tel: 403-220-5346; *Fax:* 403-284-2054
e-mail: asrinfo@ucalgary.ca
URL: www.chem.ucalgary.ca/asr
Overview: A organization founded in 1964
Description: The non-profit sulfur research organization focuses upon the following areas of research: the environmental aspects of gas & sulfur industries, the handling & transportation of elemental sulfur, the recovery of sour natural gas, & Claus plant operations.

Alberta Water Research Institute (AWRI)
Manulife Place, #2410, 10180 - 101 St., Edmonton AB T5J 3S4
Tel: 780-701-5406; *Fax:* 780-420-0018
URL: www.waterinstitute.ca
Overview: A organization founded in 2007
Description: Administered through the Alberta Ingenuity Fund, the Alberta Water Research Institute coordinates research to support Alberta's water strategy. The provincial water strategy contains goals such as healthy aquatic ecosystems, a safe & secure drinking water supply, & a reliable water supply for a sustainable economy. The Institute's activity areas include strategic research programs, joint tesearch collaboration, strategic opportunity studies, technology development & commercialization, & education & outreach.

Arctic Institute of North America (AINA)
University of Calgary, 2500 University Dr. NW, Calgary AB T2N 1N4
Tel: 403-220-7515; *Fax:* 403-282-4609
e-mail: arctic@ucalgary.ca
URL: www.arctic.ucalgary.ca
Overview: A organization founded in 1945
Description: A multi-disciplinary research institute of the University of Calgary, the Arctic Institute of North America aims to advance the study of the North American & circumpolar Arctic region. The Institute provides information about the region's environmental, physical, & social conditions. Examples of research projects are as follows: the Beaufort Sea project for climate change - impact & adaptation to climate change for fish & marine mammals in the Canadian Beaufort Sea; wildlife, environment, & resource management, & the role of traditional & local knowledge; & human ecology & the impact of chemical pollutants on Arctic communities.

Biogeoscience Institute (BGS)
Biosciences Bldg., University of Calgary, #186, 2500 University Dr. NW, Calgary AB T2N 1N4
Tel: 403-220-5355; *Fax:* 403-673-3671
e-mail: jmbuchan@ucalgary.ca
URL: www.bgs.ucalgary.ca
Previous Name: Kananaskis Field Stations; G8 Legacy Chair in Wildlife Ecology
Description: The Biogeoscience Institute focuses research studies in the Canadian Rockies & surrounding areas, in order to increase understanding of ecosystem processes in the region. Field stations are located in the Kananakis Valley & the Sheep River Provincial Park. Examples of research projects include hot trees & melting snow in the Rockies, collapse & recovery of recreational fisheries, & altitudinal gradients of stable isotopes in lee-slope precipitation in the Canadian Rocky Mountains. Research is used to affect environmental & natural resource policies.

Canadian Building Energy End-Use Data & Analysis Centre (CBEEDAC)
Department of Economics, University of Alberta, #8-14 Tory Bldg., Edmonton AB T6G 2H4
Tel: 780-492-4134; *Fax:* 780-492-3300
e-mail: cbeedac@ualberta.ca
URL: www.ualberta.ca/~cbeedac
Description: The Canadian Building Energy End-Use Data & Analysis Centre is engaged in the provision of building energy data. The data is used by the Canadian residential, commercial, & institutional sectors.

Canadian Circumpolar Institute (CCI)
University of Alberta, #1-37, Pembina Hall, Edmonton AB T6G 2H8
Tel: 780-492-4512; *Fax:* 780-492-1153
e-mail: ccinst@gpu.srv.ualberta.ca
URL: www.uofaweb.ualberta.ca/polar
Description: The interdisciplinary centre conducts research to contribute to the development of sustainable communities & to increase understanding of northern Canada, the Arctic, & Antarctica. Examples of research include climate change in the Arctic, rivers & lakes, & wildlife habitats under stress.

Canadian Energy Research Institute (CERI)
#150, 3512 - 33rd St. NW, Calgary AB T2L 2A6
Tel: 403-282-1231; *Fax:* 403-284-4181
URL: www.ceri.ca
Overview: A organization founded in 1975
Description: An independent, non-profit research organization, the Canadian Energy Research Institute is engaged in the study of energy economics & related environmental issues. Environmental issues involve production, transportation, & consumption. Research teams operate within the areas of oil, natural gas, electricity, & energy / environment. An example of research includes oil sands supply & carbon costs & the impact of low GHG intensity methods for oil sands development.

Canmet Energy Technology Centre (CETC - Devon)
Devon
Devon Research Centre, #202A, 1 Oil Patch Dr., Devon AB T9G 1A8
Tel: 780-987-8682; *Fax:* 780-987-5349
e-mail: croy@nrcan.gc.ca
Description: The Canmet Energy Technology Centre in Devon focuses on oil sands & heavy oil, in the development of cleaner fossil fuels & related technologies.

Center for Earth Observation Sciences (CEOS)
Department of Earth & Atmospheric Sciences, University of Alberta, #1-26 Earth Sciences Bldg., Edmonton AB T6G 2E3
Tel: 780-492-9870; *Fax:* 780-492-2030
e-mail: ceos@ualberta.ca
URL: www.ceos.ualberta.ca
Description: The University of Alberta Center for Earth Observation Sciences is a multi-disciplinary research network, which monitors environmental changes & resource management, & formulates sustainable development policies. Examples of monitoring activities include changes in biodiversity, the effects of forest fires, & snow cover & land ice.

Centre for Applied Business Research in Energy & the Environment (CABREE)
c/o Richard Dixon, University of Alberta, 3-23, School of Business, Edmonton AB T6G 2R6
Tel: 780-248-1650
e-mail: richard.dixon@ualberta.ca
URL: www.business.ualberta.ca/cabree
Description: The independent research centre provides applied economic analysis to affect public policy. The Centre for Applied Business Research in Energy & the Environment focuses upon the following research areas: climate change issues, electricity restructuring, & energy markets.

Centre for Enhanced Forest Management (CEFM)
Department of Renewable Resources, University of Alberta, #442, Earth Sciences Bldg., Edmonton AB T6G 2E3
URL: www.cefm.rr.ualberta.ca
Description: The Centre for Enhanced Forest Management at the University of Alberta is engaged in research to contribute to the sustainable management & productivity of northern forests. The Centre works to develop & test forestry practices that will enhance wood production & values such as biodiversity, watershed, wildlife, & recreation. Areas of research are as follows: forest soils; silviculture & reclamation; forest management & protection; forest genetics & tree improvement; & growth & yield.

Centre for Environmental Engineering Research & Education (CEERE)
Schulich School of Engineering, University of Calgary, 2500 University Dr. NW, Calgary AB T2N 1N4
Tel: 403-220-2881
e-mail: ceere@ucalgary.ca
URL: www.eng.ucalgary.ca/CEERE
Description: The following are some research projects conducted by the Centre for Environmental Engineering Research & Education at the University of Calgary: Nanotechnology for the environment; Industrial & hazardous waste management technology; Sustainable landfills; Air pollution assessment & control technologies; Energy sector contaminated site remediation; Renewable energy; & Clean air & clean water technology.

Centre for Intelligent Mining Systems (CIMS)
Department of Computing Science, University of Alberta, #351, Computer Science Centre, Edmonton AB T6G 2E1
Tel: 780-492-6365
e-mail: cims@cs.ualberta.ca
URL: www.cs.ualberta.ca/~cims
Description: The Centre for Intelligent Mining Systems is engaged in exploratory research in intelligent systems for the oil sands mining industry. Research is conducted to develop intelligent systems technology to improve the surface mining process, by minimizing the environmental footprint & increasing efficiencies.

Edmonton Waste Management Centre of Excellence (EWMCE)
Solid Waste Research & Development Facility, #310, 13111 Meridian St., Edmonton AB T6S 1G9

Research Centres / Edmonton Waste Management Centre of Excellence

Tel: 780-496-7316; Fax: 780-944-5709
e-mail: ewmce@edmonton.ca
URL: www.ewmce.com
Description: The Edmonton Waste Management Centre of Excellence is engaged in the following activities related to waste management & environmental practices: research, technology development, & training. Research takes place in the following areas: solid waste, wastewater, & energy from waste. The Centre of Excellence strives to develop sustainable solutions for both local & global applications.

Edmonton Waste Management Centre of Excellence
Edmonton - Meridian St.
Administration & Training Centre, #100, 13111 Meridian St., Edmonton AB T6S 1G9
Tel: 780-496-6879

Edmonton Waste Management Centre of Excellence
Edmonton - 50th St.
Wastewater Research & Training Centre, 10977 - 50th St., Edmonton AB T6A 2E9
Tel: 780-496-4332; Fax: 780-944-5757

Environmental Research & Studies Centre (ERSC)
University of Alberta, #3-23, Business Bldg., Edmonton AB T6G 2R6
Tel: 780-492-5825; Fax: 780-492-3325
e-mail: ersc@ualberta.ca
URL: www.ualberta.ca/~ersc
Overview: A organization founded in 1990
Description: The Environmental Research & Studies Centre promotes interdisciplinary, inter-university, & international environmental research.

Imperial Oil - Alberta Ingenuity Centre for Oil Sands Innovation (COSI)
University of Alberta, #572, Department of Chemical Chemical & Materials Engineering, Edmonton AB T6G 2M9
URL: www.engineering.ualberta.ca/COSI.cfm
Description: The Imperial Oil-Alberta Ingenuity Centre for Oil Sands Innovation at the University of Alberta strives to improve oil sand operations. The Centre works to develop technology in oil sands mining, extraction, & upgrading, for cleaner & less expensive oil sands operations. Examples of the Centre's projects include the reduction of the amount of water used in oil sands extraction, the minimization of the surface footprint in the mining process, & the reduction of the amount of energy used in upgrading bitumen.

Institute for Sustainable Energy, Environment, & Economy (ISEEE)
Earth Sciences Bldg., University of Calgary, #1040, 2500 University Dr. NW, Calgary AB T2N 1N4
Tel: 403-220-6100; Fax: 403-220-2400
e-mail: info@iseee.ca
URL: www.iseee.ca
Overview: A organization founded in 2003
Description: The Institute for Sustainable Energy, Environment, & Economy is engaged in the development & implementation of energy & environment related initiatives at the University of Calgary. Interdisciplinary research is conducted at the Institute for the advancement of sustainable energy, the environment, & the economy. Areas of focus include energy & environment systems & modelling, applied geoscience, alternative energy, hydrocarbon recovery & upgrading, & business, legal & policy aspects of energy & the environment.

Institute for Sustainable Energy, Environment, & Economy (EESG)
Calgary - ISEEE Energy & Environmental Systems Group
Earth Sciences Bldg., University of Calgary, #602, 2500 University Dr. NW, Calgary AB T2N 1N4
Tel: 403-220-8872; Fax: 403-210-3894
e-mail: eespinfo@ucalgary.ca
URL: www.ucalgary.ca/EES
Description: The Energy & Environmental Systems Group at the University of Calgary researches problems that arise from the interaction of energy systems with the environment. The Group's research is interdisciplinary & policy-relevant. Examples of research include the life cycle assessment of oil sands technologies project & the development of materials to improve the conversion of solar energy into electrical energy.

International Resource Industries & Sustainability Centre (IRIS)
Scurfield Hall, Haskayne School of Business, University of Calgary, 2500 University Dr. NW, Calgary AB T2N 1N4
Tel: 403-220-5685
URL: www.haskayne.ucalgary.ca/haskaynefaculty/research/centres/iris
Description: The International Resource Industries & Sustainability Centre is engaged in interdisciplinary sustainability research of resource-based industry management practices & their impacts on environmental & social issues. Examples of research include the management of limited water resources, & the development & implementation of successful climate change mitigation & adaptation strategies.

Macleod Institute
#223, 20 Coachway Rd. SW, Calgary AB T3H 1E6
Tel: 403-240-2573; Fax: 403-246-1852
e-mail: macleod@macleodinstitute.com
URL: www.macleodinstitute.com
Overview: A organization founded in 1995
Description: An independent organization, affiliated with the University of Calgary, the Macleod Institute is engaged in environmental management, performance benchmarking, policy & program development, business process transformation, & program evaluations. In the area of environmental management, the Institute delivers climate change strategies, guides to environmental practices, risk communication plans, micro-power distributed energy options, & environmental performance measures.

Miistakis Institute for the Rockies
c/o Environmental Design, Professional Faculties Bldg., U. of Calgary, #2157, 2500 University Dr. NW, Calgary AB T2N 1N4
Tel: 403-220-8968; Fax: 403-210-3859
e-mail: institute@rockies.ca
URL: www.rockies.ca
Overview: A organization founded in 1995
Description: A non-profit corporation, affiliated with the University of Calgary, the Miistakis Institute for the Rockies' area of concern is the Crown of the Continent, which is an international ecosystem with the Waterton-Glacier International Peace Park at its core. The Crown of the Continent covers areas of Alberta, British Columbia, & Montana. The Institute engages in research programs that reflect conservation issues in the region. Examples of programs include a literature eeview of golf course impacts on wildlife; spatial analysis of residential expansion in the Crown of the Continent ecosystem; & recreation & wildlife in the Rockies of southwestern Alberta.

Northern Forestry Centre (NoFC)
5320 - 122nd St., Edmonton AB T6H 3S5
Tel: 780-435-7210; Fax: 780-435-7359
e-mail: webmaster@nofc.cfs.nrcan.gc.ca
Description: The Canadian Forest Service centre carries out research in areas such as biodiversity, climate change, ecology & ecosystems, forest & landscape management, & silviculture & regeneration. Examples of research projects are as follows: climate change impacts on the productivity & health of aspen; fire & forest dynamics under climate change scenarios; reconstruction of natural fire regimes; impacts of fire & harvesting on soils & site productivity; & human dimensions of biodiversity conservation in the Foothills Model Forest.

Northern Forestry Centre
Prince Albert
Saskatchewan Liaison Office, #250, 1288 Central Ave., Prince Albert AB S6V 4V8
Tel: 306-953-8548; Fax: 306-953-8649

Oil Sands Tailing Research Facility (OSTRF)
c/o Devon Research Centre, One Oil Patch Dr., Devon AB T9G 1A8
URL: www.ostrf.com
Description: The Oil Sands Tailings Research Facility was established to provide research to develop environmentally superior tailings disposal options. To improve tailings management in the oil sands industry, the Facility works with the Canadian Oil Sands Network for Research & Development Extraction Research Group. Examples of research projects include water treatment options & their application to oil sands operations for recycling & safe discharge, & advanced treatment of oil sands tailings water.

Pipeline Engineering Center
c/o Dr. R. Hugo, Department of Mechanical & Manufacturing Engineering, 2500 University Dr. NW, Schulich School of Engineering, U. of Calgary, Calgary AB T2N 1N4
Tel: 403-220-5770
Description: The Pipeline Engineering Center is engaged in the maintenance & management of pipelines, the development of new pipeline technologies, & project management. Some areas of research include improvements in pipeline safety & environmental control, hydrogen & carbon dioxide transmission, & new coatings synthesis.

Prairie & Northern Laboratory for Environmental Testing (PNLET)
Northern Forestry Centre, NRCan,, 5320 - 122 St., Edmonton AB T6H 3S5
Tel: 780-435-7335; Fax: 780-435-7268
Description: The Prairie & Northern Laboratory for Environmental Testing consists of an ecotoxicology laboratory & chemistry laboratories. Examples of specialization include sediment studies for the Water Survey of Canada's National Sediment Program, ozone depleting substances, & phosphate in detergent guidelines related to the Fisheries Act. Its work supports the Canadian Environmental Protection Act & the Fisheries Act, as well as other federal government departments & prairie provincial governments.

Prairie Northern Wildlife Research Centre
Edmonton
#200, 4999 - 98 Ave., Edmonton AB T6B 2X3
Tel: 780-951-8853; Fax: 780-495-2615

Sustainable Forest Management Network (SFMN) / Réseau de gestion durable des forêts
#3-03, Civil Engineering Bldg., University of Alberta, Edmonton AB T6G 2G7
Tel: 780-492-6659; Fax: 780-492-8160
e-mail: info@sfmnetwork.ca
URL: www.sfmnetwork.ca
Description: The non-profit Canadian research group is engaged in conducting interdisciplinary, university-based research related to sustainable forest management. The following are examples of research projects: climate change vulnerability & adaptation for forest management in Canada; eEcological & economic trade-off analysis of conservation strategies for woodland caribou; & evaluation of the potential effect of insect outbreaks on sustainable forest management.

British Columbia

Alex Fraser Research Forest (AFRF)
72 South 7th Ave., Williams Lake BC V2G 4N5
Tel: 250-392-2207; Fax: 250-398-5708
URL: www.forestry.ubc.ca/resfor/afrf/index.htm
Overview: A organization founded in 1987
Description: Part of the Faculty of Forestry at the University of British Columbia, the Alex Fraser Research Forest has conducted more than 200 research projects in the Gavin Lake block & the Knife Creek block. The region provides a demonstration of integrated resource management, involving forestry, cattle, wildlife, & tourism.

Aleza Lake Research Forest Society (ALRF)
3333 University Way, Prince George BC V2N 4Z9
Tel: 250-960-6339; Fax: 250-960-5851
URL: alrf.unbc.ca
Description: The university-based, multidisciplinary, outdoor research facility studies the ecosystem & resource management of the wet sub-boreal spruce biogeoclimatic zone. Areas of research include environmental monitoring in small forest tenures, biological diversity, climate change, & partial cut harvest systems.

Aquatic Ecosystems Research Laboratory (AERL)
Fisheries Centre, University of British Columbia, 2202 Main Mall, Vancouver BC V6T 1Z4
Tel: 604-822-2731; Fax: 604-822-8934
e-mail: office@fisheries.ubc.ca
URL: www.fisheries.ubc.ca
Description: The Aquatic Ecosystems Research Laboratory is engaged in multidisciplinary research, which focuses upon conserving aquatic life, restoring fisheries, & rebuilding ecosystems. The Fisheries Centre consists of the following research units: Sea Around Us, to assess the impacts of fisheries; Fisheries Economics Research Unit; Back to the Future, to study the restoration of aquatic ecosystems & sustainable fishing; Project Seahorse, to advance marine conservation; Marine Mammal Research Unit; Quantitative Modeling Group, to develop mathematical models to assist biologists & resource managers; & Aboriginal Fisheries, to find how the First Nations of BC could contribute their knowledge towards fisheries conservation & management.

Research Centres / Bamfield Marine Sciences Centre

Bamfield Marine Sciences Centre (BMSC)
100 Pachena Rd., Bamfield BC V0R 1B0
Tel: 250-728-3301; *Fax:* 250-728-3452
e-mail: info@bms.bc.ca
URL: www.bms.bc.ca
Overview: A organization founded in 1972
Description: Established by the Western Canadian Universities Marine Sciences Society, the research & training facility supports coastal & marine research.

Biodiversity Research Centre
University of British Columbia, 6270 University Blvd., Vancouver BC V6T 1Z4
Tel: 604-822-0862; *Fax:* 604-822-2416
e-mail: biodiversity.centre@ubc.ca
URL: www.zoology.ubc.ca/biodiversity
Description: The Biodiversity Research Centre seeks to understand & conserve the diversity of life. Biological diversity is researched, from genes to ecosystems. Examples of the Centre's projects are as follows: conservation biology, fisheries management, & population & community ecology.

Biometeorology & Soil Physics Group of The University of British Columbia (BIOMET)
Faculty of Land & Food Systems, Univeristy of British Columbia, #266B, 2357 Main Mall, Vancouver BC V6T 1Z4
URL: www.landfood.ubc.ca/biomet/index.htm
Description: The University of British Columbia's Biometeorology & Soil Physics Group is engaged in the monitoring of carbon dioxide, water & energy exchanges between the atmosphere & forests. The Group focuses upon the effects of climate variability & disturbance on carbon sequestration. Some projects are as follows: CO_2, H_2O, & energy exchange between Douglas-fir west-coast temperate forests & the atmosphere; & the impact of mountain pine beetles on CO_2, H_2O, & energy exchange between northern lodgepole pine forests & the atmosphere.

British Columbia Environmental & Occupational Health Research Network (BCEOHRN)
c/o Henry Harder, Associate Professor, University of Northern BC, 3333 University Way, Prince George BC V2N 4Z9
Tel: 250-960-6506; *Fax:* 250-960-5744
e-mail: patherton@bceohrn.ca
URL: www.bceohrn.ca
Overview: A organization founded in 2005
Description: The BC Environmental & Occupational Health Research Network facilitates interdisciplinary research in the area of occupational & environmental health.

Canadian Centre for Climate Modelling & Analysis (CCCma)
Ocean, Earth & Atmospheric Sciences Bldg., University of Victoria, PO Box 3065, Stn. CSC, #203A, 3800 Finnerty Rd., 2nd Fl., Victoria BC V8W 3V6
Tel: 250-363-8228; *Fax:* 250-363-8247
e-mail: wwwfeedback@cccma.ec.gc.ca
URL: www.cccma.ec.gc.ca
Description: A division of the Climate Research Branch of Environment Canada, the Canadian Centre for Climate Modelling & Analysis conducts research in the following main areas: sea-ice modelling, coupled & atmospheric climate modelling, the carbon cycle, & climate variability & predictability.

Center for Metallurgical Process Engineering (CMPE)
The University of British Columbia, #309, 6350 Stores Rd., Vancouver BC V6T 1Z4
Description: The interdisciplinary research centre at the University of British Columbia is engaged in the development of advanced metallurgical processes & products. Researchers work to develop metallurgical processing technologies & practices which focus upon improved sustainability & efficiency.

Centre for Aquaculture & Environmental Research (CAER)
4160 Marine Dr., West Vancouver BC V7V 1N6
Description: A collaborative effort between the federal Department of Fisheries & Oceans & the University of British Columbica, the Centre for Aquaculture & Environmental Research specializes in aquaculture & coastal research. The Centre's research into sustainable aquaculture & marine ecosystems concentrates on the following main topics: salmon migration physiology & ecology; coastal habitat issues; biotechnology & genomics; & aquatic animal nutrition.

Centre for Environmental Research in Minerals, Metals, & Materials (CERM3)
Norman B. Keevil Institute of Mining Engineering, University of BC, 6350 Stores Rd., Vancouver BC V6T 1Z4
Tel: 604-822-6217; *Fax:* 604-822-5599
URL: www.cerm3.mining.ubc.ca
Overview: A organization founded in 2000
Description: The Centre for Environmental Research in Minerals, Metals, & Materials works to understand & solve environmental problems caused by mining activity. The Centre is comprised of the following research facilities: The Environmental Quality Laboratory; The Mine Health & Safety Laboratory; The Bioremediation & Reclamation Laboratory; The Energy & Mining Laboratory; The Mine Automation & Environmental Simulation Laboratory; & The Environmental Technology Laboratory.

Centre for Forest Biology
University of Victoria, PO Box 3020, Stn. CSC, Victoria BC V8W 3N5
Tel: 250-721-7119; *Fax:* 250-721-6611
e-mail: forbiol@uvic.ca
URL: web.uvic.ca/~forbiol
Description: The University of Victoria's Centre for Forest Biology carries out research related to the adaptation of trees & their interactions with the environment, with an emphasis upon forest regeneration & forest biotechnology. Examples of research include plant-pest interactions, carbon sequestration by forests & soils, water relations & gas exchange, & plant stress physiology.

Centre for Global Studies (CFGS)
University of Victoria, PO Box 1700, Stn. CSC, Victoria BC V8W 2Y2
Tel: 250-472-4337; *Fax:* 250-472-4830
URL: www.globalcentres.org
Overview: A organization founded in 1998
Description: The Centre for Global Studies studies issues such as the environment, sustainable development, international governance & finance, & security. Examples of research projects include low carbon, building capacity to manage aquaculture in Thailand, & climate change adaptation & mitigation.

Centre for Global Studies (PCIC)
Victoria - Pacific Climate Impacts Consortium
C Wing, Sedgewick Bldg., University of Victoria, PO Box 1700, Stn. CSC, Victoria BC V8W 2Y2
Tel: 250-721-6236; *Fax:* 250-721-7217
e-mail: climate@uvic.ca
URL: www.pacificclimate.org
Overview: A organization founded in 2005
Description: A division of the University of Victoria's Centre for Global Studies, the Pacific Climate Impacts Consortium delivers climate system information, with a focus upon North America's Pacific Northwest. The Consortium works toward adaptation & the reduction of vulnerability to climate change, climate variability, & extreme weather events. The Pacific Climate Impacts Consortium studies sectors which face impacts of climate change, such as water resources, forestry, biodiversity, agriculture, & health.

Centre for Health & Environment Research (CHER)
c/o School of Environmental Health, University of British Columbia, 2206 East Mall, 3rd Fl., Vancouver BC V6T 1Z3
Tel: 604-827-5622; *Fax:* 604-822-9588
URL: www.cher.ubc.ca
Description: Comprised of a multidisciplinary team of investigators, the Centre for Health & Environment Research is engaged in the research & prevention of diseases, which are caused by hazards in outdoor & indoor environments.

Centre for Natural Hazard Research (CNHR)
Technical & Sciences Complex, Dept. of Earth Sciences, Simon Fraser U., 8888 University Dr., Burnaby BC V5A 1S6
Tel: 778-782-4924; *Fax:* 778-782-4198
URL: www.sfu.ca/cnhr
Description: Simon Fraser University's Centre for Natural Hazard Research is engaged in the physical & social scientific research of geophysical processes, such as climate change, landslides, floods, snow avalanches, volcanism, earthquakes, & tsunamis. In the area of climate change, for example, the Centre studies how some natural disasters, such as floods & landslides, occur more often due to global warming. Research, into land use planning, critical infrastructure, hazardous waste, & emergency planning, leads to sustained improvements to the environment & society through policy-making.

Centre for Sustainable Community Development (CSCD)
West Mall Complex, Simon Fraser University, #2622, 8888 University Dr., Burnaby BC V5A 1S6
Tel: 778-782-5849; *Fax:* 778-782-5473
e-mail: scdadmin@sfu.ca
URL: www.sfu.ca/cscd
Previous Name: Community Economic Development Centre
Overview: A organization founded in 1989
Description: Simon Fraser University's Centre for Sustainable Community Development conducts research to support the sustainable development of communities. Research considers the relationship between economic factors & the natural environment, health, housing, education, & the arts.

Centre for Wildlife Ecology (CWE)
Department of Biological Sciences, Simon Fraser university, 8888 University Dr., Burnaby BC V5A 1S6
Tel: 778-782-5958; *Fax:* 778-782-3496
URL: www.sfu.ca/biology/wildberg
Description: A collaboration between Simon Fraser University & the Canadian Wildlife Service, the Centre for Wildlife Ecology conducts research in wildlife ecology. Research aids in meeting conservation challenges. Examples of research include Triangle Island seabird research, landbird ecology, avian reproduction & environmental change, & the sustainable shellfish aquaculture initiative.

Chemical Ecology Research Group (CERG)
Department of Biological Sciences, Simon Fraser University, 8888 University Dr., Burnaby BC V5A 1S6
Tel: 778-782-4392; *Fax:* 778-782-3496
URL: web.mac.com/ckeeling/CERG
Overview: A organization founded in 1981
Description: Simon Fraser University's Chemical Ecology Research Group studies semiochemicals, with a focus upon insect pests in forestry & agriculture. Examples of research are the mountain pine beetle & the ambrosia beetle, which cause damage to forests. Research aids government laboratories & industrial companies in the provision of biological pest control.

Clean Energy Research Centre (CERC)
University of British Columbia, 2360 East Mall, Vancouver BC V6T 1Z3
Tel: 604-827-4342
e-mail: cerc@cerc.ubc.ca
URL: www.cerc.ubc.ca
Description: The University of British Columbia's Clean Energy Centre strives to reduce the environmental impact of energy use, by investigating technologies which will provide sustainable energy. Examples of research projects are as follows: reducing energy loss from coking & fouling; biomass storage, handling & processing; hydrogen generation; & clean burning engines.

Cooperative Resource Management Institute (CRMI)
c/o School of Resource & Environmental Management, Simon Fraser U., 8888 University Dr., Burnaby BC V5A 1S6
Tel: 778-782-3074; *Fax:* 778-782-4968
e-mail: dallaway@sfu.ca
URL: www.rem.sfu.ca/crmi
Overview: A organization founded in 1998
Description: The Cooperative Resource Management Institute conducts multidisciplinary research in resource management, such as the areas of water, fisheries, forestry, & wildlife management.

Co-operative Resource Management Institute in Resource & Environmental Management (CRMI)
c/o SAFE Division, School of Resource & Environment Management, Simon Fraser University, Burnaby BC V5A 1S6
Tel: 604-666-1995
Description: Fisheries & Oceans Canada's SAFE Division, at Simon Fraser University, carries out research activities in the following areas related to salmonids: incubation, rearing, feeding behaviour, migration, & their habitat. Research is conducted in coastal & interior British Columbia, & the Yukon. Examples of the SAFE Division's research projects are as follows: the impacts of energy generation on adult salmon migration; & the effects of timber harvesting on fish habitat.

Cultus Lake Salmon Research Laboratory
4222 Columbia Valley Hwy., Cultus Lake BC V2R 5B6
Description: The Cultus Lake Salmon Research Laboratory conducts research on factors which affect the freshwater life-cycle stages of Pacific salmon. The Fisheries & Oceans Canada research facility consists of many laboratories, such as the radioisotope laboratory & the inorganic chemistry laboratory.

Research Centres / Environment Canada

Cultus Lake Salmon Research Laboratory also features artificial streams & ponds, plus an experimental hatchery.

Environment Canada (CCCMA)
Canadian Centre for Climate Modelling & Analysis
Bob Wright Centre, University Of Victoria, PO Box 1700, Stn. CSC, Victoria BC V8W 2Y2 Canada
URL: www.cccma.bc.ec.gc.ca
Description: CCCMA is a division of the Climate Research Branch of Environment Canada. The Centre is engaged in research on atmospheric climate modelling, sea-ice modelling, climate variability & predictability, the carbon cycle, & other climate issues.

Evolutionary & Behavioural Ecology Research Group
Department of Biological Sciences, Simon Fraser University, 8888 University Dr., Burnaby BC V5A 1S6
URL: www.sfu.ca/biology/berg
Overview: A organization founded in 1989
Description: Simon Fraser University's Evolutionary & Behavioural Ecology Research Group studies behaviours of organisms, such as plants, insects, fish, birds, & mammals, & their relationship with the environment. An example of research is behaviour & conservation biology, in association with Simon Fraser University's Centre for Wildlife Ecology.

Food & Resource Economics Group of The University of British Columbia (FRE Group)
Faculty of Land & Food Systems, University of British Columbia, #329, 2357 Main Mall, Vancouver BC V6T 1Z4
Tel: 604-822-1219; Fax: 604-822-2184
e-mail: agdean@interchange.ubc.ca
URL: www.landfood.ubc.ca/fre
Previous Name: Agricultural Economics
Description: The University of British Columbia Group researches policy & economic issues related to food markets, renewable natural resources, & the environmnent. In the area of natural resource economics, examples of research include biodiversity & wildlife habitat. Examples of research within the area of environmental economics are ground water contamination & climate change.

Habitat Conservation Trust Foundation (HCTF)
PO Box 9354, Stn. Prov Govt., #100, 333 Quebec St., Victoria BC V8W 9M1
Tel: 250-387-9853; Fax: 250-952-6684
Toll-Free: 800-387-9853
URL: www.hctf.ca
Previous Name: Habitat Conservation Trust Fund
Description: Habitat Conservation Trust Foundation supports projects to maintain & enhance fish & wildlife habitats in British Columbia. Examples of conservation projects funded by the Foundation include the following: informational, educational, & stewardship projects; land acquisition for conservation purposes; & the restoration of native freshwater fish & wildlife populations & habitats.

I.K Barber Enhanced Forestry Laboratory (EFL)
Bldg. 12, University of Northern British Columbia, #11-103, 3333 University Way, Prince George BC V2N 4Z9
Tel: 250-960-6498
URL: www.unbc.ca/efl
Overview: A organization founded in 2000
Description: The Enhanced Forestry Lab at the University of Northern British Columbia conducts controlled environmental research.

Institute for Coastal & Oceans Research (ICOR)
Technology Enterprise Facility, University of Victoria, PO Box 1700, Stn. CSC, #132, 2300 McKenzie Ave., Victoria BC V8W 2Y2
Tel: 250-721-8848; Fax: 250-472-4100
e-mail: icor@uvic.ca
URL: http://icor.uvic.ca
Previous Name: Centre for Earth & Ocean Research
Description: Ocean & coastal issues, plus related policy matters, are the focus of research conducted & coordinated by the Institute for Coastal & Oceans Research. An example of a research project is coasts under stress, which analyzed the impacts of socio-environmental restructuring on the environment, health, & communities.

Institute for Integrated Energy Systems (IESVic)
University of Victoria, PO Box 3055, Stn. CSC, Victoria BC V8W 3P6
Tel: 250-721-6295; Fax: 250-721-6323
e-mail: iesvic-request@iesvic.uvic.ca
URL: www.iesvic.uvic.ca
Overview: A organization founded in 1989
Description: The University of Victoria's Institute for Integrated Energy Systems studies sustainable energy systems. Areas of research include hydrogen technology, fuel cell science & technology, energy systems analysis & economics, & sustainable energy systems integration. Its research leads to the development of technologies for the adoption of sustainable, clean energy.

Institute for Resources, Environment & Sustainability (IRES)
Aquatic Ecosystem Research Laboratory, University of British Columbia, #429, 2202 Main Mall, Vancouver BC V6T 1Z4
Tel: 604-822-7725; Fax: 604-822-9250
e-mail: rmesgrad@ires.ubc.ca (Student Inquiries); webmaster@ires.ubc.ca
URL: www.ires.ubc.ca
Description: The interdisciplinary research institute at the University of British Columbia studies environmental & sustainability issues in order to foster sustainable futures. Research is conducted in the following areas: local & global environmental change; water, ecosystems & communities; & energy, technology, health, & society. The Institute for Resources, Environment & Sustainability carries out its research by working with governmental organizations, NGOs, local enterprises & international businesses.

Institute of Ocean Sciences (IOS)
PO Box 6000, 9860 West Saanich Rd., Sidney BC V8L 4B2
Tel: 250-363-6517
Description: Affiliated with Fisheries & Oceans Canada, the scientific facility is engaged in research on the coastal waters of the following regions: British Columbia, the western Canadian Arctic, the Northeastern Pacific Ocean, & the navigable fresh waters east to the Alberta border. The Institute of Ocean Sciences contributes to the restoration & management of coastal ecosystems.

John Prince Research Forest (JPRF)
c/o S. Grainger, Ecosystem Science/Mgmt. Program, U. of Northern BC, #8-313, 3333 University Way, Prince George BC V2N 4Z9
Tel: 250-648-3322
URL: researchforest.unbc.ca/jprf/jprf.htm
Overview: A organization founded in 1999
Description: Located in north central British Columbia, the John Prince Research Forest is jointly managed by the University of Northern British Columbia & the Tl'azt'en First Nation. Interdisciplinary research is conducted. Examples of research include a bat ecology study, forest health & bark beetle infestation treatment methods, & leave-tree survival & wind damage after partial cutting in the upland SBS forests.

Kahiltna Research Group
#108 125A, 1030 Denman St., Vancouver BC V6G 1R8
URL: www.kahiltna.org
Description: The Vancouver location of the Kahiltna Research Group is a branch of the group at California State University Long Beach. In British Columbia, the Kahiltna Research Group is associated with the Centre for Wildlife Ecology at Simon Fraser University. The Group is engaged in research of ecological topics, with a focus on marine ecology. An example of research is the migration of shorebirds. The Kahiltna Research Group provides information to government, agencies, & non-profit organization to assit the ecologically related work.

Liu Institute for Global Issues
The University of British Columbia, 6476 NW Marine Dr., Vancouver BC V6T 1Z2
Fax: 604-822-6966
e-mail: liu.institute@ubc.ca
URL: www.ligi.ubc.ca
Description: The Liu Institute for Global Issues is engaged in interdisciplinary, policy-relevant research in the following areas: the environment, peace & security, development, justice, & health. Examples of environmental projects are as follows: Climate Science, Equity & Development: The Role of International Institutions in Capacity Building for Climate Change; Risks & Benefits of Nanotechnology; & Risk, Regulation & Controversy: Agricultural Biotechnology in Developing Countries.

Natural Resources & Environmental Studies Institute (NRESI)
University of Northern British Columbia, 3333 University Way, Prince George BC V2N 4Z9
e-mail: nresi@unbc.ca
URL: www.unbc.ca/nres/institute_overview.html
Description: The University of Northern British Columbia's Natural Resources & Environmental Studies Institute promotes interdisciplinary research related to natural resource systems & human uses of the environment. The Institute focuses upon northern regions. Areas of research include ecological patterns & processes, earth systems & dynamics, & societal structures & values. Examples of research include habitat effects on behaviour & reproduction in forest generalist birds, the rehabilitation of petroleum wellsites, & the Prince George sustainable landscaping initiative.

Norman B. Keevil Institute of Mining Engineering
University of British Columbia, 6350 Stores Rd., Vancouver BC V6T 1Z4
Tel: 604-822-2540; Fax: 604-822-5599
e-mail: info@mining.ubc.ca
URL: www.mining.ubc.ca
Description: The University of British Columbia's NBK Institute of Mining Engineering conducts research which promotes sustainability & improved working processes in the mining industry. Research projects range from mine safety to environmental issues. Examples of research are as follows: environmental research in minerals, metals, & materials; environmental services; & remote-monitoring systems for environmental protection.

North Pacific Marine Science Organization (PICES)
c/o Institute of Ocean Sciences, PO Box 6000, 9860 West Saanich Rd., Sidney BC V8L 4B2
Tel: 250-363-6366; Fax: 250-363-6827
e-mail: secretariat@PICES.int
URL: www.pices.int
Overview: A organization founded in 1992
Description: The intergovernmental scientific organization coordinates marine research in the North Pacific & its surrounding seas. The following countries are members of the North Pacific Marine Science Organization: Canada, the United States of America, the Russian Federation, the People's Republic of China, Japan, & the Republic of Korea.

Pacific Biological Station (PBS)
3190 Hammond Bay Rd., Nanaimo BC V9T 6N7
Tel: 250-756-7000; Fax: 250-756-7053
e-mail: paclibrarypbs@dfo-mpo.gc.ca; seminar@pac.dfo-mpo.gc.ca
URL: www.pac.dfo-mpo.gc.ca/sci/pbs
Overview: A organization founded in 1908
Description: As a research facility of Fisheries & Oceans Canada, the fisheries research centre concentrates its studies on the following waters: British Columbia's coastal waters, the Western Arctic, the Northeast Pacific Ocean, & the navigable waters east to the Manitoba, Saskatchewan border. The Pacific Biological Station's research contributes to the following areas: stock assessment, fish productivity, habitat, ocean science, & marine environment.

Pacific Environmental Science Centre (PESC)
2645 Dollarton Hwy., North Vancouver BC V7H 1B1
Description: A federal laboratory of Environment Canada, The Pacific Environmental Science Centre is engaged in testing the quality of water, sediments, soil, & biota. The testing contributes to research in environmental protection, shellfish water quality, emergency response, & environmental quality monitoring. The Centre partners with Health Canada, BC Environment, Fisheries & Oceans Canada, Transport Canada, & the University of Victoria. Its clients include municipal & territorial governments & First Nations.

Pacific Forestry Centre (PFC)
506 West Burnside Rd., Victoria BC V8Z 1M5
Tel: 250-363-0600; Fax: 250-363-0775
e-mail: webmaster@pfc.cfs.nrcan.gc.ca
Description: The Canadian Forest Service centre conducts research in the following areas: biodiversity, ecology & ecosystems, entomology, & forest & landscape management. Examples or research projects in the Pacific Region are as follows: stand development following mountain pine beetle outbreaks in south-central British Columbia; application of Landsat Satellite Imagery to monitor land-cover changes at the Athabasca Oil Sands; & investigating the effectiveness of mountain pine beetle mitigation strategies.

Pacific Geoscience Centre
PO Box 6000, 9860 West Saanich Rd., Sidney BC V8L 4B2
Tel: 250-363-6500; Fax: 250-363-6565
Also Known As: Geological Survey of Canada Pacific (Sidney)
Description: The Pacific Geoscience Centre conducts research in the following areas: Marine Geoscience, to study the the coastal marine environment; Earthquakes Canada; & Geodynamics, to investigate the movement of the Earth's crust. An example of one of the Centre's projects is the Georgia Basin Geohazards Initiative, to provide research to aid in environmental & resource management decision making.

Pacific Wildlife Research Centre (PWRC)
5421 Robertson Rd., Delta BC V4K 3N2
Tel: 604-940-4700; Fax: 604-946-7022
e-mail: greenlane.pyr@ec.gc.ca
Description: The mission of the Pacific Wildlife Research Centre is the management & protection of wildlife, endangered species, & migratory birds & their habitats. The Centre also strives to maintain biological diversity.

Pulp & Paper Centre
The University of British Columbia, 2385 East Mall, Vancouver BC V6T 1Z4
Tel: 604-822-8560; Fax: 604-822-8563
e-mail: ppc-info@ppc.ubc.ca
URL: www.ppc.ubc.ca
Description: The Pulp & Paper Centre hosts collaborative research programs between the Pulp & Paper Research Institute of Canada (Paprican) & the University of British Columbia. Examples of environmental research include waste water & solids treatment, air emissions, life cycle assessment, & fouling & condensates.

Quesnel River Research Centre (QRCC)
PO Box 28, Likely BC V0L 1N0
URL: www.unbc.ca/qrrc
Description: The University of Northern British Columbia's Quesnel River Research Centre is engaged in research projects on the Quesnel River. Examples of research projects are as follows: northern hydrometeorological processes & their impacts; factors related to spawning site locations in interior Fraser coho salmon; & the effect of landscape disturbance, from factors such as forestry, agriculture, & mining, & climate change, on the behaviour of water, sediment & chemicals in the environment.

Soil - Water Environmental Group of The University of British Columbia
Faculty of Land & Food Systems, University of British Columbia, #227, 2357 Main Mall, Vancouver BC V6T 1Z4
Description: The University of British Columbia Group is involved in the research of human & natural processes which affect land & water resources. Examples of the Soil - Water Environmental Group's research are as follows: climate & land use changes on water resources, non-point source pollution, & land use impacts on water & soil quality.

Soil - Water Environmental Laboratory of The University of British Columbia (SWEL)
MacMillan Bldg., Faculty of Land & Food Systems, University of BC, #112A, 2357 Main Mall, Vancouver BC V6T 1Z4
Tel: 604-822-6360
URL: www.landfood.ubc.ca/swel
Description: The University of British Columbia Laboratory is a cooperative effort of the Faculty of Land & Food Systems, the Faculty of Forestry's Forest Resources Management, & the College for Interdisciplinary Studies' Institute for Resources, Environment & Sustainability. It carries out research related to soil, water, organic materials, & air.

Tree Ring Lab
c/o Dr. K.J. Lewis, College of Science & Management, U. of Northern BC, #LABB 212, 3333 University Way, Prince George BC V2N 4Z9
URL: www.unbc.ca/dendrolab
Description: Examples of research conducted by the University of Northern British Columbia's Tree Ring Lab are as follows: change in Douglas fir sensitivity to climate variation in British Columbia; the influence of disturbance agents on mature spruce-subalpine fir forests in central British Columbia; & wood decay & degradation in lodgepole pine killed by mountain pine beetles.

Water & Climate Impacts Research Centre (W-CIRC) / Centre de Recherche sur les Eaux et d'Impacts du Climat (CREIC)
Social Sciences & Mathematics Bldg., University of Victoria, PO Box 3060, Stn. CSC, 3800 Finnerty Rd., Victoria BC V8W 3R4
URL: www-circ.uvic.ca
Overview: A organization founded in 2002
Description: Created as a result of an agreement between the University of Victoria & Environment Canada's National Water Research Institute, the Water & Climate Impacts Research Centre's studies include the hydrologic & ecological impacts of atmospheric change & variability. Research focuses upon the following areas: groundwater systems, lake heat & energy budgets of lakes, floods & droughts, river & lake ice, aquatic ecology, alpine & reservoir water supplies, & forest hydrology.

Manitoba

Centre for Forest Interdisciplinary Research (C-FIR)
c/o Department of Geography, University of Winnipeg, #5L13, 515 Portage Ave., Winnipeg MB R3B 2E9
Tel: 204-786-9435
URL: www.cfir.uwinnipeg.ca
Description: The research centre at the University of Winnipeg conducts interdisciplinary research in the following areas: forest ecosystems, forestry, the human uses of forests, & forest values. Examples of research projects have included forest growth response to climate change, the influence of long term insecticide spraying on forest structure, & climate & fire relationships in the central & eastern boreal forest.

Freshwater Institute Science Laboratory (FWI)
501 University Cres., Winnipeg MB R3T 2N6
Tel: 204-983-5000
Description: Fisheries & Oceans Canada's Freshwater Institute Science Laboratory in Winnipeg is the regional headquarters of the Central & Arctic Region. The research facility features a solar warehouse, an ozone waste treatment facility, & a water treatment facility. Research activities are conducted in the key areas of freshwater & marine fisheries, & aquatic biology. Programs are carried out in freshwater science, oceans management, Arctic research, fisheries management, & fish habitat management.

Great Lakes Environmental Research Laboratory (GLERL)
4840 S. State Rd., Ann Arbor MI 48108-9719 USA
Tel: 734-741-2235; Fax: 734-741-2055
e-mail: www.glerl@noaa.gov OR: margaret.lansing.noaa.gov
URL: www.glerl@noaa.gov
Description: The Research Laboratory, founded in 1974, is under the aegis of the U.S. National Oceanic and Atmospheric Administration & is mandated to conduct high quality research & provide leadership on issues concerning the Great Lakes & marine coastal environments. The focus of research is on the physical environment of the Great Lakes, water quality & quantity, human health, fish recruitment & productivity, & invasive species affecting the Lakes. GLERL collaborates with Canadian scientists & with institutions such as Environment Canada, Fisheries & Oceans Canada, the Canadian Ice Service & the Canadian Hydrographic Service, & conducts research in the Canadian waters of the Lakes as well as in Canada's inland lakes.

Prairie Northern Wildlife Research Centre
Winnipeg
#150, 123 Main St., Winnipeg MB R3C 4W2
Tel: 204-983-5259; Fax: 204-983-5248

Rural Development Institute (RDI)
McMaster Hall Complex, Brandon University, 270 - 18th St., Lower Concourse, Brandon MB R7A 6A9
Tel: 204-571-8515; Fax: 204-725-0364
e-mail: rdi@brandonu.ca
URL: www.brandonu.ca/rdi
Overview: A organization founded in 1989
Description: The not-for-profit research & development organization conducts multi-disciplinary academic & applied research on rural issues. Topics of research include environmental & agro-economic issues, rural / northern health & well-being, rural adaptation & change, & policy & program research & development.

New Brunswick

Aquaculture Collaborative Research and Development Program (ACRDP)
Maritime Region
St. Andrews Biological Station, 531 Brandy Cove Rd., St. Andrews NB E5B 2L9 Canada
Tel: 506-529-5882; Fax: 506-851-2079
Description: The Aquaculture Collaborative Research and Development Program (ACRDP) is an initiative of the Department of Fisheries and Oceans to increase the level of collaborative research. The ACRDP seeks to increase research in optimizing fish production, optimizing fish health, and optimizing environmental sustainability.

Aquaculture Collaborative Research and Development Program
531 Brandy Cove Rd., St. Andrews NB E5B 2L9 Canada

Atlantic Forestry Centre (AFC)
PO Box 4000, 1350 Regent St. S, Fredericton NB E3B 5P7 Canada
Tel: 506-452-3500; Fax: 506-452-3525
e-mail: afcinquiries@nrcan.gc.ca
URL: cfs.nrcan.gc.ca/regions/afc
Description: The Atlantic Forestry Centre (AFC) is a research facility under National Resources Canada based out of Fredericton, New Brunswick and Corner Brook, Newfoundland. The AFC conducts research projects in biodiversity, effects of air pollution and climate change, forest health, pest management, genetics, and risk analyses to advance forest ecosystem sustainability.

Atlantic Laboratory for Environmental Testing (ESC)
Morton Ave. & University Ave., Moncton NB E1A 6S8 Canada
Tel: 506-851-2622; Fax: 506-851-6608
Description: The Atlantic Region Environmental Science Centre is based out of the Université de Moncton Campus. The Centre conducts research in a variety of areas including the toxicity of pesticides and nonylphenol, studies on amphibians, studies on sand shrimp, and other areas. The Centre houses a chemistry laboratory that focuses on pesticides, oil analysis, and toxicology testing.

Coastal Zones Research Institute Inc. (CZRI)
Université de Moncton, Campus de Shippagan, 232B, ave de l'Eglise, Shippagan NB E8S 1J2 Canada
Tel: 506-336-6600; Fax: 506-336-6601
e-mail: info@irzc.umcs.ca
URL: www.irzc.umcs.ca
Description: The Coastal Zones Research Institute Inc. (CZRI) is a private non-profit institution affiliated with the Université de Moncton and established in 2002. The Institute promotes a multidisciplinary approach that focuses on three main areas of research: aquaculture, fishery and marine products, and peat and peatlands. The Institute also conducts research on the sustainable development of coastal zones.

Eastern Canada Soil and Water Conservation Centre (CCSE)
1010 ch. De l'Eglise, Grand Falls NB E3Y 2X9 Canada
Tel: 506-475-4040; Fax: 506-475-4030
e-mail: ccse-swcc@umce.ca
URL: www.ccse-swcc.nb.ca
Description: The Eastern Canada Soil and Water Conservation Centre is a non-governmental organization affiliated with Université de Moncton, Campus d'Edmundston. The Centre is dedicated to the promotion of sustainable natural resource management for the agriculture industry in Eastern Canada. The Centre specializes in soil and water conservation, environmental planning, sustainable development, climate change and greenhouse gas emissions, and studies of production systems.

Gulf Fisheries Centre
PO Box 5030, Moncton NB E1C 9B6 Canada
Tel: 506-851-6206; Fax: 506-851-2378
Description: The Gulf Fisheries Centre is a research facility of the Canada Department of Fisheries and Oceans based in New Brunswick. The Centre focuses on research in aquaculture and environmental sciences, fisheries sciences and aquatic resources, and oceans and habitat projects. Specific research areas include studies of indigenous species, stock assessment and population biology, and studies on the ecosystems of the Gulf of St. Lawrence.

Huntsman Marine Science Centre (HSMC)
1 Lower Campus Rd., St. Andrews NB E5B 2L7 Canada
Tel: 506-529-1200; Fax: 506-529-1212
e-mail: huntsman@huntsmanmarine.ca
URL: www.huntsmanmarine.ca
Overview: A organization founded in 1970
Description: The Huntsman Marine Science Centre (HSMC) was established in 1970 through a consortium of 20 Universities and various Government departments. The HSMC is dedicated to research and education in the field of marine science for the benefit of both the private and public sector. One of it's key

Research Centres / Huntsman Marine Science Centre

research projects is the banding of birds to study the impact of habitat changes on indigenous bird species. The HSMC also operates a public aquarium in addition to research facilities.

Huntsman Marine Science Centre
Atlantic Reference Centre
1 Lower Campus Rd., St. Andrews NB E5B 2L7 Canada
Tel: 506-529-1203; *Fax:* 506-529-1212
e-mail: arc@mar.dfo-mpo.gc.ca
URL: www.huntsmanmarine.ca/html/arc.html
Description: The Huntsman Marine Science Centre and Fisheries and Ocean Canada (DFO) created the Atlantic Reference Centre (ARC) in 1984 to archive samples of Canadian Atlantic marine life collected by research surveys and as a source of taxonomic information. The ARC and DFO collaborate on marine biodiversity research and planning. Services provided by the ARC include sample processing, specimen identification, and research services for government, academic, private, and public organizations.

Maritime College of Forest Technology
Hugh John Fleming Forestry Centre, 1350 Regent St., Fredericton NB E3C 2G6 Canada
Tel: 506-458-0653; *Fax:* 506-458-0652
e-mail: info@mcft.ca
URL: www.mcft.ca
Description: The Maritime College of Forest Technology was established in 1946 under joint funding from the Provinces of Nova Scotia and New Brunswick to better improve the forestry industries of maritime provinces. The programs the College offers cover a range of topics, including forest ecology, wildlife taxonomy, fish and wildlife management, wildfire science, forest harvesting, and siviculture. The College makes use of the Noonan Forest for field research, as well as on-site facilities.

Mount Allison University
Coastal Wetlands Institute
Department of Geography, 65 York St., Sackville NB E4L 1E4 Canada
Tel: 506-364-2428; *Fax:* 506-364-2625
URL: www.mta.ca/research/macwi
Description: Research facility at Mount Allison University focused on the study of coastal wetlands at the biological, chemical, and physical level. The Institute seeks to promote and conduct research on the scientific, social, and economic aspects of coastal wetlands while enhancing understanding of coastal wetlands in eastern Canada.

Mount Allison University
62 York St., Sackville NB E4L 1E2 Canada

St. Andrews Biological Station (SABS)
531 Brandy Cove Rd., St. Andrews NB E5B 2L9 Canada
Tel: 506-529-8854; *Fax:* 506-529-5862
URL: www.mar.dfo-mpo.gc.ca/sabs
Description: The St. Andrews Biological Station (SABS) was established in 1908 and carries out research via Fisheries and Oceans Canada. SABS performs studies in Aquaculture and Biological Interactions, Coastal Ocean Research, Population Ecology, and other areas.

St. Andrews Biological Station (CIAS)
Centre for Integrated Aquaculture Science
531 Brandy Cove Rd., St. Andrews NB E5B 2L9 Canada
Tel: 506-529-5866; *Fax:* 506-529-5862
Overview: A organization founded in 2007
Description: Established in 2007, the Centre for Integrated Aquaculture Science (CIAS) operates via the St. Andrews Biological Station with a focus on developing and researching methods and techniques to improve production of Canadian aquaculture while minimizing the impact of Aquaculture in the aquatic environment.

Southern Gulf of St. Lawrence Coalition on Sustainability
057 pavillion P.A. Landry, Université de Moncton, Moncton NB E1A 3E9 Canada
Tel: 506-858-4495; *Fax:* 506-863-2000
e-mail: coord@coalition-sgsl.ca
URL: www.coalition-sgsl.ca
Description: The Southern Gulf of St. Lawrence Coalition on Sustainability is a non-profit organization seeking to promote an environmentally, economically, and socially sustainable Southern Gulf of St. Lawrence. The Coalition seeks to promote awareness and education on sustainability issues by supporting community initiattives, monitoring progress, as well as working with local science and research organizations. The Coalition's Science, Research & Habitat working group seeks to establish indicators for project monitoring and evaluation.

University of New Brunswick (CRI)
Canadian Rivers Institute
Biology Department, PO Box 4400, Fredericton NB E3B 5A3 Canada
Tel: 506-452-6208; *Fax:* 506-453-3583
URL: www.unb.ca/research/institutes/cri
Description: Research institute specializing in aquatic science. The CRI is focused primarily on water resources conservation, protection, restoration, and sustainable use.

University of New Brunswick
New Brunswick Cooperative Fish and Wildlife Unit
Faculty of Forestry and Environmental Management, PO Box 44555, Fredericton NB E3B 6C2 Canada
Tel: 506-453-4929; *Fax:* 506-453-3538
URL: www.unbf.ca/forestry/centers/cwru.htm
Overview: A organization founded in 1989
Description: Cooperative research project focused on fish and wildlife resource information, including specific studies on wildlife, with a focus on enhancing conservation efforts.

University of New Brunswick
Environment & Sustainable Development Centre
University of New Brunswick, PO Box 4400, Fredericton NB E3B 5A3 Canada
Tel: 506-453-4886; *Fax:* 506-453-4883
e-mail: enviro@unb.ca
URL: www.unb.ca/enviro
Description: Research centre focused on natural resource management, with projects assessing the integration of biophysical and socioeconomic approaches to ecological problem solving

University of New Brunswick
Greater Fundy Ecosystem Project
PO Box 4400, Fredericton NB E3B 5A3 Canada
URL: www.unbf.ca/forestry/centers/fundy/index.htm
Description: Research centre focused on providing research, monitoring, and scientific support for conservation and sustainability efforts in New Brunswick.

University of New Brunswick
Groundwater Studies Group
Department of Civil Engineering, PO Box 4400, Fredericton NB E3B 5A3 Canada
URL: www.unb.ca/civil/hydro/water.htm
Description: Research organization based out of the University of New Brunswick focused primarily on water resources management. The group works on technical, manegerial, and environmental aspects of these issues including hydrogeology, groundwater quality, and contamination.

University of New Brunswick
Forest Watershed Research Centre
PO Box 4400, Fredericton NB E3B 5A3 Canada
URL: watershed.for.unb.ca
Description: Research centre through the Faculty of Forestry and Environmental Management at the University of New Brunswick. The centre focuses on sustainable forest management projects including water quality testing, hydrology modeling, trail and route optimization, and soil studies.

University of New Brunswick
Centre for Coastal Studies and Aquaculture
PO Box 5050, 100 Tucker Park Rd., Saint John NB E2L 4L5 Canada
Tel: 506-648-5605; *Fax:* 506-648-5650
e-mail: coastal@unbsj.ca
URL: www.unbsj.ca/coastal
Description: The Centre for Coastal Studies and Aquaculture was established in 1985 at the Saint John Campus of the University of New Brunswick. The Centre performs multidisciplinary research projects in the field of coastal studies and aquaculture primarily in the Bay of Fundy. The University conducts both in-house research at it's laboratory and library facilities and offshore research on the Mary-O vessel.

University of New Brunswick
Tweedale Centre
Laboratory for Forest Soils and Environmental Quality, 1350 Regent St., Fredericton NB E3C 2G6 Canada
Tel: 506-458-7817; *Fax:* 506-453-3574
URL: www.unbf.ca/forestry/centers/lfseq.htm
Description: The Tweedale Centre was established in 1987 to serve the forest sector in the Atlantic region. It has provided operational support directly to centres of planting stock production; seed orchards and Christmas tree growers through its analytical services programs and indirectly through research and development. The Centre's second focus is on the impacts of forestry practices and industrial activities on soil, watersheds and water quality.

University of New Brunswick
PO Box 4400, Fredericton NB E3B 5A3 Canada

University of New Brunswick
Environment and Sustainable Development Research Centre
PO Box Box 4400, Fredericton NB E3B 5A3 Canada
e-mail: enviro@unb.ca
URL: www.unb.ca
Description: The Environment & Sustainable Development Research Centre supports sustainable resource management and development through applied integrated research; innovative environmental and experimental education; outreach in communities; and through mutually beneficial partnerships with a variety of actors.

Newfoundland and Labrador

C-Core Innovative Engineering Solutions
Captain Robert A. Bartlett Building, Morrisey Rd., St. John's NL A1B 3X5 Canada
Tel: 709-737-8354; *Fax:* 709-737-4706
e-mail: info@c-core.ca
URL: www.c-core.ca
Description: C-Core provides engineering services worldwide with a focus on solutions for the Energy industry. Specific areas of expertise include issues encountered in offshore oil and gas production, mining, pulp and paper, and gas transmission, with a focus on assessing and mitigating risk from ice environments.

Centre of Environmental Excellence (CEE)
c/o Sir Wilfred Grenfell College, 10 University Dr., Corner Brook NL A2H 6P9 Canada
URL: www.ceenl.ca
Description: The Newfoundland Centre of Environmental Excellence (CEE) is a research institute based in Western Newfoundland. The CEE is focused on environmental research in the field of sustainability and economic growth. The CEE focuses on Sustainable Forestry, Sustainable Tourism, and Sustainable Municipal and Rural Infrastructure ad key areas of research and development projects.

Community - University Research for Recovery Alliance (CURRA)
Memorial University of Newfoundland, St. John's NL A1C 5S7 Canada
Tel: 709-737-7244; *Fax:* 709-737-7530
URL: www.bonnebay.mun.ca/curra/curra_home.htm
Description: Five-year research program based in Memorial University dedicated to developing strategies for the recovery of fish stocks and fishery communities by examining a variety of topics in social, economic and environmental areas.

Institute for Environmental Monitoring and Research (IEMR)
PO Box 1859, Stn. B, 114 Hamilton River Rd., Happy Valley-Goose Bay NL A0P 1E0 Canada
Tel: 709-896-3266; *Fax:* 709-896-3076
e-mail: iemr@iemr.org
URL: www.iemr.org
Description: The Institute for Environmental Monitoring and Research was established in 1995 at the recommendation of an independent Environmental Assessment panel to review the ecological effects of flight training conducted at Canadian Forcesd Base Goose Bay. The IEMR specifically conducts research into indigenous wildlife, contaminants, and ecosystem impacts related to low-level flights in the Labrador area.

Memorial University of Newfoundland (MI)
Fisheries & Marine Institute
Office of Research and Development, PO Box 4920, 155 Ridge Rd., St. John's NL A1C 5R3 Canada
Tel: 709-778-0766
URL: www.mi.mun.ca
Description: Multidisciplinary research institute with research centres focusing on Aquaculture and Seafood Development, Sustainable Aquatic Resources, Marine Simulation, and Ocean Technology, as well as projects in conjunction with the international branch of the Marine Institute (MI International)

Memorial University of Newfoundland (MII)
Marine Institute International
Marine Institute - Memorial University, PO Box 4920, St. John's NL A1C 5R3 Canada
Tel: 709-778-0484; *Fax:* 709-778-0371
e-mail: miintl@mi.mun.ca
URL: www.mi.mun.ca/mi_international
Description: International research institute based out of Memorial University's Marine Institute. Over 85 marine research projects have been carried out through MI International in over 35 countries. Areas of research include fisheries resource management, marine environment, food safety, aquaculture, and others.

Memorial University of Newfoundland
Institute for Biodiversity, Ecosystem Science & Sustainability
c/o Sir Wilfred Grenfell College, University Drive, Corner Brook NL A2H 6P9 Canada
Tel: 709-639-7590; *Fax:* 709-639-7591
e-mail: ibes@swgc.mun.ca
URL: www.ibes.swgc.mun.ca
Description: The Institute for Biodiversity, Ecosystem Science & Sustainability (IBES) is a research initiative within Memorial University's Sir Wilfred Grenfell College and the Newfoundland & Labrador Department of Environment and Conservation. The IBES broadly focuses on research in the fields of natural resource conservation, management, and sustainability and specifically in sustainable development, ecosystems ecology, climate change, population ecology, fisheries & aquaculture science, natural resource management, and urban planning and design.

Memorial University of Newfoundland
Fisheries Conservation Group
Marine Institute - Memorial University, PO Box 4920, St. John's NL A1C 5R3 Canada
Tel: 709-778-0318; *Fax:* 709-778-0669
URL: fishcons.mi.mun.ca
Description: The Fisheries Conservation Group is a research group created at the Fisheries and Marine Institute of Memorial University in 1996, to develop an independent fisheries research and training program with a focus on the fisheries ecosystems of the Northwest Atlantic. The Group focuses on researching groundfish stocks in Atlantic Canada, the ecology of commercial fisheries, and collaboration with fishers and industry.

Memorial University of Newfoundland
Ocean Sciences Centre
Memorial University of Newfoundland, St. John's NL A1C 5S7 Canada
Tel: 709-737-3708; *Fax:* 709-737-3220
URL: www.mun.ca/osc
Description: The Ocean Sciences Centre (OSC) is a cold ocean research facility operated in conjunction with Memorial University. The Centre houses laboratories where research is conducted on the North Atlantic fishery industry, aquaculture, oceanography, ecology, behavior and physiology. The Centre also performs research on a variety of organisms; from bacteria to mammals.

Memorial University of Newfoundland
Bonne Bay Marine Station
PO Box 69, Norris Point NL A0K 3V0 Canada
Tel: 709-458-2550; *Fax:* 709-458-2605
URL: www.bonnebay.mun.ca
Description: The Bonne Bay Marine Station is a research and teaching facility operated by Memorial University and the Gros Morne Co-operating Association. The Station provides services for research in marine ecosystems. Research projects and areas include aquaculture, marine ecology/biology, habitat sensitivity, ecology of indigenous species, oceanography, and ocean dynamics.

Memorial University of Newfoundland
AquaNet
Ocean Sciences Centre, St. John's NL A1C 5S7 Canada
Tel: 709-737-3245; *Fax:* 709-737-3500
e-mail: info@aquanet.ca
URL: www.aquanet.mun.ca
Description: AquaNet was established in 1999 as a collaborative research network for Universities, government, industry and non-government organisations. The Network seeks to foster a sustainable aquaculture sector in Canada through research and education. The Network focuses on research in sustainability, marine and fresh water resources and ecology of indigenous species.

Memorial University of Newfoundland (ARDF)
Aquaculture Research and Development Facility
Ocean Sciences Centre, St. John's NL A1C 5S7 Canada
Tel: 709-737-8691
URL: www.osc.mun.ca/ardf
Description: The Aquaculture Research and Development Facility carries out research in collaboration with industry partners. The Facility houses numerous state-of-the-art research and training facilities, including a sea water system designed for temperature-controlled flow-through and water circulation, as well as hatcheries, 15 silos ranging in size from 1000 litres to 12,000 litres, and outdoor cages. The Facility's research is focused largely on fish species and biodiversity.

Memorial University of Newfoundland (CCFI)
Canadian Centre for Fisheries Innovation
PO Box 4920, St. John's NL A1C 5R3 Canada
Tel: 709-778-0517; *Fax:* 709-778-0516
e-mail: ccfi@mi.mun.ca
URL: www.ccfi.ca
Description: The Canadian Centre for Fisheries Innovation (CCFI) is a non-profit organization owned by Memorial University of Newfoundland and funded by Atlantic Innovation Fund. The Centre provides the tools of scientific research and technology to the fishing industry. The Centre focuses research on aquaculture, harvesting, processing, biotechnology, and resource sustainability.

Memorial University of Newfoundland
PO Box 4200, St. John's NL A1C 5S7 Canada

Northwest Atlantic Fisheries Centre
PO Box 5667, St. John's NL A1C 5X1 Canada
Tel: 709-772-4355; *Fax:* 709-772-6100
Description: The Northwest Atlantic Fisheries Centre is a research facility used through the Canadian Department of Fisheries and Oceans. The Centre conducts research in a variety of fields related to the fisheries industry, including habitat research and assessment, oceanography, environmental and habitat management, aquaculture, ecology and population dynamics, parasitology, and toxicology.

Petroleum Research Atlantic Canada (PRAC)
INCO Innovation Centre - Memorial University, #IIC-3067, 3rd Fl., St. John's NL A1C 5S7 Canada
Tel: 709-737-2626; *Fax:* 709-737-8807
URL: pr-ac.ca
Description: Petroleum Research Atlantic Canada (PRAC) is a non-profit research organization formed by industry, academic, and government parties dedicated to funding and facilitating petroleum-related research and development in Atlantic Canada. Areas of research include projects in environmental sustainability and assessment, gas development, ice management, geosciences, and energy policy.

Northwest Territories

Great Lakes Research Consortium (GLRC)
College of Environmental Science & Forestry, SUNY, 1 Forestry Dr., 253 Baker Labs, Syracuse NY 13210 USA
Tel: 315-470-6720; *Fax:* 315-470-6970
e-mail: glrc@esf.edu
URL: www.esf.edu/glrc/
Description: GLRC is comprised of 18 New York universities & 9 Canadian affiliates (McMaster University, Brock University, University of Ottawa, University of Toronto, University of Guelph, University of Waterloo, University of Windsor, Queens University, & Ryerson University). The focus is on collaborative research & education on aspects of Great Lakes ecology, environmental concerns, & issues such as Great Lakes security. The Consortium hosts an annual conference, develops & delivers seminars, & publishes research.

Prairie Northern Wildlife Research Centre
Iqaluit
PO Box 1870, 939 Federal Rd., Iqaluit NU X0A 0H0
Tel: 867-975-4642; *Fax:* 867-975-4645

Nova Scotia

Acadia University (ACER)
Acadia Centre for Estuarine Research
War Memorial House, PO Box 115, 23 Westwood Ave., Wolfville NS B4P 2R6 Canada
Tel: 902-585-1113; *Fax:* 902-585-1054
URL: science.acadiau.ca/cer
Overview: A organization founded in 1985

Description: Research facility with a focus on estuaries and nearshore coastal waters. The Centre is focused primarily in the Bay of Fundy, Gulf of Maine, and Georges Bank, as well as various international projects through Acadia University. Projects include environmental impact studies, sediment and soil erosion studies, and research of wildlife activities.

Acadia University
The Arthur Irving Academy for the Environment
Acadia University, PO Box 90, 52 University Dr., Wolfville NS B4P 2R6 Canada
Tel: 902-585-1311; *Fax:* 902-585-1055
e-mail: academy@acadiau.ca
URL: academy.atlanticwebfitters.ca
Description: Centre for interdisciplinary scholarship, education, and environmental advocacy. The centre focuses on sustainability and funding of research projects in the field of environmental sustainability

Acadia University
Morton Center
Department of Earth and Environmental Science, Wolfville NS B4P 2R6 Canada
URL: ees.acadiau.ca/content/morton
Description: The Morton Center at Acadia University is an academic research facility focused on promoting public understanding of environmental issues. The Center focuses research in five areas of study: biodiversity and ecosystems, earth systems, social ecology, environmental conditions monitoring, and sustainability.

Acadia University (ACGCER)
Atlantic Centre for Global Change and Ecocystem Research
Acadia University, Wolfville NS B4P 2R6 Canada
URL: gradstudies.acadiau.ca/acgcer
Description: The Atlantic Centre for Global Change and Ecosystem Research (ACGCER) is an interdisciplinary research group based out of Acadia University. The ACGCER seeks to conduct environmental research to understand the impact of climate change on the Atlantic region and how the public, government, and industry can meet these challenges. Research areas at the ACGCER include genetics, population biology, ecology, and both terrestrial and aquatic ecosystems.

Acadia University
K.C. Irving Environmental Science Centre
Acadia University, PO Box 48, 32 University Ave., Wolfville NS B4P 2R6 Canada
Tel: 902-585-5242; *Fax:* 902-585-1034
URL: kcirvingcentre.acadiau.ca
Description: The K.C. Irving Environmental Science Centre opened in 2002 at Acadia University. The Centre is intended for the study of the natural environment, concentrating on the ecology of the native flora of the Acadia Forest Region of northeastern North America. The Centre functions as both a research and teaching facility with classrooms, labs, and conference capabilities. The Centre is also home to the six-acre Harriet Irving Botanical Gardens which features a collection of native plants including rare and endangered species.

Acadia University
Centre for Wildlife and Conservation Biology
Patterson Hall, Acadia University, Wolfville NS B0P 1X0 Canada
Tel: 902-585-1469; *Fax:* 902-585-1059
e-mail: tom.herman@acadiau.ca
URL: biology.acadiau.ca/gen/cwcb.html
Description: The Centre for Wildlife and Conservation Biology (CWCB) at Acadia University was established in 1992. The goal of the Centre is to integtate research and education to promote the importance of biodiversity stewardship. The Centre works in conjutction with the Biology Department of Acadia University, focusing on research in protected areas management, forestry and wildlife, and species at risk.

Acadia University
Wolfville NS B4P 2R6 Canada

Acadia University
Morton Centre
Heckman's Island, Lunenburg NS Canada
URL: ees.acadiau.ca/content/morton/index.html
Description: The Centre is currently focusing on collecting baseline data using Environment Canada's protocol Ecological Monitoring and Assessment Network (EMAN). The following five focus research areas will branch out from there: Social Ecology, Earth Systems, Biodiversity & Ecosystems, Environmental

Research Centres / Atlantic Coastal Action Program

Conditions Monitoring, and Applied Sustainability. In the future the centre will develop methods to share knowledge with the Acadia University faculty and the general public within the county and island.

Atlantic Coastal Action Program (ACAP)
Queen Square, 45 Alderney Rd., 16th Fl., Dartmouth NS B2Y 2N6 Canada
Tel: 902-426-8679; Fax: 902-426-6348
Description: The Atlantic Coastal Action Program is a community-based program established by Environment Canada in 1991 with the purpose of restoring and sustaining watersheds and coastal areas in Atlantic Canada. The ACAP is made up of 16 local non-profit organizations. The ACAP participates in numerous research studies including assessments of local ecosystems, biomonitoring, water quality monitoring, studies of indigenous species, and water systems studies.

Atlantic Cooperative Wildlife Ecology Research Network (ACWERN)
Acadia University, Biology Department, Wolfville NS B4P 2R6 Canada
Tel: 902-585-1287; Fax: 902-585-1059
URL: landscape.acadiau.ca/acwern
Description: Government/University research partnership with research projects in the field of wildlife ecology and species at risk with the goal of relating research results to tangible problems in ecological conservation.

Atlantic Environmental Prediction Research Initiative (AEPRI)
c/o Dalhousie University, Halifax NS B3H 3J5 Canada
URL: www.ns.ec.gc.ca/msc/as/as_aepri.html
Description: The Atlantic Environmental Prediction Research Initiative was established by Environment Canada's Meteorological Research Branch in Halifax, Nova Scotia. The Initiative is a collaborative research agency through Dalhousie University, the Canadian Meteorological Centre, McGill University, and other organizations. Research is focused largely on improving existing meteorological prediction systems, as well as assessment tools for environmental damages, such as oil spills.

Bedford Institute of Oceanography (BIO)
PO Box 1006, 1 Challenger Dr., Dartmouth NS B2Y 4A2 Canada
URL: www.bio.gc.ca
Description: The Bedford Institute of Oceanography (BIO) is Canada's largest centre for ocean research, established in 1962. BIO performs targeted research through the Canadian Department of Fisheries and Oceans, the Geological Survey of Canada, the Department of National Defence, and Environment Canada. The research done at BIO ranges from navigational charts, fisheries studies, and offshore resource studies.

Cape Breton University
Institute for the Development of Energy & Sustainability
c/o Cape Breton University, 1250 Grand Lake Rd., Sydney NS B1P 6L2 Canada
Description: Established in 2003 in response to the exploration of Nova Scotia's offshore petroleum industry. The Centre provides resources for the establishment of academic programs, infrastructure, and other projects. The Centre has also established three labs; the Shell Canada Operations Lab, a Petroluem Simulation Lab, and the Cape Breton University Fluid Flow and Measurement Lab.

Cape Breton University
PO Box 5300, 1250 Grand Lake Rd., Sydney NS B1P 6L2 Canada

Centre for Applied Petroleum Sciences
St. Francis Xavier University, PO Box 5000, Antigonish NS B2G 2W5 Canada
Tel: 902-867-2396; Fax: 902-867-2414
URL: www.stfx.ca/caps/index.htm
Description: Multidisciplinary research institute working in areas related to the oil and gas industry with researchers from Dalhousie, Lakehead, Guelph, and other Canadian Universities. Current research projects include biofilms, colloids, and high-performance computing.

Centre for Marine Environmental Prediction (CMEP)
c/o Dalhousie University, Halifax NS B3H 3J5 Canada
URL: www.cmep.ca
Description: The Centre for Marine Environmental Prediction (CMEP) was founded in 1998 with the mission of researching marine environmental changes for the improvement of forecasting technologies and public education. The Centre is based out of Dalhousie University, and has projects focused on flooding forecasts and risk assessment, as well as ongoing research in the North Atlantic Basin and Scotian Shelf.

Centre for Ocean Model Development for Applications (COMDA)
Bedford Institute of Oceanography, PO Box 1006, Dartmouth NS Canada
Tel: 902-426-8232
Description: The Centre for Ocean Model Development for Applications (COMDA) was established to provide national leadership, coordination and advice in areas of ocean model development through the Department of Fisheries and Oceans. Research projects include the Canadian Network of Operational Oceanography Systems, the Canadian Operational Network for Coupled Environmental Prediction Systems, and the Canada-Newfoundland Operational Ocean Forecasting System.

Centre for Offshore Oil and Gas Environmental Research (COOGER)
Bedford Institute of Oceanography, PO Box 1006, Dartmouth NS B2Y 4A2 Canada
Tel: 902-426-1440
URL: www.dfo-mpo.gc.ca/science/coe-cde/cooger-crepge/index-eng.htm
Description: Fisheries and Oceans Canada established the Centre for Offshore Oil and Gas Environmental Research (COOGER) to coordinate the department's nation-wide research into the environmental and oceanographic impacts of offshore petroleum exploration, production and transportation.

Coastal CURA
c/o St. Mary's University, 923 Robie St., Halifax NS B3H 3C3 Canada
Tel: 902-420-5003; Fax: 902-496-8101
e-mail: coastalcura@smu.ca
URL: www.coastalcura.ca
Description: Five-year research project that consists of eight Maritime-based partners including Universities, First Nations partners, and Community organizations. The goal of the project is to implement a community-based governance of coastal resources. Research projects include local ecosystem research, ocean resource management, and fisheries.

Dalhousie University
Environment, Sustainability & Society Program
Henry Hicks (A&A) Building, Room 332, 6299 South St., Halifax NS B3H 4R2 Canada
Tel: 902-494-2211
e-mail: sustainability@dal.ca
URL: sustainability.dal.ca
Description: Conducts research through 140 faculty members in a variety of fields including Marine Biology, the Ocean Tracking Network, Marine and Environmental Law. Projects in conjunction with other departments include climate change and renewable energy research with the Department of Engineering, green building with the Department of Architecture, impact on health with the Faculty of Medicine, and sustainability with the Faculty of Management

Dalhousie University
Centre for Water Resources Studies
PO Box 1000, Office D-514, 1360 Barrington St., Halifax NS B3J 2X4 Canada
Tel: 902-494-6070; Fax: 902-494-3105
e-mail: cwrs@dal.ca
URL: centreforwaterresourcesstudies.dal.ca
Description: The Centre for Water Resources Studies (CWRS) was established in 1981 at Dalhousie University to apply the research resources of the University to water resource concerns in Atlantic Canada. The Centre conducts research in sewage disposal, technology for water supply, watershed acidification, water and wastewater treatment, and international development. The Centre also has research panels on sewage disposal, drinking water quality, erosion and sediment control, and rain water cisterns.

Dalhousie University
Aquatron Laboratory
Life Sciences Centre, Halifax NS B3H 4J1 Canada
Tel: 902-494-3874
e-mail: aquatron@dal.ca
URL: aquatron.dal.ca
Description: The Aquatron Laboratory is an aquatic research facility at Dalhousie University. The facility houses a 684,000 litre pool tank, a 117,000 litre tower tank, a behavioural observation tank, and 18 independent wet labs. Research conducted at the Aquatron Laboratory ranges from aquaculture to wildlife studies to marine fisheries.

Dalhousie University
Energy at Dalhousie
A-200, Sexton Campus, PO Box 1000, 1360 Barrington St., Halifax NS B3J 2X4 Canada
Tel: 902-494-3669
URL: energy.dal.ca
Description: Energy at Dalhousie was created to coordinate and maximize collaborative research in the field of renewable energy resources. The aim of Energy at Dalhousie is to play a leading role in researching new energy sources and their impact on the environment, the economy, and society at large. Specific research areas include energy conservation, efficiency, and sustainability.

Dalhousie University
Halifax NS B3H 3J5 Canada

East Coast Ecosystems Research Organization
PO Box 36, Freeport NS B0V 1B0 Canada
Description: East Coast Ecosystems Research Organization is a charitable organization dedicated to education and research about natural processes and human involvement in nature. Since 1986, East Coast Ecosystems has been conducting research in collaboration with the New England Aquarium in the Bay of Fundy and on the Southern Scotian Shelf to study the seasonal distribution, abundance, and behavior of the endangered North Atlantic right whale. The Organization's goal is to compile the scientific evidence and foster the public support to encourage the federal government to develop sound practices of ocean management to ensure the recovery and the survival of the North Atlantic right whale.

Eastern Scotian Shelf Integrated Management Initiative (ESSIM)
Bedford Institute of Oceanography, PO Box 1006, Dartmouth NS B2Y 4A2 Canada
Tel: 902-426-9900; Fax: 902-426-3855
e-mail: essim@mar.dfo-mpo.gc.ca
Description: The Eastern Scotian Shelf Integrated Management (ESSIM) Initiative is a collaborative ocean management and planning process led by Fisheries and Oceans Canada (DFO) under Canada's Oceans Act. The goal of the Initiative is to develop and implement an Integrated Ocean Management Plan for the region. The Initiative's primary objectives are collaborative governance, sustainable use, and healthy ecosystems, and collaborates with government, aboriginal groups, ocean industry, conservation groups, communities, and University researchers.

ecoNova Scotia for Clean Air and Climate Change
PO Box 442, 5151 Terminal Rd., Halifax NS B3J 2P8 Canada
Tel: 902-424-8269; Fax: 902-424-0503
e-mail: econovascotia@gov.ns.ca
URL: http://www.gov.ns.ca/econovascotia
Previous Name: Nova Scotia EcoTrust for Clean Air and Climate Change
Description: ecoNova Scotia is a joint effort by the Nova Scotia Department of Energy and the Nova Scotia Department of Environment aimed at promoting innovation and research in the field of clean air and environmental sustainability in Nova Scotia. The program intends to support initiatives by Nova Scotians that reduce greenhouse gas emissions and other air pollutants in accordance with Nova Scotia's Environmental Goals and Sustainable Prosperity Act.

Environmental Sciences Research Centre (ESRC)
Physical Sciences Complex, St. Francis Xavier University, PO Box 5000, 1 West St., Antigonish NS B2G 2W5 Canada
Tel: 902-867-2326; Fax: 902-867-2414
URL: esrc.stfx.ca
Overview: A organization founded in 2004
Description: Multidisciplinary research and training centre based out of St. Francis Xavier University. Areas of research include climate change, aquatic and soil biochemistry, marine ecology and climate change, hydrogeology and water resources, renewable energies, environmental monitoring, and climatology.

Fishermen & Scientists Research Society (FSRS)
PO Box 25125, Halifax NS B3M 4H4 Canada
URL: www.fsrs.ns.ca
Description: The Fishermen and Scientists Research Society (FSRS) is a non-profit organization that seeks to develop a network of fishermen and scientists concerned with the long-term sustainability of the fishing industry in Atlantic Canada.

The FSRS's research projects include studies on fish habitats, fish diet studies, tagging projects, ecosystem studies, and reproduction studies.

Geological Survey of Canada (GSC)
Atlantic
Bedford Institute of Oceanography, PO Box 1006, 1 Challenger Dr., Dartmouth NS B2Y 4A2 Canada
Fax: 902-426-4848
e-mail: jacob.verhoef@nrcan-rncan.gc.ca
URL: gsc.nrcan.gc.ca/org/atlantic
Description: The Geological Survey of Canada Atlantic (GSC) is Canada's principal marine geoscience facility, a branch of the Canadian Department of Natural Resources. The GSC Atlantic conducts research in marine and petroleum geology, geophysics, marine geoscience, geochemistry, and geotechnology. Research projects are split into two streams: the Marine Environmental Geoscience Subdivision, which studies the environmental impact of development and processes, and the Marine Resources Geoscience Subdivision, which studies the geology of the region to evaluate its oil and gas potential.

Geological Survey of Canada
CoastWeb
Bedford Institute of Oceanography, PO Box 1006, 1 Challenger Dr., Dartmouth NS B2Y 4A2 Canada
Tel: 902-426-7736; *Fax:* 902-426-4104
URL: gsc.nrcan.gc.ca/coast
Description: The CoastWeb department of the Geological Survey of Canada conducts research pertinent to Canada's coastline. Major areas of research include coastal evolution, sea level changes, storm impacts, cliff and coastal monitoring, and climate change and adaptation.

Geological Survey of Canada
BASIN Database
Bedford Institute of Oceanography, PO Box 1006, 1 Challenger Dr., Dartmouth NS B2Y 4A2 Canada
URL: basin.gsca.nrcan.gc.ca
Description: The BASIN Database is a project that streamlines geological, geophysical, and engineering information for petroleum exploration in offshore northern and eastern Canada. BASIN collects data from past explorations, research projects, and seismic surveys from the petroleum industry and government sources.

GPI Atlantic
535 Indian Point Rd., Glen Haven NS B3Z 2T5 Canada
Tel: 902-823-1944; *Fax:* 902-826-7088
e-mail: info@gpiatlantic.org
URL: www.gpiatlantic.org
Description: GPI Atlantic was founded in 1997 and is an independent, non-profit research and education organization dedicated to the development of the Genuine Progress Index (GPI), a means of measuring social, economic, and environmental assets for use in future planning and sustainability. The GPI measures time use, living standards, natural capital, human impact on the environment, and social capital and as an alternative to the Gross Domestic Product (GDP) measurement system.

The Halifax STAR Project
c/o St. Mary's University, 923 Robie St., Halifax NS B3H 3C3 Canada
Tel: 902-420-5472
URL: www.halifaxstarproject.ca
Description: The Halifax Space-Time Activity Research (STAR) Project conducts space-time research via GPS and other methods. The Project's aim is to use this research to benefit other researchers and urban planners to plan communities that improve the economic, environmental, social, and public health of the area. The STAR project is conducted by the Time-Use Research Program of St. Mary's University, in partnership with the Halifax Regional Municipality.

National Research Council Institute for Marine Biosciences (NRC-IMB)
1411 Oxford St., Halifax NS B3H 3Z1 Canada
Tel: 902-426-8332; *Fax:* 902-426-9413
e-mail: communications.imb@nrc-cnrc.gc.ca
URL: imb.nrc.gc.ca
Description: One of 19 institutes of the National Research Council, the Institute for Marine Biosciences (NRC-IMB) is a multidisciplinary research facility focused on marine bioproducts. The NRC-IMB primarily does research in three areas: Bioanalytical Chemistry, Marine Bioactives, and Functional Genomics. The NRC-IMB partners with numerous organizations, including private industry, other Government agencies, and academic organizations.

Nova Scotia Department of Natural Resources
Renewable Resources Branch
Founders Square, PO Box 698, 1701 Hollis St., Halifax NS B3J 3M8 Canada
URL: www.gov.ns.ca/natr/thedepartment/renewable.asp
Description: The Renewable Resources Branch of Natural Resources Nova Scotia provides policy, planning and program development in the area of management and conservation of forests, parks, and wildlife resources in Nova Scotia. The Branch coordinates research and development projects aimed at improving resource management and sustainability goals.

Nova Scotia Department of Natural Resources
1701 Hollis St., Halifax NS B3J 3M8 Canada

Offshore Energy Research (OER)
Bank of Montreal Bldg., PO Box 2664, #400, 5151 George St., Halifax NS B3J 3P7 Canada
Tel: 902-424-8479; *Fax:* 902-424-0528
Toll-Free: 888-257-8688
e-mail: oeer@offshoreenergyresearch.ca
URL: www.offshoreenergyresearch.ca
Description: The OER is a government funded research project working in conjunction with St. Francis Xavier University, Acadia University, Cape Breton University, and the Nova Scotia Department of Energy established in 2006. The aim of the OER is to support offshore energy research in Nova Scotia. The objective of the OER is to research and assess the potential impacts of petroleum exploration, development and production and renewable energy technologies on the marine environment.

Prairie Northern Wildlife Research Centre
Yellowknife
Northern Conservation Division, Diamond Plaza, #301, 5204 - 50th Ave., 3rd Fl., Yellowknife NT X1A 1E2
Tel: 867-669-4700; *Fax:* 867-873-8185

St. Francis Xavier University
Marine Ecology Lab
Department of Biology, Antigonish NS B2G 2W5 Canada
Tel: 902-867-5289; *Fax:* 902-867-2389
URL: people.stfx.ca/rscrosat
Description: The Marine Ecology Lab at St. Francis Xavier University is focused on research of the ecology of marine rocky shores. Research projects include species diversity, environmental stress, ecosystem biodiversity, species interactions, and ecological theory.

St. Francis Xavier University
PO Box 5000, Antigonish NS B2G 2W5 Canada

St. Georges Bay Ecosystem Project
c/o St. Francis Xavier University, PO Box 5000, Antigonish NS B2G 2W5 Canada
URL: www.stfx.ca/research/gbayesp
Description: Interdisciplinary and collaborative research project working towards improved marine resource management, focused on researching the marine and human ecology of St. Georges Bay.

St. Mary's University
Community Based Environmental Monitoring Network
Department of Geography, Burke Building, Room 204A, 923 Robie St., Halifax NS B3H 3C3 Canada
Tel: 902-491-6243; *Fax:* 902-496-8213
e-mail: environmental.network@smu.ca
URL: www.envnetwork.smu.ca
Description: Environmental monitoring research network. The network is geared towards public participation and transparency in environmental monitoring systems and cooperation among organizations committed to environmental stewardship. The network also offers equipment and facilities at Saint Mary's University for environmental organizations. Projects include the monitoring of water and air quality.

St. Mary's University (CEAR)
Centre for Environmental Analysis and Remediation
Science Building, St. Mary's University, #501, 923 Robie St., Halifax NS B3H 3C3 Canada
Tel: 902-496-8798; *Fax:* 902-420-5261
e-mail: cear@smu.ca
URL: fgsr.smu.ca/cear
Description: Established in 2000 as a research facility at St. Mary's University. The laboratory specializes in chemical analysis in the areas of chromatography, mass spectrometry and element analysis technologies. These technologies can be used for the separation and purification of compounds, structural and identification of organic compounds, identification of unknown substances, and quantification of elements and compounds.

St. Mary's University
Office of Aboriginal & Northern Research
Gorsebrook Research Institute, 5960 Inglis St., Halifax NS B3H 1K8 Canada
Tel: 902-420-5668; *Fax:* 902-496-8135
e-mail: gorsebrook@smu.ca
URL: www.smu.ca/administration/gorsebrook/north.html
Description: The Office of Aboriginal and Northern Research was established at St. Mary's University through the Gorsebrook Research Institute in 2006. The Office maintains a collaboration between the Innu First Nation and Environment Canada. The Office works with both First Nation and Government researchers to develop First Nation solutions to ecological issues in the area.

St. Mary's University
923 Robie St., Halifax NS B3H 3C3 Canada

Ontario

Canada. Fisheries & Oceans Canada
200 Kent St., Ottawa ON K1A 0E6 Canada

Canadian Network of Toxicology Centres (CNTC)
University of Guelph, Bovey Bldg., 2nd Fl., Gordon St., Guelph ON N1G 2W1 Canada
Tel: 519-824-4120; *Fax:* 519-837-3861
e-mail: dwarner@uoguelph.ca
URL: www.uoguelph.ca/cntc
Description: The Canadian Network of Toxicology Centres (CNTC) is a national network of collaborating researchers from academia and government. The Network conducts environmental health-related research along well articulated and planned themes of interdisciplinary research. Implicit in the CNTC approach is a commitment to joint, interactive efforts, centralized planning, project accountability for both intellectual and financial objectives, and regular reporting of research progress beyond the usual publication in scientific journals.

Canadian Water Network (CWN)
200 University Ave. West, Waterloo ON N2L 3G1 Canada
Tel: 519-888-4567; *Fax:* 519-883-7574
e-mail: gmeyer@cwn-rce.ca
URL: www.cwn-rce.ca
Description: The Canadian Water Network (CWN) was created as one of Canada's Networks of Centres of Excellence (NCE), to build a network that develops opportunities related to the provision of safe, clean water. In collaboration with universities, government and industry, the CWN has developed a variety of scientific projects and initiatives that address key water-related issues facing Canadians while embracing strong multidisciplinary and multi-sectoral partnerships.

Canmet Energy Technology Centre (CETC)
Ottawa Research Centre, Natural Resources Canada, 1 Haanel Dr., Ottawa ON K1A 1M1
TTY: 613-996-4397
e-mail: canmetenergy@nrcan.gc.ca
URL: www.canmetenergy-canmetenergie.nrcan-rncan.gc.ca
Description: Natural Resources Canada's Canmet Energy is engaged in the research of clean energy & the development of clean energy technology. The energy research centre works to develop & deploy clean energy technologies in order to reduce air & greenhouse gas emissions & to improve the health of Canadians.

Centre of Excellence for Earth and Environmental Technologies
#200, 156 Front St. West, Toronto ON M5J 2L6 Canada
Tel: 416-861-1092; *Fax:* 416-971-7164
Toll-Free: 866-759-6014
URL: www.oce-ontario.org/Pages/COEEarth.aspx?COE=EA
Description: The Centre of Excellence for Earth and Environmental Technologies helps Ontario organizations compete by adopting innovative, environmentally responsible solutions. The Centre facilitates the development and execution of R&D that drives commercially viable outcomes contributing to clean air, water, land, and smart infrastructures.

Environment Canada (CCCSN)
Canadian Climate Change Scenarios Network
AIRD, Atmospheric Sci. & Tech. Directorate, Sci. & Tech. Branch, 4905 Dufferin St., Toronto ON M3H 5T4 Canada

Fax: 416-739-4297
URL: cccsn.ca
Description: Launched in 2005 & supported by the Adaptation and Impacts Research Division (AIRD), CCCSN is a national network that supports research into the impacts of climate change, provides technical assistance for downscaling & impacts & adaptation research, & offers training in the use of research tools developed by AIRD. Offices in each region of Canada.

Environment Canada
Meteorological Service of Canada. Atmospheric Science & Technology Directorate. Climate Research Branch
4905 Dufferin St., Toronto ON M3H 5T4 Canada
Tel: 416-739-4869; *Fax:* 416-739-5700
URL: www.msc-smc.ec.gc.ca/acsd/
Description: The Branch is engaged in research into cold-climate processes in the climate system, with a focus on energy & water cycles, land surface process modelling, development & validation of climate processes in hydrological & atmospheric models, climate/cryosphere interactions & processes; remote sensing of climate variables, & assessment of errors in in-situ measurements & their compatibility over time. Climate monitoring, analysis & prediction, & climate system modelling are two important goals/activities.

Environment Canada
Meteorological Service of Canada. Atmospheric Science & Technology Directorate. Air Quality Research Branch
4905 Dufferin St., Toronto ON M3H 5T4 Canada
Tel: 416-739-4836; *Fax:* 416-739-4224
URL: www.msc.ec.gc.ca/aqrb/
Description: The Branch brings together the largest group of atmospheric specialists in Canada, studying the chemistry & physics of the atmosphere as it pertains to acid rain, as well as aspects of air pollution such as acid deposition & oxidants, hazardous air pollutants, particulate matter, stratospheric ozone depletion, & greenhouse gases buildup. Activities include modelling, systematic measurements, & process research. The Branch is comprised of a Modelling & Integration division, a Measurements & Analysis division, a Processes Research division, & an Experimental Studies division.

Environment Canada
Meteorological Service of Canada. Atmospheric Science & Technology Directorate. Adaptation & Impacts Research Group
4905 Dufferin St., Toronto ON M3H 5T4 Canada
Tel: 416-739-4271; *Fax:* 416-739-4297
URL: www.msc-smc.ec.gc.ca/airg/
Description: The Branch is engaged in collaborative, multidisciplinary research into the socio-economic impacts of atmospheric change on Canadians & their ecosystems, viable adaptive responses to these impacts, the relationships between atmospheric changes in terms of their impacts, maladaptations & barriers to adaptive change.

Environment Canada (ESTC)
Environmental Protection Service. Science & Technology Branch. Environmental Science & Technology Centre
335 River Rd., Ottawa ON K1A 0H3 Canada
Tel: 613-991-5633; *Fax:* 613-998-0004
URL: www.etc.ec.gc.ca
Description: The Centre collaborates with the private, public & academic sectors to provide research which focusses on science & technology for environmental protection. Specifically, the Centre researches & provides new knowledge in the areas of pollution measurement, prevention, control & remediation of both air pollution & hazardous materials or oil spills, & provides the relevant sampling & analytical expertise for these areas. The Centre is comprised of 5 divisions: Analysis & Air Quality, Biological Methods, Emergencies Science & Technologies, Emissions Research & Measurement, & Green Technologies.

Geological Survey of Canada
580 Booth St., Ottawa ON K1A 0E4 Canada

Guelph Turfgrass Institute & Environmental Research Centre
328 Victoria Rd. South, RR#2, Guelph ON N1H 6H8 Canada
Tel: 519-767-5009; *Fax:* 519-766-1704
e-mail: info@guelphturfgrass.ca
URL: www.guelphturfgrass.ca
Description: The Institute, established in 1987 as the first of its kind in Canada, has a mandate to conduct research on turfgrass, provide extension services & professional development to members of the Ontario turfgrass industry, & to foster interest in turfgrass science as both a program of study & career choice for students. Research at the Institute continues the University of Guelph's recognized expertise in turfgrass science & focuses on environmental aspects such as pesticide use, evaluation of grass species, seed varieties & seeding methods, fertility & management programs, & the biological & cultural control of diseases & weeds. Staff at the Institute provide consulting & diagnostic services, publish factsheets & research reports, provide public demonstration project assistance, & expert testimony. Meeting facilities are available. The G.M. Frost Research & Information Centre is located on site.

Health Canada
Environmental Health Research Division
Jeanne Mance Bldg., Tunney's Pasture, Ottawa ON K1A 0K9 Canada
Tel: 613-957-2991; *Fax:* 613-941-5366
e-mail: info@hc-sc.gc.ca
URL: www.hc-sc.gc.ca
Description: In concert with the Assembly of First Nations, First Nations & Inuit Health Branch, & the Dept. of Indian Affairs & Northern Development, the Division conducts, coordinates & funds contaminants-related research; coordinates the replacement or upgrading of diesel-fuel tanks & the remediation of fuel oil contaminated sites on First Nations reserves across Canada; provides lab services supporting the research; & coordinates & manages First Nations & Inuit Health Branch drinking water-related research & analysis of First Nations drinking water quality data.

Health Canada
Environmental Health, Science & Research Bureau
Jeanne Mance Bldg., Tunney's Pasture, Ottawa ON K1A 0K9 Canada
e-mail: info@hc-sc.gc.ca
URL: www.hc-sc.gc.ca
Description: The Bureau's mandate is to reduce the negative impacts of environmental exposures on the health of Canadians through research, surveillance, monitoring, epidemiological investigations & emergency planning. It generates data in support of regulatory programs & interprets & formulates it so that it is useful to policy makers, conducts studies to investigate the effects of contaminants on human health, identifies vulnerable populations as well as potential hazards, provides expert advice, develops more effective testing & research tools for hazard identification, & provides chemical emergency preparedness & response capacity through the Safe Environment Programme.

Health Canada
Tunney's Pasture, Ottawa ON K1A 0K9 Canada

The Jane Goodall Institute of Canada
Earth Sciences Bldg., University of Toronto, #1046/1047A, 5 Bancroft Ave., Toronto ON M5S 1C1 Canada
Tel: 416-978-3711; *Fax:* 416-978-3713
Toll-Free: 888-882-4467
e-mail: info@janegoodall.ca
URL: www.janegoodall.ca
Description: JGI Canada is one of 23 offices of the Institute located around the world. Its mission is to support wildlife research, education & conservation. Research continues to focus on Dr. Goodall's groundbreaking work on chimpanzee behaviour, as well as the environmental & human impacts on chimpanzee habitat & species wellbeing. The Institute's Roots & Shoots education program supports environmental & humanitarian education & projects, with an emphasis on a community-centred approach. The University of Toronto's Centre for Environment is a key partner.

Lakehead University (BRI)
Biorefining Research Initiative
Rm. 3001D, 1294 Balmoral St. Bldg., 955 Oliver Rd., Thunder Bay ON P7B 5E1 Canada
Tel: 807-343-8844; *Fax:* 807-343-8240
URL: lubri.lakeheadu.ca
Description: The BRI is engaged in research into biorefining, an important alternative to the refining of fossil oil, with an emphasis on developing new technologies, solutions & products. Specifically, the research will focus on bioconversion: the conversion of cellulose in forest biomass into biofuels (ethanol, methane), other bio-based chemicals & bioenergy; chemical conversion: production of chemicals from forest biomass by thermochemical processes; & forest microbiota: chemicals, including pharmaceuticals, enzymes & microbial agents for bioremediation.

Lakehead University (ATRC)
Aquatic Toxicity Research Centre
Lakehead University, 955 Oliver Rd., Thunder Bay ON P7B 5E1 Canada
Tel: 807-343-8110; *Fax:* 807-343-8023
URL: lucas.lakeheadu.ca/atrc/
Description: The Centre is engaged in regulatory testing-monitoring of the effects of effluents on aquatic organisms from pulp & paper mills, mines & related industrial discharges in Northwestern Ontario. Testing services, which includes acute testing with rainbow trout & water fleas, are available to industry & government. The Centre is a member of the Lakehead University Centre for Analytical Services (LUCAS).

Lakehead University
Environmental Laboratory
#CB3022, Centennial Bldg., Lakehead University, 955 Oliver Rd., Thunder Bay ON P7B 5E1 Canada
Tel: 807-343-8662; *Fax:* 807-343-8023
URL: lucas.lakeheadu.ca/luel/
Description: The Laboratory, a member of the Lakehead University Centre for Analytical Services (LUCAS), provides chemical analysis of soils, foliage, water, & wastewater, & supports research & teaching at Lakehead University.

Lakehead University
Forest Resources & Soils Testing Laboratory
Lakehead University, 955 Oliver Rd., Thunder Bay ON P7B 5E1 Canada
Tel: 807-343-8639
e-mail: soilslab@lakeheadu.ca
URL: lucas.lakeheadu.ca/forest/
Description: The Lab, a member of the Lakehead University Centre for Analytical Services (LUCAS), provides reliable testing of soils, vegetation & nutrients. It collaborates with business, industry & researchers to enhance entrepreneurial activity & encourages & supports research in Northern Ontario.

Lakehead University (LUNE)
Lakehead University Nutrient Ecology Laboratory
Lakehead University, 955 Oliver Rd., Thunder Bay ON P7B 5E1 Canada
Tel: 807-343-8110; *Fax:* 807-343-8023
URL: lucas.lakeheadu.ca/lune/
Description: Established in 2003, the Laboratory supports water quality research in lakes, streams & wetlands in Northwestern Ontario, & offers hands-on training to University students with an interest in freshwater ecosystems. The Lab is a member of the Lakehead University Centre for Analytical Services (LUCAS).

Lakehead University (LUCAS)
Lakehead University Centre for Analytical Services
Rm. 0001A, 1294 Balmoral Bldg., Lakehead University, 955 Oliver Rd., Thunder Bay ON P7B 5E1 Canada
Tel: 807-343-8110; *Fax:* 807-343-8023
URL: lucas.lakeheadu.ca
Description: The Centre brings together internationally recognized scientists & research teams, & supports research & training.

Lakehead University
955 Oliver Rd., Thunder Bay ON P7B 5E1 Canada

Laurentian University (CFEU)
Cooperative Freshwater Ecology Unit
Biology Dept., Laurentian University, 935 Ramsay Lake Rd., Sudbury ON P3E 2C6 Canada
Tel: 705-671-3861; *Fax:* 705-671-3857
e-mail: livingwithlakes@laurentian.ca
URL: www.laurentian.ca
Description: The Co-op Unit was formed in partnership with the Ontario Ministries of Natural Resources, & Environment, & it collaborates also with Vale Inco, Xstrata Nickel, the City of Sudbury & other universities & research agencies. The research focus is on restoration ecology of acid & metal damaged waters in Northeastern Ontario, & issues such as climate change, invasive species, urban development, trace contaminants, aquaculture, loss of biodiversity & the general health of aquatic ecosystems. In addition to the research program, the Unit provides water monitoring & reporting services, & supports education, teaching & training. The Living with Lakes Centre will form the hub of activities in the future.

Laurentian University
Elliot Lake Research Field Station
Willet Green Miller Center Section, #A-5030, 935 Ramsey Lake Rd., Sudbury ON P3E 2C6 Canada

Tel: 705-675-1151; Fax: 705-675-4838
URL: www.elrfs.org
Description: The Field Station houses the Analytical Services Laboratory, which supports research into the effects of low-level radioactivity, resulting from uranium mine waste tailings, on the environment. Services include lab testing for a range of inorganic & radionuclide substances such as soil, manure, plant & animal tissue, effluent, & environmental monitoring & research.

Laurentian University
935 Ramsey Lake Rd., Sudbury ON P3E 2C6 Canada

McMaster University (MIEH)
McMaster Institute of Environment & Health
1280 Main St. West, Hamilton ON L8S 4K1 Canada
Tel: 905-525-9140; Fax: 905-524-2400
URL: www.mcmaster.ca/mieh/
Description: Established in 1996, MIEH facilitates collaborative, interdisciplinary research into the complex relationships between human health & the environment. The Institute communicates its findings to policy & decision makers, the general public & other stakeholders & offers expertise & consultation on environmental health issues, particularly to the City of Hamilton. It also cooperates with local boards of education, the Hamilton Industrial Environmental Association, local citizen groups, as well as all levels of government. The Institute supports & encourages education & study at all levels.

McMaster University
1280 Main St. West, Hamilton ON L8S 4L8 Canada

Mushkegowuk Environmental Research Centre (MERC)
36 Birch St. South, Timmins ON P4N 2A5 Canada
Tel: 705-268-1123; Fax: 705-268-3282
e-mail: csutherland@vianet.ca
URL: www.merc.ontera.net
Description: The Mushkegowuk Environmental Research Centre (MERC) is a First Nation owned independent agency that undertakes and coordinates research relating to the environmental and natural resources with a focus on the Western James Bay basin in Ontario.

National Water Research Institute (NWRI)
PO Box 5050, 867 Lakeshore Rd., Burlington ON L7R 4A6 Canada
Tel: 905-336-4625; Fax: 905-336-6444
URL: www.ec.gc.ca/inre-nwri/default.asp?lang=En&n=7CE9E3AC-1
Description: Canada's preeminent freshwater research facility. With partners in the Canadian and international science communities, NWRI conducts a comprehensive program of ecosystem-based research and development in the aquatic sciences.

Ontario Centre for Environmental Technology Advancement (OCETA)
#201A, 2070 Hadwen Rd., Mississauga ON L5K 2C9 Canada
Tel: 905-822-4133
e-mail: oceta@oceta.on.ca
URL: www.oceta.on.ca
Description: A private sector, not-for-profit organization that assists in the process of commercialization of new environmental technologies and supports sustainable economic development both domestically and internationally. OCETA focuses on four business areas: information services, technology commercialization, technology verification, and sustainable development.

Queen's University (QIEEP)
Queen's Institute for Energy and Environmental Policy
Policy Studies Bldg., Queen's University, 138 Union St., Rm. 237, Kingston ON K7L 3N6 Canada
Tel: 613-533-6000; Fax: 613-533-6875
URL: www.queensu.ca/qieep/
Description: The Institute aims to produce recommendations on energy & environmental policy that is of use to governments & the public. It assists with information gathering & securing research-related funding, & seeks general funding as well. A multi-disciplinary approach that results in high quality, timely & relevant research is a focus.

Queen's University (CWE)
Centre for Water and the Environment
Ellis Hall, Suite 149, Queen's University, 58 University Ave., Kingston ON K7L 3N6 Canada
Tel: 613-533-6438; Fax: 613-533-2320
e-mail: cwe@appsci.queensu.ca
URL: www.cwe.queensu.ca
Description: The CWE's mission is to conduct collaborative, multidisciplinary research, & to develop innovative solutions to water issues in general, & in particular the problem of pollution contaminated water & its impacts on public health. Researchers are drawn from various fields, including health care, the private sector, conservation authorities, & non-governmental organiztions. A 5-year expansion plan includes construction of a large water & environment research lab, as well as a climate change lab.

Queen's University
GeoEngineering Centre
Ellis Hall, Rm. 101, Queen's University, Kingston ON K7L 3N6 Canada
Tel: 613-533-6370; Fax: 613-533-2128
e-mail: info@geoeng.ca
URL: www.geoeng.ca
Description: A collaborative venture founded in 2001, the Centre brings together researchers from engineering departments at Queen's University & Royal Military College to develop knowledge & innovative solutions in the areas of geotechnical, geohydrological, geochemical & geosynthetics engineering. Specific research & project areas include groundwater & remediation; soil mechanics; geoenvironmental concerns such as soil & water pollution, solid waste management; geomechanics; geosynthetics (the effects of polymeric & other types of material as they contact soil or rock); & geochemistry.

Queen's University
99 University Ave., Kingston ON K7L 3N6 Canada

University of Guelph (GIE)
Guelph Institute for the Environment
University of Guelph, Guelph ON N1G 2W1 Canada
Tel: 519-824-4120
e-mail: gie@uoguelph.ca
URL: gie@uoguelph.ca
Description: The Institute, a unit of the Faculty of Environmental Science, opened in 2007 with a mandate to utilize the University of Guelph's recognized expertise on environmental issues & to foster opportunities for dialogue with government agencies on environmental challenges such as water resources management, waste management, heavy metal pollution, & climate change. The focus is on facilitating communication among researchers, government, & the wider community, with a view to enhancing problem solving & policy making. GIE hosts meetings, conferences & workshops on the issues, bringing together experts from on & off campus, & encourages student involvement with environmental policy & research.

University of Guelph (AC)
The Aquaculture Centre
Dept. of Animal & Poultry Science, University of Guelph, 491 Gordon St., Guelph ON N1G 2W1 Canada
Tel: 519-824-4120; Fax: 519-767-0573
e-mail: aquacntr@uoguelph.ca
URL: www.aps.uoguelph.ca/~aquacentre
Description: The Aquaculture Centre, opened in 1990, coordinates research, extension & educational activities & liaises with other provincial & national aquaculture institutions to facilitate information & technology transfer to the private sector. Services include troubleshooting a range of non-diagnostic problems faced by commercial farmers, & providing information & training. The Centre's staff also contribute to industry & government committees looking into issues such as pathogen control, fish health legislation, policy development regarding waste management, species for culture, pharmaceutical usage, product quality control, performance measures, & educational/training programs in aquaculture. While assisting with technology transfer, The Centre also acts as an advocate for balanced, sustainable development of the aquaculture industry in Ontario & in Canada.

University of Guelph (CESRF)
Controlled Environment Systems Research Facility
Ontario Agricultural College, Guelph ON N1G 2W1 Canada
Tel: 519-824-4120; Fax: 519-837-0442
e-mail: info@ces.uoguelph.ca
URL: www.ces.uoguelph.ca
Description: CESRF is engaged in whole plant research, & provides a controlled environment for the measurement of plant growth, gas exchange, volatile organic compound evolution, & nutrient remediation. The facility is comprised of 24 sealed environment chambers, with several variable pressure plant growth hypobaric chambers capable of sustaining a vacuum. The facility is useful to a diverse clientele, including those doing research into plant physiology, growth & production, in the aerospace, chemical, plant production & academic fields, to name a few. Facility staff offer expertise in plant physiology, environment analysis & sensor technology. CESRF's Space & Advanced Life Support Agriculture program contributes to the efforts of plant research at the Canadian Space Agency. In addition, a biofiltration lab utilizing plant-microbe interactions from green plants is used to investigate potential solutions to air quality problems.

University of Guelph (BIO)
Biodiversity Institute of Ontario
University of Guelph, 50 Stone Rd. East, Guelph ON N1G 2W1 Canada
Tel: 519-824-4120
URL: www.biodiversity.ca
Description: Established in 2007 & funded by the Canada Foundation for Innovation & other supporting organizations, The Biodiversity Institute of Ontario takes a multidisciplinary approach to research into species identity, genetic variation, ecological roles & ecosystem processes, with a view to answering pressing concerns such as endangered species, particulary in S. Ontario. The Institute is comprised of 4 main research divisions: the Canadian Centre for DNA Barcoding (first organization of its kind in the world - see www.barcodeoflife.org); Experimental Ecosystems (oversees the Limnotron, a controlled environment facility & the world's largest aquatic mesocosm facility); the OAC Herbarium, engaging in plant barcoding research (see www.uoguelph.ca/foibis/); & the OAC Insect Collection, an important heritage collection for North American species. Digital education programs for students & the general public are another important focus (see the links to Canada's Aquatic Environment, & Canada's Polar Life).

University of Guelph (CLAWS)
Centre for Land and Water Stewardship
Richards Bldg., University of Guelph, Guelph ON N1G 2W1 Canada
Tel: 519-824-4120
e-mail: claws@uoguelph.ca
URL: www.uoguelph.ca/~claws/
Description: The Centre evolved from the former Centre for Soil & Water Conservation, established in 1986, & is engaged in research into sustainable use of land & water resources. Agricultural practices, nutrient management, water quality, conservation of natural areas, & stewardship policies & programs are a focus. Recent research has concentrated on areas such as manure management practices & their effect on water quality, modeling of on-farm nitrogen use, land trusts & their role in conservation, reforestation in S. Ontario, & conservation planning for rural landowners.

University of Guelph
50 Stone Rd. East, Guelph ON N1G 2W1 Canada

University of Ottawa (CAREG)
Center for Advanced Research in Environmental Genomics
Dept. of Biology, University of Ottawa, 20 Marie Curie St., Ottawa ON K1N 6N5 Canada
Tel: 613-562-5800; Fax: 613-562-5486
URL: www.careg.uottawa.ca
Description: CAREG began in 2000 as a group of researchers in environmental biology, fish physiology, & molecular evolution but has evolved to include researchers outside the Dept. of Biology. The research focuses on the effects of enviromental stressors on genome function & expression, with a view to developing solutions to problems of environmental biology.

University of Ottawa (CREM)
Centre for Research on Environmental Microbiology
University of Ottawa, 451 Smyth Rd., Rm. 4119, Ottawa ON K1H 8M5 Canada
Tel: 613-562-5800; Fax: 613-562-5452
e-mail: crem@uottawa.ca
URL: www.medicine.uottawa.ca/crem/
Description: CREM's research endeavours are focused on how human pathogens get into the environment & survive there; the environmental factors affecting pathogen survival & transport & the potential for human exposure; how the spread of infections may be interrupted through the application of environmental control measures to water, air, food, waste, etc. Specific interests include the treatment & disinfection of drinking water,

the microbiological quality of potable & recreational waters, food safety, survival & transport of pathogens in wastewater & soil, biomedical waste management & monitoring, & other areas.

University of Ottawa (IE)
Institute of the Environment
555 King Edward Ave., Ottawa ON K1N 6N5 Canada
Tel: 613-562-5895; Fax: 613-562-5873
e-mail: ieuo@uottawa.ca
URL: www.ie.uottawa.ca
Description: The Institute, founded in 1999, is mandated to facilitate interdisciplinary research on the environment, both on & off campus, & to identify & encourage new areas of environmental research & educational endeavour. Current research foci include biodiversity conservation, impacts of climate change, freshwater conservation, environmental assessment, toxicants & ecosystem health, & Aboriginal community health.

University of Ottawa
Sustainable Prosperity Research and Policy Network
555 King Edward Ave., Ottawa ON K1N 6N5 Canada
Tel: 613-562-5800
URL: www.sustainableprosperity.ca
Description: The Network, founded in 2007, brings together leaders from academia & business to facilitate dialogue, generate innovative ideas, & produce research & policy tools to help build a productive Canadian economy while taking strong account of sustainability. The Network's perspective is that market forces can be used to enhance & work FOR (not against) the environment, & can provide incentive to individual consumers & businesses to lower their environmental footprint.

University of Ottawa
75 Laurier Ave. East, Ottawa ON K1N 6N5 Canada

University of Toronto
Centre for Environment
#1016V, 33 Willcocks St., Toronto ON M5S 3E8 Canada
Tel: 416-978-3475; Fax: 416-978-3884
e-mail: centre.environment@utoronto.ca
Description: The Centre for Environment brings undergraduate & graduate students, faculty, & the general public to an understanding of environmental initiatives at the University of Toronto. These include degree programs in Environmental Studies, as well as certificate programs & professional development, workshops, & environmental research at all levels. A collaborative, interdisciplinary approach to research in the areas of applied environmental science, environment & health, environmental & energy policy, ethics, & environment & international development is a focus. The Centre collaborates with the Jane Goodall Institute, the United Nations, & the University's Sustainability Office, & is responsible for the Environmental Research Database, a repository of research spanning a range of topics by student & faculty researchers.

University of Toronto
Diamond Environmental Research Group
45 St. George St., Toronto ON M5S 3G3 Canada
Tel: 416-978-1586; Fax: 416-946-5992
URL: faculty.geog.utoronto.ca/mdiamond/
Description: The Research Group focuses on the dynamics of organic & inorganic contaminants in lakes, urban areas, aquatic food-webs & indoor environments. Mathematical modelling, analytical chemistry, & lab & field studies in the areas of aquatic systems (air, water, sediment), & multimedia movement (air, water, soil, sediment, vegetation & impervious surfaces) are activities of interest. The Group collaborates with the provincial Ministry of Environment, Environment Canada & the City of Toronto.

University of Toronto
Ecohydrology Research Group
Dept. of Geography, Univ. of Toronto Mississauga, 3359 Mississauga Rd. North, Mississauga ON L5L 1C6 Canada
Tel: 905-569-4649; Fax: 905-828-5273
URL: eratos.erin.utoronto.ca/branfireun/
Description: The Group is engaged in collaborative research projects on wetlands & mercury cycling, with a focus on the peatlands of the Hudson Bay lowlands, mercury cycling in Ontario watersheds, & hydrology & biogeochemistry of small watersheds in Western Mexico.

University of Toronto
Centre for GeoInformatics
Dept. of Geography, Univ. of Toronto Mississauga, 3359 Mississauga Rd. North, South Bldg., Mississauga ON L5L 1C6 Canada
Tel: 905-828-5462; Fax: 905-828-5273
URL: eratos.erin.utoronto.ca/gis/
Description: The Centre is mandated to research the utility & development of select spatial analysis tools & extensions to GIS, in order to discover solutions to cultural & environmental challenges. Current research projects include a study to analyze the spatial distribution of fish in the Credit River, & a study to determine if there is a link between exposure to urban development & the increase in the presence of invasive species as these pertain to woodlots in Mississauga.

University of Toronto (CGCS)
Centre for Global Change Science
Dept. of Physics, University of Toronto, 60 St. George St., Toronto ON M5S 1A7 Canada
Tel: 416-978-2933; Fax: 416-978-8905
URL: www.cgcs.utoronto.ca
Description: The Centre's focus is on research into climate models & dynamics, atmospheric chemistry & global change, global change & the biosphere & hydrosphere/cryosphere, & global change & space-based remote sounding.

University of Toronto
Centre for Biocomposites & Biomaterials Processing
Fac. of Forestry, University of Toronto, 33 Willcocks St., Toronto ON M5S 3B3 Canada
Tel: 416-946-3191; Fax: 416-978-3834
URL: www.forestry.utoronto.ca/research/bbp/
Description: The Centre focuses on research into engineered wood & natural fibre composite materials, with an emphasis on engineering principles, & physico-chemical & biological phenomena involved in designing sustainable engineered products from wood residues & agro-fibers.

University of Toronto (SOCAAR)
Southern Ontario Centre for Atmospheric Aerosol Research
University of Toronto, 200 College St., Toronto ON M5S 3E5 Canada
Description: The Centre is engaged in collaborative, interdisciplinary research into air quality, specifically on how aerosols impact the environment & human health. SOCAAR brings together researchers from the medical field, engineering, & atmospheric chemistry, & partners with government & industry.

University of Toronto
Sustainability Office
Rm. 208, South Borden Bldg., University of Toronto, 487 Spadina Cres., Toronto ON M5S 2J7 Canada
Tel: 416-978-6792
e-mail: sustainability@utoronto.ca
URL: sustainability.utoronto.ca
Description: Established in 2004, the Office is mandated to address sustainability issues on campus; to facilitate student, faculty & staff environmental stewardship; to develop & implement energy & resource conservation projects; to establish baselines & targets, & monitor progress; to develop & integrate University policies to increase energy & resource conservation efforts; & to develop networks & partnerships with external organizations with similar aims.

University of Toronto
27 King's College Circle, Toronto ON M5S 1A1 Canada

University of Waterloo
Ecological Restoration Group
Fac. of Environment, University of Waterloo, 200 University Ave. West, Waterloo ON N2L 3G1 Canada
Tel: 519-888-4567; Fax: 519-746-2031
URL: www.environment.uwaterloo.ca/research/ecological_restoration/
Description: The Group conducts research, teaches, & promotes community involvement in ecological restoration, rehabilitation & management. Projects have included the Quetico Provincial Park Resource Survey; gravel pit rehabilitation at the Stanley Park Optimist Natural Area in Kitchener, ON; a marsh restoration project in Iraq; & rehabilitation of industrial land for Cytec Canada Inc. Facilities include GIS (Geographic Information Systems) & remote sensing labs, an ecology lab, natural gardens & reserves, & the RS Dorney Ecology Garden which features native species. The Group works closely with the Quetico Foundation, the Nature Conservancy of Canada, the Cruickston Charitable Research Reserve, the Heritage Resources Centre, Hydro One, the University of Guelph, & municipalites, conservation authorities & corporations.

University of Waterloo (IC3)
Interdisciplinary Centre on Climate Change
University of Waterloo, 200 University Ave. West, Waterloo ON N2L 3G1 Canada
Tel: 519-888-4567
URL: www.environment.uwaterloo.ca/research/ic3/
Description: The Centre aims to contribute to the science of climate change & its impacts on human life. Using leading edge systems, technologies & numerical modeling, researchers from diverse disciplines (Environment, Engineering, Mathematics, Sciences) focus on various spatial & temporal scales in their work. Core research themes include atmospheric science, cryospheric science, human dimensions of climate change, observing systems & modeling, & water, ecosystems, & biogeochemical cycling. The Centre also provides education & outreach to the public, particularly to high school & undergraduate students, & liaises with government & industry as appropriate. For information on cryospheric research, consult The Canadian Cryosphere Information Network, as well as the link to the State of the Canadian Cryosphere page at www.ccin.ca.

University of Waterloo
200 University Ave. West, Waterloo ON N2L 3G1 Canada

University of Windsor (LEMN)
Lake Erie Millenium Network
c/o Dept. of Biol. Sci./GLIER, University of Windsor, Windsor ON N9B 3P4 Canada
Tel: 519-253-3000; Fax: 519-971-3609
URL: www.lemn.org
Description: The Network was formed in 1998 by scientists at the University of Windsor, the National Water Research Institute (Burlington, ON), the F.T. Stone Lab at Ohio State University, & the U.S. E.P.A at Grosse Ile, MI, in order to coordinate research into the ecological challenges & concerns regarding Lake Erie. It endeavours to summarize the current environmental status of the Lake; document the research & management needs of users & agencies; develop a framework for a research network to ensure a coordinated effort in the collection & dissemination of data that will address the research & management needs.

University of Windsor
401 Sunset Ave., Windsor ON N9B 3P4 Canada

Upper Lakes Environmental Research Network (ULERN)
SSM Innovation Centre, 1520 Queen St. E., NW 307, Sault Ste. Marie ON P6A 2G4 Canada
Tel: 705-942-7927; Fax: 705-942-6169
URL: www.ulern.on.ca
Description: ULERN provides opportunities for collaboration & networking among environmental organization members doing research. The Network sources potential funding for projects, facilitates partnerships to address environmental & natural resource impacts on human health, coordinates funding applications, provides project management services, coordinates access to wage subsidy programs to help environmental organizations hire students & provides payroll administration services for student hires, coordinates workshops & conferences.

Wilfrid Laurier University
Cold Regions Research Centre
Dept. of Geography & Environmental Studies, Wilfrid Laurier University, 75 University Ave. West, Waterloo ON N2L 3C5 Canada
Tel: 519-884-0710; Fax: 519-725-1342
URL: info.wlu.ca/~wwwgeog/ColdRegions4/
Description: Founded in 1988, the Centre's research focus is on Arctic & mountain glaciology, hydrology, geochemistry, resource management, parks planning, & other aspects of Cold Regions. The approach is collaborative & interdisciplinary.

Wilfrid Laurier University (IWS)
Laurier Institute for Water Science
Wilfrid Laurier University, 75 University Ave. West, Waterloo ON N2L 3C5 Canada
Tel: 519-884-0710
URL: www.wlu.ca
Description: The Institute is engaged in collaborative, multidisciplinary research in the areas of hydrological sciences, ecological & biogeochemcial sciences, & public policy & management. The focus is on the effects of climate change on water resources, sustainability of healthy aquatic & coastal ecosystems, & development of policy & regulations relating to water use.

Wilfrid Laurier University
75 University Ave. West, Waterloo ON N2L 3C5 Canada

York University (IRIS)
  Institute for Research & Innovation in Sustainability
  347 York Lanes, York University, 4700 Keele St., Toronto ON M3J 1P3 Canada
  Tel: 416-736-2100; *Fax:* 416-736-5837
  e-mail: irisinfo@yorku.ca
  URL: www.yorku.ca/irisinfo/
  Description: Established in 2004, IRIS is a university-wide, interdisciplinary institute with a focus on collaborative research into the environmental, scientific, economic, social & cultural aspects of sustainability. Past research projects have included an inventory of York University's trees, & a study & recommendations to the Government of the NWT on a strategy for monitoring invasive species. Among other endeavours, current research will focus on food sustainability at York University, a study of white-tailed deer in London, ON, & an assessment of invasive species in Ontario.

York University
4700 Keele St., Toronto ON M3J 1P3 Canada

Prince Edward Island

Canadian Cooperative Wildlife Health Centre (CCWHC)
  Atlantic Region
  Atlantic Veterinary College, 550 University Ave., Charlottetown PE C1A 4P3 Canada
  Tel: 902-628-4314; *Fax:* 902-566-0871
  URL: atlantic.ccwhc.ca
  Description: The Canadian Cooperative Wildlife Health Centre (CCWHC) is a cooperative effort encompassing all five Canadian Veterinary Colleges. The Cooperative seeks to apply veterinary medical sciences to the field of wildlife conservation and management in Canada. Additionally, the Cooperative is dedicated to developing knowledge of wildlife health and disease through research and education. Recent projects of the Atlantic branch include studies of raccoons and skunks in maritime provinces, beached whale recovery, and studies on birds in the Maritime region.

University of Prince Edward Island (PEI HRI)
  Prince Edward Island Health Research Institute
  #504, Dalton Hall, 550 University Ave., Charlottetown PE C1A 4P3 Canada
  Tel: 902-894-2812; *Fax:* 902-894-2811
  e-mail: peihri@upei.ca
  URL: peihri.upei.ca
  Description: The Prince Edward Island Health Research Institute is a research and knowledge resource centre on human health. The mission of the Institute is to support, promote, and enhance research on health in Prince Edward Island, including environmental factors. Projects include human development, cancer research, nutrition, drugs and environmental exposures, and other areas that fall under Health, Wellness and the Environment.

University of Prince Edward Island
550 University Ave., Charlottetown PE C1A 4P3 Canada

Québec

Canada. Fisheries & Oceans Canada
  Maurice Lamontagne Institute
  PO Box 1000, 850, route de la Mer, Mont-Joli QC G5H 3Z4 Canada
  Tel: 418-775-0500; *Fax:* 418-775-0542
  e-mail: info@dfo-mpo.gc.ca
  URL: www.qc.dfo-mpo.gc.ca
  Description: The Institute is mandated to provide the Canadian government with a scientific basis for the conservation of living marine resources, the protection of the marine environment, & safe maritime navigation. Research into fisheries, marine mammals, oceanography, & habitats of the Estuary & Gulf of St. Lawrence & Northern Québec is carried out, as is environmental monitoring & assessment.

Canmet Energy Technology Centre (CETC - Varennes)
  Varennes
  Varennes Research Centre, CP 4800, 11615, boul Lionel-Boulet, Varennes QC J3X 1S6
  Description: The Canmet Energy Technology Centre in Varennes manages the RETScreen International Clean Energy Decision Support Centre. The Varennes Research Centre also directs programs in renewables, buildings & communities, & industrial processes. Examples of research projects are as follows: photovoltaic systems in buildings & stand-alone photovoltaic systems, integration of decentralized energy resources, industrial systems optimization, intelligent buildings, efficient refrigeration applications, & recommissioning.

Centre de recherche industrielle du Québec (CRIQ) / Quebec Centre for Industrial Research
  POLE Québec Chaudière-Appalaches, Place Iberville Deux, #300, 1175, av Lavigerie, Québec QC G1V 4P1 Canada
  Tel: 418-681-9700; *Fax:* 418-681-1535
  e-mail: info@pole-qca.ca
  URL: www.pole-qca.ca
  Description: While a major emphasis of research is on industrial equipment & productivity, eco-efficiency & innovation through sustainable industrial practices are an important focus. Among a number of projects, a study of recycling & reclamation of composite waste material is being developed.

Centre géoscientifique de Québec
  c/o CGC-Québec & INRS Eau Terre Environnement, 490, rue de la Couronne, Québec QC G1K 9A9 Canada
  Tel: 418-654-2604; *Fax:* 418-654-2615
  URL: www.cgq-qgc.ca
  Description: The focus of research is on socio-economic issues as they relate to aspects of environmental geoscience (climate change, environmental geodynamics, remediation of contaminated sites, etc.), regional geology, & georesources (groundwater, minerals, fossil fuels). The Centre is the result of a partnership between government & academia.

Environment Canada (CRIACC)
  Centre de Ressources en Impacts et Adaptation au Climat et à ses Changements
  Place Bonaventure, Portail Nord-Est, #7810, 800, rue de la Gauchetière ouest, Montréal QC H5A 1L9 Canada
  Fax: 514-282-2264
  e-mail: climat.quebec@ec.qc.ca
  URL: www.criacc.qc.ca
  Description: Provides reports & resources on the impacts of climate change in Québec.

Environment Canada
  Meteorological Service of Canada. Atmospheric Science & Technology Directorate. Meteorological Research Branch
  2121, rte Transcanadienne, Dorval QC H9P 1J3 Canada
  Tel: 514-421-4771; *Fax:* 514-421-2106
  URL: www.msc-smc.ec.gc.ca/acsd/
  Description: The Branch is engaged in meteorological research, with a focus on remote sensing, severe weather, atmospheric processes, & weather prediction. The goal of research is to provide the science required to improve weather predicting. The Branch is comprised of a Data Assimilation & Satellite Meteorology division, a Numerical Prediction Research division, & a Cloud Physics Research division.

Environment Canada
  Place Vincent Massey, 351 St. Joseph Blvd., 8th Fl., Gatineau QC K1A 0H3 Canada

Environmental Health Research Network
  Institut national de la recherche scientifique, 531, boul des Prairies, Laval QC H7V 1B7 Canada
  e-mail: rrse@uquebec.ca
  URL: www.rrse.ca
  Description: The Environmental Health Research Network, funded by the Fonds de la recherche en santé du Québec (FRSQ), brings together virtually all Québec university researchers working in the environmental health field. The aim of environmental health research, which is preventive in nature, is to characterize the impact of chemical and physical contaminants of the environment as health determinants.

McGill University (ASCC)
  Avian Science and Conservation Centre
  Macdonald Campus, McGill University, 21,111 Lakeshore Rd., Ste-Anne-de-Bellevue QC H9X 3V9 Canada
  Tel: 514-398-7760; *Fax:* 514-398-7990
  URL: http://ascc.mcgill.ca
  Description: Established in 1973, the centre's purpose is to foster a greater understanding of the biology, conservation, and management of birds through a multipurpose program of research and education. Major areas of Research research include behaviour, ecology, nutrition, toxicology, reproductive physiology, and parasitology of captive and wild birds, as well as captive breeding and management of endangered species.

McGill University
  Brace Centre for Water Resources Management
  Dept. of Civil Engineering & Applied Mechanics, 817 Sherbrooke West, Montréal QC H3A 2K6 Canada
  Tel: 514-398-6870; *Fax:* 514-398-7361
  e-mail: brace@mcgill.ca
  URL: www.mcgill.ca/brace
  Description: The Brace Centre for Water Resources Management brings together staff from several McGill faculties, to undertake research, teaching, specialized training, and policy and strategic studies in water resources management, both in Canada and internationally.

McGill University (GEC3)
  Global Environmental & Climate Change Centre
  805 Sherbrooke St. West, Montréal QC H3A 2K6 Canada
  Tel: 514-398-3759; *Fax:* 514-398-1381
  e-mail: mansi@geog.mcgill.ca
  URL: www.mcgill.ca/gec3
  Description: The Global Environmental and Climate Change Centre (GEC3) is a cross-disciplinary, multi-university research centre bringing together more than 40 researchers from six Quebec universities (McGill University, Université de Montréal, Université du Québec à Montréal, Université de Sherbrooke, Université Laval, Université du Québec à Rimouski) to study processes, modelling and impact of environmental and climate change.

McGill University (CINE)
  Centre for Indigenous Peoples' Nutrition and Environment
  Macdonald Campus, McGill University, 21,111 Lakeshore Rd., Ste-Anne-de-Bellevue QC H9X 3V9 Canada
  Tel: 514-398-7544; *Fax:* 514-398-1020
  e-mail: cine@cine.mcgill.ca
  URL: www.mcgill.ca/cine
  Description: This Centre was created at McGill University in response to a need expressed by Aboriginal peoples for participatory research and education to address concerns about the integrity of their traditional food systems. Deterioration in the environment has adverse impacts on the health and lifestyles of indigenous peoples, in particular health and nutrition as derived from food and food traditions. CINE is a university-based endeavour to assist indigenous peoples in dealing with their concerns related to traditional food systems, nutrition and the environment.

McGill University
  James Administration Bldg., 845 Sherbrooke St. West, Montréal QC H3A 2T5 Canada

Ouranos
  Tour Ouest, 19e étage, 550, rue Sherbrooke ouest, Montréal QC H3A 1B9 Canada
  Tel: 514-282-6464; *Fax:* 514-282-7131
  e-mail: webmestre@ouranos.ca
  URL: www.ouranos.ca
  Description: Ouranos is a non-profit consortium of 250 scientists & others doing research in the areas of climate science & adaptation to climate change. The focus is on developing new knowledge on climate change & its socioeconomic & environmental impacts, with a view to providing solid information to decision & policy makers.

Québec. Ministère du Développement durable, de l'Environnement et des Parcs
  Centre d'expertise hydrique
  Édifice Marie-Guyart, Aile René-Lévesque, 1er étage, 675, boul René-Lévesque est, Québec QC G1R 5V7 Canada
  Tel: 418-521-3866; *Fax:* 418-643-6900
  e-mail: cehq@mddep.gouv.qc.ca
  URL: www.cehq.gouv.qc.ca
  Description: The Centre was created in 2001 & is mandated to operate public dams & water level stations. It also provides expertise & data in hydrology & hydraulics to support the operations of the Ministry, by gathering & collating data, & by developing forecasting models for water systems. The Centre prepares legal documents pertaining to land surveying work, for the purposes of delineating ecological reserves & floristic zones.

Québec. Ministère du Développement durable, de l'Environnement et des Parcs
  Édifice Marie-Guyart, 675, boul. René-Lévesque Est, 29e étage, Québec QC G1R 5V7 Canada

Université du Québec
  Institut national de la recherche scientifique - Centre-Eau Terre Environnement

Research Centres / Université du Québec

490, rue de la Couronne, Québec QC G1K 9A9 Canada
Tel: 418-654-2524; Fax: 418-654-2600
e-mail: info@ete.inrs.ca
URL: www.inrs-ete.uquebec.ca
Description: A university research group dedicated to higher research into water & earth resources, with a focus on sustainable development issues, conservation & effective resource management. Issues such as environmental risk factors, pollution/contamination, climate change, remediation solutions are current research areas.

Université du Québec
475, rue du Parvis, Québec QC G1K 9H7 Canada

Université du Québec à Montréal
Centre d'étude de la forêt
PO Box 8888, Stn. Centre-ville, Montréal QC H3C 3P8 Canada
Tel: 514-987-3000; Fax: 514-987-4647
URL: www.cef-cfr.ca
Description: The Centre for Forest Research brings together researchers from across universities in Québec in a collaborative endeavour to provide research into forest ecosystems, forest management & silviculture. The focus is on integrating scientific knowledge with an innovative approach in order to more effectively & sustainably manage forests in the province.

Université du Québec à Montréal
Institut des sciences de l'environnement
PO Box 8888, Stn. Centre-ville, Montréal QC H3C 3P8 Canada
Tel: 514-987-4717; Fax: 514-987-4718
e-mail: ise@uqam.ca
URL: www.ise.uqam.ca
Description: Brings together students, faculty & researchers in a collaborative, interdisciplinary research endeavour, with a focus on environment & human health, urban ecosystems, forest & water management, & climate change & its effects on the environment.

Université du Québec à Montréal (ESCER)
Centre pour l'étude et la simulation du climat à l'échelle régionale
PO Box 8888, Stn. Centre-ville, Montréal QC H3C 3P8 Canada
Tel: 514-987-3000; Fax: 514-987-6853
URL: www.escer.uqam.ca
Description: The Centre is engaged in research on climate change, with a specific focus on numeric modelling studies, regional impacts, & hydrology & hydrogeology issues.

Université du Québec à Montréal (MDCR)
Réseau canadien en modélisation et diagnostics du climat régional
Centre ESCER, PO Box 8888, Stn. Centre-ville, Montréal QC H3C 3P8 Canada
Tel: 514-987-3000; Fax: 514-987-6853
URL: www.mrcc.uqam.ca
Description: The Network brings together researchers from UQAM's Centre ESCER, Ouranos, the University of Victoria, & Environment Canada with the aim of developing & evaluating a Canadian Regional Climate Model, an appropriate diagnostic tool to analyze high-resolution climate data, & to make the Model available to other researchers working in the field of regional climate change.

Université du Québec à Montréal
PO Box 8888, Stn. succursale Centre-ville, Montréal QC H3C 3P8 Canada

Saskatchewan

Canadian Centre for Health & Safety in Agriculture (CCHSA)
Royal University Hospital, University of Saskatchewan, PO Box 120, Stn. Royal University Hospital, #3608, 103 Hospital Dr., Wing 3E, Saskatoon SK S7N 0W8
Tel: 306-966-8286; Fax: 306-966-8799
e-mail: canadian.centre@usask.ca
URL: www.cchsa-ccssma.usask.ca
Overview: A organization founded in 2006
Description: The Canadian Centre for Health & Safety in Agriculture focuses upon public health issues related to the agricultural rural ecosystem. Examples of research projects are as follows: cross-Canada study of pesticides & health; grainhandlers, genetic polymorphisms, & respiratory health; & prairie ecosystem study.

Canadian Cooperative Wildlife Health Centre
University of Saskatchewan, 52 Campus Dr., Saskatoon SK S7N 5B4 Canada

Canadian Plains Research Center
Research Park, University of Regina, 3737 Wascana Pkwy., Regina SK S4S 0A2
Tel: 306-585-4758; Fax: 306-585-4699
Toll-Free: 866-874-2257
e-mail: canadian.plains@uregina.ca
URL: www.cprc.ca
Description: The research institute at the University of Regina is engaged in the interdisciplinary study of issues relevant to Canadian prairie life. Examples of research projects are as follows: rural community water conservation, & institutional adaptations to climate change.

Centre for Northern Agroforestry & Afforestation
c/o Ken Van Rees, Dept. Of Soil Science, University of Saskatchewan, 51 Campus Dr., Saskatoon SK S7N 5A8
Tel: 306-966-6853; Fax: 306-966-6881
e-mail: ken.vanrees@usask.ca
URL: www.saskagroforestry.ca
Description: The Centre for Northern Agroforestry & Afforestation strives to advance the sustainable agroforestry industry. Agroforestry research focuses upon shelterbelts, silvopastures, & riparian buffer zones. Afforestation research involves plantation production of fast-growing hardwood & softwood species. A willow research program was implemented to study willow production for biomass energy. Scientific research by the Centre contributes to a growing economy & a healthier environment.

Centre for Sustainable Infrastructure Research (NRC-CSIR)
#301, 6 Research Dr., Regina SK S4S 7J7
Tel: 306-780-3208
e-mail: CSIR-CRID@nrc-cnrc.gc.ca
URL: irc.nrc-cnrc.gc.ca/csir/index_e.html
Description: Part of the National Research Council of Canada, the Centre for Sustainable Infrastructure Research engages in multi-disciplinary research to develop technologies to address the environmental, economic, & social aspects of infrastructure sustainability. The Centre works toward the goal of sustainability in plannning, construction, operation, maintenance, rehabilitation, & decommissioning.

National Hydrology Research Centre (NHRC)
11 Innovation Blvd., Saskatoon SK S7N 3H5
Overview: A organization founded in 1986
Description: A centre of the National Water Research Institute, the National Hydrology Research Centre focuses upon water-related issues of public concern to sustain freshwater ecosystems & natural resources. The Centre monitors stream & river levels throughout Canada.

Prairie Northern Wildlife Research Centre
Canadian Wildlife Service, 115 Perimeter Rd., Saskatoon SK S7N 0X4
Tel: 306-975-4087; Fax: 306-975-4089
Overview: A organization founded in 1966
Description: Affiliated with Environment Canada, the Prairie Northern Wildlife Research Centre is involved in research related to prairie & northern wildlife ecology & conservation. Examples of research include the impacts of forestry upon birds, & the effects of pesticides on wildlife. The Centre also focuses upon migratory birds & their habitat, such as prairie waterfowl, songbirds, shorebirds, & Arctic-nesting geese.

University of Regina
3737 Wascana Pkwy., Regina SK S4S 0A2 Canada

University of Regina (EQAL)
Environmental Quality Analysis Laboratory
265 Laboratory Building, Regina SK S4S 0A2 Canada
Tel: 306-585-4890; Fax: 306-337-2410
URL: www.uregina.ca/science/eqal/
Description: A non-profit research and analysis laboratory that provides advanced analytical and data interpretation services primarily in the fields of environmental science. The lab is available for University of Regina research projects as well as other academic units and non-academic institutions.

Yukon Territory

Yukon College
PO Box 2799, 500 College Dr., Whitehorse YT Y1A 5K4 Canada

Yukon College
Northern Research Institute
500 College Dr, Room A1104, Whitehorse YT Y1A 5K4 Canada
Tel: 867-668-8772; Fax: 867-456-8672
e-mail: nri@yukoncollege.yk.ca
URL: www.yukoncollege.yk.ca/nri/
Description: Announced in 1989, the institute was conceived as a northern centre to promote, coordinate and perform research activities that complement the college's goal of pursuing excellence in all areas of Yukon and Northern Studies. It provides research services and support to the college and other organizations.

Websites

Alberta Environmental Network (AEN)
URL: www.aenweb.ca
Description: The AEN's purpose is to facilitate the sharing of information and resources among member groups, and to assist them in the taking of common action. AEN shares information with the general public and, where warranted, interested stakeholders. AEN facilitates member group meetings and the participation of member groups in meetings and consultation with government and/or industry.

Alternative Energy News
URL: www.alternative-energy-news.info
Description: A comprehensive set of online resources designed to raise public awareness and encourage debate about renewable energy technologies. Dedicated to providing an open and comprehensive collection of discussions, information, media and news promoting the research and development of renewables.

Alternatives
URL: http://alternativesjournal.ca
Description: Published since 1971, Alternatives is Canada's oldest environmental magazine. It is also a registered charity. Delivers analysis and debate on Canadian and world environmental issues, the latest news and ideas, as well as profiles of environmental leaders who are making a difference.

British Columbia Environmental Network (BCEN)
URL: www.ecobc.org
Description: The BCEN was established in 1981. The BCEN is a network of BC community-based non-profit organizations who work on environmental issues and solutions to environmental problems.

Bureau of International Recycling
URL: www.bir.org
Description: Founded in 1948, BIR is a non-profit-making, non-governmental organisation which represents the world's recycling industry, covering in particular ferrous and non-ferrous metals, paper, and textiles.

Canada Web Directory: Science and Environment
URL: http://dirs.educationcanada.com/cat/346777
Description: Resource that allows education career seekers to find employers seeking to fill teaching jobs and other education related employment.

Canadian Arctic Resources Committee (CARC)
URL: www.carc.org
Description: CARC is a citizens' organization dedicated to the long-term environmental and social well being of northern Canada and its peoples. We believe in the application of sustainable development and the precautionary principle. Our policy and advocacy work is grounded in solid scientific and socio-economic research and experience.

Canadian Association for Renewable Energies
URL: www.renewables.ca
Description: The national association which promote feasible applications (as opposed to specific technologies) for green power, green fuels and green heat.

Canadian Association Of Physicians For The Environment (CAPE)
URL: www.cape.ca
Description: CAPE is a membership organization for health professionals. It works to protect the environment in order to protect human health. CAPE is concerned about Ecosystem Health, Human Health and Sustainable Development.

Canadian Council of Ministers of the Environment (CCME)
URL: www.ccme.ca
Description: CCME is comprised of the environment ministers from the federal, provincial and territorial governments. These 14 ministers normally meet at least once a year to discuss national environmental priorities and determine what to be carried out under the auspices of CCME. The Council seeks to achieve positive environmental results, focusing on issues that are national in scope and that require collective attention by a number of governments. CCME aims to assist its members to meet their mandate of protecting Canada's environment.

Canadian Environmental Assessment Agency
URL: www.ceaa-acee.gc.ca
Description: The Canadian Environmental Assessment Agency is a federal body accountable to the Minister of the Environment. The Agency works to provide Canadians with high-quality environmental assessments that contribute to informed decision making, in support of sustainable development.

Canadian Environmental Certification Approvals Board (CECAB)
URL: www.cecab.org
Description: The Canadian Environmental Certification Approvals Board (CECAB) is responsible for the certification of environmental practitioners in Canada. The 9-member CECAB Board oversees final approval of all candidates.

Canadian Environmental Directory
URL: www.greyhouse.ca/environ.htm
Description: The Canadian Environmental Directory is Canada's most complete and only national listing of environmental associations and organizations, government regulators and purchasing groups, product and service companies, special libraries, and more!

Canadian Environmental Grantmakers' Network (CEGN)
URL: www.cegn.org
Description: The Canadian Environmental Grantmakers' Network (CEGN) is a membership group of private, community, public and corporate foundations, and government and corporate funding programs that give grants in support of the Canadian environment. CEGN works to develop an effective network of environmental grantmakers in Canada by facilitating information-sharing, collaboration, training and professional development, research, and communications.

Canadian Environmental Law Association (CELA)
URL: www.cela.ca
Description: The Canadian Environmental Law Association (CELA) is a non-profit, public interest organization established in 1970 to use existing laws to protect the environment and to advocate environmental law reforms.

Canadian Environmental Literacy Project (CELP)
URL: www.celp.ca
Description: The mandate of the Canadian Environmental Literacy Project (CELP) is to develop open-access curriculum materials in support of teaching environmental studies in universities, colleges, and high schools in Canada. The focus is on materials that address Canadian issues within local, regional or international contexts.

Canadian Environmental Network (RCEN)
URL: www.cen-rce.org
Description: For more than thirty years, the Canadian Environmental Network (RCEN) has been facilitating networking between environmental organizations and others who share its mandate - To Protect the Earth and Promote Ecologically Sound Ways of Life. The RCEN works directly with concerned citizens and organizations striving to protect, preserve and restore the environment, and to affect how society thinks about environmental issues.

Canadian Environmental Solutions Directory (CES)
URL: www.ic.gc.ca/eic/site/ces-sec.nsf/eng/Home
Description: Canadian Environmental Solutions (CES) is an online searchable database that includes more than 2 658 export and export-ready Canadian companies who provide innovative technologies and expertise to address the environmental challenges faced by every sector of the economy.

Canadian Environmental Technology Advancement Corp. West (CETAC-WEST)
URL: www.cetacwest.com
Description: CETAC-WEST is a private sector, not-for-profit corporation committed to helping small and medium-sized enterprises (SMEs) engaged in the development and commercialization of new environmental technologies. Established in 1994 by Environment Canada, CETAC-WEST delivers its services to SMEs in the four western provinces through its office in Calgary. The corporation has formed linkages between technology producers, industry experts, and investment sources to facilitate this process.

Canadian Forest Seedling Nurseries and Services Directory
URL: www.for.gov.bc.ca/nursery/extensn/NurseryDirectory.htm

Canadian Institute for Environmental Law and Policy (CIELAP)
URL: www.cielap.org
Description: Founded in 1970, CIELAP is an independent, not-for-profit research and education organization. CIELAP performs environmental research that is accurate, balanced, and evidence-based, and uses its findings to encourage laws, policies, and decisions in Canada that support the environment. We are registered as a Canadian charity.

Canadian Nuclear Safety Commission (CNSC)
URL: www.nuclearsafety.gc.ca
Description: The Canadian Nuclear Safety Commission (CNSC) protects the health, safety and security of Canadians as well as the environment, and respects Canada's international commitments on the peaceful use of nuclear energy. CNSC was established in 2000 under the Nuclear Safety and Control Act and reports to Parliament through the Minister of Natural Resources. CNSC was created to replace the former Atomic Energy Control Board (AECB), which was founded in 1946.

Canadian Organic Growers
URL: www.cog.ca
Description: Canadian Organic Growers Inc. is Canada's national membership-based education and networking organization representing farmers, gardeners, consumers and supporters in all provinces and territories. Its mission is to lead local and national communities towards sustainable organic stewardship of land, food and fibre while respecting nature, upholding social justice and protecting natural resources.

Canadian Parks and Wilderness Society (CPAWS)
URL: www.cpaws.org
Description: The Canadian Parks and Wilderness Society (CPAWS) is Canada's pre-eminent, national community-based voice for public wilderness protection. Since 1963 CPAWS has taken a lead role in establishing two-thirds of Canada's protected wild spaces — an area over seven times the size of Nova Scotia.

Canadian Partnership for Children's Health and Environment (CPCHE)
URL: www.healthyenvironmentforkids.ca
Description: The Canadian Partnership for Children's Health and Environment (CPCHE) is an affiliation of groups with overlapping missions to improve children's environmental health in Canada. Working across traditional boundaries, CPCHE provides common ground for organizations working to protect children's health from environmental contaminants.

Canadian Renewable Fuels Association (CRFA)
URL: www.greenfuels.org
Description: Founded in 1984, the Canadian Renewable Fuels Association (CRFA) is a non-profit organization with a mission to promote the use of renewable fuels for transportation through consumer awareness and government liaison activities. The CRFA membership is composed of representatives from all levels of the ethanol and biodiesel industry, including: grain and cellulose ethanol producers, biodiesel producers, fuel technology providers, and agricultural associations.

Canadian Society of Environmental Biologists (CSEB)
URL: www.cseb-scbe.org
Description: The Canadian Society of Environmental Biologists is a non-profit registered society, whose primary focus is to further the conservation and prudent management of Canada's natural resources based on sound ecological principles. Members are professionally-trained biologists and biology students, from the wide range of environmental biology disciplines.

Canadian Solar Industries Association
URL: www.cansia.ca

Websites / Canadian Wildlife Service

Description: CanSIA works to strengthen the Canadian solar industry, increase the professionalism of companies, foster domestic and international markets, and promote the use of renewable energies.

Canadian Wildlife Service
URL: www.cws-scf.ec.gc.ca
Description: The Canadian Wildlife Service (CWS), part of Environment Canada, handles wildlife matters that are the responsibility of the federal government. These include protection and management of migratory birds, nationally significant habitat and endangered species, as well as work on other wildlife issues of national and international importance. In addition, CWS does research in many fields of wildlife biology.

Canadian Wind Energy Association
URL: www.canwea.ca
Description: CanWEA's Mission is to represent the wind energy community, and to support the appropriate development and application of all aspects of wind energy including the promotion of a suitable policy environment to create a vibrant Canadian wind energy market driven by consumer choice.

Carolinian Canada
URL: www.carolinian.org
Description: Carolinian Canada is a coalition of non-government organizations and government agencies with a common interest in the conservation of biodiversity within Ontario's Carolinian Life Zone. Carolinian Canada is Canada's most heavily populated and productive landscape and as a consequence is also home to more rare and endangered species than any other region of the country. Carolinian Canada has developed "The Big Picture", a digital bioregional map that portrays the recovery efforts needed to rebuild a sustainable natural heritage system in southwestern Ontario.

CEPA Environmental Registry
URL: www.ec.gc.ca/CEPARegistry
Description: The CEPA Environmental Registry gives Canadians the opportunity to learn more about how the federal government administers the Canadian Environmental Protection Act, 1999 (CEPA 1999) and invites industries, individuals, interest groups and others to participate in the public consultations and decision-making processes that take place under the Act.

Clean Air Foundation (CAF)
URL: www.cleanairfoundation.org
Description: The Clean Air Foundation is dedicated to developing, implementing and managing public engagement programs and other strategic initiatives that lead to measurable emissions reductions, to improve air quality and protect the climate.

Clean Air Strategic Alliance (CASA)
URL: www.casahome.org
Description: The Clean Air Strategic Alliance (CASA) was established in March 1994 as a new way to manage air quality issues in Alberta. CASA, a non-profit association, is a multi-stakeholder partnership, composed of representatives selected by industry, government and non-government organizations.

Click4Carbon
URL: www.click4carbon.com
Description: Click4Carbon is an environmentally friendly website that offers consumers and businesses an eco friendly alternative when looking for and purchasing products and services on the internet.

Climate Project - Canada
URL: www.climateprojectcanada.org
Description: The Climate Project-Canada is a non-profit organization and registered Canadian charity dedicated to educating the public about climate change through presentations by trained volunteers. The website is a comprehensive online support system and interactive community with a professional team of online communications and environmental specialists.

Coalition for Alternatives to Pesticides (CAP)
URL: www.cap-quebec.com
Description: CAP is non-profit organization founded in December 1999 by a group of people affected by pesticide spraying. The mission of the Coalition for Alternatives to Pesticides (CAP) is to raise province-wide public awareness on the issue of pesticides by joining together interested groups and individuals throughout Quebec, by creating ties with similar organizations throughout North America and overseas, and with the dissemination of relevant information about pesticides and their alternatives.

Committee on the Status of Endangered Wildlife in Canada (COSEWIC)
URL: www.cosewic.gc.ca
Description: The Committee on the Status of Endangered Wildlife in Canada (COSEWIC) determines the national status of wild Canadian species, subspecies, varieties or other designatable units that are suspected of being at risk of extinction or extirpation. COSEWIC uses a process based on science and Aboriginal or community knowledge to assess wildlife species at risk. All native mammals, birds, reptiles, amphibians, fish, arthropods, molluscs, vascular plants, mosses and lichens are included in COSEWIC's current mandate.

David Suzuki Foundation
URL: www.davidsuzuki.org
Description: Non-profit organization dedicated to finding innovative solutions to help conserve the natural world. Since 1990, the David Suzuki Foundation has worked to find ways for society to live in balance with the natural world that sustains us. Focusing on four program areas - oceans and sustainable fishing, climate change and clean energy, sustainability, and the Nature Challenge - the Foundation uses science and education to promote solutions that conserve nature and help achieve sustainability within a generation.

Directory of Consultants in Occupational and Environmental Health & Safety
URL: www.ohao.org/PDF/07_consultants.pdf
Description: The Occupational Hygiene Association of Ontario (OHAO) has provided this directory as a source document for those who may wish to retain the services of a consultant.

Earth Day Canada (EDC)
URL: www.earthday.ca
Description: Earth Day Canada (EDC) is a national environmental communications organization mandated to improve the state of the environment by empowering Canadians to achieve local solutions. Since 1991, EDC has been coordinating Earth Day/Earth Month events, and creating successful community programs and award-winning artistic and media projects.

Earth Energy Society of Canada (EESC)
URL: www.earthenergy.ca
Description: The Earth Energy Society of Canada was incorporated to represent the domestic earth energy (ground-source / geothermal heat pump) industry, with a mission to promote quality installations and to promote earth energy technology as a viable economic and environmental option in Canada's energy scenario. It is responsible for developing and delivering adequate and relevant training for practitioners, and promoting the applications on economic and environmental bases.

EarthTrends
URL: http://earthtrends.wri.org
Description: Online collection of information regarding the environmental, social, and economic trends that shape our world. Committed to the principle that accurate information drives responsible decisions by governments and individuals, EarthTrends offers the public a large breadth of statistical, graphic, and analytical data in easily accessible formats.

Ecojustice
URL: www.ecojustice.ca
Description: Ecojustice, formerly Sierra Legal Defence Fund, is Canada's leading non-profit organization of lawyers and scientists devoted to protecting the environment. Since 1990, they have helped hundreds of groups, coalitions and communities expose law-breakers, hold governments accountable and establish powerful legal precedents in defence of our air, water, wildlife and natural spaces.

EcoKids
URL: www.ecokids.ca
Description: EcoKids is Earth Day Canada's environmental education program for youth who care about the planet. Since 1994, the EcoKids Program has empowered Canadian youth with environmental knowledge and hands-on activities, and presented this information in fun, exciting ways that increase awareness and encourage active community involvement.

Ecological Monitoring and Assessment Network (EMAN)
URL: www.eman-rese.ca
Description: The Ecological Monitoring and Assessment Network (EMAN) is made up of linked organizations and individuals involved in ecological monitoring in Canada to better detect, describe, and report on ecosystem changes. The network is a cooperative partnership of federal, provincial and municipal governments, academic institutions, aboriginal communities and organizations, industry, environmental non-government organizations, volunteer community groups, elementary and secondary schools and other groups/individuals involved in ecological monitoring. Environment Canada's Ecological Monitoring and Assessment Network Coordinating Office (EMAN CO) is mandated to work collaboratively with the EMAN partners in improving the effectiveness of ecosystem monitoring to ensure informed decision-making and to create environmental awareness among Canadians.

EcoLogo
URL: www.ecologo.org
Description: Founded in 1988 by the Government of Canada but now recognized world-wide, EcoLogo is North America's largest, most respected environmental standard and certification mark. EcoLogo provides customers - public, corporate and consumer - with assurance that the products and services bearing the logo meet stringent standards of environmental leadership. EcoLogo certifies environmental leaders in over 120 product and service categories, helping customers find and trust the world's most sustainable products.

Encyclopedia of Earth
URL: www.eoearth.org
Description: Electronic reference website about the Earth, its natural environments, and their interaction with society.

Energy Probe
URL: www.energyprobe.org
Description: Energy Probe is a consumer and environmental research team, active in the fight against nuclear power, and dedicated to resource conservation, economic efficiency, and effective utility regulation.

EnviroJobs
URL: www.canadianenvironmental.com/envirojobs
Description: The Job Board that environmental professionals across Canada have been using since March 2001.

Environmental Contaminants
URL: www.hc-sc.gc.ca/ewh-semt/contaminants/index-eng.php
Description: The Health Canada Environmental Contaminants website provides information on Health Canada's work on this issue.

Environmental Industries
URL: www.ic.gc.ca/eic/site/ea-ae.nsf/eng/Home
Description: This site offers information on the Canadian environment industry and highlights the efforts of the Government of Canada and its partners to promote the growth and increased competitiveness of the Canadian environment industry.

Environnement Canada
URL: www.ec.gc.ca
Description: Environment Canada's mandate is to preserve and enhance the quality of the natural environment; conserve Canada's renewable resources; conserve and protect Canada's water resources; forecast weather and environmental change; enforce rules relating to boundary waters; and coordinate environmental policies and programs for the federal government. The Department employs about 6000 people and has an annual budget of over half a billion dollars. Approximately 60 percent of its workforce and 80 percent of its budget is devoted to science and technology activities. Environment Canada's national headquarters are located in Gatineau, Quebec. It has offices in some 100 communities across the country.

ETV Canada
URL: www.etvcanada.ca
Description: Canada's Environmental Technology Verification Program was established in 1997 by Environment Canada to provide a mechanism for the independent performance verification of environmental technologies. ETV Canada is the independent verification organization which manages Canada's Environmental Technology Verification Program under a license agreement with Environment Canada. ETV Canada offers a reliable assessment process for verifying the environmental

performance claims associated with projects and programs, as well as technologies and technological processes.

Evergreen
URL: www.evergreen.ca
Description: Evergreen is a registered national charity founded in 1991. They are a national non-profit environmental organization with a mandate to bring nature to our cities through naturalization projects.

Friends of the Earth Canada (FoE)
URL: www.foecanada.org
Description: FoE is a voice for the environment, nationally and internationally, working with others to inspire the renewal of our communities and the earth, through research, education and advocacy. Affiliated with one of the largest international environmental networks — Friends of the Earth International — which has over 70 sister organizations around the world working for a healthy environment.

Great Lakes Fishery Commission
URL: www.glfc.org
Description: The Great Lakes Fishery Commission was established by the Convention on Great Lakes Fisheries between Canada and the United States in 1955. The Commission has two major responsibilities: To develop coordinated programs of research on the Great Lakes, and, on the basis of the findings, to recommend measures which will permit the maximum sustained productivity of stocks of fish of common concern; and To formulate and implement a program to eradicate or minimize sea lamprey populations in the Great Lakes.

Great Lakes Information Network (GLIN)
URL: www.great-lakes.net
Description: The Great Lakes Information Network (GLIN) is a partnership that provides one place online for people to find information relating to the binational Great Lakes-St. Lawrence region of North America. GLIN offers a wealth of data and information about the region's environment, economy, tourism, education and more.

Green Communities Canada
URL: www.gca.ca
Description: Green Communities Canada is a national network of community-based non-profit organizations that deliver innovative environmental programs and services, with a focus on household and community action. Green Communities Canada supports member organizations in working together to achieve environmental sustainability, including healthy ecosystems and communities, sustainable resource use, and clean air, water, and soil.

Green Ontario
URL: www.greenontario.org
Description: Green Ontario is a gateway site to Ontario's conservation and environmental movement. The site is produced and managed by The Conservation Council of Ontario. It is compiled through our ongoing research into Ontario's conservation issues and activities. The site structure reflects our efforts to promote a coordinated conservation movement across Ontario.

The Green Pages
URL: www.thegreenpages.ca
Description: Provides a web-based network where Canadian organizations and community groups can voice their opinions, share information and maintain valuable connections with like-minded people. An interactive resource for environmental information, highlighting the latest environmental news, events, and stories from across Canada in one place.

Greening Government
URL: www.greeninggovernment.gc.ca
Description: GreeningGovernment is an electronic information system developed by the Government of Canada for the World Wide Web. It is designed to provide a one-window access to sustainable development in government operations knowledge in the Government of Canada.

Greenpeace Canada
URL: www.greenpeace.org/canada
Description: Greenpeace is an independently funded organization that works to protect the environment. Greenpeace seeks to Protect biodiversity in all its forms; Prevent pollution of the Earth's oceans, land, air and fresh water; End all nuclear threats; Promote peace, global disarmament and non-violence.

Greenpower Canada
URL: www.greenpowercanada.org
Description: Greenpower Canada is a Toronto-based non-profit youth organization that inspires and empowers young people to take leadership locally and globally to achieve socio-economic development through conservation and environmental initiatives. Since its inception in 2001, Greenpower has reached thousands of youth through numerous conferences and workshops. Internationally, Greenpower has established a rural energy program to promote socio-economic development in Orissa, India as well supporting numerous community conservation awareness activities.

Intergovernmental Panel on Climate Change (IPCC)
URL: www.ipcc.ch
Description: The IPCC is a scientific intergovernmental body set up by the World Meteorological Organization (WMO) and by the United Nations Environment Programme (UNEP). The IPCC was established to provide the decision-makers and others interested in climate change with an objective source of information about climate change. The IPCC does not conduct any research nor does it monitor climate related data or parameters. Its role is to assess on a comprehensive, objective, open and transparent basis the latest scientific, technical and socio-economic literature produced worldwide relevant to the understanding of the risk of human-induced climate change, its observed and projected impacts and options for adaptation and mitigation.

International Joint Commission
URL: www.ijc.org/en/home/main_accueil.htm
Description: Canada and the United States created the International Joint Commission because they recognized that each country is affected by the other's actions in lake and river systems along the border. The two countries cooperate to manage these waters wisely and to protect them for the benefit of today's citizens and future generations.

International Union for Conservation of Nature (IUCN)
URL: www.iucn.org
Description: Helps the world find pragmatic solutions to our most pressing environment and development challenges. It supports scientific research, manages field projects all over the world and brings governments, non-government organizations, United Nations agencies, companies and local communities together to develop and implement policy, laws and best practice. IUCN is the world's oldest and largest global environmental network - a democratic membership union with more than 1,000 government and NGO member organizations, and almost 11,000 volunteer scientists in more than 160 countries. IUCN's work is supported by over 1,000 professional staff in 60 offices and hundreds of partners in public, NGO and private sectors around the world. The Union's headquarters are located in Gland, near Geneva, in Switzerland.

Learning for a Sustainable Future (LSF)
URL: www.lsf-lst.ca
Description: Founded in 1991 by a diverse group of youth, educators, business leaders, government and community members, Learning for a Sustainable Future is a non-profit Canadian organization created to integrate Education for Sustainable Development into the curricula at all grade levels in Canada.

LiveScience
URL: www.livescience.com
Description: LiveScience is a science news website run by Imaginova Corporation. Stories and editorial commentary are commonly syndicated to major news outlets, such as Yahoo!, MSNBC, AOL, and Fox News.

Manitoba Eco-Network
URL: www.mbeconetwork.org
Description: Manitoba Eco-Network promotes positive environmental action by connecting people and groups in our communities. Manitoba Eco-Network is an umbrella for environmental non-governmental organizations (ENGO's) throughout the province.

Manitoba Environment Companies Directory
URL: www.gov.mb.ca/trade/globaltrade/environ/allcompanies.html
Description: Manitoba environmental companies listed by sectors.

Meteorological Service of Canada (MSC)
URL: www.msc-smc.ec.gc.ca/contents_e.html
Description: The Meteorological Service of Canada is Canada's source for meteorological information. The Service monitors water quantities, provides information and conducts research on climate, atmospheric science, air quality, ice and other environmental issues, making it an important source of expertise in these areas.

MiningWatch Canada
URL: www.miningwatch.ca
Description: MiningWatch Canada (MWC) is a pan-Canadian initiative supported by environmental, social justice, Aboriginal and labour organisations from across the country. It addresses the urgent need for a co-ordinated public interest response to the threats to public health, water and air quality, fish and wildlife habitat and community interests posed by irresponsible mineral policies and practices in Canada and around the world.

My Sustainable Canada
URL: www.mysuscan.org
Description: My Sustainable Canada is a national not-for-profit organization that serves as a policy advocate for sustainable consumption solutions. The My Sustainable Canada Team embodies decades of experience with specific expertise in conducting policy research, managing programs and promoting behaviour changes that collectively inform our understanding of the sustainable consumption challenges facing Canada.

National Geographic
URL: http://environment.nationalgeographic.com/environment
Description: National Geographic's Mission Programs support critical expeditions and scientific fieldwork, encourage geography education for students, promote natural and cultural conservation, and inspire audiences through new media, vibrant exhibitions, and live events.

Natural Resources Canada (NRCan)
URL: www.nrcan-rncan.gc.ca
Description: Natural Resources Canada (NRCan) seeks to enhance the responsible development and use of Canada's natural resources and the competitiveness of Canada's natural resources products. We are an established leader in science and technology in the fields of energy, forests, and minerals and metals and use our expertise in earth sciences to build and maintain an up-to-date knowledge base of our landmass. NRCan develops policies and programs that enhance the contribution of the natural resources sector to the economy and improve the quality of life for all Canadians.

Natural Step Canada
URL: www.naturalstep.ca
Description: The Natural Step Canada is part of an international non-profit that uses a science-based, systems framework to help organizations and communities understand and move towards sustainability. TNS Canada engages in education, training, community outreach, advisory services, research.

Nature Canada
URL: www.naturecanada.ca
Description: Nature Canada is a member-based non-profit conservation organization. Their network includes 40,000 supporters and more than 350 naturalist organizations across Canada. Their mission is to protect and conserve wildlife and habitats in Canada by engaging people and advocating on behalf of nature.

Nature Challenge for Kids
URL: www.davidsuzuki.org/kids
Description: This David Suzuki Foundation website starts out with ten simple ways you can protect nature, followed by four challenge activities that offer first-hand experience with the natural world. The "Cool Links" page connects with other environmental websites.

Nature Conservancy of Canada
URL: www.natureconservancy.ca
Description: The Nature Conservancy of Canada (NCC) is Canada's leading national land conservation organization. We are a private, non-profit group that partners with corporate and individual landowners to achieve the direct protection of our most important natural treasures through property securement (donation, purchase, conservation agreement and the relinquishment of other legal interests in land) and long-term stewardship of our portfolio of properties. Since 1962, NCC and its partners have helped to conserve more than 2 million acres

(over 800,000 hectares) of ecologically significant land nationwide.

NatureServe Explorer
URL: www.natureserve.org/explorer
Description: Authoritative source for information on more than 70,000 plants, animals, and ecosystems of the United States and Canada. Explorer includes particularly in-depth coverage for rare and endangered species.

New Brunswick Environmental Network (NBEN)
URL: www.nben.ca
Description: The New Brunswick Environmental Network (NBEN), established in 1991, is a communication network that links together over 70 non-profit environmental organizations. The role of the NBEN is to improve communication and co-operation among environmental groups and between these groups, government and industry. The NBEN provides educational opportunities for its member and associate groups and encourages the growth of the environmental movement in New Brunswick. The NBEN is not an advocacy group and does not take positions on any issue.

Newfoundland and Labrador Environmental Network (NLEN)
URL: www.nlen.ca
Description: The Newfoundland and Labrador Environment Network was established in 1990 as a branch of the Canadian Environment Network. A non-advocacy member-based organization that serves more than 40 member groups throughout the province. The goal of the NLEN is to facilitate communication between non-government environmental organizations and assist with initiatives through non-advocacy means. We also work to position the NLEN as a point of contact for municipalities, government departments, media and the public on environmental issues.

Nova Scotia Environmental Network (NSEN)
URL: www.nsen.ca
Description: The Nova Scotia Environmental Network (NSEN) was founded in 1991 and is a registered non-profit organization under the Society Act of Nova Scotia. Their mission is to connect environmental and health organizations together to conserve and enhance our natural environment and achieve a sustainable future for Nova Scotia.

Ontario Environment Business Directory
URL: www.envirodirectory.on.ca
Description: Ontario's rapidly growing environment industry is recognized as a national and international leader in providing environmental goods and services. Companies with a facility in Ontario that provide environmental goods and services are invited to register on this Web site free of charge. This site includes a search feature and can be used to identify solution providers and strategic partners.

Ontario Environment Industry Association (ONEIA)
URL: www.oneia.ca
Description: Established in 1991, ONEIA is the business association representing the interests of the environment industry in Ontario. ONEIA has a membership of over 200 product and service companies, institutes, universities and governments.

Ontario Environment Network (OEN)
URL: www.oen.ca
Description: A non-profit, non-governmental network coordinating the efforts of over 500 Ontario environmental groups working towards and promoting protection of the environment. The OEN offers many services: we provide a central referral service for anyone seeking environmental information, organize workshops and conferences, publish resource materials, facilitate issue-specific caucuses, and maintain a database of Ontario environmental groups as well as a delegate database for public consultations.

Ontario Environmental Directory
URL: www.oen.ca/dir
Description: Here you can find hundreds of environmental groups, organizations, agencies and websites across Ontario, Canada. Search by name, location or area of interest.

Ottawa Environmental Grants Directory
URL: www.ottawa.ca/residents/funding/enviro/index_en.html
Description: The purpose of this directory is to enable community groups, school groups, environmental groups, non-profit groups, rural landowners, and farmers with the ability to ACT! This directory will aid groups in locating funding opportunities for a wide range of environmental projects.

Parks Canada
URL: www.pc.gc.ca
Description: On behalf of the people of Canada, they protect and present nationally significant examples of Canada's natural and cultural heritage and foster public understanding, appreciation and enjoyment in ways that ensure their ecological and commemorative integrity for present and future generations.

Pembina Institute
URL: www.pembina.org
Description: The Pembina Institute envisions a world in which our immediate and future needs are met in a manner that protects the earth's living systems; ensures clean air, land and water; prevents dangerous climate change, and provides for a safe and just global community. Their mission is to advance sustainable energy solutions through innovative research, education, consulting and advocacy.

People and Planet
URL: www.planetfriendly.net
Description: People and Planet is a unique gateway to environment, sustainability and conservation, across Canada and beyond. We provide Canada's largest green events calendar; Canada's most popular and effective green job listings; plus a growing number of green volunteer listings. In addition to this, our sites include thematic green gateways on themes ranging from climate change, to local/organic food and agriculture, sustainable living, green business, renewable energy, etc. We also do a lot of behind-the-scenes work to connect, empower, and bring people together over themes of environment and sustainability in Canada.

Pollution Probe
URL: www.pollutionprobe.org
Description: Pollution Probe is a Canadian environmental organization that defines environmental problems through research, to promote understanding through education, and presses for practical solutions through advocacy.

PollutionWatch
URL: www.pollutionwatch.org
Description: PollutionWatch is a source for information about pollutants that facilities release and transfer in communities including: toxic pollutants (such as benzene, lead, dioxins and furans); Criteria Air Contaminants (pollutants that cause smog and acid rain); and, greenhouse gases (air pollutants that lead to climate change).

Prince Edward Island Eco-Net
URL: www.peieconet.org
Description: The Prince Edward Island Eco-Net is a not-for-profit, non-governmental network of groups on Prince Edward Island that care about the environment. The organization was originally formed in 1991 and was formally incorporated as a co-operative in 2000. The PEI Eco-Net is non-advocacy and thus does not take stands on particular issues. Instead it helps its member groups with the work they do through the sharing of information and provision of administrative and technical support.

Resource Library for the Environment and the Law
URL: www.ecolawinfo.org
Description: This website contains the catalogue of their collection database, including numerous topical research files. The collection reflects the multidisciplinary nature of many environmental issues with a focus on environmental law and policy. Topic areas of particular strength include environmental assessment and land use planning, environmental law, protection of the Great Lakes, pesticides and other toxic substances, international trade and investment issues, environmental health, waste management and water quality and quantity.

Royal Canadian Geographical Society (RCGS)
URL: www.rcgs.org
Description: The Royal Canadian Geographical Society is dedicated to imparting a broader knowledge and deeper appreciation of Canada - its people and places, its natural and cultural heritage and its environmental, social and economic challenges. The Society is one of Canada's largest non-profit educational organizations and is funded primarily by membership fees and generous donations. The Society's Board of Governors and its program committees are comprised entirely of volunteers.

Saskatchewan Eco-Network (SEN)
URL: www.econet.sk.ca
Description: The Saskatchewan Eco Network (SEN) is a non-profit, non-government organization that connects environmentalists - within the province and across Canada - promoting active networking among member groups. SEN can be considered Saskatchewan's "one-stop shopping centre" for the general public, journalists, and government departments and agencies looking for information on environmental issues and for contacting members of environmental groups.

Saskatchewan's Green Directory
URL: www.saskatchewangreendirectory.org
Description: There's a growing awareness in Saskatchewan of the environmental impacts of what we buy. People want to choose well, but it's hard to get information about what's available, or where to purchase. The Green Directory is designed to provide that information.

Science and Technology for Canadians
URL: www.science.gc.ca
Description: Lists websites of interest to Canadians.

Secrétariat des organismes environnementaux du Québec
URL: www.soeq.org
Description: Le Secrétariat des organismes environnementaux du Québec a pour objectif de susciter la création de liens entre les organisations environnementales désireuses de travailler sur des enjeux communs à l'échelle québécoise, canadienne et internationale. Le Secrétariat assume en ce sens des fonctions similaires à ceux des dix autres réseaux provinciaux et territoriaux du Canada associés au Réseau Canadien de l'environnement (RCEN). Son mandat, ses activités, les ressources et les services qu'il offre aux groupes membres sont menés avec le souci constant de respecter les champs d'expertise des autres groupes et réseaux du Québec.

Sierra Club Canada
URL: www.sierraclub.ca
Description: Sierra Club Canada is a member-based organization that empowers people to protect, restore and enjoy a healthy and safe planet. Sierra Club of Canada has been active in Canada since 1963. The national office of Sierra Club of Canada was established in Ottawa in 1989. Sierra Club of Canada has several major national campaigns with four program areas: Health and Environment, Protecting Biodiversity, Atmosphere and Energy, and Transition to a Sustainable Economy.

Silent Spring Institute
URL: www.silentspring.org
Description: Silent Spring Institute builds on a unique partnership of scientists, physicians, public health advocates, and community activists to identify and break the links between the environment and women's health, especially breast cancer.

Society Promoting Environmental Conservation (SPEC)
URL: www.spec.bc.ca
Description: Founded in 1969, The Society Promoting Environmental Conservation (SPEC) is a non-profit charitable organization that addresses environmental issues in British Columbia, with a particular focus on urban communities in Lower Mainland and the Georgia Basin. Works to raise public awareness on environmental issues and encourage policies and practices that lead to urban sustainability.

Species at Risk Public Registry
URL: www.sararegistry.gc.ca
Description: The Public Registry is your source for news, information, and documents related to species at risk in Canada. This web site has been designed to help you better understand Canada's approach to protecting and recovering species at risk, learn about species at risk and what's being done to help them, and get involved in decision making and recovery activities. The Public Registry fulfills the requirement under the Species at Risk Act (SARA) for the Minister of the Environment to establish a public registry for the purpose of facilitating access to SARA-related documents.

Statistics Canada
URL: www.statcan.gc.ca
Description: Statistics Canada, a member of the Industry Portfolio, produces statistics that help Canadians better understand their country-its population, resources, economy, society and culture.

Stewardship Canada
URL: www.stewardshipcanada.ca
Description: The Stewardship Canada web portal exists to support a stewardship knowledge network in response to the premise that information is essential to good stewardship.

Tree Canada
URL: www.treecanada.ca
Description: Tree Canada is a not-for-profit, charitable organization established in 1992. Under the direction of a 10-member volunteer Board of Directors, Tree Canada provides education, technical assistance, resources and financial support through working partnerships to encourage Canadians to plant and care for trees in rural and urban areas.

Tree of Life
URL: http://tolweb.org/tree/phylogeny.html
Description: The Tree of Life Web Project is a collection of information about biodiversity compiled collaboratively by hundreds of expert and amateur contributors. Its goal is to contain a page with pictures, text, and other information for every species and for each group of organisms, living or extinct.

United Nations Environment Programme (UNEP)
URL: www.unep.org
Description: Their mission is to provide leadership and encourage partnership in caring for the environment by inspiring, informing, and enabling nations and peoples to improve their quality of life without compromising that of future generations.

USC Canada
URL: http://usc-canada.org
Description: USC Canada promotes vibrant family farms, strong rural communities, and healthy ecosystems around the world. With engaged Canadians and partners in Africa, Asia, and Latin America, we support programs, training, and policies that strengthen biodiversity, food sovereignty, and the rights of those at the heart of resilient food systems - women, indigenous peoples, and small-scale farmers.

Voteforenvironment
URL: www.voteforenvironment.ca
Description: VoteForEnvironment.ca was designed by Canadians who believe what the vast majority of the world's scientists have told us. That we are out of time and we must start to reduce our fossil fuel pollution now to save the planet from dangerous climate change.

Western Canada Wilderness Committee
URL: www.wildernesscommittee.org
Description: The Western Canada Wilderness Committee was founded in BC in 1980, and is now the largest membership-based, citizen-funded wilderness preservation organization in Canada. Across the country, the Wilderness Committee has more than 30,000 members and an additional support base of 30,000 donors.

Wildlife conservation Society Canada (WCS)
URL: www.wcscanada.org
Description: WCS Canada was incorporated as a conservation organization in Canada in July 2004. Its mission is to save wildlife and wildlands by improving our understanding of and seeking solutions to critical problems that threaten key species and large wild ecosystems throughout Canada. It implements and supports comprehensive field studies that gather information on wildlife needs and then seeks to resolve key conservation problems by working with a broad array of stakeholders, including local community members, conservation groups, regulatory agencies, and commercial interests. It also provides technical assistance and biological expertise to local groups and agencies that lack the resources to tackle conservation dilemmas. Major issues addressed to date include protected-area design, wildlife monitoring and recovery, ecosystem restoration, integrated landscape management and community-based conservation.

Wildlife Preservation Canada
URL: www.wptc.org
Description: Wildlife Preservation Canada saves animals on the brink of extinction. Since 1985, they've been saving critically endangered species - species whose numbers in the wild are so low that a great deal more than habitat protection is required to recover them. Their programs include research, captive breeding, reintroduction, habitat stewardship, and public education - each a crucial part of species recovery.

World Environment Library
URL: www.nzdl.org/fast-cgi-bin/library?a=p&p=about&c=envl
Description: Contains 400 publications (45,000 pages) of ideas and solutions in the fields of Agriculture, Biodiversity, Climate Change, Environmental Impact Assessment, Energy, Health, Natural Resources, Policy, Sustainable Development, Waste Management and Water.

World Wildlife Fund Canada
URL: http://wwf.ca
Also Known As: WWF-Canada
Description: World Wildlife Fund Canada (WWF-Canada) was founded in 1967 by Senator Alan MacNaughton, and has become one of the country's leading conservation organizations, enjoying the active support of more than 150,000 Canadians. As a member of the WWF global network, they actively contribute to the achievement of the organization's mission: To stop the degradation of the planet's natural environment and to build a future in which humans live in harmony with nature.

Worldwatch Institute
URL: www.worldwatch.org
Description: The Worldwatch Institute is an independent research organization recognized by opinion leaders around the world for its accessible, fact-based analysis of critical global issues. Its mission is to generate and promote insights and ideas that empower decision makers to build an ecologically sustainable society that meets human needs.

Yukon Environmental Network (YEN)
URL: http://yukonenvironetwork.blogspot.com
Description: The Yukon Environmental Network is a not-for-profit, non-governmental network of groups in the Yukon that care about the environment.

Zoocheck Canada
URL: www.zoocheck.com
Description: Zoocheck Canada is a national animal protection charity established in 1984 to promote and protect the interests and well-being of wild animals. Zoocheck has also provided vital support to the efforts of individuals, organizations and governments throughout Canada and around the world as they work to address wildlife problems and issues in their own regions.

SECTION 5
Master Indexes

Included in this section:
- *Entry Name Index* 1221
- *Executive Name Index* 1261

Entry Name Index

A

A&A Environmental Consultants Inc., 63
A&C Produits Chimiques Americains Ltée, 63
A. A. Boscariol and Associates Limited, 63
A. Lanfranco & Associates Inc., 63
A.C. Carbone Canada Inc., 63
A.C. Plastiques Canada, 63
A.D. Allen Chemistry Library, 1156
A.H. Lundberg Systems Ltd., 63
A.H. Roy & Associates Ltd., 64
A1 Sewage Services (1989) Limited, 64
AA Environmental & Associates, 64
AAA Petroleum Contracting Ltd., 64
AADCO Automotive Inc., 64
AB Mechanical Ltd., 64
Abandonrite, 64
ABB Inc. (Canada), 64
ABBA Pump Parts & Service, 64
Abbeywood Associates Inc., 64
Abbotsford, 679
Abbotsford Campus Library, 1110
Abbott Laboratories Limited, 1184
Abbott Strategies, 64
ABCO Industries Ltd., 64
Abcott Construction Ltd., 65
ABGG Technologies Inc., 65
Abitibi, 746
Abitibi-Consolidated Inc., 65
Abitibi-Ouest, 746
ABL Environmental Consultants, 65
Aboriginal Affairs, 580
Aboriginal Affairs Secretariat, 584
Aboriginal Affairs Unit, 632
The Aboriginal Funds for Species at Risk, 1045
Aboriginal Policy & Governance, 528
Aboriginal Policy & Operations, 659
Aboriginal Relations Branch, 587
Abydoz Environmental, 65
AC Environmental Services, 65
AC Plastiques Canada Inc., 65
Academic & Experience Requirements Committee of the Association of Ontario Land Surveyors, 631
Acadia Consultants & Inspectors Ltd., 65
Acadia Environmental Society, 813
Acadia University, 1205, 1137, 1033
Acadian Entomological Society, 813
ACAP Saint John, 1042
Accommodation Services, 588
Accurassay Laboratories, 65
Accurate Industrial Waste Limited, 66
Accutest Laboratories Ltd., 66
Accuworx Inc., 66
ACDEG International Inc., 66
ACE Vegetation Control Service Ltd., 66
Acer Environmental Services Ltd., 66
ACG Technology Ltd., 66
Acklands-Grainger Inc., 66
Ackroyd LLP Barristers & Solicitors, 1054
ACM Environmental Corporation, 66
Acme Engineering Products Ltd., 66
ACME Vacuum Cleaner Co. Ltd., 67
ACO Container Systems Ltd., 67
Acorus Restoration Native Plant Nursery, 67
Acoustic Solutions Ltd., 67
Acoustical Association Ontario, 813
Acquisitions Branch, 558
Acres & Associated Environmental Ltd., 67
Acsion Industries Inc., 67
Action Nord Terre, 813
Action on Smoking & Health, 813
Action to Restore a Clean Humber, 813
Action Volunteers for Animals, 813
Action: Environment, 813
Activation Laboratories Ltd., 67
Active Chemicals Ltd., 67
Acton, 746
Acuren Inc., 1104
Acute & Emergency Services, 659
Addiction & Mental Health Services Division, 594

Addictions Foundation of Manitoba, 588
Addy Environmental Services Inc., 68
Adhawk Communications Inc., 68
ADI Group, 1127
ADI Group Inc., 68
Adjala-Tosorontio, 724
Adkinson & Associates, 68
Administration & Finance Division, 587
Administrative Services Division, 589
Adult Community Corrections, 621
Advance Engineered Products Ltd., 68
Advance Laboratories Ltd., 69
Advanced Biotechnology Inc., 69
Advanced Coolant Technologies Inc., 69
Advanced Environmental Water Technologies Inc., 69
Advanced Foods & Materials Network, 813
Advanced Technology Industries Division, 563
Adventis Technologies, 69
Adventus Canada Inc., 69
Advertising Review Board, 626
Advisory Council on Drinking Water Quality & Testing Standards, 623
Advisory Council on the Status of Women, 641
Advisory Council on Workplace Safety & Health, 589
Aearo Canada Ltd., 69
AECOM Canada Ltd., 69
Aecon Group Inc., 71
Aercoustics Engineering Limited, 71
AERDE Environmental Research, 71
Aeroflo Inc., 71
Aerospace Engineering Test Establishment, 1103
Aerospace Industries Association of Canada, 813
Aerospace Technology Campus, 1115
Aerospace, Defence & Marine Branch, 543
AeroTek Manufacturing Ltd., 71
Aerzen Canada Surpresseurs Compresseurs inc., 71
AESL Instrumentation inc., 72
AET Group Inc., 72
Aevitas Inc., 72
AF Pollution Abatement Systems Inc., 72
Affaires économiques internationales, 648
Affaires économiques régionales, 648
Affaires policières, 653
African Coelacanth Ecosystem Programme, 813
African Violet Society of Canada, 813
African Wildlife Foundation, 813, 1040
Ag EnviroTech Inc., 72
Ag-West Bio Inc., 72
Ag-WestBio Inc., 1189
AGAT Laboratories Ltd., 72
Agence d'évaluation des technologies et des modes d'intervention en santé, 652
Agence de l'efficacité énergétique, 650
Agencies Division, 634
Aggregate Producers' Association of Ontario, 813
AGM Steel Industries Ltd., 73
AGO Environmental Electronics Ltd., 73
Agra Earth & Environmental Limited, 1104
AGRECOM inc., 73
Agreements Management, 584
Agri-Business Expansion Division, 565
Agri-Environment, 585
Agri-Environment Policy Bureau, 510
Agri-Environment Services Branch, 507
Agri-Food & Rural Development Division, 585
Agri-Food Council, 656
Agri-Food Innovation & Adaptation, 585
Agri-Food Laboratories, 73
Agri-Industry Development & Innovation Division, 585
AGRI-SX, 73
AGRICORP, 619
Agricultural Alliance of New Brunswick, 813
Agricultural Groups Concerned About Resources & the Environment, 814
Agricultural Implements Board, 656
Agricultural Institute of Canada, 814
Agricultural Institute of Canada Foundation, 814, 1043
Agricultural Insurance Corporation, 636
Agricultural Land Commission, 574

Agricultural Producers Association of Saskatchewan, 814
Agricultural Research Institute of Ontario, 619
Agricultural Societies, 584
Agricultural Technology Centre, 73
Agriculture & Agri-Food Canada, 507, 1147
Agriculture & Agri-Food Development, 637
Agriculture & Bio-Economy Division, 591
Agriculture Branch, 665
Agriculture Financial Services Corporation, 564
Agriculture Operations, 574
Agriculture Policy & Regulatory Division, 637
Agriculture Producers Association of New Brunswick, 1127
Agriculture Research Division, 564
Agriculture Resource Division, 637
Agriculture Services, 609
Agriculture, Food & Rural Affairs Tribunal, 619
Agrifoods Branch, 603
Agrium Inc., 1099
Agrodev Canada Inc., 73
Agrosysts Ltée, 73
AIC Associated Industrial Controls Ltd., 73
AIC Sullivan's Environmental Services, 73
Aikins, MacAulay & Thorvaldson LLP, 1063
AIM Environmental Group, 74
Aimco Solrec Ltd., 74
AimGlobal Technologies Company, Inc., 74
AiMS Environmental, 74
Ainley Group, 74
Ainsworth Inc., 74
Air & Waste Management Association, 814
Air Control Engineering Inc., 74
Air Liquide Canada Ltée, 74
Air Movement Services Ltd., 75
Air Phaser Environmental Ltd., 75
Air Policy & Climate Change Branch, 624
Air Products Canada Ltd., 75
Air Quality Branch, 612
Air Quality Management Section, 586
Air Solutions Inc., 75
Air Trac Corp., 75
Air Transport Association of Canada, 814
AIRCOM Technologies Inc., 75
Aircraft Appliances & Equipment Ltd., 75
Aircraft Certification, 1147
Aircraft Services Directorate, 1147
Aird & Berlis LLP, 1072
Airdrie, 670
Airmaster Sales Ltd., 75
Airports, 608
AirScience Inc., 76
Airspace Action on Smoking & Health, 814
Airtechni Inc., 76
Airtest Technologies Inc., 76
Airzone One Ltd., 76
Ajax, 537, 705
Aker Chemetics, 76
Aker Kvaerner Chemetics Inc., 1117
Aker Metals (Toronto), 76
Akerley Campus, 1135
AKZO Nobel Chemicals Ltd., 76
Alameda Agricultural Society, 815
Alan A. Smith Inc., 76
Alan Willis & Associates, 76
ALARA Industrial Hygiene Services Ltd., 76
Alaron Instruments Inc., 76
Alberni Valley Outdoor Club, 815
Alberni-Clayoquot, 676
Alberta & Northwest Territories Lung Association, 815
Alberta & Territories Regional Office, 508
Alberta Aboriginal Relations, 563
Alberta Advanced Education & Technology, 562
Alberta Agricultural Economics Association, 815
Alberta Agricultural Research Institute, 562
Alberta Agriculture & Rural Development, 563
Alberta Apprenticeship & Industry Training Board, 563
Alberta Aquaculture Association, 815
Alberta Association of Agricultural Societies, 815
Alberta Association of Landscape Architects, 815
Alberta Association of Municipal Districts & Counties, 815

Entry Name Index

Alberta Beef Producers, 815
Alberta Biodiversity Monitoring Institute, 1199
Alberta Bottle Depot Association, 816
Alberta Branches, 512
Alberta Building Envelope Council (South), 816
Alberta Camping Association, 816
Alberta Canola Producers Commission, 816
Alberta Capital Region Wastewater Commission, 757
Alberta Centre for Boreal Studies, 816
Alberta Centre for Livestock Genomics, 564
Alberta Centre for Surface Engineering & Science, 1199
Alberta Chamber of Resources, 816
Alberta Children's Hospital Library, 1099
Alberta Cogenerators Council, 816
Alberta Community Development, 1110
Alberta Conservation Association, 816, 1039
Alberta Conservation Tillage Society II, 816
Alberta Construction Association, 816
Alberta Council on Admissions & Transfer, 563
Alberta Dept. of Energy, 1099
Alberta Development Officers Association, 816
Alberta Economic Development Authority, 566
Alberta Ecotrust Foundation, 1039
Alberta Emergency Management Agency, 571
Alberta Employment & Immigration, 566
Alberta Energy, 567
Alberta Environment, 568
Alberta Environmental Appeals Board, 567
Alberta Environmental Network, 1213, 816
Alberta Environmental Rubber Products Inc., 77
Alberta Falconry Association, 816
Alberta Farm Fresh Producers Association, 816
Alberta Farmers' Market Association, 817
Alberta Film Commission, 572
Alberta Fish & Game Association, 817
Alberta Forest Products Association, 817
Alberta Forestry Association, 817
Alberta Foundation for the Arts, 572
Alberta Government Library, 1104
Alberta Grain Council, 564
Alberta Greenhouse Growers Association, 817
Alberta Greens, 817
Alberta Health & Wellness, 568
Alberta Health Services, 569
Alberta Historical Resources Foundation, 572, 817
Alberta Hospital Edmonton, 1104
Alberta Housing & Urban Affairs, 569
Alberta Human Rights & Citizenship Commission, 572
Alberta Infrastructure, 569
Alberta Ingenuity Centre for In Situ Energy, 1199
Alberta Ingenuity Fund, 568
Alberta Innovates - Health Solutions, 562
Alberta Institute of Agrologists, 817
Alberta International & Intergovernmental Relations, 570
Alberta Irrigation Projects Association, 818
Alberta Justice, Office of the Chief Medical Examiner, 1104
Alberta Lake Management Society, 818
Alberta Land Surveyors' Association, 818, 1104
Alberta Learning Information Service, 563
Alberta Livestock & Meat Agency, 564
Alberta Lottery Fund, 1039
Alberta Medical Association, 818
Alberta Milk, 818
Alberta Motor Transport Association, 818
Alberta Municipal Affairs, 570
Alberta Municipal Government Board, 570
Alberta Native Plant Council, 818
Alberta Occupational Health Nurses Association, 818
Alberta Organic Producers Association, 818
Alberta Plastics Recycling Association, 818
Alberta Prion Research Institute, 562
Alberta Professional Outfitters Society, 819
Alberta Public Affairs Bureau, 571
Alberta Public Health Association, 819
Alberta Real Estate Foundation, 1039
Alberta Recreation & Parks Association, 819
Alberta Recycling Management Authority, 567
Alberta Region, 534
Alberta Research Council, 569, 1104
Alberta Rural Municipal Administrators Association, 819
Alberta Safety Council, 819
Alberta Science & Research Authority, 562
Alberta Service Alberta, 571
Alberta Society of Professional Biologists, 819
Alberta Society of Surveying & Mapping Technologies, 819

Alberta Special Areas Board, 571
Alberta Speleological Society, 820, 1099
Alberta Sport, Recreation, Parks & Wildlife Foundation, 572, 1039
Alberta Sulphur Research Ltd., 1199, 820
Alberta Sustainable Resource Development, 571
Alberta Tourism, Parks, Recreation & Culture, 572
Alberta Transportation, 573
Alberta Trappers' Association, 820
Alberta Underwater Council, 820
Alberta Urban Municipalities Association, 820
Alberta Used Oil Management Association, 567
Alberta Utilities Commission, 567
Alberta Utilities Consumer Advocate, 573
Alberta Water & Wastewater Operators Association, 820
Alberta Water Council, 820
Alberta Water Research Institute, 1199
Alberta Water Well Drilling Association, 820
Alberta Wilderness Association, 820
Alberta Wilderness Resource Centre, 1099
Alberta Workers' Compensation Board, 566
Alberta-NWT-Nunavut, 541
Alberta-Pacific Forest Industries Inc., 77
Alcan International Ltée., 1168
Alchemist Transport Inc., 77
ALCO Gas & Oil Production Equipment Ltd., 77
Alcohol & Gaming Commission of Ontario, 626
Alcohol & Gaming Division, 612
Alcohol Countermeasure Systems Corp., 77
Alcore Fabricating Corp., 77
Aldergrove Daylily Society, 820
Aldworth Engineering Inc., 77
Alenag Brokers, 77
Alex Fraser Research Forest, 1200
Alex Milne Associates Ltd., 77
Alexander Boome Consulting Engineering, Ltd., 78
Alexander Graham Bell Historic Site of Canada, 552
Alexander Holburn Beaudin & Lang, LLP, 1057
Aleza Lake Research Forest Society, 1200
Alfa Laval Inc., 78
Alfa Plastics Inc., 78
Algoma Manitoulin Environmental Awareness, 820
Algoma University College, 1154
Algonquin College of Applied Arts & Technology, 1147
Algonquin Forestry Authority - Huntsville, 631
Algonquin Forestry Authority - Pembroke, 631
Algonquin Power Income Fund, 78
Alimentation, 646
All Treat Farms Limited, 78
All Waste Removal Inc., 78
ALL-TECH Environmental Services Ltd., 78
All-Weld Company Limited, 79
All-Wood Fibre Ltd., 79
Allan Fyfe Equipment Limited, 79
Alldec Trading Ltd., 79
AllerGen NCE Inc., 820
Allergy Asthma Information Association, 821
Allergy, Asthma & Immunology Society of Ontario, 821
Allergy/Asthma Information Association, 1164
Alliance Envelope Ltd., 79
Alliance for Sustainability, 821
Alliance for the Wild Rockies, 821
Alliance of Foam Packaging Recyclers, 821
Allianz Madvac Inc., 79
Alloy Fab Ltd., 79
Allyn & Betty Taylor Library, 1143
Alma, 733
Alnor Industries Ltd., 79
Alnwick-Haldimand, 724
Alouette Field Naturalists, 821
Alpha Controls & Instrumentation, 79
Alpha Industrial Services, 79
AlphaNuclear Company, 80
Alpine Club Environment Fund, 1039
Alpine Environmental Ltd., 80
Alpine Garden Club of BC, 821
Alrange Container Services, 80
ALS Environmental, 80
Alsek Renewable Resource Council, 665
Alstom Canada Inc., 80
Alta-Fab Structures Ltd., 81
Altamar International Inc., 81
ALTECH Environmental Consulting Ltd., 81
ALTECH Technology Systems Inc., 81
Altek Power Corporation, 81
Alternative Energy & Market Development, 593

Alternative Energy News, 1213
Alternative Fuel Systems (2004) Inc., 81
Alternative Service Delivery Secretariat, 581
Alternatives, 1213
Alternatives Journal: Canadian Environmental Ideas & Action, 1193
Altus Capital Planning Inc., 81
Aluma Systems Inc., 82
The Aluminum Association, 821
Amaircare Corporation, 82
Amalgamated Conservation Society, 821
Amberg Corp. - Environmental & Regulatory Consultants, 82
Ambio Biofiltration Ltd., 82
Ambler & Co. Inc., 82
AMC - Agricultural Manufacturers of Canada, 822
AMEC, 82
AMEC Inc., 1099
American Association for the Advancement of Science, 822
American Association of Botanical Gardens & Arboreta, 822
American Association of Bovine Practitioners, 822
The American Association of Petroleum Geologists, 822
American Birding Association, 822
American Cave Conservation Association, 822
American Council for an Energy-Efficient Economy, 823
American Farmland Trust, 823
American Fisheries Society, 823
American Forest & Paper Association, 823
American Industrial Hygiene Association, 823
American Iron & Steel Institute, 823
American Lung Association, 823
American Medical Association, 823
American National Standards Institute, 532
American Ornithologists' Union, 824
American Planning Association, 824
American Plastics Council, 824
American Public Works Association, 824
American Rivers, 824
American Society for Environmental History, 824
American Society of Heating, Refrigerating & Air Conditioning Engineers, 824
American Society of Mechanical Engineers, 824
American Society of Mining & Reclamation, 825
American Society of Plant Biologists, 826
American Society of Plumbing Engineers, 826
American Society of Safety Engineers, 826
American Water Resources Association, 826
American Water Works Association, 826
American Wildlands, 827
American Zoo & Aquarium Association, 827
Americas Strategy, 531
AMETEK Process Instruments, 84
Amherst, 537
Amherstburg, 705
Les AmiEs de la Terre de Québec, 827
Les Amis du Jardin botanique de Montréal, 827
Amity Plastics Ltd., 84
AMKO Systems Inc., 84
Amos, 733
AN-GEO Environmental Consultants Ltd., 84
Anachem Ltd., 84
Anachemia Canada Inc., 85
Anadarko Canada Corp., 1099
Analyse et expertise régionales, 647
Analytical Services Branch, 594
The Anchorage, 597
Anco Chemicals Inc., 85
Anderson Water Systems, 85
Anderson, Greg W.. Barrister, Solicitor, Notary, 1071
André Simard et associés ltée, 85
Andrews' Scenic Acres, 85
Andritz Bird, 85
Anex Distributors Ltd., 86
Angus, Butler Engineering Ltd., 86
Animal Alliance of Canada, 827
Animal Care Review Board, 621
Animal Defence & Anti-Vivisection Society of BC, 827
Animal Defence League of Canada, 827
Animal Nutrition Association of Canada, 827
Animal Welfare Foundation of Canada, 827, 1043
Annapolis County, 696
Annapolis Field Naturalist Society, 828
Annapolis Valley Peat Moss Co. Ltd., 86
Anrep Krieg Desilets Gravelle Ltd., 86
Antarctic & Southern Ocean Coalition, 828
Antelope Land Services Inc., 86

Entry Name Index

Anthrafilter Media & Coal Ltd., 86
Anticorrosion Materials & Technologies Inc., 86
Antigonish, 537
Antigonish County, 696
Antoine-Labelle, 747
Antymniuk & Antymniuk, 1063
Apex Geoscience Ltd., 86
Apex Industries Inc., 86
Apollo Environmental Systems Corporation, 87
Les Appalaches, 749
Appeal Panel for Home Care, 588
Appeals Commission for Alberta Workers' Compensation, 566
Appin Associates, 87
Applied Aquatic Research Ltd., 87
Applied Groundwater Research Ltd., 87
Applied Oxidation Technologies Inc., 87
Applied Research & Development Branch, 633
Applied Science Technologists & Technicians of British Columbia, 828
Apprenticeship & Occupational Certification Board, 595
Approvals Branch, 593
APS Aviation Inc., 87
Aqua Dam & Diversion Ltd., 87
Aqua Data Inc., 87
Aqua Tech Sales & Marketing Inc., 88
Aqua Terre Solutions Inc., 88
Aqua-Guard Spill Response Inc., 88
Aqua-Pak Styro Containers Ltd., 88
Aqua-Plus, 88
Aqua-Rehab Inc., 88
Aqua-Tex Scientific Consulting Ltd., 88
Aquaculture, 639
Aquaculture & Fisheries Research Initiative Inc., 637
Aquaculture Association of Canada, 828
Aquaculture Association of Nova Scotia, 828
Aquaculture Branch, 599
Aquaculture Collaborative Research and Development Program, 1203
AquaMetrix Inc., 88
AquaNet - Network in Aquaculture, 828
Aquareal Water Systems Inc., 88
AQUASOL EnviroTech Ltd., 89
Aquasolution Technologies Inc., 89
Aquateck Ltd., 89
Aquaterre Inc., 89
Aquatic Ecosystems Research Laboratory, 1200
Aquatic Life Ltd., 89
AquaTox Testing & Consulting Inc., 89
ARAM Systems Ltd., 89
Arbrux Limited, 89
ARC Geobac Group Inc., 89
ARC Vegreville Library & Information Centre, 1109
ArcelorMittal Dofasco, 90
Arch Industries, 90
Archaeological Institute of America, 828
Archer Chemical, 90
Archipelago Marine Research Ltd., 90
The Architectural Conservancy of Ontario, 828
Architectural Heritage Society of Saskatchewan, 828
Architecture & Fine Arts Library, 1122
Archives of Ontario, 626
Arctic Council, 763, 829
Arctic Goose, 525
Arctic Goose Joint Venture, 763
Arctic Institute of North America, 1199, 829
ArcticNet Inc., 829
Ardgowan National Historic Site of Canada, 552
Ardenteuil, 747
Argentine Republic, 767
Argo Protective Coatings Inc., 90
Argus Telecom International Inc., 90
ARISE Technologies Corporation, 90
Arjay Engineering Ltd., 91
Ark Envirotech Inc., 91
ARK II, 829
Arlat Technology, 91
Armatek Controls Limited, 91
Armstrong Engineering & Land Surveying Inc., 91
Armstrong Monitoring Corp., 91
Armtec Construction Products, 91
Arnprior, 537
Arpi's Industries Canada Ltd., 92
Arrakis Consultants Inc., 92
Array Systems Computing Inc., 93
Arrow Speed Controls Ltd., 93

Arrowsmith Naturalists, 829
Art Gallery of Ontario, 621
Arthabaska, 747
Artillery Park National Historic Site of Canada, 554
Arts Development, 598
Arusha Centre Society, 829
Asbeguard Equipment Inc., 93
ASCO Canada, 93
Ashland Canada, 93
Ashtead Technology Rentals, 93
ASI Group Ltd., 93
Asia Pacific Foundation of Canada, 575, 829
Asia Pacific Trade Council, 575
Asia Pacific, Trade, & Investment Division, 575
Asia-Pacific Centre for Environmental Law, 829
ASL Environmental Sciences Inc., 94
Assaynet Canada Inc., 94
Assembly of First Nations, 829
Assessment & Planning Appeal Board, 594
Assessment Appeal Board, 663
Assessment Appeal Tribunal of the Northwest Territories, 607
Assessment Services, 615
Asset Management Division, 608
Assets Management Directorate, 534
Assiniboia, 540
Assiniboine Community College, 1121
Assistant Deputy Minister & Chief Engineer Office, 597
Associated Agencies, Boards & Commissions, 616
Associated Engineering Group Ltd., 94
Associated Environmental Site Assessors of Canada, 829
Associated Tube Industries, 94
Association canadienne des sciences régionales, 830
Association chasse et pêche du Lac Brébeuf, 830
Association d'isolation du Québec, 831
Association de chasse et pêche nordique, inc., 831
Association de l'exploration minière de Québec, 831
Association de la santé et de la sécurité des pâtes et papiers et des industries de la forêt du Québec, 831
Association des Allergologues et Immunologues du Québec, 831
Association des Aménagistes Régionaux du Québec, 831
Association des architectes paysagistes du Québec, 831
Association des chefs en sécurité incendie du Québec, 831
Association des consultants et laboratoires experts, 831
Association des directeurs généraux des municipalités du Québec, 831
Association des embouteilleurs d'eau du Québec, 831
Association des enterprises spécialiseés en eau du Québec, 832
Association des entomologistes amateurs du Québec inc., 832
Association des expositions agricoles du Québec, 832
Association des fermières de l'Ontario, 832
Association des ingénieurs municipaux du Québec, 832
Association des ingénieurs-conseils du Québec, 832
Association des ingénieurs-professeurs des sciences appliquées, 832
Association des jardineries du Québec, 832
Association des jardins du Québec, 832
Association des jeunes ruraux du Québec, 832
Association des médecins biochimistes du Québec, 833
Association des médecins spécialistes en santé communautaire du Québec, 833
Association des microbiologistes du Québec, 833
Association des technologues en agroalimentaire, 833
Association du camionnage du Québec inc., 833
Association for Mineral Exploration British Columbia, 833, 1117
Association for Mountain Parks Protection & Enjoyment, 833
Association francophone pour le savoir, 833
Association médicale du Québec, 833
Association minière du Québec, 834
Association of Alberta Agricultural Fieldmen, 834
Association of American Geographers, 834
Association of Applied Geochemists, 834
Association of British Columbia Forest Professionals, 834
Association of British Columbia Land Surveyors, 834
Association of Canada Lands Surveyors, 834
Association of Canadian Ergonomists, 834
Association of Canadian Port Authorities, 834
Association of Canadian Universities for Northern Studies, 834
Association of Certified Engineering Technicians & Technologists of Prince Edward Island, 835
Association of Consulting Engineering Companies - New Brunswick, 835
Association of Engineering Technicians & Technologists of Newfoundland & Labrador, 835
Association of Environmental Engineering & Science Professors, 835

Association of Equipment Manufacturers - Canada, 835
Association of Fish & Wildlife Agencies, 835
Association of Great Lakes Outdoor Writers, 835
Association of Independent Corrugated Converters, 836
Association of International Automobile Manufacturers of Canada, 836
Association of Local Public Health Agencies, 836
Association of Major Power Consumers in Ontario, 836
Association of Manitoba Land Surveyors, 836
Association of Manitoba Municipalities, 836
Association of Municipal Administrators of New Brunswick, 836
Association of Municipal Administrators, Nova Scotia, 836
Association of Municipalities of Ontario, 836, 1156
Association of New Brunswick Land Surveyors, 837
Association of Newfoundland Land Surveyors, 837
Association of Nova Scotia Land Surveyors, 837
Association of Ontario Land Economists, 837
Association of Ontario Land Surveyors, 631, 837
Association of Postconsumer Plastic Recyclers, 837
Association of Power Producers of Ontario, 837
Association of Prince Edward Island Land Surveyors, 837
Association of Professional Biology, 837
Association of Professional Community Planners of Saskatchewan, 838
Association of Professional Engineers & Geoscientists of Saskatchewan, 838
Association of Professional Engineers of the Yukon Territory, 838, 839
Association of Professional Engineers, Geologists & Geophysicists of the Northwest Territories & Nunavut, 839
Association of Professional Geoscientists of Ontario, 839
Association of Quantity Surveyors of Alberta, 839
Association of Registered Professional Foresters of New Brunswick, 839
The Association of Science and Engineering Technology Professionals of Alberta, 840
Association of Supervisors of Public Health Inspectors (Ontario), 840
Association of the Chemical Profession of Ontario, 840
Association of University Forestry Schools of Canada, 840
Association of World Citizens & World Citizens Foundation, 840
Association of Yukon Communities, 840
Association paritaire pour la santé et la sécurité du travail - Services automobiles, 840, 841
Association pour la prévention de la contamination de l'air et du sol, 841
Association pour la protection des intérêts des consommateurs de la Côte-Nord, 841
Association pour la santé publique du Québec, 841
Association professionnelle des géographes du Québec, 841
Association professionnelle des ingénieurs du gouvernement du Québec (ind.), 841
Association provinciale des constructeurs d'habitations du Québec inc., 841
Association québécoise d'urbanisme, 841
Association québécoise de l'industrie de la pêche, 841
Association québécoise de la gestion parasitaire, 841
Association québécoise de lutte contre la pollution atmosphérique, 841
Association québécoise des organismes de coopération internationale, 842
Association québécoise du gaz naturel, 842
Association québécoise du transport aérien, 842
Association québécoise du transport et des routes inc., 842
Association québécoise pour l'évaluation d'impacts, 842
Association québécoise pour l'hygiène, la santé et la sécurité du travail, 842
Association québécoise pour la maîtrise de l'énergie, 842
Association sectorielle - Fabrication d'équipement de transport et de machines, 842
Asta Sales & Marketing Ltd., 94
ATCO Group, 94
ATCO Power, 95
ATD Waste Systems Inc., 95
Athabasca Regional Waste Management Services Commission, 757
Athabasca University, 1099
Atkinson, Davies Inc., 95
Atlantic, 542, 522, 534
Atlantic Acoustical Associates, 95
Atlantic Air Cleaning Specialists Ltd., 95
Atlantic Canada Centre for Environmental Science, 842
Atlantic Canada Opportunities Agency, 510
Atlantic Canada Sustainability Initiative, 1042
Atlantic Canada Water & Wastewater Association, 842

Entry Name Index

Atlantic Canadian Organic Regional Network, 843
Atlantic Coastal Action Program, 1206
Atlantic Cooperative Wildlife Ecology Research Network, 1206
Atlantic Dairy Council, 843
Atlantic Engineering Consultants Ltd., 95
Atlantic Environmental Prediction Research Initiative, 1206
Atlantic Environmental Training & On-Site Services Inc., 95
Atlantic Food & Horticulture Research Centre, 509
Atlantic Forestry Centre, 1203, 550
Atlantic Industrial Services, 95
Atlantic Industries Ltd., 95
Atlantic Laboratory for Environmental Testing, 1203
Atlantic Newsprint Company, 96
Atlantic Orient Canada Inc., 96
Atlantic Packaging Products Ltd., 96
Atlantic Pest Control Association, 843
Atlantic Pilotage Authority Canada, 560
Atlantic Planners Institute, 843
Atlantic Poly Liners Inc., 97
Atlantic Provinces Association of Landscape Architects, 843
Atlantic Provinces Council on the Sciences, 843
Atlantic Provinces Trucking Association, 843
Atlantic Purification Systems, 97
Atlantic Region, 516, 534, 1135
Atlantic Regional Library, 1135
Atlantic Regional Office, 508
Atlantic Salmon Federation, 843, 1126
The Atlantic Salmon Journal, 1194
Atlantic Soils & Associated Management Ltd., 97
Atlantic Turfgrass Research Foundation, 843
Atlantic Wind Power Corp. Ltd., 97
Atlantic/Nunavut Region, 546
Atlas Polar Company Limited, 97
Atlin Campus, 1110
Atmospheric Science & Technology, 524
Atomic Energy of Canada Limited, 511
Atomic Energy of Canada Ltd., 549, 1139
Atotech Canada Ltd., 97
Atrion International Inc., 97
ATS Scientific Inc., 97
Auditing Association of Canada, 844
Auditor General of Canada, 526, 511
Augustana Faculty, 1103
Aulavik National Park of Canada, 555
Aurora, 633, 706
Aurora College, 1133
Aurora College - Thebacha Campus, 1033
Aurora College. Aurora Research Institute, 1133
Aurora Environmental Consulting Ltd., 97
Aurora Instruments Ltd., 98
Aurora Research Institute, 605
Ausable Bayfield Conservation Foundation, 844, 1043
Australian Association for Environmental Education, 844
Austring, Fendrick, Fairman & Parkkari, 1091
Auto-Chlor Inc., 98
AUTO21 - The Automobile of the 21st Century, 844
Automatic Controls Ltd., 98
Automotive & Industrial Materials Branch, 543
Automotive Industries Association of Canada, 844
Automotive Parts Manufacturers' Association, 844
Automotive Recyclers of Canada, 844
Auyuittuq National Park of Canada, 555
Avalon, 601
Avalon & Eastern, 599
Avalon Mechanical Consultants Ltd., 98
Avani Oxygen Water Corporation, 98
Avensys Inc., 98
Avenue Industrial Supply Co. Ltd., 98
Avery Dennison Canada Inc., 98
The Avian Preservation Foundation, 844, 1040
Aviation & Forest & Fire Management Branch, 632
Aviation, Forest & Fire Management Branch, 633
Avicultural Advancement Council of Canada, 844
Avignon, 747
Avmor Ltd., 99
Avoca-tec Environmental Services Inc., 99
Aware Learning Technologies, 99
AWI, 99
Axford Agencies BC Ltd., 99
Axion Technologies, 99
AXOR Experts-Conseils Inc., 99
AXYS Analytical Services Ltd., 99
Aylmer, 633
Aysix Technologies, 100
Az-Tec Reclaim Ltd., 100

Azco Industries Ltd., 100
AZZ Blenkhorn & Sawle Limited, 100

B

B & R Engineering Co. Ltd., 100
B.D. Rae Waste Management, 100
B.J. Bear Grain Company Ltd., 100
Babcock & Wilcox Canada Ltd., 100
Babcock Supply Ltd., 100
Backup-Power.ca, 101
Bacon Donaldson & Associates Ltd., 101
Bacta-Pur, 101
BAE Newplan Group Ltd., 101
Baffin, 618
Baie Comeau, 530
Baie-Comeau, 647, 733
Baker & Baker, 1057
Baker & McKenzie LLP, 1072
Ballard Power Systems Inc., 101
Bamfield Marine Sciences Centre, 1201
Bancomext, 531
Bancroft, 537
Bancroft Gem & Mineral Club, 844
Bancroft Light & Power Company (2000) Ltd., 101
Bancroft Western Sales Ltd., 101
Banff National Park of Canada, 555
Banff Park Museum National Historic Site of Canada, 555
Bank Fishery National Heritage Exhibit, 552
Bank of Canada, 526
Banyan Chains Inc., 101
Bar U Ranch National Historic Site of Canada, 555
Barbados, 767
Barbeau, Evans, Goldstein, 1057
Barenco Inc., 101
Barrat & Associates Inc., 101
Barrett Sales Ltd., 102
Barrie, 706
Barrie Agricultural Society, 844
Barrie Branch, 513
Barrington Environmental Services, 102
Barrington Industrial Services Limited, 102
Barrow Bay & District Sports Fishing Association, 844
Barry Spalding - Moncton Office, 1064
Barry Spalding - Saint John Office, 1065
Bartle & Gibson Co. Ltd., 102
Bartlet & Richardes LLP, 1081
Bartley Silver Co. Inc., 102
Bas St-Laurent, 515
Bas-Saint-Laurent, 540
Bas-Saint-Laurent - Gaspésie - Iles-de-la-Madeleine - Saguenay - Lac Saint Jean, 644
Bas-Saint-Laurent Model Forest, 845
Bas-Saint-Laurent - Gaspésie et Iles-de-la-Madeleine, 653
Bas-Saint-Laurent-Gaspésie-Iles-de-la-Madeleine, 655
Bas-St-Laurent, 644
BASF Canada Inc., 103
Les Basques, 749
Bass Engineering Systems Technology, 103
Bathurst Branch, 512
Bathurst Campus, 1126
Bathurst Regional Office, 593
Bathurst, 690
Batiscan, 747
Batoche National Historic Site of Canada, 555
The Battery Broker Environmental Services Inc., 391
Battle of the Châteauguay National Historic Site of Canada, 554
Battle of the Restigouche National Historic Site of Canada, 555
Battle of the Windmill National Historic Site of Canada, 554
Battlefords Agricultural Society, 845
Bay D'Espoir, 603
Bay of Fundy Ecosystem Project, 1042
Bay St George Campus, Stephenville Crossing Building, 1133
Bayer CropScience, 103
Bayer Inc., 103
Bayfield Institute, 527
Baymag Inc., 103
BC & Yukon, 531
BC Air Filter Ltd., 103
BC Games Society, 583
BC Hydro, 103
BC/Yukon Regional Headquarters, 536
BCHazman Management Ltd., 103
BCL Landview Systems Inc., 103
BDM Supply Limited, 103

BDR Machinery Ltd., 103
BDS Laboratories, 104
Beaconsfield, 734
Beament Green, 1070
Beasy Nicoll Engineering Ltd., 104
Beaton Institute, 1134
Beauce-Sartigan, 747
Beaudry, Bertrand Avocats, 1082
Beaufort-Delta, 606
Beauharnois, 734
Beauharnois-Salaberry, 747
Beaulier Inc., 104
Beaver Regional Waste Management Services Commission, 757
Beaver River Regional Waste Management Commission, 757
Beaverhill Bird Observatory, 845
Bebbington Industries, 104
Bécancour, 734, 747
BECK Drilling and Environmental Services Ltd., 104
Beckie Hydrogeologists (1990) Ltd., 104
Becquerel Laboratories Inc., 104
Bedard Tankers Inc., 104
Bedeque Bay Environmental Management Association, 845, 1045
Bedford, 537
Bedford Institute of Oceanography, 1206, 527, 1135
The Beer Store, 391
Behrick Enterprises Inc., 104
Beijing, 565
Bélanger, Sauvé, 1082
Belfab Inc., 104
Bell Canada, 1170
Bell Helicopter Textron, 1169
Bellechasse, 747
Belleville, 706
Belleville Area, 625
Bellevue House National Historic Site of Canada, 554
Beloeil, 734
Belzberg Library, 1117
Bema Co. Ltd., 104
Bémalux Inc., 105
Bengough Agricultural Society, 845
Benjamin Moore & Co. Ltd, 105
Bennett Environmental Inc., 105
Bennett Jones LLP - Calgary Office, 1049
Benson Chemicals Limited, 105
Benson Myles, 1065
Bentofix Technologies Inc., 105
Bercan Environmental Resources Inc., 105
Bercha Group, 105
Berg Chilling Systems Inc., 105
Bernard & Partners, 1057
Bernard Darveau Ingénieur, 105
Bérubé & Pion, SENCRL, 1089
Besnier, Dion & Rondeau, 1089
Bestobell AquaTronix Limited, 106
Bethune Memorial House National Historic Site of Canada, 554
Béton Provincial Ltée, 106
Bétonel Limitée, 106
Beulah Tec Limited, 106
Beverage Container Management Board, 567
Beverly & Qamanirjuaq Caribou Management Board, 541
BEX Engineering Limited, 106
BFC Bagotville, 545
BFC Montréal, 545
BFC Valcartier, 546
BFI Canada Inc., 106
BG Controls Ltd., 107
BGR Oilfield Services Incorporated, 107
BH Engineering Systems Ltd., 107
Biantco Environmental Services Inc., 107
Bibliothèque canadienne de l'agriculture - Sainte-Foy, 1184, 1177
Bibliothèque centrale, 1170
Bibliothèque d'aménagement, 1170
Bibliothèque de botanique - L'Institut de recherche en biologie végétale, 1170
Bibliothèque de chimie, 1170
Bibliothèque de didacthèque, 1170
Bibliothèque de droit, 1170
Bibliothèque de droit Brian-Dickson, 1147
Bibliothèque de droit et publications gouvernementales, 1184
Bibliothèque de géographie, 1177
Bibliothèque de musique, 1185
Bibliothèque de physique, 1170
Bibliothèque des sciences, 1171
Bibliothèque des sciences de la santé, 1171, 1147, 1185
Bibliothèque des sciences et de génie, 1185

Entry Name Index

Bibliothèque des sciences humaines et sociales, 1177
Bibliothèque des sciences juridiques, 1171
Bibliothèque et Archives nationales du Québec (BAnQ), 645
Bibliothèque paramédicale, 1171
Bibliothèque scientifique Charles-Auguste-Gauthier, 1177
Big Bear Pumping Inc., 107
Big Country Waste Management Commission, 757
Big Rideau Lake Association, 845
Bigelow-Liptak of Canada, 107
Bigfoot Systems Inc., 107
Binbrook Agricultural Society, 845
Bio-Contrôle inc., 107
Bio-dynamic Agricultural Society of British Columbia, 845
Bio-Limno Research & Consulting, 107
Bio-Software Inc., 108
Bio-Terre Systems Inc., 108
Biodiversity Research Centre, 1201
Bioforj Environmental Services, 108
Biogénie, 108
Biogeoscience Institute, 1199
Biolab Inc., 108
Biomation, 108
Biomax Inc., 108
Biomedical Branch Library, 1117
Biometeorology & Soil Physics Group of The University of British Columbia, 1201
Biopacific Diagnostic Inc., 109
Biophilia Inc., 109
Biophysical Society of Canada, 845
BIOQuébec, 845
BIOREM Inc., 109
Biorex Inc., 109
BioSolve of Canada Ltd., 109
BioSource Solutions Inc., 109
BIOTECanada, 845
Biotech Solutions, 109
Biotechnology Research Institute, 546
Biothermica, 109
Birchall Northey, 1072
Birchwood Environment Management Inc., 109
Bird Studies Canada, 845
Birks Co., 110
Bishop & McKenzie LLP, 1049, 1054
Bishop Falls, 603
Bishop's University, 1185, 1034, 1035
Bissett Resource Consultants Ltd., 110
Black & Decker Canada Inc., 110
Black Creek Conservation Project, 845
Black Duck, 525
Black Duck Joint Venture, 763
Blackbox Automation Inc., 110
Blainville, 734
Blais, Roger avocat inc, 1082
Blake, Cassels & Graydon LLP - Calgary, 1049
Blake, Cassels & Graydon LLP - Toronto, 1072
Blake, Cassels & Graydon LLP - Vancouver, 1057
Blaney McMurtry LLP, 1073
Blind River Refinery, 1139
Blomidon Naturalists Society, 846
Blower Engineering Inc., 110
Blowmoulding Technologies Inc., 110
Blue Water Agencies Ltd., 110
Blue-Zone Technologies Ltd., 110
Bluenose Coastal Action Foundation, 1042
Bluewater Environmental Inc., 110
Bluewater Recycling Association, 846
BMT Fleet Technology Ltd., 111
Board of Canadian Registered Safety Professionals, 846
Board of Examiners under the Scaler's Act, 595
Boart Longyear Inc., 111
BOC Canada Limited, 111
Bodycot Analex Inc., 113
Boehringer Ingelheim (Canada) Ltd., 1167
Boilersmith Ltd., 113
Bois Blanc Island Lighthouse National Historic Site of Canada, 554
Boisbriand, 734
Boishébert & Beaubears Shipbuilding National Historic Sites of Canada, 552
Bolger and Associates Ltd., 113
BOMA Environmental & Safety Inc., 113
Bombardier Inc./Canadair Aerospace & Defence Groups, 1171
Bonaventure, 747
Bonavista Campus Learning Resource Centre, 1130
Bonn Agreement, 846
Boojum Research Ltd., 113

Bora Laskin Law Library, 1156
Borden Ladner Gervais LLP - Calgary, 1049
Borden Ladner Gervais LLP - Montréal, 1082
Borden Ladner Gervais LLP - Ottawa, 1070
Borden Ladner Gervais LLP - Toronto, 1073
Borden Ladner Gervais LLP - Vancouver, 1058
Border Chemical Company Ltd., 114
BOS Engineering & Environmental Services Inc., 114
Both Belle Robb Ltd., 114
Boucher Precast Concrete Ltd., 114
Bouctouche, 592
Boughton Law Corporation, 1058
Boundary Organic Producers Association, 846
Boutillette Parizeau et Associés inc., 114
Bow Valley Waste Management Commission, 757
Bowater Canadian Forest Products Inc., 114
Bowen Nature Club, 846
Bowie Environmental Edge Management & Assessment Ltd., 114
Bowie Pumps of Canada Ltd., 114
Bowser Technical Inc., 114
Boyne Clarke, 1067
BP Canada Energy Company, 114
BP Trading Ltd., 114
BPG Graphics Solutions, 114
BPR, 115
Brace Centre for Water Resources Management, 115
Bracebridge, 537, 706
Bracebridge Generation Ltd., 115
Bracken Health Sciences Library, 1142
Bradex Industrial Services Ltd., 115
Bradford West Gwillimbury, 706
Bradford White Canada Inc., 115
Brampton, 706
Brampton Branch, 513
Brampton Engineering Inc., 115
Brampton Horticultural Society, 846
Branch Library, 1147
Brandon, 689
Brandon Branch, 512
Brandon Mining Engineering Office, 590
Brandon Regional Health Centre, 1121
Brandon Research Centre, 509, 1122
Brandon University, 1122, 1033
Brant, 626, 698
Delhi Industries Inc., 115
Brantford, 537, 707, 115
Brantford Campus, 1139
Brantford Disposal Service, 115
Brantford Lapidary & Mineral Society Inc., 846
Les Bras d'Fer Gingras Inc., 267
Brass Craft Canada Ltd., 115
Bratty & Partners LLP, 1081
Braymo Energy Corporation, 116
Brazeau Seller LLP, 1070
Breast Cancer Action, 846
Breast Cancer Society of Canada, 846
Brendar Environmental Inc., 116
Brenntag Canada Inc., 116
Brereton Field Naturalists' Club Inc., 846
BRI International Inc., 116
Brian Clark Architect, 116
Brighton, 620
Brim Pumps & Systems Ltd., 116
Brincad Technologies Inc., 116
Brisbin & Sentis Engineering Inc., 116
Bristar Containment Industries Ltd., 117
British Columbia & Yukon, 541
British Columbia 2010 Olympic & Paralympic Games Secretariat, 578
British Columbia Agriculture Council, 846, 1040
British Columbia Assessment Authority, 582
British Columbia Association for Regenerative Agriculture, 846
British Columbia Association of Agricultural Fairs & Exhibitions, 847
British Columbia Bottle Depot Association, 847
British Columbia Branches, 512
British Columbia Camping Association, 847
British Columbia Cattlemen's Association, 847
British Columbia Conservation Foundation, 847, 1040
British Columbia Construction Association, 847
British Columbia Environment Industry Association, 847
British Columbia Environmental & Occupational Health Research Network, 1201
British Columbia Environmental Assessment Office, 577, 578
British Columbia Environmental Network, 1213, 847

British Columbia Farm Industry Review Board, 574, 847
British Columbia Farm Machinery & Agriculture Museum Association, 847
British Columbia Ferry Services, 1120
British Columbia Ferry Services Inc., 583
British Columbia Food Technologists, 847
British Columbia Fruit Growers' Association, 848
British Columbia Fuchsia & Begonia Society, 848
British Columbia Ground Water Association, 848
British Columbia Health & Human Services, 1120
British Columbia Herb Growers Association, 848
British Columbia Housing, 1110
British Columbia Hydro, 580, 1110
British Columbia Hydro Bridge Coastal Restoration Program, 1040
British Columbia Innovation Council, 575
British Columbia Institute of Agrologists, 848
British Columbia Institute of Technology (BCIT), 1110, 1029, 1030
British Columbia Labour Relations Board, 581
British Columbia Landscape & Nursery Association, 848
British Columbia Lodging & Campgrounds Association, 848
British Columbia Lottery Corporation, 576
British Columbia Lung Association, 848
British Columbia Marine Trades Association, 849
British Columbia Medical Association, 849
British Columbia Ministry of Economic Development, 1120
British Columbia Ministry of Energy & Mines, 1120
British Columbia Ministry of Environment, 1120
British Columbia Nature (Federation of British Columbia Naturalists), 849
British Columbia Office of the Police Complaint Commissioner, 582
British Columbia Paint Manufacturers' Association, 849
British Columbia Pension Corporation, 574
British Columbia Progress Board, 575
British Columbia Provincial Emergency Program, 582
British Columbia Ready Mixed Concrete Association, 849
British Columbia Recreation & Parks Association, 849
British Columbia Region, 534
British Columbia Regional Office, 508
British Columbia Salmon Farmers Association, 849
British Columbia Shellfish Growers Association, 849
British Columbia Society of Landscape Architects, 850
British Columbia Spaces for Nature, 850
British Columbia Sustainable Energy Association, 850
British Columbia Technology Industries Association, 850
British Columbia Timber Sales, 579
British Columbia Transit, 583
British Columbia Transmission Corporation, 583
British Columbia Treaty Commission, 573
British Columbia Trucking Association, 850
British Columbia Utilities Commission, 584, 1117
British Columbia Water & Waste Association, 850
British Columbia Waterfowl Society, 850
British Columbia Women's Institutes, 850
British Columbia Wood Specialities Group Association, 851
British Council - Canada, 851
Broadway Campus Library, 1117
Broan Canada Ltd., 117
Brock, 724
Brock University, 1153
Brockville, 537, 707
Brockville Campus, 1139
Brodeur, Boileau, 1089
The Brofield Group, 391
Brome-Missisquoi, 747
Brookfield Power, 117
Brooklin Concrete Products Ltd., 117
Brooks, 671
Brooks Campus, 1099
Brossard, 540
Brossard Branch, 513
Brosz & Associates, 117
Brown Strachan Associates, 117
Brownlee LLP, 1054
Bruce, 627, 698
Bruce A. Brown Associates Limited, 117
Bruce Peninsula Environment Group, 851
Bruce Peninsula National Park, 554
Bruce Sutherland & Associates Ltd., 117
The Bruce Trail Conservancy, 851
Brunei Darussalam, 767
Brunet Ltée, Tuyaux de béton, 117
Bryco Environmental, 117
Brytex Building Systems Inc., 117
BSI Management Systems Canada Inc., 118

Entry Name Index

BSM North America, 118
Bubble Technology Industries Inc., 118
Buchan, Lawton, Parent Ltd., 118
Buchanan Environmental, 118
Buckham Transport Ltd., 118
Buckhorn Canada Inc., 118
Buffalo Lake Naturalists Club, 851, 1109
Building & Fire Safety, 657
Building Code Commission, 630
Building Materials Evaluation Commission, 630
Building Supply Industry Association of British Columbia, 851
Buildings Group, 597
Bulkley Valley Naturalists, 851
Bulkley-Nechako, 676
Burchell Hayman Parish, 1067
Burchell, MacDougall, 1067, 1068
Burden Management & Design Ltd., 118
Bureau d'audiences publiques sur l'environnement, 646
Bureau de Normalisation du Québec, 118
Bureau des projets Centres hospitaliers universitaires de Montréal, CHUM, CUSM et CHU Sainte-Justine, 652
Bureau du coroner, 652
Bureau of International Recycling, 1213, 851
Bureaux de la protection de la faune/Regional Wildlife Protection Offices, 651
Burin Campus Library, 1130
Burke Mountain Naturalists, 851
Burlew, Edward L., 1072
Burlington, 537, 707
Burlington / Halton Branch, 513
BurlingtonGreen Environmental Association, 852
Burnaby, 536, 679
Burnaby Bag & Burlap Ltd., 118
Burnaby Hospital, 1110
Burnaby-Fraser, 517
Burnet, Duckworth & Palmer LLP, 1050
Burns, Fitzpatrick, Rogers & Schwartz, 1058
Burrard Inlet Environmental Action Program & Fraser River Estuary Management Program, 852
Burton Ronald W. Lawyers, 1067
Busch Systems International Inc., 118
Busch Vacuum Technics Inc., 119
Business & Fiscal Planning Branch, 624
Business & Trade Statistics, 559
Business Access Canada, 559
Business Council of British Columbia, 852
Business Development Bank of Canada, 512
Business Financial Support & Corporate Services, 592
Business Funding Group Inc., 119
The Business Link Business Service Centre, 515
Business Management Division, 630
Business Service & Rural Utilities Sector, 564
Business Services Division - Financial Services, 585
Butler's Barracks c/o Fort George National Historic Site, 554
BV SORBEX, Inc., 119
BVA Systems Ltd./Vibro-Acoustics, 119
BW Technologies by Honeywell, 119
Byram Industrial Services Ltd., 119
Bytown Marine Ltd., 119

C

C F Reclamation & Fresh Water Services, 119
C V Environmental Services, 119
C-Core Innovative Engineering Solutions, 1204
C-Max Transportation Equipment, 119
C.D. Howe Institute, 893, 1157
C.D. Sonter Ltd., 119
C.E. Jones & Associates Ltd., 119
C.G. Industrial Specialties, Ltd., 119
C.J. MacLellan & Associates Inc., 120
C.J. Pink Ltd., 120
C.R. Wall Co. Inc., 120
C.V. Environmental Services, 120
C3 Environmental Group, 120
C5 Plus Ltd., 120
Cactus Environmental Services Ltd., 120
CadhamHayes Systems Inc., 120
Cadman Power Equipment, 120
The Cadmus Group, 391
Caduceon Environmental Laboratories, 120
CAE Electronics Ltd., 1184
Caframo Co. Ltd., 121
CAHFIL FARR (Canada Inc.), 121
Cain Lamarre Casgrain Wells - Alma, 1082

Cain Lamarre Casgrain Wells - Amos, 1082
Cain Lamarre Casgrain Wells - Amqui, 1082
Cain Lamarre Casgrain Wells - Chicoutimi, 1082
Cain Lamarre Casgrain Wells - Drummondville, 1082
Cain Lamarre Casgrain Wells - Montréal, 1083
Cain Lamarre Casgrain Wells - Québec, 1087
Cain Lamarre Casgrain Wells - Rimouski, 1089
Cain Lamarre Casgrain Wells - Sept-Iles, 1089
Cain Lamarre Casgrain Wells - Val-d'Or, 1089
Cal's Eco Depot, 121
Caledon, 707
Caledon Laboratory Chemicals Inc., 121
Calgary, 671, 121
Calgary Area Branch, 512
Calgary Centre, 535
Calgary East, 535
Calgary Engineering & Environmental Services, 1099
Calgary Field Naturalists' Society, 852
Calgary Foundation, 1039
Calgary Health Region, 1099
Calgary Horticultural Society, 852
Calgary Library, 1100
Calgary Library & Information Centre, 1100
Calgary Metal (1985) Ltd., 121
Calgary North, 535
Calgary North Branch, 512
Calgary South Branch, 512
Calgary Utilities & Environmental Protection, 1100
Calgary Zoological Society, 852, 1100
Calgon Carbon Corp., 121
Calibre Strategic Services Inc., 121
California Institute of Public Affairs, 852
Callrich Eco Services Inc., 122
Calta Computer Systems Ltd., 122
Camatec, 122
Cambrian College, 1155
Cambridge, 617, 537, 707
Cambridge Materials Testing Limited, 122
Cameco Corporation, 1189
Cameron Science & Technology Library, 1104
Camosun College, 1120, 1030
Campbell Lea, 1082
Campbell Marr, 1063
Campbell River, 679
Campbell River Campus Library, 1111
Campbell Scientific (Canada) Corp., 122
Campbell's Concrete Ltd., 122
Campground Owners Association of Nova Scotia, 852
Camping Québec, 852
Campus Alberta Quality Council, 563
Campus d'Edmundston, 1126
Campus de Bathurst, Bibliothèque, 1126
Campus de Campbellton, Bibliothèque, 1126
Campus de Charlesbourg, 1177
Campus de Dieppe, Bibliothèque, 1126
Campus de Shippagan, 1130
Campus Notre-Dame-de-Foy, 1182
Camrose, 535, 671
Camvac Inc., 122
Can Ecosse Engineering, 122
Can-Am Border Trade Alliance, 892
Can-Am Instruments Ltd., 122
Can-Aqua Inc., 123
Can-Aqua International Ltée, 123
Can-Cell Industries Inc., 123
Can-K Artificial Lift Systems Inc., 123
Can-Ross Environmental Services Ltd., 123
Canada Beef Export Federation, 852
Canada Border Services Agency, 514
Canada Business, 514
Canada Centre for Inland Waters, 1139
Canada Centre for Remote Sensing - Geomatics Canada, 551
Canada Colors & Chemicals Ltd., 123
Canada Composting Inc., 123
Canada Council for the Arts, 519
Canada Deposit Insurance Corporation, 526
Canada Dept. of National Defence & the Canadian Forces, 1148
Canada East Equipment Dealers' Association, 852
Canada Economic Development for Québec Regions, 515
Canada Employment Insurance Commission, 535
Canada Firearms Centre, 557
Canada Foundation for Innovation, 1043
Canada Green Building Council, 853
Canada Heat Pumps, 123
Canada Industrial Relations Board, 535

Canada Institute for Scientific & Technical Information (CISTI), 1148
Canada Investment & Savings, 526
Canada Lands Company, 560
Canada Mortgage & Housing Corporation, 560, 516, 1148
Canada Post Corporation, 560
Canada Public Service Agency, 562
Canada Revenue Agency, 526, 516, 1148
Canada Safety Council, 853
Canada Science & Technology Museum, 1148
Canada Science & Technology Museum Corporation, 519, 516
Canada Trade Mission to Mexico, 531
Canada Transport Emergency Centre, 561
Canada Water Supply Ltd., 123
Canada Web Directory: Science and Environment, 1213
Canada's Research-Based Pharmaceutical Companies (Rx&D), 853
Canada-Manitoba Infrastructure Secretariat, 588
Canada-Newfoundland Offshore Petroleum Board, 603, 763, 853, 1131
Canada-Nova Scotia Offshore Petroleum Board, 610, 763, 853
Canada-Saskatchewan Irrigation Diversification Centre, 508
Canada. Fisheries & Oceans Canada, 1211, 1207
Canada/Manitoba Business Service Centre, 515
Canada/New Brunswick Business Service Centre, 515
Canada/Newfoundland & Labrador Business Service Centre, 515
Canada/Nova Scotia Business Service Centre, 515
Canada/Nunavut Business Service Centre, 515
Canada/NWT Business Service Centre, 515
Canada/Ontario Business Service Centre, 515
Canada/Prince Edward Island Business Service Centre, 515
Canada/Saskatchewan Business Service Centre, 515
Canada/Yukon Business Service Centre, 515
Canada-Alberta Municipal Rural Infrastructure Fund, 1039
Canadax Industrial Group Limited, 123
Canadian 4-H Council, 854
Canadian Academy of Engineering, 854
Canadian Acoustical Association, 854
Canadian Advanced Technology Alliance, 854
Canadian Aeronautics & Space Institute, 854
Canadian Agri-Marketing Association (Alberta), 855
Canadian Agri-Marketing Association (Manitoba), 855
Canadian Agricultural Economics Society, 854
Canadian Agricultural Safety Association, 854
Canadian Agriculture Library (Summerland), 1116
Canadian Agriculture Library - Kentville, 1137
Canadian Agriculture Library - Lethbridge, 1108
Canadian Agriculture Library - Saskatoon, 1189
Canadian Air Transport Security Authority, 560
Canadian Airports Council, 855
Canadian Animal Health Institute, 855
Canadian Aquaculture Industry Alliance, 855
Canadian Archaeological Association, 855
Canadian Arctic Resources Committee, 1213
Canadian Associated Air Balance Council, 855
Canadian Association for Health Services & Policy Research, 855
Canadian Association for Humane Trapping, 855
Canadian Association for Laboratory Accreditation Inc., 856
Canadian Association for Laboratory Animal Science, 856
Canadian Association for Mine & Explosive Ordnance Security, 856
Canadian Association for Renewable Energies, 1213, 856
Canadian Association for Research in Nondestructive Evaluation, 856
Canadian Association for Studies in Co-operation, 856
Canadian Association of Agri-Retailers, 856
Canadian Association of Animal Health Technologists & Technicians, 856
Canadian Association of Chemical Distributors, 857
Canadian Association of Drilling Engineers, 857
Canadian Association of Equipment Distributors, 857
Canadian Association of Fire Chiefs, 857
Canadian Association of Geographers, 857
Canadian Association of Geophysical Contractors, 857
Canadian Association of Medical Biochemists, 857
Canadian Association of Members of Public Utility Tribunals, 857
Canadian Association of Mining Equipment & Services for Export, 858
Canadian Association of Oilwell Drilling Contractors, 858, 1100
Canadian Association of Palynologists, 858
Canadian Association of Petroleum Landmen, 858
Canadian Association of Petroleum Producers, 858
Canadian Association Of Physicians For The Environment, 1213
Canadian Association of Physicians for the Environment, 858
Canadian Association of Professional Heritage Consultants, 858

Entry Name Index

Canadian Association of Recycling Industries, 858
Canadian Association of Swine Veterinarians, 859
Canadian Association of Zoos & Aquariums, 859
Canadian Association on Water Quality, 859
Canadian Automobile Association, 859
Canadian Avalanche Association, 859
Canadian Bar Association, 860
Canadian Benthic Ltd., 124
Canadian Bioethics Society, 860
Canadian Bison Association, 860
Canadian Botanical Association, 860
Canadian Botanical Conservation Network, 860
Canadian Bottled Water Association, 860, 1153
Canadian Broadcasting Corporation, 519
Canadian Building Energy End-Use Data & Analysis Centre, 1199
Canadian Bus Association, 860
Canadian Camping Association, 860
Canadian Cancer Society, 861
Canadian Cancer Society Research Institute, 861
Canadian Carbonization Research Association, 861
Canadian Cartographic Association, 861
Canadian Cattle Breeders' Association, 861
Canadian Cattlemen's Association, 861
Canadian Centre for Biodiversity, 519
Canadian Centre for Climate Modelling & Analysis, 1201
Canadian Centre for Emergency Preparedness, 861
Canadian Centre For Energy Information, 1100
Canadian Centre for Energy Information, 861
Canadian Centre for Fisheries Innovation, 861
Canadian Centre for Health & Safety in Agriculture, 1212
Canadian Centre for Occupational Health & Safety, 535, 517, 862
Canadian Centre for Policy Alternatives, 862
Canadian Centre for Pollution Prevention, 862, 1156
The Canadian Chamber of Commerce, 862
Canadian Chamber of Commerce in Mexico, 531
Canadian Chemical Producers' Association, 862
Canadian Circumpolar Institute, 1199, 862
Canadian Circumpolar Library, 1104
Canadian Clay Products Inc., 124
Canadian Clean Power Coalition, 862
Canadian Co-operative Wool Growers Ltd., 864
Canadian Coalition for Nuclear Responsibility, 862
Canadian Coast Guard, 527
Canadian College of Health Leaders, 863
Canadian Commercial Corporation, 517
Canadian Concrete Pipe Association, 863
Canadian Construction Association, 863
Canadian Consulting Agrologists Association, 863
Canadian Consumer Specialty Products Association, 863
Canadian Cooperative Wildlife Health Centre, 1211, 1212
Canadian Council for International Co-operation, 864
Canadian Council for Tobacco Control, 864
Canadian Council of Chief Executives, 864
Canadian Council of Directors of Apprenticeship, 535
Canadian Council of Food & Nutrition, 864
Canadian Council of Forest Ministers, 763, 864
Canadian Council of Grocery Distributors, 864
Canadian Council of Independent Laboratories, 864
Canadian Council of Land Surveyors, 864
Canadian Council of Ministers of the Environment, 1213, 763, 865
Canadian Council of Motor Transport Administrators, 865
Canadian Council of Professional Fish Harvesters, 865
Canadian Council of Technicians & Technologists, 865
Canadian Council on Animal Care, 865
Canadian Council on Ecological Areas, 865
Canadian Council on International Law, 865
Canadian Dairy Commission, 507
Canadian Dam Association, 865
Canadian District Energy Association, 866
Canadian Drives Inc., 124
Canadian Eagle Recyclers, Inc., 124
Canadian Electricity Association, 866
Canadian Emissions Ltd., 124
Canadian Energy Efficiency Alliance, 866
Canadian Energy Pipeline Association, 866
Canadian Energy Research Institute, 1199, 866, 1100
Canadian Environmental Assessment Agency, 1213, 517
Canadian Environmental Auditors Inc., 124
Canadian Environmental Certification Approvals Board, 1213, 866
Canadian Environmental Directory, 1213
Canadian Environmental Grantmakers' Network, 1213, 867
Canadian Environmental Group, 124
Canadian Environmental Law Association, 1213, 867
Canadian Environmental Literacy Project, 1213
Canadian Environmental Network, 1213, 867

Canadian Environmental Protection, 1193
Canadian Environmental Solutions Directory, 1213
Canadian Environmental Technology Advancement Corporation - West, 1213, 867
Canadian Farm Animal Care Trust, 867
Canadian Farm Writers' Federation, 867
Canadian Federation of Agriculture, 867
Canadian Federation of Earth Sciences, 867
Canadian Federation of Engineering Students, 868
Canadian Federation of Humane Societies, 868
Canadian Federation of Independent Grocers, 868
Canadian Federation of Woodlot Owners, 868
Canadian Fertilizer Institute, 868
Canadian Fibre, 124
Canadian Fire Safety Association, 868
Canadian Fishery Consultants Ltd., 124
Canadian Fluid Power Association, 868
Canadian Food Inspection Agency, 507, 518
Canadian Forces College, 546
Canadian Forces Medical Group Headquarters, 1148
Canadian Forces Northern Area Headquarters, 1133
Canadian Forest Seedling Nurseries and Services Directory, 1213
Canadian Forest Service, 549
Canadian Forestry Association, 868
Canadian Forestry Association of New Brunswick, 869
Canadian Foundation for Climate & Atmospheric Sciences, 869
Canadian Foundation for Climate and Atmospheric Sciences, 1043
Canadian Foundry Association, 869
Canadian Gas Association, 869
Canadian General Standards Board, 559, 869, 124
Canadian Genetic Diseases Network, 869
Canadian GeoExchange Coalition, 869
Canadian Geographic, 1193
Canadian Geophysical Union, 869
Canadian Golf Superintendents Association, 870
Canadian Grain Commission, 507, 1122
Canadian Ground Water Association, 870
Canadian Hay Association, 870
Canadian Health Food Association, 870
Canadian Health Libraries Association, 870
Canadian Heavy Oil Association, 871
Canadian Hemerocallis Society, 871
Canadian Heritage, 519, 1167
Canadian Home Builders' Association, 871
Canadian Home Builders' Association - British Columbia, 871
Canadian Horticultural Council, 871
Canadian Horticultural Therapy Association, 871
Canadian Hurricane Centre, 524
Canadian Hydraulics Centre, 548
Canadian Hydro Developers, Inc., 124
Canadian Hydrogen & Fuel Cell Association, 871
Canadian Hydrographic Association, 871
Canadian Hydrographic Service, 528
Canadian Hydropower Association, 872
Canadian Ice Service, 524
Canadian Industrial Transportation Association, 872
Canadian Injured Workers Alliance, 872
Canadian Innovation Centre, 872
The Canadian Institute, 872
Canadian Institute for Energy Training, 872
Canadian Institute for Environmental Law & Policy, 1213, 872
Canadian Institute for Health Information, 872
Canadian Institute for NDE, 872, 1140
Canadian Institute for Photonics Innovations, 873
Canadian Institute of Biotechnology, 1148
Canadian Institute of Chartered Accountants, 873
Canadian Institute of Energy, 873
Canadian Institute of Food Science & Technology, 874
Canadian Institute of Forestry, 874
Canadian Institute of Geomatics, 874, 1149
Canadian Institute of Mining, Metallurgy & Petroleum, 874
Canadian Institute of Planners, 875
Canadian Institute of Plumbing & Heating, 875
Canadian Institute of Public Health Inspectors, 875
Canadian Institute of Resources Law, 875, 1100
Canadian Institute of Steel Construction, 875
Canadian Institute of Traffic & Transportation, 875
Canadian Institutes of Health Research, 533, 519, 1043
Canadian Intellectual Property Office, 544
Canadian Intergovernmental Conference Secretariat, 763, 875
Canadian Intergovernmental Relations, 659
Canadian International Council, 876
Canadian International Development Agency, 529, 519
Canadian International Grains Institute, 529

Canadian Iris Society, 876
Canadian Labour Congress, 876
Canadian Land Forces Command & Staff College, 546
Canadian Land Reclamation Association, 876
Canadian Law & Society Association, 876
Canadian Liquids Processors Limited, 124
Canadian Lumbermen's Association, 876
Canadian Lung Association, 876
Canadian Manufacturers & Exporters, 876
Canadian Maritime Law Association, 877
Canadian Marketing Association, 877
Canadian Meat Council, 877
Canadian Meat Science Association, 877
Canadian Medical & Biological Engineering Society, 877
Canadian Medical Association, 877
Canadian Meteorological & Oceanographic Society, 878
Canadian Meteorological Centre, 1167
Canadian Micro-Mineral Association, 879
Canadian Mineral Analysts, 879
Canadian Mineral Society, 879
Canadian Mining Industry Research Organization, 879
Canadian Museum of Civilization, 519
Canadian Museum of Nature, 519, 518, 1149
The Canadian National Committee for Irrigation & Drainage, 879
The Canadian Network for Environmental Education & Communication, 879
Canadian Network for Vaccines & Immunotherapeutics, 879
Canadian Network of Toxicology Centres, 1207, 879
Canadian Nuclear Association, 879
Canadian Nuclear Safety Commission, 1213, 520, 1149
Canadian Nuclear Society, 880
Canadian Nursery Landscape Association, 880
Canadian Oil Heat Association, 880
Canadian Organic Growers, 1213
Canadian Organic Growers Inc., 880, 1149
Canadian Organic Livestock Association, 881
Canadian Ornamental Plant Foundation, 881, 1043
Canadian Pacific Railway, 1100
Canadian Paint & Coatings Association, 881
Canadian Pallet Council, 881
Canadian Paper Recyclers, 124
Canadian Pari-Mutuel Agency, 507
Canadian Parks & Recreation Association, 881
Canadian Parks & Wilderness Society, 881
Canadian Parks and Wilderness Society, 1213
Canadian Parks Partnership, 881
Canadian Partnership for Children's Health and Environment, 1213
Canadian Patient Safety Institute, 881
Canadian Pest Management Association, 882
Canadian Petroleum Engineering Inc., 124
Canadian Petroleum Law Foundation, 882
Canadian Physiological Society, 882
Canadian Phytopathological Society, 882
Canadian Plains Research Center, 1212
Canadian Plastics Industry Association, 882
Canadian Plastics Sector Council, 882
Canadian Plywood Association, 882
Canadian Polar Commission, 520
Canadian Polystyrene Recycling Alliance, 882
Canadian Portable Structures (1992) Ltd., 125
Canadian Ports Clearance Association, 882
Canadian Precast / Prestressed Concrete Institute, 883
Canadian Printing Industries Association, 883
Canadian Printing Ink Manufacturers Association, 883
Canadian Process Control Association, 883
Canadian Public Health Association, 883
Canadian Public Health Association - NB/PEI Branch, 883
Canadian Public Health Association - NWT/Nunavut Branch, 883
Canadian Public Works Association, 883
Canadian Pulp & Paper Network for Innovation in Education & Research, 883
Canadian Radiation Protection Association, 883
Canadian Radio-television & Telecommunications Commission, 519
Canadian Recycling Equipment & Systems Ltd., 125
Canadian Remote Sensing Society, 884
Canadian Renewable Energy Association, 884
Canadian Renewable Fuels Association, 1213, 884
Canadian Respiratory Health Professionals, 884
Canadian Rock Mechanics Association, 884
Canadian Rose Society, 884
Canadian Safety Equipment Inc., 125
Canadian Sanitation Supply Association, 884
Canadian Science Writers' Association, 884

Entry Name Index

Canadian Seabed Research Ltd., 125
Canadian Security Intelligence Service, 557
Canadian Seed Growers' Association, 884
Canadian Seed Trade Association, 884
Canadian Sheep Breeders' Association, 885
Canadian Sheet Steel Building Institute, 885
Canadian Shield Foundation, 1041
Canadian Society for Analytical Sciences & Spectroscopy, 885
Canadian Society for Bioengineering, 885
Canadian Society for Civil Engineering, 885
Canadian Society for Horticultural Science, 885
Canadian Society for Industrial Engineering, 885
Canadian Society for International Health, 885
Canadian Society for Mechanical Engineering, 885
Canadian Society for Medical Laboratory Science, 886
Canadian Society for the Study of Practical Ethics, 886
Canadian Society of Agronomy, 886
Canadian Society of Air Safety Investigators, 886
Canadian Society of Allergy & Clinical Immunology, 886
Canadian Society of Animal Science, 886
The Canadian Society of Biochemistry, Molecular & Cellular Biology, 886
Canadian Society of Clinical Chemists, 886
Canadian Society of Environmental Biologists, 1213, 887
Canadian Society of Exploration Geophysicists, 887
Canadian Society of Landscape Architects, 887
Canadian Society of Microbiologists, 887
Canadian Society of Petroleum Geologists, 887
Canadian Society of Plant Physiologists, 887
Canadian Society of Safety Engineering, Inc., 888
Canadian Society of Soil Science, 888
Canadian Society of Zoologists, 888
Canadian Soil & Climate Protection Corp., 125
Canadian Solar Industries Association, 1213
Canadian Solar Industries Association Inc., 888
Canadian Space Agency, 520
Canadian Space Society, 888
Canadian Sphagnum Peat Moss Association, 888
Canadian Standards Association, 888
Canadian Steel Construction Council, 889
Canadian Steel Partnership Council, 889
Canadian Steel Producers Association, 889
Canadian Sugar Beet Producers' Association Inc., 889
Canadian Sugar Institute, 1156
Canadian Swine Breeders' Association, 889
Canadian Swine Exporters Association, 889
Canadian Technical Tape Ltd., 125
Canadian Tourism Commission, 543
Canadian Trade Commissioner Service, 530
Canadian Transportation Agency, 560, 520, 1167
Canadian Transportation Research Forum, 889
Canadian Trucking Alliance, 889
Canadian University College, 1108
Canadian Urban Transit Association, 889, 1156
Canadian Urethane Foam Contractors Association, 890
Canadian Urethane Manufacturers Association, 890
Canadian Veterinary Medical Association, 890
Canadian Water & Wastewater Association, 890
Canadian Water Conditioning Inc., 125
Canadian Water Network, 1207, 890
Canadian Water Quality Association, 890, 1156
Canadian Water Resources Association, 891
Canadian Well Logging Society, 891
Canadian Wheat Board, 558, 507, 1123
Canadian Wildlife, 1193
Canadian Wildlife Federation, 891, 1149
Canadian Wildlife Service, 1214, 523, 1129, 1045
Canadian Wind Energy Association, 1214
Canadian Wind Energy Association Inc., 891
Canadian Wood Council, 891
Canadian Wood Fibre Centre, 550
Canadian Wood Pallet & Container Association, 892
Canadian Wood Preservers Bureau, 892
Canadian Worcester Controls Ltd., 125
CanadianEnvironmental.com, 125
Canadians for Ethical Treatment of Food Animals, 892
Canadians for Responsible & Safe Highways, 892
CanAsia Environmental & Engineering Ltd., 125
Canatec Consultants Ltd., 125
Canbar Inc., 126
Canberra Company, 126
Cancer Care Ontario, 628
Cancer Research Society, 892
Cancoppas Limited, 126
CanDetec Inc., 126

Candiac, 734
Canentec Inc., 126
CanHemp Corporation, 126
Canmet Energy Technology Centre, 1199, 1207, 1211
CANMET Energy Technology Centre, 551
CANMET Energy Technology Centre-Devon, 551
CANMET Energy Technology Centre-Ottawa, 551
CANMET Energy Technology Centre-Varennes, 551
CANMET Information Centre, 1149
CANMET Mineral Technology Branch, 552
Canmore, 535, 671
Canning & Pitt Associates Inc., 126
Cannington Group, 126
CanNorth Environmental Services Inc., 126
Canon Canada Inc., 126
Canrom Photovoltaics Inc., 126
Canso Islands National Historic Site of Canada, 552
Canspect Corporation, 127
Cansult Maunsell Limited, 127
Cantech Inspections Ltd., 127
CanTox Environmental Inc., 127
CanTox Health Sciences International, 1144
Canviro, 127
Canwest Pumping Systems Ltd., 127
Cape Breton, 610, 695
Cape Breton Development Fund Corporation, 543
Cape Breton District Health Authority, 1137
Cape Breton Highlands National Park of Canada, 553
Cape Breton University, 1206, 1137, 1033
Cape Dorset, 617
Cape Spear National Historic Site of Canada, 553
Capilano College, 1114
Capital Environmental Resource Inc., 127
Capital H2O Systems Inc., 128
Capital Health, 1135
Capital Projects Division, 641, 569
Capital Region, 610
Capital Region Northeast Water Services Commission, 757
Capital Region Parkland Water Services, 757
Capital Region Southwest Water Services Commission, 757
Capital Region Vegreville Corridor Water Services Commission, 757
Capital Regional District, 676
Capitale-Nationale, 643
Capitale-Nationale et Chaudière-Appalaches, 651
Capitale-Nationale, Chaudière Appalaches et Nunavik, 653
Capitale-Nationale, Chaudières-Appalaches, 653
Capitale-Nationale-Chaudières-Appalaches, 651
Capricorn Control Technologies Ltd., 128
Caraquet, 592
Carbonear Campus Library, 1130
Cardel Construction Ltd., 128
Cardinal Biologicals Ltd., 128
Care First Aid Training Inc., 128
Career Advancement Employment, 128
Careful Hand Laundry & Dry Cleaners Ltd., 128
Cariboo, 677
Carillon, 552
Carillon Barracks National Historic Site of Canada, 554
CARIS, 128
Caristrap International Inc., 128
Caritas Health Group, 1104
Carleton County Law Association, 892
Carleton Martello Tower National Historic Site of Canada, 553
Carleton Place, 537
Carleton University, 1149, 1034
Carlo Gavazzi (Canada) Inc., 128
Carlyle, 540
Carmacks Renewable Resource Council, 665
Carmanah Technologies Corp., 129
Carole Burnham Consulting, 129
Carolinian Canada, 1214
Carolinian Canada Coalition, 892
Carp Agricultural Society, 892
Carrier Canada Ltd., 129
Carrying Capacity Network, 892
Carscallen Leitch LLP, 1050
Carson Safety & Environmental Services, 130
Carswell Consulting Engineers Ltd., 130
Carthy Foundation, 1039
Cartier Chemicals Ltd., 130
Cartier-Brébeuf National Historic Site of Canada, 554
Cartothèque, 1185
Cartridge Care Canada, 130
Cartwright, 603

Casa Loma Campus, 1156
Casa Loma ESL Resource Centre, 1157
Cascade Environmental Resource Group. Ltd., 130
Cascades Fine Papers Group Inc., 130
Cascades Inc., 130
Cascades Recovery Inc., 130
Cascades Resource, 131
Cassels Brock & Blackwell LLP, 1074
Caster-Rack Systems Ltd., 131
Castle Building Centres Groups Ltd., 131
Castle Hill National Historic Site of Canada, 553
Castle-Crown Wilderness Coalition, 892
Cat Tech Canada Company, 131
Catalyst Paper Corp., 132
Catherine Berris Associates Inc., 132
Catherine Donnelly Foundation, 1043
Cathy's Crawly Composters, 132
Catterall & Wright, 132
Cave & Basin National Historic Site of Canada, 555
CB Engineering, Inc., 132
CBCL Limited, 132
CBR Products - Canadian Building Restoration Products Inc., 133
CCI Thermal Technologies Inc., 133
CCL/IBI, 23
CCR Technologies Ltd., 133
CCS Income Trust, 133
CD Nova, 134
Cecon Limited, 135
CEDA International Corporation, 135
CEF Consultants Ltd., 135
CÉGEP d'André-Laurendeau, 1169
CÉGEP de Baie-Comeau, 1166
CÉGEP de Beauce-Appalaches, 1183
CÉGEP de Chicoutimi, 1166
CÉGEP de Drummondville, 1167
CÉGEP de Granby, 1168
CÉGEP de Jonquière, 1168
CÉGEP de l'Abitibi-Témiscamingue, 1182
CÉGEP de la Pocatière, 1177
CÉGEP de Lévis-Lauzon, 1169
CÉGEP de Marie-Victorin, 1171
CÉGEP de Matane, 1169
CÉGEP de Rimouski, 1181
CÉGEP de Rivière-du-Loup, 1181
CÉGEP de Saint-Hyacinthe, 1183
CÉGEP de Saint-Laurent, 1184
CÉGEP de Sainte-Foy, 1178
CÉGEP de Sept-Îles, 1184
CÉGEP de Sherbrooke, 1185
CÉGEP de Sorel-Tracy, 1186
CÉGEP de St-Jérôme, 1184
CÉGEP de Trois-Rivières, 1186
CÉGEP de Victoriaville, 1187
CÉGEP du Vieux-Montréal, 1171
CÉGEP Limoilou, 1178
CÉGEP Régional de Lanaudière à Joliette, 1168
CÉGEP St-Jean-sur-Richelieu, 1183
Cegerco - GCL Inc., 135
Cegertec Experts-Conseils, 135
Celfort Construction Materials Inc., 135
CEM Specialties Inc., 135
Cemcorp Ltd. Consulting Engineers, 135
Cement Association of Canada, 893
Cengea Solutions Inc., 136
CENSOL Inc., 136
Centennial College of Applied Arts & Technology, 1157
Center for Earth Observation Sciences, 1199
Center for Health, Environment & Justice, 893
Center for Metallurgical Process Engineering, 1201
Center for Plant Conservation, 893
Central, 622, 612, 614, 602, 592, 569, 610
Central & Arctic, 527
Central & Northern Vancouver Island, 536
Central (Gimli), 586
Central (Winnipeg), 586
Central British Columbia Railway & Forest Industry Museum Society, 893
Central Canadian Federation of Mineralogical Societies, 893
Central Elgin, 724
Central Interior Logging Association, 893
Central Kootenay, 677
Central Management Services, 659
Central Newfoundland Regional Health Centre, 1131
Central Okanagan, 677
Central Okanagan Naturalists Club, 893

Entry Name Index

Central Ontario Orchid Society, 893
Central Peace Regional Waste Management Commission, 757
Central Plains, 585
Central Region - Capital Health, IWK Health Centre, 613
Central Reproductions Ltd., 136
Central Saanich, 686
Central Valley Naturalists, 893
Le Centre Culturel franco-manitobain/Franco-Manitoban Cultural Centre, 587
Centre d'excellence en sciences agricoles et biotechnologiques, 1128
Centre d'expertise en analyse environnementale du Québec, 648
Centre d'expertise hydrique du Québec, 648
Centre de contrôle environnemental du Québec, 647
Centre de documentation, 1171
Centre de documentation (Génie), 1178
Centre de formation en entreprise et récupération, 893
Centre de recherche et de développement sur les aliments, 1183
Centre de recherche industrielle du Québec, 1211, 648, 1178
Centre de santé et de services sociaux de Laval, 1169
Centre de santé et de services sociaux Richelieu-Yamaska, 1183
Centre de service des Mines (Capitale-Nationale), 650
Centre de services partagés, 654
Centre de Toxicologie du Québec, 136
Centre des études collégiales - Carleton, 1166
Centre des Iles, 1167
Centre for Applied Business Research in Energy & the Environment, 1199
Centre for Applied Petroleum Sciences, 1206
Centre for Aquaculture & Environmental Research, 1201, 528
Centre for Developing Area Studies, 1171
Centre for Enhanced Forest Management, 1199
Centre for Environmental Engineering Research & Education, 1199
Centre for Environmental Research in Minerals, Metals, & Materials, 1201
Centre for Forest Biology, 1201
Centre for Forest Interdisciplinary Research, 1203
Centre for Global Studies, 1201
Centre for Health & Environment Research, 1201
Centre for Indigenous Environmental Resources, 893
Centre for Intelligent Mining Systems, 1199
Centre for Marine Environmental Prediction, 1206
Centre for Medicine, Ethics & Law, 893
Centre for Natural Hazard Research, 1201
Centre for Newfoundland Studies, 1131
Centre for Northern Agroforestry & Afforestation, 1212
Centre for Ocean Model Development for Applications, 1206
Centre for Offshore Oil and Gas Environmental Research, 1206
Centre for Rural Sustainability, 1042
Centre for Surface Transportation Technology, 548
Centre for Sustainable Community Development, 1201
Centre for Sustainable Infrastructure Research, 1212
Centre for Wildlife Ecology, 1201
Centre géoscientifique de Québec, 1211
Centre hospitalier de l'Université de Montréal Hôtel-Dieu, 1171, 1172
Centre hospitalier des Vallées de l'Outaouais Hôpital de Hull, 1167
Centre hospitalier régional du Grand-Portage, 1182
Centre hospitalier universitaire de Sherbrooke Hôtel-Dieu, 1185
Centre of Environmental Excellence, 1204
Centre of Excellence for Earth and Environmental Technologies, 1207
Centre québécois de formation aéronautique, 1183
Centre québécois du droit de l'environnement, 894
Centre régional de santé et de services sociaux Rimouski, 1181
Centre spécialisé des Pêches - Grande-Rivière, 1168
Centre Wellington, 724
Centre-du-Québec, 643
Century Environmental Services, 136
Century Environmental Systems, 136
Century Plastics Ltd., 136
CenturyVallen, 136
CEPA Environmental Registry, 1214
Cercles des jeunes naturalistes, 894
Cereal Research Centre, 509
CertainTeed Insulation Canada, Inc., 137
Certified Organic Associations of British Columbia, 894
Certified Technicians & Technologists Association of Manitoba, 894
Ceta-Research Inc., 894
Cetac-West, 137
CFB Borden, 545
CFB Cold Lake, 545
CFB Comox, 545
CFB Edmonton, 545
CFB Esquimalt, 545
CFB Gagetown, 545
CFB Gander, 545
CFB Goose Bay, 545
CFB Greenwood, 545
CFB Halifax, 545
CFB Kingston, 545
CFB Moose Jaw, 545
CFB North Bay, 545
CFB Petawawa, 545
CFB Shilo, 545
CFB Suffield, 546
CFB Trenton, 546
CFB Winnipeg, 546
CFS Alert, 546
CFS Leitrim, 546
CFS Masset, 546
CFS St. John's, 546
CH2M Hill Canada Limited, 1157, 137
CH2M HILL Canada Ltd., 137
Chalk River Laboratories, 511
Challenger Geomatics Ltd., 138
Chamard & Associés, 138
Chamber of Mineral Resources of Nova Scotia, 894
Chamber of Mines of Eastern British Columbia, 894, 1113
Chambly, 552, 734
Champion Moyer Diebel, 138
Champlain-Saint Lambert, 1184
Changements climatiques, 647
Chapleau (Fire Management & Area Office), 632
Char Developments Ltd., 138
The ChariTREE Foundation, 1040
Charland Thermojet Inc., 138
Charles Simon Architect & Planner, 138
Charlesworth & Associates, 138
Charlevoix, 747
Charlevoix-Est, 747
Charlottetown, 732
Charlottetown Branch, 513
Chartered Institute of Logistics and Transport in North America, 894
Chartis Insurance Company of Canada, 138
Chartwell Consultants Ltd., 138
Châteauguay, 735
Chatham-Kent, 537, 724
Chatham-Kent Health Alliance, 1139
Chatwin Engineering Ltd., 138
Chaudière - Appalaches (Saint-Romuald) Regional Branch, 513
Chaudière-Appalaches, 651, 644, 649, 655, 643
Cheiron Resources Ltd., 139
Chem Action Inc., 139
Chem Experts Inc., 139
Chem Solv, 139
Chemco Inc., 139
Chemcorp Industries Inc., 139
Chemical Ecology Research Group, 1201
Chemical Emission Management Services, 139
Chemical Institute of Canada, 894
Chemical Safety Training Associates, 139
ChemiGreen Inc., 139
Cheminées Sécurité Internationale Ltée, 139
Cheminfo Services Inc., 139
Chemline Plastics Ltd., 139
Chemrec, 140
Chemspec Inc, 140
Les Chenaux, 749
CHEP Canada, 140
Cherkewich, Ron, 1089
Chester District, 697
Chetwynd Campus, 1111
Chevron Canada Resources, 1100
CHI Canada Inc., 140
Chibougamau, 530
Chicoutimi, 517
Chief Financial Officer Sector, 542
Chief Informatics Office, 543
Chief Information Office, 581
Chief Information Officer, 522
Chilkoot Trail National Historic Site of Canada, 555
Chilliwack, 680
Chilliwack Campus, Library, 1111
Chilliwack Field Naturalists, 895
Chisholm, Fleming & Associates, 140
Chown, Cairns LLP, 1071
Christian Farmers Federation of Ontario, 895
Christmas Tree Farmers of Ontario, 895
Chromatographic Specialties Inc., 140
Chrysotile Institute, 895
CHUQ-CHUL, 1178
Church & Trought Inc., 140
Churchill Falls (Labrador) Corporation Limited, 601
Churchill Northern Studies Centre, 1122
CHUS Hôtel-Dieu, 1185
CIAL Group, 141
CIBA Spécialités Chimiques Canada inc., 141
CIMA+, 141
Cimatec Environmental Engineering Inc., 141
The Cintec Group, 391
Cintube Ltd., 141
Circul-Aire Inc., 141
Cirrus Environmental Services Inc., 141
Citizen Scientists, 895
Citizen Service Branch, 535
Citizens for a Safe Environment, 895
Citizens For Renewable Energy, 895
Citizens' Clearinghouse on Waste Management, 895
Citizens' Environment Alliance of Southwestern Ontario, 895
Citizens' Environment Watch, 895
Citizens' Opposed to Paving the Escarpment, 895
Citizenship & Heritage Sector, 519
City Farmer - Canada's Office of Urban Agriculture, 895
City Hospital, Saskatoon, 1189
City Metal Manufacturing Inc., 141
City of Edmonton, 1039
CIVICUS: World Alliance for Citizen Participation, 896
Civil Aviation Technical Reference Centre, 1128
Civtech Engineering & Surveying Ltd., 141
CLA Experts-Conseils, 142
Clamex Environnement Inc., 142
Clarence-Rockland, 708
Clarenville, 536
Clarenville Campus Learning Resource Centre, 1130
Clariant (Canada) Inc., 142
Clarington, 724
Clark Drummie, 1065
Clark Wilson LLP, 1058
Claus Engineering (1986) Ltd., 142
Clayton Research Associates Ltd., 142
Clean Air & Water Centre, 142
Clean Air Directorate, 523
Clean Air Foundation, 1214, 896, 1043
Clean Air Services Inc., 142
Clean Air Strategic Alliance, 1214, 567, 896
Clean Annapolis River Project, 896, 1042
Clean Earth Solutions Ltd., 142
Clean Energy Research Centre, 1201
Clean Environment Commission, 586
Clean Harbors Energy & Industrial Services Corp., 142
Clean North, 896, 1154
Clean Nova Scotia, 896, 1135, 1043
Clean Ontario, 143
Clean Water Action, 896
Cleanit Greenit Compost System, 143
Clear Environmental Products, 143
Clearstone Engineering Ltd., 143
Cleartech Industries Inc., 143
Clearview, 725
ClearView Geophysics Inc., 143
Clearview Packaging Inc., 143
Clearwater County, 669
Clemmer Technologies Inc., 143
Click4Carbon, 1214
Client Services, 620, 581
Clifton Associates Ltd., 144
Climate Action Network - Canada, 896
Climate Change & Environmental Services, 593
Climate Change Central, 144
Edmonton, 672, 144
Climate Change Impacts & Adaptation Directorate, 551
Climate Control Systems Inc., 144
Climate Institute, 896
Climate Project - Canada, 1214
Climatizer Insulation Inc., 144
Cline, Backus, Nightingale & McArthur, LLP, 1071
Clintar Groundskeeping Services, 144
Clinton, 620
Clivus Multrum Canada Ltd., 144
Cloverdale Paint Inc., 144
Club des ornithologues de Québec inc., 896

Entry Name Index

Clubs 4-H du Québec, 897
CMC Electronics Inc., 1184
CMD Insurance Services Inc., 144
CMEL Enterprises Ltd., 144
CML Northern Blower Inc., 144
CMS: Crisis Management Specialists Inc., 145
Co-operative Branch, 615
Co-operative Resource Management Institute in Resource & Environmental Management, 1201
CO2 Solution, 145
Coady International Institute, 897, 1134
Coalition for Alternatives to Pesticides, 1214
Coalition for Education in the Outdoors, 897
Coalition of Rail Shippers, 897
Coalition to Save the Elms, 897
Coast Forest Management Ltd., 145
Coast Forest Products Association, 897
Coast Paper Ltd., 145
Coast River Environmental Services Ltd., 145
Coast, 579
Coastal BioAgresearch Ltd., 145
Coastal CURA, 1206
Coastal Ecosystems Research Foundation, 897, 1040
Coastal Ocean Associates Inc., 145
Coastal Zones Research Institute Inc., 1203, 145
Coaticook, 747
Cobham Tracking & Locating Ltd., 145
Cobourg, 537, 708
Cochrane, 627, 671, 725
Cochrane (Fire Management Office), 632
CODE, 897
Coen Canada Inc., 146
Coffey Geotechnics Inc., 146
COGENCanada, 146
Cogent Environmental Solutions Ltd., 146
Cohen Highley LLP, 1069
Colchester County, 697
Cold Lake, 672
Cold Lake Regional Utility, 757
Cole Harbour Rural Heritage Society, 897
Cole-Parmer Canada Inc., 146
College & Careers Development Branch, 605
Collège André-Grasset, 1172
Collège Bourget, 1181
Collège d'Ahuntsic, 1172
Collège d'Alma, 1166
Collège de Maisonneuve, 1172
Collège de Rosemont, 1172
Collège de Saint-Félicien, 1182
Collège Édouard-Montpetit, 1169
Collège Français, 1172
Collège Jean-de-Brébeuf, 1172
Collège Laflèche, 1186
Collège Lasalle, 1172
Collège Lionel-Groulx, 1182
Collège Mérici, 1178
Collège Montmorency, 1169
Collège O'Sullivan, 1172
College of Alberta Professional Foresters, 897
College of Applied Biology British Columbia, 897
College of New Caledonia, 1115
College of the North Atlantic, 1133
College of the North Atlantic, Corner Brook Campus, 1130
College of the Rockies, 1111, 1030
College of Veterinarians of Ontario, 619
Collège Shawinigan, 1184
Collège St-Jean-Vianney, 1173
Collège Stanislas inc, 1177
Collège universitaire de St-Boniface, 1123
Les Collines-de-l'Outaouais, 749
Collingwood, 708
Colour Innovations Print Inc., 146
Columbia Basin Trust, 575
Columbia Power Corporation, 574
Columbia-Shuswap, 677
Colwood, 680
Combustion & Energy Systems Ltd., 146
Comco Manufacturing Ltd., 146
Comcor Environmental Limited, 146
Comenco Systems Inc., 147
Comfort King Doors & Windows Ltd., 147
Comité conjoint de chasse, de pêche et de piégeage, 650
Comité consultatif de l'environnement Kativik, 647
Comité de déontologie policière, 652
Comité maritime international, 898

Commands, 545
Commerce Court Educational Resources, 1146
Commercial & Consumer Products Directorate, 558
Commercial Acquisition & Supply Management Sector, 558
Commercial Solutions Inc., 147
Commercialization Division, 565
Commissaire à la déontologie policière, 653
Commissaire à la santé et du bien-être, 652
Commissaire de l'industrie de la construction, 655
Commissariat des incendies, 653
Commission de gestion des déchets solides de la péninsule Acadienne (COGEDES), 758
Commission de gestion enviro ressources du Nord-Ouest (COGERNO), 758
Commission de l'équité salariale, 655
Commission de la construction du Québec, 655
Commission de la santé et de la sécurité du travail, 1173
Commission de la santé et de la sécurité du travail du Québec, 655, 652
Commission de protection du territoire agricole du Québec, 646
Commission de reconnaissance des associations d'artistes et des associations de producteurs, 645
Commission de toponymie du Québec, Bibliothèque (Library), 1178
Commission des biens culturels du Québec, 645
Commission des lésions professionnelles, 655
Commission des normes du travail, 655
Commission des relations du travail, 655
Commission des transports du Québec, 654
Commission for Environmental Cooperation, 525, 763, 898, 1045
Commission for Public Complaints Against the Royal Canadian Mounted Police, 557
Commission for Sustainable Development, 764, 898
Commission municipale du Québec, 642
Commission québécoise des libérations conditionnelles, 653
Commissioner of the Environment & Sustainable Development, 511
Committee on the Status of Endangered Wildlife in Canada, 1214, 523
Common Business Services, 581
Commonwealth Association of Surveying & Land Economy, 898
Commonwealth Engineers' Council, 898
Commonwealth Forestry Association - Canadian Chapter, 898
Commonwealth Geographical Bureau, 898
Commonwealth Human Ecology Council, 898
Commonwealth of Australia, 767
Communications, 592
Communications & Consultations Branch, 507
Communications & Information Technology Ontario, 898
Communications Branch, 620
Communications Bureau, 530
Communications Research Centre Canada, 543
Communications Security Establishment, 545
Communications Services Branch, 631
Communications Services Manitoba, 587
Communications, Energy & Paperworkers Union of Canada, 899
Communicopia.Net Internet Inc., 147
Communities Economic Development Fund, 584
Communities of Tomorrow, 1046
Community & Economic Development Committee of Cabinet Secretariat, 585
Community & Hospital Infection Control Association Canada, 899
Community & Labour Development, 641
Community & Population Health Division, 569
Community - University Research for Recovery Alliance, 1204
Community Care Branch, 659
Community Development, 663, 639
Community Development Trust, 575
Community Health Nurses of Canada, 899
Community Land Use Planning Services, 589
Community Programs Directorate, 534
Community Resource Services Ltd., 147
Community Safety, 621
Community Safety & Partnerships Branch, 557
Community, Learner & Industry Connections Division, 563
Comox, 680
Comox Valley, 530, 677
Comox Valley Community Foundation, 1040
Competition Bureau, 543
Competition Tribunal, 543
Compliance & Enforcement, 580
Compliance & Field Services, 658
Compliance Division, 577
Compo Recycle, 147
Compo-Haut-Richelieu inc., 147

Compost Council of Canada, 899
Compost Management, 147
Composite Manufacturing Corp., 147
Les Composts du Québec inc., 268
Compressed Gas Association, Inc., 899
CompreVac Inc., 147
Comptank Corp., 147
Compteurs Lecomte Ltée, 148
Compusult Limited, 148
Comstock Canada Ltd., 148
Hamilton, 711, 725, 148
Con Cast Pipe, 148
CON-SPACE Communications Ltd., 148
Con-Tank Installations Ltd., 148
Con-Test, A Division of Contamination Containment Technology Inc., 148
Con-V-Air Inc., 148
Conair Group Inc., 148
Concept Controls Inc., 148
Conception Bay South, 693
Concerned Educators Allied for a Safe Environment, 899
Concordia Hospital, 1123
Concordia University, 1035
Concordia University College of Alberta, 1104, 1029
Concordia University Libraries, 1173
Condor Engineering Ltd., 149
Conestoga College Institute of Technology & Advanced Learning, 1143
Conestoga-Rovers & Associates, 149
Confederation College, 1155
The Conference Board of Canada, 899
Conference of New England Governors & Eastern Canadian Premiers, 764, 900
Conformance Check Inc., 149
Connections Research, 150
Connexions Information Sharing Services, 900, 1157
Connor Architects & Planners, 150
Conor Pacific Environmental Technology Inc., 150
Conporec Inc., 150
Conseil Canadien des Électrotechnologies, 900
Conseil consultatif du travail et de la main d'oeuvre, 655
Conseil de l'industrie forestière du Québec, 900
Conseil de la recherche forestière du Québec, 900
Conseil de la science et de la technologie, 648
Conseil de la transformation agroalimentaire et des produits de consommation, 900
Conseil des arts et des lettres du Québec, 645
Conseil des monuments et sites du Québec, 900
Conseil des services essentiels du Québec, 655
Conseil du médicament, 652
Conseil patronal de l'environnement du Québec, 901
Conseil québécois sur le tabac et la santé, 901
Conseil régional de l'environnement de la Gaspésie et des Îles-de-la-Madeleine, 901
Consent & Capacity Board, 628
Conservation & Environment Library, 1123
Conservation & Protection Directorate, 528
Conservation Branch, 623
Conservation Council of New Brunswick, 901, 1127, 1042
Conservation Council of Ontario, 901
Conservation Division, 658
Conservation Foundation, 901, 1043
Conservation Halton Foundation, 901, 1043
Conservation International, 901
Conservation Officer Services, 665
Conservation Ontario, 901
Conservation Programs Division, 586
Conservation Review Board, 621
The Conserver Group Inc., 391
Conserver Society of Hamilton & District, 902
Consolidated Envirowaste Industries Inc., 150
Consolidated Giroux Environment Inc., 150
Constant America Inc., 150
Construction & Maintenance Branch, 589
Construction & Operations Branch, 636
Construction Association of New Brunswick Inc., 902
Construction Association of Prince Edward Island, 902
Construction Specifications Canada, 902
Construction Val-d'Or Ltée, 150
Consultants Enviroconseil inc., 150
Les Consultants Eoletech S.Q. Inc., 268
Consultants Filion, Hansen & Associés Inc., 150
Les Consultants LBCD, 268
Consultants Mésar inc., 150
Les Consultants RSA, 268

Entry Name Index

Consultations & Communications Branch, 526
Consultative Group on International Agricultural Research, 902
Consulting & Audit Canada, 558
Consulting Engineers of Alberta, 902
Consulting Engineers of British Columbia, 903
Consulting Engineers of Manitoba Inc., 903
Consulting Engineers of Nova Scotia, 903
Consulting Engineers of Ontario, 903
Consulting Engineers of Saskatchewan, 903
Consulting Engineers of Yukon, 903
Consulting Foresters of British Columbia, 903
Consumaj, 151
Consumer & Commercial Affairs Branch, 600
Consumer & Safety Services, 663
Consumer Health Organization of Canada, 903
Consumer Policy Institute, 903
Consumers International, 903
Consumers' Association of Canada, 904
Conterm Inc., 151
Continental Conveyor Ontario Ltd., 151
Continuing Care, 613
Contor Terminals Inc., 151
Control Fire Systems, 151
Control Microsystems, 151
Control Techniques Drives Inc., 151
Les Contrôles PROVAN Associés Inc., 268
Convoyeurs B.M.G. inc., 151
Conway Davis Gryski, 1074
Conway Disposal Ltd., 151
Cook Engineering, 151
Cook Roberts LLP, 1062
Cooperative Resource Management Institute, 1201
Coquitlam, 536, 680
The Cord Group Ltd., 392
Cormorant Ltd., 152
Corner Brook, 693
Corner Brook Branch, 512
Corner Brook Pulp & Paper Ltd., 152
Cornwall, 537, 708
Cornwall Area, 625
Cornwall Campus, 1140
Corolon Coatings & Corrosion Control Technologies Inc., 152
Coroners Service of British Columbia, 582
Corporate & Community Finance, 594
Corporate & Financial Services, 660
Corporate & Provincial Program Support, 588
Corporate Management, 507
Corporate Management & Services Sector, 550
Corporate Management Division, 624, 634
Corporate Planning & Services Division, 621
Corporate Planning Branch, 630
Corporate Policy, Legislation, & Intergovernmental Relations, 580
Corporate Services, 568, 574, 594
Corporate Services & Direct Services Division, 628
Corporate Services & Fleet Management, 597
Corporate Services Division, 635, 577
Corporate Services Group, 560
Corporate Stakeholder Relations, 535
Corporate Strategic Services Division, 571
Corporate Support Division, 569
Corporation d'hébergement du Québec, 652
Corporation des entreprises de traitement de l'air et du froid, 904
Corporation des maîtres mécaniciens en tuyauterie du Québec, 904
Corporation des officiers municipaux agréés du Québec, 904
Correctional Service of Canada, 557
Correctional Services, 621
Corrections Branch, 582
Corrosion Service Company Limited, 152
Corrpro Canada, Inc., 152
Corrugated Steel Pipe Institute, 904
Cosmopolitan Industries Limited, 152
Côte-Nord, 643, 540, 651
Coteau-du-Lac National Historic Site of Canada, 555
Cottonwood Consultants Ltd, 1100
Cottonwood Consultants Ltd., 152
Couchiching Institute on Public Affairs, 904
Council for a Smoke-Free PEI, 904
Council of Atlantic Premiers, 609, 764, 904
Council of Canadian Fire Marshals & Fire Commissioners, 904
Council of Forest Industries, 905
Council of Great Lakes Governors, 905
Council of Marine Carriers, 905
Council of Ministers of Education & Training, 609
Council of Ontario Construction Associations, 905

Council of Outdoor Educators of Ontario, 905
Council of Science Editors, 905
Council of the Haida Nation - Haida Fisheries Program, 905
Council on Hemispheric Affairs, 905
Counterspil Research Inc., 153
Countryside Disposal Service Ltd., 153
Courtenay, 680
The Cousteau Society, 905
Covertech Fabricating Inc., 153
Cowansville, 735
Cowater International Inc., 153
Cowichan Campus, 1112
Cowichan Valley, 677
Cowichan Valley Naturalists' Society, 905
Cox and Palmer - Charlottetown, 1082
Cox and Palmer - Fredericton, 1064
Cox and Palmer - Halifax, 1067
Cox and Palmer - St. John's, 1065
CP Environmental Technologies, 153
CPC Tuyauteries Canada Ltée, 153
CPP/OAS BC/Yukon Processing Centre, 536
Craig Hydrogeologic Inc., 153
Cramer Nursery Inc., 153
Cranbrook, 680
Cranbrook Branch, 512
Crandall Engineering Ltd., 153
Crane Energy Flow Solutions, 153
Crane Operators Appeal Board, 611
Crease Harman & Company, 1062
Credit Union Deposit Guarantee Corporation, 600
Credit Valley Conservation Foundation, 905, 1043
Credit Valley Hospital, 1145
Creelman Agricultural Society, 905
Creston Campus, 1111
Crompton Co./Cie, 1140
Crompton Technology Inc., 153
Crop Technology, 620
CropLife Canada, 905
Croplife International, 906
Crops & Livestock Research Centre, 509
Crops Branch, 585
Crosbie Industrial Services Ltd., 153
Crossman Machinery Co. Ltd., 154
Crown Assets Distribution Centre, 558
Crown Fibre Tube Inc., 154
Crown Land Administration, 574
Crown Lands Record Centre, 614
Crown Packaging Ltd., 154
Crown Publications, Inc., 154
Crown Shred & Recycling, 154
Crown Timber Board of Examiners, 631
CSA International, 1157
Cues Canada, 154
Cultural Services Branch, 667
Culture & Community Development Division, 565
Culture & Heritage, 604, 617
Culture, Heritage & Libraries, 638
Culture Division, 616
Culture Policy, Programs & Services Division, 622
Culture, Heritage & Recreation Programs Division, 587
Cultus Lake Salmon Research Laboratory, 1201
Cumberland County, 697
Cumulative Environmental Management Association, 906
Cunningham Sheet Metal Works Inc., 154
Cunningham, Swan, Carty, Little & Bonham LLP, 1069
Curtis Environmental & Engineering Inc., 154
Curtis Reclamation Service Ltd., 154
CUSO-VSO, 906
Custom Environmental Services Ltd., 154
Cutler-Hammer Canada, 154
Cyanide Destruct Systems Inc., 155
Cyntech Corporation, 155
Cypher International Ltd., 155
Cypress Hills Regional College, 1191
Cypress Sales Partnership, 155
Cyr Engineering Ltd., 155
Czech Republic, 767

D

D'Arcy & Deacon LLP, 1063
D'Autray, 747
D. Besner & Associates Inc., 155
D. Greenfield Associates Ltd., 156
D.G. Taylor Inc., Consulting Ecologist Division, 156

D.M. Wills Associates Limited, 156
D.R. Estey Engineering Ltd., 156
Da-Lee Dust Control, 156
Dagex Inc., 156
Daigneault, avocats inc., 1083
Dairy & Swine Research & Development Centre, 509
Dakins Engineering Group Ltd., 156
Dalco Wastewater Specialists Inc., 156
Dalhousie University, 1206, 1033, 1034
Dalhousie University Libraries, 1135
Dalynn Biologicals Inc., 156
Dana Porter Library, 1164
Danatec Educational Services Ltd., 156
Danfoss Inc. - Electric Floor Heating Division, 157
Danfoss Inc. - Hydronic Heating Division, 157
Dangerous Goods Advisory Council, 906
Dangerous Goods Control & Rail Safety, 570
Daniel & Partners LLP, 1072
Daniel Fauteux Environnement inc., 157
Darke Marketing Inc., 157
Dartmouth, 537
Dartmouth Appliance Repair, 157
Dartmouth Metals & Bottles Ltd., 157
Dashwood Industries Ltd., 157
DATA Group of Companies, 157
The DATA Group of Companies, 392
Data Tech Environmental Services, 157
Datarite, 157
Daubois Inc., 158
Dauphin, 536
Dave Vallieres & Associates Inc., 158
David A. McLean & Associates, 158
David Suzuki Foundation, 1214, 906, 1040
David Winton Bell Memorial Library, 1153
Davies Howe Partners, 1074
Davies Ward Phillips & Vineberg LLP, 1074
Davies Ward Phillips & Vineberg S.E.N.C.R.L., s.r.l., 1083
Davis & Company LLP, 1091, 1066
Davis Campus, 1139
Davis Centre Library, 1164
Davis Controls Ltd., 158
Davis LLP - Calgary, 1050
Davis LLP - Edmonton, 1054
Davis LLP - Montréal, 1083
Davis LLP - Toronto, 1074
Davis LLP - Vancouver, 1058
Dawson College, 1173
Dawson Creek, 680
Dawson District Renewable Resource Council, 665
Dawson Historical Complex National Historic Site of Canada, 555
Daybar Industries Ltd., 158
DB Geoservices Inc., 158
DBC Environmental Services Ltd., 158
DBM6/LSTL Building, 1149
DBS Environmental, 158
DCL International Inc., 158
DDH Environnement ltée, 159
DEB Canada, 159
Decibel Consultants Inc., 159
Decommissioning Consulting Services Limited, 159
Dectron Internationale, 159
Dedicated Plastic Tanks Inc., 159
Defence Construction Canada, 558, 520
Defence R & D Canada - Atlantic, 1135
Defence R & D Canada - Ottawa, 1149
Defence R & D Canada - Suffield, 1109
Degussa Canada Inc., 159
Deh Cho, 605
Dekka Resins Inc., 159
DEL Warehousing Inc., 160
Del-Air Systems Ltd., 160
Delcan Water, 160
Delivery Services Division, 566
Dell Tech Laboratories Ltd., 160
Delorme, LeBel, Bureau, s.e.n.c., 1089
The Delphi Group, 392
Delta, 686
Delta Aerial Surveys Ltd., 160
Delta Piping Products Canada Inc., 160
Demers MetalFab Inc., 160
Demesa Inc., 160
Demilec Inc., 160
Democratic Socialist Republic of Sri Lanka, 769
Dendron Resource Surveys Inc., 161
Denoco Energy Systems Ltd., 161

Entry Name Index

Denso North America Inc., 161
Department of Aboriginal Affairs & Intergovernmental Relations, 604
Department of Agriculture, 636, 609
Department of Agriculture, Aquaculture & Fisheries, 591
Department of Business New Brunswick, 592
Department of Communities, Cultural Affairs & Labour, 638
Department of Community & Government Services, 617
Department of Culture, Language, Elders & Youth, 617
Department of Economic & Rural Development, 610
Department of Economic Development & Transportation, 617
Department of Education, Culture & Employment, 605
Department of Energy, 611, 592
Department of Environment, 611, 618
Department of Environment & Conservation, 598
Department of Environment & Natural Resources, 605
Department of Environment, Energy & Forestry, 638
Department of Executive & Intergovernmental Affairs, 618
Department of Fisheries & Aquaculture, 609, 599
Department of Fisheries, Aquaculture & Rural Development, 639
Department of Government Services, 599
Department of Health, 640, 594, 613
Department of Health & Community Services, 601
Department of Health & Social Services, 618, 606
Department of Health Promotion & Protection, 613
Department of Industry, Tourism & Investment, 606
Department of Innovation & Advanced Learning, 640
Department of Innovation, Trade & Rural Development, 601
Department of Intergovernmental Affairs, 613
Department of Justice, 161
Department of Justice Canada, 161
Department of Labour & Workforce Development, 614
Department of Labrador & Aboriginal Affairs, 602
Department of Local Government, 594
Department of Municipal & Community Affairs, 607
Department of Municipal Affairs, 602
Department of Natural Resources, 595, 614, 602
Department of Post-Secondary Education, Training & Labour, 595
Department of Public Safety, 596
Department of Public Works & Services, 608
Department of Service Nova Scotia & Municipal Relations, 615
Department of Supply & Services, 597
Department of the Environment, 593
Department of the Provincial Treasury, 642
Department of Tourism, 641
Department of Tourism & Parks, 597
Department of Tourism, Culture & Heritage, 616
Department of Tourism, Culture & Recreation, 604
Department of Transportation, 597, 608
Department of Transportation & Infrastructure Renewal, 616
Department of Transportation & Public Works, 641
Department of Transportation & Works, 604
Department of Wellness, Culture & Sport, 597
Departmental Planning & Financial Administration Directorate, 534
Dependable Turbines Ltd., 161
Deputy Minister's Office, 620, 507
Deputy Minister, MGS, Associate Secretary of the Cabinet & Secretary of Mgmt Board of Cabinet, 626
Des Moulins - Lanaudière (Terrebonne) Regional Branch, 513
Deschênes Drilling Ltd., 161
Deschênes et Fils Ltée., 161
Dessau, Inc., 162
Deuce Disposal Ltd., 162
Deux-Montagnes, 735, 747
Développement durable, 648
Développement régional et développement durable, 646
Devon Canada Corporation, 1100
Devon Library & Information Centre, 1103
DeVry Institute of Technology, 1101
Dewar Insulations Ltd., 162
Dewar Pacific Projects Ltd., 162
DGH Engineering, 162
DGM Inc., 163
Diacon Technologies Ltd., 163
Diagnostic Engineering Inc., 163
Diagnostix Ltd., 163
Diana M. Priestly Law Library, 1120
Diane Beckett, 163
Dieppe, 691
Digby, 537
Digicon Building Control Solutions, 163
Digital Land Resources, 163
Dillon Consulting Ltd., 163
Dimplex North America, 164
DINOFLEX Manufacturing Ltd., 164

Dionex Canada Limited, 164
Direct Marketing Association, 906
Direct Sellers Association of Canada, 906
Direct Separation Solutions, 164
Direction générale de la Sûreté du Québec, 653
Directions régionales/Regional Offices, 644
Directory of Consultants in Occupational and Environmental Health & Safety, 1214
Disease Prevention & Health Protection Unit, 660
District Agricultural Offices, 637
District Health Authorities 1, 2 & 3 (Western Nova Scotia), 1138
Diversified Waste Solutions, 164
Divex Marine, 164
DJA Environmental Consultants Inc., 164
dmg world media (Canada) Inc., 164
Doctors Manitoba, 906
Doctors Nova Scotia, 906
Dofasco Inc., 1140
Doherty's Hydraulic Oil Recycling, 164
Dol Hydroseeding Inc., 164
Dolbeau-Mistassini, 735
Domaine Label & Trim Inc., 164
Le Domaine-du-Roy, 749
Dominican Republic, 767
Dominion Recycling Ltd., 165
Domtar Inc., 165
Donalco Inc., 165
Donald Olynyk, Acoustical Engineer, 165
Donald W. Craik Engineering Library, 1123
Donald-Petzel Memorial Library, 1178
Donnelly & Murphy, 1068
Donner Canadian Foundation, 1043
Donovan & Company, 1059
Double Industries & Trading, 165
Double T Equipment Ltd., 165
Doucette Library of Teaching Resources, 1101
Dougan & Associates, 165
Douglas Brothers, 165
Douglas College, 1114, 1030
Douglas, Barwick Inc., 165
Dove Environmental Services Inc., 165
Downtown Campus Library, 1117
DPL Group, 166
Dr. D.A. Thompson Memorial Library, 1126
Dr. Everett Chalmers Regional Hospital, 1127
Draeger Safety Canada Ltd., 166
DRDC Valcartier, R&D pour La defense Canada, Valcartier, 1186
Dredge No. 4 National Historic Site of Canada, 555
Drexan Energy Systems Inc., 166
Drilling Fluids Treatment Systems Inc., 166
Drinking Water Management Division, 624
Drinking Water Program Management Branch, 624
Drive Clean Office, 624
Drive Safety, Research & Traffic Safety Initiative, 570
Driver Control Board, 663
DRL Environmental Services, 166
Droycon Bioconcepts Inc., 166
DRS Earthwise Society, 906
Drug Plan & Extended Benefits, 660
Drug Strategy & Controlled Substances Programme, 534
Drummond, 747
Drummondville, 530, 735
Drummondville Branch, 513
Dryden, 537
DST Consulting Engineers, 166
DSS Marine Inc., 167
DTE Industries Ltd., 167
Ducks Unlimited Canada, 906, 1122
Ducks Unlimited Inc., 907
Duerden & Keane Consultants Inc., 167
Dufferin, 627, 699
Dufour Scott Phelps & Mason, 1090
DuMoulin, Boskovich, 1059
Duncan & Craig LLP, Lawyers & Mediators, 1055
Dundas, 627
Dundas-Jafine Inc., 167
Dunsford & Scott, 1056
DuPont Canada Inc., 167
Dural Industries, 167
Durex Steel & Alloy Industries Ltd., 167
Durham, 627, 699
Durham (Whitby) Branch, 513
Durham Avicultural Society of Ontario, 907
Durham College of Applied Arts & Technology, 1147
Durmitor Inc., 167

Dutab, 167
DynaMotive Energy Systems Corporation, 167
Dynamotive Energy Systems Corporation, 168
Dynapompe Inc., 168

E

E.A.I. Technologies Inc., 168
E.B. Tobe Enterprises, 168
E.H. Hanson Engineering Group Ltd., 168
E.I. duPont Canada Company, 1145
E.K. Gillin & Associates Inc., 168
E.K. Williams Law Library, 1123
E2 Management Corporation, 168
E2D Laboratory, 168
e3 Solutions Inc., 168
EAGLE (Environmental-Aboriginal Guardianship through Law & Education), 907
Eagle Home Inspection Services Inc., 168
Earth & Environmental Technologies (ETech), 168
Earth Day Canada, 1214, 907
Earth Energy Society of Canada, 1214, 907
Earth First! Journal, 907
Earth Island Institute, 907
Earth Sciences Sector, 550
Earth Voice, 907
Earthbound Environmental Inc., 168
Earthcycle, 169
EarthFx Inc., 169
Earthguard Environmental Group Inc., 169
earthRight Solar Products, 169
Earthroots, 907
EarthSave Canada, 1117
Earthsave Canada, 907
EarthTrends, 1214
Earthwatch Europe, 907
Earthworks Technology Inc., 169
East African Wild Life Society, 907
East Coast Aquatics, 169
East Coast Ecosystems Research Organization, 1206
East Gwillimbury, 708
East Kootenay, 677
East Kootenay Chamber of Mines, 907
East, 592
Eastcan Geomatics, 169
Eastern, 610, 630, 602, 603, 586, 621, 629
Eastern & Southern Africa, 544
Eastern Canada Orchid Society, 907
Eastern Canada Soil and Water Conservation Centre, 1203
Eastern Cereal & Oilseed Research Centre Library, 509, 1149
Eastern Division Library/Bibliothèque de la division de l'est, 1178
Eastern Environmental Services Ltd., 169
Eastern Habitat, 525
Eastern Habitat Joint Venture, 764
Eastern Office, 600
Eastern Ontario Model Forest, 908
Eastern Region - Guysborough Antigonish Strait, Cape Breton, 613
Eastern Republic of Uruguay, 769
Eastern Scotian Shelf Integrated Management Initiative, 1206
Eastern Wind Power Inc., 169
Eastman, 585
Eastwest Synergies Inc., 169
Eaton Hydro Developers Inc., 169
EBA Engineering Consultants Ltd., 169
Eccleston LLP, 1075
ECE Group - a Division of Conestoga-Rovers & Associates, 170
Echo Environmental, 170
Eckel Industries, 170
ECL Envirowest Consultants Ltd., 170
Eco Canada, 170
Éco Entreprises Québec, 908
ECO Fuel Systems Inc., 170
Eco Waste Solutions, 170
Eco Week.ca, 1193
Eco Wood Products, 170
Eco-Guide International, 170
Eco-North Laboratories, 171
Eco-Tec Ltd., 171
ECO-TEK Ecological Technologies Inc., 171
Eco2 Systems Inc., 171
EcoAction, 523
Ecocern Inc., 171
EcoCompliance.ca, 1193
Ecodyne Ltd., 171

Entry Name Index

EcoEthic Inc., 171
EcoFlame International Inc., 171
Ecofluid Systems Inc., 171
Ecoforestry, 1193
Ecoforestry Institute Society, 908
Ecojustice, 1214
Ecojustice Canada, 908, 1117
EcoKids, 1214
Ecolad Corp., 172
École nationale d'aérotechnique, 1183
École nationale de police du Québec, 653
École nationale des pompiers du Québec, 653
École polytechnique de Montréal, 1173
EcoLog Information Resources Group, 172
Ecological Agriculture Projects, 908
Ecological Farmers Association of Ontario, 908
Ecological Monitoring and Assessment Network, 1214
Ecological Reserves Advisory Committee, 586
Ecological Services Division, 591
Ecological Society of America, 908
Ecologistics Research Services, 1155, 172
EcoLogo, 1214
Ecology Action Centre, 908
Ecology North, 908
Ecology Products International, 172
Ecomark Ltd., 172
ECOMatters Inc., 172
Economic & Policy Analysis, 528
Economic Competitiveness Division, 575
Economic Development, 617
Economic Development Division, 620
Economics & Competitiveness Division, 565
Economics & Trade, 580
Economics & Transportation I&IT Cluster, 636
Econotech Services Ltd., 1112, 172
ecoNova Scotia for Clean Air and Climate Change, 1206
EcoPerth, 908
ECORC Plant Research Library, 1150
EcoSource Mississauga, 908
Ecosystem Science, 528
Ecosystems Branch, 578
Ecotainer Sales Inc., 172
EcoTec Environmental Consultants Inc., 172
Ecotech Planners & Advisors Inc., 172
EcoVu Analytics, 173
EDA Collaborative Inc., 173
EDC Regional Offices, 525
EDM Consultants Ltd., 173
EDM Environmental Design & Management Ltd., 173
Edmonton & NWT, 517
Edmonton - Provincial Nominee Program, 565
Edmonton Branch, 512
Edmonton Canada Place, 535
Edmonton Meadowlark, 535
Edmonton North, 535
Edmonton Planning & Development Dept. Library, 1105
Edmonton South, 535
Edmonton South Branch, 512
Edmonton Space & Science Foundation, 909, 1039
Edmonton Transportation & Streets Dept., 1105
Edmonton Waste Management Centre of Excellence, 1199, 1200
Edmundston, 536, 691
Edmundston Branch, 512
Edson, 535
Education & Culture, 605
Education & Outreach Branch, 624
Educational Program Innovations Centre, 173
Edwards, 173
Edwards, Kenny & Bray LLP, 1059
ÉEM inc., 173
EEP Engineered & Environmental Products Inc., 173
EFC Control Inc., 173
Efficiency Engineering Inc., 173
Efficiency NB, 593
EFR Disposal, 173
Egetec Enterprises Inc., 174
Eggum, Abrametz, Eggum, 1090
Egmond Associates Ltd., 174
EIL Environmental Services, 174
EITNL/Earth Information Technologies (nfld) Limited, 174
The EJLB Foundation, 1046
El-Rayes Environmental Corp., 174
Elasto Valve Rubber Products Inc., 174
Elecsar Engineering Co. Ltd., 174
Electric Motor Service (1979) Ltd., 174

Electric Vehicle Council of Ottawa Inc., 909
Electric Vehicle Society of Canada, 909
Electricity & Alternative Energy, 576
Electricity Distributors Association, 909
Electricity Resources Branch, 551
Electricity, Alternative Energy, & Carbon Capture & Storage Division, 567
Electro-Air Canada, 174
Electro-Federation Canada Inc., 909
Electro-Mecanik Inc., 175
Electronic Commerce Branch, 543
Electronic Warfare Associates - Canada, Ltd., 175
Electronics Product Stewardship Canada, 909
Electronics-recycling.com, 175
Elemental Research Inc., 175
Elford Environmental, 175
Elgin, 627, 699
Elgin Pure Water Supply, 175
ELI Eco Chemical Technologies Inc., 175
Elite Technologies Inc., 175
Elizabeth Dafoe Library, 1123
Elizabethtown-Kitley, 725
Elk Island National Park of Canada, 555
Ellett Industries, 176
Elliot Lake, 538, 709
Elliott & Elliott Limited Consulting Engineers, 176
Elmec Engineering Ltd., 176
Elmridge Engineering Inc., 176
Elmtree Environmental Ltd., 176
Elora Environment Centre, 909
Elsa Wild Animal Appeal of Canada, 909
Les Emballages Polyform inc., 268
Embassy of Mexico in Canada, 531
Emco, 176
Emco Wheaton Corp., 176
Emerge Knowledge Design Inc., 176
Emergency Health Services, 613
Emergency Management & National Security Branch, 557
Emergency Management BC, 582
Emergency Management Ontario, 621
Emergency Measures Organization, 608, 664, 589
EmerGeo Solutions Inc., 176
Emergex Planning Inc., 176
Emerson Electric Canada Limited, 177
Emery International Developments, 177
Emery Jamieson LLP, 1055
EMP Environmental Management & Protection Corporation, 177
Empire Dynamic Structures Ltd., 177
Employment Development Agency, 640
Employment Practices Branch, 629
Employment Standards Board, 638
Employment Standards Division, 590
Employment Standards Tribunal, 581
EMS Technologies, 178
EnCana Corporation, 1101
Encana Corporation, 178
Encyclopedia of Earth, 1214
Endangered Species Advisory Committee, 586
Endress+Hauser Canada Ltd., 178
Endswell Foundation, 1040
Eneco Industries Ltd., 178
Enercombustion Ltd., 179
Enercorp Instruments Ltd., 179
Eneready Products Ltd., 179
Énergie, 650
Énergie Solaire Québec, 909
Energy & Environment Industries Branch, 543
Energy & Minerals, 639
Energy Action Council of Toronto, 909
Energy Branch, 603
Energy Climate Change & Green Strategy Initiatives Branch, 590
Energy Conservation Contractors Warranty Corporation, 179
Energy Corporate Policy, 664
Energy Council of Canada, 909
Energy Development Initiative, 590
Energy Diversification Research Laboratory, 1186
Energy Future Division, 567
Energy Management, Markets & Climate Change, 611
Energy Ottawa, 179
Energy Policy Sector, 550
Energy Probe, 1214
Energy Probe Research Foundation, 910, 1157, 1043
Energy Resources Conservation Board, 567
Energy Resources Conservation Board (ERCB), 1101
Energy Solutions Centre, 664

Energy Systems & Design Limited, 179
Energy Technology Products Ltd., 179
Energy, Minerals & Metals Information Centre, 1150
Enermodal Engineering Ltd., 179
Enerplan Consultants Ltd., 179
Enerscan Consultants Limited, 179
Enervac Corp., 180
Enforcement, 632
Enforcement Branch, 523
Enforcement Division, 615
Enforcement Program/Conservation Officer Service, 578
Enform: The Safety Association for the Upstream Oil & Gas Industry, 910
Engine Control Systems, 180
Engineered Air, 180
Engineering & Computer Science Library, 1157
Engineering & Land Use Planning, 602
Engineering & Operations Division, 589
Engineering & Science Library, 1142
Engineering Branch, 1150
The Engineering Institute of Canada, 910
Engineering Library, 1127, 1189
Engineering Management Services Croscan, 180
Engineering Standards Branch, 636
Engineers Canada, 910
Engineers Without Borders, 910
EnGlobe Corp., 180
Les Engrais Naturels McInnes Inc./McInnes Natural Fertilizers Inc., 268
ENMAX Corporation, 181
Enmet Canada Ltd., 181
ENPAR Technologies Inc., 181
EnRel Energy Group, 181
Entara Consulting Services Ltd., 181
Entech Environmental Consultants Ltd., 181
Entech Laboratories, 181
Entegrity Wind Systems Inc., 181
Enterprise Cape Breton Corporation, 543
Enterprise Saskatchewan, 662
Enterprise Steel Fabricators Ltd., 181
Entomological Society of Alberta, 910
Entomological Society of British Columbia, 910, 1112
Entomological Society of Manitoba Inc., 910
Entomological Society of Ontario, 911, 1140
Entomological Society of Saskatchewan, 911
Entraco, 181
Les Entreprises Forlam, 268
Les Entreprises Julien Inc., 268
Entretien M. Perron inc. (SANI-TRI), 181
Entropex, 182
Entropic Energy Inc., 182
ENV Treatment Systems Inc., 182
Envir'eau Puits Inc., 182
Envirem Technologies Inc., 182
EnvirInfo, 182
Enviro Clean Ltd., 182
Enviro Rentals, 182
Enviro Scan Technologies Inc., 182
Enviro Vault Ltd., 182
Enviro Waste Ltd., 182
Enviro Waste Management Services Ltd., 182
Enviro Wood Recovery Systems Ltd., 182
Enviro-Accès Inc., 911
Enviro-Care Services, 182
The Enviro-Connect, 392
Enviro-Gun Ltd., 182
Enviro-Klean Technologies Inc., 182
Enviro-Met Engineering, 183
Enviro-Pack Material Handling, 183
Enviro-RISQUE Inc., 183
Enviro-Safe Chemicals Canada Inc., 183
Enviro-Sol Plus, 183
Enviro-Solutions Ltd., 183
Enviro-Systèmes Inc., 183
EnviroCare Environmental Services Ltd., 183
Envirochem Services Inc., 183
Enviroconseil, 183
Envirogain Inc., 184
Envirogard Products Ltd., 184
Envirogineering, 184
EnviroGuard Ltd., 184
EnviroJobs, 1214
EnviroLine, 1193, 184
EnviroMed Detection Services, 184
EnviroMetal Technologies Inc., 184

Entry Name Index

Envirometrex, 184
EnvironChem Engineering Consultants, 184
Environment & Forestry, 662
Environment Accounts & Statistics Division, 559
Environment Branch, 599
Environment Canada, 1211, 1208, 1207, 1202, 521, 1167
Environment Canada Library, Downsview, 1157
Environment Canada Regional Directors General, 522
Environmental & Natural Areas Management, 612
Environmental & Sustainable Development Services Directorate, 559
Environmental Abatement Council of Ontario, 911
Environmental Accident Protection Inc., 184
Environmental Action Barrie, 911
Environmental Advisory Council, 639
Environmental Advisory Group, 185
Environmental Affairs, 561
Environmental Allies Inc., 185
Environmental Appeal Board, 577
Environmental Approvals Branch, 587
Environmental Assessment & Approvals Branch, 625
Environmental Assessment Branch, 612, 658
Environmental Assessment Division, 599
Environmental Assurance Division, 568
Environmental Bankers Association, 911
Environmental Bill of Rights Office, 624
Environmental Biodetection Products Inc., 185
Environmental Building Science Inc., 185
Environmental Careers Organization of Canada, 911
The Environmental Coalition of PEI, 911
Environmental Coalition of Prince Edward Island, 1045
Environmental Commissioner of Ontario, 626, 1157
Environmental Communications Options, 185
Environmental Consultants & Engineers, 185
Environmental Contaminants, 1214
Environmental Defence, 911
Environmental Defense, 911
Environmental Disposal Concepts Inc., 185
Environmental Dynamics Inc., 185
Environmental Economics International, 185
Environmental Education, 612
Environmental Education Ontario, 912
Environmental Educators' Provincial Specialist Association, 912
Environmental Effects Monitoring Office, 524
Environmental Health, 640
Environmental Health Association of Ontario, 912
Environmental Health Foundation of Canada, 912, 1040
Environmental Health Research Network, 1211
Environmental Health Services, 666
Environmental Industries, 1214
Environmental Industry Associations, 912
Environmental Information Association, 912
Environmental Innovations & Emerging Sciences Branch, 624
Environmental Law Centre, 1105
Environmental Law Centre (Alberta) Society, 1055
The Environmental Law Centre (Alberta) Society, 912
Environmental Law Institute, 912
Environmental Management, 593, 578
Environmental Management Division, 568
Environmental Managers Association of British Columbia, 912
Environmental Monitoring & Compliance, 612
Environmental Monitoring & Reporting Branch, 624
Environmental Plastics Advisory Service, 185
Environmental Policy & Programs Branch, 620
Environmental Programs, 665
Environmental Protection, 618
Environmental Protection & Audit Division, 658
Environmental Protection Agency: Office of Acquisition Management, 532
Environmental Protection Division, 605, 577
Environmental Protection Operations Directorate, 523
Environmental Protection Review Canada, 521
Environmental Protection UK, 912
Environmental Quality, 578
Environmental R&D Capital Corporation, 185
Environmental Remediation Equipment Inc., 185
Environmental Reporting Systems Limited, 186
Environmental Research & Studies Centre, 1200
Environmental Response Centre, 568
Environmental Review Tribunal, 623
Environmental Reviews, 1193
Environmental Sciences & Standards Division, 624
Environmental Sciences Research Centre, 1206
Environmental Services Association of Alberta, 912
Environmental Services Association of Nova Scotia, 913

Environmental Services Group, 616
Environmental Solutions Remediation Services, 186
Environmental Stewardship Branch, 522
Environmental Stewardship Division, 586, 568, 577
Environmental Structures, 186
Environmental Studies Association of Canada, 913
Environmental Trade & Innovation, 612
Environmental Training Institute, 186
Environmental Waste International, 186
Environmental Youth Alliance, 913
Environmentalists For Nuclear Energy (Canada) Inc., 913
Environnement Canada, 1214
Environnement ESA Inc., 186
Environnement Godin Inc., 186
Environnement jeunesse, 913
Environova Planning Group Inc., 186
Enviropac Inc., 186
Enviroplast inc, 187
EnviroPower Equipment Marketing Inc., 187
EnviroSan Products Ltd./SOLUTION 2000, 187
Enviroservices Inc., 187
Envirosoil Ltd., 187
EnviroSORT Inc., 187
Envirosphere Consultants Ltd., 187
Envirosystems Inc., 187
Envirotec Services Incorporated, 187
Envirotech Associates Limited, 187
Envirotech Engineering, 187
Envirotech Nisku Inc., 188
Envirotech Pollution Controls Ltd., 188
Envirotest Inc., 188
Envirotray Ltd., 188
EnviroZine, 1193
Envision Compliance, 188
Envision Planning Solutions Inc., 188
Envision Sustainability Tools, 188
ENVision...synergy, 188
Envitech Automation Inc., 188
EOA Scientific System Inc., 188
Éocycle Technologies Inc., 188
EPA Certified Clean Ltd., 188
EPCOR, 1105
EPCOR Energy Services Inc., 188
EPEC Consulting (Sask) Ltd., 189
EPI Environmental Products Inc., 189
Epistream Consulting Inc, 189
EPS Wood Products Ltd., 189
Epsilon Chemicals Ltd., 189
Equipement Labrie Ltee, 189
Equipements Lapierre Inc., 189
Les Équipements Vibrotech Inc., 268
Eric Marshall Aquatic Research Library (Central and Artic Library), 1123
Erickson & Partners, 1072
Eriksson Sediment Systems Inc., 189
Erin, 709
Erin Consulting Ltd., 189
Esco Engineering, 189
ESI Environmental Sensors Inc., 189
Espanola, 538
Esquimalt, 686
ESRI Canada Ltd., 190
ESRS Environmental Solution, 190
Essa, 725
Essex, 627, 709, 699
Est-de-la-Montérégie, 654
Est-de-Montréal, 540
Estco Battery Management Inc., 190
Estevan, 540, 754
Estrie, 515
Estrie et Montérégie, 653
Estrie, Centre-du-Québec, 653
Estrie-Montréal-Montérégie et Laval-Lanaudière-Laurentides, 651
Estuaire et Eaux intérieures, 645
ETC Group, 913
Les Etchemins, 749
EthicScan Canada, 190
ETV Canada, 1214, 190
Eucania International Inc., 190
European Association of Geoscientists & Engineers, 913
European Geosciences Union, 913
European Solidarity Towards Equal Participation of People, 913
European Space Agency, 913
Eurovac, 191
Ever Green Recycling, 191

Evergreen, 1215, 914, 1043
Evergreen Regional Waste Management Services Commission, 757
Everts-Lind Enterprises, 191
Evolutionary & Behavioural Ecology Research Group, 1202
EVS Environment Consultants Ltd., 1114
eWaterTek Inc., 191
Executive Forum on Climate Change, 914
Exova, 191
Experimental Fusion Facility, 191
Expert Systems Inc., 191
Expertise hydrique, analyse & évaluations environnementales, 647
Experts-Conseils BMST inc., 192
Experts-Conseils CEP Inc., 192
Exploitation Santec Inc., 192
Exploration & Geological Services, 660
Explore Plus Duct Cleaning Ltd., 192
Explorer's Club (Canadian Chapter), 914
Expo agricole de Chicoutimi, 914
Expocrete Concrete Products Ltd., 192
Export Development Canada, 525, 192
ExTech Environmental Services Inc., 192
Extox Industries Inc., 192

F

F.C. O'Neill, Scriven & Associates Ltd., 193
F.E. Myers, 193
Fabco Plastics Wholesale (Ontario) Limited, 193
Fabcon Canada Ltd., 193
Fabricated Plastics Ltd., 193
Fair Canada Engineering Ltd., 193
Falconbridge Limited, 1140
Falls Brook Centre, 914
Fanchem Ltd., 193
Fanshawe College of Applied Arts & Technology, 1143
Faraci Engineering, 194
Farm Credit Canada, 507
Farm Financial Programs Branch, 507
Farm Lands Ownership Board, 584
Farm Machinery Board, 584
Farm Practices Protection Board, 585
Farm Products Marketing Council, 585
Farm Radio International, 914
Farm Safety Association Inc., 1140
Farm Stress Unit, 656
Farmers' Advocate of Alberta, 564
FarmFolk/CityFolk Society, 914
Farris Industries Canada, 194
Farris, Vaughan, Wills & Murphy LLP, 1059
Fasken Martineau - Calgary, 1050
Fasken Martineau - Montréal, 1083
Fasken Martineau - Québec, 1087
Fasken Martineau - Toronto, 1075
Fasken Martineau - Vancouver, 1059
Fastco Equipment Corporation, 194
Faszer Farquharson & Associates Ltd., 194
Fathom Five National Marine Park of Canada, 554
Faune Québec, 650
FaunENord, 914
FCX NH Valves, 194
Federal Bridge Corporation Limited, 560
Federal Contaminated Sites & Solid Waste Landfills Inventory, 562
Federal Democratic Republic of Ethiopia, 767
Federal House in Order, 764
Federal Republic of Germany, 767
Federated Co-operatives Ltd., 194
Fédération d'agriculture biologique du Québec, 914
Fédération des agricultrices du Québec, 914
Fédération des associations pour la protection de l'environnement des lacs inc., 914
Fédération des producteurs de cultures commerciales du Québec, 915
Fédération des sociétés d'horticulture et d'écologie du Québec, 915
Federation of Alberta Naturalists, 915
Federation of Calgary Communities, 915
Federation of Canadian Municipalities, 915, 1044
Federation of Malaysia, 768
Federation of Northern Ontario Municipalities, 915
Federation of Nova Scotian Heritage, 915
Federation of Ontario Cottagers' Associations, 915
Federation of Ontario Naturalists, 1157
Federation of Prince Edward Island Municipalities Inc., 915

Federation of Saskatchewan Surface Rights Association, 916
Fédération québécoise de camping et de caravaning inc., 916
Fédération québécoise de la montagne et de l'escalade, 916
Fédération québécoise des chasseurs et pêcheurs, 916
Fédération québécoise des coopératives forestières, 916
Fédération Québécoise des Municipalités, 916
Fédération québécoise du canot et du kayak, 916
Fédération québécoise pour le saumon atlantique, 916
FEMCO International, 194
Fenco Shawinigan Engineering Limited, 194
Fergus, 620
Ferguson Simek Clark, 194
Ferland & Bélair, 1082
Ferme R&B Fafard Inc., 194
Fero Waste & Recycling Inc., 195
Ferti-Val Inc., 195
Fiducie Desjardins, 195
Field Botanists of Ontario, 916
Field Law - Calgary, 1050
Field Law - Edmonton, 1055
Field Law - Yellowknife, 1066
Field Services Division, 631
Fielding Chemical Technologies Inc., 195
Film & Bag Federation, 916
Film & Sound Commission, 664
Film Nova Scotia, 610
Filter Innovations Inc., 195
Filtration Seco Inc., 195
Filtrum Inc., 195
Finance, 588
Finance & Administration, 528, 641
Finance & Administration Branch, 661
Finance & Administration Division, 582
Finance & Business Services Branch, 631
Finance & Corporate Branch, 522
Finance & Management Services Department, 583
Finance Canada, 526
Finance, Accounting, Banking & Compensation Branch, 558
Financial & Corporate Services, 580
Financial & Management Services, 606
Financial Accountability Division, 569
Financial Consumer Agency of Canada, 526
Financial Institutions, 612
Financial Management Branch, 621
Financial Transactions & Reports Analysis Centre of Canada, 526
Finnex Agencies Ltd., 195
Fire Management & Forest Protection, 658
Fire Marshal's Office, 638, 664
Fire Prevention Canada, 916
Fire Safety Commission, 621
FIRETAK Manufacturing Ltd., 195
Firing Industries Ltd., 195
First Nations & Inuit Health Branch, 533
First Nations & Métis Relations, 563
First Nations Environmental Network, 916
First Nations Tax Commission, 541
First Nations University of Canada, 1187, 1035
First Stage Enterprises Inc., 196
Firwin Corporation, 196
Fiscal Management, 642
Fisgard Lighthouse National Historic Site of Canada, 556
Fish & Wildlife Branch, 595, 633, 578
Fish & Wildlife Compensation Program, 1040
Fish & Wildlife Division, 572
Fish & Wildlife Heritage Commission, 631
Fish Harvesters Resource Centres, 917
Fisher Environmental Ltd., 196
Fisher Scientific Ltd., 196
Fisheries & Aquaculture Loan Board, 610
Fisheries & Aquaculture Management, 527
Fisheries & Marine Institute, 1132
Fisheries & Oceans Canada, 526, 1150
Fisheries & Sealing, 618
Fisheries Branch, 599
Fisheries Council of Canada, 917
Fisheries Council of Canada - British Columbia Representative, 917
Fisheries Division, 592
Fisheries Resource Conservation Council, 527
Fisheries, Environment & Biodiversity Science, 528
Fishermen & Scientists Research Society, 1206
Fishermen and Scientists Research Society, 917
Five Hills Health Region, 1187
Five Seasons Comfort Limited, 196
Le Fjord-du-Saguenay, 749

Flakeboard Company Ltd., 196
Flax Canada 2015, 917
Flax Council of Canada, 917
Fleet, 528
Fleet Management Division, 615
Fleming LLP, Barristers & Solicitors, 1051
Flett Research, 196
Flexahopper Plastics Ltd., 196
Flexo Products Ltd., 196
FLIR Systems, Inc., 197
Floorworks Inc., 197
Flowers Canada, 917
Flowmatic Holdings Inc., 197
Flowmetrix Technical Services Inc., 197
Flowserve Canada Corp. - Pump Division, 197
Flowserve Inc., 197
FLSmidth Canada Ltd., 197
Fluidcare Ltd., 197
Fluor Canada, 197
Fluor Constructors International Inc., 198
Fluorosense Inc., 198
Flush Quip, 198
Flygt Canada, 198
FMA Heritage Resources Consultants Inc., 198
Focal Technologies Inc., 198
Focus Environmental Group Inc., 198
Focus Industries, 198
Focus Surveys Inc., 198
Folio Instruments Inc., 199
Foncier Québec, 650
Fondation de la faune du Québec, 650, 917
Fondation des partenaires de la Biosphère de Montréal, 917
Fondation Hydro-Québec pour l'environnement, 917, 1046
Fondation québécoise du cancer, 917
Fondation québécoise en environnement, 918
Fonds d'action québécois pour le développement durable, 1046
Fonds de la recherche en santé du Québec, 648
Fonds québécois de la recherche sur la nature et les technologies, 648
Fonds québécois de la recherche sur la société et la culture, 648
Fontaine International Corp., 199
Food & Consumer Products of Canada, 918
Food & Resource Economics Group of The University of British Columbia, 1202
Food Development Centre, 585, 1122
Food Directorate, 534
Food Industry Competitiveness Branch, 620
Food Inspection Branch, 620
Food Processors of Canada, 918
Food Research & Development Centre, 509
Food Safety & Environment Division, 619
Food Safety Division, 564
Food Safety Programs Branch, 620
Food Technology Centre, 640
Foodservice & Packaging Institute, 918
Foothills No. 31, 669
Foothills Regional Services, 757
Foothills Research Institute, 918
Fored BC, 918
Foreign Affairs, 529
Foreign Affairs & International Trade Canada, 529
Forest Action Network, 918
Forest Analysis & Inventory Branch, 579
Forest Appeals Commission, 579
Forest Ecosystem Management Division, 603
Forest Engineering & Industry Services Division, 603
Forest Management Branch, 595, 633, 665
Forest Management Division, 606
Forest Practices Board, 579
Forest Practices Branch, 579
Forest Products Association of Canada, 918
Forest Products Association of Nova Scotia, 919
Forest Protection Limited, 595, 199
Forest Resources, 603
Forest Service Branch, 658
Forest Stewardship, 579
Forest Technology Systems Ltd., 199
Foresteel Industries Inc., 199
Forestry Branch (Newfoundland Forest Service), 603
Forestry Division, 572, 615
Forestry Innovation Investments, 579
Forests Division, 633
Forêt Québec, 650
Forges du Saint-Maurice National Historic Site of Canada, 555
Forillon National Park of Canada, 555

The Forks National Historic Site of Canada, 557
Forsythe Lubrication Associates Ltd., 199
Fort Amherst/Port-La-Joye National Historic Site of Canada, 553
Fort Anne National Historic Site of Canada, 553
Fort Battleford National Historic Site of Canada, 556
Fort Beauséjour National Historic Site of Canada, 553
Fort Chambly National Historic Site of Canada, 555
Fort Edward National Historic Site of Canada, 553
Fort Erie, 709
Fort Frances, 538
Fort Garry Industries Ltd., 199
Fort George National Historic Site of Canada, 554
Fort Langley National Historic Site of Canada, 556
Fort Lennox National Historic Site of Canada, 555
Fort Malden National Historic Site of Canada, 554
Fort McNab National Historic Site of Canada, 553
Fort Mississauga National Historic Site of Canada, 554
Fort Nelson Campus, 1112
Fort Qu'Appelle Indian Hospital, 533
Fort Rodd Hill National Historic Site of Canada, 556
Fort St. James National Historic Site of Canada, 556
Fort St. John, 681
Fort St. John Branch, 512
Fort St. John Campus, 1112
Fort St. Joseph National Historic Site of Canada, 554
Fort Saskatchewan, 672
Fort Saskatchewan Fish & Game Association, 919
Fort Storage Warehousing & Distribution, 200
Fort Témiscamingue National Historic Site of Canada, 555
Fort Walsh National Historic Site of Canada, 556
Fort Wellington National Historic Site of Canada, 554
Fortier 2000 Ltée, 200
Fortifications of Québec National Historic Site of Canada, 555
Fortress of Louisbourg National Historic Site, 553
FortWhyte Alive, 919
Foundation for Educational Exchange Between Canada & the United States of America, 919
Foundation for Environmental Conservation, 919, 1039
Foundation for International Environmental Law & Development, 919, 1039
FP Innovations - Paprican Division, Vancouver, 1117
FP Innovations Forintek Division, 1117
FPInnovations, 919, 1177, 200
FracFlow Consultants Inc., 201
Francophone Secretariat, 573
Frank T. Ross & Sons Ltd., 201
Frank's Alternate Energy, 201
Franz Environmental Inc., 201
Frappier & Génier Conseillers, 201
Fraser Basin Council, 577
Fraser Environmental Services, 201
Fraser Milner Casgrain LLP - Calgary, 1051
Fraser Milner Casgrain LLP - Edmonton, 1055
Fraser Milner Casgrain LLP - Ottawa, 1070
Fraser Milner Casgrain LLP - Toronto, 1075
Fraser Milner Casgrain LLP - Vancouver, 1060
Fraser Milner Casgrain S.E.N.C.R.L./LLP, 1083
Fraser Valley, 677
Fraser Valley Labour Council, 919
Fraser-Fort George, 678
Fred Cressman Sales Inc., 201
Frederick Goertz Ltd., 201
Fredericton, 691
Fredericton Branch, 512
Fredericton Fish & Game Association, 919
Fredericton Region Solid Waste Commission, 758
Fredericton Regional Office, 593
Freedom of Information & Privacy, 629
Freight Carriers Association of Canada, 920
French Republic, 767
Freshwater Fish Marketing Corporation, 527
Freshwater Fisheries Society of British Columbia, 920
Freshwater Institute, 528
Freshwater Institute Science Laboratory, 1203
Frey & Associates Engineering Ltd., 201
Frickie Creek Consulting Corp., 201
Friends of Abandoned Pets, 920
The Friends of Algonquin Park, 920
Friends of Animals, 920
The Friends of Awenda Park, 920
The Friends of Bon Echo Park, 920
The Friends of Bonnechere Parks, 920
The Friends of Charleston Lake Park, 920
Friends of Clayoquot Sound, 920
Friends of Devonian Botanic Garden, 920

Entry Name Index

Friends of Ecological Reserves, 920
Friends of Ferris, 920
The Friends of Frontenac Park, 920
The Friends of Killarney Park, 920
The Friends of MacGregor Point, 920
Friends of Mashkinonje Park, 921
Friends of Mount Revelstoke & Glacier, 921
The Friends of Nancy Island Historic Site & Wasaga Beach Park, 921
Friends of Nature Conservation Society, 921
Friends of Oak Hammock Marsh, 921
The Friends of Pinery Park, 921
The Friends of Presqu'ile Park, 921
The Friends of Rondeau Park, 921
The Friends of Sandbanks Park, 921
Friends of Short Hills Park, 921
The Friends of Sleeping Giant, 921
Friends of the Delta Marsh Field Station, 921
Friends of the Earth Canada, 1215, 921
Friends of the Earth International, 921
Friends of the Forestry Farm House Inc., 921
Friends of the Greenbelt Foundation, 1044
Friends of the Oldman River, 921
Friends of the Stikine Society, 921
Friends of the Trent-Severn Waterway, 922
The Friends of West Kootenay Parks Society, 922
Friesen Tokar Architects, Landscape & Interior Designers, 201
Frontenac, 627, 699
Frontenac Environmental Ltd., 202
Frontline Associates Conference Coordinators, 922
Frost Campus, School of Environmental & Natural Resources Sciences, 1143
FS Partners, 202
FSI International Services Ltd., 202
Fuel Maker Corp., 202
Fugro Airborne Surveys, 202
Fugro Jacques GeoSurveys Inc., 203
Fuller Austin Insulation Inc., 203
Fulton & Company LLP, Lawyers & Trade-Mark Agents, 1056
Fulton Engineered Specialties Inc., 203
Fundy Compost Inc., 203
Fundy Engineering & Consulting Ltd., 203
Fundy Model Forest, 922
Fundy National Park of Canada, 553
Fundy Region Solid Waste Commission, 758
The Fur Council of Canada, 922
Fur Institute of Canada, 922
The Fur Trade at Lachine National Historic Site of Canada, 555
Fur-Bearer Defenders, 922
Furriers Guild of Canada, 922
Fusionex inc., 203
FWR Ecoresource Consultants Ltd., 203

G

G & G Computer Services, 203
G. Landry Vacuum Services Ltd., 203
G.A. Borstad Associates Ltd., 203
G.I. Russell & Co. Ltd., 203
G.P. Lewis Library, 1145
G.R. Kelly Environmental Services, 203
G.T. Wood Co. Ltd., 204
G3 Consulting Ltd., 204
Gabonese Republic, 767
Gabriel Dumont Institute of Native Studies & Applied Research, 1188
GAEA Technologies, 204
Gage Environmental Management Inc., 204
GAIA Power Inc., 204
Galaxy Pallets Ltd., 204
Gallagher Library of Geology & Geophysics, 1101
Gallason Industrial Cleaning Services Inc., 204
Gambo, 603
Gamsby & Mannerow Ltd., 204
Gananoque, 538
Ganapathi & Company, 1060
Ganaraska Hiking Trail Association, 922
Gandalf Consulting Ltd., 204
Gander, 599, 694
Gander Campus Library & Career Exploration Centre, 1431
GAP EnviroMicrobial Services Inc., 204
The Garden Clubs of Ontario, 922
Garden Institute of Alberta, 922
Gardiner, Roberts LLP, 1075
Gary Steacy Dismantling Limited, 204

Gas Liquids Engineering Ltd., 205
Gas Processing Association Canada, 922
Gasmac Inc., 205
Gaspé, 651, 735
Gaspésie, 645
Gaspésie-Iles-de-la-Madeleine, 643, 540, 515, 651
Gaspésie/Iles-de-la-Madeleine, 644, 649
Gaston Marcil, Consultant, 205
Gatineau, 529, 735
Gatineau Branch, 513
Gator International, 205
Gazoduc Trans Québec & Maritimes Inc., 1166
GDG Environnement Ltée, 205
GE Ground Engineering Ltd., 205
GE Multilin, 205
GE Water & Process Technologies, 205
GEA Barr-Rosin Inc., 205
GEA Westfalia Separator Canada, Inc., 205
Gem & Mineral Club of Scarborough, 922
Gemcom Software International Inc., 205
Gemini Twins Consulting Ltd., 206
Gemite Products Inc., 206
Gemteck Environmental Software Ltd., 206
Genaire Limited, 1146
GENEQ Inc., 206
General Filtration, 206
General Medical Library, 1141
General Paint Ltd., 206
General Scrap Partnership, 206
General Services Administration, 532
Generation PV Inc., 207
Genetics Society of Canada, 922
Genex Swine Group, 207
Genics Inc., 207
Génie Audio inc., 207
Genilab Environnement Inc., 207
Génius Conseil Inc., 207
Genivar, 207
Genome Canada, 923
Genor Recycling Services, 209
Gensco Equipment (1990) Ltd., 210
Gentec Inc., 210
Genus Loci Ecological Landscapes Inc., 210
Genzyme Canada Inc., 210
Geo Environmental Engineering - Geocon SNC-Lavalin, 210
Geo-Logic Inc., 210
Geochemical Society, 923
Geocor Engineering Inc., 210
Geodetic Software Systems/Geomatics Information Center, 211
Geographic Dynamics Corp., 211
Geographic Information Branch, 633
Geographic, Statistical and Government Information Centre, 1150
GeoInsight Corporation, 211
Geolab Inc., 211
Geological Association of Canada, 923
Geological Services, 615
Geological Survey, 603
Geological Survey of Canada, 1207, 1208, 550
Geomarine Associates Ltd., 211
Geomatics for Informed Decisions Network, 923
Geomatics Industry Association of Canada, 923
Geonics Limited, 211
Géophysique GPR International Inc., 211
George Brown College of Applied Arts & Technology, 1157
George Cedric Metcalf Charitable Foundation, 1044
George Grant Consulting, 211
George Kelk Corporation, 211
Georges Island National Historic Site of Canada, 553
Georges P. Vanier Library, 1173
Georgetown, 538
Georgian Bay Islands National Park of Canada, 554
Georgian Bluffs, 725
Georgian College of Applied Arts & Technology, 1138
Georgina, 709
Geosoft, 212
Geosolutions Consulting Inc., 212
Geostat Systems International Inc., 212
Geotechnical Society of Edmonton, 923
Geowest Environmental Consultants, 212
Geraldton, 538
Gerard V. La Forest Law Library, 1127
Gerry Brushett Enterprises Limited, 212
Gerstein Science Information Centre, 1158
Gestion Eaux Richelieu Inc., 212
GET Industries Inc., 212

Gevity Group Inc., 212
GHG Reductions Directorate, 523
Gilbert McGloan Gillis, 1065
Gilchrist & Company, 1057
GILFAB, 212
Gitwangak Battle Hill National Historic Site of Canada, 556
GL&V - Groupe Laperrière & Verreault Inc., 212
Glace Bay, 537
Glacier National Park of Canada, 556
Glaholt LLP, 1075
Glass Packaging Institute, 923
Glengarry, 627
Glenn Group Ltd., 213
GLM Tanks & Equipment Ltd., 213
Global Change Strategies International Co., 213
Global Contract Inc., 213
Global Dewatering Ltd., 213
Global Engineering & Testing Ltd., 213
Global Facman Entreprises Inc., 213
Global Issues, 529
Global Operations & Chief Trade Commissioner, 530
Global Repair Ltd., 213
Global Sensor Systems Inc., 213
Global, Environmental & Outdoor Education Council, 924
GlobalTox International Consultants Inc., 213
GLOBE Foundation, 924
The GLOBE Foundation of Canada, 1040
Globetron Controls Inc., 214
Glos Associates Inc., 214
Go for Green, 924
GO Transit, 635
Goderich, 538
Godfrey Associates Ltd., 214
Golden Horseshoe Health Libraries Association, 924
Golden Maple Leaf (Hangzhou) Technology Consulting Co. L, 214
Golder Associates Ltd., 1145, 214
Good, Donald R., 1070
Goodmans LLP, 1075
Gore Bay, 620
Gorman Nason, 1065
Gorman-Rupp of Canada Ltd., 215
Goss Gilroy Inc., 215
Gough Risk Management Ltd., 215
Goulbourn Stittsville Sanitation Ltd., 215
Gourley Construction Ltd., 215
Gouvernement du Québec, 642
Gouw Quality Onions Ltd., 215
Government House Foundation, 573
Government of Alberta, 562
Government of British Columbia, 573
Government of Manitoba, 584
Government of New Brunswick, 591
Government of Newfoundland & Labrador, 598
Government of Nova Scotia, 609
Government of Ontario, 619
Government of Prince Edward Island, 636
Government of Saskatchewan, 655
Government of the Northwest Territories, 604
Government of the Nunavut Territory, 617
Government of the Yukon Territory, 663
Government Printing Office, 532
Government Publications, 215
Government Purchasing Information, 558
Government Services, 588
Government Services Branch, 600
Gowling Lafleur Henderson LLP - Calgary, 1051
Gowling Lafleur Henderson LLP - Kanata, 1069
Gowling Lafleur Henderson LLP - Toronto, 1075
Gowling Lafleur Henderson LLP - Vancouver, 1060
Gowling Lafleur Henderson S.E.N.C.R.L./LLP, 1084
GPEC Global Corp., 215
GPEC International Ltd., 215
GPI Atlantic, 1207
Graecam Incorporated, 216
Graham Wilson & Green, Barristers & Solicitors, Notaries, Mediators, 1068
Grain Elevator & Processing Society, 924
Grain Elevators Corporation, 636
Grain Financial Protection Board, 619
Granby, 735
Granby Branch, 513
Grand Falls, 599
Grand Falls Regional Office, 593
Grand Falls-Windsor, 600, 694
Grand Falls-Windsor Branch, 512

Entry Name Index

Grand Falls-Windsor Campus Library, 1131
Grand Manan Whale & Seabird Research Station, 924
Grand Manan Wildlife Association, 924
Grand Pré National Historic Site of Canada, 553
Grand River Conservation Foundation, 924, 1044
Grande Prairie, 535, 672
Grande Prairie Branch, 512
Grande Prairie No. 1, 669
Grande Prairie Regional College, 1107
Le Granit, 749
Grant MacEwan University, 1105
Grasslands National Park of Canada, 556
Grasslands Naturalists, 925
Gratec Ltd., 216
Gravenhurst, 709
Graymont Inc., 216
Great Lakes Branch, 633
Great Lakes Commission, 764, 925
Great Lakes Environmental Research Laboratory, 1203
Great Lakes Fishery Commission, 1215
Great Lakes Forestry Centre, 550, 1154
Great Lakes Information Network, 1215
Great Lakes Institute for Environmental Research, 925
Great Lakes Pilotage Authority, 560
Great Lakes Regional Office, 545
Great Lakes Research Consortium, 1205
The Great Lakes Research Consortium, 925
Great Lakes Safety Products Inc., 216
Great Lakes United, 925
Great Northern Recycling Inc., 216
Great Western Containers Inc., 216
Greatario Industrial Storage Systems Ltd., 217
Greater Napanee, 709
Greater Saint John Community Foundation, 1042
Greater Sudbury / Grand Sudbury, 710
Greater Toronto Rose & Garden Society, 925
Greater Toronto Water Garden & Horticultural Society, 925
Green Action Centre, 925
The Green Brick Road, 925
Green Calgary, 925
Green Communities Canada, 1215, 925
Green Gables Heritage Place, 553
Green Island Recycling Ltd., 217
Green Key Solutions Inc., 217
Green Kids Inc., 925
Green Living Magazine, 1193
Green Ontario, 1215
The Green Pages, 1215
Green Party of British Columbia, 926
Green Party of Canada, 926
The Green Party of Manitoba, 926
Green Party of New Brunswick, 926
The Green Party of Ontario, 926
Green Plan Ltd., 217
Green Policy Branch, 658
Green Roofs for Healthy Cities, 926
Green Soils Inc., 217
Green Tourism Association, 926
Green Turtle Technologies Ltd. (Canada), 217
Greenbridge Management Inc., 217
Greenest City, 926
Greenfield Research Inc., 217
Greenflow Environmental Services Inc., 217
Greenhouse & Processing Crops, 1141
Greenhouse & Processing Crops Research Centre, 509
Greening Government, 1215, 764
Greenland Corporation, 217
Greenland International Consulting Inc., 218
Greenpeace Canada, 1215, 926
Greenpeace International HQ, 926
Greenpeace USA, 926
Greenpower Canada, 1215
Greenspace Alliance of Canada's Capital, 926
Greenview Regional Waste Management Commission, 757
GreenWare Environmental Systems Inc., 218
Greenwind Power Corp., 218
Greenwood & Associates, 218
The Greer Galloway Group Inc., Engineers & Planners, 392
Greif Bros. Canada Inc., 218
Grenville, 627
Grey, 627, 700
Grey House Publishing Canada, 218
Greyline Instruments Inc., 218
Greystone Energy Systems Inc., 218
Griffin Laboratories Corporation, 218

Griffiths Muecke Associates, 218
Grimsby, 710
Gro-Bark (Ontario) Ltd., 218
Grondin, Poudrier, Bernier, 1087
Gros Morne National Park of Canada, 553
Grosse Ile & the Irish Memorial National Historic Site of Canada, 555
Groundfish Enterprise Allocation Council, 926
GroundTech Solutions, 219
Groupe Bau-Val, 219
Groupe Berlie-Falco Inc., 219
Groupe Bouffard, 219
Groupe Chagnon International, 219
Groupe Conseil Bellefeuille, Samson et Associés, 219
Groupe Consulteaux Inc., 219
Groupe de recherche en écologie sociale, 926
Groupe Deschênes, 219
Groupe DHB Inc., 219
Groupe EnvirAqua, 219
Le Groupe Forces, 265
Groupe GLD Inc., Experts-Conseils, 219
Le Groupe Leblond & Bouchard/Daniel Arbour et associes, 265
Le Groupe Légerlite inc., 265
Le Groupe Pétrolier OLCO Inc., 265
Groupe RSW inc., 220
Groupe S.M. International Inc., 220
Le Groupe Sani Marc, 265
Groupe Séguin, 220
Groupe SM inc., 220
Groupe Sodinco inc., 221
Groupe SOLROC, 221
Groupe Stavibel Inc., 221
Groupe Teknika, 221
Groupe Tremca inc., 221
Groupe-Conseil TDA, 221
Grundfos Canada Inc., 221
Gryphon International Engineering Services Inc., 222
GSC - Quebec Library, 1179
GSI Environnement Inc., 222
Guardian Industries Canada Corp., 222
Guelph, 538, 710
Guelph Chemical Laboratories, 222
Guelph Food Research Centre, 509
Guelph Turfgrass Institute & Environmental Research Centre, 1208
Guelph-Eramosa, 725
Guertin Brothers Coatings and Sealants Ltd., 222
Guild Contracting Specialists Inc., 222
Guildline Instruments Limited, 222
Gulf, 527
Gulf Fisheries Centre, 1203, 528
Gulf Islands National Park Reserve of Canada, 556
Gulf of Georgia Cannery National Historic Site of Canada, 556
Gulf of Maine Council on the Marine Environment, 764, 927
Gull Island Power Co. Ltd., 601
Gunn Centre, 569
Guspro Inc., 223
Gwaii Haanas National Park Reserve & Haida Heritage Site of Canada, 556

H

H. Broer Equipment Sales and Service, 223
H. Pickard & Associates, 223
H.E. Bent Services Ltd., 223
H.H. Angus & Associates, 1158
H.L. Blachford Ltd., 223
H.R. MacMillan Space Centre Society, 930
H2Flow Equipment Inc., 223
H2O Innovation Inc., 223
Habitat Acquisition Trust, 927
Habitat Conservation Trust Foundation, 1202
Habitat Management, 528
Habitat Studio & Workshop Ltd., 223
Hagersville Recycling & Auto Wrecking Ltd., 223
Haileybury Campus, 1140
Hakmet Ltd., 223
Haldimand, 627, 700
Haley Industries Ltd., 223
Halford Pallet Recyclers Ltd., 224
Haliburton, 627, 700
Halifax Branch, 513
Halifax C&D Recycling, 224
Halifax Citadel National Historic Site of Canada, 553
Halifax Field Naturalists, 927

Halifax Regional Municipality, 695
The Halifax STAR Project, 1207
Hallmark Insurance Brokers Ltd., 224
Halltech Environmental Inc., 224
Halton, 627, 700
Halton Hills, 710
Halton-Peel, 625
Hamilton Branch, 513
Hamilton Central/East, 538
Hamilton Community Energy, 224
Hamilton Geological Society, 927
Hamilton Health Sciences, 1141
Hamilton Incubator of Technology, 927
Hamilton Industrial Environmental Association, 927
Hamilton Mountain, 538
Hamilton Naturalists' Club, 927
Hamiota District Health Centre, 1122
Hammond Manufacturing, 224
HAMON Custodis-Cottrell Canada, Inc., 224
Hamworthy-Peabody Combustion Canada Inc., 224
Hanley & District Agricultural Society, 927
Hanna Instruments Canada Inc., 224
Hanna Paper Fibres Ltd., 224
Hanover, 690
Hanson Pressure Pipe, 225
Hants East District, 697
Hants West District, 697
Happy Harry's Used Building Material, 225
Happy Valley-Goose Bay, 537
Harbour Grace, 600
Harbour Metal Recycling Ltd., 225
Harbour Remediation & Transfer Inc., 225
Hardy Filtration, 225
Hardy Stevenson & Associates, 225
Harmony Foundation of Canada, 927, 1040
Harold Marcus Ltd., 225
Harris & Roome Supply Limited, 225
Harris Industrial Testing, 226
Harry Gamble Shipyard, 226
Hashemite Kingdom of Jordan, 768
Hassco Industries Inc., 226
Hastings, 627, 700
Hatch, 1145
Hatch Energy, 1146
Hatch Ltd., 226
Hatfield Group, 226
Haul-All Equipment Ltd., 227
Le Haut-Richelieu, 749
Le Haut-St-François, 749
Le Haut-St-Laurent, 749
Hawk Migration Association of North America, 927
Hawkesbury, 538, 711
Hawthorne Cottage National Historic Site of Canada, 553
Hayward Gordon Ltd., 227
Hazard Alert Training & Supplies Canada Inc., 227
Hazard Control Systems Inc., 227
Hazardous Materials Information Review Commission, 533
Hazardous Materials Management Magazine, 227
Hazco Environmental Services Ltd., 227
Hazelmere Research Ltd., 228
Hazmark Inc., 228
Hazmasters Environmental Controls Inc., 228
Healing Arts Radiation Protection Commission, 628
Health & Safety Conference Society of Alberta, 927
Health Authorities, 580
Health Boards Secretariat, 628
Health Canada, 1208, 533, 1150
Health Canada, Health Products & Food Branch, 1150
Health Disciplines Board, 569
Health Facilities Review Committee, 569
Health Human Resources Strategy Division, 628
Health Libraries Association of British Columbia, 928
Health Policy, 533
Health Policy & Service Standards Division, 569
Health Products & Food Branch, 533
Health Promotion, 660
Health Protection, 580
Health Quality Council, 659
Health Registration & Vital Statistics, 660
Health Sciences Association of Alberta, 928
Health Sciences Association of Saskatchewan, 928
Health Sciences Library, 1101, 1141, 1189, 1132
Health Sector Information Management / Information Technology, 580
Health Services, 628

Entry Name Index

Health System Planning, 580
Health System Strategy Division, 629
Health Workforce Division, 569
Healthcare Information & Management Systems Society, 928
Healthcare Policy, 534
Healthy Environments & Consumer Safety Branch, 533
Healthy Homes Consulting, 228
Healthy Indoors Partnership, 928
Hearst, 632
Heating, Refrigeration & Air Conditioning Institute of Canada, 928
Hebco International Inc., 228
HEC Group, 228
HEC Montréal, 1173
HECS Library, 1150
Heelis, Williams, Little & Almas LLP, Barristers & Solicitors, 1072
Heenan Blaikie LLP - Calgary, 1051
Heenan Blaikie LLP - Ottawa, 1070
Heenan Blaikie LLP - Toronto, 1075
Heenan Blaikie LLP - Vancouver, 1060
Heenan Blaikie LLP - Victoria, 1062
Heenan Blaikie S.E.N.C.R.L./SRL - Québec, 1087
Heenan Blaikie S.E.N.C.R.L/SRL, 1084
Heenan Blaikie S.E.N.C.R.L/SRL - Sherbrooke, 1089
Heenan Blaikie S.E.N.C.R.L/SRL - Trois-Rivières, 1089
Helen McCrea Peacock Foundation, 1044
Helimax Energy Inc., 228
Hellenic Republic, 767
Hemisphere Engineering Inc, 1105
Hemispheres Environmental Consulting Inc., 229
Hemmera Envirochem Inc., 229
Hénaire, Louis, 1089
Henderson Medical Library, 1141
Henderson Paddon & Associates Ltd., 229
Henlex Inc., 229
Henry A. Wallace Center for Agricultural & Environmental Policy at Winrock International, 929
Henry Kortekaas & Associates Inc., 229
Henry Kroeger Regional Water Services Commission, 757
Herb Society of Manitoba, 929
Herby Enterprises Ltd., 229
Hercules SLR Inc., 229
Heritage, 598
Heritage Agricultural Society, 929
Heritage Association of Antigonish, 929
Heritage Canada Foundation, 929
Heritage College, 1168
Heritage Division, 616
Heritage Foundation of Newfoundland & Labrador, 929
Heritage Grants Advisory Council, 587
Héritage Montréal, 929, 1173
Heritage Research Associates Inc., 230
Heritage Society of British Columbia, 929
Heritage Trust of Nova Scotia, 929
Heritage Winnipeg Corp., 930
Heron Instruments, 230
Herring Cove, 597
Herzberg Institute of Astrophysics, 547
HETEK Solutions Inc., 230
Hewlett Packard (Canada) Co., 230
HFP Acoustical Consultants Corp., 231
HGC Engineering, 231
Hi-Country Environmental Services Ltd., 231
Hi-Point Industries (1991) Ltd., 231
Hi-Q Developments Ltd., 231
Hibon Inc., 231
Hickling Arthurs Low Corp., 231
Hicks Morley Hamilton Stewart Storie LLP, 1069, 1070, 1076
Higher Education, 641
Highland Equipment Ltd., 231
Highway 14 Regional Water Services, 757
Highway 43 East Waste Commission Services, 757
Highway Engineering Branch, 589
Highway Maintenance, 642
Highway Operations, 616
Highway Traffic Board/Motor Transport Board, 588
Highways, 608
Highways Department, 583
Hike Metal Products Ltd., 231
Hike Ontario, 930
Hilderman Thomas Frank Cram & Associates, 232
Hiltz & Seamone Co. Ltd., 232
Historic Sites & Monuments Board of Canada, 552
Historica Research Limited, 232
Hitachi Canadian Industries Ltd., 232
HLS Ecolo, 232

HMI Construction Inc., 232
HMI Hoyme Manufacturing Inc., 232
HMI Industries, 232
HMO Limited, 232
Hodgson Russ LLP, 1077
Holland College, 1165
Hollimex Products Ltd., 232
Home Hardware Stores Ltd., 232
Homelessness Partnering Secretariat, 535
Homewood Health Centre, 1140
Honey Electric Ltd., 233
Honeywell Ltd., 233
Hong Kong, 565
Hook & Smith, 1063
Hooper Welding Enterprises Ltd., 233
Hope for Wildlife Society, 930
Horizon Environment Inc., 233
Horizons Systems Group Inc., 233
Horner Associates Limited, 233
Horticultural Research Institute of Ontario, 1164
Horticulture Nova Scotia, 930
Horticulture Research & Development Centre, 509
Horton CBI Ltd., 233
Horton Tree Farms, 233
Hoskin Scientific Ltd., 233
Hospital Appeal Board, 580
Hospital for Sick Children, 1158
Hot Zone Training Consultants Inc., 233
Hotsy Pressure Washers Ltd., 233
Hotz Environmental Services Inc., 233
Housing Division, 630
Howard Marten Fluid Technologies Inc., 234
Howard Ryan Kelford Knott & Dixon, 1068
Howard Ryan Kelford Knott & Dixon, Barristers & Solicitors, 1071
Howell Fleming LLP, 1071
Howell-Mayhew Engineering Inc., 234
HQN Industrial Fabrics Inc., 234
HSE Integrated, 234
Hughes, Amys LLP, 1077
Human Resources & Corporate Services, 527
Human Resources & Skills Development Canada, 534
Human Resources Branch, 522, 507, 631
Human Resources, Strategies & Programs, 528
Humber College Institute of Technology & Advanced Learning, 1158
Hume, Forrest C., Law Corporation, 1060
Hunter & Associates, 235
Hunter Litigation Chambers, 1060
Huntsman Corporation Canada Inc., 235
Huntsman Marine Science Centre, 1203, 1204
Huntsville, 711
Hurlburt Construction Limited, 235
Huron, 627, 701
Huron Wind Ltd. Partnership, 235
Huron Window Corporation, 235
HurterConsult Inc., 235
Husky Oil Operations Ltd., 1101
Hutchins Caron & Associates, 1060
Hutchins Caron & Associés, 1085
Hy-Grade Geoscience, 235
Hy-Grade Precast Concrete, 235
Hycal Environmental Sciences, 1101
Hydralogic Systems Inc., 235
Hydraulic Systems Ltd., 235
Hydro Dyne Inc., 236
Hydro One, 622, 236
Hydro One Inc., 629
Hydro Québec, 650
Hydro Vision America, 236
Hydro-Com Technologies Ltd., 236
Hydro-Logic Environmental Inc., 236
Hydro-Mechanical Sales Ltd., 236
Hydro-Québec, 649, 1173
Hydro-Québec CapiTech, 649
Hydro-Québec International, 649
Hydrogenics Corporation, 236
Hydrogéo Plus Inc., 236
Hydrogéochem Environnement Inc., 236
Hydrogeological Consultants, 236
Hydromantis Inc., 237
Hydromega Energy Inc., 237
Hydroqual Laboratories Ltd., 237
Hydroxyl Systems Inc., 237
Hygrex-Spehr Industries, 237
Hymopack Ltd., 237

Hyperspectral Data International Inc., 237
Hyprescon Inc., 237

I

I.G. Micromed Environmental Inc., 237
I.K Barber Enhanced Forestry Laboratory, 1202
IBI Group, 1158, 238
IBM Canada Ltd., 1144
ICC The Compliance Center Inc., 238
ICC The Compliance Centre Inc., 238
Icefield Instruments Inc., 238
ICF International Canada Inc., 238
ICI Paints (Canada) Inc., 238
ICOMOS Canada, 930
ICT Services Manitoba, 591
IEG Consultants Ltd., 238
IG Machine & Fibers Ltd., 238
Ile-de-Montréal, 515
Iles-de-la-Madeleine, 645
Imalog Inc., 238
Imbitive Technologies Canada, Inc., 238
Immigration & Multiculturalism Division, 590
Immigration Division, 566
IMO Pump Inc., 239
IMP Liquid Meters & Petroleum Services, 239
Impact Environmental Services Ltd., 239
The Impact Group, 392
Impact Microbiology Services, 239
Imperial Oil - Alberta Ingenuity Centre for Oil Sands Innovation, 1200
Imperial Oil Limited, 1158
Imperial Oil Resources Limited, 1101
Implementation Branch, 542
Impro, 239
IMTT-Newfoundland Ltd., 239
IMTT-Québec Ltd., 239
In Tech Risk Management Inc., 239
In!Flame Fireplaces Inc., 239
Incinolet Products, 239
Inco Technical Services Limited, 1145, 239
INCOM Manufacturing Group, 240
InCoretec Inc., 240
Indachem Inc., 240
Indaco Manufacturing Limited, 240
INDECO Strategic Consulting Inc., 240
Independent Electricity System Operator, 622, 629
Independent Lumber Dealers Co-operative, 930
Independent Power Producers Association of British Columbia, 930
Independent Power Producers Society of Alberta, 930
Indian & Northern Affairs Canada, 541
Indian Agricultural Program of Ontario, 930
Indian Head Research Farm, 1187
Indian Oil & Gas Canada, 541
Indoor Air Quality Ottawa, 240
Industrial Accident Prevention Association, 1145
Industrial Accident Victims Group of Ontario, 930
Industrial Combustion Equipment Ltd., 240
Industrial Ecology Corp., 240
Industrial Forestry Service Ltd., 240
Industrial Gas Users Association Inc., 930
Industrial Marine Power Engineering Group, 240
Industrial Materials Institute, 547
Industrial Plastics Fabricators Ltd., 240
Industrial Scientific Corporation, 241
Industrial Technology Centre, 590, 1123
Industrial Thermo Polymers Ltd., 241
Industrial Truck Association, 931
Les Industries Cascades Ltée, 269
Industries de Moules et Plastiques VIF, 241
Les Industries Fournier Inc., 269
Industries Machinex Inc., 241
Industry Canada, 543
Industry Development & Food Safety Sector, 564
Industry Division, 622
Industry Relations Branch, 633
Industry Sector, 543
Industry Training Authority, 574
Infectious Diseases, 629
Infectious Diseases Society of America, 931
Info entrepreneurs, 515
InfoMine Inc., 241
Inform Consulting Services Ltd., 241
INFORM Inc., 931

Entry Name Index

Informatics Circle of Research Excellence, 563
Information & Business Services, 612
Information Centre (Calgary), 1101
Information Geographical Branch, 633
Information Management & Technology Services, 528
Information Systems Branch, 507
Information Technology Services Branch, 558
Information Technology Services Division, 582
Information Technology Shared Services, 642
Infotech Canada Inc., 241
Infrastructure Canada, 544
Infrastructures et finances municipales, 643
Infrastructures et technologies, 654
Infrasutucture Ontario, 634
Infratech Corporation, 241
Ingersoll, 711
Ingersoll District Nature Club, 931
Ingersoll-Rand Canada Inc., 241
Ininew Project Management Inc., 241
Inland Aquatics, 241
Inland Technologies Inc., 242
Innergy Tech, 242
Innisfil, 711
InNOVACorp, 610
Innovatech Québec, 648
Innovation & Competitiveness Division, 619
Innovation and Energy Technology Sector, 551
Innovation Management Association of Canada, 931
Innovation technologique, 649
Innovation, Research & Advanced Technologies Branch, 601
Inproheat Industries Ltd., 242
INRS - Université du Québec, CGC - Québec, 1179
Inscan Contractors (Ontario) Inc., 242
Inside Education, 931
Insitu Contractors Inc., 242
Insituform Technologies Ltd. - Edmonton, 242
Insituform Technologies Ltd. - Hamilton, 242
Insituform Technologies Ltd. - Montréal, 242
Inspec-Sol Inc., 242
InspecTech, 243
Inspection Services Branch, 638
Instantel, 243
Institut de l'Énergie et de l'environnement de la francophonie, 1179
Institut de l'énergie et de l'environnement de la Francophonie, 931
Institut de recherche en biologie végétale, 932
Institut de recherche Robert-Sauvé en santé et en sécurité du travail, 932
Institut de technologie agro-alimentaire de Saint-Hyacinthe, 1177, 1183
Institut maritime du Québec, 1181
Institut Maurice-Lamontagne, 528, 1170
Institut national de santé publique du Québec, 652
Institut Teccart Inc., 1174
Institute for Aerospace Research, 547
Institute for Biodiagnostics, 547
Institute for Biological Sciences, 547
Institute for Chemical Process & Environmental Technology, 547
Institute for Coastal & Oceans Research, 1202
Institute for Environmental Monitoring and Research, 1204
Institute for Fuel Cell Innovation, 547
Institute for Information Technology, 547
Institute for Integrated Energy Systems, 1202
Institute for Local Self-Reliance, 932
Institute for Marine Biosciences, 547
Institute for Microstructural Sciences, 547
Institute for National Measurement Standards, 548
Institute for Nutrisciences & Health, 548
Institute for Ocean Technology, 548
Institute for Research in Construction, 548, 1150
Institute for Research on Public Policy, 932
Institute for Resources, Environment & Sustainability (IRES) at the University of British Columbia (UBC), 1202, 1030
Institute for Risk Research, 932
Institute for Sustainable Energy, Environment, & Economy, 1200
Institute for Work & Health, 932
Institute of Electrical & Electronics Engineers Inc. - Canada, 932
Institute of Environmental Research Inc., 243
Institute of Food Technologists, 932
Institute of Industrial Engineers, 933
Institute of Ocean Sciences, 1202, 528, 1116
Institute of Packaging Professionals, 933
Institute of Population & Public Health, 519
Institute of Power Engineers, 933
Institute of Scrap Recycling Industries, Inc., 933
Institute of Space & Atmospheric Studies, 933
Institute of Technology Campus, 1135
Institute of Transportation Engineers, 933
Institute of Urban Studies, 934, 1124
Institution nationale & sociétés d'État, 645
Institution of Mechanical Engineers, 934
Integra Environmental Inc., 243
Integra Technologies Ltd., 243
Integran Technologies Inc., 243
Integrated Business Management, 528
Integrated Catalyst Engineering Inc., 244
Integrated Community Services, 606
Integrated Ecosystem Management Directorate, 523
Integrated Environmental Planning Division, 626
Integrated Environments Ltd., 244
Integrated Explorations, 244
Integrated Metal Products, 244
Integrated Resource Management, 244
Integrated Service Delivery, 615
Integrated Technical Support, 528
Integrated Vegetation Management Association of British Columbia, 934
Intelex Technologies Inc., 244
Inter-American Development Bank, 532
Inter-regional Intervention & Partnership, 516
Intera Engineering Ltd., 244
Interbath of Canada Ltd., 244
Interface FLOR Commercial, 244
Interforest Inc., 244
Intergovernmental Affairs Directorate, 534
Intergovernmental Committee on Urban & Regional Research (ICURR), 934, 1158
Intergovernmental Panel on Climate Change, 1215
Intergovernmental Relations, 570
Interior Weather Services Ltd., 245
InterLink Business Management Inc., 245
Internal Administrative Services Division, 629
International Affairs, 522
International Affairs Directorate, 534
International Agricultural Exchange Association, 934
International Air Transport Association, 934
International Arctic Science Committee, 934
International Association for Bear Research & Management, 934
International Association for Earthquake Engineering, 934
International Association for Ecology, 934
International Association for Environmental Hydrology, 935
International Association for Great Lakes Research, 935
International Association for Impact Assessment - Western & Northern Canada, 935
International Association for Public Participation, 935
International Association of Agricultural Economists, 935
International Association of Educators for World Peace, 935
International Association of Environmental Analytical Chemistry, 935
International Association of Fire Fighters (AFL-CIO/CLC), 935
International Association of Hydrogeologists - Canadian National Chapter, 935, 936
International Association of Science & Technology for Development, 936
International Association of Sedimentologists, 936
International Atomic Energy Agency, 936
International Bar Association, 936
International Bio-Recovery Corp., 245
International Bottled Water Association, 936
International Business Development, Investment & Innovation, 530
International Business Opportunities Centre, 530
International Centre for Conservation Education, 936
International Centre for Sustainable Cities, 936
International Civil Aviation Organization, 1174
International Coalition of Fisheries Associations, 936
International Commission of Agricultural & Biosystems Engineering, 937
International Commission on Irrigation & Drainage, 937
International Commission on Occupational Health, 937
International Commission on Radiological Protection, 937
International Confederation for Thermal Analysis & Calorimetry, 937
International Cooling Systems Inc., 245
International Cooperative Alliance, 937
International Council for Applied Mineralogy, 937
International Council for Archaeozoology, 937
International Council for Laboratory Animal Science, 937
International Council for Local Environmental Initiatives, 937
International Council of Associations for Science Education, 938
International Council of Environmental Law, 938
International Council on Monuments & Sites, 938
International Development Research Centre, 544, 938
International Energy Foundation, 938
International Ergonomics Association, 938
International Erosion Control Association, 938
International Federation for Cell Biology, 939
International Federation for Housing & Planning, 939
International Federation for Medical & Biological Engineering, 939
International Federation of Hydrographic Societies, 939
International Federation of Landscape Architects, 939
International Federation of Organic Agriculture Movements, 939
International Federation of Surveyors, 939
International Financial Centre British Columbia, 575
International Flying Farmers, 939
International Fund for Animal Welfare Canada, 939
International Genetics Federation, 939
International Geographic Union, 939
International Geographical Union - Canadian Committee, 939
International Geosynthetics Society, 940
International Heavy Haul Association, 940
International Institute for Applied Systems Analysis, 940
International Institute for Conservation of Historic & Artistic Works, 940
International Institute for Energy Conservation, 940
International Institute for Sustainable Development, 940, 1124
International Institute of Concern for Public Health, 940
International Institute of Fisheries Economics & Trade, 940
International Irrigation Systems Ltd., 245
International Joint Commission, 1215, 544, 1150
International Joint Commission (Canadian Section), 529
International Labour Organization, 940
International Law Association - Canadian Branch, 940
International Lilac Society, 941
International Marine Salvage Inc., 245
International Maritime Organization, 941
International Network for Environmental Management, 941
International Nuclear Law Association, 941
International Occupational Safety & Health Information Centre, 941
International Ocean Institute, 941
International Oceans Institute of Canada, 941
International Organization for Standardization, 941
International Peat Society, 941
International Peat Society - Canadian National Committee, 941
International Permafrost Association, 941
International Plant Nutrition Institute, 942
International Plant Propagators Society, Inc., 942
International Primary Care Respiratory Group, 942
International Primate Protection League, 942
International Relations, 570
International Research Group on Wood Protection, 942
International Resource Industries & Sustainability Centre, 1200
International Road Dynamics Inc., 245
International Sanitary Supply Association, Inc., 942
International Security Branch & Political Director, 529
International Society for Ecological Economics, 942
International Society for Ecological Modelling, 942
International Society for Environmental Ethics, 942, 943
International Society for Evolutionary Protistology, 943
International Society for Plant Pathology, 943
International Society for Rock Mechanics, 943
International Society for Soil Mechanics & Geotechnical Engineering, 943
International Society of Arboriculture, 943
International Society of Biometeorology, 943
International Society of Citriculture, 943
International Society of City & Regional Planners, 943
International Society of Indoor Air Quality & Climate, 943
International Society of Limnology, 944
International Soil Reference & Information Centre, 944
International Solar Energy Society, 944
International Solid Waste Association, 944
International Submarine Engineering Ltd., 245
International Titanium Association, 944
International Trade Canada, 530
International Union for Conservation of Nature, 1215, 944
International Union of Biological Sciences, 945
International Union of Food Science & Technology, 945
International Union of Forest Research Organizations, 945
International Union of Geodesy & Geophysics, 945
International Union of Microbiological Societies, 945
International Union of Nutritional Sciences, 945
International Union of Pure & Applied Chemistry, 945
International Union of Soil Sciences, 945

Entry Name Index

International Water Association, 946
International Water Supply Ltd., 245
International Whaling Commission, 946
International Wildlife Coalition, 946
International Wildlife Rehabilitation Council, 946
International WWOOF Association, 946
Interprovincial Corrosion Control Co. Ltd., 246
Interra Environmental Inc., 246
Intersciences Inc., 246
Intertek Systems Certification, 246
Interurban Campus, 1120
Interwest Property Services (1991) Ltd., 246
Inuktun Services Ltd., 246
Invensys Systems Canada Inc., 246
Inverarden House National Historic Site of Canada, 554
Inverness County, 697
Investigations & Enforcement Branch, 625
Investigative Science Inc., 247
Investissement Québec, 648
Investment & Economic Analysis, 607
Investment & Trade Division, 622
Investment Agriculture Foundation of British Columbia, 1040
Investment, Export & Business Development, 592
Iogen Corp., 247
IPAC Inc., 247
IPEC Industries Ltd., 247
Ipex Inc., 247
IPL Inc., 247
Iqaluit, 698
iQmetrix, 247
IRC Integrated Resource Consultants Inc., 247
IRC International Water & Sanitation Centre, 946
Ireland Business Partnership, 601
IRIS Environmental Systems Inc., 248
Iron Ore Company of Canada, 248
Irrigation Canal Power Co-operative Ltd., 248
Irrigation Council, 564
Irving Forest Services Limited, 248
ISCA Management Ltd., 248
Island Clean Air Inc., 248
Island Investment Development Inc., 640
Island Nature Trust, 946, 1045
Island Regulatory & Appeals Commission, 641
Island Technologies Inc., 248
Island Waste Management Corporation, 641
Islands Organic Producers Association, 946
Islands Trust, 575
ISOVision, 248
Ispat Sidbec inc., 1167
Italian Republic, 768
ITM Instruments, 248
ITRES Research Ltd., 248
Ivey International Inc., 249
Ivvavik National Park of Canada, 556

J

J&B Engineering Inc., 249
J&F Waste Systems Inc., 249
J&M Industrial Engineering & Sales Ltd., 249
J. Walter Company Ltd., 249
J.D. Mollard & Associates Ltd., 249
J.E. Coulter Associates Ltd., 249
J.K. Engineering Ltd., 249
J.L. Richards & Associates Limited, 250
J.M. Turcotte ltée, 250
J.R. Cousin Consultants Ltd., 250
J.R. Tinderblox, 250
J.W. Bird & Company Ltd., 250
Jack Atkinson & Associates, 250
Jack Miner Migratory Bird Foundation, Inc., 946, 1044
Jacobs Canada Inc., 1101
Jagger Hims Limited, 250
Jamaica, 768
James N. Allan Campus, 1155
The Jane Goodal Institute of Canada, 946
The Jane Goodall Institute for Wildlife Research, Education & Conservation, 946
The Jane Goodall Institute of Canada, 1208, 946
Janin Atlas Inc., 251
Jannock Steel Fabricating Co., 251
Jardin Botanique de Montréal, 1174
Jardin zoologique du Québec, 946
Les Jardins-de-Napierville, 749
Jasco Research Ltd., 251

Jasper Environmental Association, 947
Jasper National Park of Canada, 556
JB Laboratories Ltd., 251
Jenike & Johanson, Ltd., 251
Jes-Chem Ltd., 251
Jetvac Inc., 251
JFA James Floyd Associates Ltd., 252
JFM Environmental Ltd., 252
JKM Custom Fabricating Ltd., 252
JM Science Canada Inc., 252
JMB Research Ltd., 252
JNE Consulting Ltd., 252
Jodek Industries Ltd., 252
Joe Johnson Equipment Inc., 252
John & Dotsa Bitove Family Law Library, 1144
John Alexander Weir Memorial Law Library, 1105
John B. Ridley Research Library, 1138
John Brooks Company Ltd., 252
John H. Daniels Faculty of Architecture, Lanscape & Design, 1158
John McMullen & Associates, 252
John Meunier Inc., 253
John Prince Research Forest, 1202
John Thurston Machine Ltd., 253
John W. Scott Health Sciences Library, 1105
John Zubick Ltd. Scrap Metals, 253
Johns Manville Canada Inc., 253
Joint Centre for Bioethics, 947
Joint Venture Coordinators, 525
Joli-Cour Lacasse Avocats, 1088
Joliette, 736, 747
Jomac Canada Inc., 253
Jones Group Engineering Ltd., 253
Jonquière Tax Centre, 517
Joseph & Co. Inc., 253
Jour de la Terre Québec, 1046
Journal of Environmental Engineering and Science, 1193
JTU Consulting, 253
Jubilee Rose Enterprises Ltd., 253
Junior Farmers' Association of Ontario, 947
Just Homes, 253
justenvironment, 254
Justice Institute of British Columbia, 1114
Justice Technology Services Division, 621

K

K&D Pratt Group Inc., 254
K-Tech Services Ltd., 254
K.T. Enviro Clean Inc., 254
Kaehne Consulting Ltd., 254
Kafko Manufacturing Ltd., 254
Kahiltna Research Group, 1202
Kahn Zack Ehrlich Lithwick, 1057
Kaizen Environmental Services Inc., 254
Kalyn Siebert Canada Inc., 254
Kam Biotechnology Ltd., 254
Kamloops, 681
Kamloops Branch, 512
Kamloops Exploration Group, 947
Kamloops Naturalist Club, 947
Kamloops Range Research Unit, 1112
Kamloops Scrap Iron Ltd., 254
Kamloops Wildlife Park Society, 947
Kamouraska, 748
Kang Construction Ltd., 255
Kanotech Information Systems Ltd., 255
Kanuka Thuringer LLP, Barristers & Solicitors, 1090, 1091
Kappler Canada, 255
Kapuskasing, 538
Kason, 255
Katch Kan Limited, 255
Kavanagh & Associates Ltd., 255
Kawartha Lakes, 711
Kawartha World Issues Centre, 947, 1152
Kay, McVey, Smith & Carlstrom LLP, 1056
KBL Land Use Consulting Ltd., 255
KBM Forestry Consultants Inc., 255
KBR Canada, 255
KBU Environmental Technologies Inc., 255
KC Environmental Group Ltd., 256
KEDCO Constructors Ltd., 256
Kejimkujik National Park of Canada, 553
Kel-Ann Organics, 256
Kelowna, 536, 681
Kelowna Branch, 512

Kemel Cartons (1973) Ltd., 256
Kemic Bioresearch Laboratories Ltd., 256
Kemira Water Solutions Canada Inc., 256
Kemptville, 620
Ken Noftell Drilling Services, 256
Ken Summers Biological Services, 256
Keneco Environmental Services Inc., 256
Kennebecasis Naturalists' Society, 947
Kenora, 726
Kenora Branch, 513
Kent, 627
Kent County Solid Waste Commission, 758
Kent Engineering Ltd., 256
Kentain Products Ltd., 256
Kentville, 537
Kernic Systems Inc., 257
Kerr Wood Leidal Associates Ltd., 257
Keyano College, 1107
Keystone Agricultural Producers, 947
Keystone Environmental Ltd., 257
Keywood Entreprises Ltd., 257
KGS Group Inc., 257
Kimco Steel Sales Limited, 257
Kincardine, 726
Kinder Morgan Canada Inc., 257
The Kindness Club, 947
Kinectrics Inc., 257
Kinetics Noise Control Inc., 257
King, 726
King Campus, 1142
King Metal Fabricators Ltd., 258
The King's University College, 1106, 1029
Kingdom of Belgium, 767
Kingdom of Denmark, 767
Kingdom of Morocco, 768
Kingdom of Norway, 768
Kingdom of Saudi Arabia, 768
Kingdom of Spain, 769
Kingdom of Sweden, 769
Kingdom of Thailand, 769
Kingdom of the Netherlands, 768
Kings County, 696
Kings County Region Solid Waste Commission, 758
Kingstec Campus, 1137
Kingston, 712
Kingston Branch, 513
Kingston Field Naturalists, 947
Kingston General Hospital, 1142
Kingston Lapidary & Mineral Club, 947
Kingston Martello Towers, 554
Kingston R & D Centre, 1142
Kingsville, 712
Kirkland Lake, 538
Kirkland Lake Campus, 1143
Kirwin LLP, 1055
Kitchener, 712
Kitchener-Waterloo, 517
Kitchener-Waterloo Branch, 513
Kitchener-Waterloo Field Naturalists, 947
Kitikmeot, 618
Kitimat, 687
Kitimat Valley Naturalists, 947
Kitimat-Stikine, 678
Kivalliq, 618
Klajnerman Contracting Corp., 258
Kleinfeldt Consultants Limited, 258
Klohn Crippen Berger Ltd., 1118, 258
Klondike Placer Miners' Association, 947
Kluane National Park & Reserve of Canada, 556
KMK Consultants Limited, 258
KMW Systems Inc., 258
Kneehill Regional Water Services Commission, 757
Knight Piésold Ltd., 258
Knowaste LLC, 259
Knowledge Enterprises Branch, 591
KnowTech Environmental Inc., 259
Koch Engineering Co. Ltd., 259
Kodiak Environmental Limited, 259
Kodiak Oilfield Services, 259
Koers & Associates Engineering Ltd., 259
Komline-Sanderson, 259
The Kongsgaard-Goldman Foundation, 1046
Kongskilde Limited, 259
Konica Minolta Business Solutions (Canada) Ltd., 259
Kootenay Boundary, 678

Entry Name Index

Kootenay National Park of Canada, 556
Kouchibouguac National Park of Canada, 553
KPMG Performance Registrar Inc., 260
KPS & Associates, 260
Kraemer Tool & Manufacturing Co. Ltd., 260
Kraftur Engineering Inc., 260
Kraus Global Inc., 260
Kruger Inc., 260
KSB Pumps Inc., 261
KSH Solutions Inc. (KSH), 1174
KW Gaspé Ltd. Partnership, 261
Kwantlen University College, 1112
KWH Pipe, 261
Kyocera Mita Canada Ltd., 261

L

L&K International Training, 261
L&M Engineering Ltd., 261
L&M Feed Services, 261
L'Anse aux Meadows National Historic Site of Canada, 553
L'Assomption, 736, 748
L'Érable, 748
L'Héritage canadien du Québec, 929
L'Islet, 748
L.E. Washington Sales Ltd., 261
L.W. Ward Limited, 261
La Cité Collégiale, 1151
La Côte-de-Beaupré, 748
La Côte-de-Gaspé, 748
La Fédération des producteurs de bois du Québec, 914
La financière agricole du Québec, 646
La Haute-Côte-Nord, 748
La Haute-Gaspésie, 748
La Haute-Yamaska, 748
La Jacques-Cartier, 748
La Maison du 21e siècle, 1193
La Matapédia, 748
La Mauricie National Park of Canada, 555
La Mitis, 748
La Nouvelle-Beauce, 748
La Prairie, 736
La République, 597
La Rivière-du-Nord, 748
La Ronge, 540
La Ronge Compliance Area, 658
La Tuque, 530, 736
La Vallée-de-l'Or, 748
La Vallée-de-la-Gatineau, 748
La Vallée-du-Richelieu, 748
La Verendrye, 536
Lab-Élite limitée, 261
Labatt Breweries Canada, 1144
Labelle, Ryan, Genipro Inc., 261
Labexcel Inc., 262
Laboratoire de Canalisation Souterraines Inc., 262
Laboratoire des technologies de l'énergie (LTE) de Shawinigan, 649
Laboratoires d'Expertises de Québec Ltée, 262
Laboratoires de recherche et d'essais de Varennes, 649
Les Laboratoires S.L. inc., 269
Les Laboratoires Shermont Inc., 269
Laboratory & Scientific Services Directorate, 1151
Laboratory Services Branch, 624
Labour, 535
Labour & Legislative Development, 595
Labour Management Services, 630
Labour Relations & Mediation Division, 661
Labour Relations Board, 638, 566, 661
Labour Relations Board & Construction Industry Panel, 611
Labour Services, 612
Labour Standards, 661
Labour Standards Division, 612
Labour Standards Tribunal, 611
Labrador, 602, 599
Labrador City, 601
Labrador Southeast Coastal Action Program Inc., 1042
Labrador West Campus, 1131
Labrador West, 537
Labrie Environmental Group, 262
Labtronics, 262
Lac-Saint-Jean-Est, 749
LaCas Consultants Inc., 262
Lachine, 552
Lachute, 736

Lacombe County, 669
Lacombe Research Centre, 509, 1108
Lacombe Waste Services, 262
LADEN Steel Fabricators Inc., 262
The Ladies of the Lake, 947
Lady Davis Institute for Medical Research of the Sir Mortimer B. Davis - Jewish General Hospital, 1174
Lafarge Canada Inc., 1174, 262
Lafarge Dundas Quarry, 262
Laidlaw Carriers Inc. - Van Division, 262
Laidlaw Foundation, 1046
Laidlaw Medical Services, 263
Lajemmerais, 749
Lake Abitibi Model Forest, 948
Lake Charlotte Sanitation, 263
Lake of the Woods Control Board, 586
Lake Simcoe Region Conservation Foundation, 948, 1044
Lake Winnipeg Stewardship Board, 588
Lakehead Scrap Metal, 263
Lakehead University, 1208, 1146, 1156, 263
Lakeland College, 1109
Lakeland Protective Wear Inc., 263
Lakeland Regional Waste Management Services Commission, 757
Lakes Environmental Software, 263
Lakeshore, 712
Lakeshore Campus, 1159
Lakeshore Recycling, 263
Lalonde Geraghty Riendeau Lapierre, 1089
Lamarre Perron Lambert Vincent, 1085
Lambert Somec inc., 263
Lambton, 627, 701
Lambton College of Applied Arts & Technology, 1154
Lambton Scientific, 263
Lambton Shores, 726
Lambton Wildlife Incorporated, 948
Lamont County Regional Solid Waste Commission, 757
Lanark, 627, 701
Lanaudière, 643
Land & Environment, 642
Land & Resource Issues, 562
Land & Sea Environmental Consultants Ltd., 264
Land Administration, 614
Land Compensation/Surface Rights Board, 572
Land Force Atlantic Area (Headquarters), 545
Land Force Central Area (Headquarters), 545
Land Force Western Area (Headquarters), 545
Land Improvement Contractors of Ontario, 948
Land Services Branch, 614
Land Trust Alliance, 948
Land Use Policy Branch, 625
Land, Corporate & Appellate Services Division, 641
LandOwner Resource Centre, 1144
Lands & Forests Division, 658
Lands & Resources Branch, 659
Lands & Trusts Services, 542
Lands & Waters Branch, 633
Lands Administration, 608
Lands Branch, 665
Landscape Alberta Nursery Trades Association, 948
Landscape Newfoundland & Labrador, 948
Landscape Nova Scotia, 948
Landscape Ontario Horticultural Trades Association, 948
Landscope Consulting Corp., 264
Lane Environment Limited, 264
Lang Michener LLP - Ottawa, 1070
Lang Michener LLP - Toronto, 1077
Lang Michener LLP - Vancouver, 1060
Langara College, 1118, 1030
Langford, 681
Langley, 681, 687
Langley Branch, 512
Langley Campus, 1113
Langley Field Naturalists Society, 948
Langlois Kronström Desjardins, 1085, 1088
Lansdowne Outdoor Recreational Development Association, 948
Lantech Drilling Services Inc., 264
Lanxess Inc. - Sarnia, 1154
Lapointe Rosenstein Marchand Melançon, 1085
Lapp-Hancock Associates Limited, 264
Larose & Fils Ltée, 264
LaSalle, 713
Lasec Enterprises Ltd., 264
Laser Diagnostic Instruments International Inc., 264
LaserNetworks Inc., 264

Laserworks Computer Services, 264
Latimat Inc., 265
Latin America & the Caribbean, 544
Laurentian Forestry Centre, 550, 1179
Laurentian Pilotage Authority, 560
Laurentian University, 1208, 1209, 1155
Laurentides, 643
Les Laurentides, 749
Laurentides - Outaouais - Abitibi-Témiscamingue, 644
Laurentides-Lanaudière, 654
Laurier House National Historic Site of Canada, 554
Laval, 736
Laval - Laurentides - Lanaudière, 515
Laval Branch, 513
Laval, Lanaudière et les Laurentides, 644
Laval, Lanaudière, Laurentides, 653
Laval-Lanaudière-Laurentides, 651
Laval-Mille-Iles, 654
Lavaltrie, 736
Lavery, de Billy - Montréal, 1085
Lavery, de Billy - Ottawa, 1070
Lavery, de Billy - Québec, 1088
Lavo Inc., 265
Law Enforcement & Policing Branch, 557
Law Library, 1102, 1189, 265
Lawrence, Lawrence, Stevenson, 1068
Lawson Lundell LLP - Calgary, 1051
Lawson Lundell LLP - Vancouver, 1060
Lawson Lundell LLP - Yellowknife, 1066
Layfield Geosynthetics & Industrial Fabrics Ltd., 265
Lazier Hickey Langs O'Neal, 1068
Lea International Ltd., 266
Lea-Der Coatings (614248 Alberta Ltd.), 266
LEAD Canada Inc., 948
Leamington, 538, 726
Learning Branch, 535
Learning for a Sustainable Future, 1215
Lebanese Republic, 768
Lecompte Engineering Ltd., 266
Lécuyer et Fils Ltée, 266
Leduc, 673
Leduc County, 669
Lee & Lee, 1063
Leeds, 627
Leeds & Grenville, 726
Leeson Canada Ltd., 266
Leferink Transfer Ltd., 266
Legal Information Society of Nova Scotia, 1135
Legal Services, 551, 568, 507
Legal Services Branch, 621
Legaré F., Ing. Forestier Conseil, 266
Legend Power Systems Inc., 266
Legislation & Compliance Services, 609
Legislative Services, 592
LEHDER Environmental Services Ltd., 267
LEM Laboratory Inc., 267
Lennox, 627
Lennox & Addington, 701
Lennox Drum Ltd., 267
Lennox Industries (Canada) Ltd., 267
Leon's Insulation, 267
Lesperance Mendes, 1061
Lesser Slave Lake Regional Waste Management Services Commission, 757
Lester B. Pearson College of the Pacific, 1121
Lethbridge, 673
Lethbridge & District Japanese Garden Society, 948
Lethbridge Branch, 512
Lethbridge Community College, 1108
Lethbridge Community Foundation, 1039
Lethbridge Naturalists' Society, 948
Lethbridge Regional Waste Management Services, 757
Lethbridge Regional Water Services Commission, 757
Lethbridge Research Centre, 509
Levac Robichaud Leclerc Associates Ltd., 270
Levelton Consultants Ltd., 270
Lévis, 736
Lévis Forts National Historic Site of Canada, 555
Leviton Canada, 270
Levitt-Safety Limited, 270
Levy's Machine Works Ltd., 271
Levy, Alan D., 1077
Lewisporte, 603
LEX Scientific Inc., 271
Lexcan Industrial Supply Ltd., 271

CANADIAN ENVIRONMENTAL RESOURCE GUIDE 2011-2012

Entry Name Index

Lexmark Canada Inc., 271
LGL Limited Environmental Research Associates, 271
LH - Division of Full Circle Organics Inc., 272
Libraries of Niagara College, 1165
Library & Archives Canada, 519
Library (Burnaby), 1110
Library (Edmonton), 1105
Library (Vancouver), 1118
Licence Appeal Tribunal (LAT), 626
License Suspension Appeal Board/Medical Review Committee, 588
Licensing & Inspections, 656
Life Rhythm Corporation, 272
Life Sciences Industries Branch, 544
Life Sciences Library, 1174
Lifeforce Foundation, 949, 1040
LifeSciences British Columbia, 949
Lifewater Canada, 949
Light Solar Wind Manufacturing, 272
Lincoln, 713
Linda Willcox Whetung Professional Corporation, 1071
Lindsay, 538
Lindsay Iron & Metal Inc., 272
Lindsay Kenney LLP, 1056, 1061
Lineman's Testing Laboratories of Canada Limited, 272
Link-Pipe Inc., 272
LINPAC Ropak Packaging, 272
Linpro Petroleum Services Ltd., 272
Liqui-Box Canada Inc., 272
Liquor Distribution Branch, 582
Lister Industries Ltd., 273
Listowel, 538
Liu Institute for Global Issues, 1202
Live Green Toronto, 1044
LiveScience, 1215
Livestock Financial Protection Board, 619
Livestock Medicines Advisory Committee, 619
Livestock Technology, 620
Living Resources Inc., 273
LJM Environmental Consulting, 273
Lloydminster, 535, 673, 754
Lloydminster Agricultural Exhibition Association, 949
LOB Blasting Mat, 273
Local Governance & Community Infrastructure, 594
Local Government & Planning Policy Division, 630
Local Government Department, 575
Local Government Development Division, 584
Local Government Management Association of British Columbia, 949
Local Government Services Division, 571
Local Service District, 594
Lockerbie & Hole Contracting Ltd., 273
Loewen Welding & Manufacturing Ltd., 273
Logan Geotech, 273
Logiball Inc., 273
Logistics, Electrical, Fuel & Transportation Directorate, 558
Lojen Industrial Cleaning Ltd., 273
London, 566, 713
London - Centre for Automotive Materials and Manufacturing, 548
London Area Health Libraries Association, 949
London Branch, 513
London Health Sciences Centre, 1144
London Regional Resource Centre for Heritage & the Environment, 949
Long Environmental Consultants, 273
Long Lake Regional Waste Management Commission, 757
Longueuil, 540, 737
Longueuil Branch, 513
Longwood Forestry Services Ltd., 273
Loomers Pumping Services Ltd., 274
Loopstra Nixon LLP, 1077
Loraday Environmental Products Ltd., 274
Lord & Partners Ltd., 274
Lotbinière, 750
Lotek Wireless Inc., 274
Lotowater Technical Services Inc., 274
Louis S. St-Laurent National Historic Site of Canada, 555
Lovell & Associates, 274
Low-Level Radioactive Waste Management Office, 511
The Lowe-Martin Group, 392
Lower Churchill Development Corporation Ltd., 601
Lower Fort Garry National Historic Site of Canada, 556
Loyalist College of Applied Arts & Technology, 1138
Loyalist, 727
LTS Sales Ltd., 274

Lubrication Engineers of Canada Ltd., 274
Lucas-Milhaupt Toronto, 274
Lumber & Building Materials Association of Ontario, 949
Lunenburg District, 697
Lupien Rosenberg Consultants Inc., 274
LURA Consulting, 275
LVM Inc., 275
Lynk Electric Ltd., 276
Lynn Canyon Ecology Centre, 950
Lyreco Office Products, 276

M

M&E Engineering Ltd., 276
M&L Testing Equipment (1995) Ltd., 276
M+A Environmental Consultants, 276
M.J. International Inc., 276
M.J. Labelle Co. Ltd., 276
M.R. Gordon Consulting Inc., 276
M.S. Thompson & Associates Ltd., 276
M.S.D.A. Inc., 277
Mabarex inc., 277
Mac Industrial Exhaust Shop, 277
MacAuley Group Ltd., 277
Maccaferri Canada Ltd., 277
MacDonald & Fils Inc., 277
Macdonald Campus Library, 1182
MacDonald Dettwiler & Associates Ltd., 1115
MacDonald, Dettwiler & Associates Ltd., 277
MacDonnell Group, 277
MacEwen Petroleum Inc., 277
Machida Mack Shewchuk Meagher LLP, 1052
Machine Knife Co., 278
Machinerie Laurin Inc., 278
MacInnis, Kenneth Associates, 1067
MacKenzie Fujisawa LLP, 1061
Mackenzie Regional Waste Management Commission, 757
Mackenzie Valley Environmental Impact Review Board, 541
Mackenzie Valley Pipeline Office, 607
MacLachlan McNab Hembroff, 1056
MacLeod & Grant Ltd., 278
Macleod Dixon LLP, 1052, 1077
Macleod Institute, 1200, 950
MacMillan & Associates, 278
MacPherson Brown Ltd., 278
MacPherson Leslie & Tyerman LLP - Calgary, 1052
MacPherson Leslie & Tyerman LLP - Regina, 1090
MacPherson Leslie & Tyerman LLP - Saskatoon, 1090
Macquarie Power & Infrastructure Income Fund, 278
Macrotek Inc., 278
Maddocks Industrial Filter Division, 278
Madorin, Snyder LLP, 1069
Magnetrol International Ltd., 278
Magnor, Division of Magchem, 278
Magnum Industries Ltd., 278
Magog, 737
Magotteaux Ltée, 278
Magwood, Van De Vyvere, Thompson, & Grove-McClement LLP, 1081
Mainetti Canada Inc., 278
Maintenance & Engineering Society of The Canadian Institute of Mining, Metallurgy & Petroleum, 950
Maitland Engineering, 279
Major Water Treatment Tech Ltd., 279
MakLoc Buildings Inc., 279
Malaspina University-College, 1113
Malnar Industries Ltd., 279
Malroz Engineering Inc., 279
Malton, 538
Management Horizons, 279
Management Services, 575
Management Services Branch, 582
Management Services Division, 575
Mancorp Industrial Sales Ltd., 279
Mandel Scientific Co. Inc., 279
Manicouagan, 750
Manitoba (NWT & Nunavut), 531
Manitoba Aboriginal & Northern Affairs, 584
Manitoba Agricultural Services Corporation, 585
Manitoba Agriculture, Food & Rural Initiatives, 584
Manitoba Arts Council, 587
Manitoba Association of Health Information Providers, 950
Manitoba Association of Landscape Architects, 950
Manitoba Branches, 512
Manitoba Bureau of Statistics, 585

Manitoba Camping Association, 950
Manitoba Cattle Producers Association, 950
Manitoba Centennial Centre Corporation, 587
Manitoba Christmas Tree Grower Association, 950
Manitoba Civil Service Commission, 589
Manitoba Competitiveness, Training & Trade, 585
Manitoba Conservation, 586
Manitoba Conservation Districts Commission, 591
Manitoba Council for International Cooperation, 950
Manitoba Crop Diversification Centre, 508
Manitoba Culture, Heritage, Tourism & Sport, 587
Manitoba Dept. of Conservation, Environment Canada & Canadian Council of Ministers of the Environment, 1124
Manitoba Dept. of Science, Technology, Energy & Mines, 1124
Manitoba Drug Standards & Therapeutics Committee, 588
Manitoba Eco-Network, 1215
Manitoba Eco-Network Inc., 950, 1124
Manitoba Education, Research & Learning Information Networks, 590
Manitoba Environment Companies Directory, 1215
Manitoba Environmental Industries Association Inc., 951
Manitoba Ethnocultural Advisory & Advocacy Council, 589
Manitoba Farm Mediation Board, 585
Manitoba Film & Sound Recording Development Corporation, 587
Manitoba Film Classification Board, 587
Manitoba Floodway Authority, 588
Manitoba Forestry Association Inc., 951
Manitoba Geological Survey, 590
Manitoba Habitat Heritage Corporation, 588
Manitoba Health & Healthy Living, 587
Manitoba Health Appeal Board, 588
Manitoba Health Research Council, 590
Manitoba Healthy Child Office, 588
Manitoba Heritage Council, 587
Manitoba Horse Racing Commission, 585
Manitoba Hydro, 588, 1124, 1041
Manitoba Infrastructure & Transportation, 588
Manitoba Institute of Agrologists, 951
Manitoba Intergovernmental Affairs, 589
Manitoba Labour & Immigration, 589
Manitoba Labour Board, 590
Manitoba Land Value Appraisal Commission, 588
Manitoba Liquor Control Commission, 589
Manitoba Lung Association, 951
Manitoba Milk Prices Review Commission, 585
Manitoba Minimum Wage Board, 590
Manitoba Model Forest, 951
Manitoba Municipal Administrators' Association Inc., 951
Manitoba Municipal Board, 589
Manitoba Museum, 587, 1124
Manitoba Naturalists Society, 1124
Manitoba Ozone Protection Industry Association, 951
Manitoba Professional Planners Institute, 951
Manitoba Public Health Association, 951
Manitoba Region, 534
Manitoba Regional Lily Society, 951
Manitoba Regional Office, 508
Manitoba Round Table for Sustainable Development, 586
Manitoba Science, Technology, Energy & Mines, 590
Manitoba Seniors & Health Aging Secretariat, 588
Manitoba Tobacco Reduction Alliance, 952
Manitoba Trucking Association, 952
Manitoba Underwater Council, 952
Manitoba Water & Wastewater Association, 952
Manitoba Water Services Board, 588
Manitoba Water Stewardship, 591
Manitoba Water Well Association, 952
Manitoba Wildlife Federation, 952
Manitoba Women's Advisory Council, 590
Manitoba Workers' Compensation Board, 591
Manitoba/Saskatchewan Region, 534
Manitoulin, 627, 727
Manoir Papineau National Historic Site of Canada, 555
Mansfield & Rodney Printing Ltd., 279
Map and Data Library, 1159
Map Library, 1159, 1121
Maple Engineering & Construction Canada Ltd., 279
Maple Reinders Environmental Ltd., 279
Maple Ridge, 687
Mapping Information Branch, 551
Mapping Services Branch - Geomatics Canada, 551
Maps, Data & Government Information Centre (MADGIC), 1142
Mar Cor Purification, 280
Maratek Environmental Inc., 280
Marathon, 538

Entry Name Index

Marbek Resource Consultants Ltd., 280
Marbicon Inc., 280
Marcel Baril Ltée, 280
Marconi National Historic Site of Canada, 553
Maria-Chapdelaine, 750
Marianopolis College, 1174
Marie Rousseau, ING, 280
Marine Atlantic Inc., 560
Marine Campus, 1114
Marine Environmental Data Service, 529
Marine Fisheries & Seafood Services, 640
Marine Programs, 528
Marine Safety Directorate, 561
Maritime Auto Salvage, 280
Maritime College of Forest Technology, 1204, 1127
Maritime Electric Company Ltd., 280
Maritime Forces Atlantic (Headquarters), 545
Maritime Forces Pacific (Headquarters), 545
Maritime Geothermal Ltd., 280
Maritime Microbiologicals Inc., 281
Maritime Paper Products Ltd., 281
Maritime Provinces Harness Racing Commission, 609
Maritime Soil Ltd., 281
Maritime Testing Ltd., 281
Maritime Ultrasonic Cleaning Inc., 281
Maritimes, 527
Maritimes Health Libraries Association, 952
Market & Industry Services Branch, 508
Market & Industry Services Branch Regional Offices, 508
Market Development Branch, 620
Marketing, Aboriginal & Community Relations, 576
Markham, 713
Markham Branch, 513
Markham Campus, 1144
Markland Specialty Engineering Ltd., 281
Marmot Recovery Foundation, 952, 1040
Marriotts Container Rental Ltd., 281
Marsh Instrumentation Inc., 281
Marshall & Lamperson, 1057
Marsulex Inc., 281
Martec Ltd., 281
Martin Sheppard Fraser LLP, 1070
Martin Whalen Hennebury Stamp, 1066
Marvin Silbert & Associates, 282
Mascouche, 737
Maskinongé, 750
Les Maskoutains, 749
Massey Drive, 603
Master Builders Technologies Ltd., 282
Master Insulators' Association of Ontario Inc., 952
Masternet Ltd., 282
Matane, 738, 750
Matawinie, 750
Matco Ltd., 282
Material Resource Recovery Inc., 282
Materials & Manufacturing Ontario, Division of OCE Inc., 952
Matériauthèque, 1186
Matheson & Murray, 1082
Matrix Energy, 282
Matrix Photocatalytic Inc., 282
Matrix Solutions Inc., 282
Mattson, Mark O., 1077
Mauricie, 515, 540
Mauricie - Centre-du-Québec - Estrie, 644
Mauricie et Centre-du-Québec, 644
Mauricie, Centre-du-Québec, 653
Mauricie-Centre-du-Québec, 655, 651
MAUSER, 283
Max Bell Foundation, 1039
Maxim Power Corp, 283
Maxxam Analytics Inc., 283
Maxxam Analytics Ltd., 283
Mayer Heritage Consultants Inc., 284
Mayo District Renewable Resources Council, 665
Mayo General Hospital, 533
McAtee Safety & Environmental Health Services Ltd., 284
MCC Industrial Services Ltd, 284
McCaffery Mudry Pritchard LLP, Barristers & Solicitors, 1052
McCarthy Tétrault LLP - Calgary, 1052
McCarthy Tétrault LLP - Montréal, 1086
McCarthy Tétrault LLP - Ottawa, 1070
McCarthy Tétrault LLP - Québec, 1088
McCarthy Tétrault LLP - Toronto, 1077
McCarthy Tétrault LLP - Vancouver, 1061
McClymont & Rak Engineers, Inc., 284

McCordick Glove & Safety Inc., 284
McCullough O'Connor Irwin LLP, 1061
McDougall Gauley, 1089, 1090
McElhanney Consulting Services Ltd., 284
McGill University, 1211, 1174, 1035
McGregor Model Forest, 952
McIlwraith Field Naturalists, 953
McInnes Cooper, 1064, 1067, 1066
McKell Marketing Ltd., 285
McKenzie Lake Lawyers LLP, 1069
McKerlie Solar Systems, 285
The McLean Foundation, 1044
McLennan Ross LLP, 1053, 1055, 1066
McMaster University, 1209, 1141
McMichael Canadian Art Collection, 621
McMillan Binch Mendelsohn - Montréal, 1086
McMillan Binch Mendelsohn - Toronto, 1077
McNair & Marshall Planning & Development Consultants, 285
McNamara Construction Company, 285
MCR Environmental Consulting, 285
MCW Custom Energy Solutions, 285
MDA Space, 1182
MDI Waste Management Inc., 285
MDS Sciex, 285
Meadow Lake, 540
Meadow Lake Compliance Area, 658
Meaford, 727
MEC Systems Inc., 286
Mechanical Contractors Association of Alberta, 953
Mechanical Contractors Association of British Columbia, 953
Mechanical Contractors Association of Canada, 953
Mechanical Contractors Association of Manitoba, 953
Mechanical Contractors Association of Newfoundland & Labrador, 953
Mechanical Contractors Association of Nova Scotia, 953
Mechanical Contractors Association of Ontario, 953
Mechanical Contractors Association of Prince Edward Island, 953
Mechanical Contractors Association of Saskatchewan Inc., 953
Medgate Inc., 286
Mediation & Arbitration Board, 576
Medical Eligibility Committee, 628
Medical Reform Group of Ontario, 1159
Medical Services, 660, 580
Medical Services Commission, 580
Medical Society of Prince Edward Island, 953
Medicine Hat, 535, 673
Medicine Hat Branch, 512
Medicine Hat College, 1109
Medina Construction Limited, 286
Meewasin Valley Authority, 953
Megalab Inc., 286
Megasecur Inc., 286
Mékinac, 750
Melfort, 540
Melfort Agricultural Society, 953
Melville & District Agri-Park Association Inc., 953
Membrex Ltée, 286
Memorial University of Newfoundland, 1205, 1204, 1132, 286, 1033
Memphrémagog, 750
Menart S.L. Inc., 286
Mental Health & Addiction Services, 613
Meo & Associates Inc., 286
MEP Environmental Products Ltd., 286
The MEP Environmental Products Ltd., 392
Mequipco Ltd., 286
Merchant Law Group LLP - Calgary, 1053
Merchant Law Group LLP - Edmonton, 1055
Merchant Law Group LLP - Saskatoon, 1090
Merchant Law Group LLP - Victoria, 1062
Merchant Seamen Compensation Board, 535
Merchants of Green Coffee, 286
Merck Frosst Canada Inc., 1168
Merley Chains Ltd., 287
Merlin Plastics Supply Inc., 287
MERX, 558
Mesa Forestry & Environmental Services Ltd., 287
Mesh Technologies Inc., 287
Metacor International Inc., 287
Metafix, 287
Metallurgy & Materials Society of the Canadian Institute of Mining, Metallurgy & Petroleum, 954
Metcon Sales & Engineering Ltd., 287
Météoglobe Canada Inc., 287
Meteorological Service of Canada, 1215, 522

Metex Corp. Ltd., 287
Métis Settlements Appeal Tribunal, 563
Métis Settlements Ombudsman Office, 563
Metocean Data Systems Limited, 287
Metro Recycling, 287
Metro Toronto Convention Centre Corporation, 635
Metro Vancouver, 678
Metro Vancouver (formerly Greater Vancouver Regional District), 1110
Metrographic Green Print, 287
Métropole, 643
Métropolitain Valve Inc., 288
Metropolitan Consulting Inc., 288
Metrovan Hotsy Equipment Ltd., 288
Metso Automation Canada Ltd., 288
Mexico, 565
MF Paints, 288
MFL Occupational Health Centre, 1124
MGM Management, 288
MICCA Paints Inc., 288
Miceli & Frères Ltée, 288
Michael Holliday & Associates, 288
Michael Wall & Sons Enterprises Ltd., 288
Michel Lavallée, 289
Michelin North America (Canada) Inc., 289
The Michener Institute for Applied Health Sciences, 954, 1162
Micro-Watt Control Devices Ltd., 289
Micrologic Ltd., 289
Middle East & North Africa, 544
Middlesex, 701
Middlesex Centre, 727
Middlesex East, 627
Middlesex Federation of Agriculture, 954
Midhurst, 633
Midland, 538, 713
MIE Consulting Engineers Ltd., 289
Mifab Canada, 289
MIG Engineering Ltd., 289
Miistakis Institute for the Rockies, 1200
Mike Fuller Electric Ltd., 289
Mikro-Tek Inc., 289
Miles, Davison LLP, 1053
Military Police Complaints Commission, 545
Millar Western Forest Products Ltd., 290
Millar-Williams Hydronics Ltd., 290
Millard Health, 1105
Millarville Racing & Agricultural Society, 954
Millennium Water Management Ltd., 290
Miller Environmental Corp., 290
Miller Thomson LLP - Calgary, 1053
Miller Thomson LLP - Edmonton, 1055
Miller Thomson LLP - Markham, 1069
Miller Thomson LLP - Montréal, 1086
Miller Thomson LLP - Toronto, 1077
Miller Thomson LLP - Vancouver, 1061
Miller Thomson LLP - Waterloo, 1081
Miller Waste Systems, 290
Milton, 538, 714
Minas Basin Pulp & Power Company Limited, 290
Mineral Development & Lands Branch, 634
Mineral Policy & Business Development, 590
Mineral Resources, 664
Mineral Resources Division, 590
Mineral Society of Manitoba, 954
Mineralogical Association of Canada, 954
Minerals & Metals Sector, 551
Minerals Management Division, 614
Minerals Resources Branch, 614
Minerals, Oil & Gas Division, 607
Minerals, Policy & Planning Division, 595
Mines, 650
Mines & Aggregates Safety & Health Association, 954, 1146
Mines & Minerals Division, 634
Mines Branch, 603, 590
Mingan Archipelago National Park Reserve of Canada, 555
Minganie, 750
Minimum Wage Board, 661
Mining & Lands Commissioner, 631
Mining & Minerals, 576
Mining Association of British Columbia, 954
Mining Association of Canada, 955
Mining Association of Manitoba Inc., 955
Mining Board, 590
Mining Industry Human Resources Council, 955
Mining Society of Nova Scotia, 955

Entry Name Index

Mining Suppliers, Contractors & Consultants Association of BC, 955
MiningWatch Canada, 1215, 955
Minister's Advisory Council for Arts & Culture, 621
Ministère de l'Agriculture, des Pêcheries et de l'Alimentation, 645
Ministère de la Culture, des Communications & de la Condition féminine, 644
Ministère de la Santé et des Services sociaux, 651
Ministère de la Sécurité publique, 652
Ministère des Affaires municipales et Occupation du territoire, 642
Ministère des Ressources naturelles et de la Faune, 649
Ministère des Services gouvernementaux, 653
Ministère des Transports, 654
Ministère du Développement durable, de l'Environnement et des Parcs, 646
Ministère du Développement économique, de l'Innovation et de l'Exportation, 648
Ministère du Tourisme, 654
Ministère du Travail, 655
Ministerial Advisory Committee on Multiculturalism, 595
Ministry of Agriculture, 574
Ministry of Agriculture, Food & Rural Affairs, 619
Ministry of Community Safety & Correctional Services, 621
Ministry of Community, Sport & Cultural Development, 574
Ministry of Culture, 621
Ministry of Economic Development & Trade, 622
Ministry of Energy and Infrastructure, 622
Ministry of Energy, Mines & Petroleum Resources, 576
Ministry of Environment, 623, 576
Ministry of Forests, Lands & Natural Resource Operations, 578
Ministry of Government Services, 626
Ministry of Health & Long-Term Care, 628
Ministry of Health Services, 580
Ministry of Healthy Living & Sport, 583
Ministry of Jobs, Tourism, & Innovation, 575
Ministry of Labour, 629
Ministry of Labour, Citizens' Services & Open Government, 581
Ministry of Municipal Affairs & Housing, 630
Ministry of Natural Resources, 631
Ministry of Northern Development, Mines & Forestry, 634
Ministry of Public Safety & Solicitor General, 582
Ministry of Research & Innovation, 635
Ministry of Tourism, 635
Ministry of Transportation, 635
Ministry of Transportation & Infrastructure, 583
Miniveil Air Systems, 290
Mirabel, 738
Miramichi, 691
Miramichi Campus Library, 1128
Miramichi Regional Office, 593
Miramichi River Environmental Assessment Committee, 1042
Mirarco Mining Innovation, 290
Mirus International Inc., 290
Misericordia Community Hospital, 1106
Misericordia Health Centre, 1124
Mission, 687
Mission Campus at Heritage Park Centre Library, 1113
MissionHGE inc., 291
Mississauga, 529, 714
Mississauga Branch, 513
Mississauga East, 538
Mississauga Laboratory, 291
Mississauga West, 538
Mississippi Mills, 714
Mississippi River Power Corp., 291
Mitlenatch Field Naturalists Society, 955
Mitsubishi Canada Ltd., 291
MK Plastics Corp., 291
MKG Imaging Solutions Inc., 291
MLC Associés Inc., 292
MMM Group, 292
Mobile Augers & Research Ltd., 292
Model Forest of Newfoundland and Labrador, 955
Mohawk College of Applied Arts & Technology, 1141
Mohawk-McMaster Institute for Applied Health Sciences, 1141
Mold & Bacteria Consulting Laboratories (MBL) Inc., 292
Momentum Conveyors, 292
Monalt Environmental Inc., 292
Moncton / Ville de Moncton, 691
Moncton Branch, 512
Moncton Campus, Library, 1128
Moncton Regional Office, 593
Mondo Products Company Limited, 292
Mondry Del Zotto et associés inc., 292
Monitrex Engineering Ltd., 293

Monsanto Canada Inc., 293
Monserco Ltd., 293
Monster Polymers Inc., 293
Mont-Laurier, 738
Mont-St-Hilaire, 738
Montague/Souris, 637
Montcalm, 750
Montérégie, 515, 653, 644
Montérégie - Secteur Est, 645
Montérégie et Montréal, 651
Montérégie-Rive-Sud, 517
Montmagny, 738, 750
Montréal, 738
Montréal - Laval - Lanaudière, 645
Montréal Branch, 513
Montréal Centre-Ville/Sud-ouest-de-Montréal, 540
Montréal et de l'Ouest, 654
Montréal Field Naturalists Club, 955
Montréal Gem & Mineral Club, 955
Montréal General Hospital, 1174
Montréal, Laval, Lanaudière et Laurentides, 653
Montrose Technologies Inc., 293
Monty, Coulombe, 1089
Monument Lefebvre National Historic Site of Canada, 553
Moore-Stewart, Robert, 1062
Moose Factory General Hospital, 533
Moose Jaw, 540, 754
Moose Jaw Wildlife Federation, 955
Morden, 536
Morelli Chertkow LLP, Lawyers, 1056
Morency Avocats, 1088
Morgan Falls Power Company, 293
Morrison Environmental Limited, 293
Morrison Hershfield, 293
Morval, 294
Motherwell Homestead National Historic Site of Canada, 556
Les Moulins, 750
Mount Allison University, 1204, 1129, 1033
Mount Pearl, 694
Mount Revelstoke National Park of Canada, 556
Mount Royal College, 1102
Mount Sinai Hospital, 1159
Mount Waddington, 678
Mountain Equipment Co-op (Environment Fund Grants), 1040
Mountain Valley Geophysics, 294
Mountain View County, 669
Mountain View Regional Waste Management Commission, 757
Mountain View Regional Water Services, 758
Movac Mobile Vacuum Services Ltd., 294
Mowat Fabrication Ltd., 294
MPI Drilling, 294
Mr. Gas Ltd., 294
MR2-McDonald & Associates, 294
MSA: Mine Safety Applicances Company, 294
MSU Mississauga Ltd., 294
MTE Consultants Inc., 294
Muddy River Technologies Inc., 294
Mueller Canada, 295
Muis Controls Ltd., 295
Multi Recyclage S.D. Inc., 295
Multi-Materials Stewardship Board, 599
Multi-Stage Filter, 295
Multiculturalism Secretariat, 590
Multitel Inc., 295
Multiview Locates Inc., 295
Munich, 565
Municipal Affairs, 638
Municipal Affairs Consulting, 295
Municipal Engineers Association, 955
Municipal Equipment & Operations Association (Ontario) Inc., 955
Municipal Finance Branch, 631
Municipal Recyclers Ltd., 295
Municipal Services Division, 616
Municipal Services Offices, 630
Municipal Waste Association, 955
Municipalities Newfoundland & Labrador, 956
The Murphy Foundation Incorporated, 1041
Murray Krovats Agency Ltd., 295
Musée d'art contemporain de Montréal, 645
Musée de la civilisation, 645
Musée national des beaux-arts du Québec, 645
Mushkegowuk Environmental Research Centre, 1209
Muskoka, 627, 702
Muskoka Containerized Services Ltd., 295
Muskoka Lakes Association, 956

Musquodoboit Trailways Association, 956
Muttart Tufts Dewolfe & Coyle, 1068
MW Metal Spinning & Stamping Ltd., 295
MWA Consultants, 295
MWH Canada Inc., 295
My Sustainable Canada, 1215

N

N-T Enterprise Inc., 296
N. Vandenassem & Associate, 296
N.A.T.S. Nursery Ltd., 296
N.L. Sobey & Associates Limited, 296
N.R. Murphy Ltd., 296
N.S. Bauman Ltd., 296
NACE International, 956
NAFTA Office of Mexico in Canada, 531
Nahanni National Park Reserve of Canada, 556
Nahum Gelber Law Library, 1174
NAID Canada, 956
Nalco Canada Co., 296
Nanaimo, 681, 678
Nanaimo Branch, 512
Nanaimo Community Foundation, 1041
Nanaimo Field Naturalists, 956
Napanee, 538
Napier Environmental Technology, 296
Napier-Reid Ltd., 297
Napoleon Appliance Corp., 297
NAR Environmental Consultants Inc., 297
Nardei Fabricators Ltd., 297
Natech Environmental Services, 297
The Nation, 731
National Aboriginal Forestry Association, 956
National Air Photo Library, 1151
National Arts Centre, 519
National Association for Environmental Education (UK), 956
National Association for Environmental Management, 956
National Association for Information Destruction, 956
National Association for PET Container Resources, 957
National Association of Environmental Professionals, 957
National Association of the Chemistry Industry, 957
National Audubon Society, Inc., 957
National Battlefields Commission, 519
National Building Envelope Council, 957
National Capital Commission, 545, 1151
National Capital Region, 1151
National Centre for Small Communities, 957
National Climate Data & Information Archive, 524
National Coalition Against the Misuse of Pesticides, 957
National Council for Science & the Environment, 957
National Defence Canada, 545
National Electronic Procurement Assistance Center, 533
National Energy Board, 549, 546, 1102
National Energy Conservation Association, 957, 1125
National Energy Equipment Inc., 297
National Environmental Health Association, 957
National Farmers Union, 958
National Film Board of Canada, 519
National Gallery of Canada, 519
National Geographic, 1215
National Ground Water Association, 958
National Guidelines & Standards Office, 524
National Horse Protection League, 958
National Hydrology Research Centre, 1212, 524
National Hydrology Research Centre, National Water Research Institute, 1189
National Institute of Nanotechnology, 548
National Instruments Canada, 297
National Laboratory of Environmental Testing, 525
National Land & Water Information Service, 510
National Marine Manufacturers Association Canada, 958
National Parks Conservation Association, 958
National Parks Directorate, 552
National Parole Board, 557
National Process Equipment Inc., 298
National Recycling Coalition, 958
National Research Council Canada, 546
National Research Council Institute for Marine Biosciences, 1207
National Round Table on the Environment & Economy, 523, 548
National Search & Rescue Secretariat, 549
National Solid Wastes Management Association, 958
National Sunflower Association of Canada, 958
National Technical Information Service, 532
The National Testing Laboratories Ltd., 393

Entry Name Index

National Waste Services, 298
National Water Research Institute, 1209, 525
National Wildlife Federation, 958
Native Investment & Trade Association, 959
Native Orchid Conservation Inc., 959
Natural Forces Technologies Inc., 298
Natural Health Practitioners of Canada, 959
Natural Heritage, 599
Natural History Society of Newfoundland & Labrador, 959
Natural Life, 1193
Natural Resources & Environment Branch, 543
Natural Resources & Environmental Studies Institute, 1202
Natural Resources Canada, 1215, 549, 1151, 1044
Natural Resources Canada Library - Earth Sciences (Vancouver), 1118
Natural Resources Canada, Canadian Forest Service, 1127
Natural Resources Conservation Board, 572
Natural Resources Management Division, 633
Natural Resources Union, 959
Natural Sciences & Engineering Research Council of Canada, 552
Natural Sciences Library, 1189
Natural Step Canada, 1215
Nature Canada, 1193, 1215, 959, 1151
Nature Challenge for Kids, 1215
Nature Conservancy of Canada, 1215
The Nature Conservancy of Canada, 959
Nature Manitoba, 959
Nature NB, 960
Nature Nova Scotia (Federation of Nova Scotia Naturalists), 960
Nature Québec, 960
Nature Saskatchewan, 960
Nature Trust of New Brunswick, 960, 1042
Nature Vancouver, 960
Nature's Environmental Products Inc., 298
Nature's Friend Environmental, 298
Nature's Mate Distribution Inc., 298
NatureServe Explorer, 1216
Navajo Metals, 298
Naylor Engineering Associates Ltd., 298
NB Board of Commissioners of Public Utilities, 597
NB Coal Limited, 299
NBCC, 595
NCL Envirotek Inc., 299
NCR Canada Ltd. - Systemedia Division, 299
Near North Laboratories Inc., 299
Nearshore Atlantic, 601
NEDCO, 299
Nederman Canada Ltd., 299
Neighborhood Recycling, 299
Neil John Maclean Health Sciences Library, 1125
Neilson Excavation, 299
NEK Environmental Technologies Inc., 299
Nelligan O'Brien Payne, 1068, 1069, 1071, 1081
Nelson, 536
Nelson Environmental Inc., 299
Nelson Environmental Remediation Ltd., 299
Nelson Environmental Services, 299
Nelson-Superior Consultants Ltd., 300
Nemato Inc., 300
Neo Valves, 300
Nepisiguit Salmon Association, 960
Nepisiguit-Chaleur Solid Waste Commission, 758
The Neptis Foundation, 1044
Neptune Technology Group (Canada) Ltd., 300
Nertec Design Inc., 300
Nestlé Purina PetCare, 300
Net Safety Monitoring Inc., 300
NetPlus-HazMat Tracker, 300
Nett Technologies Inc., 300
Network Environmental Services Inc., 300
Nevin Sadlier-Brown Goodbrand Ltd., 300
New Brunswick, 546
New Brunswick Agricultural Insurance Commission, 591
New Brunswick Arts Board, 598
New Brunswick Branches, 512
New Brunswick Community College, 1127
New Brunswick Community Colleges, 595
New Brunswick Dept. of Environment, 1128
New Brunswick Dept. of Wellness, Culture & Sport, 1129
New Brunswick Emergency Measures Organization, 596
New Brunswick Environment Industry Association, 960
New Brunswick Environmental Network, 1216, 960, 1042
New Brunswick Environmental Trust Fund, 1042
New Brunswick Farm Products Commission, 591
New Brunswick Federation of Woodlot Owners Inc., 961

New Brunswick Film, 598
New Brunswick Forest Products Association Inc., 961
New Brunswick Forest Products Commission, 595
New Brunswick Fruit Growers Association Inc., 961
New Brunswick Ground Water Association, 961
New Brunswick Human Rights Commission, 595
New Brunswick Industrial Development Board, 592
New Brunswick Institute of Agrologists, 961
New Brunswick Lung Association, 961
New Brunswick Medical Society, 961
New Brunswick Mining Association, 961
New Brunswick Museum, 598, 1129
New Brunswick Power Group of Companies, 595
New Brunswick Regional Office, 510
New Brunswick Research & Productivity Council, 596
New Brunswick Round Table on Environment & Economy, 593
New Brunswick Salmon Council, 961
New Brunswick Salmon Growers Association, 961
New Brunswick Society of Certified Engineering Technicians & Technologists, 961
New Brunswick Soil & Crop Improvement Association, 961
New Brunswick Transportation Authority, 597
New Brunswick Wildlife Federation, 962
New Brunswick Wildlife Trust Fund, 1042
The New Directions Group, 962
New East Consulting Services Ltd., 301
New Era Farms Ltd., 301
New Liskeard, 538
New Tecumseth, 714
New Trend Environmental Services, 301
New West Gypsum Recycling Inc., 301
New Westminster, 682
New World Generation Inc., 301
Newalta Corporation, 301
Newfoundland & Labrador Association of Landscape Architects, 962
Newfoundland & Labrador Association of Technology Companies, 962
Newfoundland & Labrador Board of Commissioners of Public Utilities, 604
Newfoundland & Labrador Branches, 512
Newfoundland & Labrador Camping Association, 962
Newfoundland & Labrador Construction Association, 962
Newfoundland & Labrador Dept. of Forest Resources & Agrifood, 1130
Newfoundland & Labrador Dept. of Government Services, 1131
Newfoundland & Labrador Dept. of Health & Community Services, 1132
Newfoundland & Labrador Dept. of Innovation, Trade & Rural Development, 1132
Newfoundland & Labrador Dept. of Natural Resources, 1132
Newfoundland & Labrador Emergency Measures Organization, 598
Newfoundland & Labrador Environmental Industry Association, 962
Newfoundland & Labrador Federation of Agriculture, 962
Newfoundland & Labrador Film Development Corporation, 604
Newfoundland & Labrador Forest Protection Association, 962
Newfoundland & Labrador Health Boards Associations, 601
Newfoundland & Labrador Health Libraries Association, 963
Newfoundland & Labrador Housing Corp., 1132
Newfoundland & Labrador Hydro, 601, 1132
Newfoundland & Labrador Institute of Agrologists, 963
Newfoundland & Labrador Lung Association, 963
Newfoundland & Labrador Medical Association, 963
Newfoundland & Labrador Outfitters Association, 963
Newfoundland & Labrador Public Health Association, 963
Newfoundland & Labrador Regional Office, 511
Newfoundland & Labrador Safety Council, 963
Newfoundland & Labrador Wildlife Federation, 963
Newfoundland & Labrador Workplace Health, Safety & Compensation Commission, 604
Newfoundland and Labrador Environmental Network, 1216
Newfoundland Aquaculture Industry Association, 963
Newfoundland Design Associates Limited, 302
Newfoundland Horticultural Society, 963
Newfoundland Ocean Industries Association, 1132
Newfoundland/Labrador Ground Water Association, 964
Newmac Manufacturing Inc., 303
Newmarket, 538, 714
Newpark Environmental Services, 303
Nexen Inc., 1102
Next Environmental, 303
NextEnergy Inc., 303
Nexus Solutions Inc., 303

NI Plastique Inc., 303
Niagara, 625, 702
Niagara Analytical Inc., 303
Niagara Energy Products Limited, 303
Niagara Environmental Dynamics, 303
Niagara Escarpment Commission, 631
Niagara Falls, 538, 715
Niagara Falls Nature Club, 964
Niagara North, 627
Niagara Parks Botanical Gardens School of Horticulture, 1146
Niagara Parks Commission, 635
Niagara Peninsula Conservation Foundation, 964, 1044
Niagara Peninsula Geological Society, 964
Niagara Recycling, 303
Niagara South, 627
Niagara Waste Systems Ltd., 303
Niagara Water Conditioning Ltd., 303
Niagara-on-the-Lake, 715
Niblett Environmental, 304
Nichols Applied Management, 304
Nichols Environmental (Canada) Ltd., 304
Nickel Institute, 964, 1159
Nicola Valley Institute of Technology, 1113
Nicola Valley Institute of Technology (NVIT), 1030
Nicolet, 647
Nicolet-Yamaska, 750
Niijkiwenhwag - Friends of Lake Superior Park, 964
Nilex Inc., 304
Nilfisk-Advance Canada Company, 304
NIM Disposals Limited, 304
Nimbus Water Systems, 304
Nimegeers, Schuck, Wormsbecker & Bobbitt, 1091
Nipawin, 540
Nipigon, 632
Nipissing, 627, 727
Nipissing Environmental Watch, 964
Nippissing University/Canadore College, 1146
Nisymco Inc., 304
Nixon Wenger, 1062
Noel Rochette et Fils Inc., 305
NOIA, 964
Noise Solutions Inc., 305
Nolar Industries Ltd., 305
Non-Insured Health Benefits Directorate, 534
Non-Smokers' Rights Association, 964
Nor-Alta Environmental Services Ltd., 305
NORA, An Association of Responsible Recyclers, 964
Noram Engineering & Constructors Ltd., 305
Norampac Inc., 305
Noranda Earth Sciences Library, 1159
Nord-de-Montréal, 540
Nord-du-Québec, 643, 515
Nordevco Associates Ltd., 305
Nordic Systems Corporation, 305
NORDIKeau Inc., 305
Norditrade Inc., 305
Norfolk, 627, 702
Norfolk County Agricultural Society, 964
Norfolk Disposal Services Limited, 305
Norfolk Field Naturalists, 964
Norjohn Transfer System Limited, 305
Norm Shropshall & Sons Ltd., 305
Normal Farm Practices Protection Board, 619
Norman B. Keevil Institute of Mining Engineering, 1202
Normcan, 306
NorQuest College, 1106
Norseman Plastics Ltd., 306
Nortec S.G.S. Inc., 306
North 43 Lagoon Commission, 758
North American Association for Environmental Education, 964
North American Bird Conservation Initiative Canada, 523, 764, 965
North American Development Bank, 531
North American Native Plant Society, 965
North American Packaging Association - Canada, 965
North American Recycled Rubber Association, 965
North American Society for Oceanic History, 965
North American Waterfowl Management Plan, 523, 525, 765, 965
North Battleford, 754
North Bay, 538, 715
North Bay Branch, 513
North Central Local Government Association, 965
North Cowichan, 687
North Dundas, 727

CANADIAN ENVIRONMENTAL RESOURCE GUIDE 2011-2012　　　1245

Entry Name Index

North Forty Mile Regional Waste Management Services Commission, 758
North Glengarry, 727
North Grenville, 728
North Interlake, 585
North Island College Library, 1111
North Okanagan, 678
North Okanagan Naturalists Club, 965
North Okanagan Organic Association, 965
North Pacific Marine Science Organization, 1202
North Parkland, 585
North Peace Regional Landfill Commission, 758
North Perth, 715
North Red Deer River Water Services Commission, 758
North Saanich, 687
North Safety Products Canada, 306
North Saskatchewan Watershed Alliance, 966
North Shore, 536
North Shore Forest Products Marketing Board, 966
North Shore Management Systems Inc., 306
North Shuswap Naturalists, 966
North Slave, 605
North Sydney, 537
North Vancouver, 688, 682
North Vancouver Branch, 512
North West Environmental Group, 306
North York, 529
North Yukon Renewable Resources Council, 665
North/South Consultants Inc., 306
Northeast Avalon ACAP, Inc., 966
Northeast Organic Farming Association, 966
Northeast Pigeon Lake Regional Services Commission, 758
Northeast Region, 632
Northeast, 569
Northeastern, 636, 630, 586
Northeastern Region, 610
Northeastern Resource Recovery Ltd., 307
Northern Windows, 307
Northern, 621, 612, 622
Northern Affairs, 542
Northern Alberta & BC, 508
Northern Alberta Development Council, 566
Northern Alberta Health Libraries Association, 966
Northern Alberta Institute of Technology, 1106
Northern Alternate Power Systems, 307
Northern BC & Yukon, 517
Northern Bridge and Mat Rentals Ltd., 307
Northern College of Applied Arts & Technology, 1156
Northern Development, 592
Northern Development Branch, 573
Northern Development Division, 634
Northern Development Initiative Trust, 575
Northern Field Services, 658
Northern Forestry Centre, 1200, 550, 1106
Northern Interior, 579
Northern Interior Vegetation Management Association, 966
Northern Lakes College - Grouard Campus, 1108
Northern Lakes College - Slave Lake, 1109
Northern Lakes College, 1111
Northern Lights Energy Systems, 307
Northern Lights Health Library Association, 966
Northern Lights Regional Health Centre, 1107
Northern Native Fishing Corporation, 966
Northern Oil & Gas Branch, 543
Northern Ontario Aquaculture Association, 966
Northern Ontario Region, 516
Northern Petroleum Services, 307
Northern Prospectors Association, 966
Northern Region, 534
Northern Region - Colchester East Hants, Cumberland, Pictou, 613
Northern Saskatchewan, 508
Northern Steel Industries, 307
Northland Power, 307
NorthPoint Energy Solutions, 307
Northstar Trade Finance Inc., 532
Northumberland, 627, 702
Northumberland Salmon Protection Association, 966
Northumberland Solid Waste Commission, 758
Northwatch, 966
Northway-Photomap Inc., 307
Northwest Atlantic Fisheries Centre, 1205, 1132
Northwest Coalition for Alternatives to Pesticides, 966
Northwest Community College Library, 1116
Northwest Metal Recycling, 307

Northwest Occupational Health & Safety, 307
Northwest Region, 632
Northwest River, 603
Northwest Territories, 542
Northwest Territories & Nunavut Workers Compensation Board, 619
Northwest Territories & Nunavut Workers' Compensation Board, 608
Northwest Territories Apprenticeship, Trade & Occupations Certification Board, 605
Northwest Territories Association of Communities, 967
Northwest Territories Association of Landscape Architects, 967
Northwest Territories Branches, 512
Northwest Territories Business Development & Investment Corporation, 607
Northwest Territories Construction Association, 967
Northwest Territories Geoscience Office, 605
Northwest Territories Legislative Assembly, 1134
Northwest Territories Power Corporation, 608
Northwest Territories Public Works & Services, 1134
Northwest Territories Recreation & Parks Association, 967
Northwest Territories Remote Sensing Centre, 607
Northwest Territories Resources, Wildlife & Economic Development, 1134
Northwest Territories Water Board, 608
Northwest Wildlife Preservation Society, 967
Northwest, 592, 569
Northwestern, 630, 586
Northwestern Ontario Health Libraries Association, 967
Northwestern Ontario Municipal Association, 967
Norvac Industrial Services, 307
Norwesco Canada Ltd., 308
Norwich, 728
Not Far From The Tree, 967
Notra Inc., 308
Notre Dame Bay Memorial Health Centre, 1133
Notre Development Corp., 308
Notre-Dame-des-Lourdes, 536
Nouvelle Technologie (TEKNO) Inc., 308
Nova Chemicals Corporation, 308
NOVA Chemicals Ltd., 1102
Nova Envirocom, 308
Nova Forest Alliance, 967, 1043
Nova Magnetics Burgmann Ltd., 308
Nova PB Inc., 308
Nova Scotia, 541
Nova Scotia Advisory Commission on AIDS, 613
Nova Scotia Agricultural College, 1137, 1034
Nova Scotia Branches, 513
Nova Scotia Business Inc., 610
Nova Scotia Cattle Producers, 967
Nova Scotia Community College, 1136
Nova Scotia Crop & Livestock Insurance Commission, 609
Nova Scotia Daylily Society, 967
Nova Scotia Department of Natural Resources, 1207
Nova Scotia. Dept. of Natural Resources, 1043
Nova Scotia Dept. of Natural Resources, 1136
Nova Scotia Dept. of Transportation & Public Works, 1136
Nova Scotia Emergency Management Office, 610
Nova Scotia Environment & Labour, 1136
Nova Scotia Environmental Network, 1216, 967, 1043
Nova Scotia Farm Loan Board, 609
Nova Scotia Farm Practices Board, 609
Nova Scotia Federation of Agriculture, 968
Nova Scotia Fish Packers Association, 968
Nova Scotia Forest Technicians Association, 968
Nova Scotia Forestry Association, 968
Nova Scotia Fruit Growers' Association, 968
Nova Scotia Geomatics Centre, 615
Nova Scotia Ground Water Association, 968
Nova Scotia Institute of Agrologists, 968
Nova Scotia Lung Association, 968
Nova Scotia Mackerel Association, 968
Nova Scotia Municipal Finance Corporation, 615
Nova Scotia Natural Products Marketing Council, 609
Nova Scotia Nature Trust, 968
Nova Scotia Power, an Emera Company, 308
Nova Scotia Public Interest Research Group, 968
Nova Scotia Regional Office, 511
Nova Scotia Safety Council, 968
Nova Scotia Salmon Association, 969
Nova Scotia Securities Commission, 611
Nova Scotia Swordfish Fishermen's Association, 969
Nova Scotia Tourism Partnership Council, 616
Nova Scotia Utility & Review Board, 616

Nova Scotia Utility and Review Board, 613
Nova Scotia Wild Flora Society, 969
Nova Scotian Institute of Science, 969
Novapet Inc., 308
Novatech Controls, Inc., 309
Nove Environnement Inc., 309
Novitherm Canada Inc., 309
NPS Pharmaceuticals, 1159
NRC Information Centre, 1166
NRC Information Centre - Halifax, 1136
NRC Information Centre - St John's, 1133
NRC Information Centre - Saskatoon, 1189
NRC Information Centre Montréal, 1174
NRI Industries, 309
NS Archives & Records Management, 616
NS Primary Forest Products Marketing Board, 614
NSERC/Petro-Canada Chair for Women in Science & Engineering, 969
NSF-ISR, 309
Nu-Air Ventilation Systems Inc., 309
Nu-Plast Polymers International, 309
Nu-West Services Ltd., 309
Nuclear Awareness Project, 1164
Nuclear Information & Resource Service, 969
Numet Engineering Ltd., 309
Nunavut, 542, 518
Nunavut Arctic College, 1138
Nunavut Business Credit Corporation, 617
Nunavut Dept. of Environment, 1138
Nunavut Emergency Management, 618
Nunavut Harvesters Association, 969
Nunavut Impact Review Board, 542
Nunavut Planning Commission, 542
Nunavut Research Institute, 1138
Nunavut Water Board, 542
Nusco Supply & Manufacturing Inc., 309
NWT & Nunavut Chamber of Mines, 969
NWT Arts Council, 605

O

O'Connor Associates Environmental Inc., 310
O'Connor MacLeod Hanna LLP, 1070
O'Connor Tanks Ltd., 310
O'Halloran Campbell Consultants Limited, 310
O'Leary, 540
O-I Canada Corp., 310
Oak Bay, 688
Oak Environmental Inc., 310
Oak Ridges Moraine Foundation, 1044
Oakhill Environmental, 310
Oakridge Environmental Ltd., 310
Oakside Chemicals Ltd., 311
Oakville, 538, 715
Oakville Community Centre for Peace, Ecology & Human Rights, 969
Oasis Bags, 311
Occupational & Environmental Medical Association of Canada, 969
Occupational Health & Safety, 629
Occupational Health & Safety Advisory Council, 612
Occupational Health & Safety Appeal Panel, 612
Occupational Health & Safety Branch, 601, 629
Occupational Health & Safety Council, 566
Occupational Health & Safety Division, 613
Occupational Health Clinics for Ontario Workers, 969
Occupational Health Nurses of British Columbia, 969
Occupational Hygiene Association of Ontario, 969
The Ocean Conservancy, 969
Ocean Net, 970
Ocean Sciences, 529
Ocean Steel & Construction Ltd., 311
The Oceanography Society, 970
Oceans & Habitats, 527
Oceans & Marine Fisheries Division, 577
Oceans Directorate, 528
Oceans Ltd., 311
OCL Services Ltd., 311
Octagon Environmental Services, 311
ODIM Brooke Ocean, 311
Oetiker Limited, 311
Office de vente des produits forestiers du Madawaska, 970
Office des personnes handicapées du Québec, 652
Office of Audit & Evaluation, 508
Office of Conservation & Strategic Policy, 622

Entry Name Index

Office of Consolidated Hearings, 623
Office of Consumer & Regulatory Affairs, 623
Office of Corporate Services, 623
Office of Drinking Water, 591
Office of Energy Conservation, 662
Office of Energy Efficiency, 552
Office of Energy Research & Development, 551
Office of Energy Supply, 623
Office of Greening Government Operations, 559, 970
Office of Protocol, 529
Office of the Attorney General, 637
Office of the Chief Information Officer & Community Services I&IT Cluster, 622
Office of the Chief Medical Officer of Health, 613
Office of the Commissioner of Review Tribunals, 535
Office of the Communications Security Establishment Commissioner, 545
Office of the Comptroller, 642
Office of the Corporate Chief Information Officer, 626
Office of the Employer Advisor, 629
Office of the Fire Commissioner, 602, 590, 657
Office of the Fire Marshal, 608, 596, 1159
Office of the Provincial Health Officer, 583
Office of the Queen's Printer, 600
Office of the Registrar of Lobbyists, 562
Office of the Superintendent of Bankruptcy, 544
Office of the Superintendent of Financial Institutions, 526
Office of the Superintendent of Motor Vehicles, 582
Office of the Worker Advisor, 629
Office of the Worker's Advocate, 661
Office of Tobacco Control Program, 534
Offset Systems Directorate, 524
Offshore Design Associates Ltd., 311
Offshore Energy Environmental Research Association, 970
Offshore Energy Research, 1207
Ogilvie Scientific Inc., 311
Ogilvy Renault LLP/S.E.N.C.R.L., s.r.l. - Toronto, 1053, 1086, 1071, 1088, 1078
Oil & Gas, 576
Oil & Gas Commission, 576
Oil & Gas Management, 664
Oil & Gas Mineral Resources, 664
Oil Museum of Canada, 1146
Oil Sands Strategy & Operations, 567
Oil Sands Tailing Research Facility, 1200
Oil Spill Control Services Canada, 311
Okanagan College, 1112, 1030
Okanagan Similkameen Parks Society, 970
Okanagan Water Basin Board, 1041
Okanagan-Similkameen, 678
Okotoks, 674
Old Port of Québec Interpretation Centre, 555
Oldham Engineers Inc., 312
Olds College, 1109, 1029
Oliver-Osoyoos Naturalists, 970
OMB (Americas) Forged Steel Valves, 312
Omega Public Works, 312
Omega Recycling Technologies, 312
ON Nature, 1193
One Sky: Canadian Institute of Sustainable Living, 970
ONEIA - Ontario Environment Industry Association, 970
Ontario, 518
Ontario Agri Business Association, 970
Ontario Agri-Food Education Inc., 970
Ontario Agricultural Training Institute, 970
Ontario Arts Council, 621
Ontario Association for Geographic & Environmental Education, 971
Ontario Association for Impact Assessment, 971
Ontario Association of Agricultural Societies, 971
Ontario Association of Certified Engineering Technicians & Technologists, 971
Ontario Association of Landscape Architects, 971
Ontario Automotive Recyclers Association, 971
Ontario Branches, 513
Ontario Building Solutions, 312
Ontario Camps Association, 971
Ontario Cattlemen's Association, 971
Ontario Centre for Environmental Technology Advancement, 1209
Ontario Centre of Excellence for Photonics, 971
Ontario Centres of Excellence, 312
Ontario Centres of Excellence - Centre for Earth & Environmental Technologies, 972
Ontario Civilian Commission on Police Services, 621
Ontario Clean Air Alliance, 972

Ontario Clean Water Agency, 623
Ontario Commercial Fisheries' Association, 972
Ontario Community Transit Association, 972
Ontario Concrete Pipe Association, 972
Ontario Corn Producers' Association, 972
Ontario Creamerymen's Association, 972
Ontario Dairy Council, 972
Ontario Daylily Society, 972
Ontario Delphinium Club, 972
Ontario Electrical League, 972
Ontario Energy Association, 973
Ontario Energy Board, 622, 1159
Ontario Environment Business Directory, 1216
Ontario Environment Industry Association, 1216, 973
Ontario Environment Network, 1216
Ontario Environmental Directory, 1216
Ontario Environmental Network, 973
Ontario Environmental Training Consortium, 312
Ontario Farm & Country Accommodations Association, 973
Ontario Farm Animal Council, 1140
The Ontario Farm Animal Council, 973
Ontario Farm Products Marketing Commission, 619
Ontario Federation of Agriculture, 973
Ontario Federation of Anglers & Hunters, 973, 1153
Ontario Field Ornithologists, 973
Ontario Film Review Board, 626
Ontario Fire Buff Associates, 973
Ontario Food Processors Association, 973
Ontario Food Terminal Board, 619
Ontario Forest Industries Association, 974
Ontario Forestry Association, 974
Ontario Forestry Safe Workplace Association, 1146
Ontario Fruit & Vegetable Growers' Association, 974
Ontario Geographic Names Board, 631
Ontario Geological Survey, 634
Ontario Good Roads Association, 974
The Ontario Greenhouse Alliance, 974
Ontario Ground Water Association, 974
Ontario Growth Secretariat, 634
Ontario Healthy Communities Coalition, 974
Ontario Heritage Trust, 622, 974
Ontario Highway Transport Board, 635
Ontario Horticultural Association, 974
Ontario Hospital Association, 975
Ontario Housing Corporation, 630
Ontario Industrial Fire Protection Association, 975
Ontario Institute of Agrologists, 975
Ontario Labour Relations Board, 629
Ontario Library Service - North, 622
Ontario Lumber Manufacturers' Association, 975
Ontario Lung Association, 975
Ontario Marine Operators Association, 975
Ontario Media Development Corporation, 622
Ontario Medical Association, 975
Ontario Mental Health Foundation, 628
Ontario Mining Association, 976
Ontario Ministry of Economic Development & Trade, 1159
Ontario. Ministry of Energy & Infrastructure, 1044
Ontario Ministry of Environment, 1160
Ontario Ministry of Health & Long-Term Care, 1160
Ontario Ministry of Municipal Affairs & Housing, 1160
Ontario Ministry of Natural Resources, 1153
Ontario Ministry of Northern Development & Mines, 1155
Ontario Ministry of Transportation, 1154
Ontario Moose & Bear Allocation Advisory Committee, 631
Ontario Municipal Human Resources Association, 976
Ontario Municipal Management Institute, 976
Ontario Municipal Water Association, 976
Ontario Nature, 976
Ontario Northland, 634
Ontario Occupational Health Nurses Association, 976
Ontario Parks, 633
Ontario Parks Association, 976
Ontario Parole & Earned Release Board, 621
Ontario Pension Board, 626
Ontario Petroleum Institute Inc., 976, 1144
Ontario Pipe Trades Council, 977
Ontario Place Corporation, 635
Ontario Plumbing Inspectors Association, 977
Ontario Police Arbitration Commission, 621
Ontario Pollution Control Equipment Association, 977
Ontario Power Authority, 622
Ontario Power Generation, 622, 634, 1160, 312
Ontario Printing & Imaging Association, 977
Ontario Professional Fire Fighters Association, 977

Ontario Professional Foresters Association, 977
Ontario Professional Planners Institute, 977
Ontario Prospectors Association, 977
Ontario Provincial Police, 621
Ontario Public Health Association, 977
Ontario Public Interest Research Group, 978
Ontario Public Interest Research Group - Toronto/Downtown Women's Centre, 1160
Ontario Racing Commission, 626
Ontario Refrigeration & Air Conditioning Contractors Association, 978
Ontario Region, 534
Ontario Regional Library, 1160
Ontario Regional Office, 508
Ontario Rental Housing Tribunal, 630
Ontario Respiratory Care Society, 978
Ontario Review Board, 628
Ontario Rock Garden Society, 978
Ontario Safety League, 978, 1145
Ontario Sawdust Supplies, 312
Ontario Science Centre, 622, 1160
Ontario Sewer & Watermain Construction Association, 978
Ontario Shared Services, 628
Ontario Small Urban Municipalities, 978
Ontario Society for Environmental Education, 978
Ontario Society for Environmental Management, 978
Ontario Society of Nutrition Professionals in Public Health, 979
Ontario Society of Professional Engineers, 979
Ontario Soil & Crop Improvement Association, 979
Ontario Soybean Growers, 979
Ontario Streams, 979
Ontario Sustainable Energy Association, 980
Ontario Tender Fruit Producers, 980
Ontario Tire Dealers Association, 980
Ontario Tourism Marketing Partnership Corporation, 635
Ontario Traffic Conference, 980
Ontario Trails Council, 980, 1153
The Ontario Trillium Foundation, 1044
Ontario Trillium Foundation, 622
Ontario Trucking Association, 980
Ontario Urban Forest Council, 980
Ontario Vegetation Management Association, 981
Ontario Waste Management Association, 981
Ontario Waste Materials Exchange, 312
Ontario Water Works Association, 981
Ontario Wheat Producers' Marketing Board, 981
Ontario Woodlot Association, 981
Ontor Ltd., 312
Onyx Chemical Cleaning, 313
Opcon Pacific Recycling Ltd., 313
Operational Commands, 545
Operations, 515, 579
Operations Division, 615
Operations Sector, 544
OPSEU Pension Trust, 626
Optech Inc., 313
Optikon Corp. Ltd., 313
Optimira Controls, 313
Option Environnement Inc., 313
Opus DaytonKnight Consultants Ltd., 313
Opus International Consultants (Canada) Ltd., 313
Orangeville, 538, 716
Orchid Cellmark ULC, 314
Ordan Thermal Products Ltd., 314
Ordre des agronomes du Québec, 981
Ordre des arpenteurs-géomètres du Québec, 981
Ordre des chimistes du Québec, 981
Ordre des ingénieurs du Québec, 981
Ordre des ingénieurs forestiers du Québec, 981
Ordre des technologues professionnels du Québec, 982
Ordre des urbanistes du Québec, 982
Organic Crop Improvement Association (International), 982
Organic Crop Improvement Association - New Brunswick, 982
Organic Crop Improvement Association - Québec & Ontario, 982
Organic Crop Producers & Processors Ontario Inc., 982
Organic Farm Services, 314
Organic Producers Association of Manitoba Co-operative Inc., 982
Organic Resource Management Inc., 314
Organic Trade Association, 982
Organic Verification Organization of North America, 982
Organization for Economic Cooperation & Development, 982
Organization of CANDU Industries, 982
Orillia, 538, 716
Orillia Campus, 1147
Oro-Medonte, 728

Entry Name Index

Ortech Environmental Inc., 314
Orwak Waste Systems Inc. - Canada, 314
OSB Services, 314
Osgoode Hall Law School, 1160
Oshawa, 538, 716
Osler, Hoskin & Harcourt LLP - Calgary, 1053
Osler, Hoskin & Harcourt LLP - Toronto, 1079
Osler, Hoskin & Harcourt S.E.N.C.R.L./LLP, 1086
OSPAR Commission, 983
Osram Sylvania Ltd., 314
Ottawa, 716
Ottawa & Nunavut, 516
Ottawa Branch, 513
Ottawa Centre, 538
Ottawa Congress Centre, 635
Ottawa Duck Club, 983
Ottawa East, 538
Ottawa Engineering Ltd., 315
Ottawa Environmental Grants Directory, 1216
Ottawa Environmental Law Clinic, 983
Ottawa Field-Naturalists' Club, 983
Ottawa Government Services Centre, 538
Ottawa Hospital, 1151
Ottawa Hospital - Civic Campus, 1151
Ottawa Hospital-Riverside Campus, 1151
Ottawa Orchid Society, 983
Ottawa River Regulation Planning Board, 631
Ottawa Safety Council, 983
Ottawa Valley Health Libraries Association, 983
Ottawa Valley Rock Garden & Horticultural Society, 983
Ottawa West, 539
Ottawa-Carleton, 627
Ottenheimer Baker, 1066
Ouest-de-la-Montérégie, 654
Ouest-de-Montréal, 540
Ouranos, 1211
Outaouais, 517
Outaouais, Abitibi-Témiscamingue et Nord-du-Québec, 653
Outdoor Writers of Canada, 983
Outerbridge Miller Sefton, 1079
Outokumpu Technology Ltd., 315
Outward Bound Canada, 983
Overwatch Consulting, 315
Owen G. Carney Ltd., 315
Owen Sound, 539, 717
Owen Sound Campus, 1152
Owen Sound Transportation Company Ltd., 634
Oxegen Inc., 315
Oxford, 627, 728
Oxford County Geological Society, 983, 1156
Ozocan Corporation, 315
Ozogram Inc., 315
OZZ Corporation, 315

P

P. Machibroda Engineering Ltd., 315
P.J. Cluff Architect Inc., 315
P.J. Hannah Equipment Sales Corp., 315
P.J.B. Duffy & Associates, 316
Pacesetter Sales & Associates Inc., 316
Pacific & Yukon Region - Vancouver, 1118
Pacific & Yukon Region - Whitehorse, 1191
Pacific & Yukon: Yukon Office, 522
Pacific Agri-Food Research Centre, 509
Pacific Biological Station, 1202, 528, 1113
Pacific Coast, 525
Pacific Engineering Inc., 316
Pacific Environmental Consulting & Occupational Hygiene Services, 316
Pacific Environmental Science Centre, 1202
Pacific Forestry Centre, 1202, 550, 1121
Pacific Geoscience Centre, 1203
Pacific Institute for Advanced Study, 316
Pacific Metals Recycling International, 316
Pacific NorthWest Economic Region, 983
Pacific Peoples Partnership, 983
Pacific Phytometric Consultants, 316
Pacific Pilotage Authority, 560
Pacific Region, 517, 546, 1110, 1118
Pacific Regional Library, 1118
Pacific Rim National Park Reserve of Canada, 556
Pacific Salmon Commission, 1118
Pacific Salmon Foundation, 1041
Pacific States/British Columbia Oil Spill Task Force, 765, 984

Pacific Urchin Harvesters Association, 984
Pacific Wildlife Research Centre, 1203
Packaging Association of Canada, 984
Pacwill Environmental, 317
Paddle Canada, 984
Paddy's Pond, 604
Pageau Morel & associés, inc., 317
The Paint Recycling Company, 393
Paladin Environmental Consulting Services Ltd., 317
Palais des congrès de Montréal, 654
Pall (Canada) Limited, 317
Pam Wight & Associates, 317
Pan American Center for Sanitary Engineering & Environmental Sciences, 984
Pan Tec Inc., 317
Panama Enterprises (1990) Inc., 317
Panasonic Canada Inc., 317
Panos Canada, 984
Panos London, 984
Panos Washington, 984
Panther Environmental IInc., 317
PAP Engineering Services, 317
Paper & Paperboard Packaging Environmental Council, 984
Paper Packaging Canada, 984
Papiers Perkins, 317
Papineau, 750
Par Excellence Developments, Inc., 318
Para Paints, 318
Paracel Laboratories Ltd., 318
Paradigm Environmental Technologies Inc., 318
Paragon Soil & Environmental Consulting Inc., 318
Parameter Control Ltd., 318
Paramount Emergency Planners Ltd., 318
Parc Aquarium du Québec, 1179
Conserval Engineering Inc., 318
Paris, France, 318
Parish Geomorphic Ltd., 318
Parkes Scientific Canada Inc., 318
Parkland County, 670
Parklane Computer Systems, 319
Parks & Conservation Areas, 618
Parks & Natural Areas Division, 599
Parks & Protected Areas, 578
Parks & Recreation Division, 615
Parks & Recreation Ontario, 984
Parks Branch, 658
Parks Canada, 1216, 552
Parks Yukon, 666
Parks, Conservation, Recreation & Sport Division, 565
Parkson Corporation, 319
Parksville, 682
Parkvalley Consulting Ltd., 319
Parlee Beach, 597
Parlee McLaws LLP, 1053, 1055
Parry Sound, 539, 728
Parsons Commercial Technology Group Inc., 319
Parti Vert du Québec, 985
Partners FOR the Saskatchewan River Basin, 985
Partners in Flight, 523
Partnerships Department, 583
The Pas, 536
Pasadena, 604
Passenger Transportation Board, 583
Passport Canada, 529
Pat Dwyer Construction Inc., 319
Paterson, MacDougall LLP, Barristers, Solicitors, 1079
Patterson Industries (Canada) Ltd., 319
Patterson Law, 1067, 1068
Patton Cormier & Associates, 1069
Paul F. Wilkinson & Associates Inc., 319
Paul G. Chénard, 319
Paul Martin Law Library, 1165
Pavillon Félix-Leclerc, 1168
Pay Equity Commission, 612, 629
Les Pays-d'en-Haut, 750
PBR Laboratories Inc., 319
PCB Disposal Inc., 319
PCI Geomatics Group Inc., 320
PDK Projects Inc., 320
Peace & Environment Resource Centre, 985, 1151
Peace Parkland Naturalists, 985
Peace River, 678
Peace Valley Environment Association, 985
Pearl & Associates, 1086
Pebblestone Multi-Services Inc., 320

Pêches et aquaculture commerciales, 645, 1167
Peco Filters Ltd., 320
Pedocan Land Evaluation Ltd., 320
Peel, 627, 703
Peel Scrap Metal Recycling Ltd., 320
Pegasus Industrial Specialties Inc., 320
The PEI Energy Corp., 393
PEI Energy Corporation, 639
PEI Museum & Heritage Foundation, 638
Peintures Denalt, 320
Les Peintures Sico inc., 269
Pelham, 717
Pelmar Engineering Ltd., 320
Pembina, 585
Pembina Institute, 1216
The Pembina Institute, 985
The Pembina Institute for Appropriate Development, 1103
Pembroke, 717
Pembroke Area Field Naturalists, 985
Pembroke Environmental Services Ltd., 320
Pembroke Campus, 1152
Pencon Equipment Co., 321
Pender Island Field Naturalists, 985
Peninsula Field Naturalists, 985
Penn Refrigeration Ltd., 321
Penny & Casson Co., 321
Pension Appeals Board, 535
Pension Commission of Manitoba, 590
Pension Regulation Division, 613
Penticton, 682
Penticton Campus, 1114
People and Planet, 1216
People for the Ethical Treatment of Animals, 985
People's Democratic Republic of Algeria, 767
People's Law School, 985
People's Republic of Bangladesh, 767
People's Republic of China, 767
Pepi Sewage Disposal Service, 321
Pepin Prevention des Pertes Inc., 321
Pepper Compressed Air & Gas Ltd., 321
Percy E. Moore Hospital, 533
Performance Fluid Equipement Inc., 321
Perkin Elmer Optoelectronics, 1187
PerkinElmer Life & Analytical Sciences Canada Inc., 321
Perley-Robertson, Hill & McDougall LLP, 1071
Perth, 539, 627, 703
Perth Campus, 1152
Perth East, 728
Pest Management Association of Alberta, 985
Pest Management Regulatory Agency, 533
Pesticide Action Network North America, 985
Pesticide Education Network, 985
Pesticides Advisory Committee, 624
Pesticides Regulatory Program, 639
Petawawa, 717
Peter Lougheed Centre Library, 1102
Peter T. Mitches & Associates Limited; Project Managers & Consulting, 321
Peterborough, 718, 703
Peterborough Branch, 513
Peterborough Field Naturalists, 985
Peto MacCallum Ltd., 321
Petrifond Foundation Co. Ltd., 322
Petro Laboratories Inc., 322
Petro Sep Membrane Technologies Inc., 322
Petro-Canada Lubricants, 322
Petroleum, 590
Petroleum & Natural Gas, 660
Petroleum Enviro Services, 322
Petroleum Human Resources Council of Canada, 986
Petroleum Industry Training Service, 1102
Petroleum Products Division, 608
Petroleum Research Atlantic Canada, 1205, 986
Petroleum Resources Branch, 552
Petroleum Services Association of Canada, 986
Petroleum Society of CIM, 986
Petroleum Tank Management Association of Alberta, 986
Petroleum Technology Alliance Canada, 986
Petromax Ltd., 322
Petrozyme Technologies Inc., 322
Pfizer Canada, Inc., 1169
Pharmaceutical Services, 580
Pharmatox Inc., 322
Phason Electronics, 322
PHH ARC Environmental Ltd., 322

Entry Name Index

Philip Doyle Manufacturing Inc., 323
Philom Bios Inc., 323
Phoenix Biomedical Products Inc., 323
Phoenix Contact Ltd., 323
Phoenix Engineering Inc., 323
Photech Environmental Solutions, 323
Physicians for a Smoke-Free Canada, 986
Physics Library, 1160
Pickering, 718
Pickering & Ajax Citizens Together for the Environment, 986
Pickering Naturalists, 986
Picton, 539
Pictou County, 698
Pierre-De Saurel, 750
Pigeon Lake Regional Chamber of Commerce, 986
Pigmalion Environmental Services Group, 323
Piikuni Utilities Corp., 323
Pildysh Technologies Inc., 323
Pilot Performance Resources Management Inc., 324
Pinch Group, 324
Pincher Creek, 565
Pinchin Environmental Ltd., 324
Pincourt, 739
Pine Beetle Epidemic Response, 575
Pink Larkin, 1064
PINTER & Associates Ltd., 324
Pioneer Envelopes Ltd., 325
Pioneer Petroleums, 325
Pipe Line Contractors Association of Canada, 987
Pipe Specialties Canada, 325
Pipeline Engineering Center, 1200
Pisces Environmental Consulting Services Ltd., 325
Pitblado LLP, 1063
Pitch-In Alberta, 987
Pitch-In Canada, 987
Piteau Associates, 325
Pitt Meadows, 683
Placentia, 537
Placentia Campus Learning Resource Centre, 1131
Plad Équipement Ltée, 325
Plains Environmental Inc., 325
Plan-it Environmental Consulting Ltd., 325
Planetary Association for Clean Energy, Inc., 987
Planification, performance et qualité, 643
Planning & Development Division, 630
Planning & Engineering Initiatives Ltd., 325
Planning & Evaluation Branch, 658
Planning & Inspection Services, 638
Planning & Policy, 608
Planning & Product Branch, 597
Planning Alliance, 326
Planning Institute of British Columbia, 987
Planning Secretariat, 614
Plant Biotechnology Institute, 548
Plant Engineering & Maintenance Association of Canada, 987
Plant Health Regulatory Program, 637
Plant Products Co. Ltd., 326
Plasma Environmental Technologies Inc., 326
Plast-Ex International Inc., 326
Plasti-Fab Ltd., 326
Plastic Loose Fill Council, 987
Plasticair Inc., 326
Plastichem Consulting, 326
Plastics America, 326
Plastiglas Industries Limited, 326
Les Plastiques Simport Ltée, 270
Plastrec Inc., 326
Plein Disposal, 326
PlymoVent Canada Inc., 326
Pneus Métro Inc., 326
Poch, Harry Environmental Lawyer, 1079
Point Clark Lighthouse National Historic Site of Canada, 554
Point Four Systems Inc., 326
Point Pelee National Park, 1143
Point Pelee National Park of Canada, 554
Pointe Claire, 529
Pointe-au-Père Lighthouse National Historic Site of Canada, 555
Pointe-Claire Branch, 513
Pointe-Claire Technology Centre, 327
Pol R Enterprises Inc., 327
Pol-E-Mar Inc., 327
Polar Bear Health Equipment Supplies, 327
Polar Continental Shelf Project, 551
Polaris Corporate Services Inc., 327
Policing & Community Safety Branch, 582

Policy, 527
Policy & Administration, 638
Policy & Communications Branch, 544
Policy & Consumer Protection Services Division, 626
Policy & Corporate Services Division, 570
Policy & Environment Sector, 564
Policy & Planning, 516
Policy & Planning Branch, 660
Policy & Planning Coordination Branch, 633
Policy & Planning Division, 636
Policy & Programs Division, 619
Policy & Strategic Direction Sector, 542
Policy Coordination Division, 603
Policy Development, 621
Policy Development & Planning, 593
Policy Development & Planning Branch, 599
Policy Group, 560
Policy, Coordination & Liaison, 528
Policy, Legislation & Communications, 606
Policy, Legislation & Communications Division, 606
Policy, Planning & Priorities Directorate, 534
Policy, Planning & Public Affairs, 595
Policy, Program Development & Dispute Resolution Services, 629
Policy, Strategic Development & Intergovernmental Relations, 597
Politiques, 643
Politiques et recherche, 644
Politiques et sécurité en transport, 655
Politiques et sociétés d'État, 648
Politiques, patrimoine, muséologie & communications, 645
Pollutech Environmental Ltd., 1146
Pollutech Group of Companies Inc., 327
Pollution Prevention, 599
Pollution Prevention Branch, 587
Pollution Prevention Directorate, 524
Pollution Prevention Division, 639
Pollution Probe, 1216
The Pollution Probe Foundation, 987, 1044
PollutionWatch, 1216
Polychem Products Ltd., 328
Polyland Industries Ltd., 328
Polyrama Plastics (1987) Ltd., 328
Polystyrene Packaging Council, 987
Pomeroy Consulting Engineers Limited, 328
Pompaction inc., 328
Pompage Express M.D. Inc., 328
Pompco inc., 328
Pompe Saguenay Enr., 328
Pompex Inc., 328
Pond Inlet, 617
Pontiac, 751
Poole Althouse, Barristers & Solicitors, 1065
Population & Public Health, 583
Population Connection, 987
Population Growth Secretariat, 591
Population Health, 606
Population Health Branch, 660
Population Secretariat, 641
Porcupine Caribou Management Board, 542
Port Alberni, 683
Port Alberni Regional Campus Library, 1114
Port Aux Basques, 537
Port aux Basques Campus Library, 1131
Port Colborne, 718
Port Coquitlam, 683
Port Hardy Centre, 1115
Port Hawkesbury, 537
Port Hope, 728
Port Moody, 683
Port of Entry Inc., 328
Port Royal National Historic Site of Canada, 553
Port Saunders, 604
Port-au-Choix National Historic Site of Canada, 553
Porta-Mini Systems, 328
Portage College, 1108
Portage la Prairie, 536
Portage La Prairie, 689
Portneuf, 751
Portuguese Republic, 768
POS Bio-sciences, 1190
Post Secondary Excellence Division, 563
Poscor Group, 328
Positive Results Environmental Management Ltd., 328
Potash Corporation of Saskatchewan Inc., 1190
Potato Research Centre, 510, 1128
Potatoes NB, 987

Pottinger Gaherty Environmental Consultants Ltd., 328
Powell River, 683, 679
Powell River Campus, 1115
Power Grow Systems Inc., 329
Power Ignition & Controls, 329
Power Plant Supply Co., 329
Power Suction Services Ltd., 329
Power Vac of Nova Scotia, 329
Power-Pacific Poles Ltd., 329
Powerex Corp., 580
Powerscreen of Canada Ltd., 329
Powersmiths International Corp., 329
Powertech Labs Inc., 580, 1116, 329
Poyry (Vancouver) Inc., 329
PPG Canada, Inc., 330
Prairie & Northern, 522, 561
Prairie & Northern Laboratory for Environmental Testing, 1200
Prairie & Northern Region - Edmonton, 1106
Prairie & Northern Region - Yellowknife, 1134
Prairie & Northern: Manitoba Office, 522
Prairie & Territories Region, 516
Prairie Agricultural Machinery Institute, 656, 988, 1187
Prairie Association for Water Management, 1108
Prairie Conservation Forum, 988
Prairie Farm Rehabilitation Administration, 1188
Prairie Fruit Growers Association, 988
Prairie Geomatics Ltd., 330
Prairie Habitat, 525, 765
Prairie Northern Wildlife Research Centre, 1200, 1205, 1212, 1203, 1207, 1190
Prairie Region, 517, 518, 1190
Prairie Western Reclamation & Consturction Inc., 330
Prairies & Northern Region, 519
Pratt & Whitney Canada Inc., 1169
Praxair Canada Inc., 330
Praxis Environmental, 330
Praxis Inc., 330
Precision Assessment Technology Corp., 330
Precision Chemical Manufacturing Ltd., 330
Precision Identification Biological Consultants, 330
Precision Industrial Ltd., 330
Precisioneering Ltd., 330
Premier Envelope, 331
Premier Plastics Ltd., 331
Premier Tech Environment, 331
Premier Tech Environnement / Division municipale, commerciale et ind, 331
Premier's Economic Advisory Council, 585
Premier's Technology Council, 575
Prescott, 539
Prescott & Russell, 729
Prescott Paper Products Inc., 331
Presentey Engineering Products Ltd., 331
Preston Phipps Inc., 331
Pretal, 332
Pribusin Inc., 332
PricewaterhouseCoopers Management Consultants, 332
Pridy Associates, 332
Priestly Demolition Inc., 332
Primary Care & Healthy Living, 588
Primex Packaging Services, 332
Prince Albert, 540, 754
Prince Albert Model Forest Association Inc., 988, 1187
Prince Albert National Park of Canada, 556
Prince Edward, 627, 703
Prince Edward Island, 541
Prince Edward Island Aquaculture Alliance, 988
Prince Edward Island Branches, 513
Prince Edward Island Business Development Inc., 640
Prince Edward Island Cattle Producers, 988
Prince Edward Island Cultured Mussel Growers Association, 988
Prince Edward Island. Dept. of Environment, Energy & Forestry, 1045
Prince Edward Island Dept. of Provincial Treasury, 1165
Prince Edward Island Eco-Net, 1216, 988
Prince Edward Island Emergency Measures Organization, 638
Prince Edward Island Federation of Agriculture, 988
Prince Edward Island Finfish Growers Association, 988
Prince Edward Island Fishermen's Association, 988
Prince Edward Island Food Technology Centre, 1165
Prince Edward Island Forest Improvement Association, 988
Prince Edward Island Ground Water Association, 988
Prince Edward Island Institute of Agrologists, 989
Prince Edward Island Lending Agency, 640
Prince Edward Island Lotteries Commission, 642

Entry Name Index

Prince Edward Island Lung Association, 989
Prince Edward Island National Park of Canada, 553
Prince Edward Island Public Service Commission, 642
Prince Edward Island Regional Office, 511
Prince Edward Island Salmon Association, 989
Prince Edward Island Wildlife Federation, 989
Prince Edward Island Workers Compensation Board, 642
Prince George, 536, 683
Prince George Backcountry Recreation Society, 989
Prince George Branch, 512
Prince George Naturalists, 989
Prince George Recycling & Environmental Action Planning Society, 989
Prince George Regional Forest Exhibition Society, 989
Prince of Wales Fort National Historic Site of Canada, 556
Prince of Wales Tower National Historic Site, 553
Prince Philip Drive Campus Library, 1133
Prince Rupert, 684
Prism Chemicals Inc., 332
Private Forest, 639
Private Motor Truck Council of Canada, 989
Private Vocational Schools Advisory Council, 563
Pro-Lab Diagnostics, 333
ProAgri Consulting Limited, 333
Probe International, 989
Probyn & Company Inc., 333
Proceco Ltd., 333
Procedair Industries Inc., 333
Process Innovations Canada Inc., 333
Proctor & Gamble Inc., 333
Procurement Allocation Directory, 559
Procyon Consulting Inc., 333
Product Care Association, 989
Product Safety Programme, 534
Production Development, 639
Products BCM Ltée BCM, 333
Produits Chimiques Handy Ltée, 333
Les Produits Environnementaux Atlas, 270
Produits Ferpac Ltée, 333
Proeco Enviroservices Ltd., 333
Professional & Specialized Services, 630
Professional & Technical Programs, 559
Professional Engineers & Geoscientists Newfoundland & Labrador, 989
Professional Engineers Ontario, 990
Professional Fish Harvesters Certification Board, 599
Professional Resources Inc., 334
Program Development Division, 615
Program Evaluation & Fiscal Relations, 642
Program Management & Corporate Services, 615
Program Management Branch, 636
Program Operations Branch, 544
Program Planning & Coordination, 529
Programs Branch, 551
Programs Group, 561
Progress Land Services Ltd., 334
Project Assessment Branch, 594
Project Engineering Limited, 334
Prolab Technolub, 334
Proline Filter Systems Inc., 334
Promag Enviro Systems Ltd., 334
Promens Canada Inc., 334
Promet Environmental Group Ltd., 334
ProMinent Fluid Controls Ltd., 334
Promosalons Canada, 334
Propane Gas Association of Canada Inc., 990
Properties Division, 570
Property Management Agency, 666
ProPower Equipment Ltd., 335
ProSep Inc., 335
Proserco Inc., 335
Proshred Security, 335
ProSolve Consulting Ltd., 335
Prospectors & Developers Association of Canada, 990, 1160
Protected Areas, 612
Protected Areas Association of Newfoundland & Labrador, 990
Protection & Emergency Services, 656
Protective Services, 664
Proto Manufacturing Ltd., 335
Province House National Historic Site of Canada, 553
Provincial Airlines Ltd. - Environmental Services Division, 335
Provincial Disaster Assistance Program, 657
Provincial Environmental Services Inc., 335
Provincial Forest, 639
Provincial Highways Management, 636

Provincial Partitions Ltd., 335
Provincial Planning Branch, 638
Provincial Services Division, 587
Provincial-Municipal Support Services, 589
ProViro Instrumentation Inc., 335
PRT Inc., 336
PSC Analytical Services, 336
The Public Affairs Association of Canada, 990
Public Forest Council, 639
Public Health, 588
Public Health & Medical Services, 594
Public Health Agency of Canada, 533
Public Health Association of British Columbia, 990
Public Health Association of Nova Scotia, 991
Public Health Division, 629
Public Health Library, 1152
Public Health Services, 1190
Public Health, Wellness, & Children & Youth Services, 601
Public Lands & Forests Division, 572
Public Legal Education Association of Saskatchewan, Inc., 991
Public Legal Information Association of Newfoundland, 991
Public Petroleum Data Model Association, 991
Public Safety, 613
Public Safety Canada, 557
Public Safety Division, 571, 621
Public Sector Pension Investment Board, 562
Public Service Commission of Canada, 519
Public Service Labour Relations Board, 562
Public Utilities Board of the Northwest Territories, 608
Public Works, 616
Public Works & Government Services Canada, 558, 1168
Public Works & Planning Division, 642
Les Publications du Québec, 270
Publications Ontario, 336
Pukaskwa National Park of Canada, 554
Pullan Kammerloch Frohlinger, 1064
Pulp & Paper Centre, 1203
Pulp & Paper Research Institute of Canada (PAPRICAN), 1177
Pulp & Paper Technical Association of Canada, 991
Pumps & Systems, 336
Purchasing Branch, 662
Pure Energy Battery Inc., 336
Pure Energy Inc., 336
Puresource Inc., 337
Purifics ES Inc., 337
Pushor Mitchell LLP, Lawyers & Trade-Mark Agents, 1056
PWC Pure Water Corporation, 337
Pylon Electronics, 337
Pylon Electronics Inc., 337
Pyradia Inc., 337
Pyrotech Mfg. Corp., 337

Q

Q-Air Environmental Controls Ltd., 337
QCA Laboratories Inc., 337
Qikiqtaaluk, 618
QIT-Fer et Titane inc, 1186
QMI-SAI Global, 337
QSDM Inc., 338
Quad-Lock Building Systems Ltd., 338
Quality Fabricating & Supply Limited, 338
Quality Matters Inc., 338
Quantum Murray LP, 338
QUASAR, 338
Quatic Industries Inc., 338
Quatrex Environnement inc., 338
Quatrosense Environmental Ltd., 338
Québec, 546, 561, 520, 740
Québec (Grande Allée ouest) Branch, 513
Québec (Lebourgneuf) Branch, 514
Québec - Chaudière - Appalaches, 516
Québec - Chaudière-Appalaches, 645
Québec 4-H, 991
Québec Branches, 513
Québec Conseil de la science et de la technologie, 1179
Québec et de l'Est, 655
Québec Farmers' Association, 991
Québec Lung Association, 991
Québec Ministère de l'agriculture, des pêcheries et de l'alimentation, 1179
Québec Ministère de la santé et des services sociaux, 1179
Québec Ministère de la Sécurité Publique - Direction des Communications, 1175
Québec Ministère des affaires municipales et des Régions, 1179

Québec Ministère des Ressources naturelles et de la Faune, 1179
Québec Ministère des transports, 1180
Québec Ministère du Développement durable, de l'Environnement et des Parcs, 1180
Québec Ministère du Développement économique, de l'Innovation et de l'Exportation, 1180
Québec Office des personnes handicapées, 1175
Québec Oiseaux, 1193
Québec Public Interest Research Group - McGill, 991
Québec Régie de l'assurance-maladie, 1180
Québec Region, 517, 534
Quebec Regional Library, 1169
Québec Regional Office, 508
Quebec Young Farmers' Provincial Federation, 1182
Québec. Ministère du Développement durable, de l'Environnement et des Parcs, 1211
Québec-Labrador Foundation (Canada) Inc., 991, 1046
Quebecor World Concord, 338
Queen Elizabeth II Hospital, 1108
Queen's Printer, 338, 339
Queen's Printer & Document Publishing Centre, 339
Queen's Printer Subscriptions, 339
Queen's University, 1209, 1142, 1034
Queenston Heights & Brock's Monument, 554
Quest University Canada, 1030
Quesnel, 688
Quesnel Naturalists, 992
Quesnel River Research Centre, 1203
QuestAir Technologies Inc., 339
Quester Tangent Corp., 339
Quetico Foundation, 992, 1044
Quidi Vidi Rennie's River Development Foundation, 992, 1042
Quinte West, 718
Quispamsis, 692
Quorum Growth Inc., 339
Quttinirpaaq National Park of Canada, 556
Qwatro Corporation, 339

R

R Plus Industries Alberta Inc., 339
R&R Drilling Supply Ltd., 339
R. Howard Webster Library, 1175
R.A. Campbell & Associates, 339
R.A. Kirby Sales Inc., 339
R.A. Murray International Limited, 340
R.B. Intermark Inc., 340
R.D. Cookson Disposal Ltd., 340
R.G. Robinson & Associates (Barrie) Ltd., 340
R.H. Loucks Oceanology, 340
R.J. Burnside & Associates Limited, 340
R.J. Lévesque et Fils Ltée, 341
R.U. Kistritz Consultants Ltd., 341
R.V. Anderson Associates Limited, 1161, 341
Rabies Advisory Committee, 631
Racal Protection Canada, 341
Racan Carrier, 341
Radiation Environmental Management Systems Inc., 341
Radiation Safety Institute of Canada, 992, 1160
Radiodetection (Canada) Ltd., 341
Raging River Power & Mining Inc., 341
Rail Safety Directorate, 561
RailPower Technologies Corp., 341
Rainforest Action Network, 992
Rainforest Alliance, 992
Rainy River, 627, 729
RAM Forest Products Inc., 342
RAM Lining Systems Inc., 342
Ramsay Lampman Rhodes, 1056
Ramsay Machine Works Ltd., 342
Rapid-Eau Technologies, 342
Rare Breeds Canada, 992
Ratcliff & Company LLP, 1057
Raw Materials Corporation, 342
Rawdon Industries Ltd., 342
Rawdon Technologies Ltd., 342
Ray Electric Ltd., 342
Raymond James Financial Inc., 342
Rayovac Canada Inc., 342
Raypak Canada Ltd., 342
Rayplex Limited, 342
RBR Ltd., 343
Real Estate Foundation of British Columbia, 1041
Réal Huot Inc., 343
Real Property Branch, 558

Entry Name Index

Real Property Contracting Directorate, 559
Rebuts Solides Canadiens Inc., 343
Rechargeable Battery Recycling Corporation, 343
Recherche, innovation, science et société, 649
Recovery Technologies Inc., 343
Recreation New Brunswick, 992
Recreation Newfoundland & Labrador, 992
Recubec Inc., 343
Récupération Nord-Ben Inc., 343
Recyc-Haul Waste Management Inc., 343
Recyclage Alexandria Recycline (Équipe), 343
Recyclage d'Alluminium Québec, 343
Recyclage PF Inc., 343
The Recycle Systems Company Inc., 393
Recyclenet Corporation, 343
Recycling Canada, 1193
Recycling Council of Alberta, 993
Recycling Council of British Columbia, 993
Recycling Council of Ontario, 993
Recycling Product News, 1193
Red Bay National Historic Site of Canada, 553
Red Deer, 517, 535, 674
Red Deer Branch, 512
Red Deer College, 1109, 1029
Red Deer County, 670
Red Deer River Naturalists, 993
Red Devil Drain Service, 343
Red Lake, 632
Red Oak Industries Inc., 343
Red River, 585
Red River Apiarists' Association, 1122
Red River College, 1125
Redeemer University College, 1034
Redstone Associates Ltd., 343
REDUCT & Lobbe Technologies Inc., 344
Reference Resource Centre, 1165
Refined Specialty Chemicals Inc., 344
Refreshments Canada, 993
Refrigerant Services Inc., 344
Refrigeration & Air Conditioning Contractors Association of Manitoba, 993
Refrigeration Service Engineers Society (Canada), 994
Régie d'aqueduc de Grand Pré, 759
Régie d'aqueduc intermunicipale des Moulins, 759
Régie d'aqueduc intermunicipale paroisse St-Pie et Notre-Dame-de-St-Hyacinthe, 759
Régie d'aqueduc Richelieu-Centre, 759
Régie d'assainissement des Coteaux, 759
Régie d'assainissement des eaux de Chandler, Pabos et Pabos Mills, 759
Régie d'assainissement des eaux de la région sherbrookoise, 759
Régie d'assainissement des eaux de la Vallée du Richelieu, 759
Régie d'assainissement des eaux du bassin de la Prairie, 759
Régie d'assainissement des eaux du Haut-Richelieu, 759
Régie d'assainissement des eaux Richelieu/Saint-Laurent, 759
Régie d'assainissement des eaux usées de Piedmont, St-Sauveur et St-Sauveur-des-Monts, 759
Régie d'assainissement des eaux usées Rougemont/St-Césaire, 759
Régie d'assainissement des eaux usées Terrebonne/Mascouche, 759
Régie de l'assurance maladie du Québec, 652
Régie de l'eau de l'Ile Perrot, 759
Régie de l'énergie, 650
Régie des alcools, des courses et des jeux, 653
Régie des marchés agricoles et alimentaires du Québec, 646
Régie du bâtiment du Québec, 655
Régie du cinéma, 645
Régie du logement du Québec, 642
Régie Intermunicipale Argenteuil-Deux-Montagnes, 759
Régie intermunicipale d'alimentation en eau potable du Bas-St-François, 759
Régie intermunicipale d'approvisionnement en eau potable Henryville/Venise, 759
Régie intermunicipale d'aqueduc de la vallée de Châteauguay, 759
Régie intermunicipale d'aqueduc du Bas-Richelieu, 759
Régie intermunicipale d'aqueduc et d'égout de Lotbinière-Centre, 759
Régie intermunicipale d'aqueduc Richelieu-Yamaska, 759
Régie intermunicipale d'assainissement de Daveluyville, 760
Régie intermunicipale d'élimination de déchets solides de Brome-Missisquoi, 760
Régie intermunicipale d'enfouissement sanitaire de Charlevoix-Est, 760

Régie intermunicipale de gestion des déchets du Bas St-François, 760
Régie intermunicipale de gestion intégrée des déchets Bécancour-Nicolet-Yamaska, 760
Régie intermunicipale de l'aqueduc de Saint-Antoine, 760
Régie intermunicipale de l'eau de Deux-Montagnes, 760
Régie intermunicipale de l'eau de la Vallée du Richelieu, 760
Régie intermunicipale de l'eau potable Varennes, Ste-Julie, St-Amable, 760
Régie intermunicipale de l'Est de Portneuf, 760
Régie intermunicipale de récuperation des Hautes-Laurentides, 760
Régie intermunicipale de traitement de l'eau potable Saint-Romuald/Saint-Jean, 760
Régie intermunicipale de traitement des déchets de Matawinie, 760
Régie intermunicipale des déchets de CJLLR, 761
Régie intermunicipale des déchets de la Rouge, 761
Régie intermunicipale des déchets solides de la Lièvre, 761
Régie intermunicipale du comté de Beauce-Sud, 761
Regina, 754
Regina & District Labour Council, 994
Regina North Central, 540
Regina Qu'Appelle Health Region - Wascana Rehabilitation Centre, 1188
Regina Qu'Appelle Health Region Library Services - Regina General Hospital, 1188
Regina Wildlife Federation, 994
Région du Québec, 1180
Regional & Corporate Services Division, 635, 622
Regional Agricultural Services Division, 585
Regional Development, 601
Regional Development Corporation, 596
Regional Envelope, 344
Regional Environmental Services, 593
The Regional Health Authorities of Manitoba, 994
Regional Offices, 618
Regional Operations Division, 586
Regional Petroleum Products Recycling Ltd., 344
Regional Power Inc., 344
Regional Services Branch, 614
Registered Professional Foresters Association of Nova Scotia, 994
Registrar General Branch, 626
Registry of Deeds, 615
Registry of Joint Stock Companies, 615
Registry of Motor Vehicles, 615
Regroupement des associations forestières régionales du Québec, 994
Regroupement QuébecOiseaux, 994
Regulatory & Operational Services, 591
REHAU Industries Inc., 344
Reinforced Plastic Systems Inc., 344
Relations du travail, 644
Reliance Geological Services Inc., 344
Remediation Branch, 593
RemedX Remediation Services Inc., 344
Remedy Energy Services Ltd., 344
René Gervais Inc., Consultants, 1166, 345
Renewable Energy Services Inc., 345
Renewable Natural Resources Foundation, 994, 1041
Renewable Resources, 595
Renewable Resources Branch, 614
Renfrew, 627, 539, 704
Renick, Jim Law Office, 1068
Renovators Resource Inc., 345
RenuWater Centre, 345
Repentigny, 540, 740
Republic Environmental Systems (Fort Erie) Ltd., 345
Republic of Austria, 767
Republic of Bolivia, 767
Republic of Bulgaria, 767
Republic of Cameroon, 767
Republic of Chile, 767
Republic of Colombia, 767
Republic of Costa Rica, 767
Republic of Croatia, 767
Republic of Cuba, 767
Republic of Cyprus, 767
Republic of Ecuador, 767
Republic of El Salvador, 767
Republic of Finland, 767
Republic of Guatemala, 767
Republic of Guyana, 767
Republic of Hungary, 768

Republic of Iceland, 768
Republic of India, 768
Republic of Indonesia, 768
Republic of Ireland, 768
Republic of Ivory Coast, 768
Republic of Kazakhstan, 768
Republic of Korea, 768
Republic of Latvia, 768
Republic of Mali, 768
Republic of Mozambique, 768
Republic of Panama, 768
Republic of Peru, 768
Republic of Poland, 768
Republic of Romania, 768
Republic of Senegal, 768
Republic of Singapore, 769
Republic of the Philippines, 768
Republic of Trinidad & Tobago, 769
Republic of Tunisia, 769
Republic of Turkey, 769
Republic of Venezuela, 769
Republic of Zambia, 769
Rescan Environmental Services Ltd., 345
Research & Business Development Library, 1142
Research & Commercialization Division, 635
Research & Corporate Services Division, 619
Research & Development Institute for the Agri-Environment, 994
Research & Innovation Division, 563
Research Branch, 508, 579
Research Centres, 509
Research Department Information Resources, 1154
Research Electronics (Reselco) Ltd., 345
Research Facility, 345
Réseau environnement, 994
Réseau québécois des groupes écologistes, 994
Resource & Economic Policy, 660
Resource Assessment & Royalties, 611
Resource Conservation Manitoba, 1125
Resource Development Policy Division, 567
Resource Efficient Agricultural Production, 995
Resource Environmental Associates, 345
Resource Inventory & Modeling, 639
The Resource Library for the Environment and the Law, 1162
Resource Library for the Environment and the Law, 1216
Resource Management & Irrigation, 564
Resource Management Directorate, 528
Resource Management Division, 615, 576
Resource Processing Industries Branch, 544
Resource Recycling Inc., 995
Resource Revenue & Operations Division, 567
Resource Stewardship Branch, 658
Resource Stewardship Division, 609
Resource Systems Inc., 345
Resource Tenure & Engineering, 580
Resources for Global Sustainability, 995
Restigouche Solid Waste Corporation, 758
Restoration Environmental Contractors - Restoration Consultants, 346
Retail Council of Canada, 995
Rexdale Disposal Ltd., 346
Reynolds, Mirth, Richards & Farmer LLP, 1056
Rheinmetall Canada Inc., 1183
Rhododendron Society of Canada, 995
Ribbons Recycled Inc., 346
Rice Engineering & Operating Ltd., 346
Richard Ivey Foundation, 995, 1044
Richard Kadulski Architect, 346
Richards Buell Sutton LLP, 1062
Richelieu-Yamaska, 540
Richmond, 529, 684
Richmond Agricultural Society, 995
Richmond Campus, 1115
Richmond County, 698
Richmond Hill, 539, 718
Richmond Hill Naturalists, 995
Richmond Specialty Mushroom Farms Ltd., 346
RICHWAY Environmental Technologies Ltd., 346
Rick & Associates, 1071
Ricoh Canada Inc., 347
Rideau, 552
Rideau Environmental Action League, 995
Rideau Trail Association, 995
Rideau Valley Conservation Authority, 995
Rideau Valley Field Naturalists, 995, 1152
Ridgeline Environment Inc., 347

Entry Name Index

Ridgetown, 620
Riding Mountain National Park of Canada, 556
Riel House National Historic Site of Canada, 556
Rimbey Fish & Game Association, 996
Rimouski, 517, 740
Rimouski Branch, 514
Rimouski-Neigette, 753
Riopelle Griener Professional Corporation, 1070, 1072
Rioux Bossé Massé Moreau, 1089
Risk Check Environmental Ltd., 347
Ritch Durnford, Lawyers, 1067
Rive-Sud-de-Québec, 540
Riverview, 692
Riverview Hospital, 1115
Rivière-du-Loup, 741, 753
RMS Enviro Solv Inc. Québec, 347
RMS Instruments Ltd., 347
Roach, Schwartz & Associates, Barristers & Solicitors, 1079
Road Licensing & Safety, 608
Road Safety & Motor Vehicle Registration, 561
Road User Safety Division, 636
Robar, 347
Robb Engineering Ltd., 347
Robert Hornal & Associates Ltd., 348
Robert J. Redhead Limited, 348
Robert Laurin, 348
Robert-Cliche, 753
Robertson Environmental Services Ltd., 348
Robertson Stromberg Pedersen LLP, 1091
Roberval, 741
Robicheau's Pumping Service, 348
Robinson Consultants Inc., 348
Robinson Sheppard Shapiro LLP, 1086
Robinson Solutions, 348
Roche ltée, Groupe-conseil, 348
Le Rocher-Percé, 749
Rochester Midland Ltd., 349
Rockwell Automation Canada Inc., 349
Rocky Mountain Environmental Ltd., 350
Rocky Mountain House National Historic Site of Canada, 556
The Rocky Mountain Institute, 996
Rocky Mountain Naturalists, 996
Rocky View No. 44, 670
Rockyview Hospital Library, 1102
Roctest Ltée, 350
Rocvent Inc., 350
Roddickton, 604
Rodrigue Métal Ltée, 350
Roger LaRue Enterprises Ltd., 350
Roley Construction, 350
Romatec Incorporated, 350
ROMOR Atlantic Limited, 351
Ron Robinson Limited, 351
Ron Wedman Engineering Services, 351
Ronco Protective Products, 351
Rondar Inc., 351
Ronel Engineering Ltd., 351
Rose Mechanical Water Systems Inc., 351
Rosemère, 741
Rosenberg & Rosenberg, 1062
Rosenbloom & Aldridge, 1062
Roseridge Waste Management Services Commission, 758
Ross & McBride LLP, 1069
Ross Healthcare, Inc., 351
Rotblott & Sons Ltd., 352
Rothesay, 692
Rothsay, 352
Rotork Controls (Canada) Ltd., 352
Roussillon, 753
Rouville, 753
Rouyn-Noranda, 517, 741
Rouyn-Noranda Branch, 514
Rowan Williams Davies & Irwin Inc., 352
Roxul Inc., 353
Roy Northern Environmental Ltd., 353
Royal Agricultural Winter Fair Association, 996
Royal Botanical Gardens, 622, 996, 1139
Royal Canadian Geographical Society, 1216
The Royal Canadian Geographical Society, 996
Royal Canadian Mint, 560
Royal Canadian Mounted Police, 557
Royal Canadian Mounted Police External Review Committee, 557
Royal City Field Naturalists, 996
Royal Columbian Hospital - Simon Fraser Health Authority, 1114
Royal Envelope Ltd., 353
Royal Military College, 546
Royal Military College of Canada, 1142
Royal Ontario Museum, 622
Royal Ontario Museum Libraries, 1161
Royal Roads University, 1121, 1030, 1031
Royal Saskatchewan Museum, 657
The Royal Society of Canada, 996
Royal Tyrrell Museum of Palaeontology, 1104
Royal Victoria Hospital, 1175
Royalpak Inc., 353
RP Graphics Group, 353
RPC, 353
RPR Environmental Inc., 353
RST Instruments Ltd., 354
RSP International Inc., 354
The Rubber Association of Canada, 997
Rubber Manufacturers Association, 997
Rubber Rock Resources, 354
Rubicon Environmental Inc., 354
Rudiger Enterprises Ltd., 354
Ruiter Valley Land Trust, 997
Rural & Co-operatives Secretariat, 510
Rural Development, 575
Rural Development Institute, 1203
Rural Municipal Administrators' Association of Saskatchewan, 997
Rural Secretariat, 620
Russell, 627, 729
Russell Christie LLP, 1070
Russell NDE Systems Inc., 354
Russian Federation, 768
Ruth's Daughters of Canada, 997
RWDI AIR Inc., 354
Ryan Premises National Historic Site, 553
Ryerson University, 1161

S

S.A. Armstrong Limited, 354
S.L. Ross Environmental Research Ltd., 1152
Saanich, 688
Sabatini Earth Technologies Inc., 354
Sable Island Preservation Trust, 1043
Sable Offshore Energy Inc., 354
SACO Technologies, Inc., 354
Safe Drinking Water Branch, 624
Safe Environments Programme, 534
Safe Workplace Promotion Services Ontario, 997
Safety & Security Group, 561
Safety Codes Council, 571
Safety Express Ltd., 355
Safety Plus Inc., 355
Safety Projects International Inc., 355
Safety Services, 596
Safety Services Manitoba, 997
Safety Services New Brunswick, 997
Safety-Kleen Canada Inc., 355
Saguenay, 529, 741
Saguenay - Lac-Saint-Jean, 516
Saguenay - Lac-Saint-Jean - Côte-Nord, 646
Saguenay St. Lawrence Marine Park of Canada, 555
Saguenay-Lac-Saint-Jean, 643, 540, 644, 651
Saguenay-Lac-Saint-Jean et Côte-Nord, 653
Saguenay-Lac-Saint-Jean-Chibougamau, 655
Saguenay/Lac-Saint-Jean, 649
Sahtu, 605
SAIC Canada, 355
Saint John, 692
Saint John Animal Rescue League, 998
Saint John Branch, 512
Saint John Campus Library, 1129
Saint John Naturalists' Club, 998
Saint John Regional Office, 593
Saint Mary's University, 1034
Saint-Basile-le-Grand, 741
Saint-Charles-Borromée, 753
Saint-Constant, 742
Saint-Eustache, 742
Saint-Félicien, 742
Saint-Georges, 742
Saint-Hyacinthe, 742
Saint-Jean-sur-Richelieu, 742
Saint-Jérôme, 540, 743
Saint-Jérôme Branch, 514
Saint-Laurent, 530
Saint-Laurent Branch, 514
Saint-Lazare, 743
Saint-Léonard Branch, 514
Saint-Lin-Laurentides, 743
Saint-Ours, 552
Saint-Pierre-Jolys, 536
St. Albert, 674
St. Andrews, 690
St. Andrews Biological Station, 1204, 528, 1129
St. Andrews Blockhouse National Historic Site of Canada, 553
St. Andrews Campus, 1129
St. Andrews Rectory National Historic Site of Canada, 557
St Anthony Campus Library, 1131
St Boniface General Hospital, 1125
St Catharines, 517
St. Catharines, 529, 719
St Catharines Branch, 513
St. Catharines Hydro Generation Inc., 356
St Catherines, 539
St. Clair, 729
St Clair College of Applied Arts & Technology, 1165
St. Clair Parks Commission, 635
Sainte-Anne-de-Bellevue, 552
Sainte-Anne-des-Monts, 647
Sainte-Anne-des-Plaines, 743
Sainte-Catherine, 743
Sainte-Julie, 743
Sainte-Marie, 647, 743
Sainte-Thérèse, 540, 744
St. Francis Xavier University, 1207, 1034
St Francis-Xavier University, 1134
St. George, 592
The St. George Co. Ltd., 393
St. George Power LP, 356
St. George's, 604
St. Georges Bay Ecosystem Project, 1207
St James Library/Learning Commons, 1161
St. John's, 694
St. John's Branch, 512
St. John's Clean & Beautiful, 998
St John's Department of Planning, 1133
St. John's Tax Centre, 516
St Joseph's Health Care, London, 1144
St Joseph's Hospital (Hamilton), 1141
St Joseph's Hospital (Saint John), 1129
St. Lawrence Centre, 525
St Lawrence College, 1143
St. Lawrence Islands National Park of Canada, 554
St. Lawrence Parks Commission, 635
St Mary's River Association, 998
St Mary's University, 1136, 1029
St. Mary's University, 1207
St. Marys Cement Inc., 356
St Michael's Hospital, 1161
St Paul, 535
St. Paul, 565
St Paul's Health Sciences Library, 1118
St Paul's Hospital (Grey Nuns) of Saskatoon, 1190
St. Peters, 552
St. Peters Canada National Historic Site of Canada, 553
St Thomas, 539
St. Thomas, 719
SAL Engineering Ltd., 356
Salaberry-de-Valleyfield, 744
The Salamander Foundation, 1044
Salmon Arm, 684
Salmon Arm Bay Nature Enhancement Society, 998
Salmon Arm Campus, 1116
Salmon Preservation Association for the Waters of Newfoundland, 998
Salt Institute, 998
Saltcoats Agricultural Society, 998
Sambrabec Inc., 356
Samco Resources & By-Products, 356
Sanbec, 356
Sanders Resource Manage Inc., 356
Sandhill Disposal & Recycling Inc., 356
Sandwell Engineering Inc., 356
Sanexen Environmental Services Inc., 357
Sani Gestion ONYX, 357
Sanitherm Engineering Limited, 357
Sanix Incorporated, 357
Sanofi Pasteur Limited, 1161
Santé publique, 652
Santinel Inc., 357
SAR Engineering, 357

Entry Name Index

Sarafinchin Associates Ltd., 358
SARCAN Recycling, 358
Sarnia, 539, 719
Sarnia-Lambton Environmental Association, 998, 1154
Sask Film, 657
Sask Heritage Foundation, 657
Saskatchewan & Manitoba, 546
Saskatchewan Advanced Education, Employment & Labour, 661
Saskatchewan Agriculture, 655
Saskatchewan Applied Science Technologists & Technicians, 998
Saskatchewan Archives Board, 657
Saskatchewan Arts Board, 657
Saskatchewan Assessment Management Agency, 656
Saskatchewan Association of Agricultural Societies & Exhibitions, 999
Saskatchewan Association of Landscape Architects, 999
Saskatchewan Association of Rehabilitation Centres, 999
Saskatchewan Association of Rural Municipalities, 999
Saskatchewan Branches, 514
Saskatchewan Camping Association, 999
Saskatchewan Coalition for Tobacco Reduction, 999
Saskatchewan Communications Network, 657
Saskatchewan Conservation Data Centre, 658
Saskatchewan Construction Safety Association Inc., 999
Saskatchewan Corrections, Public Safety & Policing, 656
Saskatchewan Crop Insurance Corporation, 656
Saskatchewan Eco-Network, 1216, 999
Saskatchewan Emergency Management Organization, 657
Saskatchewan Energy & Resources, 660
Saskatchewan Environment, 657, 1187
Saskatchewan Environmental Industry & Managers' Association, 999
Saskatchewan Environmental Society, 1000, 1190
Saskatchewan First Nations & Métis Relations, 658
Saskatchewan Forest Centre, 1187
Saskatchewan Forestry Association, 1000
Saskatchewan Government Relations, 659
Saskatchewan Government Services, 662
Saskatchewan Ground Water Association, 1000
Saskatchewan Health, 659, 1188
Saskatchewan Health Libraries Association, 1000
Saskatchewan Herb & Spice Association, 1000
Saskatchewan Highway Traffic Board, 660
Saskatchewan Highways & Infrastructure, 660
Saskatchewan Highways & Transportation, 1188
Saskatchewan Institute of Applied Science & Technology, 1188
Saskatchewan Katahdin Sheep Association Inc., 1000
Saskatchewan Land Surveyors' Association, 1000
Saskatchewan Lands Appeal Board, 656
Saskatchewan Livestock Association, 1000
Saskatchewan Lotteries Trust for Sport, Culture & Recreation, 657
Saskatchewan Lung Association, 1000
Saskatchewan Medical Association, 1001
Saskatchewan Mining Association, 1001
Saskatchewan Northern Affairs, 661
Saskatchewan Nursery Landscape Association, 1001
Saskatchewan Outdoor & Environmental Education Association, 1001
Saskatchewan Parks & Recreation Association, 1001
Saskatchewan Power Corporation (SaskPower), 661
Saskatchewan Public Health Association Inc., 1001
Saskatchewan Region, 534
Saskatchewan Regional Office, 508
Saskatchewan Research Council, 662, 1190
Saskatchewan Safety Council, 1001
Saskatchewan Science Centre, 657
Saskatchewan Soil Conservation Association, 1001
Saskatchewan Stock Growers Association, 1001
Saskatchewan Tourism, Parks, Culture, & Sport, 657
Saskatchewan Trade & Export Partnership Inc., 660, 1002
Saskatchewan Trucking Association, 1002
Saskatchewan Urban Municipalities Association, 1002
Saskatchewan Waste Reduction Council, 1002
Saskatchewan Water Corporation (SaskWater), 662
Saskatchewan Watershed Authority, 658, 1187
Saskatchewan Wildlife Federation, 1002
Saskatchewan Workers' Compensation Board, 661, 663
Saskatchewan's Green Directory, 1216
Saskatoon, 754
Saskatoon Campus Library, 1190
Saskatoon Compliance Area, 658
Saskatoon Research Centre, 510
Saskatoon Wildlife Federation, 1002
SaskEnergy Incorporated, 662
Saskferco Products Inc., 358

SaskPower, 358
SaskPower Corporation, 1188
SaskPower Shand GreenHouse, 661
SaskTel, 1188
Sass Manufacturing Ltd., 358
SatCon Power Systems (Canada), 358
Satlantic, 358
Saugeen Shores, 719
Sault, 552
Sault Area Hospital, 1154
Sault College of Applied Arts & Technology, 1154
Sault Naturalists, 1002
Sault Ste. Marie, 632, 720
Sault Ste Marie, 539
Sault Ste Marie Branch, 513
Save Ontario Shipwrecks, 1002
Saxe, Dianne, 1079
Scales Bioresource Consulting Ltd., 358
Scarborough, 530
The Scarborough Hospital - General Campus, 1162
The Scarborough Hospital - Grace Campus, 1162
Scarfone Hawkins LLP, 1069
SCC Environmental, 358
Scepter Manufacturing Co. Ltd., 358
SCG Industries Ltd., 358
Schlegel Canada Inc., 359
Schlumberger Oilfield Services, 359
Schlumberger Water Services, 359
Schneider Electric Canada Inc., 359
School of Architecture, 1139
School of Community Government, 608
Schulich Library of Science & Engineering, 1175
Schwank Group, 359
Scicorp Systems Inc., 359
Science & Engineering Division, 1118
Science & Forestry Library, 1128
Science & Information Branch, 634
Science & Information Resources Division, 633
Science & Risk Assessment Directorate, 524
Science & Technology Branch, 522
Science & Technology Strategies, 524
Science Alberta Foundation, 1002, 1039
Science and Technology for Canadians, 1216
Science Horizons: Environment Canada's Youth Internship Program, 524
Science Library, 1111
Science North, 622
Science Procurement Directorate, 559
Science Sector, 527
Science/Engineering Library, 1143
Sciences & Planning, 593
Sciences & Reporting Branch, 594
Sciences & Technology Library, 1125
Sciencetech Inc., 359
Scientific Instrumentation Ltd., 360
Scimus Inc., 360
Scintrex Ltd., 360
Scitax Advisory Partners LLP, 360
Scotia Plastics, 360
Scotia Recycling Ltd., 360
Scott & Stewart Forestry Consultants, 360
Scott Resource Services Inc., 360
Scott Tank Cleaning Co. Ltd., 360
Scott Venturo LLP, 1053
Scugog, 729
SDS Drilling Ltd., 360
SEA Engineering Company Inc., 360
Sea Lamprey Control Centre, 1155
Sea Scan International Inc., 361
Sea Shepherd Conservation Society, 1002
Sea Shepherd Conservation Society - USA, 1002
Seaboard Industrial Supply Co. Ltd., 361
Seacom International Inc., 361
Seaforth Engineering Group Inc., 361
Seagull Foundation, 1003, 1043
Seal Cove Campus Library, 1130
SEAL-OGIC Innovations Corp., 361
Sealcon Liner Systems Inc., 361
Sealtech Restorations Inc., 361
Sears Canada Inc., 361
SeCan Association, 1003
Secrétariat à l'accès aux services en langue anglaise et aux communautés ethnoculturelles, 652
Secrétariat à la politique linguistique, 645
Secrétariat des organismes environnementaux du Québec, 1216

Secretariat of Environment & Natural Resources, 531
Secter Environmental Resource Consulting, 361
Secteur du Québec de la Force terrestre, 545
Secteurs stratégiques et des projets économiques, 648
Sector Compliance, 625
Sectoral Policy Analysis, 526
Secural Inc., 361
Sécurité civile et Sécurité incendie, 653
Security & Emergency Preparedness Directorate, 561
Sedac Inc., 361
Sedore Stoves Canada, 361
SEEDS Foundation, 1003, 1039
Seeds of Diversity Canada, 1003
Seeker Green Products Ltd., 361
SEG Engineering Inc., 362
Seguro Projects Inc., 362
SEI Industries Ltd., 362
Self-Government Branch, 542
Selkirk, 536
Selkirk College, 1111, 1031
Selkirk Renewable Resources Council, 665
Semco Systems Limited, 362
Semi-Arid Prairie Agricultural Research Centre, 1191
Semiarid Prairie Agricultural Research Centre, 510
Sendex Environmental Corp., 362
Seneca College of Applied Arts & Technology, 1161
Seneca@York Campus, 1161
SENES Consultants Limited, 362
Seniors for Nature Canoe Club, 1003
Seniors' Secretariat, 613
Sensible Life Products, 362
Seoul, 566
Seprotech Systems Inc., 363
Sept-Iles, 647, 744
Sept-Rivières, 753
Septo-Clean Co. Ltd., 363
The Sernas Group Inc., 393
Servco Environmental Solutions Inc., 363
Service BC, 581
Service Canada, 535
Service Canada Centres, 535
Service de l'urbanisme, 1175
Service de rebuts Soulanges inc., 363
Service Delivery, 616
Service Development & Implementation Office, 636
Service New Brunswick, 596
ServiceMaster of Canada, 363
ServiceOntario, 626
Services, 597
Services & Specialized Acquisitions Management Sector, 559
Services & Technology Acquisition Management Sector, 559
Services à la gestion, 643
Services à la gestion & au milieu terrestre, 648
Services administratifs, 644
Services correctionnels, 653
Services d'Évaluation Santé/Toxicologie Inc., 363
Services de santé et médecine universitaire, 644
Services industriels Newalta, 363
Services Industries Branch, 544
Services Matrec inc., 363
Services Québec, 653, 654
Servicestat Ltd., 363
Settlement Surveys Ltd., 364
Seven Oaks General Hospital, 1125
Severn, 729
Severn Sound Environmental Association, 1003
SEW Eurodrive Co. of Canada Ltd., 364
Sexton Design & Technology Library, 1136
SGE Hatch Ltd., 364
SGS Canada Inc., 364
SHAD Valley International, 1003
SHAL Consulting Engineers Ltd., 365
Shared Vision, 1194
Sharp Electronics of Canada Ltd., 365
Shaunavon, 537
Shaver Industries Inc., 365
Shaw Precast Solutions, 365
Shawinigan, 744
Shawinigan-Sud Tax Centre, 517
Sheet Metal & Air Conditioning Contractors' National Association, 1003
Sheet Metal Contractors Association of Alberta, 1003
Shelburne, 537
Sheldons Engineering Inc., 365
Shell Canada Limited, 1102, 365

Entry Name Index

Shell Environmental Fund, 1039
Shelterbelt Centre, 508
SHER-PAC Container Systems Ltd., 365
Sherbrooke, 651, 744
Sherbrooke Branch, 514
Sheridan Institute of Technology and Advanced Learning, 1146
Sheridan Park Site, 1145
Sherwin-Williams Canada Inc., 365
Shibley Righton LLP, 1079, 1081
Shibogama Interim Planning Board, 631
Shigawake Organics Ltd., 365
Shipbuilding Association of Canada, 1003
Shook, Wickham, Bishop & Field, 1056
Showa-Best Glove, Inc., 366
Shred-It, 366
Shuswap Naturalists, 1003
SIAST Kelsey Campus, 1190
SIAST Palliser Campus, 1187
SIAST Wascana Campus, 1188
Sick Building Solutions, 366
Sico, 366
Sidney, 684
Siemens Building Technologies, Ltd., 366
Siemens Milltronics Process Instruments Inc., 366
Siemens Water Technologies, 367
Sierra Club, 1003
Sierra Club Canada, 1216
Sierra Club of British Columbia, 1004
Sierra Club of Canada, 1004
Sierra Club of Canada - Ontario Chapter, 1004
Sierra Club of Canada - Prairie Chapter, 1004
Sierra Youth Coalition, 1004
Sigma Engineering Ltd., 367
Signal Hill National Historic Site of Canada, 554
Sika Canada Inc., 367
Silent Spring Institute, 1216
Silex Innovations Inc., 367
Silliker Canada Co., 367
Silliker JR Laboratories, ULC, 367
Silo Clean International, 367
Silva Forest Foundation, 368
Silvana Import Trading Inc., 368
Silver King Campus, 1114
Silvicon Services Inc., 368
Simark Controls Ltd., 368
Simcoe, 539, 628, 704
Simcoe Engineering Group Limited, 368
Simcoe Plastics Ltd., 368
Similkameen Naturalist Club, 1004
Similkameen Okanagan Organic Producers Association, 1004
Simon Fraser University, 1111, 368, 1031
SimplexGrinnell, 368
SimpsonWigle LAW LLP, 1068, 1069
Sinanni Inc., 369
Sinclair Technologies, 369
Single Window Service, 640
Singleton Urquhart LLP, 1062
Sinnott Farm Services Ltd., 369
Sintra Inc., 369
Sioux Lookout, 632
Sioux Lookout Zone Hospital, 533
Sir F.G. Banting Research Centre, 1152
Sir George-Étienne Cartier National Historic Site of Canada, 555
Sir John Johnson National Historic Site of Canada, 554
Sir Mortimer B. Davis Jewish General Hospital, 1175
Sir Sandford Fleming College of Applied Arts & Technology, 1153
Sir Wilfred Grenfell College, 1131, 1033
Sir Wilfrid Laurier National Historic Site of Canada, 555
Sirmilik National Park of Canada, 556
Siskind, Cromarty, Ivey & Dowler LLP, 1069
Sittler Environmental, 369
Sittler Excavating Ltd., 369
Sittler's Manufacturing, 369
Skeena Valley Naturalists, 1004
Skeena-Queen Charlotte, 679
Skelton Brumwell & Associates Inc., 369
Sky Generation, 369
Skylark Controls, 370
SL Ross Environmental Research Ltd., 370
Slave Lake, 535
Sleegers Engineering Inc., 370
Slope Indicator Canada, 370
Slovak Republic, 769
SLR Consulting Ltd. (Canada), 370
Small & Medium Enterprise Division, 635

Small & Medium Enterprises Sector, 559
Small Business BC, 583, 515
Small Business Development, 585
Small Water Users Association of BC, 1004
Smart Commute, 1004
Smart Systems for Health, 628
Smart Turner Pumps, 370
Smith & Andersen Consulting Engineering, 370
Smith, Kenneth W., Barrister & Solicitor, 1071
Smith-Ennismore-Lakefield, 729
Smith-Way Ltd., 371
SmithBrook Waste Management Services Inc., 371
Smiths Detection, 371
Smiths Falls, 539
Smoke-Free Nova Scotia, 1004
Smoking & Health Action Foundation, 1004
Smoky River Regional Waste Management Commission, 758
Smoky River Regional Water Management Commission, 758
SMS Engineering Ltd., 371
SNC-Lavalin Engineers & Constructors Inc., 1161
SNC-Lavalin Environment Inc., 371
SNC-Lavalin Group Inc., 371
SNC-Lavalin inc., 1175
Snowcap Waters Ltd., 371
Social Development, 541
Social Development Policy Office, 580
Social Investment Organization, 1004
Socialist People's Libyan Arab Jamahiriya, 768
Socialist Republic of Vietnam, 769
Société d'énergie de la Baie-James, 649
Société d'énergie de la rivière Ste-Anne/AXOR, 371
Société d'entomologie du Québec, 1005
Société d'habitation du Québec, 642
Société d'Horticulture et d'Écologie de Prévost, 1005
Société de conservation de la Baie de l'Isle-Verte, 1005
Société de coopération pour le développement international, 1005
Société de développement de la Baie James, 650
Société de développement des entreprises culturelles, 645
Société de développement économique du Saint-Laurent, 1005
Société de l'assurance automobile du Québec, 654
Société de la Place des Arts de Montréal, 645
Société de protection des plantes du Québec, 1005
Société de télédiffusion du Québec (Télé-Québec), 645
Société des établissements de plein air du Québec, 1005
Société des établissements en plein air du Québec, 647
Société des roses du Québec, 1005
Société des traversiers du Québec, 654
Société du Centre des congrès de Québec, 654
Société du Grand Théâtre de Québec, 645
Société du port ferroviaire Baie-Comeau-Hauterive, 654
Société générale de financement du Québec (SGF), 648, 1175
Société habitation du Québec, 1175
Société immobilière du Québec, 654
Société Laurentide inc., 371
Société Provancher d'histoire naturelle du Canada, 1006
Société québécoise d'assainissement des eaux, 1006
Société québécoise de récupération et de recyclage, 647, 1006
Société québécoise de spéléologie, 1006, 1176
Société québécoise des hostas et des hémérocalles, 1006
Société québécoise du dahlia, 1006
Société québécoise pour la défense des animaux, 1006
Society for Canadian Women in Science & Technology, 1006
Society for Conservation Biology, 1006
Society for Ecological Restoration International, 1007
Society for Environmental Graphic Design, 1007
Society for Organic Urban Land Care, 1007
Society for Research on Nicotine & Tobacco, 1007
Society for Socialist Studies, 1007
Society of Canadian Ornithologists, 1007
Society of Chemical Industry - Canadian Section, 1008
Society of Environmental Toxicology & Chemistry, 1008
Society of Fire Protection Engineers, 1008
Society of Petroleum Engineers, 1008
Society of Professional Engineers & Associates, 1008
Society of the Plastics Industry, Inc., 1008
Society of Toxicology, 1008
Society of Toxicology of Canada, 1009
Society Promoting Environmental Conservation, 1216, 1009
Socio Policy & Programs Branch, 542
Socodec Inc., 371
Softrisk Technologies Ltd., 372
Soil & Water Conservation Society, 1009
Soil - Water Environmental Group of The University of British Columbia, 1203

Soil - Water Environmental Laboratory of The University of British Columbia, 1203
Soil Conservation Council of Canada, 1009
Soil, Plant & Feed Laboratory, 603
Soils & Crops Research & Development Centre, 510
Solaction Inc., 372
Solar & Sustainable Energy Society of Canada Inc., 1009
Solar Solutions Inc., 372
Solarmart, 372
Solcan Ltd., 372
Solenco Environnement inc., 372
Soleno Inc., 372
Solid Waste & Recycling, 1194
Solid Waste Association of North America, 1009
Solid Waste Reclamation Inc., 372
Solignum, 372
Solignum Inc., 372
Solinov Inc., 373
Solinst Canada Ltd., 373
Solmax International Inc., 373
Solmax-Texel Geosynthetics Inc., 373
Solmers Internationale Experts-Conseils Inc., 373
Soloway, Wright LLP, 1071
Sols Consultants Ltée, 373
Solution 3R, 373
Somenos Marsh Wildlife Society, 1009
Sonepar Canada, 373
Sonic Environmental Solutions Inc., 373
Sonic Soil Sampling Inc., 374
Sonic Technology Solutions Inc., 374
Sonitec Inc., 374
sonnevera international corp., 374
Sonoco Recycling Ltd., 374
Soper's, 374
SOQUEM INC., 1180
Sorel-Tracy, 745
Soren Construction Ltd., 374
SOTAR Inc., 374
Les Sources, 750
Souris, 540
Souris Valley Industries Ltd., 374
Sous-ministre associé & Forestier en chef, 651
South, 569, 592
South Asia, 544
South Campus, 1106
South Dundas, 730
South Forty Waste Services Commission, 758
South Frontenac, 730
South Glengarry, 730
South Huron, 730
South Interlake, 585
South Lake Simcoe Naturalists, 1010
South Parkland, 585
South Peel Naturalists' Club, 1010
South Stormont, 730
South West Solid Waste Commission, 759
South-East Regional Health Authority, 1128
Southeast and East Asia, 544
Southeast Environmental Association, 1010
Southeast, 592, 622
Southern, 570, 621
Southern Alberta, 508
Southern Alberta Health Libraries Association, 1010
Southern Alberta Institute of Technology, 1103
Southern Crop Protection & Food Research Centre, 510, 1164
Southern Gulf of St. Lawrence Coalition on Sustainability, 1204
Southern Interior, 579, 517
Southern Interior Development Initiative Trust, 575
Southern Interior Local Government Association, 1010
Southern Ontario Library Service, 622
Southern Ontario Orchid Society, 1010
Southern Ontario Region, 517
Southern Ontario Seismic Network, 1010
Southern Ontario Waste Inc., 374
Southern Region, 632
Southern Saskatchewan, 508
Southern Vancouver Island, 536
Southwell Controls Ltd., 374
Southwest, 622, 585
Southwestern, 636
Southwestern Flowtech & Environmental Ltd., 374
Southwestern Shore/Valley, 610
Spanach Construction Ltd., 375
SPD Sales Ltd., 375
Special Initiatives, 592

Entry Name Index

Specialty Technical Publishers, 375
Species at Risk Public Registry, 1216
Spectrum Resource Group Inc., 375
Spectrum, Information Technologies & Telecommunications, 544
Spencer-Lemaire Industries Ltd., 375
SPG Hydro International Inc., 375
Sphag Sorb (Canada) Inc., 375
Sphere Research Corp., 375
SPI Industries Inc., 375
SpilKleen, 375
Spill Management Inc., 376
Spills Action Centre, 625
Sport, Recreation & Youth, 608
Sprayaway Marine Services Ltd., 376
Sprecher + Schuh Inc., 376
Spriet Associates London Ltd., 376
Spring Air Silver Services Ltd., 376
Springdale, 604
Springfield, 690
Springwater, 730
Sproule Associates Limited, 1103
Spruce Grove, 674
Sprung Instant Structures Ltd., 376
Squamish, 688
Squamish-Lillooet, 679
SRB Controls Inc., 376
SRI Petro Chemical Inc., 376
SRK Consulting (Canada) Inc., 376
SRP Control Systems Ltd., 377
SRT Soil Remediation Technologies, 377
SS Keno National Historic Site of Canada, 556
SS Klondike National Historic Site of Canada, 556
SSI Schaefer Systems International Ltd., 377
Stabilis Environment Inc., 377
Stablex Canada Inc., 377
Standards Council of Canada, 543, 559
Standards Development Branch, 624
Stanley Park Ecology Society, 1010
Stantec Inc., 377
Stanton, 606
Startco Engineering Ltd., 378
State of Israel, 768
State of Kuwait, 768
Statiflo Inc., 379
Statistics Canada, 1216, 559
Status of Women, 661, 590
Status of Women Canada, 519
Statutory Publications, 379
Staveley Services Canada Inc., 380
Steacie Institute for Molecular Sciences, 548
Steacie Science and Engineering Library, 1161
Stedtnitz Maritime Technology Ltd., 379
Steel Recycling Institute, 1010
Steinbach, 536
Stem Cell Network, 1010
Stemmer Steel Craft Industries Limited, 379
Stephenville, 601
Sterling Power Systems, 379
Sterling Press, 379
Stewardship Branch, 593
Stewardship Canada, 1217
Stewart & Turner, 1067
Stewart Group, 379
Stewart McKelvey Stirling Scales - Fredericton, 1064
Stewart McKelvey Stirling Scales - Halifax, 1067
Stewart McKelvey Stirling Scales - Moncton, 1064
Stewart McKelvey Stirling Scales - Saint John, 1065
Stewart McKelvey Stirling Scales - St. John's, 1066
Stikeman Elliott LLP - Calgary, 1053
Stikeman Elliott LLP - Montréal, 1087
Stikeman Elliott LLP - Ottawa, 1071
Stikeman Elliott LLP - Toronto, 1079
Stikeman Elliott LLP - Vancouver, 1062
Stitt Feld Handy Group, 1080
STOBEC Inc., 379
Stockholm Environment Institute, 1010
StonCor Canada, 379
Stones Carbert Waite Wells LLP, 1054
Stoney Creek Campus, 1155
Stora Enso North America, 379
Stork Bronswerk Inc., 380
Stormceptor Canada Inc., 380
Stormont, 628
Stormont, Dundas & Glengarry, 730
Strait Area Campus, 1137

Strait Engineering Ltd., 380
Strasser Alloy Steels Ltd., 380
Strata Environmental Ltd., 380
Strata Soil Sampling Inc., 380
Strategic Corporate Services Division, 566
Strategic Forestry Initiative Division, 572
Strategic Industries, 602
Strategic Industries & Business Development Branch, 602
Strategic Industry Development, 574
Strategic Infrastructure, 581
Strategic Initiatives Division, 567
Strategic Leadership Forum, The Toronto Society for Strategic Management, 1010
Strategic Policy, 522
Strategic Policy Branch, 625, 636
Strategic Policy Division, 577
Strategic Priorities & Planning, 528
Strategic Support & Integration Division, 568
Strategic Transportation Initiatives, 573
Strategies for the Environment, 380
Strategy & Business Planning Division, 565
Stratem Inc., 380
Stratford, 539, 720
Stratford Branch, 513
Strathcona County, 1109, 670
Strathcona Park Lodge & Outdoor Education Centre, 1010, 1111
Strathroy-Caradoc, 731
Stratos Inc., 380
Straub Tadco Inc., 380
Stringer, Brisbin, Humphrey Management Lawyers, 1080
Structural Pest Management Association of Ontario, 1010
Strum Environmental, 381
Stuart Energy USA, 381
Stuart Hunt & Associates, 381
Sturgeon County, 670
SUBBOR, 381
Subsidiaries/Filiales, 649
Succursale de Québec, 1180
Sudbury, 539
Sudbury Branch, 513
Sudbury District, 731
Sudbury Rock & Lapidary Society, 1011, 1155
Sudbury Tax Centre, 516
Sugarloaf, 597
Suimon Engineering Canada Ltd., 381
Sultech Consulting Ltd., 381
Sumas Environmental Services Inc., 381
Summa Engineering Ltd., 381
Summerhill Group, 381
Summerland, 689
Summerside, 540, 733
Summerside Tax Centre, 516
Summit Structures, 382
Sun Prairie Organic, 382
Sun Ross Energy Systems Ltd., 382
Sunarc of Canada Inc., 382
SunBridge Wind Power, 382
Suncor Energy Foundation, 1039
Suncor Energy Products, 382
Suncor Inc., 1103
Suncurrent Industries Inc., 382
Sundog Energy Management, 382
Sunergy Systems Ltd., 382
Sunmotor International Ltd., 382
Sunnybrook Health Sciences Centre - Sunnybrook Campus, 1162
Sunoco Inc., 382
SunOpta, 382
Sunset Solar Systems Ltd., 382
Sunshine Coast Natural History Society, 1011
Sunshine Coast, 679
Supervac 2000, 383
Supplier Registration Information, 559
Supply & Services Division, 589
Supply Chain Management, 628
Supply Services, 666
Supremex Inc., 383
Surface Rights Board, 590
Surpac Minex (Canada) Ltd., 383
Surrey, 684
Surrey Branch, 512
Surrey Campus, 1116
Surrey Library, 1116
Surrey Memorial Hospital, 1116
Surrey Tax Centre, 517
Survalent Technology Corporation, 383

Surveys & Mapping, 608
Surveys Division, 615
Sustainable Agriculture Resources, 637
Sustainable Buildings Canada, 1011
Sustainable Development Innovations Fund, 1041
Sustainable Development Technology Canada, 1011
Sustainable EDGE Ltd., 383
Sustainable Energy Technologies Ltd., 383
Sustainable Forest Management Network, 1200
Sustainable Forestry Initiative, 1011
Sustainable Planning Branch, 594
Sustainable Resource & Environmental Management, 572
Sustainable Resource Management Branch, 587
Sustainable Resources, 665
Sustainable Resources Management Group, 383
The Sustainable Times, 1194
Sustainable Urban Development Association, 1011
SustaiNet Software Solutions Inc., 383
Sutherland Excavating Ltd., 384
Sutherland-Schultz Inc., 384
Sutts, Strosberg LLP, 1082
Swan Hills Treatment Centre, 384
Swan River, 536
Swift Current, 540, 755
Swift Current Agricultural & Exhibition Association, 1011
Swift Current Compliance Area, 658
Swift Current Creek Watershed Stewards, 1011
Swish Maintenance Ltd., 384
Swiss Confederation, 769
Swiss Environment & Safety Inc., 384
Sydenham Field Naturalists, 1011
Sydney Branch, 513
Sydney Environmental Resources Ltd., 384
Sydney Tar Ponds Agency, 616
Sylvain Léger, 384
Sylvain, Parent, Gobeil, 1089
Sylvametrics Consulting, 384
Symbion Consultants, 384
Symbiose Consultants inc, 385
Symplastics Ltd., 385
Syncrude Canada Ltd., 1106
Syndel International Inc., 385
Synex International Inc., 385
Syrian Arab Republic, 769
System Ecotechnologies Inc., 385
System Evaluation & Accountability Office, 580
Systems Plus, 385

T

T. Buck Suzuki Environmental Foundation, 1041
T-G Burgmann, 385
T. Harris Environmental Management Inc., 385
T.D. Rooke Associates Ltd., 385
T.D. ThermoDesign, 386
Taco Canada Ltd., 386
Taipei, 566
Talisman Energy Inc., 1103
Talkie Tooter Canada Ltd., 386
Talon Projects Inc., 386
Tang G. Lee Architect, 386
Tank-Craft Ltd., 386
Tankless Water Heater Company, 386
Tankman, 386
Tanknology Canada Inc., 386
Tanks-A-Lot Ltd., 386
TankTek Environmental Services Ltd., 386
Tansley Associates Environmental Services, 387
Tarandus Associates Limited, 387
Target Recycling Inc., 387
Tax Commission, 615
Tax Policy Branch, 526
Tax Services Offices, 516
Taxicab Board, 588
Tay, 731
Taylor Mazier Associates, 387
Taylor Munro Energy Systems Inc., 387
TD Friends of the Environment Foundation, 1011, 1044
TEAM-1 Environmental Services Inc., 387
Tech Sales Co., 387
Techint Goodfellow Technologies Inc., 387
Technel Engineering Inc., 387
Technical & Regulatory Services Division, 641
Technical Library, 1188
Technical Reference Centre, 1162

Entry Name Index

Technical Services Division, 564
Technical Services Library, 1135
Technisol Environnement, 388
Technology & Business Solutions, 631
Technology PEI Inc., 640
Technology Services, 571
Technology, Research & Innovation Division, 576
TechNova, 1011
Techstar Plastics Inc., 388
Teck Cominco Metals Ltd., 1116
Teck Resources, 1118
Teckn-O-Laser, 388
TECSULT inc, 1176
Tecsult Inc., 388
Tecumseh, 720
Tekmar Control Systems Ltd., 389
Teknion Corporation, 389
Tekran Canada, 389
Telamode, 389
Télé-Université, 1180
Telefilm Canada, 519
Teleflex Canada Ltd., 389
Tellus Institute, 1011
Temagami Community Foundation, 1044
Témiscamingue, 753
Témiscouata, 753
Temiskaming Environmental Action Committee, 1012
Templeman Menninga LLP, 1068
Temprite Industries Ltd., 389
Tenure & Revenue, 579
Tera Environmental Consultants (Alta) Ltd., 389
Terasen Waterworks, 389
TeraWind Ltd., 389
Terex Ltd., 389
Terinex International Ltd., 389
Terminal City Iron Works Ltd., 389
Terra Experts Conseils Inc., 390
Terra Nova National Park of Canada, 554
Terrace, 685
Terrace Branch, 512
TerraChoice Environmental Marketing, 390
Terracon Geotechnique Ltd., 390
Terrafix Geosynthetics Inc., 390
TerraLink Horticulture Inc., 390
Terralog Technologies Inc., 390
Terrapex Environmental Ltd., 390
Terratec Environmental Ltd., 390
Terratech, 390
Terratechnik Environmental Limited, 391
Terratlantic Engineering Ltd., 391
Terrebonne, 745
Territoire, 650
Territoires, 643
Territorial Board of Revision, 607
Tertec Enterprises Inc., 391
Teshmont Consultants LP, 1125
Teslin Renewable Resource Council, 665
Testwell Instruments, 391
TetrES Consultants Inc., 391
Texel Géomembrane Inc., 391
Thames Campus Resource Centre, 1139
Thames Centre, 731
Thames Region Ecological Association, 1012
Theodor D. Sterling & Associates Ltd., 393
Thérèse-de-Blainville, 753
Thérèse-de-Blainville (Boisbriand) Regional Branch, 514
Therm-O-Comfort Co. Ltd., 393
Thermal Energy International Inc., 394
Thermal Environmental Comfort Association, 1012
Thermal Hydronics Supply Ltd., 394
Thermal Insulation Association of Alberta, 1012
Thermal Technics Corporation, 394
Thermo Design Engineering Ltd., 394
Thermo Dynamics Ltd., 394
Thermo Electric (Canada) Ltd., 394
Thermo Electron Corp., 394
Thermo-Cell Industries Ltd., 394
Thermon Heat Tracing Services, 394
Thermotech Windows Ltd., 394
Thetford Mines, 540, 745
Thimm Engineering Inc., 395
Thoman Soule LLP, Lawyers, 1069
The Thomas Sill Foundation Inc., 1042
Thompson, 690
Thompson Dorfman Sweatman LLP, 1064

Thompson Engineering Consultants Ltd., 395
Thompson River University, 1031
Thompson Rivers University, 1112
Thompson Rosemount Group, 395
Thompson, Cariboo, Shuswap Health Sciences Library, 1112
Thompson-Nicola, 679
Thomson & Howe Energy Systems Inc., 395
Thomson Technology Inc., 395
Thomson, Rogers, 1080
Thor Global Enterprises Ltd., 395
Thorhild Regional Waste Management Services Commission, 758
Thorhild Regional Water Services Commission, 758
Thorold, 727
3M Canada Company, 1144, 395
360 Energy Inc., 395
Thunder Bay, 721, 731
Thunder Bay Branch, 513
Thunder Bay Field Naturalists, 1012
Thurber Engineering Ltd., 395
Thurber Group, 1121
Thuro Inc., 396
Tides Canada Foundation, 1041
Tiger-Vac International Inc., 396
Tillsonburg, 539, 721
Timber Export Advisory Committee, 579
Timberline Trail & Nature Club, 1012
Timiskaming, 628, 731
Timmins, 625, 721
Timmins Branch, 513
Tinari Energy Management Services Inc., 396
TIR Systems Ltd., 396
Tire Stewardship BC Association, 1012
Tiru Canada Inc., 396
Titan Logix Corp., 396
Titles & Offshore, 576
TJ Consulting Ltd., 396
Tlicho, 606
TLT Co-Vent, 396
TMK IPSCO Inc., 397
Tobacco Strategy for Nova Scotia, 613
Tokyo, 566
Tomark Compliance Centre, 397
Tomlinson Environmental Services, 397
TOR Geoscience Corp., 397
Tornatech, 397
Toromont Caterpillar, 397
Toromont Energy Ltd., 398
Toronto, 721
Toronto (Finch Ave. West) Branch, 513
Toronto (King St.) Branch, 513
Toronto (Metropolitan Land Titles), 628
Toronto (Metropolitan Registry), 628
Toronto (Milner Ave.) Branch, 513
Toronto Atmospheric Fund, 1044
Toronto Biotechnology Initiative, 1012
Toronto Botanical Garden, 1162
Toronto Canada Quay, 539
Toronto East General Hospital, 1162
Toronto Entomologists Association, 1012
Toronto Environmental Alliance, 1012
Toronto Etobicoke, 539
Toronto Field Naturalists, 1012
Toronto Health Libraries Association, 1012
Toronto Lakeside, 539
Toronto Lawrence Square, 539
Toronto Ornithological Club, 1012
Toronto Parks & Trees Foundation, 1045
Toronto Public Health, 1162
Toronto Rehab, 1162
Toronto Renewable Energy Co-operative, 1013
Toronto Scarborough, 539
Toronto Sheet Metal Contractors Association, 1013
Toronto Transportation Society, 1013
Toronto Urban Development Services City Planning, 1162
Toronto West, 517
Toronto Western Hospital, 1162
Toronto Willowdale, 539
Toronto Zoo, 1013, 1163
Torrie Smith Associates Inc., 398
Torys LLP, 1080
Toshiba of Canada Ltd., 398
Total Combustion Inc., 398
Total Comfort Solution Inc., 398
Total Safety Canada Inc., 399
Totten Sims Hubicki Associates Ltd., 399

Touchie Engineering, 399
Tourism, 604
Tourism & Parks, 607
Tourism Branch, 667
Tourism Development, 641
Tourism Division, 616
Tourism Marketing, 641
Tourism Marketing & Heritage Division, 566
Tourism Policy & Development Division, 635
Tourism Saskatchewan, 660
Tourism Secretariat & Travel Manitoba, 587
Townsend Engineering, 399
The Township of Muskoka Lakes Ratepayers' Association, 1013
ToxCo Waste Management Ltd., 399
Toxicology Centre, 399
Toxics Watch Society of Alberta, 1013
Toxprobe Inc., 399
TPE Technologies Inc., 399
T.R. Meighen Family Foundation, 1045
TRACC (NB), 400
Tract Consulting Inc., 400
Trade & Export Development Branch, 602
Trade & International Relations, 659
Trade Centre Limited, 610
Trade Law Bureau, 531
Trade Policy & Negotiations, 531
Traders Metal Company Ltd., 400
Trafalgar Campus Library, 1146
Training & Development Services, 400
Trans Canada Trail Foundation, 1013
Trans Canada Yellowhead Highway Association, 1013
Transalta Utilities, 400
TransAlta Utilities Corporation, 1103
TransCanada PipeLines Limited, 1103
Transchem Inc., 400
Transco Plastic Industries, 400
Transcontinental Energy Saving Products Inc., 400
Transcontinental Printing Inc., 400
Transform Compost Systems Ltd., 400
Transformation Alimentaire Québec, 645
TransGas Limited, 662, 400
Translation Bureau, 558
Transport Action Canada, 1013
Transport Canada, 560, 1152, 1045
Transport Dangerous Goods Directorate, 561
Transportation, 618, 589
Transportation & Civil Engineering, 573
Transportation Appeal Tribunal of Canada, 560
Transportation Association of Canada, 1013, 1152
Transportation Development Centre, 560
Transportation Health & Safety Association of Ontario, 1163
Transportation Planning & Policy Department, 583
Transportation Policy Branch, 636
Transportation Policy Division, 589
Transportation Safety Board, 573
Transportation Safety Board - Calgary, 573
Transportation Safety Board of Canada, 560, 561
Transportation Safety Services, 573
Transportation Services, 604
Transway Systems Inc., 400
Travel Alberta, 573
Treasury Board of Canada, 561
Treaties & Aboriginal Government, 542
Trecan Combustion Ltd., 400
Tree Canada, 1217
Tree Canada Foundation, 1013, 1045
Tree Improvement Branch, 580
Tree of Life, 1217
Tree Ring Lab, 1203
Treeline Well Abandonment & Reclamation Ltd., 401
Trees Ontario, 1045
Trellcan Rubber Ltd., 401
Tremblay, Bois, Mignault & Lemay, 1089
Tremcar inc., 401
Tremco Ltd., 401
Trent Hills, 731
Trent Metals Ltd., 401
Trent University, 1153, 1034
Trent-Severn Waterway, 552
Trenton, 539
Tri Village Regional Sewage Services, 758
Tri-Arrow Industrial Recovery Inc., 401
Triangle Fluid Controls Ltd., 401
Trihedral Engineering Limited, 401
Trillium Gift of Life Network, 628

Trillium Health Centre-Mississauga Site, 1145
Trimax Residuals Management Inc., 401
Trinity Western University, 1113, 1031
Triple M Fiberglass Mfg. Ltd., 401
Triple M Metal, 402
Triton Consultants Ltd., 402
Triton Engineering Services Ltd., 402
Triton Environmental Consultants Ltd., 1116, 402
Trivalent Data Systems Ltd., 402
Trivar Inc., 402
TriWaste Services Inc., 402
Trois-Rivières, 517, 745
Trois-Rivières Branch, 514
Trojan Technologies Inc., 402
Trout Unlimited Canada, 1013
Trow Consulting Engineers Ltd., 403
Troy-Ontor Inc., 404
Truck Loggers Association, 1014
Truro, 537, 696
Truro Branch, 513
Truro Campus, 1137
Trux Route Management Systems Inc., 404
Try Recycling Inc., 404
TTA Technology Training Associates Ltd., 404
Tuktut Nogait National Park of Canada, 557
Tunnelling Association of Canada, 1014
TurboSonic Inc., 404
Turcal, 404
Turkstra Mazza Associates, 1069
Turner Foundation, Inc., 1041
Turtle Island Recycling Co., 404
Twin Falls Limited Partnership, 404
Twin Falls Power Corporation, 601
Two Hills Regional Waste Management Commission, 758
2cg Inc., 404
2R Services Inc., 404
Tyler Research Instruments Corp., 404

U

U-pak Disposal Ltd., 405
U.S. Filter/Asdor Ltd., 405
U.S. Green Building Council, 1016
U.S. Steel Canada, 1141
Ukkusiksalik National Park of Canada, 557
Ukraine, 769
Ultra-Chem Industries Ltd., 405
UMA Engineering Ltd., 1106
UMA Group Ltd., 405
Underwater Archaeological Society of British Columbia, 1014
Underwriters' Laboratories of Canada, 405
UNEP - World Conservation Monitoring Centre, 1014
Unies Limited, 405
UniFold Shelters Ltd., 405
Unilever Canada Foundation, 1045
Union Carbide/Pétromont, 1176
Union des cultivateurs franco-ontariens, 1014
Union des municipalités du Québec, 1014
Union des producteurs agricoles, 1014
Union Gas Ltd., a Duke Energy Company, 1140
Union internationale des architectes, 1014
Union mondiale pour la nature - Bureau de Montréal, 1014
Union of British Columbia Municipalities, 1014, 1116
Union of Nova Scotia Municipalities, 1015
Union québécoise pour la conservation de la nature, 1180
Unisearch Associates Inc., 405
United Arab Emirates, 769
United Kingdom of Great Britain & Northern Ireland, 769
United Mexican States, 768
United Nations Association in Canada, 1015
United Nations Conference on Trade & Development, 1015
United Nations Development Program, 1015
United Nations Environment Programme, 1217, 1015
United Nations Environment Programme - Convention on Biological Diversity, 1176
United Nations Industrial Development Organization, 1015
United Oil Services, 406
United Republic of Tanzania, 769
United Safety Ltd., 406
United States Embassy in Canada, 532
United States Section, 545
Universal Drum Reconditioning Company, 406
Universal Filter Media, 406
Universal Handling Equipment Company Limited, 406
Universal Industries, 406

Université d'Ottawa, 1152
Université de Hearst, 1141
Université de l'Alberta Bibliothèque Saint-Jean, 1107
Université de Moncton, 1129
Université de Montréal, 1176
Université de Sherbrooke, 1185
Université du Québec, 1211, 1212, 406
Université du Québec à Chicoutimi, 1166
Université du Québec à Montréal, 1212, 1176
Université du Québec à Rimouski, 1181, 1035
Université du Québec à Trois-Rivières, 1186, 1035
Université du Québec École de technologie supérieure, 1176
Université du Québec en Abitibi-Témiscamingue, 1182
Université du Québec INRS - Institut Armand-Frappier, 1169
Université du Québec Institut national de la recherche scientifique, INRS-Urbanisation, Culture et Société, 1180, 1176
Université Laval, 1181
Université Sainte-Anne, 1134
University College of the Fraser Valley, 1110
University College of the North, 1122
University Health Network, 1163
University Map Library, 1154, 1164
University of Alberta, 1107, 1029
University of Alberta Dept. of Physiology, 1107
University of Alberta Dept. of Rural Economy, 1107
University of Alberta J.P. Das Developmental Disabilities Centre, 1107
University of Alberta School of Native Studies, 1107
University of British Columbia, 1119
University of British Columbia (UBC), 1031, 1032
University of Calgary, 1103, 1029
University of Guelph, 1209, 1140
University of Guelph Collège d'Alfred, 1138
University of Guelph Kemptville College, 1142
University of Guelph Ridgetown Campus, 1153
University of Lethbridge, 1108, 1029
University of Manitoba, 1033
University of Manitoba Libraries, 1125
University of New Brunswick, 1204, 1128
University of Northern British Columbia (UNBC) & University of British Columbia (UBC), 1115, 1032
University of Ottawa, 1209, 1210, 1034
University of Prince Edward Island, 1211, 1166, 1034
University of Regina, 1212, 1035
University of Regina Library, 1189
University of Saskatchewan, 1191, 406, 1035
University of Sudbury, 1155
University of Toronto, 1210
University of Toronto at Mississauga, 1145
University of Toronto Innis College, 1163
University of Toronto Libraries, 1163
University of Toronto Massey College, 1163
University of Toronto Scarborough Library, 1163
University of Victoria (UVic), 1032
University of Victoria Libraries, 1121
University of Victoria School of Health Information Science, 1121
University of Waterloo, 1210, 1164, 1034
University of Western Ontario Dept. of Geography, 1144
University of Western Ontario Libraries, 1144
University of Windsor, 1210, 1165
The University of Winnipeg, 1033
University of Winnipeg, 1125
University Technologies International, 406
UNOTEC, 407
Unterman McPhail Associates, 407
UPI Inc., 407
Upper Lakes Environmental Research Network, 1210
Upper Thames River Conservation Authority, 1015
Urban & Regional Information Systems Association, 1015
Urban Development Institute of Canada, 1016
Urban Ecology Centre of Montréal, 407
Urban Impact Recycling Ltd., 407
Urban Municipal Administrators' Association of Saskatchewan, 1016
Urban Pest Management Council of Canada, 1016
Urban Strategic Initiatives, 589
Urban Systems Ltd., 407
Urecon Ltée, 408
Urgel Delisle & Associés inc., 408
Urgences-santé Québec, 652
URS Canada Inc., 408
US Commercial Service in Canada, 532
USC Canada, 1217
Utility Risk Management Ltd., 408
UV Pure Technologies, 408

Uxbridge, 731
Uxbridge Conservation Association, 1016

V

V. Fournier & Associates, 408
V.J. Rice Concrete Ltd., 408
Vacuum Products Canada Inc., 408
Val d'Or, 530
Val Temp Sales Ltd., 409
Val-d'Or, 746
Le Val-St-François, 749
Vale Inco, 1163
Valerie Falls Limited Partnership, 409
Valhalla Wilderness Society, 1016
Valley Associates Inc., 409
Valley Comfort Systems Inc., 409
Valley Solid Waste Commission, 759
Valley Waste Resource Management, 409
Valleys North, 585
The Van Horne Institute for International Transportation & Regulatory Affairs, 1016
Vanbots Construction Corp., 409
Vancouver, 685
Vancouver Aquarium Marine Science Centre, 1119
Vancouver Branch, 512
Vancouver City Savings Credit Union, 1041
Vancouver Coastal Health Authority, 1119
Vancouver Community College, 1119
Vancouver Community Services Group, 1119
Vancouver Electric Vehicle Association, 1016
Vancouver Foundation, 1041
Vancouver Fraser Port Authority, 409
Vancouver Gear Works Ltd., 409
Vancouver Island, 517
Vancouver Island University, 1032, 1033
Vancouver Museum, 1119
Vancouver Regional Construction Association, 1016
VanDusen Botanical Garden Association, 1016
VanDusen Gardens Library, 1119
Vanport Sterilizers Inc., 409
Vansco Electronics Ltd., 409
Vanscoy & District Agricultural Society, 1016
Varcon Inc., 409
Varennes, 746
Varian Canada Inc., 410
Vaudreuil-Dorion, 540, 746
Vaudreuil-Soulanges, 753
Vaughan, 722
Vaughan Branch, 513
Vecteur Environnement, 1194
Vegetable Growers' Association of Manitoba, 1016
Vegewax Candleworx Ltd., 410
Vehicle Safety & Carrier Services, 570
Velan Inc., 410
Vemco Ltd., 410
Venables Machine Works Ltd., 410
Venerus International Purification Inc., 410
Venmar CES, Inc., 410
Venmar Ventilation Inc., 410
Ventax Robot Inc., 410
Ventes Techniques Nimatec inc., 411
Venture Foam Products Inc., 411
Veolia ES Canada Industrial Services Inc., 411
Veolia Water Canada, 412
Verdyol Mulch of Canada Ltd., 412
Vermilion Forks Field Naturalists, 1016
Vermilion River Naturalist Club, 1016
Verner, 620
Vernon, 685
Vernon Campus, 1120
Versatech Industries Inc., 412
Versatech Products Inc., 412
Versatile Measuring Instruments Inc., 412
Vestar, 412
Vestas Canada, 413
Via Disposal Services Ltd., 413
VIA Rail Canada Inc., 560
Via-Sat Data Systems, 413
Vibec International Inc., 413
Victaulic Co. of Canada Ltd., 413
Victoria, 628, 685
Victoria Branch, 512
Victoria Foundation, 1041
Victoria General Hospital (Winnipeg), 1126

Entry Name Index

Victoria Lapidary & Mineral Society, 1017
Victoria Natural History Society, 1017
Victoria Orchid Society, 1017
Victoriaville, 746
Viessmann Manufacturing Company Inc., 413
Vineland, 620
The Vinyl Institute, 1017
VIQUA - A Trojan Technologies Company, 413
Virden, 591
Viridis Environmental Inc., 413
Vision Quest - TransAlta's Wind Business, 413
Vision Quest Windelectric Inc., 414
Visionwall Corporation, 414
Vitafoam Products Canada Ltd., 414
Vital Statistics, 616, 606, 580
Vital Statistics Division, 600
Viterra Inc., 414
Vizon SciTec Inc., 414
Voghel Inc., 414
Voice Construction Ltd., 414
Voteforenvironment, 1217
Voyageur Trail Association, 1017
VQUIP Inc., 414
Vulcan & District Fish & Game Club, 1017
Vulcan District Waste Commission, 758
Vuntut National Park of Canada, 557
VWR International, LLC, 414

W

The W. Garfield Weston Foundation, 1017, 1045
W. Ralston (Canada) Inc., 414
W. Sodin (Gravity) Ltd., 414
W.B. Beatty & Associates, 414
W.D. Cookson Ltd., 415
W.F. Baird & Associates Coastal Engineers Ltd., 415
W.G. Shaw & Associates, 415
W.J. Sheldrick Sanitation Ltd., 415
W.K. Kellogg Health Sciences Library, 1137
W.L. Whelan Environmental Consultants Ltd., 415
W.R. Graham Services Ltd., 415
W.T. McGinn & Associates Ltd., 415
Wabush, 604
Wainbee Limited, 415
Wakefield Acoustics Ltd., 416
Walinga Inc., 416
Walker Industries Holdings Ltd., 416
Walker Technologies Corporation, 416
Walker, Nott, Dragicevic Associates Limited, 1163
Walkerton, 539
Walkerton Clean Water Centre, 624
Wallace Meschishnick Clackson Zawada, 1091
Wallace, Van Egmond Spankie Inc., 416
Wallaceburg, 539
Walsh Wilkins Creighton LLP, 1054
Walter & Duncan Gordon Foundation, 1045
Walter Dow Associates Ltd., 416
Walter Hitschfeld Geographic Information Centre, 1177
Wanuskewin Heritage Park, 657
Wapusk National Park of Canada, 557
Warco Process Technologies, 416
Ward Chemical, 416
Ward Chipman Library, 1129
Wardrop Engineering Inc., 416
Warmer Bulletin - Residua Ltd., 1017
Warren Tettensor Amantea LLP, 1054
Warren's Imaging & Dryography Inc., 417
Wasaga Beach, 722
Wascana Recycling & Resource Recovery Corp., 417
Waskada, 591
Waste Alternatives Inc., 417
Waste Logic Inc., 417
Waste Management of Canada, 417
Waste Management Policy Branch, 625
Waste Opportunities Inc., 420
Waste Resource Containers, 420
Waste Services (CA) Inc., 420
Wasteco, 421
Wastequip Cusco, 421
Waswanipi Cree Model Forest, 1017
Water & Climate Impacts Research Centre, 1203
Water & Earth Science Associates Ltd., 421
Water & Wastewater Branch, 612
Water Conservation Company Ltd., 421
Water Environment Association of Ontario, 1017

Water Environment Federation, 1017
Water Management Division, 639
Water Matrix, 421
Water Pik Canada, 422
Water Policy Branch, 625
Water Resource Consultants Ltd., 422
Water Resources, 599
Water Science & Technology, 524
The Water Shed, 393
Water Stewardship Division, 578
The Waterbird Society, 1018
WaterCan, 1018
Waterford Group, 422
Waterfront Development Corporation Ltd., 610
Waterfront Regeneration Trust, 1163
Waterline Environmental Inc., 422
Waterloo, 628, 722, 704
Waterloo Barrier Inc., 422
Waterloo Biofilter Systems Inc., 422
Waterloo Concrete Products, 422
Waterloo Evaporateurs Inc., 422
Waterloo Regional Heritage Foundation, 1018
Waterous Power Systems, 422
Waterra Pumps Limited, 423
Waters Limited, 423
Watershed Sentinel, 1194
Waterstone Law Group LLP, 1056
Waterton Lakes National Park of Canada, 557
Waterton Natural History Association, 1018
Watson & Associates Economists Ltd., 423
Watson Petroleum Services Ltd., 423
Watson Process Systems, 423
Watts, Griffis & McOuat Limited, 1163
Wavefront Technology Solutions Inc., 423
Wawa, 632
WDA Consultants Inc., 423
Weather & Environmental Monitoring, 524
Weather & Environmental Prediction & Services, 524
Weaver, Simmons LLP, 1072
Web Engineering Ltd., 423
Weed Science Society of America, 1018
The Weeden Foundation, 1042
Weiler, Maloney, Nelson, 1072
Weir Power & Industrial, 424
WeirFoulds LLP, 1081
Well To Wire Emissions Control Inc., 424
Welland, 539, 722
Wellington, 628, 540, 705
Wellington North, 732
Wellmaster Pipe & Supply, 424
Wellness, Sport, & Community Development, 598
Wellons Canada, 424
Wentworth, 628
Wenvor Technologies Inc., 424
West & Central Africa, 544
West Coast Environmental Law Research Foundation, 1018, 1119, 1041
West Coast Spill Supplies Ltd., 424
West Elgin Nature Club, 1018
West Grey, 732
West Kootenay Naturalists Association, 1018
West Lincoln, 732
West Nipissing, 732
West Penetone Inc., 424
West Point Products Canada, 424
West Prince, 637
West Vancouver, 689
Wesman Salvage, 425
West, 592
West-Lock Fastener Corp., 425
Westburne Canada, 425
Westchem Mfg. Ltd., 429
Westech Industrial Ltd., 429
Westeel, 429
Westend Regional Sewage Services, 758
Western, 602, 599, 586, 614, 612, 518, 520
Western Bio Resources Consulting Ltd., 429
Western Canada Tire Dealers Association, 1018
Western Canada Water, 1019
Western Canada Wilderness Committee, 1217, 1019
Western Canadian Shippers' Coalition, 1019
Western Canadian Spill Services Ltd., 429
Western Development Museum, 657, 1191
Western Economic Diversification Canada, 562
Western Employers Labour Relations Association, 1019

Western Health Care Corporation, 1131
Western Industrial Services Ltd., 429
Western Red Cedar Lumber Association, 1019
Western Region - South Shore Health, South West Health, Annapolis Valley Health, 613
Western Retail Lumber Association, 1019
Western Scrap Metals, 429
Western Silvicultural Contractors' Association, 1019
Western Site Technologies Inc., 430
Western Solutions 2000 Ltd., 430
Western Subsea Technology Ltd., 430
Western Transportation Advisory Council, 1019
Westest, 430
The Westford Group Inc., 393
Westhoff Engineering Resources Inc., 430
Westland Plastics Ltd., 430
Westland Resource Group Inc., 430
Westlock Regional Waste Management Commission, 758
Westmorland-Albert Solid Waste Corporation, 759
Westmount Campus, 1107
Westport Innovations Inc., 430
Westra & Associates Inc., 430
Westworth Associates Environmental Ltd., 430
Wetaskiwin, 674
Wetaskiwin County No. 10, 670
Weyburn, 540
Weyburn Agricultural Society, 1019
Weyburn Wildlife Federation, 1019
Weyerhaeuser Company Ltd., 430
whatIf? Technologies Inc., 431
Wheatland Regional Centre Inc. & SARCAN Recycling, 431
Wheelabrator Canada Co., 431
Whisco Ltd., 431
Whitby, 530, 723
Whitchurch-Stouffville, 723
Whitchurch-Stouffville Recycling Group, 1019
White Rock, 686
Whitecourt Fish & Game Association, 1019
Whitecourt Power Limited Partnership, 431
Whitehorse, 755
Whitehorse General Hospital, 533
Whitman Benn Group, 431
WHMIS Inc., 431
Whole Village, 1019
Wickwire Holm, 1068
Wiebe Environmental Services Inc., 431
Wilbur & Wilbur, 1065
Wilcorp Manufacturing, 431
Wild Bird Care Centre, 1020
Wild Rose Agricultural Producers, 1020
Wild Rose Foundation, 573
Wilderness Canoe Association, 1020
Wilderness Tourism Association, 1020
Wildlife, 606
Wildlife & Ecosystem Protection, 587
Wildlife & Landscape Science, 525
Wildlife conservation Society Canada, 1217
Wildlife Division, 599, 615
Wildlife Habitat Canada, 1020
Wildlife Haven Rehabilitation Centre, 1020
Wildlife Management, 618
Wildlife Preservation Canada, 1217, 1020
Wildlife Rescue Association of British Columbia, 1020
Wilfrid Laurier University, 1210, 1211, 1165
Wilkinson Heavy Precast Ltd., 431
William Alexander & Associates Ltd., 432
The William and Flora Hewlett Foundation, 1041
William C. Wonders Map Collection, 1107
William Dam Seeds Ltd., 432
William R. Lederman Law Library, 1143
William R. Newman Library, 1126
Williams Engineering Inc., 432
Williams Lake, 686
Williams Lake Campus, 1121
Williams Lake Field Naturalists, 1020
Williams Milton Roy, 432
Willis Energy Services Ltd., 432
Willms & Shier Environmental Lawyers LLP, 1081
Willms Construction Ltd., 432
Willow Beach Field Naturalists, 1020
Willow Creek Regional Waste Management Services Commission, 758
Willowglen Systems Inc., 432
Wilmot, 732
Wilson Laycraft, 1054

Entry Name Index

Winchurch Environmental Inc., 432
Wind Energy Institute of Canada, 639, 432
Wind Energy Solutions Canada, 432
Wind Power Inc., 433
Windfall Ecology Centre, 1021
Windigo Interim Planning Board, 631
Winds & Voices Environmental Services Inc., 433
Windsor, 537, 723
Windsor Barrel & Drum Ltd., 433
Windsor Branch, 513
Windsor Pump Co. Ltd., 433
Windsor Regional Hospital - Metropolitan Campus, 1165
Winnipeg, 690
Winnipeg Branch, 512
Winnipeg Centre, 536
Winnipeg Foundation, 1042
Winnipeg Northeast, 536
Winnipeg Research Centre, 1126
Winnipeg St. Boniface, 536
Winnipeg Southwest, 536
Winnipeg Tax Centre, 517
Winnipeg Water & Waste Dept., 1126
Winnipeg West Branch, 512
Wishart Law Firm LLP, 1071
Wittmann Canada, Inc., 433
WJF Instrumentation (1990) Ltd., 433
Wolch, Hursh, deWit & Watts, 1054
Women & Environments International Magazine, 1194
Women's College Hospital, 1163
Women's Environment & Development Organization, 1021
Women's Healthy Environments Network, 1021
Wood Buffalo, 670
Wood Buffalo Environmental Association, 1021
Wood Buffalo National Park of Canada, 557
Wood Energy Technology Transfer Inc., 1021
Wood Laboratory Ltd., 433
Wood Manufacturing Council, 1021
Wood Preservation Canada, 1021
Woodington Systems Inc., 433
Woodside National Historic Site of Canada, 554
Woodstock, 539, 723
Woodstock Campus, 1165
Woodstock Campus, Library, 1130
Woodstock Field Naturalists, 1021
Woodward & Company, 1063
Woodward Biomedical Library, 1119
Woolwich, 732
Workers' Advisers Program, 612
Workers' Compensation Appeal Tribunal, 581
Workers' Compensation Board, 581
Workers' Compensation Board Northwest Territories, 1134
Workers' Compensation Board of Alberta, 1107
Workers' Compensation Board of British Columbia, 584
Workers' Compensation Board of Nova Scotia, 612, 617
Workforce Planning Branch, 660
Workforce Planning Office, 624
Workforce Supports Division, 566
WorkLab Inc., 433
Workplace Hazardous Materials Information System, 534
Workplace Health & Public Safety, 534
Workplace Health, Safety & Compensation Commission of New Brunswick, 595, 598
Workplace Safety & Health Division, 590
Workplace Safety & Insurance Board, 629, 636
Workplace Skills, 541
Workplace Standards Division, 566
Workplace Technology Services, 581
Works Branch, 604
World Agroforestry Centre, 1021
World Aquaculture Society, 1021
World Association of Industrial & Technological Research Organizations, 1021
The World Bank Group, 532
World Blue Chain for the Protection of Animals & Nature, 1021
World Business Council for Sustainable Development, 1021
World Coal Institute, 1022
World Ecology Enviro Store Ltd., 433
World Energy Council, 1022
World Environment Library, 1217
World Federalist Movement, 1022
World Federation of Ukrainian Engineering Societies, 1022
World Fuel Cell Council, 1022
World Future Society, 1022
World Health Organization, 1022
World Meteorological Organization, 1022
World Nuclear Association, 1022
World Organization of Building Officials, 1022
World Packaging Organization, 1023
World Petroleum Congress, 1023
World Resources Institute, 1023
World Safety Organization, 1023
World Society for Ekistics, 1023
World Society for the Protection of Animals, 1023
World Wildlife Fund - Canada, 1023
World Wildlife Fund - USA, 1023
World Wildlife Fund Canada, 1217
Worldware Enterprises Ltd., 433
Worldwatch Institute, 1217, 1023
WorleyParsons Canada Ltd., 433
WORX Environmental Products Inc., 434
Wotherspoon Environmental Inc., 434
Woznuk Brothers Ltd., 434
WPI Safety & Environmental Consultants, 434
WRS Environmental, 434
WSH Laboratories Ltd., 434
WWF International, 1024
WWOOF Canada, 1024
Wyckomar Inc., 434
Wynn's Canada Ltd., 435
Wynyard, 540

X

XCG Consultants Ltd., 435
Xeneca Power Development Inc., 435
Xerox Canada Ltd., 435
Xerox Research Centre of Canada, 1146
Xylon Biotechnologies Ltd., 435

Y

Yarmouth, 537
Yarmouth Branch, 513
Yarmouth District, 698
Yellowknife, 695
Yellowknife Branch, 512
Yellowquill College, 1126
YES Environment Technologies Inc., 435
Yoho National Park of Canada, 557
York, 705
York Disposal Service Ltd., 435
York Factory National Historic Site of Canada, 557
York Fluid Controls Ltd., 435
York Redoubt National Historic Site of Canada, 554
York Region, 628
York University, 1211, 1034
York University Glendon College Campus, 1163
York University Libraries, 1164
York-Durham, 625
Yorkton, 755
Young, Anderson, 1062
Youth Challenge International, 1024
Yugo-Tech, 435
Yukon, 542
Yukon Branches, 514
Yukon Chamber of Mines, 1024, 1191
Yukon College, 1036, 1212, 1191
Yukon College Northern, 1036
Yukon Community Services, 663
Yukon Conservation Society, 1024, 1191
Yukon Dept. of Energy, Mines & Resources, 1191
Yukon Dept. of Environment, 1191
Yukon Development Corporation, 664
Yukon Economic Development, 664
Yukon Energy Corporation, 664
Yukon Energy Solutions Centre, 1191
Yukon Energy, Mines & Resources, 664
Yukon Environment, 665
Yukon Environmental Network, 1217, 1024
Yukon Finance, 666
Yukon Fish & Game Association, 1024
Yukon Fish & Wildlife Management Board, 665
Yukon Geological Survey, 665
Yukon Health & Social Services, 666
Yukon Highways & Public Works, 666
Yukon Land Use Planning Council, 665
Yukon Lottery Commission, 663
Yukon Motor Transport Board, 666
Yukon Public Health Association, 1024
Yukon Public Legal Education Association, 1024
Yukon Tourism & Culture, 667
Yukon Tourism Education Council, 1024
Yukon Workers' Compensation Health & Safety Board, 667, 1192

Z

Z-Tech/Geogard Inc., 435
Zazula Process Equipment Ltd., 436
Zbeetnoff Agro-Environmental Consulting, 436
ZCL Composites Inc., 436
Zell Oilfield Service Ltd., 436
Zep Manufacturing Company of Canada, 436
Zephyr Alternative Power, 437
Zephyr North, 437
Zeton Inc., 437
Zimmark Inc., 437
Zodiac Fabrics Inc., 437
Zoocheck Canada, 1217
ZOOCHECK Canada Inc., 1025
Zoological Society of Manitoba, 1025
Zoological Society of Montréal, 1025
Zorbit Technologies Inc., 437
Zurn Industries Limited, 437

Executive Name Index

A

Aaslepp, Rein, Manager, Nemato Inc., 300
Abbot, Sue, Vice-President, Nature Nova Scotia (Federation of Nova Scotia Naturalists), 960
Abbott, Bill, Manager, TEAM-1 Environmental Services Inc., 387
Abbott, Duncan A., Mississippi Mills, 714
Abbott, George, Minister, 580
Abbott, Jim, Parliamentary Secretary to the Minister of Interna, 519
Abbott, John, Executive Vice-President, Shell Canada Limited, 365
Abbott, Rob, CEO, Canadian Genetic Diseases Network, 869
Abbott, Rob, Founder, Abbott Strategies, 64
Abbott, Wade, General Manager, Atlantic Industries Ltd., 95
Abdel-Aziz, Ahab, Partner, Heenan Blaikie LLP - Toronto, 1075
Abdel-Barr, B.Comm., J.D., Khaled S., Partner, Lawson Lundell LLP - Vancouver, 1060
Abdula, Amyn M., Stikeman Elliott LLP - Vancouver, 1062
Abel, John, Aurora, 706
Abernethy, Jim, Mayor, Clarington, 724
Abeytunga, Patabendi K., Vice-President, 517
Ableson, Serena, Assistant Law Librarian, Akitsiraq Law School, Diana M. Priestly Law Library, 1120
Abouchar, Juli, Willms & Shier Environmental Lawyers LLP, 1081
Abraham, Brian E., Fraser Milner Casgrain LLP - Vancouver, 1060
Abrahamson, Randy, Manager, Mifab Canada, 289
Abrams, Gary, President, Schneider Electric Canada Inc., 359
Abrams, Jeffrey A., City Clerk, Vaughan, 722
Abushawashi, Salem, Superintendent, Wood Buffalo, 780-697-3600, 670
Abusow, Kathy, President & Chief Executive Officer, Sustainable Forestry Initiative, 1011
Abutaleb, Nikki, Office Administrator, Island Clean Air Inc., 248
Abzinger, Sue, Manager, Medical Library, Royal Columbian Hospital - Simon Fraser Health Authority, 1114
Accettone, Paolo, Project Engineer, Safety Plus Inc., 355
Accursi, Gary, Pelham, 717
Acharya Van Horne, Sheila, Borden Ladner Gervais LLP - Calgary, 1049
Achenbach, Heidi, Manager, Hants East District, 902-758-2299, 697
Ackerman, Hy, President, Metro Recycling, 287
Ackles-Dold, Simon C., Associate, Genus Loci Ecological Landscapes Inc., 210
Acorn, Joe, Chair, 608
Acquaah, Paul, Manager, Dillon Consulting Ltd., 163
Acre, Lynn, Elgin, 699
Acton, Bill, President/CEO, Parkson Corporation, 319
Acton, Dale, Managing Director, Nu-West Services Ltd., 309
Acton, Gordon P., Wishart Law Firm LLP, 1071
Acton, Kevin, Manager, SARCAN Recycling, 358
Adair, David, Owen Sound, 717
Adam, Arlene, Librarian, Saskatchewan Watershed Authority, 1187
Adam, Colin, Branch Manager, McElhanney Consulting Services Ltd., 285
Adam, Gerry, Fire Chief, Oak Bay, 250-592-9121, 688
Adam, Howard, President, SustaiNet Software Solutions Inc., 206, 384
Adam, Robert-André, Associé, Cain Lamarre Casgrain Wells - Val-d'Or, 1089
Adam, Sylvie, Saint-Hyacinthe, 742
Adams, Eve, Peel, 714, 703
Adams, Gord, District Chair, Muskoka, 702
Adams, John, Deputy Warden, Essex, 519-326-7010, 699
Adams, John M., Mayor, Leamington, 726
Adams, Joseph L., Vice-President/Manager, Sleegers Engineering Inc., 370
Adams, K., Carrier Canada Ltd., 129
Adams, Karen, Director of Libraries, University of Manitoba Libraries, 1125
Adams, Karen, Director, Library Services & Information Resources, University of Alberta, 1107
Adams, Mark A., Sr. Project Manager, ECL Envirowest Consultants Ltd., 170
Adams, Maureen, General Manager, Financial Services, Cornwall, 708
Adams, Muriel, Acting General Manager, Ag-West Bio Inc., 72
Adams, Patricia, President, Energy Probe Research Foundation, 1157
Adams, Richard H.G., Thompson Dorfman Sweatman LLP, 1064
Adams, Rob, Dufferin, 699
Adams, Rob, Mayor, Orangeville, 716
Adams, Stephen, Councillor, Halifax Regional Municipality, 695
Adams, Tom, Halton, 700
Adams, Tom, Executive Director, Energy Probe Research Foundation, 1157
Adams, Tom, Town & Regional Councillor, Oakville, 715
Adams, Tracy, Director, Corporate Communications & Marketing, Oshawa, 716
Adams, Virginia, Dept Head, Library Public Services, Vancouver Community College, 1119
Adams, William, President, Estco Battery Management Inc., 190
Adamson, Dan, General Manager, McGregor Model Forest, 952
Adamson, Lee, Manager, International Maritime Organization, 941
Adamson, Shona, Sr. Consultant, INDECO Strategic Consulting Inc., 240
Adamson, Susanne, Terralog Technologies Inc., 390
Adams-Webber, Thomasin, Systems & Clinical Services Librarian, Hospital for Sick Children, 1158
Adant, Pierre, Responsable, Bibliothèque des sciences et de génie, 1185
Adant, Pierre, Responsable, Bibliothèque sciences et génie, Université de Sherbrooke, 1186
Addario, Martin J., Partner, Hicks Morley Hamilton Stewart Storie LLP, 1076
Addison, Emily, Membership Coordinator, Ontario Society for Environmental Education, 978
Addurahman, Ross, Manager, Ferguson Simek Clark, 194
Addy, John, President, Addy Environmental Services Inc., 68
Adelaar, Martin, Principal/Secretary, Marbek Resource Consultants Ltd., 280
Adey, Sheldon, Conestoga-Rovers & Associates, 149
Adkin, Rob, Secretary-Treasurer, Freshwater Fisheries Society of British Columbia, 920
Adkins, Robert J.M., Thompson Dorfman Sweatman LLP, 1064
Adkins, Sam, McCarthy Tétrault LLP - Vancouver, 1061
Adkins, Tom, Director, Emerson Electric Canada Limited, 177
Adkinson, Donald, President/CEO, Adkinson & Associates, 68
Adolfo, Quesada, Trade Commissioner, 767
Adrien, Michel, Maire, Mont-Laurier, 738
Ady, Cindy, Associate Minister, 572
Afanasiev, Victor B., President/CEO, Aeroflo Inc., 71
Afatsawo, Laura, Library Technician, University College of the North, 1122
Agar, Glen W., Thompson Dorfman Sweatman LLP, 1064
Agar, Jeff, St. Clair, 519-862-5062, 729
Agbeti, Michael, Principal, Bio-Limno Research & Consulting, 108
Aggas, Roger, Registrar, Registered Professional Foresters Association of Nova Scotia, 994
Aghjayan, Ara, Comptroller, Conterm Inc., 151
Agioritis, John, MacPherson Leslie & Tyerman LLP - Saskatoon, 1090
Aglukkaq, Leona, Minister, Health, 533
Agnew, Jocelyne, Bibliotechnicienne, La Cité Collégiale, 1151
Agnolin, Jennifer, Willms & Shier Environmental Lawyers LLP, 1081
Agre, Peter C., Chair, American Association for the Advancement of Science, 822
Agyar, Hakan, Senior Quality Assurance Advisor, The Lowe-Martin Group, 392
Ahearn, Margaret, Chief, CANMET Information Centre, CANMET Information Centre, 1149
Ahearn, Margaret, Head Librarian, Natural Resources Canada, 1151
Ahearn, Margaret, Head of Library, Energy, Minerals & Metals Information Centre, 1150
Ahern, Steve, Baie-Comeau, 418-296-2245, 733
Ahmed, Fatimah, Librarian, The Scarborough Hospital - Grace Campus, 1162
Ahuja, Hira, President, Educational Program Innovations Centre, 173
Ahuja, Kelley, Chief Administrative Officer, Institute of Food Technologists, 933

Ai Hue, Zhang, General Manager, Brampton Engineering Inc., 115
Aikenhead, Sherri, Director, 614
Aikens, Ann, Renfrew, 613-584-2000, 704
Aikens, John, Head, 596
Aime, Rachelle, Vice-President, Manitoba Wildlife Federation, 952
Ainley, Simon, Chairman, Ainley Group, 74
Ainley, William M., Senior Partner, Davies Ward Phillips & Vineberg LLP, 1074
Ainscough, Brian, Contact, All Waste Removal Inc., 78
Ainsley, Johanne, Directeur, Westburne Canada, 426
Ainsley, Mike P., Vice-President, Ainley Group, 74
Ainslie, Paul, Toronto, 721
Ainsworth, Bonnie J., Barrie, 706
Aird, Judy, Volunteer Director, VanDusen Botanical Garden Association, 1016
Aitchison, Scott, District & Town Councillor, Huntsville, 711
Aitken, Elizabeth, Acting Regional Manager, Calgary Health Region, 1099
Aitken, Mark, Chief Administrative Officer, Simcoe, 704
Aitken, Mark, Director, 607
Aiton, Alison, Director, 597
Aiton, David, Manager, 636
Akamphuber, Harry, Manager, Liqui-Box Canada Inc., 272
Akeeagok, David, Deputy Minister, 617
Aker, John, Regional Councillor, Oshawa, 716
Aker, John R., Durham, 699
Akerman, Q.C., John R.M., Burchell, MacDougall, 1068
Akermann, Markus, CEO, World Business Council for Sustainable Development, 1021
Akesuk, Olayuk, Minister, 618
Akin, Kosetorunu, Trade Commissioner, 769
Akpalialuk, Mary, Iqaluit, 698
Akrigg, Dave, Supervisor, Parks Operations, Thorold, 905-227-6544, 720
Alaica, Jake, President, Cancoppas Limited, 126
Alarie, Pierre, Vice-President, 517
Alati, John, Davies Howe Partners, 1074
Alavy, Sam, President & Chief Executive Officer, Canadian Polystyrene Recycling Alliance, 882
Albach, Gary, President, 568
Albanese, Damian, Director, Transportation, Peel, 703
Albanese, Laura, Parliamentary Assistant, 621
Albanese, Michael, President, H2Flow Equipment Inc., 223
Alberico, John, General Manager, RWDI AIR Inc., 354
Albert, Dan, Systems Sales Director, ICC The Compliance Centre Inc., 238
Albert, Jo-Anne, Hastings, 700
Albert, Johanne, Secrétaire, Campus d'Edmundston, 1126
Albert, John, Sales Contact, Rotork Controls (Canada) Ltd., 352
Albert, Martin (Tin), Edmundston, 691
alberta ecotrusaintfounda, Alberta Ecotrust Foundati, Calgary, AB, 1039
Albizzati, Ryan, Chief Financial Officer, Micro-Watt Control Devices Ltd., 289
Albright, Garth A., CFO & Corporate Secretary, Gemcom Software International Inc., 206
Alcott, Bob, Manager, Schwank Group, 359
Alde, Kreg, Matrix Solutions Inc., 282
Alden, Rolph, President, General Paint Ltd., 206
Alder, Sheridan L., Librarian, Southern Crop Protection & Food Research Centre, 1164
Aldred, Richard, Manager, Trivalent Data Systems Ltd., 402
Aldworth, George, President, Aldworth Engineering Inc., 77
Alexander, Dana, Manager, Public Affairs, Canadian Institute of Biotechnology, 1148
Alexander, Earl, Manager, Universal Handling Equipment Company Limited, 406
Alexander, Garry, Project Assessment Director, 578
Alexander, Greg, General Manager, Community Services, Thunder Bay, 807-625-2315, 721
Alexander, Ken, Manager, Bartle & Gibson Co. Ltd., 102
Alexander, Lawrence, Heenan Blaikie LLP - Victoria, 1062
Alexander, Lincoln, Chair, 622
Alexander, Matthew, President, Colour Innovations Print Inc., 146
Alexander, Michael, President, KPMG Performance Registrar Inc., 260

Executive Name Index

Alexander, Pat, Reeve, Clearwater County, 669
Alexander, Scott, Director, 605
Alexander, Stephen, General Manager, Planning, Parks & Recreation Serv, Cornwall, 708
Alexander, Steve, Executive Director, Association of Postconsumer Plastic Recyclers, 837
Alexander, Timothy P., Blaney McMurtry LLP, 1073
Alexanderson, Miguel Benedetto, President, National Association of the Chemistry Industry, 957
Alexandra, Laverdure, Trade Commissioner, 768
Alexandre, Misty, Robertson Stromberg Pedersen LLP, 1091
Alexandrowicz, John-Paul, Partner, Hicks Morley Hamilton Stewart Storie LLP, 1076
Alexeev, Lev, Stikeman Elliott LLP - Montréal, 1087
Aleyaseen, Val, Chair, Society of Professional Engineers & Associates, 1008
Alfieri, Jocelyn, Laboratory Director, Silliker Canada Co., 367
Algeo, Jim, President, WJF Instrumentation (1990) Ltd., 433
Alger, Carmen, Fleming LLP, Barristers & Solicitors, 1051
Algie, Roger H., Owner, Just Homes, 253
Al-Hashimi, Ahmad, Chief Executive Officer, AA Environmental & Associates, 64
Ali, Ashgar, DEB Canada, 159
Ali Khan, Abbas, Fraser Milner Casgrain LLP - Toronto, 1075
Alico, Bill, President/COO, Showa-Best Glove, Inc., 366
Alizadeh, Ala, Vice-President, Marketing & Business Development, 511
Alksnis, John, Sales Manager, National Energy Equipment Inc., 297
Allan, Don, Manager, Engineering Branch, East Gwillimbury, 708
Allan, Kim, Director, Mission, 604-820-3764, 687
Allan, Nancy, Minister, 589
Allan, Philip B., Director, Library Services, Canadian Forces Medical Group Headquarters, 1148
Allan, Ron, Vice-President, TurboSonic Inc., 404
Allan, Steve, Director, Public Works, Lanark, 701
Allan, Steve, Manager, Alberta Recreation & Parks Association, 819
Allard, André, Responsable, Centre hospitalier de l'Université de Montréal Hôtel-Dieu, 1172
Allard, Jean-Luc, Vice President, SNC-Lavalin Environment Inc., 371
Allard, Jeannot, Directeur, Saguenay, 741
Allard, Ken, Superintendent, Thompson, 204-677-7900, 690
Allard, Louis-Paul, Président, Fondation québécoise en environnement, 918
Allard, Louise, Chef, Division du Traitement des fonds documentair, Université Laval, 1181
Allard, Michel, Victoriaville, 819-752-6362, 746
Allard, Paul, Directeur général, Blainville, 450-434-5209, 734
Allard, Remi, President, British Columbia Ground Water Association, 848
Allard, Yves, Controller, Pompco inc., 328
Allard Strutt, Suzanne, Chief Executive Officer, British Columbia Recreation & Parks Association, 849
Allard-Gignac, Josette, Shawinigan, 744
Allas, Toivo, Manager, Metro Vancouver, 678
Allcock, William F., County Manager, Norfolk, 702
Allemano, Gregory O., President/CEO, Ecodyne Ltd., 171
Allen, Barry, President, Souris Valley Industries Ltd., 374
Allen, Brian, Contact, Indachem Inc., 240
Allen, Greg, Senior Associate, Sustainable EDGE Ltd., 383
Allen, Greg J., Alexander Holburn Beaudin & Lang, LLP, 1057
Allen, Ian, Manager, Harris & Roome Supply Limited, 226
Allen, Kim, Chief Building Official, Oro-Medonte, 728
Allen, Mary, Chief Executive Officer, Allergy Asthma Information Association, 821
Allen, Michael S., Partner, Stikeman Elliott LLP - Vancouver, 1062
Allen, Neil, Ciculation Supervisor, Engineering & Computer Science Library, 1157
Allen, Paul, Vice-President, Stantec Inc., 378
Allen, Peter L., President/CEO, Thermo Dynamics Ltd., 394
Allen, Scott, Engineer, Enervac Corp., 180
Allen, Scott, Vice President, Enervac Corp., 180
Allen, Terry, Commissioner, Fire Services, Cambridge, 707
Allen, Thomas A., Sherbrooke, 744
Allford, R. Bruce, Burnet, Duckworth & Palmer LLP, 1050
Allgaier, Anne, Treasurer & Contact, Health Libraries Association of British Columbia, 928
L'Allier, Renée-Claude, Greffière, Argenteuil, 747
Allingham, Doug, Exec. VP, AECOM Canada Ltd., 69
Allingham, Doug, President, Totten Sims Hubicki Associates Ltd., 399

Allingham, Jana, Library Assistant, Campbell River Campus Library, 1111
Allison, Andrea, Librarian, John B. Ridley Research Library, 1138
Allison, Andrew C., City Solicitor, Pickering, 905-420-4626, 718
Allison, Brad, Biologist, Lakehead University, 263
Allison, G., Director, Building Services & Chief Building Offic, Barrie, 706
Allison, Ken, President, Ottawa Field-Naturalists' Club, 983
Allison, Lawrence, Chief Administrative Officer, Saugeen Shores, 719
Allmand, Warren, Conseiller, Loyola, Montréal, 738
Allsion, Lawrence, Chief Administrative Officer, Innisfil, 711
Almas, Sara J., Clerk, Collingwood, 708
Almond, Simon, Fire Chief, Uxbridge, 905-852-3393, 731
Alsgard, Stewart, Mayor, Powell River, 683
Alter, Matthew R., Partner, Borden Ladner Gervais LLP - Toronto, 1073
Althouse, Dennis, Superintendent, Yellowknife, 867-766-5512, 695
Althouse, Q.C., D. Paul, Partner, Poole Althouse, Barristers & Solicitors, 1065
Alton, Michelle A., Associate, Hicks Morley Hamilton Stewart Storie LLP, 1076
Alvarenga, Rosibel, Contact, Society of Toxicology, 1009
Alvarez, Héctor, Chef des services publics, Université de Moncton, 1129
Alvarez, Pierre, Chair, Canadian Centre for Energy Information, 861
Alves, Ana, Vice-President, Finance & Manager, Tornatech, 397
Alway, Richard M., Chair, 552
Alyea, Alexis, Davis LLP - Toronto, 1074
Alyea, Jim, Quinte West, 613-475-1519, 718
Alyea, Monica, Prince Edward, 703
Alyman, Terry, Director, Recreation & Parks, Halton Hills, 710
Amantea, Joseph B., Partner, Warren Tettensor Amantea LLP, 1054
Amar, Dror, Manager, Sunarc of Canada Inc., 382
Amar, Serge, Associé, Langlois Kronström Desjardins, 1085
Amaroso, Debbie, Mayor, Sault Ste. Marie, 705-759-7550, 720
Amato, Guido, General Manager, Coast Paper Ltd., 145
Amaya, Jauregui, Trade Commissioner, 769
Ambeault, Bruce, Vice-President, Contracts, 511
Amblard, Jody, President, AIC Associated Industrial Controls Ltd., 73
Ambler, Anthony, President, Swish Maintenance Ltd., 384
Ambler, Brian, President, Ambler & Co. Inc., 82
Ambrosone, Giulio, Vice-President, 574
Ambrozy, Samantha, Heenan Blaikie LLP - Toronto, 1075
Ambwani, Virender, Director, 596
Ameln, Maureen Von, Sales Coordinator, SSI Schaefer Systems International Inc., 377
Amerongen, Peter, President, Habitat Studio & Workshop Ltd., 223
Ames, Doris, President, Native Orchid Conservation Inc., 959
Amesse, Normand, Salaberry-de-Valleyfield, 450-371-6895, 744
Amey, Vern, Director, Public Works, Greater Napanee, 709
Amiel, B., President, J. Walter Company Ltd., 249
Amin, Fareed, Deputy Minister, 622
Aminata, Ly Faye, Trade Commissioner, 769
Amnotte, Céline, Directrice, Bibliothèque de droit, 1170
Amorosi, M., Director, Human Resources, Guelph, 710
Amsterdam, Cynthia, Partner, Heenan Blaikie LLP - Toronto, 1051, 1075
Amyot, Denise, President/CEO, 516
Anagnostakos, Louis, President, Turtle Island Recycling Co., 404
Anaka, Mike, PricewaterhouseCoopers Management Consultants, 332
Anawak, Jack, Ambassador for Circumpolar Affairs, Arctic Council, 829
Ancheta, Barbara, Contact, Atlin Campus, 1110
Anctil, Marc André, President, Logiball Inc., 273
Anctil, Martin, Chemical Engineer, Nove Environnement Inc., 309
Andersen, Harold K., Partner, Stikeman Elliott LLP - Calgary, 1053
Anderson, Barry, Supervisor, Westburne Canada, 426
Anderson, Bill, Managing Director, Eco-Tec Ltd., 171
Anderson, Bob, Bathurst, 506-548-3536, 690
Anderson, Bruce L., Executive Director, Human Resources, Toronto, 416-397-4112, 721
Anderson, Bryan, Edmonton, 780-496-8130, 672
Anderson, Clayton, Principal, FWR Ecoresource Consultants Ltd., 203
Anderson, Danny R., Partner, MacPherson Leslie & Tyerman LLP - Saskatoon, 1090

Anderson, Darryl, Specialist, Secter Environmental Resource Consulting, 361
Anderson, David, Wellington, 519-343-3883, 705
Anderson, David, President/CEO, 584
Anderson, Elaine, Research Assistant, 520
Anderson, Ellen, Mayor, Grey, 700
Anderson, Glenn, Branch manager, Gamsby & Mannerow Ltd., 204
Anderson, Glenn, Vice-President, Gamsby & Mannerow Ltd., 204
Anderson, Guy, Councillor, Kincardine, 519-396-3529, 726
Anderson, Ian, President, Kinder Morgan Canada Inc., 257
Anderson, Jack, Regional Sales Manager, REHAU Industries Inc., 344
Anderson, Jim, Director, Cochrane, 403-851-2560, 671
Anderson, John, Triangle Fluid Controls Ltd., 401
Anderson, John, Head of Library, Atlantic Salmon Federation, 1126
Anderson, John F., Partner, Stikeman Elliott LLP - Vancouver, 1062
Anderson, Ken, Director, Grande Prairie, 780-538-0302, 672
Anderson, Leslie, Asst. Deputy Minister, 666
Anderson, Lloyd M., Manager, Crown Fibre Tube Inc., 154
Anderson, Patricia, Director, Suncor Energy Products, 382
Anderson, Paula, Land Administrator, Antelope Land Services Inc., 86
Anderson, Pete, Manager, FS Partners, 202
Anderson, Robert S., Farris, Vaughan, Wills & Murphy LLP, 1059
Anderson, Rodney, Founding President, Environmentalists For Nuclear Energy (Canada) Inc., 913
Anderson, Roger, Regional Chair & Chief Executive Officer, Durham, 699
Anderson, Ron, Councillor, Wasaga Beach, 722
Anderson, Roxanne, PricewaterhouseCoopers Management Consultants, 332
Anderson, Ryan, Treasurer, Ontario Printing & Imaging Association, 977
Anderson, Shannon, General Manager, Peace River, 678
Anderson, Tom, Manager, Cowichan Valley, 677
Anderson, Trevor, Publication Manager, Energy Conservation Contractors Warranty Corporation, 179
Anderson, W. Victor, Executive Vice-President, Delcan Water, 160
Anderson, William A., Sec.-Treas., International Society for Environmental Biotechnology, 942
Anderson, B.A., J.D., Greg W., Anderson, Greg W.. Barrister, Solicitor, Notary, 1071
Anderton, Joan, Chief Administrative Officer, Richmond Hill, 905-771-2505, 718
Andison, Alan, Chair, 577
Andison, Mark, Director, Kootenay Boundary, 678
Andoney, Linda, Coordinator, Environmental Services, Lennox & Addington, 701
Andrahennadi, Ruwandi, President, Entomological Society of Saskatchewan, 911
André, McArdle, Secretary, Canadian Intergovernmental Conference Secretariat, 763
Andreae, Christopher, President, Historica Research Limited, 232
Andreatta, Brenda, Clerk, LaSalle, 713
Andres, Reg J., Vice-President, R.V. Anderson Associates Limited, 341
Andrew, Joan C., Deputy Minister, 621
Andrew, John, Environmental Lab Manager, Stewart Group, 379
Andrew, Murray, Executive Director, Saskatchewan Livestock Association, 1000
Andrew, Tom, Farris Industries Canada, 194
Andrews, Chris, Office Manager, Trow Consulting Engineers Ltd., 403
Andrews, Mark R., Partner, Ottenheimer Baker, 1066
Andrews, Steve, President, Nemato Inc., 300
Andrews, Warren, Manager, Lethbridge, 673
Andrews, Q.C., Robert B., Partner, Ottenheimer Baker, 1066
Andreychuk, Nick, Grimsby, 710
Andrus, Ken, Chief Building Official, Port Hope, 905-885-2415, 728
Andrusiak, Ed, Manager, Metro Vancouver, 678
Andrychuk, Q.C., Leonard D., Partner, MacPherson Leslie & Tyerman LLP - Regina, 1090
Anema, Kim, CAO, Squamish, 604-815-5004, 688
Angelo, Chris, Director, Public Works, Quinte West, 613-392-7151, 718
Angelo, Peter, Director, Public Works, Port Hope, 905-885-2431, 728

Executive Name Index

Angelo, P.Eng., Joe, Manager, Public Works Department Projects, Prince Edward, 703
Angeloni, Denise, Scientific Information Specialist, Ontario Ministry of Environment, 1160
Angelopoulos, Basile, Laval, 736
Angers, Jacques, Director, Genivar, 207
Angers, Luc, Gatineau, 735
Angers, Viviane, Bibliothécaire, Bibliothèque paramédicale, 1171
Angrove, Doug, Fire Chief, Victoria, 250-920-3353, 685
Anguish, Brad, Director, Halifax Regional Municipality, 695
Angus, George, President, Fisher Scientific Ltd., 196
Angus, George, Sr. Vice-President & Chief Operating Officer, Sustainable Development Technology Canada, 1011
Angus, Iain, Councillor at Large, Thunder Bay, 721
Angus, Tim, President, Thermal Energy International Inc., 394
Anic, Predrag, Fleming LLP, Barristers & Solicitors, 1051
Anker, Mark, Manager, North 43 Lagoon Commission, 757, 758
Annand, Jim, Manager, Lunenburg District, 902-541-1325, 697
Annis, Eleanor, Catalogue Librarian, University of Northern British Columbia, 1115
Anseeuw, Paul, Regional Manager, Vestar, 413
Ansell, Peter, Manager, Westburne Canada, 427
Anselmo, Hélène, Supervisor of Processing, Laurentian University, 1155
Anstey, Q.C., B.Sc., LL.B, Wayne, Deputy CAO, Halifax Regional Municipality, 902-490-4426, 695
Antaya, Ken, Mayor, LaSalle, 713
Ante, Lorraine, Vice-President, MEC Systems Inc., 286
Anthony, Annette, Librarian, Northwest Atlantic Fisheries Centre, 1132
Anthony, Leland, Warden, Yarmouth District, 698
Anthony, Mike, North Bay, 715
Anthony, Monica, Office Manager, AMEC, 84
Anthony, Richard, Manager, Kinetics Noise Control Inc., 258
Anthony-Malone, Kristin, Manager, Canadian Avalanche Association, 859
Antill, Sally, Administrator, International WWOOF Association, 946
Antler, Susan, Contact, Rechargeable Battery Recycling Corporation, 343
Antler, Susan, Executive Director, Compost Council of Canada, 899
Anton, Suzanne, Vancouver, 604-873-7248, 685
Antoniw, Karna, Reference Librarian, The King's University College, 1106
Antunes, Fred, Treasurer, Saskatchewan Environmental Industry & Managers' Association, 1000
Anwar, Faisal, Officer, Yorkton, 306-786-1747, 755
Anyaoku, Emeka, President, WWF International, 1024
Apold, Robert, Contact, Natural Forces Technologies Inc., 298
Apon, Fred, Unit Manager, AMEC, 82
Apostle, Nicholas J., Commissioner, Community Services, Sault Ste. Marie, 720
Apostolatos, Gerry, Associé, Langlois Kronström Desjardins, 1085
Appel, Larry, Director, Economic Development, Stratford, 720
Applebaum, Michael, Maire d'arrondissement, Montréal, 738
Applejohn, Andrew, Director, 605
Applejohn, Andrew, Institute Director, Aurora College. Aurora Research Institute, 1133
Appollinaro, Frank, Vice-President, Cannington Group, 126
Apps, Deborah, President & CEO, Trans Canada Trail Foundation, 1013
Apps, Rachel, Library Technician & Publications Officer, Defence R & D Canada - Ottawa, 1149
Aquilina, Dan, Director, Planning & Development, Port Colborne, 718
Aquin, Elizabeth, Senior Vice-President, Petroleum Services Association of Canada, 986
Araujo, Jackie, General Manager, Spruce Grove, 780-962-7617, 674
Arboleda Ramirez, Julio N., Partner, Borden Ladner Gervais LLP - Calgary, 1049
Arbour, Adele, Director, Planning & Building Services, Thorold, 720
Arbour, Dave, Manager, Westburne Canada, 429
Arbour, Lyne, Directrice générale, Matawinie, 750
Arbour, Roch, Directeur, Saint-Jean-sur-Richelieu, 450-357-2238, 742
Arbuckle, Kathryn, Head, John Alexander Weir Memorial Law Library, 1105
Arbuckle, R., Marketing Manager, NEDCO, 299
Arcand, Cliff, Contact, Clemmer Technologies Inc., 143
Arcand, Jean, Pneus Métro Inc., 326
Arcand, Pierre, Ministre, 646

Arcaro, Sherry, Chair, Municipal Waste Association, 955
Arcaro, Sherry, Manager, Environmental Services, Peterborough, 703
Arch, Arlene, Thorold, 720
Archambault, Daniel, Regroupement des associations forestières régionales du Québec, 994
Archambault, Isabelle, Secteur de la consultation, Bibliothèque des sciences humaines et sociales, 1177
Archambault, Jean, Vice President, Roctest Ltée, 350
Archambault, Louis, Président, Entraco, 181
Archambault, Marc, Chef entreposage et exploitation des fonds documen, Hydro-Québec, 1173
Archambault, Peter, Weaver, Simmons LLP, 1072
Archambault, Pierre, Directeur, Longueuil, 737
Archer, Cynthia, University Librarian, York University Libraries, 1164
Archer, Jennifer, Borden Ladner Gervais LLP - Vancouver, 1058
Archer, CMA, Ed, General Manager, Corporate Services, Barrie, 706
Archibald, Alan, Vice-President, Sonic Soil Sampling Inc., 374
Archibald, Bruce, Deputy Minister, 619
Archibald, Dale, President, St Mary's River Association, 998
Archibald, Deborah, Director, 607
Archibald, Helen, Secretary, Blomidon Naturalists Society, 846
Archibald, James, Director, Waste Management, Waterloo, 704
Archibald, Jane, Head, Technical Services, Dalhousie University Libraries, 1135
Archibald, John, President, Sonic Soil Sampling Inc., 374
Archibald, Louise, Senior Library Technician, Pacific Region, 1118
Archibald, Tom, General Manager, Foothills Research Institute, 918
Arcouette, Daniel, President/CEO, Enviro-Systèmes Inc., 183
Arcuri, Ken, Director, Central Okanagan, 250-868-5227, 677
Ardellini, Danny, President/COO, National Waste Services, 298
Arel, Raymond, Préfet, Pierre-De Saurel, 750
Argue, Andrea V., Kanuka Thuringer LLP, Barristers & Solicitors, 1091
Argue, Bob, Executive Director, EcoPerth, 908
Ariens, John, Director of Development, Planning & Engineering Initiatives Ltd., 325
Ariens, John, Vice President, Planning & Engineering Initiatives Ltd., 325
Arisman, Audrey, Executive Director, Western Canada Water, 1019
Arisq, Hans, Manager, Touchie Engineering, 399
Arklie, Sandra, Library Supervisor, Stoney Creek Campus, 1155
Armand, Bernard, Coordonnateur, Saint-Constant, 742
Armeneau, Dwayne, President/CEO, AGM Steel Industries Ltd., 73
Armour, Greg, Field Supervisor, North Okanagan, 678
Armstrong, Allan, North Dundas, 727
Armstrong, Bill, London, 713
Armstrong, Bruce, Fire Chief, Russell, Russell, 729
Armstrong, Bryan, Manager, KC Environmental Group Ltd., 256
Armstrong, Charles A., President/CEO, S.A. Armstrong Limited, 354
Armstrong, Fraser, Site Engineer, Geocor Engineering Inc., 211
Armstrong, J. Craig, Chief Operating Officer & Executive Vice-President, Millar Western Forest Products Ltd., 290
Armstrong, James C., Executive Vice President, S.A. Armstrong Limited, 354
Armstrong, Jeff E., Secretary, Henderson Paddon & Associates Ltd., 229
Armstrong, John F., General Manager, Armstrong Engineering & Land Surveying Inc., 91
Armstrong, Kent, Canadian Divisional Sales Manager, Draeger Safety Canada Ltd., 166
Armstrong, Les, Mayor, Wilmot, 732
Armstrong, Robert, Director, Planning & Building, Meaford, 727
Armstrong, S., Director, Emergency Services, Guelph, 710
Armstrong, Sandra, Librarian, Assiniboine Community College, 1121
Armstrong, Shawn, Fire Chief, Guelph-Eramosa, 519-824-6590, 725
Armstrong, QC, B.A.,M.Sc., Brad, Partner, Lawson Lundell LLP - Vancouver, 1060
Arnaquq, Naullaq, Asst. Deputy Minister, 617
Arnkvarn, Michael, Greatario Industrial Storage Systems Ltd., 217
Arnold, Debra, Director, Legal Services & Regional Solicitor, Waterloo, 704
Arnold, Frank, Associate Financial Advisor, Pinch Group, 324
Arnold, Fred T., ELI Eco Chemical Technologies Inc., 175
Arnold, Fred T., CEO, ELI Eco Chemical Technologies Inc., 175

Arnold, Harriet, Coordinator, Information Research & Instruction, Northern Alberta Institute of Technology, 1106
Arnold, Jack, Langley, 681
Arnold, Jean, Executive Director, Falls Brook Centre, 914
Arnold, Paula, Marketing Manager, dmg world media (Canada) Inc., 164
Arnold, Richard, President, Hotsy Pressure Washers Ltd., 233
Arnold, Rick, President/CEO, Flowmatic Holdings Inc., 197
Arnold, Steve, Lambton, 701
Arnold, Steve, Mayor, St. Clair, 519-867-3333, 729
Arnold, Susan, Partner, Heenan Blaikie LLP - Vancouver, 1060
Arnold, Susan P., Partner, Heenan Blaikie LLP - Victoria, 1062
Arns, Keith, CAO, Conception Bay South, 693
Arrison, Norman, President/CEO, WHMIS Inc., 431
L'Arrivee, Jean, President, Saskatchewan Katahdin Sheep Association Inc., 1000
Arscott, Lorne, Fire Chief, Bradford West Gwillimbury, 706
Arsenault, Corinne, PEB, Université Sainte-Anne, 1135
Arsenault, Cynthia, Konica Minolta Business Solutions (Canada) Inc., 259
Arsenault, Cynthia, Marketing Communicatons Specialist, Stormceptor Canada Inc., 380
Arsenault, Eric, Fire Chief, Moncton / Ville de Moncton, 506-857-8800, 691
Arsenault, Jean-Luc, Quality Control, Géophysique GPR International Inc., 211
Arsenault, Jim, Director of OSH & Traffic Training, Safety Services New Brunswick, 998
Arsenault, Mario, Saint-Constant, 742
Arsenault, Nicole, Le Groupe Sani Marc, 266
Arsenault, Patricia, Sr. Vice-President, Clayton Research Associates Ltd., 142
Arsenault, Philip, Vice-President, Optech Inc., 313
Arsenault, Steve, ITM Instruments, 248
Arseneau, Bernard, Vice-President, 597
Arseneau, Robert L., Contact, Maritime Soil Ltd., 281
Arseneau, Vincent, Sainte-Thérèse, 744
Arsenault, Céline, Botaniste/bibliothécaire, Jardin Botanique de Montréal, 1174
Arseneault, Donald, Minister, 595
Arseneault, Eric, Executive Secretary, Canadian Mineral Analysts, 879
Arshinoff-Foss, Jordan, Sales Contact, Great Western Containers Inc., 216
Arthur, Bill, Chief Administrative Officer & Clerk, Perth, 703
Arthur, Michael, Chief Building Official, Kingsville, 712
Arthur, Tracey, Acting City Clerk, Langley, 604-514-2803, 681
Arthur, Tracey, City Clerk, White Rock, 604-541-2212, 686
Arthurs, David, President, Hickling Arthurs Low Corp., 231
Arthurs, Donald R., Cassels Brock & Blackwell LLP, 1074
Arvisais, Conrad R., City Clerk, Brandon, 204-729-2207, 689
Asbreuk, Lisa M., McCarthy Tétrault LLP - Calgary, 1052
Ascherl, Peter, Partner, Fasken Martineau - Toronto, 1075
Asgarpour, Soheil, President, Petroleum Technology Alliance Canada, 986
Ash, Cathy, Library Technician, L.A. Bown Bldg LRC, College of the North Atlantic, 1133
Ash, J.Stephen, Branch Manager, Jagger Hims Limited, 251
Ash, Matt, Director, Public Works, Perth, 703
Ashby, Doug, President, Char Developments Ltd., 138
Ashby, Renrick, Ajax, 705
Ashcroft, Robert, Osler, Hoskin & Harcourt LLP - Calgary, 1053
Ashcroft, Susan, Collections Librarian, Douglas College, 1114
Ashe, Kevin, City Councillor, Pickering, 718
Ashley, Duncan, Loyalist, 727
Ashley, Greg, Manager, Delcan Water, 160
Ashley, Jim, Manager, Hants East District, 697
Ashlie, Cheryl, Maple Ridge, 687
Ashmore, Ron, Kawartha Lakes, 711
Ashoughian, Gohar, University Librarian, University of Northern British Columbia, 1115
Ashton, Dan, Chair, Okanagan-Similkameen, 678
Ashton, Dan, Mayor, Penticton, 682
Ashton, Steve, Minister, 589
Asimakopulos, Marika, Reference Librarian, Schulich Library of Science & Engineering, 1175
Askin, C.F., President, Positive Results Environmental Management Ltd., 328
Aslett, Kim, President, Northern Lights Health Library Association, 966
Aslett, Kimberley, Head, Library, Sault Area Hospital, 1154
Asmae, Amrouche, Trade Commissioner, 768
Asmundson, Brent, Coquitlam, 680
Assandri, Daniel, Country Manager, ABB Inc. (Canada), 64
Asselin, Brigitte, Saint-Lazare, 743

Executive Name Index

Asselin, Frédéric, Terrebonne, 745
Asselin, Marc, Alma, 418-668-8923, 733
Asselin, Paul, Terrebonne, 745
Asselin, Philippe, Morency Avocats, 1088
Asselin, Pierre, Exec. VP, AECOM Canada Ltd., 69
Asselin, Pierre, Vice-President, Tecsult Inc., 388
Assmann, Stephen, President, ACO Container Systems Ltd., 67
Aston, M., President, Network Environmental Services Inc., 300
Aston, Tim, Officer, Canadian Foundation for Climate & Atmospheric Sciences, 869
Atcheson, Aaron E., Partner, Miller Thomson LLP - Toronto, 1078
Atchison, Donald J., Mayor, Saskatoon, 306-975-3202, 754
Atebe, James, Mayor, Mission, 687
Atfield, Cliff, Brant, 698
Atkin, Rick, Councillor, Leamington, 726
Atkins, Jayne, CEO, FS Partners, 202
Atkins, Lisa, President, Society for Organic Urban Land Care, 1007
Atkins, Rick, Manager, Agricultural Technology Centre, 73
Atkins, Robert, President, Micrologic Ltd., 289
Atkinson, Cheryl, Policy Specialist, EPCOR Energy Services Inc., 189
Atkinson, Colin J.W., President, Atkinson, Davies Inc., 95
Atkinson, Gary, Manager, Waterous Power Systems, 423
Atkinson, John, Owner, Jack Atkinson & Associates, 250
Atkinson, Keith, General Manager, Coast Forest Management Ltd., 145
Atkinson, Lorne, Chair, Cansult Maunsell Limited, 127
Atkinson, Pat, Operations Manager, dmg world media (Canada) Inc., 164
Atkinson, Ron, Economic Development Officer, Charlottetown, 732
Atkinson, Tim, Librarian, Technical Services, University of British Columbia, 1119
Atkinson, CGA, B., Director, Recreation, Facilities, & Culture, Grimsby, 710
Atleo, Shawn, National Chief, Assembly of First Nations, 829
Attirgi, Nabil, President, Bedard Tankers Inc., 104
Attrill, Sue, Chilliwack, 680
Attwood, Jim, Midland, 713
Atwater, Wayne, Councillor, Kings County, 696
Atwell, Gordon, Sales Representative, Kruger Inc., 260
Atwood, Corinne, Executive Director, British Columbia Bottle Depot Association, 847
Atwood, Dave, Manager, Westburne Canada, 426
Atwood-Petkovski, Janet, Commissioner, Legal & Administrative Services, Vaughan, 722
Au, Anthony, Treasurer, Petroleum Society of CIM, 986
Au, Dominic, Principal & Manager, Gryphon International Engineering Services Inc., 222
Aubé, Gaétan, Saint-Lazare, 743
Aube, Renata, Secretary to the Deputy Minister, 616
Aubin, Alain, Bibliothécaire, Québec Ministère du Développement durable, de l'Environnement et, 1180
Aubin, Gervaise, Technicienne en documentation, prêt, référence, tr, CÉGEP de Jonquière, 1168
Aubut, Marcel, Partner, Heenan Blaikie S.E.N.C.R.L/SRL, 1084
Aubut, Q.C., Marcel, Partner, Heenan Blaikie S.E.N.C.R.L./SRL - Québec, 1087
Auch, Derrick K., Davis LLP - Calgary, 1050
Audet, Aline, Administrative Assistant, ABGG Technologies Inc., 65
Audet, Louise, Directrice générale, Rimouski-Neigette, 753
Audy, Stéphane, Vice-President, Groupe Berlie-Falco Inc., 219
Auger, André, Maire, Saint-Lin-Laurentides, 743
Auger, Daniel, Asst. Deputy Minister, 608
Auger, France, Victoriaville, 819-758-7330, 746
Auger, Patrick, Manager, Les Plastiques Simport Ltée, 270
Auger, Sylvie, Technicienne en documentation, Collège Lasalle, 1172
Auger, Trevor, Chief Engineering Technologist, Langford, 681
Augimeri, Maria, Toronto, 721
Auguste, Laurent, President/CEO, Veolia Water Canada, 412
Augustyn, Dave, Niagara, 702
Augustyn, Dave, Mayor, Pelham, 717
Aujla, Raj, President, CanAsia Environmental & Engineering Ltd., 125
Aumon, William, Vice-President, Versatile Measuring Instruments Inc., 412
Aumond, Mike, Deputy Minister, 608
Aumuller, Paul M., President/Owner, Safety Plus Inc., 355
aurora college thebacha c, Aurora College - Thebacha, Fort Smith, NT, 1033
Austin, Dave, Whitehorse, 755

Austin, Lorraine, Marketing, Spencer-Lemaire Industries Ltd., 375
Austin, Lucy, Executive Director, 607
Austin, Mark, Partner, Osler, Hoskin & Harcourt LLP - Toronto, 1079
Austin, Rick, Port Hope, 728
Austin, Thomas P., President, ABL Environmental Consultants, 65
Autut, Stephanie, Executive Director, 542
Avery, Alan E., Manager, Sumas Environmental Services Inc., 381
Avery, Judith S., Director, Public Works, Brock, 724
avian preservation founda, The Avian Preservation Fo, Chemainus, BC, 1040
Avon, Lauria, Vice-President, Eucania International Inc., 191
Avrahami, Leeora, Ogilvy Renault LLP/S.E.N.C.R.L, s.r.l. - Toronto, 1078
Awad, Michelle C., McInnes Cooper, 1067
Awad, Mitchell, President, Ecolad Corp., 172
Axford, Don, Axford Agencies BC Ltd., 99
Axworthy, Mary, Director, Calgary, 671
Ayers, Q.C., Edward A., Partner, Borden Ladner Gervais LLP - Toronto, 1073
Aylward, Bronda, Director, Mount Pearl, 709-748-1096, 694
Aylward, Rhoda, Stikeman Elliott LLP - Toronto, 1079
Aylwin, Josée, Technicienne, Collège Laflèche, 1186
Ayotte, Daniel, Partner, Borden Ladner Gervais LLP - Montréal, 1082
Ayres, James, Cassels Brock & Blackwell LLP, 1074
Ayrhart, Ross, National Account Sales Manager, Wynn's Canada Ltd., 435
Ayyad, Hanna, President, Canadian Soil & Climate Protection Corp., 125
Ayzenberg, Luda, Director, 667
Aziz, Shahid, Engineering, EnRel Energy Group, 181
Azizi, Frank, Representative, Mifab Canada, 289

B

Babbitt, Bruce, Chairman, World Wildlife Fund - USA, 1023
Babchishin, Donna, Director, 570
Babcock, Brian A., Partner, Weiler, Maloney, Nelson, 1072
Babcock, Janet, Commisssioner, Planning Services, Cambridge, 707
Babcock, John, Director, 656
Babec, Christine, Reference Librarian, Justice Institute of British Columbia, 1114
Babenic, John, President/CEO, Maxim Power Corp., 283
Babicki, Matt, Principal Engineer, QuestAir Technologies Inc., 339
Babicz, Walter, Corporate Officer, Prince George, 250-561-7605, 683
Babin, Joanne, Library Assistant, Nova Scotia Environment & Labour, 1136
Babineau, Florence, General Manager, Kent County Solid Waste Commission, 758
Babinski, Marc A., Partner, Borden Ladner Gervais LLP - Montréal, 1083
Babki, Bob, Lethbridge, 673
Babstock, Reg A., CEO, Newfoundland Design Associates Limited, 303
Babulic, Jon, Chief Administrative Officer, Barrie, 706
Bach, Ralph, Chair, St. Andrews, 690
Bachand, André, Manager, Public Works, North Glengarry, 727
Bache, Geoff, Director, Environmental Services, Muskoka, 702
Bachetti, Joe, Tecumseh, 519-979-3339, 720
Bachinski, John, Managing Director, 567
Bachman, Mel, Manager, Engineered Air, 180
Bachmann, John, Manager, Wainbee Limited, 415
Bachmann, Mark, Chief Financial Officer, Zep Manufacturing Company of Canada, 436
Bachop, Steve, Director, 582
Bacic, Mia, Partner, McCullough O'Connor Irwin LLP, 1061
Back, Gabrielle, Vice-Chair, National Association for Environmental Education (UK), 956
Backer, Joan, Librarian, Conservation & Environment Library, 1123
Backhouse, Paul, Lindsay Kenney LLP, 1061
Backman, Anna, Client Services Officer, NRC Information Centre - Halifax, 1136
Backman, Larry, Pinchin Environmental Ltd., 324
Badawey, Vance, Niagara, 702
Badawey, Vance, Mayor, Port Colborne, 718
Badger, Chris, Chief Operating Officer, Vancouver Fraser Port Authority, 409

Badger, Gerald, Préfet, Le Val-St-François, 749
Badia, Giovanna, Librarian, Royal Victoria Hospital, 1175
Badiuk, Randy, Manager, Harold Marcus Ltd., 225
Badke, Bill, Head, Theology, Trinity Western University, 1113
Badurina, David, Ogilvy Renault LLP/S.E.N.C.R.L., s.r.l. - Toronto, 1078
Baechler, Joni, London, 713
Baer, Richard, Chair, Library Services, Camosun College, 1120
Baer, Wallace E., President, Enform: The Safety Association for the Upstream Oil & Gas Industr, 910
Bagdade, Jeffrey, VP, Opus International Consultants (Canada) Ltd., 314
Bagh, Signe, Director, Kelowna, 681
Bagley, Jim, PHH ARC Environmental Ltd., 322
Bagnato, Charlie, Bruce, 698
Bagnell, James G., President, Inland Technologies Inc., 242
Bagnell, Shara, Officer, Health & Safety, Dufferin, 699
Baguley, Barb, Mayor, Innisfil, 711
Bahamin, Poupak, Partner, Heenan Blaikie S.E.N.C.R.L/SRL, 1084
Bahry, Evan, Executive Director, Independent Power Producers Society of Alberta, 930
Baiden, Brent, President, Avoca-tec Environmental Services Inc., 99
Baier, Maria, Innisfil, 711
Baig, Mirza, Specialist, YES Environment Technologies Inc., 435
Baigrie, Jeff A., Pitblado LLP, 1063
Bailao, Ana, Toronto, 721
Bailey, Ann, Supervisor, Prince George, 683
Bailey, Gwen, Coordinator, Library Systems, Malaspina University-College, 1113
Bailey, Jeffrey D., Office Manager, Golder Associates Ltd., 215
Bailey, Laverne, Prince Edward, 703
Bailey, Marg, General Manager, Vernon, 685
Bailey, Margaret, Director, 518
Bailey, Rick, Director, Brandon, 689
Bailey, Robert, Essex, 519-978-0974, 699
Bailey, Susan, Marketing Director, Haul-All Equipment Ltd., 227
Baillargeon, Danièle, Bibliothécaire professionnelle, CÉGEP de Trois-Rivières, 1186
Baillargeon Bouchard, Geneviève, Ogilvy Renault LLP/S.E.N.C.R.L., s.r.l. - Québec, 1088
Baillie, A.W., IBI Group, 238
Baillie, Ronald, Warden, Pictou County, 698
Bain, Grant, Director, Prince George, 250-561-7616, 683
Bain, John, Director, Nordic Systems Corporation, 305
Bain, Kevin, City Clerk, London, 713
Bain, Kevin, Regional Clerk, Niagara, 702
Bain, Mac, North Bay, 715
Bain, Mark W. S., Torys LLP, 1080
Bain, Tom, Essex, 519-728-2394, 699
Bain, Tom, Mayor, Lakeshore, 712
Baines, Simon C., Partner, Osler, Hoskin & Harcourt LLP - Calgary, 1053
Baird, B., President, W.F. Baird & Associates Coastal Engineers Ltd., 415
Baird, James R., Commissioner, Saint John, 506-658-2835, 692
Baird, Jim, Commissioner, Development Services, Markham, 905-475-4875, 713
Baird, Roger, Director, 518
Baird, CET, CMMIII, Ec.D., Christopher D., General Manager, Planning & Economic Development, Norfolk, 702
Bajer, Robin, Associate, Miller Thomson LLP - Toronto, 1078
Bajzik, Marc, Vice-President, Integra Environmental Inc., 243
Bake, R., Marsh Instrumentation Inc., 281
Baker, Allyson L., Clark Wilson LLP, 1058
Baker, Amy, Chief of Staff, 715
Baker, Analyn, Librarian, Seven Oaks General Hospital, 1125
Baker, Barry A., Vice-President, Trihedral Engineering Limited, 401
Baker, Bill, Essex, 709
Baker, Bob, President, Nepisiguit Salmon Association, 960
Baker, Brett, Counsel, Heenan Blaikie LLP - Toronto, 1075
Baker, Cal, Chair, Northeast Avalon ACAP, Inc., 966
Baker, David R., President, Phoenix Engineering Inc., 323
Baker, Doug, General Manager, Public Works, & Town Engineer, Midland, 713
Baker, G.R., Director, Simcoe Engineering Group Limited, 368
Baker, Geoffrey D., Carscallen Leitch LLP, 1050
Baker, Jack S., President, Agrodev Canada Inc., 73
Baker, Janice, City Manager & Chief Administrative Officer, Mississauga, 714
Baker, Jason, Brockville, 707
Baker, Jill, Librarian, St Lawrence College, 1143
Baker, Jim, Director, Human Resources, Brockville, 707

Executive Name Index

Baker, Joe, Manager, Clearwater County, 669
Baker, Jonathan B., Baker & Baker, 1057
Baker, Ken, Chief Executive Officer, 579
Baker, Ken, Mayor, Lloydminster, 754
Baker, Lorraine, ILL Assistant, Health Sciences Library, 1101
Baker, Marie, Strathroy-Caradoc, 731
Baker, Mark, Contact, Western Solutions 2000 Ltd., 430
Baker, Mark, Manager, Masternet Ltd., 282
Baker, Maurice, Manager, IMTT-Newfoundland Ltd., 239
Baker, Mike, CH2M Hill Canada Limited, 137
Baker, Rachel, Coordinator, Universal Handling Equipment Company Limited, 406
Baker, Rick, Vice-President, Plastiglas Industries Limited, 326
Baker, Robert B., Sr. Vice-President, Totten Sims Hubicki Associates Ltd., 399
Baker, Stephen, Vice-President, 518
Baker, Steve, President/CEO, Plastiglas Industries Limited, 326
Baker, Tom, General Manager, Republic Environmental Systems (Fort Erie) Ltd., 345
Baker, William V., Deputy Minister, 557
Baker, Q.C., John A., Founding Partner, Ottenheimer Baker, 1066
Baker, Q.C., Michael, Minister Responsible, 617
Baker, Q.C., Wendy A., Partner, Miller Thomson LLP - Vancouver, 1061
Bakken, Mark, Administrator, Langley, 604-533-6002, 687
Bakker, MA, Linda, Coordinator, Wildlife Rescue Association of British Columbia, 1020
Baksa, Diane, Information Technologist, Inco Technical Services Limited, 1145
Bakshi, Vivek, Fraser Milner Casgrain LLP - Toronto, 1075
Balakrishnan, Desmond, Lang Michener LLP - Vancouver, 1060
Balasubramanian, V. (Bala), Roach, Schwartz & Associates, Barristers & Solicitors, 1079
Balcerczyk, Diane, Advertising/Marketing Manager, Performance Fluid Equipement Inc., 321
Balcerczyk, George, President, Performance Fluid Equipement Inc., 321
Balcom, Frank, Chair, 609
Balcom, Lesley, Associate Director, Learning & Research Services, University of New Brunswick, 1128
Balcombe, Gordon, Vice-President, Rawdon Technologies Ltd., 342
Baldasserra, Domenic, President, Via Disposal Services Ltd., 413
Baldazzi, Cris, Aquatic Biologist, Fraser Environmental Services, 201
Balderstone, Lorna, Library/Records Clerk, British Columbia Housing, 1110
Baldry, Dale, General Manager, Terminal City Iron Works Ltd., 390
Baldwin, Graham, Director, InfoMine Inc., 241
Baldwin, Matthew, City Planner, Langford, 681
Baldwin, Ryan, President, Monsanto Canada Inc., 293
Baldwin, B.A., J.D., Chris G., Partner, Lawson Lundell LLP - Vancouver, 1060
Baldwin-Sands, Lori, Alderman, St. Thomas, 719
Balfour, Bill, Executive Director, Ontario Water Works Association, 981
Balfour, Jim, President, Dillon Consulting Ltd., 163
Balfour, Scott C., President & Chief Financial Officer, Aecon Group Inc., 71
Baliski, Scott, Sr. Project Manager, Lockerbie & Hole Contracting Ltd., 273
Balkham, Carroll, Contact, Circulation & Journals, Science/Engineering Library, 1143
Balko, Ed, Manager, Toromont Caterpillar, 397
Ball, Donald, President, DB Geoservices Inc., 158
Ball, Elizabeth, Librarian, Silver King Campus, 1113
Ball, James K., Sutts, Strosberg LLP, 1082
Ball, Jason, Osler, Hoskin & Harcourt LLP - Toronto, 1079
Ball, Jerry, Director, Transportation & Environmental Services, Oro-Medonte, 728
Ball, John, Chief Financial Officer, Velan Inc., 410
Ball, Stephen, Contact, Conestoga-Rovers & Associates, 149
Ball, Steven, President, Restoration Environmental Contractors - Restoration Consultants, 346
Ball, Vivienne M., Willms & Shier Environmental Lawyers LLP, 1081
Ballamingie, Patricia, Vice-President, Environmental Studies Association of Canada, 913
Ballantyne, Donna, Smith-Ennismore-Lakefield, 729
Ballantyne, Kathy, Manager, Parks & Facilities, Brant, 698
Ballantyne, Meena, Assistant Deputy Minister, 533

Ballantyne, Robert, Executive Member, British Columbia Spaces for Nature, 850
Ballantyne-Scott, Brooke, Vice-President, Health Libraries Association of British Columbia, 928
Ballard, Chris, Aurora, 706
Ballard, Q.C., Donna, Assistant Deputy Minister, 602
Ballem, Penny, City Manager, Vancouver, 604-873-7625, 685
Ballermann, Elisabeth, President, Health Sciences Association of Alberta, 928
Ballinger, Jack, Durham, 699
Balmer, Steve, President/COO, Napier Environmental Technology, 296
Balsam, Dee, Manager, 665
Balsdon, Jason, Branch Manager, Jagger Hims Limited, 251
Baltacioglu, Yaprak, Deputy Minister, 544
Baltgailis, Karen, Executive Director, Yukon Conservation Society, 1024
Bambrough, Denise L., Partner, Borden Ladner Gervais LLP - Toronto, 1073
Bamford, Mike, Secretary, Saint John Naturalists' Club, 998
Bamford, Pat, Timmins, 721
Banack, Darren, Operations Manager, Two Hills Regional Waste Management Commission, 758
Banack, Hart, President, British Columbia Camping Association, 847
Banasch, Barb, Circulation Supervisor, Medicine Hat College, 1109
Bancroft, Bob, President, Nature Nova Scotia (Federation of Nova Scotia Naturalists), 960
Bancroft, Lee G., Executive Manager, Bancroft Western Sales Ltd., 101
Bancroft, Q.C., James, Davis LLP - Calgary, 1050
Bandyopadhyay, Debanjan, SENES Consultants Limited, 362
Banfai, Geza, Partner, Heenan Blaikie LLP - Toronto, 1075
Banfai, Geza R., Blaney McMurtry LLP, 1073
Banfield, B.A., Chown, Cairns LLP, 1071
Bangma, Janet, Head Librarian, Health Sciences Library, 1189
Banham, Fred, CAO, Peace River, 250-784-3208, 678
Banks, A., Manager, Ordan Thermal Products Ltd., 314
Banks, Doug, Fire Chief, Parksville, 250-954-4671, 682
Banks, John, Matrix Solutions Inc., 282
Banks, Mary Jane, Clerk, Rothesay, 692
Banks, Susannah, General Manager, New Brunswick Soil & Crop Improvement Association, 962
Banks, William M., President, Institution of Mechanical Engineers, 934
Bannister, Albert, Middlesex, 701
Bannister, Carl, CAO, Salmon Arm, 684
Bannister, Dave, Vice-President, R.J. Burnside & Associates Limited, 340
Bannister, Jacqueline, Director, 520
Banno, Robert T., Davis LLP - Vancouver, 1059
Bannon, David J., Partner, Ogilvy Renault LLP/S.E.N.C.R.L., s.r.l. - Toronto, 1078
Bannon, Jeff, City Planner, Stratford, 720
Bannon, Phil, Councillor, Whitchurch-Stouffville, 723
Banting, Wendy, President/CEO, Secural Inc., 361
Bapna, Manish, Exec. Vice-President & Managing Dir, World Resources Institute, 1023
Baptista, Hazel, Executive Assistant, Alfa Laval Inc., 78
Baqi, Anowara, CFO, Sierra Club of Canada, 1004
Baratta, Lisa, Director, Western Transportation Advisory Council, 1019
Baraya, Raymond, President, Kyocera Mita Canada Ltd., 261
Barbe, Manon, Mairesse d'arrondissement/Conseillère de la ville, Montréal, 738
Barbe, Peter, President, Arbrux Limited, 89
Barbeau, André, Trésorier, Gatineau, 735
Barbeau, Jacques, Greater Sudbury / Grand Sudbury, 710
Barbeau, Madeleine, Greffière, Lavaltrie, 736
Barbeau, Marc B., Associé, Stikeman Elliott LLP - Montréal, 1087
Barber, Allan F., President, JKM Custom Fabricating Ltd., 252
Barber, Bob, Fire Chief, St. Thomas, 719
Barber, Daniel, Singleton Urquhart LLP, 1062
Barber, Ed, Manager, Recreation, Smith-Ennismore-Lakefield, 705-292-8774, 729
Barber, Jennifer, Vice-President, Hydrogenics Corporation, 236
Barber, Karen, Library Technician, Kirkland Lake Campus, 1143
Barber, Wendy, Coordinator, Library Services, Manitoba Dept. of Conservation, Environment Canada & Canadian Cou, 1124
Barberini, Ivano, President, International Cooperative Alliance, 937
Barbondy, Jim, Sales Agent, Danatec Educational Services Ltd., 157
Barcelo, Sylvie, Sous-ministre, 644

Barclay, Kevin, Executive Director, Canadian Association for Health Services & Policy Research, 855
Barclay, William W., Reynolds, Mirth, Richards & Farmer LLP, 1056
Bard, Carol, FCX NH Valves, 194
Bardai, Naheed, Partner, MacPherson Leslie & Tyerman LLP - Saskatoon, 1090
Bardak, Lydia, Yellowknife, 695
Bardonnex, Don, Manager, Red Deer County, 670
Barenie, Mark, Chief Financial Officer, Institute of Food Technologists, 933
Barfoot, Alan, Mayor, Grey, 725, 700
Barfoot, Carol, Georgian Bluffs, 725
Barg, Carl, Director, Flygt Canada, 198
Baribeau, Pierre-L., Lavery, de Billy - Montréal, 1085
Barich, Phyllis, Coordinator, Off Campus & Media Services, Red River College, 1125
Baril, Cécile, Agente de bureau, Collège Laflèche, 1186
Baril, Guy, Contact, Marcel Baril Ltée, 280
Baril, Jean-Yves, President, Marcel Baril Ltée, 280
Baril, Robert, Vice-President, Marcel Baril Ltée, 280
Barker, Geoff, Manager, Sumas Environmental Services Inc., 381
Barker, Jim, President/CEO, Commercial Solutions Inc., 147
Barker, John, Wascana Recycling & Resource Recovery Corp., 417
Barker, Mike, President, Donalco Inc., 165
Barker, Steve, CFO & Vice-President, World Resources Institute, 1023
Barker, Susan, Digital Services & Reference Librarian, Bora Laskin Law Library, 1156
Barkhouse, Jackie, Councillor, Halifax Regional Municipality, 695
Barkhouse, Laura, Coordinator, Lunenburg District, 697
Barkley, Brian, General Manager, Eastern Ontario Model Forest, 908
Barkley, Dennis, Manager, Westburne Canada, 425
Barkley, Johanna, Treasurer, South Stormont, 730
Barkley, Sharon, Milton, 714
Barkman, Les, Abbotsford, 679
Barkwell, Rob, Manager, Sustainable Development Technology Canada, 1011
Barless, Bob, Vice-President, Alliance Envelope Ltd., 79
Barlott, Paul J., President, BCL Landview Systems Inc., 103
Barlow, Gary, President, Canadian Recycling Equipment & Systems Ltd., 125
Barlow, Geoffrey, Lincoln, 713
Barlow, Shawn, Photech Environmental Solutions, 323
Barlow, William, Chair, 588
Barnable, Paul, Director, Corner Brook, 709-637-1548, 693
Barnard, John, Director, Acsion Industries Inc., 67
Barnes, Bill, Contact, Western Site Technologies Inc., 430
Barnes, Brandon, Burnet, Duckworth & Palmer LLP, 1050
Barnes, Brent, Ainley Group, 74
Barnes, Brent, Fire Chief, Arthur, Wellington North, 519-848-3500, 732
Barnes, D., Chief Administrative Officer, Caledon, 707
Barnes, Dawna, Specialist, Red Deer County, 670
Barnes, Debbie, Marketing Manager, Firing Industries Ltd., 196
Barnes, Dianne, Administrative Assistant, 617
Barnes, Dianne, Manager, Westburne Canada, 426
Barnes, Gary, President, Western Site Technologies Inc., 430
Barnes, Kathryn M., Councillor at Large, Moncton / Ville de Moncton, 691
Barnes, Kevin, Director, 637
Barnes, Linda, Richmond, 684
Barnes, Rex, Mayor, Grand Falls-Windsor, 694
Barnet, Barry, Minister, 611
Barnett, Chris, Davis LLP - Toronto, 1074
Barnett, Linda, Head of Public Services, Health Sciences Library, 1132
Barnett, Linda, Secretary, Newfoundland & Labrador Health Libraries Association, 963
Barnett, Phil, Superintendent, Oak Bay, 250-598-4501, 688
Barnett, Steve, Chief Financial Officer, 584
Barnsley, Joseph D., Pitblado LLP, 1063
Baron, David, General Manager, Cowater International Inc., 153
Baron, Mark, President, Cowater International Inc., 153
Baron, Walter, Manager, LTS Sales Ltd., 274
Barone, Sam, FCILT Treasurer, Chartered Institute of Logistics and Transport in North America, 894
Barr, Michele, Manager, Building & Planning, Kincardine, 726
Barraclough, Cori L., Freshwater Ecologist, Aqua-Tex Scientific Consulting Ltd., 88
Barraclough, Graham, CFO, Stemmer Steel Craft Industries Limited, 379

CANADIAN ENVIRONMENTAL RESOURCE GUIDE 2011-2012

Executive Name Index

Barraclough, Joe, Director, Environmental Services Association of Alberta, 912
Barrat, Olga, Principal, Barrat & Associates Inc., 102
Barratt, Karen, Manager, Library Services, Sault College of Applied Arts & Technology, 1154
Barré, Bernard, Saint-Hyacinthe, 742
Barré, Louis, President, Mabarex inc., 277
Barré, Louis, Vice-President, Canadian Institute for Health Information, 872
Barrett, Alvin, Manager, Harris & Roome Supply Limited, 226
Barrett, Andy, Group CEO, SRK Consulting (Canada) Inc., 376
Barrett, Ann, Coordinator, Electronic Services, W.K. Kellogg Health Sciences Library, 1136
Barrett, Bruce, Vice-President, 583
Barrett, Catherine, Executive Director, Ever Green Recycling, 191
Barrett, Christine, Administrator/ Account Representative, Daybar Industries Ltd., 158
Barrett, Fred, Contact, Barrett Sales Ltd., 102
Barrett, Hyacinth, Contact, Circulation Services, The King's University College, 1106
Barrett, Ian, Executive Director, Ontario Agricultural Training Institute, 970
Barrett, Julie, Treasurer & Deputy-Clerk, Essa, 725
Barrett, Larry C., President, Emerson Electric Canada Limited, 177
Barrett, Lynn, Technician, Noranda Earth Sciences Library, 1159
Barrett, Mark, Officer, 642
Barrett, Mike, Lennox Industries (Canada) Ltd., 267
Barrett, Robin, Chief Consultant, Hi-Q Developments Ltd., 228, 231
Barrett, Roderick F., Managing Partner, Stikeman Elliott LLP - Toronto, 1079
Barrette, Bruno, Associé, Stikeman Elliott LLP - Montréal, 1087
Barriault, Michel, Directeur général, Matane, 738
Barrick, David, Regional Councillor, Port Colborne, 718
Barrie, Patti L., Municipal Clerk, Clarington, 724
Barriere, Rhett, Vice-President, Folio Instruments Inc., 199
Barrington, Suzelle, Academic Staff, Brace Centre for Water Resources Management, 115
Barrington-Moss, Gail, General Manager, St. Albert, 674
Barron, Tracy, Director, 603
Barron Jr., Pat, Coordinator, Provincial Airlines Ltd. - Environmental Services Division, 335
Barrow, Dave, Mayor, Richmond Hill, 718
Barrow, David, York, 705
Barr-Telford, Lynn, Director, 559
Barry, Ellen, Deputy Minister, 597
Barry, Leo, Contact, IMO Pump Inc., 239
Barry, Mary Pat, Manager, Edmonton, 780-496-8191, 672
Barry, Robert, Secretary, Newfoundland Aquaculture Industry Association, 963
Barry, Q.C., David G., Barry Spalding - Saint John Office, 1065
Barry, Q.C., John P., Barry Spalding - Saint John Office, 1065
Barry, Q.C., T. Arthur, Stewart McKelvey Stirling Scales - Halifax, 1067
Barsby, Dennis, Sales Representative, Ontor Ltd., 313
Barsi, Ron G., Principal, Golder Associates Ltd., 214
Bartel, Patricia, Library Staff, Ontario Ministry of Transportation, 1154
Bartle, Bart, Chair, Ontario Society of Nutrition Professionals in Public Health, 979
Bartlett, Brian, Peterborough, 703
Bartlett, Leroy, Haldimand, 700
Bartlett, Linda, Executive Director, Newfoundland & Labrador Environmental Industry Association, 962
Bartley, Peter C., President/CEO, Bartley Silver Co. Inc., 102
Bartley, Richard, Councillor, Whitchurch-Stouffville, 723
Bartolucci, Rick, Minister, 621
Barton, Brian, Président, Association québécoise des organismes de coopération internationa, 842
Barton, Gary J., Prescott & Russell, 729
Barton, Manson, Superintendent, Drainage, North Glengarry, 727
Barton, Tony, Chair, Bruce Peninsula Environment Group, 851
Barutciski, Miles, President, International Law Association - Canadian Branch, 940
Basey, John, City Solicitor, Victoria, 250-361-0588, 685
Bashir, Naseem, President, Williams Engineering Inc., 432
Basi, K., Coordinator, Burnaby, 679
Basic, Sandra, Manager, CertainTeed Insulation Canada, Inc., 137
Baskin, Mary, Manager, Fur Institute of Canada, 922
Basler, Gayl, Executive Assistant, 661
Bass, Jim, President, Bass Engineering Systems Technology, 103

Bass, Ted, Vice-President, Genex Swine Group, 207
Bassam, Roger, North Vancouver, 688
Bassan, Daniela F., Stewart McKelvey Stirling Scales - Halifax, 1067
Bassermann, Don, Prince George, 683
Bassett, Dawn, Librarian, Canadian Grain Commission, 1123
Bassett, Dawn, Manager, Content & Information Resources, Vancouver Aquarium Marine Science Centre, 1119
Bassi Kellett, Sheila, Asst. Deputy Minister, 608
Bassios, A., Commissioner, Planning, Richmond Hill, 718
Bastaja, John, Chief Information Officer, Maple Ridge, 604-467-7479, 687
Bastein, Daniel, Manager, Flygt Canada, 198
Bastiani, Corina, Sorel-Tracy, 450-743-8484, 745
Bastien, Rowena, Supervisor, Cariboo, 677
Batchelor, Mike, Regional Operating Vice-President, Aluma Systems Inc., 82
Batdorf, Kevin, Development Engineer, YES Environment Technologies Inc., 435
Bate, Lisa, Chair, Canada Green Building Council, 853
Bateman, Brian, Manager, Focus Industries, 198
Bateman, Jordan, Langley, 687
Bateman, Robert, Director, Alberta Government Library, 1104
Bateman, Tom, County Engineer, Essex, 699
Bates, Bryan, Exec. Vice-President & COO, BW Technologies by Honeywell, 119
Bates, Chris, Operations Manager, SGS Canada Inc., 364
Bates, Derek, City Manager, Prince George, 250-561-7607, 683
Bates, Ed, General Counsel & Secretary, 584
Bates, Fred, Chair, Comox Valley, 677
Bates, Garth, Manager, Valley Comfort Systems Inc., 409
Bates, J., Vice President, Bema Co. Ltd., 105
Bates, Jocelyne, Mairesse, Sainte-Catherine, 743
Bates, Jocelyne, Préfète, Roussillon, 753
Bates, Martin, Chief Executive Officer, Expocrete Concrete Products Ltd., 192
Bates, Michael, President, Bema Co. Ltd., 105
Bates, Monique, Managing Director, Dagex Inc., 156
Bath, Debbie, Durham, 699
Bathurst, Gordon, Sr. Vice-President, Metafix, 287
Batt, Kelly, Manager, Tillsonburg, 721
Battista, Mario, Conseiller d'arrondissement, St-Léonard-Ouest, Montréal, 738
Battista, Renaldo, President, Canadian Association for Health Services & Policy Research, 855
Battiste, Angela, Information Specialist, Saskatchewan Environment, 1187
Batty, Jane, Edmonton, 672
Baty, Brian, Niagara, 702
Bau-Coote, Maria, Councillor, Niagara-on-the-Lake, 715
Bauer, Al, President, Alnor Industries Ltd., 79
Bauer, Christian, Vice-President, Alnor Industries Ltd., 79
Bauer, Evelyn, Treasurer, Mineral Society of Manitoba, 954
Bauer, Jack, Vice-President, Mineral Society of Manitoba, 954
Bauer, Paul, President, The MEP Environmental Products Ltd., 393
Bauld, Jim, Manager, Halifax Regional Municipality, 902-490-6606, 695
Bauman, Wayne, Plant Manager, N.S. Bauman Ltd., 296
Bauman, Willard, President, N.S. Bauman Ltd., 296
Baumgartner, Todd, Plant Manager, CCS Income Trust, 134
Bausinger, Lynda, Acting General Manager, Elora Environment Centre, 909
Bauslaugh, H. Roy, Treasurer, Norwich, 728
Bauthus, Fred, Chief Administrative Officer, Elliot Lake, 709
Bavis, Kirk, President, Enerplan Consultants Ltd., 179
Bax, Herb, President, KBM Forestry Consultants Inc., 255
Bax, Ken, Manager, Abandonrite, 64
Baxter, Gary, Essex, 699
Baxter, Leona V., Pushor Mitchell LLP, Lawyers & Trade-Mark Agents, 1056
Baxter, Rose, Deputy Minister, 602
Bayard, Rick, Facility Manager, Hyprescon Inc., 237
Baydala, Allan, Chief Financial Officer, Vancouver Fraser Port Authority, 409
Bayer, R. Martin, Weaver, Simmons LLP, 1072
Bayne, Chad, Partner, Osler, Hoskin & Harcourt LLP - Toronto, 1079
Bayne, Ken, General Manager, Vancouver, 685
Baynham, Chuck, Armtec Construction Products, 92
Bazin, Lawrence, Vestar, 412
Bazin, Q.C., Jean, Fraser Milner Casgrain S.E.N.C.R.L./LLP, 1084
Bazinet, Jean-Pierre, Lévis, 736
Baziuk, Morris, President/CEO, Flush Quip, 198

Baziuk, Ursula, Sales, Flush Quip, 198
Beach, Cynthia, Commissioner, Sustainability & Growth, Kingston, 712
Beacham, Warren, Treasurer, Conserver Society of Hamilton & District, 902
Beadman, Tim P., Chief, Emergency Services, Greater Sudbury / Grand Sudbury, 710
Beakley, Bruce, Director, Human Resources, Renfrew, 704
Beal, Les, Contact, Digicon Building Control Solutions, 163
Beale, Suzanne, Acting Director, Whitby, 723
Bealle, D.F., President, CD Nova, 134
Beaman, Roger T., Thomson, Rogers, 1080
Beamer, Andrew, Peterborough, 718
Beamish, Christine, Co-Director, Ceta-Research Inc., 894
Beamish, Dennis, Vice-President, Roxul Inc., 353
Beamish, Peter, Co-Director, Ceta-Research Inc., 894
Bean, Gary, Precision Assessment Technology Corp., 330
Bean, John, Vice-President, CCS Income Trust, 134
Bean, Stephen, Thurber Engineering Ltd., 396
Beard, Colleen, Map Librarian, University Map Library, 1154
Beard, Mark R., Pitblado LLP, 1063
beard, Peter, Manager, Toromont Caterpillar, 398
Beasley, Gerald, University Librarian, Concordia University Libraries, 1171
Beatch, Rebecca, Alexander Holburn Beaudin & Lang, LLP, 1057
Beaton, Bill, President, Lotowater Technical Services Inc., 274
Beaton, Fabian, Westech Industrial Ltd., 429
Beaton, Jack, Chief of Police, Calgary, 403-206-5900, 671
Beattie, Bob, Island Clean Air Inc., 248
Beattie, Brian S., Sr. Vice-President, CHEP Canada, 140
Beattie, D.M., Senior Environmental Engineer, Long Environmental Consultants, 273
Beattie, David, Vice President, ADI International Inc., ADI Group Inc., 68
Beattie, Karen, Bennett Jones LLP - Calgary Office, 1049
Beattie, Leslie, Librarian, Red Deer College, 1109
Beattie, Mick, Plant Manager, Sciencetech Inc., 359
Beattie, Norman, Coordinator, Reference, Red River College, 1125
Beatty, Brad, Stratford, 720
Beatty, Brian, President, W.B. Beatty & Associates, 415
Beatty, David E., Brockville, 707
Beatty, Lynn, Coordinator, Economic Development, Petawawa, 717
Beatty, Suzanne, Manager, Human Resources, Midland, 713
Beaubier, Aidan, Librarian, Semi-Arid Prairie Agricultural Research Centre, 1191
Beauchamp, Gaetan, Engineering Manager, Lecompte Engineering Ltd., 266
Beauchamp, John, Ogilvy Renault LLP/S.E.N.C.R.L., s.r.l. - Toronto, 1078
Beauchamp, Kevin, Office Manager, Golder Associates Ltd., 215
Beauchamp, Line, Ministre, 649
Beauchamp, Pierre, President & CEO, Les Consultants LBCD, 268
Beauchamp, Réal, Directeur général adjoint, Shawinigan, 744
Beauchemin, André, Directeur général, La Vallée-de-la-Gatineau, 748
Beauchemin, Charlene, Director, 663
Beauchemin, Manon, VP, Iron Ore Company of Canada, 248
Beauchemin, Michel, Directeur, Québec, 740
Beauchemin, Paul, Vice-President/Partner, Envirochem Services Inc., 183
Beauchesne, Gaetan, Municipal Engineer, Lecompte Engineering Ltd., 266
Beauchesne, Notaire; OMA, Hélène, Greffière, Saint-Hyacinthe, 450-778-8317, 742
Beaudet, Alain, President, 519
Beaudet, Jean, Lennox Industries (Canada) Ltd., 267
Beaudet, Maurice, Sr. Group Engineer, Beaulier Inc., 104
Beaudin, Denis, Sec.-Trés., Régie intermunicipale de gestion des déchets solides des Anses, 760
Beaudin, Geneviève, Heenan Blaikie S.E.N.C.R.L/SRL, 1084
Beaudoin, Alain, Director General, 543
Beaudoin, Claude, Vaudreuil-Dorion, 746
Beaudoin, Guy-Lin, Directeur général, Vaudreuil-Soulanges, 753
Beaudoin, Jean, President, Biomax Inc., 108
Beaudoin, Marie-Andrée, Mairesse d'arrondissement, Montréal, 738
Beaudoin, Pierre, Partner, Lavery, de Billy - Québec, 1088
Beaudouin, Jean, President, Conporec Inc., 150
Beaudry, Gilles, Conseiller d'arrondissement, Anjou Ouest, Montréal, 738
Beaudry, Gilles, Director, Rodrigue Métal Ltée, 350
Beaudry, Guylaine, Director, R. Howard Webster Library, 1175

Executive Name Index

Beaudry, Marie-Andrée, Associée, Stikeman Elliott LLP - Montréal, 1087
Beaudry, Marie-Claude, Technicienne en documentation, CÉGEP Limoilou, 1178
Beaudry, Patrice, Vice-President, RailPower Technologies Corp., 342
Beaudry, Pierre, Principal, Golder Associates Ltd., 214
Beaudry, Q.C., Harold P., Counsel, Weaver, Simmons LLP, 1072
Beaulé, Gilles, Directeur, 655
Beaulé, Yannick, Asst. Sales Manager, Pompaction inc., 328
Beaulieu, Anne, Québec, 740
Beaulieu, Ben, Edmundston, 691
Beaulieu, Claude, Directeur général, Mékinac, 750
Beaulieu, Daniel, Bibliothécaire de référence, Collège universitaire de St-Boniface, 1123
Beaulieu, Daniel, Préfet, Argenteuil, 747
Beaulieu, Denis, Trois-Rivières, 745
Beaulieu, France, Shawinigan, 744
Beaulieu, Jean-Marie, Manager, 520
Beaulieu, Louis, President/CEO, Sambrabec Inc., 356
Beaulieu, Louise, Greffière, Lachute, 736
Beaulieu, Maryna, Bibliothécaire, Bibliothèque de géographie, 1177
Beaulieu, Normand, Chief Administrative Officer & Treasurer, Hawkesbury, 711
Beaulieu, Pierre, Partner, Heenan Blaikie S.E.N.C.R.L./SRL - Québec, 1087
Beaulne, Michel A., Hawkesbury, 711
Beaumier, Michel, Borden Ladner Gervais LLP - Toronto, 1073
Beaumier, Pierre, Exec. Vice-President, Maxxam Analytics Inc., 283
Beaumier, Rénald, Directeur, Bibliothèque centrale, 1170
Beaumier, Rénald, Directeur, Bibliothèque centrale, Université du Québec à Montréal, 1176
Beaumont, D. Robert, Partner, Osler, Hoskin & Harcourt LLP - Toronto, 1079
Beaumont, Huguette, Technicienne en documentation, Centre de recherche industrielle du Québec, 1178
Beaumont, Sylvie, Alma, 418-668-0919, 733
Beauparlant, Alain, Shawinigan, 744
Beaupré, Adrien, Sec.-Trés., Régie intermunicipale de gestion des déchets solides de Saint-Via, 760
Beaupre, Daniel, Director, Rodrigue Métal Ltée, 350
Beaupré, Denis, Bélanger, Sauvé, 1082
Beaupré, Jean-Marie, Directeur général, Saint-Basile-le-Grand, 741
Beaupré, Marie-Josée, Terrebonne, 745
Beaupré, Paul, Conseiller d'arrondissement, Champlain-L'île-des-S, Montréal, 738
Beauregard, Jean, Chambly, 450-658-2213, 734
Beauregard, Nathalie, Partner, Osler, Hoskin & Harcourt S.E.N.C.R.L./LLP, 1086
Beausoleil, Richard, Director, Public Works, Essex, 709
Beaveridge, Ralph, Michelin North America (Canada) Inc., 289
Beavers, Janet, Librarian, Northern Lights College, 1112
Beazley, Frank, Chief, Halifax Regional Municipality, 902-490-6500, 695
Beazley, Mike, Academic Librarian, Acadia University, 1138
Bebbington, Tony, CEO, Bebbington Industries, 104
Bebee, Ron, President/Site Manager, The Battery Broker Environmental Services Inc., 391
Bechamp, Richard, Chief Building Official, Petawawa, 717
Béchard, Anne-Marie, Cain Lamarre Casgrain Wells - Québec, 1087
Béchard, Gaétan, Directeur général, Shawinigan, 744
Bechard, Marjolaine, Services Publics, CÉGEP de Victoriaville, 1187
Bechard, Mary Ellen, Coordinator, Windsor Regional Hospital - Metropolitan Campus, 1165
Beck, Bary, Director, Lethbridge, 673
Beck, Christian, Vice-President, GDG Environnement Ltée, 205
Beck, John M., Chairman/CEO, Aecon Group Inc., 71
Beck, Marlene, Library Technician, Interlibrary Loans & Special N, Humber College Institute of Technology & Advanced Learning, 1158
Beckel, Murray, Chief Building Official & Planner, Loyalist, 727
Becker, Barry, Director, Port Coquitlam, 683
Becker, Joanna, Head, Technical Services, AMEC Inc., 1099
Becker, Keith, Vice-President, Econotech Services Ltd., 172
Becker, Norma, Librarian, Econotech Services Ltd., 1112
Becker, Steven, CEO, Syndel International Inc., 385
Beckett, Bob, Fire Chief, Langford, 250-478-9555, 681
Beckett, Diane, President/CEO, Diane Beckett, 163
Beckett, George, Associate University Librarian, Health Sciences, Health Sciences Library, 1132

Beckett, Janet, Clerk, Port Colborne, 718
Beckett, Ken, Fire Chief, East Gwillimbury, 708
Beckett, Robert, President, Central Canadian Federation of Mineralogical Societies, 893
Beckett, Robert, Vice-President, Numet Engineering Ltd., 309
Beckett, Tim, Fire Chief, Kitchener, 519-741-2495, 712
Becking, Ken, Director, Public Works, Kawartha Lakes, 711
Beckingham, John D., CEO & Sr. Ecologist, Geographic Dynamics Corp., 211
Beckley, Michael, President & CEO, HLS Ecolo, 232
Beckley, Michael, President/CEO, Hydralogic Systems Inc., 235
Beckman, David, President, Zeton Inc., 437
Beckman, Kimberly L., Davies Howe Partners, 1074
Beckstrom, Bruce, A.H. Lundberg Systems Ltd., 63
Beckwith, Martin, Coordinator, Technical Services & Systems, Red River College, 1125
Bédard, Chantal, Greffière, L'Assomption, 736
Bédard, Joëlle, Acquisitions, Québec Ministère de la santé et des services sociaux, 1179
Beddome, James, President, The Green Party of Manitoba, 926
Bede, Gilbert, Librarian, Systems & Acquisitions, Okanagan College, 1112
Bedeau, Keri E.D., Borden Ladner Gervais LLP - Toronto, 1073
Bedford, S., Director, Planning & Development, Niagara-on-the-Lake, 715
Bedford, Tom, Manager, Ambulance Services & Emergency Programs, Lennox & Addington, 701
Bedford, B.A., LL.B., Andrew P., Partner, Lawson Lundell LLP - Calgary, 1051
Bedi, Shailoo, Head, Access Services, University of Victoria Libraries, 1121
Beechinor, Jim, Exec. Vice-President, AMEC, 82
Beecroft, Diane, Treasurer, Lloydminster, 780-875-6184, 673
Beeler, Jim, Chief Superintendent, Environmental Services, North Grenville, 728
Beeman, Robb D., Partner, Heenan Blaikie LLP - Calgary, 1051
Beer, Don, Fire Chief, Abbotsford, 604-853-2281, 679
Beffort, Doug, Area Councillor, Caledon, 707
Beggs, Gail, Deputy Minister, 623
Beggs, Paul, President, International Society of Biometeorology, 943
Bégin, Ghislain, Administrateur, Régie d'assainissement des eaux de la Vallée du Richelieu, 759
Bégin, Jean-Noel, Vice-Président, Electro-Mecanik Inc., 175
Bégin, Richard, Directeur, Saint-Jérôme, 743
Bégin Giroux, Carol, Québec, 740
Behie, Q.C., Peter C.P., Partner, Ramsay Lampman Rhodes, 1056
Behman, Heather K.M., Executive Director, 564
Behrens, Elizabeth, Associate University Librarian, Sir Wilfred Grenfell College, 1130
Behrick, David A., President, Behrick Enterprises Inc., 104
Behrns, Julie, Mayor, North Perth, 715
Behrns, Julie, Warden & Councillor, Perth, 703
Beier, Wolfgang, Manager, North Vancouver, 604-983-7392, 682
Beijal, Vivek, Vice-President, Cengea Solutions Inc., 136
Beil, Janet, Director, Skeena-Queen Charlotte, 679
Bein, Michael, Software Architect, Torrie Smith Associates Inc., 398
Beisel, Colin, Manager, Westburne Canada, 425
Beke, Paul A., Burnet, Duckworth & Palmer LLP, 1050
Bekolay, Tim, Prairie Region Manager, National Energy Equipment Inc., 297
Bélair, Jo-Anne, Secteur du répertoire de vedettes-matière, Université Laval, 1181
Bélair, Sylvain, Bélanger, Sauvé, 1082
Bélanger, André, Sorel-Tracy, 450-742-9587, 745
Bélanger, Anne, Lavery, de Billy - Montréal, 1085
Bélanger, Denise, Responsable, Périodiques, Collège de Maisonneuve, 1172
Bélanger, Donald, Rimouski, 740
Bélanger, François, Mirabel, 738
Bélanger, Gaston, Directeur général, Bécancour, 734
Bélanger, Gaston, Sec.-Trés., Régie intermunicipale d'assainissement de Daveluyville, 760
Bélanger, Ghislain, Directeur, Repentigny, 450-470-3150, 740
Bélanger, Guy, Directeur, Québec, 740
Bélanger, Jacques, Robinson Sheppard Shapiro LLP, 1087
Bélanger, Louis P., Associé, Stikeman Elliott LLP - Montréal, 1087
Bélanger, Louise, Fasken Martineau - Montréal, 1083
Bélanger, Marcel, Greffier, Saint-Jérôme, 736
Belanger, Maria, Library Technician, Northwest Atlantic Fisheries Centre, 1132
Bélanger, Michel, Directeur général, Les Laurentides, 749

Belanger, Michel, Vice President, Anachemia Canada Inc., 85
Bélanger, Michel, Vérificateur général, Lévis, 418-839-2002, 736
Bélanger, Micheline, Présidente, 655
Belanger, Nicholas, Industries Machinex Inc., 241
Bélanger, Nicole, Bibliotechnicienne, Centre régional de santé et de services sociaux Rimouski, 1181
Belanger, Peter, Account Manager, Hy-Grade Precast Concrete, 235
Bélanger, Pierre, Directeur-général, Régie intermunicipale d'aqueduc du Bas-Richelieu, 759
Bélanger, Pierre, Technicien en documentation, CÉGEP de Marie-Victorin, 1171
Bélanger, Richard, Maire d'arrondissement/Conseiller de la ville, Montréal, 738
Bélanger, Walter, Béton Provincial Ltée, 106
Bélanger, Yves, Granby, 735
Bélanger, Étienne, Manager, Forest Products Association of Canada, 918
Bélanger-Cadieux, Nicole, Responsable, acquisitions, CÉGEP de Marie-Victorin, 1171
Belcourt, Ron, Director, Recreation Services, Springwater, 730
Belcourt, Wayne, Branch Manager, Peto MacCallum Ltd., 322
Belczewski, Dan, Sr. Engineer, Bissett Resource Consultants Ltd., 110
Beldié, Jean-Jacques, Laval, 736
Belec, Lise, Sales Representative, Danfoss Inc. - Electric Floor Heating Division, 157
Belhumeur, Jean, President/COO, Leviton Canada, 270
Belhumeur, Marilyn, Librarian, Gabriel Dumont Institute of Native Studies & Applied Research, 1188
Belich, Mel, Chairman, The Van Horne Institute for International Transportation & Regula, 1016
Bélisle, Amélie, Heenan Blaikie S.E.N.C.R.L/SRL, 1084
Bélisle, André, Conseiller de ville, Pointe-aux-Trembles, Montréal, 738
Bélisle, André, Président, Association québécoise de lutte contre la pollution atmosphérique, 842
Bélisle, Serge, Directeur, Québec, 418-641-6292, 740
Bélisle Dutil, Lise, Longueuil, 737
Bélisle, CGA, Gilles, Trésorier, Drummondville, 819-478-6559, 735
Bélisle, OMA, Jean, Directeur, Saint-Hyacinthe, 450-778-8387, 742
Beliveau, Jean-Louis, President, Les Emballages Polyform inc., 268
Béliveau, Nicole, Longueuil, 737
Bell, Allan, Associate University Librarian, Information Techno, University of Waterloo, 1164
Bell, Bob, Guelph, 710
Bell, Connie, Manager, Oil Museum of Canada, 1146
Bell, David, Saxe, Dianne, 1079
Bell, Dennis, Foreman, Squamish, 688
Bell, Donald R.M., Davis LLP - Vancouver, 1074, 1059
Bell, Fran, Director, Corporate Services, Brant, 698
Bell, Gary K., President, Skelton Brumwell & Associates Inc., 369
Bell, James G.M., Davis LLP - Calgary, 1050
Bell, Janis, CAO, Cariboo, 677
Bell, Jeff, President, Manitoba Water Well Association, 952
Bell, Jim, Chief Building Official, Saugeen Shores, 719
Bell, Jim, President, Hydro-Mechanical Sales Ltd., 236
Bell, John, Shibley Righton LLP, 1079
Bell, Lynn, Director, 569
Bell, Norman A., Vice-President, Henderson Paddon & Associates Ltd., 229
Bell, Pat, Minister, 575
Bell, Pierre, Trésorier, Cowansville, 735
Bell, Ron, President, Association of Manitoba Municipalities, 836
Bell, Sarah Jane, Coordinator, Southeast Environmental Association, 1010
Bellamy, Mark, Principal, Stantec Inc., 378
Bellavance, Pierre C., Partner, Heenan Blaikie S.E.N.C.R.L/SRL - Québec, 1087
Belle, G. Carlo, President, Both Belle Robb Ltd., 114
Belleau, Shannon, Manager, Dillon Consulting Ltd., 164
Belleforte, Solange, Manager, Kamloops, 681
Belle-Isle, Manon, Planner, Hawkesbury, 711
Belleli, Hasmig, Conseillère, Ahuntsic, Montréal, 738
Bellemare, Christian, Directeur général, Saint-Eustache, 450-974-5280, 742
Bellemare, Ginette, Trois-Rivières, 745
Bellemare, Marie-Claude, Fasken Martineau - Montréal, 1083
Bellemare, Marie-Claude, Partner, Heenan Blaikie S.E.N.C.R.L/SRL, 1084
Belley Perron, Julie, McCarthy Tétrault LLP - Montréal, 1086

Executive Name Index

Bellhouse, Susan, Office Administrator, Manitoba Naturalists Society, 1124
Belli, Fabio, Greater Sudbury / Grand Sudbury, 710
Bellinger, Deborah A., Nelligan O'Brien Payne, 1071
Bellisle, Robin, Manager, G3 Consulting Ltd., 204
Belliveau, Paul N., Dieppe, 506-855-2637, 691
Belliveau, Sterling, Minister, 611
Belliveau, V.J., President, A.H. Roy & Associates Ltd., 64
Belliveau, Q.C., Robert G., McInnes Cooper, 1067
Bell-LeNoury, Carol, General Manager, EcoLog Information Resources Group, 172
Bellward, Bonny, Library Assistant, Edmonton Planning & Development Dept. Library, 1105
Belo, Jefferey C., Milton, 714
Belter, Dale, Contact, Comstock Canada Ltd., 148
Belton, John, Manager, Vancouver Gear Works Ltd., 409
Beltzner, Klaus, Treasurer, Transport Action Canada, 1013
Belyea, Paul, Sr. Engineer, AMEC, 83
Belzile, Sylvie, Directrice, Université de Sherbrooke, 1186
Bénard, Denis, Gestionnaire, Veolia ES Canada Industrial Services Inc., 411
Benarroch, Lison, VP, Groupe S.M. International Inc., 220
Benedetti, Bob, Maire, Beaconsfield, 734
Benedetti, Guy, Directeur général, Longueuil, 737
Benedetto, Paul, City Manager, Leduc, 673
Benedict, Eileen, Chair, Bulkley-Nechako, 250-692-3195, 676
Benjelloun, Rida, Secteur recherche et développements numériques, Université Laval, 1181
Benke, Larry M., Managing Director, WorleyParsons Canada Ltd., 434
Benkovich, Nick, Director, Water & Wastewater, Greater Sudbury / Grand Sudbury, 710
Benner, Steve, President, Envirogineering, 184
Bennett, Bruce, Acres & Associated Environmental Ltd., 67
Bennett, Clarence L., Stewart McKelvey Stirling Scales - Fredericton, 1064
Bennett, Daryl, Mayor, Peterborough, 718
Bennett, Dwight, CAO, Hants West District, 697
Bennett, George, Technical Sales Representative, Frontenac Environmental Ltd., 202
Bennett, John, Executive Director, Sierra Club of Canada, 1004
Bennett, John, Manager, 520
Bennett, Kearon J., President, Ottawa Engineering Ltd., 315
Bennett, Ken, Manager, North Vancouver, 604-990-2445, 688
Bennett, R., Contact, Entomological Society of British Columbia, 1112
Bennett, Sally, Director, Social Services, Middlesex, 701
Bennett, Wanda, Manager, Corporate Communications, Newmarket, 714
Bennett, Wayne, Councillor, Riverview, 506-386-3295, 692
Bennett Cook, Diane, Truro, 696
Bennewies, Dan, Manager, Boilersmith Ltd., 113
Bennington, Ken, Dufferin, 699
Benoit, C., PHH ARC Environmental Ltd., 322
Benoit, Gil, Treasurer, Sudbury Rock & Lapidary Society, 1011
Benoit, Jacques, Sr. Vice President/General Manager, SNC-Lavalin Environment Inc., 371
Benoît, Luc, President & CEO, Tecsult Inc., 388
Benoit, Manon, Agente de bureau, Comptoir de prêt, CÉGEP St-Jean-sur-Richelieu, 1183
Benoit, Éric, Manager, Flygt Canada, 198
Benson, Dianne, Financial Contact, Society for Research on Nicotine & Tobacco, 1007
Benson, Kim, Chair, 575
Benson, Matthew, Heenan Blaikie LLP - Toronto, 1075
Benson, Michael A., Contact, Conestoga-Rovers & Associates, 149
Benson, Vic, Senior Project Manager, Abcott Construction Ltd., 65
Bensoussan, Aimé, CEO, Groupe SOLROC, 221
Bent, Henry Everett, President/CEO, H.E. Bent Services Ltd., 223
Benteau, Steven, Director, 595
Bentley, Bob, Niagara, 702
Bentley, Brian, General Manager, Saskatoon, 306-975-2575, 754
Bentley, Lynne, Director, Humber College Institute of Technology & Advanced Learning, 1158
Bentley, Robert N., Mayor, Grimsby, 905-945-2710, 710
Bentley, Ross A., Blake, Cassels & Graydon LLP - Calgary, 1049
Bentz, Mark, Ward Councillor, Thunder Bay, 721
Bepple, Nancy, Kamloops, 681
Berard, Maureen, Manager, Yorkton, 306-786-1710, 755
Bérard, Yves, Sorel-Tracy, 450-746-8671, 745
Berardicurti, Lou, District Manager, BFI Canada Inc., 107
Berardinetti, Michelle, Toronto, 721

Bercha, F.G., President, Bercha Group, 105
Bercier, Pierre, Président, Union des cultivateurs franco-ontariens, 1014
Bercovitch, Morley, Councillor, Wasaga Beach, 722
Berdin, Julie, President/General Manager, Arpi's Industries Canada Ltd., 92
Berdnikoff, Loïc, Lavery, de Billy - Montréal, 1085
Berdowski, Ted, President, Structural Pest Management Association of Ontario, 1011
Beres, Dave, Councillor, Tillsonburg, 721
Beresford, Q.C., Harvey A., Partner, Hicks Morley Hamilton Stewart Storie LLP, 1076
Berezowskyj, Stephen J., Partner, Singleton Urquhart LLP, 1062
Berezuk, Gerry, Chair, 588
Berfelz, Patricia, Clerk, North Perth, 519-292-2062, 715
Berg, Sandy, Councillor, Kingston, 712
Berg, Victor, National Sales Manager, Equipement Labrie Ltee, 189
Bergan, Terry, President & CEO, International Road Dynamics Inc., 245
Berge, John, President, Durex Steel & Alloy Industries Ltd., 167
Berger, Bertrand, Préfet, Avignon, 747
Berger, Craig M., Director, Society for Environmental Graphic Design, 1007
Bergeron, Carole, Chef de service, Commission de la santé et de la securité du travail, 1173
Bergeron, Christine, Technicienne en documentation, CÉGEP St-Jean-sur-Richelieu, 1183
Bergeron, Gaétan, Directeur, Saguenay, 741
Bergeron, Ghislain, Chef technicien, Régie d'assainissement des eaux usées de Boischatel, L'Ange-Gardi, 759
Bergeron, Jacques, Vérificateur général, Montréal, 738
Bergeron, Jean, Directeur général, La Prairie, 450-444-6619, 736
Bergeron, Jean-François, President, NORDIKeau Inc., 305
Bergeron, Jean-Paul, Directeur général, Convoyeurs B.M.G. inc., 151
Bergeron, Jean-Sébastien, Cain Lamarre Casgrain Wells - Chicoutimi, 1082
Bergeron, Luc, Les Laboratoires Shermont Inc., 269
Bergeron, Luc, Directeur général, Saint-Félicien, 418-679-2100, 742
Bergeron, Marthe, Responsable, Référence et periodiques, CÉGEP de la Pocatière, 1177
Bergeron, Martine, Langlois Kronström Desjardins, 1085
Bergeron, Nicole, Sherbrooke, 744
Bergeron, Pierre, Directeur, Mont-St-Hilaire, 738
Bergeron, Richard, Associé, Cain Lamarre Casgrain Wells - Chicoutimi, 1082
Bergeron, Richard, Conseiller de ville, De Lorimier, Montréal, 738
Bergeron, CA, MBA, M.Sc., Jacques, Vérificateur général, Montréal, 738
Bergeson, Cara, Publisher & Conference Manager, Resource Recycling Inc., 995
Bergey, Richard, Manager, Quesnel, 688
Berggren, Don, President, Berg Chilling Systems Inc., 105
Berggren, R. Lorne, Chair & CEO, Berg Chilling Systems Inc., 105
Bergheim, Dennis, Manager, Evergreen Regional Waste Management Services Commission, 757
Bergin, PhD, Patrick J., President/CEO, African Wildlife Foundation, 813
Bergmann, S., Head, Canadian Bottled Water Association, 1153
Bergner, B.A., LL.B., Keith, Partner, Lawson Lundell LLP - Vancouver, 1060
Bergsma, John, Commissioner, Corporate Services, Niagara, 702
Beriau, Tania, Development Director, Sierra Club of Canada, 1004
Berkenbosch, Wendy-Anne, Davis LLP - Edmonton, 1055
Berkovich, Stuart J., President/CEO, Array Systems Computing Inc., 93
Berliner, Lloyd I., Patterson Law, 1068
Berloni, Gianni, General Manager, Polychem Products Ltd., 328
Bermingham, Tim W., Blake, Cassels & Graydon LLP - Toronto, 1072
Bernard, Diane, Executive Secretary to the Minister, 611
Bernard, Francine, Bibliothécaire, Bibliothèque canadienne de l'agriculture - Sainte-Foy, 1177
Bernard, Fred, Operations Manager, Eco Wood Products, 78, 170
Bernard, Manon, Directrice générale, Vaudreuil-Dorion, 746
Bernard, Max R., Partner, Heenan Blaikie S.E.N.C.R.L/SRL, 1084
Bernard, Rupert, Miramichi, 691
Bernard, Réal, Granby, 735

Bernard, Scotty, Chair, Northumberland Solid Waste Commission, 758
Bernard, Stella, President, Refined Specialty Chemicals Inc., 344
Bernard, Terence H., Charlottetown, 732
Bernard, Yann, Associé, Langlois Kronström Desjardins, 1085
Bernatchez, Anik, Heenan Blaikie S.E.N.C.R.L./SRL - Québec, 1087
Bernatchez, Danielle, Directrice, Baie-Comeau, 418-296-8128, 733
Bernatchez, Gaétan, Directeur général, Avignon, 747
Bernatchez, Gilles, Technicien en documentation, Centre spécialisé des Pêches - Grande-Rivière, 1168
Bernier, André, Chair, Pulp & Paper Technical Association of Canada, 991
Bernier, Claude, Maire, Saint-Hyacinthe, 450-778-8302, 742
Bernier, Denis, Director, Enviroconseil, 183
Bernier, Hélène, Bibliothécaire, Bibliothèque des sciences et de génie, 1185
Bernier, Janice, President, Regina & District Labour Council, 994
Bernier, Jean-Luc, Officer, ArcticNet Inc., 829
Bernier, Jean-Pierre, Engineer, Hebco International Inc., 228
Bernier, Maurice, Préfet, Le Granit, 749
Bernier, Mike, First Vice President, North Central Local Government Association, 965
Bernier, Mike, Mayor, Dawson Creek, 680
Bernier, Monique, Vice-Chair, Canadian Remote Sensing Society, 884
Bernier, Pierre, Director General, 522
Bernier-Genest, Carle, Conseiller, Marie-Victorin, Montréal, 738
Bernier-Monzon, Alexander, Assistant, Hanna Instruments Canada Inc., 224
Beros, Greg, Richmond Hill, 718
Berris, Catherine, President/CEO, Catherine Berris Associates Inc., 132
Berry, Gerald (Jerry), City Manager, Nanaimo, 250-755-4401, 681
Berry, Joffre, President, JMB Research Ltd., 252
Berry, Lawrence, President, Hamworthy-Peabody Combustion Canada Inc., 224
Berry, Shawn, Brandon, 689
Berry, Steve, Grimsby, 905-945-2578, 710
Berry, Susan, Manager, Roseridge Waste Management Services Commission, 758
Berry, William J., Director, Kelowna, 681
Bertell, PhD., Rosalie, Founder, International Institute of Concern for Public Health, 940
Bertelsen, Siri, Planner, Fraser Valley, 677
Berthellette, Denis, Directeur d'Exploitation, Régie intermunicipale de l'eau de Deux-Montagnes, 760
Berthelot, Jean-Marie, Vice-President, Canadian Institute for Health Information, 872
Berthelot, Yvan, Saint-Jean-sur-Richelieu, 450-349-0685, 742
Berthiaume, Claude, Greater Sudbury / Grand Sudbury, 710
Berthiaume, Michel, Sorel-Tracy, 450-742-0267, 745
Berthiaume, Phillip, Planner, Emergency Measures, Essex, 699
Berthiaume, Rene, Prescott & Russell, 729
Berthiaume, Rene, Mayor, Hawkesbury, 711
Berthiaume, Réjean, Président, Pageau Morel & associés, inc., 317
Berthiaume, Sylvain, Directeur général, Lajemmerais, 749
Berthiaume, M.Sc., OMA, Jean-Luc, Greffier, Sainte-Thérèse, 744
Berthiume, Denis, Manager, Area Water Services, Tecumseh, 720
Berthold, Luc, Maire, Thetford Mines, 745
Bertles, Kevin, Manager, Vernon, 685
Bertoia, Stan, Commissioner, Community Services Department, Oshawa, 716
Bertol, Michèle, Director, Iqaluit, 867-979-6363, 698
Bertolini, Renzo, Manager, 517
Bertossi, Henry, Partner, Heenan Blaikie LLP - Toronto, 1075
Bertram, Carolyn, Minister, 638
Bertrand, Anne E., General Manager, ARC Geobac Group Inc., 90
Bertrand, Claude, Greffier, Blainville, 450-434-5215, 734
Bertrand, Denis, Laval, 450-978-5876, 736
Bertrand, Gilles, Directeur général, Magog, 819-843-2880, 737
Bertrand, Ginette, Municipal Clerk, Russell, 729
Bertrand, Gordon, Head, Systems & Support Services, St Francis-Xavier University, 1134
Bertrand, Jean G., Ogilvy Renault LLP/S.E.N.C.R.L., s.r.l. - Montréal, 1086
Bertrand, Justin, Heenan Blaikie LLP - Ottawa, 1070
Bertrand, Luc, Geotechnical Engineer, Les Laboratoires Shermont Inc., 269

Executive Name Index

Bertrand, Nicole, Director, Calgary, 121
Bertrand, Rémi, Directeur général, Pontiac, 751
Bertrand, Sylvie, Reader's Services Assistant, Canada Science & Technology Museum, 1148
Bertrand, Wendy, Operations Manager, FCX NH Valves, 194
Bérubé, Andrée-Claude, McCarthy Tétrault LLP - Montréal, 1086
Bérubé, Daniel, Communications, Université Laval, 1181
Bérubé, François, Associé, Cain Lamarre Casgrain Wells - Amqui, 1082
Bérubé, Gilles, Val-d'Or, 746
Bérubé, Jean-Sébastien, President & CEO, GDG Environnement Ltée, 205
Bérubé, Marcel, Saint-Georges, 742
Bérubé, Paul C., Bérubé & Pion, SENCRL, 1089
Berube, Robert, Vice-President, TurboSonic Inc., 404
Bérubé, Serge, Conseiller pédagogique, Collège de Saint-Félicien, 1183
Berube, Serge, Technical Specialist, Decibel Consultants Inc., 159
Berze, Frank, Middlesex Centre, 727
Bes, Bill M., City Councillor, Woodstock, 723
Besner, Dave, President, D. Besner & Associates Inc., 156
Besnier, Hubert, Besnier, Dion & Rondeau, 1089
Besserer, Dean, Vice-President, Apex Geoscience Ltd., 86
Best, Cathie, Town Clerk, Oakville, 715
Best, Colin, Halton, 700
Best, Colin, Local & Regional Councillor, Milton, 714
Best, Margarett R., Minister, 629
Best, Ray, Prince Edward, 703
Bestwick, William Leslie (Bill), Nanaimo, 681
Beswick, Bette, Registrar, Alberta Society of Professional Biologists, 819
Betts, Greg, Administrator, North Okanagan, 250-550-3714, 678
Betts, Ted, Blake, Cassels & Graydon LLP - Toronto, 1072
Bevan, Andy, Director, 605
Bevan, Lori M., Macleod Dixon LLP, 1052
Beverage, Becky, Office Manager, Plastiglas Industries Limited, 326
Bevilacqua, Maurizio, York, 705
Bevilacqua, Maurizio, Mayor, Vaughan, 722
Beynon, Douglas, President/CEO, Unisearch Associates Inc., 406
Bezaire, John, Huron, 701
Bezaire, Steven, Lakeshore, 712
Bezak, Stafford, Manager, Waterous Power Systems, 422
Bharati, Raj, Willms & Shier Environmental Lawyers LLP, 1081
Bhat, Ph.D, FCSME, Rama B., President, Canadian Society for Mechanical Engineering, 886
Bhattacharya, P.Eng., Nirmal, Municipal Engineer, Central Saanich, 250-652-4444, 686
Bhushan, Bharat, Sr. Research Scientist, Kam Biotechnology Ltd., 254
Bialkowski, Mark, Manager, Human Resources, Dufferin, 699
Bianchini, Sandy, Executive Secretary, 520
Biard, André, Saint-Eustache, 450-473-2214, 742
Bibeau, Yvon, Sorel-Tracy, 450-746-8987, 745
Bickell, Jana, Library Technician, Orillia Campus, 1147
Biderman, David, General Counsel & Director, National Solid Wastes Management Association, 958
Biderman, Matthew A., Paterson, MacDougall LLP, Barristers, Solicitors, 1079
Bidyk, Brian, Partner, Heenan Blaikie LLP - Calgary, 1051
Bielaczyk, Scott, Operations Manager, Ecotech Planners & Advisors Inc., 172
Bienvenu, Richard, SOTAR Inc., 374
Bieri, Ernest, CEO, Waterloo Evaporateurs Inc., 422
Bieri, Jacques, Vice-President, Waterloo Evaporateurs Inc., 422
Bies, Michel, Contact, Divex Marine, 164
Biesenthal, Betty, Director of Publicity, The Friends of Bonnechere Parks, 920
Bifolchi, Nina, Councillor, Wasaga Beach, 722
Big Bull, William, Project Coordinator, Piikuni Utilities Corp., 323
Bigeard, Eric, CEO, Lyreco Office Products, 276
Bigelow, Juanita, Administrator, Truro, 696
Biggar, Michael, President, Willow Beach Field Naturalists, 1020
Bigger, John, Chair, Fredericton Region Solid Waste Commission, 758
Biggs, Wayne G., Biologist, Westland Resource Group Inc., 430
Bigler, Joseph A., President, MSA: Mine Safety Applicances Company, 294
Bignell, Dave, President & Chief Executive Officer, Siemens Milltronics Process Instruments Inc., 366
Bignell, Robert, Executive Director, Ontario Tire Dealers Association, 980
Bigras, Martin, Deux-Montagnes, 735

Bigras, Steven, Executive Director, 520
Bigué, Ann M., McCarthy Tétrault LLP - Montréal, 1086
Bilanski, Marlys, General Manager, Saskatoon, 306-975-3206, 754
Biljan, Tyrone, Regional Recycling Manager, Rechargeable Battery Recycling Corporation, 343
Billett, Doug, Director, 656
Billey, Brett, Micro-Watt Control Devices Ltd., 289
Billey, Clayton, Manager, Metso Automation Canada Ltd., 288
Billings, Keith, President, Integrated Metal Products, 244
Billington, Charles, Executive Director, Rideau Valley Conservation Authority, 995
Bilodeau, A., Carrier Canada Ltd., 129
Bilodeau, Danielle, Directrice, Lévis, 418-839-2002, 736
Bilodeau, Louis, Directeur général, Saint-Hyacinthe, 742
Bilodeau, Nancy, Greffière, Coaticook, 747
Bilodeau, Raymond, Préfet, Nicolet-Yamaska, 750
Bilodeau, Sandra, Morency Avocats, 1088
Bilodeau, Serge, Directeur général, Le Granit, 749
Bilodeau, Yvan, Président-directeur général, 647
Bilsky, Ray, Rayplex Limited, 343
Bilton, William (Bill), Lambton, 701
Binda, Roberto, Branch Leader, Urban Systems Ltd., 407
Binder, Michael, President, 520
Binder, Richard, Manager, Calgary, 671
Binet, Carole, Directrice générale adjointe, La Nouvelle-Beauce, 748
Binet, Michel, Directeur, Longueuil, 737
Binette, Serge, Marketing Manager, Canadian Technical Tape Ltd., 125
Bingaman, Jim, Director, 656
Binnie, Brenda, President, Union of British Columbia Municipalities, 1015
Binnington, Cynthia, Assistant Deputy Minister, 545
Binns, Dawn, Contact, Council for a Smoke-Free PEI, 904
Binns, Shawn, Director, Recreation & Community Services, Oro-Medonte, 728
Birch, Rick, Equipment Rental Manager, ASL Environmental Sciences Inc., 94
Birch, Sean, President, Geotechnical Society of Edmonton, 923
Birch, P.Eng., Rowan, Assistant City Engineer, Vancouver, 604-873-7280, 685
Bird, Andrea, Manager, Bartle & Gibson Co. Ltd., 102
Bird, Carl, Director, Yellowknife, 867-920-5666, 695
Bird, F. Keith, Halton, 700
Bird, F. Keith, Town & Regional Councillor, Oakville, 715
Bird, Gwen, Associate University Librarian, Collection Service, Simon Fraser University, 1111
Bird, Kathryn J., Associate, Hicks Morley Hamilton Stewart Storie LLP, 1076
Birdi, Paul, Sr. Project Engineer, Aerzen Canada Surpresseurs Compresseurs inc., 72
Birkbeck, Geoffrey, Chief Executive Officer, Comstock Canada Ltd., 148
Birks, Michael, President, Birks Co., 110
Birns, Larry, Director, Council on Hemispheric Affairs, 905
Biron, Michèle D., Conseillère d'arrondissement, Norman-McLaren, Montréal, 738
Biron, Yvan, Lavery, de Billy - Montréal, 1085
Birshtein, Nili, Stikeman Elliott LLP - Toronto, 1079
Birt, Charles, President, Sandwell Engineering Inc., 357
Birtz, Frédéric, Directeur des opérations, Association provinciale des constructeurs d'habitations du Québec, 841
Bischoff, Angela, Director, Ontario Clean Air Alliance, 972
Bish, Lucille, Director, Community Services, Waterloo, 704
Bishop, Bill, Director, Human Resources, Lennox & Addington, 701
Bishop, Donavon (Von), Manager, Saanich, 688
Bishop, Gart, Chair, Kennebecasis Naturalists' Society, 947
Bishop, Janet, Assistant, New Brunswick Dept. of Wellness, Culture & Sport, 1129
Bishop, Jeff, Coordinator, Forest Products Association of Nova Scotia, 919
Bishop, John, Branch Manager, BC Air Filter Ltd., 103
Bishop, Liz, Acting Chief Librarian, Ryerson University, 1161
Bishop, William J., Mayor, Rothesay, 692
Bishop, C.A., Robert, Treasurer & Director, St. John's, 709-576-8696, 694
Bishop, P.Ag, Gary, President/Treasurer, Newfoundland & Labrador Institute of Agrologists, 963
Bishop, Q.C., Donald G., Bishop & McKenzie LLP, 1054
Bisset, Laura K., Davis LLP - Toronto, 1074
Bissett, K.R. (Dick), President, Bissett Resource Consultants Ltd., 110
Bissett, Scott, Director, Armstrong Monitoring Corp., 91

Bisson, Lucie, Sainte-Julie, 743
Bisson, Phillipe, Archives Technician, National Air Photo Library, 1151
Bissonnet, Michel, Maire d'arrondissement, Montréal, 738
Bissonnet, Yvette, Conseillère de ville, Saint-Léonard, Montréal, 738
Bissonnette, Alain, Directeur, Finances/Trésorier, Longueuil, 737
Bissonnette, Leo, Organic Resource Management Inc., 314
Bissonnette, Marcel, Manager, Miller Environmental Corp., 290
Bissoon, Devin, Sales Manager, Refined Specialty Chemicals Inc., 344
Bissoon, Frank, General Manager, Refined Specialty Chemicals Inc., 344
Bittar, M.Sc., Patricia, Conseillère de ville, Norman-McLaren, Montréal, 738
Bizier, Gilles, Bibliothécaire, Laurentian Forestry Centre, 1179
Bizimana, Bernard, Directeur, Services techniques & informatisés, HEC Montréal, 1173
Bizio, Albert, Commissioner, Medicine Hat, 403-529-8229, 673
Bjorgaard, Ken, Director, Mission, 687
Bjornerud, Bob, Minister, 656
Bjornerud, Bob, Minister Responsible, 656
Bjornson, Pam, Director General, 546
Bjornson, Pam, Director, Business Affairs, Canada Institute for Scientific & Technical Information (CISTI), 1148
Bjornson, Peter, Minister, 587
Blachford, John, Manager, BDS Laboratories, 104
Blachford, John, President, H.L. Blachford Ltd., 223
Black, David R., McCaffery Mudry Pritchard LLP, Barristers & Solicitors, 1052
Black, Gary, P.J. Hannah Equipment Sales Corp., 316
Black, Linda, Director, Winnipeg, 690
Black, Malcolm, President, Blackbox Automation Inc., 110
Black, Michael J., Heenan Blaikie LLP - Calgary, 1051
Black, Nancy E., Distance & Document Delivery Librarian, University of Northern British Columbia, 1115
Black, Patricia, Directrice, Bibliothèque des arts et musique, Université du Québec à Montréal, 1176
Black, Steven L., Timmins, 721
Black, Q.C., Douglas J., Fraser Milner Casgrain LLP - Calgary, 1051
Black, Q.C., J. Robert, Brownlee LLP, 1054
Blackburn, Diane, Manager, Recycling Council of Ontario, 993
Blackburn, Luc, Saguenay, 741
Blackburn, Norman, Maire, Lavaltrie, 736
Blackburn, Norman, Préfet, D'Autray, 747
Blackburn, Q.C., E.A. Nelson, Chair, 611
Blackett, Glenn C., Carscallen Leitch LLP, 1050
Blackhurst, Ross, Conseiller d'arrondissement, Sault-St-Louis, Montréal, 738
Blackman, Wendy, President, Cartridge Care Canada, 130
Blackmore, Bob, Sales Engineer, Folio Instruments Inc., 199
Blackmore, Bonnie, Manager, Community Services, Wellington, 705
Blackmore, David, Director, St. John's, 709-576-8701, 694
Blackmore, Vance, Middlesex, 701
Blades, Mike, Landfill Manger, CCS Income Trust, 134
Blaikie, Bill, Minister, 586
Blaikie, Peter M., Founding Partner, Heenan Blaikie S.E.N.C.R.L/SRL, 1084
Blain, David, Director, Chilliwack, 604-793-2841, 680
Blain, Isabelle, Vice-President, 552
Blair, Christine, Councillor, Colchester County, 697
Blair, David F., Partner, Heenan Blaikie S.E.N.C.R.L./SRL - Québec, 1087
Blair, Hugh, Contact, Ozocan Corporation, 315
Blair, Iain, Documentalist, Centre for Developing Area Studies, 1171
Blair, K. Alan, Gowling Lafleur Henderson LLP - Vancouver, 1060
Blairs, Mark, Kason, 255
Blais, Alain, President, Sonitec Inc., 374
Blais, Donald, Directeur, Québec Ministère des transports, 1180
Blais, Hervé, Préfet, Bellechasse, 747
Blais, Jules, President, Bémalux Inc., 105
Blais, Laurent, La Prairie, 736
Blais, Marcel (Pat), Tecumseh, 519-735-2686, 720
Blais, Richard, Vice-President & Manager, Waters Limited, 423
Blais, Roger, Blais, Roger avocat inc, 1082
Blais, Réjean, Technical Director, René Gervais Inc., Consultants, 1166
Blais, Stephen, Ottawa, 716
Blaize, Ted, Manager, Conterm Inc., 151
Blake, Erik, President, Icefield Instruments Inc., 238
Blake, Melissa, Mayor, Wood Buffalo, 670
Blake, Phil, President/CEO, Bayer Inc., 103

Executive Name Index

Blake, Scott, Fire Chief, Lincoln, 713
Blake, Tim, Fire Chief, Trent Hills, 705-653-1234, 731
Blakely, Bernie, Business Development, Ocean Steel & Construction Ltd., 311
Blakely, Jane, Director, Fredericton, 691
Blakely, Robert, Chair, 571
Blakeman, P., Carrier Canada Ltd., 129
Blakey, Carol, Principal, Cheiron Resources Ltd., 139
Blakey, D., The Greer Galloway Group Inc., Engineers & Planners, 392
Blakey, Steve, Contact, The Greer Galloway Group Inc., Engineers & Planners, 392
Blakney, John F., Fraser Milner Casgrain LLP - Ottawa, 1070
Le Blanc, Denis, Varennes, 746
Blanchard, Carmel, Technicienne en administration, Québec Ministère des Ressources naturelles et de la Faune, 1180
Blanchard, Ghislain, Director General, 520
Blanchard, Jim, Head, Reference Service, Elizabeth Dafoe Library, 1123
Blanchard, Laurent, Conseiller, Hochelaga, Montréal, 738
Blanchard, Pierre-Luc, Directeur, Sainte-Julie, 450-922-7142, 743
Blanchet, Bernard, Conseiller d'arrondissement, J.-Émery-Provost, Montréal, 738
Blanchet, Sylvain, Bibliothécaire, Québec Ministère du Développement durable, de l'Environnement et, 1180
Blanchette, Bertrand, Co-President, Groupe Berlie-Falco Inc., 219
Blanchette, Dany, Gestionnaire, Veolia ES Canada Industrial Services Inc., 411
Blanchette, Denis, Gowling Lafleur Henderson S.E.N.C.R.L./LLP, 1084
Blanchette, Frédéric, Associé, Lapointe Rosenstein Marchand Melançon, 1085
Blanchette, Ray, Partner, Servicestat Ltd., 364
Blanchette, Shirley, Library Technician, City Hospital, Saskatoon, 1189
Blaney, Paul, President, Kingston Lapidary & Mineral Club, 947
Blank, Irwin, CEO, 656
Blanleil, Andre F., Kelowna, 681
Blanleil, Rene M., Fire Chief, Kelowna, 681
Blaszak, Derek, McElhanney Consulting Services Ltd., 285
Blau, J., President, Saskatchewan Coalition for Tobacco Reduction, 999
Blazina, Sandy, Document Delivery Specialist, Gallagher Library of Geology & Geophysics, 1101
Blicker, tTacey, Contact, International Titanium Association, 944
Blight, Murray, Brandon, 689
Blize, Val, Contact, Alberta Conservation Tillage Society II, 816
Block, David, City Planner, Terrace, 250-615-4028, 685
Block, Q.C., Randall W., Partner, Borden Ladner Gervais LLP - Calgary, 1049
Bloess, Rainer, Ottawa, 613-580-2472, 716
Blokker, Peter, Project Manager, Esco Engineering, 189
Blomfield, Kate, Ratcliff & Company LLP, 1057
Bloome, Mark, Operations Manager (Atlantic), Lantech Drilling Services Inc., 264
Bloomer, David, Commissioner, Infrastructure & Transportation Serv, Oakville, 715
Bloomfield, Clare, Deputy Mayor, Middlesex Centre, 727
Blouin, Gaétan, President, Sani Gestion ONYX, 357
Blouin, Michel, Lavery, de Billy - Montréal, 1085
Blouin, Monique, Technicienne en documentation, Québec Conseil de la science et de la technologie, 1179
Blouin, Pierre, Québec, 740
Bloxom, Cecilia, Director, Canadian Patient Safety Institute, 881
Blue, Q.C., Ian A., Cassels Brock & Blackwell LLP, 1074
Blues, Frank, Manager, Prince George, 250-561-7503, 683
Blumenthal, Jerry, Councillor, Halifax Regional Municipality, 695
Blythe, Don, Chair, Tire Stewardship BC Association, 1012
Boa, Mae, Executive Director, 656
Boag, David, Director, Maple Ridge, 604-467-7344, 687
Boag, Thomas, President & Sr. Fish Biologist, Applied Aquatic Research Ltd., 87
Boal, Gary, Superintendent, Waste Site, North Grenville, 728
Boan, Daniel A., Partner, Borden Ladner Gervais LLP - Toronto, 1073
Boase, Shannon, Founder & President, Earthcycle, 169
Bobbie, Brian, President, ALTECH Environmental Consulting Ltd., 81
Bobbitt, Judith, President, Oceans Ltd., 311
Bochar, Quentin, Manager, Sturgeon County, 780-939-8325, 670
Bock, Johanne, Directrice-générale, Régie intermunicipale des déchets de la Rouge, 761
Bock, Theodor E., Aikins, MacAulay & Thorvaldson LLP, 1063

Bocking, Cheri, Lang Michener LLP - Vancouver, 1060
Bockstegers, Ute, Chief Financial Officer/Head, Bayer Inc., 103
Bodak, Trudy, Map Librarian, Map Library, 1159
Boddez, Gary, Deputy Minister, 573
Boddy, Brent, Asst. Deputy Minister, 617
Boddy, Ian C., Owen Sound, 717
Bodechon, Allen, Police Chief, Saint John, 506-648-3200, 692
Bodnar, Greg, Director, Coast Paper Ltd., 145
Bodnarek, Q.C., Ray, Deputy Minister & Deputy Attorney General, 570
Bodner, Ron, Port Colborne, 718
Bodtker, Nils, President & CEO, Great Western Containers Inc., 216
Boduch, Walt, General Manager, Wyckomar Inc., 435
Boettcher, Richard, Manager, Degussa Canada Inc., 159
Boffice, Anthony, Châteauguay, 450-699-4613, 735
Bogaski, Doug, Library Service Assistant, Winnipeg Water & Waste Dept., 1126
Bohna, Tom, CEO, Happy Harry's Used Building Material, 225
Bohnet, Gary, Deputy Minister, 605
Boies, Karine, Cain Lamarre Casgrain Wells - Chicoutimi, 1082
Boileau, Alexandre, Fraser Milner Casgrain S.E.N.C.R.L./LLP, 1084
Boileau, André, Laval, 736
Boileau, Chantal, Librarian, Quebec Regional Library, 1169
Boileau, Diane, Directrice, Longueuil, 737
Boileau, Mark, Manager, Economic Development, Cornwall, 708
Boily, Lucien, Alma, 418-669-1070, 733
Boily, Martin, Vice-President, Kruger Inc., 260
Bois, Charles W., Partner, Miller Thomson LLP - Vancouver, 1061
Bois, Hans, Associé, Langlois Kronström Desjardins, 1088
Boisaubert, Philip, Director, Produits Ferpac Ltée, 333
Boisseau, Pierre, President, Métropolitain Valve Inc., 288
Boisselle, Marc, Associé directeur régional, Cain Lamarre Casgrain Wells - Drummondville, 1082
Boisson, Chantal, Maccaferri Canada Ltd., 277
Boisson, Chantal, Territory Manager, Green Turtle Technologies Ltd. (Canada), 217
Boissonneault, Marie-Josée, Directrice, Deux-Montagnes, 735
Boissonneault, Paul, Fire Chief, Brant, 698
Boisvenue, John Paul, Stablex Canada Inc., 377
Boisvenue, Marc, Sales & Marketing, Chemrec, 140
Boisvert, Alain, Business Development Director, GSI Environnement Inc., 222
Boisvert, Claire, Directrice, Services techniques, Université du Québec à Montréal, 1176
Boisvert, Daniel, President & Forest Engineer, Nove Environnement Inc., 309
Boisvert, Denis, Directeur, Université du Québec à Rimouski, 1181
Boisvert, Denis, Directeur général, Pierre-De Saurel, 750
Boisvert, Diane, Vice President, Argus Telecom International Inc., 90
Boisvert, Elaine, Marketing Administrator, Argus Telecom International Inc., 90
Boisvert, Johanne, Acquisitions, CÉGEP de Drummondville, 1167
Boisvert, Léo, Rouyn-Noranda, 741
Boisvert, Pierre, Sherbrooke, 744
Boitier, Dominique, Sales & Marketing, Fugro Airborne Surveys, 203
Boivin, Ben, Muskoka, 702
Boivin, Bernard, Siège #2, Saint-Félicien, 742
Boivin, Christian, Aquateck Ltd., 89
Boivin, Claude, President, Labrie Environmental Group, 189, 262
Boivin, Jean-François, Directeur général, Saguenay, 418-698-3320, 741
Boivin, Michel, Sous-ministre, 654
Boivin, Mélanie, Cain Lamarre Casgrain Wells - Québec, 1087
Boivin, Philippe, McCarthy Tétrault LLP - Québec, 1088
Boivin, Pierre, McCarthy Tétrault LLP - Québec, 1088
Boivin, Thomas, President/Senior Environmental Biologist, Hatfield Group, 227
Bojin, Minda, Chief, Metadata & Cataloguing Services, Public Works & Government Services Canada, 1168
Bokenfohr, Daniel R., McLennan Ross LLP, 1055
Boland, Bruce, Librarian, Newfoundland & Labrador Dept. of Forest Resources & Agrifood, 1130
Boland, Bruce, Senior Vice-President, 634
Boland, Leo, President, Pembroke Area Field Naturalists, 985
Bolander, Pat, Information Technician, EnCana Corporation, 1101
Bolanos-Shaw, Kerry, Vice-President, Adventus Canada Inc., 69
Bolch, Mike, Manager, Powell River, 679

Bolduc, Bertrand, Président, BIOQuébec, 845
Bolduc, Martin, Regional Director General, Québec Region, 514
Bolduc, Yves, Ministre, 652
Bolen, John, General Manager, CCL/IBI, 133
Bolger, P.Jeremy, Partner, Borden Ladner Gervais LLP - Montréal, 1083
Bolger, Pat, President, Bolger and Associates Ltd., 113
Bolger, T.B. (Brent), President & Technical Director, Brendar Environmental Inc., 116
Bolivar-Getson, Carolyn, Minister, 614
Bolone, Harold, Director, CCL/IBI, 133
Bolt, Trevor, Regional Manager, Varcon Inc., 410
Bolton, David, Middlesex, 701
Bolton, Kari, Director, Quesnel, 688
Bolton, Lori, Director, Human Resources, Orillia, 716
Bolton, Steve, Manager, Labtronics, 262
Bombardier, Michel, Magog, 737
Bombay, Harry M., Executive Director, National Aboriginal Forestry Association, 956
Bomhof, Rick, Director, Mission, 604-820-3736, 687
Boncori, Anthony, Chief Building Official, West Lincoln, 732
Bond, Alan J., Clerk-Treas., Antigonish County, 696
Bond, Bonnie, Chair, Seagull Foundation, 1003
Bond, Joshua, Riopelle Griener Professional Corporation, 1072
Bond, Meredith, President, Zorbit Technologies Inc., 437
Bond, Shirley, Minister, 576
Bond, Tim, Fire Chief, North Grenville, 728
Bondy, Cheryl, Clerk & Deputy-Treasurer, Essex, 709
Bondy, Marc, LaSalle, 713
Bondy, Sherry, Essex, 709
Bone, Christopher, President, Rotork Controls (Canada) Ltd., 352
Bone, Scott, Manager, Prince George, 250-561-7511, 683
Bonfini, Jeremy, Healthcare Information & Management Systems Society, 928
Bonhomme, Robert, Partner, Heenan Blaikie S.E.N.C.R.L/SRL, 1084
Bonin, Lionel, Director of Library, Laurentian University, 1155
Bonin, Pauline, Secrétaire, CÉGEP de Drummondville, 1167
Boniwell, Simon, Sales Manager, Geonics Limited, 211
Bonnah, Victor, Co-Founder, President & CEO, Infotech Canada Inc., 241
Bonneau, André, Directeur, Gatineau, 735
Bonner, Bruce, D.M. Wills Associates Limited, 156
Bonner, Bruce, President, D.M. Wills Associates Limited, 156
Bonner, Penny S., Senior Partner, Ogilvy Renault LLP.S.E.N.C.R.L., s.r.l. - Toronto, 1078
Bonnet, Olivier, Canadian Director, International Fund for Animal Welfare Canada, 939
Bonnette, Rick, Halton, 700
Bonnette, Rick, Mayor, Halton Hills, 710
Bonneville, Denis, Cain Lamarre Casgrain Wells - Alma, 1082
Bonneville, M. Daniel, Président, Camvac Inc., 122
Bonora, Doris., Reynolds, Mirth, Richards & Farmer LLP, 1056
Bonser, Steve, Manager, Environmental Division, CD Nova, 135
Bonura, Joseph J., Chief Building Offical, Brock, 724
Boodman, Martin, McCarthy Tétrault LLP - Montréal, 1086
Boogaards, R., General Manager, Comox Valley, 677
Boome, Alexander J., President, Alexander Boome Consulting Engineering, Ltd., 78
Boone, Daniel M., Managing Partner, Stewart McKelvey Stirling Scales - St. John's, 1066
Boorn, Andy, President, MDS Sciex, 286
Booth, Jim, Acting Assistant Commissioner & Comptroller, 552
Booth, Michael, Manager, Atlantic Newsprint Company, 96
Boothe, Paul, Deputy Minister, 522
Bootsma, Marty, Chair, Columbia-Shuswap, 677
Bootsma, Marty, Mayor, Salmon Arm, 684
Boras, Keith, Manager, Lacombe County, 669
Bordeleau, Lynda A., Perley-Robertson, Hill & McDougall LLP, 1071
Bordeleau, Yves, Shawinigan, 744
Borden, Charmaine, Librarian, Truro Campus, 1137
Borden, Rick P., Partner, Macleod Dixon LLP, 1052
Borges, Felix R., President/CEO, Prism Chemicals Inc., 333
Le Borgne, Louis, Bibliothécaire, Bibliothèque centrale, 1170
Borja, Robert, Tech Sales Co., 387
Bork, Greg, President, FLIR Systems, Inc., 197
Born, Peter, Manager, Toromont Caterpillar, 397
Bornehag, Carl-Gustaf, Treasurer, International Society of Indoor Air Quality & Climate, 943
Bornes, Glenn, Branch Manager, Fort Garry Industries Ltd., 200
Bornmann, Barbara, Executive Assistant, International Sanitary Supply Association, Inc., 942

Executive Name Index

Borodacz, Marusia, Team Leader, Ontario Ministry of Environment, 1160
Borooah, Ann, Executive Director, Toronto Building, & Chief Buil, Toronto, 416-397-4446, 721
Borowicz, QC, JP, CA (Hon, Frank S., Counsel, Davis LLP - Vancouver, 1059
Borrell, Ian H., Vice-President, BIOREM Inc., 109
Borret, Alan, Design/Engineering, Hike Metal Products Ltd., 232
Borstad, Gary, President, G.A. Borstad Associates Ltd., 203
Bortolotti, Sandra, Operations Manager, AUTO21 - The Automobile of the 21st Century, 844
Borud, Dave, President & General Manager, Northerm Windows, 307
Bos, Art, President, BOS Engineering & Environmental Services Inc., 114
Boscariol, A.A., Principal, A. A. Boscariol and Associates Limited, 63
Bose, Robert, Surrey, 604-591-4624, 684
Boshcoff, Ken, Councillor at Large, Thunder Bay, 721
Boshyk, Andrika, Assistant Director, Social Investment Organization, 1004
Boskovich, Joseph A., DuMoulin, Boskovich, 1059
Bosnar, Miro, President, Geonics Limited, 211
Bossy, Ronald, Conseiller d'arrondissement, St-Paul-Émard, Montréal, 738
Boston, Brad, President, Mondo Products Company Limited, 292
Boston, Steve, Owner, Mondo Products Company Limited, 292
Bostrom, Harvey, Deputy Minister, 584
Boswall, R. Glen, Clark Wilson LLP, 1058
Botelho, Daniel, Bratty & Partners LLP, 1081
Bothwell, George, Senior Vice-President, External Relations & Commun, 511
Bottos, Lorie, City Solicitor, Sault Ste. Marie, 720
Botwright, Dave, Partner, Sanitherm Engineering Limited, 357
Botz, Peter, Lang Michener LLP - Vancouver, 1060
Bouchard, Catherine, Greffière, Granby, 450-776-8275, 735
Bouchard, Christian, Directeur général, Maria-Chapdelaine, 750
Bouchard, Claude, Directeur, Saguenay, 741
Bouchard, Daniel, Partner, Lavery, de Billy - Québec, 1088
Bouchard, Francine, Québec, 740
Bouchard, François, Associé, Langlois Kronström Desjardins, 1082, 1088
Bouchard, Georges, Saguenay, 741
Bouchard, Gérard, Président, Fédération d'agriculture biologique du Québec, 914
Bouchard, Hervé, Rivière-du-Loup, 741
Bouchard, Jacques, Président, Société québécoise du dahlia, 1006
Bouchard, Jean, Mirabel, 738
Bouchard, Jean Pierre, Plant Manager, Bennett Environmental Inc., 105
Bouchard, Jean-Claude, Lévis, 736
Bouchard, Jean-Yves, Planner Vice President, Le Groupe Leblond & Bouchard/Daniel Arbour et associes, 265
Bouchard, Laure, Administratrice, Cercles des jeunes naturalistes, 894
Bouchard, Louise, Saint-Jérôme, 450-432-9625, 743
Bouchard, Martial, President & Directeur Général, Products BCM Ltée BCM, 333
Bouchard, Monique, Administratrice, Cercles des jeunes naturalistes, 894
Bouchard, Nicolas, Directeur général, Deux-Montagnes, 735
Bouchard, Pierre, President, Les Consultants RSA, 268
Bouchard, Pierre, Trésorier, La Tuque, 736
Bouchard, Rodrigue, Technicien en documentation, Collège de Saint-Félicien, 1183
Bouchard, Stéphanie, Directrice, Saint-Eustache, 450-974-5220, 742
Bouchard, Sylvain, Representative, Les Emballages Polyform inc., 268
Bouchard, Sylvie, Directrice, Repentigny, 450-470-3800, 740
Bouchard Jr., Jacques, Partner, Heenan Blaikie S.E.N.C.R.L/SRL, 1084
Boucher, Andre, Manager, AlphaNuclear Company, 80
Boucher, Bill, Vice-President, Air Transport Association of Canada, 814
Boucher, Gilbert Kurt, Magog, 819-868-2006, 737
Boucher, Isabelle, Directrice administrative, Filtrum Inc., 195
Boucher, Jean Denis, Associé, Robinson Sheppard Shapiro LLP, 1086
Boucher, Marcel, Chief Financial Officer, Genivar, 207
Boucher, Normand, Mayor, Medicine Hat, 403-529-8181, 673
Boucher, Paul, President, Boucher Precast Concrete Ltd., 114
Boucher, Sylvain, Sous-ministre adjoint, 643

Boucher, Sylvie, Parliamentary Secretary for Status of Women, 560
Boucher, Yvon, Gatineau, 735
Boudreau, Clément, Thetford Mines, 418-423-2257, 745
Boudreau, Dan, Superintendent, Drainage, Essex, 709
Boudreau, Hélène, Dieppe, 506-866-2739, 691
Boudreau, Janice, Directrice, Université Sainte-Anne, 1135
Boudreau, John, Warden, Richmond County, 698
Boudreau, Lionel, Responsable, bibliothèque, Centre des Iles, 1167
Boudreau, Omer, Vice-President, 518
Boudreau, Pierre A., Councillor at Large, Moncton / Ville de Moncton, 691
Boudreau, René, Director, 659
Boudreau, Robert, Sintra Inc., 369
Boudreau, Yvon, Baie-Comeau, 418-296-2672, 733
Boudreault, Danielle, Technicienne en documentation, CÉGEP de Baie-Comeau, 1166
Boudreault, Sonia, Siège #5, Saint-Félicien, 742
Boudreault, Yves, Tremblay, Bois, Mignault & Lemay, 1089
Boudreaux, Don, Chair, Tri Village Regional Sewage Services, 758
Bouffard, Denis, Greffier, Terrebonne, 745
Bouffard, Martin, Morency Avocats, 1088
Bouffard, Norbert, Contact, Groupe Bouffard, 219
Boughton, Brenda, Metro Vancouver, 678
Bougie, Bernard, Saint-Jérôme, 450-431-7227, 743
Bougie, Trevor, South Glengarry, 730
Bouillet, Raymond, Vice-President & Director, Brisbin & Sentis Engineering Inc., 116
Boulais, Roger, President, EFC Control Inc., 173
Boulanger, André, Président, 649
Boulanger, Benoît, Secrétaire, Association des expositions agricoles du Québec, 832
Boulanger, Pierre, Project Engineer, Ottawa Engineering Ltd., 315
Boulay, Denise, Resp., Prêt et des équipements audiovisuels, CÉGEP de Drummondville, 1167
Boulay, Pierre, Directeur, Régie intermunicipale de traitement de l'eau potable Saint-Romual, 760
Boulerice, Serge, Directeur, Saint-Jean-sur-Richelieu, 450-359-2529, 742
Boulet, Jean, Partner, Heenan Blaikie S.E.N.C.R.L/SRL - Trois-Rivières, 1089
Boulet, Marcel, Directeur, Collège universitaire de St-Boniface, 1123
Boulet, Mychelle, Bibliothécaire, Bibliothèque des sciences, 1170
Boulianne, Blandine, Greffière, Mont-Laurier, 738
Boulianne, Maureen, Team Leader, Library Client Services, Transport Canada, 1152
Boulier, Rick, Manager, Squamish, 604-815-5015, 688
Boulos, Karim, Conseiller d'arrondissement, Peter-McGill, Montréal, 738
Boulton, Mark, Honorary Director, International Centre for Conservation Education, 936
Boulton, Richard, Manager, North Vancouver, 604-990-3804, 688
Boulva, Olivier, Stikeman Elliott LLP - Montréal, 1087
Bouma, Roger, City Councillor, Oshawa, 716
Bourbonnais, Ginette, Director, Genivar, 207
Bourbonnais, Jacques, La Prairie, 736
Bourbonnais, Luc, Fasken Martineau - Montréal, 1083
Bourchier, B.A., LL.B., Kinji C., Partner, Lawson Lundell LLP - Vancouver, 1060
Bourdeau, Millie, Director, Public Safety & Enforcement, Russell, 729
Bourden, David, Conestoga-Rovers & Associates, 149
Bouret, Lucie, Technicienne en documentation, CÉGEP St-Jean-sur-Richelieu, 1183
Bourgault, Jean-Daniel, Bibliothécaire, Université du Québec Institut national de la recherche scientifiq, 1181
Bourgault, Jean-Daniel, Head Librarian, INRS - Université du Québec, CGC - Québec, 1179
Bourgeois, Anne, Bibliothécaire, Bibliothèque centrale, 1170
Bourgeois, Annie, Langlois Kronström Desjardins, 1085
Bourgeois, Daniel, Moncton / Ville de Moncton, 691
Bourgeois, Jean, CEO, Labrie Environmental Group, 189, 262
Bourgeois, Pierre, Directeur, Saint-Jérôme, 743
Bourget, Louis, Directeur général, La Vallée-de-l'Or, 748
Bourgie, Jean-Luc, Fire Chief, Embrun, Russell, 729
Bourgon, Rick, Customer Service Manager, Sumas Environmental Services Inc., 381
Bournival, Carmen, Technicienne en documentation, Matériauthèque, 1186
Bourns, Elizabeth, Director, Human Resources, Oakville, 715

Bourque, Alain, Chef, Bibliothèque des sciences humaines et social, Bibliothèque des sciences humaines et sociales, 1177
Bourque, Céline, Technicienne en documentation, Collège Shawinigan, 1184
Bourque, Germain, Directeur, Westburne Canada, 429
Bourque, Guy, Manager, Nestlé Purina PetCare, 300
Bourque, Jean A., General Manager, Commission de gestion enviro ressources du Nord-Ouest (COGERNO), 758
Bourque, Michael, Vice-President, Canadian Chemical Producers' Association, 862
Bourque, Nancy, Information Specialist, Research Department Information Resources, 1154
Bouse, Rota, Manager, National Capital Commission, 1151
Boushy, Dave, City / County Councillor, Sarnia, 719
Boushy, David, Lambton, 701
Boussey, M., Carrier Canada Ltd., 130
Boutcher, Priscilla, Corner Brook, 693
Bouthillier, Mario, Vice-President, Belfab Inc., 104
Bouthillier, Paul, President, Lavo Inc., 265
Boutilier, Bob, General Manager, Edmonton, 780-496-2808, 672
Boutilier, Cecil, Manager, Harris & Roome Supply Limited, 225
Boutin, Bertrand, Siège #1, Saint-Félicien, 742
Boutin, Jacques, Trésorier, Sainte-Marie, 743
Boutin, Louise, Associée, Langlois Kronström Desjardins, 1085
Boutin, Marc-André, Davies Ward Phillips & Vineberg S.E.N.C.R.L., s.r.l., 1083
Boutin, Nancy, Trésorière, Roberval, 741
Bouvette, Sylvie, Partner, Borden Ladner Gervais LLP - Montréal, 1083
Bouvier, Louise, Greffière, Chambly, 734
Bouvier, Maurice, Executive Director, 584
Bouw, John, Vice-President, Alberta Greenhouse Growers Association, 817
Bowa, George, Director, Engineering & Public Works, Stratford, 720
Bowden, Jim, Acting Clerk Administrator, Langford, 681
Bowden, Jim, Manager, Nanaimo, 681
Bowen, Derek, President, BEX Engineering Limited, 106
Bowen, Pete, Orillia, 716
Bowen, Strachan, President, Elmridge Engineering Inc., 176
Bowen, Susan, Head, Technical Services, Merck Frosst Canada Inc., 1168
Bower, Bill, President, Ottawa Duck Club, 983
Bower, Richard, Blue-Zone Technologies Ltd., 110
Bower, Robert J., Manager, Delcan Water, 160
Bower, CAE, Tim, National Association of Environmental Professionals, 957
Bowers, Charles, Principal, Scott & Stewart Forestry Consultants, 360
Bowhay, Bob, General Manager, WorleyParsons Canada Ltd., 434
Bowie, James S., President, Bowie Environmental Edge Management & Assessment Ltd., 114
Bowler, Aaron J., Aikins, MacAulay & Thorvaldson LLP, 1063
Bowles, Brendan D., Glaholt LLP, 1075
Bowles, Peter, President, Royal Envelope Ltd., 353
Bowles, Ron, Director, Terrace, 205-638-4725, 685
Bowman, Brad, President, NAR Environmental Consultants Inc., 297
Bowman, Corin, Lang Michener LLP - Vancouver, 1060
Bowman, D., Carrier Canada Ltd., 129
Bowman, Jerry, Vice-President, Institute of Food Technologists, 933
Bowman, Laura, Staff Counsel, Environmental Law Centre (Alberta) Society, 1055
Bowman, Michael H.D., Partner, Osler, Hoskin & Harcourt LLP - Toronto, 1079
Bowman, Morley, Essex, 709
Bowser, Alan, Vice-President, Komline-Sanderson Ltd., 259
Bowser, Dara G., President, Bowser Technical Inc., 114
Bowyer, Craig, President, CB Engineering, Ltd., 132
Box, Gordon, President, Contor Terminals Inc., 151
Boyce, Egerton, Belleville, 706
Boyce, Gerry, Deputy Mayor, North Dundas, 727
Boyce, Steven, Moncton / Ville de Moncton, 691
Boychuk, Nelson, Vice-President, Alberta Farm Fresh Producers Association, 816
Boychuk, Q.C., Christopher C., McDougall Gauley, 1090
Boyd, Barry, Marketing, Light Solar Wind Manufacturing, 272
Boyd, Bill, Minister, 659
Boyd, Bill, Minister Responsible, 659
Boyd, Chuck, Branch Manager, Zep Manufacturing Company of Canada, 436
Boyd, Linda, Library Technician, Sunnybrook Health Sciences Centre - Sunnybrook Campus, 1162

Executive Name Index

Boyd, Lynne, Librarian, Canadian Agriculture Library (Summerland), 1116
Boyd, Mike, Police Chief, Edmonton, 780-421-3333, 672
Boyd, Shari L., Brownlee LLP, 1054
Boyd, Stephanie, Associate Director, Bell Canada, 1170
Boyd, Wayne, Project Consultant, WPI Safety & Environmental Consultants, 434
Boyd, Wes, Executive Director, 583
Boyd, William C., Managing Partner, Ottenheimer Baker, 1066
Boyd, Q.C., Keith D., Kanuka Thuringer LLP, Barristers & Solicitors, 1090
Boyer, Daniel, Wainwright Librarian, Nahum Gelber Law Library, 1174
Boyer, François, Saint-Jérôme, 450-224-1148, 743
Boyer, Michel, Manager, Gorman-Rupp of Canada Ltd., 215
Boyer, Norm, Sales Manager, Comfort King Doors & Windows Ltd., 147
Boyer, Ph.D, Greg, Executive Director, The Great Lakes Research Consortium, 925
Boyes, Richard, Fire Chief, Oakville, 715
Boykiw, Donald, Partner, Osler, Hoskin & Harcourt LLP - Calgary, 1053
Boyko, Lorne, Haldimand, 700
Boyle, D., Chief Administrative Officer, Haldimand, 700
Boyle, David, President, Maritime Microbiologicals Inc., 281
Boyle, Greg, National Director, Sierra Youth Coalition, 1004
Boyle, Judy, Five Hills Health Region, 1187
Boyle, PhD, Glenn J., Executive Director, Wildlife Rescue Association of British Columbia, 1020
Boynton, Rod, Innisfil, 711
Bozic, Joseph, Chair, NAID Canada, 956
Bozzato, Andrew, Stikeman Elliott LLP - Toronto, 1079
Brace, John, Director, Northland Power, 307
Bracewell, Phil, Manager, Engineered Air, 180
Bracken, Deb, Treasurer, South Frontenac, 730
Bracko, Len, St. Albert, 780-458-6478, 674
Bradbury, Wanda, Manager, Polar Bear Health Equipment Supplies, 327
Braden, Kelly, Director, Portage La Prairie, 204-239-8350, 689
Bradet, Denis, Grondin, Poudrier, Bernier, 1087
Bradford, P. Ross, Executive Director, Alberta Society of Professional Biologists, 819
Bradley, Brian, Principal, Unies Limited, 405
Bradley, Chris, Director, Public Works, Peterborough, 703
Bradley, Francis, Vice-President, Canadian Electricity Association, 866
Bradley, Gordon M., McCaffery Mudry Pritchard LLP, Barristers & Solicitors, 1052
Bradley, James J., Minister, 630
Bradley, Janet, Borden Ladner Gervais LLP - Ottawa, 1070
Bradley, John, Manager, Colour Innovations Print Inc., 146
Bradley, Mike, Lambton, 701
Bradley, Mike, Mayor, Sarnia, 719
Bradley, Monica, Treasurer, Alberta Association of Agricultural Societies, 815
Bradley, Rinnie, Executive Director, Prince Edward Island Cattle Producers, 988
Bradley, Sophie, Library Technician, Saskatoon Campus Library, 1190
Bradley, Sylvia, Orangeville, 716
Bradshaw, Garrick, Director, Vancouver, 685
Bradshaw, Graham, Head, Collection Development, University of Toronto Libraries, 1163
Bradshaw, Jeff, President, Canadian Camping Association, 860
Bradshaw, Kris, Coordinator, Federated Co-operatives Ltd., 194
Bradt, Robert R., Manager, Fire Services & Fire Chief, Leamington, 726
Brady, Alan, Manager, Halifax Regional Municipality, 302-835-9566, 695
Brady, David W., Partner, Hicks Morley Hamilton Stewart Storie LLP, 1076
Brady, Emily, President, International Society for Environmental Ethics, 943
Brady, Mark, Manager, Flygt Canada, 198
Brady, Peter, McCarthy Tétrault LLP - Toronto, 1077
Braet, Mark S., President, Environmental Accident Protection Inc., 185
Bragg, Michael, Chief Administrative Officer & Clerk, Oxford, 728
Braid, Larry, Muskoka, 702
Braid, Ron, Head, Reference, Trinity Western University, 1113
Braithwaite, Alison, Director, Walker Industries Holdings Ltd., 416
Braithwaite, Jack, Counsel, Weaver, Simmons LLP, 1072
Braithwaite, William J., Senior Partner, Stikeman Elliott LLP - Toronto, 1079

Brake, Phil, National Coordinator, Canadian Injured Workers Alliance, 872
Branch, Donald, Vice-President, M.S. Thompson & Associates Ltd., 276
Branchaud, Rick, Office Manager, Golder Associates Ltd., 214
Branco, John, Operator, West Lincoln, 732
Brand, John, Business Manager, Acklands-Grainger Inc., 66
Brand, Marc, Sales Manager, Alpha Controls & Instrumentation, 79
Brander, Lin, Public Services Librarian, Kwantlen University College, 1113
Brander, R. Bruce, Burnet, Duckworth & Palmer LLP, 1050
Brandon, Barry, Operations Manager, Optikon Corp. Ltd., 313
Brandt, Derik, Chief Administrative Officer, South Glengarry, 730
Branscombe, Nancy Ann, London, 713
Branson, Dave, President, Geosolutions Consulting Inc., 212
Brant, Steve, Manager, Delcan Water, 160
Brant, William J., Chair, Indian Agricultural Program of Ontario, 930
Brassard, Bernie, Exec. Vice-President, Maxxam Analytics Inc., 283
Brassard, John, Barrie, 706
Brassard, Matt, Branch Leader, Urban Systems Ltd., 408
Brassard, Monique, Lavery, de Billy - Montréal, 1085
Brassard, Pierre, Greffier, Saguenay, 741
Brassard, Raynald, Cain Lamarre Casgrain Wells - Chicoutimi, 1082
Bratina, Bob, Mayor, Hamilton, 711
Bratty, Lola, Councillor, Gravenhurst, 709
Braul, Waldemar, Fraser Milner Casgrain LLP - Vancouver, 1060
Brault, Christiane B., Director, Finance, Russell, 729
Braun, Barry, Commissioner, Recreation, Parks, & Culture Departm, Prince Edward, 703
Braun, Darcy, Principal Engineer, AC Environmental Services, 65
Braun, Jeff, Manager, Dillon Consulting Ltd., 163
Braun, John R., Aikins, MacAulay & Thorvaldson LLP, 1063
Braun, Ronald K., Managing Director, VIQUA - A Trojan Technologies Company, 413
Braun-Jackson, Jeff, Office Manager & Researcher, Ontario Professional Fire Fighters Association, 977
Brauss, Michael, President, Proto Manufacturing Ltd., 335
Bray, Charles, Chief Building Official, The Nation, 731
Bray, Shirley, Director, Alberta Wilderness Resource Centre, 1099
Brayford, Susan, Manager, Library Operations, Southern Alberta Institute of Technology, 1103
Brayton, Earl F., Elizabethtown-Kitley, 613-345-2650, 725
Brazeau, Luce, Responsable, Référence, Bibliothèque de physique, 1170
Brazier, Dan, Manager, Colwood, 250-474-4133, 680
Brearley, Scott, Singleton Urquhart LLP, 1062
Breau, P.Eng., Pierre A., Municipal Engineer & Director, Lunenburg District, 902-541-1331, 697
Breault, Alain, McMillan Binch Mendelsohn - Montréal, 1086
Breault, Brenda, Commissioner, Corporate Services, & Treasurer, Mississauga, 714
Breault, Richard, VP, Groupe S.M. International Inc., 220
Brebeau, Martine, Head, Information Resources, FPInnovations, 1177
Brebner, Ian, Middlesex, 701
Brecher, Ronald, Principal, GlobalTox International Consultants Inc., 214
Breckenridge, Peggy, Simcoe, 704
Breen, Danny, St. John's, 709-576-2332, 694
Breen, Elizabeth, Partner, Stikeman Elliott LLP - Toronto, 1079
Breen, Kevin, Director, St. John's, 709-576-8213, 694
Breier, Liz, Library Technician, Sir Mortimer B. Davis Jewish General Hospital, 1175
Breivik, Erik, Manager, Universal Handling Equipment Company Limited, 406
Bremermann, Eric H., Partner, Stikeman Elliott LLP - Toronto, 1079
Bremner, David, Sr. Project Manager, Restoration Environmental Contractors - Restoration Consultants, 346
Bremner, Don, President, Abcott Construction Ltd., 65
Bremner, Don, Vice President, Restoration Environmental Contractors - Restoration Consultants, 346
Bremner, Tom, Chief, Truro, 696
Brenders, Peter, President & CEO, BIOTECanada, 845
Brendle-Moczuk, Daniel, Instruction Librarian, Thompson Rivers University, 1112
Brennan, Bob B., President/CEO, 588
Brennan, David, Senior Vice-President, 634
Brennan, Edward, Division Manager, Donalco Inc., 165
Brennan, Jim, Chief, Winnipeg, 690

Brennan, John, Erin, 727, 709
Brennan, John G., Strathroy-Caradoc, 731
Brennan, Krystal, Coordinator, Wildlife Rescue Association of British Columbia, 1020
Brennan, Mary Ellen, Director, American Industrial Hygiene Association, 823
Brennan, Mary S., Clerk & Director, Council Services, Essex, 699
Brennan, Nola, Librarian, Institute of Technology Campus, 1135
Brennick, John, President, Campground Owners Association of Nova Scotia, 852
Brennom, Stephen, Vice-President, Cat Tech Canada Company, 132
Brent, Meade, Deputy Minister, 601
Brenton, Janelle, Cataloguer, Nova Scotia Agricultural College, 1137
Bresee, Carl, Loyalist, 727
Bresee, Kim, Director, Planning & Building, Sarnia, 719
Bresee, Ric, Loyalist, 727
Bresner, Barry H., Senior Partner, Borden Ladner Gervais LLP - Toronto, 1073
Bressan, Robert, Contact, Conestoga-Rovers & Associates, 149
Bretherick, Ross, Agent, Terrace, 250-615-4036, 685
Breton, Francine, Directrice générale, La Jacques-Cartier, 748
Breton, Jean-Louis, Vice-President, Groupe Sodinco inc., 221
Breton, Nicole, Directrice générale, Abitibi-Ouest, 746
Breton, Patrice, Director, Sustainable Development Technology Canada, 1011
Breton, Pierre, Granby, 735
Brett, Dave, Fire Chief, Gander, 709-651-5928, 694
Brett, David J., Gowling Lafleur Henderson LLP - Calgary, 1051
Brett, Jim, Contact, Entomological Society of Ontario, 1140
Brett, Mary, Adjala-Tosorontio, 519-941-5828, 724
Breu, Michael, President, Environmental Information Association, 912
Brewer, Andrea, Ogilvy Renault LLP/S.E.N.C.R.L., s.r.l. - Toronto, 1078
Brewer, Dave, Sales Manager, Robar, 347
Brewer, Gisèle, Coordinator, Integra Technologies Ltd., 243
Brewer, Jane, Waterloo, 704
Brewer, Jane, Regional Councillor, Cambridge, 707
Brewer, Jill, Director, St. John's, 709-576-8405, 694
Brewster, Dana, Manager, Engine Control Systems, 180
Brewster, Janet, Acting Executive Director, 619
Breyfogle, Donna, Associate Director, Collections, University of Manitoba Libraries, 1125
Briant, Wayne, Manager, Saskatoon, 754
Brice, Susan, Saanich, 688
Bricker, Brad, Sr. Environmental Scientist, LGL Limited Environmental Research Associates, 271
Brickman, Q.C., G.V., Thompson Dorfman Sweatman LLP, 1064
Bridal, Patti, Manager, Vernon, 685
Brideau, Marthe, Responsable, Bibliothèque des sciences de la santé, 1185
Brideau, Marthe, Responsable, Bibliothèque sciences de la santé, Université de Sherbrooke, 1186
Bridge, Ed, Marketing, General Filtration, 206
Bridges, Barry D., McDougall Gauley, 1089
Bridges, Vance, Summerside, 733
Brien, Louis P., Associé, Lapointe Rosenstein Marchand Melançon, 1085
Brière, Christian, Directeur, Lévis, 418-839-2002, 736
Brière, Jules, Partner, Lavery, de Billy - Québec, 1088
Brière, Yvon, La Prairie, 736
Brigden, Gary, Manager, Northwest Metal Recycling, 307
Briggs, Colin, Chief Administrative Officer, St. Catharines, 719
Brignall, Ben, Manager, Waterous Power Systems, 422
Brillant, Clothilde, Responsable, Acquisitions, CÉGEP de Chicoutimi, 1166
Brillon, Sherri, Exec. Vice-President/CFO, Encana Corporation, 178
Brimo, René J., President, R.B. Intermark Inc., 340
Brindamour, Céline, Val-d'Or, 746
Brindle, Derek A., Chair, 580
Brindle, Q.C., Derek A., Counsel, Singleton Urquhart LLP, 1062
Bringloe, Chris, Secretary, 595
Brink, Jack, President, Canadian Archaeological Association, 855
Brinkman, John S., President/CEO, Imbitive Technologies Canada, Inc., 239
Brinley, David, General Counsel & Vice-President, Shell Canada Limited, 365
Brinza, Daniel, Borden Ladner Gervais LLP - Toronto, 1073
Briscoe, Raye-Anne, Renfrew, 613-432-2885, 704
Brisebois, Guy, Executive Director, Auditing Association of Canada, 844

Executive Name Index

Brisebois, Jimmy, Directeur-général, Régie intermunicipale des déchets solides de la Lièvre, 761
Brisebois, Stephen, Châteauguay, 514-914-4945, 735
Brisette, Viviane, Agente de bureau, Collège de Maisonneuve, 1172
Brisson, Christine, Baie-Comeau, 418-295-2883, 733
Brisson, Gilles, Associé, Groupe Stavibel Inc., 221
Brisson, Janice, Library Assistant, British Columbia Ministry of Energy & Mines, 1120
Brisson, Pierre-Félix, President, Aquasolution Technologies Inc., 89
Britten, Steve, Director, Specialty Technical Publishers, 375
Britton, Frank, General Manager, YES Environment Technologies Inc., 435
Britton, Shirley, Manager, YES Environment Technologies Inc., 435
Broad, James, CEO, Hallmark Insurance Brokers Ltd., 224
Broad, Owen, President, Boundary Organic Producers Association, 846
Broad, Peter, President, Enviro-Met Engineering, 183
Broadbent, Garett, Director, Leduc County, 780-955-6404, 669
Broadhead, Wes, St. Albert, 674
Broadley, David, Manager, SAIC Canada, 356
Brobbel, Mark, Manager, Dillon Consulting Ltd., 163
Brocanier, Gil, Mayor, Cobourg, 708
Brochu, André, Président-directeur général, 655
Brochu, Louida, Sherbrooke, 744
Brock, Doug, President, Caledon Laboratory Chemicals Inc., 121
Broderick, D., Manager, Recreation, Community Services, & Centenn, Gravenhurst, 709
Brodeur, Jacques, Team Lead, Cataloguing and Library System Administ, Canadian Heritage, 1167
Brodeur, Lindor, Brodeur, Boileau, 1089
Brodeur, Randy, Vice-President, Fuller Austin Insulation Inc., 203
Brodeur Comeau, Louise, Granby, 735
Brodie, Chris, Manager, Knight Piésold Ltd., 259
Brodie, Malcolm, Metro Vancouver, 678
Brodie, Malcolm D., Mayor, Richmond, 684
Brodkin-Schneider, Lonnie, Associée, Miller Thomson LLP - Montréal, 1086
Broekema, Paul, Walinga Inc., 416
Broer, Marcel, General Manager, H. Broer Equipment Sales and Service, 223
Broer, S.D., Vice-President, H. Broer Equipment Sales and Service, 223
Broman, Soren, President, Soren Construction Ltd., 374
Bromby, Daniel, Reference Librarian, Bishop's University, 1185
Bromley, Jennifer, Librarian, Pembrook Campus, 1152
Bromley, Steven R., Chair/CEO, SunOpta, 382
Bromley, Yvon, Laval, 736
Bronicheski, David, CFO, Managing Director, Algonquin Power Income Fund, 78
Bronsard, Michel, Trois-Rivières, 745
Bronsema, Jamie, Director, Strategic & Business Services, Oshawa, 716
Brooker, Ian D.M., Vice-President/General Manager, Bradford White Canada Inc., 115
Brooker, Michael, Vice-President, Bradford White Canada Inc., 115
Brooker, Q.C., Michael R., Burchell, MacDougall, 1068
Brooks, Barry, Manager, Cook Engineering, 152
Brooks, Beverley, Manager, SIAST Palliser Campus, 1187
Brooks, Bob, Yellowknife, 695
Brooks, Donald, Secretary, 656
Brooks, Fred, Sr. Manager, Cape Breton, 902-563-5510, 695
Brooks, Harvey, Deputy Minister, 664
Brooks, Jake, Executive Director, Association of Power Producers of Ontario, 837
Brooks, John E., Partner, Hicks Morley Hamilton Stewart Storie LLP, 1076
Brooks, Leo, Whitman Benn Group, 431
Brooks, Rod, Ortech Environmental Inc., 314
Brooks, Ross, President, Precision Industrial Ltd., 330
Brooks, Yolanda, Coordinator, Wildlife Rescue Association of British Columbia, 1020
Broomhead, Mike, Wellington, 519-323-1981, 705
Brophy, David, Manager, 517
Brophy, Sean, President/CEO, Opus DaytonKnight Consultants Ltd., 313
Brosemer, Kathleen, Chair, Clean North, 1154
Brossard, Christian J., Associé, Miller Thomson LLP - Montréal, 1086
Brosseau, Nicole, Account Inquiries & Billing, Herby Enterprises Ltd., 229
Brosz, Helmut G., President & CEO, Brosz & Associates, 117

Broten, Laurel C., Parliamentary Assistant, 628
Brothers, Diana, Councillor, Kings County, 696
Brotzel, Glen, Operations Manager, National Energy Equipment Inc., 297
Brouard, Julie, Communications Manager, Air Liquide Canada Ltée, 75
Broughton, Christine, Clerk & Director, Woolwich, 732
Broughton, Mike, Milton, 714
Brouillard, Gaétan, Contact, E.A.I. Technologies Inc., 168
Brouillard, Jean-François, Associé, Cain Lamarre Casgrain Wells - Drummondville, 1082
Brouillette, Alain, Directeur, Trois-Rivières, 819-372-4642, 745
Brouillette, Alain, Manager, Pretal, 332
Brouillette, Marc, Associé, Cain Lamarre Casgrain Wells - Sept-Iles, 1089
Brouwer, Ken, Managing Director, Knight Piésold Ltd., 259
Browaty, Jeff, Winnipeg, 204-986-5196, 690
Browitt, Terry, President, Terinex International Ltd., 389
Brown, Alan, Director, Engineering, Markham, 905-415-7507, 713
Brown, Allan, Contact, Rubber Rock Resources, 354
Brown, Allison, Coordinator, AllerGen NCE Inc., 821
Brown, Andy, Chief Administrative Officer, North Grenville, 728
Brown, Art, Fire Chief, Mississippi Mills, 714
Brown, B.A., President/CEO, Bruce A. Brown Associates Limited, 117
Brown, Bill, Fugro Airborne Surveys, 202
Brown, Bob, Managing Director, Thermon Heat Tracing Services, 394
Brown, Brice, Contact, HETEK Solutions Inc., 230
Brown, Cathy, Agent, Alfa Plastics Inc., 78
Brown, Chad J., McLennan Ross LLP, 1055
Brown, Chris, Director, Finance Services, Oshawa, 716
Brown, Craig, General Manager, Globetron Controls Inc., 214
Brown, David, Partner, Brown Strachan Associates, 117
Brown, Denise, London, 713
Brown, Denise, Office Administrator, Valley Solid Waste Commission, 759
Brown, Dwight, General Manager, Medicine Hat, 673
Brown, Fred, Contact, TeraWind Ltd., 389
Brown, G.M., Vice-President, Pollutech Group of Companies Inc., 327
Brown, Garry, Principal, SMS Engineering Ltd., 371
Brown, Garry, Town Clerk & Director, Gander, 694
Brown, Gary, CFO, TIR Systems Ltd., 396
Brown, Gary R., Saugeen Shores, 719
Brown, George, Stratford, 720
Brown, Gerardette, Secretary, Beaton Institute, 1134
Brown, Gordon, Manager, Campbell River, 679
Brown, Gordon, Vice-President, CanTox Environmental Inc., 127
Brown, Graham, President, ADI Systems Inc., ADI Group Inc., 68
Brown, Ian, President, PerkinElmer Life & Analytical Sciences Canada Inc., 321
Brown, Ian C.R., City Manager, Orillia, 716
Brown, James R., Osler, Hoskin & Harcourt LLP - Toronto, 1079
Brown, Janet, Chair, Skeena-Queen Charlotte, 679
Brown, Jim, Chatham-Kent, 724
Brown, Joanna, Coordinator, New Brunswick Environmental Network, 961
Brown, John, City Manager, Brantford, 707
Brown, Karl, Vice-President, Waste Alternatives Inc., 417
Brown, Kathryn, Director, 545
Brown, Kent, Exec. Vice-President & CFO, Canadian Hydro Developers, Inc., 124
Brown, L.G., President, Envirotech Nisku Inc., 188
Brown, Levinia, Minister, 617
Brown, Lucy, General Manager, Health & Family Services, Chatham-Kent, 724
Brown, Lyn, Director, Catalyst Paper Corp., 132
Brown, Malcolm, Associate Deputy Minister, 549
Brown, Margaret, Serials & Government Publications Librarian, Kwantlen University College, 1113
Brown, Mark, District Arborist, North Vancouver, 688
Brown, Matt, London, 713
Brown, Michael A., Interforest Inc., 244
Brown, Michael A., Parliamentary Assistant, 635
Brown, Mike, Foreman, Hants East District, 902-261-2178, 697
Brown, Mike, Treasurer, Registered Professional Foresters Association of Nova Scotia, 994
Brown, Orville, Clearview, 725
Brown, Pat, Ajax, 705
Brown, Peter, Mayor, Airdrie, 670
Brown, Peter G., Academic Staff, Brace Centre for Water Resources Management, 115

Brown, Phil, General Manager, Shelter, Support, & Housing Admin, Toronto, 416-392-7885, 721
Brown, Richard, Minister, 639
Brown, Rick, Services Technician, Orillia Campus, 1147
Brown, Robert, President, BP Trading Ltd., 114
Brown, Russ J., General Manager, Bissett Resource Consultants Ltd., 110
Brown, Scott, Director, 656
Brown, Sharlene, Chair, Westend Regional Sewage Services, 758
Brown, Sharon, University Librarian, Wilfrid Laurier University, 1165
Brown, Susan H., Fraser Milner Casgrain LLP - Ottawa, 1070
Brown, Q.C., Geoffrey E.J., Partner, Stewart McKelvey Stirling Scales - St. John's, 1066
Browne, Graham, Vice-President, ArcelorMittal Dofasco, 90
Browne, Murray, Woodward & Company, 1063
Browne, B.A.(Hons.), LL.B, Louis, Regina, 306-531-5151, 754
Brown-Harper, Lynne, Vice-President, PCI Geomatics Group Inc., 320
Browning, Rob, Chief Administrative Officer, Chatham-Kent, 724
Brownlee, Barry, South Stormont, 613-537-9753, 730
Brownlow, Jennifer, Reference Librarian, Malaspina University-College, 1113
Brownoff, Judy, Saanich, 688
Brownridge, Jerymy, Director, 573
Brownstein, Bonnie, Librarian, Mines & Aggregates Safety & Health Association, 1146
Brubacher, Les, Aquateck Ltd., 89
Bruce, Grant, Vice-President/Senior Chemist, Hatfield Group, 227
Bruce, James P., Senior Associate, Global Change Strategies International Co., 213
Bruce, Jeffrey, Chair, Green Roofs for Healthy Cities, 926
Bruce, Jim, SAIC Canada, 356
Bruce, Jim, College Librarian, Nicola Valley Institute of Technology, 1113
Bruce, Jim, Representative, Soil & Water Conservation Society, 1009
Bruce, John J., Partner, Hicks Morley Hamilton Stewart Storie LLP, 1076
Bruce, Kathy, Plant Manager, ToxCo Waste Management Ltd., 399
Bruce, Leo, Corner Brook, 693
Bruce, Lynne, Manager, Stewart Group, 379
Bruce, Russ, President, Gem & Mineral Club of Scarborough, 922
Bruce-Veitch, Heather, Director, Iron Ore Company of Canada, 248
Bruchet, Susan, Public Services & Electronic Resources Librarian, Kwantlen University College, 1113
Bruckert, Sabine, General Cousel & Vice-President, Velan Inc., 410
Bruckner, Roy, Products Specialist, Konica Minolta Business Solutions (Canada) Inc., 259
Bruckschwaiger, Darren, Councillor, Cape Breton, 695
Bruehlmann, Sabina, Project Manager, University Technologies International, 407
Brujins, Peter, President/CEO, BIOREM Inc., 109
Brûlé, Pierre-Marcel, Coordonnateur, CÉGEP Régional de Lanaudière à Joliette, 1168
Brulot, Myriam, Donovan & Company, 1059
Brumwell, Scott W., Vice-President, Skelton Brumwell & Associates Inc., 369
Brun, Jean, Account Manager, Premier Envelope, 331
Brun, Pascal J., President, CHI Canada Inc., 140
Brunas, Shane, Acting Vice-President, 546
Brundrige, Rick, Manager, Cariboo, 677
Bruneau, Anne, Directrice, Institut de recherche en biologie végétale, 932
Bruneau, Gérard, Préfet, Les Chenaux, 749
Brunelle, Daniel, Directeur, Bécancour, 734
Brunet, Bernard, Marketing Manager, Brunet Ltée, Tuyaux de béton, 117
Brunet, Jean, Branch Manager, Safety-Kleen Canada Inc., 355
Brunet, Jim, Manager, Safety-Kleen Canada Inc., 355
Brunet, Laurent, Contact, GILFAB, 212
Brunet, Martin, Inspecteur municipal, Amos, 733
Brunet, Michel A., Fraser Milner Casgrain S.E.N.C.R.L./LLP, 1084
Brunet, Paul G., Greffier & Directeur général, Châteauguay, 735
Brunet, Randy U., Partner, MacPherson Leslie & Tyerman LLP - Regina, 1090
Brunet, Stephen J., Mayor, Bathurst, 506-548-2171, 690
Brunetti, Brian, Exec. Vice President, AGAT Laboratories Ltd., 73

Executive Name Index

Bruni, Marchy, Sault Ste. Marie, 720
Bruni, Steven, Vice-President, Stablex Canada Inc., 377
Brunk, Don, Perth East, 728
Brunning, Fay K., Borden Ladner Gervais LLP - Ottawa, 1070
Bruno, Mike, USA Operations, Terralog Technologies Inc., 390
Brunt, Brenda M., Clerk, South Dundas, 730
Brunt, Glenn, Vice-President, F.C. O'Neill, Scriven & Associates Ltd., 193
Brushett, G., President, Gerry Brushett Enterprises Limited, 212
Bruton, Elizabeth, Reference/Electronic Services Librarian, John & Dotsa Bitove Family Law Library, 1143
Brutto, Italo, Commissioner, Engineering & Public Works, Richmond Hill, 905-771-8830, 718
Bruun, Anders, Campbell Marr, 1063
Bruynooghe, Donna, Treasurer, Saskatchewan Katahdin Sheep Association Inc., 1000
Bruziewicz, Andy, City Councillor, Sarnia, 719
Bryan, Bruce, Leeds & Grenville, 726
Bryan, Tim, Thurber Engineering Ltd., 396
Bryan-Pulham, Paul, Chief Administrative Officer, Woodstock, 723
Bryant, Chris, Director, 610
Bryant, D.L., Principal, Keystone Environmental Ltd., 257
Bryant, John K., President, Bryco Environmental, 117
Bryant, Judy, London, 713
Bryant, Kevin, Supervisor, Parkland County, 670
Bryant, Mark, Reference & Information Literacy Librarian, Humber College Institute of Technology & Advanced Learning, 1158
Bryant, B.A., M.P.A., Bonny, General Manager, Regina, 754
Bryar, Raymond, General Manager, Nepisiguit-Chaleur Solid Waste Commission, 758
Bryce, Bill, Chair, The Friends of West Kootenay Parks Society, 922
Bryce, R.N., Sharron, Regina, 306-949-5025, 754
Bryden, J. Douglas, President, The Township of Muskoka Lakes Ratepayers' Association, 1013
Bryden, Mary A., Chair, Rideau Valley Conservation Authority, 995
Bryden, Melissa, Lindsay Kenney LLP, 1061
Brydges, Barbara, Director, Doucette Library of Teaching Resources, 1101
Brydges, Kevin, Environmental Coordinator, Nanaimo, 250-755-4460, 681
Bryks, Janice, Acquisitions Assistant, Portage College, 1108
Bryson, Dan, Vice-President, Treeline Well Abandonment & Reclamation Ltd., 401
Bubbar, Kundan, Chief Building Inspector, Kamloops, 681
Bubelis, Paul, Chair, Earth Day Canada, 907
Bucci, Vince, Brantford, 707
Buccilli, Lina, Librarian, Ontario Energy Board, 1159
Buchanan, Audrey, Senior Engineer, Truro, 696
Buchanan, Buck, Red Deer, 403-343-6550, 674
Buchanan, David, General Manager, Neo Valves, 300
Buchanan, Douglas B., Q.C., Davis LLP - Vancouver, 1059
Buchanan, Kenneth, Councillor, North Perth, 715
Buchanan, Randy D., President, Buchanan Environmental, 118
Buchanan, Robert, Vice-President, LGL Limited Environmental Research Associates, 272
Buchanan, Q.C., Douglas, Davis LLP - Toronto, 1074
Buchholz, Doug, Officer, North Okanagan, 678
Buchholzer, Michael, Manager, Yorkton, 306-786-1771, 755
Buchinski, Marie H., Bennett Jones LLP - Calgary Office, 1049
Buchnea, Alex, President/CEO, Scimus Inc., 360
Buchner, Lynn, Director, Corporate Services, Oxford, 728
Buchowski, Stan, President, Corolon Coatings & Corrosion Control Technologies Inc., 152
Buchowski, Stan E., President, Anticorrosion Materials & Technologies Inc., 86
Buck, Dani, Controller, D.M. Wills Associates Limited, 156
Buck, Evelyn, Aurora, 706
Buck, Gordon A., Alexander Holburn Beaudin & Lang, LLP, 1057
Buck, Rhonda, Administrator, Building & Planning, Erin, 709
Buckham, William A., President, Buckham Transport Ltd., 118
Buckingham, Janice, Partner, Osler, Hoskin & Harcourt LLP - Calgary, 1053
Buckle, Stephen, Director, Celfort Construction Materials Inc., 135
Buckler, Jim, Vice-President & CFO, Industrial Ecology Corp., 240
Buckley, Henry, Vice-President / General Manager, Acklands-Grainger Inc., 66
Buckley, Penné, Executive Assistant, 596
Buckway, Bev, Mayor, Whitehorse, 867-668-8626, 755

Buczynski, James, Campus Librarian, Seneca@York Campus, 1161
Budd, Bill, Director, Moncton / Ville de Moncton, 691
Budd, Jason, Manager, Westburne Canada, 427
Bueble, Richard, Pildysh Technologies Inc., 323
Buehler, Charles H., Chairman/CEO, Organic Resource Management Inc., 314
Buehlow, David, Contact, Twin Falls Limited Partnership, 404
Bugala, Michael, Milton, 714
Bugden, David, Director, TerraChoice Environmental Marketing, 390
Bugden, Lydia S., Stewart McKelvey Stirling Scales - Halifax, 1067
Bugley, Rennie, CAO, Cumberland County, 697
Buhlman, J.M., WeirFoulds LLP, 1081
Buholzer, Bill, Young, Anderson, 1062
Buisson, Andre, President, Société Laurentide inc., 371
Buist, Clive, Director, Parks & Recreation, Niagara-on-the-Lake, 715
Buist, Rick, Treasurer, Green Roofs for Healthy Cities, 926
Bujold, Mario, Directeur général, Conseil québécois sur le tabac et la santé, 901
Bujold, Monette, Secrétaire adjointe-administrative, Conseil régional de l'environnement de la Gaspésie et des Iles-de, 901
Bujold, Yvan, Associé, Cain Lamarre Casgrain Wells - Rimouski, 1089
Bulat, Dan, Partner, Envirotech Engineering, 188
Bulbrook, Vince, Vice-President/CFO, AADCO Automotive Inc., 64
Bulbuck, Troy, President/CEO, Alpine Environmental Ltd., 80
Bulla, Paul, Vice-President, Comcor Environmental Limited, 146
Bullen, J., Carrier Canada Ltd., 129
Bullock, Chris, President, Western Bio Resources Consulting Ltd., 429
Bullock, Greg, President, Ontario Ground Water Association, 974
Bullock, Peter, Manager, Environmental Services, North Bay, 715
Bullock, Richard, Chair, British Columbia Farm Industry Review Board, 574, 847
Bullock, Timothy, Managing Partner, SimpsonWigle LAW LLP, 1069
Bullough, Vaughn, President, Manitoba Environmental Industries Association Inc., 951
Bulman, Dorthy, Treasurer & Deputy Clerk, Adjala-Tosorontio, 724
Bulpitt, Don, Manager, Lethbridge, 673
Bundschuh, Jim, Director, Financial Services, Elgin, 699
Bundy, Steve, Sales Manager, C.J. Pink Ltd., 120
Bunke, Brad, Branch Manager, Gamsby & Mannerow Ltd., 204
Bunnell, Q.C., Everett L., Partner, Macleod Dixon LLP, 1052
Bunron, Louis, Landfill Manager, CCS Income Trust, 134
Bunting, Kathy, Clerk, Middlesex, 701
Buntsma, Everett, Director, Operations & Emergency Services, Pickering, 905-420-4624, 718
Bunz, Karen, Manager, Quad-Lock Building Systems Ltd., 338
Buott, Gerry, Councillor, Colchester County, 697
Buoy, Lana, Enviro Scan Technologies Inc., 182
Bur, Justin, VP East, Transport Action Canada, 1013
Burak, Monika, Coordinator, Alberta Society of Professional Biologists, 819
Burbidge, Bryan, Fire Chief, King, 726
Burbidge, Danny, Directeur, Val-d'Or, 746
Burch, Jeff, St. Catharines, 905-988-3695, 719
Burcher, Lise, Guelph, 710
Burchill, Derek, Miramichi, 691
Burden, Bill, Librarian, Prince Edward Island Dept. of Provincial Treasury, 1165
Burden, Ken, Executive Director, Corporate Services, Niagara Falls, 715
Burden, Trina, Business Resource Manager, Corner Brook, 709-637-1558, 693
Bureau, Claude, Directeur général, Sept-Iles, 418-964-3201, 744
Bureau, Ginette, Président-directeur général, Société québécoise de récupération et de recyclage, 1006
Bureau, Marc, Maire, Gatineau, 819-595-7100, 735
Bureau, Paul, Delorme, LeBel, Bureau, s.e.n.c., 1089
Bureau, Suzanne, Director, Collection & Metadata Services, Canada Institute for Scientific & Technical Information (CISTI), 1148
Burge, Todd, Manager, Fort Saskatchewan, 780-992-6255, 672
Burgess, Joan, Director, New Westminster, 682
Burgess, John, Director, Library & Educational Resources, Keyano College, 1107
Burgess, Patrick, Gowling Lafleur Henderson LLP - Calgary, 1051

Burgess, Robin, Finance/Administration, United Nations Environment Programme, 1015
Burgess, Steve, Executive Director, 518
Burke, D. Kevin, Cox and Palmer - Halifax, 1067
Burke, Heather, Director, Housing, Wellington, 705
Burke, Jim, Aquateck Ltd., 89
Burke, Joan, Minister, 598
Burke, John, President, Foodservice & Packaging Institute, 918
Burke, Michael, Managing Director, Corporate Services, North Bay, 715
Burke, Patrick, Fire Chief, Niagara Falls, 715
Burke, Richard, President & CEO, Veolia ES Canada Industrial Services Inc., 411
Burke, Sabrina, Cataloguer, Champlain-Saint Lambert, 1184
Burke, Steve, President, The Water Shed, 393
Burke, Valerie, Markham, 905-479-7747, 713
Burkett, Brian W., Heenan Blaikie LLP - Toronto, 1075
Burkett, Mike H., Mayor, Severn, 729
Burkhardt, Tracey, Director, 594
Burlew, Edward L., Burlew, Edward L., 1072
Burley, Dave, Manager, Canada-Newfoundland Offshore Petroleum Board, 853
Burley, Dwight, Deputy Mayor & Councillor, Grey, 725, 700
Burling, Linda, Clerk, Kingsville, 712
Burlingham, Ralph, General Manager, Schlegel Canada Inc., 359
Burnett, David, President, Trecan Combustion Ltd., 401
Burnett, Marian, Librarian, College of the North Atlantic, Corner Brook Campus, 1130
Burnett, Q.C., William J., Thompson Dorfman Sweatman LLP, 1064
Burney, Derek, Chair, 596
Burnham, Carole, Sr. Consultant, Carole Burnham Consulting, 129
Burnham, Erica, Head of Library Services, Macdonald Campus Library, 1182
Burnham, Kent G., Partner, Nixon Wenger, 1062
Burnham, L., Director, Public Works, Operations, & Engineering, St. Clair, 729
Burns, Angela, Librarian, Energy Resources Conservation Board (ERCB), 1101
Burns, Chris, Public Services Librarian - Degrees & Research, Kwantlen University College, 1113
Burns, Greg W., Port Hope, 728
Burns, Hope V., Director, Central Saanich, 686
Burns, Jim, Warden & Councillor, Lambton, 701
Burns, Robert, President, Proceco Ltd., 333
Burns, Robert J., Associate, Heritage Research Associates Inc., 230
Burns, Sandy, Treasurer, Victoria Lapidary & Mineral Society, 1017
Burns, Steven, CEO, Notra Inc., 308
Burns, Terry, LaSalle, 713
Burns, Tim, President, The Vinyl Institute, 1017
Burns, Trevor, Territory Manager, Green Turtle Technologies Ltd. (Canada), 217
Burnside, Dave, Director, Engineering Services, Saugeen Shores, 719
Burnside, John, President, R.J. Burnside & Associates Limited, 340
Buron, Paul, Executive Vice-President & Chief Financial Officer, 512
Burpee, Jim, Executive Vice-President, 634
Burpee, Terry, Sec.-Treas., New Brunswick Ground Water Association, 961
Burrage, Q.C., Donald, Deputy Minister, 602
Burrell, Gordon, Manager, Red Oak Industries Inc., 343
Burrell, Terry, City Councillor, Sarnia, 719
Burrell, W. Bruce, Fire Chief, Calgary, 403-287-4255, 671
Burridge, Linda, University Librarian, Brandon University, 1122
Burris, Peggy, Prince Edward, 703
Burrough, Josy, Manager, Grande Prairie, 780-538-0476, 672
Burroughs, Gary, Niagara, 702
Burroughs, Gary, Regional Councillor, Niagara-on-the-Lake, 715
Burrows, Barbara, Collections Coordinator, John Alexander Weir Memorial Law Library, 1105
Burrows, Fred, Fire Chief, Fort St. John, 250-785-4333, 681
Burrows, Holly-Ann, Manager, British Columbia Recreation & Parks Association, 849
Burrows, Scott, Laboratory Manager, Caduceon Environmental Laboratories, 120
Burry, Aaron, General Manager, Community & Social Services, Ottawa, 716
Bursey, G. Glenn, Vice-President, FracFlow Consultants Inc., 201

Executive Name Index

Bursey, Leigh Z., Brockville, 707
Burston, Merle, Chair, Ontario Rock Garden Society, 978
Burt, Dennis, Hydro-Mechanical Sales Ltd., 236
Burt, Ed, Contact, Algoma Manitoulin Environmental Awareness, 820
Burt, Graeme, Partner, Planning Alliance, 326
Burt, Patricia, Head Librarian, Red River College, 1125
Burt, Thomas, General Manager, TankTek Environmental Services Ltd., 387
Burton, Alstair H. A., Thomson, Rogers, 1080
Burton, Andrew J.G., Davis LLP - Vancouver, 1074, 1059
Burton, Barry, Regional Manager, Fort Garry Industries Ltd., 200
Burton, Dave, Warden & Councillor, Haliburton, 705-448-9355, 700
Burton, Rick, Assistant Deputy Minister, 656
Burton, Rob, Halton, 700
Burton, Rob, Mayor, Oakville, 715
Burton, Ronald W., Burton Ronald W. Lawyers, 1067
Burton, Terri, Director, Emergency Services, Muskoka, 702
Burton, Tom, Essex, 519-979-2339, 699
Burtt, Edward H., President, American Ornithologists' Union, 824
Burtt, Rob, Sales Engineer, EEP Engineered & Environmental Products Inc., 173
Burtwell, Jeff, Branch Manager, CenturyVallen, 137
Busby, Lorraine, Associate University Librarian, Information Resour, University of Western Ontario Libraries, 1144
Busby, Mathew, District Sales Manager, Buckhorn Canada Inc., 118
Busch, Craig, President/CEO, Busch Systems International Inc., 119
Busch, C.G.A., Carol, Treasurer & General Manager, Finance, Thunder Bay, 807-625-2242, 721
Bush, Fraser, Macleod Dixon LLP, 1052
Buss, Karin E., Ackroyd LLP Barristers & Solicitors, 1054
Bussière, Hélène, Bibliothécaire, Bibliothèque centrale, 1170
Bussière, Jean, Research Editor, Canadian Association for Research in Nondestructive Evaluation, 856
Bussières, Yvon, Québec, 740
Butcher, Jim, Assoc. Vice-President, 518
Butcher, Tim, Manager, Crane Energy Flow Solutions, 153
Butland, Steve, Sault Ste. Marie, 720
Butler, B., Constable, Moncton / Ville de Moncton, 691
Butler, Bill, Director, Kings County, 902-690-6137, 696
Butler, Bill, President, Hi-Point Industries (1991) Ltd., 231
Butler, Brenda, Library Technician, Yukon Dept. of Energy, Mines & Resources, 1191
Butler, Dave, Manager, Cook Engineering, 152
Butler, John, Treasurer, Peterborough, 703
Butler, Kim, Supervisor, Association of Alberta Agricultural Fieldmen, 834
Butler, M.A., Vice-President & General Manager, Polyland Industries Ltd., 328
Butler, R.M., President, Dewar Pacific Projects Ltd., 162
Butler, Ray, Director, 597
Butler, Terry, North Grenville, 728
Butler, RN, BN, MPA, Evelyn, Administrative Manager, Community Health Nurses of Canada, 899
Butler-Jones, David, Chief Public Health Officer, 533
Butorin, Dmitry, Manager & Director, TMK IPSCO Inc., 397
Butters, Barbara, Port Colborne, 905-834-4005, 718
Butters, Brian, President, Purifics ES Inc., 337
Butters, David, President, Association of Power Producers of Ontario, 837
Buttigieg, Bryan J., Partner, Miller Thomson LLP - Toronto, 1078
Button, Tom, Contact, Anex Distributors Ltd., 86
Button, Tom, Sales Manager, Ecotainer Sales Inc., 172
Butts, Floyd, Manager, SGE Hatch Ltd., 364
Butts, Gerald, President & CEO, World Wildlife Fund - Canada, 1023
Butts, Richard, Deputy City Manager, Toronto, 416-338-7200, 721
Buus, Erik, Contact, R.J. Burnside & Associates Limited, 340
Buwalda, Sandie, Coordinator, Alberta Fish & Game Association, 817
Buxton, Philip, Director, Corporate Services, Stratford, 720
Buzunis, M.Eng., PMP, P.E, Byron, Urban Construction Manager, Lethbridge, 403-320-3975, 673
Bych, Casper, Lang Michener LLP - Vancouver, 1060
Bycraft, Suzanne, Manager, Richmond, 604-233-3338, 684
Bye, Chris, Plant Manager, CCS Income Trust, 134
Byers, Barbara, Executive Vice-President, Canadian Labour Congress, 876
Byers, Bob, President, Alberta Professional Outfitters Society, 819

Byers, Grant, Sr. Vice President/General Manager, SNC-Lavalin Environment Inc., 371
Byers, Sharron, Truro, 696
Byette, Michel, Directeur général, Trois-Rivières, 819-372-4608, 745
Bylsma, Mark, Niagara, 702
Byres, Nicole M., Clark Wilson LLP, 1058
Byrick, Katherine L., Partner, Borden Ladner Gervais LLP - Toronto, 1073
Byrne, Geraldine, Vice-President, Suncurrent Industries Inc., 382
Byrne, John, Chief Administrative Officer, Lambton Shores, 726
Byrne, Melissa, Coordinator, Newfoundland & Labrador Outfitters Association, 963
Byrnes, Robyn L., Accounting, Blower Engineering Inc., 110
Byrnes, William O.R., Plant Manager, Blower Engineering Inc., 110
Byrnes, Jr., Tom, Vice-President, Blower Engineering Inc., 110
Byrnes. Sr., Thomas S., President/CEO, Blower Engineering Inc., 110
Byvelds, Steven, Mayor, Stormont, Dundas & Glengarry, 730
Byvelds, Steven J., Mayor, South Dundas, 730

C

Cabajsky, Rick, Sales Contact, Rotork Controls (Canada) Ltd., 352
Cabel, Lisa C., Borden Ladner Gervais LLP - Toronto, 1073
Cable, Dan, Director, 667
Caboret, Daniel, PricewaterhouseCoopers Management Consultants, 332
Cabrera-Rivera, Orlando, Program Manager, Commission for Environmental Cooperation, 525, 898
Cacchione, Richard, Président, 649
Cacciotti, Dan, Area Supervisor, AMEC, 83
Cadaret, Denis, Vice President, AXOR Experts-Conseils Inc., 99
Cade, James R., Senior Partner, Ogilvy Renault LLP/S.E.N.C.R.L., s.r.l. - Toronto, 1078
Cadham, John S., President, CadhamHayes Systems Inc., 120
Cadieux, Robert, Laval, 450-978-5866, 736
Cadieux, Stephanie, Minister, 581
Cadigan, Robert, President & CEO, NOIA, 964
Cadman, David, Vancouver, 604-873-7244, 685
Cadman, David, President, International Council for Local Environmental Initiatives, 937
Cadoret, Nicole, Biologist, Prolab Technolub, 334
Cadorette, Pierre, Camatec, 122
Cadotte, A.P., Vice-President, Laidlaw Medical Services, 263
Cadotte, Alan P., President & CEO, Newalta Corporation, 301
Caetano, Lucy, Commis, Bibliothèque de géographie, 1177
Cafaro, Philip J., Vice-President, International Society for Environmental Ethics, 943
Cafferty, Mary Rae, Director, 666
Cahill, Robert B., Executive Director, Fur Institute of Canada, 922
Caines, Jennifer, Treasurer, Newfoundland Aquaculture Industry Association, 963
Caines, Kevin, Executive Director, 616
Cain-Lough, Cynthia, Technician, Kingston R & D Centre, 1142
Cairns, Jim, Contact, Environmental Plastics Advisory Service, 185
Cairns, Sandy, District Councillor, Gravenhurst, 709
Cairns, Scott, Chief Geologist, 607
Cairns, Stephen, Commissioner, Finance & Corporate Services, Muskoka, 702
Caisse, Normand, Longueuil, 737
Caissy, Richard, Rimouski, 740
Cajic, Natalie, Specialist, Canadian Health Food Association, 870
Cajolet, Thérèse, Greffière, Drummondville, 819-478-6554, 735
Caldarelli, Frances, Greater Sudbury / Grand Sudbury, 710
Calder, David, General Manager, Corporate Services, Waterloo, 519-747-8542, 722
Calderone, Maria, Conseillère d'arrondissement, Rivière-des-Prairies, Montréal, 738
Caldwell, Douglas, President, ISCA Management Ltd., 248
Caldwell, Earl, President, Nu-Air Ventilation Systems Inc., 309
Caldwell, Fran, President, Brampton Horticultural Society, 846
Caldwell, Rob, Manager, Information Services, Toronto Botanical Garden, 1162
Caldwell, Q.C., Douglas A., Patterson Law, 1068
Calendino, Pietro, Burnaby, 679
Callaghan, Cathy, Information Services Librarian, University of Prince Edward Island, 1166
Callaghan, Dan, Pembroke, 717
Callaghan, Deb, Erin, 709
Callaghan, Eileen, Director, 641
Callaghan, Mary Ellen, Manager, Campbell River, 679

Callahan, Bob, City Councillor, Brampton, 706
Callahan, Shelly, Manager, Westburne Canada, 427
Callan, Jill, Chair, 581
Callander, Bob, Farris Industries Canada, 194
Callbreath, Deborah, Chair, Canadian Health Food Association, 870
Callery, Raymond, Chief Administrative Officer, Greater Napanee, 709
Callihoo, Michael W., Bennett Jones LLP - Calgary Office, 1049
Calver, Wayne, Fire Chief, Loyalist, 727
Calvo Sorando, José-Pedro, General Secretary, International Association of Sedimentologists, 936
Cambray, Fernande, Branch Manager, Anachemia Canada Inc., 85
Cambrin, Harry Riva, Municipal Manager, Foothills No. 31, 669
Came, Frank, Vice-President, British Columbia Environment Industry Association, 847
Cameron, Allan, Director, Richmond, 604-276-4096, 684
Cameron, Ashley, Contact, Atlantic Soils & Associated Management Ltd., 97
Cameron, Bernard, Mississippi Mills, 714
Cameron, Brian, Applications Engineer, Performance Fluid Equipement Inc., 321
Cameron, Bruce, Director, 611
Cameron, Clayton, Director, Public Works, Severn, 729
Cameron, Dave, Strathroy-Caradoc, 731
Cameron, Ewart, General Manager, WorleyParsons Canada Ltd., 434
Cameron, George G., Graham Wilson & Green, Barristers & Solicitors, Notaries, Mediato, 1068
Cameron, Glenn, Partner, Stikeman Elliott LLP - Calgary, 1053
Cameron, Grant, Executive Director, Alberta Plastics Recycling Association, 819
Cameron, Hugh J., Partner, Stewart McKelvey Stirling Scales - Fredericton, 1064
Cameron, Ian, Directeur, Abitibi-Ouest, 746
Cameron, Jean R., Executive Coordinator, Pacific States/British Columbia Oil Spill Task Force, 984
Cameron, Kathleen, Manager, Sunset Solar Systems Ltd., 383
Cameron, Matthew, Stikeman Elliott LLP - Toronto, 1079
Cameron, Nancy, Medical Officer of Health, Huron, 701
Cameron, Rod, Manager, Operations, Mississippi Mills, 714
Cameron, Russ, Fire Chief, Colwood, 680
Cameron, Scott, Manager, Red Deer, 403-342-8100, 674
Cameron, Susan, Head, User Services, St Francis-Xavier University, 1134
Camp, David K., Partner, Borden Ladner Gervais LLP - Vancouver, 1058
Campagna, Galliano, Manager, Westburne Canada, 426
Campagna, Marc, Terrebonne, 745
Campbell, Alex, Deputy Minister, 619
Campbell, Allan V., Minister, 640
Campbell, April, Manager, Westburne Canada, 428
Campbell, Archie, Lennox Industries (Canada) Ltd., 267
Campbell, Bev, Prince Edward, 703
Campbell, Bob, Clerk, Clearview, 725
Campbell, Brian, Project Manager, Bristar Containment Industries Ltd., 117
Campbell, Bruce, Vice-President, 629
Campbell, Carolyn, Executive Director, British Columbia Ready Mixed Concrete Association, 849
Campbell, Colin, Markham, 713
Campbell, Don, Manager, FS Partners, 202
Campbell, Donald, Manager, Flygt Canada, 198
Campbell, Donna, Manager, Colchester County, 697
Campbell, Doug, Manager, Portage La Prairie, 204-239-8373, 689
Campbell, Gail, Orangeville, 716
Campbell, Gerard, General Manager, Campbell's Concrete Ltd., 122
Campbell, Glenn, Kawartha Lakes, 711
Campbell, Gord, Alderman, St. Thomas, 719
Campbell, Gordon, Councillor, Kincardine, 519-396-8075, 726
Campbell, Gregory, Executive Vice-President, Hazco Environmental Services Ltd., 227
Campbell, Gérald, Superintendent, Public Works, Hawkesbury, 711
Campbell, Heather, ILL Clerk, Canada Dept. of National Defence & the Canadian Forces, 1148
Campbell, Jackie, Saxe, Dianne, 1079
Campbell, James W., President/CEO, EPEC Consulting (Sask) Ltd., 189
Campbell, Jocelyn Ann, Conseillère, Saint-Sulpice, Montréal, 738

CANADIAN ENVIRONMENTAL RESOURCE GUIDE 2011-2012

Executive Name Index

Campbell, Kaitryn, Librarian, Ottawa Hospital-Riverside Campus, 1151
Campbell, Ken W., Vice-President, R.V. Anderson Associates Limited, 341
Campbell, Kent, Deputy Minister, 660
Campbell, Léo, Président, Convoyeurs B.M.G. inc., 151
Campbell, Margaret, Librarian, Chatham-Kent Health Alliance, 1139
Campbell, Marty, Coordinator, Red Deer County, 670
Campbell, Mary, Renfrew, 613-623-5756, 704
Campbell, Mel, Leeds & Grenville, 726
Campbell, Michael C., President, SCG Industries Ltd., 359
Campbell, Neil, Associate University Librarian, Law, University of Victoria Libraries, 1121
Campbell, Neil A., Law Librarian & Associate Professor, Diana M. Priestly Law Library, 1120
Campbell, Norm, CEO, Saskatchewan Parks & Recreation Association, 1001
Campbell, Patric, General Manager, Canadian Seabed Research Ltd., 125
Campbell, Rita, Librarian, St Francis-Xavier University, 1134
Campbell, Robert, Delta, 604-948-0623, 686
Campbell, Robert, Director, Library Services, Cape Breton University, 1137
Campbell, Robin B., Regional Solicitor, Cape Breton, 902-563-5045, 695
Campbell, Ron, CEO, Proshred Security, 335
Campbell, Ryan, President, R.A. Campbell & Associates, 339
Campbell, Sandy, Collection Coordinator, Cameron Science & Technology Library, 1104
Campbell, Suzzette, Library Assistant, DeVry Institute of Technology, 1101
Campbell, Vern, General Manager, CML Northern Blower Inc., 145
Campbell, Q.C., Harry S., Burnet, Duckworth & Palmer LLP, 1050
Campbell, Q.C., Karen A., Cox and Palmer - Charlottetown, 1082
Campbell-Platt, Geoffrey, President, International Union of Food Science & Technology, 945
Campeau, Stephanie, Communications Manager, AUTO21 - The Automobile of the 21st Century, 844
Campion, Frank, Welland, 722
Campitelli, Lenny, President, J&F Waste Systems Inc., 249
Campitelli, Rob, Controller, National Waste Services, 298
Campo, Gary, Woodward & Company, 1063
Canac Marquis, Suzanne, Directrice générale adjointe, Québec, 740
canadaalberta municipal r, Canada-Alberta Municipal, Edmonton, AB, 1039
canadian foresaintseedlin, Canadian Forest Seedling, 1213
Candy, Eileen, Library Technician, Alberta Hospital Edmonton, 1104
Cane, D.D.B., President, Simcoe Engineering Group Limited, 368
Cane, CMO, Diane, County Clerk, Northumberland, 702
Canfield, Brian R., Farris, Vaughan, Wills & Murphy LLP, 1059
Cann, John, President, R&R Drilling Supply Ltd., 339
Cannan, Kevin, Treasurer, Environmental Information Association, 912
Cannella, Tony, Director, Engineering Services, Clarington, 724
Canning, Darlene, Computer Services Librarian, Schulich Library of Science & Engineering, 1175
Canning, Glen M., Midland, 713
Canning, Stratford, Partner, Canning & Pitt Associates Inc., 126
Cannon, Charles A., President/CEO, Rubber Manufacturers Association, 997
Cannon, Heather, Environmental Planner, Environova Planning Group Inc., 186
Cannon, Lawrence, Minister, Foreign Affairs, 529
Cannon, Mike, Vice-President, Carmanah Technologies Corp., 129
Cannon, R. Carl, Chief Administrative Officer, Port Hope, 728
Cansfield, Donna H., Minister, 631
Cant, Michael, Manager, Totten Sims Hubicki Associates Ltd., 399
Cantello, Geoffrey, Nelligan O'Brien Payne, 1071
Cantelo, Kelly, Program Officer, 637
Cantin, François, Maire, Blainville, 450-434-5203, 734
Cantin, Louis, Manager, Chem Action Inc., 139
Cantin, Marie-Claude, Partner, Lavery, de Billy - Montréal, 1085
Cantin, Marie-Claude, President/CEO, Bacta-Pur, 101
Cantin, Maxime, Associé, Ogilvy Renault LLP/S.E.N.C.R.L., s.r.l. - Québec, 1088
Cantin, Michel, Bélanger, Sauvé, 1082
Cantin, Paul-Roger, Saguenay, 741
Cantin, Robert, Saint-Jean-sur-Richelieu, 450-349-6661, 742

Cantrell, Rick, Vice-President & Chief Operating Officer, Sustainable Forestry Initiative, 1011
Canyon, Ryan, Project Director, Smart Commute, 1004
Caouette, Pierre, Cain Lamarre Casgrain Wells - Québec, 1087
Capaldi, Grahaem H., President, Environmental Reporting Systems Limited, 186
Cape, Geoff, Executive Director, Evergreen, 914
Caplan, David, Minister, 628
Caplan, Tyana R., Stewart McKelvey Stirling Scales - Halifax, 1067
Capozi, Robert, New Brunswick Contact, Gulf of Maine Council on the Marine Environment, 927
Capozio, Nicola, Engineering President, NCL Envirotek Inc., 299
Capparelli, Pat, Executive Vice-President, Shred-It, 366
Capuano, Mike, Chair, Canadian Medical & Biological Engineering Society, 877
Carbert, Blair R., Founding Partner, Stones Carbert Waite Wells LLP, 1054
Carbonaro, David, Partner, Heenan Blaikie LLP - Toronto, 1075
Card, Leah C., Fulton & Company LLP, Lawyers & Trade-Mark Agents, 1056
Card, Michael, Contact, Canadian Eagle Recyclers, Inc., 124
Cardell, Craig, Branch Manager, Fort Garry Industries Ltd., 200
Cardell, Robert, General Manager & Vice-President, Marsulex Inc., 281
Cardiff, Len, Manager, Westburne Canada, 428
Cardin, Louis, Sec.-Trés., Régie d'assainissement des eaux Richelieu/Saint-Laurent, 759
Cardinal, Bernard, Beloeil, 450-467-7127, 734
Cardinal, Mark, Manager, Parkland County, 670
Cardona, Sophie, Manager, INFORM Inc., 931
Cardozo, Robin, CEO, 622
Carefoot, Rick, Chief Building Official, Meaford, 727
Carella, Tony, Vaughan, 722
Carere, Christina, Contact, Vacuum Products Canada Inc., 408
Carette, Roger, Maire, Saint-Georges, 742
Cargnelli, Joseph, Chief Technology Officer, Hydrogenics Corporation, 236
Caricofe, Erin, Program Assistant, Henry A. Wallace Center for Agricultural & Environmental Policy a, 929
Carignan, Claude, Maire, Saint-Eustache, 450-974-5014, 742
Carignan Lefebvre, Nicole, Saint-Eustache, 450-623-5730, 742
Carl, Mark, Welland, 722
Carle, Rod, General Manager, New Westminster, 682
Carley, P.Eng., Neal, Assistant City Engineer, Vancouver, 604-873-7360, 685
Carlile, Cathryn, General Manager, Richmond, 604-276-4068, 684
Carlin, Nancy, Library Technician, Alberta Children's Hospital Library, 1099
Carline, Johnny, CAO, Metro Vancouver, 678
Carlos, Lindo da Silva, Trade Commissioner, 768
Carlson, Darren W., McDougall Gauley, 1090
Carlson, George, Peel, 714, 703
Carlson, Harold, Chairperson, Alberni Valley Outdoor Club, 815
Carlson, Jack, Manager, SGE Hatch Ltd., 364
Carlson, Jeff, Lethbridge, 403-360-7550, 673
Carlson, Joel, Manager, Miller Environmental Corp., 290
Carlson, Ken, Director, Wetaskiwin County No. 10, 780-361-6340, 670
Carlson, Matthew, Officer, Newfoundland & Labrador Federation of Agriculture, 962
Carlston, B.A., M.A., Jason, General Manager, Regina, 754
Carlyle, Bob, Branch Manager, Fort Garry Industries Ltd., 200
Carlyle, Bob, OE Sales Manager, Fort Garry Industries Ltd., 200
Carlyle, Phyllis, General Manager, Richmond, 604-276-4104, 684
Carlyly, Elaine, Director, 666
Carman, Jayne, Clerk & Coordinator, Council Committee, Brant, 698
Carmichael, Robert W., Cox and Palmer - Halifax, 1067
Carmichael, Russ, Director, Maple Ridge, 604-467-7363, 687
Carmichael, Wayne, Manager, Henderson Paddon & Associates Ltd., 229
Carmody, James, Petawawa, 717
Carnegie, Dan, Director, Human Resource Services, Oshawa, 716
Carnegie, Robert, Clerk & Director, Chilliwack, 604-793-2910, 680
Carney, Owen G., President, Owen G. Carney Ltd., 315
Carol, Turner, Integra Environmental Inc., 243
Caron, Christian, La Prairie, 736
Caron, Denis, President, 596
Caron, Eric, President & CEO, Groupe Tremca inc., 221
Caron, Gaétan, Chair/CEO, 546

Caron, Gilbert, Directeur général, Robert-Cliche, 753
Caron, Gilles, Directeur, Université du Québec à Chicoutimi, 1166
Caron, Gisele, Agent, Burnaby, 679
Caron, Marie-Michèle, Director, Multitel Inc., 295
Caron, Mario, Directeur général, La Nouvelle-Beauce, 748
Caron, Michel, Chair, Groupe Tremca inc., 221
Caron, Michel, Directeur, Sherbrooke, 819-821-5630, 744
Caron, Michel, Président, MissionHGE inc., 291
Caron, Monique, Hutchins Caron & Associés, 1085
Caron, Terri, Chief Administrative Officer, New Tecumseth, 714
Caron, s.m.a., André, Directeur général de Québec & de l'Est, 654
Carothers, Leslie, President, Environmental Law Institute, 912
Carozzi, Mila, Senior Information Agent, Shell Canada Limited, 1102
Carpenter, A.W, Fasken Martineau - Calgary, 1050
Carpenter, David, Account Manager, ESRI Canada Ltd., 190
Carpenter, Richard, Brantford, 707
Carpenter, Scott, Manager, PRT Inc., 336
Carpenter, Stephen, President/CEO, Enermodal Engineering Ltd., 179
Carpentier, Vincent, Field Sales Rep., National Instruments Canada, 298
Carr, Blaine, Operations Manager, Canadian Seabed Research Ltd., 125
Carr, Denis, Cornwall, 708
Carr, Gary, Regional Chair, Halton, 905-825-6115, 700
Carr, Hillary, Manager, Canada Revenue Agency, 1148
Carr, John, Contact, Ecology North, 908
Carr, Roger, Vice-President, Eriksson Sediment Systems Inc., 189
Carr, S., Central Elgin, 724
Carr, Scott, Chief Executive Officer, Jasco Research Ltd., 251
Carr, Scott, Vice-President, Jasco Research Ltd., 251
Carr, Stuart, Secretary-Treasurer, Canadian Society of Allergy & Clinical Immunology, 886
Carr, Susan, General Manager, Prince Albert Model Forest Association Inc., 988
Carr, Terry, Test Technician, Westest, 430
Carra, Gian-Carlo, Calgary, 403-268-2430, 671
Carr-Harris, J.Bruce, Borden Ladner Gervais LLP - Ottawa, 1070
Carrick, Mark, Deputy Mayor & Councillor, LaSalle, 713
Carrier, Chris, Simcoe, 704
Carrier, Daniel, Directeur, Longueuil, 737
Carrier, Dave, Advance Engineered Products Ltd., 69
Carrier, Geneviève, Cain Lamarre Casgrain Wells - Québec, 1087
Carrier, Hélène, Cain Lamarre Casgrain Wells - Québec, 1087
Carrier, Hélène, Directrice, Université d'Ottawa, 1152
Carrier, Jean, Associé, Stikeman Elliott LLP - Montréal, 1087
Carrier, Marie-Claude, Associé, Langlois Kronström Desjardins, 1088
Carrier, Paul, Responsable, Référence, Pêches et aquaculture commerciales, 1167
Carrier, Réjean, Directeur général, 650
Carriere, Henri P., Manager, Calibre Strategic Services Inc., 122
Carriere, Jeff, VP, Fort Garry Industries Ltd., 199
Carrière, Louis, Partner, Heenan Blaikie S.E.N.C.R.L./SRL - Québec, 1087
Carrière, Marc, Directeur général, Argenteuil, 747
Carrière, Mathilde, Fraser Milner Casgrain S.E.N.C.R.L./LLP, 1084
Carrière, Mireille, Longueuil, 737
Carrière, Patrick, Supervisor, Waste Water Treatment Facility, Cornwall, 708
Carrière, Robert, Saint-Jérôme, 450-432-5629, 743
Carrière, Thierry, Owner & President, Industries de Moules et Plastiques VIF, 241
Carrières, Michel, Maire, Saint-Basile-le-Grand, 741
Carrigan, Bryan, District Manager, BFI Canada Inc., 106
Carrigan, Keith A., CEO & Vice-Chairman, BFI Canada Inc., 106
Carrington, Richard, Klohn Crippen Berger Ltd., 258
Carroll, Aileen M., Minister, 621
Carroll, Daniel P., Field Law - Edmonton, 1055
Carroll, Gary, Director, Engineering Services, Oshawa, 716
Carroll, Joanna, Blaney McMurtry LLP, 1073
Carroll, Maureen, President, Matco Ltd., 282
Carroll, Neil, Director, Planning & Development, Pickering, 905-420-4617, 718
Carroll, Shelley, Toronto, 721
Carroll, Sherry, Port Coquitlam, 683
Carruthers, Amy J., Partner, Lawson Lundell LLP - Vancouver, 1060

Executive Name Index

Carruthers, Arden, Director, Public Works, & Fire Chief, Morewood, North Dundas, 727
Carruthers, Brian, General Manager, Williams Lake, 250-392-1763, 686
Carruthers, Dave, Fire Chief, Clearview, 725
Carruthers, Mitch, Treasurer, Clearview, 725
Carscallen, Q.C., Stanley, Carscallen Leitch LLP, 1050
Carsley, Timothy R., Partner, Borden Ladner Gervais LLP - Montréal, 1083
Carson, Breen, Manager, Climatizer Insulation Inc., 144
Carson, Dave, Construction Manager, Ambler & Co. Inc., 82
Carson, Greig, Contact, Sears Canada Inc., 361
Carson, Lorne, Partner, Osler, Hoskin & Harcourt LLP - Calgary, 1053
Carson, Tim, Chief Executive Officer, Alberta Association of Agricultural Societies, 815
Carsten, Tudor, Davis LLP - Toronto, 1074
Carswell, Harry, President, Carswell Consulting Engineers Ltd., 130
Carswell, John, Vice-President, Carswell Consulting Engineers Ltd., 130
Carswell, Robert, Sec.-Treas., Carswell Consulting Engineers Ltd., 130
Carswell-Alexander, Patricia, St. Clair, 519-864-4006, 729
Carteaux, William R., President, Society of the Plastics Industry, Inc., 1008
Carten, Michael, President, Sustainable Energy Technologies Ltd., 383
Carter, Bruce, Manager, Penny & Casson Co., 321
Carter, David C., President & Sr. Geologist, Hy-Grade Geoscience, 235
Carter, Fran, President, British Columbia Fuchsia & Begonia Society, 848
Carter, Jennifer, General Manager, M&L Testing Equipment (1995) Ltd., 276
Carter, Jim, Comptroller, 545
Carter, Jim, Senior Financial Officer, 564
Carter, John, Manager, Westburne Canada, 428
Carter, Mae, Reference Resource Clerk, Reference Resource Centre, 1165
Carter, Margaret, Principal, Heritage Research Associates Inc., 230
Carter, Ray, Manager, Dillon Consulting Ltd., 164
Carter, Ruby, Senior Negotiator, 602
Carter, Steve, Vice President, Gemcom Software International Inc., 206
Carter, T., Manager, Moncton / Ville de Moncton, 506-853-3535, 691
Carter, William D.T., Senior Partner, Borden Ladner Gervais LLP - Toronto, 1073
Cartier, Jean-Yves, Conseiller de ville, Saint-Paul-Émard, Montréal, 738
Cartwright, Barbara, Chair, The Jane Goodal Institute of Canada, 946
Cartwright, Thomas, Fire Chief, Port Colborne, 718
Carty, Mike, PricewaterhouseCoopers Management Consultants, 332
Caruana, Joseph, Director, Community Services, Clarington, 724
Caruk, Kelly, MacPherson Leslie & Tyerman LLP - Saskatoon, 1090
Carvell, Dorothea, Manager, Transit, North Bay, 715
Cary, W.N., CEO, Gator International, 205
Carzoli, Paul, Maire, Saint-Lazare, 743
Casabon, François, Coordonnateur Services des technologies de l'infor, Campus Notre-Dame-de-Foy, 1182
Casacia, Lucy, Managing Partner, Adventis Technologies, 69
Casaletto, Rick, Manager, Toromont Caterpillar, 397
Casaletto, Vic, VP, Toromont Caterpillar, 398
Casaubon, Marie-Josée, Présidente, Association des Aménagistes Régionaux du Québec, 831
Casavant, Ginette, Technicienne, Université du Québec Institut national de la recherche scientifiq, 1176
Casciaro, Marlène, Director, Genivar, 207
Case, Ray, Director, 605
Case, Todd, Lambton, 701
Case, Todd, Chair, 635
Casement, Kevin, Vice-President, University Technologies International, 407
Casey, Andrew, Vice-President, Forest Products Association of Canada, 918
Casey, Karen, Minister, 613
Casey, Margaret, Muskoka, 702
Casey, Pam, Research Information Specialist, NPS Pharmaceuticals, 1159
Casey, Patrick, Director, Corporate Communications, York, 705

Casey, Ron, Mayor, Canmore, 671
Casey, Tom, Vice-President, Nardei Fabricators Ltd., 297
Casey, Q.C., Michael F., Field Law - Calgary, 1051
Cash, Sean, President, Alberta Agricultural Economics Association, 815
Cass, Fred D., Aird & Berlis LLP, 1072
Cass, Paul, Vice-President, Ballard Power Systems Inc., 101
Cassel, Karen, Head, Serials & Electronic Acquistions, York University Libraries, 1164
Casselman, Bob, City Manager, Brockville, 707
Casselman, Judy, Niagara, 702
Casselman, Lyle, Environmental Auditor, M.S. Thompson & Associates Ltd., 276
Cassidy, Myles, Manager, Emergency Services & Chief, Fire, Cornwall, 708
Cassidy, Paul R., Blake, Cassels & Graydon LLP - Vancouver, 1057
Cassidy, Terry R.F., Quinte West, 613-395-2031, 718
Cassista, Carl, President & CEO, Axion Technologies, 99
Castagner, Alain, Préfet, Le Haut-St-Laurent, 749
Castell, Barb, Staff, Millarville Racing & Agricultural Society, 954
Castonguay, Ghislain, Directeur, Saint-Lazare, 743
Castravelli, Chris, Founder, ProViro Instrumentation Inc., 336
Castrilli, Mauro, Coordinator, Transportation, Middlesex Centre, 727
Castro, Pilar, Manager, 559
Castro-Wunsch, Kirsten, Managing Director, Cleanit Greenit Compost System, 143
Castro-Wunsch, Kristen, President, KC Environmental Group Ltd., 256
Caswell, Dianne, Exec. Assistant/Office Manager, 611
Catalano, Mike, Geonics Limited, 211
Catania, PhD, P.Eng., Peter J., Chair, International Energy Foundation, 938
Catelin, Milton, Chief Executive, World Coal Institute, 1022
Catellier, Marcel, Préfet, Montmagny, 750
Catellier, Maryse, Vice-président exécutif, Camping Québec, 852
Caterer, Gerry, Director, Planning, Adjala-Tosorontio, 724
Caterina, Tony, Edmonton, 780-496-8333, 672
Caterini, Rose, City Clerk, Hamilton, 711
Cathcart, Neal, Peterborough, 703
Cathers, Brad, Minister, 664
Cathro, Mike, President, Kamloops Exploration Group, 947
Catley-Carlson, Margaret, Honorary President, Panos Canada, 984
Cattaneo, Joseph J., President, Glass Packaging Institute, 923
Caudwell, Stephen G., President & Owner, Wasteco, 421
Caughlin, Bunny, Officer, Breast Cancer Society of Canada, 846
Causton, Christopher M., Mayor, Oak Bay, 688
Cavan, Laurie, General Manager, Surrey, 604-598-5765, 684
Cavanagh, Paul, Unit Manager, AMEC, 84
Cavanaugh, Darlene, Director, Alberta Farmers' Market Association, 817
Cavanaugh, Ron, Councillor, Colchester County, 697
Cavender, Peter, Branch Manager/Director of Mining, North America, Anachemia Canada Inc., 85
Cavers, Douglas E., CAO, Hanover, 690
Cawker, Joel, Vice President/General Manager, Sandwell Engineering Inc., 357
Cayen, Pat, Fire Chief, Fire Rescue Services, Sarnia, 719
Céclier, Michèle, Saint-Jérôme, 450-438-1073, 743
Celestian, Leong, Trade Commissioner, 767
Céline, Jacob, Sec.-Trés., Régie de l'eau de l'Ile Perrot, 759
Cerilli, Renata, Director, Enviroplast inc, 187
Cerit, Errol, Senior Director, Food & Consumer Products of Canada, 918
Cernile, Carol, Research Library Technician, U.S. Steel Canada, 1141
Cerny, Mark, Regional Manager, Babcock & Wilcox Canada Ltd., 100
Cesari, Vincenzo, Conseiller d'arrondissement, Cecil-P.-Newman, Montréal, 738
Ceschi-Smith, Marguerite, Brantford, 707
Cesconetto, Fabio, St. Marys Cement Inc., 356
Cessford, Jim, Chief Constable, Delta, 604-946-3729, 686
Chabot, Alain, President, Aqua Data Inc., 88
Chabot, Andre, Calgary, 403-268-2430, 671
Chabot, Andy, Executive Director, Cancer Research Society, 892
Chabot, Annie, Directrice générale, Association des jeunes ruraux du Québec, 832
Chabot, François, Contact, Golder Associates Ltd., 215
Chabot, Josiane, Présidente, Association des jeunes ruraux du Québec, 832
Chabot, Ricky, McCordick Glove & Safety Inc., 284
Chabot, Rock, Vice-President, Envirogain Inc., 184

Chabot, Sylvain, Associé, Ogilvy Renault LLP/S.E.N.C.R.L., s.r.l. - Québec, 1088
Chaboyer, Jan, Brandon, 689
Chacalias, Brad, Manager, Movac Mobile Vacuum Services Ltd., 294
Chadbourn, Jean, Administrative Assistant, Mines & Aggregates Safety & Health Association, 954
Chadwick, Ian, Collingwood, 708
Chadwick, Mike, Chief Constable, Saanich, 250-475-4321, 688
Chafe, Dan, Director, 602
Chafe, Dermot, Director, Gander, 709-651-5912, 694
Chaffe, Donna, Coordinator, Human Resources, Perth East, 728
Chagnon, Claude, Vice-President, MLC Associés Inc., 292
Chagnon, Daniel, Directeur, Sainte-Julie, 450-922-7122, 743
Chagnon, Jules, Coordonnateur, CÉGEP de Victoriaville, 1187
Chaiken, MD, Barry P., Chair, Healthcare Information & Management Systems Society, 928
Chaillez, Lise, Bibliothécaire, École nationale d'aérotechnique, 1183
Chaîné, Yves, Bélanger, Sauvé, 1082
Chaisson, J. Robert, Vice-President, Nepisiguit Salmon Association, 960
Chaisson, Linda, Corner Brook, 693
Chalmers, Cameron, Director, Squamish, 604-815-5010, 688
Chalmers, Jeff, Assistant General Manager, Pure Energy Inc., 336
Chalmers, Kathryn I., Senior Partner, Stikeman Elliott LLP - Toronto, 1080
Chalmers, Marshall, Mayor, Camrose, 671
Chalmessin, Desimil, Superintendent, Dieppe, 691
Chamaillard, André, Hawkesbury, 711
Chamard, Jean-Louis, President, Chamard & Associés, 138
Chamaschuk, Shelly, Reynolds, Mirth, Richards & Farmer LLP, 1056
Chamberlain, Adam, Partner, Borden Ladner Gervais LLP - Toronto, 1073
Chamberlain, Chris, President/CEO, ARAM Systems Ltd., 89
Chamberlain, Darren, Manager, Elmtree Environmental Ltd., 176
Chamberlain, H., Director, Financial Services, Fort Erie, 709
Chamberlain, Jan, Owen Sound, 717
Chamberlain, Susi, Coordinator, 596
Chamberland, Geneviève, Heenan Blaikie S.E.N.C.R.L/SRL - Sherbrooke, 1089
Chamberland, Patricia, Bibliotechnicienne, CHUQ-CHUL, 1178
Chamberland, Serges, Directeur général adjoint, Saguenay, 741
Chamberlin, George K., Principal, Procyon Consulting Inc., 333
Chambers, Carolin, Lead, Monsanto Canada Inc., 293
Chambers, Dale, General Manager, SCG Industries Ltd., 359
Chambers, Douglas B., Executive Vice-President, SENES Consultants Limited, 362
Chambers, Judy, Coordinator, Moncton Campus, Library, 1128
Chambers, Robert, Brant, 698
Chambers, Stephen, President, Dell Tech Laboratories Ltd., 160
Chambers, Stuart W., McLennan Ross LLP, 1055
Chambers, Thane, President, Northern Alberta Health Libraries Association, 966
Chambers, B.Comm., LL.B., Gordon R., Partner, Lawson Lundell LLP - Vancouver, 1060
Champ, Martyn, President, Dimplex North America, 164
Champagne, André, Directeur, Services informatiques, Université du Québec à Montréal, 1176
Champagne, Claude, Directeur, Symbiose Consultants inc, 385
Champagne, Louis-Philippe, Thetford Mines, 418-335-7119, 745
Champagne, Luc, Thetford Mines, 418-338-2812, 745
Champagne, Mélanie, Borden Ladner Gervais LLP - Montréal, 1083
Champagne, Pierre, Partner, Heenan Blaikie LLP - Ottawa, 1070
Champagne, Raymond, Directeur, Terrebonne, 450-492-2433, 745
Champagne, Sylvain, Directeur, Services à la clientèle, HEC Montréal, 1173
Chan, Godwin, Richmond Hill, 718
Chan, Kathy, Treasurer, Spruce Grove, 674
Chan, Liza, Research Librarian, John W. Scott Health Sciences Library, 1105
Chan, Michael, Technical Representative, Dalynn Biologicals Inc., 156
Chan, Peter, Office Manager, Trow Consulting Engineers Ltd., 403
Chandler, Claudia, Chemical Info Specialist, Aker Kvaerner Chemetics Inc., 1117
Chandler, Don, President, Vancouver Electric Vehicle Association, 1016
Chandler, Eric, Manager, Planning, New Tecumseth, 714

CANADIAN ENVIRONMENTAL RESOURCE GUIDE 2011-2012   1277

Executive Name Index

Chandler, Harry, Director, 629
Chandler, Trevor, President, Landscope Consulting Corp., 264
Chandler, R.N., Sonya, Victoria, 685
Chandra, Jim, Country Manager, Sandwell Engineering Inc., 357
Chang, Frank, President, Plast-Ex International Inc., 326
Chang, Jimmy, Divison Vice-President, Silliker JR Laboratories, ULC, 367
Chang, Lily, General Manager, Plast-Ex International Inc., 326
Chang, Richard, Burnaby, 679
Channon, Keith, Program Manager, Commission for Environmental Cooperation, 898
Chantal, Claude, Président, Association des entomologistes amateurs du Québec inc., 832
Chapados, Ghislain, Responsable, Prêt et Photocopie, Pêches et aquaculture commerciales, 1167
Chaperon, Johanne, Bibliotechnicienne, Centre hospitalier de l'Université de Montréal Hôtel-Dieu, 1172
Chapman, Bob, Durham, 699
Chapman, Bob, Regional Councillor, Oshawa, 716
Chapman, Bruce, Executive Director, Groundfish Enterprise Allocation Council, 926
Chapman, Dan, City Treasurer & General Manager, Financial Servic, Kitchener, 519-741-2357, 712
Chapman, Dan, Treasurer, Woolwich, 732
Chapman, Gail, CAO, Bulkley-Nechako, 250-692-3195, 676
Chapman, Lee, Research & Development, Target Recycling Inc., 387
Chapman, Paul, Director, Planning Services, St. Catharines, 719
Chapman, Peter M., Principal, Golder Associates Ltd., 214
Chapman, Philip M., Ritch Durnford, Lawyers, 1067
Chapman, Robert D., McCarthy Tétrault LLP - Ottawa, 1071
Chapman, Shad A., Brownlee LLP, 1054
Chapman, Q.C., Anthony L., Cox and Palmer - Halifax, 1067
Chappele, David, Manager, PRT Inc., 336
Chappell, Barry, Summerside, 733
Chappell, Charles L., Aikins, MacAulay & Thorvaldson LLP, 1063
Chappell, John, President, Sealcon Liner Systems Inc., 361
Chapple, Paul, Vice-President, HLS Ecolo, 232
Chaput, Carl, Ozogram Inc., 315
Chaput, Claudia, Val-d'Or, 746
Chaput, Rhéaume, Fire Chief, Belleville, 706
Charabin, Gail, Library Assistant, Canadian Agriculture Library - Saskatoon, 1189
Charanduk, Brian, Treasurer, Alberta Association of Landscape Architects, 815
Charbonneau, Gary, Director, Wilmot, 732
Charbonneau, George, President, Canadian Association of Swine Veterinarians, 859
Charbonneau, Guy, VP, Groupe S.M. International Inc., 220
Charbonneau, Luke, Deputy Mayor & Councillor, Saugeen Shores, 719
Charbonneau, Paul, Director, Emergency & Transportation Services & Ch, Frontenac, 699
Charbonneau, Roland, Préfet, La Rivière-du-Nord, 748
Charbonneau, Suzanne, Longueuil, 737
Charest Knoetze, Claire, Technicienne en documentation, Campus d'Edmundston, 1126
Charest, André, Directeur, Victoriaville, 819-758-0651, 746
Charest, Jean-Guy, Préfet, Kamouraska, 748
Charest, Lynda, Directrice générale, Régie intermunicipale de gestion des déchets de la région Maskout, 760
Charette, Jon, Office Manager, Armatek Controls Limited, 91
Charette, Louis, Partner, Lavery, de Billy - Montréal, 1085
Charette, Ross, Manager, Les Plastiques Simport Ltée, 270
Charette, Tammy, Staff, Aircraft Services Directorate, 1147
charitree foundation, The ChariTREE Foundation, Bowen Island, BC, 1040
Charky, Gabriel, CEO, Allianz Madvac Inc., 79
Charland, Claude, General Manager, Charland Thermojet Inc., 138
Charland, Robert, Longueuil, 737
Charland, Roger, SMTE, CÉGEP de Beauce-Appalaches, 1183
Charland-Lallier, Maryève, Présidente, Conseil régional de l'environnement de la Gaspésie et des Iles-de, 901
Charlebois, Cézanne M., McKenzie Lake Lawyers LLP, 1069
Charlebois, Jack H., Midland, 713
Charlebois, Mario, Technical Director, Demilec Inc., 161
Charlebois, Michel, President, Enviroplast inc, 187
Charlesbois, Daniel, Maire, Beauharnois, 734
Charlesworth, David L., President, Charlesworth & Associates, 138
Charlton, Anne, Director, Calgary, 403-268-3888, 671
Charlton, David, Principal, Stantec Inc., 378
Charneux, Roland, Directeur général et Vice-président, Pageau Morel & associés, inc., 317

Charney, Richard J., Senior Partner, Ogilvy Renault LLP/S.E.N.C.R.L., s.r.l. - Toronto, 1078
Charpentier, Brigitte, Contact, Les Peintures Sico inc., 269
Charron, Denis, Directeur général, Rouyn-Noranda, 741
Charron, Eric, President, Les Laboratoires Shermont Inc., 269
Charron, Jean-Pierre, Préfet, Témiscamingue, 753
Charron, Lyne, Responsable, PEB, La Cité Collégiale, 1151
Charron, Noëllline, Technicienne en documentation, Collège Jean-de-Brébeuf, 1172
Charron, Pierre, Saint-Eustache, 450-473-8054, 742
Charron, Pierre R., Directeur général, La Côte-de-Gaspé, 748
Chart, Ted., Project Director, Decommissioning Consulting Services Limited, 159
Chartier, Gene, Commissioner, Planning & Public Works, Scugog, 729
Chartier, Michelle, Responsable, services techniques, Collège Édouard-Montpetit, 1169
Chartier, Ray Raymond, Partner, Macleod Dixon LLP, 1052
Chartrand, Denis, Manager, Whitchurch-Stouffville, 723
Chartrand, Jean-Pierre, Clarence-Rockland, 708
Chartrand, Melanie, Lavery, de Billy - Montréal, 1085
Chartrand, Pierre, CLA Experts-Conseils, 142
Chartrand, Pierre, Vice-President, 519
Chase, Doug, City Manager, Miramichi, 691
Chase, Michael, President, International Erosion Control Association, 938
Chase, Rick, Vice-President, Consolidated Envirowaste Industries Inc., 150
Chase, Stephen, Deputy Mayor & Councillor, Saint John, 692
Chase, Stephen A., Fredericton, 691
Chase-Mobus, Pamela, Acting Head, Circulation, Sexton Design & Technology Library, 1136
Chassie, Dan, President, Halifax C&D Recycling, 224
Chassie, Lee-Anne, General Manager, Halifax C&D Recycling, 224
Chaston, Brent, General Manager, Inscan Contractors (Ontario) Inc., 242
Châteauneuf, Hugues, President, Beaulier Inc., 104
Chatters, Philip F., President, Greenland Corporation, 218
Chatterton, Deborah, Director, Klohn Crippen Berger Ltd., 258
Chatwin, Brian, President/CEO, Chatwin Engineering Ltd., 138
Chatwin, Randall C., Lawson Lundell LLP - Vancouver, 1061
Chaulk, Brad, President, EDM Consultants Ltd., 173
Chaulk, Brad, Technical Services, KBM Forestry Consultants Inc., 255
Chaulk, Derrick, Manager, Flygt Canada, 198
Chaves, Patricia, Secretariat, Commission for Sustainable Development, 898
Chawrun, Carol, Director, 572
Chay, J., Carrier Canada Inc., 129
Chayer, Nathalie, Deux-Montagnes, 735
Chayer, Yves, Directeur, Montmagny, 418-248-5813, 738
Chaykowski, Miles, Contact, IMO Pump Inc., 239
Chayra, Melanie, Secretariat, Canadian Medical & Biological Engineering Society, 877
Chaytor, Q.C., Sandra R., Cox and Palmer - St. John's, 1065
Chebat, Joe, Representative, Canadian Drives Inc., 124
Chedrawy, Tony, President, Metocean Data Systems Limited, 287
Cheetham, Bob, Manager, Economic Development, Leeds & Grenville, 726
Chelsky, Brian, President, Careful Hand Laundry & Dry Cleaners Ltd., 128
Chemnitz, Shelley, Director, Financial Management Services, St. Catharines, 719
Chen, Denno, Lang Michener LLP - Toronto, 1077
Chenard, Doreen, Manger, Maritime Testing Ltd., 281
Chénard, Paul G., Contact, Paul G. Chénard, 319
Cheng, Harry, Operations Manager, Wheelabrator Canada Co., 431
Chenier, Dan, General Manager, Parks, Recreation & Cultural Serv, Ottawa, 716
Chenier, Denis, Branch Manager, Safety-Kleen Canada Inc., 355
Chénier, J. Raymond (Ray), Board Chair, Manitoulin-Sudbury District Services, Sudbury District, 705-862-7850, 731
Chenier, Mike, Manager, Metso Automation Canada Ltd., 288
Chénier, A.M.C.T., Roland, Town Clerk, Georgina, 709
Chenoweth, Brian, Information Specialist, Kingston R & D Centre, 1142
Cherepa, Melissa, Manager, Career Advancement Employment, 128
Cherepak, Glen, Sales Contact, Rotork Controls (Canada) Ltd., 352
Cherneski, Irv, Chair, Foothills Regional Services, 757

Chernis, Terry, Manager, Sir F.G. Banting Research Centre, 1152
Cherniwchan, Clarke N., President, Aurora Environmental Consulting Ltd., 97
Chernos, David P., Torys LLP, 1080
Chernushenko, David, Ottawa, 716
Cherry, David, Regional Sales Manager, Hibon Inc., 231
Cherry, John, President, Atlantic Packaging Products Ltd., 96
Chérubin, Ulrick, Maire, Amos, 733
Chesebrough, Jeff, Chief Operating Officer, Cimatec Environmental Engineering Inc., 141
Chesebrough, Rick, Fire Chief, South Frontenac, 730
Chester, Simon, Partner, Heenan Blaikie LLP - Toronto, 1075
Chestney, Dan, Foreman, Estevan, 306-634-1829, 754
Cheung, F., CAO, Langley, 604-514-2805, 681
Cheung, Ray, Division President, Silliker JR Laboratories, ULC, 367
Chevalier, Chuck, Manager, Public Works, Lakeshore, 712
Chevalier, Michel, Manager, Wastewater & Drainage Operations, Ottawa, 716
Chevalier, René, Greffier, Sorel-Tracy, 745
Chevalier, Éric, Directeur, Trois-Rivières, 819-372-4603, 745
Cheveldayoff, Ken, Minister, 661
Cheverie, Mel, Chief Building Inspector, Charlottetown, 732
Chevrette, Danielle, Directrice générale, Sainte-Catherine, 743
Chevrette, Denis, Contact, Fiducie Desjardins, 195
Chevrette, Mario, President, Cancer Research Society, 892
Chevrier, Andrée, Director, 518
Chevrier, Dan, Manager, Emergency Medical Services (EMS) Division, Leeds & Grenville, 726
Chevrier, Pierre, Directeur général, Salaberry-de-Valleyfield, 450-370-4800, 744
Chew, Patricia, Executive Director, West Coast Environmental Law Research Foundation, 1018
Chiarelli, Rick, Ottawa, 613-580-2478, 716
Chiasson, Cindy, Executive Director, The Environmental Law Centre (Alberta) Society, 912
Chiasson, Claude, Associate Director, Bathurst Campus, 1126
Chiasson, Trevor, Plant Manager, Engineered Air, 180
Chick, Diane, McKenzie Lake Lawyers LLP, 1069
Chick, Timothy P., Davis LLP - Calgary, 1050
Chiesa, Dino, Chair, 516
Child, Peter, Co-founder, Investigative Science Inc., 247
Childress, Amy, President, Association of Environmental Engineering & Science Professors, 835
Chilton, John, Executive Manager, International Association of Hydrogeologists, 935
Chilukuri, Sarathi, Manager, Wastequip Cusco, 421
Chin, Allison, President, Sierra Club, 1003
Chin, Ron A., Farris, Vaughan, Wills & Murphy LLP, 1059
Ching, Eng K., Regional Librarian, Ontario Regional Library, 1160
Chinks, Mattie, President, Avmor Ltd., 99
Chiocchio, Pat, Welland, 722
Chiodi, Tracet, Manager, Westburne Canada, 426
Chipeur, Gerald D., Partner, Miller Thomson LLP - Toronto, 1078
Chipeur, Q.C., Gerald D., Partner, Miller Thomson LLP - Calgary, 1053
Chirico, Peter, North Bay, 715
Chirico, T., Durmitor Inc., 167
Chirita, Tana, Information Technician, Ontario Ministry of Environment, 1160
Chisholm, Bill, President, Acres & Associated Environmental Ltd., 67
Chisholm, Bob, Director, Chisholm, Fleming & Associates, 140
Chisholm, Cathy, Information Services Librarian, Cape Breton University, 1137
Chisholm, Damon, Lang Michener LLP - Vancouver, 1060
Chisholm, Ken, VP, Great Western Containers Inc., 216
Chisholm, Ronald, Minister, 609
Chisholm, William, Managing Director, Chisholm, Fleming & Associates, 140
Chislett, Donna, Director, 615
Chislett, Geneva, Controller, Iqaluit, 867-979-5610, 698
Chittick, Angela, Clerk, Smith-Ennismore-Lakefield, 705-292-9507, 729
Chiu, Alex, Markham, 713
Chiu, Bo, Office Manager, Trow Consulting Engineers Ltd., 403
Chiu, Bo, Vice-President, Trow Consulting Engineers Ltd., 403
Chiu, Jung-Kay, Partner, Ogilvy Renault LLP/S.E.N.C.R.L., s.r.l. - Toronto, 1078
Chiu, Marian, Chief Scientist, 549
Chlala, Lynne, Borden Ladner Gervais LLP - Montréal, 1083
Cho, Raymond, Toronto, 721
Choinière, Denis, Granby, 735
Cholette, André, Directeur général, Chambly, 734

Executive Name Index

Chomlak, Kerra, Executive Director, Clean Air Strategic Alliance, 568, 896
Chompuech, Pattiya, RICHWAY Environmental Technologies Ltd., 347
Chong, Ida, Minister, 575
Chong, Jerry, Director, Richmond, 604-276-4064, 684
Chong, Stephen, Area Manager, AMEC, 83
Chong, P. Eng., Tony, CAO, Port Coquitlam, 683
Chopra, Anil, Manager, Semco Systems Limited, 362
Chopra, Hira, Chair, Alberni-Clayoquot, 250-723-2146, 676
Choquette, Carolyne, Academic Staff, Brace Centre for Water Resources Management, 115
Choquette, Réal, Administrative Director, ArcticNet Inc., 829
Choquette, Réal, Network Manager, Geomatics for Informed Decisions Network, 923
Chorloton, Q.C., Megan, Alexander Holburn Beaudin & Lang, LLP, 1057
Chornoby, Warren B., Stewart McKelvey Stirling Scales - Halifax, 1067
Chou, Henry, Client Services Officer, NRC Information Centre - Saskatoon, 1189
Choudhri, Shurjeel, Senior Vice-Presdient/Head, Bayer Inc., 103
Choueiri, Mario J., International Law Association - Canadian Branch, 940
Chouinard, Jocelyn, Manager, Veolia ES Canada Industrial Services Inc., 411
Chouinard, Marie-Claude, Sec.-Trés., Régie intermunicipale de gestion des déchets de l'Islet-Sud, 760
Chourke, David, President, NetPlus-HazMat Tracker, 300
Chow, Allan, Chair, 586
Chow, Campbell, Thurber Engineering Ltd., 396
Chow, Christopher, Manager, University Technologies International, 407
Chow, George, Metro Vancouver, 685, 678
Chow, George, Unit Manager, AMEC, 83
Chowaniec, Joe, Director, Environmental Services Association of Alberta, 912
Chrétien, Michel, Director, Emergency Services, Prescott & Russell, 729
Chripounoff, Stefan, Langlois Kronström Desjardins, 1085
Chrisfield, Jeff, CFO, African Wildlife Foundation, 813
Christen, Alexander, Executive Forum on Climate Change, 914
Christens, Elaine, Curatorial Assistant, Toronto Zoo, 1163
Christensen, Mark A., Stikeman Elliott LLP - Calgary, 1053
Christian, Bernie, City Treasurer, Timmins, 721
Christian, Kevin, Regional Sales Manager, Draeger Safety Canada Inc., 166
Christian, Paul, Sault Ste. Marie, 720
Christian, B.A.Sc., LL.B., Jeff, Partner, Lawson Lundell LLP - Vancouver, 1061
Christiansen, Carolyn R., Associate, Nixon Wenger, 1062
Christiansen, Ian, Manager, Brandon, 689
Christianson, Brian, Senior Associate, Stantec Inc., 378
Christie, Douglas S., Russell Christie LLP, 1070
Christie, Phil, President, European Association of Geoscientists & Engineers, 913
Christine, Luttmann, Trade Commissioner, 767
Christopher, Chris A., Blake, Cassels & Graydon LLP - Calgary, 1049
Christopher, Taso, Belleville, 706
Chrysler, Judy, Director, Skeena Valley Naturalists, 1004
Chtaneva, Anastassia, McCarthy Tétrault LLP - Québec, 1088
Chu, Barbara, Librarian, Physics Library, 1160
Chu, Jim, Chief Constable, Vancouver, 604-717-3321, 685
Chu, Lambert, Director, Burnaby, 604-294-7460, 679
Chua, Fernando, Director, Summa Engineering Ltd., 381
Chubb, Timothy, Partner, Stikeman Elliott LLP - Toronto, 1080
Chuddy, Barry, President/CEO, 574
Chugh, Pawan, CEO, 607
Church, David, Director, Forest Products Association of Canada, 918
Church, Matthew, Director, Evergreen, 914
Churchill, Aubrey, Lanark, 701
Churchill, Lloyd, Hastings, 700
Churchill-Smith, Q.C., Bruce, Partner, Borden Ladner Gervais LLP - Calgary, 1049
Chute, Jim, CAO, Dawson Creek, 680
Cia, Patricia, Coordinator, Technical Services & Library Systems, Langara College, 1118
Cicon, Guy, Director/City Engineer, Port Alberni, 683
Ciepiela, Ed, Marketing Manager, Power Grow Systems Inc., 329
Cimino, Joe, Greater Sudbury / Grand Sudbury, 710
Cimon, Alexandre, Cain Lamarre Casgrain Wells - Val-d'Or, 1089
Cimon, Pierre, Associé principal, Ogilvy Renault LLP/S.E.N.C.R.L., s.r.l. - Québec, 1088

Cindea, Tinca, Caristrap International Inc., 128
Cinq-Mars, Kevin, Vice-President, Tomlinson Environmental Services, 397
Cinq-Mars, Marie, Mairesse d'arrondissement/Conseillère de la ville, Montréal, 738
Ciplin, Heide, Information Analyst, AquaTox Testing & Consulting Inc., 89
Cirella, Frank, Petawawa, 717
Ciuciura, Ivan, Director, Durham Emergency Management Office, Durham, 905-430-2792, 699
Civak, Bob, Managing Director, Materials & Manufacturing Ontario, Division of OCE Inc., 952
Clackson, Colin D., Wallace Meschishnick Clackson Zawada, 1091
Clahane, Pat, General Counsel, 614
Clain, Q.C., Levi E., Stewart McKelvey Stirling Scales - Moncton, 1064
Clair, Bill, Works Superintendent, Charlottetown, 902-629-4015, 732
Clairmont, Lynda, Assistant Deputy Minister, 557
Clairmont, Mark, Muskoka, 702
Clamen, Murray, Secretary, 545
Clapham, Ward, RCMP Officer-in-Charge, Richmond, 604-207-4741, 684
Clapp, R. Jim, Commissioner, Finance Department, Durham, 699
Clapperton, Ken, Fire Chief, Baltimore, Hamilton, 725
Clapperton, Maureen, Directrice, HEC Montréal, 1173
Clarahan, Gregory L., President, Visionwall Corporation, 414
Clare, Kristan, Vice-President, Rawdon Industries Ltd., 342
Clark, Alan, Engineer, Prince George, 250-561-7617, 683
Clark, Andrew, Sales Coordinator, Denso North America Inc., 161
Clark, Bart, Manager, Sturgeon County, 780-939-0600, 670
Clark, Becky, Library Assistant, University of Guelph Ridgetown Campus, 1153
Clark, Bill, Vice-President, Lockerbie & Hole Contracting Ltd., 273
Clark, Brad, Hamilton, 711
Clark, Brian, President/CEO, Brian Clark Architect, 116
Clark, Bruce, CFO, Hydralogic Systems Inc., 235
Clark, Christy, Premier, 573
Clark, Dean, Fire Chief, Yorkton, 306-786-1795, 755
Clark, Dennis, Director, Mission, 687
Clark, Dorothy, Pol R Enterprises Inc., 327
Clark, Doug, Principal, EcoTec Environmental Consultants Inc., 172
Clark, Elaine, Clerk, Ingersoll, 711
Clark, Garry, Contact, Northern Prospectors Association, 966
Clark, Garry, Executive Director, Ontario Prospectors Association, 977
Clark, Graham, Fire Chief, Foothills No. 31, 669
Clark, Jim, General Manager, Kamloops Scrap Iron Ltd., 254
Clark, Jim, President, Sphag Sorb (Canada) Inc., 375
Clark, Keith E., Lang Michener LLP - Vancouver, 1060
Clark, Ken, Aird & Berlis LLP, 1072
Clark, Larry, Pelham, 717
Clark, Norm, Hastings, 700
Clark, Pat, Chilliwack, 680
Clark, Paul, Librarian, Dr. Everett Chalmers Regional Hospital, 1127
Clark, Peggy, CAO, White Rock, 686
Clark, Peggy, City Manager, White Rock, 686
Clark, Peter, Ottawa, 716
Clark, Peter, Vice-President & General Manager, Haley Industries Ltd., 224
Clark, Richard E., Senior Partner, Stikeman Elliott LLP - Toronto, 1080
Clark, Robert (Bob), Manager, Pelmar Engineering Ltd., 320
Clark, Ron, Aird & Berlis LLP, 1072
Clark, Sarah, Administrator, Certified Organic Associations of British Columbia, 894
Clark, Scott, Manager, Victoria, 250-361-0265, 685
Clark, Stu, Earthbound Environmental Inc., 169
Clark, B.Ed., M.E.S., Charlie, Saskatoon, 754
Clark, Q.C., D. Ross, Davis LLP - Vancouver, 1059
Clarke, A. Thomas, Edwards, Kenny & Bray LLP, 1059
Clarke, Al, SAIC Canada, 356
Clarke, B., Carrier Canada Ltd., 130
Clarke, Basil, Simcoe, 704
Clarke, Cynthia, Associate Director, Watson & Associates Economists Ltd., 423
Clarke, Cynthia D., Borden Ladner Gervais LLP - Toronto, 1073
Clarke, D. Bruce, Burchell Hayman Parish, 1067
Clarke, Dennis N., McInnes Cooper, 1066
Clarke, Dominic T., Blaney McMurtry LLP, 1073
Clarke, Don, Chatham-Kent, 724

Clarke, Douglas W., Gowling Lafleur Henderson S.E.N.C.R.L./LLP, 1084
Clarke, Grant, Office Manager, Golder Associates Ltd., 215
Clarke, Greg, COO, Energy Ottawa, 179
Clarke, Helen, Associate Vice Provost, Collections & Technical Se, University of Calgary, 1103
Clarke, Henry, Peterborough, 718
Clarke, Jim, Manager, St. John's, 709-576-8541, 694
Clarke, John, President, MPI Drilling, 294
Clarke, Murray, CAO/Corporate Administrator, Sidney, 250-656-1139, 684
Clarke, Robert, University Librarian, Trent University, 1153
Clarke, Scott W.N., Blake, Cassels & Graydon LLP - Calgary, 1049
Clarke, Steve, Co-Founder & CIO, Infotech Canada Inc., 241
Clarke Walker, Marie, Executive Vice-President, Canadian Labour Congress, 876
Clarke, Q.C., O. Noel, McInnes Cooper, 1066
Clarkin, Greg, Manager, Caduceon Environmental Laboratories, 120
Clarkson, Chris, Director, Camrose, 780-672-9195, 671
Clarkson, John, Deputy Minister, 590
Clarotto, RN, BN, MHS, Anne, Treasurer, Community Health Nurses of Canada, 899
Claude, Léger, Senior Advisor, Canadian Council of Forest Ministers, 763
Claudia Paola, Gutierrez Chaves, Trade Commissioner, 767
Clausen, P. Eng, Greg, General Manager, Infrastructure Services, Greater Sudbury / Grand Sudbury, 710
Claveau, Clayton, COO, Hygrex-Spehr Industries, 237
Claveau, Jean-Marie, Préfet, Le Fjord-du-Saguenay, 749
Clavet, Marie-Eve, Lavery, de Billy - Québec, 1088
Claxton, Edward B., Associé, Stikeman Elliott LLP - Montréal, 1087
Clay, Jennifer, Director, Orchid Cellmark ULC, 314
Clay, Paul R., President, Seacom International Inc., 361
Claybo, Don, Manager, Delta, 604-952-3640, 686
Clayton, Frank A., President, Clayton Research Associates Ltd., 142
Clayton, Fred, Branch Manager, Totten Sims Hubicki Associates Ltd., 399
Clayton, Mary, Director, Canadian Avalanche Association, 859
Clazie, David, Treasurer & Director, Finance, Quinte West, 718
Cleall, Jennifer L., Davis LLP - Edmonton, 1055
Clearwater, Karen L., Thompson Dorfman Sweatman LLP, 1064
Cleary, Bas, Director, 599
Cleary, Jacques, Saguenay, 741
Cleary, Patrick S., Alexander Holburn Beaudin & Lang, LLP, 1057
Cleland, Sue, Contact, Babcock Supply Ltd., 101
Clelland, Lawrence, Klohn Crippen Berger Ltd., 258
Clemens, Brian, Director, Nanaimo, 250-755-4431, 681
Clemens, Herman, Director, Water & Sewer Operations, Muskoka, 702
Clemens, Joel, Treasurer, Electric Vehicle Society of Canada, 909
Clemens, Terry, Hastings, 700
Clement, Bernadette, Cornwall, 708
Clement, Brian, Manager, Engineering, St. Thomas, 719
Clement, Dan, Springwater, 730
Clément, Jean-Sébastien, Gowling Lafleur Henderson S.E.N.C.R.L./LLP, 1084
Clément, Louis, Partner, Borden Ladner Gervais LLP - Montréal, 1083
Clement, Marc, President & CEO, CanHemp Corporation, 126
Clement, Steve, District Councillor, Bracebridge, 706
Clement, Steven, Muskoka, 702
Clement, Tony, Minister, Industry, 543
Clements, John, Head, 639
Clements, Rose, Interlending & Acquisitions, District Health Authorities 1, 2 & 3 (Western Nova Scotia), 1138
Clements, Simon A., Partner, Borden Ladner Gervais LLP - Toronto, 1073
Clément-Talbot, Catherine, Conseillère d'arrondissement, Montréal, 738
Clerk, Jean E., Partner, Heenan Blaikie S.E.N.C.R.L/SRL, 1084
Clermont, André, Directeur des opérations, Premier Tech Environnement / Division municipale, commerciale et, 331
Clermont, Denis, Directeur général, Témiscamingue, 753
Clermont, Marc, Director, Public Works, Prescott & Russell, 729
Clermont, Michel, Directeur, Westburne Canada, 428
Clermont, Sylvie, Laval, 736
Cléroux, Pierre, Laval, 736
Cleveland, Randy, Director, Kelowna, 681
Cleveland, Scott, Manager, Harris & Roome Supply Limited, 226

Executive Name Index

Clevett, Stephen, Chief Executive Officer, Optimira Controls, 313
Cliche, Bernard, Associé, Langlois Kronström Desjardins, 1088
Cliche, Colombe, Directrice, Montréal, 738
Cliche, Ghyslain, Thetford Mines, 418-335-9267, 745
Cliff, Grahame, Vice-President, World Wildlife Fund - Canada, 1023
Cliffe, Michelle, Communications Manager, World Society for the Protection of Animals, 1023
Clifford, Bill, Director, Anachemia Canada Inc., 85
Clifford, Connie, Librarian, Misericordia Community Hospital, 1106
Clifford, Connie, Manager, Learning Resources, Caritas Health Group, 1104
Clifford, Tom, Stratford, 720
Clifton, Phil, Divisional Managing Director, Weir Power & Industrial, 424
Clifton, Wayne, Founder & President, Clifton Associates Ltd., 144
climate project canada, Climate Project - Canada, 1214
Cline, Q.C., Thomas A., Cline, Backus, Nightingale & McArthur, LLP, 1071
Clinton, Peter, Head, Systems, University of Toronto Libraries, 1163
Clipsham, Fred, Regina, 306-757-8212, 754
Clisby, Larry, Manager, MakLoc Buildings Inc., 279
Clive, Bob, Director, Riverview, 506-387-2031, 692
Cloete, Jack, Financial Controller, National Energy Equipment Inc., 297
Clohecy, Jane, Commissioner, Planning & Development Services, Oakville, 715
Clonda, Georges, Chef de bibliothèque, Bibliothèque de botanique - L'Institut de recherche en biologie v, 1170
Close, Karen, Director, Human Resource Services, York, 705
Close, Rob, Branch Leader, Urban Systems Ltd., 408
Closson Duquette, Marie-Noëlle, Sainte-Thérèse, 744
Clouatre, Lyle, General Manager, Envirotec Services Incorporated, 187
Clouston, Jennifer, Manager, MICCA Paints Inc., 288
Cloutier, Alain, Directeur, Val-d'Or, 746
Cloutier, Bernard, General Manager, Procedair Industries Inc., 333
Cloutier, Claudette, Manager, Gallagher Library of Geology & Geophysics, 1101
Cloutier, Colette, President, Gemini Twins Consulting Ltd., 206
Cloutier, Dany, Trésorier, Club des ornithologues de Québec inc., 896
Cloutier, Denise, Mascouche, 450-968-0325, 737
Cloutier, Henri, Préfet, La Côte-de-Beaupré, 748
Cloutier, Jean-François, Conseiller d'arrondissement, Fort-Rolland, Montréal, 738
Cloutier, Jean-Sébastien, Ogilvy Renault LLP/S.E.N.C.R.L., s.r.l. - Québec, 1088
Cloutier, Nicolas X., Davies Ward Phillips & Vineberg S.E.N.C.R.L., s.r.l., 1083
Cloutier, O'Neil, Treasurer, Canadian Council of Professional Fish Harvesters, 865
Cloutier, Patrick, Solenco Environnement inc., 372
Cloutier, Sylvie, Saint-Eustache, 450-974-9379, 742
Cloutier, Yvon, President/Director of Engineering, Biotech Solutions, 109
Clow, Bob S., Director, 641
Clubb, Warren, Exhibits Curator, Western Development Museum, 1191
Cluett, Mike, Milton, 714
Cluff, Pamela, President, P.J. Cluff Architect Inc., 315
Clugston, Ted, Medicine Hat, 403-526-8760, 673
Clyburn, Garth, Planner II, Edmonton, 780-496-6209, 672
Clyde, Marion, Office Manager, Rockwell Automation Canada Inc., 349
Coady, Joseph, Director, Charlottetown, 732
Coak, Robert, Director, Greenland Corporation, 218
Coallier, Louis, Partner, Miller Thomson LLP - Toronto, 1078
Coates, Don, Muskoka, 702
Coates, Kim, Scugog, 729
Coates, Tamela J., Fraser Milner Casgrain LLP - Calgary, 1051
Cobb, Kasia, Supervisor, Westburne Canada, 427
Cobb, Larry, Partner, Stikeman Elliott LLP - Toronto, 1080
Cobbett, Wayne, Principal, Robicheau's Pumping Service, 348
Cobden, Catherine, Vice-President, Forest Products Association of Canada, 918
Cobean, C.M.O., Bettyanne, Clerk-Treasurer, Bruce, 698
Coben, Chris, Superintendent, Quesnel, 688
Cober, Bill, King, 726
Coburn, Rick F., Partner, Borden Ladner Gervais LLP - Toronto, 1073
Cocci, Albert, ADI Group Inc., 68

Cochran, Sherry, Project Engineer, PINTER & Associates Ltd., 325
Cochrane, Brian, Superintendent, Fredericton, 506-460-2230, 691
Cochrane, Doug, Chair, Canadian Patient Safety Institute, 881
Cochrane, Harold, D'Arcy & Deacon LLP, 1063
Cochrane, Linda, General Manager, Edmonton, 780-496-5804, 672
Cochrane, Meredith, Executive Director, Citizens' Environment Watch, 895
Cochrane, Scott, Rothesay, 692
Cochrane, Wayne, Engine Control Systems, 180
Cochrane, William E., CAO, Oak Bay, 688
Cockburn, Jean, Electronic Resources Librarian, Douglas College, 1114
Cocker, Jonathan, Baker & McKenzie LLP, 1072
Cockerill, Sarah, Director, Fort St. John, 681
Cockrall, Q.C., Terrence A., Counsel, Parlee McLaws LLP, 1055
Codd, Michael, CFO, L&K International Training, 261
Coderre, Serge, President, Enviroservices Inc., 187
Coe, David, Chair, Sonic Technology Solutions Inc., 374
Coe, Lorne Earl, Regional Councillor, Whitby, 723
Coe, Lorne Earle, Durham, 699
Coffey, Ken, Owner, Micro-Watt Control Devices Ltd., 289
Coffey, M., President, Net Safety Monitoring Inc., 300
Cogan, Q.C., Frederick, Counsel, Brazeau Seller LLP, 1070
Cogswell, Eric, General Manager, Pacwill Environmental, 317
Cohen, Adele, Librarian, Canadian Wildlife Service, 1129
Cohen, Alan K., Soloway, Wright LLP, 1071
Cohen, Earl S., McMillan Binch Mendelsohn - Montréal, 1086
Cohen, Glenn, President, Alberta Environmental Rubber Products Inc., 77
Cohen, J., President, TLT Co-Vent, 397
Cohen, Leonard, President, Canadian Technical Tape Ltd., 125
Cohen, Maurice, Conseiller d'arrondissement, Côte-de-Liesse, Montréal, 738
Cohen, Mitchell, Blake, Cassels & Graydon LLP - Calgary, 1049
Cohen, Pamela, Vice-President, 584
Cohen, Paul, Vice-President, Canadian Technical Tape Ltd., 125
Cohen, Robert L., President, Traders Metal Company Ltd., 400
Cohen, Susan, Executive Director, The W. Garfield Weston Foundation, 1017
Colasante, Tim, Manager, Engineering Services, Quinte West, 718
Colasanti, Ron, Kingsville, 712
Colbert, Gerry, Councillor at Large, St. John's, 709-576-7689, 694
Colborne, Christine, Director, 597
Colborne, Kelly P., Stones Carbert Waite Wells LLP, 1054
Colbourne, Junior, Vice-President, Cecon Limited, 135
Cole, Alison, Office Manager, EarthSave Canada, 1117
Cole, Avril, Macleod Dixon LLP, 1077
Cole, Barry, Director, Transit Services, Oakville, 715
Cole, Bonnie, Manager, Saanich, 688
Cole, Gerry, Supervisor, Corner Brook, 709-637-1232, 693
Cole, Glen, Principal Resource Geologist, SRK Consulting (Canada) Inc., 377
Cole, Glenn, Manager, Technical Information Programs, Transportation Association of Canada, 1152
Cole, Hollis, Chief Executive Officer, Acadia Consultants & Inspectors Ltd., 65
Cole, Hollis B., President/CEO, ADI Group Inc., 68
Cole, Kevin, Director, Leduc, 673
Cole, Mike, President, Fugro Jacques GeoSurveys Inc., 203
Cole, Roger, Deputy Mayor & Councillor, Greater Napanee, 613-354-3664, 709
Coleman, Brian, Brant, 698
Coleman, Fran, Muskoka, 702
Coleman, Fran, District & Town Councillor, Huntsville, 711
Coleman, Gary, Manager, Control Techniques Drives Inc., 151
Coleman, James H., Partner, Macleod Dixon LLP, 1052
Coleman, John M., Acting Vice-President, 546
Coleman, Mary Ann, Executive Director, New Brunswick Environmental Network, 961
Coleman, Michele, Contact, NB Coal Limited, 299
Coleman, Terry, Deputy Minister, 656
Coleman, Tim, Director, 607
Coleman, B.A., M.B.A., LL, Chris, Victoria, 685
Coleman, Q.C., James H., Partner, Macleod Dixon LLP, 1077
Coles, Dave, President, Communications, Energy & Paperworkers Union of Canada, 899
Coletta, Ray, Secretary/Project Manager, RAM Lining Systems Inc., 342
Colgan, George, President, Prescott Paper Products Inc., 331
Colhoun, Bob, Muskoka, 702

Colhoun, Bob, District Councillor, Gravenhurst, 709
Collard, Guy, Greffier, Laval, 450-978-3950, 736
Collard, Jim, Councillor, Niagara-on-the-Lake, 715
Collard, Paul, Fort Erie, 709
Colle, Josh, Toronto, 721
Collett, Al, Elliot Lake, 709
Collette, Michelle, Manager, Human Resources, Innisfil, 711
Collette, Monique, President, 510
Colley, Michelle L., Stones Carbert Waite Wells LLP, 1054
Colley-Urquhart, Diane, Calgary, 403-268-2430, 671
Collie, Donald R., Davis LLP - Vancouver, 1059
Collier, C., Manager, Whitby, 723
Collier, C., Vice-President, J. Walter Company Ltd., 249
Collier, Ken, President, Society for Socialist Studies, 1007
Collier, Norm, Sales Manager, Brim Pumps & Systems Ltd., 116
Collier, Shaun, Regional Councillor, Ajax, 705
Collin, Brigitte, Varennes, 746
Collin, Catherine, Mairesse, Sainte-Anne-des-Plaines, 743
Collin, Marie-Claude, Blainville, 734
Collings, William, Vice-President, Quester Tangent Corp., 339
Collingwood, Jennifer, Director, 602
Collins, Chad, Hamilton, 711
Collins, Faye, President, Ontario Daylily Society, 972
Collins, Felix, Minister, 602
Collins, Jim, General Manager, British Columbia Farm Industry Review Board, 847
Collins, Joe, Director, whatIf? Technologies Inc., 431
Collins, Joseph, National Sales Manager, Nederman Canada Ltd., 299
Collins, Leann, Marketing Manager, LEM Laboratory Inc., 267
Collins, Linda, Mayor, Springwater, 730
Collins, Lori, Head of Reference, Bedford Institute of Oceanography, 1135
Collins, Norval, President & Founder, CEF Consultants Ltd., 135
Collins, Paul, Lang Michener LLP - Toronto, 1077
Collins, Peter L., Field Law - Calgary, 1051
Collins, Rob, Director, Fire & Emergency Services, Port Hope, 905-885-5323, 728
Collins, Wally, St. John's, 709-576-8584, 694
Collison, Marvin, Receptionist, Council of the Haida Nation - Haida Fisheries Program, 905
Collison, Thor, Contact, Skeena-Queen Charlotte, 679
Collopy, Thomas, Macleod Dixon LLP, 1052
Collyer, Chris, Chief Operator, Environmental Services, Meaford, 727
Collyer, Tim, Huron, 701
Colman-Sadd, Vanessa, Director, 600
Colosimo, Frank, Manager, Red Deer, 403-342-8238, 674
Colpitts, Lorne, COO, 588
Colpron, Daniel, Président, Association des embouteilleurs d'eau du Québec, 832
Colthurst, Casey, Manager, Area Parks & Horticulture, Tecumseh, 720
Columbus, Kerry, Director, Community Services, Innisfil, 711
Columbus, Michael J., Norfolk, 702
Comazzetto, Anthony, Professional Engineer, Urban Systems Ltd., 407
Comeau, Felix J.E., Chairman and CEO, Alcohol Countermeasure Systems Corp., 77
Comeau, Hugh L., Bathurst, 506-548-2255, 690
Comeau, Ian, General Manager, Restigouche Solid Waste Corporation, 758
Comeau, Jacques, Directeur, Baie-Comeau, 418-296-8142, 733
Comeau, Louise, Executive Forum on Climate Change, 914
Comeau, Sylvain, Technisol Environnement, 388
Comeau, Yvon, Councillor at Large, Dieppe, 506-388-3245, 691
Comerford, Rick, Regional Director General, Greater Toronto Area Re, 514
Comis, Debbie R., City Clerk, Burnaby, 604-294-7290, 679
Comiskey, Ted J., Oxford, 519-462-2697, 728
Comiskey, Ted J., Mayor, Ingersoll, 711
Commisso, Tim, City Manager, Thunder Bay, 807-625-2224, 721
Companion, Lori Anne, Assistant Deputy Minister, 602
Compartino, Nancy, Technicienne en documentation, traitement document, CÉGEP de Jonquière, 1168
Compeau, Cynthia, Director, Public Works, Brant, 698
Compton-Smith, Carole, Director, Douglas College, 1114
Compton-Taylor, Valerie, Membership Secretary, International Institute for Conservation of Historic & Artistic W, 940
Comtois, Marcel, Director, Genivar, 208
Conacher, Q.C., Roy B., Cunningham, Swan, Carty, Little & Bonham LLP, 1069
Conant, Bernadette, Director of Programs, Canadian Water Network, 890
Condotta, Robert, Lincoln, 713

Executive Name Index

Conley, Gordon G., Riopelle Griener Professional Corporation, 1072
Conlin, Brian, Principal, Golder Associates Ltd., 214
Conn, Berni, President, Friends of Abandoned Pets, 920
Connell, Anne, Archival Clerk, Beaton Institute, 1134
Connell, Frances J., Director, Vancouver, 604-873-7506, 685
Connelly, Neil, General Manager, Nanaimo, 678
Connolly, Brian, Principal Mining Engineer, SRK Consulting (Canada) Inc., 377
Connolly, Douglas, Director, 600
Connor, Greg, Sales Manager, Metocean Data Systems Limited, 287
Connor, Peter, Architect & Sr. Consultant, Connor Architects & Planners, 150
Connor, Scott, Manager, TEAM-1 Environmental Services Inc., 387
Connors, Elena, Director, Impact Microbiology Services, 239
Connors, Gregory J., McInnes Cooper, 1066
Connors, Paul, Executive Director, Newfoundland & Labrador Federation of Agriculture, 962
Connors, Steven T., Brownlee LLP, 1054
Conquest, Stan, Manager, Quatrosense Environmental Ltd., 338
Conrad, Brent, Vice-President, SRT Soil Remediation Technologies, 377
Conrad, Cathy, City Clerk, North Bay, 715
Conrad, Doug, Manager, Harbour Metal Recycling Ltd., 225
Conrad, Robert, President, Nova Scotia Mackerel Association, 968
Conroy, April, Coordinator, Northumberland Solid Waste Commission, 758
Conroy, R., Supervisor, Parks & Facilities, Pembroke, 717
Constant, Carmel, Trésorier, Mont-St-Hilaire, 738
Constantini, Bernard, Longueuil, 737
Contini, John S., Lang Michener LLP - Toronto, 1077
Conuny, Sheila, Sales Manager, Q-Air Environmental Controls Ltd., 337
Convery, Ian, Branch Manager, Safety-Kleen Canada Inc., 355
Convery, Mark A., Senior Partner, Ogilvy Renault LLP/S.E.N.C.R.L., s.r.l. - Toronto, 1078
Conway, Dawn, Executive Director, Canadian Foundation for Climate & Atmospheric Sciences, 869
Conway, Teresa, President/CEO, 580
Cook, Bob, Fire Chief, Burnaby, 604-294-7195, 679
Cook, Dianne, Collection Development Librarian, Queen's University, 1142
Cook, Eric, Executive Director, RPC, 353
Cook, Eric, President, Abydoz Environmental, 65
Cook, Eric, Secretary-Treasurer, New Brunswick Environment Industry Association, 960
Cook, Ethel M., Administrator, Cantech Inspections Ltd., 127
Cook, Florrie, Head Librarian, Calgary Library, 1100
Cook, Jim, Fire Chief, West Vancouver, 604-925-7370, 689
Cook, John B. (Jack), Partner, Osler, Hoskin & Harcourt LLP - Toronto, 1079
Cook, John R., Secretary, 579
Cook, Ken, Canwest Pumping Systems Ltd., 127
Cook, Kerry, Mayor, Williams Lake, 686
Cook, Lauren E., Lawson Lundell LLP - Vancouver, 1061
Cook, Lynn, Executive Director, 573
Cook, Michele, Eastern Region Librarian, Northwest Community College Library, 1116
Cook, Roger, Director, Forest Products Association of Canada, 918
Cook, Tom, Adjala-Tosorontio, 705-424-2065, 724
Cook, Tracy, Manager, Barrington Industrial Services Limited, 102
Cook, BA, Misha, Executive Director, Pitch-In Canada, 987
Cook, P.Eng., Eric, Executive Director, 596
Cooke, Carl, Contact, Westchem Mfg. Ltd., 429
Cooke, Dwight, Manager, Bartle & Gibson Co. Ltd., 102
Cooke, Everett, Fire Chief, Grande Prairie No. 1, 780-567-5590, 669
Cooke, Gord, President, Air Solutions Inc., 75
Cooke, Patrick M., Director, Trihedral Engineering Limited, 401
Cooke, Robert, Directeur, Lévis, 418-839-2002, 736
Cookson, James D., Vice-President, W.D. Cookson Ltd., 415
Cookson, Robert D., President, R.D. Cookson Disposal Ltd., 340
Cookson, Vera E., President, W.D. Cookson Ltd., 415
Coolen, Mike, Manager, Sable Offshore Energy Inc., 354
Cooley, Dennis, Deputy Minister, 667
Cooley, Ken, Associate University Librarian, IT & Technical Ser, University of Victoria Libraries, 1121
Coombs, Ken, Deputy Superintendent, Quesnel, 688
Coombs, Marc, Northumberland, 702
Coombs, Robert, Deputy Minister, 602
Coombs, Shelly, Coordinator, Canadian Liquids Processors Limited, 124
Coon, David, Chair, Climate Action Network - Canada, 896
Coon, Robert, CAO, Rocky View No. 44, 670
Cooney, P.Eng., Adam, President, Environmental Services Association of Nova Scotia, 913
Cooper, A., Manager, MCC Industrial Services Ltd, 284
Cooper, A., Vice-President, Highland Equipment Ltd., 231
Cooper, Joel, Chair, Niijkiwenhwag - Friends of Lake Superior Park, 964
Cooper, Ken, President, SAR Engineering, 358
Cooper, Lynn, Manager, Westburne Canada, 425
Cooper, Mark, Director, 568
Cooper, Mike, Councillor, Colchester County, 697
Cooper, Peter J., President, Cambridge Materials Testing Limited, 122
Cooper, Rosalind H., Partner, Fasken Martineau - Toronto, 1075
Cooper, S., PHH ARC Environmental Ltd., 322
Cooper, Sandra, Simcoe, 704
Cooper, Sandra, Director, 519
Cooper, Sandra, Mayor, Collingwood, 705-446-4704, 708
Cooper, Tyler, Sales Representative, Avensys Inc., 98
Coote, Joan, Communications Support Coordinator, Newfoundland Ocean Industries Association, 1132
Copeland, Craig, Mayor, Cold Lake, 672
Copeland, Dan, Fire Chief, Delta, 604-952-3119, 686
Copeland, Lynn, Dean of Library Services, Simon Fraser University, 1111
Copestake, Peter, President, Big Rideau Lake Association, 845
Coplen, Larry, Fire Chief & Coordinator, Community Emergency Mana, Fort Erie, 709
Copley, Christine, Senior Manager, World Coal Institute, 1022
Copperthwaite, Sid, Alberta Representative, ACO Container Systems Ltd., 67
Coppola, Saverio (Sam), Partner, Borden Ladner Gervais LLP - Montréal, 1083
Corbeil, Huguette, Saint-Hyacinthe, 742
Corbeil, Pierre, Ministre, 646
Corbett, C.M., General Manager, 631
Corbett, Helen, Director, Climate Change Central, 144
Corbett, John, Commissioner, Planning, Design & Development, Brampton, 706
Corbett, Leland P., Partner, Stikeman Elliott LLP - Calgary, 1053
Corbett, Ron, Senior Associate, Hardy Stevenson & Associates, 225
Corbett, Tracy, Senior Manager, Capital Regional District, 250-360-3244, 676
Corbett, Q.C., William T., Field Law - Calgary, 1051
Corbin, Henri, Sainte-Julie, 743
Corbo, Nicola, Borden Ladner Gervais LLP - Montréal, 1083
Corbusier, Pascal, Magotteaux Ltée, 278
Cordato, Marlene, Boisbriand, 734
Cordell, Scott H., President, Geocor Engineering Inc., 210
Cordiner, Shirley, Niagara, 702
Cordsva, Eduardo, Vice-President, Techint Goodfellow Technologies Inc., 387
Corfe, Christine, Director, Langley, 604-533-6015, 687
Corke, Sue, Deputy City Manager, Toronto, 416-338-7205, 721
Corkill, Larry, Sales Manager, Cues Canada, 154
Corley, Richard, Blake, Cassels & Graydon LLP - Toronto, 1072
Cormack, Alison, Information Services Officer, British Columbia Utilities Commission, 1117
Cormier, Chantal, Vice-President, Canadian Association of Animal Health Technologists & Technicians, 856
Cormier, Elizabeth, Patton Cormier & Associates, 1069
Cormier, Fay A., Chief Civil Engineer, J.L. Richards & Associates Limited, 250
Cormier, Gerry, Mayor, Miramichi, 691
Cormier, Kurt, Rothsay, 352
Cormier, Linda, Mairesse, Matane, 738
Cormier, Lucien, Building Inspector, Bathurst, 690
Cormier, Mathieu, Adjoint au directeur des études, CÉGEP de Saint-Laurent, 1184
Cormier, Michel, Vice-President, Crandall Engineering Ltd., 153
Cormier, Pierre, Prèfet, Minganie, 750
Corne, Ian, Nilex Inc., 304
Cornell, Trevor, Chief Operating Officer, 590
Cornfield, Bob, Manager, Engineered Air, 180
Cornfield, Charlie, Mayor, Campbell River, 679
Cornforth, Brian, Fire Chief, Lethbridge, 403-320-3800, 673
Cornish, Barbara, Partner, Singleton Urquhart LLP, 1062
Cornwall, Chris, President, Alrange Container Services, 80
Cornwallace, Simon, Contact, Slope Indicator Canada, 370
Corpuz, Bernadette, Borden Ladner Gervais LLP - Toronto, 1073
Corr, Aaron, Parish Geomorphic Ltd., 318
Corr, Tom, President & CEO, Ontario Centres of Excellence - Centre for Earth & Environmental, 972
Corra, Richard, Regional Manager, Vestar, 412
Corrente, Edmund, President, Versatile Measuring Instruments Inc., 412
Corrigan, Derek, Metro Vancouver, 678
Corrigan, Derek, Mayor, Burnaby, 679
Corrigan, Larry, Scugog, 729
Corriveau, André, Chief Medical Officer of Health, 569
Corriveau, Denis, Beloeil, 450-464-2435, 734
Corriveau, François, Greffier, Baie-Comeau, 418-296-8109, 733
Corriveau, Josée, Responsable, Collège de Rosemont, 1172
Corriveau, Robert, President, Canadian Institute for Photonics Innovations, 873
Corry, Julie, Hutchins Caron & Associés, 1085
Corson, Jennifer, President, Renovators Resource Inc., 345
Cortvriendt, Chris, Manager, Waterous Power Systems, 423
Cory, Lance, Summit Structures, 382
Cory, Neil, District Sales Manager, ESRI Canada Ltd., 190
Cosens, Mark, Alderman, St. Thomas, 719
Cosentino, Frank, Director, Summa Engineering Ltd., 381
Cosentino, Joseph, Goodmans LLP, 1075
Cosette, Claude, Vice-President, Cascades Inc., 130
Cosgrove, Julie, Coordinator, Kawartha World Issues Centre, 947
Cosgrove, Mike, Manager, Gorman-Rupp of Canada Ltd., 215
Cosgrove, William J., Président, 646
Cosmescu, Shannon, Secretary, Shell Canada Limited, 365
Cosmides, Shelli, Manager, Draeger Safety Canada Ltd., 166
Cossarini, Danielle, Librarian, Selkirk College, 1111
Costello, Bill, President, Walker Industries Holdings Ltd., 416
Costello, Cecily, Treasurer, International Association for Bear Research & Management, 934
Costello, Keith, Superintendent, Corner Brook, 709-637-1595, 693
Costello, Matthew, Secretary, Conservation International, 901
Costelo, Debbie, Public Services Librarian, Nova Scotia Community College, 1136
Costigan, Doug, Director, Edmonton, 780-496-4956, 672
Costley, Jo-Ann, Pinchin Environmental Ltd., 324
Côté, Alexandre, Victoriaville, 819-357-3272, 746
Côté, André, Greffier, Dolbeau-Mistassini, 735
Côté, André J., Maire, Candiac, 734
Côté, François, Vice-President, Lupien Rosenberg Consultants Inc., 275
Côté, Gilbert, Longueuil, 737
Cote, Gilbert, Director, Esquimalt, 686
Côté, Gilles, Directeur général adjoint, Longueuil, 737
Côté, Jacques, CFO, 520
Côté, Jean-Noël, Vice-President & Director of Engineering, Les Consultants LBCD, 268
Côté, Jean-Pierre, Directeur général, Université de Montréal, 1176
Cote, Jonathan, New Westminster, 682
Côté, Karl, Vice-President, Sinanni Inc., 369
Côté, Louis-Antoine, Heenan Blaikie S.E.N.C.R.L./SRL - Québec, 1087
Côté, Léonard, Préfet, Lac-Saint-Jean-Est, 749
Côté, Marie-José, Grondin, Poudrier, Bernier, 1087
Côté, Mario, Coordonnateur, CÉGEP de Rimouski, 1181
Côté, Nathalie, Client Service and Circulation Representative, Canadian Heritage, 1167
Côté, Richard, Québec, 735, 740
Coté, Richard V., Vice-President, Commercial, 511
Coté, Venence (Ven), President/CEO, ZCL Composites Inc., 436
Cote, Victor, General Manager, Finance & Corporate Services, London, 713
Côté, Yvan, Project Manager, Boutillette Parizeau et Associés inc., 114
Côté, Yvon, Directeur, Génius Conseil Inc., 207
Côté, Éric, Directeur, Rivière-du-Loup, 418-867-6663, 741
Cotter, Brent, Sales and Marketing Manager, Direct Separation Solutions, 164
Cotter, Catherine, Reference & Instruction Librarian, Gerard V. La Forest Law Library, 1127
Cotter, David, Director of Communications, Canadian Water Network, 890
Cotter, Thomas, Secretary, Canadian Centre for Energy Information, 861
Cotterill, Robert, City Manager, Prince Albert, 306-953-4300, 754
Cotton, Glen, Regional Manager, Century Environmental Services, 136
Cotton, Jacques, Sous-ministre, 652
Cotton, Ross, Manager, Planning, Innisfil, 711

Master Indexes

CANADIAN ENVIRONMENTAL RESOURCE GUIDE 2011-2012 1281

Executive Name Index

Cottrell, Cathy, Sr. Energy Efficiency Advisor, Yukon Energy Solutions Centre, 1191
Cottrell, Lois, Library Technician, St Joseph's Hospital (Hamilton), 1141
Cottrell, Tom, IWMP Coordinator, North Saskatchewan Watershed Alliance, 966
Coudé, Dany, Trésorier, Saint-Félicien, 742
Coughlan-Lambly, Judith, Head of Technical Services, W.K. Kellogg Health Sciences Library, 1136
Coulombe, Alexandre, Technisol Environnement, 388
Coulombe, Denis, Directeur, Saguenay, 741
Coulombe, Guylain, Saint-Hyacinthe, 742
Coulombe, Louis, Associé, Cain Lamarre Casgrain Wells - Chicoutimi, 1082
Coulombe, Raymond, Baie-Comeau, 418-589-8930, 733
Coulombe, Robert, Président, Union des municipalités du Québec, 1014
Coulombe, Simon, Directeur, Lavaltrie, 736
Coulombe, Solange, Technicienne en documentation, CÉGEP de Trois-Rivières, 1186
Coulson, Cassie, Coordinator, Water & Sewer, Saugeen Shores, 719
Coulson, Marg, City Clerk, Vancouver, 604-873-7266, 685
Coulson, Neall, Sun Prairie Organic, 382
Coulter, J.C., President, Cemcorp Ltd. Consulting Engineers, 136
Coulter, John E., President, J.E. Coulter Associates Ltd., 249
Coulter, M.A., Managing Director, Cemcorp Ltd. Consulting Engineers, 136
Coulter, Pam, Director, Community Services, Owen Sound, 717
Coulter, B.Sc., Sandy, Acting Director, Operations - Water, Wastewater &, Barrie, 706
Coumans, Ph.D., Catherine, Research Coordinator, MiningWatch Canada, 955
Countway, Norman, Vice-President, Satlantic, 358
Courchesne, Guy, Laval, 450-978-6888, 736
Courchesne, Michelle, Ministre, 653
Courchesne, Michelle, Ministre responsable de l'Administration gouvernem, 655
Courchesne, Serge, Trésorier, Sainte-Catherine, 743
Courchesne, Suzanne, Partner, Borden Ladner Gervais LLP - Montréal, 1083
Courchesne, Yves, Directeur, Québec, 418-641-6203, 740
Courchesne, Yvon, Vice-President & Biologist, Nove Environnement Inc., 309
Courneya, Kevin, Vestar, 413
Cournoyer, Claude, Trésorier, Fédération québécoise de camping et de caravaning inc., 916
Cournoyer-Proulx, Magali, Partner, Heenan Blaikie S.E.N.C.R.L/SRL, 1084
Coursey, Ruth, Chief Administrative Officer, Lakeshore, 712
Court, Bruce, Saint John, 692
Court, Ivan, Mayor, Saint John, 692
Courteau, Micheline, Trois-Rivières, 745
Courtney, Bob, Contact, Shaver Industries Inc., 365
Courtois, Catherine, Marketing, Société Laurentide inc., 371
Courville, Isabelle, Présidente, 649
Cousin, Jerry, President, J.R. Cousin Consultants Ltd., 250
Cousineau, Carole, Greffière, Sainte-Catherine, 743
Cousineau, Marie, Heenan Blaikie S.E.N.C.R.L/SRL, 1084
Cousins, Barry, Vice-President, Arpi's Industries Canada Ltd., 92
Cousins, Brian, Director, Finance & Treasurer, Belleville, 706
Cousins, Bruce, Vice-President/CFO, Ballard Power Systems Inc., 101
Cousins, Gary, Director, Planning, Wellington, 705
Cousteau, Francine, President, The Cousteau Society, 905
Coutanche, Mel, Oro-Medonte, 705-835-5728, 728
Coutney, Frank, County Administrator, Wetaskiwin County No. 10, 670
Coutney, Frank, Manager, Northeast Pigeon Lake Regional Services Commission, 758
Couto, Sandra, Manager, British Columbia Recreation & Parks Association, 849
Coutu, Aurel, Owner/Manager, Lindsay Iron & Metal Inc., 272
Coutu, Heather, Lindsay Iron & Metal Inc., 272
Couture, Daniel, Pompex Inc., 328
Couture, Danielle, Plastiglas Industries Limited, 326
Couture, Dianne, Bibliotechnicienne, Centre hospitalier des Vallées de l'Outaouais Hôpital de Hull, 1167
Couture, Eric, Partner, Miller Thomson LLP - Toronto, 1078
Couture, Jacqueline, Director, 552
Couture, Karine, Bibliothécaire responsable, Bibliothèque de droit et publications gouvernementales, 1184
Couture, Karine, Responsable, Bibliothèque droit et publications go, Université de Sherbrooke, 1186
Couture, Patrick, Vice-President, Le Groupe Sani Marc, 265

Couture, Yves, Directeur, Centre de formation en entreprise et récupération, 893
Couture Bordeleau, Suzanne, Val-d'Or, 746
Couturier, Anne, Trésorière, Magog, 737
Couturier, Marie, Manager, Yellowknife, 695
Covington, Charlene, Director, Kelowna, 681
Cowan, Art, Presiding Member, 590
Cowan, David J., Lang Michener LLP - Vancouver, 1060
Cowan, Deanna, Head of Reference, Life Sciences Library, 1174
Cowan, J.G., WeirFoulds LLP, 1081
Cowan, Larry, Strathroy-Caradoc, 731
Cowan, Nick, Director, Cardinal Biologicals Ltd., 128
Cowan, Todd, Mayor, Woolwich, 732
Cowbourne, Derek, Vice-President, 629
Cowell-Poitras, Jane, Conseillère de ville, Montréal, 738
Cowie, Phillip, Directeur, Marketing, Industrial Combustion Equipment Ltd., 240
Cowles, Roger, President, Association of the Chemical Profession of Alberta, 840
Cowper, Daniel, Borden Ladner Gervais LLP - Vancouver, 1058
Cowsill, Rick, City Councillor, Cambridge, 707
Cox, Bryan, Executive Director, Youth Challenge International, 1024
Cox, Charles, Truro, 696
Cox, Judith, Simcoe, 704
Cox, Judith, Deputy Mayor & Councillor, Severn, 729
Cox, Lynette, Assistant Deputy Minister, 522
Cox, Tim, Superintendent, Swift Current, 306-778-2748, 755
Coxhead, William, Director, Parks & Recreation, London, 713
Coxworthy, Paul L., Partner, Stewart McKelvey Stirling Scales - St. John's, 1066
Coyne, Kevin, President/CEO, e3 Solutions Inc., 168
Coyne, Michael, Systems Librarian, Thompson Rivers University, 1112
Cozzi, P.Eng., Daniel, Director, Roads & Works Operations, Oakville, 715
Crabbe, Darrell, Executive Director, Saskatchewan Wildlife Federation, 1002
Crabtree, Donna M., Soloway, Wright LLP, 1071
Crack, Grant, Mayor, Stormont, Dundas & Glengarry, 730
Crack, Grant E., Mayor, North Glengarry, 727
Cracknell, Linda, Head, Acquisitions & Serials, Wilfrid Laurier University, 1165
Craddock, David, Partner, Macleod Dixon LLP, 1052
Craddock, Jay, Manager, Arlat Technology, 91
Craggs, Karen, Deputy Treasurer, Orangeville, 716
Craib, Linda, Admin Coordinator & Sr. Researcher, Conservation Foundation, 901
Craig, Dana, Map Library Assistant, Map Library, 1159
Craig, Doug, Waterloo, 710, 704
Craig, Doug, Mayor, Cambridge, 519-740-4517, 707
Craig, Gary, Branch Manager, Totten Sims Hubicki Associates Ltd., 399
Craig, Gary, Regional Manager, Thermon Heat Tracing Services, 394
Craig, Glen, Labratory Supervisor, Maxxam Analytics Ltd., 284
Craig, Glen W., Project Manager/Technical Sales, Maxxam Analytics Ltd., 283
Craig, H. Douglas, Contact, Craig Hydrogeologic Inc., 153
Craig, John N., Bennett Jones LLP - Calgary Office, 1049
Craig, Kenneth, Councillor at Large, Kincardine, 519-396-8767, 726
Craig, Kevin, Kelowna, 681
Craig, Liam, Bracebridge, 706
Craig, Martin, Manager, Dekka Resins Inc., 159
Craig, B.A., LL.B., Gordon M., Partner, Lawson Lundell LLP - Vancouver, 1061
Craik, Bill, Executive Director, Health Sciences Association of Saskatchewan, 928
Craik, Sharon, Information Agent, Shell Canada Limited, 1102
Crake, Del, Bradford West Gwillimbury, 706
Cram, Heather, Principal, Hilderman Thomas Frank Cram & Associates, 232
Cram, Mart, Vice-President, 663
Cramer, Garth, Director, 623
Cramerstetter, Walter, Contact, Cramer Nursery Inc., 153
Crandall, David, Vice-President, Acadia Consultants & Inspectors Ltd., 65
Crane, Ian, Director, Chilliwack, 604-793-2906, 680
Crane, Lee-Ann, CAO & Manager, East Kootenay, 677
Crane, Rebecca, Ogilvy Renault LLP/S.E.N.C.R.L., s.r.l. - Toronto, 1078
Cranna, Derek A., Field Law - Edmonton, 1055
Cranston, Fred, Chief Financial Officer, Bennett Environmental Inc., 105

Cranston, Robert R., Lang Michener LLP - Toronto, 1077
Crantz, Wade, Branch Manager, CenturyVallen, 137
Craveiro, John, Manager, Capital Regional District, 250-360-3164, 676
Craven, Jarrod, Area Superintendent, Thames Centre, 731
Craven, Jarrod, Superintendent, Thames Centre, 731
Craven, Rick, Halton, 707, 700
Craven, Wayne, Medicine Hat, 673
Crawford, Dean, Partner, Heenan Blaikie LLP - Vancouver, 1060
Crawford, Dwane, Manager, Development, South Glengarry, 730
Crawford, Elizabeth J., Coordinator, Moncton Campus, Library, 1128
Crawford, Gary, Toronto, 721
Crawford, John, Oro-Medonte, 705-487-3373, 728
Crawford, Kara L., Thompson Dorfman Sweatman LLP, 1064
Crawford, Kate, Borden Ladner Gervais LLP - Toronto, 1073
Crawford, Linda, Supervisor, CRL Library, Atomic Energy of Canada Ltd., 1139
Crawford, Lloyd, General Manager, Del-Air Systems Ltd., 160
Crawford, Marilyn, Ajax, 705
Crawford, Patricia, Head of Library, British Columbia Hydro, 1110
Crawford, Paul, Manager, Langley, 604-533-6056, 687
Crawford, Peter, Contact, A&A Environmental Consultants Inc., 63
Crawford, Peter, Director, Courtenay, 680
Crawford, Scott, Durham, 699
Crawford, Steve, CEO, MEC Systems Inc., 286
Crawford, Traceyann, Contact, Ontario Ministry of Environment, 1160
Crayford, Mindy, Director, 665
Creber, David, Manager, Dillon Consulting Ltd., 164
Cree, Lysane, Hutchins Caron & Associés, 1085
Creech, Lori, Manager, Alberta Beef Producers, 815
Creeden, Gary, VP & General Manager, Gorman-Rupp of Canada Ltd., 215
Creery, David, City Engineer, Woodstock, 723
Creighton, Mary, Director, Recreation & Culture Services, Oshawa, 716
Creighton, Q.C., J. Ronald, Patterson Law, 1068
Crelinston, Jeffrey, President, The Impact Group, 392
Crépault, Hubert, Cain Lamarre Casgrain Wells - Québec, 1087
Creron, Joe, Director, Kelowna, 681
Cressman, Doug, CEO, Trout Unlimited Canada, 1014
Cressman, Fred, President, Fred Cressman Sales Inc., 201
Crew, Marjorie, Chatham-Kent, 724
Crewson, Ed, Dufferin, 699
Cribbett, Barbara, Treasurer, Markham, 905-475-4735, 713
Crichton, Chad, Coordinator, Reference, Research & Instruction, University of Toronto Scarborough Library, 1163
Crichton, Ian, Severn, 729
Crighton, Michelle G., McLennan Ross LLP, 1055
Crilly, Tom, Office Manager, Trow Consulting Engineers Ltd., 403
Cripps, Joan M., Miramichi, 691
Crisanti, Vincent, Toronto, 721
Criscenti, Louise, Treasurer, Geochemical Society, 923
Crist, Brian, Director, Whitehorse, 867-668-8301, 755
Critch, Felix, Manager, Harris & Roome Supply Limited, 226
Critchley, Valerie, City Clerk, Windsor, 519-255-6868, 723
Crittenden, Guy, Editor, Hazardous Materials Management Magazine, 227
Crochetière, Simon, Longueuil, 737
Crocker, Donald, Director, Fire & Rescue Services, Central Elgin, 724
Croitoru, Nancy, President & Chief Executive Officer, Food & Consumer Products of Canada, 918
Crome, David, Director, Planning Services, Clarington, 724
Cronier, Ernie, Chief Building Official, Port Colborne, 718
Cronier, Karen, Technician, Planning, Petawawa, 717
Cronkite, Paul, Office Manager, Whisco Ltd., 431
Crook, Andrew, Project Manager, Clean Air Services Inc., 142
Crook, Phil, Managing Director, Clean Air Services Inc., 142
Crooks, Rob, Manager, Westburne Canada, 427
Crosbie, Michael J., McInnes Cooper, 1066
Crosbie, Norm, Manager, Westburne Canada, 425
Crosbie, P.C., Q.C., O.C., John C., Cox and Palmer - St. John's, 1065
Crosbie-Larmon, Lisa, Director, Human Resources, Lanark, 701
Crosby, Edward, Chief Executive Officer, Comcor Environmental Limited, 146
Crosby, Paul, Maxxam Analytics Ltd., 284
Cross, Fraser, General Manager, Republic Environmental Systems (Fort Erie) Ltd., 345
Cross, John, Manager, Emergency Services, Kingston, 712
Cross, Larry, Mayor, Sidney, 684

Cross, Larry, President, Structural Pest Management Association of British Columbia, 1010
Cross, Mark, Specialist, Waste Diversion Operations, Peterborough, 703
Cross, Ted, Chair & CEO, Canadian Innovation Centre, 872
Cross, William, Vice-President, LGL Limited Environmental Research Associates, 271
Crossan, Marci, Manager, Comox Valley, 677
Crossan, Owen, President, Medina Construction Limited, 286
Crossman, Norman H., Chair, Westmorland-Albert Solid Waste Corporation, 759
Crossman, Tony, Partner, Miller Thomson LLP - Vancouver, 1078, 1061
Croswell, Blair, Manager, Staveley Services Canada Inc., 379
Croteau, Nicolas, Heenan Blaikie S.E.N.C.R.L./SRL - Québec, 1087
Croteau, Yvan, President/CEO, Génie Audio inc., 207
Croudace, Mark, Group Executive, Coffey Geotechnics Inc., 146
Crough, Stephen, Manager, Public Works, Smith-Ennismore-Lakefield, 705-292-8621, 729
Crouse, Nolan, Mayor, St. Albert, 780-459-1606, 674
Crowdis, Ray, Director, DPL Group, 166
Crowe, Marianne, Manager, Central Kootenay, 677
Crowe, Robert, Product Manager, Electro-Air Canada, 175
Crowe, Ron, Acting Deputy Minister & Assistant Deputy Minister, 659
Crowe, Terry, Manager, Richmond, 604-276-4139, 684
Crowe, P.Eng., Brian, Assistant City Engineer, Vancouver, 604-873-7313, 685
Crowfoot, Strater, CEO & Executive Director, 541
Crown, Wes, Director, Tay, 731
Crown, Wes, Director, Planning & Development, Midland, 713
Crowther, Douglas E., Fraser Milner Casgrain LLP - Calgary, 1051
Crowther, Sherry, Librarian, Lester B. Pearson College of the Pacific, 1121
Croxford, Steve, Manager, Associated Engineering Group Ltd., 94
Croy Vanwely, Marcia, Head, Library Services, Pacific Region, 1118
Crozier, Brian, Director, Community Services, Huntsville, 711
Crozier, Jim, Harris & Roome Supply Limited, 226
Cruickshank, Jill, Manager, National Environmental Health Association, 957
Cruickshank, Murray, President, Neighborhood Recycling, 299
Cruikshank, Bernie, President, Friends of the Forestry Farm House Inc., 921
Cruikshank, Ron, Executive Director, 665
Crum, Liz, Library Clerk, Reserves, AV Resources, Overdues, Lakeshore Campus, 1159
Cryderman, Hilton, Chief Building Official & Administrator, Planning, South Stormont, 730
Cubitt, M.S.W., Garry H., Chief Administrative Officer, Durham, 699
Cudmore, Bruce, EDA Collaborative Inc., 173
Cudney, Robert, Director, Cimatec Environmental Engineering Inc., 141
Cuff, Lynn, College Librarian, D.S.B. Fowlow Bldg LRC, College of the North Atlantic, 1133
Cuff, Lynn, Librarian III, Bay St George Campus, Stephenville Crossing Building, 1133
Cui, David, Technical Director, Watson Process Systems, 423
Cuke, Teresa, Technical Reference Centre Librarian, Technical Reference Centre, 1162
Culham, Allan, Vice-President, 520
Culhane, Mike, Head, Library & Internet Services, Institute for Research in Construction, 1150
Culhane, Pat, Belleville, 706
Cullen, Brian, CAO, Pictou County, 698
Cullen, Louis-Paul, Ogilvy Renault LLP/S.E.N.C.R.L., s.r.l. - Montréal, 1086
Cullen, Peter J., Associé, Stikeman Elliott LLP - Montréal, 1087
Culley, Sandy, Library Technician, Henderson Medical Library, 1141
Cullimore, D. Roy, President, Droycon Bioconcepts Inc., 166
Cullis, Tara, President, David Suzuki Foundation, 906
Culliton, Keith, Stratford, 720
Cumming, Neil A., Exec. Vice-President, Levelton Consultants Ltd., 270
Cummings, Greb, Deputy Minister, 606
Cundy, C., Director, St. Albert, 674
Cunliffe, M.J.(Pemme), McLennan Ross LLP, 1055
Cunningham, Andrea, Head, Reference, St Joseph's Hospital (Saint John), 1129

Cunningham, Christy, Secretary, Association of Consulting Engineering Companies - New Brunswick, 835
Cunningham, Dale, Field Law - Edmonton, 1055
Cunningham, Paul, CEO, Energy Systems & Design Limited, 179
Cunningham, Rob, Assistant Deputy Minister, 655
Cunningham, Sandy, Collingwood, 708
Curcio Lister, Debra, Partner, Miller Thomson LLP - Toronto, 1055, 1078
Curley, John P., Timmins, 721
Curran, Ed, Director, Lunenburg District, 902-541-1336, 697
Curran, Sean, Manager, Atlantic Newsprint Company, 96
Currie, Adrian R., Field Law - Edmonton, 1055
Currie, Doug W., Minister, 640
Currie, Grant, Manager, Human Resources, Prince Edward, 703
Currie, Gregg, College Librarian, Selkirk College, 1111
Currie, Linda, Aquatic Biologist, Fraser Environmental Services, 201
Currie, Mike, President, Kerr Wood Leidal Associates Ltd., 257
Currier, Jay, Chief Administrative Officer & Town Manager, Bradford West Gwillimbury, 706
Currins, Judy, Kawartha Lakes, 711
Curry, Gail, Instruction/Data Librarian, University of Northern British Columbia, 1115
Curry, Traci, Specialist, ProAgri Consulting Limited, 333
Curtis, Alison, Coordinator, Collection Development, Langara College, 1118
Curtis, Bill, Director, 666
Curtis, Cliff, Commissioner, Works Department, Durham, 699
Curtis, Craig, City Manager, Red Deer, 403-342-8156, 674
Curtis, Donna, Head, NRC Information Centre - Halifax, 1136
Curtis, Mark S., Executive Director, The Avian Preservation Foundation, 844
Curtis, Martin, Manager, Westburne Canada, 426
Curtis, Mary Grace, Coordinator, Airdrie, 780-948-0246, 670
Curtis, Rick, Executive Director, Alberta Recreation & Parks Association, 819
Curtis, William E., President & General Manager, Curtis Environmental & Engineering Inc., 154
Curwin, Claude, Councillor, Riverview, 506-860-6873, 692
Cusano, John R., Gowling Lafleur Henderson LLP - Calgary, 1051
Cusano, Luigi A., Partner, Stikeman Elliott LLP - Calgary, 1053
Cuschieri, David, Macleod Dixon LLP, 1052
Cusinato, Curtis A., Partner, Stikeman Elliott LLP - Toronto, 1080
Cusson, Gilles, Coordonnateur, CÉGEP de Chicoutimi, 1166
Cutajar, Dennis, Commissioner, Economic Development & Communication, Brampton, 706
Cutcliffe, Tracey, Deputy Minister, 638
Cuthbertson, John H., Burnet, Duckworth & Palmer LLP, 1050
Cuthill, Cody, General Manager, Normcan, 306
Cutler, Annette, Secretary, Environmental Action Barrie, 911
Cutrone, Michel, President, MICCA Paints Inc., 288
Cvitan, Anni, Administration, Bradex Industrial Services Ltd., 115
Cybulsky, Tyler, Branch Manager, Fort Garry Industries Ltd., 200
Cynthia, Wright, Chair, North American Bird Conservation Initiative Canada, 765
Cyr, André, Repentigny, 450-585-3410, 740
Cyr, Art, Vice-President, Industrial Thermo Polymers Ltd., 241
Cyr, Caroline, Sec.-Trés., Batiscan, 747
Cyr, Claude, Préfet, Le Rocher-Percé, 749
Cyr, Donna, Director, Finance, Brockville, 707
Cyr, Gilles, President/CEO, Supremex Inc., 383
Cyr, Kyle, Clarence-Rockland, 708
Cyr, Roger E., President, Cyr Engineering Ltd., 155
Cyr, Roger N., General Manager, Barrington Industrial Services Limited, 102
Cyr, Thérèse, Responsable, Didacthèque, Université du Québec en Abitibi-Témiscamingue, 1182
Czerwinski, Melinda, Coordinator, Asia Pacific Foundation of Canada, 829

D

D'Addio, Grace, Finance Manager, Grundfos Canada Inc., 222
D'Agostino, Stephen J., Thomson, Rogers, 1080
D'Amboise, Marion, Librarian, Hatch Energy, 1146
D'Amour, Normand, Associé, Miller Thomson LLP - Montréal, 1086
D'Andrea, Donna M., Partner, Hicks Morley Hamilton Stewart Storie LLP, 1076
D'Angela, Henry, Niagara, 702
D'Angela, Henry, Regional Councillor, Thorold, 720
D'Angelo, Joseph C., Lang Michener LLP - Toronto, 1077

d'Anglejan-Chatillon, Alix, Associée, Stikeman Elliott LLP - Montréal, 1087
D'Anjou, Réal, Groupe EnvirAqua, 219
D'Aoust, Jeannic, Trésorière, Lachute, 736
D'Autremont, Dan, Minister, 662
d'Entremont, Nil, President, Nova Scotia Nature Trust, 968
D'Entremont, Rick, Superintendent, Works, Woodstock, 723
D'Eon, MPH, P.Eng, Willard, Secretary-Treasurer, Atlantic Canada Water & Wastewater Association, 842
d'Etcheverry, Philippe, Lavery, de Billy - Montréal, 1086
D'Hondt, P.Eng., Eric R., General Manager, Public Works & Environmental Serv, Norfolk, 702
D'Onofrio, Joe, Manager, Red Deer County, 670
D'Sa, Peter, Territory Sales Manager, Lineman's Testing Laboratories of Canada Limited, 272
D'Silva, Alan, Partner, Stikeman Elliott LLP - Toronto, 1080
D'Souza, Rudy, Manager, Squamish-Lillooet, 679
da Silva, Joann, Library Technician, Winnipeg Water & Waste Dept., 1126
Dabner, Samuel S., Fulton & Company LLP, Lawyers & Trade-Mark Agents, 1056
Daemen, Harry, Manager, C.J. MacLellan & Associates Inc., 120
Daeninck, Tom, Manager, Coast Paper Ltd., 145
Dagenais, Benoit, Director, Enviroservices Inc., 187
Dagenais, Daniel Alain, Partner, Lavery, de Billy - Montréal, 1085
Dagenais, Marc, Partner, Lavery, de Billy - Montréal, 1085
Dagenais, Pierre R., Partner, Ogilvy Renault LLP/S.E.N.C.R.L., s.r.l. - Toronto, 1078
Dagicour, Florence, Fasken Martineau - Montréal, 1083
Daher, Bechara, Manager, Building Services, Leamington, 726
Daher, Joe, Canada Branch Mgr., National Instruments Canada, 298
Dahl, Denis, Saguenay, 741
Dahlie, Rita, Head, Woodward Biomedical Library, 1119
Dahlie, Rita, Interim Head, Biomedical Branch Library, 1117
Daicos, Steve, President, Optikon Corp. Ltd., 313
Daigle, Guy, Trois-Rivières, 745
Daigle, Jean-Luc, Lévis, 736
Daigle, Jean-Marc, Partner, Genus Loci Ecological Landscapes Inc., 210
Daigle, Louis, Directeur, Sherbrooke, 819-821-5623, 744
Daigle, Pierre, Ombudsman, 545
Daigle, Suzanne, Responsable, Publications gouvernementales, Université du Québec en Abitibi-Témiscamingue, 1182
Daigneault, Robert, Daigneault, avocats inc., 1083
Dainard, Gary, Director, Cardinal Biologicals Ltd., 128
Dalacu, Nick, Canrom Photovoltaics Inc., 127
Dale, Denise, Public Services Librarian & Archives, Kwantlen University College, 1113
Dale, Frank, Peel, 714, 703
Dale, Kathleen, Director, Planning & Development, Lincoln, 713
Daley, Jill, Ogilvy Renault LLP/S.E.N.C.R.L., s.r.l. - Toronto, 1078
Dalgity, Garry, Mississippi Mills, 714
Dalgleish, Laverne, CEO, National Energy Conservation Association, 179, 1125
Dalgleish, Laverne, Treasurer, Manitoba Ozone Protection Industry Association, 951
Dalgleish, Ryan, Contact, National Energy Conservation Association Inc., 957
Dalgleish, Ryan, Manager, National Energy Conservation Association, 1125
Dalgleish, Stuart, Director & City Assessor, Calgary, 403-268-4609, 671
Dalgleish, Tim, Plant Manager, CCS Income Trust, 134
Dalgleish, Q.C., Terence, Davis LLP - Calgary, 1050
Dalimonte, Tony, Deputy Mayor & Councillor, Haldimand, 700
Dalke, Dean L., Davis LLP - Vancouver, 1059
Dallaire, Bernard, Directeur, Alma, 418-669-5059, 733
Dallaire, Catherine, Assistant City Manager, Moncton / Ville de Moncton, 691
Dallaire, Jean Patrick, Langlois Kronström Desjardins, 1088
Dallaire, Jean-Philippe, Senior Counsel, 544
Dallaire, Jody, Councillor at Large, Dieppe, 506-387-8738, 691
Dallaire, Pierre, Beaudry, Bertrand Avocats, 1082
Dalrymple, Barry, Councillor, Halifax Regional Municipality, 695
Dalrymple, Mike, Executive Director, 568
Dalta, Sumona, Manager, Optech Inc., 313
Dalton, Art, Owner/Manager, Prairie Geomatics Ltd., 330
Dalton, Danny, Project Manager, Clean Air Services Inc., 142
Dalton, Joan, Associate University Librarian, University of Windsor, 1165
Daly, John, Clerk & Director, Corporate Services, Springwater, 730
Dalziel, Monica, Director, Salmon Arm, 684
Dam, René, President/CEO, William Dam Seeds Ltd., 432

Executive Name Index

Damiani, Domenic, Partner, Borden Ladner Gervais LLP - Toronto, 1073
Daminato, Paul, CAO, New Westminster, 682
Damkjar, Eric, Vice-President, Canadian Archaeological Association, 855
Dammrich, Thomas, President, National Marine Manufacturers Association, 958
Damoff, Pam, Town Councillor, Oakville, 715
Damore, Mike, Sales Manager, Ecotainer Sales Inc., 172
Damphousse, Martin, Varennes, 746
Damus, Martin, Canadian Coordinator, 523
Danaher, Ross, Director, Educational Resources, Loyalist College of Applied Arts & Technology, 1139
Dance, Peter, Director, Public Works, Orillia, 716
Danch, Frank M., Port Colborne, 718
Dandonneau, François, Gowling Lafleur Henderson S.E.N.C.R.L./LLP, 1084
Dandurand, Mirelle, Dutab, 167
Dandurand, Robert, Vice-President, Genivar, 207
Dane, Brent, Fire Chief, Brandon, 204-729-2404, 689
Dane, Ratliff, Director, Commission for Environmental Cooperation, 763
Daneault, Hélène, Mairesse, Rosemère, 741
Daneliuk, John, General Manager, Provincial Environmental Services Inc., 335
Dang, Derek, Richmond, 684
Dang-Anh, Thu, Trade Commissioner, 769
Daniel, Emil, Manager, Fisheries & Oceans Canada, 1150
Daniel, Yolanda, Vice-President, Acklands-Grainger Inc., 66
Daniel, Q.C., Harry J., Daniel & Partners LLP, 1072
Daniela, Oyague, Trade Commissioner, 769
Daniel-Ivad, Josef, Vice President, Pure Energy Inc., 336
Daniel-Ivad, Josef, Vice-President, Pure Energy Battery Inc., 336
Daniels, Caroline, Systems & Web Librarian, Kwantlen University College, 1113
Daniels, Dan, Deputy Minister, 605
Daniels, J., General Manager, Servco Environmental Solutions Inc., 363
Daniels, AMCT, Susan M., City Clerk, Thorold, 720
Danis, Luc, Director, Aqua-Rehab Inc., 88
Dankowich, Stephen, Executive Director, Oakville Community Centre for Peace, Ecology & Human Rights, 969
Dansereau, Claire, Deputy Minister, 527
Dansereau, Jean-Pierre, Directeur, La Fédération des producteurs de bois du Québec, 914
Dansereau, Mike, Contact, Western Site Technologies Inc., 430
Danshin, William, President, PWC Pure Water Corporation, 337
Danson, Howard, Scugog, 729
Danyluk, Ray, Minister, 569
Danziger, Richard, Director, Development Services, Kawartha Lakes, 711
Daoust, Nathalie, Council Secretary, 525
Daoust, Robert, Director, Proceco Ltd., 333
Daoust, Serge, Directeur, Repentigny, 450-470-3600, 740
Daoust, Yves, Préfet, Beauharnois-Salaberry, 747
Darby, Gail, Librarian, New Brunswick Dept. of Environment, 1128
Darcel, Colin, President, Maratek Environmental Inc., 280
Darch, Dave, Director, Public Works & Engineering, Renfrew, 613-732-4353, 704
Dargewitcz, Rob, Treasurer, Shell Canada Limited, 365
Darke, Frank, Contact, Darke Marketing Inc., 157
Darling, Don, Director, Summerland, 689
Darling, Margaret, Library Manager, Kingston General Hospital, 1142
Darling, Peter D., Ritch Durnford, Lawyers, 1067
Darlow, Melanie, Coordinator, African Coelacanth Ecosystem Programme, 813
Darrach, Ian, Exec. Vice-President, AMEC, 82
Darragh, Alec, Supervisor, Quesnel, 688
Darroch, Kim, Manager, Development Services, Lakeshore, 712
Darrow, David, Deputy Minister, 616
Dart, Graham, Director, Human Resources, St. Thomas, 719
Darveau, Bernard, President, Bernard Darveau Ingénieur, 105
Daschuk, George, President, Envirotech Pollution Controls Ltd., 188
Dash, Cheryl, Secretary, Prairie Conservation Forum, 988
DaSilva, Ser, Manager, Veolia ES Canada Industrial Services Inc., 441
Daskewech, Frank, Director, Grande Prairie, 780-538-0350, 672
Dattani, Dipak, Supervisor, Burnaby, 604-294-7771, 679
Daudelin, Michel, Directeur, Westburne Canada, 426
Daum, Kevin, Contact, Environmental Building Science Inc., 185
Daunais, Pierre-Paul, Stikeman Elliott LLP - Montréal, 1087
Dauphin, Claude, Maire d'arrondissement, Montréal, 738

Dauphinee, Richard B., Warden, Hants West District, 697
Dausett, Brad, Manager, Roads, Strathroy-Caradoc, 731
Dausett, Steve, Strathroy-Caradoc, 731
Dave, Burley, Manager, Canada-Newfoundland Offshore Petroleum Board, 763
Dave, Neil, President, Tract Consulting Inc., 400
Davey, Brad, Vice-President, ArcelorMittal Dofasco, 90
Davey, Ian, Director, Corporate Services, Cobourg, 708
Davey, James R., President, Enviro-Safe Chemicals Canada Inc., 183
Davey, Scott, Kitchener, 712
David, Beverly, President, Five Seasons Comfort Limited, 196
David, Beverly, President/CEO, Electro-Air Canada, 175
David, Camil, Technicien en documentation, Bibliothèque des sciences, 1171
David, Caroline, Marketing & Sales Manager, Five Seasons Comfort Limited, 175, 196
David, Claude, Manager, Dillon Consulting Ltd., 163
David, Mallette, Trade Commissioner, 768
David, Marie-Claude, Stikeman Elliott LLP - Montréal, 1087
David-Evans, Maria, Deputy Minister, 563
Davidson, Al, Partner, David A. McLean & Associates, 158
Davidson, Alex, Manager, Water Division, Brant, 698
Davidson, Bob, Manager, YES Environment Technologies Inc., 435
Davidson, Brett, President/CEO, Wavefront Technology Solutions Inc., 423
Davidson, Catherine, Associate University Librarian, Collections, York University Libraries, 1164
Davidson, Dan, Deputy Mayor & Councillor, Innisfil, 711
Davidson, Darla, Librarian, Civil Aviation Technical Reference Centre, 1128
Davidson, Jim, Commissioner, Corporate Services, York, 705
Davidson, Larry, President, Kodiak Oilfield Services, 259
Davidson, Laurie, Exec. Vice-President, AMEC, 82
Davidson, Lawrence, EarthFx Inc., 169
Davidson, Marsha, Executive Director, Breast Cancer Society of Canada, 846
Davidson, Maureen, Library Technician (Cataloguing), College of the Rockies, 1111
Davidson, Sarah, Administrator, British Columbia Association for Regenerative Agriculture, 847
Davidson, Shawn, Clearview, 725
Davidson, Susan, President, British Columbia Association for Regenerative Agriculture, 847
Davidson, Trina, Supervisor, Westmorland-Albert Solid Waste Corporation, 759
Davidson-Fisher, Irene, CEO, Trans Canada Yellowhead Highway Association, 1013
Davidson-Meyn, Heather, Sr. Consultant, INDECO Strategic Consulting Inc., 240
Davie, Lucille, Volunteer, Five Hills Health Region, 1187
Davies, Anton E., Vice President, Rowan Williams Davies & Irwin Inc., 353
Davies, Brian, President, Brincad Technologies Inc., 116
Davies, Carolyn, Amherstburg, 705
Davies, David, Contact, Forest Protection Limited, 199
Davies, David C., General Manager, 595
Davies, Don, McCarthy Tétrault LLP - Calgary, 1052
Davies, Don G., Partner, Macleod Dixon LLP, 1052
Davies, Jeffrey L., Davies Howe Partners, 1074
Davies, Karen, Director, Human Resources, Meaford, 727
Davies, Michael, Partner, Heenan Blaikie LLP - Toronto, 1075
Davies, Myra, Library Technician, Royal Victoria Hospital, 1175
Davies, Stuart, President, North/South Consultants Inc., 306
Davies, Terrence, Acting Director, Canadian General Standards Board, 869
Davies, Terrence, Director, Canadian General Standards Board, 124
Davies, Todd R., Alexander Holburn Beaudin & Lang, LLP, 1057
Davies, B.A., M.A., Glen, City Manager, Regina, 306-777-7314, 754
Davies, P.Eng., Brian, Assistant City Engineer, Vancouver, 604-873-7348, 685
Davis, Amy, Administration Coordinator, Novapet Inc., 308
Davis, Ashley, President, Alfa Laval Inc., 78
Davis, Bill, Haliburton, 705-457-1196, 700
Davis, Elizabeth, Library Technician, Royal Tyrrell Museum of Palaeontology, 1104
Davis, James C., Senior Partner, Stikeman Elliott LLP - Toronto, 1080
Davis, Janet, Toronto, 721
Davis, John, Councillor, Huntsville, 711
Davis, Lisa, Project Coordinator, Pitch-In Canada, 987
Davis, Lynn, Director, Hants West District, 902-798-6900, 697

Davis, Martha, President, Earth Island Institute, 907
Davis, Paul, President, GPEC Global Corp., 215
Davis, Rob, EcoEthic Inc., 171
Davis, Rolph A., Chair, LGL Limited Environmental Research Associates, 271
Davis, Ron, Officer, Medicine Hat, 403-529-8359, 673
Davis, Roxanne M., Stones Carbert Waite Wells LLP, 1054
Davis, Russell, Manager, Staveley Services Canada Inc., 379
Davis, Seth, Manager, Geochemical Society, 923
Davis, Steve, President, Independent Power Producers Association of British Columbia, 930
Davis, Susan, Coordinator, Yukon Environmental Network, 1024
Davis, Terry R., Partner, Parlee McLaws LLP, 1053
Davis, Tom, Director, 568
Davison, Amy, Partner, Borden Ladner Gervais LLP - Vancouver, 1058
Davison, Betty, Office Manager, British Columbia Nature (Federation of British Columbia Naturalis, 849
Davison, Carolyn, Director, 613
Davison, Doug, President/CEO, ITRES Research Ltd., 249
Davison, Gary, Frontenac, 699
Davison, Gary C, Mayor, South Frontenac, 730
Davison, Naomi, Georgina, 709
Davy, Peter, Administrative Manager, Dol Hydroseeding Inc., 164
Davy, Peter, Manager, Verdyol Mulch of Canada Ltd., 412
Dawe, Geoff, York, 705
Dawe, Geoff, Mayor, Aurora, 706
Dawe, Lori, Director, Parliamentary Affairs, 522
Dawe, Sean, Director, 602
Dawe, Sue, Clerk & Director, Corporate Services, Port Hope, 728
Dawson, Bryan T., President/CEO, Aircraft Appliances & Equipment Ltd., 75
Dawson, Joe, Regional Manager, Electronic Warfare Associates - Canada, Ltd., 175
Dawson, John, McCarthy Tétrault LLP - Toronto, 1077
Dawson, Scott A., Farris, Vaughan, Wills & Murphy LLP, 1059
Dawtre, E. Bernard, Manager, Environmental Services, Norfolk, 702
Day, Barry, Deputy Minister, 569
Day, Becky, Thorold, 720
Day, Bill, City Treasurer, St. Thomas, 719
Day, Brian, General Manager, Campbell Scientific (Canada) Corp., 122
Day, Brian A., Executive Director, North American Association for Environmental Education, 964
Day, Byron, President, Aevitas Inc., 72
Day, Byron, Vice-President, Aevitas Inc., 72
Day, Chris, Chief, Corporate Communications, Ottawa, 716
Day, David L., Director, Calgary, 403-268-3668, 671
Day, Deborah, Director, Victoria, 250-361-0511, 685
Day, Dennis, Chair, 583
Day, Elizabeth, Director, 600
Day, Frédérick T., Contact, Global Facman Entreprises Inc., 213
Day, Janet, Library Technician, South Campus, 1106
Day, Jill, Supervisor, Technical Services, Grant MacEwan University, 1105
Day, John W.R., Cassels Brock & Blackwell LLP, 1074
Day, Joseph, Director, 600
Day, Mark, Director, Finance & Treasurer, Greater Napanee, 709
Day, Robert D., Executive Director, Renewable Natural Resources Foundation, 994
Day, Tom, Chief Executive Officer, West Point Products Canada, 425
Day, Q.C., Frederick A., McLennan Ross LLP, 1055
Dayday, Henry, Director, PINTER & Associates Ltd., 325
Daykin, Ernie, Mayor, Maple Ridge, 687
Daykin, Margot, Asst. Manager, Richmond, 604-276-4130, 684
Dayton, Tim, General Manager, Aqua-Pak Styro Containers Ltd., 88
De Baeremaeker, Glenn, Toronto, 721
De Boer, Gerald, Vice President/Project Manager, RAM Lining Systems Inc., 342
de Boer, Y. (Ike), Coordinator, Pitt Meadows, 604-465-2425, 683
De Bonis, Elaine, Operations Manager, Davis Campus, 1139
De Caria, Joseph, Executive Secretary, Acoustical Association Ontario, 813
De Ciccio, Franco, Contact, Conterm Inc., 151
De Cicco, John, Kamloops, 681
De Clerck-Floate, Rose, President, Entomological Society of Alberta, 910
De Courval, Lise, Technicienne en documentation, École nationale d'aérotechnique, 1183
De Feo, Alberto, CAO, Williams Lake, 250-392-1775, 686
De Freitas, Douglas R., President, Kaizen Environmental Services Inc., 254

Executive Name Index

De Gagne, Don, CAO, Summerland, 689
De Giovanni, Vivian, Executive Director, Municipal Waste Association, 955
de Grandpré, Nathalie, Directice générale, Minganie, 750
De Groot, George, Director, Public Works & Environmental Services, Tecumseh, 720
de Gruchy, Margy, Ecologist, Dougan & Associates, 165
de Haan, Betty, Chief Administrative Officer & Clerk, South Stormont, 730
de Hoop, James, Director, Community & Family Services, Kingston, 712
De Koster, Christophe, Partner, Heenan Blaikie S.E.N.C.R.L/SRL, 1084
de la Sablonniere, Lucie, Spécialiste en moyen techniques d'enseignement, Collège André-Grasset, 1172
de Lange, David, Sr. Associate, Praxis Inc., 330
de Launière, Olivier, Directeur, Saint-Félicien, 418-679-0313, 742
De Leeuw, Johan, Director, Wind Energy Solutions Canada, 433
De Luca, Mike, Contact, Aqua Terre Solutions Inc., 88
de Marsh, Peter, President, Canadian Federation of Woodlot Owners, 868
de Montmorency, David De, President, Rapid-Eau Technologies, 342
De Olivia, Jose, Intertek Systems Certification, 246
De Palma, Vincent R., President & Chief Executive Officer, Shred-It, 366
De Sua, Giovanni, Borden Ladner Gervais LLP - Montréal, 1083
De Sylva, Joseph, Gatineau, 735
De Vita, Bruno, Alexander Holburn Beaudin & Lang, LLP, 1057
De Vries, Sean, Manager, Panasonic Canada Inc., 317
de Vries, P.Eng, Ron, Senior Vice-President, 521
De Vuono, Anthony (Tony), Senior Vice-President & Chief Technology Officer, 511
de Wit, Mélanie, Borden Ladner Gervais LLP - Toronto, 1074
Deacon, Mary, Vice-President, World Wildlife Fund - Canada, 1023
Deacon, Q.C., John E., D'Arcy & Deacon LLP, 1063
Deakin, Ian, Strasser Alloy Steels Ltd., 380
Deal, Heather, Metro Vancouver, 685, 678
Dean, Jan, Manager, Strata Soil Sampling Inc., 380
Dean, John, Principal, C5 Plus Ltd., 120
Dean, Kelliann, Deputy Minister, 616
Dean, Linda J., Chief Administrative Officer, Dufferin, 699
Dean, Martin, Plant Manager, CCS Income Trust, 134
Dean, Rob, Site Operations Supervisor, Fundy Region Solid Waste Commission, 758
Dean, Sven, President, GroundTech Solutions, 219
DeAngelis, Michael, City Manager, Vaughan, 722
Deans, Dan, Ottawa, 613-580-2480, 716
Deans, Rosemary, Coordinator, Manitoba Environmental Industries Association Inc., 951
Dear, Donald W., McLennan Ross LLP, 1053
Dearing, Garry, Reeve, Wetaskiwin County No. 10, 670
Dearth, Betty, Librarian, Industrial Technology Centre, 1124
DeAth, S. Samuel, Founder & Chief Executive Officer, Sensible Life Products, 362
DeBaker, April, Director, American Water Works Association, 826
Debbah, Karim, Bibliothécaire, Bibliothèque des sciences, 1170
Debenham, David, Lang Michener LLP - Ottawa, 1070
Debicki, Ruth, Librarian, Sudbury Rock & Lapidary Society, 1155
Debicki, Ruth, Vice-President, Sudbury Rock & Lapidary Society, 1011
Debieuvre, Frédéric, Contact, Société d'énergie de la rivière Ste-Anne/AXOR, 371
Debnath, P.Ag., Samir, Registrar, Newfoundland & Labrador Institute of Agrologists, 963
Debney, Dennis, Intelex Technologies Inc., 244
deBoer, Nick, Area Councillor, Caledon, 707
DeBoer, William, Manager, Onyx Chemical Cleaning, 313
Debono, Bernie, General Manager, Norfolk Disposal Services Limited, 305
Debono, Louis, President, Norfolk Disposal Services Limited, 305
deBortoli, R., Director, Operations, Elliot Lake, 709
DeBow, Richard E., Barry Spalding - Moncton Office, 1064
deBruyn, Garth, General Manager, ProMinent Fluid Controls Ltd., 334
DeBussac, R., Carrier Canada Ltd., 129
Decaire, Brian J., SimpsonWigle LAW LLP, 1069
Décarie, Suzanne, Conseillère d'arrondissement, Pointe-aux-Trembles, Montréal, 738
Decaro, Terry, Production Manager, N.R. Murphy Ltd., 296
Decary, Claude, Président/directeur général, Boutillette Parizeau et Associés inc., 114

Décary, c.r., Michel, Associé, Stikeman Elliott LLP - Montréal, 1087
Dechaine, Nathalie, Officer, Saanich, 250-475-5475, 688
Dechant, Brent, Chair, North Peace Regional Landfill Commission, 758
Deck, Darrell, General Manager, Comco Manufacturing Ltd., 146
deCocq, Julian, Clerk, Cochrane, 671
DeCoste, Genevieve, Superintendent, Truro, 696
Decter Hirst, Shari, Mayor, Brandon, 689
DeCudlo, Garry, Vice-President, ELI Eco Chemical Technologies Inc., 175
Dee, Cecilia, Supervisor, Bombardier Inc./Canadair Aerospace & Defence Groups, 1171
Deegan, Dick, Vice-President, Triangle Fluid Controls Ltd., 401
Deering, Keith, Assistant Deputy Minister, 603
Defrancesca, Rosanna, Vaughan, 722
deFreitas, Doug, Kaizen Environmental Services Inc., 254
Defreltas, Chris, Head of Technical Services, Connexions Information Sharing Services, 1157
DeGagne, Justin, Treasurer, Health & Safety Conference Society of Alberta, 927
DeGagne, Mark, Branch Manager, McElhanney Consulting Services Ltd., 284
Degazio, Dan, Manager, Economic Development, Welland, 722
DeGroot, Anne Marie, Systems Administrator, Southern Alberta Institute of Technology, 1103
DeGurse, Jim, St. Clair, 729
deHaan, Harold, Engineer, Development, Woodstock, 723
Dehondt, John, Lambton Shores, 726
DeHooge, John, Fire Chief, Waterloo, 722
Deighton, Anne, Chief Librarian, Lakehead University, 1156
Deising, Mike, Director, 570
Deitch, Sydney, President, Calta Computer Systems Ltd., 122
Dejak, Mike, Sales, Eco-Tec Ltd., 171
Dekker, Chris, Interim Chief Executive Officer, 662
Del Grande, Mike, Toronto, 721
Del Mastro, Dean, Parliamentary Secretary to the Minister of Canadia, 519
Del Vecchio, Matt, Vice-President, Avmor Ltd., 99
Del Zotto, Ezio, President, Mondry Del Zotto et associés inc., 292
Delage, Benoît, Saint-Jérôme, 450-436-6134, 743
Delâge, Cyrille, Commissaire, 653
Delage, Johanne, Saint-Hyacinthe, 742
Delâge, Marc, Grondin, Poudrier, Bernier, 1087
Delaloye, Cindy, Sec.-Treas., Canadian Meat Science Association, 877
Delaney, Patrick J., Vice-President, Petroleum Services Association of Canada, 986
Delaney, Tom, Contact, Polaris Corporate Services Inc., 327
Delanty, Peter, Northumberland, 722
Delaunay, Jean-Marie, Préfet, La Haute-Côte-Nord, 748
Delegarde, Evonne, South Dundas, 613-652-1388, 730
Delgaty, Blake, Regional Director General, Pacific Region, 514
Deline, Tom, Hastings, 700
Délisle, Diane, Sherbrooke, 744
Delisle, Jean-François, Cain Lamarre Casgrain Wells - Chicoutimi, 1082
Delisle, Pierre, Président, 642
Delisle, Urgel, President/CEO, Urgel Delisle & Associés inc., 408
Delisle-Beaulieu, Simon, Heenan Blaikie S.E.N.C.R.L/SRL - Sherbrooke, 1089
Dell, Brian K., Wilson Laycraft, 1054
Dell, David A., Torys LLP, 1080
Della Croce, Luisa, Director, Child Care Services, Wellington, 705
Delmage, Doug, Chief Building Inspector, Camrose, 780-672-4428, 671
Delmonico, Tony, Fire Chief, Coquitlam, 680
Delnea, Wes, Branch Manager, CenturyVallen, 137
Delogu, Rick, CEO/CFO, Ventax Robot Inc., 411
DeLong, Kathleen, Associate Director, Finance & Human Resources, University of Alberta, 1107
DeLong, Linwood, Collections Coordinator, University of Winnipeg, 1126
Delongchamp, Diane, Aide bibliothécaire/Collections, Université de l'Alberta Bibliothèque Saint-Jean, 1107
DeLorey, Herbert J., Warden, Antigonish County, 696
Delorme, Silvie, Directrice, Université Laval, 1181
Delorme, Yvan, Directeur, Montréal, 738
DeLoyde, Leo, General Manager, Development & Infrastructure, Burlington, 707
Deluney, Joanne, Librarian, Clarenville Campus Learning Resource Centre, 1130
DeMaleco, Paul, CEO, Nature's Environmental Products Inc., 298
Demaray, Max, Huron, 701

Demarcke, Janet, Manager, Chilliwack, 604-792-9311, 680
DeMarco, Elisabeth (Lisa), Partner, Macleod Dixon LLP, 1077
DeMars, John, Clerk & Director, Administration, St. Clair, 729
Demars, Tina, Information Specialist, Lanxess Inc. - Sarnia, 1154
Dembek, Barbara, Director, Building & Planning, Stratford, 720
Demeriez, Gary, Sales Manager, EIL Environmental Services, 174
Demers, André, Québec, 740
Demers, Annette, Reference Librarian, Paul Martin Law Library, 1165
Demers, Darrell, Lea-Der Coatings (614248 Alberta Ltd.), 266
Demers, David, CEO, Westport Innovations Inc., 430
Demers, Don, Director, Fort St. John, 681
Demers, Isabelle, Lévis, 736
Demers, Jean, Directeur, Victoriaville, 819-758-1571, 746
Demers, Jean-Louis, Bibliothécaire en chef, CÉGEP de la Pocatière, 1177
Demers, Jean-Louis, Responsable, CÉGEP St-Jean-sur-Richelieu, 1183
Demers, Marie-C., Librarian, Union Carbide/Pétromont, 1176
Demers, Steeves, Chambly, 514-250-9960, 734
Demers, CA, Laval, Conseiller de ville, Côte-de-Liesse, Montréal, 738
Demharter, Stefan, General Manager, Millar Western Forest Products Ltd., 290
Demidow, Mirek, Principal, Avalon Mechanical Consultants Ltd., 98
Demirkan, David, McInnes Cooper, 1067
Demofsky, Brianna, MacPherson Leslie & Tyerman LLP - Regina, 1090
Demond, Charles, President, Atlantic Wind Power Corp. Ltd., 97
DeMont, Paul, Operator, Hants West District, 697
Dempsey, Donna, Executive Director, Film & Bag Federation, 916
Dempsey, James B., Specialist, Cormorant Ltd., 152
Denault, Marc, Sherbrooke, 744
Denault, Yvon, Bélanger, Sauvé, 1082
Denbigh, Brian, Manager, Nanaimo, 681
Denburg, Judah, CEO & Scientific Director, AllerGen NCE Inc., 821
Denine, Dave, Minister, 602
Denis, Pierre, Partner, Lavery, de Billy - Montréal, 1085
Denis, Rob, Scicorp Systems Inc., 359
Denis, Q.C., Jonathan, Minister, 569
Denneron, Rita, Resource Library Technician, Workers' Compensation Board Northwest Territories, 1134
Dennis, Monica, Treasurer, Salmon Arm, 684
Dennison, Brian, Manager, Cowichan Valley, 677
Dennison, Don, Vice-President, Nature Trust of New Brunswick, 960
Dennison, Jack, Halton, 707, 700
Denny, Jack, President, Chamber of Mines of Eastern British Columbia, 894
Denolf, Debbie, Administrative Assistant, Edmonton Transportation & Streets Dept., 1105
Denomme, Mike, Principal, LEHDER Environmental Services Ltd., 267
Denoon, Norm, Vice-President, Nusco Supply & Manufacturing Inc., 310
Denouden, Kim, Waterloo, 704
Densmore, Kathy, Administrative Support, 594
Denstedt, Q.C., Shawn, Partner, Osler, Hoskin & Harcourt LLP - Calgary, 1053
Dente, Vittorio, Manager, Vancouver Gear Works Ltd., 409
Denyes, Jackie, Belleville, 706
Denys, Leo, General Manager, Infrastruture & Engineering Syste, Chatham-Kent, 724
Denys, Rob, Manager, Estevan, 306-634-1821, 754
Denzel, Gene, Treasurer, Richmond Hill Naturalists, 995
Deon, Judy, Library Director, Silver King Campus, 1113
Dépelteau, Jean-Pierre, Fraser Milner Casgrain S.E.N.C.R.L./LLP, 1084
Dépin, Marc-André, President/CEO, Norampac Inc., 305
DePlancke, Lynne, Norwich, 728
DePoe, Robert N., McCarthy Tétrault LLP - Calgary, 1052
Deprez, Paul, President, Nordevco Associates Ltd., 305
Der, Bruce, President, A.H. Lundberg Systems Ltd., 63
Derbyshire, Bill, Councillor, Leamington, 726
Dergousoff, Debbie, Treasurer, Society for Socialist Studies, 1007
Derksen, Dave, Chair, Mountain View Regional Waste Management Commission, 757
Derkuch, Jeff, President, Sonepar Canada, 373
Derman, Vic, Saanich, 688

Executive Name Index

Dermer, M. Jeffrey, Partner, Borden Ladner Gervais LLP - Toronto, 1073
Dermer, Mitch, Singleton Urquhart LLP, 1062
Dermott, Blake, General Manager, Trimax Residuals Management Inc., 401
Deros, Mary, Conseillère, Parc-Extension, Montréal, 738
deRosenroll, John, Chief Administrative Officer, Kincardine, 519-396-3018, 726
Deroy, Alain, Technologue senior, Génius Conseil Inc., 207
Deroy, Rena, Agente de bureau, Institut maritime du Québec, 1181
Dervis, Kemal, Administrator, United Nations Development Program, 1015
Déry, Alain, Technicien en documentation, Centre de santé et de services sociaux Richelieu-Yamaska, 1183
Dery, Armande, Technicienne en documentation, documents audio-vis, CÉGEP de Jonquière, 1168
Dery, Daniel, President, Megasecur Inc., 286
Déry, Gaston, Vice President, Roche ltée, Groupe-conseil, 348
Dery, Michael A., Alexander Holburn Beaudin & Lang, LLP, 1057
DeRyck, Susan, Manager, Golder Associates Ltd., 214
Des Chênes, Isabelle, Vice-President, Forest Products Association of Canada, 918
Des Trois Maisons, Michèle, Laval, 736
Desaulniers, Marc, Technisol Environnement, 388
Desautels, Erin, Coordinator, Surrey, 604-501-5158, 684
Desautels, Marc, Nova PB Inc., 308
Desbarats, Q.C., Robert, Partner, Osler, Hoskin & Harcourt LLP - Calgary, 1053
Deschambault, Claude, General Manager, Biogénie, 108
DesChamp, Tim, Operations Supervisor, Skeena-Queen Charlotte, 679
Deschamps, Chantal, Mairesse, Repentigny, 450-470-3103, 740
Deschamps, Chantal, Préfète, L'Assomption, 748
Deschamps, Joanne, Technicienne en documentation, CÉGEP de Granby, 1168
Deschamps, Johanne, Officer, Breast Cancer Society of Canada, 846
Deschamps, Louise, Bibliotechnicienne, Centre hospitalier de l'Université de Montréal Hôpital Notre-Dame, 1172
Deschamps, Marcel, Châteauguay, 450-699-1120, 735
Deschamps, Richard, Conseiller de ville, Sault-St-Louis, Montréal, 738
Descheneaux, Josée, Responsable, Collège O'Sullivan, 1173
Deschênes, Carole, Baie-Comeau, 418-589-8734, 733
Deschenes, D., MacDonald & Fils Inc., 277
Deschênes, Georges, Greffier, Rivière-du-Loup, 418-867-6715, 741
Deschênes, Gilles, President, Deschênes Drilling Ltd., 161
Deschênes, Jacques, Chair, Groupe Deschênes, 219
Deschênes, Joel, Contact, Clamex Environnement Inc., 142
Deschênes, Martin, President & CEO, Groupe Deschênes, 219
Deschênes, Martine, Adjointe administrative, Association pour la santé publique du Québec, 841
Deschênes, Vicky, Director, 593
Descoteau, Dale, General Manager, Medicine Hat, 403-529-8108, 673
Descoteau, David, Manager, Bartle & Gibson Co. Ltd., 102
Descotes, Don, Sales Manager, Armtec Construction Products, 92
Desforges, Alain-Claude, Bélanger, Sauvé, 1082
Desforges, Marc, Manager, Westburne Canada, 427
Desgagnes, Christine, Library Assistant, Fisheries & Oceans Canada, 1150
Desgagnes, N., Engineer, Chamard & Associés, 138
Desgagnés, Richard L., Ogilvy Renault LLP/S.E.N.C.R.L., s.r.l. - Montréal, 1086
Desgagnés, Serge, Manager, Kruger Inc., 260
Desgroseillers, Allan, Director, NetPlus-HazMat Tracker, 300
Deshaies, Suzanne, Trésorière, Laval, 450-978-5700, 736
Desjardins, Aurèle, Gatineau, 735
Desjardins, Barbara, Mayor, Esquimalt, 686
Desjardins, Guy, Clarence-Rockland, 708
Desjardins, Jacques, Directeur, Westburne Canada, 426
Desjardins, Jacques Y., Partner, Lavery, de Billy - Ottawa, 1070
Desjardins, Jean-Pierre, Directeur, Saint-Lin-Laurentides, 743
Desjardins, Johanne, Technicienne en documentation, CÉGEP de Saint-Laurent, 1184
Desjardins, Kathy, Director, West Lincoln, 732
Desjardins, Luc, President, Les Engrais Naturels McInnes Inc./McInnes Natural Fertilizers Inc, 268
Desjardins, Marc, President, Canadian Associated Air Balance Council, 855
Desjardins, Marc-André, Vice President, AXOR Experts-Conseils Inc., 99
Desjardins, Michel, Longueuil, 737
Desjardins, Pierre, Directeur, Trois-Rivières, 819-372-4626, 745
Desjardins, Robert Y., Directeur, Shawinigan, 744
Desjardins, Roger, Fire Chief, South Stormont, 730
Desjardins, Stéphane, Longueuil, 737
Desjardins, Yves, Directeur général, 653
Desjarlais, Sue, LaSalle, 713
Deslandes, Marcel, Directeur, Régie intermunicipale de traitement de l'eau potable Saint-Romual, 760
Deslauriers, Denis, Directeur, Québec, 418-641-6239, 740
Deslauriers, Michel, Ingénieur, Experts-Conseils BMST inc., 192
Desmarais, Angie, Port Colborne, 718
Desmarais, R.J., Vice-President, Laidlaw Medical Services, 263
Desmarais, Robert, Directeur général, Brome-Missisquoi, 747
Desmarais, Serge, Directeur, Génius Conseil Inc., 207
Desmet, Dominique, Directeur, La Haute-Yamaska, 748
Desmeules, Justine, FaunENord, 914
Desmeules, Michel, Contact, C.R. Wall Co. Inc., 120
Desnoyers, Robert, President, Hamilton Community Energy, 224
DeSousa, Ed, Treasurer & Director, Corporate Services, Halton Hills, 710
DeSousa, FCA, Alan, Maire d'arrondissement, Montréal, 738
Despres, C., Director, Moncton / Ville de Moncton, 506-859-2608, 691
Desrochers, Daniel L., General Manager, Leon's Insulation, 267
Desrochers, Mélissa, Vice-présidente, Association de l'exploration minière de Québec, 831
Desrochers, Paul, Director of Operations, Pol R Enterprises Inc., 327
Desrochers, Yvan, Managing Partner, Utility Risk Management Ltd., 408
DesRoches, Alan, Marketing Manager, DPL Group, 166
Desroches, Daniel, Directeur général, Saint-Jean-sur-Richelieu, 450-357-2383, 742
Desroches, Steve, Ottawa, 613-580-2751, 716
Desrosiers, Françoise, Périodiques et service de consultation, CÉGEP de Drummondville, 1167
Desrosiers, Jean-Guy, Maire, Montmagny, 738
Desrosiers-Harvey, Mylaine, Ogilvy Renault LLP/S.E.N.C.R.L., s.r.l. - Québec, 1088
Dessureault, Carmen, Bibliotechnicienne, Québec Office des personnes handicapées, 1175
Dessureault, Pierre, Contact, Chemco Inc., 139
Desveaux, Kim, Councillor, Cape Breton, 695
Detheridge, Claire, Councillor, Cape Breton, 695
DeThomasis, Tony, Superintendent, Roads & Parks, Amherstburg, 705
Detière, Laurence, Davies Ward Phillips & Vineberg S.E.N.C.R.L., s.r.l., 1083
Deuel, John, Manager, Engineered Air, 180
Deutsch, Thomas J., Lang Michener LLP - Vancouver, 1060
Deveau, Marcel, Vice-President, O'Halloran Campbell Consultants Limited, 310
Deveault, Hélène, Greffière, Nicolet-Yamaska, 750
Deveaux, Nicole, CFO, North Vancouver, 604-990-2234, 688
Devenis, Peter, President, Envision Planning Solutions Inc., 188
Deverall, Rob, President, ALS Environmental, 80
Devereaux, Barbara, Library Technician, Port aux Basques Campus Library, 1131
Devereux, Jeremy J., Partner, Ogilvy Renault LLP/S.E.N.C.R.L., s.r.l. - Toronto, 1078
Deverman, Ron, President, National Association of Environmental Professionals, 957
DeViet, Aina, Middlesex Centre, 727
Devine, Kim, Communications Officer, 639
Devine, Patrick J., Fraser Milner Casgrain LLP - Toronto, 1075
Devine, Ted, Secretary, Association of Supervisors of Public Health Inspectors (Ontario), 840
Devine, B.A., Kim, Charlottetown, 732
Devins, John, President, Sandhill Disposal & Recycling Inc., 356
Devion, Catherine, Coordinator, Circulation & Access, University of Toronto Scarborough Library, 1163
Devitt, Crosby, Research Manager, Ontario Soybean Growers, 979
Devlin, Calvin, President, Cal's Eco Depot, 121
Devlin, Corbin D., McLennan Ross LLP, 1055
Devlin, Robert, General Manager, Mondo Products Company Limited, 292
Devos, Henry, McElhanney Consulting Services Ltd., 285
Devost-Rivard, Monique, Coordonnatrice, Collège de Maisonneuve, 1172
DeVries, Andrew, Director, Forest Products Association of Canada, 918
DeVries, J., Director, Building Services, & Chief Building Offi, Richmond Hill, 718
DeVries, Marvin R., President/CEO, Trojan Technologies Inc., 403
Dewancker, John, Director, Environmental Services, & City Engineer, St. Thomas, 719
Dewar, Edgar, Chair, Southeast Environmental Association, 1010
Dewar, Karen, Director, Genome Canada, 923
Dewar, Keith, Deputy Minister, 640
Dewar, Keith, Director General, 545
Dewar, Matthew L., Lang Michener LLP - Toronto, 1077
Dewar, Scott, President, Dewar Insulations Ltd., 162
Dewasha, Mervin, CEO, R.J. Burnside & Associates Limited, 340
Dewey, Krista, Director, Hants East District, 697
Dewhirst, R., Director, Fire Services, St. Clair, 729
DeWilde, John, Pottinger Gaherty Environmental Consultants Ltd., 329
Dex, Daniel D., Lang Michener LLP - Vancouver, 1060
Dexter, David, Treasurer & Director, Financial Services, Richmond Hill, 718
Dextraze, Dave, Director, Wetaskiwin County No. 10, 780-361-6230, 670
Dey Nuttall, Anita, Associate Director, Canadian Circumpolar Institute, 862
Dhaliwal, Raj, Osler, Hoskin & Harcourt LLP - Toronto, 1079
Dhaliwal, Sav, Metro Vancouver, 679, 678
Dhaliwal, MD, Dhali, Chair, Manitoba Tobacco Reduction Alliance, 952
Dhillon, Vicky, City Councillor, Brampton, 706
Dhir, Sandeep K., Field Law - Edmonton, 1055
Di Biase, Michael, York, 705
Di Biase, Michael, Regional Councillor, Vaughan, 722
Di Campo, Pierre, Bibliothécaire, Centre de recherche et de développement en horticulture, 1183
Di Cesare, Marco, Representative, Ventes Techniques Nimatec inc., 411
Di Felice, Dolores, Partner, Borden Ladner Gervais LLP - Toronto, 1073
Di Giorgio, Frank, Toronto, 721
Di Gironimo, Lou, General Manager, Toronto Water, Toronto, 416-392-8200, 721
Di Lorenzo, Rick, Milton, 714
Di Loreto, Steve, Director, Waterous Power Systems, 422
Di Lullo, Michael, Clerk & Manager, Corporate Services, South Huron, 730
Di Muccio, Maddie, Newmarket, 714
Di Persio, Barb, Director HR, Northern Lights Regional Health Centre, 1107
Di Piazza, Ivo, Maire, Baie-Comeau, 418-296-8101, 733
Di Piazza, Ivo, Préfet, Manicouagan, 750
Di Pietro, Joseph, Conseiller d'arrondissement, Pointe-aux-Prairies, Montréal, 738
Dia Touré, Fatimata, Directrice, Institut de l'énergie et de l'environnement de la Francophonie, 931
Diadelfo, Angelo, President, Environmental Remediation Equipment Inc., 186
Diamant, Peter, Chair, 589
Diamond, Denise, Bibliothécaire, Bibliothèque paramédicale, 1171
Diamond, Nancy, Durham, 699
Diamond, Nancy, Regional Councillor, Oshawa, 716
Diamond, Stephen, McCarthy Tétrault LLP - Toronto, 1077
Dian, Martosoebroto, Trade Commissioner, 768
DiBarbora, Lisa, Virtual Services Librarian, Humber College Institute of Technology & Advanced Learning, 1158
Dibbelt, Dan, Executive Director, 566
Dicaire, Lorraine, Russell, 729
Dicerni, Richard, Deputy Minister, 543
DiCesare, D.J., President/CEO, Atlantic Engineering Consultants Ltd., 95
DiCiocco, Tony, Manager, Engineering Services, Lakeshore, 712
Dick, Bruce, Vice-President, Expocrete Concrete Products Ltd., 192
Dick, Dennis, Councillor, Niagara-on-the-Lake, 715
Dick, Georges P., President/CEO, Groupe RSW inc., 220
Dick, MSW, Kenneth C.R., General Manager, Social & Health Services, Lambton, 701
Dickerson, Doug, City Councillor, Pickering, 718
Dickie, Rob, President, Nichols Environmental (Canada) Ltd., 304
Dickie, Q.C., Gregory W., Partner, Ottenheimer Baker, 1066
Dickinson, Daniel M., Director, BFI Canada Inc., 106
Dickinson, Dawn, Contact, Grasslands Naturalists, 925
Dickinson, Evan, Stikeman Elliott LLP - Calgary, 1053
Dickinson, Geoff, Contact, Terratlantic Engineering Ltd., 391
Dickinson, Jan, Executive Director, London Regional Resource Centre for Heritage & the Environment, 949
Dickinson, Ron, Director, Kelowna, 681

Executive Name Index

Dickinson, Ross, President, Eneco Industries Ltd., 178
Dicks, Kirk, Manager, Veolia ES Canada Industrial Services Inc., 412
Dicks, Terry, Fire Chief, Norfolk, 519-426-4115, 702
Dickson, Cathy, Vice-President, Health Sciences Association of Saskatchewan, 928
Dickson, James M., Stewart McKelvey Stirling Scales - Halifax, 1067
Dickson, Jeff, Branch Manager, Maitland Engineering, 279
Dickson, Kelly, Library Technician, Natural Resources Canada, Canadian Forest Service, 1128
Dickson, Linda, Coordinator, Community Emergency Management, Wellington, 519-846-8058, 705
Dickson, Louise, Library Technician, Nexen Inc., 1102
DiClemente, Lucio, President, The Beer Store, 391
DiCosimo, Joanne, President/CEO, 518
Diegel, Leslie A., Manager, Administration, Canadian Association of Oilwell Drilling Contractors, 1100
Diehl, Randy H., CAO, Kamloops, 250-828-3498, 681
Diemer, Dan, Lakeshore, 712
Diemer, Tom, President, Great Lakes Safety Products Inc., 216
Diemer, Ulli, Head, Connexions Information Sharing Services, 1157
Dieners, Claus, Operations Manager, Fabco Plastics Wholesale (Ontario) Limited, 193
Dies, Joanne, Ajax, 705
Dietrich, Jim, Huron, 701
Dietrich, Ken, Foreman, Wilmot, 732
Dietrich, Shawn, Calgary Sales Manager, Endress+Hauser Canada Ltd., 178
Dietrick, Linda, Acting University Librarian, University of Winnipeg, 1126
Dietzler, Tim, Fieldman, Rocky View No. 44, 403-520-1271, 670
DiFlavio, Nick, Grimsby, 905-309-4133, 710
DiFolco, Sylviane, Directrice, Repentigny, 450-470-3400, 740
Digby, Karl, Supervisor, Mount Waddington, 678
Diges, Carmen, McMillan Binch Mendelsohn - Toronto, 1077
DiGiovanni, Dan, Chief Administrative Officer, Kingsville, 712
Di-Giovanni, Franco, Sr. Air Quality Manager, Airzone One Ltd., 76
Dignan, Annette, Librarian, Metro Vancouver (formerly Greater Vancouver Regional District), 1110
Dignan-Rumble, Debi, Brantford, 707
Digout, Louis, CAO, Richmond County, 698
Diguer, Christine, Montréal Office Manager, Québec-Labrador Foundation (Canada) Inc., 991
Dilkens, Drew, Windsor, 723
Dillard, Sylvie, Présidente-directrice générale, 648
Dillon, Eddie, Chair, 608
Dimarco, Tony, Welland, 722
Dimond, Michael F., President, CHEP Canada, 140
Dinel, Pierre, Directeur, Westburne Canada, 427
Dineley, S. Luke, Borden Ladner Gervais LLP - Vancouver, 1058
Dinino, Tony, Envirochem Services Inc., 183
Dinovitzer, Aaron, President, BMT Fleet Technology Ltd., 111
Dinsdale, Henry Y., Partner, Heenan Blaikie LLP - Toronto, 1075
Dinwoodie, Murray, City Manager, Surrey, 604-591-4441, 684
Diodati, Jim, Mayor, Niagara Falls, 715
Dion, Chantale, Documentaliste, Gazoduc Trans Québec & Maritimes Inc., 1166
Dion, Ginette, Information Specialist, Fisheries & Oceans Canada, 1150
Dion, Joseph, Director, 520
Dion, Jérôme, Director, SPG Hydro International Inc., 375
Dion, Marc, Sous-ministre, 646
Dion, Olivia, Coordinator, H2O Innovation Inc., 223
Dion, Raymond, Québec, 740
Dion, Serge, Châteauguay, 450-691-6088, 735
Dion-Audette, Nicole, Saint-Hyacinthe, 742
Dionne, Benoît, Sherbrooke, 744
Dionne, François, President, Socodec Inc., 372
Dionne, Paul, Director, Edmundston, 506-739-2103, 691
Dioszeghy, Jozsef, Director, North Vancouver, 604-990-3828, 688
Diotte, Kerry, Edmonton, 672
Diotte, Marie-Josée, Responsable, Service du prêt, Campus de Shippagan, 1130
DiPasquale, Bart, Amherstburg, 705
DiPietro, Barbara, Vice-President, Conservation International, 901
Diponio, Pete, Regional Director General, Windsor - St. Clair Reg, 514
Dipple, John A., Partner, MacPherson Leslie & Tyerman LLP - Regina, 1090

Dirk, Pat, President, Association of Alberta Agricultural Fieldmen, 834
Dirks, Jeff, General Manager, Biogénie, 108
Dischiavi, Tony, Imalog Inc., 238
Dishan, Brad, Librarian, St Joseph's Health Care, London, 1144
Distasio, Jino, Director, Institute of Urban Studies, 934
Dittaro, Donna, CAO, Rainy River District Social Services Administ, Rainy River, 729
Diveky, Janet, Library Technician, Northwest Territories Public Works & Services, 1134
Dixon, Belinda, Administrative Assistant, Pollutech Environmental Ltd., 1146
Dixon, Dave, Environmental Manager, Warren's Imaging & Dryography Inc., 417
Dixon, Neil, Supervisor, Waste Management, Cornwall, 708
Dixon, Robert, Commissioner, Corporate & Financial Services, Newmarket, 714
Djeffal, Salah, Manager, Bubble Technology Industries Inc., 118
Djokic, Mirela, Public Services Librarian, Kwantlen University College, 1113
Djurdevic, Joco, President, Yugo-Tech, 435
Djurfors, Iris, Librarian, Environmental Law Centre, 1105
Doan, Donald, Oxford, 519-863-2709, 728
Doan, Donald, Mayor, Norwich, 728
Doan, Doug, Assistant Deputy Minister, 607
Doan-Crider, Diana, Secretary, International Association for Bear Research & Management, 934
Dobbin, Bradley S., Stones Carbert Waite Wells LLP, 1054
Dobell, Colin, President, Inuktun Services Ltd., 246
Dobni, George, Managing Director, 656
Dobrowolski, Greg, Manager, Dawson Creek, 250-784-3619, 680
Dobson, Bill, Lanark, 701
Dobson, Mary, Information Services Librarian, Cape Breton University, 1137
Dobush, Tim, CEO, Geosoft, 212
Docherty, Valerie E., Minister, 641
Dochstader, Jim, President/CEO, Ecotech Planners & Advisors Inc., 172
Dockerty, Steve, President, Romatec Incorporated, 350
Dodd, Sheila, Supervisor, Whitehorse, 867-668-8660, 755
Dodds, Karen, Executive Director, 533
Dodge, Dawn, St. Catharines, 905-934-9138, 719
Dodge, William, President & CEO, Graymont Inc., 216
Dodic, Rajko, Mayor, Lethbridge, 403-320-3823, 673
Dodson, Mark, Executive Vice President, Daybar Industries Ltd., 158
Doehler, Joachim G., President, Greater Toronto Water Garden & Horticultural Society, 925
Doelle, Meinhard, Stewart McKelvey Stirling Scales - Halifax, 1067
Doepker, Sharon, Librarian, Prairie Agricultural Machinery Institute, 1187
Doerksen, Darlene, Chief Executive Officer, Yukon Tourism Education Council, 1024
Doge, Trish, Director, Vancouver, 604-873-7011, 685
Doherty, Cliff, Director, Squamish, 688
Doherty, Edward, Minister, 597
Doherty, Jean, Communications Officer, 638
Doherty, Ken, Director, Community Services, Peterborough, 718
Doherty, Myron, Pacific Regional Manager, ESRI Canada Ltd., 190
Doherty, Myron, Regional Manager, ESRI Canada Ltd., 190
Doherty, Tracey, Contact, Lexmark Canada Inc., 271
Doiron, Brian, Owner, B.D. Rae Waste Management, 100
Doiron, Cheryl A., Deputy Minister, 613
Dol, Joe, President, Dol Hydroseeding Inc., 164
Dol, Roger, Seeding Manager, Dol Hydroseeding Inc., 164
Dolbec, Gilles, Maire, Saint-Jean-sur-Richelieu, 450-357-2095, 742
Dolbec, Gilles, Préfet, Le Haut-Richelieu, 749
Dolbec, Jean-François, Partner, Heenan Blaikie S.E.N.C.R.L./SRL - Québec, 1087
Dolberg, Andy, Executive Director, British Columbia Agriculture Council, 846
Dolberg, Andy, Manager, British Columbia Farm Industry Review Board, 847
Dolcetti, Jerry, Commissioner, Engineering & Planning, Sault Ste. Marie, 720
Dolezsar, Richard, Executive Director, Urban Municipal Administrators' Association of Saskatchewan, 1016
Dollin, Lynn, Innisfil, 711
Dolter, Michael, CAO, Corner Brook, 709-637-1532, 693
Dombrowski, Alain, Directeur régional, ESRI Canada Ltd., 190
Dombrowsky, Leona, Minister, 619

Dominell, Ralph, Fire Chief, Orillia, 716
Dominelli, Fern, Chief Administrative Officer, Manitoulin-Sudbury D, Sudbury District, 731
Dominelli, Nick, Director, Powertech Labs Inc., 329
Domke, Dave, Manager, Winnipeg, 690
Domorski, Paul, President/CEO, EMS Technologies, 178
Dompierre, Richer, Conseiller, Louis-Riel, Montréal, 738
Don, Gary, Territory Sales Manager, National Energy Equipment Inc., 297
Don, Margaret, Membership Secretary, Ottawa Valley Rock Garden & Horticultural Society, 983
Don, Osmond, Secretary, Conference of New England Governors & Eastern Canadian Premiers, 764
Don, Osmond, Secretary to Council, Council of Atlantic Premiers, 764
Donaghy, David, CAO, Springfield, 690
Donahue, Madeleine, Partner, Macleod Dixon LLP, 1077
Donais, Daniel, Ingénieur, Experts-Conseils BMST inc., 192
Donais, Michel, Pompage Express M.D. Inc., 328
Donaldson, Keith, Director, Apex Industries Inc., 87
Donaldson, Paisley, Mayor, Gravenhurst, 705-689-8334, 709
Donaldson, Wanda, Hastings, 700
Donat, Naomi, Manager, Northern Interior Vegetation Management Association, 966
Donnelly, Darren T., Clark Wilson LLP, 1058
Donnelly, Fin, Coquitlam, 688
Donnelly, Frank, Chief Technology Officer, RailPower Technologies Corp., 342
Donnelly, Margaret, Research & Cataloguing Librarian, Yukon Dept. of Energy, Mines & Resources, 1191
Donnelly, Mike, Manager, Nanaimo, 678
Donnelly, Sean, Vice-President, ArcelorMittal Dofasco, 90
Donoghue, Brenna, Director of Operations, Engineers Without Borders, 910
Donoghue, Christine, Assistant Deputy Minister, 549
Donoghue, Joe, Councillor, Gravenhurst, 709
Donohoe, P.Geo, Howard, Executive Director & Registrar, Association of Professional Geoscientists of Nova Scotia, 839
Donovan, Allan, Donovan & Company, 1059
Donovan, Jeremy, Pinchin Environmental Ltd., 324
Donovan, Jim, Fire Chief, Elizabethtown-Kitley, 725
Donovan, Jim, Project Manager, Halifax Regional Municipality, 902-490-1742, 695
Donovan, Terry, Public Services Librarian, Portage College, 1108
Donovan, B.Sc., LL.B., Mary Ellen, Director, Halifax Regional Municipality, 902-490-4226, 695
Doody, Michael J.J., Timmins, 721
Doody, Peter K., Borden Ladner Gervais LLP - Ottawa, 1070
Dooks, William, Minister, 616
Dooley, Sarah Jane, Reference & Liaison Librarian, Sexton Design & Technology Library, 1136
Dooley, Thomas P., Aikins, MacAulay & Thorvaldson LLP, 1063
Dooling, Lisa, Executive Lead, 574
Doomekamp, Marten, Eastern Branch Manager, EcoTec Environmental Consultants Inc., 172
Doon, Mary, Librarian, St. Andrews Campus, 1129
Doran, Cheryl, Chair, Greenspace Alliance of Canada's Capital, 926
Doran, Dec, Owner/Operator, Oil Spill Control Services Canada, 311
Doran, Martin, Sales Manager, Hanson Pressure Pipe, 225
Doray, Raymond, Partner, Lavery, de Billy - Montréal, 1085
Doré, Robert, Director, Research & Development Institute for the Agri-Environment, 994
Doricic, Susan, Library Technician, Teck Resources, 1119
Dorion, Guy, Tecumseh, 519-735-8580, 720
Dorion, Q.C., Marc N., McCarthy Tétrault LLP - Québec, 1088
Doris, Jack, Peterborough, 718
Dornan, Bev, Langley, 687
Dorosz, Wanda, CEO & Managing Partner, Quorum Growth Inc., 339
Dort-MacLean, Ann, President, Wood Buffalo Environmental Association, 1021
Dorval, Christine, Library Technician, Northern College of Applied Arts & Technology, 1156
Dos Santos, Isabel, Conseillère d'arrondissement, Jeanne-Mance, Montréal, 738
Doss, Joseph K., President, International Bottled Water Association, 936
Dossetor, John, Lead, Monsanto Canada Inc., 293
Dostie, Paul E., Vice-President, Douglas Brothers, 165
Doucet, André, City Manager, Bathurst, 506-548-0733, 690
Doucet, André, Gestionnaire, Veolia ES Canada Industrial Services Inc., 411
Doucet, Brian, Maritime Paper Products Ltd., 281

Executive Name Index

Doucet, Claude, Directeur, Gatineau, 735
Doucet, Claude, Sec.-Trés., Régie intermunicipale d'assainissement des eaux du Trois-Rivières, 760
Doucet, Lola, City Clerk, Bathurst, 506-548-0417, 690
Doucet, Luce, Greffière, Saint-Basile-le-Grand, 741
Doucet, Marc, Greffier, Rimouski, 418-724-3125, 740
Doucet, Patrick, Sylviculture Manager, North Shore Forest Products Marketing Board, 966
Doucet, Paul-René, Directeur, Saint-Félicien, 742
Doucet, Suzanne, Librarian, Dr. D.A. Thompson Memorial Library, 1126
Doucet, Yvon A., Port Colborne, 718
Doucette, Catherine, Officer, Fundy Region Solid Waste Commission, 758
Doucette, Patricia, Manager, Library Services, Holland College, 1165
Doucette, Sarah, Toronto, 721
Doug, Bunting, Manager, Westburne Canada, 427
Dougall, Janine, Director, Bulkley-Nechako, 250-692-3195, 676
Dougan, Elaine, Executive Director, 571
Dougan, James, Principal & Sr. Ecologist, Dougan & Associates, 165
Doughty, Claude, Muskoka, 702
Doughty, Claude, Mayor, Huntsville, 711
Douglas, Allen, Plant Manager, CCS Income Trust, 134
Douglas, Anne, Director, 572
Douglas, Barry, Treasurer, Niagara Peninsula Geological Society, 964
Douglas, Brian, Deputy Minister, 636
Douglas, Darryl, Borden Ladner Gervais LLP - Calgary, 1049
Douglas, Dave, Director, Powell River, 683
Douglas, Heather, Partner, Borden Ladner Gervais LLP - Toronto, 1073
Douglas, John, Managing Director/CEO, Coffey Geotechnics Inc., 146
Douglas, Ken, President, Delta Aerial Surveys Ltd., 160
Douglas, Marianne S., Director, Canadian Circumpolar Institute, 862
Douglas, Murray W., Kanuka Thuringer LLP, Barristers & Solicitors, 1090
Douglas, Vern, Director, Building & By-law Enforcement, Orangeville, 716
Douglas, William T., Fire Chief, Pickering, 905-839-9968, 718
Dove, Larry J., President, Dove Environmental Services Inc., 166
Dover, Pegi, Executive Director, Canadian Environmental Grantmakers' Network, 867
Dow, John R., Partner, Stikeman Elliott LLP - Toronto, 1080
Dowd, Holly, Town Clerk, Niagara-on-the-Lake, 715
Dowdall, Terry, Simcoe, 704
Dowdall, Terry, Deputy Mayor & Councillor, Essa, 705-423-1154, 725
Dowding, Ian, CEO, Anco Chemicals Inc., 85
Dowell, Eric, Director, Fire & Emergency Services, Severn, 729
Dowey, Sandra, City Clerk, North Vancouver, 682
Dowler, James A., Alexander Holburn Beaudin & Lang, LLP, 1057
Dowling, Ron, Summerside, 733
Downe, Don, Warden, Lunenburg District, 697
Downer, James, Simcoe, 704
Downes, Rick, Councillor, Kingston, 712
Downie, Karin, Access Service Manager, Durham College of Applied Arts & Technology, 1147
Downing, Debra, Contact, Canada-Newfoundland Offshore Petroleum Board, 1131
Downs, Carolyn, City Clerk, Kingston, 712
Downs, Darcy, President, Levy's Machine Works Ltd., 271
Downs, Susan, Director, Corporate Services & Chief Librarian, Innisfil, 711
Downs, Warren H., Davis LLP - Vancouver, 1059
Dowson, Bill, Huron, 701
Doyle, Cassie J., Commissioner, 552
Doyle, Cassie J., Deputy Minister, 549
Doyle, Colin, Director, Saanich, 250-475-5447, 688
Doyle, Glen, Acting Director, 640
Doyle, Heather, Manager, Petroleum Services Association of Canada, 986
Doyle, Jean-Guy, Controller, MICCA Paints Inc., 288
Doyle, Jim, Field Law - Calgary, 1051
Doyle, Martin, Troy-Ontor Inc., 404
Doyon, Luc, Chairman & CEO, Air Liquide Canada Ltée, 75
Doyon, Roger, Directeur, Westburne Canada, 428
Dozzi, Brent, Manager, West Vancouver, 604-925-7157, 689
Dozzi, Christina A., Carscallen Leitch LLP, 1050
Drabinsky, Howard M., Lang Michener LLP - Toronto, 1077
Drackley, Don, Associate, IBI Group, 238

Draeger, Martin, Manager, Schlumberger Water Services, 359
Dragasevich, John, President, Filter Innovations Inc., 195
Dragasevich, Maureen, Manager, Filter Innovations Inc., 195
Drager, Q.C., Paul P., Partner, Macleod Dixon LLP, 1052
Drainville, André, Directeur, Boisbriand, 734
Dramalis, Dan, President, EnviroGuard Ltd., 184
Drance, Jonathan S., Partner, Stikeman Elliott LLP - Vancouver, 1062
Drapeau, Micheline, Directrice, Bibliothèque des sciences juridiques, 1171
Drapeau, Robert, President, Construction Val-d'Or Ltée, 150
Drapeau, Steven, Administrator, Construction Val-d'Or Ltée, 150
Drapeau, Suzanne, Responsable, Centre hospitalier régional du Grand-Portage, 1182
Drapeau-Miles, Monique, Executive Director, 591
Draper, Dennis, Senior Policy Advisor, 626
Draude, June, Minister, 659
Draude, June, Minister Responsible, 661
Drechsler, Marie, Manager, Universal Handling Equipment Company Limited, 406
Drescher, Gay, Director, Rothesay, 692
Drescher, Richard, Vice-President, CMD Insurance Services Inc., 144
Dresen, Deborah L., Davis LLP - Edmonton, 1055
Dresher, Drew, Sr. Vice-President, CH2M Hill Canada Limited, 137
Drew, Bobbie, Durham, 699
Drew, Bobbie, Regional Councillor, Scugog, 729
Drew, Dorothy, Librarian, Southern Crop Protection & Food Research Centre, 1164
Drew, Ralph, Metro Vancouver, 678
Drewry, Q.C., Richard B., Emery Jamieson LLP, 1055
Drexler, Julianna, Head Librarian, York University Glendon College Campus, 1164
Drinkwater, Bryan, Manager, Tillsonburg, 721
Driol, Chris, President, Health Sciences Association of Saskatchewan, 928
Driscoll, Murray, Mayor, Quispamsis, 506-849-5992, 692
Drolet, Christian, Partner, Heenan Blaikie S.E.N.C.R.L./SRL - Québec, 1088
Drolet, Normand, Associé, Cain Lamarre Casgrain Wells - Québec, 1088
Drolet, René, Director, 549
Drope, Heather, Sec.-Treas., Nova Scotia Wild Flora Society, 969
Droppo, Q.C., Dallas L., Blake, Cassels & Graydon LLP - Calgary, 1049
Drouin, Caroline, Secrétaire générale et Directrice, 646
Drouin, Guy, President, Biothermica, 109
Drouin, Hugh A., Commissioner, Social Services Department, Durham, 699
Drouin, Jacques L., President/CEO, ProSep Inc., 335
Drouin, Nicole, Greffière, Pincourt, 739
Drouin, Paul, President, Option Environnement Inc., 313
Drouin, Paule, SMTE-Bibliothécaire, CÉGEP de Lévis-Lauzon, 1169
Drouin, Roger, Technical Sales, Avoca-tec Environmental Services Inc., 99
Drouin, Régis, Saint-Georges, 742
Drouin, Serge, Directeur général, Candiac, 734
Drover, John, Director, 599
Drumhiller, Earnest (Hank), Vice-President & General Manager, Operations, 511
Drumm, Joe, Durham, 699
Drumm, Joe, Regional Councillor, Whitby, 723
Drummond, Sheila, Reference Librarian, Medicine Hat College, 1109
Drury, Gib, Chairman, Canada Beef Export Federation, 852
Drysdale, Karl, Director, Technology Services, London, 713
Du Plessis, Claude, Président, Geostat Systems International Inc., 212
Du Sault, Carole, Conseillère, Étienne-Desmarteau, Montréal, 738
Dubé, Diane, Sec.-Trés., Régie intermunicipale d'assainissement des eaux de Sainte-Thérèse, 760
Dubé, Diane, Vice-President, Export Development Canada, 192
Dubé, François, Director, Technology & Research Services, Canada Institute for Scientific & Technical Information (CISTI), 1148
Dubé, Jacques, City Manager, Moncton / Ville de Moncton, 506-853-3498, 691
Dubé, Jean, Directeur général, Lévis, 418-839-2002, 736
Dubé, Michel, Edmundston, 691
Dubé, Paul, Chief Executive Officer, Newfoundland & Labrador Association of Technology Companies, 962
Dubé, Sylvie, Référence-PEB, CÉGEP de Lévis-Lauzon, 1169

Dubeau, Anita, Simcoe, 704
Dubeau, Colin, Nelligan O'Brien Payne, 1071
Dubeau, Michel, President/CEO, Santinel Inc., 357
Duben, Michael, General Manager, Community & Protective Services, Windsor, 723
Dubenofsky, Deborah, City Manager, Brampton, 706
Dubernet, L., Administrative Assistant, Canadian Council for Tobacco Control, 864
Dublanko, Deryld, Manager, Leduc County, 780-955-2469, 669
Dubois, Bev, Saskatoon, 754
Dubois, Christian G., Conseiller de ville, Montréal, 738
Dubois, Claire, Chef de bibliothèque, Bibliothèque de physique, 1170
Dubois, Daniel, Directeur, Saint-Hyacinthe, 742
Dubois, Gaetane, Administrative Assistant, Ontario Forestry Safe Workplace Association, 1146
Dubois, Guy, Chef de police, Terrebonne, 745
Dubois, Laval, Directeur général, Bécancour, 747
Dubois, Maxine, Éocycle Technologies Inc., 188
Dubois, Nathalie, Director, 598
Dubois, Susie, Sec.-Trés., Régie d'assainissement des eaux usées Rougemont/St-Césaire, 759
Dubois, Sylvain, Directeur, Laval, 450-978-6888, 736
Dubois, Yves A., Partner, Borden Ladner Gervais LLP - Montréal, 1083
Dubois-Flynn, Geneviève, Director, 519
Dubrick, Geoff, Manager, Wilmot, 732
Dubuc, Martine, Vice-President, 518
DuBuc, Michel, Firing Industries Ltd., 196
DuBuc, Michel, President, Firing Industries Ltd., 195
Dubuc-Johnson, Lorraine, Sept-Iles, 744
Ducas, Ada, Head Librarian, Neil John Maclean Health Sciences Library, 1125
Ducey, Aloysius, Owner, BSM North America, 118
Ducharme, Alain, Corporate Vice President, Cascades Resource, 131
Ducharme, Gaetan, Vice-President, Vibec International Inc., 413
Ducharme, Melanie, Municipal Clerk & Planner, West Nipissing, 705-753-2250, 732
Ducharme, René, Rouyn-Noranda, 741
Duchene, Michael, Project Director, EnviroMetal Technologies Inc., 184
Duchesne, Benoit M., Partner, Heenan Blaikie LLP - Ottawa, 1070
Duchesne, Caroline, Directrice, Conseil régional de l'environnement de la Gaspésie et des Iles-de, 901
Duchesne, Robin, Contact, Gestion Eaux Richelieu Inc., 212
Duchesneau, Bernard, Rouyn-Noranda, 741
Duckworth, David, Director, Kamloops, 681
Duckworth, Harry, President, Friends of the Delta Marsh Field Station, 921
Ducros, Francoise, Acting Vice-President, 520
Duczek, Loree, Public Education Coordinator, East Kootenay, 677
Dudas, Janice, Library Technician, Metro Vancouver (formerly Greater Vancouver Regional District), 1110
Duddeck, Cathy, Halton, 700
Duddeck, Cathy, Town & Regional Councillor, Oakville, 715
Dudley, Bruce, Sr. Vice-President, The Delphi Group, 392
Dudley, Michael, Research Associate, Institute of Urban Studies, 1124
Dudley, Scott, President/CEO, Armstrong Monitoring Corp., 91
Dueck, Annette E.F., Stikeman Elliott LLP - Vancouver, 1062
Dueck, Judy, Metro Vancouver, 687, 678
Dueck, Marnie, Municipal Clerk, Cranbrook, 680
Duerden, Colin, Manager, Duerden & Keane Consultants Inc., 167
Duff, John P., CEO, Eastcan Geomatics, 169
Duff, Shannie, Deputy Mayor & Councillor, St. John's, 709-576-8583, 694
Duff, Sheila, Technical Files Clerk, Canada-Newfoundland Offshore Petroleum Board, 1131
Duffy, Bill, Simcoe, 704
Duffy, Carol Anne, CEO, 642
Duffy, Chris, Director, 582
Duffy, Patrick, Stikeman Elliott LLP - Toronto, 1080
Duffy, Patrick, President, P.J.B. Duffy & Associates, 316
Dufort, Richard, Greffier & Directeur général, Saint-Lin-Laurentides, 743
Dufour, Christine, Directrice générale, Le Fjord-du-Saguenay, 749
Dufour, Eric J., Partner, Borden Ladner Gervais LLP - Toronto, 1073
Dufour, Geoff, Dufour Scott Phelps & Mason, 1090

Dufour, Jean-Pierre, Adjoint à la direction des études, CÉGEP de Jonquière, 1168
Dufour, Marie-Christine, Grondin, Poudrier, Bernier, 1087
Dufour, Marie-Hélène, Fraser Milner Casgrain S.E.N.C.R.L./LLP, 1084
Dufour, Michel, Branch Manager, Services industriels Newalta, 363
Dufresne, Alain, Manager, 521
Dufresne, Pierre, General Manager, ICI Paints (Canada) Inc., 238
Dufresne, Pierre, Sales, Romatec Incorporated, 351
Dufresne, Richard, Canadian Sales Vice-President, Stablex Canada Inc., 377
Dufton, Bob, Group Leader, AMEC, 83
Dugas, Arnold, Directeur général, Association sectorielle - Fabrication d'équipement de transport e, 842
Dugas, Ginette, Conseillère en ressources documentaires, Service de l'urbanisme, 1175
Dugas, Roberta, Chair, 598
Duggan, Lou, Systems Librarian, Cape Breton University, 1137
Dugré, Frédéric, President/CEO, H2O Innovation Inc., 223
Duguay, Monique, Manager, Nestlé Purina PetCare, 300
Duguay, Pat, Library Administration/Admin. Assistant, University of Winnipeg, 1126
Duguid, Brad, Minister, 619
Duhaime, Lynne, Coordinator, West Nipissing, 732
Duhaime, Pierre, President/CEO, SNC-Lavalin Group Inc., 371
Duhamel, Sylvie, Secrétaire du service, Ispat Sidbec inc., 1167
Duignan, Bob, City Manager, Oshawa, 905-436-5622, 716
Duimovich, George, Database Management, Natural Resources Canada, 1151
Dujardin, Michael, Controller, Canadian Hydrogen & Fuel Cell Association, 871
Dujlovic, Edward, Executive Director, Community Services, Niagara Falls, 715
Dujmovich, Christine-Louise, Librarian, Reference & Electronic Resources, Justice Institute of British Columbia, 1114
Duke, Laura E., Lawson Lundell LLP - Vancouver, 1061
Dukes, Nancy, Contact, Great Lakes Forestry Centre, 1154
Dul, Donna, Secretary, 587
Dulmage, Paul, Warden & Councillor, Lanark, 701
Dulude, France, Associée, Robinson Sheppard Shapiro LLP, 1087
Dulude, Marc, Exec. Vice-President, IMTT-Québec Ltd., 239
Dumanowski, Robert C., Medicine Hat, 673
Dumas, Angelo, Project Manager, Construction Val-d'Or Ltée, 150
Dumas, Jocelin, Sous-ministre, 655
Dumont, Donald, Victoriaville, 819-758-9169, 746
Dumont, Jean-René, Contact, Experts-Conseils CEP Inc., 192
Dumont, Marie-Josee, Wellons Canada, 424
Dumont, Rino, BPR, 115
Dumouchel, Bernard, Director General, Canada Institute for Scientific & Technical Information (CISTI), 1148
Dumouchel, Mona, Trésorière, Vaudreuil-Dorion, 450-424-8532, 746
Dumoulin, Guy, Lévis, 736
Dumoulin, Louis, Manager, Flygt Canada, 198
Dumoulin, Nicole, Directrice, Gatineau, 735
Dumoulin, Paul, Vaudreuil-Dorion, 746
Dumoulin, Ray-Marc, Saint-Hyacinthe, 742
Dunbar, Brian, President, Eastern Canada Orchid Society, 907
Dunbar, David, Inproheat Industries Ltd., 242
Dunbar, Peter, Director, Leisure Services, Collingwood, 708
Dunberry, Éric, Ogilvy Renault LLP/S.E.N.C.R.L., s.r.l. - Montréal, 1086
Duncan, Eric, Mayor, North Dundas, 730, 727
Duncan, George, CAO, Richmond, 604-276-4336, 684
Duncan, George, President, A&A Environmental Consultants Inc., 63
Duncan, Janne, Partner, Macleod Dixon LLP, 1077
Duncan, Jim, Co-Chair, 586
Duncan, Linda, Executive Director, Prince Edward Island Aquaculture Alliance, 988
Duncan, Matt, Councillor, North Perth, 715
Duncan, Pierre, Professionnel, Institut de technologie agro-alimentaire de la Pocatière, 1177
Duncan, Rob, Contact, Accurassay Laboratories, 63, 65
Duncan, Ph.D, Ian, President & Chair, Animal Welfare Foundation of Canada, 827
Dundas, Bruce, Fire Chief, Langley, 604-514-2881, 681
Dunderdale, Kathy, Minister, 603
Dunets Wills, Anna, Associate, Planning Alliance, 326
Dunlop, Jane, Severn, 729
Dunlop, Karen, Director, Public Works, North Grenville, 728

Dunlop, Paula, Director, Canadian Gas Association, 869
Dunn, Pat, Kawartha Lakes, 711
Dunn, Pat, Minister, 613
Dunn, Robin, Chief Administrative Officer, Oro-Medonte, 728
Dunn, Tanya, Executive Assistant, Ontario Centres of Excellence - Centre for Earth & Environmental, 972
Dunnill, Wilma, Library/Data Technician, Crompton Co./Cie, 1140
Dunphy, B.A., Paul, Director, Halifax Regional Municipality, 695
Dunsford, L.G., Dunsford & Scott, 1056
Dunsky, Ilan, Partner, Heenan Blaikie S.E.N.C.R.L/SRL, 1084
Dunsmoor, W.A., President & General Manager, All-Weld Company Limited, 79
Dupelle, Maurice, Cornwall, 708
DuPerré, Nicole, Technicienne en documentation, Collège d'Alma, 1166
Duplessis, Alexandre, Laval, 736
Duplessis, Guylène, Vaudreuil-Dorion, 746
Duplessis, Josée, Conseillère d'arrondissement, De Lorimier, Montréal, 738
Duplin, Jean-Pierre, Trésorier, Sainte-Julie, 450-922-7062, 743
Dupoint, Jacques, Sous-ministre adjoint, 646
Dupont, C., Consultant, Aqua-Plus, 88
Dupont, Josée, Directrice générale (par intérim), 654
Dupont, Normand, Blainville, 734
Dupont, Patrice, Information Specialist, NRC Information Centre, 1166
Dupont, Pierre A., Trois-Rivières, 745
Dupont, Robert, Shawinigan, 744
Dupont, Yvan, Chairman, AXOR Experts-Conseils Inc., 99
Dupont-Freill, Lori, Manager, Canadian Liquids Processors Limited, 124
Dupuis, Jean-Marc, Deputy Minister, 591
Dupuis, Marie-Hélène, Responsable, Services d'accès à l'information, École polytechnique de Montréal, 1173
Dupuis, Mario, FCX NH Valves, 194
Dupuis, Norm, Director, Alberta Forest Products Association, 817
Dupuis, Ron, Greater Sudbury / Grand Sudbury, 710
Duquette, Robert, Chef de division, Montréal, 738
Durance, Cynthia, President, Precision Identification Biological Consultants, 330
Durand, Simon, Directeur général, Union des cultivateurs franco-ontariens, 1014
Durando, Paola, Librarian, Public Services, Bracken Health Sciences Library, 1142
Durisin, Michael N., Bratty & Partners LLP, 1081
Durkin, Paul, President, Gryphon International Engineering Services Inc., 222
Durley, John, Pelham, 717
Durocher, André, Partner, Fasken Martineau - Montréal, 1083
Durocher, Claude, Coordonnateur, Services gestion documentaire, Université du Québec à Rimouski, 1181
Durocher, Claude, General Manager, Schlumberger Oilfield Services, 359
Durocher, Raphael, Radiation Technician, Monserco Ltd., 293
Durovick, Randy, Manager, Saskatchewan Parks & Recreation Association, 1001
Durrell, Melissa, Waterloo, 722
Dusdal, Herb, Director, Terrace, 250-615-4030, 685
Dussault, Chantal, Archivist, Canadian Museum of Nature, 1149
Dussault, Louis-Marie, Adjoint à la directrice, Collège Édouard-Montpetit, 1169
Dust, Theresa, City Solicitor, Saskatoon, 306-975-3270, 754
Dutchak, Kathleen, Services & Systems Librarian, British Columbia Institute of Technology, 1110
Dutfield, James H., Owner/Manager, The Brofield Group, 391
Dutil, Camil, President/CEO, Envirogain Inc., 184
Dutil, Marie-Ôve, Saint-Georges, 742
Dutil, Robert, Ministre, 652
Dutrisac, Evelyn, Greater Sudbury / Grand Sudbury, 710
Duval, Jean-Jacques, Président, Nouvelle Technologie (TEKNO) Inc., 308
Duval, Linda, President, Masternet Ltd., 282
Duval, Luc, Director, Vaudreuil-Dorion, 450-455-7636, 746
Duval, Luc, Director, Public Works & Engineering, Timmins, 721
Duval, Marc, Bibliothécaire consultant, QIT-Fer et Titane inc, 1186
Duval, Marie-Jeanne, Ogilvy Renault LLP/S.E.N.C.R.L., s.r.l. - Québec, 1088
Duval, Raymond, Directeur général, Rivière-du-Loup, 753
Duvall, Scott, Hamilton, 711
Dvorkin, Gary, President/CEO, Peel Scrap Metal Recycling Ltd., 320
Dvorkin, Richard, President, Calgary Metal (1985) Ltd., 121
Dwight, Stephen, Vice-President, Unisearch Associates Inc., 406
Dwyer, Brett, Manager, North Vancouver, 604-990-2247, 688

Dwyer, Pat, Pat Dwyer Construction Inc., 319
Dwyer, Peter, Senior Partner, William Alexander & Associates Ltd., 432
Dyble, John, Deputy Minister, 583
Dyck, Mark, Sales Representative, Fort Garry Industries Ltd., 200
Dyck, Philip A., Partner, Nixon Wenger, 1062
Dyer, Craig, Treasurer, Wellington, 705
Dyer, Dave, Chief Engineer, Prince George, 250-561-7663, 683
Dyer, Fiona, Manager, Library Services, Lethbridge Community College, 1108
Dyke, Gary, CAO, City Clerk, & Manager, Corporate & Economic D, Quinte West, 718
Dykhyuzen, Diane, Office Manager, Metrovan Hotsy Equipment Ltd., 288
Dykie, Jr., Peter, Bradford West Gwillimbury, 706
Dykstra, Bert, Huron, 701
Dykstra, Mark, Director, Environment & Parks Services, Waterloo, 519-747-8611, 722
Dymond, Doug, Manager, Columbia-Shuswap, 677
Dysart, J.E. Britt, Partner, Stewart McKelvey Stirling Scales - Fredericton, 1064
Dysart, Robert M., Stewart McKelvey Stirling Scales - Moncton, 1065
Dyson, Carson, Vice-President, Universal Handling Equipment Company Limited, 406
Dyson, Russell, City Clerk, Port Alberni, 683
Dziuba, Mike, Sales Manager, Transway Systems Inc., 400

E

Eadie, Alison, Barrie, 706
Eadie, Ross, Winnipeg, 690
Eagles, Christopher W., Partner, Borden Ladner Gervais LLP - Vancouver, 1058
Eagleson, Phil, Fire Chief, Saugeen Shores, 719
Eamon, Rick, Vice-President, M.S. Thompson & Associates Ltd., 276
Earle, Jeffery, Brockville, 707
Earle, Rick, Director, Burnaby, 604-294-7360, 679
Earle, Stephen, President, Anco Chemicals Inc., 85
Earle, Yvonne, Legislative Librarian, 617
East, Andrea M., Clark Wilson LLP, 1058
East, Ken, Vice-President & Director of Sales, Horton CBI Ltd., 233
Easterbrook, Bonnie, Controller, 517
Eastwood, M., Carrier Canada Ltd., 129
Eastwood, Paul, Reynolds, Mirth, Richards & Farmer LLP, 1056
Eastwood, Peter J., President, Chartis Insurance Company of Canada, 138
Easwaran, Linda, Controller, Wasteco, 421
Eaton, John, East Gwillimbury, 708
Eaton, John, Head Librarian, E.K. Williams Law Library, 1123
Eaton, Q.C., J. David B., McInnes Cooper, 1066
Eawgeweh, Shahrokh, Vice-President, Kinectrics Inc., 257
Ebbett, Gwendolyn, University Librarian, University of Windsor, 1165
Ébengué, J-F., Manager, Nortec S.G.S. Inc., 306
Eberle, David, Chairman, 663
Eberschlag, Robert W., Partner, Macleod Dixon LLP, 1077
Eby, Kevin, Director, Community Planning, Waterloo, 704
Eccles, Julie, General Manager, Zoological Society of Manitoba, 1025
Eccles, Kevin, Mayor, Grey, 732, 700
Eccleston, Marion, President, Oxford County Geological Society, 983, 1156
Eccleston, B.A., LL.B., Kenneth P., Partner, Eccleston LLP, 1075
Eckel, Alan, President, Eckel Industries, 170
Eckenfelder, Margaret, Director, North Vancouver, 604-990-2398, 688
Eckford, L., Treasurer & Deputy Clerk, Pembroke, 717
L'Écuyer, Daniel, Directeur général, Repentigny, 450-470-3110, 740
L'Écuyer, Isabelle, Heenan Blaikie S.E.N.C.R.L/SRL - Québec, 1088
Edde, Robert, DST Consulting Engineers, 167
Eddy, Ron, Mayor, Brant, 698
Edelman, Tim, President & CEO, GE Ground Engineering Ltd., 205
Eden, Ken, Fire Chief, Niagara-on-the-Lake, 715
Eder, Peter, President/CEO, Thermotech Windows Ltd., 395
Eder, Tim A., Executive Director, Great Lakes Commission, 925
Edey, David, General Manager, Edmonton, 780-496-7201, 672
Edgar, Ted, President/CEO, Can-Ross Environmental Services Ltd., 123

Executive Name Index

Edge, Brent, Supervisor, Penticton, 682
Edgecombe, Don, Director, 545
Edgington, Paul, CAO, Squamish-Lillooet, 679
Edgson, Kevin, Chief Financial Officer & Vice-President, Millar Western Forest Products Ltd., 290
Edie, Q.C., Donald C., Carscallen Leitch LLP, 1050
Edinger, H. David, Partner, Heenan Blaikie LLP - Vancouver, 1060
Edjericon, Richard, Chair, 542
Edmanson, Bill, President, Trent Metals Ltd., 401
Edmond, James G., Thompson Dorfman Sweatman LLP, 1064
Edmonds, Debbie, Town Clerk, Halton Hills, 710
Edmonds, Michael, Unit Manager, AMEC, 83
Edmondson, Al, Middlesex, 701
Edmondson, Al, Mayor, Middlesex Centre, 727
Edmondson, Debra E., Librarian, ADI Group, 1127
Edmunds, Eileen, Librarian, Powell River Campus, 1112, 1115
Edmunds, Eileen, Regional Campus Librarian, Powell River Campus, 1112, 1115
Edwards, Carole, Treasurer, Burke Mountain Naturalists, 851
Edwards, Cheryl A., Stringer, Brisbin, Humphrey Management Lawyers, 1080
Edwards, Cheryl A., Partner, Heenan Blaikie LLP - Toronto, 1075
Edwards, Don, President, Malnar Industries Ltd., 279
Edwards, Donald B., Partner, Borden Ladner Gervais LLP - Calgary, 1049
Edwards, Garry M., Clarence-Rockland, 708
Edwards, Gary, Plant Manager, CCS Income Trust, 134
Edwards, Glen, Councillor, Colchester County, 697
Edwards, Gord, Executive Director, Alberta Water Council, 820
Edwards, James S., Chair, ZCL Composites Inc., 436
Edwards, Jean Marc, Associate University Librarian, Information System, Concordia University Libraries, 1173
Edwards, John H., Mississippi Mills, 714
Edwards, Mike, Collingwood, 708
Edwards, Nancy, Manager, Vemco Ltd., 410
Edwards, Paul, Gowling Lafleur Henderson LLP - Calgary, 1051
Edwards, Randy, Terrapex Environmental Ltd., 390
Edwards, Sally, Director, Kamloops, 250-828-3413, 681
Edwards, Shane, Manager, Bartle & Gibson Co. Ltd., 102
Edwards, Steve, Manager, Whitby, 723
Edwards, William, Commissioner, Saint John, 506-658-2911, 692
Edwardson, Dean, General Manager, Sarnia-Lambton Environmental Association, 998
Edzerza, John, Minister, 665
Eegeesiak, Joamie, Officer, Iqaluit, 867-979-6363, 698
Eeles, David A., Partner, Macleod Dixon LLP, 1052
Egan, Kevin A., McKenzie Lake Lawyers LLP, 1069
Egan, Timothy M., President & Chief Executive Officer, Canadian Gas Association, 869
Eger, Jeff, Executive Director, Water Environment Federation, 1017
Egerton, Alfred, President, Egetec Enterprises Inc., 174
Egerton, Teresa, Inside Sales Manager, Puresource Inc., 337
Eggers, Doris, Director, 605
Eggertson, CAE, Bill, Executive Director, Canadian Association for Renewable Energies, 856
Eggleston, Tom, Director, Showa-Best Glove, Inc., 366
Eggleton, Cliff, Manager, Operations, Perth, 703
Eggum, Krista L.L., Eggum, Abrametz, Eggum, 1090
Egli, Graham K., Corporate Director, Sandwell Engineering Inc., 357
Egli, Keith, Ottawa, 716
Ehaloak, Sharon, Executive Director, 542
Ehgoetz, Rhonda, Perth East, 728
Ehmann, Q.C., James S., Kanuka Thuringer LLP, Barristers & Solicitors, 1090
Ehnes, Phil, Terminal City Iron Works Ltd., 390
Ehrlich, Alan, President, International Association for Impact Assessment - Western & North, 935
Ehrlich, Karl F., Vice-President, Bacta-Pur, 101
Eichenbaum, Tom, Director, Engineering, Burlington, 707
Eichenberger, Kathy, Project Assessment Director, 578
Eichenlaub, Naomi, Librarian, Technical Services, Royal Roads University, 1121
Eichler, Glenn, Regional Sales Manager, Wastequip Cusco, 421
Eid, Bassem, Vice President, BAE Newplan Group Ltd., 101
Eidemiller, Betty, Contact, Society of Toxicology, 1009
Eisan, Darryl C., Director, 614
Eisenhauer, J.D., CEO, ABCO Industries Ltd., 64
Eisner, Chantelle L., McDougall Gauley, 1090
Eisner, Ken, Assistant Sales Manager, Reinforced Plastic Systems Inc., 344
ejlb foundation, The EJLB Foundation, Montréal, QC, 1046

Eke, David, Mayor, Niagara-on-the-Lake, 715
El Ktaibi, Hicham, Sales Representative, GENEQ Inc., 206
Eladis, Constantine (Taki), Chair, Sustainable Buildings Canada, 1011
Elbaz, Andrew, Heenan Blaikie LLP - Toronto, 1075
El-Chantiry, Eli, Ottawa, 613-580-2475, 716
Elder, Darcy, Superintendent, Wood Buffalo, 780-799-7475, 670
Elder, David, Heenan Blaikie LLP - Calgary, 1051
Elder, Ken, Contact, Public Works, Centre Wellington, 519-846-9801, 724
Elder, Peter H., Director General, 520
Elder, Robert, President, Ontor Ltd., 313
Elderbroom, Bruce, Sales Agent, Danatec Educational Services Ltd., 157
Eldridge, Cyril, Manager, Powersmiths International Corp., 329
Elford, Robin K., Contact, Elford Environmental, 175
Elgar, Allan, Halton, 700
Elgar, Allan, Town & Regional Councillor, Oakville, 715
Elgersma, Amy, Director, Iqaluit, 867-979-5616, 698
El-Hallak, Mona, Senior Technical Director, ETV Canada, 190
Elhard, Wayne, Minister, 660
Elhard, Wayne, Provincial Secretary, 659
El-Hawary, Ferial, President, BH Engineering Systems Ltd., 107
Eliason, Jennifer, Executive Director, Habitat Acquisition Trust, 927
Eliasson, Hugh, Deputy Minister, 585
Elkins, Brad, Media Contact, ICI Paints (Canada) Inc., 238
Ell, David, Iqaluit, 698
Ell, John, President, ATCO Power, 95
Ellard, Bob, Vice-President, Stantec Inc., 378
Ellefsen, Harold, Directeur, Saint-Jean-sur-Richelieu, 742
Ellenwood, D., Director, Burnaby, 604-294-7450, 679
Ellerby, Robert, Controller, MKG Imaging Solutions Inc., 291
Ellerman, Brian, President, Condor Engineering Ltd., 149
Ellett, Claire E., Lang Michener LLP - Vancouver, 1060
Ellett, John S., President, Ellett Industries, 176
Elliot, Bill, Mayor, Wetaskiwin, 674
Elliot, Chris, Manager, Westburne Canada, 427
Elliot, Jeffrey, Partner, Stikeman Elliott LLP - Toronto, 1080
Elliot, John, Manager, Nanaimo, 681
Elliott, Bill, President/CEO, FortWhyte Alive, 919
Elliott, Chris, Sales Manager, Quester Tangent Corp., 339
Elliott, Claude, Mayor, Gander, 694
Elliott, Craig, General Manager, Finance & Administration, Simcoe, 704
Elliott, Cy, Manager, Elliott & Elliott Limited Consulting Engineers, 176
Elliott, David B., Port Colborne, 718
Elliott, Dylan, General Manager, Raw Materials Corporation, 342
Elliott, Gordon, Chair, Lakeland Regional Waste Management Services Commission, 757
Elliott, J., Manager, Comox Valley, 677
Elliott, Julie, Research Technician, Lakehead University, 263
Elliott, K.W., President, International Marine Salvage Inc., 245
Elliott, Mark, St. Catharines, 719
Elliott, Mark, Vice-President, Smiths Detection, 371
Elliott, Shari D., Graham Wilson & Green, Barristers & Solicitors, Notaries, Mediato, 1068
Elliott, Tim, Librarian, AMEC Inc., 1099
Elliott, Wayne, President, Raw Materials Corporation, 245, 342
Elliott-Spencer, M.B.A.,, Patricia, Treasurer & Director, Finance, Oakville, 715
Ellis, Aimee, Head, Library Services, Yukon Dept. of Energy, Mines & Resources, 1191
Ellis, Amber, Executive Director, Earthroots, 907
Ellis, Bob, Director, 660
Ellis, Bruce, Manager, SimplexGrinnell, 368
Ellis, C., Carrier Canada Ltd., 130
Ellis, Chris, Blaney McMurtry LLP, 1073
Ellis, D. Roy, President, Claus Engineering (1986) Ltd., 142
Ellis, Faron, Lethbridge, 673
Ellis, G. Henry, Gowling Lafleur Henderson LLP - Vancouver, 1060
Ellis, Glen, Library Technician, Winnipeg Water & Waste Dept., 1126
Ellis, Jim, Deputy Minister, 568
Ellis, Neil R., Mayor, Belleville, 613-967-3267, 706
Ellis, Patrick, Acting Associate University Librarian, Health Scie, W.K. Kellogg Health Sciences Library, 1136
Ellis, Richard H., University Librarian, Memorial University of Newfoundland, 1132
Ellis, Roberta, Vice-President, 584
Ellis, S., Manager, Economic Development, Recreation, & Touri, Pembroke, 717
Ellis, Vic, President, Ecology Products International, 172

Ellison, Michelle M., Ratcliff & Company LLP, 1057
Ellison, Q.C., W. Ross, Davis LLP - Vancouver, 1059
Ellmann, Peter, President, Lister Industries Ltd., 273
Ellmen, Eugene, Executive Director, Social Investment Organization, 1004
Ellsworth, Barry, Manager, Corner Brook, 709-637-1509, 693
Ellsworth, Curling, Group Leader, AMEC, 84
Ellsworth, Stephen, Templeman Menninga LLP, 1068
Elmslie, Doug, Kawartha Lakes, 711
Elnekave, Ruth, Stikeman Elliott LLP - Toronto, 1080
Elo-Sheperd, Brian, Director, Social Services, Lennox & Addington, 701
Eloyan, Noushig, Conseillère, Bordeaux-Cartierville, Montréal, 738
El-Rayes, Hamdy, President, El-Rayes Environmental Corp., 174
Elsdon, Stan R., President, Emco Wheaton Corp., 176
Elsey, Ken, President/CEO, Canadian Energy Efficiency Alliance, 866
Elston, John, Fire Chief & Supervisor, Emergency Services, Middlesex Centre, 727
Elsworth, P.Eng., Brian, Fire Chief, Milton, 714
El-Tahan, Mona, President/CEO, InCoretec Inc., 240
Eltom, Jeff, Executive Director, British Columbia Environment Industry Association, 847
Elton, Robert G., President/CEO, 580
Elyea, Trent, Fire Chief, Collingwood, 708
Emakpor, Tobor, Davis LLP - Toronto, 1074
Emakpor, Tobor, Partner, Osler, Hoskin & Harcourt LLP - Toronto, 1079
Emanuel, Chris, Newmarket, 714
Emanuels, Roger, Coordinator, New Westminster, 604-527-4540, 682
Embleton, Norm, Chief Information Officer, 607
Embree, Ken, Knight Piésold Ltd., 259
Emenau, Kevin, Contact, Conestoga-Rovers & Associates, 149
Emerson, Carolyn J., Chair, NSERC/Petro-Canada Chair for Women in Science & Engineering, 969
Emerson, Ron, Graecam Incorporated, 216
Emery, Alan, CFO, Emery International Developments, 177
Emery, Dave, Principal, Stantec Inc., 378
Emery, James, CEO, Emery International Developments, 177
Emery, John, Chair, Emery International Developments, 177
Emery, Martin, Manager, Westburne Canada, 426
Emery-Carter, Janice, Manager, Food & Consumer Products of Canada, 918
Emes, Aaron S., Torys LLP, 1080
Emin, Donna, Administration, Fundy Compost Inc., 203
Emm, Michael G., Councillor, Whitby, 723
Emmerson, Dana, President/CEO, Environmental Disposal Concepts Inc., 185
Emmerson, Wayne, York, 705
Emmerson, Wayne, Mayor, Whitchurch-Stouffville, 723
Emmett, Brian, Vice-President, Archipelago Marine Research Ltd., 90
Emmott, Harry, President, Ontario Association of Agricultural Societies, 971
Emms, Laurie, Director, Annapolis County, 902-584-2188, 696
Emon, Danielle, Library Technician, Technical Services, Loyalist College of Applied Arts & Technology, 1139
Emon, Peter, Renfrew, 613-752-2222, 704
Emond, Carol, PricewaterhouseCoopers Management Consultants, 332
Émond, François, Directeur du Cabinet, 646
Émond, Majella, Préfet, La Haute-Gaspésie, 748
Émond, Renée, President/CEO, Biolab Inc., 108
Emond, Ron, Warden & Councillor, Hastings, 700
Empey, Heather, Educations Services Librarian, University of Northern British Columbia, 1115
Emry, Greg, Marketing Manager, SEI Industries Ltd., 362
Enarson, Jeremy, Acting City Engineer, Camrose, 671
Enderle, Paul, Provincial Partitions Ltd., 335
Endersby, Beverly, Manager, Mission, 604-820-3732, 687
Endres, Henry, President, Annapolis Valley Peat Moss Co. Ltd., 86
Endres, Kyle, Managing Director, Annapolis Valley Peat Moss Co. Ltd., 86
Enewold, Kate, Library Systems Administrator, Silver King Campus, 1113
Engel, Paul, Director, 520
Engelberts, Joe, Manager, Williams Lake, 686
Engen, Terry, Reeve, Lacombe County, 669
England, Amy, Durham, 699
England, Amy, Regional Councillor, Oshawa, 716
England-Bizjak, Sally, Secretary, 630

Executive Name Index

English, Bob, Chief, Emergency Medical Services (EMS), Peterborough, 703
English, Ernest C., President, Bentofix Technologies Inc., 105
English, M.P.A., Dan, CAO, Halifax Regional Municipality, 902-490-6430, 695
English-Barbour, Melissa, HSEQ Coordinator, K&D Pratt Group Inc., 254
Engman, Eva, Librarian, Collections & Cataloguing, Okanagan College, 1112
Enlund, Bob, Sales Representative, Farris Industries Canada, 194
Ennamorato, Fred, Manager, Lennox Industries (Canada) Ltd., 267
Ennamorato, Nick, Manager, Lennox Industries (Canada) Ltd., 267
Ennis, Mike, Councillor, Kings County, 902-542-5217, 696
Enns, Carol, Librarian, Brandon Research Centre, 1122
Enns, Don, President & Chief Executive Officer, Maxxam Analytics Ltd., 283
Enns, Herb, Councillor, Leamington, 726
Enser, Maureen, Executive Director, Urban Development Institute of Canada, 1016
Epema, Eric, Manager, Eurovac, 191
Epp, Elmer, Manager, Crown Shred & Recycling, 154
Epp, Jake, Chair, 312, 634
Epp, Tracey L., Pitblado LLP, 1063
Epstein, Joyce, Manager, Parks, Recreation & Culture, New Tecumseth, 714
Erceg, Joe, General Manager, Richmond, 604-276-4083, 684
Eresman, Randy, President/CEO, Encana Corporation, 178
Erfan, Ahmad, Alexander Holburn Beaudin & Lang, LLP, 1057
Erhardt, Brad, Rothsay, 352
Eric, Theriault, Advisor, Canada-Nova Scotia Offshore Petroleum Board, 763
Erickson, Q.C., John W., Erickson & Partners, 1072
Erikson, Pam, President, Aldergrove Daylily Society, 820
Eriksson, Lars, President, Eriksson Sediment Systems Inc., 189
Erin, Windibank, Treasurer, Environmental Studies Association of Canada, 913
Erlor, Eugene, Secretary, Altamar International Inc., 81
Ermeta, Nicholas, City Councillor, Cambridge, 707
Ernest, Akpoue, Trade Commissioner, 768
Escobar, Miguel, President, O-I Canada Corp., 310
L'Espérance, Chantal, Sherbrooke, 744
L'Espérance, Daniel, Terrebonne, 745
Estep, Laura K., Fraser Milner Casgrain LLP - Calgary, 1051
Estey, D.R., President, D.R. Estey Engineering Ltd., 156
Estill, Glen, President/CEO, Sky Generation, 370
Estock, Rita, Senior Manager, Capital Regional District, 250-360-3011, 676
Estrela, Rosa, Manager, Great Western Containers Inc., 216
Etherington, Frank, Kitchener, 712
Éthier, Michel, Sales/Marketing Director, EFC Control Inc., 173
Ettehadieh, Ali, Genivar, 208
Etzinger, Bernard, Acting Director General, 520
Eugeni, Josette, Manager, Transportation Planning, Windsor, 723
Eugeni, Paolo, KMK Consultants Limited, 258
Euler, David, Director, Sewer & Water, North Bay, 715
Evan, Lloyd, Acting Executive Director, Commission for Environmental Cooperation, 763
Evanchuk, Doug I., McLennan Ross LLP, 1055
Evans, Angela, Officer, Saanich, 250-475-1775, 688
Evans, Brian, Executive Vice-President, 518
Evans, Carolynne, Municipal Clerk, Esquimalt, 686
Evans, Craig, Manager, Waterous Power Systems, 422
Evans, Darin, ADI Group Inc., 68
Evans, David D., Executive Director, Society of Fire Protection Engineers, 1008
Evans, Dwight, Oro-Medonte, 705-325-1653, 728
Evans, Iris, Minister, 570
Evans, K.A., Principal, Keystone Environmental Ltd., 257
Evans, Ken, Lambton Shores, 726
Evans, Les, President/CEO, Titan Logix Corp., 396
Evans, Majorie, Contact, Action: Environment, 813
Evans, Mary Anne, Director, Information Services, Lennox & Addington, 701
Evans, P.A. (Paul), Contact, EBA Engineering Consultants Ltd., 170
Evans, Paul, Co-CEO & Chair, Asia Pacific Foundation of Canada, 829
Evans, Randy, Superintendent, Pitt Meadows, 604-465-2435, 683
Evans, Rosalie, General Manager, Corporate Services & City Solicit, Thunder Bay, 807-625-2405, 721
Evans, Steve, Hayward Gordon Ltd., 227
Evans, Steve, Director, Planning & Economic Development & Deputy, Middlesex, 701
Evans, Thomas, Treasurer, International Society for Plant Pathology, 943
Evenson, Evan, Principal, Techint Goodfellow Technologies Inc., 387
Everett, Kevin, Contact, Linpro Petroleum Services Ltd., 272
Everett, Linda, Group Leader, Pulp & Paper Research Institute of Canada (PAPRICAN), 1177
Everett, Q.C., B.A., LL.B, William M., Partner, Lawson Lundell LLP - Vancouver, 1061
Evers, Paul, Director, Associated Tube Industries, 94
Everson, Peter, Executive Director, 518
Ewa, Gawron-Dobroczynska, Trade Commissioner, 768
Ewart, M. John, Howell Fleming LLP, 1071
Ewasiuk, Q.C., Rick, Reynolds, Mirth, Richards & Farmer LLP, 1056
Ewing, Carmen, Chair, Smoky River Regional Waste Management Commission, 758
Ewing, Don, President, Statiflo Inc., 379
Ewles, James, General Manager, Raw Materials Corporation, 342
Exner, Scott A., Partner, MacPherson Leslie & Tyerman LLP - Calgary, 1052
Exposti, Anthony, Treasurer, Canada Green Building Council, 853
Extavour, Doris, Library Assistant, Toronto Rehab, 1162
Exton, Denise, Associate Commissioner, Strathcona County, 780-464-8291, 670
Eydt, George J., Partner, Hodgson Russ LLP, 1077
Eyram, Christer, President, BDR Machinery Ltd., 104
Ezako, Bryan, Executive Director, Manitoba Camping Association, 950
Ezard, Gary W., Sec.-Treas./Principal, Triton Engineering Services Ltd., 402
Ezekiel, Ron, Fasken Martineau - Vancouver, 1059

F

Faas, Joe, Chatham-Kent, 724
Faber, Alexandre, Sec.-Trés., Régie intermunicipale de gestion des déchets de la Rive-Sud de Qu, 760
Fabian, Nelson, Executive Director, National Environmental Health Association, 957
Fabien, Marc-André, Fasken Martineau - Montréal, 1083
Fabienne, De Kimpe, Trade Commissioner, 767
Fabro, Andrew, Chief Librarian, Pacific & Yukon Region - Vancouver, 1118
Fabro, Andrew, Head Librarian, Canadian Wildlife Service, 1129
Facette, Jim, President/CEO, Canadian Airports Council, 855
Fader, Dwayne, Sales Manager, Hercules SLR Inc., 229
Fadum, Hans, Coordinator, Technical Services, Malaspina University-College, 1113
Fafard, Real, Associate, Ferme R&B Fafard Inc., 195
Fagan, Carol, Office Manager, Kamloops Range Research Unit, 1112
Fage, Ernest, Minister Responsible, 611
Faggion, Jean-Claude, Application Specialist, Les Équipements Vibrotech Inc., 268
Fagnan, Mary, Contact, Yellowquill College, 1126
Fair, Cal, Sales Manager, Quatic Industries Inc., 338
Fair, John E., President, Fair Canada Engineering Ltd., 193
Fair, Ross, General Manager, Community Services, London, 713
Fairbaird, Dave, Managing Partner, Stratos Inc., 380
Fairbanks, Mike R., International Water Supply Ltd., 245
Fairbrother, Wayne, Partner, Templeman Menninga LLP, 1068
Fairchild, Tracy, Manager, Velan Inc., 410
Faircloth, Jennifer, Partner, Borden Ladner Gervais LLP - Calgary, 1049
Faires, Paul, Secretary, Ontario Farm & Country Accommodations Association, 973
Fairey, Elaine, Associate University Librarian, Simon Fraser University, 1111
Fairfax, Jennifer, Osler, Hoskin & Harcourt LLP - Toronto, 1079
Fairgrieve, Jim, President, Echo Environmental, 170
Fairhurst, Sean, McLennan Ross LLP, 1053
Fairhurst, Sean, Counsel, MacPherson Leslie & Tyerman LLP - Calgary, 1052
Fairlie, Jim, Chief Administrative Officer, Strathroy-Caradoc, 731
Fairlie, Joanne, Asst. Deputy Minister, 666
Fairman, H. Shayne, Austring, Fendrick, Fairman & Parkkari, 1091
Fairweather, Steven, Commisssioner, Corporate Services, Cambridge, 707
Fakotakis, Eleni, Conseillère d'arrondissement, Mile-End, Montréal, 738
Falardeau, Julie, Ogilvy Renault LLP/S.E.N.C.R.L., s.r.l. - Québec, 1088
Falcioni, Robert, Director, Roads & Transportation, Greater Sudbury / Grand Sudbury, 710
Falcon, Kevin, Minister, 578
Falcone, Joe, Vice-President, Ontario Sawdust Supplies, 312
Falcone, Rosanne, President, Ontario Sawdust Supplies, 312
Falconer, Alex, CFO/Chair, Plasma Environmental Technologies Inc., 326
Falconi, Bob, Marketing, Rayovac Canada Inc., 342
Falevich, Julia, Heenan Blaikie LLP - Toronto, 1075
Falkenstein, Arthur, President, Arch Industries, 90
Fallis, Brian, Peterborough, 703
Fallu, Yves, Ingénieur Associé, Experts-Conseils BMST inc., 192
Falvo, Paul, Yellowknife, 695
Fancy, Holly, Director, 610
Fansher, Brenda, Library Manager, Ecologistics Research Services, 1155
Fanthome, Rick, President, Emco, 176
Farag, Suzanne M., Nelligan O'Brien Payne, 1071
Farago, Azure-Dee A., Kanuka Thuringer LLP, Barristers & Solicitors, 1090
Farah, Brigitte, Manager, Metallurgy & Materials Society of the Canadian Institute of Minin, 954
Farand, Gilles, Préfet, Vaudreuil-Soulanges, 753
Farber, Tamara, Partner, Miller Thomson LLP - Toronto, 1078
Farbridge, Karen, Mayor, Guelph, 519-837-5643, 710
Farbrother, Simon, Chief Administrative Officer, Waterloo, 519-747-8702, 722
Farbrother, Simon, City Manager, Edmonton, 780-496-8231, 672
Farinacci, Alvaro, Conseiller de ville, Cecil-P.-Newman, Montréal, 738
Faris, Graeme, General Manager, Comox Valley, 677
Farley, Bryan, Director, Triple M Metal, 402
Farman, Olga, Lavery, de Billy - Québec, 1088
Farmer, Brian, President, Powerscreen of Canada Ltd., 329
Farmer, David, Borden Ladner Gervais LLP - Calgary, 1049
Farmer, David J., McLennan Ross LLP, 1053
Farmer, Robert A., Bishop & McKenzie LLP, 1054
Farmer, FAICP, Paul, Executive Director, American Planning Association, 824
Farmer, Q.C., Allan, Reynolds, Mirth, Richards & Farmer LLP, 1056
Farmery, Dick, Contact, Bancroft Gem & Mineral Club, 844
Farmilo, Irenka, Officer, Canadian Foundation for Climate & Atmospheric Sciences, 869
Farquhar, Brian, Manager, Cowichan Valley, 677
Farquhar, Tom, Elliot Lake, 709
Farquharson, James, Principal, Faszer Farquharson & Associates Ltd., 194
Farr, Bruce K., General Manager, Emergency Medical Services, & EMS, Toronto, 416-397-9240, 721
Farr, Jason, Hamilton, 711
Farrah, Georges, Président et Directeur général, 654
Farrar, David P.S., Stewart McKelvey Stirling Scales - Halifax, 1067
Farraway, Robert, Manager, Westburne Canada, 428
Farrell, Druh, Calgary, 403-268-2475, 671
Farrell, Gary A., Sec.-Treas., R.V. Anderson Associates Limited, 341
Farrell, Jack, Water Resource Engineer & Regulatory Specialist, Secter Environmental Resource Consulting, 361
Farrell, Jerry H., Counsel, Fraser Milner Casgrain LLP - Toronto, 1075
Farrell, John, Interim Administrator, Skeena-Queen Charlotte, 679
Farrell, R., Carrier Canada Ltd., 129
Farrell-Cordon, Jennifer, Secretary, Ontario Association for Geographic & Environmental Education, 971
Farren, Bill, Saint John, 692
Farrow-Lawrence, Jacquie, Clerk, Annapolis County, 696
Fassbender, Peter, Mayor, Langley, 681
Fast, Don, Deputy Minister, 575
Fast, Duane, President, Fastco Equipment Corporation, 194
Fast, Kenton, Campbell Marr, 1063
Fasthuber, Otto F., Vice-President, SSI Schaefer Systems International Ltd., 377
Faszer, Clifford, President, Faszer Farquharson & Associates Ltd., 194
Fata, Frank, Sault Ste. Marie, 720
Faubert, Claude, Director General, 516
Faubert, Gisèle, Bibliothécaire, Bibliothèque centrale, 1170
Faucher, Guy, Directeur général, Val-d'Or, 746
Faucher, Hélène, Préfète, Les Appalaches, 749

Executive Name Index

Faucher, Patrice, Directeur, Granby, 450-776-8824, 735
Faulds, Q.C., P. Jon, Field Law - Edmonton, 1055
Faulkner, Brian, General Manager, WorleyParsons Canada Ltd., 434
Faulks, Lyle, Tech Sales Co., 387
Fauteux, Arthur, Maire, Cowansville, 735
Fauteux, Arthur, Préfet, Brome-Missisquoi, 747
Fauteux, Daniel, Directeur, Daniel Fauteux Environnement inc., 157
Fauteux, Kim, Communications Officer, 549
Fava, Jean, President, Neilson Excavation, 299
Fawaz, Ramzi, Senior Vice-President, Operations, 511
Fawcett, David, Deputy Mayor & Councillor, Grey, 700
Fawcett, Debbie, Dufferin, 699
Fawcett, Jeff, Brandon, 689
Fawcett, Jim, Managing Partner, Utility Risk Management Ltd., 408
Fawcus, Ingrid, Director, 664
Fay, Andrea, Clerk, Midland, 713
Fay, Peter, City Clerk, Brampton, 905-874-2100, 706
Faye, Terry, Vice-President, JTU Consulting, 253
Fazio, Al, Deputy Mayor & Councillor, Lakeshore, 712
Fear, Janet, Reference, Trafalgar Campus Library, 1146
Fearrey, Murray, Haliburton, 705-457-2557, 700
Feasby, David, Applications Specialist, Firing Industries Ltd., 195
Featherstone, Mike, President, Pacific Urchin Harvesters Association, 984
Fecenko, Mark J., Partner, Borden Ladner Gervais LLP - Toronto, 1073
Fecteau, Michel, Québec, 740
Fecteau, Sylvain, Vice-President, Broan Canada Ltd., 117
Fedak, Grace, Treasurer, Alberta Farm Fresh Producers Association, 816
Feddema, Simon, President, Grundfos Canada Inc., 222
Federko, Peter, CEO, 663
Fedirchuk, Gloria, Managing Principal, FMA Heritage Resources Consultants Inc., 198
Fedko, Sarah, Coordinator, Campus Information Literacy, University of Toronto Scarborough Library, 1163
Fedoruk, John, General Manager, Medicine Hat, 403-529-8176, 673
Fedrizzi, S. Richard, President & CEO, U.S. Green Building Council, 1016
Fedun, Wayne W., Partner, Macleod Dixon LLP, 1052
Fedy, BA, Barb, Director, Social Services, Grey, 700
Feehely, Paul, Superintendent, Public Works, Bradford West Gwillimbury, 706
Feenstra, Stan, President, Applied Groundwater Research Ltd., 87
Fehr, Brodie, Corporate Sales, Huron Window Corporation, 235
Fehr, Dennis, Coordinator, Johns Manville Canada Inc., 253
Fehr, Jake, Manager, Solar Solutions Inc., 372
Fehr, Rod, Manager, Engineered Air, 180
Fehr, Victor, General Manager, Huron Window Corporation, 235
Feicht, Trevor, Manager, Swift Current, 755
Feick, John, Executive Chair, Matrix Solutions Inc., 282
Feldberg, Peter, Fasken Martineau - Calgary, 1050
Feldman, Jay, Executive Director, National Coalition Against the Misuse of Pesticides, 957
Felicetti, Serge, Director, Business Development, Niagara Falls, 715
Felker, Kevin, Canon Canada Inc., 126
Felker, Kurtis, Manager, Nanaimo, 250-756-5317, 681
Fell, Barbara, Publications Manager, Nickel Institute, 1159
Fell, Todd, Manager, Dougan & Associates, 165
Fellin, Phil, Vice-President/Manager, Airzone One Ltd., 76
Fellini, Dan, Georgina, 709
Fellows, Bob, Impro, 239
Felske, Honey, Sales Director, Hygrex-Spehr Industries, 237
Feltham, Dana, Head, Reference, Newfoundland Ocean Industries Association, 1132
Feltham, Kim, Library & Records Coordinator, Klohn Crippen Berger Ltd., 1118
Felx, Yolande, SMTE, CÉGEP de Saint-Laurent, 1184
Fendrick, Robert, Director, Whitehorse, 867-668-8612, 755
Fenelius, Johan, Manager, Strata Soil Sampling Inc., 380
Fenety, Peter, Chair, South West Solid Waste Commission, 759
Feng, Vivian, Coordinator, Reference & Instructional Services, Langara College, 1118
Fenger, Michael, President, Friends of Ecological Reserves, 920
Fenik, John, Lanark, 701
Fennell, Lloyd, City Manager, Sarnia, 719
Fennell, Susan, Mayor, Brampton, 706
Fennell, Susan, Mayor & Councillor, Peel, 703

Fennema, Conrad, President, Alberta Fish & Game Association, 817
Fenner, Linda, Manager, Society of Environmental Toxicology & Chemistry, 1008
Fenske, Dana, Project Engineer, PINTER & Associates Ltd., 325
Fenske, Dennis, Director, Thompson, 690
Fenson, Brad, Coordinator, Alberta Fish & Game Association, 817
Fentie, Dennis, Minister, 666
Fentie, Dennis, Minister Responsible, 664
Fenton, Paul, President, Canadian Drives Inc., 124
Fenton, Ryan, Contact, Canadian Drives Inc., 124
Fenton, Thomas A., Aird & Berlis LLP, 1072
Fenwick, Bill, General Manager, Parks, Facilities, & Leisure Serv, Welland, 722
Fenwick, Paul, General Manager, Sunshine Coast, 679
Feral, Priscilla, President, Friends of Animals, 920
Ferchichi, Aline, President, Kam Biotechnology Ltd., 254
Ferchichi, Karim, Vice-President, Kam Biotechnology Ltd., 254
Ferchichi, Mongi, CEO, Kam Biotechnology Ltd., 254
Fercho, Ed, President, Canadian Petroleum Engineering Inc., 125
Fercho, Mark, Manager, Prince George, 250-561-7698, 683
Ferdinand-Grant, Ita, Librarian, Casa Loma Campus, 1156
Ferdinands, Ken, Councillor, Whitchurch-Stouffville, 723
Fergusen, Rob, SEI Industries Ltd., 362
Ferguson, Alex, Commissioner & Chief Executive Officer, 576
Ferguson, Catherine, Metro Vancouver, 678
Ferguson, Catherine, Mayor, White Rock, 686
Ferguson, Denzil, Mississippi Mills, 714
Ferguson, Donald, Deputy Minister, 594
Ferguson, Frances, Macleod Dixon LLP, 1052
Ferguson, James A., Aikins, MacAulay & Thorvaldson LLP, 1063
Ferguson, Janet, Treasurer, Lambton Shores, 726
Ferguson, Janette, City Clerk, Grande Prairie, 780-538-0314, 672
Ferguson, Jim, Branch Manager, CenturyVallen, 137
Ferguson, Jonathan, Secretary, Save Ontario Shipwrecks, 1002
Ferguson, Ken, Simcoe, 704
Ferguson, Ken, Mayor, Clearview, 705-446-2323, 725
Ferguson, Lloyd, Hamilton, 711
Ferguson, Lonnie, General Manager, Pictou County, 902-396-5062, 698
Ferguson, R.F., Industrial Manager, NEDCO, 299
Ferguson, Reg, President, Hazard Alert Training & Supplies Canada Inc., 227
Ferguson, Rob, Severn, 729
Ferguson, Rob, Divisional Manager, Surpac Minex (Canada) Ltd., 383
Ferguson, Scott, Interim President/CEO, 610
Ferguson, Scott A., Bathurst, 506-547-8993, 690
Ferguson, Steve, Langley, 687
Ferguson, William A., MacKenzie Fujisawa LLP, 1061
Ferguson, B.A., M.P.A, L, Clara C., Associate, Lawson Lundell LLP - Calgary, 1051
Fergusson, Jim, Huron, 701
Ferko, Lorina, Manager, Caduceon Environmental Laboratories, 121
Ferland, Huguette, Degussa Canada Inc., 159
Ferland, Michel, Ferland & Bélair, 1082
Fernadez, Leila, Science Librarian, Steacie Science and Engineering Library, 1161
Fernandes, Yvonne, Kitchener, 712
Fernandez, Francisco, Technical, UNOTEC, 407
Fernandez, Vada, Purchasing Officer, Charlottetown, 732
Fernández Ugalde, José Carlos, Manager, Commission for Environmental Cooperation, 898
Fernández Ugalde, José Carlos, Program Manager, Commission for Environmental Cooperation, 898
Ferrier, Jo-Anne, City Treasurer, Winnipeg, 690
Ferries, Tom, President & CEO, National Energy Equipment Inc., 297
Ferris, Laïla, Responsable, Information et gestion documentaire, Université du Québec à Chicoutimi, 1166
Ferry, Jennifer, Thorold, 720
Ferstman, Leonard, Librarian, University of Toronto Innis College, 1163
Fesnak, Vera, Head of Access Services, Wilfrid Laurier University, 1165
Feth, Kevin S., Field Law - Edmonton, 1055
Fetter, Colin R., Brownlee LLP, 1054
Fetzner, Joanne, Manager, Association of Environmental Engineering & Science Professors, 835
Feuer, Gabor, Library IT Manager, Durham College of Applied Arts & Technology, 1147

Fewer, Ellen C., Library Technician, Central Newfoundland Regional Health Centre, 1131
Fiacco, Pat, Mayor, Regina, 754
Fiander, Anna, Regional Librarian, Bedford Institute of Oceanography, 1135
Fickes, Jack, President/CEO, Bigfoot Systems Inc., 107
Fiddament, A., Carrier Canada Ltd., 129
Fiddy, Chuck, Supervisor, Water & Wastewater, St. Thomas, 719
Field, Colleen, Assistant Head, Centre for Newfoundland Studies, 1131
Field, John C., Partner, Hicks Morley Hamilton Stewart Storie LLP, 1076
Field, Ken, Access Services Librarian, Trent University, 1153
Field, Paul J., Partner, Ogilvy Renault LLP/S.E.N.C.R.L., s.r.l. - Toronto, 1078
Field, Richard K., Director, Sunarc of Canada Inc., 382
Fielding, David, City Engineer, Sarnia, 719
Fielding, Jeff, Chief Administrative Officer, London, 713
Fielding, Scott, Winnipeg, 204-986-5848, 690
Fields, David, Fire Chief, Windsor, 723
Fields, David T., Fire Chief, Windsor Fire & Rescue Service, Windsor, 519-253-6573, 723
Fierheller, Robert, Manager, PPG Canada, Inc., 330
Fife, Denis, Mayor, Stormont, Dundas & Glengarry, 700
Figueira, Filipe, Director, Paradigm Environmental Technologies Inc., 318
Filby, Brendan, Regional Manager, Canada Colors & Chemicals Ltd., 123
File, Patricia A., Midland, 713
Filiatrault, Dionne, Executive Director, 542
Filion, Gilles, Chairman, John Meunier Inc., 253
Filion, Gilles, Contact, Consultants Filion, Hansen & Associés Inc., 150
Filion, Gilles, President/CEO, Prosperco Inc., 335
Filion, John, Toronto, 721
Filipov, Rob, Manager, Engineering Services, Tecumseh, 720
Filipovic, Dusanka, President, Blue-Zone Technologies Ltd., 110
Fillion, Clément, Directeur général, Bellechasse, 747
Filmer, Cam, Executive Director, 582
Finaley, Heath, Senior Librarian, Ontario Ministry of Natural Resources, 1153
Finall, Alice, Mayor, North Saanich, 687
Finamore, Sandy, Elliot Lake, 709
Finch, Bob, Soper's, 374
Finch, David, Grimsby, 905-945-4545, 710
Finch, Q.C., F. Stephen, Miller Thomson LLP - Waterloo, 1081
Find, Doris, Receptionist, Ontario Environmental Training Consortium, 312
Findlater, Stewart M., Director, Thames Centre, 731
Findlay, Caroline, Blake, Cassels & Graydon LLP - Vancouver, 1057
Findlay, Ian, Guelph, 710
Findura, John, Regina, 306-536-4250, 754
Fine, Joanna, Heenan Blaikie LLP - Toronto, 1075
Finer, Brian B., Bratty & Partners LLP, 1081
Fink, Tanis, Chief Librarian and Director, King Campus, 1142
Finkelstein, David N., Partner, Stikeman Elliott LLP - Toronto, 1080
Finlay, Shauna, Fraser Milner Casgrain LLP - Edmonton, 1055
Finlayson, Blair R., General Manager & President, SRB Controls Inc., 376
Finlayson, G. Barry, Lang Michener LLP - Vancouver, 1060
Finlayson, Michael G., D'Arcy & Deacon LLP, 1063
Finlayson, Nancy, Founder, Garden Institute of Alberta, 922
Finlayson, Shiona, President, Canadian Printing Ink Manufacturers Association, 883
Finley, William, Northumberland, 702
Finley, B.A., M.B.A., Diane, Minister, Human Resources & Skills Development, 534
Finn, David, President, Petroleum Research Atlantic Canada, 986
Finn, Dianne, Contact, Shaver Industries Inc., 365
Finn, Helen, Greffière, Beaconsfield, 734
Finn, Ph.D., P.Geo., Greg, President, Association of Professional Geoscientists of Ontario, 839
Finnbogason, Thomas, President/Partner, Envirochem Services Inc., 183
Finnegan, Leo P., Mayor, Prince Edward, 703
Finnerty, Ken, North Grenville, 728
Finnerty, Pat C., Blake, Cassels & Graydon LLP - Calgary, 1049
Finney, Lana J., Davis LLP - Toronto, 1074
Finnie, John, General Manager, Nanaimo, 250-390-6560, 678
Finnie, John, Manager, Nanaimo, 250-390-6560, 678
Finnie, Rod, Warden & Councillor, Wellington, 519-833-2380, 705
Finucan, Ken, Genor Recycling Services, 210
Finucan, Ken, Executive Manager, Lakeshore Recycling, 263

Executive Name Index

Fiot, Gerard, VP, Groupe S.M. International Inc., 220
Firat, MSc., Murat, President, Canadian Medical & Biological Engineering Society, 877
Firlotte, Frederick W., President, Golder Associates Ltd., 214
Firlotte, Rick, President, Golder Associates Ltd., 214
Firnesz, John, Program Manager, Saskatchewan Parks & Recreation Association, 1001
Firth, Leslie, Assistant Librarian, Systems, Carleton University, 1149
Fisch, Bill, Regional Chair & Councillor, York, 705
Fischer, Allyson M., Partner, Hicks Morley Hamilton Stewart Storie LLP, 1076
Fischer, Rhonda, Treasurer, Perth East, 728
Fiset, Martin, Laval, 450-978-6560, 736
Fish, Nancy, Manager, Library, Ontario Power Generation, 1160
Fisher, Anita, Manager, Universal Filter Media, 406
Fisher, Anne, Information Services Librarian, Cape Breton University, 1137
Fisher, Darrell, ADI Group Inc., 68
Fisher, Darren, Councillor, Halifax Regional Municipality, 695
Fisher, David A., Founder & President, Fisher Environmental Ltd., 196
Fisher, Denise, Corporate Administrator, Terrace, 250-638-4722, 685
Fisher, Ewen S., Director, IBI Group, 238
Fisher, Jeff, Deputy Executive Director, Urban Development Institute of Canada, 1016
Fisher, John C., Chief Operating Officer, T. Harris Environmental Management Inc., 385
Fisher, Roger, Plant Products Co. Ltd., 326
Fisher, Will, Vice-President, Institute of Food Technologists, 933
Fisher, P.Eng, Darrell, Director, Atlantic Canada Water & Wastewater Association, 843
Fishlock, Robert M., Blake, Cassels & Graydon LLP - Toronto, 1072
Fisk, John, Director, Henry A. Wallace Center for Agricultural & Environmental Policy a, 929
Fitch, Bruce, Minister Responsible, 597
Fitch, Gavin S., McLennan Ross LLP, 1053
Fittes, Dale, Plant Manager, CCS Income Trust, 134
Fittes, Tyler, Plant Manager, CCS Income Trust, 134
Fitzgerald, Charlie, Vice-President, West Point Products Canada, 425
Fitzgerald, Christine, Executive Vice-President, 519
Fitzgerald, Dorothy, Director, Health Sciences Library, 1141
Fitzgerald, Paul, Partner, Ogilvy Renault LLP/S.E.N.C.R.L., s.r.l. - Toronto, 1078
Fitzpatrick, Ian, Coordinator, Mission, 604-820-5390, 687
Fitzpatrick, Ian, Fire Chief, Mission, 604-820-5390, 687
Fitzpatrick, Joe, Officer, Summerland, 689
Fitzpatrick, Kelley C., Director, Flax Canada 2015, 917
Fitzpatrick, Paul, Chief Administrative Officer, Cornwall, 708
Fixter, Kristina, Contact, Urban Pest Management Council of Canada, 1016
Fjeldsted, John, Executive Director, Manitoba Environmental Industries Association Inc., 951
Fjellstrom, Terry, Principal, L&M Engineering Ltd., 261
Flageol, Denis, General Manager, Universal Handling Equipment Company Limited, 406
Flaherty, B.A., LL.B., James Michael (Jim), Minister, Finance, 526
Flaman, Derek S., McCarthy Tétrault LLP - Calgary, 1052
Flanagan, Cathy, Director, 641
Flanagan, James P., McLennan Ross LLP, 1053
Flanagan, Koovian, Deputy Minister, 619
Flanagan, W. Frank, Director, Fredericton, 691
Flannery, Steve, General Manager, Material Resource Recovery Inc., 282
Flatt, Don, President/CEO, The National Testing Laboratories Ltd., 393
Flavell, Q.C., C.J. Michael, Lang Michener LLP - Ottawa, 1070
Flavin, Christopher, President, Worldwatch Institute, 1023
Fleck, John, Director, Human Resource Services, Ajax, 705
Fleck, Susan, Director, 605
Flecker, Karl, Director, Canadian Labour Congress, 876
Fleeton, Robert D., President, KMK Consultants Limited, 258
Flegel, Neil, Strathroy-Caradoc, 731
Fleischhacker, Dean, President, Recyc-Haul Waste Management Inc., 343
Fleishmann, Jo, President, Ronco Protective Products, 351
Fleming, Allan W., Environmental Sales, CD Nova, 134
Fleming, Andrew, Senior Partner, Ogilvy Renault LLP/S.E.N.C.R.L., s.r.l. - Toronto, 1078
Fleming, Angus, Director, Cape Breton, 902-563-5058, 695

Fleming, Gerry R., Partner, Stewart McKelvey Stirling Scales - St. John's, 1066
Fleming, Scott, Branch Manager, CenturyVallen, 136
Fleming, Stephen, Clerk, Kelowna, 250-469-8500, 681
Fleming, Susan, Library Technician, College of the Rockies, 1111
Fleming, W.B., Vice-President, CD Nova, 134
Flemming, Jon, Director, Forest Products Association of Canada, 918
Flemming, Tom, Head of Public Services, Health Sciences Library, 1141
Flesher, Hugh, Manager, Emerson Electric Canada Limited, 177
Fletcher, Bev, Library Technician, SaskTel, 1188
Fletcher, Bob, Lanark, 701
Fletcher, Greg, Administrator, Mount Waddington, 678
Fletcher, Kris, Regional Clerk & Director, Council & Administrativ, Waterloo, 704
Fletcher, LauraLee, Office Manager, Enermodal Engineering Ltd., 179
Fletcher, Paul, President, Somenos Marsh Wildlife Society, 1009
Fletcher, Paula, Toronto, 721
Fletcher, Peter, Executive Manager, Occupational Hygiene Association of Ontario, 969
Fletcher, Sharon, Director, Mission, 604-820-3752, 687
Fletcher, Steve, Executive Director, Ontario Automotive Recyclers Association, 971
Flett, Robert, President/CEO, Flett Research, 196
Fleury, Lois, Sec.-Treas., Régie intermunicipale de gestion des déchets des Chutes-de-la-Cha, 760
Fleury, Mathieu, Ottawa, 716
Fleury, Odile, Library Technologist, Eastern Division Library/Bibliothèque de la division de l'est, 1178
Fleury, Richard, Directeur général, Laval, 736
Flewelling, Debra, Information Technology Librarian, Douglas College, 1114
Flewelling, John, Manager, CBCL Limited, 133
Flewwelling, Morris, Mayor, Red Deer, 403-342-8154, 674
Flick, Kim, Manager, Vernon, 685
Flicker, John, President/CEO, National Audubon Society, Inc., 957
Flindall, Robert, Director, Engineering & Public Works, King, 726
Flipsen, Frank, Fire Chief, North Glengarry, 727
Flitton, Bill, City Clerk, Abbotsford, 604-864-5603, 679
Flood, Barrie, President, RemedX Remediation Services Inc., 344
Flood, Charles F., President, BFI Canada Inc., 106
Flor, Nick, Vice-President, Imbibitive Technologies Canada, Inc., 239
Flores, Rene, Contact, YES Environment Technologies Inc., 435
Florizone, Dan, Deputy Minister, 659
Flowers, Anne-Marie, Directrice générale, Bonaventure, 747
Flowers, Mark, Davies Howe Partners, 1074
Floyd, Gary C., Lang Michener LLP - Vancouver, 1060
Floyd, James, Owner, JFA James Floyd Associates Ltd., 252
Fluhrer, Mark, Director, Recreation Culture & Community Services, Belleville, 706
Fluker, Bryon, Chatham-Kent, 724
Flynn, Carney, General Manager, Power Vac of Nova Scotia, 329
Flynn, Donna, Executive Assistant, SustaiNet Software Solutions Inc., 384
Flynn, Kevin, President, Southern Interior Local Government Association, 1010
Flynn, Terry, Councillor, Niagara-on-the-Lake, 715
Flynn, Thomas, Peterborough, 703
Fobes, Caroline, Counsel, 557
Foerster, Mark, Manager, Aqua Terre Solutions Inc., 88
Fogal, Jane, Halton, 700
Fogal, Jane, Regional Councillor, Halton Hills, 710
Fogarassy, Tony, Clark Wilson LLP, 1058
Fogarty, Justin R., Counsel, Heenan Blaikie LLP - Ottawa, 1070
Fogarty, Michael, Orillia, 716
Fogarty, Richard, President, New Trend Environmental Services, 301
Fogel, Daniel B., Partner, Hicks Morley Hamilton Stewart Storie LLP, 1076
Fogg, Brian, Group Leader, AMEC, 83
Foisy, Gary, Superintendent, Water Services, Leamington, 726
Foley, Bob, Director of Library Services, Malaspina University-College, 1113
Foley, John, General Manager, Tomlinson Environmental Services, 397
Foley, Patricia, Health Sciences Librarian, Cape Breton District Health Authority, 1137
Foley, Patti, Peel, 703
Foley, Patti, Regional Councillor, Caledon, 707
Foley, Theresa, Advisor, Urban Systems Ltd., 407

Folland, Barry, Emergency Measures Officer, 638
Fonberg, Robert, Deputy Minister, 545
fondation hydroquebec pou, Fondation Hydro-Québec po, Montréal, QC, 1046
fonds d'action quebecois, Fonds d'action québécois, Québec, QC, 1046
Fong, Forry, Manager, AiMS Environmental, 74
Fong, Janis, Manager, Leduc County, 669
Fonger, Steve, President, Middlesex Federation of Agriculture, 954
Fonseca, Chris, Peel, 714, 703
Fonseca, Peter, Minister, 629
Fontaine, Alain, Gestionnaire, Veolia ES Canada Industrial Services Inc., 411
Fontaine, François, Ogilvy Renault LLP/S.E.N.C.R.L., s.r.l. - Montréal, 1086
Fontaine, François, Vice-President, Fontaine International Corp., 199
Fontaine, Jean, Saint-Jean-sur-Richelieu, 450-346-3063, 742
Fontaine, Jean-Marie, Partner, Borden Ladner Gervais LLP - Montréal, 1083
Fontaine, Liza, Purchasing Manager, Fort Garry Industries Ltd., 200
Fontaine-Deshaies, Johane, Longueuil, 737
Fontana, Joe, Mayor, London, 713
Fooks, Cathy, Chair, The Michener Institute for Applied Health Sciences, 954
Foran, Allan F., Aikins, MacAulay & Thorvaldson LLP, 1063
Foran, John W., Minister, 596
Foran, Kirk, Director, Corporate Services, Lakeshore, 712
Foran, Patricia A., Aird & Berlis LLP, 1072
Foran, S.G., WeirFoulds LLP, 1081
Foran, Q.C., Frank R., Borden Ladner Gervais LLP - Calgary, 1049
Foran, Q.C., James E., Aikins, MacAulay & Thorvaldson LLP, 1063
Forbes, Alison, Stikeman Elliott LLP - Toronto, 1080
Forbes, Douglas J., Thompson Dorfman Sweatman LLP, 1064
Forbes, Glenn, Product Support Manager, Toromont Caterpillar, 398
Forbes, Tammy, Director, 573
Forcier, Françoise, Solinov Inc., 373
Forcillo, Sammy, Conseiller de ville, Ste-Marie-St-Jacques, Montréal, 738
Ford, Daniel A., Torys LLP, 1080
Ford, Doug, Toronto, 721
Ford, John, Treasurer & Manager, Financial Services, Norfolk, 702
Ford, Karen, Manager, Earth & Environmental Technologies (ETech), 168
Ford, Michael, McCarthy Tétrault LLP - Calgary, 1052
Ford, Michael, Engineer, StonCor Canada, 379
Ford, P.J. (Jim), Manager, St. John's, 709-576-8294, 694
Ford, Rob, Director, Finance & Treasurer, Ajax, 705
Ford, Rob, Mayor, Toronto, 721
Ford, Wendy, Corporate Controller, Bennett Environmental Inc., 105
Forder, M.Sc, Doug, Field Supervisor, Ontario Streams, 979
Foreman, Sean, Partner, Wickwire Holm, 1068
Forest, Bruce, Director, Chester District, 902-275-1312, 697
Forest, Daniel, Vice-President, Les Contrôles PROVAN Associés Inc., 268
Forest, Serge, Sherbrooke, 744
Forest, Éric, Maire, Rimouski, 418-724-3126, 740
La Forest, C.C., Q.C., Gérard V., Counsel, Stewart McKelvey Stirling Scales - Fredericton, 1064
Forfar, Don, Reeve, St. Andrews, 690
Forget, Claude, District Manager, BFI Canada Inc., 107
Forget, Gérald, Mirabel, 738
Forget, Jean-Yves, Directeur général, Mont-Laurier, 738
Forget, Lucien, Directeur, Services à la clientèle, administration, Université du Québec à Trois-Rivières, 1186
Formanek, Edwin, President, Wheelabrator Canada Co., 431
Formanek, Paula, Office Manager, Trow Consulting Engineers Ltd., 403
Formusa, Laura, President/CEO, 629
Fornari, Marco, Manager, Prince George, 250-561-7509, 683
Forrest, Grant, Responsable, Référence, CÉGEP de Saint-Laurent, 1184
Forrest, Ian, Perth, 703
Forrest, Ian, Mayor, Perth East, 728
Forrest, Ken, Manager, Fredericton, 506-460-2110, 691
Forrest, Mike, Port Coquitlam, 683
Forsey, John, Manager, Westburne Canada, 425

Executive Name Index

Forstbauer, Mary, President, Bio-dynamic Agricultural Society of British Columbia, 845
Forster, Cindy, Niagara, 702
Forster, Elizabeth J., Blaney McMurtry LLP, 1073
Forster, John, Assistant Deputy Minister, 544
Forster, Mac, Director, Swift Current, 306-778-2740, 755
Forsyth, Harold G., Kent Engineering Ltd., 256
Forsyth-Arbour, Dee, CEO, Forsythe Lubrication Associates Ltd., 199
Forsythe, Bob, President, Forsythe Lubrication Associates Ltd., 199
Fortier, Benoît, Directeur, Shawinigan, 744
Fortier, Dan, Welland, 722
Fortier, Jean-Marc, Associé, Robinson Sheppard Shapiro LLP, 1087
Fortier, Louis, Scientific Director, ArcticNet Inc., 829
Fortier, Manon, Directrice générale (par intérim) & Greffière, Beauharnois, 734
Fortier, Manon, Présidente, Clubs 4-H du Québec, 897
Fortier, Martin, Executive Director, ArcticNet Inc., 829
Fortier, Matthew, Regional Manager, ON North & East, TD Friends of the Environment Foundation, 1011
Fortier, Michael J., Torys LLP, 1080
Fortier, Suzanne, President, 552
Fortier, Vincent, Directeur, Trois-Rivières, 819-372-4627, 745
Fortier, Violaine, Responsable, Collège Jean-de-Brébeuf, 1172
Fortin, Caroline, Head, Systems & Technical Services, Bombardier Inc./Canadair Aerospace & Defence Groups, 1171
Fortin, Christian, Maire, Batiscan, 747
Fortin, Claude, Vice-President, Nova PB Inc., 308
Fortin, Dominique, Directeur, Lévis, 418-839-2002, 736
Fortin, Dominique, Sous-ministre associée, 646
Fortin, Hélène, Greffière, Matawinie, 750
Fortin, Jacques, Saguenay, 741
Fortin, Jacques, Directeur, Saint-Charles-Borromée, 753
Fortin, Jeanne, Associée, Lapointe Rosenstein Marchand Melançon, 1085
Fortin, Madeleine, Sous-ministre adjointe & Directrice générale, 646
Fortin, Manon, Directrice générale, Le Val-St-François, 749
Fortin, Marcel, GIS & Map Librarian, Map and Data Library, 1159
Fortin, Martine, Secrétaire, Régie intermunicipale de gestion des déchets solides de l'Anse-à-, 760
Fortin, Myriam, Stikeman Elliott LLP - Montréal, 1087
Fortin, Normand, Conseiller d'arrondissement, Ovide-Clermont, Montréal, 738
Fortin, Pierre, Maritime Paper Products Ltd., 281
Fortin, Pierre, Technicien, CÉGEP de Victoriaville, 1187
Fortin, Serge, Préfet, Témiscouata, 753
Fortin, Sophie, Sec.-Trés., Régie intermunicipale d'assainissement du canton de Metgermette, 760
Fortin, Valerie, Collections Librarian, Life Sciences Library, 1174
Fortin, Vivian, Volunteer, Five Hills Health Region, 1187
Fortin, B.A., LL.B., M.Ed, Dean, Mayor, Victoria, 250-361-0200, 685
Fortin-Carrière, Denise, Technicienne en documentation, Bibliothèque des sciences, 1171
Fortman, Fred J., Executive Director, American Society of Safety Engineers, 826
Fortner, John F., Ingersoll, 711
Forward, M.Sc., P.Eng., Richard, General Manager, Infrastructure, Development & Cul, Barrie, 706
Foskett, Tom, General Manager, Terex Ltd., 389
Fossey, Ken, Director, Swan Hills Treatment Centre, 384
Foster, Adrian, Local Councillor, Clarington, 724
Foster, Chris, Operations Manager, Leon's Insulation, 267
Foster, David, Simcoe, 704
Foster, David, Deputy Mayor & Councillor, Wasaga Beach, 722
Foster, David G., Executive Director, American Cave Conservation Association, 822
Foster, Doug, Director, Cape Breton, 902-563-5070, 695
Foster, Joan, University Coordinator/Career Counsellor, Cypress Hills Regional College, 1191
Foster, John, International Sales, Wheelabrator Canada Co., 431
Foster, Ken, Vice-President, Insituform Technologies Ltd. - Edmonton, 242
Foster, Kevin, Fire Chief, Midland, 713
Foster, Lynn, Richmond Hill, 718
Foster, Mélanie C., Technicienne en documentation, CÉGEP de Baie-Comeau, 1166
Foster, Robert, Centre Wellington, 713, 724
Foster, Ron, Auditor General, Oshawa, 716
Foster, Wendy, Business Manager, International Association for Great Lakes Research, 935
Fothergill, Piers, Vice-President, Tera Environmental Consultants (Alta) Ltd., 389
Fotopulos, Helen, Mairesse d'arrondissement, Montréal, 738
Foubister, Jim, Lambton, 701
Foubister, Jim, City / County Councillor, Sarnia, 719
Fougère, Roland, Chair, Kent County Solid Waste Commission, 758
Fougere, B.A.(Hons.), M.S, Michael, Regina, 306-789-5586, 754
Foulds, Andrew, Ward Councillor, Thunder Bay, 721
Fouquet, Guy, Groupe SM inc., 221
Fournier, Claude, Vice-President, Horizon Environment Inc., 233
Fournier, Elizabeth, Contact, A&A Environmental Consultants Inc., 63
Fournier, Elizabeth, Vice-President, Notre Development Corp., 308
Fournier, Gaston, Responsable, Services techniques, Université du Québec École de technologie supérieure, 1176
Fournier, Geneviève, Lavery, de Billy - Montréal, 1085
Fournier, Jean-Charles, Directeur, Rimouski, 418-724-3111, 740
Fournier, Jocelyne, Prêt et acquisitions, Pêches et aquaculture commerciales, 1167
Fournier, Karine, Head, Reference, Bibliothèque des sciences de la santé, 1147
Fournier, Michel, Multi Recyclage S.D. Inc., 295
Fournier, Sébastien, Greffier, Gaspé, 735
Fournier, Vincent, President, V. Fournier & Associates, 408
Fournier, Q.C., Dan P.E., Blake, Cassels & Graydon LLP - Calgary, 1049
Fournier-Viger, David, Bibliothécaire et référence, CÉGEP de l'Abitibi-Témiscamingue, 1182
Fournier-Viger, David, Conseiller en documentation, Université du Québec en Abitibi-Témiscamingue, 1182
Fourtané Bordonado, Louise, Mascouche, 450-474-0847, 737
Fouts, Chris, Contact, Bancroft Gem & Mineral Club, 844
Fowler, Deborah, Librarian, Toronto Urban Development Services City Planning, 1162
Fowler, Ian, General Manager, Moncton / Ville de Moncton, 691
Fowler, Kim, Director, Victoria, 250-361-0290, 685
Fowler, Trevor S., Partner, Lindsay Kenney LLP, 1056
Fowlie, Joanne, Business Librarian, Georgian College of Applied Arts & Technology, 1138
Fox, Charlie, Langley, 687
Fox, David, Head, Information Technology Services & Technical, University of Saskatchewan, 1191
Fox, Harold, Inproheat Industries Ltd., 242
Fox, Jim, Sales, Neo Valves, 300
Fox, Rosemary, Chair, British Columbia Nature (Federation of British Columbia Naturalis, 849
Fox, Stephen, Director, Financial & Physical Services, Lennox & Addington, 701
Fox, Stephen A., CFO, 596
Fox-Mellway, Linda, Calgary, 403-268-2430, 671
Foxton, Bruce, Operations Manager, Inland Aquatics, 242
Foy, Christine, Manager, Westburne Canada, 427
Foy, Malcolm, Sr. Environmental Scientist, LGL Limited Environmental Research Associates, 272
Foy, Rock, Director, Human Resources, Timmins, 721
Fradet, Benoit, Laval, 736
Fradette, Denis, Sec.-Trés., Régie intermunicipale d'assainissement des eaux usées des Desjard, 760
Fradette, Isabelle, Greffière, Lotbinière, 750
Fradette, Jocelyn, Alma, 418-480-1359, 733
Fraenkel, Amy, Regional Director, United Nations Environment Programme, 1015
Fragedakis, Mary, Toronto, 721
Frahm, Jennifer, Singleton Urquhart LLP, 1062
Fraiberg, Jeremy, Partner, Osler, Hoskin & Harcourt LLP - Toronto, 1079
Frail, Kim, Bibliothécaire/Services publics, Université de l'Alberta Bibliothèque Saint-Jean, 1107
Frain, Seamus, Manager, Sanix Incorporated, 357
Fralick, Barb, Manager, Human Resources, Springwater, 730
Frame, Grant, President, Environmental Consultants & Engineers, 185
Frame, Mark, Director, North Cowichan, 687
Fran, Rosmarie, Administration, Parish Geomorphic Ltd., 318
France, John, CAO, Sunshine Coast, 604-885-6800, 679
Franceschi, Susan, Chief Membership Officer, American Water Works Association, 826
Franceschini, Anthony P., Director, Stantec Inc., 377
Francis, Bart, President, Tremco Ltd., 401
Francis, Donna, Corner Brook, 693
Francis, Eddie, Mayor, Windsor, 723
Francis, Karol, Rimouski, 740
Francis, Paul, Vice-President, Northway-Photomap Inc., 307
Francisco, Rodriguez, Trade Commissioner, 767
Francisco, Tony, Manager, Environmental Services, Lakeshore, 712
Francoeur, Alain, Directeur, Lévis, 418-839-2002, 736
Francoeur, Marthe, Bibliothécaire, Pavillon Félix-Leclerc, 1168
François, Coté, Trade Commissioner, 767
Francois, J.P., Operations, Terratechnik Environmental Limited, 391
Francois, Twyla, Head, Canadians for Ethical Treatment of Food Animals, 892
Franey, Ron, Director, Conception Bay South, 693
Frank, Brenda, Executive Vice-President & General Counsel, Shred-It, 366
Frank, Brian E., President & CEO, BP Canada Energy Company, 114
Frank, Darrell, Forester, North Cowichan, 250-746-3104, 687
Frank, Gordon, Acting Administrator, Greenview Regional Waste Management Commission, 757
Frank, Gordon, CAO, Cold Lake, 672
Frank, Jeffrey, Principal, Hilderman Thomas Frank Cram & Associates, 232
Frank, Jillian, Heenan Blaikie LLP - Vancouver, 1051, 1060
Frank, Leslie, HFP Acoustical Consultants Corp., 231
Frank, Robert I., Partner, Macleod Dixon LLP, 1077
Frank, Terry, Vice-President, Semco Systems Limited, 362
Frankish, Charles, President, Canadian Society of Allergy & Clinical Immunology, 886
Frankland, Todd, President/Owner, Provincial Partitions Ltd., 335
Franklin, Adam, Regional Sales Manager, Wastequip Cusco, 421
Franklin, Sharon, Finance/Administrative Director, Center for Health, Environment & Justice, 893
Frankling, Freddie, Vice-President, GLOBE Foundation, 924
Franks, Maria, Executive Director, Legal Information Society of Nova Scotia, 1136
Frankum, Ken, Chair, Electro-Federation Canada Inc., 909
Fransen, S., Carrier Canada Ltd., 130
Franson, Dan, Director, H.L. Blachford Ltd., 223
Franssen, Gary, Manager, Nanaimo, 681
Franz, Thomas, President, Franz Environmental Inc., 201
Franzin, Bill, President, American Fisheries Society, 823
Frappier, Chantal, Récupération Nord-Ben Inc., 343
Frappier, Pierre, President, Frappier & Génier Conseillers, 201
Fraser, Alain, Hawkesbury, 711
Fraser, Allan, Superintendent, Comox, 250-339-2421, 680
Fraser, Brian, Vice President/General Manager, Layfield Geosynthetics & Industrial Fabrics Ltd., 265
Fraser, Bruce, Chair, 579
Fraser, Derek, Manager, AGAT Laboratories Ltd., 73
Fraser, Don, Vice-President, AADCO Automotive Inc., 64
Fraser, Gail, Analyst, Canadian Pacific Railway, 1100
Fraser, Gail, Head of Acquisitions, W.K. Kellogg Health Sciences Library, 1136
Fraser, Hugh, Deputy Director, Delta, 686
Fraser, James W., Director, 584
Fraser, Janet, Bibliographic & Collection Services Librarian, Ward Chipman Library, 1129
Fraser, Jim, Director, Conestoga-Rovers & Associates, 149
Fraser, John, Secretary-Treasurer, Mississippi River Power Corp., 291
Fraser, John G., President, Avensys Inc., 98
Fraser, Joseph, Acting Executive Officer, 611
Fraser, Kathleen, Director, Chilliwack, 604-792-9311, 680
Fraser, Marjie, Director, Parks & Forestry Operations, Vaughan, 722
Fraser, Mike, President, GAEA Technologies, 204
Fraser, Richard A., Vice President, Sandwell Engineering Inc., 357
Fraser, Ron, City Councillor, Woodstock, 723
Fraser, Sheila, Auditor General, 511
Fraser, Terri, Head, Regional Library & Records Services, Prairie & Northern Region - Edmonton, 1106
Fraser, Tim, Manager, Apex Industries Inc., 87
Fraser, Tony, North Dundas, 727
Fratesi, B.A., LL.B., Joseph M. (Joe), Chief Administrative Officer, Sault Ste. Marie, 705-759-5347, 720
Freamo, Joe, Chief Audit Executive, 549
Freathy, Paul, Managing Director, Rowan Williams Davies & Irwin Inc., 353
Fréchette, Lionel, Préfet, Arthabaska, 747
Fréchette, Pierre E., Conseiller d'arrondissmnt., St-Henri-Pte-Bourgogne, Montréal, 738
Fréchette, Yves, Directeur, Victoriaville, 746
Frede, Carla, Webmaster, The Van Horne Institute for International Transportation & Regula, 1016
Frederick, Catherine, Director, Human Resources, Ottawa, 716

1294 GUIDE DES RESSOURCES ENVIRONNEMENTALES CANADIENNES 2011-2012

Executive Name Index

Frederick, G. Marcille, Director of Library Services, The King's University College, 1106
Fredette-Thériault, Danielle, Officer, Human Resources, Hawkesbury, 711
Fredrickson, Bryan, Head, Acquisitions, Law Library, 1189
Freedman, Bonnie, Borden Ladner Gervais LLP - Toronto, 1073
Freedman, Robert C., Cook Roberts LLP, 1062
Freedman, Ron, Vice-President, The Impact Group, 392
Freelan, Jeffery L., Blaney McMurtry LLP, 1073
Freeman, Diane, Waterloo, 722
Freeman, Fred, Deputy Mayor & Councillor, Ingersoll, 711
Freeman, James, Matrix Solutions Inc., 282
Freeman, Sally, Quinte West, 613-965-6769, 718
Freeman, Stefan, Head, Bayer Inc., 103
Freeman, Susan, Lanark, 701
Freeman, P.Eng., Roger, Engineer, Hants East District, 697
Freer, Marnie, Principal, LEHDER Environmental Services Ltd., 267
Frégeau, Robert, Boisbriand, 734
Frei, Alex, Westech Industrial Ltd., 429
Freiburger, Larry, COO, AET Group Inc., 72
Freiburger, Scott, President/CEO, Eco2 Systems Inc., 72, 171
Freiburger, William, Treasurer & Commissioner, Finance, Sault Ste. Marie, 705-759-5349, 720
Freire, Thierry, Contact, Le Groupe Forces, 265
Freisen, John, President, Canadian Ground Water Association, 870
Freitag, Dale, Manager, Lacombe County, 669
Freitag, Shane, Partner, Borden Ladner Gervais LLP - Toronto, 1073
Freitaq, Dale, Planner & Development Officer, Lacombe County, 669
French, Brenda, Treasurer, Kincardine, 519-396-3468, 726
French, Brian, Maritime Paper Products Ltd., 281
French, Harry, Director, Ontario Sustainable Energy Association, 980
French, Lew, Treasurer, Ontario Association for Geographic & Environmental Education, 971
French, Ron, Fire Chief, Central Saanich, 250-544-4227, 686
French, Woodrow, Mayor, Conception Bay South, 693
Frenette, Denise, Vice-President, Finance & Corporate Services, 510
Frenette, Guy, Bibliotechnicien, Jardin Botanique de Montréal, 1174
Frenette, Marie-Christine, Heenan Blaikie S.E.N.C.R.L/SRL, 1084
Frenette, Mathieu, Health Physicist, Monserco Ltd., 293
Frenette, Yvon, Val-d'Or, 746
Frère, Philippe, Partner, Lavery, de Billy - Montréal, 1085
Fretz, Art, President, Transcontinental Energy Saving Products Inc., 400
Freund, Cliff, President, Manitoba Christmas Tree Grower Association, 950
Frey, Denise, Manager, Hitachi Canadian Industries Ltd., 232
Frey, Joseph G., Chair, Explorer's Club (Canadian Chapter), 914
Friars, Kate, Director, Victoria, 250-361-0355, 685
Friary, Dave, Acting Director, Operations - Roads, Parks & Fleet, Barrie, 706
Fricke, Gary, Sales Contact, HETEK Solutions Inc., 230
Friedel, Chanoch, President, Global Contract Inc., 213
Friedland, Tom, Goodmans LLP, 1075
Friedmann, Daniel E., President/CEO, MacDonald, Dettwiler & Associates Ltd., 277
Friedrich, Elliott, President/General Manager, Progress Land Services Ltd., 334
Friel, Chris, Mayor, Brantford, 519-756-2242, 707
Friel, Christine, Office Administration, E.K. Gillin & Associates Inc., 168
Friend, Bill, Vice-President, Sharp Electronics of Canada Ltd., 365
Friesen, Dave, Manager, C.G. Industrial Specialties, Ltd., 120
Friesen, Ken, Vice-President, Earthbound Environmental Inc., 169
Friesen, Morley, Manager, FS Partners, 202
Friesen, Rudy P., Principal, Friesen Tokar Architects, Landscape & Interior Designers, 202
Friesen, Tara, Sr. Specialist, Chilliwack, 604-792-9311, 680
Frigon, Chantal, Directrice, Saint-Hyacinthe, 450-778-8304, 742
Frigon, Florence, Présidente, Société d'Horticulture et d'Écologie de Prévost, 1005
Frigon, Guy, Blainville, 734
Friley, Joel S., Partner, Macleod Dixon LLP, 1052
Frinton, Peter, Metro Vancouver, 678
Frissell, Sharon E., Chair, Kamloops, 681
Frith, Steve, Branch Leader, Urban Systems Ltd., 407

Fritz, Linda, Head, Research Services, University of Saskatchewan, 1191
Fritz, Richard (Rick) D., Executive Director, The American Association of Petroleum Geologists, 822
Fritzler, Marvin, Chair, 562
Frizzell, Brad, Principal, Stantec Inc., 378
Frizzell, Garth, Prince George, 683
Froats, Doug, Coordinator, Waste Management, North Dundas, 727
Froc, Gene, Manager, AMEC, 83
Froehlich, Robert J., Macleod Dixon LLP, 1052
Frohlinger, Thomas, Pullan Kammerloch Frohlinger, 1064
From, Wesley D., Vice-President, Trojan Technologies Inc., 403
Froot, Tim, Plant Manager, CCS Income Trust, 134
Frosst, Myles, CEO, Agricultural Institute of Canada Foundation, 814
Frosst, Taun, Saugeen Shores, 719
Frost, David, Contact, Weir Power & Industrial, 424
Frost, Stan, Deputy Mayor & Councillor, Cobourg, 708
Fryer, Terry, Manager, Maple Ridge, 604-467-7450, 687
Fudge, P.Eng, John, Executive Director, Association of Consulting Engineering Companies - New Brunswick, 835
Fuerth, David, Sales & Marketing Manager, KWH Pipe, 261
Fuerth, Shaun, Director, Information Technology, Tecumseh, 720
Fugère, Marlette, Sherbrooke, 744
Fulcher, Bruce, VP, Novitherm Canada Inc., 309
Fulford, Allison, Head, Technical Services, Sexton Design & Technology Library, 1136
Fulford, John E., Vice-President, MDS Sciex, 286
Fullarton, Jonathan, Manager, CBCL Limited, 133
Fuller, Chrystal, Manager, Kings County, 902-690-6173, 696
Fuller, Cliff, Fire Chief, Red Deer County, 670
Fuller, Mike, Contact, Mike Fuller Electric Ltd., 289
Fullerton, Jane, Brockville, 707
Fulton, B.A., LL.B., Brian D., Partner, Lawson Lundell LLP - Vancouver, 1061
Fumiko, Kitano, Second Secretary (Commercial) & Trade Commissioner, 769
Fung, Aileen, Research Services Assistant, EPCOR, 1105
Fung, David T., CEO, ACDEG International Inc., 66
Fung, Peter, Manager, Tillsonburg, 721
Fung, Ray, Director, West Vancouver, 689
Funk, Eldon, Territory Manager, Waterous Power Systems, 423
Funke, Brian, Superintendent, East Kootenay, 677
Funke, Lee, Managing Director, 571
Funt, Christopher R.C., Lawson Lundell LLP - Vancouver, 1061
Fuoco, Russ, Director, Saanich, 250-475-5472, 688
Furfaro, Jim J., Guelph, 710
Furgason, Jean, Library Clerk, Hamiota District Health Centre, 1122
Furgiuele-Percy, Karen, Director, Canadian Pest Management Association, 882
Furlan, Patrice, Directeur, Saint-Hyacinthe, 450-778-8320, 742
Furlong, Arnold, Partner, ODIM Brooke Ocean, 311
Furlong, Patrick J., Davis LLP - Vancouver, 1059
Furness, Steve, Manager, Economic Development & Tourism, Owen Sound, 717
Furtney, Gloria, Librarian, Genaire Limited, 1146
Fuso, Paul, WorkLab Inc., 433
Fütterer, Dieter, Vice-President, International Arctic Science Committee, 934
Fuzakas, T., Manager, Aqua Terre Solutions Inc., 88
Fydirchuk, Alan, General Manager, Facililties & Fleet, Thunder Bay, 807-684-2774, 721
Fyfe, Alastair, Vice-President, Allan Fyfe Equipment Limited, 79
Fyfe, Steve, Lennox Industries (Canada) Ltd., 267
Fyfe, Trina, Northern Health Sciences Librarian, University of Northern British Columbia, 1115
Fyfe-Fortin, Mariette, Vice-President, 517

G

Gaal, Alex, Manager, Soper's, 374
Gaal, Bill, Manager, Prince George, 250-561-7691, 683
Gaal, Mary-Lynn, Head, Reference, Merck Frosst Canada Inc., 1168
Gabanni, Farida, Senior Director, 613
Gabor, Q.C., Robert T., Aikins, MacAulay & Thorvaldson LLP, 1063
Gaboury, Marc, Fisheries Biologist/Restoration Ecol, LGL Limited Environmental Research Associates, 271
Gabriel, Robert, Niagara, 702
Gabriele, Rénald, Vaudreuil-Dorion, 746
Gabruck, Kelly, Manager, Westburne Canada, 429

Gach, Dale, Regional Operations Manager, National Energy Equipment Inc., 297
Gachignard, Christian, President & Chief Executive Officer, Eucania International Inc., 191
Gadonneix, Pierre, Chair, World Energy Council, 1022
Gadoury, Lynda, Bibliothécaire, Bibliothèque des sciences juridiques, 1171
Gaedecke, Gabrielle, Library Technician, Ontario Ministry of Health & Long-Term Care, 1160
Gaerdes, Fritz C., Alexander Holburn Beaudin & Lang, LLP, 1057
Gaertner, Wendy, Aurora, 706
Gaetz, Sharon, Mayor, Chilliwack, 680
Gagich, Vince, President/CEO, Provincial Environmental Services Inc., 335
Gagné, Denis, Sorel-Tracy, 450-742-6481, 745
Gagné, Gervais, Sept-Iles, 744
Gagné, Hélène, Greffière, Sainte-Marie, 743
Gagné, Jean M., Fasken Martineau - Québec, 1087
Gagné, Jocelyne, Partner, Lavery, de Billy - Montréal, 1085
Gagné, Lise, Technicienne en documentation, Institut maritime du Québec, 1181
Gagné, Martin R., Fasken Martineau - Québec, 1087
Gagné, Michel, McCarthy Tétrault LLP - Montréal, 1086
Gagné, Michel, Directeur général, Rosemère, 741
Gagné, Pierre, Vice-président, Association des embouteilleurs d'eau du Québec, 832
Gagné, Richard, Director General, 518
Gagné, Serge, Directeur, Sept-Iles, 418-964-3215, 744
Gagné, Simon, Partner, Heenan Blaikie S.E.N.C.R.L/SRL, 1084
Gagné, Sylvain, Saint-Jérôme, 450-436-5357, 743
Gagné-Giguère, Suzanne, Library Team Leader-Eastern Network, Bibliothèque canadienne de l'agriculture - Lennoxville, 1184
Gagne-Lalonde, Lyne, Technicienne en documentation, University of Guelph Collège d'Alfred, 1138
Gagnier, Drew, Vice-President, Napier Environmental Technology, 296
Gagnier, Francis, Vice-President & Sales Manager, Pompaction inc., 328
Gagnier, Sylvain, President & General Manager, Pompaction inc., 328
Gagnon, Alain, Greffier, Salaberry-de-Valleyfield, 450-370-4304, 744
Gagnon, D., Director, Economic Development, Elliot Lake, 709
Gagnon, Eric, Operations Supervisor, Services industriels Newalta, 363
Gagnon, Francis, Sherbrooke, 744
Gagnon, François, Directeur, Thetford Mines, 745
Gagnon, François, General Manager, Biogénie, 108
Gagnon, François, Vérificateur général, Québec, 740
Gagnon, Frederic, Bibliothécaire, Commission de toponymie du Québec, Bibliothèque (Library), 1178
Gagnon, Gaétan, Saint-Jean-sur-Richelieu, 450-347-3209, 742
Gagnon, Gerald, Director, 666
Gagnon, Hélène, Specialist, Scientific Information, Boehringer Ingelheim (Canada) Ltd., 1167
Gagnon, Jacques, Victoriaville, 819-758-8511, 746
Gagnon, Jeannot, Directeur, Roberval, 741
Gagnon, Ken, Manager, Guelph-Eramosa, 725
Gagnon, Lise, Mascouche, 450-474-4501, 737
Gagnon, Luc, Treasurer & Director, Financial Services, Tecumseh, 720
Gagnon, Lucille, Ateliers de production, CÉGEP de Drummondville, 1167
Gagnon, M. Michel, Président, Camvac Inc., 122
Gagnon, Marc, President, Biorex Inc., 109
Gagnon, Marc-A., Président, 646
Gagnon, Marc-André, Saguenay, 741
Gagnon, Marie-Andrée, Lavery, de Billy - Montréal, 1085
Gagnon, Michael, Secretary, 607
Gagnon, Michel, Directeur général, Drummond, 747
Gagnon, Michel, Gestionnaire, Veolia ES Canada Industrial Services Inc., 412
Gagnon, Michel, President & CEO, Henlex Inc., 229
Gagnon, Michel, Siège #6, Saint-Félicien, 742
Gagnon, Michel C., Directeur général, L'Assomption, 748
Gagnon, Nicolas, Partner, Lavery, de Billy - Montréal, 1085
Gagnon, Pierre, Recyclage d'Alluminium Québec, 343
Gagnon, Réginald, Beloeil, 514-569-4500, 734
Gagnon, Suzy, Trésorière, Dolbeau-Mistassini, 735
Gagnon, Yolande, Senior Library Assistant, Circulation & Serials Ma, Gerard V. La Forest Law Library, 1127
Gagnon, Yrieix, T. Harris Environmental Management Inc., 385
Gagnon, ing., Michel, Président, Association professionnelle des ingénieurs du gouvernement du Qué, 841

CANADIAN ENVIRONMENTAL RESOURCE GUIDE 2011-2012

Executive Name Index

Gagnon-Bourget, Marianne, Cain Lamarre Casgrain Wells - Amos, 1082
Gagnon-Goupil, Sylvie, Responsable, périodiques, CÉGEP de Marie-Victorin, 1171
Gaherty, William, Vice-President, Pottinger Gaherty Environmental Consultants Ltd., 329
Gajdostik, Ward, President, MCR Environmental Consulting, 285
Gal, Ruthann, Manager, 605
Galal, Osman, Secretary General, International Union of Nutritional Sciences, 945
Galambos, Michael Z., Ganapathi & Company, 1060
Galanti, Horacio, Director, Fort St. John, 681
Galardo, Catherine, Langlois Kronström Desjardins, 1085
Galardo, Pierre, Associé, Langlois Kronström Desjardins, 1085
Galati, Robert, President/CEO, Penn Refrigeration Ltd., 321
Galbraith, David, Head, Scientific Development, Royal Botanical Gardens, 1139
Galbraith, David A., Executive Director, Canadian Botanical Conservation Network, 860
Galbraith, E., Engineering, Ingersoll-Rand Canada Inc., 241
Galbraith, Shayne, Director, Saint John, 506-658-2852, 692
Gale, Kevin, Prince Edward, 703
Gale, Norm, Chief, Emergency Medical Services, Thunder Bay, 807-625-3259, 721
Gale, Steve, Contact, DST Consulting Engineers, 167
Galea, Dave, Director, Edmonton, 780-944-6420, 672
Galgay, Frank, St. John's, 709-576-8577, 694
Galinis, Ted, General Manager, Durham Region Transit, Durham, 699
Galio, Charlie, Vice-President, Canadian Paper Recyclers, 124
Gall, John, Sales Representative, Kafko Manufacturing Ltd., 254
Gall, Murray, Territory Manager, Waterous Power Systems, 423
Gall, Q.C., Peter A., Partner, Heenan Blaikie LLP - Victoria, 1060, 1062
Gallaccio, Barbara, City Clerk, Welland, 722
Gallagher, Fred, Vision Quest - TransAlta's Wind Business, 414
Gallagher, Kevin, Vice-President, TerraChoice Environmental Marketing, 390
Gallagher, Lincoln, President, Soper's, 374
Gallagher, Ryan C., Hume, Forrest C., Law Corporation, 1060
Gallagher Jette, Pat, Rothesay, 692
Galland, Karel, President, Ecofluid Systems Inc., 172
Gallant, Brent, Summerside, 733
Gallant, Bryan L., Stones Carbert Waite Wells LLP, 1054
Gallant, Patricia, Academic Librarian, Acadia University, 1138
Gallaway, Gregg, Owner/Operations Manager, Gallason Industrial Cleaning Services Inc., 204
Gallery Dilworth, Leslie, Chief Executive Officer, Society for Environmental Graphic Design, 1007
Gallivan, Q.C., Daniel F., Cox and Palmer - Halifax, 1067
Gallo, John, Aurora, 706
Galloway, Bob, Chief, Leduc County, 780-955-7099, 669
Galloway, Kelly, Kitchener, 712
Galloway, Tom, Waterloo, 704
Galloway, CMO, Mike, Clerk, Essa, 725
Galpin, Dennis, Manager, Westburne Canada, 427
Galway, Leslie, CEO, 604
Gamache, François, President, Foresteel Industries Inc., 199
Gamache, Ginette, Directrice générale, Association québécoise du gaz naturel, 842
Gambacort, Shelley, Director, Kelowna, 681
Gambino, Vince, President, Aercoustics Engineering Limited, 71
Gamble, Harry, Owner, Harry Gamble Shipyard, 226
Gamble, Lyn, Head, Systems, Health Canada, Health Products & Food Branch, 1150
Gamble, Paul, Secretary/President & CEO, The Michener Institute for Applied Health Sciences, 954
Gamble, S., Fire Chief, Port Coquitlam, 683
Gamble, Wendy, Contact, Clearview Packaging Inc., 143
Gamble Scruton, Peggy, OFC Manager, Harry Gamble Shipyard, 226
Gamma, Tim, President, International Society of Arboriculture, 943
Gammage, Anne, Office Manager, Ontario Ground Water Association, 974
Gammon, Anne-Marie, Bathurst, 506-545-6821, 690
Ganann, John, Fire Chief, West Lincoln, 905-957-3361, 732
Ganapathi, Nathan S., Ganapathi & Company, 1060
Ganapathy, Murali, Manager, SENES Consultants Limited, 362
Gangur, Lawrence, Director, Environmental Services, Russell, 729
Gant, Alex, Chief Administrator, Uxbridge, 731
Gantefoer, Rod, Minister, 658
Gaouette, Johanne, Directrice générale, La Haute-Yamaska, 748
Garand, Bernard, President, Pompco inc., 328
Garand, François, Blainville, 734
Garceau, François, Directeur, Shawinigan, 744
Garceau, Louis-André, Greffier, Repentigny, 450-470-3130, 740
Garcia, Roberto, Coordinator, Ontario Sustainable Energy Association, 980
Garcia, Sherry, Library Coordinator, Nicola Valley Institute of Technology, 1113
Garde, Timothy J., Office Manager, Golder Associates Ltd., 215
Garde, Ty, Principal, Golder Associates Ltd., 214
Garden, Q.C., A. Robson, Counsel, MacPherson Leslie & Tyerman LLP - Calgary, 1052
Gardham, Bruce, Senior Librarian, Toronto Public Health, 1162
Gardhouse, Joe, Collingwood, 708
Gardiner, Ed, CEO, Novatech Controls, Inc., 309
Gardiner, George, Area Sales Manager, Argus Telecom International Inc., 90
Gardiner, Penny, Facilities Director, Hamilton Incubator of Technology, 927
Gardiner, Syd, Cornwall, 708
Gardiner, BSc, RVT, Sheila, Administrator, Wildlife Rescue Association of British Columbia, 1020
Gardner, Grant, Chair, The Canadian Network for Environmental Education & Communication, 879
Gardner, Greg, Mayor, Squamish, 688
Gardner, Lucie, Directrice générale, Université du Québec à Montréal, 1176
Gardner, Tom, Haliburton, 705-489-3703, 700
Gardner, William S., Pitblado LLP, 1063
Gardner-Barclay, Susan, Director General, 527
Gareau, Denis, Sr. Vice-President, Comstock Canada Ltd., 148
Gareau, Laurent F., Office Manager, Golder Associates Ltd., 215
Gareau, Sophie, Greffière, Val-d'Or, 746
Gareau, CA, AMCT, John J., Treasurer, North Dundas, 727
Garets, FHIMSS, Dave, Executive VP & President/CEO, Healthcare Information & Management Systems Society, 928
Garfinkel, John P., Executive Director, International Sanitary Supply Association, Inc., 942
Garfinkel, Josh, Campaign Director, Earthroots, 907
Garibaldi, Bill, Director, Water Services, Waterloo, 519-747-8605, 722
Gariépy, Jean, Directeur et chef, Saint-Constant, 742
Gariépy, Jean-Pierre, Directeur, Laval, 450-662-4242, 736
Garis, Len, Fire Chief, Surrey, 604-541-4011, 684
Garland, Art, Business Development, Nelson Environmental Remediation Ltd., 299
Garlough, Hugh, Manager, Public Works, South Dundas, 730
Garneau, Claude, Alma, 418-668-3694, 733
Garneau, Céline, Associée, Langlois Kronström Desjardins, 1085
Garner, David A., Managing Partner, Alexander Holburn Beaudin & Lang, LLP, 1057
Garner, Diana L., City Clerk, Calgary, 403-268-5861, 671
Garner, Jeremy, Superintendent, Fort St. John, 681
Garner, Mike, Commissioning Engineer, Muddy River Technologies Inc., 295
Garnett, Joyce C., University Librarian, University of Western Ontario Libraries, 1144
Garnier, Charles, Préfet, Les Pays-d'en-Haut, 750
Garon, Denis, Sous-ministre & dirigeante principale de l'informa, 653
Garrett, Crae, Partner, Macleod Dixon LLP, 1052
Garrington, Diane, Coordinator, Communications, St. Catharines, 719
Garrison, Elizabeth, Manager, Transit Operations, Belleville, 706
Garrity, Michael T., Executive Director, Alliance for the Wild Rockies, 821
Garrod, Bruce, Head Librarian, Noranda Earth Sciences Library, 1159
Garson, Allen H., Partner, Heenan Blaikie LLP - Toronto, 1075
Gartshore, Louise, City Clerk, Woodstock, 723
Garvin, Susan, Librarian, Teshmont Consultants LP, 1125
Garychuk, Gregg, President, Expert Systems Inc., 192
Gascon, Benoît, Associé, Miller Thomson LLP - Montréal, 1086
Gascon, Marc, Maire, Saint-Jérôme, 743
Gaspar, Ed, Yard Manager, Hagersville Recycling & Auto Wrecking Ltd., 223
Gass, Cheryl, Treasurer, Saint John Naturalists' Club, 998
Gates, Donna, Principal, James N. Allan Campus, 1155
Gates, Jenny, Editor, The Bulletin, Manitoba Naturalists Society, 1124
Gates, Jim, Treasurer, Middlesex, 701
Gates, Steve, Facility Manager, Hyprescon Inc., 237
Gates, Wayne, City Councillor, Niagara Falls, 715
Gatien, Daniel, Chief Administrative Officer & Clerk, Clarence-Rockland, 708
Gatward, Joan, Brant, 698
Gau, Mike, Manager, Whitehorse, 867-668-8333, 755
Gaucher, Gilles, Beloeil, 450-446-5576, 734
Gaudart, Raymond, Coordinator, Kootenay Boundary, 678
Gaudes, Kathie, Library Technician, Peter Lougheed Centre Library, 1102
Gaudet, Charlene, Director, 518
Gaudet, Jean J., Councillor at Large, Dieppe, 506-854-8409, 691
Gaudet, John D., Vice-President, Maritime Electric Company Ltd., 280
Gaudet, Marc, Contact, Conestoga-Rovers & Associates, 149
Gaudet, Ronald, Rouyn-Noranda, 741
Gaudette, Michel, Contact, Dynapompe Inc., 168
Gaudor, Guy, Granby, 735
Gaudreau, Josée, Technicienne en documentation, Campus Notre-Dame-de-Foy, 1182
Gaudreau, Louis, Responsable, Référence, CÉGEP de Chicoutimi, 1166
Gaudreau, Léopold, Sous-ministre adjoint, 646
Gaudreault, Annie, Directrice, Québec, 740
Gaudreault, Jean, Directeur, Mirabel, 450-475-8656, 738
Gaudreault, Michel, Directeur administratif, Université de Montréal, 1176
Gaudreault, Réjean, Maire, La Tuque, 736
Gaudreault, Sylvie, Saguenay, 741
Gaudry, Michelle, Policy Coordinator, Burrard Inlet Environmental Action Program & Fraser River Estuary, 852
Gaul, Alain, Davies Ward Phillips & Vineberg S.E.N.C.R.L., s.r.l., 1083
Gauley, Q.C., David (Tom) E., McDougall Gauley, 1090
Gaulin, Céline, Chief Administrative Officer, 552
Gaulin, Diane, Responsable, Services techniques, Université de Hearst, 1142
Gaulin, Marty, General Manager, WorleyParsons Canada Ltd., 434
Gauthier, Daniel, Mirabel, 738
Gauthier, Danielle, Partner, Heenan Blaikie S.E.N.C.R.L/SRL - Sherbrooke, 1089
Gauthier, Danielle, Secrétaire & acquisitions, CÉGEP St-Jean-sur-Richelieu, 1183
Gauthier, Danny, Sales Representative, Services industriels Newalta, 363
Gauthier, Denis, Assistant Deputy Minister, 526
Gauthier, Denis, Vice-President, Products BCM Ltée BCM, 333
Gauthier, Elizabeth, Manager, Human Resources, Prescott & Russell, 729
Gauthier, Gaby, Sept-Iles, 744
Gauthier, Jacques, President & CEO, LVM Inc., 275
Gauthier, Ken, Branch Leader, Urban Systems Ltd., 408
Gauthier, Lise, Présidente, Association des jardineries du Québec, 832
Gauthier, Louise, Boisbriand, 734
Gauthier, Michel, Saint-Jean-sur-Richelieu, 450-515-9846, 742
Gauthier, Paul, General Manager, Saskatoon, 754
Gauthier, Pierre, President/CEO, Alstom Canada Inc., 80
Gauthier, Robert, Analyste, CÉGEP d'André-Laurendeau, 1169
Gauthier, Robert, Directeur, Westburne Canada, 427
Gauthier, S., Carrier Canada Ltd., 130
Gauthier, MBA, OMA, Jean-François, Greffier, Sainte-Julie, 450-922-7050, 743
Gauthieu, Michel, Director, NRC Information Services, Canada Institute for Scientific & Technical Information (CISTI), 1148
Gautreau, Yvon, Vice-Chair, Westmorland-Albert Solid Waste Corporation, 759
Gauvin, Hélène, Lavery, de Billy - Québec, 1088
Gauvin, Jacques, Président, Conseil de la recherche forestière du Québec, 900
Gauvin, Line, Technicienne en documentation, Québec Ministère de l'agriculture, des pêcheries et de l'alimenta, 1179
Gauvin, Mira, McCarthy Tétrault LLP - Montréal, 1086
Gauvreau, Chantal, Directrice générale, Sainte-Thérèse, 744
Gauvreau, Chantal, Sec.-Trés., Régie intermunicipale d'assainissement des eaux de Rosemère et de, 760
Gavin, Jerry, Director, 636
Gavins, Margaret, Partner, Heenan Blaikie LLP - Toronto, 1075
Gay, Amanda, Library Technologist, FP Innovations Forintek Division, 1118
Gay, Judy, Georgian Bluffs, 725
Gaynor, Kathy, Information Services Librarian, Thompson Rivers University, 1112
Gazky, Sue, Vice-President & Business Manager, Rochester Midland Ltd., 349
Gazurek, Eva, Heenan Blaikie S.E.N.C.R.L/SRL, 1084
Gazzola, John, Kitchener, 712
Gee, Barry, Director, LifeSciences British Columbia, 949
Gee, Ian, President, Premier Envelope, 331

1296 GUIDE DES RESSOURCES ENVIRONNEMENTALES CANADIENNES 2011-2012

Executive Name Index

Geehan, Elizabeth, Head, Technical Services, Health Canada, Health Products & Food Branch, 1150
Geere, Richard, I.G. Micromed Environmental Inc., 237
Geesing, Dieter, Project Manager, Transform Compost Systems Ltd., 400
Gehrels, Jim, President, Lifewater Canada, 949
Geiger, Jochen, AMETEK Process Instruments, 84
Geleta, Richard K., President & Director/Senior Engineer, Brisbin & Sentis Engineering Inc., 116
Geleynse, Bart, Manager, RBR Ltd., 343
Gelinas, Frank, General Manager, Corporate Services, Norfolk, 702
Gélinas, Michel, Président-fondateur, Fondation québécoise du cancer, 917
Gelly, Sylvie, Directrice générake, Régie intermunicipale de gestion des déchets du Bas St-François, 760
Gemmell, John, Lanark, 701
Gemmell, Tom, Division Manager, Municipal Works, Cornwall, 708
Gendebien, Daniel, Director, Tornatech, 397
Gendron, Alain, Secteur de la circulation, Bibliothèque des sciences humaines et sociales, 1177
Gendron, Irene V., General Counsel, 518
Gendron, Jean Pierre, Directeur, Sainte-Thérèse, 744
Gendron, Lucie, Directrice générale, Saint-Lazare, 743
Gendron, Lucie, Responsable, Cartothèque, 1185
Gendron, Mike, Châteauguay, 514-829-1986, 735
General, K., General Manager, Corporate Services, Haldimand, 700
General Manager, Bruce, Director, Peace River, 678
Généreux, Bernard, Préfet, Le Domaine-du-Roy, 749
Généreux, Bernard, Président, Fédération Québécoise des Municipalités, 916
Genest, Yvan, Directeur général, Les Pays-d'en-Haut, 750
Gennings, Keegan, Chief Building Official, Pelham, 717
Geoghegan, Tony, Regional Director General, Niagara - Fort Erie Reg, 514
Georgakopoulos, John, Willms & Shier Environmental Lawyers LLP, 1081
Georgas, Jim, Contact, R.J. Burnside & Associates Limited, 340
George, Brian F., Regional Director, Williams Engineering Inc., 432
George, Kevin, Councillor, Kingston, 712
Georgeff, Lynn, Manager, Human Resources, Newmarket, 714
Georgescu, Adina-Cristina, Miller Thomson LLP - Montréal, 1086
Georgetti, Ken, President, Canadian Labour Congress, 876
Georgieff, Alex L., Commissioner, Planning Department, Durham, 699
Georgiou, Demetri, Office Manager, Trow Consulting Engineers Ltd., 403
Geraghty, D., Lalonde Geraghty Riendeau Lapierre, 1089
Geraghty, Shannon, Treasurer, South Dundas, 730
Gerardi, Paul, English Language Contact, Crompton Technology Inc., 153
Gerbasi, Jenny, Winnipeg, 204-986-5878, 690
Gerber, Fred, Manager, LINPAC Ropak Packaging, 272
Gerbis, Michael, President/CEO, The Delphi Group, 392
Gerencher, Eva, Senior Environmental Scientist, URS Canada Inc., 408
Gerke, Gerry, Manager, Custom Environmental Services Ltd., 154
Germain, Claude, Sales Representative, GENEQ Inc., 206
Germain, Diane, President, Hydrogéochem Environnement Inc., 236
Germain, Lizette, Bibliothécaire, CHUQ-CHUL, 1178
Germain, Marc-André, Heenan Blaikie S.E.N.C.R.L/SRL - Trois-Rivières, 1089
Germain, Marie-France, Présidente, 648
German, Richard B., Sr. Principal, Decommissioning Consulting Services Limited, 159
Germano, Joe, Manager, Road & Traffic, North Bay, 715
Germundson, John G., System Administrator, Transport Canada, 1152
Gerow, Ronald, Warden & Councillor, Peterborough, 703
Gerrand, Karl, Sr. Vice-President, Viterra Inc., 414
Gerrard, Paul, Saanich, 688
Gerrard, Peter, Executive Director, Cosmopolitan Industries Limited, 152
Gerrard, Philip, Chief Building Official, North Grenville, 728
Gerretsen, John, Minister, 623
Gerretsen, Mark, Mayor, Kingston, 712
Gerry, David, Head, AquaMetrix Inc., 88
Gerry, Mongey, Trade Commissioner, 768

Gershon, MD, FIDSA, Anne, President, Infectious Diseases Society of America, 931
Gerspacher, Melvin, Managing Partner, Robertson Stromberg Pedersen LLP, 1091
Gervair, Michael, Sr. Vice-President, Business Develop, ATCO Group, 95
Gervais, René, President, René Gervais Inc., Consultants, 345
Gervais, Ronald, Pembroke, 717
Gervais, Trent, Fire Chief, Peterborough, 718
Gettinby, MA, MCIP, RPP,, Thomas G., Municipal Clerk, Brock, 724
Getty, Mel, Councillor, Tillsonburg, 721
Gévry, Jacques, Granby, 735
Geysens, Roger, Norfolk, 702
Ghandi, Zaim, Director, Petro Sep Membrane Technologies Inc., 322
Gherbaz, Sabrina A., Torys LLP, 1081
Ghikas, Q.C., Gerald W.J., Senior Partner, Borden Ladner Gervais LLP - Vancouver, 1058
Gho, Joseph G., Chairman & CEO, EPI Environmental Products Inc., 189
Ghoche, Camille, President, Megalab Inc., 286
Ghonima, FCILT, Hazem, CEO, Chartered Institute of Logistics and Transport in North America, 894
Ghosh, A., Director, Space & Photonics, Experimental Fusion Facility, 191
Giampaolo, Michael, President, Triple M Metal, 402
Giannou, Chris, President, Hercules SLR Inc., 229
Giansante, Piero, Marketing Manager, Endress+Hauser Canada Ltd., 178
Giard, Jean-Luc, Sec.-Trés., Régie d'aqueduc intermunicipale paroisse St-Pie et Notre-Dame-de-, 759
Giard, Marc, Greffier, Varennes, 746
Giaschi-Pacini, Lori-Lynn, District Councillor, Bracebridge, 706
Giasson, Serge, Directeur, Québec, 740
Gibb, David, Manager, Westburne Canada, 426
Gibb, Diane, Conseillère, Pierre-Foretier, Montréal, 738
Gibb, Roger S., Vice-President/General Manager, Stablex Canada Inc., 377
Gibbon, Brian, Contact, Brereton Field Naturalists' Club Inc., 846
Gibbons, Ed, Edmonton, 672
Gibbons, J. Shawn, CH2M Hill Canada Limited, 137
Gibbons, Jack, Chair, Ontario Clean Air Alliance, 972
Gibbons, Luc, Siège #4, Saint-Félicien, 742
Gibbs, Don, President, Tekmar Control Systems Ltd., 389
Gibbs, Lois Marie, Executive Director/Founder, Center for Health, Environment & Justice, 893
Gibbs, Mitchell, Manager, TEAM-1 Environmental Services Inc., 387
Gibeau, Guy, Adjoint au directeur des études, CÉGEP de Saint-Laurent, 1184
Gibeau, Jean-Marc, Conseiller de ville, Ovide-Clermont, Montréal, 738
Giberson, Peter, Owner, Dartmouth Metals & Bottles Ltd., 157
Gibson, Bill, Director, Fire Services, & Fire Chief, Strathroy-Caradoc, 731
Gibson, Dan, Manager, Focal Technologies Inc., 198
Gibson, Dean, Director, New Westminster, 682
Gibson, Dean, President, British Columbia Recreation & Parks Association, 849
Gibson, Grant, City Councillor, Brampton, 706
Gibson, Jean, Treasurer, Nature Nova Scotia (Federation of Nova Scotia Naturalists), 960
Gibson, Kevin D., McInnes Cooper, 1067
Gibson, Mark, Plant Manager, LINPAC Ropak Packaging, 272
Gibson, Simon, Abbotsford, 679
Gibson, Tim, Director, Building Approvals & Inspections, East Gwillimbury, 708
Gibson, Q.C., Brock W., Chair, Blake, Cassels & Graydon LLP - Calgary, 1049
Gibson-MacDonald, Norma, Manager, 517
Gick, Natialie, Campus Librarian, Surrey Library, 1116
Giddens, Peter, Lang Michener LLP - Toronto, 1077
Giercke, Ron K., President, Mesh Technologies Inc., 287
Giersch, Lynn, Business Manager, Manitoba Water Well Association, 952
Giertuga, Trevor, Ward Councillor, Thunder Bay, 721
Giesbrecht, Michael, Manager, Mission, 604-820-3756, 687
Giesbrecht, Peter, Manager, The National Testing Laboratories Ltd., 393
Gifford, Brian, Chair, 572
Gignac, Clément, Ministre, 648
Gignac, Jo-Anne, Windsor, 723
Gignac, Pierre, Directeur, Québec, 418-641-6210, 740
Gignac, Pierre, Senior Vice-President, 525

Gignac, Sue, Treasurer, Midland, 713
Giguère, Chantale, Directrice, Québec, 740
Giguère, Chantale, Directrice générale adjointe, Québec, 740
Giguère, Suzanne, Sous-ministre, 654
Gil, George, Sr. Research Scientist, Kam Biotechnology Ltd., 254
Gilbart, Bryan, Vice-President, Envirogard Products Ltd., 184
Gilbert, André, Val-d'Or, 746
Gilbert, Anne, Chatham-Kent, 724
Gilbert, Annick, Fasken Martineau - Québec, 1087
Gilbert, Charles, District Sales Manager, Babcock & Wilcox Canada Ltd., 100
Gilbert, Cheryl, Heenan Blaikie S.E.N.C.R.L/SRL - Sherbrooke, 1089
Gilbert, Christian, Sales Representative, Armtec Construction Products, 92
Gilbert, Clermont, President/CEO, Environnement Godin Inc., 186
Gilbert, Eric, Chair, Ontario Tire Dealers Association, 980
Gilbert, Glen, President, Canadian Seabed Research Ltd., 125
Gilbert, Gwen, Bruce, 698
Gilbert, Jay, City Clerk, Coquitlam, 680
Gilbert, Kevin, Outside Sales Representative, C.G. Industrial Specialties, Ltd., 120
Gilbert, Leslie, Sec.-Treas., Heritage Society of British Columbia, 929
Gilbert, Michel, Maire, Mont-St-Hilaire, 738
Gilbert, Owen, Manager, GLM Tanks & Equipment Ltd., 213
Gilbert, Richard, President, Météoglobe Canada Inc., 287
Gilbert-Collet, Alice, Bibliotechnicienne, Acquisitions, Collège universitaire de St-Boniface, 1123
Gilborn, R.J. Daniel, Borden Ladner Gervais LLP - Calgary, 1049
Gilby, Stuart C.B., Burchell Hayman Parish, 1067
Gilchrist, Doug, Director, Kelowna, 681
Gilchrist, Jim, President, Career Advancement Employment, 128
Gilchrist, Kathleen, Municipal Clerk, Huntsville, 711
Gilders, Ross, Manager, 596
Giles, B., Secretary, Saskatchewan Coalition for Tobacco Reduction, 999
Giles, Gerry, Chair, Cowichan Valley, 677
Giles, Greg, Superintendent, Mission, 604-820-3765, 687
Giles, John, Manager, Solid Waste, Kingston, 712
Giles, John M., President, EnviroPower Equipment Marketing Inc., 187
Giles, Kevin, Manager, PRT Inc., 336
Giles, L.A., City Clerk & Director, Information Services, Guelph, 710
Giles, Marshall, Director, 610
Giles, Michael A., Chief Building Official, Dufferin, 699
Gill, Alex, Executive Director, Ontario Environment Industry Association, 970, 973
Gill, Bruce, President, Entomological Society of Ontario, 911
Gill, Ed, Managing Director, Operations & Transportation, Orangeville, 716
Gill, Harvinder, Manager, Recycling Council of British Columbia, 993
Gill, Moe, Metro Vancouver, 678
Gill, Mohindar (Moe), Abbotsford, 679
Gill, Paul, General Manager, Maple Ridge, 687
Gill, Rob, General Manager, York Disposal Service Ltd., 435
Gill, Tom, Surrey, 604-591-4634, 684
Gillard, Debbie, City Clerk, Yellowknife, 867-920-5646, 695
Gillard, Todd, Cascades Recovery Inc., 131
Gilles, Russell, Co-ordinator, Altamar International Inc., 81
Gillespie, C., Carrier Canada Ltd., 129
Gillespie, Eric, Director, Transit Services, Waterloo, 704
Gillespie, R.K., Commissioner, Employee & Business Services, Peel, 703
Gillespie, Ted, City Manager, Wetaskiwin, 674
Gillette, Gordon, Manager, Cariboo, 677
Gillette, Patrick, President/COO, Xeneca Power Development Inc., 435
Gillezeau, Jeannette, Vice-President, Clayton Research Associates Ltd., 142
Gilligan, Steve, Sales Manager, Cancoppas Limited, 126
Gilliland, Peter, Lambton, 701
Gilliland, Peter, Deputy Mayor & Councillor, St. Clair, 519-862-3534, 729
Gilliland, William G., Fraser Milner Casgrain LLP - Calgary, 1051
Gillingham, Ed, Parts Manager, Toromont Caterpillar, 397
Gillis, Alex, Mississippi Mills, 714
Gillis, Anne Marie, City / County Councillor, Sarnia, 719
Gillis, Anne Marie, Deputy Warden, Lambton, 701
Gillis, Jim, DPL Group, 166
Gillis, Malcolm, Manager, Cape Breton, 695

CANADIAN ENVIRONMENTAL RESOURCE GUIDE 2011-2012   1297

Executive Name Index

Gillis, Mary, Circulation Clerk, Defence R & D Canada - Atlantic, 1135
Gillis, Ralph, Director, North Saanich, 687
Gillis, Tom, Director, Foothills No. 31, 669
Gillis, William, Officer, Inverness County, 697
Gillis, P.Eng., Edward, Director, Hants East District, 697
Gillott, Roger, Partner, Osler, Hoskin & Harcourt LLP - Toronto, 1079
Gilmer, Jeffrey S., Port Hope, 728
Gilmet, Roy, Howard Marten Fluid Technologies Inc., 234
Gilmore, Carolyn, Coordinator, Dawson College, 1173
Gilmore, John R., Bennett Jones LLP - Calgary Office, 1049
Gilmore, Karl, Senior. Vice-President, Tera Environmental Consultants (Alta) Ltd., 389
Gilmour, Bradley S., Bennett Jones LLP - Calgary Office, 1049
Gilmour, Ray, Deputy Minister, 570
Gilroy, Ernie, CEO, 588
Gingras, Appollinaire, President, Les Bras d'Fer Gingras Inc., 268
Gingras, Liliane E., Davis LLP - Toronto, 1074
Gingras, Paul, Directeur, La Mitis, 748
Gingras, Serge, Technicien en audiovisuel, Campus Notre-Dame-de-Foy, 1182
Gingras, Serge, Vice-President, Les Bras d'Fer Gingras Inc., 268
Gingras, Vincent, Joli-Cour Lacasse Avocats, 1088
Ginter, Marvyl, Library Technician, Manitoba Dept. of Conservation, Environment Canada & Canadian Cou, 1124
Giofu, P.Eng, Antonietta, Engineer, Environmental Services, Amherstburg, 705
Gionet, André, Head, Potato Research Centre, 1128
Gionet, Jean-Marie, Chair, Commission de gestion des déchets solides de la péninsule Acadien, 758
Gionet, Pierre, Directeur général, Lachute, 736
Giovannetti, Thomas F., Engineer, Civtech Engineering & Surveying Ltd., 142
Girard, Brian, Treasurer, Society of Professional Engineers & Associates, 1008
Girard, Carol, Directeur, Saguenay, 741
Girard, Denis, Coordonnateur, Saint-Charles-Borromée, 753
Girard, Jacques, Directeur, Bureau de Normalisation du Québec, 118
Girard, Jean, Lévis, 736
Girard, Jean-Claude, Morency Avocats, 1088
Girard, Jean-François, Président, Centre québécois du droit de l'environnement, 894
Girard, Jocelyn, Président-Directeur général (par-intérim) & Vice-p, 654
Girard, José, Directeur, Repentigny, 450-470-3860, 740
Girard, Leonard, General Manager, Azco Industries Ltd., 100
Girard, Marlène, Directrice, Repentigny, 450-470-3140, 740
Girard, Norman, Laval, 736
Girard, Patrick, Associé, Stikeman Elliott LLP - Montréal, 1087
Girard, Pierre, Directeur général, Charlevoix-Est, 747
Girard, Raymond, Manager, Calgary Metal (1985) Ltd., 121
Girard, Valérie, Communication Coordinator, Seeds of Diversity Canada, 1003
Giroday, Lesley A., Ratcliff & Company LLP, 1057
Girotti, Dominic, President & Owner, Hy-Grade Precast Concrete, 235
Girouard, Jean-Marc, Président, Exploitation Santec Inc., 192
Girouard, Marcie, Executive Director, 515
Giroux, Claude, Sec.-Trés., Régie intermunicipale de l'eau de la Vallée du Richelieu, 760
Giroux, François, President, Gentec Inc., 210
Giroux, Ghislaine, Web & Library Assistant, International Civil Aviation Organization, 1174
Giroux, Jeanette, Library Technician, Thames Campus Resource Centre, 1139
Giroux, Lee, Director, 656
Giroux, Mario, Directeur, Saguenay, 741
Giroux, Michel, Préfet, La Jacques-Cartier, 748
Girvitz, Ronald S., Wilson Laycraft, 1054
Gish, Ann, Librarian, Grande Prairie Regional College, 1108
Gislason, Thora, Librarian, Metro Vancouver (formerly Greater Vancouver Regional District), 1110
Gittings, Dave, Town Councillor, Oakville, 715
Given, Bill, Mayor, Grande Prairie, 672
Gjerek, Martin, Sales Manager, Fabco Plastics Wholesale (Ontario) Limited, 193
Glab, Arthur, Manager, Engineering, Leamington, 726
Gladden, Bob, Manager, Toromont Caterpillar, 397
Gladu, Claude, Maire, Longueuil, 737
Gladu, Robert, Longueuil, 737
Glaholt, Duncan W., Glaholt LLP, 1075

Glaholt, Randal, Sr. Wildlife Biologist/Partner, Tera Environmental Consultants (Alta) Ltd., 389
Glaister, Bill, Coordinator of Faculty of Education Curriculum Lab, University of Lethbridge, 1108
Glanville, William H., Vice-President & COO, International Institute for Sustainable Development, 940
Glanville, Q.C., G. Mort, McKenzie Lake Lawyers LLP, 1069
Glasgow, Ian, CAO, Hants East District, 697
Glaspell, Barry L., Partner, Borden Ladner Gervais LLP - Toronto, 1073
Glass, Ian, Librarian, Ducks Unlimited Canada, 1122
Glassco, Michael, Operations Manager, Theodor D. Sterling & Associates Ltd., 393
Glassford, Don, Chief Administrative Officer, Brant, 698
Gleason, Mary J., Partner, Ogilvy Renault LLP/S.E.N.C.R.L., s.r.l. - Ottawa, 1071
Gleason, Mary Lynn, Partner, Borden Ladner Gervais LLP - Toronto, 1073
Gleave, Stephen F., Partner, Hicks Morley Hamilton Stewart Storie LLP, 1076
Gleddie, Sandy, Philom Bios Inc., 323
Gleddie, Sanford, Vice-President, Philom Bios Inc., 323
Gleig, Tim, Director, Kitimat, 687
Glen, Jim, Vice-President, Central Canadian Federation of Mineralogical Societies, 893
Glenn, Daniel K., Principal, Glenn Group Ltd., 213
Glenn, Ray H., General Manager, Global Sensor Systems Inc., 213
Glenn-Graham, Daniel, Kitchener, 712
Gliener, Isidor, President, Acoustic Solutions Ltd., 67
globe foundation of canad, The GLOBE Foundation of C, Vancouver, BC, 1040
Glos, C., President & Chief Engineer, Glos Associates Inc., 214
Glos, J.L., Vice-President, Glos Associates Inc., 214
Glos, Martin, Vice-President, Glos Associates Inc., 214
Glover, Bill, Councillor, Kingston, 712
Glover, Robert, Manager, ACO Container Systems Ltd., 67
Glowacki, Dan, Supervisor, Westburne Canada, 429
Glowacki, Monina A.P., Thompson Dorfman Sweatman LLP, 1064
Gnassi, Bruno, University Librarian, Mount Allison University, 1129
Gobbi, Norm, Chief Operator, Prince George, 250-562-4578, 683
Gobeil, Bertrand, Morency Avocats, 1088
Gobeil, Francis, Directeur, Trois-Rivières, 819-370-6700, 745
Gobeil, Michel, Directeur, Mascouche, 737
Godavari, Norma, Head, Donald W. Craik Engineering Library, 1123
Godbout, Steven, Regional Manager, Varcon Inc., 409
Goddard, Chuck, Manager, Maple Ridge, 604-467-7487, 687
Godding, Randy, President, Ontario Building Solutions, 312
Godfredson, Egan, Plant Superintendent, Border Chemical Company Ltd., 114
Godfrey, Grant W., President/CEO, Godfrey Associates Ltd., 214
Godfrey, Ian, Partner, Heenan Blaikie LLP - Toronto, 1075
Godfrey, Irene, Supervisor, Diana M. Priestly Law Library, 1120
Godhe, Pat, President, Canadian Organic Livestock Association, 881
Godin, Gastien, General Director, Coastal Zones Research Institute Inc., 145
Godin, Paul, General Engineer, Bathurst, 690
Godin, Pierre, Directeur, Shawinigan, 744
Godin, Pierre, Directeur général, La Rivière-du-Nord, 748
Godin, Stéphane, Exec. VP & COO, Graymont Inc., 216
Godmaire, Hélène, Director, Great Lakes United, 925
Godolphin, Jocelyn, Associate University Librarian, Collection Service, Concordia University Libraries, 1173
Godreau, Guy, Joli-Cour Lacasse Avocats, 1088
Goebel, Nancy, Head Librarian, Augustana Faculty, 1103
Goebel, Randy, President/CEO, 563
Goehring, Brenda, Manager, BC Hydro, 103
Goertz, Gretchen, Technical Services Librarian, Douglas College, 1114
Goettler, Vaughn, CEO, Blue-Zone Technologies Ltd., 110
Goetz, Bill, Bruce, 698
Goetz, John C., Burnet, Duckworth & Palmer LLP, 1050
Gogal, Sandra A., Partner, Miller Thomson LLP - Toronto, 1078
Gogolev, Mikhail, AGRECOM inc., 73
Gohn, Jennifer, Manager, Human Resources, Orangeville, 716
Golay, Nathalie, Donovan & Company, 1059
Gold, Mitchell, Executive Director, International Association of Educators for World Peace, 935
Goldbach, Mark, Office Manager, Golder Associates Ltd., 214
Goldberg, Jed, President, Earth Day Canada, 907
Goldberg, Joel, Partner, Heenan Blaikie S.E.N.C.R.L/SRL, 1084

Goldberg, Tanya M., Partner, Borden Ladner Gervais LLP - Toronto, 1073
Goldberg, Tracey J., Director, Eco Waste Solutions, 170
Goldblatt, Harold, President, Hagersville Recycling & Auto Wrecking Ltd., 223
Goldblatt, Jerry, Non Ferrous Manager, Hagersville Recycling & Auto Wrecking Ltd., 223
Goldenberg, Jonathan L., D'Arcy & Deacon LLP, 1063
Goldfuss, Kevin, Director, Williams Lake, 250-392-1783, 686
Goldhaber, Martin, President, Geochemical Society, 923
Goldie, Andrew, Director, Parks & Recreation, Centre Wellington, 724
Golding, Bill, Partner & Operations Manager, Silvicon Services Inc., 368
Golding, Greg, Manager, SimplexGrinnell, 369
Golding, Kevin, President, Rothsay, 352
Goldring, Rick, Halton, 700
Goldring, Rick, Mayor, Burlington, 905-335-7607, 707
Goldsmith-Jones, Pamela, Metro Vancouver, 678
Goldsmith-Jones, Pamela, Mayor, West Vancouver, 689
Goldstein, Annette, Vice-President, MW Metal Spinning & Stamping Ltd., 295
Golem, Dave, Hastings, 700
Golembiewski, David, District Sales Rep., National Instruments Canada, 298
Goloff, Theodore, Associé, Robinson Sheppard Shapiro LLP, 1087
Golota, Kara-Lee, Vice-President, RBR Ltd., 343
Golton, Dave, General Manager, Laidlaw Carriers Inc. - Van Division, 262
Gomery, Sally A., Partner, Ogilvy Renault LLP/S.E.N.C.R.L., s.r.l. - Ottawa, 1071
Gomes, Robert J. (Bob), President & CEO, Stantec Inc., 377
Gomez, Antonio, Director, Climate Control Systems Inc., 144
Goncalves, Francisco, McElhanney Consulting Services Ltd., 285
Gonnsen, Karl, President, Metropolitan Consulting Inc., 288
Gonzalez, Francisco, VP, Integran Technologies Inc., 244
Gonzalez, Yvette, CEO, Northwest Territories Association of Communities, 967
Gonzalez, P. Eng., Robert, General Manager, Richmond, 604-276-4000, 684
Goobie, Roger, Area Supervisor, Armtec Construction Products, 91
Goobie, Tony, Sales Contact, Rotork Controls (Canada) Ltd., 352
Gooch, Daniel-Robert, Director, Canadian Airports Council, 855
Gooch, Mike, Director, Development Services, Huntsville, 711
Good, Donald R., Good, Donald R., 1070
Good, Rick, Plant Manager, CCS Income Trust, 134
Goodacre, Rick, Executive Director, Heritage Society of British Columbia, 929
Goodall, Geoff, Director, Williams Lake, 250-392-1766, 686
Goodall, Gerald W., Consultant, Edmonton, 780-496-3729, 672
Goodall, DBE, Jane, Founder, The Jane Goodal Institute of Canada, 946
Goode, Steve, Fire Chief, Erin, 709
Gooderham, David A., Alexander Holburn Beaudin & Lang, LLP, 1057
Goodeve, Colin, Committee Administrator, Kitchener, 712
Goodfellow, Eileen, Head of Technical Services, Concordia University College of Alberta, 1105
Goodfellow, Howard D., President, Techint Goodfellow Technologies Inc., 387
Goodfellow, Ian, Director, Finance & Treasurer, Bradford West Gwillimbury, 706
Goodfellow, Ian, Treasurer, Innisfil, 711
Gooding, Ted, President, College of Alberta Professional Foresters, 897
Goodings, Karen, Chair, North Central Local Government Association, 678, 965
Goodlet, James, Vice-President & Manager, Frederick Goertz Ltd., 201
Goodman, Jeffrey, Partner, Heenan Blaikie LLP - Toronto, 1075
Goodman, Kim, Manager, Environmental Information Association, 912
Goodwin, Randall, Environmental Scientist, Kodiak Environmental Limited, 259
Goodyear, Michael, Executive Director, Churchill Northern Studies Centre, 1122
Goosen, Keith, Cypress Sales Partnership, 155
Goosen, Keith, Sales Contact, Rotork Controls (Canada) Ltd., 352
Goraczko, Adalbert W., President, Sols Consultants Ltée, 373
Goranson, Paul, Director, Red Deer, 403-342-8162, 674

Executive Name Index

Gorber, Donald M., President & CEO, SENES Consultants Limited, 362
Gordon, Adrian, President & Chief Executive Officer, Canadian Centre for Emergency Preparedness, 861
Gordon, Alan, President & CEO, Altus Capital Planning Inc., 82
Gordon, Charles, President & Chief Executive Officer, Siemens Water Technologies, 367
Gordon, Colin G., Director, 607
Gordon, David, Leeds & Grenville, 726
Gordon, David, Mayor, North Grenville, 728
Gordon, François, Gestionnaire, Veolia ES Canada Industrial Services Inc., 411
Gordon, Gordon, Manager, American Society of Plant Biologists, 826
Gordon, Isabel, Director, North Vancouver, 682
Gordon, Jim, Executive Officer, 612
Gordon, Judy, Chair, North Red Deer River Water Services Commission, 758
Gordon, Judy, Coordinator, Foothills No. 31, 669
Gordon, Martin, VP, Opus International Consultants (Canada) Ltd., 314
Gordon, Mike, M.R. Gordon Consulting Inc., 276
Gordon, Neil, Vice-President, Bruce Sutherland & Associates Ltd., 117
Gordon, P.Eng., Jim, General Manager, Abbotsford, 604-864-5556, 679
Gordon-Cooper, Marilyn, Contact, Foothills No. 31, 669
Gordon-Dillane, MPA, CAE, Sheila, Director, Ontario Respiratory Care Society, 978
Gore, Robert, Collections Librarian, Kwantlen University College, 1113
Gorham, Thomas, President & Managing Partner, Envision Compliance, 188
Gorley, Al, President, McGregor Model Forest, 952
Gorman, J.C., Burden Management & Design Ltd., 118
Gorman, James, Deputy Minister, 576
Gorman, Ken, President, Association of Supervisors of Public Health Inspectors (Ontario), 840
Gorman, M.C., Vice-President, Atlantic Engineering Consultants Ltd., 95
Gormely, Bryan, Director, Canadian Gas Association, 869
Gormley, Daniel, Goodmans LLP, 1075
Gorr, Joel, FCX NH Valves, 194
Gorrie, Fraser, President, Bio-Software Inc., 108
Gorsline, Dayle, Library Technician, Acquisitions & Electronic Reso, Loyalist College of Applied Arts & Technology, 1139
Gorsuch, Wanda, Head, David Winton Bell Memorial Library, 1153
Goshulak, Ted, University Librarian, Trinity Western University, 1113
Goss, Q.C., William B., Partner, Stewart McKelvey Stirling Scales - Saint John, 1065
Gosselin, Benoît, Technical Support, ABGG Technologies Inc., 65
Gosselin, Denis, Directeur, Régie intermunicipale de traitement de l'eau potable Saint-Romual, 760
Gosselin, François, Directeur général, Les Basques, 749
Gosselin, Gérard, Président, ABGG Technologies Inc., 65
Gosselin, Ian, Associé, Ogilvy Renault LLP/S.E.N.C.R.L., s.r.l. - Québec, 1088
Gosselin, Lucie, Daigneault, avocats inc., 1083
Gosselin, Serge, Magog, 819-843-8203, 737
Gosselin, Guy, Adjoint à la direction - Gestion des collections, Université du Québec École de technologie supérieure, 1176
Goswami, Jayashree, Heenan Blaikie LLP - Toronto, 1076
Gottardi, Mick, Director, Squamish, 604-815-5011, 688
Gottschlich, Lee, President & General Manager, GLM Tanks & Equipment Ltd., 213
Goucher, Judith, Director/CFO, 608
Goudey, Stephen, President, Hydroqual Laboratories Ltd., 237
Goudreau, Hector, Minister, 570
Goudreau, M. Michel, President, Camvac Inc., 122
Goudreault, Pierre, President, Le Groupe Sani Marc, 265
Gouge, Raymond, Cain Lamarre Casgrain Wells - Québec, 1087
Gougeon, Nicole, Secrétaire-trésorière, 650
Gough, George, President, Gough Risk Management Ltd., 215
Gough, John, Manager, GLOBE Foundation, 924
Goulbourne, Damian, Niagara, 702
Gould, Ken, Manager, West Grey, 732
Gould, Linda D., Executive Director, 595
Gould, Mel, President/COO, AimGlobal Technologies Company, Inc., 74
Gould, Seymour J., Quality Manager, Nolar Industries Ltd., 305
Goulet, Denis, Managing Director/Country Manager, Safety-Kleen Canada Inc., 355

Goulet, Gilbert, Préfet, Maria-Chapdelaine, 750
Goulet, Lise, Secrétaire, Collège de Saint-Félicien, 1183
Goulet, Richard, Maire, Granby, 450-776-8228, 735
Goulet, Sylvie, Bibliothécaire, Bibliothèque des sciences, 1171
Goundrey, D. John, Alexander Holburn Beaudin & Lang, LLP, 1057
Goupil, Bruno, President/CEO & Manager, Tornatech, 397
Gour, Pierre, Maire, L'Assomption, 736
Gourde, Jacques, Parliamentary Secretary, 558
Gourdeau, Gaston, General Manager, Saskatoon, 754
Gourdeau, Gaston, Manager, Saskatoon, 754
Gourley, Philippa, Secretary-Treasurer, Council of Canadian Fire Marshals & Fire Commissioners, 904
Gourley, Tim, President, Gourley Construction Ltd., 215
Gourley-Davis, Jane M., Patterson Law, 1068
Gouron, Raymond, VP, National Energy Equipment Ltd., 297
Gouveia, Wayne, Vice-President, Air Transport Association of Canada, 814
Gouw, Kyle, Farm Manager, Gouw Quality Onions Ltd., 215
Gouw Jr., Casey, Sales & Controller, Gouw Quality Onions Ltd., 215
Gow, Harry, President, Canadians for Responsible & Safe Highways, 892
Gowanlock, Doug, Vice Deputy Mayor, Saugeen Shores, 719
Gower, Les, CFO/Corporate Secretary, e3 Solutions Inc., 168
Gowing, Brian, Manager, SimplexGrinnell, 369
Goyer, Daniel, Saint-Eustache, 450-974-9104, 742
Goyer, Jean-Luc, Contact, Groupe Bau-Val, 219
Goyette, Jacques, Longueuil, 737
Goyette, René, Trois-Rivières, 745
Grace, Dib, Trade Commissioner, 768
Grace, John, Huron, 701
Grace, Richard, President, AXYS Analytical Services Ltd., 100
Grady, Emily, Manager, Canadian Avalanche Association, 859
Grady, James, Sales Coordinator, Transcontinental Printing Inc., 400
Grady, Mary, Muskoka, 702
Grady, Michael, Manager, EFR Disposal, 174
Graesser, Q.C., R.A., Reynolds, Mirth, Richards & Farmer LLP, 1056
Graf, Andy, Superintendent, Water, Essex, 709
Graf, Q.C., Terence G., McDougall Gauley, 1090
Graham, Andrew, Manager, Ontario Soil & Crop Improvement Association, 979
Graham, Bill, Owner, W.R. Graham Services Ltd., 415
Graham, Brett, Sales Manager Infrastructure, Armtec Construction Products, 92
Graham, Bruce, President, Cengea Solutions Inc., 136
Graham, Caroline, Treasurer, Aquaculture Association of Canada, 828
Graham, Darcelle, Executive Director, National Sunflower Association of Canada, 958
Graham, David, Director, Kelowna, 681
Graham, Doug, Whitehorse, 755
Graham, Evelyn, Serials Technician, Keyano College, 1107
Graham, George, President, Airtest Technologies Inc., 76
Graham, Jamie, Chief Constable, Victoria, 250-995-7217, 685
Graham, Jeffrey T., President, Henderson Paddon & Associates Ltd., 229
Graham, Jim, South Dundas, 613-543-3588, 730
Graham, Jim, Manager, Pol R Enterprises Inc., 327
Graham, Jim, President, Try Recycling Inc., 404
Graham, Jordan S., Fredericton, 691
Graham, Know, Coordinating Committee Member, Pacific States/British Columbia Oil Spill Task Force, 765
Graham, Malcolm, Manager, Metro Vancouver, 678
Graham, Mark S., Director, 518
Graham, Mike, Exec. Vice-President/President, Encana Corporation, 178
Graham, Pete, President/CEO, CCR Technologies Ltd., 133
Graham, Sheridan, General Manager, Strategic Services & Corporate Pr, Peterborough, 703
Graham, Tracy, Klajnerman Contracting Corp., 258
Graham Crook, Graham, Project Manager, Clean Air Services Inc., 142
Graham, Q.C., Douglas A., Partner, Macleod Dixon LLP, 1052
Graham, Q.C., Glenda F., Partner, Macleod Dixon LLP, 1052
Granatier, Ann, Secretary, Canadian Iris Society, 876
Granda, Paul R., Gowling Lafleur Henderson S.E.N.C.R.L./LLP, 1084
Grandbois, Gisèle, President & Chief Executive Officer, Research & Development Institute for the Agri-Environment, 994
Grande, Maria L., Thompson Dorfman Sweatman LLP, 1064

Grande, Nicole, Administrative Coordinator, Saskatchewan Trade & Export Partnership Inc., 1002
Grandmont, Alain, Executive Vice-President, Abitibi-Consolidated Inc., 65
Grandy, Bruce N., Deputy Mayor & Councillor, Fredericton, 691
Granek, Fred, Chief Operating Officer, Canadian Centre for Pollution Prevention, 862
Granger, André, Vice President, Vansco Electronics Ltd., 409
Granger, Heidi, Fasken Martineau - Vancouver, 1059
Granger, Lucie, Directrice Générale, Association pour la santé publique du Québec, 841
Granger, Richard, Purchasing Manager, Quebecor World Concord, 338
Granovsky, Dahra, Vice President, Atlantic Packaging Products Ltd., 96
Grant, Alan, Executive Director, 609
Grant, Bradley B., Partner, Stikeman Elliott LLP - Calgary, 1053
Grant, Carry, Manager, Cold Lake, 780-594-3776, 672
Grant, Danny, Partner, Interwest Property Services (1991) Ltd., 246
Grant, Ed, Mount Pearl, 694
Grant, George, President, George Grant Consulting, 211
Grant, Glen, Cornwall, 708
Grant, Glenn, Operations Manager, Kamloops Wildlife Park Society, 947
Grant, James W., CEO, Bruce Sutherland & Associates Ltd., 117
Grant, Janet L., Stewart McKelvey Stirling Scales - St. John's, 1066
Grant, John, Durham, 699
Grant, John, Regional Councillor, Brock, 724
Grant, Larry, Triple M Fiberglass Mfg. Ltd., 401
Grant, Laura, Contact, Greater Toronto Water Garden & Horticultural Society, 925
Grant, Marc, Town Councillor, Oakville, 715
Grant, Marven, City Treasurer & Director, Fredericton, 691
Grant, Peter, Office Manager, MacLeod & Grant Ltd., 278
Grant, Richard J.C., Gowling Lafleur Henderson LLP - Calgary, 1051
Grant, Robyn A., Partner, Borden Ladner Gervais LLP - Toronto, 1073
Grant, Shane, Greater Napanee, 613-354-5529, 709
Grant, Winanne, Chief Administrative Officer, Springwater, 730
Grant, Q.C., Bruce C., Partner, Stewart McKelvey Stirling Scales - St. John's, 1066
Grant, Q.C., Robert G., Stewart McKelvey Stirling Scales - Halifax, 1067
Grantham, Jacques, Directeur, Québec, 740
Gratton, Glen, Rothsay, 352
Gratton, Luc, Associé, Miller Thomson LLP - Montréal, 1086
Gratton, Luc, Partner, Miller Thomson LLP - Toronto, 1078
Grauer, Randy, Manager, Saskatoon, 754
Gravani, PhD, Robert, President, Institute of Food Technologists, 933
Gravel, Alain, Directeur général, Les Appalaches, 749
Gravel, Bernard, President, Airtechni Inc., 76
Gravel, Renald, Coordonnateur, Joliette, 736
Gravel, Valérie, Présidente, Société de protection des plantes du Québec, 1005
Graveley, Patrick, Manager, PRT Inc., 336
Gravelle, Joyce, South Glengarry, 730
Gravelle, Maurice J., Manager, Kamloops, 250-828-3463, 681
Gravelle, Michael, Minister, 634
Gravelle, Paul, Treasurer, Deputy CAO, & Director, Finance, Oro-Medonte, 728
Gravenor, Gaël C., Fasken Martineau - Montréal, 1083
Graves, David A., McInnes Cooper, 1067
Graves, Michael, Chief Administratiivve Officer & Clerk, Norwich, 519-879-6568, 728
Graves, Patrick, K&D Pratt Group Inc., 254
Graves, Wendell, City Clerk, St. Thomas, 719
Gray, Barbara, President, Golden Horseshoe Health Libraries Association, 924
Gray, Beth, President, Environmental Bankers Association, 911
Gray, Brian, Osler, Hoskin & Harcourt LLP - Toronto, 1079
Gray, Brian W., Senior Partner, Ogilvy Renault LLP/S.E.N.C.R.L., s.r.l. - Toronto, 1078
Gray, Connie, Councillor, Wasaga Beach, 722
Gray, David J., President, Elemental Research Inc., 175
Gray, Donna L., Director, Organizational Development & Performance, Ottawa, 716
Gray, Marge, Reference Library Technician, South Campus, 1106
Gray, Sandy, City Administrator, Courtenay, 680
Gray, Terry, Manager, Ferguson Simek Clark, 194
Gray, P.C., C.C., Q.C., Herb, Chair & Commissioner, 545
Graziani, Walter, President, Comcor Environmental Limited, 146

Executive Name Index

Graziosi, Jack, Director, Engineering Services, Vaughan, 722
Grbesic, Ivan, Partner, Stikeman Elliott LLP - Toronto, 1080
Greason, David, Vice-President, 598
Greatrix, Susan, City Clerk, Waterloo, 519-747-8705, 722
Greaves, Al, Manager, United Oil Services, 406
Greaves, Jeff, President, North Shore Management Systems Inc., 306
Greaves, Kurt, Treasurer & Director, Finance, Lanark, 701
Greaves, Susan, GIS/Map Librarian, Maps, Data & Government Information Centre (MADGIC), 1142
Greeley, Neville, Mayor, Corner Brook, 709-637-1537, 693
Green, Allan C., Managing Director, SGE Hatch Ltd., 364
Green, Audrey R., Renfrew, 613-432-4848, 704
Green, Dave, Manager, Portage La Prairie, 204-239-8325, 689
Green, Donald, Manager, Environmental Services, Collingwood, 708
Green, E. Marshall, Graham Wilson & Green, Barristers & Solicitors, Notaries, Mediato, 1068
Green, Ilja, Technical Services Assistant, Canadian Urban Transit Association, 1156
Green, Jack, Manager, Transportation, Orillia, 716
Green, Jim, Chief Administrative Officer, Muskoka, 702
Green, John, Wellington, 519-638-2126, 705
Green, Kent W., President, Campbell's Concrete Ltd., 122
Green, Lisa, Marketing, Testwell Instruments, 391
Green, Nancy, Director, Social Services, Lanark, 701
Green, Philip E.J., President, Greenbridge Management Inc., 217
Green, Ray, Chief Administrative Officer, Oakville, 715
Green, Rick, Metro Vancouver, 678
Green, Rick, Mayor, Langley, 687
Green, Shari, Prince George, 683
Green, Thelma, Manager, 596
green pages, The Green Pages, 1215
Green, Q.C., John M., McInnes Cooper, 1066
Greenan, Gerard, Attorney General, 637
Greenan, L. Gerard, Minister, 638
Greenaway, Andrew, Chief Building Official, Lincoln, 713
Greenberg, Arlene, Chief Medical Librarian, Sir Mortimer B. Davis Jewish General Hospital, 1174, 1175
Greenberg, Brian, Floorworks Inc., 197
Greenberg, Jonathan D., Counsel, Heenan Blaikie LLP - Vancouver, 1060
Greenberg, Tyler, Architect Contact, BMT Fleet Technology Ltd., 111
Greene, Dale, General Manager/Secretary, Richmond Agricultural Society, 995
Greene, Jeff, City Planner & Team Leader, Airdrie, 403-948-8848, 670
Greene, Steve, Branch Manager, CenturyVallen, 137
Greenfield, D., President, D. Greenfield Associates Ltd., 156
Greenfield, Donald E., Bennett Jones LLP - Calgary Office, 1049
Greenfield, Harley, Meaford, 519-538-2570, 727
Greenlaw, Glenn, Chair, South West Solid Waste Commission, 759
Greenspoon, Joan, Director, NIM Disposals Limited, 304
Greenwood, Aleteia, Head, Science & Engineering Division, 1118
Greenwood, Barbara, Niagara, 702
Greenwood, Barbara, Regional Councillor, Niagara Falls, 715
Greenwood, Ellen, President, Greenwood & Associates, 218
Greenwood, Les, Director, Tremco Ltd., 401
Greenwood, Tony, Northern Area Manager, Zell Oilfield Service Ltd., 436
Greer, Crystal, City Clerk, Mississauga, 714
Greer, John, Chair, Canadian Concrete Pipe Association, 863
Greer, John, General Manager, Shaw Precast Solutions, 365
Greer, John, Vice-President, North Safety Products Canada, 306
Greer, Larry, Fire Chief, Rothesay, 506-848-6604, 692
Greer, Sandra, President/CEO, Vemco Ltd., 410
Greetham, Georgia, Coordinator, Yukon Conservation Society, 1024
Greffe, Jacques, Vice-President, 517
Gregg, Brian, Chief Administrative Officer, Essex, 699
Gregg, Miles, Manager, Toromont Caterpillar, 398
Gregg, Mora, Head of Library, William R. Newman Library, 1126
Grégoire, Gilles, Longueuil, 737
Grégoire, Ginette, Directrice, Traitement et accès aux documents, Université de Montréal, 1176
Grégoire, Louis-Pierre, Heenan Blaikie LLP - Ottawa, 1073, 1070
Grégoire, Simon, Partner, Borden Ladner Gervais LLP - Montréal, 1083
Gregor, Dennis J., President, CanDetec Inc., 126
Gregorchuk, John, Managing Secretary, Canadian Mineral Analysts, 879

Gregorwich, Don, Secretary, Alberta Farm Fresh Producers Association, 816
Gregorwich, Joan, Contact, Alberta Farm Fresh Producers Association, 816
Gregory, Glen, Greatario Industrial Storage Systems Ltd., 217
Gregory, Sara J., Lawson Lundell LLP - Vancouver, 1061
Greig, Howard, Mayor, Grey, 700
Greig, John, President, Canadian Farm Writers' Federation, 867
Greig, Tracy, Vice-President, Supply Chain, 511
Greig, Warren, Supervisor, Calgary, 121
Grellette, Leo, Director, Building Standards, Vaughan, 722
Grenier, Chantal, General Manager, Prolab Technolub, 334
Grenier, Denis, Directeur, Westburne Canada, 428
Grenier, Donald, Préfet, Matane, 750
Grenier, Glenn, Lang Michener LLP - Toronto, 1077
Grenier, Jacques, CEO, AXOR Experts-Conseils Inc., 99
Grenier, Jean R., Regional Manager, Parkson Corporation, 319
Grenier, Jean-Guy, President, Prolab Technolub, 334
Grenier, Kateri-Anne, Associée, Ogilvy Renault LLP/S.E.N.C.R.L., s.r.l. - Québec, 1088
Grenier, Keri T., Clark Wilson LLP, 1058
Grenier, Mario, Directeur général, Le Rocher-Percé, 749
Grenier, Paul, Welland, 722
Grenier, Pierre, Fraser Milner Casgrain S.E.N.C.R.L./LLP, 1084
Grenier, Sylvie, Responsable, Abitibi-Ouest, 746
Gres, Edward, President/CEO, Bradex Industrial Services Ltd., 115
Gretener, Nicholas M., Bennett Jones LLP - Calgary Office, 1049
Grey, Deb, Reference Librarian, John & Dotsa Bitove Family Law Library, 1144
Greyson, Devon, President, Health Libraries Association of British Columbia, 928
Grice, Craig, Haldimand, 700
Grier, Brian, Acquisitions Clerk, Canada Dept. of National Defence & the Canadian Forces, 1148
Grier, Dave, Director, 662
Grier, Norma, Executive Director, Northwest Coalition for Alternatives to Pesticides, 966
Grieveson, Steve, Vice-President, The Lowe-Martin Group, 392
Griffin, Bruce L., Community Emergency Planner, Barrie, 706
Griffin, Derek, Project Assessment Director, 578
Griffin, Kim, Manager, Maritime Electric Company Ltd., 280
Griffin, Laura, President, CanadianEnvironmental.com, 125
Griffin, P., Vice-President, Gas Liquids Engineering Ltd., 205
Griffin, Ward, CEO, The Lowe-Martin Group, 392
Griffith, Gillian, Librarian, Outreach Services, Bracken Health Sciences Library, 1142
Griffith, Jennifer, Donovan & Company, 1059
Griffith, Scott, Fire Chief, Innisfil, 711
Griffiths, Dave, Director, Calgary, 671
Griffiths, David A., President, Dagex Inc., 156
Griffiths, John, Organic Resource Management Inc., 314
Griffiths, Lesley, Partner, Griffiths Muecke Associates, 218
Griffiths, C.E.T., Gareth, Manager, St. John's, 709-576-8440, 694
Grimaldi, Mary Ann, Welland, 722
Grimaud, Andrea, Officer, Canadian Society for Civil Engineering, 885
Grimes, Brenda B., Cox and Palmer - St. John's, 1065
Grimes, Mark, Toronto, 721
Grindley-Ferris, Lee, Corporate Sales, Specialty Technical Publishers, 375
Grineage, Linda, Library Technician, Thames Campus Resource Centre, 1139
Gripp, Roger D., D'Arcy & Deacon LLP, 1063
Gripton, Roger, Vice-President, Napoleon Appliance Corp., 297
Grisé, Ginette, Laval, 736
Grisley, Kerry, Co-Manager, Alberta Fish & Game Association, 817
Griss, Paul, Co-ordinator, The New Directions Group, 962
Grist, A.D. (Tony), Sales Manager, All-Weld Company Limited, 79
Grist, Michael, President, MKG Imaging Solutions Inc., 291
Griswold, Elizabeth, Executive Director, Canadian Bottled Water Association, 860
Grodinsky, Daniel, Borden Ladner Gervais LLP - Montréal, 1083
Groen, Sharon, President, Niagara Peninsula Geological Society, 964
Groff, Douglas, Director, The DATA Group of Companies, 392
Grof-Iannelli, Martie, Manager, Library & Media Services, Fanshawe College of Applied Arts & Technology, 1143
Groleau, Jean, Fraser Milner Casgrain S.E.N.C.R.L./LLP, 1084
Grondin, Andre, Region Manager, HAMON Custodis-Cottrell Canada, Inc., 224

Grondin, Dwayne, Superintendent, Sewer & Watermain, Amherstburg, 705
Grondin, François, McCarthy Tétrault LLP - Montréal, 1086
Grondin, François, Partner, Borden Ladner Gervais LLP - Montréal, 1083
Grondin, Gilles, Conseiller, Vieux-Rosemont, Montréal, 738
Grondin, Guy, Marketing Manager, Stablex Canada Inc., 377
Grondin, Julie, Lavery, de Billy - Montréal, 1085
Grondin, Marcel, Directeur général, Saint-Georges, 742
Grondin, Sylvie, Sous-ministre associé, 653
Grondin, c.r., c.q., Henri, Avocat, Langlois Kronström Desjardins, 1088
Groody, P.Eng., Paul, Commissioner, Saint John, 506-658-4455, 692
Groot, Chris, President, Land Improvement Contractors of Ontario, 948
Groot, Dave, Sales Representative, Armtec Construction Products, 92
Grootendorst, Peter, Director, Maple Ridge, 604-463-5221, 687
Groppini, Guido, Branch Manager, Fort Garry Industries Ltd., 200
Groshak, Steve, Manager, Coast Paper Ltd., 145
Gross, Benjamin David, Partner, Lavery, de Billy - Montréal, 1085
Gross, H.P., President, Next Environmental, 303
Gross, Margaret, Manager, MDA Space, 1182
Grosshauser, Dan, General Manager, Waste Management of Canada, 418
Grossi, Jeff, COO, Pinchin Environmental Ltd., 324
Grossi, Robert, York, 705
Grossi, Robert, Mayor, Georgina, 709
Grossman, Andrew, Partner, Ogilvy Renault LLP/S.E.N.C.R.L., s.r.l. - Toronto, 1078
Groulx, Christine, Clerk, Hawkesbury, 711
Groulx, Gilles, National Sales Manager, ATS Scientific Inc., 97
Groulx, Marie-Josée, Director, 592
Grout, Kim, Director, Pitt Meadows, 604-465-2420, 683
Grove, Jim, Plant Manager, CCS Income Trust, 134
Grove, Margaret, University Librarian, Brock University, 1153
Grove-McClement, Tammy W., Magwood, Van De Vyvere, Thompson, & Grove-McClement LLP, 1081
Grover, John H., Fulton & Company LLP, Lawyers & Trade-Mark Agents, 1056
Groves, Brett, President, Sydenham Field Naturalists, 1011
Groves, Kent, Specialist, ProAgri Consulting Limited, 333
Groves, Tom, Sales Representative, Ontor Ltd., 313
Growden, Rick, General Manager, Waste Management of Canada, 418
Grubb, Richard, President, Arlat Technology, 91
Gruchalla-Wesierski, Tad, Partner, Macleod Dixon LLP, 1052
Gruending, Dennis, Contact, Canadian Labour Congress, 876
Gruenefeld, George, President, Outdoor Writers of Canada, 983
Grunau, Ted, Chair, Intelex Technologies Inc., 244
Grundberg, Jeneane S., Brownlee LLP, 1054
Grundy, Kyle, President, B.J. Bear Grain Company Ltd., 100
Gruninger, CGA, S., Town Treasurer & Director, Finance, Grimsby, 710
Grushcow, Jeremy, Partner, Ogilvy Renault LLP/S.E.N.C.R.L., s.r.l. - Toronto, 1078
Gryski, Chester, Conway Davis Gryski, 1074
Grzenda, Karen, General Manager, MEP Environmental Products Ltd., 286
Guay, Frédéric, Sous-ministre adjoint, 646
Guay, Harold, Maire, Sainte-Marie, 743
Guay-Boivin, Lorraine, Longueuil, 737
Guberney, Derek, Sales Manager, Con Cast Pipe, 148
Gudbjartsson, Loren, Contact, Kraftur Engineering Inc., 260
Guénard, Georges, Préfet, La Matapédia, 748
Guénette, Jean-Sébastien, Directeur général, Regroupement QuébecOiseaux, 994
Guenther, John, Building Inspector, North Vancouver, 604-985-7761, 682
Guenther, Mary Ann, Coordinator, Library Services, North Island College Library, 1111
Guenther, Mary Anne, Coordinator, Library Services, Port Alberni Regional Campus Library, 1114
Guenther, Noreen, First Vice-President, Southern Interior Local Government Association, 1010
Guérette, Anne, Québec, 740
Guergis, David, Simcoe, 704
Guergis, David, Mayor, Essa, 705-424-0698, 725
Guergis, Tony, Simcoe, 704
Guergis, Tony, Warden & Councillor, Simcoe, 704
Guérin, Claude, Directeur, Lévis, 418-839-2002, 736
Guérin, Marcel, Directeur, Alma, 418-669-5111, 733

Executive Name Index

Guérin, Nathalie, Directrice, Beloeil, 734
Guérin, Nathalie, Trésorière, La Prairie, 450-444-6603, 736
Guérin, Serge, Président-directeur général, 648
Guertin, Catherine, Partner, Borden Ladner Gervais LLP - Montréal, 1083
Guertin, Charles, Vice-President, Guertin Brothers Coatings and Sealants Ltd., 222
Guertin, Jocelyne, Laval, 736
Guertin, Phil, President, Guertin Brothers Coatings and Sealants Ltd., 222
Guertin, Richard, Superintendent, Water Treatment Plant, Hawkesbury, 711
Guglielmi, Anthony, President, Enervac Corp., 180
Guibord, Marcel, Prescott & Russell, 729
Guibord, Marcel, Mayor, Clarence-Rockland, 613-446-4856, 708
Guibord, Marcel, Representative, Aqua Data Inc., 88
Guice, Robert, Executive Vice-President, Shred-It, 366
Guichon Jr., Dave. A., Partner, Macleod Dixon LLP, 1052
Guidoin, Steve, President, Wastequip Cusco, 421
Guilbault, David, Fire Chief, Kawartha Lakes, 711
Guilbault, Nathalie, Director, FPInnovations, 200
Guilbeault, Melanie, Microbiologist, MacDonald & Fils Inc., 277
Guild, Jeff, Manager, Noram Engineering & Constructors Ltd., 305
Guillemette, Yves, Directeur général adjoint, Saint-Eustache, 742
Guillot, Patrick, Director, SPG Hydro International Inc., 375
Guillou, Christian, Computer Services, Douglas College, 1114
Guimond, Lucie, Partner, Heenan Blaikie S.E.N.C.R.L/SRL, 1084
Guimond, Pierre, President & Chief Executive Officer, Canadian Electricity Association, 866
Guimont, François, Deputy Minister, 558
Guinan, William C., Partner, Borden Ladner Gervais LLP - Calgary, 1049
Guindon, Benoit, Division Manager, Ontor Ltd., 313
Guindon, Denis, Vice-President, Dessau, Inc., 162
Gulka-Tiechko, Myron, Clerk, Moose Jaw, 754
Gullacher, David, General Manager, Westest, 430
Gullacher, David, President/CEO, 656
Gullberg, Edward, McLennan Ross LLP, 1066
Gulliford, Jim, Executive Director, Soil & Water Conservation Society, 1009
Gullino, M. Lodovica, President, International Society for Plant Pathology, 943
Guluzian, Leon G., President & General Manager, Intersciences Inc., 246
Guluzian, Suzanne, Controller & VP, Intersciences Inc., 246
Gumbs, Diane, Director, 621
Gundry, Michael, Manager, Totten Sims Hubicki Associates Ltd., 399
Gunn, Brian, President, Wilderness Tourism Association, 1020
Gunn Jr., Angus M., Partner, Borden Ladner Gervais LLP - Vancouver, 1058
Gunning, Bill, Manager, Poyry (Vancouver) Inc., 330
Gunning, Katherine, Essex, 699
Gunther, George K., President, Geo-Logic Inc., 210
Gunther, Michael S., Brownlee LLP, 1054
Guoth, Tom, Conestoga-Rovers & Associates, 149
Guoth, Tom, Contact, Conestoga-Rovers & Associates, 149
Guptill, Nancy, Chair, 642
Gural, Dave, Vice-President, The MEP Environmental Products Ltd., 393
Gurnham, Q.C., Peter W., Chair, 617
Gurría, Angel, Secretary General, Organization for Economic Cooperation & Development, 982
Gusev, Aleks, Chair, Wilderness Canoe Association, 1020
Gushue, Kevin, Manager, St. John's, 709-567-8545, 694
Gussin, Anthony, Corporate Marketing Manager, Trow Consulting Engineers Ltd., 403
Gustafson, Jim, CAO, Central Kootenay, 677
Gustafson, Wayne, Regional Director, Williams Engineering Inc., 432
Gustafson, Q.C., Karl E., Lang Michener LLP - Vancouver, 1060
Guthrie, Cam G., Guelph, 710
Gutierrez, Anne Marie, Director, 631
Gutman, Jonathan, Partner, Borden Ladner Gervais LLP - Toronto, 1073
Gutowski, Janet, Warden & Councillor, Frontenac, 699
Gutzman, Vance, Renfrew, 613-584-3114, 704
Guy, Louise, Bibliotechnicienne, Québec Régie de l'assurance-maladie, 1180
Guy, Mark, Director, Recreation & Culture, North Dundas, 727
Guzy, Janusz, Owner, G & G Computer Services, 203
Guzzardi, Virginia, Research Analyst, TransCanada PipeLines Limited, 1103
Gwin, James L., Sprayaway Marine Services Ltd., 376
Gwin, James L., President, Sprayaway Marine Services Ltd., 376
Gyabronka, Steve, President, Elmec Engineering Ltd., 176
Gysel, Lisa, Librarian, Thompson, Cariboo, Shuswap Health Sciences Library, 1112

H

Haac, Norman, President, Genor Recycling Services, 210
Haaf, Chad M., McDougall Gauley, 1090
Haag, Ivan, Manager, PRT Inc., 336
Haalboom, Jean, Waterloo, 704
Haanstra, J., Vice-President, Maple Engineering & Construction Canada Ltd., 279
Haar, Jonathan, President & CEO, Eastern Wind Power Inc., 169
Haas, Denise, Chief Financial Officer, 662
Haas, Jennifer, Department Head, Information Services & Resources,, Davis Centre Library, 1164
Habberfield, Lois, Reeve, Rocky View No. 44, 670
Habenicht, Gerfried, Manager, International Solid Waste Association, 944
Haber, G. Jeffrey, President, National Centre for Small Communities, 957
Haberl, Andrew, Sales Director, Procedair Industries Inc., 333
Habkirk, Bob, Elgin, 699
Hacault, Antoine F., Thompson Dorfman Sweatman LLP, 1064
Hacault, Marcel L., Executive Director, Canadian Agricultural Safety Association, 854
Hache, Angie, City Clerk, Greater Sudbury / Grand Sudbury, 705-674-4455, 710
Hachey, Gary, Manager, R.V. Anderson Associates Limited, 341
Hackenbrook, Ken, Georgina, 709
Hackenschmidt, Gerald, Director, Annapolis County, 902-532-3135, 696
Hackett, Bob, Pembroke, 717
Hackett, Carrie, Resource Centre Librarian, Environmental Commissioner of Ontario, 1157
Hackett, G., Director, Community Services, St. Clair, 729
Hacking, John A., Treasurer, Wilmot, 732
Hackman, Arlin, Vice-President, World Wildlife Fund - Canada, 1023
Hackney, Ruth, Simcoe, 704
Hackson, Virginia, York, 705
Hackson, Virginia, Mayor, East Gwillimbury, 708
Hadavi, M., Sales Manager, KSB Pumps Inc., 261
Haddad, April, Institute Librarian, Justice Institute of British Columbia, 1114
Haddad, Gilbert, Chief Operating Officer, Terratech, 391
Haddad, Rick, Manager, Crown Shred & Recycling, 154
Haddad, Rolla, Librarian, Canada Revenue Agency, 1148
Haddock, Lorie, Dufferin, 699
Haden, Andy, Manager, Parkland County, 670
Haeberle, Jim, President & General Manager, Nor-Alta Environmental Services Ltd., 305
Haener, Sylvia, Assistant Deputy Minister & Solicitor General, 607
Haga, B.Sc., Rick, Executive Director, Carleton County Law Association, 892
Hagan, Bob, Vice President/General Manager, Atlantic Packaging Products Ltd., 96
Hagen, Troy, Chief, Regina, 306-777-6500, 754
Hager, David, Lang Michener LLP - Toronto, 1077
Hager, Terry, County Commissioner, Lacombe County, 669
Haggart, Roy, Brant, 698
Haggarty, Penny, Collections Librarian, Thompson Rivers University, 1112
Hahn, Dianne, Clerk, Swift Current, 755
Haichert, Colleen, Library Technician, St Paul's Hospital (Grey Nuns) of Saskatoon, 1190
Haig, Roy, Manager, Engineering, Haliburton, 700
Haigh, Liz, Director, American Water Works Association, 826
Haigh, Q.C., David R., Burnet, Duckworth & Palmer LLP, 1050
Haight, Laura, Deputy Mayor & Councillor, Kincardine, 519-396-5204, 726
Haile, Jeremy, President, Knight Piésold Ltd., 259
Haince, Valérie, Greffière, Sept-Iles, 418-964-3205, 744
Hainer, Joanne, Executive Officer, Yukon Chamber of Mines, 1191
Haines, Margaret, University Librarian, Carleton University, 1149
Hainnu, Phoebe, Deputy Minister, 617
Hains, Bradley, Vice-President, The DATA Group of Companies, 392
Haire, Bruce, New Tecumseth, 714
Haischt, H.W., President & General Manager, Patterson Industries (Canada) Ltd., 319
Hakala, Mika, President, Hakmet Ltd., 223
Hakim, Harry, Director, Parks & Recreation, Essex, 709

Halat, Marim, Chief Financial Officer, Matrix Solutions Inc., 282
Halberstadt, Alan, Windsor, 723
Halbert, David, Manager, Canadian Water Conditioning Inc., 125
Halcrow, Cynthia, Town Clerk, Mississippi Mills, 714
Halcrow, Dawn, Director, Finance, Elliot Lake, 709
Halde, Jean, Contact, DDH Environnement ltée, 159
Halde, Jean-René, President & Chief Executive Officer, 512
Haldenby, Don, Contact, The Westford Group Inc., 393
Haldenby, Don, President, ÉcoFlame International Inc., 171
Hale, Alison, Librarian, Library Services, Canadian Transportation Agency, 1167
Hale, Frances, Treasurer & Director, Finance, North Perth, 519-292-2045, 715
Hale, Jennifer, Plant Products Co. Ltd., 326
Hale, Larry, Manager, FS Partners, 202
Hale, Robin, President, Canadian Association of Zoos & Aquariums, 859
Hales, David, General Manager, Spruce Grove, 780-962-7622, 674
Hales, David, President, Grand River Conservation Foundation, 924
Hales, Roy, Director, Cranbrook, 680
Hales, Sid, Manager, Barrington Environmental Services, 102
Haley, Carol, Vice President, Anachemia Canada Inc., 85
Haley, Joanne, General Manager, Community Services, South Glengarry, 730
Haley, Roger, Leeds & Grenville, 726
Halfyard, Job, President, Newfoundland Aquaculture Industry Association, 963
Halifax, Margaret, Director, 661
Halkett, Stephen, Vice-President, Silex Innovations Inc., 367
Hall, Andrew G., Vice-President, QuestAir Technologies Inc., 339
Hall, Basil, Councillor, Kings County, 696
Hall, Bob, Peterborough, 718
Hall, Carl, Wellington, 519-846-5235, 705
Hall, Cassandra, Director, Communications & External Relations, Association for Mineral Exploration British Columbia, 1117
Hall, Charmaine, Executive Assistant to the Deputy Minister, 667
Hall, Chris, Director, North Cowichan, 687
Hall, Dave, Langley, 681
Hall, David, President, ProSolve Consulting Ltd., 335
Hall, Karin, Collections Librarian, Capilano College, 1114
Hall, M., Director, Planning & Development, Caledon, 707
Hall, Max, City Administrator, Yellowknife, 867-920-5624, 695
Hall, Murray K., President, Halltech Environmental Inc., 224
Hall, Nancy, Head, Monograph Acquisitions, York University Libraries, 1164
Hall, Randy, Secretary, Petroleum Tank Management Association of Alberta, 986
Hall, Steve, President, Mirarco Mining Innovation, 290
Hall, Tom, Registrar, 607
Hall, P.Eng., Rob, Director, Sidney, 250-656-4502, 684
Halldorson, Dwayne, Manager, Saanich, 250-475-5574, 688
Hallett, Ron, Founder, UV Pure Technologies, 408
Hallgren, Bibi, Office Manager, Trellcan Rubber Ltd., 401
Halliday, C.H., Fire Chief, Grimsby, 710
Halliday, Jim, Sec.-Treas., Barrow Bay & District Sports Fishing Association, 845
Halliday, Karen, Health Sciences Librarian, Georgian College of Applied Arts & Technology, 1138
Halliday, Sandra, Librarian, Public Services/Circulation Supervisor, Bracken Health Sciences Library, 1142
Hallman, Ron, Centre Wellington, 724
Hallman, Ron, Director General, 552
Halloran, Brenda, Waterloo, 704
Halloran, Brenda, Mayor, Waterloo, 722
Hallsor, Bruce, Crease Harman & Company, 1062
Halperin, Jesse, Lindsay Kenney LLP, 1061
Halpin, Matthew J., Partner, Ogilvy Renault LLP/S.E.N.C.R.L, s.r.l. - Ottawa, 1071
Halsey-Brandt, Evelina, Richmond, 684
Halsey-Brandt, Greg, Richmond, 684
Halsey-Brandt, Sue, Richmond, 684
Halstead, William, GM, Campbell River, 679
Halvorson, Herman, Chair, North Okanagan, 678
Halwachs, J. Ken, Vice Chair & Chief Engineer, Stemmer Steel Craft Industries Limited, 379
Halward, Doug, CEO, Consolidated Envirowaste Industries Inc., 150
Hamad, Sam, Ministre, 654
Hamblin, P.Eng., Brian, City Manager, Camrose, 671
Hamel, André, Lévis, 736
Hamel, Andréanne, Responsable, Union québécoise pour la conservation de la nature, 1180
Hamel, Chantal, Greffière, La Côte-de-Beaupré, 748

Executive Name Index

Hamel, Line, Conseillère de ville, St-Henri-Petite-Bourgogne-Pt, Montréal, 738
Hamel, Lucie, Coordonnatrice, Collège Laflèche, 1186
Hamer, Alfred, Manager, Waterous Power Systems, 422
Hamer, Doug, Chief, Riverview, 506-387-2201, 692
Hames, Sandra, City Councillor, Brampton, 706
Hamid, Zeeshan, Milton, 714
Hamill, David, Chief Executive Officer, ICI Paints (Canada) Inc., 238
Hamill, John, Medicine Hat, 403-526-7196, 673
Hamilton, Brenda, Township Clerk, Loyalist, 727
Hamilton, Charles, Administrator, Columbia-Shuswap, 677
Hamilton, Coreen, Sr. Scientist, AXYS Analytical Services Ltd., 100
Hamilton, D., Superintendent, Okanagan-Similkameen, 678
Hamilton, Dave, Contact, Golder Associates Ltd., 214
Hamilton, Dawn, Coordinator, Breast Cancer Society of Canada, 846
Hamilton, Debbie, Acting Commission Manager, Thorhild Regional Waste Management Services Commission, 758
Hamilton, Debbie, Manager, Thorhild Regional Water Services Commission, 758
Hamilton, Don, Markham, 713
Hamilton, Don, Information Technology Manager, Wilfrid Laurier University, 1165
Hamilton, Douglas, McCarthy Tétrault LLP - Toronto, 1077
Hamilton, Erica, Commission Secretary, 584
Hamilton, John, Manager, Engineering, Norfolk, 702
Hamilton, Lawrence, President, Enviro-Klean Technologies Inc., 183
Hamilton, Neil, President/CEO, 585
Hamilton, Peter E., Partner, Stikeman Elliott LLP - Toronto, 1080
Hamilton, Rachel J., Davis LLP - Edmonton, 1055
Hamilton, Rick, Mayor, Elliot Lake, 709
Hamilton, Ron, Quinte West, 613-392-5369, 718
Hamilton, Scott, Delta, 604-599-9261, 686
Hamilton, William A., Owner, Canada Heat Pumps, 123
Hamilton Upham, Jennifer J., Patterson Law, 1068
Hamlyn, Barbara, Librarian, Notre Dame Bay Memorial Health Centre, 1133
Hamlyn, Carl, Manager, Toromont Caterpillar, 397
Hamm, Vicki May, Magog, 819-347-7409, 737
Hammer, Lorne, Principal, Canadian Petroleum Engineering Inc., 125
Hammond, Robert F., Chair & CEO, Hammond Manufacturing, 224
Hammond, Susan, Executive Director, Silva Forest Foundation, 368
Hammond, Thomas, Program Manager, 525
Hammonds, David, Professional Resources Inc., 334
Hampson, Susan, Norwich, 728
Hanacek, Megan, Managing Director & Registrar, Association of Professional Biology, 837
Hanbidge, Donn, Sr. Vice-President & CFO, Ontario Power Generation, 312
Hanbridge, Donn, Senior Vice-President & CFO, 634
Hanchar, John M., Director, Memorial University of Newfoundland, 286
Hancock, Dave, Minister, 566
Hancock, Jim, Fire Chief, Richmond, 604-303-2700, 684
Hancock, John, Scugog, 729
Hancock, Kimberly, Director, Library Services, Western Health Care Corporation, 1131
Hancock, Peter, CEO, Chartis Insurance Company of Canada, 138
Hand, Clem, Manager, Yellowknife, 867-920-5617, 695
Hand, Jeffrey A., Partner, Singleton Urquhart LLP, 1062
Handfield, Normand, Manager, Kruger Inc., 260
Handlon, Richard J., Pitblado LLP, 1063
Handrahan, Phil, Director, Charlottetown, 732
Handy, Frank, Stitt Feld Handy Group, 1080
Handzic, Kember, Emery Jamieson LLP, 1055
Hanellin, Luc, NCL Envirotek Inc., 299
Hanert, Caireen E., Partner, Heenan Blaikie LLP - Calgary, 1051
Haney, Harry, Chair, 564
Haney, Ted, President, Canada Beef Export Federation, 852
Hanick, David, Partner, Osler, Hoskin & Harcourt LLP - Toronto, 1079
Hankey, Aleksandra, Librarian, POS Bio-sciences, 1190
Hankinson, James F., President/CEO, 634
Hanlan, Paul, Supervisor, Spruce Grove, 674
Hanley, Jim, Manager, New Brunswick Salmon Growers Association, 961
Hanlon, Debbie, St. John's, 709-576-2383, 694

Hanlon, P.Eng., Peter J., Manager, Saint John, 506-658-2811, 692
Hanly, Dave, Director, Planning & Development, Perth, 703
Hanmer, Gregory P., Miller Thomson LLP - Waterloo, 1081
Hanmore, George, Director, Fire & Emergency Services, Greater Napanee, 709
Hann, Tom, Councillor at Large, St. John's, 709-576-8219, 694
Hanna, Jack, Springwater, 730
Hanna, Ron, Senior Technologist, Glenn Group Ltd., 213
Hanna, Sandy, Sr. Program Officer, Foundation for Educational Exchange Between Canada & the United S, 919
Hanna, Terry, Vice-President, Mifab Canada, 289
Hanna, Tim, Director, Recreation & Leisure Services, Strathroy-Caradoc, 731
Hanna, W. Brad, McMillan Binch Mendelsohn - Toronto, 1077
Hannaberg, Mark, Sales Representative, Armtec Construction Products, 92
Hannah, Brent, Canadian Safety Equipment Inc., 125
Hannah, K.W., Vice-President, Godfrey Associates Ltd., 214
Hannah, Peter, President, P.J. Hannah Equipment Sales Corp., 316
Hannah, Roy, Manager, Westburne Canada, 425
Hannam, John S., City Clerk, Thunder Bay, 807-623-2238, 721
Hannam,, Scott, Executive Manager, ALS Environmental, 80
Hannan, Gerry, Manager, Vitafoam Products Canada Ltd., 414
Hannay, Dave, Chief Science Officer, Jasco Research Ltd., 251
Hanneson, Dave, President, Biomation, 108
Hannon, Andrew, Manager, Westburne Canada, 426
Hannon, Jim, Coordinator, Cumberland County, 902-667-2313, 697
Hannon, Kevin, Project Engineer, Kavanagh & Associates Ltd., 255
Hansen, Brian, Environmental Technologist, Middlesex Centre, 727
Hansen, Bruce, President, Nelson-Superior Consultants Ltd., 300
Hansen, Evelyn, Library Technician, Class Bookings, ILL & Special, Lakeshore Campus, 1158
Hansen, Jim, District Service Manager, Rondar Inc., 351
Hansen, Linda, Electronic Services Librarian, Ward Chipman Library, 1129
Hansen, Margarita, President, Altamar International Inc., 81
Hansen, Peter, President, Pacific Environmental Consulting & Occupational Hygiene Services, 316
Hansen, Ron, Regional Manager, Fort Garry Industries Ltd., 200
Hansen, S., Manager, Parks & Open Space Development, Fort Erie, 709
Hansen, Sarah D., Associate, Miller Thomson LLP - Toronto, 1078
Hansen, Sarah D., Partner, Miller Thomson LLP - Vancouver, 1061
Hansen, Tony, Canadian Emissions Ltd., 124
Hansen, M.Sc., P. Geo.,, Kristin E., Treasurer, Association of Professional Geoscientists of Ontario, 839
Hansford, Ron, Gowling Lafleur Henderson LLP - Calgary, 1051
Hanson, David, Program Manager, Recycling Council of Ontario, 993
Hanson, Elson H., President/CEO, E.H. Hanson Engineering Group Ltd., 168
Hanson, Randy, Exec. VP & COO, International Road Dynamics Inc., 245
Hanson, Ron, Director, Engineering & Operations, Port Colborne, 718
Hanson, Tracy, Councillor, Whitby, 723
Hantho, Jon, CEO, Maxxam Analytics Inc., 283
Hara, O.C., LLD, Arthur, Chair, 575
Harasen, Paul J., Kanuka Thuringer LLP, Barristers & Solicitors, 1090
Harbell, James W., Partner, Stikeman Elliott LLP - Toronto, 1080
Harber, Don, General Manager, Hotz Environmental Services Inc., 234
Harcourt, Clint S., Partner, Waterstone Law Group LLP, 1056
Hardacre, Elizabeth, Librarian, Science Library, 1110
Hardcastle, Cheryl M., Deputy Mayor & Councillor, Tecumseh, 519-817-4864, 720
Harden, Hugh, Vice-President, Kinder Morgan Canada Inc., 257
Harder, Brian, President, Fraser Valley Labour Council, 919
Harder, Jan, Ottawa, 613-580-2473, 716
Hardie, Steve, Director, Parks & Recreation, North Perth, 519-292-2055, 715
Harding, Gregory S., Partner, Stewart McKelvey Stirling Scales - Saint John, 1065
Harding, Harry, Minister, 600
Harding, John, Chair, Canadian Association of Swine Veterinarians, 859
Harding, Reece, Young, Anderson, 1062

Harding, Richard, Director, Nanaimo, 250-755-7516, 681
Hardman, Andrew, Manager, Crown Fibre Tube Inc., 154
Hardman, Donna, Compliance Officer, Water & Waste Water Administra, Kincardine, 519-396-4660, 726
Hardwicke-Brown, Mungo, Blake, Cassels & Graydon LLP - Calgary, 1049
Hardy, David R., Principal, Hardy Stevenson & Associates, 225
Hardy, John L., Director, Educational Resources, George Brown College of Applied Arts & Technology, 1158
Hardy, Lisa, Executive Director, Alberta Association of Agricultural Societies, 815
Hardy, Neal, Chair, 656
Hardy, Paul, President, HQN Industrial Fabrics Inc., 234
Hardy, Paula, Library Technician, Thompson, Cariboo, Shuswap Health Sciences Library, 1112
Hardy, Réjean, Contact, Hardy Filtration, 225
Hardy, Sandra, Deputy Minister, 587
Hare, Geoffrey C., Chair/CEO, 520
Harel, Mario, Directeur et Chef, Gatineau, 735
Hargesheimer, Erika, General Manager, Calgary, 403-268-5636, 671
Hargrave, Heather, Coordinator, Agricultural Groups Concerned About Resources & the Environment, 814
Hargrave, Rob, Councillor, Whitchurch-Stouffville, 723
Hargreaves, Tara, Scientist & Coordinator, Radiation Safety Institute of Canada, 992
Hargrove, Herb, General Manager, Andritz Bird, 85
Hargrove, Lyle, President, Occupational Health Clinics for Ontario Workers, 969
Hargrove, Pamela G., City Clerk, Fredericton, 691
Harju, Mel, Director, Maintenance & Engineering Society of The Canadian Institute of Mi, 950
Harker, Harry, Director, Red Deer County, 670
Harker, Jim, Kamloops, 681
Harkness, John, Service Manager, Hibon Inc., 231
Harkness, Michelle, Coordinator, AllerGen NCE Inc., 821
Harley, Jayne, Library Clerk, Homewood Health Centre, 1140
Harley, Rob, By-law Enforcement Officer & Manager, Campbell River, 679
Harling, Ann, Secretary-Treasurer, Canadian Public Health Association - NB/PEI Branch, 883
Harman, Donna A., President & Chief Executive Officer, American Forest & Paper Association, 823
Harman, L., Vice-President, Enform: The Safety Association for the Upstream Oil & Gas Industr, 910
Harmon, Patrica Anne, Library Manager, Crompton Co./Cie, 1140
Harmon, Rod, Manager, Dawson Creek, 250-782-3114, 680
Harms, Colin, District Manager, BFI Canada Inc., 106
Harmsen, Dolf, President, Ontario Woodlot Association, 981
Harmsworth Dow, Joan, Library Technician, Regina Qu'Appelle Health Region - Wascana Rehabilitation Centre, 1188
Harned, Chris, Supervisor, Fundy Region Solid Waste Commission, 758
Harner, Todd, Manager, Great Western Containers Inc., 216
Harney, Margo, Library Technicien, Aurora College, 1133
Harnick, Elise, Engineer, Cochrane, 403-851-2575, 671
Harnois, Pierre, Principal, Golder Associates Ltd., 214
Harper, Bill, New Westminster, 682
Harper, Brad, Contact, Pebblestone Multi-Services Inc., 320
Harper, David E., Planner, Westland Resource Group Inc., 430
Harper, Duff, Blake, Cassels & Graydon LLP - Calgary, 1049
Harper, Dufferin R., Partner, Wickwire Holm, 1068
Harper, Judy, Head, Sciences & Technology Library, 1125
Harper, Robert A., Administrator, Alberni-Clayoquot, 676
Harper, Scott, CEO, Wind Energy Institute of Canada, 432
Harpin, Denis, Responsable, Référence, Bibliothèque de botanique - L'Institut de recherche en biologie v, 1170
Harpley, Paul, President, South Lake Simcoe Naturalists, 1010
Harquail, J. Paul M., Partner, Stewart McKelvey Stirling Scales - Saint John, 1065
Harrigan, Brendan, Contact, DST Consulting Engineers, 166
Harrington, James R., President, AGO Environmental Electronics Ltd., 73
Harrington, Kim, Customer Service Representative, Process Innovations Canada Inc., 333
Harrington, Terry, Manager, Water Department, Woodstock, 723
Harris, Chris, Ogilvy Renault LLP/S.E.N.C.R.L., s.r.l. - Calgary, 1053
Harris, Clayton D., Deputy City Manager & Commissioner, Finance & Corp, Vaughan, 722
Harris, David, President/CEO, Kinectrics Inc., 257
Harris, Donna, Acquisitions Librarian, Dawson College, 1173
Harris, Doug, Director, Human Resources, Bruce, 698
Harris, Gary, President, Harris Industrial Testing, 226

Executive Name Index

Harris, Glenn, Senior Manager, Capital Regional District, 250-360-3090, 676
Harris, J, Manager, Terrace Office, Triton Environmental Consultants Ltd., 402
Harris, J.A., President, International Water Supply Ltd., 245
Harris, Jason J., Miramichi, 691
Harris, Kent, Senior Vice-President & Chief Financial Officer, 511
Harris, Lynne, Abbotsford, 679
Harris, Maria, Metro Vancouver, 678
Harris, Mark, Director, Environmental Services, Strathroy-Caradoc, 731
Harris, Matthew J., St. Catharines, 719
Harris, Michael, Chair, EnGlobe Corp., 181
Harris, Mike, PricewaterhouseCoopers Management Consultants, 332
Harris, Paul, Red Deer, 674
Harris, Raymond E.A., Project Consultant, WPI Safety & Environmental Consultants, 434
Harris, Trevor J., Chair & CEO, T. Harris Environmental Management Inc., 385
Harrison, Chris, President, Opus International Consultants (Canada) Ltd., 314
Harrison, Colin, Contact, Weir Power & Industrial, 424
Harrison, Donald, Managing Director, 562
Harrison, Douglas, Partner, Stikeman Elliott LLP - Toronto, 1080
Harrison, Douglas K., Edwards, Kenny & Bray LLP, 1059
Harrison, Eleanor, Haliburton, 705-489-2128, 700
Harrison, Fabian, Librarian, SIAST Kelsey Campus, 1190
Harrison, Grant, Manager, PRT Inc., 336
Harrison, Jean, President, Aqua Data Inc., 87
Harrison, Jim, Quinte West, 613-392-9437, 718
Harrison, M. Lynne, Thompson Dorfman Sweatman LLP, 1064
Harrison, Pauline, Saint-Eustache, 450-473-8141, 742
Harrison, Rick, Chief, Fire, Brock, 724
Harrison, Sarah, Osler, Hoskin & Harcourt LLP - Toronto, 1079
Harrison, Sarah, Director, 578
Harrison, Tej, Librarian, SIAST Kelsey Campus, 1190
Harrity, Lisa, Director, 596
Harrold, Jim, City Manager, Owen Sound, 717
Hart, Brad, Senior Estimator, Donalco Inc., 165
Hart, Glenn, Minister, 666
Hart, Glenn, Minister Responsible, 667
Hart, Jim, Executive Director, Municipal Licensing & Standard, Toronto, 416-392-8445, 721
Hart, John, Senior Technical Advisor, Conestoga-Rovers & Associates, 149
Hart, T.H., General Manager, Canbar Inc., 126
Hart, Tammy, Deputy Mayor & Councillor, South Stormont, 730
Hart, Ted, Partner, Envirotech Engineering, 188
Hart, Terry, Clerk Administrator, North Glengarry, 727
Hart, Thomas E., McInnes Cooper, 1067
Harten, Ron, General Manager, Hamilton Community Energy, 224
Hartfiel, Yvonne, Business Development, Pomeroy Consulting Engineers Limited, 328
Hartford, D. Wayne, President/CEO, Pure Energy Inc., 336
Hartholt, Andrew, Chief Building Official, Erin, 709
Hartke, Jan A., Executive Director, Earth Voice, 907
Hartley, Darryl, Director, Western Site Technologies Inc., 430
Hartley, Diana, Executive Officer, 612
Hartley, Terry, Director, Nanaimo, 250-755-4427, 681
Hartman, Eva Wyszkowski-, CEO, Fluor Canada, 197
Hartman, Steve, President, Industrial Thermo Polymers Ltd., 241
Hartmann, Franz, Executive Director, Toronto Environmental Alliance, 1012
Hartmann, Rina, Account Manager, Geosoft, 212
Hartson, Jane, Specialist, Waters Limited, 423
Hartwell, Vern, Chair, 572
Harty, Steven J., Senior Engineer, GE Ground Engineering Ltd., 205
Harvey, Andrew, Contact, Cyanide Destruct Systems Inc., 155
Harvey, Dave, National Sales Manager, National Process Equipment Inc., 298
Harvey, Lorne, Assistant Deputy Minister, 563
Harvey, Robert (Bob) P., Councillor, Halifax Regional Municipality, 695
Harvey, Stephen, Middlesex Centre, 727
Harvey, Sue, Managing Director, Vancouver, 604-871-6001, 685
Harvey, Sylvie, Directice générale, Coaticook, 747
Harvey, Valerie, Director, Parks & Recreation, Brockville, 707
Harvey, Q.C., Christopher, MacKenzie Fujisawa LLP, 1061
Harvey-Renner, Shannon, Manager, Langley, 604-533-6121, 687
Harvie, Alan, Partner, Macleod Dixon LLP, 1052

Harvie, Dwayne, Project Engineer, Wood Buffalo, 780-743-7855, 670
Harvie, George, CAO, Delta, 604-946-3212, 686
Harwood, Jeff, Brandon, 689
Harwood, Sat D., Lesperance Mendes, 1061
Hashey, Q.C., David T., Cox and Palmer - Fredericton, 1064
Haskins, Tania, Director, American Water Works Association, 826
Haslett, Mark, University Librarian, University of Waterloo, 1164
Hass, Lisa, Town Manager, Erin, 709
Hassan, Ahmed, Manager, Hassco Industries Inc., 226
Hassan, David A., President, Hassco Industries Inc., 226
Hassard, Brenda, Administrator, Boart Longyear Inc., 111
Hassard, Q.C., Richard J., Counsel, Gardiner, Roberts LLP, 1075
Haswell, Deborah, Mayor, Owen Sound, 717
Hatch, Shawn, Davis LLP - Vancouver, 1059
Hatcher, P.Eng., Scott, Director, Rothesay, 506-848-6668, 692
Hatfield, Percy, Windsor, 723
Hatfield, Q.C., Bruce D., Cox and Palmer - Fredericton, 1064
Hatherton, David, President, NextEnergy Inc., 303
Hattat, Frank, Tanknology Canada Inc., 386
Hatten, Valerie, Librarian, Ontario Science Centre, 1160
Hattle, Tom, Contact, Recyclenet Corporation, 343
Hatton, Bruce, Lennox Industries (Canada) Ltd., 267
Hatzis, Patrick, Vice-President, Osram Sylvania Ltd., 315
Hau, Edward, Bibliographic & Computing Services Librarian, Calgary Library, 1100
Hauge, Dallas, Vice-President, Willowglen Systems Inc., 432
Haugh, Liz, Vice-President, Ontario Public Health Association, 978
Haughn, Chad, Director, Chester District, 697
Hauk, Ryan, Macleod Dixon LLP, 1077
Haulena, Peter, Analytical Services Manager, Accutest Laboratories Ltd., 66
Hausmann, Peter, Chair, Land Trust Alliance, 948
Hauswald, Karin, Marketing & Sales Coordintor, Care First Aid Training Inc., 128
Haverstock, Scott, President, Atlantic Poly Liners Inc., 97
Havixbeck, Paula, Winnipeg, 690
Hawco, Alan, President, Rawdon Technologies Ltd., 342
Hawes, Michael K., Executive Director, Foundation for Educational Exchange Between Canada & the United S, 919
Hawke, Tony, Terrapex Environmental Ltd., 390
Hawkings, Alicia, Information Analyst, EnCana Corporation, 1101
Hawkins, Donald B., Scarfone Hawkins LLP, 1069
Hawkins, Mike, Director, Associated Tube Industries, 94
Hawkins, Patrick J., Partner, Borden Ladner Gervais LLP - Toronto, 1073
Hawkins, Robert, President, Del-Air Systems Ltd., 160
Hawkins, Susan, Executive Director, Prince Edward Island Eco-Net, 988
Hawksworth, George, Delta, 604-946-4740, 686
Hawley, Mark K., Vice-President, BIOREM Inc., 109
Hawn, Laurie, Parliamentary Secretary to the Minister of Nationa, 545
Hawn, Robert, Sales Representative, DTE Industries Ltd., 167
Hawrychuk, Shelley, Coordinator of Collection Services, University of Toronto at Mississauga, 1145
Hawryluk, Allan A., Senior Vice-President, Strategic Contracting, 511
Hawrysh, Brian, CEO, British Columbia Wood Specialities Group Association, 851
Hay, D. Brian, Principal, CMS: Crisis Management Specialists Inc., 145
Hay, David, President/CEO, 596
Hay, Eli, Chief Executive Officer, Nisymco Inc., 305
Hay, Gerry, Trainer, Rocky Mountain Environmental Ltd., 350
Hay, Greg, Executive Director, Pulp & Paper Technical Association of Canada, 991
Hay, James Alexander (Sandy), County Planner, Leeds & Grenville, 726
Hay, John, Fire Chief, Thunder Bay, 721
Hay, Joyce, Acquisitions Coordinator, Canada Science & Technology Museum, 1148
Hay, Nairn, General Manager, Fundy Model Forest, 922
Haybarger, Allen, National Sales Manager, Dundas-Jafine Inc., 167
Hayden, Bradley J., Partner, Macleod Dixon LLP, 1052
Hayden, Dana, Deputy Minister, 575
Hayden, Jack, Minister, 564
Hayden, Jay, Partner, Heenan Blaikie LLP - Victoria, 1060, 1062
Hayden, Terry, Asst. Deputy Minister, 664
Hayes, Bill, CH2M Hill Canada Limited, 137
Hayes, Bill, Sr. Vice-President, CH2M Hill Canada Limited, 137

Hayes, Jessica, Alcohol Countermeasure Systems Corp., 77
Hayes, Patrick, Senior Project Manager, Abcott Construction Ltd., 65
Hayes, Pierre, Sec.-Trés., Régie d'assainissement des eaux usées de la Basse-Lièvre, 759
Hayes, B.Comm., CA, Lorella M., Chief Financial Officer & Treasurer, Greater Sudbury / Grand Sudbury, 710
Hayes, P. Eng, Robert, Town Engineer, LaSalle, 713
Hayles, Des, Principal, LEHDER Environmental Services Ltd., 267
Hayman, George, Service Manager, National Energy Equipment Inc., 297
Hayne, Kirsten M.L., Brownlee LLP, 1054
Haynes, Jim, Vice-President, 601
Haynes, Mike, Scientific Director, Radiation Safety Institute of Canada, 992
Hays, Fred, Policy Analyst, Alberta Beef Producers, 815
Hayward, Christine, Interim Director, Health Sciences Library, 1101
Hayward, John, President, Hayward Gordon Ltd., 227
Haywood-Farmer, Stewart, Manager, PRT Inc., 336
Hazel, Jane, Director General, 533
Hazell, Stephen, General Counsel & Director of Environmental Assess, Marbek Resource Consultants Ltd., 280
Hazen, Guylaine, Technicienne en documentation, Québec Ministère de l'agriculture, des pêcheries et de l'alimenta, 1179
Hazlett, Brian, Supervisor, Kings County, 902-690-6198, 696
Hea, James A., Brownlee LLP, 1054
Heakes, Edward A., Partner, Macleod Dixon LLP, 1077
Heal, Andrew J., Blaney McMurtry LLP, 1073
Heald, Chris, Systems Administrator, West Coast Environmental Law Research Foundation, 1119
Healey, Colleen, Manager, Planning & Development, Essa, 725
Healey, Kevin, Directeur régional, Harold Marcus Ltd., 225
Healey, Martha A., Partner, Ogilvy Renault LLP/S.E.N.C.R.L., s.r.l. - Ottawa, 1071
Healing, Alison, President, Conserver Society of Hamilton & District, 902
Healy, Edith, Responsable, référence, Université du Québec École de technologie supérieure, 1176
Healy, Finbarr, Reference Librarian, Canadian Heritage, 1167
Heaps, Wally, Branch Manager, ICC The Compliance Centre Inc., 238
Heapy, Ernest, Vice President, 662
Heard, Stuart, President, Vermilion River Naturalist Club, 1017
Hearn, David, Managing Director, Scitax Advisory Partners LLP, 360
Hearn, Patricia, Director, 600
Hearns, Geoff, Manager, Tremco Ltd., 401
Heath, Jack, York, 705
Heath, Jack, Deputy Mayor & Regional Councillor, Markham, 905-475-4872, 713
Heath, Paul, Peterborough, 703
Heathcote, Tyler, President, Ridgeline Environment Inc., 347
Hebblethwaite, Russ, President/CEO, Enviro Vault Ltd., 182
Hebblethwaite, Tyler, Field Sales, Enviro Vault Ltd., 182
Hebert, Brenda, Senior Partner, Stikeman Elliott LLP - Toronto, 1080
Hebert, Erica, Associate Reference Librarian, Concordia University College of Alberta, 1105
Hébert, France, Saint-Constant, 742
Hébert, Guillaume, Associé, Lapointe Rosenstein Marchand Melançon, 1085
Hébert, Jean, Environmental Engineer, Lecompte Engineering Ltd., 266
Hébert, Jean, Partner, Lavery, de Billy - Montréal, 1085
Hebert, Larry, Councillor at Large, Thunder Bay, 721
Hebert, Marc, Manager, Consolidated Giroux Environment Inc., 150
Hébert, Martin, Contact, Les Emballages Polyform inc., 268
Hebert, Michael S., Beament Green, 1070
Hébert, Michelle, Directrice générale adjointe, Saint-Jean-sur-Richelieu, 742
Hébert, Olivier, Heenan Blaikie S.E.N.C.R.L./SRL - Québec, 1088
Hébert, Paul, Executive Director, Mining Industry Human Resources Council, 955
Hébert-Erban, Madeleine, Bibliothécaire, Bibliothèque centrale, 1170
Hecke, Michele A., Blaney McMurtry LLP, 1073
Hecker, Kathy, Library Contact, Chetwynd Campus, 1111
Hector, Dorothy, Councillor, Kingston, 712
Hedges, H.G., Contact, Rhododendron Society of Canada, 995
Heeney, David, President, INDECO Strategic Consulting Inc., 240

Executive Name Index

Heffel, Patricia, Director, Health Sciences Association of Alberta, 928
Heggie, Carla, President, Nova Scotia Daylily Society, 967
Hehn, T., Carrier Canada Ltd., 129
Heidenheim, Lorna, Executive Director, Ontario Healthy Communities Coalition, 974
Heidt, Myles, Saskatoon, 754
Heighton, Ronnie, Vice-President, Canadian Council of Professional Fish Harvesters, 865
Heil, Robert J., Chief Administrative Officer, Port Colborne, 718
Heilbrunn, Lila, Director, Library & Learning Resources, Vancouver Community College, 1117, 1119
Heiman, Mary-Ellen, Director, Canadian Centre for Emergency Preparedness, 861
Heiman, Tyrone, Manager, Veolia ES Canada Industrial Services Inc., 411
Heimann, Allen, Medical Officer of Health, Windsor, 723
Heinbuch, Lorraine (Lori), Clerk, Wellington North, 732
Heino, Alex, President, ATS Scientific Inc., 97
Heinsen, Patrick, Partner, Borden Ladner Gervais LLP - Calgary, 1049
Heinz, Heinrich, Thurber Engineering Ltd., 395
Heinz, Michael, Chief Executive Officer, CIBA Spécialités Chimiques Canada inc., 141
Heissler, Gunnar, Sr. Technical Consultant, ECE Group - a Division of Conestoga-Rovers & Associates, 170
Heit, Brian, Niagara, 702
Helbronner, Valerie, Torys LLP, 1081
Helfrich, Jerry, President, Angus, Butler Engineering Ltd., 86
Helin, Calvin, President, Native Investment & Trade Association, 959
Hellinga, Jack, CH2M Hill Canada Limited, 137
Helmuth, Antje, Head Librarian, British Columbia Health & Human Services, 1120
Hemingway, Heather, Contact, Foothills No. 31, 669
Hémond, Jacques, Préfet, Les Sources, 750
Hempen, Tom, Newmarket, 714
Hemsley, Paul, President, Hemmera Envirochem Inc., 229
Hénaire, Louis, Hénaire, Louis, 1089
Hénault, André, Maire, Saint-Charles-Borromée, 753
Hénault, André, Préfet, Joliette, 747
Hénault, Andrée, Conseillère de ville, Montréal, 738
Hénault, Cécile, Repentigny, 450-654-3046, 740
Hénault, Manon D., Longueuil, 737
Hénault, Raymond, Repentigny, 450-581-0319, 740
Henderson, Barbara, Niagara, 702
Henderson, Barry, Diversion & Recycling Programs, J&F Waste Systems Inc., 249
Henderson, Ben, Edmonton, 780-496-8146, 672
Henderson, Bob, President, Matrix Photocatalytic Inc., 282
Henderson, Bonnie, Stratford, 720
Henderson, Christopher, Chairman, The Delphi Group, 392
Henderson, Dale, London, 713
Henderson, David L., Mayor, Brockville, 707
Henderson, Ian, Inside Sales, Asbeguard Equipment Inc., 93
Henderson, Jim, Life Sciences Librarian, Life Sciences Library, 1174
Henderson, John, Cobourg, 708
Henderson, Julie, Financial Administrator, Ontario Soil & Crop Improvement Association, 979
Henderson, Kevin, Director, Dawson Creek, 250-784-3622, 680
Henderson, Merrill A., Moncton / Ville de Moncton, 691
Henderson, Pat, Pacesetter Sales & Associates Inc., 316
Henderson, Pat, Western Canada Sales Manager, Pacesetter Sales & Associates Inc., 316
Henderson, Phil J., Partner, Stikeman Elliott LLP - Toronto, 1080
Henderson, Ric, Director, Red Deer County, 670
Henderson, Ron, Essa, 705-424-9752, 725
Hendricken, Sue, Manager, Charlottetown, 902-368-1025, 732
Hendricks, Duncan, Office Manager, Golder Associates Ltd., 214
Hendry, Bev, Chief Administrative Officer, Scugog, 729
Hendry, Wayne, Director, 600
Hendsbee, David, Councillor, Halifax Regional Municipality, 695
Hendy, Fred, Assistant Manager, Squamish, 688
Hendy, Gary R., Project Engineer, Jagger Hims Limited, 250
Hener, Darrell, Vice-President, Proeco Enviroservices Ltd., 333
Heney, J. Rick, Fulton & Company LLP, Lawyers & Trade-Mark Agents, 1056
Henke, Keray, Deputy Minister, 566
Henkel, Ric, WRS Environmental, 434
Henley, David G., Stewart McKelvey Stirling Scales - Halifax, 1067
Hennebery, Phil, Technical Representative, Can-Am Instruments Ltd., 122
Hennebury, Bruce, Director, 610

Hennebury, Krista, Executive Director, Environmental Managers Association of British Columbia, 912
Hennigar, G. Wayne, Director & CEO, HETEK Solutions Inc., 230
Henning, Joanne, Associate University Librarian, Reference & Collec, University of Victoria Libraries, 1121
Henrickson, Linda, Manager, Red Deer County, 670
Henrie, André, Clarence-Rockland, 708
Henrie, Pierre-Paul, Partner, Ogilvy Renault LLP/S.E.N.C.R.L., s.r.l. - Ottawa, 1071
Henriksson, Lars, President, Norditrade Inc., 305
Henry, Cameron, Executive Director, 563
Henry, France, Director, Biorex Inc., 109
Henry, Jeff, Waterloo, 722
Henry, John, Mayor, Oshawa, 716
Henry, Nick, National Sales Manager, Phoenix Contact Ltd., 323
Henry, Patricia, Library Technician, Manitoba Museum, 1124
Henry, R. Falconer, Triton Consultants Ltd., 402
Henry, Scott, Rothsay, 352
Henry, Todd, Vice-President, Integrated Explorations, 244
Henry, C.M.O., Glen, Director, Corporate Services, Owen Sound, 717
Hensen, Phil, Manager, Dekka Resins Inc., 159
Henze, Harald, Treasurer, Electro-Federation Canada Inc., 909
Hepburn, James, Treasurer, Prince Edward, 703
Hepner, Linda, Metro Vancouver, 684, 678
Heppell, Fernand, Directeur général, Les Etchemins, 749
Heppner, Nancy, Minister, 658
Heppner, Nancy, Minister Responsible, 658
Herasymuik, Greg, Office Manager, Golder Associates Ltd., 214
Herback, D., Fire Chief, Pembroke, 717
Herbert, Jason K., Davis LLP - Vancouver, 1059
Herchenson, Lorna, Int'l Corresponding Secretary, British Columbia Fuchsia & Begonia Society, 848
Heredia Fragoso, Marco Antonio, Head, Commission for Environmental Cooperation, 898
Heredia Fragoso, Marco Antonio, Program Manager, 525
Heredy, Laszlo, Chief Scientist, Plasma Environmental Technologies Inc., 326
Hergart, Lars, Engine Control Systems, 180
Herity, John, Director, Union mondiale pour la nature - Bureau de Montréal, 1014
Herle, Damian, Manager, Camrose, 671
Herle, Neil, Osler, Hoskin & Harcourt LLP - Calgary, 1053
Herlovitch, Alex, Director, Planning & Development, Niagara Falls, 715
Herman, Alexander, Langlois Kronström Desjardins, 1085
Herman, Ashley, Site Manager, Green Soils Inc., 217
Herman, Brett, Vice-President, Firwin Corporation, 196
Herman, Karen, Chatham-Kent, 724
Herman, Les, Manager, Guspro Inc., 223
Herman, Miriam, Vice-President, Firwin Corporation, 196
Herman, Paul, President, Firwin Corporation, 196
Hermann, Hans, Senior Manager, Commission for Environmental Cooperation, 898
Hermann, Hans, Senior Program Manager, Commission for Environmental Cooperation, 898
Hermanutz, Roni, Manager, Health Sciences Association of Alberta, 928
Hermosilla, Daniel, Contact, KBM Forestry Consultants Inc., 255
Hernandez, Helios, Secretary, 586
Hernblad, Darcy, Fire Chief, Yellowknife, 867-766-5501, 695
Hernen, Steve, Director, Protective Services, Huntsville, 711
Heron, Anne Louise, Chief Administrative Officer, Lincoln, 713
Heron, Cathy, St. Albert, 674
Herone, Marilee, Manager, Saskatchewan Wildlife Federation, 1002
Héroux, André, Directeur, Saint-Lin-Laurentides, 743
Héroux, André, President & CEO, EnGlobe Corp., 181
Herr, Laban, General Manager, Laidlaw Carriers Inc. - Van Division, 262
Herrington, Christine, Northumberland, 702
Herritt, Perry, Manager, Harris & Roome Supply Limited, 225
Herscovitch, Pearl, Coordinator, Access Services, Mount Royal College, 1102
Hershenfield, Jeff, Stikeman Elliott LLP - Toronto, 1080
Hertzberg, Norm, General Manager, Peco Filters Ltd., 320
Hervieux, Margot, Contact, Peace Parkland Naturalists, 985
Herwig, Laurel, Executive Director, 518
Herzberg, Curtis, County Manager, Red Deer County, 670
Hesch, Rob, Manager, Westburne Canada, 429
Hesham, Ganem, Trade Commissioner, 768
Heshka, Harvey, Area Sales Manager, Argus Telecom International Inc., 90
Heshka, Renee, Senior Manager, Tansley Associates Environmental Services, 387

Hesterman, Larry, President, Magnum Industries Ltd., 278
Hettinga, Hilary, Director, Central Okanagan, 250-868-5241, 677
Hétu, Marie-Josée, Partner, Heenan Blaikie S.E.N.C.R.L/SRL - Trois-Rivières, 1089
Hetu, Susan, Executive Director, 657
L'Heureux, Brigitte, Bibliotechnicienne, Référence et service du prêt, Collège universitaire de St-Boniface, 1123
Hewitson, Phil, Director, Transportation, Waterloo, 519-747-8630, 722
Hewitt, Daniel, Principal Consultant, SRK Consulting (Canada) Inc., 377
Hewitt, Dennis, President, Terrafix Geosynthetics Inc., 390
Hewitt, Dianne, Web Development Librarian, Douglas College, 1114
Hewitt, Ron, Councillor at Large, Kincardine, 519-395-2774, 726
Hewko, Allen, President, Cactus Environmental Services Ltd., 120
Hewlett, Diane, Manager, Kitimat, 687
Hewson, Don G., Director, Romatec Incorporated, 350
Heyck, Mark, Yellowknife, 695
Heydon, Dan, Fire Chief, New Tecumseth, 714
Hibbs, Art, CH2M Hill Canada Limited, 137
Hicik, Andrew, Manager, Sidney, 684
Hicken, Curt, Executive Director, Association of Great Lakes Outdoor Writers, 835
Hickerson, H. Thomas, University Librarian, University of Calgary, 1103
Hickey, Christopher, Cox and Palmer - St. John's, 1065
Hickey, John, Minister Responsible, 602
Hickey, Tom, Director, Nanaimo, 681
Hickie, Darryl, Minister, 656
Hickman, Charles, Manager, 596
Hickman, Sandy, Councillor at Large, St. John's, 709-576-8045, 694
Hickman, Stephanie S., Cox and Palmer - St. John's, 1065
Hicknell, Dave, President, Gamsby & Mannerow Ltd., 204
Hicknell, David, Branch Manager, Gamsby & Mannerow Ltd., 204
Hicks, Barb, President, Rideau Environmental Action League, 995
Hicks, Brian A.Q., Moncton / Ville de Moncton, 691
Hicks, D., CEO, MMM Group, 292
Hicks, E., Associate, MMM Group, 292
Hicks, Paul, Coordinator, Planning, Strathroy-Caradoc, 731
Hicks, Robin, North Vancouver, 688
Hicks, Steven, Fredericton, 691
Hicks, Tim, District Sales Manager, Babcock & Wilcox Canada Ltd., 100
Hickson, Jim, Owner, Sterling Press, 379
Hie, Isobel, Mayor, Hamilton, 725
Hie, Randy, Chief, Buckham Transport Ltd., 118
Hiebert, Brian F., Managing Partner, Davis LLP - Vancouver, 1059
Hierlihy, Tim, Director, 666
Hietapakka, Al, Regional Sales & Service Manager, KMW Systems Inc., 258
Higgelke, Peter, Consulting Forester, KBM Forestry Consultants Inc., 255
Higgins, Charles L.K., Fasken Martineau - Toronto, 1075
Higgins, Glen, Manager, 618
Higgins, Larry, Supervisor, Water & Sewer, Niagara-on-the-Lake, 715
Higgins, Michael, Associate Financial Advisor, Pinch Group, 324
Higgins, Patricia (Patty), Saint John, 692
Higgins, Rod, Assistant General Manager, Moncton / Ville de Moncton, 691
Higginson, E., Greyline Instruments Inc., 218
Higo, Ron, Director, Port Moody, 604-469-4542, 683
Higson, Robert, Director, Riverview, 506-387-2023, 692
Hilchey, Karen, Saint-Georges, 742
Hildebrand, Cynthia, Director, Tillsonburg, 721
Hildebrand, Martin, President, Nelson Environmental Inc., 299
Hildebrandt, John, Renfrew, 613-756-2747, 704
Hildebrandt, Karen, Library Systems Coordinator, Concordia University College of Alberta, 1105
Hilderley, Patrice, Treasurer, Woodstock, 723
Hilderman, Garry, Principal, Hilderman Thomas Frank Cram & Associates, 232
Hill, Andrew, Orillia, 716
Hill, Bill, Dufferin, 699
Hill, Chris, President, Canatec Consultants Ltd., 126
Hill, Claude, Directeur général, Fondation québécoise en environnement, 918
Hill, Darren, Saskatoon, 754
Hill, Dave, Managing Director, Thurber Engineering Ltd., 395
Hill, Dave, Superintendent, Summerland, 689

Executive Name Index

Hill, David, President/CEO, Eneready Products Ltd., 179
Hill, Doug, Contact, AIC Sullivan's Environmental Services, 74
Hill, James, Executive Vice-President, Sonic Technology Solutions Inc., 374
Hill, James, President, HSE Integrated, 234
Hill, Jim, President, Alberta Farm Fresh Producers Association, 816
Hill, Joel, Manager, RPC, 353
Hill, John, Fort Erie, 709
Hill, Judy, Senior Assistant, CanTox Health Sciences International, 1144
Hill, Ken, Mayor, Russell, 729
Hill, Kevin, Director, Parks, Recreation & Culture, Greater Napanee, 709
Hill, Krista F., Torys LLP, 1081
Hill, Mark, Landfill Manager, CCS Income Trust, 134
Hill, Mark, Manager, Westburne Canada, 426
Hill, Michael, President, Save Ontario Shipwrecks, 1002
Hill, Murray, Director, 610
Hill, N., Carrier Canada Ltd., 129
Hill, Tina H., Ogilvy Renault LLP/S.E.N.C.R.L., s.r.l. - Ottawa, 1071
Hill Laroque, Lucie, Laval, 736
Hiller, Marc, Directeur par intérim de la bibliothèque, École polytechnique de Montréal, 1173
Hiller, Marc, Responsable, Développement des collections, École polytechnique de Montréal, 1173
Hillier, Brent, Executive Vice-President, Siemens Water Technologies, 367
Hillier, Wad, General Manager, Plains Environmental Inc., 325
Hillman, Brian, Director, Planning & Building Services, Tecumseh, 720
Hillmer, Randy, Manager, Lakeland Protective Wear Inc., 263
Hillock, Pam, Clerk, Dufferin, 699
Hilsen, Agnes S., Municipal Clerk, North Vancouver, 604-990-2207, 688
Hilton, Al, Deputy Minister, 659
Hilton, D.C., Manager, Kamloops, 681
Hilton, John N., President, Decommissioning Consulting Services Limited, 159
Hilton, Kim, Manager, Langley, 681
Hilton, Mike, Branch Manager, Plad Équipement Ltée, 325
Hilton, Susanne, Councillor, Whitchurch-Stouffville, 723
Hilton, B.A., Melissa, Charlottetown, 732
Hiltz, Darrell, CAO, Chester District, 697
Hims, Andrew G., Branch Manager, Jagger Hims Limited, 251
Hims, Andrew G., Principal, Jagger Hims Limited, 250
Hince, Anne-Marie, Library Assisntant, Royal Victoria Hospital, 1175
Hincks, Terry, Regina, 306-949-9690, 754
Hinde, Doug, Regional Sales Manager, Wastequip Cusco, 421
Hines, Michael A., Partner, Hicks Morley Hamilton Stewart Storie LLP, 1076
Hinrichs, Rob, Vice-President & Chief Actuary, 636
Hinton, Paddy, Coordinator, Mount Waddington, 678
Hipfner, Scott, McLennan Ross LLP, 1055
Hipwell, Dawn, Director, Purchasing, Fleet, & Property, Simcoe, 704
Hirning, Lorraine, Serials Technician, Athabasca University, 1099
Hirsch, Brian, General Manager, Point Four Systems Inc., 327
Hirst, Christopher E., Alexander Holburn Beaudin & Lang, LLP, 1057
Hirst, Q.C., Thomas E., Partner, Macleod Dixon LLP, 1052
Hirtle, Ken, President, Nature Trust of New Brunswick, 960
Hiscock, Diane, General Manager, Fraser-Fort George, 678
Hisey, Brenda, Director, Camrose, 780-672-4428, 671
Hittinger, Mike, Coordinator, Sturgeon County, 780-939-8339, 670
Hixson, Carol, University Librarian, University of Regina Library, 1189
Hjorth, Alan, Manager, Human Resources, Thunder Bay, 807-625-2585, 721
Hluchan, T.H., President, SHAL Consulting Engineers Ltd., 365
Hnatick, Lynn E., Partner, MacPherson Leslie & Tyerman LLP - Saskatoon, 1090
Hnatiuk, Ron, Organic Resource Management Inc., 314
Hnetka, Bob, Director, SARCAN Recycling, 358
Ho, Alan, Markham, 713
Ho, Carrie G., Kanuka Thuringer LLP, Barristers & Solicitors, 1090
Ho, David Y.F., Principal, AN-GEO Environmental Consultants Ltd., 84
Hoar, John, Sr. Trade Policy Analyst, 614
Hoar, Nancy L., Moncton / Ville de Moncton, 691

Hobbins, John, Law Librarian, Nahum Gelber Law Library, 1174
Hobbs, Katherine, Ottawa, 716
Hobbs, Keith, Mayor, Thunder Bay, 721
Hobbs, Kristen, Manager, Human Resources, Leeds & Grenville, 726
Hobbs, Randy, Director, Canadian Pest Management Association, 882
Hobday, Tina, Associée, Langlois Kronström Desjardins, 1085
Hobson, Richard, Manager, Fort Saskatchewan, 780-992-6205, 672
Hobson, Robert, Chair, Central Okanagan, 677
Hobson, Robert Douglas, Kelowna, 681
Hocher, Josef, Partner, Osler, Hoskin & Harcourt LLP - Calgary, 1053
Hochstein, Sandra, Information Literacy Librarian, Douglas College, 1114
Hockin, Jeremy H.H., Partner, Parlee McLaws LLP, 1056
Hockmann, Bruno, President, B & R Engineering Co. Ltd., 100
Hodes, Jonathan L.S., Clark Wilson LLP, 1058
Hodge, Brett, Head, AquaMetrix Inc., 88
Hodge, Charlie, Kelowna, 681
Hodge, Jamie, City Engineer, Cranbrook, 680
Hodge, Kevin, Brant, 698
Hodge, Mark, General Manager, Western Canada, Benjamin Moore & Co. Ltd, 105
Hodges, Dale, Calgary, 403-268-2445, 671
Hodges, Ken W., Manager, Delcan Water, 160
Hodgett, Simon, Partner, Osler, Hoskin & Harcourt LLP - Toronto, 1079
Hodgins, Paul, Middlesex, 701
Hodgins, Robert A., Partner, Singleton Urquhart LLP, 1062
Hodgins, Tom, Commissioner, Development Services Department, Oshawa, 716
Hodgins, Winston, President/CEO, 590
Hodgkinson, Charlie, CEO, AADCO Automotive Inc., 64
Hodgkinson, Dennis, President, DGH Engineering, 108, 163
Hodgson, Amanda, Secretary, Ottawa Valley Health Libraries Association, 983
Hodgson, Bill, Niagara, 702
Hodgson, Bill, Mayor, Lincoln, 713
Hodgson, David, Kawartha Lakes, 711
Hodgson, James A., Senior Partner, Ogilvy Renault LLP/S.E.N.C.R.L., s.r.l. - Toronto, 1078
Hodgson, John, Manager, Edmonton, 780-496-5658, 672
Hodgson, Paul, Sales Manager, Enervac Corp., 180
Hodgson, Randy, Manager, Westburne Canada, 428
Hodgson, Wesley, Middlesex, 701
Hodkinson, Roger, Honorary Chair, Action on Smoking & Health, 813
Hodson, Gary, Lennox & Addington, 613-354-3664, 701
Hoekenga, Virginia, Deputy Director, National Association for Environmental Management, 956
Hoeppner, Christine, Digital Resources & Aquisitions Coordinator, University of Winnipeg, 1126
Hoermann, Lesley, Head, Reference, Natural Resources Canada, 1151
Hoeve, Ed, Contact, EBA Engineering Consultants Ltd., 170
Hoevenaars, Tony, President & Chief Executive Officer, Mirus International Inc., 291
Hofer, Mike, Coordinator, Fraser Valley, 677
Hofer, Mike, Environmental Technician, Mission, 604-820-3736, 687
Hofer, Mike, Manager, Fraser Valley, 677
Hoff, Elvind, President, Trellcan Rubber Ltd., 401
Hoff, Vern, Chair, 564
Hoffbauer, Michael, Director, LEX Scientific Inc., 271
Hoffman, Bruce, Clerk, Georgian Bluffs, 725
Hoffman, Derek D., McDougall Gauley, 1090
Hoffman, Eric, General Manager, Activation Laboratories Ltd., 67
Hoffman, F. Owen, President/Director, SENES Consultants Limited, 362
Hoffman, Jason, President, Occupational Hygiene Association of Ontario, 969
Hoffman, Rob, Superintendant, Nusco Supply & Manufacturing Inc., 310
Hoffman, Robert, President, whatIf? Technologies Inc., 431
Hoffstrom, Bob, McElhanney Consulting Services Ltd., 285
Hofhuis, Sylvia, Elgin, 699
Hofhuis, Sylvia, Mayor, Central Elgin, 519-782-3541, 724
Hofland, June, Guelph, 710
Hofman, Wayne, Coordinator, LR Computer Services, Northern Alberta Institute of Technology, 1106
Hogan, Christine, Vice-President, 520
Hogan, Rob, Foreman, Iqaluit, 867-975-8509, 698
Hogan, BSc, Geoff, Director, Information Technology, Grey, 700

Hogarth, Al, Maple Ridge, 687
Hogarth, Geoff, Director, Pioneer Petroleums, 325
Hogarth, Timothy W., President/CEO, Pioneer Petroleums, 325
Hogg, Brenda, York, 705
Hogg, Brenda, Regional & Local Councillor, Richmond Hill, 718
Hogg, Gordon, Minister of State, 576
Hogg, Henry, Lennox & Addington, 613-336-0227, 701
Hogg, Linda J., Lang Michener LLP - Vancouver, 1060
Hogg, Melissa, Stikeman Elliott LLP - Toronto, 1080
Hogg, Q.C., John M., Morelli Chertkow LLP, Lawyers, 1056
Hoglund, Nikii, Manager, North Vancouver, 604-983-7388, 682
Hogue, Denis, Sales, Société Laurentide inc., 371
Hogue, Marie-Josée, Partner, Heenan Blaikie S.E.N.C.R.L/SRL, 1084
Hogue, Michèle-E., Directrice générale, Les Amis du Jardin botanique de Montréal, 827
Holan, Gary A., Brownlee LLP, 1054
Holborn, Richard W., Division Head, Municipal Property & Engineering Di, Pickering, 90-542-0463, 718
Holbrook, John, General Manager, Primex Packaging Services, 332
Holden, Gary, President/CEO, ENMAX Corporation, 181
Holden, Rick, President, EcoSource Mississauga, 908
Holder, Barbara, Librarian, FP Innovations Forintek Division, 1118
Holder, Dan, Fire Chief, Sidney, 250-656-2121, 684
Holder, William D., Clark Wilson LLP, 1058
Holdom, Bill, Nanaimo, 681
Holl, Bill, Chief Commercial Officer, Zep Manufacturing Company of Canada, 436
Holland, Andrew, Director, 597
Holland, Clifford L., President, Spill Management Inc., 376
Holland, George H., President/CEO, Douglas Brothers, 165
Holland, John, Pinchin Environmental Ltd., 324
Holland, John, President, PHH ARC Environmental Ltd., 322
Holland, Roger E., Partner, Singleton Urquhart LLP, 1062
Holland, Rudy, Superintendent, Swift Current, 306-778-2755, 755
Holland, Ruth A., General Manager, Spill Management Inc., 376
Holländer, Tibor, Partner, Heenan Blaikie S.E.N.C.R.L/SRL, 1084
Hollands, Neil, Director, Brooks, 671
Hollett, Fred, Director, 598
Hollett, Fred, Fire Commissioner, 602
Hollick, John, Chief Executive Officer, Paris, France, 318
Holliday, Michael G., Senior Partner, Michael Holliday & Associates, 288
Holliday, Ray, Chief Building Official, West Grey, 732
Holling, Lee, Director, Community & Development Services, Lakeshore, 712
Hollinger, Ed, Perth, 703
Hollingworth, Q.C., Alan S., Gowling Lafleur Henderson LLP - Calgary, 1051
Hollmann, Dieter, Manager, Degussa Canada Inc., 159
Holloway, Irene, Vice President, Anachemia Canada Inc., 85
Holloway, Kate, Director, Ontario Sustainable Energy Association, 980
Holman, Geoffrey, Director, Municipal Works, Niagara Falls, 715
Holman, Ronald E., Leeds & Grenville, 726
Holmes, Andrew, Vice-President, Piteau Associates, 325
Holmes, Diane, Ottawa, 613-580-2484, 716
Holmes, Doug, General Manager, Nanaimo, 250-755-4488, 681
Holmes, Jane, Coordinator, Spruce Grove, 674
Holmes, Jeff, Manager, Mountain View County, 669
Holmes, Marcia, Technical Services Technician, Portage College, 1108
Holmes, Tracy, Vice-President, Jenike & Johanson, Ltd., 251
Holmes, Tyla, Reference & Instruction Services Librarian, Hospital for Sick Children, 1158
Holmlund, John, Executive Chair, Focus Surveys Inc., 199
Holodniuk, Wes, Manager, Wood Buffalo, 780-743-7931, 670
Holowatiuk, Gary, Director, New Westminster, 682
Holschuh, Carmen I., Wildlife Biologist & Environmental Planner, Westland Resource Group Inc., 430
Holt, Neil, Vice-President, CEM Specialties Inc., 135
Holtby, Bill, City Manager, St. Albert, 780-459-1607, 674
Holtby, Quinn, President, Katch Kan Limited, 255
Holtze, Keith, President, AquaTox Testing & Consulting Inc., 89
Holtzman, Tammy, District Manager, BFI Canada Inc., 107
Holub, Geoffrey D., Gowling Lafleur Henderson LLP - Calgary, 1051
Holyday, Doug, Toronto, 721
Holyoke, Andy, Superintendent, Fredericton, 691
Holyoke, Francesca, Head Librarian, Science & Forestry Library, 1128

Executive Name Index

Holzschuster, Alfred, Manager, International Solid Waste Association, 944
Hombek, Richard, President, Caduceon Environmental Laboratories, 120
Homenick, Ken, Director, SARCAN Recycling, 358
Homenuck, Peter, Sr. Principal, Institute of Environmental Research Inc., 243
Homes, Adam, Director, Lloydminster, 780-875-8332, 673
Homick, Devin, Manager, FS Partners, 202
Hong, S. Len, President/CEO, 517
Honsinger, Sandra, Library Technician, Boehringer Ingelheim (Canada) Ltd., 1167
Hoobin, Dan, President, Les Contrôles PROVAN Associés Inc., 268
Hood, David, Chair, Public Petroleum Data Model Association, 991
Hood, Louisa, Director, Canadian Electricity Association, 866
Hoogkamer, Dawne, Library Technician, Government Documents/Statistic, Humber College Institute of Technology & Advanced Learning, 1158
Hook, Alexandra, Librarian, Aurora College, 1133
Hook, Sheril, Coordinator of Instructional Services, University of Toronto at Mississauga, 1145
Hooker, Lee, Manager, Mifab Canada, 289
Hooley, Q.C., David W., Cox and Palmer - Charlottetown, 1082
Hooper, Chris, Sales Manager, Hooper Welding Enterprises Ltd., 233
Hooper, Ron, Local Councillor, Clarington, 724
Hooper, Ross, President, Hooper Welding Enterprises Ltd., 233
Hooper, Q.C., John G.M., Lang Michener LLP - Ottawa, 1070
Hope, Bill, General Manager, Buckham Transport Ltd., 118
Hope, Dave, Chair, 619
Hope, David, President, Canadian Council of Independent Laboratories, 864
Hope, Randy, Mayor & Chief Executive Officer, Chatham-Kent, 519-436-3219, 724
Hope, Tony, Simcoe, 704
Hopkins, Ann, Director, Port Alberni, 683
Hopkins, Frank, Owner, Power Plant Supply Co., 329
Hopkins, Kathy, Director, Lethbridge, 403-320-3015, 673
Hopkins, Susan, Concerned Educators Allied for a Safe Environment, 899
Hoppe, Bob, General Manager, Hanson Pressure Pipe, 225
Hopper, Darrin, Manager, H2Flow Equipment Inc., 223
Hopper, Earl, Maxxam Analytics Ltd., 284
Hopper, Rodney, Touchie Engineering, 399
Hopper, Rodney, Manager, R.V. Anderson Associates Limited, 341
Hopwood, Jerry, Vice-President, Product Development, 511
Hora, Zuzka, Manager, Information Centre Team, Industrial Accident Prevention Association, 1145
Horan, Chad, Manager, Public Works, New Tecumseth, 714
Horan, Wendy, Coordinator, Squamish-Lillooet, 679
Hordyk, Carl, Bradford West Gwillimbury, 706
Horgan, Michael, Deputy Minister, 526
Hori, Dennis, Fulton & Company LLP, Lawyers & Trade-Mark Agents, 1056
Horkey, Bill, President, Pumps & Systems, 336
Horlin, Bruce, Lanark, 701
Horn, Paul, Councillor, North Perth, 715
Horn, Samantha G., Partner, Stikeman Elliott LLP - Toronto, 1080
Hornal, Robert, President, Robert Hornal & Associates Ltd., 348
Horncastle, Peter, Manager, Harris & Roome Supply Limited, 226
Horne, Amy, Recycling Coordinator, Grande Prairie, 780-538-0452, 672
Horne, Bonnie, Coordinator, Access & Information, Gerstein Science Information Centre, 1158
Horne, Marian, Minister, 666
Horne, Rob, Commissioner, Planning, Housing & Community Servic, Waterloo, 704
Hornell, James, Regional Director, Performance & Accountablity, Central Newfoundland Regional Health Centre, 1131
Horning, George H., Vice-President & Secretary, Cansult Maunsell Limited, 127
Horosko, Barry A., Bratty & Partners LLP, 1081
Horrigan, Kim, Director, Development Services, Bracebridge, 706
Horrobin, B.Comm, CA, AMC, Cheryl L., Director, Finance & Business Services, Leamington, 726
Horrocks, Maureen, Coordinator, Saskatchewan Wildlife Federation, 1002
Horrocks, Thomas, ADI Group Inc., 68
Horsborough, Allan, CFO, 613
Horsfall, Penelope, Secretary, 630

Horsfall, Wilmer, Treasurer, Annapolis Field Naturalist Society, 828
Horsfield, Grace, Officer, Parkland County, 670
Horsman, Gorden, Secretary, Atlantic Turfgrass Research Foundation, 843
Horsman, Linda, Executive Assistant, 596
Horst, Roger, Blaney McMurtry LLP, 1073
Horswill, Jeffrey D., Davis LLP - Vancouver, 1059
Horton, Brian, Senior Director, Corporate Services, Peterborough, 718
Horton, Harold, General Manager, Horton Tree Farms, 233
Horton, Lenore, Photo Technician, National Air Photo Library, 1151
Horton, Pamela, Partner, Macleod Dixon LLP, 1077
Horvath, Fred, Director, Operations, Clarington, 724
Horvath, Karine, Directrice générale, Charlevoix, 747
Horvath, Peter, Manager, Operations Services, Aurora, 706
Horwood, Sue, Treasurer, Director, Finance, Asset Management & S, Hastings, 700
Hosein, Roland, Chair, Institute for Work & Health, 932
Hoskin, Lyle, General Manager, Machine Knife Co., 278
Hoskins, R. Craig, Partner, Macleod Dixon LLP, 1052
Hotchkiss, Tricia, Library Services Assistant, Fort St. John Campus, 1112
Houde, Annie, Regional Office Manager, Organic Crop Improvement Association - Québec & Ontario, 982
Houde, Hélène, Bibliothécaire, Université du Québec Institut national de la recherche scientifiq, 1176
Houde, Marc, Manager, Golder Associates Ltd., 214
Hough, Ralph, Simcoe, 704
Hough, Ralph, Deputy Mayor & Councillor, Oro-Medonte, 705-835-2770, 728
Houghton, Ed, Executive Director, Public Works, Collingwood, 708
Houlding, Julian, COO & Chief Technical Officer, InfoMine Inc., 241
Houle, Jean, Associé principal, Ogilvy Renault LLP/S.E.N.C.R.L., s.r.l. - Québec, 1088
Houle, Jocelyne, Gatineau, 735
Houle, Louis, Librarian, Schulich Library of Science & Engineering, 1175
Houle, Normand, Chambly, 450-658-0362, 734
Houle, Réal, Trésorier, Val-d'Or, 746
Houle, Sylviane, Bibliothécaire, CÉGEP de Saint-Hyacinthe, 1183
Houle, Yvan, Partner, Borden Ladner Gervais LLP - Montréal, 1083
Hourdequin, Marion, Treasurer, International Society for Environmental Ethics, 943
Housdorff, Cathy, Director, 564
House, Betty, Coordinator, New Brunswick Salmon Growers Association, 961
Houston, Des, President, Mississippi River Power Corp., 291
Houston, Ian J., Partner, Borden Ladner Gervais LLP - Toronto, 1073
Houston, Jamie, Director, Parks, Recreation, & Leisure Services, North Bay, 715
Houston, Mark T., Burnet, Duckworth & Palmer LLP, 1050
Houston, Pauline, General Manager, Community Services, Kitchener, 519-741-2646, 712
Houston, Stuart, Mayor, Spruce Grove, 674
Hovington, Fabien, Saguenay, 741
Howard, Jack, Far Eastern Librarian, Royal Ontario Museum Libraries, 1161
Howard, Jim, Scugog, 729
Howard, John, Chair, Canadian Association of Physicians for the Environment, 858
Howard, Linda, Librarian, Surrey Memorial Hospital, 1116
Howard, Paul T., Howard Ryan Kelford Knott & Dixon, Barristers & Solicitors, 1071
Howard, Rick, President, Ontario Camps Association, 971
Howard, Sheila, Librarian, Interurban Campus, 1120
Howard, Warren, Councillor, North Perth, 715
Howarth, Stewart, Manager, PRT Inc., 336
Howat, Ian, Director, Nanaimo, 506-755-4405, 681
Howe, Bill, Vice-President, Barrow Bay & District Sports Fishing Association, 844
Howe, Brian, President, HGC Engineering, 231
Howe, Fred, President, Thomson & Howe Energy Systems Inc., 395
Howe, Shirley, Deputy Minister, 566
Howell, Ceri, Vice President, Armtec Construction Products, 91
Howell, D. Gordon, President, Howell-Mayhew Engineering Inc., 234
Howell, Rita, Librarian, Lakeshore Campus, 1158

Howes, Donna, Section Manager, North Vancouver, 604-990-2450, 688
Howes, Gordon, President, Folio Instruments Inc., 199
Howie, Alan, Secretary, Kingston Lapidary & Mineral Club, 947
Howie, Gord, City Manager, Prince Rupert, 684
Howie, Kent D., Partner, Borden Ladner Gervais LLP - Calgary, 1049
Howison, Suzanne, Bibliothécaire, Collège Français, 1172
Howitt, Al, Asta Sales & Marketing Ltd., 94
Howland, Brad, Vice-President, Eastern Environmental Services Ltd., 169
Hoyme, Clifford, President & General Mgr., HMI Hoyme Manufacturing Inc., 232
Hoyt, Q.C., Leonard T., McInnes Cooper, 1064
Hoyt-Hallett, Bonny, Deputy Minister, 593
Hribar, Darren B., Partner, Macleod Dixon LLP, 1052
Hrycan, David, Deputy Minister, 666
Hrycan, Len, Director, Kamloops, 681
Hsu, Raymond, President, Comenco Systems Inc., 147
Huang, Alice S., President, American Association for the Advancement of Science, 822
Huang, Martin, Vice-President, 583
Huang, Rubin, AMETEK Process Instruments, 84
Huang, Yanfen, RICHWAY Environmental Technologies Ltd., 346
Huard, Marie-Douce, Cain Lamarre Casgrain Wells - Québec, 1087
Huart, Michel, Langlois Kronström Desjardins, 1085
Hubbard, William, Plant Ecologist & Manager, Secter Environmental Resource Consulting, 361
Hubbell, John, General Manager, Calgary, 671
Hubburmin, Alannah, Jubilee Rose Enterprises Ltd., 253
Huber, Anthony, Manager, Westburne Canada, 428
Huber, Diane, Saugeen Shores, 719
Huber, Paula, Section Manager, North Vancouver, 604-990-2328, 688
Huber, Rob, Manager, Wastequip Cusco, 421
Hubert, Lyndon, Les Entreprises Julien Inc., 268
Hubert, Mark, Vice-President, Forest Products Association of Canada, 918
Hubert, Paul, London, 713
Hubick, Lisa, Public Services Librarian & Public Relations, Kwantlen University College, 1113
Hubley, Allan, Ottawa, 716
Huck, John J., President, McCordick Glove & Safety Inc., 284
Huck, Phil, VP, McCordick Glove & Safety Inc., 284
Hucul, Darin, Principal Engineer, AC Environmental Services, 65
Hudacin, Joe, Loyalist, 727
Huddlestan, Al, Chair, Mount Waddington, 678
Hudon, Claudette, Granby, 735
Hudon, Gaétan, Directeur général, Montcalm, 750
Hudson, Benjamin, Stikeman Elliott LLP - Calgary, 1054
Hudson, Clarence, Director, 607
Hudson, Roy H., Davis LLP - Calgary, 1050
Hudson, Q.C., Douglas, City Solicitor, Lethbridge, 673
Hue, Sebastien, Projects Manager, Ferti-Val Inc., 195
Huehn, Don, President, Barrow Bay & District Sports Fishing Association, 845
Huet, Patricia, Directrice générale, Manicouagan, 750
Huff, Bob, Chief Information Officer, American Water Works Association, 826
Huff, Donald W., President, Environmental Communications Options, 185
Huffman, Arnold, Milton, 714
Huffman, P.Eng., Robert, Manager, North Vancouver, 604-990-3861, 688
Huges, Harry, Simcoe, 704
Hugget, Bill, Vice-President, Ainley Group, 74
Huggins, Norman D., CH2M Hill Canada Limited, 137
Hughes, Alana K., Fulton & Company LLP, Lawyers & Trade-Mark Agents, 1056
Hughes, B., Chief Building Official, Pembroke, 717
Hughes, Barb, Director, Emery International Developments, 177
Hughes, Dan, Manager, Charlottetown, 732
Hughes, Darryl, Performance Fluid Equipement Inc., 321
Hughes, Harry, Mayor, Oro-Medonte, 728
Hughes, John, City Solicitor, Medicine Hat, 403-529-8350, 673
Hughes, Kim, Director, 593
Hughes, Lynn, Library Technician (Copyright), College of the Rockies, 1111
Hughes, M., Service Manager, Mancorp Industrial Sales Ltd., 279
Hughes, Nicholas R., McCarthy Tétrault LLP - Vancouver, 1061
Hughes, Philip, Instructor/Librarian, Maritime College of Forest Technology, 1127
Hughes, Ralph M., Director, Squamish, 688
Hughes, Rob, Senior Project Manager, Stantec Inc., 378

Executive Name Index

Hughes, Shawn, Vice-President, Ontario Association for Geographic & Environmental Education, 971
Hughes, Terrance M., McCarthy Tétrault LLP - Calgary, 1052
Hughes, Terrance M., Partner, Macleod Dixon LLP, 1052
Hughes, Yvette, Unit Manager, AMEC, 82
Hughes Power, Mary, Director, 642
Hughes, B.A., LL.B., Krista L., Associate, Lawson Lundell LLP - Calgary, 1051
Hughes, MD, FIDSA, James M., Vice-President, Infectious Diseases Society of America, 931
Hughson, Bruce, Manager, Transportaton & Solid Waste, Loyalist, 727
Hugo, J. Francis, Principal, Entara Consulting Services Ltd., 181
Hugo, Ken, Hydrogeologist, Sabatini Earth Technologies Inc., 354
Hui, Katherina, Librarian, Edmonton Planning & Development Dept. Library, 1105
Hui, Stephen, President, Industrial Marine Power Engineering Group, 240
Huisman, Rudy, Director, Financial Services, Kawartha Lakes, 711
Hull, Jack, General Manager, Capital Regional District, 250-474-9604, 676
Hull, Jeanette, Environmental Contact, Huntsman Corporation Canada Inc., 235
Hull, Keith, Collingwood, 708
Hull, Phil, Campus Librarian, Orillia Campus, 1147
Hullah, Bill, President, Cardinal Biologicals Ltd., 128
Hulshof, Herman, Director, 661
Hum, Debbie, Councillor, Halifax Regional Municipality, 695
Humber, Allyn, Director, Calgary, 403-268-2702, 671
Humbert, Mark, Manager, AMEC, 83
Humble, Jeffrey, Director, Yellowknife, 867-920-5633, 695
Humble, Randy, Director, Sidney, 250-655-5418, 684
Humble, Robbi, Coordinator, Saskatchewan Environmental Industry & Managers' Association, 1000
Hume, Forrest Clyde, Hume, Forrest C., Law Corporation, 1060
Hume, Peter, Ottawa, 613-580-2488, 716
Hume, Trevor, GIS Manager, EDM Environmental Design & Management Ltd., 173
Humes, Paul, Vice President, National Ground Water Association, 958
Humm, Barbara, Vice-President, Mandel Scientific Co. Inc., 279
Humphrey, Jeff, Technologist, Rothesay, 692
Humphreys, Travis, Manager, Westburne Canada, 427
Humphreys, Wayne, Manager, Westburne Canada, 427
Humphries, Colleen, Supervisor, Corner Brook, 709-637-1553, 693
Humphries, Sandra, Aurora, 706
Humphris, P.Eng., Doug, Manager, Metro Vancouver, 678
Humphry, Ross, President, Canadian Safety Equipment Inc., 125
Hung, Benjamin, Chief Technology Officer, Array Systems Computing Inc., 93
Hung, Jeff, Contact, YES Environment Technologies Inc., 435
Hungerford, Peter, Manager, Economic Development & Corporate Planning, Sarnia, 719
Hunniford, Brent, Manager, Westburne Canada, 429
Hunston, Jeff, Secretary-Treasurer, Canadian Archaeological Association, 855
Hunt, Christian, Electronics-recycling.com, 175
Hunt, Gerard, Chief Administrative Officer, Kingston, 712
Hunt, Harlene, Manager, Quesnel, 688
Hunt, John, Norfolk, 702
Hunt, Lawrie, Chair, St. Andrews, 690
Hunt, Malcolm, Director, Planning & Development Services, Peterborough, 718
Hunt, Marvin, Metro Vancouver, 684, 678
Hunt, Randy, Owner/Operator, Big Bear Pumping Inc., 107
Hunt, Raymond G., Walsh Wilkins Creighton LLP, 1054
Hunt, Rory, Canadian Safety Equipment Inc., 125
Hunt, Stuart, Principal Consultant, Stuart Hunt & Associates, 381
Hunt, Ted, Officer, Economic Development, Norwich, 728
Hunt, Wayne, General Manager, Community Programs & Infrastructu, East Gwillimbury, 708
Hunt, MCIP, RPP, Thom, City Planner, Windsor, 723
Hunter, Amanda J., Partner, Hicks Morley Hamilton Stewart Storie LLP, 1076
Hunter, Clay, Paterson, MacDougall LLP, Barristers, Solicitors, 1079
Hunter, David, Branch Manager, J.L. Richards & Associates Limited, 250
Hunter, Donna, Director, Finance & Administration & Treasurer, Essex, 709
Hunter, Eric, Vice-President, Laidlaw Medical Services, 263
Hunter, Garry T., President, Hunter & Associates, 235
Hunter, Henry, Regional Director, Williams Engineering Inc., 432

Hunter, Jennifer, Assistant, Marine Campus, 1114
Hunter, Jim, Director, Transportation Construction, Simcoe, 704
Hunter, Keith, Warden, Cumberland County, 697
Hunter, Lynn, Victoria, 685
Hunter, Michael, Environmental Coordinator, North Vancouver, 604-990-4224, 682
Hunter, Nigel Derek, Executive Director, East African Wild Life Society, 907
Hunter, Pat G., President, Comfort King Doors & Windows Ltd., 147
Hunter, Paul, Fire Chief, Thames Centre, 731
Hunter, Robert, President/CEO, Carrier Canada Ltd., 129
Hunter, Roger, Director, Yorkton, 306-786-1730, 755
Hunter, Wayne, Saanich, 688
Hunter, FAICP, Robert B., President, American Planning Association, 824
Huntley, Judy, Exective Director, Castle-Crown Wilderness Coalition, 892
Huot, Pierre, Directeur, Québec, 418-641-6193, 740
Huot, Réal, Founder, Réal Huot Inc., 343
Huppé, Joanne, Communications Advisor, 552
Hurd, Michael, Chair, Ontario Society of Nutrition Professionals in Public Health, 979
Hurdle, Lanie, Director, Recreation & Leisure Services, Kingston, 712
Hurdon, Charles E., Partner, Ogilvy Renault LLP/S.E.N.C.R.L., s.r.l. - Ottawa, 1071
Hurlburt, Kate L., Emery Jamieson LLP, 1055
Hurlburt, Mark, President, Hurlburt Construction Limited, 235
Hurlburt, Richard, Minister, 615
Hurlburt, Q.C., William, Counsel, Reynolds, Mirth, Richards & Farmer LLP, 1056
Hurley, John, Gowling Lafleur Henderson S.E.N.C.R.L./LLP, 1084
Hurley, Ryan, Clerk Typist, 598
Hurrle, Brenda, Lanark, 701
Hurst, Chris, Head, Systems, Brandon University, 1122
Hurst, Jon, Councillor, Halton Hills, 710
Hurst, Laurie, Acting CAO, Esquimalt, 686
Hurst, Michael A., Fraser Milner Casgrain LLP - Calgary, 1051
Hurst, Susan, Librarian, Defence R & D Canada - Ottawa, 1149
Hurst, Wayne, Essex, 519-736-7646, 699
Hurst, Wayne, Mayor, Amherstburg, 519-736-7646, 705
Hurt, Tim, Vice-President & General Manager, Toromont Caterpillar, 397
Hurt, Tim, VP Southwest Region, Toromont Caterpillar, 398
Hurter, Robert W., President/CEO, HurterConsult Inc., 235
Hurtubise, Marc, Grondin, Poudrier, Bernier, 1087
Husband, Bob, Manager, Brass Craft Canada Ltd., 116
Huseby, Brian, Plant Manager, CCS Income Trust, 134
Huska, Susan, Manager, Universal Handling Equipment Company Limited, 406
Husoy, Tracy, Manager, Metro Vancouver, 678
Hussack, Brad, President, Mequipco Ltd., 286
Hussey, Al, District Manager, Muskoka Containerized Services Ltd., 295
Hussey, John, Chief Administration Officer, Iqaluit, 867-979-5666, 698
Huston, Dale, Reference Librarian, Champlain-Saint Lambert, 1184
Huston, Jeff, Branch Manager, Safety-Kleen Canada Inc., 355
Huston, Justin, Nova Scotia Contact, Gulf of Maine Council on the Marine Environment, 927
Huston, Mark, PHH ARC Environmental Ltd., 323
Hutchen, Wesley, Operations Manager, Oak Environmental Inc., 310
Hutcheon, Jill, President & CEO, 636
Hutcherson, Christine, Director, National Solid Wastes Management Association, 958
Hutcheson, Larissa, General Manager, Capital Regional District, 250-360-3000, 676
Hutchings, Brian, Commissioner, Social Services, Niagara, 702
Hutchings, Deborah L.J., McInnes Cooper, 1066
Hutchings, Jeffrey, Chair, 523
Hutchings, Pat, Woodward & Company, 1063
Hutchings, Rhea, Sustainable Development Officer, Corner Brook, 709-637-1574, 693
Hutchings, Q.C., Joseph S., Partner, Poole Althouse, Barristers & Solicitors, 1065
Hutchins, Peter W., Associé, Hutchins Caron & Associés, 1085
Hutchinson, Bill, Minister, 659
Hutchinson, Harry, Deputy Chief Building Official & Superintendent, D, South Stormont, 730
Hutchinson, Jocelyn, Regina, 306-584-1739, 754
Hutchinson, Kristine, Manager, 619

Hutchinson, Lynden, Chair, South Forty Waste Services Commission, 758
Hutchinson, Marilyn, Officer, Nanaimo, 250-755-4465, 681
Hutchinson, Rob, Councillor, Kingston, 712
Hutt, David G., Burchell Hayman Parish, 1067
Hutt, Howard W., President, Electric Vehicle Society of Canada, 909
Hutt, Jonathan, VP, Matrix Solutions Inc., 282
Huttema, Ken, Chilliwack, 680
Hutton, Andrew, Overseas Sales, Napier-Reid Ltd., 297
Hutton, John, City Councillor, Brampton, 706
Hutton, Jon, Director, UNEP - World Conservation Monitoring Centre, 1014
Hutton, Susan M., Partner, Stikeman Elliott LLP - Ottawa, 1071
Hwang, Dianna S., Alexander Holburn Beaudin & Lang, LLP, 1057
Hwang, Fontaine, Library Technician, Natural Resources Canada Library - Earth Sciences (Vancouver), 1118
Hyde, Andrea, Librarian, Seal Cove Campus Library, 1130
Hyland, Maureen, Collections Development & Technical Services Libra, Humber College Institute of Technology & Advanced Learning, 1158
Hyndman, Ec.D.(F), MCIP R, Stephen G., Chief Administrative Officer, Belleville, 706
Hynes, Theresa, Library Technician, Martin Gallant Bldg LRC, College of the North Atlantic, 1133
Hypes, Rennie, Manager, BAE Newplan Group Ltd., 101
Hyslop, Bob, Councillor, Riverview, 506-866-2273, 692
Hyvärinen, Anne, Secretary, International Society of Indoor Air Quality & Climate, 943
Hyvarinen, Joy, Director, Foundation for International Environmental Law & Development, 919

I

Iacovelli, Antonio, Miller Thomson LLP - Montréal, 1086
Iafrate, Marilyn, Vaughan, 722
Ialenti, Pascal, President, Venmar Ventilation Inc., 410
Iannello, Sal, General Manager, Engineering, Public Works, & Tran, Welland, 722
Iannicca, Nando, Peel, 714, 703
Iannucci, Americo (Mike), Sales Manager, Daybar Industries Ltd., 158
Ibey, John, Loyalist, 727
Ibrahimi, Ali, Manager, Toronto Biotechnology Initiative, 1012
Iezzoni, Véronique, Partner, Heenan Blaikie S.E.N.C.R.L/SRL, 1084
Ignasiak, Les, Director, T.D. ThermoDesign, 386
Ilczyszyn, Frank, Owner/Manager, Frank's Alternate Energy, 201
Illing, David, CEO, Forest Technology Systems Ltd., 199
Illman, Ruth, Lambton Shores, 726
Ilnyckyj, Oleh W., Partner, Miller Thomson LLP - Vancouver, 1061
Ilsa, Stuart-Muirk, Trade Commissioner, 767
Imad, Arafat, Trade Commissioner, 769
Imata, Katsuji, Deputy Secretary General, CIVICUS: World Alliance for Citizen Participation, 896
Imhoff, Ken, Manager, 656
Immonen, Peter, General Manager, Traders Metal Company Ltd., 400
Impey, Isabelle, Chair, 660
Impey, Patrice, Chief Financial Officer & General Manager, Human R, Vancouver, 604-873-7011, 685
Inch, Sam, Librarian, Miramichi Campus Library, 1128
Infantino, James V., Conseiller de ville, Marie-Clarac, Montréal, 738
Ing, Lianne, Vice-President, Bubble Technology Industries Inc., 118
Inga-Lill, Olsson, Trade Commissioner, 769
Ingham, Steve, Manager, Coast Paper Ltd., 145
Inglis, Bob, Councillor, Halton Hills, 710
Inglis, John, McCarthy Tétrault LLP - Toronto, 1077
Ingram, Cathy, Manager, Penticton, 250-490-2412, 682
Ingram, Joyce, Executive Director, 572
Ingram, Sarah, Programs Manager, The Van Horne Institute for International Transportation & Regula, 1016
Ingratta, Sandra, Director, Financial Services, Kingsville, 712
Injodey, Andrew I., Vice-President/Treasurer, Peto MacCallum Ltd., 321
Inkel, Nicole, Directrice générale, Les Jardins-de-Napierville, 749
Inkinen, Tomi, Library Technician, Library (Burnaby), 1110
Innes, Jean, Wellington, 519-846-8460, 705
Innes, Professor, John, Regional Director, Commonwealth Forestry Association - Canadian Chapter, 898
Ioannidis, Bil, Kitchener, 712

Executive Name Index

Ioannoni, Carolynn, City Councillor, Niagara Falls, 715
Ionita, Marinela, Manager, University Technologies International, 407
Iorfida, Dean, City Clerk & Director, Council Services, Niagara Falls, 715
Ip, Samantha, Clark Wilson LLP, 1058
Ippen, Mike, Manager, Saanich, 250-475-1775, 688
Ippolito, Nick, Chief Building Official, Springwater, 730
Ircandia, John L., Partner, Borden Ladner Gervais LLP - Calgary, 1049
Iredale, Q.C., John N., Gowling Lafleur Henderson LLP - Calgary, 1051
Ireland, Michael, Acting Director, Information Access & Delivery, Canada Institute for Scientific & Technical Information (CISTI), 1148
Ireland, T.J., City Administrator & Planner, Prince Rupert, 684
Irena, Cirpuse, Trade Commissioner, 768
Irg, Mike, Manager, Alberni-Clayoquot, 250-720-2710, 676
Ironmonger, Kathryn, Clerk, Erin, 709
Irvine, Melissa, Process/Compliance Analyst, Wellington North, 732
Irving, Catherine, Librarian, Coady International Institute, 1134
Irving, D., Manager, St. Albert, 674
Irving, Donna P., City Clerk, Sault Ste. Marie, 705-759-5388, 720
Irving, John, Vice-President & General Counsel, 583
Irvin-Ross, Kerri, Minister, 588
Irwin, Albert, President, IPEC Industries Ltd., 247
Irwin, Betty, Whitehorse, 755
Irwin, Doug, Clerk & Director, Corporate Services, Oro-Medonte, 728
Irwin, Elizabeth, Library Assistant, Powertech Labs Inc., 1116
Irwin, Jason J., Miles, Davison LLP, 1053
Irwin, Larry, Director, Information Technology, Collingwood, 708
Irwin, N.A., Chair/Director, IBI Group, 238
Irwin, Peter A., Senior Consultant, Rowan Williams Davies & Irwin Inc., 353
Irwin, P.Eng, Steve, Vice-President, 521
Isaac, Kim, Director of Library Services, University College of the Fraser Valley, 1110
Isaac, Thomas F., McCarthy Tétrault LLP - Vancouver, 1052, 1061
Isabel, Denis, President, Enviroconseil, 183
Isabella, Louis, Treasurer, Allergy Asthma Information Association, 821
Isabelle, Eric, Gestionnaire, Veolia ES Canada Industrial Services Inc., 412
Isabelle, Eric, Manager, Veolia ES Canada Industrial Services Inc., 411
Isbester, Marg, Greater Napanee, 709
Ische, Allen, President, Trux Route Management Systems Inc., 404
Isenberg, Harold, Sales Manager, Allan Fyfe Equipment Limited, 79
Isfeld, Randy, Director, Williams Lake, 250-392-1778, 686
Islam, Tareq, Director, Fraser Valley, 677
Isleifson, Len, Brandon, 689
Isley, R., Carrier Canada Ltd., 130
Ismail, Nae, Director, EnRel Energy Group, 181
Isman, Van, Deputy Minister, 657
Israel, Greg, Regional Sales Manager, Fort Garry Industries Ltd., 200
Ivanoff, Paul, Partner, Osler, Hoskin & Harcourt LLP - Toronto, 1079
Ivarsson, Bernt, President, Rocvent Inc., 350
Iverson, R., Manager, Northern Petroleum Services, 307
Ives, Paul, Mayor, Comox, 680
Iveson, Don, Edmonton, 780-496-8132, 672
Ivey, George A., President & CEO, Ivey International Inc., 249
Ivey, Richard W., Secretary-Treasurer, Richard Ivey Foundation, 995
Ivey, Rosamond, Chair, Richard Ivey Foundation, 995
Iwachewski, Ed, Manager, Lakehead University, 263
Iwaskiw, Liz, Lethbridge, 673

J

Jaber, Jay, Unit Manager, AMEC, 83
Jablonski, Heather, Town Planner, Essex, 709
Jaboeuf, Lee, Nilex Inc., 304
Jack, Anawak, Ambassador for Circumpolar Affairs, Arctic Council, 763
Jack, Bob, Supervisor, New Westminster, 604-526-4691, 682
Jack, Brian, Clemmer Technologies Inc., 144
Jack, Don, Partner, Heenan Blaikie LLP - Toronto, 1076
Jack, Jason, Manager, Great Western Containers Inc., 216
Jack, Patty, Manager, Muddy River Technologies Inc., 295
Jack, Peter, President, Muddy River Technologies Inc., 295
Jackie, Q.C., Larry R., Senior Partner, Borden Ladner Gervais LLP - Vancouver, 1058
Jackiw, Randy, CEO, 619
Jacklin, Brant, General Manager, Alloy Fab Ltd., 79
Jackman, Bradley, Supervisor, AMEC, 83
Jackman, Clyde, Minister, 604
Jackson, Andrew, Director, Canadian Labour Congress, 876
Jackson, Bob, Manager, Besse Information & Learning Commons, Ryerson University, 1161
Jackson, Brian, Simcoe, 704
Jackson, Brian H., Barrie, 706
Jackson, Craig, Coordinator, Ontario Sustainable Energy Association, 980
Jackson, Dale, Technical Sales Representative, ACG Technology Ltd., 66
Jackson, Gayle, City Clerk, Orillia, 716
Jackson, Gayle, Director, Parksville, 250-954-4660, 682
Jackson, Gina, Manager, Human Resources, Port Hope, 905-885-4544, 728
Jackson, Greg, President, ACG Technology Ltd., 66
Jackson, Ian, Coordinator, Ontario Sustainable Energy Association, 980
Jackson, John, Coordinator, Citizens' Clearinghouse on Waste Management, 895
Jackson, Kathryn, Manager, HECS Library, 1150
Jackson, Laura, Executive Director, Protected Areas Association of Newfoundland & Labrador, 990
Jackson, Lois, Metro Vancouver, 678
Jackson, Lois, Chair, Metro Vancouver, 678
Jackson, Lois, Chairman of the Board, Western Transportation Advisory Council, 1019
Jackson, Lois E., Mayor, Delta, 604-946-3210, 686
Jackson, Patricia D. S. (Trisha), Torys LLP, 1081
Jackson, Reg, Fire Chief, Bewdley, Hamilton, 725
Jackson, Roger, Executive Director, 567
Jackson, Susan, Head, Maps, Data & Government Information Centre, Carleton University, 1149
Jackson, Tim, President, Aquaculture Association of Canada, 828
Jackson, Tom, Hamilton, 711
Jackson, Wayne, Director, Utility Services, Peterborough, 718
Jackson-Chapman, Heather, Mayor, St. Thomas, 719
Jacob, Gibby, Chair, EAGLE (Environmental-Aboriginal Guardianship through Law & Educat, 907
Jacobs, Jake, Officer, 576
Jacobs, Neil L., Partner, Stewart McKelvey Stirling Scales - St. John's, 1066
Jacobs, Pamela, Associate University Librarian, Collection Resourc, Brock University, 1153
Jacobs, Patric, Treasurer, International Association of Sedimentologists, 936
Jacobsohn, Alice, Director, National Solid Wastes Management Association, 958
Jacobson, Joel, Metcon Sales & Engineering Ltd., 287
Jacovella, Diane, Vice-President, 520
Jacques, Danielle, Acting Director, Agriculture & Agri-Food Canada, 1147
Jacques, Luce, Trésorière, Rosemère, 741
Jacques, Mélanie, Fraser Milner Casgrain S.E.N.C.R.L./LLP, 1084
Jacques, Ronald, Coordonateur, Régie d'aqueduc Richelieu-Centre, 759
Jacubo, Gerry, Executive Director, 571
Jacyno, Ed, Mayor, Pembroke, 717
Jadoo, Dave, French Language Contact, Crompton Technology Inc., 153
Jaffray, Carol, Head, Cataloguing, University of Toronto Libraries, 1163
Jagani, Mohamed, President, AiMS Environmental, 74
Jagger, Brian D., Branch Manager, Jagger Hims Limited, 250
Jagger, Douglas E., Principal, Jagger Hims Limited, 250
Jago, Charles, Chair, 577
Jagoe, Ken, Yard Supervisor, Halifax C&D Recycling, 224
Jahnke, David B., Wallace Meschishnick Clackson Zawada, 1091
Jail, Louis-Noël, Chef du service, Information et documentation, Institut de l'Énergie et de l'environnement de la francophonie, 1179
Jain, Anup, Area Manager, Avensys Inc., 98
Jaine, Mark, Executive-Vice-President, Intelex Technologies Inc., 244
Jakob, Thomas, President, Pan Tec Inc., 317
Jaksetic, Ed, National Project Manager, Nederman Canada Ltd., 299
Jakul, Don, PHH ARC Environmental Ltd., 322
Jakul, Don, Vice-President, PHH ARC Environmental Ltd., 322
Jalbert-Jacques, Carmen, Thetford Mines, 418-338-1901, 745
Jalil, Abdul, Director, 656
Jamart, Perry, Sales Manager, Simark Controls Ltd., 368
Jambakhsh, Ray, Contact, DST Consulting Engineers, 167
Jamer, P.Eng., Murray, Director, Fredericton, 691
James, Byron, Deputy Minister, 595
James, Chris, General Manager, Lambton Scientific, 264
James, Dennis J., Patterson Law, 1068
James, Eric, Technician, Noranda Earth Sciences Library, 1159
James, Gord, Kawartha Lakes, 711
James, Graeme, Kelowna, 681
James, J. Malcolm, President, Lambton Scientific, 264
James, Lisa J., President, Environmental Advisory Group, 185
James, Robert, President, Auto-Chlor Inc., 98
James, Robert G., Acting Secretary General, 546
James, Robert P., Partner, Parlee McLaws LLP, 1056
James, Teri, Langley, 681
James, Tina, Associate Director, Facilities & Administration, University of Alberta, 1107
Jameson, Grant A., Senior Partner, Ogilvy Renault LLP/S.E.N.C.R.L., s.r.l. - Ottawa, 1071
Jamieson, Carolyn, Lambton, 701
Jamieson, Carolyn, Deputy Mayor & Councillor, Lambton Shores, 519-296-5810, 726
Jamieson, Derrick, CEO, 609
Jamieson, Elisha C., Associate, Hicks Morley Hamilton Stewart Storie LLP, 1076
Jamieson, J. Wayne, Chief Administrative Officer, Bruce, 698
Jamieson, N., General Manager, St. Albert, 674
Jamieson, Stuart, Minister, 597
Jammal, Ramzi, Executive Vice-President/Chief Regulatory Operatio, 520
Jancik, Milos, President/CEO, Electro-Federation Canada Inc., 909
Janczak, Daniel, Vice-President, ArcelorMittal Dofasco, 90
Janeau, Mireille, Directrice, Développement collections et acquisiti, Université de Montréal, 1176
Janecki, Zyg, Kitchener, 712
Janega, Rick, General Manager, Nova Scotia Power, an Emera Company, 308
Janelle, André, Vice-President, Magnor, Division of Magchem, 278
Janes, Glenn, Marketing, Hi-Point Industries (1991) Ltd., 231
Janes, Robert J.M., Cook Roberts LLP, 1062
Jang, Kerry, Vancouver, 604-873-7621, 685
Janik, Sophie, Responsable, Québec Office des personnes handicapées, 1175
Janisse, Len, Lakeshore, 712
Janits, Julius, District Sales Manager, Buckhorn Canada Inc., 118
Janke, J.R., Manager, 631
Janke, Laura, Treasurer, Haliburton, 700
Jankura, Rick, Laidlaw Carriers Inc. - Van Division, 262
Janower, Lori, Library Services Coordinator, Manitoba Dept. of Science, Technology, Energy & Mines, 1124
Janson, Gilles, Bibliothécaire, Bibliothèque centrale, 1170
Janson, Karlis, General Manager, Geo Environmental Engineering - Geocon SNC-Lavalin, 210
Jantz, Barry, Director, Powell River, 683
Janz, Cameron, Chief Operating Officer, Aqua-Guard Spill Response Inc., 88
Janzen, Barbara, Library Coordinator & Public Services Librarian, College of the Rockies, 1111
Janzen, Dave, Manager, Waterous Power Systems, 422
Janzen, Diane, Chilliwack, 680
Janzen, Ray, Engineering Technician, Thompson, 204-677-7905, 690
Janzen, Tamara, Contact, Alberta Bottle Depot Association, 816
Jardine, Marjory, Librarian, Vancouver Coastal Health Authority, 1119
Jardine, Marjory, Librarian, Reference & Instruction, Justice Institute of British Columbia, 1114
Jardine, Todd, Manager, Veolia ES Canada Industrial Services Inc., 412
Jarrell, Shannon, Advisor, Western Canadian Spill Services Ltd., 429
Jarvis, Daniel R., Davis LLP - Vancouver, 1059
Jarvis, Daphne G., Partner, Borden Ladner Gervais LLP - Toronto, 1073
Jarvis, Greg, Chief, 545
Jarvis, Julie, Librarian, MacDonald Dettwiler & Associates Ltd., 1115
Jasim, Saad, CEO, 624

Executive Name Index

Jasim, Saad, President, Ontario Water Works Association, 981
Jasper, Marianna, Lawson Lundell LLP - Vancouver, 1061
Jauron, Guy, Directeur général, Memphrémagog, 750
Javadi, Saeed H.S., President, Sumas Environmental Services Inc., 381
Jealouse, Jutta, President/CEO, Stewart Group, 379
Jean, André, Directeur, Granby, 450-776-8366, 735
Jean, Brian, Parliamentary Secretary, 544
Jean, Diane, Sous-ministre, 646
Jean, Jean-Paul, Westech Industrial Ltd., 429
Jean, Louis-Joseph, Directeur général, Expo agricole de Chicoutimi, 914
Jean, Marcel, Saguenay, 741
Jean, Maurice, Director, Biorex Inc., 109
Jean, Michel, Directeur général, Fédération québécoise pour le saumon atlantique, 916
Jean, Pierre, Director, 520
Jean, Sylvie, Directrice, Saguenay, 741
Jean R., Cameron, Executive Coordinator, Pacific States/British Columbia Oil Spill Task Force, 765
Jean-Claude, Diplo, Trade Commissioner, 768
Jeanes, David, President, Transport Action Canada, 1013
Jeannotte, Hélène, Conseillère pédagogique et bibiothécaire, CÉGEP de Jonquière, 1168
Jeannotte, Réal, Maire, Beloeil, 450-467-4679, 734
Jeanvoine, Margaret, Library Clerk, FPInnovations, 1177
Jeaurond, René, Recyclage Alexandria Recyclinge (Équipe), 343
Jebb, Donna, New Tecumseth, 714
Jedynak, Paul, Sales, AMKO Systems Inc., 84
Jeerakathil, Rangi G., Partner, MacPherson Leslie & Tyerman LLP - Saskatoon, 1090
Jefferies, Cindy, Red Deer, 403-302-3706, 674
Jefferies, Mary, Leader, 568
Jefferson, Susan D., Commission Administrator, 641
Jeffery, Bob, Midland, 713
Jeffery, Geoff, Weaver, Simmons LLP, 1072
Jeffery, Steven P., Blaney McMurtry LLP, 1073
Jeffrey, Ann, Lévis, 736
Jeffrey, Rick, President/CEO, Coast Forest Products Association, 897
Jelley, Paul R., Deputy Provincial Treasurer, 642
Jelson, Joe, Hanna Paper Fibres Ltd., 224
Jenkins, David, President, Quatrosense Environmental Ltd., 338
Jenkins, Donald W., Orillia, 716
Jenkins, Jodie, Belleville, 706
Jenkins, Katherine, Contact, Technical Services/Acquisitions & Catalog, The King's University College, 1106
Jenkyns, Jocelyn, General Manager, Victoria, 250-361-1000, 685
Jennings, Ken, Osler, Hoskin & Harcourt LLP - Toronto, 1079
Jensen, A., Manager, Port Coquitlam, 683
Jensen, Allan, Technical Manager, A.H. Lundberg Systems Ltd., 63
Jensen, Colleen, Director, Red Deer, 403-342-8323, 674
Jensen, Eric, Sunmotor International Ltd., 382
Jensen, Josh, Contact, Weir Power & Industrial, 424
Jensen, Kevin, Coordinator, Lethbridge, 403-330-5108, 673
Jensen, Len, Manager, North Vancouver, 604-990-3845, 688
Jensen, BA, MPL, MCIP, RP, Mark B, Director, Community & Development Services, Timmins, 721
Jepson, Christopher, Regional Manager, Vestar, 412
Jervis, P.Eng., Tim, Manager, Metro Vancouver, 678
Jeske, Catherine Buntain, Scarfone Hawkins LLP, 1069
Jesse, Chad W., McDougall Gauley, 1089
Jessome, Don, Les Entreprises Julien Inc., 268
Jesson, Claudia, Acting Municipal Clerk, Delta, 604-946-4141, 686
Jessop, Karl, Associé, Cain Lamarre Casgrain Wells - Québec, 1087
Jette, Guy, Acting Superintendent, Wood Buffalo, 780-799-7486, 670
Jette, Q.C., M. Robert, Clark Drummie, 1065
Jetten, Ben A., Blake, Cassels & Graydon LLP - Toronto, 1072
Jewcyzk, Stephen, Director, Mount Pearl, 709-748-1029, 694
Jibb, Scott, Chief Building Official, Hamilton, 725
Jilek, Jeff, Chief Building Official, St. Thomas, 719
Jillian, Senkiw, Third Secretary & Trade Commissioner, 767
Jim, Comtois, Federal House in Order, 764
Jim, Mohninger, Federal House in Order, 764
Jimenez, Patricia, Manager, Zorbit Technologies Inc., 437
Jimmie, Le Fresne, Councillor, Colchester County, 697
Jinks, Roger, President, AMEC, 82
Jitka, Hoskova, Trade Commissioner, 767
Jiwani, Bashir, Treasurer, Canadian Bioethics Society, 860
Jmaeff, Victor, Vice-President, 574

Joanisse, David, Partner, Heenan Blaikie S.E.N.C.R.L/SRL, 1084
Joannette, Denis, Deux-Montagnes, 735
Jobe, Bengt, Project Development, KMW Systems Inc., 258
Jobin, Tania C., Tecumseh, 519-735-9286, 720
Jobson, Brian, Director, Rocky View No. 44, 670
Jochmann, John S., CEO, Tankman, 386
Joe, Randy, Director, Haley Industries Ltd., 224
Joelson, Derwin, President, Lea-Der Coatings (614248 Alberta Ltd.), 266
Joelson, Leah, Sec.-Treas., Lea-Der Coatings (614248 Alberta Ltd.), 266
Johannesen, Greg, J.W. Bird & Company Ltd., 250
Johannson, Lynn, President, E2 Management Corporation, 168
John, Gerretsen, President, Canadian Council of Ministers of the Environment, 763
John, Goswell, General Manager, Alfa Laval Inc., 78
John, Winterbourne, Trade Commissioner, 768
Johns, Brad, Councillor, Halifax Regional Municipality, 695
Johns, Cheryl, Clerk, Orangeville, 716
Johns, Garth S., Commissioner, Human Resources, Durham, 699
Johnsen, Thomas, Pacwill Environmental, 317
Johnson, Adrian, Librarian, Prairie Region, 1190
Johnson, Annette, Finance Officer, 642
Johnson, Brenda, Hamilton, 711
Johnson, Brian, Sr. Technologist, CBCL Limited, 133
Johnson, Brian I., President/Senior Chemist, Niagara Analytical Inc., 303
Johnson, Byron, CAO, Quesnel, 688
Johnson, Carl, Vice-President, BW Technologies by Honeywell, 119
Johnson, Celia, Davis LLP - Toronto, 1074
Johnson, Charlene, Minister, 599
Johnson, Charles, President, AquaMetrix Inc., 88
Johnson, Cyril, Alberni-Clayoquot, 250-726-7088, 676
Johnson, Dale, President, Wind Power Inc., 433
Johnson, David, Executive Secretary, OSPAR Commission, 983
Johnson, Deborah, Chief of Protocol, 659
Johnson, Deborah, Executive Director, 659
Johnson, Dewayne, Director, Soil & Water Conservation Society, 1009
Johnson, Diane, Bibliotechnicienne, Traitement, catalogage, sys. i, Collège universitaire de St-Boniface, 1123
Johnson, Edward, Associate & Professional Engineer, Western Site Technologies Inc., 430
Johnson, F., President, RBR Ltd., 343
Johnson, Gary, President, Maritime Paper Products Ltd., 281
Johnson, Glen, Contact, EnviroPower Equipment Marketing Inc., 187
Johnson, Greg A., D'Arcy & Deacon LLP, 1063
Johnson, Jane, Director, American Water Works Association, 826
Johnson, Jeff, Co-Owner & Operator, Momentum Conveyors, 292
Johnson, Jeff, Sales Manager, Joe Johnson Equipment Inc., 252
Johnson, Joanne, Eastern Sales Manager, Puresource Inc., 337
Johnson, Joe, President/CEO, Joe Johnson Equipment Inc., 252
Johnson, Kay, Head, Reference & Circulation Services, Athabasca University, 1099
Johnson, Ken, President, Newmac Manufacturing Inc., 303
Johnson, Mark, Owner/Sales Manager, Gallason Industrial Cleaning Services, Inc., 204
Johnson, Michael A., Lakes Environmental Software, 263
Johnson, Mike, Deputy Minister, 666
Johnson, Mike, Plant Manager, CCS Income Trust, 134
Johnson, Moya, Councillor, Halton Hills, 710
Johnson, Nick, Co-Owner & Operator, Momentum Conveyors, 292
Johnson, Owen A., McCarthy Tétrault LLP - Calgary, 1052
Johnson, Patricia, Reference Specialist, Gallagher Library of Geology & Geophysics, 1101
Johnson, Paul, Director, 656
Johnson, Peter, Chair, 520
Johnson, Pierre-Marc, Counsel, Heenan Blaikie S.E.N.C.R.L/SRL, 1084
Johnson, Rebecca, Councillor at Large, Thunder Bay, 721
Johnson, Rob, Coordinator, Forestry, Wellington, 705
Johnson, Robert, Executive Director, National Association for Information Destruction, 956
Johnson, Robert, President/Microbiologist, Bioforj Environmental Services, 108
Johnson, Sheila, Public Services Librarian, Maps, Data & Government Information Centre (MADGIC), 1142
Johnson, Stephanie A., Vice-President, Niagara Analytical Inc., 303

Johnson Jr., Joe, Vice-President, Joe Johnson Equipment Inc., 252
Johnson, Q.C., Cal, Burnet, Duckworth & Palmer LLP, 1050
Johnston, Alan, Halton, 700
Johnston, Alan, Town & Regional Councillor, Oakville, 715
Johnston, Bill, President, The Jane Goodall Institute for Wildlife Research, Education & Con, 946
Johnston, Bob, Manager, Waterous Power Systems, 423
Johnston, Brenda A., D'Arcy & Deacon LLP, 1063
Johnston, Cliff, Director, St. John's, 709-576-8383, 694
Johnston, Dan, Burnaby, 679
Johnston, Dave, Huron, 701
Johnston, Dave, President, Metrovan Hotsy Equipment Ltd., 288
Johnston, David, Director, Development Services, Brant, 698
Johnston, Donald B., Aird & Berlis LLP, 1072
Johnston, Elizabeth, Library Assistant, Toronto Rehab, 1162
Johnston, Joe, Vice-President, Nilfisk-Advance Canada Company, 304
Johnston, John, Elizabethtown-Kitley, 613-342-8952, 725
Johnston, John, Sec.-Treas., Land Improvement Contractors of Ontario, 948
Johnston, Kathleen, Head of Acquisitions, Olds College, 1109
Johnston, Ken, Richmond, 684
Johnston, Kent, Estimator/Project Coordinator, Western Industrial Services Ltd., 429
Johnston, Lindsay, Circumpolar Librarian & Public Service Mgr, Canadian Circumpolar Institute, 862
Johnston, Marlene, East Gwillimbury, 708
Johnston, Norman, Sous-ministre adjoint & Directeur général, 646
Johnston, Paul, Manager, Charlottetown, 902-894-5208, 732
Johnston, R. Brock, Clark Wilson LLP, 1058
Johnston, Ralph B., Chair, Northeast Pigeon Lake Regional Services Commission, 758
Johnston, Ray, General Manager, N.R. Murphy Ltd., 296
Johnston, Robert, Exec. VP, AECOM Canada Ltd., 69
Johnston, Robert A., Renfrew, 613-432-6271, 704
Johnston, Therell W., President, TJ Consulting Ltd., 396
Johnston, Tim, Mayor, Thompson, 690
Johnston, Tom, Alderman, St. Thomas, 719
Johnston, C.E.T., John D., Director, Operations, Owen Sound, 717
Johnston, P.Eng., Gord, President, Consulting Engineers of Alberta, 902
Johnstone, Audrey, Clerk, Wasaga Beach, 722
Johnstone, Betty A., Aikins, MacAulay & Thorvaldson LLP, 1063
Johnstone, David J., Deputy Minister, 597
Johnstone, Diana, Nanaimo, 681
Johnstone, Greg, President, Pharmatox Inc., 322
Johnstone, Kirk, In charge, Atlantic Region, 1135
Jolicoeur, Catherine, SMTE, CÉGEP du Vieux-Montréal, 1171
Jolicoeur, Darquise, Beaudry, Bertrand Avocats, 1082
Jolicoeur, Elizabeth, General Manager, Calgary Horticultural Society, 852
Joli-Coeur, Jacques, Québec, 740
Jolicoeur, Manon, Partner, Heenan Blaikie S.E.N.C.R.L/SRL, 1084
Jolicoeur, Marc, Borden Ladner Gervais LLP - Ottawa, 1070
Jolicoeur, Michel, Thermon Heat Tracing Services, 394
Jolin, Michel, Associé, Langlois Kronström Desjardins, 1088
Joll, Kevin, Manager, Red Deer, 403-342-8225, 674
Jolley, Don, Fire Chief, Pitt Meadows, 683
Joly, Linda, Commis bibliothèque, Université du Québec Institut national de la recherche scientifiq, 1176
Joly, Pascal, Urbaniste, Acton, 746
Joncas, Paul, Directeur général, Baie-Comeau, 418-296-8104, 733
Joncas, Rodrigue, Rimouski, 740
Jones, Anita, Executive Director, 661
Jones, Audra, Director, Edmonton, 780-496-1790, 672
Jones, Beth, Associate Director & Manager, Green Communities Canada, 925
Jones, Bill, Director, Public Works, Saugeen Shores, 719
Jones, Bill, Manager, Hyperspectral Data International Inc., 237
Jones, Bill, President/CEO, LTS Sales Ltd., 274
Jones, Brad, President, Maritime Ultrasonic Cleaning Inc., 281
Jones, Brian, Director, Public Works Services, Newmarket, 714
Jones, Carol E., Principal, C.E. Jones & Associates Ltd., 119
Jones, Charlene, Program & Service Manager, Red Deer College, 1109
Jones, Chris K., Director, 641
Jones, Christopher, Vice-President, Council of Canadian Fire Marshals & Fire Commissioners, 904
Jones, Cory, Branch Manager, CenturyVallen, 137

Executive Name Index

Jones, David, Map Librarian, William C. Wonders Map Collection, 1107
Jones, David, President/Director, Xylon Biotechnologies Ltd., 435
Jones, Doug, Managing Director, Environmental & Development Ser, Orangeville, 716
Jones, Doug, President, Business Funding Group Inc., 119
Jones, Graham, Manager, RBR Ltd., 343
Jones, H. Robert, Vice-President, A&A Environmental Consultants Inc., 63
Jones, Harold, Staff, Canadian Institute of Geomatics, 1149
Jones, Harry, Fire Chief, Brockville, 707
Jones, Ian C., Singleton Urquhart LLP, 1062
Jones, J.D., President, MIE Consulting Engineers Ltd., 289
Jones, James, Peterborough, 703
Jones, James, Manager, Castle Building Centres Groups Ltd., 131
Jones, Jeff, Branch Manager, Accutest Laboratories Ltd., 66
Jones, Jim, York, 705
Jones, Jim, Regional Councillor, Markham, 905-479-7757, 713
Jones, Joel B., Borden Ladner Gervais LLP - Calgary, 1049
Jones, Lance, Streets Maintenance Supervisor, Charlottetown, 732
Jones, Lee Anne E., Vice-President, Ontario Water Works Association, 981
Jones, Lindsay M., McDougall Gauley, 1090
Jones, Mary-Ellen, Jones Group Engineering Ltd., 253
Jones, Paul, Town Clerk, Whitby, 723
Jones, Peter F.M., Paterson, MacDougall LLP, Barristers, Solicitors, 1079
Jones, Ray, Calgary, 403-268-2430, 671
Jones, Rich, Manager, J. Walter Company Ltd., 249
Jones, Rich, Sales Manager, Nett Technologies Inc., 300
Jones, Robert, Manager, Alldec Trading Ltd., 79
Jones, Ronald, Windsor, 723
Jones, Stacy, Program Coordinator, Ontario Waste Materials Exchange, 312
Jones, Stan, Vice-President, Sales & Marketing & Regional Sales, Wastequip Cusco, 421
Jones, Susan, General Manager, Emergency & Protective Services, Ottawa, 716
Jones, Thomas, Sr. Vice-President & CFO, BW Technologies by Honeywell, 119
Jones, Tom, Manager, Dillon Consulting Ltd., 163
Jones, Warren, CAO, Cowichan Valley, 677
Jones, Wayne, General Manager, Canwest Pumping Systems Ltd., 127
Jones, Wayne, Head, Technical Services, Queen's University, 1142
Jones, Wendy, Vice-President, LTS Sales Ltd., 274
Jones Gordon, Barb, Executive Director, 612
Jonson, Derek, Partner, Ramsay Lampman Rhodes, 1056
Joos, Steve, Manager, Westburne Canada, 428
Jopling, Gord, Fire Chief, Smith-Ennismore-Lakefield, 705-292-7282, 729
Jordan, Colleen, Durham, 679, 678, 699
Jordan, Colleen, Regional Councillor, Ajax, 705
Jordan, Jack, Deputy Mayor & Councillor, Adjala-Tosorontio, 519-941-6687, 724
Jordan, Ken, Sales & Technical Marketing Manager, Chromatographic Specialties Inc., 140
Jordan, Shawn, Environmental Coordinator, Walker Industries Holdings Ltd., 416
Jordan, Sheila, Director, UMA Group Ltd., 405
Jordan, Trish, Lead, Monsanto Canada Inc., 293
Jorgensen, Randy, Councillor, Gravenhurst, 709
Jorgenson, Jeff, General Manager, Saskatoon, 754
Jorhannsen, Thor, President, Thor Global Enterprises Ltd., 395
Jory, John, Contact, Bémalux Inc., 105
Joseph, Sidney, CEO, AiMS Environmental, 74
Josephson, Katie, Director, Victoria, 250-361-0210, 685
Josey, Joseph, Manager, Guild Contracting Specialists Inc., 222
Joshi, Deepak, Director, Winnipeg, 690
Joshi, Sanjay, Partner, Ogilvy Renault LLP/S.E.N.C.R.L., s.r.l. - Toronto, 1078
Joslin, D., Director, Recreation & Culture, Richmond Hill, 718
Joslin, Jennifer, Library Technician, Pacific Region, 1110
Jotcham, Jim, President, Marbicon Inc., 280
jour de la terre quebec, Jour de la Terre Québec, Montréal, QC, 1046
Journal, Larry F., Brockville, 707
Journault, Denyse, Directrice, Sainte-Julie, 450-922-7092, 743
Jovanovic, D. Stephen, Bartlet & Richardes LLP, 1081
Jowett, Craig, President & Inventor, Waterloo Biofilter Systems Inc., 422
Jowett, Ed, President, Canadian Iris Society, 876
Jowett, Gregory T., Antymniuk & Antymniuk, 1063
Jowett, Robin, Contact, Waterloo Barrier Inc., 422
Jowett, Robin, Manager, Waterloo Biofilter Systems Inc., 422
Joyal, Christiane, Trésorière, Sainte-Anne-des-Plaines, 743
Joyal, Danielle, Directrice générale, D'Autray, 747
Joyal, Gentiane, Fraser Milner Casgrain S.E.N.C.R.L./LLP, 1084
Joyce, Gavin, Director, North Vancouver, 604-990-2336, 688
Joyce, Gordon, Senior Manager, Capital Regional District, 250-474-9621, 676
Joyce, Jim, Lennox Industries (Canada) Ltd., 267
Joyce, Martha, Head, Media Services, Fanshawe College of Applied Arts & Technology, 1143
Joyce, Percy, Officer, Corner Brook, 709-637-1544, 693
Joyce, Randy, Branch Manager, Fort Garry Industries Ltd., 200
Joyner, Douglas, Mayor, West Lincoln, 732
Joys, Jack, Director, Millar Western Forest Products Ltd., 290
Juby, Bill J., Peterborough, 718
Jude, Bijingsi, Trade Commissioner, 767
Judge, Ross, Counsel, Weiler, Maloney, Nelson, 1072
Judge, Vince, Deputy Mayor & Councillor, North Perth, 715
Judith, Baguley, Trade Commissioner, 768
Juhasz, Jin, Director, Dundas-Jafine Inc., 167
Juillet, Yves, Technicien en documentation, CÉGEP d'André-Laurendeau, 1169
Julien, Carole, Responsable, Institut Teccart Inc., 1174
Julien, Lisette, Technicienne en documentation, CÉGEP d'André-Laurendeau, 1169
Julien, Nadia, Office Manager, Logibail Inc., 273
Jull, Russell, Norwich, 728
Juneau, Ray, Plant Manager, CCS Income Trust, 134
Juneau, Raymond, Vice-President, Laboratoires d'Expertises de Québec Ltée, 262
Jungeblut, Gert, General Manager, Alfa Plastics Inc., 78
Junger, Robin, Associate Deputy Minister & Executive Director, 578
Junkert, Manfred, President, Alcore Fabricating Corp., 77
Junkin, Brian, Kawartha Lakes, 711
Junkin, Steve, Plant Manager, MSU Mississauga Ltd., 294
Junkin, Virginia, President, MSU Mississauga Ltd., 294
Jupp, George, Chair, District of Nipissing Social Services Admin, Nipissing, 877-829-5121, 727
Jurk, John, Manager, Kernic Systems Inc., 257
Justason, Don, Manager, Harris & Roome Supply Limited, 226
Juteau, Nathalie, Présidente, Association québécoise de la gestion parasitaire, 841
Jutras, Jacques, Secrétaire, Régie d'assainissement des eaux du Haut-Richelieu, 759
Jutras, Michel, Responsable, Trois-Rivières, 745
Juzkiw, Olena, Secretary, Recycling Council of Alberta, 993

K

Kaai, Wanjiku, Librarian, Public Services, Lakeland College, 1109
Kaal, Lonnie, Director, Yorkton, 306-786-1721, 755
Kaardal, Randy J., Senior Counsel, Hunter Litigation Chambers, 1060
Kabasele, Daniel, Châteauguay, 450-699-4883, 735
Kachur, Richard, City Clerk, Winnipeg, 204-986-2428, 690
Kaczur, Cheryl, Branch Manager, Canwest Pumping Systems Ltd., 127
Kadla, Tom, Supervisor, Prince George, 250-561-7575, 683
Kadulski, Richard, President/CEO, Richard Kadulski Architect, 346
Kadwell, Dave, Grimsby, 905-945-8259, 710
Kaehn, Art, Chair, Fraser-Fort George, 678
Kaehn, Art, Second Vice President, North Central Local Government Association, 965
Kaehne, Jerry, CEO, Kaehne Consulting Ltd., 254
Kafri, Jake, Vice-President, Metro Recycling, 287
Kagan, Jamie A., Thompson Dorfman Sweatman LLP, 1064
Kagan, Rachel, Senior Director, Food & Consumer Products of Canada, 918
Kahlil, George, Quality Control, MICCA Paints Inc., 288
Kahn, Jonathan W., Blake, Cassels & Graydon LLP - Toronto, 1072
Kahwa, Henne, Manager, Library Services, Public Works & Government Services Canada, 1168
Kaiser, Andrea, Councillor, Niagara-on-the-Lake, 715
Kaiser, K., Secretary, Hamilton Geological Society, 927
Kalimootoo, Christopher, Director, Engineering & Environmental Services, East Gwillimbury, 708
Kalin, Margarete, President & Research Director, Boojum Research Ltd., 113
Kalivas, Barbara, Director, Planning & Development, Elizabethtown-Kitley, 725
Kalivas, Mike, Brockville, 707
Kalka, Ron, President, Air Trac Corp., 75
Kallideen, Marlon, Commissioner, Community Services, Vaughan, 722
Kalmakoff, David, Hutchins Caron & Associés, 1085
Kalmbach, Dave, Manager, Generation PV Inc., 207
Kalmbach, Eric, President, Generation PV Inc., 207
Kalmbach, Jason, Manager, Generation PV Inc., 207
Kalra, Aarash, Librarian, SNC-Lavalin Engineers & Constructors Inc., 1161
Kalvee, Debbie, Associate University Librarian, Services, Brock University, 1153
Kambeitz, Darrell, Police Chief, Camrose, 671
Kamennof-Sine, Lana, Librarian, Kingstec Campus, 1137
Kamenz, Marvin, Municipal Planner, Comox, 250-339-1118, 680
Kamerman, Linda, Commissioner, 631
Kaminski, Bernard, Partner, Cypress Sales Partnership, 155
Kaminski, Zbigniew, Vice-President, InspecTech, 243
Kammerer, Joan, Resource Support Services, Allyn & Betty Taylor Library, 1143
Kamnitzer, David, IBI Group, 238
Kamp, Randy, Parliamentary Secretary to the Minister of Fisheri, 527
Kampitsch, Ronald E., Merchant Law Group LLP - Edmonton, 1053, 1055
Kamski, Steven, VP, McCordick Glove & Safety Inc., 284
Kanani, Zahida, Manager, GLOBE Foundation, 924
Kanapathi, Logan, Markham, 905-479-7748, 713
Kandyba, Michel, Maire, Pincourt, 739
Kane, Barbara, Clerk, Adjala-Tosorontio, 724
Kane, Donna, Vice President, 663
Kane, Q.C., John J., Bishop & McKenzie LLP, 1054
Kane, Q.C., T. Gregory, Partner, Stikeman Elliott LLP - Ottawa, 1071
Kanellakos, Steve, Deputy City Manager, Ottawa, 716
Kang, Alvin, President/CEO, Kang Construction Ltd., 255
Kang, Anne, Burnaby, 679
Kangles, Nick J., Senior Partner, Ogilvy Renault LLP/S.E.N.C.R.L., s.r.l. - Calgary, 1053
Kango, Natsiq, Iqaluit, 698
Kani, Mario, President, Sustainable EDGE Ltd., 383
Kanigan, Richard, Administrator, Comox, 680
Kao, Jack, President, Global Engineering & Testing Ltd., 213
Kapa, Dubravka, Director, Georges P. Vanier Library, 1173
Kapila, Mukesh, Vice-President, SCC Environmental, 358
Kaplun, Rolf N., Davis LLP - Vancouver, 1059
Kaptein, Shelley, President, Herb Society of Manitoba, 929
Karakatsanis, Catherine, Senior Vice-President, Morrison Hershfield, 293
Karakochuk, Mel, CFO & VP, International Road Dynamics Inc., 245
Karamanos, Mary, Senior Vice President, Human Resources, 512
Karas, Ted, Firwin Corporation, 196
Karass, Audrey, President, Caristrap International Inc., 128
Karayannides, George J., Partner, Heenan Blaikie LLP - Toronto, 1076
Karbusicky, Rhona, Librarian, EVS Environment Consultants Ltd., 1114
Karch, Danny, Director, Sustainable Forestry Initiative, 1011
Kardash, Adam, Partner, Heenan Blaikie LLP - Toronto, 1076
Karg, Ludwig, Chair, International Network for Environmental Management, 941
Kargut, Sigrid, Public Services Librarian, Kwantlen University College, 1113
Kariel, Douglas, Head, Technical Services & Systems, Athabasca University, 1099
Karin, Ahmed, Ph.D., Sec.-Treas., National Council for Science & the Environment, 957
Karkut, Neil N., McDougall Gauley, 1090
Karn, Bruce, Borden Ladner Gervais LLP - Toronto, 1073
Karpa, Nelson, Director, Winnipeg, 690
Karpluk, Les, Fire Chief, Prince Albert, 306-953-4200, 754
Karst, Garry, Vice-President, Ferguson Simek Clark, 194
Karsten, Bill, Councillor, Halifax Regional Municipality, 695
Kary, Dale, Project Coordinator, Lacombe County, 669
Kary, Ryan R., Borden Ladner Gervais LLP - Calgary, 1049
Kashyap, Pram, Manager, Delcan Water, 160
Kaske, Wolfgang, Director, Notra Inc., 308
Kassa, Hamish, Coordinator, Columbia-Shuswap, 677
Kassi, Hassan, COO/President, Avensys Inc., 98
Kassirer, Jay, President, Healthy Indoors Partnership, 928
Katadotis, Peter, Manager, Genor Recycling Services, 210
Katayama, Mikio, President & Chief Operating Officer, Sharp Electronics of Canada Ltd., 365

Executive Name Index

Katayama, Tsuneo, President, International Association for Earthquake Engineering, 934
Katchur, Gale, Contact, Fort Saskatchewan, 672
Katchur, Gale, Mayor, Fort Saskatchewan, 672
Kath, Shelley L., Fasken Martineau - Montréal, 1083
Kathol, Todd W., Field Law - Calgary, 1051
Katic, Dennis, Manager, 521
Katschor, Andy, Acting Director, Esquimalt, 686
Katschor, Andy, Manager, Esquimalt, 686
Katz, David, CEO, Sustainable Resources Management Group, 383
Katz, Sam, Mayor, Winnipeg, 204-986-2171, 690
Katz, Sharon, Manager, 605
Katzman, Ronna, Niagara, 702
Kaufman, R., Treasurer, Deputy CAO, & Director, Corporate Servi, Caledon, 707
Kaufmann, Gabrielle C., Field Law - Calgary, 1051
Kaulback, Terri, General Manager, Great Northern Recycling Inc., 216
Kavanagh, Benjamin J., Benson Myles, 1065
Kavanagh, Sean, President, Kavanagh & Associates Ltd., 255
Kavanagh, Shawn M., Cox and Palmer - St. John's, 1065
Kay, Jackie, Contact, R.J. Burnside & Associates Limited, 340
Kay, Jim, General Manager, Hamilton Emergency Services, Hamilton, 711
Kay, Katherine, Partner, Stikeman Elliott LLP - Toronto, 1080
Kay, Robert C., Chair, 517
Kaye, Glenn, President, Maritime Geothermal Ltd., 280
Kayes, Brian, Director, Brandon, 689
Kazakoff, Greg, Vice-President, Hydroxyl Systems Inc., 237
Kazakoff, Richard, Branch Manager, Fort Garry Industries Ltd., 200
Kazakoff-Lane, Carmen, Contact, ILL/OCLS, Brandon University, 1122
Kazaz, Charles, Fasken Martineau - Montréal, 1083
Kazaz, Charles, Partner, Fasken Martineau - Toronto, 1075
Kean, Mark, Founder, Mikro-Tek Inc., 290
Kean, Ross, Head, 353, 596
Keaney, P. Berk, Weaver, Simmons LLP, 1072
Kearney, Simon, Langlois Kronström Desjardins, 1088
Kearns, Stephanie A., Ratcliff & Company LLP, 1057
Kearsey, John, Sales Manager, TMK IPSCO Inc., 397
Keating, David, Fire Chief, Miramichi, 506-623-2225, 691
Keating, Jim, Vice-President, 601
Keating, John, Chief Executive Officer, Canadian Hydro Developers, Inc., 124
Keating, Matt, Manager, Bartle & Gibson Co. Ltd., 102
Keating, Shane A., Calgary, 403-268-2430, 671
Keats, Don, Deputy Minister, 601
Keays, Glenn, President, Birchwood Environment Management Inc., 109
Keays, Ryan W., Macleod Dixon LLP, 1052
Keays, Sharon, Financial Officer, Birchwood Environment Management Inc., 109
Kedrosky, Dave, Contact, KEDCO Constructors Ltd., 256
Kedzierski, Carl, Manager, LTS Sales Ltd., 274
Keech, Larry, Chief Administrative Officer & Clerk, Lennox & Addington, 701
Keefe, Greg, Chair, 615
Keefe, Terry, Director, 640
Keefe, Terry, General Manager, Waterous Power Systems, 422
Keefer, Bowie, Principal Scientist, QuestAir Technologies Inc., 339
Keeley, Brent, Vice-President, WORX Environmental Products Inc., 434
Keeley, Steve, Director, Public Works, Huntsville, 711
Keeling, David, President, HETEK Solutions Inc., 230
Keen, Alex R., President, ALTECH Technology Systems Inc., 81
Keen, Matthew, Osler, Hoskin & Harcourt LLP - Calgary, 1053
Keenainak, Rosemary, Deputy Minister, 617
Keenan, Daniel R., Fredericton, 691
Keenan, Glenn, General Manager, Toromont Caterpillar, 397
Keenan, Gregory A., President, Canadian Paper Recyclers, 124
Keenan, Patrick, Director, Planning, St. Thomas, 719
Keenan, Steve D., Office Manager, Golder Associates Ltd., 215
Keene, George, City Manager, Airdrie, 670
Keenlyside, David L., Executive Director, 638
Keesing, Don, Administrative Coordinator, Nuclear Information & Resource Service, 969
Kefalas, Dennis, Director, Yellowknife, 867-920-5639, 695
Keffer, Rob, Deputy Mayor & Councillor, Bradford West Gwillimbury, 706
Kehl, Gerry, Perth, 703
Kehler, Connie, Executive Director, Saskatchewan Herb & Spice Association, 1000

Kehoe, John, Howard Marten Fluid Technologies Inc., 234
Kehoe, Patrick F., Orillia, 716
Kehoe, Sheila, Treasurer, North Grenville, 728
Kehren, Bill, President, Fabco Plastics Wholesale (Ontario) Limited, 193
Keighley, Roy, General Manager, Dekka Resins Inc., 159
Keir, Dave, Vice-President, Millar Western Forest Products Ltd., 290
Keir, Jack, General Manager, Fundy Region Solid Waste Commission, 758
Keirstead, Robin, University Archivist, University of Western Ontario Libraries, 1144
Keiser, Al, Manager, Saanich, 250-475-1775, 688
Keith, Channon, Program Manager, Commission for Environmental Cooperation, 764
Keith, John A., Cox and Palmer - Halifax, 1067
Keith, Landra, Manager, Canada-Nova Scotia Offshore Petroleum Board, 763
Keith, Mary, St. George Power LP, 356
Keizer, Charles, Torys LLP, 1081
Keizer, Danny, Chief Information Officer, 597
Kelch, Mike, City Councillor, Sarnia, 719
Kelford, Shane A., Howard Ryan Kelford Knott & Dixon, Barristers & Solicitors, 1071
Kelk, Peter, President, George Kelk Corporation, 212
Kell, Rob, Manager, Dillon Consulting Ltd., 163
Kellas, Hugh, Manager, Metro Vancouver, 678
Keller, Kerri, Administration, Target Recycling Inc., 387
Keller, Mark, Contact, Saskatoon, 754
Keller, Werner H., Sutts, Strosberg LLP, 1082
Keller, Wolf, Director, Calgary, 403-268-6752, 671
Kellerman, Jacob, General Manager, WorleyParsons Canada Ltd., 434
Kellerman, Jay C., Partner, Stikeman Elliott LLP - Toronto, 1080
Kelley, Cheryl, Director, Economic Development, Bracebridge, 706
Kelley, Jeff, Sales Contact, Rotork Controls (Canada) Ltd., 352
Kelley, Shannon L., Parlee McLaws LLP, 1053
Kellgren, Q.C., Kristjana E., Brownlee LLP, 1054
Kellington, Carolyn, Manager, Community Planning & Development Branch, East Gwillimbury, 708
Kelln, Doug, President/CEO, 662
Kellum, Doug, Councillor, North Perth, 715
Kelly, Bill, Fire Chief, Trent Hills, 731
Kelly, Cheryl, Osler, Hoskin & Harcourt LLP - Calgary, 1053
Kelly, Craig, Director, Works & Transportation Services, Oshawa, 716
Kelly, Dale, Vice-President, 662
Kelly, Dan, Fire Chief, Winchester, North Dundas, 727
Kelly, Dave, Vice-President, Wardrop Engineering Inc., 417
Kelly, David A.J., Fredericton, 691
Kelly, Denis, Regional Clerk, York, 705
Kelly, Dennis P., Director, 611
Kelly, Dorothy, Huron, 701
Kelly, Douglas B., Soloway, Wright LLP, 1071
Kelly, Glenn, President & CEO, CO2 Solution, 145
Kelly, Graham, Medicine Hat, 403-527-1891, 673
Kelly, Greg, Contact, G.R. Kelly Environmental Services, 204
Kelly, Harlan, Vice President, Opus DaytonKnight Consultants Ltd., 313
Kelly, Howard, Terminal Manager, IMTT-Newfoundland Ltd., 239
Kelly, Ian D., Principal, SMS Engineering Ltd., 371
Kelly, Jennifer, Osler, Hoskin & Harcourt LLP - Toronto, 1079
Kelly, Joe, Manager, Trent Hills, 705-653-1480, 731
Kelly, Kristine, Manager, Saanich, 250-475-5539, 688
Kelly, Linda, Director, Water Environment Federation, 1017
Kelly, Margaret, Vice-President, Canadian Environmental Technology Advancement Corporation - West, 867
Kelly, Mark, Clerk, Grand Falls-Windsor, 709-489-0422, 694
Kelly, Martin, Office Manager, Golder Associates Ltd., 214
Kelly, Mike, Manager, Westburne Canada, 425
Kelly, Norm, Toronto, 721
Kelly, Pat, Library Technician, Gabriel Dumont Institute of Native Studies & Applied Research, 1188
Kelly, Stephen T., Fredericton, 691
Kelly, Ted, President/CEO, Oakside Chemicals Ltd., 311
Kelly, Trish, General Manager, Agri-Food Laboratories, 73
Kelly, Will, Director, DPL Group, 166
Kelly, M.B.A., Peter J., Mayor, Halifax Regional Municipality, 902-490-4010, 695
Kelsch, Ray, District Fire Chief (St. Andrews Central), St. Andrews, 204-738-2607, 690
Kelsey, Len, Chair/CEO, 584
Kelso, R., Manager, Wasaga Beach, 722
Kelson, Chris, CEO, Risk Check Environmental Ltd., 347

Kelterborn, Ross, Waterloo, 704
Kembel, Beth, City Clerk, Lloydminster, 780-871-8328, 673
Kemel, Marvin, President, Kemel Cartons (1973) Ltd., 256
KemeysJones, Shirley, Director, 607
Kemmere, Albert, Reeve, Mountain View County, 669
Kemmett, Sue, Coordinator, Yukon Conservation Society, 1024
Kemp, Joanne, Director, Learning Resource Centre, Grant MacEwan University, 1105
Kendall, Anouk, Vice-President, IRIS Environmental Systems Inc., 248
Kendall, Sandra, Director, Library Services, Mount Sinai Hospital, 1159
Kendrick, Kathleen J., Associate, Miller Thomson LLP - Toronto, 1053, 1078
Kenea, Nasir, Chief Information Officer, Markham, 905-475-4733, 713
Kennard, Laurie, Treasurer & Director, Finance, Springwater, 730
Kennedy, Barry, Vice-President, Lynk Electric Ltd., 276
Kennedy, Craig, Superintendent, Corner Brook, 709-637-1607, 693
Kennedy, Desiree, Director, Financial Services, Kingston, 712
Kennedy, Doug, Manager, Brass Craft Canada Ltd., 116
Kennedy, Jacky, Director, Green Communities Canada, 925
Kennedy, Joseph, Coordinator, North Okanagan, 678
Kennedy, Lorna, Executive Secretary, 614
Kennedy, Michael, Principal, Stantec Inc., 378
Kennedy, Michele, Clerk, Whitchurch-Stouffville, 723
Kennedy, Pat, Director, Emergency Services, Haliburton, 700
Kennedy, Patrick, Executive Director, 631
Kennedy, Priscilla E.S.J., Davis LLP - Edmonton, 1055
Kennedy, Robert, Sales & Marketing, Flexahopper Plastics Ltd., 196
Kennedy, S., Carrier Canada Ltd., 129
Kennedy, Wendy, Associate University Librarian, Information Servic, University of Western Ontario Libraries, 1144
Kennedy, Ph.D., Kathryn, President & Executive Director, Center for Plant Conservation, 893
Kenneweg, Wes, President/CEO, Draeger Safety Canada Ltd., 166
Kenney, Daniel E., Davis LLP - Calgary, 1050
Kenney, Jason, Minister, Citizenship, Immigration, & Multicultura, 520
Kenny, Bea, Port Colborne, 905-834-7685, 718
Kenny, Brenda, President, Canadian Energy Pipeline Association, 866
Kenny, Diane, Executive Director, 609
Kenny, Line, Technicienne en documentation, prêt, CÉGEP de Jonquière, 1168
Kenny, Mark, Manager, Hydro-Mechanical Sales Ltd., 236
Kenny, Scott, Director, Port Alberni, 683
Kenny, Tara, Library Technician, Manitoba Eco-Network Inc., 1124
Kenny, Wallace M., Partner, Hicks Morley Hamilton Stewart Storie LLP, 1076
Kent, Ann, Chair, Canadian Horticultural Therapy Association, 871
Kent, Clarence D., President, Kent Engineering Ltd., 256
Kent, Cory, Lang Michener LLP - Vancouver, 1060
Kent, Peter, Minister, Environment, 522
Kentner, David, Councillor, Halton Hills, 710
Kenward, Peter H., McCarthy Tétrault LLP - Vancouver, 1061
Kenyon, Jim, Minister, 664
Kenyon, Jim, Minister Responsible, 666
Keough, Loyola G., Bennett Jones LLP - Calgary Office, 1049
Keoycga, Tony, Manager, Springfield, 204-444-4119, 690
Ker, Tony, CEO, Director, Ridgeline Environment Inc., 347
Kerc, Pawel, Contact, Saskatoon, 306-975-2486, 754
Kerekes, Helen, Vice-President, Niagara Peninsula Geological Society, 964
Kerekes, Richard, Director, Canadian Pulp & Paper Network for Innovation in Education & Resea, 883
Kerfoot, Michael, Sunergy Systems Ltd., 382
Kerford, Michael, Vice-President, Environmental Careers Organization of Canada, 911
Kerklaan, John, President & CEO, St. Catharines Hydro Generation Inc., 356
Kern, Michael, Business Development, ECE Group - a Division of Conestoga-Rovers & Associates, 170
Kerr, Brian, President, Ecologistics Research Services, 172
Kerr, D.M., Chown, Cairns LLP, 1071
Kerr, Doug, Director, Public Works, Lincoln, 713
Kerr, Holly, Manager, Petroleum Services Association of Canada, 986
Kerr, Jim, CEO, Delcan Water, 160
Kerr, Keith, Lanark, 701

CANADIAN ENVIRONMENTAL RESOURCE GUIDE 2011-2012   1311

Executive Name Index

Kerr, Randy, Senior Systems Analyst, G.A. Borstad Associates Ltd., 203
Kerr, Shawn, Manager, Great Western Containers Inc., 216
Kerr, Shelagh, President/CEO, Electronics Product Stewardship Canada, 909
Kerr, Skip, Treasurer, Environmental Services Association of Alberta, 912
Kerr, Stephen, Director, 608
Kerr, P.Eng., Kevin, Director, Miramichi, 506-623-2020, 691
Kerrio, Vince A., City Councillor, Niagara Falls, 715
Kershaw, Herb, Managing Director, Bestobell AquaTronix Limited, 106
Kersten, Elisabeth K., Senior Associate, California Institute of Public Affairs, 852
Kerton, Marilyn K., Fredericton, 691
Kerwin, Dave, Newmarket, 714
Kerwin, M.Scott, Partner, Borden Ladner Gervais LLP - Vancouver, 1058
Keshmiri, Mehrdad, Sr. Research Scientist, Kam Biotechnology Ltd., 254
Keskinen, Peter, Macquarie Power & Infrastructure Income Fund, 278
Keskinen, Peter, Contact, Whitecourt Power Limited Partnership, 431
Kesler, Dave, Contact, R.J. Burnside & Associates Limited, 340
Kester, Ben, Director, Uxbridge, 731
Kester, Rick, Director, Engineering & Development Services, Belleville, 706
Kester, P.Eng, Rick A., President, Municipal Engineers Association, 955
Kestler, Ulrike, Public Services Librarian, Kwantlen University College, 1113
Kett, Carolyn J., Town Clerk, Fort Erie, 709
Kett, Terry, Greater Sudbury / Grand Sudbury, 710
Kettleson, Wayne, President, Spring Air Silver Services Ltd., 376
Kettner, Joel, Chief Medical Officer of Health, 588
Keyes, Artur J., Director, Extox Industries Inc., 193
Keyes, Kathryn, Director, 545
Keys, David, Contact, Redstone Associates Ltd., 344
Keys, Rick, Operations Manager, Premier Envelope, 331
Khan, Abbas, VP, Osram Sylvania Ltd., 315
Khan, Haseen, Acting Director, 599
Khan, Max, Town Councillor, Oakville, 715
Khan, Parveen, Vice President, SNC-Lavalin Group Inc., 371
Kharouba, Dianne, Director, Bibliothèque des sciences de la santé, 1147
Khatter, Kapil, President, Canadian Association of Physicians for the Environment, 858
Kheng-Lian, Koh, Director, Asia-Pacific Centre for Environmental Law, 829
Khoraych, Mireille, Associate, Hicks Morley Hamilton Stewart Storie LLP, 1076
Khouri, Anastassia, Coordinator, Walter Hitschfeld Geographic Information Centre, 1176
Kiang, Karen, Borden Ladner Gervais LLP - Toronto, 1073
Kibala, Cody, Site Supervisor, Armtec Construction Products, 92
Kidd, Matt, Manager, Universal Handling Equipment Company Limited, 406
Kidd, Richard, Lanark, 701
Kidd, Ron, Chair, Highway 43 East Waste Commission Services, 757
Kidnie, Rod, Manager, All Treat Farms Limited, 78
Kiefer, Karl, City Councillor, Cambridge, 707
Kieley, Chris, Deputy Minister, 603
Kiell, David, Executive Director, Landscape Newfoundland & Labrador, 948
Kielly, Carole, Manager, Association of Power Producers of Ontario, 837
Kiernan, Jim, Hanna Paper Fibres Ltd., 224
Kiernan, Thomas C., President, National Parks Conservation Association, 958
Kieswetter, Murray, Manager, Parks Operations, Waterloo, 519-747-8607, 722
Kilabuk, Jimmy, Iqaluit, 698
Kilabuk, Lena, Acting Director, 618
Kilback, Keith D., Managing Partner, Kanuka Thuringer LLP, Barristers & Solicitors, 1090
Kilby, Shelley, Operations, Ontario Petroleum Institute Inc., 1144
Kileel, Joseph J., President, Crandall Engineering Ltd., 153
Kilfoil, Terry, Rothesay, 692
Kilger, Bob, Mayor, Cornwall, 708
Kilgour, Dave, Greater Sudbury / Grand Sudbury, 710
Kilgour, Ian, Manager, Planning Services, North Bay, 715
Killacky, Gary, Chief Technical Officer, Legend Power Systems Inc., 267

Killam, Dick, Councillor, Kings County, 696
Killebrew, Martha, Treasurer, Association of World Citizens & World Citizens Foundation, 840
Killen, Carl, Saint John, 692
Killick-Dzenick, Cherisse, Reynolds, Mirth, Richards & Farmer LLP, 1056
Killingbeck, Karl, Sales Manager, Merley Chains Ltd., 287
Killingsworth, Colleen, President, Canadian Centre For Energy Information, 1100
Killins, Shawn, Chief Building Official, North Bay, 715
Killoran, Frank, President & CEO, National Process Equipment Inc., 298
Killoran, Maureen, Partner, Osler, Hoskin & Harcourt LLP - Calgary, 1053
Killoran, Shawn, Manager, Water & Wastewater Operations, South Glengarry, 730
Kilpatrick, Mike, Coordinator, East Coast, Promens Canada Inc., 334
Kilty, Colleen, Manager, Canadian Labour Congress, 876
Kim, Sooin, Faculty Services Librarian, Bora Laskin Law Library, 1156
Kimber, Jeanne, Group Leader, Information Centre, EnCana Corporation, 1101
Kimery, Clint, Facility Manager, Enviro-Gun Ltd., 182
Kimmel, Terry, Vice-President, Canadian Hydrogen & Fuel Cell Association, 871
Kimmons, Sean, President, Water Matrix, 422
Kimnach, Kim, Executive Director, American Society of Plant Biologists, 826
Kinastowski, Anna, City Solicitor, Toronto, 416-392-0080, 721
Kinch, Blair, Sr. Superintendent, Charlottetown, 732
Kinchlea, Richard, Director, Canadian Centre for Emergency Preparedness, 861
King, Barbara, Library Technician, D.S.B. Fowlow Bldg LRC, College of the North Atlantic, 1133
King, Bill, Manager, Planning Services, Essex, 699
King, Brad, Manager, CEM Specialties Inc., 135
King, Brian, President & Environmental Geologist, Oakridge Environmental Ltd., 310
King, Brian J., Miramichi, 691
King, Brian W., Chatham-Kent, 724
King, Bruce H., Pitblado LLP, 1063
King, Catherine, Pelham, 717
King, Derek J., Brownlee LLP, 1054
King, Devon, Library Branch Supervisor, Interurban Campus, 1120
King, Elinor, Commercial Sales, Niagara Recycling, 303
King, Gary, Chief Administrative Officer & Deputy Clerk, Peterborough, 703
King, Geraldine, Manager, St. John's, 709-576-8613, 694
King, Heather, Delta, 604-946-4141, 686
King, Jamie R., Councillor, Niagara-on-the-Lake, 715
King, Jean, Head, Acquisitions, Health Canada, 1150
King, Jennie, Manager, Satlantic, 358
King, Jim, Chief Administrative Officer, Cambridge, 519-740-4683, 707
King, John, Manager, Lethbridge, 403-320-3884, 673
King, Linda, Maple Ridge, 687
King, Lucille, Town Clerk, Aurora, 905-727-3123, 706
King, Matt, Director, 663
King, Michael W., Sr. Vice-President, WorleyParsons Canada Ltd., 434
King, Mike, Sales Agent, Clear Environmental Products, 143
King, Patricia, General Manager, Fishermen and Scientists Research Society, 917
King, Peter, Executive Director, American Public Works Association, 824
King, Richard J., Partner, Ogilvy Renault LLP/S.E.N.C.R.L., s.r.l. - Toronto, 1078
King, Robin, Transportation Engineer, St. John's, 709-576-8232, 694
King, Rosemary, District Councillor, Gravenhurst, 709
King, Shelley, Secretary, Aquaculture Association of Canada, 828
King, Q.C., Roger B., Campbell Marr, 1063
Kings, Larry M., Brantford, 707
Kingsbury, Rob, Environmental Manager, Lacombe Waste Services, 262
Kingsley, Curt, Manager, North Saanich, 687
Kingston, Brad, Chair, Maintenance & Engineering Society of The Canadian Institute of Mi, 950
Kingston, Gerald H., CAO, Fraser Valley, 677
Kingston, K. Andrew, President/CEO, DynaMotive Energy Systems Corporation, 168
Kingston, Mary, Director, 617

Kingswood, Glen, Vice-President, Capital Environmental Resource Inc., 127
Kinley, John L., CEO, AECOM Canada Ltd., 69
Kinnaird, Helga, Manager, Technology & Curriculum Innovation Operat, Northern Alberta Institute of Technology, 1106
Kinsman, Brian, Truro, 696
Kinsman, Mary, Director, 639
Kipp, Jim, Nanaimo, 681
Kipp, Jim, Coordinator, Nanaimo, 250-753-4572, 681
Kirby, C.W. Daniel, Partner, Osler, Hoskin & Harcourt LLP - Toronto, 1079
Kirby, Heather, Manager, Green Communities Canada, 925
Kirby, Richard, President, R.A. Kirby Sales Inc., 340
Kirby, Robert, Prescott & Russell, 729
Kirby, Sarah M., McInnes Cooper, 1067
Kirbyson, John, Director, Penticton, 250-490-2426, 682
Kirchner, Matthew F., Partner, Ratcliff & Company LLP, 1057
Kirk, Art, Regional Vice-President, National Energy Equipment Inc., 297
Kirk, Mike, General Manager, Richmond, 604-276-4142, 684
Kirkby, Jan, Director, Pender Island Field Naturalists, 985
Kirkby, Melanie, Director, Finance & Treasurer, Elizabethtown-Kitley, 725
Kirkham, Roderick, Lang Michener LLP - Vancouver, 1060
Kirkland, Dick, Lambton, 701
Kirkpatrick, Kent, City Manager, Ottawa, 716
Kirolos, Hany, Director, Strategy & Economic Development, Barrie, 706
Kirschner, Tony, Vice-President, Precision Assessment Technology Corp., 330
Kirsh, Harvey, Senior Partner, Osler, Hoskin & Harcourt LLP - Toronto, 1079
Kiru, Tony, Partner, Heenan Blaikie LLP - Toronto, 1076
Kirvan, Mary-Anne, Senior Counsel / Strategic Policy Advisor, 557
Kirwin, BA, LLB, Mark M., Kirwin LLP, 1055
Kiselbach, Daniel L., Partner, Miller Thomson LLP - Vancouver, 1078, 1061
Kishchuk, Boris, President, Engineering Management Services Croscan, 180
Kishchuk, Daniel, Vice-President, Engineering Management Services Croscan, 180
Kiss, Jim, Farmers' Advocate, 564
Kissack, Graham, Environment, Catalyst Paper Corp., 132
Kissinger, S.A., Lynn Canyon Ecology Centre, 950
Kissner, Bob, Fire Chief, Kingsville, 712
Kistritz, Ron U., Principal, R.U. Kistritz Consultants Ltd., 341
Kitai, Anton, President, Montrose Technologies Inc., 293
Kitamura, Yutaka, Secretary, International Commission of Agricultural & Biosystems Engineering, 937
Kitchen, Brian, Director, 666
Kitchen, Brian, Vice-President, Pioneer Petroleums, 325
Kitchen, John, President/CEO, PRT Inc., 336
Kitchen, Lynn, Deputy Corporate Administrator, Parksville, 682
Kitchen, Paul, General Sales Manager, Ecodyne Ltd., 171
Kitsul, Dale T., Manager, White Rock, 604-541-2181, 686
Kitteringham, Kimberly, Town Clerk, Markham, 905-475-4729, 713
Kjartanson, Kelly, Manager, Winnipeg, 690
Klacko, David, Borden Ladner Gervais LLP - Toronto, 1073
Klashinsky, Rod, Vice-President, International Road Dynamics Inc., 245
Klassen, Darryl, General Sales Manager, MEC Systems Inc., 286
Klassen, Gary, General Manager, Edmonton, 780-496-6050, 672
Klassen, Gordy, President, Alberta Trappers' Association, 820
Klassen, Merlin, Fire Chief, Wetaskiwin, 780-361-4429, 674
Klassen, Mike, Manager, Westburne Canada, 426
Klassen, Peter W., Crease Harman & Company, 1062
Klassen, R., Sales Representative, Energy Technology Products Ltd., 179
Klatt, David, Executive Director, 657
Klaus, Jerry, General Manager, Waterworks, Markham, 713
Klauwers, Tony, General Manager, Medicine Hat, 673
Kleespies, Michael, Sales Representative, Rice Engineering & Operating Ltd., 346
Klein, James, Stikeman Elliott LLP - Toronto, 1080
Klein, Marty, Councillor, Tillsonburg, 721
Klein, Michel, Executive Director, Canadian Network for Vaccines & Immunotherapeutics, 879
Kleinau, S. (Ziggy), Coordinator, Citizens For Renewable Energy, 895
Kleinlagel, Ron, Manager, Westburne Canada, 425
Klie, John, Fire Chief, Kitimat, 687
Klimchuk, Heather, Minister, 571
Klimkait, Rob, Manager, Bradex Industrial Services Ltd., 115

Klinck, John, Muskoka, 702
Klingenberg, Bill, Chief Building Official, Georgian Bluffs, 725
Klingender, Franz, Curator, 516
Kloeze, Harold, Chair, 619
Klohn, Hans W., President, Ocean Steel & Construction Ltd., 311
Kloiber, Frank W., Principal, Amberg Corp. - Environmental & Regulatory Consultants, 82
Kloss, Kelly, Acting CAO, Wood Buffalo, 780-743-7023, 670
Klotz, Devin, Contact, Venables Machine Works Ltd., 410
Knapman, D., President/CEO, York Fluid Controls Ltd., 435
Knapp, John, Deputy Minister, 564
Knechtel, Ken, Contact, Shaver Industries Inc., 365
Knegt, Leigh, Area Supervisor, AMEC, 83
Knell, Graham, Coordinator, North Vancouver, 604-990-3806, 688
Knelsen, Barny, Contact, Biantco Environmental Services Inc., 107
Kneteman, Ross D., Bishop & McKenzie LLP, 1054
Knicklebein, Mat, Iqaluit, 698
Knight, Anthony H.S., Lang Michener LLP - Vancouver, 1060
Knight, Bob, Director, Health & Social Services, Kawartha Lakes, 711
Knight, Brian, Regional Sales Manager, Joe Johnson Equipment Inc., 252
Knight, Cheryl, Executive Director & CEO, Petroleum Human Resources Council of Canada, 986
Knight, David, Partner, Macleod Dixon LLP, 1077
Knight, Elizabeth, Head, Reference Services, Carleton University, 1149
Knight, John, Québec Representative, ACO Container Systems Ltd., 67
Knight, Simon, President/CEO, Climate Change Central, 144
Knight, T., Manager, Comox Valley, 677
Knight, Tom, Sr. Vice-President, UMA Group Ltd., 405
Knoblock, Laura, City Clerk, Leduc, 673
Knoedler, Ron, Greenwind Power Corp., 218
Knoll, Jeff, Halton, 700
Knoll, Jeff, Town & Regional Councillor, Oakville, 715
Knott, Brian, Clerk & Solicitor, Sarnia, 719
Knott, Steve, Fire Chief, Petawawa, 717
Know, Graham, Coordinating Committee Member, Pacific States/British Columbia Oil Spill Task Force, 984
Knowler, Sandra M., Lang Michener LLP - Vancouver, 1060
Knowles, Anna, Acting Clerk, East Gwillimbury, 708
Knowles, David, Superintendent, Dieppe, 691
Knox, Brian, County Engineer, Bruce, 698
Knox, D. Anthony, McCarthy Tétrault LLP - Vancouver, 1061
Knox, Eddy, Manager, Hydraulic Systems Ltd., 236
Knox, Glen R., County Clerk, Simcoe, 704
Knox, Harold, Chief Building Official, Wellington North, 732
Knox, Jerry, Managing Director, Community Services, North Bay, 715
Knox, Maggie, Manager, North Okanagan, 678
Knox, Q.C., Andrew C., O'Connor MacLeod Hanna LLP, 1070
Knuever, Steffen, Vice-President & Sales & Marketing Manager, Tekmar Control Systems Ltd., 389
Knutsen, D.E., President, Cook Engineering, 152
Knutson, Don, Acting Commissioner, Medicine Hat, 403-529-8231, 673
Kobayashi, Denny, Director, 664
Kobeluck, Darlene, Manager, Pigeon Lake Regional Chamber of Commerce, 986
Kober, Gary Lee, Chief Librarian, Montréal General Hospital, 1174
Koch, Alanna, Deputy Minister, 656
Koch, Ellen, Alex Milne Associates Ltd., 78
Koch, Fred, Manager, Crane Energy Flow Solutions, 153
Koch, Fred, Site Leader, Flowserve Canada Corp. - Pump Division, 197
Koch, Henry, President, Ag EnviroTech Inc., 72
Koch, Katherine, Librarian, South Campus, 1106
Kochan, Don, CAO, Canmore, 671
Kochan, Don, Director, Canmore, 671
Kochanoff, Peggy, Illustrator & Graphic Designer, Environova Planning Group Inc., 186
Kochanoff, Stan, President, Environova Planning Group Inc., 186
Kochany, Joe, Nature's Mate Distribution Inc., 298
Kochany, Josephine, Nature's Mate Distribution Inc., 298
Kocialek, Tim, Director, Roads & Public Work, Mississippi Mills, 714
Kociolek, Peter, Contact, EnviroPower Equipment Marketing Inc., 187
Kodousek, Nancy, Director, Water Services, Waterloo, 704
Koehle, L., Director, Public Works & Engineering, Caledon, 707
Koehler, Marlaine, Contact, Waterfront Regeneration Trust, 1163

Koehn, Erwin, Sales Manager, Premier Envelope, 331
Koenderman, Paul P., Exec. Vice-President & CEO, Aecon Group Inc., 71
Koepke, C.M.O., Marion, City Clerk, Owen Sound, 717
Koers, D.A., President, Koers & Associates Engineering Ltd., 259
Kohler, Jeff, Alderman, St. Thomas, 719
Kohnert, Nicole, Manager, North Okanagan, 678
Kohut, Jim, Manager, Kraus Global Inc., 260
Kojima, Yorihiko, President & Chief Executive Officer, Mitsubishi Canada Ltd., 291
Kokko, John, Enermodal Engineering Ltd., 179
Kokot, Glenn, Manager, Toshiba of Canada Ltd., 398
Kolach, Marnie, Maxxam Analytics Ltd., 284
Kolasa, William J., Clerk & Director, Corporate Services, Lincoln, 713
Kolb, Emil, Regional Chair & Councillor, Peel, 703
Kolind, Mike, General Manager, Central Canada, Benjamin Moore & Co. Ltd, 105
Koller, Hermann, Managing Director, International Solid Waste Association, 944
Kolodziechuk, Walter, Dufferin, 699
Kolomeychuk, Richard, President, Envirometrex, 184
Kolybabi, Deanie, Executive Director, EAGLE (Environmental-Aboriginal Guardianship through Law & Educat, 907
Komanchuk, John, Commissioner, Medicine Hat, 403-529-8354, 673
kongsgaardgoldman foundat, The Kongsgaard-Goldman Fo, Seattle, WA, 1046
Konig, Ron, Product Support Manager, Toromont Caterpillar, 398
Konkin, Doug, Deputy Minister, 577
Konopelky, Tina, Client Services Technician, National Air Photo Library, 1151
Kontzamanis, Demetrios, Chair, KGS Group Inc., 257
Kooistra, Peter, Hastings, 700
Koop, Donald, Assistant Deputy Minister, 662
Koopmans, Sim, Treasurer, Petroleum Tank Management Association of Alberta, 986
Kopach, Chad, Blaney McMurtry LLP, 1073
Kopke, Deon, Vice-President, Specialty Technical Publishers, 375
Kopp, Tony, Manager, Vernon, 250-545-1361, 685
Koppe, Lou W., Contact, West-Lock Fastener Corp., 425
Koppe, Maxine, Executive Director, North Central Local Government Association, 965
Kopystynski, Adrian, General Manager, Pitt Meadows, 604-467-2432, 683
Korbutt, Orest, Chair, 573
Korell, Alan, Managing Director, Engineering, Environmental & Wo, North Bay, 715
Korey, Marie, Librarian, University of Toronto Massey College, 1163
Kormann, Ted, Operations Manager, Lennox Drum Ltd., 267
Kormylo, G., Carrier Canada Ltd., 130
Korolnek, Debbie, Director, Engineering Services, Bradford West Gwillimbury, 706
Korotki, B.A., A.M.C.T., Terrence, Administrator-Clerk & Coordinator, Alnwick-Haldimand, 724
Kort, Kees W., Hicks Morley Hamilton Stewart Storie LLP, 1069
Kortegast, Peter, Business Manager, Opus International Consultants (Canada) Ltd., 314
Kortekaas, Henry, Principal, Henry Kortekaas & Associates Inc., 229
Kortright, Bob, President, Toronto Field Naturalists, 1012
Korzeniowski, Jan, President, J.K. Engineering Ltd., 250
Kosak, Alvin R., Brownlee LLP, 1054
Kosch, John, President/CEO, AMKO Systems Inc., 84
Kositsky, Mel, Langley, 687
Koski, Mike, Vice-President, Trow Consulting Engineers Ltd., 404
Kosmenko, Gordon, Contact, Arrow Speed Controls Inc., 93
Kosmidis, Elizabeth, Associate, Hicks Morley Hamilton Stewart Storie LLP, 1076
Kosolowski, John A., Duncan & Craig LLP, Lawyers & Mediators, 1055
Kosowan, Leo, President, Norvac Industrial Services, 307
Kossivas, Georgina, Vice-President, Finance, 511
Kosten, April, Stikeman Elliott LLP - Calgary, 1054
Kosterman, Robert, Chief, Spruce Grove, 780-962-4496, 674
Kostic, Kosta, Partner, Heenan Blaikie S.E.N.C.R.L/SRL, 1084
Kostiuk, Elaine, Clerk, North Battleford, 754
Kosztyo, George, Terrapex Environmental Inc., 390
Kotak, Brian, General Manager, Manitoba Model Forest, 951
Kotkas, Alex, Fasken Martineau - Calgary, 1050
Kottmann, Hariolf, Chief Executive Officer, Clariant (Canada) Inc., 142

Koufogiannakis, Denise, Head, Reference, John W. Scott Health Sciences Library, 1105
Koughan, William S., Russell Christie LLP, 1070
Kouicem, Acène, President, Genilab Environnement Inc., 207
Koutroubis, Jim, Director, Engineering Services, Newmarket, 714
Kovacevic, Michelle, Director General, 533
Kovach, Gloria, Guelph, 710
Kovacs, Ed, Commisssioner, Transportation & Public Works, Cambridge, 707
Kovacs-Reid, Melissa, Coordinator, Waste Management, Dufferin, 699
Kovaks, Ernie, Director, F.E. Myers, 193
Koval, Patricia, Chair, World Wildlife Fund - Canada, 1023
Koversky, Wayne, Agent, Thompson, 204-677-7973, 690
Kowall, Mark, Director, Associated Tube Industries, 94
Kowbel, Christine J., Lawson Lundell LLP - Vancouver, 1061
Kozak, Frederick, Reynolds, Mirth, Richards & Farmer LLP, 1056
Koziol, Judy, North Bay, 715
Kozlik, Ken, Vice-President, 629
Kozlowski, Ronald, Vice-President, Canadian Worcester Controls Ltd., 125
Kraag, Scott, Torys LLP, 1081
Kraatz, Sandra, Director, 569
Kraemer, Larry, Bruce, 698
Kraemer, Larry, Mayor, Kincardine, 519-395-3130, 726
Kraemer, Lynda, Purchasing, Kraemer Tool & Manufacturing Co. Ltd., 260
Kraemer, Philipp, President/CEO, Kraemer Tool & Manufacturing Co. Ltd., 260
Kraemer, Rosemarie, Vice-President, Kraemer Tool & Manufacturing Co. Ltd., 260
Krafczyk, Aaron, Micro-Watt Control Devices Ltd., 289
Kraft, Kenneth David, Partner, Heenan Blaikie LLP - Toronto, 1076
Kraft, Norman, General Manager, Niagara Recycling, 303
Krahn, Mark, Manager, Pildysh Technologies Inc., 323
Krajewska, Ewa, Borden Ladner Gervais LLP - Toronto, 1073
Kralt, John A., Lincoln, 713
Kramer, Gabrielle K., Partner, Borden Ladner Gervais LLP - Toronto, 1073
Kramer, Jim, Manager, T.D. ThermoDesign, 386
Kramer, Larry, Manager, Finnex Agencies Ltd., 195
Kramer, Stuart, President, 663
Kramp, Stephan M., Deputy Mayor & Councillor, Midland, 713
Kranc, Sandra, City Clerk, Oshawa, 716
Krannitz, Pam, Canadian Board Member, Society for Conservation Biology, 1006
Krantz, Gordon, Halton, 700
Krantz, Gordon A., Mayor, Milton, 714
Krantz, Kevin, Supervisor, Westburne Canada, 426
Kranz, Lutz, Executive Vice President, Siemens Water Technologies, 367
Krause, Murry, Prince George, 683
Krebs, Ron, Director, American Plastics Council, 824
Krechowicz, Rich, Owner, Callrich Eco Services Inc., 122
Kreese, Brent, Branch Manager, Fort Garry Industries Ltd., 200
Kreiger, Ken, Director, Saanich, 250-475-5422, 688
Krejci, David, Executive Vice-President, Grain Elevator & Processing Society, 924
Krentz, Hugh, Chair, 559
Kress, Don, President, Par Excellence Developments, Inc., 318
Kress, Vicky, Administrator, Alberta Irrigation Projects Association, 818
Kreutzer, Vitold, President, Citizens For Renewable Energy, 895
Krich, Peter, Fire Chief/Deputy Director, Emergency Management, Camrose, 671
Krieg, John, Partner/President, Anrep Krieg Desilets Gravelle Ltd., 86
Krieger, Mike, Manager, Westburne Canada, 427
Kriksic, Frank, General Manager, Rowan Williams Davies & Irwin Inc., 353
Krischke, Greg, Mayor, Leduc, 673
Kristbjorg, Agustsdottir, Trade Commissioner, 768
Kristensen, Neills, Executive Director, Friends of Mount Revelstoke & Glacier, 921
Kristensson, Sven, President/CEO, Nederman Canada Ltd., 299
Kristine, Randall, Second Secretary (Commercial & Development), Trade, 767
Kristjáansson, Kristjáan, President, International Arctic Science Committee, 934
Kristoffy, Nick, Treasurer & Administrator, Whitchurch-Stouffville, 723
Kriviak, Gary, CH2M Hill Canada Limited, 137
Krmpotich, Joe, Sault Ste. Marie, 720

Executive Name Index

Kroeker, Harry, Second Vice-President, Southern Interior Local Government Association, 1010
Kroft, P. Jason, Partner, Stikeman Elliott LLP - Toronto, 1080
Krohman, Kenneth V., MacKenzie Fujisawa LLP, 1061
Kropninski, Sherry, Library Technician, Port Alberni Regional Campus Library, 1114
Kroshus, Jim, Coordinator, Saskatchewan Wildlife Federation, 1002
Krpan, Nick R., Vice President, Sandwell Engineering Inc., 357
Kruger, Gail, Vice President, 663
Kruger, Joseph, Chair/CEO, Kruger Inc., 260
Kruger, Rod, Manager, Woolwich, 732
Kruhlak, Ronald M., McLennan Ross LLP, 1055
Krupa, Henry, Lang Michener LLP - Toronto, 1077
Krupat, Howard, Partner, Heenan Blaikie LLP - Toronto, 1076
Krupp, Fred, President, Environmental Defense, 911
Krushell, Kim, Edmonton, 780-496-8128, 672
Krushelnicki, Bruce, Director, Planning & Building, Burlington, 707
Kruysse, Marten, Officer, Kootenay Boundary, 678
Krysac, Robert, Chief Financial Officer & Vice-President, 574
Krysiak, Peter K., Brownlee LLP, 1054
Krystal, Steve, Manager, Capital Programs & Traffic Engineering Br, East Gwilliambury, 708
Krywulak, Chris, President/CEO, iQmetrix, 247
Kteily, Edward, Vice-President, Vibec International Inc., 413
Kub, John, Secretary, Manitoba Ozone Protection Industry Association, 951
Kubiak, Janice, Corporate Manager, Human Resources, Oxford, 728
Kucy, Verna, Manager, Delta, 604-946-3281, 686
Kuczera, E., Director, Public Works, Niagara-on-the-Lake, 715
Kuehl, Gary A., International Water Supply Ltd., 245
Kuepfer, Wes, Manager, Public Works, Perth East, 728
Kuhl, George, Senior Planner, Lethbridge, 403-327-3926, 673
Kuhlmann, Dietrich, Treasurer, Alberta Greenhouse Growers Association, 817
Kukkonen, David, Plant Manager, Engineered Air, 180
Kulawik, Lucinda, Librarian, Canadian Energy Research Institute, 1100
Kulik, John, McInnes Cooper, 1067
Kulp, Dale, Director, Public Works, Elizabethtown-Kitley, 725
Kulscar, Pat, Chair, Mackenzie Regional Waste Management Commission, 757
Kumagai, Toshiko, Branch Manager, Sanix Incorporated, 357
Kumitch, Bruce, Territory Manager, Waterous Power Systems, 423
Kummling, Beth, Director of Business Development, ELI Eco Chemical Technologies Inc., 175
Kumpula, Jim, Sr. Vice-President, Summit Structures, 382
Kunc, Frank, President, RAM Lining Systems Inc., 342
Kundrik, Larry, Aquateck Ltd., 89
Kundur, Prabha, President, Powertech Labs Inc., 329
Kunin, Roslyn, Chair, 584
Kuntz, Allison G., Macleod Dixon LLP, 1052
Kuntz, Greg, Vice-President, Saskatchewan Environmental Industry & Managers' Association, 1000
Kuntz, Ken, Director, Delta, 604-952-3537, 686
Kuntze, Don, Quinte West, 613-962-6122, 718
Kunyk, T.W., President & General Manager, Bowie Pumps of Canada Ltd., 114
Kunyk, Terry, President, Rice Engineering & Operating Ltd., 346
Kunz, George, Supervisor, Peace River, 678
Kupferberg, Minel, President, MK Plastics Corp., 291
Kupferschmidt, William, Vice-President & General Manager, Research & Devel, 511
Kupila, Wendell, President, Capricorn Control Technologies Ltd., 128
Kupka, Jim, Director, Camrose, 780-672-5513, 671
Kupper, Angela, Contact, Agra Earth & Environmental Limited, 1104
Kuran, Peter, Acting General Manager, Vancouver, 685
Kurji, Karim, Medical Officer of Health & Director, Public Healt, York, 705
Kurli, Sudhakar, Hydrogeologist, Henderson Paddon & Associates Ltd., 229
Kuropas, Joe, Sales Manager, Eastern Region, Epsilon Chemicals Ltd., 189
Kurowski, George, Chair, Manitoba Ozone Protection Industry Association, 951
Kuryk, Paula, Treasurer, Recycling Council of Alberta, 993
Kuryllowicz, Peter, President & CEO, Testwell Instruments, 391
Kurylo, Sandra, Director, White Rock, 686
Kurz, Jeanne, President, TTA Technology Training Associates Ltd., 404

Kusec, Igor E., Specialist, K-Tech Services Ltd., 254
Kushner, Joseph, St. Catharines, 905-685-1817, 719
Kuski, Deron A., Partner, MacPherson Leslie & Tyerman LLP - Regina, 1090
Kusterman, Hubert Max, CEO, Quad-Lock Building Systems Ltd., 338
Kuszniryk, Nick, President, Plan-it Environmental Consulting Ltd., 325
Kutney, Gerald, COO, All-Wood Fibre Ltd., 79
Kutryk, E.A., President, Drilling Fluids Treatment Systems Inc., 166
Kutschke, CA, James D., Treasurer & Deputy Clerk, Renfrew, 704
Kutyba, P.Eng., Jim, General Manager, Infrastructure & Development Serv, Lambton, 701
Kutz, Michelle, Contact, Golder Associates Ltd., 214
Kuyek, Nial, General Manager, Agricultural Producers Association of Saskatchewan, 814
Kuypers, Fred, Quinte West, 613-392-8588, 718
Kuzmina, Elena, Head Librarian, Natural Resources Canada Library - Earth Sciences (Vancouver), 1118
Kuzyk, Robert, Manager, R.V. Anderson Associates Limited, 341
Kvill, Randy, Curator, Agriculture & Documentary Collections, Alberta Community Development, 1110
Kvisle, Daina, Osler, Hoskin & Harcourt LLP - Calgary, 1053
Kvitek, Josef, Contact, Enviro-Care Services, 182
Kwan, K., Director, Development, Richmond Hill, 718
Kwasek, Lisa, McKenzie Lake Lawyers LLP, 1069
Kwiatkowski, Marvin, Director, Terrace, 250-615-4041, 685
Kwinter, Larwrence M., Partner, Borden Ladner Gervais LLP - Calgary, 1049
Kwok, Emily, Contact, Golder Associates Ltd., 215
Kwok, Philip, Vice-President, Brampton Engineering Inc., 115
Kyle, Robert J., Commissioner, Health Department & Medical Officer, Durham, 699
Kyle, Rosanne M., Partner, Miller Thomson LLP - Toronto, 1078
Kyle, Stuart, Superintendent, Swift Current, 306-778-2748, 755
Kyluik, Linda, Treasurer, Leduc, 673
Kynoch, Brent, Managing Director, Environmental Information Association, 912
Kyte, Kevin, Associé, Stikeman Elliott LLP - Montréal, 1087
Kyte, Paul, Quinte West, 613-967-2134, 718
Kyvetos, Joanne, Technician, Donald-Petzel Memorial Library, 1178

L

Laakso, Stephen, President, SpilKleen, 376
Laar, Win, Contact, Niagara Falls Nature Club, 964
Laarhuis, S., Chief Legislative Officer, St. Albert, 674
Labadie, Jean-Yves, Beloeil, 450-446-0347, 734
Labarge, Simon, Heenan Blaikie S.E.N.C.R.L/SRL, 1084
Labas, Gerry, COO, Medicine Hat, 403-529-8222, 673
Labatte, Eric, Contact, Climate Control Systems Inc., 144
Labatte, Tina, Contact, Climate Control Systems Inc., 144
Labbate, Eric, Founder & President, Climate Control Systems Inc., 144
Labbé, André, Préfet, Robert-Cliche, 753
Labbé, Gaétan, Directeur, Sherbrooke, 819-821-5555, 744
Labbé, Pierrette, Technicienne en documentation, Québec Ministère des Ressources naturelles et de la Faune, 1180
Labeau, Pierre-Christian, Ogilvy Renault LLP/S.E.N.C.R.L., s.r.l. - Québec, 1088
Labeaume, Régis, Maire, Québec, 418-641-6434, 740
Labelle, Darcy, Sales Manager, M.J. Labelle Co. Ltd., 276
LaBelle, Lionel, President & CEO, Saskatchewan Trade & Export Partnership Inc., 1002
LaBelle, Lionel, President/CEO, 660
Labelle, Marcel J., President, M.J. Labelle Co. Ltd., 276
Labelle, Sophie, Technicienne en documentation, Bibliothèque de géographie, 1177
Labelle-Gelinas, Denise, City Clerk, Cornwall, 708
Laberge, Paulin, Chair, CON-SPACE Communications Ltd., 148
Laberge, Philippe, Lévis, 736
Laberge, Pierre, Bibliothécaire, Centre québécois de formation aéronautique, 1183
Labonté, Benoît, Maire d'arrondissement, Montréal, 738
Labonté, M. Robyn, Président, Camvac Inc., 122
LaBossiere, Keith D., Thompson Dorfman Sweatman LLP, 1064
labrador southeasaintcoas, Labrador Southeast Coasta, Port Hope Simpson, NL, 1042
Labrèche, Manon, Saint-Jérôme, 450-432-2733, 743
Labrecque, Annie-Claude, Heenan Blaikie S.E.N.C.R.L./SRL - Québec, 1088

Labrecque, Dan, Commissioner, Environment, Transportation, & Plann, Peel, 703
Labrecque, Daniel, Repentigny, 450-841-2437, 740
Labrecque, Jean-Luc, Terrebonne, 745
Labrecque, Michel, Conseiller de ville, Mile-End, Montréal, 738
Labrecque, Mike, Deputy CAO, Halifax Regional Municipality, 902-490-1520, 695
Labrecque, Nancy, Directrice générale, Montmagny, 750
Labrecque, Roger, Sherbrooke, 744
Labreque, Aline, Bibliotechnicienne, Québec Ministère du Développement économique, de l'Innovation et, 1180
Labreque, Jacques, Director, H2O Innovation Inc., 223
Labrie, Daniel, Gestionnaire, Veolia ES Canada Industrial Services Inc., 411
Labrie, Geneviève, Secrétaire, Société d'entomologie du Québec, 1005
LaCas, Brian, Senior River Engineer & Hydrologist, LaCas Consultants Inc., 262
Lacasse, Bill, Manager, Lou Romano Water Reclamation Plant, Windsor, 519-253-7217, 723
Lacasse, Claude, Terrebonne, 745
Lacasse, Michel, Directeur général, Boisbriand, 734
Lacey, Peter, VP West, Transport Action Canada, 1013
Lachaine, Yvon, Operations Manager, National Energy Equipment Inc., 297
Lachambre, Alain, Executive Vice-President, Teckn-O-Laser, 388
Lachambre, Martine, Vérificatrice générale, Laval, 450-978-8715, 736
Lachance, Dany, Sherbrooke, 744
Lachance, Ghislain, Directeur, Trois-Rivières, 745
Lachance, Julien, Sherbrooke, 744
Lachance, Marcel, Saint-Jérôme, 450-432-4399, 743
Lachance, Monique, Directrice, 644
Lachance, Philippe, Sales Coordinator, Anachemia Canada Inc., 85
Lachance, René, Directeur, Saint-Jérôme, 743
Lachance, Roger, Director, West Nipissing, 732
Lachance, Réjeanne, Directrice, 654
Lachance, Stéphanie, Cain Lamarre Casgrain Wells - Val-d'Or, 1089
Lachance, Sylvain, Conseiller, Villeray, Montréal, 738
Lachapelle, André, Directeur général adjoint, Longueuil, 737
Lachapelle, Éric, Directeur général, Saint-Jérôme, 743
Lachcik, Richard, Partner, Macleod Dixon LLP, 1077
Lachevrotière, André, Operations Manager, Barrington Industrial Services Limited, 102
Lachmaniuk, Lesia, Manager, Ontario Water Works Association, 981
LaCivita, Patricia, Coordinator, Collections & Information Management, University of Toronto Scarborough Library, 1163
Lacoix, Ginette, Directrice, Saint-Eustache, 450-974-5070, 742
Lacoix, Marc, Sous-ministre, 643
Lacombe, Jean-Pierre, Directeur, Longueuil, 737
Lacombe, Johanne, Executive Director, Go for Green, 924
Lacombe, Pierre, Directeur, Granby, 450-776-8344, 735
Lacombe-Gauthier, Michèle, Sorel-Tracy, 450-746-7710, 745
Lacount, Jamie, Manager, SpilKleen, 376
Lacourse, Terri, Editor, Canadian Association of Palynologists, 858
Lacourte, Carole, Senior Manager, Canadian Pacific Railway, 1100
Lacroix, Claude, Trois-Rivières, 745
Lacroix, Claude, Partner, Lavery, de Billy - Québec, 1088
Lacroix, Gilles, Varennes, 746
Lacroix, Jean, Président/directeur général, Association québécoise pour la maîtrise de l'énergie, 842
Lacroix, Norbert, Président, Club des ornithologues de Québec inc., 896
Lacy, Alison, Torys LLP, 1081
Ladd, Carla, Chief Administrative Officer, Kitchener, 519-741-2350, 712
Ladd, Ken, Associate Dean, University of Saskatchewan, 1191
Ladd, Ted, Treasurer, Land Trust Alliance, 948
Laden, Francine, Sec.-Treas., International Society for Environmental Epidemiology, 942
Ladner-Beaudry, Wendy, Co-Chair, 583
Ladouceur, Anne, Lévis, 736
Ladouceur, Felix, Manager, Westburne Canada, 427
Ladouceur, Hélène, Directrice, Longueuil, 737
Ladouceur, Marie-Élaine, Marketing Agent, Premier Tech Environment, 331
Ladouceur, Michael, Simcoe, 704
Ladouceur, Nels, Manager, Muddy River Technologies Inc., 295
Ladret, Frances, CAO, Powell River, 679

Executive Name Index

Laferrière, Denise, Gatineau, 735
Lafferty, Jackson, Minister, 605
Lafferty, Tom, Belleville, 706
Laffin, Michael, Blake, Cassels & Graydon LLP - Calgary, 1049
Laflamme, Conrad, Langlois Kronström Desjardins, 1088
Laflamme, Guy, Facility Manager, Hyprescon Inc., 237
Laflamme, Paul, Saint-Lazare, 743
Laflamme, Yves, Sr. Vice-President, Abitibi-Consolidated Inc., 65
Laflammme, Sophie, Greffière, Saint-Constant, 742
Laflèche, Guylain, Municipal Planner, The Nation, 731
LaFleche, Paul, Deputy Minister, 609
Lafleur, Marc, General Manager, AIRCOM Technologies Inc., 75
LaFleur, Natalie, Librarian, Alberta Justice, Office of the Chief Medical Examiner, 1104
Lafleur, Nicole, KW Gaspé Ltd. Partnership, 261
Lafleur, Paul, Chairman, BPR, 115
Lafond, Andre, President, Les Plastiques Simport Ltée, 270
Lafond, Anne, Technicienne en documentation, Québec Ministère de l'agriculture, des pêcheries et de l'alimenta, 1179
Lafond, Pierre, Directeur, Westburne Canada, 426
LaFontaine, Manon, Technicienne en documentation, Québec Ministère de la santé et des services sociaux, 1179
Lafontaine, Nicole, Longueuil, 737
LaForest, Chris, Director, Planning, Bruce, 698
Laforest, Joanne, Bibliothécaire, CÉGEP de Rivière-du-Loup, 1181
Laforest, Réjean, Saguenay, 741
LaForest, Suzy, Technicienne en documentation, Québec Ministère de l'agriculture, des pêcheries et de l'alimenta, 1179
Laforet-Fliesser, RN, BSc, Yvette, Officer, Community Health Nurses of Canada, 899
Laforge, Richard, Technicien, CÉGEP de St-Jérôme, 1184
LaForge, Troy, Green Key Solutions Inc., 217
Lafortune, Sylvain, Président/Directeur général, Compo Recycle, 147
Lafortune, Sylvie, Coordinator of ILL & Cataloguing, Laurentian University, 1155
Lafortune-Bélair, Maude, Lavery, de Billy - Montréal, 1085
Laframboise, André, Gatineau, 735
LaFrance, David B., Executive Director, American Water Works Association, 826
Lafreniere, Denis, Manager, West Nipissing, 732
Lafreniere, Patricia, Pembroke, 717
Lafrenière, Pierre B., Président, 648
Lafreniere, Robert, Sous-ministre, 652
LaFreniere, Tim, City Planner, North Battleford, 754
Lagacé, Michel, Préfet, Rivière-du-Loup, 753
Lagan, Kevin, Director, Courtenay, 250-703-4860, 680
Laghi, Brian, Director, 549
Laglagaron, Delia, Deputy CAO, Metro Vancouver, 678
Lagore, Doug, City Manager, Spruce Grove, 674
Lagran, Terry, Acquisitions Technician, Medicine Hat College, 1109
Lahaye, André, Directeur, Régie d'aqueduc de Grand Pré, 759
Lahey, Brian, Councillor, Cape Breton, 695
Lahey, Catherine A., Managing Partner, Stewart McKelvey Stirling Scales - Saint John, 1065
Lahti, Kenneth J., Vice-Pres. & CFO, Graymont Inc., 216
Lai, Mike, Manager, Saanich, 250-475-5492, 688
Laidlaw, Andy, General Manager, Nanaimo, 250-756-5346, 681
Laidlaw, Jeff, King, 726
Laidlaw, Maggie, Guelph, 710
Laing, Michele, Branch Head, School of Architecture, 1139
Laing, Richard, Director, West Vancouver, 689
Laing, Sharon, Director, Human Resources, Markham, 905-475-4725, 713
Laird, Duane, President, DRS Earthwise Society, 906
Laird, J., Director, Environmental Services, Guelph, 710
Laître, Denis, Salaberry-de-Valleyfield, 450-373-0954, 744
Laity, Peter, Sales Manager, Levy's Machine Works Ltd., 271
Lajamie, Chantal, Technicienne, documentation, Collège Lionel-Groulx, 1182
Lajoie, Andrée, Technicienne en documentation, Campus Notre-Dame-de-Foy, 1182
Lajoie, Fernand, Trois-Rivières, 745
Lake, Bonnie, Owner, Elgin Pure Water Supply, 175
Lake, Darlene, Co-ordinator, Document Services, Bracken Health Sciences Library, 1142
Lake, Harold, President/CEO, Elgin Pure Water Supply, 175
Lake-Kavanagh, Jackie, Director, 602
Lakinsky, Eugène, Responsable, Division recherche et diffusion, Québec Ministère de la santé et des services sociaux, 1179
Lakshman, G., President, System Ecotechnologies Inc., 385
Lalach, Jeanne, Contact, AKZO Nobel Chemicals Ltd., 76
Lalande, François, Marketing Specialist, Demilec Inc., 161

Lalande, Guy, Saint-Jérôme, 450-438-2021, 743
Lalande, Jacqueline, Systems Librarian, Fisheries & Oceans Canada, 1150
Lalande, Jean-Francois, General Manager, Innergy Tech, 242
Lalande, Michel, Office Manager, Trow Consulting Engineers Ltd., 403
Lalande, Normand, Trésorier, Saint-Basile-le-Grand, 741
Lalande, Paulette, Préfète, Papineau, 750
Laliberté, Jean-Marie, Québec, 740
Laliberte, Marc, Vice-President, Gentec Inc., 210
Laliberté, Sylvain, Directeur, Westburne Canada, 426
Laliberté, Sylvie, Technicienne en documentation, Québec Ministère des Ressources naturelles et de la Faune, 1180
Lalji, Amyn F., Partner, Miller Thomson LLP - Vancouver, 1061
Lalli, Dominic, District Sales Rep., National Instruments Canada, 298
Lally, Paraic, Vice-President, Roxul Inc., 353
Lalonde, André, Interlibrary Loans Technician, Canadian Heritage, 1167
Lalonde, Germain, Saint-Eustache, 450-472-5890, 742
Lalonde, Gord, Commissioner, Corporate Services, Oakville, 715
Lalonde, Jean-Yves, Prescott & Russell, 729
Lalonde, Marc, Bélanger, Sauvé, 1082
Lalonde, Marie, Administrative Assistant, International Joint Commission, 545, 1151
Lalonde, Michel, President, Groupe Séguin, 220
Lalonde, Michel, Président, Génius Conseil Inc., 207
Lalonde, Patrick, Recubec Inc., 343
Lalonde, Robert, Préfet, Maskinongé, 750
Lalonde, Serge, Fraser Milner Casgrain S.E.N.C.R.L./LLP, 1084
Lalonde, Vincent, General Manager, Surrey, 604-591-4011, 684
Lalonde, P. Eng., Vincent, Manager, Surrey, 604-591-4146, 684
Lalumière, Claude, EnvirInfo, 182
Lalumière, Denis, Sous-ministre adjoint, 652
Lam, Ander, President, Double Industries & Trading, 165
Lam, Carolyn, Associate Director, Seneca College of Applied Arts & Technology, 1161
Lam, Florence, Information Specialist, Ontario Ministry of Municipal Affairs & Housing, 1160
Lam, Helena, Administrator, Link-Pipe Inc., 272
Lam, Henry, Information Specialist, Sunnybrook Health Sciences Centre - Sunnybrook Campus, 1162
Lam, Joe, President, Polyland Industries Ltd., 328
Lam, John C., Vice-President, ABL Environmental Consultants, 65
Lam, Tuyet, Medical Library Technician, Peter Lougheed Centre Library, 1102
LaMarca, Joe, Treasurer, Association of Supervisors of Public Health Inspectors (Ontario), 840
Lamarche, Marie-Claude, Terrebonne, 745
Lamarre, Anne-Louise, Ogilvy Renault LLP/S.E.N.C.R.L., s.r.l. - Montréal, 1086
Lamarre, Claude, Chef du service des ressources documentaires, Québec Ministère de la santé et des services sociaux, 1179
Lamarre, François, Cain Lamarre Casgrain Wells - Montréal, 1083
Lamarre, Isabelle, Coordonnatrice, Service de soutien à l'apprentissa, Collège d'Ahuntsic, 1172
Lamarre, Louis, Blainville, 734
Lamarre, Martin, Contact, Les Entreprises Forlam, 268
Lamarre, Paul, Lamarre Perron Lambert Vincent, 1085
Lamarre, Robert, Manager, Building & Planning, Smith-Ennismore-Lakefield, 729
Lamb, Gary R., Bradford West Gwillimbury, 706
Lamb, Susan, CEO, Meewasin Valley Authority, 953
Lambert, Bertrand, Victoriaville, 819-752-5388, 746
Lambert, David, Circulation Librarian, Capilano College, 1114
Lambert, Deborah, Library Manager, The Scarborough Hospital - General Campus, 1162
Lambert, Frederic, President, Control Techniques Drives Inc., 151
Lambert, Gabrielle, Director of Operations, STOBEC Inc., 379
Lambert, Jeff, Fire Chief, Port Moody, 683
Lambert, Lawrence A., President, Applied Oxidation Technologies Inc., 87
Lambert, Lise, Présidente, 654
Lambert, Phil, Acting Deputy Minister, 662
Lambert, Phillip, Director, Operations, Thorold, 905-227-3535, 720
Lambert, Ron, Fire Chief, Nanaimo, 250-755-7550, 681
Lambert, Tony, Halton, 700
Lambert, Tony, Local & Regional Councillor, Milton, 714
Lambert, William M., President & Chief Executive Officer, MSA: Mine Safety Appliances Company, 294

Lambert, C.E.T., Darnell, Director, Engineering & Construction, Oakville, 715
Lambright, Randy, Manager, Kamloops, 681
Lambrou, Angella, Computer Services Librarian, Life Sciences Library, 1174
Lamkey, James F., Clerk, Miramichi, 691
Lamm, Chris, Concerned Educators Allied for a Safe Environment, 899
Lammers, Rachel R., Morelli Chertkow LLP, Lawyers, 1056
Lamont, Elizabeth, Chief Librarian, Royal Victoria Hospital, 1175
Lamont, Sharon, Director, Organizational Services, University of Waterloo, 1164
Lamontagne, Annick, Technicienne en documentation, Québec Ministère de la santé et des services sociaux, 1179
Lamontagne, Eric, President/CEO, Sedac Inc., 361
Lamontagne, Jean, General Manager, Surrey, 604-591-4441, 684
Lamontagne, Michel, Sherbrooke, 744
Lamontagne, Paule, Présidente, Les Amis du Jardin botanique de Montréal, 829
Lamontagne, Serge, Menart S.L. Inc., 286
Lamontagne, CA, MBA, Robert, Directeur, Montréal, 738
Lamothe, Jane, Head, Natural Sciences Library, Natural Sciences Library, 1189
Lamoureux, Jean, Saint-Jean-sur-Richelieu, 450-348-5014, 742
Lamoureux, Lorraine, Technicienne, CÉGEP de St-Jérôme, 1184
Lamoureux, Todd, Manager, Westburne Canada, 427
Lampart, Tony, Executive Director, 591
Lampman, Jonathan W., Counsel, Ramsay Lampman Rhodes, 1056
Lampron, Denis, Shawinigan, 744
Lamy, André, Gestionnaire, Veolia ES Canada Industrial Services Inc., 411
Lancaster, Blair, Halton, 707, 700
Lancaster, Greg, Manager, Facilities & Parks, Lincoln, 713
Lancaster, Joyce, Executive Secretary, Weed Science Society of America, 1018
Lancaster, Marty, Oro-Medonte, 728
Landa, Eveline, Head, NRC Information Centre Montréal, 1174
Landell, Bob, Principal, Avalon Mechanical Consultants Ltd., 98
Landers, David, CAO, Cochrane District Social Services Administrat, Cochrane, 705-268-7722, 725
Landers, Shawn, President, Opus International Consultants (Canada) Ltd., 314
Landes, Barb, Contact, Imperial Oil Resources Limited, 1101
Landis, Sian, Librarian, Selkirk College, 1111
Landmaid, Ken, Chair, South West Solid Waste Commission, 759
Landon, Edwin O., Executive Director, Institute of Packaging Professionals, 933
Landon, Gordon, York, 705
Landon, Gordon, Regional Councillor, Markham, 905-415-7534, 713
Landra, Keith, Manager, Canada-Nova Scotia Offshore Petroleum Board, 853
Landreth, Cathryn, Acting Utilities Consumer Advocate, 573
Landreville, François, Directeur général, Le Haut-St-Laurent, 749
Landry, Anna, Director, Human Resources, Muskoka, 702
Landry, Cédric, Conseiller en documentation, Campus de Shippagan, 1130
Landry, Dan, Branch Manager, Mequipco Ltd., 286
Landry, Daniel, Secretary, Canadian Council of Professional Fish Harvesters, 865
Landry, Denis, Minister, 597
Landry, Emanuelle, Contact, GSI Environnement Inc., 222
Landry, Gary, ADI Group Inc., 68
Landry, Greg, Vice-President, Fabricated Plastics Ltd., 193
Landry, Gérard, Québec, 740
Landry, Isabelle, Heenan Blaikie S.E.N.C.R.L./SRL - Québec, 1088
Landry, Jacques, Directeur, Portneuf, 751
Landry, Joe, Owner, G. Landry Vacuum Services Ltd., 203
Landry, Karen, Town Clerk & Director, Administration, Caledon, 707
Landry, Linda, Secrétaire général (par intérim), 648
Landry, Lise, Mairesse, Shawinigan, 744
Landry, Lynda, President, Laboratoire de Canalisation Souterraines Inc., 262
Landry, Maurice, Manager, Brooks, 671
Landry, Nicole, Responsable, Services techniques et de consultatio, CÉGEP de Drummondville, 1167
Landry, P. John, Davis LLP - Vancouver, 1059
Landry, Peter, Director, Viridis Environmental Inc., 413

Executive Name Index

Landry, Pierre, Contact, The Paint Recycling Company, 393
Landry, Pierre, President, New Brunswick Environment Industry Association, 960
Landry, René (Pepsi), Moncton / Ville de Moncton, 691
Landry, Ross, Minister & Attorney General, 614
Landry, Stephen, COO, Advance Laboratories Ltd., 69
Landry, Stephen, Operations Manager, Epsilon Chemicals Ltd., 189
Landry, Yves, Trois-Rivières, 745
Landry-Altmann, Joscelyne, Greater Sudbury / Grand Sudbury, 710
Lane, Patricia A., President, Lane Environment Limited, 264
Lane, Paul, Deputy Mayor & Councillor, Mount Pearl, 694
Lane, R., General Manager, Community Services, Haldimand, 700
Lane, Richard, Director, Recreation & Community Services, St. Catharines, 719
Lane, Ron, Vice-Chair, North Forty Mile Regional Waste Management Services Commission, 758
Lane, Summer, Borden Ladner Gervais LLP - Vancouver, 1058
Laneville, David, Director, Information Technology, Timmins, 721
Lanfranco, Alan M., Principal, A. Lanfranco & Associates Inc., 63
Lang, André, Edmundston, 691
Lang, Archie, Minister, 663
Lang, F. Stuart, Alexander Holburn Beaudin & Lang, LLP, 1057
Lang, Jim, Coordinator, Squamish, 688
Lang, Peter, General Manager, Western Red Cedar Lumber Association, 1019
Lang, Rick, Contact, Vacuum Products Canada Inc., 408
Lang, Robert, BFI Canada Inc., 106
Lang, Robert, Chief Financial Officer, PCI Geomatics Group Inc., 320
Lang, Shari, Coordinator, Trent Hills, 731
Lange, Tina, Kamloops, 681
Langelier, André, Coordonnateur, Gatineau, 735
Langen, Dennis P., Macleod Dixon LLP, 1052
Langen, Scott, Executive Director, 657
Langford, Chessy, Environmental Scientist, Emergex Planning Inc., 177
Langford, Francesca, Coordinator, Squamish, 604-815-5021, 688
Langill, John, Manager, Bartle & Gibson Co. Ltd., 102
Langille, Jim, CAO, Truro, 696
Langille, Robin, President, Northwest Territories Recreation & Parks Association, 967
Langille, Roger, Vice President, Inland Technologies Inc., 242
Langille, Steven, Branch Manager, J.L. Richards & Associates Limited, 250
Langlais, Robert, Fire Chief, Bathurst, 506-548-0439, 690
Langlands, Sandra, Reference/Research Unit Coordinator, Gerstein Science Information Centre, 1158
Langley, Carolyn, Clerk, West Lincoln, 732
Langley, Douglas G., Executive Vice-President, Delcan Water, 160
Langlois, Bruno, Responsable, Analyste information, Université du Québec à Rimouski, 1181
Langlois, David, President, Argo Protective Coatings Inc., 90
Langlois, Denis, Préfet, Portneuf, 751
Langlois, Donald, Préfet, L'Érable, 748
Langlois, Jean, Repentigny, 450-585-4285, 740
Langlois, Pierre, Partner, Heenan Blaikie S.E.N.C.R.L/SRL, 1084
Langlois-Brouillette, Sylvie, Repentigny, 514-295-8376, 740
Langthorne, William, Executive Director, 600
Langton, Terri, Manager, Westburne Canada, 428
Lankester, Janis, Clerk, Haldimand, 700
Lanni, Gino, Directeur, Génius Conseil Inc., 207
Lanoue, Réal, Directeur, Terrebonne, 745
Lanouette, Noël, Directeur, Rouyn-Noranda, 741
Lansbergen, Paul, Director, Forest Products Association of Canada, 918
Lanteigne, Wayne, Howard Marten Fluid Technologies Inc., 234
Lantz, Bruce, Mayor, Fort St. John, 681
Lantz, B.Sc., Rob, Charlottetown, 732
Lanz, Douglas, President, Air Phaser Environmental Ltd., 75
Lapalme, Monique, Documentation Librarian II, Bell Helicopter Textron, 1170
Lapenseé, Robert, Marketing, Génie Audio inc., 207
Laperle, Yollande, Director, Student Services, Cornwall Campus, 1140
Laperrière, Claude, Directeur général, Sainte-Julie, 450-922-7102, 743
Laperrière, François, Vice-President, Travaux Publiques, Cegerco - GCL Inc., 135
Lapierre, Alain, Directeur général, Sept-Rivières, 753
Lapierre, Jean-Jacques, Laval, 736

LaPierre, Louis, Review Officer, 521
Lapierre, Mireille, Assistance à l'usager, Bibliothèque des sciences de la santé, 1185
Lapierre, Perrine, Directrice générale, Thérèse-de-Blainville, 753
Lapierre, Rhona, Corporate Librarian, Manitoba Hydro, 1124
Lapierre, T., Manager, Human Resources, Pembroke, 717
Lapierre, Terry, Chief Administrative Officer, Pembroke, 717
Lapierrière, Marc, Bélanger, Sauvé, 1082
Laplante, Jean-Pierre, Directeur général, Témiscouata, 753
Laplante, Maurice, Cain Lamarre Casgrain Wells - Drummondville, 1082
Laplante, Paul, Contact, ACME Vacuum Cleaner Co. Ltd., 67
Lapointe, Bruno, Regional Director, Les Laboratoires Shermont Inc., 269
Lapointe, Denis, Maire, Salaberry-de-Valleyfield, 450-370-4819, 744
Lapointe, François, Greffier, Saint-Jean-sur-Richelieu, 450-357-2077, 742
Lapointe, Julie, Cain Lamarre Casgrain Wells - Sept-Iles, 1089
Lapointe, Louise, Québec, 740
Lapointe, Manon, Service du prêt, Université du Québec en Abitibi-Témiscamingue, 1182
Lapointe, Marie, Directrice, Rivière-du-Loup, 418-867-6711, 741
Lapointe, Pierre, President/CEO, FPInnovations, 200
Lapointe, Roger, Préfet, Antoine-Labelle, 747
Lapointe, Sylvie, Directrice générale, Sherbrooke, 819-821-5618, 744
LaPorte, Blake, Senior Technician, Lakehead University, 263
Laporte, Guy, Branch Manager, Totten Sims Hubicki Associates Ltd., 399
Laporte, Jean L., COO, 561
Laporte, Line, Directrice générale, Joliette, 747
Laporte, Manon, ETV Canada, 190
Laporte, Manon, Présidente-directrice générale, Enviro-Accès Inc., 911
Laporte, Sylvain, Supervisor, Calgary, 121
Lapp, Ken, President/CEO, Westech Industrial Ltd., 429
Lapper, Robert, Deputy Minister, 581
Laprise, Lucie, Responsable, acquisitions/périodique, CÉGEP de l'Abitibi-Témiscamingue, 1182
Laprise, Sébastien, Associé, Langlois Kronström Desjardins, 1088
Lapworth, Roger, Town Councillor, Oakville, 715
Laramée, François, Directeur, Longueuil, 737
Laramée, Gilles, Exec. Vice President/CFO, SNC-Lavalin Group Inc., 371
Larcombe, P., Partner, Symbion Consultants, 385
Lardjane, Mahmoud, Manager, Canadian Society for Civil Engineering, 885
Laredo, Serge, Lennox Industries (Canada) Ltd., 267
Largy, Pierre, Directeur général, Roussillon, 753
Larivière, Jacques, President, Demilec Inc., 161
Larkin, Bill, Director, Winnipeg, 690
Larkin, J. Stephen, President, The Aluminum Association, 821
Larmand, Andrew J., Martin Sheppard Fraser LLP, 1070
Larmour, Craig, Director, Planning Services, Pelham, 717
Larmour, Matt, Contact, SUBBOR, 381
Larmour, Sharon, Treasurer & Director, Financial Services, Central Elgin, 724
Larner, Caren, Librarian, E.I. duPont Canada Company, 1145
Laroche, Ben, President, Council of Canadian Fire Marshals & Fire Commissioners, 904
Laroche, Martin, Vice-President, Dessau, Inc., 162
LaRoche, Philippe, President/CEO, STOBEC Inc., 379
Larochelle, Charles, Sous-ministre adjoint, 646
Larochelle, Dany, Siège #3, Saint-Félicien, 742
Larochelle, Denis, Directeur, Salaberry-de-Valleyfield, 450-370-4820, 744
Larocque, Claude, Directeur, Shawinigan, 744
LaRocque, Judith A., Deputy Minister, 519
Larocque, Manon, Director, 520
Larocque, Paul, Préfet, Thérèse-de-Blainville, 753
Larocque, Reno, Serials Assistant, Portage College, 1108
Laroque, Ronald L., President, Ozocan Corporation, 315
Larose, Denis, Directeur, Repentigny, 450-470-3620, 740
Larose, Diane, Bélanger, Sauvé, 1082
LaRose, Jean, President, Larose & Fils Ltée, 264
Larose, Manon, General Manager, Larose & Fils Ltée, 264
Larose, Michel, Directeur, Saint-Jérôme, 753
Larouche, Alain, Baie-Comeau, 418-589-2107, 733
Larouche, Daniel, Directeur, Saguenay, 741
Larouche, Jim, Welland, 722
Larouche, Marguerite, Vice-président, Club des ornithologues de Québec inc., 896
Larouche, Marina, Saguenay, 741

Larouche, Michel, Maire, Roberval, 741
Larouche, Nicole, Lévis, 736
Larouche, Réjean, General Manager, Envitech Automation Inc., 188
Larouche, Sabin, Directeur général, Lac-Saint-Jean-Est, 749
Larrivée, Pierre, Partner, Heenan Blaikie S.E.N.C.R.L./SRL - Québec, 1088
Larson, Max R., Triton Consultants Ltd., 402
Larson, Sandy, Mayor, Swift Current, 755
Larsson, J., President, Miniveil Air Systems, 290
LaRue, Fred, Vice-President, Roger LaRue Enterprises Ltd., 350
Lash, Jonathan, President, World Resources Institute, 1023
Laskarzewska, Barbara, Pottinger Gaherty Environmental Consultants Ltd., 329
Lasnier, Caroline, Comptable, Régie intermunicipale d'élimination de déchets solides de Brome-M, 760
Lasnier, Philippe, Saint-Jean-sur-Richelieu, 450-347-1299, 742
Lassaad, Bourguiba, Trade Commissioner, 769
Last, Iva, Executive Director, Manitoba Water & Wastewater Association, 952
Lastiwka, Larry, FCX NH Valves, 194
Lasuik, Tim, Vice-President, J.R. Cousin Consultants Ltd., 250
Latam, Wayne, Executive Manager, Alberta Society of Surveying & Mapping Technologies, 820
Latchford, Sandy, Prince Edward, 703
Latendresse, Marc, Directeur, Sherbrooke, 744
Latendresse, Michel, Longueuil, 737
Lathan, Gina, Sales Manager, Hy-Grade Precast Concrete, 235
Lathan, Susan, Regional Clerk & Director, Council Services, Halton, 700
Lathem, Andy S., Director, 611
Lathlin, Oscar, Minister, 584
Latimer, Doug, President, Latimat Inc., 265
Latimer, Eric, Treasurer, Canadian Association for Health Services & Policy Research, 855
Latimer, Shelly, National Sales Manager, Latimat Inc., 265
Latimer, Q.C., Kevin, Cox and Palmer - Halifax, 1067
Latko, Mary Ann, Director, American Industrial Hygiene Association, 823
Latourelle, Alan, CEO, 552
Latta, Sharyl, Library Techinician, University College of the North, 1122
Lattimore, Ted, CEO, Carmanah Technologies Corp., 129
Latulippe, Éric, Associé, Langlois Kronström Desjardins, 1088
Lau, Joseph, Vice-President, Engineering & Technical Delivery, 511
Lau, Ron, President, Ronel Engineering Ltd., 351
Lau, Sebastian, Manager, General Scrap Partnership, 206
Laubenstein, Glen, CAO, Winnipeg, 690
Laudan, Dirk, Partner, Borden Ladner Gervais LLP - Vancouver, 1058
Laughren, Thomas B., Mayor, Timmins, 721
Laughton, Richard, President, CENSOL Inc., 136
Laurell, Ari, Sales & Marketing, UNOTEC, 407
Laurence, Robert A., Vaudreuil-Dorion, 746
Laurendeau, Jacques, Magog, 819-843-3244, 737
Laurens, Barb, Manager, ASI Group Ltd., 94
Laurent, Francine, Présidente & Directrice générale, 648
Laurent, Jacques, Partner, Borden Ladner Gervais LLP - Montréal, 1083
Lauret, Jean-Claude, Nertec Design Inc., 300
Laurette, Bill, President, Atlantic Environmental Training & On-Site Services Inc., 95
Lauridsen, John, CFO, Kongskilde Limited, 259
Laurie, Dave, Director, Public Works, Huron, 701
Laurin, Denis, President, Machinerie Laurin Inc., 278
Laurin, Guy, Mirabel, 738
Laurin, Jamie, Russell, 729
Laurin, Joanne, Communications Officer, 545
Laurin, Jules, Production Foreman, Ray Electric Ltd., 342
Laurin, René, Maire, Joliette, 736
Laurin, Robert, Principal, Robert Laurin, 348
Laustrup, Karen, Manager, Port Coquitlam, 604-927-5430, 683
Lautenbach, Bill, General Manager, Growth & Development, Greater Sudbury / Grand Sudbury, 710
Lautsch, Karen, Executive Director, 656
Lauzon, Anne, Sainte-Thérèse, 744
Lauzon, Hélène, Présidente, Conseil patronal de l'environnement du Québec, 901
Lauzon, Jacques, Director, Megasecur Inc., 286
Lauzon, Louis, Sainte-Thérèse, 744
Lauzon, Marc, Maire, Deux-Montagnes, 450-473-8898, 735
Lauzon, Marc, Préfet, Deux-Montagnes, 747
Lauzon, Marcelle, Technicienne en documentation, Campus de Charlesbourg, 1177

Executive Name Index

Lauzon, Michel, Mirabel, 738
Lauzon, Roxanne, Greffière, Papineau, 750
Lauzone, Marie-Christine, Heenan Blaikie S.E.N.C.R.L/SRL, 1084
Lavallée, Alexandra, Responsable, CÉGEP Limoilou, 1178
Lavallée, André, Maire d'arrondissement, Montréal, 738
Lavallée, Chantal, Associée, Cain Lamarre Casgrain Wells - Chicoutimi, 1082
Lavallée, Lise, Assistante en bibliothèque, Centre de recherche et de développement en horticulture, 1183
Lavallée, Marcel, Sorel-Tracy, 450-742-3101, 745
Lavallée, Mario, Boisbriand, 734
Lavallée, Myriam, Heenan Blaikie S.E.N.C.R.L/SRL - Trois-Rivières, 1089
Lavallee, P., Manager, J. Walter Company Ltd., 249
Lavallee, P.P., IBI Group, 238
Lavallée, Pierre, President/CEO, BPR, 115
Lavalley, Janice, Chief Administrative Officer, Smith-Ennismore-Lakefield, 729
Laverdière, Marc R., Scientific Director, Research & Development Institute for the Agri-Environment, 994
Laverdière, Réal, Préfet, L'Islet, 748
Laverdure, Paul, Library Director, University of Sudbury, 1155
Lavergne, Albert, Reynolds, Mirth, Richards & Farmer LLP, 1056
Lavergne, Christine, Executive Advisor to the Deputy Minister, 527
Lavergne, M. Pierre-Louis, Président, Camvac Inc., 122
Lavergne, Rick, Directeur général, L'Érable, 748
Lavers, John W., Partner, Ottenheimer Baker, 1066
Laverty, Cory, Acting Head, Reference, Queen's University, 1142
Laverty, Glenn, President/CEO, Ricoh Canada Inc., 347
Lavignasse, Nancy, Chief Financial & Admin. Officer, Integran Technologies Inc., 244
Lavigne, Marc, Manager, Valley Associates Inc., 409
Lavigne, Robert, President/CEO, Nova PB Inc., 308
Lavigueur, Philippe, Responsable, Référence, Collège Montmorency, 1169
Lavigueur-Thériault, Josée, Conseillère d'arrondissement, Desmarchais-Crawford, Montréal, 738
Lavoie, Daniel, Associate Assistant Deputy Minister, 557
Lavoie, Denis, Maire, Chambly, 734
Lavoie, Diane, Beloeil, 450-464-3095, 734
Lavoie, Dominique, Directrice (par intérim), 654
Lavoie, Guy, Directeur général, Kamouraska, 748
Lavoie, Gérald, Trésorier, Amos, 733
Lavoie, Jeannette, Blainville, 734
Lavoie, Marc, President, Canadian Hay Association, 870
Lavoie, Mario, Directeur général, La Matapédia, 748
Lavoie, Michel, Préfet, Les Jardins-de-Napierville, 749
Lavoie, Mylène, Conseillère pédagogique en bibliothéconomie, CÉGEP de Drummondville, 1167
Lavoie, Patrick J., President/CEO, Atrion International Inc., 97
Lavoie, Sylvie, Directrice, Shawinigan, 744
Law, Daniel R., Partner, Fasken Martineau - Toronto, 1075
Law, Debra, Manager, Campbell River, 679
Law, John, Deputy Minister, 660
Law, Margaret, Assoc. Dir., Science/Technology & Health Sciences, John W. Scott Health Sciences Library, 1105
Law, Margaret, Associate Director Libraries, Cameron Science & Technology Library, 1104
Law, Myrna, Sales Coordinator, Anachemia Canada Inc., 85
Law, Richard, President, ACE Vegetation Control Service Ltd., 66
Law, Sam, Director, Information Technology, Lanark, 701
Lawee, Philip, Contact, Hydromega Energy Inc., 237
Lawless, Janice, Membership Coordinator, Saskatchewan Trade & Export Partnership Inc., 1002
Lawless, Justin, Coordinator, Prince Edward Island Cattle Producers, 988
Lawlor, Ann, Councillor, Halton Hills, 710
Lawlor, Sean, North Bay, 715
Lawrance, Rob, Environmental Planner, Nanaimo, 250-755-4483, 681
Lawrence, Bruce A., Partner, Borden Ladner Gervais LLP - Calgary, 1049
Lawrence, Chris, Yard Supervisor, Halifax C&D Recycling, 224
Lawrence, Elizabeth, Director, St. John's, 709-576-8203, 694
Lawrence, George, Simcoe, 704
Lawrence, Paul, President, General Filtration, 206
Lawrence, Simon, Director, Colwood, 250-478-5541, 680
Lawrie, Darryl, Construction Manager, Abcott Construction Ltd., 65
Laws, Todd, CADD/Tech, Long Environmental Consultants, 273
Lawson, Andrea, Administrator, Human Resources, Wellington, 705
Lawson, Cindy, Director, Recreation, Loyalist, 727

Lawson, Sandra, General Manager, Engineering & Operational Service, Brantford, 707
Lawson, Steve, Coordinator, First Nations Environmental Network, 916
Lawson, Steve, Manager, Kitimat, 687
Lawson, Tim, Partner, Heenan Blaikie LLP - Toronto, 1076
Lawton, Catherine, Librarian, Fisheries & Marine Institute, 1132
Lawton, Jane, Executive Director, The Jane Goodall Institute of Canada, 946
Laxdal, John, Regional Manager, AMEC, 82
Laxdal, John, Unit Manager, AMEC, 83
Laycock, Anthony, Executive Director, Wood Energy Technology Transfer Inc., 1021
Laycock, Glen, Warren's Imaging & Dryography Inc., 417
Laycraft, Q.C., James B., Founding Partner, Wilson Laycraft, 1054
Layte-Liston, Gina, Environmental Coordinator, Prince George, 250-614-7824, 683
Layton, Mike, Toronto, 721
Layzell, Rick, Chair, National Marine Manufacturers Association Canada, 958
Lazar, Avrim, President & Chief Executive Officer, Forest Products Association of Canada, 918
Lazarnko, David, President, Canadian Agri-Marketing Association (Manitoba), 855
Lazarou, Elizabeth, Manager, Suncor Energy Products, 382
Lazier, Thomas E., Lazier Hickey Langs O'Neal, 1068
Lazure, Mario, Directeur général, Sorel-Tracy, 745
Lazzarin, Darcy, General Manager, Williams Lake, 686
Le, Trisha, Urban Planner, Lloydminster, 673
Lea, Q.C., William G., Campbell Lea, 1082
Leach, John D., Clerk, Innisfil, 711
Leach, Meagan, Director, Iqaluit, 867-979-6363, 698
Leach, Ray, President, Waste Alternatives Inc., 417
Leaf, Ron, County Manager, Clearwater County, 669
Leahy, Doug, President, Eagle Home Inspection Services Inc., 168
Leahy, Douglas, Treasurer, Penticton, 682
Leahy, Jim, CEO, Automatic Controls Ltd., 98
Leake, Greg, Director, 658
Leamen, Paull N., Soloway, Wright LLP, 1071
Lean, Ernie, Manager, J.W. Bird & Company Ltd., 250
Leape, James P., Director General, WWF International, 1024
Leard, Neal L.D., Partner, Stewart McKelvey Stirling Scales - Saint John, 1065
Leary, Kelvin, Deputy Minister, 665
Leathem, Thomas, Director, Delta, 604-946-3380, 686
Leavens, Richard, Executive Director, Association for Mountain Parks Protection & Enjoyment, 833
Leavitt, Bernice, Supervisor, Technical Services, Canadian University College, 1108
Lebel, Denis, Minister of State, Economic Development Agency of, 515
Lebel, Denise, Technicienne, CÉGEP de St-Jérôme, 1184
Lebel, Elisabeth, Chef, Centre de documentation, Collège Lasalle, 1172
Lebel, Jean, Director, 544
LeBel, Peter, Director, Whitby, 723
LeBlanc, Candace, Sr. Admin. Coordinator, 662
Leblanc, Carole, Agente de bureau, Comptoir de prêt, CÉGEP St-Jean-sur-Richelieu, 1183
Leblanc, Christian, Asst. Manager, Technisol Environnement, 388
LeBlanc, Dave, Councillor, Cape Breton, 695
LeBlanc, Diane, Agente de bureau, Centre des études collégiales - Carleton, 1166
LeBlanc, Elphège, Sec.-Trés., Responsable de l'alimentation en eau p, Régie intermunicipale d'approvisionnement en eau potable de l'île, 759
LeBlanc, Frank, Manager, SGE Hatch Ltd., 364
LeBlanc, Fred, President, Ontario Professional Fire Fighters Association, 977
LeBlanc, Gary, General Manager, Commission de gestion des déchets solides de la péninsule Acadien, 758
LeBlanc, George H., Mayor, Moncton / Ville de Moncton, 506-856-4343, 691
LeBlanc, Jacques, Director, Dieppe, 691
LeBlanc, Jean G., Mayor, Dieppe, 691
Leblanc, Jean-Claude, Représentant, CPC Tuyauteries Canada Ltée, 153
LeBlanc, John, President, Lantech Drilling Services Inc., 264
LeBlanc, Kenny, Chief Worker Adviser, 612
LeBlanc, Marie, Manager, Northumberland Solid Waste Commission, 758
LeBlanc, Paul J., Executive Vice-President, 510

LeBlanc, Paul J.L., Dieppe, 506-853-3974, 691
Leblanc, Rachelle, Responsable, Audiovidéothèque, CÉGEP de Drummondville, 1167
LeBlanc, Roger J., Dieppe, 506-850-1604, 691
LeBlanc, Roland, ADI Group Inc., 68
LeBlanc, Roland, President, Acadia Consultants & Inspectors Ltd., 65
LeBlanc, Ron, Pinchin Environmental Ltd., 324
Leblanc, Stéphane, Project Manager, Solmax-Texel Geosynthetics Inc., 373
LeBlanc-Comeau, Réjeanne, Acquisitions, Université Sainte-Anne, 1167
Leblond, André, Préfet, Les Basques, 749
Leblond, François, Directeur, Baie-Comeau, 418-296-8358, 733
LeBlond, Isidore J., Director, Canadian Council of Technicians & Technologists, 865
Leblond, Robert, Planner Vice President, Le Groupe Leblond & Bouchard/Daniel Arbour et associes, 265
Leblond, Ron, Vice-President & General Manager, Monserco Ltd., 293
LeBlond, Q.C., Charles A., Stewart McKelvey Stirling Scales - Moncton, 1065
Leboeuf, Marie-Josée, Chef de service, Prêt et traitement des collection, Bibliothèque des sciences de la santé, 1171
Leboeuf, Yves, Vice-President, 518
Lebreton, Clarence, Asst. Deputy Minister, 597
LeBreton, Paul M., Chair, 598
Lebrun, Gilles, Varennes, 746
Lebrun, Marilyn, Clerk, South Glengarry, 730
Lebrun-Ginn, Lucie, Office Administrator, Canadian Institute of Geomatics, 874
Lebuis, Francis, President/COO, Aqua Data Inc., 87
Lecamp, Janet, Director, 666
Lechner, Bill, President, Canadian Micro-Mineral Association, 879
Lechow, Clifford, District Manager, BFI Canada Inc., 107
Leckie, David, Director, Roads & Transportation, London, 713
Leclair, Rosemarie, President/CEO, Energy Ottawa, 179
Leclerc, André, Pol-E-Mar Inc., 327
Leclerc, Anne-Marie, Directrice générale, 654
Leclerc, Chantal, Bibliothécnicienne, CÉGEP de Rivière-du-Loup, 1182
Leclerc, France, Greffière, Bécancour, 734
Leclerc, Jean-Claude, Vice-President, Celfort Construction Materials Inc., 135
Leclerc, Liette, Responsable, Traitement documentaire, Université du Québec en Abitibi-Témiscamingue, 1182
Leclerc, Marc, Coordonnateur, CÉGEP de Saint-Hyacinthe, 1183
Leclerc, Monique, Trois-Rivières, 745
Leclerc, Réal, Terrebonne, 745
LeClerc, Serge, Legislative Secretary to the Minister of Correctio, 656
Leclerc, Stéphane, Treasurer, Levac Robichaud Leclerc Associates Ltd., 270
Lecompte, Jacques, President, Lecompte Engineering Ltd., 266
Lecompte, Mark, Technical Advisor, Lecompte Engineering Ltd., 266
Lecomte, François, President/CEO, Compteurs Lecomte Ltée, 148
Ledingham, G. Brett, McDougall Gauley, 1090
LeDrew, Bevin, President, LEM Laboratory Inc., 267
Leduc, Claude, President, Groupe Sodinco inc., 221
Leduc, Dan J., Partner, Ogilvy Renault LLP/S.E.N.C.R.L, s.r.l. - Ottawa, 1071
Leduc, Jacques, Directeur, Sherbrooke, 819-821-5677, 744
Leduc, James, Mayor, Bradford West Gwillimbury, 706
Leduc, Jean, Chief Administrative Officer, Russell, 729
Leduc, Jean-Jacques, Salaberry-de-Valleyfield, 450-371-5099, 744
Leduc, Marc, Fire Chief, Greater Sudbury / Grand Sudbury, 710
Leduc, Philip, Leader, Westest, 430
Leduc, Pierre-Yves, Associé, Stikeman Elliott LLP - Montréal, 1087
Ledwell, Keith, Contact, FLIR Systems, Inc., 197
Lee, Chin, Toronto, 721
Lee, Chris, President, LH - Division of Full Circle Organics Inc., 272
Lee, Clifford J., Mayor, Charlottetown, 732
Lee, Darryl, City Clerk, Brantford, 707
Lee, E. Jung, Partner, Macleod Dixon LLP, 1052
Lee, Howard, President, Diagnostix Ltd., 163
Lee, Jack, President, Consulting Engineers of British Columbia, 903
Lee, Jack, Vice President, Opus DaytonKnight Consultants Ltd., 313

Executive Name Index

Lee, Ken-Beck, President/CEO, New East Consulting Services Ltd., 301
Lee, Norman, Director, Waste Management, Peel, 703
Lee, Pat, Norwich, 728
Lee, Raelene L., Partner, Ottenheimer Baker, 1066
Lee, Robert, President, Versatech Industries Inc., 412
Lee, Sandy, Minister, 606
Lee, Serena, SimpsonWigle LAW LLP, 1068
Lee, Tang G., Professor of Architecture, Tang G. Lee Architect, 386
Lee, Vivian, Coordinator, Canadian Space Society, 888
Lee Dalton, Diana, Chair, 610
Lee, BSc.,B.A.,M.A.,LL.B., Michael L., Partner, Lawson Lundell LLP - Vancouver, 1061
Lee, Q.C., Brock G., Lee & Lee, 1063
Lee-Bun, Turney, Branch Manager, Peto MacCallum Ltd., 321
Lee-Bun, Turney, President, Peto MacCallum Ltd., 321
Leeder, Dianne, Treasurer, Huntsville, 711
Leedham, Bill, Sr. Environmental Engineer, Naylor Engineering Associates Ltd., 299
Leekha, Peter, Managing Director, Sandwell Engineering Inc., 357
Leeman, Robert, President, EITNL/Earth Information Technologies (nfld) Limited, 174
Leenhouts, Pieter, Vice-President, Ontario Woodlot Association, 981
Lees, Christine, District Clerk, Muskoka, 702
Lees, Jeff G., Port Hope, 728
Lees, Mike, President, Babcock & Wilcox Canada Ltd., 100
Leese, Dave, Contact, Lansdowne Outdoor Recreational Development Association, 948
Leeson, Patricia, Gowling Lafleur Henderson LLP - Calgary, 1051
Lefaivre, Thérèse, Director, Community Services, Clarence-Rockland, 708
Lefebvre, Gabriel, Borden Ladner Gervais LLP - Montréal, 1083
Lefebvre, Guy, Manager, Flygt Canada, 198
Lefebvre, Guylaine, Directrice régionale, Fusionex inc., 203
Lefebvre, Joan, Trois-Rivières, 745
Lefebvre, Madeleine, University Librarian, St Mary's University, 1136
Lefebvre, Michel, Terrebonne, 745
Lefebvre, Roger, Président, 646
Lefebvre, Sylvie, Environmental Consultant, Pepin Prevention des Pertes Inc., 321
Leferink, Bert, President, Leferink Transfer Ltd., 266
Leflar, Dave, City Clerk, Medicine Hat, 403-529-8234, 673
Lefrançois, Carol, Bibliothécaire, DRDC Valcartier, R&D pour La defense Canada, Valcartier, 1186
Lefrançois, Guy, Bibliothécaire/Directeur, Campus d'Edmundston, 1126
Lefrançois, Paul, President, Technisol Environnement, 388
Lefton, Hartley, Lang Michener LLP - Toronto, 1077
Lefton, Jay A., Senior Partner, Ogilvy Renault LLP/S.E.N.C.R.L., s.r.l. - Toronto, 1078
Legailt, Marc, Superintendent, The Nation, 731
Légaré, Francine, Laval, 736
Legaré, François, Executive Director, Legaré F., Ing. Forestier Conseil, 266
Legault, Claudine, Bibliothécaire, Collège St-Jean-Vianney, 1173
Legault, David, Directeur, Repentigny, 450-470-3840, 740
Legault, Francine, Partner, Heenan Blaikie S.E.N.C.R.L/SRL, 1084
Legault, Jacques, Agent de liaison, Régie d'assainissement des Coteaux, 759
Legault, Leonard, President & Co-Founder, All-Wood Fibre Ltd., 79
Legault, Marcel, Saugeen Shores, 719
Legault, Pierre, Gowling Lafleur Henderson S.E.N.C.R.L./LLP, 1084
Legault, Richard, President & CEO, Brookfield Power, 117
Legault, Wendy, Managing Director, All-Wood Fibre Ltd., 79
Legault, FCILT, Gilles, Chair, Chartered Institute of Logistics and Transport in North America, 894
Legault-Bernier, Ginette, Laval, 736
Legé, Christine, Stikeman Elliott LLP - Montréal, 1087
Legendre, Renaud, Thetford Mines, 418-423-2349, 745
Léger, Claude, Directeur général, Montréal, 738
Léger, Claude, Senior Advisor, Canadian Council of Forest Ministers, 864
Leger, Denis, Commissioner, Corporate Services, Kingston, 712
Leger, Linda, Collections Librarian, Malaspina University-College, 1113
Leger, Marc, Deputy Minister, 596
Leger, Maurice, Vice-President, Stantec Inc., 378

Léger, Sylvain, Sylvain Léger, 384
Léger, M.Sc., MLIS, Lori W., Manager of Library Services, South-East Regional Health Authority, 1129
Legere, Delaina, Sales, Tanknology Canada Inc., 386
Legge, John A., Partner, Heenan Blaikie LLP - Vancouver, 1060
Legge, Michael, Treasurer, Brock, 724
Leggett, Casey L., Borden Ladner Gervais LLP - Vancouver, 1058
Leggett, Marsha, Councillor at Large, Kincardine, 519-368-7644, 726
Leggett, Mike, Councillor, Kincardine, 519-396-4529, 726
Leggott, Mark, University Librarian, University of Prince Edward Island, 1166
LeGoffe, Bob, Executive Director, SARCAN Recycling, 358
Legrand, Stéphane, Saint-Jean-sur-Richelieu, 450-545-9515, 742
Legris, Yves, Saint-Jérôme, 450-438-1076, 743
Lehman, Jeff, Mayor, Barrie, 705-792-7900, 706
Lehmann, Quenton, Manager, Saanich, 250-475-5441, 688
Lehoux, Geneviève, Technicienne, Collège Lafllèche, 1186
Lehoux, Marc-André, Directeur, Saint-Basile-le-Grand, 741
Lehoux, Richard, Préfet, La Nouvelle-Beauce, 748
Leibovici, Karen, Edmonton, 780-496-8120, 672
Leifso, Perry, Aquateck Ltd., 89
Leigh, Andria, Director, Development Services, Oro-Medonte, 728
Leighton, Catherine, Coordinator, Recycling Council of Ontario, 993
Leipnitz, Lori, Director, Cochrane, 403-851-2510, 671
Leis, Don, President, International Flying Farmers, 939
Leishman, Joan, Director, Gerstein Science Information Centre, 1158
Leishman, Scott, Manager, Bartle & Gibson Co. Ltd., 102
Leitch, Dave, Manager, Cowichan Valley, 677
Leitch, Donald N., Chief Administrative Officer & Clerk, Central Elgin, 724
Leitch, Doug, Manager, International Sales, Armtec Construction Products, 91
Leitch, Frederick E., Thoman Soule LLP, Lawyers, 1069
Leite, Darrin W., Director, Langley, 604-514-2806, 681
Leitold, Daina, Tour Manager, Green Kids Inc., 925
Leitold, Michael A., Roach, Schwartz & Associates, Barristers & Solicitors, 1079
Lejeune, Guylaine, Sept-Iles, 744
Lelièvre, François, Directeur, Shawinigan, 744
Lelièvre, Gaétan, Directeur général, Gaspé, 735
Lelievre, Martin, Directeur général, L'Assomption, 736
Lelievre, Steve, Head Librarian, Engineering Library, 1127
Lemaire, Alain, Lévis, 736
Lemaire, Alain, President & CEO, Papiers Perkins, 131, 318
Lemaire, Alain, President/CEO, Cascades Inc., 130
Lemaire, Carole, Greffière, Candiac, 734
Lemay, André, Tremblay, Bois, Mignault & Lemay, 743, 1089
Lemay, Christine, Bibliothécaire, Institut Maurice-Lamontagne, 1170
LeMay, Helen, Sales Coordinator, Megasecur Inc., 286
Lemay, Jean-Paul, Régie intermunicipale d'aqueduc et d'égout de Lotbinière-Centre, 418-728-3976, 759
Lemay, Jeannot, Repentigny, 450-585-6594, 740
Lemay, Louise, Boisbriand, 734
Lemay, Luc, Engineer, Groupe Sodinco inc., 221
Lemay, Marie, CEO, 545
Lemay, Mario, Sainte-Julie, 743
Lemay, Paul, Chief Building Official, Mississippi Mills, 714
Lemay, Paul, Directeur, Laval, 450-662-4343, 736
Lemay, Treena, Petawawa, 717
LeMay, William L., Partner, Hicks Morley Hamilton Stewart Storie LLP, 1076
LeMesurier, James F., Partner, Stewart McKelvey Stirling Scales - Saint John, 1065
Lemieux, Dan, Sr. Deputy Fire Chief, Grande Prairie, 780-538-0398, 672
Lemieux, Fred M., Director, RSP International Inc., 354
Lemieux, Frédéric, Directeur général, Dolbeau-Mistassini, 735
Lemieux, John F., Fraser Milner Casgrain S.E.N.C.R.L./LLP, 1084
Lemieux, Kevin, Contact, Weir Power & Industrial, 424
Lemieux, Luc, Préfet, Beauce-Sartigan, 747
Lemieux, Martine, Secteur du soutien informatique et administratif, Université Laval, 1181
Lemieux, Michel, Directeur, Trois-Rivières, 819-372-4621, 745
Lemieux, Robert, Président-directeur général, 647
Lemieux, Roger, St. Albert, 780-460-7223, 674
Lemieux, Ron, Minister, 588

Lemieux, CA, OMA, Jacques, Trésorier, Salaberry-de-Valleyfield, 450-370-4320, 744
Lemire, Brian, COO, Emery International Developments, 177
Lemire, Jacques, Longueuil, 737
Lemire, Phil, Fire Chief, White Rock, 604-541-2122, 686
Lemke, Gary, Lennox Industries (Canada) Ltd., 267
Lemke, Norm, Chief Administrative Officer & Clerk, Renfrew, 704
Lemmens, Matti, Borden Ladner Gervais LLP - Calgary, 1049
Lemoine, Pierre C., Rebuts Solides Canadiens Inc., 343
Lemoing, Denis, Director, AIRCOM Technologies Inc., 75
Lemon, Cynthia, Meaford, 519-376-1013, 727
Lemon, Doug, Manager, Flygt Canada, 198
Lemon, Louise, Deputy Minister, 597
Lemon, Peter, Owen Sound, 717
Lenaerts, Vincent, President, Bodycot Analex Inc., 113
Lenders, Taryn, President, Southern Alberta Health Libraries Association, 1010
Lenehan, Don, Councillor at Large, Riverview, 506-386-4483, 692
Lenfesty, Tracy, Head librarian, Nova Scotia Dept. of Natural Resources, 1136
Lenhardt, Larry, Organic Crop Producers & Processors Ontario Inc., 982
Lennox, Jerry, President, Lennox Drum Ltd., 267
Lennox, Ray, Vice-President, Lennox Drum Ltd., 267
Lennox, Robert, Georgian Bluffs, 725
Lenser, Elise, Stikeman Elliott LLP - Toronto, 1080
Lenters, M.Sc.Pl., MCIP,, Harold, Director, Planning & Building, Georgina, 709
Lentsch, Joanne, DuMoulin, Boskovich, 1059
Lentz, Norm, Renfrew, 613-758-2061, 704
Leonard, Carol Anne, Vice-President, Pipe Specialties Canada, 325
Leonard, Frank, Mayor, Saanich, 250-475-5510, 688
Leonard, John, President/CEO, TRACC (NB), 400
Leonard, Marjory, Treasurer, Collingwood, 708
Leonard, Mike, Chief Building Official, Oshawa, 716
Leonard, Ray, Manager, Penny & Casson Co., 321
Leonard, Robert, President, Pipe Specialties Canada, 325
Leonard, Wish, Manager, Circulation Services, Resource Sharing, University of Waterloo, 1165
Lepage, André, Partner, Heenan Blaikie S.E.N.C.R.L/SRL - Québec, 1088
Lepage, Claire, Deputy Minster, 593
Lepage, Jean-François, Partner, Lavery, de Billy - Montréal, 1085
Lepage, Lisette, Québec, 740
Lepage, Michel, Président, Société Provancher d'histoire naturelle du Canada, 1006
Lepage, Mike, Project Director, RWDI AIR Inc., 354
LePage, Pierre, Bélanger, Sauvé, 1082
Lepage, Serge, Greffier & Directeur général, Sainte-Anne-des-Plaines, 743
Lepage, Sylvain, Associé, Cain Lamarre Casgrain Wells - Québec, 1087
Lepage-Gareau, Louise, Treasurer, Prescott & Russell, 729
Lépine, Ernest, Laval, 450-978-8777, 736
Lepine, Peter A., Superintendent, Coquitlam, 604-945-1550, 680
Lepp, Dave, Niagara, 702
Leppard, Sally, President/CEO, LURA Consulting, 275
Leprette, Hannah, Library Assistant, Port Alberni Regional Campus Library, 1114
Leptick, Steve, Interim President/CEO, International Bio-Recovery Corp., 245
Lerat, Phyllis G., Head, Library, Saskatoon Campus Library, 1190
Lerat, Phyllis G., University Librarian, First Nations University of Canada, 1188
Leriche, Peter, President, Reliance Geological Services Inc., 344
Leroux, Andy, Branch Manager, CenturyVallen, 136
Leroux, Debbie, Clerk & Officer, Uxbridge, 731
Leroux, Doug, Simcoe, 704
Leroux, Gilles, President, Decibel Consultants Inc., 159
LeRoux, P.Eng., R., Director, Public Works, Grimsby, 710
Leroy, Denise, Acting Head, Library Services, Northern Forestry Centre, 1106
Lesage, Raymond, Sous-ministre adjoint, 654
Lesarge, Chris, Assistant to Head, William R. Lederman Law Library, 1143
Leshner, Alan I., Chief Executive Officer, American Association for the Advancement of Science, 822
Lesiuk, Barry, President, Interra Environmental Inc., 246
Lesiuk, Steven L., Singleton Urquhart LLP, 1062
Leskie, Victoria, Clerk, Prince Edward, 703
Leskiw, Leonard, President, Paragon Soil & Environmental Consulting Inc., 318

Executive Name Index

Leslie, Bill, Manager, Universal Handling Equipment Company Limited, 406
Leslie, Glenn F., Partner & General Counsel, Blake, Cassels & Graydon LLP - Toronto, 1072
Leslie, Kathleen, Manager, Kings County, 902-690-6155, 696
Lesniak, Ken, Chair, 570
Lesperance, Maureen, Coordinator, Planning, Lakeshore, 712
Lesperance, Robert J., Lesperance Mendes, 1061
Lesperance, Yvon, Vice President & Region Manager, Armtec Construction Products, 92
Lessard, Caroline, Coordonnatrice, Collège Shawinigan, 1184
Lessard, Claude, Sept-Iles, 744
Lessard, Daniel, Saint-Georges, 742
Lessard, Daniel, Directeur, Québec, 740
Lessard, Isabelle, Conseillère, Les Composts du Québec inc., 268
Lessard, Jean-Yves, Directeur, Alma, 733
Lessard, Jocelyn, Directeur général, Fédération québécoise des coopératives forestières, 916
Lessard, Laurent, Ministre, 643
Lessard, Martin, Directeur général, Victoriaville, 746
Lessard, Pierre-Olivier, Langlois Kronström Desjardins, 1088
Lesser, Gord, Ingersoll, 711
Lessif, John, Oxford, 728
Lessif, John, Mayor, Tillsonburg, 721
Lesueur, David D., Brockville, 707
Letalik, Norman G., Partner, Borden Ladner Gervais LLP - Toronto, 1073
Letellier, Sylvie, Director General, 549
Letendre, André, Québec, 740
Lethbridge, Sid, Principal, LEHDER Environmental Services Ltd., 267
Létourneau, Anne, Québec, 740
Létourneau, Bernard, Directeur général, Montmagny, 738
Létourneau, Pierre, Executive Vice-President, Labrie Environmental Group, 262
Létourneau, Raymond, Saint-Constant, 742
Létourneau, Rocky G., Welland, 722
Lettre, Christian, Victoriaville, 819-357-8573, 746
Leung, Cindy, Director, GLOBE Foundation, 924
Leung, Mark, Borden Ladner Gervais LLP - Vancouver, 1058
Levac, Claude, Prescott & Russell, 729
Levac, Johanna (Annie), Treasurer, North Glengarry, 727
Levac, Neil, President, Levac Robichaud Leclerc Associates Ltd., 270
Levac, Norm, General Manager, Infrastructure & Municipal Works, Cornwall, 708
Levac, Rheal, Superintendent, West Nipissing, 732
Levak, Natalie, Newpark Environmental Services, 303
Levasseur, Angele, Contact, GILFAB, 212
Levasseur, Denis, Responsable, Web, Université du Québec École de technologie supérieure, 1176
Leveillé, Marie-Eve, Borden Ladner Gervais LLP - Montréal, 1083
Leveillé, Yvon, President, Teckn-O-Laser, 388
Léveillée, Réjean, Sales Manager, Les Bras d'Fer Gingras Inc., 268
Levene, Adam L., Aikins, MacAulay & Thorvaldson LLP, 1063
Lever, Todd, Timmins, 721
Leverman, Phil, President, Envirosystems Inc., 187
Levert, Lyne, Boisbriand, 734
Lévesque, André, Vice-President & COO, Les Laboratoires Shermont Inc., 269
Lévesque, Anne-Marie, Lavery, de Billy - Montréal, 1085
Lévesque, Bill, Deputy Minister, 592
Lévesque, Clermont, Terrebonne, 745
Levesque, D., Director, Calgary, 121
Lévesque, Denis, Directeur général, Terrebonne, 745
Lévesque, Gaston, Directeur, La Nouvelle-Beauce, 748
Lévesque, Ghislain, Maire, Sept-Iles, 744
Lévesque, Ghislain, Préfet, Sept-Rivières, 753
Lévesque, Johanne, Director, Community Sustainability, Ottawa, 716
Lévesque, Karine, Bibliothécaire, Institut de technologie agro-alimentaire de Saint-Hyacinthe, 1183
Lévesque, Keith, Coordinator, ArcticNet Inc., 829
Lévesque, Louis, Deputy Minister, 529
Lévesque, Marie-Andrée, Daigneault, avocats inc., 1083
Lévesque, Martial, Sept-Iles, 744
Lévesque, Maxime, R.J. Lévesque et Fils Ltée, 341
Lévesque, Michel, Chef de service, Québec Ministère de l'agriculture, des pêcheries et de l'alimenta, 1179
Lévesque, Nancy, Director, Thompson Rivers University, 1112
Lévesque, Serge, Sept-Iles, 744
Lévesque, Yves, Maire, Trois-Rivières, 745

Lévesque, CA, André, Directeur, Montmagny, 418-248-3361, 738
Levesque-Finn, Sylvie, President, 597
Levi, John, Mayor, Mississippi Mills, 714
Levin, Michael, Chief Engineer, Mirus International Inc., 291
Levine, Dan, Sales Contact, Warco Process Technologies, 416
Levine, Neil, Contact, Suncor Energy Products, 382
Leviten-Reid, Ph.D., Catherine, President, Canadian Association for Studies in Co-operation, 856
Levitt, Bruce, President/CEO, Levitt-Safety Limited, 271
Levitt, Darryl, Counsel, Macleod Dixon LLP, 1077
Levitt, Howard A., Lang Michener LLP - Toronto, 1077
Levy, Chico, Saint-Lazare, 743
Levy, Eric M., Partner, Heenan Blaikie S.E.N.C.R.L/SRL, 1084
Levy, Isra, Medical Officer of Health, Ottawa, 716
Levy, Michael H., Director, Polystyrene Packaging Council, 987
Lévy, Yolette, Val-d'Or, 746
Levy, B.A., LL.B., Alan D., Levy, Alan D., 1077
Lew, Shirley, Coordinator, Library Systems, Vancouver Community College, 1119
Lewandowski, Richard, General Manager, Endress+Hauser Canada Ltd., 178
Lewin, David, Chair, Canadian Clean Power Coalition, 862
Lewis, B., Supervisor, Roads & Fleet, Pembroke, 717
Lewis, Brian, General Manager, Genzyme Canada Inc., 210
Lewis, Bryan, Councillor, Halton Hills, 710
Lewis, Dave, Executive Director, Truck Loggers Association, 1014
Lewis, David H., President, Ecocern Inc., 171
Lewis, Don, Mayor, Grey, 700
Lewis, Don J.W., Manager, Planning & Enforcement, South Dundas, 730
Lewis, Gerard, CAO, Mount Pearl, 709-748-1025, 694
Lewis, Judy, General Manager, Abbotsford, 604-864-5532, 679
Lewis, Karen, Manager, Corporate Communications & Strategic Init, Thunder Bay, 807-625-3859, 721
Lewis, Margaret, Clerk, Thames Centre, 731
Lewis, Michael, Chair, Rainy River District Social Services Admini, Rainy River, 729
Lewis, Michelene, Marketing Specialist, Geosoft, 212
Lewis, Mo, Commissioner, Finance, Brampton, 706
Lewis, Trevor, Director, Public Works, Dufferin, 699
Lewis, Vivian, Associate University Librarian, Services, McMaster University, 1141
Lewis, Wayne, Vice-President, Canadian Fishery Consultants Ltd., 124
Lhussier, Philippe, CEO, Anderson Water Systems, 85
Li, Frank, Manager, Napier-Reid Ltd., 297
Li, Joe, York, 705
Li, Joe, Regional Councillor, Markham, 713
Li, Leonard, President, RICHWAY Environmental Technologies Ltd., 346
Li, Lilian, Information/Technology Librarian, Medicine Hat College, 1109
Liang, Dong C., President, Aurora Instruments Ltd., 98
Liang, Fay, General Manager, Aurora Instruments Ltd., 98
Liber, K., Director, Toxicology Centre, 399
Liber, Karsten, Director, University of Saskatchewan, 406
Librecz, Brenda, Commissioner, Community & Fire Services, Markham, 905-479-7761, 713
Lichach, Kevin, General Manager, Community Services, Norfolk, 702
Lichtenwald, Kyle, Vice-President, Saskatchewan Outdoor & Environmental Education Association, 1001
Liddy, Deacon, Contact, Conestoga-Rovers & Associates, 149
Liddy, Paul, President/CEO, Suncurrent Industries Inc., 382
Lidgren, Roy, Vice-Mayor, Sturgeon County, 780-939-8250, 670
Lidsler, S., Chief Executive Officer, Wheatland Regional Centre Inc. & SARCAN Recycling, 431
Lieber, CAE, H. Stephen, President & Chief Executive Officer, Healthcare Information & Management Systems Society, 928
Lieff, Norman B., Senior Partner, Ogilvy Renault LLP/S.E.N.C.R.L., s.r.l. - Ottawa, 1071
Liefso, Janet, Certification Manager, Organic Producers Association of Manitoba Co-operative Inc., 982
Liegey, Yvan, President, John Meunier Inc., 253
Liepert, Ron, Minister, 567
Lif, Sten S., Chief Administrative Officer, Kenora District Serv, Kenora, 807-223-2100, 726
Ligard, Owen, Director, Beaver Regional Waste Management Services Commission, 757
Light, Eric, Acting Vice-President, 663
Lightfoot, Shaune, Director, Human Resources, Hastings, 700
Lighthall, Peter, Vice-President, AMEC, 82
Lileikis, Walt, Plant Manager, Sleegers Engineering Inc., 370

Lilley, Lance, Planner, Fraser Valley, 677
Lilya, Panova, Trade Commissioner, 768
Lim, David, President, Pacific Engineering Inc., 316
Lim, Eileen, Chief, Client Services, Public Works & Government Services Canada, 1168
Lim, Hoong, Librarian, Burnaby Hospital, 1110
Lim, Joe, President, Island Clean Air Inc., 248
Lim, Monica, Section Head, AECL Library Services, Atomic Energy of Canada Ltd., 1139
Lim, Susan, Library Clerk, Acuren Inc., 1104
Lima, Felipe, CFO, St. Marys Cement Inc., 356
Limaye, Vidya, Vice-President, MacDonnell Group, 277
Limbrick, Bill, Vice-President, 629
Limoges, Julie, Technicienne de la documentation, Québec Ministère des affaires municipales et des Régions, 1179
Lin, Jeffrey, Vice-President, DynaMotive Energy Systems Corporation, 168
Lin, Richard, Chair, DynaMotive Energy Systems Corporation, 168
Lincourt, Jean-Philippe, Lavery, de Billy - Montréal, 1085
Lind, Carol, Coordinator, East Kootenay, 677
Lind, Richard, President/CEO, Everts-Lind Enterprises, 191
Lindahl, Lori, Vice-President, Vancouver Fraser Port Authority, 409
Lindauer, Martha, Contact, Society of Toxicology, 1009
Linde, Lorette, Librarian/Records Administrator, Calgary Utilities & Environmental Protection, 1099, 1100
Lindeman, Katherine E., McCaffery Mudry Pritchard LLP, Barristers & Solicitors, 1052
Linder, Al, President, Western Scrap Metals, 430
Lindsay, Craig, President, Pacesetter Sales & Associates Inc., 316
Lindsay, David, Deputy Minister, 634
Lindsay, David L., Deputy Minister, 631
Lindsay, Herbert J., President, Herby Enterprises Ltd., 229
Lindsay, J.G., President, Canadian Benthic Ltd., 124
Lindsay, Matthew R., Managing Partner (Calgary), Fraser Milner Casgrain LLP - Calgary, 1051
Lindsay, Tim, Manager, Waterous Power Systems, 423
Lindsay, Tim G., Manager, Waterous Power Systems, 422
Lindsay Luby, Gloria, Toronto, 721
Lindsay, Q.C., Richard B., Founding Partner, Lindsay Kenney LLP, 1061
Lindsey, M.C., Sales Manager, Patterson Industries (Canada) Ltd., 319
Linett, Amanda, Partner, Stikeman Elliott LLP - Toronto, 1080
Linfield, Gerald, Inform Consulting Services Ltd., 241
Lingnau, Brian, Manager, Sealcon Liner Systems Inc., 361
Link, David, Director, Alberta Historical Resources Foundation, 817
Linkert, Mary Ruth, Administrator, McMaster University, 1141
Linkie, Dave, Chief Administration Officer, North Bay, 715
Linnen, Bill, Manager, Operations, Peterborough, 703
Linteau, Denis, Président, Lambert Somec inc., 263
Linton, Ed, Officer, Cloverdale Paint Inc., 144
Linton, Jeff, Executive Director, Alberta Bottle Depot Association, 816
Linzey, Doug, Secretary, Nature Nova Scotia (Federation of Nova Scotia Naturalists), 960
Lion, John, Sales Manager, Vansco Electronics Ltd., 409
Lipman, Richard, President, Wood Manufacturing Council, 1021
Lipman, Rosemarie, Stikeman Elliott LLP - Toronto, 1080
Lippert, Glen, President, Kentain Products Ltd., 256
Lippert, Wayne, Mayor, Vernon, 685
Lippold, Karen, Head of Information Services, Memorial University of Newfoundland, 1132
Lippoway, David, Regional Manager, Fort Garry Industries Ltd., 200
Lipsett, Colin G.W., Davis LLP - Edmonton, 1055
Lipton, Becky, Coordinator, Alberta Farmers' Market Association, 817
Lischynsky, Terry, Manager, Waterous Power Systems, 423
Liskowich, Mark, Principal Consultant, SRK Consulting (Canada) Inc., 376
Lister, Scott, Treasurer, Alberta Camping Association, 816
Liszka, Alexander, Macleod Dixon LLP, 1077
Liteplo, Jonathan M., Burnet, Duckworth & Palmer LLP, 1050
Lithwick, Marvin, Partner, Kahn Zack Ehrlich Lithwick, 1057
Litschko, Chris, President/CEO, Bracebridge Generation Ltd., 115
Little, Allan, Superintendent, Drainage, & Construction Inspector, Lambton Shores, 726
Little, Andrew M., Weaver, Simmons LLP, 1072
Little, Christopher, Conseiller, Denis-Benjamin-Viger, Montréal, 738

Executive Name Index

Little, Doug, Simcoe, 704
Little, Doug, Deputy Mayor & Councillor, Adjala-Tosorontio, 705-435-9020, 724
Little, Doug, Vice-President, 583
Little, H.A. Patrick (Pat), Heelis, Williams, Little & Almas LLP, Barristers & Solicitors, 1072
Little, Mike, North Vancouver, 688
Little, Robert W., Partner, Hicks Morley Hamilton Stewart Storie LLP, 1076
Little, Q.C., R.A., Cunningham, Swan, Carty, Little & Bonham LLP, 1069
Littlejohns, Caroline, Bibliothécaire, SNC-Lavalin inc., 1175
Litton, KayLynn G., Partner, Macleod Dixon LLP, 1052
Litzenberger, Tanya, Blaney McMurtry LLP, 1073
Liu, Catro, Richmond Hill, 718
Liu, Phyllis, Technical Services Librarian, Kwantlen University College, 1113
Liu, Wei, RICHWAY Environmental Technologies Ltd., 347
Livey, John, Chief Administrative Officer, Markham, 905-479-7755, 713
Livings, John, Armatek Controls Limited, 91
Livingston, Bruce, Chair, Canadian Parks Partnership, 881
Livingston, Dan, PRT Inc., 336
Livingston, Kathleen, Executive Director & COO, Saskatchewan Environmental Industry & Managers' Association, 1000
Livingston, Mark, Manager, Westburne Canada, 427
Livingstone, David, Project Coordinator, 609
Livingstone, Gary, President/CEO, Opcon Pacific Recycling Ltd., 313
Livingstone, Greg, General Manager, Opcon Pacific Recycling Ltd., 313
Livingstone, Steve, Vice-President, Franz Environmental Inc., 201
Lizotte, Jean Marie, Marketing Contact, Enviroservices Inc., 187
Lizotte-MacPherson, Linda, Commissioner & CEO, 516
Llewellyn, Dennis, Chamber Manager, Chamber of Mines of Eastern British Columbia, 894
Llewellyn, Jason, Director, Bulkley-Nechako, 250-692-3195, 676
Llewellyn, Scott, Conestoga-Rovers & Associates, 149
Llewellyn-Thomas, Kathleen, Commissioner, Transportation Services, York, 705
Lloyd, B., Coordinator, Northwatch, 966
Lloyd, Dale, Councillor, Kings County, 696
Lloyd, David, Customer Service Director, Weyerhaeuser Company Ltd., 430
Lloyd, Duncan, Chair, Lethbridge Regional Water Services Commission, 757
Lloyd, Evan, Acting Executive Director, Commission for Environmental Cooperation, 898
Lloyd, Evan, Executive Director, 525
Lloyd, Gordon, Vice-President, Canadian Chemical Producers' Association, 862
Lloyd, Kevin, Collingwood, 708
Lloyd, Richard, Director, Kings County, 902-690-6111, 696
Lloyd, Rick, Deputy Mayor & Councillor, Collingwood, 708
Lloyd, Stephen, Fraser Milner Casgrain S.E.N.C.R.L./LLP, 1084
Loan, Marilyn, Manager, Human Resources, King, 726
Lobb, T., Carrier Canada Ltd., 130
Lobo, Suzana A., Ogilvy Renault LLP/S.E.N.C.R.L., s.r.l. - Toronto, 1078
Locat, Gilles, Directeur, Matawinie, 750
Locatelli, Lou, Contact, Church & Trought Inc., 140
Locatelli, Lou, Vice Chair, Canadian Environmental Certification Approvals Board, 867
Lochhead, Mary, Head Librarian, Architecture & Fine Arts Library, 1122
Locke, Anita, Smith-Ennismore-Lakefield, 729
Locke, Herb, General Manager, Tri-Arrow Industrial Recovery Inc., 401
Locke, Jeffrey W., Fulton & Company LLP, Lawyers & Trade-Mark Agents, 1056
Locke, Jim, Mount Pearl, 694
Locke, Jim, Deputy Mayor & Councillor, South Dundas, 730
Locke, Michael, Coordinator, Western Canadian Spill Services Ltd., 429
Lockerby, CPP, Vivianne, Supervisor, Brandon, 689
Locking, Mark, Director, Airdrie, 670
Lockyer, Gord, Treasurer & Director, Financial Management & Repor, Niagara, 702
Lodermeier, Phil, Supervisor, Lacombe County, 669
Lodge, Andy W., Barry Spalding - Saint John Office, 1065
Lodge, Malcolm, Chief Technical Officer, Entegrity Wind Systems Inc., 181
Lodge, Malcolm A., Founder & President, Island Technologies Inc., 248

Lodge, W.O., MacDonald & Fils Inc., 277
Lodick, G., Environment Coordinator, Bema Co. Ltd., 105
Loeper, Garry, Sr. Project Manager, Notra Inc., 308
Loeppky, Byron, Partner, Macleod Dixon LLP, 1077
Loewen, Dave, Abbotsford, 679
Loewen, Ernie, President, Loewen Welding & Manufacturing Ltd., 273
Loewen, Stan, Manager, TerraLink Horticulture Inc., 390
Loewen, Tom, District Manager, BFI Canada Inc., 106
Loewenberg, Madeleine L.S., Ogilvy Renault LLP/S.E.N.C.R.L., s.r.l. - Toronto, 1078
Loewig, Hans, Chief Administrative Officer, Guelph, 519-837-5602, 710
Logan, David, Purchasing Agent, Saint John, 506-658-2930, 692
Logan, Fred, Logan Geotech Inc., 273
Logan, Kerrie J., Partner, Macleod Dixon LLP, 1052
Logan, Kim, Alberta Cogenerators Council, 816
Logan, Penny, Manager, Library Services, Capital Health, 1135
Loh, Andrew, Partner, Borden Ladner Gervais LLP - Vancouver, 1058
Lohse, Andy, Principal, SMS Engineering Ltd., 371
Loiacono, Joseph, Manager, Sanexen Environmental Services Inc., 357
Loiselle, Nicole, Directrice générale, Deux-Montagnes, 747
Loiselle, Rick, President, Ontario Fire Buff Associates, 973
Lojk, Robert, Director, 520
Loken, Dave, Edmonton, 672
Lokken, Diana, General Manager, Capital Regional District, 250-360-3010, 676
Lombardi, David, President, Seaforth Engineering Group Inc., 361
Lombardi, Paula, Siskind, Cromarty, Ivey & Dowler LLP, 1069
Lommer, Josh, MacPherson Leslie & Tyerman LLP - Saskatoon, 1090
London, Ron, Vice-President, Crown Packaging Ltd., 154
London, Q.C., Jack R., Counsel, Pitblado LLP, 1063
Lonergan, Guy, President, GEA Barr-Rosin Inc., 205
Lonergan, Robert M., Fasken Martineau - Vancouver, 1059
Loney, J. David, President, Anthrafilter Media & Coal Ltd., 86
Long, Bob, Langley, 687
Long, Garth, Chair, Kings County Region Solid Waste Commission, 506-433-1341, 758
Long, R.J., President, Long Environmental Consultants, 273
Long, Steve, Manager, Westburne Canada, 428
Long, Zane, Manager, Kings County, 696
Longard, Sharon, Reference, Dalhousie University Libraries, 1135
Longley, Ann L., Municipal Clerk, Kings County, 696
Longo, Angela, Deputy Minister, 635
Longo, Pat, Head, Cataloguing Services, Brock University, 1153
Longon, Jennifer, New Brunswick Dept. of Wellness, Culture & Sport, 1129
Longpré, Denis, Manager, Environment, Clarence-Rockland, 708
Longpré, François, Partner, Borden Ladner Gervais LLP - Montréal, 1083
Looby, Maureen A., Director, Public Works & Engineering, Middlesex Centre, 727
Look, Joe, Plant Manager, CCS Income Trust, 134
Looker, Norman, Vice-President, Cowater International Inc., 153
Loomer, Garnet, Contact, Loomers Pumping Services Ltd., 274
Loopstra, Al, President, Capital Environmental Resource Inc., 127
Loopstra, Q.C., C.M., Loopstra Nixon LLP, 1077
Looy, Linde, Aquatic Biologist, Fraser Environmental Services, 201
Lopatka, Sharon, Director, 571
Lopez, Henry, Manager, Petromax Ltd., 322
Loptson, Scott, McElhanney Consulting Services Ltd., 285
Loranger, Bruce, Manager, Westburne Canada, 427
Loranger, Christian, Directeur, Westburne Canada, 428
Lord, Alain, Shawinigan, 744
Lord, Andrew, Davis LLP - Toronto, 1074
Lord, Doug, President/CEO & Chair, Xerox Canada Ltd., 435
Lord, Guy, Partner, Osler, Hoskin & Harcourt S.E.N.C.R.L./LLP, 1086
Lord, Martin, Vice-President, GDG Environnement Ltée, 205
Lordon, Nancy, Miramichi, 691
Lorek, Annette, AV Librarian, Capilano College, 1114
Lorenz, Heidi, Councillor, Gravenhurst, 709
Lorenzato, Diane, Asst. Deputy Minister, 558
Lorimer, Peter R., President, Loraday Environmental Products Ltd., 274
Lorion, Johanne, Technicienne en documentation, CÉGEP St-Jean-sur-Richelieu, 1183
Lorje, B.A., M.A., Pat, Saskatoon, 754

Loroff, Brad, Manager, Transit, Thunder Bay, 807-684-2187, 721
Loroway, Jason, Sales, AMKO Systems Inc., 84
Lorraine, Maclauchlan, Sec.-Treas., Entomological Society of British Columbia, 910
Lortie, Jacques, Director, Public Works, Parks, & Recreation, Russell, 729
Lorusso, Carl J., Vice-President & General Manager, Wasteco, 421
Losier, Gary, Director, Quispamsis, 506-849-5749, 692
Losier, Marc, Director, Bathurst, 690
Lothian, Rob, Co-Owner, IRIS Environmental Systems Inc., 248
Lotimer, Jim, President, Lotek Wireless Inc., 274
Lott, Jeff, Superintendent & Officer-in-Charge, Nanaimo, 250-754-2345, 681
Lotzkar, Mark, President/General Manager, Pacific Metals Recycling International, 316
Loubier, Alain, Québec, 740
Loucks, Ronald H., President, R.H. Loucks Oceanology, 340
Louden, Blake, VP, Matrix Solutions Inc., 282
Louden, Brian, Edmonton Area Manager, BECK Drilling and Environmental Services Ltd., 104
Loughead, Bill, Innisfil, 711
Lougheed, Del, General Manager, General Scrap Partnership, 207
Lougheed, Doug, Innisfil, 711
Loughlin, Rita, Records/Information Manager, Sproule Associates Limited, 1103
Louie, Raymond, Metro Vancouver, 685, 678
Louis Chamard, Jean, Vice-President, Alenag Brokers, 77
Loukes, Peter, Director, Operations, Markham, 905-475-4894, 713
Loukidelis, David, Deputy Attorney General, 574
Lounsberry, Bob, Manager, Engineered Air, 180
Lourie, Bruce, Executive Director & President, Richard Ivey Foundation, 995
Love, David, Executive Director, Conservation Foundation, 901
Love, Grant, Fire Chief, North Bay, 715
Love, Peter, Chief Energy Conservation Officer, 622
Love, William, Manager, The Battery Broker Environmental Services Inc., 391
Lovegrove, Wendy, Secretary, Brampton Horticultural Society, 846
Lovelace, W. Scott, Chief Executive Officer, International Heavy Haul Association, 940
Lovell-Stanners, Ruth, Mayor, Grey, 700
Lovelock, Marty, Chief Librarian, Health Canada, 1150
Lovett, Lynn, Acting Senior General Counsel, 527
Lovshin, Mark, Northumberland, 702
Lovshin, Mark, Deputy Mayor & Councillor, Hamilton, 725
Low, David R., Chair, Hickling Arthurs Low Corp., 231
Low, Keith, Coordinator, Teck Resources, 1119
Low, Terry, Peterborough, 703
Lowe, Frederick Gordon, Calgary, 403-268-2430, 671
Lowe, H., President, Numet Engineering Ltd., 309
Lowe, Howard, Howard Marten Fluid Technologies Inc., 234
Lowe, John, Burnet, Duckworth & Palmer LLP, 1050
Lowe, Steve, Treasurer, Atlantic Turfgrass Research Foundation, 843
Lowery, Jamie, Commissioner, Community Services, Brampton, 706
Lowey, Mark, Editor, EnviroLine, 184
Lowman, Sandra, Regional Librarian, Natural Resources Canada, Canadian Forest Service, 1127
Lowndes, Carol, Secretary-Treasurer, Canadian Organic Livestock Association, 881
Lowrie, Jim, Director, New Westminster, 682
Lowry, Bill, Lennox & Addington, 613-583-2412, 701
Lowry, Bill, Deputy Reeve, Loyalist, 727
Lowry, Bill, Reeve, Loyalist, 727
Lowry, Linda, Head, Reference, Brock University, 1153
Lowry, Lynda, General Manager/COO, 585
Lowry, Mark, President, Ontario Association for Geographic & Environmental Education, 971
Lowry, Paul J., Partner, Borden Ladner Gervais LLP - Vancouver, 1058
Loyer, Marcel, Rouyn-Noranda, 741
Lozynsky, M. Kristen, Bennett Jones LLP - Calgary Office, 1049
Lu, George, General Manager, Golden Maple Leaf (Hangzhou) Technology Consulting Co. L, 214
Lu, Jennifer, Library Technician, British Columbia Ministry of Energy & Mines, 1120
Lubberts, Don, Fort Erie, 709
Lubberts, Walter, Technical Support Manager, Wynn's Canada Ltd., 435

Lubeck, Darren, Manager, North Peace Regional Landfill Commission, 758
Lubka, Lidia, Publisher/Editor, EcoLog Information Resources Group, 172
Lucas, Jean, Director, Eco Waste Solutions, 170
Lucas, Pat, Vice-President, Maxim Power Corp, 283
Lucas, Scott, Vice-President, Bentofix Technologies Inc., 105
Lucas, Shaune, Greater Napanee, 709
Lucas, B.A., Phillipe, Victoria, 685
Luce, Peter J., Director, R.J. Burnside & Associates Limited, 340
Lucey, William Patrick, President & Sr. Aquatic Ecologist, Aqua-Tex Scientific Consulting Ltd., 88
Luciani, Ted, Mayor, Thorold, 720
Lucier, Chris, Manager, Countryside Disposal Service Ltd., 153
Lucier, Chris or Pat, Countryside Disposal Service Ltd., 153
Lucier, Lawrence, Director, Countryside Disposal Service Ltd., 153
Lucier, Pat, Director, Countryside Disposal Service Ltd., 153
Luck, Ken, Director, Spruce Grove, 674
Lucot, Joe, President & Chief Operating Officer, West Point Products Canada, 425
Lucuik, Mark, Director, Morrison Hershfield, 293
Lucyshen, Ron, District Fire Chief (St. Andrews North), St. Andrews, 204-389-2004, 690
Lucyshyn, Troy, Leader, Westest, 430
Ludington, David, Councillor, North Perth, 715
Ludwig, Harry J., Partner, Macleod Dixon LLP, 1052
Ludwig, Paula, Library Technician, Vancouver Coastal Health Authority, 1119
Luff, Andy, Kawartha Lakes, 711
Luff, David, Treasurer, Canadian Centre for Energy Information, 861
Lui, Javis, Manager, Canadian Hydrogen & Fuel Cell Association, 871
Lui, Matthew, Borden Ladner Gervais LLP - Calgary, 1049
Luis, Cedeno, Trade Commissioner, 768
Lukacs, Joe, ETV Canada, 190
Lukacs, Joe, President/CEO, Canadian Environmental Technology Advancement Corporation - West, 137, 867
Luke, Charlie, Norfolk, 702
Lukka, Rishi, District Sales Rep., National Instruments Canada, 298
Luksun, Basil, Director, Burnaby, 604-294-7432, 679
Lum, Ann, Information Specialist, Imperial Oil Limited, 1158
Lumey, Lisa, Treasurer, Entomological Society of Alberta, 910
Lumsden, Dave, President, St. Marys Cement Inc., 356
Lunardo, Domenic, Commissioner, Community Services, Oakville, 715
Lunau, Cindy, Milton, 714
Lund, Peter, Chair, Halifax Regional Municipality, 695
Lund, Peter, Councillor, Halifax Regional Municipality, 695
Lund, Stephen, President/CEO, 610
Lund, P.Eng., Steve, Director, Tillsonburg, 721
Lundrigan, Glenn, Branch Manager, Safety-Kleen Canada Inc., 355
Lundrigan, Jennifer E., Stewart McKelvey Stirling Scales - St. John's, 1066
Lundy, Jonathan, Senior Vice-President, General Counsel & Corporate, 511
Lungle, May, Administrator, Boundary Organic Producers Association, 846
Lunney, Al, Lanark, 701
Lupien, Pierre, Technisol Environnement, 388
Lupien, Pierre, Asst. Manager, Technisol Environnement, 388
Lupton, Margaret E., Oxford, 519-485-2490, 728
Lura, Ken, Superintendent, Fort Saskatchewan, 780-992-6247, 672
Lurdes, Magneli, Trade Commissioner, 768
Lush, Teresa, Manager, Inland Technologies Inc., 242
Lussier, Catherine, Borden Ladner Gervais LLP - Montréal, 1083
Lussier, Guy, Rothsay, 352
Lussier, Richard, Controller, Canadian Electricity Association, 866
Lussier, Serge, Secretary-Treasurer, Canadian Association of Zoos & Aquariums, 859
Luszka, John R., Commissioner, Human Resources, Sault Ste. Marie, 720
Luton, B.A., John, Victoria, 685
Lutter, Lorelei, Director, Maxxam Analytics Ltd., 284
Luty, Jason, Nilex Inc., 304
Lutz, Douglas, McInnes Cooper, 1067
Lutzac, Marjorie, Coordinator, Moncton Campus, Library, 1128
Luyben, Jean, Library Instruction, Trent University, 1153
Luzak, Bruno, President, Associated Environmental Site Assessors of Canada, 829

Lyall, Drew, Executive Director, Stem Cell Network, 1010
Lyle, Dale, City Manager, Portage La Prairie, 689
Lyle, Garth, Summerside, 733
Lynch, Allen, Manager, West Vancouver, 604-984-9730, 682, 689
Lynch, Allen, Section Manager, North Vancouver, 604-984-9730, 688
Lynch, Barrie, Coquitlam, 680
Lyne, Joseph, Manager, Walker Industries Holdings Ltd., 416
Lyng, Joseph, Manager, Niagara Waste Systems Ltd., 303
Lynn, B.R., Marketing, Continental Conveyor Ontario Ltd., 151
Lynn, David, President/CEO, Continental Conveyor Ontario Ltd., 151
Lynn, John, Fire Chief, Barrie, 706
Lynn, W.D., Sales, Continental Conveyor Ontario Ltd., 151
Lyon, Duncan, Vice-President, Nemato Inc., 300
Lyons, Audrey, Acquisitions/Cataloguing, ARC Vegreville Library & Information Centre, 1109
Lyons, Beverley, Librarian, Saint John Campus Library, 1129
Lyons, Catherine, Goodmans LLP, 1075
Lyons, Michael, Secretary-Treasurer, British Columbia Environment Industry Association, 847
Lyons, Michel, Varennes, 746
Lyrette, Jacques, CEO, APS Aviation Inc., 87
Lyris, Primo, Commercial Officer, 767
Lysak, Travis, Borden Ladner Gervais LLP - Calgary, 1049
Lysakowski, George, Regional Manager, Velan Inc., 410
Lysyk, Stephanie P., Borden Ladner Gervais LLP - Vancouver, 1058
Lysyk, Tom, City Clerk, Lloydminster, 754

M

M., Calcott, Ambassador, 769
Ma, Cathy, Macleod Dixon LLP, 1077
Ma, Fung Ling, Director, Eco Canada, 170
Maaskant, John, Chairman, The Ontario Farm Animal Council, 973
Maass, Barbara, Bibliothécaire, Succursale de Québec, 1176, 1180
Maat, Derk Z., Vice-President, GPEC Global Corp., 215
Maayoufi, J.M., SDM, J. Walter Company Ltd., 249
Mabberi-Mudonyi, John, Director, Iqaluit, 867-979-5675, 698
Mabee, Jim, President, Ontario Horticultural Association, 975
Maber, Glenn, President, Triple M Fiberglass Mfg. Ltd., 401
MacAlpine, Andrew, Perth East, 728
MacArthur, Greg, Truro, 696
MacArthur, Q.C., Colin R., Aikins, MacAulay & Thorvaldson LLP, 1063
Macatee, Gordon, Deputy Minister, 580
MacAulay, Douglas, Sherbrooke, 744
MacAulay, Duart, Warden, Inverness County, 697
Macaulay, John, Manager, 596
Macaulay, Neil, President, Mac Industrial Exhaust Shop, 277
MacAuley, Kenneth M., President, MacAuley Group Ltd., 277
MacBride, Barry, Director, Winnipeg, 690
MacCallum, Brenda, Public Education Officer, Fundy Region Solid Waste Commission, 758
MacCallum, Greg, Manager, 642
MacCaskill, J.E., Regional Treasurer & Commissioner, Corporate Servi, Halton, 700
MacCharles, Quentin, President, Airmaster Sales Ltd., 75
MacCormac, Donald G., Chair, 638
MacCready-Williams, Nancy, CEO, 617
MacCuish, George A., Vice-President, JNE Consulting Ltd., 252
MacDiarmid, Hugh, President & Chief Executive Officer, 511
MacDonald, Aaron, Director, Summerside, 733
Macdonald, Brock, Executive Director, Recycling Council of British Columbia, 993
Macdonald, Cameron, Director, Publishing (NRC Research Press), Canada Institute for Scientific & Technical Information (CISTI), 1148
MacDonald, Carol, Head, Access Services, University of Regina Library, 1189
MacDonald, Carol, Vice-President, 597
MacDonald, Cathy, Dean of Learner Resources, Surrey Campus, 1113, 1115, 1116
MacDonald, Colleen, Manager, Parks, Cemeteries & Environment, Huntsville, 711
MacDonald, Dan, Nilex Inc., 304
MacDonald, Dan, President & CEO, 610
MacDonald, Darren, Manager, 642
Macdonald, Dave, Manager, Sherwin-Williams Canada Inc., 365
MacDonald, David, Charlottetown, 732
MacDonald, Ed, President, Maritime Auto Salvage, 280

MacDonald, Elaine, Cornwall, 708
MacDonald, Francine, President, MacDonald & Fils Inc., 277
MacDonald, Geoff, Planning Director, Chester District, 697
MacDonald, George, Councillor, Cape Breton, 695
MacDonald, Hilda, Councillor, Leamington, 726
MacDonald, Ian, Councillor, Riverview, 506-386-8756, 692
MacDonald, J., General Manager, Moncton / Ville de Moncton, 691
MacDonald, J. Ewen, General Manager, Infrastructure Services, South Glengarry, 730
MacDonald, Jackie, Regional Librarian, District Health Authorities 1, 2 & 3 (Western Nova Scotia), 1138
MacDonald, Jamie, North Glengarry, 727
MacDonald, Joan, Director General, 520
MacDonald, John B., Director, 641
MacDonald, Keith, Prince Edward, 703
MacDonald, Kemp, Municipal Planner, Antigonish County, 696
MacDonald, Ken, Technical Representative, Can-Am Instruments Ltd., 122
MacDonald, Kevin, Director, Cape Breton, 902-563-5051, 695
MacDonald, Linda, Executive Director, 609
MacDonald, Margaret F., Deputy Minister, 614
MacDonald, Mike, Director, Cantech Inspections Ltd., 127
MacDonald, Nathan B., Director, Electronics Product Stewardship Canada, 909
MacDonald, Norman, Manager, GENEQ Inc., 206
MacDonald, P.D. (Don), Partner, Borden Ladner Gervais LLP - Vancouver, 1058
Macdonald, Paul, Fire Chief, Essa, 725
MacDonald, Randy, Fire Chief, Charlottetown, 732
MacDonald, Reg, Owner, Honey Electric Ltd., 233
MacDonald, Robert, Vice-President, MacDonald & Fils Inc., 277
MacDonald, Rod, Vice-President, Noise Solutions Inc., 305
MacDonald, Rodney, Minister, 613
MacDonald, Ross A., Managing Partner, Stikeman Elliott LLP - Vancouver, 1062
Macdonald, Sandie, Essa, 705-424-6844, 725
Macdonald, Scott, President, Noise Solutions Inc., 305
Macdonald, Scott, President/General Manager, Envirogard Products Ltd., 184
MacDonald, Steve, Vice-President, Maritime Paper Products Ltd., 281
Macdonald, Thomas, Goodmans LLP, 1075
MacDonald, Tim, College Librarian, Northwest Community College Library, 1116
Macdonald, Tim, Owner, Hydro Dyne Inc., 236
MacDonald, William L., Clark Wilson LLP, 1058
MacDonald, Q.C., Alexander, Cox and Palmer - St. John's, 1065
MacDonald, Q.C., George W., McInnes Cooper, 1067
Macdonald, Q.C., Mark E., Stewart McKelvey Stirling Scales - Halifax, 1067
Macdonald, Q.C., Webster, Blake, Cassels & Graydon LLP - Calgary, 1049
MacDonald-Donovan, Jennifer, Communications Officer, 642
MacDonald-Pratt, Elizabeth, Co-ordinator, Circulation & Reserve, Bracken Health Sciences Library, 1142
Macdonell, Doug, Coquitlam, 680
MacDougall, Bev, Lambton, 701
MacDougall, Bev, City / County Councillor, Sarnia, 719
MacDougall, Bruce, Deputy Mayor & Councillor, Summerside, 733
MacDougall, Cindy, Emergency Measures Officer, 638
MacDougall, Colleen, Executive Director & Registrar, Natural Health Practitioners of Canada, 959
MacDougall, Donald, Deputy Superintendent, 607
MacDougall, Donna, Clerk, Kincardine, 726
MacDougall, Gary, Director, 607
Macdougall, Glenn, Director, Learning and Teaching Services, Algonquin College of Applied Arts & Technology, 1167
MacDougall, Jack, Leader, Green Party of New Brunswick, 926
MacDougall, Ken, Sales Manager, Armtec Construction Products, 92
MacDougall, P.J., Head, Reference, University of Toronto Massey College, 1163
MacEachern, Carna, Executive Director, Wood Buffalo Environmental Association, 1021
MacEachern, Melissa, Deputy Minister, 641
MacEachern, Mike, Simcoe, 704
MacEachern, Mike, Mayor, New Tecumseth, 714
MacEachern, Ronald, Acting Fire Chief, Mount Forest, Wellington North, 519-323-1441, 732
MacEwen, Kathy, Information & Promotion Assistant, Prince Edward Island Food Technology Centre, 1166
MacEwen, Philip, President, Canadian Society for the Study of Practical Ethics, 886

Executive Name Index

MacEwen, Richard, Contact, Conestoga-Rovers & Associates, 149
MacFadyen, Sterling, Deputy Mayor & Councillor, Charlottetown, 732
Macfarlane, Bruce, Corporate Secretary, 596
MacFarlane, Courtney, Donovan & Company, 1059
MacFarlane, Craig, City Solicitor, Surrey, 684
MacFarlane, Gordon, Director, Summerside, 733
MacFarlane, John D., JM Science Canada Inc., 252
MacFarlane, Ron, Director, 613
MacGillivray, Ernest, Director, 596
MacGillivray, Paula, Library Resource Manager, Syncrude Canada Ltd., 1106
MacGregor, Andrew, Manager, The DATA Group of Companies, 392
MacGregor, Bill, Abbotsford, 679
Macgregor, Bruce, Chief Administrative Officer, York, 705
MacGregor, Scott R., Chair, 594
Machan, James L., President, J&B Engineering Inc., 249
MacHattie, Ian, General Manager, L&M Feed Services, 261
Machibroda, Paul, President, P. Machibroda Engineering Ltd., 315
Machibroda, Ray, Manager, P. Machibroda Engineering Ltd., 315
Machida, N.K., Machida Mack Shewchuk Meagher LLP, 1052
Machum, D. Geoffrey, Stewart McKelvey Stirling Scales - Halifax, 1067
MacInnes, Campbell, Principal, Unies Limited, 405
MacInnes, Doug, Development Officer, Hants West District, 697
MacInnes, Sheldon, Celtic Music Researcher, Beaton Institute, 1134
MacInnis, Debbie, Paralibrarian/Head of Circulation, Cape Breton University, 1137
MacInnis, Kenneth, MacInnis, Kenneth Associates, 1067
Macintosh, Andy, Fire Chief, Orangeville, 716
Macintosh, Don, Fraser Milner Casgrain LLP - Toronto, 1075
MacIntyre, Dale, Vice-President, Safety-Kleen Canada Inc., 355
MacIntyre, Michael, Planning Manager, Grande Prairie, 780-538-0440, 672
Maciocia, Cosmo, Maire d'arrondissement, Montréal, 738
MacIsaac, Cathy, Director, 616
MacIsaac, Norma, Director, 614
MacIsaac, Pat, Chief, North Battleford, 754
MacIver, Don, Dufferin, 699
Mack, Scott, Director, Fort Saskatchewan, 780-992-6573, 672
MacKarl, K.W., Fire Chief, Whitby, 905-668-3312, 723
MacKay, Andrew S., Alexander Holburn Beaudin & Lang, LLP, 1057
MacKay, Art, Manager, Policy Planning, Belleville, 706
MacKay, Cam, St. Albert, 674
Mackay, Crystal, Executive Director, The Ontario Farm Animal Council, 973
MacKay, Grant, General Manager, Medicine Hat, 403-529-8239, 673
Mackay, John, Director, North Cowichan, 250-746-3103, 687
MacKay, Kimberly J., Cox and Palmer - St. John's, 1065
MacKay, Lori, General Manager, Coquitlam, 604-927-3000, 680
MacKay, Peter Gordon, Minister, National Defence, 545
Mackay, Stuart R., McKenzie Lake Lawyers LLP, 1069
MacKay, Tara A., Torys LLP, 1081
MacKay, Q.C., R. Neil, Partner, MacPherson Leslie & Tyerman LLP - Saskatoon, 1090
MacKay, Q.C., O.C., Harold H., Counsel, MacPherson Leslie & Tyerman LLP - Regina, 1090
Mackay-Dunn, Doug, North Vancouver, 688
Mackay-Dunn, Q.C., Hector, Chair, 575
MacKeigan, Eion, General Manager, Petroleum Enviro Services, 322
MacKeigan, Mike, Manager, Cape Breton, 695
MacKell, Bryan, Director, Planning & Development, Simcoe, 704
MacKenzie, Ann, President/CEO, 610
MacKenzie, Ann, Vice-President, Ottawa Field-Naturalists' Club, 983
MacKenzie, Carol, Manager, Pictou County, 902-396-1495, 698
Mackenzie, D., President, Gas Liquids Engineering Ltd., 205
MacKenzie, Daphne J., Partner, Stikeman Elliott LLP - Toronto, 1080
MacKenzie, Dave, Parliamentary Secretary to the Minister of Public, 557
MacKenzie, Don, Director, Maritime Paper Products Ltd., 281
MacKenzie, Doug, Director, Truro, 696
MacKenzie, Douglas J., Campbell Marr, 1063
MacKenzie, J. Darren, Superintendent, Irrigation & Drainage, Niagara-on-the-Lake, 715
MacKenzie, Joe, Treasurer, Mount Waddington, 678

Mackenzie, Judy, Librarian, FP Innovations - Paprican Division, Vancouver, 1117
MacKenzie, Karen, Councillor, Colchester County, 697
Mackenzie, Kimberley, Executive Director, Lake Simcoe Region Conservation Foundation, 948
MacKenzie, Mark, Wellington, 519-338-2641, 705
MacKenzie, Rory, Manager, Westburne Canada, 428
Mackenzie, Russ, Vice-President, Stantec Inc., 377
Mackey, Paul, Director, St. John's, 709-576-8303, 694
Mackie, James, Haliburton, 613-339-1714, 700
MacKinlay, Shaune, Manager, Halifax Regional Municipality, 695
MacKinley, Ron W., Minister, 641
MacKinnon, Bernie, Director, Cape Breton, 902-563-5132, 695
MacKinnon, Birt, Acting Director, 640
MacKinnon, Corey, Heenan Blaikie LLP - Toronto, 1076
MacKinnon, Don, President, Ribbons Recycled Inc., 346
MacKinnon, Ian, General Manager, F.E. Myers, 193
MacKinnon, Jamie, Fire Chief, Kincardine, 726
MacKinnon, Rob, Secretary-Treasurer, Ontario Ground Water Association, 974
MacKinnon, Scott, Vice-President, Greystone Energy Systems Inc., 218
Mackintosh, Grace, Associate, Miller Thomson LLP - Toronto, 1078
Macklem, John, Kawartha Lakes, 711
Macklem, Paul, General Manager, Kelowna, 681
Macklem, Tiff, Associate Deputy Minister & G-7 Deputy for Canada, 526
MacKnight, Barry, Police Chief & Director, Fredericton, 506-460-2300, 691
MacKnight, Scott, President, OCL Services Ltd., 264, 311
MacLachlan, Janet, Research Librarian, Inco Technical Services Limited, 1145
MacLachlan, Thomas B., MacLachlan McNab Hembroff, 1056
MacLachlans, Janet, Supervisor, Information & Office Services, Inco Technical Services Limited, 1145
MacLaren, Leslie, Acting President, 609
MacLatchy, Paul, Director, Strategy, Environment, & Communications, Kingston, 712
MacLaughlan, Craig D., CEO/Deputy Head, 611
MacLean, Brian, ADI Group Inc., 68
MacLean, Brian, Director, Geomembrane Technologies Inc., ADI Group Inc., 68
MacLean, Bruce D., Director, Planning, Development, & Sustainability, Halton Hills, 710
MacLean, Chad, Manager, Monserco Ltd., 293
MacLean, Colin, President, 610
MacLean, Don, Metro Vancouver, 678
MacLean, Don, Mayor, Pitt Meadows, 604-465-2416, 683
MacLean, Elaine, Head, Technical Services, St Francis-Xavier University, 1134
MacLean, Eleanor, Biology Librarian, Life Sciences Library, 1174
MacLean, Glenn, Manager, Engineered Air, 180
Maclean, James R., Heenan Blaikie LLP - Calgary, 1051
MacLean, John, CAO, Kootenay Boundary, 678
MacLean, Lana, Librarian, Strait Area Campus, 1137
Maclean, Lorne, Contact, Endress+Hauser Canada Ltd., 178
MacLean, Michael, Director, Leduc County, 780-955-6416, 669
MacLean, Norm, Wildlife Ecologist, LGL Limited Environmental Research Associates, 272
MacLean, Paul, President, ÉEM inc., 173
MacLean, Scott, Vice-President, Satlantic, 358
MacLean, Steven, President & Chief Astronaut, 520
MacLean, Theresa, Library Clerk, Seal Cove Campus Library, 1130
MacLean, P. Eng, Steve, Deputy Minister, 641
MacLellan, Bernie, Huron, 701
MacLellan, Donald, Assistant City Manager, Moncton / Ville de Moncton, 691
MacLellan, Edwin, Environmental Planner, C.J. MacLellan & Associates Inc., 120
MacLellan, James W., Partner, Borden Ladner Gervais LLP - Toronto, 1073
Macleod, Angela, Corporate Secretary, Canadian Electricity Association, 866
Macleod, April, Kitimat Valley Naturalists, 947
MacLeod, Colin, Unit Manager, AMEC, 83
MacLeod, Darren, Managing Director, K&D Pratt Group Inc., 254
MacLeod, Don, Crossman Machinery Co. Ltd., 154
MacLeod, Douglas L., Graham Wilson & Green, Barristers & Solicitors, Notaries, Mediato, 1068
MacLeod, Edgar, Police Chief, Cape Breton, 902-563-5095, 695
MacLeod, Gael, Calgary, 403-268-2430, 671
MacLeod, Gary, General Manager, DBC Environmental Services Ltd., 158

MacLeod, Gordon, Councillor, Cape Breton, 695
MacLeod, Hugh, CEO, Canadian Patient Safety Institute, 881
MacLeod, Iain, Chair, Hawk Migration Association of North America, 927
MacLeod, James D., Manager, Whitehorse, 867-668-8351, 755
MacLeod, Jim, Councillor, Cape Breton, 695
MacLeod, Jody, Manager, CBCL Limited, 133
MacLeod, Lynda, Library Technician, Periodicals, Government Docume, Lakeshore Campus, 1159
Macleod, Sheena, Treasurer & Manager, Coquitlam, 680
MacLeod, Wayne, President, Hazard Control Systems Inc., 227
MacMaster, Ken, Vice-President, Manitoba Wildlife Federation, 952
Macmillan, Hector, Northumberland, 702
MacMillan, Hector, Mayor, Trent Hills, 731
MacMillan, Jason, Technologist, Richmond County, 902-226-3989, 698
MacMillan, Luke, Representative, Calgary, 121
Macmillan, Margy, Coordinator, Information Services, Mount Royal College, 1102
MacMillan, Norman, Ministre délégué, 654
MacMillan, Ron, President, Rocky Mountain Environmental Ltd., 350
Macmillan, Ron, President & Deputy Minister, 666
MacMillan, Tom, Contact, MacMillan & Associates, 278
MacMillan, Tom, President, Northeastern Resource Recovery Ltd., 217, 307
MacMillan, Vicki, Liberal Arts/University Studies Librarian, Georgian College of Applied Arts & Technology, 1138
MacMillan, Wayne, Lincoln, 713
MacNamara, Y., Sales Coordinator, Bema Co. Ltd., 105
MacNaughton, John A., Chair, 512
MacNeil, Graham, Sales Contact, Rotork Controls (Canada) Ltd., 352
MacNeil, James D., Boyne Clarke, 1067
MacNeill, Kevin D., Partner, Heenan Blaikie LLP - Toronto, 1070, 1076
MacNeill, Sandy, Manager, Fredericton, 506-460-2200, 691
MacPhail, Ann, Head, Resource Centre, Perth Campus, 1152
MacPhail, Malcolm, Senior Manager, Capital Regional District, 250-360-3052, 676
MacPhee, Carrie M., Manager, Saanich, 688
MacPhee, Scott, Manager, Hunter & Associates, 235
Macpherson, Crawford, Director, Colchester County, 697
MacPherson, Glen, Director, Chilliwack, 604-792-9311, 680
MacPherson, James C., Calibre Strategic Services Inc., 122
MacPherson, James C., President, Calibre Strategic Services Inc., 122
MacPherson, Natalie, Information Resources Manager, Nova Scotia Environment & Labour, 1136
MacPherson, Seonaid, Executive Director, 659
MacQuarrie, John, Deputy Minister, 639
MacQuarrie, Wayne, CEO, 393, 639
MacQuarrie, Wayne, Director, 639
MacRae, Brian, City Manager, Brandon, 204-729-2204, 689
MacRae, Jack, Manager, Little River Pollution Control Plant, Windsor, 519-948-1751, 723
MacRae, Wayne C., Executive Officer, Canadian Ground Water Association, 870
Mac-Seing, Valérie, Associée, Stikeman Elliott LLP - Montréal, 1087
MacSweyn, Eric, North Glengarry, 727
MacTavish, John, Lanark, 701
MacVicar, Heather, General Manager, Employment & Social Services, Toronto, 416-392-8952, 721
MacWilliam, Alexander G., Fraser Milner Casgrain LLP - Calgary, 1051
Madaire, Patricia, Librarian, Eastern Cereal & Oilseed Research Centre Library, 1149
Maddalena, Michael, Burchell, MacDougall, 1067
Madden, John, President, Barrie Agricultural Society, 844
Madden, Steve, Manager, Grande Prairie No. 1, 780-532-7393, 669
Madden, Tom, Director, Prince George, 250-561-7644, 683
Madden, Tony, Orillia, 716
Maddever, Wayne, CEO/President, Plasma Environmental Technologies Inc., 326
Maddigan, Robert, Principal Civil Engineer, Ferguson Simek Clark, 194
Maddocks, Derrick, Director, 599
Maddocks, J., Vice-President, Gas Liquids Engineering Ltd., 205
Maddox, Ken, McElhanney Consulting Services Ltd., 285
Maddy, Jim, President & CEO, American Zoo & Aquarium Association, 827
Madeley, June, Secretary, Society for Socialist Studies, 1007

Executive Name Index

Madill, Patricia M., Regional Clerk, Durham, 699
Madjar, Henri, President, Terratech, 391
Madoff, Pamela, Victoria, 685
Madorin, Q.C., W.H.P., Managing Partner, Madorin, Snyder LLP, 1069
Madramootoo, Chandra A., Academic Staff, Brace Centre for Water Resources Management, 115
Madsen, David T., Partner, Borden Ladner Gervais LLP - Calgary, 1049
Maekawan, Takaaki, Secretary General, International Commission of Agricultural & Biosystems Engineering, 937
Maes, William R., University Librarian, Dalhousie University Libraries, 1135
Magar, Marc, Marketing, Matrix Energy, 282
Magaw, Ken G., President, Promag Enviro Systems Ltd., 334
Magaw, Mike, Manager, Promag Enviro Systems Ltd., 334
Magdalena, Goranova, Trade Commissioner, 767
Magditsch, Alexander, Vice-President, Comcor Environmental Limited, 146
Magee, Lucy, Director, 617
Maghneih, Al, Windsor, 723
Maginn, Gerry, Sales Manager, Transcontinental Printing Inc., 400
Magliozzi, Stefano, Sr. Project Manager, Con-Tank Installations Ltd., 148
Magloughlen, P.Eng., Robert, Director, Engineering & Public Works, Georgina, 709
Magnin, Gérard, President, AirScience Inc., 76
Magnusson, Renee, Contact, CON-SPACE Communications Ltd., 148
Magon, Magdalene, President, Victoria Lapidary & Mineral Society, 1017
Magri, Joe, Conseiller de ville, Rivière-des-Prairies, Montréal, 738
Magrum, Nancy, Director, 605
Maguire, Ron, Frontenac, 699
Magusin, Elaine, Reference Services Librarian, Athabasca University, 1099
Magwood, George C., Magwood, Van De Vyvere, Thompson, & Grove-McClement LLP, 1081
Magyar, Len, Commissioner, Development, Woodstock, 723
Mahabir, T., SHAL International President, SHAL Consulting Engineers Ltd., 365
Mahanna, Mike, Manager, National Association for Environmental Management, 956
Mahar, Christine, Director, 663
Maher, Janet, Administrator, Medical Reform Group of Ontario, 1159
Maher, M., Controller, MCC Industrial Services Ltd, 284
Maheux, Marcel, Rouyn-Noranda, 741
Maheux, Pierre, Québec, 740
Maheux, Serge, Production Coordinator, Rodrigue Métal Ltée, 350
Mahgroub, Nayef., Environmental Engineer, McClymont & Rak Engineers, Inc., 284
Mahler, James W., Scarfone Hawkins LLP, 1069
Mahoney, Brenda, Reference & Electronic Resources Librarian, Algonquin College of Applied Arts & Technology, 1147
Mahoney, Erin, Commissioner, Environmental Services, York, 705
Mahoney, Katie, Peel, 714, 703
Mahoney, Kevin, Chair, 583
Mahoney, P.C., Steven W., Chair, 636
Mahony, Dennis E., Torys LLP, 1081
Mahony, Heather, Woodward & Company, 1063
Mahood, Garfield, Executive Director, Smoking & Health Action Foundation, 1004
Maidment, Glenn, Secretary, Tire Stewardship BC Association, 1012
Maier, Robert, Vice-President, Environmental Waste International, 186
Maieron, Lou, Wellington, 519-833-2559, 705
Maieron, Lou, Mayor, Erin, 709
Maihot, Réal, Gestionnaire, Veolia ES Canada Industrial Services Inc., 412
Mailhot, Michel, Granby, 735
Mailhot, Michel, Directeur, Repentigny, 450-470-3700, 740
Mailloux, Jacques, Acting Chief Information Officer, 520
Mailly, Donald, Mascouche, 450-966-1413, 737
Maimets, Lembit, President, Link-Pipe Inc., 272
Maimets, Olev, Sales Engineer, Link-Pipe Inc., 272
Maimon, Catherine, Manager, National Solid Wastes Management Association, 958
Main, Grant, Deputy Minister, 583
Main, Roy, Chief Administrative Officer, Charlottetown, 732
Mainguy, Raymond, Joli-Cour Lacasse Avocats, 1088

Mains, Dawn, Trade-mark Agent, Heenan Blaikie LLP - Calgary, 1051
Mains, Dwight, Vice President, Robinson Solutions, 348
Mainville, Pierre, Conseiller d'arrondissement, Ste-Marie-St-Jacques, Montréal, 738
Mainville, Robert, Manager, Anachem Ltd., 84
Mair, Julia J., Director, INFORM Inc., 931
Maisonville, Robert, Director, Corporate Services & Treasurer, Essex, 699
Maitland, Jim, Officer, Port Coquitlam, 683
Maitland, Karen, Coordinator, Ecological Farmers Association of Ontario, 908
Majeau, Jean, Vice-President, Kruger Inc., 260
Majek, Steve, Director, Wetaskiwin County No. 10, 780-361-6226, 670
Majid, Carey, Executive Director, 602
Major, Dan, Supervisor, Parks, Woodstock, 723
Major, Jean-Denis, Président, Consumaj, 151
Major, Marie-France, Lang Michener LLP - Ottawa, 1070
Major, Paula, GAIA Power Inc., 204
Major, Tim, General Manager, General Scrap Partnership, 207
Mak, Shirley, Secretary, Asia-Pacific Centre for Environmental Law, 829
Makarewicz, Grace, Director, Library Services, Langara College, 1118
Makaro, Wade, Manager, Bartle & Gibson Co. Ltd., 102
Maki, Duane, General Manager, Spectrum Resource Group Inc., 375
Makowski, Ann, Chief Operating Officer, Society for Environmental Graphic Design, 1007
Makuch, Stanley M., Cassels Brock & Blackwell LLP, 1074
Malatches, John, McCordick Glove & Safety Inc., 284
Malayil, Koshy, Analytical Divisions Manager, Kaizen Environmental Services Inc., 254
Malboeuf, Rick, Milton, 714
Malcolm, Brian, Sales Manager, Fanchem Ltd., 194
Malcolm, David, President/CEO, Malroz Engineering Inc., 279
Malcolm, Q.C., Robert T., Partner, Macleod Dixon LLP, 1052
Maldoff, Eric, Partner, Heenan Blaikie S.E.N.C.R.L/SRL, 1084
Maldoff, Gerry, President, Hympopack Ltd., 237
Male, Jeff, Branch Manager, Leeson Canada Ltd., 266
Malec, Mike, Sales Manager, IPEC Industries Ltd., 247
Malecha, Fran, Chief Operating Officer, Viterra Inc., 414
Malenfant, Pauline, Assistante, Institut de l'Énergie et de l'environnement de la francophonie, 1179
Maley, Shawn, Asst. Deputy Minister, 617
Malick, James, Exec. Vice-President/Director, SLR Consulting Ltd. (Canada), 370
Malinowski, Lyle, Service Manager, Fort Garry Industries Ltd., 200
Mallam, John, Vice-President, 601
Mallet, James, McLennan Ross LLP, 1055
Mallett, Daniel, Director, Canadian Labour Congress, 876
Mallett, Ed, President & CEO, ETV Canada, 190
Mallett, Lea Ann, Executive Director, EcoSource Mississauga, 908
Mallette, Sylvain, Saint-Eustache, 450-472-2519, 742
Malley, Diane F., President, PDK Projects Inc., 320
Malley, Mark, Manager, Harris & Roome Supply Limited, 226
Malley, Michael J. (Tanker), Miramichi, 691
Mallon, Amanda, Yellowknife, 695
Mallory, Carolyn, Resource Centre Coordinator, Nunavut Dept. of Environment, 1138
Mallory, Steven, President, Longwood Forestry Services Ltd., 274
Malloy, Kevin, Asst. Deputy Minister, 615
Malloy, Kevin, Deputy Minister, 615
Malone, David M., President, 544
Maloney, Elaine L., Managing Editor, Canadian Circumpolar Institute, 862
Maloney, Rick, Bracebridge, 706
Maloney, Sean, Vice-President, Mirarco Mining Innovation, 290
Maloni, Laurie, President, Oasis Bags, 311
Maloni, Seema, Vice-President, Oasis Bags, 311
Malott, Pam, Chief Administrative Officer, Amherstburg, 705
Maltais, Dave A., Dieppe, 506-855-4299, 691
Maltais, Francine, Directrice, Saguenay, 741
Maltais, Patrice, Directeur General, Les Consultants RSA, 268
Malyk, Mike, Librarian, Winnipeg Research Centre, 1126
Mammoliti, Giorgio, Toronto, 721
Mamon, D., Co-Chair, Highland Equipment Ltd., 231
Man, Christine, Lang Michener LLP - Vancouver, 1060
Manager, David Milbury General, Sales, Whisco Ltd., 431
Mancell, Garry E.P., Davis LLP - Vancouver, 1059
Manchester, Mike, Brock, 724

Manchia, Sergio, Director, Planning & Engineering Initiatives Ltd., 325
Manconi, John, General Manager, Public Works, Ottawa, 716
Mancuso, Dan, Vice-President, Export Development Canada, 192
Mancuso, Lily, Container Sales & Service, Contor Terminals Inc., 151
Mandarin, Frank, Sales Manager, Armtec Construction Products, 92
Mandel, Stephen, Mayor, Edmonton, 780-496-8100, 672
Manderville, Christopher B., Partner, Heenan Blaikie LLP - Calgary, 1051
Mandlowitz, Jason E., VP, Consulting Services, Hicks Morley Hamilton Stewart Storie LLP, 1076
Mandrusiak, Jason, Branch Manager, CenturyVallen, 136
Mandryk, Brad, District Manager, BFI Canada Inc., 106
Mandzuk, Trent, Manager, Yorkton, 306-786-1760, 755
Manevich, Alejandro, Heenan Blaikie LLP - Toronto, 1076
Manfield, Normand, Vice-President, Turcal, 404
Mangan, Eddie, Manager, Powerscreen of Canada Ltd., 329
Mange, Derers, Electronics-recycling.com, 175
Mangiardi, Bruno, Chief Information Officer, Greater Sudbury / Grand Sudbury, 710
Mangin, Patrice, Chair, Canadian Pulp & Paper Network for Innovation in Education & Resea, 883
Mangione, Joe, Vice-President, Trow Consulting Engineers Ltd., 403
Manhas, Sukhbir, Young, Anderson, 1062
Maniatis, Dimitri, Associé, Langlois Kronström Desjardins, 1085
Manickam, Vivek, Senior Health Physicist, Monserco Ltd., 293
Manion, Evelyn, Manager, Henry Kroeger Regional Water Services Commission, 757
manitoba econetwork, Manitoba Eco-Network, 1215
Manjak, Scott, Mayor, Cranbrook, 680
Manji, Alnoor, President/CEO, Horizon Environment Inc., 233
Manley, C., General Manager, Planning & Economic Development, Haldimand, 700
Manley, L.J., Director, Simcoe Engineering Group Limited, 368
Manlow, Scott, Fire Chief, Prince Edward, 703
Mann, Brian, Manager, Westburne Canada, 426
Mann, Janice, City Clerk, Saskatoon, 306-975-3240, 754
Mann, Kevin, Chief Financial Officer, American Water Works Association, 826
Mann, Margaret, Manager, 591
Mann, Norman, Elliot Lake, 709
Mann, Sheila K., McCaffery Mudry Pritchard LLP, Barristers & Solicitors, 1052
Mann, P.Eng., W.F., Director, Planning & Development, Milton, 714
Mannell, Alan, Manager, Engineering, Pelham, 717
Manning, A. Julia, Reference, Ontario Ministry of Transportation, 1154
Manning, David, Head of Acquisitions, St Mary's University, 1136
Manning, Graham, Pinchin Environmental Ltd., 324
Manning, Paul M., Willms & Shier Environmental Lawyers LLP, 1081
Manning, B.A., LL.B., LL., Lewis L., Partner, Lawson Lundell LLP - Calgary, 1051
Manojlovich, Slavko, Assistant to Librarian, Systems & Planning, Memorial University of Newfoundland, 1132
Manolakis, Emmanuel, Gowling Lafleur Henderson S.E.N.C.R.L./LLP, 1084
Manser, Scott, Ortech Environmental Inc., 314
Mansfield, Larry, Sales Representative, Armtec Construction Products, 92
Manson, Alan, ISAS Secretary, Institute of Space & Atmospheric Studies, 933
Manson, Fred, CAO, Parksville, 250-954-4666, 682
Manson, Gary, Manager, Maple Ridge, 687
Manson, John, City Engineer, Langford, 681
Mansueti, Ernie, Director, North Cowichan, 687
Mansz, Paul, Vice-President, Saint John Naturalists' Club, 998
Mantas, Peter, Partner, Heenan Blaikie LLP - Ottawa, 1070
Mantei, Jim, General Manager, Vancouver Gear Works Ltd., 409
Mantesso, Rosanne, General Manager, Human Resources, Welland, 722
Mantessp, Mike, Chief Building Official, Welland, 722
Manzo, Denis, Fraser Milner Casgrain S.E.N.C.R.L./LLP, 1084
Manzo, Frank, Sault Ste. Marie, 720
Mao, Ted, Vice-President, Trojan Technologies Inc., 403
Mar, Jack, Mayor, Central Saanich, 686
Mar, John, Calgary, 403-268-2430, 671
Maragno, Jean, Manager, Library Services, St Joseph's Hospital (Hamilton), 1141
Maraj, John, Sales Manager, Wilcorp Manufacturing, 431

Executive Name Index

Maranda, Daniel, Directeur, Québec, 418-641-6164, 740
Maranda, Dominique, Lévis, 736
Maranda, Lynn, Curator of Anthropology, Vancouver Museum, 1119
Maranda, Robert, Lévis, 736
Maranda, Suzanne, Head, Bracken Health Sciences Library, 1142
Marano, Marie, Director, Corporate Services, Clarington, 724
Marceau, Louise, Technicienne en documentation, CÉGEP de Sherbrooke, 1185
Marceau, Paul, Vice-président, 652
Marcellin, Robert, Administrator, Kitimat-Stikine, 678
Marcellus, R.W., President, CMEL Enterprises Ltd., 144
March, Evan, General Manager, Tank-Craft Ltd., 386
March, Rick, Manager, Bartle & Gibson Co. Ltd., 102
Marchand, Catherine, Executive Director, Intergovernmental Committee on Urban & Regional Research (ICURR), 1158
Marchand, Denis, Directeur, Varennes, 746
Marchand, Denis, Responsable, Varennes, 746
Marchand, Gilles, Shawinigan, 744
Marchand, Jocelyne, Commis, CÉGEP de St-Jérôme, 1184
Marchand, Leonard S., Fulton & Company LLP, Lawyers & Trade-Mark Agents, 1056
Marchand, Nicole, Sainte-Julie, 743
Marchand, Paul-André, Thetford Mines, 418-335-9871, 745
Marchiori, Dennis, Director, Yellowknife, 867-920-5661, 695
Marcil, Gaston, Consultant, Gaston Marcil, Consultant, 205
Marcil, Rosaire, Directeur général, Rouville, 753
Marck, B.A., LL.B, William J., Chief Administrative Officer, Leamington, 726
Marco Antonio, Heredia Fragoso, Head, Commission for Environmental Cooperation, 764
Marcoccia, J. Frank, Principal, JFM Environmental Ltd., 252
Marcos, Denis, Vice-President, Comptank Corp., 148
Marcotte, Chenoa, Secretary, Global, Environmental & Outdoor Education Council, 924
Marcotte, Gilles, Québec, 740
Marcotte, Nathalie, Executive Secretary, 545
Marcotte, Richard, Maire, Mascouche, 737
Marcotte, Stéphane, Gestionnaire, Veolia ES Canada Industrial Services Inc., 412
Marcoux, Alain, Directeur général, Québec, 740
Marcoux, Christiane, Saint-Jean-sur-Richelieu, 450-347-5277, 742
Marcoux, Claude, Directeur, Sherbrooke, 819-821-5901, 744
Marcum, Larry, Manager, National Environmental Health Association, 957
Marcus, Denis, President, Harold Marcus Ltd., 225
Marecak, Ted, Chief Building Official, Belleville, 706
Margot, Edwards, Trade Commissioner, 767
Marguerita, Niada, Trade Commissioner, 767
Mariage, Frank, Associé, Miller Thomson LLP - Montréal, 1086
Marimpietri, Tito-Dante, Durham, 699
Marimpietri, Tito-Dante, Regional Councillor, Oshawa, 716
Marineau, Leon, Vice-President, Cascades Inc., 130
Marineau, Léon, Vice-President, Cascades Inc., 130
Marini, Lou, Zorbit Technologies Inc., 437
Marion, Guylaine, Bibliothécaire, Québec Ministère de la Sécurité Publique - Direction des Communic, 1175
Marion, Marcelle, Legal Officer, 525
Marion, Michael A., Partner, Borden Ladner Gervais LLP - Calgary, 1050
Mariotte, Michael, Executive Director, Nuclear Information & Resource Service, 969
Marisett, Brian, Prince Edward, 703
Mark, Alan, Senior Partner, Ogilvy Renault LLP/S.E.N.C.R.L., s.r.l. - Toronto, 1078
Mark, Chris, Director, Parks & Open Space, Oakville, 715
Mark, Frank, Stratford, 720
Mark, Larry R., Az-Tec Reclaim Ltd., 100
Mark, Rachel, Director, 618
Markgraf, Herb, Vice-President, PRT Inc., 336
Markin, Quentin, Partner, Stikeman Elliott LLP - Toronto, 1080
Markotich, Gary, Contact, Church & Trought Inc., 141
Marks, Andrew, Timmins, 721
Marks, Paul, President, EnviroSan Products Ltd./SOLUTION 2000, 187
Marks, Raissa, Coordinator, New Brunswick Environmental Network, 961
Marks, T., Deputy Mayor & Councillor, Central Elgin, 724
Marks, Tom, Elgin, 699
Markwell, Jason C., Partner, Ogilvy Renault LLP/S.E.N.C.R.L., s.r.l. - Toronto, 1078
Marleau, Lyle, Contact, Terrace, 250-635-6871, 685
Marlo, P.Eng., Ceri, Manager, Maple Ridge, 604-467-7482, 687

Marmen, Bobby, Conseiller pédagogique, CÉGEP de Matane, 1169
Marmen, Claude, Sr. Vice-President, Conporec Inc., 150
Maroosis, George, North Bay, 715
Marotte, Ginette, Conseillère de ville, Champlain-L'Île-des-Soeurs, Montréal, 738
Marotz, Karen, Head Librarian, Belzberg Library, 1117
Marples, Ian R., President, Alcohol Countermeasure Systems Corp., 77
Marpole, Kevin, Manager, Saskatchewan Environmental Industry & Managers' Association, 1000
Marques, Al, Division Manager, T-G Burgmann, 385
Marquis, Daniel, Bibliothécaire professionnel, CÉGEP de Granby, 1168
Marquis, Dany, Technicienne en documentation, Campus d'Edmundston, 1126
Marquis, David, Brock, 724
Marquis, Jean Guy, Edmundston, 691
Marquis, Pierre, HMI Construction Inc., 232
Marquis, Robert, Terra Experts Conseils Inc., 390
Marr, S., Central Elgin, 724
Marr, Scott, Manager, Westburne Canada, 428
Marra, Bill (Biagio), Windsor, 723
Marrie, Megan, Manager, Kanotech Information Systems Ltd., 255
Marriott, Kevin, Owner, Marriotts Container Rental Ltd., 281
Marriott, Robert E., Davis LLP - Vancouver, 1059
Marriott, Thomas D., Brownlee LLP, 1054
Marrison, Anna L., Partner, Borden Ladner Gervais LLP - Toronto, 1073
Marrs, Bob, New Tecumseth, 714
Marsales, Claudia, Manager, Waste Management, Markham, 713
Marsden, Stan, Sr. Vice-President, Medgate Inc., 286
Marsden, C.H.R.P., C.M.M., Claire, Manager, Human Resources, Georgina, 709
Marsh, David, Manager, 3M Canada Company, 395
Marsh, Jack, Director, Quesnel, 688
Marsh, John, Head, Ontario Trails Council, 1153
Marsh, Mike, Vice-President, 661
Marsh, Nigel, Contact, Office of Greening Government Operations, 970
Marshall, Barbara, Environmental Contact, McNair & Marshall Planning & Development Consultants, 285
Marshall, Bill, President, Walter Dow Associates Ltd., 416
Marshall, Dave, Director, Oak Bay, 688
Marshall, Douglas H., Marshall & Lamperson, 1057
Marshall, George, Niagara, 702
Marshall, Harry J., President, Water & Earth Science Associates Ltd., 421
Marshall, Ian, Ultra-Chem Industries Ltd., 405
Marshall, Ian, Marketing, Ultra-Chem Industries Ltd., 405
Marshall, K. Bradford, Executive Director, 593
Marshall, Karen, Director, Library, University of Western Ontario Libraries, 1144
Marshall, Kerri, Manager, Environment, Thunder Bay, 807-625-2836, 721
Marshall, P., Manager, Gas Liquids Engineering Ltd., 205
Marshall, Sharon, Director, Finance, Erin, 709
Marshall, Tom, Minister & President, Treasury Board, 599
Marshall, Tom, Vice President, Sandwell Engineering Inc., 357
Marshall, Q.C., John J., Partner, Macleod Dixon LLP, 1052
Marsland, Ken, Anco Chemicals Inc., 85
Marsman, Arnie, Director, Planning & Development Svs., & Chief Bui, Middlesex Centre, 727
Marstaller, Tom, Superintendent, Red Deer, 403-342-8238, 674
Marston, Twila, Hamilton, 725
Martel, Donald, Directeur général, Nicolet-Yamaska, 750
Martel, Gaetan, Directeur operations, Régie intermunicipale d'élimination de déchets solides de Brome-M, 760
Martel, Mario W., President/CEO, Roche Itée, Groupe-conseil, 348
Martel, P., Manager, J. Walter Company Ltd., 249
Martel, Sylvain, Trésorier, Saint-Lin-Laurentides, 743
Martell, Mark, General Manager, Caster-Rack Systems Ltd., 131
Martell, Michael W., O'Halloran Campbell Consultants Limited, 310
Martell, Paul, Laval, 736
Marteniuk, Jay, Manager, Maxxam Analytics Inc., 283
Martens, Charles, Superintendent, Blind River Refinery, 1139
Martens, Christine, Specialist, Scientific Information, Boehringer Ingelheim (Canada) Ltd., 1167
Martens, Doug, District Manager, BFI Canada Inc., 106
Martens, Doug, Branch Manager, Fort Garry Industries Ltd., 200
Martens, Ernie, General Manager, Northern Steel Industries, 307

Martens, Marilyn, Office Manager, Saskatchewan Soil Conservation Association, 1001
Martens, Tony, Director, Mountain View County, 669
Martin, Andrew, Planner & Officer, Wilmot, 732
Martin, André, Directeur, Saguenay, 741
Martin, André, Président-directeur général, Fondation de la faune du Québec, 650, 917
Martin, Angela, President, Friends of Mashkinonje Park, 921
Martin, Barratt, Sr. Trade Commissioner, 768
Martin, Christopher D., Lindsay Kenney LLP, 1061
Martin, David, Owner, GET Industries Inc., 212
Martin, David, Responsable, acquisitions, Université de l'Alberta Bibliothèque Saint-Jean, 1107
Martin, David H., Research Director, Nuclear Awareness Project, 1164
Martin, Debbie, Vice-President, 574
Martin, Derek, Executive Vice-President, CEDA International Corporation, 135
Martin, Douglas, Niagara, 702
Martin, Douglas G., Mayor, Fort Erie, 709
Martin, Ed, President/CEO, 601
Martin, Fernand, Directeur, Québec, 418-641-6160, 740
Martin, Gayle, Metro Vancouver, 681, 678
Martin, George, President, Douglas, Barwick Inc., 165
Martin, Glenn, Executive Director, Consulting Engineers of British Columbia, 903
Martin, Greg, Corporate Secretary, Westmorland-Albert Solid Waste Corporation, 759
Martin, Isabelle, Vice-President, GDG Environnement Ltée, 205
Martin, Jacques P., Mayor, Edmundston, 691
Martin, Jim, General Manager, Fraser-Fort George, 678
Martin, Joan, Librarian, Canadian Agriculture Library - Saskatoon, 1189
Martin, John, Lennox Industries (Canada) Ltd., 267
Martin, John, City Treasurer & CFO, Moncton / Ville de Moncton, 506-853-3566, 691
Martin, John, Director, Human Resources, Belleville, 706
Martin, Lloyd, Environmental Engineer, Carson Safety & Environmental Services, 130
Martin, Lorne, Manager, CBCL Limited, 133
Martin, Luciano, Executive Director, Action to Restore a Clean Humber, 813
Martin, Mary, Surrey, 604-591-4622, 684
Martin, Maureen, Head of Technical Services, Bedford Institute of Oceanography, 1135
Martin, Michael, President, Valley Associates Inc., 409
Martin, Narelle, Consultant, Hemispheres Environmental Consulting Inc., 229
Martin, Neil, City Clerk, Director & Associate Commissioner, St. John's, 709-576-8446, 694
Martin, Patrice, Gatineau, 735
Martin, Paul D., Operations Manager, PDK Projects Inc., 320
Martin, Pierre, Cain Lamarre Casgrain Wells - Québec, 1087
Martin, Rhona, Chair, Columbia-Shuswap, 677
Martin, Rhonda, Executive Assistant, Joint Centre for Bioethics, 947
Martin, Rick, Vice-President, Thomson Technology Inc., 395
Martin, Ronald J.E., President, Danatec Educational Services Ltd., 157
Martin, Rosaire, Saint-Hyacinthe, 742
Martin, Réjean, Greffier, Thetford Mines, 745
Martin, Sara, Library Services Coordinator, Woodstock Campus, Library, 1130
Martin, Scott, Contact, EBA Engineering Consultants Ltd., 170
Martin, Steve, Shawinigan, 744
Martin, Stewart, Muskoka, 702
Martin, Tom, Executive Vice-President, National Parks Conservation Association, 958
Martin, Trent, Manager, Westburne Canada, 427
Martin, Wendy, Manager, Green Space, Collingwood, 708
Martin, William, CFO, Marsulex Inc., 281
Martinak, David, Vice-President, Smiths Detection, 371
Martindale, Graeme D., Partner, Borden Ladner Gervais LLP - Vancouver, 1058
Martineau, André, Vice-President, General Manager, Laidlaw Medical Services, 263
Martineau, Brenda, Coordinator, Employee Relations, Loyalist, 727
Martineau, Ron, President & COO, Fuller Austin Insulation Inc., 203
Martineau, Yves, Associé, Stikeman Elliott LLP - Montréal, 1087
Martineau, Yvon, Laval, 736
Martinez, Karla, Manager, Association of Power Producers of Ontario, 837
Martinez, Roy, Director, American Water Works Association, 826

Executive Name Index

Martinez, Soraya, Conseillère, Saint-Michel, Montréal, 738
Martiuk, Roman, City Manager, Burlington, 707
Martland, Q.C., John G., Bennett Jones LLP - Calgary Office, 1049
Martyn, S., Central Elgin, 724
Martyniuk, Larry, Manager, Wheelabrator Canada Co., 431
Marzinzik, Nicole, Coordinator, North Okanagan, 678
Masella, Brigitte, Manager, Paul F. Wilkinson & Associates Inc., 319
Maser, Bill, Manager, LTS Sales Ltd., 274
Masi, Joe, Executive Director, Association of Manitoba Municipalities, 836
Maskell, Cathy, Associate University Librarian, University of Windsor, 1165
Maskell, Kathi, Mayor, Grey, 700
Maslen, Lynden, Manager, Calgon Carbon Corp., 121
Masnyk, Bob, President, Enviropac Inc., 186
Mason, Carol, CAO, Nanaimo, 678
Mason, Dave, Regional Manager, Danfoss Inc. - Hydronic Heating Division, 157
Mason, James, President, Poyry (Vancouver) Inc., 330
Mason, Karen, Director, 664
Mason, Kirk, Borden Ladner Gervais LLP - Calgary, 1050
Mason, Mary, Associate Librarian, Queen's University, 1142
Mason, S., Vice-President, Seaforth Engineering Group Inc., 361
Mason, Stan, Co-owner, Atlantic Orient Canada Inc., 96
Mason, Stan, Contact, Morgan Falls Power Company, 293
Mason, Tony J., Vice-President, Bytown Marine Ltd., 119
Masry, Salem, President/CEO, CARIS, 128
Masschaele, Brian, Director, Community & Cultural Services, Elgin, 699
Massé, David, Stikeman Elliott LLP - Montréal, 1087
Masse, Gary, National Sales Manager, Puresource Inc., 337
Massé, Guillaume, Engineer, Les Consultants RSA, 268
Masse, Jean, Sept-Iles, 744
Masse, Martin G., Lang Michener LLP - Ottawa, 1070
Masse, Mary, Clerk, Lakeshore, 712
Masse, Ray, Director, 631
Massé, Richard, Président-directeur général, 652
Massé, Yvan, Executive Vice President, Consultants Mésar inc., 151
Massee, Tyler, Manager, Campbell River, 679
Massicotte, Michael G., Partner, Borden Ladner Gervais LLP - Calgary, 1050
Massicotte, Normand, Sec.-Trés., Régie intermunicipale de l'eau potable Varennes, Ste-Julie, St-Am, 760
Massicotte, S., Head, Systems, Aerospace Engineering Test Establishment, 1103
Massicotte, Samuel, Heenan Blaikie S.E.N.C.R.L./SRL - Québec, 1088
Massinon, Rene, Director, CH2M HILL Canada Ltd., 138
Masson, Aarin, Director, 561
Masson, Eve, Sec.-Trés., Régie d'aqueduc de Grand Pré, 759
Masson, Marie-Geneviève, Associée, Langlois Kronström Desjardins, 1085
Masson, Robert, Président, Société de développement économique du Saint-Laurent, 1005
Masson, Réjean, Préfet, Coaticook, 747
Masson, Stéphane, Coordonateur scientifique, Parc Aquarium du Québec, 1179
Mastalerz, Tammy, Manager, Westburne Canada, 428
Masters, Andrew, Exec. Vice-President, Maxxam Analytics Inc., 283
Masters, Bill, Councillor, Colchester County, 697
Masters, Charles (Alfie), Vice President, Argus Telecom International Inc., 90
Matchim, Cluny, Director, Gander, 709-651-5914, 694
Mate, M. John, Cox and Palmer - St. John's, 1065
Matesic, Gina, Guelph-Humber Librarian, Humber College Institute of Technology & Advanced Learning, 1158
Mathany, Ian, Borden Ladner Gervais LLP - Toronto, 1073
Matheson, Catherine, General Manager, Community Development, Greater Sudbury / Grand Sudbury, 710
Matheson, George, Principal, Marbek Resource Consultants Ltd., 280
Matheson, Jeremy, Perth East, 728
Matheson, Terry, Officer, Hants East District, 697
Mathews, Michael, President, Waste Resource Containers, 420
Mathewson, C.G.A., Rebecca, Director, Administrative Services, Georgina, 709
Mathieson, Daniel, Mayor, Stratford, 519-271-2783, 720
Mathieu, Andre, Director, CIMA+, 141
Mathieu, José, President/CEO, RailPower Technologies Corp., 342
Mathieu, Micheline, Terrebonne, 745

Matichuk, Adam, Coordinator, Saskatchewan Wildlife Federation, 1002
Matichuk, Marianne, Mayor, Greater Sudbury / Grand Sudbury, 705-674-4455, 710
Matlock, Matt, Executive Director, Western Canada Tire Dealers Association, 1018
Matlow, Josh, Toronto, 721
Matson, Dana, Manager, Toromont Caterpillar, 398
Matson, Darrell, General Manager, Transportation & Works, Thunder Bay, 721
Matt, Jonathan, EPCOR Energy Services Inc., 189
Matte, Caroline, Partner, Borden Ladner Gervais LLP - Montréal, 1083
Matte, Jean, Directeur général, Rimouski, 418-724-3171, 740
Matte, Jean-Marie, Québec, 740
Mattern, Douglas, President, Association of World Citizens & World Citizens Foundation, 840
Mattheos, Sarantos, Thompson Dorfman Sweatman LLP, 1064
Matthews, Dan, General Manager, Laidlaw Carriers Inc. - Van Division, 262
Matthews, Dave, Supervisor, Red Deer, 674
Matthews, Erin, Vice President & General Manager, Vanbots Construction Corp., 409
Matthews, Fay, President, Newfoundland & Labrador Public Health Association, 963
Matthews, Joanne, Collections & Acquisitions Librarian, University of Northern British Columbia, 1115
Matthews, Karen, General Manager, Norfolk County Agricultural Society, 964
Matthews, Kevin, President, Canada Composting Inc., 123
Matthews, Larry, General Manager, Laidlaw Carriers Inc. - Van Division, 262
Matthews, Mary, Reference Services Librarian, Douglas College, 1114
Matthews, Michael, President, Caster-Rack Systems Ltd., 131
Matthews, R., Central Elgin, 724
Matthews-Malone, Betty, Director, Water & Wastewater Services, Niagara, 702
Mattice, Randy, Economic Development Officer, Stratford, 720
Mattie, H. Basil, President & Owner, Strait Engineering Ltd., 380
Mattinson, David, President, Hazco Environmental Services Ltd., 134, 227
Mattiussi, Ronald, City Manager, Kelowna, 681
Mattson, Mark O., Mattson, Mark O., 1077
Matysio, Cecile, Exec. Assistant, 661
Maudsley, Jim, Mayor, Thames Centre, 731
Maudsley, Jim, Warden & Councillor, Middlesex, 701
Mauer, Marvin, DEB Canada, 159
Mault, Francine, Clarence-Rockland, 708
Maunaga, Suzana, Head, Cataloguing, Trinity Western University, 1113
Maurice, Denis, Directeur, Mirabel, 450-475-2010, 738
Maurice, Joe, Vice-President, Ontario Association for Geographic & Environmental Education, 971
Mauro, Bill, Parliamentary Assistant, 631
Mauro, Joe, Lethbridge, 673
Mauro, Maria J., Director, Finance, Thorold, 720
Mauro, Pat, Manager, Engineering, Thunder Bay, 807-625-3022, 721
Maves, Bart, City & Regional Councillor, Niagara Falls, 715
Maves, MD, MBA, Michael D., Exec. Vice President & CEO, American Medical Association, 824
Mavin, Bob, Chief Financial Officer, Waterloo, 519-747-8722, 722
Mavrikos, Adia, Director, Colwood, 680
Mavrinac, Mary Ann, Chief Librarian, University of Toronto at Mississauga, 1145
Mawdsley, William, Director, 605
Max, Ruelokke, P.Eng, Chair & CEO, Canada-Newfoundland Offshore Petroleum Board, 763
Maxwell, James F., Partner, Macleod Dixon LLP, 1052
Maxwell, Michael (Max), Principal, Golder Associates Ltd., 214
Maxwell, Tom, Vice President, Aevitas Inc., 72
May, Judy, Vice-President, 661
May, Shelley, Coordinator, Ontario Parks Association, 976
May, Steve, Director, Corner Brook, 709-637-1541, 693
May, P.Eng., Don, Manager, Thompson-Nicola, 679
Maybee, Ross, General Manager, Valley Waste Resource Management, 409
Mayberry, David, Oxford, 728
Maycock, Warren, Dufferin, 699
Maycock, Warren, Deputy Mayor & Councillor, Orangeville, 716
Mayer, Daniel, Maire, Lachute, 736
Mayer, Daniel, Président, Régie Intermunicipale Argenteuil-Deux-Montagnes, 759

Mayer, Robert G., President, Mayer Heritage Consultants Inc., 284
Mayes, Kim, Chair, British Columbia Food Technolgists, 848
Mayes, Mike, Treasurer, Newmarket, 714
Mayhew, William J., Vice-President, Howell-Mayhew Engineering Inc., 234
Maynard, Hugh, Secretary-Treasurer, Canadian Farm Writers' Federation, 867
Maynard, Robert J., Principal Engineer, Aurora Environmental Consulting Ltd., 97
Maynard, P.Eng, Alan, Director, 641
Mayne, Chris, North Bay, 715
Mayne, Ed, Mayor, Parksville, 682
Mayne, Michael, Deputy Minister, 640
Mayne, Michael, Interim Chief Executive Officer, 640
Mayne, Rob, Director, Kelowna, 681
Maynes, Clifford, Executive Director, Green Communities Canada, 925
Mayo, Jeff, Omega Public Works, 312
Mayo, Roger, Sales Manager, Performance Fluid Equipement Inc., 321
Mayovsky, Grant H., Partner, Borden Ladner Gervais LLP - Vancouver, 1058
Mazen, El-Khatib, Trade Commissioner, 768
Mazereeuw, John, Manager, Trimax Residuals Management Inc., 401
Mazereeuw, Roger, Service Manager, WJF Instrumentation (1990) Ltd., 433
Mazerolle, Robert, Manager, Harris & Roome Supply Limited, 225
Mazur, Paulette, Cataloguing Technician, Manitoba Hydro, 1124
Mazza, Guido, Director, Building Services, Greater Sudbury / Grand Sudbury, 710
Mazza, Martin, Councillor, Niagara-on-the-Lake, 715
Mazzaferro, George, President, RP Graphics Group, 353
McAdam, Charlotte, Librarian, St. Andrews Biological Station, 1129
McAlea Major, Veronica, Director, Human Resources, London, 713
McAleese, Kerry, Marketing Manager, Kernic Systems Inc., 257
McAllister, P.Eng, David, President, Association of Consulting Engineering Companies - New Brunswick, 835
McAlpine, Dawn, City Clerk, Barrie, 705-739-4204, 706
McAmmond, Laurie, Executive Director, 582
McAra, Dave, Manager, Saanich, 250-475-5432, 688
McArdle, André, Secretary, Canadian Intergovernmental Conference Secretariat, 875
McAree, Marc, Willms & Shier Environmental Lawyers LLP, 1081
McArthur, Cory, President, Monsanto Canada Inc., 293
McArthur, Ian, President, Burke Mountain Naturalists, 851
McArthur, Peter J.G., Partner, Miller Thomson LLP - Vancouver, 1061
McArthur, Wendell, Director, Engineering, Barrie, 706
McAskill, James, O'Connor MacLeod Hanna LLP, 1070
McAtee, C., President, McAtee Safety & Environmental Health Services Ltd., 284
McAuley, Robert, Director, Planning & Development, Innisfil, 711
McAuley, Steve, Director, Thames Centre, 731
McAuley, P.Eng., Patrick, Commissioner, Public Works & Transportation, Sault Ste. Marie, 720
McAvoy, Lynette, Director, Health Sciences Association of Alberta, 928
McBain, Dale, Mayor, Moose Jaw, 754
McBeath, Suzanne, Librarian, Teck Resources, 1119
McBride, Ian R., Davies Ward Phillips & Vineberg LLP, 1074
McBride, Truper, Mayor, Cochrane, 671
McCabe, Darcy, Operations Manager, Mar Cor Purification, 280
McCabe, Denise E., Fulton & Company LLP, Lawyers & Trade-Mark Agents, 1056
McCabe, Don, President, Soil Conservation Council of Canada, 1009
McCabe, John, President/CEO, Argus Telecom International Inc., 90
McCabe, Tim, General Manager, Planning & Economic Development, Hamilton, 711
McCachen, Michael, Blake, Cassels & Graydon LLP - Calgary, 1049
McCaffrey, George T., President, J.L. Richards & Associates Limited, 250
McCall, Carol E., Paterson, MacDougall LLP, Barristers, Solicitors, 1079
McCall, Mike, Manager, Accurate Industrial Waste Limited, 66
McCallion, Hazel, Mayor, Mississauga, 714
McCallion, Hazel, Mayor & Councillor, Peel, 703

Executive Name Index

McCallum, David R., President, M+A Environmental Consultants, 276
McCallum, Joseph C., Heelis, Williams, Little & Almas LLP, Barristers & Solicitors, 1072
McCamley, John A., President/CEO, New West Gypsum Recycling Inc., 301
McCamley, John A. (Tony), General Manager, New West Gypsum Recycling Inc., 301
McCance, John, Secretary:, Ontario Prospectors Association, 977
McCann, Kathryn, Commissioner, Corporate Services, Scugog, 729
McCann, BAS, AMCT, Kathryn, Chief Administrative Officer, Brock, 724
McCann-Hiltz, Diane, Secretary, Alberta Agricultural Economics Association, 815
McCarten, W. Paul, Partner, Borden Ladner Gervais LLP - Toronto, 1073
McCarter, Katherine S., Executive Director, Ecological Society of America, 908
McCarthy, Daniel, Director, Energy, Environment Policy, & Coordinati, 510
McCarthy, Jane, Vice-President, 636
McCarthy, John, President, Salmon Preservation Association for the Waters of Newfoundland, 998
McCarthy, Stuart, Investor Relations & Communications, Thermal Energy International Inc., 394
McCartney, Leah, Project Manager, University Technologies International, 407
McCarty, Marion, Librarian, Buffalo Lake Naturalists Club, 1109
McCarver, Wayne, General Manager, Integra Technologies Ltd., 243
McCaskill, Keith, Chief of Police, Winnipeg, 690
McCaslin, Jo-Anne, Clerk, North Dundas, 727
McCaughan, D., Director, Operations, Guelph, 710
McCauley, Gordon C., Chair, Hallmark Insurance Brokers Ltd., 224
McCauley, John, President, Ontario Association for Impact Assessment, 971
McCauley, Pamela, Vice-President, Hotz Environmental Services Inc., 234
McCaw, Dan, Hastings, 700
McCaw, Darren, President, Control Fire Systems, 151
McCharles, John, Lambton, 701
McClare, Christine, Coordinator, Hants West District, 697
McClellan, David, Manager, Aqua Terre Solutions Inc., 88
McClelland, Chris, Manager, Engineered Air, 180
McClinton, P.Ag., Blair, Executive Manager, Saskatchewan Soil Conservation Association, 1001
McCloskey, Joanne, Head of Acquistions, Calgary Library, 1100
McCloskey, Peter F., Charlottetown, 732
McClure, Gord, Area Councillor, Caledon, 707
McClure, Neville J., Partner, Stikeman Elliott LLP - Vancouver, 1062
McCluskey, Gloria, Councillor, Halifax Regional Municipality, 695
McColeman, Norma, Summerside, 733
McColl, Ian, Executive Vice-President, Aker Metals (Toronto), 76
McCollough, Jean, Greffier, Saint-Georges, 742
McCollum, Vicki, Librarian, Yukon Dept. of Environment, 1191
McComb, Brian, Director, Planning, Hastings, 700
McConaghy, Scott, Fredericton, 691
McConchie, Corinne, Systems & Technical Services Librarian, University College of the Fraser Valley, 1110
McConkey, Sandy, Springwater, 730
McConnell, Gord, Lanark, 701
McConnell, Mary, Associate University Librarian, Planning & Adminis, University of Calgary, 1103
McConnell, Merle, Chief, Health Canada, Health Products & Food Branch, 1150
McConnell, Pam, Toronto, 721
McConomy, Brent, Sales Director, Hayward Gordon Ltd., 227
McCooey, Mark, President, SEI Industries Ltd., 362
McCooeye, Timothy, Quality Control Manager, Accutest Laboratories Ltd., 66
McCoombs, Michael J., Miramichi, 691
McCorkell, Byron, Director, Kamloops, 250-828-3850, 681
McCormack, Hilary, Manager, Human Resources, New Tecumseth, 714
McCormack, Nancy, Head, Law Library, William R. Lederman Law Library, 1143
McCormack, Neil, Business Manager, Ontario Pipe Trades Council, 977
McCormack, Renald, Contact, Envir'eau Puits Inc., 182
McCormack, Stuart C., Managing Partner, Stikeman Elliott LLP - Ottawa, 1071

McCormick, Gary, Reference Librarian, Bishop's University, 1185
McCormick, Morris, Division Manager, Environment, Cornwall, 708
McCormick, Penny, Director, 611
Mccormick, Raymond P., Sr. VP & CFO, IMP Liquid Meters & Petroleum Services, 239
McCormick, Q.C., Carman G., Stewart McKelvey Stirling Scales - Halifax, 1067
McCoubrey, David, Coordinator, Annapolis County, 696
McCourt, Pat, Hamilton, 725
McCoy, QC, Elaine, President, Macleod Institute, 950
McCracken, Ken, President, A&C Produits Chimiques Americains Ltée, 63
McCracken, Lynn, Library Technician, Information/ILL, Loyalist College of Applied Arts & Technology, 1139
McCrae, James, Brandon, 689
McCrank, Michael, Préfet, Pontiac, 751
McCrank, Q.C., P.Eng, Neil, Chair, 567
McCrank, Q.C., P.Eng, Neil, Counsel, Borden Ladner Gervais LLP - Calgary, 1050
McCray, Kevin, Executive Director, National Ground Water Association, 958
McCrea, Linda, Contact, Vacuum Products Canada Inc., 408
McCreary, Dan, Brantford, 707
McCreary, Randall, Reynolds, Mirth, Richards & Farmer LLP, 1056
McCrory, Colleen, Executive Director, Valhalla Wilderness Society, 1016
McCrossan, David, President, Cannington Group, 126
McCuaig, Bruce, Deputy Minister, 635
McCuaig, Mary J., Clerk, The Nation, 731
McCue, Richard, Systems Administrator, Diana M. Priestly Law Library, 1120
McCue, Robert D., McCarthy Tétrault LLP - Calgary, 1052
McCullagh, Corwin, Director, Lloydminster, 780-871-8340, 673
McCulloch, Mark, Manager, 617
McCulloch, Rob, Borden Ladner Gervais LLP - Calgary, 1050
McCullogh, Q.C., Kenneth B., Partner, Stewart McKelvey Stirling Scales - Saint John, 1065
McCullough, Rick, Director, Regina, 754
McCullough, Rob, Director, Environmental Services, Simcoe, 704
McCully Collier, Marie, President, Public Health Association of Nova Scotia, 991
McCunn, Timothy J., Borden Ladner Gervais LLP - Ottawa, 1070
McCurdy, Earle, President, Canadian Council of Professional Fish Harvesters, 865
McCutcheon, David, Fraser Milner Casgrain LLP - Toronto, 1075
McDade, Q.C., Greg J., Managing Partner, Ratcliff & Company LLP, 1057
McDermid, Hugh, Perth East, 728
McDermid, Ryan, Operations Manager, The Recycle Systems Company Inc., 393
McDermott, Eamon, Vice-President, Canadian Federation of Engineering Students, 868
Mcdermott, Marilyn, Information Services Coordinator, Mohawk College of Applied Arts & Technology, 1141
McDermott, Ron, Essex, 519-776-8150, 699
McDermott, Ron, Mayor, Essex, 519-776-8150, 709
McDermott, Sean, Director, Horizons Systems Group Inc., 233
McDiarmid, Q.C., Robert W., Morelli Chertkow LLP, Lawyers, 1056
McDonald, Al, Mayor, North Bay, 715
McDonald, Art, Regional Manager, Vestar, 412
McDonald, Bob, Program Coordinator, Cowichan Valley, 677
McDonald, Brock, Director, Maple Ridge, 604-467-7370, 687
McDonald, Bruce, Delta, 604-946-4141, 686
McDonald, Carol, Director, Ecojustice Canada, 908
McDonald, Carol, Director of Admin. & Human Resources, Ecojustice Canada, 1117
McDonald, Charles, Director, Development Services, Greater Napanee, 709
McDonald, Connie, Library Technician, Information, Loyalist College of Applied Arts & Technology, 1139
McDonald, Dale, Director, Summerland, 695
McDonald, Dallas, Contact, Heating, Refrigeration & Air Conditioning Contractors Association, 928
McDonald, Dalton, Mayor, Alnwick-Haldimand, 905-349-2747, 724
McDonald, Donald J., County Engineer, Stormont, Dundas & Glengarry, 730
McDonald, Everett, Reeve, Grande Prairie No. 1, 669
McDonald, Gayla, Clerk & Manager, Administration, New Tecumseth, 714
McDonald, Gerard, Vice-President, 601

McDonald, Jon, Manager, New Westminster, 604-521-6594, 682
McDonald, Kate, Energy Coordinator, The Environmental Coalition of PEI, 911
McDonald, Lori, Clerk, Bracebridge, 706
McDonald, Madeline, Manager, Mount Waddington, 250-956-3301, 678
McDonald, Marie, Director General, 545
McDonald, Mark G., Chief Administrative Officer, Elgin, 699
McDonald, Morgan, Environmental Contact, Taylor Munro Energy Systems Inc., 387
McDonald, Paul, Contact, Bradford White Canada Inc., 115
McDonald, Paul M., Cox and Palmer - St. John's, 1065
McDonald, Rodger, Principal Engineer, MR2-McDonald & Associates, 294
McDonald, Stephen, Chief Administrative Officer, South Dundas, 730
McDonald, Steve, Marketing Manager, Nett Technologies Inc., 300
McDonald, Q.C., Daniel J., Burnet, Duckworth & Palmer LLP, 1050
McDonell, Chris, Deputy Mayor & Councillor, North Glengarry, 727
McDonell, Jim, Mayor, South Glengarry, 730
McDonell, Paul, Burnaby, 679
McDonell, Robert J., Farris, Vaughan, Wills & Murphy LLP, 1059
McDonnell, Glenn S., Contact, Sigma Engineering Ltd., 367
McDonnell, John C., Brownlee LLP, 1054
McDonnell, Neil, COO, TIR Systems Ltd., 396
McDonnell, Paul A., Partner, Miller Thomson LLP - Vancouver, 1061
McDonough, Fergal J., Photech Environmental Solutions, 323
McDougall, Barbara, Chair, 544
McDougall, Bill, Operations, UNOTEC, 407
McDougall, Dan, CAO, Colchester County, 697
McDougall, Ian, Director, Recreation & Culture Services, Newmarket, 714
McDougall, John R., South Frontenac, 730
McDougall, John R., President, 546
McDougall, Mike, President, Klondike Placer Miners' Association, 947
McDougall, Raymond A., Partner, Stikeman Elliott LLP - Toronto, 1080
McDougall, T. Micheal, Kanuka Thuringer LLP, Barristers & Solicitors, 1090
McDougall, Terry, Executive Director, Niagara Peninsula Conservation Foundation, 964
McDowell, Lisa A., Partner, Stikeman Elliott LLP - Calgary, 1054
McDowell, Mary, Map Library Assistant, Map Library, 1159
McDowell, Patricia, Vice-President, 520
McEachen, Terry, General Manager, Fraser-Fort George, 678
McEachran, Jon, City Councillor, Sarnia, 719
McElderry, Howard, Co-founder, Archipelago Marine Research Ltd., 90
McElhanney, Dave, McElhanney Consulting Services Ltd., 284
McElhanney, William L., Ackroyd LLP Barristers & Solicitors, 1054
McElligott, RPBio., Paul, President, College of Applied Biology British Columbia, 897
McElveny, Darcy, Manager, PRT Inc., 336
McElveny, Dave, Manager, PRT Inc., 336
McElwain, Brian, President, Muskoka Lakes Association, 956
McElwain, Kirk, Centre Wellington, 724
McEvoy, Jamie, New Westminster, 682
McEwan, Q.C., J. Kenneth, Farris, Vaughan, Wills & Murphy LLP, 1059
McEwen, Clayton, Lennox & Addington, 613-354-4883, 701
McEwen, Jeff, Coordinator, Engineering, North Grenville, 728
McEwen, Q.C., David F., Alexander Holburn Beaudin & Lang, LLP, 1057
McFadden, Bruce, Manager, Flygt Canada, 198
McFadden, Michael G., Partner, Ogilvy Renault LLP/S.E.N.C.R.L., s.r.l. - Toronto, 1078
McFadden, Sue, Peel, 714, 703
McFadyen, Alan B., Managing Director, Western Canadian Spill Services Ltd., 429
McFadyen, Linda, Deputy Minister, 589
McFall, Mary Jane, Brockville, 707
McFarland, Bob, Director, Community Services, Woodstock, 723
McFarland, Dana, University Librarian, Royal Roads University, 1121
McFarland, Lorie, Manager, Utilities, Loyalist, 727
McFarland, Sean, Office Manager, Golder Associates Ltd., 214
McFarlane, Anne, Vice-President, Canadian Institute for Health Information, 872
McFarlane, Bruce, President/CEO, Galaxy Pallets Ltd., 204

Executive Name Index

McFarlane, James, President, International Submarine Engineering Ltd., 245
McFarlane, Maryse, Coordinator, 597
McFarlane, Q.C., John S., Stewart McKelvey Stirling Scales - Halifax, 1067
McFayden, Lee, Director, Similkameen Naturalist Club, 1004
McFayden, Ross A., Thompson Dorfman Sweatman LLP, 1064
McGarry, David, President/Operations Manager, Elecsar Engineering Co. Ltd., 174
McGarry, Mike, Sr. Engineer, Cowater International Inc., 153
McGaughey, Anne, Reference Librarian, York University Glendon College Campus, 1164
McGeary, Jim, Area Supervisor, Armtec Construction Products, 92
McGee, David, Manager, Canada Science & Technology Museum, 1148
McGee, Karen, Coordinator, Human Resources, Smith-Ennismore-Lakefield, 729
McGee, Larry, Director, Net Safety Monitoring Inc., 300
McGee, Ric, Mayor, Kawartha Lakes, 711
McGee, P.Eng., GSC, Randy, Vice-President, 521
McGhan, Eric, Deputy Minister, 572
McGhee, Ken, Dufferin, 699
McGill, Sean, Director, Delta, 604-946-3218, 686
McGill, P.Eng., James D., Executive Director, Canadian Association for Mine & Explosive Ordnance Security, 856
McGillis, Bryan, Mayor, South Stormont, 730
McGillivray, Dan, Managing Director, Ontario Centres of Excellence, 312
McGillivray, Dennis, Sales, FLSmidth Canada Ltd., 197
McGillvray, Roger, Clearview, 725
McGilvray, Kate, Blake, Cassels & Graydon LLP - Toronto, 1072
McGinn, Michael, President, W.T. McGinn & Associates Ltd., 415
McGinn, Patrick, Vice-President, W.T. McGinn & Associates Ltd., 415
McGinn, Sean, Coordinator, Alberni-Clayoquot, 250-720-2714, 676
McGinnis, Gregs T., Partner, Heenan Blaikie LLP - Toronto, 1076
McGinty, Shannon K., McCaffery Mudry Pritchard LLP, Barristers & Solicitors, 1052
McGlashon, Glenn J., Director, Planning & Development Services, Cobourg, 708
McGoldrick, Elizabeth, Library Assistant, Defence R & D Canada - Ottawa, 1149
McGowan, Joe, Director, Cranbrook, 250-489-0240, 680
McGowan, John P., Cassels Brock & Blackwell LLP, 1074
McGowan, Rob, Manager, Parkland County, 670
McGrath, Beth M.W., Ottenheimer Baker, 1066
McGrath, Bob, Director, Human Resources, North Bay, 715
McGrath, John, Information Technology Services Coordinator, Grant MacEwan University, 1105
McGrath, Karen, Manager, Library Services, Libraries of Niagara College, 1165
McGrath, Margie, Secretary, Quispamsis, 506-849-5745, 692
McGrath, Rosalie E., Partner, Ottenheimer Baker, 1066
McGrath, Q.C., Dalton W., Blake, Cassels & Graydon LLP - Calgary, 1049
McGregor, Ellen, President, Fielding Chemical Technologies Inc., 195
McGregor, Gerald, Kawartha Lakes, 711
McGregor, Tom, Chatham-Kent, 724
McGregor, CMA, C.P.P., Violet, Manager, Surrey, 604-591-4011, 684
McGrogan, Andy, Police Chief, Medicine Hat, 403-529-8410, 673
McGueire, Gerry, Chair, Willow Creek Regional Waste Management Services Commission, 758
McGugan, Debbie, Head, Reference Services, Grant MacEwan University, 1105
McGugan, Don, Lambton, 701
McGuinty, Gordon E., President, Notre Development Corp., 308
McGuire, Darren, Partner, Borden Ladner Gervais LLP - Montréal, 1083
McGuire, Mike, Lead, Monsanto Canada Inc., 293
McGuire, Peter, Saint John, 692
McGuire, Veronica, Executive Director, 518
McHaffie, Nicholas P., Partner, Stikeman Elliott LLP - Ottawa, 1071
McHarg, Troy, Clerk, Milton, 714
McHattie, Brian, Hamilton, 711
McIllwraith, Peter, Secretary, Citizens For Renewable Energy, 895
McIlmoyle, Jim, Manager, Trent Hills, 731
McIlveen, Nyle C., Vice-President, Geo-Logic Inc., 210
McIlwain, Greg, Lang Michener LLP - Toronto, 1077

McInnes, Allan J., President, Bercan Environmental Resources Inc., 105
McInnes, J. David, Field Law - Edmonton, 1055
McInnes, Mike, Chair, Ontario Printing & Imaging Association, 977
McInnis, Bert, whatIf? Technologies Inc., 431
McInnis, Steve, Director, Mountain View County, 669
McInroy, Peter, Chair, Musquodoboit Trailways Association, 956
McIntosh, Betty, New Westminster, 682
McIntosh, Betty, Chief Administrative Officer, Clerk, & Treasurer, Hamilton, 725
McIntosh, George, Foreman, Cold Lake, 780-639-3604, 672
McIntosh, James A., Director, Wasaga Beach, 705-429-2540, 722
McIntosh, Julia, Chief, Departmental Library, Environment Canada, 1168
McIntosh, Keith, District Manager, BFI Canada Inc., 107
McIntyre, Bruce, PricewaterhouseCoopers Management Consultants, 332
McIntyre, Bruce E., Global Forest & Paper Practice, PricewaterhouseCoopers Management Consultants, 332
McIntyre, James, Elgin, 699
McIntyre, Jim, General Manager, Coquitlam, 604-927-3000, 680
McIntyre, Sandi, Kingsville, 712
McIntyre, Trevor, Director, IBI Group, 238
McIsaac, Steve, Executive Director, Inside Education, 931
McIver, Brian, Vice-President, Nova PB Inc., 308
McIver, Colin J., Fraser Milner Casgrain LLP - Vancouver, 1060
McIver, Karen, Director, Saskatchewan Outdoor & Environmental Education Association, 1001
McIver, Milt, Bruce, 698
McIvor, Kelly, President, Saskatchewan Health Libraries Association, 1000
McIvor, R.A. (Dick), Treasurer, Maintenance & Engineering Society of The Canadian Institute of Mi, 950
McKague, Patti, Director, Corporate Communications, Waterloo, 519-747-8748, 722
McKague, William G., President, Gro-Bark (Ontario) Ltd., 219
McKay, Barb, Wellington, 519-822-2984, 705
McKay, Brian, Director, Finance, Sarnia, 719
McKay, Cameron, Manager, Public Works, Leamington, 726
McKay, Corinne, General Manager, Northern Native Fishing Corporation, 966
McKay, Diena, Sales, Northern Lights Energy Systems, 307
McKay, Don E., Oxford, 519-462-2697, 728
McKay, Gordon A., Mayor, Midland, 713
McKay, Ian, General Manager, Sturgeon County, 780-939-8337, 670
McKay, John, Regional Director, Williams Engineering Inc., 432
McKay, Ken, Contact, Foothills No. 31, 669
McKay, Laurence, Owner, Northern Lights Energy Systems, 307
McKay, Ron, Perth, 703
Mckay, Scott, Head of Technical Services, Olds College, 1109
McKay, Stephen, President, Quester Tangent Corp., 339
McKeage, Sue, Director, 613
McKean, Malcolm, General Manager, Abandonrite, 64
McKearney, John, General Manager & Fire Chief, Vancouver, 604-665-6051, 685
McKee, John, Office Manager, Trow Consulting Engineers Ltd., 403
McKee, Michael, Manager, Acme Engineering Products Ltd., 67
McKeever, Lesley, Senior Vice-President, Food & Consumer Products of Canada, 918
McKeever, Patrick, President, Lojen Industrial Cleaning Ltd., 273
McKeich, Cynthia, Campus Librarian, King Campus, 1142
McKell, Bruce, McKell Marketing Ltd., 285
McKelvey, Michael K., Partner, Borden Ladner Gervais LLP - Toronto, 1073
McKelvey, Peter, President, Fundy Engineering & Consulting Ltd., 203
McKelvey, Q.C., E. Neil, Counsel, Stewart McKelvey Stirling Scales - Saint John, 1065
McKelvie, Dan, National Marketing Manager, Leeson Canada Ltd., 266
McKend, Michael, President, Chromatographic Specialties Inc., 140
McKenna, Brian J., Vice-Chair, 641
McKenna, Bruce A., Lang Michener LLP - Toronto, 1077
McKenna, Earl D., Councillor, Colchester County, 697
McKenna, John, President & Chief Executive Officer, Air Transport Association of Canada, 814
McKennan, CMA, Bill, Director, Kings County, 902-690-6130, 696
McKenney, Mark, President, MGM Management, 288
McKenzie, Bill, South Glengarry, 613-347-3254, 730

McKenzie, Carol, Clerk, Lambton Shores, 726
McKenzie, J.Scott, Principal, Golder Associates Ltd., 214
McKenzie, Janet, Vice President, Eco2 Systems Inc., 171
McKenzie, Kathryn, Medical Library Technician, Rockyview Hospital Library, 1102
McKenzie, Nicole, Secretary, Entomological Society of Ontario, 911
McKenzie, Robert, Program Specialist, 584
McKenzie, Rory, Supervisor, Bulkley-Nechako, 250-692-3195, 676
McKenzie, Susan, Chief Administrative Officer, Clearview, 725
McKenzie, Tom, Police Chief, Lethbridge, 403-327-2210, 673
McKenzie, Vince J., Fire Chief, Grand Falls-Windsor, 709-489-0431, 694
McKeown, David, Medical Officer of Health, Toronto, 416-338-7820, 721
McKeown, Frank, District Manager, BFI Canada Inc., 107
McKercher, Susan, Directrice générale, Saint-Constant, 742
McKerlie, David W., President/CEO, McKerlie Solar Systems, 285
McKernan, J. Michael, Vice-President, TetrES Consultants Inc., 391
McKim, John, General Manager, Pol-E-Mar Inc., 327
McKinlay, Duncan, Deputy Mayor & Councillor, Grey, 700
McKinlay, Linda, Lakeshore, 712
McKinley, Scott, Executive Scientific Director, AquaNet - Network in Aquaculture, 828
McKinney, John M., President, Project Engineering Limited, 334
McKinnon, Andrew, Director, Truro, 696
McKinnon, Brian, Ward Councillor, Thunder Bay, 721
McKinnon, Cameron S., Burchell, MacDougall, 1068
McKinnon, Colin D., Scott Venturo LLP, 1053
McKinnon, Curtis, Manager, Normcan, 306
McKinnon, D., Vice-President, TLT Co-Vent, 397
McKinnon, Debbie, Director, Finance, Barrie, 706
McKinnon, Gerry, Manager, Surrey, 604-590-4011, 684
McKinnon, Mark, Executive Vice-President, Ontario Professional Fire Fighters Association, 977
McKinnon, R., Manager, Safety Projects International Inc., 355
McKinnon, Robert J., Fraser Milner Casgrain LLP - Calgary, 1051
McKnight, Andrew, Marketing Manager, Jomac Canada Inc., 253
McKnight, David T., Alexander Holburn Beaudin & Lang, LLP, 1057
McKnight, Donald, FCILT Executive Director, Chartered Institute of Logistics and Transport in North America, 894
McKnight, Geoff, Director, Planning & Development, Bradford West Gwillimbury, 706
McKnight, Jeff, Manager, Toromont Caterpillar, 398
McKnight Duralia, Ann, Manager, Human Resources, Perth, 703
McKyes, Edward, Associate Director, Brace Centre for Water Resources Management, 115
McLachlan, Glenda, Executive Director, Quetico Foundation, 992
McLachlan, Jim, Director, 549
McLachlan, Ross, Acting Director, 664
McLaren, Ed, Director, Dundas-Jafine Inc., 167
McLaren, Gene, Director, Engineering Services, Ingersoll, 711
McLaren, Graeme, Project Assessment Director, 578
McLaren, Leslie, Marketing Service Manager, Roxul Inc., 353
McLaren, Ross, Director, 611
McLarty, D., Town Clerk, Richmond Hill, 718
McLarty, Q.C., Allan L., Fraser Milner Casgrain LLP - Calgary, 1051
McLauchlan, George, Director, Calgary, 403-268-2201, 671
McLauchlin, Robert, Supervisor, Anadarko Canada Corp., 1099
McLaughlin, David, President & CEO, 549
McLaughlin, Donald, Technician, Bathurst, 690
McLaughlin, Hélène, Directrice de la bibliothèque, Campus de Shippagan, 1130
McLaughlin, Patricia, Manager, Veolia ES Canada Industrial Services Inc., 411
McLaughlin, Shaun J., Mississippi Mills, 714
McLay, Brenda, Director, Near North Laboratories Inc., 299
McLean, Bill, Durham, 699
McLean, Bill, Regional Councillor, Pickering, 718
McLean, Charles W., Lakeshore, 712
McLean, Dan, Deputy Mayor & Councillor, Springwater, 730
McLean, Darrel, General Manager, Reinforced Plastic Systems Inc., 344
McLean, Darrin, Director, Richmond County, 902-226-3988, 698
McLean, Dave, President, David A. McLean & Associates, 158
McLean, Greg, Sales, Wyckomar Inc., 435
McLean, John, Foreman, Cold Lake, 780-594-3776, 672
McLean, Jonathan M., Senior Counsel, Stikeman Elliott LLP - Vancouver, 1062

Executive Name Index

McLean, Larry, Branch Coordinator, Toromont Caterpillar, 398
Mclean, Mike, Vice-President, Expocrete Concrete Products Ltd., 192
McLean, Roy, Reeve, Foothills No. 31, 669
McLean, Stewart, Chilliwack, 680
McLean, Tom, President, Ontario Vegetation Management Association, 981
McLean, William R., Partner, Borden Ladner Gervais LLP - Toronto, 1073
mclean foundation, The McLean Foundation, Toronto, ON, 1044
McLean-Leroux, Chantal, Treasurer, Clarence-Rockland, 708
McLellan, David, General Manager, Vancouver, 604-276-4083, 685
McLellan, Jennifer, Chair, Elora Environment Centre, 909
Mclellan, Jillian, Office Administrator, Yukon Fish & Game Association, 1024
McLellan, Walter, Municipal Clerk, Kitimat, 687
McLelland, Andrea, Information Resources Librarian, Health Sciences Library, 1141
McLennan, Mike, Director, Power Suction Services Ltd., 329
McLennan, Paul, Guelph Branch Manager, Gamsby & Mannerow Ltd., 204
Mclennan, Rex, Chief Financial Officer, Viterra Inc., 414
McLeod, Andrew, Manager, East Kootenay, 677
McLeod, Barbara, Clerk, Wilmot, 732
McLeod, Bob, Minister, 607
McLeod, Bob, Minister Responsible, 608
McLeod, Darcy, Director, Yorkton, 306-786-1750, 755
McLeod, Dave, Ingersoll, 711
McLeod, David, Welland, 722
McLeod, Donald J., McCarthy Tétrault LLP - Calgary, 1052
McLeod, Ian, Deputy Mayor & Councillor, South Glengarry, 730
McLeod, Michael, Minister, 608
McLeod, Michael, President, Bancroft Light & Power Company (2000) Ltd., 101
McLeod, N., Principal, Catterall & Wright, 132
McLeod, Roderick M., Counsel, Miller Thomson LLP - Toronto, 1078
McLeod, Scott, Fire Chief, Pelham, 717
McLeod, Scott, Sales and Project Engineer, Aerzen Canada Surpresseurs Compresseurs inc., 72
McLeod, Sheldon, Secretary, Manitoba Environmental Industries Association Inc., 951
McLeod, Q.C., Roderick M., Miller Thomson LLP - Markham, 1069
McLeod-Hill, Lori, CFO, HSE Integrated, 234
McLevy, Grant, Director, Human Resources, Grey, 700
McLoughlin, O'Shein, Manager, Harris & Roome Supply Limited, 225
McMackin, Q.C., Gerald S., Partner, Stewart McKelvey Stirling Scales - Saint John, 1065
McMahan, Ron, President/CEO, Airzone One Ltd., 76
McMahon, Beth, Executive Director, Atlantic Canadian Organic Regional Network, 843
McMahon, Colleen, Manager, Competitive Intelligence, SaskTel, 1188
McMahon, Gale, Assistant, Fraser Valley, 677
McMahon, James, Haliburton, 705-286-2801, 700
McMahon, Jim, Vice-President, CCS Income Trust, 134
McMahon, Mary-Margaret, Toronto, 721
McMahon, Mike, Fire Chief, Chesterville, North Dundas, 727
McMahon, Ron, Director, 618
McManaman, Jim, Owen Sound, 717
McManus, Karen, Librarian, Information Centre (Calgary), 1101
McManus, Kerry, Stratford, 720
McManus, Neil, Director, Northwest Occupational Health & Safety, 307
McMartin, Pierre, Beaudry, Bertrand Avocats, 1082
McMeekin, Bruce J., Partner, Miller Thomson LLP - Toronto, 1078
McMeekin, J. Bruce, Miller Thomson LLP - Markham, 1070
McMillan, Bob, Perth, 703
McMillan, Bob, Deputy Mayor & Councillor, Perth East, 728
McMillan, Duncan, Sales Contact, Flowserve Canada Corp. - Pump Division, 197
McMillan, Emmerson, President, 637
McMillan, Grant, General Manager & City Treasurer, Brandon, 204-729-2209, 689
McMillan, N., Manager, Townsend Engineering, 399
McMillan, Rory, Chair, Kenora District Services Board of Directors, Kenora, 807-468-4383, 726
McMillan, Sharon, Middlesex Centre, 727
McMinn, Nancy, Parks Superintendent, Charlottetown, 732
McMorris, Don, Minister, 659

McMullan, Brian, Niagara, 702
McMullan, Brian, Mayor, St. Catharines, 905-688-5600, 719
McMullen, Bruce, KMK Consultants Limited, 258
McMullen, John, President, John McMullen & Associates, 253
McMullen, Ken, Director, Fire Services, Tecumseh, 720
McMullin, Ron, Executive Director, Alberta Irrigation Projects Association, 818
McMurray, Barb, Bracebridge, 706
McMurray, François, Chargé de projet, Exploitation Santec Inc., 192
McMurtry, Q.C., William R., Blaney McMurtry LLP, 1073
McNabb, Carol, Head, Technical Services, Georgian College of Applied Arts & Technology, 1138
McNabb, Larry, Nanaimo, 681
McNair, Alan, Partner, McNair & Marshall Planning & Development Consultants, 285
McNair, Alice, Chair, Red Deer College, 1109
McNairn, Deborah, Development Analyst, ETV Canada, 190
McNally, Gary, Sales Manager, Enercorp Instruments Ltd., 179
McNally, R. Andy, IBI Group, 238
McNally, P.Eng., Patrick, General Manager, Environmental Engineering Service, London, 713
McNamara, Gary, Essex, 519-735-6654, 699
McNamara, Gary, Mayor, Tecumseh, 519-735-6654, 720
McNaught, Hugh, Information & Library Services Manager, Sanofi Pasteur Limited, 1161
McNaughtan, Sheila, Reynolds, Mirth, Richards & Farmer LLP, 1056
McNaughton, William K., National Leader, Environmental, Borden Ladner Gervais LLP - Vancouver, 1058
McNee, Rhonda, Manager, Waterous Power Systems, 423
McNeely, Andrew, Manager, Whitchurch-Stouffville, 723
McNeely, J.B., Manager, Kamloops, 250-828-3463, 681
McNeil, Bob, Director, Cape Breton, 902-563-5066, 695
McNeil, James E. (Jim), Principal, Val Temp Sales Ltd., 409
McNeil, John, Manager, Forestry & Cemetery Services, Oakville, 715
McNeil, L., Senior Researcher, Robert Hornal & Associates Ltd., 348
McNeil, Lee, Councillor, Cape Breton, 695
McNeil, Lucie, Secretary, Option Environnement Inc., 313
McNeil, Pippa, Co-Coordinator, Whitehorse, 867-668-8312, 755
McNeill, Dan, Manager, East Kootenay, 677
McNeill, Terry, President, Oak Environmental Inc., 310
McNeilly, Kent, Manager, Energy Systems & Design Limited, 179
McNichol, Ann, Sr. Associate, Praxis Inc., 330
McNicoll, Dan, Office Manager, Trow Consulting Engineers Ltd., 403
McNish, Jeff, Manager, Halford Pallet Recyclers Ltd., 224
McNiven, Al, Director, North Okanagan, 250-550-3664, 678
McNiven, Bruce, Partner, Heenan Blaikie S.E.N.C.R.L/SRL, 1084
McNulty, Bill, Richmond, 684
McNulty, Michael, Technical Manager, ProMinent Fluid Controls Ltd., 334
McNulty, Pat, Manager, Transportation, Belleville, 706
McPhadden, Ian, President/CEO, Ag-West Bio Inc., 72
McPhail, Allan G., South Frontenac, 730
McPhail, Barbara E., Principal, Unterman McPhail Associates, 407
McPhail, Patricia, Cox and Palmer - Charlottetown, 1082
McPhail, Scott, Customer Service, Radiodetection (Canada) Ltd., 341
McPhail, P.Eng., Roy, Presiding Member, 590
McPhee, Dave, Officer, Leduc County, 780-955-4541, 669
McPhee, Laura, Marketing Consultant, Maritime Geothermal Ltd., 280
McPhee, Steve, Industrial Sales Manager, K&D Pratt Group Inc., 254
McPherson, Brent, Lang Michener LLP - Toronto, 1077
McPherson, Jane, Treasurer & Director, Financial Services, Strathroy-Caradoc, 731
McPherson, Jim, Meaford, 519-538-0859, 727
McQuade, Colleen, Marketing Coordinator, ASL Environmental Sciences Inc., 94
McQuaker, Randall, Executive Director, Green Action Centre, 925
McQueen, James G., Director, Corporate Services, Milton, 714
McQueen, Marilyn, Manager, FS Partners, 202
McQueen, Nairn, Vice-President, 629
McQuillan, Edward, Operator, Hants East District, 697
McRadu, Grant, CAO, West Vancouver, 604-925-7002, 689
McRae, Don, Minister, 574
McRae, Ken, Mayor, Port Alberni, 683
McRae, Maria, Ottawa, 613-580-2486, 716

McRae, Marshall, CFO/Secretary/Vice-President, CCS Income Trust, 134
McReynolds, B.A., LL.B., D. Shawn, Managing Partner, Davies Ward Phillips & Vineberg LLP, 1074
McRobert, David, In-House Counsel/Senior Policy Advisor, 626
McTaggart, Dale, Municipal Engineer, Salmon Arm, 684
McTaggart, Keith, General Manager, Lucas-Milhaupt Toronto, 274
McTavish, Bruce, Associate, Zbeetnoff Agro-Environmental Consulting, 436
McTavish, Robert J., Perth, 703
McTurk, David, President, Earthworks Technology Inc., 169
McVey, Geoff, Manager, Forest, Leeds & Grenville, 726
McVicar, James, Partner, Heenan Blaikie LLP - Toronto, 1076
McWhinnie, Ken, CH2M Hill Canada Limited, 137
McWilliams, Dan, Peterborough, 718
Meade, Aidan J., McInnes Cooper, 1067
Meade, Brent, Deputy Minister, 604
Meade, Kathy, Manager, Human Resources, Sarnia, 719
Meade, Sharon L., Event Coordinator, Green Tourism Association, 926
Meadows, Lyndsay, Research Technician, Ecologistics Research Services, 172
Meadows, Teresa, Associate, Miller Thomson LLP - Toronto, 1078
Mealing, Greg, Superintendent, Summerland, 689
Mearns, Bridget, Lethbridge, 673
Measures, Doug, Clearview, 725
Mech, Konrad, Co-Founder & Vice-President, Drexan Energy Systems Inc., 166
Meckling, Brent A., Davis LLP - Vancouver, 1059
Medemblik, Butch, Walinga Inc., 416
Medemblik, Terry, Walinga Inc., 416
Medhora, Rohinton, Vice-President, 544
Medhurst, Beth, Senior Vice-President, Human Resources, 511
Medley, Murray, Fire Chief, Bracebridge, 706
Medves, Gian, Acting Chief Librarian, Bora Laskin Law Library, 1156
Medway, Mike, Manager, Westburne Canada, 428
Meech, Judith, Secretary-General & Treasurer, International Union of Food Science & Technology, 945
Meed Ward, Marianne, Halton, 700
Meeder, Anneli, Librarian, Triton Environmental Consultants Ltd., 1116
Meehan, Charles, Director, 621
Meehan, Kerry, President/CEO, Konica Minolta Business Solutions (Canada) Inc., 259
Meehan, Q.C., Eugene, Lang Michener LLP - Ottawa, 1070
Meeker, Mike, President, Northern Ontario Aquaculture Association, 966
Megarity, Eric, Fredericton, 691
Megaw, Lyall, Vice-President, Waterous Power Systems, 422
Meggison, Natalie, Librarian, Heritage College, 1168
Meggs, Geoff, Vancouver, 604-873-7011, 685
Megill, Ph.D, William, Research Director, Coastal Ecosystems Research Foundation, 897
Mehdi, Husain, General Manager, Kinectrics Inc., 257
Mehlenbacher, Mark, Director, Fire & Emergency Management Services, St. Catharines, 719
Mehranvar, Ladan, Borden Ladner Gervais LLP - Toronto, 1073
Mehta, Ram, President & CEO, PBR Laboratories Inc., 319
Meier, Fred, Deputy Minister, 586
Meilleur, Guy, Directeur, Saint-Jérôme, 743
Meilleur, Hubert, Maire, Mirabel, 738
Meilleur, Hélène, Director, Genome Canada, 923
Meindl, Patricia, Librarian, A.D. Allen Chemistry Library, 1156
Meisenheimer, Peter, Executive Director, Ontario Commercial Fisheries' Association, 972
Melançon, Paul A., Associé, Lapointe Rosenstein Marchand Melançon, 1085
Melançon-Bolduc, Ginette-Denyse, Responsable, Référence, Bibliothèque d'aménagement, 1170
Melanson, Eric, Regional Manager, ESRI Canada Ltd., 190
Melanson, Marc, Chief Administrative Officer, Dieppe, 691
Melanson, Marc, Director, Dieppe, 691
Melanson, Pat, Library Clerk, Canadian Agriculture Library - Kentville, 1137
Meldrum, Heidi L., Parlee McLaws LLP, 1053
Meldrum, Stephen, Director, Pure Energy Inc., 336
Meldrum, Stephen, President & General Manager, Pure Energy Battery Inc., 336
Meldrum, Steve, CEO, Eco Waste Solutions, 170
Melendy, William, ADI Group Inc., 68
Melenka, Mike, General Manager, Active Chemicals Ltd., 68

Executive Name Index

Melhoff, Lindsay A., Kanuka Thuringer LLP, Barristers & Solicitors, 1091
Melhorn, Margaret, Secretary & Comptroller General, 606
Meli, Jody, Manager, Lethbridge, 673
Melkic, Al, President & Research Director, Integrated Explorations, 244
Mellan, Archie L., South Dundas, 730
Mellett, Cathy, Acting Municipal Clerk, Halifax Regional Municipality, 902-490-4210, 695
Mellick, Marie, Secretary, Brantford Lapidary & Mineral Society Inc., 846
Melling, Michael, Davies Howe Partners, 1074
Mellis, Dave, Treasurer, British Columbia Ground Water Association, 848
Mellish, Robert L., Patterson Law, 1068
Mellott, John D., Plastic Loose Fill Council, 987
Mellouli, Zeïneb, Lavery, de Billy - Montréal, 1085
Melnick, Christine, Minister, 591
Melnyk, Peter, Manager, Engineered Air, 180
Meloche, Crystal B., LaSalle, 713
Meloche, Pierre-Paul, Mirabel, 738
Meloche, Richard, Essex, 519-776-5726, 709, 699
Meloche, s.m.a., André, Directeur, 654
Melrose, Jayme, Contact, Nova Scotia Public Interest Research Group, 968
Melrose, Simon, Oceans Ltd., 311
Melville, Bill, President, Canadian Pest Management Association, 882
Melville, Bob, Executive Vice-President, Estco Battery Management Inc., 190
Melville, Bryan, Manager, Westburne Canada, 427
Melymuk, Thomas E., Director, Office of Sustainability, Pickering, 905-420-4625, 718
Ménard, Bertrand P., Associé, Stikeman Elliott LLP - Montréal, 1087
Menard, Cathy, Administrator & Deputy Chief Coroner, 607
Menard, Dan, Treasurer, Alberta Aquaculture Association, 815
Ménard, Dominique, Partner, Heenan Blaikie S.E.N.C.R.L/SRL, 1084
Ménard, Françoise, Bibliothécaire professionnelle, Collège Lionel-Groulx, 1182
Ménard, Gaétan, Saint-Lazare, 743
Ménard, Gaétan, Sec.-Treas., Communications, Energy & Paperworkers Union of Canada, 899
Ménard, Ghislain, Directeur général, Papineau, 750
Ménard, Louise, Greffière, Saint-Félicien, 742
Menard, Louise, Office Manager, Golder Associates Ltd., 214
Ménard, Michel, Directeur, Salaberry-de-Valleyfield, 450-370-4750, 744
Ménard, Michel G., Associé, Lapointe Rosenstein Marchand Melançon, 1085
Ménard, Nicole, Ministre, 654
Ménard Dumas, Pierre-Olivier, Heenan Blaikie S.E.N.C.R.L./SRL - Québec, 1088
Menard, A.Sc.T., B.Tech, Jeff, Chief Building Official, Thorold, 720
Mendicino, Dave, North Bay, 715
Meneray, Mark, Commissioner, Legislative & Planning Services & Co, Halton, 700
Menna, Ted, Sales & Marketing Manager, Napoleon Appliance Corp., 297
Mennill, Dave, Elgin, 699
Mentzelopoulos, Athana, Executive Director, 575
Menzi, Robert G., CFO & Executive Vice-President, The Jane Goodall Institute for Wildlife Research, Education & Con, 946
Menzies, Robert, Plant Manager, CCS Income Trust, 134
Meo, Raffaele, President, Meo & Associates Inc., 286
Merali, Raheem, President, Pioneer Envelopes Ltd., 325
Meraw, Vince, President, Aqua Dam & Diversion Ltd., 87
Mercer, Brian, Manager, Hi-Point Industries (1991) Ltd., 231
Mercer, Chris, President, Adhawk Communications Inc., 68
Merchant, Adil, Contact, Vacuum Products Canada Inc., 408
Mercier, Alain, General Manager, Transit Services, Ottawa, 716
Mercier, Chuck, Mayor, Scugog, 729
Mercier, Guy, Directeur général, 650
Mercier, Guy, Président, Association professionnelle des géographes du Québec, 841
Mercier, Jacques, Vice-President, Groupe RSW inc., 220
Mercier, Jean, Directeur, Victoriaville, 819-758-1571, 746
Mercier, Lise T., Associate, Ross Healthcare, Inc., 352
Mercier, Maurice, Directeur, Sainte-Marie, 743
Mercier, Michel, President, Noel Rochette et Fils Inc., 305
Mercier, Ralph, Québec, 740
Mercier, Trent J., Macleod Dixon LLP, 1052
Mercier-Filteau, Nathalie, Stikeman Elliott LLP - Montréal, 1087

Mercure, Claire, Marketing Director, Waterloo Evaporateurs Inc., 422
Mercure, Julie, Marketing Manager, Mandel Scientific Co. Inc., 279
Mercure, Stéphane, Directeur, CD Nova, 135
Mercury, Q.C., A.J. (Telly)., Aikins, MacAulay & Thorvaldson LLP, 1063
Meredith, Dave, Director, Operations & Environmental Services, Ajax, 705
Meredith, Jane, Contact, The Ladies of the Lake, 947
Meredith, Mimi, Manager, Society of Environmental Toxicology & Chemistry, 1008
Meredith, Steve, Trecan Combustion Ltd., 401
Mereu, R.F., Administrator, Southern Ontario Seismic Network, 1010
Meringer, Steve, Fire Chief, Oshawa, 716
Meritet, Clothilde, Contact, Promosalons Canada, 335
Merkel, Garry, Chair, 575
Merkley, Ray, Director, Parks & Recreation, Orillia, 716
Meronek, Q.C., Brian J., D'Arcy & Deacon LLP, 1063
Merrall, Denis, Director, Emergency Services, Middlesex, 701
Merritt, Chris, Technical Sales, P.J. Hannah Equipment Sales Corp., 316
Merritt, Jim, Chair, 623
Merritt, Sue-Ellen, Chair, West Lincoln, 732
Mersereau, Guy, Vice-President/General Manager, CenturyVallen, 136
Mersereau, Jennifer, Client Services Officer, NRC Information Centre - St John's, 1133
Merswolke, Paul, President, New World Generation Inc., 301
Mertens, Peter, Prince Edward, 703
Mertes, Bill, Executive Vice President, Siemens Water Technologies, 367
Mertn, Rudolf, Vice-President, A.C. Carbone Canada Inc., 63
Mertn, Jr., Karl, General Manager, A.C. Carbone Canada Inc., 63
Mertn, Sr., Karl, President/CEO, A.C. Carbone Canada Inc., 63
Merulla, Sam, Hamilton, 711
Meschishnick, Gary A., Wallace Meschishnick Clackson Zawada, 1091
Messely, Louis, Secrétaire, Club des ornithologues de Québec inc., 896
Messely, Maryse, Responsable, Bibliothèque, Collège Mérici, 1178
Messervey, Virginia, Executive Secretary, 611
Messicotte, Danielle, Technicienne en documentation, CÉGEP d'André-Laurendeau, 1169
Messier, Pierre-Paul, Salaberry-de-Valleyfield, 450-373-5459, 744
Mestinsek, Michael, Partner, Stikeman Elliott LLP - Calgary, 1054
Metauro, Al, Chief Executive Officer, Cascades Recovery Inc., 131
Metcalf, Alan, Manager, Parksville, 250-954-4667, 682
Metcalf, Cameron, Head, Geographic, Statistical and Government Information Centre, 1150
Metcalf, Craig, Director, Culture & Heritage, Orillia, 716
Metcalfe, B. Patrick, D'Arcy & Deacon LLP, 1063
Metcalfe, James A., President & CEO, Cansult Maunsell Limited, 127
Metcalfe, Mary, Director, Public Health & Emergency Services, Oxford, 728
Metcalfe, S.A., WeirFoulds LLP, 1081
Metcalfe, Vern, VP & General Manager, North Safety Products Canada, 306
Metha, Y.B., Manager, Enervac Corp., 180
Methot, Benoit, President, Multitel Inc., 295
Methot, Christa, Coordinator, Westmorland-Albert Solid Waste Corporation, 759
Méthot, Josée, Directrice générale, Réseau environnement, 994
Métivier, Edmée, Executive Vice-President, Financing & Consulting, 512
Metzger, Thom, Director, National Solid Wastes Management Association, 958
Meunier, Guy, Senior VP & COO, LVM Inc., 275
Meunier, Luc, Président & Chef de la direction, 652
Meunier, Philippe, Coordonnateur, Beauharnois-Salaberry, 747
Meunier, Pierre B., Fasken Martineau - Montréal, 1083
Meurant, Philippe, Directeur, Lévis, 418-839-2002, 736
Mew, Bev, Head, Information Services, Defence R & D Canada - Suffield, 1108
Meyer, Andrew, Coordinator, Community Development, Strathroy-Caradoc, 731
Meyer, Kelly, Oro-Medonte, 728
Meyerhans, Urs, Group Executive, Coffey Geotechnics Inc., 146
Meyers, Judith, Librarian, Calgary Library, 1100

Meyette, Paul, Director, Red Deer, 674
Mezzapelli, Rob, Area Councillor, Caledon, 707
Mia, Yen, Second Secretary (Commercial) & Trade Commissioner, 768
Miachika, P.Eng, David L., Partner, Borden Ladner Gervais LLP - Vancouver, 1058
Miah, Farid, Manager, Sunnybrook Health Sciences Centre - Sunnybrook Campus, 1162
Micak, James, Sr. Vice-President, Institute of Environmental Research Inc., 243
Miceli, Dominic, Directeur général, Miceli & Frères Ltée, 288
Michael, Helen, Coordinator, Resource Sharing, Gerstein Science Information Centre, 1158
Michaeline, Narcisse, Trade Commissioner, 769
Michaels, Lisa, Marketing Services, BOC Canada Limited, 111
Michalchuk, Gary, President, EIL Environmental Services, 174
Michaluk, Garry, Area Supervisor, Armtec Construction Products, 92
Michaluk, RPBio., Linda, Executive Director, College of Applied Biology British Columbia, 897
Michaud, Denis, Lavery, de Billy - Québec, 1088
Michaud, Frédérick, Directeur général, Arthabaska, 747
Michaud, Félix, Greffier, Montmagny, 738
Michaud, Gabriel, Directeur général, Les Maskoutains, 749
Michaud, Gerard, Société de conservation de la Baie de l'Isle-Verte, 1005
Michaud, Ginette, Responsable, Services techniques, CÉGEP de Rimouski, 1181
Michaud, Guy, Director, Information Technology & Chief Informati, Ottawa, 716
Michaud, Josée, Coordinator, ArcticNet Inc., 829
Michaud, Marc, Acting Chief Administrative Officer, Edmundston, 691
Michaud, Michael, Director, Planning, Clarence-Rockland, 708
Michaud, Pierre, Chair, Commission de gestion enviro ressources du Nord-Ouest (COGERNO), 758
Michaud, Pierre, Vice President, Avensys Inc., 98
Michaud-Oystryk, Nicole, Head, Elizabeth Dafoe Library, 1123
Michel, Joe, Président, Chemrec, 140
Michnik, Brad, Executive Director, Saskatchewan Trade & Export Partnership Inc., 1002
Mick, C., Supervisor, Water & Sewer, Pembroke, 717
Mick, Pat, Sault Ste. Marie, 720
Mickelson, A., Principal, Catterall & Wright, 132
Miclette, Cheryl, Clerk, Pelham, 717
Middlebrook, G., Chief Building Official, Caledon, 707
Middler, Anne, Coordinator, Yukon Conservation Society, 1024
Middleton, Janice, Contact, The Garden Clubs of Ontario, 922
Middleton, Lorne, Manager, Oak Bay, 250-592-7275, 688
Miedema, Robert, Boyne Clarke, 1067
Miele, Frank, Chief Administrative Officer, Meaford, 727
Mifflin, Elinor, Clerk, Chatham-Kent, 724
Mifflin, Heather, Treasurer, Brant, 698
Mighetto, Lisa, Executive Director, American Society for Environmental History, 824
Mighton, Christine, Senior Technologist, Urban Systems Ltd., 407
Mignacco, Dominique, President, CAHFIL FARR (Canada Inc.), 121
Mignault, Jocelyne, Responsable, Services techniques, CÉGEP de la Pocatière, 1177
Migué, Robert, Directeur, Val-d'Or, 746
Mihai, Adina, Helimax Energy Inc., 229
Mihailidi, Helen A., Bratty & Partners LLP, 1081
Mihalick, Roy, Chief Operator, Squamish, 688
Mihelcic, Ken, President/Geophysicist, ClearView Geophysics Inc., 143
Mihevc, Joe, Toronto, 721
Miki, Raymond G., Brownlee LLP, 1054
Mikkelborg, Kris, Vice President, Tansley Associates Environmental Services, 387
Miklic, Don, President, Victoria Orchid Society, 1017
Milani, Q.C., Michael W., McDougall Gauley, 1090
Milburn, Dan, Manager, Prince George, 250-561-7614, 683
Milczyn, Peter, Toronto, 721
Miles, Diana, Vice-President, 584
Miles, Gael, Peel, 703
Miles, Gael, Regional Councillor, Brampton, 706
Miles, Jon, Designer, Firwin Corporation, 196
Miles, Richard, Minister, 593
Mileuski, Stan, Marketing Director, Sols Consultants Ltée, 373
Milicia, Joe, Treasurer, LaSalle, 713
Militano, Carmine, CH2M Hill Canada Limited, 137
Millan, Larry, Vice-President, Manitoba Wildlife Federation, 952
Millar, Claudette, Waterloo, 704

Executive Name Index

Millar, Claudette, Regional Councillor, Cambridge, 707
Millar, H. MacKenzie, President & Chief Executive Officer, Millar Western Forest Products Ltd., 290
Millar, Janet, Director, Millar Western Forest Products Ltd., 290
Millar, John, Principal, Coast River Environmental Services Ltd., 145
Millar, Malcolm, Director, Summerside, 733
Millar, W.A.D., WeirFoulds LLP, 1081
Millard, Margot, Instructional Services Librarian, Mount Royal College, 1102
Millbank, Jennifer, Ramsay Lampman Rhodes, 1056
Millen, Ron, Peterborough, 703
Millen, Roy W., Blake, Cassels & Graydon LLP - Vancouver, 1057
Miller, Alex, President, ESRI Canada Ltd., 190
Miller, Barb, Information Technician, EnCana Corporation, 1101
Miller, Bruce, President, Morrison Hershfield, 293
Miller, Cherry, Technician, Commerce Court Educational Resources, 1146
Miller, Chris, Vice-President, Campground Owners Association of Nova Scotia, 852
Miller, D., Commissioner, Corporate & Financial Services, Richmond Hill, 905-771-8830, 718
Miller, Dave, Manager, Waterous Power Systems, 423
Miller, David, Assistant Deputy Minister, 544
Miller, David, Business Manager, MWA Consultants, 295
Miller, David, President, ToxCo Waste Management Ltd., 399
Miller, Dennis, Chair, Enform: The Safety Association for the Upstream Oil & Gas Industr, 910
Miller, Diana, Customer Service/Inside Sales, Temprite Industries Ltd., 389
Miller, Dusty, Sales Agent, Danatec Educational Services Ltd., 157
Miller, Gord, Commissioner, 626
Miller, Gordon, Head, Library Services & Scientific Archives, Pacific Biological Station, 1113
Miller, Greg S., Partner, Lindsay Kenney LLP, 1061
Miller, Jack, Belleville, 706
Miller, Jeffery W., Cox and Palmer - St. John's, 1065
Miller, Jim, Elizabethtown-Kitley, 613-924-9542, 725
Miller, Jim, C.O.L.T. Director, Strathcona Park Lodge & Outdoor Education Centre, 1111
Miller, Jim, Manager, ABBA Pump Parts & Service, 64
Miller, Joan, Vice-President & General Manager, Waste Management, 511
Miller, Joe, Director, Vision Quest Windelectric Inc., 414
Miller, John, Manager, Building Standards & Chief Building Offic, New Tecumseth, 714
Miller, Keith F., Burnet, Duckworth & Palmer LLP, 1050
Miller, Ken, Plant Manager, Engineered Air, 180
Miller, Kevin, Chief Administrative Officer, LaSalle, 713
Miller, Mark E., Executive Director, Manitoba Ozone Protection Industry Association, 951
Miller, Michael, Vice-President, Parkson Corporation, 319
Miller, Mike, Manager, Harris & Roome Supply Limited, 226
Miller, Ray, Secretary-Treasurer, Ontario Water Works Association, 981
Miller, Richard, Fire Chief, Scugog, 729
Miller, Rob, CFO & Vice-President, PRT Inc., 336
Miller, Rob, President, Wittmann Canada, Inc., 433
Miller, Robert J., McCarthy Tétrault LLP - Vancouver, 1061
Miller, Ron, Fire Chief, Prince Rupert, 250-624-5115, 684
Miller, Ross, Vice-President, Bruce Sutherland & Associates Ltd., 117
Miller, Sarah, Coordinator and Researcher, The Resource Library for the Environment and the Law, 1162
Miller, Scott Rusty, Senior Partner, Ogilvy Renault LLP/S.E.N.C.R.L., s.r.l. - Calgary, 1053
Miller, Sherree, Circulation Assistant, Nova Scotia Agricultural College, 1137
Miller, Steve, St. Clair, 519-677-5676, 729
Miller, Wayne, Chief Administrative Officer, Essex, 709
Miller, Q.C., David A., Stewart McKelvey Stirling Scales - Halifax, 1067
Miller-Sanford, Brenda, Business Operations Manager, Ontario Corn Producers' Association, 972
Millette, Claude, Gatineau, 735
Millette, Denis, President, Hydrogéo Plus Inc., 236
Millette, Réjean, Président, Société québécoise des hostas et des hémérocalles, 1006
Milley, Craig, Manager, Lethbridge, 403-320-3961, 673
Milley, Gary, Executive Director, Recreation Newfoundland & Labrador, 992
Millman, Jay, Vice-President, Process Innovations Canada Inc., 333

Millman-Wilson, Doreen, Manager, Library Services, Toronto Rehab, 1162
Milloy, John, Minister, 635
Mills, Chris, Director, Infrastructure Services & Town Engineer, Halton Hills, 710
Mills, Douglas G., Burnet, Duckworth & Palmer LLP, 1050
Mills, Janine, Paralibrarian (Cataloguing), Cape Breton University, 1137
Mills, Ken, Managing Parnter, Blake, Cassels & Graydon LLP - Calgary, 1049
Mills, Lindsay, Coordinator, Planning, South Frontenac, 730
Mills, Rick, Technical Sales Representative, Frontenac Environmental Ltd., 202
Mills, Robert, Thurber Engineering Ltd., 396
Mills, Sarah, Manager, Recycling Council of Ontario, 993
Mills, W.R. (Bill), Mayor, Truro, 696
Mills, Walt, Director, St. John's, 709-576-8658, 694
Mills, Ph.D., Edward, Research Director, The Great Lakes Research Consortium, 925
Millward, Al, Contact, Telamode, 389
Milman, Warren B., McCarthy Tétrault LLP - Vancouver, 1061
Milne, Andrew, Cataloguing Librarian, Dawson College, 1173
Milne, Bill, President, Alex Milne Associates Ltd., 78
Milne, Bob, General Manager, Atlantic Air Cleaning Specialists Ltd., 95
Milne, Brian, Deputy Mayor & Councillor, Grey, 700
Milne, Ian, Manager, Portage La Prairie, 204-239-8349, 689
Milne, Rick, Simcoe, 704
Milne, Rick, Deputy Mayor & Councillor, New Tecumseth, 714
Milnes, Heather, Regional Manager, ESRI Canada Ltd., 190
Milnthrop, Ross, GM, Campbell River, 679
Milobar, Mary Ann, President, Kamloops Wildlife Park Society, 947
Milobar, Peter, Chair, Thompson-Nicola, 679
Milobar, Peter, Mayor, Kamloops, 681
Miltenberger, J. Michael, Minister, 605
Miltenberger, J. Michael, Minister Responsible, 609
Milton, Scott, Director, 664
Minchau, Mitch, Supervisor, Cariboo, 677
Minchuk, Gerald, Director, Langley, 604-514-2815, 681
Miner, Jean-Claude, Chief Building Official, Hawkesbury, 711
Miner, Jerry, Manager, Library & Information Services, Canadian Agriculture Library - Kentville, 1137
Ming, Peter, Manager, West Nipissing, 732
Mingie, Christine, Lang Michener LLP - Vancouver, 1060
Mingo, Verna, Head, Acquisitions/Serials, Nova Scotia Agricultural College, 1137
Minielly, Gord, Lambton, 701
Minielly, Gord, Mayor, Lambton Shores, 519-786-4629, 726
Minion, Robin, Manager, Library Services, Olds College, 1109
Minks, Ron, Director, Calgary, 121
Minnan-Wong, Denzil, Toronto, 721
Minnille, Rick, Mississippi Mills, 714
Mintha, Zig, Renfrew, 613-628-3101, 704
Min-yang Wang, Eric, Secretary General, International Ergonomics Association, 938
Miousse, Denis, Sept-Iles, 744
Miranda, Luis, Maire d'arrondissement/Conseiller de la ville, Montréal, 738
Mirau, Dan, Library Director, Concordia University College of Alberta, 1105
Mireault, Suzanne, Greffière, Mirabel, 450-475-2002, 738
Miron, Huguette, Technicienne, Collège de Maisonneuve, 1172
Miron, Luc, Vice President Sales and Marketing, A&C Produits Chimiques Americains Ltée, 63
Mirth, Q.C., Sonny, Reynolds, Mirth, Richards & Farmer LLP, 1056
Mirza, Khurshid, Sr. Vice-President, Trow Consulting Engineers Ltd., 403
Misek-Evans, Margaret, Corporate Manager, Community & Strategic Planning, Oxford, 728
Mish, Janette, Vice-President, Saskatchewan Katahdin Sheep Association Inc., 1000
Miskiman, Lloyd, Fire Chief, Summerland, 689
Misra, Kara, Manager, British Columbia Recreation & Parks Association, 849
Misra, Mickey, Entech Laboratories, 181
Mistry, Reena, Secretary, British Columbia Food Technolgists, 848
Misura, Frank, Manager, Rocky View No. 44, 670
Mitcham, Paul, Commissioner, Community Services, Mississauga, 714
Mitchell, A.C., President & Senior Partner, Triton Environmental Consultants Ltd., 402
Mitchell, Alex, City Clerk, Cambridge, 519-740-4680, 707

Mitchell, Allan, Chief Financial Officer, Dillon Consulting Ltd., 163
Mitchell, Andy, Deputy Reeve, Smith-Ennismore-Lakefield, 729
Mitchell, Brad S., McDougall Gauley, 1090
Mitchell, Carol, Sr. Environmental Engineer, Naylor Engineering Associates Ltd., 299
Mitchell, David, Manager, Flygt Canada, 198
Mitchell, Don, Durham, 699
Mitchell, Don, Regional Councillor, Whitby, 723
Mitchell, Donald G., Conway Davis Gryski, 1074
Mitchell, Elaine, Director, Conception Bay South, 693
Mitchell, Garner, Acting President & CEO, 661
Mitchell, Garner, Vice-President, 661
Mitchell, Gary, Manager, Degussa Canada Inc., 159
Mitchell, Gerry, Branch Manager, Peto MacCallum Ltd., 322
Mitchell, Gregg, Vice-President, African Wildlife Foundation, 813
Mitchell, Jane, Waterloo, 704
Mitchell, Jeffrey P., Partner, Borden Ladner Gervais LLP - Toronto, 1073
Mitchell, Joan, Archives Librarian, Wilfrid Laurier University, 1165
Mitchell, Ken, Manager, Waterous Power Systems, 422
Mitchell, Lisa, President, LJM Environmental Consulting, 273
Mitchell, Lynn, Partner, Heenan Blaikie LLP - Toronto, 1076
Mitchell, Mark, Manager, AllerGen NCE Inc., 821
Mitchell, Mark, Regional Manager, Vestar, 413
Mitchell, Mark S., Lang Michener LLP - Toronto, 1077
Mitchell, Murray, Sales Manager, M&L Testing Equipment (1995) Ltd., 276
Mitchell, Parker, Co-CEO, Engineers Without Borders, 910
Mitchell, Ron, Treasurer, Uxbridge, 731
Mitchell, Ruth, Sec.-Treas., Binbrook Agricultural Society, 845
Mitchell, Tom, Archivist, Brandon University, 1122
Mitchell, Tom, President & CEO, Ontario Power Generation, 312
Mitchelmore, Lorraine, President, Shell Canada Limited, 365
Mitropoulos, Efthimios E., Secretary General, International Maritime Organization, 941
Mittermeier, Russell A., President, Conservation International, 901
Mittlestead, Carol, Acting Dean & Associate Librarian, Durham College of Applied Arts & Technology, 1147
Mitty, Earl, Advance Engineered Products Ltd., 69
Mizener, Mike, President, M&L Testing Equipment (1995) Ltd., 276
Moch, Darcy D., Bennett Jones LLP - Calgary Office, 1049
Moddle, Phillip M., Office Manager, Golder Associates Ltd., 214
Modenesi, George, Coordinator, Reference, Capilano College, 1114
Moe, Matthew, Contact, Organic Verification Organization of North America, 982
Moen, Harold, Director, Magnum Industries Ltd., 278
Moen, Keith, Manager, 661
Moen, Lindsey, Coordinator, Canadian Hydro Developers, Inc., 124
Moen-Nijssen, Phyllis, Library Technician, Cameco Corporation, 1189
Moeser, Ron, Toronto, 721
Moffat, Kirk, Contact, Fort Storage Warehousing & Distribution, 200
Moffat, Larry, General Manager, Toromont Caterpillar, 397
Moffat, Mark, Sales Manager, Genor Recycling Services, 210
Moffatt, Alida, Director, Finance, Loyalist, 727
Moffatt, Craig, Sales & Marketing, N.R. Murphy Ltd., 296
Moffatt, Dave, Contact, Flakeboard Company Ltd., 196
Moffatt, Jan, Library & Information Services Coordinator, C.D. Howe Institute, 1157
Moffatt, Julian, Vice-President, e3 Solutions Inc., 168
Moffatt, Louis, Conseiller, Claude-Ryan, Montréal, 738
Moffatt, Michael, Director, Human Resources, Simcoe, 704
Moffatt, Scott, Ottawa, 716
Mogianesi, Michael, Regional Manager, Velan Inc., 410
Mogus, Jason, President & CEO, Communicopia.Net Internet Inc., 147
Mohamed, Simba, Technical, York Fluid Controls Ltd., 435
Mohammed, Peter, President, Integrated Vegetation Management Association of British Columbia, 934
Mohammed, Wahid, Sales Manager, Aimco Solrec Ltd., 74
Moher, Karl, Peterborough, 703
Moher, Michael R., Partner, Macleod Dixon LLP, 1077
Mohns, Tom, Deputy Mayor & Councillor, Petawawa, 717
Mohr, Dan, Branch Manager, Jagger Hims Limited, 251
Mohr, Daniel S., Project Engineer, Jagger Hims Limited, 250
Mohr, Gary, Executive Vice-President, Canadian Centre for Emergency Preparedness, 861
Moignard, Rick, President/CEO, Gemcom Software International Inc., 206

Executive Name Index

Moir, Scott, Customer Service Manager, Safety-Kleen Canada Inc., 355
Moisan, Jérémie-Nicolas, McCarthy Tétrault LLP - Montréal, 1086
Mok, Vicky, Head, Technical Services, Acquisitions & Systems, Fanshawe College of Applied Arts & Technology, 1143
Molby, Kim, Vice President, Armtec Construction Products, 92
Molcar, Karl, President, Climatizer Insulation Inc., 144
Molgat, Lucie, Director, Csi Project Managment Office, Canada Institute for Scientific & Technical Information (CISTI), 1148
Molinari, Mike, Director, Parks & Environmental Services, Oshawa, 716
Molinari, Patrick A., Heenan Blaikie S.E.N.C.R.L/SRL, 1084
Mollard, J.D., President, J.D. Mollard & Associates Ltd., 249
Moloci, Matthew G., Scarfone Hawkins LLP, 1069
Mologne, Lew, President, ProSep Inc., 335
Moloney, Terry, President & CEO, PCI Geomatics Group Inc., 320
Molyneaux, John, Director, Emergency Services, & Fire Chief, Newmarket, 714
Molyneux, Jim, Field Works Coordinator, Charlottetown, 732
Mombourquette, David, Pink Larkin, 1064
Mombourquette, Derek, Councillor, Cape Breton, 695
Mona, Ashkar, Trade Commissioner, 768
Monaghan, Brian, Marketing, Hydromantis Inc., 237
Monaghan, Joanne, Mayor, Kitimat, 687
Monast, Daniel, Chambly, 514-978-5405, 734
Monasterios, Ingrit, Chief, Information Resource Management, Agriculture & Agri-Food Canada, 1147
Moncion, Daniel, IT Technician, University of Sudbury, 1155
Moncur, Robert H., City Manager, Burnaby, 604-294-7110, 679
Mondor, Françoise, Coordonnatrice, Association québécoise pour l'évaluation d'impacts, 842
Mondry, Richard V., Sec.-Treas., Mondry Del Zotto et associés inc., 292
Monette, Bob, Ottawa, 613-580-2471, 716
Monette, René, Directeur, Salaberry-de-Valleyfield, 450-370-4390, 744
Money, J. Stuart, Burnet, Duckworth & Palmer LLP, 1050
Mongeau, Lucie, Greffière, Boisbriand, 734
Mongeau, Éric, Associé, Stikeman Elliott LLP - Montréal, 1087
Mongrain, Claude, Rimouski, 740
Mongrain, Diane, Responsable du centre d'information, Alcan International Ltée., 1168
Mongrain, Jocelyne, Magog, 819-847-1577, 737
Mongrain, Lucien, Préfet, Mékinac, 750
Monk, Alan L., Davis LLP - Vancouver, 1059
Monk, Craig, Marketing, Thermal Technics Corporation, 394
Monk, Dan, Manager, Envirosoil Ltd., 187
Monk, Dave, Lakeshore, 712
Monk, Tony, President, Thermal Technics Corporation, 394
Monreal, Maria-Luisa, Directrice générale, Association québécoise des organismes de coopération internationa, 842
Monro, H. Alec B., President, Wildlife Preservation Canada, 1020
Monro, Joanne, Officer, Health Sciences Association of Alberta, 928
Monson, Cathie, Coordinator, Alberta Water & Wastewater Operators Association, 820
Monster, Rod, Founder & President, Monster Polymers Inc., 293
Monster, Sterling, Vice-President, Monster Polymers Inc., 293
Montague, Ken, Councillor, Whitby, 723
Montague, Len, General Manager, Universal Handling Equipment Company Limited, 406
Montague, Neville, Manager, Engine Control Systems, 180
Montague, Stephen, Brandon, 689
Montambault, Gilles, Inspecteur municipal de voirie, Joliette, 736
Monteiro, Frank, City Councillor, Cambridge, 707
Monteith, Janet, Coordinator, Technical Services, Mount Royal College, 1102
Monteith, Peter, CAO, Chilliwack, 604-793-2903, 680
Monteith, Scott, President, Stormceptor Canada Inc., 380
Montgomerie, Duff, Deputy Minister, 613
Montgomery, Gordon D., Dufferin, 699
Montgomery, Katrina, Library Technician, Orillia Campus, 1147
Montgomery, Margaret, Clerk, Trent Hills, 731
Montgomery, N., President, Lubrication Engineers of Canada Ltd., 274
Montgomery, Reilly, General Manager, Training & Development Services, 400
Montgomery, Sean, Foreman, Wilmot, 732
Montgomery, Shelagh, Yellowknife, 695
Montgomery, Tom, KMK Consultants Limited, 258
Montieth, Jamie A., Director, MIG Engineering Ltd., 289
Montminy, Eve, Technicienne en documentation, Laurentian Forestry Centre, 1179

Montmorency, Nicolas, Conseiller de ville, Pointe-aux-Prairies, Montréal, 738
Montpetit, Jacqueline, Mairesse d'arrondissement, Montréal, 738
Montreuil, Luc, Gatineau, 735
Monty, Vivienne, Reference Librarian, York University Glendon College Campus, 1164
Monuk, Larry, Reference Clerk, Canada Dept. of National Defence & the Canadian Forces, 1148
Moodle, Phil, Office Manager, Golder Associates Ltd., 215
Mooi, Anne, Director, West Vancouver, 604-925-7206, 689
Moon, David J., Electrical Engineering Associate, Aldworth Engineering Inc., 77
Moon, Jeffrey, Head, Maps, Data & Government Information Centre, Maps, Data & Government Information Centre (MADGIC), 1142
Moon, Joshua P., Perley-Robertson, Hill & McDougall LLP, 1071
Mooney, Darcy, Coordinator, Columbia-Shuswap, 677
Mooney, Darrell, Contact, MacEwen Petroleum Inc., 278
Mooney, Pat Roy, Executive Director, ETC Group, 913
Moore, André, Director, 614
Moore, Anita, Town Clerk, Newmarket, 714
Moore, Carole, Chief Librarian, University of Toronto Libraries, 1163
Moore, Christine, Contact, Greater Toronto Rose & Garden Society, 925
Moore, Christine, Senior Scientist, CanTox Environmental Inc., 127
Moore, Deirdre, Librarian, Eastern Division Library/Bibliothèque de la division de l'est, 1178
Moore, Don, Manager, Lexcan Industrial Supply Ltd., 271
Moore, Dwayne, Principal, The Cadmus Group, 391
Moore, Elaine, Peel, 703
Moore, Elaine, Regional Councillor, Brampton, 706
Moore, Fred, President, Nusco Supply & Manufacturing Inc., 310
Moore, Gary, President, Victaulic Co. of Canada Ltd., 413
Moore, Gerry, CEO, 641
Moore, Greg, Metro Vancouver, 678
Moore, Greg, Mayor, Port Coquitlam, 604-927-5498, 683
Moore, Harold, President, GeoInsight Corporation, 211
Moore, James, District Manager, BFI Canada Inc., 106
Moore, James, Minister, Canadian Heritage & Official Languages, 519
Moore, Jason, Contact, Accurassay Laboratories, 65
Moore, Jennifer, Treasurer & Director, Finance, Northumberland, 702
Moore, John, Vice-President & General Manager, Harris & Roome Supply Limited, 225
Moore, Kathryn, Librarian, Lacombe Research Centre, 1108
Moore, Kenneth, Chairman, Algonquin Power Income Fund, 78
Moore, Larry, Vice-President, Electro-Federation Canada Inc., 909
Moore, Monica, Founding Director, Pesticide Action Network North America, 985
Moore, P.J., IBI Group, 238
Moore, Patrick, Honorary Chair, Environmentalists For Nuclear Energy (Canada) Inc., 913
Moore, Patti, General Manager, Health & Social Services, Norfolk, 702
Moore, Robert, Sales, Neo Valves, 300
Moore, Tim, Chief Building Official, Pickering, 905-420-4617, 718
Moore, Wayne, President, Bruce Sutherland & Associates Ltd., 117
Moores, Gregory A.C., Partner, Stewart McKelvey Stirling Scales - St. John's, 1066
Moores, Richard, Executive Director, Fish Harvesters Resource Centres, 917
Moore-Stewart, Robert, Moore-Stewart, Robert, 1063
Moorhouse, Richard, Exec. Director, Ontario Heritage Trust, 974
Moorman, P.Eng., Wayne, Manager, Nanaimo, 678
Moquin, Ken, Chambly, 450-658-8124, 734
Morabito, Aldo, Chief Financial Officer, Comstock Canada Ltd., 148
Morabito, Mark J., President, Tankless Water Heater Company, 386
Morais, Mario, Repentigny, 450-654-4018, 740
Moran, Dave, General Foreman, Bathurst, 690
Moran, M. Patrick, Partner, Hicks Morley Hamilton Stewart Storie LLP, 1076
Moran, Tim, President, Pollutech Group of Companies Inc., 327
Moran, Tim S., Vice-President (Sarnia), Pollutech Group of Companies Inc., 327
Morand, Pierre-Étienne, Heenan Blaikie S.E.N.C.R.L./SRL - Québec, 1088
Morasiewicz, Ryan W., Miller Thomson LLP - Vancouver, 1061

Morassutti, Paul J., Partner, Osler, Hoskin & Harcourt LLP - Toronto, 1079
Morawski, Matthew M., Miller Thomson LLP - Vancouver, 1061
Morden, Garry W., Fire Chief, Mississauga, 714
Morden, Mike, Maple Ridge, 687
Morden, Tammy, Coordinator, Human Resources, Port Colborne, 718
More, Lucy, Contact, Nimbus Water Systems, 304
More, Lucy N., Marketing/Manager of Operations, Nimbus Water Systems, 304
More, Russel R., President/CEO, Nimbus Water Systems, 304
Moreau, Gilles, Rioux Bossé Massé Moreau, 1089
Moreau, Manuel, Director, Kemira Water Solutions Canada Inc., 256
Moreau, Marcel, Directeur général, La Mitis, 748
Moreau, Serge, Administration, Kirkland Lake Campus, 1143
Moreault, Liette, Bibliothécaire, Bibliothèque des sciences juridiques, 1171
Morehouse, D., Director, Moncton / Ville de Moncton, 691
Moreira, William, Stewart McKelvey Stirling Scales - Halifax, 1068
Morelli, Bernie, Hamilton, 711
Morello, Emanuele, Contact, MF Paints, 288
Morency, Monique, Personnel, Centre de documentation (Génie), 1178
Moreton, Jim, Sales Manager, Border Chemical Company Ltd., 114
Moretti, Carolina, Markham, 905-479-7751, 713
Morgan, David, Director, Summerside, 733
Morgan, David, Vice-President, TetrES Consultants Inc., 391
Morgan, Dennis, Vice-President & Project Engineer, Via-Sat Data Systems, 413
Morgan, John K., President/CEO, Zep Manufacturing Company of Canada, 436
Morgan, John W., Mayor, Cape Breton, 695
Morgan, Lloyd, President, Nova Scotia Forest Technicians Association, 968
Morgan, Nigel, Owner, Poscor Group, 328
Morgan, Susan, Library Technician, Royal Victoria Hospital, 1175
Morgan, Trish, Library Systems Support, Bracken Health Sciences Library, 1142
Morgan, Q.C., Don, Minister & Attorney General, 661
Moriarty, Gerry, Sales, Banyan Chains Inc., 101
Morier, Rolland, VP, Iron Ore Company of Canada, 248
Morin, Bastien, Directeur, Saint-Eustache, 450-974-5284, 742
Morin, Denis, Victoriaville, 819-357-7821, 746
Morin, Denise, Bibliotechnicienne, CHUQ-CHUL, 1178
Morin, Francine, Préfète, Les Maskoutains, 749
Morin, Gaétan, Préfet, Matawinie, 747
Morin, Jean, Grondin, Poudrier, Bernier, 1087
Morin, Linda, Sous-ministre adjointe, 643
Morin, Michel, Terrebonne, 745
Morin, Michel, Maire, Rivière-du-Loup, 418-867-6625, 741
Morin, Patrice, Partner, Borden Ladner Gervais LLP - Montréal, 1083
Morin, Patrick, Sainte-Thérèse, 744
Morin, Pierre, Responsable, Saint-Constant, 742
Morin, Roland, Responsable, Gatineau, 735
Morin, Véronique, Lavery, de Billy - Montréal, 1086
Morin-Corbeil, Johanne, Bibliothécaire responsable, Université de Hearst, 1142
Morisset, Sasha D., Stewart McKelvey Stirling Scales - Moncton, 1065
Morissette, Brenda, Library Technician, Haileybury Campus, 1140
Morissette, M. Jean, Président, Camvac Inc., 122
Morissette, Marcel, Maire, Régie intermunicipale de gestion des déchets solides des Etchemin, 760
Morissette, Yves, Sec.-Trés., Régie intermunicipale de gestion des déchets solides de la région, 760
Morley, Gordon, District Planner & Approving Officer, Summerland, 689
Morley, Susan, Manager, CSA International, 1157
Morneau, Jean, Directeur, Saguenay, 741
Morneault, Gérald G., Edmundston, 691
Moro, Frank, Executive Vice-President, International Lilac Society, 941
Moro, Marcia, Contact, Parsons Commercial Technology Group Inc., 319
Morocco, Joyce, City Councillor, Niagara Falls, 715
Moroskat, Sharon, Manager, Consulting Engineers of Alberta, 902
Moroz, Michele, President, Canadian Association of Animal Health Technologists & Technicians, 856
Moroz, Neill, Fire Chief, Kamloops, 250-372-3311, 681

Executive Name Index

Moroziuk, Mitch, Director, Penticton, 682
Morris, Andrew, Vice-President, R.J. Burnside & Associates Limited, 340
Morris, Anthony (Tony), Partner, Macleod Dixon LLP, 1052
Morris, Dan G., McDougall Gauley, 1090
Morris, Dave, Manager, Campbell River, 679
Morris, David, Vice President, Institute for Local Self-Reliance, 932
Morris, David C., CAO, Tillsonburg, 721
Morris, Fred, Centre Wellington, 724
Morris, John J., Partner, Borden Ladner Gervais LLP - Toronto, 1073
Morris, Kate, Branch Manager, ICC The Compliance Centre Inc., 238
Morris, Malcolm, Director, Envirotest Inc., 188
Morris, Malcolm, Director, Transportation, Kingston, 712
Morris, Marion, Clerk, Centre Wellington, 724
Morris, Patric, Manager, Semco Systems Limited, 362
Morris, Paul, Principal, Acorus Restoration Native Plant Nursery, 67
Morris, Ross, Sec.-Treas., Pacific Urchin Harvesters Association, 984
Morris, Sara R., Secretary, American Ornithologists' Union, 824
Morrish, Douglas, Director, Development Services, Leamington, 726
Morrison, Bill, General Manager, Seaboard Industrial Supply Co. Ltd., 361
Morrison, Brian, Secretary-Treasurer, Prince Edward Island Cattle Producers, 988
Morrison, David, CEO, 664
Morrison, Del, Executive Director, Alberta Water & Wastewater Operators Association, 820
Morrison, Don, President, South Peel Naturalists' Club, 1010
Morrison, Frank, Sales Manager, Bigelow-Liptak of Canada, 107
Morrison, Fred, President, Envirotray Ltd., 188
Morrison, Gary D.D., Partner, Heenan Blaikie S.E.N.C.R.L/SRL, 1084
Morrison, Harvey L., McInnes Cooper, 1067
Morrison, Heather G., Chief Health Officer, 640
Morrison, Holly, Treasurer, Georgian Bluffs, 725
Morrison, Jennifer, Manager, Whitby, 905-655-4571, 723
Morrison, Jim, Vice-President/General Manager, Buckhorn Canada Inc., 118
Morrison, Joan, Instructional Librarian, NorQuest College, 1106
Morrison, John D., Lang Michener LLP - Vancouver, 1060
Morrison, Kelly, Director, Petroleum Services Association of Canada, 986
Morrison, Ken A., President, R.V. Anderson Associates Limited, 341
Morrison, Kirk, Engineer, Lloydminster, 673
Morrison, Marolyn, Mayor, Peel, 707, 703
Morrison, Matt, Executive Director, Pacific NorthWest Economic Region, 983
Morrison, Patricia L., Partner, Borden Ladner Gervais LLP - Calgary, 1050
Morrison, Paul, CEO, Hyperspectral Data International Inc., 237
Morrison, Paul, President/COO, ADI Group Inc., 68
Morrison, Paul, Vice-President, Acadia Consultants & Inspectors Ltd., 65
Morrisseau, Joe, Executive Director, 584
Morrissette, Mike, President, Dangerous Goods Advisory Council, 906
Morrissey, Denyse, Director, Parks, Recreation, & Culture, Niagara Falls, 715
Morrissey, J., Manager, Life Rhythm Corporation, 272
Morrissey, John, President, DRL Environmental Services, 166
Morrissey, Krista, Executive Director, Conservation Council of New Brunswick, 1127
Morrissey O'Ryan, Michelle, Vice-President, 629
Morrow, Mike, President, EmerGeo Solutions Inc., 176
Morrow, Stuart B., Davis LLP - Vancouver, 1059
Mortelliti, Cleve, King, 726
Mortelliti, Cleve, Mayor, King, 726
Mortimer, Patricia, Vice-President, 546
Mortimer, Simon E., Partner, Hicks Morley Hamilton Stewart Storie LLP, 1076
Mortimore, Amy A., Clark Wilson LLP, 1058
Morton, Cathy, East Gwillimbury, 708
Morton, Cheryl, Director, American Industrial Hygiene Association, 823
Morton, Chris, General Manager, Systems Plus, 385
Morton, Cynthia, Deputy Minister, 629
Morton, Dawn, Manager, Annapolis Valley Peat Moss Co. Ltd., 86
Morton, Ian, Partner, Summerhill Group, 381

Morton, Marshall, Manager, Clearwater County, 669
Morton, Ted, Minister, 572
Mortoza, Tarafder, Sr. Trade Commissioner, 767
Moseley, F. Colin, Chair, American Forest & Paper Association, 823
Moser, D.W., President, Triangle Fluid Controls Ltd., 401
Moser, John, General Manager, Planning & Growth Management, Ottawa, 716
Moses, Jim, General Manager, ExTech Environmental Services Inc., 192
Moses, Ken, CAO, Yarmouth District, 698
Mosher, Bill, Chief Director, Halifax Regional Municipality, 695
Mosher, Kathy, Head Librarian, Champlain-Saint Lambert, 1184
Mosher, Linda, Councillor, Halifax Regional Municipality, 695
Mosher, Scott, President, Landscape Nova Scotia, 948
Moshiri, Laleh, Borden Ladner Gervais LLP - Toronto, 1073
Moskoff, Hirschel, CIO, eWaterTek Inc., 191
Moskovitch, Dale, Sales, Century Plastics Ltd., 136
Moss, Eileen, Vice-President, Kingston Lapidary & Mineral Club, 947
Moss, Janet, Head Law Librarian, Gerard V. La Forest Law Library, 1127
Moss, Keith, President/CEO, Sonepar Canada, 373
Moss, Q.C., Armand J., Bishop & McKenzie LLP, 1049
Mostacci, R., Director, Community & Development Services, Fort Erie, 709
Mosteko, Nancy, Administrator, Waters Limited, 423
Mostowich, John, Boughton Law Corporation, 1058
Mostowy, Tom, Director, Romatec Incorporated, 351
Mostyn, Chris, Manager, PRT Inc., 336
Mostyn, Mitchell, Davis LLP - Toronto, 1074
Motard, Pauline, McCarthy Tétrault LLP - Québec, 1088
Motard, Richard, Châteauguay, 450-699-6141, 735
Mott, Cathy, Ingersoll, 711
Mott, Joe, Saint John, 692
Moucachen, Tony, President, Merlin Plastics Supply Inc., 287
Mouland, Tracy, Library Technician, Bonavista Campus Learning Resource Centre, 1130
Mould, Anne, Director, 607
Moulder, Roy, Manager, New Westminster, 604-527-4632, 682
Moulton Tennison, Melissa, Burnet, Duckworth & Palmer LLP, 1050
mountain equipment coop (, Mountain Equipment Co-op, Vancouver, BC, 1040
Mourie, Bill, General Manager, Spring Air Silver Services Ltd., 376
Mousley, Brian, Superintendent, Port Alberni, 683
Mousseau, Sharon, Lanark, 701
Mousseau, Yvon, Directeur général, Lavaltrie, 736
Moutsatsos, Steve S., Weaver, Simmons LLP, 1072
Moutsatsos, Tom, Partner, Hicks Morley Hamilton Stewart Storie LLP, 1076
Mowat, D., Medical Officer of Health, Peel, 703
Mowat, Farley, Honorary Chair, Sea Shepherd Conservation Society - USA, 1003
Mowat, Kirk, President, Mowat Fabrication Ltd., 294
Mowbray, Jan, Milton, 714
Moxey, Sue, Director, Williams Lake, 250-392-1774, 686
Moy, Laura, Clerk & Director, Staff Services, Tecumseh, 720
Moyaert, Leon, President, Prince Edward Island Finfish Growers Association, 988
Moyes, Alan, Director, 578
Moyle, Pat, Chief Administrative Officer, Halton, 700
Moysa, Susan, Reference Coordinator, Cameron Science & Technology Library, 1104
Mozayani, Natalia, Program Manager, Radiation Safety Institute of Canada, 992
Mozur, Mike, Executive Director, Society of Environmental Toxicology & Chemistry, 1008
Mpofo, Penias, Géophysique GPR International Inc., 211
Mrazek, Q.C., Margaret, Reynolds, Mirth, Richards & Farmer LLP, 1056
Mroczek, Chris, Director, Hydromantis Inc., 237
Mryglod, Des, Manager, Leduc County, 669
Mucklow, Jim, Manager, Wardrop Engineering Inc., 417
Mudry, T.T. (Tom), McCaffery Mudry Pritchard LLP, Barristers & Solicitors, 1052
Muecke, Cristin, President, Canadian Public Health Association - NB/PEI Branch, 883
Mueller, B., Vice-President, ISCA Management Ltd., 248
Mueller, Brad, Manager, Dillon Consulting Ltd., 164
Mueller, Jim, President/Director, Adventus Canada Inc., 69
Mueller, Steve, President, Survalent Technology Corporation, 383
Mugas, Michael, President, Niagara Environmental Dynamics, 303

Muggah, Sean A., Partner, Borden Ladner Gervais LLP - Vancouver, 1058
Muggeridge, Derek, President, Offshore Design Associates Ltd., 311
Muggeridge, H.M., Secretary, Offshore Design Associates Ltd., 311
Muir, Brent J., Partner, Miller Thomson LLP - Toronto, 1078
Muir, Dave, Manager, Whitehorse, 867-668-8391, 755
Muir, David, Chief Administrative Officer, Riverview, 506-387-2021, 692
Muir, Gavin R., Howell Fleming LLP, 1071
Muir, J. Brent, Associé, Miller Thomson LLP - Montréal, 1086
Muir, Robert, Blaney McMurtry LLP, 1073
Muirhead, Kathy, PHH ARC Environmental Ltd., 322
Muirhead, Mike, President, Western Subsea Technology Ltd., 430
Mukasa, Samuel, Vice-President, Geochemical Society, 923
Mulcahy, John, General Manager, McNamara Construction Company, 285
Mulcahy, Pat, Manager, Campbell River, 679
Mulder, Lynne, Red Deer, 403-341-6418, 674
Mulder, Zoelita (Zo), Treasurer, Kitimat, 687
Muldoon, Dan, General Manager, Nova Scotia Power, an Emera Company, 308
Mullally, Catherine, Director, Halifax Regional Municipality, 695
Mullan, Joe, Ainley Group, 74
Mullan, Joe, President & CEO, Ainley Group, 74
Mullan, Q.C., Derek J., Clark Wilson LLP, 1058
Mullaney, Carol, Treasurer, Regina & District Labour Council, 994
Mullen, Jane, Office Manager, Rare Breeds Canada, 992
Mullen, Peter W., President, Kemic Bioresearch Laboratories Ltd., 256
Muller, Joy, Manager, Seneca@York Campus, 1144, 1161
Muller, Pavel, President, Toxprobe Inc., 399
Muller, Ted, Principal, EDA Collaborative Inc., 173
Muller, EMT-P, ABCP, Peter, Emergency Management Officer (Planning), Edmonton, 780-496-1530, 672
Mullett, Norma, Rothesay, 692
Mulligan, Brock, Director, Alberta Forest Products Association, 817
Mulligan, Jeff, Mayor, Lloydminster, 673
Mulligan, Terry B., Executive Director, Mining Suppliers, Contractors & Consultants Association of BC, 955
Mulligan, Tom, Commissioner, Works & Transportation, Brampton, 706
Mullin, Bill, Manager, Petrozyme Technologies Inc., 322
Mullin, Brent, Chair, 581
Mullin, Brian, Mayor, Grey, 700
Mullin, Jeff, Director, Hydromantis Inc., 237
Mullin, Pat, Chair, Credit Valley Conservation Foundation, 905
Mullin, Patricia, Peel, 714, 703
Mullins, Carolyn, Grimsby, 710
Mulroy, J. Michael, Lang Michener LLP - Toronto, 1077
Mulvihill, Brian J., President, Brim Pumps & Systems Ltd., 116
Mumaw, Sterling, Industrial Sales, Summit Structures, 382
Muncaster, Sheilagh, Manager, Westburne Canada, 428
Munday, Brian, Executive Director, Alberta Land Surveyors' Association, 1104
Mundee, Dean, Executive Secretary, 593
Munden, L. Martina, Patterson Law, 1068
Mundle, Todd, Associate University Librarian, Simon Fraser University, 1111
Munn, D. Lawrence, Clark Wilson LLP, 1058
Munn, Geoff, J.W. Bird & Company Ltd., 250
Munn, Geoff, President, J.W. Bird & Company Ltd., 250
Munn, Karen, Librarian, Falconbridge Limited, 1140
Munns, Kevin, Marketing, Eco-Tec Ltd., 171
Munns-Audet, Sherri, Director, Corporate Communications, Durham, 714
Munoz, Debora, Prince George, 683
Munoz, Eeva, Assistant University Librarian, Allyn & Betty Tayl, Allyn & Betty Taylor Library, 1143
Munro, James R., Lang Michener LLP - Vancouver, 1060
Munro, Lorraine, Contact, J.R. Tinderblox, 250
Munro, Shawn M., Bennett Jones LLP - Calgary Office, 1049
Munroe, Roger, Manager, Cape Breton, 902-563-5182, 695
Mural, Fred, President, Northway-Photomap Inc., 307
Murchison, Ann, Librarian, Donald-Petzel Memorial Library, 1178
Murdoch, Cheryl, Haliburton, 705-286-1701, 700
Murdock, Dean, Saanich, 688
Murgoi, Dumitrou, M.S.D.A. Inc., 277
Muri, Lisa, North Vancouver, 688
Murison, Laurie, Managing Director, Grand Manan Whale & Seabird Research Station, 924

Executive Name Index

Murisso, Don, Office Manager, Vestar, 413
Murphy, Amanda, Vice-President, Infotech Canada Inc., 241
Murphy, Brian, Project Assessment Director, 578
Murphy, Charlie, Director, Planning & Development Services, Quinte West, 613-392-7151, 718
Murphy, David, Cornwall, 708
Murphy, Francis, Val-d'Or, 746
Murphy, Gerry, Commissioner, Planning Services Department, Prince Edward, 703
Murphy, Gerry, Manager, Planning & By-law Enforcement, & Chief Bu, North Glengarry, 727
Murphy, Grant, Director, Engineering Services, Kitchener, 519-741-2410, 712
Murphy, James D., Burnet, Duckworth & Palmer LLP, 1050
Murphy, Joann, Associate University Librarian, University of Northern British Columbia, 1115
Murphy, John, Executive Vice-President, 634
Murphy, John G., Partner, Borden Ladner Gervais LLP - Montréal, 1083
Murphy, Karen, Library Technician, General Medical Library, 1140
Murphy, Katherine, Borden Ladner Gervais LLP - Calgary, 1050
Murphy, Kathleen C., Thompson Dorfman Sweatman LLP, 1064
Murphy, Lisa, Executive Director, 641
Murphy, Lynne, University Librarian, St Francis-Xavier University, 1134
Murphy, Martha, Librarian, Office of the Fire Marshal, 1159
Murphy, Michael B., Minister, 594
Murphy, Mike, Thorold, 720
Murphy, Mike, Vice-President, CBCL Limited, 132
Murphy, Norman, President/CEO, N.R. Murphy Ltd., 296
Murphy, Paul, Director, Paul Martin Law Library, 1165
Murphy, Paul, President/CEO, 629
Murphy, Peter, Vice-President, 598
Murphy, Raymond, President, Montréal Field Naturalists Club, 955
Murphy, Rebecca, Clerk & Director, Corporate & Legal Services, Greater Napanee, 709
Murphy, Sharon, Head, Engineering & Science Library, Engineering & Science Library, 1142
Murphy, Suzanne, Treasurer, International Union of Nutritional Sciences, 945
Murphy, Terry, CAO, Summerside, 733
Murphy, Tim, ADI Group Inc., 68
murphy foundation incorpo, The Murphy Foundation Inc, Winnipeg, MB, 1041
Murphy, CMO, Greg, Chief Administrative Officer & Manager, Public Wor, Essa, 725
Murphy, Q.C., D.J., Donnelly & Murphy, 1068
Murphy, Q.C., George L., Partner, Poole Althouse, Barristers & Solicitors, 1065
Murray, Chris, City Manager, Hamilton, 905-540-5420, 711
Murray, Craig, Acting Vice-President, 662
Murray, Craig, Vice-President, 662
Murray, D.M., President, Clean Air & Water Centre, 142
Murray, Dale B., President/Principal, Triton Engineering Services Ltd., 402
Murray, Dale B., Principal, Triton Engineering Services Ltd., 402
Murray, Dave, Chief Building Official, Thames Centre, 731
Murray, Dave, Manager, Coast Paper Ltd., 145
Murray, Doug, Director, Public Works, Hamilton, 725
Murray, Doug, Manager, Bowater Canadian Forest Products Inc., 114
Murray, Greg, Enercombustion Ltd., 179
Murray, Jeffrey, Osler, Hoskin & Harcourt LLP - Toronto, 1079
Murray, John, Senior Associate, Hardy Stevenson & Associates, 225
Murray, Karen, Library Technician, Hamilton Health Sciences, 1141
Murray, Keith, Director, Alberta Forest Products Association, 817
Murray, Linda, Orillia, 716
Murray, Michèle, Blainville, 734
Murray, Mike, Chief Administrative Officer, Waterloo, 704
Murray, Mike, General Manager, Maple Ridge, 687
Murray, Pat, Treasurer, Newfoundland & Labrador Public Health Association, 963
Murray, Patty G., Partner, Hicks Morley Hamilton Stewart Storie LLP, 1076
Murray, Paul, Director, Saanich, 250-475-5521, 688
Murray, Raymond-Marie, Rimouski, 740
Murray, Richard A., President, R.A. Murray International Limited, 340
Murray, Shawn, Manager, Coast Paper Ltd., 145
Murray, Steve, Coordinator, Economic Development, & Manager, Tour, Kincardine, 726

Murray, Susan, Executive Director, Forest Products Association of Canada, 918
Murray, Wade, Regina, 306-596-1035, 754
Murray, William A., President, Promet Environmental Group Ltd., 334
Murray, MD, FIDSA, Barbara E., Treasurer, Infectious Diseases Society of America, 931
Murray, Q.C., M. Lynn, Matheson & Murray, 1082
Murrell, Iris, Secretary, 588
Murrell, Robert, President, Pepi Sewage Disposal Service, 321
Murry, Sean, Treasurer, Canadian Mineral Analysts, 879
Murry, Sean, Vice-President, Anachemia Canada Inc., 85
Musch, Kathy, Customer Service, Zodiac Fabrics Inc., 437
Muschalla, Frank, Technical Sales Representative, Canviro, 127
Musgrove, James B., Lang Michener LLP - Toronto, 1077
Mussallem, Jack, Mayor, Prince Rupert, 684
Mussatto, Darrell, Metro Vancouver, 678
Mussatto, Darrell R., Mayor, North Vancouver, 682
Mustard, Cameron, President & Senior Scientist, Institute for Work & Health, 932
Mustard, Jeff, Superintendent, Spruce Grove, 780-962-7624, 674
Mustard, Paul, Director, Transportation & Environmental Services, St. Catharines, 719
Musto, Mitha, Trade Commissioner, 767
Mutchmor, Samantha, Executive Director, Coalition to Save the Elms, 897
Muter, Brad, General Manager, Waste Management of Canada, 418
Muthukrishnan, Rajan, Contact, Weir Power & Industrial, 424
Mutrie, Dean F., President, Tera Environmental Consultants (Alta) Ltd., 389
Muttart, Geoffrey P., Muttart Tufts Dewolfe & Coyle, 1068
Mutter, Paul, Sales Manager, Zodiac Fabrics Inc., 437
Mutton, Miriam, Cobourg, 708
Muturi, Elisheba, Secretary, Health Libraries Association of British Columbia, 928
Muzzi, Jeff, Manager, Forestry Services, Renfrew, 613-735-3204, 704
Muzzi, Matt, Branch Manager, Safety-Kleen Canada Inc., 355
Myatt, Mike, Director, Community Services, Saugeen Shores, 719
Myers, Daryl, Supervisor, Antigonish County, 902-863-4744, 696
Myers, Don, President, King Metal Fabricators Ltd., 258
Myers, Randy, President, Hazmasters Environmental Controls Inc., 228
Myers, Ronald, President/CEO, AF Pollution Abatement Systems Inc., 72
Myers, Sidney, Technical Services Librarian, Capilano College, 1114
Myers, Susan, Sault Ste. Marie, 720
Myerscough, Alison, Municipal Planner, Sidney, 250-655-5419, 684
Myers-Gerrits, Joanne, Manager, AF Pollution Abatement Systems Inc., 72
Myette, Michael, Director, 611
Myles, Robert, Longueuil, 737
Myles, Q.C., R. Wayne, Benson Myles, 1065
Mynzak, Greg, Manager, Bartle & Gibson Co. Ltd., 102
Myra, Pamela, Clerk, Chester District, 697
Myrol, David, McLennan Ross LLP, 1055
Myskiw, Finley, Contact, Aquatic Life Ltd., 89

N

Naccarato, D. John, Senior Partner, Ogilvy Renault LLP/S.E.N.C.R.L., s.r.l. - Ottawa, 1071
Nadalin, Sil, Engineer, Design & Construction, Woodstock, 723
Nadati, Flora, Manager, AA Environmental & Associates, 64
Nadeau, Aldéo D., Edmundston, 691
Nadeau, Charles, Associé, Stikeman Elliott LLP - Montréal, 1087
Nadeau, Daniel, Director, 518
Nadeau, Elisabeth, Assistant Deputy Minister, 557
Nadeau, Jacques, Victoriaville, 819-758-8530, 746
Nadeau, Marie-José, Présidente, Fondation Hydro-Québec pour l'environnement, 917
Nadeau, Nicole, Responsable, Québec Ministère du Développement économique, de l'Innovation et, 1180
Nadeau, Steven, Administrator, Ontario Soil & Crop Improvement Association, 979
Nadeau, ing., MBA, Brigitte, Directrice generale, Régie intermunicipale d'élimination de déchets solides de Brome-M, 760
Nadel, Steven, Executive Director, American Council for an Energy-Efficient Economy, 823
Nadiger, Bill, Librarian, Aerospace Technology Campus, 1115

Nadiger, Bill, Librarian, Transportation, British Columbia Institute of Technology, 1110
Nadiger, Bill, Marine Engineer Reference Librarian, Marine Campus, 1114
Nadorozny, Doug, Chief Administrative Officer, Greater Sudbury / Grand Sudbury, 710
Naffin, Daron K., Bennett Jones LLP - Calgary Office, 1049
Nagaraj, Gopinath, Syndel International Inc., 385
Nagel, Stephanie, Treasurer & Director, West Lincoln, 732
Nagelbach, Melissa, Singleton Urquhart LLP, 1062
Nagle, Debbie, Chief Officer, 580
Nagoya, Kevin, Director of Public Works & Infrastructure, Cold Lake, 672
Nagus, Gordon, Partner, Cypress Sales Partnership, 155
Nagy, Erin, Library Clerk, Fort Nelson Campus, 1112
Nagy, Robin, Manager, Client Services, Health Canada, 1150
Nahirnik, Todd, Ackroyd LLP Barristers & Solicitors, 1054
Nahmias, Ahron, President, Metcon Sales & Engineering Ltd., 287
Naidoo, Nalini, Manager, Yellowknife, 867-920-5675, 695
Naing Win, Naig, Sr. Research Scientist, Kam Biotechnology Ltd., 254
Nair, Bondy S., Manager, Canadian Drives Inc., 124
Naish, Cam L., South Frontenac, 730
Naka, Ernie, Terminal City Iron Works Ltd., 390
Naka, Les, Manager, Estevan, 306-634-1818, 754
Nakamoto, Kevin, Intertek Systems Certification, 246
Nakamura, Tamotsu, President, Canon Canada Inc., 126
Nakonechny, Lorne, President, FCX NH Valves, 194
Nakoneshny, Philip W., Director, 584
Nalli, Marco, Manager, Kyocera Mita Canada Ltd., 261
Nantais, Réjean, Trésorier, Lavaltrie, 736
Nantel, Johanne, Trésorière, Mont-Laurier, 738
Nantel, Marc, Director, Ontario Centre of Excellence for Photonics, 972
Napper, Lonny, Lambton, 701
Nardei, Robert, President, Nardei Fabricators Ltd., 297
Nash, David R., McKenzie Lake Lawyers LLP, 1069
Nash, Patricia, Municipal Clerk, Bradford West Gwillimbury, 706
Nason, Gary C., Administrator, Central Saanich, 686
Nataros, Rod, Owner, N.A.T.S. Nursery Ltd., 296
Nathoo, Alnoor (Al), Vice-President, Peto MacCallum Ltd., 321
Nathwani, Jay, Osler, Hoskin & Harcourt LLP - Toronto, 1079
Nation, Chris, Municipal Solicitor, Saanich, 688
Nattaq, Simon, Iqaluit, 698
Nattress, Frances, President, Canadian Meat Science Association, 877
nature trusaintof new bru, Nature Trust of New Bruns, Fredericton, NB, 1042
Natynczyk, Walt, Chief of the Defence Staff, 545
Naud, André, Président, Action Nord Terre, 813
Nauth, Vishnu, Representative, Mifab Canada, 289
Naylor, Dave, President, Naylor Engineering Associates Ltd., 299
Nazareth, Andrew, General Manager, Richmond, 604-276-4095, 684
Nazir, Muhammad, President, Model Forest of Newfoundland and Labrador, 955
NcClure, Dave, Manager, Toromont Caterpillar, 397
Neal, John, Durham, 699
Neal, John, Regional Councillor, Oshawa, 716
Neals-Bolinger, Sarah, Archivist/Research Technician, Ecologistics Research Services, 172
Neas, Gisèle, Responsable, Audiovidéothèque, Université du Québec en Abitibi-Témiscamingue, 1182
Neate, Bob, Manager, Waterford Group, 422
Neate, John H., Senior Associate, ETV Canada, 190
Neault, Maurice (Moe), Saskatoon, 754
Nedelkopoulos, Ted, Director, Sonic Soil Sampling Inc., 374
Neehall, Roy, Manager, Edmonton, 780-496-5405, 672
Neeland, Donald K., Field Law - Edmonton, 1055
Neely, Colleen, Head, Technical Services, Carleton University, 1149
Neely, George, Ark Envirotech Inc., 91
Neff, Paul, Reference Librarian, Augustana Faculty, 1103
Neff, Robert L., President, International Irrigation Systems Ltd., 245
Neighbor, Mark, Lang Michener LLP - Vancouver, 1060
Neil, Joan, Contact, West Elgin Nature Club, 1018
Neilas, Peter, Vice-President, Associated Tube Industries, 94
Neill, Jim, Councillor, Kingston, 712
Neilsen, Carole, President, DBS Environmental, 158
Neilson, Chris, Senior Manager, Capital Regional District, 250-360-3282, 676
Neilson, David, Manager, Buckham Transport Ltd., 118
Neilson, George, President, Lacombe Waste Services, 262

Executive Name Index

Nelligan, Richard, T. Harris Environmental Management Inc., 385
Nelligan, Q.C., LSM, D.U., John, Nelligan O'Brien Payne, 1071
Nellis, Ed, Manager, Westburne Canada, 426
Nellis, Richard, Kleinfeldt Consultants Limited, 258
Nelson, Darryl, President, Nelson Environmental Remediation Ltd., 299
Nelson, David, Peterborough, 703
Nelson, Gordon, Chair, Carolinian Canada Coalition, 892
Nelson, Gordon, Vice President, AGAT Laboratories Ltd., 73
Nelson, Greg, Milton, 714
Nelson, Jean, Secretary, Land Trust Alliance, 948
Nelson, Jennifer, Manager, Partners FOR the Saskatchewan River Basin, 985
Nelson, Larry J., Fasken Martineau - Vancouver, 1059
Nelson, Marcia, Deputy Minister, 569
Nelson, Mike, President/CEO, Nelson Environmental Services, 300
Nelson, Mike, Principal, Cascade Environmental Resource Group. Ltd., 130
Nelson, Paul, Coordinator, Esquimalt, 250-414-7125, 686
Nelson, Paul, Fire Chief, Esquimalt, 250-414-7126, 686
Nelson, Phillip J., President, Council of Marine Carriers, 905
Nelson, Ron, Environmental Coordinator, Fundy Region Solid Waste Commission, 758
Nelson, Ronald R., Brownlee LLP, 1054
Nelson, S., Head, Reference, Aerospace Engineering Test Establishment, 1103
Nelson, Warren, Vice-President, Nelson Environmental Remediation Ltd., 299
Nelson, Wendy, Executive Director, Urban & Regional Information Systems Association, 1015
Nemeth, Dianne, City Clerk, Lethbridge, 403-320-3821, 673
Nenshi, Naheed K., Mayor, Calgary, 403-268-5622, 671
Nepstad, Carl, Fire Chief, New Westminster, 682
Nepszy, Chris, Director, Infastructure & Development, Essex, 709
neptis foundation, The Neptis Foundation, Toronto, ON, 1044
Nepton, Annie, Directrice, Chambly, 734
Nerman, Howard P., Pitblado LLP, 1063
Néron, Bruno, Grondin, Poudrier, Bernier, 1087
Néron, Marie-Claude, Cain Lamarre Casgrain Wells - Chicoutimi, 1082
Nesbitt, Cathy, Founder, Cathy's Crawly Composters, 132
Nestor, Rob, Librarian, First Nations University of Canada, 1188
Nethery, BES, MCIP, RPP, Rick, Director, Planning, Newmarket, 905-953-5321, 714
Netser, Patterk, Minister, 617
Nettlefold, Brian, Executive Director, Nippissing University/Canadore College, 1146
Nettleton, Gordon, Partner, Osler, Hoskin & Harcourt LLP - Calgary, 1053
Neu, Joseph, Vice-President, Electro-Federation Canada Inc., 909
Neubauer, M., Director, Finance, Guelph, 710
Neudorf, Russell, Deputy Minister, 608
Neufeld, Brian, General Manager, Engineered Air, 180
Neufeld, Jack, WORX Environmental Products Inc., 434
Neufeld, Richard, Minister, 576
Neufeld, Richard A., Fraser Milner Casgrain LLP - Calgary, 1051
Neufeld, Rob, GM, Campbell River, 679
Neufeld, Ron, Manager, Campbell River, 679
Neufeld, Stephanie, President, Alberta Lake Management Society, 818
Neufeldt, Dennis, President, Haul-All Equipment Ltd., 227
Neugebauer, Peter, Director, Yellowknife, 867-920-5660, 695
Neuheimer, Joel, Director, Forest Products Association of Canada, 918
Neumann, David E., Brantford, 707
Neumann, Randy, Secretary, Environmental Services Association of Alberta, 912
Neumer, Nathan, Director, Dynamotive Energy Systems Corporation, 168
Neveu, Marie-Josée, Library Services, Energy Diversification Research Laboratory, 1186
Neville, John, CEO, Quester Tangent Corp., 339
Neville, Richard R., Davis LLP - Toronto, 1074
Newark, Mike, Chief Building Official, Guelph-Eramosa, 725
Newbery, George, Operations Manager, Rochester Midland Ltd., 349
Newbigging, Mike, Hydromantis Inc., 237
Newbigging, Mike, President, Hydromantis Inc., 237
Newbold, K. Bruce, Président, Association canadienne des sciences régionales, 830
Newby, Richard, Plant Manager, CCS Income Trust, 134

Newcomb, Chris, President, McElhanney Consulting Services Ltd., 284
Newell, Bill, CAO, Okanagan-Similkameen, 678
Newell, Peter S., Senior Partner, Ogilvy Renault LLP/S.E.N.C.R.L., s.r.l. - Toronto, 1078
Newell, Wayne, Director, Infrastructure Services, Ottawa, 716
Newkirk, Ingrid E., President, People for the Ethical Treatment of Animals, 985
Newland, Helen, Fraser Milner Casgrain LLP - Toronto, 1075
Newlove, Rick, Essa, 705-458-1337, 725
Newlove, Rick, General Manager, Corporate Services, Simcoe, 704
Newman, David G., Pitblado LLP, 1063
Newman, Deborah, Deputy Minister, 621
Newman, Judy, Office Manager, Seeds of Diversity Canada, 1003
Newman, Louise, Manager, Canadian Society for Civil Engineering, 885
Newman, Mike, Organics, Lambton Scientific, 264
Newman, Phil, Director, Leduc County, 780-955-6413, 669
Newman, Q.C., Forbes, Gowling Lafleur Henderson LLP - Calgary, 1051
Newton, Janet, Councillor, Kings County, 696
Newton, Karen, Development Officer, Chester District, 697
Newton, Mark, Group Executive, Coffey Geotechnics Inc., 146
Newton, Paul, President, Western Canada Tire Dealers Association, 1018
Newton, Peter A., Warden, Annapolis County, 696
Newton, Scott, Manager, Mississippi River Power Corp., 291
Newyear-Ramirez, Jo Anne, Assist. University Librarian, Collections & Schola, University of British Columbia, 1119
Ng, David, RICHWAY Environmental Technologies Ltd., 347
Ng, Joe, President, JNE Consulting Ltd., 252
Ng, Judy, Library Technician, The Scarborough Hospital - General Campus, 1162
Ng, Rodney, Vice-President, Industrial Marine Power Engineering Group, 240
Ngo, Young, General Manager, Kinectrics Inc., 257
Nguyen, Minh-Thu, Responsable, Services techniques, École polytechnique de Montréal, 1173
Nguyen, V.T.V., Director, Brace Centre for Water Resources Management, 115
Nguyen, Vy-Khanh, Bibliothécaire, Centre de documentation, 1171
Niblett, Philip, President/CEO, Niblett Environmental, 304
Nichol, Gail, Librarian, Engineering & Computer Science Library, 1157
Nichol, Kevin, President, Toronto Transportation Society, 1013
Nicholas, Richard, Intertek Systems Certification, 246
Nicholls, David, Sales Manager, Epsilon Chemicals Ltd., 189
Nicholls, Pat, Head, Systems, University of Manitoba Libraries, 1125
Nichols, Barrie, President, Asbeguard Equipment Inc., 93
Nichols, Dave, Director, Grand Falls-Windsor, 709-489-0450, 694
Nichols, Lee, Principal, Terracon Geotechnique Ltd., 390
Nichols, Peter, Partner, Nichols Applied Management, 304
Nichols, Sarah, Information Specialist, Ontario Ministry of Municipal Affairs & Housing, 1160
Nicholson, Jeff, Manager, Waterous Power Systems, 423
Nicholson, Jim, General Manager, Transcontinental Printing Inc., 400
Nicholson, Mike, City Councillor, Oshawa, 716
Nicholson, P.Eng, Ensor, Chair, Atlantic Canada Water & Wastewater Association, 842
Nicholson, Q.C., G. Fred, Clark Drummie, 1065
Nickel, Paul, Stratford, 720
Nickel, William A., McDougall Gauley, 1090
Nickels, Steve, Fire Chief, Meaford, 727
Nickerson, Susan L., Partner, Hicks Morley Hamilton Stewart Storie LLP, 1076
Nickes, Carol, Assistant Librarian, Canadian University College, 1108
Nicol, Don, Contact, R.J. Burnside & Associates Limited, 340
Nicol, Don, Manager, AMEC, 82
Nicol, John, Chief of Staff, Regina, 754
Nicol, John, Chief Administrative Officer, Thorold, 720
Nicol, Peter, Sr. Vice-President, CH2M Hill Canada Limited, 137
Nicolet, Roger, Préfet, Memphrémagog, 750
Nicoll, Lorelei, Councillor, Halifax Regional Municipality, 695
Nicoll, Murray, Contact, Beasy Nicoll Engineering Ltd., 104
Nicolson, Bev, Planner, Georgian Bluffs, 725
Niebergall, Kevin, Branch Manager, C.G. Industrial Specialties, Ltd., 120
Nield, Liz, Consultant, LURA Consulting, 275
Nielsen, Kim, Manager, Clearwater County, 669

Nielsen, Leah, Coordinator, Canadian Centre for Pollution Prevention, 862
Nielsen, Peter, Secretary, Oxford County Geological Society, 983
Nielsen, Udo, President, Dendron Resource Surveys Inc., 161
Nielsen, Q.C., Allan D., Partner, Borden Ladner Gervais LLP - Calgary, 1050
Nieuwenburg, Roy A., Clark Wilson LLP, 1058
Nightingale, Dave, Director, 607
Nigro, Mario, Blake, Cassels & Graydon LLP - Toronto, 1072
Nihei, Kathy, Founder, Wild Bird Care Centre, 1020
Nijboer, Gordon, Manager, Brendar Environmental Inc., 116
Nijman, Gary M., Alexander Holburn Beaudin & Lang, LLP, 1057
Nikiforov, Dmitry, Acting Manager, Systems & Media, Centennial College of Applied Arts & Technology, 1157
Nikkel, Terry, Director, Information Services & Systems, Ward Chipman Library, 1129
Nikolajev, Igor, President, Gemite Products Inc., 206
Nimmo, Tomás L., President, Organic Farm Services, 314
Nirenberg, Jami, Coordinator, Food & Consumer Products of Canada, 918
Niro, Linda, Vice-President, Export Development Canada, 192
Niro, Rick, Sault Ste. Marie, 720
Niro, M.Sc., Perry, Directeur général et chef de la dir, BIOQuébec, 845
Nishimura, Warren B., Blake, Cassels & Graydon LLP - Calgary, 1049
Nissan, Sandra, Partner, Ogilvy Renault LLP/S.E.N.C.R.L., s.r.l. - Toronto, 1078
Nitkin, David, President/CEO, EthicScan Canada, 190
Nittritz, Mani, Director, Cantech Inspections Ltd., 127
Niven, Michael B., Carscallen Leitch LLP, 1050
Nix, K.R., Acting CAO, Treasurer & Director, Whitby, 723
Nixon, Alan, North Vancouver, 688
Nixon, Brian, President/CEO, Vizon SciTec Inc., 414
Njagi Runguma, Sebastian, Manager, CIVICUS: World Alliance for Citizen Participation, 896
Noakes, Steve, Planner, North Okanagan, 678
Nobert, Conrad, President, Toxics Watch Society of Alberta, 1013
Noble, Al W., National Sales Manager, F.E. Myers, 193
Noble, Bruce A., City Solicitor, Fredericton, 691
Nobréga, Gérard, Responsable du centre de documentation, Québec Ministère du Développement durable, de l'Environnement et, 1180
Nodrick, Dennis, Chief, Portage La Prairie, 204-239-8340, 689
Noel, Amos, Trade Commissioner, 769
Noël, André, Trois-Rivières, 745
Noël, Bernard, Saguenay, 741
Noel, Denis, Reynolds, Mirth, Richards & Farmer LLP, 1056
Noël, François, President, Filtrum Inc., 195
Noël, Gilles, Directeur général adjoint, Québec, 740
Noël, Jean, Office Manager, Trow Consulting Engineers Ltd., 403
Noftall, Karen, President, Quality Matters Inc., 338
Noftell, Ken, Owner/Operator, Ken Noftell Drilling Services, 256
Noiseux, André, General Manager, Solmax-Texel Geosynthetics Inc., 373
Nolan, Liana, Medical Officer of Health, Waterloo, 704
Nolan, Mark, Registrar, Alberta Association of Landscape Architects, 815
Nolan, Michael, Director, Emergency Services, Renfrew, 704
Nolan, Philip, Partner, Lavery, de Billy - Montréal, 1086
Nolan, Stephen, Librarian, Carbonear Campus Library, 1130
Nolan, Esq., Stephen J., Chair, American Lung Association, 823
Nolan, MA, DPhil, Fergal, President & Chief Executive Officer, Radiation Safety Institute of Canada, 992
Nolet, Guy, Directeur général, Amos, 733
Noll, George, Novatech Controls, Inc., 309
Nols, Jacques, Partner, Lavery, de Billy - Montréal, 1086
Noon, Blake, Vice-President & General Manager, Eckel Industries, 170
Noonan, Ken, Director, Facilities Management & Fleet Services, Waterloo, 704
Noone, Fran, Information Specialist, Teck Cominco Metals Ltd., 1117
Noordermeer, Jim, Principal & Manager, Gryphon International Engineering Services Inc., 222
Norburn, Jeff, Director, Quesnel, 688
Norcross, Richard, New Tecumseth, 714
Nordick, D'Arcy, Partner, Stikeman Elliott LLP - Toronto, 1080
Nordman, Grant, Winnipeg, 204-986-5920, 690
Norie, Jim, Senior Planner, Landscope Consulting Corp., 264
Norman, David, Deputy Minister, 600
Norman, Peter, Head, Systems, Newfoundland Ocean Industries Association, 1132

Executive Name Index

Norman, Randy G., Marine Environmental Technologist, Cormorant Ltd., 152
Norman, Q.C., David M., Cox and Palmer - Fredericton, 1064
Normand, Jérôme, Directeur général, Environnement jeunesse, 913
Normand, Louis, Directeur général, Sainte-Marie, 743
Normand, Patrice, Sec.-Trés., Régie d'assainissement des eaux usées de Piedmont, St-Sauveur et, 759
Normand, Richard, Vice-President, Lambert Somec inc., 263
Normandin, Pierre, Directeur (par intérim), 646
Normandin, Yves, Vice-President, BFI Canada Inc., 106
Norquay, Don, Deputy Minister, 591
Norris, Christopher, Manager of Technical Services, Canadian Urban Transit Association, 1156
Norris, Gary, Manager, Brantford Disposal Service, 115
Norris, Gord, Chief Administrative Officer, Collingwood, 708
Norris, Ian, Director, Calgary, 403-974-4876, 671
Norris, Max, President, Joseph & Co. Inc., 253
Norris, Rob, Minister, 661
Norris, Rob, Minister Responsible, 661
Norris, Robin-Lee, Miller Thomson LLP - Waterloo, 1081
Norris, Robin-Lee A., Partner, Miller Thomson LLP - Toronto, 1078
Norris-Kirk, Valerie, Development Coordinator, Grande Prairie, 780-513-5236, 672
Norsworthy, Lori, LADEN Steel Fabricators Inc., 262
North, Brad, Contact, Terrace, 250-615-4032, 685
North, Linda, Library Clerk, Nexen Inc., 1102
Northcott, Jim, City Councillor, Woodstock, 519-539-3698, 723
Northey, Rodney V., Birchall Northey, 1072
Norton, Debbie, President, Northumberland Salmon Protection Association, 966
Norton, Doug, Vice-President, Environmental Waste International, 186
Norton, Michele, Circulation Assistant, Portage College, 1108
Nosal, Robert, Commissioner & Medical Officer of Health, Halton, 700
Nottley, Mike, Secretary-Treasurer, HQN Industrial Fabrics Inc., 234
Nouch, Agako, Vice-President, Ingersoll-Rand Canada Inc., 241
Noulty, Rob, Manager, Bubble Technology Industries Inc., 118
Nouvet, Dominique A., Cook Roberts LLP, 1062
nova foresaintalliance, Nova Forest Alliance, Stewiacke, NS, 1043
nova scotia dept of natur, Nova Scotia. Dept. of Nat, Kentville, NS, 1043
Novak, Lesley, Vice-President, AquaTox Testing & Consulting Inc., 89
Novak, Mary, Durham, 699
Novak, Mary, Regional Councillor, Clarington, 724
Novak, Patrick, President, Environmental Managers Association of British Columbia, 912
Novak, Paul, Gemite Products Inc., 206
Novokowski, Ray, President/CEO, EcoVu Analytics, 173
Nowack, R.E. (Bob), Chairman & Chief Executive Officer, Conor Pacific Environmental Technology Inc., 150
Nowak, Ed, Fire Chief, Owen Sound, 717
Nowicki, Victor K., President, ARC Geobac Group Inc., 90
Noye, Trevor J.L., Vice-President, Trojan Technologies Inc., 403
Nucci, Steve, Cancoppas Limited, 126
Nugent, Bill, Director & Solicitor, 570
Nugent, John, City Solicitor, Saint John, 506-658-2860, 692
Nugent, Q.C., Ross A.L., Thompson Dorfman Sweatman LLP, 1064
Nunes, Ana, Conseillère, Jeanne-Sauvé, Montréal, 738
Nunn, Cara, North Okanagan Organic Association, 966
Nunziata, Frances, Toronto, 721
Nurse, David W., Manager, Flygt Canada, 198
Nuttall, Alexander, Barrie, 706
Nuttall, Evan, Partner, Borden Ladner Gervais LLP - Calgary, 1050
Nuttall, Robert, President, Explore Plus Duct Cleaning Ltd., 192
Nuttall, Robert W., Vice-President, ArcelorMittal Dofasco, 90
Nyce, Harry, Board Chair, Kitimat-Stikine, 678
Nyland, Jennifer S., Lawson Lundell LLP - Vancouver, 1061

O

O'Brien, Allan R., Nelligan O'Brien Payne, 1071
O'Brien, Anthony, Contact, Golder Associates Ltd., 214
O'Brien, Brad, Publisher, Hazardous Materials Management Magazine, 227
O'Brien, Dan, Sanitherm Engineering Limited, 357
O'Brien, David, Blake, Cassels & Graydon LLP - Toronto, 1072
O'Brien, Dianne, Prince Edward, 703
O'Brien, Fred J., President/CEO, Maritime Electric Company Ltd., 280
O'Brien, Michael G., Fredericton, 691
O'Brien, Robert, Founder/Chair, Ocean Net, 970
O'Brien, Sean, President, Acklands-Grainger Inc., 66
O'Byrne, Simone, Information Specialist, Ontario Ministry of Environment, 1160
O'Callaghan, Kevin, Fasken Martineau - Vancouver, 1059
O'Carroll, Colm, President, Epsilon Chemicals Ltd., 189
O'Carroll, Colm, President/CEO, Advance Laboratories Ltd., 69
O'Connell, David J., President, Dalynn Biologicals Inc., 156
O'Connell, Jennifer, Durham, 699
O'Connell, Jennifer, Regional Councillor, Pickering, 718
O'Connor, Brian, Medical Health Officer, North Vancouver, 688
O'Connor, Dennis, President, Denoco Energy Systems Ltd., 161
O'Connor, Gerri Lynn, Mayor, Uxbridge, 731
O'Connor, James A., Regional Manager & Sarnia Site Manag, DuPont Canada Inc., 167
O'Connor, Joe, CAO, Inverness County, 697
O'Connor, Joe, Director, Inverness County, 902-787-3502, 697
O'Connor, John, Associé, Langlois Kronström Desjardins, 1088
O'Connor, Larry, Mayor, Brock, 724
O'Connor, M. Rick, City Clerk & Solicitor, Ottawa, 716
O'Connor, Michael, Founder & President, O'Connor Associates Environmental Inc., 310
O'Connor, Neil, Air Liquide Canada Ltée, 75
O'Connor, P., Regional Solicitor & Director, Legal & Risk Manage, Peel, 703
O'Connor, Rita, Contact, Regional Petroleum Products Recycling Ltd., 344
O'Connor, Tim, President, U-pak Disposal Ltd., 405
O'Connor, Q.C., C.Arb., F, Christopher J., Partner, Borden Ladner Gervais LLP - Vancouver, 1058
O'Dea, John V., McInnes Cooper, 1066
O'Dell, Gerard, Managing Director, SGS Canada Inc., 364
O'Donnell, Danna, COABC Representative, Boundary Organic Producers Association, 846
O'Donnell, Edward, Supervisor, Water, Bradford West Gwillimbury, 706
O'Donnell, Mike, Regina, 306-545-7300, 754
O'Donnell, Rosemary F., Manager, Lanxess Inc. - Sarnia, 1154
O'Farrell, Jeff, Deputy Minister, 663
O'Fee, John, Kamloops, 681
O'Grady, Jennifer, Vice-President, Terrapex Environmental Ltd., 390
O'Hagan, James, Senior Partner, William Alexander & Associates Ltd., 432
O'Halloran, Dan, President, O'Halloran Campbell Consultants Limited, 310
O'Hara, Erril, Regional Sales Manager, Celfort Construction Materials Inc., 135
O'Hearn, Anne, Contact, FS Partners, 202
O'Keefe, Dennis, Mayor, St. John's, 709-576-8477, 694
O'Keefe, John, Principal, Aercoustics Engineering Limited, 71
O'Keefe, Owen, Supervisor, Water Purification Plant, Cornwall, 708
O'Keefe, Ross, Pinchin Environmental Ltd., 324
O'Krafka, Harold, Director, Wilmot, 732
O'Krane, Dale, Manager, Sumas Environmental Services Inc., 381
O'Leary, Dennis, President & Sr. Quaternary Geologist, Geowest Environmental Consultants, 212
O'Leary, Dennis M., Aird & Berlis LLP, 1072
O'Leary, Michael, Director, Antigonish County, 696
O'Leary, Mike, Councillor, Halton Hills, 710
O'Leary, Sheilagh, Councillor at Large, St. John's, 709-576-8567, 694
O'Loughlin, Chloe, Executive Member, British Columbia Spaces for Nature, 850
O'Melia, Steven J., Associate Counsel, Miller Thomson LLP - Toronto, 1078
O'Neil, Melony, Director, 599
O'Neil, Mike, Operations Manager, Connor Architects & Planners, 150
O'Neil, Peggy, Manager, London Health Sciences Centre, 1144
O'Neil, CAE, Peter J., Executive Director, American Industrial Hygiene Association, 823
O'Neill, Gavin, Contact, Conestoga-Rovers & Associates, 149
O'Neill, James, Contact, Conestoga-Rovers & Associates, 149
O'Neill, Leona, Manager, 600
O'Neill, Sean, Lang Michener LLP - Vancouver, 1060
O'Neill, Sean, Manager, Canadian Liquids Processors Limited, 124
O'Neill, Suzanne, Head, Reference & Public Services, Fanshawe College of Applied Arts & Technology, 1143
O'Neill, Terry, Pembroke, 717
O'Neill, C.M.M. III, Bill, Director, Emergency Services & Fire Chief, Georgina, 709
O'Regan, Fred, President, International Fund for Animal Welfare Canada, 939
O'Reilly, Adrienne A., Heenan Blaikie LLP - Calgary, 1051
O'Reilly, Patrick, Kawartha Lakes, 711
O'Rielly, Alastair, Deputy Minister, 599
O'Riley, Chris, Senior Vice-President, 580
O'Rourke, Barry, President, Compusult Limited, 148
O'Rourke, Jim, Manager, Public Works, Kincardine, 726
O'Rourke, Kerri Ann, Clerk, Perth East, 728
O'Shannassy, Julia, Matrix Solutions Inc., 282
O'Shaugnessy, Leslie, Cornwall, 708
O'Shea, Paul, CFO, DATA Group of Companies, 157
O'Sullivan, Siobhan, Lang Michener LLP - Vancouver, 1060
O'Toole, Colleen, Principal, Connections Research, 150
O'Toole, C.G.A., Cathie, Director, Halifax Regional Municipality, 695
Oakes, Coralee, Councillor & Member, Quesnel, 688
Oakes, David, Director, Economic Development & Tourism Services, St. Catharines, 719
Oakes, Larry, Owner/Senior Advisor, Resource Systems Inc., 346
Oakley, Russ, Chair, Squamish-Lillooet, 679
Oakman, Debra, CAO, Comox Valley, 677
Obal, Taras, Manager, Canviro, 127
Obed, Letia, Director, 618
Obee, Tamara, Officer, Human Resources, Oro-Medonte, 728
Oberg, Glen, Manager, Victoria, 250-361-0271, 685
Obhrai, Deepak, Parliamentary Secretary to the Minister of Foreign, 529
Oblin, Rhonda, General Manager, Waswanipi Cree Model Forest, 1017
Octavian, Bonea, Trade Commissioner, 768
Oda, Beverley J. (Bev), Minister, International Cooperation, 519
Odell, David, President/CEO, The DATA Group of Companies, 392
Odell, David M., President/CEO, DATA Group of Companies, 157
Odum, Marvin, Chair, Shell Canada Limited, 365
Oehr, Klaus, President, Hazelmere Research Ltd., 228
Oele, Laura, Manager, Westburne Canada, 426
Officer, Paul, Fire Chief, Elliot Lake, 709
Ofoha, Bert, Consultant, HMO Limited, 232
Ogale, Aruna, Executive Director, Ontario Camps Association, 971
Ogilvie, Jim, President, Ogilvie Scientific Inc., 311
Ogilvie, Louise, Vice-President, Canadian Institute for Health Information, 872
Ogilvie, R., Vice-President, Enform: The Safety Association for the Upstream Oil & Gas Industr, 910
Ogilvie, Trent, President, Roxul Inc., 353
Ogle, Q.C., James J., Wolch, Hursh, deWit & Watts, 1054
Ogryzlo, Jon, Sec.-Treas., Environmental Careers Organization of Canada, 911
Ohlmann, Hans-Armin, President, Ventax Robot Inc., 411
Ohnysty, Dean, Director, Leduc County, 780-955-4535, 669
Ohreen, Paula, Vision Quest Windelectric Inc., 414
Oickle, Scott, Contact, Clemmer Technologies Inc., 143
Okalik, Paul, Minister, 618
Oke, Ken, Warden & Councillor, Huron, 701
Okerman, Rob, General Manager, Advanced Coolant Technologies Inc., 69
Okoli, Rem, Manager, Canadian Soil & Climate Protection Corp., 125
Olafson, David, Contact, Prince Edward Island Salmon Association, 989
Olddale, Jane, System Design/Marketing, Frank's Alternate Energy, 201
Oldham, Eamonn, President, Oldham Engineers Inc., 312
Oldham, John, President, Arrow Speed Controls Ltd., 93
Olds, D. Mason, Vice-President & General Manager, Canon Canada Inc., 126
Oleniuk, Terri-Lee V., Osler, Hoskin & Harcourt LLP - Calgary, 1053
Oleszkiewicz, Wanda, Librarian, Husky Oil Operations Ltd., 1101
Olexiuk, Paula, Partner, Osler, Hoskin & Harcourt LLP - Calgary, 1053
Oliphant, Monica V., President, International Solar Energy Society, 944
Olive, Pat W., Commissioner, Economic Development & Tourism, Durham, 800-413-0017, 699
Oliver, Debbie, Coordinator, Waters Limited, 423
Oliver, Don, Treasurer, Central Canadian Federation of Mineralogical Societies, 893
Oliver, Jim, Norfolk, 702

Executive Name Index

Oliver, Joan, Library Technician, St Clair College of Applied Arts & Technology, 1165
Oliver, Norman, Manager, Tansley Associates Environmental Services, 387
Oliver, Richard, Macleod Dixon LLP, 1077
Oliver, Walter, Fire Chief, Iqaluit, 867-976-5657, 698
Olivier, Marie, Responsable, Collège Stanislas inc, 1177
Ollenberger, Mike, Plant Manager, CCS Income Trust, 134
Olley, Stuart M., Partner, Stikeman Elliott LLP - Calgary, 1054
Olmstead, Steven, Manager, Squamish-Lillooet, 679
Olscamp, Michael, Minister, 591
Olsen, Clarinda, Head, Science/Engineering Library, ILL & Reference, Science/Engineering Library, 1143
Olsheski, Contance C., Lang Michener LLP - Toronto, 1077
Olsiak, Catherine A., SimpsonWigle LAW LLP, 1069
Olsmats, Carl, General Secretary, World Packaging Organization, 1023
Olson, Karen, Information Management, UMA Engineering Ltd., 1106
Olson, Pamela, Librarian, Institute of Ocean Sciences, 1116
Olson, Pat, ITM Instruments, 248
Olson, Stan, Head, Acquisitions & Systems, Trinity Western University, 1113
Olson, Q.C., E. William, Thompson Dorfman Sweatman LLP, 1064
Olthafer, Lars, Blake, Cassels & Graydon LLP - Calgary, 1049
Olyan, Arnold, Burnet, Duckworth & Palmer LLP, 1050
Olynyk, Donald, Donald Olynyk, Acoustical Engineer, 165
Olynyk, B.Sc., M.Sc., LL., John M., Administrative Partner, Lawson Lundell LLP - Calgary, 1051
Olyslager, Patricia E., Burnet, Duckworth & Palmer LLP, 1050
Ondyak, Jim, President, Silliker Canada Co., 367
Oness, Marley, Municipal Engineer, Okotoks, 403-938-8930, 674
Ono, Herbert I., Lang Michener LLP - Vancouver, 1060
Ono, Steven, City Engineer, North Vancouver, 682
ontario ministry of energ, Ontario. Ministry of Ener, Toronto, ON, 1044
ontario trillium foundati, The Ontario Trillium Foun, Toronto, ON, 1044
oogemans, Scott, Director, 583
Oosterhof, John, Dufferin, 699
Opitz, Mike, Vice-President LEED, U.S. Green Building Council, 1016
Oppedisano, Salvatore, President, Lupien Rosenberg Consultants Inc., 243, 275
Oram, Julie C., City Clerk & Director, Corporate Services, Belleville, 613-967-3271, 706
Oram, Peter, Vice-President, Conestoga-Rovers & Associates, 149
Oranchuk, Debbie, Library Assistant, Northern Forestry Centre, 1106
Orawan, Chandrangsu, Trade Commissioner, 769
Orchard, Brenda, Chief Administrative Officer, Annapolis County, 696
Orchard, Q.C., Vincent R., Senior Counsel, Borden Ladner Gervais LLP - Vancouver, 1058
Orduz, Tania, General Manager, Assaynet Canada Inc., 94
Ordyniec, Krystyn, Scarfone Hawkins LLP, 1069
Organ, Ken, Partner, Goss Gilroy Inc., 215
Orlandini, Rosa, Manager, Walter Hitschfeld Geographic Information Centre, 1176
Orlando, Cabrera-Rivera, Program Manager, Commission for Environmental Cooperation, 764
Orlikow, John, Winnipeg, 204-986-5236, 690
Orme, William, Chief, United Nations Development Program, 1015
Ormerod, David W., President, Sylvametrics Consulting, 384
Ormerod, Rose Mary, Library Head, Thurber Group, 1121
Orms, FACHE, CAE, R. Norris, Exec. VP & COO & Executive Director, Healthcare Information & Management Systems Society, 928
Orr, David, Marketing, Scott Tank Cleaning Co. Ltd., 360
Orr, Fay, Deputy Minister, 572
Orr, Fay, Mental Health Patient Advocate, 569
Orr, Wayne, Clerk & Administrator, South Frontenac, 730
Orser, Stephen, London, 713
Orsi, Angelo, Mayor, Orillia, 716
Orthner, Judy, Co-Director, 656
Osanic, Lisa, Councillor, Kingston, 712
Osberg, Lyle, Sales Manager, Ellett Industries, 176
Osborn, Tom, Alberta & BC Sales Manager, Endress+Hauser Canada Ltd., 178
Osborne, Bruce, Manager, 610
Osborne, Michael, President, Terrapex Environmental Ltd., 390
Osborne, Ray, Supervisor, Whitehorse, 867-668-8669, 755

Osborne, Tom, General Manager, Nanaimo, 678
Osborne, P.Eng., Cathie, Manager, Halifax Regional Municipality, 902-490-4093, 695
Osepchook, Felicity, Head, New Brunswick Museum, 1129
Osepchook, Felicity, Manager, New Brunswick Dept. of Wellness, Culture & Sport, 1129
Osinchuk, Linda, Mayor, Strathcona County, 670
Osmar, Peter, Vice President, M.J. Labelle Co. Ltd., 276
Osmond, Don, Secretary, Conference of New England Governors & Eastern Canadian Premiers, 900
Osmond, Don, Secretary to Council, Council of Atlantic Premiers, 904
Osmond, Raymond, Director, Mount Pearl, 709-748-1027, 694
Osmun, Barry, Maccaferri Canada Ltd., 277
Ossington, Rita, Tecumseh, 519-735-8251, 720
Oster, Tim, Vice-President, British Columbia Ground Water Association, 848
Osterman, Bob, New Westminster, 682
Ostermann, David, Secretary, Entomological Society of Manitoba Inc., 910
Osterreicher, Angela, President, Manitoba Association of Health Information Providers, 950
Osther, Jennifer, Librarian, IBI Group, 1158
Ostola, Larry S., Director General, 552
Ostraat, Ken, Director, Summerland, 689
Ostrowski, Richard, Facilities & Program Administrator, Ontario Petroleum Institute Inc., 1144
Ostrowski, Steve, Vice-President, UniFold Shelters Ltd., 405
Oswald, Patricia, President, Canadians for Ethical Treatment of Food Animals, 892
Oswald, Ron, Bruce, 698
Oswald, Theresa, Minister, 588
Oswick-Kearney, Tammy, Provincial Coordinator, Quebec Young Farmers' Provincial Federation, 1182
Osyany, Andrew, Secretary, Ontario Rock Garden Society, 978
Otis, Michael, County Planner, Stormont, Dundas & Glengarry, 730
Ott, L., Sales Coordinator, Parkson Corporation, 319
Ottema, Gerry, President, Wyckomar Inc., 435
Otto, Brenda, Officer, Trent Hills, 731
Otto, Paul, Associate University Librarian, Information Techno, McMaster University, 1141
Otton, Tim, President, Napier-Reid Ltd., 297
Ottoni, C.A., Angelo, Vice-President, 521
Oud, Joanne, Collections & Acquistions Dept. Head, Wilfrid Laurier University, 1165
Ouellet, Alain, President, Integrated Catalyst Engineering Inc., 244
Ouellet, Benoît, Directeur, Rivière-du-Loup, 418-862-0906, 741
Ouellet, Caroline, Manager, Westburne Canada, 428
Ouellet, Colette, Directrice, Sherbrooke, 819-821-5572, 744
Ouellet, Cécile, Chambly, 450-658-2045, 734
Ouellet, Diane, Bibliotechnicienne, CÉGEP de Rivière-du-Loup, 1182
Ouellet, Jean-Clément, Préfet, La Mitis, 748
Ouellet, Jean-François, Saint-Constant, 742
Ouellet, Nathalie, SMTE, Collège de Maisonneuve, 1172
Ouellet, Pierre, Grondin, Poudrier, Bernier, 1087
Ouellet, Suzanne, Greffière, Gatineau, 735
Ouellet, Suzanne, Sec.-Trés., Régie intermunicipale d'approvisionnement en eau potable Henryvil, 759
Ouellet, Sylvain, Greffier, Québec, 418-641-6212, 740
Ouellett, Iris, Library Manager, Defence R & D Canada - Atlantic, 1135
Ouellette, Dan, Director, Powell River, 683
Ouellette, Luke, Minister, 573
Ouellette, Peter, Manager, Westburne Canada, 428
Oughton, Martin J., Regional Operations Leader, Underwriters' Laboratories of Canada, 405
Ouimet, François H., Associé, Stikeman Elliott LLP - Montréal, 1087
Oulds, Larry, Manager, Dillon Consulting Ltd., 163
Oulton, Daniel L., Burchell, MacDougall, 1068
Oulton, Mark S., Hunter Litigation Chambers, 1060
Oussoren, Harry, President, Insitu Contractors Inc., 242
Outhit, Tim, Councillor, Halifax Regional Municipality, 695
Outos, Jim, Contact, Canberra Company, 126
Overbeek, Christian, Président, Fédération des producteurs de cultures commerciales du Québec, 915
Overholt, Deborah H., Managing Partner, Borden Ladner Gervais LLP - Vancouver, 1058
Owen, Brian, Associate University Librarian, Simon Fraser University, 1111
Owen, Gordon T., Chief Enforcement Officer, 522
Owen, Richard C., Counsel, Stikeman Elliott LLP - Toronto, 1080

Owen, Robert G., Partner, Borden Ladner Gervais LLP - Vancouver, 1058
Owen, Teo, Senior Trade Commissioner, 767
Owen, Victoria, Head Librarian, University of Toronto Scarborough Library, 1163
Owens, Dennis C., Vice-President, Biotech Solutions, 109
Owens, Geoff, Coordinator, Access Services, Mount Royal College, 1102
Owens, Rob, Fire Chief, Campbell River, 679
Oxford, James, Director, Mount Pearl, 709-748-1028, 694
Oxley, Michael J., Vice-President & CFO, DuPont Canada Inc., 167
Ozolins, Dorothy, Librarian, KSH Solutions Inc. (KSH), 1174
Ozunko, Randy, Program Specialist, 584

P

P.Ag., Wesley Wall, President, Genics Inc., 207
Pabst, Linda, King, 726
Pabst, Rick, Field Law - Edmonton, 1055
Pace, William R., Executive Director, World Federalist Movement, 1022
Pachereva, John D., Lincoln, 713
Packard, James D., President, Pacwill Environmental, 317
Padurean, John, Estimator, Monalt Environmental Inc., 292
Padwick, James, Ogilvy Renault LLP/S.E.N.C.R.L., s.r.l. - Toronto, 1078
Pagani, Richard, President, Conterm Inc., 151
Paganucci, Al, Allianz Madvac Inc., 79
Paganuzzi, Peter, President, Petrifond Foundation Co. Ltd., 322
Page, Devon, Executive Director, Ecojustice Canada, 1117
Pagé, Frédéric, Lavery, de Billy - Montréal, 1086
Pagé, Jean-François, Partner, Heenan Blaikie S.E.N.C.R.L/SRL - Sherbrooke, 1089
Pagé, Normand, Mascouche, 450-966-6326, 737
Page, Rick, Director, New Westminster, 682
Page, Victoria, Sec.-Treas., Alberta Aquaculture Association, 815
Page, PhD, Stacey, Officer, Canadian Bioethics Society, 860
Pageau, Marc, Directeur, Gatineau, 735
Pageot, Hervé, Daigneault, avocats inc., 1083
Pages, Barry, Chair, Skeena-Queen Charlotte, 679
Pagtakhan, Mike, Winnipeg, 204-986-8401, 690
Pahl, Roselyn, Sec.-Treas., North Forty Mile Regional Waste Management Services Commission, 758
Pahlke, Darryl, Contact, Andritz Bird, 85
Paiement, Bertrand, Associé, Lapointe Rosenstein Marchand Melançon, 1085
Paiement, Corey, Director, Salmon Arm, 684
Paiement, Roger, Daigneault, avocats inc., 1083
Paillard, Cedric, Vice-President, Air Transport Association of Canada, 814
Paillé, Mario, SMTE, Collège de Maisonneuve, 1172
Paine, Jeff, Templeman Menninga LLP, 1068
Pakalnis, Peter, Principal, LEHDER Environmental Services Ltd., 267
Pakenham, Dennis, Morency Avocats, 1088
Pakenham, Robert E., Howell Fleming LLP, 1071
Pakes, Tom, F.E. Myers, 193
Pakrul, Robert W., Alexander Holburn Beaudin & Lang, LLP, 1057
Palacio, Cesar, Toronto, 721
Paladines, Melissa, Staff, Credit Valley Hospital, 1145
Palamar, Bill, President, Aqua Tech Sales & Marketing Inc., 88
Palayew, Dan, Partner, Heenan Blaikie LLP - Ottawa, 1070
Palczynski, Richard, President, EnvironChem Engineering Consultants, 184
Palermo, Rosie, Contact, Domaine Label & Trim Inc., 165
Palestini, Laura, Conseillère d'arrondissement, Sault-St-Louis, Montréal, 738
Palleschi, Paul, Peel, 703
Palleschi, Paul, Regional Councillor, Brampton, 706
Palleson, Martin L., Gowling Lafleur Henderson LLP - Vancouver, 1060
Palmay, P.Eng, Frank, Lang Michener LLP - Toronto, 1077
Palmer, Bob, Lunenburg District, 902-543-8650, 697
Palmer, Colin, Chair, Powell River, 679
Palmer, Deborah, Technical Services Librarian, Ontario Ministry of Natural Resources, 1153
Palmer, Sam, Vice-President, Thermon Heat Tracing Services, 394
Palmer, William, Manager, Cheminfo Services Inc., 139
Palmeter, Aubrey, President/CEO, Whitman Benn Group, 431
Palumbo, Felicia, National Marketing Support Assistant, Konica Minolta Business Solutions (Canada) Inc., 259

Executive Name Index

Palumbo, Gino, President & CEO, Integran Technologies Inc., 244
Pamel, Peter G., Partner, Borden Ladner Gervais LLP - Montréal, 1083
Pammett, Dianne, Information Specialist/Head, NRC Information Centre - Saskatoon, 1189
Panabaker, Dave, Hastings, 700
Panabaker, Dave, General Manager, Medicine Hat, 403-529-8288, 673
Panahi, Kami, Director, Avoca-tec Environmental Services Inc., 99
Panas, Gordon, President/CEO, Lockerbie & Hole Contracting Ltd., 273
Pander, Sean, Acting Manager, Vancouver, 604-871-6619, 685
Pandey, R.N., Guelph Chemical Laboratories, 222
Pandit, Ph.D., Nitin, President, International Institute for Energy Conservation, 940
Panek, L.A., Vice-President, Environment, Mississauga Laboratory, 291
Panek, Les, Sr. Vice-President, AMEC, 82
Panetta, Vince M., Hicks Morley Hamilton Stewart Storie LLP, 1069
Pankratz, Darryl G., Alexander Holburn Beaudin & Lang, LLP, 1057
Pankratz, Harley, Manager, AMEC, 84
Panneton, Alexandre, Heenan Blaikie S.E.N.C.R.L/SRL, 1084
Pantelmann, Wolfgang, President & Senior Project Consultant, WPI Safety & Environmental Consultants, 434
Panz, Eric, President, Inproheat Industries Ltd., 242
Panz, Gus, Exec. Vice-President, Inproheat Industries Ltd., 242
Panz, Steven, Vice-President, Inproheat Industries Ltd., 242
Panzer, Rob, General Manager, Planning & Development, London, 713
Papa, Nick, Richmond Hill, 718
Papaiz, Denise, Senior Manager, Corporate Communications, Niagara, 702
Le Pape, Daniel, Directeur général, Portneuf, 751
Papin, Dominique, Bibliothécaire professionnelle, CÉGEP de Trois-Rivières, 1186
Papp, Peter, Pelham, 717
Pappas, Christopher D., Sr. Vice-President/COO, Nova Chemicals Corporation, 308
Pappas, Dean, Peterborough, 718
Pappas, Ernie S., Vice-President, 662
Pappas, Stephanie, Technology & Communications, Saskatchewan Trade & Export Partnership Inc., 1002
Pappas, Q.C., Chrys, Thompson Dorfman Sweatman LLP, 1064
Pappert, A., Director, Community Services, Guelph, 710
Paquet, Claude, Partner, Heenan Blaikie S.E.N.C.R.L/SRL, 1084
Paquet, Patrick, Québec, 740
Paquet, Pierre, Partner, Miller Thomson LLP - Toronto, 1078
Paquet, Sarah, Senior General Counsel, 558
Paquet, Serge, Saint-Georges, 742
Paquet, Éric, Directeur général, Beauce-Sartigan, 747
Paquette, Denis, Manager, Westburne Canada, 426
Paquette, Denise, Mascouche, 450-966-6044, 737
Paquette, Germain, Trésorier, Mirabel, 450-475-2003, 738
Paquette, Jean, Vice-President, 520
Paquette, Patrice, Saint-Eustache, 450-974-1120, 742
Paquette, René, Associé, Langlois Kronström Desjardins, 1085
Paquette, Serge, Blainville, 734
Paquette, Yan, Langlois Kronström Desjardins, 1088
Paquin, Chantal, Technician, INRS - Université du Québec, CGC - Québec, 1179
Paquin, Chantal, Technicienne, Université du Québec Institut national de la recherche scientifiq, 1181
Paquin, Emery, Board Member, 608
Paquin, Jacques, Directeur général, La Haute-Gaspésie, 748
Paquin, Jean, Vice-President, Sanexen Environmental Services Inc., 357
Paquin, Pierre B., Bélanger, Sauvé, 1082
Paquin, Serge, Sherbrooke, 744
Paquin, Éric, Vice-President, Horizon Environment Inc., 233
Paradis, Brigitte, Client Services Officer, NRC Information Centre, 1166
Paradis, Christian, Minister responsible, 515
Paradis, Christian, Minister, Natural Resources, 549
Paradis, Claude, President, Recyclage PF Inc., 343
Paradis, François, Sales Representative, Armtec Construction Products, 92
Paradis, Jean, Greffier, Alma, 733
Paradis, Jean-Luc, Contact, Chem Experts Inc., 139
Paradis, Louise, Bibliothécaire, Bibliothèque paramédicale, 1171
Paradis, Monique, Bibliothécaire professionnelle, CÉGEP de Trois-Rivières, 1186

Paradis, Patrick, President, Quatrex Environmental inc., 338
Paradis, Paul D., Partner, Ross & McBride LLP, 1069
Paradise, CAE, Connie, Director, American Industrial Hygiene Association, 823
Parashar, Surendra, Director, 520
Paraszczak, Jacek, Director, Maintenance & Engineering Society of The Canadian Institute of Mi, 950
Paré, Daniel, IBI Group, 238
Paré, Frédéric, Stikeman Elliott LLP - Montréal, 1087
Paré, Jim, Manager, KBM Forestry Consultants Inc., 255
Pare, Michael, District Manager, BFI Canada Inc., 106
Paré, Mike, FCILT Secretary, Chartered Institute of Logistics and Transport in North America, 894
Paré, Pierre, President, Industries Machinex Inc., 241
Paré, Véronique, Secteur des acquisitions, Université Laval, 1181
Parent, Gabriel, Vaudreuil-Dorion, 746
Parent, Jean-Guy, Sylvain, Parent, Gobeil, 1089
Parent, Jennifer, Division Head, Human Resources, Pickering, 905-420-4627, 718
Parent, Louis, Directeur, Saint-Jérôme, 743
Parent, Marcel, Maire d'arrondissement/Conseiller de la ville, Montréal, 738
Parent, Mark, Minister, 609
Parent, Maurice, ITM Instruments, 248
Parent, Paul-Eugène, Président, Régie intermunicipale de l'Est de Portneuf, 760
Parets, Otto, Vice-President, Alberta Plastics Recycling Association, 819
Parghi, Ira G., Partner, Borden Ladner Gervais LLP - Toronto, 1073
Parimeter, Lee, President, EnviroMed Detection Services, 184
Paris, Jim, Manager, Flygt Canada, 198
Paris, Percy, Minister, 610
Parisé, Maurice, President/CEO, GENEQ Inc., 206
Parisé, Rene, Vice-President, GENEQ Inc., 206
Pariseau, Lucie, Associée, Ogilvy Renault LLP/S.E.N.C.R.L., s.r.l. - Québec, 1089
Parish, John D., Director, Parish Geomorphic Ltd., 318
Parish, Rob, Manager, Chemline Plastics Ltd., 139
Parish, Steve, Durham, 699
Parish, Steve, Mayor, Ajax, 705
Parisien, Gloria, Director, 656
Parisien, Stéphane P., Chief Administrative Officer & Clerk, Prescott & Russell, 729
Parissi, Mauro, Chief Financial Officer, Dectron Internationale, 159
Park, Jason, Fraser Milner Casgrain LLP - Toronto, 1075
Park, Matthew A., Kanuka Thuringer LLP, Barristers & Solicitors, 1090
Park, Stephen, Directeur, Bibliothèque sciences juridiques, Université du Québec à Montréal, 1176
Park, Q.C., J. Jay, Partner, Macleod Dixon LLP, 1052
Parke, Joel, Vice-President, Vanbots Construction Corp., 409
Parker, Brian, Senior Landscape Architect, Glenn Group Ltd., 213
Parker, Bruce J., President & CEO, Environmental Industry Associations, 912
Parker, Bruce J., President & Chief Executive Officer, National Solid Wastes Management Association, 958
Parker, Chris, Councillor, Kings County, 696
Parker, Darell, Fire Chief, Ingersoll, 711
Parker, G.G., Chown, Caims LLP, 1072
Parker, Garth E., Gowling Lafleur Henderson LLP - Calgary, 1051
Parker, Glenn, Manager, Proctor & Gamble Inc., 333
Parker, John, Toronto, 721
Parker, Linda G., McCarthy Tétrault LLP - Vancouver, 1061
Parker, Malcolm, St. Albert, 674
Parker, Michael, Principal/Sr. Fisheries Biologist, East Coast Aquatics, 169
Parker, Pamela, Executive Director, New Brunswick Salmon Growers Association, 961
Parker, Randy, Supervisor, Westburne Canada, 426
Parker, Rob, Pinchin Environmental Ltd., 324
Parker, Robert, Vice-President, Montrose Technologies Inc., 293
Parker, Ryan, Lethbridge, 403-380-4848, 673
Parker, Scott D., Executive Director, NORA, An Association of Responsible Recyclers, 964
Parker, Sharon, Vice-President, International Road Dynamics Inc., 245
Parker, Steve, President & CEO, Flexo Products Ltd., 196
Parkes, Lance, President, Parkes Scientific Canada Inc., 319
Parkes, Trevor, Senior Planner, Esquimalt, 686
Parkin, Alan, Director, North Battleford, 306-445-1740, 754
Parkinson, Bryan, Manager, J.L. Richards & Associates Limited, 250
Parkinson, David, Unit Manager, AMEC, 83

Parks, David, Director, Planning & Development, Severn, 729
Parks, Dawn, Manager, National Environmental Health Association, 957
Parks, Richard, Prince Edward, 703
Parmar, K., Vice-President, W.T. McGinn & Associates Ltd., 415
Parnell, Lesley, Peterborough, 718
Parnwell, Lindsay, Engineer, Lloydminster, 673
Parpinel, Gary, Regional Manager, Romatec Incorporated, 350
Parps, Lew, VP, Grundfos Canada Inc., 222
Parr, Dana, Planner, Pitt Meadows, 604-465-2497, 683
Parr, Jeff, Deputy Minister, 589
Parr, R., President, Atlas Polar Company Limited, 97
Parra, Mariela, Corporate Librarian, Devon Canada Corporation, 1101
Parran, Shachar, CEO, GEA Barr-Rosin Inc., 205
Parrish, Doug, Director, Leduc, 780-980-7124, 673
Parrott, Denise, Technical Services Librarian, Nova Scotia Community College, 1136
Parrott, William, Deputy Minister, 599
Parrotta, Danielle M., Burnet, Duckworth & Palmer LLP, 1050
Parry, Barbara, Lab Services Manager, Newalta Corporation, 301
Parry, Tom, Chief Building Official & Director, Whitchurch-Stouffville, 723
Parschin-Rybkin, Q.C., Tamara, Vice-President/Legal General Counsel & Corporate S, 517
Parsons, Albert, Manager, Harris & Roome Supply Limited, 225
Parsons, Bob, Acting Director, Port Moody, 683
Parsons, Bob, Fire Chief, Tillsonburg, 519-842-2905, 721
Parsons, Colin, Chair, Trow Consulting Engineers Ltd., 403
Parsons, Greg, Manager, Swift Current, 755
Parsons, Nancy, Secretary to the Deputy Minister, 614
Parsons, Ryan, Borden Ladner Gervais LLP - Vancouver, 1058
Parsons, Sheldon, Chatham-Kent, 724
Parsons, Sue, Information Resources Officer, Canadian Institute of Resources Law, 1100
Parsons, Tom, Engineer, King Metal Fabricators Ltd., 258
Partington, Lynne, Head, Bibliographic Control, University of Manitoba Libraries, 1125
Partington, Peter, Regional Chair & Councillor, Niagara, 702
Partridge, Judi, Hamilton, 711
Paruch, Ray, Councillor, Cape Breton, 695
Pasay, Vic, Chair, Roseridge Waste Management Services Commission, 758
Pascoe Merkley, Maureen, Director, Planning, Brockville, 707
Pascolo, Rita, Library Technician, Engineering Branch, 1150
Pasieka, James, Partner, Heenan Blaikie LLP - Calgary, 1051
Passer, Ron, President, Accurate Industrial Waste Limited, 66
Passerieux, Catherine, Bibliothécaire, Bibliothèque centrale, 1170
Passero, Stephen, Fort Erie, 709
Pasternak, James, Toronto, 721
Pastoric, George S., Hydro-Logic Environmental Inc., 236
Pastro, Mike, General Manager, Abbotsford, 604-864-5651, 679
Pasuta, Robert, Hamilton, 711
Pataky, Julius, Vice-President, 583
Patel, Arman, Executive Director, Flowers Canada, 917
Patel, Pesh, Team Leader, NOVA Chemicals Ltd., 1102
Patel, Rujuta, Partner, Macleod Dixon LLP, 1052
Patel, Sydney, Thermo Electric (Canada) Ltd., 394
Patenaude, Etienne, International Sales, Westech Industrial Ltd., 429
Patenaude, Jean-Claude, Saint-Hyacinthe, 742
Patent, Maurice, ITM Instruments, 248
Paterak, Richard, Peel, 703
Paterak, Richard, Regional Councillor, Caledon, 707
Paterson, Bryan, Councillor, Kingston, 712
Paterson, D. Brad, Chief Financial Officer, Wavefront Technology Solutions Inc., 423
Paterson, David J., President & CEO, Abitibi-Consolidated Inc., 65
Paterson, Gilles A., Treasurer & Director, Corporate Services, Pickering, 905-420-4634, 718
Paterson, Jim, General Manager, Kelowna, 681
Paterson, John, Councillor, Leamington, 726
Paterson, Krystyna, Manager, 621
Paterson, Murray, Vice-President, Huron Wind Ltd. Partnership, 235
Paterson, Thom, Clearview, 725
Patey, Catherine, Geologist, Newfoundland & Labrador Dept. of Natural Resources, 1132
Patlik, Howard R., Vice-President, J.E. Coulter Associates Ltd., 249
Patmore, Darren, Director, Parks, Recreation & Culture, North Grenville, 728
Patmore, Steven, Branch Manager, CenturyVallen, 136

Executive Name Index

Paton, Richard, President & CEO, Canadian Chemical Producers' Association, 862
Paton, Terry, Provincial Comptroller, 658
Patricia, Wilson, Trade Commissioner, 769
Patrick, Bill, Regional Manager, Velan Inc., 410
Patrick, Denise, Accounts Manager, AGM Steel Industries Ltd., 73
Patrick, Eric, Manager, AGM Steel Industries Ltd., 73
Patrie, Chris, Elliot Lake, 709
Patriquin, Tim, Group Manager, Stormceptor Canada Inc., 380
Patrizia, Giuliotti, Trade Commissioner, 768
Patry, Daniel, Directeur général, Lotbinière, 750
Patry, Linda, Chef, Services dév des collections et référence, Bibliothèque de droit, 1170
Pattern, George, Head, Technical Services, Pacific Biological Station, 1113
Patterson, Alex, President, Mifab Canada, 289
Patterson, Brenda, General Manager, Parks, Forestry, & Recreation, Toronto, 416-392-8182, 721
Patterson, Cal, Simcoe, 704
Patterson, Cal, Mayor, Wasaga Beach, 722
Patterson, Gord, Chief Operating Officer, The Sernas Group Inc., 393
Patterson, J. Pitman, Partner, Borden Ladner Gervais LLP - Toronto, 1073
Patterson, James, Coordinator, Acadia Environmental Society, 813
Patterson, Janet, Chief Administrative Officer, District Social Serv, Parry Sound, 705-746-7777, 728
Patterson, John, Warden, Hants East District, 697
Patterson, Rae-Lynne, Manager, Library Services, Nunavut Arctic College, 1138
Patterson, Scott, Fire Chief, Mountain, North Dundas, 727
Patteson, Julian, Commissioner, Buildings & Property Management, Brampton, 706
Pattison, Scott, Officer, Health Sciences Association of Alberta, 928
Pattje, Fred, Nanaimo, 681
Patton, Alan R., Patton Cormier & Associates, 1069
Patton, Brad, Fire Chief, Centre Wellington, 724
Patton, Ed, Secretary, Maintenance & Engineering Society of The Canadian Institute of Mi, 950
Pätzold, Karen, Librarian, Gander Campus Library & Career Exploration Centre, 1131
Pau, Tiffany, Library Coordinator, MFL Occupational Health Centre, 1124
Pau Woo, Yuen, President & Co-CEO, Asia Pacific Foundation of Canada, 829
Paul, David C., Director, Economic Development, Brockville, 707
Paul, France, Responsable, Services techniques, Université de Sherbrooke, 1186
Paul, James S., President/CEO, 521
Paul, John, President, Transform Compost Systems Ltd., 400
Paul, Myra, Administrative Assistant, Canadian Energy Pipeline Association, 866
Paul, Robert, President/CEO, EOA Scientific System Inc., 188
Paul, Réjean, President & CEO, Géophysique GPR International Inc., 211
Paul, Sacha R., Thompson Dorfman Sweatman LLP, 1064
Paula, Caldwell, Senior Trade Commissioner, 768
Paula, Solari, Trade Commissioner, 767
Pauley, Andrew, VP & General Manager, HETEK Solutions Inc., 230
Paulin, Jos J., President, Preston Phipps Inc., 331
Paulin, Mark, Vice President, Preston Phipps Inc., 331
Paulissen, Al, President, Wenvor Technologies Inc., 424
Paulmier, Irene M., Head Librarian, Lafarge Canada Inc., 1174
Pauloski, Linda, Manager, Dofasco Inc., 1140
Paulsen, B.A., LL.B., Tiffany, Saskatoon, 754
Paulson, Dianne, Secretary, Health & Safety Conference Society of Alberta, 927
Paulson, Garry, President, Startco Engineering Ltd., 379
Paura, C. Mario, Partner, Stikeman Elliott LLP - Toronto, 1080
Pauzé, Lee, General Manager, The Friends of Algonquin Park, 920
Pavlis, Robert, President, Labtronics, 262
Pavone, Sergio, Maire, Châteauguay, 735
Pawluk, Brad, Superintendent, St. Andrews, 690
Pawson, Owen D., Partner, Miller Thomson LLP - Vancouver, 1061
Payer, Francine, Repentigny, 450-582-7711, 740
Payne, Alton, President, Newalta Corporation, 301
Payne, Carol, Library Staff, Nova Scotia Dept. of Natural Resources, 1136
Payne, D., Carrier Canada Ltd., 130

Payne, Geoff, Office Manager, 595
Payne, Hilary, Windsor, 723
Payne, L.E., Director, Corporate Services & City Solicitor, Guelph, 710
Payne, Marty, Manager, CCS Income Trust, 134
Payne, Richard H., President/CEO, American Birding Association, 822
Payne, Thomas D., President, Macrotek Inc., 278
Payne, W.D., President/CEO, Energy Technology Products Ltd., 179
Pazdzior, Josie, President, Ottawa Valley Rock Garden & Horticultural Society, 983
Pazzano, Nadia, Stringer, Brisbn, Humphrey Management Lawyers, 1080
Peach, Brenda, Library Technician, Carbonear Campus Library, 1130
Peach, Ches, Principal, Roley Construction, 350
Peach, C.A., Michelle, City Treasurer, Mount Pearl, 694
Peacock, Steven, Director, Public Works, Cobourg, 708
Peake, Janet, Muskoka, 702
Peana, Cornel, Singleton Urquhart LLP, 1062
Pearce, Andrew D., Director, Development & Transportation Engineering, Vaughan, 722
Pearce, Diane, Chief Administrative Officer, Loyalist, 727
Pearce, Jeff, Manager, Westburne Canada, 428
Pearce, R. Kenneth S., Blake, Cassels & Graydon LLP - Toronto, 1072
Pearce, Will, CAO, Cranbrook, 680
Pearcy, Douglas, Peterborough, 703
Pearl, Reevin, Pearl & Associates, 1086
Pearsell, Grant, Director, Edmonton, 780-496-6080, 672
Pearson, Céline, Gestionnaire, Veolia ES Canada Industrial Services Inc., 411
Pearson, Jean, Contact, Anadarko Canada Corp., 1099
Pearson, Keith, President, World Packaging Organization, 1023
Pearson, Les, Medicine Hat, 673
Pearson, Madeline, Peterborough, 703
Pearson, Maria, Hamilton, 711
Pearson, Mark, Director General, 549
Pearson, Ron, Contact, Yukon Public Health Association, 1024
Peary, George, Metro Vancouver, 678
Peary, George, Mayor, Abbotsford, 679
Pease, Chris, CAO, Colwood, 680
Pease, Judy, Director, Community Services, Lincoln, 713
Peat, John P., President, Canadian Hemerocallis Society, 871
Pecchioli, Ron, Director, Ronco Protective Products, 351
Peck, Frank, Director, Red Deer County, 670
Peck, Steven, President, Green Roofs for Healthy Cities, 926
Peddle, Derek R., Chair, Canadian Remote Sensing Society, 884
Pedersen, Bob, Manager, Poyry (Vancouver) Inc., 330
Pedersen, Leigh, Morelli Chertkow LLP, Lawyers, 1056
Pedersen, Rick, Vice-President & General Manager, Conair Group Inc., 148
Pedersen, Soren, President, International Commission of Agricultural & Biosystems Engineering, 937
Pederson, Gordon, Director, Chilliwack, 604-792-9311, 680
Pederson, Lori, Library Assistant, Aerospace Technology Campus, 1115
Pederson, Randy L., Vice-Presdent, Visionwall Corporation, 414
Pedlar, Matthew K., Civil Engineer Technologist, Geocor Engineering Inc., 210
Pedlar, Rob, Manager, Westburne Canada, 426
Pedneault, Jean-Rock, Alma, 418-662-6223, 733
Peer, Glen, Vice-President/General Manager, Leeson Canada Ltd., 266
Peever, Jacynthe, Business Administrator, Lake Abitibi Model Forest, 948
Pegoraro, Liz, Coordinator, Information Support, Northern Alberta Institute of Technology, 1106
Peirone, Barth, Maccaferri Canada Ltd., 277
Péladeau, Claire, Executive Administrative Assistant, 521
Pelchat, Carole, Archiviste, Gestionnaire de documents, Collège universitaire de St-Boniface, 1123
Pelchat, Diane, Trésorière, Repentigny, 450-470-3200, 740
Pelensky, Ron, Manager, Mackenzie Regional Waste Management Commission, 757
Peleshytyk, Rick, Office Manager, Golder Associates Ltd., 214
Pelkey, Gerald, President, Acer Environmental Services Ltd., 66
Pelkey, Pierrette, Aide-bibliothécaire, New Brunswick Community College, 1128, 1127
Pelkman, Steve, Strathroy-Caradoc, 731
Pellant, Mike, Director, Richmond, 604-276-4092, 684
Pellegrini, Steve, York, 705
Pellegrino, Ted, Planner, Kitimat-Stikine, 678

Peller, Peter, Public Services Librarian, Thompson Rivers University, 1112
Pellerin, Johanne, Technicienne en documentation, Bibliothèque des sciences juridiques, 1171
Pellerin, Paul A., Moncton / Ville de Moncton, 691
Pellerin, Stephen, Vice-President, URS Canada Inc., 408
Pelletier, Claude, Rivière-du-Loup, 741
Pelletier, Claude A., Directeur général, Office de vente des produits forestiers du Madawaska, 970
Pelletier, Clem A., President/CEO, Rescan Environmental Services Ltd., 345
Pelletier, Céline, Adjointe au Directeur des études, Collège André-Grasset, 1172
Pelletier, Denis M., Edmundston, 691
Pelletier, Francine, Bibliothécaire, CÉGEP de Sherbrooke, 1185
Pelletier, Germain, Environmental Officer, Neilson Excavation, 299
Pelletier, Jean-Marie, Chair, Potatoes NB, 987
Pelletier, Joanne, Bibliotechnicienne, Service du prêt entre biblioth, Collège universitaire de St-Boniface, 1123
Pelletier, Ken, Vice-President, ALCO Gas & Oil Production Equipment Ltd., 77
Pelletier, Louise, Pilote du système Unicorn, Université Laval, 1181
Pelletier, Marie, Directrice, Matane, 738
Pelletier, Michel, Davies Ward Phillips & Vineberg S.E.N.C.R.L., s.r.l., 1083
Pelletier, Michel, Directeur général, L'Islet, 748
Pelletier, Noël, Président, Association québécoise d'urbanisme, 841
Pelletier, Pierre, Directeur, Laval, 450-662-4600, 736
Pelletier, Suzanne, Officer Manager, Herby Enterprises Ltd., 229
Pelletier-Giroux, Dominique, Cain Lamarre Casgrain Wells - Québec, 1087
Pelley, Robert, Senior Negotiator, 602
Pellis, Paul, Deputy Minister, 571
Pelly, W.Douglas, Principal, Golder Associates Ltd., 214
Peltier, Denyse, Repentigny, 450-581-5733, 740
Peltier-Rivest, Patrice, Repentigny, 450-657-1255, 740
Pelton, Tina, Office Manager, Fanchem Ltd., 194
Peluso, Anthony, Eastern Canada Operations Manager, SEW Eurodrive Co. of Canada Ltd., 364
Pender, Kelly, Chief Administrative Officer, Huntsville, 711
Pendlebury, Zena, Midland, 713
Pendleton, Leon, World Ecology Enviro Store Ltd., 433
Peng, Christopher R., Partner, Heenan Blaikie LLP - Calgary, 1051
Peng, Douglas, Vice-President, Sciencetech Inc., 359
Penhorwood, Jan, Chair & Public Services Librarian, Kwantlen University College, 1113
Penman, Barrie, Fire Chief, North Vancouver, 604-980-5021, 682
Penman, Brian, Chair, Conservation Halton Foundation, 901
Pennachetti, Joseph, City Manager, Toronto, 416-392-3551, 721
Pennell, Tracey, Cox and Palmer - St. John's, 1065
Penner, Barry, Attorney General, 574
Penner, Barry, Minister, 577
Penner, Blair, Director, Waste Logic Inc., 417
Penner, Bob, Contact, Shaver Industries Inc., 365
Penner, Darrell, Port Coquitlam, 683
Penner, Irv, Journal Chair, Ecoforestry Institute Society, 908
Penner, Nancy M., Counsel, Parlee McLaws LLP, 1053
Penner, B.Ed., M.Ed., Glen, Saskatoon, 754
Penney, Geoffrey K., Partner, Ottenheimer Baker, 1066
Penney, J., Carrier Canada Ltd., 129
Penney, Jacqueline A.M., McInnes Cooper, 1066
Penney, Kerry, Manager, Yellowknife, 695
Penney, Ronald, City Solicitor & City Manager, St. John's, 709-576-8557, 694
Penney, Stephen F., Partner, Stewart McKelvey Stirling Scales - St. John's, 1066
Penny, Bill, President, Penny & Casson Co., 321
Penny, Dave, T. Harris Environmental Management Inc., 385
Penny, Joss, Executive Director, British Columbia Lodging & Campgrounds Association, 848
Pentland, R.S. (Ray), President, Water Resource Consultants Ltd., 422
Pentney, William F., Associate Deputy Minister, 545
Pepall, Jennifer, Chief, 544
Pepevnak, Thomas F., Partner, Borden Ladner Gervais LLP - Calgary, 1050
Pepin, Gilles, Maire, Saint-Constant, 742
Pépin, Hubert, Partner, Heenan Blaikie S.E.N.C.R.L/SRL - Sherbrooke, 1089
Pepin, Joel, General Manager, Denso North America Inc., 161
Pepin, Luc, Chief, Les Peintures Sico inc., 270

Executive Name Index

Pepin, Michel, President, Pepin Prevention des Pertes Inc., 321
Pépin, Robert, Directeur, Saguenay, 741
Pépin, Robert, Directeur/Chef, Joliette, 450-759-5222, 736
Pepin, Véronique, Responsable de la bibliothèque, TECSULT inc, 1176
Pepin, Y., Carrier Canada Ltd., 129
Pe-Piper, G., Contact, Atlantic Canada Centre for Environmental Science, 842
Pepper, David, Director, Library Services, British Columbia Institute of Technology, 1110
Pepper, Steve, Manager, Westburne Canada, 428
Peraya, Michael, Singleton Urquhart LLP, 1062
Percival, Michael J., Partner, Miller Thomson LLP - Vancouver, 1061
Percival, Robert L., Partner, Ogilvy Renault LLP/S.E.N.C.R.L., s.r.l. - Toronto, 1078
Percy, Alan, Controller, Priestly Demolition Inc., 332
Percy, Eamonn, President/COO, 581
Percy, Jon, President, Annapolis Field Naturalist Society, 828
Percy, Mary, Director, Human Resources, Peterborough, 703
Percy, Steven W., Chair, Wavefront Technology Solutions Inc., 423
Perdue, Simon, Senior Sales Representative, Armtec Construction Products, 92
Pereira, Frank S., President, Industrial Plastics Fabricators Ltd., 241
Perera, Noel, President, GPEC International Ltd., 216
Perey, André B., Blake, Cassels & Graydon LLP - Toronto, 1072
Perez, Benjamin, Vice-President, Survalent Technology Corporation, 383
Perez, José, Director, Coen Canada Inc., 146
Periche, Nathalie, Technical Director, Aqua Data Inc., 87
Perkins, Andrew, Director, Power Suction Services Ltd., 329
Perkins, Janice, EcoFlame International Inc., 171
Perkins, Michael J., Partner, Borden Ladner Gervais LLP - Calgary, 1050
Perkins, Pat, Mayor, Whitby, 723
Perks, Al R., Regional Manager, R.V. Anderson Associates Limited, 341
Perks, Gord, Toronto, 721
Perks, John, Senior Engineer, Planning & Engineering Initiatives Ltd., 325
Perlin, D., Chief Administrative Officer, Halton Hills, 710
Perlini, Arthur, Academic Dean & Library Director, Algoma University College, 1154
Perlmutter, Tom, Government Film Commissioner & Chair, 546
Perlotto, Dennis, General Manager, AIM Environmental Group, 74
Pernarowski, David, Mayor, Terrace, 685
Peron, Martin, General Manager, Sedac Inc., 361
Peros, Matthew, President, Canadian Association of Palynologists, 858
Perozzo, Q.C., Ron, Deputy Minister & Deputy Attorney General, 589
Perras, Andre, Manager, Guildline Instruments Limited, 223
Perras, Carolyne, Présidente, Association québécoise pour l'hygiène, la santé et la sécurité du, 842
Perras, Delmar, Chair, 567
Perras, Jean, Préfet, Les Collines-de-l'Outaouais, 749
Perrault, Guy, Québec, 740
Perrault, Jean, Maire, Sherbrooke, 819-821-5969, 744
Perreault, Denis, Responsable, Division catalogage et gestion des do, Québec Ministère de la santé et des services sociaux, 1179
Perreault, Jean, Coordonnateur, Papineau, 750
Perreault, Rhéaume, Partner, Heenan Blaikie S.E.N.C.R.L/SRL, 1084
Perreault, Richard, Blainville, 734
Perreault, Roger, Air Liquide Canada Ltée, 75
Perreault, Sophie, Ogilvy Renault LLP/S.E.N.C.R.L., s.r.l. - Montréal, 1086
Perreault-Théberge, Denise, Sainte-Thérèse, 744
Perrelli, Carmine, Richmond Hill, 718
Perri, B.Sc., M.A., Dominic, Conseiller de ville, St-Léonard-Ouest, Montréal, 738
Perrier, Michel, Directeur général, Pincourt, 739
Perrin, Larry, Firwin Corporation, 196
Perrin, Lloyd, Director, Physical Services, Central Elgin, 724
Perrin, Robert, Davis LLP - Calgary, 1050
Perrino, Janice, Mayor, Summerland, 689
Perron, Benoit, Président, Énergie Solaire Québec, 909
Perron, Christian, Manager, Prolab Technolub, 334
Perron, Claude, Entretien M. Perron inc. (SANI-TRI), 182
Perron, Jacques, Partner, Lavery, de Billy - Montréal, 1086
Perron, Jean, Saint-Georges, 742

Perron, Jean, Chair, Restigouche Solid Waste Corporation, 758
Perron, Nicole, Bibliothécaire, Bibliothèque centrale, 1170
Perron, Suzanne, La Prairie, 736
Perrotte, Claude, Directeur, Blainville, 450-434-5237, 734
Perruzza, Anthony, Toronto, 721
Perry, Alan, President, Canadian Fishery Consultants Ltd., 124
Perry, Alan, President/CEO, CBCL Limited, 132
Perry, Bert, Director, 664
Perry, Chrysten E., Partner, Macleod Dixon LLP, 1052
Perry, Claude, Regional Manager, FCX NH Valves, 194
Perry, David G., Partner, Singleton Urquhart LLP, 1062
Perry, Don, Plant Manager, Sleegers Engineering Inc., 370
Perry, Edwin, Head, Research Services, University of Regina Library, 1189
Perry, Gord, Lambton, 701
Perry, Jane, Librarian, Union Gas Ltd., a Duke Energy Company, 1140
Perry, Jim F., President/CEO, Alternative Fuel Systems (2004) Inc., 81
Perry, Joan, Secretary, British Columbia Ground Water Association, 848
Perry, Lawrence W., President, Alenag Brokers, 77
Perry, Rick, Fire Chief, Estevan, 306-634-1850, 754
Persad, Vashti, Administrative Coordinaor, Ontario Public Interest Research Group - Toronto/Downtown Women's, 1160
Pertile, Lawrence, President, Aqua-Guard Spill Response Inc., 88
Peskett, Daniel R., Brownlee LLP, 1054
Pessione, Heather, Borden Ladner Gervais LLP - Toronto, 1073
Petelle, Marie-Andrée, Sainte-Thérèse, 744
Peter-Cherneff, Brigitte, Institute Librarian, Aerospace Technology Campus, 1115
Peterman, Terry W., Lang Michener LLP - Ottawa, 1070
Peters, Ann, Executive Director, Northwest Wildlife Preservation Society, 967
Peters, Bill, National Director, Canadian Association of Zoos & Aquariums, 859
Peters, Diane, Acting Head of Reference, Wilfrid Laurier University, 1165
Peters, Frank, Business Unit Manager, AIM Environmental Group, 74
Peters, Herbert J., Aikins, MacAulay & Thorvaldson LLP, 1063
Peters, James, Director, Summerside, 733
Peters, Jerald D., Principal, Friesen Tokar Architects, Landscape & Interior Designers, 202
Peters, Jim, Director, Trent Hills, 731
Peters, Judy, Corporate Relations Officer, 662
Peters, Leona, Coordinator, Guildline Instruments Limited, 223
Peters, Rod, Manager, Roy Northern Environmental Ltd., 353
Peters, Rod D., First Nations Manager, Henderson Paddon & Associates Ltd., 229
Peters, Roland, Branch Manager, CenturyVallen, 137
Petersen, Carol, Manager, Alberta Recreation & Parks Association, 819
Petersen, Gordon, Contact, Urban Systems Ltd., 407
Petersen, Gordon, President & Treasurer, Castle-Crown Wilderness Coalition, 892
Petersen, Tara L., Partner, Warren Tettensor Amantea LLP, 1054
Peterson, Anne, Delta, 604-946-4141, 686
Peterson, Bob, Kingsville, 712
Peterson, Eric, Chief Administrative Officer, Severn, 729
Peterson, Jeff, Contact, DST Consulting Engineers, 166
Peterson, Laura-Ann, Coordinator, Manitoba Camping Association, 950
Peterson, Michael M., McMillan Binch Mendelsohn - Toronto, 1077
Peterson, Tom, Manager, Veolia ES Canada Industrial Services Inc., 411
Petit, Monique, Technicienne, CÉGEP de St-Jérôme, 1184
Petitclerk, René, Manager, Armatek Controls Limited, 91
Petlic, John, Republic Environmental Systems (Fort Erie) Ltd., 345
Petrachenko, Donna, Assistant Deputy Minister, 527
Petrachenko, Michael, Welland, 722
Petrie, Dale, General Manager, Ontario Soybean Growers, 979
Petrie, P. Douglas, Willms & Shier Environmental Lawyers LLP, 1081
Petrie, Richard G., Partner, Stewart McKelvey Stirling Scales - Fredericton, 1064
Petrie, Q.C., J. Gordon, Partner, Stewart McKelvey Stirling Scales - Fredericton, 1064
Petrullo, Tim, In!Flame Fireplaces Inc., 239
Petryk, Laurel M., Lang Michener LLP - Vancouver, 1060
Pettes, Cindy, Administrator, 607

Petti, Felice, Manager, Strategic & Environmental Services, Ottawa, 716
Pettie, Alan T., Burnet, Duckworth & Palmer LLP, 1050
Pettigrew, Gerald, Manager, Operations, Bathurst, 506-548-0410, 690
Pettman, Allan J., President/Partner, Greenflow Environmental Services Inc., 217
Pettus, C., Site Manager, Power Grow Systems Inc., 329
Peverett, Jane, President/CEO, 583
Pfaff, Vanessa R., McLennan Ross LLP, 1053
Pfannenstiel, Vern, President, American Society of Mining & Reclamation, 825
Pfau, Herb, Superintendent, Grande Prairie No. 1, 780-532-7393, 669
Pham, Jean-Pierre, Bennett Jones LLP - Calgary Office, 1049
Pham, Thao, Vice-President, 518
Pham, Thu, Treasurer, British Columbia Food Technolgists, 848
Phan Nguyen, Ngoc Thanh, Bibliothécaire, Bibliothèque centrale, 1170
Phaneuf, Linda, Directrice générale, Beauharnois-Salaberry, 747
Phaneuf, Tim, Air Liquide Canada Ltée, 75
Pharand, Rachel, Secretary, University of Sudbury, 1155
Phare, Merrell Ann, President, Winds & Voices Environmental Services Inc., 433
Phare, Merrell-Anne, Executive Director, Centre for Indigenous Environmental Resources, 893
Pharoah, Joyce, Coordinator of Library, Homewood Health Centre, 1140
Pheasey, Fred, President, Global Dewatering Ltd., 213
Phelan, Daniel, Manager, Collection Services, Ryerson University, 1161
Phelan, Philip, Information Services Administrator, Alberta Land Surveyors' Association, 1104
Phelps, Greg, Mayor, Courtenay, 680
Philion, Pierre, Gatineau, 735
Philip, Andrew, CH2M Hill Canada Limited, 137
Philipow, Wanda, Coordinator, Technical Services, Keyano College, 1107
Philippon, André, Rouyn-Noranda, 741
Phillip, Andrew, President, CH2M Hill Canada Limited, 137
Phillips, Alison, Environmental Management Representative, Lord & Partners Ltd., 274
Phillips, Barbara, Head, Information Services, St Francis-Xavier University, 1134
Phillips, Bert, Principal, Unies Limited, 405
Phillips, Beth, Director, Foodservice & Packaging Institute, 918
Phillips, Bill, St. Catharines, 905-937-7752, 719
Phillips, Bruce, Manager, 596
Phillips, Chantal, Head Librarian, University of Guelph Ridgetown Campus, 1153
Phillips, Daryl, Manager, Parkland County, 670
Phillips, Holly, Library Technician, Toronto Rehab, 1162
Phillips, Irene, Vice-President, Victoria Lapidary & Mineral Society, 1017
Phillips, James D., President & CEO, Can-Am Border Trade Alliance, 892
Phillips, Jason, Manager, Westburne Canada, 427
Phillips, John, Director, Public Works, Ingersoll, 711
Phillips, John, Project Manager, Priestly Demolition Inc., 332
Phillips, Kim, City Clerk, Burlington, 905-335-7698, 707
Phillips, Laurie, Sales, AXYS Analytical Services Ltd., 100
Phillips, Lorne, General Manager, Outokumpu Technology Ltd., 315
Phillips, Wayne, Executive Director, Canadian Dam Association, 865
Philpott, Gerard, Vice-President, Phoenix Engineering Inc., 323
Philpott, Kerry, Office Manager, Sustainable EDGE Ltd., 383
Phimister, Jim, President/CEO, Barenco Inc., 101
Phipps, Malcolm, Director, QMI-SAI Global, 338
Phyper, John David, Principal, Conformance Check Inc., 150
Piaggio, Ken, Vice-President, TIR Systems Ltd., 396
Le Piane, John, Sales Manager, Mainetti Canada Inc., 279
Pianosi, Jim, Sales Manager, Solinst Canada Ltd., 373
Picard, David, Principal, Clearstone Engineering Inc., 143
Picard, François, Québec, 740
Picard, Jim, Manager, Bartle & Gibson Co. Ltd., 102
Picard, Pierre, Heenan Blaikie S.E.N.C.R.L./SRL - Québec, 1088
Picard, Rejean, Chair, The Ontario Greenhouse Alliance, 974
Picard Lavoie, Ginette, Québec, 740
Picco, Ed, Minister, 618
Picco Garland, Deborah, Executive Director, Quidi Vidi Rennie's River Development Foundation, 992
Piché, Francine, Coordonnatrice, service des ressources documentair, CÉGEP de Sainte-Foy, 1178

Executive Name Index

Piché, Ronald, President & General Director, Groupe Consulteaux Inc., 219
Piché, Réjean, Vice-Président, Nouvelle Technologie (TEKNO) Inc., 308
Piché, Stéphane, Saint-Jérôme, 450-432-2791, 743
Pichet, Jacques, President, Magnor, Division of Magchem, 278
Pichette, Denis, Technicien, Collège de Maisonneuve, 1172
Pichette, Jacques, Directeur général, La Côte-de-Beaupré, 748
Pichette, Janyse L., Directrice générale, Maskinongé, 750
Pichette, Jean-François, Associé, Langlois Kronström Desjardins, 1088
Pichette, Martin, Partner, Lavery, de Billy - Montréal, 1086
Pick, Arthur, Administrator, 609
Pickard, Hubert E., Owner, H. Pickard & Associates, 223
Pickard, Jim, Leeds & Grenville, 726
Pickard, Jim, Mayor, Elizabethtown-Kitley, 613-342-5721, 725
Pickard, Steve, Chatham-Kent, 724
Picken, Heather M., Lawrence, Lawrence, Stevenson, 1068
Picken, Jim, North Glengarry, 727
Pickering, Brad, Deputy Minister & Deputy Solicitor General, 571
Pickering, Jane, Director, Maple Ridge, 604-467-7471, 687
Pickersgill, Michael T., Torys LLP, 1081
Pickett, Marty, Executive Director, The Rocky Mountain Institute, 996
Pickett, Todd, Land Management Officer, Corner Brook, 709-637-1544, 693
Pickles, David, City Councillor, Pickering, 718
Picotte, Michel, Préfet, Rouville, 753
Pidduck, Steve, Contact, Andritz Bird, 85
Pidgeon, Ann-Marie, Marketing Department, Kyocera Mita Canada Ltd., 261
Pidwerbecki, Nester, Durham, 699
Pidwerbecki, Nester, Regional Councillor, Oshawa, 716
Piérard, Sylvie, Greffière, Beloeil, 734
Piercey, Colin D., Stewart McKelvey Stirling Scales - Halifax, 1068
Pierobon, Nancy, Health Sciences Librarian, Humber College Institute of Technology & Advanced Learning, 1158
Pieroway, Bob, Contact, BioSource Solutions Inc., 109
Pierre-Louis, Edith, Public Relations, Services d'Évaluation Santé/Toxicologie Inc., 363
Pierre-Roy, Sébastien, Heenan Blaikie S.E.N.C.R.L/SRL - Sherbrooke, 1089
Pierrestiger, Frédéric, Associé, Stikeman Elliott LLP - Montréal, 1087
Piescic, Dan, Director, Engineering & Infrastructure Services, Lakeshore, 712
Pietrangelo, Michael, Manager, Tomatech, 397
Pietrangelo, Victor, City Councillor, Niagara Falls, 715
Piette, Jean, Ogilvy Renault LLP/S.E.N.C.R.L., s.r.l. - Montréal, 1086
Piette, Jean, Associé principal, Ogilvy Renault LLP/S.E.N.C.R.L., s.r.l. - Québec, 1089
Pietz, Bill, Sales, Advance Engineered Products Ltd., 68
Pigeon, Ghislain, Fire Chief, Hawkesbury, 711
Pigeon, Gilbert, Préfet, Rimouski-Neigette, 753
Pigeon, Martin, Saint-Jérôme, 450-436-1787, 743
Pignoli, Frank, Scarfone Hawkins LLP, 1069
Pihowich, Tony, Manager, Human Resources, Woodstock, 723
Pike, Alexandria J., Davies Ward Phillips & Vineberg LLP, 1074
Pike, Jeff, President, Canviro, 127
Pike, Val, President, Yukon Public Health Association, 1024
Pikel, John, Treasurer, Manitoba Environmental Industries Association Inc., 951
Pilarski, Joseph, Chairman/CEO, Earthguard Environmental Group Inc., 169
Pildysh, Mike, President, Pildysh Technologies Inc., 323
Pile, David, Operations Manager, AeroTek Manufacturing Ltd., 71
Pilger, Charles, Sr. Occupational Hygienist, ALARA Industrial Hygiene Services Ltd., 76
Pilger, Marguerite, Sr. Occupational Hygienist/Project Manager, ALARA Industrial Hygiene Services Ltd., 76
Pilger, Terry, Muskoka, 702
Piliounis, Richard, Engineering Manager, ECE Group - a Division of Conestoga-Rovers & Associates, 170
Pilip, Ken, Registrar, Consulting Engineers of Alberta, 902
Pilkington, Bill, Senior Vice-President & Chief Nuclear Officer, 511
Pillai, Ranj, Whitehorse, 755
Pilley, Brooke, Contact, Lakehead University, 263
Pilling, Peter, President, Tomark Compliance Centre, 397
Pillo-Blocka, Francey, President & CEO, Canadian Council of Food & Nutrition, 864
Pillon, Ed, Fire Chief, Essex, 519-776-6476, 709
Pillon, Robert (Bob), Amherstburg, 705
Pillon-Abbs, Tracey, Manager, Planning Services, Leamington, 726
Pilon, Alain, Gatineau, 735
Pilon, Dan, Manager, Public Works, South Stormont, 730
Pilon, Daniel, Directeur général, Les Moulins, 750
Pilon, Darlene, Manager, Canadian Council of Technicians & Technologists, 865
Pilon, Guy, Maire, Vaudreuil-Dorion, 746
Pilot, Jayne, President/CEO, Pilot Performance Resources Management Inc., 324
Pilote, Pascal, Alma, 418-480-1417, 733
Pinard, Alain, Director, Planning, Kitchener, 519-741-2426, 712
Pinard, Suzanne, Technicienne en documentation, CÉGEP de Sept-Iles, 1184
Pinault, Michel, Directeur général, Granby, 450-776-8232, 735
Pinch, Brian, Senior Financial Advisor, Pinch Group, 324
Pinchin, Don, President & Owner, Pinchin Environmental Ltd., 324
Pincock, Doug, Founder & Chair, Vemco Ltd., 410
Pincott, Brian, Calgary, 403-268-2430, 671
Pincott, Sylvia, Contact, Pender Island Field Naturalists, 985
Pine, James, Chief Administrative Officer & Clerk, Hastings, 700
Pineo, Robert H., Patterson Law, 1068
Pingue, Antonio, Vice-President, Horizon Environment Inc., 233
Pink, Chris, President, C.J. Pink Ltd., 120
Pink, Michael, Contact, Kel-Ann Organics, 256
Pinks, Stuart, CEO, Canada-Nova Scotia Offshore Petroleum Board, 853
Pinksen, Steve, Director, 618
Pinnell, Richard Hugh, Manager, University Map Library & Branch Library S, University Map Library, 1164
Pinsent, Celine, Partner, Goss Gilroy Inc., 215
Pinsent, Michael, Town Manager, Grand Falls-Windsor, 709-487-0407, 694
Pinsonneault, Steve, Chatham-Kent, 724
Pintar, Mike, Fire Chief, Timmins, 721
Pinter, Lawrence, CEO, PINTER & Associates Ltd., 325
Pio, Maurizio, Manager, Westburne Canada, 428
Pipe, Gary, Director, Public Works & Superintendent, Drainage, North Perth, 519-292-2066, 715
Piper, Leanne, Guelph, 710
Pipon, Sharon, Manager, Pfizer Canada, Inc., 1169
Pippard, Dan, Director, Newalta Corporation, 301
Pippus, Greg, PHH ARC Environmental Ltd., 322
Piquette, Claude B., Conseiller, Joseph-Beaubien, Montréal, 738
Pires, Sandra, Manager, CIVICUS: World Alliance for Citizen Participation, 896
Pirillo, Tony, Supervisor, Prince George, 250-614-7830, 683
Pirri, Paul, Aurora, 706
Pisciutta, Albino, Owner, Fero Waste & Recycling Inc., 195
Piskovic, Michael, Associate, Meo & Associates Inc., 286
Pitcher, Barry, Cascades Recovery Inc., 131
Pitchford, Amanda, Collections/Reference Librarian, North Island College Library, 1111
Pitchford, Simon, Vice-President, MDS Sciex, 286
Pitman, Paul, AGRECOM inc., 73
Pitre, Benoit, Degussa Canada Inc., 159
Pitre, Sheila, Terrapex Environmental Ltd., 390
Pitre, Stéphane, Partner, Borden Ladner Gervais LLP - Montréal, 1083
Pitt, Robert, Partner, Canning & Pitt Associates Inc., 126
Pittman, Lyle, PricewaterhouseCoopers Management Consultants, 332
Pittman, Miles, Treasurer, Canadian Petroleum Law Foundation, 882
Pittman, Miles F., Partner, Ogilvy Renault LLP/S.E.N.C.R.L., s.r.l. - Calgary, 1053
Pittman, Neil F., Partner, Ottenheimer Baker, 1066
Pitura, Wayne, President, Talon Projects Inc., 386
Pivonik, Edward, President, ENV Treatment Systems Inc., 182
Pizzardi, Dennis, Vice-President, Carlo Gavazzi (Canada) Inc., 129
Pizzuto, Frank, City Manager, Abbotsford, 604-864-5501, 679
Plain, Richard, Vice-President, Waterous Power Systems, 422
Plamondon, Guy, Directeur des ventes & marketing, Electro-Mecanik Inc., 175
Plamondon, Susan, Chief Administrative Officer, Georgina, 709
Plamping, Doug, CAO, Mountain View County, 669
Plancke, C.E.T., Andrew, Director, Municipal Services, Kingsville, 712
Plant, Paul D., City Councillor, Woodstock, 723
Plante, Agathe, Agente de secrétariat, Institut de technologie agro-alimentaire de la Pocatière, 1177
Plante, Alain, Greffier, Amos, 733
Plante, Carmen L., Bishop & McKenzie LLP, 1054
Plante, Chris, Sales Agent, Danatec Educational Services Ltd., 157
Plante, Gilles, Préfet, La Vallée-du-Richelieu, 748
Plante, Jean, Principal, Archer Chemical, 90
Plante, Léon, Saint-Hyacinthe, 742
Plante, Michel, Director, Le Groupe Sani Marc, 265
Plante, Robert, Laval, 736
Plantenga, Stansje, President, Ruiter Valley Land Trust, 997
Plastow, Kristine, Librarian, Red Deer College, 1109
Plate, Jason, Howard Marten Fluid Technologies Inc., 234
Platel, Sydney, Vice-President, Versatile Measuring Instruments Inc., 412
Plater, L. Greg, Partner, Stikeman Elliott LLP - Calgary, 1054
Platt, Janice, Director, Human Resources, Kawartha Lakes, 711
Plavac, Bill, Secretary, Central Canadian Federation of Mineralogical Societies, 893
Playfair, Richard, Director, Fire & Emergency Services, Oro-Medonte, 728
Pleadwell, Derek, Chair, 597
Pleasance, Rod, Project Engineer, Squamish, 604-815-5016, 688
Plein, Adolph, President, Plein Disposal, 326
Pletch, Q.C., Robert B., Chairman, MacPherson Leslie & Tyerman LLP - Regina, 1090
Pletcher, Fred R., Partner, Borden Ladner Gervais LLP - Vancouver, 1058
Pletsch, Carolyn, Project Director, Ontario Agricultural Training Institute, 970
Plett, Kathy, Associate Director, College of New Caledonia, 1115
Plewa, Rick, Secretary & Communication Officer, Environmental Bankers Association, 911
Plewes, Bill, Director, Building Services, Collingwood, 708
Pley, Tim, Fire Chief, Port Alberni, 250-724-1351, 683
Plouffe, Sandra, Circulation Assistant, South Campus, 1106
Plourde, Alain, Directeur général, Association paritaire pour la santé et la sécurité du travail - H, 840
Plourde, Marcel, Secteur du catalogage, Université Laval, 1181
Plourde, Mario, President/CEO, Cascades Fine Papers Group Inc., 130
Plummer, Stephen, President & CEO, IMP Liquid Meters & Petroleum Services, 239
Plunkett, Eva, Inspector General, 557
Plut, Martin, InspecTech, 243
Poch, Harry, Poch, Harry Environmental Lawyer, 1079
Pockar, Robert, President & CEO, Matrix Solutions Inc., 282
Pockey, Michelle, Fasken Martineau - Vancouver, 1059
Podbielski, Ron, Executive Director, 662
Podniewicz, Ed, Chief Building Official & Administrator, Zoning, North Perth, 519-292-2058, 715
Podowski, Darrell W., Lang Michener LLP - Vancouver, 1059, 1060
Podruzny, David, Vice-President, Canadian Chemical Producers' Association, 862
Poehlmann, Thyson, Engineer, Nett Technologies Inc., 300
Poffenroth, Q.C., Robert W., Fraser Milner Casgrain LLP - Calgary, 1051
Pohrebniuk, Patricia, Program Administrator, Manitoba Christmas Tree Grower Association, 950
Poirer, Rheal, President, Major Water Treatment Tech Ltd., 279
Poirer, Roger, Contact, Conestoga-Rovers & Associates, 149
Poirier, Claude, Corporate Legal Counsel, 597
Poirier, Fernand, Dave Vallieres & Associates Inc., 158
Poirier, Ghislain, Président, Association de l'exploration minière de Québec, 831
Poirier, Gilberte, Responsable, CHUS Hôtel-Dieu, 1185
Poirier, Gérald, Québec, 740
Poirier, Gérard, Laval, 450-978-6888, 736
Poirier, J. David, Director, Summerside, 733
Poirier, Jean, Greffier, Victoriaville, 746
Poirier, Jean-Guy, Préfet, Bonaventure, 747
Poirier, Jean-Sébastien, Greffier, La Tuque, 736
Poirier, Katherine, Partner, Borden Ladner Gervais LLP - Montréal, 1083
Poirier, Marc, Manager, PRT Inc., 336
Poirier, Martin, Responsable, Bibliothèque de musique, 1185
Poirier, Michel, Partner, Heenan Blaikie S.E.N.C.R.L/SRL, 1084
Poirier, Rhéal, Acting Secretary to Council, 609
Poirier, Roger, Vice-President, Conestoga-Rovers & Associates, 149
Poirier, Sylvain, Partner, Heenan Blaikie S.E.N.C.R.L/SRL, 1084
Poirier, Théo, Gestionnaire, Veolia ES Canada Industrial Services Inc., 411
Poirier, Yvelle, Executive Secretary, 609
Poirier Rivard, Denise, Saint-Constant, 742
Poissant, Dave, Director, Carrier Canada Ltd., 129
Poissant, Germain, Saint-Jean-sur-Richelieu, 450-347-8703, 742

1340 GUIDE DES RESSOURCES ENVIRONNEMENTALES CANADIENNES 2011-2012

Executive Name Index

Poisson, Pierre D., Vérificateur général, Longueuil, 737
Poitras, Denis, Terrebonne, 745
Poitras, Jacques E., Longueuil, 737
Poitras, Richard, Directeur, Québec, 418-641-6231, 740
Pol, BES, MCIP, RPP, Calvin, Director, Planning, Building, & Enforcement, North Dundas, 727
Polak, John C., President, TerraChoice Environmental Marketing, 390
Polak, Mary, Minister, 583
Polakoff, Jeff, Deputy Minister, 608
Polet, Mark, President, Ecomark Ltd., 106, 172
Polet, Terri, CEO, Ecomark Ltd., 106, 172
Polhill, Bud, London, 713
Poling, George, Sr. Vice-President, Rescan Environmental Services Ltd., 345
Poling, Jan, Vice-President, General Counsel & Secretary, American Forest & Paper Association, 823
Poliquin, Manon, Sec.-Trés., Régie intermunicipale de gestion intégrée des déchets Bécancour-N, 760
Polis, J. Chris, Corporate Product Manager, Imbibitive Technologies Canada, Inc., 239
Pollard, Adriane, Manager, Saanich, 688
Pollard, Ken, President, CP Environmental Technologies, 153
Pollmueller, Andreas, Vice President, Allianz Madvac Inc., 79
Pollock, Andrew, Director, Waste Management Services, Niagara, 702
Pollock, Bruce, Partner, Stikeman Elliott LLP - Toronto, 1080
Pollock, Dan, Regional Manager, Jomac Canada Inc., 253
Pollock, David, Director, White Rock, 604-541-2181, 686
Pollock, Glenn, Port Coquitlam, 683
Pollock, John, Contact, Settlement Surveys Ltd., 364
pollution probe foundatio, The Pollution Probe Found, Toronto, ON, 1044
Polsky, Larry, Windsor Barrel & Drum Ltd., 433
Polsky, Ron, Windsor Barrel & Drum Ltd., 433
Polson, Rory G., Burnet, Duckworth & Palmer LLP, 1050
Polysou, Nick, Manager, AMEC, 83
Polysou, Nick, Unit Manager, AMEC, 83
Pomerleau, Serge, Sales Director, Demilec Inc., 161
Pomeroy, Julia, Borden Ladner Gervais LLP - Montréal, 1083
Pomfret, William, President, Safety Projects International Inc., 355
Pominville, Cahl, Clerk, North Grenville, 728
Pommer, Leslie, Coordinator, Customer Services & Concession, Strathroy-Caradoc, 731
Pon, Leola W., Associate, Hicks Morley Hamilton Stewart Storie LLP, 1076
Ponich, Wally, Director, Acklands-Grainger Inc., 66
Pontbriand, France, Bibliothécaire, Centre de santé et de services sociaux de Laval, 1169
Pontone, Dante, President/CEO, 623
Pontus, Larry, Public Trustee, 607
Pook, Dennis, Manager, Guspro Inc., 223
Poole, Dave, Manager, Dillon Consulting Ltd., 163
Poole, Derek, Branch Manager, Safety-Kleen Canada Inc., 355
Poole, Don, Manager of Planning, Charlottetown, 732
Poole, Grace, Treasurer, Oxford County Geological Society, 983
Poole, Jeremy M., Alexander Holburn Beaudin & Lang, LLP, 1057
Poole, Ron, CAO, Terrace, 685
Poon, Debra, Counsel, McCarthy Tétrault LLP - Calgary, 1053
Poon, Don C.K., Managing Director, SAL Engineering Ltd., 356
Poonja, Amin, President, Pest Management Association of Alberta, 985
Poot, Peter, Secretary, Greater Toronto Water Garden & Horticultural Society, 925
Pootmans, Richard, Calgary, 403-268-2430, 671
Pope, Doug, Manager, North Vancouver, 604-983-7337, 682
Pope, Frank, Treasurer, Ottawa Field-Naturalists' Club, 983
Pope, Richard, Manager, Dillon Consulting Ltd., 164
Pope, Q.C., Dale B., Davis LLP - Vancouver, 1059
Popik, John, President, Nett Technologies Inc., 300
Popoff, Barry, Manager, SimplexGrinnell, 368
Popovich, N., Manager, Development Services, Gravenhurst, 709
Popowich, Douglas M., Fire Commissioner, 590
Porasz, Ed, M&E Engineering Ltd., 276
Porlier, Pascal, Cain Lamarre Casgrain Wells - Val-d'Or, 1089
Porozni, Greg, Chair, 564
Portafaix, Thierry, President, Janin Atlas Inc., 251
Portelance, Alain, Blainville, 734
Portelance, Johanne, Hawkesbury, 711
Portelance, Luc, Executive Vice-President, 514
Porteous, Nelson, Coordinator, Annapolis County, 902-532-3141, 696
Porter, Dean A., Poole Althouse, Barristers & Solicitors, 1065

Porter, Earl, Mayor, Portage La Prairie, 689
Porter, Eric, J. Walter Company Ltd., 249
Porter, Karen, Treasurer, Fraser Valley Labour Council, 919
Porter, Shirley, Accounting, Light Solar Wind Manufacturing, 272
Porter, Steve, Contact, 658
Porteus, Murray, Chair, 619
Portner, Christopher, Partner, Osler, Hoskin & Harcourt LLP - Toronto, 1079
Portz, Ted, Vice-President, Soper's, 374
Poruchny, Rita, President, Global, Environmental & Outdoor Education Council, 924
Posavad, Anna, Financial Manager, Regional Power Inc., 344
Poscente, Mike, Director, 572
Posehn, Daryl, Sr. Vice-President, 400, 662
Poston, Brian C., MacKenzie Fujisawa LLP, 1061
Poth, Lorraine, Director, Red Deer, 674
Pothier, Marc, Associé, Miller Thomson LLP - Montréal, 1086
Pothier-Comeau, Cécile, Bibliothécaire, Université Sainte-Anne, 1135
Potma, Dick, Owner, Solarmart, 372
Potolicki, Grant, Founder & President, Green Plan Ltd., 217
Potter, Paul, President, The Cord Group Ltd., 392
Potter, Stephen, Managing Director, SL Ross Environmental Research Ltd., 370
Potter, P.Eng., Frank, Acting CEO, 616
Pottier, Anne, Associate University Librarian, Collection Resourc, McMaster University, 1141
Pottinger, Edmund L., President, Pottinger Gaherty Environmental Consultants Ltd., 329
Pottinger, Helen, Library Technician, Brockville Campus, 1139
Pottle, Patty, Minister Responsible, 602
Pottle-Fewer, Karen, Library Technician, Labrador West Campus, 1131
Pottruff, Q.C., Betty Ann, Executive Director, 661
Potts, Arthur, Founder & Principal, Municipal Affairs Consulting, 295
Potts, Michael, President & CEO, The Rocky Mountain Institute, 996
Potts, Robert J., Blaney McMurtry LLP, 1073
Potvin, Christiane, Technicienne en documentation, DRDC Valcartier, R&D pour La defense Canada, Valcartier, 1186
Potvin, Denis, Vice-President, Conporec Inc., 150
Potvin, Gilles, Maire, Saint-Félicien, 742
Potvin, Jacinthe, Assistante, Institut de l'Énergie et de l'environnement de la francophonie, 1179
Potvin, Lorraine, Vice-President/CFO, RailPower Technologies Corp., 342
Potvin, Marie, Conseillère, Robert-Bourassa, Montréal, 738
Pouget, Diane, Amherstburg, 705
Poulet, Isabelle, Sainte-Julie, 743
Poulette, François, Trésorier et Directeur, Sherbrooke, 819-821-5490, 744
Poulin, André, Gestionnaire, Veolia ES Canada Industrial Services Inc., 412
Poulin, Annette, City Solicitor, St. Catharines, 719
Poulin, Bernard, Directeur, Mirabel, 450-475-2001, 738
Poulin, Bernard, President & CEO, Groupe S.M. International Inc., 220
Poulin, Clément, Directeur, Saint-Georges, 742
Poulin, Ghislain, Directeur général, Les Collines-de-l'Outaouais, 749
Poulin, Gilles, Directeur, Trois-Rivières, 819-372-4604, 745
Poulin, Jacques, Directeur général, Rivière-du-Loup, 418-867-6707, 741
Poulin, Marc, Maire, Magog, 819-843-2880, 737
Poulin, Pierre, Directeur, Westburne Canada, 425
Poulin, Roger, President, Sudbury Rock & Lapidary Society, 1011
Poulin, Roger, Vice-President, Ontario Prospectors Association, 977
Poulin, Sonia, Directrice, Bibliothèque de droit Brian-Dickson, 1147
Poulin, M.Eng., P.Eng., Martin, Treasurer, Canadian Medical & Biological Engineering Society, 877
Poulin-Marcotte, Denise, Magog, 819-843-1146, 737
Pouliot, Michel, Vice-President, Biogénie, 108
Pouliot, Mignonne, Saint-Constant, 742
Pouliot, Renée, Technicienne en documentation, Collège Shawinigan, 1184
Pouliot, Robert Y., Sherbrooke, 744
Powell, Glenn, Director, Ontario Water Works Association, 981
Powell, Helen, Head, Public Services, Sexton Design & Technology Library, 1136

Powell, John, Branch Manager, CenturyVallen, 137
Powell, Martin, Commissioner, Transportation & Works, Mississauga, 714
Powell, Murray, Brant, 698
Powell, Sarah V., Davies Ward Phillips & Vineberg LLP, 1074
Powell, Tony, Applications Manager, Purifics ES Inc., 337
Powell, B.A., LL.B., Sarah V., Partner, Davies Ward Phillips & Vineberg LLP, 1074
Powelson, Susan, Director, Regina Qu'Appelle Health Region Library Services - Regina General, 1188
Power, Chris, Acting Chair, 617
Power, Derm, President, Dominion Recycling Ltd., 165
Power, Geoff, Manager, Columbia-Shuswap, 677
Power, Glenda, Director, 601
Power, Gregory J., Associate, Hicks Morley Hamilton Stewart Storie LLP, 1076
Power, Henry, President/Operator, Power Vac of Nova Scotia, 329
Power, Michelle, Saint-Jean-sur-Richelieu, 514-449-9614, 742
Power, Richard, Chief Development Officer, Lloydminster, 780-871-8335, 673
Power, Steve, COO, Crosbie Industrial Services Ltd., 154
Powers, Andrew, Osler, Hoskin & Harcourt LLP - Toronto, 1079
Powers, Chris, Fire Chief, Whitchurch-Stouffville, 723
Powers, Jack, CFO, Delcan Water, 160
Powers, Linda, Contact, Yukon Workers' Compensation Health & Safety Board, 1192
Powers, Russ, Hamilton, 711
Powers, Sean, Manager, Bartle & Gibson Co. Ltd., 102
Powers, Q.C., R. Greg, Fasken Martineau - Calgary, 1050
Prakash, V., Int'l Sales Manager, Enervac Corp., 180
Prange, Laurie, Cataloguing Librarian, Yukon College, 1191
Prapavessis, Karen, Manager, H.L. Blachford Ltd., 223
Prason, Sholem, Contact, Teknion Corporation, 389
Prather, Valerie R., Bennett Jones LLP - Calgary Office, 1049
Pratt, Rick, Manager, North Vancouver, 604-990-2312, 688
Pratte, Guy J., Partner, Borden Ladner Gervais LLP - Montréal, 1083
Prazmowski, George, Director, CadhamHayes Systems Inc., 120
Preachuk, Art, Fieldman, Red Deer County, 670
Précourt, Diane, Sec.-Trés., Régie intermunicipale d'alimentation en eau potable du Bas-St-Fra, 759
Preda, Adina, Brownlee LLP, 1054
Preece, Warren, Director, 591
Prefontaine, E., President, Stratem Inc., 380
Prefontaine, Gabrielle, University Archivist/FIPPA Coordinator, University of Winnipeg, 1126
Prégent, Sophie, Lavery, de Billy - Montréal, 1086
Preibe, D., Carrier Canada Ltd., 129
Preiner, Norbert, Thorold, 720
Prénoveau, Marie-Andrée, Directrice, Éco Entreprises Québec, 908
Prentice, Bill, Manager, Brooks, 403-362-3146, 671
Prentice, Robert, Commissioner, Community Services, Newmarket, 714
Presch, Sabine, President, DINOFLEX Manufacturing Ltd., 164
Prescott, Gordon, Manager, Squamish, 688
Prescott, Michel, Conseiller de ville, Jeanne-Mance, Montréal, 738
Presentey, Nicole, General Manager, Presentey Engineering Products Ltd., 331
Presnell, Jackie, Secretary, Saskatchewan Environmental Industry & Managers' Association, 1000
Presseau, Christine, Président, Cercles des jeunes naturalistes, 894
Presser, G.S., President, Acme Engineering Products Ltd., 67
Presser, Robert, Vice-President, Acme Engineering Products Ltd., 67
Pressman, Amy, Davis LLP - Toronto, 1074
Presti, Patricia, Campus Librarian, Markham Campus, 1144
Prestley, Janet, Director, Fort St. John, 681
Preston, David C., Manager, Fenco Shawinigan Engineering Limited, 194
Preston, Kathy, Project Director, RWDI AIR Inc., 354
Preston, Shirley, Deputy Clerk, Trent Hills, 731
Preston, Tracey, President, Ontario Printing & Imaging Association, 977
Preston, Q.C., Bill D., Robertson Stromberg Pedersen LLP, 1091
Prettejohn, Susan, Elizabethtown-Kitley, 613-498-2842, 725
Pretty, Scott, Operations Manager, BECK Drilling and Environmental Services Ltd., 104
Preuss, Karl, Director, Delta, 604-946-3230, 686
Prevost, Denys, Fire Chief, Welland, 722
Prevost, Louis, Director, Planning & Forestry, Prescott & Russell, 729

Executive Name Index

Prévost, Marc, Associé, Robinson Sheppard Shapiro LLP, 1087
Prévost, Pierre, Directeur général par intérim, Union des municipalités du Québec, 1014
Prévost, Stéphanie, Directrice générale, Sept-Iles, 744
Prevost, Y.G., Environmental Engineer, Les Laboratoires Shermont Inc., 269
Price, Alf A., Corporate Controller, Sandwell Engineering Inc., 357
Price, Bill, President, African Violet Society of Canada, 813
Price, Brenda, Cataloguer & Head, ILL, Bombardier Inc./Canadair Aerospace & Defence Groups, 1171
Price, Gary, City Councillor, Cambridge, 707
Price, Jackie, Pribusin Inc., 332
Price, Jamie, Director, Racal Protection Canada, 341
Price, John, Assistant, Civil Aviation Technical Reference Centre, 1128
Price, Kevin O., Technical Consultant, Cormorant Ltd., 152
Price, Maureen, Campus Librarian, Mohawk-McMaster Institute for Applied Health Sciences, 1141
Price, Ron, Manager, Coquitlam, 680
Price, Wayne, Coordinator, Cranbrook, 680
Pride, Calvin, President, Ambio Biofiltration Ltd., 82
Pridy, Donald, Managing Principal, Pridy Associates, 332
Priel, Joe-Anne, General Manager, Community Services, Hamilton, 711
Priest, Bill, Maritime Paper Products Ltd., 281
Priest, Margot, Chief Review Officer, 521
Priestley, Charles, Chair, Beaverhill Bird Observatory, 845
Priestly, Ryan, President, Priestly Demolition Inc., 332
Prieur, André, Directeur, Génius Conseil Inc., 207
Prieur, Danielle, Coordonnatrice, Salaberry-de-Valleyfield, 450-370-4875, 744
Prima, Robert, Acting Fire Marshall, 618
Primeau, Gaëtan, Conseiller, Tétreaultville, Montréal, 738
Prince, Cameron, Vice-President, 518
Prince, Clarence, Councillor, Cape Breton, 695
prince edward island econ, Prince Edward Island Eco-, 1216
prince edward island dept, Prince Edward Island. Dep, Charlottetown, PE, 1045
Princz, Marina, Librarian, VanDusen Gardens Library, 1119
Pringle, Bob, Deputy Mayor & Councillor, Grey, 700
Pringle, Eric K., Vice-President, Hemmera Envirochem Inc., 229
Pringle, Sherri, Library Technician, Owen Sound Campus, 1152
Pringle, B.S.W., M.S.W., Bob, Saskatoon, 754
Prior, Susan, Librarian, Prince Philip Drive Campus Library, 1133
Prior, Susan, Librarian III, St Anthony Campus Library, 1131
Prior, Tom, Consultant, N. Vandenassem & Associate, 296
Priorello, Pat, President/CEO, PAP Engineering Services, 317
Pritchard, Andrew, Senior Partner, Ogilvy Renault LLP/S.E.N.C.R.L., s.r.l. - Ottawa, 1071
Pritchard, Heather, Execxutive Director, FarmFolk/CityFolk Society, 914
Pritchard, Ian, Wardrop Engineering Inc., 417
Pritchard, J.P. (Scott), McCaffery Mudry Pritchard LLP, Barristers & Solicitors, 1052
Pritchard, Rob, General Manager, Calgary, 403-268-2042, 671
Pritchard, Robert, Contact, Yukon Public Legal Education Association, 1024
Pritchard, Sonya, Director, Parks & Recreation, Orangeville, 716
Probyn, Stephen, President, Probyn & Company Inc., 333
Probyn, Steven, Macquarie Power & Infrastructure Income Fund, 278
Procopio, Angelo, Branch Manager, CenturyVallen, 137
Proctor, Donna, Inside Sales, Mancorp Industrial Sales Ltd., 279
Proestos, Angelo, Managing Director, Cheminfo Services Inc., 139
Profit, Sherra, Chair, 639
Prokop, Valerie, Manager, Canadian Gas Association, 869
Prokopchuk, Shauna, Coordinator, Alberta Society of Professional Biologists, 819
Prokopenko, Bob, Manager, Nanaimo, 681
Prokopiak, Angela, Director, 544
Pronovost, Janet, Office Manager, National Aboriginal Forestry Association, 956
Pronovost, Michel, Directeur, Westburne Canada, 427
Prosser, Helen, Coordinator, Library Services, Northern Lakes College - Slave Lake, 1108, 1109
Prosser, Q.C., Leslie W., Managing Partner, Robertson Stromberg Pedersen LLP, 1091
Prosterman, Paul, Ogilvy Renault LLP/S.E.N.C.R.L., s.r.l. - Montréal, 1086
Proudfoot, LL.B., LL.M., Clifford C., Partner, Lawson Lundell LLP - Vancouver, 1061
Proudfoot, Q.C., Gordon F., Boyne Clarke, 1067
Proudley, Herbert, Director, Tay, 731

Proudlock, R. Lorne, Sr. Vice-President & CFO, Cansult Maunsell Limited, 127
Proulx, Alain, Sales, Lavo Inc., 265
Proulx, Bertrand, Président, Consultants Mésar inc., 151
Proulx, Claude, Directeur général, Drummondville, 819-478-6557, 735
Proulx, Dominique, President, Arrakis Consultants Inc., 93
Proulx, Francis, Rimouski, 740
Proulx, Marc, VP, Great Western Containers Inc., 216
Proulx, Mario, Cain Lamarre Casgrain Wells - Montréal, 1083
Prout, Tom, Secretary/General Manager, Ausable Bayfield Conservation Foundation, 844
Provençal, Hector, Préfet, Les Etchemins, 749
Provencher, Francis, Coordonnateur, Rouville, 753
Provencher, Jean-Yves, Saguenay, 741
Provencher, Marie-France, Présidente, Centre de formation en entreprise et récupération, 893
Provencher, Mario, Rouyn-Noranda, 741
Provencher, Mario, Maire, Rouyn-Noranda, 741
Provencher, Yvan, Directeur général, Les Sources, 750
Provenzano, Marcel, Fire Chief, Sault Ste. Marie, 720
Provost, Dominic, Directeur général, Le Haut-St-François, 749
Provost, Paul-Emil, Directeur, Bureau systèmes, Université de Montréal, 1176
Provost, Ronald, Préfet, Les Laurentides, 749
Provost, ing., Claude, Responsable, Varennes, 746
Prowse, Michael, Barrie, 706
Prud'homme, Louis, Directeur général, Mirabel, 450-475-2000, 738
Prud'homme, Yves, Préfet, Montcalm, 750
Prudhomme, Rachel, Director, West Nipissing, 732
Prussky, Alan, President, SHER-PAC Container Systems Ltd., 365
Prychitko, Ron, Sales Manager, Armtec Construction Products, 92
Pryke, Susan, Muskoka, 702
Pryke, Susan, Acting Chair, Muskoka, 702
Pryor, Miranda, Executive Director, Newfoundland Aquaculture Industry Association, 963
Prysliak, JeanAnne, Coordinator, Saskatchewan Wildlife Federation, 1002
Puchalski, Irene, Librarian, John H. Daniels Faculty of Architecture, Lanscape & Design, 1158
Puddester, Leigh, President, K&D Pratt Group Inc., 254
Puertas, Ralph, President, Zep Manufacturing Company of Canada, 436
Pueyo, Jacques, Contact, AGRI-SX, 73
Puffalt, Jim, City Manager, Estevan, 306-634-1803, 754
Puga, Robin, Vice-President, Canadian Association for Studies in Co-operation, 856
Pugh, Garth, Manager, 657
Pugh, Paul, Ward Councillor, Thunder Bay, 721
Pugh, Perry, Vice-President, Fuller Austin Insulation Inc., 203
Puhl, Darvin E., President, Rondar Inc., 351
Pukteris, Marek, Library Technician, Lady Davis Institute for Medical Research of the Sir Mortimer B., 1174
Pulleyblank, Marcia, Librarian, Casa Loma ESL Resource Centre, 1157
Pullia, Renato, Treasurer & Director, Corporate Services, Perth, 703
Puopolo, Paul, President & CEO, Planning & Engineering Initiatives Ltd., 325
Pupatello, Sandra, Minister, 622
Pupo, Cari, Director, Financial Services, Pelham, 717
Purcell, Carl, President, Nova Scotia Salmon Association, 969
Purcell, Catherine, Director, Parks, Recreation, & Culture, King, 726
Purcell, François, Conseiller, Saint-Édouard, Montréal, 738
Purcell, Michael, Systems Librarian, University of Northern British Columbia, 1115
Purchase, Bruce, Director, Colchester County, 697
Purdon, Colleen, Owen Sound, 717
Purdy, John, Manager, Focal Technologies Inc., 198
Purdy, Q.C., Raymond C., Managing Partner, Brownlee LLP, 1054
Purser, Don, National Secretary, Institute of Power Engineers, 933
Putnam, Ian G., Partner, Stikeman Elliott LLP - Toronto, 1080
Puttick, Norm, Niagara, 702
Putz, Dan, Manager, Westburne Canada, 426
Putz, CGA, David, City Manager, Yorkton, 306-786-1703, 755
Pyatt, Bill, Chief Administrative Officer, Northumberland, 702
Pybus, Kathy L., Burnet, Duckworth & Palmer LLP, 1050
Pyke, Stephen, Senior Environmental Engineer, Project Engineering Limited, 334

Pynn, Paul, Project Manager/Engineer, Atlantic Orient Canada Inc., 96

Q

Qadri, Shad, Ottawa, 613-580-2476, 716
Qirbi, Taha, President, Canspect Corporation, 127
Quaglia, Alexander, President, Sciencetech Inc., 359
Quail, Nick, Technical Manager, The St. George Co. Ltd., 393
Quail, Peter, President, The St. George Co. Ltd., 393
Quail, Rick, Municipal Manager, Okotoks, 403-938-8900, 674
Quarshie, Liz, Deputy Minister, 658
quebeclabrador foundation, Québec-Labrador Foundatio, Montréal, QC, 1046
Queen, Gord, Kingsville, 712
Quemby, Mark, Bracebridge, 706
Quenneville, C., Treasurer & Director, Finance, St. Clair, 729
Quenneville, Mathieu, Lavery, de Billy - Montréal, 1086
Quenneville, Richard, Director, T. Harris Environmental Management Inc., 385
Quenneville, Richard, Sec.-Treas., Occupational Hygiene Association of Ontario, 969
Quesnel, Alicia K., Burnet, Duckworth & Palmer LLP, 1050
Quesnel, Normand, Partner, Heenan Blaikie S.E.N.C.R.L/SRL, 1084
Quick, Tim, President & Director, Environmental Studies Association of Canada, 913
Quigg, Janice L., Associate, Eccleston LLP, 1075
Quigley, Barbara A., City Clerk & Director, Moncton / Ville de Moncton, 691
Quigley, Steve, Secretary, Conestoga-Rovers & Associates, 149
Quinlan, Maureen, Partner, Heenan Blaikie LLP - Toronto, 1076
Quinn, Barry, Secretary-Treasurer, Ontario Professional Fire Fighters Association, 977
Quinn, Frank, General Manager, Maple Ridge, 687
Quinn, Glenna, Head, Collection Development, St Francis-Xavier University, 1134
Quinn, Peter, McCarthy Tétrault LLP - Toronto, 1077
Quinn, Robert, President/COO, Comstock Canada Ltd., 148
Quinn, Scott, Project Engineer, Kings County, 902-690-6194, 696
Quinn, Stephen, President/CEO, Interior Weather Services Ltd., 245
Quinn, Thomas J., Chief Administrative Officer, Pickering, 905-420-4648, 718
Quinton-Campbell, Patricia, Burnet, Duckworth & Palmer LLP, 1050
Quiquero, Susan, Manager, Edwards, 173
Quirie, Margaret, Director, Ottawa Hospital, 1151
Quirion, Diane, Responsable, Bibliothèque sciences humaines, Université de Sherbrooke, 1186
Quirion, France, Registrar/Director, Student Affairs, Cambrian College, 1155
Quirion, Georges, Manager, J.L. Richards & Associates Limited, 250
Quirion, Irma, Saint-Georges, 742
Quirion, Patrick, Trésorier, Candiac, 734
Quirk, Tony, President, Q-Air Environmental Controls Ltd., 337
Quoika-Stanka, Wanda, Reference Services Coordinator, John Alexander Weir Memorial Law Library, 1105
Quraeshi, Saeed, Les Consultants Eoletech S.Q. Inc., 268

R

Raaen-Gossell, Erin, Emery Jamieson LLP, 1055
Raaymakers, Marty L., President, MIG Engineering Ltd., 289
Rabinovitch, Paul A., Graham Wilson & Green, Barristers & Solicitors, Notaries, Mediato, 1068
Rabnett, Mark, Hospital Librarian, St Boniface General Hospital, 1125
Raboud, J.P., Process Specialist, Mabarex inc., 277
Racca, Roberto, Chief Communications Officer, Jasco Research Ltd., 251
Rachold, Volker, Executive Secretary, International Arctic Science Committee, 934
Racicot, Patrice, Partner, Lavery, de Billy - Montréal, 1086
Racine, Lynda, Technicienne en documentation, Québec Ministère des Ressources naturelles et de la Faune, 1180
Racine, Pierre, Directeur, Saguenay, 741
Racine, Simon, Gatineau, 735
Racine, Ted J., Head, Laboratory & Scientific Services Directorate, 1151
Radford, Phil, Executive Director, Greenpeace USA, 926
Radman, Ljiljana, Library Technician, Hatch, 1145
Radnidge, Ian, Director, Delta, 604-946-3279, 686

Executive Name Index

Radnoff, Diane, President, Health & Safety Conference Society of Alberta, 927
Radu, Mihai, Service & Technical Contact, Rotork Controls (Canada) Ltd., 352
Radvanyi, Shawn, Manager, New West Gypsum Recycling Inc., 301
Rae, Dan, Vice-President, 597
Rae, G., General Manager, Public Works, Haldimand, 700
Rae, Scott, Manager, Wastequip Cusco, 421
Rae, Q.C, Douglas G.S., Fasken Martineau - Vancouver, 1059
Rahilly, Tony, Director General, 546
Rahman, Zobayur, Unit Manager, AMEC, 83
Rahn, Jeff, Manager, Peace River, 678
Raiche, Wayne, General Manager, Loewen Welding & Manufacturing Ltd., 273
Railer, Carol, Production & Advertising Manager, Canadian Institute of Geomatics, 1149
Raimondo, Frank, Administrator, Cowichan Valley, 677
Raina, Bob, Unit Leader, MWH Canada Inc., 296
Raine, R.Michael, Principal, Golder Associates Ltd., 214
Raine, Rich, Lennox Industries (Canada) Ltd., 267
Rainham, Daniel, Contact, Praxis Environmental, 330
Rainville, Guy, Chef, Parti Vert du Québec, 985
Rainville, Simon, Cain Lamarre Casgrain Wells - Québec, 1087
Raitt, Lisa, Minister, Labour, 534
Rajewski, Gord, Regional Director, Williams Engineering Inc., 432
Rajotte, George, President, Western Industrial Services Ltd., 429
Rajotte, Joe, District Manager, BFI Canada Inc., 107
Rajpal, Dee, Partner, Stikeman Elliott LLP - Toronto, 1080
Rak, Lad J., Vice-President, McClymont & Rak Engineers, Inc., 284
Rakochey, Robert A., Partner, Macleod Dixon LLP, 1052
Ralf, Phil, General Manager, Laidlaw Carriers Inc. - Van Division, 262
Ralph, Paul, Director, Planning Services, Oshawa, 716
Ralston, Caroline, Manager, Westburne Canada, 426
Ramamoorthy, Balachandran, Manager, AZZ Blenkhorn & Sawle Limited, 100
Ramani, Venkat, Manager, Infrastructure, Lambton Shores, 726
Ramarui, Jennifer, Executive Director, The Oceanography Society, 970
Ramji, Karim, Donovan & Company, 1059
Rammelaere, Sylvia, Director, Finance & Performance Service, Lakeshore, 712
Ramon, Yazon, Trade Commissioner, 768
Ramos, Ben, Manager, Recycling Council of British Columbia, 993
Ramotar, Jay, Deputy Minister, 569
Ramsay, David B.N., Pitblado LLP, 1063
Ramsay, Donna, Associate, LINPAC Ropak Packaging, 272
Ramsay, Gregory H.P., President, Ramsay Machine Works Ltd., 342
Ramsay, Richard, Associé, Langlois Kronström Desjardins, 1088
Ramsay, Wray, Superintendent, Drainage, Norwich, 519-879-6568, 728
Ramsey, Allan, Business Manager, Ecology Products International, 172
Ramsey, Doug, Manager, Wardrop Engineering Inc., 417
Ramsey, Virginia, President, INFORM Inc., 931
Rana, Kulbir, Secretary-Treasurer, British Columbia Bottle Depot Association, 847
Rancier, Sarah, Stikeman Elliott LLP - Toronto, 1080
Rancourt, Daniel, Préfet, Abitibi-Ouest, 746
Rancourt, Dominique, Controller, Coen Canada Inc., 146
Rancourt, Gilles, Heenan Blaikie S.E.N.C.R.L./SRL - Québec, 1088
Rancourt, Jocelyn F., Associé, Ogilvy Renault LLP/S.E.N.C.R.L., s.r.l. - Québec, 1089
Rand, Barry, Peterborough, 703
Randa, Lorne I., Brownlee LLP, 1054
Randall, Jeff, Manager, Versatech Products Inc., 412
Randell, Darrell, St. Clair, 519-627-3764, 729
Raney, Dave, District Manager, BFI Canada Inc., 106
Rang, Sarah, Partner, Environmental Economics International, 185
Rang Zhou, Jenny, Library Technician, Saskatchewan Environment, 1187
Rangeley, Robert, Vice-President, World Wildlife Fund - Canada, 1023
Rankin, Jude, 1st National Vice President, Institute of Power Engineers, 933
Rankin, Reg, Councillor, Halifax Regional Municipality, 695
Rankin, Shawn, Principal, Indoor Air Quality Ottawa, 240

Rankin, Q.C., T. Murray, Partner, Heenan Blaikie LLP - Victoria, 1060, 1062
Rapallo, Andrea, President, City Metal Manufacturing Inc., 141
Rapchak, Les, President, Tech Sales Co., 387
Raphaël, Dina, Partner, Lavery, de Billy - Montréal, 1086
Raponi, Larry, President, Nolar Industries Ltd., 305
Raponi, Michael, Sales, Nolar Industries Ltd., 305
Rapp, Cameron, General Manager, Development Services, Waterloo, 519-747-8763, 722
Rapp, Linda, Manager, Whitehorse, 867-668-8325, 755
Rappolt, Marg, Deputy Minister, 621
Raschke, Vera, Legislative Librarian, Northwest Territories Legislative Assembly, 1134
Rashid, Asaf, Contact, Nova Scotia Public Interest Research Group, 968
Rashid, Humayun, Reference Librarian & Cataloguer, Bora Laskin Law Library, 1156
Raskin, Paul, President & Director, Tellus Institute, 1011
Rasmussen, Hans, Resident Manager, Kongskilde Limited, 259
Rasmussen, Johanne, Chef de bibliothèque, Bibliothèque paramédicale, 1171
Rasode, Barinder, Surrey, 604-591-4011, 684
Rassam, Ghassan N., Executive Director, American Fisheries Society, 823
Rastin, Ken, Elliot Lake, 709
Rathbone, Geoff, General Manager, Solid Waste Management Services, Toronto, 416-392-4715, 721
Rathwell, Don, Warden & Councillor, Renfrew, 613-646-2282, 704
Ratle, Réginald, President, Membrex Ltée, 286
Ratliff, Dane, Director, Commission for Environmental Cooperation, 898
Ratté, Hélène, Bibliotechnicienne, La Cité Collégiale, 1151
Ratté, Pierre, Directeur, Saint-Jérôme, 743
Ratzlaff, Linda, Coordinator, Rocky View No. 44, 403-520-8166, 670
Rauh, CMC, Susan, Corporate Officer, Port Coquitlam, 683
Rauma, Jorma, Director, Power-Pacific Poles Ltd., 329
Raun, Vaino, Manager, R.V. Anderson Associates Limited, 341
Rautenkranz, Frank, Librarian, Canadian Nuclear Safety Commission, 1149
Raven, Ken, Manager, Intera Engineering Ltd., 244
Ravinsky, Carl M., Partner, Lavery, de Billy - Montréal, 1086
Rawlins, Rey, Sales, Advanced Biotechnology Inc., 69
Rawlins, Rey, Sales Representative, Double T Equipment Ltd., 165
Rawson, Julie, Executive Director, Northeast Organic Farming Association, 966
Ray, Doug, Director, Public Works, Haliburton, 700
Ray, Geoff, Executive Director, Northwest Territories Recreation & Parks Association, 967
Ray, Larry, President/CEO, Ray Electric Ltd., 342
Ray, Rahul E., Planner, Westland Resource Group Inc., 430
Ray, Steven, Vice-President, Ray Electric Ltd., 342
Rayburn, Bill, Chief Administrative Officer, Middlesex, 701
Raycroft, Lorne, Manager, Douglas, Barwick Inc., 165
Raycroft, Rob, Manager, Whitchurch-Stouffville, 723
Rayment, Jennifer, Library Technician, Periodicals, Humber College Institute of Technology & Advanced Learning, 1158
Raymer, Richard B., Partner, Hodgson Russ LLP, 1077
Raymond, Colette, Executive Vice-President Operations, Shred-It, 366
Raymond, Diane, Directrice, Bibliothèque des sciences de la santé, 1171
Raymond, Kathryn A., Boyne Clarke, 1067
Raymond, Ken, Sales, Neo Valves, 300
Raynard, Melissa, Hospital Librarian, Concordia Hospital, 1123
Rayneault, Nathaly, Greffière, Saint-Lazare, 743
Rayner, Wally, President, Ontario Prospectors Association, 977
Raynor, Ric, Director, Quesnel, 688
Rea, Carlo, Owner, Technel Engineering Inc., 388
Rea, Matthew, Davies Howe Partners, 1074
Reaburn, Ross A., Counsel, Borden Ladner Gervais LLP - Calgary, 1050
Read, Claire, Vice-President, Panama Enterprises (1990) Inc., 317
Read, Jack, President, Panama Enterprises (1990) Inc., 317
Ready, Suzanne, Chargée de l'information, Association sectorielle - Fabrication d'équipement de transport e, 842
Ready, Q.C., Kenneth A., McDougall Gauley, 1090
Reali, Mary, Director, Recreation & Culture, Vaughan, 722
Rear, Dean, Director, Pitt Meadows, 604-465-2449, 683
Reardon, Kenneth V., President & General Manager, Atlantic Purification Systems, 97

Reardon, Terry D., Vice-President, Atlantic Purification Systems, 97
Reashor, Ken, Acting Director, Halifax Regional Municipality, 695
Reay, Harold, Administrator, Central Okanagan, 677
Rebane, Blair A., Partner, Borden Ladner Gervais LLP - Vancouver, 1058
Rebbapragada, Aditya, Ogilvy Renault LLP/S.E.N.C.R.L., s.r.l. - Toronto, 1078
Redden, Bob, President, Environmental Dynamics Inc., 185
Redden, Paul, Canadian Portable Structures (1992) Ltd., 125
Reddigan, Linda, Librarian, Placentia Campus Learning Resource Centre, 1131
Reddin, Ellie, Director, 637
Redekopp, Michelle R., Aikins, MacAulay & Thorvaldson LLP, 1063
Redford, Alison, Minister & Attorney General, 570
Redford, Donald, President, Pigmalion Environmental Services Group, 323
Redhead, Robert J., President, Robert J. Redhead Limited, 348
Redmond, Marina, City Clerk, Corner Brook, 709-637-1534, 693
Redmond, B.A., Daniel (Danny) J., Charlottetown, 1078
Reece, Karen, Library Technician, Acquisitions, Lakeshore Campus, 1159
Reed, Craig, Director, Lambton College of Applied Arts & Technology, 1154
Reed, David, President/CEO, ITM Instruments, 248
Reed, Gordon A.D., Principal, Abbeywood Associates Inc., 64
Reed, Josh, Contact, Abandonrite, 64
Reed, K., Contact, Scotia Plastics, 360
Reed, Linda, Chief Administrative Officer, Peterborough, 718
Reed, Mark, General Manager, Pro-Lab Diagnostics, 333
Reed, Wendy S., Counsel, Heenan Blaikie LLP - Toronto, 1076
Reeder, Andrew, Manager, Okanagan-Similkameen, 678
Reedie, Penny, Associate Chief, 545
Reehill, Paul, Sales & Marketing Manager, Therm-O-Comfort Co. Ltd., 394
Rees, B., Manager, Comox Valley, 677
Reese, David, Project Manager, University Technologies International, 407
Reesor, Lauri A., Associate, Hicks Morley Hamilton Stewart Storie LLP, 1076
Reeve, Dean, Executive Vice-President, 662
Reeve, Jim, Superintendent, Drainage, Middlesex Centre, 727
Reeves, Andrew, Coordinator, Recycling Council of Ontario, 993
Reeves, Greg, General Manager, Arjay Engineering Ltd., 91
Reeves, Greg, Sales Manager, Enmet Canada Ltd., 181
Reeves, Mark R., President, Can-Am Instruments Ltd., 122
Reeves, Richard J., CEO, Can-Am Instruments Ltd., 122
Reeves, Rick, President & CEO, Arjay Engineering Ltd., 91
Reeves, Russ, President, EPA Certified Clean Ltd., 188
Reeves, Todd, ProMinent Fluid Controls Ltd., 334
Regalado, MISt, MA, Sophie M., Chair, Northwestern Ontario Health Libraries Association, 967
Regehr, Bradley D., D'Arcy & Deacon LLP, 1063
Regehr, Dave, Thurber Engineering Ltd., 396
Regier, Terry, President, Thermal Environmental Comfort Association, 1012
Regimbald, Gisèle, Director, 591
Regis, Batista-Lemaire, Trade Commissioner, 767
Regnaud, Marc, Co-President, Groupe Berlie-Falco Inc., 219
Reich, Kathy, CFO, Alpine Environmental Ltd., 80
Reiche, Delia, Middlesex, 701
Reichert, Donald, Supervisor, Victoria, 250-361-0417, 685
Reid, Alison, President, Newfoundland & Labrador Health Libraries Association, 963
Reid, Angela, Kelowna, 681
Reid, Bill, Director, Romatec Incorporated, 351
Reid, Brian, Chief Building Official, Property Standards, Norwich, 728
Reid, David R., Davis LLP - Vancouver, 1059
Reid, Dean, Sr. Project Manager, CBCL Limited, 133
Reid, Donna, City Councillor, Cambridge, 707
Reid, Doug, Research Scientist, Lakehead University, 263
Reid, James R., Davies Ward Phillips & Vineberg LLP, 1074
Reid, Keith, Quinte West, 613-398-7991, 718
Reid, Mae, Metro Vancouver, 680, 678
Reid, Margaret E., Librarian, Technical Services Library, 1136, 1135
Reid, Meaghen, Clerk, Guelph-Eramosa, 725
Reid, Pierre, Directeur, Montréal, 738
Reid, Ron, President, Strata Soil Sampling Inc., 380
Reid, Tom, Deputy Minister, 595
Reid, Trevor, Director, Babcock & Wilcox Canada Ltd., 100
Reid, Twila E., Partner, Stewart McKelvey Stirling Scales - St. John's, 1066

CANADIAN ENVIRONMENTAL RESOURCE GUIDE 2011-2012

Executive Name Index

Reid, Q.C., Wendy E., Cox and Palmer - Charlottetown, 1082
Reidel, Helga, Chief Administrative Officer, Windsor, 519-255-6349, 723
Reilly, Maureen, Researcher, Uxbridge Conservation Association, 1016
Reilly, Sue, Enermodal Engineering Ltd., 179
Reilly, Terry, Director, Archives & Special Collections, University of Calgary, 1103
Reimer, Andrea, Metro Vancouver, 685, 678
Reimer, Garth P., Campbell Marr, 1063
Reimer, Greg, Deputy Minister, 576
Reimer, Karl, Project Engineer, ENPAR Technologies Inc., 181
Reimer, Linda, Coquitlam, 680
Reimer-Heck, Q.C., Beth, Counsel, Borden Ladner Gervais LLP - Calgary, 1050
Reinders, F.J., Chairman, Maple Reinders Environmental Ltd., 279
Reinders, Gerry, Manager, Wasaga Beach, 705-429-0412, 722
Reinders, M., President, Maple Engineering & Construction Canada Ltd., 279
Reinders, Mike, President, Maple Reinders Environmental Ltd., 279
Reinert, Richard, Manager, Environmental Services, Belleville, 706
Reinhart, Ellen, Contact, Wildlife Preservation Canada, 1020
Reinhart, Heidi, Ogilvy Renault LLP/S.E.N.C.R.L., s.r.l. - Toronto, 1078
Reis, Darrell, Fire Chief, Perth East, 728
Reiter, Burt, President, Eurovac, 191
Reiter, Charlie, Manager, Eurovac, 191
Reitzel, Brian, Councillor, Kingston, 712
Relton, Chris, Director, Invensys Systems Canada Inc., 246
Rémillard, Gil, Counsel, Fraser Milner Casgrain S.E.N.C.R.L./LLP, 1084
Rempel, George, President/CEO, TetrES Consultants Inc., 391
Rempel, Roger, Associate, TetrES Consultants Inc., 391
Rempel, Sharon, Founder & Project Manager, Garden Institute of Alberta, 922
Renaud, Albert, President/CEO, Ainsworth Inc., 74
Renaud, Eleanor, Elizabethtown-Kitley, 613-275-2091, 725
Renaud, Fernande, Responsable, Périodiques, La Cité Collégiale, 1151
Renaud, Guy, Directeur général adjoint, Québec, 740
Renaud, Jean-Pierre, Trésorier, Granby, 450-776-8287, 735
Renaud, Mark, Deputy Mayor & Councillor, Tillsonburg, 721
Renaud, Michael, Vice-President, The Lowe-Martin Group, 392
Renaud, Ray, LaSalle, 713
Renaud, Sophie, Directrice, Université du Québec INRS - Institut Armand-Frappier, 1169
Renaud, Sophie, Responsable, Université du Québec Institut national de la recherche scientifiq, 1181
Renaud, Tom, Supervisor, Public Works, Petawawa, 717
Renfer, Andre, Asst. Manager, Technisol Environnement, 388
Renick, J. James, Renick, Jim Law Office, 1068
Rennehan, George, Vice-President, Nova Scotia Swordfish Fishermen's Association, 969
Renner, Rob, Minister, 568
Rennie, Elizabeth, Williams Lake Campus Librarian, Williams Lake Campus, 1121
Rennie, Nancy, Hydrogeologist, W.B. Beatty & Associates, 415
Renouf, Charlie, Corner Brook, 693
Renton, Darin R., Partner, Stikeman Elliott LLP - Toronto, 1080
Renwick, Ron L., General Manager, Irrigation Canal Power Co-operative Ltd., 248
Reny, Gilles, Grondin, Poudrier, Bernier, 1087
Repa, Ed, Director, National Solid Wastes Management Association, 958
Resch, Peter, Assessment Librarian, University of Regina Library, 1189
Ressler, Bill, Chair, North Forty Mile Regional Waste Management Services Commission, 758
Restau, Ed, Sales Manager, Phason Electronics, 322
Retter, Bert, Manager, Eurovac, 191
Reu, G., Central Elgin, 724
Reum, Rod, President, Altek Power Corporation, 81
Revill, Alan, Chief Building Inspector, South Frontenac, 730
Rew, Paul, President, Rubicon Environmental Inc., 354
Rey, Christelle, Contact, Promosalons Canada, 335
Reycraft, Doug, Middlesex, 701
Reyes, Katrina, Heenan Blaikie LLP - Toronto, 1076
Reynard, Barry, Director, Dawson Creek, 250-784-3605, 680
Reynolds, Archie, General Manager, Norjohn Transfer System Limited, 305
Reynolds, Bill, Division Business Manager, Engineered Air, 180

Reynolds, Harry, Vice-President, International Association for Bear Research & Management, 934
Reynolds, Jane, Chief Administrative Officer, Kawartha Lakes, 711
Reynolds, Jennifer, Director, Community Services, Milton, 714
Reynolds, John D., Lang Michener LLP - Vancouver, 1060
Reynolds, R. Bruce, Partner, Borden Ladner Gervais LLP - Toronto, 1074
Reynolds, Stephen, Division Head, Culture & Recreation, Pickering, 905-420-4620, 718
Rhea, Pelides, Trade Commissioner, 767
Rheault, Dan, Engineering & New Product Development, Maritime Geothermal Ltd., 280
Rhodes, Rick, Hydro One, 236
Rhodes, Terry, Supervisor, Westburne Canada, 428
Rhong Zhou, Jenny, Library Technician, Saskatchewan Forest Centre, 1187
Rhyno, Art, Head, Systems Department, University of Windsor, 1165
Ribeiro, Sara C., Corp. Administrator, Central Saanich, 686
Ribière, Michelle, Bibliothécaire, CÉGEP de Sainte-Foy, 1178
Ricchetti, Leonard, McMillan Binch Mendelsohn - Toronto, 1077
Ricci, Tony M., Chief Financial Officer, EmerGeo Solutions Inc., 176
Ricciardi, Nicola, Field Engineer, National Instruments Canada, 298
Ricciardi, Savio, Vice-President, Racan Carrier, 341
Rice, David, Counsel, Miller Thomson LLP - Vancouver, 1062
Rice, Garth, Brandon, 689
Rice, James, Manager, Vernon, 685
Rice, Kerri, Manager, Area Recreation, Tecumseh, 720
Rice, Richard M., D'Arcy & Deacon LLP, 1063
Rice, T.J., Manager, V.J. Rice Concrete Ltd., 408
Rice, V.J., President, V.J. Rice Concrete Ltd., 408
Rich, Bob, Chief Constable, Abbotsford, 604-864-4724, 679
Rich, John R., Partner, Ratcliff & Company LLP, 1057
Richard, A., Director, Moncton / Ville de Moncton, 691
Richard, Cathy, Research Assistant, 614
Richard, Denyse, Deputy Town Clerk, Riverview, 506-387-2043, 692
Richard, Dorothy, Library Technician, Saskatoon Campus Library, 1190
Richard, Frédérik, NI Plastique Inc., 303
Richard, Geneviève, Secrétaire, Société de protection des plantes du Québec, 1005
Richard, Guy, Logiball Inc., 273
Richard, Jennifer, Head, Research Services, Acadia University, 1138
Richard, L., Manager, Port Coquitlam, 683
Richard, Laura Lee, Director, Port Coquitlam, 683
Richard, Le Bars, Second Secretary & Vice-Consul & Sr. Trade Commiss, 767
Richard, Maurice, Maire, Bécancour, 734
Richard, Maurice, Préfet, Bécancour, 747
Richard, Roger, Maire, Victoriaville, 819-758-1571, 746
Richards, Brad, Deputy Mayor & Councillor, Strathroy-Caradoc, 731
Richards, Dave, Office Manager, Trow Consulting Engineers Ltd., 403
Richards, Doug, General Manager, Flowserve Inc., 197
Richards, Ed, President, Engine Control Systems, 180
Richards, Greg, President, Metallurgy & Materials Society of the Canadian Institute of Minin, 954
Richards, Joe, Manager, Veolia ES Canada Industrial Services Inc., 411
Richards, Lisa, Ritch Durnford, Lawyers, 1067
Richards, Michael D., D'Arcy & Deacon LLP, 1063
Richards, Pam, Manager, St Michael's Hospital, 1161
Richards, Sarah, Manager, Canadian Hydrogen & Fuel Cell Association, 871
Richards, Steve, President, UniFold Shelters Ltd., 405
Richardson, Adam, Technical Marketing Manager, Intersciences Inc., 246
Richardson, Cynthia, Director, 518
Richardson, Dan, General Counsel, Environmental Bankers Association, 911
Richardson, Dana, Interim Deputy Minister, 630
Richardson, David, President, Precisioneering Ltd., 331
Richardson, Donna, Associate University Librarian, Sexton Design & Technology Library, 1136
Richardson, Douglas, Executive Director, Association of American Geographers, 834
Richardson, Douglas, Partner, Stikeman Elliott LLP - Calgary, 1054
Richardson, Faye, Director, Leisure Services, Georgina, 709

Richardson, Francis, Mayor, Meaford, 519-538-5998, 700, 727
Richardson, Harold, District Manager, BFI Canada Inc., 106
Richardson, Ian, Executive Vice-President, Conestoga-Rovers & Associates, 149
Richardson, J. Mark, Lang Michener LLP - Toronto, 1077
Richardson, Jim, Manager, Westburne Canada, 427
Richardson, John L., President, Premier Plastics Ltd., 331
Richardson, Karen, Program Manager, 525
Richardson, Mark, Sec.-Manager, Canadian Council on Ecological Areas, 865
Richardson, Matt, Councillor, North Perth, 715
Richardson, Peter, Sales Manager, Trecan Combustion Ltd., 401
Richardson, Ron, Service Engineer, Folio Instruments Inc., 199
Richardson, Stephen, Associate Deputy Minister, 526
Richardson, Stephen, General Manager, TRACC (NB), 400
Richardson, Terry, Manager, Harris & Roome Supply Limited, 226
Richardson, W. John, Exec. Vice-President, LGL Limited Environmental Research Associates, 271
Richelhoff, Jerald, Vice-President, Health & Safety Conference Society of Alberta, 927
Richer, Michel, Directeur, Sherbrooke, 819-821-5514, 744
Richer, Pierrette, Bibliothécaire, Bibliothèque centrale, 1170
Richer, Yves, Président, SPG Hydro International Inc., 375
Richer La Flèche, Erik, Associé, Stikeman Elliott LLP - Montréal, 1087
Richet, Bruce, Sr. Vice-President, UMA Group Ltd., 405
Richmond, Al, Chairperson, Cariboo, 677
Richmond, Dave, General Manager, Waste Management of Canada, 418
Richter, Kim, Langley, 687
Rick, W. John, Managing Partner, Rick & Associates, 1071
Rick Zanussi, Rick, Chair, Parry Sound, 728
Rickard, Don, President, Overwatch Consulting, 315
Ricker, Don, Haldimand, 700
Ricker, Gary, Supervisor, West Lincoln, 732
Ricketts, Bill, President/COO, Satlantic, 358
Rickford, Greg, Parliamentary Secretary for Official Languages, 519
Rico, Melissa A., Stones Carbert Waite Wells LLP, 1054
Riddell, Archie, Project Assessment Director, 578
Riddell, J., Director, Community Design & Development Services, Guelph, 710
Riddell, M. Gatz, Executive Vice-President, American Association of Bovine Practitioners, 822
Ridley, Kevin, President, EMP Environmental Management & Protection Corporation, 177
Ridley, Michael, Chief Librarian, University of Guelph, 1140
Riediker, Martin, Chief Technology Officer, CIBA Spécialités Chimiques Canada inc., 141
Riel, Alain, Gatineau, 735
Riel, Keith G., Peterborough, 718
Rielly, Brian, Executive Vice-President, Comstock Canada Ltd., 148
Riemer, Pierce, Director General, World Petroleum Congress, 1023
Riendeau, Yvan, Saint-Constant, 742
Rierden, Andi, Vice-President, Annapolis Field Naturalist Society, 828
Rifkind, Lewis, Coordinator, Yukon Conservation Society, 1024
Rigby, Sheldon, Supervisor, New Westminster, 604-517-5416, 682
Rigby, Stephen, President, 514
Rigby, Tim, Niagara, 702
Riggs, Bert, Archivist, Centre for Newfoundland Studies, 1131
Riggs, Q.C., Christopher G., Partner, Hicks Morley Hamilton Stewart Storie LLP, 1076
Rigney, B.Sc., MBA, Donald, Mayor, Sturgeon County, 780-921-3041, 670
Rilett, John, Vice-President, Climate Change Central, 144
Riley-Arenburg, Catherine, Office Manager, Acorus Restoration Native Plant Nursery, 67
Rimanic, Leo, Vice-President, Versatech Products Inc., 412
Rimbaud, Pascal, Firwin Corporation, 196
Rimer, Philip M., Fraser Milner Casgrain LLP - Ottawa, 1070
Rimes, Dave, Leader, Airdrie, 403-948-8402, 670
Rimmer, Brian, Supervisor, Parkland County, 670
Rimmer, Leah D., Boyne Clarke, 1067
Rinaldis, Angela, Associate, Miller Thomson LLP - Toronto, 1078
Rinaldo, Noella C., Timmins, 721
Rincón Mejía, Eduardo A., Secretary, International Solar Energy Society, 944
Rindahl, Bob, Fire Chief, Swift Current, 306-778-2760, 755
Rinfret, Francis, Varennes, 746
Ring, Grant, President/CEO, NorthPoint Energy Solutions, 307

Executive Name Index

Ringuette, Manon, Insituform Technologies Ltd. - Montréal, 242
Rink, Kimron D., President, ECO-TEK Ecological Technologies Inc., 171
Rink, Perry, Project Manager, ECO-TEK Ecological Technologies Inc., 171
Rintjema, Dianne, Lincoln, 713
Rintoul, Neil, Huron, 701
Riopel, Christian, Directeur, La Vallée-de-l'Or, 748
Riopel, Jacques, Préfet, Abitibi, 746
Riopel, Jean-Marie, Responsable SMTE, CÉGEP de Sorel-Tracy, 1186
Riopel, Ray, Director, BC Air Filter Ltd., 103
Riopelle, Robert M., Riopelle Griener Professional Corporation, 1070
Rioux, Rhonda, Directrice, Québec, 418-641-6181, 740
Rioux, Robert, Saint-Jérôme, 450-438-2057, 743
Rioux, Yvon, Directeur, Amos, 733
Ripley, Bob, City Treasurer, Orillia, 716
Ripley, Goro, Systems Librarian, Trent University, 1153
Ripley, Herb, President, Hyperspectral Data International Inc., 237
Rirchardson, A.C., President, InspecTech, 243
Risling, Rod, Manager, Red Deer, 674
Risse, Nicole, Coordinator, Ontario Sustainable Energy Association, 980
Rissling, Lois, District Manager, BFI Canada Inc., 106
Ritacca, Gaspare, Manager, Planning & Development, King, 726
Ritcey, Joan, Head, Centre for Newfoundland Studies, 1131
Ritchie, Cathie, Clerk, Lanark, 701
Ritchie, Erika, Environmental Manager, PINTER & Associates Ltd., 325
Ritchie, Jeff, Senior Manager, Nanaimo, 681
Ritchie, Perry, Springwater, 730
Ritchie, Rachael, Head, 596
Ritchie, Reginald C., Chair, Annapolis County, 696
Ritchie, Richard, Manager, Sandwell Engineering Inc., 357
Ritchie, Tim, Sales Contact, Rotork Controls (Canada) Ltd., 352
Ritchie, CGA, Wayne, Director, Financial Services, Owen Sound, 717
Ritchie, Q.C., Walter L., Thompson Dorfman Sweatman LLP, 1064
Ritchot, Renee D., Alexander Holburn Beaudin & Lang, LLP, 1057
Ritsma, Martin, Stratford, 720
Rittenhouse, Steve, Canadian Safety Equipment Inc., 125
Rittenhouse, Tiffany, Canadian Safety Equipment Inc., 125
Ritvo, Harriet, President, American Society for Environmental History, 824
Ritz, John, Fire Chief, Wilmot, 732
Rivard, Marc, Exec. Vice-President, Genivar, 207
Rivard, Martin, Director, Bétonel Limitée, 106
Rivard, Yves, Director, By-law Enforcement, Clarence-Rockland, 708
Rivera, Soraya, Manager, Association of Power Producers of Ontario, 837
Riverin, Johanne, Vice-présidente, Société québécoise de récupération et de recyclage, 1006
Rivers, Nelson, President, Avenue Industrial Supply Co. Ltd., 98
Rivest, André, Greater Sudbury / Grand Sudbury, 710
Rivette, André, Cornwall, 708
Riviere, John L., President/CEO, Metafix, 287
Rivière, Richard, Directeur, Westburne Canada, 427
Rizzo, Sam, Lennox Industries (Canada) Ltd., 267
Roach, Charles C., Roach, Schwartz & Associates, Barristers & Solicitors, 1079
Roach, Gregory, Asst. Deputy Minister, 610
Roach, Kikélola, Roach, Schwartz & Associates, Barristers & Solicitors, 1079
Roach, Omar, ADI Group Inc., 68
Roark, Tim, Treasurer, Environmental Health Foundation of Canada, 912
Robb, George, President/Project Manager, Robb Engineering Ltd., 347
Robb, Gordon, President, COGENCanada, 146
Robbins, D. Richard, Cox and Palmer - St. John's, 1065
Robbins, David, Woodward & Company, 1063
Robbins, G.H., Director, Inco Technical Services Limited, 239
Robbins, Jeff, Environmental Manager, Zell Oilfield Service Ltd., 436
Robbins, Jim, President, Electronic Warfare Associates - Canada, Ltd., 175
Robbins, Larry Mansfield, Chatham-Kent, 724
Robbins, Ted, Senior Manager, Capital Regional District, 250-360-3061, 676
Robbins, Tobin, Partner, Heenan Blaikie LLP - Vancouver, 1060

Robblee, William, President, Greystone Energy Systems Inc., 218
Roberge, Alain, Bibliothécaire en chef, Université de Moncton, 1129
Roberge, Claude L., President & CEO, North Safety Products Canada, 306
Roberge, Jason, Branch Manager, CenturyVallen, 137
Roberge, Johanne, Technicienne, Collège Laflèche, 1186
Robert, François, Conseiller, Jacques-Bizard, Montréal, 738
Robert, Marcel, Maire, Sorel-Tracy, 745
Robert, Nicole, Préfète, Le Haut-St-François, 749
Robert, Yvonne L., Administrator-Clerk, Elizabethtown-Kitley, 725
Robert, Ing., dsa., André-P., Directeur-général, Régie d'assainissement des eaux de la région sherbrookoise, 759
Roberts, Brian E., Partner, Borden Ladner Gervais LLP - Calgary, 1050
Roberts, Brian G., President, BGR Oilfield Services Incorporated, 107
Roberts, Carter S., President, World Wildlife Fund - USA, 1023
Roberts, Cliff, General Manager, Chartwell Consultants Ltd., 138
Roberts, Corey, Brandon, 689
Roberts, Ed, President, Conestoga-Rovers & Associates, 149
Roberts, Florence, Whitehorse, 755
Roberts, Gayle, Admin. Assistant, 638
Roberts, Gord, Elecsar Engineering Co. Ltd., 174
Roberts, Gord, Geophysicist, Fugro Airborne Surveys, 202
Roberts, Gord, Vice-President/Engineering Manager, Elecsar Engineering Co. Ltd., 174
Roberts, Heather, Librarian, Newfoundland & Labrador Dept. of Health & Community Services, 1132
Roberts, Jayne R., Parlee McLaws LLP, 1053
Roberts, Jeff, Manager, Hi-Point Industries (1991) Ltd., 231
Roberts, Jeff, Vice-President, MK Plastics Corp., 291
Roberts, Julia, Manager, Dillon Consulting Ltd., 163
Roberts, Kathryn, Coordinator, Collection Services, Bora Laskin Law Library, 1156
Roberts, Liz, Superintendent, 584
Roberts, Mark, Director, 664
Roberts, Richard, President, Praxis Inc., 330
Roberts, Rory M., President, In Tech Risk Management Inc., 239
Roberts, Susan, Director, 602
Roberts Jones, Bonnie, Heenan Blaikie LLP - Toronto, 1076
Roberts Thorne, Wendy E., President, Biophilia Inc., 109
Roberts, Q.C., Darrell W., Counsel, Miller Thomson LLP - Vancouver, 1062
Robertson, Allan, President, Halifax Field Naturalists, 927
Robertson, Andrew R., Partner, Macleod Dixon LLP, 1052
Robertson, Andy, Exec. Chair, President & CEO, InfoMine Inc., 241
Robertson, Angus, Deputy Minister, 664
Robertson, Bill, Manager, Newalta Corporation, 301
Robertson, Bill, Mayor, Okotoks, 674
Robertson, Bill, Partner, Servicestat Ltd., 364
Robertson, Bob, Vice-President, Diagnostix Ltd., 163
Robertson, Craig, Manager, Wiebe Environmental Services Inc., 431
Robertson, Craig, President, Environmental Services Association of Alberta, 912
Robertson, D., Lynn Canyon Ecology Centre, 950
Robertson, Dale, Contact, Paracel Laboratories Ltd., 318
Robertson, Dale, President, Enerscan Consultants Limited, 180
Robertson, Dave, Manager, Okotoks, 403-938-8952, 674
Robertson, Doug, Chief Building Official, Wilmot, 732
Robertson, Doug, Superintendent, Public Works Department, Sarnia, 719
Robertson, Earl, President, L&K International Training, 261
Robertson, Ed, Assistant Director, Victoria, 250-361-0457, 685
Robertson, Geoff, FCX NH Valves, 194
Robertson, George, Huron, 701
Robertson, George, Mayor, South Huron, 730
Robertson, Glenn, CAO, Mission, 604-820-3704, 687
Robertson, Grant, Chair, British Columbia Bottle Depot Association, 847
Robertson, Gregor, Metro Vancouver, 678
Robertson, Gregor, Mayor, Vancouver, 604-873-7621, 685
Robertson, Guy, Librarian, Library (Vancouver), 1118
Robertson, Helen Lee, Liaison/Document Delivery, Health Sciences Library, 1101
Robertson, Hugh, Director, Chem Solv, 139
Robertson, Ian, CEO, Algonquin Power Income Fund, 78
Robertson, Ian, Principal, Robertson Environmental Services Ltd., 348
Robertson, Jack, District Fire Chief (St. Andrews South), St. Andrews, 204-757-4748, 690
Robertson, Jessie, Library Technician, Cornwall Campus, 1140

Robertson, Marie, Directrice, La Cité Collégiale, 1151
Robertson, Marlene, Librarian, Nexen Inc., 1102
Robertson, Peter, Principal, Chem Solv, 139
Robertson, Ross, Branch Manager, CenturyVallen, 137
Robertson, Sandy, CEO, Canada Water Supply Ltd., 123
Robertson, Q.C., Reynold A., Robertson Stromberg Pedersen LLP, 1091
Robey, Herbert L., Contact, Cyanide Destruct Systems Inc., 155
Robiaee, Al, Contact, A&A Environmental Consultants Inc., 63
Robichaud, Anne-Marie, Secrétaire, Centre québécois du droit de l'environnement, 894
Robichaud, Carmel, Minister, 594
Robichaud, Christian, Vice-President, Levac Robichaud Leclerc Associates Ltd., 270
Robichaud, Karen, Treasurer, Association of Consulting Engineering Companies - New Brunswick, 835
Robichaud, Lynn, Senior Coorindator, Environmental Services, Burlington, 707
Robichaud, Paul, Minister Responsible, Business New Brunswick, 596, 592
Robicheau, Claire, Comptoir de prêt, Université Sainte-Anne, 1135
Robillard, Denis, Laval, 736
Robillard, Diane, Directrice, Sorel-Tracy, 745
Robillard, Lise, Library Assistant, ECORC Plant Research Library, 1150
Robillard, Paul, Principal/Treasurer, Marbek Resource Consultants Ltd., 280
Robin, Hockaday, Specialist, Soil & Water Conservation Society, 1009
Robin, Jackie, Director, Ag-West Bio Inc., 72
Robin, Jackie, Director, Communications, Ag-WestBio Inc., 1189
Robins, David L., Sutts, Strosberg LLP, 1082
Robins, E.W., President/CEO, Cartier Chemicals Ltd., 130
Robins, Michael, Senior Vice-President, Restructuring, 511
Robinson, Andy J., President, Robinson Consultants Inc., 348
Robinson, Art, President, Sick Building Solutions, 366
Robinson, Bill, Commissioner, Engineering & Public Works, Vaughan, 722
Robinson, Bill, Sec.-Treas., Foothills Regional Services, 757
Robinson, Bill W.L., South Frontenac, 730
Robinson, Brent, MacPherson Leslie & Tyerman LLP - Saskatoon, 1090
Robinson, Carla, Administrative Director, Sea Shepherd Conservation Society - USA, 1003
Robinson, Charles, Manager, Worldware Enterprises Ltd., 433
Robinson, Christine, Chief Administrative Officer & Clerk, West Grey, 732
Robinson, D.S., Chief Administrative Officer, Cobourg, 708
Robinson, Darcy, Manager, Westburne Canada, 428
Robinson, Dusty L., McDougall Gauley, 1090
Robinson, Eric, Minister, 587
Robinson, Georges, Repentigny, 450-654-9746, 740
Robinson, Gilles, Magog, 819-843-2364, 737
Robinson, Gord, Local Councillor, Clarington, 724
Robinson, Jaye, Toronto, 721
Robinson, John, President, New Brunswick Soil & Crop Improvement Association, 962
Robinson, Joy, Office Manager, Brim Pumps & Systems Ltd., 116
Robinson, Keith, Superintendent, Chilliwack, 604-702-4086, 680
Robinson, Lawrence (Lanny) N., Alexander Holburn Beaudin & Lang, LLP, 1057
Robinson, Lee, Manager, Infrastructure Services, Brant, 698
Robinson, Lisa J., Davis LLP - Vancouver, 1074, 1059
Robinson, Lucy, Manager, Recycling Council of Ontario, 993
Robinson, Martin, President, Anachemia Canada Inc., 85
Robinson, Michael, President, Robinson Solutions, 348
Robinson, Nika, Laing Michener LLP - Vancouver, 1060
Robinson, Peter, CEO, David Suzuki Foundation, 917
Robinson, Peter J., President & CEO, Integrated Resource Management, 244
Robinson, Ralph, Town Councillor, Oakville, 715
Robinson, Rick, Commission Manager, Lethbridge Regional Water Services Commission, 757
Robinson, Rob, Principal, Stantec Inc., 378
Robinson, Ron, Branch Manager, Totten Sims Hubicki Associates Ltd., 399
Robinson, Ron, Fire Chief, Medicine Hat, 403-502-8006, 673
Robinson, Ron, President, R.G. Robinson & Associates (Barrie) Ltd., 340
Robinson, Ron R., President, Ron Robinson Limited, 351
Robinson, S. Eric, President/CEO, SPI Industries Inc., 375
Robinson, Selina, Coquitlam, 680
Robinson, Q.C., Christopher C., McInnes Cooper, 1067

Executive Name Index

Robison, Brett, Vice-Presient, Sick Building Solutions, 366
Robitaille, Alain, Associé, Langlois Kronström Desjardins, 1088
Robitaille, Anne, Responsable des acquisitions, Université du Québec Institut national de la recherche scientifiq, 1181
Robitaille, Anne, Technician, INRS - Université du Québec, CGC - Québec, 1179
Robitaille, Charles-Antoine, Gowling Lafleur Henderson S.E.N.C.R.L./LLP, 1084
Robitaille, Jean-Marc, Maire, Terrebonne, 745
Robitaille, Jean-Marc, Préfet, Les Moulins, 750
Robitaille, Louis, Contact, Plastrec Inc., 326
Robitaille, Steeve, Associé, Stikeman Elliott LLP - Montréal, 1087
Roblin, Andrew, President/CEO, Cimatec Environmental Engineering Inc., 141
Robson, Dean, Director, Swift Current, 755
Robson, Joan, Councillor, Halton Hills, 710
Robson, Laurie M., Partner, Borden Ladner Gervais LLP - Calgary, 1050
Robson, Patrick, Commissioner, Integrated Community Planning, Niagara, 702
Rocca, Onorio, President, RMS Instruments Ltd., 347
Rocca, Tony, Manager, Westburne Canada, 429
Rocchetti, Paul, President, Via-Sat Data Systems, 413
Rocchi, Sarah, VP, Opus International Consultants (Canada) Ltd., 314
Roche, Michael V., Alexander Holburn Beaudin & Lang, LLP, 1057
Rochefort, Bob, Division Sales Manager, Engineered Air, 180
Rocheleau, René, Les Contrôles PROVAN Associés Inc., 268
Rochelle, Anna, Director, Recycling Council of British Columbia, 993
Rochette, Louis, Partner, Lavery, de Billy - Québec, 1088
Rochon, Dianne, Responsable, CÉGEP d'André-Laurendeau, 1169
Rochon, Jean-Marc, Salaberry-de-Valleyfield, 450-377-2774, 744
Rochon, Michael, Principal, Cogent Environmental Solutions Ltd., 146
Rochon, Yves, Sales Manager, Nortec S.G.S. Inc., 306
Rock, Sabrina, Manager, 521
Rockström, Johna, Executive Director, Stockholm Environment Institute, 1010
Rockwell, Alan T., McInnes Cooper, 1064
Rockwell, F.S., Medical Health Officer, North Cowichan, 687
Rockwood, Linda, Director, Emergency Medical Services, Perth, 703
Rockwood, Paul, Director, Port Moody, 683
Rodenberg, Frances, Honorary Secretary, Animal Welfare Foundation of Canada, 827
Rodey, J., Chief Administrative Officer, St. Clair, 729
Rodger, J. Mark, Senior Partner, Borden Ladner Gervais LLP - Toronto, 1074
Rodger, R.J., President/CEO, Wainbee Limited, 415
Rodgers, Kirk, Office Manager, Golder Associates Ltd., 215
Rodgerson, Maurice (Moe), Chair & CEO, 641
Rodic, Vera, Information Specialist, G.P. Lewis Library, 1145
Rodier, Ryan, MacPherson Leslie & Tyerman LLP - Saskatoon, 1090
Rodin, Dan, Chief Financial Officer, Prince Rupert, 684
Rodney, Steve, Contact, Mansfield & Rodney Printing Ltd., 279
Rodney, RN, PhD, Patricia, President, Canadian Bioethics Society, 860
Rodricks, Larry, Vice President, Sonic Environmental Solutions Inc., 373
Rodrigue, Claude, President, Rodrigue Métal Ltée, 350
Rodrigue, Marcel, Directeur, Lévis, 418-839-2002, 736
Rodrigue, Pierre, Rouyn-Noranda, 741
Rodrigues, Peter, Durham, 699
Rodrigues, Peter, Regional Councillor, Pickering, 718
Rodrique, Patrick, Director, MICCA Paints Inc., 288
Roe, Brent, Associate University Librarian, York University Libraries, 1164
Roe, Kelly, Manager, Malnar Industries Ltd., 279
Roebuck, L. David, Partner, Heenan Blaikie LLP - Toronto, 1076
Roehler, Mark, Principal, LEHDER Environmental Services Ltd., 267
Roeland, Grant, CFO, Central Kootenay, 677
Roelfson, Brad, Manager, Guelph-Eramosa, 725
Roelofsen, Patrick, Vice-President, Diagnostic Engineering Inc., 163
Rogachevsky, Bram, Donovan & Company, 1059
Rogan, W.A., County Administrator, Grande Prairie No. 1, 669
Rogers, Ben, President, Canadian Petroleum Law Foundation, 882
Rogers, Brian, Klohn Crippen Berger Ltd., 258
Rogers, Brian, Chief Financial Officer, North Bay, 715
Rogers, Carolyn, President & CEO, Hydroxyl Systems Inc., 237
Rogers, Cindy, Manager, North Vancouver, 604-990-2217, 688
Rogers, Dan, Mayor, Prince George, 683
Rogers, Dave, General Manager, Da-Lee Dust Control, 156
Rogers, David, Chief Building Official, Trent Hills, 731
Rogers, David, President/Founder, BCHazman Management Ltd., 103
Rogers, David N., Gilbert McGloan Gillis, 1065
Rogers, Gerald, Deputy Mayor & Councillor, Grey, 700
Rogers, James, By-Law Officer, Forest Conservation, Northumberland, 705-799-2470, 702
Rogers, James E., Chairman, President & CEO, World Business Council for Sustainable Development, 1021
Rogers, Karen M., Partner, Heenan Blaikie S.E.N.C.R.L/SRL, 1084
Rogers, Linda, Collections Librarian, Kwantlen University College, 1113
Rogers, R. Ben, Partner, Ogilvy Renault LLP/S.E.N.C.R.L., s.r.l. - Calgary, 1053
Rogers, Wayne, Branch Manager, CenturyVallen, 136
Rohde, Colleen, City Clerk, Port Moody, 604-469-4505, 683
Rojas, Alukie, Deputy Minister, 618
Rojek, Tony, President, T.D. ThermoDesign, 386
Rojo, Alejandra, President, Port of Entry Inc., 328
Roland, Floyd, Minister, 605
Roland, Floyd K., Minister Responsible, 608
Roland, Rossi, Trade Commissioner, 767
Rolfe, Derrick, Managing Director, Environmental R&D Capital Corporation, 185
Rolland, Emmanuelle, Partner, Borden Ladner Gervais LLP - Montréal, 1083
Rollings, Jeffrey, Planning Tech, Long Environmental Consultants, 273
Rollins, Caron, Associate Law Librarian, Diana M. Priestly Law Library, 1120
Rollo, Sean, Treasurer, Canadian Pest Management Association, 882
Rolnick, Abe, President & CEO, Scintrex Ltd., 360
Rolston, Garry, President & CEO, Lapp-Hancock Associates Limited, 264
Roman, Ann, Librarian, Akerley Campus, 1135
Romanick, Dana L., Alexander Holburn Beaudin & Lang, LLP, 1057
Romanko, Patti, Instructional Services Librarian, Douglas College, 1114
Romanow, Ivan, Director, Sonepar Canada, 373
Rombouts, Tony, Manager, Waterous Power Systems, 423
Romeike, H., Manager, Proctor & Gamble Inc., 333
Romeo, Calderon, Trade Commissioner, 767
Romer, S., Office Manager, Power Grow Systems Inc., 329
Ronan, Paul, Executive Director, Ontario Parks Association, 976
Rondeau, Jim, Minister, 590
Rondeau, Pierre, Préfet, La Vallée-de-la-Gatineau, 748
Ronning Mains, Cheryl, Librarian Chief, Information Services, Western Reg, Canadian Agriculture Library - Lethbridge, 1108
Ronson, Peter, Contact, Toromont Energy Ltd., 398
Roome, Rebecca, Deputy Minister, 598
Rooney, Kevin, Partner, Heenan Blaikie LLP - Toronto, 1076
Rooney, Mike, Contact, Montréal Gem & Mineral Club, 955
Rooney, Steve, Commercial Solutions Inc., 147
Roop, Ateesh, Office Manager, Golder Associates Ltd., 214
Roos, Hank, President, Central Valley Naturalists, 893
Root, Mayne, Executive Director, Alberta Motor Transport Association, 818
Roozen, Harold A., Chairman/CEO, CCI Thermal Technologies Inc., 133
Rop, John, Treasurer, Fort Saskatchewan, 672
Roppel, Randy, Councillor, Kincardine, 519-368-7792, 726
Rorison, Al, President, Pyrotech Mfg. Corp., 337
Rosa, Orlando M., Wishart Law Firm LLP, 1071
Rosalba, Cruz, Trade Commissioner, 768
Rosati, Gino, York, 705
Rosati, Gino, Regional Councillor, Vaughan, 722
Rose, B.R., City Solicitor, Burnaby, 604-294-7382, 679
Rose, Bonnie, President, Canadian Standards Association, 888
Rose, C. Brian, President, Archaeological Institute of America, 828
Rose, Chris, Principal, Rose Mechanical Water Systems Inc., 351
Rose, Dave, Manager, Harris & Roome Supply Limited, 226
Rose, Don, General Counsel & Corporate Secretary, 574
Rose, Elizabeth, Library Technician, Kirkland Lake Campus, 1143
Rose, Frank, Treasurer, Newfoundland Horticultural Society, 963
Rose, James, Supervisor, Westburne Canada, 426
Rose, Mark, General Manager, Layfield Geosynthetics & Industrial Fabrics Ltd., 265
Rose, Mark, Librarian, Intergovernmental Committee on Urban & Regional Research (ICURR), 1158
Rose, Martin, Director, British Council - Canada, 851
Rose, Mary, Orangeville, 716
Rose, Ramona, Head, Archives/Special Collections, University of Northern British Columbia, 1115
Rose, Stephen, Director, 664
Rose, Steven, Director, Malroz Engineering Inc., 279
Rose, Tammy, Manager, Drinking Water Services, Ottawa, 716
Rose, Tom, President/CEO, Layfield Geosynthetics & Industrial Fabrics Ltd., 265
Rose, R.P.F., Craig D., Davis LLP - Edmonton, 1055
Roseblade, Leslie, Quinte West, 718
Rosehart, Chris (Chrissy), Councillor, Tillsonburg, 721
Rosen, Eric Bertil, President, KMW Systems Inc., 258
Rosen, Gregg, Vice-President, Kimco Steel Sales Limited, 257
Rosen, Hillel W., Davies Ward Phillips & Vineberg S.E.N.C.R.L., s.r.l., 1083
Rosen, Lorna, City Manager, Fort Saskatchewan, 672
Rosen, Michael, President, Tree Canada Foundation, 1013
Rosenberg, David M., Rosenberg & Rosenberg, 1062
Rosenberg, John, Manager, Salmon Arm, 684
Rosenberg, Morris, Deputy Minister, 529
Rosenberg, P.S., Rosenberg & Rosenberg, 1062
Rosenberg, Sheryl A., Thompson Dorfman Sweatman LLP, 1064
Rosenbloom, Donald J., Rosenbloom & Aldridge, 1062
Rosenstein, Mark M., Associé, Lapointe Rosenstein Marchand Melançon, 1085
Rosenthal, Peter M., Roach, Schwartz & Associates, Barristers & Solicitors, 1079
Rosenthal, Susan, Davies Howe Partners, 1074
Ross, Adele, Video Librarian, Ontario Safety League, 1145
Ross, Alan L., Partner, Borden Ladner Gervais LLP - Calgary, 1050
Ross, Alex, Sales, Busch Vacuum Technics Inc., 119
Ross, Amanda, Librarian, Outreach Services, Bracken Health Sciences Library, 1142
Ross, Bernie, CEO, Frank T. Ross & Sons Ltd., 201
Ross, Blake, President, Frank T. Ross & Sons Ltd., 201
Ross, Brian D., Fulton & Company LLP, Lawyers & Trade-Mark Agents, 1056
Ross, Cathy, Coordinator, Information Resources, Talisman Energy Inc., 1103
Ross, Cyrus, Howard Marten Fluid Technologies Inc., 234
Ross, Dan, Assistant Deputy Minister, 545
Ross, Dave, Contact, FLIR Systems, Inc., 197
Ross, David J., Lang Michener LLP - Vancouver, 1060
Ross, Douglas, Manager, BVA Systems Ltd./Vibro-Acoustics, 119
Ross, George, Deputy Minister, 635
Ross, Ian, Manager, Westburne Canada, 426
Ross, John, President, Sun Ross Energy Systems Ltd., 382
Ross, Ken, Sales Manager, MakLoc Buildings Inc., 279
Ross, Laura, Legislative Secretary to the Minister of Health, 659
Ross, Linda, Westech Industrial Ltd., 429
Ross, Line, Directrice générale, Matane, 750
Ross, Lloyd, President, Demers MetalFab Inc., 160
Ross, Lynn, Sr. Consultant, MWA Consultants, 295
Ross, M. David, Associate, Hicks Morley Hamilton Stewart Storie LLP, 1076
Ross, Marc, President, Ross Healthcare, Inc., 352
Ross, Mike, Midland, 713
Ross, N. Michael, Corporate Contact, Ross Healthcare, Inc., 352
Ross, Nancy, Chair, British Columbia Food Technolgists, 848
Ross, Patricia, Abbotsford, 679
Ross, Patricia, Chair, Fraser Valley, 677
Ross, Robert, Director, Mission, 604-820-3751, 687
Ross, Robert, Vice-President, Waste Services (CA) Inc., 420
Ross, Roger, Manager, Westburne Canada, 428
Ross, Stephen R., Partner, Miller Thomson LLP - Vancouver, 1062
Ross, William, President & CEO, Sundog Energy Management, 382
Ross, C.A., Judy, Executive Director, 597
Rosser, Doug, President, First Stage Enterprises Inc., 196
Rosset, Jason, President, Accuworx Inc., 66
Rosseth, Lynn, Director, Foodservice & Packaging Institute, 918
Rossi, Dionysios, Borden Ladner Gervais LLP - Vancouver, 1058
Rossi, Mauro, General Manager, Rexdale Disposal Ltd., 346
Rossi, Rocco, Manager, Clearview Packaging Inc., 143
Rossi, Tony, Manager, Konica Minolta Business Solutions (Canada) Inc., 259

1346 GUIDE DES RESSOURCES ENVIRONNEMENTALES CANADIENNES 2011-2012

Executive Name Index

Rossini, Robert, Head of Circulation, Brock University, 1154
Rossini, Roberto, General Manager, Finance & Corporate Services, Hamilton, 711
Ross-Smith, Denny, Executive Director, Small Water Users Association of BC, 1004
Ross-Zuj, Joanne, Mayor, Centre Wellington, 519-846-0213, 724
Ross-Zuj, Joanne, Warden & Councillor, Wellington, 519-846-0213, 705
Rotblott, Howard, Principal, Rotblott & Sons Ltd., 352
Rotenburger, Dale, Branch Manager, CenturyVallen, 137
Roter, George, Co-CEO, Engineers Without Borders, 910
Roth, Barbara, Director, Leisure, Transit & Facilities, Barrie, 706
Roth, Bernie J., Fraser Milner Casgrain LLP - Calgary, 1051
Roth, Dennis B., Ackroyd LLP Barristers & Solicitors, 1054
Roth, Sandra, President, Living Resources Inc., 273
Roth, Wayne, Waterloo, 704
Rotherham, Duncan, Vice-President, ICF International Canada Inc., 238
Rothkop, Rami, Chair, Silva Forest Foundation, 368
Rothschild, David W., Davis LLP - Montréal, 1083
Rotrand, Marvin, Conseiller, Snowdon, Montréal, 738
Rotvold, Marguerite, Chair, Kootenay Boundary, 250-449-2222, 678
Rougeau, Joe, Manager, Westburne Canada, 427
Roughley, Dennis, Simcoe, 704
Rougvie, Carol, Secretariat, International Society for Environmental Epidemiology, 942
Rouleau, Alain, Directeur, Sorel-Tracy, 745
Rouleau, Denis, Vice-Chief of Defence Staff, 545
Rouleau, Jean-François, Sherbrooke, 744
Rounds, Gloria, Library Contact, Northern Lights College, 1112
Rouse, Anderson, Coordinator, Ontario Healthy Communities Coalition, 974
Rouse, Peggy, Clerk, Meaford, 727
Rouse, Shelley, Cascades Recovery Inc., 131
Rousseau, André, Associé, Lapointe Rosenstein Marchand Melançon, 1085
Rousseau, Bernard, Ingénieur Associé, Experts-Conseils BMST inc., 192
Rousseau, Denis, Forestry Technician, Legaré F., Ing. Forestier Conseil, 266
Rousseau, Marie, Marie Rousseau, ING, 280
Rousseau, Michel, Sous-ministre adjoint, 646
Rousseau, Normand, President, GILFAB, 212
Rousseau, Philippe C., Davies Ward Phillips & Vineberg LLP, 1074
Roussel, Céline, Responsable, Services techniques, CÉGEP de Chicoutimi, 1166
Roussel, Lucie F., Mairesse, La Prairie, 450-444-6618, 736
Rousselle, Eugene, Manager, Consolidated Giroux Environment Inc., 150
Rousselle, Yves, Director, Physical Services, Clarence-Rockland, 708
Roussy, Benoît, Sec.-Trés., Régie intermunicipale de gestion des déchets solides de New Richm, 760
Roussy, François, Maire, Gaspé, 735
Roussy, François, Préfet, La Côte-de-Gaspé, 748
Roux-Guindon, Johanne, Library Technician, Ontario Ministry of Northern Development & Mines, 1155
Rouzier, Michael, Bibliothécaire, La Cité Collégiale, 1151
Rowcliffe, Devon, Librarian, Vancouver Community Services Group, 1119
Rowden, Forrest, Cobourg, 708
Rowe, Kenneth C., Executive Chair, IMP Liquid Meters & Petroleum Services, 239
Rowe, Kevin, Librarian, Canadian Forces Northern Area Headquarters, 1133
Rowe, Mae, Councillor, Cape Breton, 695
Rowe, May, Chair, Long Lake Regional Waste Management Commission, 757
Rowell, Greg, Manager, Library Services, Riverview Hospital, 1115
Rowland, Jeff, Fire Chief, Prince George, 250-561-7670, 683
Rowland, Jill, Librarian, Pacific Regional Library, 1118
Rowlands, Gareth, Acting Manager, West Vancouver, 604-985-3500, 689
Rowlands, William A., Lang Michener LLP - Toronto, 1077
Rowney, David, Director, AMEC, 82
Roxburgh, Bruce, Manager, Green Communities Canada, 925
Roy, Bernard, Directeur général, La Vallée-du-Richelieu, 748
Roy, Christiane, Vice-President, Option Environnement Inc., 313
Roy, Christopher, Senior Strategist, Communicopia.Net Internet Inc., 147
Roy, Claude, Directeur, Études, Campus Notre-Dame-de-Foy, 1182

Roy, Daniel (Danny), Bathurst, 506-546-1588, 690
Roy, Denis, President, Vibec International Inc., 413
Roy, Diane, Librarian, Rheinmetall Canada Inc., 1183
Roy, Diane, Regional Sales Manager, Anachemia Canada Inc., 85
Roy, Diane, Sales Manager, Atlantic Packaging Products Ltd., 96
Roy, Doug, President, Roy Northern Environmental Ltd., 353
Roy, Elizabeth, Councillor, Whitby, 723
Roy, François, Directeur, Trois-Rivières, 819-372-4602, 745
Roy, Fred, Technical Sales Manager, Ontario, Epsilon Chemicals Ltd., 189
Roy, Gilles, Président, Electro-Mecanik Inc., 175
Roy, Jean, Chambly, 450-447-6152, 734
Roy, Jean-François, Directeur, Lévis, 418-839-2002, 736
Roy, Jean-Pierre, Coodonnateur, Télé-Université, 1180
Roy, Marcel, Directeur, Québec, 418-641-6240, 740
Roy, Marlene, Information Resources Coordinator, International Institute for Sustainable Development, 1124
Roy, Martin, Pompe Saguenay Enr., 328
Roy, Michel, Directeur général, Abitibi, 746
Roy, Michel, Engineer, Vibec International Inc., 413
Roy, Nicolas, Fraser Milner Casgrain S.E.N.C.R.L./LLP, 1084
Roy, Patrick, Engineering Project Director, Rodrigue Métal Ltée, 350
Roy, Roger, Longueuil, 737
Roy, Roger, Controller, Deschênes Drilling Ltd., 161
Roy, Roger, President, New Brunswick Ground Water Association, 961
Roy, Ron, Operations Manager, Barrington Industrial Services Limited, 102
Roy, Stéphane, Associé, Lapointe Rosenstein Marchand Melançon, 1085
Roy, Suzanne, Mairesse, Sainte-Julie, 450-922-7053, 743
Roy, Suzanne, Préfète, Lajemmerais, 749
Roy Marinelli, Danielle, Mairesse, Lévis, 736
Royal, Danielle, Partner, Stikeman Elliott LLP - Toronto, 1080
Royal, Mark, Clearview, 725
Royce, Diana, Chief Operating Officer & Managing Director, AllerGen NCE Inc., 821
Roy-Diclemente, Tara, East Gwillimbury, 708
Royer, Gaetan, City Manager, Port Moody, 683
Royer, Lucien, Director, Canadian Labour Congress, 876
Royle, Valerie, President/CEO, 667
Roz, Jim, Bigelow-Liptak of Canada, 107
Rozdeba, Derrick, Manager, Bayer CropScience, 103
Roziere, Jeff, Director, Brandon, 204-573-6480, 689
Ruaro, Carol Ann, Document Control/Library, AMEC Inc., 1099
Ruberto, Aldo. V., Councillor at Large, Thunder Bay, 721
Rubin, Greg, Librarian, Saskatchewan Health, 1188
Rubin, Mark A., Executive Director, Society of Petroleum Engineers, 1008
Rubin, Nancy G., Stewart McKelvey Stirling Scales - Halifax, 1068
Rubis, Darryl, Manager, Capital Region Southwest Water Services Commission, 757
Ruby, Peter, Goodmans LLP, 1075
Rudd, Diane, Membership Contact, British Columbia Fuchsia & Begonia Society, 848
Rudd, Kerry, President/CEO, Associated Engineering Group Ltd., 94
Rudderham, Robert, Head, F.C. O'Neill, Scriven & Associates Ltd., 193
Ruddock, Richard, President, Chemline Plastics Ltd., 139
Rudiak, Ron, Secretary, Red River Apiarists' Association, 1122
Rudichuk, Rick, Manager, Great Western Containers Inc., 216
Rudiger, Emil, Manager, Rudiger Enterprises Ltd., 354
Rudnicki, Joe, Manager, Waterous Power Systems, 423
Rudolph, Jake, CAO, Pitt Meadows, 604-465-2413, 683
Rudolph, Mark S., President, justenvironment, 254
Rudy, Harold, Executive Director, Ontario Soil & Crop Improvement Association, 979
Rudyk, Jim, Executive Vice-President & Chief Financial Officer, Shred-It, 366
Rudyk, Marta, Manager, Communications & Coordinator, AllerGen NCE Inc., 821
Rudzevicius, Diane, Acting Chief, Library Systems, Agriculture & Agri-Food Canada, 1147
Ruel, Michel, President, Elite Technologies Inc., 176
Ruel, Serges, Granby, 735
Ruel, Simon, Heenan Blaikie S.E.N.C.R.L./SRL - Québec, 1088
Ruelokke, Max, Chair/CEO, 603
Ruelokke, P.Eng, Max, Chair & CEO, Canada-Newfoundland Offshore Petroleum Board, 853
Ruest Jutras, Francine, Mairesse, Drummondville, 735
Ruest Jutras, Francine, Préfète (par intérim), Drummond, 747

Ruese, Pete, General Manager, Talkie Tooter Canada Ltd., 386
Ruffel, Paul, President, EBA Engineering Consultants Ltd., 169
Ruffell, J.P. (Paul), Contact, EBA Engineering Consultants Ltd., 170
Ruffman, Alan, President, Geomarine Associates Ltd., 211
Rugeroni, Mike, Manager, Toromont Caterpillar, 398
Ruggero, Sue, Administrator, Ontario Society for Environmental Management, 978
Ruggles, Bob, Associate Deputy Minister, 658
Rule, James, CAO, Maple Ridge, 604-463-5221, 687
Rule, Michele, Kelowna, 681
Rule, TJ, Contact, R.J. Burnside & Associates Limited, 340
Rulff, Mike, President, Jenike & Johanson, Ltd., 251
Rumbolt, Deon, Supervisor, Corner Brook, 709-637-1552, 693
Runciman, Mark, CEO, Royal Botanical Gardens, Royal Botanical Gardens, 1139
Runciman, Mark C., Executive Director, Royal Botanical Gardens, 996
Rundle, B., Manager, Arts & Culture, Gravenhurst, 709
Rung, Sandy, Chair, Waterloo Regional Heritage Foundation, 1018
Runge, Dave, District Manager, Insituform Technologies Ltd. - Hamilton, 242
Runnalls, David, President/CEO, International Institute for Sustainable Development, 940
Rupke, Gerry, Lambton Shores, 726
Rupke, Jack, King, 726
Ruscio, Robert, President, Thermal Hydronics Supply Ltd., 394
Rusinek, Joseph, Vice-President, Nu-Plast Polymers International, 309
Rusk, Richard J., Associé, Stikeman Elliott LLP - Montréal, 1087
Ruskowksy, Wilf, Manager, Waterous Power Systems, 423
Rusnak, Jim, CFO, Metro Vancouver, 678
Russell, Alan, President, Jetvac Inc., 252
Russell, Andy, Director, Zurn Industries Limited, 437
Russell, Dave, President, Russell NDE Systems Inc., 354
Russell, Gord, Director, Planning Services, Collingwood, 708
Russell, Gordon I., President, G.I. Russell & Co. Ltd., 203
Russell, Henry, New Brunswick Contact, Gulf of Maine Council on the Marine Environment, 764
Russell, Janet E., Partner, Scott Venturo LLP, 1053
Russell, Lloyd, Regional Treasurer & Commissioner, Finance, York, 705
Russell, Shari, Coordinator, Canadian Centre for Pollution Prevention, 862
Russell, W. Benjamin, Bishop & McKenzie LLP, 1054
Russell, MEd., IPMA-CP, Pauline, Officer, Human Resources, Leamington, 726
Russell, Q.C., Wharton D., Russell Christie LLP, 1070
Russon, Nicholas N., Stewart McKelvey Stirling Scales - Fredericton, 1064
Ruston, David, Sales, Cantech Inspections Ltd., 127
Ruta, Michael P., Deputy CAO/CFO, Winnipeg, 690
Rutagengwa, Jean-Claude, Tenchical Sales Rep, National Instruments Canada, 298
Rutherford, Heather, Chief Building Official, Essa, 725
Rutherford, Mike, Vice-President, Nusco Supply & Manufacturing Inc., 310
Rutledge, Brian, Executive Director, National Audubon Society, Inc., 957
Rutley, Angela, Manager, Water & Sewer Department, North Dundas, 727
Rutley, Leanne F., Associate, Nixon Wenger, 1062
Ruttan, David, Senior Associate, Charlesworth & Associates, 138
Ruttan, Garry, President/CEO, Systems Plus, 385
Ruttan, John, Mayor, Nanaimo, 250-754-4251, 681
Ruttan, Kyle, CFES President, Canadian Federation of Engineering Students, 868
Ruttan, Mark O., Director, North Cowichan, 687
Ruttman, Kelly, Manager, Environmental Information Association, 912
Rutwind, Stan, Assistant Deputy Minister, 563
Rutz, Murray, Petawawa, 717
Ryall, Rick, Fire Chief, Chilliwack, 604-792-9311, 680
Ryan, Alain, Sales Manager, Labelle, Ryan, Genipro Inc., 262
Ryan, Bill, Financial Officer, 520
Ryan, Dave, Mayor, Pickering, 905-420-4600, 718
Ryan, Dennis, Fasken Martineau - Vancouver, 1059
Ryan, Dennis J., Partner, Stewart McKelvey Stirling Scales - St. John's, 1066
Ryan, Diane, President, Breast Cancer Action, 846
Ryan, Elizabeth, Manager, National Association for Environmental Management, 956
Ryan, Greg, Manager, FS Partners, 202
Ryan, Jerry, CAO, Cape Breton, 695

Executive Name Index

Ryan, Kuffner, Trade Commissioner, 767
Ryan, Larry, Chief Financial Officer, Waterloo, 704
Ryan, Marty, President & Sales Manager, Canadian Portable Structures (1992) Ltd., 125
Ryan, Maureen E., Partner, Stewart McKelvey Stirling Scales - St. John's, 1066
Ryan, Michelle, Team Lead, Library Client Services, Canadian Heritage, 1167
Ryan, Neil, Director, Biogénie, 108
Ryan, Patrick, President, Labelle, Ryan, Genipro Inc., 262
Ryan, M.B.A., CMA, FCMA, Scott, Manager, Charlottetown, 732
Ryan, Q.C., William L., Stewart McKelvey Stirling Scales - Halifax, 1068
Ryder, Tim, Officer, Monserco Ltd., 293
Ryder-Lahey, Pamela, Director, 602
Rydholm, Linda, Ward Councillor, Thunder Bay, 721
Rykse, Harriet, Research & Instructional Services, Allyn & Betty Taylor Library, 1143
Ryneveld, Q.C., Dirk, Police Complaint Commissioner, 582

S

Saab, Richard J., Project Engineer, Aldworth Engineering Inc., 77
Saarela, Jari E., President, ACM Environmental Corporation, 66
Sabar, Karimah Es, President, LifeSciences British Columbia, 949
Sabino, Darren, Manager, Emco Wheaton Corp., 176
Sablinskas, D.L., President, Fabricated Plastics Ltd., 193
Sabourin, Dennis, Executive Director, National Association for PET Container Resources, 957
Sabourin, M.J. (Marc), Contact, EBA Engineering Consultants Ltd., 170
Sabourin, Pierre, Fire Chief, Clarence-Rockland, 708
Sabourin, Theresa, Petawawa, 717
Sabusco, Michael, Partner, Macleod Dixon LLP, 1077
Saccary, Kevin, Councillor, Cape Breton, 695
Sacco, Antonio, Manager, REHAU Industries Inc., 344
Sacco, Dom, General Manager, BG Controls Ltd., 107
Sacher, Brad, Manager, Winnipeg, 690
Sacre, Hettie, Manager, Atlantic Purification Systems, 97
Sadikman, Jacob A., Osler, Hoskin & Harcourt LLP - Toronto, 1079
Sadilkova, Regina, Manager, Powell River, 683
Sadler, John, Director, John & Dotsa Bitove Family Law Library, 1143
Sadler, Sherry, Coordinator, Canadian Aquaculture Industry Alliance, 855
Sadlier-Brown, Timothy L., President, Nevin Sadlier-Brown Goodbrand Ltd., 301
Sadlowski, Julian, Mayor, North Battleford, 754
Sager, Bob, Hastings, 700
Sager, Joy, Coordinator, Alberta Society of Professional Biologists, 819
Saikaley, Jeff, Heenan Blaikie LLP - Ottawa, 1070
Saindon, Louise, Présidente, Fédération québécoise de camping et de caravaning in, 916
Saindon, Yves, Greffier, Montréal, 514-872-3007, 738
Sainsbury, Fran, New Tecumseth, 714
Saint, Barbara, Head, St Paul's Health Sciences Library, 1118
St. Amand, Christian, Service Québec, Hibon Inc., 231
St. Amand, Pierre, Director, Universal Handling Equipment Company Limited, 406
St. Amant, Mike, City Treasurer, London, 713
St. Amour, François, Prescott & Russell, 729
St. Amour, François, Mayor, The Nation, 731
Saint-Charles, Mario, Deux-Montagnes, 735
St. Clair, Colleen Cassady, Canadian Board Member, Society for Conservation Biology, 1006
saintfrancis xavier unive, St. Francis Xavier Univer, Antigonish, NS, 1034, 1207
St. Godard, Jo-Anne, Executive Director, Recycling Council of Ontario, 993
St. Hilaire, Gil, General Manager, Toromont Caterpillar, 397
St. John, Jennifer, Analyst, Canadian Pacific Railway, 1100
St. John, Muriel, Reference Librarian, E.K. Williams Law Library, 1123
St. Louis, David, Director, Community Services, Stratford, 720
St. Louis, Keri, Head, Acquisitions, Aerospace Engineering Test Establishment, 1103
Ste-Marie, Louis, Associé, Ogilvy Renault LLP/S.E.N.C.R.L., s.r.l. - Québec, 1089
Saint-Marseille, Gilles, Deux-Montagnes, 735
St. Onge, Gary, Mayor, Estevan, 754
St. Onge, Yvon, Vice President/Project Manager, RAM Lining Systems Inc., 342

St. Peter, Leigh, The Paint Recycling Company, 393
St. Pierre, Donald, Russell, 729
St. Pierre, Jean, President, Service de rebuts Soulanges inc., 363
Saint-Pierre, Jean-Paul, Prescott & Russell, 729
St. Pierre, John, Treasurer, Nature Trust of New Brunswick, 960
Saint-Pierre-Beaulieu, Gisèle, Rimouski, 740
Saito, Pat, Peel, 714, 703
Sajecki, Ed, Commissioner, Planning & Building, Mississauga, 714
Sajewycz, Mark, Partner, Ogilvy Renault LLP/S.E.N.C.R.L., s.r.l. - Toronto, 1078
Sajko, Paul R., General Manager, Thermo Dynamics Ltd., 394
Sajur, Gene, Sales, Penn Refrigeration Ltd., 321
Saker, Kurtis, Contact, Golder Associates Ltd., 214
salamander foundation, The Salamander Foundation, Toronto, ON, 1044
Salci, R.T. (Ted), Niagara, 702
Salem, Andrew E., Fraser Milner Casgrain LLP - Toronto, 1075
Salembier, Q.C., Gordon A., Fraser Milner Casgrain LLP - Edmonton, 1055
Sales, J.W. (Jim), General Manager, Community Operations, Barrie, 706
Salhia, Susan, Supervisor, SP Library, Sheridan Park Site, 1145
Salisbury, Ted, General Manager, Community Development Services, Brantford, 707
Salkeld, Mark, President & Chief Executive Officer, Petroleum Services Association of Canada, 986
Sallee, Brent, Vice-President, West Point Products Canada, 425
Salloch, Dean, Manager, Semco Systems Limited, 362
Salloum, Doug, Executive Director, Canadian Society for Civil Engineering, 885
Salmaso, Darryl, Investigation Officer, 520
Salmon, Brett, Director, Planning, Centre Wellington, 724
Salmon, Jim, Consultant, Zephyr North, 437
Salmon, Karen A., Partner, Borden Ladner Gervais LLP - Calgary, 1050
Salmon, Ruth, Executive Director, Canadian Aquaculture Industry Alliance, 855
Salmons, Andrew, Milton, 714
Salter, David, Director, 604
Salter, H., Director, Legal & Legislative Services & Town Soli, Fort Erie, 709
Salter, Sue, Aquatic Biologist, Fraser Environmental Services, 201
Saltman, Roger, President, American Association of Bovine Practitioners, 822
Salus, Roger, Library Technician, Millard Health, 1105
Salusbury, Tim, Pacific Environmental Consulting & Occupational Hygiene Services, 316
Samis, Mark, Vice-President, ESRS Environmental Solution, 186, 190
Sampson, Joe, Manager, St. John's, 694
Sampson, Margaret, President, Ottawa Valley Health Libraries Association, 983
Sampson, Marina E., Fraser Milner Casgrain LLP - Toronto, 1075
Sampson, Tom, Deputy Chief, Calgary, 671
Sams, Frank, Manager, Parks & Facilities, Norfolk, 702
Sams, Robert, Senior Sales Manager, Atlantic Canada, Armtec Construction Products, 92
Samson, Anie, Mairesse d'arrondissement, Montréal, 738
Samson, Bertrand, Groupe Conseil Bellefeuille, Samson et Associés, 219
Samson, Daniel, Greffier, Rouyn-Noranda, 741
Samson, Gilbert, Sec.-Trés., Régie d'assainissement des eaux du bassin de la Prairie, 759
Samson, Julie, Langlois Kronström Desjardins, 1088
Samson, Larry, Coordinator, Campbell River, 679
Samson, Michel, Treasurer & Deputy Clerk, South Glengarry, 730
Samson, Paul, Director General, 520
Samuelson, Darel Grant, Blake, Cassels & Graydon LLP - Calgary, 1049
Samusevich, Alla, Coordinator, Consulting Engineers of British Columbia, 903
Sananikone, Malivahn, Responsable, Référence, Bibliothèque de chimie, 1170
Sanborn, Pat, General Manager, Layfield Geosynthetics & Industrial Fabrics Ltd., 265
Sanchioni, Fortunato, Contact, Master Builders Technologies Ltd., 282
Sand, Jerry, President/CEO, Alpha Controls & Instrumentation, 79
Sandberg, Marla, Sales/Order Desk, HMI Hoyme Manufacturing Inc., 232

Sander, Guy, Vice-President, W.T. McGinn & Associates Ltd., 415
Sander, Henry, Clerk-Treasurer & Director, Corporate Services, Severn, 729
Sanders, Richard, President, Sanders Resource Manage Inc., 356
Sanders, Vicki, Saanich, 688
Sanders, P.Eng, Doug R., Partner, Borden Ladner Gervais LLP - Vancouver, 1058
Sanderson, Heather, Librarian, Information Literacy, St Mary's University, 1136
Sanderson, Heather A., Counsel, MacPherson Leslie & Tyerman LLP - Calgary, 1052
Sanderson, John, Peel, 703
Sanderson, John, Regional Councillor, Brampton, 706
Sanderson, John, Principal, Southern Ontario Waste Inc., 374
Sanderson, Les, Principal, Southern Ontario Waste Inc., 374
Sanderson, Terry, Director, Social Services & Social Housing, Bruce, 698
Sanderson, Q.C., B.A., LL, Chris W., Partner, Lawson Lundell LLP - Vancouver, 1061
Sanderson, Q.C., Dale G., Davis LLP - Vancouver, 1059
Sandham, Phil, Vice-President, 662
Sandhu, Amandeep, Lang Michener LLP - Vancouver, 1060
Sandhu, Raj, Bradford West Gwillimbury, 706
Sanford, Fred, Director, 614
Sanford, Steve, Product Manager, Rochester Midland Ltd., 349
Sanford, Tim, President, Nova Magnetics Burgmann Ltd., 308
Sangarapillai, Ubey, Manager, Hallmark Insurance Brokers Ltd., 224
Sangret, Marcy, Planning Manager, Delta, 604-946-3219, 686
Sangster, Scott W., Fraser Milner Casgrain LLP - Calgary, 1051
Sanjeeva, Sellahewe, Trade Commissioner, 769
Sankey, John, Contact, Pesticide Education Network, 985
Sansom, Timothy, Manager, Flygt Canada, 198
Sansregret, Marc-André, Associé, Langlois Kronström Desjardins, 1085
Santos, Maria, Supervisor, The National Testing Laboratories Ltd., 393
Santos, Nelson, Mayor, Kingsville, 712
Santos, Nelson, Warden & Councillor, Essex, 519-733-9936, 699
Sapi, Louis, Secretary - Treasurer, The Jane Goodal Institute of Canada, 946
Sapsford, Ron, Deputy Minister, 628
Saracino, Bob, Niagara, 702
Sarafinchin, Murray G., President, Sarafinchin Associates Ltd., 358
Sarah, Powles, Trade Commissioner, 767
Sargeant, Terry, Chair, 586
Sarkar, Harry, President, Chemcorp Industries Inc., 139
Sarmiento, Kim, General Manager, Barrie Agricultural Society, 844
Sarracini, Diane, Office Manager, North American Recycled Rubber Association, 965
Sarrazin, Marie-Claude, Borden Ladner Gervais LLP - Montréal, 1083
Sarrazin, Michel, Directeur, Terrebonne, 745
Sarrazin, Paul, Préfet, La Haute-Yamaska, 748
saskatchewan econetwork, Saskatchewan Eco-Network, 1216
Sather, Steven M., Thurber Engineering Ltd., 396
Saucier, Mario, CFO, EnGlobe Corp., 181
Saucier, Mario, Vice-président, Association québécoise pour l'hygiène, la santé et la sécurité du, 842
Sauder, Jane, Library Technician, Women's College Hospital, 1162, 1163
Saul, Lloyd, President, Saskatchewan Environmental Industry & Managers' Association, 189, 1000
Saul, Mike, Treasurer, Salmon Arm Bay Nature Enhancement Society, 998
Saul, R. Patrick, Alexander Holburn Beaudin & Lang, LLP, 1057
Saulit, Ken, Manager, Parkland County, 670
Saulnier, Joane, Directrice générale, Le Haut-Richelieu, 749
Saulnier, Marcel, Secretary, Canadian Association for Health Services & Policy Research, 855
Saunby, Linda, Coordinator, Food & Consumer Products of Canada, 918
Saunders, Adrian, Contact, Atlantic Industrial Services, 95
Saunders, Bob, Sales Manager, SPI Industries Inc., 375
Saunders, Cathy, Chief Administrative Officer & Clerk, Middlesex Centre, 717
Saunders, D., Manager, Public Works & Operations, Gravenhurst, 709
Saunders, Dave, President, Lea International Ltd., 266
Saunders, David, Mayor, Colwood, 680
Saunders, Gerry, Vice-President, Ogilvie Scientific Inc., 311

Executive Name Index

Saunders, J. Owen, Executive Director, Canadian Institute of Resources Law, 1100
Saunders, Jeff, Director, Grand Falls-Windsor, 709-489-0427, 694
Saunders, John W., Partner, Hicks Morley Hamilton Stewart Storie LLP, 1076
Saunders, Loretta, Office Manager, Dangerous Goods Advisory Council, 906
Saunders, Ronona, Contact, Metallurgy & Materials Society of the Canadian Institute of Minin, 954
Saunders, Sally, Clerk, Peterborough, 703
Saunders, Sonya, Director, 607
Saunders, Troy, Lennox Industries (Canada) Ltd., 267
Saunderson, Jim, Executive Director, 562
Saundry, Ph.D., Peter D., Executive Director, National Council for Science & the Environment, 957
Saurette, Ray, Fire Chief, Squamish, 688
Sauriol, Alain, President, Sanexen Environmental Services Inc., 357
Sauriol, Colleen, Manager, Planning, Building, & Parking Authority, Pembroke, 717
Sauriol, Gilles, Boisbriand, 734
Sauriol, Jean-Pierre, President, Dessau, Inc., 162
Sauriol, Mélanie, Heenan Blaikie S.E.N.C.R.L/SRL, 1084
Sauser, Daniel, Technicien, SOQUEM INC., 1180
Sauvageau, Sylvain, Deux-Montagnes, 735
Sauvé, André, Saint-Constant, 742
Sauvé, Diane, Bibliothécaire, Université du Québec INRS - Institut Armand-Frappier, 1169
Sauvé, Hugues, Directeur, Westburne Canada, 429
Sauvé, Isabelle, Greffière, Sherbrooke, 819-821-5500, 744
Sauvé, Jean-Marc, Directeur (par intérim), 648
Sauvé, Jennifer, Public Services Librarian, College of New Caledonia, 1115
Sauvé, Jocelyne, Administrative Assistant, British Council - Canada, 851
Sauvé, Josiane, Spécialiste, Moyen et techniques d'enseignement, Collège Shawinigan, 1184
Sauvé, Marc, Heenan Blaikie LLP - Ottawa, 1070
Sauvé, Marie-Lise, Longueuil, 737
Sauvé, Robert, Sous-ministre, 650
Sauvé, Roger, Director, Greater Sudbury Transit, Greater Sudbury / Grand Sudbury, 710
Savage, Alicia, Simcoe, 704
Savage, Alicia, Deputy Mayor & Councillor, Clearview, 725
Savage, David, Vice-President, Aearo Canada Ltd., 69
Savage, Graham, Manager, Nanaimo, 681
Savage, Joanne, Mayor, West Nipissing, 732
Savage, Richard, Fire Chief, West Nipissing, 732
Savard, André, Conseiller d'arrondissement, Desmarchais-Crawford, Montréal, 738
Savard, Carl, Saguenay, 741
Savard, Gabriel, Directeur, Québec, 418-522-3511, 740
Savard, Jean-Guy, Beloeil, 450-467-2545, 734
Savard, Marc, Directeur général, Association provinciale des constructeurs d'habitations du Québec, 841
Savard, Marco, Saint-Jean-sur-Richelieu, 450-349-0473, 742
Savard, Martine, Greffière, Magog, 737
Savard, Michel, Superintendent, Wood Buffalo, 780-799-7490, 670
Savard, Patrick, Directeur général, Mont-St-Hilaire, 738
Savard, Pierre, Gestionnaire, Veolia ES Canada Industrial Services Inc., 411
Savard, Robert, Salaberry-de-Valleyfield, 450-371-1173, 744
Savard, Roger, President & CEO, Groupe Chagnon International, 219
Savard, Suzie, Autre personnel, Québec Ministère de la Sécurité Publique - Direction des Communic, 1175
Savard, CA, MBA, Denis, Directeur, Montréal, 738
Savaria, Donald, Sainte-Julie, 743
Savary, S., Chemist/Toxicologist, Services d'Évaluation Santé/Toxicologie Inc., 363
Savidov, Nick, Secretary, Alberta Greenhouse Growers Association, 817
Savill, Liz, Chief Administrative Officer & Clerk, Frontenac, 699
Savini, Jennifer G., Templeman Menninga LLP, 1068
Savoie, Denise, Bibliothécaire, Campus de Campbellton, Bibliothèque, 1126
Savoie, Léandre, Sec.-Trés., Régie d'assainissement des eaux de Chandler, Pabos et Pabos Mills, 759
Savoie, Patrick, Sales, Matrix Energy, 282
Savoie, Philippe, Marketing & Sales Contact, Les Laboratoires Shermont Inc., 269
Savoie, Sarah-Anne, Heenan Blaikie S.E.N.C.R.L/SRL, 1085
Savoie, Tim, Director, Port Moody, 604-469-4545, 683

Savoie Jourdain, Reina, Baie-Comeau, 418-296-5231, 733
Saw, Janine B., Executive Director, British Columbia Association of Agricultural Fairs & Exhibitions, 847
Sawa, Paul, Library Manager, Canada Dept. of National Defence & the Canadian Forces, 1148
Sawatzky, Q.C., Murray R., McDougall Gauley, 1090
Sawchuk, Dellarae, Manager, Langley, 604-533-7327, 687
Sawchuk, Mike, Enviro-Solutions Ltd., 183
Sawden, I., Carrier Canada Ltd., 129
Sawers, Jim, Regional Manager, Vestar, 412
Sawh, Dianne, Librarian, CH2M Hill Canada Limited, 1157
Saxe, Dianne, Saxe, Dianne, 1079
Sayant, Alice, Vice President, 591
Sayle, Leanne, Director, 640
Scagel, Rob, Principal Consultant, Pacific Phytometric Consultants, 316
Scaini, Mike, Metals, Lambton Scientific, 264
Scales, Pete, President, Scales Bioresource Consulting Ltd., 358
Scalzo, Primo A., Manager, Cook Engineering, 152
Scandlan, Gary, Associate Director, Watson & Associates Economists Ltd., 423
Scaplen, Nicole, Marketing Coordinator, Oceans Ltd., 311
Scarfo, Maria, Blaney McMurtry LLP, 1073
Scarfone, James A., Scarfone Hawkins LLP, 1069
Scarlett, Lynne, Lab Supervisor, Rochester Midland Ltd., 349
Scarpitti, Frank, York, 705
Scarpitti, Frank, Mayor, Markham, 905-475-4702, 713
Scarrow, Jim, Mayor, Prince Albert, 754
Scerbak, Greg, City Manager, Grande Prairie, 780-538-0312, 672
Sceviour, Paul, Environmental Engineer, Cecon Limited, 135
Schachler, Juergen G., President/CEO, ArcelorMittal Dofasco, 90
Schaedlich, Frank, President, Tekran Canada, 389
Schaefer, R.A. (Bob), Sales Manager, Triple M Fiberglass Mfg. Ltd., 401
Schaer, Lilian, Executive Director, Agricultural Groups Concerned About Resources & the Environment, 814
Schafer, Lore, President, Ontario Farm & Country Accommodations Association, 973
Schafer, Steve, Director, Library Services, Athabasca University, 1099
Schafer, Stewart, Director, North Battleford, 754
Schaffer, Don, Manager, Victoria, 250-361-0549, 685
Schaffner, MD, FIDSA, William, Secretary, Infectious Diseases Society of America, 931
Schafler, Michael, Fraser Milner Casgrain LLP - Toronto, 1075
Schaitberger, Harold A., General President, International Association of Fire Fighters (AFL-CIO/CLC), 935
Scharfe, Lynn, Representative, Draeger Safety Canada Ltd., 166
Schatz, Leah A., Partner, MacPherson Leslie & Tyerman LLP - Saskatoon, 1090
Schauer, Helmut, CEO, Proceco Ltd., 333
Schedler, Mike, Technical Advisor, National Association for PET Container Resources, 957
Scheiffert, Kathy, Library Technician, Misericordia Health Centre, 1125
Scheifley, Doug, Contact, Clemmer Technologies Inc., 143
Schell, Andrew, Manager, Environmental Services, Orillia, 716
Schell, Charlie, Plant Manager, CCS Income Trust, 134
Schell, Liz, Councillor, Kingston, 712
Schellenberg, David, President & CEO, Conair Group Inc., 148
Schellenberg, Heidi, Circulation Clerk, Keyano College, 1107
Schembri, J., Officer, Environmental Progress, Caledon, 707
Schenher, Bonnie, City Clerk, Yorkton, 755
Schentag, S., Coordinator, Medicine Hat, 403-502-8593, 673
Schepers, Nancy, Deputy City Manager, Ottawa, 716
Schepper, Josée, Manager, Merck Frosst Canada Inc., 1168
Scherer, Hans, Nova Magnetics Burgmann Ltd., 308
Scherer, Paul, Milton, 714
Scherman, Chris S., Stikeman Elliott LLP - Calgary, 1054
Schermerhorn, Gord, Mayor, Greater Napanee, 613-354-0429, 709
Schermerhorn, Gord, Warden & Councillor, Lennox & Addington, 613-354-4883, 701
Scherzer, BES, MCIP, RPP, Randy, Director, Planning & Development, Grey, 700
Schildroth, Fred, Saugeen Shores, 719
Schill, Jack, President/CEO, Jes-Chem Ltd., 251
Schille, Ed, Manager, Cosmopolitan Industries Limited, 152
Schimke, Errol, Green Key Solutions Inc., 217
Schindelka, Dana, Davis LLP - Calgary, 1050
Schindler, M.Eng., P.Eng., John, President & Chair, Ontario Society of Professional Engineers, 979
Schira, Rainer, Reference Librarian, Brandon University, 1122
Schlaht, Rudy, Manager, Westburne Canada, 427

Schlange, H., Chief Administrative Officer, Fort Erie, 709
Schlereth, Mike, Manager, Toromont Caterpillar, 397
Schlereth, Mike, Vice-President, Toromont Caterpillar, 398
Schlosser, Greg, Director, Human Resources, Essex, 699
Schmid, Taryn, Librarian, Reference & Instruction, Salmon Arm Campus, 1116
Schmidt, Brad, Vice-President, PCI Geomatics Group Inc., 320
Schmidt, Janine, Trenholme Director of Libraries, McGill University, 1174
Schmidt, Jerry, Contact, EBA Engineering Consultants Ltd., 170
Schmidt, Karl, President/CEO, Enercombustion Ltd., 179
Schmidt, Katharina, Supervisor, Viessmann Manufacturing Company Inc., 413
Schmidt, Mark A., Davis LLP - Vancouver, 1059
Schmidt, Mayo, President & Chief Executive Officer, Viterra Inc., 414
Schmidt, Rob, Deputy Mayor & Councillor, Leamington, 726
Schmidt, Robert, Essex, 519-326-7443, 699
Schmidt, Thomas, Commissioner, Transportation & Environmental Servi, Waterloo, 704
Schmidtke, Klaus, Contact, Conestoga-Rovers & Associates, 149
Schmidtmeyer, Andy, Manager, Lambton Scientific, 264
Schmitt, Douglas G., Alexander Holburn Beaudin & Lang, LLP, 1057
Schmitt, Steve, Brant, 698
Schmuck, Derek A., Partner, SimpsonWigle LAW LLP, 1068
Schneeberger, Dan, Sec.-Treas., Tekran Canada, 389
Schneider, Linda, Manager, Conestoga College Institute of Technology & Advanced Learning, 1143
Schneider, Lorne, Vice-President, Calta Computer Systems Ltd., 122
Schneider, Marilyn, Secretary-Treasurer, Manitoba Water Well Association, 952
Schneider, Meredith, Councillor, North Perth, 715
Schneider, Richard, Executive Director, Alberta Centre for Boreal Studies, 816
Schnurr, Amy, Executive Director, BurlingtonGreen Environmental Association, 852
Schoettler, Brad, Branch Manager, Fort Garry Industries Ltd., 200
Schofield, Faye, Technical Services Technician, Durham College of Applied Arts & Technology, 1147
Schofield, Jonathan, President, AeroTek Manufacturing Ltd., 71
Schofield, Kim, Director, 607
Schofield, Lloyd, President, F.C. O'Neill, Scriven & Associates Ltd., 193
Schofield, RN, MSc(T), Ruth, Secretary, Community Health Nurses of Canada, 899
Schollaardt, Steve, Manager, Westburne Canada, 426
Scholl-Buckwald, Steve, CFO & Managing Director, Pesticide Action Network North America, 985
Scholtens, Reuben, Manager, Terratec Environmental Ltd., 390
Scholz, Janet, Manager, University Technologies International, 407
Schonewille, J., Director, Building & Enforcement, Grimsby, 710
Schoonover, Jason, Communications Director, Explorer's Club (Canadian Chapter), 914
Schramm, Laurier, President/CEO, 662
Schramm, Laurier L., President & CEO, Saskatchewan Research Council, 1190
Schramm, B.Comm., LL.B., Jerrold W., Partner, Lawson Lundell LLP - Vancouver, 1061
Schreiner, Gord, Fire Chief, Comox, 250-339-2432, 680
Schriemer, Joceline, Legislative Secretary to the Minister of Health, 659
Schroder, Jorn, Contact, Environmental Structures, 186
Schroeder, Janice, Director, 566
Schroeder, Ryan, Kaizen Environmental Services Inc., 254
Schroeninger, Marco, Manager, Beaver River Regional Waste Management Commission, 757
Schroer, J., Natech Environmental Services, 297
Schroeter, Ingrid, Vice-President, Napoleon Appliance Corp., 297
Schroeter, Wolfgang, President, Napoleon Appliance Corp., 297
Schroter, Craig, Manager, Westburne Canada, 427
Schrum, Mike, Secretary, Environmental Information Association, 912
Schryer, Brigitte, Director, 518
Schryver, Donna, Secretary, Saskatchewan Katahdin Sheep Association Inc., 1000
Schulman, Dave, Senior Associate, Hardy Stevenson & Associates, 225
Schulte, Deb, York, 705
Schulte, Deb, Regional Councillor, Vaughan, 722

Executive Name Index

Schultz, Henry K., Senior General Counsel & Head, Legal Services, 560
Schumacher, Det, Councillor, Huntsville, 711
Schumacher, Susan, Marketing Specialist, Hayward Gordon Ltd., 227
Schuster, Michael, Commissioner, Social Services, Waterloo, 704
Schwan, Angie, Supervisor, Westburne Canada, 428
Schwanke, Dallas, Controller, HMI Industries, 232
Schwanky, T.J., Executive Director, Outdoor Writers of Canada, 983
Schwartz, Bryan P., Associate Counsel, Pitblado LLP, 1063
Schwartz, Mark D., Secretary, International Society of Biometeorology, 943
Schwartz, Phillip, Fire Chief & Coordinator, West Grey, 732
Schwartz, Sandra, Vice-President, Canadian Electricity Association, 866
Schwartz, Stephen Z., Burns, Fitzpatrick, Rogers & Schwartz, 1058
Schwartzel, Ellen, Senior Policy Advisor, 626
Schwartzentruber, Grant, Chief Building Official, Perth East, 728
Schwarzer, Rick, Chief Administrative Officer, Orangeville, 716
Schwass, Dave, President, Alberta Plastics Recycling Association, 819
Schweiger, Larry J., President & CEO, National Wildlife Federation, 958
Schweiger, Sabine, Co-Coordinator, Whitehorse, 867-668-8312, 755
Schwendinger, Glenn, Chief Administrative Officer, Perth East, 728
Schyven, Melissa, Stikeman Elliott LLP - Toronto, 1080
Scian, Karen, Waterloo, 722
Scigliano, Marisa, Technical Services Librarian, Trent University, 1153
Scissons, Daniel, Treasurer & Deputy Clerk, Petawawa, 717
Scissons, Ray, Chief Building Official, Elizabethtown-Kitley, 725
Sclisizzi, Martin, Partner, Borden Ladner Gervais LLP - Toronto, 1074
Scollan, Anna-Léa, Vice-présidente, Centre québécois du droit de l'environnement, 894
Scomazzon, Dave, Contact, R.J. Burnside & Associates Limited, 340
Scordo, Frank R., Fulton & Company LLP, Lawyers & Trade-Mark Agents, 1056
Scott, Alison, Deputy Minister, 611
Scott, Anne, Technical Services Librarian, Dawson College, 1173
Scott, Bill, President, Newfoundland & Labrador Environmental Industry Association, 962
Scott, Cynthia M., Boyne Clarke, 1067
Scott, Dan, Systems Librarian, Laurentian University, 1155
Scott, Dave, Vice President, 591
Scott, David, Operations Manager, Durex Steel & Alloy Industries Ltd., 167
Scott, Don, Manager, Westburne Canada, 427
Scott, Doug, Superintendent, Roads, North Grenville, 728
Scott, Gavin, General Manager, Custom Environmental Services Ltd., 154
Scott, George, Trading Manager, SRI Petro Chemical Inc., 376
Scott, Greg, Manager, Red Deer, 403-342-8159, 674
Scott, Herb, Leeds & Grenville, 725, 726
Scott, Hugh, Vice-President, MPI Drilling, 294
Scott, Jeff, Councillor, Kingston, 712
Scott, Jim, President, Scott Resource Services Inc., 360
Scott, John, Essex, 709
Scott, John, Chair & CEO, 599
Scott, John, Sales Manager, Harold Marcus Ltd., 225
Scott, John, Vice-Chair, 520
Scott, Ken, District Service Manager, Rondar Inc., 351
Scott, Laurence H., Managing Director, Clivus Multrum Canada Ltd., 144
Scott, Les, Pembroke, 717
Scott, Maggie, Librarian, Library (Edmonton), 1105
Scott, Murray, Huron, 701
Scott, Paul, Director of Projects, Stuart Energy USA, 381
Scott, S.M., Dunsford & Scott, 1056
Scott, Shaun, Principal, Scott & Stewart Forestry Consultants, 360
Scott, Tom, Asst. General Manager, Leon's Insulation, 267
Scott, Trina, Director, Victoria, 250-361-0229, 685
Scott, Wendy, Librarian, H.H. Angus & Associates, 1158
Scott, Wes, Group Sales Manager, dmg world media (Canada) Inc., 164
Scott, P.Eng., Greg, City Engineer, White Rock, 686
Scott-Brown, Miles, Principal, Integrated Environments Ltd., 244

Scouten, M., Vice-President, Vermilion Forks Field Naturalists, 1016
Screawn, Tom, K.T. Enviro Clean Inc., 254
Screpnek, D., General Manager, St. Albert, 674
Scripnick, Gary, Timmins, 721
Scruton, Dan, President, Integra Environmental Inc., 243
Scruton, Steven A., Stewart McKelvey Stirling Scales - St. John's, 1066
Scull, John, Vice-President, Cowichan Valley Naturalists' Society, 905
Scullion, Gérald, Maire, Alma, 418-669-5005, 733
Scupham, Tom, Manager, LTS Sales Ltd., 274
Sczesny, John, Contact, CCR Technologies Ltd., 133
Seaborn, Michelle, Grimsby, 710
Seager, John, President & CEO, Population Connection, 987
Seager, Randy, Manager, Wenvor Technologies Inc., 424
Seale, Linda, Site Manager, John W. Scott Health Sciences Library, 1105
Seale, Sandra M., City Clerk, Brockville, 707
Seaman, Thead, Saugeen Shores, 719
Seamans, Ann, Councillor at Large, Riverview, 506-386-4558, 692
Seamone, D.A., Principal, Hiltz & Seamone Co. Ltd., 232
Searle, Yvonne, President, Mineral Society of Manitoba, 954
Sears, Cathy, Library Assistant, Coady International Institute, 1134
Seaward, Dennis, J.W. Bird & Company Ltd., 250
Seaward, Ken, Manager, Aluma Systems Inc., 82
Sebastiano, Rocco M., Partner, Osler, Hoskin & Harcourt LLP - Toronto, 1079
Secord, Peter, St. Catharines, 905-937-0044, 719
Secord, Richard C., Ackroyd LLP Barristers & Solicitors, 1054
secretariat du organisme, Secrétariat des organisme, 1216
Secter, Jonathan, Principal & Ecologist, Secter Environmental Resource Consulting, 361
Secter, Jordan, Landscape Architect & Environmental Planner, Secter Environmental Resource Consulting, 361
Seddon, Laura, Director, 607
Sedgewick, Tim, Contact, Saskatoon, 754
See, Jeff, Executive Director, Organic Crop Improvement Association (International), 982
Seebruch, Carol A., Information Resources Coordinator, Jacobs Canada Inc., 1102
Seech, Alan G., CEO/Director, Adventus Canada Inc., 69
Seed, Leonard, Sr. Lab Scientist, ENPAR Technologies Inc., 181
Seegmiller, Doug, District Manager, Klohn Crippen Berger Ltd., 258
Seel, June, Manager, Library Systems, University of Toronto at Mississauga, 1145
Seetner, Irene, Quality Registrar Inc., NSF-ISR, 309
Sefi, Ramin, Director, Langley, 604-533-6059, 687
Sefton, Cynthia R.C., Outerbridge Miller Sefton, 1079
Segal, Elizabeth (Betsy), Singleton Urquhart LLP, 1062
Segsworth, Mark, Manager, Public Works, South Frontenac, 730
Séguin, Benoit, Directeur, Développement, svs techniques et inform, Université du Québec à Trois-Rivières, 1186
Séguin, Benoit, Responsable, systèmes, Université du Québec à Trois-Rivières, 1186
Séguin, François, Vaudreuil-Dorion, 746
Séguin, Jean, Sous-ministre adjoint, 643
Séguin, Lise, Supervisor of Circulation, Laurentian University, 1155
Seguin-Forget, Sylvette, Chief, Purchasing, Administration & Systems, Public Works & Government Services Canada, 1168
Seidel, Christina, President, sonnevera international corp., 374
Seidel, Q.C., Robert A., National Managing Partner, Davis LLP - Edmonton, 1055
Seiler, Terry, Perth, 703
Seili, Joe, Huron, 701
Seiling, Ken, Regional Chair & Councillor, Waterloo, 519-575-4585, 704
Seiling, Mike, Director, Building, Kitchener, 519-741-2669, 712
Seitz, Gary, Treasurer & Director, Finance, Ingersoll, 711
Sekora, Lou, Coquitlam, 680
Selby, Alan, Treasurer, Dufferin, 699
Selcho, Laura, Course Registrar, Alberta Water & Wastewater Operators Association, 820
Seldman, Neil, President, Institute for Local Self-Reliance, 932
Selfe, Brian, Partner, Greenflow Environmental Services Inc., 217
Selhke, Jerry, President Elect, American Water Resources Association, 826
Seligmann, Aria, Communications Coordinator, Northwest Coalition for Alternatives to Pesticides, 966
Seligmann, Peter, Chair & CEO, Conservation International, 901
Selinger, Gregory F., Minister responsible, 588

Sellars, John, Director, Parks, Recreation, & Culture, Scugog, 729
Selzler, Robert W., Vice-President, Gemcom Software International Inc., 206
Semenchuk, Glen, Executive Director, Cumulative Environmental Management Association, 906
Semenoff, Wally, Manager, Delta, 604-946-3384, 686
Semmens, Pete, Executive Vice President, Comstock Canada Ltd., 148
Semple, Dave, Director, Richmond, 604-244-1206, 684
Senay, Gregory R., Fire Chief, Vaughan, 722
Sénécal, Francine, Conseillère, Côte-des-Neiges, Montréal, 738
Sénécal, Jean-Guy, Terrebonne, 745
Sénécal, Maurice, Préfet, Lotbinière, 750
Sénécal, Yves, La Prairie, 736
Sénécal-Tremblay, Marie, Directrice générale (par intérim), Héritage Montréal, 929
Senis, Sherry, Smith-Ennismore-Lakefield, 729
Sennuck, Bruce, Vice-President, Niagara Water Conditioning Ltd., 304
Sense, Peter, Director, Community & Corporate Services, Port Colborne, 718
Sentenne, Justine, Protectrice de la personne, 649
Sentner, Max, Branch Manager, National Energy Equipment Inc., 297
Separi, Kayvan, Contact, Vacuum Products Canada Inc., 409
Seppo, Vihersaari, Trade Commissioner, 767
Serafini, Ersilia, Executive Director, Clean Air Foundation, 896
Sereda, Rick, Fire Chief & Director, Leduc, 673
Serres, Donat, La Prairie, 736
Serrurier, Raymond, Clarence-Rockland, 708
Servant, Michel, Partner, Lavery, de Billy - Montréal, 1086
Servos, Mark, Scientific Director, Canadian Water Network, 890
Severin, Gary, Pembroke, 717
Severinsky, Ivan, Manager, AMEC, 83
Severinsky, Ivan, Unit Manager, AMEC, 83
Sévigny, Bernard, Sherbrooke, 744
Sévigny, Catherine, Conseillère de ville, Peter-McGill, Montréal, 738
Sévigny, Serge, President/CEO, Bio-Contrôle inc., 107
Seviour, Colm St. Roch, Partner, Stewart McKelvey Stirling Scales - St. John's, 1066
Seward Carpenter, Kerri Lynn, Matheson & Murray, 1082
Sewell, Gwendolyn, Director, Kitimat, 687
Sewerin, Cris, Librarian, Engineering & Computer Science Library, 1157
Sexsmith, Cal, Manager, Saskatoon, 754
Sexsmith, Doug, President/CEO, 591
Sexsmith, Wendy, Chief Scientist, 533
Seyed Mahmoud, Donna, Associate University Librarian, University of Lethbridge, 1108
Seymour, Nola Kate, President & CEO, International Centre for Sustainable Cities, 936
Sferrazza, Carmen, President, ASI Group Ltd., 94
Sha, Zukang, Secretary-General, Commission for Sustainable Development, 764
Shaban, Richard H., Senior Partner, Borden Ladner Gervais LLP - Toronto, 1074
Shafaat, Noghat, Assistant, CanTox Health Sciences International, 1144
Shaffer, Jeff, Peel Scrap Metal Recycling Ltd., 320
Shaffer, Marvin, Contact, Transco Plastic Industries, 400
Shahab, Saqib, President, Saskatchewan Public Health Association Inc., 1001
Shaigec, Rodney, Mayor, Parkland County, 670
Shallow, Sandra, Library Technician, Burin Campus Library, 1130
Shamie, Stephen J., Managing Partner, Hicks Morley Hamilton Stewart Storie LLP, 1076
Shan, Umesh (Mason), Heenan Blaikie LLP - Calgary, 1051
Shanchayan, Shan B., Project Engineer, Ambio Biofiltration Ltd., 82
Shand, Dennis, Superintendent, Thames Centre, 731
Shand, J.A., President, KnowTech Environmental Inc., 259
Shane, Ken, National Sales Manager, F.E. Myers, 193
Shane, Michael P., Partner, Richards Buell Sutton LLP, 1062
Shaner, Karan, Assistant Deputy Minister & Attorney General, 607
Shanfield, Joy, Information Resources Specialist, Toronto Rehab, 1162
Shanks, Jamie, Executive Director, Recreation New Brunswick, 992
Shannon, Bill, Senior Estimator, Donalco Inc., 165
Shannon, Bob, Chair, 591
Shannon, Richard, Chief Administrative Officer, Prince Edward, 703

Executive Name Index

Shannon, P.Eng, Colleen M., Partner, Borden Ladner Gervais LLP - Toronto, 1074
Shantz, J. David, Executive Director, Municipal Engineers Association, 955
Shantz, Paul D., Counsel, Fraser Milner Casgrain LLP - Toronto, 1075
Shapiro, J., Chair, CanTox Environmental Inc., 127
Shapiro, Ralph, President, Huntsman Corporation Canada Inc., 235
Shapton, Larry, General Manager, Ontario Wheat Producers' Marketing Board, 981
Sharma, Devi, Winnipeg, 690
Sharma, H.D., President, Radiation Environmental Management Systems Inc., 341
Sharma, Niki, Donovan & Company, 1059
Sharma, Rakesh, Water Treatment Engineer, Henderson Paddon & Associates Ltd., 229
Sharma, Samit, GAIA Power Inc., 204
Sharman, Paul, Halton, 707, 700
Sharp, Ed, Manager, Environmental Services, Brant, 698
Sharp, Glenn, Engineer, Abydoz Environmental, 65
Sharp, Lisa, Chief Financial Officer, Sonic Technology Solutions Inc., 374
Sharpe, Andy, Peterborough, 703
Sharpe, Barry, Mayor, Welland, 722
Sharpe, Brian, Vice-President, Masternet Ltd., 282
Sharpe, Doreen, President, Friends of Ferris, 920
Sharpe, Eric, Manager, East Kootenay, 677
Sharpe, Eric, Superintendent, East Kootenay, 677
Sharpe, Jeff, Burnet, Duckworth & Palmer LLP, 1050
Sharpe, Kenneth L., Director, Riverview, 506-387-2035, 692
Sharpe, Vicky J., President & Chief Executive Officer, Sustainable Development Technology Canada, 1011
Sharren, Martin, Executive Vice-President, Alberta Fish & Game Association, 817
Shartal Levinthal, Sarah, Roach, Schwartz & Associates, Barristers & Solicitors, 1079
Shaughnessy, Richard, President, International Society of Indoor Air Quality & Climate, 943
Shaver, Diane, Head, Aerospace Engineering Test Establishment, 1103
Shaver, Mark, Contact, Shaver Industries Inc., 365
Shaw, Chad, Sales Representative, Armtec Construction Products, 92
Shaw, Cory, Manager, Crown Shred & Recycling, 154
Shaw, David E., Treasurer, American Association for the Advancement of Science, 822
Shaw, Gary, Director, Transportation & Public Safety, Grey, 700
Shaw, Glen, Executive Director, Soil Conservation Council of Canada, 1009
Shaw, Gord, Manager, Brooks, 671
Shaw, Jack, President & CEO, Bennett Environmental Inc., 105
Shaw, Jack, President/CEO, Crown Shred & Recycling, 154
Shaw, James F., President, Canadian Plywood Association, 882
Shaw, Karen, Osler, Hoskin & Harcourt S.E.N.C.R.L./LLP, 1086
Shaw, Kevin, Director, Engineering Services, Greater Sudbury / Grand Sudbury, 710
Shaw, Mike, Associate Deputy Minister, 659
Shaw, Pam, Deputy Manager, Nanaimo, 250-390-6510, 678
Shaw, Robert, Vice-President, Vancouver Electric Vehicle Association, 1016
Shaw, Rod, President/CEO, Total Comfort Solution Inc., 399
Shaw, Ronald R., Chief Administrative Officer, Stratford, 720
Shaw, Shellee, Vice-President/COO, Total Comfort Solution Inc., 399
Shaw, Terry, Vice-President, Les Engrais Naturels McInnes Inc./McInnes Natural Fertilizers Inc, 268
Shaw, W.G., President, W.G. Shaw & Associates, 415
Shaw, William J., McDougall Gauley, 1090
Shawcross, Chuck, Assistant Deputy Minister & Chief Information Offi, 522
Shawcross, S.W., IBI Group, 238
Shaw-Daigle, Christine, Head of Library, Victoria General Hospital (Winnipeg), 1126
Shawlee, Walter, President, Sphere Research Corp., 375
Shay, Gary D., Town Manager, Grimsby, 710
Shay, Greg, Director, Yarmouth District, 698
Shea, Daniel (Dan) P., President/CEO, ARISE Technologies Corporation, 90
Shea, Don, Rothesay, 692
Shea, Edison J., Deputy Attorney General, 637
Shea, Gail, Minister, Fisheries & Oceans, 527
Shea, Scott, President, Voice Construction Ltd., 414
Shea, Shawn, CEO, 638
Sheahan, Ann-Marie, McCarthy Tétrault LLP - Montréal, 1086

Sheahan, Cillian D., Poole Althouse, Barristers & Solicitors, 1065
Shearing, Bill, Coordinator, Emergency Management, South Dundas, 730
Shearmur, Richard, Vice-président, Association canadienne des sciences régionales, 830
Shedd, Phil, Superintendent, Quispamsis, 506-849-5742, 692
Shedd, Regina, Reference Specialist, Gallagher Library of Geology & Geophysics, 1101
Sheedy, Mark, Vice-President, R.J. Burnside & Associates Limited, 340
Sheehan, Humphrey, Chief Executive Officer, 591
Sheehan, Jim, Environmental Technician, Maple Ridge, 604-467-7499, 687
Sheehan, Ken, Branch Manager, Leeson Canada Ltd., 266
Sheehan, Terry, Sault Ste. Marie, 720
Sheeran, Ruth, Assistant University Librarian, Bishop's University, 1185
Sheffer, F.G., President, Mancorp Industrial Sales Ltd., 279
Sheffer, G.N., Operations Manager, Mancorp Industrial Sales Ltd., 279
Sheffer, K.G., Sales Manager, Mancorp Industrial Sales Ltd., 279
Shefman, Alan, Vaughan, 722
Sheikh, Nasir, Municipal Engineer, Foothills No. 31, 669
Sheikh, Sabeen, Blake, Cassels & Graydon LLP - Calgary, 1049
Shek, P.Eng, Patrick, Chief Building Inspector, Burnaby, 679
Sheldon, BSc, Lani, Team Leader, Wildlife Rescue Association of British Columbia, 1020
Sheldrake, Mark, Operations Manager, W.J. Sheldrick Sanitation Ltd., 415
Sheldrake, Stanley J., General Manager, W.J. Sheldrick Sanitation Ltd., 415
Shelford, Jeremy, Lang Michener LLP - Vancouver, 1060
Shelly, David R., Nelligan O'Brien Payne, 1071
Shelp, Gene, President/CEO, ENPAR Technologies Inc., 181
Shelton, Robert N., Chief Administrative Officer, Newmarket, 714
Shepard, Merrill, Donovan & Company, 1059
Shepard, Roger T., Ritch Durnford, Lawyers, 1067
Shepherd, Gary, Councillor at Large, North Glengarry, 727
Shepherd, Leslie, Director, Works, Planning Services, & Asset Manage, Leeds & Grenville, 726
Shepherd, Sharon, Mayor, Kelowna, 681
Shepley, Tanya, Marketing Director, Hygrex-Spehr Industries, 237
Sheppard, Greg R., Operations Manager, Big Country Waste Management Commission, 757
Sheppard, Margo, Executive Director, Nature Trust of New Brunswick, 960
Sheppard, Marie Leigh, Library Technician, Northern College of Applied Arts & Technology, 1156
Sheppard, Maureen, Technical Services & Systems Librarian, Algonquin College of Applied Arts & Technology, 1147
Sheppard, Sally, Deputy Minister, 667
Sheppard, P.Eng., John P., Manager, Halifax Regional Municipality, 902-490-6958, 695
Shepstone, Carol, Head, Access Services, University of Saskatchewan, 1191
Shergill, Ranju, CAO, Alpine Environmental Ltd., 80
Sheridan, Ann, Business Manager, ECO-TEK Ecological Technologies Inc., 171
Sheridan, John, President/CEO, Ballard Power Systems Inc., 101
Sheridan, Wesley J., Provincial Treasurer, 642
Sheridan, William J.V., Lang Michener LLP - Toronto, 1077
Sherk, L., Officer, Community Economic Development, Gravenhurst, 709
Sherkat, Maryam, Borden Ladner Gervais LLP - Vancouver, 1058
Sherkey, Gary, Vice-President, 629
Sherman, Keith, Executive Director, Severn Sound Environmental Association, 1003
Sherrard, Rick, Director, Hants West District, 697
Sherrott, Geoffrey M., Edwards, Kenny & Bray LLP, 1059
Sherry, Cameron W., President, Enviro-RISQUE Inc., 183
Sherry, Loyd, Nanaimo, 681
Sherry, Winnifred, Vice-President, Enviro-RISQUE Inc., 183
Sherwin, Larry E., Cobourg, 708
Sherwin, Ross, Instructional Services Librarian, Mount Royal College, 1102
Sherwin, B.Comm., CA, Garth, City Manager, Lethbridge, 673
Sheutiapik, Elisapee, Mayor, Iqaluit, 698
Shewchuk, Leo, Regional Manager, Velan Inc., 410
Shewfelt, Deb, Huron, 701
Shewfelt, Dennis, City Manager, Whitehorse, 867-668-8650, 755
Shewfelt, Lorne, National President, Institute of Power Engineers, 933
Shields, Barbara M., Aikins, MacAulay & Thorvaldson LLP, 1063

Shields, Douglas G., Davis LLP - Vancouver, 1059
Shields, Martin, Mayor, Brooks, 671
Shier, Donna S.K., Willms & Shier Environmental Lawyers LLP, 1081
Shier, E. Mitchell, Counsel, Heenan Blaikie LLP - Calgary, 1051
Shigetomi, Elaine, President, Care First Aid Training Inc., 128
Shillabeer, Dave, Sec.-Treas., Koers & Associates Engineering Ltd., 259
Shilliday, Corey, Contact, Aqua Terre Solutions Inc., 88
Shin, Jay C.H., Partner, Borden Ladner Gervais LLP - Vancouver, 1058
Shiner, David, Toronto, 721
Shinkle, Matt, K&D Pratt Group Inc., 254
Shipley, Doug, Barrie, 706
Shirley, Brad, Fire Chief, Salmon Arm, 250-803-4064, 684
Shirley, Robert, Vice-Chair, Credit Valley Conservation Foundation, 905
Shirreff, Michael D., Singleton Urquhart LLP, 1062
Shirreff, Rhonda R., Heenan Blaikie LLP - Toronto, 1076
Shirzadi, Fred, President/CEO, Carlo Gavazzi (Canada) Inc., 129
Shiu, Julia, Information Analyst/Researcher, Association of Municipalities of Ontario, 1156
Shkazofsky, I., Director, Fusion, Experimental Fusion Facility, 191
Shkurhan, Glen, Professional Engineer, Urban Systems Ltd., 407
Shoemaker, Heather, Manager, Metro Vancouver, 678
Shoemaker, Wes, Deputy Minister, 574
Shoiry, Paul, Québec, 740
Shoiry, Pierre, President/CEO, Genivar, 207
Shoji, Bryan, General Manager, Sunshine Coast, 679
Shoniker, Tim, Director, 666
Shore, Howard, Markham, 713
Shore, Linda, Manager, Metro Vancouver, 678
Shorey, Jim, Technical Services, CD Nova, 134
Short, Robert B., Director, Whitby, 723
Shortreed, John, Director, Institute for Risk Research, 932
Shorts, Mike, General Manager, Triangle Fluid Controls Ltd., 401
Shortt, Gerald, Meaford, 519-538-2648, 727
Shortt, Kevin, President, Canadian Space Society, 888
Shostak, Jim, Plant Manager, Swan Hills Treatment Centre, 384
Shoukry, Sonia, President, InterLink Business Management Inc., 245
Shouldice, Robert R., Partner, Borden Ladner Gervais LLP - Vancouver, 1058
Shrieves, Richard, Partner, Heenan Blaikie LLP - Victoria, 1060, 1062
Shrimpton, Mark, Principal, Community Resource Services Ltd., 147
Shropshall, Don, President, Norm Shropshall & Sons Ltd., 306
Shropshall, Wayne, General Manager, Norm Shropshall & Sons Ltd., 306
Shropshire, Don, General Manager. Community Development & Planning, Chatham-Kent, 724
Shropshire, Gary, Manager, Community Parks & Programs Branch, East Gwillimbury, 708
Shrum, John, Branch Manager, Fabricated Plastics Ltd., 193
Shugar, Donna, Chair, Sunshine Coast, 679
Shugart, Ian, Deputy Minister of Human Resources & Skills Develo, 534
Shular, Richard, Fort Erie, 709
Shully, Allen, Director, Zorbit Technologies Inc., 437
Shulman, Tammy, Partner, Borden Ladner Gervais LLP - Montréal, 1083
Shutiak, Wayne, Branch Manager, Fort Garry Industries Ltd., 200
Shuttleworth, Valerie, Director, Planning & Urban Design, Markham, 713
Shuturma, Jim, Manager, Engineered Air, 180
Shybunka, Brad, COO/Director, Ridgeline Environment Inc., 347
Shynkaruk, Darren, Manager, Calgary, 121
Sibbald, John, Coordinator, Halifax Regional Municipality, 902-490-5527, 695
Sicard, Robert P., President & CEO, UPI Inc., 407
Sicotte, Paul, President, UNOTEC, 407
Siddiquee, Yursa, Partner, Ogilvy Renault LLP/S.E.N.C.R.L., s.r.l. - Toronto, 1078
Sidey, Carolyne, Manager, Xerox Research Centre of Canada, 1146
Sidhom, Nasif, N-T Enterprise Inc., 296
Sidhu, Gurshan, District Sales Rep., National Instruments Canada, 298
Sidhwa, Phil, Vice-President, Terratec Environmental Ltd., 390
Sidlofsky, James C., Partner, Borden Ladner Gervais LLP - Toronto, 1074
Sieben, Gerry, General Manager, Bacon Donaldson & Associates Ltd., 101

Executive Name Index

Siebert, Erica, General Manager, Canadian Liquids Processors Limited, 124
Siegel, Eric D., President/CEO, 525
Siemens, Jol, President, Saskatchewan Outdoor & Environmental Education Association, 1001
Siemon, Bill, Huron, 701
Sigalet, Jennifer, Director, Library Services, Vernon Campus, 1119
Siglet, S., Carrier Canada Ltd., 129
Sigmundson, Danny Jo, CAO, St. Andrews, 690
Sigouin, C. Nicole, Partner, Ogilvy Renault LLP/S.E.N.C.R.L., s.r.l. - Toronto, 1078
Sigouin, Luc, Directeur, Université du Québec en Abitibi-Témiscamingue, 1182
Sikora, Jason, Manager, Tansley Associates Environmental Services, 387
Silani, Larry, Director, Planning & Development Services, LaSalle, 713
Silbermann, Hanan S., President/Technical Manager, Pelmar Engineering Ltd., 320
Silbert, Marvin D., President, Marvin Silbert & Associates, 282
Silkie, Rand, President, Remedy Energy Services Ltd., 345
Silliphant, Dave, Touchie Engineering, 399
Sills, Gary, Executive Director, Cimatec Environmental Engineering Inc., 141
Sills, Michael, President, Canentec Inc., 126
Silva, Sylvia, National Sales Manager, North America, Hydro Vision America, 236
Silveira, Peter, Barrie, 706
Silver, Steven, Chief Administrative Officer, Leeds & Grenville, 726
Silvester, Robin, President/CEO, Vancouver Fraser Port Authority, 409
Silvestri, Bruno, Treasurer & General Manager, Financial & Corporate, Welland, 722
Silzer, Laur'Lei, Co-Director, 656
Silzer, Laur'Lei, Director, 661
Simanovskis, Ilmar, Director, Public Works, Aurora, 706
Simard, André, President, André Simard et associés ltée, 85
Simard, Christian, Directeur général, Nature Québec, 960
Simard, Danielle, Rouyn-Noranda, 741
Simard, Denis, Directeur, Saguenay, 741
Simard, Estelle, Greffière, Mont-St-Hilaire, 738
Simard, Fabienne, Technicienne en documentation, publications sériée, CÉGEP de Jonquière, 1168
Simard, Georges, Maire, Dolbeau-Mistassini, 735
Simard, Guy, Directeur général, Alma, 733
Simard, Jean-Eudes, Saguenay, 741
Simard, Jean-Luc, Préfet, Charlevoix-Est, 747
Simard, Joachim, President, Les Laboratoires S.L. inc., 269
Simard, Joanie, Ogilvy Renault LLP/S.E.N.C.R.L., s.r.l. - Québec, 1089
Simard, Patrice, Sylvain, Parent, Gobeil, 1089
Simard, Raoul, Saguenay, 741
Simard, Serge, Ministre, 650
Simard, Stéphane, Magog, 819-843-6389, 737
Simard, Virginie, Lavery, de Billy - Montréal, 1086
Simard-Pageau, France, Technicienne, documentation, Collège Mérici, 1178
Simcik, Matt F., President, International Association for Great Lakes Research, 935
Simek, Stefan, President, Ferguson Simek Clark, 194
Simmering, Stephen G., Principal, Golder Associates Ltd., 214
Simmonds, Tony, Manager, Westburne Canada, 426
Simmons, Crystal, Liaison, Wildlife Rescue Association of British Columbia, 1020
Simmons, Daniel W., Partner, Ottenheimer Baker, 1066
Simmons, Joann, Commissioner, Community & Health Services, York, 705
Simmons, Rick D., Ross & McBride LLP, 1069
Simmons, Q.C., James C., Weaver, Simmons LLP, 1072
Simms, Randy, Mayor, Mount Pearl, 694
Simms, Stephen, President/CEO, Environmental Waste International, 186
Simon, Charles, Principal, Charles Simon Architect & Planner, 138
Simon, Donald (Tony), President & Chief Executive Officer, Seguro Projects Inc., 362
Simon, Judy, Vice-President, INDECO Strategic Consulting Inc., 240
Simon, Philippe, President, Sinanni Inc., 369
Simon, Thierry, Vice-President, Groupe Berlie-Falco Inc., 219
Simond, Raymond, Communications Manager, Flygt Canada, 198
Simonds, Rob, Fire Chief, Saint John, 506-658-2910, 692

Simoneau, Jacques, Executive Vice President, Investments, 512
Simoneau, Marc, Québec, 740
Simoneau, Marcel, Directeur, Bibliothèque des sciences, 1170
Simoneau, Marcel, Directrice, Bibliothèque des sciences, Université du Québec à Montréal, 1176
Simons, Derek R., President, Kernic Systems Inc., 257
Simons, Shirley, Brant, 698
Simpson, Bob, Group Executive, Coffey Geotechnics Inc., 146
Simpson, Brian, Superintendent, Red Deer, 674
Simpson, Debra, Library Associate, University of Guelph Kemptville College, 1142
Simpson, Don, City Solicitor, Red Deer, 674
Simpson, Donna, Office Clerk, University of Alberta Dept. of Physiology, 1107
Simpson, Geoff, Director, Energy Ottawa, 179
Simpson, Jeff, President, Aquatic Life Ltd., 89
Simpson, Jennifer, Executive Director, International Titanium Association, 944
Simpson, John, Director, Grande Prairie No. 1, 780-513-3950, 669
Simpson, John, Marketing & Sales Manager, Thermo Electron Corp., 394
Simpson, Ken, Innisfil, 711
Simpson, Kenneth, Executive Director, Union of Nova Scotia Municipalities, 1015
Simpson, L., Vice-President, Kruger Inc., 260
Simpson, Mark, Lambton Shores, 726
Simpson, Mark, General Manager, Layfield Geosynthetics & Industrial Fabrics Ltd., 265
Simpson, Mark, Operations Coordinator, Grande Prairie, 780-538-0442, 672
Simpson, Neil, Marketing/Sales, Kam Biotechnology Ltd., 254
Simpson, Richard, Innisfil, 711
Simpson, Robert J., Fraser Milner Casgrain LLP - Calgary, 1051
Simpson, Ron, Bradford West Gwillimbury, 706
Simpson, Steven, President/Quality Assurance Manager, Becquerel Laboratories Inc., 104
Simpson Campbell, Shari, Director, Green Tourism Association, 926
Simpson, MBA, P.Ag., Susan, President, Agricultural Institute of Canada Foundation, 814
Simser, Gary, Technician, Regulatory Water / Wastewater Complian, North Grenville, 728
Simulik, Marian, City Treasurer, Ottawa, 716
Simundsson, Elva, Regional Librarian, Eric Marshall Aquatic Research Library (Central and Artic Library), 1123
Sinanan, Carol, Instructional Services Librarian, Mount Royal College, 1102
Sinclair, Don, General Manager, Development & Legal Services, East Gwillimbury, 708
Sinclair, Douglas, Manager, Pomeroy Consulting Engineers Limited, 328
Sinclair, Gavin, Partner, Heenan Blaikie LLP - Toronto, 1076
Sinclair, Jane, General Manager, Health & Cultural Services, Simcoe, 704
Sinclair, Jill, Assistant Deputy Minister, 545
Sinclair, Karen, Manager, Abbotsford, 604-557-4416, 679
Sinclair, Laura, Vegewax Candleworx Ltd., 410
Sinclair, Pierrette, Counsel, Borden Ladner Gervais LLP - Montréal, 1083
Sinclair, William J., Founder & Director, Fluorosense Inc., 198
Sinclair, Q.C., P. Michael, Managing Partner, Thompson Dorfman Sweatman LLP, 1064
Singer, Aaron B., Clark Wilson LLP, 1058
Singer, Cathy, Partner, Ogilvy Renault LLP/S.E.N.C.R.L., s.r.l. - Toronto, 1078
Singer, Evan, Vice-President, Canadian Federation of Engineering Students, 868
Singer, Marvin, Partner, Macleod Dixon LLP, 1077
Singer Neuvelt, Carol, Executive Director, National Association for Environmental Management, 956
Singh, Naresh, Acting Vice-President, 520
Singh, Paul, Kitchener, 712
Singleton, Darryl, Vice-President, Aqua Tech Sales & Marketing Inc., 88
Singleton, Michael, Executive Director, Sustainable Buildings Canada, 1011
Singleton, Q.C., John R., Partner, Singleton Urquhart LLP, 1062
Singleton, Q.C., Robyn W., Chief Commissioner, Strathcona County, 780-464-8100, 670
Sinnott, Curtis, Sinnott Farm Services Ltd., 369
Sipos, Kathy, Manager, West Lincoln, 732
Sirett, Robin M., McCarthy Tétrault LLP - Vancouver, 1061
Sirko, Ariana, Technical Services Librarian, E.K. Williams Law Library, 1123

Sirois, Daniel C., Weaver, Simmons LLP, 1072
Sirr, Mark, Treasurer & Manager, Finance, New Tecumseth, 714
Sisco, David R., Secretary-Treasurer, Planning & Engineering Initiatives Ltd., 325
Siscoe, Mathew D., St. Catharines, 719
Sisson, Gord, Director, 656
Sisson, John R., Chief Administrative Officer, Bracebridge, 706
Sitland, D., Manager, Operations, Pembroke, 717
Sittler, Clark, Plant Manager, CCS Income Trust, 134
Sittler, Richard, Operations, Sittler Environmental, 369
Sittler, Steven, General Manager, Sittler Environmental, 369
Sittler, Steven, President, Sittler Excavating Ltd., 369
Situm, Milan, P.Geophysicist, Géophysique GPR International Inc., 211
Siva, Amelia, Executive Director, Canadian Plastics Sector Council, 882
Sivilotti, Paul, Manager, Sherwin-Williams Canada Inc., 365
Siwanowicz, Hellen L., Lang Michener LLP - Toronto, 1077
Sixsmith, Paul, President/CEO, Plasticair Inc., 326
Siydock, Mark, Facility Manager, BFI Canada Inc., 106
Sjoberg, C.M.A., Brent, General Manager, Regina, 754
Sjolie, Q.C., Barry A., Brownlee LLP, 1054
Sjostrom, Mary, Mayor, Quesnel, 688
Skakun, Brian, Prince George, 683
Skauge, Cliff, Clerk, Prince Albert, 754
Skeele, Tom, Executive Director, American Wildlands, 827
Skeels, Melinda J., Ratcliff & Company LLP, 1057
Skelling, Joanne, Greffière, Cowansville, 735
Skelton, Brooke, Head of Cataloguing, Wilfrid Laurier University, 1165
Skene, Gord, President, Paradigm Environmental Technologies Inc., 318
Skene, Michael A., Partner, Borden Ladner Gervais LLP - Vancouver, 1058
Skernolis, Ed, Executive Director, National Recycling Coalition, 958
Skiera, Jim, Executive Director, International Society of Arboriculture, 943
Skinner, Brian J., Chief Administrative Officer, Ajax, 705
Skinner, Douglas B., McInnes Cooper, 1066
Skinner, Randy, Brock, 724
Skinner, Robin, Environmental Planner, East Gwillimbury, 708
Skinner, Shawn, Minister, 601
Skinner, Susan, Co-Manager, Alberta Fish & Game Association, 817
Skipper, Barbara, Manager, UPI Inc., 407
Skirrow, Paul, Vice-President, Semco Systems Limited, 362
Skogster, Mauri, Manager, Finnex Agencies Ltd., 195
Skolrood, B.A., LL.B., LL, Ron A., Partner, Lawson Lundell LLP - Vancouver, 1061
Skorayko, Stanley, Vice-President, Canon Canada Inc., 126
Skrobica, Mike, Vice-President, Air Transport Association of Canada, 814
Skrupski, Peter, Reeve, Springfield, 204-444-2970, 690
Skull, J.R., President, Westeel, 429
Slade, David, Senior Vice-President, 510
Slater, Bill, General Manager, Westmorland-Albert Solid Waste Corporation, 759
Slater, Cody, President & CEO, BW Technologies by Honeywell, 119
Slater, Curtis, Director, HMI Industries, 232
Slater, John, Chair, North Okanagan, 678
Slater, Ron, Chair, Information & Instruction, Laurentian University, 1155
Slattery, C.A., J. William, Director, 612
Slauenwhite, Tammy, President, RenuWater Centre, 345
Slavik, Jerome M., Ackroyd LLP Barristers & Solicitors, 1054
Sled, Phil, Simcoe, 704
Sleiman, Ed, Windsor, 723
Slemp, Jay J., Chair, 571
Slik, Lori, Prince Edward, 703
Sliwinski, John, Manager, OSB Services, 314
Sloan, Carol, Manager, Westburne Canada, 426
Sloan, Hugh, Director, Fraser Valley, 677
Sloan, Linda, Edmonton, 780-496-8122, 672
Sloan, Michael, Vice President, Napier Environmental Technology, 296
Sloan, William, Leeds & Grenville, 726
Sloane, Dawn Marie, Councillor, Halifax Regional Municipality, 695
Sloat, Buck, Haldimand, 700
Sloboda, Susanne, Robertson Environmental Services Ltd., 348
Slobodan, D., Director, Courtenay, 680
Slobogan, Karen, EPCOR Energy Services Inc., 189

Executive Name Index

Slocombe, John, Branch Manager, Gamsby & Mannerow Ltd., 204
Slocombe, John, Treasurer, Gamsby & Mannerow Ltd., 204
Slone, Dan, Secretary, Green Roofs for Healthy Cities, 926
Slyster, Donna, Sr. Vice-President & Chief Information Officer, CHEP Canada, 140
Smailes, Rob, Manager, North Okanagan, 678
Smale, Kim, Manager, Westburne Canada, 429
Smale, Patrick, President, E.K. Gillin & Associates Inc., 168
Smallhorn, Charles, President, Mainetti Canada Inc., 279
Smallhorn, Ed A., President, SEA Engineering Company Inc., 361
Smallwood, Michael, Vice-President, Aker Metals (Toronto), 76
Smardon, Richard, Co-Director, The Great Lakes Research Consortium, 925
Smart, Robert, Deputy Minister, 604
Smart, Rosemary, Intl Marketing Programs Coordinator, Canadian Swine Exporters Association, 889
Smaye, Sheldon, Contact, Solignum Inc., 372
Smeaton, Willian (Bill), Niagara, 702
Smelko, Mark, President, M.S. Thompson & Associates Ltd., 276
Smellie, James H., Gowling Lafleur Henderson LLP - Calgary, 1051
Smerchanski, Dennis, General Manager, Border Chemical Company Ltd., 114
Smereka, Barry, Manager, Bartle & Gibson Co. Ltd., 102
Smilar, Debbie, Office Manager, Golder Associates Ltd., 214
Smiley, Penny, Commissioner, Human Resources, Waterloo, 704
Smith, A.R., President/CEO, Banyan Chains Inc., 101
Smith, Alan, Business Manager, Fort Storage Warehousing & Distribution, 200
Smith, Alan, Contact, BMT Fleet Technology Ltd., 111
Smith, Alan A., President/CEO, Alan A. Smith Inc., 76
Smith, Andrew, Borden Ladner Gervais LLP - Toronto, 1074
Smith, Anne, Secretary-Treasurer, Canadian Remote Sensing Society, 884
Smith, Archie, Inside Technical Sales, Romatec Incorporated, 350
Smith, Arthur, Head, Library & Archives, Royal Ontario Museum Libraries, 1161
Smith, B., Economic Development Officer, Wasaga Beach, 705-429-3847, 722
Smith, Bill, Sales Agent, Danatec Educational Services Ltd., 157
Smith, Bradley A., Partner, Weiler, Maloney, Nelson, 1072
Smith, Brandon, Manager, E2 Management Corporation, 168
Smith, Brenda, Access Services Librarian, Thompson Rivers University, 1112
Smith, Brian, CAO, Kings County, 902-690-6131, 696
Smith, Bruce, Executive Director, Island Nature Trust, 946
Smith, Byard A., Executive Director, 597
Smith, Cameron, Simcoe Engineering Group Limited, 368
Smith, Carl, President/CEO, Rechargeable Battery Recycling Corporation, 343
Smith, Charles B., President, Boilersmith Ltd., 113
Smith, Christina, President, Calgary Horticultural Society, 852
Smith, Christine, Director, 663
Smith, Clyde, Councillor, Whitchurch-Stouffville, 723
Smith, D.I., Corporate Partner, Smith & Andersen Consulting Engineering, 370
Smith, David, General Manager, Recreation & Leisure Services, Waterloo, 519-747-8739, 722
Smith, David, President, Highland Equipment Ltd., 231
Smith, Deanna, Branch Manager, CenturyVallen, 136
Smith, Don, Chief Administrative Officer, Niagara-on-the-Lake, 715
Smith, Don, Sales, Smith-Way Ltd., 371
Smith, Doug, Director, Emergency Services, Bruce, 698
Smith, Doug, President, Entropic Energy Inc., 182
Smith, Douglas O., Partner, Borden Ladner Gervais LLP - Toronto, 1074
Smith, Ed, Fire Chief, North Perth, 519-292-2053, 715
Smith, Elliot A., Osler, Hoskin & Harcourt LLP - Toronto, 1079
Smith, Eric, Councillor, Kings County, 696
Smith, Eric A.H., President & CEO, PCB Disposal Inc., 320
Smith, Fred A., Director, North Vancouver, 604-990-4206, 682
Smith, Gary, BMT Group, Regional Director, BMT Fleet Technology Ltd., 111
Smith, Gary, Manager, Kings County, 902-690-6117, 696
Smith, Gary, President, AAA Petroleum Contracting Ltd., 64
Smith, Glen, Sales Representative, Armtec Construction Products, 72
Smith, Gordon, Manager, Harris & Roome Supply Limited, 226
Smith, Gordon, Vice-President, MacDonald & Fils Inc., 277
Smith, Gordon (Shorty), Fire Chief, Dawson Creek, 250-784-3635, 680

Smith, Graydon, Muskoka, 702
Smith, Graydon, Mayor, Bracebridge, 706
Smith, Gregory C., Partner, Miller Thomson LLP - Vancouver, 1062
Smith, Harvey, Winnipeg, 204-986-5951, 690
Smith, Howard F., Chief Administrative Officer, North Dundas, 727
Smith, Ian, Director, Cochrane, 403-851-2530, 671
Smith, Ian, Director, Community Services, Sarnia, 719
Smith, Ian, General Manager, Comox Valley, 677
Smith, Jack, Plant Manager, LINPAC Ropak Packaging, 272
Smith, Jacques, Salaberry-de-Valleyfield, 450-371-4975, 744
Smith, James W., President, Apollo Environmental Systems Corporation, 87
Smith, Jamie, New Tecumseth, 714
Smith, Janette, Commissioner, Health Services, Peel, 703
Smith, Jim, Councillor, Halifax Regional Municipality, 695
Smith, Jim, Division Head, Technical Services/Research, Prince Edward Island Food Technology Centre, 1166
Smith, Jim, President, KGS Group Inc., 257
Smith, John, Abbotsford, 679
Smith, John, Director, 596
Smith, John D., Director, 518
Smith, Judy, CAO, Torrie Smith Associates Inc., 398
Smith, Kara, Heenan Blaikie LLP - Toronto, 1076
Smith, Keith, Contact, Red Devil Drain Service, 343
Smith, Kelly, Chief Building Official, Orillia, 710
Smith, Lawrence, Waterstone Law Group LLP, 1056
Smith, Lee, Fire Chief, Niagara Falls, 715
Smith, Lewis T., Partner, Stikeman Elliott LLP - Toronto, 1080
Smith, Linda, Executive Director, 661
Smith, Linda, Manager, Therm-O-Comfort Co. Ltd., 394
Smith, Lisa, Manager, Human Resources, Huntsville, 711
Smith, Lorraine, Acquisitions/Cataloguing Librarian, Bishop's University, 1185
Smith, Lorraine, Manager, Library & Information Services, Greenhouse & Processing Crops, 1141
Smith, Mark, General Manager, Development Services, Thunder Bay, 807-625-2544, 721
Smith, Martin, Vice-President, Boojum Research Ltd., 113
Smith, Mary, Peterborough, 703
Smith, Mary, Reeve, Smith-Ennismore-Lakefield, 729
Smith, Mike, Mayor, Saugeen Shores, 719
Smith, Mike, Warden & Councillor, Bruce, 698
Smith, Mindy, Director, Port Coquitlam, 683
Smith, Monique M., Minister, 635
Smith, Neil, Manager, Mount Waddington, 678
Smith, Paul, Chief of Police, Charlottetown, 732
Smith, Paul N.K., Partner, Lawson Lundell LLP - Yellowknife, 1066
Smith, Peter, Chair, 635
Smith, Peter, President, Canadian Environmental Group, 124
Smith, Peter W., Vice-President, Zeton Inc., 437
Smith, Phil, President, Australian Association for Environmental Education, 844
Smith, R.L. (Bud), President & Chief Executive Officer, Brampton Engineering Inc., 115
Smith, Randall W., Cox and Palmer - St. John's, 1065
Smith, Rich, General Manager, Alberta Beef Producers, 815
Smith, Richard, ADI Group Inc., 68
Smith, Richard, President, SmithBrook Waste Management Services Inc., 371
Smith, Rick, Executive Director, Environmental Defence, 911
Smith, Rob, Manager, Westburne Canada, 427
Smith, Robert, Director, Economic Development & Tourism Marketing, Haliburton, 700
Smith, Robert, Manager, Athabasca Regional Waste Management Services Commission, 757
Smith, Roger F., Partner, Macleod Dixon LLP, 1052
Smith, Ron, Superintendent, Public Works, Norwich, 728
Smith, Russ, Manager, Medicine Hat, 403-529-8188, 673
Smith, Scott, Planner, Port Alberni, 683
Smith, Sid, Technologist, Sinclair Technologies, 369
Smith, Sybil, Director, New Brunswick Salmon Growers Association, 961
Smith, Syd, CEO, Nortec S.G.S. Inc., 306
Smith, Terry, Chief Coroner, 582
Smith, Terry, General Manager, ALL-TECH Environmental Services Ltd., 78
Smith, Wayne, Chief Statistician of Canada, 559
Smith, William, Sherbrooke, 744
Smith, NCMN, FHIMSS, Carla, Executive Vice-President, Healthcare Information & Management Systems Society, 928
Smith, PhD, MBA, FIFST, James (Jim), Executive Director, 640
Smith, Q.C., B.A.R., Fraser Milner Casgrain LLP - Calgary, 1051

Smith, Q.C., Harold M., Partner, Stewart McKelvey Stirling Scales - St. John's, 1066
Smith, Q.C., Lawrence E., Bennett Jones LLP - Calgary Office, 1049
Smith, Q.C., Phyllis A., Emery Jamieson LLP, 1055
Smith, Q.C., William H., McCarthy Tétrault LLP - Calgary, 1053
Smith, Q.C., Winston F., Hook & Smith, 1063
Smith, RPF, Peggy, Senior Advisor, National Aboriginal Forestry Association, 956
Smithard, Lynda, Coordinator, URS Canada Inc., 408
Smithen, Jon S., Heenan Blaikie LLP - Toronto, 1076
Smithers, Anne, Head, Technical & Document Services, Bracken Health Sciences Library, 1142
Smith-Morken, Kelly, Manager, Westburne Canada, 426
Smith-Robinson, Colleen, Executive Director, Ontario Agri-Food Education Inc., 970
Smithson, Diane, Chief Administrative Officer, Mississippi Mills, 714
Smithson, Margaret, President, Occupational Health Nurses of British Columbia, 969
Smitten, Ron, Chair, 573
Smockum, Brad, Georgina, 709
Smola, Jake, Waterloo, 704
Smordin, Don, Head, Armstrong Monitoring Corp., 91
Smyth, France, Bibliothécaire, New Brunswick Community College, 1128, 1127
Smyth, Jamie, Economic Development Officer, King, 726
Smyth, Joan, Sanitherm Engineering Limited, 357
Smyth, Michael, Partner, Heenan Blaikie LLP - Toronto, 1076
Smyth, Peter, Technical Representative, Can-Am Instruments Ltd., 122
Smyth, Richard, Partner, Sanitherm Engineering Limited, 357
Smythe, Karen, Stratford, 720
Snarr, Wes, Chief Financial Officer & Treasurer, Centre Wellington, 724
Snelgrove, Cathy, General Manager, Brandon, 204-729-2145, 689
Snelgrove, Lloyd, Minister, 568
Snell, Deanna, Registrar, Calgary Zoological Society, 1100
Snider, Dick, Engineer, LTS Sales Ltd., 274
Snider, George, Interim Manager, Lesser Slave Lake Regional Waste Management Services Commission, 757
Snider, Sue, Dufferin, 699
Snook, Donnie, Saint John, 692
Snow, Catherine, Clerk, Quispamsis, 506-849-5738, 692
Snow, Ernie, Owner, EPS Wood Products Ltd., 189
Snow, Larry, President, G.T. Wood Co. Ltd., 204
Snowball, Bill, Fire Chief, Fire & Emergency Services, Markham, 905-305-5982, 713
Snure, Ted, General Manager & City Engineer, Brandon, 204-729-2214, 689
Snyder, Al M., Vice-President, 588
Snyder, Barbara, Director, Esquimalt, 686
Snyder, Frank, President & Gen. Mgr., Novitherm Canada Inc., 309
Snyder, Joan, Chair, British Columbia Nature (Federation of British Columbia Naturalis, 849
Snyder, Stephen G., President & CEO, Transalta Utilities, 400
Sobeski, Pat, Oxford, 728
Sobeski, Pat, Mayor, Woodstock, 723
Sobey, Newton, President, N.L. Sobey & Associates Limited, 296
Sobol, Isaac, Chief Medical Officer of Health, 619
Sobol, Isaac, President, Canadian Public Health Association - NWT/Nunavut Branch, 883
Sobol, Nick, Paralibrarian (Serials), Cape Breton University, 1137
Sobotta, A., Co-General Manager, Phoenix Contact Ltd., 323
Sobsey, Richard, Contact, University of Alberta J.P. Das Developmental Disabilities Centre, 1107
Soczka, Rob, General Manager, Verdyol Mulch of Canada Ltd., 412
Soderberg, Allan, President, Sultech Consulting Ltd., 381
Sodin, W., President, W. Sodin (Gravity) Ltd., 414
Soetens, René, President, Con-Test, A Division of Contamination Containment Technology Inc., 148
Sohi, Amarjeet, Edmonton, 780-496-8148, 672
Sokach, Brad, Director, Public Works, Springwater, 730
Sokalsky, Steven, Heenan Blaikie LLP - Toronto, 1076
Sokol, Bob, Director, West Vancouver, 604-925-7058, 689
Sokolowski, Terri, Anachem Ltd., 84
Sol, Ruth, President, Western Transportation Advisory Council, 1019
Solano, Paolo, Legal Officer, 525
Soldo, Edward, Manager, Operations & Compliance, St. Thomas, 719

Executive Name Index

Soligo, Michael J., President/CEO, Rowan Williams Davies & Irwin Inc., 353
Soliman, Walied, Partner, Ogilvy Renault LLP/S.E.N.C.R.L., s.r.l. - Toronto, 1078
Sollazzo, Madeleine, Laval, 736
Solmes, Paul, Coordinator, Peace River, 678
Solomon, Lawrence, Executive Director, Consumer Policy Institute, 903
Solomon, Lawrence, Managing Director, Energy Probe Research Foundation, 1157
Solomon, Milimbo, Trade Commissioner, 769
Soltis, Kathleen, Director, Prince George, 683
Solyma, Alice, Head, Library Services, Pacific Forestry Centre, 1121
Somers, Diane, Rosenberg & Rosenberg, 1062
Somers, Janice, Information Specialist, Ontario Ministry of Economic Development & Trade, 1160
Somerton, Lisa, Manager, Westburne Canada, 426
Somerville, Chris, Clerk, King, 726
Somerville, Clark, Halton, 700
Somerville, Clark A., Regional Councillor, Halton Hills, 710
Somerville, M.A., Director, Centre for Medicine, Ethics & Law, 894
Somerville, Scott, Chief Administrative Officer, King, 726
Sommerfeldt, Dale, Vice-President, Scientific Instrumentation Ltd., 360
Sonego, P. Eng., Mario, City Engineer, Windsor, 723
Song, Hiju, Manager, Consulting Engineers of Alberta, 902
Song, J.J., Manager, Canadian Fibre, 124
Sonnenberg, Harold, Norfolk, 702
Sonnenburg, Ed, Lanark, 701
Sonntag, Calvin., President, Philom Bios Inc., 323
Sooknanan, Joey, Supervisor, Wastequip Cusco, 421
Soomro, Maqsood A., Milton, 714
Sopel, Mark, Project Manager, Elecsar Engineering Co. Ltd., 174
Sopotiuck, Don, Electronics Technician, Frank's Alternate Energy, 201
Sorba, Jake, Director, Maple Ridge, 604-467-7317, 687
Sorenson, Hugo, President, Toromont Caterpillar, 397
Sorieul, Françoise, Secteur des collections spéciales, Bibliothèque des sciences humaines et sociales, 1177
Sorochan, Q.C., Donald J., Partner, Miller Thomson LLP - Vancouver, 1062
Sosiak, Lyne, Sales Coordinator, Caristrap International Inc., 128
Sosnoski, Gary, Commissioner, Corporate Resources, Waterloo, 704
Soubeyrand, Françoise, Technicienne, SNC-Lavalin inc., 1175
Soucy, René, Directeur général, Thetford Mines, 745
Soulard, Pierre L., Partner, Ogilvy Renault LLP/S.E.N.C.R.L., s.r.l. - Toronto, 1078
Soulis, C., Carrier Canada Ltd., 129
South, George, General Manager, Miller Waste Systems, 290
Southcott, Richard F., Stewart McKelvey Stirling Scales - Halifax, 1068
Southern, Nancy C., President/CEO, ATCO Group, 94
Southern, Ronald D., Chairman, ATCO Group, 94
Southwell, Mike, Manager, Inuktun Services Ltd., 246
Sowers, Rhonda, Contact, Ontario Federation of Anglers & Hunters, 1153
Sowik, Jane, City Clerk, Surrey, 604-591-4113, 684
Spadoni, Robert, Director, Finance, Lincoln, 713
Spafford, Gordon, Principal, Unies Limited, 405
Spalding, Q.C., Howard A., Barry Spalding - Saint John Office, 1065
Spangler, Ray, Office Manager, Trow Consulting Engineers Ltd., 403
Sparanese, Peter, General Manager, Victoria, 250-361-0292, 685
Sparkes, Judy, Secretary, Central Ontario Orchid Society, 893
Sparks, Clive, Fire Chief, Whitehorse, 867-668-8383, 755
Sparks, S., Director, Moncton / Ville de Moncton, 691
Sparling, Gabriela, Deputy Minister, 605
Spasoff, Christopher W., McLennan Ross LLP, 1055
Spatafora, Vito, York, 705
Spatafora, Vito, Regional & Local Councillor, Richmond Hill, 718
Spears, Paul, Orillia, 716
Speck, Troy, General Manager, Corporate Services, Kitchener, 519-741-2279, 712
Spector, Charles R., Fraser Milner Casgrain S.E.N.C.R.L./LLP, 1084
Speel, Janis, Vice-President, Niblett Environmental, 304
Speer, Christina, Chair, Niijkwenhwag - Friends of Lake Superior Park, 964
Speevak, Dena, Chief, Information Services, Agriculture & Agri-Food Canada, 1147
Spehr, Erwin, President, Hygrex-Spehr Industries, 237

Speight, Connie, Executive Secretary, Cumberland County, 697
Speirs, Craig, Maple Ridge, 687
Speller, Liz, Environmental Planner, LGL Limited Environmental Research Associates, 271
Spence, Daniel, Director, Sierra Club of Canada, 1004
Spenceley, Bill, President & CEO, Flexahopper Plastics Ltd., 196
Spencer, Anna, Head of Acquisitions, Concordia University College of Alberta, 1105
Spencer, Geoffrey L., Benson Myles, 1065
Spencer, Heather, Coordinator, Food & Consumer Products of Canada, 918
Spencer, Henry A., President & General Manager, Spencer-Lemaire Industries Ltd., 375
Spencer, Rob, Secretary, Rawdon Technologies Ltd., 342
Spencer, Robert D., Vice-President, Trihedral Engineering Limited, 401
Spencer, Shirley, Manager, Saskatchewan Highways & Transportation, 1188
Spensieri, Aldo, Vice-President, West Point Products Canada, 425
Speranzini, Joseph G., Scarfone Hawkins LLP, 1069
Sperduti, Frank J., Partner, Borden Ladner Gervais LLP - Toronto, 1074
Spetgang, Shai, Manager, ONEIA - Ontario Environment Industry Association, 970
Spettigue, Doug, Human Resource Officer, Middlesex, 701
Spicer, Robert M., President/General Manager, RMS Enviro Solv Inc. Québec, 347
Spicer, Q.C., Wylie, McInnes Cooper, 1067
Spidell, Heather, Director, 610
Spierkel, Karen, Director, 519
Spiers, Graeme, Director, Mirarco Mining Innovation, 290
Spiewak, Ron, Secretary-Treasurer, Ontario Tire Dealers Association, 980
Spillman, Ron, HFP Acoustical Consultants Corp., 231
Spina, Marg, Kamloops, 681
Spink, Ed, CEO, TurboSonic Inc., 404
Spiratos, Nelu, President/CEO, Produits Chimiques Handy Ltée, 333
Spitale, Lisa, Director, New Westminster, 682
Spitzke, Richard, President, Fort Garry Industries Ltd., 199
Spitzke-Kent, Robyn, Executive VP, Fort Garry Industries Ltd., 200
Sponga, Joe, Newmarket, 714
Sponton, Shawn, PRT Inc., 336
Spooner, Neil, District Manager, ESRI Canada Ltd., 190
Spothelfer, Pascal E., President & CEO, British Columbia Technology Industries Association, 850
Spracklin, Q.C., Wayne F., Partner, Ottenheimer Baker, 1066
Spraggs, Richard, Director, Public Works, Clearview, 725
Sprague, Andrew, Communications Officer, 641
Sprague, Lesley, City Clerk, Elliot Lake, 709
Spray, Frank, Manager, Romatec Incorporated, 350
Sproule, Althea, Librarian, Canada Revenue Agency, 1148
Sprovieri, John, Peel, 703
Sprovieri, John, Regional Councillor, Brampton, 706
Spruill, Vikki N., President & CEO, The Ocean Conservancy, 969
Spry, Barbara, Treasurer, Port Hope, 728
Spry, Keith, Manager, Westburne Canada, 427
Spurr, Mary, Secretary, Health Sciences Association of Saskatchewan, 928
Spyker, Dave, Executive Vice President, Siemens Water Technologies, 367
Squire, Mike, Manager, Parksville, 250-954-4698, 682
Squires, Dave, Regional Manager, Electronic Warfare Associates - Canada, Ltd., 175
Sracek, Ondrej, AGRECOM inc., 73
Srinath, Ingrid, Secretary General, CIVICUS: World Alliance for Citizen Participation, 896
Srivastava, Raman, Director, 518
Staatz, Merlene, Contact, Technical Services, Serials, Interlibrary, The King's University College, 1106
Stacey, Arthur J., Thompson Dorfman Sweatman LLP, 1064
Stacey, Mark C., Partner, Singleton Urquhart LLP, 1062
Stacey, Steve, Raging River Power & Mining Inc., 341
Stachoski, Lyndon, Clerk, Estevan, 754
Stack, Derek, Executive Director, Great Lakes United, 925
Stack, Len, St. Catharines, 719
Stack, Luke, Kelowna, 681
Stack, Walter, Renfrew, 613-623-4231, 704
Stady, Judy, Supervisor, Interlibrary Loan, Athabasca University, 1099
Staeben, Brent, Director, 597
Staeben, Paul, Pinchin Environmental Ltd., 324
Stafford, Doug, Branch Manager, Leeson Canada Ltd., 266

Stafford-Veale, Scott, Account Manager, ESRI Canada Ltd., 190
Stainsby, Jonathan, Partner, Heenan Blaikie LLP - Toronto, 1076
Stakern, Doug, AMETEK Process Instruments, 84
Stam, Chuck, Chilliwack, 680
St-Amant, Robert, Chef de section, University of Guelph Collège d'Alfred, 1138
St-Amour, Lysane, Information Specialist, Pratt & Whitney Canada Inc., 1169
St-Amour, Patrick, Greffier, Rosemère, 741
St-Amour, Wayne, Executive Director, Offshore Energy Environmental Research Association, 970
Standford, Victoria, Librarian, Newfoundland & Labrador Hydro, 1132
Standing, Jesse, Manager, SimplexGrinnell, 369
Standish, Ronald, Director, Wastewater & Treatment, London, 713
Stanfield, Ross, President, East Kootenay Chamber of Mines, 907
Stanford, Jay, Director, Environmental Programs & Solid Waste, London, 713
Stanhope, Joseph, Chair, Nanaimo, 678
Staniland, Tauna M., Stewart McKelvey Stirling Scales - St. John's, 1066
Stanker, Glenn, Engineer, Prince George, 250-561-7757, 683
Stanley, Alan, Coordinator, Nanaimo, 678
Stanley, Douglas C., President/CEO, 598
Stanley, Gary, Chair, 635
Stannard, Glenn, Chief of Police, Windsor, 723
St-Antoine, Jean, Greffier, Vaudreuil-Dorion, 746
Stanton, Andy, President, Hike Metal Products Ltd., 232
Stanton, Michael, Scarfone Hawkins LLP, 1069
Stanton, Paul, Director, White Rock, 686
Stanton, Paul, Manager, Campbell River, 679
Staples, Pete, Fire Chief, Harwood, Hamilton, 725
Stapleton, Paul R., City Administrator, Fredericton, 691
Stark, Daniel J., Executive Director, American Association of Botanical Gardens & Arboreta, 822
Stark, John E., Partner, Stikeman Elliott LLP - Vancouver, 1062
Stark Leader, Myrna, Vice-President, Canadian Farm Writers' Federation, 867
St-Arnaud, Claire, Conseillère, Maisonneuve-Longue-Pointe, Montréal, 738
Starr, John, Vice-President, Covertech Fabricating Inc., 153
Starr, Lea, Associate University Librarian, Public Services, University of British Columbia, 1119
Starr, Peter, Vice-President, Wasteco, 421
Starr, Ron, Peel, 714, 703
Stasiewicz, Brian E., Vice-President, Marsulex Inc., 281
Stasiuk, Nancy, Library Technician, Alberta Dept. of Energy, 1099
Stauble, Heather, Kawartha Lakes, 711
Staudt, Wayne, Director, Cranbrook, 680
St-Croix, Dave, Trésorier, Gaspé, 735
Steacy, Gary, President, Gary Steacy Dismantling Limited, 204
Stead, Graham, Contact, Oxford County Geological Society, 1156
Stebbins, Shawn, Co-founder, Archipelago Marine Research Ltd., 90
Steblin, Peter, City Manager, Coquitlam, 680
Steckler, Ed, Production Manager, Cosmopolitan Industries Limited, 152
Steckley, Bob, Fort Erie, 709
Stecyk, Sharon, Executive Assistant, Alberta Land Surveyors' Association, 1104
Stedtnitz, Sigrun, Vice-President, Stedtnitz Maritime Technology Ltd., 379
Stedtnitz, Wolfgang, President, Stedtnitz Maritime Technology Ltd., 379
Stedwill, Hilary, MacPherson Leslie & Tyerman LLP - Regina, 1090
Stedwill, R., Manager, SaskPower, 358
Steedman, Robert, Professional Leader, 546
Steel, Alan, Managing Director, Alberta Professional Outfitters Society, 819
Steele, Bill, Port Colborne, 905-834-4483, 718
Steele, Dave, Chairperson, Pickering & Ajax Citizens Together for the Environment, 986
Steele, Don, Secretary, Natural History Society of Newfoundland & Labrador, 959
Steele, H. Barbara, Surrey, 604-591-4623, 684
Steele, Sally, Coordinator, Lunenburg District, 902-543-2913, 697
Steele, Todd, Lennox & Addington, 613-379-5664, 701
Steen, Thomas, Winnipeg, 690
Steeves, George, Director, Algonquin Power Income Fund, 78
Steeves, Gord, Winnipeg, 204-986-5088, 690

Executive Name Index

Steeves, Jim, Superintendent, Riverview, 506-387-2027, 692
Steeves, Karl, Thermon Heat Tracing Services, 394
Steeves, Lucas, Manager, Greystone Energy Systems Inc., 218
Steeves, Peter, Contact, Geodetic Software Systems/Geomatics Information Center, 211
Steeves, Rob, Sales, Flexahopper Plastics Ltd., 196
Stefanchuk, Don, Pinchin Environmental Ltd., 324
Stefaniuk, John D., Thompson Dorfman Sweatman LLP, 1064
Stefanson, Grant A., D'Arcy & Deacon LLP, 1063
Stefenelli, Nicole, General Manager, Urban Impact Recycling Ltd., 407
Steffen, Preusser, Trade Commissioner, 767
Steffes, Collin, Manager, Sturgeon County, 780-939-8275, 670
Stein, Allan, Acting Vice-President, Natural History Society of Newfoundland & Labrador, 959
Steinberg, Jeff, Warco Process Technologies, 416
Steinberg, Jeff, Sales, Warco Process Technologies, 416
Steiner, David P., Chief Executive Officer, Waste Management of Canada, 407
Steiner, Jessica, Recovery Biologist, Wildlife Preservation Canada, 1020
Steiner, John, Branch Leader, Urban Systems Ltd., 408
Steinhoff, Wayne, President, Osram Sylvania Ltd., 314
Steinman, Ned A., Partner, Ogilvy Renault LLP/S.E.N.C.R.L., s.r.l. - Toronto, 1071, 1078
Steinwender, Ron, Manager, Public Works, Kingsville, 712
Stempski, Frank, Vice-President & General Manager, Aqua Tech Sales & Marketing Inc., 88
Stenger, Geoffrey, Borden Ladner Gervais LLP - Calgary, 1050
Stepaniuk, Darin, Director, 568
Stephan, Chris, Red Deer, 674
Stéphane, Beaulieu, Counsellor (Commercial) & Sr. Trade Commissioner, 769
Stephen, David C., Sr. Vice-President, Cansult Maunsell Limited, 127
Stephens, Alan, Chair, Synex International Inc., 385
Stephens, Bob, Application Specialist, Integra Environmental Inc., 243
Stephens, Carla, Director, Kelowna, 681
Stephens, Dave, Vice-President, Mequipco Ltd., 286
Stephens, Gail, City Manager, Victoria, 250-361-0202, 685
Stephens, Lynda, Meaford, 519-538-1189, 727
Stephens, Robert, Chair, 619
Stephenson, Brian, Councillor, Tillsonburg, 721
Stephenson, Cheryl, Librarian, 3M Canada Company, 1144
Stephenson, Dan, FCX NH Valves, 194
Stephenson, Darrell J., Partner, Stewart McKelvey Stirling Scales - Saint John, 1065
Stephenson, Gord, Micro-Watt Control Devices Ltd., 289
Stephenson, Kevin, City Manager, Brooks, 671
Stephenson, Rob, Chief Technical Officer, Paradigm Environmental Technologies Inc., 318
Stephenson, Q.C., Rod E., Aikins, MacAulay & Thorvaldson LLP, 1063
Stepovy, John, Acoustic Solutions Ltd., 67
Sterling, Art, Chatham-Kent, 724
Sterling, Elia, President, Theodor D. Sterling & Associates Ltd., 393
Sterling, Lorelei, Administrative Assistant, Kamloops Range Research Unit, 1112
Steuart, Nathan, Engineering Technician, Thompson, 690
Stevely, Mike, Manager, Whitehorse, 867-334-2100, 755
Stevens, Cindy, Tech Services Assistant, Nova Scotia Agricultural College, 1137
Stevens, Emile, Contact, Electric Vehicle Society of Canada, 909
Stevens, Jacquelyn, Willms & Shier Environmental Lawyers LLP, 1081
Stevens, Jennifer, St. Catharines, 905-641-5744, 719
Stevens, Jim, Director, Transit, Sarnia, 719
Stevens, Kristopher, Executive Director, Ontario Sustainable Energy Association, 980
Stevens, Mark, Senior Associate, Hardy Stevenson & Associates, 225
Stevens, Ron, Severn, 729
Stevens, Shane, Supervisor, Westburne Canada, 429
Stevens, Spencer, Library Technician, Alberta Children's Hospital Library, 1099
Stevens, Tom, City Manager, Campbell River, 679
Stevenson, Amy, Vice-President, 574
Stevenson, Brian, Controller, LaserNetworks Inc., 264
Stevenson, Colleen T., Macleod Dixon LLP, 1052
Stevenson, Deanne, Cascades Recovery Inc., 131
Stevenson, Garry, President, Tunnelling Association of Canada, 1014
Stevenson, J. Scott, Assistant Deputy Minister, 545

Stevenson, Jim, Calgary, 403-268-2430, 671
Stevenson, Patrice, Librarian, Canadian Museum of Nature, 1149
Stevenson, Romeyn, Iqaluit, 698
Stevenson, Tim, Vancouver, 604-873-7247, 685
Stevenson, Tom, General Manager, Keneco Environmental Services Inc., 256
Steves, Harold, Metro Vancouver, 684, 678
Steward, Paul, Program Director, Cobham Tracking & Locating Ltd., 146
Stewart, Alan F., President, Piteau Associates, 325
Stewart, Andrea, Director, Library Services, Nova Scotia Community College, 1136
Stewart, Basil L., Mayor, Summerside, 733
Stewart, Carolyn, Coordinator, Penticton, 682
Stewart, Christopher J., Stewart McKelvey Stirling Scales - Moncton, 1065
Stewart, Clint, General Manager, Barrington Industrial Services Limited, 102
Stewart, Delia, Inside Sales Manager, GE Multilin, 205
Stewart, Don, President, Millarville Racing & Agricultural Society, 954
Stewart, George, Director, 642
Stewart, Ian, Contact, Sunoco Inc., 382
Stewart, Ian, Vice-President, EBA Engineering Consultants Ltd., 169
Stewart, Janice, Secretary, Ontario Society of Nutrition Professionals in Public Health, 979
Stewart, Jim, President/CEO, UMA Group Ltd., 405
Stewart, John C., D'Arcy & Deacon LLP, 1063
Stewart, Kenneth W., President, Can Ecosse Engineering, 122
Stewart, Kim, Vice-Chair, Ontario Printing & Imaging Association, 977
Stewart, Mary-Lou, CEO, 611
Stewart, Murray J., President, Energy Council of Canada, 909
Stewart, Patrick L., President, Envirosphere Consultants Ltd., 187
Stewart, Ralph, President, Scott & Stewart Forestry Consultants, 360
Stewart, Ray, Chief Officer, 103, 580
Stewart, Richard, Metro Vancouver, 678
Stewart, Richard, Mayor, Coquitlam, 680
Stewart, Robert C., Stewart & Turner, 1067
Stewart, Sandra, Information Manager, CanTox Health Sciences International, 1144
Stewart, Scott, General Manager, Community Services, Burlington, 707
Stewart, Tammy, Renfrew, 613-586-2526, 704
Stewart, Wes, Branch Manager, Fabricated Plastics Ltd., 193
Stewart, Wes, Sales Manager, Fabco Plastics Wholesale (Ontario) Limited, 193
Stewart, William (Bill), General Manager, Fire Services & Fire Chief, Toronto, 416-338-9051, 721
Stewart, C.E.T., Scott, General Manager, Public Works, Hamilton, 711
St-Gelais, Bernard, Manager, Electro-Mecanik Inc., 175
St-Georges, Andrée, Présidente, 655
St-Hilaire, Lyne, Bibliothécaire - Archiviste, Collège Jean-de-Brébeuf, 1172
Stibrany, Sandra, Manager, Prince George, 250-561-7677, 683
Sticklee, Bruce, Northern Ontario Representative, ACO Container Systems Ltd., 67
Stiffler, Gail, Kingsville, 712
Stiles, Tom, Hayward Gordon Ltd., 227
Stiles, Wally, Minister, 595
Stillman, Mitchell, Chief Administrative Officer & Clerk, Petawawa, 717
Stilwell, Bill, President, Laidlaw Medical Services, 263
Stilwell, Brian W., Burchell, MacDougall, 1068
Stinchfield, Rhyne, Director, Quad-Lock Building Systems Ltd., 338
Stintz, Karen, Toronto, 721
Stirling, Jim, Chair, Hamilton Industrial Environmental Association, 927
Stirling, Jim, General Manager, ArcelorMittal Dofasco, 90
Stirpe, Paul A., Sales Manager, Survalent Technology Corporation, 383
Stirtzinger, Craig A., City Manager, Welland, 722
Stiver, James, Director, Planning, Orangeville, 716
Stiver, Lisa J., Thompson Dorfman Sweatman LLP, 1064
Stix, Al, President, Brytex Building Systems Inc., 118
Stix, Darrell, Controller, Brytex Building Systems Inc., 118
St-Jean, Jacques, Laval, 736
St-Jean, Luc, Mirabel, 738

St-Jean, Monique, Chef de bibliothèque, Bibliothèque d'aménagement, 1170
St-Jean, Sylvie, Mairesse, Boisbriand, 734
St-Laurent, Jacques, Commis specialisé en approvisionnements, Université du Québec à Rimouski, 1181
St-Laurent, Jacques, Directeur, Trois-Rivières, 819-372-4642, 745
St-Laurent, Marc, Rimouski, 740
St-Laurent, Marc, Directeur, Longueuil, 737
St-Laurent, Serge, Stablex Canada Inc., 377
St-Louis, Carl, Directeur, Sainte-Anne-des-Plaines, 743
St-Louis, Chantal, Secteur de l'aide à la recherche, Bibliothèque des sciences humaines et sociales, 1177
St-Louis, Michel, Saint-Lazare, 743
St-Louis, Pierre, Vice-président, Association québécoise de la gestion parasitaire, 841
St-Martin, Michel, Sec.-Trés., Régie intermunicipale d'aqueduc Richelieu-Yamaska, 759
Stobbs, Bob, Executive Director, Canadian Clean Power Coalition, 862
Stobie, Jim, Vice President, Brampton Engineering Inc., 115
Stock, Anthony P., President, Target Recycling Inc., 387
Stock, Emily A., Alexander Holburn Beaudin & Lang, LLP, 1057
Stockdale, Dave, Whitehorse, 755
Stockenstrom, Hannelie G., Clark Wilson LLP, 1058
Stocker, Simon, Director, European Solidarity Towards Equal Participation of People, 913
Stockla, Ken, Contact, Cartridge Care Canada, 130
Stockman, Rick, Commissioner, Corporate Services Department, Oshawa, 716
Stocks, David, Vice-President, BMT Fleet Technology Ltd., 111
Stockton, Paul, Manager, SGE Hatch Ltd., 364
Stoddart, Dave, Vice-President & General Manager, Neptune Technology Group (Canada) Ltd., 300
Stogre, Richard, Manager, Powell River, 683
Stokaluk, Bill, Manager, Waterous Power Systems, 423
Stokes, Alex, Contact, Alberta Falconry Association, 816
Stokes, Bryson A., Blake, Cassels & Graydon LLP - Toronto, 1072
Stokoe, Michael, Burchell, MacDougall, 1068
Stolch, Klaus, Office Manager, Trow Consulting Engineers Ltd., 403
Stoll, Scott, Aird & Berlis LLP, 1072
Stolz, Angela, McDougall Gauley, 1090
Stolz, Cameron, Prince George, 683
Stomp, Tamara, Deputy Mayor & Councillor, Kingsville, 712
Stone, Barry, Chair, Atlantic Turfgrass Research Foundation, 843
Stone, Jim, New Tecumseth, 714
Stone, Karen, Director, 614
Stone, Larry, Chair, Kason, 255
Stone, Laurence, President, Kason, 255
Stone, Neil, Chief Engineer, Esco Engineering, 189
Stonehewer, Judith, Chief Librarian, Marianopolis College, 1174
Stonely, Martin, President, Ventes Techniques Nimatec inc., 411
Stonely, Stéphane, Vice-President, Ventes Techniques Nimatec inc., 411
Stoner, Ruth, Librarian, Niagara Parks Botanical Gardens School of Horticulture, 1146
Stones, Ginger, Director General, 545
St-Onge, François, Directeur, Shawinigan, 744
St-Onge, Jean, Executive Vice President, Consultants Mésar inc., 151
St-Onge, Jean-François, Conseiller, Sault-au-Récollet, Montréal, 738
St-Onge, Pierre, Directeur général, Les Chenaux, 749
Stopforth, Sylvia, Head, Archives, Trinity Western University, 1113
Stork, Rod, Chair, 619
Storms, Todd, Ogilvy Renault LLP/S.E.N.C.R.L., s.r.l. - Ottawa, 1071
Storrier, Brian, Director, Mission, 604-820-5355, 687
Storteboom, Rudy, Langley, 681
Storz, Dina Alengi, Administrator, International Association for Public Participation, 935
Stothart, Sandra, Coordinator, Planning, Hamilton, 725
Stott, Rod, Environmental Planner, Maple Ridge, 604-467-7390, 687
Stougiannos, Lampros, Heenan Blaikie S.E.N.C.R.L/SRL, 1085
Stoute, Anna, Reference Librarian, Macdonald Campus Library, 1182
Stover, Tim, Manager, StonCor Canada, 379
Stowe, Del, South Frontenac, 730
Stoyanova, Penka, Health Sciences Librarian, Credit Valley Hospital, 1145
Stoyles, Lucy, Mount Pearl, 694

Executive Name Index

St-Pierre, Alain, Longueuil, 737
St-Pierre, André, Châteauguay, 450-692-4979, 735
St-Pierre, Christine, Ministre, 644
St-Pierre, Diane, Responsable, Bibliothèque scientifique Charles-Auguste-Gauthier, 1177
St-Pierre, Gaétan, Rivière-du-Loup, 741
St-Pierre, Gilles, President/General Manager, Les Entreprises Julien Inc., 268
St-Pierre, Marc, Président, Association de chasse et pêche nordique, inc., 831
St-Pierre, Réal, Saint-Hyacinthe, 742
St-Pierre, Rébecca, Langlois Kronström Desjardins, 1085
St-Pierre, Vincent, Ogilvy Renault LLP/S.E.N.C.R.L., s.r.l. - Québec, 1089
Strachan, Lynn M., Barrie, 706
Strachan, Robert, Partner, Brown Strachan Associates, 117
Strahl, Charles (Chuck), Minister, Transport, Infrastructure, & Communities, 544
Straight, Geoff, Vice-President, Wilderness Tourism Association, 1020
Strain, Kerry, Library Assistant, Campbell River Campus Library, 1111
Strandberg, Paul, General Manager, Fugro Airborne Surveys, 203
Strang, Robert, Chief Public Health Officer, 613
Strange, Kit, Director, Warmer Bulletin - Residua Ltd., 1017
Les Strange, Terrell, Librarian, British Columbia Ferry Services, 1120
Stranges, Jenny, President/CEO, Recovery Technologies Inc., 343
Strangway, Stephen, Kawartha Lakes, 711
Strano, Anita, Director, Wasteco, 421
Stratton, Q.C., David J., Davis LLP - Edmonton, 1050, 1055
Straughan, Andy, Vice-President, Longwood Forestry Services Ltd., 274
Straus, Paul, President & CEO, Home Hardware Stores Ltd., 232
Strauss, William, Waterloo, 704
Strawn, Brian, Sales Manager, Asbeguard Equipment Inc., 93
Streatch, Robert, Director, Cumberland County, 902-667-3029, 697
Streatch, Steve, Councillor, Halifax Regional Municipality, 695
Streich-Poser, Kim, Commissioner, Social Services, Sault Ste. Marie, 720
Strenkowski, Mike, Branch Manager, Leeson Canada Ltd., 266
Strgacic, Ivana, President, Strategies for the Environment, 380
Stribling, John, Chair, Lamont County Regional Solid Waste Commission, 757
Strickland, Cecily Y., Partner, Stewart McKelvey Stirling Scales - St. John's, 1066
Strickland, Sean, Waterloo, 704
Strickland, Sheri, Media Relations Coordinator, 595
Stright, Larry, RCMP Inspector, Campbell River, 679
Stritesky, Vlad, President, Trow Consulting Engineers Ltd., 403
Strobele, Kurt A., President & CEO, Hatch Ltd., 226
Strobl, Herbert, Contact, British Columbia Herb Growers Association, 848
Strohman, Nigel, President, Manitoba Regional Lily Society, 952
Strombert, Krista, Reference Librarian, Yukon College, 1191
Stronach, Bruce, President, Century Environmental Systems, 136
Strong, Kim, President, Maritime Testing Ltd., 281
Strong-Duffin, Kathy, Manager, Calgary, 403-268-4699, 671
Stroock, Lucy, Concerned Educators Allied for a Safe Environment, 899
Stroock, Lucy, Sec.-Treas., Concerned Educators Allied for a Safe Environment, 899
Stroud, Nancy, Reference Clerk, Canada Dept. of National Defence & the Canadian Forces, 1148
Strum, Bruce, President, Strum Environmental, 381
Struthers, J. Douglas, Leeds & Grenville, 726
Struthers, Sandra, Chief Financial Officer, Hydro One, 236
Stuart, D. Craig, Senior Scientist, Becquerel Laboratories Inc., 104
Stuart, David, CAO, North Vancouver, 604-990-2209, 688
Stuart, Pinks, CEO, Canada-Nova Scotia Offshore Petroleum Board, 763
Stuart, Russ, Sales Manager, Atlantic Packaging Products Ltd., 96
Stuart, Tim, Branch Manager, Totten Sims Hubicki Associates Ltd., 399
Stubbard, S., Sales, Bowie Pumps of Canada Ltd., 114
Stubbard, Scott, Manager, Rice Engineering & Operating Ltd., 346
Stubbert, Wesley, Councillor, Cape Breton, 695

Stubbings, Ken, Coordinator, Emergency Management, Northumberland, 702
Stuchlik, Vladimir, Manager, Azco Industries Ltd., 100
Stuhldreier, Lucia M., Aikins, MacAulay & Thorvaldson LLP, 1063
Stumpf, Kevin, Manager, FS Partners, 202
Stumph, David, Executive Director, Council of Science Editors, 905
Sturchio, Neil, Secretary, Geochemical Society, 923
Sturge, Derrick, Vice-President, 601
Sturhahn, Gunther, General Manager, Coast Paper Ltd., 145
Stutz, John, Chair, Bow Valley Waste Management Commission, 757
Suarez, Steve, Partner, Osler, Hoskin & Harcourt LLP - Toronto, 1079
Suave, M., Carrier Canada Ltd., 129
Subba, Bhim, Director, Green Communities Canada, 925
Sucharda, Peter, Engineer, Elasto Valve Rubber Products Inc., 174
Suddard, Darlene, Coordinator, Water & Waste Water Compliance, Port Colborne, 718
Sue-Tang, Joe, President, Nexus Solutions Inc., 303
Suffron, Bob, Coordinator, Kings County, 902-690-6153, 696
Sugden, Ian, Director, Planning & Development, Orillia, 716
Sugden, Lori, Map Curator, Map Library, 1121
Suhan, Carol, Coordinator, Central Okanagan, 250-469-6259, 677
Suissa, Moshe, President, Omega Recycling Technologies, 312
Suissa, Sam, Vice-President, Omega Recycling Technologies, 312
Sulliman, Celeste, Director, 609
Sullivan, Brad, Supervisor, Waste Water, Bradford West Gwillimbury, 706
Sullivan, Charlene, Director General, Human Resources, 510
Sullivan, Dan, Deputy Mayor & Councillor, Grey, 700
Sullivan, Gerry, Coordinator, Newfoundland & Labrador Federation of Agriculture, 962
Sullivan, H. Gary, Saint John, 692
Sullivan, James M., Blake, Cassels & Graydon LLP - Vancouver, 1057
Sullivan, Kaye, Deputy Executive Director/COO, American Public Works Association, 824
Sullivan, Mike, Cascades Recovery Inc., 131
Sullivan, Susan, Minister, 601
Sullivan, Terry, Marketing, Johns Manville Canada Inc., 253
Sullivan, William (Bill), Manager, North West Environmental Group, 306
Sullivan Curley, Q.C., Shauna, Deputy Minister, 638
Sullivan-Corney, Judith, Deputy Minister, 613
Sully, Lorne, Manager, Saskatoon, 754
Sulman, Douglas, Chatham-Kent, 724
Sulymko, Terry, Director, Learning Resource Centre, The Michener Institute for Applied Health Sciences, 1162
Sumel, Adam, President/CEO, Sonic Environmental Solutions Inc., 373
Sumel, Adam R., President/CEO, Sonic Technology Solutions Inc., 374
Summers, Alan, Senior Manager, Capital Regional District, 250-260-3080, 676
Sun, Wei Kiat, Singleton Urquhart LLP, 1062
Sundara, Khamsing, Directeur, CÉGEP de Sept-Iles, 1184
Sunell, Greg, President, Synex International Inc., 385
Sunley, Bruce, Vice-President & General Manager, Raypak Canada Ltd., 342
Sunnen, Paul, President, Guspro Inc., 223
Surbey, James W., Senior Partner, Borden Ladner Gervais LLP - Calgary, 1050
Surdhar, Perry, Manager, Sumas Environmental Services Inc., 381
Surette, David, Vice-President, Export Development Canada, 192
Surette, John, Thermo-Cell Industries Ltd., 394
Surlyk, Finn, President, International Association of Sedimentologists, 936
Surprenant, Sylvie, Mairesse, Sainte-Thérèse, 744
Susak, Bill, General Manager, Coquitlam, 604-927-3000, 680
Sushma, Gera, Trade Commissioner, 769
Sutcliffe, Greg, Muskoka, 702
Sutcliffe, John, Executive Director, Canadian Council of Professional Fish Harvesters, 865
Sutcliffe, Tony, Vice-President & General Counsel, Ricoh Canada Inc., 347
Sutherland, Blake, President, Sutherland Excavating Ltd., 384
Sutherland, Bonnie, Executive Director, Nova Scotia Nature Trust, 968
Sutherland, Bruce, Chair, 575

Sutherland, Donald G., Director, 641
Sutherland, Jo-Anne, Admin. Assistant, 610
Sutherland, John, Contact, Heating, Refrigeration & Air Conditioning Contractors Association, 928
Sutherland, Peter, President, Tanknology Canada Inc., 386
Sutherland, Robert, Manager, Yukon College, 1191
Sutherland, Ron, Amherstburg, 705
Sutherland, Shelley, Treasurer, Saskatoon, 754
Sutin, Richard S., Senior Partner, Ogilvy Renault LLP/S.E.N.C.R.L., s.r.l. - Toronto, 1078
Sutter, Kevin, Manager, Estevan, 754
Sutton, John, Amherstburg, 705
Sutton, Roxanne, Librarian, Labrador West Campus, 1131
Sutton, Tim, North Grenville, 728
Sutts, Q.C., Clifford N., Sutts, Strosberg LLP, 1082
Sutwin, John, Sales, Light Solar Wind Manufacturing, 272
Suvega, Paul, Asst. Deputy Minister, 618
Suzanne, Steensen, Trade Commissioner, 767
Suzuki, David, Chair, David Suzuki Foundation, 906
Svarich, Brigitte, Director, Energy Council of Canada, 909
Sveinson, Lynn, Chief Operating Officer, Climate Change Central, 144
Svelnis, Ingrid, Director, Uxbridge, 731
Swabey, Ted, General Manager, Nanaimo, 250-755-4429, 681
Swallow, Darin, Manager, Westburne Canada, 425
Swan, Andrew, Minister, 585
Swan, Carole, President, 518
Swan, Heather, Manager, Corporate Services, Saskatchewan Trade & Export Partnership Inc., 1002
Swan, Joe, London, 713
Swan, Neal, Area Sales Manager, Argus Telecom International Inc., 90
Swandel, Justin, Winnipeg, 204-986-6824, 690
Swanepoel, Marinus, University Librarian, University of Lethbridge, 1108
Swanson, James, Ainley Group, 74
Swanson, Janice, Office Manager, Enviro Vault Ltd., 182
Swanson, Kevin, Director, Brooks, 403-362-2331, 671
Swanson, Marnie, University Librarian, University of Victoria Libraries, 1121
Swanson, Matthew, Borden Ladner Gervais LLP - Vancouver, 1058
Swanson, Tom, Vice-President, Whitman Benn Group, 431
Swaren, Kristine, Librarian, Canadian Organic Growers Inc., 1149
Swaren, Tyler, Matrix Solutions Inc., 282
Swartman, R.K., President, Solcan Ltd., 372
Swartz, L. Brian, Sr. Vice-President, Aecon Group Inc., 71
Swayzer, Natalie, Executive Director, The Canadian Network for Environmental Education & Communication, 879
Sweeney Marsh, Joan, Manager, Library Services, Sheridan Institute of Technology and Advanced Learning, 1146
Sweet, Bob, Renfrew, 613-687-5536, 704
Sweet, Robert, Mayor, Petawawa, 717
Sweet, Ron, Manager, YES Environment Technologies Inc., 435
Sweet, B.A., LL.B, Brian R., Municipal Clerk, Corporate Counsel & Director, Cor, Leamington, 726
Sweetapple, Graham, Contact, Lasec Enterprises Ltd., 264
Sweetland, Barb, Manager, Alberta Beef Producers, 815
Sweetland, Clarence O., Mayor, Riverview, 506-386-1703, 692
Sweetland, Mary Beth, Vice-President, People for the Ethical Treatment of Animals, 985
Sweig, Laurie, Cascades Recovery Inc., 131
Sweiger, Lori, Treasurer, Saugeen Shores, 719
Swetlishoff, Andy, Director, Thompson-Nicola, 679
Swiatek, George, President, DCL International Inc., 159
Swiddle, Steve, Leader, Westest, 430
Swidnicki, Joni, City Clerk, Regina, 306-777-7262, 754
Swift, Kelly, Director, Pitt Meadows, 683
Swift, Leah, Researcher, R.V. Anderson Associates Limited, 1161
Swigger, Phil, Vice-President, National Waste Services, 298
Swinden, Kevin, Sales Agent, Danatec Educational Services Ltd., 157
Swinimer, CVPM, Hope, Founder & Director, Hope for Wildlife Society, 930
Swinkin, Gerald S., Blake, Cassels & Graydon LLP - Toronto, 1072
Swiss, James J., President, Swiss Environment & Safety Inc., 384
Switzer, C.M., Chair, 624
Switzer, G. Ross, Partner, Borden Ladner Gervais LLP - Vancouver, 1058
Switzer, Lloyd, Partner, whatIf? Technologies Inc., 431

Executive Name Index

Switzer, Sheldon, Director, Building Services & Chief Building Offic, Oakville, 715
Swoboda, Don, President/COO, Eaton Hydro Developers Inc., 169
Swords, Colleen, Associate Deputy Minister, 541
Sykes, Stephanie J., Partner, Heenan Blaikie LLP - Toronto, 1076
Sylvain, Mario, Directeur, La Vallée-de-l'Or, 748
Sylvester, Bruce, Vice-President, Radiation Safety Institute of Canada, 992
Sylvester, Peter, President, 518
Sylvester, Robert, Essex, 519-727-3849, 699
Sylvestre, Bruno, Langlois Kronström Desjardins, 1088
Sylvestre, Chantal, Partner, Heenan Blaikie S.E.N.C.R.L/SRL, 1085
Sylvestre, Michel G., Ogilvy Renault LLP/S.E.N.C.R.L., s.r.l. - Montréal, 1086
Sylvestre, Pierrick, Greffier, Joliette, 736
Symington, Bob, President, British Columbia Environment Industry Association, 847
Symington, Jo-Ann, Coordinator, Red Deer County, 670
Symington, Robert, Hydrogeologist, Gandalf Consulting Ltd., 204
Symmonds, Philip D. A., Torys LLP, 1081
Symon, Forbes, Director, Planning & Development, North Grenville, 728
Syms, Laura, Information Services Librarian, Cape Breton University, 1137
Synnott, Matthew, Stikeman Elliott LLP - Calgary, 1054
Synthia, Dodig, Trade Commissioner, 767
Sypniewski, Ted, Serials & Acquisitions Officer, Canadian Museum of Nature, 1149
Szaraz, Georges, Sr. VP, EnGlobe Corp., 181
Szarka, Chris, Regina, 306-551-2766, 754
Szel, Marcella, Chairman (Executive Committee), Western Transportation Advisory Council, 1019
Szep, Jutta, Librarian, Walker, Nott, Dragicevic Associates Limited, 1163
Szeto, James, Chief Chemist, Petro Laboratories Inc., 322
Szilos, Agnes, Director, Oak Bay, 250-595-7946, 688
Szladow, Adam J., President, REDUCT & Lobbe Technologies Inc., 344
Szollosy, Dave, Georgina, 709
Szot-Sacawa, Anna, Circulation Coordinator, Bora Laskin Law Library, 1156
Szucs, Janette, Coordinator, Parkland County, 670
Szumski, Roman, Vice-President, 546
Szwarc, David, Chief Administrative Officer, Peel, 703
Szybalski, D., Coordinator, Sustainability, Halton Hills, 710
Szymko Thiele, Corinne, President, Resources for Global Sustainability, 995

T

t buck suzuki environment, T. Buck Suzuki Environmen, New Westminster, BC, 1041
Tabak, Leon, Operations, Pelmar Engineering Ltd., 320
Tachuk, Rick, Director, Canadian Council of Technicians & Technologists, 865
Tadros, Wendy A., Chair, 561
Tafelmeyer, Marlys, Director, 656
Tagami, Reiko, Information & Resolutions Coordinator, Union of British Columbia Municipalities, 1116
Taggart, Marcia, McCarthy Tétrault LLP - Toronto, 1077
Taggart, Tom, Councillor, Colchester County, 697
Taillefer, Claudine, Administration & Information Officer, 519
Taillon, Andrew D., Cox and Palmer - Halifax, 1067
Taillon, Denis, Directeur général, Le Domaine-du-Roy, 749
Tainturier, Laurent, President, BASF Canada Inc., 103
Tait, B. Douglas, Thompson Dorfman Sweatman LLP, 1064
Tait, Deb A., Oxford, 728
Tait, Deb A., City / County Councillor, Woodstock, 519-421-7449, 723
Tait, Glenn D., McLennan Ross LLP, 1066
Tak, Devendra, Manager, CIVICUS: World Alliance for Citizen Participation, 896
Tak, John W., President & Chief Executive Officer, Canadian Hydrogen & Fuel Cell Association, 871
Takahashi, Bruce, President, Nilfisk-Advance Canada Company, 304
Takahashi, O., President/General Manager, MCC Industrial Services Ltd, 284
Takhar, Harinder S., Minister, 626
Talavera, Fernando R., Director, Eastwest Synergies Inc., 169
Talbot, Jean, Directeur (par intérim), 653
Talbot, Sandra J., Oxford, 519-539-6685, 728

Talbot, Sandra J., City / County Councillor, Woodstock, 519-788-0639, 723
Talbot, Scott, Laidlaw Carriers Inc. - Van Division, 262
Talbot, Scott, General Manager, Laidlaw Carriers Inc. - Van Division, 262
Talbot, Steve, Executive Director, Forest Products Association of Nova Scotia, 919
Talbot, Todd, President, Brass Craft Canada Ltd., 116
Talbot, Yvan, Sec.-Trés. & Directeur général, Acton, 746
Talbot, Yves, Finance Director, Solaction Inc., 372
Talen, Fred, Director, 605
Talley, David, Project Manager, Niagara Environmental Dynamics, 303
Tallon, Gregory J., Thompson Dorfman Sweatman LLP, 1064
Tallon, Jan, Manager, Learning Centres & LRC Operations, Centennial College of Applied Arts & Technology, 1157
Tallon, Wayne, Director, Fredericton, 691
Talon, Terry, General Manager, Social Services, Simcoe, 704
Talvitie, Rick, Branch Manager, Totten Sims Hubicki Associates Ltd., 399
Tam, Andrew W.H., Lang Michener LLP - Toronto, 1077
Tammy, Griffith, Trade Commissioner, 767
Tan, Darlene, Reference Librarian, Fisheries & Oceans Canada, 1150
Tancrède, Dominique, Greffière, Matane, 738
Tang, Jun, Director, Babcock & Wilcox Canada Ltd., 100
Tanguay, Bernard F., Sherbrooke, 744
Tanguay, Huguette, Bibliothécaire, Bibliothèque centrale, 1170
Tanguay, Marco, Thetford Mines, 418-338-8819, 745
Tanguay, Marlene, Documentaliste, Société générale de financement du Québec (SGF), 1175
Tanner, Richard C., Scott Venturo LLP, 1053
Tansley, Mark G., President, Tansley Associates Environmental Services, 387
Tansony, Reg, General Manager, Markland Specialty Engineering Ltd., 281
Tanton, Tim, Engineer, North Saanich, 687
Tanton, Tim, Senior Manager, Capital Regional District, 250-474-9611, 676
Tanyan, Jean Mario, Sales Manager, Ashtead Technology Rentals, 93
Tapak, Laraine, Director, Learning Resources, Confederation College, 1156
Tapardjuk, Louis, Minister, 617
Tapp, Len, Division Manager, Transit, Cornwall, 708
Tapuska, Edward W., Partner, Borden Ladner Gervais LLP - Calgary, 1050
Taraschuk, Rick, Sales Agent, Danatec Educational Services Ltd., 157
Tarbotton, Michael R., President, Triton Consultants Ltd., 402
Tardif, Danielle, Chef, Dév. collections/référence, Bibliothèque des sciences de la santé, 1171
Tardif, Denis, Rivière-du-Loup, 741
Tardif, Jean-Guy, Greffier, Roberval, 741
Tardif, Margaret, Chair, Smoky River Regional Water Management Commission, 758
Tardif, Sylvie, Trois-Rivières, 745
Tardif, Yves, Hydrogeology/Environment, Laboratoires d'Expertises de Québec Ltée, 262
Tardiff, Deb, Coordinator, Manitoba Environmental Industries Association Inc., 951
Taria, D., Carrier Canada Ltd., 129
Tarita, Teri, Librarian, Pacific Salmon Commission, 1118
Tarnawsky, Peter, General Manager, Sturgeon County, 780-939-8344, 670
Tarnowsky, Gordon L., Fraser Milner Casgrain LLP - Calgary, 1051
Tarry, Greg, Manager, Canadian Association of Zoos & Aquariums, 859
Taschereau, Charles, Associé, Ogilvy Renault LLP/S.E.N.C.R.L., s.r.l. - Québec, 1089
Taschuk, Q.C., Peter P., McLennan Ross LLP, 1055
Tasker, Ryan, Manager, Mondo Products Company Limited, 292
Tassé, Alain, Conseiller de ville, Desmarchais-Crawford, Montréal, 738
Tassé, Denis, Gatineau, 735
Tastad, Mary, Reference Librarian, Law Library, 1189
Tate, James P., Partner, Ratcliff & Company LLP, 1057
Tathe, Vik, Manager, Monserco Ltd., 293
Tatsuoka, Fumio, President, International Geosynthetics Society, 940
Tattrie, Brenda, Manager, Sydney Environmental Resources Ltd., 384
Tavender, Q.C., E. David D., Fraser Milner Casgrain LLP - Calgary, 1051

Tay, Derrick C., Senior Partner, Ogilvy Renault LLP/S.E.N.C.R.L., s.r.l. - Toronto, 1078
Taylor, Allen, Warden & Councillor, Dufferin, 699
Taylor, Andy, Commissioner, Corporate Services, Markham, 905-475-4705, 713
Taylor, Barry, President, Taylor Mazier Associates, 387
Taylor, Blair S., O'Connor MacLeod Hanna LLP, 1070
Taylor, Bob, Mayor, Colchester County, 697
Taylor, Brad, Chief Financial Officer, Expocrete Concrete Products Ltd., 192
Taylor, Brian, Manager, Halifax Regional Municipality, 902-490-6388, 689, 695
Taylor, Brooke D., Minister, 616
Taylor, Crispin, Executive Director, American Society of Plant Biologists, 826
Taylor, D.G., Consulting Ecologist, D.G. Taylor Inc., Consulting Ecologist Division, 156
Taylor, Don, President/CEO, Pepper Compressed Air & Gas Ltd., 321
Taylor, Elaine, Minister, 667
Taylor, G. Bruce, Aikins, MacAulay & Thorvaldson LLP, 1063
Taylor, J., Director, Planning Services Department, Barrie, 706
Taylor, Jeremy, Contact, R.J. Burnside & Associates Limited, 340
Taylor, Jim, Councillor, Kings County, 696
Taylor, John, York, 707, 700, 705
Taylor, John, Manager, Whitehorse, 867-668-8318, 755
Taylor, John, Regional Councillor, Newmarket, 714
Taylor, Ken, CFO, Proshred Security, 335
Taylor, Lidia, Collection Development Librarian, CANMET Information Centre, 1149
Taylor, Lynn, City Manager, Thompson, 690
Taylor, Mark, Ottawa, 729, 716
Taylor, Mark, General Manager, Abbotsford, 604-859-3134, 679
Taylor, Nancy, Treasurer & Director, Finance, Clarington, 724
Taylor, Nimette, Office Manager, MSU Mississauga Ltd., 294
Taylor, P. Alanna, Cox and Palmer - Charlottetown, 1082
Taylor, Paul, President, Compost Management, 147
Taylor, Peter, Chair, British Columbia Food Technolgists, 848
Taylor, Rennie, President, Central Ontario Orchid Society, 893
Taylor, Richard, Executive Director, Union of British Columbia Municipalities, 1014
Taylor, Rob, Principal, RST Instruments Ltd., 354
Taylor, Robert C., Blaney McMurtry LLP, 1073
Taylor, Sandy, Manager, Plastiglas Industries Limited, 326
Taylor, Stan, General Manager, Integrated Explorations, 244
Taylor, Stephen, Contact, Enviro Waste Ltd., 182
Taylor, Ted, Senior Accounts, KWH Pipe, 261
Taylor, Trevor, Acting Minister, 599
Taylor, MSW, Andrew, Manager, Environmental Health & Prevention Service, Lambton, 701
Taylor, Q.C., Martin, Hunter Litigation Chambers, 1060
Taylor-Prime, Dawn, Regional Librarian, Environment Canada Library, Downsview, 1157
Tchegus, R.P., Cunningham, Swan, Carty, Little & Bonham LLP, 1069
Teal, Jeffrey C., Scarfone Hawkins LLP, 1069
Teal, John, Regional Councillor, Fort Erie, 709
Teasdale, Guy, Chef, Division Services soutien et développement, Université Laval, 1181
Teasdale, Jacques, Québec, 740
Teasdale, Sylvia, University Librarian, Bishop's University, 1185
Teatero, Barbara, Associate Librarian, Queen's University, 1142
Ted Smith, W.E. Ted, Brock, 724
Tedesco, Ralph, President/CEO, Nova Scotia Power, an Emera Company, 308
Tegart, Gerald, Deputy Minister & Deputy Attorney General, 661
Teggarty, Lisa, Deputy Treasurer, Terrace, 685
Tegler, Scott, Fire Chief, Woodstock, 723
Teichroeb, Jay, General Manager, Abbotsford, 604-864-5525, 679
Teitelbaum, Michael S., Partner, Hughes, Amys LLP, 1077
Telego, D. Jeff, Co-Executive Director, Environmental Bankers Association, 911
Telego, Tacy, Co-Executive Director, Environmental Bankers Association, 911
Telesnicki, Mark J., Principal, Golder Associates Ltd., 214
Telfer, Lindsay, Chapter Director, Sierra Club of Canada - Prairie Chapter, 1004
Telford, Dan, Senior Manager, Capital Regional District, 250-360-3064, 676
Tell, Christine, Minister, 657
Tellier, Gisèle, Head, Acquisitions, Bombardier Inc./Canadair Aerospace & Defence Groups, 1171
Tellier, Jean-Yves, Directeur, Québec, 740
Temple, Lauren, Blake, Cassels & Graydon LLP - Toronto, 1073

Executive Name Index

Temple, Laurie, Secretary, Regina & District Labour Council, 994
Templeton, J. Alex, Cox and Palmer - St. John's, 1065
Templeton, Jamie, Stikeman Elliott LLP - Vancouver, 1062
Temprile, Dan, General Manager, Public Health, Safety, & Social S, Brantford, 707
Tenasco-Banerjee, Sheila, Acting Director General, 520
Tencha, Gary, McElhanney Consulting Services Ltd., 285
Tennant, Richard G., President, Vanport Sterilizers Inc., 409
Ter Harmsel, Johan, Zeton Inc., 437
Termeer, Walter, CEO, Fundy Compost Inc., 203
Ternent, Steve, Treasurer, Langford, 681
Terpstra, Mike, Program Manager, Ontario Soil & Crop Improvement Association, 979
Terrio, Pat, Vice-President, Pure Energy Inc., 336
Terroux, Peter, Principal Consultant, Atlantic Acoustical Associates, 95
Tersigni, John, Executive Director, The Green Brick Road, 925
Tersigni, Santino, General Manager, Maccaferri Canada Ltd., 277
Terziano, Karin, Councillor, Huntsville, 711
Teskey, John, Director of Libraries, University of New Brunswick, 1128
Teskey, Q.C., Robert H., Field Law - Edmonton, 1055
Tessier, Claudette, Longueuil, 737
Tessier, Céline, McMillan Binch Mendelsohn - Montréal, 1086
Tessier, Paula, Mount Pearl, 694
Tessier, Philippe-André, Associé, Robinson Sheppard Shapiro LLP, 1087
Tessier, Pierre, Directeur général, 648
Tessier, Raymond, Saint-Eustache, 450-472-3951, 742
Tessler, Susan, Director, 588
Testa, Robert, Director General, 545
Testulat, Jacques, Sherbrooke, 744
Teti-Tomassi, Clementina, Conseillère d'arrondissement, Marie-Clarac, Montréal, 738
Tetlichi, Joe, Chair, 542
Tetrault, Laurent, CAO, Springfield, 690
Tetreau, Kristy, Supervisor, AMEC, 82
Tétreault, Jean-Claude, Executive Director, Association of Canada Lands Surveyors, 834
Tetreault, Richard, Chambly, 450-658-4282, 734
Tewsley, John T., Vice-President, Geo-Logic Inc., 210
Thake, William (Bill) L., Leeds & Grenville, 726
Tham, Carmen, Lindsay Kenney LLP, 1061
Thangaraj, Arun, Director General, 520
Thayer, Cindy, General Manager, Community Services, Lambton, 701
Thé, Jesse L., President, Lakes Environmental Software, 263
Théberge, Gilles, Directeur, Westburne Canada, 428
Theberge, Jocelyn, Contact, Conestoga-Rovers & Associates, 149
Théberge, Nicolas, Ingénieur Associé, Experts-Conseils BMST inc., 192
Théberge, Simon, Lévis, 736
Thelitz, Mike, Manager, PRT Inc., 336
Thellen, Claude, Scientific Director, Centre de Toxicologie du Québec, 136
Theobald, Dorothy, Director, Human Services, Leeds & Grenville, 726
Theodorakis, Tom, Lang Michener LLP - Vancouver, 1060
Theodore, Kevin, Manager, Lethbridge, 403-320-3088, 673
Theoharopoulos, George, Manager, 521
Théorêt, Jean-Paul, Président, 650
Thériault, Alain, Directeur général adjoint, Québec, 740
Theriault, Donat, Director, 597
Theriault, Eric, Advisor, Canada-Nova Scotia Offshore Petroleum Board, 853
Thériault, François, Directeur général, Saint-Charles-Borromée, 753
Thériault, Hugues, Marketing & Sales, Aquaterre Inc., 89
Thériault, Jacques, Rivière-du-Loup, 741
Thériault, Jean, Baie-Comeau, 418-296-8637, 733
Thériault, Lise, Ministre, 655
Thériault, Lyn, Mairesse d'arrondissement, Montréal, 738
Thériault, Manon, Greffière, La Prairie, 450-444-6625, 736
Thériault, Paulette, Moncton / Ville de Moncton, 691
Theriault, Pierre, Operations Manager, Fredericton Region Solid Waste Commission, 506-453-9932, 758
Thériault, Yves, Trésorier, Alma, 733
Thérien, Frank, Gatineau, 735
Therriault, Dominique, Technicienne agricole, Institut de technologie agro-alimentaire de la Pocatière, 1177
Therrien, Armand, Manager, R.V. Anderson Associates Limited, 341
Therrien, Carole, President, LEAD Canada Inc., 948

Therrien, Claude, Operator, Régie d'aqueduc intermunicipale des Moulins, 759
Theurer, Susanne, Director, Okanagan-Similkameen, 678
Thevenot, Ken, Fire Chief, Thompson, 204-677-7915, 674, 690
Thibaudeau, Jérôme, Directeur, 646
Thibaudeau, Louise, Directrice, Université du Québec École de technologie supérieure, 1176
Thibault, Charles Olivier, Heenan Blaikie S.E.N.C.R.L/SRL, 1085
Thibault, Daniel, Directeur général adjoint, Trois-Rivières, 819-372-4649, 745
Thibault, Denis, Cornwall, 708
Thibault, Germain, President/CEO, Environnement ESA Inc., 186
Thibault, Julie, Heenan Blaikie LLP - Ottawa, 1070
Thibault, Melanie, ILL Technician, ARC Vegreville Library & Information Centre, 1109
Thibault, Myriam, Bibliothécaire, Québec Office des personnes handicapées, 1175
Thibault, Pierre, President, Solaction Inc., 372
Thibault, Raymond, Président-directeur général (par intérim), 650
Thibeault, Solange, Technicienne en documentation, CÉGEP de Trois-Rivières, 1186
Thibodeau, Michel, Hawkesbury, 711
Thie, Jean, Executive Director, Canadian Institute of Geomatics, 874
Thiessen, Gary, Manager, Great Western Containers Inc., 216
Thiessen, Trevor, Vice-President, Philom Bios Inc., 323
Thifault, Patrick, Boisbriand, 734
Thiffeault, Stephane, General Manager, Corporate Services, Lambton, 701
Thimm, Harold, President, Thimm Engineering Inc., 395
Thirlwall, David, Associate University Librarian, Personnel & Commun, Concordia University Libraries, 1173
Thistle, Q.C., James L., McInnes Cooper, 1066
Thivierge, Jacques, Vice President, Roche ltée, Groupe-conseil, 348
Thivierge, Lynda, Bibliothécaire, SNC-Lavalin inc., 1175
Thivierge, Michel, Clarence-Rockland, 708
Thoem, Peter, Burlington, 707
Thom, Q.C., Jeffrey N., Associate Counsel, Miller Thomson LLP - Calgary, 1053
Thomas, Alison, Clerk, Tay, 731
Thomas, Brian, President, Delta Piping Products Canada Inc., 160
Thomas, Cory, Summerside, 733
Thomas, Derrick, Chief Administrative Officer, West Lincoln, 732
Thomas, Gregory P., President, G3 Consulting Ltd., 204
Thomas, Ian, Manager, Delta Piping Products Canada Inc., 160
Thomas, James C., Principal, Hilderman Thomas Frank Cram & Associates, 232
Thomas, Jennifer, Chair, Grande Prairie Regional College, 1108
Thomas, Jim, President, Refrigerant Services Inc., 344
Thomas, Kimberly, Technology Librarian, Georgian College of Applied Arts & Technology, 1138
Thomas, Lori, Director, Manitoba Wildlife Federation, 952
Thomas, Mike, Manager, Eco Wood Products, 78, 170
Thomas, Misty, Manager, British Columbia Recreation & Parks Association, 849
Thomas, Norm, Director, 629
Thomas, Percival, Manager, Water & Wastewater Systems, Orillia, 716
Thomas, Sébastien, Stikeman Elliott LLP - Montréal, 1087
Thomas, Thomas, President, Double T Equipment Ltd., 69, 165
Thomas, Vic, Senior Vice-President, Willowglen Systems Inc., 432
thomas sill foundation in, The Thomas Sill Foundatio, Winnipeg, MB, 1042
Thomas, Q.C., Bruce A., Cassels Brock & Blackwell LLP, 1074
Thomassen, Roy, Chief Building Inspector, Central Saanich, 686
Thomassen, Roy, Director, Oak Bay, 688
Thomlinson, Janelle, Director, Environmental Careers Organization of Canada, 911
Thompon, Scott G., Partner, Hicks Morley Hamilton Stewart Storie LLP, 1077
Thompson, Allan, Peel, 703
Thompson, Allan, Regional Councillor, Caledon, 707
Thompson, Amanda, Sales Coordinator, Anachemia Canada Inc., 85
Thompson, Andrew L., Thompson Dorfman Sweatman LLP, 1064
Thompson, Beth, Councillor, Quispamsis, 506-849-2852, 692
Thompson, Bob, Chair, Skeena-Queen Charlotte, 679

Thompson, Bob, Project Manager, Elecsar Engineering Co. Ltd., 174
Thompson, Brent, President, Wardrop Engineering Inc., 417
Thompson, Brian, Muskoka, 702
Thompson, Brian, District & Town Councillor, Huntsville, 711
Thompson, Bruce L., President, Thompson Engineering Consultants Ltd., 395
Thompson, Brycen, Manager, Harris & Roome Supply Limited, 226
Thompson, Chidinma, Borden Ladner Gervais LLP - Calgary, 1050
Thompson, Claudia, National President, Natural Resources Union, 959
Thompson, Dave, PricewaterhouseCoopers Management Consultants, 332
Thompson, David, Scarfone Hawkins LLP, 1069
Thompson, David, Director, Engineering Services, Loyalist, 727
Thompson, David A., Boyne Clarke, 1067
Thompson, Debbie, Lennox & Addington, 613-378-1553, 701
Thompson, Doug, Ottawa, 613-580-2490, 716
Thompson, Doug, Manager, Water Operations, Hamilton, 725
Thompson, Frank, General Manager, Biotech Solutions, 109
Thompson, Garnet, Belleville, 706
Thompson, Gordon, General Manager, Alberta Capital Region Wastewater Commission, 757
Thompson, Ian, Deputy Minister, 610
Thompson, Jeremy, Medicine Hat, 403-504-5647, 673
Thompson, Joanne, Vice-President, W.B. Beatty & Associates, 415
Thompson, Jocelyne, Associate Director, Collections Services, University of New Brunswick, 1128
Thompson, John, Prince Edward, 727, 703
Thompson, John, CEO, Hazco Environmental Services Ltd., 227
Thompson, Ken, Technical Sales Representative, SRI Petro Chemical Inc., 376
Thompson, Linda, Warden & Councillor, Northumberland, 702
Thompson, Linda M., Mayor, Port Hope, 728
Thompson, Mark S., Partner, Singleton Urquhart LLP, 1062
Thompson, Michael, Toronto, 706, 721
Thompson, Nancy, Muskoka, 702
Thompson, Nigel J., Aikins, MacAulay & Thorvaldson LLP, 1063
Thompson, Patsy, Director General, 520
Thompson, Richard P., Gilchrist & Company, 1057
Thompson, Rick, Vice-President, Le Groupe Sani Marc, 265
Thompson, Robert, Director, Library Computing Services, York University Libraries, 1164
Thompson, Robert, Supervisor, Grand Falls-Windsor, 709-489-0421, 694
Thompson, Robert M., General Manager, Prince Rupert, 250-627-0954, 684
Thompson, Ryan, Georgian Bluffs, 725
Thompson, Stephen, General Manager, Economic Development & Tourism, Port Colborne, 718
Thompson, Wendy, Deputy Secretary, Alberni-Clayoquot, 250-720-2706, 676
Thompson, BScN, MSc, CCHN, Kate, President, Community Health Nurses of Canada, 899
Thompson, Q.C., Peter C.P., Borden Ladner Gervais LLP - Ottawa, 1070
Thomson, Barry, President/CEO, Cecon Limited, 135
Thomson, Bob, President, Thomson Technology Inc., 395
Thomson, Dave A., Lincoln, 713
Thomson, David R., President, Challenger Geomatics Ltd., 138
Thomson, Denis, Vice-President, LGL Limited Environmental Research Associates, 271
Thomson, Douglas, McCarthy Tétrault LLP - Toronto, 1077
Thomson, Helen, Clerk, Stormont, Dundas & Glengarry, 730
Thomson, Jim, Chair, 575
Thomson, Joan, Clerk, Stratford, 720
Thomson, Joyce, Librarian, Collections Development, St Mary's University, 1136
Thomson, Larry, Vice-Chair, Lethbridge Regional Waste Management Services, 757
Thomson, Mary, Librarian, CMC Electronics Inc., 1184
Thomson, Patricia, Executive Director, Stanley Park Ecology Society, 1010
Thomson, Paul, Director, Moncton / Ville de Moncton, 691
Thomson, Rick, Le Groupe Sani Marc, 266
Thomson, Robert, Executive Director, 664
Thomson, Steve, Minister, 579
Thomson, Wayne, City Councillor, Niagara Falls, 715
Thorassie, Albert, Chair, 541
Thorbourne, James, President, KBL Land Use Consulting Ltd., 255

Executive Name Index

Thorburn, Mary, Secretary/Manager, Environmental Abatement Council of Ontario, 911
Thordarson, John D., President/CEO, Scott Tank Cleaning Co. Ltd., 360
Thorkelsson, Rodd C., Brownlee LLP, 1054
Thorne, Arlene, Contact, Vacuum Products Canada Inc., 409
Thorne, Chris, Graphics Arts Sales Associate, Metafix, 287
Thorneloe, Karen, Reference Librarian, Bishop's University, 1185
Thornhill, Alan D., Executive Director, Society for Conservation Biology, 1006
Thornhill, Danny, Sales Manager, Provincial Partitions Ltd., 335
Thornton-Joe, B.A., Charlayne, Victoria, 685
Thorpe, Donald, General Manager, Planning & Development Services, Welland, 722
Thorpe, Mark, Klohn Crippen Berger Ltd., 258
Thorpe, Mark, Officer, Guelph-Eramosa, 725
Thorpe, Mary, Manager, Human Resources, Waterloo, 722
Thorpe, Tim, Sales Engineer, Folio Instruments Inc., 199
Thrasher, Marilyn, Marketing Manager, GE Multilin, 205
Thrasher, Ross, Director of Library Services, Mount Royal College, 1102
Thrasher, Q.C., R.J. Jack, Partner, Osler, Hoskin & Harcourt LLP - Calgary, 1053
Thring, David E., Lang Michener LLP - Toronto, 1077
Thurgood, David, President, Brantford, 115
Thurston, Lance, Chief Administrative Officer, Grey, 700
Thususka, Michael, Director, Summerside, 733
Thwaites, Candace, Clerk, Gravenhurst, 709
Thwaites, Joe, President, Taylor Munro Energy Systems Inc., 387
Thwaites, Stephen, Marketing, Thermotech Windows Ltd., 395
Tibbo, Dave, Director, Conception Bay South, 693
Tickell, Brad, Library Technician, Petroleum Industry Training Service, 1102
Tickell, Crispin, Chair (Emeritus), Climate Institute, 896
Tidball, John R., Miller Thomson LLP - Markham, 1070
Tidball, John R., Partner, Miller Thomson LLP - Toronto, 1078
Tidy, David, Metcon Sales & Engineering Ltd., 287
Tidy, Steve, Manager, Waterous Power Systems, 423
Tiemstra, Harold, President, Can-Cell Industries Inc., 123
Tiemstra, Karl, Vice-President, Can-Cell Industries Inc., 123
Tiemstra, Warren, Vice-President, Can-Cell Industries Inc., 123
Tierney, James M., Chair, Great Lakes Commission, 925
Tierney, Tim, Ottawa, 716
Tiessen, Sean, Coordinator, Iqaluit, 698
Tigert, Bill, Director, Social Services, Stratford, 720
Tiggelaar, Jordan, Manager, Bartle & Gibson Co. Ltd., 102
Tilford, Wendy, Deputy Minister, 622
Tillard, Ian, Whitman Benn Group, 431
Tilley, Bruce, St. John's, 709-576-8643, 694
Tiltman, Connie, Library Technician, Woodstock Campus, 1165
Tim, Elder, Executive Director, Great Lakes Commission, 764
Timken Jr., Ward J., Chair, American Iron & Steel Institute, 823
Timlin, James, Chief Administrative Officer, Ingersoll, 711
Timm, P.Eng., Tom, General Manager, Vancouver, 604-873-7300, 685
Timmenga, Hubert J., Associate, Zbeetnoff Agro-Environmental Consulting, 436
Timmerman, Martin, Superintendent, Roads, Georgian Bluffs, 725
Timmings, Carol, President, Ontario Public Health Association, 978
Timmins, Barry, Laidlaw Medical Services, 263
Timmons, Richard, President/CEO, Guildline Instruments Limited, 223
Timms, D. Bruce, Niagara, 702
Timuss, Steve, Director, Maxxam Analytics Ltd., 283
Timuss, Steve, Marketing & Sales Coordinator, Maxxam Analytics Ltd., 283
Tin, Tony, Electronic Resources Librarian, Athabasca University, 1099
Tinari, Nancy, Sales Director, Pacific Institute for Advanced Study, 316
Tinari, Nancy, Vice-President, Tinari Energy Management Services Inc., 396
Tinari, Paul D., Director, Tinari Energy Management Services Inc., 396
Tinari, Paul D., President/Director, Pacific Institute for Advanced Study, 316
Tingey, Douglas V., Fasken Martineau - Toronto, 1075
Tingey, Ian, Vice-President, SpilKleen, 376
Tingley, Richard, Corporate Secretary & General Counsel, 598
Tinguely, Thérèse, Aide-bibliothécaire, Collège universitaire de St-Boniface, 1123
Tink, Lisa, Manager, Alberta Recreation & Parks Association, 819

Tinker, Jon, Executive Director, Panos Canada, 984
Tinker, Scott W., President, The American Association of Petroleum Geologists, 822
Tinlin, Mark, South Frontenac, 730
Tinney, Carl, Hastings, 700
Tipping, CMA, Scott, Director, Corporate Services, Niagara-on-the-Lake, 715
Tison, Denis, District Sales Manager, National Instruments Canada, 298
Titcomb, Bert, Manager, Transport Action Canada, 1013
Titerle, James A., McCarthy Tétrault LLP - Vancouver, 1061
Tittler, Konrad R., President, Diacon Technologies Ltd., 163
Titus, Christopher, Councillor at Large, Saint John, 692
Tkatch, Brett J., Blaney McMurtry LLP, 1073
Tlustos, Paul, Contact, Cutler-Hammer Canada, 154
Tobe, Edith B., Environmental Consultant, E.B. Tobe Enterprises, 168
Tobert, P.Eng., Owen, City Manager, Calgary, 671
Tobin, Barb, North Grenville, 728
Tobin, John J., Torys LLP, 1081
Tobler, Patrick, Branch Manager, Environmental Dynamics Inc., 185
Tocchet, Andy, Vice President/General Manager, Atlantic Packaging Products Ltd., 96
Tocher, Barb, Erin, 709
Todd, Barry, Deputy Minister, 584
Todd, Dinnis, Guelph, 710
Todd, Donna, Cobourg, 708
Todd, Eugene, Director, Parks, Recreation, & Culture, Port Hope, 905-753-2230, 728
Todd, Ken, Chief Administrative Officer, Niagara Falls, 715
Todd, Kenneth R., City Clerk & Director, Corporate Services, St. Catharines, 719
Todd, Kevin, Director, 607
Todd, Lesley, Clerk, Leeds & Grenville, 726
Todd, Shane, Heenan Blaikie LLP - Toronto, 1076
Todd, P.Ag., Sandy, Treasurer, Agricultural Institute of Canada Foundation, 814
Toderian, Brent, Director, Vancouver, 604-873-7011, 685
Todgham Cherniak, Cyndee, Lang Michener LLP - Toronto, 1077
Toews, A., Vice-President, Gas Liquids Engineering Ltd., 205
Toews, Lorraine, Head, Public Services, Health Sciences Library, 1101
Toews, Maureen, Librarian, Red Deer College, 1109
Toews, Stan, Reeve, Hanover, 690
Toews, Vic, Minister, Public Safety, 514
Toews-Neufeldt, Lynette, Reference Services Coordinator, Concordia University College of Alberta, 1105
Tofflemire, John, Director, Community Services, Leamington, 726
Toffoli, Oliver, CFO, Thermal Energy International Inc., 394
Tolensky, Peter M., Clark Wilson LLP, 1058
Toma, Greg, CAO, Thompson-Nicola, 679
Tomasini, Chris, Librarian, Orillia Campus, Lakehead University, 1146
Tomkow, Pat, Manager, Capital Region Vegreville Corridor Water Services Commission, 757
Tomlin, Judy, Director, 663
Tomm, Ian, Executive Director, Canadian Avalanche Association, 859
Tompkins, Trent, Coordinator, Parkland County, 670
Tomsons, Sandra, Vice-President, Canadian Society for the Study of Practical Ethics, 886
Ton, Peter, Marketing & Sales Manager, Alcore Fabricating Corp., 77
Tondreau, Rémy, Conseiller d'arrondissement, Anjou Est, Montréal, 738
Tonogai, Blake, Partner/Owner, ACG Technology Ltd., 66
Toole, Philip E., Fire Chief & Deputy Director, Fredericton, 506-460-2500, 691
Toomey, Sarah, Acting Chief Librarian, Royal Military College of Canada, 1143
Tooms, Roger, Manager, Kitimat-Stikine, 250-615-6100, 678
Toon, Donald, Owner, Heron Instruments, 230
Toplack, Stephen, President, C V Environmental Services, 119
Toplack, Stephen A., President, C.V. Environmental Services, 120
Topley, Michael G., Principal Engineer & President, Horner Associates Limited, 233
Topolnisky, Bruce, Manager, Bartle & Gibson Co. Ltd., 102
Topp, Anne, Manager, Saanich, 250-475-1775, 688
Topp, Christina, Vice-President, World Wildlife Fund - Canada, 1023
Topp, Graham, Vice President, 663

Topping Jr., John C., President/CEO, Climate Institute, 896
Torcoletti, Gene, President, Atotech Canada Ltd., 97
Torkar, Brian W., Principal, Friesen Tokar Architects, Landscape & Interior Designers, 202
Torlone, Joanne, Contact, Nature's Environmental Products Inc., 298
Torlone, Joe, Chief Administrative Officer, Timmins, 721
Torrance, Michael, Ogilvy Renault LLP/S.E.N.C.R.L., s.r.l. - Toronto, 1078
Torrance-Perks, John, Director, Planning & Engineering Initiatives Ltd., 325
Torrie, Ralph, President, Torrie Smith Associates Inc., 398
Toscher, Martha, Coordinator, Health & Safety, Port Colborne, 718
Tosh, Gordon, Wellington, 519-856-9056, 705
Tosh, Shawn, Manager, Springfield, 204-444-2241, 690
Tosto, Anna M., McCarthy Tétrault LLP - Ottawa, 1071
Toth, Andrew, President, Metex Corp. Ltd., 287
Toth, Andy, Manager, Swift Current, 306-778-2787, 755
Toth, Angela, Clerk & Director, Corporate Services, Strathroy-Caradoc, 731
Toth, Cindy, Director, Environmental Policy, Oakville, 715
Toth, Julius, Contact, IMO Pump Inc., 239
Totland, Murray, City Manager, Saskatoon, 754
Totten, Margaret, Manager, Saint John, 506-658-2990, 692
Touchette, Josée, Assistant Deputy Minister, 545
Touchette, Marc, Conseiller d'arrondissement, Champlain-L'île-des-S, Montréal, 738
Tougas, François E.J., Lang Michener LLP - Vancouver, 1060
Tough, Michael, National Sales Manager, Leeson Canada Ltd., 266
Toupin, Sylvain, Cain Lamarre Casgrain Wells - Montréal, 1083
Tourangeau, Marc, Hawkesbury, 711
Tourangeau, Marc, Greffier, Saint-Eustache, 742
Tourangeau, Michel, Associé, Lapointe Rosenstein Marchand Melançon, 1085
Tourigny, George, Manager, Great Western Containers Inc., 216
Tourigny, R. Michael, Lang Michener LLP - Vancouver, 1060
Tourigny, Thérèse, Directrice générale, Fédération des sociétés d'horticulture et d'écologie du Québec, 915
Tourville, Pierre, Rimouski, 740
Tousaw, Jane, Director, Planning, Haliburton, 700
Tousaw, Scott, Director, Planning & Development, Huron, 701
Tousignant, Sylvain, Terrebonne, 745
Tousignant, Yves, Directeur général, La Tuque, 736
Toussaint, Attiave, Les Produits Environnementaux Atlas, 270
Tout, Mike, Manager, Roads Operations, Brant, 698
Tout, Raymond T., Mayor, Wellington North, 732
Tovell, James, General Manager, Coast Paper Ltd., 145
Tovey, Jim, Peel, 714, 703
Townley, John L., Bennett Jones LLP - Calgary Office, 1049
Townsend, Doug, Manager, Canmore, 403-678-1586, 671
Townsend, Phillip, Director, Halifax Regional Municipality, 695
Townsend, Gary, President, Toronto Sheet Metal Contractors Association, 1013
Towriss, Colonel, Pembroke, 717
Toyota, Jack, General Manager, OMB (Americas) Forged Steel Valves, 312
Tozer, Scott, Contact, DST Consulting Engineers, 166
Tozzi, Ralph, Manager, Invensys Systems Canada Inc., 246
tr meighen family foundat, T.R. Meighen Family Found, Toronto, ON, 1045
Traballo, Ramon, Consultant/Diver, MIE Consulting Engineers Ltd., 289
Tracey, Karen, Executive Director, Northern Ontario Aquaculture Association, 966
Tracey, Matt, Manager, Water & Wastewater, Quinte West, 718
Trachsel, Walter, Wellington, 519-323-2794, 705
Trachu, Kandis, Customer Service, Thermon Heat Tracing Services, 394
Trafford, Richard J., Miller Thomson LLP - Waterloo, 1081
Trahan, Fernand, Maire, Val-d'Or, 746
Trahan, Fernand, Préfet, La Vallée-de-l'Or, 748
Trahan, J. Bernie, Director, Calgary, 403-268-1122, 671
Trainer, Marie, Mayor, Haldimand, 700
Traini, Chris, County Engineer, Middlesex, 701
Trasente, Diana, Director, Environmental Remediation Equipment Inc., 186
Trask, Andrea, Coordinator & Educator, Hants East District, 697
Trask, Ruth E., Stewart McKelvey Stirling Scales - St. John's, 1066
Trasolini, Franco E., Davis LLP - Vancouver, 1059
Trasolini, Joe, Metro Vancouver, 678
Trasolini, Joe, Mayor, Port Moody, 604-469-4501, 683

Executive Name Index

Trattner, Paula, Partner, Osler, Hoskin & Harcourt LLP - Toronto, 1079
Trautmann, Ron, Manager, Carrier Canada Ltd., 129
Travale, Dennis, Mayor, Norfolk, 702
Travers, Scott, President & Chief Operating Officer, Minas Basin Pulp & Power Company Limited, 290
Traverse, Margaret, Manager, The Enviro-Connect, 392
Travis, Cliff, Chair, Central Peace Regional Waste Management Commission, 757
Trawin, David A., Director, Kamloops, 250-828-3473, 681
Traynor, Michael, Deputy Mayor & Councillor, Meaford, 519-376-8791, 700, 727
Treacy, Brian, Lead, Monsanto Canada Inc., 293
Treacy, Heather L., Fraser Milner Casgrain LLP - Calgary, 1051
Treadwell, Bill, Miramichi, 691
Treffry, Keith, Director, Earth Day Canada, 907
Treidler, B., General Manager, St. Albert, 674
Trelford, Roberta, Coordinator, Community Emergency Management, & Hea, Kincardine, 726
Tremblay, Alain, Directeur général, La Haute-Côte-Nord, 748
Tremblay, André, Cain Lamarre Casgrain Wells - Montréal, 1083
Tremblay, Annie, Cain Lamarre Casgrain Wells - Chicoutimi, 1082
Tremblay, Chantal C., McCarthy Tétrault LLP - Montréal, 1086
Tremblay, Christine, Directrice, Saguenay, 741
Tremblay, Christyne, Sous-ministre, 648
Tremblay, Claude, Saguenay, 741
Tremblay, Daniel, Vice-President, Tremcar inc., 401
Tremblay, Denis, Chef de division, Montréal, 738
Tremblay, Dominic, Cain Lamarre Casgrain Wells - Chicoutimi, 1082
Tremblay, Dominic, Préfet, Charlevoix, 747
Tremblay, Dominique, Director, Planning, Russell, 729
Tremblay, Donald, Exec. Vice-President & CFO, Brookfield Power, 117
Tremblay, Donald, Head, Les Laboratoires S.L. inc., 269
Tremblay, Eric, Vice-President, Equipement Labrie Ltee, 189
Tremblay, Frederic, Chemline Plastics Ltd., 140
Tremblay, Frédéric, Alma, 418-668-5014, 733
Tremblay, Gilles H., Président, 647
Tremblay, Guy, Responsable, Informatique, Université du Québec à Chicoutimi, 1166
Tremblay, Gérald, Directeur, Rivière-du-Loup, 418-862-2121, 741
Tremblay, Gérald, Maire, Montréal, 514-872-3101, 738
Tremblay, Jacques, Morency Avocats, 1088
Tremblay, Jacques, President, Tremcar inc., 401
Tremblay, Jacques A., Sous-ministre adjoint, 643
Tremblay, Jean, Maire, Saguenay, 418-698-3330, 741
Tremblay, Jean, Sec.-Trés., Régie d'assainissement des eaux de la Vallée du Richelieu, 759
Tremblay, Louis-Michel, Associé, Miller Thomson LLP - Montréal, 1086
Tremblay, Louise, Partner, Miller Thomson LLP - Toronto, 1078
Tremblay, Luc, Directeur général, Mascouche, 737
Tremblay, Luc, Sec.-Trés., Régie d'assainissement des eaux usées Terrebonne/Mascouche, 759
Tremblay, Lucien, Directeur général, 653
Tremblay, Madeleine, Documentaliste, Centre des études collégiales - Carleton, 1166
Tremblay, Marcel, Conseiller, Notre-Dame-de-Grâce, Montréal, 738
Tremblay, Martine, Cain Lamarre Casgrain Wells - Alma, 1082
Tremblay, Michel, Maire, Varennes, 746
Tremblay, Philippe, Partner, Heenan Blaikie S.E.N.C.R.L/SRL, 1085
Tremblay, Pierre A., Directeur, Saguenay, 741
Tremblay, René, Directeur, Lévis, 418-839-2002, 736
Tremblay, Richard, General Manager, Eastern Canada, Benjamin Moore & Co. Ltd, 105
Tremblay, Ron, Director, Building & Bylaws, Newmarket, 714
Tremblay, Réjean, Vice-président exécutif, Lécuyer et Fils Ltée, 266
Tremblay, Sabin, Directeur général adjoint, Lévis, 418-839-2002, 736
Tremblay, Serge, Directeur, Montréal, 738
Tremblay, Sylvain, Directeur, Thetford Mines, 745
Tremblay, Yves, Varennes, 746
Tremblay, Yves, Sales, Service & Technical Contact, Rotork Controls (Canada) Ltd., 352
Tremblay Blanchette, Denise, Québec, 740
Tremorin, Andy, Contact, Comstock Canada Ltd., 148
Trent, Eric, Roctest Ltée, 350
Trépanier, Denys, General Manager, Aquaterre Inc., 89
Trépanier, Janic, SMTE - Responsable, Collège d'Alma, 1166
Treu, Andrew, Coordinator, Red Deer County, 670

Treusch, Andrew, Assoc. Deputy Minister, 558
Trevors, Robert B., Miramichi, 691
Trew, David, Executive Director, North Saskatchewan Watershed Alliance, 966
Trickey, Marianne, Historian, Rideau Valley Field Naturalists, 1152
Triffo, Ron, Chair, 569
Triffo, Ronald P., Chairman, Stantec Inc., 377
Trifon, Larry, Bratty & Partners LLP, 1081
Trihey, Stephan H., Partner, Heenan Blaikie S.E.N.C.R.L/SRL, 1085
Trillo, Sandi, Secretary, Greenest City, 926
Trim, Charlie, Regional Councillor, Clarington, 724
Trim, N., Chief Financial Officer & Commissioner, Corporate, Peel, 703
Trimble, J.R. (Richard), Contact, EBA Engineering Consultants Ltd., 170
Trip, Luke, Program Manager, Commission for Environmental Cooperation, 898
Tripiciano, Dario, Intelex Technologies Inc., 244
Tripp, Michael, District Manager, BFI Canada Inc., 107
Tripp, R., Director, Infrastructure Services, Fort Erie, 709
Tripp, P.Eng., Douglas, President, Canadian Institute for Energy Training, 872
Trippler, Aaron, Director, American Industrial Hygiene Association, 823
Trites, Darren, President, DSS Marine Inc., 167
Trocakstad, Sandy, Sec.-Treas., Lethbridge Regional Waste Management Services, 757
Trojan, Michael, Chief Administrative Officer, Niagara, 702
Trombetta, Katie, Niagara, 702
Trood, Barry, Foreman, Wellington North, 519-848-5327, 732
Trotman, Ian, Vice-President, Life Extension Projects & Project, 511
Trott, Guy, Library Manager, Calgary Library & Information Centre, 1100
Trott, John, Woodlands Conservation Officer & Weed Inspector, Middlesex, 701
Trottier, Donna, Coordinator, Red Deer County, 670
Trottier, Jacques, Head of Circulation, University of Sudbury, 1155
Trottier, Roger, Conseiller d'arrondissement, Montréal, 738
Trought, John, Contact, Church & Trought Inc., 140
Troup, Lynda K., Thompson Dorfman Sweatman LLP, 1064
Troyer, Andrew, Manager, FS Partners, 202
Trudeau, Dennis, Manager, Nanaimo, 678
Trudeau, Marie-Josée, Cain Lamarre Casgrain Wells - Montréal, 1083
Trudeau, Mélanie, Cain Lamarre Casgrain Wells - Sept-Iles, 1089
Trudeau, Stephan Scott, Davis LLP - Montréal, 1083
Trudel, Claude, Maire d'arrondissement/Conseiller de ville, Montréal, 738
Trudel, Denise, Québec, 740
Trudel, Marie-France, Québec, 740
Trudel, Raymond, Bibliothécaire responsable, CÉGEP de St-Jérôme, 1184
Trudel, Sandy, Officer, Brandon, 689
Trudel, Sylvain, Shawinigan, 744
Trudelle, A., Product Sales & Marketing Manager, Ingersoll-Rand Canada Inc., 241
Trueman, Stephen, City Solicitor, Moncton / Ville de Moncton, 691
Trump, Grant, President & CEO, Eco Canada, 170
Trump, Grant S., President/CEO, Environmental Careers Organization of Canada, 911
Truscott, Joe, Acting Project Assessment Director, 578
Trussler, Doug, Chief, North Vancouver, 604-990-3653, 688
Tryon, Gerry, Bracebridge, 706
Trypis, Steve, Operating Manager, BPG Graphics Solutions, 115
Tryssenaar, Sherry, CFO & Vice-President, QuestAir Technologies Inc., 339
Trzeciak, Jeffrey, University Librarian, McMaster University, 1141
Trzyna, Thaddeus C., President, California Institute of Public Affairs, 852
Tsafarti, Amichai, Controller, Joseph & Co. Inc., 253
Tsafarti, David, Operations Manager, Joseph & Co. Inc., 253
Tsakopoulos, Tom C., Graham Wilson & Green, Barristers & Solicitors, Notaries, Mediato, 1068
Tsang, Edward, President, Zephyr Alternative Power, 437
Tse, Hau Sing, Senior Vice-President, 519
Tse, Mark, Chair, Petroleum Tank Management Association of Alberta, 986
Tsikayi, Hilary, Director, Langley, 604-533-6156, 687
Tso, Henry, Contact, RICHWAY Environmental Technologies Ltd., 346

Tsounis, Nak, President, Safety Express Ltd., 355
Tsui, Stephen, Principal, Stantec Inc., 378
Tucci, Ben, City Councillor, Cambridge, 707
Tucci, Lou, Vice President, Royal Envelope Ltd., 353
Tuck, Wayne, Manager, Whitehorse, 867-668-8306, 755
Tucker, Andrew, Director, Nanaimo, 250-754-4251, 681
Tucker, John, Supervisor, Nelson Environmental Remediation Ltd., 299
Tucker, Karen, Director, 592
Tucker, Lynn, Administration, RMS Instruments Ltd., 347
Tucker, Mary, Manager, 598
Tucker, Ralph, Chair, 604
Tucker, Reada, Accountant, Services d'Évaluation Santé/Toxicologie Inc., 363
Tucker, Ross, Manager, Parks & Recreation, St. Thomas, 719
Tuckett, Nancy, Director, Planning & Development, Springwater, 730
Tuckey, Bryan, Commissioner, Planning & Development Services, York, 705
Tudhope, Roger, Office Manager, Trow Consulting Engineers Ltd., 403
Tuer, Greg, Executive Director, 661
Tufenkji, Nathalie, Associate Director, Brace Centre for Water Resources Management, 115
Tuff, Julia, Chief Building Official, Russell, 729
Tuffrey, Keith, Vice-President, Comstock Canada Ltd., 148
Tufgar, R., Branch Manager, Totten Sims Hubicki Associates Ltd., 399
Tufgar, Ray, Vice-President, Totten Sims Hubicki Associates Ltd., 399
Tugman, Laurie, President & CEO, Marsulex Inc., 281
Tuhtar, Dinko, Contact, A&A Environmental Consultants Inc., 63
Tuhtar, Dinko, Sr. Environmental Engineer, BOMA Environmental & Safety Inc., 113
Tulk, Harold, Fire Chief, Kingston, 712
Tulk, Jennifer, Director, 602
Tullis, Carole, Manager, Health Sciences Library, Toronto East General Hospital, 1162
Tulloch, Dave, Director, 661
Tume, Vincent, Secretary, Society of Professional Engineers & Associates, 1008
Tunteng, Verki, Heenan Blaikie LLP - Toronto, 1076
Tupling, Jack, Director, Public Works, Orangeville, 716
Tupper, David V., Blake, Cassels & Graydon LLP - Calgary, 1049
Turchan, Glenn, Executive Vice-President, Conestoga-Rovers & Associates, 149
Turchyn, Greg, Vice-President, Wardrop Engineering Inc., 417
Turck, David, Port Hope, 728
Turco, Lou, Sault Ste. Marie, 720
Turcotte, Dawna, Campus Librarian, Fort St. John Campus, 1112
Turcotte, Denis, President, J.M. Turcotte ltée, 250
Turcotte, Guy, Directeur général, Fortier 2000 Ltée, 200
Turcotte, Mathieu, Associé, Miller Thomson LLP - Montréal, 1086
Turcotte, Michael Louis, Président, 649
Turcotte, Robert, Bibliothécaire, Campus de Dieppe, Bibliothèque, 1126
Turcotte, Robert, Business Development, Géophysique GPR International Inc., 211
Turcotte, Roger, Sec.-Trés., Régie intermunicipale du comté de Beauce-Sud, 761
Turenne, L., Project Coordinator, Western Industrial Services Ltd., 429
Turgeon, Richard, Directeur, Westburne Canada, 429
Turgeon, Sylvie, Rouyn-Noranda, 741
Turgeon, Yves, Partner, Heenan Blaikie S.E.N.C.R.L/SRL, 1085
Turkheim, Richard, Executive Director, 661
Turkstra, Herman, Partner, Turkstra Mazza Associates, 1069
Turlea, Ovidiu, Territory Manager, Silex Innovations Inc., 367
Turmel, André, Fasken Martineau - Montréal, 1083
Turmel, André, Président, Fondation des partenaires de la Biosphère de Montréal, 917
Turmel, Roland, Technicien, PEB, Québec Ministère du Développement durable, de l'Environnement et, 1180
Turnbull, Phil, Medicine Hat, 673
Turnbull, Susan, Commissioner, Corporate Services & Finance, Prince Edward, 703
Turner, Annie, Bibliothécaire, Québec Ministère des Ressources naturelles et de la Faune, 1180
Turner, Don, Regional Planner, Powell River, 679
Turner, Frank, Partner, Osler, Hoskin & Harcourt LLP - Calgary, 1053
Turner, Greg J., Stewart & Turner, 1067
Turner, Heather, Director, North Vancouver, 604-983-6305, 682
Turner, John, Assistant Deputy Minister, 545
Turner, Juliann, Contact, Knowaste LLC, 259

Executive Name Index

Turner, Malcolm C., Newfoundland & Labrador Camping Association, 962
Turner, Patrick, President, Valley Comfort Systems Inc., 409
Turner, Shannon, President, Public Health Association of British Columbia, 990
Turner, Shawn, Manager, Westburne Canada, 429
Turner, Tammy, Director, 642
Turner, Tanya, Planner, Quesnel, 688
Turner, Thomas W., Pitblado LLP, 1063
Turner, Wendy, Manager, Legal Information Line & Lawyer Referral, Legal Information Society of Nova Scotia, 1136
turner foundation, inc, Turner Foundation, Inc., Atlanta, GA, 1041
Turner-Davis, Timothy, Manager, Ferguson Simek Clark, 194
Turpin, Barry, Prince Edward, 703
Turpin, Chad, Deputy City Manager, Burnaby, 604-294-7110, 679
Turrittin, Tony, Secretary, Transport Action Canada, 1013
Turyk, Jason, Manager, Westburne Canada, 427
Tuson, Eric, KMK Consultants Limited, 258
Tustian, Joyce, General Manager, Edmonton, 780-442-6356, 672
Tutkaluk, Judy, Marketing Executive, Dimplex North America, 164
Tuttosi, Trevor, General Manager, Organic Producers Association of Manitoba Co-operative Inc., 982
Tuytel, Neo J., Bernard & Partners, 1057
Twa, Q.C., Allan R., Burnet, Duckworth & Palmer LLP, 1050
Twaddle, Bill, Owen Sound, 717
Tweedie, James, Director, Castle-Crown Wilderness Coalition, 892
Tweedie, Jim, Director, Canadian Gas Association, 869
Tweel, B.A., Mitchell G., Charlottetown, 732
Twinney, Jane, Newmarket, 714
Twolan, Mitch, Bruce, 698
Twomey, Jim, Executive Vice-President, 634
Tyagi, Dev, General Manager, Public Works, Windsor, 723
Tyers, Bryan, Manager, Comstock Canada Ltd., 148
Tyler, Jonathan, President & CEO, Tyler Research Instruments Corp., 404
Tyler, Kenneth J., Partner, Borden Ladner Gervais LLP - Vancouver, 1058
Tyler, Robert, Chair, 656
Tyler, Robert L., Aikins, MacAulay & Thorvaldson LLP, 1063
Tyler, Scott, Regional Sales Manager, Joe Johnson Equipment Inc., 252
Tyler, Susan, Administrator, Organic Crop Improvement Association - New Brunswick, 982
Tyler, Terry, President, Cat Tech Canada Company, 132
Tyner, Ross, Director, Library Services, Okanagan College, 1112
Tynes, Raymond, Truro, 696
Tyre, Bob, Regional Manager, ASI Group Ltd., 94
Tyson, Q.C., Marian F., Deputy Minister, 614
Tziatis, Andrea, Manager, Universal Handling Equipment Company Limited, 406

U

Uauy, Richard, President, International Union of Nutritional Sciences, 945
Udala, Berne, Supervisor, Penticton, 250-490-2550, 682
Uleryk, Elizabeth, Director, Hospital for Sick Children, 1158
Ullyot, Kim, Manager, Library & Info Services, Northwest Territories Resources, Wildlife & Economic Development, 1134
Ulmi, Sandi, Vice-Chair, British Columbia Farm Industry Review Board, 847
Ulrich, Lise, Agente de bureau, Acquisitions, Collège de Maisonneuve, 1172
Umedaly, Mossadiq S., Chair, 580
Ummenhofer, Michael, Agent, Penticton, 250-490-2555, 682
Underdown, Géraldine, Executive Director, 549
Underhay, Bruce, Manager, Yellowknife, 867-669-3404, 695
Underhill, Brian, Director, 574
Underhill, Harley, Director, Human Resources, Elgin, 699
Underhill, Jane, King, 726
Underwood, Chris, Manager, Vancouver, 604-873-7992, 685
Underwood, Peter, Deputy Minister, 614
Underwood, Tim, President, The Recycle Systems Company Inc., 393
Unger, Jason, Staff counsel, Environmental Law Centre (Alberta) Society, 1055
Unger, Marc, Borden Ladner Gervais LLP - Montréal, 1083
Unger, Mervin Wayne (Merv), Nanaimo, 681
Unger, Willie M., President, Comco Manufacturing Ltd., 146
universite du quebec a ri, Université du Québec à Ri, Rimouski, QC, 1035
universite du quebec a tr, Université du Québec à Tr, Trois-Rivieres, QC, 1035
Unkerskov, Ken, President, KBU Environmental Technologies Inc., 256
Unterman, Richard M., Principal, Unterman McPhail Associates, 407
Unvoas, Arlene, Executive Director, Swift Current Creek Watershed Stewards, 1011
Unyi, Richard, Director, Raw Materials Corporation, 342
Upper, T-Jay, Contact, The Beer Store, 391
Urbain, Carole, Directrice, Bibliothèque de géographie, 1177
Urbanowicz, Debbie, Pelham, 717
Urbanski, Adelina, Commissioner, Social & Community Services, Halton, 700
Urbonas, Arnold, Vice-President, PBR Laboratories Inc., 319
Urch, Phil, Supervisor, Westburne Canada, 428
Urisk, Jasmine, President, JTU Consulting, 253
Urkow, Diane, Manager, Camrose, 671
Urmetzer, Burk, Commercial Solutions Inc., 147
Urquhart, Roger, Hatch Ltd., 226
Urquhart, Scott, Manager, Trimax Residuals Management Inc., 401
Urquhart, Sharon M., Alexander Holburn Beaudin & Lang, LLP, 1057
Urquhart, Q.C., Glenn A., Counsel, Singleton Urquhart LLP, 1062
Urzada, Tami, Cascades Recovery Inc., 131
Useche, Aurelio, Vice-President, Dectron Internationale, 159
Usher, Harold, London, 713
Usova, Tatiana, Directrice, Université de l'Alberta Bibliothèque Saint-Jean, 1107
Uteck, Sue, Councillor, Halifax Regional Municipality, 695
Utley, John K., Brantford, 707

V

Vaadeland, Merv, Supervisor, Kodiak Oilfield Services, 259
Vaccaro, Angie, Reference Librarian, Manitoba Hydro, 1124
Vachon, Claire, Partner, Heenan Blaikie LLP - Toronto, 1076
Vachon, Gaétan, Thetford Mines, 418-335-9543, 745
Vachon, Marc, Thetford Mines, 418-334-0340, 745
Vachon, Roger, Directeur, Sherbrooke, 819-821-5726, 744
Vadacchino, Michael, Conseiller d'arrondissement, Cecil-P.-Newman, Montréal, 738
Vadeboncoeur, Mélanie, Lavery, de Billy - Ottawa, 1070
Vaes, Peter, Manager, North Safety Products Canada, 306
Vail, Q.C., Walter D., Cox and Palmer - Fredericton, 1064
Vaillancourt, Chantal, VP, Oxegen Inc., 315
Vaillancourt, Cindy, McCarthy Tétrault LLP - Montréal, 1086
Vaillancourt, Daryl, North Bay, 715
Vaillancourt, Gilles, Maire, Laval, 736
Vaillancourt, Jérôme, Québec, 740
Vaillancourt, Serge, Chef de division, Montréal, 738
Vaisey, Douglas, Librarian, Reference & Research, St Mary's University, 1136
Valade, Liette, Director, Recreation & Culture, Hawkesbury, 711
Valcic, Mark, General Manager, Corporate & Financial Services &, East Gwillimbury, 708
Valcourt, Alphé, Sales Representative, Deschênes Drilling Ltd., 161
Valdes, Miguel, Branch Manager, Anachemia Canada Inc., 85
Valente, Michael J., Scarfone Hawkins LLP, 1069
Valente, Tony, Vice President, Canon Canada Inc., 126
Valentine, Thomas E., Partner, Macleod Dixon LLP, 1052
Valentinis, Fulvio, Windsor, 723
Valin, Jean, Director General, 560
Valiquette, CGA, OMA, Dominique, Trésorier, L'Assomption, 736
Vallee, Don, Regional Manager, Jomac Canada Inc., 253
Vallée, Kim, Senior Library Technician, Lakehead University, 1146
Vallée, Louis, Sous-ministre adjoint, 644
Vallee, Mary E., Graham Wilson & Green, Barristers & Solicitors, Notaries, Mediato, 1068
Vallée, Michel, Directeur, Longueuil, 737
Vallée, Serge, Vice-President, Biolab Inc., 108
Vallières, Dominique, Lavery, de Billy - Montréal, 1086
Vallières, Martine, Directrice générale, Beloeil, 734
Vallis, Q.C., Jeffrey D., Partner, Borden Ladner Gervais LLP - Calgary, 1050
Vallisse, Karen, Marketing Coordinator, K&D Pratt Group Inc., 254
Valmstead, Liv, Reference Librarian, Architecture & Fine Arts Library, 1122
van Aanhout, Michael, President, Stratos Inc., 380
Van Bakel, John, Perth, 703
Van Bibber, Pat, Chair, 665
Van Bruinessen, Marian, Treasurer, Frontenac, 699
Van Buren, Mark, Director, Engineering, Kingston, 712
Van Buul, Ken, Manager, Parkland County, 670
Van Bynen, A.J. (Tony), York, 705
Van Bynen, Tony, Mayor, Newmarket, 905-898-2876, 714
Van Dam, Tony, Director, Fire & Emergency Services, Springwater, 730
Van Damme, Laird, Consulting Forester, KBM Forestry Consultants Inc., 255
Van de Voorde, P., President, TPE Technologies Inc., 400
Van de Voort, Colleen, Borrower Services Librarian, Kwantlen University College, 1113
van der Bank, Johan, Manager, Red Deer County, 670
van der Lee, Jean C., Field Law - Calgary, 1051
van der Linden, Mike, Manager, Sidney, 684
Van Der Raadt, Paulie, Unit Manager, AMEC, 83
van der Werf, Paul, President, 2cg Inc., 404
Van Diepenbeek, Ben, Huron, 701
Van Doesburg, John, Administrator, Mountain View Regional Water Services, 758
Van Doesburg, John, Manager, Kneehill Regional Water Services Commission, 757
Van Dusen, George, Forest Management Superintendent, Corner Brook Pulp & Paper Ltd., 152
Van Dyk, Heidy, Norfolk, 702
Van Dyk, Luke, Landfill Manager, CCS Income Trust, 134
Van Dyk, Marie, Director, Saanich, 688
Van Eerden, Evert, Chair, Freshwater Fisheries Society of British Columbia, 920
Van Egmond, John, President, Wallace, Van Egmond Spankle Inc., 174, 416
Van Esbroeck, Jeanette, Research & Cataloguing Librarian, Yukon Dept. of Energy, Mines & Resources, 1191
van Gelder, Patrick, Business Unit Director, Genzyme Canada Inc., 210
Van Hellemond, Andy, Guelph, 710
Van Herk, Case, County Commissioner, Sturgeon County, 780-939-8345, 670
van Hierden, John, Vice-President, Canadian Hay Association, 870
Van Hoi, Hoang, Technical Manager, Mabarex inc., 277
Van Horne, Ronald G., Chief Administrative Officer, Lambton, 701
Van Houdt, Gerry, Manager, Petro Sep Membrane Technologies Inc., 322
van Kampen, Dwight, Controller & Vice-President, Shell Canada Limited, 365
Van Kooten-Bossence, Kristy, Ingersoll, 711
van Lierop, Martin, President/CEO, Agrosysts Ltée, 73
van Manen, Frank, President, International Association for Bear Research & Management, 934
Van Meerbergen, Paul, London, 713
Van Mierlo-West, Peggy, Director, Community Services, Lambton Shores, 726
van Niekerk, Jan, Senior Manager, Capital Regional District, 250-474-9655, 676
van Nostrand, John, Partner, Planning Alliance, 326
Van Omme, Herman, Superintendent, Charlottetown, 902-628-6647, 732
Van Overberghe, Joe, Trustee, Ontario Petroleum Institute Inc., 1144
van Oyen, Bob, President, Research & Development Institute for the Agri-Environment, 994
Van Randen, Ed, Director, 665
van Rikxoort, Rick, Owner, Southwell Controls Ltd., 374
Van Scheik, Joyce, Librarian, Canadian University College, 1108
Van Slyke, Victor, President, ATD Waste Systems Inc., 95
Van Tighem, Gordon, Mayor, Yellowknife, 695
Van Veen, Walter, Contact, Conestoga-Rovers & Associates, 149
van Velzen, M.Sc., P.Biol, Kevan, Manager, Calgary, 403-250-6448, 671
Van Vliet, Kevin, Manager, Canmore, 403-678-1545, 671
Van Wachem, Gerry, President, Advance Engineered Products Ltd., 68
van Walsum, Nell, Secretary, International Association of Hydrogeologists - Canadian National, 936
van Warmerdam, Paul, President & CEO, KWH Pipe, 261
Van Weelden, Hank, Vice-President, Alta-Fab Structures Ltd., 81
Van Wely, Theo, President, AIM Environmental Group, 74
van Woudenberg, Walter, Founder & CEO, Nilex Inc., 304
Van Wyck, Donna, Clerk, Wellington, 705
Van Wyck, Larry, Superintendent, Roads, Erin, 709
Van Wyngaarden, Robert, Principal, Golder Associates Ltd., 214
Van Ymeren, Sandra E., McKenzie Lake Lawyers LLP, 1069

Executive Name Index

Vana, Peter, Associate Commissioner, Strathcona County, 780-464-8188, 670
Vanbiesbrouck, Barry, Manager, Thames Campus Resource Centre, 1139
VanCasteren, Dave, Manager, Venture Foam Products Inc., 411
Vance, Bradley N., Counsel, MacPherson Leslie & Tyerman LLP - Regina, 1090
Vance, Elzina, Acting Manager, Long Lake Regional Waste Management Commission, 757
Vance, R. Lane, Treasurer & Manager, Financial Services, Smith-Ennismore-Lakefield, 729
Vancha, Colleen, Sr. Vice-President, Viterra Inc., 414
Vandal, Daniel, Winnipeg, 204-986-5206, 690
Vandal, Thierry, Président-directeur général, 649
VanDam, Robert, President, Alberta Greenhouse Growers Association, 817
Vandeloo, Joe, Assistant University Librarian, Administrative Ser, University of Western Ontario Libraries, 1144
Vanden Eynden, Alain, Magog, 819-843-1706, 737
Vanden Hoek, Jim, Frontenac, 699
Vandenassem, David J., Consultant, N. Vandenassem & Associate, 296
Vandenassem, Nicholas, President, N. Vandenassem & Associate, 296
Vander Stelt, Jan C., Brantford, 707
Vanderbeek, Peter, Chief Building Official, Woolwich, 732
Vanderburgh, Eileen E., Alexander Holburn Beaudin & Lang, LLP, 1057
Vanderby, Leo, Controller, Elmec Engineering Ltd., 176
Vanderfluit, Sean D., Clark Wilson LLP, 1058
Vanderheyden, Joanne, Middlesex, 701
Vanderheyden, Joanne, Mayor, Strathroy-Caradoc, 731
Vanderlinden, Doug, President, VQUIP Inc., 414
VanDerMeulen, Jackie, Heenan Blaikie LLP - Toronto, 1076
Vanderpas, John, Vice-President/General Manager, St. Marys Cement Inc., 356
Vandervecht, Dylan, Osler, Hoskin & Harcourt LLP - Calgary, 1053
Vandervoort, Cheryl, Manager, Human Resources, Quinte West, 718
Vanderwell, Gary, President, Burnaby Bag & Burlap Ltd., 118
Vandewal, Ron W., South Frontenac, 730
VanGenderen, Albert, Secretary Treasurer, Canadian Hay Association, 870
Vanier, Léopold, Secrétaire, Régie intermunicipale d'aqueduc de la vallée de Châteauguay, 759
Vankoughnet, Ron, Supervisor, Roads & Landfill, Greater Napanee, 709
VanLeuvenhage, Jerry, Specialist, Brantford, 115
Vanriel, Peter, General Manager, CanNorth Environmental Services Inc., 126
VanSchouwen, Adrian, Vice President/General Manager, Sandwell Engineering Inc., 357
VanSchubert, Rob, General Manager, Environmental Dynamics Inc., 185
Vanslyke, Jason, General Manager, Mowat Fabrication Ltd., 294
Vanstone, Greg, Municipal Solicitor, Delta, 604-946-3213, 686
Vanstone, Nancy, Deputy Minister, 611
Vanthuyne, Cory, Yellowknife, 695
VanVeen, Walter, Conestoga-Rovers & Associates, 149
VanZant, Paul, Vice-President, Ontario Association for Geographic & Environmental Education, 971
Vardi, Gideon, Vice-President, GEA Barr-Rosin Inc., 205
Vardon, Bruce E., Principal, Triton Engineering Services Ltd., 402
Vardy, Elizabeth, Vice-President, Varcon Inc., 409
Vardy, Matt, Manager, Varcon Inc., 409
Vardy, T.M. (Tom), President, Varcon Inc., 409
Varga, Bill, Essex, 699
Varghese, Mary, OHS Resource Librarian, Newfoundland & Labrador Dept. of Government Services, 1131
Varin, Normand, Sainte-Julie, 743
Varns, Riley, Alberni-Clayoquot, 250-726-7176, 676
Varro, Alex, President, Thuro Inc., 396
Vaseux, Jean, Roctest Ltée, 350
Vasic, Dragan, Contact, Arrow Speed Controls Ltd., 93
Vass, Len, Peterborough, 718
Vastag, Robert, Manager, Dillon Consulting Ltd., 163
Vatcher, Ian, President, Panasonic Canada Inc., 317
Vatri, Rick, Manager, Engineering, New Tecumseth, 714
Vaughan, Adam, Toronto, 721
Vaughan, Steve, Partner, Heenan Blaikie LLP - Toronto, 1076
Vaxvick, Adam, Contact, Venables Machine Works Ltd., 410
Vaykovich, D., Coordinator, Okanagan-Similkameen, 678
Vázquez-Gálvez, Felipe Adrián, Executive Director, Commission for Environmental Cooperation, 898

Veale, Mel, Middlesex, 701
Vecchiarelli, Andy, Manager, Atotech Canada Ltd., 97
Veer, Tara, Red Deer, 403-358-3568, 674
Vegh, Tom, Newmarket, 714
Veillard, Jeremy, Vice-President, Canadian Institute for Health Information, 872
Veillette, Lucie, Responsable, Amos, 733
Veillette, Michel, Trois-Rivières, 745
Veilleux, Charles A., Morency Avocats, 1088
Veilleux, Denise, Secrétaire, Régie intermunicipale d'assainissement de la Haute-Bécancour, 760
Veilleux, Francis, President, Bluewater Recycling Association, 846
Veilleux, Paule, Associé, Langlois Kronström Desjardins, 1088
Veilleux, Ruth, Associée, Lapointe Rosenstein Marchand Melançon, 1085
Veilleux, Réjean, Saint-Hyacinthe, 742
Veinotte, Jennifer, Recycling Coordinator, Chester District, 697
Veitch, Keith, Combustion & Energy Systems Ltd., 146
Veith, Angela, Waterloo, 722
Vejvoda, Berenica, Data Librarian, Map and Data Library, 1159
Vellone, John A.D., Borden Ladner Gervais LLP - Toronto, 1074
Venerus, Angelo, President, Venerus International Purification Inc., 410
Vengelisti, Diana, CH2M Hill Canada Limited, 137
Veniot, Barry, Supervisor, Bathurst, 506-548-0700, 690
Venne, Serge, Vice President/General Manager, Sandwell Engineering Inc., 357
Venneri, Frank, Conseiller, François-Perrault, Montréal, 738
Vens, Henry A., President, Envirotech Associates Limited, 187
Venus, Jason, Branch Manager, CenturyVallen, 136
Verbeek, Linda, President, Alpine Garden Club of BC, 821
Verberve, Richard, Manager, Boilersmith Ltd., 113
Vercouteren, Frank, Chatham-Kent, 724
Verdy, Alexandre, Greffier, Deux-Montagnes, 735
Verge, Darrin, President, ROMOR Atlantic Limited, 351
Verge, Elizabeth, Conseillère d'arrondissement, Canal, Montréal, 738
Vergeer, Henry C., President, CEM Specialties Inc., 135
Verhagen, Annette, Vice-President, Citizens For Renewable Energy, 895
Verissimo, Nelson, Customer Service Manager, Wynn's Canada Ltd., 435
Verleun, Peter, Chair, Prince Edward Island Cattle Producers, 988
Vermeire, Marc, Operations Manager, St. Marys Cement Inc., 356
Vermes, Peter, Straub Tadco Inc., 381
Vermette, Denys, Vice-President, 544
Vermette, B.Sc., MBA, Maryse, Présidente-directrice générale, Éco Entreprises Québec, 908
Vermeulen, Bram, President/CEO, St. Marys Cement Inc., 356
Vernon, David, Osler, Hoskin & Harcourt LLP - Toronto, 1079
Veronneau, Lorraine, Agente de bureau, Matériauthèque, 1186
Verreault, Laurent, CEO, GL&V - Groupe Laperrière & Verreault Inc., 212
Verreault, Lucie, Directrice, Bibliothèque sciences de l'éducation, Université du Québec à Montréal, 1176
Verreault, Richard, Président & Chef de la direction, 654
Verret, Conrad, Québec, 740
Verret, Pierre, Beloeil, 450-467-0630, 734
Verret, Steeve, Québec, 740
Verrier, Michel, Vice-President, Cheminées Sécurité Internationale Ltée, 139
Verry, Tim, Library Assistant, Winnipeg Research Centre, 1126
Verschueren, Christian, Director General, Croplife International, 906
Verville, Mario, Directeur, Saint-Jean-sur-Richelieu, 450-359-2400, 742
Vessey, Karen, Officer, 591
Vetter, Mary A., Secretary-Treasurer, Canadian Association of Palynologists, 858
Veuger, Julian, County Constable, Lacombe County, 669
Vézina, Alain, Bibliothécaire, CÉGEP de Marie-Victorin, 1171
Vézina, Gilles, Sec.-Trés., Régie intermunicipale des déchets de CJLLR, 761
Vézina, Jean-François, Fraser Milner Casgrain S.E.N.C.R.L/LLP, 1084
Vézina, Luc, Sainte-Thérèse, 744
Vézina, Martin, Director, Biolab Inc., 108
Vézina, Sébastien, Partner, Lavery, de Billy - Montréal, 1086
Vice, John, Vice-Chair, Conservation Halton Foundation, 901
Vician, Peter, Deputy Minister, 607
Vickers, Cheryl, Chair, 576

Vickers, Darwin, Operations Supervisor, Barrington Industrial Services Limited, 102
Vida, Shady, President, HMI Industries, 232
Vidershpan, Valery, Manager, Canadian Council of Technicians & Technologists, 865
Vidrascu, Emil, Partner, Lavery, de Billy - Montréal, 1086
Vien, Dominique, Ministre déléguée, 652
Viens, Françoise H., Trois-Rivières, 745
Viergutz, Kevin, Manager, Lethbridge, 673
Vigeant, Virginie, Heenan Blaikie S.E.N.C.R.L/SRL, 1085
Vigneau, Isabelle, Agente de bureau, Centre des Îles, 1167
Vigneault, Diane, Présidente, Société des roses du Québec, 1006
Vigneault, Jean-Paul, Mechanical Seal Consultant, DGM Inc., 163
Vignet, Sylvie, Rivière-du-Loup, 741
Vigod, Toby, Chair, 623
Vigon, Bruce, Manager, Society of Environmental Toxicology & Chemistry, 1008
Villalobos, Ignacio, Corporate Controller, Flowserve Canada Corp. - Pump Division, 197
Villard, Cecil, Director, 640
Villard, Cecil F., Charlottetown, 732
Villecourt, Guy, President, Similkameen Okanagan Organic Producers Association, 1004
Villemaire, Donna, Kawartha Lakes, 711
Villeneuve, Claude, Partner, Heenan Blaikie S.E.N.C.R.L/SRL - Sherbrooke, 1089
Villeneuve, Dave, Branch Manager, Lockerbie & Hole Contracting Ltd., 273
Villeneuve, Jacques, Sec.-Trés., Régie d'assainissement des eaux usées de Boischatel, L'Ange-Gardi, 759
Villeneuve, Jean-Pierre, Directeur, Université du Québec, 406
Villeneuve, Judy, Metro Vancouver, 684, 678
Villeneuve, Lina, Relationniste, Les Laboratoires S.L. inc., 269
Villeneuve, Mario, Directeur des ventes, Fortier 2000 Ltée, 200
Villeneuve, Normand, Engineer, Les Consultants RSA, 268
Villeneuve, Paul, Epistream Consulting Inc, 189
Villeneuve, Pierre, Mascouche, 450-474-3626, 737
Villeneuve, Réjean, Engineer, Les Consultants RSA, 268
Villiard, Luc, Partner, Lavery, de Billy - Montréal, 1086
Vinals, José, Bibliothécaire, Québec Conseil de la science et de la technologie, 1179
Vince, Kim, Coordinator, Comcor Environmental Limited, 146
Vincent, Denis, Vaudreuil-Dorion, 746
Vincent, Doug, Chief Enforcement Officer, Iqaluit, 867-979-6363, 698
Vincent, Graham, Director, Transportation Planning, Waterloo, 704
Vincent, Jan, Vice-President, Alldec Trading Ltd., 79
Vincent, Marcel, Estimator/Project Coordinator, Western Industrial Services Ltd., 429
Vincent, Neil, Huron, 701
Vincent, Pat, CAO, Parkland County, 780-968-8411, 670
Vincent, Ryan, CEO, Oxegen Inc., 315
Vincent, Yves, Greffier, Shawinigan, 744
Vincent, Q.C., Robert G., Partner, Stewart McKelvey Stirling Scales - Saint John, 1065
Vincze, Georgette, Librarian, Abbott Laboratories Limited, 1184
Vine, Kevin, Branch Manager, Safety-Kleen Canada Inc., 355
Vinet, Suzanne, President, 515
Viney, Gupta, Trade Commissioner, 768
Virdiramo, Joe, Ward Councillor, Thunder Bay, 721
Virdo, Paul, Milton, 714
Virdo, Tony, General Manager, Contor Terminals Inc., 151
Virginillo, Alexis, Business Research Librarian, Agrium Inc., 1099
Virtue, Judson E., Partner, Macleod Dixon LLP, 1052
Visneskie, Janice, Renfrew, 613-757-2300, 704
Visser, Karen, Access Services Coordinator, Concordia University College of Alberta, 1105
Visser, Walt, Centre Wellington, 724
Vitaterna, Andrew, Manager, ASI Group Ltd., 94
Vitiello, Tom, Chair, Annapolis County, 696
Vivian, Gordon, President, CCS Income Trust, 134
Vizbar, R., General Manager, Medicine Hat, 403-529-8312, 673
Vlasak, Yanick, Partner, Heenan Blaikie S.E.N.C.R.L/SRL - Sherbrooke, 1089
Vlieg, Gary, Director, Langley, 681
Voakes, Randy, Essex, 709
Voce, Graham, Executive Secretary, International Institute for Conservation of Historic & Artistic W, 940
Vocilka, Michael G., Environmental Waste International, 186
Vocino, Pierre, La Prairie, 736
Vogan, John, President, EnviroMetal Technologies Inc., 184

Executive Name Index

Vogan, Raymond, Director, Regional Affairs, 510
Vogel, Charlie, Branch Manager, Leeson Canada Ltd., 266
Vogel, Dolores, Coordinator, Promens Canada Inc., 334
Vogel, Paul G., Cohen Highley LLP, 1069
Voghel, Jean-Yves, Voghel Inc., 414
Vogl, K., Director, Planning, Grimsby, 710
Vogler, Connie, Library Technician, Westmount Campus, 1107
Voight, Michael, Plant Manager, CCS Income Trust, 134
Voisard, Philippe, Conseiller, Ste-Geneviève, Montréal, 738
Vokac, Irene, Manager, Transport Canada, 1152
Vokes, Stephen, Director, Operations, Meaford, 727
Vokes, C.M.O., Sharon, County Clerk & Director, Council Services, Grey, 700
Volberg, Walter, Point Four Systems Inc., 327
Volesky, Boya, President, BV SORBEX, Inc., 119
Volkanova, Victoria, Chef du service des systèmes informatisés, Université de Moncton, 1129
Volkers, Jeff, General Manager, Optimira Controls, 313
Volkow, Nick, Burnaby, 679
Voller, William, Manager, National Air Photo Library, 1151
Volpatti, Selina, Regional Councillor, Niagara Falls, 715
von Doellen, Eric, Manager, Del-Air Systems Ltd., 160
von Lonski, Ulrike, Director of Communications, World Petroleum Congress, 1023
von Rüti, Rebecca R., Davis LLP - Vancouver, 1059
von Sass, Carola, Director, Alberta Forest Products Association, 817
Voncina, Gordon, Manager, Port Coquitlam, 683
Voordouw, Jan, Executive Director, Panos Washington, 984
Vorobiev, Alexandre, President, Laser Diagnostic Instruments International Inc., 264
Vos, Bill, Director, Central Okanagan, 250-868-5232, 677
Vos, John, General Manager, Kelowna, 681
Vosburg, Bill, Vice-President, Intertek Systems Certification, 246
Voswinkel, Judith, Executive Assistant to the Deputy Minister, 664
Vout, Kathryn J., Town Clerk, Grimsby, 905-945-9634, 710
Vowel, Bonnie, Elgin, 699
Voysey, Andrea, Marketing Director, Carmanah Technologies Corp., 129
Vradenburg, Leigh, Thermo-Cell Industries Ltd., 394
Vrbanovic, Berry, Kitchener, 712
Vrebosch Merry, Tanya, North Bay, 715
Vriezen, Chris, Supervisor, Quispamsis, 506-849-5734, 692
Vukelic, Snezana, Manager, Information Services, Association of Municipalities of Ontario, 1156
Vukmanich, Jim, Supervisor, Calgary, 121
Vynohrad, Vera, Partner, Macleod Dixon LLP, 1077
Vyskocil, Thomas, President, Diagnostic Engineering Inc., 163

W

w garfield weston foundat, The W. Garfield Weston Fo, Toronto, ON, 1045
Waddell, Bonnie R., Chief Librarian, Nova Scotia Agricultural College, 1137
Waddell, Donna, Director, Charlottetown, 732
Waddell, Gary, Vice-President, Ontor Ltd., 313
Waddell, Linda, Vice President, National Marine Manufacturers Association, 958
Waddell, Michael S., Chief Administrative Officer, Stormont, Dundas & Glengarry, 730
Wadden, Glenn, President, Trihedral Engineering Limited, 401
Waddy, Susan, Manager, Aquaculture Association of Canada, 828
Wade, Catherine, Partner, Heenan Blaikie LLP - Vancouver, 1060
Wade, Deirdre L., Barry Spalding - Saint John Office, 1065
Wade, Doug, Fire Chief, Langley, 604-532-7509, 687
Wade, Joy, Vice-President, Aquaculture Association of Canada, 828
Waedt, Helmut, Principal, SMS Engineering Ltd., 371
Wafa, Herzallah, Trade Commissioner, 768
Wagenaar, Randy, Sales Representative, Benson Chemicals Limited, 105
Waggott, George, Lang Michener LLP - Toronto, 1077
Wagland, Peter, Chief Administrative Officer, Lanark, 701
Wagner, Andreas, Principal, Golder Associates Ltd., 214
Wagner, Philippa, President, Recycling Council of Alberta, 993
Wagner, Rob, Pinchin Environmental Ltd., 324
Wagner, Robert, President, Qwatro Corporation, 339
Wahl, Darren, Cascades Recovery Inc., 131
Wahn, Dave, Sr. Planner, Central Kootenay, 677
Waisglass, Howard, Porta-Mini Systems, 328
Waisman, Tully, President/CEO, Emergex Planning Inc., 177

Waite, Michael A., Partner, Stones Carbert Waite Wells LLP, 1054
Waiting, Kendall W., Carscallen Leitch LLP, 1050
Wakabayashi, Doug, Director, 660
Wakaluk, Mike, Manager, LTS Sales Ltd., 274
Wake, Rowena, Library Assistant, British Columbia Ministry of Economic Development, 1120
Wake, Tyler, MacPherson Leslie & Tyerman LLP - Saskatoon, 1090
Wake, W.S., Western Operations Manager, SEW Eurodrive Co. of Canada Ltd., 364
Wakefield, Carol, Treasurer, Bracebridge, 706
Wakefield, Clair W., President, Wakefield Acoustics Ltd., 416
Wakim, Albert, Vice-President, H2Flow Equipment Inc., 223
Walden, Janet, Vice-President, 552
Walden, Jim, Muskoka, 702
Waldie, P.Geo., Andrea Y., APGO Executive Director & Registrar, Association of Professional Geoscientists of Ontario, 839
Waldman, Dave, President, The Conserver Group Inc., 392
Waldroff, Richard, South Stormont, 730
Waldvogel, Blair, President/CEO, General Scrap Partnership, 206
Wales, Leah, Director of Business Operations & Special Events, St Lawrence College, 1143
Walker, Al, President, Walker Technologies Corporation, 416
Walker, Ann, Library/Technical Assistant, Perkin Elmer Optoelectronics, 1187
Walker, Bill, President & CEO, Safety Services New Brunswick, 998
Walker, Cheryl A., Thompson Dorfman Sweatman LLP, 1064
Walker, Cheryl Lyn, President, Society of Toxicology, 1009
Walker, Craig, Manager, Charlottetown, 902-629-4014, 732
Walker, Graham, Partner, Borden Ladner Gervais LLP - Vancouver, 1058
Walker, Greg, Manager, Westburne Canada, 427
Walker, Jim, Chair, Marmot Recovery Foundation, 952
Walker, John, Territory Manager, Green Turtle Technologies Ltd. (Canada), 217
Walker, Keith, Chief Librarian, Medicine Hat College, 1099, 1109
Walker, Mike, President, Koch Engineering Co. Ltd., 259
Walker, Patricia A., Treasurer, Oak Bay, 688
Walker, R.F.G., President, Bytown Marine Ltd., 119
Walker, Robert, Clearview, 725
Walker, Robert, Client Services Manager, Accutest Laboratories Ltd., 66
Walker, Robert S., Assistant Deputy Minister, 545
Walker, Russell, Councillor, Halifax Regional Municipality, 695
Walker, Ted, Chief Administrative Officer, Midland, 713
Walker, Tim, Regional Manager, ESRI Canada Ltd., 190
Walker, Tom, Mayor, North Cowichan, 687
Walker, B.A.H., B.Ed.,, Jennifer, Head Librarian, Carleton County Law Association, 892
Walker-Renshaw, Barbara J., Partner, Borden Ladner Gervais LLP - Toronto, 1074
Wall, Calvin, Vice-President, Genics Inc., 207
Wall, Dennis, President/CEO, LADEN Steel Fabricators Inc., 262
Wall, Marilyn, Secretary, Sierra Club, 1003
Wall, Wayne, Manager, Portage La Prairie, 204-239-8359, 689
Wall, Wesley, Director, Michael Wall & Sons Enterprises Ltd., 289
Wallace, Carol, Association Secretary, American Birding Association, 822
Wallace, Derek, Officer, Wilmot, 732
Wallace, George, Director, Planning & Development, Kingston, 712
Wallace, Ian C., Partner, Stewart McKelvey Stirling Scales - St. John's, 1066
Wallace, John, President, Pomeroy Consulting Engineers Limited, 328
Wallace, Mark, President & CEO, Medgate Inc., 286
Wallace, Patricia, Kamloops, 681
Wallace, Ray, Adjala-Tosorontio, 905-936-3116, 724
Wallace, Rob, Media Contact, Home Hardware Stores Ltd., 232
Wallace, Rosemary, Langley, 681
Wallace, Shari, Director, Vancouver, 685
Wallace, Stephen, Associate Deputy Minister, 519
Walling, Mary Ellen, Executive Director, British Columbia Salmon Farmers Association, 849
Wallis, Cliff, Botanist, Cottonwood Consultants Ltd., 153
Wallis, Cliff, Environmental Researcher, Cottonwood Consultants Ltd, 1100
Wallis, Katherine, Director, Learning Resource Centres, Georgian College of Applied Arts & Technology, 1138
Wallis, Keith, Technical Sales, Romatec Incorporated, 351

Wallis, Peter C., President & CEO, The Van Horne Institute for International Transportation & Regula, 1016
Wallmann, Christine, Library Technician, Canadian Grain Commission, 1123
Wallrap, Albert, Borden Ladner Gervais LLP - Toronto, 1074
Walman, Kylie E., Borden Ladner Gervais LLP - Vancouver, 1058
Walmsley, D.A., Senior Environmental Planner, Long Environmental Consultants, 273
Walsh, Barry, Manager, Toromont Caterpillar, 397
Walsh, Bob, Manager, CBCL Limited, 133
Walsh, Dave, Superintendent, Maple Ridge, 604-463-6251, 687
Walsh, Denis, Kamloops, 681
Walsh, Gord, Branch Manager, National Energy Equipment Inc., 297
Walsh, John, Mount Pearl, 694
Walsh, Kimberley A., Partner, Stewart McKelvey Stirling Scales - St. John's, 1066
Walsh, Margaret, Hastings, 700
Walsh, Marie, Director, Cape Breton, 902-563-5014, 695
Walsh, Mike, Manager, Berg Chilling Systems Inc., 105
Walsh, Mike, President, Envision Sustainability Tools, 188
Walsh, Robert, Executive Director, Canadian Council for Tobacco Control, 864
Walsh, Rose, Program Coordinator, Fish Harvesters Resource Centres, 917
Walsh, Terry, Director, Brooks, 671
Walsh, Tom, Simcoe, 704
Walsh, Tom, Mayor, Adjala-Tosorontio, 905-729-2132, 724
Walsh, Tracy, Library Technician, Riverview Hospital, 1115
Walsh, P.Eng., Kelly, Director, Community & Infrastructure Services, Pelham, 717
Walter, John, Executive Director, 559
Walter, Norman, Chair, East Kootenay, 677
Walter, Tim, Manager, Wastequip Cusco, 421
Walters, Gary, CFO & Exec. Vice-President, AMEC, 82
Walters, Janice, Administrative Assistant, 641
Walters, John, President, Hallmark Insurance Brokers Ltd., 224
Walters, Len, Manager, Langley, 604-514-2912, 681
Walters, Nathan, Marketing Director, Katch Kan Limited, 255
Walters, Philip, Barbeau, Evans, Goldstein, 1057
Walters, Wanda, Administrator, Carleton County Law Association, 892
Walton, Ben, Inside Sales, Norseman Plastics Ltd., 306
Walton, Janice H., Blake, Cassels & Graydon LLP - Vancouver, 1057
Walton, Richard, Director, Metro Vancouver, 678
Walton, Richard, Mayor, North Vancouver, 604-990-2208, 688
Walton, Robert, Director, Public Works, Oxford, 728
Walton, Ron, Director, Public Works & Municipal Engineer, Bracebridge, 706
Walton, Shelby, Entegrity Wind Systems Inc., 181
Walzak, Albert, Director, 614
Wamala, George, Manager, Forest Products Association of Canada, 918
Wambolt, Brian, Manager, Maritime Paper Products Ltd., 281
Wan, Albert, Product Manager, Precisioneering Ltd., 331
Wandler, Albert, Manager, Waterous Power Systems, 423
Wandzura, P.Eng., Dorian, General Manager, Regina, 754
Wang, Jiabin, Head of Library, Engineering & Computer Science Library, 1157
Wang, Ningyan (Sandy), Lang Michener LLP - Vancouver, 1060
Wang, Ren, Director, Consultative Group on International Agricultural Research, 902
Wang, Weina, President, Toronto Health Libraries Association, 1012
Wannamaker, Bob, Quinte West, 613-392-8548, 718
Wannamaker, Brian, President, Sea Scan International Inc., 361
Waqué, Stephen F., Senior Partner, Borden Ladner Gervais LLP - Toronto, 1074
Warburton, D., Triton Environmental Consultants Ltd., 402
Warburton, Dave, Manager, Prince George Office/GIS Manager, Triton Environmental Consultants Ltd., 402
Ward, Al, President/COO, Alberta-Pacific Forest Industries Inc., 77
Ward, Barry J., Barrie, 706
Ward, Bertrand A., Conseiller de ville, Montréal, 738
Ward, Bonnie, Director, Recreation, Ingersoll, 711
Ward, Charles, Director, Salmon Arm, 684
Ward, Dave, Fire Chief, Saanich, 250-475-5423, 688
Ward, Grant, Langley, 687
Ward, Julie P., Marketing Rep., Safety Plus Inc., 355
Ward, Keith, Commissioner, Human Services, Peel, 703
Ward, Lance W., President, L.W. Ward Limited, 261
Ward, Lloyd, Owner, United Oil Services, 406
Ward, Mike, Aquateck Ltd., 89

Executive Name Index

Ward, Nancy, Director, Council of Great Lakes Governors, 905
Ward, Philip, President/COO, Lockerbie & Hole Contracting Ltd., 273
Ward, Robert G., Edwards, Kenny & Bray LLP, 1059
Ward, Samantha, Professional Engineer, Urban Systems Ltd., 407
Ward, W. Peter, University Librarian, University of British Columbia, 1119
Warden, David, Alderman, St. Thomas, 719
Warden, Donald, Fire Chief, Wasaga Beach, 705-429-5281, 722
Warden, Vince A., Vice-President, 588
Wardhaugh, Ron, Chief Building Official, Quinte West, 718
Wardlaw, Steve, General Manager, Fugro Airborne Surveys, 202
Wardrop, Dave, Director, Winnipeg, 690
Wardroper, Lawrence, Head, Systems, CANMET Information Centre, 1149
Wareham, Wendy, Coordinator, Health Resource Centre, Brandon Regional Health Centre, 1122
Warford, P.Eng., James, Coordinator, Corner Brook, 709-637-1626, 693
Wargel, Eric, Director, Public Works & Deputy CAO, Adjala-Tosorontio, 724
Wark, Robyn, Planner, Burnaby, 604-294-7297, 679
Warland, Simon, Manager, Quatrosense Environmental Ltd., 338
Warman, Philip R., President/CEO, Coastal BioAgresearch Ltd., 145
Warn, Louise, Administrator, Water Compliance, Erin, 709
Warne, Ron, Director, Planning & Development Services, Port Hope, 905-885-2415, 728
Warner, Brad, Coordinator, Northern Steel Industries, 307
Warner, Ilana, Acting Chairperson, 589
Warner, Jim, President, Martec Ltd., 281
Warner, John E., Manager, Eco-North Laboratories, 171
Warner, Michele, Borden Ladner Gervais LLP - Toronto, 1074
Warner, Patrick, Head, Lending Services Division, Memorial University of Newfoundland, 1132
Warner, Q.C., J. Philip, Bishop & McKenzie LLP, 1054
Warnica, Carolyn, Information Specialist, Hatch, 1145
Warnica, Glenn, President, Ontario Tire Dealers Association, 980
Warnock, Richard, President, Alberta Motor Transport Association, 818
Warnock, Scott, Simcoe, 704
Warnock, Scott, Mayor, Tay, 731
Warren, Chris, Director, Vancouver, 604-873-7011, 685
Warren, Glen, Manager, Warren's Imaging & Dryography Inc., 417
Warren, Jamie, Officer, Newfoundland & Labrador Federation of Agriculture, 962
Warren, Katrina E., Poole Althouse, Barristers & Solicitors, 1065
Warren, Lynne, Library Technician, Public Health Services, 1190
Warren, Mike, Manager, Kamloops, 681
Warren, Pat, Kawartha Lakes, 711
Warren, R.B., WeirFoulds LLP, 1081
Warring, Bob, Sales Manager, Precision Chemical Manufacturing Ltd., 330
Warrington, Richard, Vice-President, Canadian Society of Allergy & Clinical Immunology, 886
Warsaba, Ronald M., Kanuka Thuringer LLP, Barristers & Solicitors, 1090
Warsh, Ronna, General Manager, Windsor, 723
Wartenberg, Daniel, President, International Society for Environmental Epidemiology, 942
Wartman, Brandon, Manager, EHS Compliance, Grimsby, 905-309-2016, 710
Warwick, Graham, Warden & Councillor, Elgin, 699
Washington, Larry, President, L.E. Washington Sales Ltd., 261
Washuta, Greg, St. Catharines, 905-938-5123, 719
Washuta, Steve, President, W.J. Sheldrick Sanitation Ltd., 415
Wasilewski, Barb, President, Manitoba Public Health Association, 951
Wass, Tom, Sales Manager, Material Resource Recovery Inc., 282
Wastle, Brian, Vice-President, Canadian Chemical Producers' Association, 862
Wasylenko, Karen, Treasurer, Health Sciences Association of Saskatchewan, 928
Waterman, Kevin, Director, Gander, 709-651-5928, 694
Waterman, R. Nairn, Lang Michener LLP - Toronto, 1077
Waterman, R.S., Vice-President & General Manager, NEDCO, 299
Waters, Natalie, Computer & Instructional Services Librarian, Schulich Library of Science & Engineering, 1175
Waters, Noel, Director, Roads & Waste Management, Muskoka, 702
Waters, Ross, President, C.G. Industrial Specialties, Ltd., 120

Wathen, Graham, Manager, Veolia ES Canada Industrial Services Inc., 411
Watkin, Ken, Judge Advocate General, 545
Watkins, Brian, Sault Ste. Marie, 720
Watkins, Ron, President, Canadian Steel Partnership Council, 889
Watkins, Tom, Manager, Capital Regional District, 250-360-3030, 676
Watkiss, Roger, Partner, Macleod Dixon LLP, 1077
Watkiss, Ulli S., City Clerk, Toronto, 416-392-8010, 721
Watling, Brian, Renewable Energy Services Inc., 345
Watson, Cam, President, Watson & Associates Economists Ltd., 423
Watson, Christopher J., MacKenzie Fujisawa LLP, 1061
Watson, Cindy, Library Technician, Owen Sound Campus, 1152
Watson, Daniel, Deputy Minister, 562
Watson, David, General Manager, Calgary, 403-268-2601, 671
Watson, Don, Managing Partner, Utility Risk Management Ltd., 408
Watson, Ed, President, Watson Petroleum Services Ltd., 423
Watson, Eric, Sales & Marketing, Temprite Industries Ltd., 389
Watson, Eric, Sales and Marketing Consultant, Comenco Systems Inc., 147
Watson, Gladys, Director, Learning & Resource Centres, Centennial College of Applied Arts & Technology, 1157
Watson, Harold R., O'Connor MacLeod Hanna LLP, 1070
Watson, Jeff, Councillor, Gravenhurst, 709
Watson, Jim, Mayor, Ottawa, 716
Watson, Joel, Partner, Heenan Blaikie LLP - Toronto, 1076
Watson, John, Project Estimator, Donalco Inc., 165
Watson, Ken, City Manager, Port Alberni, 683
Watson, Kenneth, Treasurer, Gravenhurst, 709
Watson, Matthew, Chief Executive Officer, ESI Environmental Sensors Inc., 190
Watson, Misty R., Stewart McKelvey Stirling Scales - Saint John, 1065
Watson, Paul, Founder & President, Sea Shepherd Conservation Society - USA, 1003
Watson, Peter, Chair, 635
Watson, Peter, Deputy Minister, 567
Watson, R. Jack, Clerk, Timmins, 721
Watson, Rob, Director, U.S. Green Building Council, 1016
Watson, Sheri, Sales & Marketing Correspondent, Elemental Research Inc., 175
Watson, Tom, Vice-President/Senior Biologist, Triton Environmental Consultants Ltd., 402
Watt, Cam, Owner, Advanced Coolant Technologies Inc., 69
Watt, Jim, Contact, MDI Waste Management Inc., 285
Watt, Shelley, Group Leader, National Energy Board, 1102
Watt, Sue, Project Engineer, Environmental Advisory Group, 185
Watters, Bronwyn, Deputy Minister, 607
Watters, Clayton, Director, Engineering Services, Elgin, 699
Watters, Paul J., Mississippi Mills, 714
Watters, Shawn, Centre Wellington, 724
Watterton, Greg, Treasurer & Deputy Clerk, Middlesex Centre, 727
Wattsworth, Ann L., Cassels Brock & Blackwell LLP, 1074
Watton, Caroline C., McInnes Cooper, 1066
Watts, Bryan, President/CEO, Klohn Crippen Berger Ltd., 258
Watts, Dianne, Metro Vancouver, 678
Watts, Dianne L., Mayor, Surrey, 604-591-4126, 684
Watts, Jennifer, Councillor, Halifax Regional Municipality, 695
Watts, Kenneth W., O'Connor MacLeod Hanna LLP, 1070
Watts, Michael, Partner, Osler, Hoskin & Harcourt LLP - Toronto, 1079
Watts, Sharon, President/CEO, 533
Wauchope, Gord, Simcoe, 704
Waugh, Alan, Library Systems User Analyst, Mount Royal College, 1102
Waugh, Don, Contact, Chemical Safety Training Associates, 139
Wauters, Eugene, Chair, Lethbridge Regional Waste Management Services, 757
Waxman, Douglas A., Vice-President, Solid Waste Reclamation Inc., 372
Waxman, Michael S., President, Solid Waste Reclamation Inc., 372
Waxman, Morris J., Chair, Solid Waste Reclamation Inc., 372
Way, Dave, President, Earthsave Canada, 907
Way, Leanne E., Madorin, Snyder LLP, 1069
Wayne, Mike, Circulation & ILL, Canadian Museum of Nature, 1149
Wayner, Danial D., Vice-President, 546
Waytuck, Brett, Head, Public Services & Education, Bracken Health Sciences Library, 1142
Weadon, Bryn, Assistant Deputy Minister, 545

Wearn, Marion, Oxford, 728
Weary, Walter, Secretary-Treasurer, Toronto Field Naturalists, 1012
Weaver, Bill, Chatham-Kent, 724
Weaver, Donald J., Gowling Lafleur Henderson LLP - Vancouver, 1060
Weaver, Tim, Schwank Group, 359
Webb, G.P., General Manager, Ingersoll-Rand Canada Inc., 241
Webb, Horace, Manager, Toromont Caterpillar, 398
Webb, Nicola, General Manager, Surrey, 684
Webb, Ron, General Manager, Medicine Hat, 403-529-8310, 673
Webb, B.Sc., LL.B., Ian D., Partner, Lawson Lundell LLP - Vancouver, 1061
Webb, P.Eng., Chris, Manager, Engineering Services, Owen Sound, 717
Webber, Allen, Warden, Chester District, 697
Webber, Andrew, Manager, Kitimat-Stikine, 678
Webber, Ford H., Owner, Lake Charlotte Sanitation, 263
Webber, Judy, Event Planner/Financal Officer, Union of Nova Scotia Municipalities, 1015
Webber, Len, Minister, 563
Weber, Bill, Lambton Shores, 726
Weber, Clare, President, C-Max Transportation Equipment, 119
Weber, Dave, Supervisor, Customer Relations, Southern Alberta Institute of Technology, 1103
Weber, David, Director, Richmond, 604-276-4007, 684
Weber, Larry, Manager, Westburne Canada, 425
Weber, Markus, Deputy Minister, 619
Weber, Meagan, Collections Librarian, Mount Royal College, 1102
Weber, Reg, Commisssioner, Community Services, Cambridge, 707
Webser, Rick, Springwater, 730
Webster, Bruce, General Manager, Canadian Sugar Beet Producers' Association Inc., 889
Webster, Dave, Regional Service Manager, National Energy Equipment Inc., 297
Webster, George T., Minister, 636
Webster, Gord, PricewaterhouseCoopers Management Consultants, 332
Webster, Joy, Adjala-Tosorontio, 705-434-0355, 724
Webster, Kenneth, Director, Viessmann Manufacturing Company Inc., 413
Webster, Peter, Librarian, Information Services, St Mary's University, 1136
Webster, Reg D., President, The Sernas Group Inc., 393
Webster, Thomas R., Chief Administrative Officer, East Gwillimbury, 708
Weckworth, Harold, Renfrew, 613-628-2080, 704
Wedge, Richard, Director, 640
Wedman, Gord, Pacific Environmental Consulting & Occupational Hygiene Services, 316
Wedman, Ron, Owner, Ron Wedman Engineering Services, 351
Weeber, Peter, Fire Chief, Terrace, 685
Weeda, Jim, Sales & Marketing Manager, Westeel, 429
weeden foundation, The Weeden Foundation, New York, NY, 1042
Weeger, Tim, President, Nalco Canada Co., 296
Weekley, Robert, Editor, Electric Vehicle Society of Canada, 909
Weemaes, Robert F., Directeur général, Gatineau, 735
Wees, Eric, Acting Director, Canadian Heritage, 1167
Wegleitner, Garry, President, BECK Drilling and Environmental Services Ltd., 104
Wehmeir, Tina Marie, Chief Development Officer & Senior VP, Institute of Food Technologists, 933
Weigelt, JoAnne, Clerk, Northern Lights Regional Health Centre, 1107
Weighill, Clive, Police Chief, Saskatoon, 306-975-8300, 754
Weila, Rashmi, Vice-President, Pigmalion Environmental Services Group, 323
Weinberg, Hal, Metro Vancouver, 678
Weiner, Marni, Director, Medgate Inc., 286
Weinstein, Q.C., Joel A., Aikins, MacAulay & Thorvaldson LLP, 1063
Weinwurm, Paul, President, 2R Services Inc., 404
Weir, Bryan, Director, Planning, Peterborough, 703
Weir, Dixon A., General Manager, Environmental Services, Ottawa, 716
Weir, Gord, Director, Emergency & Fire Services, Clarington, 724
Weir, J. Graham, Chair, Graymont Inc., 216
Weir, Joanne, Secretary, Canada Green Building Council, 853
Weir, Wally, Contact, Talkie Tooter Canada Ltd., 386
Weiru, Leslie, University Chief Librarian, Université d'Ottawa, 1152

Executive Name Index

Weiser, Nick H.M., Fulton & Company LLP, Lawyers & Trade-Mark Agents, 1056
Weiser, Paul M., General Manager, Busch Vacuum Technics Inc., 119
Weisman, Paul, Sales Manager, Wasteco, 421
Weismiller, Marv, Acting Director, 662
Weiss, Allan, Chief, Cold Lake, 780-594-4494, 672
Weiss, Carry, Sales Executive, Hymopack Ltd., 237
Weisz, Jonathan B., Torys LLP, 1081
Welbourne, Bruce, Water Resource Manager, Valerie Falls Limited Partnership, 409
Welch, Andy, Marketing Manager, Dendron Resource Surveys Inc., 161
Welch, Marianne, Reference/Collections Librarian, John & Dotsa Bitove Family Law Library, 1143
Welch, Tom, General Manager, Tanks-A-Lot Ltd., 386
Welde, Allison, Director, Sustainable Forestry Initiative, 1011
Weldon, Cam, Chief Financial Officer & Deputy City Manager, Toronto, 416-392-8773, 721
Welke, Jeff, Executive Director, 659
Welland, Matt, Novatech Controls, Inc., 309
Wellington, Paul, Opus DaytonKnight Consultants Ltd., 313
Wells, Andy, Chair & CEO, 604
Wells, Damon, Director, Public Works, Kingston, 712
Wells, Guy, Associé, Cain Lamarre Casgrain Wells - Chicoutimi, 1082
Wells, Harry, Republic Environmental Systems (Fort Erie) Ltd., 345
Wells, Janet, Exec. Vice-President, Qwatro Corporation, 339
Wells, John, Norfolk, 702
Wells, Joseph F., Principal, Integrated Environments Ltd., 244
Wells, Patrick, Secretary, Northeast Avalon ACAP, Inc., 966
Wells, Peter E.J., Lang Michener LLP - Toronto, 1077
Wells, Simon R., Davis LLP - Vancouver, 1059
Wells, Stan, Councillor, Wasaga Beach, 722
Wells, Q.C., Gregory S., Stones Carbert Waite Wells LLP, 1054
Welner, Darren, Coordinator, Scotia Recycling Ltd., 360
Welsh, Gary, General Manager, Transportation Services, Toronto, 416-392-8431, 721
Welsh, Laurel, Acting Executive Director, 658
Welsh, Mario, Partner, Heenan Blaikie S.E.N.C.R.L./SRL - Québec, 1088
Weltrowska, Margaret, Fraser Milner Casgrain S.E.N.C.R.L./LLP, 1084
Wende, David B., Alexander Holburn Beaudin & Lang, LLP, 1057
Wendt, Steve, Director, North American Waterfowl Management Plan, 965
Wentzell, Kevin, Supervisor, Lunenburg District, 902-543-2991, 697
Weppler, Kevin, Director, Finance, Grey, 700
Werenka, Brad J., Macleod Dixon LLP, 1052
Wergeland, Leif, Saanich, 688
Werier, Michael D., D'Arcy & Deacon LLP, 1063
Werklund, Dave, President/CEO/Chair, CCS Income Trust, 134
Werle, Dirk, Partner & Geoscientist, AERDE Environmental Research, 71
Werner, Naef, Trade Commissioner, 769
Wernick, Michael, Deputy Minister, 541
wesaintcoasaintenvironmen, West Coast Environmental, Vancouver, BC, 1041
Weslowski, Karen L., Partner, Miller Thomson LLP - Vancouver, 1062
Wesseling, Frank, Director, Cochrane, 403-851-2570, 671
West, Brad, Port Coquitlam, 683
West, Dale, Collingwood, 708
West, Heather, Acting Director of Library Services, Saskatchewan Institute of Applied Science & Technology, 1188
West, Jim, Office Manager, Trow Consulting Engineers Ltd., 404
West, John B., Senior Partner, Ogilvy Renault LLP/S.E.N.C.R.L., s.r.l. - Toronto, 1078
West, John S., Henderson Paddon & Associates Ltd., 229
West, Rob, Senior Environmental Scientist, Oakridge Environmental Ltd., 310
West, Virginia M., Deputy Minister, 629
Westby, Stan, CAO, Powell River, 683
Westell, Mary, Assoc. University Librarian, Info. Technology & Sc, University of Calgary, 1103
Westendorp, Glenn, Superintendent, Comox, 250-339-2485, 680
Westerby, Jo-Anne, Director, Library Resource Centre, Mohawk College of Applied Arts & Technology, 1141
Westersund, Q.C., Lowell A., Fraser Milner Casgrain LLP - Calgary, 1051
Westheuser, Pat, Chair, British Columbia Nature (Federation of British Columbia Naturals, 849
Westlake, Jim, Monitrex Engineering Ltd., 293

Westlake, Ron W., Director, Kelowna, 681
Westland, John, Office Manager, Golder Associates Ltd., 214
Westmacott, Penny, Director, Library Information Technology Services, University of Western Ontario Libraries, 1144
Westman, Denine, Manager, 572
Westoff, Dennis R, President/Chief Engineer, Westhoff Engineering Resources Inc., 430
Westra, Robert, President, Westra & Associates Inc., 430
Westwood, Eleanor, Manager, 517
Wetmore, W., Senior Vice-President, Enform: The Safety Association for the Upstream Oil & Gas Industr, 910
Wetsch, Frank, Manager, Medicine Hat, 403-529-8227, 673
Wetston, Q.C., Howard, Chair, 622
Wettstein, Karl, Guelph, 710
Weyer, Udo, President, WDA Consultants Inc., 423
Whalen, Darlene, Vice-Chair, 604
Whalen, Dianne C., Minister, 604
Whalen, Ed, General Manager, QUASAR, 338
Whalen, Fred, Councillor, Kings County, 696
Whalen, Fred, Warden, Kings County, 902-690-6132, 696
Whalen, Jim, Manager, Plasti-Fab Ltd., 326
Whalen, Joann, Academic Staff, Brace Centre for Water Resources Management, 115
Whalen, Tim, Thorold, 720
Whalen, Tony J., Fredericton, 691
Whaley, Blaine, Director, Cantech Inspections Ltd., 127
Whaley, David, Chair, Ontario Wheat Producers' Marketing Board, 981
Whaley, John, Reeve, Leduc County, 669
Whaley, Mark, Waterloo, 722
Wharton, Anne, Coordinator, IBM Canada Ltd., 1144
Wheat, John, Brant, 698
Wheatley, Terry, Branch Manager, Safety-Kleen Canada Inc., 355
Wheaton, Neville, Fire Chief, Corner Brook, 709-637-1615, 693
Wheeler, Bruce, Executive Director, Society for Research on Nicotine & Tobacco, 1007
Wheeler, Danny, York, 705
Wheeler, Danny, Deputy Mayor & Regional Councillor, Georgina, 709
Wheeler, Jan, Executive Director, 580
Wheeler, Mark, General Manager, Simark Controls Ltd., 368
Wheeler, Mark, Partner, Borden Ladner Gervais LLP - Toronto, 1074
Wheeler, Sue, Director, Maple Ridge, 604-467-7308, 687
Wheeler, Todd, Lennox Industries (Canada) Ltd., 267
Wheeler, William L., President, Simcoe Plastics Ltd., 368
Whelan, David C., Managing Partner, Borden Ladner Gervais LLP - Calgary, 1050
Whelan, Jim, Peterborough, 703
Whelan, John, Fire Chief, Quinte West, 613-392-6567, 718
Whelan, John, Librarian, Grand Falls-Windsor Campus Library, 1131
Whelan, Rob, Laboratory Manager, PSC Analytical Services, 336
Whelan, Tensie, Executive Director, Rainforest Alliance, 992
Whelan, W.L., General Manager, W.L. Whelan Environmental Consultants Ltd., 415
Whelan, Wendy, Borden Ladner Gervais LLP - Toronto, 1074
Whelly, Zetta G., Librarian, St Joseph's Hospital (Saint John), 1129
Whiddon, Alison, Collections Management, Natural Resources Canada, 1151
Whight, Jim, Maritime Paper Products Ltd., 281
Whitby, Laurence, Vice-President, Blue-Zone Technologies Ltd., 110
Whitby, Scott, Partner, MacPherson Leslie & Tyerman LLP - Calgary, 1052
Whitcombe, Brad, Wellington, 519-623-7970, 705
White, Alexandra L., Associate, Miller Thomson LLP - Toronto, 1078
White, Angela, Secretary-Treasurer, Canadian Society for the Study of Practical Ethics, 886
White, Bernie, Municipal Clerk, Cape Breton, 902-563-5010, 695
White, Bill, Chief Administrative Officer, Georgian Bluffs, 725
White, Bob, Councillor, Colchester County, 697
White, Chris, Wellington, 519-856-0450, 705
White, Chris, Mayor, Guelph-Eramosa, 725
White, Craig, Vice-President, Newalta Corporation, 301
White, D'Arcy, President, Strata Environmental Ltd., 380
White, Danny, Manager, Bathurst, 690
White, Dave, Supervisor, Roads & Transportation, St. Thomas, 719
White, Doug, Simcoe, 704
White, Doug, Mayor, Bradford West Gwillimbury, 706
White, Doug, President, Wellmaster Pipe & Supply, 424

White, George, Manager, Whitehorse, 867-668-8345, 755
White, George H., President, All Treat Farms Limited, 78
White, Glenn, Senior Planner, Oro-Medonte, 728
White, Gordon, Vice-President, 520
White, Grant, Director, Yellowknife, 867-920-5636, 695
White, Janice, Technical Librarian, Aircraft Services Directorate, 1147
White, Jeff, Head Librarian, Aircraft Certification, 1147
White, John, Grondin, Poudrier, Bernier, 1087
White, John, President, Taco Canada Ltd., 386
White, Judie, General Manager, Aevitas Inc., 72
White, Judy, Office Manager, Canadian Plywood Association, 882
White, Kimara, Library Technician, Brooks Campus, 1099
White, Linda, Clerk, Saugeen Shores, 719
White, Lynda, Wellington, 519-848-2806, 705
White, Mary, Manager, Dillon Consulting Ltd., 164
White, Marybelle, Library Coordinator, Potash Corporation of Saskatchewan Inc., 1190
White, Mildred, Director, Rocky Mountain Naturalists, 996
White, Nick, Contact, CON-SPACE Communications Ltd., 148
White, Nigel, Treasurer & Director, Corporate Services, Leeds & Grenville, 726
White, Peggy, Interim Associate University Librarian, Client Ser, University of Calgary, 1103
White, Peter, President, Society of Professional Engineers & Associates, 1008
White, Peter A., President, Hot Zone Training Consultants Inc., 233
White, Robert G. (Bob), President, BRI International Inc., 116
White, Sandy, London, 713
White, Scott, Manager, Trent Hills, 731
White, Stephen, Lang Michener LLP - Toronto, 1077
White, Terry, Branch Manager, IMP Liquid Meters & Petroleum Services, 239
White, Tim, General Manager, Comstock Canada Ltd., 148
White, Tony, Commissioner, Engineering & Public Works, Muskoka, 705-645-6764, 702
White, Troy, Branch Manager, Fort Garry Industries Ltd., 200
White, William A., CAO, District of Nipissing Social Services Adminis, Nipissing, 705-474-2151, 727
White, William B., President, DuPont Canada Inc., 167
White, Q.C., Robert B., Davis LLP - Edmonton, 1055
White, Q.C., TEP, George L., Patterson Law, 1068
Whitehall, Q.C., Ivan C., Counsel, Heenan Blaikie LLP - Ottawa, 1070
Whitehead, Bob, President, Association of Great Lakes Outdoor Writers, 835
Whitehead, Brian, Vice-President, Air Transport Association of Canada, 814
Whitehead, Chris, Director, Energy Ottawa, 179
Whitehead, Ian, Branch Manager, McElhanney Consulting Services Ltd., 284
Whitehead, Karen, Treasurer, Global, Environmental & Outdoor Education Council, 924
Whitehead, Richard, Peel, 703
Whitehead, Richard, Regional Councillor, Caledon, 707
Whitehead, Terry, Hamilton, 711
Whitehouse, Paul, Director, Whitchurch-Stouffville, 723
Whitehouse, Paul, Manager, Chilliwack, 604-792-9311, 680
Whitelaw, Jan, Vice-President, justenvironment, 254
Whiteside, J.J. Paul, New Tecumseth, 714
Whiteway, Kenneth, Law Librarian, Law Library, 1189
Whiteway, Sandra, Laboratory Supervisor, LEM Laboratory Inc., 267
Whitford, Chris, Plant Manager, CCS Income Trust, 134
Whitford, Dean, President/CEO, Kanotech Information Systems Ltd., 255
Whiting, Patty, Chair, 566
Whitley, Stuart, Deputy Minister, 666
Whitman, Rick, President, Blomidon Naturalists Society, 846
Whitmarsh, Graham, Deputy Minister, 578
Whitmarsh, Rhonda, Treasurer, Mississippi Mills, 714
Whitney, Doug, Quinte West, 613-392-4779, 718
Whitney, Edward B., Chair, American Rivers, 824
Whitney, Greg, Responsable, Systèmes informatisés, École polytechnique de Montréal, 1173
Whitney, Hugh, Director, 603
Whittaker, Brady, President & Chief Executive Officer, Alberta Forest Products Association, 817
Whittaker, Paul, Deputy Minister, 570
Whittingham, Ed, Executive Director, The Pembina Institute, 985
Whittingham, Marc, President, 517
Whittington, Cindy, Comptroller, KBM Forestry Consultants Inc., 255

Executive Name Index

Whittington, Grant, Chief Administrative Officer, Wilmot, 732
Whitton, P.M., Sales Manager, Farris Industries Canada, 194
Whitty, Patrick, General Manager, RPR Environmental Inc., 354
Whitty, Robert, President, Bartle & Gibson Co. Ltd., 102
Whitwham, Rob, Director, Prince George, 250-561-7608, 683
Whyatt, Chris, Mayor, Yorkton, 755
Whynot-Lohnes, April, Officer, Lunenburg District, 697
Whyte, D. Alan, Hicks Morley Hamilton Stewart Storie LLP, 1069
Whyte, Ian, Coordinator of Public Services, University of Toronto at Mississauga, 1145
Whyte, Ian W., President/CEO, ECL Envirowest Consultants Ltd., 170
Whyte, Joanne, Incinolet Products, 239
Whyte, W., Manager, Comox Valley, 677
Whytock, John, Director, 631
Wichenko, Grant, President/CEO, Appin Associates, 87
Wickenheiser, Les, General Manager, Medicine Hat, 403-529-8327, 673
Wickens, Mel, Manager, Toromont Caterpillar, 398
Wickersham, Tom, Lethbridge, 403-381-1521, 673
Wickett, Robert V., MacKenzie Fujisawa LLP, 1061
Wickett, Sarah, Health Informatics Librarian, Bracken Health Sciences Library, 1142
Wickham, Daniel A.J., Partner, Shook, Wickham, Bishop & Field, 1056
Wickins, Hélène, Library Assistant, North Island College Library, 1111
Wicks, Roger, Chair, World Coal Institute, 1022
Wicks, Sheri H., Partner, Ottenheimer Baker, 1066
Wideman, Earl, Fire Chief, Woolwich, 519-664-2237, 732
Wideman, Jim, Waterloo, 704
Wideman, Jim, Administrator/Secretary, 619
Widla, Walter, President, Fulton Engineered Specialties Inc., 203
Wiebe, Dale, Pinchin Environmental Inc., 324
Wiebe, John D., President & Chief Executive Officer, GLOBE Foundation, 924
Wiebe, Reg, Coordinator, Manitoba Wildlife Federation, 952
Wiebe, Victor G., Engineering Librarian, Engineering Library, 1189
Wiener, Neil, Partner, Heenan Blaikie S.E.N.C.R.L/SRL, 1085
Wiener, Robin K., President, Institute of Scrap Recycling Industries, Inc., 933
Wiens, Eric, Principal, Stantec Inc., 378
Wiens, Paul, University Librarian, Queen's University, 1142
Wiercinska, Grazyna, Library Technician, Women's College Hospital, 1163
Wight, Pamela A., President, Pam Wight & Associates, 317
Wight, Wanda, President, Recreation Newfoundland & Labrador, 992
Wightman, Clive, Director, Winnipeg, 690
Wigle, Q.C., Wendell S., Senior Partner, Hughes, Amys LLP, 1077
Wijewickreme, Nilmini, Chair, British Columbia Food Technolgists, 848
Wilbee, Tamara, County Clerk & Coordinator, Human Resources, Haliburton, 700
Wilbur, Dave, Prince George, 683
Wilbur, Stephen P., Wilbur & Wilbur, 1065
Wilcox, Bill, Branch Manager, Totten Sims Hubicki Associates Ltd., 399
Wilcox, Debi, City Clerk, Pickering, 718
Wilcox, Ian, General Manager, Upper Thames River Conservation Authority, 1015
Wilcox, Linda, President, London Area Health Libraries Association, 949
Wild, Errol, Agent, Kamloops, 681
Wildey, Steve, General Manager, Anthrafilter Media & Coal Ltd., 86
Wildfong, Bob, Executive Director, Seeds of Diversity Canada, 1003
Wildinson, Lanette, Stikeman Elliott LLP - Toronto, 1080
Wile, Mary, Councillor, Halifax Regional Municipality, 695
Wiles, David M., President, Plasticchem Consulting, 326
Wiley, Mary, Communications Coordinator, Ontario Soybean Growers, 979
Wiley, Tom, Georgian Bluffs, 725
Wilford, Donald, Managing Director, Ontario Centre of Excellence for Photonics, 972
Wilgosh, Arlene, Deputy Minister, 588
Wilhelm, Dave J., Project Manager, MTE Consultants Inc., 294
Wilhelm, Robert, Perth, 703
Wilk, Steve, Pinchin Environmental Ltd., 322, 324
Wilk, Steve, Regional Manager, PHH ARC Environmental Ltd., 322
Wilke, Connie, Marketing Coordinator, QSDM Inc., 338

Wilke, Vivienne, General Manager, Surrey, 604-591-4011, 684
Wilker, Jeffrey J., Thomson, Rogers, 1080
Wilkie, Ann, Vice-President, CBCL Limited, 132
Wilkie, Jim, President, AB Mechanical Ltd., 64
Wilkin, T.J., Cunningham, Swan, Carty, Little & Bonham LLP, 1069
Wilkins, Brian, Director, 596
Wilkins, Gillian, Borden Ladner Gervais LLP - Toronto, 1074
Wilkins, Pamela, Ministry Librarian, British Columbia Ministry of Environment, 1120
Wilkins, Robert, Borden Ladner Gervais LLP - Montréal, 1083
Wilkins, Susan, Vice-President, Pottinger Gaherty Environmental Consultants Ltd., 329
Wilkinson, Anna, Ogilvy Renault LLP/S.E.N.C.R.L., s.r.l. - Toronto, 1079
Wilkinson, B., President, Matrix Energy, 282
Wilkinson, Brian, General Manager, Matrix Energy, 282
Wilkinson, Donna, Executive Director, Saskatchewan Camping Association, 999
Wilkinson, Jim, President, Wilkinson Heavy Precast Ltd., 432
Wilkinson, Jonathan, President/CEO, QuestAir Technologies Inc., 339
Wilkinson, Marianne, Ottawa, 613-580-2474, 716
Wilkinson, Paul F., President, Paul F. Wilkinson & Associates Inc., 319
Wilkinson, Val, Mississippi Mills, 714
Will, Sharon, President, Pigeon Lake Regional Chamber of Commerce, 986
Willard, Darlene, Office Manager, Labtronics, 262
Willcock, Michael, D'Arcy & Deacon LLP, 1063
Willcocks, Gordon, McCarthy Tétrault LLP - Toronto, 1077
Willcox Whetung, Linda Louise, Linda Willcox Whetung Professional Corporation, 1071
Willemse, Lisa, Director of Communications, Stem Cell Network, 1010
Willes, Robert J., President, CanTox Environmental Inc., 127
Willett, Arthur, Executive Director, 527
Willett, Terry, President, Parameter Control Ltd., 318
Willett, Terry, President & CEO, Canadian Water Conditioning Inc., 125
william and flora hewlett, The William and Flora Hew, Menlo Park, CA, 1041
Williams, A.R., President, Millar-Williams Hydronics Ltd., 290
Williams, Albert, CEO, BAE Newplan Group Ltd., 101
Williams, Angela, Lab Manager, Integrated Explorations, 244
Williams, Bruce, Chair, Fur Institute of Canada, 922
Williams, Carma, North Glengarry, 727
Williams, D.R., Vice-President, Hammond Manufacturing, 224
Williams, Darren G., Merchant Law Group LLP - Victoria, 1062
Williams, Elaine, Executive Director, Wildlife Preservation Canada, 1020
Williams, Elizabeth, Macleod Dixon LLP, 1052
Williams, Jack R., Field Law - Yellowknife, 1066
Williams, Jacline, Directrice générale, Antoine-Labelle, 747
Williams, James, Chair, 635
Williams, Jeremy, Orangeville, 716
Williams, John, Division Manager, Bigelow-Liptak of Canada, 107
Williams, John R., Mayor, Quinte West, 866-987-2694, 718
Williams, Kevin, Director, Community Services, Kawartha Lakes, 711
Williams, Laura, General Manager, Central British Columbia Railway & Forest Industry Museum Society, 893
Williams, Lorrie, New Westminster, 699
Williams, Mark, General Manager (Ontario), Lantech Drilling Services Inc., 264
Williams, Matthew G., Ritch Durnford, Lawyers, 1067
Williams, Mick, Manager, Dillon Consulting Ltd., 163
Williams, Norm, Westech Industrial Ltd., 429
Williams, Peter, Director, Simon Fraser University, 368
Williams, Rachael, Technical Manager, International Solid Waste Association, 944
Williams, Rick, Commissioner, Community Services, Muskoka, 705-645-2412, 702
Williams, Rick L., Partner, Borden Ladner Gervais LLP - Vancouver, 1058
Williams, Robin C., Commissioner, Public Health & Medical Officer of H, Niagara, 702
Williams, Siân, Executive Officer, International Primary Care Respiratory Group, 942
Williams, Terry J., Fraser Milner Casgrain LLP - Edmonton, 1055
Williams, Wayne, Fire Chief, Penticton, 250-492-4209, 682
Williamson, Barry, Young, Anderson, 1062
Williamson, Bruce, St. Catharines, 905-934-2787, 719
Williamson, Dave, Principal, Cascade Environmental Resource Group. Ltd., 130

Williamson, Don, Fire Chief, Lakeshore, 712
Williamson, Gary, Superintendent, Wellington North, 732
Williamson, Vicki, Dean, University of Saskatchewan, 1191
Williamson, Q.C., Hugh D., Partner, Borden Ladner Gervais LLP - Calgary, 1050
Willing, Terry, Director, Building & Licensing, Kingston, 712
Willingshofer, Pamela, Secretary, Fraser Valley Labour Council, 919
Willis, Alan D., President, Alan Willis & Associates, 76
Willis, Bill, Owner, CBR Products - Canadian Building Restoration Products Inc., 133
Willis, Paul, Contact, Willis Energy Services Ltd., 432
Willis, Scott, Contact, Sedore Stoves Canada, 361
Williston, J. Brian, Director, 584
Willmer, Jeff, General Manager, Development & Technical Services, Kitchener, 712
Willms, David, Willms Construction Ltd., 432
Willms, John R., Willms & Shier Environmental Lawyers LLP, 1081
Willnecker, Andrew, Director, Aircraft Appliances & Equipment Ltd., 75
Wilman, Mary Ekho, Iqaluit, 698
Wilson, Barbara, Clerk, Huron, 701
Wilson, Barry, Spring Air Silver Services Ltd., 376
Wilson, Barry, Production Manager, Spring Air Silver Services Ltd., 376
Wilson, Bill, Coordinator, Operations, Perth East, 728
Wilson, Bob, Manager, St. John's, 709-576-8238, 694
Wilson, Brad, Environmental & Operational Services, Belleville, 706
Wilson, Bruce, International Water Supply Ltd., 246
Wilson, Christopher J., Director, Alcohol Countermeasure Systems Corp., 77
Wilson, Daryl, President/CEO, Hydrogenics Corporation, 236
Wilson, Dave, Grimsby, 905-309-0905, 710
Wilson, David S., Blaney McMurtry LLP, 1073
Wilson, Donald J., Davis LLP - Edmonton, 1050, 1055
Wilson, Doug, Manager, Fraser Valley, 677
Wilson, Frank, President, Fredericton Fish & Game Association, 919
Wilson, Fred, Manager, SimplexGrinnell, 368
Wilson, Garth, Curator, 516
Wilson, Glen, Director, 596
Wilson, Gordon, General Manager, Fredericton Region Solid Waste Commission, 506-444-0960, 758
Wilson, Harrison, Manager, Ocean Steel & Construction Ltd., 311
Wilson, Ian, President, Nilex Inc., 304
Wilson, Jack, Renfrew, 613-584-3114, 704
Wilson, James C., President, Active Chemicals Ltd., 68
Wilson, Jim, Chief Administrative Officer, Haliburton, 700
Wilson, Jim, President, Saint John Naturalists' Club, 998
Wilson, John R., Elgin, 699
Wilson, Judy L., Blake, Cassels & Graydon LLP - Toronto, 1073
Wilson, June E., Information Broker, Ontario Ministry of Transportation, 1154
Wilson, L. Michael, President/CEO, Atlantic Industries Ltd., 95
Wilson, L.A., President, Zimmark Inc., 437
Wilson, Liane, Content Administrator, R.V. Anderson Associates Limited, 1161
Wilson, Linda, Officer, Economic Development, South Dundas, 730
Wilson, Malcolm, General Manager, Consolidated Giroux Environment Inc., 150
Wilson, Marianne, Contact, Waterloo Biofilter Systems Inc., 422
Wilson, Mark, Treasurer, Saskatchewan Outdoor & Environmental Education Association, 1001
Wilson, Mel, PricewaterhouseCoopers Management Consultants, 332
Wilson, Patrick, President, Blue Water Agencies Ltd., 110
Wilson, Patti, Public Services Coordinator, University College of the Fraser Valley, 1110
Wilson, Paul C., Fasken Martineau - Vancouver, 1059
Wilson, Peter, Chief Executive Officer, 640
Wilson, Ralph, Branch Manager, National Energy Equipment Inc., 297
Wilson, Robert, Wellington, 519-843-3329, 705
Wilson, Sarah, Manager, Schlumberger Oilfield Services, 359
Wilson, Scott, Orangeville, 716
Wilson, Scott, Chief Administrative Officer, Wellington, 705
Wilson, Shawn, Thorold, 720
Wilson, Sherry, Councillor at Large, Riverview, 506-386-1133, 692
Wilson, Steve W., Partner, Borden Ladner Gervais LLP - Calgary, 1050

Executive Name Index

Wilson, Tammy, CAO, Lunenburg District, 697
Wilson, Tom, Councillor, Cape Breton, 695
Wilson, Tom, Regional Manager, Vestar, 413
Wilson, P. Eng., Rob, Manager, Surrey, 604-591-4276, 684
Wilson, P.Geo., Stephen, Vice-President, Association of Professional Geoscientists of Ontario, 839
Wilson, Q.C., Donald K., Managing Partner, MacPherson Leslie & Tyerman LLP - Regina, 1090
Wilson, Q.C., Earl C., Wolch, Hursh, deWit & Watts, 1054
Wilton, Karen, Manager, Information Centre, Centre de recherche et de développement sur les aliments, 1183
Wilton, Robert C., President, Clintar Groundskeeping Services, 144
Winch, Jordan D., Partner, Ogilvy Renault LLP/S.E.N.C.R.L., s.r.l. - Toronto, 1079
Wind, David, Yellowknife, 695
Wind, Rick, Director, 605
Windeatt, Mark, Sales, CML Northern Blower Inc., 145
Windle, Patrick, President, R Plus Industries Alberta Inc., 339
Windle, Patrick V., McInnes Cooper, 1064
Wing, Devlin, Branch Manager, Mequipco Ltd., 286
Wing, Janice, City Councillor, Niagara Falls, 715
Wing, Sandra, Vice-President, 518
Wingrave, Al, Technical Sales, Romatec Incorporated, 351
Wingrove, Tom, Sr. Vice-President, UMA Group Ltd., 405
Wingrove, Trevor, General Manager, Coquitlam, 680
Winkler, Mark, President, Associated Tube Industries, 94
Winkler, Tom, Chief Strategic Development Officer, Vancouver Fraser Port Authority, 409
Winser, Nigel, Executive Director, Earthwatch Europe, 907
Winsor, Rod, Unit Manager, AMEC, 83
Winsor, Roderick S.W., Blaney McMurtry LLP, 1073
Winter, Alan D., Fasken Martineau - Vancouver, 1059
Winterbottom, Marcia, Electronic Resources-Systems Librarian, Toronto Rehab, 1162
Winters, Brian, President, Proeco Enviroservices Ltd., 333
Winters, Rick, Manager, Operations, Georgian Bluffs, 725
Wintersinger, Josie, Erin, 709
Winthrop, John, Chair, American Farmland Trust, 823
Wipperman, Kristy, Office Manager, Certified Organic Associations of British Columbia, 894
Wise, Mandi, Coordinator, Alberta Recreation & Parks Association, 819
Wise, Rick, Vice-President, CCS Income Trust, 134
Wiseman, Graham, Bathurst, 506-548-3600, 690
Wiseman, Graham, Chair, Nepisiguit-Chaleur Solid Waste Commission, 758
Wiseman, Ross, Minister, 601
Wiseman, Tom, CFO, Total Combustion Inc., 398
Wishart, Bruce W., President, Whisco Ltd., 431
Wishart, Rick, Treasurer, The Canadian Network for Environmental Education & Communication, 879
Wishart, Robin, Manager, Port Coquitlam, 683
Wisking, Susan, Director General, Communications, 510
Wismer, Beth, General Manager, Indian Agricultural Program of Ontario, 930
Wisniewski, Jeremy, Heenan Blaikie S.E.N.C.R.L/SRL, 1085
Withey, Tim, Councillor, Huntsville, 711
Witmer, Mike, Manager, Westburne Canada, 426
Witmer, Scott, Waterloo, 722
Witney, Maureen, Librarian Coordinator, Capilano College, 1114
Wittlin, Leslie, Partner, Heenan Blaikie LLP - Toronto, 1076
Wiun, David, City Auditor, Edmonton, 780-496-8315, 672
Wivcharuk, Jody, Burnet, Duckworth & Palmer LLP, 1050
Wiwchar, Randy, Director, Courtenay, 680
Wlad, Russell, Principal, Stantec Inc., 378
Wock, Greg, Manager, Estevan, 306-634-1823, 754
Wolf, Pam, City Councillor, Cambridge, 707
Wolf, Uli, Solid Waste Services Supervisor, Grande Prairie, 780-538-0360, 672
Wolfe, John, CEO, Management Horizons, 279
Wolfe, John, Manager, Conformance Check Inc., 150
Wolfenden, Dave, Executive Director, Outward Bound Canada, 983
Wolff, Erin, MacPherson Leslie & Tyerman LLP - Regina, 1090
Wolff, Janine, Administrative Assistant, AMEC, 83
Wolfsgruber, Richard, Manager, Career Advancement Employment, 128
Wolfson, Stanley, Executive Director, American Society of Plumbing Engineers, 826
Wolkoff, Aaron, President, Waters Limited, 423
Wolski, Darryl, Coordinator, Airdrie, 403-948-0246, 670
Wong, Andrew, Partner, Osler, Hoskin & Harcourt LLP - Toronto, 1079
Wong, Bill, President, WSH Laboratories Ltd., 434

Wong, Cindy, Library Techician, IBI Group, 1158
Wong, Edward P., Office Manager, Trow Consulting Engineers Ltd., 403
Wong, Frank, Red Deer, 403-347-6514, 674
Wong, Glenn, Pacific Environmental Consulting & Occupational Hygiene Services, 316
Wong, Joyce, Department Chair, Langara College, 1118
Wong, Kevin, Executive Director, Canadian Water Quality Association, 891
Wong, Leslie, Blake, Cassels & Graydon LLP - Toronto, 1073
Wong, Paul, President, Capital H2O Systems Inc., 128
Wong, Reg, Manager, Bartle & Gibson Co. Ltd., 102
Wong, Richard, Partner, Osler, Hoskin & Harcourt LLP - Toronto, 1079
Wong, Sharon, Blake, Cassels & Graydon LLP - Toronto, 1073
Wong, Sylvester, Vice-President, 609
Wong, Tom, Vice-President, Industrial Plastics Fabricators Ltd., 241
Wong-Chor, Trevor, Davis LLP - Calgary, 1050
Wong-Tam, Kristyn, Toronto, 721
Woo, L.Y., Vice-President, Fabricated Plastics Ltd., 193
Woo, Sue-Ann, Cataloguer & Library System Administrator, Canadian Heritage, 1167
Woo, Willie, Durham, 699
Woo, Willie, Local Councillor, Clarington, 724
Wood, Andrew, Municipal Engineer, Maple Ridge, 604-467-7496, 687
Wood, Bev, Clerk & Manager, Council Services, Norfolk, 702
Wood, Brian, President, Con Cast Pipe, 148
Wood, Bruce, City Councillor, Oshawa, 716
Wood, Dan, Manager, Parks & Recreation, Kingsville, 712
Wood, David M., Partner, Stikeman Elliott LLP - Calgary, 1054
Wood, Doug, General Manager, ATCO Group, 95
Wood, Glen, Director, DuPont Canada Inc., 167
Wood, Harvey, Manager, Waterous Power Systems, 422
Wood, Jim, Mayor, Red Deer County, 403-350-2152, 670
Wood, John M., President, Veolia Water Canada, 412
Wood, Leslie, Department Secretary, University of Victoria School of Health Information Science, 1121
Wood, Michael K., Chief Administrative Officer, Centre Wellington, 724
Wood, Robert, CFO, BIOREM Inc., 109
Wood, Tim, Administrator, Saanich, 250-475-5555, 688
Wood, Vincent, General Foreman, Bathurst, 506-548-0444, 690
Wood, CMA, Stuart, Director, Financial Services & Treasurer, Chatham-Kent, 724
Woodacre, Kendall, General Manager, Medicine Hat, 403-502-8081, 673
Woodcock, Loretta, Executive Member, British Columbia Spaces for Nature, 850
Woodford, John, Director, Hants East District, 902-758-2715, 697
Woodin, Melanie, Secretary, Canadian Physiological Society, 882
Woodland, Chris A., Partner, MacPherson Leslie & Tyerman LLP - Saskatoon, 1090
Woodland, Mandy L., Cox and Palmer - St. John's, 1066
Woodland, Robert, Director, Victoria, 250-361-0203, 685
Woodmass, Steve, Principal, Stantec Inc., 378
Woodruff, Anthony, Brock, 724
Woodruff, Janet P., Chief Financial Officer & Vice-President, 583
Woodruff, Norris, General Manager, GE Multilin, 205
Woodruff, Rich, Quarry Manager, Lafarge Dundas Quarry, 262
Woods, Blair, President, National Sunflower Association of Canada, 958
Woods, Brad, Borden Ladner Gervais LLP - Vancouver, 1058
Woods, Cheryl, Map Curator, University of Western Ontario Dept. of Geography, 1144
Woods, Cindy, South Stormont, 730
Woods, Gary, Hamilton, 725
Woods, J. Patrick, City Manager, Saint John, 506-658-2913, 692
Woods, James, Director, Steel Recycling Institute, 1010
Woods, Jim, President, Amaircare Corporation, 82
Woods, John, Vice-President, Minas Basin Pulp & Power Company Limited, 290
Woods, Kit, Superintendent, Pollution Control Centre, Leamington, 726
Woods, Mark, Secretary, International Society for Environmental Ethics, 943
Woods, Reid, President, Manitoba Wildlife Federation, 952
Woodside, Brad S., Mayor, Fredericton, 506-460-2085, 691
Woodsworth, Ellen, Vancouver, 604-873-7245, 685
Woodward, Christina, Manager, Trillium Health Centre-Mississauga Site, 1145
Woodward, E. Jack, Woodward & Company, 1063

Woodward, Sharolynn, Manager, Yellowknife, 867-920-5651, 695
Woodworth, Earl, Building Inspector, Chester District, 697
Wookey, Russell G., D'Arcy & Deacon LLP, 1063
Woolcott, Robert, Manager, Alfa Plastics Inc., 78
Wooldridge, Edward A., Partner, Heenan Blaikie LLP - Calgary, 1051
Wooldridge, Sheila, Advisor, Western Canadian Spill Services Ltd., 429
Woolley, Jonathan M., Thompson Dorfman Sweatman LLP, 1064
Woolsey, Vernon, Energy Systems & Design Limited, 179
Worden, Sean, ProPower Equipment Ltd., 335
Work, Timothy, Président, Société d'entomologie du Québec, 1005
Workman, Peter, Environmental Health Consultant, 619
Worman, Dave, Manager, Capital Region Northeast Water Services Commission, 672, 757
Worsfold, Richard D., Director, Earth & Environmental Technologies (ETech), 168
Worsley, Julian, Partner, Heenan Blaikie LLP - Toronto, 1076
Worsley, Lynn, Officer, Human Resources, Saugeen Shores, 719
Wort, Andrew, General Manager, New Era Farms Ltd., 301
Worth, Monique, Mairesse d'arrondissement/Conseillère de la ville, Montréal, 738
Wortley, Stephen D., Lang Michener LLP - Vancouver, 1060
Wosnuk, George, President, Woznuk Brothers Ltd., 434
Wotherspoon, Darrell, Vice-President, Canadian Organic Livestock Association, 881
Wotherspoon, Paul, President, Wotherspoon Environmental Inc., 434
Wotten, Wilma, Scugog, 729
Wowchuk, Rosann, Minister, 584
Woynorowski, F., Carrier Canada Ltd., 129
Woznow, Ron, Executive Director, Advanced Foods & Materials Network, 813
Wray, Laureen, President, Alberta Camping Association, 816
Wrezel, Mira, Librarian, Golder Associates Ltd., 1145
Wright, Andrew, Siskind, Cromarty, Ivey & Dowler LLP, 1069
Wright, AnnMarie, Canviro, 127
Wright, Arlene, City & County Councillor, Owen Sound, 717
Wright, Arlene, City/County Councillor, Grey, 700
Wright, Arlene, Warden & Councillor, Grey, 700
Wright, Bob, Welland, 722
Wright, Carolyn A., Burnet, Duckworth & Palmer LLP, 1050
Wright, Christa, Coordinator, Newfoundland & Labrador Federation of Agriculture, 962
Wright, Christine, Manager, Caduceon Environmental Laboratories, 121
Wright, Cynthia, Chair, North American Bird Conservation Initiative Canada, 965
Wright, Don, Diversified Waste Solutions, 164
Wright, Doug, County Manager, Leduc County, 780-955-6400, 669
Wright, Douglas, Cox and Palmer - St. John's, 1066
Wright, Elizabeth, Secretary, Newfoundland & Labrador Public Health Association, 963
Wright, Forrest, CAO, Highway 14 Regional Water Services, 757
Wright, Gary, Board Chair, Central Kootenay, 677
Wright, Gary, Executive Director, City Planning, & Chief Planner, Toronto, 416-392-8772, 721
Wright, Gerald, Manager, Logan Geotech Inc., 273
Wright, Jim, General Manager, Hooper Welding Enterprises Ltd., 233
Wright, John, President & Chief Executive Officer, Canadian Institute for Health Information, 872
Wright, John C., Director, Building Standards, Markham, 905-475-4712, 713
Wright, Joseph H., Non-Executive Chairman, BFI Canada Inc., 106
Wright, Ken, Inproheat Industries Ltd., 242
Wright, Kenneth M., Soloway, Wright LLP, 1071
Wright, Michael, Port Coquitlam, 683
Wright, Nancy, Vice-President, GLOBE Foundation, 924
Wright, Tyson W., Project Engineer, Geocor Engineering Inc., 210
Wright, W., Principal, Catterall & Wright, 132
Wright, Wayne, Metro Vancouver, 678
Wright, Wayne, Mayor, New Westminster, 604-527-4522, 682
Wright Eastley, Teresa, Librarian, SaskPower Corporation, 1188
Wright-Laking, Nancy, City Clerk, Peterborough, 718
Wrobel, Dave, Brantford, 707
Wrubleski, Sheldon, Sales Manager, WJF Instrumentation (1990) Ltd., 433
Wrycraft, John, Manager, SimplexGrinnell, 369

Executive Name Index

Wu, Christina, Librarian, Vale Inco, 1163
Wu, Edward, President, Electronics-recycling.com, 175
Wu, Franklin, Chief Administrative Officer, Clarington, 724
Wulff, Dave, National Sales Manager, Radiodetection (Canada) Ltd., 341
Wurzer, Greg, Reference Librarian, Law Library, 1189
Wusatz, Susan, Librarian, TransAlta Utilities Corporation, 1103
Wutzke, Maurice, Assistant Manager, Squamish, 688
Wyant, B.A., LL.B., Gordon, Saskatoon, 754
Wyatt, Merle, Chair, Vulcan District Waste Commission, 758
Wyatt, Russ, Winnipeg, 204-986-8087, 690
Wyatt, Shannon L., Brownlee LLP, 1054
Wyckham, Robert, Sanix Incorporated, 357
Wylde, Jonathan, Head, Clariant (Canada) Inc., 142
Wyman, Dody, President, International Wildlife Rehabilitation Council, 946
Wyndham, Lois, Librarian, Hamilton Health Sciences, 1141
Wyndham, Lois, Team Leader, Library Services, Henderson Medical Library, 1140, 1141
Wynia, Michael, Director, Planning & Development, Clearview, 725
Wynick, Robert H., MacKenzie Fujisawa LLP, 1061
Wynne, Derrick, Sales Manager, R.A. Kirby Sales Inc., 340
Wyntjes, Dianne, Red Deer, 674
Wysocki, W., Partner, Symbion Consultants, 385
Wyss, Sam, General Manager, Oetiker Limited, 311

X

Xénopoulos, Ianny, Fasken Martineau - Québec, 1087

Y

Yada, Rick, Chair, International Union of Food Science & Technology, 945
Yada, Ph.D., Rickey, Scientific Director, Advanced Foods & Materials Network, 813
Yagerter, David, Chair/CEO, HSE Integrated, 234
Yake, David E., Director, DuPont Canada Inc., 167
Yake, Marianne, President, Richmond Hill Naturalists, 995
Yakemchuk, Les, Vice-president, Treeline Well Abandonment & Reclamation Ltd., 401
Yale, Darcie C., D'Arcy & Deacon LLP, 1063
Yamada, Gary, CFO & VP, Great Western Containers Inc., 216
Yamashita, Allan, City Engineer & General Manager, Leduc, 673
Yamashita, Colleen, Scarfone Hawkins LLP, 1069
Yamich, Martin, Chief Administrative Officer, Pelham, 717
Yanch, E. Helen, Operations Manager, The Friends of Bon Echo Park, 920
Yanch, Helen, Lennox & Addington, 613-336-8774, 701
Yanchula, MCIP, RPP, Jim, Manager, Urban Design & Community Development, Windsor, 723
Yanew, Tony, McCordick Glove & Safety Inc., 284
Yang, Michael, RICHWAY Environmental Technologies Ltd., 346
Yang, Tong, District Sales Rep., National Instruments Canada, 298
Yao, Colin, Stikeman Elliott LLP - Toronto, 1080
Yardley, Jonathan, President, Heritage Society of British Columbia, 929
Yaremchuk, Dean, Director, Portage La Prairie, 689
Yarnold, David, Executive Director, Environmental Defense, 911
Yaschuk, Brent, Contact, Concept Controls Inc., 148
Yasmin, Chong, Trade Commissioner, 768
Yates, Carl, Manager, Entropex, 182
Yates, Terry, Chair, 622
Yates, Tom, General Manager, Fraser-Fort George, 678
Yates, M.A.Sc., P.Eng., Carl D., General Manager, Halifax Regional Municipality, 902-490-4827, 695
Yates, Q.C., C. Kemm, Blake, Cassels & Graydon LLP - Calgary, 1049
Yaworski, Q.C., Brian, Davis LLP - Calgary, 1050
Yeager, Penny L., MacPherson Leslie & Tyerman LLP - Saskatoon, 1090
Yeates, Glenda, Deputy Minister, 533
Yee, Brenda, Head, Technical Services, College of New Caledonia, 1115
Yelder, Joseph, President, Snowcap Waters Ltd., 371
Yelich, Lynne, Minister of State (Western Economic Diversificatio, 562
Yeo, Emmett, Kawartha Lakes, 711
Yeomans, Greg, Treasurer & Commissioner, Saint John, 506-658-2951, 692
Yergeau, Michel, Partner, Lavery, de Billy - Montréal, 1086
Yerxa, Kelly G., O'Connor MacLeod Hanna LLP, 1070

Yetman, Marion, President, Community & Hospital Infection Control Association Canada, 899
Yeung Racco, Sandra, Vaughan, 722
Ying, Tony, Treasurer, Conestoga-Rovers & Associates, 149
Yobp, CAE, Vicky, Director, American Industrial Hygiene Association, 823
Yogendrakumar, M. (Yogi), Principal, Golder Associates Ltd., 214
Yon-Ho, Choi, Trade Commissioner, 768
Yonker, Jonathan, Library Systems & Technologies, Brock University, 1154
Yorg-Turner, Lonna, Director, Global Contract Inc., 213
York, Larry W., South Frontenac, 737
Yoshimura, Manabu, Secretary General, International Association for Earthquake Engineering, 934
Younan, Marion, Chair & President, Youth Challenge International, 1024
Young, Anne Marie, Manager, Economic Development, Frontenac, 699
Young, Barry, President & CEO, Lord & Partners Ltd., 274
Young, Bob, Estimator, Dewar Insulations Ltd., 162
Young, Charlotte, Director of Practice, ENVision...synergy, 188
Young, Charlotte, Senior Associate, Hardy Stevenson & Associates, 225
Young, Crawford, President, Spectrum Resource Group Inc., 375
Young, David, Librarian, University College of the North, 1122
Young, David Duncan, McInnes Cooper, 1064
Young, David N.W., Lang Michener LLP - Toronto, 1077
Young, Don A., Executive Vice-President, Ducks Unlimited Inc., 907
Young, Donald, Director, Finance, King, 726
Young, Donavon, Assistant Deputy Minister, 563
Young, Geoff, Board Chair, Capital Regional District, 250-385-5711, 676
Young, George, Muskoka, 702
Young, Gordon B., President, Keywood Entreprises Ltd., 257
Young, Hugh J., Bathurst, 506-548-1815, 690
Young, J., Carrier Canada Ltd., 129
Young, Jim, Manager, Operations, Haliburton, 700
Young, Joan M., Lang Michener LLP - Vancouver, 1060
Young, Kevin, President, Armtec Construction Products, 91
Young, Margot, Senior Planner, EDM Environmental Design & Management Ltd., 173
Young, Pat, Vice-President, earthRight Solar Products, 169
Young, Patricia, Librarian, Vancouver Coastal Health Authority, 1119
Young, R. Wayne, Manager, Operational Services, Innisfil, 711
Young, Raymond E., Young, Anderson, 1062
Young, Rick, Fire Chief, Stratford, 720
Young, Robert, Contact, Sea Lamprey Control Centre, 1155
Young, Ron, President, earthRight Solar Products, 169
Young, Scott, Muskoka, 702
Young, Scott, District Councillor, Bracebridge, 706
Young, Steve, Specialist, Westland Resource Group Inc., 430
Young, Stewart, Mayor, Langford, 681
Young, Tom, Rothesay, 692
Young, Tracy, Administrative Resources Coordinator, St. Albert, 780-458-2020, 674
Young, Wayne D., General Manager, Lake Abitibi Model Forest, 948
Young, Wynne, Deputy Minister, 661
Young, B.A., Ph.D., Geoff, Victoria, 685
Young, P.Eng, Danny, CEO, Ontario Society of Professional Engineers, 979
Young, Q.C., John A., Boyne Clarke, 1067
Younger, Stu, Air Liquide Canada Ltée, 75
Younker, Barrie, J.W. Bird & Company Ltd., 250
Yourkowski, Yvonne, Manager, Westburne Canada, 428
Youzwa, Pat, President/CEO, 661
Yu, Soomin, Marketing, New East Consulting Services Ltd., 301
Yu, Veronica, President & CEO, Canadian Oil Heat Association, 880
Yudelson, Jerry, Marketing Director, Pacific Institute for Advanced Study, 316
Yuen, Thomas, Coordinator, Econotech Services Ltd., 172
Yujnovich, Zoë, President & CEO, Iron Ore Company of Canada, 248
Yule, Jim, Sales, John Thurston Machine Ltd., 253
Yury, Mardak, Trade Commissioner, 769
Yusishen, Tim, President, Solar Solutions Inc., 372
Yussuff, Hassan, Secretary-Treasurer, Canadian Labour Congress, 876
Yusuf, Sam, Alderman, St. Thomas, 719

Z

Zablocki, Martin, Vice-President/CFO, 517
Zabrovsky, Andrew N., Associate, Hicks Morley Hamilton Stewart Storie LLP, 1077
Zacharias, John, President, Celfort Construction Materials Inc., 135
Zacharias, Mark, Executive Director, Geomatics for Informed Decisions Network, 923
Zacher, Glenn, Partner, Stikeman Elliott LLP - Toronto, 1080
Zachow, Darrin, Manager, Advanced Coolant Technologies Inc., 69
Zacks, Nadine S., Associate, Hicks Morley Hamilton Stewart Storie LLP, 1077
Zacks, Q.C., David, Blake, Cassels & Graydon LLP - Vancouver, 1057
Zadeh, Saba, Borden Ladner Gervais LLP - Toronto, 1074
Zahynacz, I., Director, Port Coquitlam, 683
Zaidi, Tammi, Contact, Enviro Wood Recovery Systems Ltd., 182
Zaied, Khaled, General Manager, Zurn Industries Limited, 437
Zaine, Mike, Vice-President/Regional Manager, Lockerbie & Hole Contracting Ltd., 273
Zajdel, Saulie, Conseiller, Darlington, Montréal, 738
Zakarow, Peter, Chair, 621
Zakutney, MHSc, PEng, CCE, Tim J., Chair, Canadian Medical & Biological Engineering Society, 877
Zalai, Conrad, Marketing Manager, QSDM Inc., 338
Zalepa, Jr., Gary, Councillor, Niagara-on-the-Lake, 715
Zalesak, Rudy, President, Hi-Country Environmental Services Ltd., 231
Zalezsak, Ella-Fay, Coordinator, Technical Services, Vancouver Community College, 1119
Zalmanowitz, Q.C., Barry, Fraser Milner Casgrain LLP - Edmonton, 1055
Zaltsberg, Ernst, AGRECOM inc., 73
Zalyvadna, I., Supervisor, Wood Laboratory Ltd., 433
Zambito, Robert L., Conseiller d'arrondissement, St-Léonard-Est, Montréal, 738
Zammit, Kathy, Commissioner, Corporate Services, Brampton, 706
Zammit, Michelle, Conseillère d'arrondissement, Anjou Centre, Montréal, 738
Zamojc, M., Commissioner, Public Works, Halton, 700
Zander, Daryl, Principal, LEHDER Environmental Services Ltd., 267
Zanello, Enio, President & General Manager, MakLoc Buildings Inc., 279
Zanetti, Chris, Councillor, Huntsville, 711
Zaozirny, Q.C., John B., McCarthy Tétrault LLP - Calgary, 1053
Zapernick, Perry, Manager, Engineered Air, 180
Zapotichny, Lorne, Police Chief, New Westminster, 682
Zapp, Angela, Manager, Neptune Technology Group (Canada) Ltd., 300
Zappone, Gary, President, Alchemist Transport Inc., 77
Zarlenga, P.Eng, Lou, Manager, Public Services, Amherstburg, 705
Zasada, Adam I., Clark Wilson LLP, 1058
Zavislake, Brad, Merchants of Green Coffee, 287
Zawada, Craig A., Wallace Meschishnick Clackson Zawada, 1091
Zawadski, Brian, Executive Director, Nunavut Harvesters Association, 969
Zawislak, Tim W., President, Waterous Power Systems, 422
Zbeetnoff, Darrell M., Principal, Zbeetnoff Agro-Environmental Consulting, 436
Zdebiak, Rodney J., Partner, Stewart McKelvey Stirling Scales - St. John's, 1066
Zealand, Gord, Executive Director, Yukon Fish & Game Association, 1024
Zebedee, Ed, Director, 617
Zebroff, Yuri, Administrator, Similkameen Okanagan Organic Producers Association, 1004
Zed, Q.C., Peter T., Barry Spalding - Saint John Office, 1065
Zehr, Carl, Waterloo, 704
Zehr, Carl, Mayor, Kitchener, 712
Zehr, Keith, President, Stemmer Steel Craft Industries Limited, 379
Zeitler, Dennis L., Chief Financial Officer & Senior Vice-President, MSA: Mine Safety Appliances Company, 294
Zeitlin, June, Executive Director, Women's Environment & Development Organization, 1021
Zeller, Les, President, Zell Oilfield Service Ltd., 436
Zelunka, David, General Manager, Gensco Equipment (1990) Ltd., 210
Zerr, Nadine, Library Officer, Technical Library, 1188

Zettle, Randy M., Borden Ladner Gervais LLP - Toronto, 1074
Zhang, Karen, Electronics-recycling.com, 175
Zheng, Jeff Yenyou, President, CFO & Director, AQUASOL EnviroTech Ltd., 89
Ziccardi, Dominic, President, Lab-Élite limitée, 261
Zieba, Richard, Director, 607
Zieba, Richard, President, Anachem Ltd., 84
Ziegler, Kenneth K.E., Robertson Stromberg Pedersen LLP, 1091
Zielinksi, Ewa, Coordinator, Pylon Electronics Inc., 337
Zigayer, Nicholas, Manager, SimplexGrinnell, 369
Zikovsky, claire, Associée, Stikeman Elliott LLP - Montréal, 1087
Zimarino, Stefania, Library Technician, Seven Oaks General Hospital, 1125
Zimmer, Terri, Librarian, R.V. Anderson Associates Limited, 1161
Zimmerling, Todd, President/CEO, Alberta Conservation Association, 816

Zimmerman, Debbie M., Niagara, 702
Zimmerman, Peter, Head, Information Services Department, University of Windsor, 1165
Zimmerman, Susan, Executive Director, 519
Zinck, Laura, Information Librarian, Keyano College, 1107
Zinkhofer, Bernhard, Lang Michener LLP - Vancouver, 1060
Zinter, Barbara, Communications Researcher, Suncor Inc., 1103
Zipay, John, Commissioner, Planning, Vaughan, 722
Zito, Madeline, Director, Corporate Communications, Vaughan, 722
Zivot, Louis J., Lang Michener LLP - Vancouver, 1060
Zizian, Raymond, Directeur, Saint-Jérôme, 743
Znamirowski, Barbara, Government Publications, Maps & Lab, Trent University, 1153
Zoet, Richard, Alberni-Clayoquot, 250-728-1237, 676
Zoldy, Derek, Treasurer, Tunnelling Association of Canada, 1014
Zorbas, Steve, City Treasurer, Burlington, 707

Zrobok, Dawn, Library Assistant, University of Alberta Dept. of Rural Economy, 1107
Zsuzsanna, Matyus, Trade Commissioner, 768
Zubick, Bruce, Vice-President, John Zubick Ltd. Scrap Metals, 253
Zubick, George, President, John Zubick Ltd. Scrap Metals, 253
Zucchetti, R.M., Director, Simcoe Engineering Group Limited, 368
Zurawel, Peter, IBI Group, 238
Zurfluh, Wilma, Staff, Buffalo Lake Naturalists Club, 1109
Zurowski, Laura J., Fraser Milner Casgrain LLP - Calgary, 1051
Zwicker, Bernie, President, Millennium Water Management Ltd., 290
Zwozdesky, Gene, Minister, 569
Zyzniewski, Randy, Manager, Waterous Power Systems, 423

Canada Info Desk

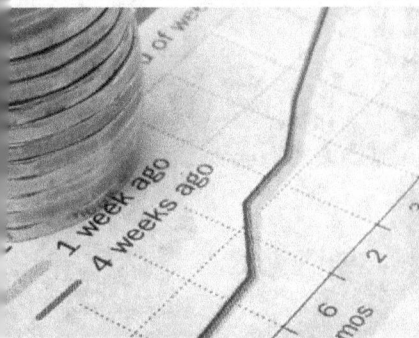

Canada Info Desk integrates Grey House Canada's best-selling directories into a single online Canadian resource—making it the most comprehensive directory database in Canada. The easy-to-use Web interface gives users instant access to thousands of organizations, contacts, facts and figures about Canadian business, government and society.

Start your search here
Canada Info Desk can be found on the desktops of Canada's finest libraries and institutions and on desks and shelves in libraries and institutions all accross Canada. Professional researchers can search by fielded data to pinpoint information on the spot. Students can quickly track down organizations or people, locate addresses, analyze activities or even job hunt using the extensive listings. Invaluable to business professionals, Canada Info Desk is an excellent tool to pinpoint contacts or prospects, identify partner groups, search for promotional opportunities and export custom lists in seconds.

Design your own custom lists, why wait?
Save time and money with this unique and valuable resource. Canada Info Desk database gives you the option to define and extract your own lists in seconds. Whether you need contact, mail or e-mail lists, Canada Info Desk can pull together the information quickly and export it in a variety of formats to where you need it most… your desktop.

Innovative interface with enhanced functionality
Canada Info Desk gives users the ability to limit their search many different ways including the original database source, subject category and location. Researchers can choose between a complex Expert Search or a simple Quick Search.

KEY ADVANTAGES OF CANADA INFO DESK:
- seamlessly cross-database search all database content or content subsets
- generate and export customized lists for contact data, marketing, or research collection
- regular ongoing changes are added to the Web version on a monthly basis.
- conduct a quick search with fields common to all databases, or build a complex Boolean expert search query
- customize results by searching for records that are head offices, have e-mail, phone, fax or websites, promote conferences, produce publications, or are mailing list compliant
- save time by saving search results for future reference
- mark records in the results list or full record and then view, print, e-mail or export
- link directly to websites or e-mail addresses

Subscribers can search based on more general record categorization, including:

- arts and culture
- awards
- business and finance
- Canadians and society
- communications
- education
- environment
- governments
- health
- industry
- labour
- law and justice
- meetings
- public services
- religion
- science and nature
- sports and recreation
- transportation
- utilities

For more information please contact Grey House Publishing Canada by Tel.: 1-866-433-4739 or (416) 644-6479
Fax: (416) 644-1904 or via E-mail: info@greyhouse.ca • www.greyhouse.ca

Canadian Almanac & Directory

THE DEFINITIVE RESOURCE FOR FACTS & FIGURES ABOUT CANADA, INCLUDING 2006 CENSUS RESULTS!

The Canadian Almanac & Directory has been Canada's most authoritative sourcebook for over 160 years. Published annually since 1847, it continues to be widely used by publishers, business professionals, government offices, researchers, information specialists and anyone needing current, accessible information on every imaginable topic relevant to those who live and work in Canada.

A directory and a guide, the Canadian Almanac & Directory provides the most comprehensive picture of Canada, from physical attributes to economic and business summaries, leisure and recreation. It combines textual materials, charts, colour photographs, the 2006 Canadian Census findings and directory listings with detailed profiles, all verified and organized for easy retrieval. The Canadian Almanac & Directory is a wealth of general information, displaying national statistics on population, employment, CPI, imports and exports, as well as images of national awards, Canadian symbols, flags, emblems and Canadian parliamentary leaders.

For important contacts throughout Canada; for any number of business projects or for that once-in-a-while critical fact; the Canadian Almanac & Directory will help you find the leads you didn't even know existed—quickly and easily!

PRINT OR ONLINE - QUICK AND EASY ACCESS TO ALL THE INFORMATION YOU NEED!

Available in hardcover print or electronically via the Web, the Canadian Almanac & Directory provides instant access to the people you need and the facts you want every time. Canadian Almanac & Directory print edition is verified and updated annually. Regular ongoing changes are added to the Web version on a monthly basis. The Web version allows you to narrow your search by using index fields such as name or type of organization, subject, location, contact name or title, and postal code.

Create your own contact lists! For a small additional fee, online subscribers can instantly generate their own contact lists and export them into spreadsheets for further use. A great alternative to high cost list broker services.

All the information you'll ever need, organized into 17 distinct categories for easy navigation!

Almanac – a fact-filled snapshot of Canada including History, Geography, Economics and Vital Statistics.

Arts & Culture – includes 9 topics from Galleries to Zoos.

Associations – thousands of organizations arranged in 139 different topics, from Accounting to Writers.

Broadcasting – Canada's major Broadcasting Companies, Provincial Radio and Television Stations, Cable Companies, and Specialty Broadcasters.

Business & Finance – Accounting, Banking, Insurance, Canada's Major Companies and Stock Exchanges.

Education – arranged by Province and includes Districts, Government Agencies, Specialized and Independent Schools, Universities and Technical facilities.

Government – spread over three sections, with a Quick Reference Guide, Federal and Provincial listings, County and Municipal Districts and coverage of Courts in Canada.

Health – Government agencies, hospitals, community health centers, retirement care and mental health facilities.

Law Firms – all Major Law Firms, followed by smaller firms organized by Province and listed alphabetically.

Libraries – Canada's main Library/Archive and Government Departments for Libraries, followed by Provincial listings and Regional Systems.

Publishing – Books, Magazines and Newspapers organized by Province, including frequency and circulation figures.

Religion – broad information about religious groups and Associations from 21 different denominations.

Sports – Associations for 93 single sports, with detailed League and Team listings.

Transportation – complete listings for all major modes.

Utilities – Associations, Government Agencies and Provincial Utility Companies.

For more information please contact Grey House Publishing Canada by Tel.: 1-866-433-4739 or (416) 644-6479
Fax: (416) 644-1904 or via E-mail: info@greyhouse.ca • www.greyhouse.ca

Canadian Parliamentary Guide

YOUR NUMBER ONE SOURCE FOR ALL GENERAL FEDERAL ELECTIONS RESULTS!

Published annually since before Confederation, the Canadian Parliamentary Guide is an indispensable directory, providing biographical information on elected and appointed members in federal and provincial government. Featuring government institutions such as the Governor General's Household, Privy Council and Canadian legislature, this comprehensive collection provides historical and current election results with statistical, provincial and political data.

The Canadian Parliamentary Guide is broken down into 5 comprehensive categories:

Monarchy - biographical information on Her Majesty Queen Elizabeth II, The Royal Family and the Governor General

Federal Government - a separate chapter for each, Privy Council, Senate, House of Commons including a brief description of the institution, its history in both text and chart format and a list of current members, followed by un-paralleled biographical sketches*

General Elections - 2 chapters
1867 - 2006
- information is listed alphabetically by province then by riding name
- notes on each riding include: date of establishment, date of abolition, former division, later divisions etc. followed by election year and successful candidate's name and party
- by-election information follows

2008
- information for the 2008 elections is organized in the same manner but also includes information of all the candidates who ran in each riding, their party affiliation and the number of votes won

Provincial and Territorial Governments
Each provincial chapter includes:
- statistical information
- description of Legislative Assembly
- biographical sketch of the Lieutenant Governor
- list of current Cabinet Members
- dates of Legislatures since Confederation
- current Members and Constituencies
- biographical sketches*
- general election and by-election results

Courts: Federal - each court chapter includes: a description of the court (Supreme, Federal, Federal Court of Appeal, Court Martial Appeal and Tax Court), its history, a list of its judges followed by biographical sketches*

* Biographical Sketches follow a concise yet in-depth format:
- *Personal Data*: place of birth, education, family information
- *Political Career*: political career path and services
- *Private Career*: work history, organization memberships, military history

AVAILABLE IN PRINT AND NOW ONLINE!

Available in hardcover print, the Canadian Parliamentary Guide is also available electronically via the Web, providing instant access to the government officials you need and the facts you want every time. Whereas the print edition is verified and updated annually, the Web version is updated on a monthly basis. Use the Web version to narrow your search with index fields such as institution, province and name.

Create your own contact lists! Online subscribers can pay a small fee to instantly generate their own contact lists and export information into spreadsheets for further use. A great alternative to high cost list broker services!

For more information please contact Grey House Publishing Canada by Tel.: 1-866-433-4739 or (416) 644-6479
Fax: (416) 644-1904 or via E-mail: info@greyhouse.ca • www.greyhouse.ca

Associations Canada

ASSOCIATIONS CANADA: MAKES RESEARCHING ORGANIZATIONS QUICK AND EASY

In addition to spending over $1 billion annually on transportation, conventions and marketing, Canadian associations spend millions more in the pursuit of membership interests.

Associations Canada is an easy to use compendium providing detailed indexes, listings and abstracts on over 18,000 local, regional, provincial, national and international organizations, identifying location, budget, founding date, who's in charge, scope of activity and funding source - just to name a few.

POWERFUL INDEXES HELP YOU TARGET THE ORGANIZATIONS YOU WANT

There are a number of criteria you can use to target specific organizations. Organized with the user in mind, Associations Canada is broken down into a number of indexes to help you find what you're looking for quickly and easily.

Subject Index - listing of Canadian and foreign association headquarters, alphabetical by subject and keyword

Acronym Index - an alphabetical listing of acronyms and corresponding Canadian and foreign associations, in both official languages

Budget Index - Canadian associations, alphabetical within eight budget categories

Conferences & Conventions Index - meetings sponsored by Canadian and foreign associations, alphabetical by conference name

Executive Name Index - alphabetical listing of key contacts of Canadian associations, for both headquarters and branches

Geographic Index - listing of headquarters, branch offices, chapters and divisions of Canadian associations, alphabetical within province and city

Mailing List Index - associations that offer mailing lists, alphabetical by subject

Registered Charitable Organizations Index - listing of associations that are registered charities, alphabetical by subject

PRINT OR ONLINE - QUICK AND EASY ACCESS TO ALL THE INFORMATION YOU NEED!

Available in hardcover print or electronically via the Web, Associations Canada provides instant access to the people you need and the facts you want every time. Whereas the print edition is verified and updated annually, ongoing changes are added to the Web version on a monthly basis. Use the Web version to narrow your search by using index fields such as name or type of organization, subject, location, contact name or title, and postal code.

Create your own contact lists! Online subscribers can pay a small fee to instantly generate their own contact lists and export them into spreadsheets for further use. A great alternative to high cost list broker services.

Associations Canada provides complete access to these highly lucrative markets:

Travel & Tourism
- Who's hosting what event... when and where?
- Check on events up to three years in advance

Journalism and Media
- Pure research - What do they do? Who is in charge? What's their budget?
- Check facts and sources in one step

Business
- Target your market, research your interests, compile profiles, and identify membership lists
- Warm-up cold calls with all the background you need to sell your product or service
- Preview prospects by budget, market interest or geographic location

Association Executives
- Look for strategic alliances with associations of similar interest
- Spot opportunities or conflicts with convention plans

Research & Government
- Scan interest groups or identify charities in your area of concern
- Check websites, publications and speaker availability
- Evaluate mandates, affiliations and scope

Libraries
- Refer researchers to the most complete Canadian association reference anywhere

---

For more information please contact Grey House Publishing Canada by Tel.: 1-866-433-4739 or (416) 644-6479
Fax: (416) 644-1904 or via E-mail: info@greyhouse.ca • www.greyhouse.ca

Financial Services Canada

UNPARALLELED COVERAGE OF THE CANADIAN FINANCIAL SERVICES INDUSTRY

With corporate listings for over 17,000 organizations and hard-to-find business information, Financial Services Canada is the most up-to-date source for names and contact numbers of industry professionals, senior executives, portfolio managers, financial advisors, agency bureaucrats and elected representatives.

Financial Services Canada is the definitive resource for detailed listings—providing valuable contact information including: name, title, organization, profile, associated companies, telephone and fax numbers, e-mail and website addresses. Use our online database and refine your search by stock symbol, revenue, year founded, assets, ownership type or number of employees.

POWERFUL INDEXES HELP YOU LOCATE THE CRUCIAL FINANCIAL INFORMATION YOU NEED.

Organized with the user in mind, Financial Services Canada contains categorized listings and four easy-to-use indexes:

Alphabetic - financial organizations listed in alphabetical sequence by company name

Geographic - financial institutions and their branches broken down by town or city

Executive Name - all officers, directors and senior personnel in alphabetical order by surname

Corporate Website/E-mail - an invaluable aid to the ever-expanding Internet world

Reduce the time you spend compiling lists, researching company information and searching for e-mail addresses. Whether you are interested in contacting a finance lawyer regarding international and domestic joint ventures, need to generate a list of foreign banks in Canada or want to contact the Toronto Stock Exchange—Financial Services Canada gives you the power to find all the data you need.

PRINT OR ONLINE - QUICK AND EASY ACCESS TO ALL THE INFORMATION YOU NEED!

Available in hardcover print or electronically via the Web, Financial Services Canada provides instant access to the people you need and the facts you want every time.

Financial Services Canada print edition is verified and updated annually. Regular ongoing changes are added to the Web version on a monthly basis.

The Web version allows you to narrow your search by using index fields such as name or type of organization, subject, location, contact name or title, and postal code.

Create your own contact lists! Online subscribers have the option to pay a little more to instantly generate their own contact lists and export them into spreadsheets for further use. A great alternative to high cost list broker services.

Access to Current Listings for...

Banks and Depository Institutions
- Domestic and Savings banks
- Foreign banks and branches
- Foreign bank representative offices
- Trust companies
- Credit unions/Caisses populaires

Non-Depository Institutions
- Bond rating companies
- Collection agencies
- Credit card companies
- Financing and loan companies
- Trustees in bankruptcy

Investment Management Firms including securities and commodities
- Financial planning/ investment management companies
- Investment dealers
- Investment fund companies
- Pension/money management companies
- Stock exchanges
- Holding companies

Insurance Companies including federal and provincial
- Reinsurance companies
- Fraternal benefit societies
- Mutual benefit companies
- Reciprocal exchanges

Accounting and Law
- Accountants
- Actuary consulting firms
- Law firms (specializing in finance)

Major Canadian Companies
- Key financial contacts for public, private and crown corporations
  Government
- Federal, provincial, and territorial contacts

Publications Appendix
- Leading publications serving the financial services industry

For more information please contact Grey House Publishing Canada by Tel.: 1-866-433-4739 or (416) 644-6479
Fax: (416) 644-1904 or via E-mail: info@greyhouse.ca • www.greyhouse.ca

Libraries Canada

GAIN ACCESS TO COMPLETE AND DETAILED INFORMATION ON CANADIAN LIBRARIES

Libraries Canada brings together the most current information from across the entire Canadian library sector, including libraries and branch libraries, educational libraries, regional systems, resource centres, archives, related periodicals, library schools and programs, provincial and governmental agencies, and associations.

As the nation's leading library directory for over twenty years, the Libraries Canada gives you access to almost 10,000 names and addresses of contacts in these institutions. Also included are valuable details such as library symbol, number of staff, operating systems, library type and acquisitions budget, hours of operation - all thoroughly indexed and easy to find.

Available in print and online, Libraries Canada delivers easily-accessible, quality information that has been verified and organized for easy retrieval. Five easy-to-use indexes assist you in navigating the print edition while the online version utilizes multiple index fields that help you get results.

INSTANT ACCESS TO CANADIAN LIBRARY SECTOR INFORMATION

Developed for publishers, advocacy groups, computer hardware suppliers, Internet service providers and other diverse groups which provide products and services to the library community; associations that need to maintain a current list of library resources in Canada; research departments, students and government agencies which require information about the types of services and programs available at various research institutions; Libraries Canada will help you find the information you need - quickly and easily.

EXPERT SEARCH OPTIONS AVAILABLE WITH ONLINE VERSION...

Available on Grey House Canada's CIRC interface, you can choose between Expert and Quick search to pinpoint information. Designed for both novice and advanced researchers, you can conduct simple text searches as well as powerful Boolean searches, plus you can narrow your search by using index fields such as name or type of institution, headquarters, location, area code, contact name or title, and postal code. Save your searches to build on at a later date or use the mark record function to view, print, e-mail or export your selected records.

Create your own contact lists! Online subscribers have the option to pay a little more to instantly generate their own contact lists and export them into spreadsheets for further use. A great alternative to high cost list broker services.

Libraries Canada gives you all the essentials for each institution:

- name, address, contact information and key personnel, number of staff;
- collection information, type of library, acquisitions budget, subject area, special collections;
- user services, number of branches, hours of operation, ILL information, photocopy and microform facilities, for-fee research, Internet access;
- systems information, details on electronic access, operating and online systems, Internet and e-mail software, Internet connectivity, access to electronic resources;
- additional information including associations, publications and regional systems.

With almost 60% of the data changing annually it has never been more important to have the latest version of Libraries Canada.

**For more information please contact Grey House Publishing Canada by Tel.: 1-866-433-4739 or (416) 644-6479
Fax: (416) 644-1904 or via E-mail: info@greyhouse.ca • www.greyhouse.ca**

Governments Canada

THE MOST COMPLETE AND COMPREHENSIVE GUIDE TO LOCATING PEOPLE AND PROGRAMS IN CANADA

Governments Canada provides regularly updated listings on federal, provincial —territorial and municipal government departments, offices and agencies across Canada. Branch and regional offices are also included, along with all associated agencies, boards, commissions and crown corporations.

Listings include contact name, full address, telephone and fax numbers, as well as e-mail addresses.

Produced by the professional editors of the accredited Canadian Almanac & Directory, you can be sure of our commitment to superior indexing and accuracy.

AN INNOVATIVE INTERFACE WITH ENHANCED FUNCTIONALITY

Available via Grey House Canada's CIRC interface, Governments Canada allows users to conduct their research by choosing to perform an Expert or Quick search to access the data they need quickly and easily.

- *Cross-database search* - all seven directory sources (with subscription) can be seamlessly searched at the same time, separately or in any combination.
- *Downloading capabilities* - option to generate contact lists by exporting records into spreadsheets or mailing labels in Microsoft® Word, CSV or text format at the click of a button.
- *Monthly Updates* - regular ongoing changes are added to the Web version on a monthly basis.
- *Designed for both novice and advanced researchers* - users can conduct a quick search with fields common to all six databases, or build a complex Boolean search using Expert search.
- *More search options* - researchers can customize their results by searching for records with: e-mail, telephone, URL, fax and mailing list compliance.
- *Mark Records* - get the information you need by marking records in either the Results list or the Full Record Display and view, print, e-mail or download them separately.
- *Embedded links to websites and e-mail addresses* - allows users to gain further perspective on an issue or organization.

Access the key decision-makers in all levels of Government including:

- Cabinets/Executive Councils
- Elected Officials/Constituencies
- Governors General/Lieutenant
- Governors/Territorial Commissioners
- PrimeMinisters/Premiers /Government Leaders
- Auditor General/Provincial Auditors
- Electoral Officers
- Departments/Agencies
- Administration

For more information please contact Grey House Publishing Canada by Tel.: 1-866-433-4739 or (416) 644-6479 Fax: (416) 644-1904 or via E-mail: info@greyhouse.ca • www.greyhouse.ca

INFORMATION FORM

PHOTOCOPY THIS FORM FOR CONVENIENCE

CHANGE TO LISTING

PAGE NUMBER: DIRECTORY:

_____

NAME OF ORGANIZATION:

_____
_____

PLEASE CHANGE OUR LISTING TO REFLECT THE FOLLOWING:

_____
_____
_____
_____
_____
_____

NEW LISTING:

WE ARE NOT REPRESENTED IN THE DIRECTORY. HERE IS THE INFORMATION ON OUR ASSOCIATION/ORGANIZATION/ GOVERNMENT BODY: (Please examine the guidelines in the front of the directory and the entries of similar organizations for an indication of how best to present your data).

_____
_____
_____
_____
_____

WE WOULD LIKE TO SEE MORE INFORMATION ON:

_____
_____

MAIL INFORMATION TO:
GREY HOUSE PUBLISHING CANADA
555 RICHMOND ST., W, SUITE 301, PO Box 1207
TORONTO, ONTARIO M5V 3B1

E-MAIL TO:
INFO@GREYHOUSE.CA

FAX INFORMATION TO:
THE EDITOR
(416) 644-1904

Mailing List Services

As a boutique provider of mailings lists, Grey House Canada specializes in the areas below to ensure a *high level* of accuracy. Our clients return time to us time and time again because of the reliability and customer service. We'll work with you to develop a campaign that provides results. No other list services will work as closely as we do to meet your unique needs.

Grey House Canada Custom Mailing Lists:
- *Associations* - the most extensive list of Canadian Associations available, featuring all professional, trade and business organizations together with not-for profit groups.
- *Arts & Culture* - the definitive source of key prospects in various Canadian arts and cultural outlets.
- *Education* - the most comprehensive list of educational institutions and organizations in Canada.
- *Health Care / Hospitals* - includes all major medical facilities with chief executives.
- *Lawyers* - key prospects for a number of direct mail offers.
- *Media* - the definitive source of key prospects in various Canadian media outlets, offering the top business managers and/or publishers.
- *Environmental* - a complete profile of the Canadian Environmental scene, constantly revised for the annual Canadian Environmental Directory.
- *Financial Services* - a list of key contacts from the full range of Canada's financial services industry.
- *Government Key Contacts* - a list of key Government contacts, maintained by the Canadian Almanac & Directory, Canada's standard institutional reference for over 160 years.
- *Libraries* - the most unique and complete list of government, special and public libraries available.
- *Major Canadian Companies* - listings of Canada's largest private, public and crown corporations with major key contacts of the top business decision-makers.

Availability
Lists are available on CD, labels, and via e-mail. They are provided on a one-time use basis or for a one year lease.
For a quotation on tailor made lists to suit your needs, inquire using the contact information listed below.

For more information please contact Grey House Publishing Canada by Tel.: 1-866-433-4739 or (416) 644-6479
Fax: (416) 644-1904 or via E-mail: info@greyhouse.ca • www.greyhouse.ca

CANADIAN DIRECTORIES ORDER FORM

QTY	TITLE	PRINT	ONLINE
	CANADIAN ALMANAC & DIRECTORY 2011	$350.00	Please call for quote
	CANADIAN ENVIRONMENTAL RESOURCE GUIDE 2011/12	$365.00	Please call for quote
	ASSOCIATIONS CANADA 2011	$375.00	Please call for quote
	FINANCIAL SERVICES CANADA 2011/12	$355.00	Please call for quote
	LIBRARIES CANADA 2011/12	$275.00	Please call for quote
	CANADIAN PARLIAMENTARY GUIDE 2011	$229.00	Please call for quote
	GOVERNMENTS CANADA (updated monthly)	N/A	Please call for quote
	CANADA INFO DESK (updated monthly)	N/A	Please call for quote

PLEASE NOTE:
- Prices are stated in Canadian dollars. All prices are subject to change without notice. N/A = Not Available
- To purchase print directories online visit our website – www.greyhouse.ca
- Orders shipped outside Canada are charged in US dollars

COMMENTS:

METHOD OF PAYMENT:

☐ **CHEQUE/MONEY ORDER**
Please make cheque/money order payable to Grey House Publishing Canada for total amount including shipping & handling and all applicable taxes. (Please call to confirm total)

☐ **CREDIT CARD**
  ☐ VISA   ☐ MASTERCARD   ☐ AMEX

CARD NUMBER:
EXPIRY DATE:
SIGNATURE:

☐ **BILL MY COMPANY/ORGANIZATION**
PO # IF APPLICABLE

BILL TO INFORMATION:

NAME
TITLE/DEPT.
ORGANIZATION
ADDRESS
CITY
PROV   POSTAL CODE
PHONE   FAX
E-MAIL

SHIP TO INFORMATION: (if different from above)

NAME
TITLE/DEPT.
ORGANIZATION
ADDRESS
CITY
PROV   POSTAL CODE
PHONE   FAX
E-MAIL

☐ **STANDING ORDER PLAN**
Please book my standing order for future annual print editions. With an automatic renewal, I'll save 10% off subsequent orders.

APPLICABLE TAXES
- 5% GST applies to AB, MB, SK, QC, YT, NT, NU & PE
- 12% HST applies to BC
- 13% HST applies to NB, NL & ON
- 15% HST applies to NS

SHIPPING & HANDLING
$20.00 for a single directory,
$4.00 each additional directory
(Canadian & US Orders).

International Orders – call for rates. Subject to customs, duty & tax at customer's expense.

GREY HOUSE PUBLISHING CANADA

555 Richmond St. West
Suite # 301, PO Box 1207
Toronto, ON M5V 3B1

PHONE
(866) 433-4739

FAX
(416) 644-1904

E-MAIL
info@greyhouse.ca